Film Reviews
1907-1980

A SIXTEEN-VOLUME SET,

Including an Index to Titles

Garland Publishing, Inc.
New York and London
1983

Contents

OF THE SIXTEEN-VOLUME SET

1. *1907–1920*

2. *1921–1925*

3. *1926–1929*

4. *1930–1933*

5. *1934–1937*

6. *1938–1942*

7. *1943–1948*

8. *1949–1953*

9. *1954–1958*

10. *1959–1963*

11. *1964–1967*

12. *1968–1970*

13. *1971–1974*

14. *1975–1977*

15. *1978–1980*

16. *Index to Titles*

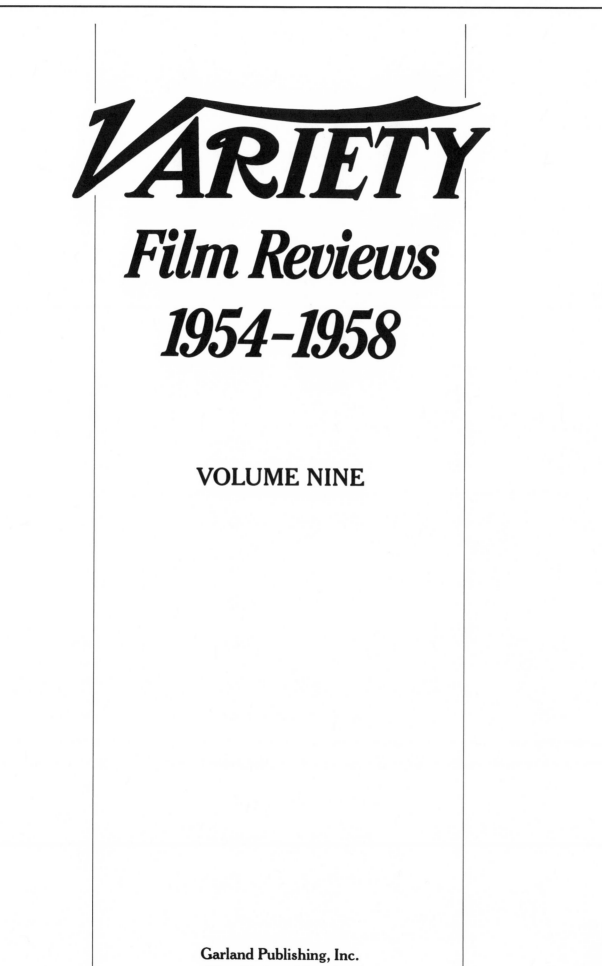

VARIETY

Film Reviews
1954-1958

VOLUME NINE

Garland Publishing, Inc.
New York and London
1983

Library of Congress Cataloging in Publication Data
Main entry under title:

Variety film reviews.
   Includes index.

   1. Moving-pictures—Reviews.   I. Daily variety.
PN1995.V34   1982   791.43′75   82-15691
ISBN 0-8240-5200-5 (v. 1)
ISBN 0-8240-5208-0 (v. 9)

Manufactured in the United States of America

Printed on acid-free,
250-year-life paper

User's Guide

The reviews in this collection are published in chronological order, by the date on which the review appeared. The date of each issue appears at the top of the column where the reviews for that issue begin. The reviews continue through that column and all following columns until a new date appears at the top of the page. Where blank spaces occur at the end of a column, this indicates the end of that particular week's reviews. An index to film titles, giving date of review, is published as the last volume in this set.

1954

The French Line
(3-D MUSICAL-COLOR)

3-D musical with hot possibilities from blue-nose controversy and censorably costumed four-minute dance by Jane Russell. Without hotspot, only mild, talky tuner with mostly distaffer appeal.

Hollywood.

RKO release of Edmund Grainger production. Stars Jane Russell; co-stars Gilbert Roland, Arthur Hunnicutt; features Mary McCarthy, Joyce MacKenzie, Paula Corday, Scott Elliott, Craig Stevens. Directed by Lloyd Bacon. Screenplay, Mary Loos, Richard Sale; based on a story by Matty Kemp, Isabel Dawn; camera (Technicolor), Harry J. Wild; editor, Robert Ford; musical supervision, C. Bakaleinikoff; music arranged and conducted by Walter Scharf; dance numbers staged by Billy Daniel; songs, Josef Myrow, Ralph Blane, Robert Wells. Previewed Dec. 29, '53. Running time, **102 MINS.**

Mary Carson .... Jane Russell
Pierre .... Gilbert Roland
"Waco" Mosby ...... Arthur Hunnicutt
Annie Farrell .... Mary McCarty
Myrtle Brown .... Joyce MacKenzie
Celeste .... Paula Corday
Bill Harris .... Scott Elliott
Phil Barton .... Craig Stevens
Katherine Hodges .... Laura Elliot
Francois .... Steven Ceray
First Mate .... John Wengraf
George Hodges ...... Michael St. Angel
Donna Adams .... Barbara Darrow
Kitty Lee .... Barbara Dobbins

The censorship controversy stirred up over "The French Line" by its lack of a Production Code seal gives the RKO release a natural edge for ballyhoo and ticket sale possibilities. Actually, except for a four-minute, censorably costumed dance by Jane Russell, it is a rather mild, gabby, fashion parade in 3-D that will appeal mostly to distaffers. Exhibs willing to join Howard Hughes in sidestepping the industry's code regulations would seem to be in line for a fancy b.o. buck—as long as the controversy continues to be fanned and the aforementioned four-minute scene stays in.

Miss Russell is well equipped by nature to fulfill the demands of the costuming by Michael Woulfe and Howard Greer, and on that count, when seen through the polaroids, eyes will pop as she shakes and quakes to "Looking for Trouble." The outfit she wears has been variously described as a bikini affair, but beach bikinis rarely have such an inquiring camera thrusting inquisitive lenses forward at such strategic angles. The number gives every male a front box seat for a burley show, and they will enjoy it if they have stayed through the 95-minute talkfest that preceeds it.

This concern with the mammary is notable through the film's 102 minutes in the casting of well-chosen femmes and in their costuming, but not to any censorable extreme except in the "Trouble" unmber. Matching, maybe even surpassing, Miss Russell for size is Mary McCarty, who plays the star's chum in the plot, joins her on singing "The Gal From Texas," a lightly costumed production number, and solos "By Madame Firelle," a fashion display of Michael Woulfe gowns that provides something for the distaff ticket-buyers to pop their eyes at. It's unfortunate, however, that Miss McCarthy, the only true musical comedy singer in the cast, is used so sparingly.

Outside of these various treats for the eyes in costuming, Technicolor tints and interesting settings, the picture is not strong on what generally passes for b.o. entertainment. The plot is the long-worked one about a rich girl who wants to be loved for herself and goes incognito as a working frail to find the right man. It's an okay basis for a musical if ingenuously handled, but there is little of the imaginative displayed in Lloyd Bacon's direction or in the screenplay by Mary Loos and Richard Sale. Once in a while a snappy quip breaks through the long passages of verbiage that strain too hard to be smart talk. And in line with the film's principal concern, these snappy quips are bosom-conscious, even to the point of having Miss Russell called "Chesty."

The score has nine tunes. The 10th song was the title number but it has been clipped. Miss Russell starts the song session on the numbers by Joseph Myrow, Ralph Blane and Robert Wells by singing "Well, I'll Be Switched" while taking a bath. Later in the footage she does "What Is This That I Feel?" while intoxicated on Black Velvets, and then joins Miss McCarthy on "Texas" before warming up to the hot finale "Trouble."

Gilbert Roland, who plays a French lover with verve, has "With a Kiss," done, naturally, to a roomful of girls; "Comment Alles Vous," a lesson in good neighborliness, and "Wait 'Til You See Paris." The ninth tune is "Poor Andre," serving as a production dance for Billy Daniel, who staged all of the terp numbers.

Miss Russell is an eye-pleaser, and she can be a good musical comedy actress ("Gentlemen Prefer Blondes") when given material and direction. Roland's suave way with the ladies helps his character of the French lover who pursues oil-rich Miss Russell for herself, not her millions. Arthur Hunnicutt tells tall tales as Miss Russell's oil partner and guardian. Among the lookers assembled to add bosom emphasis are Joyce MacKenzie, Paula Corday, Laura Elliott and others who shape up correctly. Scott Elliott, Craig Stevens, Michael St. Angel are among the male casters having little to do.

Edmund Grainger's production guidance is excellent in mustering outstanding physical attractions for the show. His choice of cleffers Myrow, Blane and Wells for the tunes was good, too. However, the listenable songs are rather poorly sung by the principals. Harry J. Wild's 3-D color lensing is topnotch, as are the background music arrangements by Walter Scharf.

Brog.

The Glenn Miller Story
(MUSIC-COLOR)

Sentiment and swing keynoting appealing but lengthy biopic. James Stewart, June Allyson and hearty boxoffice.

Hollywood, Jan. 5.

Universal release of Aaron Rosenberg production. Stars James Stewart, June Allyson; features Charles Drake, George Tobias, Henry Morgan; guest stars, Frances Langford, Louis Armstrong, Gene Krupa, Ben Pollack, the Archie Savage Dancers, the Modernaires. Directed by Anthony Mann. Written by Valentine Davies, Oscar Brodney; camera (Technicolor), William Daniels; editor, Russell Schoengarth; dance director, Ken Williams; musical direction, Joseph Gershenson; musical adaptation, Henry Mancini; technical consultant, Chummy MacGregor. Previewed Dec. 10, '53. Running time, **115 MINS.**

Glenn Miller .... James Stewart
Helen Miller .... June Allyson
Don Haynes .... Charles Drake
Si Schribman .... George Tobias
Chummy MacGregor .... Henry Morgan
Herself .... Frances Langford
Himself .... Louis Armstrong
Himself .... Gene Krupa
Himself .... Ben Pollack
Themselves ..The Archie Savage Dancers
Themselves .... The Modernaires
Polly Haynes .... Marion Ross
Mr. Miller .... Irving Bacon
Mrs. Miller .... Kathleen Lockhart
General Arnold .... Barton MacLane
Mr. Krantz .... Sig Ruman
Joe Becker .... Phil Garris
Mr. Burger .... James Bell
Mrs. Burger .... Katherine Warren

Sentiment and swing feature this biopic treatment on the life of the late Glenn Miller, and in it Universal has a boxoffice winner. James Stewart and June Allyson is strong marquee combination so their presence with the Miller music and the exploitation push U will give, means hearty ticket sales in the keys and elsewhere.

The Miller music, heard in some 20 tunes throughout the production, is still driving, rhythmic swing at its best. It will be enjoyed, both nostalgically and for its impact in comparison with present-day style. Paradoxically, although U is tied tight to Decca, the film is getting an advance promotional assist from RCA Victor, which has been pushing a plush, fancy-priced Miller album. Decca is issuing the sound track set.

The Aaron Rosenberg supervision makes excellent use of the music to counterpoint a tenderly projected love story, feelingly played by Stewart and Miss Allyson. The two stars, who clicked previously as a man-wife team in "The Stratton Story," have an affinity for this type of thing. Stewart's acting mannerisms are less in evidence in this than in his usual film roles. Both players have the advantage of sympathetic direction from Anthony Mann, who gives the subject understanding guidance, and a screen story by Valentine Davies and Oscar Brodney that is an expert blend of incidents in the Miller band career with behind-the-baton personal highlights.

With all of its many praiseworthy points, the film has its flaws, too. The principal complaint heard voiced at the special press premiere staged by U was against the picture's length, which is a long one hour and 55 minutes. This running time results from cramming too much into the show and from dwelling too long on some sections that could have been speeded up by a montage treatment. Also commented on by press preem guests was the odd absence of Tex Beneke, who gained band fame with Miller and led the outfit for several years after the maestro's death. There is no hint of Beneke in the film.

The first 70 minutes of the picture is given over to Miller's search for a sound in music arrangement that would be his trademark and live after him. Blended with this search is his absentee courtship of Helen Burger, whom he had decided was the girl for him while a student at the University of Colorado. Time of the story start is 1925, when Miller joined the Ben Pollack outfit at Venice, Calif. It then follows him cross-country to New York, his marriage and through abortive attempts to found his own band. The new sound comes at Si Shribman's State Ballroom in Boston, when the trumpet lead accidentally splits his lip at rehearsal and "Moonlight Serenade" is played with a clarinet lead.

Remaining 45 minutes covers the rocketing Miller fame, his enlistment when World War II starts and the service band's playing for overseas troups. The finale is a real tear-jerker that will have every femme, and not a few males, unabashedly drying eyes as the maestro's family listens in at home to a special Christmas Day broadcast to the States from Paris, 10 days after Miller disappeared on a flight from London to Paris.

Highlighting the romantic swing phases of the presentation are such songs identified with Miller as "Serenade," "String of Pearls," "St. Louis Blues March," "In the Mood," "Little Brown Jug," "Pennsylvania 6-5000," "Tuxedo Junction," "American Patrol," "Chattanooga Choo Choo," "I Know Why," "At Last" and "National Emblem March." The only new tune in the film is the "Love Theme," composed by Henry Mancini. It is heard at various times throughout.

One of the big musical moments in the footage has nothing to do with the Miller music. It is a red-hot jam session that has Louis Armstrong, Gene Krupa, Trummy Young, Babe Austin, Cozy Cole, Marty Napoleon, Barney Bigard and Arvell Shaw socking "Basin Street Blues." Sequence is dated 1928 and laid in Harlem's Connie's Inn. Enriching the sound of the sequence is the Technicolor lensing by William Daniels. His photography is noteworthy in all of the footage.

To match the topflight performances of Stewart and Miss Allyson, the picture has some strong thesping by featured and supporting players, as well as guest star appearances. Henry Morgan stands out as Chummy MacGregor, Miller's 88'er. Charles Drake is good as Don Haynes, the band's manager, as are James Bell and Katherine Warren, and Irving Bacon and Kathleen Lockhart, doing the respective parents of Miss Burger and Miller. George Tozias as Shribman; Barton MacLane as Gen. Hap Arnold, and the players impersonating band members.

Playing themselves are Pollack, Armstrong, Krupa, Babe Russin, the only members of the original Miller band to appear personally, Frances Langford and the Modernaires. The latter two are spotlighted in a reenactment of an overseas service show.

Backing the unusually strong human elements, as well as the music, are topnotch technical assists from Daniels' lensing, Joseph Gershenson's musical direction and the musical adaptation by Henry Manicini, on through the art direction, settings, costumes and editing. Serving as technical consultant was Chummy MacGregor.

Brog.

The Long, Long Trailer
(SONGS—COLOR)

TV's "I Love Lucy" team romps through a gay comedy. Good for plenty of laughs and an exploitation natural.

Metro release of Pandro S. Berman production.. Stars Lucille Ball, Desi Arnaz; features Marjorie Main, Keenan Wynn, Gladys Hurlburt, Moroni Olsen, Bert Freed, Madge Blake, Walter Baldwin, Oliver Blake, Perry Sheehan. Directed by Vincente Minnelli. Screenplay, Albert Hackett, Frances Goodrich; based on Clinton Twiss novel; camera (Ansco color), Robert Surtees; editor, Ferris Webster; music, Adolph Deutsch. Previewed Dec. 31, '53, in N.Y. Running time, **96 MINS.**

Tacy Collini .... Lucille Ball
Nicholas Collini .... Desi Arnaz
Mrs. Hittaway .... Marjorie Main
Policeman .... Keenan Wynn
Mrs. Bolton .... Gladys Hurlbut
Mr. Tewitt .... Moroni Olsen
Foreman .... Bert Freed
Aunt Anastacia .... Madge Blake
Uncle Edgar .... Walter Baldwin
Mr. Judlow .... Oliver Blake
Bridesmaid .... Perry Sheehan

For those itching to explore the wideopen spaces in a trailer, as well as those who've been hoping For Lucille Ball and Desi Arnaz, TV's toprated "I Love Lucy" team, to be transported to a larger screen. Metro has concocted this merry little ditty that ought to go over big at the b.o. It's a lighthearted, genuinely funny comedy that lapses into slapstick at the drop of a hat and shows both stars to best advantage.

In a way, "The Long, Long Trailer" is an apt title. The trailer is one of the stars of the picture, and it's well cast at that. At the same time, and perhaps inevitably so, the film provides one continuous plug for the shiny house-on-wheels which Miss Ball and Arnaz alternately use as a prop and a set.

Whatever exhibs may have to say about TV as competition, in this case it's certainly working to their advantage. There are few places in the country where the Ball-Arnaz combination isn't known, and the picture's theme will intrigue the audience as to its comedy potential. Nor will they be disappointed.

Not a trick has been missed in squeezing the laughs from every conceivable situation. In fact, the picture takes the couple from the moment they see the trailer they want — it costs them about five times as much as they intended to spend — through a series of adventures and misadventures to the point where Miss Ball is ready to sell their "house" and leave Arnaz in the process.

Like the "I Love Lucy" TV show, "The Long, Long Trailer" strings together situation comedy without a letup, barely giving the audience a chance to catch its breath. After a somewhat slow start, the team really hits its pace. Some of their antics involving the trailer are priceless.

Both Miss Ball and Arnaz deliver sock performances. Their timing is perfect and the dialog provided by Albert Hackett and Frances Goodrich is clever. Miss Ball occasionally gives in to the temptation of being overly cute but, judging again by TV, this shouldn't bother the audience. Arnaz has a sure touch and provides a perfect balance to his wife's antics. His brief delivery of "Breezin' Along with the Breeze" with Miss Ball, and of a short comedy number with a Latin touch, is pleasing and well integrated.

Rest of the cast easily gets into the spirit of the thing. Keenan Wynn has an all-too-brief part as a policeman and Marjorie Main gets laughs as the eager-beaver trailerite. Vincente Minnelli's direction accentuates the nonsensical aspect of the story. At the same time, he wisely lets the camera roam through Yosemite National Park for some pretty exciting views.

Ansco color is good in the outdoor settings but doesn't give true reproduction in the fleshtones and in some of the interior shots. Pandro S. Berman endowed the film with his usual production values. Music by Adolf Deutsch provides a good background and Robert Surtees' camera handling has real merit.   *Hift.*

Border River
(COLOR)

Generally-marketable escapist fare. Well-made actioner, starring Joel McCrea and Yvonne De Carlo, has good b.o. outlook.

Universal-International release of Albert J. Cohen production. Stars Joel McCrea and Yvonne De Carlo. Directed by George Sherman. Screenplay, William Sackheim and Louis Stevens from a story by Stevens; camera (Technicolor), Irving Glassberg; editor. Frank Gross. Previewed in N.Y., Dec. 30, '52. Running time, 80 MINS.
```
Clete Mattson ............. Joel McCrea
Carmelita Carias ..... Yvonne De Carlo
General Calleja........Pedro Armendariz
Newlund ................ Howard Petrie
Annina .................... Erika Nordin
Captain Vargas ....... Alfonso Bedoya
Baron Von Hollden .......Ivan Triesault
Sanchez .................. George Lewis
Fletcher ................. George Wallace
Anderson ............... Lane Chandler
Crowe ................. Charles Horvath
Lopez ................... Nacho Galindo
```

This is generally - marketable, staple escapist fare, handsomely photographed in Technicolor and mounted with the proper action ingredients. Universal is an acknowledged master in turning out this type of picture, and "Border River" is one of the company's better efforts. As a result, satisfactory returns are to be anticipated.

U's cameras move south of the border to record an incident tied in with the U.S. Civil War. It involves the purchase of arms and ammunition for the Confederacy. Joel McCrea, as a Confederate major on the purchasing mission, and Yvonne De Carlo, as a Mexican beauty, satisfactorily fulfill the demands of the William Sackheim and Louis Stevens screenplay. Writers have provided a number of interesting situations, well stacked with the necessary fisticuffs and romance. Director George Sherman carries out his assignment with precision and Albert J. Cohen's overall production supervision is a definite asset. This isn't the kind of picture that will make any "10 Best" list, but it's a throughly professional job, loaded with the values producthungry exhibs are clamoring for.

With the South's plight growing more desperate at the closing stages of the Civil War, McCrea and a band of cohorts steal $2,000,-000 in gold bullion from a Union mint. McCrea crosses the Rio Grande and in the anything-goes-for-cash town of Zona Libre seeks to make a deal for ammunition and supplies for the Rebel army. News of the loot in his possession travels fast and he is accosted by various nefarious characters bent on annexing the gold for their own use. These include a renegade Mexican general, the general's doublecrossing German advisor, a couple of ordinary crooks, and a private eye in the employ of the union forces.

Miss De Carlo is seen as the general's girl friend and co-owner of the local cafe. McCrea's idealism restores her own sense of justice, which had given way to cynicism brought about by the death of her father and brother in political skirmishes. Pedro Armendariz is effective as the cruel and sinister general and Ivan Triesault is fine in the role of the smooth-talking double-dealing German. Alfonso Bedoya scores as one of the general's aides although the part is a familiar one.

Irving Glassberg's camera work is first-rate, capturing some lush scenic views which is bound to receive some "oh" and "ah" responses from audiences.   *Holl.*

Femmes De Paris
(Women of Paris)
(FRENCH)
Paris.

Corona release of Hoche production. Stars Michel Simon. Directed by Jean Boyer. Screenplay, Alex Joffe, Ray Ventura, Boyer; dialog, Jean Marsan; camera, Charles Suin; editor, Robert Giordoni; music, Paul Misraki. At Olympia, Paris. Running time, 90 MINS.
```
Charles ................. Michel Simon
Giselle ................. Brigitte Auber
Lucien ................... Henri Genes
Inspector ........... Bernard Lajarrige
Wife .. ............. Germaine Kerjean
```

Film uses the gimmick of a staid astronomer turned loose in a lush nitery to work in a flock of acts, guest stars as well as unfold a simple story of the professor at odds with nature in the raw in nightlife. Film emerges as pleasant fare for the local trade with the Michel Simon name for pull. For the U. S. this gives nothing as a musical or as a straight pic because of its forced premise. It might do in special situations, the plethora of unclad lovelies providing an exploitation peg.

A famed astronomer discovers an exploding star in his telescope, and while trying to phone his colleagues overhears a girl's voice saying she will kill herself if her lover doesn't show up at a nightclub that night. The kindly professor is upset and when a series of calls to the club and police is of no avail, he goes himself to try to save the unknown femme. He gets mixed up in dope smuggling racket, a flock of predatory nitery gals. This gives a means of unloading numerous acts. It also brings in Patachou for a neat song stint and local comedian, Robert Lamoureux. There are plenty of the bare breasts on view plus some comic moments.

Director Jean Boyer has given this the bread-and-butter treatment, lacking verve and invention for the musical bits.

Michel Simon does well by his professor role. Brigitte Auber is cute as the suicidal dame and Henri Genes gets laughs as the harassed club owner. Lensing and editing are standard as is Paul Misraki's music.   *Mosk.*

Ansiedad
(Anxiety)
(MEXICAN; SONGS)
Mexico City, Dec. 29.

Distribuidora Mexicana de Peliculas release of a Producciones Zacarias production. Stars Libertad Lamarque and Pedro Infante; features Irma Dorantes and Arturo Soto Rangel. Directed by Miguel Zacarias. Screenplay, Miguel Zacarias and Edmundo Baez; camera, Gabriel Figueroa. Music, Manuel Esperon. At Cine Mexico, Mexico City. Running time, 101 MINS.

Co-starring of two warblers, Libertad Lamarque, Argentinian tango singer, and Pedro Infante, pop song expounder, along with favorite Agustin Lara, No. 1 romantic song writer, was a smart production move. Despite a queer but engrossing story, the gifted direction of Miguel Zacarias plus these favorites make the pic one of the best Mexican films of 1953. Zacarias does well as producer, writer and director. Same is true of Infante as an impractical trouper but self-made pro entertainer and glassy aristocrat. Miss Lamarque increases her popularity as a singer and thespian.

This tale about a tango singer, violently widowed to face a seeming deadead with a young son, who inherits the family yen for trouping, is nicely unfolded. Then there is the other scion who inclines to

commerce with quick coin a positive yen. The clashes of the trio in theatres and parlors lead into some of the best numbers of Agustin Lara, particularly "El Farolito," known in the U. S., and "Vera Cruz." Infante does very well with the former while Miss Lamarque sells the latter, in a tropical setting featuring dancing damsels.

"Ansiedad" played three top local cinemas day-date, and was clicko with distaffers.   *Doug.*

She Couldn't Say No

Amusing comedy on how a rich girl upsets a small Arkansas town with her generosity. Robert Mitchum, Jean Simmons; medium b.o. chances.

Hollywood, Jan. 12.

RKO release of Robert Sparks production. Stars Robert Mitchum, Jean Simmons. Arthur Hunnicutt; features Edgar Buchanan, Wallace Ford, Raymond Walburn, Jimmy Hunt, Ralph Dumke, Hope Landin, Gus Schilling, Eleanor Todd, Pinky Tomlin. Directed by Lloyd Bacon. Screenplay, D. D. Beauchamp, William Bowers, Richard Flournoy; based on a story by Beauchamp; camera, Harry J. Wild; editor, George Amy; music, Roy Webb; musical director, C. Bakaleinikoff. Previewed Jan. 6, '54. Running time, 88 MINS.

Doc	Robert Mitchum
Corby	Jean Simmons
Otey	Arthur Hunnicutt
Ad Meeker	Edgar Buchanan
Joe	Wallace Ford
Judge Holbert	Raymond Walburn
Digger	Jimmy Hunt
Sheriff	Ralph Dumke
Mrs. McMurtry	Hope Landin
Ed Gruman	Gus Schilling
Sally	Eleanor Todd
Elmer Wooley	Jinky Tomlin

A pleasant round of folksy comedy is unspooled in "She Couldn't Say No" and the general audiences in regular situations should find it amusing. Jean Simmons and Robert Mitchum, two names not usually associated with comedy, supply marquee draft for playdates, as well as being facile foils for the chuckles.

Story idea is concerned with an oil heiress' return to a small Arkansas town to repay the people who had chipped in to supply the medical aid that saved her life when she was a tiny girl. As she begins to bestow material rewards on the citizens reactions quite the reverse of what she expected takes place and it isn't long before the town of Progress has been swollen far beyond its capacity by milling mobs of strangers who have arrived to get in on the mysterious handouts. Alarmed at the situation, the heiress reveals her identity, calls off the largess and decides to become a citizen of Progress as the wife of the town doctor.

As the doctor and heiress, respectively, Mitchum and Miss Simmons deliver likeably and with a good feel for comedy. Latter goes in more for titters and quiet chuckles than guffaws, although the footage contains some of that variety of mirth, too, under Lloyd Bacon's capable direction. He works up the best points of the script by D. D. Beauchamp, William Bowers and Richard Flournoy and keeps the plot unfolding at a steady pace.

Arthur Hunnicutt, as the third star of the Robert Sparks production, heads the list of town characters. He gets his laughs as the village drunk, a pleasant sort of tippler whom Progress understands and accepts. Edgar Buchanan, storekeeper; Wallace Ford, veterinarian; Raymond Walburn, justice of peace; Ralph Dumke, sheriff; Hope Landin, boarding house operator; Pinky Tomlin, mailman; Gus Schilling, ailing farmer, and Eleanor Todd, village belle on the make for the bachelor doc, all get into the pleasantries that ensue and do their bits to make them amusing. Young Jimmy Hunt has his moments, too, as Mitchum's fishing chum and confidante.

Harry J. Wild's photography, the Roy Webb score, the editing and small town settings are among the technical assists capably backing the entertainment. *Brog.*

The Million Pound Note
(BRITISH-COLOR)

Gregory Peck in Mark Twain story of Strange Wager; Peck name should give this satire a good chance in U. S.

London, Jan. 4.

General Film Distributors release of Group Films production. Stars Gregory Peck; features Ronald Squire, A. E. Matthews, Wilfrid Hyde White, Jane Griffiths. Directed by Ronald Neame. Screenplay, Jill Craigie; camera, Geoffrey Unsworth editor, Clive Donner; music, William Alwyn. At Gaumont Theatre, London, Dec. 29, '53. Running time, 92 MINS.

Henry Adams	Gregory Peck
Portia Lansdowne	Jane Griffiths
Oliver Montpelier	Ronald Squire
Duchess of Cromarty	Joyce Grenfell
Rock	Reginald Beckwith
Hastings	Hartley Power
Lloyd	Brian Oulton
Ambassador	Wilbur Evans
Mr. Reid	Maurice Denham
Parsons	John Slater
Roderick Montpelier	Wilfred Hyde White
Duke of Cromarty	Hugh Wakefield
Bank Director	Ernest Thesiger

Mark Twain's classic story of the penniless American who is given a million pound bank note in a wager and succeeds in keeping it intact for a month, makes gentle screen satire which should rate as a moderate boxoffice grosser in the British market where its quota ticket will prove a valuable additional asset. For U. S. consumption, the Gregory Peck starring tag will be its principal exploitation feature, and should help in obtaining widespread exhibition.

Lensed in Technicolor with Edwardian settings providing a fascinating background, the yarn suffers from the protracted exploitation of one basic joke. It is sustaining and amusing for a time, but there are very few single gags that can successfully hold up for 92 minutes. "Note" is not an exception.

The plot is based on a bet between two brothers (Ronald Squire and Wilfred Hyde White) that a man with a million pound bank note in his possession could live on the fat of the land for a month without having to break into it. The guinea pig for their wager is Gregory Peck, a penniless American stranded in London. And, sure enough, he finds this an open sesame to food, clothes, hotels and, naturally, society. Even when he buys some comparatively worthless shares there is a stock exchange boom, but suddenly there is a suspicion of a hoax. The bank note cannot be produced to an inquisitive reporter, and there follows a wild scene of irate creditors and disillusioned investors.

Throughout the narrative, there is a pleasant degree of humor and a simple romantic theme. The basic idea is good for a few chuckles and there are some nice laugh situations derived from the dumb performance of Reginald Beckwith as a speechless, penniless weightlifter who assists Peck.

The acting attains an all-round level of competence and, apart from a characteristic performance by the male star, there is a highly satisfactory portrayal by Jane Griffiths in the romantic lead. A. E. Matthews, vet of the British screen, gives a sterling study of an elderly duke who is edged out of his suite by the upstart millionaire. Hartley Power, as head of the gold mine, and Wilbur Evans, as the American Ambassador, top a reliable lineup of feature players. Ronald Neame has directed the piece smoothly. The technical credits are standard. *Myro.*

Three Young Texans
(SONG—COLOR)

Formula outdoor feature in color for programmer market, with youthful casting emphasis in Mitzi Gaynor, Keefe Brasselle, Jeffrey Hunter.

Hollywood, Jan. 11.

20th-Fox release of Panoramic (Leonard Goldstein) production. Stars Mitzi Gaynor, Keefe Brasselle, Jeffrey Hunter; features Harvey Stephens, Dan Riss, Michael Ansara, Aaron Spelling, Morris Ankrum, Frank Wilcox. Directed by Henry Levin. Screenplay, Gerald Drayson Adams; from a story by William MacLeod Raine; camera (Technicolor), Harold Lipstein; editor, William Murphy; musical direction, Lionel Newman; song, Newman and Eliot Daniel. Previewed Jan. 8, '54. Running time, 77 MINS.

Rusty Blair	Mitzi Gaynor
Tony Ballew	Keefe Brasselle
Johnny Colt	Jeffrey Hunter
Jim Colt	Harvey Stephens
Sheriff Carter	Dan Riss
Apache Joe	Michael Ansara
Catur	Aaron Spelling
Jeff Blair	Morris Ankrum
Bill McAdoo	Frank Wilcox
Mrs. Colt	Helen Wallace
Thorpe	John Harmon
Tomas	Alex Montoya

Formula outdoor action in Technicolor is offered for the programmer market in "Three Young Texans." There's a casting emphasis on youth in the starring trio of Mitzi Gaynor, Keefe Brasselle and Jeffrey Hunter.

Film is Panoramic's second for 20th-Fox release and the outdoor accoutrements show up well in color to give the picture sight values that are considerably better than the story treatment, direction and most of the trouping. Plot per se is okay but neither direction nor writing make much of it. Dialog is very cliche. Of the starring trio only Hunter turns in a worthwhile performance, and without much help from either Henry Levin's direction or the screenplay by Gerald Drayson Adams.

Brasselle and Hunter are cowpokes on the ranch of Miss Gaynor's dad, Morris Ankrum, which lies on the Texas side of the Rio Grande. When Harvey Stephens, railroad telegrapher and father of Hunter, gets involved with some Mexican crooks, Hunter robs the train of a $50,000 Army payroll to prevent his dad from doing the same thing with the bad boys. He intends to return the money but Brasselle finds and re-hides it and from then on things are concerned with Hunter's trying to get it back and stay clear of the sheriff. Windup finds everyone forgiven, and Brasselle dead in the finale fight that wipes out the below-the-border bad men.

The baddies are portrayed by Michael Ansara, Aaron Spelling and Frank Wilcox in typical fashion. Dan Riss, as the sheriff, Stephens and Ankrum are among the character players who help the action when permitted.

"Just Let Me Love You," song by Lionel Newman, who did the musical direction, and Eliot Daniel is warbled by Vivian Marshall in a saloon sequence and there is a Latune spotted without credit in a Mexican cantino scene. Harold Lipstein gives the Leonard Goldstein excellent color lensing and the other technical credits are okay. *Brog.*

Crime Wave

Cops-and-robbers melodrama for general program datings.

Warner Bros. release of Bryan Foy production. Stars Sterling Hayden, Gene Nelson, Phyllis Kirk; features Ted de Corsia, Charles Buchinsky, Jay Novello, James Bell, Dubb Taylor, Gayle Kellogg, Mack Chandler. Directed by Andre de Toth. Screenplay, Crane Wilbur; adapted by Bernard Gordon and Richard Wormser from story by John and Ward Hawkins; camera, Bert Glennon; editor, Thomas Reilly; music, David Buttolph. Previewed June 30, '53. Running time, 73 MINS.

Det. Lieut. Sims	Sterling Hayden
Steve Lacey	Gene Nelson
Ellen	Phyllis Kirk
"Doc" Penny	Ted de Corsia
Hastings	Charles Buchinsky
"Dr." Otto Hessler	Jay Novello
Daniel O'Keefe	James Bell
Gus Snider	Dubb Taylor
Kelly	Gayle Kellogg
Sully	Mack Chandler
Johnny	Timothy Carey
Mark	Richard Benjamin

This cops-and-robbers melodrama will fill the demand for general program bookings, being suitable for top or bottom of the bill according to the situation. It is actionful and properly paced for the subject matter, although implausibly characterized.

Sterling Hayden, as a tough cop; Gene Nelson, a parolee trying to go straight, and Phyllis Kirk, his wife, topline in the Bryan Foy production and respond acceptably to the demands of Andre de Toth's direction. Hayden's character, and one or two of the hoods spotted in the plot, are overdrawn, but so is the story presentation, so the flamboyance is not too much out of place.

Script by Crane Wilbur stirs up a stock brew of situations and dialog. Nelson's parole is placed in jeopardy when three crooks escape from San Quentin and move in on him in Los Angeles. Ted de Corsia, trio leader, insists Nelson join in a bank heist and he apparently accepts to save his wife from the bad boys. When the job comes off, the police are on hand, the crooks are wiped out and Nelson gets a stern lecture from toothpick-chewing Hayden about calling in the law when things go wrong, rather than attempting to handle tough situations unaided.

There's nothing original about the mobster types created, nor much freshness in the directorial handling, but for the booking level at which the film is slanted the tough action is okay. Among the characters on the wrong side of the law giving Nelson trouble are de Corsia, Charles Buchinsky, Jay Novello and Timothy Carey, the latter a ludicrously frightening psycho in whose custody Miss Kirk is placed during the bank holdup. James Bell is the most natural player as the parole officer.

Picture was adapted by Bernard Gordon and Richard Wormser from a Satevepost story by John and Ward Hawkins. Bert Glennon's lensing is low-key and expert and the editing by Thomas Reilly is a trim 73 minutes. *Brog.*

Drums of Tahiti
(3-D—COLOR)

Tiresome 3-D South Seas adventure tale, long on talk, short on action.

Hollywood, Dec. 22.

Columbia release of Sam Katzman production. Stars Dennis O'Keefe, Patricia Medina; features Francis L. Sullivan. Directed by William Castle. Screenplay, Douglas Heyes, Robert E. Kent; from a story by Kent; camera (Technicolor), Lester H. White; editor, Jerome Thoms. Previewed Dec. 18, '53. Running time, 73 MINS.

Mike Macklin	Dennis O'Keefe
Wanda Spence	Patricia Medina
Pierre Duvois	Francis L. Sullivan
Angelo	George Keymas
Mawaii	Sylvia Lewis
Gay Knight	Cicely Browne
Shoreham	Raymond Lawrence

Seventy minutes of banal talk and three minutes of action just about sums up "Drums of Tahiti," a tiresome South Seas adventure feature in 3-D and color. The tints are good, the depth treatment okay, but any other possible plus factors are missing. It will just get by in programmer bookings.

Dennis O'Keefe and Patricia Medina, both likeable performers, are wasted in the star spots, as is the Technicolor commitment. The plotting is very involved and completely skips logic as it spins a hackneyed tale about an American who buys a bride in San Francisco to conceal the fact he is smuggling in a shipment of guns to be used to drive the French out of Tahiti. Period is 1877, although some of the props in the picture aren't.

Francis L. Sullivan is the island's prefect of police matching wits with O'Keefe. All he is required to do is to spot long passages of dialog while acting like a jovial, but smart, Frenchman. None of the unfortunate principals involved, however, is as smart as the weather and mother nature. A tropic hurricane and an erupting volcano take care of the guns, effectively smashing the proposed revolution so that O'Keefe, his purchased bride, Miss Medina, and Sullivan can continue their conversational relations on a friendly basis.

George Keymas plays a henchman on O'Keefe's schooner. Sylvia Lewis is a shapely island dancer whose curves look good in 3-D. Cicely Browne is a Barbary Coast friend who helps in the hero's marriage to Miss Medina. Frances Brandt does the island queen and Raymond Lawrence is the island's British representative.

The volcano eruption and hurricane that occupy approximately three minutes of footage are okay technical effects in the Sam Katzman production. William Castle's direction faced the impossible task of making something out of the script by Douglas Heyes and Robert E. Kent, based on a story by Kent. Lester H. White's photography and the other technical assists are okay.

Brog.

L'Envers du Paradis
(Other Side of Paradise)
(FRENCH)

Paris, Jan. 5.

Columbia release of Pafico production. Stars Eric Von Stroheim; features Etchika Choureau. Written and directed by Edmond T. Greville. Camera, L. H. Burel; editor, J. Feyte. At Alhambra, Paris. Running time, **100 MINS.**

O'Hara .... Eric Von Stroheim
Violaine .... Etchika Choureau
Blaise .... Jacques Sernas
Michele .... Dora Doll
Inspector .... Jacques Castelot
Countess .... Denice Vernac

Film is an offbeat entry that exerts interest in its locale and strange assortment of characters in a little southern French town. Though motivations are intriguing, this falls into melodrama because of the narrative style of the pic. This has the name of Eric Von Stroheim for possible dualer or special slotting for the US, but lacks the force and cohesion for any heavier dates.

This concerns a strangely assorted group of characters holed up in an isolated hilltop city in the Riviera district of France. There is an old sea captain, who has never been to sea and lives in an alcoholic reverie of an uncertain past; a countess who has nightly parties and shows porno pix at her villa; a young writer and his alcoholic wife, and a young tubercular girl who has a love in her life before dying. Production subordinates these colorful people to a whodunit style of unfoldment when the wife of the young writer is killed while the alcoholic captain, the sick young girl and the writer confess the deed.

Director-writer Edmond T. Greville has not been consistent with himself, and direction has a tendency to take short cuts and play off forced suspense to the detriment of the central theme. Location lensing benefits the production value. Von Stroheim brings a touch of poignance to his strange role of sea captain. Etchika Choureau emerges as the outstanding young find of the season in a beguiling, innocent portrayal of a dreamy young adolescent at grips with love and death. Remainder of cast is adequate, with lensing good and editing helping to keep the involved proceedings coherent.

Mosk.

Spice of Life
(French)

Arthur Mayer Edward Kingsley release of Gaumont Cinemaphonic production. Stars Noel-Noel; features Bernard Blier, Jean Tissier. Directed by Jean Dreville. Screenplay, Noel-Noel; camera, Louis Burel; editor, Jean Featy. At 55th Street Playhouse, N.Y., starting Dec. 28, '53. Running time, **72 MINS.**

(In French; English Titles)

French comic Noel-Noel does virtually a one-man show in "Spice of Life" as he gives a lecture on variegated types of public and private bores. He is always the man encountering these bores or pests excepting in one instance. Many of the pestiferous characters he points up are so exaggerated they become caricatures. Picture can cut no swath at the American boxoffice because this droll type of humor will mean little except at a few, smaller, arty theatres.

With Moliere as his inspiration, Noel-Noel tries to bridge the gap between his gallery of pests with trick camera work, odd gadgets and a lecture podium which provides the rack on which to air his pet peeves. There's the practical joker, the femme who drives an auto badly, the friend who always phones at dinner-time, the hail-fellow-well-met greeter who is such a bore Noel-Noel tries to avoid him in the street, the stranger he meets in a barroom who acts like he knows him (but whom he can't place), the moisture-spluttering acquaintance he encounters in the subway and the gesturing talker who dramatizes his story while walking down the street. Bernard Blier is the only outside character of consequence. He is the man who plans an elaborate tryst only to have it broken up by a plumber and a talky friend (Jean Tissier).

A trick blackboard writes automatically as the lecturer (Noel-Noel) outlines a specific type of pest. It prankishly suggests that the lecturer might be some sort of a bore. And that's about the way it turns out after 40-minutes. More or less the same idea has been done several times previously in U. S. shorts, possibly with more adroitness, and in English. There are some puppet and cartoon passages but they amount to little. Camera work of Louis Burel is topflight, but almost wasted on such a trivial subject.

This feature film won a couple of French prizes, presumably several years back since this obviously was produced two or three years ago.

Wear.

It Should Happen to You

Judy Holliday toplining slick, big city, comedy; excellent prospects.

Hollywood, Jan. 12.

Columbia release of Fred Kohlmar production. Stars Judy Holliday; co-stars Peter Lawford; introduces Jack Lemmon; features Michael O'Shea, Vaughn Taylor, Connie Gilchrist, Walter Klavun, Whit Bissell and guest panelists Constance Bennett, Ilka Chase, Wendy Barrie, Melville Cooper. Directed by George Cukor. Story and screenplay, Garson Kanin; camera, Charles Lang; editor, Charles Nelson; score, Frederick Hollander; musical director, Morris Stolhoff. Previewed Oct. 29, '53. Running time, **86 MINS.**

Gladys Glover .... Judy Holliday
Evan Adams, III .... Peter Lawford
Pete Sheppard .... Jack Lemmon
Brod Clinton .... Michael O'Shea
Entrikin .... Vaughn Taylor
Mrs. Riker .... Connie Gilchrist
Bert Piazza .... Walter Klavun
Scur Man .... Heywood Hale Broun

A generous helping of fun for the payees is projected in this very slick comedy toplining Judy Holliday. She is reunited with director George Cukor and scripter Garson Kanin, a trio that clicked big with "Born Yesterday," and the reunion is all to the good for the customers. The boxoffice prospects are excellent, particularly in the key runs.

The laugh range in the smooth Fred Kohlmar production is from soft titters to loud guffaws as Cukor's smartly timed direction sends the players through hilarious situations. Plot is about a small town girl who comes to the big city to make a name for herself. Right there story familiarity stops. Fresh angles belt the risibilities while dialog is adult, almost racy at times.

As the Gladys Glover of the plot, Miss Holliday has a romp for herself, and she gets major assists in the comedy from Peter Lawford, Jack Lemmon, the latter making his major screen bow, Michael O'Shea and the others in the cast.

Gladys has a different angle to flashing her name in the best places. With her meager savings she rents a signboard on Columbus Circle and has her name emblazoned thereon. This quest for fame sets off a lot of repercussions. She becomes a television celebrity under the tutoring of promoter O'Shea, endorses all manner of goods, signs autographs and generally is acclaimed by the mob which blindly figures she must be someone important. During all the excitement she is pursued romantically by Lawford, head of a soap company, whose real purpose behind the amor is to get the Columbus Circle sign to ballyhoo his own products. Also in the amatory chase is Lemmon, poor but honest maker of documentary films, who has a hard time keeping his romance with the new celebrity on even keel. True love triumphs, however, after the customers' funnybones have had just about all the punishment they can stand.

Miss Holliday posing for photographic art on a pair of skis, participating in a military ceremony, or fighting off Lawford's wolfish advances is sheer fun. So are her fights with Lemmon, posturing for a worshipping public or giving a stilted reading of a her fame story on tv. Lemmon scores strongly in his film appearance, farcing to a fare-thee-well without forcing. Lawford comes over well as the conceited wolf and O'Shea is good as the sharpie out for a quick buck. Seen briefly as video panelists are Constance Bennett, Ilka Chase, Wendy Barrie and Melville Cooper.

On the technical end, the picture has been slickly mounted to show off the story and players. Charles Lang's photography is very good. Jean Louis' costumes for Miss Holliday are extremely smart. The score by Frederick Hollander, directed by Morris Stoloff, gives the comedy mood an assist. Editing and other credits are top grade.

Brog.

The Command
(COLOR)

First CinemaScope feature western. Guy Madison and strong boxoffice outlook.

Warner Bros. release of David Weisbart production. Stars Guy Madison, Joan Weldon, James Whitmore; features Carl Benton Reid, Harvey Lembeck, Ray Teal, Bob Nichols, Don Shelton. Directed by David Butler. Screenplay, Russell Hughes; adaptation, Samuel Fuller; from a SatEvePost novel by James Warner Bellah; camera (WarnerColor), Wilfrid M. Cline; editor, Irene Morra; score, Dimitri Tiomkin; musical direction, Ray Heindorf. Previewed Jan. 13, '54. Running time, **94 MINS.**

Capt. MacClaw .... Guy Madison
Martha .... Joan Weldon
Sgt. Elliot .... James Whitmore
Col. Janeway .... Carl Benton Reid
Gottschalk .... Harvey Lembeck
Dr. Trent .... Ray Teal
O'Hirons .... Bob Nichols
Major Gibbs .... Don Shelton
Capt. Forsythe .... Gregg Barton
Cpl. Fleming .... Boyd "Red" Morgan
Mr. Pellegrini .... Zachary Yaconelli
Mrs. Pellegrini .... Renata Vanni
Trooper Nikirk .... Tom Monroe

As the first feature western entry under the CinemaScope label, "The Command" has an edge in the outdoor market and should roll up important grosses. In addition to the ticket sale strength it gains from the anamorphic lensing, its chances are further helped by a fundamentally sound cavalry-versus-Indians plot and highly charged action footage.

Actually, the picture was lensed under the brand of the anamorphic process originally known as Vistarama—later as WarnerScope. With Warners' subsequent tieup with 20th-Fox for CinemaScope, it was decided to send the film out with the Westwood label. All anamorphics have a 2.66 to one ratio so the only difference in results comes from the quality of the lense used.

In "Command," picture clarity is lacking in many scenes except for center screen, but as attention is concentrated there the fuzziness around the edges is of little consequence to the entertainment. Where squeeze-lensing plays its big part is in the finale 11-minute running fight between Indians and a wagon train, the sequence gains great impact as the action spreads across the wide screen, virtually making participants of an audience. It's the best such scene since the stagecoach-Indians brawl in "Stagecoach."

Guy Madison, who had 3-D as a big peg for his Warners debut in "Charge at Feather River," gets another break because of the anamorphic treatment on his second starring western. Two such starts give him a strong shove upwards. He turns in a thoroughly able job of the heroics under David Butler's direction. Latter handles the Russell Hughes screenplay expertly for action, particularly in the latter half when the film takes on more movement, and his staging of the climax is a humdinger.

Madison is an Army medical captain unexpectedly assuming command of a cavalry troop after its regular commander is killed. Story is concerned with how he improvises battle tactics to defeat attacking Indians, wins the respect of his men and saves a wagon train, as well as two companies of infantry, before the action curtain is rung down. Plot is from James Warner Bellah's SatEvePost novel, as adapted by Samuel Fuller.

David Weisbart's production supervision is good in the use of the cast, outdoor accoutrements and action values. All are put together in a manner that will please the western fan, as well as offering rugged entertainment for others. Joan Weldon is practically the only femme of importance in the east, doing nicely as a practical nurse with the wagon train. Her character, as well as the others, are more or less to type, but perfectly suitable to the pioneer action. James Whitmore does well by his role of tough sergeant, as do Harvey Lambeck, griping trooper; Carl Benton Reid, explosive infantry commander; Ray Teal, Bob Nichols, Don Shelton and the others.

Wilfrid M. Cline handles the WarnerColor cameras for bold action effect as well as pictorial sweep, sharpening the picture's visual impact. Dimitri Tiomkin has tuned a robust score to the action, helping the fast movement, and it has been directed by Ray Heindorf for the best blending with plot development. Stereophonic sound is very good in the running action sequences, but of little value elsewhere. *Brog.*

Jivaro
(COLOR)

Okay adventure fare for general runs favoring escapist entertainment, with Fernando Lamas and Rhonda Fleming for marquee dressing.

Hollywood, Jan. 18.

Paramount release of a Pine-Thomas production. Stars Fernando Lamas, Rhonda Fleming; co-stars Brian Keith. Directed by Edward Ludwig. Screenplay, Winston Miller; story, David Duncan; camera, Lionel Lindon; editor, Howard Smith; music, Gregory Stone. Previewed Jan. 13, '54. Running time, **93 MINS.**

Rio	Fernando Lamas
Alice Parker	Rhonda Fleming
Tony	Brien Keith
Pedro	Lon Chaney
Jerry Russell	Richard Denning
Maroa	Rita Moreno
Kovanti	Marvin Miller
Vinny	Morgan Farley
Sylvester	Pascual Pena
Jacque	Nestor Paiva
Padre	Charles Lung
Edwards	Gregg Barton
Umari	Kay Johnson
Native Woman	Rosa Turich
Sylvester's Wife	Marian Mostick
Locket Native	Richard Bartell
Indian Girl	Eugenia Paul

This adventure yarn, colored with action and romance in a South American setting, will stack up okay in the general runs, particuarly for the escapist trade. Film's fictional story line provides a picturesque backdrop, and its 93 minutes of showy Technicolor footage is enhanced by names of Fernando Lamas and Rhonda Fleming for marquee voltage.

The producers, William H. Pine and William C. Thomas, have accorded feature, which takes its tag from name of a tribe of head hunters, with their usual brand of values which have paid off in the past, even sending a camera crew to the Amazon for background shots. Direction by Edward Ludwig is rugged enough to overcome the stereotyped aspects of plot, and his use of the Amazon footage contributes to the melodramatic effect.

The romantic adventuring concerns Lamas, a tough South American who operates a jungle trading post not far distant from the Jivaro country, and Miss Fleming, who arrives from California to wed the fiance she hasn't seen in two years. Unwilling to disillusion gal that the man she thinks is a rubber plantation owner actually has turned into a drunken drifter intent on finding a gold treasure hidden in forbidden Jivaro territory, Lamas finds himself falling for femme. When it's heard that fiance and a party been killed by Indians, Lamas, accompanied by heroine and others who want the gold, goes in search of the missing treasure-seekers, and barely gets back with femme after being attacked by Jivaros.

Lamas projects his hard-hitting character successfully, and Miss Fleming, beautiful in tints, is an acceptable heroine, benefitting by some slick closeups. Co-starred is an interesting newcomer, Brian Keith, who brawls with Lamas in a couple of fights after going on the make for femme. Pascual Pena as Lamas' Indian assistant is a brief standout, and Richard Denning, the fiance, and Lon Chaney, another trader, also have a few good moments.

Technical departments are well handled, Lionel Lindon's color photography and art direction by Hal Pereira and Earl Hedrick the most effective. *Will.*

Boy From Oklahoma
(COLOR)

Folksy, humorous western with Will Rogers Jr., Nancy Olson. Entertaining filmfare for oats market.

Hollywood, Jan. 14.

Warrer Bros. release of David Weisbart production. Stars Will Rogers, Jr., Nancy Olson; features Lon Chaney, Anthony Caruso, Wallace Ford, Clem Bevans, Merv Griffin. Directed by Michael Curtiz. Screenplay, Frank Davis, Winston Miller; from a SatEvePost story by Michael Fessier; camera (WarnerColor), Robert Burks; editor, James Moore; music, Max Steiner. Previewed Jan. 11, '54. Running time, **87 MINS.**

Tom Brewster	Will Rogers, Jr.
Katie Brannigan	Nancy Olson
Crazy Charlie	Lon Chaney
Barney Turlock	Anthony Caruso
Wally Higgins	Wallace Ford
Pop Pruty	Clem Bevans
Steve	Merv Griffin
Paul Evans	Louis Jean Heydt
Pete Martin	Sheb Wooley
Shorty	Slim Pickens
Billy the Kid	Tyler MacDuff
Johnny Neil	Skippy Torgerson
Joe Downey	James Griffith
Harry	Charles Watts

This is a folksy, humorous western reminiscent of some of the old Will Rogers starrers, although not as broad, and it should prove entertaining filmfare in the feature oater market. Will Rogers Jr., takes to the treatment in good style, as does his co-star Nancy Olson, and both will be liked.

A competent job of bringing out the best points of the presentation is done under David Weisbart's production guidance and the WarnerColor tints add to the visual attraction of the outdoor values. Michael Curtiz' direction is a decided assist to the manner in which the story and players come off, his handling developing humor to counterpoint the thriller action with a touch that is just right.

The script by Frank Davis and Winston Miller, from a SatEvePost story by Michael Fessier, shows what happens to Rogers when he drifts through a small western town and dallies long enough to become sheriff, solve a murder, bust up a bad gang and win himself a girl. Plot gimmick is that he's a peaceable man who doesn't carry a gun and has to have at his heroics with only a lariat and a prayer. Both stand him in good stead, as does a native shrewdness that helps him best the baddies, even when the odds are might uneven. Deft handling in all departments keeps the doings on a believable level.

Rogers Jr.'s homespun playing carbon's his late father's to some extent, although, as noted, not so broadly, and his physical likeness to the parent should jog the memories of the oldsters. Miss Olson dons the range wear; the part requires attractively and counts in helping Rogers show to advantage. Lon Chaney has only one scene, that of the town drunk gone beserk, and he makes it register strongly.

Anthony Caruso, leader of the town crooks, is excellent, and the picture has further acting assists from Wallace Ford, Clem Bevans, Louis Jean Heydt, Sheb Wooley, Slim Pickens and, in particular, James Griffith. Latter hasn't much to say but is noticed in every scene.

Robert Burks handles his color cameras well and the score by Max Steiner is apt to the western plotting. Technical assists are competent. *Brog.*

Taza, Son of Cochise
(2-D, 3-D-COLOR)

Beautifully photographed Indian-U. S. Cavalry actioner okay for general runs.

Hollywood, Jan. 19.

Universal-International release of a Ross Hunter production. Stars Rock Hudson, Barbara Rush; features Gregg Palmer, Bart Roberts, Morris Ankrum, Gene Iglesias. Directed by Douglas Sirk. Screenplay, George Zuckerman; story-adaptation, Gerald Drayson Adams; camera, Russell Metty; editor, Milton Carruth; music, Frank Skinner. Previewed Jan. 15, '54. Running time, **79 MINS.**

Taza	Rock Hudson
Oona	Barbara Rush
Captain Burnett	Gregg Palmer
Naiche	Bart Roberts
Grey Eagle	Morris Ankrum
Chato	Gene Iglesias
Cy Hegan	Richard Cutting
Geronimo	Ian MacDonald
General Crook	Robert Burton
Sgt. Hamma	Joe Sawyer
Lt. Willis	Lance Fuller
Lt. Richards	Brad Jackson
Skinya	James Van Horn
Kocha	Charles Horvath
Lobo	Robert Hoy
Location Bit	Barbara Burck
Tiswin Charlie	Dan White

Following in the type of outdoor feature UI has found acceptable in general runs, "Taza, Son of Cochise" is a colorful Indian-U.S. Cavalry entry alternating between hot action and passages of almost pastoral quality which can expect okay grosses. Name of Rock Hudson will help it through all situations.

Beautifully lensed in Technicolor, this Ross Hunter production will be released in either 2-D or 3-D, dependant upon wishes of the exhib. In either medium film can stand on its own, effective use being made of the latter to provide some legitimate thrills. The spectacular scenery of Moab, Utah, furnishes a particularly apropos background for unfoldment of the George Zuckerman script, and Douglas Sirk's direction is forceful, aimed at making every scene an eye-filling experience.

This is the story of the great Apache chief's son, who promises at his father's deathbed he will try to keep the peace that Cochise so painstakingly made with the whites. He is opposed here by his younger brother, who attempts to win the tribe over to Geronimo and take to the warpath again. When Geronimo comes to the San Carlos reservation, where Taza captains an Apache police force, for temporary haven, the brother and Geronimo plot a giant break with guns purchased from a renegade trader. They nearly wipe out a column of pursuing cavalry, headed by Gen. Crook, before Taza and his own Apaches show up and restore peace to the territory.

Rock Hudson suffices in action demands of his role of Taza, but character is none too believable. Barbara Rush, co-starring as the daughter of Morris Ankrum, one of Geronimo's followers, is in for romantic purposes and handles part well. Gregg Palmer is strongly cast as a cavalry captain who strikes up a friendship with Taza; Bart Roberts is the fractious brother and Ian MacDonald plays Geronimo with a sneer. Jeff Chandler, who was Cochise in studio's "Battle at Apache Pass," repeats character for the single death-bed scene, without screen credit. Balance of cast is stock.

Russell Metty's color camera work stands out among the technical credits, and Bernard Herzbrun and Emrich Nicholson's art direction catches the flavor intended. Frank Skinner's music score, too, strikes the right note. *Whit.*

Riders to the Stars
(COLOR)

Intelligently - turned - out science-fictioner which may be exploited for satisfactory returns.

Hollywood, Jan.15.

United Artists release of an Ivan Tors production. Stars Lundigan, Herbert Marshall, Richard Carlson, Martha Hyer, Down Addams. Directed by Richard Carlson. Screenplay, Curt Siodmak; camera, Stanley Cortez; editor, Herbert L. Strock; music, Harry Sukman. Previewed Jan. 14, '54. Running time, **80 MINS.**

Richard Stanton	William Lundigan
Dr. Donald Stanton	Herbert Marshall
Jerry Lockwood	Richard Carlson
Jane Flynn	Martha Hyer
Susan Manners	Dawn Addams
Walter Gordan	Robert Karnes
Dr. Delmar	Lawrence Dobkin
Dr. Drayden	George Eldredge
Dr. Warner	Dan Riss
Dr. Klinger	Michael Fox
Mr. O'Herli	King Donovan
Kenneth Wells	Kem Dibbs
Sidney Fuller	James K. Best
Archibald Guiness	John Hedloe

Exploitation aspects of this science-fiction entry are high, its imaginative subject being given expert treatment right down the line. Followers of this type of film will find it intelligently handled and it stands a good chance to rack up better-than-average returns in both the exploitation and general program field. Film would benefit, however, by tighter editing, to eliminate conversational drags and snap up the action.

Major premise of the Curt Siodmak original, revolving around a rocket ship flying into space and capturing a meteor in flight, is carefully developed into a legitimate story, which Richard Carlson, also co-starred, directs in knowhow style for slick entertainment. Effect is considerably heightened by Color Corporation of America's above average tints, vitalizing the action visually as well as emotionally.

When Government technicians recover fragments of a rocket which hurtled into the sky at 18,000 m.p.h., pieces of the most refined steel which crumble because of crystallization, they realize they must devise some sort of shield to protect space travel against bombardments of cosmic rays. They plan to accomplish this by capturing meteors flying 150 miles above the earth, performed by specially constructed rocket ships flying a few miles faster than meteors travelling 18,000 m.p.h. which scoop them into a compartment in nose of the ship. Meteors then will be returned to earth for study before they are burned away by air-friction.

William Lundigan plays a young flyer-scientist chosen to handle one of the ships, and Carlson and Robert Karns two others. Narrative shows them being trained for the job, and finally their takeoff to pursue approaching meteors. Lundigan is successful in a thrilling climax, but the other two are lost, Carlson when his ship goes off course and shoots out into space, Karns when his ship disintegrates.

Cast generally is competent, with Lundigan most outstanding in a persuasive role. He generates romantic interest with Martha Hyer, scientist-assistant to Herbert Marshall, Lundigan's father and head of the dangerous scientific experiment. Both present excellent performances, and also giving good accounts of themselves are Carlson and Karnes, Dawn Addams in a brief appearance as a model, Lawrence Dobkin, George Eldredge and Dan Riss.

Ivan Tors provides slick production mounting. On the technical end, Stanley Cortez' color photography is impressive, Jerome Pycha, Jr.'s art direction atmospheric and Harry Sukman's musical score suitable. *Whit.*

Jubilee Trail
(SONGS—COLOR)

Pretentious pioneer feature in color, with sufficient action exploitation pegs to shape well for regular Republic market.

Hollywood, Jan. 15.

Republic release of Joseph Inman Kane production. Stars Vera Ralston, Joan Leslie, Forrest Tucker, John Russell, Ray Middleton, Pat O'Brien; features Buddy Baer, Jim Davis, Barton MacLane, Richard Webb. Directed by Kane. Screenplay, Bruce Manning; based on the novel by Gwen Bristow; camera (Trucolor), Jack Marta; editor, Richard L. Van Enger; music, Victor Young; songs, Young, Sidney Clare, Gwen Bristow. Previewed Jan. 13, '54. Running time, **103 MINS.**

Florinda	Vera Ralston
Garnet	Joan Leslie
John Ives	Forrest Tucker
Oliver Hale	John Russell
Charles Hale	Ray Middleton
Texas	Pat O'Brien
Handsome Brute	Buddy Baer
Silky	Jim Davis
Bartlett	Barton MacLane
Captain Brown	Richard Webb
Rinardi	James Millican
Dona Manuela	Nina Varela
Don Rafael Velasco	Martin Garralaga
Pablo	Charles Stevens
Whitey	Jack Elam

A pretentious epic of the pioneer west, "Jubilee Trail" spends more time sprawling over its lengthy 103 minutes than in the brawling action it needs to sustain complete interest. However, it is furbished with enough exploitation pegs to give it good prospects in the Republic market.

Film is dressed in Trucolor hues, and they are very good, particularly in the outdoor scenes. Other physical values of the presentation are excellent, too, but the creditable points are rather lost in a rambling screenplay that dwells too often on talky, static sequences. Bruce Manning scripted from Gwen Bristow's novel of the same title, and uses more of the tome's material than is good for quick-moving motion picture purposes. Result is loss of clarity.

Generally, the conflict is a family one. John Russell has married Joan Leslie, an act that upsets his older brother, Ray Middleton, who had dreamed of adding to his California lands by marrying Russell into a native family. Shortly after Russell and bride arrive at the old homestead, the groom is killed and Miss Leslie moves into Los Angeles to have her baby. Thereafter Middleton makes spasmodic appearances on the scene trying to get the baby and is finally killed by Pat O'Brien, drunken old doc who is lying on his own death bed. During all this Miss Leslie has picked up a new suitor, Forrest Tucker, and he's around for the finale clinch to edge out Richard Webb, another suitor who seeks to marry the pretty widow. Mixed in as a friend of Miss Leslie's is Vera Ralston, saloon singer who has fled a New York murder rap.

Of the six billed as stars of the picture, Miss Leslie and Tucker show to the most advantage, the femme being particularly moving and sincere, as well as comely. Four songs fall to Miss Ralston's character and they include the title number, on which Buddy Baer, a character pursuing the singer, joins. "Clap Your Hands," "A Man Is a Man" and "Saying No." Sidney Clare and Victor Young did the cleffing, with Miss Bristow aiding the lyrics on the latter. Young also composed and conducted the background score.

As associate producer-director, Joe Kane moves the picture slowly over most of the way, although belting the few action sequences with a good punch. He could have used more such moments. Jack Marta's lensing is on the credit side, as are the settings and costumes. Editing leaves much to be desired. *Brog.*

Go, Man, Go
(SONG)

Sports drama starring Harlem Globetrotters with okay chances in program field.

Hollywood, Jan. 14.

United Artists release of Anton M. Leader production. Stars the Harlem Globetrotters and Dane Clark; features Patricia Breslin, Sidney Poitier. Directed by James Wong Howe. Original screenplay, Arnold Becker; camera, Bill Steiner; editor, Faith Elliott; score composed and conducted by Alex North; song, Sy Oliver and Mike Shore. Previewed Jan. 12, '54. Running time, **82 MINS.**

Abe Saperstein	Dane Clark
Sylvia Saperstein	Pat Breslin
Inman Jackson	Sidney Poitier
Zack Leader	Edmon Ryan
James Willoughby	Bram Nossen
Papa Saperstein	Anatol Winogradoff
Mama Saperstein	Celia Boodkin
Fay Saperstein	Carol Sinclair
Sam	Ellsworth Wright
Slim	Slim Gaillard
Ticket Seller	Frieda Altman
MC	Mort Marshall
Secretary	Jean Shore
1st Bathing Beauty	Jule Benedic
2nd Bathing Beauty	Jerry Hauer
Announcers	Marty Glickman, Bill Stern
Appraiser	Lew Hearn
Irma Jackson	Ruby Dee

and
The Harlem Globetrotters
as Themselves

The Harlem Globetrotters have another go at motion picture stardom in "Go, Man, Go," and just as they are the big attraction in basketball, so will they be the sales point for this United Artists release. Slightly more than two years ago Columbia released "The Harlem Globetrotters" and it did well in its field. There's no apparent reason why this one should not enjoy a similar popularity in the program market.

The production by Anton M. Leader tackles the story from the angle of Abe Saperstein's long fight to make a place in organized basketball for his all-Negro team. While the concentration is on the coach's dedicated drive, James Wong Howe's able direction does not neglect those parts of the film for which the public will pay — the incredible feats of the team as it shows its mastery of the game and the showmanly touches that contribute to its enormous draw. In fact, the footage could have used even more scenes of the hoopsters in action. There's a storybook finale in which the "Trotters" win their first league tournament in the final minutes of play, exciting action enough for most any sports or film fan.

Dane Clark portrays Saperstein in the original screenplay by Arnold Becker and gets over the motivations of the characters rather well. Plot shows the hard going of years of barnstorming before the team was able to force the big leagues to take notice of it. That a good portion of the problems had to do with race is put over in the picture without direct mention or soapboxing of minority theme. Outside of the scenes of the hoopsters in action, one interesting phase of the plot shows how they adopted the clowning that made them big boxoffice. A shoestring operation didn't permit many substitute players, so each teammate would show off his specialty for several minutes in each quarter while the others rested — all the time keeping the ball in play.

Pat Breslin is charming as Sylvia Saperstein, the girl who married the basketball zealot. Sidney Poitier is good as Inman Jackson, an original "Trotter" star who sticks with the coach through all the trouble. Also acceptable are Edmon Ryan, sportswriter; Bram Nossen, principal heavy as the big-leaguer opposing the Negro team's entry into organized basketball; Anatol Winogradoff, Celia Boodkin, Ruby Dee and, of course, the Globetrotters themselves. Slim Gaillard is spotted to give some voyt to the Sy Oliver-Mike Shore title tune during a party sequence.

Bill Steiner's lensing is excellent in catching the excitement of court play. Some of the camera angles would seem to wear the Howe trademark for filming sports. Alex North's score is topnotch, emphasizing a rhythmic jazz mood that fits with the Globetrotter personality. This is particularly noticeable in his treatment of "Sweet Georgia Brown" whenever the stars are clowning. *Brog.*

The Cowboy
(SONGS-COLOR)

Arrestingly lensed documentary on the American cowboy not quite qualifying as art house material. Best suited as off-beat supporter for feature western bills.

Hollywood, Dec. 31.

Lippert Pictures release of documentary produced, directed, photographed (Eastern Color) by Elmo Williams. Written by Lorraine Williams; told by Tex Ritter, Bill Conrad, John Dehner, Larry Dobkin; editor, Williams; technical advise, ~~Ole Bill~~ Fraker; songs, Axel Johnson and Lorraine Williams; sung by Ritter and Curly Wiggins; music composed and conducted by Carl Brandt. Previewed Dec. 29, '53. Running time, **68 MINS.**

The life and times of the American cowboy are documented in this special production made by Elmo Williams for Lippert Pictures release. While there are some situations where it might be sold as a special art subject, it doesn't quite qualify as sureseater material and it will find its best level as an offbeat supporter for feature western bills.

Williams, who last year won an Oscar for his editing on "High Noon," turns producer, director, editor and cameraman with "The Cowboy" to document the rise of the legendary western symbol. While his handling on the first three functions is commendable, it is on the lensing that the picture is really outstanding. Photographed in Eastman Color, the scenes are arresting in composition and pictorial sweep, having much of the flavor of such master painters of the old west as Remington.

The simple narrative, written by Williams, goes back to the days of the early west to show how the cowboy started, his duties then, through the years, and now. Range lore has always held a fascination for a goodly portion of male filmgoers and this production caters to that fascination with a solid authenticity as Williams pokes his cameras at selected sites and types in Mexico, New Mexico, Arizona and Texas.

The narration is realistic as spoken by Tex Ritter, Bill Conrad, John Dehner and Larry Dobkin. Furthering the western feel are songs by Axel Johnson and Lorraine Williams. "The Meadowlark" and "Cowboy Saturday Night" are sung by Curly Wiggins, while Ritter sings "Dodge City Trail." The background score is another of the picture's strong points, the cleffing and conducting by Carl Brandt catching the range mood. Williams could have used his editorial shears for further tightening of some scenes, but the fans of cowboy lore will not quarrel with their length. *Brog.*

Quand Tu Liras Cette Lettre
(WHEN YOU READ THIS LETTER)
(FRENCH)

Paris, Jan. 12.

Marceau release of Titanus-Jad-Lux production. Stars Juliette Greco, Philippe Lemaire. Directed by Jean-Pierrre Melville. Screenplay, Jacques Deval; camera, Henri Alekan; editor, Marinette Cadiz. At Francais, Paris. Running time, **100 MINS.**

Therese	Juliette Greco
Max	Philippe Lemaire
Denise	Irene Galter
Irene	Yvonne Sanson
Mâmie	Claude Borelli
Barman	Robert Dalban
Bellhop	Daniel Cauchy

Measured pace of this film makes it seem pretentious instead of giving it the drive that the essentially hardboiled story demands. Story of the love affair between an avaricious skirt chaser and a would-be nun is given a weighty symbolic treatment that does not ring true because the character-drawing is vague. This looks to be in for fair biz here, but for the U. S. its chances are slim. Sole value would be in special spots, with exploitation possible.

Philippe Lemaire, a young mechanic who preys on women, encounters Juliette Greco, a novice in a convent who has gone back to secular life to care for her young sister, Irene Gatter. He forcefully seduces the young girl. Miss Greco forces him into proposing to the girl at the point of a gun. He falls in love with Miss Greco and finally talks her into leaving with him. An ironic twist has Lemaire falling under the train in a banal accident which ends the film.

Jean-Pierre Melville's heavy-handed direction puts too much emphasis on the depth of character which is not inherent. The monotoned speaking, the overemphatic character insistence, and too many symbolic incidents cut into the meaty portions of the narra-

tive. Miss Greco, the ex-existentialist singer, here essays the role of the future nun with too much grimness, but is telling in the later dramatic portions. Lemaire overdoes the vile villain, and by the time regeneration begins it is difficult to see what the army of femmes sees in this shallow puppet. Miss Galter and Yvonne Sanson are fine as the young innocent and the sensual woman of the world, respectively. Henri Alekan gives this well-contrasted lensing.
Mosk.

L'Ennemi Public No. 1
(Public Enemy No. 1)
(FRENCH)

Paris, Jan. 12.

Cocinor release of Cite Films-Fides-Peg production. Stars Fernandel; features Zsa Zsa Gabor, Jean Marchat, David Opatoshu. Directed by Henri Verneuil. Screenplay, Jean Manse, Michel Audiard from story by Max Favalelli; dialog, Audiard; music, Raymond Legrand, Nino Rota; camera, Armand Thirard; editor, Christian Gaudin. At Marignan, Paris. Running time, **110 MINS.**

Joe Calvet .... Fernandel
Lola .... Zsa Zsa Gabor
Peggy .... Nicole Maurey
Sheriff .... Alfred Adam
Attorney .... Jean Marchat
W. W. Stone .... Saturnin Fabre
Slim .... David Opatoshu
Parker .... Tino Buazelli
Warden .... Louis Seigner

This is the film which saw the crew and stars going to N. Y. for the exteriors, but any other resemblance between this and a U. S. gangster film or parody is purely coincidental. The idea of an insignificant type taken for a public enemy is not new and this adds no refreshing touches to this type of parody. As is, this will do well here on the Fernandel monicker. For the U. S., it would make a good programmer with Fernandel and Zsa Zsa Gabor names. This is out for arties.

Story has Fernandel as a near-sighted demonstrator of sporting equipment in a big N. Y. department store. When the manager insists that he take off his glasses he practically wrecks the store and is fired. He gets the wrong raincoat in a film theatre. It turns out to belong to a killer, and there is a gun in the pocket. He loses his glasses and takes out the gun in a subway which leads to his arrest. The police tag him as the leader of a big gang and the moll of the gang passing him off as the real leader to allay suspicions of the mob from the mysterious unknown leader. From there on, it follows the expected pattern but the satire never really comes across.

Ordinary direction of Henri Verneuil does not cover up the script inadequacies, and the French view of U. S. habits is only funny over here. Fernandel has trouble creating a whole comic character out of this melange but gets a few chuckles through his expressive mugging. Miss Gabor is Miss Gabor as the head moll. Nicole Maurey has nothing much to do as an early gal-friend. David Opatoshu turns in a nice bit as a dim but kindly killer. Made as an English version, this might also do for dualers.
Mosk.

Pane, Amore, E Fantasia
(Bread, Love and Imagination)
(ITALIAN)

Genoa, Jan. 12.

Titanus release of a Marcello Girosi-Titanus production. Stars Vittorio DeSica, Gina Lollobrigida. Directed by Luigi Comencini. Screenplay, Comencini and Ettore Margadonna from story by Margadonna; camera, Arturo Gallea; music, Alessandro Cicognini. Previewed in Genoa. Running time, **87 MINS.**

Antonio Carotenuto .... Vittorio DeSica
La Bersagliera .... Gina Lollobrigida
Annarella .... Marise Merlini
Don Emidio .... Virgilio Riento
Stelluti .... Roberto Risso

The producers will please both the crix and general public with this item, a tasteful, well-acted comedy which is thoroughly pleasing. Pic should get a fine run on local screens, and rates as a neat export package as well.

Film opens with arrival of a new constabulary marshal in a small Italian village. Entree sets a romantic quartet in motion, with the marshal (Vittorio DeSica) wishing an end to his bachelor career and chasing the village midwife (Marise Merlini) and, not succeeding, then switching to the local spitfire (Gina Lollobrigida), who in turn is in love with the marshal's assistant (Roberto Risso). Love game goes back and forth among the foursome, with considerable village kibitzing, until the marshal gets the midwife and boy gets gal. Pace is rapid, but allows some amusing sketches of rustic types. Among many amusing bits are the veneration of "miraculous" banknote which shows up unexpectedly in the poor gal's home and the marshal's arrival in town.

DeSica properly overplays his blustering role, never taking himself too seriously, all to good effect. Virgilio Riento is fine as the priest who also helps untangle the romantics. Miss Merlini makes a solid, believable suitee to DeSica's marshal; Roberto Risso is well cast as the shy private in love with the spitfire; and dozens of minor roles are brightly filled to round out the picture.

But its Miss Lollobrigida who steals the proverbial show with her best performance to date, an instinctive, animal portrayal of the town hooligan, basically a good gal whose spendid looks and primitive manners mislead people into believing she's a ne'er-do-well. Performance alone will rate the pic much attention.
Hawk.

Punktchen Und Anton
(AUSTRIAN)

Berlin, Dec. 29.

Herzog release of Rhombus-Film Ring-Film production. Stars Paul Klinger, Hertha Feiler, Heidemarie Hatheyer, Sabine Eggerth and Peter Feldt. Directed by Thomas Engel. Screenplay, Maria Osten-Sacken and Thomas Engel, based on novel by Erich Kastner; camera, Franz Weihmayr; music, Herbert Trantow and Heino Gaze. At Marmorhaus, Berlin. Running time, **92 MINS.**

Punktchen .... Sabine Eggerth
Anton .... Peter Feldt
Herr Pogge .... Paul Klinger
Frau Pogge .... Hertha Feiler
Frau Gast .... Heidemarie Hatheyer
Bertha, cook .... Annie Rosar
Fraulein Andacht .... Jane Tilden
Robert, the crook .... Hans Putz
Driver .... Michael Janisch
Klepperbein .... Klaus Kaap

This film has been ably adapted from the novel of the same title by Erich Kastner, one of Germany's most imaginative writers, and looms as an outstanding production. Although pic mainly concerns children, it also appeals to the older generation since there is enough tongue-in-cheek dialog to balance with the kid stuff. Low-budget film may also enjoy considerable U. S. patronage.

"Punktchen and Anton" are two kids who are great friends. She is the daughter of a rich stocking manufacturer while he is a poor youngster in a fatherless household. The girl neglected by her too party-conscious mother, secretly helps her little friend by selling matches so he can support his sick mother. All ends okay when the boy prevents a burglary of Punktchen's luxurious household, with the girl's parents then realizing that it's better to dedicate themselves more to their child.

Standout is a new face, Sabine Eggerth, as the girl Punktchen. She is a lovable teenager with real promise. Anton is played by Peter Feldt, also new to the German screen. These youngsters practically steal the pic with their heartwarming performances. Paul Klinger, Hertha Feiler and Heidemarie Hatheyer competently portray the principal adults. Jane Tilden and Annie Rosar provide fine comedy lines.

Thomas Engel's direction keeps the whole thing easy smoothly. He deserves particular praise for the adroit handling of the young players. Very much on the plus side is Herbert Trantow's accompanying music, with utilization of the now popular "Egon," song by Heino Gaze. Franz Weihmayr's lensing is fine.
Hans.

Koenigliche Hoheit
(His Royal Highness)
(GERMAN—COLOR)

Munich, Jan. 12.

Schorcht release of Filmaufbau-production. Stars Dieter Borsche and Ruth Leuwerik; with Herbert Hubner, Lil Dagover, Paul Bildt, Gunther Luders, Mathias Wieman, Heinz Hilpert and Paul Henckels. Directed by Dr. Hans Braun. Screenplay, based on Thomas Mann's novel, by Georg Hurdalek, Hans Homberg and Erika Mann; camera, Werner Krien; music, Mark Lothar. Previewed in Munich. Running time, **90 MINS.**

Author Thomas Mann came out with a strong verbal and written endorsement for this tinter version of his novel and apparently he had every reason to be pleased. Film shows German production at its current best, although it still lacks the genial touch once to be found in German top pix.

Director Dr. Hans Braun has turned Mann's story of the discreet and respectable love between a Prussian-educated German prince and an American heiress into a tender, subtle film which moves along at a not-too-exciting pace. The heavy debts of his puppet state with its Biedermeir-facade threaten to kill the German-American romance, but a fairy-tale change for the better leads to an happy ending.

Ruth Leuwerik is the femme star as a very Europeanized American girl. She is no longer of Indian descent, as in the novel, but of German parentage. Dieter Borsche, a rather stiff but sympathetic actor, is playing perhaps his best role, as a rather shy, lonely prince.

Gevaertcolor helps in bringing the slightly decadent but enjoyable "Gemutlichkeit" of the pre-first world war Germany to the screen. Supporting cast is carefully selected of top stage actors.

With Thomas Mann and the German-American theme, this should be a draw for arty clientele.
Hard.

Sor Intrepida
(Path to the Kingdom)
(SPANISH)

Master release of Aspa production. Stars Dominique Blanchar; features Julia Caba Alba, Jose Nieto, Margarita Robles, Francisco Rabel. Directed by Rafael Gil. Screenplay, Vicente Escriva; camera, Alfredo Fraile; music Juan Quintero, Joaquin Rodrego and Joaquin Turina; English subtitles and narrative by Walter Klee, George Caputo. Previewed Dec. 9, '53, New York. Running time, 95 **MINS.**

George Caputo, head of Master Films, apparently rushed "Sor Intrepida" (literally, "Sister Unafraid") to capitalize on the Yule season. But it's chiefly for the arties and Latino houses.

Made a year ago in Spain, it concerns itself with the tribulations of a successful singer turned nun. Vicente Escriva's script endows the French Dominique Blanchar with consummate faith and an unfailing ability to blunder successfully through a series of contrived situations. She teaches a paralytic boy to walk through her patience and kindness (virtues which she learns very quickly) in the face of censure from insistent, unthinking medical superiors who noisily hold that he must be "forced" to that end. In so doing they drive the boy to near paranoia before Miss Blanchar takes over; she sings her way through six records to get the necessary money to alleviate the Order's financial problems; she helps redeem the soul of a whiskyed cynic on his death bed by pushing Christmas forward a couple of weeks; and she convinces an indomitable aunt, who has millions, to leave them to the church.

Despite the obvious resorting to stereotyped characters, the simplicity of some of the dialog between Sister Maria and the boy, occasionally between her and the other nuns, and the quiet observation of the premature Yule celebration, are rewarding.

The camera work by Alfredo Fraile, although flaky, was done mostly in soft tones befitting the religious atmosphere. Miss Blanchar speaks her lines in French, but thanks to excellent dubbing in Spanish it goes relatively unnoticed. Unnamed voice dubbed in for Miss Blanchar's during the musical sequences deserves mention—whoever it was sang in a clear, direct soprano that adds credulity to the bit that Sister Maria was once a successful singer.

Script continues to confuse, particularly when he has Sister Maria senselessly walk into the face of fun-shooting bandits—an act tantamount to self-destruction, something the Catholic church is eminently against. Director Rafael Gil did as well as he could with the script material available. He was too realistic, however, when he included a "Dr. Kildare" scene at clinical.

O Destino Em Apuros
(Destiny in Trouble)
(BRAZILIAN)

Rio de Janeiro, Jan. 5.

U.C.B. release of a Multifilms production. Stars Beatriz Consuelo, Helio Souto, Paulo Autran; features Armando Cuoto, Jaime Barcelos, Waldemar Seyssel. Directed by Ernesto Remani. Camera, H. B. Corell; music, Francisco Mignoni. At Rian, Rio de Janeiro. Running time, **87 MINS.**

Brazil's first feature-length tinter deserved a better fate than this. Color system employed is Ansco. It gives the whole pic a delicate pastel shade although colors are frequently blurred. Lens work is clean but totally uninspired.

Story is that of Destiny come to earth along the lines of "Here Comes Mr. Jordan," but is infantile both in conception and execution. It lacks the logic of a fairy tale or the strength to put over its main theme. Obvious lack of attention to local detail robs the Sao Paulo location scenes of their genuineness.

A few musical numbers are forcefully injected into the plot. Also a reason has to be found to permit Beatriz Consuelo, prima ballerina of Rio's Municipal theatre, to dance a few times—so a dream is provided. Some interior

sets are unusually luxurious as compared wth prevailing standards. Performance of cast is below average. *Urja.*

Top Banana
(COLOR-MUSICAL)

Amusing stage musical transferred literally intact to screen. Happy outlook.

United Artists release of Albert Zugsmith-Ben Peskay production. Stars Phil Silvers; features Rose Marie, Danny Scholl, Judy Lynn. Directed by Alfred E. Greene. Based on Broadway musical of same name. Script, Gene Towne; music and lyrics, Johnny Mercer; musical direction, Harold Hastings and Albert Glasser; dances, Ronald Sinclair; camera, William Bradford. Tradeshown in N.Y., Jan. 7, '54. Running time, 100 MINS.
Jerry Biffle .... Phil Silvers
Betty Dillon .... Rosé Marie
Cliff Lane .... Danny Scholl
Sally Peters .... Judy Lynn
Vic Davis .... Jack Albertson
Pinky .... Joey Faye
Moe .... Herbie Faye
Mr. Parker .... Bradford Hatton
Walter .... Walter Dare Wahl
Danny .... Dick Dana
Little Man .... Johnny Trama
Dancer .... Gloria Smith
Dancer .... George Marci

"Top Banana" is a funny moving picture, in color, with music, with zip, and with Phil Silvers. It may also be something of a saga of independent production and financing, and of somebody's, presumably Al Zugsmith's, flair for promotion. At a guess it might have made a better profile for the New Yorker magazine than "Red Badge of Courage."

What gives special significance to "Top Banana" is that it "violated" most of the conventions of making screen musicals. Very little, seemingly, was conceded to the cameras or the scenario department. Instead, the picture was a "direct" shooting of a stage entertainment, practically intact. It looked like there were no more than half a dozen sets taken bodily out of the theatrical crates used for the road tour after "Top Banana" left the Winter Garden, N.Y.

Will this considerable success in literal transference of a stage property open Hollywood eyes and lead to imitations? Arch Oboler started more with a lot less. If this is shoestring picturemaking, let the shoestring be dipped in gold and mounted. Seldom has a dark horse laughed so deeply from the belly.

Of course there is an explanation. Over a period of many months, on Broadway and on tour, a group of professional funnymen, star and stooges, built up an accumulation of gags and sight business and tested throwaways which together with a terrific pace added up to a surefire entertainment property. With a singleminded devotion to tampering as little as possible with success, director Alfred E. Greene cannily managed the metamorphosis into celluloid. It will add to his trade prestige, for this is making it against what must have seemed uphill odds.

Primary credit must go to the superb antics and incredible drive of Phil Silvers. He is the living prototype of the "Top Banana" (burlesque lingo for head comic) which he plays. Thanks to his comic virtuosity and professional authority, this film runs a long 100 minutes without running down. The sustained tempo of the proceedings covers up lack of scene changes and whatever small criticisms the fast schedule and the quick takes leave open to the captious. It is readily forgivable that some lip sync work could be better, or that some of the players and legit chorines, new to studios, looked directly at the camera on occasion. So what? Let it suffice that there are plenty of laughs.

The plot would fit a thimble. The romance is a light breeze only. Musically not much can be said for

Johnny Mercer's unhighlighted score. The chorus girls are nice looking but Hollywood lovelies are possibly lovelier, and Hollywood dance scenes are certainly lavisher. This is a roadshow fun show on tinted stock. Color Corp. of America need offer no apologies for the technical job. Camera work, sound, and other craftwork are of straightaway professionalism.

It would be difficult to single out the various second and third bananas who most help Silvers in his menagerie of nonstop hoksters. Familiar show biz talents, but little known to picture fans, are present. Walter Dare Wahl, always a deadpan acrobatic comic of vast experience; Joey Faye, and Herbie Faye, and Johnny Trana, and the two femme leads, Rose Marie and Judy Lynn, do véry nicely in the new medium.

Oldtimers will perhaps remark that the tried and true corn is re-proving its worth, even though vast throngs may laugh and not know they are witnessing something once known as burlesque and deader than the Columbia Wheel.

"Top Banana" needs selling, because weak on names, but the word-of-mouth ought to be helpful and the final tally should be very pleasant, for all the holders of mortgages, percentage payoffs and private hopes of repeating with the format. *Land.*

Hell Below Zero
(BRITISH-COLOR)

Arctic murder mystery; Alan Ladd's latest British-made meller looks like a sturdy b.o. bet.

London, Jan. 19.
Columbia release of Warwick Production. Stars Alan Ladd; features Joan Tetzel, Basil Sydney, Stanley Baker. Directed by Mark Robson. Screenplay by Alec Coppel & Max Trell from noval, "The White South," by Hammond Innes with adaptation by Richard Maibaum; camera, John Wilcox; editor, John Guthridge; music, Clifton Parker. At Plaza, London, Jan. 13, '54. Running time, 90 MINS.
Duncan Craig .... Alan Ladd
Judie Nordahl .... Joan Tetzel
Bland .... Basil Sydney
Erik Bland .... Stanley Baker
Capt. MacPhee .... Joseph Tomelty
Dr. Howe .... Niall MacGinnis
Gerda Petersen .... Jill Bennett
Miller .... Peter Dyneley
Kathleen .... Susan Rayne
Sandeborg .... Philo Hauser
Larsen .... Ivan Craig
Manders .... Paddy Ryan

This new Alan Ladd starrer is a vigorous action drama which should pay sturdy dividends at the boxoffice. Apart from the marquee lure of the star, the production has obvious exploitation possibilities which should enhance its results.

Aside from the virility of the story, this has an attractive and unusual locale in the Antarctic. The snowy wastes take on a menacing look when lensed through Technicolor cameras. There is also an interesting sidelight on the technique and economics of whale fishing.

The yarn describes the way in which Ladd signs on as first-mate to a whaler to help Joan Tetzel learn the real cause of her father's death. Reports from the Antarctic to London suggested he committed suicide, having thrown himself overboard while the ship was at anchor. She suspects foul play, and is determined to find the truth. It is soon evident that suspicion is well founded. Stanley Baker, a skipper of one of the whalers and the son of the dead man's partner, finds the finger of suspicion pointed towards him. At first he tries to

bluff it out; but when that fails he rams the ship in which Ladd and Miss Tetzel are sailing, thus hoping to do away with his accusers. It ends with a grim chase and fight over the Antarctic wastes.

The screenplay aims at maximum action and Mark Robson's direction adequately capitalizes these sequences. There is a lively episode depicting a storm at sea; Ladd's one-man defeat of a gang of thugs in the bowels of a factory ship and finally the ramming of the whaler and the subsequent fight.

It is all handled in characteristic robust vein. Throughout the proceedings Ladd remains as the tough and sincere friend who is out to see justice done. It is a typically virile performance. Miss Tetzel has a pleasant style and manner and shows herself an actress who combines charm and ability. Basil Sydney and Stanley Baker, as father and son, are too obviously heavies. Their roles have been delineated without any subtlety. Support parts have been carefully selected and Joseph Tomelty, Niall MacGinnis and Jill Bennett top an experienced cast.

John Wilcox has contributed a fine job of Technicolor camerawork. Pic seems to need more scissoring. *Myro.*

Alaska Seas

Dull action programmer on salmon fishing with mild prospects generally.

Hollywood, Jan. 20.
Paramount release of Mel Epstein production. Stars Robert Ryan, Jan Sterling, Brian Keith, Gene Barry; features Richard Shannon, Ralph Dumke, Ross Bagdasarian, Fay Roope, Timothy Carey, Peter Coe. Directed by Jerry Hooper. Screenplay, Geoffrey Homes, Walter Doniger; based on a story by Barrett Willoughby; camera, William C. Mellor; editor, Archie Marshek; music direction, Irvin Talbot. Previewed Jan. 18, '54. Running time, 78 MINS.
Matt Kelly .... Robert Ryan
Nicky .... Jan Sterling
Jim Kimmerly .... Brian Keith
Verne Williams .... Gene Barry
Tom Erickson .... Richard Shannon
Jackson .... Ralph Dumke
Joe .... Ross Bagdasarian
Walt Davis .... Fay Roope
Wycoff .... Timothy Carey
Grego .... Peter Coe

"Alaska Seas" is burdened with a tiresome story line that telegraphs every move ahead. There are some excellent shots of glaciers and a salmon fishing fleet at work, but the tempo is drearily slow and seldom does plot hold the spectator. Even with the lure of Robert Ryan and Jan Sterling for marquee dressing, picture will have to be sold hard for average results in the action market.

Mel Epstein gives film suitable physical values in his production supervisory capacity, but screenplay by Geoffrey Homes and Walter Doniger is filled with banal dialog and situation cliches which bore rather than divert. Direction by Jerry Hooper consequently fails to be any more than adequate, the show being a familiar one to most audiences.

Ryan, top-billed, plays an unscrupulous Alaskan salmon fisherman who doesn't mind using his best friend, Brian Keith, to win latter's fiance, Miss Sterling, for himself. As a fisherman, too, he's as crooked as they come, mobbing salmon traps of their fish, and is responsible for Keith losing his boat under a glacier avalanche. These elements are juggled around for an old-fashioned yarn of retribution and right-winning-out, Ryan finally meeting a just end when he deliberately steers a fellow-heavy's boat toward a glacier, to protect Keith, and the craft is crushed in the ice.

Ryan plays the role for all that it's worth, but it's so unsympathetic that little interest attaches. Miss Sterling, occasionally looking as though she's wearing a fright wig, does what she can with her character, and Keith is almost absurdly noble in letting his fiance make up her mind about whom she wants to marry. Gene Barry is okay as a thieving cannery operator, and Ross Bagdasarian and Peter Coe stand out in the supporting cast as fishermen.

Technical departments are capably handled, William C. Mellor's camera work and process photography by Farciot Edouart and Wallace Kelley most interesting.

Whit.

Gypsy Colt
(COLOR)

Okay programmer for general situations. Teaming of remarkable horse, Gypsy, and moppet star Donna Corcoran, makes entry a natural for the kid trade.

Metro release of William Grady Jr. and Sidney Franklin Jr. production. Stars Donna Corcoran, Ward Bond, Frances Dee and Gypsy. Directed by Andrew Marton. Screenplay, Martin Berkeley; based on a story by Eric Knight; camera (Ansco), Harold Lipstein; editor, Conrad A. Nervig; music, Rudolph G. Kopp. Previewed in N.Y. Jan. 20, '54. Running time, 72 **MINS.**

Meg MacWade	Donna Corcoran
Frank MacWade	Ward Bond
Em MacWade	Frances Dee
Wade Y. Gerald	Larry Keating
Hank	Lee Van Cleef
Phil Gerald	Bobby Hyatt
Pancho	Nacho Galindo
Rodolfo	Rodolfo Hoyos Jr.
Pedro	Bobby Dominguez
Tony	Joe Dominguez
Carl	Jester Hairston
Pat	Peggy Maley

Sentimental attachment to animals, particularly to dogs and horses, has almost become a tradition in American films. Pix audiences remember affectionately such wonder dogs as Rin-Tin-Tin and Lassie and the remarkable horses of the western heroes, such as Champion and Silver. Through the efforts of Metro, a new name will be added to this select society. It belongs to a horse; a beautiful, young, black colt dubbed Gypsy.

This thoroughbred emerges as the star of "Gypsy Colt," a low-budgeter, especially judged from Metro's usual standards. Exhibs, who have experienced success with this type of stuff in the past, will find this a natural. Otherwise, it appears destined for programmer spots. It rates, however, as a good Saturday afternooner, having sock appeal for the kiddie trade.

Gypsy is teamed with moppet actress Donna Corcoran. He is the property of the MacWade family (Ward Bond, Frances Dee and young Miss Corcoran) who live in an unidentified western farming community periled by a serious drought. The horse is the special property of the youngster. She rides him to school each morning and he picks up his mistress promptly at three every day. In fact, the villagers set their clocks as the colt breezes through town every afternoon at the same time.

With water growing scarcer and in a desperate need of money, Bond is forced to sell the horse to the Gerald Racing Stables, headed by Larry Keating. Gypsy's mistress, though heart-broken, is somewhat reconciled to the situation when apprised of the family's difficulties. However, the horse desperately misses his young mistress, and from a racetrack 500 miles distant, he breaks away and begins a remarkable journey home. He outwits various pursuers, out to get a $1,000 reward for his capture, and arrives weary, dirty and bleeding exactly at three at the schoolhouse to meet Miss Corcoran.

Of course, things are worked out neatly so that Gypsy and Miss Corcoran can remain together. And the situation is helped no end by the timely arrival of rain.

Martin Berkeley screenplay based on a story by Eric Knight is trite, but not without appeal within the defined category. The production values are firstrate and Harold Lipstein's Ansco color filming has captured some beautiful scenic values. Andrew Marton's direction is okay.

Gypsy is the true star but Miss Corcoran is agreeably cute as his young mistress and Miss Dee and Bond are convincing as her parents. Other good performances are turned in by Keating, as the racing stable owner; Lee Van Cleef, as a surly groom; Bobby Hyatt, as Keating's young son, and Bobby Dominquez, as a young Mexican.

Holl.

Killers From Space

Routine science-fiction entry for fair returns in exploitation market.

Hollywood, Jan. 22.

RKO release of a W. Lee Wilder production. Features Peter Graves, James Seay, Steve Pendleton, Barbara Bestar. Directed by Wilder. Screenplay, Bill Raynor; story, Myles Wilder; camera, William H. Clothier; editor, William Faris; music, Manuel Compinsky. Previewed Jan. 15, '54. Running time, 71 **MINS.**

For the exploitation market this science-fiction entry indicates fair returns, but is a routine affair where more adroit handling might have upped it to a true chiller. Film's major premise is imaginative enough—plans of superman from another planet to destroy earthmen. Simply hasn't been developed sufficiently to matter.

Certain interest accrues in the W. Lee Wilder production when an American nuclear scientist, Peter Graves, meets a few of the advance guard from the planet Astron Delta, but otherwise the action doesn't hold much attraction. Graves, killed in a plane crash during atomic bomb experiments at Soledad Flats, Nevada, and brought back to life through the skill of the Astronians, is mesmerized into delivering into their hands top secret atomic info. Through his knowledge that the basis of their power is electricity he is able to blow up their under earth lab before they can accomplish their object.

Acting demands are few and Wilder makes no particular effort for characterizations in his direction. Graves is acceptable as the scientist who knows the world is in grave danger, but other theps are lost in stock roles. Topping cast are James Seay as an Army colonel; Steve Pendleton, FBI man; Barbara Bestar, Graves' wife; Frank Gerstle, another scientist. Technical credits are average.

Whit.

Jesse James Vs. The Daltons
(COLOR)

Contrived western with come-on title.

Hollywood, Jan. 22.

Columbia release of a Sam Katzman production. Stars Brett King, Barbara Lawrence; features James Griffith, Bill Phipps, John Cliff, Rory Mallinson, William Tannen, Richard Garland, Nelson Leigh. Directed by William Castle. Screenplay, Robert E. Kent; adaptation, Samuel Newman; story, Edwin Westrate; camera, Lester H. White; editor, Viola Lawrence; music, Mischa Bakaleinikoff. Previewed Jan. 19, '54. Running time, **65 MINS.**

Joe Branch	Brett King
Kate Manning	Barbara Lawrence
Bob Dalton	James Griffith
Bill Dalton	Bill Phipps
Grat Dalton	John Cliff
Bob Ford	Rory Mallinson
Emmett Dalton	William Tannen
Gilkie	Richard Garland
Father Kerrigan	Nelson Leigh
Corey Bayless	Raymond Largay

An overly-contrived western with occasional fast gunplay but more often burdened with static dialog, "Jesse James vs. The Daltons" is an obvious pitch to cash in on exploitation possibilities of the title, which has nothing to do with plot.

Plot premises around a young gunman, an outcast of society because he's reputed to be Jesse James' son, attempting to prove whether this is true. He throws in with the Daltons, through a peculiar line of reasoning, in the hope they may lead him to Jesse, whom he thinks is still alive. Daltons are wiped out in a wild-shooting climax, but hero meanwhile has learned he isn't the dead outlaw's son and can take his place in society.

Brett King throws a fast gun in lead role, measuring up generally to demands, and Barbara Lawrence co-stars in okay fashion. Supporting cast is headed by James Griffith, persuasive as Bob Dalton, and John Cliff is the heavy as another Dalton on the make for femme. Rory Mallinson is in briefly as Bob Ford, who settles hero's problem as to his identity, and Nelson Leigh is a priest.

Sam Katzman accords film suitable production values but overlooked a good plot line, for which William Castle's direction suffers accordingly. In the gun scenes, however, he delivers. Tops in the technical credits is Lester H. White's interesting color photography.

Whit.

Highway Dragnet

Program melodrama for routine playdates. Lightweight entertainment.

Hollywood, Jan. 20.

Allied Artists release of Jack Jungmeyer Jr., production; co-producers, A. Robert Nunes, Roger Corman. Stars Richard Conte, Joan Bennett, Wanda Hendrix; features Reed Hadley, Mary Beth Hughes, Iris Adrian, Harry Harvey, Tom Hubbard, Frank Jenks. Directed by Nathan Juran. Screenplay, Herb Meadow, Jerome Odlum; added dialog, Tom Hubbard, Fred Eggers; from a story by U. S. Anderson, Roger Corman; camera, John Martin; editor, Ace Herman; music, Edward J. Kay. Previewed Jan. 19, '54. Running time, **70 MINS.**

Jim	Richard Conte
Mrs. Cummings	Joan Bennett
Susan	Wanda Hendrix
White Eagle	Reed Hadley
Terry	Mary Beth Hughes
Dolly	Iris Adrian
Carson	Harry Harvey
Ben	Tom Hubbard
Marine	Frank Jenks
Truck Driver	Murray Alper
Officer	Zon Murray
Cop	House Peters Jr.
2nd Inspector	Joseph Crehan
Inspector	Tony Hughes
2nd Officer	Ball Hale
Al	Fred Gabourie

"Highway Dragnet" represents the joint efforts of four producers and six writers, but they all came up short so this collaborative effort will have to be satisfied with routine programmer dates. Selling points lie chiefly in the possible marquee lure of its star names—and a title that Jack Webb might like to put behind bars.

Taken from a story by U. S. Anderson and Roger Corman, the script is by Herb Meadow and Jerome Odlum, with some added dialog thrown in by Tom Hubbard and Fred Eggers. Plot is strictly one-dimensional and the writing doesn't help it.

Richard Conte plays an ex-Marine who is the number one suspect in the Las Vegas murder of ex-model Mary Beth Hughes. He escapes from the police and, by a remarkable coincidence, hitches a ride with mag photog Joan Bennett and her model, Wanda Hendrix. By her actions audience soon gets the idea Miss Bennett killed Miss Hughes because the latter had driven the photog's husband to suicide. It takes excessive footage while Conte, with the two femmes in tow, continues fleeing and the cops continue chasing before Miss Bennett finally confesses and Conte and Miss Hendrix are in each other's arms.

The three leads do what they can with their roles, which isn't much, and of the trio, it's Miss Hendrix who fares best. Reed Hadley is good as the cop, as is Miss Hughes. There's also a flashy bit by Iris Adrian as a lunch counter waitress.

Production via William F. Broidy (executive producer), Jack Jungmeyer Jr. (producer), A. Robert Nunes and Roger Corman (co-producers) is sloppy, which somehow seems to be heightened by Nathan Juran's direction. John Martin's camera work is okay, ditto the musical backing by Edward J. Kay.

Neal.

Dragon's Gold

Poorly-made meller for programmer market.

Hollywood, Jan. 22.

United Artists release of Aubrey Wisberg, Jack Pollexfen production. Stars John Archer, Hillary Brooke; features Noel Cravath, Dayton Lumis, Merrill Stone, Marvin Press. Directed and written by Wisberg and Pollexfen; camera, Stanley Cortez; editor, Fred Feitshans Jr.; music, Albert Glasser. Previewed Jan. 21, '54. Running time, **70 MINS.**

Mack Rossiter	John Archer
Vivian Crosby	Hillary Brooke
General Wong Kai Hai	Noel Cravath
Donald McCutcheon	Dayton Lumis
Conway	Merrill Stone
Cheng	Marvin Press
Rickshaw boy	Eric Colmar
Nico	Frank Yaconelli
Chinese youth	Wyatt Ordung
Sikh constable	Reginald Singh
Police sergeant	Roy Engel
Police officer	Gilbert Frye
Chinese girl	Leemoi Chu
Lu Sim	Wong Ahtarre
Edna Purleigh	Juney Ellis
Reverend Marlowe	Bruce Payne
Major Curzon	Keith Hitchcock
Madame Curzon	Ernestine Barrier
Sen	Philip Van Zandt
Li Tom	Anthony Joachim
Eustace Crosby	Mauritz Hugo
Howard Montgomery	Charles Victor
Concubine	Esther Lee
Sing Wah	Joseph Kim
Board member	Harvey Dunn
Second concubine	Audrey Lau
Chinese mercenary	David Chow

There's little in the way of entertainment here, but with small exhibs clamoring for secondary product it will rate some programmer bookings.

Aubrey Wisberg and Jack Pollexfen are responsible for writing, directing and producing the melodrama. Their joint efforts in each department are very poor, even for a small-budgeted feature. Script is conversational, action contrived, production values nil and there is no chance for a performance from any of the cast.

John Archer is an investigator for a New York bonding company who junkets to Hong Kong to locate $7,000,000 in gold that has been missing for 10 years. The man to whom the money has been entrusted is supposed to have reappeared, but Archer is finally able to prove it's just a trick by an outlawed Chinese general to get the gold, plus equal payment from the bonding company. Archer finds the loot in a fish pond and wins the love of the missing man's widow, Phyllis Brooke, as his reward.

Technical credits come over with the impact that would be expected of a quick shooting schedule and minimum budget expenditure.
Brog.

The Kidnappers
(BRITISH)

Two standout moppet performances make this jell; sturdy for U.S. arty houses.

London, Jan. 12.
General Film Distributors release of a Nolbandov-Parkyn production. Stars Duncan Macrae, Adrienne Corri, Jon Whiteley, Vincent Winter. Directed by Philip Leacock. Screenplay, Neil Paterson; camera, Eric Cross; editor, John Trumper; music, Bruce Montgomery. At Gaumont, London. Running time, **93 MINS.**
Grandaddy .... Duncan Macrae
Grandma .... Jean Anderson
Kirsty .... Adrienne Corri
William Bloem .... Theodore Bikel
Harry .... Jon Whiteley
Davy .... Vincent Winter
Jan Hooft (snr) ...... Francis de Wolff
Arron McNab .... James Sutherland
Andrew McCleod .... John Rae
Dominie .... Jack Stewart
Tom Cameron .... Jameson Clark
Sam Howie ...r........ Eric Woodburn
Jan Hooft (jnr) ...... Christopher Beeny
Archibald Jenkins ...... Howard Connell

The main asset of this British production rests in two outstanding moppet performances by Vincent Winter & Jon Whiteley which lift the film from a conventional rut to make it enchanting. Lack of stellar names will be a handicap in selling to the public, but constructive exploitation could make this a sturdy boxoffice proposition on the U.S. art house circuit.

The two juvenile performers, one of whom is without previous stage or film experience, completely dominate the yarn. Rarely, if ever, have there been such moppet portrayals without a trace of precociousness. They act like vets, speak their lines audibly and with understanding, and completely capture the spirit of the story. Their handling is a tribute to director Philip Leacock.

The story is set in Nova Scotia at the beginning of the century and the underlying theme is of a feud between the Scottish and the Boers. Into this unhappy atmosphere are brought the orphan grandchildren of a stern, almost inhuman Scottish Canadian (Duncan Macrae). The youngsters, too, are taught to hate the Boers. For the two orphans it is an unhappy menage but they are able to get a measure of happiness when they find a year-old baby and take it under their wing.

Although the adult roles are intelligently played by an admirable team of British artists, their performances are dwarfed by the natural charm exuded by the two kids, young Winter and Whiteley. Macrae typifies the strict Puritan while Jean Anderson, as his wife, succeeds in bringing some humanism into his character. Adrienne

Corri adequately suggests his rebellious daughter and, with Theodore Bikel, as a Dutch doctor, provides an underlying touch of romance.
Myro.

La Passeggiata
(The Walk)
(ITALIAN-COLOR)

Genoa, Jan. 19.
20th-Fox release of a Film Costellazione production. Stars Renato Rascel, Valentina Cortese; features Paolo Stoppa, Giuseppe DeMartino, Suzanne Levesy, Anna Maria Bottini. Directed by Renato Rascel. Screenplay, Rascel, Cesare Zavattini, Fabbri, Guerra, Prosperi, Vasile, Rossi, Curdi; from Gogol's "Nevski Prospective"; camera, Venceslao Vich; sets, Gianni Polidori; music, Militello. At Verdi, Genoa. Running time, **101 MINS.**

Pic is a commendable first effort by comedian Renato Rascel in the field of film direction (he has directed his own stage revues), and a near-successful attempt to follow up the whimsical comedy, "The Overcoat," Rascel's recent hit. It looks only fair on home grounds, but should click in some other European dates, and rates a U.S. arty o.o.

Rascel plays a timid and sentimental college prof who falls for a gal he meets in a park, refusing to believe she's a prostitute even after she has made the point quite evident. She lives in his dreams as a princess and in his life as the long-sought true love. She accepts his invitations only out of self-interest, still smiling at his candor and innocence. But finally, during an outing on which she's joined by her fellow-workers, she cracks up and decides to start a new life back home.

Despite the obvious plot developments, pic is given the proper tone and is well acted by Rascel and Valentina Cortese. Latter never has been better nor more eye-filling than in this color-lensed pic. Her portrayal of the prostie longing for the better life gives a cliche new vitality. Paolo Stoppa has some nice bits as a despotic college dean. Rascel is onscreen almost throughout, and succeeds in making almost all the moments credible despite the role. His love for the girl has its comic as well as its tender movements. Color lensing by Venceslao Vich is strong. *Hawk.*

Du bist die Welt fuer mich
(You Are the World for Me)
(AUSTRIAN)

Vienna, Jan. 5.
Sascha release of Ernst Marischka production. Stars Rudolf Schock; features Annemarie Dueringer. Directed and written by Ernst Marischka. Camera, Sepp Ketterer; sets, Fritz Jueptner; musical direction, Anton Profes. At Kuenstlerhaus Kino, Vienna. Running time, **100 MINS.**

This biopic of Richard Tauber will please a musically sophisticated audience. It generally lacks movement, but is filled with the songs which Tauber made famous.

Rudolf Schock makes a highly effective Tauber and gets a neat assist from Annemarie Dueringer, as the only femme in Tauber's life at least in this pic. Script, in unfolding his career, has him returning home to marry the girl, only to find her on her deathbed. Fritz Imhoff as the manager and Richard Romanovsky, the singing teacher, contribute some humor. Remainder of cast was carefully chosen.

Lots of Franz Lehar music plus the title song "You Are the World For Me," composed by Richard

Tauber in the early '30's should please music lovers.

Ernest Marischka's direction is excellent. Synchronization of old Tauber disks is so well done it is difficult to tell who is actually singing. Lensing by Sepp Ketterer is standard. Orch background music is provided by the Vienna Symphonic under Wilhelm Schuechter.
Maas.

Red Garters
(MUSICAL-COLOR)

Stylized musical spoof on westerns. Pluggable as something different, but good returns not assured.

Hollywood, Feb. 1.
Paramount release of Pat Duggan production. Stars Rosemary Clooney, Jack Carson, Guy Mitchell, Pat Crowley, Gene Barry, Cass Daley; introducing Joanne Gilbert; features Frank Faylen, Reginald Owen, Buddy Ebsen, Richard Hale. Directed by George Marshall. Written by Michael Fessier; camera (Technicolor), Arthur E. Arling; editor, Arthur Schmidt; special photographic effects, John P. Fulton; musical direction and vocal adaptations, Joseph J. Lilley; choreography, Nick Castle; songs, Jay Livingston and Ray Evans. Previewed Jan. 25, '54. Running time, **91 MINS.**
Calaveras Kate ...... Rosemary Clooney
Jason Carberry .... Jack Carson
Reb Randall .... Guy Mitchell
Susanna .... Pat Crowley
Rafael .... Gene Barry
Minnie Redwing .... Cass Daley
Billy Bucket .... Frank Faylen
Judge Winthrop .... Reginald Owen
Ginger Pete .... Buddy Ebsen
Dr. J. Pott Troy .... Richard Hale
Sheila Winthrop .... Joanne Gilbert

The screen western takes a highly stylized musical spoofing in "Red Garters." If the public is willing to go along with something different in the form of film presentation then Paramount has a winner. However, it will take a lot of plugging and other hard selling to focus ticket-buying attention on this offering so good returns are by no means assured.

The Pat Duggan production rates a bow for novelty in conception and for the courage to attempt something different in features. Unfortunately, in the writing and direction, laugh attempts miss just about as often as they hit. Whether there are enough bullseyes to make the public buy it and talk favorably about it remains to be seen. In its favor is a good score with 11 songs by Jay Livingston and Ray Evans, all delivered excellently by the singing members of the cast.

In form, "Red Garters" is more of a musical comedy stage play than a motion picture, in that it does not make use of the camera to create a semblance of real life with real settings. Actually, about the closest description of the look worn by the picture wiuld be that it resmbles a live-action UPA cartoon. This is particularly true of its seeming flatness, in the use of only suggestions of scenery and props, and in the monotones of its colorings. Props, colors and action are so arranged as to attempt a depth illusion without 3-D. It is only an illusion that will elude most viewers, even if attention is called to it, largely because most of the scenes seem to lack a horizon.

The picture serves to showcase the established singing talents of Rosemary Clooney and Guy Mitchell, and the newer voice of Joanne Gilbert, although, as a showcasing, this newcomer has only one song, done well. That Mitchell's "Dime and a Dollar" will be a big plug number is seen in the fact that it rates three reprises after its initial introduction to the footage. The title tune, sold by Miss Clooney, is heard three times and a special situation number, "Robin Randall," gets a repeat. For heart quality, and the only heart in the picture, Miss Clooney's singing of "Brave Man" is the standout. Miss Gilbert's piece is "This Is Greater Than I Thought." Miss Clooney also gets off "Lady Killer," "Bad News," "Good Intentions," and joins Mitchell on "Man and Woman."

When Mitchell isn't busy with "Dime, Dollar," he sings "Meet a Happy Guy" and "Vaquero."

A running gag through the Michael Fessier screen plot is the hat-tipping each male does when the code of the west is mentioned. It's mentioned often and gets a chuckle every time. Yarn uses the vengeance formula to poke fun at the traditional western. Mitchell comes to town to avenge the death of his brother, who is being buried at a big funeral barbecue party as he arrives. Suspicion shifts from character to character, giving the hero time to pitch woe at Pat Crowley, permit Gene Barry, Cisco Kid-type, and Miss Gilbert, newly-arrived easterner, to establish a romance, and let Miss Clooney, saloon entertainer and belle of the town, shake up her hit-and-miss courtship from Jack Carson, lawyer and big-wheel in the western settlement. The three romances conclude satisfactorily and the law gets Mitchell's man.

The performance that does more than anything else to keep this show wheeling is the comedy-wise delivery of Carson. The Misses Clooney, Gilbert and Crowley are likeable within the range of the characters given them, as is Barry. Cass Daley's wonderful comedy talents are not used, although she is a co-star. Neither is Buddy Ebsen's ability. Frank Faylen is given a free hand by George Marshall's direction to ham up his coward role. So is Reginald Owen.

Arthur E. Arling rates a credit for the use of the Technicolor cameras on the settings created by the art direction of Hal Pereira and Roland Anderson. John P. Fulton did the special photographic effects and Arthur Schmidt the editing. The musical direction and vocal adaptations by Joseph J. Lilley are among the film's stronger assets. Choreography, mostly of folk dance nature, was created by Nick Castle. *Brog.*

Hell and High Water
(C'SCOPE—COLOR)

Rip-roaring high adventure feature in CinemaScope with Richard Widmark. Stout b.o. possibilities from action trade.

Hollywood, Feb. 2.

20th-Fox release of Raymond A. Klune production. Stars Richard Widmark, Bella Darvi; features Victor Francen, Cameron Mitchell, Gene Evans, David Wayne, Stephen Bekassy, Richard Loo. Directed by Samuel Fuller. Screenplay, Jesse L. Lasky Jr., and Fuller; based on a story by David Hempstead; camera (Technicolor), Joe MacDonald; special photographic effects, Ray Kellogg; editor, James B. Clark; music, Alfred Newman. Previewed Jan. 29, '54. Running time, **103 MINS.**

Adam Jones .... Richard Widmark
Denise .... Bella Darvi
Professor Montel .... Victor Francen
"Ski" Brodski .... Cameron Mitchell
Chief Holter .... Gene Avans
Dugboat Walker .... David Wayne
Neuman .... Stephen Bekassy
Fujimori .... Richard Loo
Gunner McCrossin .... Henry Kulky
Chin Lee .... Wong Artarne
Quartermaster .... Harry Carter
Welles .... Robert Adler
Carpino .... Don Orlando
Joto .... Rollin Moriyama
Torpedo .... John Gifford
Ho-Sin .... William Yip
Crew Member .... Tommy Walker
Mr. Aylesworth .... Leslie Bradley
Col. Schuman .... John Wengraf
McAuliff .... Harry Denny
Taxi Driver .... Edo Mita
Lieutenant .... Ramsey Williams
Reporter .... Robert B. Williams
Photographer .... Harlan Warde

CinemaScope and rip-roaring adventure mate perfectly in "Hell and High Water," a highly fanciful, but mighty entertaining action feature of stout boxoffice possibilities. Slambang ballyhoo angles abound so that the selling can match the melodramatics and assure hearty ticket sales in most any situation; but most particularly in those locations catering to the action trade.

20th-Fox' squeeze-lens system has been underwater before, but never within the limiting confines of a submarine (and it handles these close quarters as easily as a 1.35-to-1 lense), nor in sea battle or focused on an atomic explosion. Those are just a few of the high action moments whipped together by Raymond A. Klune's showmanly production and Samuel Fuller's direction for the satisfaction of the chimerically-minded film patron. It's topnotch escapism, played with a gutty vigorousness that gives attention-holding vitality to every scene.

As the male star, Richard Widmark takes easily to the rugged assignment, giving it the wallop needed. It is a further projection of the action-adventure type of hero he does quite often, and good. The picture introduces as a new star Polish-born, French-raised, Bella Darvi and she creates an interesting impression in her debut. The public will decide whether she is star material, but a warm personality and an ability to read lines carry her through this initial film assignment effectively.

Plot has to do with a group of individuals of many nationalities who band together to thwart a scheme to start a new world war with an atomic incident that will be blamed on the United States. These private heroes hire Widmark, a former Naval submarine officer, to command an underwater trip to the Arctic, where scientists on the voyage will check reports that a Communist atomic arsenal is being built on an isolated island.

A series of incredible adventures ensue, all of the high action type, that are meant for enjoyment, not analysis. Tense and exciting is the sequence in which Widmark's sub and a Chinese Communist sub battle it out underwater. Another thriller is the island foray made to determine radioactivity, and there are a number of others played for rugged suspense impact as the plot builds to the explosive climax when the sub crew guns down a captured U.S. bomber as it takes off to drop the atomic bomb that will touch off another war. All hell breaks loose, literally, in this scene and wraps up the picture with a tremendous finish.

Victor Francen is very good as the head scientist on the trip (Miss Darvi, as his daughter, is the other scientist). Doing well as crew members are Cameron Mitchell, Gene Evans, David Wayne (almost lost in the footage), Stephen Bekassy, Henry Kulky and others. In fact, the entire cast react competently to the derring-do demands of the screenplay by Jesse L. Lasky Jr., and Fuller, from a story by David Hempstead.

Starting with the players on an equal basis are the C'Scope lensing by Joe MacDonald, and the special photographic effects by Ray Kellogg. The underwater shots of the submarine fight and the atomic blast are outstanding, adding greatly to the action impact of the film. Alfred Newman's score is another factor in the melodramatics and James B. Clark's editing is good. *Brog.*

Beachhead
(COLOR)

Good cast names and exploitation angles provide pop market.

Hollywood, Jan. 28.

United Artists release of Aubrey Schenck Productions presentation, produced by Howard W. Koch. Stars Tony Curtis, Frank Lovejoy, Mary Murphy. Directed by Stuart Heisler. Screenplay, Richard Alan Simmons; based on the novel, "I've Got Mine" by Richard G. Hubler; camera (Technicolor print), Gordon Avil; editor, John F. Schreyer; music, Emil Newman, Arthur Lange. Previewed Jan. 22, '54. Running time, **89 MINS.**

Burke .... Tony Curtis
Sergeant Fletcher ...... Frank Lovejoy
Nina .... Mary Murphy
Bouchard .... Eduard Franz
Reynolds .... Skip Homeier
Major Scott .... John Doucette
Biggerman .... Alan Wells
Japanese Sailor
Sunshine Akira Fukunaga
The Sniper .... Dan Aoki
Malanesian .... Steamboat Mokuahi

As a standard war actioner, "Beachhead" is well equipped with the names and exploitation angles that should put it over as a popular entry in the regular market. With Tony Curtis and Frank Lovejoy heading the war heroics and the Hawaiian Islands in Technicolor, picture has enough commercial values to take care of most any general booking.

Howard W. Koch produced the Aubrey Schenck presentation for United Artists release and gives it what it needs to get by. So does Stuart Heisler's direction, which is most effective in the handling of tight suspense. Where the picture falters, critically, is in the characters and some run-of-the-mill situations into which they are tossed. The personality clashes between the principals seem rather picayunish and petulant in view of the more important issues of war.

Richard Alan Simmons' screenplay is based on Richard G. Hubler's novel, "I've Got Mine,' 'and deals with a Marine foursome on an island near Bougainville during World War II. The small group is looking for a planter, believed to have sent a message detailing Japanese mine fields. If the message is authentic, many lives will be saved when a full scale assault is launched against Bougainville. Lovejoy is the sergeant in charge of Curtis, Skip Homeier and Alan Wells. The latter two are soon killed, leaving Curtis and Lovejoy to complete the mission, verify the message and save Mary Murphy, the daughter of planter Eduard Franz, after he is killed.

When the picture is concerned with war action, even on the compact scale of the small group, suspense is gripping and most of these sequences squeeze out plenty of tight drama. Footage is less effective when the three Marines are quarreling with their sergeant, looking on him as a leader who is taking them to death all because of a previous experience on Guadalcanal when he had a platoon wiped out. Nor is the half-hearted introduction of a semi-romantic triangle between Curtis, Lovejoy and Miss Murphy any more effective or logical.

Performancewise, the three stars and the supporting players bring off their assorted types satisfactorily for regular market purposes. Gordon Avil's camera work is good, but some of the photographic and special effects are not on the same level. Particularly phoney is the beach scene between Jap gunboat, P-T boats and a gasoline fire on the surface of the sea. The score by Emil Newman and Arthur Lange is used effectively.

Ride Clear of Diablo
(SONGS-COLOR)

Audie Murphy, Dan Duryea heading good, standard western actioner with okay chances in outdoor market.

Hollywood, Feb. 2.

Universal release of John W. Rogers production. Stars Audie Murphy, Susan Cabot, Dan Duryea, Abbe Lane. Directed by Jesse Hibbs. Screenplay, George Zuckerman; added dialog, D. D. Beauchamp; story, Ellis Marcus; camera (Technicolor), Irving Glassberg; editor, Edward Curtiss; songs, Frederick Herbert and Arnold Hughes, Maria Teresa Lara. Previewed Jan. 26, '54. Running time, **80 MINS.**

Clay O'Mara .... Audie Murphy
Laurie Kenyon .... Susan Cabot
Whitey Kincade .... Dan Duryea
Kate .... Abbe Lane
Jed Ringer .... Russell Johnson
Fred Kenyon .... Paul Birch
Tom Meredith .... William Pullen
Tim Lowerie .... Jack Elam
Rev. Moorehead .... Denver Pyle

Well-plotted western action shapes this Technicolored feature oater for an okay playoff through the outdoor market. Presence of Audie Murphy and Dan Duryea as the top males will help the bookings.

Basically, the plot is standard western fare, but the characters are handled interestingly in the writing and Jesse Hibbs' direction. Production values marshalled under John W. Rogers' supervision are geared to market demands and the actionful camera of Irving Glassberg makes the most of them.

Murphy plays a modest hero out to avenge the murder of his father and kid brother. He makes the character come over with a quiet effectiveness that pleases. Duryea is an engaging heavy who decides to help the young man outwit the plot's real villains, and the manner in which he colors the character has much to do with audience interest in the story's unfoldment.

Chief dirty-workers in the Ellis Marcus story, scripted by George Zuckerman with added dialog by D. D. Beauchamp, are Russell Johnson, Paul Birch and William Pullen. The latter two are sheriff and lawyer, respectively, who masterminded the killing of Murphy's family and the rustling of the ranch's cattle with Johnson's help. The trio didn't figure on the hero, however, and when he returns to town for vengenance they do everything they can to get him killed. Murphy wises up in time and, with Duryea's help, deals out rough range justice.

Susan Cabot and Abbe Lane handle the distaff star spots to add some femme appeal to the western action. Miss Cabot is the sheriff's niece, engaged to the lawyer, but when all the shooting is over it is Murphy who has the fadeout clinch with her. Miss Lane is Johnson's sweetie, and in her role of saloon singer has a chance to chirp two tunes, of which "Wanted" is the most effective done. It was written by Frederick Herbert and Arnold Hughes. The other is "Noche De Ronda" by Maria Teresa Lara. Jack Elam, western baddie, and Denver Pyle, town parson, are two others who figure more prominently in the cast and do okay.

Technical assists on the production are good and the editing is tight at 80 minutes. *Brog.*

World for Ransom
(SONG)

Dan Duryea, tv's "China Smith," with new alias, same setting. Fair meller programmer.

Allied Artists release of Robert Aldrich, Bernard Tabakin production. Stars Dan Duryea, Gene Lockhart, Patric Knowles; features Reginald Denny, Nigel Bruce, Marian Carr, Arthur Shields, Douglas Dumbrille. Directed by Aldrich. Written by Lindsay Hardy; camera, Joseph Biroc; editor, Michael Luciano; score, Frank De Vol; song, Walter Samuels. Previewed Jan. 25, '54. Running time, 81 MINS.

Mike Callahan .... Dan Duryea
Alexis Pederas .... Gene Lockhart
Julian March .... Patric Knowles
Major Bone .... Reginald Denny
Gov. Coutts .... Nigel Bruce
Frennessey .... Marian Carr
Sean O'Conner .... Arthur Shields
Insp. McCollum ...... Douglas Dumbrille
Dancer .... Carmen D'Antonio
Wong .... Keye Luke
Chan .... Clarence Lung
Guzik .... Lou Nova

The melodramatics shaken out in "World For Ransom" are of a fair grade, which means it will get by as a supporter. "World" is feature-length version of Dan Duryea's telepic series, "China Smith," but with the actor wearing a new alias in the Oriental setting. Another point in the tv-to-pix idea is that Bernard Tabakin, producer of the video series, teamed with Robert Aldrich on the theatrical production.

Locale for the spy intrigue meller is Singapore (instead of the tv Shanghai) and Lindsay Hardy's screen story deals with the kidnapping of a nuclear scientist. Adventurer Duryea gets mixed up in the snatch because he's in love with Marian Carr, wife of Patric Knowles, renegade Englishman who did the kidnapping of Arthur Shields for Gene Lockhart. The latter is an international crook who figures the British will pay a high ransom or he will sell Shields to the Commies.

Duryea snarls more and smiles less in his Mike Callahan character than as China Smith and more of the latter would have made the adventurer type more likeable. However, he gives the footage some zing in spots and generally carries off the story for market demands. Latter half of the pic has more meller punch than the first part since it gets Duryea into action, dodging the police headed by Douglas Dumbrille and military intelligence headed by Reginald Denny while he uncovers the hiding spot of Shields and effects the rescue. He doesn't get the girl, though. She spurns him because he had to do in Knowles.

The directorial pace set by A....... ...; only sporadic movement so the action is spotty, and the script too often gets involved in dialog during the earlier moments. Lockhart, with very short footage, Knowles, Denny, Nigel Bruce, Miss Carr, Shields and Dumbrille are acceptable in doing what is required of them. Miss Carr's character sings "Too Soon," by Walter Samuels, in a night club sequence and Carmen D'Antonio is in for a dance number. Others are adequate.

Lensing, editing, background score and other behind-camera credits fit the demands of the program offering.   *Brog.*

Dragonfly Squadron

Korean war drama with familiar names of John Hodiak, Barbara Britton, Bruce Bennett to help in the program market.

Hollywood, Jan. 28.

Allied Artists release of John Champion production. Stars John Hodiak Barbara Britton, Bruce Bennett. Directed by Lesley Selander. Screenplay, Champion; camera, Harry Neumann; editor, Walter Hannemann; musical direction, Paul Dunlap. Previewed Jan. 26, '54. Running time, 82 MINS.

Major Mathew Brady....... John Hodiak
Donna Cottrell .... Barbara Britton
Dr. Cottrell .... Bruce Bennett
Dixon .... Jess Barker
Capt. MacIntyre .... Gerald Mohr
Capt. Warnowski .... Chuck Connors
Capt. Veddors .... Harry Lauter
Anne Taylor .... Pamela Duncan
Capt. Wyler .... Adam Williams
Capt. Taylor .... John Lupton
Capt. Liehtse .... Benson Fong
Capt. Wycoff .... John Hedloe

The training of a South Korean air force back in the days before the Reds from the north struck, occupies the footage of "Dragonfly Squadron." The results make for a passable program feature. Familiar names of John Hodiak, Barbara Britton and Bruce Bennett may be of some marquee help.

John Champion produced from his own screenplay and, for budget expenditure, the physical values are okay. Less can be said for the story, which spends quite a bit of time on talk between some rather formula characters in stock situations. The trouping is competent, however, particularly by Hodiak and a few others, so the offering earns a passing mark for its release designation.

Hodiak plays an Air Force major ordered to Kongju in 1950 to step up training of South Korean, who will be used as a cover while evacuation is carried out if and when the Reds strike. There's the usual cliche about the tough officer driving his men almost beyond endurance to background a romantic involvement, but none of it ever rises to any dramatic heights. The "cavalry over the hill" type of finale finds the Reds sending tanks in and just as things look real dark for those on our side, U. S. planes sweep in and blast the tanks to bits.

The romantic triangle in the war setting involves the love between Hodiak and Miss Britton, married to Bennett, a doctor. The romance had started some time before in Hawaii between the two when the husband was believed dead. To insure the fadeout clinch, Bennett dies heroically.

Among the featured players Gerald Mohr, Hodiak's operations officer; Chuck Connors, tough infantry captain, and Benson Fong, Korean officer, come off best. Jess Barker's war correspondent role seems unnecessarily obnoxious, as though the script writer had a beef against newspapermen in general.

Lesley Selander's direction fits the formula standards of the scripting. Lensing, editing and other technical contributions are okay.   *Brog.*

Front Page Story
(BRITISH)

One of best British mellers yet about Fourth Estate; absence of names for U.S. marquee may hurt in America.

London, Jan. 26.

British Lion release of Jay Lewis production. Stars Jack Hawkins, Elizabeth Allan, Eva Bartok; features Derek Farr.

Directed by Gordon Parry. Screenplay, Jay Lewis and Jack Howells from novel, "Final Night," by Robert Gaines; adaptation, William Fairchild, Guy Morgan; camera, Gilbert Taylor; editor, Bill Lewthwaite; music, Jackie Brown. At Warner, London, Jan. 20, '54. Running time, 99 MINS.

Grant .... Jack Hawkins
Susan Grant .... Elizabeth Allan
Mrs. Thorpe .... Eva Bartok
Teale .... Derek Farr
Kennedy .... Michael Goodliffe
Dr. Brukmann .... Martin Miller
Black .... Walter Fitzgerald
Julie .... Patricia Marmont
Dan .... Joseph Tomelty
Jenny .... Jenny Jones
Craig .... Stephen Vercoe
Susan's Mother .... Helen Haye
Farrow .... Michael Howard
Gentle .... Guy Middleton

"Front Page Story," as the title indicates, is a film about newspapermen and, like most screen excursions into the Fourth Estate, it's a highly dramatized picture. From the patrons' point of view is one of the best of its type to come from a British studio. With Jack Hawkins, a local b.o. favorite, as its star, it has bright prospects of substantial returns. Reaction in America and elsewhere will be less enthusiastic, although the film rates fairly general booking. Absence of names may hurt in the U.S.

The yarn is taken from Robert Gaines' novel, "Final Night," and has skillfully been adapted by William Fairchild and Guy Morgan. The film purports to present a day in the life of a national newspaper of which Jack Hawkins is the city editor. To give the story its dramatic content, the script follows through a handful of stories which will make tomorrow's news.

The mood is set by a short prolog, preceding the credit titles, in which Hawkins tells his wife (Elizabeth Allan) that he has to cancel their vacation because he cannot be spared from the office. In the news room the reporters are given their assignments. A sob sister is sent off to the East End to do a story on four kids being evicted from their home; a poetical type is sent to the Old Bailey to get exclusive rights to the life story of a woman charged with a mercy killing; and a drunken old reporter is given his comeback chance by tracking down a distinguished atom scientist who flies in from America.

Treatment of the separate news items gives the film a marked episodic flavor but the incident blends into the general plot structure with the final big story of the day, a plane crash in which Elizabeth Allan is reported among the passengers. At times the action becomes somewhat sluggish and a long harangue on the ethics of journalism could be trimmed with advantage.

Outside of these observations, the film is essentially a taut meller and the overall effect is heightened by a sterling portrayal by Jack Hawkins, who plays the part with honest sincerity. Elizabeth Allan has limited opportunities but fills her role competently while Eva Bartok, as the woman in the dock, has a substantial slice of screen time which she uses to dramatic effect without having a single line of dialog.

Derek Farr admirably portrays Hawkins' deputy, a caddish type who has had an affair with the wife of her boss. Michael Goodliffe, Martin Miller, Walter Fitzgerald and Patricia Marmont fill the major support roles with distinction.

Film has been smoothly directed by Gordon Parry with a fine lensing job from Gilbert Taylor, Arthur Lawson has reproduced an authentic newspaper office and Old Bailey settings.   *Myro.*

Villa Borghese
(ITALIAN)

Rome, Jan. 26.

Astoria Films release of Astoria and Sigma Vog production. Stars Vittorio DeSica, Eduardo De Filippo, Micheline Presle, Gerard Philipe, Anna Maria Ferrero; features Eloisia Gianni, Leda Gloria, Luigi Russo, Enzo Turco, Marizio Arena, Gugliemo Inglese. Directed by Gianni Franciolini. Screenplay, Giorgio Bassani, Ennio Flaiano and Ercole Patti from an idea by Sergio Amidei; camera, Mario Bava; editor, Adriana Novelli. Previewed in Rome: Running time, 95 MINS.

"Villa Borghese" is the name of the Central Park of Rome. Thus, the title of this pic might easily be "A Day in the Park," since that is what it is. Film carries on from early morning to late night through a series of unrelated happenings, all taking place in the Borghese Park. "Villa" is completely Italian in flavor, without problems, and should prove satisfying entertainment. It cannot miss in arty houses.

A half dozen writers have collaborated on the story from an idea suggested by Sergio Amidei, a top Italo scripter. Pace never bogs down. There are the flirtatious nursemaids, the serious young professor who is aware that he is losing his sight, and Vittorio DeSica as an oldish Lothario who makes a fool of himself over a sexy looking seamstress.

Later, the lights go on, and the flash of automobile headlights pick up the painted faces of the ladies of the evening as they search for companions. One ends up as a beauty contest winner while the other one is picked up by the police.

Producer Rudy Solmsen picked his cast with care as well as an eye for the marquee. DeSica, one of Italy's best directors, is excellent as the elderly Romeo in quest of youthful romance while Eduardo De Filippo shows pathos as the father who is over-anxious to arrange a good marriage for his lame daughter. Micheline Presle and Gerard Philipe are standout as the married woman and young lover. Anna Maria Ferrero does well in her sequence.

Gianni Franciolini's direction shows real control of all situations. Mario Bava's camera work is particularly interesting. The musical score of Mario Nascimbene is original and better than adequate.
                          Tubb.

Riot in Cell Block 11

Well-made, topical prison drama that states, articulately, pros, cons of rioting.

Hollywood, Feb. 8.

Allied Artists release of Walter Wanger production. Features Neville Brand, Emile Meyer, Frank Faylen, Leo Gordon, Robert Osterloh, Paul Frees. Directed by Don Siegel. Written by Richard Collins; camera, Russell Harlan; editor, Bruce B. Pierce; music composed and conducted by Herschel Burke Gilbert. Previewed Feb. 4, '54. Running time, **80 MINS.**

Dunn	Neville Brand
The Warden	Emile Meyer
Haskell	Frank Faylen
Carnie	Leo Gordon
The Colonel	Robert Osterloh
Monroe	Paul Frees
Reporter	Don Keefer
Gator	Alvy Moore
Schuyler	Dabbs Greer
Snader	Whit Bissell
Acton	James Anderson
Capt. Barrett	Carleton Young
Reporter	Harold J. Kennedy
Reporter	William Schallert
Russell	Jonathan Hale
Frank	Robert Patton
Mickey	William Phipps
Al	Joel Fluellen
Delmar	Roy Glenn
Mac	Joe Kerr
Manuel	John Tarangelo
Ambrose	Robert Burton

"Riot in Cell Block 11" is a hard-hitting, suspenseful prison thriller with plenty of exploitation box-office chances. It should be a strong grosser for Allied Artists and a profitable booking for those situations that take advantage of the ticket-selling opportunities in the ballyhoo angles. It has been some time since the market has had a real good prison melodrama of this voltage.

The pros and cons of prison riots are stated articulately in the Richard Collins screen story, and producer Walter Wanger uses a realistic, almost documentary, style to make his point for needed reforms in the operation of penal institutions. Don Siegel's taut direction puts these social facets on display effectively, but never minimizes the requirements for gutty, meller-action entertainment that will sustain regular audience attention.

The picture doesn't use formula prison plot. There's no inmate reformed by love or fair treatment, nor unbelieveable boy-meets-girl, gets-same angle. Nor are there any heroes and heavies of standard pattern. Instead, it deals with a riot, how it started and why, what was done to halt it, the capitulations on both sides. Finally, it runs its course and subsides, with neither side having won or lost very much, other than to bring prison conditions to public attention.

The points for reform made in the Wanger production cover overcrowding housing, poor food, the mingling of mentally well and mentally sick prisoners, the character-corroding idleness of men caged in cell blocks. These points are brought up in the riot, a thing of desperate violence led by Neville Brand and in which, either willingly or unwillingly, are involved Leo Gordon, Robert Osterloh, Dabbs Greer, Joel Fluellen, Alvy Moore, Frank Hagney and other inmates. Brand, Gordon and the others deliver forcefully and in character.

A standout performance is given by Emile Meyer, the warden who understands the prisoners' problems because he has long called for reform. Also good are Frank Faylen, politician; Paul Frees, Whit Bissell and James Anderson, who are among the guards held hostages; Carleton Young, guard captain, and each of the other cast members who contribute to the melodramatic punch of the footage.

Russell Harlan's photography counts strongly and the editing by Bruce B. Pierce also is good. Herschel Burke Gilbert composed a good score, but it is used in a formula manner to back the footage. *Brog.*

Hell's Half Acre
(SONGS)

Murder melodrama localed and lensed in Honolulu. So-so program entertainment with mild chances.

Hollywood, Feb. 5.

Republic release of John H. Auer production. Stars Wendell Corey, Evelyn Keyes, Elsa Lanchester. Directed by Auer. Written by Steve Fisher; camera, John L. Russell, Jr.; editor, Fred Allen; music, R. Dale Butts; songs, Jack Pitman and Steve Fisher. Previewed Feb. 3, '54. Running time, **90 MINS.**

Chet Chester	Wendell Corey
Dona Williams	Evelyn Keyes
Lida O'Reilly	Elsa Lanchester
Rose	Marie Windsor
Sally Lee	Nancy Gates
Ippy	Leonard Strong
Tubby Otis	Jesse White
Chief Dan	Keye Luke
Roger Kong	Philip Ahn
Frank	Robert Shield
Jamison	Clair Weidenaar
Slim Novak	Robert Costa

The Hawaiian location sites in "Hell's Half Acre" are more interesting than the routine melodramatics in its plot. The film's possibilities in the general market are about average, however, since familiar names head the cast to give an exhibitor something for the marquees in booking a double bill.

Title derives from a Honolulu skid row section, where much of the action takes place. The Steve Fisher story is a murder meller with some rather involved complications, which aren't helped by the spotty direction of John H. Auer, who also produced, or by the lack of smoothness in the editing. The players are competent and do what they can, but aren't able to add much punch to the presentation.

Wendell Corey plays an island racketeer gone respectable. When his ex-partners try blackmail, his girl friend, Nancy Gates, bumps one off and Corey takes the rap, figuring he can beat it. Into this meller setup comes Evelyn Keyes, searching for a clue that will tab Corey as the husband she believes she lost at Pearl Harbor 10 years before. While she tries to get an admission from him, Miss Gates is murdered. Corey escapes jail on several occasions to find the killer and everything is contrived confusion. At the final, Corey displays his nobleness by fixing things so the killer, Philip Ahn, will gun him down, freeing Miss Keyes for a new marriage and leaving their son to believe his dad died a hero's death at Pearl Harbor.

Elsa Lanchester co-stars with Corey and Miss Keyes, playing a Honolulu taxi-driver who befriends the girl from the mainland. Like most of the others in the cast, nothing much is made of her presence. Miss Gates comes off well as the Chinese girl friend of Corey and others are assorted meller character studies by Ahn, Leonard Strong, Jesse White, Marie Windsor and Keye Luke, the latter good as the Honolulu police chief.

John L. Russell, Jr., handled the cameras satisfactorily, using the island settings as a backdrop for the melodramatics, rather than as as Cook's tour travelog. Two grass-skirt tunes are heard, "Polynesian Rhapsody" and "Lani." Fisher and Jack Pitman collaborated on the first and Pitman did the second solo. *Brog.*

The Holly and the Ivy
(BRITISH)

An example of fine British filmaking. Strong names help give it sock appeal for the arties.

Pacemaker Pictures release of a London Films Production. Stars Ralph Richardson, Celia Johnson, Margaret Leighton, Denholm Elliott; features Hugh Williams, John Gregson, Margaret Halstan, Maureen Delaney, William Hartnell, Robert Flemyng, Roland Culver, Sally Owen. Produced by Anatole de Grunwald. Directed by George More O'Ferrall from a screenplay by Grunwald based on the Wynyard Browne play; camera, Edward Scaife; music, Malcolm Arnold. Previewed Feb. 3, '54 in N.Y. Running time, **80 MINS.**

Rev. Gregory	Ralph Richardson
Jenny Gregory	Celia Johnson
Margaret Gregory	Margaret Leighton
Mick Gregory	Denholm Elliott
Richard Wyndham	Hugh Williams
David Paterson	John Gregson
Aunt Lydia	Margaret Halstan
Aunt Bridget	Maureen Delaney
Company Sgt./Major	William Hartnell
Major	Robert Flemyng
Lord B	Roland Culver
Young Girl	Sally Owen

"The Holly and the Ivy" is the kind of quiet and yet expertly fashioned picture which, if there were more of them, would have the American arties happy and flourishing. Simplicity itself, it is acted and directed with skill and the attention to detail and character study that has endeared other British imports in the past.

If the Wynyard Browne play on which the film is based was only a moderate success on either side of the Atlantic, the film has vastly improved on the stage offering. It is tender, completely believable and, in its critical moments, touching and revealing. It also has a kind of wry sense of humor which only the British know how to poke at themselves.

Much of the credit obviously goes to the cast which reads like a who's-who of British stars. Sir Ralph Richardson, in the lead role of the elderly vicar, delivers a distinctive and captivating performance that is restrained and yet effective. Celia Johnson, as his devoted daughter, imparts to her role all her great talents, creating a character that is uniquely British and at the same time immensely likeable, Margaret Leighton etches a fine portrayal as the second daughter, the black sheep of the family, who needs security but cannot confide in her father.

Denholm Elliot is fresh and wholly competent in the difficult part of the son who finally confronts his father with the bitter truth that his being a parson has created a wall of pretense between him and the family. There are many fine bits of acting to fill out the thin story line. John Gregson, who wants to marry Miss Johnson, is an insistent suitor without being annoying. Hugh Williams registers as the quiet observer, and Margaret Halstan and Maureen Delaney, as the aunts, are a critic's delight and examples of expert type-casting.

Anatole de Grunwald, who both produced and scripted the screenplay, deserves kudos for creating his climaxes without overstating them. His characters act, move and talk with complete conviction and their quarrels, set against the stillness of a snowy Christmas Eve and the bells of Christmas Day, resolve into depth rather than surface shrillness. If anything, the film suffers a little from the overabundance of thoughtful dialogue which is a hangover from the stage version.

The story has the vicar's family assembling for the Christmas holiday. No one has a good time except Richardson who is unawares of the tension and doesn't even know that one of his daughters wants to get married and the other is on the way to becoming a drunkard. Eventually, some frank talk clears the air, particularly in a poignant scene between Richardson and Miss Leighton.

There is much praise owing George More O'Ferrell's direction which creates a fluidity of action despite limited sets. "The Holly and the Ivy" should be a favorite among artie audiences. *Hift.*

The Love Lottery
(BRITISH-COLOR)

David Niven in satirical yarn of Hollywood's star system; over imaginative treatment with spotty b.o. prospects.

London, Feb. 2.

General Film Distributors release of Ealing Studios-Michael Balcon production. Stars David Niven, Peggy Cummins, Anne Vernon, Herbert Lom. Directed by Charles Crichton. Screenplay, Harry Kurnitz from story by Charles Neilson Gattey and Zelma Bramley-Moore; camera, Douglas Slocombe; editor, Seth Holt; music, Benjamin Frankel. At Gaumont, London, Jan. 26, '54. Running time, **89 MINS.**

Rex Allerton	David Niven
Sally	Peggy Cummins
Jane	Anne Vernon
Amico	Herbert Lom
Jennings	Charles Victor
Ralph	Gordon Jackson
Winant	Felix Aylmer
Rodney Wheeler	Hugh McDermott
Stanton	Stanley Maxted
Viola	June Clyde
Gulliver Kee	John Chandos
Parsimonious	Theodore Bikel
Suarez	Sebastian Cabot
Fodor	Andrea Malandrinos

Ealing Studios, which had a run of major boxoffice hits, via a string of outstanding comedies, lately has been trying its hand at satire with less conspicuous results. This time it is a try at satirizing Hollywood's star system. But this basically amusing idea gets bogged down by super-clever treatment which will probably misfire with most types of audience. Boxoffice prospects must be rated as spotty.

The yarn, scripted by Harry Kurnitz, opens in Hollywood, moves to London and finishes in an Italian lakeside resort. In earlier sequences, it has a few satirical shafts at the picture industry which would evoke yocks from a pro audience, but the entire subject is overloaded with a series of dream sequences which delay the plot and restrict the action.

David Niven is cast as a topranking star at a Hollywood studio where he is No. 2 only to the unit's wonder dog. As a publicity sunt, a columnist dreams up the idea of a lottery with the first prize being a week with the star. In satirical vein, Niven suggests a week is not adequate and says he'll take the winner for life. While the idea is being ridiculed by press and radio, the star flies to London but once again finds himself besieged by unruly fans. So finally, almost in desperation, he takes a boat to Italy, hoping to find peace and quiet. But he did not reckon with the computation business run by Herbert Lom, who traps him into keeping his love lottery promise.

The general theme is dressed in highly imaginative style with the dream sequences intruding whenever the plot shows signs of sagging. These are aimed to portray the state of mind of a star harassed by howling fans and by an ardent female bobbysoxer who reenacts some of the romantic scenes from the films in which her hero starred. It is this girl who picks the winning ticket.

Film has a quality look and is expensively mounted, while the Lake Como locations are attractive in the Technicolor hues The acting standard is more than adequate for the yarn. Niven gives a typically smooth portrayal as the harassed star while Peggy Cummins sparkles as the adoring fan. Anne Vernon blends sophistication and charm as the beguiling statistician. Lom turns in a reliable study as the sinister and suave head of the computation setup, with Theodore Bikel as one of his assistants. Charles Victor does a flawless job as the star's valet and Felix Aylmer, in a little more than a bit, stands out as an impresario. Other roles have been filled with obvious care. *Myro.*

White Fire

British-filmed meller mystery with Scott Brady, Mary Castle; for programmer bookings.

Hollywood, Feb. 4.

Lippert Pictures release of Robert S. Baker, Monty Berman (Tempean Films) production. Stars Scott Brady, Mary Castle; features Gabrielle Brune, Ferdy Mayne, Colin Tapley, John Blythe. Directed by John Gilling. Screenplay, Paul Erickson and John Gilling; from a story by Erickson; camera, Monty Berman; editor, Marjorie Saunders; music, Stanley Black; song, Black and Barbara Killalee. Previewed Feb. 2, '54. Running time, **81 MINS.**

Gregor Stevens	Scott Brady
Yvonne Durante	Mary Castle
Lorna	Gabrielle Brune
Sartago	Ferdy Mayne
Winston	Colin Tapley
Darr	John Blythe
James Smith	Lloyd Lamble
John Durante	Julian Somers
Inspector Haley	Ballard Berkeley
Crawson	Ronan O'Casey
Charley	John Schofield
Larrry	Paul Erickson

A passably fair 81 minutes of melodramatic complications are unspooled in "White Fire," a British-made programmer which Lippert Pictures is distributing domestically. A lively pace, stepped up quite a bit from the usual British tempo, helps to carry it off and it has Scott Brady's name for the marquees in the lesser market.

Labeled a Tempean Films production, produced by Robert S. Baker and Monty Berman, the presentation has a highly contrived plot about a U.S. Merchant Marine officer (Brady) who comes to London to visit his brother, finds him three days away from execution for murder and, in the short span of time that his ship's in harbor, solves the killing, unmasks a diamond-smuggling gang and gets himself a girl. Suspects turn up in every alley, where Brady spends quite a lot of time getting badly beaten by the gang's strongarm guys. The police aid him, in a round-about manner, get the goods on Colin Tapley, the gang's mastermind who is also the attorney who defended the brother, and when his ship sails, Mary Castle, saloon singer and unwilling tool of the crooks, is aboard for the finale clinch.

John Gilling's direction keeps the script moving, but he can't do much to make it believable. Performances by Brady, Miss Castle, Tapley, and the others in the cast are adequate, considering the light demands of the screenplay by Paul Erickson and John Gilling. Technical credits are about average for this type of budget feature. Score includes a tune, "No Way Out," written by Stanley Black and Barbara Killalee. *Brog.*

Creature From the Black Lagoon
(3-D)

Well-done science-fiction horror feature guaranteed to spook the chiller fan, amuse others. Good exploitation possibilities.

Hollywood, Feb. 9.

Universal release of William Alland production. Stars Richard Carlson, Julia Adams. Directed by Jack Arnold. Screenplay, Harry Essex, Arthur Ross; story by Maurice Zimm; camera, William E. Snyder; special photography, Charles S. Welbourne; underwater sequences directed by James C. Havens; editor, Ted J. Kent; musical direction, Joseph Gershenson; makeup, Bud Westmore. Previewed Feb. 2, '54. Running time, **79 MINS.**

David Reed	Richard Carlson
Kay	Julia Adams
Mark Williams	Richard Denning
Carl Maia	Antonio Moreno
Lucas	Nestor Paiva
Dr. Thompson	Whit Bissell
Zee	Bernie Gozier
Chico	Henry Escalante

Monsters from out of space have been getting a film ride of late in science-fiction offerings, but in this 3-D hackle-raiser Universal reverts to the prehistoric. It's horror guaranteed to spook the chiller fan and amuse others. Excellent exploitation possibilities.

After the discovery of a web-fingered skeleton hand in the Amazon region, a scientific expedition heads into the steaming tropics to hunt more fossils. In the backwashes of the Amazon they come across a still living Gill Man, half-fish, half-human. While trying to study and photograph the monster, several members of the expedition lose their lives and the creature, with a human canniness, tries to prevent the party's leaving. He has become interested in the femme member of the party, even captures her at the finale, but the windup finds her freed and the monster, mortally wounded, sinking into the depths of the black lagoon to die.

The 3-D lensing adds to the eerie effects of the underwater footage, as well as to the monster's several appearances on land. The below-water scraps between skin divers and the pre-historic thing are thrilling and will pop goose pimples on the susceptible fan, as will the closeup scenes of the scaly, gilled creature. Jack Arnold's direction has done a firstrate job of developing chills and suspense, and James C. Havens rates a good credit for his direction of the underwater sequences. The frightening monster makeup was developed by Bud Westmore and Jack Kevan.

Richard Carlson, whose name is becoming almost synonymous with science-fiction films, and Julia Adams co-star in the William Alland production and carry off the thriller very well. Topnotch assists are supplied by Richard Denning, Antonio Moreno, Nestor Paiva, Whit Bissell and other cast members, including the assorted unnamed performers who enact the monster in various scenes in the footage. As befitting the Amazonian setting, Miss Adams appears mostly in brief shorts or swim suits, and the males will like what she displays.

Harry Essex and Arthur Ross put together a good chiller script from Maurice Zimm's story. Rating a nod for the 3-D lensing is William E. Snyder, plus the special photography contributed by Charles S. Welbourne. Editing and other technical credits are expertly handled. *Brog.*

World Without End
(DOCUMENTARY)

Produced by Basil Wright for the United Nations Educational, Scientific and Cultural Organization. Directors, Paul Rotha, Basil Wright; narration written by Rex Warner, spoken by Michael Gough; camera, Jose Carlos Carbajal, Adrian Jeakins. Music, Elizabeth Luytens. Running time, **60 MINS.**

Hollywood, Feb. 8.

Since the inception of the United Nations Educational, Scientific and Cultural Organization (UNESCO) several years ago, films have played an increasingly important part in making the work of the organization understandable to the peoples of the world. UN cameras have peered and pried into many sections of the globe, explaining what UNESCO is trying to do to better living conditions and raise standards in undeveloped areas.

Latest in the series of UNESCO documents that relate the progress in this direction is "World Without End," a skillful, professional job of story-telling which weaves together activities at opposite ends of the world to explain the functions of various branches of the world organization. The camera follows UN workers in Mexico and in Thailand, capturing their labors and their successes in the fields of agriculture, medicine, etc. The "one world" concept is underlined through intercutting from one part of the globe to another so that the similarity between the basic problems to be faced in Mexico and those to be faced in Thailand is readily apparent.

This intercutting is at once the strength and the weakness of the documentary. It serves its purpose well for the most part but is occasionally overdone, or so abrupt, that the transition is ragged and the comparison therefore seems forced. Film is made up of several incidents, among the most compelling being the triumph of UN medical workers over such diseases as yaws.

Film boasts some excellent camera work by Jose Carlos Carbajal, whose Mexican footage had an almost third-dimensional quality, and by Adrian Jeakins whose black-and-white work in Thailand frequently had the impact of color. Rex Warner's fine narration is well-voiced by Michael Gough. Elizabeth Luytens' score is frequently too busy. *Kap.*

Destinees
(FRENCH-ITALIAN)

Paris, Feb. 2.

Cinedis release of Franco-London production. Starr Claudette Colbert, Martine Carol, Michele Morgan, Eleanora Rossi-Drago, Raf Vallone. Directed by Marcel Pagliero, Jean Delannoy, Christian-Jaque. Camera, Robert Lefevbre, Christian Matras; editor, James Cuenet; screenplay, Jean Aurenche, Pierre Bost, Jean Ferry, Henri Jeanson, Carlo Rim, Andre Tabot. At Marignan, Paris. Running time, **105 MINS.**

Elisabeth	Claudette Çolbert
Angela	Eleanora Rossi-Drago
Jeanne	Michele Morgan
Lysistrata	Martine Carol
Cassias	Raf Vallone
Barata	Daniel Ivernel
Senator	Paola Stoppa

Three of the top commercial directors here have put together a three-sketch pic with a bundle of femme names which should insure nice returns here. This primarily distaff-appeal pic has the theme of woman and war, with one section dealing with a victim of the last war; another, with Joan of Arc, using war to fulfill her destiny, and third sketch, built around the ancient Greek comedy, "Lysistrata," used to tell the tale of the love strike that ended a war. Though two of the sketches seem part of a full-length pic, removed from context, this has names of femmes Claudette Colbert, Michele Morgan and Martine Carol for U. S. marquee appeal. This subject could make a good bet for special spotting in America.

Film isn't as varied and insouciant as predecessor, "Seven Deadly Sins," and the sketch type mounting robs the two serious ones of dramatic depth with the characters thrown into dramatic decision before they can be properly prepared. However, the racy Greek opus gives this a word-of-mouth appeal.

First sketch concerns the almost necrophilic voyage of a U.S. wife to Italy to retrieve the body of her husband buried there. She has practically abandoned life since his death. She finds her husband had been harbored by an Italo family before he was killed and that the girl of the family bore him a child. Next sketch has a moment in the life of Joan of Arc when she has been deserted by her king and soldiers.

Last section is a bawdy takeoff on "Lysistrata" in which the wives of Athens, tired of war, go on a love strike to bring their men to their senses. This is played as outright farce and though it loses some high comedy potential, it gives the film its racy moments as the sex-hungry men finally capitulate to the enticing blandishments of their spouses.

Miss Colbert is adequately reserved as the returning wife, and Marcel Pagliero's unobtrusive direction plays out this sudsy drama without letting it get too thick. Miss Morgan lends a radiant face to the Joan of Arc role which is primarily what is called for. Christian-Jaque has blandly let the female have her way in his Greek farce section and he allows Miss Carol to play the supposedly wily ringleader in an addlepated fashion which is made up for by her obvious physical attributes. Men are in the backgronud in this, though Paola Stoppa etches a nice bit as a wily senator. However, Raf Vallone is not up to the comic handling of the harassed general. Lensing and editing are in keeping with the intelligent handling of these stories. Properly handled and hypoed this may do well in the U. S. *Mosk.*

Alerte Au Sud
(Alert in the South)
(FRENCH-COLOR)

Paris, Feb. 2.

Sirius release of Netune-Sirius-Fonorama production. Stars Eric Von Stroheim, Giana Maria Canale, Jean-Claude Pascal. Directed by Jean Devaivre. Screenplay, Jean Devaivre from novel by Pierre Nord; camera, Lucien Joulin; editor, Louis Devaivre. At Lutetia, Paris. Running time, **115 MINS.**

Conrad	Eric Von Stroheim
Jean	Jean-Claude Pascal
Natalie	Giana Maria Canale
Howard	Peter Van Eyck
Michele	Lia Amanda
Colonel	Jean Murat

This is a tinter adventure film set in French Africa with shades of escionage and science fiction. Scripting and action is much too reminiscent and old hat to make this of any U. S. interest except possibly for dualers. It has Eric Von Stroheim name, is a tinter and the action needed for general situations.

Jean-Claude Pascal, a young lieutenant, sees a friend of his die as he tries to tell him of some skullduggery. All he has are a few leads to the guilty. The avenger starts out to get the guys who killed his pal. Into his snooping comes a French secret service man masquerading as an Arab rug merchant, a mysterious German gambler, a sexy lefty ballerina and assorted thugs. He gets in with the German's gang and gets entangled romantically with the ballerina. Feigning expulsion from the army, he is sent by the mob to a desert outpost presided over by a half-mad German general, who has refused to call off the war. Last-named is Eric Von Stroheim. After the usual tussels, sacrifice and torture, the cavalry, on camels, arrives in time.

The color and Morocco lensing add production dress. The direction gets in its quota of movement and mayhem in neat commercial lines. Von Stroheim manages to get some malice and depth into his silly role as the half-crazy professional soldier while Giana Maria Canale adds Italo lushness to the part of not-so-bad girl. Lensing is good as is the editing. *Mosk.*

Overland Pacific
(COLOR)

Jack Mahoney, tv's "Range Rider," heading regulation feature western for the program action market.

Hollywood, Feb. 8.
United Artists release of a World (Eddie Small) production. Stars Jack Mahoney, Peggie Castle, Adele Jergens. Directed by Fred F. Sears. Screenplay, J. Robert Bren, Gladys Atwater, Martin Goldsmith; story, Frederic Louis Fox; camera (color by Color Corp. of America), Lester White; editor, Bernard Small. Previewed Feb. 2, '54. Running time, 73 MINS.
Rose Granger .... Jack Mahoney
Ann Dennison .... Peggie Castle
Jessie Lorraine .... Adele Jergens
Del Stewart .... William Bishop
Mr. Dennison .... Walter Sande
Sheriff Haney .... Chubby Johnson
Dark Thunder .... Pat Hogan
Jason .... Chris Alcaide
Weeks .... Phil Chambers
Broden .... George Eldredge
Saber .... Dick Rich
Perkins .... House Peters Jr.

Regulation western action is run off in this feature oater and it should prove an okay entry for program bookings, mostly because of the presence of tv's "Range Rider" Jack Mahoney as the male star, and the use of color.

A World (Eddie Small) production for United Artists release and directed by Fred F. Sears, the offering lays enough stress on action to keep the outdoor fan satisfied. The Frederic Louis Fox story, which J. Robert Bren, Gladys Atwater and Martin Goldsmith scripted, puts together standard ingredients and the formula is tried and true. Only incongruous note is the fancy phraseology the principals are given to speak. Otherwise, everything is to formula and delivered acceptably.

Mahoney plays an undercover agent for the railroad, sent to Oaktown to find out what is causing trouble with the Indians and delaying the laying of the new road. When the shooting's all over, it is revealed that William Bishop, saloon owner, wants the right-of-way to swing through Oaktown, where he owns valuable property, and to that end he gives the Indians rifles and keeps them stirred

up. Mahoney has authority in his heroics and gives the picture an action-plus touch in settling the trouble and winning the love of Peggie Castle. She, too, does well by her assignment, and Bishop is a good heavy.

Adele Jergens, saloon entertainer, divides femme interest as a Bishop castoff while he tries to make time with Miss Castle. Walter Sande, railroad construction man and father of Miss Castle; Chubby Johnson, crooked sheriff; Pat Hogan, Indian chief; Chris Alcaide, gunman, and Phil Chambers, hotel proprietor, mortician and doctor for the town, are among others offering a variety of types to the western plot.

Color Corp. of America furnished the tints for Lester White's lensing and the hues are not always true, but do add to the outdoor values. Editing and other technical assists are okay. *Brog.*

Rhapsody
(MUSIC—COLOR)

Romantic soap opera with classical music background. More for the middleaged femme matinee fans than for males or younger set. Will have its selling problems.

Hollywood, Feb. 16.
Metro release of Lawrence Weingarten production. Stars Elizabeth Taylor, Vittorio Gassman, John Ericson, Louis Calhern; features Michael Chekhov, Barbara Bates, Richard Hageman. Directed by Charles Vidor. Screenplay, Fay and Michael Kanin; adaptation, Ruth and Augustus Goetz; based on the novel "Maurice Guest" by Henry Handel Richardson; camera (Technicolor), Robert Planck; editor, John Dunning; musical adaptation, Bronislau Kaper; music conducted by Johnny Green; piano solos played by Claudio Arrau; violin solos played by Michael Rabin. Previewed Feb. 11, '54. Running time, 115 MINS.
Louise Durant .... Elizabeth Taylor
Paul Bronte .... Vittorio Gassman
James Guest .... John Ericson
Nichols Durant .... Louis Calhern
Prof. Schuman .... Michael Chekhov
Effie Cahill .... Barbara Bates
Bruno Furst .... Richard Hageman
Otto Krafft .... Richard Lupino
Frau Sigerist .... Celia Lovsky
Dove .... Stuart Whitman
Mrs. Cahill .... Madge Blake
Edmund Streller .... Jack Raine
Madeleine .... Birgit Nielsen
Yvonne .... Jacqueline Duval
Student-Pianist .... Norma Nevens

"Rhapsody" is the kind of romantic soap opera set to classical music that should lure the middle-aged femme matinee trade. Also, it is the type of tears-and-torment drama that has little appeal for the younger set or the male ticket buyer. Thus, despite a lavish presentation in Technicolor, the enduring music of Rachmaninoff and Tschaikowsky, plus a good cast, the picture has its selling problems and will not find the boxoffice-going easy.

The property was acquired from Paramount by Metro for filming, along with Charles Vidor to direct. The Culver City lot has given it the "A" treatment in casting and production budget so that visually the presentation has an outstanding quality. As entertainment, however, it falters often, through stretching its pot-boiler plot over an unnecessarily long one hour and 55 minutes. The story and the characters in it haven't the depth to sustain that much running time.

The picture is based on the novel, "Maurice Gest," by Henry Handel Richardson. Fay and Michael Kanin wrote the screenplay from an adaptation by Ruth and Augustus Goetz. The writing is slick, but shallow, and rather obviously plotted along standard romantic conflict lines. Within these limits, Vidor's direction achieves good performances from the players. Music, of course, is standout as played by Claudio Arrau on Sergei Rachmaninoff's "Concerto No. 2 in C Minor" and Michael Rabin on Peter Ilyitch Tschaikowsky's "Concerto in D Major." Their piano and violin solo stints, respectively, are high artistry.

Considerable emotional anguish is stirred up in the story behind the music. Miss Taylor is a spoiled rich girl who falls in love with Vittorio Gassman, a self-sufficient violin student. This romance takes the expected turn and they split because she plays second fiddle to his fiddle. Stepping into the breach is John Ericson, selfsacrificing piano student, who gives up his career to devote himself to her and becomes a society drunk doing it. Meanwhile, Gassman has become a great success and Miss Taylor tries to get him back. To achieve this goal, she decides to push Ericson back into music and he scores.

Finale has Miss Taylor realizing that Ericson is what she has wanted all along.

The fourth star in all this is Louis Calhern, but he is only in and out on several occasions as Miss Taylor's indulgent father, too busy with his own playing to give her much time. Michael Chekhov, as a professor at the Zurich conservatory; Richard Hageman, a conductor; Barbara Bates, a playgirl musical student; Celia Lovsky and the others come through with satisfactory type performances.

Lawrence Weingarten's production supervision has mustered a number of outstanding technical aids to give the picture high voltage visual impact. Starring here are Robert Planck's photography, the settings and the costume designs by Helen Rose. The latter are unusually becoming to the unbelieveable beauty of Miss Taylor. High on the list of credits are the musical adaptation by Bronislau Kaper and Johnny Green's conducting. Also of note is the simulation of actual playing by Gassman on violin and Ericson on piano. *Brog.*

The Naked Jungle
(COLOR)

Interesting romantic drama with jungle adventure aspects and Eleanor Parker, Charlton Heston.

Hollywood, Feb. 9.
Paramount release of George Pal production. Stars Eleanor Parker, Charlton Heston. Directed by Byron Haskin. Screenplay, Philip Yordan, Ranald MacDougall; based on "Leiningen Versus the Ants" by Carl Stephenson; camera (Technicolor), Ernest Laszlo; editor, Everett Douglas; special photographic effects, John P. Fulton; process photography, Farciot Edouart; music, Daniele Amfitheatrof. Previewed Feb. 8, '54. Running time, 95 MINS.
Joanna Leiningen ...... Eleanor Parker
Christopher Leiningen...Charlton Heston
Incacha .... Abraham Sofaer
Commissioner .... William Conrad
Boat Captain .... Romo Vincent
Medicine Man .... Douglas Fowley
Gruber .... John Dierkes
Kutina .... Leonard Strong
Zala .... Norma Calderon

There's a lot of the tried-and-found-true romantic drama formula in "The Naked Jungle," an interesting feature that mixes in jungle adventure with a science-fiction touch dealing with an invading army of ants that think.

Man-against-ant fight was described in December, 1938, issue of Esquire. (Carl Stephenson's "Leiningen versus the Ants.")

The familiar names of Eleanor Parker and Charlton Heston occupy the star spots in the well adapted script by Philip Yordan and Ranald MacDougall. For Miss Parker it is a particularly good characterization, warm and human. Heston hits his stride about the halfway mark after his character opens up and becomes more human and understandable to the ticket-buyer. Up to that time he plays the part with a sombre heaviness that is too forbidding. This is the only mistake in Byron Haskin's otherwise smart, suspense-building and actionful direction.

From a rather straightforward romantic drama, the story gets into its thriller moments. A mail-order bride comes from New Orleans to bed with a man, without femme experience, who has spent 15 years hewing a profitable plantation and palatial home out of the jungles of South America. She finds he doesn't like her matter-of-fact approach to her marital obligations. The marriage situation takes a further turn for the worse when he realizes she has been married before.

As the conflict of this marital situation moves forward to a not unexpected climax, the threat of the ant invasion takes over. The dread soldier ants of South America organize in a purposeful march and descend on the plantation, putting a gripping tag on the romantic story as the austere plantation owner finds love and the will from an untouched bride to fight off successfully an insect enemy that consumes completely plant and human life as it moves across the land relentlessly.

Supporting two stars are a number of impressive featured performances. Abraham Sofaer scores as the plantation owner's chief servant, as does William Conrad, jungle-wise commissioner; Douglas Fowley, medicine man; Leonard Strong, a native; Norma Calderon, very appealing as the native girl assigned to care for the bride; Romo Vincent and John Dierkes.

Putting wallop into the interest-holding unfoldment is Ernest Laszlo's lensing, the special photographic effects by John P. Fulton and Farciot Edouart's process photography. Edith Head clothes Miss Parker most attractively, and Daniele Amfitheatrof's score is a fitting background. *Brog.*

Duffy of San Quentin

Formula prison melodrama for programmer playdates.

Hollywood, Feb. 9.

Warner Bros. release of Berman Swarttz and Walter Doniger production. Stars Louis Hayward, Joanne Dru, Paul Kelly; co-stors Maureen O'Sullivan. Direction and screenplay by Doniger; from a story by Swarttz and Doniger; based on the book "The San Quentin Story" by Clinton T. Duffy and Dean Jennings; camera, John Alton; editor, Edward Sampson Jr.; music, Paul Dunlap. Previewed Feb. 5, '54. Running time, 76 MINS.

Edward Harper .... Louis Hayward
Anne Halsey .... Joanne Dru
Warden Clinton T. Duffy...... Paul Kelly
Gladys Duffy .... Maureen O'Sullivan
Winant .... George Macready
Pierson .... Horace McMahon
Doc .... Irving Bacon
Bill .... Joel Fluellen
Frank .... Joseph Turkel
Boyd .... Jonathan Hale
Pinto .... Michael McHale
Nealy .... Peter Brocco

The programmer market will find "Duffy of San Quentin" just a passable dual bill booking. It's a slow-moving prison melodrama, developed in ordinary fashion, and there is very little of interest, even for undiscriminating audiences, in its 76 minutes.

Picture was produced independently by Berman Swarttz and Walter Doniger, with Warner Bros. taking it over for distribution. In addition to teaming as producers, Swarttz and Doniger handled the other principal functions, but none with distinction. Doniger scripted and directed from a story on which he collaborated with Swarttz. Basis for the offering is "The San Quentin Story" by Clinton T. Duffy, long warden of San Quentin, and Dean Jennings.

Plot deals with Duffy's start as warden, the reforms he introduced and the reaction of a few of the prison inmates at that time. The unfoldment is tediously paced and there are few action spots of any validity to interest wavers constantly. Such commonplace types as the man framed by a conviction-crazy prosecutor, the brutal guard, the shiv-happy inmate, the snivelling stoolie and the beautiful nurse are mixed together in the script for minor results.

Paul Kelly appears as Duffy and Maureen O'Sullivan as his understanding wife. He is competent as far as script and direction permit, as are Miss O'Sullivan, Louis Hayward, the bitter railroaded prisoner; Joanne Dru, the beautiful nurse with whom Hayward falls in love; Horace MacMahon, the brutal guard; George Macready, the prosecutor, and Peter Brocco, the stoolie. Playing other prison types are Irving Bacon, Joel Fluellen and Joseph Turkel.

Technical support of the production is okay. *Brog.*

Tennessee Champ
(COLOR)

Entertaining comedy on prizefighting and religion; above average programmer.

Hollywood, Feb. 15.

Metro release of Sol Baer Fielding production. Stars Shelley Winters, Keenan Wynn, Dewey Martin. Directed by Fred M. Wilcox. Screenplay, Art Cohn; from "The Lord In His Corner" and other stories, by Eustace Cockrell; camera (Ansco Color), George Folsey; editor, Ben Lewis; music, Conrad Salinger; theme "Weary Blues" by Harry Warren and Ralph Blane. Previewed Feb. 10, '54. Running time, 72 MINS.

Sarah Wurble .... Shelley Winters
Willy Wurble .... Keenan Wynn
Daniel Norson .... Dewey Martin
Happy Jackfield .... Earl Holliman
Luke MacWade .... Dave O'Brien
Sixty Jubel .... Charles Buchinsky
Blossom .... Yvette Dugay
J. B. Backett .... Frank Richards
Andrews .... Jack Kruschen

Prizefighting and religion get an entertaining comedy mix in "Tennessee Champ," an above-average programmer that should draw favorable comment from its playdates in the general market. The chuckles are constant in the fast 72 minutes, the trouping is nifty and the Ansco color adds visual values for the bookings.

The title hardly goes with a Shelley Winters starrer, being more suited to masculine toppers Keenan Wynn and Dewey Martin, but since story emphasis is on them it's a fitting handle for the entertainment aims. Besides the playing of these three stars and Earl Holliman, heading the featured list, the picture scores in the scripting and direction. Producer Sol Baer Fielding's overseeing is excellent, permitting the Art Cohn screenplay to play off naturally under Fred M. Wilcox's neatly valued direction. The flavor of Eustace Cockrell's "The Lord In His Corner" and other stories by the author is maintained, even though the hero has been switched from a Negro prizefighter with religion to a white character.

Wynn portrays a fast-buck fight manager who finds a new boy to fleece when he pulls Martin out of the river. With Wynn's smart management and by having the Lord in his corner, Martin comes along fast until Wynn tries to promote a crooked match and his fighter finds out about the deal and leaves the manager flat. The religious philosophy of Martin finally gets through to Wynn, he turns a new leaf and stages an honest bout between Martin and Charles Buchinsky, a man the hero believed he had killed in an early-footage scrap. The new Wynn pleases Miss Winters, his wife, and the film ends on uplift note.

Little touches of character and comedy prevail in most of the scenes to make the picture better entertainment than its normal booking slot. The three stars come over excellently and Holliman scores as a punchy fighter continually blowing a tiny, concealed harmonica. Buchinsky, Dave O'Brien, Yvette Dugay, as Martin's sweetie, Frank Richards, Jack Kruschen and others do their share towards helping the amusement.

Theme melody, "Weary Blues" by Harry Warren and Ralph Blane, is featured in the background throughout and has appeal. Conrad Salinger did the good score and George Folsey the topnotch color lensing. Other credits are competent, too. *Brog.*

Bait

Hugo Haas in another earthy meller; exploitable for the program market.

Columbia release of Hugo Haas (Robert Erlik) production. Stars Cleo Moore, Hugo Haas, John Agar. Directed by Haas. Screenplay and story, Samuel W. Taylor; additional dialog, Haas; camera, Edward P. Fitzgerald; editor, Robert S. Eisen; music, Vaclav Divina. Tradeshown, N.Y., Feb. 4, '54. Running time, 79 MINS.

Peggy .... Cleo Moore
Marko .... Hugo Haas
Ray Brighton .... John Agar
Foley .... Emmett Lynn
Webb .... Bruno Ve Sota
Waitress .... Jan Englund
Chuck .... George Keymas
Prologue .... Sir Cedric Hardwicke

"Bait" is the fourth in a series of low-budgeters that writer-producer-director-actor Hugo Haas has turned out since his "Pickup" for Columbia release started the cycle in the summer of 1951. In keeping with previous entries, his latest effort contains a generous helping of sex and melodrama.

While such time-tested ingredients obviously hold audience interest, the story of which they're components is too familiar and evident to command more than average returns from the program market. Subject, however, is an exploitable one and strong selling on this aspect may help offset the lack of marquee names in the cast.

Screenplayed by Samuel W. Taylor from his own yarn, the script is localed in the northern California mountains where eccentric prospector Haas has been seeking a "lost" gold mine for almost 20 years. Suffice to note that he locates the lode with aid of John Agar with whom he previously agreed to split 50-50 on the proceeds.

But with the glint of the gold to goad him on, Haas conceives of a diabolical scheme to murder Agar and appropriate the latter's share. He baits the trap with his (Haas') waitress-wife, Cleo Moore, and attempts to lead the younger couple into a compromising spot so Agar could be slain as "justifiable homicide." Plan backfires into his own death.

Haas, who usually collaborates on the scripting, contributed additional dialog on this one. But more than extra conversation is needed to make the Taylor story ring with realism and plausibility. In what amounts to virtually a one-man affair, Haas makes good use of his limited production values but his direction falls short of making the subject an absorbing one. His portrayal of the prospector is fair.

Agar acquits himself favorably as Haas' husky partner who for the most part restrains his instincts when femininity in the buxom shape of Miss Moore pervades the trio's one-room mountain cabin. She capably fills the moderate demands of her role and under some interesting camera angles shows that she can wear lingerie with the best of her contemporaries. Adequate support is provided by Emmett Lynn and Bruno Ve Sota, among others.

There's brief prologue to the film in which Sir Cedrick Hardwicke more or less does a "monodrama" as the devil. It's intended as some "stage-setting" for Haas' machinations and as such probably attains its objective. Camerawork of Edward P. Fitzgerald represents competent lensing especially in his shots of mountain vistas. Vaclav Divina's score blends nicely with the general mood. *Gilb.*

You Know What Sailors Are
(BRITISH—COLOR)

Amusing British comedy about a naval hoax; Okay for general exhibition in U.S.

London, Feb. 9.

General Film Distributors release of Julian Wintle production. Stars Akim Tamiroff, Donald Sinden, Sarah Lawson, Naunton Wayne. Directed by Ken Annakin. Screenplay, Peter Rogers; camera, Reginald Wyer; editor, Alfred Roome; music, Malcolm Arnold. At Odeon, Leicester Square, London, Feb. 9, '54. Running time, 89 MINS.

President of Agraria ..... Akim Tamiroff
Lt. Green .... Donald Sinden
Betty .... Sarah Lawson
Capt. Owbridge .... Naunton Wayne
Lt. Smart .... Bill Kerr
Gladys .... Dora Bryan
Prof. Pfumbaum .... Martin Miller
Admiral .... Michael Shepley
Capt. Hamilton .... Michael Hordern
Voritz .... Ferdy Mayne
Commander Voles .... Bryan Coleman
Stores Officer .... Cyril Chamberlain
Petty Officer .... Hal Osmond
Ahmed .... Peter Arne
Jasmin .... Shirley Lorrimer
Almyra .... Janet Richards
Hepzibah .... Eileen Sands
Elsie .... Marianne Stone
Lt. Andrews .... Peter Dyneley
Lt. Ross .... Peter Martyn

Lush Technicolor, luscious girls in an eastern harem and a neatly sustained joke about a naval hoax are the main boxoffice ingredients of this new British comedy which looks set for healthy returns in the home market. As pure escapist entertainment it also deserves general showing overseas, including America, where they appreciate the British weakness for laughing at themselves.

The title of the film does not give a fair impression of its story content although it may have marquee lure, particularly if exploited alongside some scenes of the beauties who decorate the picture.

The plot shows three naval officers, who have been taking on plenty of liquor, wending their way back to their ship and collecting an old perambulator frame and a pawnbroker's sign. Still in their cups, they rig these on to a visiting naval vessel. The following morning a shamefaced officer suggests that it might be a new type of radar equipment known as "998." This starts a top brass clamor for priority installation of the equipment on a British ship. While the mystery is being probed in England, the offending officer has been seconded to the foreign ship as a radar instructor and gets highly involved.

By far the best part of this is during the earlier sequences of bright quips. But it is in the latter half that the film has its main visual appeal. The screen is frequently filled by a bunch of eye-filling girls who keep the young officer a prisoner in the president's palace.

Participating in the comedy is a team of fine British performers. Akim Tamiroff's robust portrayal of the president is in sharp contrast to Donald Sinden's apprehension as the young naval officer. Sarah Lawson fills the romantic lead with charm while Naunton Wayne is good for many chuckles as a harassed senior naval officer. Dora Bryan, as the president's English wife, and Martin Miller, playing the foreign scientist, are at the head of a slick supporting cast.

Pic has been adroitly directed by Ken Annakin. George Provis has done an effective job with the sets, particularly those of the president's palace. *Myro.*

Weak and the Wicked
(BRITISH)

Authentic story of inside femme prison without bars. Suitable as dualer in U.S.

London, Feb. 9.

Associated British release of Marble Arch production. Stars Glynis Johns. Directed by J. Lee-Thompson. Screenplay, J. Lee-Thompson & Anne Burnaby in collaboration with Joan Henry; camera, Gilbert Taylor; editor, Richard Best. At Ritz, London, starting Feb. 2, '54. Running time, **88 MINS.**

Jean	Glynis Johns
Michael	John Gregson
Betty	Diana Dors
Babs	Jane Hylton
Syd Baden	Sidney James
Nellie Baden	Olive Sloane
Grandad	Eliot Makeham
Harry Wicks	A. E. Matthews
Millie	Athlene Seyler
Mabel	Sybil Thorndike
Tina	Simone Silva
Joe	Paul Carpenter

This new British film is based on the first-hand experience of Joan Henry of life in a women's prison and a reformatory without bars. The subject matter, which is taken from her novel and adapted for the screen by J. Lee-Thompson and Anne Barnaby, is a safe formula for a boxoffice meller. It will register best in situations here where the quota seal is an additional inducement. In the U.S. and other overseas markets it will serve as a dualer.

The incident and backgrounds are undoubtedly authentic but to encompass the experience of eight months in 88 minutes screen time leads to some scrappiness in the treatment. There is obviously no time to depict the boredom and isolation suffered by the femme inmates.

The focal point of the script is Glynis Johns, who plays a young girl of good family and education who is framed on a fraud charge after being unable to meet her gambling debts. Among the inmates are Diana Dors, who takes a two-year rap for her boy friend; Jane Hylton, whose baby was suffocated; Olive Sloane, an inveterate shoplifter and Sybil Thorndike, a would-be poisoner who gets nabbed for blackmail. The incidents which led to their conviction are told in short concise flashbacks.

Of particular interest to British audiences will be the scenes within the prison without bars, a country mansion taken over to give good conduct first offenders a chance to rehabilitate themselves and prepare for return to normal life. After the grim atmosphere of the conventional prison, there is an air of comparative freedom with plenty of hard work to keep the inmates busy. Script maintains an interesting narrative theme and pinpoints some of the harder regulations. J. Lee-Thompson has directed the piece vigorously and has been ably supported by a fine cast of British name performers.

Myro.

Executive Suite

Class drama with all-star cast and potent key-city prospects.

Hollywood, Feb. 23.

Metro release of John Houseman production. Stars William Holden, June Allyson, Barbara Stanwyck, Fredric March, Walter Pidgeon, Shelley Winters, Paul Douglas, Louis Calhern; features Dean Jagger, Nina Foch, Tim Considine. Directed by Robert Wise. Screenplay, Ernest Lehman; based on the novel by Cameron Hawley; camera, George Folsey; editor, Ralph E. Winters. Tradeshown Feb. 3, '54. Running time, **103 MINS.**

McDonald Walling	William Holden
Mary Blemond Walling	June Allyson
Julia O. Tredway	Barbara Stanwyck
Loren Phineas Shaw	Fredric March
Frederick Y. Alderson	Walter Pidgeon
Eva Bardeman	Shelley Winters
Josiah Walter Dudley	Paul Douglas
George Nyle Caswell	Louis Calhern
Jesse Q. Grimm	Dean Jagger
Erica Martin	Nina Foch
Mike Walling	Tim Considine
Bill Lundeen	William Phipps
Mrs. George Nyle Caswell	Lucille Knoch
Julius Steigel	Edgar Stehli
Sara Asenath Grimm	Mary Adams
Edith Alderson	Virginia Brissac
Ed Benedeck	Harry Shannon

MGM has a class drama for class bookings in this all-star offering. It is a quality presentation, certain to attract the discriminating in its key runs and, if sheer weight of marquee names means anything, will go good elsewhere.

From the trade angle, the John Houseman production is a real pro job, of a calibre that doesn't come along too often. Cameron Hawley's novel, "Executive Suite," was good reading, and Ernest Lehman has fashioned it into screen form as a dramatically interesting motion picture humanizing big business and its upper echelon personalities. Under Robert Wise's direction, the film's movement never becomes heavy and he deftly avoids the pitfalls that could have resulted in making this a ponderous show.

Eight scene-stealers vie for the star billing and each is fine, with some standing out over what amounts to standout performances by all concerned in the drama. Certainly Fredric March's characterization of the controller, a man with a bookkeeper's mind and cold drive, will be remembered among the really sock deliniations. So will William Holden's portrayal of the idealistic, but practical, young executive. Also effective as the other stars are Louis Calhern, cynical stockbroker who tries to turn misfortune to personal gain; Barbara Stanwyck, neurotic heiress; Walter Pidgeon, an executive never able to rise above a "number two" position; Paul Douglas, the hearty sales executive; June Allyson, Holden's wife, and Shelley Winters, Douglas's secretary and after-hour amour. Standing out among the featured players is Nina Foch with a performance that commands professional respect and audience sympathy. Dean Jagger, Tim Considine and the others are good.

Cameron Hawley, longtime ad mgr. of Armstrong Cork Co. of Lancaster, Pa., showed in his novel consequences of sudden death of an exective who ran a one-man company with no trained successor. The drama is built on the efforts of the several vice presidents to take over the top position, with most of the conflict in the film version centered on March, as he tries to seize power, and on Holden, as he tries to prevent the move. Climax finds Holden the winner after an impassioned speech on business ideals versus dividend payments.

Along with its other outstanding qualities, the production has the right kind of technical support to make it a class show. In this category are George Folsey's photography, the art direction and settings, the editing and special effects. Of particular note, especially in this day when dramatic scores are mostly overused, the screen's drama does not have to compete for audience attention with background music. The film has no score. Instead it uses, and most effectively, the natural background sounds that would be heard in a scene. *Brog.*

New Faces
(C'SCOPE - COLOR)

Entertaining filmization of the legit revue. Attractive and talented newcomers impress. More than satisfactory b.o. anticipated.

20th-Fox release of Edward L. Alperson production. Stars Ronny Graham, Eartha Kitt, Robert Clary and Alice Ghostly. Directed by Harry Horner. Words and music mostly by Graham, Arthur Siegel, June Carroll, Sheldon Harnick and Michael Brown. Additional words and music by Murray Grand, Elisse Boyd, Alan Melville, Herbert Farjeon, Francis Le Marque and Peter De Vries. Sketches mostly by Graham and Melvin Brooks. Additional sketches by Paul Lynde, Luther Davis and John Cleveland. Camera (CinemaScope), Lucien Ballard. Previewed at Academy of Music, N.Y., Feb. 11, '54. Running time, **98 MINS.**

Ronny Graham, Eartha Kitt, Robert Clary, Alice Ghostly, June Carroll, Virginia De Luce, Paul Lynde, Bill Mullikin, Rosemary O'Reilly, Allen Conroy, Jimmy Russell, George Smiley, Polly Ward, Carol Lawrence, John Laverty, Elizabeth Logue, Faith Burwell, Clark Ranger.

"New Faces," a spritely Broadway revue of two seasons ago, since then on tour, has been fashioned into a generally creditable CinemaScope picture. When it concentrates on the material featured in the stage production, "Faces" is at its best. Fortuntely producer Edward L. Alperson decided to devote most of the footage to the legit sketches and musical numbers. If he hadn't, "Faces" could have easily deteriorated into a commonplace backstage musical. Connecting story line, is thread thin and hardly gets in the way.

Forgetting what takes place off stage, "Faces" is genuine entertainment, featuring a group of attractive and talented newcomers (to the screen). Boxoffice ought to be more than satisfactory.

Best known of the "new faces" is Eartha Kitt, the slinky songstress who has gained recognition through her disk clicks, particularly "C'est Si Bon," "Santa Baby" and "Uskadara." Although these offerings were not part of the original revue, they have been included in the picture, wisely too, for Miss Kitt has a remarkably appealing way with a song. She also scores solidly with her much-acclaimed "Monotonous" and teams with Robert Clary for "Bal Petit Bal" both from the original Leonard Sillman production.

Miss Kitt, Clary, Ronny Graham, Alice Ghostly, June Carroll, Virginia De Luce and Paul Lynde are entrusted with the solo and featured numbers but receive able support from a group of singers and dancers.

Miss Ghostly, a clever comedienne, rates particular kudos for the "Boston Beguine," and Clary's piece de resistance is "I'm In Love With Miss Logan," the lament of a young boy smitten with his teacher. Miss De Luca is effective as the dumb blonde who's in the show because she's related to the backer. Miss Carroll is tops in her spotlight number, "Penny Candy."

Graham, very much in evidence in the stage production, is not given enough to do in the film version. He teams with Lynde and Miss Ghostly for a socko burlesque of "Death of a Salesman" and impresses in takeoffs of a Congressional investigation of jazz and a lampoon of southern writers, Truman Capote style. Lynde and Miss Ghostly also deserve more attention. In addition to the "Salesman" sketch, Lynde is hilarious as a travel lecturer relating his experiences in Africa.

The backstage story has something to do with stalling a determined creditor until a Texas angel has a chance to see the show. In addition, there's an incongruous romance between Miss De Luce, as a tall blonde from Texas, and Clary, a Frenchman who's about two heads shorter.

From the technical standpoint, the CinemaScope photography is not always satisfactory. It's an intimate revue and the vast screen seems hardly necessary. At theatre used for preview, the light source for the screen appeared inadequate. Another disconcerting factor, noticeable in one or two numbers, was the practice of cutting away from a solo performer and focusing on the reaction of another on-stage entertainer. This was especially irritating in Miss Ghostly's "Boston Beguine" number. But these are minor criticisms for what is, after all, an enjoyable picture. *Holl.*

Dangerous Mission
(3-D - COLOR)

Melodramatic thriller in 3-D and Technicolor with entertainment suitable for regular market bookings.

Hollywood, Feb. 23.

RKO release of Irwin Allen production. Stars Victor Mature, Piper Laurie, William Bendix, Vincent Price. Directed by Louis King. Screenplay, Horace McCoy, W. R. Burnett, Charles Bennett; story, McCoy and James Edmiston; camera (Technicolor), William Snyder; editor, Gene Palmer; music, Roy Webb. Previewed Feb. 18, '54. Running time, **75 MINS.**

Matt	Victor Mature
Louise	Piper Laurie
Parker	William Bendix
Adams	Vincent Price
Mary	Betta St. John
Katoonai	Steve Darrell
Mrs. Elster	Marlo Dwyer
Dobson	Walter Reed
Pruitt	Dennis Weaver
Elster	Harry Cheshire

Fair possibilities loom for this 3-D, Technicolored, melodramatic thriller in general bookings. The entertainment offered hits about an average level, overall, and it has star names that rate okay for the market.

Picture gets rolling with high promise of being a strong suspense meller, well-plotted, but settles down to a routine unfoldment about the halfway mark. Had the starting flavor been sustained, it would have been a real taut thriller set against colorful Glacier National Park, site of much of the footage. Louis King's direction gets the film moving with tight suspense and continues that air up until the script by Horace McCoy, W. R. Burnett and Charles Bennett goes formula. After that he maintains some action and thrills but they are routine.

The story opens with an afterhouse murder in a night club. The killing is inadvertently witnessed by a girl. She flees New York for Glacier National Park, hoping neither the killer's men, nor the police will catch up with her. However, both get on her trail and send agents, one acting for her safety and the other to arrange an accident that will keep her from testifying. Neither is identified to the audience so it's a tight guessing game for the audience as the suspects contact the girl and carry on resort social life. Expectancy dissipates as soon as effete Vincent Price is revealed as the gunman and Victor Mature as the D.A.'s undercover agent. Footage strives for thrills, some of which come off, and there is a harrowing chase across a glacier to climax the plot with Mature saving Piper Laurie, the witness, from Price.

These three principals, and William Bendix, a Ranger, are capable in responding to the situations into which they are tossed by the script and King's direction. Mature's heroics come over well and Miss Laurie pleases also. Betta St. John heads the featured players as an Indian girl romantically interested in Price, but it is a rather thankless role. Harry Cheshire, Walter Reed and Ken Dibbs (uncredited) who does the killer in the opening sequence are among other competents.

Irwin Allen's production guidance gets neat values from the outdoor locations and tossed in for thrill action are an avalanche, a forest fire and the glacier bit. Colorful Indian dances, typical of western resort life, and other such tourist bait are seen. The 3-D lensing in color by William Snyder is good, as is the Roy Webb score. The editing is choppy. *Brog.*

Saskatchewan
(COLOR)

Northwest Mounties versus Indians with Canadian Rockies background and average prospects. Alan Ladd, Shelley Winters for marquees.

Hollywood, Feb. 23.

Universal release of Aaron Rosenberg production. Stars Alan Ladd, Shelley Winters: features Robert Douglas, J. Carrol Naish, Hugh O'Brian, Richard Long, Jay Silverheels, Antonio Moreno. Directed by Raoul Walsh. Story and screenplay, Gil Doud; camera (Technicolor), John Seitz; editor, Frank Gross. Previewed Feb. 16, '54. Running time, **87 MINS.**

O'Rourke	Alan Ladd
Grace	Shelley Winters
Benton	Robert Douglas
Batoche	J. Carrol Naish
Smith	Hugh O'Brian
Scanlon	Richard Long
Cajou	Jay Silverheels
Chief Dark Cloud	Antonio Moreno
Lawson	George J. Lewis
Banks	Lowell Gilmore
Spotted Eagle	Anthony Caruso
Keller	Frank Chase
Merrill	Henry Wills
Brill	Robert D. Herron

The scenic splendors of the Canadian Rockies are a fitting backdrop for this Northwest Mounties versus Indians adventure tale. It has Alan Ladd as the male star and prospects for average returns in the outdoor action market. Shelley Winters is toplined, also, to give the marquee a femme name. Other than that value, though, she is completely miscast and lends a ludicrous touch to an otherwise okay actioner.

Main line of conflict has to do with how one heroic Mountie, against rules and regulations, prevented the American Sioux from arousing the friendly Canadian Cree Indians against the whites. The Aaron Rosenberg production and Raoul Walsh's direction of the Gil Doud screen story give the setup a rugged presentation that pays off with plenty of action for the outdoor fan and lenser John Seitz's uses the Technicolor cameras to make the most of the location sites.

Ladd is the Indian-raised Mountie who sees the de-arming of the friendly Crees as a stupid regulation that will help the sioux plan for mass massacre. He's proved right and has to lead the regiment in a cross-country flight, fighting off Sioux at every bend in the trail, even though his action is called mutiny. He further defies authority by re-arming his Cree friends and, with their help, saves the Mounties from total disaster. This makes him a hero instead of a mutineer.

Ladd portrays the straight-line character competently and his fans will like his derring-do. The miscast Miss Winters plays her role of a girl on the lam from the law, and who gets mixed up in all the Mountie action, with a misfit performance so out of place here it seems to have gotten into the wrong picture. Robert Douglas, Mountie inspector who finally realizes he is wrong and Ladd right; J. Carrol Naish, scout; Hugh O'Brian, the sheriff pursuing Miss Winters; Richard Long, Jay Silverheels, Antonio Moreno and the others are effective in varying degrees in putting over their assignments.

The lineup of technical credits provide the production with expert assists in carrying out the outdoor action flavor. *Brog.*

Loophole

Suspense melodrama, fairly entertaining for program dating in smaller situations.

Hollywood, Feb. 17.

Allied Artists release of Lindsley Parsons production. Stars Barry Sullivan, Charles McGraw, Dorothy Malone. Directed by Harold Schuster. Screenplay, Warren Douglas; story, George Bricker, Dwight V. Babcock; camera, William Sickner; editor, Ace Herman; music composed and conducted by Paul Dunlap. Previewed Feb. 15, '54. Running time, **79 MINS.**

Mike Donovan	Barry Sullivan
Gus Slavin	Charles McGraw
Ruthie Donovan	Dorothy Malone
Neil Sanford	Don Haggerty
Vera	Mary Beth Hughes
Tate	Don Beddoe
Mr. Starling	Dayton Lummis
Georgia	Joanne Jordan
Mr. Temple	John Eldredge
Pete Mazurki	Richard Reeves

Sufficient measure of suspense melodrama is presented in "Loophole" for it to be a fairly entertaining entry for program dating in the smaller situations. The names fit the release category, too.

Most of the footage deals with Barry Sullivan, a bank teller, trying to get out of the jam caused by the theft of $49,900 from his cage. He wouldn't have been in the trouble if he had reported the shortage immediately and having waited over the weekend to make it known, he's naturally suspect by Charles McGraw, tough bonding company investigator.

Sullivan's fired from the bank and hounded from other jobs by McGraw, but all the time keeps his eyes open for the man he believes pulled the heist. The climax is rather contrived, spoiling somewhat the good suspense and expectancy built up by Harold Schuster's direction, but Sullivan is vindicated and returns to a better bank post. Plot gimmick that gets the story underway has a cross-town teller entering Sullivan's bank with a group of examiners and walking out with the cash, and, up to the resolving of this, Warren Douglas' script from a story by George Bricker and Dwight V. Babcock maintains interest.

Producer Lindsley Parsons assembled a competent cast to enact the chief roles and they do acceptable jobs, particularly Sullivan, McGraw, Dorothy Malone, as the teller's wife; Don Haggerty, smart policeman; Don Beddoe, the crook; Mary Beth Hughes, his blonde girlfriend, and Richard Reeves, taxi operator who helps Sullivan.

William Sickner plays his cameras over Los Angeles and Malibu scenes to help the presentation's physical appearance and Paul Dunlap's score is another asset to the melodrama. *Brog.*

They Who Dare
(BRITISH-COLOR)

Dirk Bogarde in a British-made drama of a wartime Commando raid on a Greek island; okay where war pictures are still acceptable.

London, Feb. 2.

British Lion release of Mayflower Productions. Stars Dirk Bogarde, Denholm Elliott, Akim Tamiroff. Directed by Lewis Milestone. Screenplay, Robert Westerby; camera (Teechnicolor), Wilkie Cooper; editor, V. Sagovsky; music, Robert Gill. At Carlton, London, Feb. 2, '54. Running time, **100 MINS.**

Lieut. Graham	Dirk Bogarde
Sergeant Corcoran	Denholm Elliott
Capt. George One	Akim Tamiroff
Capt. George Two	Gerard Oury
Capt. Papadopoulos	Eric Pohlmann
Patroklis	Alec Mango
Nightclub singer	Kay Callard
Lieut. Poole	Russell Enoch
Girl-friend	Lisa Gastoni
Marine Boyd	Sam Kydd
Marine Barrett	Peter Burton
Sgt. Evans	David Peel
Toplis	Michael Mellinger
Marika	Anthea Leigh
Greek Woman	Eileen Way

"They Who Dare" is a dramatic flashback to last world war at the point when the British Eighth Army was ready to launch its campaign at El Alamein. The entire footage is devoted to a Commando attack on one of the Dodecanese Islands to put harassing aircraft out of action. It is a grim drama, almost unrelieved in its tension, which will appeal to audiences looking for realism in films.

Lewis Milestone has captured, in his forthright direction the basic element of a plot in which 10 Commandos are waging war against an island of 30,000 people. With a handful of time bombs these young soldiers have to put two airdromes out of action, and thus give the main fighting force a chance to proceed unharassed.

Apart from the conventional formalities, the entire incident is devoted to the trek across the mountainous island from the remote beach landing point to the main targets. For half the journey the men stay together, but at a prearranged point they divide at a tangent to attack their respective targets. They have a rendezvous at the beachhead the following night but, of the 10, only two make it and they have to swim out to the Greek U-Boat which is waiting to pick them up.

Attractive island backgrounds are enhanced by the color lensing and the trek across the mountainous country provides a vivid backcloth to the entire production. Although the incident has something of a repetitious quality, there is full dramatic content in the script. There are a couple of minor femme roles but no romance. The main acting chores are handsomely filled by Dirk Bogarde and Denholm Elliott, Akim Tamiroff, Gerard Oury and Alec Mango, as the three Greek guides; and Russel Enoch, who heads the "splinter" expedition, are at the head of the reliably competent supporting team. Eric Pohlmann gives an intriguing cameo as the skipper of the Greek U-Boat.

Robert Westerby's script has a documentary approach while Wilkie Cooper has done a solid job of Technicolor color lensing. Editing could be improved by scissoring a few hundred feet. *Myro.*

Texas Bad Man

Routine western programmer with Wayne Morris.

Hollywood, Feb. 18.

Allied Artists release of Vincent M. Fennelly production. Stars Wayne Morris; features Frank Ferguson, Elaine Riley, Sheb Wooley. Directed by Lewis D. Collins. Written by Joseph F. Poland; camera, Gil Warrenton; editor, Sam Fields; music, Raoul Kraushaar. At Fox Hollywood, Feb. 17, '54. Running time, **62 MINS.**

Walt	Wayne Morris
Gil	Frank Ferguson
Lois	Elaine Riley
Mack	Sheb Wooley
Tench	Denver Pyle
Jackson	Myron Healey
Bartender	Mort Mills
Bradley	Nelson Leigh

This is a stock western programmer for supporting bookings and in its market the name of Wayne Morris packs sufficient weight to carry it. The 62-minute running time is suitable to filling the lower rung of dual bills.

Morris plays an honest sheriff trying to prevent a crooked trio led by his dishonest dad from making off with the annual spring cleanup of gold from the local mine. Frank Ferguson is the dad, and a right smart operator, so Morris has his work cut out for him to halt the theft and bring the wrongdoers to justice.

Morris heroics come off okay and Ferguson is a smooth heavy. Elaine Riley figures only briefly as a femme interested in the sheriff. Others involved are to western type and include Sheb Wooley, Denver Pyle and Myron Healey.

Lewis D. Collins' direction of the Vincent M. Fennelly production has its slam-bang moments, but the script by Joseph F. Poland could have furnished more such scenes. Otherwise, the plot basis pans out. Lensing by Gil Warrenton and the other credits are standard for budget expenditures. *Brog.*

Le Portrait de Son Pere
(His Father's Portrait)
(FRENCH)

Paris, Feb. 9.

Columbia release of Bertho-Orsay Films production. Stars Jean Richard. Directed by Berthomieu. Screenplay, Berthomieu; dialog, Roger-Pierre; camera, Georges Million; editor, C. Natot. At Georges V, Paris. Running time, **90 MINS.**

Paul	Durand
Marie	Michele Philippe
Domino	Brigitte Bardot
Mother	Mona Goya
Director	Duvalles

Columbia has a mild programer in this comedy which starts with a good, if not new, premise. However, the edge is taken off the laughs by playing it straight, making this a hybrid entry. One of the top young comics here, Jean Richard, plays the role of a peasant thrown into an important role among the Paris elite. But he doesn't have a chance to play this for all the yocks because of the pedestrian treatment and story. This will do well here on the Richard name, but for the U. S. it is too lightweight for anything but dualers. Doubtful there, too.

A department store magnate leaves a codicil in his will giving part of his store to a son who has been brought up by his peasant mother. The son comes for his inheritance in spite of the machinations of the grasping widow. He blunders through and displays a cunning and warmth that soon makes the store a success, and brings around his estranged stepmother.

Berthomieu has tempered this conventional story with a slow pace and has glossed over the inherent comic aspects. Richard p'ays this too straight. Lensing and editing are par. *Mosk.*

Rose Marie
(C'SCOPE—COLOR)

Slow-moving version of familiar operetta, but with sufficient ingredients to make it b.o.

Metro release of Mervyn LeRoy production. Stars Ann Blyth, Howard Keel and Fernando Lamas. Features Bert Lahr and Marjorie Main. Directed by LeRoy. Screenplay, Ronald Millar and George Froeschel, based on the operetta "Rose Marie" presented by Arthur Hammerstein, book and lyrics by Otto A. Harbach and Oscar Hammerstein 2d, music by Rudolf Friml and Herbert Stothart; lyrics for screen version by Paul Francis Webster; additional music and lyrics by Friml, George Stoll and Herbert Baker; musical direction by Stoll; musical numbers staged by Busby Berkeley; camera, Paul Vogel; editor, Harold F. Kress. Previewed in N.Y., March 1, '54. Running time, 104 MINS.

Rose Marie Lemaitre	Ann Blyth
Mike Malone	Howard Keel
James Severn Duval	Fernando Lamas
Barney McCorkle	Bert Lahr
Lady Jane Dunstock	Marjorie Main
Wanda	Joan Taylor
Inspector Appleby	Ray Collins
Black Eagle	Chief Yowlachie

"Rose Marie," a perennial operetta favorite since first presented on Broadway in 1924, was first converted to the screen as a silent picture in 1928 with Joan Crawford in the leading role. Then "Rose Marie" talked and sang when Metro teamed Jeanette MacDonald and Nelson Eddy in 1936. Now the Rudolf Friml-Herbert Stothart-Otto A. Harbach-Oscar Hammerstein 2d opus is dished up as a lavish CinemaScope production complete with stereophonic sound.

C'Scope treatment adds to the production values, for the widescreen medium is ideally suited for the presentation of the Canadian northwest scenery. The views of the forests, the lakes and the mountains are breathtaking and they have been captured in beautiful Eastman color. Unfortunately "typical" operetta plot of yesteryear is sweet and occasionally sad, but with little substance. Resultantly, the current "Rose Marie" is a slow-moving offering.

Old score fares better than plot. Despite the familiarity of such Friml tunes as "Rose Marie," "Indian Love Call" and the rousing "Mounties," they all register solidly. Some additional tunes added by Friml, with lyrics by Paul Francis Webster, make pleasant listening. These include "Free to Be Free," "The Right Place for a Girl," and "I Have the Love." '

There are probably enough ingredients, however, in the film to make it a generally acceptable boxoffice attraction. Like the Moun'ies of the story who always get their man, "Rose Marie" will get its coin, but the chase won't be an entirely easy one.

Mervyn LeRoy, who produced and directed, has fine looking leads in Ann Blyth, Howard Keel and Fernando Lamas, but they fail to instill much verve or enthusiasm to the proceedings. The bright moments of the film are offered by Marjorie Main and Bert Lahr, who provide some welcome comedy relief. Lamentably, Lahr is not given enough screen time. His buffoonery in "I'm a Mountie Who Never Got His Man," by George Stoll and Herbert Baker, comes over solidly.

Miss Blyth is seen as the backwoods French-Canadian gal who has to choose between Howard Keel, the Mountie, and Lamas, "the ornery but-no-killer" trapper. Keel magnanimously releases her from any obligations and she rides off into the woods to join Lamas. There may be many in the audi-

ence who may quarrel with the ending.

There is one dance production number, staged by Busby Berkeley, an Indian festival dance completely lacking in authenticity but nevertheless an effective eye-catcher. Paul Vogel's photography is topnotch and all other technical aspects are right out of the top draw.

There is a nine-minute prologue to the film, with the Metro orchestra, under the direction of symphony conductor Alfred Wallerstein, playing the "Poet and Peasant" overture. *Holl.*

Casanova's Big Night
(SONG-COLOR)

Mild comedy with Bob Hope to give it fair b.o. chances.

Hollywood, Feb. 26.
Paramount release of Paul Jones production. Stars Bob Hope, Joan Fontaine, Basil Rathbone; co-stars Audrey Dalton, Hugh Marlowe; features Arnold Moss, John Carradine, John Hoyt, Hope Emerson, Robert Hutton, Lon Chaney, Raymond Burr, Frieda Inescort, Primo Carnera. Directed by Norman Z. McLeod. Written for the screen by Hal Kanter and Edmund Hartmann; based on a story by Audrey Wisberg; camera (Technicolor), Lionel Lindon; editor, Ellsworth Hoagland; score, Lyn Murray; song, Jay Livingston and Ray Evans. Previewed Feb. 24, '54. Running time, 85 MINS.

Pippo	Bob Hope
Francesca	Joan Fontaine
Elena	Audrey Dalton
Lucio	Basil Rathbone
Stefano Di Gambetta	Hugh Marlowe
The Doge	Arnold Moss
Minister Foressi	John Carradine
Maggiorin	John Hoyt
Duchess of Castelbello	Hope Emerson
Raphael, Duc of Castelbello	Robert Hutton
Emo	Lon Chaney
Bragadin	Raymond Burr
Signora Di Gambetta	Frieda Inescort
Corfa	Primo Carnera
Carabaccio	Frank Puglia
Signor Alberta Di Gambetta	Paul Cavanagh
Giovanni	Romo Vincent
Capt. Rugello	Henry Brandon
Signora Foressi	Natalie Schafer
2nd Prisoner	Douglas Fowley
Gnocchi	Nestor Palva
1st Prisoner	Lucien Littlefield

This is an attempt at broad comedy that misses as often as it clicks. Overall effect is very mild. Boxoffice chances, although the name of Bob Hope can be expected to help, point to fair returns only.

The laughs are spotty in the Paul Jones production, coming mostly from Hope's interpretation of a meek tailor's apprentice who finds himself forced to impersonate the notorious libertine, Casanova. The costume comedy is laid in Italy back in the 1700's and rates widescreen lensing in Technicolor to show off the period trappings. The blowup in size at the preview wasn't particularly impressive since there was a noticeable lack of definition.

Norman Z. McLeod's direction holds a loose rein on the antics, letting the situations run wild over the 85 minutes of footage to force as many laughs as possible. This was probably the best way to handle the frantic hoke offered in the script by Hal Kanter and Edmund Hartmann, based on a story by Aubrey Wisberg. Audience comment is invited by two endings on the film, one showing Hope being beheaded and the other having him best his enemies. Winding the plot up shouldn't have posed any problems for the writers as they have shown a tendency to blithely ignore all the other story holes.

Comedy basis has Hope, mistaken for Casanova, hired by Hope Emerson, a duchess, and Robert Hutton, her son, to "test" the love of Hutton's fiancee, Audrey Dalton. If successful, he is to bring back Miss Dalton's petticoat, embroid-

ered with the duchess' family crest. Chaperoning Hope on this love adventure are Joan Fontaine, a widow to whom he is attracted, and Basil Rathbone, the real Casanova's valet. Court intrigue is mixed in by having Arnold Moss, Doge of Venice, use the situation as an excuse to take over Miss Emerson's duchy, Genoa.

Comedy is not Miss Fontaine's forte, but she manages to be a pleasant sparring partner for Hope. The others in the cast work hard at laughs, sometimes scoring. Hope's best moments include a comedy duel, dancing a gavotte while dressed as a baroness, a prison sequence with Lon Chaney, and some gondola antics while singing "Tic-A-Tic-A-Tic," cleffed by Jay Livingston and Ray Evans.

Lionel Lindon handled the color cameras on the production, with John P. Fulton doing the special photographic effects. Art direction, editing and other assists are okay. *Brog.*

Phantom of Rue Morgue
(3-D COLOR)

Three-D horror feature in color for exploitation dates. Fair entertainment for thrill-chill fans.

Hollywood, Feb. 25.
Warner Bros. release of Henry Blanke production. Stars Karl Malden, Claude Dauphin, Patricia Medina, Steve Forrest. Directed by Roy Del Ruth. Screenplay, Harold Medford, James R. Webb; from Edgar Allen Poe's "Murders in the Rue Morgue"; camera (WarnerColor), J. Peverell Marley; editor, James Moore; music, David Buttolph. Previewed Feb. 23, '54. Running time, 83 MINS.

Dr. Marais	Karl Malden
Inspector Bonnard	Claude Dauphin
Jeannette Rovere	Patricia Medina
Prof. Paul Dupin	Steve Forrest
Yvonne	Allyn McLerie
Arlette	Veola Vonn
Camille	Dolores Dorn
Jacques	Anthony Caruso
Georges Brevert	Merv Griffin
Rene	Paul Richards
LeBon	Rolphe Sedan
Wardrobe Woman	Erin O'Brien-Moore
Specialty	The Flying Zacchinis

The horror in "Phantom of the Rue Morgue" is more to be taken lightly than seriously, since the shocker quality in Edgar Allen Poe's chiller tale, "Murders in the Rue Morgue," has been dimmed considerably by the passage of time. The picture is light on marquee names that will sell tickets, but has plenty of strong ballyhoo values and other commercial aspects, such as the 3-D, WarnerColor treatment, to give it good prospects for exploitation dates. Most filmgoers attracted to this kind of show should enjoy its attempts at hackle-raising, but are not likely to experience any goosepimple thrills.

Murders and gory bodies abound in the Henry Blanke production, which gives fulsome attention to the bloody violence loosed by the title's phantom. Considering the film's entertainment intent and those it will attract, the display of crushed victims is okay, but not for the squeamish. The script by Harold Medford and James R. Webb follows regulation horror lines in getting the Poe yarn on film and Roy Del Ruth's direction also is standard. Performances by Karl Malden, Claude Dauphin, Patricia Medina, Steve Forrest and the others fall into the same groove and none manages to rise above the material.

Malden is the mad scientist who has his trained ape destroy all pretty girls who spurn him. The ape is lured to the victims by bells jangling on the bracelets they wear. After Allyn McLerie, Veloa Vonn and Dolores Dorn have died violent deaths, the rather stupid police inspector played by Dauphin figures Forrest, young 'professor of psychology, is the guilty party. Forrest is jailed and Malden seems set to make time with the young man's girl, Miss Medina. Finale takes place in a zoo gone mad with escaped animals, a completely berserk Malden, an ape who has fallen for Miss Medina, and police who have seen the truth at last.

The 3-D color lensing by J. Peverell Marley is good, and puts the turn-of-the-century Paris scenes on display to full advantage. The settings have excellent period values, the score fits the melodrama and the editing is good. *Brog.*

Battle of Rogue River
(COLOR)

George Montgomery in standard cavalry versus Indians outdoor feature. Fair actioner.

Hollywood, Feb. 26.
Columbia release of Sam Katzman production. Stars George Montgomery; features Richard Denning, Martha Hyer. Directed by William Castle. Story and screenplay, Douglas Heyes; camera (Technicolor), Henry Freulich; editor, Charles Nelson. Previewed Feb. 23, '54. Running time, 70 MINS.
Major Frank Archer..George Montgomery
Stacey Wyatt .... Richard Denning
Brett McClain .... Martha Hyer
Capt. Richard Hillman....John Crawford
Sergeant McClain .... Emory Parnell
Chief Mike .... Michael Granger
Private Reed .... Freeman Morse
Corporal .... Bill Bryant
Matt Parish .... Charles Evans
Lt. Keith Ryan .... Lee Roberts
Kohler .... Frank Sully
1st Brave .... Steve Ritch
Henry .... Bill Hale
Roy .... Wes Hudman
Hamley .... Jimmy Lloyd
Major Wallich .... Willis Bouchey

Some fair action, along program lines, is kicked up in this regulation outdoor feature which has George Montgomery toplining to give it a booking assist in its market. The plot is of the cavalry versus Indians school, strictly stock, but should get by with the undiscriminating trade.

Story period is in the pre-statehood days of Oregon. Montgomery is a stern cavalry officer assigned to bring order to the Rogue River fort. Working against him in secret is Richard Denning, leader of a group of civilian volunteers, who keeps the Indians led by Michael Granger stirred up so that Oregon's rich mineral resources can be exploited by Charles Evans and other crooked businessmen. Montgomery learns the truth in time and brings the crooks to justice, establishing a lasting peace with the redskins.

The heroics of Montgomery come off acceptably and Denning also does okay with his skullduggery. Martha Hyer lends the action an attractive femme touch and there is capable support from John Crawford, Emory Parnell, Granger and the others.

The Sam Katzman production uses Technicolor for added physical values, which are passable considering budget expenditure. William Castle's direction is fairly effective in handling the players and the screen story by Douglas Heyes. Technical credits turn in standard jobs. *Brog.*

The Runaway Bus
(BRITISH)

London, Feb. 16.
Boisterous British comedy has limited U.S. appeal because lacking known-name stars.

Eros Films release of Conquest-Guest production. Stars Frankie Howerd, Margaret Rutherford, Petula Clark. Written and directed by Val Guest. Camera, Stan Pavey; editor, Doug Myers; music, Ronald Binge. At Dominion Theatre, London. Running time, 80 MINS.
Percy Lamb .... Frankie Howerd
Miss Beeston ....Margaret Rutherford
Lee Nichols .... Petula Clark
Shroeder .... George Coulouris
Henry Waterman........ Toke Townley
Peter Jones ....Terence Alexander
Janie Grey .... Belinda Lee
Detective Henley .... John Horsley
Duty Officer .... Anthony Oliver

Frankie Howerd, a British comic who recently has come to the fore, makes his screen debut in this broad, boisterous comedy which will hit the jackpot in the home market, but will have only a limited appeal overseas. This is especially true of the U.S. market because lacking known-name players.

A prolog preceding the credit titles establishes the fact that there's going to be a bullion raid on the London Airport at the first heavy fog. On the appointed day, Frankie Howerd is a relief driver who is detailed to drive a coach from one airport to another with a cargo of half-a-dozen assorted passengers and a load of gold tucked away, unknown to him, in the luggage compartment. The plot is neatly worked out as the coach slowly moves on its tortuous way through the almost impenetrable fog.

With the accent on easy laughs, the suspense angles are of secondary consideration. Atmosphere is effectively created while the mixed passenger list provides all the necessary red herrings. Apart from Howerd, there is Margaret Rutherford, as a determined battleaxe ferociously wielding an umbrella; George Coulouris, a suspicious-looking character with a foreign-sounding name; Terence Alexander in the uniform of a pilot officer, who obviously knows too much; Toke Townley, as a mild individual with a passion for garden seed catalogs; Belinda Lee, whose entire conversation is made up from the plots of paper-covered thrillers and Petula Clark, who is the official hostess. They enter into the spirit of the theme with obvious good humor, extracting the best from the story.

Film has been competently scripted and directed by Val Guest. *Myro.*

Hobson's Choice
(BRITISH)

Charles Laughton and John Mills starred in successful filmization of stage hit; highgrade art house winner.

London, Feb. 25.
British Lion release of London Films-David Lean production. Stars Charles Laughton, John Mills, Brenda de Banzie. Directed by David Lean. Screenplay, David Lean, Norman Spencer, Harold Brighouse, Wynyard Browne; camera, Jack Hildyard; editor, Peter Taylor; music, Malcolm Arnold. At Plaza, London, Feb. 24, '54. Running time, 107 MINS.
Hobson .... Charles Laughton
Willie Mossop .... John Mills
Maggie Hobson .... Brenda de Banzie
Alice Hobson .... Daphne Anderson
Vicky Hobson .... Prunella Scales
Albert Prosser .... Richard Wattis
Freddy Beenstock ...... Derek Blomfield
Mrs. Hepworth .... Helen Haye
Jim Heeler .... Joseph Tomelty
Sam Minnst .... Julien Mitchell
Tudsbury .... Gibb McLaughlin
Denton .... Philip Stainton
Ada Figgins .... Dorothy Gordon
Mrs. Figgins .... Madge Brindley
Dr. McFarlane .... John Laurie
Nat. Beenstock .... Raymond Huntley
Tubby Wadlow .... Jack Howarth
Printer .... Herbert C. Walton

There is a wealth of charm, humor and fine characterization in David Lean's latest British picture made under the Korda banner. Although the film ambles slowly to its obvious conclusion, it should have great boxoffice appeal to class audiences which appreciate better type of productions. This is also a highgrade arty theater offering which could play selected dates throughout America as well.

This period comedy, with a Lancashire setting, is essentially British in its makeup although it should prove international in appeal. Charles Laughton returned to his native country to star, and his name, coupled with John Mills, should help sell the pic.

Laughton plays the widower Hobson, a shoemaker with three unmarried daughters, one of whom is regarded as being permanently on the shelf. After all, as he is always explaining to his cronies in the saloon, she is past it at 30. But the daughter will have none of it; she railroads one of her father's assistants into marriage and together, using her brains and his skill, they set up successfully in opposition. Finally, when the old man is critically ill, with chronic alcoholism, the sneered at son-in-law returns as a partner in the business.

Dovetailed into the main plot are a number of delightful episodes with rich comedy situations. One of the best of these is the wedding night supper when the bride traps her father into providing marriage settlements for her two sisters. There are times, however, where the treatment is a shade too leisurely, and some comedy scenes are allowed to run overly long. This is a defect which can easily be remedied in a film of this length.

It was a natural piece of casting to have Laughton fill the Hobson part. Although he richly overplays every major scene, his performance remains one of the film's highlights.

Mills also makes a major contribution in his interpretation of the illiterate shoemaker's assistant who learns to assert himself. Brenda de Banzie captures top femme honors for her playing of the spirited daughter who triumphs over the ridicule of her father and sisters. These latter roles are nicely filled by Daphne Anderson and Prunella Scales while Richard Wattis and Derek Blomfield are more than adequate as their suitors.

The name supporting cast includes Helen Haye, Joseph Tomelty, John Laurie and Raymond Huntley, all of whom contribute to the picture. *Myro.*

L'Eta Dell'Amore
(The Age of Love)
(FRANCO-AMERICAN)

Rome, Feb. 9.
Diana release of a ICS-Cormoran production. Stars Marina Vlady, Pierre Michel Beck, Fernand Gravey, Aldo Fabrizi, Vittorio Sanipoli. Directed by Lionello DeFelice. Screenplay, Franco Brusati, Vittorio Novarese, DeFelice, from the play, "Mother Nature," by Andre Birabeau; music, Mario Nascimbene; camera, Mario Montuori; editor, Mario Serandrei. Tradeshown in Rome.

A touchy subject is handled with care and taste in this coproduction, shot in Rome with a mixed cast. With a stronger script, it might have gone places. As is, it looks mild for the local trade, but export offers some possibilities. Subject and treatment may help in the U.S. but it looms very limited there.

Two 15-year-olds, one the son of a well-to-do lawyer with marital troubles and the other the daughter of a widowed jailbird, fall in love. After the boy is sent away to school, the girl discovers she is pregnant. In their innocence, both kids are happy over the coming event. Only contact with their elders and efforts of police to find the child's father make them realize that their innocence is an evil thing. Pic is weak in depicting parental events, although Aldo Fabrizi has some good moments in his few appearances. *Hawk.*

The Golden Mask
(COLOR)

Better-than-average programmer with exploitable angles. Location footage of North Africa a big plus.

United Artists release of Aubrey Baring and Maxwell Setton production. (Associated British Picture Corp., Ltd. "Mayflower" Production). Stars Van Heflin, Wanda Hendrix and Eric Portman. Features Charles Goldner and Jacques Francois. Directed by Jack Lee. Screenplay, Robert Westerby; from an original story by Westerby; camera, Oswald Morris; editor, V. Sagovsky; music, Robert Gill. Previewed in N.Y., April 30, '54. Running time, **88 MINS.**

Nicholas Chapman	Van Heflin
Anne Burnet	Wanda Hendrix
Doctor Burnet	Eric Portman
Petris	Charles Goldner
Jacques Farnod	Jacques Francois
Kress	Jacques Brunius
Prof. Sir Arthur Young	Aubrey Mather
Workman	Alec Finter
Stewardess	Noelle Middleton
Doctor Farnod	Rene Leplat
Zara	Simone Silva
Concierge	Pierre Chaminade
Thankyou	Marne Maitland
Hassan	George Pastell
Spahi Officer	Arnold Diamond
Yasmin	Marie-France
Abdel	Messaoud
Spahi N.C.O.	Michael Mellinger
Mahmoud	Alec Mango
Donkey Buyer	Maxwell Setton
1st Camel Rider	Aubrey Baring

That travel can be broadening and interesting is clearly demonstrated in "The Golden Mask," which was filmed on location in North Africa. The Technicolor camera effectively captures the hubbub of Tunis, the modern sections of the city, the market place and the native quarters. It roams into a local nitery, scans the countryside taking in the ancient ruins of Carthage, travels by camel in the Sahara Desert, visits native villages, and focuses on the local residents, including an assortment of Arabs, fez-topped officials and exotic belly dancers.

As a travelog, presenting various aspects of the life and environment of North Africa, the Aubrey Baring-Maxwell Setton production is superior and more intimate than a James A. FitzPatrick two-reeler. But "Golden Mask" is not meant to be a travelog. It is offered as a feature film, complete with a story dealing with archaeology and with performers such as Van Heflin, Wanda Hendrix and Eric Portman.

Had the story been as good as the background footage, United Artists may have had a b.o. companion to "African Queen," but as it turns out, "Mask" is nothing more than a better-than average programmer. It has, however, some exploitable angles.

Stories of exploration in ancient tombs to uncover a valuable relic have been used many times. Here the search is for the lost tomb of Marcus Manilius which contains the mask of Moloch, said to be worth millions. Expedition is led by a dedicated archaeologist, played by Portman. He is accompanied by his daughter, Miss Hendrix; an American archaeologist-writer, Heflin; and the daughter's fiance, Jacques Francois.

Efforts of the adventurers are frustrated by a typical pair of villains. Charles Goldner and Jacques Brunius, who tip off every unscrupulous move in a ludicrous manner. A marauding group of desert bandits also presents a danger, but the local military, colorfully garbed and on beautiful white Arabian horses, ride to the rescue. A romance develops between Heflin and Miss Hendrix, and Francois magnanimously releases his claim. The sought-after object is, of course, found.

The principals carry off their assignments well and some fine performances are registered by Marne Maitland, as a local guide; Marie-France and Messaoud, as a couple of local nomadic kids. Oswald Morris' photography is outstanding and Jack Lee's direction is competent. *Holl.*

Ma and Pa Kettle at Home

Another amusing entry in the Kettle series with good b.o. where these comedies usually do well.

Hollywood, March 9.

Universal release of Richard Wilson production. Stars Marjorie Main, Percy Kilbride; features Alan Mowbray, Alice Kelley, Brett Halsey, Ross Elliott, Mary Wickes. Directed by Charles Lamont. Story and screenplay, Kay Lenard; camera, Carl Guthrie; editor, Leonard Weiner; musical direction, Joseph Gershenson. Previewed March 3, '54. Running time, **80 MINS.**

Ma Kettle	Marjorie Main
Pa Kettle	Percy Kilbride
Mannering	Alan Mowbray
Sally Maddocks	Alice Kelley
Elwin Kettle	Brett Halsey
Pete Crosby	Ross Elliott
Miss Wetter	Mary Wickes
Geoduck	Oliver Blake
Crowbar	Stan Ross
Billy Reed	Emory Parnell
Mrs. Maddocks	Irving Bacon

The comedy adventures of Ma and Pa Kettle are carried forward ably in this latest entry in the Universal series and a good playoff is assured in the areas where the family funsters usually find favor. What is offered here holds up the series' standard and it is good rural-slanted fun.

Marjorie Main and Percy Kilbride, stars of the series, pitch hard for and collect plenty of chuckles in running through the antics to be found in the story and screenplay by Kay Lenard. A nice touch of heart is mixed in with the laughs, especially at the climax, and Charles Lamont's direction makes sure that all facets are played to the hilt.

One of the Kettles' many offspring is a finalist in an essay contest that can win him an agricultural college scholarship. Judges Alan Mowbray and Ross Elliott plan to spend a week at the farm homes of each of two finalists to determine which will be the winner so Pa has to spruce up his ramble-shackled homestead to fool them. The humorous situations that ensue are familiar and funny, but a rain apparently spoils the son's chances when the phony improvements are washed away. However, the touching way in which the Kettles spread the Christian spirit at the climaxing Christmas party in their beatup home sways the judges so things end on a warm, folksy note.

Mowbray scores plenty of laughs as his prissy, meticulous character encounters the free-and-easy life at the Kettles. Elliott is a nice counter-balance to the Mowbray character. Brett Halsey, the son, and Alice Kelley, his neighbor girl friend; Oliver Blake and Stan Ross, the Indian pals of Pa, and the others do their parts.

Among the funnier bits in the Richard Wilson production is the fake Indian raid Pa's redskin pals pull to make Kettle look like a hero to the judges. Irving Bacon, stingy neighbor farmer, also has a good routine chasing Pa's bull away from his heifer. Lensing by Carl Guthrie and the other technical credits are well-handled. *Brog.*

A Queen's World Tour
(BRITISH—COLOR)

Feature-newsreel type film covering the Pacific part of Queen Elizebeth II's Commonwealth tour.

United Artists release of a Castleton Knight production presented by the J. Arthur Rank Organization. Associate producers, Geoffrey Scott and Cyril J. Morton. Directed by Oxley Hugham. Filmed in conjunction with the New Zealand Film Unit. Reviewed in N.Y. March 3, '54, at the Guild Theatre, N.Y. Running time, **84 MINS.**

With the 44,000-mile Commonwealth tour of Queen Elizabeth II and the Duke of Edinburgh so extensively covered by the press, this pictorial supplement in Eastman color is both welcome and a reminder of the inadequacy of the printed work to convey a real impression of such pageantry.

"A Queen's World Tour," is a lively travelogue featuring the Queen of England and her handsome husband which should have wide appeal and satisfies general American curiosity about Britain's royal couple.

It shows the Queen to be gracious, poised and most attractive even when the heat appears to be at its worst. There are revealing moments, when her usual half-smile breaks into open and friendly laughter, such as the time when she visits a New Zealand nursery and watches the children at play.

The Duke, always a few steps behind his wife as per protocol, emerges as even better looking than news photos usually picture him. He also appears slightly bored by the proceedings, for which he can't be blamed. It's too bad that the cameras weren't permitted to scout around the Gothic, the liner which carried the Queen and her consort to New Zealand and from there to Australia. Such an intimate closeup of the couple would have been revealing since, going by the footage in the picture, they barely look at one another.

The feature-length newsreel, intelligently lensed and edited, does much more than follow the Queen on her appointed rounds. It catches the enthusiasm of her people, their revelry and both the loud and solemn sides of their welcome. The best scenes are in New Zealand where the colors take on a new sparkle and the uniforms glitter and glint in the bright sun. Here the cameras follow the Queen and the Duke from sightseeing trips to visits to industrial establishments and on their train tour of the country.

There is a moving scene as the Queen opens the New Zealand parliament, the first British monarch to do so. There are shots of Elizabeth in summer dress, waiving gaily to the crowds, and of a radiant Queen in ermine at the film preem.

And there are many sidelights—the dances of the welcoming Maoris; a Scotch settler's wife view of the visit; scenes in Wellington, Aukland and Christ Church, and the Gothic steaming out of the harbor towards Australia. Before that, the couple's visit to the Fijii Islands and the two-day trip to Tonga where the British Queen met another Queen in her realm.

Quality of the color varies throughout the film from dull to excellent. Camerawork is uniformly good without departing too long from the main subject. Many delightful incidents are caught and recorded, such as the Canadian who stopped the Queen as she was about to board the Gothic with his cheery "Have a good trip maam, and when are you coming back to Canada?". Elizabeth went over to shake hands, a delightful smile on her face. Sidelights in both lensing and narration help to quicken the film's leisurely pace. *Hift.*

The Royal Symphony
(BRITISH-COLOR)

Highlights of the Coronation year in Britain. Plenty of visual appeal.

United Artists release of a Castleton Knight production presented by the J. Arthur Rank Organization. Color by Technicolor. Musical advisor, and music conducted by Sir Malcolm Sergent. Orchestra, The London Symphony Orchestra. Reviewed March 3, '54, at the Guild Theatre, N.Y. Running time, **26 MINS.**

This is the companion piece to "A Queen's World Tour" and probably the only suitable booking possibility for exhibs. It is a review of highlights of the coronation year, lensed with care and in excellent Technicolor. In the background, the London Symphony Orchestra provides some great music to underscore the pageantry on the screen.

Short starts off with a performance of the "Hallelujah" chorus from Handel's "Messiah," sung by 1,000 voices. It goes on to show such events as the Queen's return to Buckingham Palace following the Coronation, with the Royal family assembled on the balcony; the trooping of the colors and the Queen's review of the Royal Air Forces, an occasion which provides some startling shots of RAF planes both on the ground and in the air.

Most impressive sequence comes with the lensing of the Thames review, a coronation year pageantry involving barges telling the story of London. In the background, the orchestra plays parts of Handel's Water Music. The review has its f[illegible]cination even though closeups are lacking. "The Royal Symphony," apart from fitting in well with the more intimate closeup of the Queen, is a fitting review of a great year and, with obvious intent, has been crammed full of pomp and circumstance. *Hift.*

Riding Shotgun
(COLOR)

Hollywood, March 4.

Warner release of Ted Sherdeman production. Stars Randolph Scott; co-stars Wayne Morris; features Joan Weldon, Joe Sawyer, James Millican, Charles Buchinsky, James Bell, Fritz Feld, Richard Garrick. Directed by Andre de Toth. Screenplay, Tom Blackburn; story, Kenneth Perkins; camera, Bert Glennon; editor, Rudi Fehr; music, David Buttolph. Previewed March 2, '54. Running time, **74 MINS.**

Larry	Randolph Scott
Tub Murphy	Wayne Morris
Orissa Flynn	Joan Weldon
Tom Biggert	Joe Sawyer
Dan Marady	James Millican
Pinto	Charles Buchinsky
Doc Winkler	James Bell
Fritz	Fritz Feld
Walters	Richard Garrick
Bar M Rider	Victor Perrin
Hughes	John Baer
Col. Flynn	William Johnstone
Ben	Kem Dibbs
Johnny	Alvin Freeman

Audience acceptance of this Randolph Scott film will depend entirely upon whether the spectator regards it as a satire on westerns or a giddyap drama with a multitude of unintentional laughs. Whatever the reaction, the pattern is strange for a star of Scott's stature, whose heroics in the past always have been good for considerable violent action and money in the till for exhibs. It's a far cry from the standard Scott epic, not a welcome one, in which endless dialog supplants motion until the climax.

Scott is introduced as a stagecoach guard, constantly searching for a man who done him wrong. Up and down the west he travels, figuring if he rides enough stages he'll find him. He finally flushes his quarry, James Millican, an outlaw leader, who lures him away from his post so the outlaw band can attack the coach, thus resulting in the sheriff and all the gunpower of the neighboring town forming a posse to track down the bandits. Town will then be left wide open for Millican and his gang to swoop down and raid the gambling hall.

Scott, returning to town after the stage attack, is suspected of complicity, and no one but his girl and the doctor will believe him when he tries to explain it's all a scheme to hold up the gambling joint. He's forced to take refuge in a Mexican dive, and there he's holed up for much of the footage, until finale shows him escaping and downing the outlaws when they raid the town.

Andre de Toth is at a loss with the Tom Blackburn script, his usual straightforward and punchy direction at strange odds with what is handed him. Ted Sherdeman's production mounting is okay as far as physical values are concerned, and Bert Glennon's WarnerColor photography is satisfactory.

Scott tries valiantly with his role but it never comes off in the heroic style his followers have come to expect from him. Wayne Morris, his co-star, in the role of a tubby deputy sheriff who is over-padded, handles himself in okay fashion but looks like a German comic. Millican scores as the outlaw leader, Charles Buchinsky is a snakey henchman and Joan Weldon is in briefly as the romantic interest. Fritz Feld is a comedy saloon-keeper and Joe Sawyer heads the townspeople who endlessly debate hanging Scott. *Whit.*

Paris Playboys

Another in the Bowery Boys series. An adequate supporter, but not up to its predecessors.

Hollywood, March 5.
Allied Artists release of a Ben Schwalb production. Stars Leo Gorcey, Huntz Hall; features Bernard Gorcey, Veola Vonn, Steven Geray. Directed by William Beaudine. Screenplay, Elwood Ullman and Edward Bernds; camera, Harry Neumann; editor, John Fuller. Reviewed March 1, '54. Running time, 62 MINS.
Slip .... Leo Gorcey
Sach } .... Huntz Hall
Le Beau }
Louie .... Bernard Gorcey
Mimi .... Veola Vonn
Gaspard .... Steven Geray
Vidal .... John Wengraf
Celeste .... Marianne Lynn
Chuck .... David Condon
Butch .... Bennie Bartlett
Pierre .... Alphonse Martell
Cambon .... Gordon Clark

The Bowery Boys become "Paris Playboys" for this latest in their Allied Artists series. It's not up to its predecessors, yet adequate supporting fare.

The laughs don't come frequently nor with ease in the script dished up by Elwood Ullman and Edward Bernds. Main springboards, per usual, are the malaprops of Leo Gorcey and Huntz Hall's crazy antics. Yarn puts pair in the French capitol, where Hall impersonates a missing French scientist who'd been working on a formula for a super rocket fuel. Spies try trickery, even murder, to get the data, and by the time it's all over the real scientist is back;

it really doesn't matter, though, for Hall has discovered a better formula anyway.

Gorcey and Hall (in dual role) romp through it all in usual fashion, but are hindered somewhat by their material. Bernard Gorcey is okay and, as the pint-sized sidekick of the Boys, impersonates Toulouse-Lautrec in one brief scene for the film's cleverest bit. Of the supporters, it's Steven Geray, as the doctor spy, who fares best.

William Beaudine's direction of the Ben Schwab production does its best to enliven the proceedings, and sometimes succeeds. Technical credits are stock.

Paris, incidentally, is represented by one stock shot; one exterior scene resembling a French sidewalk cafe. Accents and interiors try to do the rest. *Neal.*

Stormy the Thoroughbred
(COLOR)

Deserves attention as companion feature.

Buena Vista Film Distributing Co release of Walt Disney presentation. Produced and directed by Larry Lansburgh. Written by Bill Walsh; based on a story by Jack Holt and Carolyn Coggins; camera, Floyd Crosby, Hal Ramser, and Lansburgh; editor, John Link; music, William Lava; narrated by George Fanneman. Previewed in N.Y., March 8, '54. Running time, 45 MINS.
The Vaquero .... M. R. Valdez
The Stranger .... Robert Skene
Auctioneer .... George Swinebroad
The Team .... Aiden Roark, Cecil Smith, Robert Skene, James Stimmel
Stormy .... Woodie D.

"Stormy the Thoroughbred," subtitled "With an Inferiority Complex," rates as a fine contender in the featurette division. Although the 45-minute film is listed by Buena Vista Film Distributing, the Walt Disney releasing org, as a feature, it can hardly stand up alone. But as a companion feature, it deserves attention.

Story by Jack Holt and Carolyn Coggins concerns a true-blue colt who is born out of season on a thoroughbred breeding farm in Kentucky. Although he enters the world in August, seven months later than the regular foaling season, his birthdate is listed as January 1, a rule of the official breeding associations. This makes the colt, Stormy, a misfit. Being smaller than other members of his yearling class, he is ignored by the trainers and owners.

Stormy is left behind when the other colts are sent to the famous Keenland auction sale. He is later sold to a western ranch and eventually winds up as a polo pony. He proves his true worth on the playing field and loses his "inferiority."

Film gives an excellent behind-the-scene view of a thoroughbred farm and the preparations for the race. The Technicolor photography is an asset, and the cameras have effectively caught a polo game in action. George Fenneman handles the narration of Bill Walsh's bright commentary. *Holl.*

Amore In Citta
(Love in the City)
(ITALIAN)

Genoa, March 2.
D.C.N. release of Faro Film production. Written and directed by Carlo Lizzani, Michelangelo Antonioni, Dino Risi, Federico Fellini, Cesare Zavattini, Umberto Maselli, Alberto Lattuada; script collaboration by Aldo Buzzi, Luigi Chiarini, Luigi Malerba, Tullio Pinelli, Vittorio Vettroni. Camera, Gianni di Venanzo; music,

Mario Nascimbene. At Olimpia, Genoa. Running time, 110 MINS.
EPISODES
Paid Love .... by Carlo Lizzani
Attempted Suicide ... Michelangelo Antonioni
Paradise Four Hours..... Dino Risi
Marriage Agency ...... Federico Fellini
Story of Caterina...... Zavattini-Maselli
Italians Stare .... Alberto Lattuada

This episoder is a completely unconventional series of probes into the various aspects of love in the city. Format and style make it difficult to classify, hence sales will have to depend mainly on exploitation treatment, with word-of-mouth aiding only for certain strata of public. Actually, this is not an exploitationer either, for handling is completely objective and sincere, when not slightly tongue-in-cheek. More a social document than pic entertainment, its export values appear highly speculative.

First bit, by Carlo Lizzani, is an unsensational inspection of prostitution, which stresses the human side and tragic precedents of the nightwalkers, with camera lensing actual prosties. In "Attempted Suicide," several frustrated suiciders recount their attempts at death and events and reasons which led up to these tries.

Dino Risi, with "Paradise for Four Hours," has humorously sketched an evening in a cheap Italian dancehall frequented by servant girls and sidewalk Don Juans. It's a gem of observation and provides many a chuckle. In "Marriage Agency," follows a reporter posing as a potential husband through the operation of a seamy Roman agency. Zavattini's story of Caterina is no more than a reenactment of a recent headline episode in which a poor servant girl abandons her illegitimate child in a park. Final item has a hidden camera following a set of buxom and bouncing beauties around Rome, recording stares and reactions from males, all underlined with an appropriately humorous soundtrack.

Pic is an amazing example of how real "realism" can be, and at no time is its sincerity in doubt. Musical backdrop by Mario Nascimbene is very good. *Hawk.*

Ich Und Du
(I And You)
(GERMAN)

Berlin, March 1.
Europa release of Neue Emelka Zeyn production. Stars Hardy Krueger and Liselotte Pulver. Directed by Alfred Weidenmann. Screenplay, Herbert Reinecke and Alfred Weidenmann; camera, Franz Weihmayr; music, Lothar Bruehne; sets, Franz Bi and Bruno Monden. At Gloria Palast, Berlin. Running time, 98 MINS.
Peter Erdmann .... Hardy Krueger
Brigitte .... Liselotte Pulver
Aunt Gruber .... Lucie Mannheim
Marianne .... Doris Kirchner
Charly .... Peer Schmidt
Paul .... Claus Biederstaedt
Herr Roland .... Kurt Waitzmann
The Neighbor .... Ursula Herking
Frau Erdmann...Edith Schultze-Westrum
Herr Erdmann .... Arno Paulsen

The overall improvement of German film quality is obvious in "Ich und Du," a delightful comedy about two young people and their first marriage experiences. Pic shapes as an outstanding money-maker here. Chances abroad, however, appear only spotty.

Simple story of a young couple who get divorced after a series of little quarrels which happen when young people take things too seriously. Although the story is old-hat, pic has enjoyable moments thanks to good directing, acting

and neat scripting. There are many laughs along the way.

Top honors go to Alfred Weidenmann, a relatively unknown director. His adept handling of the players is perhaps the best thing about the film. Hardy Krueger and Liselotte Pulver convincingly portray the young couple. An excellent performance is turned in by Lucie Mannheim as a helping hand in their disputes. On the technical side, Franz Weihmayr's handsome lensing is worth mentioning. *Hans.*

Salt of the Earth

Union view of mineworkers' strike. Despite artistic values its chances as b.o. entertainment is practically nil.

Independent Productions Corp. release presented with the International Union of Mine, Mill & Smelter Workers. A Paul Jarrico production. Stars Rosaura Revueltas and Juan Chacon. Features, in professional cast, Will Geer, David Wolfe, Mervin Williams and David Sarvis. In non-professional cast, Henrietta Williams, Ernest Velasquez, Angela Sanchez, Joe T. Morales, Clorinda Alderette, Charles Coleman, Virginia Jencks, Clinton Jencks, Victor Torres, E. A. Rockwell, William Rockwell, Floyd Bostick, E. S. Conerly, Mary Lou Castillo, Frank Talevera, Adolfo Barela, Albert Munoz, Alford Roos and members of the IUMMSW Local 890 in Bayard, N.M. Directed by Herbert J. Biberman. Written by Michael Wilson; music, Sol Kaplan. Previewed March 12, '54 at the Grande Theatre, N.Y. Running time, **94 MINS.**

Esperanza Quintero . Rosaura Revueltas
Ramon Quintero .... Juan Chacon
The Sheriff .... Will Geer
Barton .... David Wolfe
Alexander .... Mervin Williams
Hartwell .... David Sarvis
Teresa Vidal .... Henrietta Williams
Charley Vidal .... Ernest Velasquez
Consuelo Ruiz .... Angela Sanchez
Sal Ruiz .... Joe T. Morales
Luz Morales .... Clorinda Alderette
Antonio Morales .... Charles Coleman
Ruth Barnes .... Virginia Jencks
Frank Barnes .... Clinton Jencks
Sebastian Prieto .... Victor Torres
Vance .... E. A. Rockwell
Kimbrough .... William Rockwell
Jenkins .... Floyd Bostick
Kalinsky .... E. S. Conerly
Estella Quintero .... Frank Talevera
Alfredo .... Adolfo Barela
Vicente .... Albert Munoz
District Attorney .... Alford Roos

So much adverse publicity has preceded "Salt of the Earth" that it comes as something of a surprise to find it a good, highly dramatic and emotion-charged piece of work that, in its pictorial values at least, tells its story straight. It is, however, a propaganda picture which belongs in union halls rather than motion picture theatres where audiences come for entertainment and not lectures couched in dramatics.

It is a bitter tale that Michael Wilson has concocted here and the large cast acts it out with a conviction that obviously didn't require much prompting. The story concerns Mexican miners in a small New Mexican mining community, Zinc Town. They live in shacks without plumbing. Large families are cramped together and above them lords "the company."

A series of mine accidents prompts a strike. The company attempts to break it via acts of intimidation that include arrest and brutality. Finally, the Taft-Hartley Act is invoked. As the men quit the picketing, the women—who've been fighting for equality within the union—take over. Finally, as a sullen, threatening crowd deters the sheriff from evicting miner families, the company gives in.

One would have to become quite analytical to read the alleged "Red" line into this Paul Jarrico production. It certainly isn't on the surface even though scripter Wilson can't be accused of admiring the owners. This is reminiscent of the social problem pix Hollywood used to put out in the thirties and which since then have gone out of vogue.

The "bosses," who come in for frequent and cutting mention, are the heavies and "the company" is only out to discriminate against and exploit the workers, particularly if they're Mexican. All the police are vicious and brutal despite a lack of provocation, the reason being that they are putty in the hands of the company representatives. In this story, if not in life, all workers are noble, fearless and self-sacrificing. Such black-and-white treatment seems oddly out of place nowadays and certainly makes suspect the purposes of Jarrico and Herbert J. Biberman, the director, in tackling this subject in the first place.

It is bound to occur to anyone seeing this film that, even though it may not be Communist, it must become a triumphant argument in the hands of those whose purpose it is to vilify the United States, and that certainly includes the Communists. Because it treats a somewhat isolated situation from a distinctly biased point of view, "Salt" will do only harm to the U. S. outside the U. S.

Since it tells its message in such impassioned terms, and with such an obvious lack of objectivity, audiences and exhibs should be aware of who's behind the film. The International Union of Mine, Mill & Smelter Workers was kicked out of the CIO because of its allegedly Red-Dominated leadership. Biberman was one of the Unfriendly Ten who served a five-months jail sentence for contempt of Congress. Jarrico also has been in trouble with Congress.

Yet as a piece of film artistry, "Salt" achieves moments of true pictorial excellence. Rosaura Revueltas, a Mexican actress playing the wife of the strike leader, gives a taut, impressive performance that has real dimension. Juan Chacon, a union leader in real life, turns in a creditable acting job. Will Geer as the sheriff introduces an element of indecision as he pictures a man who doesn't altogether enjoy what he's told to do. Mervin Williams contributes a smooth bit as the mine superintendent.

Biberman's direction achieves distinctive quality. Most of the picture is in low-key, underscoring the dramatics. He concentrates on misery and violence and anger with a stark determination and a flair for realism that is designed to do much more than rouse sympathy. His shots are extremely well composed and his camera angles chosen for maximum effect. Pic locationed at Silver City, N. M., and catches the dusty desolation of the countryside.

It is hard to quarrel with the film when it speaks out against discrimination, poverty and abuse. But Biberman might well be asked what he hopes to achieve by his one-sided if provocative presentation. It is hard to believe that the situation he pictures could exist in a vacuum, without the influence of public opinion and the attention of the U. S. Bureau of Mines. "Salt" has no Production Code seal. Never applied for one, either.

Hift.

Night People
(COLOR—C'SCOPE)

Topnotch, contemporary cloak - and - dagger thriller C'Scoped against present-day Germany. Excellent b.o. prospects.

Hollywood, March 12.

20th-Fox release of Nunnally Johnson production. Stars Gregory Peck, Broderick Crawford, Anita Bjork, Rita Gam; features Walter Abel, Buddy Ebsen, Casey Adams, Jill Esmond, Peter Van Eyck, Marianne Koch, Ted Avery. Direction and screenplay by Johnson; from a story by Jed Harris and Thomas Reed; camera (Technicolor), Charles G. Clarke; editor, Dorothy Spencer; music, Cyril Mockridge; musical direction, Lionel Newman. Previewed March 10, '54. Running time, **93 MINS.**

Col. Van Dyke .... Gregory Peck
Leatherby .... Broderick Crawford
Hoffy .... Anita Bjork
Miss Cates .... Rita Gam
Foster .... Walter Abel
Sgt. McColloch .... Buddy Ebsen
Frederick S. Hobart...... Casey Adams
Frau Schindler .... Jill Esmond
Petrechine .... Peter Van Eyck
Kathy .... Marianne Koch
Johnny .... Ted Avery
Burns .... Hugh McDermott
Whitby .... Paul Carpenter
Stanways .... John Horsley
Lakeland .... Lionel Murton

This is a topnotch, exciting cloak-and-dagger thriller, modernly-paced and with excellent boxoffice chances in most of all situations. With a story setting in present-day Germany, where it was filmed, the picture has a contemporary feel that will make it catch on with all who like a modern melodrama. An added contemporary touch is CinemaScope, making it the first up-dated meller in that medium and giving it extra sales value in the big key bookings.

Nunnally Johnson gets a clean triple for his smart handling of the production, direction and scripting. The guidance is good all around, but most particularly noticeable in the effective casualness with which he treats the heavier melodramatic angles to the plot and the playing. Also, there's a political awareness in the dialog, again done with an offhand touch that is extremely effective. In the casting, too, he has chosen just the right players and drawn potent performances from them, as from stars Gregory Peck, Broderick Crawford, Anita Bjork, Rita Gam.

The screenplay is based on a story by Jed Harris and Thomas Reed, which tells of the kidnapping of a young American soldier and how a CIC officer manages to get him back safely to the western zone by being quicker-witted than the GI's captors and their agents. Peck plays the colonel and how he brings off the rescue makes for plenty of suspense-laden, and credibly conceived footage, since he has to fool the East Berlin Reds, the hangover Nazis working with them; handle Crawford, stateside industrial tycoon who has come to Berlin to see that things are done right, and quickly, to rescue his son; and placate the State Department, which wants no illegal trafficking that might have serious international repercussions. Peck and Crawford are extremely good as the top male stars.

Chief heavy in the melodrama is ably enacted by Miss Bjork, who through most her footage appears to be a friendly agent trying to help Peck. Miss Gam, not completely fooled by the agent, makes an excellent appearance as Peck's secretary. Buddy Ebsen soundly values his role of master sergeant aiding the colonel, as well as adding a number of natural chuckles. Walter Abel clicks as a cigaret-cadging medical officer. Also scoring is Casey Adams as the State Department man, while Ted Avery, the young soldier; Marianne Koch, his fraulein girl friend; Jill Esmond, whom the Reds want in exchange for Avery; Peter Van Eyck, American-Russian, and the others are very capable.

A still battle-scarred Berlin provides interesting backgrounds for the melodramatics and the C'Scoping in Technicolor by Charles G. Clarke makes valid use of the settings. It must be noted, however, that the anamorphic process was not all it should have been at the preview. Figures were inclined to distort at each side of the screen; in other shots the images were fuzzy, and there was a noticeable blur in some scenes when the cameras panned. The stereophonic sound was not allowed to distract except in opening and closing shots, when it booms out noisily. Scoring, editing and other production factors are good.

Brog.

The Maggie
(BRITISH)

Paul Douglas in Ealing comedy of small coastal craft tin Scottish Waters; for arty theatres in U.S.

London, March 2.

G.F.D. release of Ealing Studios-Michael Balcon production. Stars Paul Douglas; features Hubert Gregg, Alex Mackenzie, Abe Barker, James Copeland, Tommy Kearins. Directed by Alexander Mackendrick. Screenplay, William Rose; camera, Gordon Dines; editor, Peter Tanner; music, John Addison. At Odeon, Leicester Square, London. Running time, **93 MINS.**

Marshall .... Paul Douglas
Skipper .... Alex Mackenzie
Mate .... James Copeland
Engineer .... Abe Barker
Wee Boy .... Tommy Kearins
Pusey .... Hubert Gregg
Cambell .... Geoffrey Keen
Miss Peters .... Dorothy Alison
Reporter .... Andrew Keir
Sarah .... Meg Buchanan
Laird .... Mark Dignam

One of the small coastal colliers which ply in Scottish waters provides the main setting for this new Ealing comedy. The story of a hustling American businessman who gets involved with a leisurely-minded but crafty skipper, gives the film an Anglo-U.S. flavor. The casting of Paul Douglas provides some marquee strength and the film should rate as a good average attraction for the arty theatre circuit.

The yarn has been subtly written as a piece of gentle and casual humor. The pace is always leisurely, and the background of Scottish lakes and mountains provides an appropriate backcloth to the story. The picture has been directed without any attempt to force the pace. Fine camera work highlights the natural scenery.

The skipper of "The Maggie" is a crafty old sailor, short of cash to make his little coaster seaworthy. By a little smart practice he gets a contract to transport a valuable cargo but when a hustling American executive realizes what has happened, he planes from London to Scotland to get his goods transferred to another vessel. For the best part of 90 minutes, he is outwitted by the old sailor, sees his cargo jettisoned and even refuses to accept the return of the cash he paid in advance.

There is virtually an all-male cast with only minor bits for a few femme players. Douglas, playing the American executive, provides the perfect contract between the old world and the new. His is a reliable performance which avoids the pitfall of overacting. Alex Mackenzie makes the old skipper a lovable and sympathetic character while James Copeland and Abe Barker, as the other senior members of the crew, fit into the general pattern. Tommy Kearins as the "wee boy" on "The Maggie" plays the role with a nice impish touch. Hubert Gregg and Geoffrey Keen fill the principal supporting roles in the right spirit. They are ably supported by the remainder of the cast.

General technical credits are up to standard although a little more scissoring in later stages would be an asset.

Myro.

Drive a Crooked Road

Occasionally interesting melodramatic programmer starring Mickey Rooney.

Hollywood, March 16.

Columbia release of Jonie Taps production. Stars Mickey Rooney, Dianne Foster; features Kevin McCarthy, Jack Kelly, Harry Landers, Jerry Paris, Paul Picerni, Dick Crockett. Directed by Richard Quine. Screenplay, Blake Edwards; adapted by Quine from a story by James Benson Nablo; camera, Charles Lawton Jr.; editor, Jerome Thoms; musical director, Ross DiMaggio. Previewed March 11, '54. Running time, **83 MINS.**

Eddie Shannon .... Mickey Rooney
Barbara Mathews .... Dianne Foster
Steve Norris .... Kevin McCarthy
Harold Baker .... ack Kelly
Ralph .... Harry Landers
Phil .... Jerry Paris
Carl .... Paul Picerni
Don .... Dick Crockett
Garage Foreman .... Mort Mills
Marge .... Peggy Maley

The programmer market will find "Drive a Crooked Road" just an occasionally interesting melodrama proving that crime doesn't pay. It has been handled with fair competence through most of the footage, but it has a depressing quality and a tragic ending that will keep it from beng liked generally. It will play off as a lower-case duel dater mostly.

Story is the ages-old one about man tempted by woman into crime. Things are so set up that audiences will sympathize both with the man, and the woman who tempts him, but there's no twist that can put a happy ending on the affair so the inevitable downbeat ending is easily anticipated. Mickey Rooney appears as a woman-shy auto mechanic, expert at sports car racing, and Dianne Foster is the lure who uses nature's bait to trick him into participating in a bank holdup. Audience sympathy will be with both, mostly because they give their characters understanding histrionics that are believable.

Richard Quine directs the Jonie Taps production from his own adaptation of a story by James Benson Nablo, which Blake Edwards scripted. Since the plot line isn't going anywhere except towards its inconclusive, although moralistic, ending, the makers have spent a lot of time with incidentals, particularly in the first 43 minutes of footage. The show drags considerably in the first half, but the last half has plenty of melodramatic pacing tied in with blueprinting and executing the robbery.

Kevin McCarthy and Jack Kelly do passable chores of the New York hoods out to rob a bank in Palm Springs. For a safe getaway, they need someone to tool a hopped up jalopy over a back road through the mountains and Rooney is picked. They assign McCarthy's girl friend, Miss Foster to handle Rooney and it doesn't take her long to get him. She starts her part of the job willingly, but soon regrets it, so much so that she tries to save him at the end, resulting in the violent deaths of the two hoods, leaving she and Rooney to face the demands of justice.

Playing caricatures of the male wolf-pack, unbelievably broad in writing and direction, are Jerry Paris, Paul Picerni, ick Crockett and Mort Mills, garage mechanics who slobber and howl at every passing femme. Harry Landers fares better as another mechanic friendly to Rooney. The picture has some good road racing sequences, well-lensed by Charles Lawton, Jr., and the other technical contributors do their jobs in okay fashion. *Brog.*

Yankee Pasha
(COLOR)

Typical U sex-and-sand adventure, with Jeff Chandler, Rhonda Fleming, Technicolor and average outlook.

Hollywood, March 12.

Universal release of Howard Christie production. Stars Jeff Chandler, Rhonda Fleming; features Mamie Van Doren, Lee J. Cobb, Bart Roberts. Directed by Joseph Pevney. Screenplay, Joseph Hoffman; based on the novel by Edison Marshall; camera (Technicolor), Carl Guthrie; editor, Virgil Vogel. Previewed March 9, '54. Running time, **83 MINS.**

Jason .... Jeff Chandler
Roxana .... Rhonda Fleming
Lilith .... Mamie Van Doren
Sultan .... Lee J. Cobb
Omar-Id-Din .... Bart Roberts
Hassan Serdar .... Hal March
Elias Derby .... Tudor Owen
Richard O'Brien .... Arthur Space
Zimil .... Benny Rubin
Baidu Sa'Id .... Phil Van Zandt
Dick Bailey .... Harry Lauter
First Mate Miller .... John Day
Miss Universe ...... Christiane Martel
Miss United States ...... Myrna Hansen
Miss Japan .... Kinuko Ito
Miss Panama .... Emita Arosemena
Miss Norway ...... Synove Gulbrandsen
Miss Uruguay .... Alicia Ibanez
Miss South Africa .... Ingrid Mills
Miss Australia .... Maxine Morgan

Universal has another of its sex-and-sand adventure features in "Yankee Pasha," a type of subject with which the studio has had considerable success over the years. This one should give an average account of itself, since it is equipped with the standard ingredients, as well as having the names of Jeff Chandler, Rhonda Fleming and Technicolor for the marquees to flaunt.

Critically, it's not much of a show, being shy of story merit and reasonably credible action and performances. However, such lack has never seemed to bother the other s-and-s features. All the trappings to go with this type of highly fanciful adventure tale are supplied under Howard Christie's production supervision and Joseph Pevney's direction guides it along stock action trails that range from New England to France to Morocco.

Edison Marshall's swashbuckling novel had a lot more punch in print than it does on the screen, so Joseph Hoffman's script has only occasional flashes of imaginative action capable of holding the viewer. The derring-do concerns the rescue of Miss Fleming, New England girl, by Chandler, frontiersman, after she has been captured by Barbary pirates and sold into the Moroccan harem of Bart Roberts. Horse and sea chases, and mass and individual clashes are used to convey movement, while harem beauties are spotted at intervals for sight appeal. In regards to the Miss Universe beauties used in the film, it's a good thing for them Miss Fleming wasn't competing. On her the harem scanties and Technicolor look exceptionally good. Chandler is an acceptable hero and Roberts an okay heavy.

Mamie Van Doren, U's Monroeish blonde curve-pitcher, stirs up some chuckles as a talkative harem slave. Among some of the others getting by in their characterizations are Lee J. Cobb, sultan; Hal March, native officer who helps Chandler's rescue operations; Arthur Space, U.S. Consul in Morocco; Tudor Owen and Benny Rubin.

The color lensing by Carl Guthrie is capable in sharpening the visual values and the other technical functions are carried out expertly. *Brog.*

The Scarlet Spear
(COLOR)

Slow - moving African locationer for the secondary situations.

United Artists release of Present-Day (Charles Reynolds) production. Features John Bentley, Martha Hyer. Written and directed by George Breakston and Ray Stahl. Camera (Technicolor), Bernard Davies; editor, John Shirley; music, Ivor Slaney. Tradeshown, N.Y., March 10, '54. Running time, **78 MINS.**

Jim Barneson .... John Bentley
Christine .... Martha Hyer
Morasi .... Morasi

Africa's flora, fauna and tribal customs again come in for photographic scrutiny via "The Scarlet Spear." Any of these categories have the basic requisites of an entertaining film. But, unfortunately, this Charles Reynolds production is so slim on story and direction that it emerges as a tedious chronicle suitable only as supporting fare for the duals.

Written and directed by George Breakston and Ray Stahl, the film primarily recounts the efforts of a tribal chief to prove himself a worthy successor to his father under a long standing tradition. His assignment is a minor variation of Hercules' famed 12 labors for he's called upon to demonstrate his courage, stamina and sundry other qualities.

While chieftain Morasi is running the gauntlet as it were, he's being closely observed by district commissioner John Bentley who fears that the ritual of dipping the "scarlet spear" into the blood of an adversary will stir up tribal warfare. Final member of the three character cast is Martha Hyer who joins Bentley's vigil as a mag correspondent in seach of a story.

Bernard Davies' Technicolor camera takes over from there for the thin plot is merely a peg to hang scene upon scene of the Kenya terrain as well as views of its animal inhabitants. Some of the shots are in the best travelog tradition but others are cliched such as fights between a mongoose and a cobra.

Of the trio of players it's safe to say that the lâconic Bentley is the most impressive. Miss Hyer seems out of place in amidst the snakes and safaris while Morasi (who portrays himself) is rather colorless although he acquits himself favorably in hand-to-hand combat with snakes and other jungle denizens. Editing of John Shirley is remiss in that repetitious footage could have been trimmed considerably. Ivor Slaney's score is adequate as are other technical credits. *Gilb.*

The Good Die Young
(BRITISH)

Big Anglo-U.S. cast in tense dramatic subject; shapes as steady boxoffice proposition.

London, March 9.

IFD release of Romulus-Remus production. Stars Laurence Harvey, Gloria Grahame, Richard Basehart, Joan Collins, John Ireland, Rene Ray, Stanley Baker, Margaret Leighton, Robert Morley. Directed by Lewis Gilbert. Screenplay, Vernon Harris and Lewis Gilbert from novel by Richard Macauley; camera, Jack Asher; editor, Ralph Kemplen; music, Georges Auric. At Odeon, Leicester Square, London, March 2, '54. Running time, **98 MINS.**

Rave .... Laurence Harvey
Denise .... Gloria Grahame
Joe .... Richard Basehart
Mary .... Joan Collins
Eddie .... John Ireland
Angela .... Rene Ray
Mike .... Stanley Baker
Eve .... Margaret Leighton
Sir Francis .... Robert Morley
Mrs. Freeman .... Freda Jackson
Tod Maslin .... Lee Patterson
Dr. Reed .... Walter Hudd

There is a major lineup of talent in this independently-made British pic, but fulfillment does not quite come up to expectations Although there is basically a tense dramatic theme, the scrappy treatment, necessitated by the omnibus type of story, robs the film of some of its suspense and values. Nevertheless, with its strong marquee strength it should do steady business on either side of the Atlantic.

The yarn takes four characters, brought together by force of circumstances, who participate in an armed holdup and come to a sticky end. That they should all die in this way strikes a false note, but the twist clearly has been done to satisfy a censor's insistence that crime mustn't pay. The killing of the last two participants is particularly melodramatic, and calls for revised editing to give added conviction.

First of the four central figures is Richard Basehart, playing an ex-GI and Korean war vet, whose English wife had returned home to visit an ailing mother. He throws in his job with the intention of bringing her back but is trapped into staying. The second is Stanley Baker, a professional boxer who has decided to abandon the ring with some money saved up, but an injured hand makes him virtually unemployable. To worsen matters, his wife stood bail for her no-good brother who absconded and their savings went down the drain.

Then there is John Ireland, an American airman stationed in Britain who, while on a 48-hour pass, finds his wife (Gloria Grahame) knocking around with a British film actor. He winds up becoming a deserter. Finally, there is Laurence Harvey, an aristocratic English gent who has never done a day's work in his life. He relies on his natural charm to induce his wife to meet all his gambling and other debts. It is the last-named who conceives the holdup and talks the others into participating.

The direction focuses in turn on each of the four before the principal characters merge into the climax. The episodic treatment is smoothly handled although some of the passages have a tendency to drag. The main strength of the film rests in the quality of the acting. All principal roles are expertly played. Basehart, Miss Grahame and John Ireland, over from Hollywood, give sensitive performances. The main British contingent, headed by Harvey, Joan Collins, Baker, Margaret Leighton and (in a one-scene bit) Robert Morley, keep the local flag flying. Freda Jackson does an outstanding job as the possessive mother, while Lee Patterson contributes sterling work as the British actor who comes between Ireland and his wife. *Myro.*

The Saint's Girl Friday
(BRITISH)

Fast-moving resumption of The Saint series, with Louis Hayward again starred.

Hollywood, March 13.

RKO release of a Julian Lesser-Anthony Hinds production. Stars Louis Hayward; features Naomi Chance, Sidney Tafler, Charles Victor. Directed by Seymour Friedman. Story-screenplay, Allan MacKinnon; based on characters created by Leslie Charteris; camera, Walter Harvey; editor, James Needs; music, Ivoy Slanley. Previewed March 12, '54. Running time, **70 MINS.**

Simon Templar .... Louis Hayward
Carol Denby .... Naomi Chance

Max Lennar .... Sidney Tafler
Chief Inspector Teal...... Charles Victor
Katie French .... Jane Carr
Jarvis .... Harold Lang
Keith Merton .... Russell Enoch
Margie .... Diana Dors
Irish Cassidy .... Fred Johnson
Hoppy Uniatz .... Thomas Gallagher

This British whodunit re-casts Louis Hayward as The Saint, the Leslie Charteris character he last played for RKO in 1938, and emerges a fast entry for the program market. Excellent use has been made of London backgrounds in establishing atmosphere, and star delivers strongly in a quick-triggered role.

Jointly produced by American Julian Lesser and British Anthony Hinds, the Saint, whom a police inspector describes as not breaking the law — he merely bends it — returns to an England whose Scotland Yard resents him, at the cabled behest of a close woman friend, whom he finds dead upon his arrival. Saint is convinced her death isn't accidental, as the police claim, but planned, connected somehow with gamblers to whom she lost vast sums.

Efforts to solve the mystery leads to exciting run-ins with the River Mob, operating from a luxurious barge, and in bringing them to justice the Saint is aided by Naomi Chance, a victim of the gamblers who is paying off her indebtedness to them by luring in suckers.

Hayward handles his role in hard-hitting fashion, reminiscent of his earlier days in character, and receives satisfactory thesping assistance right down the line. Miss Chance plays his Girl Friday, Thomas Gallagher is his man, Charles Victor scores as the Yard inspector and Sidney Tafler and Fred Johnson are in as mob leaders.

Seymour Friedman makes his work as director count, and he gets good technical backing by Walter Harvey, handling the cameras, and Ivor Slanley's musical score.

Whit.

Si Versailles M'Etait Conte
(If Versailles Were Told to Me)
(FRENCH—COLOR)

Paris, March 9.

Cocinor release of Cocinex-CIM production. Written and directed by Sacha Guitry. Stars Guitry, Claudette Colbert, Georges Marchal, Jean Marais, Micheline Presle, Lana Marconi, Fernand Gravey. Camera, Pierre Montazel; editor, Raymond Lamy; music, Jean Francaix; sets, Rene Renoux. At Berlitz, Paris. Running time, **180 MINS.**

Louis XIV .... Sacha Guitry
Louis XV .... Jean Marais
Louis XIV (young) .... Georges Marchal
Madame Montespan.... Claudette Colbert
La Pompadour .... Micheline Presle
Mlle. Lavaliere .... Gisele Pascal
Ben Franklin .... Orson Welles
Marie Antoinette .... Lana Marconi
Cardinal .... Jean-Pierre Aumont
Feloton .... Jean-Louis Barrault
Moliere .... Fernand Gravey
Madame La Motte .... Gaby Morlay

In three hours Sacha Guitry has spanned the 300-year history of Versailles. This royal showplace serves as a cadre for a handpicked series of episodes in the lives of the Kings Louis XIV, XV, XVI, plus a quick tying up of the fate of this landmark up until the present day. The kaleidoscopic view takes on a cohesive air in the hands of Guitry, and this can best be described as a super-documentary, sketch pic or fragmentary eulogy to Versailles. This is fundamentally nationalistic in vein and appeal, and the bundle of star names, where practically every role hides a big star, should make this a top grosser here. For the U.S., chances are slimmer because a great deal of spectacle is sacrificed to make this a primarily intime Gallic pic. Also, great deal of shearing would be needed for the American market.

Despite the names of Claudette Colbert and Orson Welles, they only make episodic appearances. Hence, this will have to be sold on its pomp and illusion. Guitry picks out choice anecdotage to embellish the slow-moving pace.

No time is spent in its (Versailles) being built by Louis XIII, but how young Louis XIV lavished his love and care on it, and developed it into the most magnificent court in Europe is stressed. Guitry takes the lion's acting share of the vehicle as the aging Louis XIV. He gives the pic its main cohesive portion as he deftly and intelligently paints this king. The reign of the debauched Louis XV, and its fading after the unsavory death of the king only to be relit by Louis XVI with Marie Antoinette carry it to a conclusion.

Eastmancolor is kind to the rich hues of the palace except for some exteriors which tend to be bluish. In spite of the grandiose subject, Guitry's raconteur technique makes the production intime. It is this technique which takes the edge off the film for foreign situations.

Guitry is always regal as the old king while Georges Marchal and Jean Marais are fine as the younger effigies. Welles, in astonishing makeup, portrays an owly, aging Ben Franklin who comes for, and gets, aid for the American revolution. Miss Colbert bears the histrionic brunt of the affair as the conniving Montespan. Micheline Presle is graceful and lovely as Madame Pompadour. The revolution episode is weakest part of the film for it's played in comic operetta style.

Though Guitry flounders along the way, his lucid-eye view of the royal history of Versailles is a diverting affair. It should eventually make back its gigantic $750,000 outlay. The government helped in this by making Versailles available, and it proves to be the greatest production asset. This is also intended as a cultural prestige film, and, as such, definitely stands as a pleasant way of learning history. Jean Francaix's music is clever while the editing keeps this mammoth fresco always coherent. Guitry has found a lot of his old verve, charm and malicious wit and uses the film like the born story teller he is. This will have to be heavily sold hard in the U.S. for best resuults.

Mosk.

Bitter Creek
Action-packed Wild Bill Elliott western, best for star in years.

Hollywood, March 4.

Allied Artists release of Vincent M. Fennelly production. Stars Wild Bill Elliott; features Carleton Young, Beverly Garland, Claude Akins, Jim Hayward, John Harmon, Veda Ann Borg. Directed by Thomas Carr. Written by George Waggner; camera, Ernest Miller; editor, Sam Fields; music, Raoul Kraushaar. Previewed March 2, '54. Running time, **74 MINS.**

Clay Tyndall .... Wild Bill Elliott
Quentin Alien .... Carleton Young
Gail Bonner .... Beverly Garland
Vance Morgan .... Claude Akins
Dr. Prentiss .... Jim Hayward
A. Z. Platte .... John Harmon
Whitey .... Veda Ann Borg
Jerry Bonner .... Dan Mummert
Oak Mason .... John Pickard
Harley Pruett .... Forest Taylor
Sheriff .... Dabbs Greer
Joe Venango .... Mike Ragan
2nd Rider .... Zon Murray
Gunman .... John Larch
Pat Cleary .... Joe Devlin
Charles Hammond .... Earl Hodgins
Mrs. Hammond .... Florence Lake
Oak's Girl .... Jane Easton

This is good example of a western feature turned out on a moderate budget. Logical story motivations and action, excellent performances by an above-average cast and expert direction give familiar ingredients the punch needed for its market. It is Wild Bill Elliott's best in long time.

A revenge motive makes up the familiar basis for the George Waggner original screenplay, but he has plotted the action credibly and made the characters believable so the playoff under Thomas Carr's tight direction holds attention. Producer Vincent M. Fennelly has given Elliott topnotch supporting talent, most notable in Carleton Young's heavy duties and in Beverly Garland's playing of the femme lead. Her performance is considerably above the level of the usual prairie heroine.

Elliott comes to Bitter Creek to avenge the murder of his brother. The town seems willing to let the killing furore pass as by persons unknown, principally because Young, ambitious rancher, is suspicioned as having had a hand in it although there is no real evidence to link him to it. Realistic gun fights and physical brawls, as well as incidental supporting action, are logically brought on to keep the tale alive and kicking as Elliott fights his way through every effort of Young to remove him. The showdown climax is well handled and finds Elliott with Miss Garland, a girl who had believed in Young's honesty until circumstance reveals his treachery.

Ernest Miller handles the camera excellently to take care of outdoor values. Sam Fields' editing is good, as is the background score by Raoul Kraushaar

Brog.

Le Defroque
(The Unfrocked One)
(FRENCH)

Paris, March 9.

Gaumont release of SNEG-SFC-Gaumont production. Stars Pierre Fresnay. Directed by Leo Joannon. Screenplay, Joannon, Denis De La Patelliere camera, Nicolas Toporkoff; editor, Robert and Monique Isnard. At Madeleine, Paris. Running time, **120 MINS.**

Maurice .... Pierre Fresnay
Gerard .... Pierre Trabaud
Catherine .... Nicole Stephane
Mother .... Marcelle Geniat
Seminar Director .... Leo Joannon

This is a powerful offbeat pic about the crisis in faith of an unfrocked priest. It is meticulously made and benefits from excellent performances. Film is of good enough calibre for art house situations in the U.S. However, boxoffice likely will be limited due to downbeat theme.

An unfrocked priest takes refuge in mocking and finding fault with the essence of the church. In an army prison camp, he gives absolution to a dying priest out of amity, but it is taken as a sign of his still latent priesthood by a young man who is convinced of his vocation after this. He becomes a priest and tries to bring the unfrocked one back to the church. The latter has reached a point of fanaticism after the death of his mother which is attributed to him. At odds with himself, he thinks he has finally scourged himself when the young priest appears, and the unfrocked one kills him in a paroxysm of pride and anguish, and then gives himself up in donning the dead priest's frock.

Although drawn out at times, the film holds active interest throughout, and reaches high points of violence and revolt which make this film sure to be talked about. The unfrocked one's blessing of a decanter of wine in a nightclub and his final killing of the priest are points of brilliant professional work. Leo Joannon has given this good, studied direction and has also contributed a fine performance as the friend of the unfrocked one.

Pierre Fresnay brings his immense talent to bear on the anguish and hallucinations of the erring priest, making this his most complete composition to date. Pierre Trabaud holds his own as the fervid, simple young priest. Lensing is tops as in the editing.

However, this might set off polemics on differences of interpretation. But the taste and intelligence of handling should eliminate any sort of censorship or ecclesiastical differences.

Mosk.

Il Piu Comico Spettacolo Del Mondo
(Funniest Show On Earth)
(3-D—ITALIAN—COLOR)

Rome, Feb. 9.

Paramount release of a Rosa Film production. Stars Toto, Marc Lawrence, May Britt, Franca Faldini, Tania Weber. Directed by Mario Mattoli. Screenplay, Mattoli, Monicelli, Continenza, De Tuddo; camera (Ferraniacolor), Karl Struss; editor, Leo Catozzo. Running time, **80 MINS.**

Tottens .... Toto
Boss .... Marc Lawrence
Tamer .... May Britt
Trapezist .... Tania Weber
Singer .... Franca Faldini
Bastian .... Alberto Sorrentino

Paramount is releasing this would-be takeoff on "Greatest Show on Earth." With Toto, color, and a 3-D first in Italian production, returns should be good throughout Italian runs. It has considerably less to offer foreign viewers, and appears spotty at best, despite the gimmicks, for the U. S. It follows on the heels of an Italo lampoon of "Quo Vadis," titled "OK Nero" and not as good. By coincidence both are Par pix but two different local outfits made the takeoffs.

What might have been an amusing satire, as well as good spectacle in 3-D, for the most part has been turned into tame stuff because of a patchy, improvised script. Best moments are when Toto takes over with some vaude routines he's done before onstage some years back. There appears to have been an attempt at the start to take off the Cecil B. DeMille pic, characters and plot line generally following that of the Ringling epic, with Toto in the James Stewart role, Marc Lawrence as Charlton Heston, etc.

But the effort soon washes out. What emerges is some good but local comedy by Toto, some fair circus shots with 3-D angles, some brief appearances by May Britt and Tania Weber as the circus cuties, all melanged into a pic difficult to define.

Even the spotting of stars in the audience here is a repeat of "Greatest Show," with the names including Anthony Quinn, Silvana Mangano, Aldo Fabrizi and others. Karl Struss, as cameraman, has done a good job in this first local 3-D effort but experimentation is evident, and results uneven. With almost all plot strands still left dangling, pic is brought to an abrupt halt with a strange and apparently tacked-on scene depicting the evening prayer of the circus troupe.

Pic was also shot in 2-D and color, and some test first-runs as a flattie are planned.

Hawk.

Cet Homme Est Dangeureux
(This Man Is Dangerous) (FRENCH)

Paris, Feb. 2.

Sonofilm release of Sonofilm-EDIC-Lutetia production. Stars Eddie Constantine. Directed by Jean Sacha; screenplay Jacques Berland from novel by Peter Cheney; dialog, Marcel Duhamel; camera, Marcel Weiss; editor, Paulette Robert. At Balzac, Paris. Running time, **90 MINS.**

Lemmy Oaution	Eddie Constantine
Miranda	Claude Borelli
Constance	Colette Doreal
Siegella	Gregoire Aslan
Suzanne	Vera Norman
Dora	Jacqueline Pierreux

Following on the heels of the first Peter Cheney opus, "The Gun Moll Poison Ivy," here, which was nice b.o., this is another one with Eddie Constantine, U.S. warbler, again playing the tough FBI man, Lemmy Caution. This has enough intrigue, sexy femmes and fisticuffs to make this another neat program entry here. For the U.S., this is mainly for dual or secondary billing. Republic has already picked up the English version which was made at the same time.

This time Cheney's toughguy plays a gangster who has escaped from the U.S. and is on the lam in France. He is after a bank robber who, for some reason, is French, and gets involved in a proposed kidnapping after he gets a carousing American heiress in tow. After several murders, love affairs and fights, the swift-moving story ends with Lemmy victor and still in the clutches of the heiress. It ends with the promise that more is to follow. In fact, Constantine is now working in another one in this series, "Dames Get Along."

Director Jean Sacha has tried for some distinctive styling. Constantine is properly ingenious as the hard-drinking, fastfisted Caution. A bevy of gals supply the pulchritude. Colette Doreal is a looker with nice thespian ability. Lensing and editing are passable. Fights are the best mounted and conceived to come along in a Gallic pic of this kind. *Mosk.*

Rimsky-Korsakov
(RUSSIAN—COLOR)

Biopic of the Russian composer; average b.o. returns in its intended market.

Artkino release of Leningrad Film Studio production. Features Grigori Belov, Nikolai Cherkassov, L. Griasenko. Directed by G. Roshal, G. Kazansky. Screenplay, A. Abramova, G. Roshal; camera (Sovcolor), M. Magid, L. Sokolsky; music and arrangements, Y. Sviridov. At Stanley Theatre, N.Y., week beginning Feb. 27, '54. Running time, **88 MINS.**

Rimsky-Korsakov	Grigori Belov
Stasov	Nikolai Cherkassov
Mamontov	A. Borisov
Zabelt-Vrubel	L. Griasenko
Glazunov	V. Khokhryakov
Mrs. Rimsky-Korsakov	L. Sukharevskaya
Chaliapine	A. Ognivtsev
Serov	B. Kokovkin
Almazova	L. Dranovskaya
Grand Duke	F. Nikitin

Symphony Orchestra of the Kirov Opera and Ballet Theatre in Leningrad.

(In Russian; English Titles)

Billed as a "brilliant musical biography of the composer of 'Sadko,' 'Coq d'Or' and Scheherazade,'" this newest Soviet import is interesting longhair diversion but hardly measures up to its advance heralding. Market for the Leningrad Film Studio production will be largely confined to the few U. S. theatres which show Russian product.

When the film devotes itself exclusively to its cultural aspects it emerges as fine entertainment. But as usual there had to be a political sermon. Czar's cossacks shooting down the revolting masses and sundry other unsubtle scenes will be familiar to veteran viewers of Kremlin-sponsored pictures.

Moreover, this biopic of Nikolai Rimsky-Korsakov (1844-1908) is considerably abridged for it spans only the period from 1898 to shortly before the composer's death. Nevertheless there are liberal excerpts from such of his works as "Sadko," "Snow Maiden" and "Czar Saltan." These are excellently played and beautifully sung.

A decided asset to the film is the melodious voice of L. Griasenko. She's outstanding in her portrayal of the title role in "Snow Maiden." Grigori Belov, as Rimsky-Korsakov, handles the part with warmth and dignity. Balance of the cast provides fair support under the uneven direction of G. Roshal (who co-scripted) and G. Kazansky.

On the credit side is the fine work of the Kirov Opera Symphony Orchestra and Ballet Theatre as conducted by B. Haikin. Sovcolor, in which this import was lensed, appears to be improving but still lags behind the vivid hues found in Technicolor and Eastman color. Print's English titles are adequate. *Gilb.*

Appointment for Murder
(ITALIAN)

Italian Film Export release of Lux Film production. Stars Umberto Spadaro, Delia Scala. Directed by Piaccio Bandini. Screenplay, Sandro Continenza, Ennio de Concini, Mario Monicelli, Stefano Venzina, Bandini; camera, Renato del Frate, Ugo Nudi; sets Alberto Boccianti; music, Gine Marinuzzi Jr. At Cinema Giglio, N. Y., starting Feb. 18, '54. Running time, **91 MINS.**

Det. Pietrangeli	Umberto Spadaro
Silvia	Delia Scala
Aldo Manni	Andrea J. Bosic
Giorgio Morelli	Marco Vicario
Palermo	Natale Cirino
Vandina	Dorian Grey

(In Italian; English Titles)

This tedious Italian whodunit not only depicts a baffled police force but most of the time keeps the audience in doubt as to what is going on. Even the familiar impeccable performance by Umberto Spadero fails to save it from the tired, actionless story and weak thespian performances. "Appointment For Murder" shapes only as a fill-in for Italian-language houses of the U. S. It was hardly worth the bother and expense of imposing English titles.

Besides Spadaro's yeomanship work in the chief detective's role, only Delia Scala, as his daughter, and Andrea Bosic, cast as husband of the dead woman, contribute much to making the story plausible. Others in the large cast appear either bewildered by the story or the director. Actual screenplay seems to have been spoiled by having too much writers work on it. There were five, including Bandini, the director. Latter's directorial stint is way below par. *Wear.*

Prisoner of War

Grim uninspired account of North Korean atrocities.

Hollywood, March 23.

Metro release of Henry Berman production. Stars Ronald Reagan, Steve Forrest, Dewey Martin; features Oscar Homolka, Robert Horton, Paul Stewart, Henry Morgan, Stephen Bekassy. Directed by Andrew Marton. Written by Allen Rivkin; camera, Robert Planck; editor, James Newcom. Previewed March 17, '54. Aspect ratio up to 1:75-1. Running time, **80 MINS.**

Web Sloane	Ronald Reagan
Cpl. Joseph R. Stanton	Steve Forrest
Jesse Treadman	Dewey Martin
Col. Nikita I. Biroshilov	Oscar Homolka
Francis Aloysius Belney	Robert Horton
Capt. Jack Hodges	Paul Stewart
Maj. O. D. Halle	Henry Morgan
Lt. Georgi M. Robovnik	Stephen Bekassy
Col. Kim Doo Yi	Leonard Strong
Merton Tollivar	Darryl Hickman
Red Guard	Weaver Levy
Capt. Lang Hyun Choi	Rollin Moriyama
Benjamin Julesberg	Ike Jones
MVD Officer	Clarence Lung
Axel Horstrom	Jerry Paris
Lt. Peter Reilly	John Lupton
Red Guard	Ralph Ahn

This is a grim film account of the atrocities practiced on prisoners of war by North Koreans. While the incidents are well-documented in actual records by returning POWs, the presentation here is uninspired so there's little shock value or credibility to carry the picture. It doesn't figure for the entertainment market although heavy promotional efforts may buoy its chances.

Storywise, the film has all the ingredients to be a startling shocker giving the truth about POW treatment in the Korean war, but the production and direction handling gives it a "quickie" look and routine treatment that will not grip and hold an audience. Scripter Allen Rivkin interviewed many POW returnees to get the facts straight for the film story and, reportedly, all of the incidents and dialog are for real. However, they don't come out that way on the screen under Andrew Marton's direction of the Henry Berman production and many of the sequences would be laughable if the basis was not such a serious one.

Plot twist used has Ronald Reagan volunteering to check reports of brutalities. He parachutes behind enemy lines, slips into a column of G.I. prsioners and becomes one of them at a Red prison camp. Scenes of brutal beatings, calculated tortures, senseless killings and other inhumanly conceived treatments fill the footage but fail to have the intended shock value. Indoctrination lectures by Russian and North Korean officers, played by Oscar Homolka and Leonard Strong, are so broad as to be almost comic opera. A particular offender is Homolka, who gives an opera bouffe flavor to his Russian officer character. This performance points up the general lack of the kind of forceful direction the picture needs.

Steve Forrest, a defiant G.I., and Dewey Martin, a prisoner who seemingly swings over to the Reds, co-star with Reagan but none of the trio has a chance to be more than adequate. Glimpsed in feature and supporting roles among the prisoners are Robert Horton, Paul Stewart, Darryl Hickman and Ike Jones. Stephen Bekassy is a comic aide to Homolka.

The technical credits behind the production, including Robert Planck's lensing, are acceptable generally. *Brog.*

The Iron Glove
(COLOR)

Eighteenth century action costumer; okay escapist entertainment.

Columbia release of Sam Katzman production. Stars Robert Stack, Ursula Thiess; features Richard Stapley. Directed by William Castle. Screenplay, Jesse L. Lasky Jr., DeVallon Scott, Douglas Heyes from story by Robert E. Kent and Samuel J. Jacoby; camera (Technicolor), Henry Freulich; editor, Gene Havlick; music, Mischa Bakaleinikoff. Tradeshown N.Y., March 18, '54. Running time, 77 MINS.

Charles Wogan	Robert Stack
Ann Brett	Ursula Thiess
James Stuart	Richard Stapley
James O'Toole	Charles Irwin
Patrick Gaydon	Alan Hale Jr.
Duke of Somerfield	Leslie Bradley
Count DuLusac	Louis D. Merrill
Cavenly	Paul Cavanagh
King George	Otto Waldis
Princess Clementina	Rica Owen
Austrian Lieutenant	Eric Feldary
Austrian Sergeant	David Bruce
Amy	Shirley Whitney
Gretzel	Ingard Dawson

As producer Sam Katzman's latest Columbia release, "The Iron Glove" fits comfortably into his familiar romance-adventure pattern. The 18th-century period costumer on which five scripters toiled contains sufficient movement to please the action fans. Withal, it shapes up as satisfying escapist entertainment fare for the twin-bill market.

While most of the cast are unknown to the average filmgoer, Robert Stack and Ursula Thiess share top billing and provide the marquee values. Another lift stems from the fine Technicolor interiors and exteriors as lensed by Henry Freulich. Katzman's overall production values mantle the film nicely and extract maximum returns budgetwise.

The Robert E. Kent and Samuel J. Jacoby story, which Jesse L. Lasky, Jr., DeVallon Scott and Douglas Heyes screenplayed, is a lusty tale of an attempt of Scottish prince Richard Stapley to seize the throne of England's King George I. Among Stapley's chief supporters is Irish swordsman Robert Stack. On hand as femme interest is Miss Thiess.

Swordplay and chicanery are the main ingredients of the 77-minutes of footage. Although the final frame finds King George, as played by Otto Waldis, still wearing his regal trappings, there's a cheerful atmosphere for Stapley has won himself a bride and an heir follows a year later.

Performances are generally good under William Castle's breezy direction. Stack, of dashing physique, is well cast as a swashbuckler who not only rescues Stapley's kidnaped bride-to-be but wins the affections of Miss Thiess as well. She acquits herself favorably as a spy who lets her romantic inclinations interfere with business.

Stapley, as the Scottish pretender, appears too conservative and modest to give his role much realism as a candidate for the throne by force of arms. Charles Irwin and Alan Hale Jr. are effective as Stack's fellow swordsmen while Leslie Bradley and Louis D. Merrill are okay heavies. Gene Havlick's editing is tight and Mischa Bakaleinikoff's musical direction is competent. *Gilb.*

Carnival Story
(COLOR)

Good Munich-lensed drama with s.a. and carnival thrills for pop appeal and okay prospects.

Hollywood, March 23.

RKO release of Maurice and Frank King production. Stars Anne Baxter, Steve Cochran, Lyle Bettger, George Nader; features Jay C. Flippen, Helene Stanley, Adi Berber. Directed by Kurt Neumann. Screenplay, Hans Jacoby and Kurt Neumann; based on a story by Marcel Klauber and C. B. Williams; camera (AGFA Color), Ernest Haller; editors, Merrill White, Ludolf Griesbach; music composed and conducted by Willy Schmidt-Gentner. Previewed March 19, '54. Aspect ratio up to 1:65-1. Running time, **94 MINS.**

Willie	Anne Baxter
Joe	Steve Cochran
Frank	Lyle Bettger
Vines	George Nader
Charley	Jay C. Flippen
Peggy	Helene Stanley
Groppo	Adi Berber

Some sizzling sex and carnival thrills are the commercial commodities giving this King Brothers production a chance at pop appeal and good ticket sales. Strong selling will be no problem with these exploitation angles and there should be some added ballyhoo worth in the fact Munich was the site of the picture's lensing.

The independently-made film, which RKO is distributing, has an eye-brow lifting aspect or two to its sex-in-the-sawdust handling, but this treatment of elemental urges should be a selling factor. The amatory facets spring from a plot woven around a woman with three men, one of whom is bad for her. The role of the life-buffeted German girl who joins an American carnival in Munich and becomes its high-diving star is the best film part Anne Baxter has had in some time. The manner in which she handles it should awaken new interest in her talents because she makes it come over with considerable sexy zing.

Kurt Neumann's direction gets good mileage out of the principal exploitation angles to the plot. His guidance of other phases is less effective, but still satisfactory in making the most of the screenplay he wrote with Hans Jacoby from a story by Marcel Klauber and C. B. Williams. The Munich and carnival settings are colorful backgrounds for the dramatic and romantic conflicts in the plot. Real thriller sequences are the high dives from a 110-foot platform into a six-foot tank of water, although these scenes, as well as some others become repetitious after awhile.

Miss Baxter gets her carnival job after picking the pockets of Steve Cochran, the show's advance man. A sizzling affair between the two starts immediately and this animal attraction continues even after the girl learns Cochran is a thorough heel and she has married Lyle Bettger, the high-diving star of the carnival. Bettger is killed in a diving "accident" arranged by Cochran and the latter arouses the widow again long enough to make love to her and then steal the dead man's savings. A third man, George Nader, enters her life while she is recuperating from a diving injury, but Cochran turns up again, is rebuffed at last and then killed by the show's strong-man, who has had a crush on Miss Baxter all the time, leaving her free for a new life with Nader.

The sympathetic diver character from Bettger is a switch from his usual heavy roles and he sells it convincingly. Cochran appears perfectly at ease as the colorful heel. Nader has few opportunities but does them nicely. Jay C. Flippen capably does his character of the carnival owner. Helene Stanley's part of a hula dancer is almost a walkon and Adi Berber is seen as the huge, small-brained but big-muscled strongman. Others are carnival types.

Maurice and Frank King give the picture a good flavor by the overseas lensing in AGFA Color (print by Technicolor), and the tints provide sight values to the backgrounds under Ernest Haller's camera handling. Willy Schmidt-Gentner composed and conducted the score which fits the action.

Brog.

Pride of the Blue Grass
(COLOR)

Okay supporter with a race-track backdrop. Lloyd Bridges and Vera Miles topline.

Hollywood, March 20.

Allied Artists release of a Hayes Goetz production. Stars Lloyd Bridges, Vera Miles, Margaret Sheridan. Directed by William Beaudine. Story and screenplay, Harold Shumate; camera (Color Corp. of America), Harry Neumann; editor, John Fuller; music, Marlin Skiles. Previewed March 17, '54. Running time, **71 MINS.**

Jim	Lloyd Bridges
Linda	Vera Miles
Helen	Margaret Sheridan
Wilson	Arthur Shields
Danny	Michael Chapin
Hunter	Harry Cheshire
Mrs. Graves	Cecil Weston
Mr. Casey	Emory Parnell
Mrs. Casey	Joan Shawlee
Vet	Ray Walker

"Pride of the Blue Grass" travels a rather familiar track as it tells the story of Gypsy Prince, from maiden days until the nag eventually wins "the big race." There's inherent charm in the footage, however, plus neat thesping by the principals which all adds up to rate film an okay supporter.

The Harold Shumate story and screenplay pivots around Vera Miles' faith in her horse, Gypsy Prince. Arriving at the track, Miss Miles talks trainer Lloyd Bridges into stabling the animal. When horse eventually is entered in a race, it stumbles because of a loose bandage and breaks a leg. Miss Miles refuses to let horse be destroyed and the leg is set, eventually heals and Gypsy Prince goes on to win his big race. By this time, Miss Miles has also won—Bridges.

Hayes Goetz's capable production supervision is evident in film's overall treatment, while William Beaudine's direction manages to stir up and generally sustain interest. Megging also works well with the players. Bridges and Miss Miles both come over well, the latter in particular registering strongly with a marked ability and pert attractiveness. Margaret Sheridan, as third topliner, has the rather thankless role of the other woman. She's okay in the spot, however.

Performances of the supporters, as well as technical contributions, are along stock lines.

Neal.

Siege at Red River
(COLOR)

North-versus-South actioner fitting requirements of general outdoor action program market.

Hollywood, March 19.

20th-Fox release of Leonard Goldstein (Panoramic production. Stars Van Johnson, Joanne Dru; features Richard Boone, Milburn Stone, Jeff Morrow, Craig Hill. Directed by Rudolph Mate. Screenplay, Sydney Boehm: based on a story by J. Robert Bren and Gladys Atwater; camera (Technicolor), Edward Cronjager: editor, Betty Steinberg; music, Lionel Newman; song, Neuman and Ken Darby. Aspect ratio up to 1:66-1. Previewed March 15, '54. Running time, **86 MINS.**

Jim Farraday	Van Johnson
Nora Curtis	Joanne Dru
Brett Manning	Richard Boone
Benjy	Milburn Stone
Frank Kelso	Jeff Morrow
Lieutenant Braden	Craig Hill
Chief Yellow Hawk	Rico Alaniz
Sheriff	Robert Burton
Lukoa	Pilar Del Rey
Anderson Smith	Ferris Taylor
Sgt. Jenkins	John Cliff

The War Between States is being fought again in "Siege at Red River," this time in the midwest with warring Indians and a stolen Gatling gun thrown in for good measure. It's a Panoramic production, going out through 20th-Fox, and fits the overall requirements of the general outdoor actioner market, plus having the familiar names of Van Johnson, Joanne Dru and Technicolor for marquee flash.

Plot of the Leonard Goldstein production is built around the theft of the Gatling gun by Southern raiders who transport it across country in a medicine show wagon to some unnamed destination. **Rudolph Mate's direction gives a fast opening to the Sydney Boehm script, but the story pace slows thereafter until past the midway mark, when movement picks up again and builds to a rousing bang-bang climax with enough happening to satisfy the average outdoor action fan.**

Johnson and Milburn Stone are the medicine show men, and both keep their characters alive and entertaining. Miss Dru is present, attractively, as a Yankee nurse whom the pair comes across in its travels. The Indians get into the act when whip-cracking Richard Boone steals the gun, sells it to the warring redskins and then helps them attack a Union fort. Johnson, pursued by Jeff Morrow, a Pinkerton man, and Union troops led by Craig Hill, comes to the rescue of the fort. By the time this individual war is satisfactorily concluded, so is the big North-South fighting, leaving time for a finale clinch between Johnson and Miss Dru, who had been too concerned with their respective sympathies to get together romantically before the windup.

Most of the characters in the J. Robert Bren-Gladys Atwater story lean to the flamboyant, particularly Boone's, but prove acceptable to this type of show. Picture gets in its comedy licks on occasion, mostly from Johnson and Stone singing "Tapioka" as they hawk their medicine. It's powerful brew because Stone uses it in another sequence to get Miss Dru tight so he can smuggle the gun aboard her ambulance wagon.

The color lensing by Edward Cronjager is a production asset, and stands out most noticeably in the Indian attack on the fort. Lionel Newman did the score and wrote the situation tune with Ken Darby. Other technical credits are okay.

Brog.

Eight O'Clock Walk
(BRITISH)

Suspense thriller good for local consumption but underdramatized for U. S. taste.

London, March 23.

British Lion release of George King Production. Stars Richard Attenborough, Cathy O'Donnell, Derek Farr, Ian Hunter. Directed by Lance Comfort. Screenplay, Katherine Strueby, Guy Morgan; camera, Brendan Stafford; editor, Francis Bieber; music, George Melachrino. At Pavilion, London, March 16, '54. Running time, **87 MINS.**

Tom Manning	Richard Attenborough
Jill Manning	Cathy O'Donnell
Geoffrey Tanner	Ian Hunter
Peter Tanner	Derek Farr
Horace Clifford	Maurice Denham
Mr. Justice Harrington	Harry Welchman
Mr. Munro	Kynaston Reeves
Mrs. Zunz	Lilly Kann
Mrs. Evans	Eithne Dunn
Irene Evans	Cheryl Molineaux
Miss Ribden-White	Totti Truman Taylor
Mr. Pettigrew	Robert Adair
Mrs. Higgs	Grace Arnold
Ernie Higgs	David Hannaford
Edith Higgs	Sally Stephens

The title of this pic is more melodramatic than its substance. There is no eleventh-hour snatch from the gallows, but a protracted murder trial of an innocent man eventually acquitted because his counsel accidentally stumbles on a vital piece of evidence. Scenes of the famous Old Bailey and the accoutrements of justice are interesting in themselves, but are too laboriously true to life for snap entertainment purposes. It should do well locally on the star's appeal, but it lacks the speedy technique of its U. S. counterparts to attract much attention overseas.

Richard Attenborough plays a taxidriver, newly married and about to own a cab and a house of his own. On his way to work several kids delay him with April Fool tricks, and he is coaxed onto a bombed site by a small girl pretending she has lost her doll. On realizing her tears are faked and that he has again been hoaxed, he chases her in mock anger. This incident is witnessed and quoted against him when he is later charged with her murder. Several people testify he was near the spot where the body was found and circumstantial evidence piles up against him. Only his young wife and the junior counsel defending him believe his story. When illness prevents the senior counsel's attendance, the younger one takes charge.

While lunching during a court adjournment, the lawyer notices one of the male witnesses offering candy to a child in the street. Following a hunch and employing a few theatrical devices he breaks down the man's evidence on the stand and unmasks him as the real criminal.

It probably is not Attenborough's fault that he neither looks nor acts like a conventional taxi driver, but he bears the stunning burden of the monstrous accusation with convincing realism. Cathy O'Donnell is not served well with either script or camera as his Canadian wife. Her rather drab air of pathos arouses a certain amount of sympathy but is seldom really moving. The young lawyer is sincerely portrayed by Derek Farr, and Ian Hunter is admirable as his father who is counsel for the prosecution.

An excellent performance comes from Eithne Dunn as the victim's mother while Maurice Denham depicts the murderer's guile quite appropriately. Ex-musical comedy singer Harry Welchman acquits himself well as the judge who continues bravely despite personal bereavement. The youngsters are all natural, and at times amusing. Lance Comfort keeps to his usual high standard of direction.

Clem.

Rails Into Laramie
(COLOR)

Good, regulation outdoor actioner slanted for okay response in its market.

Hollywood, March 19.

Universal release of Ted Richmond production. Stars John Payne, Mari Blanchard, Dan Duryea; features Joyce Mac-

Kenzie, Barton MacLane, Ralph Dumke, Harry Shannon, Jamer Griffith. Directed by Jesse Hibbs. Screenplay, D. D. Beauchamp, Joseph Hoffman; camera (Technicolor), Maury Gertsman; editor, Ted J. Kent; song, "Laramie," sung by Rex Allen, Frederick Herbert and Arnold Hughes; musical direction, Joseph Gershenson. Aspect ratio up to 2-1. Previewed March 16, '54. Running time, 80 MINS.

Jefferson Harder	John Payne
Lou Carter	Mari Blanchard
Jim Shanessy	Dan Duryea
Heden Shanessy	Joyce MacKenzie
Lee Graham	Barton MacLane
Mayor Frank Logan	Ralph Dumke
Judge Pierce	Harry Shannon
Orrie Sommers	James Griffith
Ace Winton	Lee Van Cleef
Con Winton	Myron Healey
Pike Murphy	Charles Horvath
Grimes	George Chandler
Telegraph Operator	Douglas Kennedy
Higby	Alexander Campbell

Regulation, but well-valued, outdoor action characterizes "Rails Into Laramie" and it should draw an okay response in its market. Pace is lively with performances to match. Add Technicolor as a pictorial value.

Co-starring in the Ted Richmond production are John Payne, Mari Blanchard and Dan Duryea. The two males have familiar names and the top trio is capable in carrying the show. Payne is literally a one-man army as the hero, playing a sergeant assigned to clean up a gang headed by Duryea which is preventing the railroad from coming to Laramie. Duryea is a saloonkeeper, partnered with Miss Blanchard, who doesn't want the railroad to 'progress because the section gangs keep his business prospering.

Women's suffrage is a historical twist introduced in the script by D. D. Beauchamp and Joseph Hoffman. Male juries keep freeing Duryea and his thugs and the hero's constantly frustrated until Miss Blanchard swings to his side and organizes the first all-femme jury. Despite this distaff assist, though, it takes male heroics to bring Duryea back for his hanging after he has escaped.

Jesse Hibbs' direction stirs up plenty of visual action during the fast 80 minutes, making excellent use of the well-established characters and motivations. Payne plays his role with conviction and Duryea does another of his likeable heavies. Miss Blanchard is an attractive romantic partner for Payne. Joyce MacKenzie, as Duryea's wife, hasn't much to do. James Griffith shows up strongly as a timid marshal among the principal featured parts and others spotted to advantage include Barton MacLane, Ralph Dumke, Harry Shannon, Lee Van Cleef, Myron Healey and Charles Horvath.

Camera work by Maury Gertsman is actionful, giving the movement a neat display that helps the excitement of several chase and fight sequences, as well as a near-collision between trains. A background song, "Laramie," which Frederick Herbert and Arnold Hughes cleffed, is sung behind the title cards by Rex Allen, who does not appear in the picture. Technical credits are good. *Brog.*

Bang! You're Dead
(BRITISH)

Rural mystery outstanding for newcomer Anthony Richmond's performance; good for local b.o. and general second feature in U.S.

London, March 16.

British Lion release of Wellington Film Production. Stars Jack Warner, Derek Farr; features Veronica Hurst, Michael Medwin, Gordon Harker, Anthony Richmond. Directed by Lance Comfort. Screenplay, Guy Elmes and Ernest Borneman; camera, Brandar J. Stafford; editor, Francis Bieber; music, Eric Spear. At Gaumont Theatre, London. Running time, 88 MINS.

Bonsell	Jack Warner
Detective Grey	Derek Farr
Hilda	Veronica Hurst
Bob Carter	Michael Medwin
Mr. Hare	Gordon Harker
Cliff Bonsell	Anthony Richmond
Willy	Sean Barrett
Mrs. Moxted	Beatrice Varley
Ben Jones	Philip Saville
Sergeant Gurney	John Warwick
Jimmy Knuckle	Toke Townley

As often is the case when young children are featured in a story, in this one a moppet steals the picture. Here a nine-year-old boy, Anthony Richmond, making his screen debut, exhibits all the effortless confidence of a vet. His personality is more worth watching than the improbable story in which he is the central figure. Pic should prove a good b.o. proposition here on the draw of the male stars, and make a suitable second feature for most houses elsewhere.

Film is a whodunit in reverse, with a hue and cry for the murderer of a man after it has been revealed in prolog style that he was accidentally shot by a child. The gradual tracking down by the police and the terror of the hunted boy is tensely unreeled. His scenes with his older buddy are more convincing than those portrayed by the adults, whose dialog seems stilted.

Living in an old shanty among the woods, the small son of a logman swaggers and bosses his nearby friend, an older boy with a retarded mind. A model, helpful child to his father, he runs wild and exerts his budding authority while the boys roam the countryside. He finds an army revolver in a deserted shack and substitutes it for his own toy weapon. Holding up a neighbor he does a highwayman act demanding his watch and fires and kills the man. A quarrel over a girl resulting in bad blood causes the crime to be laid at the door of an innocent person until the investigating detective unravels the truth.

Apart from the sterling performance by Richmond and the good support by Sean Barrett, as his companion, there are excellent contributions by Jack Warner, as the boy's father; Michael Medwin, as the accused man; and Derek Farr, the sleuth. Veronica Hurst has little to do but supply the blonde distraction while Gordon Harker has a brief appearance as the local innkeeper. The production is directed with equal sense of drama and pathos. *Clem.*

An Inspector Calls
(BRITISH)

Stagey adaptation of J. B. Priestley's play; rates only moderate b.o. prospects.

London, March 16.

British Lion release of Watergate Production. Stars Alastair Sim; features Olga Lindo, Arthur Young, Brian Worth, Bryan Forbes, Eileen Moore, Jane Wenham. Directed by Guy Hamilton. Screenplay by Desmond Davis from the play by J. B. Priestley; camera, Ted Scaife; editor, Alan Osbiston; music, Francis Chagrin. At Gaumont, London. Running time, 79 MINS.

Inspector Poole	Alastair Sim
Arthur Birling	Arthur Young
Sybil Birling	Olga Lindo
Sheila Birling	Eileen Moore
Eric Birling	Bryan Forbes
Gerald Croft	Brian Worth
Eva Smith	Jane Wenham

There has been no attempt to disguise the stage original in this film version of J. B. Priestley's play. It has been treated in static fashion with the plot unspooled to the accompaniment of a succession of prolonged flashbacks. Looks only moderate at the b.o., but for British exhibs will have the advantage of a quota tag.

The story has dramatic potentialities while the plot has been skillfully developed, but the manner of presentation tends to become a little wearisome. Alastair Sim, an actor of rich comedy talent, is given few opportunities as the bogus inspector who compels every member of a prosperous midlands family to accept some share of the blame for the suicide of a poor, working girl.

The father (Arthur Young) had fired her because she was a troublemaker and had led a factory deputation for more money. The spoiled daughter (Eileen Moore) had been responsible for her dismissal from a local store in a fit of temper while the prospective son-in-law (Brian Worth) had led her off the straight and narrow and set her up in his own apartment. The mother (Olga Linda) is pictured as having denied her aid when she appeared before a charity committee for help. Finally the son (Bryan Forbes) had been forced to steal money after he learned the girl was going to have a baby by him.

As each incident is told in flashback, the moral of the play becomes clear. Society, Priestley is inferring, has a duty to perform and even the humblest citizen has a right to a place in the sun. The social aspect is soft-pedalled but is brought out by the younger and more impressionable member of the family. Although the entire cast is quite adequate, the best performance comes from Jane Wenham as the young girl. She has a refreshing personality and the quality of complete sincerity. *Myro.*

Fangs of the Wild

Mild outdoor melodrama for programmer dates.

Hollywood, March 5.

Lippert Pictures release of Robert L. Lippert, Jr., production. Stars Onslow Stevens, Margia Dean; introduces Charles Chaplin, Jr. Directed by William Claxton. Screenplay, Orville Hampton; based on a story idea by Claxton; camera, Paul Ivano; editor, Monica Collingwood; music, Paul Dunlap. Previewed March 3, '54. Running time, 72 MINS.

Roger	Charles Chaplin, Jr.
Jim	Onslow Stevens
Linda	Margia Dean
Tad	Freddy Ridgeway
Mac	Phil Tead
Deputy Sheriff	Robert Stevenson
Shep	Buck

The melodramatics in "Fangs of the Wild" play mildly and it is a barely passable lowercase programmer. Basic plot also has a familiar ring, having been seen a number of times (i.e. RKO's "The Window," etc.), but is so statically handled that a good meller punch is lacking. It's a routine dualer filler.

William Claxton direct from his own story idea, scripted by Orville Hampton, but tempoed the scenes too slowly for presentation to have much life. A kid given to tall tales witnesses a cold-blooded murder but can get no one to believe him. That basic plot this time is laid in the outdoors at a mountain hunting lodge operated by the boy's dad. The killer passes the murder off as a hunting accident and almost gets away with it until he panics and tries to kill the boy. The latter's dog, however, proves the hero when he saves the lad after a finale chase through the mountains.

Film introduces Charles Chaplin, Jr., as the killer and, while his personality indicates some promise, this is not much of a showcase for him. Onslow Stevens is the dad who doesn't believe his son, Freddy Ridgeway, and Margia Dean is Chaplin's wife and motive for the shooting. Phil Tead, the lodge's handyman, Robert Stevenson, a deputy sheriff who sounds off about careless hunters, and Buck, large collie, are the others in the melodrama.

On the technical side, the Robert L. Lippert, Jr., production has good values, such as Paul Ivano's photography, which does justice to the mountain locations. *Brog.*

Racing Blood
(COLOR-SONG)

So-so horse-racing entry for mild response in program market.

20th-Fox release of a Wesley Barry production. Stars Bill Williams, Jean Porter, Jimmy Boyd. Directed by Barry; associate producer, Edward L. Alperson Jr.; screenplay, Sam Roeca; story, Roeca, Barry; camera, John Martin; editor, Ace Herman; music, Edward J. Kay. Previewed March 15, '54. Running time, 75 MINS.

Tex	Bill Williams
Lucille	Jean Porter
David	Jimmy Bold
Gramps	George Cleveland
Mitch	John Eldredge
Doc Nelson	Sam Flint
Emerson	Fred Kohler Jr.
Wee Willie	George Steele
Mullins	Bobby Johnson
Jockey Ben	Frankie Darro

This apparently is a case of 20th-Fox getting caught with its program down and indiscriminately throwing in a low-budget release to service customers badly in need of product. Wesley Barry production, which former juve star also directed, is a listless horse-racing yarn which lacks finish even for the program market. For exploitation, there's boy platter artist Jimmy Boyd making his film bow, but at best picture will be held to lower-bracketing in double bill datings.

Footage, poorly tinted, is fashioned around twin foals sired by a racing champ on the stock farm on John Eldredge. One is born with cloven hoof, and it's decided by trainer Bill Williams, and the owner to destroy him, particularly when the vet says he'll never be any good at racing. Young Boyd, whose grandfather, George Cleveland, handyman, is detailed the task of shooting the colt, prevails upon latter to give him the small animal. They secretly rear the foal and prep him for the two-year-old classic, in which he outruns, of course, the good twin.

Williams handles himself with his usual casualness and romance is supplied rather haphazardly by Jean Porter, daughter of Eldredge, who has a yen for her father's trainer. Young Boyd is in for four songs, which he warbles capably enough, including "Pardners" and "Fa-La-Link-A-Di-Do," but as an actor he's mostly on the yelling side. Eldredge makes one of his few sympathetic appearances, smooth and easy, Cleveland is called upon for an overdose of comedy and Sam Flint is the vet who encourages young Boyd in raising the colt.

Technical credits are average. Barry co-authored original story with Sam Roeca, who scripted. *Whit.*

Devil on Horseback
(BRITISH)

Ambitious British racetrack meller; might get by as part of twin bill in U. S.

London, March 23.
British Lion release of (Group 3) John Grierson-Isobel Pargiter production. Stars Googie Withers, John McCallum, Jeremy Spenser. Directed by Cyril Frankel. Screenplay, Neil Paterson, Montagu Slater; camera, Denny Densham; editor, Sidney Stone; music, Malcolm Arnold. At London Pavilion, March 17, '54. Running time, 88 MINS.
Mrs. Cadell .... Googie Withers
Charles Roberts .... John McCallum
Moppy Parfitt .... Jeremy Spenser
Ted Fellowes .... Meredith Edwards
Scarlett O'Hara .... Liam Redmond
Darky .... Sam Kydd
Squib .... Malcolm Knight
Len .... Peter Lindsay
Reg Guest .... Eric Francis
Fred Cole .... Vic Wise
Mr. Parfitt .... Peter Swanwick
Mrs. Parfitt .... Fatty Hardy
Valet .... Arthur Lovegrove
Blacksmith .... George Rose

Group 3, a government-sponsored outfit, has become more ambitious in its choice of talent for this story, with a horseracing background. The script does not always match up with the ability of the stars; but there is a solid audience for this type of production. It should register as a reliable dualler, and may go as lower half of twin bill in U. S.

Central character in the story is a young boy (Jeremy Spenser) with a natural way of handling horses, who gets signed up as a stable lad. He soon gets his chance to ride several winners as an apprentice jockey. But the lad is bumptious and conceited. He has to be taken down a peg or two, after being found responsible for the death of one of his mounts, and forced to learn that winning a race is not always the sole answer.

This role is sincerely played by Spenser, a boy with several major film credits. He admirably suggests the conceit of youth and the humility that follows. Googie Withers and John McCallum (real life husband and wife) are nicely teamed in the romantic leads as owner and trainer although given only moderate scope. Liam Redmond, as a tippling ex-jockey, Meredith Edwards and Sam Kydd head a standard supporting cast. Cyril Frankel's direction keeps the action rolling, and makes the most of the suspense values in the script. Myro.

Le Ble En Herbe
(The Flowering Wheat)
(FRENCH)

Paris, Feb. 9.
Gaumont release of Franco-London Film production. Stars Edwige Feuillere. Directed by Claude Autant-Lara. Screenplay, Jean Aurenche, Pierre Bost, Autant-Lara from novel by Colette; camera, Robert Le Fevbre; editor, Madeleine Gug. At Colisee, Paris. Running time, 110 MINS.
Woman in White ..... Edwige Feuillere
Philippe .... Pierre-Michel Beck
Vinca .... Nicole Berger
Mother .... Renee Duvillers
Cameraman .... Louis De Funes

Claude Autant - Lara, who has made few pix of international import since his "Devil In The Flesh," goes back to the much the same source for this new offering which treats with the tribulations of first love, the coming of age and the affair of a young boy with an older woman. Here the similarity ends with the new film lacking the force and cohesion of its predecessor. It emerges as a sensitive portrayal of adolescence in the first throes of love. Film will do well here on theme and the Edwige Feuillere name. His name and an exploitable theme may help sell it in the U. S.

However, pic could stand some cutting.

This explores the growing love of two youngsters, a boy of 16 and Vinca, a 15-year-old girl, who have lived together practically as brother and sister because of the close ties of their families. However, one summer's vacation shows the beginnings of physical tension between them and the growth of love under the unseeing eyes of the parents.

A catalyst in the form of a beautiful, aging woman comes along to bring Philippe into her sensual web and initiate him, leaving him wiser. She leaves him so as to avoid involvement.

Film is steeped in literary and filmic symbols which at times give the pic an uneven quality. There is the mouse in the trap liberated by the boy, the key to his room, flashing lights of passing cars and the boudoir door of the elderly woman.

Autant-Lara has given this knowing mounting, but the film remains primarily literary in tone rather than moving. Miss Feuillere is perfect as the mysterious, sensual woman. Pierre-Michel Beck, looking like a young Freddie Bartholomew, has the coltishness for the role but lacks the intensity to detract from his more dramatic moments. Nicole Berger is the fetching, young girl on the threshold of love who emerges as a budding star here.

Lensing is fine and editing helps put over many points. Mosk.

Knock on Wood
(SONGS-COLOR)

Nifty Danny Kaye comedy with songs, dances and plenty of pop appeal.

Hollywood, March 30.
Paramount release of a Dena Productions presentation, produced, directed and written by Norman Panama and Melvin Frank. Stars Danny Kaye; co-stars Mai Zetterling; features Torin Thatcher, David Burns, Leon Askin, Abner Biberman. Camera (Technicolor), Daniel Fapp; editor, Alma Macrorie; music direction, Victor Young; songs, Sylvia Fine; choreography, Michael Kidd. Previewed March 26, '54. Running time, 103 MINS.
Jerry .... Danny Kaye
Ilse Nordstrom .... Mai Zetterling
Langston .... Torin Thatcher
Marty Brown .... David Burns
Gromek .... Leon Askin
Papinek .... Abner Biberman
Car Salesman .... Gavin Gordon
Brodnik .... Otto Waldis
Dr. Kreuger .... Steven Geray
Princess .... Diana Adams
Mama Morgan .... Patricia Denise
Audrey .... Virginia Huston
Chief Inspector Wilton ... Paul Eneland
Langston's Secretary ... Johnstone White
2nd Trenchcoat Man .... Henry Brandon
Inspector Cranford ...... Lewis Martin
(Aspect Ratio, 1.85:1)

Danny Kaye's Dena Productions unit, releasing "Knock On Wood" through Paramount, gets itself off to a good start with this nifty comedy. It's the kind of crowd-pleasing escapism into mirth that makes for pop appeal at the boxoffice and returns should be firstrate.

Madcap comedy, in familiar vein but considerably freshened by the Kaye touch, marks the triple efforts of Norman Panama and Melvin Frank as co-writers, directors and producers. Partnered with the comic in the indie outfit, they have come up with a fable about a ventriloquist, with a schizophrenetic dummy, who gets himself involved with a beautiful psychiatrist, a stolen blueprint for a weapon of war, and two rival gangs of espionage agents.

To further abet the funfest such a plot structure suggests, the makers have mixed in two wow comedy musical routines, a soft shoe terp stint to the title tune, and a romantic ballad. All of this material, plus several takeoffs by Kaye into situation laugh routines that click big, stretches the running time out to 103 minutes, which is a bit unwieldy for the general market but entirely satisfactory for the big single-bill key situations.

For the first hour and 15 minutes of film, the comedy hits a pleasant pace, highlighted with a yock here and there, before winding up in high gear for the climaxing routines and plot resolution. The big laugh sequence is Kaye becoming part of a Russian ballet troupe while it performs on stage so he can dodge espionage gunmen and the police. It runs approximately 10 minutes. Among other high spots are his singing-drinking bout to "The Drastic, Livid, History of Monohan O'Han" with a hearty group of Sons of Hibernia and his car-selling efforts, both while dodging his pursuers. All are Kaye at his funniest.

When Kaye's dummy starts talking back to him and ruining his love life, his manager, smartly played by David Burns, suggests they see a psychiatrist. Just about this time, the rival gangs are after the blueprints and one group hides the two papers in the heads of Kaye's dummys. It's a chase pattern that follows, Kaye going to

London, taking treatments from, and treating, the femme mind medico, Mai Zetterling, finding bodies of spies in his room, being pursued by police and intrigue mastermind Torin Thatcher, all the while no opportunities for comedy are overlooked. Needless to say, it comes out right for Kaye at the finale and he marries the doc, having cured her of her neuroes while getting rid of his.

Miss Zetterling, Swedish film star Hollywood-debuting here, is a charming partner to all the wild doings, and Thatcher scores as the suave heavy, as do Burns as Kaye's worried manager, Leon Askin, Abner Biberman and Otto Waldis, rival spies, and Gavin Gordon, auto salesman. Diana Adams dances with Kaye in the ballet sequence and Patricia Denise with him in a flashback when he's detailing his unhappy childhood to the medicos. Virginia Huston is seen briefly as a girl Kaye loses because of the neurotic dummy.

Sylvia Fine, in addition to the two comedy songs, also cleffed the ballad, "All About You," which Kaye sings to Miss Zetterling during a romantic stretch in the footage. The background score and musical direction by Victor Young is an asset, as is the Technicolor lensing by Daniel Fapp. Michael Kidd did the choreography. Brog.

Elephant Walk
(COLOR)

Elizabeth Taylor, Dana Andrews in Ceylon-localed romantic drama with moderate appeal and b.o. chances.

Hollywood, March 30.
Paramount release of Irving Asher production. Stars Elizabeth Taylor, Dana Andrews, Peter Finch; features Abraham Sofaer, Abner Biberman, Noel Drayton, Rosalind Ivan. Directed by William Dieterle. Screenplay, John Lee Mahin; based on the novel by Robert Standish; camera (Technicolor), Loyal Griggs; editor, George Tomasini; score, Franz Waxman. Previewed March 22, '54. Running time, 102 MINS.
Ruth Wiley .... Elizabeth Taylor
Dick Carver .... Dana Andrews
John Wiley .... Peter Finch
Appuhamy .... Abraham Sofaer
Dr. Pereira .... Abner Biberman
Planter (Atkinson) .... Noel Drayton
Mrs. Lakin .... Rosalind Ivan
Planter (Strawson) ...... Barry Bernard
Planter (Ralph) .... Philip Tonge
Planter (Gregory) ...... Edward Ashley
Planter (Chisholm) .... Leo Britt
Rayna .... Mylee Haulani
The Madhyma Lanka Mandala Dancers
(Aspect Ratio, 1.85:1)

The novelty of the Ceylon backgrounds and pictorial beauty are recommendable points in "Elephant Walk," an otherwise leisurely-paced romantic drama that strolls through an hour and 42 minutes. There's not enough dramatic wallop in the yarn to carry that much footage so, overall, the film's appeal and b.o. chances appear moderate. Exploitation may brighten its prospects somewhat, since it does have several ballyhoo factors to help the selling.

Elizabeth Taylor and Dana Andrews are the familiar names that will do the most for the picture in general release, along with the value to be obtained from the Technicolor tints that make the Irving Asher production visually attractive. Hollywood newcomer Peter Finch (seen previously in several British-made films) is the third topliner in the film and remains an unknown quantity as far as draw possibilities are concerned. He's a competent performer but, critically, one is always conscious he is acting. Miss Taylor and Andrews appear more natural in their star spots, thus have more impact.

Robert Standish's novel about life among the pekoe-planters rates a sprawling script from John Lee Mahin and direction that lacks attention-holding pace from William Dieterle. Had both of these contributors concentrated more on the dramatic points along the way and less on unnecessary detail it would have been a better show. Of interest, tradewise, is the fact that in some of the Ceylon-filmed longshots, Vivian Leigh is still seen, although not noticeably so. Illness forced the English star out of the picture after about a month of lensing, with Miss Taylor replacing.

Elephants are the sympathetic heavies in this story of a bride who comes to Ceylon from England and finds her husband, the natives and the tea plantation still under the dominance of a dead man's memory. Added to this tradition worship is the always present threat that the pachyderms may eventually succeed in wrestling back from the white usurpers the trail they had used for centuries in coming down from the wilds to water. The plantation mansion had been built across the trail by the bridegroom's strong-willed late father, who had bowed to nothing, man or beast.

The clinging to hidebound tradition, more than the elephant threat, almost defeats the bride and her personal unhappiness in the masculine world lorded over by Finch eventually turns her to Andrews, readily-available plantation overseer. An outbreak of cholera prevents her flight with Andrews and in the crisis that finds her husband being reborn and the mansion destroyed by elephants and fire, man and wife are able to again stir up their love. The only action of note in the picture is the six-minute climax when the elephants reclaim their walk.

Abraham Sofaer is type cast as the native of India who is the household majordomo. Abner Biberman is good as the doctor. Noel Drayton, Barry Bernard, Philip Tonge, Edward Ashley and Leo Britt play neighboring planters, and are presented in the picture as alcoholic morons who gather weekly in the great hall of Elephant Walk for drinking and bicycle polo. The Madhyma Lanka Mandala Dancers are seen in an interesting native ceremony dance.

Noteworthy, among the production values are Loyal Griggs' color lensing; Franz Waxman's score, and the dazzling Edith Head costumes that complement Miss Taylor's natural beauty. *Brog.*

Make Haste to Live

Excellent, femme-slanted melodramatic thriller entertainment; good b.o. outlook with stout selling.

Hollywood, March 30.

Republic release of William A. Seiter production. Stars Dorothy McGuire, Stephen McNally; features Mary Murphy, Edgar Buchanan, John Howard, Ron Hagerthy. Directed by Seiter. Screenplay, Warren Duff; based on the novel by The Gordons: camera, John L. Russell Jr.; editor, Fred Allen; music, Elmer Bernstein. Previewed March 24, '54. Running time, **90 MINS.**

Crystal Benson .... Dorothy McGuire
Steve .... Stephen McNally
Randy Benson .... Mary Murphy
Sheriff .... Edgar Buchanan
Josh .... John Howard
Hack .... Ron Hagerthy
Rudolfo Gonzales .... Pepe Hern
Spud Kelly .... Eddy Waller
Mary Rose .... Carolyn Jones
(Aspect Ratio, 1.65:1)

In the field of suspense shows, "Make Haste to Live" is a honey and should score with fans of tight, well-done, thriller entertainment. Word-of-mouth potentials look good for the femme-slanted melodramatics and will help to offset a title that is not too suggestive of the film's worth. Strong selling is indicated and can build this one to better than average returns for Republic.

The 90 minutes of footage is sustained by a constantly building expectancy that gets the most out of the logical motivations and situations in Warren Duff's expertly-crafted screenplay. Basis for the script was the novel by Mildred and Gordon Gordon, the latter a former 20th-Fox publicist, which tells of a woman faced with her past and what she does about it. Plot has substance in the fact there is justification for the re-appearing husband wanting revenge. After all, his wife had left him serve an 18-year prison term for supposedly murdering her, while she disappears to start a new life in the west with a baby daughter.

The dramatic elements are carefully developed under the producer-director guidance of William A. Seiter, with a deliberate, but never laggard, pacing that mounts to the suspenseful climax. Fine performances by Dorothy McGuire, the wife, and Stephen McNally, the husband, do their part in maintaining the drama's interest. Miss McGuire scores exceptionally well, her character having audience sympathy entirely, and McNally is back with a forceful heavy performance that exerts a powerful pull. The two play a cat-and-mouse game in a little New Mexico town as he attempts to exact revenge through their grownup daughter, now Mary Murphy. Climax is a tingler and sees McNally accidentally falling to his death as he chases Miss McGuire through the ruins of an old Indian cliff village.

Miss Murphy, aptly cast as the daughter, shows growing stature as a film personality and actress and Ron Hagerthy is good as her earnest young suitor. Edgar Buchanan characterizes a western sheriff excellently and John Howard does well by the archaeologist with whom Miss McGuire is in love.

John L. Russell's lensing, the score by Elmer Bernstein, the editing by Fred Allen and the other production assists are firstrate. *Brog.*

The Mad Magician (3-D)

Fair mystery entry for the program market.

Columbia release of Bryan Foy production. Stars Vincent Price, Mary Murphy, Eva Gabor; features John Emery, Donald Randolph, Lenita Lane, Patrick O'Neal, Jay Novello. Directed by John Brahm. Screenplay and story, Crane Wilbur; camera, Bert Glennon; editor, Grant Whytock; music, Emil Newman, Arthur Lange. Tradeshown N.Y., March 4, '54. Running time, **72 MINS.**

Gallico .... Vincent Price
Karen .... Mary Murphy
Claire .... Eva Gabor
Rinaldi .... John Emery
Ormond .... Donald Randolph
Alice Prentiss .... Lenita Lane
Bruce .... Patrick O'Neal
Mr. Prentiss .... Jay Novello

"The Mad Magician," which reportedly may be Columbia's last 3-D release, is standard horror fare for the programmer situations. Producer Bryan Foy, who turned out "House of Wax" as the first major studio feature in 3-D a year ago, has come up with a mediocre road company to his initial effort. Curiously, both of his pictures cast Vincent Price in a top role, had Crane Wilbur as scripter and Bert Glennon as cameraman. Latter, however, shared lensing chores on "Wax" with Peverell Marley.

Wilbur's current yarn threads the tale of a crazed magico who kills three persons before perishing in one of his own fiendish devices. Plot is a fairly obvious one and contains few twists that the average filmgoer will be unable to anticipate. While performances easily meet the demands of the script, a real fillip is provided via Bob Haskell's magical effects as well as special effects of David Koehler.

Amid a turn-of-the-century setting, the gloomy atmosphere abounds in such magico equipment as whirling circular saws, various masks and an incinerator designed to consume a human body. These props were intended as means of illusions but Price, who portrays the title role, used 'em for baser purposes.

Price gives a realistic interpretation of the warped magician. Mary Murphy impresses as his unsuspecting assistant but at times is too calm in face of the diabolical goings on. Eva Gabor tosses in a dash of glamor as Price's ex-wife who establishes him as the killer. John Emery scores nicely as a rival sleight-of-hander.

Others contributing good support are Donald Randolph as one of the victims, Lenita Lane as a femme novelist with an amateur Philo Vance complex, Patrick O'Neal as the detective boy friend of Miss Murphy and Jay Novello as Miss Lane's husband. John Brahm's direction shows up best in the horror sequences while Bert Glennon's 3-D camerawork throws nothing into the audience save for a few streams of water and some playing cards. Other technical credits are standard. *Gilb.*

The Miami Story

Fast paced meller with good prospects in the programmer market.

Columbia release of Sam Katzman production. Stars Barry Sullivan, Luther Adler; features John Baer, Adele Jergens. Directed by Fred F. Sears. Story and screenplay, Robert E. Kent; camera, Henry Freulich; editor, Viola Lawrence; music, Mischa Bakaleinikoff. Tradeshown, N.Y., March 25, '54. Running time, 75 **MINS.**

Mick Flagg .... Barry Sullivan
Tony Brill .... Luther Adler
Ted Delacorte .... John Baer
Gwen Abbott .... Adele Jergens
Holly Abbott .... Beverly Garland
Frank Alton .... Dan Riss
Chief Martin Belman....Damian O'Flynn
Robert Bishop .... Chris Alcaide
Johnny Loker .... Gene D'Arcy
Louie Mott .... George E. Stone
Gil Flagg .... David Kasday
Charles Earnshaw .... Tom Greenway

"The Miami Story" is a suspenseful melodrama with good b.o. prospects in the programmer market. Barry Sullivan and Luther Adler, who are cast in top roles, provide some marquee dressing while an exploitable touch is lent by the film's semi-documentary handling.

Apparently inspired by the U. S. Senate's frequent probes into crime, the Robert E. Kent script is a swiftly paced chronicle of how a gambling and white slave syndicate was supposedly smashed in Miami. A brief introduction by Florida's Sen. George A. Smathers plus liberal use of background footage of the Miami area give added authenticism to the yarn.

Aroused over two gangland killings, a citizens' "vigilante" committee hires reformed gangster Barry Sullivan to pin the goods on syndicate chief Luther Adler. In the drive to root out vice, Sullivan poses as a rival Cuban racketeer but actually is working in cooperation with Miami and Cuban police.

Action scenes in which Sullivan roughs up the opposition are well staged under the taut direction of Fred F. Sears. The ex-mobster, who's turned sleuth, relentlessly presses toward his goal and even solves a kidnapping of his own son in stride.

Sullivan, a convincing undercover man, grimly and methodically plans and executes his blueprint for smashing the syndicate. Adler, for the most part, typifies the average filmgoer's conception of an arrogant, unlettered underworld chieftain. John Baer, as Adler's youthful "pretty boy" killer, is none too impressive.

Adele Jergens, in an unsympathetic part, registers nicely as a femme heel and vice queen who fingered her own sister. Latter is ably portrayed by Beverly Garland. She, incidentally, weds Sullivan in a contrived "happy ending" which wasn't necessary. Among others lending okay support are George E. Stone, as a stoolie; Dan Riss, as a civic crusader, and Damian O'Flynn as the police chief.

Viola Lawrence edited the print down to a crisp 75 minutes, Mischa Bakaleinikoff's musical direction is a plus and Sam Katzman's sound production values are attested to by the better-than-average physical mantling this modest budgeter has been endowed. Special effects of Jack Erickson and art direction of Paul Palmentola are also worthy of mention. *Gilb.*

La Rage Au Corps
(Tempest In The Flesh)
(FRENCH)

Paris, March 23.

Corona release of Del Duca-EGC production. Stars Francoise Arnoul, Raymond Pellegrin, Philippe Lemaire. Directed by Ralph Habib. Screenplay, Jacques Companeez, Jean-Claude Aurel; adaption and dialog, Paul Andreota; camera, Roger Hubert; editor, Glansberg. At Triomphe, Paris. Running time, **95 MINS.**

Clara .... Francoise Arnoul
Tonio ....Raymond Pellegrin
Andre ....Philippe Lemaire
Greta ....Catherine Gora
Sebastian ....Balpetre
Gino ....Jean-Claude Pascal
Pole ....Gerard Pourh

Nymphomania is the exploitable item director Ralph Habib now tackles in this film. As in all his pix, Habib has turned this into a clinical piece. This emerges less than moving but capitalizes on a touchy subject. Film becomes case history of a tainted gal and is unlikely for U.S. art house patronage. It might do in special spots when heavily exploited.

Story concerns a pretty, young femme working in the canteen of a construction company. Her affliction is discovered one day when one of the men dives on her to save her from a nearby blast. Then trouble starts as men battle for her. Finally, a friend gets her to a psychiatrist after many affairs, with the usual happy ending.

Habib's lacklustre direction throws away the filmic possibilites. Francoise Arnoul is uneven as the nympho, but scores in her pash scenes. Raymond Pellegrin does fine as the confused husband while Philippe Lemaire plays his familiar roie of the ladies' man. Lensing and editing are only passable.
Mosk.

Le Chevalier De La Nuit
(The Knight of the Night)
(FRENCH)

Paris, March 23.
AGDC release of Telouet Film production. Stars Renee Saint-Cyr, Jean-Claude Pascal. Directed by Robert Darene. Screenplay, Jean Anouilh, Dareneı camera, Roger Hubert; editor, Germaine Artus; music, Jean-Jacques Grunewald. At Raimu, Paris. Running time, **90 MINS.**

Bella	Renee Saint-Cyr
Georges,	
Chevalier	Jean-Claude Pascal
Commissioner	Gregoire Aslan
Maid	Annette Poivre
Legrand	Pierre Destailles
Host	Jean Servais
Valet	Roger Blin

This pic is a half-toned, period piece that lightly plays with the supernatural in a Jekyll-and-Hyde-like theme. Treated with delicacy in the slow-moving style of a 19th century tale, this could only serve for special situations in the U.S.

This is reminiscent of the early German tales about the duality of man. Here a husband and wife have come to a period of mutual spiritual torture, the wife feeling she has lost the wonder of the first meeting with her husband. The good half of the husband and bad are depicted, finally with the good half remaining alive with her.

Director Robert Parene has given this fairy tale a light, atmospheric mounting which has atmosphere of an unreal world. Renee St. Cyr does not possess the fragility necessary for the ballerina (the wife), but Jean-Claude Pascal acquits himself well in the dual role. Lensing is diffused and just right for the mood. A haunting guitar strain by Jean-Jacques Grunenwald also helps.
Mosk.

Les Fruits Sauvages
(The Wild Fruit)
FRENCH

Paris, March 23.
Cinedis release of Filmsonor-Odeon-Agiman production. Directed by Ilerve Bromberger. Screenplay, Max Gallai, Bromberger; camera, Jacques Mercanton; editor, Mitzi D'Esterno. At Madeleine, Paris. Running time, **105 MINS.**

Maria	Estella Blain
Michel	Michel Reynal
Christine	Evelyne Ker
Hans	Roger Dumas
Frederique	Jacques Moulieres
Lolita	Talina Sauzer
Jose	Jean-Pierre Bonnefous

This story concerns a group of adolescents and children who run off when one daughter kills her drunken father after a beating. Story is not new, and general lack of direction on the story fails to bring this across dramatically. Downbeat theme and ordinary moppet handling make it dubious of art house consideration in the U.S.

After killing her drunken father, Estella Blain takes charge of her brothers and a sister, and they run away to the Italian border. Living in an abandoned village, they are helped by a young gypsy girl who brings food to them. Two passionate love affairs intervene. Finally, lack of water forces them to sneak into the village for refills. They

are discovered by the police, and jailed.

Director Herve Bromberger has mounted this carefully but has never imbued it with the intensity needed. Lensing and editing are opflight and moppets are okay but ot spontaneous. Evelyne Ker, ogers Dumas and Miss Blain emerge as future film bets. *Mosk.*

Operation Ivy
(COLOR)

Documentary of the first H-Bomb explosion.

Washington, March 31.
Civil Defense Administration release for ewsreel, television and civilian defensc. Produced by the Atomic Energy Commission and Department of Defense. Shown to press March 31, 1954, at Department of Interior, D.C. Time **28 MINS.**

"Operation Ivy" was the code name given to the hydrogen weapons test conducted at Eniwetok Atoll in November, 1952. Current pic has been released in black and white version for television, motion pictures and private use, and for special showings by the Civil Defense Administration in color.

This is a stripped down, fairly non-technical version from which all material affecting national security has been removed. Its purpose is to give the American people a picture of the horrors of thermo-nuclear warfare. Actually it falls short of its goal. Co.or, as shown to the press, was only so-so, but since the public mostly won't see the tinted version this is not too important. While the actual bomb explosion is a powerful scene, film as a whole tends to be choppy and wordy. The message given is mainly via the soundtrack, with picture, aside from the actual explosion, holding little excitement or punch.

Format is the same as the one followed earlier in documentaries made by the Government on the atom bomb explosions. Thus, there is the buildup aboard the naval vessel which is flagship of the task force conducting the test, pictures of the little island on which the H-bomb is located inside of a two-story black building, with a couple of miles of conduits leading from it to test instruments on another island of the atoll.

Then, back to the vessel as the minutes tick off, the final seconds, and then the big boom, as the bomb goes off in what was the greatest man-made explosion up to that time followed by a picture and a diagram of the damage done. A diagram shows that 14 buildings the size of the Pentagon could fit into the crater made by the explosion. There is also an explanation of how much damage would be done in New York or Washington by a comparable blast, and a final statement by Civil Defense Administrator Val Peterson.

Introduction of the film includes an excerpt of President Eisenhower making his atomic speech before the UN General Assembly on December 8, 1953. *Lowe.*

Prince Valiant
(COLOR)

C'Scoped film based on the cartoon strip hero with good b.o. prospects.

Hollywood, April 2.
20th-Fox release of Robert L. Jacks production. Stars James Mason, Janet Leigh, Robert Wagner, Debra Paget, Sterling Hayden; features Victor McLaglen, Donald Crisp, Brian Aherne, Barry Jones, Mary Philips, Howard Wendell, Tom Conway. Directed by Henry Hathaway. Screenplay, Dudley Nichols; based on King Features Syndicate's "Prince Valiant" by Harold Foster; camera (Technicolor), Lucien Ballard; editor, Robert Simpson; music, Franz Waxman. Previewed March 31, '54. Running time, **100 MINS.**

(Aspect Ratio, 2.55:1)

Sir Brack	James Mason
Aleta	Janet Leigh
Prince Valiant	Robert Wagner
Ilene	Debra Paget
Sir Gawain	Sterling Hayden
Boltar	Victor McLaglen
King Aguar	Donald Crisp
King Arthur	Brian Aherne
King Luke	Barry Jones
Queen Mother	Mary Philips
Morgan Todd	Howard Wendell
Sir Kay	Tom Conway
Small Page	Sammy Ogg
Viking Warrior Chief	Neville Brand
Seneschal	Ben Wright
Queen Guinevere	Jarma Lewis
Sir Brack's Man at Arms	Robert Adler
Gorlock	Ray Spiker
Sligon	Primo Carnera
Old Viking	Basil Ruysdael
Strangler	Fortune Gordien
Doctor	Percival Vivian
Sir Launcelot	Don Megowan
Sir Galahad	Richard Webb
Sir Tristram	John Dierkes
Herald	Carleton Young
Patch Eye	Otto Waldis
Patriarch	John Davidson
Prince Valiant, Age 12	Lloyd Ahern Jr.
Captain of Guards	Lou Nova
Prison Guards	Hal Baylor, Mickey Simpson
Viking	Eugene Roth

The cartoon strip hero comes to the screen in CinemaScope and Technicolor as a good offering for those fans who dote on the fanciful derring-do of the Arthurian period. On that basis it should hit a good b.o. pace since it has all the standard costumer ingredients, plus the presence of Janet Leigh, Robert Wagner and Debra Paget as possible attractions for the younger filmgoers.

Harold Foster's King Features strip has long been a favorite Sunday comic, and these weekly escapes into the past give an imaginative action basis for Robert L. Jacks' production guidance and the direction by Henry Hathaway. Although the picture comes in a bit overlength at 100 minutes, the direction and Dudley Nichols' scripting combine to bring it off acceptably against some rather dazzling settings, including authentic castles and sites actually lensed in England.

Heading the star list is James Mason, who plays Sir Brack, pretender to King Arthur's throne. His dirty work is excellent, whether thinking üp ambushes for Wagner, in the title role, or engaging the young hero in joust or broadsword combat. Wagner is suitable to the physical heroics demanded of his Viking prince character. The way he and Mason have at each other in the climaxing duel puts a topnotch action capper on the tale. The Misses Leigh and Paget are sisters who pair off with Wagner and Sterling Hayden, the swaggering Sir Gawain, both adding some femme charm to the footage. Hayden handles his part in okay style, as do Donald Crisp, Brian Aherne as King Arthur, Victor McLaglen and Primo Carnera.

The plot finds Wagner in exile with his royal parents after their throne was seized by Carnera. The Viking prince goes to King Arthur's court, becomes a squire to Sir Gawain, falls in love with Miss Leigh and, eventually, is able to put the finger on Mason as the mysterious Black Knight who has been scheming with Carnera's Vikings to take over King Arthur's Throne.

The jousting scenes, chase sequences over hill and dale, several seascapes, plus authentic English locales, keep up the Arthurian feel of the presentation. For rousing action, there's a giant castle fire as the daring Prince Valiant burns out a Viking lair to rescue his parents and Miss Leigh, and the climaxing broadsword engagement between Valiant and the Black Knight. All of these sequences gain interest from the Cinema-Scope treatment of Lucien Ballard's photography and the special photographic effects by Ray Kellogg. Other technical credits are good. *Brog.*

Doctor in the House
(BRITISH—COLOR)

Firstclass British comedy set in medical school; sturdy b.o. proposition.

London, March 23.

General Film Distributors release of Betty E. Box production. Stars Dirk Bogarde, Muriel Pavlow, Kenneth More, Donald Sinden. Directed by Ralph Thomas. Screenplay, Nicholas Phipps; adapted from the novel by Richard Gordon; camera, Ernest Steward; editor, Gerald Thomas; music, Bruce Montgomery. At Odeon, Leicester Square, London. Running time, 92 MINS.

Simon .... Dirk Bogarde
Joy .... Muriel Pavlow
Grimsyke .... Kenneth More
Benskin .... Donald Sinden
Isobel .... Kay Kendall
Sir Lancelot .... James R. Justice
"Taffy" .... Donald Houston
Stella .... Suzanne Cloutier
Dean .... Geoffrey Keen
Briggs .... George Coulouris
Sister Virtue .... Jean Taylor-Smith
Jessup .... Harry Locke
May .... Ann Gudrun
Rigor Mortis .... Joan Sims
Mrs. Cooper .... Maureen Pryor
Milly Groaker .... Shirley Eaton
Lecturer .... Geoffrey Sumner
Magistrate .... Nicholas Phipps

A topdraw British comedy, "Doctor in the House," is in the same boxoffice class as the recent "Genevieve," and is geared for equally hefty grosses in the domestic market. This is bright, diverting entertainment, intelligently scripted, and warmly played. Its marquee appeal may be restricted across the Atlantic but the film merits widespread showing.

Background to the story is the medical school of a London hospital. Within 92 minutes, the film spans the five years in the life of a student group. On the surface, it is a serious theme but the entire treatment has a lighthearted touch, the jokes are good and plentiful while the story abounds with ample good-humor.

The new recruit to the school is Dirk Bogarde, who is taken under the protective wing of three oldtimers who had all failed their preliminary exams. Kenneth More, Donald Sinden and Donald Houston make up a contrasted quartet who seem to have ideas on most subjects but not how to qualify as a medico. Much of the comedy incident has been clearly contrived but it is nonetheless effective, particularly in the scenes featuring James Robertson Justice as a distinguished surgeon and More. The latter is now one of Britain's most promising star bets.

Principal femme roles are nicely played by Muriel Pavlow, Kay Kendall and Suzanne Cloutier, Geoffrey Keen gives an incisive portrayal as the Dean of the medical school while Nicholas Phipps (who did the screenplay) has a nice bit as a magistrate.

For this picture, Ralph Thomas can claim one of his best directorial credits. Ernest Steward has done a handsome job of Technicolor lensing. Gerald Thomas rates kudos for slick editing. *Myro.*

West of Zanzibar
(BRITISH-COLOR)

Harry Watt adventure of ivory smugglers filmed in authentic East African locations; shapes as sturdy b.o. attraction.

London, March 24.

General Film Distributors release of Ealing Studios-Michael Balcon (in association with Schlesinger Organization) production. Stars Anthony Steel, Sheila Sim; features Edric Connor, Orlando Martins, William Simons, Martin Benson. Color by Technicolor. Story and direction, Harry Watt. Screenplay, Max Catto, Jack Whittingham; camera, Paul Beeson; editor, Peter Bezencenet; music, Alan Rawsthorne. At Odeon, Leicester Square, London, March 24, '54. Running time, 94 MINS.

Bob Payton .... Anthony Steel
Mary Payton .... Sheila Sim
Tim Payton .... William Simons
M'Kwongwi .... Orlando Martins
Ushingo .... Edric Connor
Ambrose .... David Osiell
Bethlehem .... Bethlehem Sketch
Lawyer Dhofar .... Martin Benson
Khingoni .... Peter Illing
Balf Breed .... Edward Johnson
Juma .... Juma
Wood .... Howard M. Crawford
Col. Ryan .... R. Stuart Lindsell

Since his success with "The Overlanders" some years ago, Harry Watt has developed the technique of choosing a suitable film location and finding the right story to match it. His last effort, "Where No Vultures Fly" (released as "Ivory Hunters" in U.S.) got the nod as the royal command performance film, and "West of Zanzibar" is, in effect, a sequel to that production. It should earn the same boxoffice acclaim.

Like all productions in the Watt series, "Zanzibar" was filmed entirely on location. The East African backgrounds, with wild animal life, primitive settlements and crocodile-invested swamps, provide a dramatic backcloth to the story of a small native tribe which is being corrupted by the financial temptations offered by ivory smugglers.

Entire plot is focused on the one-man attempt by Anthony Steel, a game ranger, to track down the brains behind the smuggling racket, and thus remove the source of temptation from simple native folk. His chase across the Zanzibar territory takes him in a primitive craft over rough seas, in a small canoe through rivers thick with crocodiles and rhinos and through jungle terrain where elephants are killed by native spears.

The yarn is developed as a strong adventure meller in which native customs and rivalries play an important part. There is a brief attempt to point a moral which, well-meaning though it may be, appears a little fatuous on the screen.

Steel, who was the star of "Vultures," again plays the role of the white man trying to help the natives with a measure of authority and humanity. Sheila Sim is more than adequate in the restricted role of his wife while Edric Connor plays a native chief with great dignity. Martin Benson gives an admirable portrayal of a shyster lawyer who turns out to be the smuggler's ring-leader. William Simmons has limited cope as Steel's young son.

Watt has done a vigorous job of directing and Paul Beeson's Technicolor lensing captures all the advantages of the African setting. *Myro.*

The Lone Gun
(COLOR)

Poor formula western. Very talky.

Hollywood, April 2.

United Artists release of World Films (Edward Small) production. Stars George Montgomery, Dorothy Malone; features Frank Faylen, Neville Brand. Directed by Ray Nazarro. Screenplay, Don Martin, Richard Schayer; story, L. L. Foreman; camera (Color Corp. of America), Lester White; editor, Bernard Small. Previewed April 1, '54. Running time, 74 MINS.

Cruz .... George Montgomery
Charlotte Downing .... Dorothy Malone
Fairweather .... Frank Faylen
Tray Moran .... Neville Brand
Cass Downing .... Skip Homeier
Gad Moran .... Doug Kennedy
Hort Morgan .... Robert Wilke
Mayor Booth .... Fay Roope
Charlie .... Douglas Fowley

(Aspect Ratio, 1.65:1)

This is a lack-lustre program oater making use of formula western ingredients, but with nothing much to recommend it other than the name of George Montgomery.

Action is lacking, with endless and witless talk substituting for movement, both in the direction by Ray Nazarro and in the scripting by Don Martin and Richard Schayer. Even the tints supplied by Color Corp., of America are poor.

The plot is the one about the poor but honest marshall who cleans up a cow town gang that is threatening law and order in the community. Performances are in kind. Dorothy Malone does the romantic spot opposite Montgomery, the marshall, as the sister of Skip Homeier, a lad under the thumb of the rustling Moran brothers played by Neville Brand, Doug Kennedy and Robert Wilke. Frank Faylen is a talkative gambler, Fay Roope the mayor and Douglas Fowley a bartender. *Brog.*

Dos Tipos de Cuidado
(Two Careful Fellows)
(MEXICAN; SONGS)

Mexico City, March 30.

Distribuidora Mexicana de Peliculas release of Cinematografica TeleVoz production. Stars Jorge Negrete and Pedro Infante; features Carlos Orellana, Carmelita Gonzalez, Yolanda Varela, Jose Elias Moreno. Directed by Ismael Rodriguez; screenplay, Carlos Orellana and Rodriguez. At Cines Mexico and Mariscala, Mexico City. Running time, 103 MINS.

Value of this little pic which swings mildly between romantic drama and musifilm is that it is the last of numerous pix of the late Jorge Negrete. It is the first film in which he ever co-starred with Pedro Infante, also a top singer. Production also has two of Mexico's top femme lookers, Carmelita Gonzalez and Yolanda Varela, this time excitingly costumed. Ismael Rodriguez, co-author of the script with Carlos Orellana, who doubles in the film as character comic, directs clearly and with a personal touch.

Film's locale is the Actor's Ranch, a beautifully bucolic spot near here. Picnic pranks featuring the two lookers lavishly displaying legs and lingerie, and the fishing sequences are pleasing.

Infante takes care of his singing in characteristic lusty style. In a long sequence, he is remarkably well supplemented by a girl bit player, unbilled, whose work mitigates her tasteless costuming. *Doug.*

Conflict of Wings
(BRITISH—COLOR)

Group 3 production in Eastmancolor of islanders who frustrate intrusion by Royal Air Force; a solid dualer which should appeal to arthouse trade.

London, March 30.

British Lion release of Herbert Mason-Group 3 production. Stars John Gregson, Muriel Pavlow, Kieron Moore, Niall MacGinnis. Directed by John Eldridge; screenplay, Don Sharp & John Pudney; camera, Arthur Grant; editor, Lito Carruthers; music, Philip Green. At Leicester Square Theatre, London, March 30, '54. Running time, 84 MINS.

Bill Morris .... John Gregson
Sally .... Muriel Pavlow
S Ldr. Parsons .... Kieron Moore
Harry Tilney .... Niall MacGinnis
Fanny Bates .... Sheila Sweet
Buster .... Harry Fowler
F O Control .... Howard Connell
Mrs. Thompson .... Barbara Hicks
Bookie .... Charles Lloyd Pack
Station Adjutant .... Guy Middleton
3rd Pilot .... Brian Moorehead
Soapy .... Bartlett Mullins
W Cmmdr. Rogers .... Russell Napier
Joe Bates .... Frederick Piper
Smother Brooks .... Edwin Richfield
Mrs. Trotter .... Dorothea Rundle
Range Officer .... Harold Siddons

In a mild and gentle way, there is a measure of charm which is typically British in this new Group 3 production, which in the U.S. market should carve a modest niche for itself in the arthouse circuit. Basically it is a dualer and, as such, should attract modest biz on both sides of the Atlantic.

"Conflict of Wings" is a story of simple village folk in the beautiful Norfolk country, who join in a rebellion when a local beauty spot and a veritable sanctuary of wild birdlife is earmarked as a target area for the air force. Local folk try to get their small island scheduled as a bird sanctuary, but the official from London also turns out to be a member of the so-called Ministry of Land Acquisition. They look up the history books and find that Henry VIII scheduled the area as a public preserve—but again they are overruled. Finally, they take the law into their own hands and invade the target area on the day of the first air trials.

Background to the yarn, with its attractive stretches of the countryside and colorful shots of the famed Norfolk fields, is much more effective than the plot itself. Much of the story development is naive in presentation, particularly the romantic action. Visually the film is attractive, and the all-British cast, headed by John Gregson, Muriel Pavlow, Kieron Moore and Niall MacGinnis, capably demonstrates the difference in viewpoint between legend-ridden villagers and far-sighted airmen. The conflict is never resolved although the viewpoint of both sides is adequately expressed.

John Eldridge has done an able job of direction and Don Sharp and John Pudney have captured the atmosphere in their screenplay. Arthur Grant has done a workmanlike job of Eastman color lensing. *Myro.*

The Lonely Night

Psychiatric film study suitable for special situations.

Arthur Mayer-Edward Kingsley release of Willard Van Dyke-Irving Jacoby production. Written and directed by Jacoby; narration, Frank Silvera; score, Mel Powell. Reviewed at 55th St. Playhouse, N.Y., April 1. Running time, 62 MINS.

Caroline .... Marian Seldes
Doctor .... Charles W. Moffett
The Dunnes .... The Shortall Family
The Crams .... The Gambino Family
Mac .... Val Dufour

"The Lonely Night," produced with the cooperation of the Mental Health Film Board, is an interesting documentary study of the modern approach to psychiatric problems. For its special purpose, the film succeeds as a serious, adult work which can be used as an educational aid. The pic's clinical quality, however, limits it to offbeat playdate situations.

The film is centrally focussed on the case history of a young girl, Caroline, who is under psychiatric treatment because of an acute emotional depression. The origins of her predicament as a motherless child are contrasted to the healthy atmosphere in an unrelated family via an alternation of sequences between Caroline and the Dunne family.

The encounters between Caroline and her doctor are depicted with complete scientific objectivity, sometimes even painful in showing Caroline's efforts to express herself. Pictorially, these sequences are completely static, but illustrate the doctor-patient relationship truthfully. The other details of Caroline's life are sketched in just enough to suggest the reasons for her neurotic behaviour. The film presents no specific solution for her problem but points to psychiatric treatment as the main key.

Marian Seldes, daughter of author Gilbert Seldes, plays the role of Caroline with a powerfully realistic performance that's chiefly responsible for the film's persuasiveness. As the doctor, Charles W. Moffett also handles his role credibly but has little more to do than to look grim. Others in the cast are non-professionals but the children, particularly, perform with complete naturalness.

Little dialog is used. Frank Silvera's narration explains most of the action with Mel Powell's quartet supplying the musical background. *Herm.*

Touchez Pas Au Grisbi
(Don't Touch the Coin) (FRENCH)

Paris, April 6.

Corona release of Del duca Film production. Stars Jean Gabin; features Jeanne Moreau, Dora Doll, Rene Dary, Paul Frankeur, Marilyn Bufferd, Denise Clair, Angelo Borrini. Directed by Jacques Becker; screenplay, Becker, Albert Simonin, Maurice Griffe, from a novel by Simonin; camera, Pierre Montazel; editor, Marguerite Renoir; music, Jean Weiner. At Colisee, Paris. Running time, **95 MINS.**

Max	Jean Gabin
Riton	Rene Dary
Josie	Jeanne Moreau
Lola	Dora Doll
Angelo	Angelo Borrini
Pierrot	Paul Frankeur
Betty	Marilyn Bufferd
Bouche	Denise Clair

Jacques Becker, who did such a fine job in painting the turn-of-the-century apache milieu in "Casque D'Or," now brings the same care and psychological overtones to a film on the modern racketeer element. Though behind its predecessor in story, love motif and colorful backgrounds, Becker's feeling for character and detail makes this slight and literary tale an interesting offbeat entry. Here, on Jean Gabin name and word-of-mouth, it looks to snowball into a neat grosser.

For the U.S. it is limited to arty and sureseater spots on its Gallic gang theme with word-of-mouth and Gabin name to also shape as a plus factor there. This is not of sufficient suspense and entertainment value for more general situations, for in the cops-and-robbers orbit it lacks the U.S. counterpart of pacing, action and movement.

Max, the Liar is an aging racketeer who has made a big haul in gold bullion and wants to retire. He has cultivated urbane tastes and feels the gold will let him ease into a ripe old age. However friendship, gang codes and women mess up this dream when Max's best friend gets kidnapped by a rival gang, who will only release him in return for the gold. The friend's attentions to a perfidious girl have sprung the trap. Max turns over his nest-egg but the other gang tries to wipe him out and are rubbed out in the process. Max loses the gold, which burns with the gangsters, and his only friend who is, ironically enough, killed in the scuffle.

The usual gilding of pretty girls, sultery scenes, gun fights and milieu talk abound in the film, but the element of keen insight into gang behavior puts this into a measured pacing which crescendos in a final well-staged gunfight. Becker has brought this off in spite of a puffy story and some thumbnail character aspects of some of the other people in this adventure. Gabin brings all his authority and experience to bear in making Max a sturdy, noble crook whose code carries him through a logical series of actions, though Max the man is left a bit shadowy. Jeanne Moreau turns in a neat bit as well as a moll and Rene Dary as the inarticulate aging Romeo friend is memorable in the presence and feeling he brings to the part.

Lensing and editing are firstrate and Jean Weiner's music adds to the narration in a series of cleverly cleffed themes which make the dough and Max's fatigue an integral part of the film. *Mosk.*

La Caraque Blonde
(The Blonde Gypsy) (FRENCH-COLOR)

Paris, March 23.

Fernand Rivers release of Protis Film production. Stars Tilda Thamar, Roger Pigaut, Gerard Landry. Directed by Jacqueline Audry. Screenplay, Pierre Laroche; camera, Marcel Weiss; editor, Marguerite Beauge. At Monte-Carlo, Paris. Running time, **100 MINS.**

Myra	Tilda Thamar
Antoine	Roger Pigaut
Pedro	Gerard Landry
Ginou	France Degrand
Jeannot	Didier D'Yd
Polyte	Armontel
Barcarin	Henri Poupon
Mother	Ozane Damazis

The Gamargue section of France, a flat, cattle land, has served as locale for various attempts of French filmmakers to create an oater-type of Gallic film. The latest to come-a-cropper is this one directed by Jacquelin Audry. It is a dragging, unimaginatively made film. Despite being shot on location, this gets neither the local flavor nor makes out as a good action pic. Mediocre thesping, poor pacing and familiar situations make this unsuited for the U. S. purposes. Its color is the main plus factor as well as some nudie coverting by Tilda Thamar.

Story concerns a blonde gypsy, become a famous dancer, who comes to the Camargue district for a recital. She disguises herself with a wig and runs into a handsome rice planter. Then she meets the evil Gerard Landry with whom she had once been intimate before her rise to stardom. Pic develops into a duel between the two men with the enmity between cattlemen and rice planters as a side interest.

Color is passable as is the editing, but thesping is stilted throughout. *Mosk.*

Die Letzte Bruecke
(The Last Bridge) (AUSTRIAN)

Berlin, March 23.

Columbia release of Cosmopol production. Stars Maria Schell; features Bernhard Wicki, Barbara Ruetting, Carl Moehner, Horst Haechlert, Fritz Eckhardt, Robert Meyn, Pable Mincic, Franz Eichberger, Tilla Durieux, Steffi Schwarz. Directed by Helmut Kaeutner and Gustav Gavrin. Screenplay, Helmut Kaeutner and Norbert Kunze; camera, Eleio Carniel; music, Carl de Groof. At Filmbuehne Wien, Berlin. Running time, **104 MINS.**

If there ever was a German film in recent years which could stand comparison with the realistic Italian postwar productions, it is "The Last Bridge." This Austrian picture, released by Columbia, is perhaps the most courageous European production since its plot required more than tactful and human treatment: Two enemies of the last world war, Germans and Yugoslavians on Yugoslavian soil. Filmed in association with "Ufus," Yugoslavia's filmtrade union, and against an authentic background, "Bridge" has all the qualities of a good film. It should emerge here as a big grosser, partly guaranteed by the Maria Schell name. Film seems likely for U. S. arty houses.

As seen through German eyes, pic is human and objective enough to promote understanding between foreign nations. But this is apparently a one-sided opinion since Yugoslavians feel it does not entirely do justice to them.

Central figure in the film is a young German femme medico (Maria Schell) who has been caught by partisans and compelled to take care of the wounded. She follows them, first reluctantly and then voluntarily and dies on the "last bridge" from both German and Yugoslavian gunfire. Film tries to explain the senselessness of the murderous war via her making the doctor the victim of its slaughter.

Helmut Kaeutner, as director and author, did an extraordinary job on this. It is undoubtedly his best effort since his 1946 "In Jenen Tagen" (shown in the U. S. as "Seven Journeys"). The script is unusually tight and competent. This unconventional film is far above German or Austrian run-of-the-mill productions of recent years.

Acting is superb. Maria Schell gives an impressive portrayal of the doctor. No less convincing are the others, such as Bernhard Wicki, as the partisan acting as interpreter. A lesser but very touching performance is turned in by Tilla Durieux as an old countrywoman.

Technical contributions are excellent, particularly the outdoor lensing by Eleto Carniel. *Hans.*

Caballito Criollo
(Native Pony) (ARGENTINE)

Buenos Aires, March 23.

Adoca release of the Emelco production. Directed by Ralph Pappier. Features Enrique Muino, Alberto Bello, Mario Passano, Roberto Fugazot, Margarita Corona and Lia Casanova. Original screenplay, Hugo McDougall; camera, Humberto Peruzzi; music, Alberto Ginastera; editor, Gerardo Rinaldi. At Gran Rex, in Buenos Aires. Running time, **100 MINS.**

At last an interesting subject has been picked in this film of Argentine life as it really is. However, the treatment is disappointing and the picture leaves a regret that it might have been much better.

For the most part, French-born director Ralph Pappier has sensed what aspects of local scenes, characters and customs can attract foreign audiences. He is hampered by a defective script.

What might have been a stirring yarn about the beginnings of polo as a national sport has been marred by reluctance to give due credit to its real founders, the British and Irish settlers who introduced it. They imported blood stock to improve the native strains, risked their cash on building clubs and polo grounds and became world-famous as international players and champions.

The picture's charm rests largely on the shoulders of vet actor Enrique Muino as the old campaigner and rancher who loves horses better than humans. His faith in the native pony is unbounded, his hatred of foreign influences strong. Roberto Fugazot and Margarita Corona second him ably as faithful retainers. Mario Passano is natural as the grandson, but the same can't be said of Lia Casanova, a blonde who adds the slight heart interest.

Alberto Ginastera's score is skillful, and one of the film's best features while Humberto Peruzzi's camerawork does ample justice to a wide range of exteriors.

A dubbed English version has already been made with a view to selling the picture in the U. S. *Nid.*

Avant Le Deluge
(Before The Deluge) (FRENCH)

Paris, March 30.

AGDC release of UGC-Documento Films production. Directed by Andre Cayatte; screenplay, Cayatte, Charles Spaak; dialog, Spaak; camera, Jean Bourgoin; editor, Paul Cayatte. Features Bernard Blier, Balpetre, Line Noro, Isa Miranda, Jacques Castelot, Clement Thierry, Jacques Fayet, Marina Vlady, Jean Coggio, Jacques Chabassol. At Normandie, Paris. Running time, **140 MINS.**

Francoise	Isa Miranda
Liliane	Marina Vlady
Daniel	Jean Coggio
Philippe	Clement Thierry
Richard	Jacques Fayet
Jean	Jacques Chabassol
Professor	Bernard Blier
Serge	Jacques Castelot
Mother	Line Noro
Dutiot	Balpetre

After studying the intricacies of justice in "Justice Is Done" and capital punishment in "We Are All Murderers," Andre Cayatte, ex-lawyer, now turns his searching camera on adolescent delinquency and parental responsibility. Result is a jolting social yarn which covers too much territory and has a tendency to preach to the detriment of the drama. It forces its hand in fitting everything into its legal, pamphlet-like plea. It will do well on word-of-mouth here. For the U. S., this would need special handling for arty situations, but doesn't shape big because of its downbeat theme.

The banding together of five adolescents, who decide to flee Paris to a safe desert isle after being driven to panic over fear of a new war (this in in 1950) and lack of love and comfort from their selfish parents.

They find they need money to get away and decide to rob lover of one boy's mother. But a night policeman comes along, and he is accidentally shot and killed. Two of the boys in terror slay the young Jewish boy who they think will talk. Another boy confesses after a suicide attempt, and they are put on trial.

Film uses a flashback technique at the trial as the bereft parents all question themselves, and begin to realize their guilt. Cayatte has held this literary-type film together and generated many scenes of intense feeling. Lensing and editing is tops in keeping this complicated story always intelligible. Marina Vlady lends a lovely face as the girl in the gang. Youths are all well played, with Jean Coggio as the young Jewish boy a standout. Jacques Fayet, Clement Thierry and Jacques Chabassol all do well. Adults are also finely played with Bernard Blierra moving and bewildered as the father of a daughter he no longer understands.

Much of the excess haranguing, such as the professor's countless arguments with his son on Com-

munism, possibly can be sheared away to make this more palatable for special U. S. situations.
Mosk.

L'Etrange Desir de Monsieur Bard
(Strange Desire of Mr. Bard)
(FRENCH)

Paris, March 23.
AGCD release of UGC production. Stars Michel Simon; features Yves Deniaud, Genevieve Page, Henri Cremieux, Georgette Anys, Louis De Funes. Directed by Geza Radvanyi. Screenplay, Radvanyi, Rene Barjavel, L. H. Burel; editor, Rene Le Heneff. At Normandie, Paris. Running time, 110 MINS.

Bard	Michel Simon
Donta	Genevieve Page
Antonio	Yves Deniaud
Ernest	Henri Cremieux
Julie	Georgette Anys
Shanto	Louis De Funes
Priest	Paul Frankeur

"Strange Desire of Mr. Bard," which takes the form of a great desire for a child before he dies, makes for a strange but interesting film that safely tightropes the line between downbeat drama, comedy and pathos. Although death is a prime mover in the film, it never falls into the mawkish. It is a rare type pic which might do for special situations in the U.S. This should have a nice pull here on the Michel Simon name.

Simon, as Bard, is a mature bus driver in Monte Carlo who is told that he is suffering from a heart condition and may die soon. He has to retire among a group of avaricious, conniving relatives. Realizing that nobody ever really loved him, he gets a great desire to have a child before he dies.

He wins a fortune at a casino. Then he finds a young dejected dancer and makes her the proposition to have a child. She accepts. The expected happens and Bard goes through a period of great happiness as he plans for the coming child and maps out its future.

Geza Radvanyi has given this fable a load of neat visuals which keeps up a lively series of incidents. Lensing is excellent as is the editing. Outdoor French and Italo settings add to the production value. Simon manages to make the Bard a commendable rather than a grotesque figure. Genevieve Page is appealing as the woman in the matter while Yves Deniaud adds a nice earthy balance as the carping but tender pal. Well hypoed in special slotting, this well may have a chance for U. S. coin.
Mosk.

La Neige Etait Sale
(The Snow Was Dirty)
(FRENCH)

Paris, March 30.
Marceau release of Tellus production. Stars Daniel Gelin. Directed by Luis Saslavsky. Screenplay, Saslavsky, Andre Tabet; dialog by Tabet from novel by Georges Simenon; camera, Andre Dac; editor, Isabele Elman. St. Francais, Paris, Feb. 21, '54. Running time, 110 MINS.

Frank	Daniel Gelin
Irma	Valentine Tessier
Suzy	Marie Mansart
Moune	Vera Norman
Kramer	Daniel Ivernol
Colette	Joelle Bernard
Berta	Nadine Basile
Holtz	Balpetre

Though many of prolific Georges Simenon's books have been brought to the screen, few have managed to make the transfer adequately. Present attempt was a book first and then was a hit play some seasons ago before being fashioned into a screenplay. Here, too the atmosphere and psychological insight of the Simenon work bogs down on celluloid. This turns out to be a downbeat affair of the re-

generation of a psychotic during the occupation.

This concerns the son of a prostitute who is seared by his realization of his mother's profession. When he grows up he goes to live in a bagnio which she now runs, the film unfolding during the German occupation. Pic follows the book as he kills a German officer without reason, and gets into association with a local hoodlum. Again, per the book's plot, he seduces an innocent girl and sends the hoodlum into her bedroom. He is arrested by the Gestapo but finds forgiveness from the girl before he goes to his death.

Daniel Gelin is impressive, if a bit monotonous, as the tortured, morally lost youth. Marie Mansart lends an expressive, pure countenance to the girl who loves him while Valentine Tassier is fine as the mother whose love for her son has lost him to her.

Director Luis Saslavsky has not been able to remove the literary tang from this work. Technical credits are good and the halftoned lensing is helpful in maintaining the mood of despair.
Mosk.

Boum Sur Paris
(FRENCH-SONGS)

Paris, March 30.
Marceau production and release. Directed by Maurice De Canonge; screenplay, Jacques Chabannes, Roger Feral; camera, Jean Bachelet; editor, Isabelle Elman; music, Lougiuy; with Jacques Pills, Daniele Godet, Armand Bernard, Luce Feyrer, Edith Piaf, Charles Trenet, Greco, Mouloudji, Annie Cordy, Jacqueline Francois. At Lutetia, Paris. Running time, 95 MINS.

Jean	Jacques Pills
Monique	Daniele Godet
Lola	Luce Feyrer
Father	Armand Bernard
Edith Piaf	Herself
Charles Trenet	Himself

A rather tired gimmick is the core of this Gallic quickie which manages to work in most of the top French balladists. The better known singers and a looksee at French niteries might give this some hypo value for dualers or make this a tele filler; otherwise it has little for U. S. market.

A perfume company is also making a high explosive which is put in a perfume bottle to be given to a governmental rep for testing. By mistake the bottle goes to a bazaar where it is won by a stranger. The chase through Paris starts for the explosive, with acts and niteries thus worked into the proceedings.

Director Maurice De Canonge has given this ordinary treatment, with lensing and editing on par. Plot is broken by some nice vocals by Edith Piaf, Jacqueline Francois, Charles Trenet and others. Jacques Pills, as head of the chaser, is much too flamboyant and mannered while Daniele Godet, Luce Feyrer and Armand Bernard adequately make up the support. Music is passable, but most ditties sung by the specialists are the standards.
Mosk.

Secret Document— Vienna

Arthur Davis release of Helene Davis production. Directed by Andre Haguet. Screenplay, Andre Legrand; based on novel by Maurice Dekobra; camera, Charles Bauer; music, Van Hoorebeke. At Stanley Theatre, N.Y. Running time, 90 MINS.

Florence Henning	Renee Saint-Cyr
Rudolph Henning	Frank Villard
Colonel Von Pennwitz	Howard Vernon
Marika	Nathalie Nattier
Spy	George Galley
Inspector Braun	Andre Valmy
Steward	Oliver Hussenot

(In French; English Titles)

Okay World War I spy meller for lower rung bookings at nabe foreign film houses. Running 90 minutes, picture has some moments of suspense but mostly it's routine.

An Austrian captain is convicted of being a traitor and supposedly shot as a result. His French wife convinced that her husband had been framed by his superiors as part of a psychological maneuver returns to her native country from Switzerland. Intent on avenging his death she enlists as a Mata Hari for the French. While on assignment she discovers her husband is still alive, succeeds in carrying out her instructions with his aid and escapes to Switzerland, with the hope of eventually getting back together again with her spouse.

Renee Saint-Cyr is convincing as the wife turned spy, while Frank Villard also does nicely as her husband. Howard Vernon is authoritative as an Austrian colonel, with a yen for women. Andre Valmy is properly brusque as a Germanic inspector. Other cast members handle their chores efficiently.

Andre Hague did a smooth directional job, while other production elements are satisfactory.
Jess.

Morsiussseppele
(The Bridal Wreath)
(FINNISH)

Helsinki, March 23.
Suomi-Filmi release of Risto Orko production. Stars Aino-Maija Tikkanen, Jussi Jurkka, Kerstin Nylander. Directed by Hannu Leminen. Screenplay, Erkki Koivusalo, Hannu Leminen; camera, Erkki Imberg; sets, Tapio Vilpponen. At Helsinki, Finland. Running time, 105 MINS.

The girl	Aino-Maija Tikkanen
The boy	Jussi Jurkka
Boy's mother	Kerstin Nylander

Here is one of the finest films made in Finland since the war. A simple story about a country girl and a boy student who fall in love but can't get married (the boy's father is a high dignitary) has been made into a touching, convincing film. It is competently directed by Hannu Leminen, who was in charge of the Finnish Olympic film. It is a doubtful entry for the U.S.

Leminen's eye for filmatic qualities is sharp as well as his handling of the story. He had great help from a couple of young actors.

Following a recent pattern, there is some nudity in the film but it is done so well no protests have been made against it here. This film should do well in such spots where high-quality Swedish and French films are patronized.

Lucky Me
(MUSICAL—COLOR)

Routine musical in CinemaScope with name value Doris Day to help chances.

Warner Bros. release of Henry Blanke production. Stars Doris Day, Robert Cummings. Phil Silvers; features Eddie Foy Jr., Nancy Walker, Martha Hyer, Bill Goodwin, Marcel Dalio, Hayden Rorke, James Burke. Directed by Jack Donohue. Screenplay, James O'Hanlon, Robert O'Brien, Irving Elinson; from a story by O'Hanlon; camera (WarnerColor), Wilfrid M. Cline; editor, Owen Marks; songs, Sammy Fain, Paul Francis Webster; musical direction, Ray Heindorf. Previewed April 6, '54. Running time, 99 MINS.

Candy	Doris Day
Dick	Robert Cummings
Hap	Phil Silvers
Duke	Eddie Foy Jr.
Flo	Nancy Walker
Lorraine	Martha Hyer
Thayer	Bill Goodwin
Anton	Marcel Dalio
Tommy Arthur	Hayden Rorke
Mahoney	James Burke

(Aspect ratio: 2.55-1)

A round of routine musical ingredients are featured in "Lucky Me" and it will have to depend almost entirely on the name of Doris Day to sell tickets. The singer is a proven draw, so there undoubtedly is some coin in the offing for this CinemaScope offering, but there would have been much larger returns in view had the entertainment been fresher.

The screenplay by James O'Hanlon, Robert O'Brien and Irving Elinson is a tissue of tired, often tiresome, gags and situations without redeeming imagination or originality. This pat musical format doesn't inspire Jack Donohue's direction to any heights and his handling of the Henry Blanke production is poor. Picture is so full of high and low places that the 99 minutes of footage seem overly long. The songs by Sammy Fain and Paul Francis Webster are not viewed to any particular advantage, so it is hard to determine whether they have enough merit to become pop sellers. In the film they are only so-so listening.

Song lineup gets underway with Miss Day doing a long marathon to "The Superstition Song," followed quickly by "Men" with Phil Silvers and "Parisian Pretties" with a tab line of girls. Miss Day, Silvers, Eddie Foy Jr., and Nancy Walker team on "High Hopes" and "Blue Bells of Broadway." As a solo spotlight, Miss Day has "I Speak to the Stars," which has a charm almost lost because of pretentious staging and over-arranging. "Love You Dearly" is a good ballad and "I Wanna Sing Like An Angel" a peppy finale tune. Snatches of the title number also are heard but nothing much ever comes of it in the picture.

Miami Beach is the story setting and its beauties take neatly to the squeeze-lensing. A tab show headed by Silvers is stranded in the resort city and through a series of remarkable circumstances, Silvers, Miss Day, Foy and Miss Walker are working out their debts in the kitchen of a swank hotel. Stopping at the hotel is Robert Cummings, successful songsmith who is about to stage his own musical if Martha Hyer's oilrich Texan dad, Bill Goodwin, turns angel. Everything is brought off without any surprises that might have quickened interest.

While the settings take well to the CinemaScope treatment, the players do not, many of the scenes showing the principals in an unflattering manner. Miss Day, Cummings and Silvers work hard at the co-star spots, but aren't too successful in bringing them off. Foy, the Misses Walker and Hyer, Goodwin, Marcel Dalio, Hayden Rorke and James Burke do what they can in the hit-and-miss proceedings.

Wilfrid M. Cline handled the CinemaScope cameras and the WarnerColor hues, and Owen Marks edited. Ray Haindorf directed the music, with vocal arrangements by Norman Luboff and orchestrations by Frank Comstock. *Brog.*

Det Stora Aventyret
(The Great Adventure) (SWEDISH)

Cannes, April 6.

Sandrew-Bumanfilm release of Sucksdorff-Sandrew production. Written, directed, photographed and edited by Arne Sucksdorff; commentary, Sven Bertil Norberg; music, Lars Erik Larrson. At Cannes Film Festival. Running time, 83 MINS.

Anders	Anders Norborg
Kjell	Kjell Sucksdorff
Father	Arne Sucksdorff

This is a one-man film which took two years of painstaking work to complete. Primarily a nature film, worked in with the story of two children and a pet otter, this benefits from a poetic eulogy to the simple life and change of seasons. Its offbeat qualities and slim story peg this primarily for some arty situations in the U. S.

Director Arne Sucksdorff's series of nature films have been seen in some parts of the U. S., but this is his first full-length pic. Film starts out in a forest, showing young foxes, otters and other animals, and then shifts to a nearby farm. One fox has wreaked havoc with the local livestock and the owner is out to get the fox, and finally does. Two boys save an otter from a poacher and make a secret pet of it. Finally the young boy gives away the secret and the other sets the otter free.

Excellent lensing provides exciting animal views. Pic carefully depicts the play, tragedy and cruel cycle of the forest as well as affinity of youth against man's encroachment. Editing helps the overall effect. *Mosk.*

The Desperate Women

Theme is abortion. Done without sensationalism, but likely to get that type of ballyhoo treatment.

Hollywood, April 7.

Independent release of a Samuel Newman Productions, Inc., presentation, produced by Samuel Newman and Louis B. Appleton Jr. Features Anne Appleton, Douglas Howard, Paul Hahn. Directed by Appleton Jr. Written by Newman; camera, Russ Meyer; editor, Albert Shaff; music, Melvyn Lenard. Previewed April 1, '54. Running time, 67 MINS.

Mona	Anne Appleton
Eddie	Douglas Howard
Dr. Martin	Paul Hahn
Captain Dawson	Ben Daniels
Kovacs	Samuel Newman
Flo Brown	Maria Girard
Miss Parker	Virginia Leon
Mary Jane	Karen Moore
Operator	Joseph Allen Jr.
Publisher	Robert Lee
Doctor	Theodore Marcuse
Jimmy	Richard Risso
Mr. Jones	Stanley Glenn
Mrs. Callucci	Rebecca Young
Sadie	Karen Wolfe
Contact Man	Raymond Barrett
Joe	William Sharpe
Interne	Ross Durfee
Mother	Jean McCampbell
Boy Friend	Richard Learman
Operator's Nurse	Ragna Kyle
Room Clerk	Jo Young
Barnes	Joseph Penner
Husband	Hughes Rudd
Wife	Nilli Carroll
Doctor's Nurse	Virginia Royce
Bartender	William ...
Woman	Eve Meyer
Nurse	...

(Aspect ratio: 1.33-1)

The "adults only" tag on this exploitation subject, being marketed independently by Samuel Newman Productions, Inc., carries more shock value than the film itself, which is an abortive piece of entertainment about abortions.

There's a sincere message of warning in the presentation, and it's delivered without sensationalism, and with enough restraint to warrant screening for bobby-soxers as part of their sex education. However, this very lack of sensationalism mitigates b.o. prospects in the exploitation market, which is about the only commercial outlet the picture will have.

Teenagers are warned that no medicine, drug, oil or salve yet known will halt a pregnancy, but may take a life. Case histories of all kinds of devices for abortion are run off along a story line that uses an inquiring reporter angle to tie things together. Point is made that knitting needles, umbrella ribs, falls downstairs and other forms of violence are no substitute for the advice of one's physician or clergyman (sic). Equally dangerous are the criminal abortionists who are responsible for many thousands of deaths yearly.

Newman wrote "Desperate Women" for the screen and co-produced with Louis B. Appleton, Jr. The latter directed and Russ Meyer photographed. The picture's pace is slow, even though the footage is only 67 minutes. The lensing took place in San Francisco, where a cast of suitable unknowns was rounded up to play the various types in the story. A little more strength in the performances and direction might have helped the entertainment values and chances, although, as to the latter, where strongly ballyhooed some business can result. *Brog.*

Them

Topnotch science-fiction shocker with good outlook in thriller market.

Hollywood, April 8.

Warner Bros. release of David Weisbart production. Stars James Whitmore, Edmund Gwenn, Joan Weldon, James Arness; features Onslow Stevens, Sean McClory, Chris Drake. Directed by Gordon Douglas. Screenplay, Ted Sherdeman; adaptation by Russell Hughes from a story by George Worthing Yates; camera, Sid Hickox; editor, Thomas Reilly; music, Bronislaw Kaper. Previewed April 5, '54. Running time, 93 MINS.

Sgt. Ben Peterson	James Whitmore
Dr. Harold Medford	Edmund Gwenn
Dr. Patricia Medford	Joan Weldon
Robert Graham	James Arness
Brig. Gen. O'Brien	Onslow Stevens
Major Kibbee	Sean McClory
Ed Blackburn	Chris Drake
A Little Girl	Sandy Descher
Mrs. Lodge	Mary Ann Hokanson
Capt. of Troopers	Don Shelton
Crotty	Fess Parker
Jensen	Olin Howlin

(Aspect ratio: 1.66-1)

This is a science-fiction shocker that should scare up plenty of trade in the thriller market. It has a well-plotted story, expertly directed and acted in a matter-of-fact style to rate a chiller payoff and thoroughly satisfy the fans of hackle-raising melodrama.

David Weisbart's production guidance gives the Ted Sherdeman script realistic backing to bring out all of the meller facets, and Gordon Douglas' direction maintains a constant air of expectancy that gives the thrills impact and makes the unfoldment seem fast. Film is based on Russell Hughes's adaptation of a story by George Worthing Yates.

The title monsters are mutations caused by radiation from the 1945 detonation of an atomic bomb in the desert. Over the intervening years the tiny insects affected by the lingering radiation have become fantastic creatures, ranging in size from nine feet to 12 feet. James Whitmore, sergeant in the New Mexico State Police, first gets on the track of the incredible beings. Into the picture then come Edmund Gwenn and Joan Weldon, entomologists, and James Arness, FBI man.

With the aid of Air Force officers Onslow Stevens and Sean McClory, the little group attempts to wipe out the nest of the mutated monsters with flame throwers and gas. Two of the newlyborn queen ants escape, however. One nests on a ship, destroys its crew and, in turn, the Navy destroys the ship at sea. The other queen holes up in the huge storm drains under Los Angeles and the picture's climax is concerned with the destruction of this one and her offspring. It's a real chiller-diller finale.

As the co-stars, Whitmore, Gwenn, Miss Weldon and Arness wrap up the acting chores in first-rate fashion, getting good assists from Stevens, McClory, Chris Drake, Sandy Descher, Mary Ann Hokanson, Don Sheldon, Fess Parker and Olin Howland. The latter two show up very well, the first as a pilot, booby-hatched for his "flying saucer" story, and the other as a happy drunk.

Sid Hickox's photography gets plenty of menace into the fantastic monsters. Also doing their full share at maintaining thriller impact are the score, editing, art direction and settings. *Brog.*

Southwest Passage
(3-D Color)

Actionful western feature in 3-D; good entry for outdoor market.

Hollywood, April 9.

United Artists release of Edward Small presentation. Stars Rod Cameron, Joanne Dru, John Ireland; features John Dehner, Guinn (Big Boy) Williams. Directed by Ray Nazarro. Screenplay, Harry Essex, Geoffrey Homes; story by Essex; camera (PatheColor), Sam Leavitt; editor, Grant Whytock. Previewed April 2, '54. Running time, 75 MINS.

Lilly	Joanne Dru
Edward Beale	Rod Cameron
Clint McDonald	John Ireland
Matt Carrol	John Dehner
Tall Tale	Guinn (Big Boy) Williams
Hi Jolly	Mark Hanna
Jeb	Darryl Hickman
Lieut. Owens	Stuart Randall
Doc Stanton	Morris Ankrum
Sheriff Morgan	Kenneth MacDonald
Constable Bartlett	Stanley Andrews

(Aspect ratio: 1.71-1)

Another version of how the camels came to the Great American Desert is presented in "Southwest Passage" and it's an interesting, action-filled western in 3-D and Pathecolor for the outdoor market.

Cast names are good for release intentions, having Rod Cameron, frontiersman charting a new trail to California while attempting to prove camels can be put to practical use in the west; Joanne Dru and John Ireland, the latter a bank robber with whom Miss Dru is fleeing, to head up the player list. This top trio, along with John Dehner, Guinn (Big Boy) Williams and several others respond well to the action intentions of Ray Nazarro's well-paced direction.

The Edward Small presentation through United Artists rates a good outdoor script from Harry Essex and Geoffrey Homes. Plotting has Ireland ducking a pursuing posse by passing himself off as the doctor for whom Cameron's outfit had been waiting. Miss Dru gets in on the act by posing as a femme who has lost her way and the long, trail-blazing trek across the desert starts. Menace is in several forms: Indians, who at first think the camels are some kind of gods and then attack the whites later; lack of water which hampers the journey, and Dehmer, member of Cameron's outfit who has learned Ireland is carrying his bank loot with him and wants a cut. A bloody battle around a water hole takes care of all plot angles. Ireland reforms and looks forward to a new life in the west with Miss Dru.

The 3-D color lensing by Sam Leavitt is good and blows up to widescreen without too apparent loss of definition. The editing and other technical functions also are expertly handled to help make the most of the action and outdoor settings. *Brog.*

Massacre Canyon

So-so hoss opera for the lower half of the duals

Columbia release of Wallace MacDonald production. Stars Phil Carey, Audrey Totter; features Douglas Kennedy, Jeff Donnell, Guinn Williams, Charlita, Ross Elliott. Directed by Fred F. Sears. Screenplay and story, David Lang; camera, Lester H. White; editor, Aaron Stell; music, Mischa Bakaleinikoff. Tradeshown, N.Y., April 1, '54. Running time, 66 MINS.

Lt. Richard Faraday	Phil Carey
Flaxy	Audrey Totter
Sgt. James Marlowe	Douglas Kennedy
Cora	Jeff Donnell
Peaceful	Guinn Williams
Gita	Charlita
George Davis	Ross Elliott
"Parson" Canfield	Ralph Dumke
Gonzales	Mel Welles
Running Horse	Chris Alcaide
Black Eagle	Steve Ritch
Lt. Ridgeford	John Pickard
Col. Jos. Tarant	James Flavin
Lt. Farnum	Bill Hale

An implausible story and not enough action hamper b.o. prospects of "Massacre Canyon." It's patently a low-budget oater for the lower half of the duals and the going will be slow.

There are some familiar names in the cast but they are largely wasted in the dullish yarn contrived by David Lang. Whole premise of script is based upon the attempt of Sergeant Douglas Kennedy to hustle four wagons of rifles past the redskins led by renegade warrior Steve Ritch.

Of course, the ruse is discovered and the small group of soldiers (plus a couple of women they've picked up enroute) are hard pressed to drive off the Injuns. Pace picks up at the finale when Kennedy eludes the pursuers by leading the pack train through a tunnel and safety.

Performances are generally uninspired due to the listless direction of Fred F. Sears. Phil Carey is fair in an unsympathetic role of a drunken lieutenant who professes to know it all. Kennedy is effective at times and Guinn ("Big Boy") Williams is adequate as one of the soldiers.

Audrey Totter, often a fine actress, gets no chance whatever to show her talent in the role of a femme heading west to find a beau. Likewise, Jeff Donnell hasn't much to do on the same mission. Other cast members turn in standard characterizations in keeping with the pedestrian plot. Lester White's camerawork is good as is most other technical credits. Wallace MacDonald's production values reflect the low budget. *Gilb.*

Out of This World
(TRAVELOG—COLOR)

Theodore R. Kupferman presentation of Lowell Thomas Sr. and Jr. production. Commentary written and narrated by Thomas Sr. and Jr. At the Guild Theatre, N.Y., April 15, '54. Running time, 75 **MINS.**

Public interest in exploration, as evidenced in the success of the written and filmed accounts of "The Conquest of Everest" and "Annapurna," should be sustained by "Out of This World," the film documentary of a trek some years ago to Tibet by Lowell Thomas Sr. and Jr. While lacking the dramatic impact of the mountain-climbing sagas, the Thomas adventure is nonetheless a fascinating report of an enigmatic section of the world. It rates as a natural for artic situations and as a companion feature in standard houses.

Photographed in color, "World" is at its best when it focuses on the people of the strange Asiatic country. Coupled with the interesting narrative provided and spoken by the Thomases, father and son, the film offers an insight of the people, customs and life of this little-known country which is rarely visited by Westerners. The Thomas celluloid report rates as a modern historical document since Tibet has since fallen into the hands of the Chinese Communists.

Highlights of the film include the visit to the sacred Tibetan capital city of Lhasa, a view of the young Dalai Lama and the Potala, the skyscraper center of deeply religious Tibet. The Thomases also take their cameras into the monasteries where at least one-third of the country's male population is trained for monkhood.

The Thomas expedition to Tibet took 24 days by mule train. This portion of the film appears somewhat repetitious. On the return trip to India, Thomas Sr. was injured and had to be carried all the way back in a makeshift stretcher.

The eamera work, while not of professional stature, still succeeds in capturing the scenic views and people in a wholly satisfactory manner. The Thomas visit to the "sealed kingdom" was at the invitation of the Tibetan government which wanted Thomas Sr. to bring a message of friendship to the U. S. and an appeal for help against the Communist threat.

Holl.

Indiscretion of An American Wife

Italian-filmed study of a farewell to a summer dalliance; consciously arty, but with femme appeal, Jennifer Jones, Montgomery Clift strengthening possibilities.

Hollywood, April 20.

Columbia release of Vittorio De Sica production. Stars Jennifer Jones, Montgomery Clift; features Gino Cervi, Dick Beymer. Directed by De Sica. Screenplay, Cesare Zavattini, Luigi Chiarini, Giorgio Prosperi; from the story, "Terminal Station," by Zavattini; dialog, Truman Capote; camera, G. R. Aldo; editor, Eraldo Da Roma, Jean Barker; music, Alessandro Cicognini; conducted by Franco Ferrara. Previewed April 15, '54. Running time, **63 MINS.**

Mary .... Jennifer Jones
Giovanni .... Montgomery Clift
Commissioner .... Gino Cervi
Paul .... Dick Beymer

(*Aspect ratio: 1.85 to 1*)

The plot of "Indiscretion of An American Wife" is told rather precisely in the title. It is an Italian-filmed feature, very consciously arty and foreign, but with the American star names of Jennifer Jones and Montgomery Clift and a strong appeal to the feminine to bolster its domestic possibilities. The "true romance," "true confession" type of escape fiction seems to be returning to favor and "Indiscretion" fits the classification thoroughly.

The picture was produced and directed by Vittorio De Sica from Cesare Zavattini's story, "Terminal Station." The lensing by G. R. Aldo was done in its entirety in the Stazione Termini in Rome, where the story of an American housewife saying farewell to her holiday lover takes place.

Domestic distribution rights to the picture, held by Selznick Releasing Organization, were turned over to Columbia and the footage edited down considerably from its foreign release length. In fact the trimming was so drastic Columbia ordered a musical prolog from SRO to pad out the footage, so "Indiscretion," itself running 63 minutes, has an eight-minute hitchhiker riding along. Patti Page sings "Autumn in Rome" and "Indiscretion," songs by Paul Weston and Sammy Cahn that are themed on the Alessandro Cicognini score from the main feature. She's good. So are the songs; Joe Reisman's arrangements; James Wong Howe's camera work, and the design and direction by William Cameron Menzies. However, the short is still of dubious value to the feature.

As typical of foreign film pretentions, much use is made of bits and types flowing through the busy railway terminal to color and add movement to the picture. However, these players who sustain the show aren't considered important enough to credit. Other than the stars, only two are named, Gino Cervi and Dick Beymer, but they are not identified as to characters. As the picture wears the De Sica brand, the pseudo-intellectuals will probably hail it, and it has its definite merits, along with techniques and posturings long ago discarded by Hollywood.

Outside of the agonizing moments of farewells between Miss Jones, Philadelphia housewife returning to her safe hearth, and her younger holiday lover, Clift, the story's dramatic suspense pull is developed around the couple's arrest after being discovered in an extremely compromising embrace in a secluded spot. Will she be freed in time to catch the train for Paris, or will her shame be bared to all? Script makes quite a bit of this angle before turning it loose in a final farewell scene that will really squeeze the femme tear ducts.

The stars give the drama a real pro try and the professional standards of delivery are high, even though the character interpretations will not be liked by all. Faring best is Miss Jones, managing to be just a bit dowdy and matronly in her Christian Dior costume, as would be the character she portrays. Clift is extremely intense, and somewhat more youthful in the impression he creates than necessary, as her lover. There are several very excellent prformances by the nameless cast members.

The Cicognini score, conducted by Franco Ferrara, too often is intrusive to the point of being a major distraction to the mood being sought.

Brog.

Witness to Murder
(SONG)

Standard suspense meller with Barbara Stanwyck, George Sanders, Gary Merrill to help chances generally.

Hollywood, April 14.

United Artists release of Chester Erskine production. Stars Barbara Stanwyck, George Sanders, Gary Merrill; features Jesse White, Harry Shannon, Claire Carleton, Lewis Martin, Dick Elliott, Harry Tyler, Juanita Moore. Directed by Roy Rowland. Original screenplay, Chester Erskine; camera, John Alton; editor, Robert Swink; score, composed and directed by Herschel Burke Gilbert; song by Gilbert and Sylvia Fine. Previewed April 13, '54. Running time, **81 MINS.**

Cheryl Draper .... Barbara Stanwyck
Albert Richter .... George Sanders
Lawrence Mathews .... Gary Merrill
Eddie Vincent .... Jesse White
Capt. Donnelly .... Harry Shannon
The Blonde .... Claire Carleton
Psychiatrist .... Lewis Martin
Apartment Manager .... Dick Elliott
Charlie .... Harry Tyler
Woman .... Juanita Moore
Woman's co-worker ...... Joy Hallward
The Old Lady. Adeline DeWalt Reynolds
Policewoman .... Gertrude Graner

(*Aspect ratio 1.75-1*)

The suspense thriller tricks used as a background for "Witness to Murder" play over a familiar course, resulting in a standard melodrama that, while it does have its thrills, varies little from countless other such offerings. The presence of Barbara Stanwyck, as well as George Sanders, should help the booking chances in regular release.

Chester Erskine wrote "Witness" for the screen and produced for United Artists release. Both chores are brought off professionally, even though lacking a novel or fresh touch that might have rated the presentation more than just an average mark. Roy Rowland's direction is in the same key, expertly fashioned to make the most of what's available, but adding little that is new.

Plenty of holes exist in the plot, that has Miss Stanwyck awakening from a deep sleep, rising to close a window against a storm, and seeing Sanders murder a girl in an apartment across the way. Quite often logic bows to convenience as the script goes through its paces. Gary Merrill, police lieutenant who takes the heroine's report of homicide, doesn't believe her. Nor does anyone else take her tale seriously because Sanders is a wily killer who leaves no clues scattered around. Footage finds Miss Stanwyck trying to find a friendly ear while Sanders resorts to all sorts of trickery that will convince the police she is crazy. It does seem that Erskine's writing could have found some other out to wrap up the plot than the old-hat stunt of putting the principals atop a high building where, after the prescribed heights thrills, justice triumphs.

Within this familiar framework, the performances are good, reflecting the long experience many of the players have had with this type of material. On the male side, Merrill shows up exceptionally well, even considering the police and their methods are displayed unfavorably. Sanders does another of his suave villains and Miss Stanwyck is properly panic-stricken. Jesse White is okay as Merrill's aide. Among supporting spots remembered are Claire Carleton, a looney in the psycho ward where Miss Stanwyck is being quizzed, and Juanita Moore, also an inmate, who sings the mournful blues, cleffed by Herschel Burke Gilbert and Sylvia Fine. Lensing by John Alton, Gilbert's score and other credits are handled correctly.

Brog.

Playgirl

Talky saga of the innocent country girl in the big city.

Hollywood, April 19.

Universal release of Albert J. Cohen production. Stars Shelley Winters, Barry Sullivan, Colleen Miller; features Richard Long, Gregg Palmer, Kent Taylor. Directed by Joseph Pevney. Screenplay, Robert Blees; story, Ray Buffum; camera, Carl Guthrie; editor, Virgil Vogel; musical supervision, Joseph Gershenson; song, Ray Gilbert. Previewed April 13, '54. Running time, **85 MINS.**

Fran .... Shelley Winters
Mike Marsh .... Barry Sullivan
Phyllis Matthews .... Colleen Miller
Barron Courtney .... Richard Long
Tom Burton .... Gregg Palmer
Ted Andrews .... Kent Taylor
Greta Marsh .... Jacqueline de Wit
Jonathan .... Dave Barry
Lew Martel .... Philip Van Zandt
Paul .... James McCallion
Wilbur .... Paul Richards
Anne .... Helen Beverly
Linda .... Myrna Hansen
Pam .... Mara Corday

(*Aspect ratio: 2-1*)

An updated treatment of the old plot about big-city perils facing innocents from the country is used in "Playgirl." While the results are only so-so as concerns entertainment merit, there are some exploitation angles. The $100 "party girl" angle is not the least of the selling points, even though it gets nowhere in the once-over-lightly plot treatment.

Story, despite its modern setting in New York, is more of the Roaring Twenties cycle so popular on the screen and in novels during the early and mid-thirties after 3.2 beer made a come-back. For the demands of the story and the characters that people it, Albert J. Cohen's casting is good, toplining Shelley Winters, Harry Sullivan, and newcomer Colleen Miller. Within the scope of Robert Blees' script and Joseph Pevney's direction, the performances are satisfactory, the only real fault being that none of the characters, good or bad, generates sympathy. Most promising is Miss Miller, who is undoubtedly slated for a buildup. Richard Long expertly delineates a caddish playboy, an impoverished socialite who arranges "dates" for a fee. Gregg Palmer and Kent Taylor are the others getting featured billing.

Miss Miller is the wide-eyed innocent, come to live in the big city with Miss Winters, a well-seasoned singer in love with Sullivan, photo mag publisher whose wife doesn't understand him. Palmer is an employee on the mag who gets Miss Miller a layout, the boss tries to move in on the girl, is accidentally shot in a scuffle with the jealous Miss Winters. All this ruins Miss Miller's reputation and Palmer's regard, so she becomes a party girl, is eventually involved in a gangster killing which, oddly enough, gets her back with Palmer and winds up the picture after a wounded Miss Winters announces the heroine is still an innocent babe.

The new "Lie to Me" by Ray Gilbert is sung by the Winters character and it's a listenable blues hit. Also spotted for a nitery sequence is "There'll Be Some Changes Made," oldie by Billy Higgins, W. Benton Overstreet and Herbert Edwards. Picture rates good lensing from Carl Guthrie and Joseph Gershenson's musical supervision is satisfactory.

Brog.

Untamed Heiress
(Songs)

Typical Judy Canova comedy for the corn belt.

Hollywood, April 20.
Republic release of Sidney Picker production. Stars Judy Canova; features Donald Barry, George Cleveland. Taylor Holmes, Chick Chandler, Jack Kruschen, Hugh Sanders, Douglas Fowley, William Haade, Ellen Corby. Directed by Charles Lamont. Screenplay, Barry Shipman; story, Jack Townley; camera, Reggie Lanning; editor, Arthur Roberts; score, Stanley Wilson; songs, Jack Elliott, Donald Kahn. Previewed April 16, '54. Running time, 69 MINS.

Judy .... Judy Canova
Spider Mike .... Donald Barry
Andrew (Cactus) Clayton
George Cleveland
Walter Martin .... Taylor Holmes
Eddie Taylor .... Chick Chandler
Louie .... Jack Kruschen
Williams .... Hugh Sanders
Pal .... Douglas Fowley
Friend .... William Haade
Mrs. Flanny .... Ellen Corby

(Aspect ratio: 1.66-1)

Judy Canova is about the only excuse for this two-reel comedy idea that has been stretched out to 69 minutes. However, her presence may be excused enough for the rural and small-town trade where she rates. Elsewhere, it has nothing to offer.

Three typical Canova tunes are spotted in the footage, "Welcome," which she does with a group of kids; "A Dream For Sale" and "Sugar Daddy." The gal can growl a good blue note, as demonstrated on the latter two pieces, first of which was written by Jack Elliott and Donald Kahn and the second by Elliott.

Plot is concerned with the saving of a gold hoard from Hugh Sanders, a situation in which Miss Canova finds herself because an old prospector, George Cleveland, once loved her opera-singing ma. Cleveland, with a big bankroll, hires Taylor Holmes and Chick Chandler, agents, to find the ma. Instead, they come up with the daughter because the ma is dead but find Sanders has taken charge of Cleveland's desert castle and the old man, hoping to get hold of the gold. Donald Barry and Jack Kruschen, gangsters, get into the act on the side of the heroine because of money owed them by Taylor and Chandler. It's all rather confusing and continues that way, even though Miss Canova and friends win out in a finale slapstick battle royal.

Charles Lamont gives extremely broad direction to the Sidney Picker production, working from a script by Barry Shipman, which was based on a Jack Townley story. Reggie Lanning photographed and other technical credits are average. *Brog.*

Arrow in the Dust
(COLOR-SONG)

Passable western feature in Technicolor for the outdoor action market.

Hollywood, April 14.
Allied Artists release of Hayes Goetz production. Stars Sterling Hayden, Coleen Gray; co-stars Keith Larsen. Tom Tully, Jimmy Wakely; features Tudor Owen, Lee Van Cleef, John Pickard, Carleton Young. Directed by Lesley Selander. Screenplay, Don Martin; from a novel by L. L. Foreman; camera (Technicolor), Ellis W. Carter; editor, William Austin; music, Marlin Skiles; songz, Jimmy Wakely. Previewed April 12, '54. Running time, 79 MINS.

Bart Laish .... Sterling Hayden
Christella .... Coleen Gray
Lt. King .... Keith Larsen
Crowshaw .... Tom Tully
Carqueville .... Jimmy Wakely
Tillotson .... Tudor Owen
Crew Boss .... Lee Van Cleef
Lybarger .... John Pickard
Pepperis .... Carleton Young

†Aspect ratio: 1.85-1)

Regulation western antics for the entertainment of the not-so-discriminating customer are run off in "Arrow In the Dust," making it passable filmware for the general market. There's nothing outstanding in the playing, writing or direction to pull it above the formula level and things unfold at a routine pace.

Chief star of the Hayes Goetz production, is Sterling Hayden, playing a deserting cavalry trooper who is forced by circumstance to assume the guise and authority of a major to lead a wagon train to safety. Script credit on the L. L. Foreman story goes to Don Martin, but the way events come off it appears as though the writing was ad lib, with no formal plotting before cameras started to grind. Directorial pacing of Lesley Selander isn't helped by this loose development, nor by having the character stand around and explain events. However, he pours on enough aimless shooting between whites and Indians to create a semblance of action.

Hayden, in his guise of major, joins a wagon train that has been under almost constant Indian attack. He pulls rank to keep the train on the road, as it were, fights delaying actions with the pursuing redskins and keeps a group of bad whites with the outfit under control. After the heroics have just about played out Hayden gets wise to why the redskins have been such relentless pursuers. Tudor Owen, one of the bad whites, has a wagon load of repeating rifles and ammunition which the Indians want. Hayden destroys this prize and the Indians ride away just as cavalry reinforcements arrive to escort the motley crew into Laramie. It's established that Hayden will get a short sentence for deserting and that Coleen Gray, a brave girl who cared for the wounded on the trek, will be awaiting his release.

Hayden, Miss Gray, and co-stars Keith Larsen, Tom Tully and Jimmy Wakely are adequate to the light demands. Wakely also composed and sings throughout "The Weary Stranger." Others in the cast get by.

Ellis W. Carter did the Technicolor lensing, which will blow up to widescreen for added advantages in displaying the outdoor scenery. Editing, score and other functions are okay for release intentions. *Brog.*

Nenita Unit
(PHILIPPINE)

Tokyo, April 13.
Columbia release of Luzon Theatres-Antonio G. Sanchez production. Stars Anita Linda, Danile Montes, Patricia Plata. Directed and written by Eddie Infante. Camera, Arsenio Dona; music, Aristo Avelino. Previewed in Tokyo.

(English Dialog)

The first screen treatment of the Communist Hukbalahap guerrillas of the Philippines is a low-budget production which proves that a dramatic subject can triumph over the twin handicaps of amateurish production and none-too-subtle anti-Communist propaganda weighing down the plot. Despite its shortcomings, the film's powerful theme; capable performances and camerawork hold the interest. It should have an appeal to U. S. foreign language and arty houses.

Story centers around the extermination of a large band of Huks by the girl leader, Anita Linda. Her group is called the Nenita Unit. She was captured by the Huks when younger and groomed against her will to be a guerrilla leader by another female rebel, Patricia Plata. Linda breaks with the Huks when they raid her hometown and she is ordered to shoot her own parents. Troops dispersing the raiders find Linda huddled over her dead parents, shot in cold blood by the fleeing Huks. Remainder of pic shows Nenita leading national troops to Huks' hideout. Romance enters when Nenita falls in love with a lieutenant of the national troops, Danila Montes.

As the girl leader, Miss Linda is splendid and deserves a more smoothly directed and more expensive production. Miss Plata leans heavily on Katrina Paxinou's performance in "For Whom The Bell Tolls" for her portrayal of a vigorous, crude and utterly consecrated Communist. Others in cast are satisfactory, with Montes drawing on real life experience in the Army to make his young lieutenant completely believable.

Largest fault in the development of the pic lies in the fact that it seems to have been made without considering the foreign market although to be distributed by Columbia. Producer Antonio G. Sanchez apparently thought audiences would have an intimate knowledge of the Philippines, the Huk situation and the Filipino character from the abrupt way the film plunges into the story. *Lars.*

River of No Return
(C'SCOPE-SONGS-COLOR)

Robert Mitchum, Marilyn Monroe in fairly diverting outdoor actioner that shapes to average CinemaScope chances.

Hollywood, April 23.
20th-Fox release of Stanley Rubin production. Stars Robert Mitchum, Marilyn Monroe; features Rory Calhoun, Tommy Rettig, Murvyn Vye, Douglas Spencer. Directed by Otto Preminger. Screenplay, Frank Fenton; from a story by Louis Lantz; camera (Technicolor), Joseph La Shelle; editor, Louis Loeffler; music, Cyril J. Mockridge; songs, Ken Darby, Lionel Newman. Previewed April 19, '54. Running time, 90 MINS.

Matt Calder .... Robert Mitchum
Kay Weston .... Marilyn Monroe
Harry Weston .... Rory Calhoun
Mark .... Tommy Rettig
Colby .... Murvyn Vye
Benson .... Douglas Spencer
Ben .... Don Beddoe
Trades .... Will Wright
Young Punk .... Hal Baylor

(Aspect ratio: 2.55-1)

The striking beauties of the Canadian Rockies co-star with the blonde charms of Marilyn Monroe and the masculine muscles of Robert Mitchum in the "River of No Return." The combo makes for a fairly diverting western actioner with about average possibilities in the CinemaScope market.

The competition between scenic splendors of the Jasper and Banff National Parks and entertainment values finds the former finishing slightly ahead on merit, although there's enough rugged action and suspense moments to get the Stanley Rubin production through its 90 minutes of footage. In between the high spots, Otto Preminger's directorial pacing is inclined to lag, so the running time seems overlong for the conventionally-motivated Louis Lantz story, scripted by Frank Fenton.

Mitchum and Tommy Rettig, playing father and son, pull Miss Monroe and Rory Calhoun from a river that races by their wilderness farm. Calhoun is trying to get to a settlement to file a gold claim he has won dishonestly at cards and Miss Monroe is along because she expects to marry him. Calhoun steals Mitchum's horse and gun and rides off, leaving the others at the mercy of warring Indians. Man, woman and boy take to the river on a raft to escape the redskins and, also, so Mitchum can catch up with Calhoun at the settlement. Between the river rapids, the Indians and sex, it's not an easy voyage that takes the trio downstream to town where, obviously, Mitchum and Monroe clinch for the fadeout after Calhoun has paid for his sins.

Mitchum, Miss Monroe and Calhoun perform acceptably in roles that make no great demands, each being true to their story characters: Mitchum the strong silent outdoor man, Miss Monroe a saloon singer out of place in the wilderness, and Calhoun a suave heavy. Young Rettig is good as Mitchum's motherless son. Short bits are played by Murvyn Vye, Douglas Spencer, Don Beddoe, Will Wright and Hal Baylor.

Joseph La Shelle's Technicolored lensing captures the feel of the great outdoors and enhances the production as a whole. However, the process shots are too apparent. Picture has four songs, sung by Miss Monroe. They are the title number, "I'm Gonna File My Claim," accompanied by gestures that verge on the vulgar, "One Silver Dollar" and "Down In the Meadow." Ken Darby and Lionel Newman did the good cleffing, and Newman also directed the Cyril J.

Mockridge background score. The Travilla costumes for Miss Monroe's saloon chirp character are apt, but when the femme goes outdoors in rougher garb, it's obvious there's too much of her for levis. The film's stereo sound generally listens okay, although it's used to irritating effect in the rapids-forging sequences. *Brog.*

Flame and the Flesh
(COLOR)

Lana Turner in an unusually frank portrayal (for exploitation peg) but entertainment values mediocre.

Metro release of Joe Pasternak production. Stars Lana Turner, Pier Angeli, Carlos Thompson; features Bonar Colleano, Charles Goldner, Peter Illing. Directed by Richard Brooks. Screenplay, Helen Deutsch, based on Auguste Bailly novel; camera (Technicolor), Christopher Challis; editors, Albert Akst and Ray Poulton; music, Nicholas Brodszky; lyrics, Jack Lawrence; musical direction, George Stoll. Previewed in N.Y., April 23, '54. Running time, **104 MINS.**

Madeline	Lana Turner
Lisa	Pier Angeli
Nino	Carlos Thompson
Ciccio	Bonar Colleano
Mondari	Charles Goldner
Peppe	Peter Illing
Francesca	Rosalie Crutchley
Filiberto	Marne Maitland
Marina Proprietor	Eric Pohlmann
Dressmaker	Catharina Ferraz

(*Aspect ratio*: 1.66:1)

"Flame and the Flesh" at the outset had a couple of strong points in its favor. Joe Pasternak is a producer with a sure touch for plush entertainment; Lana Turner is a star of considerable allure; Helen Deutsch has fashioned some fine scripts, and, finally, the title indicates a provocative story, potentially loaded with tension and rife with sex.

In its final form, the film still retains several exploitable assets, such as the very nature of the tramp character played by Miss Turner and the fine color which enhances the beauty of the Italian scenery. Also, exhibs likely will not pass up the comparatively rare opportunity of dangling before their patrons the prospect of seeing Miss Turner undressing to her slip.

All of which does not obscure the fact that "Flame and the Flesh" is a talky, occasionally even dull picture that misses the mark by a mile marred by an inept script and a couple of indecisive performances. Miss Turner, looking gay and wholesome rather than sultry and menacing as the part demands, overacts to the point of embarassment under Richard Brooks' direction.

Story casts her as a beautiful but broke adventuress partial to practically any men willing to take up with her. She rouses the sympathy of a young musician (Bonas Colleano) who offers her temporary lodgings. There she meets Carlos Thompson, a singer engaged to Pier Angeli. For a while Thompson manages to resist Miss Turner's taunting advances, but eventually he gives in, leaves his girl at the altar and goes off with the more experienced woman.

Since men continue to interest her, he is racked by jealousy. In the end, Colleano finds them, and Miss Turner, realizing that Thompson is her only real love, gives him up heroically by pretending to take up with a cafe owner.

Brooks' directorial handling suggests an attempt to copy the manner in which some European filmmakers might have treated such a theme. That this doesn't come off is partly the fault of Miss Deutsch's script that never let the Auguste Bailly novel come to life or permit the characters to take on real dimension. Proceedings at times almost resemble a takeoff on the European passion pix.

Miss Turner did her best to portray the scheming female who is "all woman," as she describes herself. Instead she succeeds in being pert and rather crisp and obvious, without much of the animal magnetism the character suggests. There's no denying her looks, however, and her flirtations—despite the overplaying—are fun to watch.

Newcomer Thompson handles his assignment well enough, particularly in the musical sequences which remind of the Pasternak tradition. The lines handed him by Miss Deutsch make it difficult for him to get his teeth into the part and his shows emoting by breathing heavily, a technique copied by Miss Turner in their crucial love scene. Colleano does his best with an unthankful part. Miss Angeli is a beauty and an actress deserving of better parts than this. She registered in an essentially colorless role.

If Pasternak was out of his element with this yarn, he nevertheless contributed some fine sets and some very pleasant musical interludes. Nicholas Brodzky wrote a couple of tuneful melodies including "Languida," "By Candlelight" and "Then I Loved," all well sung by Thompson. Lensing was fine but didn't show much imagination. *Hift.*

Dial M For Murder
(3-D—COLOR)

Familiar names with Hitchcock reputation for mellers help this film version of the legit hit rate attention.

Hollywood, April 27.

Warner Bros. release of Alfred Hitchcock presentation. Stars Ray Milland, Grace Kelly, Robert Cummings; features John Williams, Anthony Dawson. Directed by Hitchcock. Screenplay, Frederick Knott, as adapted from his play; camera (WarnerColor), Robert Burks; editor, Rudi Fehr; score, Dimitri Tiomkin. Previewed April 21, '54. Running time, **105 MINS.**

Tony	Ray Milland
Margot	Grace Kelly
Mark	Robert Cummings
Inspector Hubbard	John Williams
Capt. Lesgate	Anthony Dawson
The Storyteller	Leo Britt
Pearson	Patrick Allen
Williams	George Leigh
1st Detective	George Alderson
Police Sergeant	Robin Hughes

(*Aspect ratio*: 1.85-1)

The melodramatics in Frederick Knott's legit hit, "Dial M for Murder," have been transferred to the screen virtually intact, but they are not as impressive on film as they are behind the footlights. However, Alfred Hitchcock's reputation for screen suspense and the familiar name of Ray Milland as the chief exponent of suave evil sharpen the possibilities for the Warner Bros. release.

Picture was filmed in 3-D and WarnerColor. The tints are good, adding to production values, but the depth treatment is a distraction that contributes little to the meller mood. It can be shown in regular widescreen 2-D, perhaps the more acceptable projection method for the majority of its playdate prospects.

Knott adapted and scripted his play for the Hitchcock film presentation, but neglected, as did the director, to take full advantage of the screen's expansive powers. As a result, "Dial M" remains more of a filmed play than a motion picture, unfortunately revealed as a conversation piece about murder which talks up much more suspense than it actually delivers. The camera's probing eye also discloses that there's very little that's new in the Knott plotting or in the situations which he uses to play it off over a rather long 105 minutes.

Co-starring with Milland are Grace Kelly, his wife and the intended murder victim, and Robert Cummings, her lover, who has a rather fruitless part in the resolution of the melodramatics. They make up a very able trio, and within the limitations imposed by the screenplay turn in excellent performances. Hitchcock's direction makes good use of Robert Burks' mobile cameras to suggest movement and action through varying lensing angles. The scene rarely shifts from the Milland-Kelly London apartment and it is within the confines of its walls that the principals talk out the story action.

Milland plots his wife's death, figuring on using Anthony Dawson for the actual killing while he has an alibi established elsewhere. The scheme goes awry. Miss Kelly kills Dawson, whom she believes to be a housebreaker, and Milland twists facts to make it appear she committed murder to stop blackmail. Just as it seems he will get away with his new plot, John Williams, playing the inspector, tricks Milland into giving away the entire scheme, thus saving Miss Kelly from a hanging to which she had already been sentenced.

There are a number of basic weaknesses in the setup that keep the picture from being a good suspense show for any but the most gullible. Via the performances and several suspense tricks expected of Hitchcock, the weaknesses are glossed over to some extent, but not enough to rate the film a cinch winner. Dawson and Williams, both from the legit cast of the play, repeat their characters here. Dawson registers much the best on the screen, having fewer of the stagey posturings that Williams displays.

As noted, Burks' color photography is good, especially when seen flat (as was the latter part of the picture at the preview when the 3-D went bad). An unobtrusive background score by Dimitri Tiomkin supports the melodrama. *Brog.*

Fireman Save My Child
(MUSIC)

Spike Jones and City Slickers in hilariously zany slapstick for general situations.

Hollywood, April 27.

Universal release of Howard Christie production. Stars Spike Jones and His City Slickers, Buddy Hackett, Hugh O'Brian; features Tom Brown, Adele Jergens, George Cleveland, Willis Bouchey, Henry Kulky. Directed by Leslie Goodwins. Screenplay, Lee Loeb and John Grant; story by Loeb; camera, Clifford Stine; editor, Russell Schoengarth; musical supervision, Joseph Gershenson. Previewed April 14, '54. Running time, **79 MINS.**

Lt. McGinty	Spike Jones
Firemen	His City Slickers
Smokey	Burry Hackett
Smitty	Hugh O'Brian
Capt. Bill Peters	Tom Brown
Harry's Wife	Adele Jergens
Chief Rorty	George Cleveland
Mayor	Willis Bouchey
Harry	Henry Kulky
Commissioner Spencer	Harry Cheshire
Mayor's Wife	Madge Blake
Tucker	Tristram Coffin
Crane	John Cliff

(*Aspect ratio*: 2-1)

A fast session of titters, yocks and howls are loosed in "Fireman Save My Child," a hilariously zany slapstick affair starring Spike Jones and His City Slickers. It is a completely uninhibited romp of the old two-reeler school that grinds out an unrelenting attack on the risibilities. A good response to the fun seems certain in the general market and Jones and his musicmakers (sic) probably will be back at U for similar offerings.

"Fireman" started out as a vehicle for Abbott & Costello, with the Jones outfit to occupy a music-comedy place. Lou Costello's illness resulted in a rewrite, with Jones and his boys taking over the top spots while Buddy Hackett and Hugh O'Brian were recruited to handle the old A&C parts. As a team, the latter pair command a respectable share of the laughs, but it's Jones and several of his crew, most particularly Freddie Morgan, the eloquently silent banjoist, who rate the aisle-roller response.

Lee Loeb and John Grant concocted the screenplay from a story by Loeb, coming up with a session of laugh situations and repeating gag gimmicks that invite roars. In fact, any staid ticket buyer that inadvertently becomes a witness of this show will laugh even if he hates himself for it. Plot, such as it is, revolves around the motorization of a 1910 San Francisco fire station, the crew of which is made up of Jones and his Slickers, plus O'Brian and the addlepated Hackett, rookie fireman who has invented a new type of fire extinguisher.

Leslie Goodwins' direction whips the frenetics along at a swift pace and belts over the running gags for full effect as the plot maneuvers to the point where villains try to steal Hackett's formula but meet their fate in a wild finale. Such gags as having an old fire horse beating the motor truck to every blaze and the whipping of a fireman from a skidding truck into the assorted apartments of Adele Jergens and Henry Kulky enroute to every fire keep up the laugh quota, as does the immpossible haircut and pantomime of Morgan, with assists from the almost-as-ludicrous Earl Bennett.

Among the others who get into the act to good purpose are Tom Brown, George Cleveland, Willis Bouchey. Typical Jones arrangements of "Poet & Peasant Overture," "Pass the Biscuits, Mirandy," "In a Persian Market," "Dance of the Hours" and "There'll Be a Hot Time In the Old Town Tonight" are heard at intervals throughout as part of the assorted rib-ticklers producer Howard Christie has furnished the presentation. Clifford Stine's lensing and the other technical factors, including Russell Schoengarth's editing, do their part in keeping the laughs rolling. *Brog.*

John Wesley
(BRITISH-COLOR)

Fine color film on the 18th century evangelist.

Produced by Radio & Film Commission of Methodist Church in cooperation with J. Arthur Rank and Religious Films, Ltd.; no theatrical release set. Directed by Norman Walker. Screenplay, Lawrence Barrett; camera (EastmanColor), Hone Glendenning, Stanley Grant; editor, Dave Powell; music, Henry Reed. Previewed N.Y., April 22, '54. Running time, **77 MINS.**

John Wesley	Leonard Sachs
As a Child	Gerald Loha
As a Student	Neil Heayes
Rev. Samuel Wesley	Keith Pyott
Susannah Wesley	Curigwen Lewis
Charles Wesley	Derek Aylward
Peter Bohler, a Moravian	John Witty

Birth of the Methodist movement in 18th century England is dramatically chronicled in this semi-documentary film that's based upon some of the high points in the long career of John Wesley—churchman, educator and evangelist. In many respects, the picture is similar to "Martin Luther" which the Louis de Rochemont Organization produced for the Lutheran Church.

But where "Luther" is winning wide theatrical distribution and stout grosses under careful salesmanship of the de Rochemont outfit, "Wesley" won't tap such a market for some time. For, it's understood, some 500 churches which contributed toward the $200,000 production cost received "first-run" privileges over a period of months. Until this situation is resolved, it's unknown whether theatrical release will be arranged, if at all.

Moreover, the producers of the film emphasize that "It was not made as an entertainment film but as a teaching film . . . However, exhibitors have expressed delight with its entertainment qualities." Original plans provided for a 55-minute black and white picture on a small budget but the project later was expanded to 77 minutes to embrace more aspects of John Wesley's influence. Eastman color was utilized to bring about an "added effectiveness."

Another interesting facet to this celluloid venture of the Methodist Church is that J. Arthur Rank (a prominent Methodist layman) made the film at cost in Britain. Under the production guidance of Clifford Jeapes who was assigned to the project by Religious Films, Ltd., London, the film painstakingly traces John Wesley's efforts to work out his own personal salvation. After achieving this goal he not only carries his evangelism to the common man but spreads the philosophy of Methodism through educational, social service groups and other media.

Throughout the film, which Lawrence Barrett screenplayed from material amassed by historians, the subject matter is often dry and wordy. There is no sex or comedy relief, and wasn't any in Wesley's dedicated life. Accent is entirely on Wesley and his untiring devotion to his principles. The serious minded will find the theme a refreshing and enlightening one.

Educational values of the picture from the Methodist standpoint are especially heightened by the fine and moving portrayal of Wesley by Leonard Sachs. A long cast of players, practically all unknown to American filmgoers, provides excellent support under the firm direction of Norman Walker. Production values bespeak a budget far in excess of the reported $200,000 cost while the Eastman color cam-

era work of Hone Glendenning and Stanley Grant is superb. Print, incidentally is by Pathe. Other technical credits are in keeping with the general quality of the film.
Gilb.

The Fortyniners

Static western with name of Wild Bill Elliott to get by in oater situations.

Hollywood, April 23.
Allied Artists release of a Vincent M. Fennelly production. Stars Wild Bill Elliott; features Virginia Grey, Henry Morgan. Directed by Thomas Carr; screenplay, Dan Ullman; editor, Sam Fields, music, Raoul Kraushaar. Previewed April 23, '54. Running time, 71 MINS.
Sam Nelson .... Wild Bill Elliott
Stella Walker .... Virginia Grey
Alf Billings .... Henry Morgan
Ernie Walker .... John Doucette
William Norris .... Lane Bradford
Everett .... Stanford Jolley
Gambler .... Harry Lauter
1st Hotel Clerk .... Earle Hodgins
Sloane .... Dean Cromer
Burtender .... Ralph Sanford
(Aspect ratio: 1:85-1)

Over-plottage and too many story gaps without the star reduce this latest Wild Bill Elliott entry to an also-ran category, although the Elliott name will ensure some reception. Star needs better material than this.

Script twirls around Elliott, a U.S. marshal, on the trail of three men involved in the murder of another Federal agent in California of 1849. Plot development is weak, story lacking the virility necessary for a successful Elliott western. Insertion of narration to cover some of the action also is a strike against the Vincent M. Fennelly production.

Elliott is persuasive enough as he scouts the gold camps in search of a crooked gambler, Henry Morgan, who furnished two killers in the murder, but once he's found him it's Morgan who proceeds to dominate the footage from here on in. The marshal doesn't disclose his identity, posing as a gunman, and after saving Morgan from a gambling scrape attaches himself to the cardsharp in the hopes he'll drop names of the two killers. Action picks up only when star mows down one of gunmen in a face-to-face encounter.

Star makes a pitch for a good performance but doesn't stand any too much chance with material afforded him except in the few shooting scenes. Morgan, on the other hand, turns in an excellent portrayal through a strongly-developed character. Virginia Grey in a smaller role delivers convincingly as the wife of one of the killers, John Doucette, who with Lane Bradford as the other gunman score. Thomas Carr's direction isn't able to overcome rambling aspects of script by Dan Ullman.
Whit.

Living It Up
(SONGS-COLOR)

Martin & Lewis pepping up new version of 'Hazel Flagg,' legiter; (previously "Nothing Sacred," film). Good fun and prospects.

Hollywood, April 24.
Paramount release of Paul Jones production. Stars Dean Martin, Jerry Lewis; co-starring Janet Leigh, Edward Arnold; features Fred Clark, Sheree North, Sammy White. Directed by Norman Taurog. Screenplay, Jack Rose and Melville Shavelson; from the musical comedy, "Hazel Flagg," book by Ben Hecht; music, Jule Styne; lyrics, Bob Hilliard; based on a story by James Street; camera (Technicolor), Daniel Fapp; editor, Archie Marshek; music arranged and conducted by Walter Scharf; choreography, Nick Castle. Previewed April 23, '54. Running time, 94 MINS.
Steve .... Dean Martin
Homer .... Jerry Lewis
Wally Cook .... Janet Leigh
The Mayor .... Edward Arnold
Oliver Stone .... Fred Clark
Jitterbug Dancer .... Sheree North
Walter .... Sammy White
Master of Ceremonies ...... Sid Tomack
Dr. Egelhofer .... Sig Ruman
Dr. Lee .... Richard Loo
Conductor .... Raymond Greenleaf
Isaiah .... Walter Baldwin
(Aspect ratio: 1.85-1)

The durable, and adaptable, comedy originally seen in the 1937 film, "Nothing Sacred," and more recently in the Broadway musical titled "Hazel Flagg," are back on display in "Living It Up." This time the exponents are Dean Martin and Jerry Lewis, a laugh team that knows what to do with the vehicle's basic merits and which points it for a good response in most all playdates.

The screenplay by Jack Rose and Melville Shavelson requires the team to be less hectic than usual, but Lewis is still permitted to break loose with enough wild moments to sprinkle some guffaws among the chuckles. The pair handles the comedy and songs for excellent effect under Norman Taurog's well-valued direction, the pacing moves forward with very few lagging moments and, generally, it adds up to a worthwhile 94 minutes of film fun that has been expertly packaged for customer enjoyment in the Paul Jones production.

The characters in the plot have undergone more changes of sex than Christine. The late Carole Lombard did the character played here by Lewis. In the stage musical it was also feminine, as was the editor character, which is now back to masculine, as it was in the original film when played by the late Walter Connolly. The reporter role played by Fredric March in "Nothing Sacred" is now a femme in the person of Janet Leigh. No matter how it, or its characters, are shuffled and changed around, the basic comedy still endures and entertains.

Jule Styne and Bob Hilliard contributed three new songs to "Living It Up" and four were drawn from the stage musical. Most are handled by Martin, and well, with the topper being "How Do You Speak to An Angel," from the stage. Good also is the new "That's What I Like." Lewis has his vocal moments with "Champagne and Wedding Cake," plus a brief reprise of "Angel," and teams with Martin on a finale production number terper tagged "Every Street's a Boulevard." Others are "You Are the Bravest," "Money Burns a Hole

in My Pocket" and "You're Gonna Dance With Me Baby," the latter teeing off a wild jitterbug production number in which Sheree North makes her only appearance as a fringe-waving, head-shaking terper with Lewis.

Lewis plays the station master at a western flag-stop who is believed to be radio-active. Sobsister Janet Leigh convinces editor Fred Clark the poor guy should be brought to New York and given the celebrity treatment. Lewis, by now aware he's okay despite a poor diagnosis by medico Martin, comes to the big city and has a ball, all the while trying to keep the truth from Miss Leigh and her boss. Truth will out, but not until after a goodly round of laughs have been clocked.

Miss Leigh is a pretty package to add looks to the comedy and Clark socks a lot of chuckles with his editor characterization. Edward Arnold, as the mayor; Sammy White, very funny as a waiter; Sig Ruman and Richard Loo, excellent as doctors called in to examine Lewis, and the others, including Morgan, the sad-faced Bassett hound of tv fame, are good.

The Technicolor photography by Daniel Fapp heads the list of expert technical contributions. Walter Scharf arranged and conducted the music and Nick Castle staged the dances. Settings in the big city are lush.
Brog.

About Mrs. Leslie

Shirley Booth, Robert Ryan in mature drama especially slanted for distaffer interest and good b.o. prospects.

Hollywood, April 30.
Paramount release of Hal Wallis production. Stars Shirley Booth, Robert Ryan; co-stars Marjie Millar, Alex Nicol. Directed by Daniel Mann. Screenplay, Ketti Frings, Hal Kanter; from the novel by Vina Delmar; camera, Ernest Laszlo; editor, Warren Low; score, Victor Young. Previewed April 26, '54. Running time, 104 MINS.
Mrs. Vivien Leslie .... Shirley Booth
George Leslie .... Robert Ryan
Nadine Roland .... Marjie Millar
Lan McKay .... Alex Nicol
Harry Willey .... Sammy White
Mr. Poole .... James Bell
Pixie .... Eilene Janssen
Mort Finley .... Philip Ober
Fred Blue .... Henry Morgan
Marion King .... Gale Page
Mrs. Poole .... Virginia Brissac
Mr. Pope .... Ian Wolfe
Mrs. Croffman .... Ellen Corby
Barney .... Ray Teal

"About Mrs. Leslie" returns Shirley Booth to the screen in what is best termed a "woman's show." It is a picture carefully calculated to whip up distaffer sympathy for its middle-aged heroine. Since this type of romantic escapism, more frequently labelled "soap opera," is enjoying a popular market currently, "Mrs. Leslie" seems in for a good money run through its playdates. Matinees in particular should be above average.

Miss Booth's fine talent, already much honored, was a natural choice for the Hal Wallis production from the Vina Delmar novel. Also, it re-teams her with Daniel Mann as director and Ketti Frings as scripter, two artists who played significant parts in the same capacities on Miss Booth's first film starrer, "Come Back, Little Sheba." This trio, as well as co-stars Robert Ryan, Marjie Millar and Alex Nicol, make the Wallis presentation a worthwhile piece of entertainment for the femme and more mature theatregoer.

With all of its good points, though, "Mrs. Leslie" is not the kind of picture that will be completely acceptable to all types of audiences, particularly many males and the younger, more action-minded fans. To them it is apt to be a leisurely-told soaper only occasionally interesting, and sometimes quite tedious during its long 104 minutes of footage. Since the great romance in Mrs. Leslie's life is told via flashback, the emotions don't have the impact they would have had had the scenes been in the present. However, they do arouse compassion as the players interpret the well-written words and situations of scripters Ketti Frings and Hal Kanter.

The back street love in Mrs. Leslie's life is unfolded against a Beverly Hills boarding house setting (on the wrong side of Wilshire), as the middle-aged woman is stirred to remember her past by the little dramatic situations that come up with her tenants. The first flashback shows her, a third-rate singer in cheap N. Y. niteries, meeting Ryan, an aircraft industrialist, and accepting his offer of a six-week vacation in California. Each year, the couple return to the beach hideaway until war's end, when he dies of a heart attack and she buys the Bevhills house. Ryan is a splendid partner in these sequences with Miss Booth.

Of concern to the present in the plot are Miss Millar and Nicol, two rather mixed up young people. She's a former Sunset Strip nightlife girl, now in earnest about acting, and he's an ex-G.I. running away from the dominance of a rich brother-in-law. They make a fine pair as the young lovers, both showing up excellently in competition with the older players. Miss Millar, in particular, impresses. Eilene Janssen, in a stinging portrayal of a teenager; James Bell and Virginia Brissac, worried parents, and Henry Morgan, wolfish agent, are among some of the others adding to the assorted acting merits.

The Victor Young background score expertly frame's the drama's mood and the Ernest Laszlo lensing is another top credit. Miss Booth sings two oldies. "Kiss the Boys Goodbye" and "I'm in the Mood for Love" pleasantly in her saloon chirp role. *Brog.*

Johnny Guitar
(SONG-COLOR)

Joan Crawford's marquee worth to bolster only fair piece of western entertainment. Prospects spotty.

Hollywood, May 4.

Republic release (no producer credit). Stars Joan Crawford; co-stars Sterling Hayden, Mercedes McCambridge, Scott Brady; features Ward Bond, Ben Cooper, Ernest Borgnine, John Carradine, Royal Dano, Frank Ferguson, Paul Fix, Rhys Williams, Ian MacDonald. Directed by Nicholas Ray. Screenplay, Philip Yordan; camera (Trucolor), Harry Stradling; edicamera (Truecolor), Harry Stradling; editor, Richard L. Van Enger; music, Victor Young; song, Peggy Lee and Young; sung by Miss Lee. Previewed April 30, '54. Running time, **111 MINS.**

Vienna .... Joan Crawford
Johnny Guitar .... Sterling Hayden
Emma Small......Mercedes McCambridge
Dancin' Kid .... Scott Brady
John McIvers .... Ward Bond
Turkey Ralston .... Ben Cooper
Bart Lonergan .... Ernest Borgnine
Old Tom .... John Carradine
Corey .... Royal Dano
Marshal Williams .... Frank Ferguson
Eddie .... Paul Fix
Mr. Andrews .... Rhys Williams
Pete .... Ian MacDonald

(*Aspect ratio*: 1.66-1)

Joan Crawford, whose last western was Metro's "Montana Moon" in 1930, has another try at the wide open spaces with "Johnny Guitar." Like "Moon," it proves the actress should leave saddles and levis to someone else and stick to city lights for a background. "Guitar" is only a fair piece of entertainment, seemingly headed for spotty returns, even with exploitation.

The Roy Chanslor novel on which Philip Yordan based the screenplay provides this Republic release with a conventional oater basis. Had the makers played it straight it would have been much better entertainment for the masses. Instead, scripter Yordan and director Nicholas Ray become so involved with character nuances and neuroses, all wrapped up in dialog, that "Johnny Guitar" never has enough chance to rear up in the saddle and ride at an acceptable outdoor pace. It will be a major disappointment to loyal Crawford fans, even though they will give the picture some initial business.

Miss Crawford plays Vienna, strong-willed owner of a plush gambling saloon standing alone in the wilderness of Arizona. The solitude doesn't bother Vienna; she knows the railroad's coming through and she will build a whole new town and get rich. Opposing her is Mercedes McCambridge, bitter, frustrated leader of a nearby community, who has egged the ranchers and others into taking her side in the fight by using their fear of the settlers and fences that will come with the rails.

Love, hate and violence, with little sympathy for the characters, is stirred up during the overlong 111 minutes of film. Near the climax the picture takes on the appearance and rough action of a western, all of which would have been to more effective purpose had not it been so long in coming. The people in the story never achieve much depth, this character shallowness being at odds with the pretentious attempt at analysis to which the script and direction devotes so much time.

Republic's Trucolor process was used to dye the footage and under the camera-wielding of Harry Stradling the hues are an effective part of the film's sight values. *Brog.*

Blackout

Overlong, talky, lowercase meller filmed in England with Dane Clark heading cast.

Hollywood, April 16.

Lippert Pictures release of Michael Carreras (Hammer) production. Stars Dane Clark, Belinda Lee; features Betty Ann Davies, Eleanor Summerfield, Andrew Osborn, Harold Lang. Directed by Terence Fisher. Screenplay, Richard Landau; based on a novel by Helen Nielsen; camera, Jimmy Harvey; editor, Maurice Rootes; music, Ivor Slaney. Previewed April 15, '54. Running time, **87 MINS.**

Casey Morrow .... Dane Clark
Phyllis Brunner .... Belinda Lee
Alicia Brunner .... Betty Ann Davies
Maggie Doone .... Eleanor Summerfield
Lance Gorden .... Andrew Osborn
Travis .... Harold Lang
Miss Nardis .... Jill Melford
Lita Huntley .... Alvis Maben
Inspector Johnson .... Michael Golden
Ernie .... Alfie Bass

This is a gabby, overlong, import from England that has Dane Clark heading the cast as the only name known in the domestic market. Condition of the supporting feature market is such currently that the film will have no trouble getting bookings, even though it offers scant measure of entertainment.

Clark, while drunk, is hired by Belinda Lee to marry her. He blacksout, comes to the next day in the studio of artist Eleanor Summerfield, with blood on his coat, no memory of the night before's events, a missing bride and a murdered father-in-law. What to do is a constant puzzle to Clark, while what's going on is a constant puzzle to the audience, but somehow, the finale finds Clark back with his bride, whose mother has confessed she murdered to escape exposure for some charity swindles.

There's nothing the players can do with the plot as presented under the production helming of Michael Carreras, and Terence Fisher's direction is deliberate to the extreme, even for a British offering. Richard Landau scripted the Helen Nielsen novel and Jimmy Harvey photographed. Miss Lee, who toplines with Clark, is attractive and seemingly a promising talent. Miss Summerfield also is better than the material. Betty Ann Davies plays the mother and Andrew Osborn a suspect.

"St. Louis Blues" is used as a jazzy background tune for the opening pub sequence in which Clark gets himself hired. The background score was done by Ivor Slaney. *Brog.*

The Long Wait

Program meller with ballyhoo angles and familiar names to help through general run of bookings.

Hollywood, April 28.

United Artists release of Parklane (Lesser Samuels) production. Stars Anthony Quinn, Charles Coburn, Gene Evans, Peggie Castle; features Mary Ellen Kay, Shawn Smith, Dolores Donlon. Directed by Victor Saville. Screenplay, Alan Green and Lesser Samuels, from the Mickey Spillane novel; camera, Franz Planer; editor, Ronald Sinclair; music, Mario Castlenuovo-Tedesco, conducted by Irving Gertz; song, Harold Spine and Bob Russell. Previewed April 26, '54. Running time, **94 MINS.**

Johnny McBride .... Anthony Quinn
Gardiner .... Charles Coburn
Servo .... Gene Evans
Venus .... Peggy Castle
Wendy .... Mary Ellen Kay
Carol .... Shawn Smith
Troy .... Dolores Donlon
Tucker .... Barry Kelley
Lindsey .... James Millican
Packman .... Bruno Ve Sota
Bellboy .... Jay Adler
Logan .... John Daaler
Pop Henderson .... Frank Marlowe

(*Aspect ratio*: 1.75-1)

Program melodramatics, with familiar names and assorted ballyhoo angles, have been packaged in "The Long Wait" for average prospects in the general run of bookings. Had it used more clarity in the story and less footage in the telling, it would have served its release intentions more satisfactorily.

The Parklane presentation through United Artists was produced by Lesser Samuels and directed by Victor Saville from the Mickey Spillane novel. While a Spillane-type tale, it is not one of that writer's private eye mellers, but does classify as a "paper back" thriller in every other respect, right down to a man character continually clutching skimpily-clad blondes. Samuels scripted with Alan Green, but the screenplay's story points are so obscure that viewers will constantly wonder what's going on. Neither Saville's direction nor the playing is able to shed much light on the plotting.

Anthony Quinn tops the cast as an amnesia victim tricked into returning to the hometown he left two years before and doesn't remember. There he finds he has run away from a murder and robbery rap. Everyone in town knows him, including the police, but they let him stay out of jail because the accident that wiped out his memory also burned off the fingerprints from his hands. Four dames, Peggie Castle, Mary Ellen Kay, Shawn Smith and Dolores Donlon, are mixed up with the dubious hero. One of them is his old girl friend, who has undergone plastic surgery, but even after getting very familiar with each in turn he's not able to figure things out. In between the romancing he's dodging bullets flung around by Gene Evans' gang and the crime trail eventually leads to Charles Coburn, respected banker. Quinn is cleared of old charges and Miss Kay is unveiled as the sweetie who gets him at the finale.

Quinn does as much as possible with the male lead and, of the femmes, Misses Kay and Smith come over best, although Miss Castle is a sharp Venus in the plotting. Coburn is virtually wasted in an obscure role and there's not much menace in Evans or his henchmen. Franz Planer's lensing generally goes along with the meller mood, although included to get very arty in some scenes. The score and a Harold Spina-Bob Russell tune, "Once" are okay. *Brog.*

The Rocket Man

Below par juve-angled comedy.

20th-Fox release of Panoramic (Leonard Goldstein) production. Stars Charles Coburn, Spring Byington, Anne Francis, John Agar, George Winslow; features Stanley Clements, Emory Powell, June Clayworth, Don Haggerty, Beverly Garland. Directed by Oscar Rudolph. Screenplay, Lenny Bruce, Jack Henley; story, George W. George, George F. Slavin; camera, John Sertz; editor, Paul Weatherwax. Previewed in N.Y., April 21, '54. Running time, **79 MINS.**

Mayor Ed Johnson......Charles Coburn
Justice Ameilia Brown...Spring Byington
Timmy .... George Winslow
June Brown .... Anne Francis
Tom Baxter .... John Agar
Big Bill Watkins........ Emory Parnell
Bob .... Stanley Clements
Ludine .... Beverly Garland
Miss Snedley .... June Clayworth
Officer O'Brien .... Don Haggerty

(*Aspect Ratio*: 1:33 to 1)

The current juve fad for science fiction on tv is the probable reason for this 79-minute item from Leonard Goldstein's Panoramic Productions. Film is low-budget in every department including scripting and thesping and doesn't add up as adequate supporting fare.

Yarn, scripted for the screen by Lenny Bruce and Jack Henley from a story by George W. George and George F. Slavin, revolves about an orphan, who had been gifted with a magic space gun, and how he and the gun help rid a smalltown of its crooked politico and straighten out the lives of a couple of lovebirds as well as the town's mayor and the distaff justice of the peace, who had adopted him. Doubtful if even the moppets, at whom this is obviously aimed, will buy it.

Such vet thesps as Charles Coburn and Spring Byington, as the mayor and j.o.p., respectively, seem trapped in the proceedings. George Winslow, as the kid with the science fixation, fails in his efforts to be a winning screen moppet. Anne Francis and John Agar aren't much help in the romance department.

Oscar Rudolph's direction is static and the technical credits display pic's low-budget makeup. *Gros.*

Gorilla at Large
(3-D—COLOR)

Exploitation programmer with okay prospects in regular market.

Hollywood, April 30.

20th-Fox release of Panoramic (Leonard Goldstein) production, produced by Robert L. Jacks. Stars Cameron Mitchell, Anne Bancroft; features Lee J. Cobb, Raymond Burr, Charlotte Austin, Peter Whitney, Lee Marvin. Directed by Harmon Jones. Written by Leonard Praskins and Barney Slater; camera (Technicolor), Lloyd Ahern; editor, George A. Gittens; musical direction, Lionel Newman. Previewed April 27, '54. Running Time **93 MINS.**

Joey Matthews	Cameron Mitchell
Laverne Miller	Anne Bancroft
Detective Sgt. Garrison	Lee J. Cobb
Cyrus Miller	Raymond Burr
Audrey Baxter	Charlotte Austin
Kovacs	Peter Whitney
Shaughnessy	Lee Marvin
Mack	Warren Stevens
Morse	John G. Kellogg
Owens	Charles Tannen

(Aspect ratio: 1.66-1)

This Panoramic presentation through 20th-Fox is a 3-D exploitation feature in Technicolor that stacks up as a good entry for the general market at which it is aimed. It's a better grade programmer that concentrates on getting the proper values for that classification.

The thriller is fashioned around an amusement park background, which gives a colorful setting for the action developed in the expertly fashioned script by Leonard Praskins and Barney Slater, and under the directorial helming of Harmon Jones. Robert L. Jacks produced under the executive supervision of Leonard Goldstein and the picture will be available on Pola-Lite's single-strip system, so that the double-print bugaboos that plague 3-D releases will be avoided. A good case for Pola-Lite or similar systems was made at the "Gorilla" preview when the dual prints went out of sync and the last half of the film had to be shown flat.

Cameron Mitchell, law student working in the amusement park carnival, and Anne Bancroft, trapeze artist, star in the presentation and both do their parts well. Miss Bancroft cuts a fine figure in her brief, skin-tight costumes, a display that will not be overlooked by male viewers, even had their attention not been directed that way by the direction and camera angles. Lee J. Cobb, detective sergeant; Raymond Burr, carney owner and Miss Bancroft's husband; Charlotte Austin, Mitchell's sweetie, and Peter Whitney, trainer of the title monster, are the principal featured players who help put over the tale of horror and violence.

The plot rings in its meller complications with the murder of John G. Kellogg, carnival barker, apparently by Whitney's great ape. Also suspected are Burr, who had just fired Kellogg, and Cameron, who resented his attentions to Miss Austin. There's another killing and more suspicious circumstances before Miss Bancroft is revealed as the beautiful murderess. To pay her debt to society she must be rescued from the ape, who has carried her atop the roller coaster, a job Miller tackles to clear himself with the law and it puts a thriller cap on the film.

Assisting the principals are Lee Marvin, doing a good study of a talkative cop; Warren Stevens, Kellogg and Charles Tannen, as well as the performer who wears the monkey suit. Lloyd Ahern's camera angling adds interest, as do the carnival settings, the score directed by Lionel Newman and the other contributions. *Brog.*

Laughing Anne
(Anglo-U.S.)
(COLOR—SONGS)

Dull South Seas adventure based on a Joseph Conrad story; lightweight entertainment.

Hollywood, April 27.

Republic release of Herbert Wilcox production. Stars Wendell Corey, Margaret Lockwood, Forrest Tucker, Ronald Shiner. Directed by Wilcox. Screenplay, Pamela Bower; story by Joseph Conrad; camera (Technicolor), Max Greene; editor, Basil Warren; score, Anthony Collins; songs, Ted Grouya, Pierre Roche, Geoffrey Parsons. Previewed, April 22, '54. Running time, **90 MINS.**

Captain Davidson	Wendell Corey
Laughing Anne	Margaret Lockwood
Jem Farrell	Forrest Tucker
Nobby Clark	Ronald Shiner
Joseph Conrad	Robert Harris
Frenchie	Jacques Brunius
Blonde Singer	Daphne Anderson
Susan Davidson	Helen Shingler
Nicholas	Danny Green
Jacques	Harold Lang
Conrad's Companion	Edgar Norfolk
David	Sean Lynch
Davy	Gerard Lohan
Chinese Merchant	Andy Ho
Battling Bruinius	Maurice Bush
First Boxer	Dave Crowley
Second Boxer	Jack Cooper
M. of Ceremonies	Rudolph Offenbach
First Escort	Christopher Rhodes
Second Escort	John Serret
Third Escort	Michael Oldham
Pianist	Bernard Robel
Pierre	Joe Powell
Bartender	Julian Sherier
Charlie	Nandl

(Aspect ratio: 1.85-1)

Produced and directed in England for distribution by Republic, "Laughing Anne" is a stilted, old-fashioned type of adventure drama that will draw a goodly share of laughs where none is intended. Wendell Corey and Forrest Tucker are familiar names for stateside audiences, teaming with Britishers Margaret Lockwood and Ronald Shiner in the starring roles, but there is scant entertainment merit to back up their use in this overlength, slowly-paced offering.

Herbert Wilcox produced and directed from a poorly written script by Pamela Bower. Latter fails to capture any of the flavor of Joseph Conrad's story. Admittedly, Conrad is a difficult author to film, but neither the scripter nor Wilcox show much insight. As a consequence, the pace is slow, and the entertainment and performances of the programmer variety, even though the footage runs 90 minutes.

Miss Lockwood plays the title role of a Parisian singer who drifts to the South Seas with her lover, Forrest Tucker, a prizefighter who has lost the use of his hands. Across her path drifts Corey, a good man and captain of a small trading schooner. She makes a stowaway voyage with him and they fall in love, but she spurns his offer of marriage, returns to Tucker. Several years later, their paths cross again and she warns Corey that Tucker plans to rob his ship of a silver shipment. In the ensuing fight, both Miss Lockwood and Tucker are killed and Corey takes her son away to sea with him. The performances by these three are as unbelievable as the scripting. So is Shiner's work as the mate on Corey's ship. Others do small bits.

"I've Fallen in Deep Water," by Ted Grouya and Geoffrey Parsons, and "All the World Is Mine on Sunday," by Pierre Roche and Parsons, are the songs done by the Lockwood character. The Technicolor camera work by Max Greene is passable, but the process work is extremely poor. Editing permits the footage to run long over its logical length. *Brog.*

Stratford Adventure
(DOCUMENTARY)

Toronto, April 27.

Columbia release of Canadian National Film Board production. Stars Alex Guinness, Tyrone Guthrie, Irene Worth; with personnel of the Stratford (Ontario) Shakespearean Festival. Produced by Guy Glover. Directed by Morten Parker. Screenplay, Gudrun Parker; camera (Eastman), Don Wilder; editing, Douglas Tunstall; music, Louis Applebaum; sound recording, Joseph Champagne; sound editing, Kenneth Healy-Ray. University Theatre, Toronto, April 22, '54. Running time, **40 MINS.**

This color documentary, with name lure for marquee and exploitation purposes, tells the story of how an Ontario town of 19,000 people, namely Stratford, proceeded last summer to emulate its namesake in Britain to present a six-weeks' series of Shakespearean plays that had an overall 98% b.o. sale at $6 top plus tax. (Stratford, Conn. is trying currently to do likewise) "Stratford Adventure" is a dramatic and suspenseful blueprint of a venture which, with Alex Guinness starring in "Richard III" and "All's Well that Ends Well," with Tyrone Guthrie directing, saw top New York critics covering, plus considerable international publicity. For the picture, the entire cast and working personnel donated their services last summer but production costs were still over $100,000 for this State-financed documentary.

On general audience interest, coupled with superb photography, film traces the trials and growth of the Shakespearean Festival from its inception as a dream that overcame civic apathy on initial money grants, plus financial vicissitudes that were finally met by last minute five-figure sums from wealthy out-of-town donors; and then a town overflowing with heavy international tourist biz for six weeks.

Progressive story reconstructs city council debates, the securing of Tyrone Guthrie's interest and his organizing advice, his selling Alex Guinness on coming to Canada for expenses only, the rehearsals and stage action of "Richard III" and "All's Well," the ultimate presentation of a season of Shakespeare on a shoestring. On direction and color photography, the Louis Applebaum music and tight editing, "Stratford Adventure," as the metamorphosis of a small-town, is excellent as lower-case on a double bill, particularly the "art" houses anywhere. *McStay.*

Carosello Napoletano
(Neapolitan Carousel)
(ITALIAN—COLOR)

Cannes, April 27.

Lux Film production and release with Paolo Stoppa, Clelis Matania, Marie Fiore Nad a Gray, Leonide Massine, Antonio, Folco Lulli, Yvette Chauvire, Sophia Loren, Giacomo Rondinella, Alberto Bonnucci, Vittorio Caprioli, Marquis de Cuevas Ballet. Directed by Ettore Giannini; camera (Pathecolor), Piero Portalupi; sets, Mario Chiari; choreography, Massine; editor, Nicolo Lazzari. At Cannes Film Festival. Running time, **125 MINS.**

Salvatore Esposito	Paolo Stoppa
Concetta	Clelia Matania

First large-scale Italian filmusical, this pic rings the bell in all sectors and should pay off its producers handsomely for the impressive effort that went into it. By cutting off some excess weight, "Carousel" can be shaped into a tight package of laughs, color and songs for a strong value on any market and a winner at home. Its unabashed sentimental pitch is especially keyed for Italian audiences, but its buoyant good humor will act to win over new audiences. With special initial handling in U. S., film could spill over into more general runs.

An itinerant family of Neapolitan street singers provides a slight plot frame as it leads viewers through a century-spanning potpourri of song and dance in the shadow of the Vesuvius. Sentiment alternates with humor, dance and song as most-famed Neapolitan songs are given new life, sometimes straight, sometimes with tongue in cheek. Ettore Giannini wrote and directed, helping as well to coordinate the giant production effort, and deserves a large part of the credit. Leonide Massine was in charge of his Marquis de Ballet as well as being spotted in the cast, as is Spanish dancer Antonio, both for positive results.

On the vocal side, Giacomo Rondinella impresses on looks and easy-going style, while Beniamino Gigli's voice, dubbed into the track, adds extra value. Large cast is mostly spotted for short bits, all capable. But the least credit should go to cameraman Piero Portalupi's lensing in Pathecolor, a creative contrib to the pic's visual impact, co-ordinated with Mario Chiari's tasteful sets and Maria De Matteis' costuming.

Pace slackens somewhat at the halfway mark of this two-hour production, but with some generous cuts it should turn into non-letup entertainment with unusual sales values. *Hawk.*

Cronaca di Poveri Amanti
(Chronicle of Poor Lovers)
(ITALIAN)

Cannes, April 27.

Minerva Release of CSPC Production. Stars Anna Maria Fererro, Cosetta Greco, Antonella Lualdi, Marcello Mastrioianni, Wanda Capodaglio; features Bruno Berellini, Irene Cefaro, Eva Vaniceck, Gabriele Tinti, Adolfo Cosolini. Directed by Carloo Lizzani. Screenplay, Lizzani, Massimo Mida, Vasco Pratolini, from novel by Pratolini; camera, Gianni Di Venanzo. At Cannes Film Festival. Running time, **100 MINS.**

Gesuina	Anna Maria Ferrero
Elisa	Cosetta Greco
Milena	Antonella Lualdi
Ugo	Marcello Mastroianni

Filmization of the novel by Vasco Pratolini has the title plus cast weight for average Italian grosses. Reception elsewhere is uncertain.

In telling the story of the inhabitants of Vico de Corno, an alley in Florence, of their troubles with love and politics, "Cronaca," both in novel and in film form, depicts the spirit, the uncertainties and the social changes of the postwar 1920's.

As such, this is an interesting document of its times.

In showing the alley enmity between right and left, Fascism and Communism, director Lizzani sometimes rigs his scales to weight a point at the expense of objectivity, but generally the picture convinces. Pace sags a bit midway, but picks up again and patchwork of characters and plots is successfully handled once the film gets under way.

Acting is fine and underplayed. Antonella Lualdi gives a sensitive portrayal of the girl whose husband is killed by the fascists, Cosetta Greco does well as the prostie, who operates in and about the alley, and Anna Maria Ferrero is as competent as usual as the servant to the invalid woman (neatly played by Irene Cefaro) who owns the alley real estate. Marcello Mastroianni Giuliano Montaldo and Bruno Berellini stand out among the males of the cast.

Uncredited music gives period flavor to the film as does Gianni di Venezno's camerawork. *Hawk.*

Schlagerparade
(Hit Parade)
(GERMAN)

Berlin, April 20.

Herzog release of Melodie production. Stars Germaine Damar, Walter Giller and Karl Schonbock; features Maurice Chevalier, Stan Kenton orch, Margot Hielscher, Sunshine Quartet, Cornel Trio, Schoeneberger Singing Boys, Barnabas Von Geczy orch, RIAS orch, others. Directed by Eric Ode. Screenplay, Alro von Pinelli, H. F. Koellner; camera, Richard Angst; music, Heino Gaze; sets, Karl Weber and Kurt Herlth. At Marmorhaus, Berlin. Running time, **95 MINS.**

Barbara Blanc .... Germaine Damar
Walter Lorenz .... Walter Giller
Fred Pauli .... Karl Schonbock
Sherry Sommer .... Nadja Tiller
Frau Gabler .... Loni Heus
Angelika Gabler .... Renate Danz
Otto Bonnhoff .... Walter Gross
Max Balduweit .... Bully Buhlan

This so-called "German Broadway Melody" features many prominent local singers. It looms here as a terrific moneymaker. But lack of really big names in starring roles, color and pace give "Hit Parade" only mild international possibilities. Ballyhoo via the Stan Kenton orch and Maurice Chevalier, who appear in the film, may help.

Some 16 songs numbers are brought in while the thin plot unfolds. It is the story of a young composer who can't find a publisher. His girl friend finally mahages to smuggle one of his compositions into the repertoire of a prominent composer and the number happens to become the top tune of the hour. The happy ending sees the young composer finding himself acknowledged in the world of music.

The song (and also dance) presentations in "Hit Parade" are rather dull and mostly uninspired. One exception is Maurice Chevalier's "Ca Va" number. This one, in which the irresistible Frenchman uses his cocked strawhat and employs his famous laugh, is the film's climax. Margot Hielscher's "C'est la vie, Mon Ami" looms okay. But all other song and dance sequences can't stand comparison with those offered even in Hollywood's below-average musicals. The locally much-publicized appearance of Stan Kenton's band in the film is disappointing because it is on the screen less than two minutes. Some songs, including the title song, are easy on the ear; others are either public domain or not too catchy.

Direction by Eric Ode definitely lacks pace and imagination. However, he is obviously handicapped by the uninspired material provided in the scripting. The acting is so-so. Lensing by Richard Angst, however, is one of the better things about the production. *Hans.*

Karlexens Brad
(The Bread Of Love)
(SWEDISH)

Janco release of Nordisk-Tonefilm production. Directed by Arne Mattson. Screenplay, W. Semitjov, from a novel by Peder Sjogren; camera, Sven Thermaenius; editor, Lennart Landheim; music, Sven Skold. At Cannes Film Festival, April 4, '54. Running time, **90 MINS.**

Prisoner .... Folke Sundquist
Lunnaja .... Sissi Kaiser
Ledin ...., George Rydeberg
Tom .... Nils Harberg
Narrator .... Lennart Lindberg

Buteur .... Erik Hell
Mother .... Dagny Lind

Cannes, April 27.

This film is a heavyweight arty saga about a lost Finnish patrol during the Finno-Russian war of 1940. Though a bit ponderous in style, the pic exhudes a lyric quality in its harrowing tale of love and death among a group of trapped men. Offbeat qualities and expert technical aspects, direction and acting make this a good entry for special situations with crix and word-of-mouth a probable plus asset. Distribution seems limited to arty bookings.

A patrol of Finns is trapped in a bleak hut on a snow-covered plain. Two of the men see a Russian soldier communing with a full moon and one understands that he is talking to his wife. They had arranged this when he had been dragged off to war. They leave him as he burrows in the snow to probably die. However, another member of the patrol captures him, and then film fuses the real and the unreal as the prisoner relieves his meeting with his wife. The men want the Russian to get them through a mine field, but he refuses. His wife is in a group of the beseiging Russians and her voice is heard as she sings to her captive husband. One of the Finns gets to his wife and during a scuffle kills her. The prisoner kills him and escapes while others are saved by following his trail through the mine field.

Film abounds in excellent photography which captures the frozen battlefields and certain scenes such as a Finn's dash through the snow to kill a suffering horse only to be killed in return. The conflicts and relations of the men are subtly defined and directed. It builds into a moving study of men at war. Editing is fine and acting is tops. Music is a notable mood assist
Mosk.

Monsieur Ripois
(FRANCO-BRITISH)

Cannes, April 20.

Cinedis release of Transcontinental Film production. Stars Gerard Philipe; features Joan Greenwood, Natasha Parry, Margaret Johnston, Germaine Montero, Valerie Hobson. Directed by Rene Clement. Screenplay, Clement, Hugh Mills from a novel by Louis Hemon; camera, Oswald Morris; editor, Francoise Javet; music, Roman Vlad. At Cannes Film Festival. Running time, **100 MINS.**

Andre .... Gerard Philipe
Marcelle .... Germaine Montero
Catherine .... Valerie Hobson
Norah .... Joan Greenwood
Anne .... Margaret Johnston
Patricia .... Natasha Parry
Diana .... Diana Decker

"Monsieur Ripois" is a rake, a Don Juan, a victim of his times, a debauchee, but whatever he is, this film adds up to a tour-de-force in direction and thesping. A callous subject is presented in a comedic, brilliant vein. It emerges a satirical and engaging adult film which should slake arty theatre thirst in the U.S. There may be some censorship trouble, but this may be easily glossed over, and word-of-mouth and crix are sure to give this a push.

Ripois (Gerard Philipe) is a young Frenchman living in London, the film recounting his confessions to his wife's best friend, whom he thinks he loves. Ripois' life is a series of adventures with women with whom he has only a superficial contact seeming incapable of true feeling. He has a monotonous job in an office and decides to embark on a crusade to seduce his hardbitten female boss. Ripois succeeds too well and finds

her too cold and arbitrary for long association, and leaves on a new quest. He picks up a charming English gal, and her prudishness finally goes before his assidious, if detached, assault. When she considers herself engaged, he flees.

Fired from his job he spends two days in the street and in desperation picks up a streetwalker. She is French, and his youth and need seduce her also, and he becomes her dependent. He leaves her when she gets a big inheritance. His next woman is the rich widow of one of his pupils. Then the friend of his wife is the next victim as Ripois narrates his life, insisting he is sincere for the first time. She almost gives in, but leaves when another woman knocks on the door. He feigns a leap from the window to bring her back, and really falls. His wife thinks he did this for her and spends her time in his convalescence, but already Ripois has a roving eye.

Philipe touches perfection as the strangely unfeeling Ripois who walks through his ardors with too susceptible females. The femme roles are well played. Joan Greenwood, as the passionate marrying kind; Natasha Parry, as the supposed loved one; Valerie Hobson, as the wife, and Germaine Montero, as the tender prostie are all excellent. Rene Clement, responsible for such pix as "Forbidden Games" and "Walls of Malapaga," have concentrated his directorial brilliance. The film abounds in clever observation, visual nuance and smooth pacing. Lensing and editing ably help the high grade quality of this production, and its two versions are both of high order. Though made in England, this is primarily a French film in feeling, and gives a lucid Gallic-eyed view of London and its manners.
Mosk.

Sang Et Lumieres
(Blood and Light)
(FRANCO-SPANISH)
(Color)

Cannes, April 20.

Cocinor release of Cite Films-Reig production. Stars Daniel Gelin, Zsa Zsa Gabor; features Arnoldo Foa. Directed by Georges Rauquie. Screenplay, Maurice Berry, Michel Audiard from novel by Joseph Peyre; camera, Maurice Barry; editor, Christian Gaudin. At Cannes Film Festival. Running time, **100 MINS.**

Ricardo .... Daniel Gelin
Marilena .... Zsa Zsa Gabor
Naguera .... Henri Vilbert
Riera .... Arnoldo Foa
Pili .... Christine Carrere
Chispa .... Jacques Dufhilo
Federico .... Eugenio Domingo

This bullfight film adds nothing to the vernacular, with the usual tale of a toreador who wants to quit. He is hounded back into the ring by a demanding mistress and acid journalists only to meet his bloody death. Sketchy story line and characterization hampers the pic while the bullfight scenes are held to a minimum. All of which makes this of improbable value for U.S. art houses or sureseaters. It may do for special situations via the Zsa Zsa Gabor name and the exploitable quality of the subject.

Daniel Gelin has decided to quit the ring and raise bulls after the death of a friend. His demanding American mistress leaves him and a cynical journalist blasts him in his articles. But Ricardo remains firm. However, his manager and mistress scheme to get him back, and they finally succeed. He is gored in the bullring, and the girl he loves comes rushing to his side, is caught in a milling crowd and trampled to death.

Director Georges Rouquir has not been able to breathe life into his familiar characters. The film lags and expresses action by innuendo rather than moving dramatics. Gelin is properly impassive as the toreador, but Zsa Zsa Gabor is too wooden and unresponsive to give a semblance of life to the supposedly passionate Hollywood adventuress. Arnoldo Foa is the only one in character as the cynical newspaperman. Eastmancolor is adequate, lensing and editing par, with a notable lift in the final bullfight sequence which is the main appeal of this lagging film.
Mosk.

Three Coins in Fountain
(C'SCOPE-COLOR)

Story of three American girls in Rome is woven into a delightful and romantic yarn for excellent b.o. prospects.

20th-Fox release of Sol C. Siegel production. Stars Clifton Webb, Dorothy McGuire, Jean Peters, Louis Jourdan, Maggie McNamara, Rossano Brazzi; features Howard St. John, Kathryn Givney, Cathleen Nesbitt, Vincenta Padula, Mario Siletti, Alberto Morin, Dino Bolognese. Directed by Jean Negulesco. Screenplay, John Patrick from John H. Secondari novel; camera (Eastman color), Milton Krasner; editor, William Reynolds; music by Jule Styne and Sammy Cahn. Previewed in N.Y., May 7, '54. Running time, **101 MINS.**

Shadwell .... Clifton Webb
Miss Frances .... Dorothy McGuire
Anita .... Jean Peters
Prince Dino Di Cessi .. Louis Jourdan
Maria .... Maggie McNamara
Giorgio .... Rossano Brazzi
Burgoyne .... Howard St. John
Principessa .... Cathleen Nesbitt
Principessa .... Cathleen Nesbitt
Bartender .... Mario Siletti
Waiter .... Alberto Morin
Headwaiter .... Dino Bolognese
Venice Waiter .... Tony de Mario
Consulate Clerk .... Jack Mattis
Mr. Hoyt .... Willard Waterman
Ticket Agent .... Zachary Yaconelli
Baroness .... Celia Lovsky
Waiter .... Larry Arnold
Anna .... Renata Vanni
Butler .... Maurice Brierre
Maid .... Grazia Narciso
Butler .... Gino Corrado
(Aspect ratio: 2.55 to 1)

Once before, in 20th-Fox's "How To Marry a Millionaire," director Jean Negulesco CinemaScoped a trio of feminine beauties into a lucrative attraction. In "Three Coins in the Fountain" he repeats this feat but obviously has gained some experience. The film has warmth, humor, a rich dose of romance and almost incredible pictorial appeal.

Here, in the first CinemaScoper to be lensed abroad, the wide screen really comes into its own, capturing the charms of Rome and Venice as an unforgettable backdrop for this pleasant but insignificant story. It ought to earn 20th a mint at the b.o., and chances are it'll win CinemaScope a host of new friends.

For those who aren't satisfied feasting their eyes on the stunning backgrounds and the plush interior sets, 20th has provided another trio of femme stars—Dorothy McGuire, Jean Peters and Maggie McNamara—and has dressed them in smart and expensive-looking clothes. As their male counterparts they have Clifton Webb, debonnaire and fun as always; Rossano Brazzi, an appealing young Italian, and suave Louis Jourdan, appealing as the romantic lead.

Hard as they have tried to concentrate on the John Patrick script, which is far from distinguished but still comes up with some rib-tickling dialog and occasionally dramatically valid scenes taken from the John H. Secondari novel, Negulesco and cameraman Milton Krasner couldn't resist the fascination of their setting. "Coin" is introed by some absolutely magnificent lensing of Roman fountains and, later, of the Fountain of Trevi of which it is said that whoever tosses a coin into it and wishes to return to Rome will have this wish granted. Throughout the film, occasionally slowing up its action, the camera takes a leisurely look at Roman landmarks including St. Peters. The Venice shots have dramatic impact and were expertly composed.

Story introduces to Rome Miss McNamara, an American coming to take a secretarial job. She's met by Miss Peters and later introduced to her third room-mate in their sumptuous apartment, Miss McGuire. They all toss a coin in the fountain, and in varying ways, it grants them their wish.

Outstanding performances—perhaps because they are the only believable ones—are given by Miss McGuire and Webb who plays an American writer expatriate. She's his secretary. Miss McGuire, playing a not-so-young American, is excellent in every respect. Her final scene with Webb, in which she gets drunk and wades into a pool, has pathos and great appeal. Webb is seen in a familiar role and makes the most of it without being as brash as usual in his defiance of convention and his biting witticisms.

Miss Peters is the gal who falls in love with Brazzi, an Italian translator at the U. S. outfit where she works. There's a rule that company employees can't date. They're seen together and he's fired as she prepares to return to the U. S. Their love scenes are earthy in the Italian screen tradition and it's surprising that some of the lines got by the Production Code. Miss Peters has voluptuous appeal. She's also quite charming in the sequence involving her introduction to Brazzi's farmer parents.

Easily the most romantic couple are Miss McNamara, an elfine newcomer first seen in "The Moon Is Blue," and Jourdan, playing an Italian prince. Miss McNamara has **a pixie-like quality that is wholly delightful and she looms as a bright new star. Her part is hardly believable but she makes you** forget that with a crisp performance as the methodical dame out to trap her man. More than any of the others, she is the wide-eyed young American in a worldwise Rome.

Rest of the cast all does very well, from Jourdan and Brazzi down. Howard St. John is properly stuffed shirt as the boss; Cathleen Nesbitt has a standout bit as the aging Principessa looking over a prospective daughter-in-law; Kathryn Givney has good as St. John's gossipy wife.

But the greatest star of 'em all is still CinemaScope, which has never been put to better advantage. Scenes taking in the vastness of Rome and of Venice from the air or intimate closeups of the fountains come through with equal impact. Sol C. Siegel's production values contribute greatly even though the plush sets must give stay-at-homers a cockeyed idea of how the American working-gal in Rome lives and loves. The ending, too, is trite and something of a disappointment though in keeping with the fairy-tale spirit of the whole thing.

"Coins" has some excellent musical background featuring the Jule Styne-Sammy Cahn tune of the same name which sounds like a sure hit. The Eastmancolor processed by DeLuxe is extremely uneven, very good in some spots and fading in others. Dorothy Jeakins' costumes are elegantly designed. William Reynolds contributes a smooth editing job. Use of stereophonic sound, other than as an ad gimmick, can hardly be counted as one of the film's assets. Frank Sinatra's crooning (unbilled) of "Coins" in the intro is tops.

Hift.

Magnificent Obsession
(COLOR)

Jane Wyman and Rock Hudson in fine remake of Lloyd C. Douglas' inspirational novel; top grosses indicated.

Hollywood, May 4.

Universal-International release of Ross Hunter production. Stars Jane Wyman, Rock Hudson; co-stars Barbara Rush; features Agnes Moorehead, Otto Kruger, Gregg Palmer. Directed by Douglas Sirk. Screenplay, Robert Blees; based on novel by Lloyd C. Douglas, screenplay by Sarah Y. Mason, Victor Heerman; adaptation, Wells Root; camera (Technicolor), Russell Metty; editor, Milton Carruth; music, Frank Skinner; musical direction, Joseph Gershenson. Previewed April 20, '54. Running time, **107 MINS.**

Helen Phillips .... Jane Wyman
Bob Merrick .... Rock Hudson
Joyce Phillips .... Barbara Rush
Nancy Ashford .... Agnes Moorehead
Randolph .... Otto Kruger
Tom Masterson .... Gregg Palmer
Valerie .... Sara Shane
Dr. Giraud .... Paul Cavanagh
Judy .... Judy Nugent
Williams .... George Lynn
Dr. Dodge .... Richard H. Cutting
Sgt. Burnham .... Robert B. Williams
Sgt. Ames .... Will White
Mrs. Eden .... Helen Kleeb
(Aspect ratio: 2-1)

The same inspirational appeal which marked the 1935 making of Lloyd C. Douglas' bestseller is again caught in the new version of "Magnificent Obsession," with Jane Wyman and Rock Hudson undertaking the roles previously enacted by Irene Dunne and Robert Taylor. New release, which should be one of UI's top grossers of the season, is a sensitive treatment of faith told in terms of moving, human drama which packs emotional impact. For femme spectators particularly it should be a winner.

As megged by Douglas Sirk from Robert Blees' moving and understanding screenplay, the Ross Hunter production, impressively mounted, commands dramatic attention. Characters become alive and vital and infuse spiritual theme with a rare sort of beauty.

Hudson is the rich playboy responsible for Miss Wyman's blindness who renounces his past existence to devote himself to study and work, hoping as a surgeon to cure her. The role establishes him as a dramatic actor of substance. Miss Wyman benefits by a part to which she can bring deft shadings. Barbara Rush, as her stepdaughter, also turns in some expert trouping.

Film takes its title from the "magnificent obsession" which possessed a doctor for whose death Hudson is indirectly responsible. The doctor's obsession for the performance of unselfish and secret deeds is taken up by the remorseful playboy and changes his whole life. The doctor was Miss Wyman's husband, and when she is blinded in an accident while trying to avoid Hudson's attentions the young man, seeking peace of mind for what he has done, consecrates his life to helping others, particularly in devoting himself to the blind woman. In a poignant climax, he is able to save her life and restore her sight through the skill of his own surgery.

Otto Kruger as the friend who passes on the dead doctor's philosophy to Hudson is fine in a key character, Agnes Moorehead scores as the companion-nurse of the blind Miss Wyman, Gregg Palmer handles his role of Miss Rush's attorney-fiance effectively and Paul Cavanagh and Judy Nugent, respectively a doctor and a moppet, also are standouts in briefer parts.

Technically, the film is tops. Rating highest mention is the color photography by Russell Metty, art direction by Bernard Herzbrun and Emrich Nicholson, set decorations by Russell A. Gausman and Ruby R. Levitt, editing by Milton Carruth, gowns by Bill Thomas. Frank Skinner's music score, as directed by Joseph Gershenson, also is effective.

Whit.

Men of Fighting Lady
(COLOR)

Okay war actioner based on incidents in Korean war, with familiar names for top-of-the-bill bookings in program market.

Hollywood, May 10.

Metro release of Henry Berman production. Stars Van Johnson, Walter Pidgeon, Louis Calhern, Dewey Martin, Keenan Wynn, Frank Lovejoy, Robert Horton, Bert Freed; features Lewis Martin, George Cooper, Dick Simmons. Directed by Andrew Marton. Screenplay, Art Cohn; based on events published in the SatEvePost under the title of "The Forgotten Heroes of Korea" by James Michener, and "The Case of the Blind Pilot" by Cmdr. Harry A. Burns, USN; camera (Ansco), George Folsey; editor, Gene Ruggiero; technical adviser, Cmdr. Paul N. Gray, USN; score composed and conducted by Miklos Rozsa. Previewed May 5, '54. Running time, **79 MINS.**

Lt. (jg) Howard Thayer .. Van Johnson
Comdr. Kent Dowling .... Walter Pidgeon
James A. Michener .... Louis Calhern
Ens. Kenneth Schechter .... Dewey Martin
Lt. Comdr. Ted Dodson .. Keenan Wynn
Lt. Comdr. Paul Grayson .. Frank Lovejoy
Ens. Neil Conovan .... Robert Horton
Lt. (jg) Andrew Szymanski .. Bert Freed
Comdr. Michael Coughlin .. Lewis Martin
Cyril Roberts .... George Cooper
Lt. Wayne Kimbrell .... Dick Simmons
(Aspect ratio: 1.75-1)

An okay war actioner, with particular appeal to jet-minded youngsters, has been fashioned around battle incidents in the Korean war. Picture has a cast of familiar names to shape it for top-of-the-bill bookings in the regular program market, where most male viewers will probably find it interesting entertainment. Distaffers, however, will possibly vote against it.

The Henry Berman production, scripted by Art Cohn, is based on events published in the SatEvePost under the titles of "The Forgotten Heroes of Korea" by James Michener, and "The Case of the Blind Pilot" by Comdr. Harry A. Burns, USN. Latter incident is used as the action climax for the film as it re-stages one of the Navy's most dramatic rescue operations. There's good suspense to the sequence detailing how one jet pilot "talks" a blinded fellow pilot into a safe landing on a carrier deck. It would have had a lot more dramatic impact, too, had the loud music accompanying the action been skipped entirely. The whistle of wind and jet, and the talk between injured and rescuer is all the accompaniment needed to sock the sequence.

Andrew Marton's direction and the Ansco color lensing by George Folsey put action into the incidents unfolded aboard a carrier somewhere off Korea. From their ship base, jet planes make daily strikes at Communist installations and, while there's a sameness to the takeoffs, landings and strikes, the scenes are not without their thrills.

Van Johnson, the pilot who "talks in" blinded Dewey Martin, tops the all-male cast and does an able job of his heroics. Walter Pidgeon, ship's doctor; Louis Calhern, playing Michener getting his stories first-hand from Pidgeon and the men; Martin, Keenan Wynn and Frank Lovejoy, squadron leader and exponent of low-level flying, are among the more prominently-used cast members. Bert Freed rates some chuckles as the repair officer aboard ship.

Technical contributors to the picture give it an authenticity that helps sustain the 79 minutes.

Miklos Rozsa composed and conducted "Blind Flight," the piece that dominates the picture's climactic sequence. *Brog.*

Silver Lode
(COLOR)

Fair offbeat western for the action market.

RKO release of Benedict Bogeaus production. Stars John Payne, Lizabeth Scott, Dan Duryea. Directed by Allan Dwan. Original story and screenplay, Karen De Wolfe; camera (Technicolor), John Alton; editor, James Leicester; music, Louis Forbes. Tradeshown, N.Y., May 7, '54. Running time, **80 MINS.**

Dan Ballard	John Payne
Rose Evans	Lizabeth Scott
McCarty	Dan Duryea
Dolly	Dolores Moran
Sheriff Woolley	Emile Meyer
Judge Cranston	Robert Warwick
Mitch Evans	John Hudson
Johnson	Harry Carey Jr.
Kirk	Alan Hale Jr.
Wicker	Stuart M. Whitman
Paul Herbert	Frank Sully
Zachary Evans	Morris Ankrum
Rev. Field	Hugh Sanders
Mrs. Elmwood	Florence Auer
Dr. Elmwood	Roy Gordon
Lawyer Taylor	Edgar Barrier

Mob violence that erupts into a frantic man hunt should be a fine basis for a starkly dramatic film, but "Silver Lode," whose story is shaped around such a situation, falls short of developing into compelling screen fare. Its trio of cast toppers, however, offers some marquee appeal and there are several exploitable pegs on which exhibitors can sell this offbeat western in the action market.

Whole premise of the Karen De Wolfe script, which she screenplayed from her original story, is one of revenge. For Dan Duryea, whose brother was slain during a card game with John Payne, poses as a U.S. Marshal and hunts down Payne who now has become a respectable rancher. All the action takes place on a Fourth of July holiday, in a frontier days Nevada hamlet. (Exhibs attending the Tushinsky Widescreen test of RKO 86th Street a month ago got an unofficial foretaste of this release).

Mitigating the effectiveness of the yarn is the fact that its obvious from the beginning that Duryea is a fake marshal. Moreover, his exhortations Payne to comply with the warrant for his arrest become overly repetitious when stretched through most of the footage. There's some excitement in the final reel when Payne vindicates himself and exposes Duryea in a hail of gunfire but it's too late to save the credibility of the story.

Color and atmosphere of the pioneering west is nicely recaptured in several sets which represent the town of "Silver Lode." Locale, aside from its principals, is peopled with standard types of the times. Director Allan Dawn occasionally gets some realism into the performances but much of the thesping fails to be genuinely convincing.

Of the lengthy cast Payne, perhaps, contributes the best portrayal. His is a fine interpretation of the role of a wrongly accused man who disproves the charges against him. Duryea tends to overact as the snarling, overzealous "marshal." Lizabeth Scott has little to do as the town's richest gal whose marriage to Payne was interrupted by Duryea's arrival. Dolores Moran is fair as a saloon entertained. Among others lending okay support are Robert Warwick as a judge, Hugh Sanders as a minister and Emile Meyer as the sheriff.

Technicolor camerawork of John Alton capably captures the visual values in this Benedict Bogeaus production for RKO release. Editing of James Leicester, however, could have been tighter than the 80 minutes the film is permitted to run. Louis Forbes' musical score is good as is Van Nest Polglase's art direction. *Gilb.*

Melody of Love
(ITALIAN)

IFE release of Roberto Amoroso production. Stars Giacomo Rondinella, Maria Fiore, Nadia Gray. Directed by Mario Costa. Screenplay, A. G. Maiano, M. Costa, R. Amoroso; camera, Francesco Izzarelli; music, Gino Filippini. At Cinema Giglio, N.Y., starting April 17, '54. Running time, **96 MINS.**

Giacomo	Giacomo Rondinella
Maria	Maria Fiore
Don Salvatore	Giovanni Grasso
Don Raffaele	Giuseppe Porelli
Renato	Mirko Ellis
Concetta	Tina Pica
Mr. Ferrario	Carlo Romano
Dante e Beniamino	Dante e Beniamino Maggio
Nadia	Nadia Gray

(In Italian; English Titles)

"Melody of Love" is a standard Italian picture that has enough singing of high quality to make it appeal to patrons of Italian language theatres in the U.S. For other houses, this is too slow-moving to mean much at the wickets. The production boasts the singing of Giacomo Rondinella, pop singer of Radio-Rome, and the acting of Maria Fiore, star of "Two Cents Worth of Hope." Plot is too laboriously unfolded to compensate for the excellent vocalizing.

The screenplay, concocted by A. G. Maiano, M. Costa and R. Amoroso, is the by-now familiar yarn about the two young lovers who are kept from marriage by the girl's father. Latter wants her to wed a man of his own choosing, whom he is placing in his own biz in order to give the girl a well-to-do mate. There are the usual misunderstandings between the girl and her childhood sweetheart, his final decision being to make a career for himself on the stage.

Plot stresses from the outset what a marvelous voice the lad possesses so the career in musical shows fits in nicely. There is the customary final breaking-up of the romance and near-marriage to the comely femme singer. The man picked out by papa turns out to be a dope smuggler, and the young lovers are happily reunited.

Rondinella is not half bad as an actor, playing the romantic youth who is ignored by the girl's father. But it is warbling that really puts him over. Less plot meddling, and more of his singing would have helped. His sweetheart is nicely played by Miss Fiore, but one wonders why Rondinella did not fall for the beauteous Nadia Gray. Especially, since she virtually throws herself at him during his career on the stage with her. Miss Gray shows real potentialities in this pic, having the added asset of being beautiful.

Mirko Ellis makes a suave figure as the man that father has picked to be his daughter's husband—later revealed as a narcotic smuggler. Giovanni Grasso makes a pompous father, owner of the big fishing fleet while Giuseppe Porelli appears wasted in the role of musician-composer. There's a so-called team of comics, Dante and Beniamino Maggio, who figure in the plot, and try to be funny.

Mario Costa's direction is methodical and seldom original. The Maiano-Costa-Amoroso story is one of those things contrived to focus attention on Rondinella's vocalizing. Lens work by Francesco Izzarelli is okay. Music by Gino Filippini is topflight. *Wear.*

Forbidden Cargo
(BRITISH)

British-made suspense drama of dope smuggling from the Continent; should serve as useful dualler in the U. S.

London, May 4.

General Film Distributors release of Sydney Box-Earl St. John production. Stars Nigel Patrick, Elizabeth Sellars, Terence Morgan, Greta Gynt, Jack Warner features Greta Gynt, Theodore Bikel, Joyce Grenfell. Directed by Harold French. Screenplay, Sydney Box; camera, C. Pennington-Richards; editor, Anne V. Coates; music, Lambert Williamson. At Leicester Square Theatre, London. Running time, **83 MINS.**

Michael Kenyon	Nigel Patrick
Rita Compton	Elizabeth Sellars
Roger Compton	Terence Morgan
Alec White	Jack Warner
Madame Simonetta	Greta Gynt
Max	Theodore Bikel
Lady Flavin Queensway	Joyce Grenfell
Larkins	James Gilbert
Lasovic	Eric Pohlmann
Director	Michael Hordern
Holt	Martin Boddey
Attendant	Hal Osmond
Pierre Valance	Jacques Brunius

Dope smuggling from Europe is the theme of this new British film which has adequate suspense values to help it along at the boxoffice, although only moderate marquee appeal in overseas markets. It should qualify as a useful dualer in the U. S.

Written and produced by Sydney Box, the plot illustrates how customs officers get on the track of a smuggling gang after trapping a handful of men who, posing as naval men, bring contraband liquor into a remote part of the English coast. Action switches from England to the Riviera when a customs officer follows a couple of suspects. The method employed to defeat the authorities is not without interest, but there is only a modicum of surprise in the outcome.

Direction is neatly tuned to the suspense note established in the screenplay and there is enough action to sustain the plot. There is an allround thesping standard with Nigel Patrick effectively portraying the customs sleuth and Jack Warner doing reliable work as his immediate boss. Elizabeth Sellars and Terence Morgan, as brother and sister, are the two suspects and play their roles adequately. Greta Gynt has a minor part as a front for the smugglers while Theodore Bikel is a typical heavy. Joyce Grenfell contributes another of her characteristic gems as a titled bird-watcher who provides the first clue. *Myro.*

The Saracen Blade
(COLOR)

Good swashbuckler for the program market.

Hollywood, May 14.

Columbia release of Sam Katzman production. Stars Ricardo Montalban; co-stars Betta St. John; features Rick Jason, Carolyn Jones, Whitfield Connor, Michael Ansara, Edgar Barrier, Nelson Leigh, Pamela Duncan, Frank Pulaski. Directed by William Castle. Screenplay, DeVallon Scott, George Worthing Yates; based on the novel by Frank Yerby; camera (Technicolor), Henry Freulich; editor, Gene Havlick. Previewed May 13, '54. Running time, **77 MINS.**

Pietro	Ricardo Montalban
Iolanthe	Betta St. John
Enzio	Rick Jason
Elaine of Siniscola	Carolyn Jones
Frederick II	Whitfield Connor
Count Siniscola	Michael Ansara
Baron Rogliano	Edgar Barrier
Isaac	Nelson Leigh
Zenobia	Pamela Duncan
Donati	Frank Pulaski
Haroun	Leonard Penn
Maria	Nyra Monsour
Guiseppi	Edward Coch
Italian Prince	Gene D'Arcy
Gina	Poppy Deluando

(Aspect ratio: 1.85-1)

The program market will find "The Saracen Blade" a good swashbuckler. The 13th century costume actioner, filmed from the Frank Yerby novel, fills the bill for general audiences with its Technicolored derring-do and cast headed by Ricardo Montalban and Betta St. John.

Good physical values are achieved in the moderately-budgeted Sam Katzman production, although it's really pinching pennies when black-and-white stock footage is cut into the tinted pic to cover a castle siege sequence. A workmanlike script, satisfactorily motivated for marketing purposes, is furnished by DeVallon Scott and George Worthing Yates and William Castle's direction is actionful so there is seldom a lag in the 77 minutes running time.

Montalban, well-educated and trained commoner, has dedicated his life to avenging the death of his father at the hands of Michael Ansara and Rick Jason, playing the wicked Count of Seniscola and his son, respectively. The course of adventuring around the Italian countryside and during a Holy Land crusade doesn't overlook s.a. requirements, well supplied by Miss St. John, Montalban's beloved who is married to Jason, and Carolyn Jones, blonde menace whom Montalban marries as part of his scheme of revenge. After suitable time and action, Montalban has his revenge and gets the girl he loves.

Montalban carries off his lead with dash and authority. Miss St. John is a charming and believeable vis-a-vis, while Miss Jones fills all requirements for lure and menace. Jason scores strongly, among the other players as one of Montalban's rather engaging enemies. So do Whitfield Connor, as the Emperor of Europe, Ansara, Edgar Barrier, Nelson Leigh and Frank Pulaski.

Henry Freulich did the okay color lensing and Gene Havlick's editing is another expert technical credit. Settings and direction add a good note of flash to the presentation.

Secret of the Incas
(SONGS-COLOR)

Fairly good adventure drama, up-pointed by highly interesting Peruvian Andes location-lensing.

Hollywood, May 18.

Paramount release of Mel Epstein production. Stars Charlton Heston, Robert Young, Nicole Maurey, Thomas Mitchell; presenting Yma Sumac; features Glenda Farrell, Michael Pate, Leon Askin, William Henry, Kurt Katch, Edward Colmans. Directed by Jerry Hopper. Screenplay, Ronald MacDougall, Sydney Boehm; camera (Technicolor), Lionel Lindon; photography in Peru, Irmin Roberts; editor, Eda Warren; score, David Buttolph; songs, Moises Vivanco. Previewed May 17, '54. Running time, **100 MINS.**

Harry Steele	Charlton Heston
Dr. Stanley Moorehead	Robert Young
Elena Antonescu	Nicole Maurey
Kori-Tica	Yma Sumac
Ed Morgan	Thomas Mitchell
Mrs. Winston	Glenda Farrell
Pachacutec	Michael Pate
Anton Marcu	Leon Askin
Phillip Lang	William Henry
Man with Rifle	Kurt Katch
Col. Emilio Cardoza	Edward Colmans

(Aspect ratio: 1.85-1)

This is an adventure drama with a plus factor in its authentic outdoor backgrounds, obtained by location lensing high in the lofty Andes of Peru. It is a generally okay Technicolored display of intrigue and romance, with prospects for an average number of satisfactory, but not big, playdates in regular release.

Mel Epstein's production rates a highly attractive framing from the unusual visual values in the fresh Andean backgrounds. Site of much of the location shooting was Machu Picchu, authentic lost Inca city rediscovered about 40 years ago, and and an apt fit for much of the plot action in the script by Ranald MacDougall and Sydney Boehm.

Top-lining and replying with dramatic skill to the demands of the screenplay and Jerry Hopper's direction are Charlton Heston, American adventurer out to steal a fabled Incan sunburst; Thomas Mitchell, an older rogue with the same scheme; Nicole Maurey, Rumanian refugee without papers trying to get to the states; and Robert Young, head of an archaeological expedition already digging at the treasure site.

Before the plot gets down to basics, it spends considerable footage laying the groundwork, during which Heston is seen as a rather unpleasant grafter of money from unsuspecting tourists to Cuzco, Peru, while he schemes to get hold of a plane that will take him into the mountains for the treasure. During this period, Heston, a dubious hero, matches wits with Mitchell, artfully dodges advances made by touring Glenda Farrell, and uses the frightened refugee to get the needed plane. By the time the principals reach the mountains and find the treasure, Heston has reformed and gives the sunburst back to the Incas so he can get Miss Maurey.

Heston and Miss Maurey are an oddly matched pair. Neither gets any sort of goody-goody treatment in character makeup so their relationship takes a forthright turn towards s.a. now and then. Young hasn't very much to do as the archaeologist who goes for, and misses, Miss Maurey. Mitchell apparently has fun selling his crummy heavy character. Michael Pate comes over as an Incan, while Yma Sumac, real Peruvian, enacts an Incan princess, a role well-suited to background her five-octave singing of three Moises Vivanco songs, "Virgin of the Sun God," "Earthquake" and "High Andes."

The lensing in Peru was done by Irma Roberts, while Lionel Lindon, director of the pic's photography, handled the topnotch studio-filmed footage. Editing, the David Buttolph score and other technical assists are all good. *Brog.*

The Yellow Tomahawk
(COLOR)

Good cavalry-and-Indians actioner for the outdoor market.

Hollywood, May 7.

United Artists release of Schenck-Koch production, produced by Howard W. Koch. Stars Rory Calhoun, Peggie Castle; features Noah Beery, Warner Anderson, Peter Graves, Lee Van Cleef, Rita Moreno. Director, Lesley Selander. Screenplay, Richard Alan Simmons; based on a story by Harold Jack Bloom; camera (Color Corp. of America), Gordon Avil; editor, John F. Schreyer; music, Les Baxter. Previewed May 5, '54. Running time, **82 MINS.**

Adam	Rory Calhoun
Katherine	Peggie Castle
Tonio	Noah Beery
Major Ives	Warner Anderson
Sawyer	Peter Graves
Fireknife	Lee Van Cleef
Honey Bear	Rita Moreno
Keats	Walter Reed
Sergeant Bandini	Dan Riss
Corporal Maddock	Adam Williams
Willy	Ned Glass

(Aspect ratio: 1.85-1)

The cavalry and the Indians fight it out on the western front to provide "The Yellow Tomahawk" with a good supply of rugged action. It has a suspenseful story, once the footage gets by a slow start. Should please in the outdoor market.

Rory Calhoun is the male star in the Aubrey Schenck-Howard W. Koch presentation, and registers favorably in the action in his role of Indian scout. Also impressing is Peggie Castle, who's around to make the film attractive to the grownup males, and there are well-valued character roles turned in by Noah Beery, as a colorful Mexican; Warner Anderson, pompous officer; Peter Graves, a white heavy; Lee Van Cleef, sympathetic Indian menace; and Rita Moreno, Beery's Indian eyeful.

The Harold Jack Bloom story takes the redskins' side to show provocation for their attacks on a cavalry encampment and this angle is played up properly in the script by Richard Alan Simmons and under Lesley Selander's direction. Anderson is the object of Van Cleef's rage, having massacred many Indian women and children without cause and, as the plot starts, is readying to build a fort in Indian territory in violation of a treaty. Van Cleef sends him the yellow tomahawk of war via Calhoun, but Anderson's a stubborn man, even when the Indians wipe out his forces. In the end he is saved from Van Cleef by Calhoun, who leads the survivors of the Indian raid to safety, but has to kill his redskin friend to do it.

Directorial pacing gives the film plenty of fast movement and the outdoor settings are picturesquely displayed in color by Gordon Avil's lensing. Other technical departments come off okay. *Brog.*

Drums Across the River
(COLOR)

Actionful western in color with Audie Murphy, Walter Brennan, Lyle Bettger and okay possibilities in outdoor playdates.

Hollywood, May 10.

Universal release of Melville Tucker production. Stars Audie Murphy, Walter Brennan, Lyle Bettger; features Lisa Gaye, Hugh O'Brian, Mara Corday, Jay Silverheels. Directed by Nathan Juran. Screenplay, John K. Butler, Lawrence Roman; from a story by Butler; camera (Technicolor), Harold Lipstein; editor, Virgil Vogel. Previewed May 4, '54. Running time, **77 MINS.**

Gary Brannon	Audie Murphy
Sam Brannon	Walter Brennan
Frank Walker	Lyle Bettger
Jennie	Lisa Gaye
Morgan	Hugh O'Brian
Sue	Mary Corday
Taos	Jay Silverheels
Nathan Marlowe	Emile Meyer
Sheriff Jim Beal	Regis Toomey
Chief Ouray	Morris Ankrum
Billy Costa	Bob Steele
Jed Walker	James Anderson
Les Walker	George Wallace
Ralph Costa	Lane Bradford
Red Knife	Ken Teprell

(Aspect ratio: 2-1)

Plenty of rough and ready action keeps this regulation western rolling over its 77-minute course and it is satisfactory filmfare for the outdoor trade. Masculine top-liners Audie Murphy, Walter Brennan and Lyle Bettger, plus Technicolor tints, are assists that will help the bookings.

Nathan Juran's direction has quite a bit of story to contend with but doesn't let that slow down proceedings. Murphy's heroics come off well in contrast to the colorful and excellent dirty work projected by chief villain Bettger and his henchman, Hugh O'Brian. Femme interest is minor, and played that way, by Lisa Gaye, heroine and Murphy's sweetie, and Mara Corday, dance hall queen and girl friend of Bettger.

The script by John K. Butler and Lawrence Roman has Bettger trying to stir up trouble between the Utes and the whites for personal profit. He'd like to open up the Ute territory and its gold deposits, closed to the whites by treaty, on one hand and, on the other, he's scheming to rob the stage of a gold shipment and lay the blame at the doorstep of Murphy and his dad, Brennan. Things look pretty bad for the hero for awhile, but he's able to dodge a hanging arranged by the townspeople with Bettger's connivance, and expose the villain for what he really is.

Jay Silverheels, Indian chief, Emile Meyer, Regis Toomey, Morris Ankrum, Bob Steele, James Anderson are among the players who keep things jumping with action. The film, well-lensed by Harold Lipstein, musters a good round of outdoor and action values under the production helming of Melville Tucker. *Brog.*

Victory at Sea
(DOCUMENTARY)

Socko b.o. fare for small-seaters.

NBC Film Division (Henry Salomon-Robert W. Sarnoff) production. Written by Salomon with Richard Hanser; editor, Isaac Kleinerman; narrator, Alexander Scourby; music, Richard Rodgers. Previewed N.Y., May 14, '54. Running time, **97 MINS.**

Originally presented on NBC as a 26-part filmed documentary of World War II naval history, the television "Victory at Sea" has been compressed to 97 minutes for theatrical release via George J. Schaefer & Son. That's a cut from video's 13-hour running time. But despite the loss of many fine scenes of the original the edited print is still a forceful pictorial chronicle of the Allies' global sea campaigns against the Axis Powers.

Although the tv version was extensively aired this probably will aid the theatrical print's b.o. appeal rather than hinder it. For with most of the American public familiar with the film an obviously presold audience exists. Some no doubt will see the new picture to make comparisons with the originals, another market comprises those who may have missed a number of the tv episodes while still others will go on strength of word of mouth. Withal, this portends lengthy runs for small-seater situations booking the NBC Film Division production.

Originally culled from 60,000,000 feet of film from files of some 10 nations, "Sea" covers the period from the Axis' 1939 ascendancy to its defeat in 1945. Among key points captured by the cameras are the Japanese attack on Pearl Harbor, the Allied invasion of Normandy, the sweep of the U.S. fleets through the Pacific, the North African invasion, the atomic bombing of Japan and the liberation of the prisoners of Dachau, Buchenwald and other infamous concentration camps.

Throughout the theatrical footage runs the original musical score by Richard Rodgers as arranged by Robert Russell Bennett conducting the NBC Symphony Orchestra. At times, however, the soundtrack became too loud at preview caught and tended to distract from what was on the screen. This may have been due to a slipup on the part of the boothman.

Editing of Isaac Kleinerman is good when one thinks of the magnitude of the task that confronted him. Assistant film editors S. A. D'Alisera and Douglas Wood rate nods. Alexander Scourby's narration of the commentary written by Henry Salomon and Richard Hanser is unobtrusive and never detracts from the screen movement. Quality of the print is good considering the varied origin and age of the footage. *Gilb.*

Black Horse Canyon
(COLOR)

Entertaining hoss opera with Joel McCrea.

Hollywood, May 18.

Universal release of John W. Rogers production. Stars Joel McCrea, Mari Blanchard; co-stars Race Gentry; features Murvyn Vye, Irving Bacon, John Pickard, Ewing Mitchell, Pilar Del Rey. Directed by Jesse Hibbs. Screenplay, Geoffrey Homes; adaptation, David Lang; based on novel "The Wild Horse" by Lee Savage Jr.; camera (Technicolor), George Robinson; editor, Frank Gross. Previewed May 11, '54. Running time, **81 MINS.**

Del Rockwell	Joel McCrea
Aldis Spain	Mari Blanchard
Ti	Race Gentry
Jennings	Murvyn Vye
Doc	Irving Bacon
Duke	John Pickard
Sheriff	Ewing Mitchell
Juanita	Pilar Del Rey
Graves	William J. Williams

(Aspect ratio: 2-1)

The giddyap fan will find this Joel McCrea starrer a sterling outdoor entry. An uncomplicated plot, good characterizations, a pretty girl and tinted scenery, plus an actionful pace, make "Black Horse Canyon" the type of offering that plays well in the regular outdoor program spots.

As a saddle mate, McCrea draws Mari Blanchard. At first thought this seems an unlikely casting, but she earns her femme star spot with action that matches the males, plus supplying the show with looks. Also rating a top billing is young Race Gentry, who'll be well on his way to bobby-sox favor if enough of them see this oater.

Being a true hoss opera, based on Lee Savage Jr.'s novel, "The Wild Horse," the John W. Rogers production is concerned with a wild, black stallion whose mare-stealing tricks have the ranchers aroused. This outlaw equine was once the property of Miss Blanchard, stock-rancher with her uncle, Irving Bacon, and she wants him back. McCrea and Gentry, just trying to get themselves established as ranchers, want outlaw because of his potential value as a sire. That's the same reason Murvyn Vye, neighboring rancher, wants the horse. Unfortunately for him, and the wild nag, Miss Blanchard is able to enlist the help of McCrea and Gentry on her side. The stallion is captured and broken to saddle, Vye's unscrupulous attempts to gain possession come to naught and McCrea finds himself willing to settle down with a gal, but not before his young partner has had the same idea and lost out.

The performances of all concerned under Jesse Hibbs' good direction are first-rate. The script by Geoffrey Homes gives the players honest dialog to speak, helping the characterizations stay believable, and the situations in which the David Lang adaptation of the novel puts the actors are logical enough to carry the footage.

George Robinson's color photography puts the outdoor settings on display for their full picturesque values. Editing and other contributions are good. *Brog.*

Jail Bait

Shoestringer with sexsational title, no sex, and nothing else.

Howco release of an Edward D. Wood Jr. production. Producer-director-writer, Edward D. Wood Jr.; camera, Bill Thompson; editor, Charles Clement and Igor Kantor; music, Hoyt Kurtin. Stars Dolores Fuller, Lyle Talbot. Features Herbert Rawlinson, Steve Reeves, Clancy Malone, Tim Speril, Teddy Therman, Cotton Watts & Chick. Previewed at Monterey Theatre, Monterey Park, Calif., May 12, '54. Running time, 70 MINS.
(Aspect ratio: 1:33-1)

"Jail Bait" was brought in for $21,600, and the problem is to find where all the money went to. For that price, however, film is bound to show a handsome profit, and producer - director - writer Edward D. Wood, Jr., can sneer at this and other bad reviews "feature" is certain to receive.

With its title, and backed by a sexploitation campaign, film could well show hefty returns in certain houses. The "Bait" handle, however, has not yet been cleared with the MPAA title registry; likewise, its use on this work will bring about the registering of a solid protest with the MPAA by Columbia producer Sam Katzman, who registered the tag first and got it cleared by the Breen Office. Film itself was given a production code seal last year under its original title, "The Hidden Face." There's nothing whatsoever to offend—morally, that is; "jajl bait," in this case, refers to a gun which is carried illegally by the leading man.

Story concerns a young man, the son of a noted plastic surgeon, who goes wrong. He kills a night-watchman during a robbery, then is bumped off by the accomplice when he wants to confess. Accomplice has a record, and was recognized at the scene of the crime. He contacts the doctor-father and informs that he'll return the missing, and already dead, son in return for plastic surgery to his face for a change-of-appearance. Doctor discovers body of his son, however, just before starting the operation. Two weeks later, by which time the body has been disposed of, patient takes off the bandages to discover he looks exactly like—yep, the

wanted-for-murder son. Minutes thereafter, he's killed by the police while trying to escape.

Film gets okay thesping from veterans Lyle Talbot, as the police inspector, and Herbert Rawlinson (who died one day after film's completion, incidentally), as the doctor, but the newcomers don't show to advantage with the exception of Tim Speril, who's surprisingly good as the baddie.

Technically, film leaves much to be desired, the music even being from another picture.

The Monterey Theatre in Monterey Park, where film was press previewed, serves as the locale for a robbery scene in the film. You guessed it—audience felt robbed. *Neal.*

Les Intrigantes
(The Plotters)
(FRENCH)

Paris, May 11.
AGDC release of Memnon Films production. Stars Raymond Rouleau. Directed by Henri Decoin. Screenplay, Jacques Robert, Francois Boyer. Decoin from a novel by Robert; camera, Michel Kelber; editor, Denise Reiss. At Biarritz, Paris. Running time, 100 MINS.
Paul .... Raymond Rouleau
Mona .... Jeanne Moreau
Marie .... Etchika Choreau
Andrieux .... Raymond Pellegrin
Inspector .... Marcel Andre
Director .... Robert Hirsch
Star .... Jacques Charon

Film is a slick whodunit which takes place in colorful theatre backstage atmosphere. Plotting and characterization put this in a strictly commercial class with good chances on names and locale here. Film has only lightweight chances in America, but could get by on twin bills on its technical and colorful aspects.

A director is suspected of killing his partner, who fell from a catwalk, because of an anonymous letter. His wife has him hide in a nursing home, and begins to run the theatre. She falls in love with the excitement of the theatre, and gives in to the advances of the shifty ex-secretary who wrote the accusing letter. A simple, innocent secretary, in love with the boss, solves the case.

Director Henri Decoin has given this a slick mounting and concentrated on character rather than suspense. This leaves it with lack of plausibility. Backstage locale is well utilized with a bevy of beauteous gals good for exploitation possibilities. Raymond Rouleau is too detached as the maligned director, but Jeanne Moreau is excellent as the ambitious wife whose appetites and desires lead to betrayal. Etchika Choreau is a bit too mannered as the wide eyed secretary. Remainder of the cast adequately fill the backstage characters. Lensing and editing are solid. *Mosk.*

The Student Prince
(C'SCOPE-MUSICAL-COLOR)

Fresh new film version of the old operetta, with "voice" of Mario Lanza and excellent grossing prospects.

Hollywood, May 25.
Metro release of Joe Pasternak production. Stars Ann Blyth, Edmund Purdom, John Ericson, Louis Calhern; features Edmund Gwenn, S. Z. Sakall, Betta St. John, John Williams, Evelyn Varden, John Hoyt, Richard Anderson, and the singing voice of Mario Lanza as the Student Prince. Directed by Richard Thorpe. Written for the screen by William Ludwig and Sonya Levien; from the operetta with book and lyrics by Dorothy Donnelly, based on a novel and play by Wilhelm Meyer-Foerster, and music by Sigmund Romberg; camera (Ansco), Paul C. Vogel; editor, Gene Ruggiero; musical direction, George Stoll; vocal numbers conducted by Constantine Callinicos; musical numbers staged by Hermes Pan; added songs, Nicholas Brodszky and Paul Francis Webster. Previewed May 20, '54. Running time, 107 MINS.
Kathie .... Ann Blyth
Prince Karl .... Edmund Purdom
Count Von Asterburg ..... John Ericson
King of Karlsburg ..... Louis Calhern
Prof. Juttner .... Edmund Gwenn
Joseph Ruder ... S. Z. "Cuddles" Sakall
Princess Johanna ... Betta St. John
Lutz .... John Williams
Queen .... Evelyn Varden
Prime Minister .... John Hoyt
Lucas .... Richard Anderson
Von Fischtenstein .... Roger Allen
Feuerwald .... Steve Rowland
Richter .... Chris Warfield
Von Buhler .... Gilbert Legay
Head Corps Servant .. Archer MacDonald
Hubert .... Charles Davis
Willie Klauber .... John Qualen
(Aspect ratio: 2.55-1)

The venerable operetta about a royal cutup in the beer gardens of Heidelberg has been given a brand new look in this classy Joe Pasternak production via CinemaScope and Anscolor. This latest pic version is a fresh, beguiling musical, beautiful to hear and behold. It should have no trouble at the wickets as its grossing prospects appear excellent.

Along with the new look, the Metro presentation also is notable for a technical trick that makes a warm Italian tenor out of a clipped speech Britisher. The voice personality of Mario Lanza doesn't jibe with the British starch of Edmund Purdom's physical appearance, but not many will mind because the latter's acting is good, as is Lanza's singing of the gay old songs and the three new ones that have been added. Doing her own singing in a gracious, charming manner is Ann Blyth, who might not be everyone's idea of a barmaid who could charm a prince, but she's pert and pretty, plus giving the role an ingratiating performance.

William Ludwig and Sonya Levien play it straight in writing the operetta for the screen, which is probably the reason why it comes over so well. It has plenty of humor mixed in with its straight story and songs, but never goes comic opera. Richard Thorpe's direction takes the same slant and his handling is one of the better phases of the presentation. He keeps things moving at a likeable pace, whether the people are engaging in song, amour or duel.

Falling kindly on the ear are such old numbers as "Serenade," "Deep in My Heart," "Drink, Drink, Drink," "To the Inn We're Marching," "Come, Boys, Let's All Be Gay, Boys" and "Golden Days." To these Sigmund Romberg tunes for which Dorothy Donnelly did the original lyrics and Paul Francis Webster the revised ones used here, have been added three new songs by Webster and Nicholas Brodszky. They are "Beloved," "I'll Walk With God," that is given

a standout staging, and "Summertime in Heidelberg."

Louis Calhern plays, with a flourish, the king who sends his grandson, Purdom, to Heidelberg to learn how to be a man. There the young prince falls in love with Miss Blyth and is about to run away with her when the king's illness and subsequent death intervenes and the prince is forced to renounce true love and take up his kingly duties. All of this is seriously handled and obtains considerable more depth than one might think possible from such a make-believe setup.

Contributing considerably to the new life in the old plot are Edmund Gwenn, the tutor in charge of the prince; S. Z. "Cuddles" Sakall as the barmaid's uncle, and John Williams, the prince's harried valet. It's seasoned character acting the threesome gives the roles and each is very good. Betta St. John charms in the comparatively short-footaged role of the princess who is to marry Purdom. The latter gets an important career break with this major casting and shows himself to be a good performer.

Paul C. Vogel's photography, the musical direction by George Stoll, the film editing, the art direction and settings, costuming and other contributions help add the plush look to this presentation. *Brog.*

High and the Mighty
(C'SCOPE—COLOR)

Socko screen entertainment based on the Ernest K. Gann bestseller. John Wayne for smart b.o. start and hearty grossing prospects.

Hollywood, May 25.
Warner Bros. release of Wayne-Fellows production. Stars John Wayne, Claire Trevor, Laraine Day, Robert Stack, Jan Sterling, Phil Harris, Robert Newton, David Brian; features Paul Kelly, Sidney Blackmer, Julie Bishop, Gonzalez-Gonzalez, John Howard, Doe Avedon, Karen Sharpe, John Smith, Wally Brown, William Campbell, Ann Doran, John Qualen, Paul Fix, George Chandler, Joy Kim. Directed by William A. Wellman. Screenplay by Ernest K. Gann from his novel; camera (Warner-Color), Archie Stout; aerial photography, William Clothier; editor, Ralph Dawson; music composed and conducted by Dimitri Tiomkin. Previewed May 10, '54. Running time, 147 MINS.
Dan Roman .... John Wayne
May Holst .... Claire Trevor
Lydia Rice .... Laraine Day
Sullivan .... Robert Stack
Sally McKee .... Jan Sterling
Ed Joseph .... Phil Harris
Gustave Pardee .... Robert Newton
Ken Childs .... David Brian
Flaherty .... Paul Kelly
Humphrey Agnew ..... Sidney Blackmer
Lillian Pardee .... Julie Bishop
Gonzalez .... Gonzalez-Gonzalez
Howard Rice .... John Howard
Wilby .... Wally Brown
Hobie Wheeler .... William Campbell
Mrs. Joseph .... Ann Doran
Jose Locota .... John Qualen
Frank Briscoe .... Paul Fix
Ben Sneed .... George Chandler
Dorothy Chen .... Joy Kim
Toby Field .... Michael Wellman
Alsop .... Douglas Fowley
Garfield .... Regis Toomey
Ensign Keim .... Carl Switzer
Lt. Mowbray .... Robert Keys
Roy .... William DeWolf Hopper
Dispatcher .... William Schallert
Susie .... Julie Mitchum
    Doe Avedon as Spalding
    Karen Sharpe as Nell Buck
    John Smith as Milo Buck
(Aspect ratios 2.55-1)

Ernest K. Gann's gripping bestseller "The High and the Mighty" has been turned into an equally socko piece of screen entertainment in this Wayne-Fellows presentation through Warner Bros.

It is a class drama, blended with mass appeal into a well-rounded show that can catch on with most any audience. A definite ticket-selling asset is the name of John Wayne. Hearty grosses should be the rule.

There's very little that Gann left out in adapting his novel to film form. This makes for an unnecessarily long motion picture, but one that is so engrossingly told under William A. Wellman's forceful, probing direction that there can't be too much quarreling with the film's two hours and 27 minutes. Trimming, and the footage could well use it, would make the picture play faster, but it is doubtful if such trims would actually make the drama play better.

CinemaScope goes airborne, and in the bright, beautiful hues of WarnerColor, for visual emphasis. There's plenty of punch contributed by the cameras of Archie Stout, working on set mostly within the confines of a passenger plane, and by the aerial photography of William Clothier.

While Wayne is concerned in the production with Robert Fellows, a shared responsibility each brings off with distinction, and has the top star spot, he does not grab most of the footage, even though his personality dominates the film. In fact there is no picture-stealing, each player exhibiting a fine awareness of the character portrayed and socking it over.

The plot has to do with human reactions to danger as a troubled plane, carrying 22 persons, limps through stormy skies en route from Honolulu to San Francisco. Shortly after the takeoff, suspense sets in when the audience is tipped there's trouble, maybe death, aboard. Gradually the crew and then the passengers become aware of danger. Each reacts according to character, the meek become strong while the bravado of others turns sour as the frightened group sweats out the flight. All concerned make the mood so realistic that an audience is literally on the crippled plane with the players, and feels the same relief when the ship finally makes San Francisco and safety after the harrowing flight on three engines and diminishing fuel.

Virtually every member of the large cast delivers a discerning performance but the lineup is too long to give each the individual credit rated. Especially good are Wayne, the older co-pilot under the younger pilot captain, Robert Stack, Wally Brown and William Campbell, crew members, and Doe Avedon, very fine as the stewardess. Standouts among the passengers are Robert Newton, theatrical producer who finds hidden courage; Jan Sterling, faded and soiled beauty, mainland-bound to marry a man she has never seen; Claire Trevor, an aged beauty with money and memories; Paul Kelly, bitter atomic scientist; John Qualen, fiercely proud Italian-born citizen of the U.S.; Paul Fix, rich and hopelessly crippled, and Joy Kim, very fine as the Korean making her first trip to the states.

Phil Harris and Ann Doran, and Laraine Day and John Howard are good as marital pairs on the plane. So are Sidney Blackmer and David Brian, whose private fight has to be put aside when trouble strikes in flight. Karen Sharpe and John Smith are good as the newlyweds who find comfort for their fears in physical embrace as the plane staggers through the stormy night. Making a favorable impression is Gonzalez-Gonzalez, radio operator on a ship who relays the plane's message of danger.

The technical departments deliver outstandingly in backing the dramatics. The same can't be said for the score composed and conducted by Dimitri Tiomkin. It's best when kept simple and being an unobtrusive support for the drama, but too often is over-used and becomes a distraction. *Brog.*

Flight of White Heron

(BRITISH-COLOR)

Anamorphic coverage of the royal tour of the Commonwealth; tough to sell as a first feature.

London, May 18.

20th-Fox release of a Jack Ramsden production; camera, Paul Wyand; editor, Ray Perrin: commentary spoken by Leslie Mitchell; narrative, Gerald Sanger; color by Eastmancolor. At Carlton, London. Running time, **90 MINS.**

This CinemaScope coverage of highlights of the Royal Tour is a glorified travelog without achieving the dramatic impact scored by last year's Coronation epics. It particularly suffers from staleness. Many of the scenes featured have already been screened via the newsreels and shorter color films previously released. Undoubtedly this must be regarded as a tough selling proposition; its length puts it in the first-feature class and it will need exceptionally strong support to get by.

The version reviewed is an advance print. The complete version will include the last stages of the tour, and the return to London. The combined footage will run about 90 minutes.

Only a mere fraction of the immense footage shot necessarily could be included, and wholesale editing is apparent in the finished product. The treatment is scrappy and continuity is frequently forced. These weaknesses, however, do not detract from the panoramic effects captured by the anamorphic lens. The beauty of many scenes is enhanced by the widescreen process although the Eastmancolor lensing is occasionally variable.

Photographic coverage has not been unduly imaginative and the camera has focused most attention on the royal visitors. There are, in addition, several examples of native war dances which are of interest but not unusual. The stereo sound effects are frequently intriguing. *Myro.*

The Queen in Australia

(BRITISH-COLOR)

London, May 18.

General Film Distributors release of Australian government production. Produced by Stanley Hawes; editors, Ralph Sheldon, Stuart Legg; commentators, Peter Finch, Wilfred Thomas; color by Ferraniacolour. At Odeon, Leicester Square, London, May 18, '54. Running time, **71 MINS.**

This is the official record, sponsored by the Australian government, of the Queen's tour of that Commonwealth country, from the day she steamed into Sydney harbor aboard the Gothic with the Duke of Edinburgh until she left to continue her Empire tour two months later. It is a topical, well-made record which should prove to be an asset on any local program although having only spotty chances outside the British Empire.

The film has been made in Ferraniacolour and the system compares unfavorably with more familiar processes. What it lacks in this respect is, however, compensated for by intelligent editing and the compilation of a picture that avoids much of the obvious repetitive incident.

The pic is not unspooled as a chronological record, but events are put in their proper sequence to provide something of a narrative continuity.

The commentary has been briskly written without the too familiar fulsomeness which has characterized similar efforts in the past. It is sincerely narrated by a team of Aussie commentators whose accents occasionally jar on British ears. Only a minimum use is made of direct sound, and the backgrounding is kept on a distinctive key. *Myro.*

Welcome the Queen!

(BRITISH-COLOR)

London, May 25.

Associated British-Pathe release of Howard Thomas production. Editor, Lionel Hoare; music, Sir Arthur Bliss; commentary, John Pudney; commentator, Edward Ward; color by Eastmancolor. At Hammer Theatre, London, May 19, '54. Running time, **50 MINS.**

By rushing this 50-minute special of the Royal Commonwealth tour and bringing it up-to-date by including the scenes of the return to London and the procession to Buckingham Palace, Associated British-Pathe, from a topical point-of-view has a scoop. This film was pre-released last Thursday (20), and was available for world-wide presentation last Monday (24).

Allowing for the fact that the company has already issued a series of featurets on various aspects of the tour, this final record only gives a brief sketch of the earlier scenes and waits until the family reunion outside Tobruk before going into greater detail. And from that point onwards it allows the Royal children, Prince Charles and Princess Anne, to steal a great deal of the limelight, particularly with some appealing shots taken with the Barbary apes in Gibraltar.

The final return to London is given full coverage from the time the royal yacht Britannia enters the Pool of London, with the inevitable closing shots of the Royal family waving to the crowds from the balcony of Buckingham Palace.

Film derives its title from the special march composed by Sir Arthur Bliss, Master of the Queen's Musick. Commentary was penned by John Pudney and is spoken by a team of native commentators, with a typical cockney accent as the Queen sails up the Thames. Production is a credit to the team led by Howard Thomas and Terry Ashwood while the Eastmancolor lensing brings out the best of the varied backgrounds. *Myro.*

Flamenco

(SPANISH—COLOR)

Martin J. Lewis release of Suevia Films production (Edgar Neville-Cesareo Gonzales). Stars Antonio, Maria Luz, Pilar Lopez, Ballet Espanol; with Alejandro Vega, Roberto Ximenez, Monolo Vargas, Alberto Lorca, Elvira Real, Rosario Escudero, Dorita Ruiz, Pacita Tomas. Directed by Neville. Camera, Enrique Guerner; color by Cinefotocolor of Barcelona; English adaptation and titles by Walter Terry; singers, Almaden, Aurelio de Cadiz, Antonio Mairena, El Pili, El Nino de la Cantera, Manzanilla; guitarists, Maravilla, Badajoz, Rafael de Jerez, El Titi, Moralto Chico, El Poeta; music, Albeniz, Granados, Chueca, Father Soler and Popular Flamenco. Tradeshown in N. Y., May 20, '54. Running time, **79 MINS.**

(English Titles)

"Flamenco" boasts dancing by Pilar Lopez, Antonio, formerly of Rosario & Antonio; the Ballet Espanol, Maria Luz, Pacita Tomas and Roberto Ximenez; bullfighter Juan Belmonte; assorted guitarists and singers and virtually every known type of flamenco dance. But it all adds up to tedious screen fare, badly conceived, and produced and directed without inspiration or originality. Pruned down to 45 minutes or less, it might do in many arty theatres. But as is, it will have quite a limited audience even in these houses.

Lacking any plot or semblance of story, "Flamenco" comes over on the screen as a string of flamenco terps artists strutting their stuff. Several leaders in this type of dancing fail to overcome the static effect of the stilted direction. Director (co-producer) Edgar Neville might have made something of this, even without a story, if he had varied his pace and spotted his numbers with more intelligence. Front part is a series of not too interesting dances—all done to guitar accompaniment (and often vocal wailing). Later on, a smooth symph orchestra plays for the terp efforts, but by that time the monotony of the strumming has taken its toll.

Another example is that the only younger femme dancer, Maria Luz, is used extensively in a group of flamencos early in the pic. Yet, Pacita Tomas, who goes over solidly, is held until the last to do a bolero dance. And is seen only once.

Antonio, who is credited with the artistic supervision of the vehicle, is on only twice, once very early in the pic and then at the finale. It appears a waste of probably the best terpsing in the film.

With the bulk of action limited to this dancing, production naturally must lean on the color and direction to help carry the load. Neither measures up. Cinefotocolor of Barcelona is the tinter process used, and it is highly disappointing. Only the most brilliant blues come through, many majestic scenes being blurred by the washedout color. Even the smart English adaptation and titles by Walter Terry, dance critic of the N. Y. Herald Tribune, fail to make up for the dull proceedings of the picture itself. *Wear.*

The Devil's Pitchfork

(Ana-Ta-Han)

(JAPANESE)

Exploitable sex study well done except for pretentions narration.

Arlas Quality Pictures release of Daiwa production. Stars Akimi Negishi. Written, protographed and directed by Josef von Sternberg. Based on a book by Michiro Maruyama. Camera, K. Okazak; editor, M. Miyata; music, A. Ifukube. At the Plaza Theatre, N.Y., May 17, '54. Running time, **92 MINS.**

Queen Bee	Akemi Negishi
Husband	Suganuma
Drones	Sawamura, Nakayama, Fujikawa, Kondo, Miyashita
Skippers	Tsuruemon, Kikuji
At the Shamisen	Kokuriro
Homesick Ones	Tamura, Kitagawa, Suzuki
Patriot	Amikura

(In Japanese; English Narration)

This Japanese entry with English narration is a strange and engrossing tale of a group of Japanese soldiers and fisherman stranded on a remote South Pacific island. Based on a true incident which saw these holdouts "surrender" seven years after the end of War II, it tells the story of the gradual disintegration of these men as they vie for the affections of the one woman on the island.

Pic was originally titled "Ana-Ta-Han," but was changed because of difficulty in pronouncing the name.

Sex is the motivating factor in the adventure offered by Josef von Sternberg, who wrote, photographed and directed the picture. As such, it has exploitation values to make it a possibility as a secondary feature in general situations. In addition, it has artistic overtones to make it an acceptable attraction for arty houses.

Shipwrecked after a bombing by American planes, the men land at Anatahan where they find one couple, a Japanese plantation overseer and a pretty Japanese girl. At first disciplined and determined to defend the island at all costs, the castaways slowly forget their patriotism and decency and become "animals" in their desire for the lone femme. Death is the inevitable result and five are killed in fights over the "Queen Bee."

As the "Queen Bee," von Sternberg introduces a new find — luscious 19-year-old Akemi Negishi. At first standoffish in her reception of the newcomers, Miss Negishi develops into a tantalizing flirt and contributes considerably to the downfall of the men. Although true to the Japanese tradition of no kissing, the scenes between Miss Negishi and her lover of the moment are nevertheless passionately portrayed.

Film, as a whole, is sizzling adult stuff, well played by a good cast. The narration, spoken by von Sternberg himself, is too flowery and becomes pretentious hokum at times. There are slow-moving moments in the development of the yarn, but these can be overlooked in light of the overall effect. Von Sternberg delivers solid photographic values and the authentic Japanese musical background is excellent. *Holl.*

Girls Marked Danger
(Trattadella Bianche)
(ITALIAN)

I.F.E. release of a Ponti-De Laurentis production. Stars Silvana Pampanini, Eleonora Rossi Drago, Sophia Loren, Tamara Lees, Marc Lawrence, Vittorio Gassman Directed by Luigi Comencini. Story and screenplay, Massimo Patrizi, Ivo Perilli, Antonio Pietrangeli, Luigi Giscosi, Comencini; camera, Luciano Trasatti; music, Armando Trovaioli. Tradeshown in N.Y., May 13, '54. Running time, **78 MINS.**

Lucia .... Silvana Pampanini
Alda .... Eleonora Rossi Drago
Elvira .... Sophia Loren
Clara .... Tamara Lees
Maquedi .... Marc Lawrence
Michele .... Vittorio Gassman
Fanny .... Barbara Florian
Carlo .... Ettore Manni
Gancio .... Gianni Bonos
Giorgio .... Enrico M. Salerno
Linuccia .... Bruna Rossini

I. F. E. has tried its hand at dubbing "Girls Marked Danger," and has come up with an old-fashioned meller reminiscent of the best European thrillers of this sort. Pic accentuates action with a liberal dash of sex. This looks oke for arty spots and foreign-language theatres; of names Vittorio Gassman is nearest to familiar. Marc Lawrence, Silvana Pampanini, Eleonora Drago and Tamara Lees less so. Several comely girls are nice to contemplate.

Action centers around a vice king, operating in an Italian seaport city, who employs his dance hall and dance marathons to recruit girls for South American dance jobs. Everybody but the gals themselves knows they are destined for sporting houses in the Latino countries, but a couple of them wise up towards the pic's end. Don't they have any Sunday supplements in Italy?

With this as the main thesis, a daring robbery which puts some of the town's pretty thieves in the clink starts wheels turning to release the four or five men from prison. A couple of the girls decide to earn money at a dance marathon, depicted here at its worst. Apparently the modus-operandi was to sign up the femme contestants at the end of such endurance contests or when they flunk out. Pacting is for these boat trips to South America.

One girl, Miss Pampanini, is persuaded by her boy friend, Gassman, to enter a "modeling establishment" as an eacy way to obtain money. She has a chance to develop her voice, but a touch of this (and her vocalizing is okay), and she is back to her affairs with men. To complicate matters, Lawrence, a cadet of the white slave syndicate, falls for her. This permits a spicy bedroom sequence which appears modified a bit by scissoring. The gang is brought to justice but not until Miss Drago has suffered for hours in the dance marathon. She finally dies after a beating and childbirth.

Several episodes are lurid in the extreme while there is too much brutality in the scene where Miss Drago is kicked and beaten. Lawrence makes the meanest type of villain in this and other sequences, portraying a role not unlike the gangsters in American pix of the 1930's. Gassman has an unsympathetic part as an unscrupulous hanger-on for the vice syndicate, but is effective when given an opportunity. Ettore Manni, the nearest thing to a hero in the piece, is husky type but handicapped by being jailed much of the pic.

Standout femme portrayal is contributed by Miss Pampanini who displays surprising thespian ability to go along with her looks. She is the gal who chooses the "easiest way." Miss Drago suffers most of the time, but does it well. Sophia Loren is good enough in a second romantic role but difficult to keep track of because looking different in so many scenes. Miss Lees, one of the comeliest of the four principal femmes, is superb as partner of the vice king and supervisor of the "models." Support is headed by Barbara Florian, Gianni Bonos and Enrico M. Salerno.

Story and screenplay is remarkably tight in view of how many were involved in turning it out. Luigi Comencini's direction helps much to overcome some of the scripting uneveness. Armando Trovaioli's background music is excellent. Camerawork of Luciano Trasatti ranges from strong to ordinary. *Wear.*

Les Revoltes de Lomanach
(The Rebels of Lomanach)
(FRANCO-ITALIAN-COLOR)

Paris, May 11.

Gaumont release of Gaumont-Orso Film production. Stars Dany Robin, Amedeo Nazzari. Directed by Richard Pottier. Screenplay, Leo Joannon, Jacques Sigurd; dialog, Sigurd; camera (Eastmancolor), Jean Leherissey; editor, Jean Feyte. At Marignan, Paris. Running time, **90 MINS.**

Barnaud .... Amedeo Nazzari
Monique .... Dany Robin
Lomanach .... Jean Debucourt
Henriette .... Carla Del Poggio
Jean .... Michel Vitold
Chouan .... Jean Danet
Baron .... Jacques Castelot

This is the first French color pic conceived entirely for widescreen showing, and also has an added stereophonic system. Pic falls into the category of a competently-made action drama taking place after the French revolution and depicting the uprising of a group of noblemen against the new republic in the Vendee back in 1799. Love story and action are of familiar calibre, and this has some name value for France and Italy. For the U. S., this is primarily for some dualers. The widescreen might make this a likely feature for dubbing for U. S. action markets.

The leader of the republican forces, Amedeo Nazzari, has a personal reason for avenging himself on the upstart nobles because of an affront done to him by the proud daughter many years ago. The younger daughter slips off to kill him and stop the carnage, but she is disarmed and made to work for the general. Love blooms and both sides try to carry on the war despite the subdued attempts of the two to avert further bloodshed. Both are finally killed on the battlefield by the fanatics on either side.

Battle scenes are well done. The Eastmancolor is uneven in spots, but on the whole gives this a nice hue. Widescreen is well composed, but has a tendency to be blurred in many interior long shots. Dany Robin is adequately superior and loving as the spirited noblewoman while Nazzari brings stature to the role of the general torn between love and duty. Lensing and editing are okay. Crowds and production values add to the worth of the pic. *Mosk.*

Le Grand Jeu
(The Big Game)
(FRANCO-ITALIAN)
(Color)

Cannes, April 20.

Cinedis release of Speva-Rizzoli production. Stars Gina Lollobrigida, Jean-Claude Pascal, Arletty. Directed by Robert Siodmak. Camera (Eastmancolor), Michel Kelber; editor, V. Mercantan; screenplay, Charles Spaak. At Cannes Film Festival. Running time, **95 MINS.**

Helena }
Silvia } .... Gina Lollobrigida
Blanche .... Arletty
Pierre .... Jean-Claude Pascal
Mario .... Raymond Pellegrin
Fred .... Peter Van Eyck

Robert Siodmak makes his return to the French studios with this, his first film made here since 1936. It is a remake of a Jacques Feyder film done in 1935. Pic suffers from the usual remake shortcomings with this Foreign Legion story a bit oldhat, and lacking the romantic verve of yore. However, it has color and Gina Lollobrigida which should make this a neat grosser locally, but for the U.S. this is more problematical. This is not for the art house run, but could be of interest for special situations or for more general interest on its color, locale and building Gina Lollobrigida name.

Story is a bit vague, with too many coincidences to make this moving. It concerns a shady lawyer, who has spoiled his ravishing mistress by heaping luxuries on her. When he has trouble with his affairs he skips to Algeria and she never joins him. He joins up with the Foreign Legion to forget, but is haunted by her beauty. One day thinks he sees her but she is a local joy girl who resembles her exactly. She has had an accident and doesn't remember all her early life. He insists on trying to find his lost love in her, and finally they fall in love. His mistress turns up, and he sends the double off to Paris and goes back to the Legion.

The Eastmancolor is a bit uneven and garish in spots, but does full justice to the hue and complexion of Miss Lollobrigida who brings her bosomy beauty to the dual role of the loved one and the filler-in. Jean Claude Pascal is uneven as the tricky attorney who joins the Legion. Arletty plays an aging woman, patron to her soldiers, in a shuffly, sotto-voiced manner. Direction is fine but can not do much with this dated story. The characters are never fully developed enough to make this of interest for more important U.S. slotting. Lack of actual action footage in the Legion is also a drawback. *Mosk.*

Tarantella Napoletana
(MUSICAL-COLOR)

I.F.E. Releasing Corp. release of Titus Film production. Stars the Armando Curcio Company's players. Features the Gauthier Ballet with Claudia Lawrence and Teddy Barnett. Directed by Camillio Mastrocinque. Story, book, and lyrics, Armando Curcio; camera (Gaevacolor), Maciocchi, Varriani and Regis; music and arrangements, Curcio. At Cinema Verdi, N.Y., April 17, '54. Running time, **86 MINS.**

Cast: Clara Bindi, Clara Crispo, Vittorio Crispo, Dino Curcio, Renato Di Napoli, Mario Frera, Giacomo Furia, Amadeo Girard, Rosuta Pisano, Antonio La Raina, Dino Valdi, Lina Viti, Maria Paris, Gabriele Vanorio, and Nupzio Gallo.

(Italian; English Titles)

Italo excursion into musical comedy emerges as a potpourri of standard vaude acts and sketches thrown together without much rhyme or reason. There may be ingredients in this import that will appeal to Italian language audiences, but its chances for general patronage or booking in artie situations appear slim.

The picture, filmed in an Italo-developed color process known as Gaevacolor, purports to be "a joyous tribute to Naples . . . to its songs and dances . . . to the spirit of the people who teem through its picturesque streets." Unfortunately none of this emerges for the reader of the English titles. The musical numbers are undistinguished and the sketches are noticeable only by their loudness.

The offering has no story line. It consists of 16 sketches and dances, with Neapolitan songs and music. It features the players and singers of Armando Curcio's Company and the Gauthier Ballet with Claudia Lawrence and Teddy Barnett.

The color process employed is, on the whole, good, although a bluish tinge appears to predominate. The camera work lacks ingenuity. The film seems to have been filmed directly from a stage performance. *Holl.*

Quai des Blondes
(FRENCH-COLOR)

Paris, May 11.

Pathe Consortium release of P.A.C.-Hunnebelle production. Stars Michel Auclair, Barbara Laage. Directed by Paul Cadeac. Screenplay, Pierre Foucaud, Michel Audiard, Cadeac; dialog, Audiard; camera (Gevacolor), Marcel Grignon; editor, Roger Dwyre. At Balzac, Paris. Running time, **90 MINS.**

Jacques ....Michel Auclair
Barbara ....Barbara Laage
Nelly ....Madeleine Lebeau
Lucky ....Dario Moreno
Marco ....Andre Valmy
Inspector ....Rene Blancard

Another in a cycle of gangster pix here, this adds color to a few marquee names which should make for a nice general run in France. For the U. S., this is much too familiar to mean much. It also lacks names. Its locale of Marseilles and Algiers, with American cigarette contraband as its focal point, might give some exploitation values in special situations.

This concerns a young cigarette smuggler, Michel Auclair, whose boat is hijacked by a rival gang. In getting his loot and revenge, he gets mixed up with two femmes in the usual bedroom escapades, is beat up and fired upon. But he finally comes through it with a girl, and a promise to a sympathetic police inspector to go straight.

Salted into the pic are some brutal shootings, fisticuffs and gunfights. Color is unnecessary in the black and white goings-on, and tends to be faded in exteriors. Michel Auclair is good as the snide anti-hero with Barbara Laage and Madeleine Lebeau as good support. Editing is okay as is supporting cast. Direction is more than adequate. *Mosk.*

Demetrius and the Gladiators
(C'Scope-Color)

Socko followup to "The Robe" with mass appeal and hearty b.o. potential.

Hollywood, June 1.
20th-Fox release of Frank Ross production. Stars Victor Mature, Susan Hayward; co-stars Michael Rennie, Debra Paget, Anne Bancroft, Jay Robinson; features Barry Jones, William Marshall, Richard Egan, Ernest Borgnine, Charles Evans. Directed by Delmer Daves. Written by Philip Dunne; based on a character created by Lloyd C. Douglas in "The Robe"; camera (Technicolor), Milton Krasner; editors, Dorothy Spencer, Robert Fritch; music, Franz Waxman; themes from "The Robe" by Alfred Newman. Previewed May 21, '54. Running Time, 101 MINS.

Demetrius ....Victor Mature
Messalina ....Susan Hayward
Peter ....Michael Rennie
Lucia ....Debra Paget
Paula ....Anne Bancroft
Caligula ....Jay Robinson
Claudius ....Barry Jones
Glycon ....William Marshall
Dardanius ....Richard Egan
Strabo ....Ernest Borgnine
Cassius Chaerea ....Charles Evans
Kaeso ....Everett Glass
Macro ....Karl Davis
Albus ....Jeff York
Slave Girl ....Carmen de Lavallade
Varus ....John Cliff
Specialty Dancers .....Barbara James,
                       Willetta Smith
Senator ....Selmer Jackson
Cousin ....Douglas Brooks
Decurion ....Fred Graham
Magistrate ....Dayton Lummis
Flavius ....Robert E. Griffin

(Aspect ratio: 2.55-1)

"Demetrius and the Gladiators" is 20th-Fox's answer and followup to its tremendously successful "The Robe." It would be a hit even without the tie to last season's smash grosser because, in many ways, it is a show of more popular entertainment appeal. This doesn't mean "Robe"-type grosses; after all, it's not introducing CinemaScope, nor re-creating the Lloyd C. Douglas best-selling novel. It does have socko action—dramatic pull, with just enough religious overtones, to keep the boxoffice bell tolling loud and profitable.

While Douglas's fine novel from which 20th-Fox and Frank Ross filmed "The Robe" springboards this followup, it is a completely new story, beautifully fashioned with all the basics of good drama and action that can play, and quite often do, against any setting, period or modern. In the compelling Philip Dunne screen story, and under the equally compelling direction by Delmer Daves, "Demetrius" swings from "The Robe's" mysterious, religious miracle theme of the crucifixion, that pictured the establishment of a faith, to a story of the trial of a man's faith by the temptations of an attractive, amoral woman and a pagan Rome.

The opening scene of "Demetrius" is the closing scene of "The Robe," in which Marcellus and Diana, condemned to death because of their Christian beliefs, pass on the robe worn by the Crucifixion by Jesus Christ so that it can find its way to the Apostle Peter, "the big Fisherman." Later in the picture another scene from "The Robe" is used—that tremendous Crucifixion sequence in which the Greek slave Demetrius kneels at the feet of Christ, mute anguish mirrored in his face. Other than these two scenes, the same Roman settings and the overlying religious theme of Christianity's troubled beginning, "Demetrius" strides a different course than the picture to which it is a worthy successor.

Victor Mature again scores with the character of the slave in this second Frank Ross production. A mighty man is he battling three

huge tigers in the Roman arena to satisfy the mad urges of the crazy Emperor Caligula and the wicked Messalina, dueling to the death with five of Rome's best gladiators, or making love to the same wicked temptress who has temporarily caused him to forget his God. As in all basic stories, this one has a happy ending, not unwelcome after the trial by fire and brimestone through which the fallen has been dragged.

Curiously, and as first exampled in "The Robe," CinemaScope is never seen to better advantage than when mirroring the pageantry of the pagan Roman setting. It almost seems that the anamorphic lens was meant for Biblical drama. Certainly it is hard to conceive of any other photographic process doing as much with the scenes of the arena fights between man and men, and man and beast, or the sweeping panoramas of pagan court sessions and other visual fixtures of the period.

With Mature easily winning top acting honors for his splendidly project Demetrius, he is pressed by Susan Hayward as the evil Messalina, and Jay Robinson, repeating his mad, effeminate Caligula. Fine is Michael Rennie, again seen as the Apostle Peter, a man of quiet strength. Barry Jones, too, is good as the weak Claudius, elderly husband of the amoral Messalina, as are William Marshall, the huge Nubian gladiator, Richard Egan and Ernest Borgnine, arena experts. Debra Paget, the gentle Lucia who loves Demetrius, and Anne Bancroft, who tries to help them, are good without making too much impact.

A credit run-down finds Milton Krasner's photography, the music by Franz Waxman, with themes from Alfred Newman's "Robe" score, the editing, art direction, set decorations, costuming and other contributions figuring most importantly in making this a well-rounded, entertaining, motion picture. *Brog.*

Seven Brides For Seven Brothers
(C'Scope Musical-Color

Slick, entertaining country-style musical with a B'way polish, good songs, cast and word-of-mouth possibilities for sturdy takes.

Hollywood, June 1.
Metro release of Jack Cummings production. Stars Jane Powell, Howard Keel; features Jeff Richards, Russ Tamblyn, Tommy Rall, Howard Petrie, Virginia Gibson, Ian Wolfe. Directed by Stanley Donen. Screenplay, Albert Hackett, Frances Goodrich, Dorothy Kingsley; based on the story, "The Sobbin' Women" by Stephen Vincent Benet; camera (Ansco Color), George Folsey; editor, Ralph E. Winters; songs, Johnny Mercer, Gene de Paul; musical direction, Adolph Deutsch; musical supervision, Saul Chaplin; dances and musical numbers staged by Michael Kidd. Previewed May 26, '54. Running time, 102 MINS.

The Pontipee Brothers:
Adam ....Howard Keel
Benjamin ....Jeff Richards
Gideon ....Russ Tamblyn
Frank ....Tommy Rall
Daniel ....Marc Platt
Caleb ....Matt Mattox
Ephraim ....Jacques d'Amboise
The Brides:
Milly ....Jane Powell
Dorcas ....Julie Newmeyer
Alice ....Nancy Kilgas
Sarah ....Betty Carr
Liza ....Virginia Gibson
Ruth ....Ruta Kilmonis
Martha ....Norma Doggett
Rev. Elcott ....Ian Wolfe
Pete Perkins ....Howard Petrie
Harry ....Earl Barton
Matt ....Dante DiPaolo
Carl ....Kelly Brown
Ruth's Uncle ....Matt Moore
Dorcas' Father ....Dick Rich

Mrs. Bixby ....Marjorie Wood
Mr. Bixby ....Russell Simpson
(Aspect ratio: 2.55-1)

This is a happy, hand-clapping, foot-stomping, country type of musical with all the slickness of a Broadway show. It offers songs, dances and romancing in such a delightful package that word-of-mouth could talk it into solid business at the boxoffice. On merit alone, it rates sturdy returns and can be sold almost without qualifications as one of the fresher pieces of tune entertainment to hit the current market. CinemaScope and Ansco Color aid the visual assets.

Johnny Mercer and Gene de Paul provide the slick, showy Jack Cummings production with eight songs, all of which jibe perfectly with the folksy, hillbilly air maintained in the picture. Howard Keel's robust baritone and Jane Powell's lilting soprano make their songs extremely listenable. In that category is Keel's handling of the lusty "Bless Your Beautiful Hide," Miss Powell's "Wonderful, Wonderful Day," their work together and solo on "When You're In Love," which gets two reprises; the hearty "Sobbin' Women" done by Keel, and Miss Powell's "Goin' Co'tin."

The Broadway show touch comes from having Michael Kidd to stage the dances and musical numbers. A real standout is the acrobatic hoedown staged around a barn-raising shindig, during which six of the title's seven brothers vie in love rivalry with the town boys for the favor of the mountain belles. From a square dance, to acrobatics, to a spirited free-for-all brawl, it's a rousing sequence, packed with rhythmic fun and mayhem.

Cute is the brothers' embryonic dancing to "Co'tin'" as they get their first instructions in the niceties of courtship. Effective is the staging of "Sobbin'," in which, via song, older brother Keel tells his young kin the wonderful story of how some ancient Romans raided the homes of the Sabines and ran off with the women, a saga that cues the plot and title. Stylized to the extreme is the posturing ballet to "Lament." Virginia Gibson leads the brides, garbed in corsets and bloomers, in an okay song-terp blend to "June Bride." Least effective, in fact seeming almost foreign to the other staging, is "Spring, Spring, Spring," sung and danced by the brides and grooms.

With tunes and terping taking up so much of the footage there isn't too much for Stanley Donen to do except direct the story bridges between the numbers. This he does adequately enough, though he should have given the characters more depth and less broadness, particularly in the earlier sequences. What plot there is in the script by Albert Hackett, Frances Goodrich and Dorothy Kingsley, based on Stephen Vincent Benet's "The Sobbin' Women," almost plays itself, being conceived for amusement in dialog and situation. It's the story of seven brothers living on a mountain farm. The eldest gets a bride and the others decide likewise, steal their maidens and, after a snowed-in winter, the girls' parents mastermind a mass shotgun wedding.

The long and the short of the teaming of Keel and Miss Powell is that the pairing comes off very satisfactorily, vocally and otherwise. The brothers are all good, with Russ Tamblyn standing out in particular for performance and his dance work with such terpers as Tommy Rall, Marc Platt and Jacques d'Amboise. Jeff Richards also more than holds his own. Pleasing as the brides are Julie Newmeyer, Nancy Kilgas, Betty Carr, Virginia Gibson, Ruta Kilmonis and Norma Doggett. Those portraying the townspeople do their parts well.

The CinemaScope lensing by George Folsey is clear as a bell, with no movement blur or image fuzziness. Ralph E. Winters' edited the footage effectively. The musical supervision by Saul Chaplin and the musical direction by Adolph Deutsch are first-rate credits. *Brog.*

Johnny Dark
(COLOR)

Good sports car racing actioner with Tony Curtis, Piper Laurie and pop market possibilities.

Hollywood, June 1.
Universal release of William Alland production. Stars Tony Curtis, Piper Laurie, Don Taylor; features Paul Kelly, Ilka Chase, Sidney Blackmer, Ruth Hampton. Directed by George Sherman; written by Franklin Coen; camera (Technicolor), Carl Guthrie; editor, Edward Curtiss; technical advisor, H. Malle Chace. Previewed May 5, '54. Running time, 85 MINS.

Johnny Dark .... Tony Curtis
Liz .... Piper Laurie
Duke Benson .... Don Taylor
Jim Scott .... Paul Kelly
Abbie Binns .... Ilka Chase
James Fielding .... Sidney Blackmer
Miss Border-to-Border ... Ruth Hampton
Emory .... Russell Johnson
Svenson .... Joseph Sawyer
Smitty .... Robert Nichols
E. J. Winston .... Pierre Watkin
Himself .... Scat Man Crothers
Morgan .... Ralph Montgomery

(Aspect ratio: 2-1)

Sports car racing backgrounds this actionful Universal entry and its rpm output along the pop market track should be good, especially since it teams Tony Curtis and Piper Laurie to attract the younger set of ticket buyers.

Footage has plenty of thrills for the wouldbe sports car enthusiasts in such sequences as fast rides over proving ground tracks, an airport race over a fixed course, and the staged border-to-border road race that served as the story's climaxing action. Members of the real ring-and-piston set may marvel at the ingenuity and dispatch with which motion pictures bring these things off, but for the paying customers it's a good show, expertly fashioned to entertain under the production guidance of William Alland and the quickpaced direction of George Sherman.

Curtis plays the title character in Franklin Coen's screen original. He's an engineer at an independent automobile plant who suddenly gets a chance to build the sports car he has designed under company sponsorship. When he finds out the construction was just a maneuver in a fight between old-fashioned management, represented by Sidney Blackmer, and progressive stockholders, represented by Pierre Watkin, Curtis swipes the car. With his buddy Don Taylor, driving, the car comes a cropper in the airport race and the buddies fall out. This sets the stage for Curtis to drive the machine in the border-to-border (Canadian-Mexican) race and if you don't know before-hand that he finishes the race in front of Taylor you've been sleeping through too many of this type derring-do film.

Miss Laurie is pretty as a picture as the romantic prize that Curtis wins along with the race. Paul Kelly, plant foreman and Cur-

tis' supporter, Ilka Chase, another Curtis supporter and long-suffering secretary to Blackmer, and the latter give the picture some substance in performance, although the demands do not draw heavily on the trio's experience. Ruth Hampton shows up the correct lines as the scantily-clad Miss Border-to-Border who greets the drivers along the way.

The long road race is thrillingly staged to get the most reaction from the viewer. Cameras either ride the hood of a car around mountain curves, or take to the air in helicopter and plane for other thrill footage that will keep the customers on edge. Carl Guthrie did the excellent color lensing. Editing by Edward Curtiss· leaves little excess footage and the other technical assists deliver capably. *Brog.*

The Raid
(COLOR)

Stirring Civil War yarn based on true incident; particularly strong programmer.

Hollywood, May 27.
Twentieth-Fox release of a Leonard Goldstein-Robert L. Jacks production. Stars Van Heflin; co-stars Anne Bancroft, Richard Boone, Lee Marvin; features Tommy Rettig, Peter Graves, Douglas Spencer, Paul Cavanagh, Will Wright, James Best, John Dierkes, Helen Ford, Harry Hines. Directed by Hugo Fregonese. Screenplay, Sydney Boehm; screen story, Francis Cockrell; based on "Affair at St. Albans," by Herbert Ravenal Sass; camera (Technicolor), Lucien Ballard; editor, Robert Golden; music, Roy Webb. Previewed May 26, '54. Running time, 82 MINS.

Major Neal Benton......... Van Heflin
Katy Bishop .... Anne Bancroft
Captain Foster .... Richard Boone
Lieutenant Keating .... Lee Marvin
Larry Bishop .... Tommy Rettig
Captain Dwyer .... Peter Graves
Reverend Lucas........ Douglas Spencer
Colonel Tucker .... Paul Cavanagh
Banker Anderson .... Will Wright
Lieutenant Robinson .... James Best
Corporal Dean .... John Dierkes
Delphine Coates .... Helen Ford
Mr. Danzig .... Harry Hines
Captain Henderson .... Simon Scott
Lieutenant Ramsey .... Claude Akins

(Aspect ratio: 1.66-1)

Depiction of a little-known incident during the Civil War, "The Raid" stacks up as a stirring and suspenseful entry for top bracketing in the program market and should run up better than average returns. One of Leonard Goldstein's slate for 20th-Fox release, production handling by Robert L. Jacks is distinctive and Hugo Fregonese has given film particularly rugged direction, a cast headed by Van Heflin competently delineating colorful characters.

Screenplay by Sidney Boehm is based upon the raid of a small Vermont town in 1864 by a band of Confederate soldiers crossing over from Canada, to give Northerners a taste of the tragic events which have beset Southern families. Taken from Herbert Ravenal Sass' true story, "Affair at St. Albans," episode has been developed dramatically and realistically, its tense unfoldment assuring rapt audience attention during its full length. Technicolor feature should benefit by ·vord-of-mouth publicity as well as by the exploitation potential of its subject matter.

Heflin portrays a Confederate major who leads the escape of seven Rebel officers from a Union prison in northern New York. Taking temporary refuge in Canada, he returns to the hamlet of St. Albans, Vt., near border, in guise of a Montreal businessman looking for a site to set up shop, but actually to survey geography of the town for a daring venture. This is to

take the town with a handful of Confederate soldiers, sack and destroy it to divert Northern troops back to New England and thus relieve Union pressure on Gen. Lee.

Star delivers impressively as he carefully lays his plans, which nearly are stymied when a column of Union cavalry shows up minutes before the scheduled raid, delayed then for 48 hours. Heflin shades his role with fine restraint, a quality further reflected in the manner in which Fregonese helms the full progress of the planned attack.

Excellent support is afforded right down the line, headed by Anne Bancroft, a young war widow at whose boarding house Heflin takes a room; Richard Boone as a one-armed Union veteran; and Lee Marvin, a Southern officer whose fiery temper nearly wrecks the proposed raid and who is shot down by Heflin. Peter Graves and John Dierkes also stand out as Rebels, Tommy Rettig is in for a key spot as Miss Bancroft's young son who rides for Union help when the raid begins, and Will Wright is the banker. Balance of cast individually score.

Technical departments are strongly handled, Lucien Ballard's photography graphically attuned to Robert Golden's fast editing. Roy Webb's musical score fits the action patly. *Whit.*

Adventures of Robinson Crusoe
(COLOR)

Attractively done-up version of the Daniel Defoe classic that should excite and delight the juves.

United Artists release of an Oscar Dancigers-Henry Ehrlich production. Stars Dan O'Herlihy and James Fernandez; features Felipe De Alba, Chel Lopez, Jose Chavez, Emilio Garibay. Directed by Luis Bunuel. Screenplay by Phillip Roll and Bunuel, based on the Daniel Defoe story; camera (Pathecolor), Alex Phillips; editors, Carlos Savage, Alberto Valenzuela. Previewed April 26, '54 in N.Y. Running time, 90 MINS.

Robinson Crusoe .... Dan O'Herlihy
Friday .... James Fernandez
Capt. Oberzo .... Felipe De Alba
Bos'n .... Chel Lopez

(Aspect Ratio: 1.33 to 1)

"Robinson Crusoe," the Daniel Defoe classic which has thrilled and excited youngsters all over the the world for more than two centuries, has been brought to the screen by Oscar Dancigers and Henry Ehrlich with taste and a good deal of pictorial imagination. Pic, which by the very nature of the story is turned into a tour-de-force for Dan O'Herlihy as Crusoe, is a natural for the juve trade. If properly exploited, it should parlay its adventure theme into a hefty b.o. take.

Made in Mexico, "Crusoe" is the first sound and color version of the Defoe tale. Although a good part of it is taken up with the shipwreck and Crusoe's establishment of a home on the island on which he is to dwell for more than 28 years, director Luis Bunuel keeps the hero on the move but doesn't neglect to establish the torment of a man suddenly cut off from all outside communication, a dog his only companion.

There's plenty in the Defoe book to fill the screen with all sorts of activity and O'Herlihy, a graduate of Dublin's Abbey Theatre, enters with gusto into the spirit of the thing. Film realistically shows him aging through the years and he's excellent in communicating emo-

tions which screen rarely has a chance to express. All this changes, of course, when he has his run-in with the cannibals and rescues Friday from death. He gains a faithful companion whom he teaches English and the ways of civilized men as far as the primitive surroundings will permit.

O'Herlihy, with the exception of a few scenes, is completely believable, whether it's working on his house or holding conversations with flowers and insects. His performance, aided by Bunuel's expert direction and Alex Phillip's fine lensing, gives the film distinction. James Fernandez as Friday, the savage who learns to respect and love his rescuer after an initial period of uneasy suspicion and distrust, steps right out of the pages of the book. Felipe De Alba is splendid as the captain.

Pathe color comes through very well and in natural tones that provide added values. Bunuel's megging is intelligent and places the accent where it belongs, building suspense and tension as Crusoe suddenly discovers that he's sharing the island with cannibals. *Hift.*

The Caine Mutiny
(COLOR)

Forceful film treatment of the Herman Wouk bestseller; strong names, socko b.o.

Hollywood, June 8.

Columbia release of Stanley Kramer production. Stars Humphrey Bogart, Jose Ferrer, Van Johnson, Fred MacMurray; introducing Robert Francis, May Wynn. Directed by Edward Dmytryk. Screenplay, Stanley Roberts added dialog, Michael Blankfort; based on novel by Herman Wouk; camera (Technicolor), Frank Planer; special effects, Lawrence W. Butler; production design, Rudolph Sternad; editors, William A. Lyon, Henry Batista; technical adviser, Comdr. James C. Shaw; score, Max Steiner; songs, Jimmy McHugh and Clarence Gaskill, Fred Karger and Herman Wouk. Previewed June 3, '54. Running time, **123 MINS.**

Captain Queeg	Humphrey Bogart
Lt. Barney Greenwald	Jose Ferrer
Lt. Steve Maryk	Van Johnson
Lt. Tom Keefer	Fred MacMurray
Ensign Willie Keith	Robert Francis
May Wynn	May Wynn
Captain DeVriess	Tom Tully
Lt. Cdr. Challee	E. G. Marshall
Lt. Paynter	Arthur Franz
Meatball	Lee Marvin
Captain Blakely	Warner Anderson
Horrible	Claude Akins
Mrs. Keith	Katharine Warren
Ensign Harding	Jerry Paris
Chief Budge	Steve Brodie
Stilwell	Todd Karns
Lt. Cdr. Dickson	Whit Bissell
Lt. Jorgensen	James Best
Ensign Carmody	Joe Haworth
Ensign Rabbit	Guy Anderson
Whittaker	James Edwards
Urban	Don Dubbins
Engstrand	David Alpert

(*Aspect ratio*: 1.85-1)

"The Caine Mutiny" is highly recommendable motion picture drama, told on the screen as forcefully as it was in the Herman Wouk best-selling novel. For exhibitors, the Stanley Kramer production, being released by Columbia, is a topgrade booking, slated for strong boxoffice in both the class and mass markets. In the latter it has extremely good exploitation sales points, as well as star names, to attract ticket window attention.

Wouk's novel didn't reach the screen without some behind-the-scene struggle. Most necessary was Navy cooperation, an assist that didn't come easy because the United States Navy is proud of its record of never having had a mutiny and, in some quarters, it has been charged that Wouk's book put the "system" on trial. The intelligently adapted screenplay by Stanley Roberts retains all the essence of the novel, yet it is plain that it is the men of the "system" who are tried here. The result is a tremendously effective human drama that draws not a little of its wallop from the vital, understanding direction given it by Edward Dmytryk.

It's also plainly evident that the Navy cooperated to the fullest—to such an extent that the filmgoer has a much larger stake in the picture than just the price of the ticket. There's an awfully lot of his tax dollars represented in the production, too, via the Navy personnel and equipment put on proud display to further the dramatics as well as to showcase the "system" and its meaning to this country.

One of "Caine's" strongest points is its casting. While there are four stars named, actually it is an all-star cast in performances, from the top right down through the merest bit. And among these histrionics are some performances almost certain to make an Oscar bid when Academy time next rolls around. Such a one is Humphrey Bogart's Captain Queeg. It is a character portrait that will long be discussed among the pros.

Jose Ferrer, another of the stars, doesn't come in until late but takes over with a compelling performance as Lt. Barney Greenwald, the defense counsel who saves Van Johnson, third star, from court martial charges. No stock young hero here, Johnson reveals serious, deeper side of his talent with a thoughtful delinia-tion of the Caine's executive officer, Lt. Steve Maryk. Fred MacMurray, fourth topliner, also has a chance, and makes much of it, to sock over the character of Lt. Tom Keefer, the ship's intellect, brilliant on the surface, a coward underneath.

"The Caine Mutiny" is the story of a war-weary destroyer-mine-sweeper and its personnel, over which presides—by the book—Captain Queeg, a man beginning to crack from the strain of playing hero over the years while he hides deep his inferiority complex. Keefer is the first to spot the crack in Queeg's armor and he needles Maryk and the other officers into seeing it, too. Little incidents of faulty command build until, during a raging typhoon when the tired ship is in extreme danger of foundering Maryk relieves the captain, using Navy Article 184, which permits the executive officer taking over under certain emergency conditions, to do so. The ship comes through safely and Queeg has Maryk brought up on mutiny charges. Just when it seems Maryk will be found guilty unjustly, Queeg cracks under Greenwald's incisive probing, his condition revealing that Maryk's charge of unstableness was true all along.

Making a splendid impression in his major screen bow is Robert Francis, playing the young Ensign Willie Keith to perfection. Also introduced, and most favorably, is May Wynn, not new to pictures or show business, but never with such an important chance before. She and Francis carry the only romance (other than that of the sea) in the picture and his character springboards, as well as concludes, the story.

When supporting nominations come up at Academy time, certain to command attention will be Tom Tully's delightfully tough old salt, Captain DeVriess, from whom Queeg takes the Caine. Also fine are E. G. Marshal, court martial prosecutor; ship's personnel Arthur Franz, Lee Marvin and Claude Akins, excellent as unkempt gobs; Jerry Paris, Steve Brodie, Todd Karns, James Best and James Edwards, plus Warner Anderson, in charge of the court martial, Katharine Warren, Ensign Willie's rich mother; Whit Bissell, psychiatrist, and all of the others involved.

Scene after scene in the picture during the hour and one-half build-up to the court martial stand out, either for high action, drama or the beauty and grace of ships making their way proudly through the seas. However, the big dramatic wallop is the climaxing trial and, while Kramer's production supervision has trimmed the Wouk material, he could have cut even deeper. Despite the overall fine quality of the picture, it does not always sustain interest during the entire 123 minutes of running time.

The typhoon sequence will go down in the books as one of the most realistic sea storms yet staged. It's a shining credit to special effects by Lawrence W. Butler and just another of the top-drawer facets of Rudolph Sternad's production design. High on the credit list is Frank Planer's photography in Technicolor. Second unit lensing was by Ray Cory and Cary Odell did the art direction. William A. Lyon and Henry Batista share the editing credit. The Max Steiner score is well handled and two songs, "I Can't Believe That You're In Love With Me" by Jimmy Mc Hugh and Clarence Gaskill, and "Yellowstain Blues" by Fred Karger and Wouk are spotted.

Brog.

Tanganyika
(COLOR)

Routine jungle adventure with okay cast, regulation exploitation angles and average prospects generally.

Hollywood, June 8.

Universal release of Albert J. Cohen production. Stars Van Heflin, Ruth Roman, Howard Duff; feautres Jeff Morrow, Joe Comadore, Noreen Corcoran, Gregory Marshall. Directed by Andre De Toth. Screenplay, William Sackheim, Richard Alan Simmons; story by William R. Cox; (Technicolor), Maury Gertsman; editor, Al Clark. Previewed June 1, '54. Running time, **80 MINS.**

John Gale	Van Heflin
Peggy	Ruth Roman
Dan Harder (McCracken)	Howard Duff
Abel McCracken	Jeff Morrow
Andolo	Joe Comadore
Sally	Noreen Corcoran
Andy	Gregory Marshall
Nukumbi Prisoner	Naaman Brown
Head Porter	Edward C. Short

(*Aspect ratio*: 2-1)

An okay cast and regulation exploitation angles give this routine jungle adventure in Technicolor about average prospects in the more general situation. It's all done to the formula that "a tree's a tree; a rock's a rock; shoot it in Griffith Park." Name of Van Heflin, topping those of Ruth Roman and Howard Duff on the stellar list, will gain it more booking importance than the picture is actually entitled to.

Plot of the William R. Cox story has an early 1900 British East Africa setting. The script by William Sackheim and Richard Alan Simmons has Heflin leading a safari on a manhunt for Jeff Morrow, renegade murderer who is using the savage Nukumbi tribe to terrorize the jungle. During the long trek through backlot and stock footage, Duff, the killer's good brother, and Miss Roman, a school teacher, join the safari, as well as two kids, Noreen Corcoran and Gregory Marshall. Climax has Heflin tricking Morrow's natives into panic with a simulated bombardment, the heavy is killed and the hero is free to clinch with Miss Roman.

The stars and the other players are handicapped by the routine situations and pot-boiler dialog that feature the undistinguished story and script. The strain also shows in Andre De Toth's direction and makes the guidance unfold the footage over a slow 80-minute course.

The new footage lensed by Maury Gertsman for the Albert J. Cohen production isn't always a good match for the stock scenes that are cut in to simulate real, not reel, jungle. Editing and other technical contributions are adequate.

Brog.

Gog
(3-D COLOR)

Science-fiction thriller delivering fair entertainment for that category. For exploitation bookings, moderate prospects.

Hollywood, June 5.

United Artists release of Ivan Tors production. Stars Richard Egan, Constance Dowling, Herbert Marshall; features John Wengraf, Philip Van Zandt, Valerie Vernon, Steve Roberts, Byron Kane, David Alpert, Michael Fox, William Schallert. Directed and edited by Herbert L. Strock. Screenplay, Tom Taggart; added dialog, Richard G. Taylor; based on a story by Ivan Tors; camera (Color Corp. of America), Lothrop B. Worth; score, Harry Sukman. At the Paramount-Hollywood, June 5, '54. Running time, **82 MINS.**

David Sheppard	Richard Egan
Joanna Merritt	Constance Dowling
Dr. Van Ness	Herbert Marshall
Dr. Zeitman	John Wengraf
Dr. Elzevir	Philip Van Zandt
Madame Elzevir	Valerie Vernon
Major Howard	Steve Roberts
Dr. Carter	Byron Kane
Peter Burden	David Alpert
Dr. Hubertus	Michael Fox
Engle	William Schallert
Helen	Marian Richman
Marna	Jeanne Dean
Senator	Tom Daly
Vince	Alex Jackson
Girl Acrobats	Patti Taylor, Beverly Jocher
Dr. Kirby	Aline Towne
Pilot	Al Bayer
Security Guards	Andy Andrews, Julian Ludwig

A fair amount of science-fiction thriller entertainment is dished out in this United Artists release. It has sufficient ballyhoo angles to back up exploitation bookings so returns from such dates should hit a moderate level. Three-D and color may be added help, although the depth treatment should have had more gimmicks to go with this type of subject.

Ivan Tors produced for UA release, as well as writing the story on which the Tom Taggart script is based. Basic science-fiction idea is good, as are the gadgets with which it is brought off. However, the film plays a bit too slow and with more talk than necessary, so it seems the climax is a long time coming. Herbert L. Strock's direction has a tendency to slow down when involved with some rather long explanatory scenes in the script. Otherwise, it moves along satisfactorily, developing fair suspense to go with the thriller aims.

Top-lining are Richard Egan, Constance Dowling and Herbert Marshall. This trio, and the others in the cast, bring off the performances in a matter-of-fact style that fits the plotting. In addition to exploitable gadgets which abound in the footage, producer Tors has seen to it that virtually every scientist in the story is equipped with a shapely femme assistant, so sight values are strong, particularly in view of the fact that the tints by Color Corporation of America (old Cinecolor) are very good, as lensed by Lothrop B. Worth.

Egan, security agent from the Office of Scientific Investigation, is sent to a secret subterranean laboratory in New Mexico, where top scientists are working on the first space station. The work is being sabotaged and it's up to Egan to ferret out the evil-doer and bring him to justice. Assisted by Miss Dowling and Marshall, head of the project, Egan gradually pin-points the blame on Novac, the giant nuclear brain machine which controls every operation in the plant, and two five-armed robots. Seems that Novac, however, is not exactly disloyal to the U. S. Some enemy agents have secreted mechanism in it to give them control and the dirty work is being directed from a fibreglass space ship overhead. A Sabre Jet takes care of the enemy plane, the robots are destroyed and Novac's intelligence is back on the right track.

Science-minded youngsters will lap up the ultra-high frequency talk and assorted gadgeteering that goes on in the footage, as well as demonstrations of helio machines, etc. Technical contributions are excellent.

Brog.

This Is Your Army
(DOCUMENTARY-COLOR)

Movietone News presentation of documentary produced in color under the supervision of the United States Army. Producer, Edmund Reek; director, John J. Gordon; story, Joseph Kenas. Captain James Altieri; narrated by Joe King, Phil Tonken; camera, Jack Painter, Bill Storz; edited by Bill Kosh, John Hughes; score, Jack Shaindlin; project officer Major Robert T. Blauvelt; technical advisor, Captain James Altieri.
Previewed at Columbia studio, May 28, 1954. Running time, 78 MINS.

Over a period of two years the United States Army filmed a detailed, and dramatic, report of its activities. At first intended as a documentary for the Armed Forces, it is now being considered for regular theatrical distribution so the general public can see the part the Army plays in world-wide affairs. It's a big part.

There's little of Army activities overlooked in the lensing, which makes for some repetition in the footage, but the picture has an overall interest emphasized by the bigness of the subject. Fox Movietone News' Edmund Reck produced and John J. Gordon directed. Signal Corps cameras focus on more than 60 vital installations at home and overseas to record the activities and responsibilities of the Army.

Recruit training in all branches of the Army; specialization in such lines as parachute, anti-aircraft, radar, guided missile; advanced unit training stressing fire power, mobility over all types of terrain and under all kinds of situations, and new weapons that are a powerful force for peace, such as the atomic cannon, are among the film's highlights. The pictorial report also details the important part the Army plays in SHAPE and NATO overseas, with the cameras covering locations in Germany, Trieste, Turkey, Greece and Italy, as well as the Far East. Problems of supply and transportation, and those of command are shown. Of interest is the use of the telecon for communication between the Pentagon and bases.

The picture runs 78 minutes, including a prolog message from General Matthew B. Ridgway, Chief of Staff, and credited with the outstanding camera work are Jack Painter and Bill Storz. Footage has been well edited by Bill Kosh and John Hughes. The story was written by Joseph Kenas and Captain James Altieri. The latter also served as technical advisor. Joe King and Phil Tonken narrated and Jack Shaindlin provided the background score. Project officer on the film was Major Robert T. Blauvelt. *Brog.*

Monster From The Ocean Floor

Shoestringer which has story value.

Lippert release of a Palo Alto Production. Producer, Roger Corman; director, Wyott Ordung; screenplay, William Danch; camera, Floyd Crosby; production design, Ben Hayne; editor Ed Samson; music, Andre Brumer. Cast—Stars Anne Kimbell, Stuart Wade. Features Dick Pinner, Jack Hayes, Wyott Ordung, Inez Palange, David Garcia. Reviewed at Loew's State Theatre, Los Angeles, Calif., May 26, '54. Running time, 64 MINS.

(*Aspect ratio:* 1.33-1)

Here's an oddity—a well done quickie. Lensed entirely along the coast of lower California, "Monster From the Ocean Floor" boasts an interest-holding story-line, good direction and performances, with an added plus factor being a tag that's fully exploitable.

Film was made independently by Roger Corman and, shortly after completion, was purchased outright by Robert L. Lippert. Yarn pivots around American artist Anne Kimbell, vacationing in a Mexican village which has been terrorized by a sea monster, and biologist Stuart Wade, who's in the region studying plant life along the ocean floor. She's taken in by the monster tales; he calls it superstition. She eventually comes face-to-face with the sea beast while swimming, and is saved in the nick of time by Wade, who runs the giant squid-like monster's one eye with his one-man submarine to kill it. She revives in his arms, and it looks like marriage.

One of the picture's better points is the performance turned in by Anne Kimbell. She's an actress of extreme capability, a looker to boot, and should go far. As her vis-a-vis, Stuart Wade is good but still overshadowed by Miss Kimbell. Supporters have comparatively little to do save for Dick Pinner, who's okay as Wade's side-kick.

Roger Corman's production supervision has packed the footage with commercial values without going overboard, while Wyott Ordung's surprisingly good direction has drawn all suspense from the William Danch screenplay. Floyd Crosby's camera work (much of it underwater) is another plus factor, as is the musical score from Andre Brumer. Remaining technical credits are stock.

Film, incidentally, is made up completely of exteriors, with utilization of good setting making the footage belie its budget. *Neal.*

Challenge the Wild
(COLOR)

Amateur-filmed account of family stay in the far north woods; for family trade in general dual situations.

Hollywood, June 4.

United Artists release of a Frank A. Graham production; written, produced, directed and photographed by Graham. Features Edna, George and Sheilah Graham, and Zimmie-the-black-tail-fawn. Narration, Graham and Tom Gibson; spoken by Pat McGeehan; score, Marlin Skiles; song, Skiles, Les Kaufman, George Fisher. Previewed June 1, '54. Running time, 69 MINS.

(*Aspect ratio:* 1.33-1)

"Challenge the Wild" is a 69-minute account of a spring and summer spent in the northern wilderness by the Grahams—father, mother, son and daughter. Produced, directed, written and lensed by Frank A. Graham and tinted by Ansco Color, the film stacks up as okay fare for the family trade in dual situations.

Feature is amateurishly turned out but still possesses unusual material, being particularly long on animal shots. Graham gets in some better than average close-ups of Kodiak bears, grizzlies, cougars and Rocky Mountain goats. Additionally, his camera catches coyotes, moose, caribou, porcupine, deer (one of the principals in the slight story thread being a small faun). There is, too, a giant blue whale in the calving ground off Kodiak Island.

Much of the film unfolds in the northern Canadian Rockies, where the family makes its base. Flying in with their own small plane, they continue then to the Admiralty and Barron Islands, off the southern coast of Alaska, and Kodiak, where in one scene the elder Grahams bring down two huge Kodiak bears while the young daughter grinds the camera. The mother also is shown killing two large cougars with bow and arrow.

As a study of wild animals, picture is instructive. Pat McGeehan speaks the explanatory narration. *Whit.*

The Rainbow Jacket
(BRITISH-COLOR)

British racing meller with strong local cast; good for local situations but lacks marquee values for U. S.

London, May 27.

General Film Distributors release of Ealing Studios-Michael Balcon production. Stars Kay Walsh, Bill Owen, Edward Underdown, Robert Morley; features Fella Edmonds. Produced and directed by Michael Relph & Basil Dearden. Screenplay, T. E. B. Clarke; camera, Otto Heller; editor, Jack Harris; music, William Alwyn; color by Technicolor. At Odeon, Leicester Square, London May 26, '54. Running time, 100 MINS.

Lord Logan	Robert Morley
Barbara	Kay Walsh
Tyler	Edward Underdown
Georgie Craine	Fella Edmonds
Sam	Bill Owen
Voss	Charles Victor
Monica	Honor Blackman
Lord Stoneleigh	Wilfrid Hyde White
Bernie Rudd	Ronald Ward
Travers	Howard Marion Crawford
Harry	Sidney James
Gresham	Michael Trubshawe
Archie Stevens	Colin Kemball
Bruce	Sam Kydd
Adams	Herbert C. Walton
Ross	George Thorpe
Benny Loder	Michael Ripper
Valet	Eliot Makeham
Lukey	Frederick Piper
Ron Saunders	Brian Roper

Out of character with many of the recent productions which have emanated from the studio, this yarn of British horse-racing is not among the better entries from the Ealing stable. It is, however, good hokum entertainment, particularly for local audiences, with a strong cast of British name performers. Inadequate marquee lure may make it a tough-selling proposition in the U. S. market.

First-class Technicolor lensing takes fullest advantage of some finer aspects of the English countryside, and shows off the beauties of some famous local racetracks. There are virile action sequences including some fine racing scenes. The story, however, rarely matches up with the backgrounds.

It is a conventional yarn of a one-time champion jockey, warned off the course for shady practices, who is determined that his boy protege should go straight. But the kid's mother gets into financial difficulties and the boy is persuaded to pull a race. Subsequently the ex-champ gets his ticket back, but discovers that the youngster has been warned to lose the race and sacrifices his own career to get him first past the winning post.

Rising continually above the melodramatic theme, a fine cast gives the story a much needed veneer. Bill Owen does a sterling job as the ex-champ while Fella Edmonds, as the boy protege with a natural love for horses, is a promising newcomer. The best performances, however, come from Robert Morley, as an irascible owner, and from Wilfrid Hyde White, one of the stewards. Kay Walsh, within the limitations of her role, does very nicely as the boy's mother and supplies the solitary touch of romance in her association with Owen. Edward Underdown provides a reliable interpretation of the trainer, with Charles Victor supplying some neat comedy lines as his head boy. There are matching performances by others in the cast. *Myro.*

Within Man's Power
(DOCUMENTARY)

Produced for National Tuberculosis Association by Nicholas Webster and National Video Productions, Inc., Wash., D. C. Directed by Nicholas Webster; photography by Boris Kaufman; screenplay by Edward Murkland; narration by William Bancroft Mellor; sets by James Waring. Previewed in Washington, May 17, '54. Running time, 27 MINS.

This is a simplified, sugar-coated version of the progress made in the past half century toward the conquest of tuberculosis. It is made in 35m for theatrical showing and in 16m for television, on order by the National Tuberculosis Assn. to celebrate its 50th anniversary this month.

Story opens with a doctor telling a patient and his wife that the patient's X-rays show TB, but that the case can be cured because it was caught early. When the patient protests his hard luck, the doctor tells the story of early "consumption" and how medicos had no idea how to cure it.

Then the story moves along to the campaign of Dr. Lawrence Flick, in Philadelphia, to recognize and handle the disease for what it was, of Dr. Trudeau's discovery that healthy, outdoor life aided in licking the terrible "white plague," and of the early quack cures.

Finally, the National Tuberculosis Association is formed and the fight is carried successfully into the various states, so that the ailment can now be cured by proper care.

Film tells briefly and palatably about the problem, and is something which need not frighten anyone. If anything, it hits too lightly at the matter. It is a background story, with virtually nothing in the way of look at the future.

Pic is handled via simple impressionistic sets throughout the cutbacks, is cleanly photographed and pleasantly handled, but its impact is mild. *Lowe.*

Jungle Man-Eaters

Standard Jungle Jim programmer with Johnny Weissmuller for lowercase bookings.

Hollywood, May 2.

Columbia release of Sam Katzman production. Stars Johnny Weissmuller; features Karin Booth, Richard Stapley. Directed by Lee Sholem. Story and screenplay, Samuel Newman; based on the King Features Syndicate cartoon feature; camera, Henry Freulich; editor, Gene Hawlick. Reviewed at Hollywood Paramount May 19, '54. Running time, 67 MINS.

Jungle Jim	Johnny Weissmuller
Bonnie	Karin Booth
Bernard	Richard Stapley
Zuwaba	Bernard Hamilton
Latour	Gregory Gay
Kingston	Lester Matthews
Zulu	Paul Thompson
Chief Boganda	Vince M. Townsend Jr.
N'Gala	Louise Franklin

(*Aspect ratio:* 1.85-1)

Parring the course for Columbia's "Jungle Jim" entries, this latest Johnny Weissmuller starrer finds him in his familiar hero role, going through standard derring-do amidst appropriately cut in African stock footage.

Picture has a certain exploitation potential for its lowercase market in the stock footage showing a fight between a lion and a bull, in which the king of beasts gets his comeuppance from the toro before Weissmuller closes in for the hand-to-hand combat and kill.

The hero also gets in his licks in a crocodile battle for good effect.

Samuel Newman's screenplay, which Lee Sholem directs generally to good advantage, and which makes fast use of stock reelage, is woven aout the roundup of a diamond smuggler who threatens the stability of the world market after a jewel strike in the midst of the jungle. Jungle Jim, who enters the case after the natives he oversees are drawn into the heavy's machinations, is assisted by a Scotland Yard inspector, sent to Africa to investigate the matter. Plot is off to a deadly slow start but picks up after a while.

Weissmuller takes on man and beast in equal deadpan stride. Richard Stapley is convincing as the Scotland Yard man and Karin Booth is the particularly pretty doctor in love with him. Gregory Gay is a persuasive heavy, without being too villainous. Bernard Hamilton scores as Jim's chieftain friend and Lester Matthews is okay as the commissioner. Tamba the chimp is in for the usual laughs.

Henry Freulich's lensing meets the demands of the picture and Gene Havlick expertly cut in the stock footage which the Sam Katzman production uses so generously.

Whit.

Hell Raiders of the Deep
(ITALIAN—DUBBED INTO ENGLISH)

Suspenseful wartime drama reenacting the exploits of Italy's frogmen.

Italian Films Export release of a Valentia-Ponti-De Laurentis production. Stars Eleonora Rossi Drago, Pierre Cressoy; features Tino Carraro, Carlo Bellini, Girolamo Manisco, Giovanni Tadini, Luigi Ferraro, Giovanni de Fazio, Giovanni Magello, Giorgio Spaccarelli, Colombo Pamolli. Directed by Duilio Coletti. Screenplay, A. Bragadin, E. De Concini, D. Coletti camera, Aldo Tonti; underwater sequences, Tonti, Victor De Santis; music, Nino Rota. Previewed May 19, '54 in N.Y. Running time, **93 MINS.**

Marion	Eleonora Rossi Drago
Silvani	Pierre Cressoy
Paul Muller	Tino Carraro
Riccardo Gallone	Carlo Bellini

(*Aspect ratio:* 1.33 - 1)

There's plenty to hold the customers' interest in "Hell Raiders of the Deep," the Italo-made story of the daring frogmen who, in 1941, harried Allied naval units and managed to invade Alexandria to sink a British aircraft carrier. Done in documentary fashion that adds to the drama and suspense of the story, the dubbed film offers some extraordinary underwater scenes and has definite appeal particularly to action houses.

Here's an instance where dubbing should be a real asset in the U.S. market. Pic is more concerned with action than with dialog, and the English soundtrack has been so skillfully added that there's rarely any discrepancy between mouth movements and the matched lines. This leaves "Hell Raiders" with a highly unusual theme and treatment but a virtually unknown cast. There are no overt attempts at glorifying the Italo navy. Instead the film concentrates on the exploits of a small group of men engaged in suicidal activity.

Eleonora Rossi Drago is an attractive gal but her contribution to the proceedings is minor. She's cast as a spy for the undersea raiders and she ends up being shot by another spy. Pierre Cressoy makes a handsome and determined hero. He impersonates Luigi Durand De La Penne, a real-life frogman who was responsible for some daring exploits and who acted as adviser on the film. He's also seen in the underwater sequences.

Considerable suspense is generated by by director Duilio Coletti and his cameramen, Aldo Tonti and Victor De Santis, as they described the training of the frogmen and the actual attack. Final portion of the picture, showing the men riding their unique "pigs," electrically propelled 21-foot torpedos with a 12-mile cruising range above and below the surface, is as thrilling as any ever seen on the screen.

Underwater lensing is tops and has a highly realistic quality as the frogmen cut their way through protecting nets. Some teams die as depth bombs crush their lungs. Others reach their objective and blow it up by attaching explosive charges to the bottom of ships. Initial part of the film gets mired down in detail, but events soon speed up for the sock climax. If properly sold, "Hell Raiders" shapes as one of the best dubbed entries to date.

Hift.

Barefoot Battalion
(GREEK)

Interesting Greek import for art houses, but limited prospects for the general market.

Leon L. Brandt Associates release of Peter Boudoures production. Directed and edited by Gregg Tallas. Screenplay and original story, Nico Katsiotes; camera, Mixalis Gaziadis; music, Mikis Theodorakis. At Globe Theatre, N.Y., beginning May 28, '54. Running time, **89 MINS.**

Alexandra	Maria Costi
Black Marketeer	Nicos Fermas
Andrea	Vassilios Frangadakis
Niko	Antonios Voulgaris
Dimitri	Stavros Krozos
Joe	Christos Solouroglou
Martha	Ketty Gyni
Jacob	Evangelos Yiotopoulos
Thanos	George Axiotis
Professor	Kostas Rigas

(*In Greek; English Titles*)

Hunger and privation were familiar to many Greek children under the Nazi occupation. But despite their personal hardships some managed to harass the Germans in a resistance group known as the "Barefoot Battalion." For the most part these youngsters' exploits emerge as a touching material in this Peter Boudoures production which Gregg Tallas directed for release by Leon L. Brandt Associates release.

With practically all of its footage lensed on location in the Greek cities of Athens and Salonika, the film has a documentary flavor and shapes up as an interesting entry for art house bookings. Camera, too, has ably caught some striking character studies in the varied personalities of the picture's moppet players. However, this English-titled Greek import is too downbeat and much too long to rate more than average bookings in the program market.

Screenplayed by Nico Katsiotes from his own story, the yarn recounts how the "Barefoot Battalion" pulled a modern-day "Robin Hood" by stealing from the rich and the Nazis to aid both the poor and the Allied cause. Among its major deeds was helping smuggle an American pilot to Egypt and safety. But while the script makes much of this, actually the bulk of the film's dramatic effect lies in how Greece's teenage children and even tots survived in wartime by their wits of sheer necessity.

Tallas, who conceived the idea of filming the story of these children and their relationship to each other, directed his cast (only two were professionals) with a realistic touch. Youngsters are credible especially five-year-old Ketty Gyni as a hungry orphan. Her sobs for food could move even the most heartless to tears. Maria Costi and Nicos Fermas, professional players, are adequate as an undercover agent and a black market operator, respectively.

Hampered by antiquated equipment, cameraman Mixalis Gaziadis captured much of the footage in a murky effect that often detracts from sharpness and clarity. Score of Mikis Theodorakis as played by the Athens Symphony Orchestra is an asset. Production values are meager and most other technical credits are well below Hollywood standards.

Gilb.

Mam'Zelle Nitouche
(FRENCH-COLOR-SONGS)

Paris, May 25.

Lux release of Paris Film-Panitalia-Rizzoli production. Stars Fernandel, Pier Angeli. Directed by Yves Allegret. Screenplay, Marcel Achard, Jean Aurenche, Allegret from operetta by H. Meilhac, A. Milaud; camera (Eastmancolor), Armand Thirard; music, Georges Van Parys; editor, Roger Dwyre. At Marignan, Paris. Running time, **90 MINS.**

Celestin	Fernandel
Denise	Pier Angeli
Commander	Jean Debucourt
Corinne	Michele Cardoue
Adjutant	Georges Shamrat
Sergeant	Louis De Funes
Andre	Francois Guerin

This filmed turn-of-century operetta suffers from a lack of sparkle. Melange of girl's school intrigues and barracks humor never gets this off the ground. Hence, it emerges as a rather dated offering suitable for good situations here on Fernandel name. For the U. S., this is very problematical because of its lagging format. However, the names of Pier Angeli and Fernandel may be enough to get it some dates.

This concerns an organist (Fernandel) in a girl's school who leads a double life. By day, he is a demure butt of the girl's pranks, but at night he is a famous operetta writer who has a mistress in one of the leading operettas. His dual existence is crossed up when one of the girls, Miss Angeli, discovers his secret. She blackmails him into taking her with him on the night of the opera opening. Pic snowballs from there.

The girl meets a young soldier, who is really the fiance chosen by her family. She is also chased by a jealous sugar daddy. The operetta goes on with her in the lead. Fernandel gets railroaded into army barracks by mistake but finally gets back to his real life as an operetta writer.

Director Yves Allegret lacks the flair for bringing these situations to life. Fernandel is hard put to get a few laughs from his ill-conceived character. Songs are rung in indiscriminately. Miss Angeli is winsome as the young girl. Jean Debucourt is the only one in character as the apoplectic commander. Color is nicely hued and editing is good. This is the second version of this operetta, and it shows that film musical tastes have changed. Spontaneity and pace are the requisites lacking in this version.

Mosk.

L'Aventurier de Seville
(FRANCO-SPANISH) (COLOR-SONGS)

Paris, May 25.

Victory release of LPC-Benito Perojo-Mars Film production. Stars Luis Mariano. Directed by Ladislas Vajda. Screenplay, Alex Joffe, Arozamena, Jean Marsan; camera (Gevacolor), Andre Balestros; editor, Henri Taverna, Geores Natot; music, Francis Lopez, Quinterro. At the Paris, Paris. Running time, **115 MINS.**

Figaro	Luis Mariano
Pepilla	Lolita Sevilla
Rosine	Daniele Godet
Almaviva	Pierre Cour
Duke	Jean Galland
Duchess	Emma Penella
Bandot	Jose Maris Godero

Ladislas Vadja has bundled together the ingredients of this costumer into a palatable adventure opus that has color, spec and the Luis Mariano name for what looks like neat grosses on the Continent. Although a pleasing pic, its familiarity and lack of names only make this of dualer value for America, with chances for special situations on its tongue-in-cheek approach.

This concerns a barber of Seville, Figaro, with a golden voice who is kidnapped by bandits to serve as a lure for passing nobility. When he is freed, a surly nobleman recognizes his voice, and he joins the army to escape. He saves the remainder of the bandits, who have been captured, by having them join the army.

Then they are off to Puerto Rico, where a series of action episodes has them defeating the English. When he comes back to Seville he is famous, and saves a young lovely from a fortune-hunting Duke. He realizes he loves the daughter of the bandit chief and goes back to her for the happy ending.

Director Vadja has given this nice pacing and treatment. Film is aided by the general acting and dialog. Mariano is the leading popcharm singer here. Despite possessing a fine golden tenor, he lacks all the dash and agility necessary for the title role even though acquitting himself adequately. Remainder of cast is fine, with Lolita Sevilla standout as a vivacious, barefooted bandit queen whose loyalty and appeal win over the barber. Color is good and primarily even throughout, with editing okay. Spanish locale dresses up the pic production-wise.

Mosk.

Les Femmes-S'En Balancent
(Dames Get Along)
(FRENCH)

Paris, May 25.

Pathe release of CICC-Pathe Cinema production. Stars Eddie Constantine, Nadia Gray. Directed by Bernard Borderie. Screenplay, Borderie, Jacques Vilfrid from novel by Peter Cheney; camera, Jacques Lemare; editor, Jean Feyte; music, Paul Misraki. At Balzac, Paris. Running time, **110 MINS.**

Lemmy	Eddie Constantine
Henrietta	Nadia Gray
Paulette	Dominique Willms
Aymes	Jacques Castelot
Fernandez	Robert Berri
Walter	Dario Moreno
Secretary	Francois Perrot

Third Lemmy Caution film here this year, based on the skirt-chasing, scotch-drinking U.S. G-Man character of Peter Cheney, has this type of pic catching on in France. Based on its U.S. counterparts, this pushes everything three steps further. It emerges as a parody of its forerunners, with gobs of eroticism, fisticuffs, high-powered cars and general mayhem. U.S. warbler Eddie Constantine has established himself as a tough guy hero in this series. This will do fine here, but for the American market it is strictly for dualers or the actioner market where it has exploitable facets.

Only thing strained in making this pic are the muscles and the clinging bodices as Constantine tries to track down the origin of counterfeit American $1,000 bills in Italy. First bill was passed by looker Nadia Gray. He falls for her but is not deterred from brushing lips with a bevy of hungry, languorous gals who seem to turn up at every corner. Meanwhile he has a chance to beat up some gangsters in several slam-bang fight scenes. Constantine manages to put two-and-two together long after the audience has, but the pic bowls along in its familiar groove and oozes entertainment in the glib, tongue-in-cheek interp by Constantine and the many sinewy, agreeable dames.

Director Bernard Borderie gives this pace but still seems to lack the knowhow in the fight scenes. Dominique Willms and Miss Gray are tempting bait, and the unnamed femmes also register nicely. Robert Berri, as a hulking gunman, and the other cutthroats do well enough. Lensing and editing are first-rate. *Mosk.*

Le Secret de Helene Marimon
(FRANCO-ITALIAN)

Paris, May 25.
Corona release of SNC-Romana Films production. Stars Frank Villard. Isa Miranda, Carl Del Poggio. Directed by Henri Calef. Screenplay, Jacques and Gerard Willemetz, Calef from a novel by J. B. Cherrier; camera, Roger Dormoy; editor, J. Alvarez. At Biarritz, Paris. Running time, 11 MINS.

Jacques	Frank Villard
Helene	Isa Miranda
Dominique Marimom	Carla Del Poggio
Thierry	Jean Debucourt
Uncle	Andre Valmy
Farmer	Noel Roquevert
	Jacques Dynam

The title adequately pegs the type of this film. It is a sudsy story of a languishing love affair. Primarily distaff for its local appeal, there is not much in this for American chances because lacking names and the melodramatic events.

Film is told in flashback style as a testy 50-year-old engineer comes back to Paris for the first time in 30 years. Then his story unfolds as he is reminded of an old love affair. It goes back to the first World War and the meeting of the hero, then young, with a middle-aged man. He saves his life and they become friends. The young man is wounded, and on leave meets a woman with whom he falls in love. Then he finds out it is the wife of his friend, but doesn't tell her. Then he hears the husband is dead and breaks the news to her, and with it, their relationship. Pic then snaps back to the present.

Director Henri Calef has given this a slick mounting, but nothing much can be done with this rather trite story. Isa Miranda and Frank Villard play the lovers without the necessary passion. Frank Villard's aging is never convincing. Carla Del Poggio plays the daughter with freshness but lack of spirit, and is not helped by being dubbed. Lensing and editing are first-rate as are the supporting players. *Mosk.*

Cabaret
(GERMAN-SONGS)

Vienna, May 28.
Carlton release of Guenther Stapenhorst production. Stars Paul Henreid; features Eva Kerbler and Elma Karlowa. Directed by Willy Forst. Screenplay, Johannes Mario Simmel; camera, Guenther Anders; music, Willy Schmidt Gentner. At Forum, Vienna. Running time, 95 MINS.

Conrad Hegner	Paul Henreid
Leonie Lerch	Eva Kerbler
Fritz Gruenwald	Fritz Schulz
Trixie	Elma Karlowa

"Cabaret" is a modest programmer which combines routine melo-

drama with scenes of "Klein Kunst," a forerunner of present-day nightclubs. Mild entry at best for the U. S.

Written by J. M. Simmel, the screenplay is only a device used to weave in the cabarets sequence. Paul Henreid plays a chanson-composer while Eva Kerbler is his wife. Elma Karlowa is cast as the girl who breaks up the marriage. Just when they are being reconciled in the fortress Przemysl during the first World War, she is killed by a bomb.

Most of the performances are mechanical. While Henreid is halfway adequate as the songwriter, Miss Kerbler is weak as his wife. Miss Karlowa probably will do better in her next pic. Resembling Fritz Gruenwald, top-ranking cabaret ace 40 years ago, Fritz Schulz' portrayal is too stolid and lacking in humor throughout.

Only two oldtime songhits (and not the biggest) are sung during the nitery stint. Based on this film, director Willy Forst appears overrated. Instead of reminiscing on unforgettable songs, he merely "added" music. He guided the production in a downbeat key, unrelieved by humorous moments.

Guenther Anders camerawork rates a nod. *Maas.*

Princess of the Nile
(COLOR)

Regulation escapism in the Arabian Nights tradition. About average prospects in general situations.

20th-Fox release of Panoramic (Leonard Goldstein) production, produced by Robert L. Jacks. Stars Debra Paget, Jeffrey Hunter, Michael Rennie; features Dona Drake, Michael Ansara, Edgar Barrier, Wally Cassell, Jack Elam. Directed by Harmon Jones. Written by Gerald Drayson Adams; camera (Technicolor), Lloyd Ahern; editor, George Gittens; musical direction, Lionel Newman. Previewed June 9, '54. Running time, 71 MINS.

Taura the Dancer and Princess Shalimar	Debra Paget
Prince Haidi	Jeffrey Hunter
Rama Khan	Michael Rennie
Mirva	Dona Drake
Oshi	Wally Cassell
Shaman	Edgar Barrier
Capt. Kral	Michael Ansara
Basra	Jack Elam
Babu	Lester Sharpe
Hakar	Lee Van Cleef
Tut	Billy Curtis
Capt. Hussein	Robert Roark

Handmaidens: Lisa Daniels, Merry Anders, Suzanne Alexander, Jeanne Vaughn, Kitty London, Phyllis Winger, Honey Harlow, Genice Grayson, Cheryll Clarke and Bobette Bentley.
(Aspect ratio: 1.66-1)

As film fantasy in the Arabian Nights tradition, "Princess of the Nile" has about average prospects in the general market where such Technicolored offerings usually prove acceptable fare. The swashbuckling, rooftop derring-do indulged in by hero Jeffrey Hunter and the way Debra Paget wears the harem scanties required for her title role are cut to order for release intentions.

Leonard Goldstein's Panoramic production for 20th-Fox release picks up some tremendously expensive-looking sight values through use of standing sets from "The Robe." These fit perfectly into the Egyptian locale of the Gerald Drayson Adams screen story. Everything moves along a familiar pattern and at a pace geared to the demands of non-discriminating audiences under Harmon Jones' direction. The playing is acceptable, if not outstanding.

Hunter, son of the Caliph of Bagdad, stops over in Halwan while en route home after a victorious battle and finds Michael Rennie, head of a Bedouin tribe, has the city under control. When Hunter's traveling companion is wantonly killed, he determines to seek out the murderer, a pursuit that suits Miss Paget, daughter of the city's ruler, who sees a chance to free her father and his subjects from Rennie's cruel domination. She's been giving the people (male) comfort by doubling as a dancing girl in the city's chief nitery, a double life she has to reveal to Hunter. Rennie finds out, too, threatens to lay the city to waste, a move she thwarts by promising to be his bride. From this fate worse than death she is saved by the hero and the city's thieves that have gathered at his side. When the curtain rings down a royal wedding is in the offing.

Production-wise, Robert L. Jacks has made good use of the material at hand and cast the story to type. In support of Hunter, Rennie and Miss Paget are Dona Drake, one of the assorted handmaidens that help decorate the footage; Wally Cassell, a thief who calls in Jack Elam, Lee Van Cleef, Billy Curtis and Lester Sharpe to aid the hero; Edgar Barrier, court physician in Rennie's pay, and Michael Ansara, the heavy's chief henchman.

Lloyd Ahern's color lensing is good and the other technical credits capable. *Brog.*

Scotch on the Rocks
(BRITISH)

Offbeat charmer will be at home in discrimination clientele situations.

Kingsley International Pictures release of Group 3 (John Grierson, exec producer) production. Stars Ronald Squire. Kathleen Ryan, Raymond Huntley; features Sebastian Shaw, Fulton MacKay, Jean Colin, Jameson Clark, Grace Gavin, Keith Faulkner, Prunella Scales, Kynaston Reeves. Directed by John Eldridge. Screenplay, Eldridge and Alfred Shaughnessy, based on the Eric Linklater novel, "Laxdale Hall"; camera, Arthur Grant; music, Frank Spencer. Previewed N. Y. June 9. Running time, 77 MINS.

General Matheson	Ronald Squire
Catriona Matheson	Kathleen Ryan
Samuel Pettigrew, M.P.	Raymond Huntley
Hugh Marvell, M.P.	Sebastian Shaw
Andrew Flett	Fulton Mackay
Lucy Pettigrew	Jean Colin
Roderick McLeod	Jameson Clark
Mrs. McLeod	Grace Gavin
Peter McLeod	Keith Faulkner
Morag McLeod	Prunella Scales
Rev. Ian Macaulay	Kynaston Reeves
McKellaig	Andrew Keir
Nurse Connachy	Neil Ballantyne
Willie John Watt	Roddy Mcmillan

(Aspect ratio: 1.33-1)

Upon a whimsical story foundation is constructed a light and misty satire in "Scotch on the Rocks," which was bottled in England but speaks with a Highland brogue. Script twists tongue in cheek around the rocky roads of the village of Hebrides (That's in Scotland, Laddie!) and director and players, a competent lot, give it unlabored movements and charm.

Group 3 Production doubtless will do fair enough in the non-conventional class outlets, as distinguished from the general congregation theatres where names (none here) make the b.o. news. Further, this drollery brand of divertisment lacks the comedy impact required for mass audience penetration. In this respect there's not enough spirit in "Scotch."

Yarn tees off with a Parliamentary delegation on its way to quell "anarchy" in the isolated and tiny community. The rebels are the total of five automobile owners who refuse to pay the government road tax because their road is bed of rocks.

Intertwined with this is some business about rascals from Glasgow who come to poach in the Hebrides river (and cause interruption of an open-air performance of "Macbeth"); the local undertaker who is frustrated by the vitality of the clansmen and some faint suggestions of romance. All quite quaint and diverting.

Ronald Squire, Kathleen Ryan, Raymond Huntley and all other cast members behave histrionically well in the highland fling and John Eldridge managed a nice pace in calling the turns. All technical credits are okay. *Gene.*

Father Brown
(BRITISH)

Alec Guinness in adaptation of G. K. Chesterton's famed character; strong marquee appeal boosts b.o. prospects.

London, June 8.
Columbia release of Paul Finder Moss-Vivian A. Cox-Facet Production. Stars Alec Guinness; features Joan Greenwood, Peter Finch, Cecil Parker. Directed by Robert Hamer. Screenplay, Thelma Schnee and Robert Hamer; camera. Harry Waxman; editor, Gordon Hales; music, Georges Auric. At Plaza Theatre, London, June 8, '54. Running time, 91 MINS.

Father Brown	Alec Guinness
Lady Warren	Joan Greenwood
Flambeau	Peter Finch
Bishop	Cecil Parker
Insp. Valentine	Bernard Lee
Parkinson	Sidney James

Insp. Dubois ....Gerard Oury
Vicomte ....Ernest Thesiger
Secretary .... Ernest Clark
Herald ....Austin Trevor
Auctioneer ....Noel Howlett
Maharajah ....Marne Maitland
Station Sgt. ....John Salew
Insp. Wilykins ....John Horsley
Texan ....Lance Maraschal

"Fath■r Brown," the first entry by Facet Productions, a British setup headed by Paul F. Moss, is distinguished mainly by the excellent casting of the title role. Alec Guinness is a natural for the role, and his name on the marquee will help sell many tickets.

The G. K. Chesterton stories have been adapted by Thelma Schnee, who shares the screenplay credit with Robert Hamer, director of the picture. Between them they've fashioned a warm-hearted narrative based on the exploits of the eccentric priest who sets out to outwit international crooks while the police forces of London and Paris are on his tail.

As the yarn opens, Alec Guinness decides that, contrary to the Bishop's explicit instructions, it would not be safe to entrust a priceless cross to Scotland Yard in its journey from London to Rome, and decides to transport it himself. Needless to say he is outsmarted by an international thief with a reputation for stealing rare objects d'art. The crook is also a master of disguise, although Guinness penetrates his makeup after a minor slip.

Returning home in disgrace, the priest is determined to trap the criminal, not with the intention of handing him over to the police, but in the hope of being able to save his soul. Through a series of adventures in Paris and in a Burgundy castle, he succeeds in locating a room packed with rare stolen treasures and is hailed as a hero by the bishop.

This is, at all times, a gentle story, leisurely unfolded and always dominated by a masterly performance by Alec Guinness. The near-sighted priest, who learns the secrets of unarmed combat from some of the tougher members of his flock, is admirably brought to life by Guinness. His performance, good though it is, does not overshadow a first-class thesping job by Peter Finch as the international thief who likes to collect the rare treasures he cannot afford. Joan Greenwood, on the other hand, is inadequately served by the script. She has only a minor part in the plot and gets very few opportunities to display her talent. Cecil Parker also has a smallish role as the bishop, but fits it comfortably. Bernard Lee and Gerard Oury, as reps of Scotland Yard and the French Surete, do nicely as the coppers who are always on the priest's trail. Sidney James gives a robust performance as an ex-crook who has been led, rather reluctantly, onto the straight and narrow path by the star.

Production has been smoothly directed by Robert Hamer and expertly lensed by Harry Waxman. John Hawkesworth has done a fine job of design, while Gordon Hales' editing maintains the leisurely spirit of the story. *Myro.*

Secrets D'Alcove
(FRANCO-ITALIAN)

Paris, June 8.

Pathe Consortium release of Terra Film-Cormoran production. Stars Martine Carol, Richard Todd, Bernard Blier, Francois Perier, Vittorio De Sica. Directed by Henri Decoin, Jean Delannoy, Ralph Habib, G. Franciolini. Screenplay, Maurice Auberge, Roland Laudenbach, Antoine Blondin, Sergio Amedei, Janet Wolf; camera, Christian Matras, L. H. Burel; editor, Denis Reis, James Cuenet; music, Georges Van Parys. At Marignan, Paris. Running time, **110 MINS.**

Mother ....Jeanne Moreau
Soldier ....Richard Todd
Janet .... Dawn Addams
Bob ....Vittorio De Sica
Ricky .... Mouloudji
Martine .... Francoise Arnoul
Agnes ....Martine Carol
President .... Bernard Blier
Alfred ....Francois Perier

Film is a bed partner of such predecessors as "La Ronde," "Seven Deadly Sins" and "Le Plaisir" in which a central theme or gimmick is used to gather a flock of names and top directors and writers to fashion a sketch film with exploitation possibilities. This one uses four foreigners, on their way to a conference, who are sidetracked by the fog into a small cabin, dominated by a big bed. Their fatigue and the necessity of sharing the bed starts a series of reminiscenses about happenings around a bed.

Producers must have had an eye on foreign markets for this manages to be insouciant and naughty without being lascivious. This should not have any censorship difficulties in the U. S., especially after "The Miracle" and "La Ronde" groundwork. However, the sketches have a tendency to be dragged out, and the overworked idea is only saved by the stars' workmanship. Too many of the sketches skirt the banal. Some seem to be oft-told tales that would be of much more appeal between the covers of a book rather than the myriad of bedcovers in this. But this has a big name roster, many known in the U. S. Also the general theme should lend this to an extensive exploitation with word-of-mouth a probable plus factor. This is a probable good draw for art houses and special situations in the U. S.

Second sketch takes place in a plush N. Y. hotel. Vittorio De Sica, in order to divorce his wife, has hired a pretty girl, Dawn Addams, to act as correspondent by spending the night with him. This innocent affair turns to love when the American girl finds the dashing foreigner to her liking, and they are married. This episode has the sterling timing of De Sica and the pulchritude of Miss Addams.

Third item concerns a young truckdriver who helps a spoiled, rich girl change a tire on the road, and then dreams he is in bed with the girl. Francoise Arnoul emerges a worthy dream possibility, and Mouloudji is properly gauche as the truckdriver. Last bit is a racy turn-of-the-century farce item concerning the pereginations of a supposed bed of Madame De Pompadour. Delivered to a lively young courtesan, Martine Carol, by mistake, it takes her on a ride into big time political circuits since it was originally sent by the President of the Republic. Then episode gets a bit thin as the bed lurches back and forth. Martine Carol is properly saucy and inviting in her bedclothes, while Bernard Blier and Francois Perier give this a farcical air.

Technical credits are all high for this pic while the editing and lensing help bridge the story gap and gloss over the differences in tone between many of the stories. *Mosk.*

Susan Slept Here
(SONGS—COLOR)

Sock, Wacky Comedy

Hollywood, June 21.

RKO release of Harriet Parsons production. Stars Dick Powell, Debbie Reynolds; features Anne Francis. Directed by Frank Tashlin. Screenplay, Alex Gottlieb, adapted from Gottlieb-Steve Fisher play, "Susan"; camera (Technicolor), Nicholas Musuraca; editor, Harry Marker; music, Leigh Harline; special songs, Jack Lawrence; musical direction, Constantine Bakaleinikoff. Previewed June 21, '54. Running time, **00 MINS.**

Mark .... Dick Powell
Susan .... Debbie Reynolds
Isabella .... Anne Francis
Virgil .... Alvy Moore
Maude .... Glenda Farrell
Maizel .... Horace McMahon
Hanlon .... Herb Vigran
Harvey .... Les Tremayne
Marilyn .... Mara Lane
Georgette .... Maidie Norman
Dr. Rawley .... Rita Johnson
Waitress .... Ellen Corby
Janitor .... Benny Rubin
Legal Secretary .... Barbara Darrow
Cashier .... Sue Carlton
Motel Manager .... Oliver Blake
Telephone Voice .....Louella O. Parsons

Some 97 minutes of well-farced escapism is offered in "Susan Slept Here." Audiences should go along with comedy. Ingratiating cast headed by Dick Powell and Debbie Reynolds, expertly project fun. This one should encounter no booking troubles, most situations will find ticket window pace okay.

Romantic comedy is imaginatively developed, brightly trouped under Frank Tashlin's smart direction most of way. It goes stereotype in dream dance sequence that wastes approximately seven minutes. Slowing chuckles to only few titters. Occasional narrations, presumably by Academy Oscar, are also too cute. Remainder of footage, however, provides broad antics.

Al Gottlieb script, based on Gottlieb, Steve Fisher play, involves Hollywood writer Powell with juve delinquent Debbie in sort of May-October romantic affair.

Tashlin handling, and players, score strongest in scenes played strictly for Pantomime. One sure laugh getter scene is Powell watching old movie he dialoged on television. Other has Debbie watching home movies, grimancing cattily at love rival Anne Francis. Laughs in many sequences step on dialog, much of which is not heard, indicating possible need to re-edit.

Some of material approaches frankness of "Moon Is Blue." Some chuckles are sly type since battle-of-sexes stuff is open to assorted interpretations. For code purposes, Debbie remains pure through all (her delinquency only that of being left homeless by mother gone off to remarry), she manages to spoil Miss Francis' courtship of Powell and gets him for herself.

Firstrate featured, supporting players contribute much to fun. Glenda Farrell, Powell's secretary, Alvy Moore, his ex-navy buddy, being principal assists. Miss Reynolds more than holds her own in more experienced company. Also choice are Horace McMahon, and Herb Vigram as cops, Les Tremayne as worried lawyer, Rita Johnson as a psychiatrist and Mara Lane, Maidie Norman.

Jack Lawrence cleffed title tune and did "Hold My Hand" with Richard Myers. Latter heard via Don Cornell record in pic. Leigh Harlin background score is good and Nicholas Musuraca's technicolor lensing adds to plush look worn by Harriet Parsons production. *Brog.*

Return to Treasure Island
(COLOR)

Tab Hunter and Dawn Addams teamed in an actioner for the program market.

United Artists release of Aubrey Wisberg-Jack Pollexfen production. Stars Tab Hunter, Dawn Addams; features Porter Hall, James Seay, William Cottrell. Directed by E. A. Dupont. Screenplay and story, Wisberg and Pollexfen; camera (Pathecolor), William Bradford; editor, Fred Feitshans Jr.; music, Paul Sawtell. Previewed N.Y., June 18, '54. Running time, **75 MINS.**

Clive Stone .... Tab Hunter
Jamesina Hawkins .... Dawn Addams
Maximillian Harris .... Porter Hall
Felix Newman .... James Seay
Parker .... Harry Lauter
Cookie .... William Cottrell
Cardigan .... Lane Chandler
Williams .... Henry Rowland
Captain Flint .... Dayton Lumis
Long John Silver .... Robert Long
Thompson .... Ken Terrell

(*Aspect ratio*: 1.75-1)

Aubrey Wisberg and Jack Pollexfen, who specialize in modest budget action pictures, have another entry in that bracket that shapes up favorably for its intended market. For despite an implausible pulp fiction story, "Return to Treasure Island" does better than par the course in sex, gunplay, chicanery and aquatic scenery.

Obviously tailored to tastes of younger filmgoers, this United Artists release has Tab Hunter to titillate femme teenagers while redtressed Dawn Addams engagingly disports her figure and its more prominent accoutrements in a way calculated to entrance the male eye. Moreover, the stars' visual assets as well as the extensive seascapes are handed an extra lift via pleasing Pathecolor hues.

Script has Miss Addams, as owner of a treasure map, sailing to the South Seas with onetime archaeology prof Porter Hall in quest of pirate loot. But before the pieces-of-eight glint in the sunlight, Hall turns out to be a renegade of the first water. He seizes the map with the aid of James Seay who heads a rival group of treasure hunters.

Lest anyone think that Miss Addams has been cast adrift to fend for herself, bewhiskered Hunter conveniently befriends her. It develops that he'd been left for dead on the island while a member of a previous Hall-Seay expedition. Suffice to say that the now clean-shaven Hunter and his femme partner rout the heavies, find the treasure and sail romantically away against a typical FitzPatrick travelog horizon.

Hunter and Miss Addams appear to enjoy themselves in splashing through the water and making with the heroics. Their acting, however, is another matter for both read lines in an unconvincing manner. Hall is considerably better as the unscrupulous prof while Seay is fair as another wicked treasure hunter. Other players deliver stock performances as members of the Hall-Seay factions.

E. A. Dupont's direction is good in the action sequences but neither he nor the cast can be blamed if the so-called dramatic scenes fail to come off for the story is hardly a credible one. William Bradford's color lensing is effective, Paul Sawtell's score is adequate and Fred Feitshans Jr., edited to a breezy 75 minutes. The Wisberg-Pollexfen production values are okay as are other technical credits. *Gilb.*

The Desperado

Well-plotted western drama for the programmer market; toplines Wayne Morris, but outside his usual Allied Artists group.

Hollywood, June 17.

Allied Artists release of Vincent M. Fennelly production. Stars Wayne Morris; features James J. Lydon, Beverly Garland. Directed by Thomas Carr. Screenplay, Geoffrey Homes; based on a novel by Clifton Adams; camera, Joseph M. Novac; editor, Sam Fields. Previewed June 15, '54. Running time, **79 MINS.**

Sam Garrett .... Wayne Morris
Tall Cameron .... James J. Lydon
Lauren Bannerman .... Beverly Garland
Ray Novac .... Rayford Barnes
Jim Langley .... Dabbs Greer
Buck & Paul Creyton ..... Lee Van Cleef
Captain Thornton .... Nestor Paiva
Martin Novack .... Roy Bancroft
Sgt. Rafferty .... John Dierkes
Pat Garner .... Richard Shackleton
Mr. Garner .... Stanford Jolley
A Trooper .... Charles Garland
Mrs. Cameron .... Florence Lake

The carpetbag days in Texas serve as the basis for this rather interestingly developed, if somewhat dragged out, western drama. The familiar name of Wayne Morris heads the cast, although the film is not in his regular Allied Artists group of oater releases.

Principal plot motivation in the Geoffrey Homes screenplay, scripted from the novel by Clifton Adams, veers away from toplined Morris and makes his footage take second place to that given James Lydon. This deviation permits the story to develop naturally and Thomas Carr's direction takes advantage of this to get believable performances from the good cast.

Lydon and Rayford Barnes, young Texans, revolt against the carpetbag rule of the State Police, represented here by Nestor Paiva, and flee to escape persecution. Their trail crosses that of Morris, a wanted gunman, who befriends Lydon when the latter falls out with Barnes. Later, Paiva and one of his State Police are murdered by Barnes, who vengefully places the blame on Lydon. A smart marshall, Dabbs Greer, engineers Lydon's capture but at the trial joins with Morris in proving the young man's innocence and fixing the guilt on the proper party.

The characterizations all come across solidly and help to make this a considerable cut above the usual oater. In addition to the thoroughly competent male performances of those named, favorably spotted are Lee Van Cleef, playing twin killers, John Dierkes, a State Police, and others. In line with the picture's deviation from the oater formula is the presence of Beverly Garland, playing a western heroine who makes sense, storywise and otherwise.

Technical credits, from lensing by Joseph M. Novac on down, are acceptably handled. Footage is somewhat unwieldy in length at 79 minutes. *Brog.*

The Outlaw Stallion
(COLOR)

Formula outdoor actioner in color for supporting dates.

Hollywood, June 18.

Columbia release of Wallace MacDonald production. Features Phil Carey, Dorothy Patrick, Billy Gray, with Roy Roberts. Directed by Fred F. Sears. Story and screenplay, David Lang; camera (Technicolor), Lester H. White; editor, Aaron Stell. Previewed June 16, '54. Running time, **64 MINS.**

Doc Woodrow .... Phil Carey
Mary Saunders .... Dorothy Patrick
Danny Saunders .... Billy Gray
Hagen .... Roy Roberts
Wagner .... Gordon Jones
Rigo .... Trevor Bardette
Sheriff Fred Plummer.... Morris Ankrum
Truxton .... Chris Alcaide
Martin .... Robert Anderson
Mace .... Harry Harvey
Trimble .... Guy Teague

(Aspect ratio: 1.85-1)

There's little in "The Outlaw Stallion" to distinguish it from countless other outdoor sagas about a horse and a boy. It's a lowercase attraction for juve interest, nicely dyed with Technicolor tints, for the programmer market.

Story locale in the David Lang script is a remote section of Utah and the time is the present. Billy Gray and his widowed mother, Dorothy Patrick, ranch near a preserve for wild horses, the herds of which are ruled by a beautiful white stallion which the boy claims as his own. For menace the story introduces Roy Roberts as the head of a group of horse-runners, illegally corralling the wild steeds and trucking them across the state border. Roberts is using a trained black stallion in the horse-trapping trick when this nag is killed by the white stallion. Roberts determines to have the animal. For little reason, he takes the white, kidnaps the boy and his mother but is rounded up in the end.

Phil Carey is the adult lead in all this, but his role and that of Miss Patrick are so stereotyped very little can be, or is, made of them. Young Gray and Roberts, however, show up in okay fashion, as does Morris Ankrum, the reluctant sheriff with an aching back that makes it tough for him to lead a posse over the hills.

Fred F. Sears directed the Wallace MacDonald production. Having little to work with, storywise, in developing the human players, Sears' guidance uses some thrilling footage of fights between the stallions as much as possible. Lensing by Lester H. White and the other technical assists are satisfactory. *Brog.*

The Unconquered
(Documentary)

Fine biopic of Helen Keller. Good educational tieup entry.

Albert Margolies release of Nancy Hamilton production. Camera, Joe Lipkowitz; commentary by James Shute; narrator, Katharine Cornell; technical director, Richard Carver Wood; music, Morgan Lewis. At Guild Theatre, N.Y., June 15, '54. Running time, **55 MINS.**

"The Unconquered" is a moving documentary of how Helen Keller (now 72) became an inspiration to others through her valiant fight to carry on a normal life despite an affliction of infancy which left her sightless and deaf. But although this Nancy Hamilton production is an excellent chronicle of Miss Keller's life story, the subject matter is probably too depressing to qualify it for general distribution.

Picture's market appears to lie primarily in the art house field where it can benefit through word of mouth and tieups with schools, social welfare groups and women's clubs. For "The Unconquered" has a wealth of educational values that stand out as a shining example and beacon of courage not only to the handicapped but to the more fortunate as well. (Mark Twain considered Miss Keller and Napoleon the two great figures of the 19th century).

In re-tracing Miss Keller's career the film records much of her life through early photographs, newsreel clips of yesteryear and liberal footage of more contemporary scenes. Especially touching are sequences which point up the loyalty of her two lifelong companions—Annie Sullivan, who died 18 years ago, and Polly Thompson, who has been constantly at her side since then.

Throughout the picture narrator Katharine Cornell effectively reads the commentary written by James Shute. Overall editing is relatively good and the narration conveniently serves as an additional bridge where needed. Score of Morgan Lewis, too, is an asset. *Gilb.*

The Outcast
(COLOR)

Routine western, with hefty action footage to sustain general interest.

Republic (associate producer, William J. O'Sullivan) production and release. Stars John Derek, Joan Evans; features Jim Davis, Catherine McLeod, Ben Cooper. Directed by William Witney. Screenplay, John K. Butler, Richard Wormser, based on a story by Todhunter Ballard; camera (Trucolor), Reggie Lanning; editor, Tony Martinelli; music, R. Dale Butts. Previewed N.Y., June 21, '54. Running time, **90 MINS.**

Jet Cosgrave .... John Derek
Judy Polsen .... Joan Evans
Major Cosgrave .... Jim Davis
Alice Austin .... Catherine McLeod
The Kid .... Ben Cooper
Andrew Devlin .... Taylor Holmes
Mrs. Banner .... Nana Bryant
Boone Polsen .... Slim Pickens
Chad Polsen .... Frank Ferguson
Cal Prince .... James Milligan
Dude Rankin .... Bob Steele
Curly .... Nacho Galindo
Bert .... Harry Carey Jr.
Sam Allen .... Bill Walker
Zeke Polsen ...... Robert "Buzz" Henry
Asa Polsen .... Nicolas Coster

Although following a routine story line, "The Outcast" has enough action footage to sustain general interest. It's a natural for the oater fans and with John Derek and Joan Evans as stars should get okay market response. Brawling aspects of pic and femme charms of Miss Evans and Catherine McLeod are serviceable exploitation pegs.

Derek is yarn's pivot character and as such is kept pretty much on his toes. He's almost constantly either (1) whipping out his gun, (2) bruising his knuckles or (3) giving his horse a workout. Impetus behind all this action is his yen to gain control of his father's ranch which should have been his when the latter died. However, a conniving uncle (Jim Davis) forged a will and acquired the property, leaving Derek out in the cold.

The Misses Evans and McLeod are given ample spotting as romantic interests. Former is out to hook Derek, while latter is engaged to Davis. Derek gives both of them a whirl before settling down with Miss Evans. Both femmes register nicely.

Derek does a good job as a basically nice guy out to get what's rightfully his, while Davis is properly suave and menacing. James Milligan and Bob Steele are effective as a couple of hired gunmen. Other cast members fill their roles satisfactorily. William Witney's direction keeps film moving at a fairly rapid pace. *Jess.*

Mr. Hulot's Holiday
(FRENCH)

Jacques Tati, French pantomimist, in a sight comedy reminiscent of the silent film days. Has good chance for general situations in the U.S.

A G-B-D release of Fred Orain and Jacques Tati production. Stars Tati. Directed by Tati. Screenplay, Tati and Henri Marquet; camera, Jacques Mercanton and Jean Mouselle; editor Jacques Grassi. At the Fine Arts Theatre, June 16, '54. Running time, **85 MINS.**

Mr. Hulot .... Jacques Tati
Martine .... Nathalie Pascaud
The Aunt .... Michelle Rolla
The Old Maid .... Valentine Camax
The Boatman .... Louis Perrault
The Colonel .... Andre Dubois
The Hotel Proprietor .... Lucien Fregis
The Waiter .... Raymond Carl
The Stroller .... Rene Lacourt
The Stroller's Wife ... Marguerite Gerard

(French, dubbed in English)

"Mr. Hulot's Holiday," the one-man effort of French pantomimist Jacques Tati, will recall the comedies of the silent film days. The humor is based on situations, with the dialog playing a sparse and entirely secondary role. It is slapstick, pure and simple, with sight gags piled on in rapid succession, some of them hilarious, others amusing, still others so-so. It is a loosely-constructed and plotless film, but with enough laughs to earn it playdates in general situations in the United States.

Its French origin and dubbed English dialog should be no handicap, for the humor is for the eyes and it has universal appeal. The English dubbing is barely noticeable, since it is infrequently used and never employed in a closeup.

Tati, who produced, directed, wrote and stars in the film, presents the adventures of a well-intioned schnook on his vacation at a seaside resort. This Mr. Hulot is out to make the most of his two-weeks-with-pay, but every well meaning gesture ends in disaster. His tiny sports car is pushed off the road by big American automobiles, a balky dog blocks his way, his canoe collapses, he is dragged down a mountain by a heavy knapsack.

The situations do not always occur to Mr. Hulot, but he's connected in some way. A particularly funny bit is that involving the collapsing funeral wreath when Mr. Hulot's tire tube somehow finds its ways among the floral offerings. As his other adventures, Mr. Hulot's all-thumbs approach backfires in his romantic attempts. His holiday closes with a big bang, as he inadvertently touches off a fireworks display.

While Hulot is the center of the misadventures, the other middle class vacationers come in for close study, with Tati providing excellent touches. There's the business man who can't get away from his business, the retired military man who gallantly leads a picnic expedition, and the couple who take incessant walks. The individual incidents are too numerous to mention, but, on the whole, they're diverting and entertaining.

Tati has directed sharply, giving careful attention to each individual situation. The camera work and other technical aspects are good. *Holl.*

Young Wives' Tale
(BRITISH)

Wacky, British-made farce with Audrey Hepburn (seen briefly) as chief asset for U. S. theatre dates.

Hollywood, June 21.

Allied Artists release of an Associated British Picture Corp. production, produced by Victor Skutezky. Stars Joan Greenwood, Nigel Patrick, Derek Farr; features Bruce Middleton, Athene Seyler, Helen Cherry, Audrey Hepburn. Directed by Henry Cass. Screenplay, Ann Burnaby; camera, Edwin Miller; editor, E. Jarvis; music, Philip Green. Previewed June 16, '54. Running time, **78 MINS.**

Sabina .... Joan Greenwood
Rodney .... Nigel Patrick
Eve .... Audrey Hepburn
Bruce .... Derek Farr

Victor .... Bruce Middleton
Nurse Gallop .... Athene Seyler
Mary Banning .... Helen Cherry
Nurse Flott .... Fabia Drake
Valentine .... Anthony Deaner
Elizabeth .... Carol James
Nurse (Regents Park)....... Irene Handl
Nurse (Regents Park)....Joan Sanderson
Ay Yah .... Selma Vaz Dias
Taxi Driver .... Jack McNaughton
Man in Pub .... Brian Oulton
(Aspect ratio: 1.33-1)

Allied Artists has a wacky, British-lensed domestic farce in this frantic footage titled "Young Wives' Tale." By a fluke a main b.o. value for U.S. is the fact Audrey Hepburn occupies fourth feature (not star) spot in the billing.

"Tale" was made a number of years back by Victor Skutezky for Associated British, with Henry Cass directing a screenplay written by Ann Burnaby. Miss Hepburn was then an unknown. She appears in this in only seven scenes, mostly inconsequential, and the nominal stars of the farce are Joan Greenwood, Nigel Patrick and Derek Farr. The domestic comedy of errors is brought about by the post-war housing shortage in London.

Things get rather mad early in the footage and remain that way throughout, even bringing in a bedroom farce touch here and there, and there's no real solution to the house-shortage problem by the time the end rolls round, though the windup does find the two couples settling the marital misunderstandings and mixups that have resulted from the close quarters in which they live.

Performances are as freewheeling as the broad plotting. Miss Greenwood, now signed with Metro in Hollywood, also has been seen on Broadway, seems expert at the British-flavored humour, as do Patrick, Farr, Miss Cherry, Athene Seyler, the nurse; Bruce Middleton, the London lounge lizard after Miss Greenwood, and Miss Hepburn. Edwin Miller's protography and other technical ends are adequate. *Brog.*

Apache
(COLOR)

First Hecht-Lancaster release. Punchy action film treating Indians sympathetically.

United Artists release of Harold Hecht production. Stars Burt Lancaster, Jean Peters; features John McIntire, Charles Buchinsky, John Dehner, Paul Guilfoyle, Ian MacDonald, Walter Sande, Morris Ankrum, Monte Blue. Directed by Robert Aldrich. Screenplay, James R. Webb, based on novel "Bronco Apache" by Paul I. Wellman; camera (Technicolor), Leonard Doss; editor, Alan Crosland Jr. Running time, **86 MINS.**
Massai .... Burt Lancaster
Nalinle .... Jean Peters
Al Sieber .... John McIntire
Hondo .... Charles Buchinsky
Weddle .... John Dehner
Santos .... Paul Guilfoyle
Clagg .... Ian MacDonald
Lt. Col. Beck .... Walter Sande
Dawson .... Morris Ankrum
Geronimo .... Monte Blue

This initial Hecht-Lancaster release through United Artists is a rugged action saga in best Burt Lancaster style of muscle-flexing. His name and a plot that lives up to outdoor heroics suggested by title point picture for favorable reaction in market at which principally aimed.

Harold Hecht production based on history, re-telling story of a diehard Apache who waged one-man war against United States and thereafter became a tribal legend. While its roots are historic, Webb screenplay from Wellman novel, "Bronco Apache" gives it good old outdoor action punch true to western film tradition.

Main plot switch is viewing Indian from sympathetic angle, even though his knife, arrows, bullets often find their marks among white soldiers. Twist that leaves him free man at finale is fact it's a declared war between him and United States Army, just as though between nations, so he's off the hook for killings and property destruction soon as he's willing to make peace.

Lancaster and Miss Peters play their Indian roles understandingly without usual screen stereotyping. As played, these two top characters are humans, surprisingly loquacious in contrast to usual clipped redskin portrayals.

Robert Aldrich, making second start as feature film director, handles cast and action well, waste movement being eliminated and only essentials to best storytelling retained, as attested by comparatively short running time of 86 minutes. On white side of cast, John McIntire, chief scout out to capture or kill Lancaster, is very good, underplaying neatly. John Dehner, cruel Indian agent, also shows up well and excellent assists are provided by Charles Buchinsky, Indian soldier; Paul Guilfoyle, Apache father of Miss Peters who betrays Lancaster; Walter Sande, Morris Ankrum.

Outdoor locations lensed by Ernest Laszlo in color are unusually rugged and provide fine, interesting backing for picture. Alan Crosland Jr., edited crisply. David Raskin score always supports, never intrudes on, the action. *Brog.*

Garden of Evil
(C'SCOPE—SONGS—COLOR)

Gary Cooper, Susan Hayward, Richard Widmark giving moody suspense-action feature, Mexico location-lensed, star importance and business chances.

Hollywood, June 29.
20th-Fox release of Charles Brackett production. Stars Gary Cooper, Susan Hayward, Richard Widmark; features Hugh Marlowe, Cameron Mitchell, Rita Moreno, Victor Manuel Mendoza. Directed by Henry Hathaway. Screenplay, Frank Fenton; from a story by Fred Freiberger, William Tunberg; camera (Technicolor), Milton Krasner, Jorge Stahl Jr.; editor, James B. Clark; music, Bernard Herrmann; songs, Emilio D. Uranga, and Ken Darby and Lionel Newman. Previewed June 25, '54. Running time, **100 MINS.**
Hooker .... Gary Cooper
Leah Fuller .... Susan Hayward
Fiske .... Richard Widmark
John Fuller .... Hugh Marlowe
Luke Daly .... Cameron Mitchell
Singer .... Rita Moreno
Vicente Madariaga
.... Victor Manuel Mendoza
Captain .... Fernando Wagner
Priest .... Arturo Soto Rangel
Waiter .... Manuel Donde
Bartender .... Antonio Bribiesca
Victim .... Salvado Terroba
(Aspect ratio: 2.55-1)

The name value of such a star trio as Gary Cooper, Susan Hayward and Richard Widmark gives "Garden of Evil" plenty of marquee importance for top bookings. The names, plus a good assortment of exploitation angles, also give the picture better than average business chances so returns look likely to be profitable all down the line.

Not the least of the stronger points in the Charles Brackett production is the CinemaScope treatment of the location-lensing in Mexico. The new anamorphic lens greatly increases the visual impact of the outdoor scenes and becomes such an important part of the story-telling it almost overpowers the plot drama at times. Also standout are the hues in the Technicolor as caught by the photography of Milton Krasner and Jorge Stahl Jr., and many scenes appear as paintings. Only spot where anamorphic does not seem to enhance the presentation is in the special photographic effects and process work. Here the make-believe of the scenes is emphasized.

Henry Hathaway's direction has a lot of mood-setting, brooding characters and attempts at profundity to contend with in the script by Frank Fenton from a story by Fred Freiberger and William Tunberg. All of this occasionally makes it difficult to develop the kind of action an outdoor tale of violence and adventure needs, but Hathaway manages to do it often enough to carry the 100 minutes of footage.

The plot has Cooper, Widmark and Cameron Mitchell, three adventurers stranded in a small Mexican port while the ship on which they were passengers is being repaired, hired by Miss Hayward to ride with her into dangerous Indian country to free her husband, Hugh Marlowe, who is trapped in a gold mine. Also along on the trip is Victor Manuel Mendoza, Mexican strong man.

The greed of most of the ill-assorted party, the dangers of the difficult trails it must travel and the continued threat of the Indians hang over the footage like a dark, menacing cloud. Lust, too, gets in its licks to add to the drama before the party makes its rescue and starts back. The Indians begin to pick off the men, one by one, until at trail's end Widmark sacrifices himself so that Cooper and Miss Hayward, the only other survivors, can make it to safety.

Cooper, ex-sheriff from Texas; Miss Hayward, a woman whose character never becomes quite clear; Widmark, philosophical card sharp; and Mitchell, cowardly killer, handle the chief roles with the flourish and color demanded.

Also excellent is Marlowe, the husband who could see no good in his wife but is the first to try to save the party, and Mendoza, sizeable Mexican actor who turns in a fine portrayal. While only in the opening footage as a cafe singer, Rita Moreno makes her scene count while singing "La Negra Noche" by Emilio D. Uranga, and "Aqui" by Ken Darby and Lionel Newman.

With two exceptions, the technical credits are important assets to the picture. The exceptions are the already noted process work, and the Bernard Herrmann background score. In some sequences the music becomes so busy concentration on the drama is impossible, a flaw that is emphasized by many sequences that play without a single note of background score. *Brog.*

Her Twelve Men
(COLOR)

Greer Garson as femme teacher of 13 (sic) pupils in boys' school. Spotty prospects.

Hollywood, June 29.
Metro release of John Houseman production. Stars Greer Garson, Robert Ryan; co-stars Barry Sullivan; features Richard Haydn, Barbara Lawrence. Directed by Robert Z. Leonard. Screenplay, William Roberts, Laura Z. Hobson; from a story by Louise Baker; camera (Ansco Color), Joseph Ruttenberg; editor, George Boemler; music, Bronislau Kaper. Previewed June 23, '54. Running time, **90 MINS.**
Jan Stewart .... Greer Garson
Joe Hargrave .... Robert Ryan
Richard Y. Oliver Sr.....Barry Sullivan
Dr. Avord Barrett .... Richard Haydn
Barbara Dunning......Barbara Lawrence
Ralph Munsey .... James Arness
Homer Curtis .... Rex Thompson
Richard Y. Oliver Jr.......Tim Considine
Jeff Carlin .... David Stollery
Sylvia Carlin .... Frances Bergen
Roger Frane .... Ian Wolfe
Bobby Lennox .... Donald MacDonald
Kevin Clark .... Dale Hartlemen
Erik Haldeman .... Ivan Triesault
Jimmy Travers .... Stuffy Singer
Alan Saunders .... Peter Votrian
(Aspect ratio: 1.75-1)

An okay 90 minutes of family entertainment is offered in "Her Twelve Men," an Ansco Colored comedy-drama starring Greer Garson, Robert Ryan and Barry Sullivan. It is a generally amusing account of the relationship between a femme teacher and her 13 (sic) young pupils at an exclusive boys' school. The cast names and subject matter aren't commercially exciting enough to indicate much trade outside of family patronage, and the latter may be confused by the title's implications since Miss Garson's film reputation is hardly synonymous with sin.

The John Houseman production is based on a story by Louise Baker, "Miss Baker's Dozen" (a handle aptly and correctly tallying the 13 students), which William Roberts and Laura Z. Hobson put into screen form for Robert Z. Leonard to direct. Each function is carried out expertly to make the most of the material and a nice balance between heart tugs and chuckles is maintained.

Miss Garson, after a number of years of marriage, turns to teaching in a boys' school to make a new life. In doing so she gains a worthwhile purpose as well as a new love, but not until the script puts her through the special tortures that mischievous boys reserve for grownups who have not yet been accepted. The young male antics follow a pattern familiar to most parents and spark numerous warm chuckles.

Ryan, brusque lower-form prof at the school; and Sullivan, Texas oil millionaire and father of one of the problem kids, are rivals in Miss Garson's new romantic life, with Ryan winning out over riches. Neither of these more mature males figure too strongly in the plot, since emphasis is on the youngsters. Other adults include Richard Haydn, headmaster; Barbara Lawrence, seen intermittently as a rich girl chasing Ryan; James Arness, inarticulate physical instructor; Ian Wolfe, Frances Bergen and Ivan Triesault, the latter pair a. parents. All are competent.

Youngsters seemingly enjoying the make-believe not too far separated from real for them are Rex Thompson, an English encyclopedia; Tim Considine, Sullivan's son; Donald MacDonald, a lonesome little tyke; David Stollery, Dale Hartlemen, Stuffy Singer, Peter Votrian and others.

Joseph Ruttenberg's photography, the Bronislau Kaper score and other production assists are excellent. *Brog.*

Konjiki Yasha
(Golden Demon)
(JAPANESE-COLOR)

Tokyo, June 8.

A Daiei Motion Picture Co., release of Masaichi Nagata production. Stars Jun Negami, Fujiko Yamamoto. Directed by Koji Shima. Screenplay, Shima based on novel by Koyo Ozaki; camera, Michio Takahashi; music, Ichiro Saito. Previewed at Southeast Asia Film Festival, Tokyo. Running time, **95 MINS.**

(In Japanese; English Titles)

Daiei Motion Picture Co., winners of awards at Venice and Cannes festivals, has added another feather to its cap with this film which won the "Golden Harvest" award at the first Southeast Asia Film Festival held this month here.

Daiei loosed all its big guns in preparing "Golden Demon" for international competition, even pacing in the English subtitles, before its release. Made in Eastmancolor, it is based on Japan's immortal classic novel of the same name by Koyo Ozaki. It concerns the country's legendary lovers comparable to the West's Romeo and Juliet. Topnotch Daiei stars Jun Negami and ex-"Miss Japan," Fujiko Yamamoto, play the leads. Daiei prexy Masaichi Nagata guided "Demon" all the way.

Whereas the majority of Japanese prize winners previously have used ancient Japan as a strong point of appeal, this is comparatively a modern drama, being laid in the late 19th Century. It should pull well in the U. S. on general release though the sub-titles are a handicap.

Kanichi (Jun Negami), a student, is in love with Omiya (Fujiko Yamamoto). The two grow up expecting eventually to be married. However, a young millionaire Tomiyama (Eiji Funakoshi) asks for Omiya's hand and her parents force her into the marriage. Kanichi thinks Omiya has discarded him for wealth, and, in the film's biggest scene, beats and kicks her on a lonely beach. Four years later, Kanichi is seen as a money-mad usurer, who has pledged himself to revenge Omiya and the money which has taken her away from him. One of his debtors, an old woman, sets his house on fire after failing to kill him with a kitchen knife. Meanwhile, Omiya has become estranged from her rich husband. The flames which completely destroy Kanichi's house release him from the yoke of greed and restore his human emotions and eventually Omiya.

"Demon" does not sacrifice its dramatic element for the sake of color alone. Even in black and white, this would be a superb film. Negami scores as Kanichi and Miss Yamamoto displays intelligence as well as beauty. Supporting players are excellent.

The whole production staff has done superbly. Director-Scenarist Koji Shima deserves laurels for a well-balanced and convincing series of colorful scenes while cameraman Michio Takahashi has taken breathtakingly beautiful frames. Ichiro Saito has contributed an unusually fine score.

The only flaw is a minor one. English subtitles, while adequately carrying the plot, have been written with an attempt to portray the slang of the period in English. It's bad at times. *Lars.*

No Way Back
(Weg Ohne Umkehr)
(GERMAN)

Berlin, June 22.

West Film release of Trans-Rhein-Occident production. Stars Ivan Desny, Ruth Niehaus, Rene Deltgen and Karl John. Directed by Victor Vicas. Screenplay, Gerhard T. Buchholz and Vicas; camera, Klaus von Rautenfeld; editor, Ira Oberberg; music, Hans Martin Majevski. At Gloria Palast, Berlin, June 21, '54. Running time, **96 MINS.**

4Mischa .... Ivan Desny
Anna .... Ruth Niehaus
Kazanov .... Rene Deltgen
Schulz .... Karl John
Ljuba .... Lila Kedrova
Litvinski .... Sergez Belousov
Direktor Barger .... Alf Marholm
McCollough .... John Haggerty
Wassilij .... Leonid Pylaew

Winner of the all-German Oscar and a candidate for Berlin Film Festival honors, "No Way Back" represents a technical advance on recent local productions although it falls far short of average Hollywood standards. The specially prepared English version may find it tough sledding in the U.S. market. But the Berlin conception of the East-West conflict may command some attention.

Main weakness of the production is the implausibility of the script. Too often conviction is sacrificed for convenience and there are obvious weaknesses in continuity which rob the yarn of any realism. And it is difficult to believe in the principal male character, a Russian official who sacrifices his position to help a German who deliberately tried to murder him.

Action begins in 1945 in war-torn Berlin. After sufficient incident to establish the main characters, a Russian officer and a German girl, there is a seven-year lapse. The Russian comes back as the chief of a civilian delegation and immediately takes a streetcar to the west sector in search of the girl. Next morning he's hauled before the secret police chief, only to find the girl he was looking for happens to be his (police chief's) secretary. From then on, they get into endless trouble, until they eventually make a dash for freedom across the border. Even then, the girl allows herself to be lured back in an exceptionally naive way.

Victor Vicas, who came from America to direct this, his first feature, has done a creditable job, although as co-scripter he must accept his share of the responsibility for the story shortcomings. He has put the cast briskly through their paces. Ivan Desny and Ruth Niehaus give nice performances. Technically, the film is adequate, and the quality of the camerawork stands out. *Myro.*

Maenner Im Gefaehrlichen Alter
(Men at Dangerous Age)
(GERMAN)

Berlin, June 8.

Europa release of Fama production. Stars Hans Soehnker and Liselotte Pulver. Directed by Carl Heinz Schroth. Screenplay, Per Schwenzen; camera, Franz Weihmayr; music, Hans Martin Majewski; settings, Mathias Matthies. At Kiki, Berlin. Running time, **89 MINS.**

Franz Volker .... Hans Soehnker
Anna ....Liselotte Pulver
Mau, housekeeper.......... Annie Rosar
Adam Kassner, author..Wilfried Seyferth
Lil Dewohl .... Ilse Bally
Butzinsky, secretary...Guenther Jerschke

This is one of the most enjoyable comedies to come out of a German studio in months. Pic has a lightweight plot, but has witty dialog and a chuckle in nearly every foot. Film wisely avoids reiterating corny gags. It will emerge here as an outstanding grosser, and foreign prospects shape good.

Story concerns an orphan girl who, after she has grown up in a country school, finds a new home with her foster-father, a celebrated actor around 40 years old. Latter's initial fatherly affection gradually turns into love. After a series of hilarious situations and complications (the girl simply upsets the bachelor household), there is the happy ending. Although author Per Schwenzen occasionally squeezed the dialog, he has produced a refreshing variation of the basically old-hat plot.

Pretty Liselotte Pulver is excellent in transition from the young innocent gal to an attractive and comely femme. This role appears perhaps the best of her career. Hans Soehnker has the proper sense of proportion to play the old foster-father. Outstanding supporting roles are turned in by Wilfried Seyferth as an author and Guenther Jerschke, a new comedy find here, as a secretary.

Carl Heinz Schroth has kept the action fast moving with few quiet moments. Musical score, lensing and other contributions are fine. *Hans.*

L'Amour D'Une Femme
(The Love of a Woman)
(FRANCO-ITALIAN)

Paris, June 8.

Cine Selection release of LPC- Costilazione production. Stars Micheline Presle, Massimo Girotti; features, Gaby Morlay. Directed by Jean Gremillon. Screenplay, Gremillon, Rene Wheeler, Rene Fallet; camera, Louis Page; editor, Marguerite Renoir. At Studio De L'Etoile, Paris. Running time, **105 MINS.**

Marie .... Micheline Presle
Andre .... Massimo Girotti
Teacher .... Gaby Morlay
Sacristan .... Carette
Priest .... Paola Stoppa

This distaffer pic deals with the conflict of the love for work or for a man in the life af a femme doctor. Though this has a nice production and locale dress in a small island off the French coast, it is too familiar and surface in characterization to make for much U.S. interest. It has the Micheline Presle name for some dualers, but is too old hat in treatment to amount to much. Its dances even are limited here.

Miss Presle is a doctor sent to a small island to minister to the simple populace. First they resent her but she smiles through and begins to win their confidence. Love blooms with a visiting engineer, but she finally sticks to her profession.

Miss Presle brings sparkle and pathos to the role of the medico, but the cards are stacked against her in the obvious unfoldment. Massimo Girotti is okay as the lover while the village types are well rounded. Director Jean Gremillon has given this nice feeling but a lack of drama and movement. Lensing and editing are fine. *Mosk.*

Trouble in the Glen
(BRITISH—COLOR)

Herbert Wilcox-Herbert Yates co-production; Disappointing story, but marquee appeal for U.S.

London, June 15.

Republic release of Wilcox-Neagle-Yates production. Stars Orson Welles, Margaret Lockwood, Forrest Tucker, Victor McLaglen, John McCallum. Produced and directed by Herbert Wilcox; screenplay, Frank S. Nugent from story by Maurice Walsh; camera, Max Greene; editor, Reginald Beck; music, Victor Young; color by Trucolor. At Gaumont, London, June 15, '54. Running time, **91 MINS.**

Marissa .... Margaret Lockwood
Laird .... Orson Welles
Lance .... Forrest Tucker
Parlan .... Victor McLaglen
Malcolm .... John McCallum
Bishop's Wife .... Janet Barrow
Dinny Sullivan .... Eddie Byrne
Bishop .... Albert Chevalier
Villager .... George Cormack
Castillo .... Dorothea Dell
Nolly Dukes .... Archie Duncan
Dany Dinmont .... Ann Gudrun
Sheilah .... Grizelda Hervey
Policeman .... Alistair Hunter
Nurrich .... William Kelly
Luke Carnoch .... Moultrie Kelsall
McLaren .... Stevenson Lang
David .... Robin Lloyd
Alsuin .... Margaret McCourt
Keegan .... Alex McCrindle

"Trouble in the Glen" is the second picture made by Herbert Wilcox under the Republic banner, and once more he has recruited an Anglo-American cast with appeal for U.S. market. The names on the marquee may help in ticket selling but the picture is somewhat disappointing with limited entertainment appeal. The pictorial backgrounds, adequately lensed in Trucolor, prove to be one of the main assets of the pic. The magnificence of the Scottish highland scenery, filmed on location, often has a breath-taking appeal. The story, however, wrapped in some obscurity, has little of the stimulating quality of the setting.

Stripped of its trimmings, the plot describes how Orson Welles returns to his homeland from South America to become the Laird of the Glen. But he doesn't reckon with local customs and clannish intrigue, and soon finds himself in a tight situation. He closes the highway that runs through his estate and is generally in a state of seige with the locals. A one-time U.S. air force officer who had served locally during the war, returns in the person of Forrest Tucker. He tries in vain to induce a spirit of compromise, although half the battle is over when a romantic attachment develops with the Laird's daughter, played by Margaret Lockwood.

The plot develops into a tussle between Welles on one hand and the landless tinkers on the other, led by Victor McLaglen and John McCallum, as father and son. They burn the Laird in effigy, steal a prize steer and frustrate a plot to bring in a tough gang from the city. At this point, Welles admits his stubborness, and the Laird and his people are united. Throughout the story development, there is an over-sentimentalized treament of a young girl, (she turns out to be Tucker's daughter) who is a bedridden polio victim.

Frank S. Nugent's screenplay has an effective opening page when the narrative is introduced by Welles, but that standard is not maintained. And the plot drifts along rather casually. Herbert Wilcox's direction appears to have done little to remedy this defect. Miss Lockwood plays the Laird's daughter with little inspiration. However, Welles' portrayal is frequently one of the best things in the picture.

Tucker turns in a reliable performance, but Victor McLaglen is inadequately served. McCallum has a rugged appeal as the tinker and Margaret McCourt is all too sweet as the invalid child. Supporting roles are adequately filled. *Myro.*

What Every Woman Wants!
(BRITISH)

British pic lacks names for U. S. marquee; may do as dualer.

London, June 10.
Adelphi Films release of David Dent production. Stars William Sylvester, Elsy Albiin, Brenda de Banzie, Patric Donan. Directed by Maurice Elvey. Screenplay, Talbot Rothwell from Edwin Lewis's "Relations Are Best Apart"; camera, Wilkie Cooper; music, Edward Astley; editor, Robert Jordan Hill. At Rialto Theatre, London, June 10, '54. Running time, **86 MINS.**
Jim Barnes...........William Sylvester
Jane ....Elsy Albiin
Sarah ....Brenda de Banzie
Mark ....Patric Doonan
Bill ....Dominic Roche
Polly Ann ....Joan Hickson
Herbert ....Brian Rix
Doll ....Joan Sims
Tom ....Beckett Bould
Mary ....Prunella Scales
Sam ....Douglas Ives
Frank ....Edwin Richfield

This independently-made British picture has as its main setting the industrial midlands and as its problem over the impact of the housing shortage on an ordinary working class family. Narrative is related with a measure of down to earth humor. It would serve as good mass entertainment locally where its quota ticket will be a plus selling factor. The pic has value as a dualer in U. S. situations, but lack of names for American marquee will hurt.

The central characters in the plot are a young couple who, having nowhere to live, have to be content with a room with the wife's parents. The arrangement is never, never satisfactory, particularly as the domestic situation and labor troubles complicate the plot.

The answer to the query in the title is implied: Every woman wants a home of her own where she can raise her own family. This point is warmly developed by a competent cast headed by William Sylvester, as the returning soldier; Elsy Albiin and Patric Doonan, as the young husband and wife, and Brenda de Banzie, cast as the girl's mother. Dominic Roche, Joan Hickson and Brian Rix fill the major supporting parts with competence. Maurice Elvey has handled the direction with authority. *Myro.*

Weg Ohne Umkehr
(No Way Back)
(GERMAN)

Berlin, June 15.
Westfield release of Occident and Trans-Rhein-Film production. Stars Ivan Desny, Ruth Niehaus and Rene Deltgen. Directed by Victor Vicas. Screenplay, Gerhard T. Buchholtz and Victor Vicas; camera, Klaus von Rautenfeld; music, Hans-Martin Majewski; settings, Alfred Butow. Preemed at Waldbuehne, Berlin. Running time, **96 MINS.**
Michael ....Ivan Desny
Anna ....Ruth Niehaus
Kazanow ....Rene Deltgen
Schulz ....Karl John
Ljuba ....Lila Kedrowa
Litwinski ....Sergej Belousow
Director Berger............Alf Marholm

This film, which depicts the story of a Russian who quits his regime, is one of the most courageous German postwar productions. Directed by Victor Vicas, Russian-born American living in Paris, and shot against the authentic background of divided Berlin, pic appears to have good commercial prospects outside of Germany. A good ballyhoo hinge is in the fact that, while the film was being shot, fact and fiction collided when a real-life Russian deserter ran onto the picture's location right in the middle of a fictional escape scene. This story hit the newspapers all over the world.

"No Way Back" has to do with Michael (Ivan Desny) who, as a Russian officer, met a Berlin fraulein back in 1945 when the Red Army conquered the city. He had saved her. Seven years later, he returns to Berlin as a civilian and finds her as the secretary to a NKWD (Russian Secret Police) major. Both fall in love and decide to go to the western world. Russian agents, however, drag her back to East Berlin and the end sees him free but her hopelessly lost in the brutal Red world. There's no way back for either of them.

Vicas has directed this with remarkable understanding. He was greatly helped by the tight script of G. T. Buchholz who, together with Stuart Schulberg, watched the supervision. They succeeded in producing a film which has realism and suspense in every foot. However, Berlin patrons who know what's going on in their city may object to the fact that a flight from East to West Berlin is not as tough as depicted in this film.

Great performances are turned in by the principals. First of all, Ivan Desny, French actor, deserves laurels for his highly convincing portrayal of the Russian who switches sides. Ruth Niehaus, as the Fraulein, has hardly ever been better. Standout also is Rene Deltgen as the Russian major.

The fine musical score by Hans-Martin Majewski and the brilliant lensing by Klaus von Rautenfeld are further plus points about this film which, incidentally, was declared "particularly valuable" by the West German Censor Board. *Hans.*

Sins of Rome
(ITALIAN)

Italian spectacle in days of the gladiators.

Hollywood, June 18.
RKO release of a Spartacus Consortium production. Stars Massimo Girotti, Ludmilla Tcherina, Gianna Maria Canale, Yves Vincent, Carlo Ninchi, Vittorio Sanipoli. Directed by Riccardo Freda; camera, Gabor Pogany; music, Renzo Rosselini. Previewed June 18, '54. Running time, **72 MINS.**
Amitys .... Ludmilla Tcherina
Spartacus .... Massimo Girotti
Sabina .... Gianna Maria Canale
Octavius .... Yves Vincent
Crassus .... Carlo Ninchi
Rufus .... Vittorio Sanipoli
(Aspect Ratio: 1.33-1)

(English Dubbed)
This Italian import is based upon the exploits of a Roman gladiator in the year 74 B.C., who led the slaves to freedom but in a final battle between his rebels and the overwhelming Roman forces met his death on the field. Spectaclewise, film is turned out on the grand scale with thousands of extras, but is of limited appeal in U. S. A. English dialog has been dubbed for fairly good effect.

With the exception of Ludmilla Tcherina, the European ballet star, cast is entirely Italian, unknown to American audiences. While the personal story of Spartacus, the gladiator, is told, interest is focused primarily upon the action scenes, one sequence showing the gladiator single-handedly attacking several lions which threaten the life of his beloved in the arena. This and other sequences of battle and violence are ably directed by Riccardo Freda, who maintains a fast pace during much footage. Film has been indifferently edited, however, with the result much of the impact is lost.

Story itself is negligible, only enough plot appearing to weave the subject to a conclusion. Spartacus, played by Massimo Girotti, a mercenary with the Roman legions in Thrace, protests his commander's cruelty and is returned a slave to Rome, where he becomes a gladiator. The daughter of one of the Roman leaders falls for him and tries to get him for her own, but he rebuffs her, preferring to lead the slaves' revolt, during which he is finally killed.

Girotti makes the most of his role, but rivalling him in interest is Gianna Maria Canale, femme on the make, a beautiful actress who registers. Miss Tcherina, as a slave girl, presents one dance, but it isn't the type to display her best talents. Yves Vincent is the gladiator's rival for leadership, Carlo Ninchi the Roman leader and Vittorio Sanipoli head of the legionnaires responsible for Girotti's slavery.

Gabor Pogany's photography frequently is interesting and Renzo Rosselini's music score impressive. *Whit.*

King Richard and the Crusaders
(C'SCOPE—COLOR)

Sir Walter Scott's classic, 'The Talisman,' given film spectacle treatment in CinemaScope. Good cast, stout b.o.

Hollywood, July 6.
Warner Bros. release of Henry Blanke production. Stars Rex Harrison, Virginia Mayo, George Sanders, Laurence Harvey; features Robert Douglas, Michael Pate, Paula Raymond, Lester Matthews, Antony Eustrel. Directed by David Butler. Screenplay, John Twist; from Sir Walter Scott's "The Talisman"; camera (WarnerColor), J. Peverell Marley; editor, Irene Morra; music, Max Steiner; song, "Dream, Dream," by John Twist and Ray Heindorf. Previewed June 30, '54. Running time, 113 MINS.
Emir Ilderim
Sultan Salacin .... Rex Harrison
Lady Edith .... Virginia Mayo
King Richard I .... George Sanders
Sir Kenneth .... Laurence Harvey
Sir Giles Amaury ...... Robert Douglas
Marquis Montferrat ...... Michael Pate
                            Michael Pate
Queen Berengaria .... Paula Raymond
Archbishop of Tyre.....Lester Matthews
Baron de Vaux .... Antony Eustrel
King Philip of France....Henry Corden
Duke Leopold of Austria....Wilton Graff
A Dance Specialty .... Nejla Ates
Nectohanus .... Nick Cravat
Castelaine Captain .... Leslie Bradley
1st Castelaine .... Bruce Lester
2nd Castelain .... Mark Dana
3rd Castelain .... Peter Ortiz
(Aspect ratio: 2.55-1)

"The Talisman," Sir Walter Scott's classic about the third crusade, gets the full CinemaScope spectacle treatment in this box-office entry from Warner Bros. titled "King Richard and the Crusaders." It has a good cast of familiar names enacting the period escapism and the grossing prospects are stout.

As for the title, the Henry Blanke production could just as easily be called "The Saracen and the Crusaders," so thoroughly does Rex Harrison walk off with performance honors as Saladin, the sultan whose Moslem forces are pitted against the invading Christians from Europe. However, Virginia Mayo, George Sanders and Laurence Harvey (British player making his Hollywood debut) plus Robert Douglas and Michael Pate, come up with swashbuckling characterizations that also sustain the film's 113 minutes of sweeping action under David Butler's vigorous direction.

Filming of the Scott classic may give the novel renewed reading interest among the younger filmgoers who may not yet have tasted of its romantic adventures detailing the efforts of Christian nations from Europe, marshalled under the leadership of England's King Richard, to gain the Holy Grail from the Mohammedans. In addition to the fighting wiles of the crafty Moslems, King Richard must contend with the sinister ambitions of some of his entourage and these rivalries almost doom the crusade.

Blanke's production supervision of the excellent John Twist script has all of the showmanly touches needed to make the picture attractive to almost any age group among viewers. Butler's direction manages to keep a long show nearly always moving at a fast clip. Especially attractive to the action-minded will be the jousting sequences, either those showing training or those in deadly seriousness, and the bold battling is mostly concerned with combat between the forces of good and evil among the crusaders themselves. The script is especially good in its dialog, particularly that handed to Harrison.

The latter reminds of his sock deliniation in "Anna and the King of Siam" of some years back in the interpretation he gives the wily Saracen. He even has a song to sing, a charming little melody tagged "Dream, Dream" by Twist and Ray Heindorf, that is used as a courting air when he tries to convince Miss Mayo, the lovely Lady Edith, cousin of the king, that she should be the bride of the sultan so that the bloody crusade could be concluded. Miss Mayo becomes the period costumes of a lady caught in the desert with the crusaders. Sanders' King Richard has its merits, as does the villainy offered by Douglas, as the ambitious Sir Giles Amaury, and Pate, as the crafty, evil Marquis of Montferrat. There's considerable bluster of Harvey's Sir Kenneth, the Scot who serves Richard, the man, not the king, but it goes with this type of role acceptably.

J. Peverell Marley uses the CinemaScope cameras and Warner-Color to advantage in dressing up the broad movements of the picture. Anamorphic processing is an excellent treatment for this type of subject, but is so keen-eyed it shows up the falseness of scenes done before process screens. A rousing score by Max Steiner supports the action, but also sometimes competes with it. *Brog.*

Francis Joins the WACS

Amusing entry in U's 'talking mule' series; good b.o. outlook.

Hollywood, July 1.

Universal release of Ted Richmond production. Stars Donald O'Connor, Julia Adams, Chill Wills, Mamie Van Doren, Lynn Bari, ZaSu Pitts; features Joan Shawlee, Allison Hayes, Mara Corday, Karen Kadler, Elsie Holmes. Directed by Arthur Lubin. Screenplay, Devery Freeman, James B. Allardice; story, Herbert Baker; based on the character "Francis" created by David Stern; camera, Irving Glassberg; editor, Ted J. Kent, Russell Schoengarth. Previewed June 29, '54. Running time, **94 MINS.**

Peter Stirling .... Donald O'Connor
Captain Parker .... Julia Adams
General Kaye .... Chill Wills
Corp. Bunky Hilstrom .. Mamie Van Doren
Major Louise Simpson .... Lynn Bari
Lt. Valerie Humpert .... ZaSu Pitts
Sergeant Kipp .... Joan Shawlee
Lt. Dickson .... Allison Hayes
Kate .... Mara Corday
Marge .... Karen Kadler
Bessie .... Elsie Holmes
Capt. Creavy .... Olan Soule
Aide .... Anthony Radecki
Francis, the Talking Mule

(*Aspect ratio*: 2-1)

Donald O'Connor and his loquacious friend, Francis, the Talking Mule, are back for another laugh session in this Universal release. The boxoffice outlook is good, since the same type of amusing screwball comedy that has characterized the series is put forth slickly in this one.

A clerical error puts bank clerk and ex-G. I. O'Connor back into service, but in a WAC unit. His talking sidekick goes along to make certain that no chuckles will be overlooked in the bits of business concocted by Arthur Lubin's direction and by the script written by Devery Freeman and James B. Allardice from a story by Herbert Baker.

Hokum gets an added assist in this latest series entry by having Chill Wills, the voice of Francis, also playing a visible role for the first time. It sets up a number of funny complications. So does the assignment of O'Connor to the WAC unit commanded by Lynn Bari and her aide, Julia Adams. The gals see it as an attempt by Wills, commanding general, to satotage the WAC's work in camouflage, but with the help of Francis, O'Connor is able to out-mastermind Wills and the femmes so that the latter wins out in the wai games being played.

O'Connor, Wills, the Misses Adams, Bari, Mamie Van Doren and ZaSu Pitts, the latter seen again in the screwy nurse role she created for the first Francis film, plus the other casters all deliver slickly to point the Ted Richmond production for a favorable reaction from the ticket buyers.

Technical departments are expert, although footage is a mite longer than necessary at 94 minutes. *Brog.*

Valley of the Kings
(COLOR)

Robert Taylor, Eleanor Parker in Egyptian-lensed suspense feature.

Hollywood, July 6.

Metro release (no producer credit). Stars Robert Taylor, Eleanor Parker, Carlos Thompson; features Kurt Kasznar, Victor Jory, Leon Askin, Aldo Silvani, Samia Gamal. Directed by Robert Pirosh. Written by Pirosh and Karl Tunberg; suggested by historical data in "Gods, Graves and Scholars," by C. W. Ceram; camera (EastmanColor), Robert Surtees; editor, Harold F. Kress; music, Miklos Rozsa. Previewed June 3, '54. Running time, **85 MINS.**

Mark Brandon .... Robert Taylor
Ann Mercedes .... Eleanor Parker
Philip Mercedes .... Carlos Thompson
Hamed Bachkour .... Kurt Kasznar
Taureg Chief .... Victor Jory
Valentine Arko .... Leon Askin
Father Anthimos .... Aldo Silvani
Dancer .... Samia Gamal

(*Aspect ratio*: 1.75-1)

Spectators are given a tour of the land of the Nile in this suspense drama, and the backgrounds offer more freshness to the film than does the routine story. The color cameras show off settings never before lensed for a Hollywood-produced picture and provide some exploitation excitement that will help the payoff chances.

The familiar names of Robert Taylor and Eleanor Parker team to topline the cast. Also starred is newcomer Carlos Thompson, who has yet to be seen to any particular advantage in a domestic production. The story is one dealing with robbers of the tombs of the Pharaohs in Egypt, with a side angle having to do with the establishment that Old Testament accounts of Joseph in Egypt are literally true.

Some good suspense action and thrills are whipped up in the screenplay by Robert Pirosh and Karl Tunberg on the robber score during the first 70 minutes of footage. The side angle to the plot is wrapped up in the concluding 15 minutes and, while quite interesting, is anti-climactic to the main story interest. Pirosh also directed, and gives satisfactory pacing and suspense development to the material considering that it unfolds familiarly along rather easily anticipated lines.

Taylor plays a rugged American archaeologist who agrees to help Miss Parker, married to Thompson, search for the tomb of the Pharaoh, Ra-hotep. She wants to prove that her late father was right in believing the tomb will prove his theory about Joseph in Egypt. Clues turn up indicating the tomb already has been robbed and a mysterious gang, seemingly headed by sinister Kurt Kasznar, puts obstacles in the way of the search before it is revealed Thompson is the man behind the crooked goings-on. He and Taylor battle it out atop the tomb. Thompson is killed and his widow is free to have her new hero. After this, the pair goes on to uncover Ra-hotep and the theory's proof.

Plot period is 1900 and ageless wonders of the land of the Nile fit perfectly. Viewers are treated to day and night scenes of great beauty as the cameras pick up the Sphinx and Pyramids, historic Mount Sinai, the Red Sea and the Suez Canal, the vast desert, Cairo streets and buildings, Mena House, a famous hotel near the Pyramids and other landmarks.

Miss Parker and Taylor are a good lead team for the drama, but Thompson comes off only fair. Kurt Kasznar, Leon Askin, Victor Jory, doing native menaces of varying degree, are excellent in colorful parts, and Aldo Silvani acceptably plays Father Anthimos from St. Catherine's Monastery on Sinai. Samia Gamal is in for a very brief navel expose during a cafe scene.

The script was suggested by historical data in "Gods, Graves and Scholars" by C. W. Ceram. The very good camera work was contributed by Robert Surtees. Miklos Rozsa's background score is an aide to the film's mood and settings. Other technical supports are okay. *Brog.*

Duel in the Jungle
(BRITISH-COLOR)

Topheavy drama starring Jeanne Crain, Dana Andrews and David Farrar with authentic African settings. Overlong and contrived situations.

London, June 30.

Associated British-Pathe release of Marcel Hellman production starring Jeanne Crain, Dana Andrews, David Farrar with Patrick Barr, Mary Merrall, Charles Goldner, George Coulouris. Directed by George Marshall; screenplay, Sam Marx, T. J. Morrison from original story by S. K. Kennedy; camera, Edwin Hillier; editor, E. B. Jarvis; music, Mischa Spoliansky with lyric "The Night Belongs to Me" by Norman Newell; color by Technicolor. At Warner Theatre, London, June 30 '54. Running time, **105 MINS.**

Scott Walters .... Dana Andrews
Marian .... Jeanne Crain
Perry and Arthur Henderson .... David Farrar
Roberts .... Patrick Barr
Capt. Malburn .... George Coulouris
Martell .... Charles Goldner
Pitt .... Wilfrid Hyde White
Mrs. Henderson .... Mary Merrall
Lady .... Heather Thatcher
Vincent .... Michael Mataka
Clerk .... Paul Carpenter

This melodramatic story of a trek through the jungle to unearth a sadistic swindler has brought the reaction that the overseas showing of such a situation would do harm to Britain's prestige at the present time. There is plenty of scope for an entertaining story in the basic idea, but this present treatment and trite dialog prove a waste of much that is good and of the importation of Jeanne Crain and Dana Andrews for two of the leading roles. Presumed appeal will be to sensation seekers and those not already satiated with longshots of wild animal life and death lurking in the forest.

Dana Andrews plays an American insurance agent visiting London to protest at the danger risks being run by an explorer-diamond broker for whom his company holds a million dollar life policy. The firm's assurance that their chief will cease his current deep sea diving activities off Africa is followed by the news that he has been drowned. Sensing there is something phoney in the setup the investigator planes out in the wake of the dead man's secretary whom he has tried to make before learning she is engaged to her boss. She repudiates his suggestion the death report is false and claims she is going to visit her fiance's mother. He tags along on safari with death lurking through lions, snakes, leopards crocs and other jungle impedimenta until they reach journey's end and the missing man. He openly boasts of his successful fraud claiming his firm needed the dough to proceed with costly undersea probing for diamonds. He tries to kill the investigator on a lion hunt and in a terrific fight, culminating in a canoe chase over the rapids which brings the native police to round up the cornered man.

Apart from improbabilities in the story and dialog, one of the main weaknesses is the meek acceptance of the natives of the barbarous cruelty imposed upon them by the white boss whom, alone in their midst, they could have obliterated without trace. This angle is unpalatable and there is no amelioration through the possibility of insanity which could well have been implied, his mother being shown as ultra eccentric.

Jeanne Crain plays the hard to get heroine with commendable courage and Dana Andrews as the doubly pursuing pursuer registers a clearcut characterization. David Farrar does his best in the thankless role of the brutal defrauder. Excellent support is given in smaller parts by Mary Merrall, Charles Goldner, Wilfrid Hyde White, George Coulouris and Patrick Barr. Camerawork, particularly in the African sequences, is on a high level. *Clem.*

The Bowery Boys Meet The Monsters

Below par bread-and-butter entry.

Hollywood, June 30.

Allied Artists release of a Ben Schwalb production. Stars Leo Gorcey, Huntz Hall; features Bernard Gorcey, Lloyd Corrigan, Ellen Corby, John Dehner, Laura Mason, Paul Wexler, David Condon, Bennie Bartlett. Directed by Edward Bernds. Screenplay, Ellwood Ullman, Bernds; camera, Harry Neumann; editors, Lester A. Sansom, William Austin; music, Marlin Skiles. At Orpheum, L.A., June 30, '54. Running time **62 MINS.**

Slip .... Leo Gorcey
Sach .... Huntz Hall
Louie .... Bernard Gorcey
Anton .... Lloyd Corrigan
Amelia .... Ellen Corby
Derek .... John Dehner
Francine .... Laura Mason
Grissom .... Paul Wexler
Chuck .... David Condon
Butch .... Bennie Bartlett

(*Aspect ratio*: 1.85-1)

"The Bowery Boys Meet the Monsters" goes overboard on the malaproprisms which generally give zest to series in this latest release of Allied Artists' bread-and-butter program. The Ben Schwalb production is on the weak side, not up to the usual standard, with appeal even for followers of the series apt to be limited.

This time, Leo Gorcey and Huntz Hall, in their familiar zany characters, get involved in a household of madmen seeking to obtain human heads for their scientific experiments. One wants a brain with a low I.Q. for transference to the skull of a giant ape, another a head to attach to an electronic robot, controlled by a microphone. Edward Bernds' direction of his and Ellwood Ullman's screenplay matches the slapstick qualities of the thin story line, but film is badly in need of editing to eliminate duplication of action.

The two stars acquit themselves in their usual style, and have the benefit of top support. John Dehner and Lloyd Corrigan are the two scientists; Ellen Corby their sister, who wants Gorcey to feed to her pet, a man-eating tree; and Laura Mason is the niece, a vampire. Bernard Gorcey is in for his customary role of Louie, the sweetshop owner, and Paul Wexler is the butler.

On technical side, Harry Neumann's photography is standard.

Whit.

Ring of Fear
(C'SCOPE-COLOR)

Exploitable melodrama with circus background. Marred by mediocre scripting.

Hollywood, July 2.

Warner Bros .release of Wayne-Fellows production, produced by Robert M. Fellows. Stars Clyde Beatty, Pat O'Brien, Mickey Spillane; features Sean McClory, Marain Carr, John Bromfield. Directed by James Edward Grant. Written by Paul Fix, Philip MacDonald, James Edward Grant; camera (WarnerColor), Edwin DuPar; editor, Fred MacDowell; music, Emil Newman, Arthur Lange. Previewed June 22, '54. Running time, 92 MINS.

Himself	Clyde Beatty
Frank Wallace	Pat O'Brien
Himself	Mickey Spillane
Dublin	Sean McClory
Valerie St. Denis	Marian Carr
Armond St. Denis	John Bromfield
Gonzalez	Gonzalez-Gonzalez
Twitchy	Emmett Lynn
Paul Martin	Jack Strang
Shreveport	Kenneth Tobey
Suzette	Kathy Cline

(*Aspect ratio:* 2.55-1)

An assortment of good, commercial exploitation values should pull "Ring of Fear" through to profitable grosses in most general market dates. Chances would have been more assured had the sales factors been backed with a more worthwhile story. Best prospects are in the action-exploitation situations.

While Clyde Beatty, Pat O'Brien and Mickey Spillane are starred, and the presence of Beatty and Spillane are among the ballyhoo factors, there's only one performance in the footage and that by Sean McClory, Irish-brogued heavy of the piece. Had James Edward Grant's direction, and the screen story he wrote with Paul Fix and Philip MacDonald, been more decisive and aware of where it was going, this could have been a topnotch show.

McClory is seen as a homicidal maniac, always menacing but almost likeable, who is out to wreck the Clyde Beatty Circus and the marriage of Marian Carr, a girl he fancies, to John Bromfield, a jealous aerialist. His successful sabotage, using a drunken old clown, Emmett Lynn, as the tool, keeps the circus stirred up and brings in Spillane, playing himself (badly) and his cop friend, Jack Stang, to smoke out the mystery. Climax has McClory killed by a giant tiger he had loosed to kill others.

The circus footage is real, and good, especially the lion and tiger act staged by Beatty. These are the best such scenes yet filmed for a regular feature, and the CinemaScope lens helps to make them so. Aerial footage, too, has its thrills.

The Robert M. Fellows' production set up its cameras with the Beatty show to film the authentic circus flavor. It is to be regretted that this and other attempts to bring off a somewhat different motion picture were negated by a slipshod script and poorer direction. Some attempt to salvage and bolster the picture was made by re-shooting some scenes and adding others after the original lensing but this has only added to the hot-and-cold feel and still leaves the grossing possibilities up to the good ballyhoo values. Fred MacDowell edited and Edwin DuPar did the WarnerColor lensing.

Brog.

Happy Ever After
(BRITISH—COLOR)

Sparkling Irish village comedy starring David Niven, Yvonne de Carlo, Barry Fitzgerald; should have widespread b.o. appeal.

London, July 6.

Associated British-Pathe release of Mario Zampi production. Stars David Niven, Yvonne de Carlo, Barry Fitzgerald; features George Cole, Robert Urquhart, A. E. Matthews. Directed by Mario Zampi. Screenplay, Jack Davies, Michael Pertwee; camera, Stanley Pavey; editor, Kathleen Connors; music, Stanley Black with number, "My Heart Is Irish," by Michael Carr; color by Technicolor. At Ritz, London, June 29, '54. Running time, 87 MINS.

Jasper O'Leary	David Niven
Serena McGlusky	Yvonne de Carlo
Thady O' Heggarty	Barry Fitzgerald
Terence	George Cole
General O'Leary	A. E. Matthews
Kathy McGlusky	Noelle Middleton
Dr. Flynn	Robert Urquhart
Major McGlusky	Michael Shepley
Dooley	Joseph Tomelty
Lannigan	Eddie Byrne
Regan	Liam Redmond

This hilarious Irish comedy starts off with the advantage of having three Hollywood names to bolster a thin story. It is dependent for most of its laughs on situations. In addition, there is magnificent background scenery and plenty of local color to provide all associated with the brogue and the blarney. It is a natural b.o. winner here and its nationalistic appeal should find real response in the U. S.

The old town hall and local pub are the pivots of activity in a tiny hamlet, with typical rustics and gentry fulfilling the old traditions. The local Hunt has been kept going by the old squire who, despite his 80 years, still insists on leading off the meet by jumping the customary 10-foot wall. The old boy literally takes the plunge, landing in the ditch and passing out with his boots on and a twinkly eye and a bottle of grog.

This provides the framework for David Niven's arrival from England to inherit the estate and smilingly terminate all kindly customs and concessions. He claims unpaid debts verbally cancelled by his uncle, finds his tippling butler and evicts an old tenant whose minute rent the old squire had scorned to collect. Poaching, which had been genially accepted and fairly apportioned, is now taboo and everyone seethes with revolt. Lots are drawn as to who shall rub out the tyrant and every contrivance is rigged up and independently operated. Gunshot, homemade bombs, steel wire traps and ghostly manifestations all react on the perpetrators rather than their intended victim. When a new will turns up disinheriting the newcomers, the village relaxes back into its carefree normalcy.

Through all this upheaval, two love stories are faintly threaded. Yvonne de Carlo, who once ditched the young doctor, returns as an attractive widow and again queers her sister's chances with him. The dashing lord of the manor looks a far better catch so the siren transfers her wiles and sticks despite his unpopularity and loss of inheritance.

Some may regret the unpleasant character so well depicted by Niven as alien to his usual personality. Miss de Carlo coos seductively as the designing widow while Noelle Middleton yearns appealingly as the younger sister. Picture stealers are A. E. Matthews, as the old diehard general, and Barry Fitzgerald, as the old soak of a butler. Michael Shepley, George Cole, Liam Redmond, Joseph Tomelty and Eddie Byrne provide contrasting local types as the conspirators. Robert Urquhart trails a veil of sanity as the young doctor. Pic is directed with commendable compactness by Mario Zampi.

Clem.

The Seekers
(BRITISH—COLOR)

Colorful exciting pioneering story set in New Zealand, starring Jack Hawkins and Glynis Johns; better-suited to British audiences.

London, June 29.

General Film Distributors release of a Fanfare-Earl St. John-George H. Brown production. Stars Jack Hawkins, Glynis Johns; features Noel Purcell, Laya Raki, Inia Te Wiata. Directed by Ken Annakin. Screenplay, William Fairchild; camera, Geoffrey Unsworth; editor, John Cuthridge; music, William Alwyn; color, Eastmancolor. At Odeon, Leicester Square, London, June 22, '54. Running time, 90 MINS.

Philip Wayne	Jack Hawkins
Marion Southey	Glynis Johns
Paddy Clarke	Noel Purcell
Hongi Tepe	Inia Te Wiata
Peter Wishart	Kenneth Williams
Moana	Laya Raki
Awarus	Patrick Warbrick
Rangiruru	Tony Erstich
Toroa	Edward Baker
Hongi Tepe's Father	Maharaia Winiata
Sergeant Paul	Thomas Heathcote
Grayson	Norman Mitchell
Mackay	James Copeland
Capt. Bryce	Francis de Wolff
Aapiti Tohunga	Henry Gilbert

Considerable care and imagination have been lavished on this epic tale of Empire building in New Zealand, with hundreds of Maori providing authentic background. It is a powerful story of pioneering days in the last century, marred by man's weakness and betrayal. But its interpretation falls short of the author's conception, the camerawork and native players providing better value than the stars. As an adventure story in an unusual setting, it should do well locally, but as a competitor to western thrillers its chances would be minimized in the U.S.

Jack Hawkins as a ship's officer comes ashore with an old hand who speaks the native tongue. They are seized for trespassing on a sacred burial ground, but make peace with the chieftain who begs them to remain. Through trickery they fall foul of the Excisemen on their return to England and, accompanied by his bride, Hawkins decides to go back to New Zealand and make a new life. Now a justice of the peace, the ex-sailor finds fulfilment with the birth of a son, but falls to the seductive wiles of the chief's wife. One of the new settlers accidentally kills a Maori and tribal war flares up again. Despite the wrongs he has suffered, the chieftain goes to their aid but finding the young couple have perished in the holocaust rescues their baby from an underground cache. Picture ends with the landing of fresh immigrants to build up the new world.

Jack Hawkins loses his usual granitelike integrity in this role and seems out of focus as a cheating husband. He is more at ease in his scenes with the natives as a vigorous lawmaker. Glynis Johns is suitably steadfast and forgiving in the more shadowy role of his wife while Noel Purcell gives a rich character study of the tough old seadog. Kenneth Williams is well cast as the reckless youth whose disobedience causes the conflagration. Francis de Wolff is realistic as the corrupt sea captain. Laya Raki, of German-Javanese birth, makes an alluring figure as the native chief's wife and all Maori parts are in firstrate hands.

Direction of the picture is uneven, and much more convincing on its larger scale than in closeup situations.

Clem.

The Sleeping Tiger
(BRITISH)

Domestic triangle skilled dramatic treatment and general b.o. appeal.

London, June 29.

Anglo Amalgamated Film Distributors release of Nat Cohen-Stuart Levy-Insignia Films production. Stars Dirk Bogarde, Alexis Smith, Alexander Knox. Directed by Victor Hanbury. Screenplay, Derek Frye, based on novel by Maurice Moiseiwitsch; camera, Harry Waxman; editor, Reginald Mills; music, Malcolm Arnold. At Odeon, Marble Arch, London, June 21, '54. Running time, 89 MINS.

Frank Clements	Dirk Bogarde
Glenda Esmond	Alexis Smith
Dr. Clive Esmond	Alexander Knox
Inspector Simmons	Hugh Griffith
Sally	Patricia McCarron
Carol	Maxine Audley
Bailey	Glyn Houston
Harry	Harry Towb
Manager	Russell Waters
Receptionist	Billie Whitelaw

Although run through on conventional lines, with little surprise action, this pic should make for good general entertainment. It should cash in on the Hollywood names. Film should do well as a dualer in the U.S.

Like many stories adapted from books, the crux of the situation seems a long time arriving. When a psychiatrist keeps a young criminal in his home as an experiment in reclamation, instead of turning him over to the police, it is odds on there will be trouble especially when a neglected wife looms in the background. The tension mounts with the growing attachment of the unwilling guest and his hostess plus the hypocritical obstinacy on the boy's part about his earlier life.

The doctor probes with tolerance and understanding but receives ingratitude from the hoodlum who sneaks out at night to continue his plundering and makes love to the bored wife. He is shocked back to a decent remorse when his benefactor jeopardizes his career by lying to the police to alibi him in a holdup. He tells the wife he is through and plans to give himself up, when she is all set to run off with him. Enraged, the thwarted woman screams out the truth to her husband and goes after her lover only to end up in a fatal car crash.

Alexander Knox is all gentle consideration and patience as the conscientious doctor brought rudely to earth by his wife's betrayal. As the guinea pig Dirk Bogarde conveys all the ruthless disregard of principles engendered by a twisted mind. Alexis Smith is excellent as the placid wife in whom the sleeping tiger is roused, from her first haughty treatment of the unwanted visitor thrrough the gradual phases of her degradation. The trio could scarcely have been better cast. Surrounding characters are well chosen and pic is directed with a clean-cut realism.

Clem.

Skanderbeg
(RUSSIAN)

Sovexportfilm release of Mosfilm (New Albania) production. Stars Akaki Khrava. Directed by Mikhail Papava. Directed by Mary Antjaparidze, Mikhail Gomorov, Victor Stratoberdha. Screenplay, Sergei Yutkevich; camera, Evgeni Andrikenis; sets, Joseph Shpinel; music, Yuri Sviridov, Cesk Zadeja. At Stanley, N.Y., starting July 2, '54. Running time, 95 MINS.

Georgi Kastriot .... Akaki Khrava
Donika .... Besa Imani
Mamica .... Adivie Alibali
Hamza ....Semyon Sokolovsky
Dafina .... Veriko Anjaparidze
Marash .... Georgy Chernovolenko
Pal .... Naim Fresheri
Din .... Boris Tenin
Liuka .... Nikolai Bubnov
Tanush Topia .... Oleg Zhakov
Lek Dukagjin.........Geogr Rumyantsev
Sultan Murad...........Vagram Papazyan
Balaban Pasha .... Mihal Popi
Doge of Venice .....Alexander Vertinsky
Giovanni .... Nikolai Levkoyev
Laonicus .... Sergei Zakariadze

(In Russian; English Titles)

This picture won a grand prize at the 1954 Cannes Film Festival. While it has magnificent spectacle and some good acting, being one of the better films to come from Russian studios, it would be excusable to suggest that compared with "Here To Eternity" and several other strong U. S. entries at Cannes, "Skanderbeg" shapes as not more than a moving documentary, lacking any humor or much story quality.

There seems little doubt but that a biopic about Georgi Kastriot, best-known as Skanderbeg, could be made into a powerful screen vehicle. But it would require more than thrilling battle scenes interlaced with folksy dancing of the Albanian countrymen—and repeated references to the Albanian rising against the Turks. There is military opinion that Albanian patriot was one of the great soldiers of history. If so, as a hero he deserved a better fate than accorded him by this Mosfilm production.

The battle scenes, particularly the siege of a castle fortress, are the most impressive portions of this. The charge of the cavalrymen, swinging swords, is less magnificent, particularly since it has been repeatedly done in American pix. There were three directors on this vehicle, and obviously they were impressed with the enormous task confronting them in such a sweeping story.

Akaki Khrava, in the title role, is magnificent and completely dominates the picture. Others, with equally unpronounceable names, do yeoman work. Besa Imani is probably the best of the supporting cast, with Naim Frasheri and Boris Tenin refreshing as lesser characters.

The Sovcolor is as faulty as this Russian color process was more than two years ago. In some scenes, the tinting is so lacklustre, it resembles little more than a glorified sepia mixture. Blues are washed out, browns hardly recognizable and even the red hues merely a warmish orange. This however, does not prevent fine cameraing by Evgeni Andrikanis. Picture's score often is excellent but fails to cash in on the lusty battle scenes. Mikhail Papava's screenplay is routine and seldom imaginative. *Wear.*

Sommaren Med Monika
(Summer With Monica)
(SWEDISH)

Paris, June 1.

CEF release of Svensk Film production. Stars Harriet Andersson, Lars Ekborg. Directed by Ingmar Bergman. Screenplay, P. A. Fogelstrom; camera, Gunnar Fischer; editor, Tage Holmberg. At Marbeuf, Paris. Running time, 95 MINS.

Monika .... Harriet Andersson
Harry .... Lars Ekborg
Lelle .... John Harryson
Father .... Georg Skarstedt
Far .... Ake Fridell

This film follows the usual pattern of many Swedish pix in its emphasis on the summer cadre, young love and its clash with convention. There is a plastic photography finish, with a nudey scene of the young lovers in their first touch with passion. This likely will make the film a censorship hazard but this is scissorable without ruining the main theme of this love idyll. Film benefits from fine direction and thesping to make this a neat offbeater in arty situations, with obvious exploitation values.

Harriet Andersson is a headstrong, impassioned young girl whose poverty-stricken background drives her into the arms of a sensitive young boy, Lars Ekborg. The two flee on the boat of Ekborg's father, and spend a summer of young love. Camera dwells on the budding of bodily consciousness and records some compelling scenes. When hunger and nature set in against them it makes a carping primitive out of the girl, and they head for the mainland and marriage. However, the earthy Miss Andersson finally leaves Ekborg with a son and memories of a summer.

Miss Andersson emerges as a sultry, dynamic find as she firmly outlines the character and instability of Monika, the creature of a summer. Ekborg is gentle and affirmative as the loving Harry, with the other characters doing neat bits. Mood of pic limits this distribwise and is primarily for special handling. Lensing is firstrate in capturing the changing weather. Editing is fine. *Mosk.*

Das Leben Beginnt Mit 17
(Life Begins at 17)
(GERMAN)

Berlin, June 29.

Deutsche London release of Apollo production. Stars Sonja Ziemann, Paul Hubschmid and Anne-Marie Blanc. Directed by Paul Martin. Screenplay, Paul Martin and Gerda Corbett, based on a novel by Gabor von Vaszary; camera, Albert Benitz; music, Wolfgang Zeller. At Marmorhaus, Berlin. Running time, 94 MINS.

Madeleine .... Sonja Ziemann
Raymond .... Paul Hubschmid
Aline .... Anne-Marie Blanc
Lenoire .... Paul Hartmann
Clarisse .... Loni Heuser
Jacques Peronne .... Paul Hoerbiger
Adelheid .... Margarete Haagen
Sylvia .... Marina Ried
Priest .... Heinrich Gretler
Teacher .... Hilde Koerber

Refreshingly new treatment of the basically old plot about a girl's first love is used in this German film. Shot against a beautiful Swiss locale, film has good entertainment values with serious undertones balanced with the humor. Well directed and convincingly played, pic will do well with local patrons while international prospects appear better than with previous German pix of the similar theme.

Based on a novel by Gabor von Vaszary, this centers around a 14-year-old fatherless girl whose mother leaves her most of the time alone in a boarding school. Deserted by her lover, the mother is run over by a car. Feeling responsible for her death, the man takes the teenager into his household and she falls in love with him. He tells her to wait "until you're 17" when he discovers he really is in love with the orphan by that time.

Outstanding direction by Paul Martin is helped also by his work on the script. He deserves credit for the adroit handling. Handsome Swiss actor Paul Hubschmid (in Hollywood: Paul Christian) is tops and thoroughly convincing in his transition from a playboy and lady-killer to a faithful lover. Sonja Ziemann as the wide-eyed teenager, who has been doing superficial pinup type of gals so far, is much better than in her previous pix. A moving performance is turned in by Swiss actress Anne-Marie Blanc in the role of her mother. Supporting cast, composed of such well-known actors here as Paul Hoerbiger, Paul Hartmann and Hilde Koerber is strong.

Fine lensing by Albert Benitz is a real credit to this pic. Wolfgang Zeller's music is excellent. *Hans.*

Malaga
(BRITISH—COLOR)

Melodramatic dope smuggling film. Plenty of color and action make pic good for many U.S. spots.

London, June 29.

British Lion production and release. Stars Maureen O'Hara, Macdonald Carey; features Binnie Barnes, Guy Middleton, Hugh McDermott. Directed by Richard Sale. Screenplay, Robert Westerby; camera, Christopher Challis; editor, A. S. Bates; music, Benjamin Frankel; color, Technicolor. At Leicester Square Theatre, London. Running time, 84 MINS.

Joanna Dane .... Maureen O'Hara
Van Logan .... Macdonald Carey
Frisco .... Binnie Barnes
Soames Howard .... Guy Middleton
Danny Boy .... James Lilburn
Paul Dupont .... Leonard Sachs
Augie .... Harry Lane
Potts .... Bruce Beeby
Pebbles .... Eric Corrie
Jakey .... Meinhart Maur
Cronkhite .... Gerard Tichy
Rodrigo .... Mike Brendall
Richard Farrell .... Hugh McDermott
Mustapha .... Ferdy Mayne

With a good cast of names known to U.S. audiences and care obviously expended on its production, this pic remains just a secret agent imbroglio with spies and counterspies, the femme fatale and everyone chasing the wrong suspect. There is plenty of action and enough corpses to satisfy sensation seekers. It should make a second feature for most countries, but may do better in America.

Said to be based on fact, story discloses the widespread smuggling racket rampant in the Mediterranean, centering on Tangier, a free port with international police. Powerless to check the flow of illicit goods, mainly drugs, the authorities call on the services of a slinky operator who planes in ostensibly seeking a job.

The agents are unknown to each other and the girl dodges and nearly kills the man she believes top suspect. Before they disentangle themselves there are the usual hairbreadth escapes with chases and the most surprising people turning out to be either enemies or carefully camouflaged associates. A battle royal between the shore trapped criminals and the Spanish Civil Guard makes for a lusty windup.

Maureen O'Hara has all the outward attributes of a modern Mata Hari. Her unguarded reactions of surprise and alarm should have betrayed her mission from the outset. Macdonald Carey gives a straightforward portrayal of the chief operator while Binnie Barnes is richly in character as the tough owner of a gambling spot, in reality the gang leader. Supporting players give commendable performances. The pic owes much to some excellent camera shots and colorful background. *Clem.*

L'Affaire Maurizius
(FRANCO-ITALIAN)

Paris, June 29.

Franco London Film release of Franco-London-Jolly Film production. Stars Daniel Gelin, Madeleine Robinson, Eleanora Rossi-Drago, Anton Walbrook. Directed by Julien Duvivier. Screenplay, Duvivier, from a novel by Jacob Wasserman; camera, Robert Lefebvre; editor, Marthe Poncin. At Marignan, Paris. Running time, 115 MINS.

Maurizius .... Daniel Gelin
Warenne .... Anton Walbrook
Elizabeth .... Madeleine Robinson
Anna .... Eleanora Rossi-Drago
Wolf .... Charles Vanel
Etzel .... Jacques Chabassol
Father .... Denis D'Ines
Grandmother .... Berthe Bovy

Julien Duvivier has not been able to maintain the balance between his chores as director and scripter on this film. Hence, it emerges a polished, craftsmanlike production, but the story and treatment never remove the literary stigma. This combo tirade against circumstantial evidence, with overtones of the suspense and psycho drama, remains an unmoving and overlong intersection of a miscarriage of justice. Well played with smart and slick technical attributes, plus a neat list of b.o. names, this will be in for good dates here. For the U.S. this downbeat drama is limited to arty houses.

The son of a magistrate discovers that his father had been instrumental in sending a man to prison on circumstantial evidence. This overstrung young man sets out to unravel the mystery of the trial which he considers unjust. He finds the victim's father, and from him gets clue to the whereabouts of the key witness. In a series of flashbacks the case is reshown plus the incidents leading up to the murder. Maurizius (Daniel Gelin) was a brilliant young scholar who married a woman older than himself, and then fell in love with her younger sister. A sinister friend, Anton Walbrook, jealous of Maurizius, instigates the murder of the wife by the sister. The magistrate's son gets the confession from Walbrook. Meanwhile Maurizius has been pardoned, and can't face life anew when he finds the women he loved married.

It is a tribute to Duvivier's direction that he has been able to keep this literary tirade coherent, but his mannered flashbacks never make a live case. Gelin is unable to display the facets of Maurizius' character while Walbrook adds an unsavory note to his role of the Svengalish friend Madeleine Robinson has a one key role while Eleonora Rossi-Drago is nice as the strange, hypersensitive sister.

Lensing is excellent in portraying the moods of flashback and present while editing is neat. Supporting work is fine with young Jacques Chabossol emerging as a budding actor. *Mosk.*

Rear Window
(COLOR)

Socko Alfred Hitchcock suspense thriller with James Stewart and bright b.o. prospects.

Hollywood, July 13.

Paramount release of Alfred Hitchcock production and direction. Stars James Stewart; co-stars Grace Kelly, Wendell Corey, Thelma Ritter; features Raymond Burr. Screenplay, John Michael Hayes; based on the short story by Cornell Woolrich; camera, Robert Burks; editor, George Tomasini; score, Franz Waxman. Previewed July 9, '54. Running time, **112 MINS.**

Jeff	James Stewart
Lisa Fremont	Grace Kelly
Thomas J. Doyle	Wendell Corey
Stella	Thelma Ritter
Lars Thorwald	Raymond Burr
Miss Lonely Hearts	Judith Evelyn
Song Writer	Ross Bagdasarian
Miss Torso	Georgine Darcy
Woman on Fire Escape	Sara Berner
Fire Escape Man	Frank Cady
Miss Hearing Aid	Jesslyn Fax
Honeymooner	Rand Harper
Mrs. Thorwald	Irene Winston
Newly Wed	Haris Davenport

(*Aspect ratio*: 1.66-1)

A tight suspense show with a bright boxoffice outlook is offered in "Rear Window," one of Alfred Hitchcock's better thrillers. James Stewart's established star value, plus the newer potentiality of Grace Kelly, currently getting a big buildup, and strong word-of-mouth possibilities indicate sturdy grossing chances in the keys and elsewhere.

Hitchcock combines technical and artistic skills in a manner that makes this an unusually good piece of murder mystery entertainment. A sound story by Cornell Woolrich and a cleverly dialoged screenplay by John Michael Hayes provide the producer-director with a solid basis for thrill-making. Of equal importance in delivering tense melodrama are the Technicolor camera work by Robert Burks and the apartment-courtyard setting executed by Hal Pereira and Joseph MacMillan Johnson.

Hitchcock confines all of the action to this single setting and draws the nerves to the snapping point in developing the thriller phases of the plot. He is just as skilled in making use of lighter touches in either dialog or situation to relieve this tension when it nears the unbearable. Interest never wavers during the 112 minutes of footage.

Stewart portrays a news photographer confined to his apartment with a broken leg. He passes the long hours by playing peeping-tom on the people who live in the other apartments overlooking the courtyard. It's a hot, humid summer so shades are rarely drawn to block his view of intimate goings-on. In one of the apartments occupied by Raymond Burr and his invalid, shrewish wife Stewart observes things that lead him to believe Burr has murdered and dismembered the wife.

From then on suspense tightens as Stewart tries to convince Wendell Corey, a policeman buddy, his suspicions are correct. Already sold on the idea are Miss Kelly, Stewart's girl, and Thelma Ritter, the insurance nurse who comes daily to tend his needs. With their help, Stewart eventually is able to prove his point, and almost gets himself killed doing it. Adding to the grip the melodrama has on the audience is the fact that virtually every scene is one that could only be viewed from Stewart's wheelchair, with the other apartment dwellers seen in pantomine action through the photog's binoculars or the telescopic lens from his camera.

There's a very earthy quality to the relationship between Stewart and Miss Kelly. She's a Park Avenue girl not above using all her physical charms to convince Stewart they should get married. This is carried to the point where she arrives one evening set to spend the night and gives him what she calmly calls "a preview of coming attractions" by donning frilly nightgown and negligee. Both do a fine job of the picture's acting demands.

Types that one might find in a Greenwich Village apartment add interest. Miss Torso, roundly played by Georgine Darcy, is a peeping-tom's delight, particularly when she loses her strapless bra. There is a great sadness to Miss Lonely Hearts, played by Judith Evelyn, a woman with an overwhelming desire for a man, yet not knowing what to do when she coaxes one in from the streets. There's a honeymoon joke in the actions of newlyweds Rand Harper and Haris Davenport. He's seen raising the shade at intervals, only to be called back to her arms by the bride. Ross Bagdasarian, a composer; Sara Berner and Frank Cady, a couple with a little dog, and the other types glimpsed all seem like real people, and their soundless contributions give the principles top-notch support. Burr is very good as the menace, as are Corey and Miss Ritter.

The production makes clever use of natural sounds and noises throughout, with not even the good score by Franz Waxman being permitted to intrude unnaturally into the drama. *Brog.*

On the Waterfront

Dock walloper Marlon Brando turns against ruthless labor union boss in hard-hitting entertainment that augurs bright boxoffice payoff.

Columbia release of Sam Spiegel production. Stars Marlon Brando; costars Eva Marie Saint, Karl Malden, Lee J. Cobb; features Rod Steiger, Pat Henning, Leif Erickson, James Westerfield. Directed by Elia Kazan. Screenplay, Budd Schulberg, based upon Schulberg's original story which was "suggested" by Malcolm Johnson newspaper series; camera, Boris Kaufman; editor, Gene Milford; music, Leonard Bernstein. Sneak previewed at Loew's Lexington Theatre, N.Y., July 6. Running time, **108 MINS.**

Terry Malloy	Marlon Brando
Father Barry	Karl Malden
Johnny Friendly	Lee J. Cobb
Charley Malloy	Rod Steiger
"Kayo" Dugan	Pat Henning
Edie Doyle	Eva Marie Saint
Glover	Leif Erickson
Big Mac	James Westerfield
Truck	Tony Galento
Tillio	Tami Mauriello
"Pop" Doyle	John Hamilton
Mott	Heldabrand
Moose	Rudy Bond
Luke	Don Blackman
Jimmy	Arthur Keegan
Barney	Abe Simon
J.P.	Barry Macollum
Specs	Mike O'Dowd
Gillette	Marty Balsam
Slim	Fred Gwynne
Tommy	Thomas Handley
Mrs. Collins	Anne Hegira

(*Aspect ratio*: 1.85-1)

Recent longshore labor scandals serve as the takeoff point for a flight into fictionalized violence concerning the terroristic rule of a dock union over its coarse and rough, but subdued, members. "On the Waterfront" is packed with strongarm dramatics that bespeak impressive business down the line.

Budd Schulberg's script is based on his own original which in turn was "suggested" by the Malcolm Johnson articles for Scripps-Howard. It's a rousing scenario that Schulberg fashioned, with strong accent on murder and mayhem somewhat reminiscent of the picturized gangsterism of the 1920's (per early James Cagney). Schulberg greatly enhanced the basic story line with expertly-turned, colorful and incisive dialog.

Under Elia Kazan's direction, Marlon Brando puts on a spectacular show, giving a fascinating, multi-faceted performance as the uneducated dock walloper and former pug, who is basically a softie with a special affection for his rooftop covey of pigeons and a neighborhood girl back from school.

Kazan does a penetrating job of staging the fireworks and the interspersing tender meetings between Brando and the girl. Latter is Eva Marie Saint, a newcomer to films who has appeared in television and the legiter, "Trip to Bountiful." Miss Saint, in sharp contrast with the robust people and settings of "Waterfront," is fresh and delicate but with enough spirit to escape listlessness in her characterization.

Sam Spiegel's production was lensed on location in the Hoboken, N.J., area and, it appears, much of the camera turning was done in the blue-gray early morning. This gives the pic a quality of chilly realism and an apt backdrop for the story telling. No mention of Hoboken is made in the film.

Story opens with Brando unwittingly setting the trap for the murder of a longshoreman who refuses to abide by the "deaf and dumb" code of the waterfront. The victim is hurled from a rooftop because he addressed himself to an investigating crime commission.

Lee J. Cobb is all-powerful as the one-man boss of the docks. He looks and plays the part harshly, arrogantly and with authority. Another fine job is executed by Karl Malden as the local Catholic priest who is outraged to the point that he spurs the revolt against Cobb's dictatorship.

Rod Steiger, also from tv, was a good choice as Brando's brother for both incline toward the hesitant manner of speech that has been especially identified with Brando. Steiger is Cobb's "educated" lieutenant who is murdered when he fails to prevent Brando from blabbing to the crime probers. It's the shot of Steiger pinned to a wall with a grappling hook that is particularly suggestive of the stark meller stuff of a past era. Pat Henning, Leif Erickson and James Westerfield in less prominent assignments behave competently.

A part of "Waterfront" looks designed for grandstand cheers. This is the climax where Brando, although beaten almost to unconsciousness, manages to rise and lead the longshoremen to a pier job that means the end of Cobb's cutthroat reign. This is lacking in conviction. And unclear is why Cobb, having been identified as a murderer, is not immediately brought to book.

Cast in "Waterfront" is as burly a lot as likely to be encountered outside Stillman's Gym. Tony Galento, Tami Mauriello and Abe Simon are among the heavies.

Camera work (Boris Kaufman) and editing (Gene Milford) rate special mentions for some unusually effective pictorial effects. Under Kazan's megging, of course. Notable is the curtain-raising rooftop slaying and the close-ups of Brando and, alternately, Miss Marie in hushed tete-a-tetes. The one-to-the-other panning achieves eloquent intimacy.

Leonard Bernstein's music score at a couple of points pounds its way into the foreground but mostly complements the screen action well enough. Lighting is exceptionally good. *Gene.*

Return From the Sea

Pleasant companion feature combining war action and romance.

Hollywood, July 9.

Allied Artists release of Scott R. Dunlap production. Stars Jan Sterling, Neville Brand; features John Doucette, Paul Langton, John Picard, Don Haggerty, Alvy Moore, Robert Arthur, Lloyd Corrigan. Directed by Lesley Selander. Screenplay, George Waggner; story, Jacland Marmur; camera, Harry Neumann; editor, John C. Fuller; music, Paul Dunlap. Previewed July 7, '54. Running time, **79 MINS.**

Frieda	Jan Sterling
Maclish	Neville Brand
Jimmy	John Doucette
Lt. Manley	Paul Langton
Spike	John Pickard
Tompkins	Don Haggerty
Smitty	Alvy Moore
Porter	Robert Arthur
Pinky	Lloyd Corrigan
Doctor	Lee Roberts
Clarke	Robert Wood
Welch	Robert Patten
Barr	James Best
Doyle	John Tarangelo
Harris	Bell Gentry
Captain	Walter Reed

(*Aspect ratio*: 1.85-1)

Some war action with a pleasant little romance are served up in "Return From the Sea" and it should prove acceptable filmfare in the general runs, mostly as a companion feature. The cast has Jan Sterling and Neville Brand in the leads and all concerned help put over a story that will have its most appeal to the family trade.

Plot concerns a Navy veteran who's lost ashore and usually spends his leaves with a bottle. That is, until he draws one in San Diego, meets a waitress, also lonely, who cares for him during a spree. They see a future together and start saving for an avocado ranch. The dream of the future looks likely for a setback when he's badly wounded during an assignment in Korea, but George Waggner's script, from a story by Jacland Marmur, straightens everything out for a happy finale wedding and an honorable retirement.

Brand is the Navy chief and his rugged physical appearance goes with the character. Miss Sterling is the waitress and puts over the role nicely. Excellent support comes from John Doucette, as a taxicab driver, who helps the pair; and such Navy types as Paul Langton, John Picard, Don Haggerty, Alvy Moore, Robert Arthur and Walter Reed. Lloyd Corrigan, saloonkeeper, and the other casters do okay.

Lesley Selander's direction of the Scott R. Dunlap production is sometimes leisurely, sometimes spirited, generally keeping the plot unfolding acceptably. War footage, including some stock shots, generates excitement and there's a good feel to the romantic passages. Harry Neumann's photography, the editing, score and art direction are among the array of good technical assists. *Brog.*

Dawn at Socorro
(COLOR)

Western feature in color with average chances in the general outdoor actioner market.

Hollywood, July 13.

Universal release of William Alland production. Stars Rory Calhoun, Piper Laurie, David Brian, Kathleen Hughes, Alex Nicol; features Edgar Buchanan, Mara Corday, Roy Roberts, Skip Homeier, James Millican, Lee Van Cleef. Directed by George Sherman. Written by George Zuckerman; camera (Technicolor), Carl Guthrie; editor, Edward Curtiss; music supervision, Joseph Gershenson. Previewed July 6, '54. Running time, 80 MINS.

Brett Wade .... Rory Calhoun
Rannah Hayes .... Piper Laurie
Dick Braden .... David Brian
Clare .... Kathleen Hughes
Jimmy Rapp .... Alex Nicol
Sheriff Cauthen .... Edgar Buchanan
Letty Diamond .... Mara Corday
Doc Jameson .... Roy Roberts
Buddy Ferris .... Skip Homeier
Harry McNair .... James Millican
Earl Ferris .... Lee Van Cleef
Old Man Ferris .... Stanley Andrews
Tom Ferris .... Richard Garland
Vince McNair .... Scott Lee
Desk Clerk .... Paul Brinegar
Rancher .... Philo McCollough
Jebb Hayes .... Forrest Taylor

(Aspect ratio: 2-1)

Another variation on the western gunfighter is offered in "Dawn at Socorro" and it comes out as acceptable entertainment in that class. An average number of playdates, moderately profitable, in the outdoor actioner market is indicated.

The screen story by George Zuckerman deals with characters that are a bit more rounded than usually encountered in regulation western features so there seems to be some substance holding the plot together once it is fully underway. The script is inclined to talk a bit too much for an outdoor subject, but there is enough action properly spotted throughout to balance this. George Sherman's direction whips up a good pace over the 80-minute stretch and the players appear to advantage under his guidance.

Rory Calhoun plays the gunfighter-gambler in the story. How he came by his reputation is related via flashback, with an opening in Lordsburg, N.M., showing him besting the Ferris family in a street duel and then deciding to hang up his guns for keeps. Piper Laurie gets into the story when a stern father kicks her out and she decides to become a dance-hall girl in the Socorro saloon run by David Brian. She and Calhoun become acquainted while enroute to Socorro, he learns her story, tries to win both the girl and saloon away from Brian in a card game. The cards let him down, but he's the winner anyway, because both Brian and Alex Nicol, a gunman, are killed when they try to shoot Calhoun just as dawn begins to light the streets of Socorro.

The four stars all deliver their characters well. Fifth "star" of the cast is Kathleen Hughes, seen occasionally as a dance hall girl. A nifty western sheriff character is contributed by Edgar Buchanan. He gets chuckles as a worried lawman whose chief concern is to get Calhoun on the train out of Socorro before trouble starts. Other good types are delivered by Roy Roberts, Skip Homeier, James Millican, Lee Van Cleef, Mara Corday and Stanley Andrews.

The Technicolor lensing by Carl Guthrie is among the first-rate credits marshalled for the picture by William Alland's production supervision. *Brog.*

The Diamond Wizard
(BRITISH)

Cops-and-robbers mild meller with only Dennis O'Keefe's name for marquee; light U. S. boxoffice.

United Artists release of Steven Pallos production. Stars Dennis O'Keefe, Margaret Sheridan, Philip Friend. Directed by Dennis O'Keefe. Screenplay, John C. Higgins; camera, Arthur Graham; editor, Helga Cranston; music, Matyas Seiber. Tradeshown in N.Y., July 9, '54. Running time, 83 MINS.

Joe Dennison .... Dennis O'Keefe
Marlene Miller ...... Margaret Sheridan
Inspector McClaren .... Philip Friend
Thompson Blake .... Allan Wheatley
Yeo .... Francis de Wolff
Hunziger .... Eric Berry
Hoxie .... Michael Balfour
Sergeant Smith .... Ann Gudrun
Dr. Eric Miller .... Paul Hardmuth
Castlet .... Cyril Chamberlain
Lascelles .... Seymour Green

Dennis O'Keefe tries his hand as director with this picture and does fairly well for an initial effort. However, he works under the handicap of also starring in the production and trying to make an exciting meller in a British studio. Result is slow moving, with only modest boxoffice in prospect.

Feature was photographed originally for 3-D release, but is being released in the U. S. in 2-D. Probably the chase at the tag end and the gunplay would have come out better in 3-D.

"The Diamond Wizard" starts off with a million-dollar robbery in the U. S., and then suddenly moves over to London where a U. S. Federal agent has been sent to trace the stolen money and capture the robbers. The agent is O'Keefe, and his efforts along with those of Scotland Yard, finally result in unearthing the U. S. bandits together with a well-organized gang of British crooks. Latter are manufacturing large but perfect synthetic diamonds. Big plot is for the London crooks to palm off these synthetics to the American robbers for the thefted money.

Various ramifications of the modus operandi of the two gangs as well as Scotland Yard in action are methodically and often tiresomely developed. This means the real action is jammed into the final two or three reels.

O'Keefe is okay as the Federal agent although not photographed flatteringly much of the time. Margaret Sheridan, who looks like an English girl, does nicely as the American sweetheart of O'Keefe. Philip Friend makes an efficient Scotland Yard inspector. Paul Hardmuth's scientist characterization is excellent. Francis de Wolff, Alan Wheatley and Eric Berry head the large supporting cast.

Arthur Graham's lensing is standard while Helga Cranston's editing is adequate. Screenplay by John C. Higgins is uneven, with the dialog often trite. Steven Pallos has supplied proper production values while at the same time keeping the budget down. *Wear.*

Confession at Dawn
(Confesion Al Amanecer)
(CHILEAN)

Santiago, June 28.

Import-Film Chile and O.R.I. Film release of Amero-Film (Thomas Lewis) production. Stars Florence Marly, Ricardo Mendoza; features Pepe Popas, with Lautaro Murua, David Philipps, Emilio Martinez, Ernst Uthoff, Maria Elena Aliberti, Carmen Transter, Ana Maria Gomez, Stanley Burke, Art Gaston, Yvette Espinoza, Chita Marchant, Eliana Bocca, Delfina Fuentes. Directed by Pierre Chenal. Screenplay by Chenal, from three Chilean legends. Dialog by Maria Elena Gertner, David Philipps, Reynaldo Lomboy; camera, Andres Martorell; music, Alfonso Letelier, Juan Orrego Salas, Acario Cotapos. At Rex Theatre, Santiago. Running time, 80 MINS.

Stop-and-start Chilean film industry receives a shot in the arm with this pic. While on the arty side, it is a well-made production which should do well in Spanish-language countries, and possibly attract interest from some U. S. arty houses. Cast of comparative unknowns, with possible exception of Florence Marly, is an obvious drawback.

Based on three Chilean legends, this episodic pic first tells about a dawn confession of a paralytic. This in turn reveals the story of the paralytic's three daughters who fall for an itinerant engineer, their disillusionment and death. The housekeeper takes up the thread of the plot by telling about a young mining engineer who runs off in vain search of a goldmine. The third yarn is spun by the priest who repeats the legend of the ghost ship Caleuche and the beautiful blonde found unconscious on the beach.

Pierre Chenal of France has done a good job in trying to weave the three thin legends together. Although the film was made over a long period, due to various difficulties, Chenal presents a smoothly-paced job backed up by rich photography of the Chilean sea, lake and mountain regions. Thomas Lewis, an American businessman in Santiago, handled the production reins.

While Florence Marly, Chenal's wife, is starred, her role of the femme on the beach is limited to little dialog. She is easily the standout glamorwise. The three daughters of the first episode, Maria Elena Aliberti, Chita Marchant and Yvette Espinoza, do well enough alongside David Philipps, a Yank who runs an English-language weekly in Santiago, when not playacting. Philipps does well as the cynical engineer. Lautaro Murua, as the miner, and Emilio Martinez, who provides the only chuckles in the pic, turn in bangup performances.

Malta Story
(BRITISH)

British filmic tribute to the defenders of Malta in World War II. Doubtful b.o. at this late date.

United Artists release of a Peter De Sarigny-produced J. Arthur Rank presentation. Stars Alec Guinness, Jack Hawkins, Anthony Steel, Muriel Pavlow, Renee Asherson, Flora Robson. Directed by Brian Desmond Hurst. Written by William Fairchild and Nigel Balchin; camera, Robert Krasker; editor, Michael Gordon; cmusic. William Alwyn, conducted by Muir Mathieson. Previewed July 8, '54. Running time, 103 MINS.

Air Officer Commanding...Jack Hawkins
Bartlett ....Anthony Steel
Maria ....Muriel Pavlow
Melita ....Flora Robson
Joan ....Renee Asherson
Banks ....Ralph Truman
Payne ....Reginald Tate
Eden ....Hugh Burden
Control Room ....Ronald Adam
Guiseppe ....Nigel Stock
Matthews ....Harold Siddons
O'Connor ....Colin Loudan
Stripey ....Edward Chaffers
Paolo ....Stuart Burge
Hobley ....Noel Willman
Carmella ....Rosalie Crutchley
General ....Jerry Desmonde
Old Man ....Ivor Barnard
Ramsey ....Michael Medwin
Flying Officer ....Peter Bull

It must be assumed that, in "Malta Story," United Artists is attempting — with some logic — to cash in on the by now well-established b.o. name of Alec Guinness. And all would be well, were it not for the unfortunate fact that, in this particular picture, Guinness has switched characters. Film casts him in a perfectly straight part as a reconaissance pilot for the RAF, flying out of embattled Malta.

The burden of "Malta Story" thus rests on its theme, i.e. Britain's valiant defense of its Malta outpost and the suffering of the civilian and military population alike as German and Italian bombers pounded at the island day and night, exacting a fearful toll. Director Brian Desmond Hurst had some authentic newsreel material of the raids to work with, and he has woven this footage cleverly into his human drama.

But effective as it may be—and "Malta Story" has some highly dramatic moments—this type of war story no longer packs the big punch. It's like watching a slightly aged film with its characters out of relation to present times. It's doubtful that U. S. audiences are anywhere near as familiar with the siege of Malta and the heroism of its air and naval defenders as would be the British. And not even this kind of cast can make up for the dating of the product.

Guinness, a likeable fellow regardless what part he plays, isn't given much of a chance to emote and his performance therefore is slightly disappointing. In fact, Hurst appeared to be satisfied posing him mostly looking with a half-smile scanning various objects about him. However, there are a couple of lines which in their content and delivery remind of the "old" Guinness.

Rest of the cast are stereotypes of British war films. Jack Hawkins does his usual capable job as Malta's commanding air officer. Anthony Steel is handsome in a smart part; Flora Robson does the best she can as a Maltese woman whose son is eventually found to spy for the Italians; Renee Asherson is pretty as Steel's fiancee.

Curiously harsh performance is given by Muriel Pavlow as a Maltese girl with whom Guinness falls in love. Miss Pavlow's bit just doesn't ring true whether it's in her love scene or when she follows Guinness' last moments over the operations room loudspeaker.

It's fairly obviously that "Malta Story" was made primarily for domestic consumption. Screenplay by William Fairchild and Nigel Balchin lacks distinction but is fashioned primarily for visual effects and to put across the urgency of the Malta situation at that time. Robert Krasker's lensing of rubbled Valetta as well as his sea scenes and the many shots of Spitfire takeoffs and landings are competent and at times even better than that. *Hift.*

The Stranger's Hand
(BRITISH)

Conventional secret agent drama starring Valli and Trevor Howard with newcomer Richard O'Sullivan. Good general b.o. appeal.

London, July 6.

British Lion release of John Stafford-Peter Moore (in association with Graham Greene) production. Stars Trevor Howard, Alida Valli, Richard Basehart, Eduardo Ciannelli. Directed by Mario Soldati. Screenplay, Guy Elmes, Georgio Bassini, based on story by Graham Greene; camera, Enzo Serafin; Editor, Tom Simpson; music, Nino Rota. At Film House Private Theatre. Running time, 85 MINS.

Major Court .... Trevor Howard
Roberta .... Alida Valli
Joe Hamstringer ......Richard Basehart
Dr. Vivaldi .... Eduardo Ciannelli
Roger Court ....Richard O'Sullivan
British Consul ....Stephen Murray

Another mystery from the fertile pen of Graham Greene, but definitely not in the same class as "The Third Man." It has a similar theme, the disappearance of a secret agent, and is handled with a good quota of drama and suspense. The star takes little part in the action of the story, lying fallow, registering despair and immobility through drugs, with only his eyes to betray emotion and depending upon his fellow thesps for the development of the story. It should do well locally on the strength of Greene's reputation and the star appeal of

Trevor Howard. Pic may make a profitable second feature in the U.S.

Set in Venice, a stonesthrow from the trouble area of the free port of Trieste, action revolves around the inexplicable disappearance of a British Intelligence officer who fails to join his young son whom he has not seen for four years. The child waits at the hotel and gets a telephone call unmistakably from his father. He gets sympathy from the receptionist, herself a refugee, who enlists the help of Joe, her American boy friend, when the police are unsuccessful in their search.

The missing agent had hailed a friend on a waterbus who looked dazed and obvious of his surroundings, being hustled along between two men. His obvious recognition seals his own fate and he is seized and kept heavily drugged by a renegade doctor. Even when the hideout is searched the somnolent "patients" are passed off as fever cases and the boy does not recognize his father in the glazed-eyed figure with an incipient beard. By the time Joe joins the hunt the victims have been transferred to a foreign ship for transfer behind the Iron Curtain. Owing to international law a boat cannot be stopped or boarded once it has port clearance. To circumvent this Joe hides on board, starts a fire and sets off the alarm. Police and speedboat fireguards effectively take over and release the captives, but in saving the father's life the doctor gets shot.

Most of the acting opportunities fall to Alida Valli as the kindly receptionist and a new moppet Richard O'Sullivan. Eduardo Ciannelli turns in a firstrate performance as the halfhearted villainous doctor who befriends the boy unaware of his identity. Richard Basehart is realistically forthright as the Yank who pulls off a rescue.

Attractive background scenery enhances the film's appeal and the novel fireguard race makes for an exciting climax. *Clem.*

King of Coral Sea
(AUSTRALIAN)

Sydney, July 6.
British Empire Films release of Southern International production. Stars Chips Rafferty. Directed by Lee Robinson. Screenplay, Chips Rafferty and Lee Robinson; camera, Ross Wood; editor, Alex Ezard; music, Wilbur Sampson. At Film House Theatrette, Sydney. Running time, 87 MINS.
Ted King .... Chips Rafferty
Peter Merriman .... Charles Tingwell
Rusty King .... Ilma Adey
Jack Janiero .... Rod Taylor
Yusep .... Lloyd Berrell
Serena .... Frances Chin Soon
Grundy .... Reginald Lye

Okay native pic for spots where the patrons aren't too particular about screen entertainment, with strongest appeal for boxoffice away from the keys. However, doubtful for U.S.

Chips Rafferty has been in the local production biz ever since he hit the jackpot for Ealing Studios in "The Overlanders." He also went to Hollywood to play the role of an Aussie in "Desert Rats." He has some appeal here.

Story is centered around Thursday Island, hub of the Aussie pearling industry. It tells of a bid by a smuggling ring to bring prohibited migrants from Far East territory through the Torres Straits into Australia. Story skips the pearl biz angle. It's the type of yarn buyable on any bookstore for 20c. Highlight of the pic are some thrilling underwater shots near the Great Barrier Reef around Cairns.

The acting won't have much of the audience applauding. Rafferty ambles through a role suitable to his own brand of emoting. Lloyd Berrell, as Yusep, just about steals the pic. Femmes are extremely weak. Charles Tingwell, of local radio, shapes up as a good juve possibility for abroad. Photography is firstclass. "King" should find dates in England because of its unusual setting. *Rick.*

It's the Paris Life
(C'Est La Vie Parisienne)
(FRENCH)
(Color-Songs)

Paris, July 6.
Fernand Rivers release of Udisfilm-Alfred Rode production. Directed by Alfred Rode; screenplay, Jacques Companeez; camera (Gevacolor), Andre Thomas; editor, Suzanne Landberg; music, Roger Roger. At Biarritz, Paris. Running time, 100 MINS.
Cri-Cri .... Claudine Dupuis
Paul .... Philipe Lemaire
Anatole .... Raymond Bussieres
Barfleur .... Saturnin Fabre
Daniel .... Amedee
Weston .... Jean Tissier
Inventor .... Noel Roquevert
Cocotte .... Arlette Poirier

Most of the liveliness in this opus unfortunately remains in the title. Film tries to invoke the nostalgia of the "Gay 90's" and compare it with the rather jazzy modern times by going through two love affairs, one by the unsuccessful attachment of a nobleman and a singer and the other, the successful mating of their respective grandchildren in the present. Hackneyed vintage plot and the banal modern trimmings never get this off the ground, and thesping and technical aspects don't help much either. This is of questionable interest here and even less so for U.S. chances. If the lagging second part is cut away this might make it do as an exploitation pic.

Director Alfred Rode seems amateurish in creating rhythm and movement, and the editing cannot do much to overcome the simple faults of technique. Philipe Lemaire fares better as the flabby nobleman than as the jazz trumpeteer. Claudine Dupis, ex-dancer, is still better as a dancer than as a thesper. Remainder of the cast lends okay support in the costume period with Amedee scoring as a present-day cavedweller. Color is fine in early sequences but seems more washed out and uneven in later portions. Music of the good old days is still bouncy and colorful as are costumes and settings. *Mosk.*

Betrayed
(SONG-COLOR)

World War II espionage meller, lensed in Holland. Gable-Turner-Mature to help ticket sales.

Hollywood, July 19.
Metro production and release (no producer credit). Stars Clark Gable, Lana Turner, Victor Mature; co-stars Louis Calhern; features O. E. Hasse, Wilfrid Hyde White, Ian Carmichael, Niall Mac Ginnis, Nora Swinburne, Roland Culver. Directed by Gottfried Reinhardt. Screenplay, Ronald Millar, George Froeschel; camera (Eastman Color), F. A. Young; editors, John Dunning, Raymond Poulton; score composed and conducted by Walter Goehr; song, "Johnny Come Home" by Goehr and Millar. Previewed July 14, '54. Running time, 107 MINS.
Col. Pieter Deventer .... Clark Gable
Carla Van Oven .... Lana Turner
"The Scarf" .... Victor Mature
Gen. Ten Eyck .... Louis Calhern
Col. Helmuth Dietrich ...... O. E. Hasse
Gen. Charles Larraby
.... Wilfrid Hyde White
Capt. Jackie Lawson .... Ian Carmichael
"Blackie" .... Niall MacGinnis
"The Scarf's" Mother .... Nora Swinburne
Gen. Warsleigh .... Roland Culver
"Pop" .... Leslie Weston
Chris .... Christopher Rhodes
Jan's Grandmother .... Lilly Kann
Jan .... Brian Smith
Capt. Von Stanger ...... Anton Diffring

This World War II cloak-and-dagger melodrama has a lot of marquee flash in the names of Clark Gable, Lana Turner and Victor Mature to get it started. Unfortunately it fails to deliver the exciting entertainment indicated by the espionage setup. Name strength will help some, but b.o. prospects are not socko.

An unconvincing screenplay by Ronald Millar and George Froeschel has been poorly directed by Gottfried Reinhardt so the picture unfolds as a confused, often dull, meller burdened with a running time of one hour and 47 minutes. Under these burdens, three top stars contribute nothing that helps to make the plot events more believable. An occasional personality flash, a bit of action, or a well-turned phrase, comes along, but not nearly often enough to keep the overlength footage alive and interesting.

A FitzPatrick travelog look, Fitz-Patrick should excuse the expression, is worn by the presentation as a result of the location-lensing in Holland. These settings add a picturesque note, and often the pictorial values overshadow the story-telling. The Eastman Color is used effectively by F. A. Young's photography to point up the film's visual qualities.

It is the story of spies and counterspies in Holland during the Nazi occupation, telling how a Dutch Resistance leader turned against his fellow patriots when they branded his beloved mother a collaborator and stealthily led them to their deaths until killed himself.

Gable is a Dutch Intelligence officer, working with the British, who eventually brings about the traitor's downfall. Miss Turner is the widow of a wealthy Dutchman who wants a purpose in life. Mature is the dashing Resistance leader afflicted with Momism. Story even gets the trio involved in a shadowy romantic triangle while the melodramatics are being played off but it comes to naught because it is rather apparent from the beginning that Gable will wind up with the gal.

Louis Calhern, Dutch officer; O. E. Hasse, Nazi Intelligence chief; Wilfrid Hyde White and Ian Carmichael, of British Intelligence; Niall MacGinnis, Nora Swinburne and Roland Culver are among those contributing colorful lesser types

to the footage. Picture gets a good score from Walter Goehr and there is a pleasant song, "Johnny Come Home" handled by Miss Turner's character, that Goehr cleffed and to which Millar contributed the lyrics. The femme star was costumed by Balmain of Paris. *Brog.*

Beautiful Stranger
(BRITISH)

Ginger Rogers teamed with her husband, Jacques Bergerac, in her first British pic; obvious exploitation values but spotty outlook.

London, July 13.
British Lion presentation and release. Stars Ginger Rogers, Herbert Lom, Stanley Baker; features Margaret Rawlings, Eddie Byrne, Jacques Bergerac. Produced by Maxwell Setton & John R. Sloan; directed by David Miller; screenplay by Robert Westerby and Carl Nystrom from a story by Rip Van Ronkel and David Miller; camera, Ted Scaife; editor, Alan Osbiston; music, Malcolm Arnold; with "Love Is A Beautiful Stranger" sung by Lita Roza, music by Jose Ferrer, lyrics by Ketti Frings. At Leicester Square Theatre, London, July 13, '54. Running time 89 MINS.
"Johnny" Victor .... Ginger Rogers
Louis Galt .... Stanley Baker
Emil Landosh .... Herbert Lom
Pierre Clement ..... Jacques Bergerac
Marie Galt .... Margaret Rawlings
Luigi .... Eddie Byrne
Chief of Police .... Ferdy Mayne

For her first British production, Ginger Rogers is teamed with her husband, Jacques Bergerac, and this will give "Beautiful Stranger" obvious exploitation values. On its merits, however, the feature is a disappointment with a heavy melodramatic plot, and may encounter spotty returns both in Britain and the U.S.

Attractive Riviera settings against which the entire action takes place is a plus. The production generally is well mounted with elegant sets giving an expensive veneer.

The prime weakness of the picture is in the unbelievable plot which shows Ginger Rogers as a former penniless showgirl living in an expensive villa with all expenses paid by a man she hopes to marry. She soon learns, however, that his stories of an impending divorce are untrue although she never discovers that he is a crook specializing in forged golden sovereigns. After their first tiff she meets a young artist, played by Jacques Bergerac, and from then on the yarn takes the obvious course with Herbert Lom providing a few sinister comedy touches.

Ginger Rogers, always looking attractive, does her best with the part while Bergerac, in his screen debut, makes a promising beginning although there are clear thesping limitations. Herbert Lom, in an unbelievable characterization, succeeds in getting several laughs and Stanley Baker, a solid British performer, plays the big-time crook with definite overtones.

Margaret Rawlings and Eddie Byrne do their best with limited roles. David Miller's direction keeps the plot moving at a steady pace; Ted Scaife has done a fine camera job and Geoffrey Drake has designed some excellent sets. *Myro.*

Crest of the Wave
(BRITISH)

Adaptation of London stage hit ("Seagulls Over Sorrento") strong for local audiences with Gene Kelly offering effective marquee appeal in the U. S.

London, July 13.
Metro release of John Boulting production. Stars Gene Kelly with John Justin. Bernard Lee. Director, Roy Boulting. Screenplay, Frank Harvey, Roy Boulting from play by Hugh Hastings; camera, Gilbert Taylor; editor, Max Benedict; music, Mikolas Rozsa. At Empire, London, July 13, '54. Running time **92 MINS.**

Lieut. Bradville	Gene Kelly
Lieut. Wharton	John Justin
Lofty Turner	Bernard Lee
Butch Clelland	Jeff Richards
Charlie Badger	Sidney James
P. O. Herbert	Patric Doonan
Sprog Sims	Ray Jackson
Cdr. Sinclair	Patrick Barr
Haggis Mackintosh	David Orr

For their first production under the MGM banner, Roy and John Boulting have adapted the West End stage hit "Seagulls Over Sorrento" which ran for more than three years in London although it proved a dismal flop on Broadway a year or so ago. For Britain, where the title has tremendous b.o. potential, the original moniker is being retained; in the U. S. it will be released as "Crest of the Wave," the title by which it was known during filming.

With Gene Kelly in the lead, this British production has potent marquee values in the U. S. although an overplus of cockney dialog may prove a deterrent in some situations. This is particularly a failing of the opening sequences, but once the plot gets under way there is sufficient dramatic content to override it.

In its transference from stage to screen the canvas has been broadened and the plot adjusted to give it a more acceptable Anglo-U. S. flavor. It is the story about a small bunch of naval men stationed on a remote island off the north east coast of Britain who are engaged on highly dangerous research work on a new type of torpedo. At the point at which the yarn opens, the first test has proved a failure and the scientist and the naval rating with him are killed in the explosion. Because there are no loyal people with adequate knowledge of this type of work, the Admiralty brings in an American scientist in the person of Gene Kelly and a couple of U. S. ratings played by Fredd Wayne and Jeff Richards. There is another fatal test before they trace the fault.

The script plays up some feuding on both the upper and lower decks. In the wardroom one of the British officers resents the tactics of the American scientist, while in the men's messroom there is a British rating who discovers that one of the Yanks married his girl while he was away at sea. There is drama and comedy from both these situations with an effective balance usually maintained.

Under the studied direction of Roy Boulting, the all-male cast contribute solid performances. Gene Kelly fills the role of the scientist with genuine conviction, with a performance which is in complete contrast to his more familiar song-and-dance portrayals. John Justin, his adversary in the officers' mess, gives a tensed up interpretation, while Bernard Lee, Sidney James, Ray Jackson and David Orr vigorously make up the complement of naval ratings. Jeff Richards and Fredd Wayne play the two U. S. Navy men and the latter, with some of the best comedy lines, indulges in frequent scene stealing. Patric Doonan gives a polished study of an unpopular petty officer and Patrick Barr is suitably cast as the station commander. *Myro.*

River Beat

Okay lowercase thriller, lensed in England, for the general program market.

Hollywood, July 14.
Lippert Pictures release of Victor Hanbury (Abtcon) production. Stars Phyllis Kirk, John Bentley; features Robert Ayres, Leonard White, Ewan Roberts, Glyn Houston, Charles Lloyd Pack. Directed by Guy Green. Screenplay, Rex Rienits; camera, Geoffrey Faithfull; editor, Peter Graham Scott; music, Hubert Clifford. Previewed July 13, '54. Running time, **70 MINS.**

Judy Roberts	Phyllis Kirk
Dan Barker	John Bentley
Capt. Watford	Robert Ayres
Sgt. McLeod	Leonard White
Blake	Ewan Roberts
Charlie	Glyn Houston
Hendrick	Charles Lloyd Pack
Maclure	David Hurst
Nell	Margaret Anderson
Adams	Michael Balfour
Anna	Isabel George

The programmer market, currently short of passable supporting filmfare, will find this London-localed melodrama an acceptable filler. Lippert is handling the domestic release of the Abtcon production, lensed in England with an all-British cast except for femme star Phyllis Kirk.

Miss Kirk provides a casting switch to the Anglo-American film efforts Lippert usually releases. Heretofore it has been an American male in England, and mixed up with Scotland Yard and British crooks. She plays the radio operator on an American freighter docked in the Thames. Without her knowledge, she's being used to smuggle diamonds ashore by a gang that seemingly goes to an awful lot of unnecessary trouble and difficulty getting the loot off the ship.

Opposite her as a police inspector on the Thames river detail is John Bentley. He is already interested in furthering Anglo-American relations before the girl is caught with the diamonds, so his efforts to catch the real crooks have an extra meaning. The plotting is contrived and everything drops too patly into place as the 70 minutes unfold. A good old river chase serves as an action climax after the captain of the freighter, Robert Ayres, is revealed as the real big shot behind the smuggling.

While the faces will be mostly new to U. S. viewers, the players are put through situations that are no fresher than expected of this type of offering. Among the competents are Leonard White, helping Bentley; Ewan Roberts, Glyn Houston and Charles Lloyd Pack.

Guy Green directed the Victor Hanbury production with a mild pace, but gets the Rex Rienits screenplay into action for the finale chase. Photography by Geoffrey Faithfull and the other technical assists are okay. *Brog.*

Earrings of Madame De
(FRENCH)

Mediocre French fare with some artie appeal due to the marquee attraction of the Charles Boyer-Danielle Darrieux combo.

Arlan Pictures release of a Franco-London production. Stars Charles Boyer, Danielle Darrieux, Vittorio De Sica. Written by Marcel Achard and Max Ophuls; based on the Louise de Vilmorin novel; directed by Ophuls; camera, Christian Matras; music, George Van Parys. Previewed in N.Y., July 15, '54. Running time, **105 MINS.**

Monsieur De (General)	Charles Boyer
Madame De	Danielle Darrieux
Baron Donati	Vittorio De Sica

(English Titles)

Considering the star material available to Max Ophuls in "The Earrings of Madame De," it's surprising that he managed to come up with such a dull and uninspiring opus. Film lacks the touch of the more distinctive French product and, considering its lack of action and the profusion of dialog, certainly deserves trimming.

With the exception of the names, pic has little to recommend it to the U. S. market. Neither as a period piece, nor as a love story, nor as a vehicle for such popular players as Charles Boyer, Danielle Darrieux and Vittorio De Sica does it produce the kind of spark one might expect from such a talented and proven team as Ophuls and Marcel Achard who did the scripting.

Story is a conventional triangle, with Boyer as the general tolerating the flirtations of his wife, Miss Darrieux, with the baron, De Sica, until he senses that things are becoming a little too serious. There's a duel. De Sica dies, and Miss Darrieux is felled by a heart attack at almost the same moment. Unfortunately, not even this bit of melodrama is played to the hilt.

Boyer is wasted in the part of the general and he is unquestionably handicapped by Ophuls' ponderous direction which seems intent on slowing up the proceedings. Miss Darrieux is a joy to the eye but appears to be effective only when called upon to flirt. De Sica is given a chance to look distinguished and love-lorn, and that's all. Christian Matras' lensing—or else the editing—had its faults, with the camera moving alternately too slow or too fast. *Hift.*

Broken Lance
(COLOR)

Topnotch western drama, with names, entertainment values for sturdy boxoffice.

Hollywood, July 23.
20th-Fox release of Sol C. Siegel production. Stars Spencer Tracy, Robert Wagner, Jean Peters, Richard Widmark; features Katy Jurado, Hugh O'Brien, Eduard Franz. Directed by Edward Dmytryk. Screenplay, Richard Murphy; based on a story by Philip Yordan; camera (De Luxe Color), Joe MacDonald; editor, Dorothy Spencer; music, Leigh Harline; conducted by Lionel Newman. Previewed July 21, '54. Running time, **96 MINS.**

Matt Devereaux	Spencer Tracy
Joe Devereaux	Robert Wagner
Barbara	Jean Peters
Ben	Richard Widmark
Senora Devereaux	Katy Jurado
Mike Devereaux	Hugh O'Brien
Two Moons	Eduard Franz
Denny Devereaux	Earl Holliman
The Governor	E. G. Marshall
Clem Lawton	Carl Benton Reid
Van Cleve	Philip Ober
Mac Andrews	Robert Burton
O'Reilly	Robert Adler
Capitol Clerk	Robert Grandin
Prison Guard	Harry Carter
Cook	Nacho Galindo
Manuel	Julian Rivero
Court Clerk	Edmund Cobb
Judge	Russell Simpson
Clerk	King Donovan
Gateman	Jack Mather
Paymaster	George E. Stone
Rancher	John Eppers
Bailiff	Paul Kruger
Stable Owner	James F. Stone

(*Aspect ratio: 2.55-1*)

"Broken Lance" is topnotch western drama, with an importance in cast and entertainment values that foretells sturdy boxoffice returns. To these measureable sales assets is added the pictorial wallop of a CinemaScope display of panoramic scenic wonders.

The production has been handled astutely by Sol C. Siegel, particularly in the casting, which brackets the star name of Spencer Tracy with Robert Wagner, Jean Peters and Richard Widmark for marquee punch. The same care was used in picking the featured players, headed by Mexico's Katy Jurado, and these talents, under the vigorous direction of Edward Dmytryk, manage to keep the dramatics alive and interesting.

Richard Murphy scripted from a story by Philip Yordan. It's not a particularly new plot that is unfolded, nor, basically, one of top merit, but the script treatment, the direction and the playing make it come off with audience appeal.

Seems too bad so much of the story is told via an unnecessary flashback. However, there is enough force in the trouping and direction to sustain mood and interest. This is particularly true of Tracy's performance, since he has the difficult task of making alive a character already dead when the picture opens.

Film starts with Wagner's release from an Arizona prison after serving a three-year sentence. The enmity that lies between him and his three half-brothers, Widmark, Hugh O'Brian and Earl Holliman, is quickly established. Wagner had been the favorite of their dead father, a fact the other brothers resent, and also, he believes them responsible for the father's death while he was imprisoned. The scene shifts from this strong early sequence, taking place in the office of the governor, E. G. Marshall, where they all try to get him to leave the state, to the once proud family ranch, now decayed from neglect. There Wagner recalls the events that led to his imprisonment. This recapping of bygones taps 70 minutes out of the 96 minutes of footage before the hate that is in him boils over into a smashing fight to the death with

Widmark, ending the feud that has split the family and paving the way for his union with Miss Peters.

Within the flashback Tracy is shown as a domineering cattle baron, who rules his four sons and vast empire ruthlessly by his own laws. However, time is running out for him as civilization advances, and he takes the law into his own hands once too often in destroying mining property and injuring miners. Hauled into court, he is saved from prison by Wagner, who goes instead. Widmark then leads the other brothers into open revolt, precipitating Tracy's death and the break with Wagner.

It is a finely handled characterization that Tracy gives to the cattle baron. Wagner does his best work yet as the half-breed son of Tracy and Miss Jurado, and Indian princess poured in her love. Her role is endowed with a womanly understanding that is one of the film's better points. Miss Peters satisfactorily portrays the girl whom Wagner loves. Widmark's gift for menace rates a hackle-raising display, both in the climactic death batt e with Wagner and in a flashback scene in which he defies the ailing Tracy.

The featured and supporting performances are other strong points. O'Brian and Holliman, one crafty, one dumb are good as two of the brothers, and Eduard Franz plays Two Moons, an Indian, well. Marshall, the governor; Carl Benton Reid, Philip Ober, and Robert Burton are among others contributing importantly.

Scenes of breath-taking beauty, with the desert's limitless depth of vision, are captured by Joe MacDonald's exceptional use of the new C'Scope taking lens. This footage shows a grownup CinemaScope, a process that has lived up to the promise of the pioneer "The Robe." The De Luxe Color processing adds beautiful, natural tints to the footage. Other contributions, including the editing and scoring, are first-rate. *Brog.*

Pushover

Fred MacMurray in an exploitable crime meller geared for good b.o.

Columbia release of Jules Schermer (Philip A. Waxman) production. Stars Fred MacMurray, Phil Carey, Kim Novak; features Dorothy Malone, E. G. Marshall, Allen Nourse. Directed by Richard Quine. Screenplay, Roy Huggins, based upon stories by Thomas Walsh and William S. Ballinger; camera, Lester H. White; editor, Jerome Thoms; music, Arthur Morton. Previewed N.Y. July 8, '54. Running time, **88 MINS.**

Paul Sheridan .... Fred MacMurray
Lona McLane .... Kim Novak
Rick McAllister .... Phil Carey
Ann .... Dorothy Malone
Lt. Carl Eckstrom .... E. G. Marshall
Paddy Dolan .... Allen Nourse
Briggs .... Phil Chambers
Fine .... Alan Dexter
Billings .... Robert Forrest
Peters .... Don Harvey
Harry Wheeler .... Paul Richards
Ellen Burnett .... Ann Morriss

(*Aspect ratio*: 1:85-1)

"Pushover" is a cops 'n' robbers meller whose suspense holds up nicely despite its mite too long 88 minutes running time. Marquee dressing is light save for Fred MacMurray but on the whole this Columbia release is a punchy, exploitable entry geared for good b.o. returns especially in the action situations.

The Roy Huggins screenplay, based upon stories by Thomas Walsh and William S. Ballinger, more or less boils down to the case history of a plainclothes cop who succumbs to the lure of a pretty face and a bundle of stolen bank loot. While the face was probably there for the asking, the loot was hot—and when the heat came that was the end of the errant cop.

MacMurray along with fellow detectives Phil Carey and Allen Nourse are detailed to watch gun moll Kim Novak in hopes she'll lead them to Paul Richards who's on the lam with $200,000 in a bank heist. MacMurray, led on by sexy Miss Novak's suggestions, kills Richards. However, the loyal sherlocks wise up to what's going on in time to shoot down their untrustworthy colleague and break the case.

Performances are generally credible under Richard Quine's direction which moves the plot along at a good clip. MacMurray portrays the cop who goes wrong in a low key, moody delineation in keeping with the character of the role. Phil Carey impresses as a handsome alert copper who keeps his mind on his work. Miss Novak, who reportedly is being groomed by Columbia as a possible rival of Marilyn Monroe, shows possibilities in that direction.

Dorothy Malone, as a cute nurse; E. G. Marshall, as a detective lieutenant; Nourse, a vet plainclothesman who's bumped off in the line of duty, and Richards, as the bankrobber, provide competent support along with those cast in lesser roles. Lester H. White's camerawork gives the film a lift while the musical score as conducted by Morris Stoloff is another asset. This Jules Schermer production on which Philip A. Waxman was associate producer was mantled with adequate physical values. *Gilb.*

Crossed Swords
(COLOR)

Costumed swashbuckler, with Errol Flynn conducting the amatory chase of Gina Lollobrigida and other beauties. Routine escapism.

Hollywood, July 27.

United Artists release of J. Barrett Mahon-Vittorio Vassarotti (Viva Films) production. Stars Errol Flynn, Gina Lollobrigida; features Nadia Gray, Cesare Danova, Rolando Lupi, Paola Mori. Written and directed by Milton Krims. Camera (Pathecolor), Jack Cardiff. Previewed July 22, '54. Running time, **83 MINS.**

Renzo .... Errol Flynn
Francesca .... Gina Lollobrigida
Raniero .... Cesar Danova
Fulvia .... Nadia Gray
Tomasina .... Paola Mori
Pavoncello .... Roldano Lupi
Gennarelli .... Alberto Robogliati
Buio .... Silvio Bakolini
Spiga .... Renato Chiantioni
Miele .... Mimo Billi
The Duke .... Pietro Tordi
Lenzi .... Ricardo Riolo

(*Aspect ratio*: 1.75-1)

Errol Flynn leaps from window to window in this amatory adventure of a highpowered lover back in medieval Italy. It's a costumed swashbuckler offering routine escapism for undiscriminating audiences and will get its share of playdates in the general market.

Gina Lollobrigida and an assortment of other lovelies are the chased in the 83 minutes of footage. They, and the Italian landscape, are enhanced more by Jack Cardiff's striking Pathecolor photography than by Milton Krims screenplay and direction, which falls into a stock groove that leaves the corn on the cob more than the tongue in the cheek, although a spot of sly humor shows up here and there in the Flynn character.

The tiny dukedom of Sidona passes a law making it mandatory for young bachelors to marry or go to jail. This is a revolting situation to Flynn, just back from a year of romantic jousting around the country in the company of the son of the Duke of Sidona. Another conflict angle, and just as menacing, is the efforts of the dukedom's evil councillor to take over. When Flynn isn't busy with the girls and dodging through windows to escape angry husbands he takes time to put down the planned treason. When the sword battling is all over, Miss Lollobrigida, the duke's daughter, convinces the hero that marriage doesn't necessarily make amour any the less fun so the "romantic grasshopper" decides to bow to Sidona's law.

Flynn is an agile hero, either with a sword or the ladies, and Miss Lollobrigida is a fine partner for the romancing. The assortment of foreign players involved go about their characters with the required spirit and some would have shown to better advantage had Krims' script and direction been a little bit less routine. *Brog.*

The Law vs. Billy the Kid
(COLOR)

Another version of the early-day boy outlaw's career. Standard fare for the outdoor program market.

Hollywood, July 23.

Columbia release of Sam Katzman production. Stars Scott Brady, Betta St. John; features James Griffith, Alan Hale Jr., Paul Cavanagh, William Phillips, Benny Rubin, Steve Darrell, George Berkeley, William Tannen, Richard Cutting. Directed by William Castle. Story and screenplay, John T. Williams; camera (Technicolor), Henry Freulich; editor, Aaron Stell. Previewed July 15, '54. Running time, **72 MINS.**

Billy the Kid .... Scott Brady
Nita Maxwell .... Betta St. John
Pat Garrett .... James Griffith
Bob Ollinger .... Alan Hale Jr.
John H. Tunstall .... Paul Cavanagh
Charlie Bowdre....William "Bill" Phillips
Arnold Dodge .... Benny Rubin
Tom Watkins .... Steve Darrell
Tom O'Folliard .... George Berkeley
Dave Rudabaugh ...... William Tannen
Pete Maxwell .... Richard Cutting
Carl Trumble .... John Cliff
Governor Wallace .... Otis Garth
Miguel Bolanos .... Martin Garralaga
Jack Poe .... Frank Sully
Parsons .... William Fawcett
L. G. Murphy .... Robert Griffin

Another film version of the violent life of the legendary killer and it adds up to standard fare for the outdoor program market. The customers who buy this type of western feature will find that it provides the regulation amount of action to fill the bill.

Billy the Kid, played by Scott Brady, is shown as practically forced to become a killer—a dubiously sympathetic treatment usually accorded early outlaws in films. The killings in this offering, produced by Sam Katzman and directed by William Castle from a screen story by John T. Williams, start early and carry through to the end, when Billy gets his from the gun of his sheriff friend, Pat Garrett.

Story opens with Billy on the run across a county line after having killed another man in more "self defense." With him is Garrett, played by James Griffith, and they get jobs on the ranch of Paul Cavanagh. Billy promptly falls for Betta St. John, Cavanagh's niece, and incurs the enmity of Alan Hale Jr., ranch foreman, who fancies the girl himself.

This enmity, and the greed of a land-grabber, with the help of a crooked sheriff, cause the violent death of Cavanagh, and Billy goes on the prod for revenge, committing some murders himself. Garrett becomes the honest sheriff with the necessary job of bringing the kid to book. Catches up with him at a rendezvous with Miss St. John.

The performance of the key principals, plus some among the supporting players, comes off on the credit side under Castle's direction. The outdoor values are well displayed in Technicolor by Henry Freulich's lensing and the other technical credits are okay. *Brog.*

Dance Little Lady
(BRITISH-COLOR)

Broad, hokey ballet meller; dubious seller outside the U.K. but quota tag should help locally.

London, July 13.

Renown Pictures production and release. Stars Terence Morgan, Mai Zetterling, Guy Rolfe, Mandy; features Eunice Gayson, David Poole and Maryon Lane of Sadlers Wells Trust Ltd. Directed by Val Guest. Screenplay, Guest, Doreen Montgomery, based on story by R. Howard Alexander and Alfred Dunning; camera, Wilkie Cooper; editor, John Pomeroy; music, Ronald Binge; color Eastmancolor. At Gaumont, London. Running time, **87 MINS.**

Mark Gordon .... Terence Morgan
Nina Gordon .... Mai Zetterling
John Ransome .... Guy Rolfe
Jill Gordon .... Mandy
Adele .... Eunice Gayson
Poli .... Reginald Beckwith
Mme. Bayanova .... Ina de la Haye
Mr. Bridson .... Harold Laing
Mary .... Jane Aird
Mr. Matthews .... William Kendall
Mrs. Matthews .... Joan Hickson
Joseph Miller .... Alexander Gauge
Nurse .... Marianne Stone
Amaryllis .... Lisa Gastoni
Dancers......David Poole, Maryon Lane

"Dance Little Lady," a novelletish British meller about a ballerina who becomes involved in an accident on the night of her Covent Garden triumph, is broad hokum for mass consumption, with some pleasant ballet sequences to give it class veneer. At home, its quota tag will be a strong selling factor but outside Britain, it will likely prove a difficult proposition.

Production has been handsomely mounted and attractively lensed in Eastmancolor. The earlier ballet sequences have an expensive gloss and are in direct contrast to the novelletish plot development. The script is loaded with cliche-like situations, and the story unspools without any pretense towards sophistication.

Prima ballerina of the plot is Mai Zetterling who, pushed by her worthless manager husband, because he regards her as a handsome meal ticket, gets a starring engagement at the Royal Opera House, Covent Garden. At a celebration after her opening triumph, she discovers his infidelities with another dancer. Driving home from the party she becomes involved in an auto smashup. With a broken leg and severe internal injuries, she is told by the medicos she'll never dance again. Then the husband turns to the other girl as his potential meal ticket for the future, leaving with her on a Continental and American tour. The sick wife is left behind with her child and is put on the road to recovery by a sympathetic doctor (Guy Rolfe) while the infant prodigy is being trained to follow in mama's dancing footsteps. The plot takes its major melodramatic twist when the husband returns as a Hollywood talent scout determined to put the child on to the screen and take it out of the mother's care, but sacrifices his life when his plans go awry.

Although rarely suggesting the talents of a ballerina, Miss Zetterling handles the dramatic aspec' of the role with warm and precise confidence, leaving the main tearjerking angles in the very capable hands of Mandy Miller, the moppet who hit the marquee with her performance in "Mandy." Terence Morgan, once again type-cast, plays the worthless husband in obvious overtones. Rolfe gives a sincerely believable performance as the doctor while Eunice Gayson jumps into prominence with her interpretation of the other dancer who gets ditched in New York.

Film has been casually directed by Val Guest who also collaborated on the screenplay. *Myro.*

Theodora, Imperatrice Byzantine
(Theodora, Byzantine Empress)
(FRANCO-ITALIAN; COLOR)

Paris, July 20.
Lux production and release. Stars Georges Marchal, Gianna-Maria Canale. Directed by Riccardo Freda. Screenplay, Paul Antonio, Freda, Rene Wheeler; camera (Pathecolor), Rodolfo Lombardi; editor, Mario Seraiden. At Marignan, Paris. Running-time, 95 MINS.

Theodora	Gianna-Maria Canale
Justinian	Georges Marchal
Cappadoce	Henri Guisol
Andres	Roger Pigaut
Saida	Irene Pappas
Arcas	Renato Baldini
Scarpas	Carlos Sposito

Another in the spec-color cycle of Franco-Italian films unrolls in this Roman extravaganza. This recounts the loves of Theodora and Emperor Justinian in his lush Byzantine Empire. Usual chariot races and battle scenes abound in this, but lack of names and disjoined narrative of film, plus the familiar settings and story, make this of negligible chances for the U. S. At best it might do for dualers.

This has Emperor Justinian meeting Egyptian dancer Theodora in a market place when she tries to lift some of his jewelry. Love and desire flame, and to get her he finally marries her. Then she becomes a just, liberal Empress and helps foil a plot against the Emperor.

Director Riccardo Freda has 'a few moments in his battle scenes and chariot races, but otherwise lets this lusty tale flounder in pretentious dialog and slowmoving crowd scenes. Georges Marchal is haughty as the Emperor. Gianna-Maria Canale brings looks to the Theodora role, but falls short in the acting range. However, this gal is a lush type worthy of Hollywood consideration. Remainder of the cast is okay. Color lensing tends to be uneven and blueish in spots. Editing helps get movement and punch into the more hectic battle scenes. This is just another cycle pic. *Mosk.*

Zoe
(FRENCH)

Paris, July 19.
Marceau release of Marceau-Artes Film production. Stars Barbara Laage, Michel Auclair. Directed by Charles Brabant. Screenplay by Henri-Francois Rey, Brabant, from play by Jean Marsan; dialog, Marsan; camera, Henri Alekan; editor,

Maurice Serein. At Francais, Paris. Running time, 90 MINS.

Zoe	Barbara Laage
Arthur	Michel Auclair
Louis	Jean-Pierre Kerien
Madeleine	France Roche
Chantal	Yolande Laffon
Stanislas	Amedee
Father	Louis Seigner
Plouet	Jean Marchat

Gallic situation comedy falls short of aims in lacklustre direction and thesping which make these familiar shenanigans of limited pull on the star names of Barbara Laage and Michel Auclair here, but for the U.S. there isn't much in this.

A young playboy picks up a girl on his way to the family home at a resort town. She is a frighteningly direct creature who tells only the truth. When she can't find a room she moves into the boy's house, and the trouble begins. She upsets everything from domestic relations to a $1,000,000 loan the father is trying to get for a new atomic invention. After sowing all this trouble, Zoe leaves all the rabid people flailing each other while she runs off with Arthur.

Zany scripting never gets an even keel of solid comedy, and result is lagging, telegraphed comedics that soon wear thin. Lensing and editing are the main assets of this uneven film. Miss Laage as the Dulcyish character gives only a dizzy voice to the character, but never gets the comprehensive, endearing quality needed into the role. Auclair is okay in the silly role of the young man of the house, and the rest of the cast plays the absurd roles to the best of their ability. Only in character is Amedee, as a near-sighted vindictive chauffeur who shows that there was the germ of a fine comic idea in this film. *Mosk.*

Par Ordre Du Tsar
(At The Order Of The Czar)
(FRENCH; COLOR)

Paris, July 20.
Gamma release of Florida-Gamma-Oska production. Stars Michel Simon, Colette Marchand. Directed by Andre Haguet; screenplay, H. A. Legrand; camera (Gevacolor), Nicolas Hayer; editor, R. Quignon. At Marignan, Paris. Running time, 100 MINS.

Prince	Michel Simon
Carolyne	Colette Marchand
Liszt	Jacques Francois
Duchess	Lucienne Lemarchand
Grand Duke	Willy Fritsch
Servant	Jacqueline Gay

Color opus recounts a highly romantic, melodramatic episode in the life of the Hungarian composer Franz Liszt. Familiar ingredients of a pompous and far-fetched biography and stilted treatment and characterization make this primarily a local product. For the U. S., there isn't much here except for possible limited special slotting on its music theme.

Episode is Liszt's love for a Russian princess, Co'ette Marchand, who is married to a tyrannical prince who is much older than she is. The lovers decide to get her marriage annulled but the brutish husband blocks this and Liszt enters a monastery. When the husband dies it is too late because Liszt has been ordained. Sudsy affair is leavened with glimpse of the Hungarian Revolution, an orgy at the prince's house with plenty of bare bosom and some dragged-in dance routine.

Director Andre Haguet has given this good commercial mounting. Color is good with other technical aspects adequate. Michel Simon

scores in the role of the Prince, but Colette Marchand shows she is a better dancer than thesper. Jacques Francois is properly received as Liszt. Music is, of course, excellent. *Mosk.*

Sabrina

Sock romantic comedy with Humphrey Bogart, Audrey Hepburn, William Holden. Hearty b.o. possibilities.

Hollywood, Aug. 2.
Paramount release of Billy Wilder production. Stars Humphrey Bogart, Audrey Hepburn, William Holden; features Walter Hampden, John Williams, Martha Hyer, Joan Vohs. Directed by Wilder. Screenplay, Wilder, Samuel Taylor and Ernest Lehman; from the play "Sabrina Fair" by Taylor; camera, Charles Lang; editor, Arthur Schmidt; score, Frederick Hollander. Previewed July 28, '54. Running time, 112 MINS.

Linus Larrabee	Humphrey Bogart
Sabrina Fairchild	Audrey Hepburn
David Larrabee	William Holden
Oliver Larrabee	Walter Hampden
Thomas Fairchild	John Williams
Elizabeth Tyson	Martha Hyer
Gretchen Van Horn	Joan Vohs
Baron	Marcel Dalio
The Professor	Marcel Hillaire
Maude Larrabee	Nella Walker
Mr. Tyson	Francis X. Bushman
Miss McCardle	Ellen Corby

(*Aspect ratio:* 1.75-1)

A slick blend of heart and chuckles makes "Sabrina" a sock romantic comedy that should catch on at the boxoffice and rate hearty ticket sales. Word-of-mouth potential is strong and will figure importantly in building grosses.

The picture has been loaded with the Academy Award-winning names of Humphrey Bogart, Audrey Hepburn and William Holden. When paired with a stout piece of entertainment these can keep ticket windows humming. Also, the Oscar angle is presumably exploitable in pushing sales.

Picture uses the Cinderella theme that featured Samuel Taylor's play, "Sabrina Fair," excellently. It has been reworked and broadened into a class, adult comedy that will be liked by the masses. Billy Wilder, an Oscarholder himself, produced and directed, and did the nifty scripting with Taylor and Ernest Lehman. Script is long on glibly quipping dialog, dropped with a seemingly casual air, and broadly played situations. The splendid trouping delivers them with a style that will keep audiences on the alert. Leavening the chuckles are tugs at the heart, and this turning on of sentiment upon occasion is a large factor in making this picture sterling entertainment.

Basically, the plot's principal business is to get Miss Hepburn, daughter of a chauffeur in service to an enormously wealthy family, paired off with the right man. She's always been in love with playboy Holden, but ends up with Bogart, the austere, businessman brother. The change of heart is spotted by the audience before the players let on they are aware of it, too, and before the climax is reached, viewers are in for plenty of fun. The film is 112 minutes in running time, but none of them seem long after Wilder once gets going with his story. The initial lag sets things up for a fast pace thereafter.

The fun is in the playing. Bogart is sock as the tycoon with no time for gals until he tries to get Miss Hepburn's mind off Holden. The latter sells his comedy strongly, wrapping up a character somewhat offbeat for him. Miss Hepburn again demonstrates a winning talent for being "Miss Cinderella" and will have audiences rooting for her all the way.

The talent is not all among the stars. Walter Hampden, playing the father of the ill-assorted sons, smacked over many laughs, only one of which is his struggle to get the last olive out of a bottle. John Williams scores as the chauffeur who sends his daughter to Paris to become a cook and is doublecrossed when she returns a fascinating lady. Martha Hyer, Holden's fiancee, and Joan Vohs, a giggling blonde who would like to be, contribute femme charms. The supporting performances are equally smart.

Film abounds with lush production values, all expertly put on the screen by Charles Lang's photography. The background score by Frederick Hollander is another fine point in blending laughs and heart. *Brog.*

The Black Shield of Falworth
(C'SCOPE—COLOR)

Actionful swashbuckler with Tony Curtis, Janet Leigh and good boxoffice outlook.

Hollywood, Aug. 3.

Universal release of Robert Arthur, Melville Tucker production. Stars Tony Curtis, Janet Leigh, David Farrar, Barbara Rush, Herbert Marshall; features Torin Thatcher, Daniel O'Herlihy, Patrick O'Neal, Craig Hill, Ian Keith, Doris Lloyd, Rhys Williams. Directed by Rudolph Mate. Screenplay, Oscar Brodney; based on the novel "Men of Iron" by Howard Pyle; camera (Technicolor), Irving Glassberg; editor, Ted J. Kent; music supervision, Joseph Gershenson. Previewed July 27, '54. Running time, **98 MINS.**

Myles	Tony Curtis
Lady Anne	Janet Leigh
Gilbert Blunt, Earl of Alban	David Farrar
Meg	Barbara Rush
William, Earl of Mackworth	Herbert Marshall
Sir James	Torin Thatcher
Prince Hal	Daniel O'Herlihy
Walter Blunt	Patrick O'Neal
Francis Gascoyne	Craig Hill
King Henry IV	Ian Keith
Dame Ellen	Doris Lloyd
Diccon Bowman	Rhys Williams
Friar Edward	Leonard Mudie
Count de Vermois	Maurice Marsac
Sir Robert	Leo Britt
Giles	Charles Fitz Simons
Peter	Gary Montgomery
Sir George	Claud Allister
Roger Ingoldsby	Robin Camp

(*Aspect ratio:* 2.55-1)

Universal has come up with a romantic swashbuckler for its initial CinemaScoped offering and the payoff through this company's general market looks good. It teams Tony Curtis and Janet Leigh to attract the younger ticket buyers, and backs the pairing with plenty of derring-do action.

Film is shaped expertly to market demands under the co-producer function of Robert Arthur and Melville Tucker. The escapism in the Oscar Brodney screenplay is broadly developed under Rudolph Mate's direction and there's enough good costumed entertainment to give the picture appeal to all who want light, fast-moving filmfun in a fanciful vein.

"Men of Iron," novel by Howard Pyle, furnishes the basis for Brodney's script, which details the conspiracy against the throne of King Henry IV which the Earl of Alban has cooked up, and how the threat is put down by Curtis, son of a cashiered knight, with the help of Herbert Marshall, the Earl of Mackworth, and Dan O'Herlihy, son of the king. In downing the traitor, Curtis regains a noble position and the hand of Miss Leigh, the daughter of the Earl of Mackworth.

In leading up to the climactic fight between Curtis and the evil earl played by David Farrar, footage works in plenty of details on feudal life. These scenes are principally concerned with the training for knighthood of Curtis, up to this point raised as a peasant with his attractive sister, Barbara Rush. Scenes will appeal to the youthful and action-minded, as will the wall-climbing courtship carried on between Curtis and Miss Leigh, and Miss Rush and Craig Hill, a trainee friend of Curtis. Climax is a rousing sequence of bloody dueling that comes off well.

The above named players bring their roles off in the proper spirit and other worthy contributions come from Torin Thatcher, the tough Sir James under whom the embryo knights train; Patrick O'Neal, the wicked earl's brother; O'Herlihy, the Prince Hal; Ian Keith, the king; Doris Lloyd, fluttery lady-in-waiting, and Rhys Wiliams, guardian of Curtis and Miss Rush in their earlier life.

Irving Glassberg used the CinemaScope cameras and the Technicolor tints excellently to show off the good art direction and settings. Music supervision by Joseph Gershenson permits the score to compete too often with the action drama. *Brog.*

The Vanishing Prairie
(Color—Documentary)

From Walt Disney, another fine exploration of nature in the raw.

Buena Vista Films release of Walt Disney production; associate producer, Ben Sharpsteen; director, James Algar; screenplay, Algar, Winston Hibler, Ted Sears; narrated by Hibler; camera, Tom McHugh, James R. Simon, N. Paul Kenworthy Jr., Cleveland P. Grant; added photography, Lloyd Beebe, Herb Crisler, Dick Borden, Warren Garst, Murl Deusing, Olin Sewall Pettingill Jr., Stuart V. Jewell, Bert Harwell; editor, Lloyd Richardson; music editor, Al Teeter; animation effects, Joshua Meador, Art Riley; special process, Ub Iwerks; music, Paul Smith; orchestration, Edward Plumb, Joseph Dubin; filmed with the cooperation of the U.S. Department of the Interior, National Park Service, Wind Cave National Park, Yellowstone National Park, Fish and Wildlife Service, Bureau of Indian Affairs, and the Crow Indian Tribe. Previewed N.Y. July 29, '54. Running time, **71 MINS.**

In "Vanishing Prairie," Walt Disney has a wholly satisfactory followup to "Living Desert," which was his first True-Life Adventure feature. This new entry is truly a remarkable pictorial examination of wildlife in the wide open spaces of mid-U.S. It's an uncanny study of the everyday behavior of, and the fight for survival among, prairie dogs, bison, cranes, coyotes, mountain lions, various rodents and birds.

"Prairie" will follow the marketing pattern which was cut with "Desert" and there's every reason to believe it will chalk up similarly good returns.

The billing of the series is fitting, for the new pic, like its predecessor, is a genuine adventure dealing with animal existence. The audience is given an inches-away view of a 200-pound prairie feline in exquisitely agile movement, pursuing a young deer to provide sustenance for her cubs. This and other close-ups are provided by deft use of long-range cameras and, doubtless, much long waiting by the lensmen for the right material to present itself.

Glimpses of the prairie dogs, of the rodent family, are particularly intimate for the spectator is taken right through the labyrinthine tunnels which these creatures gnaw through the ground and maintain as their protective homes.

The specific sector covered lies between the Rockies and the Mississippi. The Technicolor mirroring is a decided plus that distinctly reveals the beautiful contrasting hues in the terrain and, of course, the four-footed and winged denizens of the area.

For the most part the film is "light." That is, there's not much of the horror inherent in life-or-death struggles between the animals. As a matter of fact, there's much underlining of comedic values, such as ducks coming in for pratt-sliding landings on an icy lake. Also, the musical score is cleverly in sync with the movements of the animals on view and this has delightfully humorous effect.

One scene not for the lily-livered, though, focuses on a bison yielding a new calf. The actual birth is clearly and fully in view and the stark rawness of it is strong spectacle.

The commentary is always informative and sometimes amusing. All concerned with "Prairie" (see credits above) have contributed to a film project that is both an educational experience and a fine entertainment. *Gene.*

El Grito Sagrado
(The Sacred Call)
(ARGENTINE)

Buenos Aires, July 20.

AAA release of Eduardo Bedoya's production. Stars Fanny Navarro with Carlos Cores, Eduardo Cuitino, Aida Luz, Antonia Herrero, Alba Castellanos, Luis Medina Castro, Nina Brian. Directed by Luis Cesar Amatori. Edited by Atilio Rinaldi and Ricardo Nistal. Screenplay, Pedro Miguel Obligado; camera, Francis Boeniger; editors, Atilio Rinaldi, Ricardo Nistal; music, Tito Ribero. At Gran Rex Theatre, Buenos Aires. Running time, **116 MINS.**

The producers aimed at making an epic historical romance out of this story based on true incident during Argentina's emancipation period, but, despite heavy outlay (for a pic here), they only succeeded in making a corny soap opera on celluloid. The antiquated handling creaked at the ballyhooed preem. This has scant interest for U. S. audiences although television might be interested from an educational standpoint. Pic was disappointing on its opening here.

Handling is so ancient that characters even resort to such patent devices as calling each other by full names and patronymics, Russian-style, so audiences will catch on to their identities. Moreover, yarn is told in flashback by the heroine, Mariquita Sanchez de Thompson y Mendeville. She describes to a granddaughter, rebeling against parental discipline, her own struggle against rigid Spanish custom in opposing her parents to wed Martin Thompson; the dawning of patriotism when a British invasion spurred them to defend their native soil; eventual revolt against the tyrants, emancipation of the slaves and the final arrival of independence. The picture's long footage winds up with President Sarmiento, head of a Federated Republic, honoring the aged Mariquita Thompson at Government House.

Treatment here turns a nation's birth-pangs into a heroine's personal sob story, with deep historical overtones colored by present political ideologies. The onus of "enslavers" is tossed towards Britain rather than Spain, overlooking the historically-recorded fact that officers who led the British invasion made fast friends of the colonists and urged them towards emancipation. The impact of Napoleonic wars on Argentine development is carefully avoided.

Choice of Fanny Navarro for the role of Mariquita segued from her status as president of the Entertainment Guild. Carlos Cores was a stop-gap choice for the male lead of Martin Thompson when actor Carlos Thompson deserted for Hollywood. However, he acquits himself ably in naval uniforms which enhance his fine physique. Aida Luz shows rare charm as the wife of General San Martin while Eduardo Cuitino is suitably sonorous as Fray Cayetano Rodriguez, a signer of the declaration of independence. Luis Medina Castro as the villain is leery enough for a performance in "East Lynne" of the 1800's.

Perhaps the most interesting side of the pic is the reconstruction of old Buenos Aires. In some cases interior sets are faithfully reproduced from old prints while props are borrowed from museums for greater authenticity. But the whole has been assembled with neither taste nor imagination. *Nid.*

Varietease
(COLOR)

Beautiful Productions presentation of Irving Klaw production, directed by Klaw. Stars Lili St. Cyr. Camera (Eastmancolor), Daniel Cavelli; editor, Les Orlebeck; music, Metis; song, "Broken Toy" by Ben Blosser and Irma Hollander. Previewed in N.Y. July 29, '54. Running time, **65 MINS.**

Cast: Lili St. Cyr, Cass Franklin, Monica Lane, Betty Page, Bobby Shields, Baro & Rogers, Christine Nelson, Twinnie Wallen, Shelley Leigh, Chris La Chris, Vicki Lynn.

While beauty is represented in the form of Lili St. Cyr, Irving Klaw's immodestly-named Beautiful Productions offers a film that nowhere approaches the billing. This is a burleycue film, strictly for the skid row joints that play this product. It's a hodgepodge of strips, musical numbers, and extremely unfunny comedy routines.

Klaw has two versions of this film, one for states with censorship boards and another for the non-scissors wielders. Except for Miss St. Cyr's final disrobing number, the version shown at a New York screening offers nothing that would offend the Helen Hokinson set.

Photography, sets, editing, performances (except Miss St. Cyr's) are all substandard. *Holl.*

La Chair Et Le Diable
(The Devil And The Pulpit)
(FRANCO-ITALIAN)

Paris, July 28.

Jeannic release of Isarfilm-SAFA production. Stars Viviane Romance; features Rossano Brazzi, Peter Van Eyck. Written and directed by Jean Josipovici; camera, Michel Kelber; editor, Denise Reiss. At Raimu, Paris. Running time, **90 MINS.**

Mylene	Viviane Romance
Giuseppe	Rossano Brazzi
Mathias	Peter Van Eyck
La Vieille	Titina De Filippo
Patronne	Helena Bossis

As writer and director, Jean Josipovici is at fault for fashioning this heavyhanded, bucolic love melodrama. Lack of character definition, familiar proceedings and a plodding pace make this less than palatable for both domestic and foreign chances.

This concerns an itinerant Italian worker who comes to work on a farm in Southern France. A hot-blooded ladies' man, he is taken by the taciturn, voluptuous wife of his boss. This leads to the ensuing tragedy. The farmer disappears after a fight with the worker, and when a body is found in unrecognizable state the wife and worker are accused of murder. He is executed and the wife imprisoned. Then the farmer turns up, and the townspeople run amuck and stone farmer, his wife and servant to death.

This grisly affair is handled without any imagic knowhow and is flat in rhythm and pace to make this story unbelievable and pretentious in unfoldment. Viviane Romance has brooding sensual looks, but is not up to the hauteur of the high thespic range of the proud brooding woman, while Rossano Brazzi and Peter Van Eyck, as the worker and husband, are too stilted and pompous in playing. Rest of the familiar village types are adequate, but lensing reeks of the studio and editing does not relieve the redundant pacing of this downbeat opus. *Mosk.*

Crainquebille
(FRENCH)

Paris, July 20.
Pathe release of Calamy production. Stars Yves Deniaud. Directed by Ralph Habib; screenplay, Jean Halain, from novel by Anatole France; dialog, Andre Tabet; camera, Andre Germain; editor, Madeleine Bagiau. At Imperial, Paris. Running time, **90 MINS.**
Crainquebille .... Yves Deniaud
Boy .... Christian Fourcade
Widow .... Laurence Aubry
Friend .... Pierre Mondy
Lawyer .... Claude Winter
Tramp .... Jacques Fabbri

Film is the third celluloid round for Anatole France's novel of a miscarriage of justice and the results of man's indifference to man. The Jacques Feyder version, in 1925, still remains the most moving and humane version which, though silent, eloquently depicted the life of a small merchant made the victim of a misunderstanding, and almost dying of poverty and chagrin when he becomes a social outcast.

Present version has updated the story, but more comic playing robs it of its motives, and it emerges, in its new form, as a lachrymose, uneven tale that seems dated and anachronistic. This is okay for general situations here, but has little for U.S. chances due to its stilted, downbeat tale and uneven direction and thesping.

Crainquebille has a vegetable pushcart, and is an affable, kindly old man known and liked by all his clients. A disagreeable policeman does not get along with the old merchant, who is the champion of the kids playing in the crowded streets, and when a disagreement occurs the cop arrests the old man on the charge that he had been insulted. Pic then goes through his trial and two-week imprisonment due to the hurried court activities, and then the lack of comprehension of the old clients who boycot him and almost drive him to suicide, from which he is saved by the understanding of a little boy.

Director Ralph Habib has not been able to transfer the feeling and probing humanity of the original into this, and it emerges a folksy bit that is primarily local in appeal. Yves Deniaud makes the old man a crusty figure, but never taps the pathos inherent in the misunderstood peddler. Christian Fourcade of "Little Boy Lost" (Par) overdoes the waif attitudes, and the rest of the cast is adequate. Lensing and editing are par but production smacks of too much economy, and the supposedly steaming street scenes reek of studio, and are out of keeping with the pace and theme of the story. *Mosk.*

Mano Dello Strangiero
(The Stranger's Hand)
(ITALIAN)

Rome, July 13.
Dear Film release of a Rizzoli-Milo production. Stars Alida Valli, Trevor Howard, Richard Basehart, Richard O'Sullivan, Eduardo Ciannelli. Directed by Mario Soldati. Screenplay, Giorgio Bassani. Guy Elems, from an original story by Graham Greene; camera, Enzo Serafin; music, Nino Rota; editor, Tom Simpson. At the Bernini, Rome. Running time, 100 MINS.
Roger Court .... Richard O'Sullivan
Major Court .... Trevor Howard
Roberta .... Alida Valli
John .... Richard Basehart
Bosich .... Eduardo Ciannelli

Spy meller focusing action on a small boy in a Venice locale has suspense values for general appeal plus good performances, especially by Richard O'Sullivan, as the moppet. For the U. S., cast names plus the Graham Greene authorship will help. Pic was shot in English so no dubbing problem involved.

The kid (O'Sullivan) is skedded to meet his father (Trevor Howard), an intelligence officer, in Venice. Before meeting, latter is detoured and captured by Slavic terrorists and set for secret deportation to the East. Bulk of film shows boy's efforts, aided by a friendly secretary (Alida Valli) and her sailor friend (Richard Basehart), to find his father. Search makes for colorful location sequences and enough underplayed suspense to hold audiences until the windup, which sees the liberation of the father just as ship is set to leave harbor.

Plot is just a shade coincidental, and some of action, especially concerning the terrorist group's doings, is not clear, possibly because of the producer's attempt to play neutral. Involved also is Eduardo Ciannelli, as the terrorist doctor, often torn between East and West, and the reluctant leader of the gang.

Pic is vaguely reminiscent, in feeling, of "Fallen Idol," also authored by Greene, but lacks the latter's depth of handling, despite a good, unmannered performance by O'Sullivan. Howard is good as the kid's father. Miss Valli and Basehart have relatively little to do in helping the search, with focus on the kid.

Direction could have been a bit tighter for the genre, and sometimes lags for some moralizing by the author, but general suspense values hold. Enzo Serafin's camerawork presents an unusual, offseason aspect of Venice, in keeping with pic's mood, and is effective. Good musical score by Nino Rota backdrops appropriately. *Hawk.*

Brigadoon
(C-SCOPE MUSICAL-COLOR)

Musical fantasy giving C-Scope treatment to stage hit; mixed appeal so needs strong selling.

Hollywood, Aug. 10.
Metro release of Arthur Freed production. Stars Gene Kelly, Van Johnson, Cyd Charisse; features Elaine Stewart with Barry Jones, Hugh Laing, Albert Sharpe, Virginia Bosler, Jimmy Thompson, Dody Heath. Directed by Vincente Minnelli. Screenplay, Alan Jay Lerner; based on the musical play with book and lyrics by Lerner and music by Frederick Loewe, presented on the stage by Cheryl Crawford; camera (Ansco Color), Joseph Ruttenberg; editor, Albert Akst; musical direction, Johnny Green; choreography, Gene Kelly. Previewed Aug. 6, '54. Running time, 108 MINS.
Tommy Albright .... Gene Kelly
Jeff Douglas .... Van Johnson
Fiona Campbell .... Cyd Charisse
Jane Ashton .... Elaine Stewart
Mr. Lundie .... Barry Jones
Harry Beaton .... Hugh Laing
Andrew Campbell .... Albert Sharpe
Jean Campbell ...... Virginia Bosler
Charlie Chisholm Dalrymple
.... Jimmy Thompson
Archie Beaton .... Tudor Owen
Angus .... Owen McGiveney
Ann .... Dee Turnell
Meg Brockie .... Dody Heath
Sandy .... Eddie Quillan

(*Aspect ratio: 2.55-1*)

In transferring "Brigadoon," a click as a Broadway musical play, to the screen, Metro has achieved medium success. It's a fairly entertaining tunefilm of mixed appeal. It should find a ready audience in the keys where the footlight version did well, but needs hard selling elsewhere.

Among the more noteworthy points are the score, as directed by Johnny Green, and the stagetype settings that represent the plot's Highland locale. The latter are striking examples of art direction, even though they are the major contribution to the feeling that this is a filmed stage show, rather than a motion picture musical.

Less noteworthy is the choreography by Gene Kelly, who also plays the lead male role, and his singing of the Alan Jay Lerner-Frederick Loewe songs. The dance staging is not particularly arresting, although a few of the numbers will have the desired effect on an audience, and the vocals fail to give the tunes the tonal impact needed to put them over.

Most audiences will probably go for the spirited staging of "I'll Go Home With Bonnie Jean" as a sort of community song-and-dance effort, and "The Gathering of the Clans," with swirling bagpipes and drums, that leads into "The Wedding Dance." Missing is the exciting "Sword Dance" that was an important part of the wedding number on stage. One or two songs also are eliminated, as well as several sequences that would have better explained the plot's fantasy theme.

Kelly and Cyd Charisse, the femme star, share "The Heather On the Hill" and "From This Day On" as song-and-dance production numbers and they come over fairly well. Miss Charisse scores best on "Waitin' For My Dearie," done with a group of girls. As the Highland miss of two centuries ago who captures the heart of a 20th century male, she is one of the film's better points. "It's Almost Like Being In Love" is disappointing as sung and danced by Kelly. Other numbers are "Brigadoon," "The Chase" and "Prologue."

The Lerner musical play tells of two New Yorkers who become lost while hunting in Scotland and happen on Brigadoon on the one day that it is visible every 100 years. With nights that are 100

years long, the villagers are in a mood for making merry. Besides, a wedding is to take place and Kelly and Van Johnson, the modern-day males, join in the fun. Particularly Kelly, who falls for Miss Charisse hard enough to be willing to join his sweetheart in the long ago and escape from the wear and tear of modern living.

The latter is artfully exampled in a Broadway scene when the hunters return home and are caught up in the hectic, makehaste air of New York. It is in this sequence that Elaine Stewart makes her sole appearance as the modern fiancee of Kelly and she stands out most favorably. Johnson, other than a few good quips, has a rather thankless role. Barry Jones, as the Brigadoon scholar who tells of the village's strange escape from reality, is good. So is Jimmy Thompson, the bridegroom. Hugh Laing, the disappointed suitor, is not used to any advantage. Others make appropriate appearances as Brigadoon villagers.

Vincente Minnelli directed the Arthur Freed production from a screenplay written by Lerner. Both the script and the direction bring the show off fairly well, but it is a tough thing to put fantasy on the screen solidly. The CinemaScope lensing, in Ansco Color, is handled excellently by Joseph Ruttenberg. Cedric Gibbons and Preston Ames did the smart art direction and the equally good set decorations were by Edwin B. Willis and Keogh Gleason. *Brog.*

Human Desire

Sordid romantics and murder with Glenn Ford, Gloria Grahame and Broderick Crawford. Boxoffice values spotty.

Columbia release of Lewis J. Rachmil production. Stars Glenn Ford, Gloria Grahame, Broderick Crawford; features Edgar Buchanan, Kathleen Case, Peggy Maley, Diane DeLaire, Grandon Rhodes. Directed by Fritz Lang. Screenplay, Alfred Hayes; based on novel by Emile Zola; camera, Burnett Guffey; editor, Robert Peterson; music, Daniel Amfitheatrof (conducted by Morris Stoloff). Previewed N.Y. July 29, '54. Running time, 90 MINS.
Jeff Warren .... Glenn Ford
Vicki Buckley .... Gloria Grahame
Carl Buckley ...... Broderick Crawford
Alec Simmons .... Edgar Buchanan
Ellen Simmons.......... Kathleen Case
Jean .... Peggy Maley
Vera Simmons .... Diane DeLaire
John Owens .... Grandon Rhodes
Bartender .... Dan Seymour
Matt Henley .... John Pickard
Brakeman .... Paul Brinegar
Prosecutor Gruber .... Dan Riss
Davidson .... Victor Hugo Greene
Russell .... John Zaremba
John Thurston .... Carl Lee
Lewis .... Olan Soule

(*Aspect ratio: 1.85-1*)

The audience meets some wretched characters on the railroad in this adaptation of the Emile Zola novel, "The Human Beast." Some years ago a French picturization of the work was done with heavy accent on psychological study of an alcohol-crazed killer. Although low in moral tone it still presented an arresting portrait.

This time out the development is contrived and the characters shallow. The lead names may help but heavy selling is demanded if the pic is to get by adequately.

Fritz Lang, director, goes overboard in his effort to create mood. Long focusing on locomotive speeding and twisting on the rails has obscure value for it is neither entertaining nor essential to the plot.

At the outset, Alfred Hayes' screenplay provides much conversation about the fact that Glenn Ford, who's back on the job as an engineer, had been fighting the war in Korea. There's not much point to this, considering that Ford's background has little bearing on the yarn.

Broderick Crawford, Gloria Grahame and Ford make a brooding, sordid triangle, hopelessly involved. Crawford is utterly frustrated in his effort to please his wife, Miss Grahame, and stay on an even keel with his heartless yardmaster boss. Miss Grahame is a miserable character, alternately denying and admitting she has given herself to other men. Ford dates Miss Grahame and toys with the idea of murdering her husband.

The story works itself clumsily into an actual murder situation, a recipient of Miss Grahame's charms being the victim and Crawford the slayer. Ford eventually sizes up Miss Grahame correctly and walks out on her. Climax has Crawford about to commit his second murder, this time his wife.

Lewis J. Rachmil's production is laid out well enough in the railroad settings. But the scenario, as written by Hayes and directed by Lang, lacks any genuine suspense or excitement and the players down the line impart slight conviction to their parts. Technical credits are adequate. *Gene.*

Gambler From Natchez
(COLOR)

Regulation costumed action-drama for the program market.

Hollywood, Aug. 4.

20th-Fox release of Panoramic presentation, produced by Leonard Goldstein. Stars Debra Paget, Dale Robertson; features Thomas Gomez, Lisa Daniels, Kevin McCarthy, Douglas Dick, John Wengraf, Donald Randolph, Henry Letondal, Jay Novello. Directed by Henry Levin. Screenplay, Gerald Drayson Adams, Irving Wallace; story by Adams; camera (Technicolor), Lloyd Ahern; editor, William Murphy; music, Lionel Newman. Previewed **Aug. 2, '54. Running time, 87 MINS.**

Vance Colby .... Dale Robertson
Melanie Barbee .... Debra Paget
Captain Barbee .... Thomas Gomez
Yvette Rivage .... Lisa Daniels
Andre Rivage .... Kevin McCarthy
Claude St. Germaine .... Douglas Dick
Cadiz .... John Wengraf
Pitrre Bonet .... Donald Randolph
Renard .... Henri Letondal
Garonne .... Jay Novello
Josh .... Woody Strode
Etienne .... Peter Mamakos
Raoul .... Ivan Triesault

(*Aspect ratio:* 1.66-1)

The program market should find "The Gambler From Natchez" acceptable filmfare for either top or bottom of the bill bookings. It is a fanciful action drama in costume and Technicolor that achieves generally satisfactory results for the non-discriminating trade.

Setting for the Panoramic presentation, produced for 20th-Fox release by the late Leonard Goldstein, is the crinoline days along the Mississippi, when all the gals were as sweet as magnolia blossoms and the men dispensed justice and gallantry according to a rigid code. It's strictly regulation, in plot and performance.

Debra Paget, who mixes some ginger with the magnolias, and Dale Robertson, officer son of a professional river gambler, star under Henry Levin's direction. She comes off best as the river spitfire who is instrumental in helping Robertson obtain revenge on some blooded dandies for the slaying of his father. The direction and plotting throw more color her way than to Robertson, who tries but still seems uncomfortable in his tight-pants heroics.

The Gerald Drayson Adams story, which Adams scripted with Irving Wallace, has Robertson returning from four years service in Texas under General Sam Houston to find his father murdered. The deed was done by Kevin McCarthy, who couldn't stand losing both his interest in the new river boat and his plantation to the gambler. The heavy's out to get Robertson, too, and when a henchman plunges a knife into the hero, he's saved from the river by Miss Paget.

From then on, it is a question of Robertson running down those implcated in his father's death and eventually succumbing to Miss Paget's advances, a turn of romantic event not pleasing to Lisa Daniels, who has been helping brother McCarthy's dirty work but has also fallen for the hero.

Thomas Gomez, the rotund father of Miss Paget; Douglas Dick, Miss Daniels' effete suitor; John Wengraf, one of the conspirators, and the others provide the principals with adequate support in the formula doings. Miss Paget sings "Monsieur Banjo," a public domain number, in one of several sequences in which she is costumed in fetching undergarments.

Lensing, art direction and editing are among the okay technical credits. The Lionel Newman score is overused most of the time. *Brog.*

Le Mouton A Cinq Pattes
(The Five-Legged Sheep)
(FRENCH)

Paris, Aug. 10.

Cocinor release of Raoul Ploquin-Cocinex production. Stars Fernandel. Directed by Henri Verneuil. Screenplay, Albert Valentin, adapted by Rene Barjavel; camera, Armand Thirard; editor, Christian Gaudin. Previewed in Paris. Running time, **100 MINS.**

Edouard
Alain
Bernard .... Fernandel
Etienne
Charles
Desire
Marianne .... Francoise Arnoul
Bolene .... Delmont
Pilate .... Louis De Funes
Brissard .... Noel Roquevert

Fernandel is one of the top box-office draws here, and his present producers have decided to cash in on this by casting him as a father and his quintuplet sons. Result is a gimmick pic which allows Fernandel to romp in all the roles but only stringing together a group of incidents and sketches only related by the family ties. Plot sees the town mayor trying to reunite the quints and the crotchety father for publicity purposes. Film has some good ideas and many laughs, but is weighted down by a vulgarized batch of sketches which lack the levity and tone needed for top spotting in the U. S. It has definite local appeal but its American chances are much slimmer, main appeal being the Fernandel moniker and possible word-of-mouth.

Story shows a crusty father holding a grudge against his grown quintuplet sons who had never come home after their schooling. The mayor decides to round them up to surprise the old man. So the town doctor sets off to get the quints. He unearths an effeminate if rich beautician, a poor but easy-going windowwasher with a flock of kids, a tough sea captain, a priest and an advice to lovelorn columnist. As each character is found he goes through a sketch with Fernandel, of course, doing the different brothers.

Director Henry Verneuil has vulgarized too many aspects of this, result being that much of the comic impact is lost. Fernandel has a field day, but his bag of tricks are getting familiar and he does not give each character the relief needed to give this a more overall impact. Lensing is fine as is editing. Cast is good with Louis De Funes and Francoise Arnoul excellent in support. *Mosk.*

Les Hommes Ne Pensent Qu'A Ca
(Men Think Only of That)
(FRENCH)

Paris, Aug. 3.

Gaumont release of Chavanne-Gaumont-Cinephonic production. Directed by Yves Robert. Screenplay, Jean Bellanger: adaptation and dialog, Bellanger, Jean Marsan; camera, Paul Soulignac; editor, Raymond Lamy. Features Robert, Bellanger, Jean-Marie Amato, Louis De Funes, Catherine Erard. At Balzac, Paris. Running time, **75 MINS.**

Timid Soul .... Jean Bellanger
Don Juan .... Jean-Marie Amato
Salesgirl .... Catherine Erard
Boy .... Guy Pierrauld
Girl .... Rosy Varte
Husband .... Louis De Funes
Butcher .... Jacques Fabbri
Soldier .... Yves Robert

The Yves Robert group started in the Left Bank existentialist caves and created a new type of satirical, vest pocket theatrics which had them graduating to legit and now it is trying its hand with this formula in films. This emerges as a sort of filmic essay on the various forms of seduction built around the story of a timid soul who is initiated into the mysteries of love. Though slight in film form, this engenders enough laughs to make it palatable in general situations here with word-of-mouth a factor. For the U. S., this is too sketchy for any important runs, but might be cut to make medium-length supporting pic in arty houses. It is also a fine gambit for tv.

A timid young man hasn't the nerve to approach his adored salesgirl who gives him all the opportunities. Don Juan appears to him and initiates him to the various forms of romantic aplomb and triumph. Here pic goes into a series of clever vignettes and gags on the various forms of seduction with a series of comic situations.

This lacks the class of "Hulot's Holiday," but is Gallic enough for special situations. Simple special effects are well utilized. Jean Bellanger is fine as the timid male, Jean-Pierre Amato, okay as the cantankerous, truculent Don Juan, and the others of the group do well in severs' vignettes. Louis De Funes is a comic find as the twitching, slow-boiling husband. Technical aspects are good and obvious low production nut should make this pay off here. *Mosk.*

Orage
(Storm)
(FRANCO-ITALIAN)

Paris, Aug. 3.

Cocinor release of Bellotti Film production. Stars Raf Vallone, Francoise Arnoul. Directed by Pierre Billon, Giorgio Capitini. Screenplay by Billon, from a novel by Henri Bernstein; camera, Gabor Pogany; editor, Rezo Lucedi. At Marignan, Paris. Running time, **100 MINS.**

Andre .... Raf Vallone
Francoise .... Francoise Arnoul
Elena .... Elena Varzi
Gilbert .... Giorgio Albertazzi

This film is a sudsy affair which concerns the extra-marital affair of a devoted husband who is finally sent back to his faithful wife by his upright mistress. Slow pacing, familiarity and lack of character depth put this in the distaff category. It has chance for general play dates here on the names of Raf Vallone and Francoise Arnoul. But for the U. S., it is limited to possibly a few dualers.

Andre is a sober, industrious husband who, on a business trip to Rome, is begged by his romantic brother-in-law to beg a certain young lady to return his love. Andre goes, and through a series of circumstances finds himself stranded with the girl and love blossoms. Complications arise at the return of an old suitor, but Andre cannot face life without her and decides to leave his wife. The wife calls in the girl and says she is going to have a baby. So the girl walks off into the night, leaving Andre for his wife and coming heir.

Director Pierre Billon has not been able to erase the novelettish quality of the work. Result is that the progression of the love and final reprisal is never convincing. Miss Arnoul is good in a familiar role for her as the other woman, but Elena Varzi is colorless and uneven as the wife. Vallone is betrayed by dubbing and it is only **his massive, sombre presence which keeps the role from being completely undefined. Remainder of the cast is also inadequately dubbed. Lensing and editing are good.** *Mosk.*

Schule Fuer Eheglueck
(School For Connubial Bliss)
(GERMAN)

Berlin, Aug. 3.

Union release of Oska production. Stars Liselotte Pulver and Paul Hubschmid. Directed by Toni Schelkopf and Rainer Gies. Screenplay, Franz Geiger and Peter Berneis, based on a novel by Andre Maurois; camera, Franz Koch; music, Ulrich Sommerlatte. At Kiki, Berlin. Running time, **102 MINS.**

Justus Schneemann .... Paul Hubschmid
Marianne Schneemann .... Liselotte Pulver
Tobias .... Wolf Albach-Retty
Regine .... Cornell Borchers
Billy .... Ingrid Lutz
Boris Salmon .... Alexander Golling
Kraemer .... Hermann Pfeiffer
Sabine .... Suzanne Navrath
Songstress .... Gisela Griffel

This typically German comedy has to do with two young people's love, marriage, divorce and reconciliation. Although the pic has nice production and a good cast, it probably is too familiar in treatment and too heavy with dialog to give it more than spotty chances in the U. S. market. Domestic prospects, however, are excellent.

The story, based on a novel by French writer Andre Maurois, concerns a young journalist who dreams of becoming a great author. Feeling his wife doesn't understand him, he seeks consolation and love with another woman. Latter tries to help him climb to success while his marriage, of course, flounders. But he soon finds he was better off with his wife and, taking into consideration his limited abilities, it is better to be a good journalist than a fair author. Ending sees him remarrying his former wife.

Very much on the plus side is the acting. Liselotte Pulver and Paul Hubschmid (Paul Christian), both Swiss, convincingly play the couple. Special praise goes to Miss Pulver, whose outstanding performance again justifies the fact that she currently is one of Germany's busiest stars.

A minor weakness in the production is the occasionally draggy direction by Toni Schelkopf and Rainer Gies. A little less dialog and some sophisticated touches would have helped. Technically, the film is adequate with the fine lensing. There is a catchy song which also is utilized in the background music. *Hans.*

Rumeur Publique
(Public Rumor)
(FRANCO-ITALIAN)

Paris, Aug. 3.

Sirius release of Sirius-Caretta Films production. Stars Daniel Gelin, Maria Mauban, Gian Tedeschi. Directed by Maurizio Cognati; screenplay, A. Rossi, F. Villari, Cognati; adaptation and dialog, Charles Spaak; camera, Goffredo Alessandrini; editor, Rodolfo Palermi. At Francais, Paris. Running time, 90 MINS.
Jaier .... Daniel Gelin
Star .... Maria Mauban
Egisto .... Gian Tedeschi
Actor .... Masimo Serato
Director .... C. Campanini

Franco-Italo pic is one of the examples of the horrors that can result from coproduction. Off-synch dubbing, uneven thesping, and jumpy unfoldment evidence a babel-like attempt at quickly-made film, and this will suffer in both countries. Buried in this study of the effect of a neo-realistic film on the people involved is a good offbeat idea that lacks cohesiveness and completely national treatment needed to make this palatable. This has a few names here for both France and Italy for general situations, but is not of much consequence for U. S. chances.

A journalist covers a story in a small town in which a wife has fallen down a flight of stairs and been killed. The husband is suspected. He makes a great story of this and his attempts acquit the man. He writes a scenario in which he convinces the man to play himself due to the notoriety involved. As the picture unfolds the true story comes out, and the husband finds he had been cheated on by his best friend. He goes out to kill him, but instead ends up killing the journalist who had dug into all this and exposed his shame.

Daniel Gelin is miscast as the reporter and his bad dubbing doesn't help the role any. Maria Mauban is also a good French name lost in the shuffle. Gian Tedeschi, as the husband, can't do much with an overly dramatic role and the rest of the cast is adequate. Lensing and editing cannot help this choppily-made, erratically-paced film into falling into the mood and drama of its tale. *Mosk.*

The Beachcomber
(BRITISH—COLOR)
Colorful version of Somerset Maugham South Sea Island yarn of reformation of drunken wastrel: Robert Newton and Glynis Johns do leads effectively; limited boxoffice in U.S. looms.

London, Aug. 10.

General Film Distributors release of William MacQuitty production. Stars Glynis Johns, Robert Newton, Donald Sinden. Directed by Muriel Box. Screenplay, Sydney Box, based on a story by W. Somerset Maugham; camera (Technicolor), Reginald Wyer; editor, Jean

Security Risk

Suspense feature for the programmer market. Should be moderately satisfactory.

Hollywood, Aug. 11.

Allied Artists release of William F. Broidy production. Stars John Ireland, Dorothy Malone, Keith Larsen; features Dolores Donlon, John Craven, Suzanne Ta Fel, Joe Bassett, Burt Wenland. Directed by Harold Schuster. Screenplay, Jo Pagano, John Rich; from a story by Rich; camera, John Martin; editor, Ace Herman. Previewed Aug. 9, '54. Running time, 69 MINS.
Ralph Payne .... John Ireland
Donna Weeks ....Dorothy Malone
Ted .... Keith Larsen
Peggy .... Dolores Donlon
Dr. Lanson .... John Craven
Joan Weeks .... Suzanne Ta Fel
Malone .... Joe Bassett
Burke .... Burt Wenland
Johnny .... Steven Clark
Mike .... Murray Alper
Sheriff .... Harold Kennedy
(Aspect ratio: 1.85-1)

The suspense ingredients in the plot of "Security Risk" are brought off in moderately okay fashion to meet the not too discriminating demands of the programmer market. Communist schemers and the FBI match wits in the story to give it a dateline touch, and its overall effect would have been more satisfactory had the unfoldment not been so slowly paced.

John Ireland represents the FBI in the William Broidy production, while Keith Larsen is the baddie mixed up with the Red plotters. Action takes place at Big Bear, and the resort layout furnishes a good background for what transpires as Harold Schuster's direction sends the script by Jo Pagano and John Rich through its regulation paces. Femme interest falls to Dorothy Malone, the good sister who goes for Ireland, and Dolores Donlon, her sexy, blonde bad sister, who gets herself killed for trying to turn a dishonest buck with the Commies. Latter are represented by a femme, Suzanne Ta Fel.

Ireland and the others are vacationing at Big Bear when John Craven, atomic scientist, is killed there by his assistant, Larsen, who wants some secret papers for the Bolsheviki. The murder is witnessed by Miss Donlon, who picks up the papers and then tries to sell them to the heavies. This costs her life because Larsen shoots her down when it comes time for the Commies to try their escape. Larsen is killed also, and Ireland rounds up such remaining baddies as Miss Ta Fel, Burt Wenland, Steven Clark and Murray Alper.

Performances of the three stars and the other sare brought off acceptably. The three femmes in the cast take care of temptation angles satisfactory. Joe Bassett plays the FBI chief and Harold Kennedy is seen as the helpful sheriff.

John Martin's lensing and the other technical credits are okay. *Brog.*

Barker; music, Francis Chagrin. At Leicester Square Theatre, London. Running time, 90 MINS.
Martha .... Glynis Johns
Ted .... Robert Newton
Ewart Gray .... Donald Sinden
Owen .... Paul Rogers
Tromp .... Donald Pleasence
Vederala .... Walter Crisham
Headman .... Michael Hordern
Alfred .... Auric Lorand
Captain .... Tony Quinn
Wang .... Ah Chong Choy
Headman's son .... Ronald Lewis
Amao .... Jean Rollins
Girl .... Lizabeth Rollins
Orderly .... Michael Mellinger

With the universal reputation of Somerset Maugham, plus the transatlantic popularity of Robert Newton, this latest version of one of the author's South Sea Island stories should do goodly biz in most countries. It is well adapted and suitably backgrounded, with authentic local color and all the trappings of native drums, witch doctors and the ineradicable prejudice against the white man's medicine.

Central figure is the "Honorable Ted," a disreputable remittance man idling in drunken oblivion while his money lasts. He has an eye for the local cuties and is the despair of the only other white inhabitants, a bigoted Welsh minister and his sister who conscientiously convert the heathen and heal the sick. Setup is viewed through the eyes of the new Government official, an immaculate law-enforcer who learns that his predecessor committed suicide. When the beachcomber gets out of hand and wrecks the wineshop, the newcomer keeps his threat and jails him. An outbreak of cholera brings a sense of responsibility to the drunkard who goes to a neighboring island with the Welsh girl as medical assistant and their strange, antagonistic relationship ends in marriage.

Dramatic highlights are a fight between an elephant and a crocodile and escape from death when the girl is bound by the malevolent witch doctor to be trodden underfoot by the same elephant.

Newton gives a richly human portrayal of the reformed wastrel, fitting the role capably. Glynis Johns makes an attractive figure of the single-minded missionary-cum-surgeon who hooks out an appendix with the same aplomb as she nets her reluctant mate. Paul Rogers is suitably sincere and godly as her brother while Donald Sinden looks immaculate and dignified as the impartial dispenser of justice. Of the minor roles, Donald Pleasence stands out as a native clerk and Michael Hordern as tribal headman. Excellent contributions are made by Walter Crisham, Ronald Lewis and Jean Rollins. Pic is intelligently directed by Muriel Box.

Paramount released the 1938 version of the same story (Pommer-Laughton production), similarly titled; Erich Pommer director and Charles Laughton starred.

Paris Incident
(Telegramme pour M. Herriot)
(FRENCH)
Lightweight script and slow pace limits chances in U. S.

Helene and Arthur Davis release of Mme. Goulian production. Stars Gerard Gervais, Pierrette Simonet. Directed by Henri Decoin. Story and screenplay, Alex Joffe; additional dialog, Decoin; camera, Nicholas Hayer; music, Joseph Cosma. Tradeshown in N. Y. Aug. 13, '54. Running time, 80 MINS.
Antoine .... Gerard Gervais
Amelie ....Pierrette Simonet
Police Superintendent . Olivier Hussenot
Little Boy .... Christian Fourcade
The Headmaster ....Henry Cremieux
M. Granjean ....Jacques Parride
Arthur .... Edwin Machnik
The Flowerseller ....Gemaine Michel
The Boss ....Henri Marchand
Amelie's Mother ....Margaret Zolen
The Postman .... Darnay
Sergeant Chauvin ....Alex Gordon
Etienne ....Jules Nicola

"Paris Incident" is one of those atmospheric whimsies that fall into the "could have been" category. With a less tenuous plot and a good deal of tightening, this story of a Parisian neighborhood's search for some telegrams lost by a messenger boy could have been one of those sleepers from abroad. In its present state, however, its b.o. outlook is limited to the arties.

Director Henri Decoin took a talented crew of actors into the Montmartre neighborhood and set them loose in the streets and apartments to achieve some strikingly natural shots of Parisian domesticity. But in spite of some effective moments of whimsy and sadness, the Alex Joffe screenplay bogs down badly most of the way. And while the ending (after a lost telegram to a M. Herriot, presumed to be the Speaker of the Chamber of Deputies, is found) isn't exactly telegraphed, it comes as something of a letdown.

Gerard Gervais is the youngster who on his way to deliver three telegrams runs his bike into a truck and then embarks on an all-night excursion to find the wires, lost during the accident. He's joined by Pierrette Simonet, an appealing little girl, and a flock of other interesting characters, best of which are Olivier Hussenot, Henry Cremieux, Jacques Parride and Gemaine Michel.

Both youngsters, Gervais and Miss Simonet, give remarkably poised and sensitive performances which for the most part carry the film. Decoin's direction, though it doesn't overcome the lethargy of the story, gets in its humorous moments and some bittersweet ones, and his crowd scenes, with the people of Rue Moffetard, are excellent.

Nicholas Hayer's camerawork gives an animated picture of the streets of Paris at night, and Joseph Cosma's score follows the varying moods unhaltingly and contains some excellent themes worth hearing in themselves. Harmonica played by Flore Flavcy is another plus. French title originally was "Telegramme Pour Mons. Herriot." *Chan.*

The Egyptian
(CINEMASCOPE-COLOR)

Spectacular and ambitiously mounted version of Mika Waltari's bestselling "The Egyptian," laid against a background of ancient Egypt. A showmanship special with built-in b.o. lure.

Twentieth Century-Fox release of Darryl F. Zanuck production. Stars Jean Simmons, Victor Mature, Gene Tierney, Michael Wilding, Bella Darvi, Peter Ustinov, Edmund Purdom, Judith Evelyn; features Henry Daniell, John Carradine, Carl Benton Reid, Tommy Rettig, Anitra Stevens, Donna Martell. Directed by Michael Curtiz. Screenplay, Casey Robinson and Philip Dunne; based on Mika Waltari novel of same title; camera (EastmanColor), Leon Shamroy; editor, Barbara McLean; music, Alfred Newman and Bernard Herrmann. Previewed Aug. 19, '54 in N. Y. Running time, **140 MINS.**

Merit	Jean Simmons
Horemheb	Victor Mature
Baketamon	Gene Tierney
Akhnaton	Michael Wilding
Nefer	Bella Darvi
Kaptah	Peter Ustinov
Sinuhe	Edmund Purdom
Taia	Judith Evelyn
Mikere	Henry Daniell
Grave Robber	John Carradine
Senmut	Carl Benton Reid
Thoth	Tommy Rettig
Nefertiti	Antira Stevens
Lady in Waiting	Donna Martell
First Princess	Mimi Gibson
Egyptian Dancer	Carmen de Lavallade
Nubian	Harry Thompson
Priests	George Melford, Lawrence Ryle
Libian Guards	Tiger Joe Marsh, Karl Davis
Captain	Ian MacDonald
Sinuhe (age 10)	Peter Raynolds
Officer	Michael Granger
Nubian Prince	Don Blackman
Governess	Joan Winfield
Death House Foreman	Mike Mazurki

(*Aspect ratio:* 2.55 to 1)

The decision to bring Mika Waltari's masterly, scholarly-detailed "The Egyptian" to the screen must have taken a lot of courage for this is a long way off the standard spectacle beat. The book tells a strange and unusual story laid against the exotic and yet harshly realistic background of the Egypt of 33 centuries ago, when there was a Pharaoh who believed in one god, and a physician—a man or rare quality—who through suffering and exile glimpsed a great truth and tried to live it.

In his ambitious production of "The Egyptian," Darryl F. Zanuck has not only pulled out all the stops of showmanship—the lavish production values alone insure a vast b.o. potential—but has succeeded in capturing the many fine shadings and the deeper religious meaning of the Waltari yarn. It all adds up to a solid, alluring, can't-fail merchandising package which opens exciting new vistas for the film audience. By its very nature it lends itself to a lot of razzle-dazzle for a big payoff.

This is a long picture—there are many sequences that could stand trimming easily without affecting the overall production in the least—but for the better part it's well-paced and well-balanced. It's big and splashy and sometimes breath-taking in its CinemaScoped dramatics. Yet there are many moments of genuine emotion and spiritual quality that make for contrast and the required relief.

Big coin—around $4,200,000—has been splurged on bringing ancient Egypt to life again for this picture and the results justify the expense. Quite apart from the rich and handsome costumes, the film offers a great many authentic and impressive settings, ranging from the vast and ornate throne-room and the huge outdoor altar to Aton, the one god, to the plush quarters of Nefer, the Babylonian courtesan, and the shiny expanse of the Nile. EastmanColor effects are perfect and the colors stand out in vivid and pleasing contrasts.

A big cast with good marquee appeal was picked and, under the direction of Michael Curtiz, goes through its paces with obvious enjoyment. A weak spot in the talent lineup is Bella Darvi who contributes little more than an attractive figure. Her thesping as the seductive temptress who drives Sinuhe, the physician, to ruin, is something less than believable or skilled.

In the title part, Edmund Purdom etches a strong handsome profile. As the truth-seeking doctor who grows from weakness to the maturity of a new conviction, Purdom brings "The Egyptian" to life and makes him a man with whom the audience can easily identify and sympathize. He has a pleasant, British voice that is both distinctive and very well suited to his difficult part which, in character-development, has been changed somewhat from the Waltari novel.

Jean Simmons is lovely and warm as the tavern maid who loves Purdom and wants to marry him. However, being a believer in Aton, the one god, she dies with an arrow in her breast when the priests plot to overthrow the Pharaoh. Victor Mature as the robust Horemheb, the soldier who is to become ruler, is a strong asset to the cast without infusing the soldier-leader with some of the distinctive qualities Waltari gave him in his book. A hot-tempered man, spoiling for a fight and frustrated by the Pharaoh's refusal to allow it, Mature shapes Horemheb into a colorful figure.

Michael Wilding as Akhnaton, the epileptic emperor, who dies of Sinuhe's poison with a prayer to his one god on his lips, gives a restrained performance that ranks among the best in the picture. He is the gentle, forgiving Pharaoh of "The Egyptian," and his final scene with Purdom and Mature helps shape a resoundingly effective climax. Gene Tierney is beautiful and cold, as the script requires, in the role of Sinuhe's half-sister. Judith Evelyn as the Queen Mother does herself proud in a small but important part.

A delightfully humorous portrait is delivered by Peter Ustinov as Purdom's opportunistic servant. His is one of the best performances in the picture. Megging by Curtiz keeps in mind the film's multiple facets. Where some parts tend to be ponderous, others pound with the excitement and romance of this little known era.

There is visual delight in Purdom's and Mature's lion-hunting expedition aboard a chariot with Mature killing the lion just before he attacks the praying Pharaoh. The market scene, showing workmen moving the large stone slabs for the pyramids, has an air of reality and drama. And that flair for authenticity and realism is again evident in the sequence with Purdom, realizing he has been fooled by Miss Darvi, tries to strangle her. As added inducement, Curtiz has thrown in an intriguing teaser scene showing the supposedly-naked figure of Miss Darvi reflected in the quivering waters of a pool.

Those who come looking for an exact translation of "The Egyptian" to the screen will likely leave disappointed, for—of necessity—a good part of the novel not relevant to the main story line has been skipped by scripters Casey Robinson and Philip Dunne. This in no way weakens the story which emerges clear and strong, gaining greatly from its unusual background which in itself gives the film unique stature.

"The Egyptian" is a big and important film, in every respect. And it proves beyond a doubt the tremendous advantages of CinemaScope for this type story even though not all of the book's potentials—such as its battle sequences—have been exploited. Stereophonic sound is used throughout for good results. Leon Shamroy's lensing is topnotch and makes for a series of pulse-racing effects.

Hift.

Dragnet
(COLOR)

Toprunning radio-tv program comes to films longer, bigger and in color. Stout grossing prospects.

Hollywood, Aug. 20.

Warner Bros. release of Mark VII Ltd. (Stanley Meyer) production. Stars Jack Webb; features Ben Alexander, Richard Boone, Ann Robinson. Directed by Webb. Screenplay, Richard L. Breen; camera (WarnerColor), Edward Colman; editor, Robert M. Leeds; music composed and conducted by Walter Schumann; song, Herman Saunders, Sidney Miller; technical advisor, Capt. James E. Hamilton, L.A.P.D. Previewed Aug. 18, '54. Running time, **89 MINS.**

Sgt. Joe Friday	Jack Webb
Officer Frank Smith	Ben Alexander
Captain Hamilton	Richard Boone
Grace Downey	Ann Robinson
Max Troy	Stacy Harris
Ethel Marie Starkie	Virginia Gregg
Adolph Alexander	Victor Perrin
Belle Davitt	Georgia Ellis
Jesse Quinn	James Griffith
Roy Cleaver	Dick Cathcart
Lee Reinhard	Malcolm Atterbury
Chester Davitt	Willard Sage
Ray Pinker	Olan Soule
Captain Lohrman	Dennis Weaver
Fred Kemp	James Anderson
Fabian Gerard	Monte Masters
Mr. Archer	Herb Vigran
Mrs. Caldwell	Virginia Christine
Walker Scott	Guy Hamilton
Wesley Cannon	Ramsey Williams
Lt. Stevens	Harry Bartell
Booking Sergeant	Herb Ellis
Interne	Harlan Warde

(*Aspect ratio:* 1.75-1)

"Dragnet" comes to the motion picture screen from radio and television with a pre-sold audience that could well spark it into the stout grossing category. This readymade audience, which built the see-hear electronic versions into consistently toprunning programs, will be getting the same type of show that Jack Webb stages via video and radio every week.

The big difference, of course, is that it's no longer for free, but for the price of a ticket the film version offers 90 minutes, instead of radio-tv's 30; a tremendous big-screen picture, instead of a 21-inch tube size, and some striking WarnerColor tints. Thus, with the marquee value of the title and the Webb name, b.o. results look promising.

In making the transition from radio-tv to the big screen and color, Webb's Mark VII indie production outfit has come up with a show that is spotty in entertainment results. As on video, quite a bit is made of the long, tedious toil of thorough police methods. This can be kept in hand in a 30-minute period, but when that time is tripled the pace is bound to slow to a walk often. This seems to be the principal flaw in "Dragnet's" initial screen try. Compensating, however, are good performances, a number of scenes with a real emotional quality, and some dialog that speaks up without inhibitions and scores solidly.

Under Webb's direction of the Stanley Meyer production, the film gets off on its melodramatic path with a brutal murder, committed before the main title credits are shown. Thereafter, the homicide and intelligence divisions of the L. A. Police Dept. start a widespread hunt for evidence that will pin the killing on some redhot suspects. The latter are questioned, released, questioned again, as the hunt goes on.

Detailed are police methods, new aids to crime solution, and the often dull, thankless plodding necessary before any case is broken. It doesn't seem quite right that Stacy Harris, chief suspect, has to die of a cancerous ulcer just as the police have the evidence to convict him, but as the picture is based on a real-life case, Webb's bent for "just the facts" is carried out.

Webb's direction of the Richard L. Breen screenplay is mostly a good job. He stages a four-man fight, in which he and his police sidekick, Ben Alexander, are involved, rather poorly and it may invoke unwelcome laughs. Otherwise, when sticking to terse handling of facts, or in building honest emotion, such as in the splendidly-done drunk scene by Virginia Gregg, grieving widow of the murdered hood, he brings his show off satisfactorily.

Performancewise, Webb, Alexander, plus such other video regulars as Harris, Miss Gregg, Victor Perrin, Georgia Ellis, James Griffith, topnotch as a reluctant witness, and Virginia Christine are seen to advantage. Same goes for Richard Boone, head of the intelligence division; Ann Robinson, policewoman, and most of the other casters.

Edward Colman handles the color cameras most effectively, making a number of sequences, such as the visit to the African wing of the L. A. County Museum, pictorial standouts. Walter Schumann's score plays an important part in the film's mood. Heard in one sequence is "Foggy Night in San Francisco," by Herman Saunders and Sidney Miller.

Brog.

Khyber Patrol
(COLOR)

Another action-meller localed around the Khyber Pass; acceptable supporting fare.

Hollywood, Aug. 19.

United Artists release of World Films Presentation. Stars Richard Egan, Dawn Addams, Patric Knowles. Directed by Seymour Friedman. Screenplay, Jack DeWitt; from story by Richard Schayer; camera (Color Corp. of America), Charles Van Enger; music, Irving Gertz. Previewed Aug. 12, '54. Running time, **71 MINS.**

Cameron	Richard Egan
Diana	Dawn Addams
Ahmed	Raymond Burr
Lt. Kennerly	Patric Knowles
Melville	Paul Cavanaugh
Ishak Khan	Donald Randolph
Col. Rivington	Philip Tonge
Brussard	Patrick O'Moore
Kushla	Laura Mason

(*Aspect ratio:* 1.33-1)

"Khyber Patrol" shapes up as acceptable supporting fare. Footage is in the commercial vein, and should find okay reception from the action devotees.

As scripted by Jack DeWitt, from a story by Richard Schayer, tale has Richard Egan and group literally wiping out all the unfriendly natives not taken care of by Tyrone Power in 20th-Fox's "King of the Khyber Rifles" some months ago. Hostile border tribes are out to gain control of Khyber

Pass, and the Russians are helping their fight by supplying arms and ammunition.

Opposing are the British Lancers, this group including Richard Egan, a headstrong, undisciplined captain. Egan has his troubles before it's all over, both with the enemy and also with his own men, many of whom don't approve of his tactics, but at the final fadeout the enemy has been defeated and Egan's proved he was right all along. He's also wound up with Dawn Addams, daughter of the Lancers' commander.

Egan dominates the footage throughout, turning in a neat performance that's bound to help his popularity. Miss Addams has little to do but supply the femme interest, while Patric Knowles is acceptable as the Lancer-suitor of Miss Addams until he's killed off during an attack. Raymond Burr and rest of the supporters are adequate to demands.

Direction of Seymour Friedman tends to draw out the inherent action values, and generally gives footage a good pacing. Charles Van Enger's camera work is stock, as are remainder of the technical contributions.

Film, incidentally, carries no producer credit, but was actually produced by Edward Small. It's being released under the World Films banner. *Neal.*

The Bounty Hunter
(COLOR)

Satisfactory Randolph Scott western feature in color for regular action market.

Hollywood, Aug. 24.
Warner Bros. release of Transcona Enterprises (Sam Bischoff) production. Stars Randolph Scott; features Dolores Dorn, Marie Windsor, Howard Petrie, Harry Antrim, Robert Keys. Directed by Andre de Toth. Screenplay, Winston Miller; from story by Miller and Finlay McDermid; camera (WanerColor), Edwin DuPar; editor, Clarence Kolster; music, David Buttolph. Previewed Aug. 19, '54. Running time, **79 MINS.**
Jim Kipp ....Randolph Scott
Julie Spencer.............Dolores Dorn
Alice ....Marie Windsor
Sheriff Brand ....Howard Petrie
Dr. Spencer ....Harry Antrim
George Williams..........Robert Keys
Rachin ....Ernest Borgnine
Danvers ....Dubb Taylor
Vance ....Tyler MacDuff
Harrison ....Archie Twitchell
Jud ....Paul Picerni
Ed ....Phil Chambers
Mrs. Ed.............Mary Lou Holloway
(Aspect ratio: 1.75-1)

Western action against scenic backgrounds is offered in this Randolph Scott starrer and it should please those who like outdoor features of the oater school. The action plays along a a good clip, the plot is constructed along regulation, easily-followed lines and the results are satisfactory for the market at which it is aimed.

The Transcona Enterprises production, which Warner Bros. is releasing, started out as a 3-D feature, but the depth treatment has been dropped and it goes out as a straight 2-D feature in Warner-Color for widescreen presentation. Andre de Toth directs the Sam Bischoff production with a good hand at making the story points come out even at the finale.

The Winston Miller script, from a story by Miller and Finlay McDermid, this time casts Scott as a bounty hunter—a man who makes a trade of bringing in criminals for the reward money. Here Scott is hired by Pinkerton to get three train robbers and, if possible, the

$100,000 in currency they made off with a year before. Scott plays a cagey game when he gets to Twin Forks, the town he believes the unknown robbers are holed up in, and this eventually leads to the exposure of Howard Petrie, the sheriff; Dubb Taylor, the postmaster, and, as a surprise, Marie Windsor, as the sought-after trio. When the shooting's all over, Scott finds himself the new sheriff and with a wife, Dolores Dorn, daughter of the town's doctor.

Scott takes easily to his saddle and gun chores, playing his part with authority of long experience. Script permits him to have a number of lighter moments so it's not all tight-lipped heroics. Miss Dorn looks good as the western heroine and the baddie trio wraps up its chores satisfactorily, as do others in the cast.

Color lensing by Edwin DuPar comes off well, as does the editing that holds the footage to 79 minutes. Film has a noisy score by David Buttolph. *Brog.*

Naked Alibi
(SONG)

Implausible chase melodrama; familiar names, average prospects.

Hollywood, Aug. 24.
Universal release of Ross Hunter production. Stars Sterling Hayden, Gloria Grahame, Gene Barry, Marcia Henderson; features Casey Adams, Billy Chapin, Chuck Connors, Don Haggerty, Stuart Randall. Directed by Jerry Hopper. Screenplay, Lawrence Roman; from original story, "Cry Copper," by J. Robert Bren, Gladys Atwater; camera, Russell Metty; editor, Al Clark. Previewed Aug. 17, '54. Running time, **85 MINS.**
Joseph E. Conroy.......Sterling Hayden
Marianna ....Gloria Grahame
Al Willis ....Gene Barry
Helen Willis ....Marcia Henderson
Det. Lt. Parks.........Casey Adams
Petey ....Billy Chapin
Capt. Owen Kincaide....Chuck Connors
Matt Matthews..........Don Haggerty
Chief A. S. Babcock....Stuart Randall
Tony ....Don Garrett
Felix ....Richard Beach
Irish ....Tol Avery
Gerald Frazier ....Paul Leavitt
F. J. O'Day............Fay Roope
Otto Stoltz ....Joseph Mell
(Aspect ratio: 1.85-1)

Rough and ready melodramatics, plus some lowgrade sex, are wrapped up in this highly-improbable film titled "Naked Alibi." Names heading the cast are familiar and b.o. prospects appear about average overall, since some situations in the general market can take advantage of the more obvious exploitation angles to rate it a fast play at their wickets.

Production guidance by Ross Hunter is slack in most all departments. Stronger supervision could have corrected the lack of logical plotting and given the film's physical appearance a more realistic look. Results would have been a better show because the performances, while to type, are satisfactory and the Jerry Hopper direction whips up a fairly good action pace. Lawrence Roman scripted from an original story by J. Robert Bren and Gladys Atwater.

The chase plot sees Sterling Hayden, a discharged chief of detectives, setting out to prove he was right in accusing Gene Barry of cop-killing. Barry's a psycho, but ostensibly a law-abiding small businessman. To get away from Hayden's hounding, he leaves town and heads for a border city and his girl friend, Gloria Grahame, a cheap saloon singer. It's no trouble for Hayden to follow, gain the con-

fidence of Miss Grahame, seize the killer and take him back home. He even lets Barry escape so the murder weapon will be turned up and things wind up with a rooftop chase in which Miss Grahame is killed and Barry falls to his death.

Hayden makes a good policeman and Barry's psycho killer also comes over. Miss Grahame makes as much as possible of the blatant sex so obviously spotted in her character and sings the oldie, "The Ace In the Hole," for one saloon scene. Marcia Henderson, as Barry's wife, rates scant footage. Others are okay in living up to the light demands of their assignments.

Russell Metty's lensing, art direction and other technical credits function adequately. The music supervision by Joseph Gershenson makes the background score a noisy competitor of the action. *Brog.*

White Christmas
(MUSICAL-COLOR)

First VistaVision feature with Bing Crosby and Danny Kaye; Irving Berlin score slanting for top b.o.

Hollywood, Aug. 27.
Paramount release of Robert Emmett Dolan production. Stars Bing Crosby, Danny Kaye, Rosemary Clooney, Vera Ellen; features Dean Jagger. Directed by Michael Curtiz. Screenplay, Norman Krasna, Norman Panama, Melvin Frank; songs, Irving Berlin; camera (Technicolor), Loyal Griggs; editor, Frank Bracht; music direction and vocal arrangements, Joseph J. Lilley; music associate, Troy Sanders; arrangements, Van Cleave; dances by Robert Alton. Previewed Aug. 23, '54. Running time, **120 MINS.**
Bob Wallace ....Bing Crosby
Phil Davis ....Danny Kaye
Betty ....Rosemary Clooney
Judy ....Vera Ellen
General Waverly ....Dean Jagger
Emma ....Mary Wickes
Joe ....John Brascia
Susan ....Anne Whitfield
(Aspect ratio: 1.85-1)

"White Christmas" should be a natural at the boxoffice, introducing as it does Paramount's new VistaVision system with such a hot combination as Bing Crosby, Danny Kaye and an Irving Berlin score. The debut of the new photographic process is a plus factor complementing the already solidly established draw of Crosby and Kaye.

The widescreen process has an impressive vastness, with color clarity and sharp definition that add greatly to the visual quality of a production. VV's impact, while giving a full-stage effect to this musical, should be even greater when applied to outdoor and action-drama stories. An important value is the consistent picture quality in the various projection ratios (Paramount recommends 1.85), from the standard 1.33 up to 2 to 1. The quality carries over into 2.55-1 when the VV negative is printed anamorphically for that aspect ratio projection.

The above qualities were not displayed to their fullest on the answer print used at the preview, but have been decidedly evident in demonstration showings staged previously by Paramount.

Crosby and Kaye, along with VV, keep the entertainment going in this fancifully staged Robert Emmett Dolan production, clicking so well the teaming should call for a repeat. Both Crosby and Kaye are long in the talent department and provide a lift and importance to the material scripted by Norman Krasna, Norman Panama and Melvin Frank.

The directorial handling by Michael Curtiz gives a smooth blend of music (13 numbers plus snatches of others) and drama, and in the climax creates a genuine heart tug that will squeeze tears. The standout song presentation, beautifully socked by Rosemary Clooney, is "Love, You Didn't Do Right By Me." The top song-dance number is "The Best Things Happen While You're Dancing," strikingly terped by Kaye and Vera Ellen.

"Choreography" scores through Kaye's impression of modern ballet, with Miss Ellen and John Brascia providing the jazzier counterpoint to his hilarious posturing. The full Crosby flavor is heard on "What Can You Do With a General?" and "Count Your Blessings," latter reprised by Miss Clooney. Also listening favorably are "The Old Man," an ensemble number, and the colorfully amusing "Minstrel Show Routine," including

Berlin's oldie, "Mandy," with Crosby, Kaye, the Misses Clooney and Vera Ellen and ensemble doing the musical funning. As for "White Christmas," the Berlin hit Crosby introduced in "Holiday Inn" in 1942—it's still a top hit.

On a lesser level are "Sisters," tune introducing the sister act of the two femme stars, and "Snow." Both wear a bit, although the first has a very funny reprise by the Crosby-Kaye team. "Gee, I Wish I Was Back In the Army" and "Santa Claus Routine" are other new Berlin cleffings. "Blue Skies" and "Abraham" are among some of the oldies.

The plot holding the entire affair together has Crosby and Kaye, two Army buddies, joining forces after the war and becoming a big musical team. They get together with the girls and trek to Vermont for a white Christmas. The inn at which they stay is run by Dean Jagger, their old general, and the boys put on a show to pull him out of a financial hole, at the same time finding love with the girls.

Crosby wraps up his portion of the show with deceptive ease, selling the songs with the Crosby sock, shuffling a mean hoof in the dances and generally acquitting himself like a champion. Certainly he has never had a more facile partner than Kaye against whom to bounce his misleading nonchalance. Kaye takes in stride the dance, song and comedy demands of his assignment, keeping Crosby on his toes at all times proving himself an ace entertainer of virtually unlimited talent. Miss Clooney does quite well by the story portions and scores on her song chores, while Vera Ellen is a pert terper who can also handle her lines well.

Supporting roles are few. The chief featured part is in the able hands of Jagger and his finale scene, in which he reacts like a tough general with a heart to the turnout of his old division, is fine trouping. Mary Wickes, the inn's housekeeper, gets some chuckles. Brascia figures importantly in making the production numbers come over so well. Anne Whitfield, several unbilled chorines and others do their share.

Topnotch behind-the-cameras contributions provide the show with a lavish gloss. Among them are Loyal Griggs' Technicolor photography; the dance and musical numbers staged by Robert Alton; Joseph J. Lilley's musical direction and vocal arrangements; the art direction by Hal Pereira and Roland Anderson; Edith Head's costuming, the recording and other technical aids. *Brog.*

Rogue Cop

Melodrama about a crooked cop and gang killings, with Robert Taylor, Janet Leigh; average prospects.

Hollywood, Aug. 31.

Metro release of Nicholas Nayfack production. Stars Robert Taylor, Janet Leigh, George Raft, Steve Forrest, Anne Francis; features Robert Ellenstein, Robert F. Simon, Anthony Ross, Alan Hale Jr. Directed by Roy Rowland. Screenplay, Sydney Boehm; based on novel by William P. McGivern; camera, John Seitz; editor, James E. Newcom; music, Jeff Alexander. Previewed Aug. 25, '54. Running time, **91 MINS.**

Christopher Kelvaney ..... Robert Taylor
Garen Stephanson .... Janet Leigh
Dan Beaumonte .... George Raft
Eddie Kelvaney .... Steve Forrest
Nancy Corlane .... Anne Francis
Sidney Y. Myers .... Robert Ellenstein
Ackerman .... Robert F. Simon
Father Ahearn .... Anthony Ross
Johnny Stark .... Alan Hale Jr.
Wrinkles Fallon .... Peter Brocco
Langley .... Vince Edwards
Selma .... Olive Carey
Lt. Vince D. Bardeman ... Roy Barcroft
Manny .... Dale Van Sickel
Patrolman Mullins .... Ray Teal

(Aspect ratio: 1.75-1)

The rough melodramatics in this story of a crooked cop are brought with fair results to the action fan. And because the names are good, topped by Robert Taylor, average prospects are probable generally. Picture is one of several in the current cops-'n'-robbers cycle, suggesting possibilities for those situations that like to give action audiences a double-barrelled crime bill, with this Metro entry as the uppercase booking.

The Nicholas Nayfack production gets off to a logically plotted start but doesn't remain believable for very long. Stronger supervision would have helped to hold things together better. Compensating are good performances and a rugged action pace that is stirred up by Roy Rowland's direction. Guidance makes the most of a number of violent fight sequences and the customers of this type drama will like them best. Sydney Boehm scripted from the novel by William P. McGivern.

Taylor is the rogue cop of the title, playing it with a suave toughness that fits a policeman on the take from the vested gang interests ruled over by George Raft. Footage opens with a knifing and Steve Forrest, Taylor's rookie brother, spots the killer. The big interests get into the act to force the case to be dropped. It seems the killer has something on Raft. When Taylor fails to bring Forrest into line by using money and his girl friend, Janet Leigh, the gang kills the young policeman, an act that makes a vengeful man out of the bad cop and the windup features a guns-blazing climax as Taylor fights it out with the baddies and turns state's witness to unveil the workings of the syndicate.

The satisfactory performance by all concerned almost bring the show off, and had the scripting been more logical and moral values would have had more point. Miss Leigh, a bad girl going straight, and Anne Francis, Raft's moll who is brutally used and then killed, are the principal femmes mixed up in the melodramatics. Olive Carey spots a slick delineation of a a newsie who stools for Taylor. Robert Ellenstein, a good policeman; Anthony Ross, a priest; Robert F. Simon and Alan Hale Jr., associates of Raft, and Peter Brocco, the killer in the opening sequence, come off okay.

John Seitz' lensing is lowkeyed to the melodramatics and the other credits show up acceptably. *Brog.*

Private Hell 36

Fits well into current crooked cop cycle for okay program returns.

Hollywood, Aug. 30.

Filmakers release of Collier Young production. Stars Ida Lupino, Steve Cochran, Howard Duff, Dean Jagger, Dorothy Malone. Directed by Don Siegel. Screenplay, Miss Lupino, Young; camera, Burnett Guffey; editor, Stanford Tischler; music, Leith Stevens; song, "Didn't You Know," by John Franco. Previewed Aug. 30, '54. Running time, **81 MINS.**

Lilli Marlowe .... Ida Lupino
Cal Bruner .... Steve Cochran
Jack Farnham .... Howard Duff
Captain Michaels .... Dean Jagger
Francey Farnham .... Dorothy Malone

(Aspect ratio: 1.85-1)

Current cycle of crooked cop yarns gets a good entry in "Private Hell 35," which should rack up satisfactory grosses in the program market. Film is occasionally slow-paced but the Collier Young production generally gets payoff values slugged over for okay effect by Don Siegel in his direction. Names of star lineup should boost film's chances.

Young and Ida Lupino, one of the costars, coauthored script for production and release by their own company, Filmakers. Excellent use is made of Los Angeles and Hollywood park exteriors for story purposes and film gets off to a sock start, a $300,000 N.Y. holdup-murder which picks up a year later in L.A. when a hot $50 bill turns up.

Steve Cochran and Howard Duff, detectives, are assigned the case after the note is found. First half of narrative follows their search for the man who passed it, and the second half covers the pair's reactions after Cochran has taken $80,000 in bills off the man killed in an auto chase. Cochran counts the unwilling Duff in for a 50-50 cut. They are aided in their search by Miss Lupino, a nitery singer, to whom the bill was traced after she had received it as a tip. Windup shows Duff insisting they turn the money over to the police, Cochran shooting him when they get the coin from a cache and himself being killed by his superior officer, Dean Jagger, who has been suspected of taking part of the loot.

Both Cochran and Duff turn in suitable performances and Miss Lupino is properly brassy in her entertainer role, romanced by Cochran. Dorothy Malone is okay as Duff's wife and Jagger is impressive as the detective captain.

Technical departments are well executed. Burnett Guffey's photography in particular is effective. Leith Stevens' musical score catches the proper mood. *Whit.*

A Bullet Is Waiting
(COLOR)

Slow-moving, talky piece with Jean Simmons, Rory Calhoun; needs hard selling for fair returns.

Hollywood, Aug. 16.

Columbia release of Howard Welsch production. Stars Jean Simmons, Rory Calhoun, Stephen McNally, Brian Aherne. Directed by John Farrow. Screenplay, Thames Williamson, Casey Robinson; story, Williamson; camera (Technicolor), Frank F. Planer; music, Dimitri Tiomkin; editor, Otto Ludwig. Previewed Aug. 12, '54. Running time, **83 MINS.**

Cally Canham .... Jean Simmons
Ed Stone .... Rory Calhoun
Sheriff Munson .... Stephen McNally
David Canham .... Brian Aherne

(Aspect ratio: 1.85-1)

This Columbia release, though boasting excellent color photography and a competent cast, is a slow-moving, talkative yarn which never attains realism. Returns will depend entirely upon the b.o. draw of its principals.

Film's unusually small cast of four—the fourth appearing only in the final reel or so—make their pitch in and around an isolated sheepranch cabin on the California coast. Parts are undertaken by Jean Simmons, Rory Calhoun, Stephen McNally and Brian Aherne, but even with such able performers John Farrow isn't able to direct them past the hurdles of story and script.

Plot revolves around a vindictive sheriff, McNally, and his prisoner, Calhoun, crashing their plane enroute back to Utah—where latter is to face a manslaughter rap—and forced to hole up in the cabin belonging to Miss Simmons and her English professor-father, Aherne, until the storms which make travel impossible subside. Femme is alone, father being absent for several days, and when the sheriff sees she is warming up to Calhoun he warns her not to interfere with his efforts to return his prisoner to justice.

Most of the footage concerns this conflict, presented mostly in drawn-out passages of unconvincing dialog, the femme certain that Calhoun isn't a killer at heart and McNally taking the opposite view. When the father finally returns, the four after a good deal of further talk bundle into Aherne's jeep and set out for Utah, where Calhoun presumably will get the fair trial he previously believed impossible.

Principals try hard but the over-accented parts are against them straight through and none fares well. Dimitri Tiomkin composed the score of the Howard Welsch production. *Whit*

Shield for Murder

Melodrama of a cop turned killer; for programmer bookings.

Hollywood, Aug. 30.

United Artists release of Schenck-Koch (Aubrey Schenck) production. Stars Edmond O'Brien, John Agar, Marla English; features David Hughes, Emile Meyer, Carolyn Jones. Directed by O'Brien, Howard W. Koch. Screenplay, Richard Alan Simmons and John C. Higgins; adapted by Simmons from book by William P. McGivern; camera, Gordon Avil; editor, John F. Schreyer; music, Paul Dunlap. Previewed Aug. 26, '54. Running time, **81 MINS.**

Barney Nolan .... Edmond O'Brien
Mark Brewster .... John Agar
Patty Winters .... Marla English
Ernest Sternmueller ...... David Hughes
Capt. Gunnarson .... Emile Meyer
Girl at Bar .... Carolyn Jones
Fat Michaels .... Claude Akins
Laddie O'Neil .... Larry Ryle
Cabot .... Herbert Butterfield
Packy Reed .... Hugh Sanders
Assistant D.A. .... William Schallert

(Aspect ratio: 1.75-1)

The programmer market will find "Shield for Murder" a passable thriller in the current crime melodrama cycle.

Plot of the Schenck-Koch production for United Artists release is another of those William P. McGivern tales about a cop gone bad. It has been adequately scripted by Richard Alan Simmons, who also adapted from the book, and John C. Higgins to fit the demands of the less discriminating market, but the direction by Edmond O'Brien, who stars as the bad cop, and Howard W. Koch is rather slowly paced for the action fans.

O'Brien, a detective, kills a bookmaker and lifts a $25,000 roll he is carrying as the story opens. Killing goes into the books as a homicide in the line of duty, even though the gambling syndicate spreads some dirty rumors. The murder has been witnessed by a deafmute and, when O'Brien learns this, he commits a second killing. John Agar, a young detective trained by O'Brien, gets wise and after a wild and wooly chase that has the bad cop dodging both the law and the syndicate's hatchetmen, the killer is trapped and shot down at the model home where he had hidden his loot.

Performances are to type, adequate to the melodramatics but never giving anything extra to the show. Costarring with O'Brien and

Agar is Marla English, on loan from Paramount. Her chief asset to the picture will be lobby art from her role of the cigaret girl with whom O'Brien is in love. David Hughes, the deafmute; Emile Meyer, detective captain, and Carolyn Jones, a B-girl, are among some of the others more prominently spotted in the plot.

Gordon Avil gives the presentation lowkey photography to fit with the mood of the piece and the other technical credits are average.
Brog.

Tobor the Great

Machinations of a robot in so-so science-fiction piece for average supporting fare.

Republic release of Dudley Pictures (Richard Goldstone) production. Stars Charles Drake, Karin Booth; features Taylor Holmes, Billy Chapin, Steven Geray. Directed by Lee Sholem. Screenplay, Philip MacDonald; from story by Carl Dudley; camera, John L. Russell Jr.; editor, Basil Wrangell; music, Howard Jackson. Previewed in N.Y. Aug. 26, '54. Running time, **77 MINS.**

Harrison	Charles Drake
Janice	Karin Booth
Gadge	Billy Chapin
Dr. Nordstrom	Taylor Holmes
Man with Glasses	Steven Geray
Paul	Henry Kulky
Karl	Franz Roehn
Max	Hal Baylor
Gilligan	Alan Reynolds
Dr. Gustav	Peter Brocco
Commissioner	Norman Field
First General	Robert Shayne
Admiral	Lyle Talbot
First Congressman	Emmett Vogan
Johnston	William Schallert
Secretary	Helen Winston

This melodrama is awkwardly clothed in pseudo-scientific trappings. "Tobor (robot, spelled backwards) the Great" overlooks its original but brief scientific theme for some cops-and-robbers hokum, in a talky story with stock acting that rates as supporting fare.

After a meaningless semi-documentary intro about the atom bomb and interplanetary travel, there comes this hunk of mental metal (Tobor) with extra-sensory perception. Designed to do mankind's experimental dirtywork, Tobor ends up instead building a dog-like devotion to his creator and the latter's grandson and family wipes out a band of mean but dull spies. In the interim, he threatens to become a Frankenstein because Drs. Nordstrom and Harrison (Taylor Holmes and Charles Drake) get a few wires crossed.

Billy Chapin, as the Nordstrom grandson, does his share to befuddle and later exonerate the metallic mastermind. There's thin love interest between Janice (Karin Booth) and the younger scientist, Harrison, but hand-holding is kept at minimum while playing time is mostly split between Tobor's gyrations and leering of the cloak-and-dagger team headed by the mystery man (Steven Geray).

Direction by Lee Sholem is static while camera work by John L. Russell, in some of the angle-shots particularly, is the most upbeat item in the pic.
Art.

The Golden Link
(BRITISH)

Neatly contrived whodunit with sufficient suspense to hold interest; lack of international names will relegate to lower bracket.

London, Aug. 24.

Archway Film Distributors release of Parkside-Guido Coen production. Stars Andre Morell; features Thea Gregory, Patrick Holt, Jack Watling, Marla Landi. Directed by Charles Saunders. Screenplay, Allan Mackinnon; camera, Harry Waxman; editor, Jack Slade; music, Eric Spear. At Marble Arch Pavilion, London. Running time, **83 MINS.**

Superintendent Blake	Andre Morrell
Joan Blake	Thea Gregory
Terry Maguire	Patrick Holt
Bill Howard	Jack Watling
Det. Inspector Harris	Arnold Bell
Mrs. Pullman	Olive Sloane
Sergeant Baker	Bruce Beeby
Arnold Debenham	Alexander Gauge
Norma Sheridan	Dorinda Stevens
Mrs. West	Elsie Wagstaff
Major Grey	Edward Lexy
Marla	Marla Landi

A well-knit thriller with good scripting and camerawork makes this a workmanlike mystery story providing good entertainment values. Theme is well and plausibly developed without sensationalism; it should make a good dualer on most programs.

When a girl's body crashes down from a top floor apartment into the main hallway, the obvious answer is that it's a suicide. She is a penniless out-of-work actress estranged from her husband, who lives in the building. One of the tenants, a police superintendent, takes a different view and the husband, despite a sound alibi, is suspected of murder. Although not officially in charge of the case, this police official uncovers unpleasant facts, most damning of which is that his daughter is in love with the suspect. The suspect's wife had refused a divorce, and ensuing clues point to the daughter as having equal motive and opportunity for committing the crime. She follows her lover to a secluded houseboat, unaware of planted evidence against herself, and an anonymous telephone call that notifies the police of their hideout. The tracking down of this informant unmasks the killer, a pleasant young neighbor involved with the dead actress.

Andre Morell is excellent as the harassed father torn between paternal love and sense of duty. Thea Gregory registers more faintly as his daughter while Patrick Holt does well in the rather thankless role of the suspected husband. Jack Watling provides an even more shadowy characterization as the killer. Arnold Bell vies with Andre Morell in realism as the investigating inspector. Helen Pollock contributes a correctly overacted cameo as a phoney seeress. Olive Sloane provides another gem as a roominghouse-keeper. The direction by Charles Saunders gives full value to the highlights and never strains at credulity.
Clem.

The Young Lovers
(BRITISH)

Sensitive romantic drama of young lovers caught up in the east-west conflict. Delicately directed and acted. Worthy of exhibition in the U. S.

London, Aug. 24.

General Film Distributors release of Anthony Havelock-Allan Production. Stars Odile Versois and David Knight; features Joseph Tomelty and David Kossoff. Directed by Anthony Asquith. Screenplay, George Tabori and Robin Estridge; camera, Jack Asher; editor, Frederick Wilson. At Odeon, Leicester Square, London, Aug. 24, '54. Running time, **95 MINS.**

Anna	Odile Versois
Ted	David Knight
Moffatt	Joseph Tomelty
Gregg	Paul Carpenter
Joseph	Theodore Bikel
Judy	Jill Adams
Szobek	David Kossoff
Margetson	John McClaren
Mrs. Forrester	Betty Marsden
Dr. Weissbrod	Peter Illing
Regan	Peter Dyneley
Stefan	Bernard Rebel

The political conflict between east and west is brought home poignantly in this moving, sensitive romantic drama, directed with a sympathetic hand by Anthony Asquith and delicately interpreted by Odile Versois and newcomer David Knight. A sturdy b.o. proposition, with strong exploitation possibilities which may make it a profitable entry in the U. S. market.

It is a development of the elementary boy meets girl theme. In this case, however, the boy works in the code room of the American Embassy in London; the girl is the daughter of and secretary to the minister of an Iron Curtain legation. The girl finds she's being followed; the boy's telephone messages are intercepted. Both the Embassy and the Legation fear that confidential information is getting into the hands of the wrong people, so the girl is ordered home after she's told her father she's expecting a baby and the boy is placed under arrest pending removal to Washington. In the end, they both make a successful bid for freedom.

The script adroitly emphasizes the dilemna of the young couple by explaining they come from separate worlds, and there is no third place to go. From the Embassy point of view, any man is a suspect if he keeps questionable company, while the girl is accused of betraying her country and the revolution. The plot unfolds tenderly by pinpointing the emotions of the young lovers without indulging in unnecessary politics, using rare touches of humor to relieve a tense situation with great skill.

Under Asquith's polished direction, the two leading players bring a genuine freshness to their roles, and give point to the arty touches used by the megger to bring home the sensitive side of the story.

Odile Versois and David Knight dominate the screen and elevate the plot. Joseph Tometly, David Kossoff, Paul Carpenter and Theodore Bikel play the leading support roles, each contributing a measure of sincerity and conviction. Jack Asher's camerawork is excellent. Frederick Wilson has edited with a sure touch.
Myro.

Garden of Eden
(COLOR)

Exploitation drama filmed in Florida nudist camp. Good prospects for ballyhoo b.o. in special bookings. •

Hollywood, Aug. 31.

Excelsior Pictures release of Walter Bibo production. Features Mickey Knox, Jamie O'Hara, Karen Sue Trent, R. G. Armstrong. Directed by Max Nosseck. Original screenplay by Nat Tanchuck and Nosseck; camera (Tri-Art Color), Boris Kaufman; editor, Paul Falkenberg; music, Robert McBride. Previewed Aug. 24, '54. Running time, **70 MINS.**

John Patterson	Mickey Knox
Susan Lattimore	Jamie O'Hara
Jean Lattimore	Karen Sue Trent
Jay Lattimore	R. G. Armstrong

With

Jane Rose, Paula Morris, Stephen Gray, Arch W. Johnson, Norval E. Packwood, Jane Sterling, John Royal.

A sincere, rather than sensational effort to present the case for nudism is made in "Garden of Eden." On that score, it comes off okay, since it bears the stamp of approval of the American Sunbathing Assn. As a feature release, it is obvious that it falls in the exploitation class and should capture a goodly share of the ballyhoo b.o. in the situations that book that type of subject.

Walter Bibo produced for Excelsior Pictures Corp., and uncovers the subject of nudism through the medium of a stock drama that permits the principal action to take place at the Lake Como Club in Florida. There's no particular skill shown in the direction by Max Nosseck, nor in the original script he wrote with Nat Tanchuck, although, by developing a respectable sense of humor in some portions and an okay idyllic feel in other spots, the offering gets by sufficiently. Only the most persnicketty of viewers will be offended. Most will know what they are buying and won't be looking for quality entertainment.

With few exceptions, the performers (sic) on view must be sincere healthseekers, not exhibitionists, because they have nothing to show off. Jamie O'Hara, from tv, is one of the exceptions. However, she's the heroine of the plot and viewers will have to be content with a comparatively brief unclothing in a dream sequence. Closeups throughout are from the waist up, and the medium and long shots concentrate mostly on displaying some amusingly weird posterior forms.

Plot line has Miss O'Hara, young widow, leaving the home of her gruff, business tycoon father-in-law, R. G. Armstrong. Enroute to Miami for a job, her car stalls near a nudist camp and she's rescued from difficulties by Mickey Knox, a working sunbather. Humor gets into the act when Armstrong follows and gradually becomes converted to the bare facts of the camp and turns stripper himself. Miss O'Hara looks good and Knox handles himself capably. Little Karen Sue Trent is an endearing moppet. The others seem amateurish.

Boris Kaufman (lenser of Columbia's "On the Waterfront") handles the cameras here and gets good effects with the Eastman color, printed by Tri-Art Color Corp. The Robert McBride score includes a theme song, "Let's Go Sunning," which keys the idea of the budget production.
Brog.

Le Grand Pavois
(The Big Flag)
(FRENCH)

París, Aug. 17.

Discifilm release of Discona production. Features Jean Chevrier, Marie Mansart, Marc Cassot. Directed by Jack Pinateau. Screenplay, Jean Raynaud, adapted by Pinateau, Roger Vercel; camera, Roger Arrignon; editor, Andre Gaudier. Previewed in Paris. Running time, **90 mins.**

Favrel	Jean Chevrier
Hardouin	Marc Cassot
Simone	Marie Mansart
Madeleine	Nicole Courcel
Cheruel	Raphael Patourni
Derval	Francois Patrice

"The Big Flag" is a naval flag which is used during big maneuvers of for outstanding feats. This film does plenty of flagwaving and emerges as sort of a recruiting production without enough story, atmosphere or characterization to make this of interest for any U. S. spots. For local appeal, it has a certain amount of popular draw due to its nationalistic appeal. It already has proved its appeal by copping many awards at the recent Vichy Public Film Referendum.

This concerns a navy career man who is compromised by his wife's desire to have him quit. He decides to resign after a training cruise, and creates disillusionment in a young midshipman who is also in love with his niece. This leads to the few complications of the pic. It all is wrapped up when the young man acquits himself as a hero while the career man gets reprieves from his wife.

Director Jack Pinateau has not been able to get original pacing into this while the familiar, banal shennanigans of the crew are much too dated for many spots over the world. Jean Chevrier is properly stern and commanding as the career man. Marc Cassot does all that is possible with a badly motivated role. The women are mere land silhouettes in this floating drama. Miniature used in a storm sequence is one of the best seen in a Gallic film in some time. Lensing and editing are good. *Mosk.*

Die Kleine Stadt Will Schlafen Gehn
(Little Town Will Go to Sleep)
(GERMAN)

Berlin, Aug. 24.

Prisma release of Koenig production. Stars Gustav Froehlich and Jester Naefe. Directed by Hans H. Koenig. Screenplay, Hans H. Koenig; camera, Kurt Hasse; music, Werner Bochmann. At Hill, Berlin. Running time, **90 MINS.**

Peter Bruck .... Gustav Froehlich
Ingrid Altmann .... Jester Naefe
Fraeulein Lissy .... Helen Vita
Friedrich Altmann ...... Herbert Huebner
Oskar Blume .... Gerd Froebe
Fritz Waldvogel .... Harald Paulsen
Manfred Schmidt ...... Hermann Pfeiffer
Burgermeister .... Alexander Golling
Charlotte Altmann .... Gerda Maurus
Fraeulein Von Dobereck, Ingeborg Moravski
Rita Heinrich .... Margit Symo

This German comedy refreshingly distinguishes itself from some recent ones. It has a basically good story, offers plenty of humor, a nice cast and enough tongue-in-cheek to please more fastidious patrons. Although international chances appear dubious, pic may appeal to some U. S. patronage.

In a small German town, a mail bag has disappeared (robbers took it by mistake for another bag). Seven reputable citizens feel quite embarrassed about the bag's disappearance, fearing a real scandal as some unauthorized person might read their "confidential" letters. Suspicion is cast upon the town's sculptor, who has actually nothing to do with the robbery. However, he deliberately stirs this suspicion—and this angle provides a number of complications.

Hans H. Koenig, not so well known among local directors, did a creditable job on this production and also wrote the well-balanced script. He wisely added some satirical touches and generally keeps the pic moving nicely.

Old-timer Gustav Froehlich gives a neat performance as the sculptor but is overshadowed by some wonderful supporting players, such as the late Harald Paulsen, a lawyer with bribing intentions; Herbert Huebner, as a respectable official with an unsavory romance; and Bobby Todd, a philosopher collecting photos of nudes. Jester Naefe, absent from the German screen for two years, provides the romantic interest, but does not do too well.

This low-budget film has a nice musical score by Werner Bochman who also wrote the title song. Technical contributions ably back the entertainment. Kurt Hasse's lensing is often very good. *Horn.*

Die Sonne Von St. Moritz
(The Sun of St. Moritz)
(GERMAN)

Berlin, Aug. 17.

NF relase of Berna production. Stars Signe Hasso, Winnie Markus and Karlheinz Boehm. Directed by Arthur Maria Rabenalt. Screenplay by Curt J. Braun, based on novel by P.O. Hoecker; camera, Ernst W. Kalinke; music, Bert Grund. At Delphi Palast, Berlin. Running time, 91 mins.

Dr. Robert Frank ...... Karlheinz Boehm
Gertie Selle .... Signe Hasso
Lore Engelhofer .... Winnie Markus
Yvonne Beerli .... Ingrid Pan
Paul Genzmer .... Claus Biederstaedt
Dr. Mayr .... Erik Frey
Herr Thuregg .... Heinrich Gretler

Another variation on the eternal triangle (one man and two women) is used in this German film. To give it international exploitation values, pic stars Swedish actress Signe Hasso and has mainly been shot against the Swiss Alps. Pic has the ingredients to lure the average local patron, but because of some flaws this does not look likely to appeal to U. S. patrons.

A young doctor falls in love with the wife of a dangerously ill man. Latter dies of an overdose of medicine deliberately given him by his wife. Her lover deserts his duty as a doctor and doesn't report this to authorities, but leaves her. Later, she attempts to win him back (he has meanwhile fallen for another woman) trying some blackmail. Although the dangerous woman gets killed in a bobsled accident, his doctor's conscience urges him to go to the police with his second femme sweetheart willing to wait for him.

Unfortunately, the basically interesting story has not been exploited to advantage. The storytelling lacks plausibility, too often bordering on the banal. Arthur Maria Rabenalt's direction is not very imaginative, but obviously he was handicapped by the material. Acting is varied. The most polished performance is given by Miss Hasso as the dangerous woman. Karlheinz Boehm, usually a good actor, is not more than a sympathetic doctor in this. Others, with the exception of Claus Biederstaedt, turn in more or less mechanical performances.

Technically, the film has the standards of an average German production. Some fine camera shots of the Swiss Alps are standout. *Hans.*

Bride With a Dowry
(Musical-Color)
(RUSSIAN)

Artkino release of Mosfilm production. Stars Vera Vasilieva, Vladimir Ushakov. Directed by T. Lukashevich, B. Ravenskikh. Camera, (Sovcolor), N. Vlassov, S. Shenin; music, N. Budashkin, B. Mokrousov. At Stanley, N.Y., Aug. 20, '54. Running time **105 MINS.**

Olga .... Vera Vashilieva
Maxim .... Vladimir Ushakov
Avdei Spiridonovich .... V. Dorofeyev
Vasilisa Pavlovna .... L. Kumicheva
Lyba .... G. Kozhakina
Galya .... K. Kanayeva
Muravlev .... D. Dubov
Semyon Ivanovich .... G. Ivanov
Silanti Romanovich .... A. Pribylovsky
Lukeria .... T. Peltzer
Nikolai Kurochkin, V. Doronin, of the Maly Theatre

(In Russian; English Titles)

"Bride With a Dowry" is a Russian-made musical, done in Sovcolor, with some excellent tunes as the picture's most redeeming feature. In many respects, "Bride," is the current Soviet idea of how "Oklahoma" should be done. Despite its musical comedy technique and often stagy atmosphere, this looks suitable for Russian-language houses. Because so tediously developed plus a collective-farm setup worked into the plot, it naturally won't find much favor in most other U. S. theatres.

After wasting about two reels to spot the so-called comedian and foil into the plot, yarn finally reveals Vera Vasilieva (Olga) and Vladimir Ushakov (Maxim) as sweethearts who want to get married. She is sort of sub-lieutenant on one collective farm while he is straw boss of a rival one. At their betrothal party, she walks out in a huff because her groom-to-be criticizes her farming methods.

Seeking advice from a government farm bureau expert, Vladimir mistakes a friendly clinch as faithlessness by Vera. That and a threat of frost to the barley crop keeps the vehicle moving for an additional hour or more. It is only by accident that this misunderstanding is adjusted, but before this transpires there are the usual musical comedy song interludes, ensembles and group chorusing. With a real plot and less yammering about collective farms, this really could have amounted to something. Because the music by N. Budashkin and B. Mokrousov for the most part is tuneful, a couple of the numbers have real lilt.

Miss Vasilieva, who carries most of the plot burden, not only is one of the comeliest actresses in Russian pictures but also one of their better thespians. Ushakov, who plays opposite as her sweetheart, shapes as a comer, having he-man qualities and signs of acting ability. Both try their hands at singing, but for Miss Vasilieva, another person's vocalizing appears to have been dubbed in—and not too well.

Supporting cast, all creditable, is headed by G. Kozhakina, V. Dorofeyev, L. Kuzmicheva, K. Kanayeva and D. Dubov. Nikolai Kurochkin and V. Doronin are in for specialties.

N. Vlassov and S. Shenin contribute sterling work with their cameras whenever given an opportunity. Many of their traveling shots are excellent. But neither has quence, which is confined strictly to the limits of a single, modestly-furnished room. Direction of T. Lukashevich and B. Ravenskikh too often follows the stage musical comedy technique with few touches of originality.

The Sovcolor still does not impress although more even in hues than in previous efforts. The trouble is that the reds are not reds, the browns not browns and even one sunrise scene is so unrealistic that it looks staged. However, Sovcolor now has reached the stage where it compares favorably with some recent efforts by American companies, which still are far from perfect. *Wear.*

Romeo and Juliet
(BRITISH-COLOR)

Fine production of Shakespeare's classic. Despite lack of star names, this prestige picture for the industry should qualify for extended runs.

London, Sept. 3.

General Film Distributors release of Sandro Ghenzi (in association with Joseph Janni) production. Stars Laurence Harvey, Susan Shentall, Flora Robson, Norman Wooland, Mervyn Johns; features Bill Travers, Sebastian Cabot, Lydia Sherwood. Directed and adapted by Renato Castellani; camera (Technicolor), Robert Krasker; editor, Sydney Hayers; music, Roman Vlad; costumes, Leonor Fini. At Odeon, Leicester Square, London, Sept. 1, '54. Running time, **138 MINS.**

Romeo .... Laurence Harvey
Juliet .... Susan Shentall
Nurse .... Flora Robson
Friar Laurence .... Mervyn Johns
Benvolio .... Bill Travers
Tybalt .... Enzo Fiermonte
Mercutio .... Aldo Zollo
Prince of Verone .... Giovanni Rota
Capulet .... Sebastian Cabot
Lady Capulet .... Lydia Sherwood
Paris .... Norman Wooland
Montague .... Guilio Carbenetti
Lady Montague .... Nietta Zocchi
Rosaline .... Dagmar Josipovich
Abraham .... Luciano Bodi
Friar John .... Thomas Nicholls

With this superlative production of Shakespeare's classic romantic-tragedy, the Rank studios have made a motion picture which will bring prestige to the entire industry and earn new laurels for British film-makers. The postwar "Henry V" and "Hamlet" and, more recently, the Hollywood production of "Julius Caesar" have shown that Shakespeare on the screen is boxoffice. "Romeo and Juliet" should be no exception, but needs roadshow presentation instead of the more conventional and rigid general release pattern that prevails in Britain.

It is 18 years since Metro made its version of the same play with Leslie Howard and Norma Shearer in the title roles, but this production hopes to achieve comparable fame without the use of such lustrous boxoffice names as starred in the original Irving Thalberg production. Neither Laurence Harvey nor Susan Shentall have anything like the b.o. lure of the Shearer-Howard combination, but their performances are models of integrity and in the true classical tradition.

Renato Castellani, who directed his own adaptation, has done a connoisseur's job of compression and although the complete film runs for 138 minutes it is wholly absorbing, frequently moving and always of combined treat for eye and ear. The backgrounds, filmed on location in Italy, are enhanced by the excellent use of Technicolor. The settings have a natural splendor and the costuming reaches the best standards of period design. Technically this is an almost flawless production; the action, romance and tragedy are blended with a master's touch. And the poetry of the writing, rich in its epigrammatic quality, is given a standout appeal by the all-British cast.

The balcony scene, the classic of all love passages, is played by the principals with tenderness and sensitivity. It is a rich emotional experience, never overplayed and handled with delicate restraint. This scene is a special triumph for Miss Shentall, who made her screen debut with this assignment and has already forsaken the screen for marriage. There is no visible evidence of her lack of experience; on the contrary, her youth and freshness make her interpretation of the 14-year-old heroine all the more credible. The touch of naivite that occasionally creeps across her performance might well be a subtle way of adding a little extra conviction.

Laurence Harvey, with a Shakespearean season in Stratford-on-Avon to his credit, is at all times a sure, fine performer. His diction is perfect, his bearing excellent and he plays with sincerity. The other players are dwarfed by the immensity of the two title roles, but the performances are all of matching quality and contribute to the general integrity of the production. Flora Robson, as Juliet's nurse, and Mervyn Johns, as Friar Laurence, play the top supporting parts with studied care, proving themselves once more class thespers.

Sebastian Cabot and Guilio Garbinetti, as the rival heads of the houses of Capulet and Montague, and Norman Wooland as Juliet's ill-fated wooer, Paris, play their respective parts with understanding and help to enrich this screen classic.

Robert Krasker has handled the color cameras with artistry and Sydney Hayers has done a thoroughly competent job of editing. The background music by Roman Vlad is in line with the general standard. *Myro.*

The Black Knight
(BRITISH—COLOR)

Alan Ladd in spectacular action meller; hefty grosses on both sides of the Atlantic.

London, Aug. 31.

Columbia release of Warwick production. Stars Alan Ladd and Patricia Medina; features Peter Cushing, Andre Morell, Harry Andrews. Directed by Tay Garnett. Screenplay, Alec Coppel; camera (Technicolor), John Wilcox; editor, Gordon Pilkington; music, John Addison. At Gaumont, London, Aug. 26, '54. Running time, **85 MNS.**

John	Alan Ladd
Linet	Patricia Medina
Sir Palamides	Peter Cushing
Earl of Yeonil	Harry Andrews
Sir Ontzlake	Andre Morell
Major Domo	Laurence Naismith
King Mark	Patrick Troughton
King Arthur	Anthony Bushell
Abbot	Ronald Adam
James	John Laurie
Sir Hal	Basil Appleby
Lady Ontzlake	Olwen Brookes
Queen Guenevere	Jean Lodge
Bernard	Bill Brandon
Countess Yeonil	Pauline Jameson
Apprentice	Tommy Moore
Wood Cutter	John Kelly
Troubadour	Elton Hayes

Alan Ladd joins the gallant knights at King Arthur's Round Table in this British-made action spectacle, produced in lush Technicolor and vigorously directed by Tay Garnett. Strong marquee values put the pic in the potential big gross department on either side of the Atlantic unless it suffers from the glut of subjects with the same theme.

"Black Knight," Ladd's third British film in a row under the Warwick banner, has been lensed on a lavish scale, with big-scale battle scenes as the climax to the intrigue to get Arthur off the throne. Expansive decor, magnificent rural scenery and a glimpse of Stonehenge before its destruction, are some of the scenic highlights. This compensates for the necessarily juvenile nature of the plot.

For this version of the famed legend, Ladd portrays a young swordmaker who sets out to prove he's worthy of the hand of the Earl's daughter when he's suspected of cowardice after his master's castle has been pillaged. Actually, he was giving chase to the raiders when he was thought to be running away. Coached by one of King Arthur's loyal knights in armed combat, Ladd disguises himself as a black knight and conducts an audacious one-man vendetta against the plotters, escaping from Arthur's dungeon in time to foil a Saracen plan to massacre the monarch and his army.

There's no letup in the action as the star's exploits follow in quick succession. The virility of Ladd's performance is a fine match for the demands of the script. On the other hand, Patricia Medina is not too well served by the screenplay and has limited opportunities to register as the heroine.

Peter Cushing does a sterling job as Sir Palamides, the principal villain, who wants to put the pagan King Mark of Cornwall on the throne of England. This role is played in sinister fashion by Patrick Troughton, but Anthony Bushell interprets King Arthur with too much gentility. Other principal roles are enthusiastically played by a competent team of British performers. *Myro.*

Suddenly

Unusual exploitation yarn with Frank Sinatra's name to assure interest and good grosses.

Hollywood, Aug. 31.

United Artists release of Robert Bassler production. Stars Frank Sinatra, Sterling Hayden; features James Gleason, Christopher Dark, Paul Frees, Nancy Gates, Kim Charney, Willis Bouchey, James Lilburn, Charles Smith. Directed by Lewis Allen. Screenplay, Richard Sale; camera, Charles Clarke; editor, John Schreyer, music, David Raksin. Previewed Aug. 30, '54. Running time, **75 MINS.**

John Baron	Frank Sinatra
Tod Shaw	Sterling Hayden
Pop Benson	James Gleason
Bart Wheeler	Christopher Dark
Benny Conklin	Paul Frees
Ellen Benson	Nancy Gates
Pidge Benson	Kim Charney
Dan Carney	Willis Bouchey
Wilson	Ken Dibbs
Haggerty	Clark Howatt
Jud Hobson	James Lilburn
Bebop	Charles Smith
Slim Adams	Paul Wexler
Burge	Dan White
Hawkins	Richard Collier
Driver No. 1	Roy Engel
Driver No. 2	Ted Stanhope
Kaplan	Chas. Waggenheim
Trooper	John Berandino

(*Aspect ratio*: 1.75-1)

Frank Sinatra's name will be a valuable asset in boosting the b.o. chances of this slick exploitation feature, which twirls about a fantastic plot to assassinate the President of the U.S. UA release, Robert Bassler's first indie chore since ankling 20th-Fox last year, comes through as a well-worked-out meller containing story ingredients which may be ballyed for good returns on upper half of double bills.

Taking its title from the name of the California town where the action unfolds, the Richard Sale script carries sufficient theme novelty to whet the imagination. Sinatra as a professional gunman hired to kill the President as he debarks from his special train for a few days' fishing in neighboring mountains is an offbeat piece of casting which pays off in lively interest. Thesp inserts plenty of menace into a psycho character, never too heavily done, and gets good backing from his costar, Sterling Hayden, as sheriff, in a less showy role but just as authoritatively handled. Lewis Allen's direction manages a smart piece where static treatment easily could have prevailed, and Charles Clarke's fluid photography is a further assist in maintaining attention.

Action occurs within a few hours' time on a Saturday afternoon in Suddenly, where nothing has happened for years. A group of Secret Service men, detailed to guard the President, precedes him to check the security of the station area. Almost simultaneously, Sinatra and two cohorts arrive and take over a house, overlooking the station, belonging to James Gleason, retired Secret Service operative, with the intention of using it as a sniper's post to assassinate the President. They hold Gleason, his daughter-in-law and young grandson prisoners. When Hayden and the leader of the security crew drop by, the former also is held prisoner after a gun fight in which the agent is killed and Hayden wounded.

Considerable dramatic skill is exercised in progressing the narrative from the time Sinatra seizes the house until he is killed when the President's train doesn't make its intended stop, practically all the footage unraveling inside the house. Sinatra plays his role flamboyantly, while Hayden enacts his with repression as he seeks the weak link in the other's seeming strength. Both score heavily, and they get top support from a competent cast.

Nancy Gates excels as the mother of Kim Charney, believable as the boy. Gleason is up to his usual standard, and Christopher Dark and Paul Frees sock over their parts as Sinatra's henchmen. Other parts are handpicked. John Shreyer's tight editing is a potent plus credit. *Whit.*

Three Hours to Kill
(COLOR)

Offbeat western, with Dana Andrews and Donna Reed, for okay returns.

Columbia release of Harry Joe Brown production. Stars Dana Andrews, Donna Reed, Diane Foster. Features Stephen Elliot, Richard Coogan, Laurence Hugo, James Westerfield, Richard Webb, Carolyn Jones, Charlotte Fletcher, Whit Bissell. Directed by Alfred Werker. Screenplay, Richard Alan Simmons and Roy Huggins, based on story by Alex Gottlieb; camera (Technicolor), Charles Lawton; editor, Gene Havlick. Previewed in N.Y. Sept. 3, '54. Running time, **77 MINS.**

Jim Guthrie	Dana Andrews
Laurie Mastin	Donna Reed
Chris Plumber	Dianne Foster
Ben East	Stephen Elliott
Niles Hendricks	Richard Coogan
Marty Lasswell	Laurence Hugo
Sam Minor	James Westerfield
Carter Mastin	Richard Webb
Polly	Carolyn Jones
Betty	Charlotte Fletcher
Deke	Whit Bissell
Esteban	Felipe Turich
Little Carter	Arthur Fox
Vince	Francis McDonald

In a broad sense, "Three Hours to Kill" fits into the "High Noon" school of westerns. It's an outdoorer with a lesson, castigating, as it does, mob psychology. The Richard Alan Simmons-Roy Huggins screenplay, however, undertakes too much, resulting in a conflict of themes, none of which is satisfactorily developed. It emerges as a better-than-average western, though, and should fit neatly into the programmer slot. Dana Andrews and Donna Reed provide marquee lure.

"Three Hours" further exemplifies Hollywood's departure from the "he-went-thataway" oaters by introducing a subject that will surprise veteran sagebrush viewers —the birth of an illegitimate child. It is delicately handled and the hero and heroine, in keeping with Code standards, do not enjoy a completely happy ending, apparently as atonement for their sin.

"Three Hours" provides the necessary fisticuffs and gun-slinging for action fans. The mystery angle borders on the cliche, for it's soon obvious that the guy least likely to have committed the murder is the guilty party.

Title refers to the time given Andrews, a fugitive from his town for three years, to uncover the killer for whose crime he is charged. He returns disillusioned and bitter, bearing the scar from the rope of an abortive hanging in which his friends, in a moment of mob fury, participated. The unsuccessful lynchers as well as the killer, fearing revenge and unmasking, are out to get him. The girl he left behind, played by Miss Reed, had quickly married a rival suitor when she learned of her "condition."

The townspeople fail to learn from experience, and quickly shout for a "hanging" when Andrews shoots down the real killer. Sheepishly they ask him to remain when the proper evidence is presented. Andrews, however, rides off, followed by Dianne Foster, who loyally carried the torch throughout.

Andrews is properly taciturn and menacing as the avenger. Miss Reed turns in a sensitive portrayal as the girl caught in the Enoch Arden situation and Miss Foster, a looker, is convincing as the understanding standby. Good performances are registered by Stephen Elliot, Richard Coogan, Laurence Hugo, James Westerfield, Richard Webb and Whit Bissell. Alfred Werker's direction is good on the whole, although there are occasional slow-moving moments. Technical aspects of the Harry Joe Brown production are firstrate. *Holl.*

Down Three Dark Streets

Good, documentary - styled melodrama on FBI manhunt with favorable prospects generally.

Hollywood, Aug. 31.

United Artists release of Edward Small (Arthur Gardner and Jules V. Levy) production. Stars Broderick Crawford, Ruth Roman; features Martha Hyer, Marissa Pavan, Casey Adams, Kenneth Tobey, Gene Reynolds, William Johnstone. Directed by Arnold Laven. Screenplay, the Gordon Gordons and Bernard C. Schoenfeld; based on novel, "Case File, FBI," by the Gordons; camera, Joseph Biroc; editor, Grant Whytock; music, Paul Sawtell. Previewed Aug. 26, '54. Running time, **85 MINS.**

Ripley	Broderick Crawford
Kate Martel	Ruth Roman
Connie Anderson	Martha Hyer
Julie Angelino	Marissa Pavan
Dave Millson	Casey Adams
Zack Stewart	Kenneth Tobey
Vince Angelino	Gene Reynolds
Frank Pace	William Johnstone
Barker	Harlan Warde
Uncle Max	Jay Adler
Matty Pavelich	Claude Akin
Brenda Ralles	Suzanne Alexander
Mrs. Dones	Myra Marsh
Joe Walpo	Joe Bassett
Vicki	Dede Gainor
Emil Shurk	Alexander Campbell
Kuppol	Alan Dexter
Randol	Larry Hudson

(*Aspect ratio*: 1.75-1)

In the current cycle of cops-'n'-robbers melodramas, "Down Three Dark Streets" is a better entry, thanks to a well-plotted story, believable performances and the documentary air that dominates the presentation. It's good filmfare for the situations that go in for well-made action bills and should hit a satisfactory b.o. level.

Arthur Gardner and Jules V.

Levy, responsible for last season's profitable "Vice Squad," produced and Edward Small is presenting through United Artists. They rounded up an able cast to project the melodramatics and Arnold Laven, who also directed "Vice squad," handles the reins in first rate fashion to build a suspenseful, interest-holding show.

Title comes from the three cases FBI Agent Kenneth Tobey is working on at the time he is killed. Special Agent Broderick Crawford takes over, believing the clue to the killer lies in the solution of one of the cases. The first is solved dramatically without turning up the murderer, nor does the second, but the third time is the lucky charm, and in spoiling an attempt at extortion and kidnap, Broderick gets his man.

While dealing with three distinct plot angles, any one of which would have been sufficient for a thriller, the picture is not episodic, thanks to the good scripting by the Gordon Gordons and Bernard C. Schoenfeld from the Gordons' novel "Case File, FBI." The separate plots are tied together neatly and the methodical police work carried on by the FBI is well detailed without occupying unnecessary footage in the 85 minutes of action.

Involved in the first case is Martha Hyer, very good as the moll of the "Most Wanted" Joe Bassett, who is believed to have murdered Tobey from ambush Another femme delivering with fine feeling is Marissa Pavan, blind wife of Gene Reynolds, involved with a "hot" car gang in the second case. Ruth Roman, femme star of the film, heads the interest in the third case and does an excellent job of the young widow threatened with extortion by Casey Adams, presumably a suitor for her hand but a killer and blackmailer who, besides Tobey, has slain Suzanne Alexander, another of the cast's lookers who does well by her part. From Broderick on down, the players' trouping is topnotch.

On the technical side the good credits include Joseph Biroc's lensing; the Paul Sawtell score, and editing by Grant Whytock.

Brog.

The Black Dakotas
(COLOR)

Better-than-average western for the action market.

Columbia release of Wallace MacDonold production. Stars Gary Merrill, Wanda Hendrix, John Bromfield; features Noah Beery Jr. Directed by Ray Nazarro. Screenplay, Ray Buffum, DeVallon Scott from story by Buffum; camera (Technicolor), Ellis W. Carter; editor, Aaron Stell; music, Mischa Bakaleinikoff. Tradeshown, N.Y., Sept. 2, '54. Running time, **65 MINS.**

Brock Marsh	Gary Merrill
Ruth Lawrence	Wanda Hendrix
Mike Daugherty	John Bromfield
"Gimpy" Joe Woods	Noah Berry Jr.
John Lawrence	Faye Roope
Judge Baker	Howard Wendell
Marshal Collins	Robert Simon
Warren	James Griffith
Frank Gibbs	Richard Webb
Grimes	Peter Whitney
War Cloud	John War Eagle
Black Buffalo	Jay Silverheels
Spotted Deer	George Keymas
Boggs	Robert Griffin
Stone	Clayton Moore
Burke	Chris Alcaide
Zachary Paige	Frank Wilcox

With a story that happily deviates from the conventional western, "The Black Dakotas" provides the action market with better-than-average material. Cast toppers are Gary Merrill, Wanda Hendrix and John Bromfield, while Technicolor lensing of the outdoor vistas offers an added lift to this Wallace MacDonald production.

The Ray Buffum, DeVallon Scott screenplay from Buffum's story reaches back to Civil War times when President Lincoln was attempting to smoke the peace pipe with the Sioux nation in order that Union soldiers might be freed to fight the South. However, wind of the plan gets to the Confederates who replace Lincoln's emissary to the Indians with Gary Merrill.

Merrill, in guise of a Northerner, is supposed to swipe the tribesmen's promised gold for the Southern cause and at the same time incite the Sioux to harass the loyal Dakotans. As the script builds toward the denouement, there is a wealth of fisticuffs, chicanery, skirmishes with the Injuns and hard riding before Merrill is exposed as a thief who is loyal to neither North nor South.

Ray Nazarro, an old hand at directing saddle sagas, draws ample suspense and movement from the story. Merrill carries off his role of traitor well Wanda Hendrix, who has the film's lone femme part, registers nicely as the daughter of a Southern spy. John Bromfield, owner of a stage line and engaged to Miss Hendrix, is a lusty hero.

Good support is lent by Noah Beery Jr., as a Southern sympathizer; Faye Roope, as Miss Hendrix's father, plus other cast members. Ellis W. Carter ably caught the scenic backgrounds with his Technicolor camera, while Aaron Stell edited the footage down to a tight 65 minutes in keeping with requirements of the program market. Mischa Bakaleinikoff's score is an asset, as are the modest physical values furnished by producer Macdonald.

Gilb.

The Green Scarf
(BRITISH)

Suspenseful whodunit in a French setting, with strong marquee values for local theatres; only mild prospects in U.S.

London, Aug. 31.

British Lion release of B. & A. (Bertram Ostrer & Albert Fennell) production. Stars Michael Redgrave, Ann Todd, Leo Genn; features Kieron Moore, Michael Meedwin, Jane Griffiths. Directed by George Moore O'Ferrall. Screenplay by Gordon Wellesley from novel "The Brute," by Guy Des Cars; camera, Jack Hildyard; editor, Sid Stone; music, Brian Easdale. At Plaza, London, Aug. 25, '54. Running time, **96 MINS.**

Deliot	Michael Redgrave
Solange	Ann Todd
Rodelec	Leo Genn
Jacques	Kieron Moore
Jacques (child)	Richard O'Sullivan
Solange (child)	Jane Lamb
Teral	Michael Medwin
Danielle	Jane Griffiths
Louise	Ella Milne
Madame Vauthier	Jane Henderson
Advocate-General	George Merritt
Purser	Peter Burton
Prison Governor	Tristan Rawson
Ship's Captain	Henry Caine
John Bell	Phil Brown
Goirin	Anthony Nicholls
Interpreter	Walter Horsburgh
President of Court	Evelyn Roberts
Inspector	Neil Wilson
Warder	Michael Golden
Senator Bell	Launce Maraschal
Wireless Operator	Terence Alexander

A variation of the conventional whodunit with star names for marquee, "The Green Scarf" loses some of its dramatic grip when it embarks on a series of prolonged flashbacks but has sufficient vitality (and a quota ticket) to sell it in Britain. Prospects in the American market, however, may not be more than mild.

Based on a novel by Guy Des Cars, entire action takes place in France, largely within the confines of the courtroom. Central character is a blind, deaf and dumb mute (Kieron Moore) who has risen above his physical handicaps to become author of a successful novel. He is returning from a lecture tour in America with his wife (Ann Todd) when he's discovered standing by the dead body of a passenger. He's clapped into the ship cells and by sign language, with his wife as interpreter, makes a complete confession. Back in Paris, lawyer Michael Redgrave agrees to be defense attorney after several prominent counsel have rejected the brief. In a long, often suspenseful hearing, he succeeds in establishing the innocence of his client.

Up to the point where the mute refuses to offer any defense because he's shielding his wife, the plot makes a dramatic impact. But the denouement, not effectively concealed, is too obviously contrived and carries little conviction. There are, nevertheless, several moving passages, notably the wife's confession of infidelity with the murdered man. However, the flashbacks showing the events which led to the mute's marriage and triumph as a writer are over-sentimentalized.

Michael Redgrave's interpretation of the bearded, bespectacled French lawyer is warm and colorful, with an appealing touch of over-acting. Leo Genn gives a wholly sympathetic performance while Ann Todd turns in a forceful display of emotionalism. Kieron Moore does a standout job as the mute, registering dramatically without a word of dialog. Michael Medwin, as a ship's steward and Jane Griffiths, playing Redgrave's enthusiastic assistant, top a competent team of supporting players.

George Moore O'Ferrall has directed with painstaking care. Jack Hildyard has done a reliable lensing job while Wilfrid Shingleton's settings have an authentic look. Sid Stone edited the pic intelligently.

Myro.

The French Touch
(Coiffure Pour Dames)
(FRENCH)

Times Film Corp. release of Hoche production. Stars Fernandel; features Renee Devillers, Arlette Poirier, Georges Chamarat, Blanchette Brunoy, Jane Sourza, Jose Noguero. Directed by Jean Boyer. Screenplay, Serge Veber, Boyer, from play by P. Armont and M. Gerbidon; camera, Ch. Suin; music, Paul Misraki. At World, N.Y., Sept. 1, '53. Running time, **84 MINS.**

Marius-Mario	Fernandel
Aline	Renee Devillers
Edmonde	Arlette Poirier
M. Brochand	Georges Chamarat
Mme. Brochand	Blanchette Brunoy
Denise	Jane Sourza
Admirer	Jose Noguero

(In French; English Titles)

Name of Fernandel, mobile-faced French comic who's achieved a good following among arthouse patrons, ought to project this comedy into moderate to good b.o. in the art circuit and might even bring it into some fringe houses. "The French Touch" is a remake of a 1932 Gallic-made pic based on a stage comedy. As farce, it has its surefire moments, but they're so scattered that at times Fernandel strains to wring out the laughs.

Briefly, it's the story of a sheep shearer-turned-hairdresser, with sure fingers and a quick imagination, who becomes the object of the desires (in business and romance) of Parisian womanhood. The feel of his hands on their heads throws the gals into ecstasy, and they come more for pleasure than for the hairdress. But it's when he rejuvenates a fading beauty and thus brings her husband back that he starts to achieve his real success, a shop on the Champs-Elysees.

Up to that time, he's faithful to his wife, Renee Devillers, but after that point, he's involved in all manner of amorous complications, from getting locked in rooms with middleaged cronies to nearly marrying the daughter of the woman who put him into business. The bedroom-to-bedroom routine gets tiresome after a while, and it's only the broad comedies of Fernandel himself that keep the laughs coming.

He's backed by a good supporting cast. Mlle. Devillers comes through the dullish part of the faithful wife with charm; Arlette Poirier is tart as his occasional mistress; Jane Sourza is pert as the young girl; Blanchette Brunoy looks the part of the rejuvenated benefactor, and Jose Noguero has some funny moments as a diplomat. But the screenplay which director Jean Boyer and Serge Veber adapted from the P. Armont-M. Gerbidon comedy stretches the basic theme thin to the straining point. Boyer and Fernandel milk it dry, but the cow isn't productive enough.

Chan.

Shichinin No Samurai
(The Seven Samurai)
(JAPANESE)

Venice, Aug. 31.

Toho production and release. Directed by Akira Kurosawa. Screenplay, Kurosawa, Shinobu Hashimoto, Hideo Oguni; camera, Asaichi Nakai; editor, Fumio Yanoguchi; music, Fumio Hayasaka. At Venice Film Festival. Running time, **155 MINS.**

Kikuchiyo	Toshiro Mifume
Kambei	Takashi Shimura
Gorobei	Yoshio Inaba
Kyuzo	Seiji Miyaguchi
Shino	Keiko Tsushima
Katsushiro	Ko Kimura
Gisaku	Kuniniri Kodo

High adventure and excitement ment are stamped all over this solid-core film about a group of seven Samurai warriors who save a little village from annihilation at the hands of a group of bandits in 15th Century Japan. Besides the well-manned battlescenes, the pic has a good feeling for characterization and time which makes this sort of pic not only strong for arty houses but possibly good in the actioner market.

The lone drawback is its length, which can be sheared. This production touches the little-tapped genre of the epic adventure pic. As such, it has a chance in the U.S. if specially handled. This is primarily for the key cities judging from the career of its predecessor, "Rashomon."

Bandits are waiting to attack an isolated village as soon as the rice is ripe. Some of the men go to look for help and run into a sage old Samurai warrior who consents to help them. Then follows a series of deft bits as the seven men are gathered and then head for the village to prepare defenses, train the men and get ready for the onslaught. They finally vanquish the bandits but not without losses and the coming of age of a young warrior and the people's proving worthy of themselves.

Director Akira Kurosawa has given this a virile mounting. It is primarily a man's film, with the brief romantic interludes also done with taste. Each character is firmly molded. Toshire Mifume as the bold, hairbrained but courageous warrior weaves a colossal portrait. He dominates the picture although he has an extremely strong supporting cast.

Lensing is excellent as is editing in bundling together the immense footage and making its battle scenes monumental and exciting. Music is also helpful in mood vacillating between western and eastern themes for telling effect. Style of the film is the most occidental seen in recent Japanese films but locale is still oriental in flavor. Original version, one of the biggest hits in Japan this year, was three and a half hours long.
Mosk.

La Rebelion De Los Colgados
(The Rebellion of the Hanged)
(MEXICAN)

Venice, Sept. 7.
United Artists release of Jose Kohn production. Stars Pedro Armendariz; features Adriana Carlos Moctezuma, Victor Junco, Miguel Ferriz, Jaime Fernandez. Directed by Alfredo Crevenna. Screenplay, H. Wien, from book by B. Traven; camera, Gabriel Figueroa; editor, Anton Conde. At Venice Film Fest. Running time, 90 MINS.

Candido	Pedro Armendariz
Modesta	Adriana
Felix	Carlos Moctezuma
Calso	Victor Junco
Picaro	Alvaro Matute
Gabriel	Tito Junco
Urbano	Jaime Fernandez
Severo	Miguel Ferriz

Film was made with an English version which United Artists has for U.S. distrib. It is a rugged, red-meat drama of a brutal slave mahogany camp in the wilds of Mexico of the 1900s, and its unrelenting brutality and roughness slant this primarily for the stout actioner and more offbeat market. Arty chances are slight due to downbeat theme and overemphasized violence. However, word-of-mouth should play a big part in this and proper handling should make this of value on the U.S. scene, with proable fine prospects on the Mexican front, and chances for solid offbeat cashing-in on the foreign markets.

Story concerns a peasant, Pedro Armendariz, who gets coerced into signing for work in a mahogany camp in the jungles. He goes with his children and beauteous sister. Here he runs into raw viciousness and brutality as the overworked men are whipped, hung up by their arms for hours and treated like animals by a perverted, drunken crew and bosses. Mayhem is piled up in layers of shock visual appeal and such scenes as a closeup of a terribly-lacerated back and hands, a boy's ear being sliced off, a man being blinded by thorns, and hanged and beaten men, are definitely in the belt category and not for the squeamish. Some shearing of the more rugged and repetitive terror might make this more well-knit and play off its mounting rebellion more adequately.

Director Alfredo Crevenna has given this a good pacing, but only drawback is the addition of some familiar bits with a beautiful sister and the characterization not growing with the action. Lensing and editing are fine and acting is good, with Pedro Armendariz his competent self.
Mosk.

Sierra Maldita
(Cursed Mountain)
(SPANISH)

Venice, Aug. 31.
Paramount release of Almasirio production. Stars Lina Rosales, Ruben Rojo; features, Jose Guardiola, Jose Sepulveda, Manuel Zarzo. Directed by Antonio Del Amo. Screenplay, Fernando Merino; camera, Eloy Mella, S. Perera; editor, Peptia Orduna. At Venice Film Festival. Running time, 95 MINS.

Cruz	Lina Rosales
Juan	Ruben Rojo
Lucas	Jose Guardiola
Jose	Jose Sepulveda
Emilio	Manuel Zarzo

This may not put Spain on the international pic map, but the film does emerge as one of enough individuality and color to make for good possibilities in U.S. lingo spots or even for possible special slotting. It is a folksy tale of myth and prejudice overcome by love. Despite the familiar general plot, "Cursed Mountain" possesses enough offbeat locale to make this of interest. This won the crix prize at the San Sabastian Film Fest and also repped Spain at the Venice fete.

Story deals with southern village in Spain where there is a myth that all women born in the mountain section are barren, thus preventing marriage for them. One man from the valley braves this and marries a mountain girl. He is disowned by his family. When conditions are made difficult for him, he goes off on a special charcoal collecting expedition. He takes his wife along and a villianous mountain man tries to attack her and drags her off. The husband catches him and indulges in a vicious axe fight with him. Later the wife gives birth to a child, destroying the myth, for a happy ending.

Director Antonio Del Amo has used the rugged exteriors well. Line Rosales, as the mountain gal, and Ruben Rojo, the valley man, supply subdued performances. Skullduggery of Jose Guardiola is standard as is the pic plotting. However, the lensing is fine as is editing and supporting players. Paramount has this for Spanish and South American distrib. It also may take it for U.S. subsequent runs plus any other possibilities engendered by the pic.
Mosk.

The Human Jungle
Hard-hitting police story which can be exploited for strong grosses.

Hollywood, Sept. 11.
Allied Artists release of Hayes Goetz production. Stars Gary Merrill, Jan Sterling; features Paula Raymond, Regis Toomey, Emile Meyer, Chuck Connors. Directed by Joseph M. Newman. Associate producer, Marvin Mirisch; screenplay, William Sackheim, Daniel Fuchs; story, Sackheim; camera, Ellis Carter; editors, Lester Sansom, Samuel Fields; music, Hans Salter. Previewed Sept. 10, '54. Running time, 82 MINS.

Danforth	Gary Merrill
Mary	Jan Sterling
Pat Danforth	Paula Raymond
Rowan	Emile Meyer
Geddes	Regis Toomey
Swados	Chuck Connors
Strauss	Pat Waltz
O'Neil	George Wallace
Greenie	Chubby Johnson
Cleary	Don Keefer
Bledsoe	Rankin Mansfield
Lannigan	Lamont Johnson
Karns	Leo Cleary
Ustick	Florenz Ames
Mandy	Claude Akins
Lynch	Hugh Boswell
Captain Harrison	James Westerfield

(Aspect ratio: 1.85-1)

Allied Artists can very legitimately give the same type of heavy exploitational campaign to this film to back saturation bookings, already announced, as it accorded its "Riot in Cell Block 11" earlier this year. Picture is a sock big-city police story packed with sex as well as violence and excitement and should be a hefty grosser for the studio. particularly in situations leaning toward strong melodrama.

Authoritatively produced by Hayes Goetz, who gives it honest treatment straight through, film is a welcome switch from the current trend of bad-cop pix. The politics of a metropolitan police department backdrop an almost documentary narrative which has been imaginatively directed by Joseph M. Newman with punchy overtones. William Sackheim and Daniel Fuchs' hard-hitting screenplay, based on former's original, also carries femme appeal via Jan Sterling.

Feature is marked by standout portrayals of a hand-picked cast who insert forceful realism into natural characterizations. Gary Merrill, a police captain who had passed his bar exams and is about to leave the force, is prevailed upon to head the notorious Heights district of the city, where conditions have reached the point that no one is safe. In his revitalization of his department and attempts to solve a murder he meets with opposition both from some of his own men and those above him, but finally cracks the case and whips the district into shape.

Merrill gives true meaning to his part and Miss Sterling belts over the role of a tough blonde who is used as an alibi by Chuck Connors, excellent in his characterizing of the murderer. Actress stages a clever striptease which can be used for potent promotion. Regis Toomey as Merrill's second-in-command, Lamont Johnson as a vet detective at first antagonistic to his new captain. Pat Waltz as a new plainclothesman who accidentally shoots an innocent bystander to bring city wrath down upon the captain, and Emile Meyer, the police chief, score heavily. So, too, do Paula Raymond as Merrill's patient wife, Florenz Ames, as underworld leader. and James Westerfield, aging police captain succeeded by Merrill.

Technical credits match up, Ellis Carter's cameras aiding the fast action and Lester Sansom and Samuel Fields' editing being tight. Music by Hans Salter catches the pace and David Milton's art direction gives story fine backing.
Whit.

Jesse James' Women
(COLOR—SONGS)
Exhib-made western with fair returns indicated in program market.

United Artists release of Panorama Pictures (Lloyd Royal, T. V. Garraway) production. Stars Peggie Castle, Donald Barry, Jack Beutel, Lita Baron. Directed by Barry. Screenplay, D. D. Beauchamp; camera (Eastman Color), Ken Peach; editor, Burton E. Hayes; songs, George Antheil, Stan Jones; music, Walter Greene. Previewed N.Y. Sept. 8, '54. Running time, 83 MINS.

Jesse James	Don Barry
Frank James	Jack Beutel
Waco Gans	Peggie Castle
Delta	Lita Baron
Caprice Clark	Joyce Rhed
Cattle Kate Kennedy	Betty Brueck
Angel Botts	Laura Lee
Cole Younger	Sam Keller

(Aspect ratio: 1.75-1)

Frontier outlaw Jesse James, whose six-gun feats have provided material for a half-dozen films in the past quarter century, receives a free translation in "Jesse James' Women." For this modest entry, which represents the initial production attempt of a group of Mississippi exhibitors, minimizes his outlaw traits and depicts him as a ladies' man.

Overlong at 83 minutes, nevertheless this Panorama Picture presentation has some sexy angles that offer an exploitation twist. Peggie Castle and Lita Baron, accorded star billing, are pleasant to look at in a flock of lowcut gowns that point up their visual assets. Mississippi terrain, where the film was lensed, plus the accents of most of the supporting players, add up to sales appeal in the south.

But for the general market, "James' Women" will best fit as a companion feature to stronger product. The D. D. Beauchamp screenplay is a contrived yarn minus the majestic mountain scenery found in most oaters. Moreover, a chase through a Mississippi cornfield lacks the glamor and excitement that's conjured up when hard ridin' hombres head the stage off at Eagle Pass.

Story has Donald Barry in the title role on the lam in a small Mississippi town, along with brother Frank (Jack Beutel) plus a number of other cohorts. In rapid succession Barry is enamoured of saloonkeeper Miss Castle, songstress Miss Baron, banker's daughter Joyce Rhed and cattle owner Betty Brueck. Taunted by his followers, he asserts he's merely using the femmes as a means of stealing enough coin to make the trek back west. The footage becomes rather tedious before the James boys finally hit the homeward trail.

Performances under Barry's direction are hardly credible and the film takes on the aura of a satire, although the cast was probably playing it straight. Barry portrays James much too broadly. Beutel, however, is believable as Barry's first lieutenant. Miss Castle deserves better material than she was handed here. Her knock-down and drag-out brawl with Miss Brueck, for example, is more ludicrous than dramatic.

Miss Baron, aside from her decorative values, warbles a brace of so-so romantic ballads—"Careless Lover" by George Antheil and "In the Shadows of My Heart" by Stan Jones. Other players, most of whom utilize the Southern vernacular, are fair.

United Artists release was produced by Mississippi theatreowner

Lloyd Royal and T. V. Garraway, a businessman from the same state. Camerawork of Ken Peach is inclined to be fuzzy at times and not up to the quality of some Eastman color in which this was lensed. Print, however, is by Technicolor. Editing of Burton E. Hayes could have been tighter, while Walter Greene's score often is much too fortissimo.   Gilb.

Sitting Bull
(C'SCOPE—COLOR)

Overlong cavalry-Indians yarn, for dual situations.

Hollywood, Sept. 10.
United Artists release of W. R. Frank production. Stars Dale Robertson, Mary Murphy, J. Carrol Naish; features John Litel, Iron Eyes Cody, Douglas Kennedy. Directed by Sidney Salkow; associate producer, Alfred Strauss. Screenplay, Jack DeWitt, Salkow; camera (Eastman-color), Charles Van Enger, Victor Herrera; editor, Richard Van Enger. Previewed Sept. 7, '54. Running time, 105 MINS.

Parrish .... Dale Robertson
Kathy .... Mary Murphy
Sitting Bull .... J. Carrol Naish
Crazy Horse .... Iron Eyes Cody
General Howell .... John Litel
Wentworth .... Bill Hopper
Colonel Custer .... Douglas Kennedy
O'Connor .... Bill Tennen
Sam .... Joel Fluellen
President Grant .... John Hamilton
Webber .... Tom Brown Henry
Young Buffalo .... Felix Gonzalez
Swain .... Al Wyatt

(Aspect ratio: 2.55-1)

This confused cavalry-Indians yarn based on the Sioux chief and his troubles with the whites is sorely in need of wholesale cutting and has been badly photographed in color. Feature's extreme length will make it difficult to slot in the western market, where it's suitable only for double bills. Smart exploitation on the strength of its subject and fact it's the first Indie CinemaScope production may draw in certain quarters, but business generally will be spotty.

Filmed in Mexico, the W. R. Frank production has the benefit of vast numbers of Mexicans playing Indians and U.S. cavalrymen, but static direction by Sidney Salkow, who co-scripted with Jack DeWitt, fails to make any spectacular use of such possibilities, the effect being so much useless movement. Narrative is further weakened by liberal liberties taken with history.

Plottage deals with the efforts of Dale Robertson, a cavalry major who believes in fair treatment of the Indians, trying to keep peace between the redskins and whites. On the Indians' side, there is also Sitting Bull, who has the same idea, even after many of his people have been killed by the whites. For refusing to fire on some Sioux escaping from an Indian agency, Robertson nearly is drummed out of the service, but is saved by the intervention of President U. S. Grant, with whom he served in the Civil War.

Assigned by the President to arrange a meeting with Sitting Bull, Robertson returns west and makes the contact, but while awaiting the arrival of the President, war breaks out when Custer disregards orders and moves in on the Indians. Robertson is courtmartialed and sentenced to death by a traitor when he prevents further bloodshed by leading the Indians away from the cavalry, but is again saved by Grant when Sitting Bull arrives at the fort to explain the young officer's actions.

Robertson is okay and J. Carrol Naish well-cast in the title role, but Mary Murphy is lost in femme lead. Iron Eyes Cody makes a favorable impression as Chief Crazy Horse, the Sioux war leader. Balance of cast are stock. Charles Van Enger and Victor Herrera handled the cameras.   Whit.

Two Guns and a Badge

Okay Wayne Morris entry for the oater market.

Hollywood, Sept. 9.
Allied Artists release of Vincent M. Fennelly production. Stars Wayne Morris; features Morris Ankrum, Beverly Garland, Roy Barcroft, William Phipps. Directed by Lewis D. Collins. Screenplay, Dan Ullman; camera, Joseph M. Novac; editor, Sam Fields; music, Raoul Kraushaar. Previewed Sept. 8, '54. Running time, 68 MINS.

Jim Blake .... Wayne Morris
Sheriff Jackson .... Morris Ankrum
Gail Sterling .... Beverly Garland
Bill Sterling .... Roy Barcroft
Dick Grant .... William Phipps
Wilson .... Damian O'Flynn
Allen .... Stanford Jolley
Moore .... Robert Wilke
Val Moore .... Chuck Courtney
Sharkey .... John Pickard

This Wayne Morris western stacks up as standard fare for the giddyap trade, its catchy title offering exploitation potential. While long on dialog, in its action scenes there's plenty of punch.

In a case of mistaken identity, Morris rides into the outlaw-ridden town of Outpost and is immediately made a deputy sheriff. It's believed he's the gunman the sheriff has summoned to rid the town of its vicious element and clean up rustling activity which has been depleting ranchers' stock. Although his true identity is revealed, hero stays to accomplish the job and is kept on as sheriff.

Morris delivers rather woodenly, but gets by in role with the able support of Morris Ankrum, as the sheriff; Roy Barcroft, a wealthy rancher under suspicion of heading the rustler operations, and Beverly Garland, who provides the romantic interest as latter's daughter. William Phipps is okay as the real outlaw leader and Robert Wilke scores as his aide.

Vincent M. Fennelly provides film with suitable values and Lewis D. Collins' direction is as good as the Dan Ullman script will allow. Joseph M. Novac's lensing is up to the requirements of piece and balance of technical credits also rate.   Whit.

The Angel Who Pawned Her Harp
(BRITISH)

Simple fantasy of angel on goodwill mission to earth. For supporting situations.

London, Sept. 2.
British Lion release of Sidney Cole production. Stars Felix Aylmer, Diane Cilento; features Jerry Desmonde. Directed by Alan Bromly. Screenplay by Charles Terrot and Sidney Cole; camera, Arthur Grant; editor, John Merritt; music, Anthony Hopkins. At Rialto, London, Sept. 1, '54. Running time, 76 MINS.

Joshua Webman .... Felix Aylmer
Angel .... Diane Cilento
Voice .... Robert Eddison
Parker .... Jerry Desmonde
Ned Sullivan .... Joe Linnane
Jenny Lane .... Sheila Sweet
Len Burrows .... Philip Guard
Mrs. Burrows .... Genitha Halsey
Sgt. Lane .... Edward Evans
Mrs. Lane .... Elaine Wodson
Lennox .... Alfie Bass

There have been numerous fantasies with the flight to earth of kindly spirits, and there is insufficient novel treatment in this one to create much of a stir. It is handled with a light touch, with pleasing human background, but lacks suspense interest or element of surprise. Good camerawork, plus a compact script, makes this a pleasing second feature for local houses.

In a drab area of London a benign old man runs a pawnshop with a multiplicity of oddments and a rare collection of old musical boxes and figures. He is confronted by a ravishing blonde in floating draperies who wants to hock her harp. It had been revealed through cloud shots and vocal commentary that an angel had been granted permission to visit mortals on a goodwill trip, and her first need is cash. She goes to a dogtrack, where she makes enough to live on, and proceeds to exert her benevolent influence and smooth out troubled paths in the "Passing of the Third Floor Back" tradition.

Diane Cilento, who won a film contract with Sir Alexander Korda after her performance in "The Big Knife" last year, has no great strain put on her acting abilities in this, her first screen role. She looks ethereal and attractive as the heavenly messenger, tempering her beatific demeanor with an occasional impish twinkle. Felix Aylmer is superb as the old pawnbroker and Jerry Desmonde brings a sparkle of worldly trickery as a live-wire salesman. Sheila Sweet and Philip Guard give a good account of themselves as the lovers, and Phyllis Morris contributes an excellent character study of a venomous busybody. Supporting cast makes a realistic framework to the story, and direction by Alan Bromly is simple and well defined.   Clem.

Columbus Entdeckt Kraehwinkel
(GERMAN)
(Columbus Discovers Kraehwinkel)

Berlin, Sept. 1.
Europa release of Real production. Stars Charlie Chaplin Jr., Sidney Chaplin, Paola Loew and Eva Kerbler. Directed by Alexander Paal and Ulrich Erfurth. Screenplay, Axel von Ambesser after an idea by Alexander Paal; camera, Erich Claunigk; music, Michael Jary; sets, Herbert Kirchhoff and Albrecht Becker. At Filmbuehne Wien, Berlin. Running time, 93 MINS.

Susi Merzheim .... Paula Loew
Eva Wagner .... Eva Kerbler
Jimmy Hunter .... Charlie Chaplin Jr.
Clark Hunter .... Sidney Chaplin
Maier .... Paul Westermeier
Merzheim .... Carl Wery
Wagner .... Paul Henckels
Frau Wagner .... Ursula Herking
Toni Wagner .... Harald Maresch
Luettgen .... Rudolf Platte
Wiebel .... Josef Egger

Alexander Paal's "Columbus Discovers Kraehwinkel"—a tale of two ex-GIs who, without success, try to Americanize a "gemuetliche" Teutonic small town—turns out to be rather disappointing film fare. Admittedly, it has a basically original story which might have furnished the basis for a witty film. But this one has completely been overdone. That primarily concerns this German pic's two American characters, portrayed by the Chaplin boys (Charlie Jr. and Sidney). Although both remain sympathetic all through, their portrayals of "typical" Amis are more a thing of stupidity than genuineness. It's hard to believe that modern Americans would operate as silly as displayed in "Columbus."

Despite being a substantial money-maker here, pic's chances in the U. S. appear limited. The Chaplin names may lure some curious customers to the boxoffice.

Story sees two ex-GIs return to Kraehwinkel where both have a fraulein. Their idea is to turn this cozy little town into a modern place, strictly after the American pattern. In less than no time they open a drugstore, but they soon have to realize that the people here just can't take a fancy to anything that bears the U. S. label (which, in this instance, includes jukeboxes, slot machines, obscene neckties, boogie, jazz, etc.). So they finally give up their venture. One of the boys gets his German gal while the other one has to face a total defeat: the fraulein he loves prefers a young German who, just recently returned from "those United States," has become Kraehwinkel's buergermeister.

It's actually very hard to say anything positive about this film and even hard to classify it. As a satire, if intended, it merely reveals the filmmakers' bad taste. As a comedy, gags are rather lifeless and seldom click. It's practically neither fish nor fowl. Moreover, the direction by Paal and Ulrich Erfurth is often very dragging. Number of dull moments almost makes patrons long for the pic's fadeout.

It's said that U. S. circles in Germany are raising eyebrows over this film, calling it a degrading picture of America. To a certain extent, this may be true. However, this will only affect a small group of very provincial-minded picture-goers. In all, "Columbus" is just too silly in plot and treatment to hurt the German-American relationship. Of course, it won't make any friends for the U. S. either.   Hans.

The Purple Plain
(BRITISH—COLOR)

Gregory Peck scores in British-made drama set in wartime Burma; bright b.o. prospects.

London, Sept. 14.

General Film Distributors release of Two Cities production. Stars Gregory Peck; features Win Min Than, Brenda de Banzie, Bernard Lee, Maurice Denham, Lyndon Brook, Rem Gopal Directed by Robert Parrish. Screenplay by Eric Ambler from book by H. E. Bates; camera (Technicolor), Geoffrey Unsworth; editor, Clive Donner; music, John Veale. At Odeon, Leicester Square. Running time, **100 MINS.**

Forrester	Gregory Peck
Anna	Win Min Than
Dr. Harris	Bernard Lee
Blore	Maurice Denham
Mr. Phang	Ram Gopal
Miss McNab	Brenda de Banzie
Carrington	Lyndon Brook
Aldridge	Anthony Bushell
Sgt. Brown	Jack McNaughton
Navigator Williams	Harold Siddons
Flight Lieutenant	Peter Arne
Dorothy	Mye Mye Spencer
Mrs. Forrester	Johephine Griffin
Radio Operator	Lane Meddick
Burmese Jeweller	John Tinn
Old Woman	Soo Ah Song
Nurse	Dorothy Alison

The combined writing talents of novelist H. E. Bates and scripter Eric Ambler have produced a fine dramatic vehicle for Gregory Peck's second British-made film which is set in the Burmese jungle in the last days of the war. The star's name will be a powerful selling factor on either side of the Atlantic but the pic is strong enough to stand on its own.

The well-knit yarn is given added dramatic qualities by the incisive direction of Robert Parrish and by Clive Donner's shrewd editing. They have lifted it out of the rut of ordinary war stories and have concentrated on developing a single character who, as the script puts it, is "round the bend." This role is superbly filled by Gregory Peck and his performance as the pilot with a tortured mind ranks with his best.

After vividly establishing the atmosphere and developing the principal characters, the action switches from the airstrip to mountainous terrain held by the Japs into which Peck has crashed his plane while on a routine flight with his navigator, Lyndon Brook, and a fellow officer, Maurice Denham. From that point the entire incident concentrates on their attempts to get out with Peck in an obstinate mood and insisting they should not wait by the wreckage for help but should try and reach water. After two or three days Denham shoots himself but Peck carries his injured navigator to eventual safety.

An early flashback establishes the cause of the pilot's neurosis; his wife was killed in a London airraid on their wedding night. Subsequently there are some very tender scenes played in a neighboring village community in which Peck begins a new romantic entanglement with Win Min Than, an exotic yet restrained Burmese beauty. The backgrounds, filmed in Ceylon, are lensed in lush Technicolor. The pic was made with the co-operation of the Royal Air Force. The entire cast helps to achieve the authentic atmosphere. Apart from the starring performances, there are excellent portrayals by Bernard Lee, Brenda de Banzie, Maurice Denham and Ram Gopal. *Myro.*

Four Guns to the Border
(COLOR)

Western action feature with s. a. overtones; satisfactory fare for the outdoor trade.

Hollywood, Sept. 21.

Universal release of William Alland production. Stars Rory Calhoun, Colleen Miller, George Nader, Walter Brennan, Nina Foch; features John McIntire, Charles Drake, Jay Silverheels, Nestor Paiva. Directed by Richard Carlson. Screenplay, George Van Marter, Franklin Coen: based on the story by Louis L'Amour; camera (Technicolor), Russell Metty; editor, Frank Gross. Previewed Sept. 14, '54. Running time, **82 MINS.**

Cully	Rory Calhoun
Lolly Bhumer	Colleen Miller
Bronco	George Nader
Simon Bhumer	Walter Brennan
Maggie Flannery	Nina Foch
Dutch	John McIntire
Jim Flannery	Charles Drake
Yaqui	Jay Silverheels
Greasy	Nestor Paiva
Mrs. Pritchard	Mary Field
Smitty	Robert Hoy
Evans	Robert Herron
Cashier	Reg Parton
Town Loafer	Donald Kerr

(Aspect ratio: 2 to 1)

The western action in "Four Guns to the Border" is brought off satisfactorily enough to assure the picture an okay reception in the regular market for Technicolored outdoor features. As an extra fillip, the standard ingredients are spiced with some sagebrush sex which even the pure action fan will not find amiss.

Title of the William Alland production comes from Louis L'Amour's story about four cowpokes, down on their luck, who turn to bank robbery and try for the border after their first successful job. Had they stayed on schedule everything would have worked out as planned, but they are diverted long enough to save an old gunsel and his daughter from an Indian attack. Three are killed and the fourth goes to jail, there to pay his debt to society so he can win the girl.

The screenplay by George Van Marter and Franklin Coen makes good use of the plot framework and the succession of action events have been well-staged by Richard Carlson's direction. The dramatic mood is good since it doesn't always hew the western story line in treating the usual oater cliches, and the players acquit themselves quite well in moving the plot along its 82-minute course.

Rory Calhoun and Colleen Miller are the principal stars; he as the leader of the foursome, and she as the girl. Between the planning and the execution of the robbery they have met and paired off in a rainstorm; a sequence of rather high-voltage passion not usually found in regulation western filmfare. In their respective characters they contribute a forthright tone to the footage. The presence of Miss Miller, in particular, quite often pushes the scenery, horses and males way into the background.

Walter Brennan, as Miss Miller's crusty father; John McIntire, elder member of the gang; George Nader and Jay Silverheels, friendly brawlers who complete the robber quartet, all figure importantly. Nina Foch, an old friend of Calhoun's and now married to Charles Drake, the sheriff, is okay. Drake unwittingly aids the holdout when Calhoun baits him into a fight to decoy attention from the bank while the robbery is being carried out. This is one of several real rugged physical clashes in the footage. Other casters do capable work.

The color lensing by Russell Metty is very good in handling the scenic values and other technical assists are expert, too. *Brog.*

Roogie's Bump

Dull and awkward baseball fantasy; poor b.o. prospects.

Republic Pictures release of John Bash-Elizabeth Dickenson production. Features Robert Marriot, Ruth Warrick, Robert Simon, Olive Blakeney The Brooklyn Dodgers and Ray Campanella, Billy Loes, Carl Erskine, Russ Meyer. Directed by Harold Young. Screenplay, Jack Hanley, Dan Totheroh, from story by Frank Warren, Joyce Selznick; camera, Burgi J. Contner; music, Lehman Engels. Tradeshown in New York., Sept. 15, '54. Running time, **71 MINS.**

"Roogie" Rigsby	Robert Marriot
Mrs. Rigsby, his mother	Ruth Warrick
Mrs. Andrews (Grams)	Olive Blakeney
Boxi	Robert Simon
Red O'Malley	William Harrigan
Andy	David Winters
Benji	Michael Mann
P. A. Riker	Archie Robbins
Kate	Louise Troy
Danny Doowinkle	Guy Rennie
Sports Announcer and Narrator	Tedd Lawrence
Barney Davis	Michael Keene
Dog	Robbie

THE BROOKLYN DODGERS
Roy Campanella, Billy Loes, Carl Erskine and Russ Meyer

If there's anything worse than a humorless fantasy, it's a lifeless one. "Roogie's Bump," a baseball fantasy involving a small boy and the Brooklyn Dodgers, has both characteristics, and the result is a plodding 71 minutes of awkward and maudlin muddling. Republic's b.o. prospects are exceedingly poor on this one; even if the Brooklyn Dodgers prove an attraction, word-of-mouth will kill that off. Bottom rung of the twin-bills.

A small boy, Robert Marriot, comes to live in Brooklyn with his mother, Ruth Warrick; his grandmother, Olive Blakeney and his older sister, Louise Troy. The kids won't let him play ball with them, and out of pity for him and an unrequited love for his grandmother, the ghost of Red O'Malley, a star Dodger of the past, appears to the boy and endows him with a bump on the arm that enables him to throw a ball "with the speed of light." Naturally, he lands with the Dodgers, and from then on it's a battle between Miss Warrick and Robert Simon as the Brook's manager on the one side, and Archie Robbins as the Dodgers' ambitious exploitation man on the other, to keep him from being exploited.

Proceedings and the acting are both wooden. Marriot, although appealing, brings little life to his part. Miss Warrick's and Miss Blakeney's roles are cut-and-dry, but Simon does nicely by his conscience-stricken manager role. Robbins' stint as the ballyhooer is out of a stereotyped mold, but William Harrigan as O'Malley delivers his bit in okay manner. The Jack Hanley-Dan Totheroh script holds neither charm nor humor, and Harold Young's direction does nothing to speed up the plodding action. As for the Dodgers, only Roy Campanella delivers a little bit of warmth to his screen attempt.

Production isn't much better, with some of those action shots of the Dodgers an insult to the intelligence of even the average baseball fan. Narration in one spot tells how the Brooks are in throuble while the footage shows them up at bat belting out hits, and in the climax scene, Duke Snider is shown grounding out and then coming to bat again. Editing here was exceedingly bad. Title derives from the fact that "Roogie" is the nickname for Remington, which is Marriot's name in the pic, but the title won't help the b.o. chances either. *Chan.*

L'Air De Paris
(FRENCH)

Venice, Sept. 10.

Corona release of Del Duca-Galatea production. Stars Jean Gabin, Arletty; features Roland Lesaffre, Marie Daems, Folco Lulli, Jean Paredes, Simone Paris. Directed by Marcel Carne. Screenplay, Jacques Sigurd, Carne; camera, Roger Hubert; editor, Henri Rust; music, Maurice Thiriet. At Venice Film Fest. Running time, **100 MINS.**

Victor	Jean Gabin
Blanche	Arletty
Andre	Roland Lesaffre
Corinne	Marie Daems
Angelo	Folco Lulli
Jean-Marc	Jean Paredes
Chantal	Simone Paris

"L'Air De Paris" is not very fresh, and also, unfortunately, marks the waning of one of the top authentic pre-war talents in director Marcel Carne. Familiar boxing story lacks pacing and roundness, with uneven thesping and characterization, to make this an ordinary film. It has veteran names of Arletty and Jean Gabin for local bookings, but for the U.S. it has only thesp monickers and a possibly exploitable boxing milieu for dualer chances.

It concerns an aging boxer who dreams of training a champion. He runs a little gym with his wife, and is prone to pick kids off the street and train them for nothing. This happens with a young, hungry railroad worker. He thinks that this is it and training starts in earnest. However, flaw is fact that wife wants to retire to the South and doesn't like the boy. He, in turn, gets tangled with a flashy beauty, who finally leaves him for security while he goes back to his loyal manager to try to batter his way to the top.

Director Carne has put the brunt of this boxing pic on the shoulders of thesp Roland Lesaffre, who is not ready for it, and result is a sagging, unreal affair with a neglect of the powerful acting of Gabin and Arletty. Marie Daems is untrue as the femme fatale and supporting players lack the life and clarity needed to give this punch and interest. Few boxing scenes are unimaginative and this does not bear comparison to U. S. counterparts, such as "Champion" and "The Set-Up," which had the rosinous smell and feel of the milieu. Lensing is good and editing is fair with production dress ordinary. Gabin remains undefined and Arletty also seems to be an onlooker in this unbalanced drama. *Mosk.*

La Strada
(The Road)
(ITALIAN)

Venice, Sept. 14.

Paramount release of a Ponti-DeLaurentiis production. Stars Anthony Quinn, Richard Basehart, Giulietta Masina; features Aldo Silvani. Directed by Federico Fellini. From a story by Fellini and Tullio Pinelli; screenplay, Fellini and Pinelli; camera, Otello Martelli; music, Nino Roto. At Venice Film Festival, Venice. Running time, **115 MINS.**

Zampano	Anthony Quinn
Gelsomina	Giulietta Masina
Ilmatto	Richard Basehart
Colombaioli	Aldo Silvani

This interesting pic, daring from a present-day productive standpoint, is the arty type of product which crix and the elite cry for, and distribs dislike to handle. More frequent in earlier post-war years, it is now practically a rarity. This needs strong selling and word-of-mouth. Film needs trimming before attempting a prestige release in the U. S., with the names of Anthony Quinn and Richard Basehart helpful.

Story by Federico Fellini, who also directed this picture, tells of a blunt, brutal wandering carnie performer who "buys" a girl to serve as his assistant. She's on the nutty side, but falls for him despite his many affairs with other women and his poor treatment of her. Her poetic conversations with a similarly dim-witted clown-trapezist anger the brute, who finally accidentally kills his rival in a fist fight. The death completely unbalances gal's mind, and the brute abandons her. Many years later, alone and broken, he hears someone whistle tune she used to play on trumpet, and learns she is dead. That night after a violent drunk, alone on a deserted beach, he breaks down his lifelong reserve, and his sorrow and never expressed love for the femme pours forth in conclusive tears.

Story reads badly, but is filled with pathetic and poetic moments, often is both very touching and extremely amusing. Acting by Quinn and Basehart is tops, but Giulietta Masina, one of Italy's best performers, easily steals show with her clownish mimicry, a job which should finally earn her more consistent work in local pix.

The on-the-road atmosphere, the slum area show biz aspects typical of some parts of Italian life, are realistically pictured by Fellini's story and Otello Martelli's camera, in this intelligent film. Nino Rota's music is in style, and the simple theme song has certain haunting appeal. *Hawk.*

La Romana
(Woman of Rome)
(ITALIAN)
Venice, Sept. 14.
Minerva Film release of a Ponti-De-Laurentiis-Excelsa production. Stars Gina Lollobrigida; features Daniel Gelin, Raymond Pelegrin, Pina Piovani, Xenia Valdieri, Renato Tontini, Franco Fabrizi. Directed by Luigi Zampa. Screenplay, Zampa, Alberto Moravia, Ennio Flajano from novel by Alberto Moravia; camera, Enzo Serafin; editor, Eraldo De Roma. At Venice Film Festival, Venice. Running time, 110 MINS.
Adriana .... Gina Lollobrigida
Mino .... Daniel Gelin
Gino .... Franco Fabrizi
Astarita .... Raymond Pelegrin
The mother .... Pina Piovani
Gisella .... Xenia Valdieri
Sozogno .... Renato Tontini

Title and star value will have to help this one on its way, via exploitation rather than prestige handling. Pic has Gina Lollobrigida as general marquee bait, with Daniel Gelin and Raymond Pelegrin helping French dates. Story provides many exploitable pegs. Dullish handling can only partly be overcome by a careful trimming. Pic should do business on Italian runs without critical aid or word-of-mouth. Dubbing and recutting suggested for U.S. release.

Adapted from the well-known Alberto Moravia best-seller, story is of a simple gal whose mother prods her into a lucrative nude modelling job, and later fails to keep her from seguing as a high-class prostie. Many men fall for her while she falls for the only one who doesn't want her—or won't admit his love for her. Pic ends with most men asked for or forgotten, and her only love a suicide. Gal is left with a child, with which, the finale hints, she is to start life anew. Censorial shears have been skirted throughout, and some material passed is surprisingly frank.

Pic, especially at start, successfully attains a certain period atmosphere, but soon becomes overworked and hard to believe. Cliche dialog doesn't help nor does a listless performance by Gelin as the suicide. Pelegrin is good as a lover and Renato Tontini is properly sinister as a brute. Pina Piovani, as the mother, and the others are able.

The best job is done by Gina Lollobrigida, who surmounts real odds to turn in an interesting, often moving performance. Direction fails to overcome script weaknesses only partly due to censorial trims. Enzo Serafin's photography is fine, especially in nitetime shots. *Hawk.*

Sesto Continente
(Sixth Continent)
(ITALIAN-COLOR)
Venice, Sept. 14.
Titanus release of a Delphinus Production. With Bruno Vailati, Raimondo Bucher, Enza Bucher, F. Bascrieri Salvatori, Folco Quilici. Directed by Falco Quilici. Camera (Technicolor), Quilici, Masino Manunza; commentary, Gian Gaspare Napolitano; music, Roberto Nicolosi; editor, Mario Serandrei. At Venice Festival, Venice. Running time, 95 MINS.

Uneven cutting and a commentary unsuited to American temperament somewhat mar and lessen the impact of this underwater color (Technicolor) documentary. But it contains enough valuable, beautiful material for a trimmed U. S. release. With Walt Disney's "20,000 Leagues" and another Austro-British seadepther coming up soon, release on this item should be speeded for best results. As is, it will do well on an Italian swing.

Material gathered on this Italo-sponsored trip to the islands of Dahlach, off the coast of Ethiopia, contains probably the consistently top nether-depth sequences ever filmed. Color quality throughout is excellent. Pic avoids false excitement raised by some previous pix of similar scope. Many sequences, such as the underwater harpooning of sharks and barracudas are unquestionably unstaged, authentic and exciting. On the luckier side, but just as striking, is a sequence showing how a shark's tiny pilot fish, disoriented by his ex-boss' death, finally in desperation takes up position in front of one of the frogmen's masks and "pilots" him on his way through the deep. And there is beauty too in the many unusual fish and underwater creatures, colorfully lensed in their natural habitat.

Members of the expedition play themselves, with film story essentially story of expedition. Music by Roberto Nicolosi fits underwater setting nicely. *Hawk.*

Gefangene Der Liebe
(Prisoner of Love)
(GERMAN)
Berlin, Sept. 7.
Herzog release of Rhombus & Sued production. Stars Curd Juergens. Annemarie Dueringer, Bernard Wicki. Directed by Rudolf Jugert. Screenplay, Walter Forster; camera, Bruno Mondi; music, Werner Eisbrenner; sets, Erich Kettelhut and Johannes Ott. At Gloria Palast, Berlin. Running time, 105 MINS.
Willi Kluge .... Curd Juergens
Maria .... Annemarie Dueringer
Franz Martens .... Bernard Wicki
Anni .... Mady Rahl
Max .... Paul Esser
Dr. Thomas .... Brigitte Horney
Her Mother .... Claire Reigbert
Christine .... Gabriele Strasser
Ludwig .... Fritz Benscher

This is a very good, human and generally realistic film about a woman returning from Siberian

prisonship and the new problems posed on her and her husband as she brings a baby along. Pic's courageous plot has a remarkably tight treatment of moving drama which packs emotional impact. Despite its misleading title, film should also lure class audiences here. In particular, however, it will be a good item for the femme trade. International prospects appear above average.

Sensitively directed by Rudolf Jugert, "Prisoner" is handsomely mounted and avoids tearjerking elements German pix of this type often tend to. Though loaded with dialog, film unreels without dull moments and above expert contributions by all concerned. For the sake of a more satisfying happy end, it slides into a conventional turn in the second half. Yet this hardly reduces the impressive overall effect.

Film rates highest mention for the acting. Annemarie Dueringer establishes herself as a firstrate actress via her portrayal of the woman who, after eight years of terrible hardships in Soviet prison camps, has to face lack of understanding on the part of her husband. Latter is convincingly played by Curd Juergens, while no less impressive performances are turned in by Bernhard Wicki as the other man in her life, and Brigitte Horney, who as a medico was of valuable help for the many unfortunate women in prison camps. *Hans.*

A Star Is Born
(C'SCOPE—MUSICAL—COLOR)

Boffola boxoffice, period.

Warner Bros. release of Transcona (Sid Luft) production starring Judy Garland, James Mason; features Jack Carson, Charles Bickford. Directed by George Cukor. Screenplay, Moss Hart, based on screenplay by Dorothy Parker-Alan Campbell-Robert Carson, from story by William A. Wellman and Robt. Carson. Associate producer, Vern Alves; camera (Technicolor), Sam Leavitt; special effects, H. F. Koenekamp; songs, Harold Arlen & Ira Gershwin; "Born in a Trunk" by Leonard Gershe; dances, Richard Barstow; music, Ray Heindorf; orchestrations, Skip Martin; vocal arrangements, Jack Cathcart; art, Irene and costumes, Irene Sharaff; art director, Malcolm Bert; other costumes, Jean Louis and Mary Ann Nyberg; asst. directors, Earl Bellamy, Edward Graham. Russell Llewellyn. Tradeshown N.Y., Sept. 27, '54. Running time, 182 MINS.
Esther Blodgett .... Judy Garland
Norman Maine .... James Mason
Libby .... Jack Carson
Oliver Niles .... Charles Bickford
Danny McGuire .... Tom Noonan
Starlet .... Lucy Marlow
Susan .... Amanda Blake
Graves .... Irving Bacon
Libby's Secretary .... Hazel Shermet
Glenn Williams .... James Brown
Miss Markham .... Lotus Robb
(*Aspect ratio:* 2.55-1)

"A Star Is Born" was a great 1937 moneymaker when David O. Selznick and William A. Wellman first made the Janet Gaynor-Fredric March starrer and it's an even greater picture in its filmusical transmutation. In CinemaScope, under the Judy Garland-James Mason-Sidney Luft aegis. It will not only mop up as a commercial entry; this noble production for WB release sets a number of artistic standards which may have their echoes in the intra-industry accolades that usually comes with the Ides of March.

A VARIETY review traditionally concerns itself with the boxoffice, leaving the artistic values of Oscar sweepstakes for the fan mags and columnists. But in the instance of a "comeback" personality like Judy Garland it becomes a pertinent topic of discussion. The trade, like the public, rooted for her signal, in-personal "comeback" at the Palace on Broadway, and the same values must obtain with this, her first film, and under her husband's production aegis, since leaving Metro, her young lifetime "home" lot in Culver City.

Unfolded in the showmanly Moss Hart adaptation of the 1937 original is a strong personal saga which somehow becomes, in a sense, integrated into the celluloid plot. The reel and the real-life values sometimes play back and forth, in pendulum fashion, and the unspooling is never wanting for heart-wallop and gusty entertainment values.

Just as it threatens to become a vocalisthenic tour-de-force, such as in "Born In a Trunk," the meaty plot strands pick up again, and the whole cloth reaffirms its basic dramatic pattern.

The casting is ideal; the direction sure; the basic ingredients honest and convincing all the way.

Miss Garland glitters with that stardust which in the plot the wastrel star James Mason recognizes. And her loyalties are as Gibraltar amidst the house of cards which periodically seem to collapse around her and upon him—and invariably also affect the brittle but understanding studio head, Charles Bickford.

From the opening drunken debacle at the Shrine benefit to the scandalous antics of a hopeless dipsomaniac when his wife (Miss Garland) wins the industry's top accolade, the Academy Award, there is an intense pattern of real-life mirrorings which have been so skilfully captured on the permanent celluloid record.

From the screaming-meemy fans in the lush Technicolorful reincarnation of the glittering Santa Monica Blvd. panorama to the tragic topper, as the hapless, hopeless lush of a husband walks into the Malibu surf, the three-hours plus is an authentic documentary.

(Incidentally, Selznick's original "Star" was the first film to disprove the b.o. bogey that Hollywood stories aren't commercial, just as Par's "Greatest Show On Earth" (DeMille) dittoed on behalf of circus stories, which also for a time failed to click as film fare.)

Integrated into the arresting romance-with-music—the songs are not intrusive, being plausibly spotted as "benefit" numbers or in-rehearsal routines—is perhaps the best inside stuff on the Hollywood film production scene that has ever been publicly projected. The intrastudio attitudes and exaggerations; the private and public antics of the great and the little people of the industry; the playback and musical rehearsal scenes; the flip asides ("I had a very young week last week"; or "that's Pasadena; leave it alone"); the Dr. Kildare fol-de-rol of the makeup men, including a yesman for the top facial artist; the flip cracks about the Dietrich eyebrow and the Crawford mouth; the big to-do to shoot a waving hand ("I don't wanna see your face," screams the asst. director of this bit); the first preview jitters; the sardonic studio publicity chief who has been hatefully biding his time—these are samples of the many ingredients woven into the sum total.

The Harold Arlen-Ira Gershwin numbers are tailored for the plot and not the jukeboxes although "The Man Who Got Away" is already on the road in that direction. The yesteryear standards are plausibly interlarded. Of the new songs, "Got to Have Me With You," "Somewhere There's a Someone" and "Long Face Lost" tie into the script like it was a one-man libretto creation.

There are three or four dramatic highlights that pile on top of each other in a manner which might create the suspicion of anticlimactic toppers cluttering the cinematurgy, but such is the pitch and the pyramiding that the opposite is true.

There are minor key highlights as when she assumes responsibility for the custody of her drunken husband, resulting in his 90-day City Jail term being suspended. Or that heartbreak scene when she gayly recreates a Paris-Chinese-African-cariocan "production" conceit—to the playback disk in the home phonograph—that is better than if it were given a Radio City Music Hall production.

Whatever the production delays, which allegedly piled up a near-$5,000,000 production cost, the end-results quite obviously were worth it. There is the ring of authority and a striving for as near-perfection as possible that will pay off in jackpot proportions. And for all concerned.

Mason is as likeable a "heavy" as she is as a star. Bickford's studio head concept, and Carson's impression of a publicity chief, are the real thing. A lammister from a former two-man saloon act, Tommy Noonan, will emerge with many Hollywood opportunities as an earnest young man on his way to fatter roles. The rest are secondary although Lucy Marlow, as a starlet, makes her classy chassis bit stand up and out for heftier potentials.

The veteran George Cukor directed with a sure hand from a tiptop script by Moss Hart; Richard Barlow's dance-staging; the many art, costume and decor credits; Ray Heindorf's usually capital musical job; the Technicolorful lensing which evidences wisdom when to minor-key the hues as well as full-up—all these are among the many plus values. It's a whammo 182 minutes that belies the full three-hour course of entertainment, so arresting the unfolding.

Fort Knox, move over. *Abel.*

The Barefoot Contessa
(COLOR)

Joseph L. Mankiewicz, Humphrey Bogart and Ava Gardner teamed in one for the big money.

United Artists release of Figaro production. Stars Ava Gardner, Humphrey Bogart; features Edmond O'Brien, Marius Goring, Valentina Cortesa, Rossano Brazzi, Elizabeth Sellars, Warren Stevens, Franco Interlenghi, Mari Aldon, Bessie Love, Diana Decker, Bill Frasser. Directed by Joseph L. Mankiewicz. Original screenplay by Mankiewicz; camera (Technicolor), Jack Cardiff; editor, William Hornbeck; music, Mario Nascimbene. Previewed in N.Y., Sept. 24, '54. Running time, 128 MINS.

Harry Dawes .... Humphrey Bogart
Maria Vargas .... Ava Gardner
Oscar Muldoon .... Edmond O'Brien
Alberto Bravano .... Marius Goring
Eleanora Torlato-Favrini .... Valentina Cortesa
Vincenzo Torlato-Favrini Rossano Brazzi
Jerry .... Elizabeth Sellars
Kirk Edwards .... Warren Stevens
Pedro .... Franco Interlenghi
Myrna .... Mari Aldon
Nightclub Proprietor..Alberto Rabagliati
Busboy .... Enzo Staiola
Maria's Mother .... Maria Zanoli
Maria's Father ...... Renato Chiantoni
J. Montague Brown .... Bill Fraser
Mr. Black .... John Parrish
Mr. Blue .... Jim Gerald
Drunken Blonde .... Diana Decker
Gypsy Dancer .... Riccardo Rioli
The Pretender .... Tonio Selwart
The Pretender's Wife..Margaret Anderson
Lulu McGee .... Gertrude Flynn
Hector Eubanks .... John Horne
Mrs. Eubanks .... Bessie Love
Eddie Blake .... Robert Christopher
Chambermaid .... Ann Maria Paduan
Chauffeur .... Carlo Dale

(*Aspect ratio:* 1.75-1)

Sharpness of the characters, the high-voltage dialog, the cynicism and wit and wisdom of the story, the spectacular combination of the immorally rich and the immorally sycophantic—these add up to a click feature from writer-director Joseph L. Mankiewicz. It's adult material all the way, making no compromises in focusing on the mores of its people: Hollywood filmsters, a fiscal high and mighty newly-turned producer, and unemployed, quondam Continental royalty. They're to be found at a lush party in Beverly Hills or the swank gambling casino on the Riviera.

This is a dish of ingeniously-fashioned, original entertainment for grown-up viewers. It has a strong show business flavor and a line or two that might be beyond the ken of strangers to pic-making. But its basic story elements are strong and make for substantial fare on anybody's menu. It's potent boxoffice.

Humphrey Bogart and Ava Gardner have the leads and register with great effect. But then Mankiewicz has drawn fine performances all around. And in shaping the scenario, each member of his cast is given a chance to come to the fore with at least one histrionic grandstand play. Thus each is shown to be an essential part of the plot, necessary to the well rounded, integrated whole.

Miss Gardner is the contessa of the title, "discovered" in a second-rate flamenco nitery in Madrid. The trio of discoverers: Bogart as a writer-director and determined member of Alcoholocis Ananymous; Edmond O'Brien, as a glib, nervous, perspiring combination of pressagent and (apparent) procurer, and Warren Stevens, the producer who, as he is aptly described by another player, "owns Texas and just bought California because he wants to make a picture." This is the start of Miss Gardner's career as a shining star and much-desired woman.

Mankiewicz' script frankly makes no bones about who is or isn't (but would like to be) romancing whom. Miss Gardner, for example, while refusing to satisfy the lusts of her well-heeled admirers, including Stevens and a zillionaire South American, is revealed as yielding to a guitar player from the Spanish honky tonk. Not namby-pamby either is a wedding night scene in which the Italian ex-count in whom the contessa finally has found her true love, discloses to her that war wounds inflicted in 1942 had rendered him impotent.

Importantly, there's good taste throughout. Mankiewicz eschews shock values. Every item in the development seems to inherently belong. Where the material is strong by screen standards he has presented it without hedging but still also without any ribald, undue emphasis.

The director employs off-screen voices on many occasions. Bogart, at the start, speaks from off-camera while he is seen silently observing the interment ritual for Miss Gardner at a small cemetery in an obscure Italian village. His spoken recollection of the first meeting with the contessa then leads to the actual scene. It's via this technique that Mankiewicz, with telling effect, gets across many story points.

Miss Gardner is ideal in her spot, looking every inch the femme magnetism around which all the action revolves. She's a beautifully-dimensioned knockout—the wardrobe department didn't feel too restrained—and does an impressive job of acting as the Spanish castanet hoofer who elevates to a part in the international coterie. Bogart is splendid throughout, taking part quietly and with maximum effectiveness in the twists and turns of the intriguing story. With no desire to zero in on Miss Gardner himself—he marries a script girl—he becomes her paternalistic confidante and protector and their scenes together are done with genuine feeling.

O'Brien clicks just right in the more flamboyant role of public relations man and servile aide to producer Stevens. Latter gives a quiet moodiness to the part of owner of $200,000,000. Marius Goring does a zesty job as the fabulous Latino whose turn for the dramatic spotlighting comes as, in a cleverly-staged argument, he admits to a free-wheeling life and accuses Stevens also of being a sinner but hypocritically hiding behind a mask of self-righteousness.

At times, Mankiewicz, the writer, seems over-generous in providing his characters with words. Much of the talk is fresh and incisive and doubtless will be lifted by pirates of well-turned phraseology. But there's so much of it that once in a while it gets in the way of the story. Despite which, his yarns flow smoothly with dramatic accent just in the correct, strategic places. Coming into the homestretch, though, some of the passages tend to slowness.

The Figaro production provides fitting backdrops for the international goings-on. Film, lensed in Italy, looks authentic and authoritative with its many actual places and expertly-designed sets. The dye work by British Technicolor, unusually exquisite, seems more subtle and real than most tinted photography.

Story ends as it began, at the cemetery, with Bogart this time reflecting on the climax of the life of the barefoot contessa (so billed because she liked to kick off her shoes). Rossano Brazzi, highly polished as the former Italo nobleman whom she marries, kills her and her lover as he finds them together. Ironically, the count never learned that the contessa wanted to bear a child for him even though by another man.

Score by Mario Nascimbene, mainly a thematic tune of Spanish flavor that is not identified, has value in its own right and with proper merchandising could be a salable factor for the film. Other credits are topnotch although, in the late reels, sharper editing might step up the pace.

As a footnote it might be added that Mankiewicz has been quoted as saying none of his characters is for real. This was in answer to suspicion that the moneybags producer might be an only slightly distorted mirroring of, to come right out and name him, Howard Hughes. With the aforementioned crack about his "owning Texas," the pic does tie down the point of origin of the picturized producer. Hughes, of course, is a Texan. But then lots of men who rival Fort Knox in wealth come from Texas and some move into film production. It's understood there have been some cuts in the pic to reduce any further resemblance. *Gene.*

Woman's World
(C'SCOPE—COLOR)

Hollywood at its commercial best, with names of Clifton Webb, June Allyson, Van Heflin, Lauren Bacall, Fred MacMurray, Arlene Dahl and Cornel Wilde serving as potent marquee bait.

Twentieth-Fox release of Charles Brackett production. Stars Clifton Webb, June Allyson, Van Heflin, Lauren Bacall, Fred MacMurray, Arlene Dahl and Cornel Wilde. Features Elliot Ried and Margalo Gillmore. Directed by Jean Negulesco. Screenplay by Claude Binyon, Mary Loos and Richard Sale with additional dialogue by Howard Lindsay and Russel Crouse, based on a story by Mona Williams; camera (CinemaScope), Joe MacDonald; editor, Louis Loeffler; music, Cyril J. Mockridge; song, "It's a Woman's World" by Sammy Cahn and Mockridge; sung by the Four Aces. Previewed in N.Y., Sept. 27, '54. Running time, 94 MINS.

Gifford .... Clifton Webb
Katie .... June Allyson
Jerry .... Van Heflin
Elizabeth .... Lauren Bacall
Sid .... Fred MacMurray
Carol .... Arlene Dahl
Bill Baxter .... Cornel Wilde
Tony .... Elliott Reid
Evelyn .... Margalo Gillmore
Tomaso .... Alan Reed
Jarecki .... David Hoffman
Worker—Auto Assembly..George Melford
Butler .... Eric Wilton
Cab Driver .... Edward Astran
Bellboy .... Conrad Feid
Waiter .... Marc Snow
Doorman .... Bert Stevens

Having served as an unofficial tourist bureau for Rome in "Three Coins in the Fountain," 20th-Fox, with the aid of the CinemaScope camera, is now giving the VIP treatment to New York in "Woman's World." This is the film company's paen to Gotham and, for this alone, Zanuck & Co. rate a unanimous vote of thanks from the local Chamber of Commerce and the N.Y. Visitors Bureau.

The city, fortunately, has been peopled with attractive visitors—Clifton Webb, June Allyson, Van Heflin, Lauren Bacall, Fred Mac-Murray, Arlene Dahl and Cornel Wilde, a marquee lineup that'll draw in any city, big or small. Add to these assets a slick story by Claude Binyon, Mary Loos and Richard Sale, with additional dialogue by Howard Lindsay and Russel Crouse. The result is Hollywood at its commercial best, a highly-polished product, technically and story-wise. The returns should be socko from all situations.

Comparison between "Woman's World" and Metro's recent "Executive Suite" is inevitable, since the basic story premise is similar—the behind-the-scenes scramble for the top job of a gigantic industrial firm. While the goings-on in "Executive" were more dramatic and sombre, the 20th entry takes the lighter approach and much of it is played for comedy. The wives of the men involved also play more prominent roles.

Webb, as president of Gifford Motors, a leading auto manufacturing firm, brings three of his district managers to New York for a firsthand observation, his aim being to select a successor to the recently-deceased sales manager. He invites their wives along since he believes that the right wife is just as important as the right man for the job.

There's Miss Allyson and Wilde from Kansas City, Miss Bacall and MacMurray from Philadelphia, and Miss Dahl and Heflin from Dallas. All the men in Webb's estimation are equally capable of handling the No. 1 post. The final decision rests on their wives.

Miss Allyson is a hayseed from K.C., extremely devoted to her husband and three children, bungling and embarrassed in Gotham's glamor mill, wishing to return to her home but willing to accept her fate in N.Y. if her husband wants and gets the job.

Miss Bacall is bitter and disillusioned and at the point of separation from her ambitious husband who has neglected his family for his work in an ulcer-accompanied drive for advancement.

Miss Dahl is a pushy glamor gal, not unwilling to throw her sex around to gain her aims. She believes her efforts have played a large part in the business success of her husband. She wants the N.Y. job for the glamor it represents and wastes no time going after it.

The characters of the men are also neatly etched. Wilde is honest, outspoken, and devoted to his family. MacMurray is a proud, power-hungry self-made man. Heflin is modest and quietly competent. Webb is kindly and efficiently observant despite his approach and seemingly facetious manner. The choice, of course, is left to the very end and will come as a surprise to many. Unlike "Executive Suite," in which the audience could quickly put its finger on the chosen man, "World" keeps 'em guessing.

The visit to New York of the hinterland execs and their wives gives the C'Scope camera a wonderful opportunity to wander about Gotham. It captures the city's more lush side—the beautiful skyline, the tall buildings, the area along the East River and the United Nations, Park and Fifth Avenues, the Stork Club, the Plaza Hotel, an outside glimpse of Macy's and 34th St., the approaches to the tunnels.

It makes a great trailer for America's key metropolis.

One aspect of New York life, better known to the femmes, is a particularly hilarious sequence in a so-called women's outlet store, vaguely similar to Klein's on 14th St.

While one may quibble on the plausibility of the story, there will be no quarrel with the way it's handled. The entire cast, under Jean Negulesco fine direction, contribute a performance as polished as the entire production. They're all "old pros" and give each character the delineation that is required. Since all contribute equally, it's difficult to single anyone out individually. It's team work at its best. In addition to the star names, solid performances are registered by Margalo Gillmore, as Webb's sister who aides in the o.o. of the wives, and Elliot Reid, as the tycoon's nephew who serves as guide and one-man entertainment committee.

Charles Brackett has pulled out all stops in giving the picture top-notch production values. The technical aspects, including Joe Mac-Donald's C'Scope-Technicolor lensing, are all out of the top drawer.
Holl.

This Is My Love
(SONG—COLOR)

Unconvincing distaff drama with mild prospects.

Hollywood, Sept. 28.
RKO release of Hugh Brooke production. Stars Linda Darnell, Rick Jason, Dan Duryea, Faith Domergue; features Hal Baylor, Connie Russell. Directed by Stuart Heisler. Screenplay, Hagar Wilde and Hugh Brooks; from the story "Fear Has Black Wings" by Brooke; camera (Pathe Color), Ray June; editor, Otto Ludwig; music, Franz Waxman; song, Brooke and Waxman. Previewed Sept. 23, '54. Running time, **91 MINS.**
Vida .... Linda Darnell
Glenn .... Rick Jason
Murray .... Dan Duryea
Evelyn .... Faith Domergue
Eddie .... Hal Baylor
Connie Russell .... Connie Russell
David Myer .... Jerry Mathers
Shirley Myer .... Susie Mathers
Mrs. Timberly .... Mary Young
District Attorney .... William Hopper
Investigator .... Stuart Randall
Harry .... Kam Tong
Dr. Raines .... Judo Holdren
Customer .... Carl Switzer
(Aspect ratio: 1.66-1)

Exhibitors booking "This Is My Love" will have to pitch it to the matinee-going femmes who are supposed to like unhappy soap operas. Other film shoppers will hardly take to the tears-and-torment drama. Hence, boxoffice prospects are extremely mild.

Production gets a good Pathe Color dress and first-rate lensing of the lowkey tints, but these assets are lost on a plot that comes to the screen with little real dramatic wallop and in which the performers all seem uncomfortable. Allan Dowling is presenting the Hugh Brooke production through RKO and starred are Linda Darnell, Rick Jason, Dan Duryea and Faith Domergue, all of whom can do better than they do here under Stuart Heisler's direction of the script by Brooke and Hagar Wilde, which was based on Brooke's story, "Fear Has Black Wings."

The Misses Darnell and Domergue are sisters, the latter married to Duryea, once a dancer and now a hopeless cripple. Approaching an "old maid" state, Miss Darnell goes off the deep end for Jason when he enters the story, but is afraid of her feelings until Jason and Miss Domergue start an off-hours affair. By now com-

pletely unbalanced, Miss Darnell arranges things so her sister will give Duryea a fatal dose of poison instead of his regular medicine and then strengthens a murder charge against Miss Domergue by carefully dropped remarks to the police. Finale finds her, rejected by Jason, trudging through the rain to the police station to confess all.

The stars are called upon mostly to run through hysterical tantrums and be beaten down by life and circumstance to the accompaniment of a wordy script. Hal Baylor is featured as Miss Darnell's oafish suitor and Connie Russell is in to sing the title tune, cleffed by Brooke and Franz Waxman. Latter also did the good score and Ray June contributed the excellent photography. *Brog.*

The Unholy Four

Routine whodunit for average prospects in program market.

Hollywood, Sept. 28.
Lippert release of a Michael Carreras production. Stars Paulette Goddard; co-stars William Sylvester; features Patrick Holt, Paul Carpenter, Alvys Maben, Russel Napier. Directed by Terence Fisher. Screenplay, Carreras, from novel, "Stranger at Home," by George Sanders; camera, James Harvey; editor, Bill Lenney; music, Ivor Slaney. Reviewed Sept. 24, '54. Running time, **78 MINS.**
Angie .... Paulette Goddard
Philip Vickers .... William Sylvester
Job Crandall .... Patrick Holt
Bill Saul .... Paul Carpenter
Joan Merrill .... Alvys Maben
Inspector Treherne ...... Russel Napier
Sessions .... David King Wood
Bionde .... Pat Owens
Jenny .... Kay Callard
Sergeant Johnson .... Jeremy Hawk
Brownie .... Jack Taylor
Roddy .... Kim Mills
(Aspect ratio: 1.33-1)

This British import may be helped through the program market by lure of Paulette Goddard's name, but film stacks up as a routine whodunit, slow-moving and heavy on plot. As Miss Goddard's co-star, William Sylvester garners most of the interest.

Producer Michael Carreras poses two questions in his screenplay: who slugged Sylvester, femme's husband, on the head while on a fishing trip with three friends in Portugal, resulting in a three-year lapse of memory; and who killed one of these men the night Sylvester suddenly reappears. Practically everybody in cast but the inspector comes under suspicion for one or the other deed, including Miss Goddard.

Sylvester plays his role stoically for certain dramtic effect, but femme star's character is of a rather unknown quantity throughout. Direction of Terence Fisher is plodding until a windup fight, when he manages certain realistic action. Russel Napier as the inspector stands out in support.

Alvys Maben, social secretary to Miss Goddard, is okay as a minx who tries to throw the blame for the murder on to Sylvester, and Patrick Holt is cast as the final heavy. Technical credits are standard. *Whit.*

The Shanghai Story

Republic production and release; associate producer, Frank Lloyd. Stars Ruth Roman, Edmond O'Brien; features Richard Jaeckel, Basil Ruysdael, Janine Parreau, Barry Kelley, Philip Ahn. Screenplay, Seton I. Miller and Steve Fisher; based on story by Lester Yard; camera, Jack Marte; editor, Tony Martinelli; music, R. Dale Butts. Tradeshown, N.Y., Sept. 23, '54. Running time, **90 MINS.**
Rita King .... Ruth Roman
Dr. Dan Maynard .... Edmond O'Brien
"Knuckles" Greer .... Richard Jaeckel
Ricki Dolmine .... Barry Kelley

Paul Grant .... Whit Bissell
Rev. Hollingsworth ...... Basil Ruysdael
Colonel Zorek .... Marvin Miller
Mrs. De Verno .... Yvette Dugay
Mr. De Verno .... Paul Picerni
Mrs. Merryweather .... Isabel Randolph
Major Ling Wu .... Philip Ahn
Mrs. Warren .... Frances Rafferty
Mr. Haljerson .... Frank Ferguson
Carl Hoyt .... James Griffith
Mr. Warren .... John Alvin
Mr. Chen .... Frank Puglia
Sun Lee .... Victor Sen Yung
Penny Warren .... Janine Ferreau
Junior Officer .... Richard Loo
(Aspect ratio: 1.85-1)

"The Shanghai Story," a meller localed in the Chinese metropolis, has a fair amount of suspense and action that will help this Republic entry get by satisfactorily in the twin-bill market. Fact that producer-director Frank Lloyd is a three-time Academy Award winner is a selling point while names of Ruth Roman and Edmond O'Brien are familiar to most film-goers.

Intrigue and plotting that goes on within Communist China today no doubt would provide material for dozens of good stories. Unfortunately, the Lester Yard yarn, as screenplayed by Seton I. Miller and Steve Fisher, unravels as a web of talkiness, cliches and obvious situations.

Suspecting a spy for the western powers lurks among a motley group of Europeans and Americans, Shanghai police chief Marvin Miller places them all under house arrest in a local hotel. Among those seized are Edmond O'Brien, a muscular physician who's practiced in China for years; Richard Jaeckel, seaman and international adventurer; Basil Ruysdael, a missionary, and Barry Kelley, a tycoon who's been shipping war materials to the Reds.

Also a hotel resident is willowy Ruth Roman who appears to enjoy a special status with the police. She comes and goes at will since she's Miller's romantic interest. Much footage unreels before Miss Roman turns out as an anti-Commy who aids O'Brien and Jaeckel to escape with priceless information for American military authorities. A far-fetched finale has O'Brien returning to his femme benefactor to press an affaire de coeur.

Frank Lloyd, who seems to have had an off-day on this one, seldom gets a ring of realism into performances of most cast members, probably due to the stock story he was faced with. O'Brien, however, is lusty and vigorous in his role of a hard-hitting physician. Miss Roman is adequate as the mysterious woman of glamour while Jaeckel has a salty look befitting those who follow the sea. Miller contribs a trite portrayal of the police head. Routine support is provided by Ruysdael, Kelley, White Bissell and others.

Camerawork of Jack Marta catches the proper Oriental atmosphere of the Shanghai setting. Editing of Tony Martinelli has the film overlong at 90 minutes. Another 10 minutes deleted would have sped the action considerably. Music of R. Dale Butts is unobtrusive while art direction of William E. Flannery as well as other technical credits are okay.
Gilb.

Stars of the Russian Ballet
(RUSSIAN-COLOR)

Artkino release of Lenfilm Studios production. Stars Galina Ulanova. With Bolshoi Ballet, Moscow, and Kirov Ballet, Leningrad. Directed by G. Rappaport. Camera (Sovcolor), S. Ivanov; music, B. V. Asafiev, Tchaikovsky. At the Stanley, N.Y. Running time, **80 MINS.**

SWAN LAKE

Odetta .... Galina Ulanova
Odillia .... N. M. Dudinskaya
Prince .... N. M. Sergeyev
Magician .... V. I. Vakanov

FOUNTAIN OF BAKHCHISARAI

Maria .... Galina Ulanova
Zarema .... M. M. Plisetskaya
Girei .... P. A. Gusev
Vatslav .... Y. T. Zhdanov
Nurali .... I. D. Belsky

FLAMES OF PARIS

Phillippe .... V. M. Chabuklan
Jeanne .... M. L. Gottlieb
Theresa .... Y. G. Sangovich
Gaspar .... V. I. Tsaplin
Marquis .... V. I. Smoltsov

Some striking performers, interesting ballets and the opportunity to see and study the technique and presentation of famed Russian ballet troupes in their present Soviet incarnation, are offered in this series of three ballet excerpts. To avid balletomanes, as well as those interested generally in the dance, this film is a treat. Otherwise, the pic is limited by its subject-matter and cast to selected art houses.

Film offers the familiar "Swan Lake," and two new modern works, "Fountain of Bakhchisarai" and "Flames of Paris." Leading dancers as well as the ballet corps of the Bolshoi Opera House, Moscow, and Kirov Opera House, Leningrad, participate. Production is much more lavish than the normal stage ballet in the U. S., and the color is very effective. Film exhibits some male dancers superior to our own while the gifted Galina Ulanova lives up to her previous notices as the lead in two of the three presentations.

Film's canvas allows the director to fill out details in "Swan Lake," to make the story more intelligible and appealing than it is when staged in the U. S. Camera switches from an indoor theatre stage to outdoor settings of lakes and forests, for strong effect. But it is the brilliance of Ulanova's performance as the Swan Queen that makes this segment so fine. Pantomime, soft use of arms and hands, are added to her other technical gifts, to make the role believable while the dancing techque is remarkably finished and exciting. Ulanova is ably partnered by N. M. Sergeyev, who is not only a manly prince but a dancer of superior style and surprising turns. N. M. Dudinskaya, as the false queen, is also a brilliant, virtuoso dancer and a striking, effective actress.

Ballet corps supporting the leads is interesting in its harsh precision, lacking a certain soft quality of American dancers, but otherwise is marvelously trained.

"Fountain" is an affecting, lush story of a Tartar chieftain falling in love with a Polish princess he abducts, and the tragedy of her death at the hands of the khan's former favorite. Ulanova is more maidenlike but no less appealing a dancer here while M. M. Plisetskaya, as her rival, is femininely handsome, fiery and also a fine terp artist.

"Flames of Paris" is weakest of the three works, but here too are some fine dancers, especially among the men (as V. M. Chabukiani), while M. L. Gottlieb, the heroine, does some brilliant fouettes. Crowd scenes are exciting, too. *Bron.*

Africa Adventure
(DOCUMENTARY—COLOR)

RKO release of Jay Bonafield production. Written and narrated by Robert C. Ruark. Camera (Pathecolor), Chester Kronfeld; additional cameramen, Harry Selby, Andrew Holmberg; music, Paul Sawtell; conducted by Sylvan Levin.

Tradeshown, N.Y., Sept. 20, '54. Running time, 64 MINS.

Scripps-Howard columnist Robert C. Ruark, who wrote and narrates this documentary of a three-month hunting trek into Africa, states in a foreword to the film that it was made to show the darkest continent "as it actually is . . . nothing in this picture was staged or contrived." That's a commendable statement. However, the 64 minutes of footage are patently amateurish and the RKO release will need strong selling to eke out playdates in the program market.

But with special handling the film could find acceptance in art houses. For despite its shortcomings there are a number of unusual angles to the venture which with good breaks could be translated into a profit for the exhibitor. Ruark, whose syndicated stuff appears throughout the country, no doubt will puff the picture. Moreover, while hardly a household word, his name is familiar enough to the general public to stimulate some curiosity.

In the pictorial account of the personal safari Ruark jumps off from Nairobi, British East Africa, accompanied by professional hunters Harry Selby, Andrew Holmberg and John Sutton. They're in quest of big game. Before the expedition winds up a bull elephant is bagged, a belligerent rhinoceros is downed and a crafty leopard is shot. Aside from actual shooting scenes, daily camp routine is detailed along with occasional close-ups of natives.

There will be those who will feel Ruark's picture ought to be run off before friends in the parlor on a 16m home projector. The Pathecolor in which this is filmed does not measure up to professional lensing and Ruark's commentary (witty in spots) is fuzzily recorded. Score of Paul Sawtell, while adequate for the purpose intended, occasionally muffles the narration.

Jay Bonafield carriers production credit on the film which was produced in cooperation with Voyager Productions. *Gilb.*

Caidos en el Infierno
(Descent Into Hell)
(ARGENTINE)

Buenos Aires, Sept. 2.
Argentina Sono Film production and release. Directed by Luis Cesar Amadori. Stars Laura Hidalgo; features Eduardo Cuitino, Alberto de Mendoza, Guillermo Battaglia, Domingo Sapelli, Irma Roy. Screenplay, Gabriel Pena, from M. Valbeck novel; camera, Antonio Merayo; music, Tito Ribero; editor, Jorge Garate. At Gran Rex Theatre, Buenos Aires. Running time, 112 MINS.

As the title implies, this is a melodrama of deepest dye teeming with laughter-provoking dramatic "situations," where apparently the director hoped for suspense. It is hardly credible that local producers persist in selecting this unconvincing type of story and overdoing the dramatic hues. People just don't talk and act that way and audiences know it.

The story is set in the beautiful surroundings of the Bariloche lake district, to which the black-and-white photography does scant justice, or poor celluloid was used.

A business tycoon shoots his secretary accidentally and his gold-digger, adulterous spouse persuades him to cover up the manslaughter. Blackmail by the dead girl's husband ensues till the wife bumps him off in turn, disguising her crime as defense against burglary. Remorse drives the husband

to suicide and unwittingly the wife reveals all to a police inspector.

Star Laura Hidalgo's preoccupation with her looks hampers acting, though Eduardo Cuitino strives manfully to be convincing. Alberto de Mendoza, a male juve of promise, can do little but register as a very contemptuous Cassanova. As the blackmailer, Mario Lozano hams the role of heel to laughter-raising point. *Nid.*

Beau Brummell
(COLOR)

Opulent costume drama, fairly entertaining, with good names, ballyhoo angles.

Hollywood, Oct. 5.
Metro release of Sam Zimbalist production. Stars Stewart Granger, Elizabeth Taylor, Peter Ustinov; features Robert Morley, James Donald, James Hayter, Rosemary Harris, Paul Rogers, Noel Willman. Directed by Curtis Bernhardt. Screenplay, Karl Tunberg; based on the play written for Richard Mansfield by Clyde Fitch; camera (Eastman Color), Oswald Morris; editor, Frank Clarke; music, Richard Addinsell; played by the Royal Philharmonic Orchestra, conducted by Muir Mathieson. Previewed Sept. 24, '54. Running time, 111 MINS.

Beau Brummell .... Stewart Granger
Lady Patricia .... Elizabeth Taylor
Prince of Wales ...... Peter Ustinov
King George III .... Robert Morley
Lord Edwin Mercer ..... James Donald
Mortimer .... James Hayter
Mrs. Fitzherbert ..... Rosemary Harris
William Pitt .... Paul Rogers
Lord Byron .... Noel Willman
Midger .... Peter Dyneley
Sir Geoffrey Baker ... Charles Carson
Docter Warren .... Ernest Clark
Mr. Fox .... Peter Bull
Mr. Burke .... Mark Dignam
Colonel .... Desmond Roberts
Thurlow .... David Horne
Sir Ralph Sidley ..... Ralph Truman
Mr. Tupp .... Elwyn Brook-Jones
Docter Dubois .... George De Marfaz
Docter Willis .... Henry Oscar
Mayor .... Harold Kasket

This is an opulent, fairly entertaining, period drama based on the career of England's famous dandy and amateur politician. The marquee dressing provided by the familiar names of Stewart Granger and Elizabeth Taylor, along with a number of exploitation possibilities, should shape it for okay returns.

The Sam Zimbalist production is drawn from the Clyde Fitch play which served Richard Mansfield as a legit vehicle. The lensing took place in England to give its period settings an authentic look, an intent also carried out by the British casters, so everything is in keeping through the overly long 111 minutes. Some rather obvious process scenes are permitted to contrast sharply with those that are real.

The Karl Tunberg screenplay gives Curtis Bernhardt's direction ample opportunity for romantically emotional scenes and he gets a good effect from them with his players. Also effective are several dramatic sequences dealing with the relationship between Beau Brummell and the Prince of Wales, and the final, deathbed scene that reconciles the dying dandy and his prince, now king. For those who like to be plunged at length into tearjerk, the climax is made to order. Others will find Brummell a long time dying.

General appeal for the masses probably would have been greater had the motivations behind the Brummell character played by Stewart Granger been more clearly established. As it is, one is never quite sure whether he is patriot or opportunist as he cultivates the Prince of Wales. Had he been more heel, or more hero, viewers would have known whether to love him or hate him. Result of this is to throw the major sympathy to the Prince, a more understandable person as superbly interpreted by Peter Ustinov. Miss Taylor, too, is a victim of motivation obscurity as the beauty attracted to Brummell, first turning him down and then being turned down by him when she does decide to surrender.

Plotwise, Brummell's self assurance intrigues the Prince of Wales, who sponsors him in society and listens to his advice against Prime Minister William Pitt. While under the prince's favor, Brummell rises to be something of a style-setter and favorite. In a beruffled era, he goes in for simple elegance and is well on his way to an earldom until the scheme he has cooked up to have the prince declared regent fails and the two friends fall out. Brummell flees to France and there, as the years pass, falls deathly ill. A forgiving prince—now king—searches him out and they reconcile before Brummell dies. This is Clyde Fitch history.

Excellent type performances are turned in by Robert Morley, the prince's mad father, James Hayter, Brummell's faithful valet; and Rosemary Harris, as Mrs. Fitzherbert, the woman the prince loves but cannot marry. Paul Rogers, as Pitt; James Donald, as the lord who gets Miss Taylor, and Noel Willman, as Lord Byron, are among others doing good work.

The Eastman Color, printed by Technicolor, is used to advantage by Oswald Morris' lensing. Other technical credits are capable.

Brog.

Carmen Jones
(C'SCOPE-COLOR)

Stirring, colorful film version of the smash Broadway musical; healthy b.o.

Hollywood, Oct. 1.

Twentieth-Fox release of an Otto Preminger production. Co-stars Dorothy Dandridge, Harry Belafonte, Olga James, Pearl Bailey, Joe Adams. Directed by Preminger. Screenplay, Harry Kleiner from book by Oscar Hammerstein, 2d; music, Georges Bizet, lyrics Hammerstein; camera, Sam Leavitt; editor, Louis R. Loefler. Color by DeLuxe. At Studio, Sept. 22, '54. Running time, **105 MINS.**

Carmen .... Dorothy Dandridge
Joe .... Harry Belafonte
Cindy Lou .... Olga James
Frankie .... Pearl Bailey
Myrt .... Diahann Carroll
Rum .... Roy Glenn
Dink .... Nick Stewart
Husky .... Joe Adams
Sgt. Brown .... Broc Peters
T-Bone .... Sandy Lewis
Sally .... Mauri Lynn
Trainer .... DeForest Covan

And the voices of Le Vern Hutcherson, Marilynn Horne, Marvin Hayes.

(*Aspect ratio*: 2.55-1)

As a wartime legit offering "Carmen Jones"—the modernized, all-Negro version of the opera "Carmen"—was a long-run hit both on Broadway and on the road. Now, Otto Preminger has transferred it to the screen with taste and imagination in an opulent production that has a healthy boxoffice outlook, although as an all-Negro film, it will encounter difficulty in some situations.

Preminger has made some changes from the legit version, but none of the basic elements have been removed and the sexy situations inherent in the original story are retained to make this perhaps the first picture in both CinemaScope and Sensuoscope. Excision has been skillfully handled and might even have been carried further with at least one more not too familiar aria removed to permit the film to unspool without a lag. At its present 105-minute length, it is perhaps ten minutes too long.

Harry Kleiner's screenplay closely follows the lines of the stage libretto by Oscar Hammerstein, 2d, in which Carmen is a pleasure-loving southern gal who works in a Dixie parachute factory, where Joe (Jose) is a member of the army regiment on guard duty. She lures him away from Cindy Lou (Micaela) and he deserts with her after a fatal brawl with his sergeant. Eventually, Carmen tires of him and takes up with Husky Miller (Escamillo) the fighter and Joe kills her when she refuses to return to him. In the legit version, he stabbed her; in the film, he strangles her. (Credits blithely ignore the fact that the original creator of "Carmen" was an author named Prosper Merimee. Does professional courtesy stop at the grave?)

As in the wartime legit version, the standout songs—as a result of Hammerstein's lyricizing — are "Stand Up and Fight" (the Toreador song), "I Go For You, But You're Taboo" (Habanera) and "Beat out the Rhythm on the Drums."

Preminger has directed with a deft touch, blending the comedy and tragedy easily and building his scenes to some suspenseful heights. He gets fine performances from the cast toppers, notably Dorothy Dandridge, a sultry Carmen whose performance maintains the right hedonistic note throughout, and Harry Belafonte, who is an extremely convincing Joe. Olga James is seen comparatively briefly as Cindy Lou, but makes the most of her footage and Joe Adams (a coast deejay) is good as Husky Miller. Pearl Bailey stands out as Frankie, scoring a particular triumph since she has only one song the "Drums" number with which to showcase her voice. Off-screen voices were used for Miss Dandridge, Belafonte and Adams, the standout being Marvin Hayes' handling of the latter, for the stirring "Stand Up and Fight." Dubbing throughout is excellent.

Of the supporting players, Diahann Carroll is glimpsed briefly as Myrt and Roy Glenn and Nick Stewart each turn in a fine performance as Rum and Dink, the manager and manager's manager attached to Miller.

Fine camera work by Sam Leavitt, the color by Deluxe, musical direction by Herschel Burke Gilbert, costumes by Mary Ann Nyberg and settings by Edward L. Ilou all contribute strongly to the film's appeal.

Kap.

Hansel and Gretel
(SONG—COLOR)

Unusually well done puppet film that should mop up with the moppet trade. Strong b.o. contender with proper handling.

Michael Myerberg production. Stars the voices of Anna Russell, Mildred Dunnock, Frank Rogier, Delbert Anderson, Helen Boatright, Constance Brigham and Apollo Boys' Choir. Directed by John Paul. Screenplay by Adelheid Weft; adapted by Padriac Colum; camera (Technicolor), Martin Munkacsi; settings, Evalds Dajevskis; costumes, Ida Vendicktow; editor, James F. Barclay; head animator, Joseph Horstmann; characters designed by James Summers; production manager, William F. Rodgers Jr. Previewed in N.Y. Sept. 29, '54. Running time, **75 MINS.**

Rosina Rubylips .... Ann Russell
Mother .... Mildred Dunnock
Father .... Frank Rogier
Sandman .... Delbert Anderson
Dew Fairy .... Helen Boatright
Angels and Children..Apollo Boys' Choir
Hansel & Gretel......Constance Brigham

It's been quite a while since anyone bothered making a direct pitch for the moppet trade via that trickiest of all media, the puppet picture. Now Michael Myerberg has filled the void with "Hansel and Gretel," a skilfully produced and wholly delightful puppet version of Humperdinck's tuneful opera of the same title.

Unless youngsters of today are too preoccupied with space cadet yarns to find enjoyment in simple musical fables such as this, "Hansel and Gretel" can't fail to charm its way into the hearts of many millions. It shapes as a potent b.o. contender. Here is the answer to all those parents and educators who complain that Hollywood ignores the young.

Done in exquisite Technicolor that underscores the great craftsmanship that has gone into this film, "Hansel and Gretel" is unusual not only for the tasteful and imaginative way in which it tackled its subject but also for the "actors" themselves. The Myerberg puppets—he calls them "Kinemins"—are a triumph in themselves.

For one, in decided contrast to other puppets used in films in the past, the Myerberg figures are pleasing to the eye, even beautiful. They're capable of changing their facial expressions and do, too, with very good effects. Their movements appear awkward and jerky at times, but on the whole they have remarkable grace and convey the kind of realism not achieved before. The credit goes to Myerberg and sculptor-painter James Summers who designed them. If the merits of "Hansel and Gretel" are high, the Kinemins themselves have considerable exploitation value that ought not to be overlooked by exhibitors.

The fairy tale and the Humperdinck music are the perfect subject for a puppet film and the production makes the best possible use of its opportunities. It has visual beauty, but it has also movement, and music and, from the younger set's point of view, some lively excitement in the form of the witch Rosina Rubylips who looms, but without the customary emphasis on horror. Here again, the fine moulding of the Kinemins and the deft execution of the staging help to make the story come alive without overemphasis on the more frightening part of the tale.

Every character in the film is a puppet. They take on an added human quality via the voices which, wisely, haven't been distorted but come through much as they would in the opera. Constance Brigham does herself proud in the double role of Hansel and Gretel; Anna Russell excels as the witch; Mildred Dunnock is perfectly cast as the mother and Frank Rogier does wonders with the voice of the father.

As the Sandman, Delbert Anderson gives aural support to one of the most charming scenes in the picture. Helen Boatright is just fine as the Dew Fairy, and the Apollo Boys' Choir sounds fresh and beautiful. John Paul's direction is faultless, seeing to it that the transition from stage to screen is smooth and expert in its feel for the necessary balances.

Padriac Colum, well-known Irish poet-playwright, did the screen adaptation of the play, making the dialog fit the simplicity of the situations and brightening it with occasional touches of humor. A 60-piece symphony orch plays the Humperdinck score under Franz Allers' firm batoning.

Humperdinck's opera has been a favorite all over the world for many years. In bringing it to the screen with such a fine sense for the demands of the medium, Myerberg deserves a vote of thanks from millions of youngsters who can't get to an opera house. If he cleans up with it, it'll be a just reward for a job well done.

Hift.

Passion
(COLOR)

So-so early California action drama with mild b.o. outlook.

Hollywood, Oct. 5.

RKO release of Benedict Bogeaus production. Stars Cornel Wilde, Yvonne De Carlo; features Raymond Burr, Lon Chaney, Rodolfo Acosta, John Qualen, Anthony Caruso, Frank de Kova. Directed by Allan Dwan. Screenplay, Beatrice A. Dresher, Josef Leytes; adaptation, Howard Estabrook; based on a story by Beatrice A. Dresher, Miguel Padilla, Josef Leytes; camera (Technicolor), John Alton; editor, Carl Lodato; score, Louis Forbes. Previewed Sept. 30, '54. Running time, **84 MINS.**

Juan Obreon .... Carnel Wilde
Tonya
Rosa .... Yvonne De Carlo
Rodriguez .... Raymond Burr
Castro .... Lon Chaney
Sandro .... Rodolfo Acosta
Gaspar .... John Qualen
Munoz .... Anthony Caruso
Martinez .... Frank de Kova
Colfre .... Peter Coe
Escobar .... John Dierkes
Don Domingo .... Richard Hale
Grandmother .... Rozene Kemper
Senora Carrisa .... Belle Mitchell
Manuel Felipe .... Alex Montoya
Marca .... Zon Murray
Maraquita .... Rosa Turich
Bernal .... Stuart Whitman
Don Rosendo .... James Kirkwood
Padre .... Robert Warwick

(*Aspect ratio*: 1.85-1)

Some rather routine action dramatics, in an Early California setting, are being offered under the misnomer of "Passion." It has okay star names and Technicolor, but the entertainment is such that only mild boxoffice shapes.

Cornel Wilde and Yvonne DeCarlo topline in the Benedict Bogeous production; he as the hero who takes a vengeance trail after his family is wiped out by terrorist, and she as his dead wife's twin who helps pick off the killers. Allan Dwan's direction does what it can to keep the 84 minutes of footage moving, but there are too many slow spots for the film to hold interest overall. Script by Beatrice A. Dresher and Josef Leytes, from a story they wrote with Miguel Padilla, runs to flowery, stilted dialog and the characters in it never become real.

Terrorists, led by Rodolfo Acosta, are seeking to drive out ranchers from lands claimed by Richard Hale under an ancient grant. They attack friends of Wilde's, with whom his wife and baby are staying, during the hero's absence and Raymond Burr, police head, cannot act against the killers because he lacks sufficient evidence. Wilde takes the law into his own hands and gradually picks off all the killers but Acosta. Climax of the story takes place in the snow-covered mountains between California and Nevada, with Wilde trapping a fleeing Acosta and, in turn being caught by the pursuing Burr. Acosta confesses all in time for Burr to hear and there's the fade-out promise the hero will go free.

The characters are such that the stars and others can only turn in regulation performances, adequate to the light demands made upon them. John Alton's color lensing and the other technical assists, including the background score by Louis Forbes, are handled capably.

Brog.

Bob Mathias Story

Reenactment of story of double winner of Olympics Decathlon. Athlete and wife play themselves in good family trade programmer with tieup and ballyhoo angles.

Hollywood, Oct. 5.

Allied Artists release of William E. Selwyn production. Stars Bob Mathias,

Ward Bond; features Melba Mathias, Howard Petrie, Ann Doran. Directed by Francis D. Lyon. Screenplay, Richard Collins; camera, Ellsworth Fredricks; editor, Walter Hanneman. Running time, 79 **MINS.**

Bob Mathias	Bob Mathias
Coach Jackson	Ward Bond
Melba Mathias	Melba Mathias
Dr. Mathias	Howard Petrie
Mrs. Mathias	Ann Doran
Pat Mathias	Diane Jergens
Andrews	Paul Bryar

Allied Artists has a good family programmer in story of Tulare, California, lad who twice won decathlon at Olympics games. With Bob Mathias playing himself, and actual footage from two Olympiads used, some situations may realize extra coin from exploitations opportunities.

Pic opens with Mathias, aged 17, training for 1948 Olympic tryouts at Bloomfield, N. J., then off to Wembley, England, to win with amazing 7,139 points. Narrative then carries him to prep school struggling to make up points to enter Stanford. Despite his all round prowess as college athlete on gridiron, as well as track, Mathias decision to marry childhood sweetheart, Melba, also playing herself, nearly caused him not to enter 1952 Olympics at Helsinki, where he was first athlete to win two decathlons. Racking up 7,887 points. Narrative closes with his entry into U. S. Marines.

Mathias' personality is pleasing and he fulfills acting job with less awkwardness than could be expected. Wife Melba displays good screen presence and scenes of two together are appealing. Francis D. Lyon's sympathetic direction helped amateurs over hurdles. William E. Selwyn Productions makes good use of Olympics clips of Mathias and other star athletes for strong sports interest.

Story behind track deeds is told with minimum schmaltz as scripted by Richard Collins' "Plot" is necessarily meagre. Ellsworth Fredericks lensing is also a sturdy contribution.

Ann Doran and Howard Petrie, as parents of Mathias; Ward Bond, as his highschool coach, and Diane Jergens, as kid sister, are among casters helping family entertainment values. *Brog.*

Fire Over Africa
(COLOR)

Authentic background settings of Tangier do not make up for unconvincing story.

Columbia release of Frankovich-Sale production. Stars Maureen O'Hara and Macdonald Carey. Features Binnie Barnes, Guy Middleton, Hugh McDermott and James Lilburn. Directed by Richard Sale. Screenplay, Robert Westerby; camera (Technicolor), Christopher Challis; editor, A. S. Bates; music, Benjamin Frankel. Previewed in N.Y. Sept. 23, '53. Running time, **84 MINS.**

Joanna Dane	Maureen O'Hara
Van Logan	Macdonald Carey
Frisco	Binnie Barnes
Soames Howard	Guy Middleton
Richard Farrell	Hugh McDermott
Danny Boy	James Lidburn
Augie	Harry Lane
Paul Dupont	Leonard Sachs
Mustapha	Ferdy Mayne
Pebbles	Eric Corrie
Potts	Bruce Beeby
Cronkhite	Gerard Tichy
Rodrigo	Mike Brendall
Signor Amato	Derek Sydney
Monsieur Ducloir	Jacques Cey

Macdonald Carey gets shot once in the head and twice in the chest and, without any apparent medical care, gets up to continue some hair-raising adventures. A group of customs officials, international police and secret agents from various countries are stymied in their efforts to uncover a smuggling ring in Tangier when someone gets the bright idea that what the situation needs is a beautiful femme agent. The American rep says, "Boys, your worries are over. I've got just the gal. She's on her way here now. We'll keep this thing real secret. No one will know who she is. She'll report directly to me." The U.S. rep's insistence on secrecy, however, backfires since he's knocked off before the Mata Hari arrives in the person of Maureen O'Hara.

This is some of the anachronistic dime magazine stuff dished up in "Fire Over Africa," a Mike Frankovich-Richard Sale indie production being released by Columbia. It's strictly for the bottom rung of dual situations.

The only ring of authenticity in an otherwise incredulous film is the background lensing which effectively captures Tangier and its environs. The streets and people of this exotic North African city and the scenic splendor of the harbor are caught just right by the Technicolor camera. However, the fact is that the producers did not set out to make a travelog and realistic settings do not compensate for a trite yarn.

Miss O'Hara appears out of place as a femme du monde disguised as a secret agent. Macdonald Carey, with a crewcut and some extra poundage, is equally uncomfortable as an agent disguised as a smuggler. As it turns out, he's actually Miss O'Hara's boss. They don't find out about the connection until the end when, working separately, they succeed in uncovering the ring. Binnie Barnes is seen in stereotyped role of the tough-but-heart-of-gold keeper of the local gambling dive and saloon. The villains are types familiar to this kind of product. *Holl.*

Sansho Dayu
(JAPANESE)

Venice, Sept. 7.

Daiei production and release. Directed by Kenji Mizoguchi. Screenplay, Fuji Yahiro, Yoshikata Yoda; camera, Kazuo Miyagawa; editor, Kisaku Itoh; music, Fumio Hayasaka. At Venice Film Festival. Running time, **120 MINS.**

Tamaki	Kinuyo Tanaka
Zushio	Yoshiaki Hanayagi
Anju	Kyoko Kagawa
Sansho	Eitaro Shidno
Nio	Ichiro Sugai

This is another Japanese film that has the elegance, storytelling and acting to make it fine for special spotting. Production needs cutting, but a telling tale be gotten from this.

This utilizes 11th Century Japan. It tells the story of a noble mother and her two children who are separated by river pirates. The latter sells the children to a tyrant, and the mother to a brothel. Film builds up a fine, well-ordered story as the children grow up but never forget their mother who tries desperately to escape to them. Legendry, adventure and poetry fuse to make this engrossing, if overlong film material.

Director Kenji Mizoguchi has given this a lacquered, fetching mounting. The big cast is all admirable in depicting the many characters of this tale of mother love. Kinuyo Tanaka is superb as the strong but self-effacing mother. Her two children are well played by Yoshiaki Hanayagi as the son and Kyoko Kagawa as the daughter.

Lensing has the beauty and plasticity of most Japanese product. Editing is fine. *Mosk.*

Angelika

Joseph Brenner Associates release of a Friedrich A. Mainz production. Stars Maria Schell; features Dieter Borsche, Heidemarie Hatheyer, Carl Wery, Otto Gebuhr, Franz Schafheitlin, Gerd Brudern, Lina Carstens, Claire Reigbert, Adrian Hoven, Marianne Koch, Gustav Waldau. Screenplay, Thea Von Harbou; camera, Franz Weihmayr; music, Mark Lothar. At the 68th St. Playhouse, N.Y., Sept. 26, '54. Running time, **101 MINS.**

Angelika	Maria Schell
Dr. Holl	Dieter Barsche
Helga	Heidemarie Hatheyer
Alberti	Carl Wery
Prof. Amriss	Otto Gebuhr
Prof. Godenbergh	Franz Schafheitlin
Corvus	Gerd Brudern
Frau V. Bergmann	Lina Carstens
Housekeeper	Claire Reigbert
Tonio	Adrian Hoven
Anna	Marianne Koch
Priest	Gustav Waldau

(In German; English Titles)

A run-of-the-mill, morbidly sentimental yarn, "Angelika" has the one asset of Maria Schell, the popular Swiss actress who here proves again why she's a Continental favorite. Even within the strictly limited framework of this slow and unconvincing German film, Miss Schell stands out with the kind of warm, gentle performance that makes "Angelika" a possibility for the arties.

Film on the whole is one of the slow-moving variety that probably wasn't meant for export when it was made. A Teutonic version of a radio soap-opera, it's inundated with tear-jerker scenes in a plot that'll seem old-fashioned to U.S. audiences. Pity and self-sacrifice are the pic's dominant themes, and they're milked to the last tear.

Story is about the incurably sick daughter of a wealthy man who falls in love with her young doctor. Latter is engaged to a nurse but marries the invalid out of pity. Inevitably, while he's working on a serum that cures her, he also falls in love. After a couple of crises and a series of broken hearts, there's a happy finis.

Such is the talent and personality of Miss Schell that even the trite theme, and the even triter dialog, can't subdue her appeal. Her acting has a simple charm and should have rated her Hollywood attention long ago. Opposite her, Dieter Borsche as the doctor is stiff and wooden and overly serious. Heidemarie Hatheyer as the disappointed nurse turns in a creditable performance. Carl Wery is hard to take as the worried father. Otto Gebuhr comes up with a fine caricature in the role of a professor.

Thea Von Harbou's scripts permits none of the characters to come to life and concocts the kind of situations that were the screen vogue in the thirties. "Angelika" is certain to find favor with house catering to German-language groups. Others may find it something of a bore. *Hift.*

Raspoutine
(FRENCH—COLOR)

Paris, Sept. 21.

Warner Bros. release of Radius Film production. Stars Pierre Brasseur; features Isa Miranda, Renee Faure, Jacques Berthier, Micheline Francey, Milly Vitale, Claude Laydu. Directed by Georges Combret. Screenplay, Claude Boissol, Combret; camera (Eastmancolor), Pierre Petit; editor, Germaine Fouquet. At the Lutetia, Paris. Running time, **105 MINS.**

Raspoutine	Pierre Brasseur
Czarina	Isa Miranda
Vera	Renee Faure
Attendant	Micheline Francey
Girl	Milly Vitale
Youry	Jacques Berthier

Warner Bros. has a color bauble which has some draw for general runs here on Pierre Brasseur name and locale of the life and times of the mad monk Rasputin. For the U.S., this is too stilted in direction and too flagrantly simple and jumpy in content to be of much interest except for some arty spots.

Concerning the life of Rasputin, it unfolds his rise to power in Russia via his hold on the Czar and Czarina because of his healing power over their ailing young son. Film is told in a literary manner and works in a series of orgies in depicting the earthy side of Rasputin as well as some asides into his spiritual life as it relates his rise and demise at the hands of the army.

Pierre Brasseur puts more ham than meat into his role, with his beard and presence enveloping the film into any potent it may have. Otherwise, director George Combret has encumbered this with a literary progression, the series of absurd tableaus showing the monk turned from a debauchee into a charlatan, a religious fanatic and finally into a man seriously trying to bring peace to Russia during the first World War.

Others in the cast have spotty roles. Color has a tendency to be uneven with Brasseur's face running from red to blue in ensuing scenes. A flock of nudie scenes are worked into the film with some of the Czarist orgies and Rasputin's visit to a ladies' bath. *Mosk.*

La Pensionnaire
(The Boarder)
(FRANCO-ITALIAN; COLOR)

Paris, Sept. 21.

Jeannic release of Gamma Films production. Stars Martine Carol, Raf Vallone. Directed by Alberto Lattuada. Screenplay, Lattuada, Charles Spaak; dialog, Spaak; camera (Ferraniacolor), Mario Craveri; editor, Mario Sarandei. At Balzac, Paris. Running time, **100 MINS.**

Annie-Marie	Martine Carol
Silvio	Raf Vallone
Catherine	Clelia Matania
Millionaire	Carlo Romano
Luigi	Mario Carotenuto
Businessman	Enrico Glori

"The Boarder" in this pic is a streetwalker who takes her daughter to a summer resort for a much needed vacation. Here a typical cross-sectioning of the seasiders is neatly chronicled plus a slight moral fable. Not of the distinction of "Mr. Hulot's Holiday," this remains a simple but pleasant pic with the names of Martine Carol and Raf Vallone for local audiences. For the U.S., this lacks the stature for many arties, but its color and charm could help it into some dualers.

At the seashore, the joy girl, Miss Carol, ends up at a ritzy hotel for it is the only place with an available room. She is accepted by the others, but a snoopy police chief uncovers her profession. He promises to keep it quiet if she keeps in line. A host of familiar characters are then brought in—an eccentric millionaire, an opportunist businessman and his social climbing wife, the neurotic young girl and other types. When Miss Carol is found out she suddenly is the center of social castigations. It is the sudden action of the strange millionaire which saves her from slipping back.

Director Alberto Lattuada has placed nice rhythm plus visual pace and ease into this pic. Miss Carol is fetching as the streetwalker on vacation while Vallone is properly gallant and tender as the mayor. Remainder of the cast are fine as is the color and editing. *Mosk.*

Chateaux En Espagne
(Castles In Spain)
(FRANCO-SPANISH; COLOR)

Paris, Sept. 21.
Victory Films release of Filmal-Mars-Guion production. Stars Danielle Darrieux. Written and directed by Rene Wheeler. Camera (Eastmancolor), Philipe Agostini; editor, Henri Taverna. At Francais, Paris. Running time, **95 MINS.**

Genevieve .... Danielle Darrieux
Mario .... Pepin Martin Valezquez
Maria .... Sylvia Morgan
Manuel .... Maurice Ronet
Woman .... Suzanne Dehelly

Coproduction is a novelletish story of a standard French secretary who becomes involved with a bullfighter in Spain. Although familiar complications are soft-pedaled, the characters remain vague. The few good bullfight sequences are not enough to make this of interest for the U.S. market. It has the Danielle Darrieux name for local slots, and this may have some value for U.S. dualers. Color and theme are exploitable factors.

The French secretary is caught in Spain when her employer dies on a plane enroute to Madrid. She takes it on herself to tell the brother, a bullfighter. Love grows between them despite the language barrier, but this is complicated by a jealous cousin living off the bullfighter and a proud young female, also in love with the matador. Crisis comes when bullfighter is goaded into fighting the big bulls by the proud girl. Fighter is hurt and the secretary, realizing she doesn't belong in this milieu, goes home.

Director-writer Rene Wheeler has wisely kept this a Gallic eye view of Spain and held the story reserved by working in national fetes, color and bullfights to support the familiar and rather dragging story content. Miss Darrieux just walks through her role. Pepin Vasquez is much better in the bullring than in the thespian arena. Adequate support is given the principals. Color lensing is richly toned, with editing good. *Mosk.*

The Adventures of Hajji Baba
(COLOR-SONG)

Poor C'Scoped costumer of the sex-and-sand school; a programmer in entertainment quality for the non-discriminating.

Hollywood, Oct. 7.
20th-Fox release of an Allied Artists (Walter Wanger) production. Stars John Derek, Elaine Stewart; features Thomas Gomez, Rosemarie Bowe, Paul Picerni, Donald Randolph, Amanda Blake, Linda Danson. Directed by Don Weis. Screenplay, Richard Colling; camera (De Luxe Color), Harold Lipstein; editor, William Austin; music, Dimitri Tiomkin; song, Tiomkin and Ned Washington, sung by Nat "King" Cole. Previewed Oct. 5, '54. Running time, **92 MINS.**

Hajji Baba .... John Derek
Fawzia .... Elaine Stewart
Ayesha .... Rosemarie Bowe
Osman Aga .... Thomas Gomez
Nur-El-Din .... Paul Picerni
Caliph .... Donald Randolph
Banah ....,............ Amanda Blake
Fabria .... Linda Danson

(Aspect ratios 2.55-1)

The CinemaScope treatment of story and the scantily-clad femmes that inhabit it are the chief sales appeal for "The Adventures of Hajji Baba." While romantic-action features of the sex-and-sand school usually get by okay in the program market, this one is of such poor entertainment quality that it merits no more than so-so business. Cast names are of no ticket-selling value.

While 20th-Fox is releasing, the Walter Wanger production carries an Allied Artists label. Picture probably would have had fewer selling problems in the regular AA market than it is likely to encounter with the more de luxe situations that usually buy 20th product.

Instead of projecting chimerically exciting derring-do, the Richard Collins script, and Don Weis' direction of it, is an unintentional comedy. Under these conditions not much can be expected of stars John Derek and Elaine Stewart, or such featured players as Thomas Gomez, Rosemarie Bowe, Paul Picerni and Amanda Blake. They do the best they can, which isn't enough.

All the cliches of past flowing-robe westerns are repeated in this Arabian Nights fantasy that tells how Derek, a poor Persian barber, rescues and wins Miss Stewart, a spoiled princess, from Picerni, an evil prince who is planning to conquer all of Persia. There's a blatant sex emphasis throughout that prevents the picture from being good bait for tots. In one scene Miss Blake, leader of a horde of desert Amazons, undertakes to make Derek a member of her masculine harem. In fact all the femmes seem to have a basic yen for Derek, which keeps him busy kissing and running.

The De Luxe tints, lensed by Harold Lipstein, are good, but most of the other technical contributions are just routine. Nat "King" Cole sings "Hajji Baba," plug tune by Dimitri Tiomkin and Ned Washington, but even his undeniable talents can't make much of it. Song was a source of hilarity to the preview audience with its constant vocal repetition with almost every appearance by Derek. *Brog.*

Aida
(SONGS—COLOR)

Handsomely mounted, magnificently sung screen version of the Verdi opera. Good b.o. prospects.

I.F.E. release of an Oscar film. Directed by Clemente Fracassi; screen adaptation, C. Castelli, A. Gobbi, G. Salviucci; produced by Ferruccio De Martino and Federico Teti; camera (color), Piero Portalupi; choreography (Ballet corps of the Rome Opera), Margherita Wallmann; musical supervision, Renzo Rossellini; settings, Flavio Mogherini. Previewed in N.Y., Oct.8, '54. Running time, **95 MINS.**

THE SINGERS:
Aida .... Renata Tebaldi
Amneris .... Ebe Stignani
Radames .... Guiseppe Campora
Amonasro .... Gino Bechi
Ramfis .... Giulio Neri
The Pharaoh .... Endico Formichi

THE ACTORS
Aida .... Sophia Loren
Amneris .... Lois Maxwell
Radames .... Luciano Della Marra
Amonasro .... Afro Poli
Ramfis .... Antonio Cassinelli
The Pharaoh .... Endico Formichi

Opera lovers—and their number is supposed to be steadily on the rise in the U.S.—should have a true feast day with "Aida" which IFE is releasing under the concert impresario sponsorship of S. Hurok. Here, with the screen opening the limited horizons of the opera stage, unfolds this tragic tale of old Egypt with much lustre and vitality. It's a treat for the eye and, presumably even more important, a musical contribution that stands comparison with the best.

With Hurok taking the unusual step of presenting a film in the U.S., the quality is not surprising. This "Aida" is tops in vocalizing, and the film represents a great and significant step forward in marrying the two art forms—opera and the screen—to mutual advantage.

Just how the average U.S. patron will take to this offering will likely depend on the way he's conditioned. Among operas "Aida" is among the best known. Hurok's name and prestige will count in selling the film. There may be a good deal of curiosity about how it's been managed and somewhere along the line, the snob angle, too, may enter into the appeal of the pic, again depending on how it's sold.

"Aida" posed some pretty problems and not all of them have been overcome in this version. Costuming is imaginative and is enlivened by generally satisfactory Ferrania Color. The singing and the ballet are great. But somehow the proceedings are cruelly slow for anyone more intent on watching than on listening; and the method of employing non-singing actors, with the actual voices dubbed in, works out in only some of the parts.

Of course, opera itself is meant to be sung rather than looked at. It requires the kind of overplayed dramatics which go well on a stage but would be slightly ridiculous on the screen. Director Clemente Fracassi must have realized this, for in "Aida" his actors for the most part go through their paces more intent on visual effects than on matching their physical movements to the dubbed-in voices. This is particularly true of Luciano Della Marra as Radames, who's stiff as a rod and makes no effort at all to match his emotions with those expressed by his singing partner, Giuseppe Campora.

The same, to an extent, is true of Sophia Loren as Aida and of Lois Maxwell as Amneris. Miss Loren is attractive as the Ethiopian slave girl and in many scenes manages to be believable and prop-

erly emotional. The Aida part is sung by Renata Tebaldi with all the fine and sensitive shadings it requires. Ebe Stignani, singing Amneris, the Pharaoh's proud daughter, also gives her vocal all to the role and is nothing short of magnificent in it. Miss Maxwell in acting the role, has some very fine moments, particularly in the stirring final scenes.

Probably the most convincing in the acting cast is Afro Poli as Amonarso, Aida's father. The part is sung with great power by Gino Bechi, but Poli is every inch the real performer and one might never suspect that his singing voice is dubbed in. Giulio Neri sings Ramfis and Enrico Formichi the Pharaoh with the kind of perfection that is rarely heard.

Flavio Mogherini has concocted some handsome settings for this screen "Aida" and the camera roams far for background as a narrator fills in the story. The opera is sung in Italian. Pietro Portalupi's lensing gives the production scope even though there are moments, such as Radames' triumphant homecoming, when one wishes the film had been shot for the wide screen. Action flashes, such as the battle between the Egyptians and the Ethiopians, are interspersed to provide visual relief. Likely as not, they'll prove annoying to most people since they're imposed on continuity.

Rome Opera's ballet corps, featuring Alba Arnova, Victor Ferrari and Ciro Pardo in the principal parts, performs with grace and beauty and the Italian State radio orch gives solid musical support. Film starts very slow and continues quite static for a good while. It picks up towards the end, with the finale—the lovers are buried alive—both poignant and full of desperation and sadness. It is in this last part that the film actually proves how effectively the screen can enhance the appeal of opera, with every seat a front-row view.

To reprise: "Aida" undoubtedly requires special selling to sustain results in U.S. It is, in many respects, artistry of a very high order. It's now up to exhibs to make the public recognize and appreciate it as such. *Hift.*

Senso
(ITALIAN—COLOR)

Venice, Oct. 5.
Lux Film release of a Lux Film production. Stars Alida Valli, Farley Granger. Directed by Luchino Visconti. Screenplay, Visconti, Suso Cecchi D'Amico from a story by Camillo Boito. Camera (Technicolor), G. R. Aldo, Robert Krasker; music, Anton Bruckner; editor, Mario Serandrei. English dialog by Tennessee Williams, Paul Bowles. At Venice Film Festival. Running time, **120 MINS.**

Countess Lidia Serpieri..... Alida Valli
Lt. Franz Mahler .... Farley Granger
Roberto Ussoni .... Massimo Girotti
Count Seppieri .... Heinz Moog
Laura .... Rina Morelli
Friend of Franz .... Marcella Mariani

"Senso" is an elegant, expensively-produced period, love story, set back in the Italian 1860's, and a stylist delight. Slow pace and sprawling structure of the pic in its present form (film was shown here with Italian dialog but was originally shot with an English sound track, with dialog by Tennessee Williams and Paul Bowles), may hamper it somewhat at the boxoffice. These handicaps are not quite offset, for average tastes, by its great pictorial beauty and stylish mounting. Names of Farley Granger and Alida Valli are an aid to its U.S. chances, but the pic needs plenty of selling.

Love story, in which married Venetian aristocrat Alida Valli falls for a young Austrian officer (Farley Granger), is intertwined with historical-political events of the period, the Austrian occupation, the anti-Austrian movement, the battle of Custoza, etc. Valli falls more and more in love with her officer while his interest is more financial than real. She chases him nevertheless, hides him from the Italians, helps him avoid combat and treats him to a good life in a nearby city. When she finally catches up with him and finds he's also living with a new mistress, she goes mad and denounces him to authorities who shoot him as a deserter. Pic ends on downbeat note, but the last scenes carry plenty of impact.

Luchino Visconti's direction is evident in every detail of the picture. His direction of Valli and Granger, his care for detail and backdrop atmosphere, for lighting and color, costumes and decor, his handling of the sweeping battle scenes help keep a shaky story together and give the film class. Camera job by the late G. R. Aldo and Robert Krasker in Technicolor is among the best ever seen here, both in carefully lit interiors as well as on the many location settings in Venice and vicinity. Music, taken from Anton Bruckner's Seventh Symphony, is well chosen.

Granger is fine as the unscrupulous young officer while Valli does a good job in a difficult role. Massimo Girotti, Heinz Moog and Rina Morelli top a large, able cast. In such a beautiful film, it seems a shame that the trimmings outshine the main dish (in this case the love story). Adequate scissoring is suggested. *Hawk.*

Belles of St. Trinians
(BRITISH)

Comedy based on characters created by cartoonist Ronald Searle; mainly of local interest, with only limited prospects overseas.

London, Sept. 28.

British Lion release of London Films Launder-Gilliat Production. Stars Alastair Sim; features Joyce Grensfell, George Cole, Hermione Baddeley. Directed by Frank Launder. Screenplay by Frank Launder, Sidney Gilliat, Val Valentine; camera, Stanley; editor, Thelma Connell; music, Malcolm Arnold. At Gaumont Theatre, London, Sept. 28, '54. Running time, **91 MINS.**

Clarence Fritton .... Alastair Sim
Sergeant Ruby Gates .... Joyce Grenfell
Flash Harry .... George Cole
Miss Brownder ...... Hermione Baddeley
Miss Waters .... Betty Ann Davies
Miss Brimmer .... Renee Houston
Miss Wilson .... Beryl Reid
Miss Gale .... Irene Handl
Miss Buckland .... Mary Merrall
Miss Dawn .... Joan Sims
Mdlle. de St. Emilion .... Balbina
Miss Holland .... Jane Henderson
Jackie .... Diana Day
Florrie .... Jill Braidwood
Maudie .... Annabelle Covey
Celia .... Jauline Drewett
Rosie .... Jean Langston
Kemp Bird .... Lloyd Lamble
Manton Bassett .... Richard Wattis
Eric Rowbottom-Smith ... Guy Middleton
Sultan of Makyad .... Eric Pohlmann

Inspired by Ronald Searle's cartoons, which are popular in Britain, "The Belles of St. Trinian's" must clearly expect its biggest return in the home market, where the little horrors of the girls' school are best known. But this will even prove a letdown for the Searle fans and has only modest prospects in overseas territories.

The film makes an excellent start but subsequently never lives up to the promise of the opening and initial reel. The plot is too obviously contrived, the humor is forced and the action is of a repetitive character. The awful brats created by the artist become noisy, ill-mannered brats on the screen, and the distinction is enough to rob the film of its main purpose.

By way of a story, Launder and Gilliat have concocted an involved yarn about a plot to steal the favorite horse in a big race which is foiled by the girls in the fourth form after a battle royal with the sixth form. Prime mover in the plot is the headmistress's bookmaker brother (both roles, by the way, being played by Alastair Sim) with the aid of his sixth form daughter. The headmistress has a vested interest in the proceedings as she's staked all her available capital on the favorite in the hope of wiping out an overdraft.

Unrestrained direction by Frank Launder is matched by the lively and energetic performances by most of the cast. In either role, Sim rarely reaches the comedy heights he's attained in recent films. Joyce Grenfell, however, as a police spy, posing as a games teacher, is good for plenty of laughs. Best individual contribution is by George Cole, playing a wide-shouldered wiseguy, who acts as selling agent for the homemade gin brewed in the school lab, and also as go-between for the girls and the local bookie. Hermione Baddely, Betty Ann Davis and Renee Houston have limited scope as members of the teaching staff. *Myro.*

For Better for Worse
(BRITISH—COLOR)

Light domestic comedy, suitable as dualler in U.S. market.

London, Oct. 12.

Associated British Pathe release of Associated British-Pathe Kenwood Films Production. Stars Dirk Bogarde, features Susan Stephen, Cecil Parker, Dennis Price, Eileen Herlie. Directed by J. Lee-Thompson. Screenplay by J. Lee Thompson based on Stageplay by Arthur Watkyn; camera (Eastmancolor), Guy Green; editor, Peter Taylor; music, Wally Stott; song by Sam Coslow. At Studio One, London, Sept. 27, '54. Running time, **84 MINS.**

Tony .... Dirk Bogarde
Anne .... Susan Stephen
Anne's Father .... Cecil Parker
Anne's Mother .... Eileen Herlie
Miss Mainbrace .... Athene Seyler
Debenham .... Dennis Price
Mrs. Debenham .... Pia Terri
Plumber .... James Hayter
Mrs. Doyle .... Thora Hird
Alf .... George Woodbridge
Fred .... Charles Victor
Foreman .... Sidney James

In its original stage form, this pleasing domestic comedy by Arthur Watkyn (nom-de-plume of Arthur L. Watkins, the British film censor) ran for a year and a half in the West End. The screen version looks set for steady grosses in the home market, where the quota tag will be added selling aid. Its prospects in the U.S. are limited but it should make an attractive dualler.

The screenplay by J. Lee-Thompson is faithfully modeled on the original. Although offering a broader canvas, it doesn't depart from the basic plot of a young couple who start married life without a bank balance and are living in a one-room apartment. Soon they are dodging the creditors. At times, as in the play, the subject is given a farce-like treatment, complete with all the stock characters of the theatre, but it consistently maintains its lively and well-meaning pace.

Essentially, this is an attractive family entertainment, with its homey humor and youthful exuberance held at the right level by the adroit direction of J. Lee-Thompson. The cast, headed by Dirk Bogarde, is strong for the local marquee. He is effectively teamed with Susan Stephen, a lively and appealing screen newcomer. The girl's parents are richly played by Cecil Parker and Eileen Herlie while the stock comedy cameos include those by James Hayter, as a plumber, and Thora Hird, as a cleaner. Dennis Price aptly plays the snooty manager of the apartment house.

Guy Green has done a quality job of color lensing. Michael Stringer has designed convincing settings while Peter Taylor has edited the pic competently. Sam Coslow's title song provides an attracive opening. *Myro.*

Gestaendnis Unter Vier Augen
Confession Under Four Eyes
(GERMAN)

Berlin, Oct. 1.

Deutsche London release and production. Stars Hildegard Neff and Ivan Desny. Directed by Andre Michel. Screenplay, Hugo M. Kritz, Answald Krueger and Werner J. Lueddecke; camera, Helmuth Ashley; music, Werner Eisbrenner; sets, Ernest H. Albrecht and Paul Markwitz. At Gloria Palast, Berlin. Running time, **100 MINS.**

Hilde .... Hildegard Knef (Neff)
Marmara .... Ivan Desny
Dr. Frigge .... Carl Raddatz
Jorga .... Werner Hinz
Dr. Kopp .... Franz Schafheitlin
Carol .... Stanislav Ladinek
Reporter .... Ursula Grabley
Czech .... Hans Christian Blech

In some respects this may be regarded as a film beyond the German average. It is comparatively unconventional (no happy ending), partly realistic (particularly in the outdoor scenes) and has in Hildegard Neff and Ivan Desney two internationally known stars, while there is also a plus in the direction by Frenchman Andre Michel. Due to these facts, "Confession" may have some foreign boxoffice chance. It still falls short of Hollywood's average suspense pix.

Journalist Hildegard Neff recognizes in a police photo a bracelet that once (10 years back) belonged to her. Hoping its new owner may be able to tell her about her father in Rumania, she looks him up and falls in love with him. Later, she realizes this man stole the bracelet from one of her father's employees who was determined to bring them to her. Pic's ending sees Miss Neff leave her lover, while he is confessing his misdeeds to the police.

Andre Michel's direction keeps the action rolling at full speed, although the script has a number of basic flaws. A great deal of suspense is sacrificed for convenience. Plot twists are telegraphed ahead. Moreover, it's hard to believe in Miss Neff as presented as a female Sherlock Holmes more than a journalist. Again, Ivan Desny is played much too "sympathetic." Hard to believe that he ever committed larceny.

Excellent performances are turned in by a number of supporting players, notably Werner Hinz and Hans Christian Blech.

Technically, the film is of high quality. That primarily concerns the brilliant camerawork by Helmuth Ashley, while also Werner Eisbrenner's musical score is noteworthy. *Hans.*

Phffft

Fair-enough business figures with this Judy Holliday comedy.

Columbia release of Fred Kohlmar production. Stars Judy Holliday, Jack Lemon; features Jack Carson, Kim Novak, Luella Gear, Donald Randolph, Donald Curtis. Directed by Mark Robson. Story and screenplay, George Axelrod; camera, Charles Lang; editor, Charles Nelson; music, Frederick Hollander, conducted by Morris Stoloff. Sneak previewed at Loew's 72d Street Theatre, N.Y., Oct. 14, '54. Running time, **91 MINS.**

Nina Tracy .... Judy Holliday
Robert Tracy .... Jack Lemmon
Charlie Nelson .... Jack Carson
Janis .... Kim Novak
Mrs. Chapman .... Luella Gear
Dr. Van Kessel ...... Donald Randolph
Rick Vidal .... Donald Curtis
Language Teacher .... Arny Freeman
Marcia .... Merry Anders
Tommy .... Eddie Searles

(*Aspect ratio:* 1.85-1)

Title is the product of Walter Winchell's shell game with words —put "rift" under one cover, shake well, and it emerges "phffft" from another. Pic originally was written as a play (unproduced) by George Axelrod and was fashioned for the screen by the same author.

"Phfft" is lightweight farce running from bed to verse. Various kinds of beds are the key props in the project and nimble dialog provides the suggestive accents and exclamation points. All inoffensive, though, and cleverly put together for comedy effect. Entry lacks the laugh wallop that would make it standout, but the material and staging are sufficiently ingratiating to promise okay business in most situations.

Judy Holliday and Jack Lemon, he of tv, are the married couple whose bickering leads to the great divide of Reno. Upon this matrimonial disaffiliation (all right, phfft), each seeks to put the newly-found freedom to exciting use via romantic pursuits in other directions.

Kim Novak gets across a zesty show as an accessible blonde out to cure Lemon of the post-connubial blues. Jack Carson, as a bachelor wont to boast of his success in free-wheeling romance, registers colorfully. Miss Holliday and Lemon make an attractive combo. Femme star's bouts with the French language and psychiatry in addition to the aggressive Carson are smartly-played comedy. Lemon veers more to slapstick, and proves himself a capable hand at zanyism.

Luella Gear, Donald Randolph and Donald Curtis do right well in lesser prominent spots.

Axelrod's screenplay is given breezy pacing under Mark Robson's direction. There are no lulls, it's consistently on the move. Weak point in Fred Kohlmar's production is the lack of substantial plot. Various of the scenes are "cute" but add up to a fragile whole. And the climax, which has Miss Holliday and Lemon returning to each other, is obvious from the start.

Music and all technical credits are standard. *Gene.*

The Golden Mistress
(COLOR)

Good program adventure feature on treasure-hunting in Haiti; filmed in color in the Caribbean.

Hollywood, Oct. 18.

United Artists release of Richard Kay-Harry Rybnick production. Stars John Agar, Rosemarie Bowe; features Abner Biberman, Andre Narcisse, Jacques Molant, Kiki, Pierre Blain, Shibley Talamas, Andree Contant, Napoleon, Andre Germain, and players of the National Folklore Theatre of Haiti. Directed by Joel Judge. Screenplay, Lee Hewitt, Joel

Judge; original story by Hewitt; camera (Technicolor), William C. Thompson; editor, Howard Smith; score composed and conducted by Raoul Kraushaar. Previewed Oct. 14, '54. Running time, 82 MINS.

Bill Buchanan .... John Agar
Ann Dexter .... Rosemarie Bowe
Carl Dexter .... Abner Biberman
Lenard .... Andre Marcisse
Ti Flute .... Jacques Molant
Christofe .... Kiki
The Houngan .... Pierre Blain
DuPuis .... Shibley Talamas
Domballa Soloists ..... Andre Contant, Napoleon Bernard
Untamed Spearman .... Andre Germain
And the players of the National Folklore Theatre of Haiti.

(Aspect ratio: 1.75-1)

Mix up a treasure-hunting plot with colorful Caribbean backgrounds and some voodoo magic and the results shape up as a good program entry for the general market. This United Artists release was filmed in and around Haiti and the Technicolor printing job adds to the natural scenic values that abound in the West Indies locale.

John Agar and Rosemarie Bowe enact the lead roles in the search-for-gold script furnished by Lee Hewitt and Joel Judge. The latter also directs, handling his cast and the plot in a satisfactory manner to put the picture over for the market where it will play best. Assisting the two stars and featured lead Abner Biberman are a number of native players who contribute excellently to the generally competent performance level maintained throughout.

Biberman, a fast-buck promoter, steals a voodoo idol that is half the secret to where a legendary treasure is hidden. Miss Bowe, as his daughter, is commissioned to talk Agar into using his boat to hunt for the treasure. The hero doesn't give in readily, but finally is convinced after a voodoo curse causes Biberman's death and he takes off with the girl for a near-by fishing island, where a native friend furnishes the missing clues and dies for violating voodoo vows. The couple locate the treasure island, on which is a lake in whose waters are small golden skeletons, complete with rubies and diamonds, that are buried with the voodoo tribe's dead. Agar and Miss Bowe are caught and then barely escape with their lives and no treasure. Windup finds them deciding they are treasure enough for each other.

Agar satisfactorily puts over his stalwart hero assignment. Miss Bowe's physical charms provide the location beauties with tough competition. Biberman is good and among the natives standing out are Andre Narcisse, Jacques Molant and Pierre Blain. A snake dance by Andre Contant and Napoleon Bernard, plus contributions by the players of the National Folklore Theatre of Haiti, are excellent.

Richard Kay and Harry Rybnick produced under executive producer Sam X. Abarbanel, with Edward Barison as associate. The color lensing by William C. Thompson and Raoul Kraushaar's score are among other good points.

Brog.

Bengal Brigade
(COLOR)

Rock Hudson, Arlene Dahl in okay action feature based on British-Hindu conflict in India.

Universal release of Ted Richmond production. Stars Rock Hudson, Arlene Dahl; co-stars Ursula Thiess; features Torin Thatcher, Arnold Moss, Daniel O'Herlihy, Harold Gordon. Directed by Laslo Benedek. Screenplay, Richard Alan Simmons; adaptation, Seton I. Miller; based on the novel, "Bengal Tiger," by Hall Hunter; camera (Technicolor), Maury Gertsman; editor, Frank Gross; musical supervision, Joseph Gershenson. Previewed Oct. 12, '54. Running time, 86 MINS.

Capt. Jeffrey Claybourne....Rock Hudson
Vivian Morrow .... Arlene Dahl
Latah .... Ursula Thiess
Colonel Morrow .... Torin Thatcher
Rajah Karam .... Arnold Moss
Capt. Ronald Blaine....Daniel O'Herlihy
Hari Lal .... Harold Gordon
Sgt. Major Puran Singh..Michael Ansara
Mahindra .... Leonard Strong
Bulbir .... Shepard Menken
Themselves .... Sujata and Asoka

(Aspect ratio: 2 to 1)

Rebellion against British rule in India springboards the action in this Universal offering and the fans will find it an okay feature in Technicolor. With Rock Hudson and Arlene Dahl heading the cast, film should find a good level generally, particularly in the outdoor action market.

Plot of the Ted Richmond production opens with Hudson leading a brigade of Sepoy troops into action against orders and then resigning his captaincy in the British army when he is disciplined for disobedience. He also puts aside Miss Dahl, the colonel's daughter, because of his uncertain future. When he learns of rajah Arnold Moss' scheme to drive the British from India, however, he assumes the guise of traitor to work with the enemy and, at the finale, is able to save the colonel, the daughter, and some loyal Sepoys, as well as put down the rebellion before it can get fully started.

Hudson's heroics come over well and Miss Dahl treats the eyes in her period costumes. So does Ursula Thiess as a native charmer in love with the hero. Moss is properly menacing as the rajah who would free India of the British for his own gain and Torin Thatcher shows up well as the colonel. Daniel O'Herlihy ably enacts a cowardly British captain who redeems himself at the end. Harold Gordon, Michael Ansara, Leonard Strong and Shepard Menken sell their native characters neatly. For the terp-minded, Sujata and Asoka step off some interesting native routines.

Laslo Benedek's direction expertly fashions the action for good results and a number of sequences, including a thrilling tiger hunt, come over strongly. Color photography by Maury Gertsman is an asset in putting the Richard Alan Simmons script on film. Seton I. Miller did the adaptation of Hall Hunter's novel, "Bengal Tiger." Unusual for this type of action feature is the suspense-abetting handling of the score of Joseph Gershenson. All of the thrill scenes are heightened by background music that supports, rather than dominates.

Brog.

They Rode West
(COLOR)

Early-west cavalry actioner with good values for outdoor trade.

Hollywood, Oct. 15.

Columbia release of Lewis J. Rachmil production. Stars Robert Francis, Donna Reed, May Wynn, Phil Carey; features Onslow Stevens, Peggy Converse, Roy Roberts, Jack Kelly, Stuart Randall, Eugene Iglesias, Frank DeKova, John War Eagle, Ralph Dumke. Directed by Phil Karlson. Screenplay, DeVallon Scott, Frank Nugent; based on a story by Leo Katcher; camera (Technicolor), Charles Lawton Jr.; editor, Henry Batista; score, Paul Sawtell. Previewed Oct. 8, '54. Running time, 84 MINS.

Dr. Allen Seward ...... Robert Francis
Laurie MacKaye .... Donna Reed
Manyi-ten .... May Wynn
Capt. Peter Blake .... Phil Carey
Col. Ethan Walters ..... Onslow Stevens
Mrs. Walters .... Peggy Converse
Sergeant Creever .... Roy Roberts
Lt. Raymond .... Jack Kelly
Satanta .... Stuart Randall
Red Leaf .... Eugene Iglesias
Isatai .... Frank DeKova
Chief Qanah .... John War Eagle
Dr. Gibson .... Ralph Dumke
Maria .... Julia Montoya
Lt. Finlay .... James Best
Torquay .... George Keymas
Spotted Wolf .... Maurice Jara

(Aspect ratio: 1.85-1)

The outdoor market should find "They Rode West" a handy entry. It's an early-west cavalry-actioner, fitted out in Technicolor and good values for the trade at which it is aimed.

Film is the second for Robert Francis, seen earlier in "The Caine Mutiny," as it is for May Wynn, from the same picture. Along for additional casting emphasis is Donna Reed, Oscar-winner from "From Here to Eternity," and Phil Carey, latter having appeared in a number of outdoor action features for Columbia. The careful casting, plus story values that hold up satisfactory, all go to help make the Lewis J. Rachmil production a cut above standards of most such offerings.

Plot peg in the Leo Katcher story, as scripted by DeVallon Scott and Frank Nugent, brings Francis, young medico, to a lone western cavalry outpost where his predecessors have been drunks and butchers. Feeling against doctors at the post is strong, particularly on the part of Carey, captain who lost a good friend because of butchery in surgery. Francis is gradually winning most of them over to his side until he starts caring for an epidemic on a Kiowa reservation against orders. The bad feeling that develops erupts when the Kiowas join with Comanches in an attack on the fort, but everything is righted at the finale when Francis' medical skill brings peace.

Francis is very good in his outdoor spot as the idealistic doctor and Miss Reed comes over as a flirtatious visitor at the fort. Miss Wynn also figures strongly as a white girl raised by the Kiowas, a tribe in which she believes enough to have married the chief's son. Carey does okay as the resentful officer. Others showing up satisfactorily are Onslow Stevens, post commander; Peggy Converse, his wife; Roy Roberts, Irish sergeant; Jack Kelly, Stuart Randall, Eugene Iglesias, Frank DeKova, John War Eagle, Ralph Dumke and James Best.

Charles Lawton Jr., gives the show handsome color lensing, and keeps up with the very actionful direction by Phil Karlson, who sends the story along at just the right pace. The technical assists are capable.

Brog.

Black Widow
(CINEMASCOPE-COLOR)

Smartly produced murder story with Ginger Rogers, Van Heflin, Gene Tierney and George Raft as salable names to help initial draw. Good payoff indicated.

20th-Fox release of Nunnally Johnson production. Stars Ginger Rogers, Van Heflin, Gene Tierney, George Raft; features Peggy Ann Garner, Reginald Gardiner, Virginia Leith, Otto Krueger, Cathleen Nesbitt, Skip Homeier, Hilda Simms. Directed by Johnson. Screenplay, Johnson; from story by Patrick Quentin; camera (color by De Luxe Labs) Charles G. Clarke; editor, Dorothy Spencer; music, Leigh Harline. Previewed N.Y., Oct. 20, '54. Running time, 95 MINS.

Lottie .... Ginger Rogers
Peter .... Van Heflin
Iris .... Gene Tierney
Detective Bruce .... George Raft
Nanny Ordway .... Penny Ann Garner
Brian .... Reginald Gardiner
Claire Amberly .... Virginia Leith
Ling .... Otto Kruger
Lucia .... Cathleen Nesbitt
John .... Skip Homeier
Anne .... Hilda Simms
Welch .... Harry Carter
Miss Mills .... Geraldine Wall
Sgt. Owens .... Richard Cutting
Sylvia .... Mabel Albertson
Mr. Oliver .... Aaron Spelling
Costume Designer .... Wilson Wood
Bartender .... Tony De Mario
Model .... Virginia Maples
Maid .... Frances Driver
Stage Doorman .... James P. Stone
Coal Dealer .... Michael Vallon

(Aspect ratio: 2.55-1)

The up-front reels spin off somewhat slowly as the plot groundwork is laid but once the business of murder is gotten down to "Black Widow" takes a firm and unrelenting grip on audience attention. The title is a lure, name values are strong and the subject matter represents a welcome change of pace for the widescreen, intimately played whodunits having become almost rare in the "new era" with its accent on bigness. Looks like good b.o.

Nunnally Johnson's production is attractively set in a swank upper Manhattan apartment a good deal of the way. A few scenes in Greenwich Village also are interestingly-lensed backdrops for the action. Johnson's screenplay, based on a Patrick Quentin story, has sufficient suspense as it builds to the unexpected climax.

Flashbacks are worked in smoothly in relating how a young girl comes to Gotham with a yen to break into the bigtime and winds up the murder victim. Peggy Ann Garner, as this 20-year-old aspiring writer, gives such innocence and bright-eyed eagerness to the part that a note of near incredulity is struck as it's later revealed she was a "purpose girl" capable of sordid escapades designed as stepping stones to the top.

Brought into the web spun by Miss Garner are: Ginger Rogers, a top-rung legit actress and shallow character who finds evil delight in meddling into others' lives; Van Heflin, producer of Miss Rogers' current play, whose assistance to Miss Garner backfires into odious involvement in her murder; Gene Tierney, as Heflin's wife and also a prominent stage actress, and George Raft, the detective on the prowl for a murderer.

Miss Rogers, beautifully garbed, gives an accurate portrait of a distasteful, phoney, theatrical star. Heflin gets across a competent performance as the producer who, while under pressure of the murder rap, veers to near panic as he seeks to find the missing pieces in the homicidal jigsaw puzzle. Miss Tierney, with a less significant part in the yarn, is a plenty nifty looker and nice to have around if only for decorative purposes. Particuarly well cast is Raft, authoritative and forceful as the cop who, after some gumshoe work, can spot a murderer when he sees one.

Reginald Gardiner is effectively amiable and timid as Miss Rogers' "kept" husband whose surreptitious pursuit of an identity of his own leads to illicit affairs with Miss Garner. Others show professional know-how in lesser spots, including Otto Kruger as a legit player and uncle of Miss Garner's; Virginia Leith, a Village artist who befriends Miss Garner at the start; her brother, Skip Homeier, a law student who falls for Miss Garner; Hilda Simms, sepian hatcheck girl in a dimlit Village bistro (who registers strikingly although she's in only one scene), and Cathleen Nesbitt, as the maid employed by both Miss Rogers and Miss Tierney.

Under Johnson's direction, "Widow" plays out plausibly and with some solid tense moments. The audience is kept properly confused as to who the actual murderer really is. The climatic unmasking is cleverly brought about, although left open to guesswork is how the murdered girl could have been strung up in attempt to give the crime the appearance of suicide. Also, near the final fade, Miss Rogers' hysterical embrace of her husband looks a little ludicrous.

Music nicely underscores the dramatic high points and other technical credits are highly satisfactory. However, closer scissor work might have served to correct the slowness in the early sequences. Charles G. Clarke's camera work (color by De Luxe) manages to achieve intimacy despite the big screen. There are a few instances, though, wherein closeup lensing of dialog exchanges between the story's characters must be followed in a fashion somewhat akin to watching a tennis match.

Gene.

Operation Manhunt

Spy meller with documentary flavor. Exploitation value of Igor Gouzenko (Ex-Soviet file clerk) helps fair b.o. prospects.

United Artists release of Fred Feldkamp production. Features Harry Townes, Jacques Aubuchon, Will Kuluva, Irja Jensen. Directed by Jack Alexander. Screenplay, Paul Monash; camera, Akos Farkas; narrator, Westbrook Van Voorhees. Tradeshown N.Y., Oct. 21, '54. Running time, **77 MINS.**

Igor Gouzenko .... Harry Townes
Katya Gouzenko .... Irja Jensen
Volov .... Jacques Aubuchon
Victor Collier .... Robert Goudier
Chertok .... Albert Miller
Jean Gouzenko .... Caren Shaffer
Stephen Gouzenko ...... Kenneth Wolfe
Rostovich .... Will Kuluva
Inspector Boucher .... Ovila Lagare
Epilogue .... Igor Gouzenko

Purported experiences of Igor Gouzenko, the code clerk in the Soviet Embassy in Ottawa, who exposed a Red spy ring in Canada some nine years ago, form the basis of "Operation Manhunt." Just where fiction begins and fact ends or vice versa is impossible to determine, but on the whole this United Artists release shapes up as an unpretentious meller with fair grossing prospects in the programmer market.

Writer Paul Monash, assigned to cook up a script by Matty Fox's MPTV Corp., came up with an original screenplay that throws the spotlight on Gouzenko's life as a Canadian citizen, following his break from Communism. Some domestic scenes show his romping with his two children and hiking with his wife at a snowy retreat in the Canadian hinterland.

But marring this pleasant facet of Gouzenko's existence is an attempt by the Soviet Embassy to locate him and liquidate him as a defector to the West. Their relentless search is afforded a documentary touch by location shooting in the Ottawa and Montreal areas as well as by introductory narration by narrator Westbrook Van Voorhees. Unexpected switch at the finale finds Gouzenko's assigned killer also defecting to the West.

Producer Fred Feldkamp and director Jack Alexander, long identified with the old "March of Time" series, as was narrator Van Voorhees, further accent the documentary flavor by use of a predominantly Canadian cast. Suspense builds nicely under Alexander's guidance and the players make a good try in making it all believable. Harry Townes, who portrays Gouzenko, is self-effacing yet a man of firm principles when the occasion demands it.

Jacques Aubuchon is well cast as the MVD agent assigned to kill Gouzenko; Will Kuluva is somewhat stereotyped as a Soviet colonel in charge of eliminating the ex-code clerk while Irja Jensen, as Gouzenko's wife, shows professional promise in a minor role. Supporting players competently handle the demands of the script. Camerawork of Akos Farkas, often low key, adds to the film's attempted realism. Gouzenko, himself, is on the screen at the finale in a brief epilogue.

Gilb.

Three Ring Circus
(COLOR)

Martin and Lewis in a lively Big Top comedy good for okay returns.

Hollywood, Oct. 22.

Paramount production of a Hal Wallis production. Stars Dean Martin, Jerry Lewis; co-stars Joanne Dru, Zsa Zsa Gabor; features Wallace Ford, Elsa Lanchester. Directed by Joseph Pevney. Story-screenplay, Don McGuire; camera (Technicolor), Loyal Griggs; editor, Warren Low; music, Walter Scharf. Previewed Oct. 15, '54. Running time, 103 **MINS.**

Pete Nelson .... Dean Martin
Jerry Hotchkiss .... Jerry Lewis
Jill Brent .... Joanne Dru
Saadia .... Zsa Zsa Gabor
Sam Morley .... Wallace Ford
Schlitz .... Sig Ruman
Puffo .... Gene Sheldon
Timmy .... Nick Cravat
Bearded Lady .... Elsa Lanchester

(*Aspect ratio:* 2-1)

Circus background of this expensively-mounted Hal Wallis production gives Dean Martin and Jerry Lewis slick opportunity to disport themselves along familiar lines. Handsome in Technicolor, comedy is lensed in Par's VistaVision, admirably suited to subject, which should ring up satisfactory returns for all concerned.

Authentic production values dished up by Wallis through locationing with the Clyde Beatty Circus are accorded lush definition by the VV cameras, which director Joseph Pevney uses to fine advantage in effectively catching the antics of the stars. While comics as a team are cast in characterizations somewhat less zany than in the past, Lewis as an aspiring clown who finally makes the grade carries both humorous and sometimes emotional appeal. When he's performing as an aerial artist before an imaginary audience and again while trying to make a solemn little girl in braces laugh at an orphan's benefit, he manages considerable appeal.

For his part, Martin scores in the straight role, as well as with his singing. His rendition of John Rox's "It's a Big, Wide, Wonderful World" is an attraction, and team socks over a comedy song by Jay Livingston and Ray Evans, "Hey, Punchinello," for one of highlights in film. Their co-stars, Joanne Dru and Zsa Zsa Gabor, supply plenty of flash and femme splendor in respective roles of circus owner and star aerialist, and Wallace Ford is tops as the barking but sympathetic circus manager.

The Don McGuire script projects comics straight from Army uniform to the circus, where Lewis reports as a lion tamer's assistant in the hope he'll get to be a clown. Martin tags along, catching the eye of the beautiful but temperamental trapeze artist, who makes him her "assistant." He takes over Miss Dru's place when she leaves the circus—she's in love and keeps fighting with him—but all is happiness again after the children's benefit which Martin forbids at first due to circus' time schedule. Narrative frequently gives Lewis an opportunity to display his best comedy, one of top routines catching him in the lion's cage.

In support, Sig Ruman delivers in latter scene, as the lion tamer, and Gene Sheldon is good as a drunken clown whose place Lewis takes after he's fired. Elsa Lanchester also is in for a funny sequence, as a bearded lady about to get a shave by Lewis.

Technical credits rate highly, particularly Royal Griggs' color photography. Walter Scharf's music score definitely is an assist.

Whit.

The Steel Cage

Three "featurettes" drawn from Warden Clinton T. Duffy's "The San Quentin Story" and tied together. Slow and dull.

Hollywood, Oct. 26.

United Artists release of Berman Swarttz-Walter Doniger production. Stars Paul Kelly, Maureen O'Sullivan, Walter Slezak, John Ireland, Lawrence Tierney, Kenneth Tobey, Arthur Franz; features Alan Mowbray, George E. Stone, Lyle Talbot. Directed by Doniger. Based on the book, "The San Quentin Story" by Clinton T. Duffy and Dean Jennings; screenplay of "The Hostages," Oliver Crawford, story, Doniger and Swarttz; screenplay of "The Chef," Swarttz and Doniger; screenplay of "The Face," Guy Trosper, story, Scott Littleton; camera, John Alton, Joseph Biroc; editors, Chester Schaeffer, Everett Dodd. Previewed Oct. 22, '54. Running time, **80 MINS.**

Warden Duffy .... Paul Kelly
Mrs. Duffy .... Maureen O'Sullivan
The Chef .... Walter Slezak
The Ringleaders .... John Ireland, Lawrence Tierney
Kenneth Tobey .... Arthur Franz
Alan Mowbray .... George Cooper
George E. Stone .... Ned Glass
Lyle Talbot .... Herb Jacobs
Elizabeth Fraser .... Henry Kulky
Stanley Andrews .... Charles Nolte
Morris Ankrum .... Gene Roth
Don Beddoe .... James Seay
Robert Bice .... Charles Tannen
George Chandler .... Ben Welden

While this prison trilogy has the appearance of having been initially made in separate parts for television release, it should round up a fairly satisfactory number of lowercase programmer dates as a theatrical feature. In its favor is the present shortage of secondary product for regular double bill situations and the fact that the cast has a lineup of generally familiar names.

Three separate stories are told during the 80 minutes of footage, but are tied in by using the same prison background with Paul Kelly, as Warden Clinton T. Duffy, introducing each episode. The entertainment is spotty and slowly paced as directed by Walter Doniger, and mostly on the grim side, although the opener, "The Chef," is in a lighter vein. Berman Swarttz and Doniger, co-producers on the United Artists release, did the script for this one, which has Walter Slezak, a violent-tempered chef, framed by a gourmet fellow-inmate so he would have to continue presiding over the prison kitchen. It's the best of the trio.

"The Hostages," scripted by Oliver Crawford from a story by Doniger and Swarttz, stars John Ireland and Lawrence Tierney, with Lyle Talbot, as prisoners who plot an abortive jail break and die violently. Guy Trosper scripted "The Face," a story by Scott Littleton, which concerns an agnostic painter, serving life, who finds different values, and in turn helps a young priest find himself. Kenneth Tobey plays the painter and Arthur Franz the priest.

Incidents from "The San Quentin Story," book by Duffy and Dean Jennings, are used for the trilogy and the general theme is to show the three things prisoners most want—a little comedy, freedom and spiritual solace. Helping Slezak on the comedy in the first episode are George E. Stone and Alan Mowbray. Seen briefly in this one is Maureen O'Sullivan, as Mrs. Duffy.

Lensing of the episodes was contributed by John Alton and Joseph Biroc, with Chester Schaeffer and Everett Dodd doing the editing. These credits and other technical assists are routine.

Brog.

The Lawless Rider

Good western with standard plot.

United Artists release of a Royal West production. Stars Johnny Carpenter; features Frankie Darro, Douglas Dumbrille. Directed by Yakima Canutt. Original story, screenplay by John Carpenter; camera, William C. Thompson; editor, John Fuller; music, Rudy DeSaxe; original song, "Thinking of You," by Marguerite McFarlane. Previewed in N.Y., Oct. 22, '54. Running time, **62 MINS.**

Johnny Carpenter,
Rod Tatum .... Johnny Carpenter
Jim Bascom .... Frankie Darro
Marshal Brady ...... Douglas Dumbrille
Big Red .... Frank Carpenter
Nancy James .... Noel Neill
Freno Frost .... Kenne Duncan
Sheriff Brown .... Weldon Bascom
Texas Rose Bascom ...... Rose Bascom
Tulso .... Bud Osborne
Black Jack .... Lou Roberson
Red Rooks .... Bill Coontz
Bill .... Bill Chaney
Andy .... Roy Canada
Young Marshal .... Tap Canutt
Hank Caldwell and his Saddle Kings

"The Lawless Rider" is an oats meller which follows much the accepted pattern for this type of western. It is helped by the fact that Yakima Canutt, long a star rodeo performer and typical westerner, directed the production. He gives it a taste of authenticity so often lacking in these horse operas. Pic will fit in nicely where western adventure subjects are sought by the patronage.

Besides Johnny Carpenter, the cast numbers Frankie Darro, Douglas Dumbrille and Rose Bascom, trick rope champ. At first Darro seems a bit uncongruous as a tough cowhand but he makes the transition from a city toughie into a western player with ease. Carpenter, of course, again plays a U. S. sheriff role, only that later in the picture he disguishes himself as Rod Tatum, a notorious cowboy gunman.

Carpenter also is credited with doing the original, the screenplay and helping on the production along with Alex Gordon in the latter capacity.

This follows a rather familiar pattern of cattlemen-outlaw raider pictures. Here it is a well organized group of raiders which terrorize the ranchers, killing the owners and making off with valuable cattle. And per usual, it takes the gallant Carpenter as a marshal to round up the outlaws. Yarn rings in more fisticuffs than customary in such six-shooter mellers. Some place along the line Carpenter has learned to handle his mitts as well as his revolvers and rifle. There is a slight romance between him and Miss Bascom. Latter is a forthright western femme if there ever was one.

Fact that she is so adept in manipulating the ropes and twirling the hemp naturally rings in a local vaude show at the end. This, too, serves as a climax which sees the badmen fighting it out with the reps of the law and finally winding-up in a gun battle.

Director Canutt has done a nice job in maintaining interest and injecting considerable suspense. All of his cowboy characters are hardbitten types. Carpenter is himself again, making a tough little hombre as a rough-and-tumble guardian of the law. Dumbrille fits in well as the head marshal while Miss Bascom gives evidence of learning how to act. Support is excellent, with Kenne Duncan outstanding as the undercover manipulator of the outlaws.

The two songs are typical westerns, "Thinking of You" being best. Rudy DeSaxe has provided smooth, original music. John Fuller's editing is commendable while William C. Thompson has done smart work with his camera. *Wear.*

The Anna Cross
(RUSSIAN—COLOR)

Soviet shift to "subtle" propaganda in filmization of popular Chekhov short story. Depicts upper class life in pre-revolutionary times.

Artkino Pictures release of Gorky Film Studio production. Screenplay and direction by I. Annensky, based on Anton Chekhov's story; camera (Sovcolor), G. Reisgoff; music, L. Schwartz. At Stanley Theatre, N.Y., Oct. 23, '54. Running time, **85 MINS.**
Anna .... Anna Larionova
Pyotr Leontievich, her father
                    A. Sashin-Nikolsky
Modest Alekseyevich......Mikhail Zharov
Prince .... A. Vertinsky
Princess .... N. Belevtzeva
Mavra Grigorievna .... I. Murzayeva

(In Russian; English Titles)

This newest Soviet import, although a plodding and poorly-edited film, is nevertheless a significant departure for the Russian film industry. The Red film-makers, noted for their heavy-handed propaganda pieces, have at last resorted to a degree of subtlety in the filmization of one of Chekhov's most popular short stories. It was a sensational success in Russia but, except for the curious and students of the Soviet mind, its chances in the U, S. market are practically nil.

According to a recent dispatch from the correspondent of the New York Times, "The Anna Cross" attracted lines of a block long when it opened simultaneously at 24 Moscow houses. The picture's appeal for the Russians is obvious, for here is a film which, perhaps for the first time, depicts everything that was symbolic of the regime which the Bolshevik revolu-

tion overthrew. Accustomed to a diet of farm cooperative yarns and ballet and opera films, the Russians were given a chance to see the life of the upper classes before the November days of 1917. There are noblemen and handsome officers, lavish dusk to dawn champagne parties, lush balls given by the royalty, moonlight boating parties, and gypsy singers.

The story, of course, aims to show the callousness of this pre-revolution life. It concerns a beautiful young girl who is forced to marry an old government official for his money. She becomes the belle of society and kicks over her former environment for the hedonistic life. She breezes through the snow-covered streets with her current lover while her father and two young brothers are being evicted from their home. As her sled disappears down the street with her old father stumbling and calling after her, the picture ends, leaving the audience to draw its own moral.

Anna Larionova, who portrays the Anna of the film, is a remarkable blonde looker and, if it weren't for the Iron Curtain, American producers would probably be after her. The direction is heavy and the editing, as noted previously, is extremely bad. The Sovcolor is hazy as if the entire picture were shot in a fog. *Holl.*

Last Time I Saw Paris
(COLOR)

Topflight romantic drama with strong cast names and good b.o. possibilities.

Hollywood, Nov 2.
Metro release of Jack Cummings production. Stars Elizabeth Taylor, Van Johnson, Walter Pidgeon, Donna Reed; features Eva Gabor, Kurt Kasznar, George Dolenz, Roger Moore. Directed by Richard Brooks. Screenplay, Julius J. and Philip G. Epstein and Richard Brooks; based on the F. Scott Fitzgerald short story, "Babylon Revisited"; camera (Technicolor), Joseph Ruttenberg; editor, John Dunning; score, Conrad Salinger; musical supervision, Saul Chaplin; song, "The Last Time I Saw Paris" by Jerome Kern and Oscar Hammerstein 2d. Previewed Oct. 28, '54. Running time, **116 MINS.**
Helen Ellsworth ...... Elizabeth Taylor
Charles Wills .... Van Johnson
James Ellsworth .... Walter Pidgeon
Marion Ellsworth .... Donna Reed
Lorraine Quarl .... Eva Gabor
Maurice .... Kurt Kasznar
Claude Matine .... George Dolenz
Paul .... Roger Moore
Vicki .... Sandy Descher
Mama .... Celia Lovsky
Barney .... Peter Leeds
Campbell .... John Doucette
Singer .... Odette

(Aspect ratio: 1.75-1)

"The Last Time I Saw Paris" is an engrossing romantic drama that tells a good story with fine performances and an overall honesty of dramatic purpose. It is an above-average entry for the better situations and, because of its compelling love story, set against a Paris locale, it should fare okay elsewhere, too, although the 116 minutes is a cumbersome length for the more general playdates. Such names as Elizabeth Taylor, Van Johnson, Walter Pidgeon and Donna Reed provide marquee flash and should help the bookings.

F. Scott Fitzgerald's short story, "Babylon Revisited" has been updated and revised as the basis for the potent screenplay on which director Richard Brooks shares credit with Julius J. and Philip G. Epstein. Metro acquired the script property from Paramount and it has been given class handling under the production guidance of Jack Cummings, reflecting good taste and good story-telling all down the line.

Performancewise, Miss Taylor's work as the heroine should be a milestone for her. It is her best work to date and shows a thorough grasp of the character, which she makes warm and real, not just beautiful. Brooks' direction also gets a sock response from Johnson. The latter's portrayal of the Fitzgerald hero easily lines up with his best, if not topping previous highs. Pidgeon, too, scores in what is a definite change of pace as an elderly playboy father of two beautiful daughters. Miss Reed, while with less footage than most of her co-stars, makes her character of a girl blighted by an unrequited love entirely understandable, even sympathetic.

Plot around which the dramatics spin is laid in Paris in the reckless, gay period that followed V-E Day of World War II. There, Johnson meets and marries Miss Taylor and starts a struggling existence as a day-time reporter for a news service and wouldbe author at night. Even the faith of his wife cannot balance the brand of failure he assumes after too many rejection slips and when some supposedly worthless Texas oil property suddenly gushes into wealth he becomes a playboy himself, dooming the marriage and eventually leading to the wife's death.

This story is told in one long

flashback after an opening that finds Johnson, now a published writer but no longer rich, returning to Paris to reclaim his small daughter, Sandy Descher, from the custody of Miss Reed, his sister-in-law who loves him, and her husband, George Dolenz. This ending, while some may find it rather long, is emotionally sure and will wring not a few tears from auditors. The post-war period of the footage, which occupies most of it, is rich with Parisian flavor and the script and Brooks' direction are the nearest thing yet to recreating the reckless gaiety that Fitzgerald caught in his writings.

In addition to the four stars, the picture has fine supporting work from the other casters, including Eva Gabor as a gay divorcee; Kurt Kasznar, cafe-owning friend of the married couple; Dolenz, young Miss Descher and Roger Moore as a professional romeo.

Threading through the footage and theming it with beautiful melody is the Jerome Kern-Oscar Hammerstein 2d title song, hauntingly sung by Odette. It recurs often in the Conrad Salinger score. The Technicolor photography by Joseph Ruttenberg adds tinted beauty to the picture. Also rating credit for worthy contributions are Helen Rose' gowns, the art direction and set decorations and other technical assists. *Brog.*

Athena
(MUSICAL—COLOR)

Youthful emphasis in names of Jane Powell, Edmund Purdom, Debbie Reynolds, Vic Damone to help prospects for lightweight musical escapism.

Hollywood, Oct. 29.
Metro release of Joe Pasternak production Stars Jane Powell, Edmund Purdom, Debbie Reynolds, Vic Damone, Louis Calhern; features Linda Christian, Evelyn Varden, Ray Collins, Carl Benton Reid, Howard Wendell, Virginia Gibson, Henry Nakamura. Directed by Richard Thorpe. Written by William Ludwig, Leonard Spigelgass; camera (Eastman Color), Robert Planck; editor, Gene Ruggiero; songs, Hugh Martin and Ralph Blane; music supervised and conducted by George Stoll; choreography, Valerie Bettis. Previewed Oct. 26, '54. Running time, **95 MINS.** The Sisters:
Athena .... Jane Powell
Minerva .... Debbie Reynolds
Niobe .... Virginia Gibson
Aphrodite .... Nancy Kilgas
Calliope .... Dolores Starr
Medea .... Jane Fischer
Ceres .... Cecile Rogers
Adam Calhorn Shaw.....Edmund Purdom
Johnny Nyle .... Vic Damone
Grandpa Mulvain ...... Louis Calhern
Grandma Salome Mulvain
                      Evelyn Varden
Beth Hallson .... Linda Christian
Mr. Tremaine .... Ray Collins
Mr. Griswalde .... Carl Benton Reid
Mr. Grenville .... Howard Wendell
Roy .... Henry Nakamura
Ed Perkins .... Steve Reeves
        "Mr. Universe" of 1950
Miss Seely .... Kathleen Freeman
Bill Nichols .... Richard Sabre

(Aspect ratio: 1.75-1)

The prospects for this lightweight musical will be helped generally by the emphasis on youth in the casting of Jane Powell, Edmund Purdom, Debbie Reynolds and Vic Damone to carry off the top romantic chores. There's nothing particularly outstanding in the offering, but it manages to be fairly pleasant tintuner entertainment most of the time and so should get by in the regular market.

The Joe Pasternak production spots seven tunes by Hugh Martin and Ralph Blane, several of which rate reprises, and "Chacun Le Sait" from "Daughter of the Regiment," which Miss Powell warbles most effectively. Damone's best is "The Girl Next Door." Also listening well is "Love Can Change the Stars," sung at various times by the Misses Powell and Reynolds, and Damone. "Venezia" is pretentiously presented as a big production number with Damone singing, but listening better is "Imagine," which he does with Miss Reynolds. Others are the title tune, "Vocalize" and "I Never Felt Better."

The nonsensical fun in the screen story by William Ludwig and Leonard Spigelgass shows what happens when a health faddist family of seven sisters, a physical culturist grandfather and a grandma who communes with the stars becomes involved in the lives of Purdom, stuffy young attorney, and Damone, young crooner. The latter is willing to have Miss Reynolds move in on him, even if the stars hadn't made it inevitable, but Miss Powell has more trouble swinging Purdom into line because he's a proper Bostonian with a fiancee, Linda Christian, and a budding political career. Some routine misunderstandings ensue as Richard Thorpe's direction sends the players through the involvements but the windup finds everyone properly paired off.

Assisting the younger players in excellent style are Calhern as the muscle-flexing grandpa and Evelyn Varden as the grandma. Miss Christian, too, has her moments as the fiancee, as do Ray Collins, Carl Benton Reid and Howard Wendell, Purdom's political advisors, and Henry Nakamura, the attorney's houseboy.

The Eastman tints, printed by Technicolor, show up well in the lensing by Robert Planck. The art direction is good and George Stoll's musical conducting gives the score a good beat. *Brog.*

Ricochet Romance
(SONGS)

Grassroots comedy with "Ma and Pa Kettle" format.

Universal release of Robert Arthur-Richard Wilson production. Stars Marjorie Main; features Chill Wills, Pedro Gonzales-Gonzales, Alfonso Bedoya, Rudy Vallee. Directed by Charles Lamont. Screenplay and story, Kay Lenard; camera, George Robinson; editor, Russell Schoengarth; musical supervision, Joseph Gershenson; songs, Larry Coleman Jr., Joe Darion, Norman Gimbel, J. J. Espinosa, Ernesto Lecuona, Arturo G. Gonzales. Tradeshown, N.Y., Oct. 19, '54. Running time, **80 MINS.**

Pansy Jones	Marjorie Main
Tom Williams	Chill Wills
Manel Gonzales	Pedro Gonzales-Gonzales
Alfredo Gonzales	Alfonso Bedoya
Worthington Higgenmacher	Rudy Vallee
Angela Ann Mansfield	Ruth Hampton
Claire Renard	Benay Venuta
Betsy Williams	Judith Ames
Dave King	Darryl Hickman
Timmy Williams	Lee Aaker
Miss Clay	Irene Ryan
Mr. Webster	Phillip Tonge
Mr. Daniels	Phillip Chambers
Mr. Harvey	Charles Watts
Mrs. Harvey	Marjorie Bennett

(*Aspect ratio*: 1.85-1)

Although wearing the misleading title of "Ricochet Romance," this Universal entry boils down to another comedy in the "Ma and Pa Kettle" series. For the same down-to-earth humor, long used in the "Kettles," is employed in "Romance" with virtually the same results. It should mop up in the smaller situations which cater to a grassroots clientele.

Adding to the film's "Kettle" flavor is Marjorie Main (the original "Ma Kettle"), director Charles Lamont and co-producer Richard Wilson. Both Lamont and Wilson carry credits on previous "Kettle" pix before Percy Kilbride ("Pa Kettle") "retired" from the series. Studio is currently attempting to lure Kilbride before the cameras to resume his original role in a fresh "Kettle".

The Kay Lenard story, which the writer also screenplayed, is localed on a dude ranch. With such a setting it's too obvious that the establishment would be peopled with an assortment of types on which to hang slapstick situations and other scenes too humorous to mention. There's the problem of the dissatisfied guests, no cook for the weekend, a predatory blonde boarder with designs on the male proprietor, etc.

While the material is rather thin the cast makes a good try at giving it credibility. Marjorie Main, as a replacement cook, scores handily on the laughmeter. Chill Wills generates levity as the ranch owner who prefers his magician avocation to tending to the premises. Pedro Gonzales-Gonzales and Alfonso Bedoya are amusing as a pair of Mexican employees of the ranch while Rudy Vallee contribs some wry humor as a wealthy guest fond of good cooking.

Also fitting nicely into the overall format are supporting players Ruth Hampton, Benay Venuta, Judith Ames and Darryl Hickman, among others. Some four tunes are worked into the 80 minutes of footage. Aside from the title number of "Ricochet Romance," they include "Las Altenitas," "Para Vigo Me Voy" and "Un Tequilla." Bedoya croons "Ricochet" while the Guadalajara Trio handles the rest.

Producers Robert Arthur and Richard Wilson appear to have extracted maximum values from the modest budget. Charles Lamont's direction accents the bucolic touch in the right places while George Robinson creditably lensed the venture. Editing of Russell Schoengarth is competent as is Joseph Gershenson's musical supervision and other technical credits. *Gilb.*

Drum Beat
(COLOR)

Alan Ladd in C'Scope outdoor actioner with good prospects at the b.o.

Hollywood, Nov. 2.

Warner Bros. release of a Jaguar production. Stars Alan Ladd; co-stars Audrey Dalton, Marisa Pavan; features Robert Keith, Rodolfo Acosta, Charles Bronson, Warner Anderson. Written and directed by Delmer Daves. Camera (Warnercolor), J. Peverell Marley; editor, Clarence Kolster; music, Victor Young. Previewed Oct. 28, '54. Running time, **107 MINS.**

Johnny Mackay	Alan Ladd
Nancy Meek	Audrey Dalton
Toby	Marisa Pavan
Bill Satterwhite	Robert Keith
Scarface Charlie	Rodolfo Acosta
Captain Jack	Charles Bronson
General Canby	Warner Anderson
Crackel	Elisha Cook Jr.
Manok	Anthony Caruso
Dr. Thomas	Richard Gaines
Jesse Grant	Edgar Stehli
General Grant	Hayden Rorke
Modoc Jim	Frank de Kova
Bogus Charlie	Perry Lopez
General Gilliam	Willis Bouchey
Lt. Goodsall	Peter Hansen
Capt. Alonzo Clark	George Lewis
Lily White	Isabel Jewell
Mr. Dyar	Frank Ferguson
Mrs. Grant	Peggy Converse

(*Aspect ratio*: 2.55-1)

The Modoc Indian uprising on the California-Oregon border in 1869 is the basis for this Alan Ladd outdoor action starrer. Done in CinemaScope and WarnerColor, and with the Ladd name to brighten the marquees, it should get a good boxoffice response in the outdoor market.

Picture, first for the Jaguar production unit, was produced, directed and written by Delmer Daves for Warner Bros. release. The scripting is a careful job, in the main holding to fact with some fictionizing for dramatic values. Thus, there is less of the fanciful heroics encountered in most outdoor actioners, but action hasn't been neglected, and the characters are solidly developed. While the natural lava fort used by the warring Modocs to hold off the U. S. Army still exists, Daves found better pictorial values by locationing in the Coconino National Forest of Northern Arizona. These values are strikingly displayed in the tinted C'Scope lensing by J. Peverell Marley.

Alan Ladd is seen as a frontiersman commissioned by President U. S. Grant to negotiate a peace with the rebelling Modocs led by Captain Jack, renegade redskin forcefully played by Charles Bronson (formerly Buchinsky). The peace is to be effected without force of arms, which presents two-gun Ladd with quite a problem. His first efforts are stymied by a revenge killing which touches off a massacre by Captain Jack's braves. Later, white negotiators are killed, and Ladd almost so, by redskin treachery during a parley. The President relieves the hero of the no-force edict and he eventually brings the egocentric Captain Jack to the hangman's scaffold.

Two femmes star with Ladd. Audrey Dalton does nicely as the eastern girl who comes west and winds up with the hero. Marisa Pavan scores as the Indian girl who gives her life to save Ladd. Among other featured players who stand out along with Bronson are Robert Keith, the stage driver who caused the massacre; Rodolfo Acosta, as the bloodthirsty Scarface Charlie; Warner Anderson, as General Canby; Elisha Cook, Jr., treacherous white; Anthony Caruso, a good Modoc; Richard Gaines, professional peace-maker, a n d Hayden Rorke as President Grant.

The Victor Young score is used properly and excellently to sharpen the drama. It includes a title tune sung behind the credits. The overall technical credits are good. *Brog.*

Lease of Life
(BRITISH—COLOR)

Robert Donat in leisurely-paced story of country parson with a year to live; limited b.o. prospects.

London, Oct. 19.

General Film Distributors release of Ealing Studios-Michael Balcon production. Stars Robert Donat, Kay Walsh, Denholm Elliott, Adrienne Corri. Directed by Charles Frend. Screenplay, Eric Ambler; camera (Eastmancolor), Douglas Slocombe; editor, Peter Tanner; music, Alan Rawsthorne. At Gaumont, London. Running time, **94 MINS.**

William Thorne	Robert Donat
Vera Thorne	Kay Walsh
Susan Thorne	Adrienne Corri
Martin Blake	Denholm Elliott
The Dean	Walter Fitzgerald
Headmaster	Cyril Raymond
Foley	Reginald Beckwith
Boy With Book	Robert Sandford
Verger	Frank Atkinson
Dr. Pembury	Alan Webb
Solicitor	Richard Wattis
Jeweller	Frederick Piper
Mrs. Sproatley	Vida Hope
Sproatley	Beckett Bould
Carter	Richard Leech

For many years among the top stars of the British screen, Robert Donat has restricted his film appearances in recent times because of persistent ill-health and recurrent asthma attacks. In these circumstances, it might have been considered advisable to provide a strong dramatic vehicle for him instead of the quiet and leisurely tale which is unfolded in this new Ealing production. A modest boxoffice pic for the home market, despite its quota tag, this has limited appeal in overseas territories.

The theme of "Lease of Life" is by no means unusual, although it is an offbeat piece of writing for Eric Ambler who is usually associated with suspense and action. This is a quiet tale of a country parson who finds real happiness when he is given a year to live although he has the problem of raising money to enable his daughter to take up a music scholarship in London.

The cathedral city in which the story is set and the surrounding rural communities provide a natural and attractive background. The principal characters are clearly etched and there is a faint gesture of malicious local gossip to contrast with the more serene atmosphere of the rectory. There is a side issue concerning a dying parishioner who entrusts his money to the vicar rather than allow his grasping wife to lay hands on it. But it is the vicar's wife who succumbs to temptation and steals a wad of notes to pay for her daughter's tuition. This aspect of the plot never rings true.

In a performance, which is at times reminiscent of his famous "Mr. Chips" characterization, Robert Donat dominates the screen as he plays the sick parson with an appealing sincerity and conviction. It is unfortunate that even such a forceful individual performance is unable to infuse extra life into the production.

Kay Walsh plays his wife in a sympathetic but limited way. Adrienne Corri, as their gifted daughter, is poorly served by the script and has a hard job to convince. Denholm Elliott, as her friend and teacher, has a flimsy and relatively unimportant part. Vida Hope gives a characteristically individual performance as the dying man's wife and there are good sketches by Cyril Raymond as the headmaster and Reginald Beckwith as a local reporter. *Myro.*

The Fast and the Furious

Chase meller with sports car racing theme; for lowercase programmer dates.

Hollywood, Oct. 28.

American Releasing Corp., release of Palo Alto (Roger Corman) production. Stars John Ireland, Dorothy Malone; features Bruce Carlisle, Iris Adrian, Marshall Bradford. Directed by Edwards Sampson and John Ireland. Screenplay, Jerome Odlum, Jean Howell; from a story by Roger Corman; camera, Floyd Crosby; editor, Edwards Sampson; music composed and directed by Alexander Gerens. Previewed Oct. 27, '54. Running time, **73 MINS.**

Frank Webster	John Ireland
Connie Adair	Dorothy Malone
Faber	Bruce Carlisle
Race Official	Marshall Bradford
Sally	Jean Howell
Police Sergeant	Larry Thor
Gas Station Attendant	Robin Morse
Truck Driver	Bruno DeSota
Waitress	Iris Adrian

(*Aspect ratio*: 1.75-1)

High-priced sportscar b o m b s furnish most of the action for "The Fast and the Furious," a modestly-budgeted chase meller that is slanted for lowercase programmer bookings. Racing footage is interesting but becomes repetitious and helps to string out the running time to an unnecessary 73 minutes, an unhandy length for supporting playdates.

New indie distribution outfit,

American Releasing Corp., is handling the Palo Alto production as its first of four features from the latter unit. John Ireland and Dorothy Malone topline and supply the picture with familiar names and generally competent performances. Ireland shares directorial credit with Edwards Sampson, who also edited, and they manage to bring off the Jerome Odlum-Jean Howell script satisfactorily for release aims. Producer Roger Corman furnished the story.

Ireland is seen as a fugitive from a murder frame who commandeers Miss Malone's sports car, taking her with him. To get out of the country he enters the car in a race that will finish across the border in Mexico. Meanwhile he and Miss Malone are getting romantic so windup finds him deciding to go back and fight the false charges.

Assisting in carrying the yarn are Larry Thor, police sergeant; Marshall Bradford, race official; Iris Adrian and Jean Howell, among others. Camera work by Floyd Crosby, the Alexander Gerens score and other technical credits come off okay. *Brog.*

La Grande Speranza
(The Great Hope)
(ITALIAN—COLCR)

Rome, Oct. 19.

Minerva release of Excelsa production. Stars Lois Maxwell, Renato Baldini. Directed by Duilio Coletti. Screenplay, Coletti, Oreste Biancoli, Marc'Antonio Bragadin; from story by Bragadin: camera (Ferraniacolor), Leonida Barboni; music, Nino Rota; editor, Giuliana Attenni. Previewed in Rome. Running time, 91 MINS.

Captain	Renato Baldini
Lily	Lois Maxwell
1st Mate	Folco Lulli
Officer	Carlo Bellini
Lieutenant	Aldo Bufi Landi
Johnny	Earl Cameron
Carter	Edward Flemming
Steiner	Henri Vidon
Ciccio	Carlo Delle Piane
Fernandez	Jose Jaspe
Jackie	Tom Middleton

Pacifist despite its wartime setting, this pic has patriotic, humanitarian and entertainment factors which hint a good general reception almost anywhere. An English-language version, now being prepped, may rate a general audience looksee on some American circuits with some trimming suggested to speed pace a bit. Otherwise, pic has all well-blended requisites excitement, suspense, warmth and humor for good entertainment.

Well-balanced color production, though short on exportable names, shows that Italy can turn out commercial fare of quality without running to extremes current in the exploitation market. If this film is indicative of a trend, it looks promising for local industrial stability. Story, based on true wartime events, narrates some of the adventures by an Italian submarine and its crew during the last war. On its travels, it picks up survivors of its victims, thanks to its captain's humanitarian streak.

Among these are a British nurse, a British officer, crew members of various nationalities, a writer, etc. All types are represented, and all react differently to the environment, with the Britisher rebelling, the nurse slowly warming to the Italian captain and others becoming pals with members of the crew. Xmas spirit on board is shared by all, and a general feeling of comradeship, aided by Italo's attitude to war, is nurtured and spread. The finale points to hope that this fellowship will continue after hostilities have ceased. Although slanted to the Italian side, the argument holds water thanks to underplaying of script and cast.

Renato Baldini is fine as the captain, giving the key part strength. Lois Maxwell underplays her role as the nurse with whom he's in love for good effect in her best performance to date. Folco Lulli lends his amiable personality to lighten the setting, as do comedians Paolo Panelli and Carlo Delle Piane as two playful gobs. Others contribute sober, restrained performances. Script structure is somewhat episodic, but director Duilio Coletti ties most strings together smoothly. Ferraniacolor lensing by Leonida Barboni is consistently good. Music by Nino Rota likewise is solid. *Hawk.*

Canzoni di Mezzo Secolo
(Half a Century of Songs)
(ITALIAN-COLOR)

Confusing, poorly edited cavalcade; limited b.o. in U. S.

Continental Motion Picture Corp. release of Minerva production. Stars Silvana Pampanini, Renato Rascel, Maria Fiore. Features Anna Maria Ferrero, Cosetta Greco, Olga Villi, Carlo Dapporto, Galeazzo Benti, Franco Interlenghi, Erno Crisa, Lauretta Masiero. Directed by Domenico Paolella. Screenplay, Paolella, Carlo Infascelli; camera (Ferraniacolor), Mario Damicelli; settings, Mario Chiari. Tradeshown in N. Y., Oct. 27, '54. Running time, 95 MINS.

The Mannequin	Silvana Pampanini
The Elevator Boy	Renato Rascel
The Lady	Cosetta Greco
The Window Dresser	Galeazzo Benti
Mimi	Anna Maria Ferrero
The Sceptic	Carlo Dapporto
Rosa, the Country Maid	Maria Fiore
The Painter	Erno Crisa
The Black Bird	Olga Villi
The Student	Franco Interlenghi
Siren, Cossack, Native Girl	L. Masiero
The Mister	Marco Vicaro

(In Italian; English Titles)

"Half a Century of Songs" is just that—a glorified Italian "Hit Parade" of the past 50 years, with any attempt at skillful storytelling secondary to the music. Film, in Ferraniacolor, comprises seven episodes designed to spotlight the songs of seven modern periods in Italian history and to cram as many of the songs into each episode as is physically possible without regard to coherency. As such, it's a confusing and overlong hodgepodge, and looks to only limited returns in this country.

Even the songs, many of them familiar through American adaptations, become tiresome by the time this 95-minute feature drags itself out. Film is staged flashily, and the Ferraniacolor is almost violent in intensity, and this too, becomes tiresome. In its attempt to film a spectacular musical, Minerva has so overdone things as to make it a rather dull one. To add to the confusion, the editing is poor and one can't tell where one episode leaves off and the next starts, and in some cases the characters do the singing while in others an off-screen voice cuts in as a sort of narrator.

Best of the performances are turned in by Maria Fiore as a country girl-turned-paramour and by Renato Rascel as an over-imaginative elevator operator at a Riviera hotel. Silvana Pampanini, one of the Italian stars better known to U.S. audiences, is wasted in a tearful episode of the '30s. *Chan.*

Journey to Italy
(Viaggio in Italia)
(ITALIAN)

Rome, Oct. 19.

Titanus release of a Roberto Rossellini production (in association with Sveva-Junior Films). Stars Ingrid Bergman, George Sanders. Directed by Roberto Rossellini. Screenplay, Rossellini, Vitaliano Brancati, from a story by Rossellini and Brancati; camera, Enzo Serafin; music, Renzo Rossellini; editor, Jolanda Benvenuti. Previewed in Rome. Running time, 100 MINS.

Katherine Joyce	Ingrid Bergman
Alexander Joyce	George Sanders
Tony Burton	Leslie Daniels
Natalie Burton	Natalie Ray
Prostitute	Anna Proclemer

(In Italian; English Titles)

With the aid of the English dialog version, plus marquee bait in Ingrid Bergman-George Sanders-Roberto Rossellini, this pic could be hypoed to moderate grosses perhaps topping those of previous Bergman Italian-mades. Some re-editing would help the pace considerably, with a hasty ending a sure trouble spot, since lacking proper motivation in its present form. Film as a whole alternates brilliant bits with long stretches of so-so.

Story tells of an English couple, coldy moving close to divorce because of mutual incomprehension, who inherit a house near Naples. Planning to sell it, they begin suddenly to warm to the southern climate and the boisterous humanity about them. Fadeout sees them uniting again after witnessing a miracle during a local religious procession.

Rapid change from grit to grin, especially in Sanders, who plays Miss Bergman's husband, mars the effect of the warmup process by overspeeding. Tale is unevenly told, has some unhappy bits of dialog and sometimes shows the roughout form, which for its director, is the final version.

Editing, for example, is characteristically abrupt: Whereas Miss Bergman's character, given more footage, appears much clearer in delineation, Sanders lacks the needed definition enabling proper audience participation. For instance, his interlude with a prostitute begins promisingly, but the idea is not followed through. Others in cast fill in well.

Photography by Enzo Serafin, including some hidden-camerawork, fits the moods well. Music by Renzo Rossellini helps. *Hawk.*

Les Corsaires Du Bois De Bouglogne
(Pirates of the Bois De Bouglogne)
(FRENCH)

Paris, Oct. 12.

Sofradis release of Pecefilms production. Features Raymond Bussieres, Christian Duvaleix, Arlette Poivre, Vera Norman, Jean Ozenne, Denise Grey. Written and directed by Norbert Charbonau. Camera, Pierre Petit; editor, Marinelle Cadix. At Raimu, Paris. Running time, 90 MINS.

Hector	Raymond Bussieres
Cyprian	Christian Duvaleix
Caroline	Vera Norman
Annette	Arlette Poivre
Mother	Denise Grey
Grossac	Jean Ozenne

Slapstick and satire have been pushed into some prominence in this pic. However, the few good ideas imbedded in this lack the breath of talent to bring them into solid comedy focus. Hence, it remains a haphazardly made film which is distracted from by uneven thesping and timing, poor production dress and a lack of sufficient core. As it stands it has nabe possibilities for local showings, but it does not have U.S. interest because of its low comic vein.

This is a takeoff on the recent Dr. Bombard shipwreck ocean crossing. Pic has a street singer getting his pal and gal mixed up in an attempt to try the same thing and cash in on the publicity. They get a rich girl embroiled in this and all four have to go when her father uses it as a publicity stunt. Some good moments appear on the raft, but repetitiveness and general low comedics never bring this into ribtickling gear. *Mosk.*

Giovanna D'Arco Al Rogo
(Joan at the Stake)
(FRANCO—ITALIAN)
(Color)

Rome, Oct. 19.

ENIC release of a PCA Production Cinematografici Associati-France-London Film co-production. Stars Ingrid Bergman, Tullio Carminati; features Giacinto Prandelli, Augusto Romani, Plinio Clabassi, Saturno Meletti, Agnese Dubbini, Pietro de Palma, Aldo Tenossi: voices of Miriam Pirazzini, Pina Esca, Marcella Pillo, Giovanni Acolati. Directed by Roberto Rossellini. Story and dialogue, Paul Claudel; music, Arthur Honegger; arranged and conducted by Gian Andrea Gavazzeni; orchestra, chorus and ballet of the San Carlo Opera House, Naples; camera (Gevacolor), Gabor Pogany; editor, Jolanda Benvenuti. Previewed in Rome. Running time, 80 MINS.

Pic version of the Claudel-Honegger operatic, a hit on many European stages in the Bergman-Rossellini staging, is a difficult item to classify, with "prestige" perhaps best summing it up. Solemn-paced work, though somewhat livened up by Roberto Rossellini's direction, is nevertheless not for the general trade. Very special handling, with much aid from the Ingrid Bergman name, and more limitedly the Claudel-Honegger tandem, will help it reach its audience, worldwide even if limited. Best market appears to be France, and a French version of "Joan" was shot simultaneously with the English one.

Rossellini's direction, based on his own stage production of the work, is imaginative and different from anything he has done before. Production gamble by two new producers, Giorgio Criscuolo and Franco Francese, was made possible by using cast, costumes and some of settings of the stage version. A pre-rehearsed 18-day shooting schedule permitted the film to be brough in at $100,000 despite the double version and the color budget. This total does not include the Rossellini-Bergman contribs. Words and music remain identical with the original, while the visual has been much changed.

Action takes place mainly in a cloud-banked series of stylized settings, in and from which Joan (Miss Bergman) and a priest (Tullio Carminati) watch flashbacked and present proceedings of life on earth. Action is dominated by the dialog of these two, interspersed with choruses and dances, culminating in the burning at the stake, already previewed at start via some striking shots.

Both Miss Bergman and Carminati lend conviction to Claudel's dialogues (Miss Bergman's singing is confined to a nursery-like bit). Within its strange context, Joan is sometimes moving.

Gabor Pogany gives the pic elegant color (Gevacolor) rendering, and many of the sets are striking. Pace is slow throughout. Editing, as in many of Rossellini's films, is choppy. *Hawk.*

Guacho
(Foundling)
(ARGENTINE)

Buenos Aires, Oct. 19.

Argentina Sono Film production and release. Features Tita Merello, Carlos Cores, Julia Sandoval, Enrique Chabo, Luis Medina Castro, Margarita Corona and Alejandro Rey. Directed by Lucas Demare from a novel by Concha Espina, adapted by himself and Sergio Leonardo.

Camera, Alberto Etchebehhere; sets, Gori Munoz; music, Lucas Demare; editor, Jose Serra. At Ambassador, Buenos Aires. Running time, **97 MINS.**

This is grim entertainment without hardly a single light moment. It has grossed well here because audiences were buoyed in hopes that Lucas Demare had made another "Los Isleros." He has tried to imbue the pic with the same stark realism of the previous success but fails because he makes no attempt to explain the characters which only makes everything implausible. It is hard to understand on what grounds the producers felt this had the quality to be entered at the Venice Film Festival. Not even the photography is outstanding.

In a remote fishing village, a man marries a stranger after only brief acquaintance. For a reason which goes unexplained he has tossed overboard a next door sweetheart. A foundling is left on the couple's doorstep and the wife senses it is the former sweetheart's and her husband's child, but rears both it and her own child. As her own boy is the weaker, to retain the husband's love she has him believe the stronger is hers.

Tita Merello's acting draws tears despite all the implausibilities. It is her personality alone which has kept the pic alive here. Carlos Cores seems more in character as the rough fisherman than in most roles while Julia Sandoval is decorative as the jilted girl. The cameras are never effectively handled and the whole production lacks distinction. *Nid.*

Sign of the Pagan
(C'SCOPE—COLOR)

Topflight costumed actioner on Atilla, the Hun, with entertainment values for hearty b.o. possibilities.

Hollywood, Nov. 9.

Universal release of Albert J. Cohen production. Stars Jeff Chandler, Jack Palance, Ludmilla Tcherina, Rita Gam; features Jeff Morrow, George Dolenz, Eduard Franz, Allison Hayes, Alexander Scourby, Sara Shane, Pat Hogan, Howard Petrie, Michael Ansara. Directed by Douglas Sirk. Screenplay, Oscar Brodney, Barre Lyndon; camera (Technicolor), Russell Metty; editor, Milton Carruth, Al Clark; choreography, Kenny Williams; music, Frank Skinner, Hans J. Salter; music supervision, Joseph Gershenson. Previewed Nov. 1, '54. Running time, **91 MINS.**

Marcian	Jeff Chandler
Attila	Jack Palance
Princess Pulcheria	Ludmilla Tcherina
Kubra	Rita Gam
Paulinus	Jeff Morrow
Theodosius	George Dolenz
Astrologer	Eduard Franz
Ildico	Allison Hayes
Chrysaphius	Alexander Scourby
Myra	Sara Shane
Sangiban	Pat Hogan
Gundahar	Howard Petrie
E'econ	Michael Ansara
Bleda	Leo Gordon
Tula	Rusty Wescoatt
Mirral	Chuck Roberson
Olt	Charles Horvath
Pope Leo	Moroni Olsen
Chilothe	Robo Bechi
Herculanius	Sim Iness
Valentinian	Walter Coy

(*Aspect ratio*: 2.55-1)

Universal has good action spectacle in this topflight Cinema-Scope feature. It should register heartily at the boxoffice generally. Unlike most screen spectacles, "Sign of the Pagan's" running time is a tight 91 minutes, in which the flash of the Roman Empire period is not permitted to slow down the telling of an interesting action story.

Plot deals with Atilla, the Hun, the Scourge of God, and his sweep across Europe some 1,500 years ago. Particularly noteworthy is the treatment of the barbarian in writing and direction, and in the manner in which Jack Palance interprets the character. Instead of a straight, all-evil person, he is a human being with some good here and there to shade and make understandable the bad. This single touch, almost alone, makes the Albert J. Cohen production strong screen entertainment, frosting what is otherwise a good combination of action dramatics and heroics that has been attractively packaged in Technicolor.

Douglas Sirk's direction of the excellent script by Oscar Brodney and Barre Lyndon catches the sweep of the period portrayed without letting the characters get lost in spectacle. Representing good in the plot is Jeff Chandler, centurion made a general by his princess, Ludmilla Tcherina, to fight off Atilla's advancing hordes and save Rome from a sacking. It's not the might of the sword that fells the barbarian, but the might of the Lord, the one force Atilla feared most. Picture handles this angle of Christian spirit exceptionally well.

Scope of the lensing by Russell Metty sharpens the mass action scenes of Attila and his followers on their ruthless march and has just as much impact in the more individual sequences, keeping the footage a constant visual treat. Abetting, too, is the score by Frank Skinner and Hans J. Salter, even though the stereophonic sound is so misused that it keeps up an unrelenting assault on the ears, particularly from the surround horn tracks.

With Palance scoring so solidly in his role of Attila, he makes the other performers seem less colorful, although Chandler is good as Marsian and Miss Tcherina pleasing as Princess Pulcheria, even with a dubbed speaking voice. Femme standout is Rita Gam, as the daughter of Attila who turns Christian and is killed by her father. Allison Hayes, the abused slave wife of the Hun, does well as the instrument of his death at the climax. Also impressing in their parts are Jeff Morrow, George Dolenz, Eduard Franz, Alexander Scourby and others.

Milton Carruth and Al Clark share the credit for the tight editing. The art direction by Alexander Golitzen and Emrich Nicholson, the set decorations by Russell A. Gausmah and Oliver Emert, costuming and other technical contributions are firstrate. *Brog.*

Track of the Cat
(C'SCOPE—COLOR)

Grim, outdoor melodrama with only so-so entertainment values.

Hollywood, Nov. 9.

Warner Bros. release of Wayne-Fellows production. Stars Robert Mitchum, Teresa Wright; co-stars Diana Lynn, Tab Hunter, features Beula Bondi, Philip Tonge, William Hopper, Carl Switzer. Directed by William A. Wellman. Screenplay, A. I. Bezzerides; from the novel by Walter Van Tilburg Clark; camera (WarnerColor), William H. Clothier; editor, Fred MacDowell; music, Roy Webb. Previewed Nov. 4, '54. Running time, **102 MINS.**

Curt	Robert Mitchum
Grace	Teresa Wright
Gwen	Diana Lynn
Harold	Tab Hunter
Ma Bridges	Beulah Bondi
Pa Bridges	Philip Tonge
Arthur	William Hopper
Joe Sam	Carl Switzer

(*Aspect ratio*: 2.55-1)

The novelty of lensing, in color, a picture designed to reproduce black-and-white is rather dissipated in this Wayne-Fellows production for Warner Bros. If there had been some entertainment impact to go with the photographic treatment, the combination might have paid off strongly. The outlook is not forte.

William A. Wellman is responsible for the novelty idea and directed in a manner to achieve some rather startling effects. Only color seen is the flesh tones of the characters, the green of the trees on the snow-covered Mt. Rainier location site, a red and black mackinaw and a light-colored blouse. Everything else is in tones of black and white. It gives the right "mood" to the Walter Van Tilburg Clark story, which is a "moody" piece, at best. A. I. Bezzerides scripted, getting the characters involved in a lot of dreary talk that serves to emphasis what unpleasant persons most of them are.

Story deals with a farm family of three brothers, an old-maid sister, a drunken father and a vindictive, Bible-reading mother, plus a girl from a neighboring farm who is the intended of the younger brother. As the melodrama unfolds, first the older brother, William Hopper, is killed by a mountain lion. Then the middle brother, Robert Mitchum dies in a fall while out looking for the "cat." At the finale, the younger brother, Tab Hunter, comes into manhood when he kills the lion and claims his girl, Diana Lynn. The lion is never seen in the picture and symbolizes the "cat" every man carries on his back and which must be thrown off before he is a man.

The performances are very good in realizing on the demands of direction and the story characters. Had these people been less unpleasant characters audiences would warm up more to the show, but as it is, there's little to keep them engrossed for the long 102 minutes. Each of the players named have their big scene, well done, as do Teresa Wright as the drab old maid; Beulah Bondi, the warped mother; Philip Tonge, the alcoholic father, and Carl Switzer, a wizened, old, superstitious Indian.

The C'Scope lensing by William H. Clothier is effective and the other technical assists equally good, although the editing lets the footage run long. *Brog.*

Cannibal Attack

Johnny Weissmuller action entry for the secondary situations.

Columbia release of Sam Katzman production. Stars Johnny Weissmuller; features Judy Walsh, David Bruce. Directed by Lee Sholem. Screenplay and story, Carroll Young; camera, Henry Freulich; editor, Edwin Bryant; music, Mischa Bakaleinikoff. Tradeshown N.Y. Nov. 4, '54. Running time, **69 MINS.**

Johnny Weissmuller	Johnny Weissmuller
Luora	Judy Walsh
Arnold King	David Bruce
Rovak	Bruce Cowling
Commissioner	Charles Evan
John King	Stevan Darrell
Jason	Joseph A. Allen Jr.

(*Aspect ratio*: 1:85-1)

A Johnny Weissmuller starrer, "Cannibal Attack" is standard action-adventure material for juvenile audiences. As such there's nothing pretentious about this Sam Katzman production but it will comfortably fill demands of the secondary situations.

"Attack," incidentally, originally was intended as another entry in Columbia's "Jungle Jim" series with Weissmuller portraying the title role. However, Col recently turned over the "Jim" rights to Screen Gems, its vidpix subsidiary, and as a result the star is cast as himself instead of the comic strip adventurer.

For that matter, it's understood that producer Katzman has only two more Weissmuller pictures coming up after the current release. One is completed and the other is to roll shortly. Reportedly, the onetime swim champ prefers something less strenuous now that he's somewhat older.

As for "Attack," scripter Carroll Young whipped up a fanciful tale of cobalt mysteriously disappearing in a crocodile infested river. There are numerous fights between Weissmuller, white men, natives and crocs but just what it's all about is rather confusing until shortly before the finale.

Eventually it develops that Judy Walsh, a half-caste native gal, mine owner Stevan Darrell and his henchman, Bruce Cowling, are swiping the cobalt for a foreign government. Their plot is exposed by Weissmuller after he foils the opposition with familiar heroics.

Weissmuller; although a little beefy, is still adept in the water. Miss Walsh wears a sarong with the best of 'em but her thesping is another matter. David Bruce is fair as Weissmuller's aide while so-so support is provided by Cowling, Darrell and Charles Evans, among others.

Lee Sholem's direction couldn't do much with this one, apparently the implausible story was too much of a handicap. Camerawork of Henry Freulich is okay. Much of the background, however, consists of stock shots of jungles and animals. Mischa Bakaleinikoff's score and Edwin Bryant's editing are par for the course. *Gilb.*

Snow Creature

Science fiction entry for strictly minor situations.

United Artists release of W. Lee Wilder production. Stars Paul Langton, Leslie Denison, Teru Shimada, Rollin Moriyana. Directed by Lee Wilder. Screenplay, Myles Wilder; camera, Floyd D. Crosby; editor, Jodie Copelan; music composed and conducted by Manuel Compinsky. Tradeshown, N.Y., Nov. 5, '54. Running time, 80 MINS.

Frank Parrish .... Paul Langton
Peter Wells .... Leslie Denison
Subra .... Taru Shimada
Leva .... Rollin Moriyana
Inspector Karma .... Robert Kino
Airline Manager .... Robert Hinton
Joyce Parrish .... Darlene Fields
Corey Jr .... George Douglas
Fleet .... Robert Bice
Dr. Dupont .... Rudolph Anders
Lt. Dunbar .... Bill Phipps
Edwards .... Jack Daly
Guard in Warehouse .... Rusty Westcott

"Snow Creature" is bush league science fiction. Produced on a minimum budget, picture discloses an amateurish script, pedestrian direction, repetitive footage and uniformly unconvincing performances. It may contain a few kicks for the kids but hardly ranks with the kind of stuff moppets get for free on video.

Yarn wanders from Tibet to Hollywood while going nowhere although opening promisingly enough with an expedition of an American botanist questing some offbeat species of mountain flora in India. This, however, is only the takeoff point for some unimaginative meandering into the w.k. myth of "the abominable snowman" of the Himalayas.

In this pic, the snow creature is a shaggy, and barely scarifying, giant who is captured and transported to America in a refrigerated cage. Absurdities crowd fast on each other after the U.S. immigration office refuses entry to the creature because he's not on quota. The snow man eventually escapes in Hollywood and the manhunt through the sewers of the city is of a piece with the rest of the production in its lowercase execution and lack of suspense.

Paul Langton, as the botanist; Leslie Denison, as his assistant and Teru Shimada, as a Tibetan guide, walk through their roles in colorlessly deadpan style, as does the rest of the supporting cast.

Herm.

The Happiness of Three Women
(BRITISH)

Modest Britisher given small chance in U.S. market.

London, Nov. 2.

Adelphi Films release of David Dent production. Stars Brenda de Banzie, Petula Clark, Donald Houston. Directed by Maurice Elvey. Screenplay, Eynon Evans, based on his story, "Wishing Well"; editor, Robert Jordan Hill; camera, Stan Pavey; music, Ted Astley. At Studio 1, London, Nov. 1, '54. Running time, 79 MINS.

Jane .... Brenda de Banzie
Delith .... Petula Clark
John .... Donald Houston
Irene .... Patricia Cutts
Amos .... Eynon Evans
Ann .... Patricia Burke
Peter .... Bill O'Connor
Amelia .... Gladys Hay
Morgan .... Glyn Houston
David .... Emrya Leyshon
Minister .... Hugh Pryse
Blodwen .... Jessie Evans
Busdriver .... John Lewis
Mary Lewis .... Mary Jones
Nancy .... Julie Milton
Hannah .... Eira Griffiths
Ben .... Ronnie Harris

There is a pleasant Welsh atmosphere about this modest British production with a strong local cast which will prove a valuable selling factor for the home trade. It is a light prospect for the U.S. market but should have some appeal as a dualer.

Film is based on Eynon Evans' stage play, "The Wishing Well." Action occurs in a Welsh village where a trio of unhappy women hope their problems will be solved by tossing a coin into the well. One is a too-wealthy widow, bored with her idle existence; another has lost her husband in the war; and the third finds life difficult with her husband after he had been away on military duties.

The yarn has a leisurely Welsh charm, mainly derived from the homely philosophy of the village postman who believes that he can solve other people's problems. There is also the romantic side issue of the innkeeper's paralyzed son who feels that his impending marriage to a local girl is a major mistake. Brenda de Banzie, Petula Clark, Donald Houston and Patricia Cutts head the cast in competent fashion while the author makes a promising screen debut in the role of the postman. Maurice Elvey has done a straightforward job of direction. Other credits are up to standard.

Myro.

The World Dances
(SONGS—COLOR)

International folk dancing exhibition interlaced with songs and scenic shots. Could catch on in specialized situations.

Festival Pictures release of a Brooke L. Peters production. Directed by Peters; camera (Colorama), W. Merle Connell; music, Alex Alexander; art direction, Daniel Hall; research, Chet L. Swital; editor, Connell; narrator, George Fenneman. Reviewed at the 55th St. Playhouse, N.Y., Nov. 7, '54. Running time, 70 MINS.

Featured performers by country:

America: Carolina Cotton, Merle Travis, Bob Osgood & His Hill Billies; **Cuba:** Aura San Juan, Ramon Talavera, George Dalvos, Tao Porchon; **Spain:** Antonio & Luisa Triana and the Spanish Mountain Girls; **Armenia:** Ruth St. Denis Dancers with Karoun Tootikian and Eric Ward; **France:** Mme. Etienne's French Dancers with Pauline Farrel; **Hungary:** George and Katrine Tatar, Rima Rudina on Gypsy Violin; **Mexico:** Lourdes Chavez; with Louis Gonzales and Pat Lugo Singing; **Italy:** Sy Melano, The Village Dancers; Lead by Phillys Bloom; **Ireland:** Barry O'Hara, The Irish Rovers; Lead by Edward Masterson; **Israel:** Israeli Folk Dancers; Lead by Barry Denovitz with Dvor-Isralow; **Africa:** Bob Lee House and Group with Louis P. Brown on Congo Drums; **Bavaria:** The Mountain Dancers; Lead by William Reordan, Ernest Muster; **England:** Richard Dehr, Audrey Share's English Folk Dancers; **Japan:** Mrs. Fujima's Japanese Dancers; Directed by Mrs. Fujima Kansuma; **Philippines:** Lucas Philippine Folk Dancers; Directed by Andre Lucas; **Poland:** The Gandy Dancers; Lead by Edmund L. Szablowski; **Scotland:** Scottish Dance Group; Lead by Jean MacDougall, Margaret Montgomery; **Ukrainia:** Konstantin Hopfer and Jane Mueller; the Malentjew Sisters singing; **Sweden:** Vasa Folk Dance Group; Directed by Andrew H. Wendell; **Greece:** Greek Folk Dancers with Alexandria Kappas.

An interesting idea has been carried out with some success in "The World Dances," a feature-length collection of folk music and dances from some 20 nations. Full of earthy grace and rhythm, it should appeal both to terpsichorian enthusiasts and to the various national groups that are represented here.

Produced and directed by Brooke L. Peters, the film makes a serious attempt to provide each dance team with its whys and wherefores. Apart from that, Peters has spiced his lineup with refreshing location shots from various countries and this tends to relieve the sense of monotony which creeps into the pic after a while.

Colorama process used here serves its purpose, but its hardly the best tint variety. Although the lensing work is generally good, the images aren't all sharp, particularly when there is a lot of movement. Color registration also is uneven and hues change from scene to scene.

Various folk groups are introed by tv and radio announcer George Fenneman who has a pleasant and authoritative manner of delivery. Color is particularly unkind to him.

Elaborately costumed performers from the various countries go through their routines with zest and skill. Every type of folk dance is repped—the Cuban rhumba, the Hungarian czardas, the Irish reel, the German "Schuhplattler," they're all there. Outstanding turns are by Robert Lee House who does an African ritual dance to the throbbing accompaniment of the tom tom drum; the Ruth St. Denis Dancers in an exotic Armenian "Wedding Fantasy"; George and Katrine Tatar who whirl through a fast-moving czardas, with Rima Rudina making the fiddle sob in an outstanding Magyar bit; the Lucas Philippine Folk Dancers in an intriguing Bamboo Pole dance, and, best of all, Antonio and Luisa Triana who go through some fast and furious heel work via a group of Andalusian dances. They're the highlight of the show.

U.S. contribution comes towards the latter part of the film and includes an oldfashioned square dance and vocal numbers by Carolina Cotton and Merle Travis. Considering that the pitch is for American audiences, the selection is something less than satisfying. On the whole, exhibs should find "World Dances" uniquely exploitable, particularly in neighborhoods where foreign nationalities predominate.

Hift.

Madame Du Barry
(FRANCO-ITALIAN—COLOR)

Paris, Nov. 2.

Cinedis release of Ariane-Filmsonor-Francinex-Rizzoli production. Stars Martine Carol. Directed by Christian-Jaque. Screenplay, Albert Valentin; adaptation, Valentin, Henri Jeanson, Christian-Jaque; dialog, Jeanson; camera (Eastmancolor), Christian Matras; editor, Jacques Desagneaux. At Le Paris, Paris. Running time, 110 Mins.

Madame Du Barry .... Martine Carol
Louis XV .... Andre Luguet
Count Du Barry .... Daniel Ivernel
Madame Gramont ..... Anna Maria Canale
Choisoul .... Masimo Serato
Richilieu .... Denis D'Ines
Lebel .... Jean Paredes
Madame .... Gabriel Dorziot
Guillame .... Noel Roquevert

Martine Carol continues in her gallery of great courtesans of history as she essays the shopgirl who became Louis XV's last mistress. Coproduction obviously had U.S. in mind for nary a bosom shows in this, the first time for Miss Carol. And the offbeat and shock aspects are held to the corrupt aspects of the court as the mistresses fight and struggle for the bed of the king. Lushly mounted and directed, this may have some appeal for the U.S. in special situations because the action is confined to the boudoir intrigues of the reign.

Du Barry is picked up as a shopgirl of easy virtue who is invited to the most famous bagnio of the era by its sharpeyed madame. Here she is discovered by the scheming Count Du Barry who makes her into a bauble worthy of the king. When they go to introduce her the king doesn't show, and she gets fed up and rushes off locking her mentors in a room. She runs into the king whom she goes for immediately. She is won by her freshness. Then follows intrigue to get her introduced at court, the sudden death of the King and her abolition and final beheading at the hands of the revolutionists. Pic is told in a sort of flashback method by a barker using lantern slides at a fair.

Director Christian-Jaque has played this very much tongue-in-cheek and still has given it a measure of royal lushness in the court scenes. Miss Carol plays this in a pouty manner and gives little evidence why the king went so madly for her while the sultry, bosomy Gianna-Maria Canale was nightly waiting for him. Daniel Ivernel is a dynamic, rapidly moving Du Barry while Andre Luguet is fine as the aging, lecherous king.

Lensing is fine but colors have a tendency to unbalance in certain interiors with flesh tones going bluish. Editing is good and the rich production dress is also an asset.

In short this court and bedroom charade will depend on the drumbeating that accompanies it on U.S. dates. There is talk that its corrupt eye-view of 17th century France may ban this for exportation which would be ironic because of its obvious attempt to avoid any excuse for a U.S. nix.

Mosk.

Sauerbruch
(GERMAN)

Berlin, Oct. 19.

Schorcht release of Corona production. Stars Ewald Balser, Heidemarie Hathever and Maria Wimmer. Directed by Rolf Hansen. Screenplay, Felix Luetzkendorf; camera, Helmut Ashley; music, Mark Lothar. At Gloria Palast, Berlin. Running time, 109 MINS.

Professor Sauerbruch ..... Ewald Balser
Frau Sauerbruch .... Maria Wimmer
Olga Ahrends .... Heidemarie Hathever
Secretary .... Edith Schultze-Westrum
Wendlandt .... Paul Bildt
Hindenburg .... Friederich Domin
Professor Mikulicz .... Kurt Horwitz
Sister .... Lina Carstens
Sister .... Hilde Koerber
Songstress .... Edith Plate

"Sauerbruch," biopic of the famous German surgeon who died some years ago, turns out a well-made, entertaining picture with enough emotional impact to please local audiences. Because of Sauerbruch's popularity in this country and the excellent cast, domestic b.o. prospects are excellent. Pic also may have chances outside Germany.

This centers on Sauerbruch's life after the last world war and retells in flashbacks some of his most characteristic episodes. Although this covers much of his life, it doesn't result in an episodic jerkiness and in flat character portrayals.

On the contrary, the acting is perhaps the best thing about the film. Ewald Balser's characterization of the title character is almost a masterpiece. The supporting cast is exceptionally well chosen with many fine performances resulting.

Screenplay by Felix Luetzkendorf, based on Sauerbruch's memoirs recently published in a top German magazine, is a routine one. It tends to glorify the famous medico a bit. However, "Sauerbruch" still remains as a pic ahead of the German postwar standard.

Rolf Hansen's direction is generally smooth and loses its pace only slightly towards the end. Lensing by Herbert Ashley is first-rate. The musical score and other technical contributions are also noteworthy.

Hans.

Desiree
(C'SCOPE-COLOR)

Lavishly mounted costumer with Marlon Brando's Napoleon as the center attraction. A plenty strong b.o. property.

Twentieth Century-Fox release of Julian Blaustein production. Stars Marlon Brando, Jean Simmons, Merle Oberon and Michael Rennie; features Cameron Mitchell, Elizabeth Sellars, Charlotte Austin, Cathleen Nesbitt, Evelyn Varden, Isobel Elsom, John Hoyt, Alan Napier, Nicolas Koster, Richard Deacon, Edith Evanson, Carolyn Jones, Sam Gilman, Larry Carine, Judy Lester, Richard Van Cleemput, Florence Dublin, Louis Borell, Peter Bourne, Dorothy Neumann, David Leonard, Siw Paulsson, Lester Matthews, Gene Roth, Colin Kenny, Peter Reynolds, Leonard George, Richard Garrick, Violet Rensing, A. Cameron Grant. Directed by Henry Koster. Screenplay, Daniel Taradash from the Annemarie Selinko novel; camera (color), Milton Krasner; editor, William Reynolds; art direction, Lyle Wheeler and Leland Fuller; music, Alex North, choreography, Stephen Papich. Previewed in N.Y., Nov. 8, '54. Running time, **110 MINS.**

Napoleon .... Marlon Brando
Desiree .... Jean Simmons
Josephine .... Merle Oberon
Bernadotte .... Michael Rennie
Joseph Bonaparte ..... Cameron Mitchell
Julie .... Elizabeth Sellars
Paulette .... Charlotte Austin
Mme. Bonaparte........Cathleen Nesbitt
Marie .... Evelyn Varden
Mme. Clary .... Isobel Elsom
Talleyrand .... John Hoyt
Despreaux .... Alan Napier
Oscar .... Nicolas Koster
Etienne .... Richard Deacon
Queen Hedwig .... Edith Evanson
Mme. Tallien .... Carolyn Jones
Fouche .... Sam Gilman
Louis Bonaparte .... Larry Craine
Caroline Bonaparte .... Judy Lester
Lucien Bonaparte Richard Van Cleemput
Elisa Bonaparte .... Florence Dublin
Baron Morner .... Louis Borell
Count Brahe .... Peter Bourne
Queen Sofia .... Dorothy Neumann
Barras .... David Leonard
Princess Sofia .... Siw Paulsson
Caulaincourt .... Lester Matthews
Von Essen .... Gene Roth
General Becker .... Colin Kenny
Jerome .... Peter Raynolds
Pope Pius VII .... Leonard George
Count Reynaud .... Richard Garrick
Marie Louise .... Violet Rensing
Montel .... A. Cameron Grant

(*Aspect ratio*: 2.55-1)

There is a theory in Hollywood that nothing bogs down a historical film as easily as the facts of history. It is a maxim which 20th-Fox must have had very much in mind when it CinemaScoped Annemarie Selinko's bestselling novel, "Desiree."

The "Desiree" which Julian Blaustein has produced in handsome and elaborate fashion is easily one of the best and most potent costumers to come along in this widescreen age. It is well staged, in part exceedingly well acted and on the whole faithful—in spirit at least—to the Desiree of the book who recorded in her diary the rise and fall of Napoleon and her own ascendancy from commoner to Queen of Sweden.

Unlike the book, however, the film concentrates more on people than it does on history; and while this may disappoint some, it's probably just as well from the pic's point of view. "Desiree" is dominated primarily by two things: The acting of Marlon Brando in the part of Napoleon, which rates as a masterful exhibition of thesping, and the elaborate settings and costumes which provide the film with unique grandeur and elegance.

It's very much to the credit of director Henry Koster that "Desiree," which is primarily a conversation piece, doesn't become too slow. On the contrary, in addition to packing a considerable emotional wallop in many of its scenes, the picture also inherits from the novel some of the very funny lines and situations, such as the one when Napoleon—desirous of ending the bickering between his sisters—decides to make them all princesses.

It'll matter little to the average patron whether or not the story as presented here has any historical truth to it. "Desiree" on the screen rings true and, considering the opulence of its settings and the romantic aspects of the story, the film is loaded with b.o. merits that should pay off very handsomely.

It tells the story of Desiree, daughter of a Marseilles silk merchant, who meets an impoverished general, Napoleon Bonaparte. They plan to marry. But Napoleon goes to Paris and there meets and weds the rich and influential Josephine. Desiree marries Bernadotte, one of France's most successful generals, who later splits with the Emperor and becomes regent—and finally king—of Sweden. Throughout, the paths of Desiree and Napoleon continue to cross, and the impression is given that, almost to the last, when Napoleon surrenders his sword to her and resigns himself to his last banishment, the attraction of these two people to oneanother continues. (Same general situation was used by a French film starring Sacha Guitry.)

As Napoleon, Brando draws a portrait of a man so sure of the righteousness of his cause that no sacrifice is too great in accomplishing his ends. His Napoleon is arrogant, schemeing and temperamental, and yet oddly human in his failings. Consistently underplaying the part, with only his voice betraying the tension and the intensity of his being, Brando gives every scene his personal imprint.

Jean Simmons as Desiree is lovely, innocent and naive, as prescribed. It is easy to understand men's attraction to her, and yet she doesn't emerge as a very clear character on the screen. At the end, after a very considerable range of experience, her Desiree is as wide-eyed and as unsophisticated as at the start. Nowhere does she indicate that she has matured and taken on new stature. It is a shortcoming in characterization for which both the actress and Koster must share the blame.

As Bernadotte, Miss Simmons' husband, Michael Rennie delivers a sock portrayal that should get him attention. It is a sympathetic role, and he fits it perfectly. Film doesn't bother to tell much about Bernadotte who, in his own way, was as extraordinary as Napoleon himself. (This was clearer in the French film aforesaid.)

As Josephine, Merle Oberon handled a difficult assignment in less than satisfactory fashion. Somewhat handicapped by the script, which doesn't give the character much leeway, she emerges as a puzzling personality and with a tendency to overact.

In supporting roles, Cameron Mitchell does well as Joseph Bonaparte. Elizabeth Sellars as Julie handles herself very well. Evelyn Varden plays the old servant, Marie, with conviction. Richard Deacon as Desiree's pompous brother is fine.

Daniel Taradash fashioned the screenplay which gives the cameras every chance to roam through extravagantly furnished rooms and other eye-filling settings. Color by De Luxe is rich and satisfying although, in the print viewed by this reviewer, it was oddly uneven. Milton Krasner's camera handling is expert in every respect.

Koster's direction is a distinct credit to the film. It is full of imaginative touches pointing up emotional qualities which should make "Desiree" particularly appealing to women. Add to this the lure of many magnificent gowns and handsome uniforms. The climax, fantastic as it is, is staged with classic simplicity and telling effect, revealing the loneliness of Napoleon, defeated and rejected by his own people. Thrown in here is an observation about his wanting the "United States of Europe," a somewhat naive view of this ruthless man's endeavours.

The scene symbolizing Napoleon's defeat in Russia is handled with a maximum of good sense and craftsmanship. Other parts, such as the coronation, with Napoleon crowning himself; the bit where he forces his wife to renounce their marriage, and the nocturnal waltz scene between Napoleon and Desiree are handled for strong dramatic impact. "Song from Desiree," echoes through the film but isn't sung. William Reynolds' editing is without a flaw.

Nothing has been spared by producer Blaustein to make this a truly "big" film. *Hift.*

So This Is Paris
(SONGS—COLOR)

Light musical about three gobs in Paris. Shapes up for a lively b.o.

Universal release of Albert J. Cohen production. Stars Tony Curtis, Gloria de Haven, Gene Nelson, Corinne Calvet, Paul Gilbert; features Mara Corday, Allison Hayes, Christiane Martel, Myrna Hansen, Roger Etienne, Ann Codee, Arthur Gould-Porter, Regina Dembeck, MichelleDucasse, Maithe Iragui, Lucien Plauzoles, Numa Lapeyre, Lizette Guy. Directed by Richard Quine. Screenplay, Charles Hoffman; from a story by Ray Buffum; camera (TC), Maury Gertsman; editor, Virgil Vogel; choreography, Gene Nelson and Lee Scott; songs by Pony Sherrell & Phil Moody. Previewed in N.Y., Nov. 12, '54. Running time, **96 MINS.**

Joe Maxwell .... Tony Curtis
Colette d'Avril .... Gloria de Haven
(Janie Mitchell)
Al Howard .... Gene Nelson
Suzanne Sorel .... Corinne Calvet
"Davey" Jones .... Paul Gilbert
Yvonne .... Mara Corday
Carmen .... Allison Hayes
Christiane .... Christiane Martel
Ingrid .... Myrna Hansen
Pierre Deshons .... Roger Etienne
Grand'mere Marie .... Ann Codee
Albert .... Arthur Gould-Porter
Miss Photo Flash ...... Regina Dombeck
Simone .... Michelle Ducasse
Cecile .... Maithe Iragui
Eugene .... Eugene Plauzoles
Charlot .... Numa Lapeyre
Jeannine .... Lizette Guy

(*Aspect ratio*: 1.85-1)

It's been one of the oddities of recent years that Universal, which rose to the top on escapist film fare, hasn't gone in for musicals. In "So This Is Paris" the studio makes up for lost time. It's a gay, colorful, ambitiously projected production that's long on craftsmanship if somewhat short on imagination.

On the surface, everything that's needed for a musical b.o. click is at hand. The sets are pleasant, the performances fine and the script has some very funny lines. But neither the story nor the routines have that touch of magic that would distinguish "Paris" from innumerable other pix laid out along similar lines in the past. At a time when millions are tuning in on the tv "spectaculars," that extra ingredient of invention and cleverness is almost a "must" in this type films.

All of which doesn't mean that "So This Is Paris" doesn't have considerable entertainment merits. First of all, this is the first picture in which Tony Curtis deviates from his action-film roles and proves himself a very versatile fellow. He has some ways to go as a song-and-dance man, but his performance here is completely satisfactory and he should add a considerable number of friends to his already large fan following. He's obviously having a fine time in the film, and his audience will appreciate him.

Charles Hoffman's screenplay carries out a simple idea. Three sailors—Curtis, Gene Nelson and Paul Gilbert—spend their leave in Paris. They meet up with three very different gals, one of them an American singer (played by Gloria de Haven). They stage a benefit for a couple of orphans and, having formed various romantic attachments, return to their ship.

Nelson is a hoofer of considerable talent and is given a chance for a couple of fine solos. Comedian Paul Gilbert carries off his assignment in fine style and garners plenty of laughs. Miss de Haven is pretty but tends to become overly-precious in both her dialog and her songs. Nevertheless, her numbers are carried off very well and she's a definite asset to the show.

In the smaller parts, Corinne Calvet as a man-crazy French heiress manages to exhibit her shapely figure in an erratic part; Mara Corday, Allison Hayes, Christiane Martel and Myrna Hansen are beauties fresh out of the U talent stable, and they all look properly glamorous. Ann Codee as the grandmother is good, and the kids in the film are quite charming.

There are 10 songs in "So This Is Paris," nine of them originals written by Pony Sherrell and Phil Moody. Hottest production number is staged to the tune of "I Can't Give You Anything But Love Baby," by Jimmy McHugh and Dorothy Fields. This is where Miss de Haven does her best work. The scene is a dazzler. Some of the Sherrell-Moody tunes, such as "The Two Of Us" and "If You Were There" are catchy. Their novelty, "Three Bon Vivants" has appeal and is done with much gusto by Curtis, Nelson and Gilbert. "So This Is Paris" theme song also sticks to the ear.

Richard Quine's direction keeps things moving and interlaces song, dance and romance into smooth continuity. Technicolor is up to usual high standards. "So This Is Paris" may not be a critics' picture, but it shapes up as an eye-full for the general audience. *Hift.*

Cattle Queen of Montana
(COLOR)

Barbara Stanwyck and Ronald Reagan in program western.

RKO release of Benedict Bogeaus production. Stars Barbara Stanwyck and Ronald Reagan. Features Gene Evens and Lance Fuller. Directed by Allan Dwan. Screenplay, Howard Estabrook and Robert Blees from an original story by Thomas Blackburn; camera (Technicolor), John Alton; editor, Carl Lodato; musical supervision, Louis Forbes. Previewed in N.Y., Nov. 15, '54. Running time, **88 MINS.**

Sierra Nevada Jones...Barbara Stanwyck
Farrell .... Ronald Reagan
McCord .... Gene Evans
Colorados .... Lance Fuller
Natchakoa .... Anthony Caruso
Yost .... Jack Elam
Starfire .... Yvette Dugay
Pop Jones .... Morris Ankrum
Nat .... Chubby Johnson
Hank .... Myron Healey
Powhani .... Rod Redwing

There are cowboys and Indians in "Cattle Queen of Montana"; good and bad whites, peaceful and renegade Indians, and colorful Technicolor scenery, but all these ingredients fail to make the Benedict Bogeaus production anything more than a listless and ordinary western. The names of Barbara Stanwyck and Ronald Reagan, however, should provide marquee appeal.

The Howard Estabrook and Robert Blees screenplay is short on imagination and long on cliche, and what takes place on screen appears all to familiar. In the picture's favor (but this seems to be a trend lately in Indian territory stories) is an attempt to depict the problems of the Redmen in fighting the encroachment of their land by the white settlers. The Indians are not all evil, scalp-hunting devils. There are some chiefs who fervently work for peaceful coexistence, but are frustrated by a renegade element aroused by white man's "fire water" and rifles.

Miss Stanwyck is the "Cattle Queen" of the story, a gun-totin' hard-ridin' gal determined to establish a Montana ranch stake after her father is killed by the renegades. Reagan is an undercover Army man charged with the duty of ferreting out the element inciting the Indians. Lance Fuller is the university-educated Indian chief who wants to bring peace to his tribe while Anthony Caruso is the leader of the rebel Indians. Gene Evans is the villainous rancher in cohorts with the renegades.

The performances are professionally competent, but the roles are not designed to bring out any outstanding thesping. Allan Dwan's direction is slow moving, and even the action sequences fail to bring out the necessary excitement. The technical aspects are fine. *Holl.*

The Outlaw's Daughter
(COLOR)

Above-average modestly-budgeted oater; good supporter and a natural for the nabes.

Hollywood, Nov. 16.
20th-Fox release of Alpee Pictures Corporation (Wesley Barry) production. Stars Bill Williams, Kelly Ryan, Jim Davis; features George Cleveland, Elisha Cook, Guinn (Big Boy) Williams, Sara Hayden, Nelson Leigh, George Barrows. Directed by Wesley Barry. Screenplay, Sam Roeca; camera (Color Corp. of America), Gordon Avil; editor, Ace Herman; music, Raoul Kraushaar. Reviewed Nov. 3, '54. Running time, 76 MINS.

Jess	Bill Williams
Dan	Jim Davis
Kate	Kelly Ryan
Tulsa	Elisha Cook
Lem	George Cleveland
Moose	Guinn (Big Boy) Williams
Dalton	Nelson Leigh
Mrs. Merril	Sara Hayden
Rock	George Barrows
Duke (Bartender)	Zon Murray
Mexican Dancer	Zabuda
Bank Manager	Dick Powers
Eastern Girl	Regina Gleason
Doctor	Sam Flint
Stunt Men	Paul Stader, Danny Fisher
Rider	Eugene Anderson Jr.

This modestly budgeted tale of the Old West stands quite a few notches above average for the course. With an interest-holding story-line, good performances, direction and production, "The Outlaw's Daughter" is a natural for supporting-bill booking anywhere and good enough, even, to top a bill in most nabes.

Indie produced under the Alpee Pictures Corporation banner by Wesley Barry, with Edward L. Alperson, Jr., as associate, "Daughter" was purchased several weeks ago by 20th-Fox for release. With Kelly Ryan in title role, that of outlaw James Dalton's daughter, yarn spots Bill Williams as the robber-killer, Jim Davis as the marshal. When old man Dalton is murdered by Williams, Miss Ryan moves to another town to start a new life. There she meets Davis, who promptly falls for her.

Thinking it was he who murdered her father, she spurns him and becomes interested in Wil-

liams. When Davis learns Williams' true identity and starts to arrest him, Miss Ryan helps him escape —and goes with him. She's soon an active member of the small outlaw band. Davis and posse are out after 'em, and eventually dispose of all but Miss Ryan. By this time she's discovered Williams killed her father and that a life of crime has lost its attraction. Davis offers to let her go, but she heads back to town with him for a jail stretch. That's at least a plot switch in sagebrush sagas.

Williams and Davis are authoritative and convincing, and Miss Ryan, a pert newcomer of note, shows thespic promise. She's better known, incidentally, as Sheila Connelly—now Mrs. Guy Madison. Supporting roles are well acted, with Elisha Cook particularly good as a member of Williams' band.

Producer-director Wesley Barry has a fine credit in "Daughter;" production values belie the budget, and his direction neatly packages the ingredients. Technical contributions, especially Gordon Avil's Color Corp. of America camera work, are good. *Neal.*

Karamoja
(DOCUMENTARY—COLOR)

Raw film fare, not for the squeamish; can be exploited for good b.o.

Hollywood, Nov. 11.
Hallmark release of Matt Freed production. Conceived and planned by Dr. and Mrs. William B. Treutle; camera (Eastman Color), Dr. William B. Treutle; editor, George McGuire; music, Ernest Gold. Reviewed Nov. 10, '54. Running time, 60 MINS.

(Aspect ratio: 1.33-1)

"Karamoja" is being presented through Hallmark Productions by Kroger Babb, "America's fearless showman," as he calls himself. It could well be, if this documentary of the world's "last lost tribe" is any criterion. Pic's a natural for those who like their film fare raw, and, as an exploitation attraction, should ring up hefty returns if backed by a shocker-type ad campaign.

Film was lensed by Dr. William B. Treutle who, with his bride, went into the Belgian Congo to search for and find Karamoja (Land of Lost People). He's captured well on celluloid rites and customs of this tribe of savages who live today no differently than their forefathers 6,000 years ago.

Scenes to make the squeamish squirm are many. Among them: children's teeth being knocked out by stones; holes being punched through the lower lip, with lip plugs then inserted; the dismembering of a calf, with the natives drinking its blood; the carving of insignia on the human bodies, a calf shot at close range in the neck with an arrow, and the blood streaming into a bowl held by a Karamojan. And throughout it all, the natives wearing little more than the wind—as the ads proclaim.

Photography is crude, but so are the subjects. The adequate musical score is by Ernest Gold and credited as producer is Matt Freed. *Neal.*

Half-Way to Hell
(DOCUMENTARY)

Interest - holding compilation of footage preaching anti-totalitarianism.

Hollywood, Nov. 11.
Hallmark release of Mabel Walker Willebrandt production. Coordinated by Al Rogell. Directed by Robert Snyder. Story and narration by Quentin Reynolds, originated and compiled by George Rony; musical supervision, Gene Forrell; music composed and directed by Arthur Honegger, Tibor Harsanyi and Arthur Hoerre, in association with the concert orchestra of the Paris Conservatory of Music. Reviewed Nov. 10, '54. Running time, 62 MINS.

(Aspect ratio: 1.33-1)

Here is a powerful screen preachment against totalitarianism, a graphic documentary of the deadly parallel between Hitler's Naziism, Mussolini's Fascism and Stalin's Communism. A shocker, not for the squeamish, "Half-Way To Hell" should satisfy those who like such film fare rough.

Picture, being paired on double bills with Hallmark's "Karamoja," is a compilation of newsreel footage, German films and films "smuggled" from behind the Iron Curtain. Footage is most interesting and neatly tied together.

Technical credits are good, and majority of the footage surprisingly clear. Quentin Reynolds' narration of his own story-line keeps the interest high and the emotions aroused. *Neal.*

Mourez . . . Nous Ferons Le Reste
(Die . . . We'll Do the Rest)
FRENCH—COLOR

Paris, Nov. 9.
Discina release of SNDC production. Stars Roger Nicolas. Directed by Christian Stengel. Screenplay, Stengel; adaption, Jacques Emmanuel, Eddie Petrossian, Stengel; camera (Eastmancolor), Lucien Joulin; editor, J. Marel. At Triomphe, Paris. Running time, 100 MINS.

Ulysse	Roger Nicolas
Francoise	Magali Noel
Priest	Armentel
Mathrin	Noel Roquevert
Mayor	Balpetre
Chatalaine	Suzet Mais
Notary	Jacques Emmanuel
Georges	Georges Rollin

This gimmick pic is mainly reviewed because it rings in Gallic attitudes towards the U.S. in a lame attempt at a comedy. Banal carryings-on, lagging pacing and general obviousness of situations make this of little possibility for the American market. Its chances here are also slim except for provincial spotting. Idea of having a special American week in a small French town to attract tourists is reminiscent of a Spanish pic, "Welcome, Mr. Marshall," where it was done with taste and talent. This is too ordinary to put over an essentially engaging idea.

A Paris pitchman decides to go to the U.S. and return to his village to sell his ancestral cottage, driving the Cadillac of a chauffeur friend. He is mistaken for an American millionaire and town sharpies try to profit from this by making the house a shrine of a family which made its mark in the New World. He stays on and becomes enamoured of a local, pure and fiery orphan. He introduces the idea of an American week to get visitors. When this goes big, he hits on the idea of a Forest Lawn-type cemetery. Though he is found out, the cemetery idea grows, and the town becomes rich with people demanding plots.

Director-writer Christian Stengel was obviously under a limited budget since this pic seems

strained in production value, and sports an unneeded color coating. Roger Nicolas, a good low comic, is made to play this practically straight and support is only adequate with Noel Roquevert, a centenarian who refuses to die for the cause, the only hep actor in the film. Lensing is uneven as is editing which is not helped by the so-so direction. *Mosk.*

Mambo
(ITALIAN—SONGS)

Rome, Nov. 23.

Paramount release of a Ponti-DeLaurentiis production. Stars Silvana Mangano, Michael Rennie, Vittorio Gassmann, Shelley Winters, Katherine Dunham; features Eduardo Cianelli. Directed by Robert Rossen. Screenplay, Rossen, Guido Piovene, Ivo Perilli, Ennio De Concini, from story by Perilli and De Concini; camera, Harold Rosson; costumes, Jack Pratt, Guido Coltellacci; music, Bernardo Noriega. Dave Gilbert; dances. Katherine Dunham; editor, Adriana Novelli. At Cinema Europe, Rome. Running time, 110 MINS.

Giovanna Masetti	Silvana Mangano
Count Enrico	Michael Rennie
Mario Rossi	Vittorio Gassmann
Tony Burns	Shelley Winters
Katherine Dunham	Herself

Paramount has a moneymaker in this Ponti-DeLaurentiis production, patterned in general lines after the two previous Mangano-Gassmann costarrers, "Bitter Rice" and "Anna." Similar themes, if not settings, will help, and the title is an added asset. General runs in foreign market, including the U. S., will be aided by such cast names as Michael Rennie, Shelley Winters and Katherine Dunham. Some tightening of the pace is suggested, with the first half especially vulnerable. Actors mouth English dialog and pic gets dubbed release in U. S.

Story is again near soap opera, and involves the trials of a girl who wants to be a dancer. She is torn between the pure love for a dying prince and the passionate embraces of an adventurer. For a while Giovanna (Silvana Mangano) is happy with the dance group led by Tony (Miss Winters), and soon becomes star of the show. But despite her success on returning to her home town of Venice, she falls once more under the adventurer's (Vittorio Gassmann) spell while turning down a marriage proposal by the prince (Rennie).

Learning that the prince is incurably ill, Gassmann forces her to marry him to cash in on his future inheritance. Married life, however, shows her it's the prince whom she always really loved. When he dies, she gives up the inheritance and Gassmann, returning to her other love, the dance. Like the story, the film is not for the discriminating, at least in its present form. Reportedly, it has been re-cut several times after Rossen finished it, and is said to bear little resemblance to the original.

Performances are generally good, with Rennie copping honors in a smooth, sympathetic effort as the doomed prince. Miss Mangano goes through her paces believably, and dances well.

Miss Winters contributes ably despite a vaguely drawn character, while Gassman effectively overacts his villain role in keeping with the picture's spirit. Miss Dunham and Eduardo Cianelli liven up some minor roles, with the former also contributing the pic's choreography. In an attempt to duplicate the b.o. assist given "Anna" by its "song," producers have given Miss Mangano several to sing, but she, or her dubber, does so indifferently, without the impact found in "Anna."

Some of the film's music, however, is good for a spin, and combined with the title, can help sell the pic.

The production has been well fitted technically. Harold Rosson's camerawork, especially in capturing an unusual Venice-in-winter, is expert. *Hawk.*

Cry Vengeance

Good melodrama with revenge motivation for general playdates.

Hollywood, Nov. 19.

Allied Artists release of Lindsley Parsons production. Stars Mark Stevens; features Martha Hyer, Skip Homeier, Joan Vohs. Directed by Mark Stevens. Written by Warren Douglas, George Bricker; camera, William Sickner; editor, Elmo Veron; music, Paul Dunlap. Previewed Nov. 17, '54. Running time, 81 MINS.

Vic Barron	Mark Stevens
Peggy Harding	Martha Hyer
Roxey	Skip Homeier
Lily Arnold	Joan Vohs
Tino Morelli	Douglas Kennedy
Lieut. Ryan	Don Haggerty
Marie Morelli	Cheryl Callaway
Mike Walters	Warren Douglas
Johnny Blue-Eyes	Mort Mills
Red Miller	John Doucette
Nick Buda	Lewis Martin
Emily Miller	Dorothy Kennedy

A chase that carries a vengeance-seeking man to Ketchikan, Alaska, motivates this tough melodrama, and gives it an interesting background. Allied Artists should enjoy a satisfactory payoff from it generally, since it shapes up as acceptable filmfare for those who like their mellers on the rugged side.

Mark Stevens both stars in and directed the Lindsley Parsons production and does well on both counts. He keeps attention on his character of an ex-cop out to revenge a frame and the death of his family, even though the role doesn't command as much audience sympathy as usually accrues to the screen hero. Two talented femme lookers, Martha Hyer and Joan Vohs, add topnotch distaff interest to the plotting in the screen story by Warren Douglas and George Bricker.

Stevens, released from San Quentin after serving three years on a frameup, sets out after Douglas Kennedy, whom he believes responsible for killing his wife and child in an auto explosion that disfigured the ex-detective. The trail leads to Alaska, where Stevens finds Kennedy a respected business man whose chief interest is in his young daughter, Cheryl Callaway. Kennedy is innocent of the original fix and explosion, so the crook who had arranged it sends killer Skip Homeier after Kennedy, figuring the latter's death will put Stevens back in prison for keeps. Homeier gets Kennedy, plus his own moll, Miss Vohs, but she's able to tip off the law so that Stevens avoids the new frame and is freed of his complexes. Finale indicates he will get together with Miss Hyer after the legalistics are over.

The performances of the entire cast come over in good style. Parsons' production supervision, with John H. Burrows as associate, achieves smart values for the budget through the Pacific Northwest locales and the way they are used. On the technical side, William Sickner's camera work, the editing by Elmo Veron and the score by Paul Dunlap are among the good points. *Brog.*

The Yellow Mountain
(COLOR)

Formula western feature for regulation dating in the outdoor market.

Hollywood, Nov. 23.

Universal release of Ross Hunter production. Stars Lex Barker, Mala Powers, Howard Duff; co-stars William Demarest, John McIntire; features Leo Gordon, Dayton Lummis, Hal K. Dawson, William Fawcett, James Parnell. Directed by Jesse Hibbs. Screenplay, George Zuckerman, Russell Hughes; Adaptation, Robert Blees; based on the story by Harold Channing Wire; camera (Technicolor), George Robinson; editor, Edward Curtiss; music supervision, Joseph Gershenson. Previewer Nov. 16, '54. Running time, 77 MINS.

Andy Martin	Lex Barker
Nevada Wray	Mala Powers
Pete Menlo	Howard Duff
Jackpot Wray	William Demarest
Bannon	John McIntire
Drake	Leo Gordon
Geraghty	Dayton Lummis
Sam Torrence	Hal K. Dawson
Old Prospector	William Fawcett
Joe	James Parnell

(Aspect ratio: 2-1)

The outdoor market will probably put an okay stamp on "The Yellow Mountain." It has all the well-used ingredients of the commonplace western actioner, plus a color treatment and some familiar names.

Plot is made up of formula oater-action predicaments. Jesse Hibbs' direction stirs up some regulation outdoor movement in handling story and players. Familiar motivations have Lex Barker and Howard Duff, his larcenous partner, at odds over a gold mine and a girl, Mala Powers, but getting together at the finale to defeat efforts of John McIntire to oust Miss Powers' father, William Demarest, from a supposedly worthless claim. A lot of complications, too many, feature the script by George Zuckerman and Russell Hughes, based on Robert Blees' adaptation of the Harold Channing Wire story.

Assisting the five stars through the plot chores in featured spots are Leo Gordon, McIntire's chief gunman; Dayton Lummis, Hal K. Dawson and others. Cast toppers and the others give adequate emphasis to the action requirements.

Technicolor lensing by George Robinson makes good use of the outdoor locations and the other technical assists measure up. *Brog.*

Masterson of Kansas
(COLOR)

George Montgomery in outdoor actioner suitable for the regular programmer market.

Hollywood, Nov. 17.

Columbia release of Sam Katzman production. Stars George Montgomery; features Nancy Gates, James Griffith. Directed by William Castle. Story and screenplay, Douglas Heyes; camera (Technicolor), Henry Freulich; editor, Henry Batista. Previewed Nov. 16, '54. Running time, 72 MINS.

Bat Masterson	George Montgomery
Amy Merrick	Nancy Gates
Doc Holliday	James Griffith
Dallas Corey	Jean Willes
Coroner	Benny Rubin
Charlie Fry	William A. Henry
Clay Bennett	David Bruce
Wyatt Earp	Bruce Cowling
Sutton	Gregg Barton
Virgil Earp	Donald Murphy
Mitch	Gregg Martell
Tyler	Sandy Sanders
Yellow Hawk	Jay Silverheels
Merrick	John Maxwell
Gage	Wesley Hudman
Lt. Post	Leonard Geer

Three legendary western gunmen occupy positions of prominence in this George Montgomery outdoor actioner, and the bang-bang they supply sets the offering up as an okay entry for the programmer market.

Montgomery is seen in the title role, while James Griffith does Doc Holiday, and Bruce Cowling the character of Wyatt Earp. As a sharp-shooting trio, the threesome provides the picture with sufficient interest and movement to see it through its playdates. The characterizations come over well under William Castle's direction of the screen story by Douglas Heyes, and Sam Katzman backs the pres-

entation with suitable outdoor action values.

William A. Henry heads the heavy lineup, representing cattle interests that have framed John Maxwell so that the latter will not be able to turn over rich grass lands to an Indian tribe led by Jay Silverheels. Although Masterson and Holiday are sworn enemies out to get each other, they join together to save Maxwell, mostly because the latter's daughter, Nancy Gates, is so appealing. Climax finds Masterson, Holiday and Earp moving in on a mob for a last-minute save of Maxwell from a lynching —a stunt that also averts the Indian war threatened by Silverheels if his friend were to die.

Jean Willes, Benny Rubin and David Bruce are among others in the cast who back up the outdoor action values satisfactorily. Technicolor lensing by Henry Freulich and the other technical credits are okay. *Brog.*

The Divided Heart
(BRITISH)

Real life story of adopted wartime child claimed by real mother; sincerely told but absence of marquee strength hurts U. S. chances.

London, Nov. 9.

General Film Distributors release of Ealing Studios-Michael Balcon production. Stars Cornell Borchers, Yvonne Mitchell, Armin Dahlen, Alexander Knox. Directed by Charles Crichton. Screenplay, Jack Whittingham and Richard Hughes; camera, Otto Heller; editor, Peter Bezencenet; music, Georges Auric. At Odeon, Leicester Square, London, Nov. 9, '54. Running time, 89 MINS.

Inga	Cornell Borchers
Sonja	Yvonne Mitchell
Franz	Armin Dahlen
Chief Justice	Alexander Knox
Marks	Geoffrey Keen
First Justice	Liam Redmond
Second Justice	Eddie Byrne
Josip	Theodore Bikel
Dr. Muller	Ferdy Mayne
Prof. Miran	Andre Mikhelson
Mlle. Poncet	Pamela Stirling
Toni	Michel Ray, Martin Keller
Mitzi	Krystyna Rumistrowicz
Max	Mark Guebhard
Sonja's Daughters	Gilgi Hauser, Maria Leontovitsch
Hans	Martin Stevens
Matron	Marianne Walla
Nurse	Dorit Welles
Foreman	Hans Kuhn

A human story taken from real life, "The Divided Heart" fails to tug the emotional heartstrings and ends up as little more than a conventional if convincing meller. It is a questionable b.o. proposition, with little name value to help as a selling factor on either side of the Atlantic.

Film is based on an actual story featured in "Life" in which a "blood mother" claims her son, who had legally been adopted during the war by German parents. The narrative is sincerely developed from the actual documentation of the case. It spotlights the dilemma of the American tribunal which has to decide whether the boy should remain with his foster parents or be sent to his real mother. The circumstances are mainly depicted in flashback during the hearing by the American judges.

The boy's father is shot by the Nazis after he had helped the partisans in Yugoslavia. His two daughters are taken by the Germans but his wife escapes into the woods with her infant son until the child's ill-health drives her back into the city. She is captured and sent to Auschwitz while the child goes to an orphanage. The foster parents are a childless couple and found the boy in the orphanage where he was shy and uncooperative. With tenderness and love, they make him into a friendly, healthy youngster.

The real drama comes with the court's decision to base the final verdict on the boy's own decision. Despite the fact that the child prefers to stay with his foster parents, there is a two-to-one ruling from the judges that he should be repatriated to his real mother.

At no time does the script measure up to the real heartache of the actual incident and there is rarely more than a superficial approach to this postwar problem. The cast is more than adequate, however, and Cornell Borchers and Yvonne Mitchell give stirring performances as the two mothers involved in the dilemma. Armin Dahlen is not too convincing as the other foster parent but Alexander Knox is always dign'fied as the chief justice. Other roles are intelligently filled by Geoffrey Keen, Liam Redmond, Eddie Byrne and Theodore Bikel. Charles Crichton's direction strikes a note of sincerity. Main technical credits are more than satisfactory.

Myro.

Black 13

Inferior British import for smaller situations.

Hollywood, Nov. 22.

Twentieth-Fox release of a Roger Proudlock production. Stars Peter Reynolds, Rona Anderson, Patric Barr, Lana Morris. Directed by Ken Hughes. Story, Pietro Germi; camera, Gerald Gibbs; editor, Sam Simmons. Previewed Nov. 9, '54. Running time, **75 MINS.**

Stephen .... Peter Reynolds
Claire .... Rona Anderson
Robert .... Patric Barr
Marion .... Lana Morris
Stella .... Genine Graham
..ee .... Michael Balfour
Wally .... John Forrest
Mrs. Barclay .... Viola Lyel
Professor Barclay .... Martin Walker
Inspector .... John Le Mesurier
Bruno .... Martin Benson

(*Aspect ratio*: 1.33-1)

Twentieth-Fox seemingly imported this inferior British film for exhibs who lack widescreens, and the choice isn't a happy one. Even in the smaller program market the going will be tough.

A cast of unknowns isn't helped either by story or direction in the overlong tale. Yarn unfolds in London, where the son of a college professor has turned to holdups and eventual murder, while his sister is going with a detective assigned to the series of crimes. Premise carries static development.

Peter Reynolds is the criminal, an unpleasant blighter, and Rona Anderson as the sister is as good as part will permit. Patric Barr occasionally manages an okay impression of the dick, and Lana Morris, in love with Reynolds, is notable mostly for a striking resemblance at times to Bette Davis. Genine Graham displays an interesting personality as a hardboiled nitery pianist.

Technical credits are adequate. Roger Proudlock is producer and Ken Hughes handles the direction.

Whit.

The End of the Road
(BRITISH)

Routine tearjerker; dialect and lack of marquee names will hurt U.S. chances.

London, Nov. 16.

British Lion release of Group 3 production. Features Finlay Currie, Duncan Lamont, Naomi Chance. Directed by Wolf Rilla. Screenplay, James Forsyth and Geoffrey Orme; camera, Arthur Grant; editor, Bernard Gribble; music, John Addison. At Gaumont (private theatre), London. Running time, **76 MINS.**

Works Manager .... Edward Chapman
Time-keeper .... George Merritt
Old Worker .... Eugene Leary
Old "Mick-Mack" .... Finlay Currie
Gloomy Gertie .... Edie Martin
Barney .... Duncan Lamont
Barney Wee .... David Hannaford
Molly .... Naomi Chance
Young Kennie .... Gordon Whiting
Personnel Manager.......Pauline Winter
Builder .... Michael Bird
Manager .... Tony Kilshawe
Madge .... Hinda Fenemore

This is a conventional weepie, made on a modest scale, the originality of whose story has been blurred through recent stage and radio presentations of "The Wooden Dish" (with an identical theme—a woman rebelling against the care of her aged father-in-law). It should make an acceptable dualer here, being well constructed and a commendable specimen of its type, but the dialect and lack of topliners probably will detract from its appeal in the U.S.

Story is set in the industrial Midlands, the drab environment of factory chimneys being reflected in the lives and characters of the people. A skilled old workman is retired by his firm of electroplaters, but resents being shelved and tries in vain for other work. He shares his son's home but upsets his daughter-in-law who threatens to quit unless he is sent to an institution. The husband gets fired and in desperation his father gets a job as night watchman at his old works, but loses it after a misunderstanding. His apparent inefficiency results in his probing the secret of a deterioration in a smelting vat, which restores his prestige and he takes over the post of timekeeper.

The personalities are all stock, but of real human interest, the most appealing being that of the small grandson who plays hookey to follow the distraught old man far into the night, fearful for his safety. Finlay Currie gives a grand portrait of the old diehard while Duncan Lamont registers well in the minor role of his son, torn between loyalties. The harassed wife is well played by Naomi Chance and Edward Chapman is alternately crisply officious and humanely understanding as the works manager. David Hannaford is an endearing moppet. Pic is deftly directed by Wolf Rilla.

Clem.

The Country Girl
(SONGS)

An absorbing adaptation of the Clifford Odets play with Bing Crosby, Grace Kelly and Wil'iam Holden. Strong boxoffice.

Paramount release of William Perlberg production. Stars Bing Crosby, Grace Kelly, William Holden. Directed by George Seaton. Screenplay, Seaton, adapted from the play by Clifford Odets; camera, John F. Warren; editor, Ellsworth Hoagland; musical sequences staged by Robert Alton; music, Victor Young; songs, Ira Gershwin (lyrics) and Harold Arlen (music). Previewed in N.Y., Nov. 10, '54. Running time, **104 MINS.**

Frank Elgin .... Bing Crosby
Georgie Elgin .... Grace Kelly
Bernie Dodd .... William Holden
Phil Cook .... Anthony Ross
Larry .... Gene Reynolds
Singer-Actress ..... Jacqueline Fontaine
Ed .... Eddie Ryder
Paul Unger .... Robert Kent
Henry Johnson ..... John W. Reynolds
1st Woman .... Ida Moore
Bartender .... Frank Scanell
2nd Woman .... Ruth Rickaby
1st Actor .... Hal K. Dawson
Actor .... Howard Joslin
3rd Actor .... Richard Keene
2nd Actor .... Jack Kenney
Photographer .... Charles Tannen
Actor .... Les Clark
Man .... Allan Douglas
Jimmie .... Jonathan Provost
Expressman .... Don Dunning
Expressman .... Max Wagner
Bellboy .... Bob Alden
Ralph (Dresser) .... Chester Jones
Photographer .... John Florio
Man .... Jack Roberts

An exceptionally well performed essay on an alcoholic song man, with Bing Crosby the one carrying on a bottle romance, "Country Girl" is high on boxoffice punch. It's a strong, intense show that's certain to be talked about. "Did you see Crosby (the conversations might start) as the lush?" It's a show business story that has depth and movement.

Adapted from the Clifford Odets play of the same title, William Perlberg's production comes face to face with some harsh situations with uncontrived honesty. Its key player, a quondam star induced into trying a painful comeback, is a weak, lying, excessive drinker. The ending strikes a note of spirits resistance for the character and, as it is skillfully developed in the film, this is fitting.

Rarely does a film have such striking thesp work. Grace Kelly is resolute to the hilt, conveying a certain feminine strength and courage that enable her to endure the hardships of being the boozer's wife. Bill Holden registers in sock style as the legit director determined that Crosby can stand up to the demands of the starring role in a new play. One scene of uncommon vividness has Holden, no longer take in by Crosby's lies, suddenly realizing he's in love with Miss Kelly.

Crosby pulls a masterly switch, for it is the character of the story that he projects; it is not the crooner in another shallow disguise. He immerses himself into the part with full effect, inspiring audience revulsion with his deceit and sottiness and yet engendering just enough sympathy to make his final triumph over the bottle a welcome development.

For marquee purposes, the trio of names is important to the film's commerce, of course. Add the acting, sharp and forceful direction by George Seaton of substantial story material and the sum total augurs an unmistakable boxoffice click.

"Girl" was produced on Broadway in 1950 by the late Dwight Deere Wiman with Paul Kelly, in the spot now held by Crosby, and Uta Hagen as his wife. It's effectively backgrounded and propped in the Perlberg-Seaton version and has four songs by Ira Gershwin and Harold Arlen. The bare N. Y. theatre where the show within the show is rehearsed, the Boston house which is the scene of the play's break-in, the squalid tenement apartment where Miss Kelly and Crosby are first found—these are realistically staged.

Product of the cleffers meets requirements. The four tunes fit into the pic production well enough and one, "Live and Learn," a blues number peddled by Crosby and Jacqueline Fontaine at one point, stands a fair chance of trade on its own. Robert Alton's staging of the musical numbers is adequate, too. These song spots, it should be noted, are only minorly incidental to the story.

According to a cast sheet, "Girl" has no one billed as "featured." Nearly all of the film is focused on the three stars. But Anthony Ross deserves mention; he's professionally first-rate as a hardened and unpleasant legit producer. All others show up competently.

A final word re Seaton's direction. It's incisive, apparently wringing out the full dramatic potential from each scene clearly and crisply without any pictorial or dialog excesses. All technical credits are without flaws.

Gene.

Deep In My Heart
(MUSICAL—COLOR)

Guest star-studded cast, Sigmund Romberg's music for chief values in tintuner with generally okay b.o. prospects.

Hollywood, Nov. 30.

Metro release of Roger Edens production. Stars Jose Ferrer, Merle Oberon, Helen Traubel, Doe Avedon, Walter Pidgeon, Paul Henreid, Tamara Toumanova; features Paul Stewart, Isobel Elsom, David Burns, Jim Backus, with guest stars Rosemary Clooney, Gene and Fred Kelly, Jane Powell, Vic Damone, Ann Miller, William Olvis, Cyd Charisse, James Mitchell, Howard Keel, Tony Martin, Joan Weldon. Directed by Stanley Donen. Screenplay, Leonard Spigelgass; from the book by Elliott Arnold; camera (Eastman Color), George Folsey; editor, Adrienne Fazan; music supervised and conducted by Adolph Deutsch; orchestrations, Hugo Friedhofer, Alexander Courage; choral arrangements, Robert Tucker; choreography, Eugene Loring. Previewed Nov. 24, '54. Running time, **130 MINS.**

Sigmund Romberg .... Jose Ferrer
Dorothy Donnelly .... Merle Oberon
Anna Mueller .... Helen Traubel
Lillian Romberg .... Doe Avedon
J. J. Shubert .... Walter Pidgeon
Florenz Ziegfeld .... Paul Henreid
Gaby Deslys .... Tamara Toumanova
Bert Townsend .... Paul Stewart
Mrs. Harris .... Isobel Elsom
Berrison .... David Burns
Ben Judson .... Jim Backus
Harold Butterfield ...... Douglas Fowley
Berrison Jr. .... Russ Tamblyn

(*Aspect ratio*: 1.75-1)

The musical career of Sigmund Romberg, a romanticist of song, is spread over two hours and 10 minutes in this Metro tintuner. It has a cast loaded with guest star names and the basic heart element to be found in nearly all of the Romberg music, indicating a good audience response generally. Footage makes it a problem for any but the single bill situations, although the family appeal of its music and entertainment values should see it through the smaller bookings.

Jose Ferrer, appearing as Romberg and playing him well, has an assignment with enough demands on versatility to satisfy any actor. He sings, he dances, he clowns, he romances as he brings the Romberg character to the screen in Ferrer style. Concerned with the private life of a man who gave the public many operettas and numerous songs that still have impact today, are co-stars Merle Oberon, gracious as Dorothy Donnelly; Helen Traubel, warm and friendly as Anna Mueller, and Doe Avedon, appealing as Lillian Harris, the girl who became Mrs. Romberg. Adding good featured support to these portions are Paul Stewart, as Bert Townsend; Isobel Elsom, as Mrs. Harris; Jim Backus, as Ben Judson, and Douglas Fowley, as Harold Butterfield.

The span of Romberg's life attempted and the outpouring of music in the period presented hefty problems to Roger Edens, here making his solo producer bow, but in most instances his guidance is entirely acceptable. The same problems were faced by Stanley Donen, and overcome just as well, in the direction of the wealth of material that required spotlighting simple songs and story scenes along with the big production numbers that are used to introduce some of the operettas.

The screenplay by Leonard Spigelgass, from the book by Elliott Arnold, ably backstops for the musical kaleidoscope. The script has its moments of well-developed humor and the tune portions are worked in neatly. Of the 16 numbers, including song and production, offered there's something that will appeal to everyone. Among the probable highlights are Ferrer and Miss Traubel singing and dancing "Leg of Mutton," the composer's first venture into ragtime; "Softly, As In A Morning Sunrise," sung by Miss Traubel; "I Love To Go Swimmin' With Wimmen," with Gene and Fred Kelly; an uproarously funny audition with Ferrer doing "The Very Next Girl I See," "Fat, Fat Fatima," "Jazzadadadoo" and "Girls Goodbye"; "It," solidly sold by Ann Miller; William Olvis' beautiful voice doing "Serenade" from "The Student Prince"; the surprisingly torrid and sensuous ballet done by Cyd Charisse and James Mitchell to "One Alone"; Tony Martin's singing of "Lover Come Back To Me" to Joan Weldon, and, last but not least, the closing "When I Grow Too Old To Dream" done by Ferrer.

Among other guest star appearances for special numbers are Tamara Toumanova with "I Love To Say Hello to the Boys" and a jazzy version of "Softly," Howard Keel with "Your Land and My Land," and the "Maytime" sequence with Jane Powell and Vic Damone. Miss Traubel also is heard on "You Will Remember Vienna," "Auf Wiedersehn" and "Stouthearted Men," all effective.

The Romberg music has the benefit of Adolph Deutsch's supervision, and the latter also conducted the orchestrations by Hugo Friedhofer and Alexander Courage, with choral arrangements by Robert Tucker. The art direction and settings are excellent, as are special effects and other technical contributions. Eugene Loring's choreography is good. *Brog.*

The White Orchid
(COLOR)

Routine jungle adventure, lensed in Mexico, for the general market.

United Artists release of Reginald LeBorg production. Stars William Lundigan, Peggie Castle. Directed by LeBorg. Screenplay, David Duncan and LeBorg; camera (Eastman Color), Gilbert Warrenton; editor, Jose W. Bustos; music, Antonio Diaz Conde; song, "Femme Fatale," by Chuy Hernandez, sung in English by Don Durant. Previewed Nov. 24, '54. Running time, **81 MINS.**

Robert Burton .... William Lundigan
Kathryn Williams .... Peggie Castle
Juan Cervantes ...... Armando Silvestre
Lupita .... Rosenda Monteros
Arturo .... Jorge Trevino
Miguel .... Alejandro de Montenegro
Pedro .... Miguel A. Gallardo

(Aspect ratios 1.85-1)

This search for a lost civilization deep in the jungles of Mexico is brought off in routine fashion but will serve its purpose as an attraction for the more general situations. The backgrounds, filmed in Eastman Color, provide more interest than the stock story development.

William Lundigan and Peggie Castle are the only familiar names in the cast, playing an archeologist and a photographer, respectively, who trek into the jungle with Armando Silvestre as guide to check on a story that a mysterious people are still living in the manner of the ancient Toltecs. The two males act in a rather childish manner in their love rivalry for Miss Castle and, in the end, Silvestre sacrifices himself so Lundigan and the girl can make it back to safety. Better development of the two male characters in script and direction would have kept things on a more believable plane. As it is the performances are just adequate to demands, with Silvestre doing the most to impress.

Reginald LeBorg produced and directed, as well as sharing scripting chores with David Duncan. He functions best on the production end, obtaining a good round of sight values that are pointed up by Gilbert Warrenton's camera work. There's good interest in some fiesta sequences in the early footage and they add considerable color to the film, as do some shots of ancient ruins. A tuneful background has been provided by Antonio Diaz Conde, and there is a song, "Femme Fatale," which is effectively sung in English by Don Durant in the final footage. Earlier it is done in Spanish by Alejandro de Montenegro and Miguel A. Gallardo, two of the cast members. Only femme besides Miss Castle is Rosenda Monteros. She does nice work as girl who loves Silvestre. *Brog.*

Day of Triumph
(COLOR)

Religious film with good grossing potential.

George J. Schaefer release of Century Films (James K. Friedrich) production. Directed by Irving Pichel, co-director, John T. Coyle; screenplay, Arthur T. Horman; camera (Eastman Color), Ray June; editor, Thomas Neff; music, Daniele Amfitheatrof. Previewed N.Y., Nov. 26, '54. Running time, **110 MINS.**

Zadok .... Lee J. Cobb
The Christ .... Robert Wilson
Caiaphas .... Ralph Freud
Peter .... Tyler McVey
Andrew .... Touch Connors
Cloas .... Toni Gerry
Mary Magdalene .... Joanne Dru
Judas .... James Griffith
Annas .... Everett Glass
Pilate .... Lowell Gilmore
Barabbas .... Anthony Warde
Nikator .... Peter Whitney

(Aspect ratio: 1.85-1)

The crucifixion and resurrection of Christ are brought to the screen again after 27 years in "Day of Triumph," a handsomely mounted independent production that abounds in dignity, restraint and distinction. Story of The Saviour was last done as a full-length film back in 1927 in Cecil B. DeMille's "King of Kings."

While part of the Arthur T. Horman screenplay, is admittedly fiction, most of the story has a documentary flavor and is without the familiar embellishments usually added to so-called Biblical yarns in the interest of entertainment. Thus the spirit of reverance that warms the 110 minutes of footage makes this entry more suitable for special handling and road shows instead of immediate general release.

A careful campaign much along the lines of "Martin Luther" will go a long way toward realizing the film's boxoffice potential. For enlisting the aid of the clergy and waiting for the word-of-mouth to spread around obviously should result in a pre-sold audience when the circuits and subsequent runs are reached. Moreover, although such Hollywood names as Lee J. Cobb and Joanne Dru appear in the cast they're not strong enough to carry the picture on their marquee pull.

Writer Horman, who is said to have based his screenplay upon the "scriptures and contemporary sources," recounts the story of an Israelite group known as the Zealots who strive to free the Jews from Roman bondage. In Jesus, whose wisdom and personal magnetism have fired the imagination of the people, they see a possible leader in rallying the populace to the cause.

Jesus' work among the poor, His association with the 12 disciples, His forgiveness of the penitent Mary Magdalene and His betrayal by Judas Iscariot are among the many scenes unreeled prior to the trial before Pontius Pilate and the crucifixion. "The Day of Triumph" when Christ rose from the dead, of course, provides the title of this Century Films production.

Under fine direction of the late Irving Pichel, and co-director John T. Coyle the cast ably re-creates the atmosphere of Biblical times. Lee J. Cobb is forceful and shrewd as Zadok, the Zealot leader; Joanne Dru contributes a touching performance as Mary Magdelene, the reformed prostitute whose tears washed the feet of Christ, and James Griffith is bitingly realistic as the sly and traitorous Judas.

Particularly well done is Robert Wilson's portrayal of Christ. His humble, saintly and reverent interpretation comes close to duplicating the picture of Christ as seen through the Bible. Among others who score performancewise are Lowell Gilmore as Pontius Pilate, Anthony Warde as Barabbas, the thief, and Ralph Freud as a high priest of Israel.

Producer James K. Friedrich, who's turned out a number of religious films in the past, provided "Triumph" with a wealth of physical values that would do credit to a major company. Both sets and costumes are on par with color plates out of the Bible and are especially enhanced by the excellent Eastman Color camerawork of Ray June. Print, incidentally, is by Pathe Laboratories. Thomas Neff's editing and music of Daniele Amfitheatrof are assets to the venture as are other technical credits. *Gilb.*

Le Rouge et le Noir
(The Red & Black)
(FRANCO-ITALIAN; COLOR)

Paris, Nov. 19.

Gaumont release of Franco-London-Documento production. Stars Gerard Philipe, Danielle Darrieux; features Antonella Lualdi, Jean Mercure, Jean Martinelli, Balpetre, Anna-Maria Sandri. Directed by Claude Autant-Lara. Screenplay, Jean Aurenche, Pierre Bost from novel by Stendhal; camera (Eastmancolor), Michel Kelber; editors, Madeleine Gug, Bosis Lewin; music, Paul Cloerec. At Marivaux, Paris. Running time, **170 MINS.**

Julien Sorel .... Gerard Philipe
Louise Renal .... Danielle Darreux
Mathilde .... Antonella Lualdi
Marquis De Mole .... Jean Mercure
Renal .... Jean Martinelli
Abbe Pirard .... Balpetre
Elisa .... Anna-Maria-Sandri

This is the third turn around, on film, of the great French classic, Stendhal's "Le Rouge Et Le Noir" ("The Red & The Black"). Current version serves as the most important and definitive in its name value, close transcription, size and technical and thespic glow. A filmic condensation of a story of a 19th-century opportunist who is redeemed by love, registers as episodic at times, and though uneven, in contour and emphasis, possesses a cynical adherence to the original that will be relished by French auds. But it bodes possible seal trouble in the U. S., since a like theme (i.e. "Lovers, Happy Lovers") is now having this difficulty.

Film is also the type that foreign distribs are leery of, due to cost of color prints, length and primarily arty appeal. Its treatment makes this unlikely for mass draw in the U. S. and thus not one that will take to dubbing. It has adult treatment stamped all over it, and should benefit from word-of-mouth crix.

Bookish aspect shows in the film's insistence on the social strata of the times as the catalyst of the lead's extreme cynicism. Gerard Philipe (Sorel) has a role akin to a 19th-century Ripois and makes the most of it in underlining his role and building it into a whole in spite of the episodic quality of the film. Danielle Darrieux gives poignance to the essentially vapid character of Sorel's first seduction. His advent into the home of the Marquis De Moles, where he seduces the proud and sensual Mathilde, sinuously played by Antonella Lualdi, is another savory episode. Color is excellent and well-hued throughout, and editing is fine except in a bit of hocus-pocus when a flashback to the attempt on Mme. Renal's life is made unclear. This is a touchy **film, but worth handling.** *Mosk.*

Mad About Men
(BRITISH—COLOR)

Sequel to "Miranda," with Glynis Johns again as mermaid; spotty returns forecast on either side of Atlantic.

London, Nov. 23.

General Film Distributors Ltd. release of Betty E. Box-Earl St. John production. Stars Glynis Johns, Donald Sinden, Anne Crawford, Margaret Rutherford. Directed by Ralph Thomas. Screenplay, Peter Blackmore; camera (Technicolor), Ernest Steward; editor, Gerald Thomas; music, Benjamin Frankel. At Leicester Square Theatre, London, Nov. 16, '54. Running time, **90 MINS.**

Miranda } ....Glynis Johns
Caroline }
Barbara .... Anne Crawford
Jeff .... Donald Sinden
Nurse Cary .... Margaret Rutherford
Berengaria .... Dora Bryan
Barclay .... Nicholas Phipps
Ronald .... Peter Martyn
Old Salt .... Noel Purcell
Mrs. Forster .... Joan Hickson
Viola .... Judith Furse
Madame Blanche .... Irene Handl
Mantalini .... David Hurst
Dr. Fergus .... Martin Miller
Editor .... Deryck Guyler
Pawnbroker .... Anthony Oliver
Symes .... Harry Welchman

A sequel to the successful British comedy, "Miranda," filmed a few years back, this has not strong hopes of repeating the boxoffice impact of the original. Despite an impressive local cast, it limps along rather uneasily and can only expect spotty returns. Not a strong entry for the U.S. market.

Glynis Johns again plays the role of Miranda, the mermaid. In this yarn, she is the facial double of a young school teacher who has inherited a house in Cornwall and prevails upon the new owner to take a fortnight's vacation while she comes on land in her place. As the title suggests, the mermaid is mad about men, and indulges in a succession of amorous adventures, but paves the way for a real romance when the schoolmarm returns.

There are broad comedy possibilities, and these have been fully and conventionally exploited, but there is little sparkle to the dialog. Too obvious references to such things as "this is fishy" and "whale of a good time," illustrate the pedestrian style in scripting.

Ralph Thomas has done a hearty job of direction and secured spirited performances from Miss Johns, Donald Sinden, Anne Crawford, Margaret Rutherford and other principals. Ernest Steward handles the Technicolor cameras confidently. Benjamin Frankel's music is a plus credit. *Myro.*

Escalier de Service
(Service Entrance)
(FRENCH)

Paris, Nov. 30.

Gaumont production and release. Stars Etchika Choureau, Danielle Darrieux, Jean Richard, Robert Lamoreux, Sophie Desmarets, Mischa Auer, Saturnin Fabre. Written and directed by Carlo Rim. Camera, Robert Juillard; editor, Robert Isnardin. At Broadway, Paris. Running time, 100 MINS.

Marie-Lou	Etchika Choureau
Pushkoff	Mischa Auer
Francois	Robert Lamoureux
Noelle	Danielle Darrieux
Diplomat	Jacques Morel
Wife	Sophie Desmarets
Merchant	Jean Richard
Mother	Junie Astor
Bouureau	Saturnin Fabre
Leopold	Jean-Marc Thibault
Benevuto	Marc Cassot

Carlo Rim has collected some star names to play small roles in this sketchy film depicting the adventures of a maid. Uneven quality of the pic, with dragged in reminiscences and an insipid love affair for this retiring young maid, makes this doubtful for the foreign film circuits in the U.S.. It has some star names, known in America, could serve as a dualer on the basis of monickers and Paris locale. Otherwise this looks slated more for the home market where its allusions and comedics are better understood. The maid in question, Marie-Lou, faints on the street into the arms of a young photographer. He takes her home to a communial life shared by a group of Left Bankers in an old house. Here she tells of her other jobs wherein four sketches are shown in flashback to utilize the star names. In one she has a hectic time at a phoney diplomat's home; in another, she is in a mysterious household which turns out to be that of the head Paris executioner, then into a screenwriter's home and finally with a bourgeois trio of mother, father and the son, with the men after the innocent young maid. Interwoven is her own story of her love for a young Italian painter who is chased by the police.

Writer-director Rim has depended too much on names. His slight and, at times, plodding material is not enough to give this the charm

pacing characterization and gloss needed. Etchika Choureau brings the proper ingenuousness to the maid with others in the long cast presenting silhouettes in her simple story. Lensing is fine and editing keeps things coherent. *Mosk.*

There's No Business Like Show Business
(MUSICAL-COLOR-C'SCOPE)

Irving Berlin's ode to show biz done up in fancy C'Scope trimmings. A guaranteed b.o. smash.

20th-Fox release of Darryl F. Zanuck's (Sol C. Siegel) CinemaScope production of Irving Berlin's musical. Stars Ethel Merman, Donald O'Connor, Marilyn Monroe, Dan Dailey, Johnnie Ray, Mitzi Gaynor. Directed by Walter Lang. Screenplay, Phoebe and Henry Ephron, from original by Lamar Trotti; songs, Irving Berlin; camera (DeLuxe), Leon Shamroy; dances, Robert Alton; music, Alfred and Lionel Newman; vocal arrangements, Ken Darby, Hal Schaefer; orchestrations, Bernard Mayers, Edward B. Powell, Herbert Spencer, Earle Hagen; special effects, Ray Kellogg; film editor, Robert Simpson; asst. director, Ad Schaumer. Tradeshown N.Y., Dec. 3, '54. Running time, 117 MINS.

Molly Donahue	Ethel Merman
Tim Donahue	Donald O'Connor
Vicky	Marilyn Monroe
Terrance Donahue	Dan Dailey
Steve	Johnnie Ray
Katy Donahue	Mitzi Gaynor
Lew Harris	Richard Eastham
Charles Gibbs	Hugh O'Brian
Eddie Duggan	Frank McHugh
Father Dineen	Rhys Williams
Marge	Lee Patrick
Helen—Hat Check Girl	Eve Miller
Lillian Sawyer	Robin Raymond
Stage Manager	Lyle Talbot
Kelly—Stage Doorman	George Melford
Katy's Boy Friend	Alvy Moore
Harry	Chick Chandler
Dance Director	Henry Slate
Archbishop	Nolan Leary
Geoffrey	Gavin Gordon
Katy (Age 4)	Mimi Gibson
Katy (Age 8)	Linda Lowell
Steve (Age 2)	John Potter
Steve (Age 6)	Jimmy Baird
Steve (Age 10)	William (Billy) Chapin
Tim (Age 2)	Neal McCaskill
Tim (Age 6)	Donald Gamble

This is a one-two smash for Irving Berlin, both in the same 1954-55 season; first, Paramount's "White Christmas" and now 20th's "There's No Business Like Show Business." Both are star-loaded and both are socko b.o. filmusicals.

The late Lamar Trotti's original, from which the Ephrons fashioned this screenplay, is palpably a script primed to point up the "heart" of showfolk. It gets across with authority and not a little skill despite the long arm of coincidence which comes at the finale, and by that time is warmly accepted in light of the wealth of eye-filling and compelling splash, dash and flashiness of virtually every bit and number.

The captious, of course, will observe that if this was a sample of vaudeville in its heyday then how come it became extinct? It's as super-stupendous in its lavishness and prodigious expenditure of production values as that "little nitery floorshow" in the Miami (Florida) sequences. The very nature of the Hollywood brand of filmusicals, however, has so conditioned the public to expect the ultimate in super values that this is an intra-show biz detail which only the most carping might advance.

The story line is solid albeit of familiar pattern. But could well be born of real-life show biz families like the Sam & Kitty Morton family, Jere Cohan and his brood, Eddie Foy and his flock, the three generations of the Pat Rooneys, et al.

Ethel Merman and Dan Dailey are capital as the vaudeville Donahues who bring out first one, then two, then three of their offspring for that extra bow, with a running gag, as the vaude annunciator cards change to the 3 Donahues, the 4 and finally the 5 Donahues. The punch is the Hippodrome's closing spectacle, for benefit of the Actors' Fund of America (a stunt which is being reprised for the Roxy, N. Y., premiere this week), once again reuniting the 5 Dona-

hues. Only this time Johnnie Ray is an Army chaplain; the errant Donald O'Connor in gob's garb; and Mitzi Gaynor, sentimentally suggesting young motherhood, are all there for the happy ending. That's where the fictional "long arm" gets strained.

Marilyn Monroe, the sixth co-starring marquee name, is the femme interest to the somewhat booze-fighting O'Connor.

The conflict revolves around Miss Monroe, starting first with the "Heat Wave" number which, admittedly, is perhaps even more important to her nitery routine than to the successful Donahues. O'Connor is influential in deferring to Miss Monroe, the ambitious ex-coatroom checker who has been nursing show biz ambitions, and when the prototype of the Ziegfeld-White-Carroll character (Richard Eastham) decides to star Miss Monroe, she noblesse-obliges by splitting up The Donahues and giving O'Connor and Mitzi Gaynor important possibilities in the Broadway musical, sans their parents. Incidentally, Eastham impresses as a good picture bet, and it will probably surprise in future that he's possessed of a Pinza-type voice.

Robert Alton rates a big bend along with producer Sol. C. Siegel and director Walter Lang on those lavish musical routines. From Berlin's viewpoint, they're all a song-plugger's delight. "Alexander's Ragtime Band" gets done up in super-spectrums and in UN manner, with a variety of nationalistic reprises, from Tyrolean to Scotch to French to concert grand piano treatment. It's successively staged, with all the trimmings, first by Miss Merman and Dailey; then the oompah-oompah treatment with glockenspiel and Swiss bellringers; O'Connor's clever hoot-mon version; Miss Gaynor's clicko Gallic treatment; and Johnnie Ray at the ivories.

Even up to this point the pseudo-vaude staging is so slick that the first audience reaction may be wha' hoppened?—why isn't vaude still around? (Maybe this is Hollywood's way of bringing it back!)

The title song, in actuality, gets prominence only in the Hipp finale, and even there some more of "Alexander"-is reintroduced for a real ripsnortin' windup.

In between, Miss Monroe does "After You Get What You Want You Don't Want It," another Berlin oldie, for her "audition" number (for Eastham), and her solo nitery flash is "Heat Wave." With the thoroughly professional and versatile Miss Gaynor and O'Connor they stage "Lazy." Miss Monroe's s.a. treatment of her vocal chores must be seen to be appreciated. It's not going to chase 'em away from the b.o. On the other hand, as a song salesgirl, per se, she'll never have to worry Miss Merman. She's more competitive to Mae West in her delineating.

Ethel Merman is boffo. She's a belter of a school of song stylists not to be found on every stage or before every mike. She looks youthful in the World War I idiom, and she progresses gracefully until the World War II period. Dailey, as her vis-a-vis, is an effective actor and interprets the vaudeville hoofer and father with polish and conviction.

O'Connor, Miss Gaynor and Ray, as the talented offspring of a raised-in-the-tradition vaudeville family, impress all the way. It's not all born-in-the-trunk stuff either. The Donahues board their brood in a parochial school, but the understanding headmaster recognizes the call of the resin-board in their campus behaviorism and thus the segue back to the Donahues' troup ing, en masse, is plausible.

Just as realistic is the fresh young son of a hard-working vaude team being young beyond his years in his ways with the femmes "in the profesh," and O'Connor plays it just right.

"Remember?" is a good bridge musical theme, as the quarter-of-a-century closeup of this show biz family unfolds. "Midnight Choochoo Leaves For Alabam," "Simple Melody," "You'd Be Surprised" "Pretty Girl Is Like A Melody" are interspliced for the basic vaude two-act.

Ray belts out a modern spiritual, titled "If You Believe," in a sweet-sad farewell party in the Donahues' Jersey home, before he enters the monastery. The prop church "billing" heralds the fact that "religion, too, has been booked solid and has had a long run," and Ray's inner calling to priesthood perhaps isn't as tragic as the bewildered parents thought at first.

The casting is authoritative all the way although the six costars dominate everything. Hugh O'Brian impresses as a good "new" face in his romantic bit opposite Miss Gaynor. Frank McHugh, Lee Patrick, Robin Raymond, Lyle Talbot, George Melford, Chick Chandler, Henry Slate are almost wasted in bits but make them stand up in what little they do.

Zanuck gave "Show Business" the works in every respect. The orchestral-vocal treatments of the Berlin standards are so richly endowed as to give them constantly fresh values. Even Walter Winchell's offscreen voice was enlisted for a Broadway montage show. The DeLuxe color and the Leon Shamroy CinemaScope lensing are just that, not forgetting the lush orchestral and vocal contributions by the Newman freres, Ken Darby et al. "Show Business" has everything for wide customer appeal. It'll mop up. *Abel.*

The Atomic Kid

Weak Mickey Rooney comedy for the duals.

Republic release of Mickey Rooney (Maurice Duke) production. Stars Rooney; features Robert Strauss, Elaine Davis. Directed by Leslie H. Martinson. Screenplay, Benedict Freedman and John Fenton Murray from story by Blake Edwards; camera, John L. Russell Jr.; music, Van Alexander. At Palace Theatre, N. Y., week of Dec. 3, '54. Running time, **86 MINS.**

Blix Waterberry .... Mickey Rooney
Stan Cooper .... Robert Strauss
Audrey Nelson .... Elaine Davis
Dr. Rodell .... Bill Goodwin
Dr. Pangborn .... Whit Bissell
M.P. in Hospital .... Joey Forman
Ray .... Hal March
Bill .... Peter Leeds
General Lawler .... Fay Roope
Wildcat Hopper .... Stanley Adams
Mr. Reynolds .... Robert E. Keane

(*Aspect Ratio*: 1.85-1)

With a title such as "The Atomic Kid," there should be plenty of topical interest in this Mickey Rooney production in which Rooney also stars. But although apparently designed as a comedy, the film sets off no chain reaction of humor and its market for the most part will be confined to the lower half of the duals.

The Benedict Freedman-John Fenton Murray screenplay, as fashioned from a story by Blake Edwards, is on the comic book level for the yarn's situations and general atmosphere are far fetched and forced. There's an occasional laugh as Rooney, a survivor of an atom bomb blast, cavorts through the footage. However, the levity appears to be primed for the Saturday matinee trade and most adult patrons will be bored.

With fellow prospector Robert Strauss, Rooney is searching for uranium in a remote part of Nevada. Trapped in a test area where the Army is detonating an A-bomb, Strauss escapes and Rooney miraculously lives although in the very center of the blast. This sets up some scenes in a hospital where he falls for nurse Elaine Davis. For good measure the scripters toss in some foreign spies who are dealt with by Rooney, Strauss & Co.

In this melange of slapstick Rooney romps happily. He's at his best when nonchalantly munching a peanut butter sandwich, seconds before the A-bomb goes off. Robert Strauss, a fugitive from "Stalag 17," also makes with the mirth as Rooney's man Friday but his material is thin and the funmaking fails to come off on the scale of his meaty comedy role in "Stalag."

Also involved in this Republic release are Elaine Davis (Mrs. Rooney in private life), who's pert and pulchritudinous as the nurse; Bill Goodwin, an Army doctor; Whit Bissell, another Army medico, and Joey Forman as an efficient M. P. While director Leslie H. Martinson handled some of the sequences to advantage, the banal script was too much of a hazard for him to cope with.

Production values reflect a modest budget. Camerawork of John L. Russell Jr. nicely captures the action and physical settings. Art direction of Frank Hotaling is good as is the score of Van Alexander. Maurice Duke functioned as associate producer. *Gilb.*

Destry
(SONGS—COLOR)

Good remake of twice-filmed western, this time with Audie Murphy; should click in outdoor market.

Hollywood, Dec. 2.

Universal release of Stanley Rubin production. Stars Audie Murphy, Mari Blanchard; co-stars Lyle Bettger, Thomas Mitchell; features Edgar Buchanan, Lori Nelson, Wallace Ford. Directed by George Marshall. Screenplay, Edmund H. North, D. D. Beauchamp; from a story by Felix Jackson; suggested by Max Brand's "Destry Rides Again"; camera (Technicolor), George Robinson; editor, Ted J. Kent; music supervision, Joseph Gershenson; songs, Frederick Herbert, Arnold Hughes. Previewed Dec. 1, '54. Running time, **95 MINS.**

Tom Destry .... Audie Murphy
Brandy .... Mari Blanchard
Decker .... Lyle Bettger
Rags Barnaby .... Thomas Mitchell
Mayor Sellers .... Edgar Buchanan
Martha Phillips .... Lori Nelson
Doc Curtis .... Wallace Ford
Bessie Mae Curtis .... Mary Wickes
Jack Larson .... Alan Hale Jr.
Curly .... George Wallace
Mac .... Richard Reeves
Henry Skinner .... Walter Baldwin
Eli Skinner .... Lee Aaker
Professor .... Mitchell Lawrence
Dummy .... Frank Richards
Sheriff Bailey .... Trevor Bardette
Bartender .... Ralph Peters
Cowhand .... John Doucette

(*Aspect ratio*: 2-1)

Max Brand's familiar western hero rides again under the Universal banner, and the third time around should give the company another profitable entry. The soft-spoken, gunless lawman was played by Tom Mix in 1932, and by James Stewart in 1939. This time, Audie Murphy tackles the role, and probably better fits the original Brand conception than his predecessors.

Remakes invite comparisons, but this Stanley Rubin production and those that star in it will not be compared unfavorably. While the 1939 version was geared to both the outdoor and regular feature attraction markets, this 1954 entry is mostly slanted to the western feature field and has been so well fashioned that it should have strong appeal to the action fan. George Marshall, repeating the directorial chore he handled on the 1939 version, runs the deftly plotted script off without a lag. There's humor, hard drama, suspense, romance and sex, the latter more for the grownup than the juvenile oater fan, to be found in the script by Edmund H. North and D. D. Beauchamp, taken from Felix Jackson's adaptation of the Brand novel.

Starring with Murphy as the saloon singer-bad girl is Mari Blanchard, the same character done to a turn in 1939 by Marlene Dietrich. Miss Blanchard doesn't have to take a back seat in the s.a. department and gives the role a zingy characterization that is most effective. Also, she reveals a lively way with a song that stirs the imagination, particularly in those scanty dancehall costumes she wears while selling "Empty Arms," a real bluesy torcher cleffed by Frederick Herbert and Arnold Hughes, and their "If You Can Can-Can" and "Bang! Bang!"

Murphy does exceptionally well as the quiet hero, son of a famous father, who is called in to aid Thomas Mitchell, town drunk appointed sheriff in a sardonic joke, restore law and order to the western town ruled with ruthless hand by Lyle Bettger and Edgar Buchanan. Murphy's peaceful ways draw the scorn of the toughies but he carries on without a gun until Bettger kills Mitchell. The hero then straps on his shooting iron and makes the bad men good dead ones.

The ease with which Murphy goes about his part is a big asset to the show. So is the menace projected by Bettger; the haplessness of Mitchell in his lawman spot; the slyness of Buchanan as the mayor, and the comedy by Wallace Ford and Mary Wickes. As in the 1939 "Destry" this one features a saloon brawl between femmes, this time carried out with murderous intent by the Misses Blanchard and Wickes. In for sweet young love is Lori Nelson, the girl who gets Murphy after Miss Blanchard is killed. Other good assists come from Alan Hale Jr., Walter Baldwin, Lee Aaker and Trevor Bardette.

The action, settings and costumes are brightly displayed in Technicolor by George Robinson's lensing. *Brog.*

Four Ways Out
(ITALIAN)

Italo film dubbed in English is okay entry for midweek playing or for double feature slotting. Has Gina Lollobrigida in the cast.

Carroll Pictures release of Edoardo Capolino production. Stars Gina Lollobrigida and Renato Baldini. Features Cosetta Greco, Paul Muller, Enzio Maggio, Fausto Tozzi, Tamara Lees and Emma Baron. Directed by Pietro Germi. Previewed in N.Y., Nov. 1, '54. Running time, **77 MINS.**

Daniela .... Gina Lollobrigida
Paolo .... Renato Baldini
Lina .... Corsetta Greco
Guido .... Paul Muller
Alberto .... Enzio Maggio
Luigi .... Fausto Tozzi
Tamara .... Tamara Lees
Alberto's Mother .... Emma Baron

(*Italian; Dubbed in English*)

This Italo film dubbed in English is an okay entry for midweek playing time or for double feature slotting, particularly for situations experiencing difficulty in filling out their programs. It's a good little action picture that should meet the requirements of general situations. The dubbing job is capably done, although the synchronization is not always perfect. But only the picayune will complain.

In light of the recent publicity garnered by Italo actress Gina Lollobrigida, her presence in "Four Ways Out," although in a small role, should serve as marquee lure. In addition to Miss Lollobrigida, the picture has exploitation value via the spotting of stills of Cosetta Greco and Tamara Lees, another pair of good lookers.

The "Four Ways Out" concerns the experiences of four men following their armed robbery of the receipts of a soccer statium. The men are not gangsters, but are individuals who are driven to the act by poverty. There's a former professional soccer player who's come on bad days because of a permanent injury, an impoverished artist, a young student, and a guy out of work who participates to support his wife and child.

The men separate after the robbery as the police dragnet closes in. Eventually, all are caught in different ways—suicide, murder, and surrender. The picture, filmed in Rome, has a documentary flavor as the camera chases the different individuals through the streets of the city.

To the credit of the dubbing job is the fact that the American voices appear to fit the characters portrayed. Both the Italian thesps and the American voices perform capably. Pietro Germi's direction is firstrate as is the camera work. *Holl.*

Ulysses
(ITALIAN; COLOR)

Rome, Nov. 30.

Lux Film release of Lux-Ponti-DeLaurentiis Production. Stars Kirk Douglas, Silvana Mangano; features Anthony Quinn, Rossana Podesta, Jacques Dumesnil, Daniel Invernel, Franco Interlenghi, Elena Zareschi. Directed by Mario Camerini; screenplay, Camerini, Franco Brusati, Ben Hecht, Irwin Shaw, Hugh Gray, Ennio De Consini, Ivo Ferilli; from Homer's "Odyssey." Camera (Technicolor), Hareld Rosson; editor, Leo Catozzo; music, Alessandro Cicognini. At Moderno, Rome. Running time, **130 MINS.**

Ulysses .... Kirk Douglas
Circe,
Penelope .... Silvano Mangano
Antinous .... Anthony Quinn
Nausicaa .... Rossana Podesta
Alcinous .... Jacques Dumesnil
Eurylocus .... Daniel Invernel
Telemachus .... Franco Interlenghi
Cassanda .... Elena Zareschi

A lot, perhaps too much, money has gone into the making of "Ulysses," but expense shows, and pic is headed for very strong returns at home and should register with almost equal strength abroad. Besides the epic Homeric peg, pic has an internationally balanced cast, with Yank, French and Italian elements predominant, good for locally spotted marquee lure. Also its grand-scaled content, which is given the spectacle treatment. Lack of CinemaScope or another big screen system is a drawback, though pic having been shot with widescreen composition in mind somewhat obviates. Stateside, in general release, "Ulysses" looks to become the strongest Italian grosser so far, with successful dubbing job and proper launching important factors.

Only a few of the w.k. Homeric episodes have been included in the already lengthy pic, and are told in flashback form as remembered by the hero. Featured are his love for Nausicaa; the cave of Polyphemus, the one-eyed monster; the Siren Rocks; the visit to Circe's island cave and the return to Penelope. The Trojan War, with the famed horse episode, is telescoped into a few rapid dissolves, But material covered makes for plenty of action, dominated by a virile performance by Kirk Douglas, and elegantly decked out in Technicolor by Harold Rosson's camera. Douglas gives the part an impressive reading, aided by dialog cut some notches above par for the genre.

Others include costar Silvana Mangano, a looker, as both Circe and Penelope, but unfortunately limited by both parts to expressing monotonous unhappiness until the finale. Anthony Quinn handles his bits well; Franco Interlenghi is good as Telemachus; and Sylvie as Euryclea, Daniel Ivernel as Eurylcous, Jacques Dumesnil as Alcinous, and others back ably. Rossana Podesta lends freshness and young good looks as Nausicaa. For a spectacle, the pic runs too many closeups, with longish stretches of dialog between the two principals, or soliloquized.

Rosson has handled his color camera expertly, and same goes for Shufftan's process work, especially in Polyphemus sequence. Sets are lavish and solid, and include a full-scale ship for Ulysses. Direction by Mario Camerini is expert, though sometimes unable completely to overcome the script's episodic structure. Art and costume design by Flavio Mogherini is tasteful. Alessandro Cicognini's musical score highlights the action appropriately. *Hawk.*

20,000 Leagues Under the Sea
(COLOR—C'SCOPE)

A special event for any man's theatre.

Buena Vista release of Walt Disney production. Stars Kirk Douglas, James Mason, Paul Lukas, Peter Lorre; supported by Robert J. Wilke, Carleton Young, Percy Helton, Ted de Corsia, J. M. Kerrigan, Ted Cooper. Directed by Richard Fleischer. Screenplay, Earl Fenton; from the classic by Jules Verne; camera (Technicolor), Franz Planer; special effects photography, Ralph Hammeras; underwater photography, Till Gabbani; special processes, Ub Iwerks; special effects, John Hench and Josh Meador; editor, Elmo Williams; music, Paul Smith; song, "A Whale of a Tale," by Al Hoffman and Norman Gimbel. Previewed Beekman Theatre, N.Y., Dec. 9, '54. Running time, 120 MINS.

Ned Land .... Kirk Douglas
Captain Nemo .... James Mason
Professor Aronnax .... Paul Lukas
Conseil .... Peter Lorre
Mate on "Nautilus".....Robert J. Wilke
John Howard .... Carleton Young
Captain Farragut .... Ted de Corsia
Diver .... Percy Helton
Mate on "Lincoln" .... Ted Cooper
Shipping Agent .... Edward Marr
Casey Moore .... Fred Graham
Billy .... J. M. Kerrigan

(Aspect ratio: 2.55-1)

Walt Disney is at hand with a new cinema wonder.

His production of "20,000 Leagues Under the Sea" is very special kind of picture making, combining photographic ingenuity, imaginative story telling and fiscal daring. That last, conversely, might also be termed confidence in the business.

Disney went for a bundle (say $5,000,000 in negative costs) in fashioning the Jules Verne classic. But it's the end result that Price Waterhouse wants to know about and this can be kingsized up in glamorous terms: Ultra high box-office around the world.

A mean man with a crystal ball, Verne penned "Leagues" in the pre-atomic and pre-submarine year of 1870. He wrote of a weird and wondrous submersible ship and the awesome powers of the universe. To truly capture this great adventure in a film meant an undertaking of rare dimensions; there were few precedents to be guided by.

The project has been a success. For Disney and his army of collaborators have packaged a grand assortment of exciting entertainment values. The story of the "monster" ship Nautilus, astounding as it may be, is so astutely developed that the audience immediately accepts its part on the excursion through Captain Nemo's underseas realm and partakes of its thrills and terrors. There's no quibbling about plausibility.

James Mason is the Captain, a genius who has fashioned and guides the out-of-this-world craft. Kirk Douglas is a free-wheeling, roguish harpoon artist. Paul Lukas is a kind and gentle man of science and Peter Lorre is Lukas' fretting apprentice. They have the major roles and are on camera 90% of the time, each registering with conviction.

But it is the production itself that is the star. Technical skill was lavished in fashioning the fabulous Nautilus with its exquisitely appointed interior. The underwater lensing is remarkable on a number of counts, among them being the vivid Technicolor tinting and special designing of aqualungs and other equipment to match Verne's own illustrations.

Story opens in San Francisco where maritime men have been terrorized by reports of a monstrous denizen of the seas which has been sinking their ships. An armed frigate sets out in pursuit and is itself destroyed, with Lukas,

Douglas and Lorre the survivors. They're picked up by the Nautilus which, they learn, is the nemesis of the sea merchants, an uncannily devised vessel used by Mason to satisfy his hate of warring nations and men.

Thus the audience is introduced to the wonders of Captain Nemo's and his men's life below the surface of the water.

There are some light moments, including a frolicsome chanty barytoned amusingly by Douglas. Humorous bit has Mason hosting a dinner that's enjoyed by Douglas and Lorre until they learn the delicacies of the table are sea snake, octupus, etc.

"Leagues" and CinemaScope prove highly compatible. Widescreen was a must in this widescreen era for the story and backgrounding are of vast scope and a limited cone of vision would have meant loss of some of the pictorial excitement. Some of the filming obviously was done under difficult conditions, yet all of the finished product comes through with excellent clarity. The sterophonic sound is a plus, too, adding to the onlooker's sense of participation.

Richard Fleischer's direction keeps the Disney epic moving at a smart clip, picking up interest right from the start and deftly developing each of the many tense moments. Unusually well staged is a pulse-quickening scene showing the men of the Nautilus in close-quarter combat with a giant squid.

Earl Fenton's screenplay looks to be a combination of the best in the Verne original and new material to suit the screen form. It's a fine job of writing stimulating pic fare. Technical credits — underline the underwater photography — are excellent. Of the supporting players, Robert J. Wilke is the most prominent, doing a competent job as Mason's mate. *Gene.*

Young at Heart
(SONGS-COLOR)

Topflight romantic drama with songs, Doris Day, Frank Sinatra and prosperous b.o. prospects.

Hollywood, Dec. 21.
Warner Bros. release of Henry Blanke (Arwin) production. Stars Doris Day, Frank Sinatra, Gig Young, Ethel Barrymore, Dorothy Malone; features Robert Keith, Elisabeth Fraser, Alan Hale Jr., Lonny Chapman, Frank Ferguson. Directed by Gordon Douglas. Screenplay, Julius J. Epstein, Lenore Coffee; adaptation, Liam O'Brien; from a story by Fannie Hurst; camera (WarnerColor), Ted McCord; editor, William Ziegler; new songs, Paul Francis Webster and Sammy Fain, Ray Heindorf, Charles Henderson and Don Pippin, Floyd Huddleston and Al Rinker, Mack Gordon and James Van Heusen. Previewed Dec. 7, '54. Running time, 116 MINS.

Laurie Tuttle .... Doris Day
Barney Sloan .... Frank Sinatra
Alex Burke .... Gig Young
Aunt Jessie .... Ethel Barrymore
Fran Tuttle .... Dorothy Malone
Gregory Tuttle .... Robert Keith
Amy Tuttle .... Elisabeth Fraser
Robert Neary .... Alan Hale Jr.
Ernest Nichols .... Lonny Chapman
Bartell .... Frank Ferguson
Mrs. Ridgefield .... Marjorie Bennett

(Aspect ratio: 1.65-1)

Romance in drama and song is effectively sold by Doris Day and Frank Sinatra in this slickly framed Warner Bros. offering. It looks headed for prosperous box-office, particularly in view of its appeal to the family and younger sets among the ticket buyers, who should take to the good new songs and the sock old ones, as well as the sentimental romantics that make up the story.

For both Miss Day and Sinatra,

"Young At Heart" is a topflight credit. They give the songs the vocal touch that makes them solid listening, and score just as strongly on the dramatics, seemingly complementing each other in their scenes together to make the dramatic heart tugs all the more effective.

She is first heard on " 'Til My Love Comes Back To Me," with lyrics by Paul Francis Webster to Felix Mendelssohn's "On Wings Of Songs," and follows it with "Ready, Willing and Able," by Floyd Huddleston and Al Rinker; "Hold Me In Your Arms," by Ray Heindorf, Charles Henderson and Don Pippin; and "There's A Rising Moon For Every Falling Star," by Webster and Sammy Fain. Behind the credits Sinatra sings the title tune, following up later with "Someone To Watch Over Me," "Just One of Those Things" and "One For My Baby." Miss Day and Sinatra pair on the finale "You My Love," by Mack Gordon and James Van Heusen.

The Henry Blanke production has been smoothly fashioned so there is not too strong a resemlence to the "Four Daughters" production on which it was based. The girls in that 1938 release have been reduced to three, Warner-Color has been added for gloss and, of course, the songs are newcomers to the plot. Script credit for this version goes to Julius J. Epstein and Lenore Coffee, who did the first from a story by Fannie Hurst, and Liam O'Brien did the adaptation. The writing for this version is firstrate, being well-dialoged and plotted.

Gordon Douglas' direction give the picture responsible guidance. He makes every use of the tale's sentiment, but never lets a scene get sticky, and the able cast responds to his handling with excellent work. Story details how romance comes to each of the three Tuttle sisters, played by Miss Day, Dorothy Malone and Elisabeth Fraser. The trio lives with the father, Robert Keith, and the aunt, Ethel Barrymore.

The different angles the romancing takes as the various males comes into the girls' lives color the footage, but the main concentration is on Miss Day and Sinatra, the latter a moody, frustrated musician called in by Gig Young to arrange a musical comedy the latter is writing. Miss Day and Young are engaged, but she and Sinatra elope. With no faith in himself, he can never believe she really loves him and it is only after a near-fatal, planned auto accident that almost costs his life, does he come to recognize the truth.

The Misses Malone and Fraser come over strongly as the sisters, as do Gig Young, Alan Hale Jr., and Lonny Chapman, assorted suitors. Miss Barrymore is a big asset to the cast and Keith makes his father spot a real winnig job.

Ted McCord's cameras are used to advantage on the footage and players and the other technical contributions are good. *Brog.*

Bad Day at Black Rock
(COLOR—C'SCOPE)
Tight suspense drama with western setting but no oater. Spencer Tracy, Robert Ryan to help prospects generally.

Hollywood, Dec. 14.
Metro release of Dore Schary production. Stars Spencer Tracy, Robert Ryan; co-stars Anne Francis, Dean Jagger, Wal-

ter Brennan, John Ericson, Ernest Borgnine, Lee Marvin, Russell Collins, Walter Sande. Directed by John Sturges. Screenplay, Millard Kaufman; adaptation, Don McGuire; based on a story by Howard Breslin; camera (Eastman Color), William C. Mellor; editor, Newell P. Kimlin; music, Asdre Prèvin. Previewed Dec. 8, '54. Running time, **81 MINS.**

John J. Macreedy .... Spencer Tracy
Reno Smith .... Robert Ryan
Liz Wirth .... Anne Francis
Tim Horn .... Dean Jagger
Doc Velie .... Walter Brennan
Pete Wirth .... John Ericson
Coley Trimble .... Ernest Borgnine
Hector David .... Lee Marvin
Mr. Hastings .... Russell Collins
Sam .... Walter Sande

Considerable excitement is whipped up in this suspense drama, and fans who go for tight action will find it entirely satisfactory. With the names of Spencer Tracy and Robert Ryan bellwethering the marquee values, it looks likely to give a good account of itself in the overall release if well-sold. While the story spins off in a western setting, it is not of the oater school, being a gripping drama in modern dress with a 1945 dateline for the action.

Besides telling a yarn of tense suspense, the picture is concerned with a social message on civic complacency, whether in a whistlestop or city. Fortunately for entertainment purposes, the makers have wisely underplayed this social angle so it seldom gets out of hand except in those few sequences that are inclined to be overtalky. The fact that it's there isn't likely to bother those who wouldn't receive the message anyway since they'll be pretty well wrapped up in the good plotting to be found in Millard Kaufman's script, in the tautness of John Sturges' direction that makes for exciting expectancy, and in the really sock performances turned in by the entire cast.

Basis for the smoothly valued Dore Schary production is a story by Howard Breslin, adapted by Don McGuire. To the tiny town of Black Rock, one hot summer day in 1945, comes Spencer Tracy, war veteran with a crippled left arm. He wants to find a Japanese farmer and give to him the medal won by his son in an action that left the latter dead and Tracy crippled. Instead of help in his mission, Tracy is greeted with an odd hostility and before the bad day is over his own life is endangered when he puts together the reason for the cold, menacing treatment. At the height of anti-Jap feeling after Pearl Harbor, the farmer had been killed by Robert Ryan, rancher, in a mob scene in which the other townsmen had participated.

Film is paced to draw suspense tight and keep expectancy mounting as the plot crosses the point where Tracy could have left without personal danger and plunges him into deadly menace when he becomes the hunted. Windup, however, finds the killer dead and the participants in the mob on their way to justice.

There's not a bad performance from any member of the cast, each socking their characters for full value. In addition to Tracy and Ryan, credit goes to Anne Francis, Dean Jagger, Walter Brennan, John Ericson Ernest Borgnine, Lee Marvin, Russell Collins and Walter Sande. Scene in which the one-armed Tracy beats to a bleeding pulp the gross, bullying Borgnine is one of several real tough action sequences.

The CinemaScope photography in Eastman Color by William C. Mellor is standout for showing the stark, magnificent beauties of the desert location with its mountain backdrop. Andre Previn's score is good, although overemphasized on occasion. Editing and other technical assists are expert. *Brog.*

This Is Your Army
(COLOR; DOCUMENTARY)

Movietone News production in cooperation with the United States Army sponsored by Council of Motion Picture Organizations. Produced by Edmund Reek. Associate producer, John J. Gordon; narrator, Joe King; script, James Altieri, Joseph Kenas; editors, Bill Kosh, John Hughes; cameras (Technicolor), Jack Painter, William Storz; music, Jack Shaindlin. Previewed in New York, Dec. 8, '54. Running time, **55 MINS.**

This Technicolor documentary on today's army, which will be exhibited as a public service, is more than satisfactory theatre fare. Although it's obviously a studied public relations effort on the part of the Army, it rates more attention than the usual Government handout simply because it's got an interesting story to tell and it tells it well.

"This Is Your Army" deals with the latest in weapons and personnel. It's a post-Korean War study of the service and explores every avenue of offense and defense, from the "sky-sweeper" radar-controlled anti-aircraft guns to the new atomic cannon. The 55-minute film shows the training and developments in every branch of the service from infantry on up to the Rangers. There's much that's new in it to the American public, and much that is comforting.

Topping off the content is an outstanding production job by Fox Movietone. Color footage, shot by Movietone cameramen Jack Painter and William Storz, is right in the middle of the action, and the color is excellent. Editing by Bill Kosh and John Hughes crams a maximum of information into the 55-minute running time. The James Altieri-Joseph Kenas script, though bespattered by the usual cliches, is tightly written, and Joe King's narration is excellent. Jack Shaindlin's score rides well with the footage. COMPO can take a bow for its participation too. *Chan.*

The Bamboo Prison

P.O.W. melodrama localed in North Korea. Good actioner for the programmer market.

Hollywood, Dec. 14.

Columbia release of Bryan Foy production. Stars Robert Francis, Dianne Foster, Brian Keith; features Jerome Courtland, E. G. Marshall, Earle Hyman, Jack Kelly, Richard Loo, Keye Luke, Murray Matheson, King Donovan, Dick Jones, Pepe Hern, Leo Gordon, Weaver Levy. Directed by Lewis Seiler. Screenplay, Edwin Blum, Jack DeWitt; story by DeWitt; camera, Burnett Guffey; editor, Henry Batista. Previewed Dec. 2, '4. Running time, **79 MINS.**

Sgt. Bill Rand .... Robert Francis
Tanya Clayton .... Dianne Foster
Corporal Brady .... Brian Keith
Arkansas .... Jerome Courtland
Father Francis Dolan......E. G. Marshall
"Doc" Jackson .... Earle Hyman
Slade .... Jack Kelly
Hsai Tung .... Richard Loo
Li Chung .... Keye Luke
Clayton .... Murray Matheson
Pop .... King Donovan
Jackie .... Dick Jones
Ramirez .... Pepe Hern
Pike .... Leo Gordon
Meatball .... Weaver Levy
Metaxas .... George Keymas
Cockney .... Denis Martin

(Aspect ratio: 1.85-1)

A timely topic gives this prisoner-of-war action melodrama a good chance as an entry for the general program market. It does an entertaining job that is up to all release intentions, as well as showcasing the newer talents of Robert Francis, Dianne Foster and Brian Keith, who form a starring trio that comes off acceptably in putting over the film.

While time of the action is laid during the peace treaty negotiations at Panmunjon, plot projects the thought that some of the seeming collaborators among the Reds' American prisoners are actually intelligence men carrying on dangerous assignments even now. Francis plays one of these, a man scorned by his fellow prisoners because he has succumbed to Communism as a means of getting information useful to the peace negotiations. Windup has him still staying with the Reds to continue his dangerous mission, even though it means he has to give up Miss Foster, a Russian who had aided him.

The usual prison camp antics, although with less stress on brutality, are shown during the filming under Lewis Seiler's direction. He moves the show along at a good pace, mixing the values in the script by Edwin Blum and Jack DeWitt with a practiced hand and getting easy performances from his cast. There are several twists to the story, such as having a priest a prisoner along with the soldiers, and then revealing him as a fraud hiding behind a dead father's garb to spy on the P.O.W.'s.

Working with Francis in the deadly spying job is Keith and both do well, as does Miss Foster, wife of an American traitor now propagandizing for the Russians. Murray Matheson does the traitor and E. G. Marshall appears as the phony priest. They along with Jerome Courtland, Earle Hyman, Jack Kelly, King Donovan, Dick Jones, Pepe Hern and Leo Gordon, among the prisoners, and Richard Loo and Keye Luke, chief North Korean officers, contribute capably to the makebelieve.

Bryan Foy's production supervision gives the picture all it needs to carry it in its market and the technical assists are expertly handled. *Brog.*

Devil's Harbor

Mediocre British-lensed meller for lesser bookings.

Hollywood, Dec. 14.

20th-Fox release of Charles Deane production. Stars Richard Arlen, Greta Gynt, Donald Houston, Mary Germaine; features Elspet Gray, Vincent Ball, Howard Lang, Anthony Vicars, Edwin Richfield. Directed by Montgomery Tully. Screenplay, Charles Deane; camera, Geoffrey Faithful; editor, Peter Seabourne. Previewed Dec. 10, '54. Running time, **70 MINS.**

John .... Richard Arlen
Peggy .... Greta Gynt
Mallard .... Donald Houston
Margaret .... Mary Germaine
Mrs. Mallord .... Elspet Gray
Williams .... Vincent Ball
Marne .... Howard Lang
Inspector Hunt .... Anthony Vicars
Daller .... Edwin Richfield
Bennett .... Michael Balfour
Mark .... Arnold Adrian
Enson .... Sidney Bromley
Ryan .... Stuart Saunders
Pat .... Patricia Salonika
Susie .... Doreen Holliday
Sam .... Peter Bernard

(Aspect ratio: 1.33-1)

The melodramatics in this British-made thriller that 20th-Fox is distributing come off poorly and it is best suited for fill-in bookings in the lesser situations. Only familiar name is that of Richard Arlen, balance of cast being Britishers.

Charles Deane both produced and scripted a story that tells of how Arlen, operator of a Thames River freight boat, accidentally breaks up a gang that has been stealing medicine and drugs. Arlen stops a dock fight one night and comes into possession of a mysterious package. Efforts of the gang to get it back eventually lead to the denouement. The basic plot idea furnished a good enough springboard for a program meller, but it falls apart in the script development, giving the players little to work with. Montgomery Tully's direction is no help, either, so there's no plausibility to the action.

The technical contributions are substandard. *Brog.*

The Other Woman

Hugo Haas low-budget sex thriller, again starring Haas and Cleo Moore. Looms as moderate grosser but can be circused.

20th-Fox release of Hugo Haas production. Stars Hugo Haas and Cleo Moore. Directed and written by Haas. Camera, Eddie Fitzgerald; editor, Robert S. Eisen; music, Ernest Gold. Tradeshown in N.Y., Dec. 10, '54. Running time, **81 MINS.**

Darman .... Hugo Haas
Sherry .... Cleo Moore
Ronnie .... Lance Fuller
Mrs. Darman .... Lucille Barkley
Lester .... Jack Macy
Papasha .... John Qualen
Collins .... Jan Arvan
Marion .... Carolee Kelly
First asst. director ...... Steve Mitchell
Second assistant .... Mark Lowell
Actress .... Melinda Markey

This is about the seventh Hugo Haas screen production to come from this independent producer who, as in this one, generally stars, directs and produces besides scripting. Most recently, Cleo Moore has been co-starred, which is all to the good. "The Other Woman" suggests that Haas, perhaps should not try to star, write and direct but delegate some of these tasks to others. Because this might have been much better if he had not tried to do it all by himself. Despite this criticism, this pic should suffice, has enough sex and drama for lesser situations.

Haas is a foreign director-producer, who has insured himself a job with an American film company by marrying the daughter of the producing company prexy. Action revolves around Miss Moore's efforts as an extra to get even with Haas because he rejected her work in a bit role. She gets him **into what appears to be a compromising situation, and then demands $50,000 to hush up the so-called affair. A tricky strangling scene and efforts by the police to land Miss Moore's slayer behind the bars bring action in the final** reels.

Haas is told by his father-in-law, the vet producer, that a successful picture is made up of a dash of sex, some action of thrills, comedy relief and a happy ending. Haas tells his audience he has tried to get all of these into "The Other Woman," but that he has slipped up on the happy ending since he is shown behind bars. Pic actually has these ingredients, best of which is the femme lure of Miss Moore.

Haas is good as the foreign director-producer but deserves a better story than he wrote for himself. Miss Moore, who is curvaceous, appears to be learning how to act and is satisfactory as the unsuccessful, scheming extra. Lucille Barkley as Haas' wife, hints enough promise to justify bigger roles. Lance Fuller, as Miss Moore's boyfriend, does well enough in the part of a teenage gangster. John Qualen is submerged in a lesser role but handles in his usual capable manner. Jack Macy, as the father-in-law; and Jan Arvan, as the detective, head the support.

Haas' directing is far ahead of his scripting. Robert S. Eisen has edited skillfully while the lensing of Eddie Fitzgerald is firstrate.

Wear.

Carrington V.C.
(BRITISH)

Sensitive court-martial melodrama, strong for local audiences, with David Niven's marquee value as main selling factor for U.S.

London, Dec. 9.

Independent Film Distributors (in association with British Lion) release of Remus production. Stars David Niven, Margaret Leighton, Noelle Middleton. Directed by Anthony Asquith. Screenplay by John Hunter from a play by Dorothy and Campbell Christie; editor, Ralph Kemplen; camera, Desmond Dickinson. At Warner Theatre, London, Dec. 8, '54. Running time, **105 MINS.**

Major Carrington, V.C.	David Niven
Valerie Carrington	Margaret Leighton
Capt. Alison Graham	Noelle Middleton
Major Panton	Laurence Naismith
Lt. Col. Huxford	Clive Morton
The Prosecutor	Mark Dignam
Lt. Col. Henniker	Allan Cuthbertson
Sgt. Owen	Victor Maddern
Evans	John Glyn-Jones
Major Mitchell	Raymond Francis
Judge Advocate	Newton Blick
Adjutant Rawlinson	John Chandos
The President	Geoffrey Keen
Lt.Col. Reeve	Maurice Denham
Major Broke-Smith	Michael Bates
Capt. Foljambe	Robert Bishop
Sgt. Crane	Stuart Saunders

As a legit production last season, "Carrington, V.C.," by Dorothy and Campbell Christie, made a definite impact on the West End scene as a subject of dramatic intensity. In its translation to the screen, the drama has lost none of its basic qualities, but the very nature of the subject, the court-martial of a British Army officer, must limit its appeal outside the United Kingdom. It should do sturdy business in the home market while David Niven may provide a measure of marquee value to help in its overseas selling although its prospects may be restricted.

The story is an ideal vehicle for the sensitive directorial touch for which Anthony Asquith is noted. He extracts the essential values of the plot, knows when and how to introduce a touch of comedy relief, but never allows the production to be bogged down by too obvious touches of cockney military humor. John Hunter's screenplay is basically a carbon copy of the original, taking advantage of the broader canvas of the screen but keeping the main action within the confines of the barracks, and centered on the courtmartial room. This induces a static effect which is more acceptable on the stage than in pictures.

The plot focusses on the title character, a wartime hero who has the routine job of commanding an artillery battery in peacetime. It's no secret that he is constantly feuding with his regimental commander, is in serious financial difficulties and is harassed by a wife who is desperately clamoring for money. The army authorities owe him a substantial sum on his expense account, but partly through the lack of support from his c.o. this cash is not forthcoming. And in a moment of crisis, he helps himself to army funds "to advertise a grievance." His commander orders a courtmartial and the main incident of the pic is concerned with this trial.

By keeping strictly to procedure, there is little opportunity for theatrical dramatization. The drama has to be an inherent quality of the story unfolded in the courtroom. There are the familiar side issues—the woman officer who tries to cover up and eventually admits an affair with the accused; and the hard, unsympathetic wife who deliberately falsifies her evidence when she learns of her husband's infidelity. Although there is a guilty verdict, the story ends on a confident note.

David Niven gives one of his best performances in recent times as the accused V.C. Some of his courtroom exchanges with prosecution witnesses, notably with his superior officer, are dramatic highspots of the plot. Margaret Leighton appears a bit ill-at-ease as the unsympathetic wife. Noelle Middleton, a newcomer recruited from tele, displays bright promise as the other woman. Mark Dignam turns in a smooth portrayal as the prosecuting attorney while there is a neat comedy gem from Victor Maddern. Stuart Saunders, playing court orderly, is a little larger than life as an army NCO who is a stickler for the drillbook. Allan Cuthbertson is a too obvious heavy as the regimental commander.

Desmond Dickinson has done a sterling job with the cameras while Wilfred Shingleton's barrack settings have a genuine look. Two military advisers have steered the director and scripter along orthodox lines.

Myro.

08/15
(GERMAN)

Berlin, Nov. 30.

Gloria release of Divina production. Features Hans Christian Blech, Eva Ingeborg Scholz and Wilfried Seyferth. Directed by Paul May. Screenplay, Ernst von Salomon, adapted from novel by H. H. Kirst; camera, Heinz Hoelscher; music, Rolf Wilhelm; sets, Peter Scharf. At Gloria Palast, Berlin. Running time, **110 MINS.**

Lore Schulz	Helen Vita
Elisabeth Freitag	Eva Ingeborg Scholz
Ingrid Asch	Gundula Korte
Vierbein	Paul Boesiger
Asch	Joachim Fuchsberger
Kowalski	Peter Carsten
Unteroffizier Lindenberg	Reinhard Glemnitz
Unteroffizier Wunderlich	Dietrich Thoms
Unteroffizier Rumpler	Rudolf Rhomberg
Wachtmeister Werktreu	Hans Elwenspoek
Wachtmeister Platzek	Hans Christian Blech
Hauptwachmeister Schulz	Emmerich Schrenk

This German film might be compared with "From Here to Eternity," although it doesn't quite reach the high standard of the latter. With particular regard to acting, photography and other technical contributions, "08/15" shapes as one of Germany's best postwar pix. It's a terrific money-maker here, being the most talked-about German film currently. Pic may also appeal to the U. S. market although a number of scenes, particularly some love scenes, may have trouble with the censors.

This was adapted from the same-titled German bestseller by H. H. Kirst. The title refers to the number of a German army pistol. Pic deals with German postwar army barrack life in 1939 and comes to a close shortly before the outbreak of the last world war. Mostly the film concentrates on soldier Vierbein (Paul Boesiger), the man who just doesn't regiment easily, and who finds himself often at odds with his superiors.

Unlike "Eternity" with its dramatic climax, this German production has a happy ending, even if untrue in real life. The soldier who started a private mutiny would, in the German army, certainly have ended up in stockade and not, as depicted in this pic, have been promoted to corporal. To make it even more untrue, the various ill-treaters get their punishments via transfers, while the weak soldier Boesiger finally decides to become an officer.

Story obviously attempts at a message but this is not quite clear. It's actually neither pro nor con. Most of German crix and those who dislike German militarism would have preferred a clear anti-militaristic attitude. But the filmmakers apparently attempted to shock no one, particularly not those who are in favor of a new Wehrmacht.

While the pic's first half is thoroughly realistic, it slides more into a military farce in the second part.

Nothing but praise goes to the actors most of whom are either newcomers or unknown in films. Although it is chiefly an ensemble achievement, some deserve special mention. Such as Hans Christian Blech, Emmerich Schrenk and the late Wilfried Seyferth. Paul May directed with much spirit and imagination.

Topnotch camera work is contributed by Heinz Hoelscher. Also other technical jobs are way above the German average. Incidentally, "08/15" will soon have a sequel ("08/15" At War" which has already been published) with much the same cast.

Hans.

Feuerwerk
(Fireworks)
(GERMAN—COLOR)

Berlin, Nov. 30.

Schorcht release of NDF production. Stars Lilli Palmer, Karl Schoenboeck. Directed by Kurt Hoffmann. Screenplay, Herbert Witt, Felix Luetzkendorf and Guenther Neumann, after musical comedy of same name by Eric Charell and Juerg Amstein; camera (Eastmancolor), Guenther Anders; music, Paul Burkhard; lyrics, Juerg Amstein and Robert Gilbert; sets, Werner Schlichting; costumes, Alfred Buecken. At Kiki, Berlin. Running time, **98 MINS.**

Iduna	Lilli Palmer
Obolski	Karl Schoenboeck
Anna	Romy Schneider
Robert	Claus Biederstaedt
Albert Oberholzer	Werner Hinz
Uncle Gustav	Rudolf Vogel
Kathie	Margarete Haagen
Uncle Wilhelm	Ernst Waldow
Aunt Bertha	Liesl Karlstadt
Karoline	Kaethe Haack
Aunt Paula	Lina Carstens

Here is a Teutonic film which has strong possibilities of luring the non-German public to the boxoffice. The Lilli Palmer name and the qualities of enjoyable film fare will help. Biggest ballyhoo pegs, however, are this film's songs, notably "Oh, My Papa" and the Pony-song, which have become popular in many parts of the world. "Fireworks" is West German filmaking at its current best making this one of Germany's best postwar musical comedies.

A well done screenplay after the same-titled stage hit by Eric Charell and Juerg Amstein depicts the household of a middle-class family with father celebrating his 50th birthday. All his relatives show up. As a surprise to everyone, the bad brother who ran away 20 years ago returns as a top circus director. Film's climax sees the 16-year-old niece insisting on leaving her family to become a member of her uncle's circus. There is a romance neatly woven in, some circus numbers, jealousy, slapstick and a satisfying ending.

Production offers a nice, partly witty contrast between the circus world and the middleclass folks. Its biggest plus factor is Miss Palmer. As the wife of the circus director, she turns in a charming performance. Her broken German, genuine sentiment and, in particular, her "Oh, My Papa" numbers are a rare treat. Local crix opined that no local top performer would have registered a like success. Werner Hinz is excellent as the provincial-minded father as is Karl Schoenboeck as his brother (the circus director). Able supporting players include Rudolf Vogel, Ernst Waldow and Claus Biederstaedt.

Kurt Hoffmann directed with a sure hand, being nicely helped by the well-balanced script which has enough satirical dialog to go along with the comedy situations. Guenther Anders' camera work is fine. A weakness of this production is the color (Eastmancolor) photography. Colors are often too reddish and not always clear enough.

Hans.

The Sea Shall Not Have Them
(BRITISH)

Sincerely told drama of wartime air-sea rescue operations; stout local b.o. proposition, with strong chance in U. S. market.

London, Nov. 30.

Eros Films release of Daniel Angel Production. Stars Michael Redgrave, Dirk Bogarde, Anthony Steel, Nigel Patrick, Bonar Colleano; features James Kenney, Sydney Tafler, Griffith Jones, Jack Watling. Directed by Lewis Gilbert. Screenplay, Lewis Gilbert and Vernon Harris from novel by John Harris; camera, Stephen Dade; editor, Russell Lloyd; music, Malcolm Arnold. At Gaumont Theatre, London, Nov. 30, '54. Running time, **92 MINS.**

Air Commodore Waltby	Michael Redgrave
Flight Sergeant Mackay	Dirk Bogarde
Sergeant Kirby	Bonar Colleano
Flying Officer Harding	Jack Watling
Flying Officer Treherne	Anthony Steel
Flight Sergeant Slingsby	Nigel Patrick
Corporal Skinner	James Kenney
Corporal Robb	Sydney Tafler
A.C.2 Milliken	Ian Whittaker
Group Captain Todd	Griffith Jones
Squadron Leader Scott	Guy Middleton
Squadron Leader Craif	Jack Lambert
Lieutenant Patrick Boyle	Paul Carpenter
Petty Officer Porter	Eddie Byrne
German Pilot	Anton Diffring
Mrs. Waltby	Rachel Kempson
Tebbitt	George Rose
Mrs. Tebbitt	Joan Sims
Kirby's Fiancee	Ann Gudrun

A sincere graphic story of the air-sea rescue service in the last world war, "The Sea Shall Not Have Them" has several basic ingredients of a boxoffice success: tough but believable plot, a cast too big for the average theatre marquee and exciting action sequences in the climax when the missing air crew is picked up within range of enemy shore batteries. It's quota rating is a plus factor for local exhibitors, and the pic has the quality to merit general presentation in the U. S.

The picture has been adapted from a novel by John Harris by Lewis Gilbert and Vernon Harris and their screenplay tells the story with typical British undertones, although they have etched some fruity service characters and introduced welcome bits of service humor. Gilbert's crisp and vigorous direction is well served by the taut editing by Russell Lloyd.

Action takes place during the fall of 1944 and is centered on the crew of a Hudson aircraft forced down in the North Sea after a tussle with an enemy fighter. Most important member of the crew is an air-commodore returning from enemy occupied territory with a brief case full of secrets, and when the plane is reported overdue, the whole rescue service swings into action. Bad weather halts the search from the air and engine trouble hampers a launch. But after two days and a night of exposure the four airmen are rescued off the coast of Belgium while shells are bursting all around them from the coastal artillery.

Story is adroitly unfolded as the emphasis switches from the dinghy to the launch, with occasional sketches from the shore station. The scenes of the four men drifting aimlessly and hopelessly in their small rubber craft are mainly grim and unrelieved, but the humor content is admirably provided by the assorted crew of the rescue launch.

Acting by a nearly all-male cast attains an all-round standard, led by Michael Redgrave, as the officer with a bagfull of secrets; Dick Bogarde and Bonar Colleano, as two of his fellow passengers, and by Anthony Steel and Nigel Patrick, as the skipper and his No. 2 of the rescue launch. Featured roles are expertly filled. *Myro.*

Obsession
(FRANCO-ITALIAN; COLOR)
Paris, Nov. 30.

Pathe release of Gibo-Franco-London Film production. Stars Michele Morgan, Raf Vallone; features Jean Gaven, Robert Dalban, Olivier Hussenot, Marthe Marcadier, Jacques Castelot. Directed by Jean Delannoy. Screenplay, Antoine Blondin, Roland Laudenbach. Delannoy, from novel by William Irish; camera (Eastmancolor), Pierre Montazel; editor, James Cuenet. At Marignan, Paris. Running time, **105 MINS.**

Helene	Michele Morgan
Aldo	Raf Vallone
Alex	Jean Gaven
Arlette	Marthe Marcadier
Louis	Olivier Hussenot
Inspector	Robert Dalban
Lawyer	Jacques Castelot

"Obsession" is an attempt at a pyscho-murder thriller replete with various ironic twists, but lacks the suspense and movement necessary to make a sock pic. As is, it has names of Michele Morgan and Raf Vallone for the Franco-Italo market, but there is little in this for the U. S. except for dualers or special spots on name, color and circusy locale. Otherwise it shapes as Gallic soap opera and not for the arties.

Miss Morgan and Vallone have a high trapeze act. He loves her but refrains from confessing it to her until she tells him she is going to marry. Then he blurts out he once killed a man in a fight, and that is why he never spoke to her of love. She accepts him anyway, and they are happy until a sprained arm calls for a replacement in the form of Alex, who was one of the friends of the man Vallone killed, but who was passed off as a suicide. Then the drama unfolds as Alex is killed and a friend of theirs is convicted. Miss Morgan is sure it is Vallone and turns him over to the police, only to have the man confess it was he after all. She has unwittingly given away the previous murder, and pic ends on note of justice ready to crack down on their happiness.

Director Jean Delannoy has given this a turgid mounting, and love affair is never real enough to give the film any poignance. This detracts from any suspense and action that was inherent in the pic. Miss Morgan is much too vague and stilted, and Vallone supplies only an intense silhouette to the drama. Color is superfluous in this drama, but is of even hue, and editing is fair, as is supporting cast and production gloss. *Mosk.*

Hunters of the Deep
(DOCUMENTARY-COLOR)

Exploitable entry on underwater marine life.

Distributors Corp. of America release of Tom Gries production: associate producer, Geza De Rosner. Written by Allan Dowling and Gries; narrated by Dan O'Herlihy; camera (Eastman Color), Robert Dill, Verne Pederson, Harry Pederson, Martin Akmakjian, William Fortin, Conrad Limbaugh; editor, Bill Naylor; music, George Antheil. Tradeshown N.Y. Dec. 13, '54. Running time, **62 MINS.**

Marine life under the sea is interestingly photographed in "Hunters of the Deep," a documentary in color which represents the initial release of the newly organized Distributors Corp. of America. While there is no cast as such to provide marquee values, the film is an exploitable entry and should produce profitable returns if properly sold.

Reportedly three years in the making, this Tom Gries production was culled from some 25,000 feet of film lensed in waters off southern California, lower California and the Bahamas. Highlights of the picture are excellent shots of skirmishes with sharks as well as scenes of other man-eaters such as barracuda.

The six cameramen who made the pictorial account painstakingly record the varied types of gear required by divers to explore the mysteries of the deep. Special underwater guns are put to good use by the sub-surface investigators when sharks become menacing, and the value of newly devised breathing equipment is also stressed.

An off-screen commentary, written by Allan Dowling and producer Gries and engagingly narrated by Dan O'Herlihy, augments the camera in throwing light on a world seldom seen. Film is not without humor for it amusingly shows the efforts of one member of the finny tribe to politely discourage a starfish from trespassing on his bailiwick.

As the footage unreels, the accent is entirely on the fish. Few closeups are made of the intrepid divers for the underwater scenes are apparently regarded as paramount, and rightly so. While sequences lensed in California coastal waters are absorbing what with an abundance of manta rays, octopi, sea lions and the like, the shots in the Bahamas are better photographically probably due to clearer water in that semi-tropic area.

Lensmen who toiled on the venture include Harry and Verne Pederson; Robert Dill and Conrad Limbaugh of the Scripps Institute of Oceanography; William Fortin of the Hancock Institute, and Martin Akmakjian. Their color work is very good in light of the difficult circumstances. Musical score, composed and conducted by George Antheil, at times becomes too noisy and distracts from O'Herlihy's narration. *Gilb.*

Tren Internacional
(Valparaiso Express)
(ARGENTINE)
Buenos Aires, Nov. 30.

CINCO production and release. Stars Mirtha Legrand and Alberto Closas; features Gloria Guzman, Florindo Ferrario, Tomas Simari, Enrique Chaico, Herminia Franco, Diana Ingro, Joaquin Petrosino. Directed by Daniel Tinayre, from his own story, scripted in collaboration with Arturo S. Mom. Camera, Humberto Peruzzi; sets, Alvaro Duranona y Vedia; editor, Nicolas Proserpio. At Gran Rex, Buenos Aires. Running time, **110 MINS.**

As a comedy whodunit, sprinkled with sparkling and at times startling dialog, this is a welcome change from the usual overly dramatic story choices of local studios. As second of the state-inspired "Big Five" Amalgamation of five ace directors, it marks a change for the better in native production. There is suspense, lively action and interesting locales in a switch from Buenos Aires to the snowy peaks of the Andean frontier near Chile and sea-front suburbs of Chile's port of Valparaiso.

A strong cast also helps, with both stars standout. Vet legit comedienne Gloria Guzman, in a small bit, reveals qualities which should insure a future on the local screen, while Tomas Simari, also recruited from the front ranks of legit, shines as a train conductor. Joaquin Petrosino, a newcomer, in a gangster role, is reminiscent of the late Sydney Greenstreet, but imitates the Hollywood player in a familiar mopping of the head to the point of annoyance.

Weak spots of pic are disjointed editing perhaps resulting from faulty story construction. There is also an imperfect acquaintance with socialite manners. Guests would not be so unfamiliar with evening dress as to comment pointedly on the ladies' bosoms or put their hands down them to search for lost jewels.

Closas is cast as an international crook, posing as the "Count Alfieri" while Mirtha Legrand is the Mrs. Cheney of a rival gang, who travels in his compartment across the Andes from Buenos Aires to Valparaiso. She tries to steal the necklace he has snatched from a flirtatious socialite. A psychopathic murder convict on the same train breaks loose, and when the train is held up in the Andes, the pair capture the murderer. Closas finds himself falling in love with the rival thief. After many misunderstandings, the two wed in a Chilean fishing village.

According to the American code, a defect in the story is that at no time is there sufficient stress on the axiom that crime doesn't pay.

The extent to which the government here is prepared to help native producers is shown in the use of reception and banqueting rooms of the Foreign Ministry for the socialite mansion set. The picture was entered at the Berlin Film Festival last July and at the Mar del Plata Festival previously. Its prospects are good in Spanish markets. *Nid.*

Vera Cruz
(Color-SuperScope)

Gary Cooper, Burt Lancaster in rough, rugged, Mexican-located outdoor actioner. Stout b.o.

United Artists release of Hecht-Lancaster (James Hill) production. Stars Gary Cooper, Burt Lancaster; co-stars Denise Darcel, Cesar Romero; introduces Sarita Montiel. Directed by Robert Aldrich. Screenplay, Roland Kibbee, James R. Webb; story, Border Chase; camera (Technicolor), Ernest Laszlo; editor, Alan Crosland Jr.; music, Hugo Friedhofer; orchestrations and conducting by Raul Lavista; song, Friedhofer and Sammy Cahn. Previewed Dec. 16, '54. Running time, **94 MINS.**

Trane	Gary Cooper
Erin	Burt Lancaster
Countess	Denise Darcel
Marquis	Cesar Romero
Nina	Sarita Montiel
Maximilian	George Macready
Donnegan	Ernest Borgnine
Ramirez	Morris Ankrum
Danette	Henry Brandon
Pittsburgh	Charles Buchinsky
Charlie	Jack Lambert
Tex	Jack Elam
Little-Bit	James McCallion
Abilene	James Seay
Ballard	Archie Savage
Reno	Charles Horvath
Pedro	Juan Garcia

(Aspect ratio: 2-1)

Exhibitors playing this Hecht-Lancaster production, being distributed through United Artists, should find it a stout performer at the boxoffice. It could be figured as a money film almost off the marquee pull of Gary Cooper and Burt Lancaster alone, but this initial sparkplug is backed with the kind of rough and rugged outdoor action that their fans particularly like, suggesting hefty returns all down the line.

Picture is the first release in SuperScope (the second will be RKO's "Underwater" going out in February) and the anamorphic lensing is in an eye-kindly 2 to 1 aspect ratio, entirely ample to the demand of the outdoor locationing in Mexico and to the sprawling action that features much of the footage. Scenic values, done in Technicolor, add to the overall entertainment punch of the film.

The Borden Chase story, expertly fashioned for the screen by Roland Kibbee and James R. Webb, is of the high romance school that responds aptly to the vigorous direction given it by Robert Aldrich in the James Hill production. The stress is mostly on the violence and suspenseful action bred during Mexico's revolutionary period when the Juaristas were trying to free the country of the French-supported Emperor Maximilian. Era of the hapless Hapsburg has been used before, but here it is approached via American soldiers of fortune who drifted south of the border to get in on the loot and killing. There's no politicking, however, plot merely using the setup as a springboard for some rather fanciful entertainment.

Cooper, ex-Confederate major from New Orleans, joins forces with Lancaster, western outlaw, and his gang of choice pug-uglies to escort a countess from the court of Maximilian in Mexico City to the port at Vera Cruz. It's more than the simple guard job indicated, since secretly the countess has a load of gold to be used in Europe to bring more troops to Maximilian's aid.

It doesn't take the two Yanks long to figure out the setup, both scheming to doublecross the other at the windup and claim all the money. The countess, Denise Darcel, has a doublecross in mind, too, planning to grab the gold herself and leave Maximilian's officer. Cesar Romero, holding the bag. The Juarista forces want it, too, so there are plenty excuses for violent action along the road to Vera Cruz, and by the time it's all over, Cooper has switched allegiance to Juarez, gunned down Lancaster in a final duel and gets Sarita Montiel, a fiery follower of the Juaristas, as a reward.

Besides the more obvious advantages of their star teaming, Cooper and Lancaster come through with actionful and colorful performances. Miss Montiel, of the Mexican film industry, being film-introduced stateside in this, shows up well in her U. S. debut. Miss Darcel, the subject of some overhead photography that shows off her curves, puts an acceptable flamboyance into character, and Romero brings off his spot with considerable aplomb.

Ernest Borgnine, Charles Buchinsky, Jack Lambert, James McCallion, James Seay, Archie Savage and Charles Horvath are among the toughies helping to add menace to Lancaster's gang. George Macready, as Maximilian, Morris Ankrum, as the leader of the Juarez forces, and Henry Brandon are among others contributing capably to the action.

Ernest Laszlo's cameras are used excellently to bring out the pictorial splendors of the Mexican settings, and he never misses any of the fast action in the story. Editing by Alan Crosland Jr., has figured importantly in making this a tight film. Hugo Friedhofer's score makes beautiful use of a guitar emphasis to set the mood most of the time. Also, he did the title tune with Sammy Cahn. Orchestrations and conducting by Raul Lavista is another good music credit. *Brog.*

The Violent Men
(COLOR)

Strong marquee names, CinemaScope bolstering commercial chances of otherwise conventional outdoor feature entertainment.

Hollywood, Dec. ??.

Columbia release of Lewis J. Rachmil production. Stars Glenn Ford, Barbara Stanwyck, Edward G. Robinson, Dianne Foster, Brian Keith, May Wynn; features Warner Anderson, Basil Ruysdael, Lita Milan, Richard Jaeckel, James Westerfield, Jack Kelly, Willis Bouchey, Harry Shannon. Directed by Rudolph Mate. Screenplay, Harry Kleiner; based on a novel by Donald Hamilton; camera (Technicolor), Burnett Guffey, W. Howard Greene; editor, Jerome Thoms; music, Max Steiner; conducted by Morris Stoloff. Previewed Dec. 2, '54. Running time, 95 MINS.

John Parrish	Glenn Ford
Martha Wilkison	Barbara Stanwyck
Lew Wilkison	Edward G. Robinson
Judith Wilkison	Dianne Foster
Cole Wilkison	Brian Keith
Caroline Vail	May Wynn
Jim McCloud	Warner Anderson
Tex Hinkleman	Basil Ruysdael
Elena	Lita Milan
Wade Matlock	Richard Jaeckel
Magruder	James Westerfield
De Rosa	Jack Kelly
Sheriff Martin Kenner	Willis Bouchey
Purdue	Harry Shannon
George Menefee	Peter Hanson
Jackson	Don C. Harvey
Tony	Robo Bechi
Dryer	Carl Andre
Hank Purdue	James Anderson
Mrs. Vail	Katharine Warren
Mr. Vail	Tom Browne Henry
Bud Hinkleman	Bill Phipps

(Aspect ratio: 2.55-1)

A good array of commercial values, topped by strong marquee names and CinemaScope, should stir up generally neat trade for "The Violent Men." Without this bolstering it is just a conventional feature western of the type that plays best in the outdoor market and to nondiscriminating patrons of action fare. Despite its more obvious marketable values, it's not for the plushier de luxers because the entertainment does not live up to the initial promise.

Chief performance assets in the cast are Glenn Ford and Dianne Foster, both of whom bring off their characters in acceptable fashion. Less able to make something out of the stereotypes given them are Barbara Stanwyck and Edward G. Robinson, although their seasoned ability does do more for the parts than less talented hands could have done. Two of Columbia's newer talents, Brian Keith and May Wynn, are given star billing, too, in the Lewis J. Rachmil production and prove okay with what they have to do.

The Donald Hamilton novel, on which the Harry Kleiner screenplay is based, held out the promise of an interesting action drama, but in the scripting and direction by Rudolph Mate the impact is uneven. Some scenes have all the dramatic tension needed, but others bog down in too much talk and a general static feeling that let the show lose its force. Scenically, the picture is outstanding, the anamorphic lensing by Burnett Guffey and W. Howard Greene capturing all the pictorial values of the outdoor locations.

Plot is the one about a cattle baron, now a cripple, who is driving the small ranchers and farmers out of "his" valley. Robinson plays this role, and egging him on is his grasping wife, Miss Stanwyck, and his brother, Keith, a cozy twosome carrying on an illicit romance behind Robinson's back, to the disgust of his daughter, Miss Foster. The plans for empire probably would have been successful if the baron's henchmen hadn't pushed Ford around too much. A pacifist after war service, Ford wants no more of fighting, but adopts guerrilla tactics to put down the gunslingers. In so doing he wins Miss Foster and Robinson wises up after Miss Stanwyck and Keith die violent deaths.

Two big ranch fires, a horse stampede, an ambush and the mild Ford's gunning down of Richard Jaeckel after the latter has wantonly killed Bill Phipps, one of his hands, are among the stronger sequences during which the picture makes like a good western. There are a number of well-value characters in the featured and supporting lists, such as Jaeckel's gunslinger; James Westerfield's toadying deputy and Willis Bouchey's strong sheriff, another victim of Jaeckel's gun. Lita Milan, as a Mexican girl with whom Keith dallies when he's not busy with Stanwyck, creates a good impression.

Editing by Jerome Thoms is good. So is the score by Max Steiner, although it is not used to the best advantage, being recorded much too loud for comfort. *Brog.*

The Silver Chalice
(COLOR—C'SCOPE)

Religioso themed spectacle based on Costain novel. Prospects okay for general market.

Hollywood, Dec. 17.

Warner Bros. release of Victor Saville production. Stars Virginia Mayo, Pier Angeli, Jack Palance; introduces Paul Newman; features Walter Hampden, Joseph Wiseman, Alexander Scourby, Lorne Greene. Directed by Saville. Written by Lesser Samuels; from the novel by Thomas B. Costain; camera (WarnerColor), William V. Skall; editor, George White; music, Franz Waxman. Previewed Dec. 14, '54. Running time, 142 MINS.

Helena	Virginia Mayo
Deborra	Pier Angeli
Simon	Jack Palance
Basil	Paul Newman
Joseph	Walter Hampden
Mijamin	Joseph Wiseman
Luke	Alexander Scourby
Peter	Lorne Greene
Adam	David J. Stewart
Linus	Herbert Rudley
Nero	Jacques Aubuchon
Ignatius	E. G. Marshall
Aaron	Michael Pate
Helena (girl)	Natalie Wood
Basil (boy)	Peter Raynolds
Benjie	Mort Marshall
Hiram	Booth Colman
Sosthene	Terence de Marney
Idbash	Robert Middleton
Theron	Ian Wolfe
Ephraim	Lawrence Dobkin
Ohad	Philip Tonge
Kester	Albert Dekker
Eulalia	Beryl Machin

With its religioso theme and the best-seller status of the Thomas B. Costain novel, "The Silver Chalice" should hit a respectable grossing level. This type of spectacle has a good reputation for boxoffice in the general market, where its entertainment merit is more readily accepted than in the deluxers.

Like the Costain book, the picture is overdrawn and sometimes tedious, but producer-director Victor Saville still manages to instill interest in what's going on, and even hits a feeling of excitement occasionally. The CinemaScope photography in WarnerColor, expertly done by William V. Skall, is an advantage to the presentation, as is the production design by Rolf Gerard and the art direction by Boris Leven, even though many of the settings have a modernistic feel at variance with the Biblical period of the story.

The picture serves as an introduction for film newcomer Paul Newman. He's a personable young man who will probably make an impression on the femmes. Handles himself well before the cameras. Helping his pic debut is Pier Angeli, and it is their scenes together that add the warmth to what might otherwise have been a cold spectacle. Jack Palance also registers strongly with colorful theatrics that are just the right touch, and, for glamour, Virginia Mayo dresses up the footage. Other casters, all acceptable, are used less prominently as Saville's direction unfolds the Costain story, scripted by Lesser Samuels, who also served as associate producer.

The plot portrays the struggle of Christians to save for the future the cup from which Christ drank at the Last Supper. On the side of the Christians is a Greek sculptor, played by Newman, who is fashioning a silver chalice to hold the religious symbol. On the side of evil are the decadent Romans, ruled over by an effete Nero, and Simon, the magician (a real character), played by Palance, who wants to use the destruction of the cup to further his own rise to power. In the end, right and the pure love of Newman and Miss Angeli triumph, even though the cup is lost, a disappearance that led to the prophecy by Peter (well played by Lorne Greene) that it may well reappear sometime in the future to guide a troubled, warring world back into the way of Christian principles.

There are several good action sequences in the long footage, the best being Simon's death when he commits the rather common error of overconfidence. Believing in his own supreme magic, Simon tries to fly over Rome, but falls to his death. This thriller sequence, suspensefully developed, will be a talked-about scene. A rousing score by Franz Waxman dominates the mass action moments. *Brog.*

Long John Silver
(C'Scope-Color)
(AUSTRALIAN)

Robert Newton starred in robust action-packed sequel to "Treasure Island." British b.o. looks strong but U.S. less likely.

London, Dec. 21.

20th-Fox release of Joseph Kaufman production. Stars Robert Newton; features Kit Taylor, Connie Gilchrist. Directed by Byron Haskin. Screenplay, Martin Rackin; editor, Mike Del Campo; camera, Carl Guthrie; music, David Buttolph. At Rialto Theatre, London, Dec. 15, '54. Running time, 106 MINS.

Long John Silver	Robert Newton
Jim Hawkins	Kit Taylor
Purity Pinker	Connie Gilchrist
Trip Fenner	Eric Reiman
Ned Shill	Syd Chambers
Patch	Grant Taylor
Old Stingley	John Brunskill
Big Eric	Harry Hambleton
Billie Bowlegs	Henry Gilbert
Dodd Perch	Elwyn Daniel
Harry Grip	Al Thomas
Governor Strong	Harvey Adams
Lady Strong	Muriel Steinbeck
Mendoza	Lloyd Berrell
Kling	Tony Arpino
Ironhand	Billy Kay
Sentry	Frank Ransom
Sgt. Cover	Don McNiven
Elderly Naval Officer	Charles McCallum
Israel Hands	Rodney Taylor
Father Monaster	Hans Stern
Elizabeth Strong	Thora Smith
Capt. McDougal	George Simpson Little
Young Naval Officer	John Pooley

It's only about four years or so since Robert Newton played Long John Silver in Walt Disney's British-made live actioner, "Treasure Island," and the star turns up in the same role in this anamorphic production, lensed in Australia. It's a robust melodrama in the Robert Louis Stevenson tradition and looks set for healthy grosses, particularly in situations which cater to a substantial juve trade.

The action story has been written by Martin Rackin, using some of the Stevenson characters to make it an acceptable sequel to his "Treasure Island" classic. The attractive Botany Bay locales make ideal settings, and they are enhanced by excellent color lensing.

In this new version, "Long John Silver" is still the wily, cunning, one-legged pirate with a disposition to doublecross anyone except young Master Jim Hawkins, a boy of quality, who plays such an important part in "Treasure Island." His first major adventure is to rescue the Governor's daughter from a bitter enemy, and this sequence ends with a major doublecross in which he collects the ransom and also loots the King's warehouse. He then succeeds in getting his gang of thugs on board a ship taking the boy to England, but after an unsuccessful mutiny they are all dumped on an island which turns out to be the secret headquarters of the above mentioned rival. Eventually they get to "Treasure Island" and get their hands on the missing hoard after a battle with the rival gang.

Under Byron Haskin's skilled direction, the story keeps moving at a lively tempo and the wealth of incident is developed with gusto. Once again the title part proves a natural for Robert Newton and his fruity performance is one of the picture's main entertainment elements. Kit Taylor, a screen newcomer, gives an appealing portrayal as the boy while Connie Gilchrist, the woman innkeeper with marital designs on Newton, turns in a lively contribution. Lloyd Berrell, as Long John's main adversary, gives a virile performance. The others play their roles in the robust key set by the star.

Myro.

Black Tuesday
(SONG)

Prison break melodrama, grim but expertly fashioned for fanciers of tough action.

Hollywood, Dec. 20.

United Artists release of Leonard Goldstein (Robert Goldstein) production. Stars Edward G. Robinson; features Peter Graves, Jean Parker. Directed by Hugo Fregonese. Story and screenplay, Sydney Boehm; camera, Stanley Cortez; editor, Robert Golden; score, Paul Dunlap; song, "Black Tuesday" by Robert Parrish. Previewed Dec. 17, '54. Running time, **80 MINS.**

Vincent Canelli ..... Edward G. Robinson
Peter Manning .... Peter Graves
Hatti Combest .... Jean Parker
Father Slocum .... Milburn Stone
Joey Stewart .... Warren Stevens
Frank Carson .... Jack Kelly
Ellen Norris .... Sylvia Findley
John Norris .... James Bell
Dr. Hart .... Victor Perrin
Lou Mehrtens .... Hal Baylor
Boland .... Harry Bartell
Parker .... Simon Scott
Howard Sloan .... Russell Johnson
Fiaschetti .... Phil Pine
Donaldson .... Paul Maxey
Collins .... William Schallert
Selwyn .... Don Blackman
Benny .... Dick Rich

(Aspect ratio: 1.85-1)

Some real rough melodramatics are dished out in "Black Tuesday," so it's a rather grim 80 minutes of film mostly suited to those who fancy tough action. In the program field it will get a good share of bookings so the payoff looks okay.

Edward G. Robinson makes a return to gang czar roles in this Sydney Boehm screen story and has lost none of his menacing qualities. The direction by Hugo Fregonese is hard-hitting and everything connected with the Robert Goldstein production is expertly shaped to do a good job of telling a crime yarn.

Plot concerns the break from death row in a New Jersey prison by Robinson, who takes along Peter Graves, bank robber and killer, who has $200,000 in loot stashed away as well as several hostages. The ill-assorted group is cornered on the top floor of a warehouse, from which the kill-mad Robinson plans to toss out the body of a hostage at regular intervals until the police withdraw. The police won't play, however, and violence runs high until Graves relents enough to gun down Robinson to prevent the death of a priest and then charges the law, guns blazing, to die himself.

A rather intriguing idea for a successful jail break is staged by having Robinson's girl friend, Jean Parker, and his outside hoods kidnapping a guard's daughter so he will help Robinson and Graves after they have gone into the death chamber for electrocution. It's not too implausible as set up in the Boehm script and directed by Fregonese.

The assorted characters in the plot are brought off well. More prominent among the players after Robinson, Graves and Miss Parker, are Milburn Stone, the priest; Warren Stevens, Jack Kelly, Sylvia Findley, James Bell, Victor Perrin, Hal Baylor, and the uncredited police chief who refuses to bow to gangster threats.

Stanley Cortez gives the story good lensing and the settings help put over the yarn. A title tune by Robert Parrish is used as a prisoner song early in the footage.

Brog.

Quest for the Lost City
(COLOR)

Documentary of trek by Dana and Ginger Lamb into wilds of southern Mexico. Interesting for armchair adventurers.

Hollywood, Dec. 16.

RKO release of Sol Lesser (Dorothy Howell) production. Photographed in 16m Kodachrome (35m print by Eastman Color) by Dana and Ginger Lamb. Narrative written by Dorothy Howell; narration, Hal Gibney; introduction, Tom Harmon; special photography, Nelson S. Knaggs; editor, Robert Leo; associated in production, Bill Park; score, Paul Sawtell. Previewed Dec. 14, '54. Running time, **64 MINS.**

(Aspect ratio: 1.33-1)

Armchair adventurers who mostly daydream their derring-do should find this film saga of a couple's trek into the deep jungles along the Mexican-Guatemalan border an interesting 64 minutes. It's a good supporting subject for regular twin bills.

The two hardy souls who made the junket, with only that equipment they could pack on their backs, are Dana and Ginger Lamb. Their search for a lost Maya city, a trek made under the most primitive of conditions, is heady enough vicarious adventure for those comfortably seated away from the steamy, buggy jungle.

The Lambs used a delayed action 16m camera for their filming and the Kodachrome tints have been blown up to 35m Eastman Color for release. While the lensing is not of professional photographic standards, it still comes off effectively and adds a quality of realism to the quest. An introduction by Tom Harmon and narration by Hal Gibney of the narrative written by Dorothy Howell, who also produced, clearly establishes the hardships of the junket. Robert Leo gives the film excellent editing and the Paul Sawtell score is apt to the adventuring.

Brog.

True Friends
(RUSSIAN; COLOR)

Artkino release of Mosfilm Production. Stars V. Merkuryev, Boris Churkov, A. Borisov. Directed and written by Mikhail Kalatozov. Camera, M. Magidson; music, T. Krennikov. At Stanley, N.Y., starting Nov. 12, '54. Running time, **105 MINS.**

Nestratov .... V. Merkuryev
Chizhov .... Boris Chirkov
Lapin .... A. Borisov
Nickhoda .... A. Gribov
Natalya Sergeyevna .... L. Gritsenko
Katya .... L. Shagalova

(In Russian; English Titles)

The purveyors of Russo propaganda are not in there pitching in this picture. The story has the familiar collective building program, the collective farming and collective horse-raising—and even the usual commissars of surgery, the master horse-raiser and architect chief, but "True Friends" does not hesitate to poke fun at many of the flaws in the Soviet regimented system. In fact, the entire plot turns on the master architect's laxness in handling the needs of the people. Resultantly, film is an interesting comedy-drama, with the humorous side always stressed.

Story depicts how Nestratov, the role played by V. Merkuryev, has become a pompous stuffed-shirt and inveterate speechmaker while new construction stalls and awaits his long-coming decisions. The efforts of two boyhood companions, one now the head surgeon of the land, and the other is Master Horse Trainer, to bring the top architect down to earth constitute the basis of the yarn.

The two friends, now masters in their right, inveigle the big architect to accompany them on a boat trip, not telling him it is to wind up a three-some affair on a raft. Their adventures floating down the Volga river provide most of the action. Plot manages to land the three in a typical Russian village where delays in getting material has thrown the new building program out of kilter, and a lazy local commissar has further aggravated the situation. Of course, there is a heroic deed by one of the town gals in averting a horse stampede in which she is badly injured. This enables the surgeon-general to exercise his skill, and save the femme's life.

The third member of the trio contents himself with trying to locate a former sweetheart in this same village. Maybe, the producers should have worked him into the horse-stampede scene. It would have helped. The two succeed in making the Commissar of Architecture see the errors of his ways, and establish closer contact with his people.

M. Magidson's camerawork (Sovcolor) is a bright spot in the pic. This is one of the best tinter jobs to come from Russia. Besides Merkuryev, Boris Chirkov and A. Borisov make excellent co-stars. Mikhail Kalatozov's direction, which considerably better than many Russo directorial efforts, goes far in holding interest since he seldom lets the action drag.

Wear.

Giorni D'Amore
(Days of Love)
(ITALIAN—COLOR)

Rome, Dec. 7.

Minerva release of an Excelsa Film production. Stars Marcella Mastroianni, Marina Vlady, Lucien Gallas. Directed by Giuseppe DeSantis. Story and screenplay, DeSantis, Libero de Libero, Elio Petri, Gianni Puccini; camera, Otello Martelli (Ferrania-color); color consultant, art and costume design, Domenico Purificato; music, Mario Nascimbene; editor, Gabriele Varriale. Previewed in Rome. Running time, **105 MINS.**

Pasquale .... Marcello Mastroianni
Angela .... Marina Vlady
Oreste .... Lucien Gallas
Nonno Pittro .... Giulio Cali
Francesco .... Renato Chiantoni
Priest .... Pietro Tordi
Nunziata .... Dora Scarpetta

Cluttered script on this item almost spoils a promising story idea, with resulting pic caught halfway between a serious love story and a folk comedy. Considerable trimming is needed in order to focus on essentials, with a chattery middle section especially distracting from the central story. Outlook is spotty, with Yank possibilities dependent on a good reediting job. Locally, this pic looks like a good subsequent-run grosser.

Story springs from Italian lower-class expedient, said to be widespread in country's south, of staging a pre-marital escapade to get around the payment of formal wedding expenses. The couple, with both families agreeing in secret, spends a night in countryside. Families fake a fight, and on the twosome's return a hasty informal marriage is arranged, supposedly saving face with other villagers. Pic essentially outlines this tale, with Marcello Mastoianni and Marina Vlady as the lovers who spend the night under the stars.

While the families stage a strident battle from house to house, the gal proves reluctant to meet her obligations but finally realizes she's compromised anyway and makes up with her annoyed future husband. To the detriment of the pic, concentration is on sideline stuff rather than on developing the relationship of the lovers. Director Giuseppe DeSantis ("Bitter Rice") tamely handles his explosive material, coming through only at end with a strong scene. Marina Vlady registers in all departments with her exotic young looks and charming manners, the Ferrania-color lensing especially favoring her. Marcello Mastroianni is very good as her lover while Giulio Cali and Pina Gallina make colorful family types. Color lensing by Otello Martelli is standout, especially the exteriors. Stylish but obvious sets contrast uncomfortably with other real backdrops. Mario Nascimbene has written an excellent lightweight musical score for pic.

Hawk.

Make Me an Offer
(BRITISH-COLOR)

Lightweight British offering adapted from Wolf Mankowitz novel; marquee appeal for home market but thin prospects in U. S.

London, Dec. 7.

British Lion release of Group Three (W. P. Lipscomb) presentation. Stars Peter Finch, Adrienne Corri. Directed by Cyril Frankel. Screenplay by W. P. Lipscombe from novel by Wolf Mankowitz; camera, Denny Densham; editor, Bernard Gribble; music, John Addison. At Empire, London, Dec. '54. Running time **88 MINS.**

Charlie .... Peter Finch
Nicky .... Adrienne Corri
Bella .... Rosalie Crutchley
Abe Sparta .... Finlay Currie
Wendl .... Meier Tzelniker
Sir John .... Ernest Thesiger
Charlie's father .... Wilfred Lawson
Auctioneer .... Anthony Nicholls
Fred Frames .... Alfie Bass
Armstrong .... Guy Middleton
Sweeting .... Vic Wise
Mindel .... Mark Baker
Dobbie .... Jane Wenham
Charlie as a boy .... Richard O'Sullivan
Charlie's son .... John Godden
Auctioneer's assistant ...... Eric Francis

Wolf Mankowitz was in the antique business long before he widened his activities to include novel and playwriting. 'Make Me An Offer," taken from one of his books which describes the experiences of a dealer specializing in Wedgwood pottery, presumably tells an authentic story. But the subject does not translate too happily onto the screen and is too static. The cast of local players provides some b.o. value in the local market but is not strong enough to sell in America.

W. P. Lipscomb's production and screenplay give an interesting background to the way in which expert dealers gang together and rig an auction and bid for the goods among themselves. But there is not enough substance in this yarn about a stolen Wedgwood vase which a dealer discovered in the attic of an inarticulate man.

Cyril Frankel's direction follows a pedestrian approach, and yet within the limited framework he has been moderately well served by his cast. Peter Finch provides a note of credence to the part of the dealer, and Adrienne Corri, an attractive redhead, rises above her role, which is out of character with the entire story. Rosalie Crutchley, as the dealer's wife, and Wilfred Lawson as his father turn in good average portrayals. Finlay Currie and Meier Tzelniker, as rival dealers, help to generate some excitement during the auction sequences. Other roles are up to standard.

Myro.

Lettres de Mon Moulin
(Letters From My Mill)
(FRENCH)
Paris, Dec. 7.
Gaumont release of Compagnie Mediterrannenne De Films production. Directed by Marcel Pagnol. Screenplay, Pagnol, from stories by Alphonse Daudet; camera, Willy; editor, Jacqueline Gaudin; music, Henri Tomasi. At Paris, Paris. Running time, 180 MINS.
Alphonse Daudet	Roger Crouzet
Yvette	Pierrette Bruno
Pere Gaucher	Rellys
Druggist	Fernand Sardou
Abbe	Robert Vattier
Miller	Edouard Delmont
Priest	Henri Vilbert

A breath of fresh air is let into filmhouses here with this evocation of three rustic stories of the 19th-century Gallic author, Alphonse Daudet. Marcel Pagnol has worked these three sketches into a whole, using the author as a personage who hears these tales and is even entangled in one himself. Though slow at times, indicating needed scissoring, it emerges as an engaging, simple idyll, without falling into the bucoli or mawkish, by dint of the robust humor and impish goodness breathed into it by Pagnol. Lacking the drama, thesping and more international appeal of his famed "Baker's Wife," and Marseilles trilogy ("Marius," "Fanny," "Cesar"), this pic would be more limited for U. S. chances. It looks to do fine here, but for stateside would have to be handled for special situations, with the Pagnol name and probable word-of-mouth the lure.

Daudet comes back to his native soil in the Provencal district of France and lives in an old mill, where he intends to write stories about his people. They are a pious bunch with enough human foibles and native shrewdness to make them endearing and colorful. First tale concerns an impoverished bunch of monks who manufacture a new liqueur to make them solvent and more able to do the Lord's work. Second is a legend about how the Devil stole a mass from a gourmand priest, and the last tale concerns an old miller who almost sacrifices his life in an attempt to make his neighbors believe his mill has been running for 18 years due to a mysterious, non-existent client.

Actors are little known but add to the freshness and guile of this talky but taking pic. Camerawork and editing are good and author-director Pagnol has lavished his love for the provincials without betraying the writing of Daudet. Film techniques are sacrificed for words and spirit, to make this in need of special hypoing for any U. S. payoff. *Mosk.*

Cadet-Rousselle
(FRENCH—COLOR)
Paris, Dec. 7.
Pathe release of Pathe-PAC production. Stars Francois Perier, Dany Robin. Directed by Andre Hunnebelle. Screenplay, Jean Halain, Jean-Paul Leroix; camera (Eastmancolor), Marcel Grignon; editor, Jean Feyte; music, Jean Marion. At Balzac, Paris. Running time, 115 MINS.
Cadet-Rousselle	Francois Perier
Violetta	Dany Robin
Jerome	Bourvil
Marguerite	Madeleine Lebeau
Isabelle	Christine Carrere
Berton	Noel Roquevert
Rovignol	Alfred Adam
General	Jean Parcdes
Mayor	Henri Gremieux

This film is in the genre of its predecessor, "Fanfan La Tulipe," in using the folk hero of an old song as the springboard for a parody, adventure-spec story. Though in color, it is not as colorful as "Fanfan," and has a tendency to conglomerate hits and types from various films to make this a rambling adventure story. It has many bright moments, but is too Gallic in its inference and gags to give it the universal appeal "Fanfan" had. However, it can be cut into a wieldy film which may have a chance in arty spots if well plugged.

Cadet Rousselle is in love with the mayor's daughter, but his lowly station makes him unworthy of her. He decides to go to Paris and make his fortune. On the way, the simple, honest cadet is robbed and left in the road. He is picked up by gypsies, and transfers his love to the gypsy dancer, Violetta. However, the gypsies are fronting for a group of Royalists plotting to overthrow the new Republic. The cadet innocently delivers a letter and gets involved with politics, being thrown into prison. He escapes and helps win a battle, is imprisoned, escapes again, becomes an outlaw and then a general of Napoleon. He finally marries Violetta.

Pic does have some of the rambling appeal of a folk legend and has a fine comic aspect in Bourvil as the craven, zany sidekick of Rousselle (well played by Francois Perier), whose excellent comic timing gives this most of its laughs. Director Andre Hunnebelle has mounted his chases and sword fights admirably, but has failed to give this the zest and brightness it needs. Lensing is richly hued. Editing helps the many and multiple sword rattlings and chases.

Gals are all decorative but Dany Robin is miscast as a gypsy. Support of the large cast is firstrate. Music is also too derivative. *Mosk.*

La Belle Otero
(Color—Songs)
(FRANCO-ITALIAN)
Paris, Dec. 7.
CCFC-Les Films Moderns release of Emile Natan production. Stars Maria Felix; features Jacques Berthier, Maurice Teynac, Marie Sabouret. Directed by Richard Pottier. Screenplay, Marc-Gilbert Sauvajon from memoirs of Caroline Otero; camera (Eastmancolor), Michel Kelber; editor, Andre Gaudier; music, Georges Van Parys. At Moulin Rouge, Paris. Running time, 105 MINS.
Otero	Maria Felix
Jean	Jacques Bethier
Martin	Louis Seigner
Mountfeller	Maurice Teynac
Frederic	Paolo Stoppa
Diane	Marie Sabouret
Mario	Jean-Marc Tennberg

The Gay Nineties are evoked rather sadly in this color opus. Loosely based on the life of the famed turn-of-the-century courtesan, La Belle Otero, this unreels a cliche loaded story of backstage life and love. Familiar aspects of the rags-to-riches heroine who has only one love, is not compensated for any imagination in the period work or the songs and dances. It remains an okay pic for Franco-Italo chances, but for the U.S. is limited in appeal except for possible dualers. Otherwise, it is below par compared to the same type of films that Hollywood makes so well.

Story shows Otero (Maria Felix) as a newly arrived Spanish dancer who is out of work in Paris. She forces herself on Louis Seigner, an impresario, and gets her first chance. However she is used by Jacques Bethier, a man around town, to revenge himself on a defiant mistress. With Miss Felix it is love, but he soon tires of her. Then she goes away with an American millionaire, who makes her the toast of New York. She gets fed up with his puritanical ways and heads homeward. She becomes an international star, but the boy friend is killed in a duel.

Director Richard Pottier has given this conventional trimmings, but has left the characters stilted and lifeless. The ordinary and platitudinous dialog and screenplay are no help either. Dance and song numbers are passable and color work is fine. Miss Felix brings only looks to her role while Jacques Berthier is unprepossessing as the loved one. *Mosk.*

Senhime
(The Princess Sen)
(JAPANESE—COLOR)
Tokyo, Dec. 7.
Dalei Studios release of a Masaichi Nagata production. Stars Machiko Kyo and Kenji Sugahara. Camera, Kohei Sugiyama; screenplay, Fuji Yahiro; sets, Ichizo Kajiya; music, Fumio Hayasaka. Previewed in Tokyo. Running time, 90 MINS.

Prepared for possible entry in next year's Italian film festival, "Senhime" looks to win a prize of some sort. Filmed in Eastmancolor by Daiei, the studio which has already taken international prizes with "Rashomon," "Gate of Hell" and "Golden Demon," it stars the female lead of "Rashomon" and is as visually striking as "Gate of Hell." Its story is simple and the performances are exemplary.

The Princess Sen (Machiko Kyo), grandaughter of the founder of the Tokugawa government in the 17th century, is married to another shogun to form an alliance with her father's forces. After his death, she takes to drink and promiscuity. By accident she discovers a ronin (hired soldier) (Kenji Suguhara) who has sworn to kill her for being responsible for the death of his master. She finds in him what she had lost in her husband. Torn between duty and desire, he succumbs to her charms. After a short-lived idyl, he is slain in a fight with a rival faction. She goes to a nunnery.

The Noh plays which the princess watches are corrupted to the point where they are burlesques of the original dignified performances. She lies on imported Chinese carpets over straw mats. When she dances, the sly note of the lascivious enters.

The perfectly captured atmosphere, the brilliant use of color and the provocative performance of Miss Kyo and the persuasive performance of Suguhara are pointed up by the clever direction of Keigo Kimura.

Sure to be smash in the arty houses, "Senhime" may do well in general release if the vogue for Japanese films continues. *Lars.*

The Bridges at Toko-Ri
(COLOR)

Sock war melodrama for strong response in all situations.

Hollywood, Dec. 23.
Paramount release of a William Perlberg-George Seaton production. Stars William Holden, Grace Kelly, Fredric March, Mickey Rooney; features Robert Strauss, Charles McGraw, Keiko Awaji. Directed by Mark Robson. Screenplay, Valentine Davies; based on novel by James A. Michener; camera, Loyal Griggs; aerial photography, Charles G. Clarke; editor, Alma Macrorie; music, Lyn Murray. Running time, 102 MINS.
Lt. Harry Brubacher (USNR)	William Holden
Nancy Brubacher	Grace Kelly
Rear Admiral George Tarrant	Fredric March
Mike Forney	Mickey Rooney
Beer Barrel	Robert Strauss
Commander Wayne Lee	Charles McGraw
Kimiko	Keiko Awaji
Nestor Gamidge	Earl Hollimar
Lt. (S.G.) Olds	Richard Shannon
Capt. Evans	Willis B. Bouchey

(Aspect ratio: 1.85-1)

James A. Michener's hard-hitting novel of the Korean conflict finds slick Technicolor translation in this topflight war spectacle. Rich in human emotions that accent the grim background, film emerges a distinguished piece of picture-making right down the line and should register impressively at the b.o.

Class mounting is given their production supervision by William Perlberg and George Seaton, which strikes a high level of showmanship in the bold overtones of war. Valentine Davies' brilliant screenplay cleaves faithfully to the original Michener story, even its sadly realistic ending, and the cooperation extended by the U. S. Navy in lending all-out support adds immeasurably to the picture's numerous fine qualities.

In taking advantage of the Navy's resources, aboard an aircraft carrier off the coast of Korea and through the use of planes and equipment, Mark Robson in his taut direction catches the spirit of the Navy and what it stood for in the Korean War, never losing sight, however, of the personalized story of a Navy combat flier whose last mission ends tragically. The matchless lensing, used here, is accorded further meaning through Charles G. Clarke's exciting aerial photography.

Narrative drives toward the climactic bombing by U. S. fliers of the five bridges at Toko-Ri, which span a strategic pass in Korea's interior. These are guarded with a great concentration of Communist artillery, as befitting the most vital goal in the Reds' defense. Fliers are based on a carrier in a task force off Korea in 1952, and here the story of William Holden, a reserve officer recalled to service, unfolds.

A fine flier, he is taken under the wing of the admiral, played by Fredric March, who understands his gripe of having been forced to leave his wife and children to return to the Navy. As one of the leaders in a squadron which destroys the bridges, Holden is unable to get his plane back and is killed by Reds when he crashes.

Practically every principal performance is a standout. Holden lends conviction to his character, fearful of the outcome of the mission but doggedly performing his duty, and March delivers a sock portrayal of the admiral, who is drawn to Holden because he reminds him of his two sons lost in war. As Holden's wife who brings their two daughters to Tokyo so they may be near the flier, Grace Kelly is warmly sympathetic. Mickey Rooney, the fourth star, enacts a helicopter pilot who saves fliers forced into the ocean, killed when he lands to pick up Holden after his crash. It's a smash portrayal.

In support, Charles McGraw as the flight leader is strongly cast, and Earl Holliman does yeoman service as Rooney's pal. Robert Strauss also scores as a crewman and Keiko Awaji is a pretty Jap girl, over whose affections Rooney starts a riot in Tokyo and nearly gets Holden into another riot.

Technical credits generally are tops. Loyal Griggs handles first cameras effectively, and Wallace Kelley and Thomas Tutweiler are in charge of second unit lensing. Alma Macrorie's editing is fast and tight, art direction by Hal Pereira and Henry Bumstead colorful and the music score by Lyn Murray meets the requirements of the subject. *Whit.*

Green Fire
(COLOR—SONG—C'SCOPE)

South American emerald-mining romantic adventure, with Stewart Granger, Grace Kelly, Paul Douglas and okay prospects in regular dates.

Hollywood, Dec. 28.

Metro release of Armand Deutsch production. Stars Stewart Granger, Grace Kelly, Paul Douglas; costars John Ericson; features Murvyn Vye, Jose Torvay. Directed by Andrew Marton. Written by Ivan Goff, Ben Roberts; camera (Eastman Color), Paul Vogel; editor, Harold F. Kress; song, Jack Brooks; music, Miklos Rozsa. Previewed Dec. 15, '54. Running time, **99 MINS.**

Rian X. Mitchell .... Stewart Granger
Catherine Knowland .... Grace Kelly
Vic Leonard .... Paul Douglas
Donald Knowland .... John Ericson
El Moro .... Murvyn Vye
Manuel .... Jose Torvay
Father Ripero .... Robert Tafur
Jose .... Joe Dominguez
Officer Perez .... Nacho Galindo
Dolores .... Charlita
Hernandez .... Natividad Vacio
Antonio .... Rico Alaniz
Roberto .... Paul Marion
Juan .... Robert Dominguez

A good brand of action escapism is offered in "Green Fire" for the entertainment of that substantial portion of regular film patrons who go for high romance fiction. Its story of emerald mining and romantic adventuring in South America is decorated with the names of Stewart Granger, Grace Kelly and Paul Douglas, as well as by the CinemaScope lensing and the Eastman Color tints. It should hit a profitable boxoffice stride in the overall release.

An array of story, action and visual values that will have maximum appeal to those chimerically-minded fans who like their pulp fiction well-dressed has been assembled by producer Armand Deutsch. The location-filming in Colombia insured fresh scenic backgrounds against which to play the screen story by Ivan Goff and Ben Roberts. The script supplies believable dialog and reasonably credible situations, of which Andrew Marton's good direction takes full advantage, and the picture

spins off at a fast 99 minutes.

The adventure end of the plot is served by the efforts of Granger to find emeralds in an old mountain mine; in the face of halfhearted opposition from his partner, Douglas; the more active interference of Murvyn Vye, a bandit, and the danger of the mining trade itself. Romance is served through the presence of Miss Kelly, whose coffee plantation lies at the foot of the mountain on which Granger is mining, and the attraction that springs up between these two.

The climactic stride is hit when Granger must choose between his search for wealth and the love he has found. The mining operations have changed the course of a river, threatening the plantation with flood and ruin, the rainy season is about to begin, the bandits are attacking, and dynamite is ready to blow up the mountain. The windup, excitingly staged, has Granger choosing the course of action that ends in Miss Kelly's arms.

Paul Vogel plays his cameras over the location sites and the players advantageously. Technical contributions come off well, as does the Miklos Rozsa score. Jack Brooks did the lyrics to the title tune. *Brog.*

Target Earth

Science-fiction programmer with okay idea, poorly developed.

Hollywood, Dec. 22.

Allied Artists release of Abtcon Pictures (Herman Cohen) production. Stars Richard Denning, Kathleen Crowley, Virginia Grey, Richard Reeves; features Robert Roark, Mort Marshall, Arthur Space, Whit Bissell. Directed by Sherman A. Rose. Screenplay, William Raynor; based on the story, "The Deadly City," by Paul W. Fairman; camera, Guy Roe; editor, Sherman A. Rose; special effects, Dave Koehler. Previewed Dec. 20, '54. Running time, **74 MINS.**

Frank .... Richard Denning
Nora .... Kathleen Crowley
Vicki .... Virginia Grey
Jim .... Richard Reeves
Davis .... Robert Roark
Otis .... Mort Marshall
General .... Arthur Space
Scientist .... Whit Bissell
Lieutenant .... Jim Drake
Colonel .... Steve Pendleton
Technician .... House Peters Jr.

The lesser program market will find this belated science-fiction entry a passable lowercase booking. What starts out as a promising suspense feature soon turns into an unimaginative potboiler on invaders from space so the entertainment values are lightweight.

Opening has Kathleen Crowley and Richard Denning awakening in separate parts of a city to find it strangely deserted. Their wanderings bring them together and they find another couple, Virginia Grey and Richard Reeves. The foursome holes up in a hotel, learn that the city was ordered completely evacuated when an army of robots, believed from Venus, invaded it.

After the tense kickoff of the story, it settles down to talk out most of the action, losing suspense as it moves along the 74 minutes. Wrapup finds the Army besting the robots with supersonic soundwaves, the only thing capable of cracking their armor. This is done just in time, because Denning and Miss Crowley, having escaped a psycho killer, Robert Roark, are just about to be done in by a robot. *Brog.*

The Americano
(COLOR)

Western with Brazilian background. Okay grosser for the action situations.

RKO release of Robert Stillman production. Stars Glenn Ford, Frank Lovejoy, Cesar Romero, Ursula Thiess, Abbe Lane. Directed by William Castle. Screenplay, Guy Trosper, from an original story by Leslie T. White; camera (Technicolor), William Snyder; editor, Harry Marker; musical score, Roy Webb; song, "The Americano," composed and conducted by Xavier Cugat. Previewed in N.Y., Dec. 27, '54. Running time, **85 MINS.**

Sam Dent .... Glenn Ford
Bento Hermanny .... Frank Lovejoy
Manoel .... Cesar Romero
Marianna Figuerido .... Ursula Thiess
Teresa .... Abbe Lane
Cristino .... Rodolfo Hoyos Jr.
Captain Gonzales .... Salvador Baguez
Jim Rogers .... Tom Powers
Barney Dent .... Dan White
Captain of Ship .... Frank Marlowe
Tuba .... George Navarro
Tuba's Sister .... Nyra Monsour

Despite its Latino label and its Brazilian setting, "The Americano" is an oater in the true American tradition. The shift in country nevertheless gives the picture added appeal. Combined with the action elements, the new, strange scenery filmed in Technicolor, and the names of Glenn Ford, Frank Lovejoy, Cesar Romero, Ursula Thiess, and Abbe Lane, the Robert Stillman below-the-border production should chalk up satisfactory returns in theatres that go for this type of product.

The Guy Trosper screenplay from an original story by Leslie T. White starts off with an element of suspense and partially indicates a "High Noon" quality during the opening footage. These "High" expectations, however, are dissipated as "The Americano" becomes a standard western that might have happened in Texas or Oklahoma. The basic element of conflict involves a range war with a cattle baron attempting to fight off the inroads of the farmers.

While there are production vacillations and loose ends in the story, "The Americano" emerges, on the whole, as an okay entry that can click acceptably with proper exploitation. It is helped largely by fine performances by a top-drawer cast. Ford, as a Texas cowboy, arrives in Brazil with a shipment of Brahma bulls worth $25,000. He discovers that his buyer, a South American rancher, has been murdered. With Cesar Romero, a self-styled "bandit-chaser," he sets out to deliver the bulls to the rancher's partner. It involves a trip through 50 miles of treacherous jungle and gives the camera ample opportunity to record the scenic splendor.

At the ranch, in the midst of fine cattle country, Ford runs into a range war. After a hands-off policy for three-quarters of the picture, he sides with Ursula Thiess and the small landowners. The decision is prompted by a romantic interest in Miss Thiess and an observation of the cruel methods of Frank Lovejoy, the cattle baron.

Ford scores as the unafraid American confused by the south-of-the-border goings-on. Romero is fine as the Robin Hood type of bandit who befriends Ford, and Lovejoy is properly deceiving and menacing as the villain. Miss Thiess is okay as the femme rancher and Miss Lane lends the right sexiness to her role. Rodolfo Hoyos Jr. makes a frightening henchman who carries out the overt acts of villainy.

William Castle's direction is too leisurely. Sharper pacing and cutting would have made this a tauter actioner. Technical aspects are okay. *Holl.*

1955

Prince of Players
(COLOR-C'SCOPE)

Sock dramatization of Edwin Booth's life, including a generous dose of Shakespeare. High b.o. promise with proper selling.

Twentieth Century-Fox release of a Philip Dunne production. Stars Richard Burton, Maggie McNamara, John Derek, Raymond Massey, Charles Bickford, Elizabeth Sellars, Eva Le Gallienne; features Christopher Cook, Dayton Lummis, Ian Keith, Paul Stader, Louis Alexander, William Walker, Jack Raine, Charles Cane, Betty Flint, Mae Marsh, Stanley Hall, Sarah Padden, Ruth Clifford, Ivan Hayes, Paul Frees, Ben Wright, Melinda Markey, Eleanor Audley, Percival Vivian, George Dunn, Ruth Warren, Richard Cutting, Lane Chandler, Steve Darrell, George Melford, Tom Fadden, Henry Kulky, Olan Soule. Directed by Dunne. Screenplay, Moss Hart, based on the Eleanor Ruggles book; camera (color by De Luxe), Charles G. Clarke; editor, Dorothy Spencer; music, Bernard Herrmann; special consultant on Shakespearean scenes, Miss Gallienne. Running time, **102 MINS.**

Edwin Booth	Richard Burton
Mary Devlin	Maggie McNamara
John Wilkes Booth	John Derek
Junius Brutus Booth	Raymond Massey
Dave Prescott	Charles Bickford
Asia	Elizabeth Sellars
The Queen	Eva Le Gallienne
Edwin Booth (Age 10)	Christopher Cook
English Doctor	Dayton Lummis
"King" in Hamlet	Ian Keith
Laertes	Paul Stader
John Booth (Age 12)	Louis Alexander
Old Ben	William Walker
Theatre Manager	Jack Raine
Theatre Assistant	Charles Cane
Lady Macbeth	Betty Flint
Witch in Macbeth	Mae Marsh
Abraham Lincoln	Stanley Hall
Mrs. Abe Lincoln	Sarah Padden
English Nurse	Ruth Clifford
Bernardo	Ivan Hayes
Francisco	Paul Frees
Horatio	Ben Wright
Young Lady	Melinda Markey
Mrs. Montchesington	Eleanor Audley
Polonius	Percival Vivian
Doorman	George Dunn
Nurse	Ruth Warren
Doctor	Richard Cutting
Colonel	Lane Chandler
Major Rathbone	Steve Darrell
Stage Doorman	George Melford
Trenchard	Tom Fadden
Bartender	Henry Kulky
Catesby	Olan Soule

Within recent times there has risen the notion—contested by some and endorsed by others—that the film audience, like the country at large, is in the throes of a slow but steady maturing process. "Prince of Players," one of the handsomest and most perfectly composed CinemaScope productions to date, should go a long way in answering the question.

Produced by Philip Dunne, and also his first directing chore, pic tells a powerfully dramatic story of a great American actor of the past—Edwin Booth—and, without overaccenting the issue, it weaves into its narrative also the tragic tale of Booth's brother, John Wilkes, who gained fame and infamy by assassinating Lincoln. From a pictorial point-of-view, as well as in terms of its superb performance by Richard Burton, "Prince of Players" is a true prince of a picture, making full and intelligent use of the wide C'Scope screen. It is Hollywood using its cameras to very best advantage, and the combination of these factors won't be lost on the b.o.

But "Prince" is more than just a film. It is also a serious and for the most part outstandingly successful attempt to make the stage, and specifically Shakespeare, serve the purpose of the screen. There are excerpts, staged with skill and acted masterfully, from "Richard III," "Romeo and Juliet," "Hamlet" and "King Lear." They are, in their way, a revolutionary new approach to such entertainment, or maybe they haven't been done this well before. Under the skillful guidance of Dunne, these scenes come to live with fire and drama to make great entertainment.

It is obvious that the "natural" audience for these particular ingredients is limited. Also, one or two of them are too long for comfort. Yet, if there is any truth in the assertion that the public is ready for "mature entertainment," "Prince" should be a sockeroo all over. It is an emotional portrait of a great man, and in many ways it is warm and tender and romantic. One couldn't ask for much more.

In the part of Edwin Booth, Burton proves why Britain's Old Vic rates him so highly. He is a performer of great competence, delighting in a part tailormade to his talents. On stage and off, he etches a portrayal that stands out with its fire and strength. His Booth, overshadowed by tragedy, has a firmness and sensitivity for which he deserves great credit.

In the supporting parts, Maggie McNamara has charm, even though her Juliet pales before the conviction of Burton. Their scene in the garden of a New Orleans brothel, humorous and yet tender and wistful, is a delight. Miss McNamara does better in the dramatic parts. John Derek as John Wilkes Booth (hotheaded and envious brother and assassin of Lincoln), comes up with a fine performance. Raymond Massey brings to the tragic figure of Junius Brutus Booth the elder a curious dignity which clashes with his drunken ravings. If the character is overdrawn, it is properly so. Charles Bickford, as Booth's manager, lends valuable support, and so do Elizabeth Sellars and Eva Le Gallienne, the latter seen briefly as Hamlet's mother.

Moss Hart's screenplay is balanced, taking the audience in and out of the Shakespearean scenes smoothly. The ending particularly, again thanks to a fine bit of staging and brilliant acting by Burton, has merit and winds the film at just the right note. Dunne's direction is imaginative and manages to build up tensions in what primarily is a conversation piece. It may be the job of a megging novice, but one wouldn't know it.

As a producer, Dunne has done himself proud, for this is a richly mounted production that delights the eye. Charles G. Clarke's lensing is great in every respect, and the De Luxe color is perfect. It all adds up to a very fine production. *Hift.*

Lilacs in the Spring
(BRITISH—SONGS)
(COLOR)

Herbert Wilcox filmusical starring Anna Neagle and Errol Flynn, latter making song and dance bow. Bright exploitation angles to hypo b.o. prospects.

London, Dec. 21.

Republic release of Herbert Wilcox production. Stars Anna Neagle, Errol Flynn, David Farrar; features Kathleen Harrison, Peter Graves, Helen Haye. Directed by Herbert Wilcox. Adapted from Robert Nesbitt's "The Glorious Days," by Harold Purcell; camera (Trucolor), Max Greene; editor, Reginald Beck; music, Harry Parr Davis; incidental score, Robert Fernon. At London Pavilion, Dec. 21, '54. Running time, **94 MINS.**

Carole Beaumont / Lillian Grey / Queen Victoria / Nell Gwyn	Anna Neagle
John Beaumont	Errol Flynn
Charles King / King Charles	David Farrar
Kate	Kathleen Harrison
Albert Gutman / Prince Albert	Peter Graves
Lady Drayton	Helen Haye
Old George	Scott Sanders
1st Woman	Alma Taylor
2nd Woman	Hetty King
Hollywood Director	Alan Gifford
Young Carole	Jennifer Mitchell
Very Young Carole	Gillian Harrison
Reporter	George Margo

The vehicle chosen by Anna Neagle to mark her return to the legit stage in Coronation year has been turned into a filmusical by producer - director Herbert Wilcox. Apart from a few minor cuts, it follows the pattern of the original stage success. In its screen form this is likely to have the same b.o. impact, appealing mainly to the carriage trade. In America (where it is being released by United Artists), its success will depend largely on the exploitation possibilities of Errol Flynn in his first song and dance role.

The film, like the original play, "The Glorious Days," is a cavalcade of history in which Miss Neagle plays a variety of roles including Nell Gwyn and the young Queen Victoria. In the original legit version she also played the aging Queen, but this had been omitted from the screenplay.

As the story begins, she is seen as a wartime service performer who suffers concussion during an air-raid on London and imagines herself to be Nell Gwyn, with David Farrar playing King Charles. Plot returns to the scene of the accident where she is being courted by a British soldier of German origin, and then goes to his grandmother's country house in Windsor. Another blackout, and she is Queen Victoria introducing the waltz to her court to the music of Johann Strauss.

And just to add to the variety of roles, Miss Neagle subsequently plays her own mother in the days when she was courted and married to Errol Flynn, the man who elevated her to stardom (he was lost in the crowd after the war) and then found fame and fortune in Hollywood via the birth of the talkies.

The production, with its snippets of stage musicals and spectacular dance sequences, has a colorful and opulent look; it is, however, a little obscure in its development, brashly sentimental and somewhat confusing. Miss Neagle sails through her various roles with the elegant poise for which she is renowned, discounting her attempts in song and dance fields. Errol Flynn, in a part which calls for emotional overtones, does surprisingly well and his limited attempts in the song and dance fields are worthy of commendation. David Farrar is not too well served as Miss Neagle's producer-admirer. Kathleen Harrison has a typical part as a cockney barmaid. Peter Graves, from the original stage production, plays the other suitor, and also Prince Albert.

The songs include classics of the calibre of "Lily of Laguna," "Tipperary," "Blightly," "We'll Gather Lilacs," with Noel Coward's "Dance Little Lady" and John Neat's "Lassie from Lancashire." Harry Parr Davies composed original music, with an excellent incidental score by Robert Farnon. Philip and Betty Buchel devised the imaginative dance sequences. *Myro.*

Underwater!
(SUPERSCOPE-COLOR)

Treasure-hunting under the Caribbean with aqualung-equipped Jane Russell; deep-sea diving excitement and good b.o. prospects.

Hollywood, Jan. 10.

RKO release of Harry Tatelman production. Stars Jane Russell; costars Gilbert Roland, Richard Egan, Lori Nelson; features Robert Keith, Joseph Calleia, Eugene Iglesias, Ric Roman. Directed by John Sturges. Screenplay, Walter Newman ;based on a story by Hugh King and Robert B. Bailey; camera (Technicolor), Harry J. Wild; underwater photography, Lamar Boren; editors, Stuart Gilmore, Frederic Knudtson; music, Roy Webb. Previewed Jan. 6, '55. Running time, **98 MINS.**

Theresa	Jane Russell
Dominic	Gilbert Roland
Johnny	Richard Egan
Gloria	Lori Nelson
Father Cannon	Robert Keith
Rico	Joseph Calleia
Miguel	Eugene Iglesias
Jesus	Ric Roman

(*Aspect ratio:* 2-1)

This tale of high adventure under the Caribbean puts together a number of salable entertainment features that can mean money at the boxoffice. Not the least of the commercial aspects is an aqualung-equipped Jane Russell mermaiding in the ocean depths. Her name and the generally okay excitement stirred up by the treasure-hunting plot should attract good business.

Film is RKO's first SuperScope release. The 2-to-1 aspect ratio produces a big picture excellently proportioned to show off the pictorial splendors achieved by Harry J. Wild's lensing above the water and by Lemar Boren's under the ocean. SuperScope's versatility was further demonstrated at the preview by the use of a CinemaScope projection lens, point being that the RKO-sponsored optical process is adaptable to houses already equipped for anamorphic projection.

Picture is a production first for Harry Tatelman and the showmanly round of commercial values assembled gives him a good initial credit. Even stronger overseeing could have cured some script flaws, and the sometimes slack pacing could have been helped by eliminating several unnecessary sequences. Overall, though, it's the b.o. worth that carries the most weight, and the payoff for this one should be profitable.

While Miss Russell is the main cast attraction as far as name value goes, the story is slanted towards Richard Egan, her husband, and Gilbert Roland, adventurer, who are diving for the treasure aboard a sunken galleon. Miss Russell is a fetching sight, whether plumbing the depths or lounging comfortably aboard ship. On her, skin-diving equipment seems almost superfluous, but good taste in the production doesn't make an overly obvious point of her natural attractions.

Egan and Roland handle the masculine spots easily, both having the kind of muscles that look good when bared, as well as enough acting skill to take ample care of the story heroics. Robert Keith, good as a priest with a knowledge of sunken treasure who is along on the cruise, and Lori Nelson, scantly used but good to look at, are the other principals in the treasure-questing group.

Suspense is whipped up by John Sturges' direction in detailing the threats to the little group, both above and below the waters of the Caribbean. Underneath lurk sharks and the danger the galleon will slip from its precarious perch on a submerged ledge and sink beyond reach, taking some or all of the diving trio with it. On the surface the treasure-hunters are threatened by Joseph Calleia, Cuban shark fisherman and his crew, who see the possibility of hijacking easy riches. Calleia and his crew are effective.

Sturges' direction is hampered for the first half of the footage by more dialog than the picture's pace can comfortably assimilate, but once the unnecessary talk and extraneous sequences are out of the way, the pace tightens and thrills are consistent. Work of the divers around and in the old wreck while blasting out treasure is often hackle-raising in its thrills and the Technicolor photography shows it all up in sharp, detailed beauty.

The good basis for high adventure was scripted by Walter Newman from a story by Hugh King and Robert B. Bailey. Roy Webb's score, directed by C. Bakaleinikoff is excellent, as are the Latune numbers injected here and there by Perez Prado and a small crew. Underwater sound effects add to the entertainment. *Brog.*

Svengali
(BRITISH—COLOR)
British film version of Gerald du Maurier yarn with Hildegarde Neff and Donald Wolfit starred; sombre melodrama most suitable for arty houses.

London, Jan. 4.,
Renown Pictures release of George Minter production. Stars Hildegarde Neff, Donald Wolfit, Terence Morgan. Directed by Noel Langley. Screenplay, Noel Langley, from story by George du Maurier; camera (Eastmancolor), Wilkie Cooper; editor, John Pomeroy; music, William Alwyn. At Gaumont, London. Running time, 82 MINS.
Trilby .... Hildegarde Neff
Svengali .... Donald Wolfit
Billy .... Terence Morgan
Laird .... Derek Bond
Taffy .... Paul Rogers
Gecko .... David Kossoff
Durien .... Hubert Gregg
Patrick O'Ferral .... Noel Purcell
Carrel .... Alfie Bass
Barizel .... Harry Secombe
Police Inspector .... Peter Illing
Mrs. Bagot .... Joan Haythorne
Dubose .... Hugh Cross
Dodor .... David Oxley
Lambert .... Richard Pearson

This is a heavy, sombre and dated melodrama, based on George du Maurier's well-known novel, in which Hildegarde Neff makes a highly attractive British film debut in the role of Trilby while Donald Wolfit is a very sinister Svengali. Its boxoffice prospects are questionable but this British-made pic should get by if carefully sold. It may be a difficult proposition in America where its main appeal will be in arty houses.

Wolfit took over the title role after Robert Newton walked out in the early stages of production. This is a shrewd replacement because his rich interpretation of the dominating Svengali proves a solid basis for the production. At all times he suggests the dirty, swarthy and unwholesome character whose grip on the girl remains until his last gasp.

Miss Neff, in her first British film, gives a warm and sympathetic performance as Trilby, the girl who's taken out of a saloon to become an artist's model. She falls in love with a young English artist, the plans of marriage being ruined by an interfering parent. There is some vagueness as to the way in which she falls under Svengali's power and how he makes her an internationally famous singer. But

even so there is dramatic force in these sequences, particularly in the climax when the grip is relaxed and she is unable to utter a note at a Covent Garden concert.

Terence Morgan seems a little out of character as the British artist with whom she falls in love but Derek Bond and Paul Rogers are entirely believable as his two British friends. David Kossoff gives a solid and reliable performance as Svengali's friend and violin-accompanist, with Hubert Gregg, Noel Purcell, Alfie Bass and Harry Secombe heading a safe supporting cast.

Noel Langley has vigorously directed the piece from his own script while Wilkie Cooper has done an excellent job of color lensing. William Alwyn's music is firstrate and Elisabeth Schwarzkopf's singing for Miss Neff's solo recitals is one of the artistic highspots. *Myro.*

Battle Taxi

Commonplace. Script and production makes this a dull second half.

United Artists release of Ivan Tors-Art Arthur production. Stars Sterling Hayden; features Arthur Franz and Marshall Thompson. Directed by Herbert L. Strock. Screenplay, Malvin Wald; camera, Lothrop B. Worth; editor, Jodie Copelan; music, Herman Sukman. Previewed Jan. 3, '55. Running time, 82 MINS.
Capt. Russ Edwards......Sterling Hayden
Lieut. Pete Stacy.........Arthur Franz
2nd Lieut. Tim Vernon
                        Marshall Thompson
S'Sgt. Slate Klein..........Leo Needham
Lt. Col. Stoneham...........Jay Barney
Wounded GI ....John Goddard
Lieut. Joe Kirk........Robert Sherman
Lieut. Marty Staple........Joel Marston
M'Sgt. Joe Murdock........John Dennis
Blue Boy Three-Gene....Dale Hutchinson
Lazy Joker Two.........Andy Andrews
Lieut. Smiley Jackson....Vance Skarsted
Medic Capt. Larsen........Michael Colgan
Co-Pilot Harry..Capt. Vincent McGovern

Sights are on the Korean war but this time the requisite combat wallop is in short supply. "Battle Taxi" refers to the U. S. Air Rescue Service in action. Undoubtedly there was plenty of screenplay potential in the operations of this heretofore unspotlighted adjunct to the fighting forces but "Taxi" doesn't deliver.

Ivan Tors-Art Arthur production has some exploitation value in the nature of the subject matter, this being the exploits of a helicopter element. Further, there's the line about the film having been made in cooperation with the Department of Defense. However, the finished product emerges as a lower-case programmer at most, with stock footage used liberally and in some instances not fitted in smoothly. Overall result is a pic of limited conviction, the story being no help.

Sterling Hayden has the lead as head of the air rescue squadron, part of whose job is to convince his pilots that they're on airborne missions of mercy and not to engage in grandstand heroics. Arthur Franz, as a former jet jockey now under Hayden's command, is the one who'd rather take on the enemy in combat, until he learns— without surprise to the audience— the wisdom of Hayden's counsel.

Direction by Herbert L. Strock is commonplace, and the script similarly allows no ingenuity to come through. Music and editing contribute little. *Gene.*

One Good Turn
(BRITISH)

Norman Wisdom's second British comedy; Fine for the home market but unlikely in the U.S.

London, Jan. 4.
General Film Distributors' release of Two Cities (Maurice Cowan) production. Stars Norman Wisdom, Joan Rice, Shirley Abicair, Thora Hird. Directed by John Paddy Carstairs. Screenplay, Maurice Cowan, John Paddy Carstairs, Ted Willis; camera, Jack Cox; editor, Geoffrey Foot; music, John Addison, with music and lyrics by Norman Newell and Norman Wisdom. At Dominion, London. Running time, 90 MINS.
Norman .... Norman Wisdom
Iris .... Joan Rice
Mary .... Shirley Abicair
Cook .... Thora Hird
Alec .... William Russell
Bigley .... Richard Caldicot
Tuppeny .... Marjorie Fender
Jimmy .... Keith Gilman
Matron .... Joan Ingram
Igor Petrovitch .... Harold Kasket
Cinema Manager .... Fred Kitchen Jr.
Prof. Dofee .... David Hurst
Hypnotist's Stooge ..... Michael Balfour
Gunner Mac .... Ricky McCullough

Norman Wisdom's first entry into the British film scene a year back in Maurice Cowan's production of "Trouble in Store" was one of the top grossers in the domestic market. The b.o. formula has been repeated in "One Good Turn" and the results locally probably will assume the same proportions. Notwithstanding its great hopes in the home market, the film is a dim prospect for the U.S.

Once again Wisdom is cast as the "little man" but the script gives him none of the opportunities to develop his potentialities as a British Chaplin and he has to rely on one slapstick incident after another for the laughs. In the main, these are frequently unrelated although there is a thin sort of story thread of how the star, as a sort of general factotum, saves the orphanage.

There is good measure of comic incident but little invention. The direction allows the star to run riot through a sequence of events starting with the losing of his pants and unconsciously becoming the hero of the London to Brighton walk, to a forced climax. There is plenty of pathos from Wisdom but only a small measure of artistic talent from the remainder of the cast. Joan Rice, Shirley Abicair and Thora Hird in the principal roles are bogged down by the script.

A couple of numbers, one by Norman Newell and the other by the star, provide a pleasing diversion. *Myro.*

Das Zweite Leben
(Double Destiny)
(FRENCH-GERMAN)
Frankfurt, Jan. 4.
Columbia release of Stuart Schulberg and Gilbert de Goldschmidt production (for Trans-Rhein and Madeleine Film). Stars Simone Simon, Michel Auclair, Barbara Rutting. Directed by Victor Vicas. Screenplay, Frederick Grendel, Dieter Werner, based on Jean Giraudoux story; camera, Andre Bac; editors, Ira Oberberg, Georges Klotz; music, H. M. Majewski. At Universum Theatre, Stuttgart. Running time, 90 MINS.
Siegfried .... Michel Auclair
Francoise .... Simone Simon
Sybil .... Barbara Rutting
Reinhard .... Bernard Wicki
Professor .... Rolf Gonnauckhoff
Mittelmeier .... Gert Froebe
Garreaux .... Yves Brainville

For patrons of arty films, "Double Destiny" shapes as a likely contender for 1955. Based on a Jean Giraudoux story of the last World War, called "Siegfried," it became a hit play in Paris back in the 1920's. It is planned as a stage entry in its original version this winter on Broadway. With a some-

what altered script, written by Frederick Grendel and Dieter Werner, this was done in French and German. It appears to have a good chance for U.S. arty theatres.

Plot concerns Michel Auclair, as Siegfried, a young French painter who is called into the army in the first World War. He's in love with Francoise, sweet-voiced Simone Simon. But before he can marry her, the wedding bureau closes and he plants a ring on her finger with promises of eternal love and rushes off to war, where he is shell-shocked and loses his memory.

Although the plot seems based on some unlikely coincidences (considerably lightened from the original drama which was a highly political) the excellent direction of Victor Vicas makes the story come across with feeling. Particularly outstanding are the dramatic closeups of the moment when Auclair, in search of the "wife" he believes is somewhere in Germany, realizes he is truly a man without identity, and the moving scene in which he and Simone Simon first encounter after the war. Vicas, whose directorial talents will shortly be on view in the U.S. with the opening of "No Way Back," has already been signed by 20th-Fox for his unusual work.

There are two standard performances. Miss Rutting, winner of the German Oscar for her acting, plays the "other woman" with such sensitivity that the audience almost yearns for Auclair to remain with her. Bernard Wicki, as her brother, the teacher who returns from captivity in Russia, is exceptionally fine. Miss Simon, proves a looker capable of a warm performance.

The film is a pioneer in French-German co-production which nicely balances the delicacies of national tastes. Musical and technical credits are apt supports. *Haze.*

Emperor and the Golem
(CZECHOSLOVAKIAN-COLOR)

Overlong fantasy-comedy with slim b.o. chances in the U.S.

Artkino release of Czechoslovak State Film Studio production. Features Jan Werich, Marie Vasova, Natasa Gollova, Jiri Plashy. Directed by Martin Fric. Screenplay, Jiri Brdecka and Werich; camera, Jan Stallich; music, Julius Kalas. At Stanley, N.Y., Jan. 8, '55. Running time 110 Mins.
The Emperor,
The Baker .... Jan Werich
Countess Strada .... Marie Vasova
Kathy .... Natasa Gollova
Kelley .... Jiri Plashy

As the first Czechoslovakian film to play the Stanley Theatre, N.Y., in five years, "The Emperor and the Golem" is an interesting import. For the picture as such affords an insight on the Czech film industry. As entertainment it's another matter since this overlong fantasy-comedy is tedious fare despite a few humorous scenes.

Writers Jiri Brdecka and Jan Werich drew upon Jewish legend to unfold a tale of a crazed Czech emperor enamoured of women, eternal youth, alchemy and the Golem. Latter is an artificial man, fashioned from clay, who was popularly believed around the 16th century to be a giant that would protect the Jews in times of adversity.

But instead of developing the story purely around the emperor and the Golem as the French-made version did in 1937, the Brdecka-Werich screenplay creates a situation in which a baker successfully poses as the real sovereign. Through this device the scripters attempt to introduce a variety of levity, most of which falls in the slapstick category.

Co-scripter Werich, who essays the dual role of the aging emperor and the lusty baker, provides some amusing moments and shows genuine thesping talent whether he's quaffing the elixer of youth or training a lascivious eye on a bevy of cuties who frequent the royal menage.

Marie Vesova, as the bona fide emperor's vis-a-vis, is suitably shapely and Natașa Gollova has ample feminine charms as a magician's aide who carries on a romance with the baker. Jiri Plashy scores nicely as the magico. Competent support is provided by a long cast. Direction of Martin Fric frequently wavers as though he's undecided to stress the comedy aspects or concentrate on the narrative.

Curiously, this Czechoslovak State Film Studio production contains little propaganda in contrast with the unsubtle messages usually found in Soviet-made films. However, the "message" in the "Emperor" if it can be called that tends to fit in with the present Kremlin regime's theory of "co-existence."

For prestidigitator Plashy at one point sings a little jingle which goes something like this: "We'll all live better when we share what we have . . . when we live in peace the world will be a better place for you and me." Lines such as that, of course, can be found in most children's story books. Those looking for social significance might be impressed with the final scene where the baker harnesses the Golem to provide heat for the ovens in order that the poor might have bread.

Insofar as the film's technical aspects are concerned the camerawork is of poor quality and the editing faulty. Lensed in color (presumably Sovcolor), the tints don't measure up to Technicolor or Eastman Color. Frequently the hues on print screened at the Stanley appeared washed out and ill defined. Moreover, the action and story could have been sped up considerably if 15 or 20 minutes had been trimmed from the footage. Costumes of Jiri Trnka are eye-catching. *Gilb.*

Votre Devoue Blake
(Yours Truly Blake)
(FRENCH)

Paris, Jan. 4.

Cocinor release of Cocinor-Chaillot Film Production. Stars Eddie Constantine; features Danielle Godet, Colette Doreal, Simone Paris, Jacques Dynam, Robert Dalban. Directed by Jean Laviron; technical advisor, Jerry Epstein. Screenplay, Epstein, Jacques Vilfrid; camera, Jacques Lemare; editor, Andree Feix; music, Jeff Davis. At Balzac, Paris. Running time, **100 MINS.**

Blake .... Eddie Constantine
Michele .... Danielle Godet
Stella .... Colette Doreal
Gaxton .... Jacques Dynam
Inspector .... Robert Dalban
Eliane .... Simone Paris

There is no doubt that Eddie Constantine, U. S. singer, has become a pic b.o. name to reckon with here. His series of pix, filled with mayhem and all the attributes of the U.S. gangster films, have caught on and these cheaply made films are reaping a b.o. harvest. However, the character and situations are getting repititious and a change of pace is called for. Films have the production aspects of the U.S. "B" film, and, as such, have little value for any possible Stateside chances. U.S. original is still too superior to enable these to make the necessary inroads, but this looks to follow its predecessors in take here.

In this one, Constantine is a pilot who gets mixed up in a murder case in Paris during a three-day vacation. He picks up a film star one night and next day she is accused of murder. He goes after the killers and after a record number of fights and chases proves her innocence and flies off into the blue.

Story telling is simple, but bowls along merrily, which is what they want here. Director Jean Laviron has not been able to breathe the feel of suspense and character into this, and it remains a knockabout type of gangster pic. Constantine drinks less and has fewer women in this, but his phlegm and insouciance are still the same, and he grins and batters his way through this in acceptable fashion. Danielle Godet has a hard time convincing that she is a film star, and heavies and molls are acceptable. Lensing and editing are good, and peppering of script with many visual gags pay off in some spots but are too often cliche and gratuitous. *Mosk.*

Aleko
(RUSSIAN — COLOR)

Artkino release of Lenfilm production. Stars A. Ognivisev, M. Reizen, I. Zubkovskaya. Directed by Sergei Sidelov. Screenplay, A. Abramov, G. Roshal, based on poem by A. S. Pushkin; camera, A. Nazarov; music, Sergei Rachmaninoff. At Stanley, N.Y., starting Dec. 23, '54. Running time, **61 MINS.**

Aleko .... A. Ognivisev
The Old Gypsy .... M. Reizen
Zemphyra .... I. Zubkovskaya
Young Gypsy .... S. Kuznetsov
Old Gypsy Woman ...... B. Zlatogorova

(In Russian; English Titles)

"Aleko" is described as a color-film opera based on A. S. Pushkin's poem, "Gypsies." It boasts music by Sergei Rachmaninoff and Pushkin's name, which has been associated with the better-known Russian pictures. The music often has tremendous sweep. But this picture is so badly directed and so statically produced, it's appeal will be confined to the few Russian-language arty houses in the U.S.

Basically, the yarn is this. A fresh gypsy youth loves girl. Girl is already married. But she doesn't let that deter her—so the husband kills them both, and the gypsy band moves on. The acting and lack of any action excepting the slaying scene does not in any way enhance this simple plot.

The cast is dotted with Russo prize-winning actors, three of them having copped Stalin awards. Maybe the director was jealous, for he seldom permits the thespian talents to shine. The three Russian prize grabbers, A. Ognivisev, as Aleko; M. Reizen, cast as the girl's father; and I. Zubkovskaya, the girl (wedded young woman), sing with charm, all three having excellent voices.

Whole picture plays like a filmed opera, only with even less action. One of the redeeming factors is that the color (Sovcolor) looks like the best to date, with the director (Sergei Sidelov) and cameraman A. Nazarov apparently striving for pictures—que color portraits. But that's all they are—inanimate tinted portraits. *Wear.*

Six Bridges to Cross

Cops-and-robbers melodrama around the multi-million dollar holdup in Boston. Tony Curtis and generally good exploitation prospects.

Hollywood, Jan. 14.

Universal release of Aaron Rosenburg production. Stars Tony Curtis, George Nader, Julie Adams; features Joy C. Flippen. Sal Mineo, Jan Merlin, Richard Castle, William Murphy. Directed by Joseph Pevney. Screenplay, Sydney Boehm; based on the story "They Stole $2,500,000—And Got Away With It" by Joseph F. Dinneen; camera, William Daniels; editor, Russell Schoengarth; technical adviser, Lt. Dan Moynihan, Boston Police Department; song, Jeff Chandler, Henry Mancini; vocals by Sammy Davis Jr. Previewed Jan. 4, '55. Running time, **95 MINS.**

Jerry Florea .... Tony Curtis
Edward Gallagher .... George Nader
Ellen Gallagher .... Julie Adams
Vincent Concannon ...... Jay C. Flippen
Jerry Florea (as a boy) .... Sal Mineo
Andy Norris .... Jan Merlin
Skids Radzievich .... Richard Castle
Red Flanagan .... William Murphy
Sanborn .... Kendall Clark
Sherman .... Don Keefer

(Aspect ratio: 2-1)

The exploitation boxoffice prospects for this cops-and-robbers melodrama shape up well, with name of Tony Curtis to attract the younger filmgoers.

While it's not mentioned by name, the big Brink holdup several years back in Boston will be a ballyhoo peg on which to build exploitation interest for this story of a young hood who engineers an armored car service holdup in that city. Developed from Joseph F. Dinneen's "They Stole $2,500,000—And Got Away With It," the Aaron Rosenberg production smartly avoids flashbacks, telling its story from the beginning and thereby building interest in the outcome of Curtis' life of crime from the time the plot picks him up as a juvenile delinquent on the streets of Boston. Time lapses in the young man's crime development are covered with documentary-type narration, and Curtis gives the character a good reading, rating a modicum of sympathy, even though viewers know he is unregenerated and must die at the finale.

Played up in the script by Sydney Boehm is the relationship between Curtis and George Nader, policeman, that carries through the years. Nader and his wife, Julie Adams, do what they can to straighten out the young tough but he enjoys his crime thrills and goes from one job to jail and back to another job until, near the end, feigning respectability and a desire to reform, he plots the big job, pulls it off successfully and then dies at the hands of his own gang when he decides to give back the loot so he can remain in the states.

There's a soap opera angle introduced early by establishing that a bullet wound given Curtis by Nader on his first arrest has made it impossible for the hoodlum to ever be a father. It never means very much to the inevitable outcome, even when the plot has Curtis marrying a widow with two kids when he's seeming to go straight.

Joseph Pevney's direction has the footage rolling off at a good pace and, generally, manages to get acceptable performances from the cast, although, with the stress on Curtis, Nader's cop character doesn't have a sustained forcefulness. Miss Adams isn't given much to do, nor is Jay C. Flippen and other cast members. Sal Mineo does a creditable job of playing Curtis as a youth.

Cast and credits are run off at the tag end of the film while the title song, written by Jeff Chandler and Henry Mancini, is being sung by Sammy Davis, Jr. Lensing by William Daniels helps to carry out the documentary flavor strived for in the presentation and the editing is good. *Brog.*

To Paris With Love
(BRITISH—COLOR)

Alec Guinness in lightweight British comedy with Paris setting; strong marquee main asset for U.S. market.

London, Jan. 11.

General Film Distributors release of a Two Cities-Anthony Darnborough production. Stars Alec Guinness, Odile Versois. Directed by Robert Hamer. Screenplay, Robert Buckner; camera (Technicolor), Reginald Wyer; editor, Anne V. Coates; music, Edwin Astley. At Odeon, Leicester Square, London. Running time, **78 MINS.**

Col. Sir Edgar Fraser..... Alec Guinness
Lizette Marconnet........ Odile Versois
Jon Fraser .... Vernon Gray
Victor de Colville..... Jacques Francois
Sylvia Gilbert ...... Elina Labourdette
Leon de Colville .... Austin Trevor
Georges Duprez ..... Claude Romain
Suzanne de Colville..... Maureen Davis
Aristide Marconnet .....Jacques Brunius
Madame Marconnet ..... Pamela Stirling
Madame Alvarez Mollie Hartley Milburn
Pierre .... Michael Anthony
Head Porter .... Andre Mikhelson
Night Porter .... Jacques Cey
Claude Collier

An intriguing plot situation, Alec Guinness as the star attraction and a Paris location (handsomely lensed in Technicolor), should spell sturdy b.o. biz for this pic. This Two Cities comedy, however, is too lightweight to make the grade unreservedly and will score mainly via the personal lure of the star. His marquee value, in the U.S. particularly, will be a major selling angle.

Prime weakness of the finished film is the inadequacy of Robert Buckner's screenplay. He's taken an interesting and amusing theme but has developed it in a casual and pedestrian manner. The opening scenes have a typical Guinness sparkle, but the subsequent two reels (in which the plot line is established) have a tendency to be repetitive. And with a performer of the stature of this star, it seems a little ungracious to introduce bits of commonplace farce.

The opening sequence shows Alec Guinness in the role of a British baronet arriving for a Paris vacation with his son in a Rolls Royce. The father thinks the boy has had a sheltered existence and that Paris will be "good for him"; the son, on the other hand, considers that his father has had a lonely time on his Scottish estate and could also benefit by a diversion. So papa picks up a young redhead (Odile Versois) for the boy and the son collects a more mature woman (Elina Labourdette) for his father. It doesn't work out as planned but there are some neat comedy sequences before the dual romances are sorted out.

Robert Hamer has directed with his usual skill, and once more reveals a nice flair for light comedy. The star, as is to be expected, gives a flawless performance, too often overshadowing other male members of the cast.

Odile Versois has an appealing, piquante charm and Elina Labourdette is attractive as the more mature woman. Vernon Gray gives a limp performance as the Guinness offspring, but there is a robust comedy bit by Jacques Brunius as Miss Versois' taxi-driver father.

Other supporting roles are adequately filled. *Myro.*

A Life in the Balance

Mexico City-localed and filmed melodrama. Okay programmer.

Hollywood, Jan. 18.

20th-Fox release of Leonard Goldstein (Panoramic) production. Stars Ricardo Montalban; costars Anne Bancroft, Lee Marvin; features Jose Perez, Rodolfo Acosta. Directed by Harry Horner. Screenplay, Robert Presnell Jr., Leo Townsend; from a story by Georges Simenon; camera, J. Gomez Urquiza; editors, George Gittens. George Crone; music, Raul Lavista. Previewed Jan. 13, '55. Running time, **74 MINS.**

Antonio Gomez ...... Ricardo Montalban
Maria Ibinia .... Anne Bancroft
The Murderer .... Lee Marvin
Paco Gomez .... Jose Perez
Lieutenant Fernando .... Rodolfo Acosta
Captain Saldana .... Carlos Muzquiz
Sergeant .... George Trevino
Andres Martinez .... Jose Torvay
Carla Arlotta .... Eva Calvo
Carmen Martinez .... Fanny Schiller
Dona Lucrecia .... Tamara Garina
Porter .... Pascual G. Pena
Pedro .... Antonio Carbajal
(*Aspect ratio:* 1.33-1)

This Panoramic production, being released by 20th-Fox, makes interesting use of a Mexico City background to give a somewhat different touch to its melodramatic plot. It's an okay entry for the program market.

Produced by the late Leonard Goldstein and directed by Harry Horner, filming took place in Mexico's chief city and all of the cast, with the exception of Lee Marvin, play Latins. In fact, practically all are, so there is an authentic feel to the footage, further abetted by the standard ratio, black-and-white lensing by J. Gomez Urquiza as the streets, buildings and carnival-spirited natives are put on display. Ricardo Montalban and Anne Bancroft topline the cast with Marvin, the latter as a psycho American with a religious compulsion to kill those he believes are sinners. His latest victim is a blonde in the apartment court in which Montalban, itinerant musician and widower, and his small son live. Circumstances make it appear Montalban is the guilty party, but the boy has spotted the killer and is trailing him through the city while police look for the father, himself out on the town celebrating a chance meeting with Miss Bancroft. The screenplay by Robert Presnell Jr. and Leo Townsend, from a Georges Simenon story, boils up to its climax when the killer grabs the boy and a street chase ensues, winding up on the campus and amidst the Beautiful buildings of Mexico's University as Marvin is trapped and the boy saved.

Montalban and Miss Bancroft pair capitally as the poor lovers put through a rather trying time, and Marvin does okay by the psychopathic killer. Very good as the boy is Jose Perez and among others showing up well are Rodolfo Acosta, detective lieutenant; Carlos Muzquiz, George Trevino, Jose Torvay, Eva Calvo, Fanny Schiller and Tamara Garina.

Background score by Raul Lavista is keyed to the Mexican locale and the technical assists come off capably. *Brog.*

Port of Hell

Program meller which stacks shade above the average supporter because of good acting.

Hollywood, Jan. 15.

Allied Artists release of William F. Broidy production. Stars Dane Clark, Carole Mathews, Wayne Morris; features Marshall Thompson, Marjorie Lord, Harold Peary, Otto Waldis. Directed by Harold Schuster. Screenplay, Tom Hubbard, Fred Eggers, Gil Doud; from story by Doud and D. D. Beauchamp; camera, John Martin; editor, Ace Herman; music, Edward J. Kay. Previewed Jan. 10, '55. Running time, **80 MINS.**

Pardee .... Dane Clark
Julie Povich .... Carole Mathews
Stanley Povich .... Wayne Morris
Marsh Walker .... Marshall Thompson
Kay Walker .... Marjorie Lord
Leo .... Harold Perry
Snyder .... Otto Waldis
Nick .... Tom Hubbard
Sparks .... Charles Fredericks
Parker .... Jim Alexander
Enemy Radio Operator. Victor Sen Young
(*Aspect ratio:* 1.85-1)

Cast principals give a good account of themselves thespwise in "Port of Hell" to raise film a notch above average supporting fare. There's a provocative tag for marquee purposes, along with names of Dane Clark, Carole Mathews and Wayne Morris.

Players do much to inject credible air into the rather routine melodramatics offered in script by Tom Hubbard, Fred Eggers and Gil Doud, from a story by Doud and D. D. Beauchamp. Clark plays a port warden of L.A. Harbor, a man seemingly so devoted to his duty he has no heart—that is, until Miss Mathews comes along. His ironhand rule of the office, however, results in discovery of a freighter docked in harbor with an atomic bomb aboard—to be set off within 12 hours by a Communist "detonating" ship hovering far offshore. Keeping the whole thing q.t. so as to prevent panic, Clark, with help of Wayne Morris, his former enemy and Miss Mathews' brother, tows the ship out to sea where it subsequently explodes harmlessly.

William F. Broidy has cast his production well and, under Harold Schuster's direction, most of the players fare well.

Clark gives a vigorous performance, while Miss Mathews shows up exceptionally well via a natural, yet dominating portrayal that always commands attention. Morris is okay, as are Marshall Thompson, as Clark's side-kick, and Marjorie Lord, as Thompson's spouse. Harold (The Great Gildersleeve) Peary plays a Portuguese fisherman well, and Otto Waldis is fine as a ship captain.

Technical contributions are stock, although film could stand tightening somewhat from its present 80-minute length. *Neal.*

The True and the False
(SWEDISH)

English-language film made in Sweden by Signe Hasso who produced and stars. Story and production make this a possibility only for the second half of duals.

Helene Davis Pictures release of Signe Hasso production. Stars Signe Hasso and William Langford. Directed by Michael Road. Screenplay, Bob Condon; based on "La Grande Breteche" by Honore de Balzac and "The Old Maid" by Guy de Maupassant; camera, Sven Nykvist. Previewed in N.Y. Jan. 15, '55. Running time, **79 MINS.**

Bride-to-be .... Signe Hasso
Bridegroom-to-Be ...... William Langford
In "La Grande Breteche"
Josephine de Merrit.... Signe Hasso
Louis de Merrit........William Langford
Edmond Montez .... Michael Road
Goronflot .... Stig Olin
Gertrude, chambermaid .... Lilli Kjellin
Gertrude, 50 years later..Naima Wifstrand
Innkeeper .... Ragnar Arvedson
Innkeeper's wife .... Ann Bibby
In "The Old Maid"
Agnes Maubert .... Signe Hasso
Andre Morain .... William Langford
Agnes' father .... Ragnar Arvedson
Helene .... Ruth Brady
Aunt Emilie .... Hjordis Petterson
Officer .... Stig Olin

Swedish actress Signe Hasso takes on the dual chores of producer and star in this English-language film made in her native land. To put it bluntly, Miss Hasso emerges as a better actress than producer. "The True and the False" is a dull, rambling picture. It's not for the art house, but might find a niche in dual situations experiencing difficulty in filling up their programs.

For her debut as a producer, Miss Hasso has selected two short stories by a pair of literary greats—Balzac and deMaupassant. Both yarns are essentially mood pieces, but have been presented in such a manner that they lose whatever effectiveness they might have had. The separate stories are tied together with a silly modern connecting narrative. It involves a young couple on the eve of their marriage. Kis / ; her husband-to-be good nigh., the prospective bride browses through her wedding gifts, chances on a book, and sits down to read. She selects Balzac's "La Grande Breteche."

The viewer is then confronted with a flashback as the Balzac story is unreeled. No sooner does "Bretche" gets under way when a character in the story begins telling a story, presenting the unique situation of a flashback within a flashback. The same thing occurs in the showing of deMaupassant's "The Old Maid."

After a confusing and sketchy opening, resulting in laughter from the preview audience, the Balzac yarn gets down to cases. It concerns the mystery surrounding an old, deserted French castle. It seems that the lady of the house is two-timing her husband. He unexpectedly comes home while she is entertaining her lover. The lover hides in the closet, the husband suspects and orders a servant to seal up the closet with bricks.

The de Maupassant story also involves a frustrated love affair. A young girl, guarded by a strict father, falls in love with a dashing, young officer. The officer is transferred to another post and the girl later learns that he never intended to marry her anyway, being only after a bride with money. She falls in the snow and her beauty is marred by frostbite. Later she becomes wealthy when her father dies, looks up her soldier friend, but does not accept him even when he tells her she's more beautiful than ever despite the scar. She gives all her money to the soldier and retires in seclusion.

Miss Hasso stars in all segments of the three-part yarn, and carries off her assignments well. William Langford is properly handsome and dashing as the bridegroom-to-be, the lover, and the officer. Rest of the cast carries off its duties in a matter-of-fact manner. Michael Road's direction goes off in all directions, giving the film a rather amateurish quality. technical aspects are only fair. *Holl.*

Ali-Baba
(FRENCH; COLOR)

Paris, Jan. 11.

Cinedis release of Film Cyclope production. Stars Fernandel; features Samia Gamal, Dieter Borsche, Henri Vilbert, Delmont. Directed by Jacques Becker. Screenplay, Becker, Marc Maurette, Cesare Zavattini; camera (Eastmancolor), Robert Le Febvre; editor, Marguerite Renoir; music, Paul Misraki. At Paris, Paris. Running time, **95 MINS.**

Clash between folk comedy aspect and exotic locale make the emphasis of this version of Ali-Baba's adventures an uneven pic. Spectacle is not tried for while whimsy and fantasy are also lacking. This leaves the main burden of the film on comic Fernandel's shoulders. This is not enough to make this come off, the languishing aspects making this primarily for European appeal on the Fernandel tag. For the U. S. this would have to be sold on name value and locale.

Pic is the first to be dubbed into Arabic for the large Eastern market and will easily amortize there. It lacks the adult treatment and charm for U. S. arty houses. The color cost print also rears its head, and, at best, this looks in only for special slotting for America, with the Fernandel name the best selling point.

Fernandel makes Ali-Baba a rather wily Marseillaise rather than an Oriental, and it is his mugging and playing of the crafty underling (who wins the girl in the end in spite of man's greed) that gives the pic its few laughs. Ali is sent by his brutal master to buy a wife for him who turns out to be belly dancer Samia Gamal. It is love at first sight, and he spends his time keeping her out of the clutches of his lecherous master. In looking for a present for her he gets mixed up in a raid by bandits. With his riches he buys the girl and a great house, but the bandits sneak into the party to get their gains back.

Fernandel runs the gamut of his grimaces. Director Jacques Becker has wisely let Miss Gamal's expressive anatomy speak for her for she utters only a handful of words. Becker has missed the usual verve, observation and charm he brings to a film, and this remains a nice gallery of color portraits with one massive scene as thousands follow Ali to the cave. Editing is good as are various lesser roles. *Mosk.*

Teaserama
(COLOR)

"Burlesque type" film with potential in sexploitation spots.

Beautiful Productions presentation of Irving Klaw production and release; associate producer, Paula Kramer. Stars Tempest Storm; features Betty Page, Trudy Wayne, Hedy Bey, Cherry Knight, Twinnie Wallen, Pepe & Roccio, Don Main, Chris La Chris, Vicki Lynn. Directed by Klaw. Camera (Eastman Color), Michael Slifka; editor, Les Orlebeck. Previewed N.Y., Jan. 13, '55. Running time, **69 MINS.**

"Teaserama is heralded by producer-director Irving Klaw as a "burlesque variety type revue feature. If the film even approached its billing it might be reasonably entertaining. For this low-budget venture is so woefully lacking in production values, continuity and taste that its market will be largely confined to exploitation spots specializing in "spicy pictures.

Accent on this entry is the female form. Its supplied in this instance by a contingent of some half-dozen strippers headed by

Tempest Storm. A tousle-haired redhead, she's generously supplied bosomwise. Although strategic areas are covered by bra and G-string, little is left to the imagination as she shakes and wiggles her anatomical salients.

It may be said that once you've seen Miss Storm you've seen 'em all. For the Misses Betty Page, Trudy Wayne, Chris La Chris et al also make with the strip routine, but by this time the law of diminishing returns is beginning to assert itself. Also involved in the proceedings are a pair of unbilled male burly comics and a so-so Latino terp turn tagged Pepe & Roccio.

Virtually all routines, incidentally, are done on some inlaid linoleum against a background of some yard goods hung on a wall. With exception of an occasional sofa, there are no sets or props as such. Most of the musical accompaniment sounds suspiciously like a piano, drum and a trumpet. Eastman Color camerawork of Michael Slifka, however, is fairly good considering the circumstances.

Apparently there's a market for this type product. For producer-director Klaw turned out a similar film last year titled "Varietease," and 1953 saw release of "Striporama," another picture in the same category. Withal, Harold Minsky and the Hirst circuit have nothing to fear competitionwise from "Teaserama." *Gilb.*

Das Zweite Leben
(The Second Life)
(GERMAN-FRENCH)

Berlin, Jan. 11.

Columbia release of Trans-Rhein-Madeleine production Stars Michel Auclair, Simone Simon, Barbara Ruetting, Bernhard Wicki. Directed by Victor Vicas. Screenplay, Dieter Werner, Frederic Grendel and Victor Vicas; camera, Andre Bac; music, Hans-Martin Majewski; sets, Alfred Buetow. At Cinema Paris, Berlin. **88 MINS.**

Siegfried .... Michel Auclair
Sybille .... Barbara Ruetting
Francoise .... Simone Simon
Reinhard .... Bernhard Wicki
Medico .... Rolf von Nauckhoff
Mittelmeier .... Gert Froebe

This German-French coproduction brings to the screen another variation of the old amnesia theme. It also attempts to promote understanding between the French and Germans. Pic represents high technical standards but, unfortunately, loses some of its dramatic grip via an implausible script. Although this film still has individuality, it may find it tough going at the b.o. The names of Michel Auclair and Simone Simon, however, may help its drawing power.

Based on ideas from Giraudoux's drama, "Siegfried," story concentrates on a French soldier who lost his memory from a serious wound received on a German battlefield of the last World War. Due to some mixup, he is mistakenly held for a German and continues living as such in the postwar years, unable to remember his past.

Strangely enough, he gradually becomes a "true-born" German and sets up a group of painters (he has not lost his former painting abilities) whose job it is to dedicate itself to "German culture" and to keep away any non-German art. (This group, incidentally, represents almost an unbelievable bunch of stupid, fanatic Germans who seem to be right out of Geobbels' cultural kitchen.) There is more or less a "happy" ending when the Frenchman, turned German, finds his true identity via his Parisian fiancee.

Main weakness of this basically interesting plot is the somewhat implausible central figure of the Frenchman who in his "second life" becomes a "genuine" German. Although mentally sick, he learns to speak German fluently. Also his German counterpart, a refugee from a Siberian prison camp, is hardly convincing.

Although Victor Vicas as co-scripter must also be blamed for the story's shortcomings, he deserves high praise for his directing job. As in "No Way Back," his first big pic, this also has a number of impressive scenes (particularly during the first half), which have genuine documentary flavor and give evidence of his remarkable abilities.

The acting varies. Auclair in the role of the Frenchman who lost his memory is amazingly good despite the handicaps of the script. Although lacking verve, Miss Simon as his French fiancee also is excellent. Barbara Ruetting. cast as Auclair's German girl, could have been more vivid, while Bernhard Wicki, usually a top-notch actor, seemingly became a victim of his material. As the German who returned from a Russian prison he is about the weakest in this film.

A special word of praise goes to Hans-Martin Majewski, creator of the fine musical score. Also worth mentioning is Andre Bac's exceptionally excellent camerawork. Other technical credits are sans flaws. Film, incidentally, has a German and also a French version, both being shown in Berlin. *Hans.*

Cuidado Con El Amor
(Watch Out for Love)
(MEXICAN; SONGS)

Mexico City, Jan. 11.

Producciones Zacarias production and release. Stars Pedro Infante and Elsa Aguirre; features Oscar Pulido and Eduardo (Lalo) Gonzalez. Directed and written by Miguel Zacarias. Camera, Raul Martinez Solares; music, Manuel Esperon. At Cines Olimpia and De las Americas, Mexico City. Running time, **103 MINS.**

Typically Mexican in style, development and presentation, this is the most entertaining Mexican comedy pix of the 1954 season. It's carried largely but easily by Pedro Infante's personality and singing, plus Elsa Aguirre's looks and style (she's a radiant brunette) who is superb with her simplicity in manner and dress. Miguel Zacarias' story and direction puts it over.

Catchy songs, broad comedy and mounting make this pic of wide appeal. There are no puzzles in this. Fun highspot is when Infante inadvertly seeks shelter in Miss Aguirre's bedroom while she's right at the most interesting point in undressing.

Bellylaughs are frequent in this production. Story is singularly unstriking. Again young man leaves home to seek something better, preferably a fortune, in another town. He meets a pretty girl who would mortgage the homestead by wedding a rich elderly man. But the handsome young man (Infante) unearths a treasure on the premises. Pure corn but the way it's done, this clicks nicely. *Doug.*

L'Oro Di Napoli
(The Gold of Naples)
(ITALIAN)

Rome, Jan. 11.

Paramount release of a Ponti-DeLaurentiis production. Stars Vittorio DeSica, Silvana Mangano, Sophia Loren, Eduardo DeFilippo, Toto Piero Bilancioni. Directed by Vittorio DeSica. Screenplay, Cesare Zavattini, DeSica, Giuseppe Marotta; from a collection of short stories by Marotta; camera, Carlo Montuori; editor, Eraldo Da Roma; music, Alessandro Cicognini. Previewed in Rome. Running time, **118 MINS.**

Don Saverio .... Toto
Don Carmine .... Pasquale Cennamo
Saverio's wife .... Lainella Carell
Pizzaiola .... Sophia Loren
Her husband .... Giacomo Furia
Widower .... Paolo Stoppa
Count Prospero B ...... Vittorio DeSica
Gennarino .... Piero Bilancioni
Giovanni .... Mario Passante
Teresa .... Silvana Mangano
Her husband ....Erno Crisa

Episodic pic, in five parts, sketching some slices of Neapolitan life, looks like Vittorio DeSica's first click at the boxoffice as a director. His recent thespic efforts will help this megging turn, and a large all-star cast, plus the well-known Naples locale and color, should make "Gold" pay off strongly. Names will aid foreign runs as well, but abroad pic needs very special handling for the payoff, with many typically Italian nuances sure to be lost. Slotting is only just this side of a straight arty, with some of the going heavy and possibly confusing to general audiences. There's some exploitable footage, however, concerning Silvana Mangano and Sophia Loren.

First episode tells of the rebellion of a husband to several years' abusive guesting by an aquaintance. Latter makes Toto's house his own via threat and bluster, and only gives up when a sudden heart attack gives Toto the courage to rebel. Second item is a saucy and diverting bit concerning a ring, a buxom pizza vendor (Sophia Loren) forgets at her lover's home. She tells her husband it must have fallen into a pizza, and the chase after recent customers is on, and involves colorful types. When the lover finally shows up with the ring, husband notes sadly that he bought no pizza, goes back to work with a darker outlook on his marriage.

Third fable, acted by DeSica himself, concerns a broke and aging count who tries to satisfy his craving for cards by playing with the doorman's little boy. The kid invariably beats him while bored by the old-timer's phobia. Bit is an acting gem, with both DeSica and the boy (Piero Bilancioni) standout. In next-to-last slot is the pic's dramatic item, "Teresa," which tells of a prostie's marriage of convenience to a rich man. She falls for him, forgets terms of the platonic arrangement, and leaves the house when he spurns her. Facing her grim past life once more, she goes back to husband in fadeout. Silvana Mangano gives her best performance ever in this one, lending a difficult role depth and substance. Final bit, about a joke played by a drugstore counsellor, colorfully played by Eduardo DeFilippo, and his neighbors, on a snobbish nobleman, ends the film with a laugh.

This production is probably best of a long series shot in Naples and about Neapolitans, thanks to the Marotta-Zavattini script and DeSica's tight direction, noticeable in getting top performances from non-pros and pros alike. Pace is often uncompromisingly slow, and may appear dull to those unable to catch the dialectic or lingual touches that flavor it. Episodic structure, and its limited space for development, its austere drawback. All production credits, especially Carlo Montuori's lensing, and Alessandro Cicognini's music, are tops.

Pic forms part of a series produced by Ponti-DeLaurentiis for Paramount release and/or option. Some others have been Robert Rossen's "Mambo," "Ulysses" and "La Strada." *Hawk.*

Casa Ricordi
(FRANCO-ITALIAN)
(Color)

Rome, Jan. 11.

Diana Cinematografica release of a Documento-I.G.S.—Cormoran-Franco London Film production. Stars Roland Alexandre, Miriam Bru, Andrea Checchi, Daniele Delorme, Gabriele Ferzetti, Roldano Lupi, Marcello Mataroianni, Micheline Presle, Maurice Ronet, Paolo Stoppa, Marta Toren, Fausto Tozzi. Directed by Carmine Gallone. Story and screenplay, Age, Scarpelli, Novarese, Benvenuti, Filippo, Gallone; camera (Technicolor), Marco Scarpelli; sets, Mario Chiari; editor, Niccolo Lazzari; music, Donizetti, Rossini, Bellini, Verdi, Puccini, Zandonai. At Moderno, Rome. Running time, **130 MINS.**

Gioacchino Rossini .... Roland Alexandre
Luisa Lewis .... Miriam Bru
Giuseppina Strepponi........Elisa Cegani
Giulio Ricordi .... Andrea Checchi
Maria .... Daniele Delorme
Giacomo Puccini ...... Gabriele Ferzetti
Giuseppe Verdi .... Fosco Giachetti
Tito Ricordi .... Enzo Givampietro
Giulia Grisi .... Nadia Gray
Domenico Barbaja .... Roldano Lupi
Gaetano Donizetti...Marcello Mataroianni
Virginia Marchi ...... Micheline Presle
Vincenzo Bellini .... Maurice Ronet
Giovanni Ricordi .... Paolo Stoppa
Isabella Colbran .... Marta Toren
Arrigo Boito .... Fausto Tozzi

And the voices of: Mario Del Monaco, Tito Gobbi, Gino Mattera, Renata Tebaldi, Italo Tajo, Nelly Corradi, Aldo Ferraguti, Ferdinando Lidonni, Enrico Formichi, Arturo LaPorta, Goulio Neri, Marinella Meri, Gianni Poggi, Giulietta Simonlato, Andrea Monchelli, Ken Neate, Juanita Sariman.

This elaborately staged all-star co-production in Technicolor has a guaranteed audience among music lovers anywhere, thanks to its expertly sung operatic slices while general audiences, especially in France and Italy, will be lured by the marquee weight and word-of-mouth. U. S. chances, beyond the longhair set, may be aided by the recent breach made by "Aida" although this pic needs slightly different handling. It's worth a strong try in dubbed version.

Story, more than the usual frame work, concerns the Ricordi family and the history of its music publishing house. Producers claim the story is close to authentic. But even if not, its coincidental interweaving of famed musical names makes for fine audience interest since giving the story.

Birth of the music royalty idea, and of Ricordi's publishing business, occurs when Giovanni Ricordi discovers a bunch of manuscripts in the cellar of Milan's Scala Theatre. For his future services, free, as house printer, he receives rights to these musical scores, and business grows. His confidence in some young musicians, such as Rossini, Donizetti, etc., pays off as they become masters of opera.

Film follows the pattern through succeeding generations of the Ricordi family, while sketching their relationship to other musicians such as Verdi, Puccini, Bellini, as well as private-life episodes concerning the musicos. Thus a triangle story involves Marta Toren with Rossini (Roland Alexandre) and Domenico Barbaja (Roldano Lupi). Luisa Lewis' (Miriam Bru) jealousy helps speed the death of an already ill Vincenzo Bellini (Maurice Ronet), a visit to Paris and encounter with Maria (Daniele Delorme) helps to inspire Puccini to write "La Boheme," and so on.

Handled for laughs or pathos, most of these bits are effective. Operatic excerpts from "The Barber of Seville," "Othello," "Boheme" and many others are beautifully sung and staged. However, some audiences may be disappointed in the choice of some lesser-known arias.

Acting is excellent all the way down the long credit list, with Paolo Stoppa drawing an expert Giovanni Ricordi, Miss Toren an appealing Isabella Colbran, Gabriele Ferzetti at home repeating his role of a previous Puccini biopic, and Marcello Mataroianni, Andrea Checchi, Micheline Presle and many others all adding able characterizations. Color quality, costume and set design are tasteful and expert. Sound recording is very good. *Hawk.*

Uli der Knecht
(Uli the Servant)
(SWISS)

Zurich, Jan. 11.
Beretta-Film Zurich release of Gloria-film (Oscar Dueby) production. Directed by Franz Schnyder. Screenplay, Richard Schweizer, based on novel by Jeremias Gotthelf; camera, Emil Berna; adaptation, Christian Larch. At Scala Theatre, Zurich. Running time. 114 MINS.
With Hannes Schmidhauser, Liselotte Pulver, Heinrich Gretler, Emil Hegetschweiler, Hedda Koppe, Alfred Rasser, Marianne Matti, Robert Bichler, Linda Geiser, Anneliese Egger, Max Illufler, Stephanie Glaser, Edwin Kohlund.

First local production in more than a year, this looks to be the year's biggest moneymaker here. The great boxoffice draw, already evidenced here, stems partly from the popularity of writer Jeremias Gotthelf on whose story this is based. This Gloriafilm offering makes no attempt to reach any but Swiss audiences. It is the "Swissest" of all Swiss entries so far and therefore has only limited possibilities and slim chance in the U. S.

Plot is typical peasant drama mingled with humor. Due to the high standard of the literary pattern, however, there is no false pathos whatever and characterizations are true-to-life.

Direction by Franz Schnyder is a bit uneven. Lensing by vet cameraman Emil Berna is among the main assets. Most of the outdoors have been shot this summer on location in the Bernese Oberland.

Cast names mean nothing in Anglo-U.S. market but have a certain marquee strength over here. In his first screen appearance, newcomer Hannes Schmidhauser in the title role does remarkably well. Swiss actress Liselotte Pulver, who has made herself a name in German films, is excellent as the bride-to-be. Others deserving special credit are Emil Hegetschweiler, Hedda Koppe and Heinrich Gretler, who turn in sharp-edged, believable peasant portrayals. *Mezo.*

Maedchenjahre Einer Koenigin
(Girl Days of a Queen)
(AUSTRIAN—COLOR)

Vienna, Jan. 11.
Sascha Film Co. release of Erma Film production. Stars Romy Schneider; features Adrian Hoven, Carl Ludwig Diehl. Directed and written by Ernest Marischka. Camera, Bruno Mondi; settings, Fritz Jueptner-Jonstorf; costumes, Gerdago and Leo Bei; music, Anton Profes. In Agfa color. At Apollo Kino, Vienna. Running time, 90 MINS.

Each year for decades, back to the silent film era, Ernst Marischka preems his productions on his lucky day. He did the same with "Girl Days of a Queen." This is a very amusing, human and partly realistic film about Victoria in her

teens. Exploitation possibilities for the U. S. market are good.

Story, for which Marischka is responsible, is excellent and in the best tradition, with the libretti of the many world successes he wrote. This one, too, contains laughter as well as dramatic moments. With three candidates on a list to choose a husband, Victoria, breaking all etiquette, runs off at a big party. There, incognito, she meets a German student, also incognito. He is her future hubby, Prince Albert Consort. Too bashful to propose, he must virtually be "forced" to do so.

Romy Schneider, as Victoria, and Adrian Hoven, as Prince Albert, carry this story off with rare skill. Madga Schneider, Christl Mardayn, Carl Ludwig Diehl and Paul Hoerbiger handle their roles nicely. Otto Tressler brings life to the part of the Bishop. An all-star cast, taking in even minor roles, indicates a high budget.

Eduard Strauss plays the role of his grand-uncle, Johann Strauss, in a very believable manner.

Sensitively directed by Marischka, "Queen" seldom drags. Musical score by Anton Profes is of higher standard than usual for Austrian pix. The atmosphere is realistically captured by Bruno Mondi's camera. *Maas.*

The Far Country
(COLOR)

Rugged outdoor actioner in color with James Stewart and profitable b.o. outlook.

Hollywood, Jan. 21.
Universal release of Aaron Rosenberg production. Stars James Stewart, Ruth Roman. Corinne Calvet, Walter Brennan; features John McIntire, Jay C. Flippen, Henry Morgan. Steve Brodie, Connie Gilchrist. Directed by Anthony Mann. Story and screenplay, Borden Chase; camera (Technicolor). William Daniels; editor, Russell Schoengarth. Previewed Jan. 18, '55. Running time. 96 MINS.

Jeff	James Stewart
Ronda	Ruth Roman
Renee	Corinne Calvet
Ben	Walter Brennan
Gannon	John McIntire
Rube	Jay C. Flippen
Ketchum	Henry Morgan
Ives	Steve Brodie
Hominy	Connie Gilchrist
Madden	Robert Wilke
Dusty	Chubby Johnson
Luke	Royal Dano
Newberry	Jack Elam
Grits	Kathleen Freeman
Molasses	Connie Van

(Aspect ratio: 2-1)

Rugged action is featured in "The Far Country" to go with its rugged outdoor scenery, and the results add up to film entertainment that will have a profitable trek through its playdates. Pic marks the fifth successful combination of James Stewart, as star, Aaron Rosenberg as producer, and Anthony Mann as director, the team's previous four offerings having clicked at the boxoffice.

Cast and crew locationed around the Columbia Ice Fields and in Jasper Park to get the chilly atmosphere to go with a story of the far north, set back in the pioneer days when gold was luring adventurous souls to the snow country. The location areas in Canada provide the film with beautiful, almost frighteningly rugged, scenery that makes a good backstop for the Borden Chase outdoor action plot.

Stewart arrives in this setting driving a herd of cattle, which he and his partner, Walter Brennan, figure to unload at fancy prices in the gold-crazy country around Skagway and Dawson. The partners are in trouble almost immediately, because Skagway's self-styled law, John McIntire, tries to commander the herd before it can be driven to Dawson. In the latter frontier town, Stewart finds a few good citizens trying to combat the sin and fighting brought there by saloon keeper Ruth Roman. He maintains hands-off, though, until McIntire's claim-jumpers kill Brennan. Turning civic-minded, he goes on the prod for a rousing, guns-blazing climax.

Stewart and Brennan are completely at home in this type of film and handle their characters with the expected ease. The distaff stars, Miss Roman and Corinne Calvet, a gold fields girl who gets Stewart at the finale, add quite a bit to the entertainment values. While Miss Roman's chore is that of a heavy, she doesn't make it heavy and warms the audience to her. Miss Calvet is delightful. McIntire is exceptionally good as the prime heavy, and Jay C. Flippen comes over strongly as a bottle-loving friend of the two male stars. Henry Morgan, Steve Brodie, Connie Gilchrist, Chubby Johnson are among the capable supporting players.

The Technicolor lensing by William Daniels and Russell Schoengarth's editing head the good technical credits. The score, directed

by Joseph Gershenson, is as noisy as the gunplay at times.
Brog.

Animal Farm
(BRITISH-COLOR)

Powerful preachment in color cartoon form of Orwell fable. Good for art spots but uncertain for general audiences.

RKO release of Halas-Batchelor production presented by Louis de Rochemont. Based on the George Orwell fable. Story development: Lothar Wolff, Borden Mace, Philip Stapp, John Halas, Joy Batchelor; camera (Technicolor), S. G. Griffiths; music, Matyas Seiber; narration, Gordon Heath; animal voices, Mauric Denham. At Paris Theatre, N.Y., Dec. 29, '54. Running time, 75 MINS.

Human greed, selfishness and conniving are lampooned in "Animal Farm" with the pigs behaving in a pig-like manner and the head pig, named Napoleon, corrupting and perverting an honest revolt against evil social conditions into a new tyranny as bad as, and remarkably similiar to, the old regime. In short, this cartoon feature running some 75 minutes is a sermon against all that is bestial in politics and rotten in the human will to live in luxury at the expense of slaves.

Made in Britain, the cartoon is vividly realized pictorially. The musical score, the narration, the sound effects and the editing all are of impressive imaginative quality. Although it may be a cliche for reviewers to observe "not for children," the truth may be just the opposite. It could be argued that this is very much the sort of sobering lesson about glib oratorical protestations of equality and brotherhood, and how cruel, gangster-like leaders exploit the hopes of "sincere" men, which children should be exposed to young.

But while applauding the lesson and cheering the technical skills involved in creating this unusual attraction, the boxoffice question must remain open. Presumably "Animal Farm" is for the upper middles, the art houses, the discriminating clientele. Not that anybody should have too much difficulty "understanding." Still it's just not the kind of film fare which is likely to be "popular". A wee mite on the sombre side.
Land.

Unchained

Good program melodrama, using the California Institution for Men at Chino and rehabilitation wonders performed there for factual background.

Hollywood, Jan. 24.
Warner Bros. release of Hall Bartlett production. Stars Elroy Hirsch, Barbara Hale. Chester Morris, Todd Duncan, Tim Considine; features Johnny Johnston, Peggy Knudsen. Jerry Paris, John Qualen, Bill Kennedy, Henry Nakamura. Written and directed by Hall Bartlett; suggested by Kenyon J. Scudder's "Prisoners Are People"; camera, Virgil E. Miller; editor, Cotton Warburton; music composed and conducted by Alex North; song, North and Hy Zaret. Previewed at California Institution for Men, Chino, Calif., Jan. 19, '55. Running time, 74 MINS.

Steve Davitt	Elroy Hirsch
Mary Davitt	Barbara Hale
Kenyon J. Scudder	Chester Morris
Bill Howard	Todd Duncan
Eddie Garrity	Johnny Johnston
Elaine	Peggy Knudsen
Joe Ravens	Jerry Paris
Leonard Haskins	John Qualen
Sanders	Bill Kennedy
Jerry Hakara	Henry Nakamura

Sally Haskins	Kathryn Grant
Swanson	Bob Patten
Gladstone	Don Kennedy
Mr. Johnson	Mack Williams
Police Captain	Saul Gorss
Win Davitt	Tim Considine

(*Aspect ratio:* 1.85-1)

There's a public service flavor to this melodrama that raises it a notch above the usual prison thriller. The regular program market should find it a good entry, able to handle either top or bottom of the bill according to the situation booking it. Additionally, the exploitation factors, if properly used, may get it extra coin in special playdates.

The public service aspect comes from its factual story basis and its lensing in the California Institution for Men at Chino—a prison without walls or armed guards, where inmates, from murderers on down, can pay their debts to society and at the same time retain some portion of personal dignity.

There are no uniforms, no gun towers, no lock steps, nor clanging steel doors restricting C. I. M. inmates once they have been through a brief indoctrination period at the humane institution founded, not without long struggle, by its now retiring superintendent, Kenyon J. Scudder. The latter's book, "Prisoners Are People," was the basis for the screenplay by Hall Bartlett, who also produced and directed, and the film was previewed in the prison messhall, with guests and inmates both attending.

Picture was produced independently by Bartlett, and Warner Bros. has taken on the distribution. Like Bartlett's two previous productions, "Navajo" and "Crazylegs," this entry is told in okay dramatic terms and with a simple sincerity that gets the message across while maintaining entertainment aims. To present the C.I.M. and Scudder story, the script uses Elroy Hirsch as a murderously-tempered convict transferred from stern confinement in San Quentin to the fraternity-like atmosphere of the 2,600-acre prison at Chino. In this new environment and under a different code for handling men, he gradually loses his desire to escape and determines to serve his time with good grace.

Incidents portrayed in the plot are either actual happenings or those that could have occurred in the 14 years that C.I.M. has been in operation. However, despite this basis in fact, the picture at times becomes stock, as do some of the characters, but Bartlett generally keeps it moving along a satisfactory course with fairly believeable performances by Hirsch, Todd Duncan, Johnny Johnston, Jerry Paris, John Qualen, Bill Kennedy and Henry Nakamura, inmate principals involved in the plot. Scudder is played by Chester Morris, while distaff interest falls to Barbara Hale, as Hirsch's wife, and Peggy Knudsen, girl friend of Jerry Paris. These three haven't much to do, but the femmes sell the idea of family visiting permitted on the prison's picnic grounds on weekends and holidays.

Lensing by Virgil E. Miller is good, as is the Alex North score. A title tune is sung by Duncan, who also is heard on a hymn during a sequence. *Brog.*

Jupiter's Darling
(MUSICAL-C'SCOPE-COLOR)

Satirical musicomedy* takeoff on costume actioners. Fairly entertaining with good b.o. outlook few situations; otherwise spotty.

Hollywood, Jan. 20.

Metro release of George Wells production. Stars Esther Williams, Howard Keel, Marge and Gower Champion, George Sanders; features Richard Haydn, William Demarest, Norma Varden. Directed by George Sidney. Screenplay, Dorothy Kingsley; based on the play "Road to Rome" by Robert E. Sherwood; camera (Eastman Color), Paul C. Vogel, Charles Rosher; editor, Ralph E. Winters; songs, Burton Lane, Harold Adamson; music arranged and conducted by David Rose; musical supervision: Saul Chaplin; choreography, Hermes Pan; vocal supervision, Jeff Alexander. Previewed Jan. 7, '55. Running time, **95 MINS.**

Amytis	Esther Williams
Hannibal	Howard Keel
Meta	Marge Champion
Varius	Gower Champion
Fabius Maximus	George Sanders
Horatio	Richard Haydn
Mago	William Demarest
Fabia	Norma Varden
Scipio	Douglas Dumbrille
Carthalo	Henry Corden
Maharbal	Michael Ansara
Widow Titus	Martha Wentworth
Principal Swimming Statue	John Olszewski
The Swimming Cherubs (Courtesy of Lissa Bengtson)	

As a takeoff, with satirical treatment, on costume actioners, "Jupiter's Darling" is a fairly entertaining, although a hit-and-miss, affair, that will likely have a mixed reaction at the boxoffice. It has Esther Williams in some outstanding swim numbers, and Howard Keel's robust singing, to gain it initial attention, plus a number of exploitable factors that will be of considerable aid in some of its playdates. However, the overall outlook is for spotty business, mostly because the general public may not react favorably to the spoofing of period derring-do, nor quite understand just what the makers had in mind.

Robert E. Sherwood's stage play, "Road to Rome," dealing with Hannibal's invasion of Rome served as the foundation for Dorothy Kingsley's screenplay. Behind footlights, and playing before discerning legit audiences, the satire has considerable point. On the screen, and playing to all types of audiences, the spoof is another matter. On the count of production numbers, the George Wells production has several that are outstanding, most particularly Miss Williams' two swim bits and the elephant choreography with Marge and Gower Champion.

Storywise, George Sidney's direction has created some great costumed romantic action, whenever this is handled straight, but he runs into trouble when the plot takes time out to poke fun at chimerical derring-do. There's not much his direction can do to spread the appeal for this kidding to audiences generally, although, for literary sophisticates, it will be regal fun.

The two water numbers given Miss Williams stack up with her best. One is an imaginatively staged dream ballet in which statues of Greek gods come to life to swim with her under water to the Burton Lane-Harold Adamson tune, "I Have A Dream." It is a beautiful thing to watch because of its elegant simplicity. The other carries an essential part of the story, and its chase theme is developed into taut suspense drama as she flees through vast underwater reaches from pursuing barbarians seeking to recapture her for Howard Keel's conquering Hannibal.

The Champions have two production numbers. The first, hardly worthy of notice because of its sticky coyness, is "If This Be Slav'ry," but the second, "The Life of an Elephant," in which the team works with baby and adult pachyderms, is a real audience-pleaser that will draw a full share of oh's and ah's. It's hard to beat the baby gimmick, human or animal, in a film.

For songs, the other Lane-Adamson tunes ring out satisfactorily. Keel wallops "I Never Trust A Woman" and "Don't Let This Night Get Away," both having a part in the plot, as does the rollicking "Hannibal's Victory March," used several times for comedy effect. Seventh tune is "Horatio's Narration," with music by Saul Chaplin and lyrics by George Wells. Adamson and Chaplin, which Richard Haydn, as Horatio, uses to tell the story of Hannibal's march on Rome, the ineffectual defense of the city by Fabius Maximus, played ineffectually by George Sanders, and the part the latter's fiancee, Miss Williams, plays in turning the conquering barbarian's fighting hordes and elephants away at the very point of smashing the walls of Rome. Cast principals other than those named, include William Demarest, as Hannibal's aide, and Norma Varden, Fabius' domineering mother.

Pictorial beauty abounds in the picture, thanks to the CinemaScope lensing in Eastman Color by Paul C. Vogel and Charles Rosher. The underwater scenes are particularly outstanding. Rating a nod for contributions to the lush physical layout of the picture are the set decorations by Edwin B. Willis and Hugh Hunt, the art direction by Cedric Gibbons and Urie McCleary, and the special effects by A. Arnold Gillespie and Warren Newcombe. *Brog.*

Women's Prison

Good entry for the programmer market.

Columbia release of Bryan Foy production. Stars Ida Lupino, Jan Sterling, Cleo Moore, Audrey Totter, Phyllis Thaxter, Howard Duff; features Warren Stevens, Barry Kelley, Gertrude Michael, Vivian Marshall. Directed by Lewis Seiler. Screenplay, Crane Wilbur, Jack DeWitt from story by DeWitt; camera, Lester H. White; editor, Henry Batista; music, Mischa Bakaleinikoff. Tradeshown N.Y., Jan. 20, '55. Running time, **80 MINS.**

Amelia VanZant	Ida Lupino
Brenda Martin	Jan Sterling
Mae	Cleo Moore
Joan Burton	Audrey Totter
Helene Jensen	Phyllis Thaxter
Doctor Clark	Howard Duff
Glen Burton	Warren Stevens
Warden Brock	Barry Kelley
Sturgess	Gertrude Michael
Dottie	Vivian Marshall
Saunders	Mae Clarke
Don Jensen	Ross Elliott
Grace	Adelle August
Captain Tierney	Don C. Harvey
"Polyclinic" Jones	Juanita Moore
Sarah	Edna Holland
Carol	Lynne Millan
Burke	Mira McKinney
Enright	Mary Newton
Head Nurse	Diane DeLaire
Miss Whittier	Francis Morris

Psychological aspects of life behind bars, particularly as far as femmes are concerned, get a generous probing in "Women's Prison." Film is frequently depressing but good marquee values in the cast plus its exploitable subject will help this Bryan Foy production acquit itself favorably in the programmer market.

The Crane Wilbur-Jack DeWitt screenplay, based on the latter's story, quickly establishes the setting, introduces the principal characters, then goes on to show how lives of inmates are cruelly affected by incompetence and lack of understanding of the institution's top officials. At times the melodrama runs a bit heavy. However, the scripters pull the story threads together in the final reel to wind up things on a hopeful note.

Villain of the piece is Ida Lupino, supervisor of a women's prison which adjoins a jail for men. A "border-line psychopath" who's never been able to hit it off socially with men, she takes it out on her femme inmates who apparently have done better with the opposite sex. Among objects of her ire are Phyllis Thaxter, in for automobile manslaughter; Audrey Totter, doing time for a gun possession charge and wife of convict Warren Stevens; forger Jan Sterling, et al.

Tension between Miss Lupino and the prisoners is heightened under the brisk direction of Lewis Seiler. It's an unrelieved conflict all the way despite efforts of prison doctor Howard Duff to improve conditions. While femme players in this Columbia release are far from glamorous in the drab prison garb, they register well in their respective assignments.

Miss Lupino, in portraying the heavy, makes herself intensely disliked. Duff is an easy-going physician, patient and sympathetic despite his problems. Miss Sterling scores nicely as a tough moll, Cleo Moore is a typical femme inmate and Vivian Marshall, as an ex-stripteaser gone wrong, shines in some amusing impersonations. Phyllis Thaxter contribs a fine emotional study of a woman suffering from a guilt complex. Good support is lent by Stevens, Barry Kelley and Gertrude Michael, among others.

Black-and-white camerawork of Lester H. White capably captures the grim atmosphere within the rows of cellblocks. Mischa Bakaleinikoff's musical score is in keeping with the depressing notes the picture occasionally hits. Henry Batista edited to a tight 80 minutes. Other technical credits measure up. *Gilb.*

Tender Hearts

Fine drama but will need strong selling.

Hollywood, Jan. 21.

Hugo Haas production (no release). Stars Hugo Haas; features Francesca de Scaffa, June Hammerstein, Jeffrey Stone, Ken Carlton, John Vosper. Directed and written by Haas; associate producer, Robert Erlik; camera, Eddie Fitzgerald; music, Ernest Gold; editor, Robert Eisen. Previewed Jan. 20, '55. Running time, **78 MINS.**

Valentine	Hugo Haas
Jenette	Francesca de Scaffa
June	June Hammerstein
Chauffeur	Jeffrey Stone
Jim	Ken Carlton
Mr. Hawkins	John Vosper
Mrs. Hawkins	Tracy Roberts
Butler	Tony Jochim
Foxie	Pat Goldin
Shmoe	Sid Melton
Bus Driver	Steve Mitchell

This tale of an old beggar and his performing dog stands in need of strong selling but emerges a fine piece of drama which adult audiences in particular will find engrossing. It's another four-way project for Hugo Haas, who produces, writes, directs and stars, and it may be his best yet in quality and worth. Made without a release, a policy Haas has followed in all his previous efforts, producer is now negotiating for its distribution.

An oftimes heartwarming story is woven around the idea of the mendicant, who in his cheerless cellar room lives off what his dog takes in on street corners, finally disposing of his pet to a wealthy family so pooch may have a good home after he no longer is able to care for it due to illness. Film, frequently studded with humorous touches, is a character study of a former circus clown who claims he's still acting out a part. In its delineation Haas has inserted top dialog, as well as a good sense of dramatic values.

Interesting types people the action—there's the young woman in the flat above who mothers the beggar and is as concerned about him as though he were her own father, played feelingly by June Hammerstein; Francesca de Scaffa, the tart, in a realistic portrayal; Ken Carlton, her pimp, who arranges the holdup leading to the old man's death in the belief he got a wad of money for his dog; Jeffrey Stone, chauffeur of wealthy John Vosper, in love with June. The dog, Flip, is a well-trained canine.

Haas delivers a topflight performance which surpasses past appearances, and his direction in this instance is as sound as his writing. Technical credits are superior, too, Ernest Gold's music score excellently attuned to the subject, Robert Eisen's editing tight. Rudi Feld's art direction thoroughly atmospheric and camera work by Eddie Fitgerald attaining the proper low key. Robert Erlik is credited as associate producer. *Whit.*

They Were So Young

Subject matter, mannequins in a Rio de Janeiro fashion house who find modeling the least of their "chores," makes this exploitable fare. Okay entertainment-wise.

Hollywood, Jan. 22.

Lippert release of Corona Films (Kurt Neumann) production. Stars Scott Brady, Johanna Matz, Raymond Burr; features Ingrid Stenn, Gisela Fackeldey, Kurt Meisel, Katherina Mayberg, Eduard Linkers, Gordon Howard. Directed by Neumann. Screenplay, Felix Luetzkendorf, Neumann; based on an outline by Jacques Companeez; camera, Ekkehard Kyrath; editor, Eva Kroll; music, Michael Jary. Previewed Jan. 20, '55. Running time, **80 MINS.**

Lanning .... Scott Brady
Coltos .... Raymond Burr
Eve .... Johanna Matz
Connie .... Ingrid Stenn
Lanzowa .... Gisela Fackeldey
Pasquale .... Kurt Meisel
Felicia .... Katherina Mayberg
Albert .... Eduard Linkers
Garza .... Gordon Howard
Emily .... Elizabeth Tannev
Elise .... Erica Beer
Lena .... Hanita Hallan
Vincenta .... Hannelore Axman
Bulanos .... William Trenk-Trebitsch
Manuel .... Pero Alexander
Doctor .... Joseph Dahmen
Lobos .... Gert Froebe

(*Aspect ratios* 1.85-1)

Mannequins arriving in Rio de Janeiro under contract to what purportedly is a high fashion house find modeling the least of their "chores" in this Lippert release. It's exploitable fare, and okay entertainment to boot. Backed by proper selling, returns should be on the pleasant side.

Yarn centers around Johanna Matz, beautiful mannequin from Berlin, who finds the "added duties" not to her liking. Getting nowhere with protests to police, she escapes and meets Scott Brady, American mining engineer for wealthy Brazilian bigshot Raymond Burr. Supposedly safe at the latter's hacienda, she's soon fleeing the Brazilian, however, for he turns out to be the secret owner of the fashion house. Brady, finally wised up to his boss, rescues Miss Matz and sees Burr off to jail.

Film's a good credit for producer-director Kurt Neumann, who functions well in both categories—as well as co-scripting with Felix Luetzkendorf, from a story outline by Jacques Companeez. Via well chosen locations, the film is extremely interesting scenically (although the action is supposedly all taking place in Brazil, portions of the exteriors were lensed in the swamps and jungles of Italy). All interiors were shot in Germany.

Under Neumann's direction the three costars come across well—Brady authoritative and convincing as the male topliner and Burr turning in another of his top stints as the heavy. Film marks the U. S. pic debut of Miss Matz, in this country two years ago to enact the Maggie McNamara role in the German version of "The Moon Is Blue," which was shot simultaneously with the American version. She's pert, full of warmth, and extremely talented—and, having a fine grasp of English, stacks as a good bet for Hollywood.

Foreign thesps enact the remaining roles, with the majority competent and one. Ingrid Stenn, very fine as a friend of Miss Matz' who is forced to stick it out in a life of sin until she is finally murdered. There's a slight bit of voice dubbing, but not enough to detract. Technical contributions generally hold up with American standards.

For the record, the film was shot bi-lingually—English and German—with only Miss Matz of the three topliners repeating for the latter version. *Neal.*

The Man Who Loved Redheads
(BRITISH-COLOR)

Moira Shearer starred in frothy Terence Rattigan comedy; looks set for hefty grosses in all situations.

London, Jan. 19.

British Lion release of London Films production. Stars Moira Shearer, John Justin, Roland Culver, Gladys Cooper, Denholm Elliott. Directed by Harold French. Screenplay by Terence Rattigan adapted from the play, "Who Is Sylvia?" camera (Eastmancolor), Georges Perinal; editor, Bert Bates; music, Benjamin Frankel; ballet choreography by Alan Carter, with excerpts from "The Sleeping Beauty" by Tchaikovsky. At Warner Theatre, London, starting Jan. 19, '55. Running time, **90 MINS.**

Sylvia / Daphne / Olga / Colette .... Moira Shearer
Mark .... John Justin
Oscar .... Roland Culver
Caroline .... Gladys Cooper
Denis .... Denholm Elliott
Williams .... Harry Andrews
Bubbles .... Patricia Cutts
Ethel .... Moyra Fraser
Sergei .... John Hart
Chloe .... Joan Benham
Young Mark .... Jeremy Spencer
Sidney .... Melvyn Hayes

Terence Rattigan has adapted his own stage success, "Who Is Sylvia?" into a light and wholly enjoyable British comedy. This looks set for sturdy grosses in many situations and most countries. The marquee value of Moira Shearer will be one of the pic's main selling assets in the U.S., particularly as this is her most successful effort since she made her screen debut in "The Red Shoes."

In the years since she made her bow on the screen actress, Miss Shearer's thesping qualities have improved out of all recognition, but one of her principal assets is her outstanding skill as a ballerina. In "The Man Who Loved Redheads," she has full opportunity of demonstrating her terping prowess in a handsomely mounted excerpt from Tchaikovsky's "Sleeping Beauty," skilfully choreographed by Alan Carter.

The lightweight plot opens with a scene in which a 14-year-old viscount falls in love "for eternity" with a red-headed girl a couple of years his senior. It so happens they never meet again but the peer, respectably married, a scion of the diplomatic service, never loses his taste for redheads. He has his first affair with a redhead during the first World War. So successful is his plot to separate the illicit from the domestic that he establishes a town house, under an assumed name, where a constant succession of redheaded femmes provide a stimulating diversion from the cares of the Foreign Office.

All the redheads in the plot are filled by the star and she displays a surprising facility for switching dialects, appearing first as an immature girl who sparks the lifelong passion. Subsequently she is a cockney, a Russian ballerina and finally a mannequin. The entire plot is done with a bright, nimble touch. The denouement, in which the diplomat's wife reveals she has known her husband's guilty secret all the time, allows Gladys Cooper to shine in a guest appearance.

Principal male role is filled with distinction by John Justin. Although he's allowed to age gracefully, he never loses his flair for spotting and dating a redhead. Roland Culver, repeating his original stage part, turns in a delightfully cynical performance as Justin's lifelong friend. Denholm Elliott, also guest starring, handsomely fills the role of the diplomat's son who learns the secret of his father's double life. Harold French's polished direction is matched by other technical credits. Georges Perinal has done a sterling job of Eastman color lensing while Paul Sheriff has designed handsome settings. *Myro.*

Carolina Cannonball

Slapstick trifle starring Judy Canova. Strictly for the kiddie trade and the undiscriminating.

Republic release of Herbert J. Yates presentation. Stars Judy Canova. Features Andy Clyde, Ross Elliott, Sig Ruman, Leon Askin, Jack Kruschen, Frank Wilcox. Directed by Charles Lamont. Screenplay, Barry Shipman; from a story by Frank Gill Jr.; camera, Reggie Lanning; editor, Tony Martinelli; songs, "The Carolina Cannonball" and "Wishin' and Waitin'" by Donald Kahn and Jack Elliot. Previewed in N.Y. Jan. 24, '53. Running time, **73 MINS.**

Judy .... Judy Canova
Grandpa Canova .... Andy Clyde
Don Mack .... Ross Elliott
Stefan .... Sig Ruman
Otto .... Leon Askin
Hogar .... Jack Kruschen
Professor .... Frank Wilcox

Republic's latest Judy Canova entry is a slapstick trifle, suitable only for undiscriminating clientele. It's a fantastic concoction of unbelievably silly situations stretched out for 73 minutes. It appears anachronistic in the film biz's new era. Since Republic took the trouble to make the picture, there apparently must be a market for this kind of fare.

The picture's only concession to modern times is that the story deals with the atomic age and the effort of foreign agents to steal the secrets of the U.S.'s first atomic-powered guided missle. The presentation of the enemy agents, portrayed by Sig Ruman, Leon Askin, and Jack Kurschen, as comic opera buffoons might be passed off as one big joke in more settled times. This may be taking an insignificant picture too seriously, but the reality of recent times relating to spies, enemy agents, and atomic secrets, hardly makes the subject a laughing matter. In the light of what has happened and the continuing danger, it seems a disservice to portray these agents as stupid, left-footed nincompoops.

Miss Canova and her grandfather, Andy Clyde, are the only residents of Roaring Gulch, a desert ghost town. They operate a steam-powered Toonerville trolley which connects Roaring Gulch to the mainline whistle stop. To Roaring Gulch come the agents in search of the guided missle which has landed nearby. They're trailed by Ross Elliott, who plays a U.S. Government man. Why go on? The rest is obvious. *Holl.*

Pane, Amore, E Gelosia
(Bread, Love and Jealousy)
(ITALIAN)

Rome, Jan. 18.

Titanus release of a Marcello-Girosi-Titanus production. Stars Gina Lollobrigida, Vittorio DeSica, Roberto Risso, Marisa Merlini. Directed by Luigi Comencini. Screenplay, Luigi Comencini, Vincenzo Talarico, E. M. Margadonna, from a story by E. M. Margadonna; camera, Carlo Montuori; sets, Gastone Medin; music, Allesandro Cicognini. Previewed at Metropolitan, Rome. Running time, **98 MINS.**

Maria .... Gina Lollobrigida
Antonio Carotenuto .... Vittorio DeSica
Annarella .... Marisa Merlini
Stelluti .... Roberto Risso
Paolitta .... Maria Pia Casilio
Caramella .... Tina Pica

Titanus has another boxoffice leader in this successful followup of "Bread, Love, and Dreams," which has become the top Italian grosser of all time. Topping its predecessor in performances, and nearly equalling it otherwise, "Jealousy" looks an easy repeater of "Dreams" success story, with title and star value a pre-seller. Abroad, outlook is likewise rosy, with supporters of the first installment sure to be back for more. Special U.S. slotting, with experience of initialer, should help it to comfortable returns.

Unlike most sequels, this segues where the first left off, showing the engagements of its two couples, Maria and Stelluti, Carotenuto and Annarella. Next day, as village recovers from festivities at which engagements were announced, reports start to spread among villagers, endangering the recent splices. Marshal Carotenuto's (Vittorio DeSica) gal, Annarella, (Marisa Merlini) finds the father of her child coming back to claim his family place. It is whispered that the marshal had locked up Maria (Gina Lollobrigida) in jail for extra-judicial purposes.

Situation is played for laughs, with fiance relations becoming more and more strained until the windup. This sees Maria and Stelluti (Roberto Risso) once more united while the marshal bows out to Annarella's other man. Final shot, however, shows him ogling a voluptuous newcomer, the new midwife, with obvious intent to console his recent loss.

Thesping is tongue-in-cheek and broad, with all performers repeating their previous click performances. Miss Lollobrigida is at her physical and artistic best in the village gamin role. DeSica is fine as the self-styled village Don Juan while Miss Merlini provides a competent opposite. Risso appeals to distaffers as the shy gendarme. A colorful, featured cast backs the toppers with solid performances.

E. M. Margadonna's script is lightweight all the way, only rarely becoming superficial and repetitious. Concessions to the boxoffice are many, mostly successful. The director's pacing is speedy, in keeping with the peppery dialogue, yet the production would gain via a slight trim of its length. Musical backing and other credits are topnotch in an all-round, able production job. *Hawk.*

Rittmeister Wronski
(Cavalry-Captain Wronski)
(GERMAN)

Berlin, Jan. 18.
Deutsche London release of Apollo production. Stars Willy Birgel, Irene von Meyendorff, Antje Weissgerber. Directed by Ulrich Erfurth. Screenplay, Axel Eggebrecht; camera, Igor Oberberg; music, Norbert Schultze; sets, Fritz Maurischat and Ernst Klose. At Gloria Palast, Berlin. Running time, **102 MINS.**

Wronski .... Willy Birgel
Jadwiga .... Elisabeth Flickenschildt
Ilse von Jagstfeld....Antje Weissgerber
Leonore Cronberg .... Ilse Steppat
Liane von Templin..Irene von Meyendorff
Colonel Ranke............Paul Hartmann
Dornbusch .... Claus Holm
Frau von Eichhoff......Olga Tschechowa
Major Molenbek .... Axel Monje
Major Kegel .... Volker von Collande
Colonel Maty .... Rudolf Forster
Stepan .... Ernst Schroeder
Susi .... Marina Ried

Another German spy picture, this is chiefly tailored for the local audiences. It shapes up as a very good grosser here with the Willy Birgel name a big help. Due to a hardly convincing story and other flaws, its international prospects appear meagre. The Berlin background and theme might be exploitable factors.

It all centers around a Polish ex-officer who, in the '30's, comes to Berlin to act as a spy for his government. More than easily he collects piece after piece of top secret material via the help of mostly stupid secretaries. Everything is going along fine until he falls in love with one of the girls. He gets caught by the SS and has to face the usual punishment. In order to save his and his girl's life, he accepts an offer of the Germans to work for them as a spy against Poland. He is sent back to his native country where his former Polish bosses, already informed about his new intentions, give him to understand that there is nothing left for him than to shoot himself.

The whole thing lacks realism and conviction mainly because of a morbidly, noveletish script. It's difficult to understand how military secrets could fall so easily into the hands of a spy as depicted in this.

Birgel plays the title role with an over-emphasis on noblesse. The best performance is given by Ilse Steppat who, as a secretary to a German officer, supplies the spy most of the secret stuff he wants. A remarkably, big cast of qualified local actors and actresses are in supporting roles, including Rudolf Forster, Paul Hartmann, Elisabeth Flickenschildt and Olga Tschechowa.

Igor Oberberg's camera work is very good for the most part. Norbert Schultze's score and the settings are adequate. *Hans.*

Pirates of Tripoli

Routine swashbuckler, with action predominating. Okay as a supporter.

Hollywood, Jan. 22.
Columbia release of Sam Katzman production. Stars Paul Henreid, Patricia Medina; features Paul Newlan, John Miljan, Mark Hanna, Jean Del Val, Lillian Bond, Mel Welles, Louis G. Mercier, Karl Davis, Maralou Gray. Directed by Felix Feist. Story and screenplay, Allen March; camera (Technicolor), Henry Freulich; editor, Edwin Bryant; music, Mischa Bakaleinikoff. At Pantages Theatre, Hollywood, Calif., Jan. 22, '55. Running time, **70 MINS.**

Edri-Al-Gadrian .... Paul Henreid
Karjan .... Patricia Medina
Hammid Khassan .... Paul Newland
Malek .... John Miljan
Ben Ali .... Mark Hanna
Abu Tala .... Jean Del Val
Sono .... Lillian Bond
Tomidi .... Mel Welles
The Cat .... Louis G. Mercier
Assassin .... Karl Davis
Rhea .... Maralou Gray
Keppa .... Peter Mamakos
Beggar .... William Fawcett
Zurtah .... Frank Richards
Italian Ship's Captain......Gene Borden
(Aspect ratio: 1.85-1)

Familiar swashbuckling ingredients make up the whole of "Pirates Of Tripoli," a Technicolored saga of pirates, pretty maidens and overthrown kingdoms back in the 16th Century. The action, luckily, abounds, and on this count alone film will find favor with devotees of entertainment such as this.

Patricia Medina is the princess whose kingdom is overrun by savage hordes of the evil conqueror. Paul Henreid is the pirate in Tripoli to whom she goes for help. And, together, before it's all over, they get the kingdom back and each other to boot.

Under Felix Feist's active direction, the swordplay, fights (both at sea and on land), gun battles, underwater skirmishes and such are kept prominent, undoubtedly to throw a shadow over the time-worn story-line as much as possible without it losing continuity.

Paul Henreid romps through his role in virile, deering-do fashion, while Patricia Medina gives film a pictorial asset and a competent performance. John Miljan is okay as the heavy, while stints of supporters range from bad to good.

There's a glossy coating to this Sam Katzman production, with extremely good stock shots and Henry Freulich's fine camera work adding to the quality.

Le Vicomte de Bragelonne
(FRANCO-ITALIAN)
(Color)

Paris, Jan. 18.
CFPC release of CFPC-Orso-Iris Film production. Stars Georges Marchal, Dawn Addams, Jacques Dumesnil. Directed by Fernando Cerchio. Screenplay, Roland Laudenbach, Alexandre Astruc from novel by Alexandre Dumas; camera (Eastmancolor), Lucien Jolin; editor, L. M. Azar. At Normandie, Paris. Running time, **95 MINS.**

Raoul .... Georges Marchal
Helene .... Dawn Addams
D'Artagnan .... Jacques Dumesnil
Innkeeper .... Jean Tissier
Louis XIV .... Robert Burnier
Louise .... Florence Arnaud

Another raid into the Franco-Italo cycle of color swashbucklers, this is based on a lesser-known novel of Alexandre Dumas which follows the adventures of one of the Three Musketeers' sons. Usual Royal skulduggery, familiar sword-

play and chases put this in the ordinary category with few unique aspects for any U.S. interest. Costumes, color and locale are a plus factor.

This concerns the plan of Mazarin to place the twin brother of Louis XIV, who has been locked up since his birth, on the throne and thus control France.

Color is reserved and dressy. Georges Marchal is properly dashing as the Vicomte and Dawn Addams is a sweet looking Lady De Winter. Musketeers are portly and aging as is the film. Stereophonic sound and widescreen are used in this. *Mosk.*

La Reine Margot
(The Queen Margot)
(FRANCO-ITALIAN)
(Color)

Paris, Jan. 18.
Lux release of Lux-Vendome Film production. Stars Jeanne Moreau, Armando Francioli, Francoise Rosay. Directed by Jean Dreville. Screenplay by Abel Gance from novel by Alexandre Dumas; dialog, Jean Camp, Paul Andreota; camera (Eastmancolor), Roger Hubert, Henri Alekan; editor, Gabriel Rongier. At Normandie, Paris. Running time, **125 MINS.**

Margot .... Jeanne Moreau
Count De La Mole....Armando Francioli
Catherine .... Francoise Rosay
Annibal .... Henri Genes
Charles IX .... Robert Porte
Henri de Navarre ...... Andre Versini
Anjou .... Danile Ceccaldi
Rosine .... Nicole Riche
Rene .... Louis De Funes

Still another historical fresco from the color spec cycle of the Franco-Italian production setup, this too emerges as not fullbodied enough for exceptional chances on the U. S. general market. It lacks names and C'Scope, and is not of arty house proportions. This is reminiscent of oldie costumers with intercutting between various climaxes, and keeping most history in the bedroom. However, this has a neat color dressing and enough nudity and action for local spots, but sheared of its more sensational aspects, pic looks uncertain for any American chances.

This concerns the impetuous Margot (Jeanne Moreau), daughter of Catherine (Francoise Rosay) and brother of Charles IX (Robert Porte), who is married to the Huguenot prince (Andre Versini) in order to form a bulwark for the king and ward off trouble. However, right after the marriage, the King calls for the massacre of the Huguenots and a bloodbath follows. During this debacle, a handsome count stumbles into the Margot's boudoir. It is, of course, love after the first fright. Then intrigue builds.

Miss Moreau is an engaging, feline actress but is miscast for nudie roles. She will never give Martine Carol competition in this sphere. Remainder of the cast is fine, with Miss Rosay a scheming Catherine and Porte a properly unpredictable king. Massacre has its share of bloodiness, with the nudity and love scenes not sparing the anatomy. Director Jean Dreville has not been able to make anything unusual. Eastmancolor has been well used and editing helps in the scenes of action. Production is opulent and decorative. *Mosk.*

Okasan
(Mother)
(JAPANESE)

Paris, Jan. 18.
Shintoho production and release. Stars Kinuyo Tanaka. Directed by Mikio Naruse. Screenplay, Yoko Misuki; camera, Hiroshi Suzuki; editor, Masatoshi Kato. At Studio

De LEtoile, Paris. Running time, **100 MINS.**

Mother .... Kinuyo Tanaka
Husband .... Massao Mishima
Son .... Akihiko Katayama
Daughter .... Kyoko Kagawa
Baker .... Eiji Okada

After the rash of exoticism, the first important neo-realistic Jap film has been imported here. This story of the daily life of a lower class family, told through the eyes of the daughter, has a poignant aspect due to the pointed observation, taste and treatment by the director Mikio Naruse. Film also has excellent thesp and production values. This humane film might well be a solid arty house entry in the U.S. Crix and word-of-mouth should help.

Based on a contest at Tokyo schools for the best competition on mothers, this recounts simple family crisis and life through the eyes of an adolescent girl. Modern Japan is shown with all the troubles of adjustment, young love and survival.

Director Naruse has managed to infuse a view of a people living in a general pattern of dignity and reserve. He is helped in this by a perfectly composed performance by Kinuyo Tanaka, whose dedicated mother is a classic in poise and emotion. All roles are well filled, with Kyoko Kagawa appealing as the daughter, and Eiji Okada excellent as the wooer. Lensing and editing is of high quality. *Mosk.*

Battle Cry
(COLOR—C'SCOPE)

Action film treatment on life and love among the Marines. Good boxoffice expectations.

Hollywood, Jan. 24.

Warner Bros. release. Stars Van Heflin, Aldo Ray, Mona Freeman, Nancy Olson, James Whitmore, Raymond Massey, Tab Hunter, Dorothy Malone, Anne Francis; features William Campbell, John Lupton, Justus E. McQueen, Perry Lopez, Fess Parker, Jonas Applegarth, Tommy Cook, Felix Noriego, Susan Morrow, Carleton Young, Allyn McLerie. Directed by Raoul Walsh. Screenplay, Leon M. Uris; based on his novel; camera (WarnerColor), Sid Hickox; editor, William Ziegler; original music, Max Steiner; technical adviser, Col. H. P. (Jim) Crowe, USMC. Previewed Dec. 9, '54. Running time, **147 MINS.**

Major Huxley .... Van Heflin
Andy .... Aldo Ray
Kathy .... Mona Freeman
Pat .... Nancy Olson
Sgt. Mac .... James Whitmore
General Snipes .... Raymond Massey
Danny .... Tab Hunter
Elaine .... Dorothy Malone
Rae .... Anne Francis
Ski .... William Campbell
Marion .... John Lupton
L. Q. Jones .... Justus E. McQueen
Joe Gomez .... Perry Lopez
Speedy .... Fess Parker
Lighttower .... Jonas Applegarth
Ziltch .... Tommy Cook
Crazy Horse .... Felix Noriego
Susan .... Susan Morrow
Maj. Wellman .... Carleton Young
Enoch Rogers .... Rhys Williams
A Waitress .... Allyn McLerie
Sgt. Beller .... Gregory Walcott
Mr. Walker .... Frank Ferguson
Mrs. Forrester .... Sarah Selby
Mr. Forrester .... Willis Bouchey

Amatory, rather than military, action is the mainstay of this saga of the United States Marines. This angle, in combination with a good overall service feel, indicates the younger masculine set, and their dates, will give it a profitable run. It is good motion picture entertainment that sustains interest, even if its 147 minutes running time will prove an endurance contest for the some viewers.

With all its fanciful qualities of Hollywood-staged war and a pattern that reminds of the many such service features that have gone before, it has definite heart, a sentiment that will help general appeal and usually means better than average returns at the wickets.

While overboard in length, this comes from the detailing of several sets of romantics, each interesting in itself, plus the necessary battle action to indicate the basis is rather grim warfare. The latter is at a minimum, however, since Leon Uris' screen adaptation of his own novel is more concerned with the liberties and loves of the World War II Marines with whom he served, than with actually winning the fight in the Pacific. It is the story of a group of enlisted men and their officers in a communications battalion, taking them from civilian life, through training and then to New Zealand, from which base the outfit participates in Pacific action.

Five males and four femmes draw star billing in the cast. Of the romantic pairings, the most impression is made by Aldo Ray and Nancy Olson, not only because it occupies the main portion of the film's second half after the two other principal teamings have been completed, but also because of the grasp the two stars have on their characters. Ray should boost his film stock tremendously as the northwest logger, a man as rough and raw as the trees he cuts. Miss Olson is fine as the New Zealander, a widow who already has lost a husband and brother to the war, yet still tries love again with a fighting man.

Tab Hunter gets a big break in the love department, having two femmes, Mona Freeman and Dorothy Malone, at whom to pitch some torrid wooing. This portion of the plot comes off well, too, particularly because of the zing the femmes put into their characters. Miss Malone as a lonely married woman in San Diego who goes for the young Marine, and Miss Freeman as the girl back home who gets Hunter. The latter's being alive at the ending is film magic since the definite impression that he is killed is given earlier in the footage.

John Lupton and Anne Francis spark the third romance with a sincerity that gets through to the viewer. He is a quiet, literary-minded Marine and she is a party girl. They carry out their courtship on the ferry plying between San Diego and Coronado. His basic worth even survives disclosure of her profession and a marriage is in the offing until he dies in battle.

Van Heflin brings his acting skill to the role of the major who commands the outfit, playing a martinet, who wants his boys to be tough fighting men, with an underlying kindliness that's just the right touch. His death near the end seems almost as unnecessary as Hunter's resurrection in the closing scene. James Whitmore is excellent as the master sergeant, and Raymond Massey is seen briefly, but effectively, as a Marine general. William Campbell, Justus E. McQueen, Perry Lopez, Fess Parker, Jonas Applegarth, Tommy Cook, Felix Noriego and Carleton Young each add to the good entertainment values sparked by the entire cast.

Raoul Walsh's direction has the vigor to sustain interest through the long footage. His handling is particularly effective in sharpening the mood and feel of the varied personal stories, and does as well in the broader action. Technically, however, the film is not as realistic as is desirable for this type of subject. The uniform and equipment of the men show up too unmusted and clean to be real, and some of the actual war footage cut in does not blow up well to CinemaScope size. Otherwise, the cameras do their job well under Sid Hickox' guidance and the WarnerColor tints show up excellently. Max Steiner's score is suitable background cleffing. *Brog.*

The Racers
(COLOR—C'SCOPE)

Offbeat action yarn with plenty of exciting car racing footage. Exploitation ceiling unlimited.

Twentieth Century-Fox release of Julian Blaustein production. Stars Kirk Douglas, Bella Darvi, Gilbert Roland; features Cesar Romero, Lee J. Cobb, Katy Jurado, Charles Goldner, John Hudson, George Dolenz, Agnes Laury. Directed by Henry Hathaway. Screenplay, Charles Kaufman: based on the Hans Ruesch novel; camera (color by DeLuxe), Joe MacDonald; editor, James B. Clark; special photographic effects, Ray Kellogg; technical advisers, John Fitch, Phil Hill, E. de Graffenried; song, Alex North; vocals by Peggy Lee. Previewed in N.Y. Jan. 27, '55. Running time, **112 MINS.**

Gino .... Kirk Douglas
Nicole .... Bella Darvi
Dell 'Oro .... Gilbert Roland
Carlos .... Cesar Romero
Maglio .... Lee J. Cobb
Maria .... Katy Jurado
Piero .... Charles Goldner
Michel Caron .... John Hudson
Count Salem .... George Dolenz
Toni .... Agnes Laury
Dr. Tabor .... John Wengraf
Pilar .... Richard Allan
Chata .... Francesco de Scaffa
Dehlgreen .... Norbert Schiller
Fiori .... Mel Welles
Rousillon .... Gene D'Arcy
Dell 'Oro's Mechanic .... Mike Dengate
Gatti .... Peter Brocco
Race Official .... Stephen Bekassy
Red Haired Girl .... June McCall
Luigi .... Frank Yaconelli
Janka .... Ina Anders
Nurse .... Gladys Holland
Dr. Seger .... Ben Wright
Interne .... James Barrett
Teen-age Mechanic .... Chris Randall
Premier Ballerina .... Anna Cheselka
Dr. Bocci .... Joe Vitale
Doorman .... Salvador Baguez
Race Official .... Eddie Le Baron
Cashier .... Peter Norman
Baron .... George Givot
Race Announcer .... Carleton Young

In his book "The Racers," Hans Ruesch drew a sharp and knowing portrait of that hardy, death-defying crew of men who drive in Europe's dangerous and exciting auto races. Specifically, he wrote about a boy who evolved his own curious code of ethics as he elbowed his way to the top of the profession, and about the girl who loved him, married him and left him in disillusionment.

In 20th-Fox's expertly fashioned and technically admirable screen version of "The Racers," the outlines of the basic plot are still there but the accent has, perhaps wisely, been shifted to the races themselves. With CinemaScope a mighty big plus, this makes for a healthy dose of definitely offbeat entertainment that should be a big hit with the action fans.

Again and again, the camera catches the sleek, multi-hued little racers roaring from the starting line to attain breakneck speeds over curving roads in France, Italy and Germany. There's more tension and excitement in some of those shots than in a dozen thrillers combined. Here's a case where the wide-screen offers a real sense of audience participation, in some shots almost too much so.

Joe MacDonald's lensing and Henry Hathaway's direction, whether the sweeping vistas of the Riviera, which has never looked so beautiful, or the remarkably effective closeups of the drivers fighting tenaciously for every inch of ground, call for great big bows. There are a couple of accidents staged in the picture, and particularly the one at the start, that'll have the audience on the edge of their seats. That kind of excitement hasn't been seen on the screen for some time.

Unfortunately, with the story barely a factor, there's a tendency to throw in too much of a good thing. Towards the end, the sight of the autos shooting along dangerous hairpin curves in all kinds of weather and skidding off the track becomes a little boring. Where the first ride carries almost unbearable tension, the last one is just one too many. A little pruning might be in order still.

As The Racer, Kirk Douglas givess an excellent account of himself. He is the moody, ambitious daredevil that Ruesch sketched in his book. His restlessness, his tremendous drive that makes him drunk with desire for speed and success, are communicated with skill and yet with a tendency towards underplaying which makes the part stand out clearer.

For reasons unknown, scripter Charles Kaufman has changed the Ruesch plot. Where, in the novel, the girl, fresh out of finishing school, meets her hero and marries him, in the film she's a prima ballerina. And though she quite obviously lives with him all over Europe, she never marries him. That's hardly an improvement.

Miss Darvi, handicapped by a very heavy accent, isn't given very much to do in the film although she's "on camera" most of the time. Smartly costumed throughout, her performance leaves much to wish for.

Gilbert Roland as Douglas' friend and competitor hits the right note of bravado and fear and comes through with a rousing portrayal. Cesar Romero as the racing vet has a gentle manner that is appealing, and Lee J. Cobb puts a lot of drama into the part of the boss man. Katy Jurado as Maria, Romero's woman, is good in a minor role.

John Hudson establishes himself as a very promising newcomer as Michel, the new driver, who finally wrests from Douglas not only the racing crown but also succeeds in almost winning Miss Darvi. Charles Goldner as Piero, the devoted mechanic, comes up with a sturdy characterization that has appeal.

Julian Blaustein's production, in very good color by DeLuxe, has many solid b.o. values. Since auto racing is far more popular in Europe than it's in the U.S., the film may require a special sales pitch that'll put across the thrill angle. Its settings are a joy to the eye. Ray Kellogg, who's responsible for the special photographic effects, has done an outstanding job integrating live with filmed sequences for sock results. James B. Clark's editing (as every technical aspect of the pic) is standout.

Hathaway gets the pic off to a flying start and keeps it at a reasonably even pace without being overly imaginative in playing up the romantic angles. Peggy Lee is the vocalist (never seen) for Alex North's wistful "I Belong to You" which makes a pleasant theme. The most exciting sounds in this one, though, are the roar of the engines and the screech of tires as the racers brave death in their battle for speed. *Hift.*

Many Rivers to Cross
(COLOR-C'SCOPE)

Extremely broad, sometimes funny, romantic comedy of pioneer men and women back in early Kentucky. Merits boxoffice.

Hollywood, Jan. 27.

Metro release of Jack Cummings production. Stars Robert Taylor, Eleanor Parker; features, Victor McLaglen, Russ Tamblyn, Jeff Richards, James Arness, Alan Hale Jr. Directed by Roy Rowland. Screenplay, Harry Brown, Guy Trosper; based on a story by Steve Frazee; camera (Eastman Color), John Seitz; editor, Ben Lewis; music, Cyril J. Mockridge. Previewed Jan. 21, '55. Running time, **94 MINS.**

Bushrod Gentry .... Robert Taylor
Mary Stuart Cherne .... Eleanor Parker
Cadmus Cherne .... Victor McLaglen
Fremont .... Jeff Richards
Shields .... Russ Tamblyn
Esau Hamilton .... James Arness
Luke Radford .... Alan Hale Jr.
Hugh .... John Hudson
Lige Blake .... Rhys Williams
Mrs. Cherne .... Josephine Hutchinson
Spectacle Man .... Sig Ruman
Lucy Hamilton .... Rosemary DeCamp
Banks .... Russell Johnson
Sandak .... Ralph Moody
Slangoh .... Abel Fernandez

Filmgoers who buy "Many Rivers To Cross" on the assumption it is a pioneer actioner are due for quite a surprise. Instead, it is an extremely broad, sometimes funny, comedy about the romantic di-does of settlers in early Kentucky; more particularly the amatory byplay between a matrimonially unwilling Robert Taylor and a willing—even eager—Eleanor Parker.

The slapstick treatment, in itself, is well enough handled by Roy Rowland's direction of the Jack Cummings production, but will come as such a shock to those expecting straight outdoor action that considerable footage will have passed before they warm up to the fun-poking. By the time the climax is reached, however, most viewers will have gotten into the mood. This should mean they will at least walk out chuckling at the hectic finale battle in which, together, Taylor and Miss Parker best some Indians and he surrenders to the matrimonial advantages she has been throwing at him for most of the 94 minutes of footage.

Buckskin-clad Taylor displays a sense of humor in trouping the role of a trapper whose trek to the northwest is cancelled out by Miss Parker's yen for marriage. She portrays the girl with a madness for mating with an uninhibited enthusiasm, obviously enjoying the chance to let her hair down. In the Harry Brown-Guy Trosper script, based on a story by Steve Frazee, Miss Parker frames Taylor into a shotgun wedding after he has spurned the opportunities she gives him to be a willing groom.

Taylor doesn't give up his freedom easy, though, and still heads for the northwest, but now as the hunted pursued by an angry bride. Adventures along the way, and an encounter with another freedom-loving man now in matrimonial harness, result in a gradual change of mind and he turns back, in time to rescue the bride from an Indian party and bow to the inevitable.

Playing Miss Parker's family with hoked-up, backwoodsy zest are Victor McLaglen, Russ Tamblyn, Jeff Richards, Russell Johnson and John Hudson, the father and brothers. Josephine Hutchinson is a sane note as the mother. The strapping James Arness is the kindred soul already broken to marital harness whom Taylor encounters on the trail, and Alan Hale Jr. is the suitor Miss Parker doesn't want. Others appear briefly.   Brog.

Simba
(BRITISH-COLOR)

Realistic drama set in Mau Mau country; grim entertainment with spotty returns likely.

London, Jan. 25.
General Film Distributors release of a Peter de Sarigny production. Stars Dirk Bogarde, Donald Sinden, Virginia McKenna, Earl Cameron. Directed by Brian Desmond Hurst. Screenplay, John Baines, from an original story by Anthony Perry, with additional scenes and dialog by Robin Estridge; camera (Eastmancolor), Geoffrey Unsworth; editor, Michael Gordon; music, Francis Chagrin. At Odeon, Leicester Square, London. Running time, 99 MINS.
Howard .... Dirk Bogarde
Drummond .... Donald Sinden
Mary .... Virginia McKenna
Mr. Crawford .... Basil Sydney
Mrs. Crawford .... Marie Ney
Dr. Hughes .... Joseph Tomelty
Karanja .... Earl Cameron
Headman .... Orlando Martins
Kimani .... Ben Johnson
Joshua .... Huntley Campbell
Waweru .... Frank Singuineau
Cheze .... Slim Harris
Mundati .... Clyn Lawson
Thakla .... Harry Quash
Settler at Meeting .... John Chandos
Col. Bridgeman .... Desmond Roberts
African Inspector .... Errol John
Witch Doctor .... Willy Sholanke

Spotlighting the present unrest in Kenya, this new British film focuses attention on the terror methods of the Mau Mau and the retaliatory measures for the defense of the white farmer and sympathetic Africans. This is a grim, realistic entertainment, departing from the conventional b.o. formula of escapist fare. As such, spotty returns loom, both in the home market and overseas.

The screenplay has been adapted from an original yarn by Anthony Perry. It tries to portray the anxious problems of the white farmer and loyal natives objectively. This treatment is not applied to the Mau Mau whose terrorist campaigns brook little sympathy. Running through the theme is a plea for better understanding between white man and African. Location lensing on Mount Kenya gives the film a colorful, authentic background. Story has been briskly directed by Brian Desmond Hurst and is expertly played by a skilled local cast headed by Dirk Bogarde, Virginia McKenna, and Donald Sinden. There is a particularly dignified performance by Earl Cameron as the native doctor. Other roles are intelligently handled, and round out a competently made picture.   Myro.

La Tour de Nesle
(The Tower of Nesle)
(FRANCO-ITALIAN)
(COLOR)

Paris, Jan. 25.
Fernand Rivers release of Fernand Rivers-Costellazone production. Stars Pierre Brasseur, Silvana Pampanini. Directed by Abel Gance. Screenplay, Gance, Fernand Rivers, Fuzelier from play by Alexandre Dumas, Gaillardet; camera (Gevacolor), Andre Thomas; music, Henri Verdun; editor, Louisette Hautecoeur. Previewed in Paris. Running time, 120 MINS.
Buridan .... Pierre Brasseur
Queen .... Silvana Pampanini
King .... Michel Bouquet
Philippe .... Henri Toja
Gaultier .... Paul Guers

This film marks the return of French film pioneer Abel Gance to active production after 12 years of obscurity. It was Gance who gave the French such films as "Beethoven" and the sweeping "Napleon" (which used three cameras and projected individually on one massive screen) over 20 years before Cinerama. This pic is a scorching piece of filmic bravura which uses the old Alexandre Dumas melodrama to pictorial advantage. Full of Rabelaisian truculence, spectacle, violence and full-blown thesping and direction, it amply recreates the medieval ages. It should do well here but its frank medieval orgiastic scenes and nudity will make the pic a touchy entry for the U. S. At best, it looks only ripe for specialized arty theatre showings. Sheared of its franker aspects, this would loose some of its blustering appeal.

Gance's firm hand and mounting keep this meller in line, and its period flavor of ruthlessness and vitality plus its superbly hued color aspects, make this a solid whole. However, some scissoring can make this even more engrossing by eliminating some purely gratuitous mood aspects.

Story concerns the queen who has entered into a strange perversity in having noblemen lured to the Tower of Nesle where they are greeted by three unclad lovelies, the queen being one. After some moments of revel, they are killed by a gang of cutthroats who serve as her executioners. But the blustering, colossal Buridan (Pierre Brasseur) escapes from this adventure unharmed, and holds it over the queen to become prime minister. Then he discloses that he had been her youthful lover, and it all ends in her going crazy.

Gance has forced this into a moving tapestry of medieval skullduggery with both sensational and art appeal. He has elicited fine performances from Pierre Brasseur, as the mighty and crafty Buridan, and Silvana Pampanini as the conniving, debauched queen. Costuming and production aspects are fine. Colors are pale tinted and perfect for the film mood as is the editing and music. Conception, sweep and construction are reminiscent of a bolder and more virile period of filmmaking.   Mosk.

J'Avais Sept Filles
(I Had Seven Daughters)
(FRANCO-ITALIAN)
(COLOR—SONGS)

Paris, Feb. 1.
ABCine release of Francinalp-Faro Film production. Stars Maurice Chevalier; features Paolo Stoppa, Delia Scala. Directed by Jean Boyer. Screenplay, Aldo De Benedetti, Jean Des Vallieres, Boyer; dialog, Vallieres, Serge Veber; camera (Ferranicolor), Charles Suin; music, Fred Freed; editor, A. Laurent. At Colisee, Paris. Running time, 90 MINS.
Count Andre .... Maurice Chevalier
Luisella .... Delia Scala
Linda .... Colette Ripert
Nadine .... Annick Tanguy
Maria .... Gabby Basset
Antonio .... Paolo Stoppa
Eduard .... Louis Velle
Professor .... Pasquali

Maurice Chevalier's U.S. visa vindication and the flood of legit and pic offers from there, plus his recent boff one-man show here, insure marquee value on both sides of the brink for this bright, simple comedy. Chevalier charm and a bevy of youthful beauties light up the corners of this lightweight piece which fades into the conventional and ordinary after a bright, intriguing start.

However, this makes for pleasant fare. Although not for arty U.S. houses, this could be a nice entry for special situations, and has the general entertainment qualities that might make this a neat morsel, when dubbed for wider bookings. It also shapes as a Hollywood remake musical possibility with a little working over of the script.

It's Chevalier all the way in this as he incarnates an aging, royal roue (Count Andre) writing the memoirs of his amorous escapades vaguely connected with the history of France, who gets involved with a troupe of ballet dancers. As long as Chevalier spreads his gaiety and bits of wisdom and he has a chance to chant some personalized ditties to his brood, the film is engaging. Girls are lovely, color is good and production values are fine with the other credits craftsmanlike.

The music is tailored to Chevalier's standards, but there is some background theme too reminiscent of other pix. His beaming, ingratiating self is well set off by his tightlipped valet (Paolo Stoppa) who shares vicariously in his master's exploits, and acts as moralist. Delia Scala is an eye-filling ingenue while the remaining gals are the answer to an old romantico's dreams.

Director Jean Boyer has not succeeded in getting the pace and crispness into this, with the familiar situations not helping much. However, as Chevalier sings "J'Ai Vingt Ans (I'm 20 Years Old), he single-handedly rejuvenates this oldie operetta plot to modern tempo.   Mosk.

Cinerama Holiday
(TECHNICOLOR)

Many of the same strong box-office values of original picture in Fred Waller's process. Bright outlook while raising some questions for future.

Stanley-Warner Cinerama Corp. presentation of Louis de Rochemont film. Directors, Robert Bendick, Phillipe de Lacey. Introducing Betty and John Marsh, Beatrice and Fred Troller. Adaptation, Otis Carney, Louis de Rochemont 3d; narration, John Stuart Martin; cameramen, Joseph Brun, Harry Squire; sound, Richard J. Pietschmann Jr.; Rolf Epstein; technical supervisor, Wentworth D. Fling; editors, Jack Murray, Leo Zochling, Frederich Y. Smith; art direction, Joy Batchelor, John Halas; music, Morton Gould, Van Cleave; conductor, Jack Shaindlin. Running time, 119 MINS.

In something over two years, "This Is Cinerama" has made box-office history, triggered a theatrical revolution and turned Russian propaganda red with confusion and embarrassment in Syria and Thailand. Presently running as a great novelty attraction in some 18 cities, including London and Tokyo, the Fred Waller process is now seen at the Warner Theatre, New York, in its second mounting. Immediately the question arises: can "Cinerama Holiday" be expected to duplicate the sensational financial record of the original film?

A balanced answer must run, generally, on the strong prognostication side. There are no visible omens that any point of diminishing returns hovers over the daddy of the new widescreen media. Much of the excitement remains, although there is some feeling of repeating tried-and-true pictorial effects. The sheer size of the panoramic stuff, the tremolo of the downhill rides, the adventure of roping jet-planes on the flat top of an aircraft carrier possess implicit drama. For millions of Americans such Cinerama tricks will undoubtedly be joyously reexperienced, and no quibbling.

The big question which the speculative imagination of show business cannot avoid asking is this: can the Stanley Warner auspices go on, indefinitely assured of reaping a boxoffice bonanza, without telling a story or going beyond the travelog format? The danger of diminishing returns is not immediate, but the third offering, "Seven Wonders of the World," is apparently lined up as more of the same. Well, worry about that next year.

Right off, one thing stands out. Here is the greatest trailer for travel ever produced. "Holiday" is a sock synthesis of everything Burton Holmes ever did or said in 50 years on the lecture platform. More specifically, it is the public relations coup of the decade for one carrier, namely Swissair. Switzerland ought to forgive us on our high clock tariffs after this super-sell. When they see "Cinerama Holiday" there should be yodelling and free wine on the streets of Zurich.

There is a wisp of continuity in "Holiday" unlike the predecessor film. Betty and John Marsh of Kansas City and Beatrice and Fred Troller of Zurich did an exchange student type of act, each pair of newlyweds visiting the other's hemisphere. They are reunited at the ending in New York. Meanwhile the Swiss pair, mounted on a Vespa motorcycle, has hit the far west, meeting cowpunching Apaches. Las Vegas gamblers and the cocktail crowd in San Francisco's Top O' the Mark. Against that, the American pair has a long visit in Switzerland, climbs the

Alps on Toonerville trolleys, goes sleighing, bob-sledding, watches an ice show (presumably American) outside the Suvretta House in St. Moritz and has fun on skis and in picturesque chalets where they wash down cheese fondue with the cup that cheers.

Since the second part of the show, after a 15-minute intermission, is largely made up of an extended visit to Paris, the impression grows into a conviction that the American couple really went places, did things and met people far beyond the arrangements for the Swiss pair this side—who had much tamer calls to make—for example, upon the rural folk of Louis de Rochemont's New Hampshire, at rather considerable length. The New Hampshire stuff is "justified" in the continuity on the grounds of exquisite autumnal tree colorings. It seemed a purely personal choice.

Because "Cinerama Holiday" is intended for reserved seat operation it may not be valid to hint that maybe it's overlong in footage, some 119 minutes. An intermission is a necessary physical consideration.

Naturally, certain scenes stand out. The bobsled ride, of course. And the skiorama where seemingly hundreds of devotees zig and zag and frolic all over the snowy terrain. The extremely charming children of Paris also stand out. So do some of the shots in the gambling halls of Nevada. Nor does the United States Navy fail to score. (It's next to closing, very strong and a natural segue into the slightly George M. Cohanesque patriotic fireworks finale).

Louis de Rochemont's documentary technique works fine on occasion, but is a mite on the awkward side at a few points. Negroes may or may not complain about the jazz band parade stuff from the cemetery in New Orleans. This is undoubtedly innocuous in motivation but nonetheless tends to be pretty condescending about the picturesque American "darkies." Not that there's even a hint of any word of comment which in itself could be objectionable. It's just that the only sequence showing Negroes to a Swiss couple just happens to make the Negroes "quaint" at best. Why not honor American Negroes by showing their superior types? This was a serious lack of foresight on the producer's part.

A rather strange bit of old hat "humor" crept into the continuity of the American couple in Paris, Remember this is a fresh, wholesome, newlywed pair. Comes a silly bit of business of him ducking his wife to join some Navy shipmates who appear in Paris out of nowhere. This arouses expectations of something "naughty" in the next sequence but it's all very tame, except that the shipmates have French girls with them. The expected "dive" is nothing of the sort but instead the highly posh Lido night club.

Trouble with the documentary, or real-life, technique when visiting cafes, whether in New Orleans, Las Vegas or Paris, is that the production numbers are markedly inferior to the production numbers in any, say, Metro Technicolor musical. Dullest item in the show, undoubtedly, is "Les Indes Galantes." They have better ballet at the YM-YWHA any Friday.

"Cinerama Holiday" is strong on choirs, as was "This Is Cinerama." There are choirs from Dartmouth, Annapolis and Notre Dame de Paris.

Any attempt to judiciously bestow proper credit where it is due is almost impossible on such a long and many-elemented film. The musical score of Morton Gould and Van Cleave as conducted by Jack Shaindlin is stunningly effective. Many of the sound effects throughout are unusual, although occasionally distractive. Technicolor, too, makes a giant contribution. It is also easy to suppose that Robert Bendick and Phillipe de Lacey, the directors of the units working the respective hemispheres, were little Napoleons of location ingenuity and resourcefulness. Of the heroic cameramen there are four major credits, Joseph Brun, Harry Squire, Jack Priestley and Gayne Rescher. Undoubtedly there will be shop talk aplenty among the camera, sound, color and other cinema crafts on the problems of making this production. (There were 201 days of unit shooting and 675,000 feet of film were exposed.)

And what of the "seams" on the middle panel? They still show, although some improvement has apparently been effected by engineering experiment. Some "intimacy" previously missing has been achieved.

To sum up, second time round for Cinerama is still very promising, but enough is manifest in "Holiday" to highlight upcoming hazards. Granting that this is a great vicarious travel thrill, something more will eventually have to be added. But Swissair hasn't got a thing to complain about, not a thing. *Land.*

The Long Gray Line
(COLOR-C'SCOPE)

Standout drama of West Point with class, mass appeal; fine performances by Tyrone Power, Maureen O'Hara, others; strong b.o.

Hollywood, Feb. 8.

Columbia release of Robert Arthur production. Stars Tyrone Power, Maureen O'Hara; costars Robert Francis, Donald Crisp, Ward Bond, Betsy Palmer, Phil Carey; features William Leslie, Harry Carey Jr., Patrick Wayne, Sean McClory, Peter Graves, Milburn Stone, Erin O'Brien Moore, Walter D. Ehlers, Willis Bouchey. Directed by John Ford. Screenplay, Edward Hope; based on "Bringing Up the Brass" by Marty Maher and Nardi Reeder Campion; camera (Technicolor), Charles Lawton Jr.; editor, William Lyon; music adaptation, George Duning; supervised and conducted by Morris Stoloff. Previewed Jan. 27, '55. Running time, 135 **MINS.**

Marty Maher .... Tyrone Power
Mary O'Donnell .... Maureen O'Hara
James Sundstrom Jr...... Robert Francis
Old Martin .... Donald Crisp
Capt. Herman J. Koehler... Ward Bond
Kitty Carter .... Betsy Palmer
Charles Dotson .... Phil Carey
Red Sundstrom .... William Leslie
Dwight Eisenhower...... Harry Carey Jr.
Cherub Overton .... Patrick Wayne
Dinny Maher .... Sean McClory
Corp. Rudolph Heinz....... Peter Graves
Capt. John Pershing....... Milburn Stone

"The Long Gray Line" is a standout drama on West Point with appeal for most all types of audiences. It merits and should hit a strong pace at the boxoffice, particularly in view of the favorable word-of-mouth the initial showings will create. It is frankly sentimental, very human, proudly patriotic, and quite long with its two hours and 15 minutes running time. Only a small minority will quarrel with either the unabashed sentiment or the footage.

For Tyrone Power the role of Marty Maher, Irishman through whose eyes the story is told, is a memorable one. Certainly none of his more recent film roles has had the depth or breadth that would permit full use of his considerable talent as does this one. For Maureen O'Hara, his costar, the picture also is a major credit and she brings to the role of Maher's wife her Irish beauty and seldom displayed acting ability. Both are very fine.

Robert Arthur's exceptionally well-fashioned production is based on "Bringing Up the Brass," the autobiography of Maher's 50 years at the Point which he wrote with Nardi Reeder Campion. A screenplay by Edward Hope that is full of wonderfully human touches gave just the right foundation for John Ford to show his love for country (and the Irish) with his direction. Story oscillates between unashamed sniffles and warm chuckles, Ford not being afraid to bring a tear or stick in a laugh.

In addition to spanning the 50 years Maher spent at West Point, the picture writes a patriotic history of the Academy during a period in which two World Wars fell and through which passed such cadet names as President Eisenhower, Generals Bradley, Pershing, Cousins, McNarney, Stratemeyer and Van Fleet.

Maher's story begins when he comes to West Point, fresh off the boat from Ireland, and becomes a waiter in the cadet mess hall. From there he joins the regular Army, remaining at the Point with the service troops stationed there. He worked as an athletic trainer and swimming instructor and became, with the Irish lass who married him, friend and adviser to the embryo officers who trained at the Academy during the half-century. It's what Maher, his wife and the cadets put into those years that makes this picture rich with incident and the script, the direction and playing blend it all into rewarding drama.

The cast is large, and the performances are of a quality that merit individual praise. Donald Crisp is great as Maher's father, brought to this country by the soldier's bride as a surprise. Robert Francis shows up very well as a second generation cadet, the son of Betsy Palmer and William Leslie. Miss Palmer scores as the mother and Leslie shows much promise. Ward Bond walks off with a sock rendition of the Academy's Master of the Sword (athletic director), and Phil Carey impresses as Cadet Dotson, now general. All of the others, too, are equally good, and include Harry Carey Jr., as the young Cadet Eisenhower; Patrick Wayne as Cherub Overton; Sean McClory as Maher's brother; Peter Graves, Milburn Stone, Erin O'Brien Moore, Walter D. Ehlers and Willis Bouchey.

West Point, its grounds, its buildings and its cadets in review have been strikingly lensed in CinemaScope and Technicolor by Charles Lawton Jr. The editing by William Lyon is a standout job of blending together the wealth of footage. Also important to the entertainment is the music adaptation by George Duning, which Morris Stoloff supervised and conducted. *Brog.*

White Feather
(COLOR)

Robert Wagner, Debra Paget, John Lund, Jeffrey Hunter in Indian western thriller. High quality Western.

20th-Fox release of Leonard Goldstein (Panoramic) production. Stars Robert Wagner, Debra Paget, John Lund, Jeffrey Hunter; features Hugh O'Brian, Eduard Franz, Virginia Leith, Noah Beery. Directed by Robert Webb. Screenplay, Delmer Daves, Leo Townsend, from story by John Prebble; camera, Lucien Ballard; editor, George Gittens; print by Technicolor; music, Hugh Friedhofer. Tradeshown in N.Y., Feb. 3, '55. Running time, **102 MINS.**

Josh Tanner .... Robert Wagner
Colonel Lindsay .... John Lund
Appearing Day .... Debra Paget
Little Dog .... Jeffrey Hunter
Chief Broken Hand .... Eduard Franz
Lt. Ferguson .... Noah Beery
Ann Magruder .... Virginia Leith
Magruder .... Emile Meyer
American Horse .... Hugh O'Brian
Commissioner Trenton..... Milburn Stone

Here is a well-contrived, faithfully made and intriguing picture which somewhat handicapped by lack of marquee names having top impact at the wickets. Robert Wagner, turning in one of his finest screen portrayals; Debra Paget, fetching as a comely Indian girl; and Jeffrey Hunter, excellent as a Redskin warrior, however, are not personalities established as lures to the b.o. But feature should have good word-of-mouth and shapes about as strong as "Broken Lance" as a grosser, sans the stars the latter picture boasted.

Delmer Daves-Leo Townsend's screenplay, based on the John Prebble story, about the Cheyenne Indians circa 1877 when they were being pushed out of Wyoming by the Federals is grippingly unfolded in colorful CinemaScope. Plot depicts Wagner as a surveyor who is with the vanguard of the government party (U.S. Cavalry and all) about to sweep west from Ft. Cheyenne. They are stalled until the Cheyennes agree to move from their hunting grounds to some southern area. Scripters apparently slipped up when they pointed up that gold had been found.

Film builds to climax when the big chief's son and his young fighter-pal challenge (via the arrow with whitefeather attached) the whole cavalry contingent to pitched battle. It is only through the successful intervention of Wagner and Miss Paget, the Indian girl, that a needless slaughter is averted. Wagner of course, wins the Indian beauty. The whole story is so deftly unfolded that the cornier aspects are mainly submerged. And seldom is the Redskin depicted as the villain. Rather, the plot makes the white man the aggressor.

Produced by the late Leonard Goldstein and directed by Robert Webb, the characters are all well portrayed by Wagner, Miss Paget and Hunter, last as the chief's son. Eduard Franz is superb as the venerable Indian chief, Broken Hand, while Hugh O'Brian is well chosen as Hunter's warrior pal, American Horse. Noah Beery does one of his better thespian jobs as a cavalry lieutenant, with John Lund equally adequately suited for the role of Colonel Lindsay, commander at Ft. Cheyenne.

In support, Virginia Leith makes something of the role of daughter of a drunken store proprietor, Emile Meyer. Latter is sufficiently obscene to make the character realistic.

Lucien Ballard's camera takes in the sweep of the western background and handles the traveling shots with fine effect. George Gittens has done a sharp editing job. *Wear.*

Ten Wanted Men
(COLOR)

Standard Randolph Scott western actioner in Technicolor for the outdoor market.

Hollywood, Feb. 1.

Columbia release of Harry Joe Brown (Scott-Brown) production. Stars Randolph Scott; features Jocelyn Brando, Richard Boone, Alfonso Dedoya, Donna Martell, Skip Homeier. Directed by Bruce Humberstone. Screenplay, Kenneth Gamet; story, Irving Revetch, Harriet Frank Jr.; camera (Technicolor), Wilfrid M. Cline; editor, Gene Havlick; score, Paul Sawtell. Previewed Jan. 20, 55. Running time, **80 MINS.**

John Stewart	Randolph Scott
Corinne Michaels	Jocelyn Brando
Wick Campbell	Richard Boone
Hermando	Alfonso Bedoya
Maria Segura	Donna Martell
Howie Stewart	Skip Homeier
Tod Grinnel	Clem Bevans
Frank Scavo	Leo Gordon
Jason Carr	Minor Watson
Adam Stewart	Lester Matthews
Green	Tom Powers
Sheriff Clyde Gibbons	Dennis Weaver
Al Drucker	Lee Van Cleef
Tom Baines	Louis Jean Heydt
Marva Gibbons	Kathleen Crowley
Red Dawes	Boyd "Red" Morgan
Dave Weed	Denver Pyle
Warner	Francis McDonald
Bartender	Pat Collins

Some standard oater action is turned out in "Ten Wanted Men" to fit it to the progam demands of the outdoor market. The entertainment content isn't up to the level usually reached in the action fare bearing the Scott-Brown production brand, but Randolph Scott's name gives it a booking advantage for release intentions.

Story deals with Scott's efforts to establish law and order on the particularly large slice of Arizona range he controls, now that he finds it no longer necesary to use personal force of arms to build an empire. Scott's plans do not meet with the aims of Richard Boone, a rival, but lesser, bigshot, who prefers his own law of the shooting iron and hired thug to wrestle a fortune from the range. There are a number of diverse angles to the Kenneth Gamet script, based on a story by Irving Ravetch and Harriet Frank Jr., and some of them eventually work out as things build to the climax in which right triumphs and law is established.

There is a pretentiousness in the Harry Joe Brown production to which the story development is not equal; nor is Bruce Humberstone's direction able to overcome it. On the action score, though, the handling gets in some rough and ready sequences, and the Technicolor lensing by Wilfrid M. Cline shows off the outdoor locations effectively. On a technical count, the picture has some large holes. The doubling done for Scott in the big climactic fight is painfully obvious, and, elsewhere, action and scenes are not always well matched in shifts from long to medium or close shots. Such technical carelessness is seldom encountered in major releases today.

Scott is an experienced saddle hero and does this assignment easily, while Boone puts over the villainy in good style, with an assist in that department from Leo Gordon and other hirelings. Other more prominent parts are occupied by Skip Homeier as Scott's nephew who doesn't take readily to the west; Jocelyn Brando, a widow long in love with the hero and whose wait is eventually rewarded after the business at hand is out of the way, and Donna Martell, Latin girl coveted by Boone and whose turndown of the heavy sparks some of the trouble.

Brog.

Smoke Signal
(COLOR)

Standard outdoor actioner with Colorado River's Grand Canyon location for fresh interest. A program entry.

Hollywood, Feb. 3.

Universal release of Howard Christie production. Stars Dana Andrews, Piper Laurie, Rex Reason, William Talman; features Milburn Stone, Douglas Spencer, Gordon Jones, William Schallert. Directed by Jerry Hopper. Story and screenplay, George F. Slavin, George W. George; camera (Technicolor), Clifford Stine; editor, Milton Carruth. Previewed Jan. 31, '55. Running time, **87 MINS.**

Brett Halliday	Dana Andrews
Laura Evans	Piper Laurie
Lieutenant Wayne Ford	Rex Reason
Captain Harper	William Talman
Sergeant Miles	Milburn Stone
Garode	Douglas Spencer
Corporal Rogers	Gordon Jones
Private Livingston	William Schallert
First Sergeant Daly	Robert Wilke
Private Porter	Bill Phipps
Delche	Pat Hogan
Ute Prisoner	Peter Coe

(Aspect ratio: 2-1)

Cavalry versus Indians. Added interest from being plotted and filmed in the Colorado River's Grand Canyon, the fresh location making for pleasingly rugged background.

The visual qualities of the Howard Christie production are better than the story values, but since the film is aimed at the non-discriminating action buyer the character and plot cliches get by with some vigorous direction by Jerry Hopper. Chief fault of the story and screenplay by George F. Slavin and George W. George is that it drags in some extremely formula problems of human relationship, which lesssen the main problem of a small cavalry detachment daring uncharted river rapids to escape a band of warring Indians. Up until about the halfway mark the story is proceeding satisfactorily, but goes flat thereafter.

Dana Andrews and Piper Laurie, latter the lone femme, top the cast and he's more suited to the outdoor action than is the distaffer. William Talman heads the cavalry group, and he has the double purpose of getting the outfit to safety and bringing to courtmartial Andrews, a deserted who had gone over to the redskins after they were mistreated by another officer. Rex Reason is a petulant lieutenant who resents the fact Miss Laurie is attracted to Andrews. There are several good character types among the other players, best of which is Douglas Spencer as a trapper who has joined the party.

Camera work by Clifford Stone does justice to the Grand Canyon settings and the other technical aids bring off their contributions satisfactorily.

Brog.

Abbott & Costello Meet the Keystone Kops

Abbott & Costello following to help this mild program comedy in general bookings.

Hollywood, Jan. 27.

Universal release of Howard Christie production. Stars Bud Abbott, Lou Costello; features Fred Clark, Lynn Bari, Maxie Rosenbloom. Directed by Charles Lamont. Screenplay, John Grant; story, Lee Loeb; camera, Reggie Lanning; editor, Edward Curtiss; musical direction, Joseph Gershenson. Previewed Jan. 25, '55. Running time, **79 MINS.**

Harry Pierce	Bud Abbott
Willie Piper	Lou Costello
Joseph Gorman	Fred Clark
Leota Van Cleef	Lynn Bari
Hinds	Maxie Rosenbloom
Mr. Snavely	Frank Wilcox
Cameraman	Herold Goodwin
Old Wagon Driver	Roscoe Ates
Himself	Mack Sennett
Comic	Heinie Conklin
Prop Man	Hank Mann

(Aspect ratio: 2-1)

When Bud Abbott and Lou Costello finally meet up with Mack Sennett's Keystone Kops in this program comedy a wild and amusing chase finale results. Until the old and the more contemporary funsters get together, however, it's dull filmfare that will tax the loyal of the more avid A&C fan. (Of possible utility for tieups is just-published Mack Sennett autobiography, "King of Comedy," although there's no direct relationship).

Plot period goes back to early filmmaking when puttees were standard directorial equipment so that the Mack Sennett comical cops are at least logically introduced for the windup. Howard Christie's production has a number of nostalgic values that are better than the antics the stars are put through in the John Grant script from a story by Lee Loeb. Charles Lamont's direction seems slow, until the finish, and the laughs are extremely spotty.

The early-teens yarn opens in New York with A&C being swindled by Fred Clark, who sells them the Edison studio and then flees to Hollywood. The boys take up the chase and by accident become a film comic team. Clark's larceny again crops out and he blows a job as director to flee with producer Frank Wilcox' cash. It's here that A&C are joined in pursuing the fleeing Clark and his accomplice, Lynn Bari, to the airport by the Sennett police. Their patrol wagon, the motorcycle and sidecar commandeered by the comic team, and the producer's Rolls Royce all arrive in time to nab the crooks after hectic chase footage.

Abbott & Costello, and the other casters, including Maxie Rosenbloom, Herold Goodwin, Roscoe Ates, Sennett, Heinie Conklin and Hank Mann, do what they can to generate fun.

Musical direction by Joseph Gershenson is well-tuned, often having a better sense of humor than the action it supports. Technical credits are standard.

Brog.

Timberjack
(COLOR-SONGS)

Fair adventure-melodrama for the outdoor market.

Republic release of Herbert J. Yates presentation. Stars Sterling Hayden, Vera Ralston, David Brian; features Adolphe Menjou, Hoagy Carmichael, Chill Wills. Directed by Joe Kane. Screenplay, Allen Rivkin based on novel by Dan Cushman; camera (Trucolor), Jack Marta; editor, Richard L. Van Enger; music, Victor Young; songs, Paul Francis Webster, Hoagy Carmichael, Johnny Mercer, Ned Washington, Victor Young. Tradeshown N.Y., Feb. 4, '55. Running time, **94 MINS.**

Tim Chipman	Sterling Hayden
Lynne Tilton	Vera Ralston
Croft Brunner	David Brian
Swiftwater Tilton	Adolphe Menjou
Jingles	Hoagy Carmichael
Steve Riika	Chill Wills
Poole	Jim Davis
Axe-Handle Ole	Howard Petrie
Pauquette	Jan MacDonald
Punky	Elisha Cook
Red Bush	Karl Davis
Veazie	Wally Cassell
Charley	Tex Terry
Fireman	George Marshall

(Aspect ratio: 1.85-1)

"Timberjack" is a lusty actioner geared to the needs of the outdoor market. Story hews to a familiar pattern but the picture's scenic values and a wealth of fisticuffs help mold the 94 minutes' running time into fair entertainment for the action fans.

Despite the triteness of the Allen Rivkin screenplay as adapted from a novel by Dan Cushman, the natural beauty of Glacier National Park and western Montana, where the film was lensed as a locationer is a distinct asset. Mountain vistas are eye-catching as captured by Republic's Trucolor process.

Marquee dressing isn't too stout but names of Sterling Hayden, Vera Ralston and David Brian can be regarded as famili.r in situations where Republic product usually reaches. Use of Miss Ralston as a cabaret owner-singer is a convenient means of bringing in Hoagy Carmichael as her pianist-accompanist along with several songs staged as production numbers.

Amidst a setting of the forest primeval, the script unfolds a "fight-till-death" rivalry between two lumbermen. Brian, a powerful, ruthless operator, has already slain the father of Hayden and the latter has vowed to avenge family honor and regain timber holdings wrested from the estate.

Miss Ralston, whose affections are sought by both Hayden and Brian, attempts to act as peacemaker. However, when she learns that Brian has killed her father (Adolphe Menjou) she flees to Hayden. Now grimmer than ever, Hayden bests Brian in a rifle duel for a time-honored happy fadeout.

Performances aren't too convincing. Hayden seems too restrained for the demands of his role, Miss Ralston is only adequate while Brian does a stock characterization o' the heavy. Musical sequences offer a change of pace with Miss Ralston doing most of the numbers. Among the better tunes are "He's Dead But He Won't Lie Down" by Johnny Mercer and Carmichael. There's also a title song by Ned Washington and Victor Young.

While the story occasionally lags, the physical action moves at a fast clip thanks to Joe Kane's breezy direction. Of the better portrayals provided by supporting players, Menjou is amusingly garrulous as an aging attorney, Carmichael is fine as the pianist and Howard Petrie impresses as a rough-and-tumble timberjack. Jack Marta's Trucolor camera extracted full value from the Montana terrain and other technical credits come off favorably.

Gilb.

A Race for Life

Okay programmer with European auto racing background.

Hollywood, Jan. 28.

Lippert release of a Michael Carreras production, produced by Mickey Delamar. Stars Richard Conte, Mari Aldon; features George Coulouris. Directed by Terence Fisher. Screenplay, Richard Landau; based on novel by Jon Manchip White; camera, Jimmy Harvey; editor, Bill Lenney. Reviewed Jan. 25, '55. Running time, **68 MINS.**

Peter Wells	Richard Conte
Pat Wells	Mari Aldon
Dallapiccola	George Coulouris
Bellario	Peter Illing
Guido Rizetti	Alec Mango
Lawrence	Meredith Edwards
Johnny	Jimmy Copeland
Martin	Jeremy Hawk
Brecht	Richard Marner
Gibson	Edwin Richfield
Alverez	Tim Turner

(Aspect ratio: 1.33-1)

European auto racing provides the background for this British import, its routine story line bolstered somewhat by speed sequences lensed on some of the Continent's best tracks. Starring Richard Conte and Mari Aldon, both from the American screen, film is an okay entry for minor double billing.

Script written by Richard Landau, also from Hollywood, twirls about the try of a former American racing great to stage a comeback after the war. He ties in with an Italian team, and races against the wishes of his wife, who wants her husband whole and in one piece. After leaving him when he refuses to give up the track, she returns as he's winning the Grand Prix in Piedmont, Italy, to find he's ready to follow her wish.

The two stars struggle as best they can with cliche-filled roles, but it's colorless acting at best as directed by Terence Fisher. George Coulouris, another from Hollywood, makes a valiant effort as another driver who is killed, and manages a measure of interest. Principal interest is centered on the racing scenes in final reels, where Jimmy Harvey's photography sometimes catches good effects. Mickey Delamar gave film satisfactory production mounting.
Whit.

The Coldlitz Story
(BRITISH)

Strong prisoner-of-war camp meller, based on authentic records, and filled with suspense and humor; big b.o. locally, with bright hopes overseas.

London, Jan. 25.
British Lion release of Ivan Foxwell Production. Stars John Mills, Eric Portman. Directed by Guy Hamilton. Screenplay, adaptation by Guy Hamilton, Ivan Foxwell from novel by P. R. Reid; camera, Gordon Dines; editor, Peter Mayhew; music, Francis Chagrin. At Gaumont, London, Jan. 25, '55. Running time, 97 MINS.

Pat Reid .... John Mills
Colonel Richmond .... Eric Portman
Mac .... Christopher Rhodes
Harry .... Lionel Jeffries
Jimmy .... Bryan Forbes
Robin .... Ian Carmichael
Richard .... Richard Wattis
Dick .... David Yates
Kommandant .... Frederick Valk
Priem .... Denis Shaw
Fischer .... Anton Diffring
Franz Josef .... Ludwig Lawinski
German Officer .... Carl Duering
French Colonel .... Keith Pyott
La Tour .... Eugene Deckers
Dutch Colonel .... Rudolf Offenbach
Vandy .... Theodore Bikel
Polish Colonel .... Arthur Butcher

Easily one of the best prisoner-of-war yarns to come from any studio here, "The Coldlitz Story" is a taut real life meller, based on the personal experiences of the author and conscientiously adapted and scripted by Guy Hamilton and Ivan Foxwell. This British pic has a high b.o. potential in the home market and should make the grade in most overseas situations.

Coldlitz Castle, in the heart of Saxony, was the fortress to which the German High Command sent officers who had attempted to escape from conventional prison camps. They regarded it as impregnable although they threatened the death penalty for anyone attempting to break out. And to make escape even more precarious, the Gestapo had exerted pressure on a Pole to act as a spy.

Apart from the British contingent, the Allied forces at Coldlitz included French, Dutch and Poles. On the initiative of the senior British officer (Eric Portman) a four power escape committee was formed with the object of co-ordinating all the breakout plans. An attempt to tunnel a way out of the fortress was foiled by the Gestapo stooge; a brazen try to get over the barbed wire defenses was ended

by Nazi bullets; but the initial triumph, which was the forerunner of other successful ones, came when four men, disguised as German officers, openly walked through the officers' mess and through the main gates to freedom.

Film is loaded with meaty suspense situations and neatly leavened with good-natured humor to strike an excellent balance between the grim and the natural. Under Guy Hamilton's expressive direction, the all-male cast keeps the yarn rolling at a lively pace. John Mills is in fine form as the author. Portman turns in a distinguished performance as the British colonel. Christopher Rhodes gives a sensitive portrayal of the Scottish lieutenant who authors the successful escape plan but is unable to participate because his height would create unnecessary suspicion. Frederick Valk, as the German commandant, and Theodore Bikel, as a Dutch prisoner, are on the polished supporting team. Vetchinsky has designed the settings with imaginative skill.
Myro.

Bonnes A Tuer
(Ripe For Killing)
(FRENCH)
Paris, Jan. 25.
Sirius release of EGE-CFC-Noria Film production. Stars Michel Auclair, Danielle Darrieux, Corinne Calvet. Directed by Henry Decoin. Screenplay, Decoin. Jacques De Baroncelli, J. C. Eger from novel by Pat Mac Gerr; camera, Robert Le Febvre; editor, Denise Reiss. At Biarritz, Paris. Running time, 95 MINS.

Larry .... Michel Auclair
Constance .... Danielle Darrieux
Vera .... Corinne Calvet
Maggy .... Myriam Petacci
Cecile .... Lyla Rocco
Freddy .... Jean Olivier
Forestier .... Gilles Delamare

Lowlife among the highborn is the theme of this slickly made pic which deals with a slightly mad opportunist who invites all his past and present women to a dinner at which he intends to kill one of them. Suspense is main feature lacking in this because of cardboard characterizations and obvious unfoldment. Names will make this an okay entry here. For America, this is mainly dualer fare, which means very spotty playdating.

Michel Auclair is shown as a poor boy who rises to the heights of Paris society by attaching himself to various aprons, and also doing a little blackmail via a gossip sheet. He also cheats on his wives. He invites his former wife, the present one, an estranged wife, a mistress and a future, rich fiance to a dinner party. He intends to kill one of them while dancing. During the dinner each girl has a flashback which shows up the heel qualities of the host. By the time he is ready to kill there isn't much interest left to the pic. In sudden madness, he plunges to death himself through the sawed-off railing he contrived.

Auclair plays this with a gamut of two expressions which make his character vapid. Danielle Darrieux is appealing as the conscience and near-victim while Corinne Calvet pops up in her first Gallic pic as a starlet who talks French with a U.S. accent. Others are okay. Lensing and editing are excellent. Lack of tact by director Henri Decoin gives this an unsavory rather than engrossing aspect.
Mosk.

Huis Clos
(No Exit)
(FRENCH)
Paris, Jan. 25.
Marceau production and release. Stars Arletty, Gaby Sylvia, Frank Villard. Directed by Jacqueline Audry. Screenplay, Pierre Laroche from play by Jean-Paul Sartre; camera, Robert Juillard; editor, Marguerite Beauge. At Ermitage, Paris. Running time, 90 MINS.

Inez .... Arletty
Joseph .... Frank Villard
Estella .... Gaby Sylvia
Olga .... Nicole Courcel
Valet .... Yves Deniaud
Wife .... Arlette Thomas
Florence .... Danielle Delorme

This is an attempt to transfer Jean-Paul Sartre's metaphysical play, "No Exit," to the screen.

Transposition does not help. The atmosphere of hades is rarely created with the suspension of disbelief hardly achieved. The unsavory trio, who are condemned to pass all eternity bickering and torturing each other, run hot and cold and uneven in this pic. Even if this passes the censors, its overstated Existentialist theories, static direction and vacillating thesping will not help much for U.S. chances. Too downbeat and plodding, with only chance for some possible arty spotting.

In play-form, the Sartre philosophy came out as part of the pattern. But here it is forced in endless repetition. Characters have been added to the original three character opus, both on earth as in hell, but it still remains too stagy. Actors are unstable. Most flagrant in overacting is Gaby Sylvia as the man-hungry, rich woman. Arletty has some moments as the bitter dame while Frank Villard is fairly sober as the coward. Lensing is below par and background projection is obvious. Editing is only fair. There is the Sartre and Arletty names plus the theme for exploitation purposes.
Mosk.

Une Balle Suffit . . .
(One Bullet Is Enough)
(FRANCO-SPANISH; SONGS)
Paris, Jan. 25.
AGDC release of EDIC-IFI production. Stars Georges Ulmer; features Vera Norman, Jacques Castelot, Mercedes Barranco, Andre Valmy. Directed by Jean Sacha. Screenplay, Sacha; camera, Marcel Weiss; editor, Paulette Robert; music, Ulmer, Jean Marion. At Raimu, Paris. Running time, 100 MINS.

Carmo .... Georges Ulmer
Florence .... Vera Norman
Rita .... Mercedes Barranco
Lawyer .... Jacques Castelot
Director .... Andre Valmy
Donny .... Manuel Gas

One plot would have been enough in this. But instead a blending of familiar ingredients of tough guy and prison pictures, with both light and reform characteristics, makes this an overlong hybrid. It even has songs worked in to take care of Georges Ulmer, singer-impressionist.

It is his first film stint. This shapes as a fair entry here but for U. S. it could only do as part of a twin bill.

Director Jean Sacha has tried unsuccessfully for stylization in this, and it remains only a sound secondary entry. Plot concerns a pickpocket who is framed for a murder by the gang. He is sent to prison, but he has something the gang wants and they keep after him. In jail, he sees the light and reforms when a friend of his is killed. Meanwhile, his girl is working on the outside to trap the real killers.

Sacha gives the prison scenes some fine values but it bogs down

the main premise. Georges Ulmer overacts and gives the impression of mugging a gangster role along familiar U. S. pattern. But he scores with his warbling. Supporting cast is fair with the heavies ape U. S. counterparts.

Lensing is fine as is editing. This may cash in on the gangster cycle here, but lacks the unusual tag for export impetus.
Mosk.

Papa, Maman, La Bonne Et Moi
(Papa, Mama, The Maid And I)
(FRENCH)
Paris, Jan. 25.
Cocinor release of Cocinex-Champs-Elysees Film-Lambor production. Stars Robert Lamoureux, Gaby Morlay, Fernand Ledoux. Directed by Jean-Paul Le Chanois. Screenplay, Marcel Ayme, Pierre Very; camera, Marc Fossard; editor, Emma Le Chanois. At Paris, Paris. Running time, 100 MINS.

Robert .... Robert Lamoureux
Maman .... Gaby Morlay
Papa .... Fernand Ledoux
Catherine .... Nicole Courcel
Maid .... Madeleine Barbulee
Neighbor .... Louis De Funes
Germaine .... Judith Magre
Nicole .... Francoise Hornez

As title suggests, this is a homey film. It engenders enough laughs plus the presence of one of the top young comedians, Robert Lamoureux, to insure it good local returns. However, its possibilities are limited for the U.S. because this skimpy "life with father and mother" relies too much on the idea, based on some radio programs by Lamoureux, to make it draw in America.

Lamoureux is an easygoing man who loses his job while making a pass at one of the office girls. Instead of telling his parents he gets some teaching lessons on the side. He meets a lovely young girl and romance blooms.

Director Jean-Paul Le Chanois has treated this material tastefully. Lamoureux is engaging as the son with Fernand Ledoux and Gaby Morlay making pleasant humans out of the parents despite their pat characterizations. Lensing and editing help this over its more garrulous sections.
Mosk.

Three for the Show
(MUSICAL-COLOR-C'SCOPE)

Elaborately staged comedy tuner in the old Betty Grable tradition. Okay b.o. draw.

Columbia release of Jonie Taps production. Stars Betty Grable, Marge & Gower Champion, Jack Lemmon; features Myron McCormick, Paul Harvey, Robert Bice, Hal K. Dawson. Directed by H. C. Potter. Screenplay, Edward Hope and Leonard Stern; from a W. Somerset Maugham play; camera (Technicolor), Arthur Arling; editor, Viola Lawrence; choreography, Jack Cole; original music and arrangements, George Duning; art director, Walter Holscher. Tradeshown in N. Y. Dec. 8, '54. Running time, **93 MINS.**

Julie	Betty Grable
Gwen Howard	Marge Champion
Vernon Lowndes	Gower Champion
Marty Stewart	Jack Lemmon
Mike Hudson	Myron McCormick
General Wharton	Paul Harvey
Sergeant O'Hallihan	Robert Bice
Theatre Treasurer	Hal K. Dawson

The topsy-turvy world of show biz gets another lively going over in "Three For The Show," Columbia's new entry in the CinemaScope sweepstakes. A whacky comedy, tailor-made to the talents of a good cast, it scores primarily in the song-and-dance department where the screen comes alive with a couple of highpowered and elaborately conceived production numbers.

Mostly this is Betty Grable's picture, and there's no question that, despite the passing years, she's still an entertainer with plenty of oomph who can put over a routine with sock impact. She gets plenty strong support from the dance team of Marge & Gower Champion who also double in brass in speaking parts. Miss Champion is cute and very appealing. Jack Lemmon, a comedian who knows how to punch across a line when handed one, is a big asset to the show but unfortunately isn't given enough of a chance to do his stuff.

Main trouble with the film is that it's woefully lacking in the story department. For a comedy it's also surprisingly short of good laugh lines. Based on a W. Somerset Maugham play and adapted for the screen by Edward Hope and Leonard Stern, "Three For the Show" uses a theme that must have been knocking around Hollywood since the nickelodeon days.

It's about the fellow who goes to war and is reported dead. The wife, in this instance a famous musical star, marries his best friend. Hubby number one returns, presenting his wife with a situation in which she must choose between two husbands. It takes Miss Grable an hour and a half to make up her mind, with Marge Champion waiting on the sidelines to catch one of the boys on the rebound.

To overcome this thin story, producer Jonie Taps and director H. C. Potter have put the accent on the song-and-dance end, and here no effort has been spared to fill every inch of the wide screen with production values.

Some of the sets are stunning and the music, including two George and Ira Gershwin numbers, is pleasant and well integrated. There's a succession of such sequences in which the Champions particularly do outstanding work. Dream sequence, with Miss Grable lording it over a male harem, has fine hoofing to the tune of Hoagy Carmichael's and Harold Adamson's "Down Boy." Another dream scene stars the Champions in a fine bit of interpretive dancing that's a delight to the eye.

For the most part, the transition from musical to story is done smoothly and with a degree of logic due to the show biz background which calls for a theatre setting. There's one bit of nonsense in the Grable apartment, involving the principals chasing one another, that just doesn't come off. Jack Cole's choreography otherwise is excellent.

Among the songs heard in the film are "Someone to Watch Over Me," and "I've Got a Crush on You," both by George and Ira Gershwin; "How Come You Do Me Like You Do," by Gene Austin and Roy Bergere; Lester Lee and Ned Washington's "Which One?" and "I've Been Kissed Before," by Bob Russell and Lee, which Miss Grable gives a sexy and appealing treatment.

In the smaller parts, Myron McCormick is okay as the legit producer. Paul Harvey as an air force general trying to straighten out Miss Grable's marital dilemma does a routine takeoff. Robert Bice and Hal K. Dawson are okay in small roles. Potter's direction has merit and keeps the picture properly paced. Technicolor hues are particularly good in this one and Arthur Arling's lensing shows up C'Scope to best advantage.

Question might be asked how long audiences will hold still for those big-scale dance routines. Color and the widescreen notwithstanding, the public is being fed a good deal of this on tv. There's no question that the theatre screen makes a shambles of the video spectacles, but even so there may come a point of no return. Meanwhile, "Three for the Show" ought to keep 'em happy. *Hift.*

The Glass Slipper
(MUSIC—COLOR)

The Cinderella fairy tale brought to life with whimsical charm, but moot b.o. prospects.

Hollywood, Feb. 14.

Metro release of Edwin H. Knopf production. Stars Leslie Caron, Michael Wilding; features Keenan Wynn, Estelle Winwood, Elsa Lanchester, Barry Jones, Amanda Blake, Lurene Tuttle, Lisa Daniels. Directed by Charles Walters. Screenplay, ballet librettos and lyrics by Helen Deutsch; camera (Eastman Color), Arthur E. Arling; editor, Ferris Webster; ballets by Roland Petit, featuring Ballet de Paris; music, Bronislau Kaper. Previewed Feb. 9, '55. Running time, **93 MINS.**

Ella	Leslie Caron
Prince Charles	Michael Wilding
Kovin	Keenan Wynn
Mrs. Toquet	Estelle Winwood
Widow Sonder	Elsa Lanchester
Duke	Barry Jones
Birdena	Amanda Blake
Serafina	Lisa Daniels
Cousin Loulou	Lurene Tuttle
Tehara	Liliane Montevecchi
	Ballet de Paris

(Aspect ratio: 1.75.1)

A whimsical treatment of the Cinderella fairy tale slants "The Glass Slipper" towards those ticket buyers who prefer to go outside regular types of screenfare for their film entertainment. They should find it a beguiling 93 minutes but, unfortunately for its box-office chances, the fantasy does not have the kind of popular appeal that will make the general theatre patron lay his cash down at the wickets. With special handling, it may do okay in some sure-seater dates, but the b.o. prospects are moot.

Without making too strong a comparison with "Lili," a previous small-showcase click turned out by the principals connected with this offering, it is probable the makers figured on approaching the previous film's sureseater success. While "Slipper" has charm and a somewhat similar ugly duckling-love triumphant plot, it has neither the tremendous heart impact of "Lili" nor sufficient freshness of theme treatment to duplicate that pic's acceptance.

The Cinderella fairy tale, as remembered by all, is enacted in the Helen Deutsch screenplay, telling how the poor, mistreated girl manages to overcome circumstance and the shoddy attentions of stepmother and stepsisters to win the handsome prince who lives in the village castle. The magic wishing hour of midnight is retained and, by implication only, the magic coach and its horses formed from a pumpkin and mice, and the fairy godmother, here seen as a pixilated old woman who makes dreams come true by a practical approach.

Leslie Caron, as drab and dirty as any scullery maid could have even been, is the Cinderella who rides to the castle on her dreams, magically whisked into an enchantingly gowned, diademed princess fit for the prince played by Michael Wilding. Her particular ability to be transformed from ugliness into beauty fits the character, but Wilding does not seem happily cast in his character, nor does it get over to the viewer. Estelle Winwood is quite effective as the pixilated worker of seeming magic. Others in the cast seem to be present only because there are characters to be filled. They include Keenan Wynn, as the prince's friend; Barry Jones, the duke; Elsa Lanchester, the stepmother; Amanda Blake and Lisa Daniels, the selfish stepsisters, and Lurene Tuttle as the aunt with a past.

Where "Slipper" makes its best points is in the Bronislau Kaper score and in the ballets staged by Roland Petit with the Ballet de Paris. Particularly earning attention is the "Kitchen Ballet." Also good is the allegorical death theme of the "Tehara Ballet," the final of three ballets done in dream sequences. "Take My Love" is a song with rhythmic appeal presented by itself and as a background theme throughout the footage. The ballet librettos and the lyrics for "Take" were written by Miss Deutsch, with Kaper doing the music.

The special, although limited, appeal of the picture benefits by Charles Walters' direction of the Edwin H. Knopf production, and the eye appeal is enhanced by the Eastman Kodak Color photography by Arthur E. Arling, the costuming of Helen Rose and Walter Plunkett, the art direction and set decorations that frame the action. *Brog.*

New York Confidential

Well-fashioned crime melodrama with good cast and performances to rate its bookings and an okay payoff in the regular program market.

Hollywood, Feb. 15.

Warner Bros. release of Edward Small (Clarence Greene) production. Stars Broderick Crawford, Richard Conte, Marilyn Maxwell, Anne Bancroft, J. Carrol Naish; features Onslow Stevens, Barry Kelley, Mike Mazurki, Celia Lovsky, Herbert Heyes. Directed by Russell Rouse. Original screenplay, Greene and Rouse; suggested by the bestseller by Jack Lait and Lee Mortimer; camera, Edward Fitzgerald; editor, Grant Whytock; music, Joseph Mullendore. Previewed Feb. 8, '55. Running time, **87 MINS.**

Charles Lupo	Broderick Crawford
Nick Magellan	Richard Conte
Iris Palmer	Marilyn Maxwell
Katherine Lupo	Anne Bancroft
Ben Dagajanian	J. Carrol Naish
Johnny Achilles	Onslow Stevens
Frawley	Barry Kelley
Arnie Wendler	Mike Mazurki
Mama Lupo	Celia Lovsky
James Marshall	Herbert Heyes
Morris Franklin	Steven Geray
Whitey	Bill Phillips
Gino	Henry Kulky
Martinelli	Nestor Paiva
Batista	Joe Vitale
Sumak	Carl Milletaire
Paul Williamson	William Forrest
Waluska	Ian Keith
Judge Kincaid	Charles Evans
Hartmann	Mickey Simpson
District Attorney Rossi	Tom Powers
Ferrari	Lee Trent
Larry	Lennie Bremen
Shorty	John Doucette
Dr. Ludlow	Frank Ferguson
Mrs. Wesley	Hope Landon
Senor	Fortunio Bonanova

(Aspect ratio: 1.85-1)

Among the crime exposes currently hitting the film market, "New York Confidential" stacks up as one of the better-made entries, thanks to a well-fashioned story and good performances by a cast of familiar names. While a tough, no-punches-pulled melodrama, it relies more on logical development for effect than on unsoundly motivated bare-knuckles action. It is an okay offering for the market.

Some seasoned players who know their way around in this type of plot, plus direction that makes its points without hammering them, contribute to the entertainment aims of the Warner Bros. release. Film was made idependently by Clarence Greene and Russell Rouse for Edward Small. Producer Greene and director Rouse did the original script, suggested by the bestseller by Jack Lait and Lee Mortimer, so the events dealt within the plot have an authentic ring, whether or not probable in real life.

Story tells of the rise of Richard Conte, ambitious triggerman, in the big syndicate said to control all crime under the chairmanship of Broderick Crawford. Pleased with the dispatch with which Conte takes care of his first murder assignment, the big boss pushes the killer up rapidly. Now the syndicate is purported to work to control its empire of legitimate and illegitimate businesses backgrounds the action as murders go on and big money rolls into the coffers. No one gets bigger than the syndicate, however, and when an investigation started by crimebusters reaches to Crawford, the board members order his execution, which Conte carries out efficiently and is then rubbed out himself because by now he knows too much.

Conte does a topnotch job of making a coldblooded killer seem real and Crawford is good as the chairman of the crime board, as is Marilyn Maxwell as his girl friend. Anne Bancroft, showing continuing progress and talent, scores with a standout performance of Broderick's unhappy daughter. J. Carrol Naish, Onslow Stevens and Barry Kelley, executives in the syndicate, are most effective. Notable in other roles are Mike Mazurki, Celia Lovsky, Herbert Hayes, Steven Gray, Bill Phillips, Henry Kulky, Nestor Paiva, Joe Vitale, Carl Milletaire and William Forrest.

Edward Fitzgerald's lensing and the Joseph Mullendore music are keyed to the melodramatics. Editing and other techncal assists are good. *Brog.*

East of Eden
(C'SCOPE—COLOR

Class screen treatment of the somber dramatics from John Steinbeck's novel; special handling will develop b.o. potential.

Hollywood, Feb. 15.

Warner Bros. release of Elia Kazan production. Stars Julie Harris, James Dean, Raymond Massey; features Burl Ives, Richard Davalos, Jo Van Fleet, Albert Dekker, Lois Smith, Harold Gordon, Timothy Carey. Mario Siletti, Lonny Chapman, Nick Dennis. Directed by Kazar, Screenplay, Paul Osborn; camera, (WarnerColor), Ted McCord; editor, Owen Marks; music, Leonard Rosenman. Previewed Feb. 2, '55. Running time, 114 MINS.

Abra	Julie Harris
Cal Trask	James Dean
Adam Trask	Raymond Massey
Sam	Burl Ives
Aron Trask	Richard Davalos
Kate	Jo Van Fleet
Will	Albert Dekker
Ann	Lois Smith
Mr. Albrecht	Harold Gordon
Joe	Timothy Carey
Piscora	Mario Siletti
Roy	Lanny Chapman
Rantani	Nick Dennis

Powerfully somber dramatics have been captured from the pages of John Steinbeck's "East of Eden" and put on film by Elia Kazan. It is a tour de force for the director's penchant for hard-hitting forays with life, and as such undoubtedly will be counted among his best screen efforts. Whether the type of heavy melodrama represented here will be entirely satisfying screenfare for the majority is not an easy guess. Right kind of exploitation could push it to a successful release.

It has no top screen names to help sell tickets or to attract the casual theatregoer. Thus, it seems to demand special treatment via showcase runs and other attention-focusing handling to prep it for regular release. There is material in the Steinbeck tale that lends itself to the kind of fulsome exploitation that lures the morbidly curious.

For the Kazan followers the picture has quite a bit to offer, for every scene is stamped with his style. The student of drama will be rewarded, too. To these it will not matter much that Kazan often allows style to get in the way, because the technique will be more important. Others will find that, while the subject matter is real enough, this concern with technique prevents it from taking on a full-bodied semblance to life. Here, it's the staging of a realism of mood, rather than the realism of life, that predominates.

Much pro and con probably will develop about James Dean, unknown to whom Kazan gives a full-scale introduction. It is no credit to Kazan that Dean seems required to play his lead character as though he were straight out of a Marlon Brando mold. Just how flexible his talent is will have to be judged on future screen roles, although he has a basic appeal that manages to get through to the viewer despite the heavy burden of carboning another's acting style in voice and mannerisms. It should be interesting to see what he can do as Dean.

Only the latter part of the Steinbeck novel is used in the Paul Osborn screenplay, which picks up the principals in this Salinas Valley melodrama at the time the twin sons of a lettuce farmer are graduating in the 1917 class at high-school. One son is neurotic, fancies himself unloved, while the other is likeable, well-adjusted, normal youth, interested in his girl and the development of his father's acreage.

The principal dramatic problem posed is getting the neurotic straightened out before he completely destroys himself and those who care for him. That this is eventually brought about, in the concluding scene, keeps the picture from being entirely downbeat, but this uplift comes after he has virtually wrecked his brother's moral fiber, taken the latter's girl and caused his father to have a stroke that leaves him paralyzed and facing slow death. Not overlooked as a creator of turmoil in the youth is his discovery that his mother, believed long dead, is a madam operating a house in Monterey and he uses this as an excuse for some of his wildness.

Julie Harris, well-known stage star, gives her particular style to an effective portrayal of the girl torn between the love offered by the good brother and the instinct awakened in her by the neurotic. Richard Davalos film debuts as the normal son and wins sympathy with an excellent performance. Raymond Massey is fine as the religious father who finds it difficult to understand the need that Dean, his neurotic son, has for affection.

Burl Ives, the sheriff; Jo Van Fleet, the mother; Albert Dekker, a promoter; Harold Gordon, German-born neighbor who feels the hatred of Huns caused by World War I; Timothy Carey and Lonny Chapman are among those contributing good support. Lois Smith merits special mention for the importance she gives the small part of a slattern in the house run by the mother.

The presentation is a pictorial standout by virtue of the splendid CinemaScope lensing in WarnerColor by Ted McCord. Effective also are the Leonard Rosenman score, the art direction by James Basevi and Malcolm Bert, the set decorations by George James Hopkins, the editing by Owen Marks and the other technical credits.

Brog.

New Orleans Uncensored

Pseudo-documentary melodrama for programmer bookings. Only fair entertainment in its class.

Hollywood, Feb. 15.

Columbia release of Sam Katzman production. Stars Arthur Franz, Beverly Garland; features Helene Stanton, Michael Ansara, Stacy Harris, Mike Mazurki, William Henry, Michael Granger, Frankie Ray, Edwin Stafford Nelson. Directed by William Castle. Screenplay, Orville H. Hampton, Lewis Meltzer; story, Orville H. Hampton; camera, Henry Freulich; editors, Gene Havlick, Al Clark; music conducted by Mischa Bakaleinikoff. Previewed Feb. 10, '55. Running time, 76 MINS.

Dan Corbett	Arthur Franz
Marie Reilly	Beverly Garland
Alma Mae	Helene Stanton
Zero Saxon	Michael Ansara
Scrappy Durant	Stacy Harris
Mike	Mike Mazurki
Joe Reilly	William Henry
Jack Petty	Michael Granger
Deuce	Frankie Ray
Charlie	Edwin Stafford Nelson
Ralph Dupas	Ralph Dupas
Pete Heerman	Pete Herman
Wayne Brandon	Judge Walter B. Hamlin
Al Chittenden	Al Chittenden

(*Aspect ratio*: 1.85-1)

A familiar story of racketeering and strongarm tactics among longshore unions is told in a pseudo-documentary style in "New Orleans Uncensored." The entertainment that results is only fair at best.

Much of the film was lensed dockside in New Orleans and around other picturesque sites in the Gulf port city, but there's nothing much else about the picture that's real as the script by Orville H. Hampton and Lewis Meltzer is unfolded under William Castle's direction.

Arthur Franz is the male lead, playing a young Navy vet who comes to the southern city to buy a surplus LCI and gets a dock job to help pay for it. It isn't long before he sees things not to his liking in the way Michael Ansara, a racketeer who has managed to get control of most dock hiring, operates his business of jobs, smuggling and looting. When a friend is killed and the death of another is arranged, Franz goes to the authorities, sets a trap by planting a small transmitter-oscillator in some stolen cargo and the gang is broken up.

Adding to the documentary effect tried for is the appearance of union leaders and civic officials of New Orleans in the picture. It should at least register some business for bookings in that city through this casting. Franz gives his character a workmanlike job and Ansara is a thorough villain, abetted in the strong arm work by Mike Mazurki and some others, none of whom are believable. The two femmes, Beverly Garland and Helene Stanton, both have some good moments but are generally lost in the material, as are Stacy Harris and William Henry.

Henry Freulich's photography is good and the other technical credits measure up.

Brog.

The Big Combo

Grim meller of honest cop versus syndicate for the action trade.

Hollywood, Feb. 10.

Allied Artists release of Security-Theodora (Sidney Harmon) production. Stars Cornel Wilde, Richard Conte, Brian Donlevy, Jean Wallace; features Robert Middleton, Lee Van Cleef, Earl Holliman, Helen Walker, Jay Adler, John Hoyt, Ted De Corsia, Helene Stanton. Directed by Joseph Lewis. Written by Philip Yordan; camera, John Alton; editor, Robert Eisen; music, David Raksin; piano soloist, Jacob Gimpel. Previewed Feb. 8, '55. Running time, 86 MINS.

Diamond	Cornel Wilde
Brown	Richard Conte
McClure	Brian Donlevy
Susan	Jean Wallace
Peterson	Robert Middleton
Fante	Lee Van Cleef
Mingo	Earl Holliman
Alicia	Helen Walker
Sam Hill	Jay Adler
Dreyer	John Hoyt
Bettini	Ted De Corsia
Rita	Helene Stanton
Audubon	Roy Gordon
Doctor	Whit Bissell
Bennie Smith	Steve Mitchell
Young Detective	Baynes Barron
Lab Technician	James McCallion
Photo Technician	Tony Michaels
Malloy	Brian O'Hara
Nurse	Rita Gould
Detective	Bruce Sharpe
Hotel Clerk	Michael Mark

(*Aspect ratio*: 1.85-1)

This is another saga of the honest cop who lets nothing sway him from the self-appointed task of smashing a crime syndicate and its leader. It is done with grim melodramatics that are hard-hitting despite a rambling, not too credible plot, and is cut out to order for the meller fan who likes his action rough and raw. In that market it should do okay.

In this stress on the seamier side of gangland and its denizens, the Security-Theodora production which Allied Artists is releasing gets too realistic. One torture scene in particular will shock the sensibilities and cause near-nausea. After honest cop Cornel Wilde has been tormented by gangster Richard Conte via a hearing aid plugged in his ear while the receiver is held to a radio going full blast, the cold-blooded crook forces the contents of a large bottle of hair tonic down the victim's throat. The moronic fringe of sadists will enjoy this, and all the little kiddies will be sick to their stomachs.

Since Philip Yordan's original screenplay doesn't follow a credible line, there's not much sense to the torture scene, nor to most of the motivations used to plot the course of this shocker. Even after Wilde has been subjected to the indignities by Conte and his strongarm boys, Brian Donlevy, Lee Van Cleef and Earl Holliman, pic has you believe he still can't bring the hood to justice. In addition to his desire to get Conte, Wilde also has a desire for the crook's girlfriend, Jean Wallace, but it takes some doing to get her to escape thegangster. After she does, and with the help of some hearsay evidence from Conte's wife, Helen Walker, the cop's crusade ends successfully.

Performances are in keeping with the bare-knuckle direction by Joseph Lewis and, on that score, are good. Those mentioned project the story's toughness effectively and there are some good assists to the melodramatics, notably from Helene Stanton, very good as a chorus cutie who loves Wilde and dies because of it; Jay Adler, John Hoyt, Ted De Corsia and Robert Middleton.

Lowkey photography by John Alton and a noisy, jazzy score by David Raksin are in keeping with the film's tough mood.

Brog.

Captain Lightfoot
(C'SCOPE-COLOR)

Formula period swashbuckler, lensed in Ireland with Rock Hudson title-roling to help program market prospects.

Hollywood, Feb. 15.

Universal release of Ross Hunter production. Stars Rock Hudson, Barbara Rush, Jeff Morrow; features Kathleen Ryan, Finlay Currie, Denis O'Dea, Geoffrey Toome. Directed by Douglas Sirk. Screenplay, W. R. Burnett, Oscar Brodney; story and adaptation, Burnett; camera (Technicolor), Irving Glassberg; editor, Frank Gross; music supervision, Joseph Gershenson. Previewed Feb. 7, '55. Running time, 91 MINS.

Michael	Rock Hudson
Aga	Barbara Rush
Doherty	Jeff Morrow
Lady Ann	Kathleen Ryan
Callahan	Finlay Currie
Regis	Denis O'Dea
Captain Hood	Geoffrey Toome
Lord Glen	Hilton Edwards
Waitress	Sheila Brennan
Brady	Harry Goldblatt
Shanley	Charles Fitzsimons
Lord Clonmell	Christopher Casson
Trim	Philip O'Flynn
Tim Keenan	Shay Gorman
High Steward	Kenneth MacDonald
Clagett	Robert Bernal
Cathy	Louise Studley
Tuer O'Brien	James Devlin
Willie the Goat	Mike Nolan
Big Tom	Edward Aylward
English Gentleman	Lord Mount Charles
English Lady	Lady Mount Charles

Some formula period swashbuckling is indulged in in this costume action drama, but it's prettily dressed in CinemaScope and Technicolor, with authentic Irish locales, and has the name of Rock Hudson heading the cast to help it get by in the general program market.

Producer Ross Hunter sent cast and camera crew to Ireland for on-the-scene lensing, but as far as the entertainment results are concerned, the trip was hardly worthwhile. Other than authenticity of settings for the period plot, the picture is a mild affair that manages to be no more than just fair escapism, with neither performances nor direction adding any distinction to the commonplace plotting.

Hudson is seen as a young Irish hothead who joins up with Jeff Morrow, a rebel leader, falls in love with the latter's spitfire daughter, Barbara Rush, and generally indulges in some incredible heroics that climax with his escape from prison in time to tend to the patriot forces until Morrow can recover from wounds sustained in similar derring-do. Script by W. R. Burnett and Oscar Brodney is given to a lot of high-flown dialog, delivered in an assortment of stagey Irish brogues, about the rebellion against the English. The talk keeps the film's pace slow as directed by Douglas Sirk.

The three stars can't do much to make their characters credible and most of the featured and supporting performances are in keeping. Of the featured players, Kathleen Ryan does the most to make her role of Lady Ann, Morrow's beloved, believeable.

Photographically, Irving Glassberg's CinemaScope lensing provides visual beauty, showing the Irish landscapes and ancient buildings to advantage. The background score, supervised by Joseph Gershenson, points up the Irish flavor.
Brog.

Tarzan's Hidden Jungle

Stock entry in this longlived series; interduces well-muscled Gordon Scott as the new Tarzan.

RKO release of Sol Lesser production. Stars Gordon Scott, Vera Miles, Peter Van Eyck; features Jack Elam, Charles Fredericks and Zippy (chimp). Directed by Harold Schuster. Screenplay, William Lively; suggested by the Edgar Rice Burroughs character; camera, William Whitley; editor, Leon Barsha; music, Paul Sawtell. Previewed Feb. 10, '55. Running time, **72 MINS.**

Tarzan	Gordon Scott
Jill Hardy	Vera Miles
Dr. Celliers	Peter Van Eyck
Burger	Jack Elam
Cheta	Zippy
DeGroot	Charles Fredericks
Reeves	Richard Reeves
Johnson	Don Beddoe
Malenki	Ike Jones
Witch Doctor	Jester Hairston
Suma	Madie Norman
Makuma	Rex Ingram
Lucky	Lucky

(*Aspect ratio* 1.33-1)

"Tarzan's Hidden Jungle" is a stock entry in the Edgar Rice Burrough apeman marathon produced by Sol Lesser and serves to introduce a new title hero. Gordon Scott, succeeding Lex Barker who last played the character, is a well-muscled man but seldom convincing in the part.

As usual, Tarzan is right there pitching to save the beasts of the jungle in this William Lively screenplay. A pair of hunters, who have a contract to deliver fats, skins, heads and ivory, are the heavies, and they receive rough justice when an elephant stampede tramples them to death. Intervening footage shows them accompanying a United Nations doctor who thinks they are cameramen, into savage country where he is the only white allowed. Their purpose is to drive the vast number of animals out of this territory so they can slaughter them without fear of the natives.

Tarzan defeats this intention, simultaneously saving the doctor and the latter's nurse, but it appears to be more play-acting than for real insofar as the spectator is concerned. Harold Schuster's direction rarely rises above the script deficiencies, and the insertion of stock animal footage fails to match the quality of the footage proper.

Vera Miles is the pretty nurse and Peter Van Eyck is good in his jungle doctor impersonation. Jack Elan and Charles Fredericks are well cast as the hunters. Zippy, a new Cheta, and another chimp, Lucky, are the real cuties of this show. Ike Jones handles his native role well.

Sol Lesser's production is standard for the series and technical credits are ditto.
Whit.

Die Goldene Pest
(The Golden Pestilence) (GERMAN)

Frankfurt, Feb. 8.

Allianz release of Occident production. Stars Ivan Desny, Gertrud Kuckelmann, Karlheinz Bohm. Directed by John Brahm. Screenplay by Dieter Werner after an idea of Gerhard Buchholz and Kurt Fischer; camera, Klaus von Kautenfeld; music, Hans-Martin Majeswki. At Zeil Theatre, Frankfurt. Running time, 94 MINS.

Richard Hartwig	Ivan Desny
Franziska Hellmer	Gertrud Kuckelmann
Karl Hellmer	Karlheinz Bohm
Wenzeslaw Kolowrat	Wilfried Seyferth

This film is notable for two reasons. It is the first film directed in Germany by the Hollywood megger John Brahm. Secondly, it excited flurries of protest here from groups who maintained in advance that the film was un-American. As a result of this, U.S. soldiers were not permitted to play themselves in it.

However, the pic has much more anti-German and pro-American implication. The plot concerns a small German village in which a huge U.S. regiment is stationed, with the resultant effect on the lives of the townpeople. Eager to get the GI's money, they overprice junky souvenirs, open a casino-nightclub, offer camp followers. Also dope is for sale although the only purchaser of the latter is clearly shown as a German.

Into this comes Ivan Hesny, German-born lad who has become a U.S. soldier. He is on leave at home to see his sweetheart, Gertrud Kuckelmann. Her brother has become leader of the gang preying on the U.S. troops, stealing tires and gas from the soldiers.

Pic bogs down because the characters seem poorly motivated, with both Desny and Karlheinz Bohm in the leads fighting hard with unconvincing dialog.

Action takes place mainly in the GI-filled casino, with a band and vocal background for the gangster plottings. Highpoint of laughter is a nightclub act of two femme wrestlers battling in the mud.

It is too bad Brahm wasn't given a better script for his first German venture because this one doesn't give him much chance. Music of film is a pleasant diversion.
Haze.

Chief Crazy Horse
(C'SCOPE—COLOR)

Rise and fall of Lakota-Sioux chief who downed General Custer, presenting Indians' side of story sympathetically; for regulation outdoor action market.

Hollywood, Feb. 22.

Universal release of William Alland production, co-producer, Leonard Goldstein. Stars Victor Mature, Suzan Ball, John Lund; features Ray Danton, Keith Larsen, Paul Guilfoyle, David Janssen, Robert Warwick, James Millican. Directed by George Sherman. Screenplay, Franklin Coen, Gerald Drayson Adams; story by Adams; camera (Technicolor), Harold Lipstein; editor, Al Clark; music, Frank Skinner. Previewed Feb. 15, '55. Running time, **86 MINS.**

Crazy Horse	Victor Mature
Black Shawl	Suzan Ball
Major Twist	John Lund
Little Big Man	Ray Danton
Flying Hawk	Keith Larsen
Worm	Paul Guilfoyle
Lt. Colin Cartwright	David Janssen
Spotted Tail	Robert Warwick
General Crook	James Millican
Red Cloud	Morris Ankrum
Aaron Cartwright	Donald Randolph
Jeff Mantz	Robert F. Simon
Caleb Mantz	James Westerfield
Old Man Afraid	Stuart Randall
Dull Knife	Pat Hogan
Maj. Carlisle	Dennis Weaver
Sgt. Guthrie	John Peters
He Dog	Henry Wills

The settlement of the Black Hills of Dakota is here told from the Indians' side of the fighting with a sympathetic treatment that comes off okay, and with enough action to make "Chief Crazy Horse" suitable material for the general outdoor market.

Of side interest to the presentation, and also with a sympathetic angle, is the fact Suzan Ball makes her first camera outing since her leg amputation. The doubling in scenes requiring movement is very good, and elsewhere she acquits herself well in handling the role of the bride of Victor Mature, seen in the title role as the Indian who lived out a tribal prophecy. John Lund, as a white friend to the Indian couple, is the third star of the William Alland production and also does good work.

On his deathbed a Lakota-Sioux chief predicts that a great warrior would arise in the tribe and lead it to victory over the invading whites, only to meet his death at the hands of a fellow Lakota. The Franklin Coen and Gerald Drayson Adams screenplay brings this about with sufficient dispatch for the demands of the market where this release will find its level, and gives George Sherman's direction plenty of action setups, which he plays with fast movement. Among these sequences is Crazy Horse's ambush of General Custer, and a number of other forays against the whites that pack a good action punch.

With the three topliners doing their characters in good style, the support also is firstrate. Ray Danton shows up well as the renegade Indian who murders Crazy Horse after the latter has made his peace with the soldiers led by James Millican. Keith Larsen, David Janssen, Paul Guilfoyle and Robert Warwick are others in feature spots lending capable support.

The CinemaScope lensing of outdoor locations by Harold Lipstein gives the picture scenic beauty. This is so good, however, it makes the stock footage scenes inserted here and there seem very poor, particularly since these film library scenes have not blown up to C'Scope with any clarity, appearing badly grained and fuzzy. Score by Frank Skinner is good.
Brog.

Out of the Clouds
(BRITISH-COLOR)

Semi-documentary, with new London airport as principal locale, but embodying unacceptable romantic theme, set for fair grosses.

London, Feb. 15.

General Film Distribs release of Ealing Studios-Michael Balcon production. Stars Anthony Steel, Robert Beatty, David Knight, Margo Lorenz. Directed by Michael Relph and Basil Dearden. Screenplay, John Eldridge, Michael Relph; camera (Eastmancolor), Jeff Seaholme; editor, Jack Harris; music, Richard Addinsell. At Odeon, Leicester Square, London. Running time, **88 MINS.**

Gus Randall	Anthony Steel
Nick Milbourne	Robert Beatty
Bill	David Knight
Leah	Margo Lorenz
Captain Brent	James Robertson Justice
Penny Henson	Eunice Gayson
Mrs. Malcolm	Isabel Dean
Taxi Driver	Gordon Harker
Customs Officer	Bernard Lee
Purvis	Michael Howard
Rich Woman	Marie Lohr
Her Companion	Esma Cannon
Indian	Abraham Sofaer
Jean Osmond	Melissa Stribling
Gambler	Sirney James

Filmed in semi-documentary style, "Out of Clouds" is virtually a day behind the scenes at London Airport, with a wholly unbelievable romantic theme tagged on. This weakness notwithstanding, the pic is good average entertainment and should do fair grosses.

With the new airfield as the main background, the script adroitly folows through on a few key personnel. There is Anthony Steel, the pilot with a yen for gambling who gets involved in a smuggling racket; Robert Beatty, the chief duty officer, who is waiting for the day when the medico will again pass him for flying duties; James Robertson Justice, a bearded pilot with a justifiable superstition about a particular aircraft; and Eunice Gayson, who prefers the solidity of Beatty to the gaiety of Steel. As these characterizations are developing, the script brings together David Knight and Margo Lorenz. He is an American engineer en route to Israel and she is a German-Jewish girl on her way to marry a wealthy widower in Wisconsin. Their last minute switch to fly off together almost defies acceptance.

That there is drama in the everyday life of the airport is proved convincingly; and a prolonged scene in which James Robertson Justice is being talked down by radar in dense fog is crammed with suspense. Brief glimpses of some of the ports of call, including air shots of the Pyramids and Rome present a colorful background.

Anthony Steel offers a typical light-hearted portrayal as the happy-go-lucky pilot. Robert Beatty does a believable job as the duty officer while David Knight and Margo Lorenz, both of whom perform with great delicacy, cannot overcome the inherent weaknesses of their roles. A fine portrayal of a cockney cabdriver comes from Gordon Harker while James Robertson Justice gives a vital performance as the pilot. Eunice Gayson always looks attractive as the hostess. Direction and other technical credits are up to average standard.
Myro.

Les Diaboliques
(The Diabolical Ones) (FRENCH)

Paris, Feb. 15.

Cinedis release of Filmsonor production. Stars Simone Signoret, Vera Clouzot, Paul Meurisse. Directed by H. G. Clouzot, Screenplay, Clouzot, Jerome Geromini, Rene Masson, Frederic Grendel from

novel by Thomas Marcejac, Pierre Boileau; camera, Armand Thirard; editor, Madeleine Gug. At Paris, Paris. Running time, **110 MINS.**

Nicole .... Simone Signoret
Christina .... Vera Clouzot
Michel .... Paul Meurisse
Fichet .... Charles Vanel
Drain .... Pierre Larquey
Herboux .... Noel Roquevert
Plantineau .... Jean Brochard
Raymond .... Michel Serrault

Relentless sordidness never made a great film unless it was tempered with sincerity and fervor. A mystery about H. G. Clouzot's new film, besides that of its plot, is that it got the Gallic pic Crix Delluc Prize, supposedly for the highest film achievement in the realm of originality, even before its release. This was followed up by rave notices terming the pic a masterpiece.

Although it does not have a few hallucinating bits of terror, the fact is that the film is primarily a creaky-door type melodrama, its grim, downbeat groping for suspense is arrived at by too heavy-handed a dose of brutality and gratuitous baseness, which keeps this melodrama out of the art category so fervently seen by crix here.

Big-gun launching makes it look like a hit here, with word-of-mouth and crix-lauding a help. But for the U.S., it is primarily for special situations. Its macabre aspects and lack of sympathy for the characters make this a hybrid which flounders between a blasting look at human infamy and an out-and-out contrived whodunit. For America, this will have to be pushed on shock value. Theme is one which may well run into censorship troubles.

A brutal headmaster of a private boy's school tyrannizes his frail, sickly wife, and has a mistress, a teacher at the school, with whom he has just broken off. The women band together, and driven by the steely teacher, plot to kill him, which apparently they do.

But the wife comes on his body in the bathtub, which rises as she shrieks herself to a heart-attack and death. The mistress and husband had concocted this ghastly method to kill her with immunity and also for the film fireworks. However, they are apprehended by a wily, retired police inspector.

Clouzot's interest in terror and human dreariness for its own sake has robbed this of intrinsic honesty, and it is strictly in the horror category. He has gotten a fine, if spotty performance, from his real wife, Vera, who plays the frail mate in the pic. It is Mrs. Clouzot's second film. Simone Signoret portrays a resoundingly solid competence as the powerful crime instigator. Paul Meurisse is properly despicable as the so-called victim. Other characters are also a rather vile bunch, and children are shadowly etched in this. Lensing and editing are firstrate. Charles Vanel turns in an acting gem as the shabby, knowing inspector. *Mosk.*

Untamed
(COLOR—C'SCOPE)

African adventure yarn with some flashy action footage shot in Zululand. An exploitation natural.

Twentieth Century-Fox release of a Bert E. Friedlob-William A. Bacher production. Stars Tyrone Power, Susan Hayward, Richard Egan; features Agnes Moorehead, Rita Moreno, Hope Emerson, Brad Dexter, Henry O'Neill. Directed by Henry King. Screenplay, Talbot Jennings, Frank Fenton and Michael Blankfort. Adaptation by Jennings and Bacher from the Helga Moray novel; camera (Color by De Luxe), Leo Tover; editor, Barbara McLean; music, Franz Waxman; special effects, Ray Kellogg. Previewed in N.Y. Feb. 25, '55. Running time, **111 MINS.**

Paul Van Riebeck .... Tyrone Power
Katie O'Neill .... Susan Hayward
Kurt .... Richard Egan
Shawn Kildare .... John Justin
Aggie .... Agnes Moorehead
Julia .... Rita Moreno
Maria De Groot .... Hope Emerson
Christian .... Brad Dexter
Squire O'Neill .... Henry O'Neill
Tschaka .... Paul Thompson
Jan .... Alexander D. Havemann
Joubert .... Louis Mercier
Jantsie .... Emmett Smith
Simon .... Jack Macy
Mme. Joubert .... Trude Wyler
Bani .... Louis oPllimon Brown
Maria's Children Brian Corcoran-Linda Lowell, Tina Thompson, Gary and Bobby Diamond
Grandfather Joubert .... Edward Mundy
Miss Joubert .... Catherine Pasques
Joung Joubert .... Christian Pasques
York .... Robert Adler
Capt. Richard Eaton .... John Dodsworth
Driver—Bree Street .... Alberto Morin
Schuman .... Philip Van Zandt
Young Paul .... Kevin Corcoran
Sir George Gray .... Charles Evans
Cornelius .... John Carlyle
Lady Vernon .... Eleanor Audley

(Aspect ratio: 2:55 to 1)

If one proceeds on the assumption that CinemaScope "bigness," coupled with unusual backgrounds, still works its spell on the audience, "Untamed," with all of these elements, shapes up as a healthy b.o. contender. It's a romance-laden action western with fiery Zulus supplanting the Redmen, and Boers taking the place of the western pioneers.

Unfortunately, despite some truly grandiose and eye-filling scenery and battle action staged with sock effect in the early part of the film, this Bert E. Friedlob-William A. Bacher production just isn't a very good picture. It's overlong (there are at least three different potential endings); it's more intimate scenes lack conviction, and the scripting at times borders on the amateurish, quite an accomplishment considering that it took three men—Talbot Jennings, Frank Fenton and Michael Blankfort—to whip together the screenplay.

This may easily go down as one of the greatest see-saw romances in screen history, with Tyrone Power and Susan Hayward as the alternately eager and reluctant couple. Lack of good judgment in not editing out unnecessary sequences makes the film drag in many spots and appear repetitious. Also, there are some bits that are acted in a manner to invite hilarity when none was intended. These could easily be trimmed without the slightest harm being done to the production. On the contrary, it'd be improved.

Based on the Helga Moray novel, "Untamed" in many parts is an ideal CinemaScope action vehicle and director Henry King, who spent several months in South Africa to get his backgrounds, has come up with some gusty footage. The rugged scenery, with the Boer wagons strung out in a vast, slow-moving line; the Zulu attack, with moments of real horror and great tension; the moment the Boers reach their goal—all these give the picture an occasional exciting quality and should provide the meaty action that fans savor.

Story, in the main, is concerned with the great Boer trek, when they fought and died to establish the Dutch Free State. Woven into this is the personal and turbulent love story about one of the Dutch leaders and an Irish girl who loved him on two continents. Power meets Miss Hayward in Ireland. Later she marries and induces her husband to go to South Africa to start a new life. He is killed and the romancing between Power and Miss Hayward continues to the point where she bears him a child (of which he knows nothing, having gone off to fight). In the end, in one of the most poorly acted sequences of the picture, Miss Hayward reveals to Power the origin of the child, and he slips a ring on her finger.

Miss Hayward struggles somewhat grimly with a part that would defy any actress. However, she's easy on the eye, wears some attractive period dresses and is emotional when the occasion demands. There are some scenes, such as the one when she has to sow a field and another when she gets a lengthy back massage from Power, that are obviously beyond her capacity. Also, the script's demands, that she blaze with anger one minute and melt amorously in the next, are tough on any actress when this temperamental turnabout continues through the entire film.

Power is properly rugged and in parts curiously wooden in a routine role. Like the rest, he's hindered by some of the incredible lines he's asked to speak. Richard Egan as Miss Hayward's suitor who eventually turns bully and outlaw carries a good punch and cuts a promising new screen figure. Agnes Moorehead as Miss Hayward's nurse is barely in the picture. Rita Moreno puts a lot of fire into the role of the passionate waif, Egan's girl.

Best and most exciting scenes in the picture are the ones shot in South Africa, with thousands of dancing and shouting Zulus, drummed into a frenzy, attacking the Boer wagon train. Leo Tover's lensing is done with the big CinemaScope screen in mind. Director King also threw in some extras, such as a big dust storm which topples a huge tree which in turn pins down a man whose leg has to be amputated in a somewhat gruesome scene complete with agonized yelling, etc., and a whip-duel between Power and Egan.

"Untamed" is said to have cost $3,750,000, a rather considerable investment, not all of which shows up on the screen. This isn't exactly a critics' picture, but the African adventure tag plus exploitation values should contribute to a lively b.o. showing. De Luxe tints come out just fine. *Hift.*

Blackboard Jungle

Controversial blockbuster dealing with underpaid teachers versus juvenile hoodlums. Pro and con factors promise explosive exploitation b.o.

Hollywood, Feb. 28.

Metro release of Pandro S. Berman production. Stars Glenn Ford, Anne Francis, Louis Calhern; features Margaret Hayes, John Hoyt, Richard Kiley, Emile Meyer, Basil Ruysdael, Warner Anderson, Sidney Poitier, Vic Morrow, Dan Terranova, Rafael Campos, Paul Mazursky. Direction and screenplay by Richard Brooks. Based on the novel by Evan Hunter; camera, Russell Harlan; editor, Ferris Webster; musical adaptation, Charles Wolcott. Previewed Feb. 23, '55. Running time, **100 MINS.**

Richard Dadier .... Glenn Ford
Anne Dadier .... Anne Francis
Jim Murdock .... Louis Calhern
Lois Hammond .... Margaret Hayes
Mr. Warneke .... John Hoyt
J. Y. Edwards .... Richard Kiley
Mr. Halloran .... Emile Meyer
Dr. Bradley .... Warner Anderson
Prof. Kraal .... Basil Ruysdael
Gregory W. Miller .... Sidney Poitier
Artie West .... Vic Morrow
Belazi .... Dan Terranova
Pete V. Morales .... Rafeal Campos
Emmanuel Stoker .... Paul Mazursky
Detective .... Horace McMahon
Santini .... Jameel Farah
De Lica .... Danny Dennis

(Aspect ratio: 1.75-1)

Juvenile hoodlums get a stark working over in "Blackboard Jungle," a controversial blockbuster that should ride to an explosive exploitation boxoffice before the pro and con ashes have time to settle. Its ticket-selling potential lies in the fact that the viewer will feel, and intensely, the melodramatic content, no matter whether in agreement with what is said, or how it is said. This feeling, properly stimulated by ballyhoo, can pay off at the b.o.

Director - scripter Richard Brooks, working from novel by Evan Hunter, has fashioned an angry picture that flares out in moral and physical rage at mental slovenliness, be it juvenile, mature, or in the pattern of society acceptance of things as they are because no one troubles to devise a better way.

No particular plea is made for racial tolerance. It's baldly stated and left up to the individual to accept or reject. The same treatment is accorded the school system and the shabbily-paid teachers, both those dedicated and those unable to face a more competitive world.

Other social problems are covered, too, once-over-lightly. The main issue is the juvenile bum who terrorizes schoolrooms and teachers.

To say all this, the plot introduces Glenn Ford, young Navy veteran, taking his first teaching job. His classroom is in a big city trade school, and the pupils are a cross-section of all races. As in life, a very few are strong, the rest follow-the-leader sheep, and Ford's job is to sort out the leaders, win them over, if possible, so that learning, not defiance of authority, will take its rightful place again.

These are no mischievous youths Ford deals with, but hoodlums, some of whom are already well along the road to crime. The strong among the evil element, here represented by Vic Morrow, is already beyond any reform. The good, represented by Sidney Poitier, has had no stimulus to awaken his leadership abilities because he is a Negro. Ford, Morrow and Poitier are so real in their performances under the probing direction by Brooks that the picture alternatingly has the viewer pleading, indignant and frightened before the conclusion is brought about with a hackle-raising classroom fight in which Ford and Poitier find themselves when the teacher subdues a knife-wielding Morrow.

The story uses the shocker technique of profanity, racial slur, attempted rape and similar socially unacceptable motivations for emphasis but these all belong with such a gutty topic. Also, it uses much that is obvious in character and situation, but this, because it is familiar, only lends emphasis to the dramatic points. It seems certain that controversy will develop over two teachers, beaten down from a day in class, getting drunk in a corner saloon and then falling prey to a cruel beating by their hoodlum students; over the sexual and spiritual lonesomeness of Margaret Hayes, a frightened teacher in the school and the forthright way in which her problem is stated; over the fact a teacher witnesses a crime by some of his pupils and fails to report it, and, less possibly, over the frank approach to marital relations between Ford and his pregnant wife, Anne Francis. However, all of this can be boxoffice fuel.

Pandro S. Berman's production supervision backs the Brooks approach to the picture without reservation, resulting in a film with a melodramatic impact that hits hard at a contemporary problem. The casting, too, is exceptionally good. Miss Francis is fine and believeable as the wife. Louis Calhern reads all of the forlorn bitterness of a life-beaten man into his cynical teacher character, and Miss Hayes is simply great as the sexpot teacher. John Hoyt, school principal; Richard Kiley, Emile Meyer, and hoods Dan Terranova, Rafeal Campos, Paul Mazursky and others wallop over their parts.

On the technical side, the picture has a fine lineup of talents, including Russell Harlan's stark photography, the realistic settings, the editing and the musical adaptation. Used to pinpoint drama are three recordings, with "Rock Around the Clock," played by Bill Haley and His Comets theming the jazz beat that expresses the subject. Others heard are "Invention For Guitar and Trumpet," played by Stan Kenton and his orchestra, and "The Jazz Me Blues," played by Bix Beiderbecke and His Gang.

Brog.

Man Without a Star
(COLOR—SONG)

Good western drama, highlighting action with sex and humor; profitable possibilities.

Hollywood, March 1.

Universal release of Aaron Rosenberg production. Stars Kirk Douglas, Jeanne Crain, Claire Trevor; co-stars William Campbell; features Richard Boone, Mara Corday, Jay C. Flipper Myrna Hansen. Directed by King Vidor. Screenplay, Borden Chase, D. D. Beauchamp; based on a novel by Dee Linford; camera (Teechnicolor), Russell Metty; editor, Virgil Vogel; music supervision, Joseph Gershenson; songs: "Man Without a Star" by Arnold Hughes, Frederick Herbert, sung by Frankie Laine; "And the Moon Grew Brighter and Brighter," by Jimmy Kennedy and Lou Singer. Previewed Feb. 22, '55. Running time, **89 MINS.**

Dempsey Rae	Kirk Douglas
Reed Bowman	Jeanne Crain
Idonee	Claire Trevor
Jeff Jimson	William Campbell
Steve Miles	Richard Boone
Strap Davis	Jay C. Flippen
Tess Cassidy	Myrna Hansen
Moccasin Mary	Mara Corday
Tom Cassidy	Eddy C. Waller
Latigo	Sheb Wooley
Tom Carter	George Wallace
Little Waco	Frank Chase
Mark Toliver	Paul Birch
Sheriff Olson	Roy Barcroft
Cookie	Wm. "Bill" Phillips

(*Aspect ratio*: 2-1)

Humor and sex highlight the action in "Man Without a Star," a good western feature with profitable boxoffice prospects. Kirk Douglas, in the title role, takes easily to the saddle as a tumbleweed cowpoke who has a way with a sixgun or the ladies, helping to carry off the seemingly authentic range flavor that is one of the better aspects of the presentation. This air is furthered by the story treatment and some outstanding color photography or the outdoor settings. These factors all add up to open air drama that should rate a ready reception in the regular market.

Two femmes, Jeanne Crain and Claire Trevor, hold down the distaff star spots in the Aaron Rosenberg production, and William Campbell scores in a co-star slot as the young greenhorn who learns his cowboying from Douglas and about the wrong kind of women from Miss Crain. The latter is technically skilled in her delineation of a ruthless owner of a big ranch, not above using sex in her determination to keep the range unfenced, but is not quite believable as a sexpot. Miss Trevor is back in a character she does well, playing what is, by implication, the town madam with a heart of gold, and with a soft spot in it for the wandering Douglas.

Title of the picture, ably scripted by Borden Chase and D. D. Beauchamp from a novel by Dee Linford, comes from the thought that everyone has a star to keep them steadfast and those without a purpose are doomed to wander forever. Such a man is Douglas, a saddle tramp who hates fences and who is kept moving further west as more and more range is crossed by barbed wire.

Douglas and Campbell, a range novice who has attached himself to the colorful saddle tramp, find work on the big spread operated by Miss Crain, a gal who decides Douglas is just the man to ramrod her ranch and handle house duties at night, provided he will continue to fight the small ranchers who want to save grass for winter feeding by fencing. The plot is basic western in this setup of open versus fenced land, but writing variations keep it fresh and the action high as things move towards the climax when Douglas switches sides, helps the small ranchers and then rides off in search of new, unfenced land.

King Vidor's vigorous direction of the action and the sweeping staging of the big outdoor scenes is a top asset to the entertainment values. The humor has a crude, masculine flavor just right for the raw west and the characters peopling it. A laugh gag good for considerable footage is the cowpoke speculation over the installation and use of an inside bathroom at Miss Crain's big ranch. Along with the bold humor are fights, stampedes and chases just as bold with action, and Russell Metty's camera work shows them off importantly.

Abetting the good work of the four principals is Richard Boone, a badman from Texas who moves in on the Crain spread when Douglas switches allegiance; Jay C. Flippen, the honest foreman replaced by Douglas; Myrna Hansen, daughter of small rancher Eddy Waller who ropes young Campbell; Mara Corday, one of Miss Trevor's girls; Sheb Wooley, Roy Barcroft, Bill Phillips and others.

Douglas takes banjo in hand to plink and sing "And the Moon Grew Brighter and Brighter" by Jimmy Kennedy and Lou Singer during a saloon sequence. Behind the main title, Frankie Laine's voice is heard singing the title tune, cleffed by Arnold Hughes Frederick Herbert. It's a range ballad of the "Mule Train"-"Wild Goose"-etc., school.

Brog.

The End of the Affair
(BRITISH)

Deborah Kerr and Van Johnson in Graham Greene drama with strong religious overtones; valuable star appeal but questionable b.o. hopes.

London, March 1.

Columbia release of David E. Rose production. Stars Deborah Kerr, Van Johnson, John Mills; features Stephen Murray, Nora Swinburne, Charles Goldner, Peter Cushing. Directed by Edward Dmytryk. Screenplay, Lenore Coffee from novel by Graham Greene; camera, Wilkie Cooper; editor, Alan Osbiston; music, Benjamin Frankel. At Empire Theatre, London, Feb. 23, '55. Running time, **107 MINS.**

Sarah Miles	Deborah Kerr
Maurice Bendrix	Van Johnson
lbert Parkis	John Mills
Henry Miles	Peter Cushing
Father Crompton	Stephen Murray
Mrs. Bertram	Nora Swinburne
Savage	Charles Goldner
Smythe	Michael Goodliffe
Miss Palmer	Joyce Carey
Dr. Collingwood	Frederick Leister
Landlady	Elsie Wagstaff
Lancelot Parkis	Christopher Warbey

Graham Greene's obsession for religious themes, which has dominated most of his recent plays and novels, almost gets out of hand in this filmization of his novel. And what might have been a poignant romantic drama develops into a bewildering discussion of faith versus reason. Not a particularly promising subject from a boxoffice point of view, "The End of the Affair" will need cautious selling. The marquee values of the stars will, of course, be a big help, especially in the U.S.

There is nothing subtle about the author's introduction of the religioso aspect or in the way his own strong views are allowed to grip the subject. He strikes boldly and with obvious conviction; his characters are engulfed by his belief and echo the views he so sincerely holds. That hardly makes for scintillating dialog, but does contribute to the very static nature of this over-wordy British film.

To go along with Greene, it is necessary to accept that Deborah Kerr's prayer was answered when Van Johnson, with whom she had been having an illicit love affair, was struck in a wartime air raid. She believes him to be dead but on her bended knees promises to give him up if he can be brought back to life. Actually, he returns in a few minutes, but the oath having been taken she is determined to walk out of his life and the rest of the film is a battle between her conscience and her love. Van Johnson becomes little more than an anguished onlooker.

Sitting on the sidelines most of the time is Peter Cushing as Miss Kerr's husband, a civil servant who is bewildered by his wife's mysterious coming and goings, but cannot quite bring himself to hire an inquiry agent. So Van Johnson does it for him and the scenes in which John Mills does the trailing are among the best in the picture. But their inquiry leads them to the home of a Hyde Park soap-box agnostic, whose visiting cards are distributed to the audience he harangues.

With the emphasis on the religious debate, the film takes on a static appearance and there is hardly any action throughout the footage. Instead, there's an overabundance of closeups and two shots, when barely a bright line of dialog or a smile from one of the principal characters brightens the scene.

Despite this gloomy backcloth, Miss Kerr radiates warmth and beauty. Van Johnson's performance, on the other hand, is kept to a single key, inducing an air of monotony. Only Mills, best served by the script, is able to emerge as a believeable character. Cushing's study of the husband is also kept to one plane, but there are neat contrasting cameos by Stephen Murray, as the priest who preaches faith, and by Michael Goodliffe, as the agnostic who advocates reason.

Edward Dmytryk's direction is clearly restricted by the demands of the script. Wilkie Cooper's lensing attains a high quality and Benjamin Frankel's score is effectively unobtrusive. Other technical credits are okay, but the pic could be helped by additional scissoring.

Myro.

Stranger on Horseback
(COLOR)

Okay Joel McCrea western for the general outdoor action market.

Hollywood, March 1.

United Artists release of Robert Goldstein production. Stars Joel McCrea; co-stars Miroslava; features Kevin McCarthy, John McIntire, Emile Meyer, Nancy Gates, John Carradine. Directed by Jacques Tourneur. Screenplay, Herb Meadow, Don Martin; story by Louis L'Amour; camera (Ansco Color by Pathe), Ray Rennahan; editor, William Murphy; music, Paul Dunlap. Previewed Feb. 23, '55. Running time, **65 MINS.**

Rick Thorne	Joel McCrea
Amy Lee Bannerman	Miroslava
Tom Bannerman	Kevin McCarthy
Josiah Bannerman	John McIntire
Caroline Webb	Nancy Gates
Colonel Streeter	John Carradine
Sheriff Nat Bell	Emile Meyer
Arnold Hammer	Robert Cornthwaite
Vince Webb	Walter Baldwin
Paula Morison	Jaclynne Greene

(*Aspect ratio*: 1.85-1)

Joel McCrea brings law and order to the range in "Stranger On Horseback" and the stalwart, unflinching manner with which he tackles the chore makes for good viewing for the outdoor action fan. In that market this western should fare okay.

United Artists is releasing the outdoor actioner, location-lensed in Mexico by Robert Goldstein for Leonard Goldstein Productions, and a number of factors combine to make it acceptable filmfare for the intended market. McCrea always brings an air of credibility to his western characterizations, and his work here goes a long way towards shaping the film for general acceptance. Other performances, some flamboyant, also assist the entertainment aims, as does Jacques Tourneur's good direction of the Louis L'Amour story, scripted by Herb Meadow and Don Martin.

McCrea portrays a circuit judge, who comes to a small western town in the course of making his rounds. There he finds the town and surrounding area under the feudal thumb of an oldline family headed by John McIntire. Despite wholehearted opposition and obstacles, McCrea fingers McIntire's spoiled son, Kevin McCarthy, for murder, smokes out the necessary frightened witnesses and defies the whole clan by seeing that justice is done. In doing so he even wins the grudging respect of the old cattle baron, gains the love of the latter's strong-willed niece, Miroslava, and awakens sheriff Emile Meyer to a new sense of duty.

The Mexican locations provide the story action with attractive settings, and the lensing in Ansco Color by Ray Rennahan does them justice. Trouping is generally good. McCarthy plays his role with the proper arrogance and Miroslava is good as the fiery heroine who turns against family to aid the judge. McIntire shows up excellently as the head of the feudal domain and John Carradine sparks a colorful part as attorney for the clan. Nancy Gates is an eye and acting pleaser as a witness to murder. Meyer and the others provide complete support.

Technical credits lineup first-rate on the production. *Brog.*

Big House, U.S.A.

Fair melodrama entertainment with familiar names and medium prospects for general program market.

Hollywood, Feb. 26.

United Artists release of Bel-Air (Aubrey Schenck) production. Stars Broderick Crawford, Ralph Meeker, Reed Hadley, William Talman, Lon Chaney, Charles Bronson; features Randy Farr, Roy Roberts, Willis B. Bouchey, Peter Votrian. Directed by Howard W. Koch. Written by John C. Higgins; camera, Gordon Avil; editor, John F. Schreyer; music, Paul Dunlap. Previewed Feb. 24, '55. Running time, **82 MINS.**

Rollo Lamar .... Broderick Crawford
Jerry Barker .... Ralph Meeker
James Madden .... Reed Hadley
Nurse, Emily Evans......... Randy Farr
Machinegun Mason......William Talman
Alamo Smith .... Lon Chaney
Benny Kelly .... Charles Bronson
Danny Lambert .... Peter Votrian
Chief Ranger, Erickson..... Roy Roberts
Robertson Lambert....Willis B. Bouchey

(*Aspect ratio*: 1.75-1)

The case history of a crime, from execution through to punishment, makes up the melodrama in "Big House, U.S.A." and provides a fair amount of entertainment. Film shapes to medium prospects in the general program market, where its familiar cast names should help the bookings.

A pseudo-documentary style of storytelling is used in the Bel-Air production, produced by Aubrey Schenck for United Artists release and directed by Howard W. Koch. The technique, with quite a bit of narration, slows proceedings so there seem to be rather long stretches between the good action-melodrama scenes. The script by John C. Higginss is inclined to ramble but, in general, deals with the kidnaping of a small boy camper in Royal Gorge Park, Colorado, the kid's accidental death, the payment of ransom and the follow-through by the law as it goes about bringing the criminal to justice.

Several frustrations are encountered along the way by the FBI in the person of Reed Hadley. He has the right man, Ralph Meeker, but can only send him away for extortion since the kidnaper plotted his crime well to make it look like he only used a kid's disappearance to tap a rich father's wallet. Heavies Broderick Crawford, William Talman, Lon Chaney and Charles Bronson get into the picture when Meeker is assigned to their cell block at Cascabel Island Prison. Here yarn goes off on another angle having to do with the scheme of Crawford and his henchmen to escape, taking Meeker with them to lead the way to the buried $200,000 ransom. Windup finds the law waiting the treasure-seekers and the baddies pay with their lives for their crimes.

Plenty of violence is featured throughout in some rather chilling scenes, but fits the tough characters with which the story deals. Performances are in keeping, with Meeker doing a good job of a cold-blooded crook nicknamed "The Iceman." Crawford, Talman, Chaney and Bronson also are okay heavies, while Hadley, Roy Roberts and others on the side of law prove capable. Randy Farr, as Meeker's femme accomplice, and Peter Votrian, the youthful victim, are acceptable.

Picture has a scenic advantage in being lensed by Gordon Avil in the Royal Gorge country. Cascabel Island Prison also is used as an action site. Editing, background score and other contributions are standard. *Brog.*

Wyoming Renegades

(COLOR)

Rough, tough western feature, full of action violence, for the outdoor market.

Hollywood, Feb. 25.

Columbia release of Wallace MacDonold production. Features Phil Carey, Gene Evans, Martha Hyer. Directed by Fred F. Sears. Story and screenplay, David Lang; camera (Technicolor), Lester White; editor, Edwin Bryant; music conducted by Mischa Bakaleinikoff. Previewed Feb. 21, '55. Running time, **72 MINS.**

Brady Sutton .... Phil Carey
Butch Cassidy .... Gene Evans
Nancy Warren .... Martha Hyer
Sundance .... William Bishop
Charlie Veer .... Douglas Kennedy
Sheriff McVey .... Roy Roberts
Horace Warren .... Don Beddoe
Petie Carver .... Aaron Spelling
George Curry .... George Keymas
Medford .... Harry Harvey
Whiskey Pearson .... Mel Welles
Elza Lay .... Henry Rowland
Tom McCarthy .... Boyd Stockman
Black Jack Ketchum.....A. Guy Teague
Matt Garner .... Bob Woodward
Ben Kilpatrick .... Don C. Harvey
O. C. Hanks .... John Cason
Bob Meeks .... Don Carlos

(*Aspect ratio*: 1.65-1)

A double-barrelled load of tough violence is fired at the western fan in "Wyoming Renegades" and it will find its target in the outdoor action market, where this type of feature usually proves okay program filmfare.

Phil Carey, ex-badman going straight; Gene Evans, leader of a gang of outlaw killers, and Martha Hyer, the girl who believes in Carey, hold down the featured spots in the Wallace MacDonald production and perform competently under Fred F. Sears' fast, rugged direction.

David Lang screen story is a generally good, albeit mostly familiar, framework against which to play the hard action. Main plot nub deals with Carey's efforts to shake off the prison stigma and make a new life, but when Evans' baddies hold up the town bank, Carey's again suspect and seemingly rejoins the outlaw band but only to clear his name.

Plot finale has a seldom-used twist to make it possible for Carey and Miss Hyer to find happiness. Neither the hero, the sheriff, nor any other mere man can bring this about, the deed falling to the town femmes, by now sick of masculine fumbling in dealing out gun justice. With the townsmen away on a ruse, the gals lay an ambush for Evans and his cutthroats, shooting down most and jailing the others when another raid on the bank is tried.

William Bishop, Aaron Spelling, George Keymas and others in Evans' motley outlaw crew enact their characters capably. So do Douglas Kennedy, undercover Pinkerton man; Roy Roberts, the sheriff; Don Beddoe and others on the side of law and order. Lester White's photography, and other technical work is good.

The score, conducted by Mischa Bakaleinikoff, is used here much more effectively than in most westerns, or dramas. The music never tries to compete with the action, but proves a strong support by staying behind the scenes. This intelligent treatment particularly heightens suspense in several sequences. *Brog.*

The Silver Star

Program western which overlooks action for mood; small b.o. draw.

Hollywood, Feb. 25.

Lippert release of an Earle Lyon production. Stars Edgar Buchanan, Marie Windsor, Lon Chaney, Earle Lyon, Richard Bartlett, Barton MacLane; features Morris Ankrum, Edith Evanson, Michael Whalen, Steve Rowland. Directed by Richard Bartlett. Story-screenplay, Bartlett, Ian MacDonald; camera, Guy Roe; editor, George Reid; music, Leon Klatzken; song, Jimmy Wakely. Reviewed Feb. 23, '55. Running time, **73 MINS.**

Bill Dowdy .... Edgar Buchanan
Karen .... Marie Windsor
John W. Harmon .... Lon Chaney
Gregg .... Earle Lyon
King Daniels .... Richard Bartlett
Tiny .... Barton MacLane
Childress .... Morris Ankrum
Mrs. Dowdy .... Edith Evanson
Bainey .... Michael Whalen
Shakespeare .... Steve Rowland

(*Aspect ratio*: 1.33-1)

This low-budget western depends too much on limning a man's philosophy and not enough on action to give it much chance in the action market, where it will hit less discriminating situations only. An attempt at mood seldom stacks up for western fans, who like their heroes on the positive side. Film should also be cut a good 10 to 15 minutes.

Yarn is based on a man just elected sheriff against his wishes, who doesn't believe in the killing the job requires. When three gunmen show up to kill him, ostensibly hired by his defeated political opponent, he hides out, refusing to meet them until the old sheriff he succeeded shames him by taking his gun and going after the trio.

Earle Lyon, who also produced, is colorless in the role, and balance of cast doesn't stand much chance with their roles. Edgar Buchanan tries valiantly as the retired peace-officer, as do Marie Windsor as the sheriff's beloved, Lon Chaney his defeated opponent, Richard Bartlett (also the director) the killer and Barton MacLane a blacksmith. Bartlett manages to insert some degree of fast play in a climaxing gunfight, but effect is nixed by adding an inconsequential sequence to clean up story line. *Whit.*

La Paura

(Fear)

(ITALO-GERMAN)

Rome, Feb. 22.

Minerva Film release of an Aniene-Ariston Film production. Stars Ingrid Bergman, Mathias Wiemna; features Renate Mannhart, Kurt Krueger, Elise Aulinger, Edith Schultze-Westrum, Steffie Struck, Annelore Wied. Directed by Roberto Rossellini. Screenplay, Sergio Amidei, Franz Treuberg; from novel by Stephan Zweig; camera, Carlo Carlini; music, Renzo Rossellini; editor, Yolanda Benvenuti, Walter Boos. Previewed in Rome. Running time, **83 MINS.**

Irene Wagner .... Ingrid Bergman
Albert Wagner .... Mathias Wieman
Johanna Schultze ...... Renate Mannhart
Heinrich Stolz .... Kurt Krueger

Shot in Germany by a two-country partnership, latest product of the Bergman-Rossellini tandem shapes as the best they've done together in some time, showing care in continuity and scripting unusual to the directors well-known weakness for improvised shooting. The Bergman name is still a potent sales item, which if properly pitched can help this item pay its way. Theme chosen, however, more than anything else, will keep earnings in the moderate class.

Story, based on the Stephen Zweig tome, pictures the fear introduced into the life of Irene Wagner (Ingrid Bergman), wife of a well-to-do professor, (Mathias Wieman) by a blackmailing ex-girlfriend of her young lover. Irene is driven into a fear psychosis, and threatens suicide. She is detained by her husband, and pic winds with new understanding and mutual pardon.

Script is fairly well knit and makes for some suspense but fails importantly in backdropping character. Thus, the reasons for Irene's illicit relationship remain unexplained. Acting is competent throughout, with Ingrid Bergman giving an indecisive part a good reading. Mathias Wieman impresses as her husband. Renate Mannhart is properly coarse as the blackmailer while the lover is merely sketched in by Kurt Krueger. Carlo Carlini has done an able lensing job. Renzo Rossellini's musical score adds considerably to pic's development and mood. Editing is well done. *Hawk.*

Ludwig II

(GERMAN-COLOR)

Frankfurt, Feb. 22.

Schorcht Film release of Aura production. Stars O. W. Fischer and Ruth Leuwerik. Directed by Helmut Kautner. Screenplay, Georg Hurdalek and Peter Berneis after a story by Kadidja Wederkind; camera (Technicolor), Douglas Slocombe; music by Vienna Symphony Orchestra under Herbert von Karajan. At Turm Palast, Frankfurt. Running time, **116 MINS.**

Ludwig II .... O. W. Fischer
Kaiserin Elisabeth .... Ruth Leuwerik
Princess Sophie .... Marianne Koch
Richard Wagner .... Paul Bildt
Bismarck .... Friedrich Domin
Count Holnstein .... Rolf Kutschera
Dr. Gudden .... Robert Meny
Prinz Otto .... Klaus Kinski

It is notably difficult for a nation to accept the idea that their ruler is mad, and even more difficult to adequately portray the growing madness of a king and the resultant crises for a country. But in this tragic film about Ludwig II, the results are not only admirable, but also exceptional. Although parts of the story are left to conjecture where the truth will probably never be known, and some of Ludwig's eccentricities eliminated, the film is mainly factual and a powerful one.

O. W. Fischer, who portrays Ludwig, is an extremely handsome man whose usual light roles have made him a matinee idol in Germany. Here he has broken away from this type role with an outstanding portrayal of the king. Ludwig is shown from his youth as a lover of the arts and patron of Richard Wagner, through his ill-fated love of Elizabeth, the wife of Franz Joseph, in his struggles with Bismarck, to his final dissolution in an insane asylum and his dramatic death.

Excellent performances, too, are contributed by Ruth Leuwerik as Kaiserin Elisabeth and Marianne Koch as her younger sister. Klaus Kinski, as Ludwig's younger brother, provides a fine study. Paul Bildt portrays Wagner, and the pic is given added interest by the playing of the Vienna Symphony

Orchestra under the baton of Herbert von Karajon.

Scenes of the Bavarian countryside, and the filming at the actual castle of the mad king contribute to the film's anthenticity and local audience identification. Minor flaw is that the technicians are apparently not accustomed to Technicolor, and the makeup was somewhat inexpertly applied. The film reception here tabbed this as one of the best pix made in Germany since the war. It may do well in U.S. art houses. *Haze.*

Variety Stars
(RUSSIAN)

Artkino release of Mosfilm production. Directed by Vera Stroyeva. Features Y. Timoshenko, E. Berezin, L. Mirov, M. Novitsky, Leonid Utyosov, M. Mironova, A. Menaker, Klavdia Shulzhenko, Rinna Zelyonaya, T. Savva. Screenplay, E. Pomeshchikov, V. Tipot; camera, L. Nokolayev, M. Gindin; music, I. Dunayevsky, A. Tsfasman. At Stanley, N.Y., starting Feb. 19, '55. Running time, **85 MINS.**

(In Russian; English titles)

Soviet film producers try their luck with lightweight musical fare in this pic with rather lukewarm results. Supposed to be a backstage glimpse of the Russo Variety Hall stage, it is hard to believe that Russian vaudeville is this dull and haphazard. Vera Stroyeva, who did the commendable "Grand Concert" for the Russians, directed and helped in the production of this. Pic is poor credit to her.

Initial premise in the rather sketchy story has a comedy twosome trying out for a regular job in one of the big government-run halls. It appears that the pair have won in the competition, the board of judges howls at their comedy antics (the two are actually rather funny), but nothing happens. The two are convinced they have lost out, and at about this juncture somebody apparently lost the script. Because the story meanders all over the lot—first have the two lads as emsees, then the unknown "finds" on the new bill and finally presenting a new act at the town hall.

This is all pretty confusing and seldom amusing. The scripters trot out a portly, homely songstress whose sole redeeming feature is that she can warble. Then there is a more attractive femme who is firstrate whistler, but she's not in the vaude show as herein edited. There is a topflight ballet troupe but work is marred by whirling scarfs and faulty photography. Production boasts some good acrobats and a couple of good singers but neither group would encounter much success on the American stage.

Entire vaude troupe lines up and comes forward to take a bow at the finale of the performance — far from original. Miss Stroyeva learned the hard way in this film that it takes more than just a few available acts to make a screen musical jell. The camera work for the most part is up to the high Russian standard but the music is routine, and the screenplay is just one of those things. *Wear.*

Un Fil a la Patte
(A Fly In The Ointment)
(FRENCH)
Paris, Feb. 22.

Gaumont release of Cite Films-Gaumont production. Stars Noel-Noel, Suzy Delair. Directed by Guy Lefranc. Screenplay, Noel-Noel from farce by Georges Feydeau; camera, Pierre Petit, editor, Robert

Isnardon. At Paris, Paris. Running time, **85 MINS.**
Bois D'Enghien .... Noel-Noel
Lucette .... Suzy Delair
Marceline .... Genevieve Kervine
Bouzin .... Bourvil
Cheneviette .... Henri Guisol
Baroness .... Gabrielle Dorziat

Turn-of-century farce has been filmed with a wider scope than given the usual confines of the stage. However, the clockwork mechanism and pacing of the Georges Feydeau opus loses its impact on the screen, and the characters are too personalized and broad to make for the proper comic overtones. Played in tongue-in-cheek style, this lacks laughs and emerges as not especially suited for the U.S. market.

Fly in the ointment here is a fancy, high-living music hall singer who is the present mistress of a playboy, latter now being ready to marry into a good family. But ultimately the singer weds a rich admirer, and the playboy is forgiven.

This farce falters and the dwells on the characters so long it robs them of their true farcical attitudes. However, it is amusing in spots Director Guy Lefranc has gotten some neat period angles into this, but has missed out on movement. Noel-Noel is too supercilious. Suzy Delair has guile and bounce but lacks the necessary bombast. Remainder of the cast is uneven except for Bourvil, who provides a sock characterization of the crafty lawyer, who is a songwriter on the side. Lensing and editing are good, and production dress glossy. *Mosk.*

Canaris
(GERMAN)
Berlin, Feb. 22.
Europa release of Fama productions. Stars O. E. Hasse, Adrian Hoven, Barbara Ruetting. Directed by Alfred Weidenmann. Screenplay, Herbert Reinecker after a manuscript by Erich Ebermayer; camera, Franz Weihmayr; music, Siegfried Franz. At Gloria Palast, Berlin. Running time, **113 MINS.**
Admiral Canaris .... O. E. Hasse
Hauptmann Althoff .... Adrian Hoven
Irene von Harbeck .. Barbara Ruetting
Obergruppenfuehrer Heydrich
.... Martin Held
Oberst Holl .... Wolfgang Preiss
Fernandez .... Peter Masbacher
Herr von Harbeck .... Arthur Schroeder
Baron Trenti .... Charles Regnier
Beckmann .... Franz Essel
Oberst Degenhard .... Herbert Wilk
French Captain .... Claus Miedel
Fraeulein Winter .... Alice Treff
Frau Luedtke ...... Ilse Fuerstenberg
Gestapo Official .... Oskar Lindner
Major Ullmann .... Friedrich Steig
Hauptmann Behrens .... Otto Braml

This is a remarkably well done German semi-documentary pic centering around the controversial figure of Admiral Canaris who was in charge of Germany's defenses during the Hitler era. Both technically and artistically, pic is considerably beyond the German postwar average and rates high in acting and direction. Being a sure moneymaker here, "Canaris" also appears to have the ingredients for the foreign market.

Screenplay, ably written by Herbert Reinecker from a slick manuscript by Erich Ebermayer, has to do with Admiral Canaris, boss of the German counter-intelligence corps until 1944. It effectively retells some of his most important activities under the Hitler banner. It shows how he was in touch with anti-Hitler groups, but hesitated to participate in their underground activities. Knowing what was going to happen to Germany and yet feeling unable to change the unholy situation, he got into deep inner conflicts and more and more

showed an open dislike for the regime he served.

He lost his job in 1944 and after the attempt to overthrow Hitler failed, he was put in a concentration camp.

Pic's general appeal is helped greatly by the Canaris portrayed by outstanding actor O. E. Hasse. This stage actor, who strangely enough established his film career via American pix ("Decision Before Dawn" and "I Confess,") should find more favor with Teutonic producers after this one. Another topflight performance is turned in by Martin Held, as Heydrich, the SS chieftain who mistrust and opposed Canaris. Most others give good performances but are considerably overshadowed by Hasse and Held. Not very convincing, however, are Adrian Hoven and Barbara Ruetting.

Full praise should go to Alfred Weidenmann who directed this. Still not so widely known among local directors, Weidenmann establishes himself via this film.

"Canaris" may be regarded as one of the best and most important German efforts since the war's end. *Hans.*

Hit the Deck
(C'SCOPE-MUSICAL-COLOR)

Remake of stage musical, plushily done in C'Scope, color, with youthful cast emphasis; fairly entertaining, medium b.o.

Hollywood, Feb. 27.

Metro release of Joe Pasternak production. Stars Jane Powell, Tony Martin, Debbie Reynolds, Walter Pidgeon, Vic Damone, Gene Raymond, Ann Miller, Russ Tamblyn, J. Carrol Naish; features Kay Armen, Richard Anderson, Jane Darwell, Alan King, Henry Slate. Directed by Roy Rowland. Written by Sonya Levien, William Ludwig; based on the musical play by Herbert Fields as presented on stage by Vincent Youmans, from "Shore Leave" by Hubert Osborne; camera (Eastman Color), George Folsey; editor, John McSweeney Jr.; music supervised and conducted by George Stoll; musical numbers staged by Hermes Pan; music by Vincent Youmans; lyrics by Leo Robin, Clifford Grey, Irving Caesar; orchestral arrangements by Robert Van Eps; vocal supervision by Jeff Alexander. Previewed Feb. 25, '55. Running time, **112 MINS.**

Susan Smith .... Jane Powell
Chief Boatswain's Mate Wm. F. Clark
.... Tony Martin
Carol Pace .... Debbie Reynolds
Rear Adm. Daniel Xavier Smith
.... Walter Pidgeon
Rico Ferrari .... Vic Damone
Wendell Craig .... Gene Raymond
Ginger .... Ann Miller
Danny Xavier Smith ..... Russ Tamblyn
Mr. Peroni .... J. Carrol Naish
Mrs. Ottavio Ferrari ...... Kay Armen
Lt. Jackson .... Richard Anderson
Jenny .... Jane Darwell
Shore Patrol ....Alan King, Henry Slate
Themselves .... Jubalaires

The emphasis of youth, in the person of a number of personable young players on the Metro contract list, has been put on this remake of the venerable legit musical, "Hit the Deck." Their presence, plus the plushy CinemaScope treatment, indicates medium possibilities at the boxoffice. Overall entertainment is fair and reaction will be mixed.

There's not much producer Joe Pasternak could do to refurbish the shopworn plot about three sailors on the loose, with three femmes on their mind, and the sundry complications that batter at the steadfast portals of Navy redtape and credibility. With the limitations, he has made it a pretty picture, replete with songs from the old footlight piece, complete with new lyrics, flashy production numbers and some scenically beautiful C'Scope shots of San Francisco. These factors are blended together as neatly as possible by Roy Rowland's direction, and the latter generates a good heart feel in some sequences when he can get away from weary material that hasn't much of the spark of life left.

The vintage musical takes on its best semblance to life when Debbie Reynolds and Russ Tamblyn are lending their enthusiasm, either alone or together, to the action. They particularly scored with "A Kiss Or Two" and an intriguing production number located in a fun park. The latter is a real pleaser, easily topping the several better moments in the long 112 minutes of footage.

Young and old should react favorably to the feeling projected by "Ciribiribin" as socked by Kay Armen with an assist from Jane Powell, Miss Reynolds, Vic Damone, Tony Martin and "Why, Oh Why?," which finds the Misses Powell, Reynolds and Ann Miller lamenting about men as they wait for a bus on the street of San Francisco, pleases, as does Martin's singing of "Keepin' Myself For You" to a chorus line topped by Miss Miller, and, later, "More Than You Know," again to Miss Miller. The latter's special piece is a sexy mamboed "Lady From the Bayou," while Miss Powell and Damone join on "I Know That You Know," and her solo number is "Sometimes I'm Happy." Opening and closing the show is "Hallelujah," the finale including a cast roundup. Also heard is a medley of "Join the Navy" and "Loo-Loo," serving as a situation setup for some chase comedy.

The plot, as framed by Sonya Levien and William Ludwig from the Herbert Fields musical play which Vincent Youmans presented on stage, deals with three gobs, Martin, Damone and Tamblyn, who come to San Francisco on leave; Martin to see his chorus sweetie, Miss Miller, Damone to visit his mother, Miss Armen, and Tamblyn to salute his admiral father, Walter Pidgeon. The boys mistakenly try to defend the honor of Miss Powell, Tamblyn's sister, from the designs of Gene Raymond, romeo stage star. A scrap ensues, after which Tamblyn and Miss Reynolds, a musicomedy star, develop a romance, and the remainder of the footage is giving over to the sailors dodging a comic shore patrol consisting of Alan King and Henry Slate while they straighten out the mess, their own romances and the amor between Miss Armen and J. Carrol Naish.

The girls are fetchingly costumed by Helen Rose, the entire cast and furbishings prettily photographed in Eastman Color by George Folsey, and Hermes Pan's musical numbers staging keeps the feet in time. Other technical credits are equally able. *Brog.*

Rage at Dawn
(COLOR)

Good Randolph Scott outdoor actioner with average possibilities in that market.

Hollywood, March 8.

RKO release of Nat Holt production. Stars Randolph Scott; Forrest Tucker, Mala Powers, J. Carrol Naish; features Edgar Buchanan, Myron Healey, Howard Petrie, Ray Teal, William Forrest, Denver Pyle, Trevor Bardette, Kenneth Tobey. Directed by Tim Whelan. Screenplay, Horace McCoy; story, Frank Gruber; camera (Technicolor), Ray Rennahan; editor, Harry Marker; music, Paul Sawtell. Previewed March 4, '55. Running time, **86 MINS.**

James Barlow	Randolph Scott
Frank Reno	Forrest Tucker
Laura Reno	Mala Powers
Sim Reno	J. Carol Naish
Judge Hawkins	Edgar Buchanan
John Reno	Myron Healey
Lattimore	Howard Petrie
Constable Brant	Ray Teal
Amos Peterson	William Forrest
Clint Reno	Denver Pyle
Fisher	Trevor Bardette
Monk Claxton	Kenneth Tobey
Hyronemus	Chubby Johnson
Bill Reno	Richard Garland

(*Aspect ratio:* 1.85-1)

Behind the rather odd title of "Rage At Dawn" is a good Randolph Scott western that shapes up to average possibilities in the outdoor action market. It's the story of some early-day badmen, the notorious Reno Brothers, who preceded such other baddies as the Youngers, the Daltons, etc., in a life of crime that paid off at the end of a rope, and has been put together expertly by Nat Holt for RKO release.

While western in flavor, site of the Frank Gruber story, which Horace McCoy scripted, is early Indiana, and standing in for this frontier terrain is the Columbia Historic State Park in California. Enacting the Renos are Forrest Tucker, J. Carrol Naish, Myron Healey and Richard Garland, four bad brothers who regularly raid banks and other cash boxes around the state and return to the safety of their own county, where they control the law represented by Edgar Buchanan, Howard Petrie and Ray Teal.

To bring these baddies together with Scott, special agent assigned to catch them, the plot has the hero and Kenneth Tobey posing as train robbers. They get into the Reno gang and Scott even participates in a holdup with the crooks before he stages a train heist that is to prove their downfall. With the robbers jailed, the citizens of the county become aroused enough to form a mob and lynch them just to make sure there will be no escape from justice. While probably historically correct, this finale act seems rather anti-climactic and permits the script to do a little soapboxing about the evils of mob rule.

Tim Whelan's direction scores best in the action sequences, being less competent in the more personal conflicts between characters, this latter seeming forced in contrast to the easy stride of the picture when dealing with the broader phases. Scott is a good hero, and even has a romance with Mala Powers, sister of the bad Remos, who ore capably portrayed by Tucker, Naish and the others. Buchanan, Petrie and Teal form a choice trio of political crooks and Denver Pyle does well as a good Reno.

The Technicolor lensing by Ray Rennahan is ably done and the other behind-camera assists are expertly handled. *Brog.*

Yellowneck
(COLOR)

Offbeat but overlong trip through the Florida Everglades by deserters of the Confederate Army. Doubtful b.o.

Republic release of Empire Studios production (Harlow G. Frederick). Stars Lin McCarthy, Stephen Courtleigh, Berry Kroeger, Harold Gordon, and Bill Mason. Direction and original story by R. John Hugh. Screenplay, Nat S. Linden; camera (Trucolor), Charles O'Rork; editor, William A. Slade; original music, Laurence Rosenthal. Previewed in N. Y. March 2, '53. Running time, **83 MINS.**

The Sergeant	Lin McCarthy
The Colonel	Stephen Courtleigh
Plunkett	Berry Kroeger
Cockney	Harold Gordon
The Kid	Bill Mason

"Yellowneck," the title of the Republic release, is the term used during the Civil War by the Confederate Army for a deserter. This is the story of five "yellownecks" who, for various reasons, deserted the Confederate cause and sought to escape to Cuba by way of the treacherous Florida Everglades. It's a grim, morbid yarn, overlong at 83 minutes, and of doubtful boxoffice appeal.

Filmed in the heart of the Florida Everglades by Empire Studios, it punches home effectively the feel of the jungle area—the heat, the storms, the animals, the reptiles, and the annoying bugs the men face in their aimless search for the sea where a boat is supposed to carry them to safety. But the trudge through the jungle, added to the danger of hostile Seminole Indians, appears repetitious to the point that one wants to cry out, "Enough, enough!"

In addition to the elements and the dangers of the Everglades and the Indians, the personalities of each individual member of the group play a key role in the fight for survival. There's a Colonel, addicted to drink and sick with shame for having retreated; a sergeant, disgusted with the futility of a pointless war; a young private, an idolizer and follower of the sergeant; Plunkett, a licentious thief, and Cockney, an English mercenary of low character. The battle against the jungle and the Indians has the five men at each other's throats before long.

One by one each of the men meets a horrible death. The manner of each death is presented in such a way that it's not for the squeamish. The colonel gets an arrow in the back but doesn't die until after an unpleasant delirium. A rattlesnake gets the Cockney; an alligator takes care of Plunkett; and the sergeant sinks to his end in a quagmire. The kid, practically out of his mind, gets to the sea, but there's no boat there, only the wide, empty sea.

There's apparently a moral in Nat S. Linden's screenplay of R. John Hugh's original story. There's an inkling of it in the conversations of the kid and the sergeant and has something to do with standing up and facing your responsibilities rather than running away.

"Yellowneck" has the ingredients of a good off-beat film, but its moral and obvious effort to make use of the Everglades background could have been presented dramatically in a half-hour video. The five-man cast—Lin McCarthy, Stephen Courtleigh, Berry Kroeger, Harold Gordon, and Bill Mason—carry out their assignments well. Charles O'Rork's Trucolor photography succeeds in capturing the atmosphere of the Everglades. Hugh's direction and other technical credits, including Laurence Rosenthal's music, are okay. *Holl.*

Hell's Outpost

Lusty outdoor film geared for action houses.

Hollywood, March 2.

Republic release of a Joe Kane production. Stars Rod Cameron, Joan Leslie, Chill Wills, John Russell; features Jim Davis, Ben Cooper, Kristine Miller, Taylor Holmes, Barton MacLane. Directed by Kane. Screenplay, Kenneth Gamet; based on novel, "Silver Rock," by Luke Short; camera, Jack Marta; editor, Richard L. Van Enger; music, R. Dale Butts. Reviewed March 2, '55. Running time, **89 MINS.**

Tully Gibbs	Rod Cameron
Sarah Moffit	Joan Leslie
Ben Hodes	John Russell
Kevin Russel	Chill Wills
Sam Horne	Jim Davis
Beth Hodes	Kristine Miller
Alec Bacchione	Ben Cooper
Timothy Byers	Taylor Holmes
Sheriff Olson	Barton MacLane
Mrs. Moffit	Ruth Lee
Harry Bogue	Arthur Q. Bryan
Hotel Clerk	Oliver Blake

(*Aspect ratio:* 1.66-1)

This lusty outdoor film is tailored for the requirements of the action trade, although it could be snapped up by the trimming of a good 10 minutes. The marquee strength of its four star names coupled with usually good movement should carry feature through for okay returns.

Struggle for a tungsten mine motivates the Kenneth Gamet screenplay, adapted from the Luke Short novel, "Silver Rock," with plenty of dirty work by the heavy. Yarn takes its premise from the try of a Korean vet to worm his way into an interest in the mine through claiming friendship with the owner's son, killed in the war. He's honest in trying to develop the mine, but finds stiff opposition right down the line from the man who has been trying to get it away from the owner for years.

Rod Cameron as the vet delivers his customary rugged performance and gets in a couple of gusty brawls with the heavy, played by John Russell for good effect. Joan Leslie handles the femme lead prettily, pursued by Russell but leaning romantically toward Cameron. Chill Wills, as fourth star, is the mine owner, a serious role for him, but he also gets in a song number, "Packin' the Mail," his composition. In satisfactory support are Jim Davis as a newspaper editor; Kristine Miller, sister of Russell; Ben Cooper, Cameron's pal; Taylor Holmes, a crooked lawyer, and Barton MacLane, sheriff.

Joe Kane as associate producer-director establishes a pace after a slow start which builds well to a fast climax, and Jack Marta's outdoor camera work is expert. *Whit.*

Ma and Pa Kettle At Waikiki

Strictly for the Kettle fans and last with Percy Kilbride as Pa.

Hollywood, March 8.

Universal release of Leonard Goldstein production. Stars Marjorie Main, Percy Kilbride; features Lori Nelson, Byron Palmer, Russell Johnson, Hilo Hattie, Loring Smith. Directed by Lee Sholem. Screenplay, Jack Henley, Harry Clork, Elwood Ullman; story by Connie Lee Bennett; camera, Clifford Stine; editor, Virgil Vogel; musical direction, Joseph Gershenson. Previewed March 1, '55. Running time, **79 MINS.**

Ma Kettle	Marjorie Main
Pa Kettle	Percy Kilbride
Rosie Kettle	Lori Nelson
Bob Baxter	Byron Palmer
Eddie Nelson	Russell Johnson
Mama Lotus	Hilo Hattie
Rodney Kettle	Loring Smith
Robert Coates	Lowell Gilmore
Mrs. Andrews	Mabel Albertson
Fulton Andrews	Fay Roope
Geoduck	Oliver Blake
Crowbar	Teddy Hart
Birdie Hicks	Esther Dale
Secretary to Rodney Kettle	Claudette Thornton

(*Aspect ratio:* 1.85-1)

A wacky adventure in Waikiki is used in this latest release in the Universal series to springboard a mild brand of comedy. In the territories where previous entries have built a following for these two escapees from the 1947 "The Egg and I," this one can be figured to serve its purpose.

With this release, Percy Kilbride departs the series and his Pa Kettle character, and Universal plans continuing the comedies without a father for the large brood of 15 young Kettles.

When a cousin in Waikiki gets in health and financial troubles, he sends an emergency call to Pa to come take over operations of a pineapple factory until he recovers. Pa, Ma, and oldest daughter, prettily played by Lori Nelson, head for the islands, where papa proceeds to cause an explosion in the factory, get himself kidnapped and then have all of the adventures rebound for the good.

Marjorie Main and Kilbride team in the kind of antics their fans expect, while Miss Nelson pairs romantically with Byron Palmer, a mating that doesn't get much of a play because most of the footage is given over to Pa's difficulties being a tycoon. Loring Smith plays the bombasting cousin, while Lowell Gilmore is the promoter trying to take away the canned fruit business, an abortive scheme in which Russell Johnson participates. Hilo Hattie and Charley Lung head up an island family that counterparts the Kettles.

This production by the late Leonard Goldstein actually was lensed years back, but held up in release while later comedies went out. Lee Sholom's direction does what it can with the chuckle intents of the screenplay by Jack Henley, Harry Clork and Elwood Ullman, from a story by Connie Lee Bennett. Technical credits are standard. *Brog.*

Seven Angry Men

Mild action-drama about John Brown's crusade to free the slaves. Talky and slow; a programmer.

Hollywood, March 7.

Allied Artists release of Vincent M. Fennelly production. Stars Raymond Massey, Debra Paget, Jeffrey Hunter; features Larry Pennell, Leo Gordon, John Smith, James Best, Dennis Weaver. Directed by Charles Marquis Warren. Story and screenplay, Daniel B. Ullman; camera, Ellsworth Fredricks; editor, Richard C. Meyer; music, Carl Brandt. Previewed March 3, '55. Running time, 91 MINS.

John Brown .... Raymond Massey
Elizabeth .... Debra Paget
Owen .... Jeffrey Hunter
Oliver .... Larry Pennell
White .... Leo Gordon
Frederick .... John Smith
Jason .... James Best
John Jr. .... Dennis Weaver
Salmon .... Guy Williams
Watson .... Tom Irish
Thompson .... James Anderson
Green .... James Edwards
Wilson .... John Pickard
Newby .... Smoki Whitfield
Doyle .... Jack Lomas
Col. Washington .... Robert Simon
Doctor .... Dabbs Greer
Mrs. Brown .... Ann Tyrrell
Col. Lee .... Robert Osterloh
(Aspect ratio: 1.85-1)

This Allied Artists release dips back into history for a story about John Brown's crusade to free the slaves. It fails to qualify as worthwhile entertainment, being slow and talky. Some familiar names may help, but the grossing outlook is not promising.

The Vincent M. Fennelly production stars Raymond Massey as the fanatical Brown, a cold-blooded murderer who left a path of blood across history's pages as presented in this Daniel B. Ullman screen story. While the religious fervor that moved Brown is shown, the character still seems to lack proper motivation, as do the other people and events, including the battle at Harper's Ferry, Virginia, that proved Brown's downfall. Charles Marquis Warren's direction doesn't do much probing and the portrayals are shallow.

Picture opens with Brown's efforts to get Kansas into the Union as a free state, depicting the killings that ensued, mostly retaliations on both sides. After this section of history is dealt with, plot moves on to Brown's rallying of money and supporters to wipe out slavery throughout the country, climaxing in his futile stand at Harper's Ferry when he is taken by the then Colonel Robert E. Lee and hanged for his crimes.

Jeffrey Hunter plays one of Brown's many sons, who meets and marries Debra Paget while aiding his father. These two younger players are competent, as is Massey, but the performances haven't much impact. Leo Gordon does the Rev. White who opposes Brown in Kansas; Larry Pennell, John Smith, James Best, Dennis Weaver, Guy Williams and Tom Irish are among the sons, and James Edwards portrays a Negro follower of the fanatic.

The lensing by Ellsworth Fredricks and the other technical credits are average. *Brog.*

Comte de Monte-Cristo
(Count of Monte-Cristo)
(FRANCO-ITALIAN—COLOR)
Paris, Feb. 22.

Sirius release of Jacques Roitfeld-Cineroma production. Stars Jean Marais; features Lia Amanda, Folco Lulli, Daniel Ivernel, Jacques Castelot, Roger Pigaut, Daniel Cauchy. Directed by Robert Vernay. Screenplay, Georges Neveux, Vernay from novel by Alexandre Dumas; camera (Gevacolor), Robert Juillard; editor, Monique Kirsonoff. At Broadway, Paris. Running time, 86 MINS.

This is part two, "The Vengeance," of this episodically distributed version of the well known Alexandre Dumas romantic yarn. First part, "The Treason," was released previously. Neither could stand alone for U. S. purposes and would have to be welded together for any opportunities with time run of 183 minutes naturally needing much pruning. Tale is told soundly with little film imagination, but engenders the usual interest paid any well made romantic opus. For the U.S., it is primarily for special situations.

This spans time by having Monte-Cristo relate his past adventures to his loyal follower, the man who saved him after his escape from the Chateau D'If where three treacherous enemies had put him by trumping up a charge that he was conspiring with Napoleon.

Narrative then has him tracking down the three men, and by exposure of their dastardly past leading to the murder of one and the suicide of the others. He renounces going back to his youthful love, now freed from a husband and goes off with a young Eastern Princess.

All the characters of "Vengeance" cavort in this many years later, but romantic license is taken, for none of the seems to have aged very much. Jean Marais has the proper romantic dash for the vengeful count and the heavies are well done by Jacques Castelot, as the jaundiced procurer; Roger Pigaut, as the false general, and Daniel Ivernel, as the cowardly Caderousse. Color is uneven but techincal gloss is high. There is something in this for youth appeal, and for chopping into a possible small series for tv. *Mosk.*

Verliebte Leute
(Loving Couples)
(AUSTRIAN)
Vienna, Feb. 22.

Sascha film release of Neusser-Hope production. Stars Peter Lasetti; features Hannelore Bollmann, Doris Kirchner. Directed by Franz Antel. Screenplay, Herbert Reinecker; camera, Hans Theyer; music, Lotar Olias. At Wienzeile Kino, Vienna. Running time, 90 MINS.

This modestly budgeted tale of a love affair in the beautiful Salzkammergut stands a few notches above the average. With an interest-holding story line, acceptable performances and so-so direction, "Loving Couples" is a film tending to prove that West German and Austrian coproduction may soon figure in world competition.

Peter Pasetti, has the lead role, that of a chauffeur, who meets a telephone operator, Hannelore Bollmann. He becomes convinced she is the daughter of a millionaire. Yarn gets more complicated when others further muddle the affair. Pasetti is excellent but the two femmes are routine.

Of the support, the routine funmaking is well taken care of by Oskor Sima, as the millionaire, and Hans Moser as a garage-owner. They surpass the remainer or the cast. Frank Antel directed without much imagination, but cameraman Hans Theyer showed good taste.

Lotar Olias cannot be expected to write a hit tune every time, and perhaps he couldn't do any better in this pic. Other technical details are good. *Maas.*

Revenge of the Creature
(3-D)

Mildly exciting chiller-diller with 3-D as an added exploitation gimmick.

Universal release of a William Alland production. Stars John Agar, Lori Nelson. John Bromfield; features Robert B. Williams, Nestor Paiva, Grandon Rhodes, Dave Willock, Charles Cane. Directed by Jack Arnold. Screenplay by Martin Berkeley from a story by Alland; camera, Charles S. Welbourne; editor, Paul Weatherwax; music, Joseph Gershenson; makeup, Bud Westmore. Previewed in N.Y. March 10, '55. Running time 82 MINS.

Clete Ferguson .... John Agar
Helen Dobson .... Lori Nelson
Joe Hayes .... John Bromfield
George Johnson ...... Robert B. Williams
Lucas .... Nestor Paiva
Foster .... Grandon Rhodes
Gibson .... Dave Willock
Captain of Police .... Charles Cane
(Aspect ratio: 2-1)

Considering that this is the first 3-D picture to reach the public in over a year, it's unfortunate that it's not a better one. "Revenge of the Creature," sequel to U's "Creature From the Black Lagoon," is a routine shocker with obvious appeal for the crowd that goes for the horror pix. It doesn't get much of a boost from the 3-D treatment, nor does the picture itself bring out the more spectacular aspects of the deep-dimension medium.

If credits were to be given in order of performance values, the fellow who plays the scaly monster in the film certainly would rate top billing. Expertly made up, he's the only one who looks and acts believable. Fact that he only roars and has no speaking lines helps since the script cooked up by Martin Berkeley is hardly on the expert side. There's an unusual volume of dialog that serves mostly to bridge the gaps between the action sequences that audiences presumably came to see.

There are too few of those, but some of them are staged with sock effect, with or without 3-D. Underwater scenes involving the gillman, and particularly his escape from the aquarium, have been directed by Jack Arnold for shock value and they build up tension nicely. Charles S. Welbourne's lensing in many spots is distinctive and unusual even though he makes surprisingly little use of possible 3-D effects.

In much of footage, the 3-D effects are barely noticeable. There are a couple of spots where the depth effect is remarkable, however, and it makes one wonder why the production crew didn't bother to aim for more of the same. Cast performs its routine chores in routine fashion. John Agar plays a young scientist and Lori Nelson his romantically inclined helpmate who almost dies in the clutches of the monster but is saved at the bell. Miss Nelson is easy on the eyes and looks good in a bathing suit. John Bromfield and Robert B. Williams are okay in smaller parts. Paul Weatherwax's editing is okay. *Hift.*

Canyon Crossroads

Fair meller for the outdoor action market.

United Artists release of William Joyce (Thomas Whitesell) production. Stars Richard Boschart, Phyllis Kirk; features Stephen Elliott, Russell Collins. Directed by Al Werker. Screenplay and original story, Emmett Murphy and Leonard Heideman; camera, Gordon Avile; editor, Chester Schaeffer; music, George Bassman. Tradeshown N.Y., March 1, '55. Running time, 83 MINS.

Larry Kandall .... Richard Basehart
Katherine Rand .... Phyllis Kirk
Larson .... Stephen Elliott
Dr. Rand .... Russell Collins
Pete Barnwell......Charles Waggenheim
Joe Rivers .... Richard Hale
Charlie Rivers .... Alan Wells
Mickey Rivers .... Tommy Cook
A.E.C. Clerk .... William Pullen

Apparently due to take its place with high button shoes and grandfather's moustache cup is the cliche, "thars gold in them thar hills." For now with the atomic age well underway time honored expressions of yesteryear have been displaced. At least that's the impression gained from "Canyon Crossroads," a United Artists release about a uranium hunt.

But despite the modernity afforded through use of terms as geiger counters, radioactivity and such, this William Joyce production shapes up as average fare for the outdoor action market. For the story which Emmett Murphy and Leonard Heideman screenplayed from their own original follows an obvious pattern, replete with stock characterizations and situations.

Richard Basehart's a veteran prospector down on his luck and suspicious of even those who would aid him. Stephen Elliott's a crooked mine owner who nurses a resentment of Basehart since the latter turned down a partnership deal. Along come geology prof Russell Collins and daughter Phyllis Kirk who grubstake Basehart on condition she can accompany the searchers. Of course, Elliott makes things tough for them but they ultimately wind up with a uranium lode and romance.

In keeping with things contemporary, the chases aren't confined to hard ridin' hombres who dash about canyon and mesa exclusively on hossback. For the baddies now track down honest prospectors via helicopter. At any rate there's a fair passel of suspense when Basehart whips out his six-shooter to plug away at an airborne adversary.

While the script doesn't afford the principals much opportunity performancewise, nevertheless Basehart is relatively good as the prospector who strikes it rich. Miss Kirk makes a good try but hardly seems the kind of girl who'd brave the wild terrain of mountainous Utah in company with two males. Elliott is an okay menace as Larson, the unscrupulous mine owner, and Collins is adequate as the aging prof. Routine support is provided by Charles Waggenheim, Richard Hale and Alan Wells, among others.

Direction of Al Werker makes the most of the action sequences. Production values reflect a modest budget. It's unfortunate that producer Joyce didn't see fit to invest in color lensing since the Utah canyon country obviously would have looked much better in tint than in the existing black-and-white print. On the whole, however, cameraman Gordon Avile did a competent job on the tintless stock. Other technical credits are standard. *Gilb.*

Three Cases of Murder
(BRITISH)

Three separate murder yarns. Okay entry for art houses or for second half of dual bills. One story by Somerset Maugham starring Orson Welles should help in selling.

Associated Artists Productions release of Ian Dalrymple-Hugh Perceval-Alexander Paal production. Stars Orson Welles, John Gregson, and Leueen MacGrath. Features Alan Badel, Elizabeth Sellars, Emrys Jones. Directed by Wendy Toye, David Eady, and George More O'Ferrall. Screenplay by Dalrymple, Donald Wilson, and Sidney Carroll, based on stories by Roderick Wilkinson, Brett Halliday, and Somerset Maugham. Camera, Georges Perinal; editor, G. Turney-Smith; music, Doreen Carwithen. Previewed in N.Y. March 10, '55. Running time, **99 MINS.**

In the Picture

Mr. X .... Alan Badel
Jarvis .... Hugh Pryse
Mr. Rooke .... John Salew
The Woman in the House
Leueen MacGrath
Snyder .... Eddie Byrne
The Girl .... Ann Hanslip
Connoisseur .... Harry Welchman

You Killed Elizabeth

George Wheeler .... Emrys Jones
Edgar Curtain .... John Gregson
Elizabeth Grange ......Elizabeth Sellars
Inspector Acheson .... Jack Lambert
Sgt. Mallot .... Philip Dale
Jane .... Colette Wilde
Susan .... Christina Forrest
Pemberton .... Maurice Kaufmann

Lord Mountdrago

Lord Mountdrago.......... Orson Welles
Owen .... Alan Badel
Lady Mountdrago .... Helen Cherry
Under Secretary for
Foreign Affairs ....Peter Burton
Leader of the House....Arthur Wontner
Private Secretary ...... John Humphrey
Sir James .... David Horne
Dr. Audlin .... Andre Morell
Beautiful Blonde .... Zena Marshall
Lady Connemara .... Evelyn Hail

Three short stories dealing with murder have been put together as an omnibus film under the title of "Three Cases of Murder." With one of the yarns from the pen of Somerset Maugham, and starring Orson Welles, these names help, the entire British package shapes as acceptable art house fare this side. It's not strong enough for top billing, but should fit neatly in the second half slot.

The stories fit into three different categories—supernatural, whodunit, and psychological. "In the Picture," the opener, is a macabre piece that leaves a spine-tingling effect. Based on a story by Roderick Wilkinson, it opens in a museum, then moves into an eerie house that's in one of the paintings. A weird stranger, who turns out to be the long-dead painter of the picture, escorts the museum guide into the house where there are some odd inhabitants, including a woman and a taxidermist. Latter would just as well stuff a human as a bird. Alan Badel, Leueen MacGrath, Hugh Pryse, and Eddie Byrne, the characters involved, know how to provide a scary touch.

"You Killed Elizabeth," from a story by Brett Halliday, concerns two friends, George and Edgar, childhood chums who go through school together and eventually wind up as partners in the advertising business. One is a plodder and the other a charmer. The plodder falls in love, but the girl is charmed away by the charmer. One morning she's found dead. One of the guys did it, and a last-minute O. Henry touch uncovers the murderer. Emrys Jones, John Gregson, and Elizabeth Sellars give convincing performances in this entry.

The clincher and piece de resistance is Maugham's "Lord Mountdrago" with Welles as the title character. As Foreign Secretary, Mountdrago, in a witty and devastating speech before Parliament, brings political ruin to a member of the opposition. The member vows revenge and the threat plagues Mountdrago to the point of madness. He constantly has nightmares, dreaming that his rival has placed him in awkward and ridiculous positions. The efforts of a psychiatrist fail, and Mountdrago determines to rid himself of his rival by dreaming him to death. Owen, the rival, fails to show up in Parliament. He was killed as Mountdrago dreamt, but Owen gets his revenge nevertheless.

Welles is excellent as Mountdrago as is Alan Badel as Owen. Helen Cherry registers effectively as Mountdrago's understanding wife. Wendy Toye, David Eady, and George More O'Ferrall, the directors, present each of their murders in an interesting manner. The film should please readers of mystery fiction. *Holl.*

Treasure of Ruby Hills

Complicated western suitable only for less discriminating bookings.

Hollywood, March 11.

Allied Artists release of William F. Broidy production. Stars Zachary Scott, Carole Mathews; features Barton MacLane, Dick Foran, Lola Albright, Gordon Jones, Raymond Hatton. Directed by Frank McDonald. Screenplay, Tom Hubbard, Fred Eggers; story, Louis L'Amour; camera, John Martin; editor, Ace Herman; music, Edward J. Kaye. Previewed March 11, '55. Running time, **72 MINS.**

Haney .... Zachary Scott
Sherry .... Carole Mathews
Reynolds .... Barton MacLane
Doran .... Dick Foran
May .... Lola Albright
Voyle .... Gordon Jones
Scotty .... Raymond Hatton
Emmett .... Lee Van Cleef
Hull .... Steve Darrell
Payne .... Charles Fredericks
Garvey .... Stanley Andrews
Burt .... James Alexander
Vernon .... Rick Vallen

(*Aspect ratio*: 1.85-1)

A complicated story line brought on by over-plottage reduces this Zachary Scott western to the also-ran category, a waste of good talent.

Scott, son of a dead outlaw, is intent on settling in the Arizona town of Soledad, battle zone for two warring factions each out to wrest control of the region. As the first step, he acquires the vital water rights to the valley. After the leaders of the two warring factions are killed and their men join up with the scheming foreman of another ranch, Scott in a showdown over his water rights kills the foreman and brings peace to the area.

Scott is never believable in an artificial role, and director Frank McDonald can do little with the confused script which is long on stilted dialog and many characters. Carole Mathews and Lola Albright are in for distaff interest, former romantically paired with Scott, and Raymond Hatton and Charles Fredericks are able to make some sense with their roles, beyond the reach of most of the other casters. Technical credits are standard. *Whit.*

Sombra Verde
(Green Shadow)
(MEXICAN)

Mexico City, March 8.

Peliculas Nacionales release of a Producciones Calderon production. Stars Ricardo Montalban. Features Ariadna Welter, Victor Parra, Jorge Martinez De Hayas. Directed by Roberto Gavaldon. Camera, Alex Phillips; screenplay, Ramiro Torres Septien; music, A. Carreon. At Cine Palacio Chino, Mexico City. Running time, **90 MINS.**

Rating the locale, photography, some acting and the direction of this pic is easy: it's all excellent. But the story is a real puzzle. It's neither good nor very bad. The best that can be said of it is that it does hold you, if only mildly.

"Green Shadow" unquestionably is nearly top merchandise. It is Ricardo Montalban's first since his return to Mexican pix. He does very well. He fits the role of the eager young chemist who impetuously crashes the deep jungle of deep tropical Vera Cruz state seeking a medicinal bush. "Shadow" shapes as a boxoffice champ here.

Roberto Gavaldon makes the utmost of wild scenery as director and adds poignant dialog as special writer for the film. There's a raging rapids, big snakes (one kills Jorge Martinez de Hayas, guide to Montalban) and other tragic moments for the hero. Montalban and Victor Parra, the tough medic hiding out after a scrape, mix it in a fisticuffs sequence over Parra's daughter, Ariadna Welter (Linda Christian's sister).

Miss Welter is just good as the wench secluded in the jungle who goes nearly haywire at the sight of a man. Her garb could be much more effective. And she overstresses her bare legs, even though they are nice gams.

Peccato Che Sia Una Canaglia
(Too Bad She's Bad)
(ITALIAN)

Rome, March 8.

CEI-INCOM release of a Documento Film Production. Stars Vittorio DeSica, Sophia Loren, Marcello Mastroianni. Directed by Alessandro Blasetti. Screenplay, Blasetti, Sandro Continenza, Susi Checchi D'Amico, Ennio Flaiano from a story by Alberto Moravia; camera, Aldo Giordani; music, Alessandro Cicognini. Previewed in Rome. Running time, **100 MINS.**

Lina .... Sophia Loren
Stoppani .... Vittorio DeSica
Paolo .... Marcello Mastroianni
Brunetto .... Walter Bartoletti
Inspector .... Mario Passante
Luigi .... Giacomo Furia
Watchman .... Giulio Cali

Pic combines the new boxoffice team of Sophia Loren and Vittorio DeSica with a lightweight, fast-paced comedy based on a story by top novelist Alberto Moravia. It has excellent home-market prospects. Many of the pic's local-colorful facets will fail to project abroad, but the film should do proportionately well there. A top-quality dubbing job, however, is required for foreign success.

Story entangles cabbie Marcello Mastroianni with a sometime adventuress-thief, Sophia Loren, whose father (Vittorio DeSica) is a gentleman purse-snatcher. Close to retirement age, DeSica only occasionally indulges in the profession which has filled his home with accumulated fruit of his purloinings while lending a benevolent eye to his daughter's sometimes gauche early efforts in the trade.

The cabbie's efforts to elude entanglement with the gal meet with little success, and soon he is over his neck in her troubles with the police—and falling for her personally. All is handled in featherweight manner by director Alessandro Blasetti, with a rapid-fire rhythm and a fine laugh average. Involved also are some amusing Roman vignettes.

Acting is fine in all sectors, with Miss Loren coming through with her best thesping to date, an expert—and eye-filling—portrayal of the petty thief with a mind of her own. Mastroianni is fine as the harried hack driver who continually suppresses common sense for another round with the gal in question. DeSica is extremely droll as Sophia's father. A group of colorful actors fills out the cast list.

Heading the top-drawer credit list is a neatly comic scoring by Alessandro Cicognini, with the music highlighting pic's laughable aspects. Location camerawork by Aldo Giordani is expert. *Hawk.*

Attila
(Franco-Italian)
(COLOR)

Rome, March 8.

Lux Film release of Lux-Ponti-Le Laurentiis-Lux C C. De France co-production. Stars Anthony Quinn, Sophia Loren, Henri Vidal. Directed by Pietro Fransisci. Story and screenplay, Ennio DeConcini, Primo Zeglio; camera (Technicolor), Aldo Tonti, Karl Struss; special effects, Ivor Beddoes, Stephen Grimes; dances, Gusa Geert; music, Enzo Masetti; editor, Leo Catozzo. Previewed in Rome. Running time, **87 MINS.**

Attila .... Anthony Quinn
Onoria .... Sophia Loren
Ezio .... Henri Vidal
Grune .... Irene Papas
Galla Placida .... Colette Regis
Bleda .... Ettore Manni
Hun Leader .... Christian Marquand
Valentiniano .... Claude Laydu
Onegesio .... Eduardo Ciannelli

Elaborately staged actioner looks a moderate grosser on the local market, with aid from title and cast names. For the U.S. market, where "Attila" perforce follows the Universal Jack Palance starrer (also on the Hun leader), will need strong pre-selling for like results, although the pic is styled for the general market.

Film chronicles Attila's rise to power via murder and bloodshed, which includes his own, more reasonable-minded brother, a romantic envolvement with the ambitious sister of the foppish Roman emperor, and Attila's first successful campaign to conquer Rome. At the doors of city, after defeating the Roman army and killing its leader, Attila's hordes are stopped and turned back by a miraculous intervention of Pope Leo. Pic ends on this religioso note.

Anthony Quinn makes a strong and forceful Attila while Ettore Manni is effective as the brother he murders. Sophia Loren is not done justice by either the camera or wardrobe, projects in too matronly the temptress with ambitions. Henri Vidal, Irene Papas, Claude Laydu and the large cast of French and Italo thespers go through their paces without much enthusiasm. Eduardo Ciannelli seems miscast as Onegesio.

Script is weak and talky, with pace livened somewhat by a rousing battle scene near the end. Pic has been given full-scale technical outfitting, from costuming to sets to elaborate use of extras for the battle, plus the Technicoloring. Music by Enzo Masetti is only standard. *Hawk.*

Le Avventure Di Giacomo Casanova
(The Adventures of Giacomo Casanova)
(FRANCO—ITALIAN)
(Color)

Rome, March 1.

Cel-Incom release of an Orso Film-Iris-C.F.P.C. Production. Stars Gabriele Ferzetti, Corinne Calvet, Nadia Gray, Mara Lane, Marina Vlady, Irene Galter, Carlo Campanini, Aroldo Tieri. Directed by Steno. Screenplay, Steno, Ennio Bistolfi, S. Continenza, L. Fulci, Carlo Romano, Marco Guerra; camera, (Eastmancolor), Mario Bava; editor, Giuliana Attenni. Previewed in Rome. Running time, **105 MINS.**

Giacomo Casanova .... Gabriele Ferzetti
Dolores .... Irene Galter
Teresa of Reichburg .... Nadia Gray
Barbara .... Mara Lane
Venetian beauty .... Corinne Calvet
Fulvia .... Marina Vlady
Le Duc .... Carlo Campanini
Jose Ramirez .... Aroldo Tieri
Geltrude .... Anna Amendola
Lucrezia .... Lia di Leo
Bettina .... Fulvia Franco
Angelica .... Florence Arnaud
Bragadin .... Nico Pepe
Inquisitor .... Nerio Bernardi
Members of the Rome Opera Ballet

This elegant, tasteful co-production has elements of appeal for both exploitation and class audiences in its tongue-in-cheek rendition of the great lover's adventures. Besides the title lure, a femme-weighted credit list topped by Corinne Calvet, provides marquee bait for most markets. With some trimming for pace, and a good lingual version, pic rates U.S. bids. Consistently tasteful handling of the nevertheless frankly unashamed content poses the censorship question. Cutting is no solution—either it gets by in toto or is nixed. Tough Italo censors have raised no objections to date, limiting action to placing pic in the "above 16" category.

Pic recalls some of the lover's adventures via the flashback route, while Casanova (Gabriele Ferzetti) languishes in a Spanish jail. Predatory quality of the female is stressed as woman after woman urges him on to the inevitable, while trickery helps him win the only beauty (Corinne Calvet) to resist his attentions.

Parade of pulchritude includes items from all stations in life, from heiresses to barmaids, from country gals to boudoir beauties. One thing is in common with them all—uncommon beauty, abundantly displayed. Rarely have so many lookers been assembled for one pic, nor so enticingly photographed, with all types represented. Marina Vlady, as the country girl who catches Casanova's eye on her wedding day, outshines them all with her fresh, piquant young beauty. Ferzetti is good as Casanova.

Director Steno and his fellow-scripters have fashioned Casanova's exploits into an adultly diverting boudoir gambol. The dialogue is often sparkling while the situations, even though familiar, produce chuckles. Some slow spots can be overcome by pruning. Outfittings are elegantly designed by Italy's top specialists in the field. Mario Bava's camerawork is in keeping with the taste displayed. Location lensing in Venice, Tivoli and Rome enhance the pic's eye-appeal. *Hawk.*

Five From Barska Street
(POLISH—COLOR)

Artkino release of Film Polski production. Stars Alexandra Slaska, Tadeusz Janczar. Directed by Aleksander Ford. Screenplay, Kazimierz Kozniewski from his own novel; camera, Jaroslav Tuzar, Karol Chodura; editors, W. Otocka, H. Kubik. At Stanley, N.Y., starting March 12, '55. Running time, **109 MINS.**

Hanka .... Aleksandra Slaska
Kazek .... Tadeusz Janczar
Jacek .... Andrzej Kozak
Lutek .... Tadeusz Lomnicki
Zbych .... Marian Rulka
Franek .... Wlozzimierz Skoczylas
Marek .... Mieczyslaw Stoor

(In Polish; English Titles)

"Five From Barska Street" is credited with being a grand prize winner at the Cannes Film Festival, which gives some idea to what extent the awarding of prizes at this fete has degenerated. It probably is the best effort at Polish production in some time. But this picture still remains just a meller about juvenile delinquents stemming from the last world war. Aleksander Ford, the director, won a special prize, and neither awards are comprehensible because this compares unfavorably with any number of American "B" melodramas.

Plot concerns five boys from Barska Street, who are paroled by the gendarme after being nabbed for juvenile crimes. The film blames the unsettled conditions of postwar Warsaw and the harrowing experiences the lads have had during the war for their arrest. Entire story, in a muddled sort of way, implies that the youths are afraid of the police and still feel obligated to carry out orders of an underworld gangster chief. Perhaps in Polish it becomes understandable but this comes out on the screen as a highly skeptical plank on which to rest so much of the plot.

Ultimately the boys turn on the gang, save the newly completed roadway and bridge, and apparently all ends well. But the director is undecided whether to let the hero die or live. The audience is just as confused. Per usual, with a Russian-controlled country, there is the customary hammering home about the worth of the collective state. Only here somebody slipped once and permitted some of the workers to get drunk.

Aleksandra Slaska, a rather attractive blonde, really steals this pic despite the uneven role that's been handed her. She is the teacher in a school, and part of the Worker's Party, naturally. But her moments with Tadeusz Janczar, the film's hero and delinquent who reforms, are about the most interesting part of the vehicle. Support is unusually good for such a thankless story.

Ford directs unevenly, going from a maximum of detail to hurried and uncomprehensive movement. He drags the youths of the cast through what are supposed to be the sewers of the city in one episode and then brings them back for another sequence which is even more confused than the first. Lensing of Jaroslaw Tuzar and Karol Chodura is topflight most of the time. It is not their fault that they had to use the Russian color process. *Wear.*

Le Pain Vivant
(The Living Bread)
(FRENCH)

Paris, March 8.

Corona release of Films D'Ariel production. Directed by Jean Mousselle. Screenplay, Francois Mauriac; adaptation, Mauriac, Mousselle; camera, Pierre Ancrenaz; editor, H. Schmitt; music, Michel Magne. With Francoise Golea, Jean-Francois Calve. At Madeleine, Paris. Running time, **110 MINS.**

Therese .... Francoise Golea
Valmy .... Jean-Francois Calve
Luc .... Jean Muselli
Friend .... Jacques Pierre
Father .... Lucien Nat

Francois Mauriac, leading militant Catholic writer here, makes his first incursion into film ranks with this pic. Naturally film has a religious theme. It revolves around a love that grows between a devout young girl and a young atheist of integrity and character who tries to understand the strange rival he has for the girl's love in God. She carries the cross of a bitter father and erring brother. Offbeat and sombre with a tendency towards preachiness, this is primariliy for secializbed spots. It primarily for specialized spots. It is too downbeat in theme and

Mauriac has given this a literary turn in writing, and dialog is stilted and unreal in delving into the meaning and living of Catholicism. Director Jean Mousselle has tried to compensate for this by his treatment, but his excessive camera movements, lingering shots, plus giving bystanders an ethereal onlooking aspect, does little to get the proper feel.

Jean-Francois Calve emerges a sensitive young actor as the atheist, with a probable future. Francoise Golea has the proper mystic and ethereal qualities. Others in the small cast are good. Lensing and editing are firstrate though treatment by eternally languid camera movements is overdone.

This will have some appeal to the intellectual set here and will have to be played that way in the U.S. chances. "The Living Bread," of course, is the wafer used during the Communion in the Mass. *Mosk.*

Angst
(Fear)
(GERMAN)

Berlin, March 8.

Gloria release of Ariston production. Stars Ingrid Bergman and Mathias Wiemann. Directed by Roberto Rossellini. Screenplay, Sergio Amidei and Franz Graf Treuberg after novel of same name by Stefan Zweig; camera, Peter Haller; music, Renzo Rossellini. At Cinema Paris, Berlin. Running time, **91 MINS.**

Irene Wagner .... Ingrid Bergman
Prof. Albert Wagner .... Mathias Wiemann
Joana Schultze .... Renate Mannhardt
Heinz Baumann .... Kurt Kreuger
Houseekeepeer .... Elise Aulinger

The first German Ingrid Bergman film after 16 years turns out to be slightly disappointing. Except the outstanding performance given by Miss Bergman; there is nothing new or particularly exciting about this one. In transferring Stefan Zweig's novel to the modern era, plot loses its conviction and dramatic grip. As a result, "Fear" lacks the necessary suspense. Name of Miss Bergman may lure many patrons here and probably also outside this country. The Swedish actress has not lost her natural charm and beauty.

Screenplay, by Sergio Amidei and Franz Graf Treuberg, sees Ingrid Bergman as the wife of a wealthy factory owner. Despite Miss Bergman's affection for her husband she has a lover and latter's ex-girl takes advantage to blackmail her. Fearing a scandal and the end of her marriage, La Bergman pays any demanded sum until she finds out that her own husband is behind the blackmailing. Miss Bergman feels herself driven to suicide but it's her husband who saves her from this. They realize they both have made mistakes and the couple is reconciled again.

Had it not been Miss Bergman in the femme lead, pic might have become a total flop. The few other players are considerably overshadowed by her. That also applies to Mathias Wiemann who portrays Ingrid Bergman's husband with noblesse. Renate Mannhardt, used by Wiemann as blackmailer, is okay in her few scenes, while Kurt Kreuger, Miss Bergman's lover, doesn't do too well.

"Fear" gives evidence of the artistic decline of one of wellknown postwar directors, Roberto Rossellini. In this German opus, he lacks style and roundness, and there are comparatively few scenes which have the Rossellini touch. Technically, "Fear" represents a good standard. That is especially true of the camerawork by Peter Haller, his outdoor shots being very impressive. *Hans.*

Raising a Riot
(British-Color)

So-so British comedy exploiting Kenneth More's personality; only limited b.o. prospects.

London, March 8.

British Lion release of London Films-Wessex Film production. Stars Kenneth More; features Ronald Squire, Mandy Miller. Directed by Wendy Toye. Screenplay by Ian Dalrymple, Hugh Perceval, James Matthews, from novel by Alfred Toombs; camera, Christopher Challis; editor, Albert Rule; music, Bruce Montgomery. At Plaza, London, Feb. 21, '55. Running time, **91 MINS.**

Tony	Kenneth More
Mary	Shelagh Fraser
Anne	Mandy Miller
Peter	Gary Billings
Fusty	Fusty Bentine
Grampy	Ronald Squire
Aunt Maud	Olga Lindo
Harry	Lionel Murton
Jacqueline	Mary Laura Wood
Sue	Jan Miller

The main purpose of "Raising a Riot" appears to be to exploit the personality of Kenneth More. This British star, with two major comedy hits ("Genevieve" and "Doctor in the House") to his credit, has become a major b.o. name here and this pic is nothing more than a frank admit to cash in on that. The trouble with the film is that it lacks anything like a story. It is just a single situation, moderately amusing in parts, but totally inadequate to sustain a feature pic. It has only mild b.o. outlook in the U. S.

More manages to cope with his three children while his wife goes to Canada is the basis of the yarn. They move into his father's converted windmill and from that point onwards the action illustrates the way in which the mischievous trio are constantly in and out of trouble. As completely irrelevant side issues, there is some feuding with American neighbors and a kids' tea party.

Within the strict limitations imposed by the script, the star does remarkably well. More's timing is flawless and his keen sense of humor is never allowed to flag. The three youngsters are nicely played by Mandy Miller, Gary Billings and Fusty Bentine. Ronald Squire gives some polish to his role of Gramp while Olga Lindo is admirable in a bit role as a maided aunt. Wendy Toye's direction keeps the fable rolling but she cannot disguise the fact that there is basically no plot. Other technical credits are standard. *Myro.*

A Man Called Peter
(C'SCOPE—COLOR)

Modern religioso pic on the life of the late Peter Marshall. Tender yet forthright, it shapes up for sock b.o. impact, if sold smartly.

Twentieth Century-Fox release of a Samuel G. Engel production. Stars Richard Todd, Jean Peters; features Marjorie Rambeau, Jill Esmond, Les Tremayne, Robert Burton, Gladys Hurlbut, Richard Garrick. Directed by Henry Koster. Screenplay, Eleanore Griffin; from the book by Catherine Marshall; camera (color by De Luxe), Harold Lipstein; editor, Robert Simpson; music, Alfred Newman. Previewed in N.Y. March 18, '55. Running time, **119 MINS.**

Peter Marshall	Richard Todd
Catherine Marshall	Jean Peters
Miss Fowler	Marjorie Rambeau
Mrs. Findlay	Jill Esmond
Senator Harvey	Les Tremayne
Mr. Peyton	Robert Burton
Mrs. Peyton	Gladys Hurlbut
Col. Whiting	Richard Garrick
Barbara	Gloria Gordon
Peter John Marshall	Billy Chapin
Mrs. Whiting	Sally Corner
Senator Wiley	Voltaire Perkins
Emma	Marietta Canty
Senator Prescott	Edward Earle
College Girl	Mimi Hutson
Grandmother	Agnes Bartholomew
Peter Marshall (Ages 7 & 14)	Peter Votrian
Nancy	Janet Stewart
Ruby Coleman	Ann Davis
Usher	Arthur Tovay
Maitre D'	Sam McDaniel
Jane Whitney	Betty Caulfield
Miss Crilly	Dorothy Neumann
Janitor	Oliver Hartwell
Miss Hopkins	Doris Lloyd
President	William Forrest
Miss Standish	Barbara Morrison
Dr. Black	Carlyle Mitchell
Willie	Amanda Randolph
Peter (Age 5½)	Rick Kelman
Peter (Age 6½)	Louis Torres Jr.
Mr. Briscoe	Emmett Lynn
Butler	William Walker
President of Senate	Charles Evans
Elders	Alexander Campbell, Jonathan Hole
Chaplain	Larry Kent
Holden	Roy Glenn Jr.
Nurse	Ruth Clifford
Mr. Findlay	Ben Wright
Mrs. Ferguson	Florence MacAfee
Rob Hunter	Christopher Cook
David Weed	Winsten Severn
Mrs. Pike	Maudie Prickett

(Aspect ratio: 2.55-1)

Hollywood has at times been accused of sloughing off truly spiritual values. The critics now have their answer in 20th-Fox's "A Man Called Peter," the life story of the late Peter Marshall, Protestant Minister and chaplain of the U.S. Senate.

If there is such a thing as "living religion" on the screen, moulding a message of faith, love and decency into the framework of good entertainment, producer Samuel G. Engel, director Henry Koster and scripter Eleanore Griffin have caught the essence of it in this film.

What's more, they've resisted what must have been a considerable temptation to sugarcoat this intensly personal story. Instead, they have presented it for the most part as just what it is—the portrayal of a man of God who, all his life, stood squarely on his beliefs and who, in his sermons, preached a new, vibrant, hopeful religion that had immense appeal to young and old.

"A Man Called Peter", in CinemaScope and excellent Color by De Luxe, is certainly an unusual entry and while it will reap the benefits of such a tag, it may also suffer from it unless sold carefully. Film manages to carry a message without becoming topheavy from it. It also allows itself the privilege of sacrificing some visual effects for those of the spoken word, with penetrating effect.

Again and again, the camera picks up Richard Todd as Peter Marshall mounting the pulpit to deliver the sermons for which he was famous and which drew overflow crowds Sunday after Sunday to the New York Ave. Presbyterian Church in Washington. These sermons are things of beauty and Koster and Engel deserves kudos for allowing them to run on for several minutes at a time. One thing is guaranteed—they pack such a punch and n / e so much common sense, few will be bored by them.

Todd does such a masterful job of preaching the sermons, the camera staying on him most of the time, they're almost the best thing in the picture. Marshall's religion was one all men could understand and such, too, is the message of the picture. The two sermons—one when he takes over stewardship of the Washington church and the other at Annapolis, when he talks of the meaning of death—are not only beautiful but greatly moving.

"Peter," based on Catherine Marshall's book of the same title, derives a good deal of its strength from the performance of Todd who lives the part to perfection. His Peter Marshall, an immigrant from Scotland, is a man of towering strength and great devotion to his ministry. He is completely believable even though it's unfortunate that Miss Griffin didn't choose to transplant from the book more of the small human touches which bring it humor.

There will be some who will quarrel over the casting of Jean Peters as Mrs. Marshall but on the whole she does a nice job as the devoted wife who copes with her own tragedy (tuberculosis) and later her husband's heart attack and death by deriving her strength from her belief in God. There are scenes in which she doesn't ring true, but that's in part the script's fault. At any rate, Miss Peters is easy on the eye. (She barely ages in the film.)

The minor roles have been well cast. Marjorie Rambeau as a crusty remnant of the Washington "aristocracy" who opposes Todd and his "upbeat" approach to religion, turns in a priceless bit. So does Gladys Hurlbut as a scatterbrain society dame with her heart in the right place. Les Tremayne is mild and effective as the Senator who derives from Todd's sermons the courage to oppose his political machine at home. Gloria Gordon is cute as a teenager. Jill Esmond as Todd's mother sketches a sympathetic portrayal.

Making the most of the wide screen, "Peter" features some outstanding lensing by Harold Lipstein, including radiant shots of Washington landmarks and a very beautiful one of the Lincoln memorial at night. But it isn't all preaching and scenery. Miss Griffin has worked into the script a number of incidents that variously touch the heart and uplift the soul.

There is much charm, warmth and sensitivity in Todd's and Miss Peters' courtship; in their carefree honeymoon; their introduction to Washington and Todd's deliberate flouting of the traditional in his belief that religion must have a meaning primarily for the present and the future. Inevitably, some of the scenes are highly theatrical and there is a tendency to put into words—for cinematic purposes—the most private feelings and emotions an individual can have those relating to himself and his God.

Koster's direction is unaffected and keeps the need for entertainment values in quite sharp focus. Miss Griffin's script is expert for the most part. Editing by Robert Simpson is fine except for the last reel when Todd addresses the Senate. That sequence is curiously chopped up.

Exhibs should handle "Peter" with care. It's the perfect Easter release and should attract great numbers of people who don't ordinarily see films. At the same time, even though Protestant church organizations will undoubtedly get behind it, the pic may lack "want-to-see" appeal for some who prefer their religious pix done up in more flamboyant style. To them it should be pointed out that "Peter" has a great deal of "heart", its comparative simplicity being a part of its virtues. In any case, it's a film to which 20th and the industry can point with considerable pride both at home and abroad. *Hift.*

Marty

Sock film version of a Paddy Chayefsky teleplay. Proper selling should make it a b.o. click.

United Artists release of Hecht-Lancaster production. Produced by Harold Hecht. Stars Ernest Borgnine and Betsy Blair. Directed by Delbert Mann. Screenplay by Paddy Chayefsky, from an original teleplay by Chayefsky; camera, Joseph LaShelle; editor, Alan Crosland Jr.; music, Roy Webb; song, "Hey, Marty," by Harry Warren. Previewed in N.Y. March 16, '55. Running time, **93 MINS.**

Marty	Ernest Borgnine
Clara	Betsy Blair
Mrs. Pilletti	Esther Minciotti
Catherine	Augusta Ciolli
Angie	Joe Mantell
Virginia	Karen Steele
Thomas	Jerry Paris
Ralph	Frank Sutton
The Kid	Walter Kelley
Joe	Robin Morse

If "Marty" is an example of the type of material that can be gleaned, then studio story editors better spend more time at home looking at television. Based on Paddy Chayefsky's one-shot Television Playhouse (NBC-TV) teleplay, and screenplayed by the author, "Marty" has been fashioned into a sock picture. It's a warm, human, sometimes sentimental and an enjoyable experience.

"Marty" will further point up importance of the video showcase. Several Broadway plays have derived from that source. Warner Bros. had a b.o. click in the film version of Jack Webb's tv "Dragnet" and a number of film producers are currently readying film treatments of other video entries, both series and one-shots.

"Marty" is offbeat in theme and lack of big Hollywood names will require selling both by the distributor and the theatre. But it should rack up runs in specialized houses in big cities. Word-of-mouth will bring 'em in general situations, if exhibitors give the picture the ride it deserves.

Like "On the Waterfront," it demonstrates that story, performance, and direction always count. Neither color nor new projection and sound techniques could make "Marty" any better than it is now. Although filmed on a modest budget (reportedly about $300,000), there is no evidence of any stinting in the production values, a factor the industry will note.

Despite the picture's north Bronx locale and concern with an Italian-American family, the theme is universal and many viewers may experience a degree of identification. It's a quiet, simple story. While lacking in general excitement, it's sparked with sufficient comedy.

Basically, it's the story of a boy and girl, both of whom consider themselves misfits in that they are unable to attract members of the opposite sex. The boy, sensitively played by Ernest Borgnine, is a friendly, mild-mannered guy in his thirties who feels he hasn't the handsomeness or the necessary savoire faire to impress girls. He is constantly needled by his mother, with whom he lives, and the customers at the butcher store where he works, to get married.

The girl, beautifully played by Betsy Blair, is a plain schoolteacher whom everybody is always trying to fix up with dates. Pair come together at a boy-meets-girl dance where Miss Blair is ditched by her blind date. A blossoming romance brings both out of their shells as each is able to pour out pent-up emotions to the other.

Borgnine, remembered as the sadistic sergeant in "From Here to Eternity" and the brutal heavy in "Bad Day at Black Rock," does a complete switch in his portrayal of Marty and comes through with a performance that will be recalled next time thespian awards are distributed. Miss Blair is equally impressive in her finely etched delineation of the sensitive schoolteacher.

In the selection of Esther Minciotti, as Marty's mother who first urges his marriage and then opposes it for fear of being left alone, and Augusta Ciolli as his aunt who is the unwanted mother-in-law in her son's household, Hecht-Lancaster have come up with a pair of veteran Italo-American thesps who breathe realism into their roles. Joe Mantell, as the buddy who talks down Marty's girl to protect his own impending loneliness, contributes another gem to the topnotch dramatics. Frank Sutton, Walter Kelley, and Robin Morse are excellent as neighborhood pals who talk about conquests and likely prospects for dates. Jerry Paris and Karen Steele score as a bickering husband-and-wife faced with a mother-in-law problem.

Chayesfsky has caught the full flavor of bachelor existence in a Bronx Italian neighborhood. The meetings at a bar and grill, the stag-attended dances, the discussions about girls and "what do we do tonight?" poser ring with authenticity. The film has sociological implications, but it's presented in an easy to take manner.

Delbert Mann, who directed the teleplay, dittoed on the film and deserves a large share of the credit for its overall excellence. All technical aspects are first-rate.

Holl.

Gang Busters

Dull, repetitive cops 'n' robbers affair; strictly a dualler except where exploitation efforts push it into b.o.

Film Division of General Teleradio release (via states-rights distribution) of Visual Drama Inc. presentation in association with Terry Turner. Produced by William J. Faris and William J. Clothier. Directed by Bill Karn. Features Myron Healey, Don C. Harvey, Sam Edwards, Frank Gerstle. Screenplay, Phillips H. Lord (with revisions by Karn); camera, Clothier; editor, Paris; music, Richard Aurandt. Previewed in New York, March 1, '55. Running time, **78 MINS.**

Pinson .... Myron Healey
Detective Walsh .... Don C. Harvey
Long .... Sam Edwards
Detective Fuller .... Frank Gerstle
Bennett .... Frank Richards
Aunt Jenny .... Kate MacKenna
Mike .... Rusty Wescoatt
Louie .... William Justine
Slick Harry .... Allan Ray
Truck Driver .... William Fawcett
Pool Hall Operator .... Ed Colbrook
Officer Rondeau .... Charles Victor
Doctor .... Bob Carson
Girl in Car .... Joyce Jameson
Police Officer .... Mike Ragan
1st Guard .... Ed Hinton
2d Guard .... Robert Bice

Boxoffice success of "Dragnet" apparently prompted General Teleradio, which had acquired all rights to the "Gang Busters" radio and television series, to try a picture version, its first entry in the field. Pic has had some striking successes in New England, where it's being distributed under a states-rights pattern, but it would appear it's strictly on the basis of the heavy television exploitation campaign being waged by Terry Turner (samples of the tv spots were heavy on the lurid violence aspect, thus probably accounting for some of that b.o. success). The film itself is a dull, repetitive af-

fair that falls into the dualler category except in situations where Turner and Teleradio guarantee heavy video plugging. With the kind of tv exploitation demonstrated, the film's name and the plugs could draw fair to good returns.

Essentially, the William J. Faris-William Clothier production is a string of episodes wrapped around the repeated escapes of John Omar Pinson, at one time listed as Public Enemy No. 4. It's done in semi-documentary style with lots of location shooting in Oregon and concerns Pinson's final tracking-down by a pair of persistent detectives. Sum total of the drama is repetitiveness, and after the first escape it's kind of on the dull side. Script by Phillips H. Lord, originator of the radio series, is lifeless, despite the frequent scenes of violence, and director Bill Karn's revisions, for which he gets screen credit, apparently did little good.

Myron Healey is convincing as Pinson, an arrogant type of heavy with a brilliant mind and a fund of knowledge and tricks. Don C. Harvey, as the detective, is less so, apparently more concerned with being charming than a down-to-earth cop. Frank Gerstle is a bit more natural as Harvey's sidekick. Sam Edwards good as a fanatical follower of Pinson and Frank Richards effective as a co-escapee. Remainder of the cast is good. Clothier's camerawork has a realistic touch to it, but coproducer Faris' editing is spotty and somewhat jerky. Music, composed and conducted by Richard Aurandt, fits the dramatic moods.

Producer of the picture is listed as Visual Drama Inc. in association with Turner. Visual Drama is a subsid of General Teleradio, a wholly-owned subsid of General Tire & Rubber Co. which controls the Mutual Broadcasting System and owns a number of radio and television stations, apart from some tv-film activities. Turner works for Teleradio, his exact position never having been defined, the ex-RKO exploitation chief's in complete charge of "Gangbusters."

Chan.

An Annapolis Story
(COLOR)

Strong Allied Artists entry built around the Naval Academy and the war in Korea: excellent boxoffice prospects.

Hollywood, March 21.

Allied Artists release of Walter Mirisch production. Stars John Derek, Diana Lynn; costars Kevin McCarthy. Directed by Don Siegel. Screenplay, Dan Ullman, Geoffrey Homes; story, Ullman; camera (Technicolor), Sam Leavitt; editor, William Austin; score, Marlin Skiles; songs, Joseph W. Crosley, Marlin Skiles; technical advisor, Commander Marcus L. Lowe Jr., USN. Previewed March 17, '55. Running time, **81 MINS.**

Tony .... John Derek
Peggy .... Diana Lynn
Jim .... Kevin McCarthy
Willie .... Alvy Moore
Dooley .... Pat Conway
Watson .... L. Q. Jones
Macklin .... John Kirby
Mrs. Scott .... Barbara Brown
Mrs. Lord .... Betty Lou Gerson
Connie .... Fran Bennett
Austen .... Robert Osterloh
Coach .... John Doucette
McClaren .... Don Kennedy
Announcer .... Tom Harmon
Prentiss .... Don Haggerty

(Aspect ratio: 1.85-1)

A strong bid for important playing time is made by this Allied Artists entry. It's a Technicolor feature backdropped by the U. S. Naval Academy and the war in Korea and holds high exploitation potential. The production is expensive-looking and handsomely mounted, forcefully narrated and well enacted by a cast which has John Derek, Diana Lynn and Kevin McCarthy for marquee dressing. Hefty returns in all situations look likely.

The Walter Mirisch production was lensed partially at Annapolis and aboard an aircraft carrier to give authenticity and heightened interest in its story of midshipmen in training and later when they graduate into service. Don Siegel's direction blends colorful Annapolis parade and spectacle with the tale of two brothers seriously at outs over a girl, and subsequently melodramatizes their experiences as Naval airmen over Korea for exciting effect.

The script by Dan Ullman and Geoffrey Homes, from the former's original, is a straightforward piece of writing which effectively builds up the bitterness between the two brothers, Derek and McCarthy. Miss Lynn is the girl whom McCarthy loves but loses temporarily to Derek, the younger brother, when the latter is injured at the beginning of a summer Academy cruise and has an opportunity to escort her during his post-hospitalization. This bitterness extends through graduation and later to the Orient after both get their wings. Finale has Derek saving his brother after McCarthy is shot down into the ocean off Korea.

The three principals score in their respective roles, with the sympathy going to McCarthy for the theft of his girl. Derek is smoothly persuasive in a part which allows dramatic acting. Miss Lynn is charming. Top support is afforded by Alvy Moore, Pat Conway, L. Q. Jones and John Kirby, all servicemen. Expert photography by Sam Leavitt and a particularly atmospheric score by Marlin Skiles are added assets to the film's general overall excellence. Skiles' song, "The Engagement Waltz," is basis for a romantic production number, well staged, and Joseph W. Crosley's "Navy, Blue and Gold" also provides a striking musical sequence.

Whit.

Run for Cover
(V'VISION—COLOR)

James Cagney in good combo drama-western; medium returns overall.

Paramount release of William H. Pine-William C. Thomas production. Stars James Cagney, Viveca Lindfors, John Derek; features Jean Hersholt, Grant Withers. Directed by Nicholas Ray. Screenplay, Winston Miller; from a story by Harriet Frank Jr., and Irving Ravetch; camera (Technicolor), Daniel Fapp; editor, Howard Smith; score, Howard Jackson; song, Jackson and Jack Brooks. Previewed March 15, '55. Running time, **92 MINS.**

Matt Dow .... James Cagney
Helga Swenson .... Viveca Lindfors
Davey Bishop .... John Derek
Mr. Swenson .... Jean Hersholt
Gentry .... Grant Withers
Larsen .... Jack Lambert
Morgan .... Ernest Borgnine
Scotty .... Irving Bacon
Paulsen .... Trevor Bardette
Sheriff .... Ray Teal
Mayor Walsh .... John Miljan
Harvey .... Denver Pyle
Banker .... Emerson Treacy
Doc Ridgeway .... Gus Schilling
Andrews .... Phil Chambers
Devers .... Harold Kennedy
Miller .... Joe Haworth

(Aspect ratio: 1.85-1)

Well-valued character and plot development stand n most of the time for straight giddyap action in "Run for Cover," making it more of an outdoor drama than a western. This in-between quality, while having appeal for those who are not formula-and-sixgun fans, may lessen its chances in the regular outdoor market, so overall grossing prospects appear medium at best. The appearance of James Cagney as the chief star and the use of VistaVision for the lensing are in its favor.

Production by William H. Pine and William C. Thomas for Paramount release is marked by generally smart casting and the use of fresh-appearing location sites in Colorado as the setting for the story by Harriet Frank Jr., and Irving Ravetch. Winston Miller's script provides Nicholas Ray's direction with a good basis for screen story-telling and the guidance brings out depth in the characters, plus hitting hard in the action moments.

Viveca Lindfors and John Derek co-star with Cagney and all are excellent in varied roles. Cagney takes easily to the outdoor saddle chores as a man turned wanderer after having served six years in prison on a mistaken identity rap. He performs with his usual authority, although his fans probably would have liked for him to have turned on more of the flamboyant toughness that has featured most of his past characterizations. It's still there to a degree, but quieter. Miss Lindfors does a warm, intelligent portrayal of a Swedish immigrant girl with whom the wanderer falls in love during a stay on the farm of her father, Jean Hersholt. Derek is very good as the young man in whom Cagney sees his dead son, but who has a basic weakness that prevents him from facing up to life honestly. Hersholt makes his scenes show up excellently.

This trio of leads is brought together when Cagney comes to a small western town and is mistaken, along with Derek, of being a train robber. They are nearly lynched and Derek is crippled. To make amends, the mob-minded townsters appoint Cagney sheriff with Derek as deputy. The basic flaws begin to show up in the youth. First, he permits a lynching while Cagney is away, then allows a prisoner to escape after making a deal to aid in a bank robbery. This comes out during Cagney's pursuit of the bandit gang with Derek at his side. The youth tries to kill Cagney twice and then dies himself at the finale as he is protecting the sheriff in a last-minute flash of honesty.

The cast toppers are given competent support by such players, among others, as Grant Withers, Jack Lambert, Ernest Borgnine, Irving Bacon, Trevor Bardette, Ray Teal and John Miljan. Daniel

Fapp's Technicolor lensing demonstrates the ability of Vista-Vision's lazy-eight process to capture and make real outdoor vistas. Other technical credits are good, as is the score by Howard Jackson. Latter did a title tune, sung behind the credits, with Jack Brooks. *Brog.*

Strategic Air Command
(VISTAVISION—COLOR)

Important-money addition to the "new era" picture business with exciting photography embellishing colorful subject matter and the James Stewart-June Allyson names to help further boot it home.

Omaha, March 29.

Paramount release of Samuel J. Briskin production. Stars James Stewart. June Allyson; costars Frank Lovejoy; features Barry Sullivan, Alex Nicol, Bruce Bennett, Jay C. Flippen, James Bell, Rosemary De Camp. Directed by Anthony Mann. Screenplay, Valentine Davies and Beirne Lay Jr.; from a story by Lay; camera (VistaVision-Technicolor), William Daniels; aerial photography, Thomas Tutwiler; aerial unit supervision, Paul Mantz; editor, Eda Warran; music, Victor Young; song, "The Air Force Takes Command." Young (music) and Ned Washington and Major Tommy Thomson Jr. (lyrics). Premiered at Orpheum Theatre, Omaha, March 25, '55. Running time, **110 MINS.**
Lt. Col. Robert Holland . . James Stewart
Sally Holland . . . . June Allyson
Gen. Ennis C. Hawkes . . . Frank Lovejoy
Lt. Col. Rocky Samford . . . Barry Sullivan
Ike Knowland . . . . Alex Nicol
Gen. Espy . . . . Bruce Bennett
Doyle . . . . Jay C. Flippen
Gen. Castle . . . . James Millican
Rev. Thorne . . . . James Bell
Mrs. Thorne . . . . Rosemary De Camp
Aircraft Commander . . Richard Shannon
Capt. Symington . . . . . . John R. McKee
Sgt. Bible . . . . Henry Morgan
Major Patrol Commander Don Haggerty
Radio Operator . . . . Glenn Denning
Colonel . . . . Anthony Warde
Airman . . . . Struther Martin
Nurse . . . . Helen Brown
Capt. Brown . . . . David Vaile
Capt. Johnson . . . . Vernon Rich
Duty Officer . . . . Harlan Warde
Air Force Captain
. . . . Robert House Peters Jr.
Lt. Controller . . Henry Richard Lupino
Controller Okinawa
. . . . William August Pullen
Non Com. Tech. Sgt. Stephen E. Wyman

This picturized updating of the wild blue yonder looks sure to make quick contact with tall money. Always interesting, often spectacular and, in some instances, photographically spellbinding, "Strategic Air Command" also establishes VistaVision as a major contender in the bigscreen derby.

Credit the real-life U.S. Strategic Air Command with a very large assist. Concerning Air Force technicalities, the film is on the beam. Operations of the SAC, which cooperated with Sam Briskin's production company, have full appearance of authenticity, resulting in a pic that's important document and distinguished from run-of-the-heroics service epics.

Briskin's production widens the scope of its subject material, and audience appeal, beyond the confines of strict military aeronautics. This is via interludes of SAC's influence on the intimate family life of a pilot, his wife and comes baby to make three. Some of this suggests cliche but keen dialog in the Valentine Davies-Beirne Lay Jr. script keeps it above formularized rut.

Audience mitting likely will be evoked—as it was at the Omaha preem—with some of the in-flight footage. "SAC" is at its best when off the ground. Two giant ships engaging in a refueling operation and sweeping views of a B36 with its jet engines skywriting long hyphens in blue smoke—this is visually stirring stuff. The aerial work was supervised by Paul Mantz and the tinting by Technicolor, unusually sharp, gives it more power.

Screenplay, from a story by Lay, presents James Stewart as a hotshot third baseman for the St. Louis Cardinals who's beckoned back to the Air Force, this time with the nation's great, long-range striking force. Stewart shows his usual professional competence,

stirred by the enormity and alertness of SAC, becoming increasingly enraptured with its meaning to America's welfare and finally conveying believable sincerity in trying to convince his wife that SAC is his lifetime calling.

June Allyson scores as the wife, rebelling as the SAC takes hold on her mate and then showing sympathy and understanding. She's warm and appealing.

Frank Lovejoy fits in splendidly as the commanding general, brisk, forceful and unyielding in his demands for efficiency and security. Barry Sullivan is ingratiating as a SAC lieutenant colonel and lesser parts are handled without flaw by Alex Nicol, Bruce Bennett, Jay C. Flippen, James Millican, James Bell and Rosemary De Camp.

There's no Korea, no guns popping or bombs away in "SAC." Briskin didn't want a "war picture." It's a film backgrounded with up-to-the-minute fact and as such provides good insight on U.S. retaliatory vehicles capable of getting half-way around the world with the Sunday punch of on atom or hydrogen bomb.

Anthony Mann's direction keeps "SAC" well on the move, seguing smoothly from ground operations to the high altitudes. For an actionful highlight, he wrings out good excitement particularly from Stewart's forced pancake landing in Greenland when his big jet bomber catches fire. Editing is sharp mostly, but appearing too abrupt in a couple of spots. More loitering views of the B36 and B47 on the move would have been welcome.

Victor Young's score is fitting throughout and a march, "The Air Force Takes Command," by Young (music) and Ned Washington and Major Tommy Thomson Jr. (lyrics) has the color and beat to warrant much reprising at any kind of military pageantry.

"SAC" screening was at Omaha's Orpheum Theatre which was specially rigged for V'Vision showing from a horizontally-fed projector on kingsized curved screen. The definition and lighting both were brilliant. A last-minute hitch in equipment installation caused a little screen quiver at the start but this soon disappeared.

The audio was standard but directional sound will be made available with conventional format prints. (Only a relatively few very large theatres expectedly will play "SAC" in the double-frame super-V'Vision fashion).

Gen. Curtis LeMay, four-star commander of SAC, has given the film his endorsement to the extent that his outfit will join in exhibitor promotion — providing military bands or equipment displays for the bally. This is a sell factor that shouldn't be overlooked. *Gene.*

The Prodigal
(C'SCOPE-COLOR)

The Biblical parable of the prodigal son. Lavishly treated but long and dull. Lana Turner's name to help but prospects spotty.

Hollywood, March 29.

Metro release of Charles Schnee production. Stars Lana Turner, Edmund Purdom, Louis Calhern; features Audrey Dalton, James Mitchell, Neville Brand, Walter Hampden, Taina Elg, Francis L. Sullivan, Joseph Wiseman, John Dehner, Sandra Descher, Cecil Kellaway, Philip Tonge, David Leonard, Henry Daniel, Paul Cavanagh. Directed by Richard Thorpe. Screenplay, Maurice Zimm; adaptation from the Bible story by Joe Breen Jr., and Samuel James Larsen;

camera (Eastman Color), Joseph Ruttenberg; editor, Harold F. Kress; music, Bronislau Kaper. Previewed March 16, '55. Running time, 117 MINS.
Samarra . . . . Lana Turner
Micah . . . . Edmund Purdom
Nahreeb . . . . Louis Calhern
Ruth . . . . Audrey Dalton
Asham . . . . James Mitchell
Bhakim . . . . Neville Brand
Eli . . . . Walter Hampden
Elissa . . . . Taina Elg
Bosra . . . . Francis L. Sullivan
Carmish . . . . Joseph Wiseman
Yasmin . . . . Sandra Descher
Joram . . . . John Dehner
Governor . . . . Cecil Kellaway
Barber-Surgeon . . . . Philip Tonge
Blind Man . . . . David Leonard
Ramadi . . . . Henry Daniell
Tobiah . . . . Paul Cavanagh
Caleb . . . . Dayton Lummis
Tahra . . . . Tracey Roberts
Uba . . . . Jarma Lewis
Merchant . . . . Jay Novello
Carpenter's Wife . . . . Dorothy Adams
Carpenter's Son . . . . Peter De Bear
Miriam . . . . Phyllis Graffeo
Deborah . . . . Patricia Iannone
David . . . . Eugene Mazzola
Kavak . . . . George Sawaya
Risafe . . . . Richard Devon
Lahla . . . . Ann Cameron
Faradine . . . . Gloria Dea
Lirhan . . . . John Rosser
Zubeir . . . . Charles Wagenheim
(Aspect ratio: 2.55-1)

Yet another in the Biblical cycle. Metro's treatment of the Parable of the Prodigal Son (from Luke XV.) is a bigscale spectacle, making overwhelmingly lavish use of sets, props, CinemaScoped Eastman Color and a well-populated cast. End result of all this flamboyant polish, however, is only fair entertainment due for a mixed reaction from viewers. With Lana Turner heading the cast, and on the ticket play usually accorded religioso pix, it can be figured to get some coin initially, but there isn't much to indicate any sustained draw.

The brief 22 verses in Scripture which tell the story of the prodigal who wanders from his home in pursuit of the high priestess of Astarte have been stretched to one hour and 57 minutes. Producer Charles Schnee has filled the picture so full of scene and spectacle that Richard Thorpe's direction is hard put to give it any semblance of movement, or to get life and warmth into the characters and incidents.

With rather empty characters to portray in the screenplay by Maurice Zimm from the adaptation by Joe Breen Jr., and Samuel James Larsen, the performances by Miss Turner, as the high priestess; Edmund Purdom, the prodigal; Louis Calhern, the high priest of Baal, and most of the others in the huge cast are hollow and generally uninteresting. Almost the only note of character warmth is to be found in the romance between the mute, runaway slave, James Mitchell, and the high priestess' slave as played by Taina Elg.

Most of the screen plot takes place in pagan Damascus, where the prodigal is busy spending his third of his father's wealth trying to win the priestess away from her pagan gods to be his wife. It's a standoff, though, because he will not give up his God, Jehovah, and she cannot renounce her dedication to Astarte. The pagan revelry and temple maidens dedicated to love give an exploitation angle for selling but actually come off tamely in the film. So do the love scenes between Miss Turner and Purdom.

Return of the prodigal to his home after having squandered his fortune and gone through the adventures of love, slavery and battle, and the open-handed welcome he receives is no more believable than what transpires in the preceeding footage.

Thorpe is able to wrap up most of the final 20 minutes of film in an action key, starting with the flinging of Purdom, believed a dead slave, into the vulture pit. Here he fights off a frightening carrion-eater, frees other slaves, and leads them and citizens tired of the rule of their pagan gods into a revolt that ends with the destruction of the heathen temples, the idols and the priests and priestesses that served them.

Seen briefly is Audrey Dalton, the prodigal's betrothed. Neville Brand, a menacing, shavened scalp henchman to the high priest; Walter Hampden, the Hebrew patriarch who welcomes his son back; Francis L. Sullivan, gross, conniving moneylender, and Joseph Wiseman, overplaying a Damascus beggar, are among others more prominently involved in the story.

The C'Scope lensing by Joseph Ruttenberg does a thorough job of the pictorial values furnished by cast, settings and art direction, while Bronislau Kaper provides a background score suggestive of the period. *Brog.*

Interrupted Melody

Biopic treatment of singer Marjorie Lawrence's life. Done with beautiful music, movingly romantic feeling. Word-of-mouth potential should bolster b.o. prospects. Eileen Farrell dubbed the operatic voice.

Hollywood, March 25.

Metro release of Jack Cummings production. Stars Glenn Ford, Eleanor Parker; features Roger Moore, Cecil Kellaway, Peter Leeds, Evelyn Ellis, Walter Baldwin. Directed by Curtis Bernhardt. Written by William Ludwig, Sonya Levien; based on her life story by Marjorie Lawrence; camera (Eastman Color), Joseph Ruttenberg, Paul C. Vogel; editor, John Dunning; dramatic score adapted and conducted by Adolph Deutsch; operatic recordings supervised and conducted by Walter Du Cloux; musical supervison, Saul Chaplin; operatic sequences staged by Vladimir Rosing; music adviser, Harold Gelman; Miss Parker's singng by Eileen Farrell. Previewed March 18, '55. Running time, **105 MINS.**

Dr. Thomas King	Glenn Ford
Marjorie Lawrence	Eleanor Parker
Cyril Lawrence	Roger Moore
Bill Lawrence	Cecil Kellaway
Dr. Ed Ryson	Peter Leeds
Clara	Evelyn Ellis
Jim Owens	Walter Baldwin
Mme. Gilly	Ann Codee
Himself	Leopold Sachse
Comte Claude des Vigneux	Stephen Bekassy

A fine romantic drama with beautiful music is offered in this biopic based on the career of Marjorie Lawrence. The appeal to the discriminating is excellent, and all who go for stories told from the heart will find in "Interrupted Melody" plenty of worthwhile entertainment. For the marquees it has the names of Glenn Ford and Eleanor Parker. Add to that a class ad-pub exploitation campaign and a good word-of-mouth potential.

Jack Cummings' production supervision has smoothly coordinated the many factors in the film, which has an inspirational quality in recounting how Miss Lawrence, struck down at the height of her singing career by crippling polio, was able to fight back and sing again by drawing on the strength of a devoted husband's love. Miss Parker, as the singer, and Ford, as her doctor husband, are socko, with deftly shaded performances that come to the fore under the understanding, sympathetic direction by Curtis Bernhardt. Latter had a topflight piece of screen writing to work from in the script by William Ludwig and Sonya Levien, based on her life story by Miss Lawrence.

From winning a local singing contest in her native Australia, Miss Lawrence moved on to long, hard study in Paris, then operatic success on two continents and marriage to an American doctor, with a subsequent limiting of her engagements to New York so she could be near him. However, he persuades her to accept a South American tour, and it is while fulfilling this engagement that polio strikes. Up to this point the film is full of operatic montage of nine arias, all beautifully and thrillingly staged. Among them are O Dom Fatale from "Don Carlos," The Habanera from "Carmen," the Immolation Scene from "Goetterdammerung" and Un Bel Di Vedremo from "Madame Butterfly."

Remainder of the picture is given over to the singer's struggle to overcome the depression and lack of confidence that siezes her after the illness. Here the playing and direction will wring tears, but the lump-in-throat drama has such a sensitive, honest feel that audiences will join personally in what is transpiring. How Miss Lawrence finds the courage to again face the public, after singing for the sick and mained of World War II in farflung camps, climaxes in a special Metropolitan Opera performance of "Tristan And Isolde."

Adding measurably to the musical thrills of the production is the flexible soprano of Eileen Farrell, who does the actual, offstage singing for Miss Parker's character. Great credit also is due Vladimir Rosing for his staging of the operatic sequences, the musical supervision by Saul Chapin, the supervision and conducting of the operatic recordings by Walter Du Cloux, and the contribution Adolph Deutsch makes with his adaptation and conducting of the dramatic score. Along with these musical credits, including Harold Gelman's music advising, the recording supervision by Wesley C. Miller figures importantly.

Roger Moore, as Miss Lawrence's brother; Cecil Kellaway, as her father; Peter Leeds, as a doctor friend; Evelyn Ellis, as the nurse; Walter Baldwin, Ann Codee, Leopold Sachse and Stephen Bekasay are all good, but interest seems to be concentrated almost entirely on the two stars, so thoroughly do they dominate the footage.

The picture gains in pictorial splendor from the CinemaScope lensing in Eastman Color by Joseph Ruttenberg and Paul C. Vogel. Other firstrate contributions including editing by John Dunning, the art and set direction and the costumes. *Brog.*

Shotgun
(COLOR)

Good western filmfare for general outdoor market playdates.

Hollywood, March 24.

Allied Artists release of John C. Champion production. Stars Sterling Hayden, Yvonne De Carlo, Zachary Scott; features Guy Prescott, Robert Wilke, Angela Greene, Paul Marion, John Pickard. Directed by Lesley Selander. Written by Clark E. Reynolds, Rory Calhoun; added dialog, John C. Champion, camera (Technicolor), Ellsworth Fredericks; editor, John Fuller; music composed and conducted by Carl Brandt. Previewed March 22, '55. Running time, **80 MINS.**

Clay	Sterling Hayden
Abby	Yvonne De Carlo
Reb	Zachary Scott
Thompson	Guy Prescott
Bentley	Robert Wilke
Aletha	Angela Greene
Delgadito	Paul Marion
Perez	John Pickard
Chris	Ralph Sanford
Frank	Rory Mallinson
Midge	Fiona Hale
Ed	Ward Wood
Fletcher	Lane Chandler
Greybar	Al Wyatt
Davey	Harry Harvey Jr.

(*Aspect ratio:* 1.85-1)

"Shotgun" is good western filmfare, slated to find favor with the outdoor fan generally. Familiar plot angles of vengeance and chase are freshened and the characters believeably established in a script that wastes no time going about its business. Names of Sterling Hayden, Yvonne De Carlo and Zachary Scott also go with release intentions so this one should fare satisfactorily in the action market.

Colorfully rugged outdoor locales provide the setting for the John C. Champion production and his supervision, plus good direction by Lesley Selander, a properly valued script by Clark E. Reynolds and Rory Calhoun, and competent performances by the cast, lift the offering a cut above the level of the usual program western. The action gets rugged at times, but not objectionably so because the roughness is part of the story and not just dragged in to fit the actioner rating.

When a marshal is blown in two by a double blast from a shotgun, deputy Hayden takes up the killer's trail, packing his own sawed-off, double-barrelled weapon to use on his quarry. He also totes a rifle for some Apache troublemakers along the trail and a sixgun for personal arguments. In the pursuit of the killer, Guy Prescott, Hayden is joined by Miss De Carlo, whom he rescues from an Indian stakeout, and the pair is soon joined by Scott, a bounty hunter who wants the reward on Prescott's head. The adventuring the trio is put through has a familiar ring, but under the expert freshening in the script plays well. The action climaxes when Hayden and Prescott meet in a shotgun duel to the death, and you know who rides off into the sunset with Miss De Carlo.

The three stars and Prescott are assisting on the acting end by Robert Wilke, Paul Marion and John Pickard. Angela Greene gets short shrift as the girl who didn't want Hayden to ride off on his mission of vengeance.

Ellsworth Fredricks' photography does right by the action and scenery, but the print by Technicolor used at the preview was not consistent in its hues. John Fuller's editing, Carl Brandt's score and other behind-camera credits are good. *Brog.*

Jump Into Hell

Routine programmer based on the French-Communist fighting in Indo-China. For lowercase bookings.

Hollywood, March 29.

Warner Bros. release of David Weisbart production. Stars Jack Sernas, Kurt Kasznar, Arnold Moss, Peter Ven Eyck; features Marcel Dalio, Norman Dupont, Lawrence Dobkin, Pat Blake. Directed by David Butler. Written by Irving Wallace; camera, J. Peverell Marley; editor, Irene Morra; music, David Buttolph. Previewed March 15, '55. Running time, **92 MINS.**

Capt. Guy Bertrand	Jack Sernas
Capt. Jean Callaux	Kurt Kasznar
The General	Arnold Moss
Lt. Heinrich Heldman	Peter Van Eyck
Sgt. Taite	Marcel Dalio
Lt. Andre Maupin	Norman Dupont
Maj. Maurice Bonet	Lawrence Dobkin
Gizele Bonet	Pat Blake
Jacqueline	Irene Montwill
Major Riviere	Alberto Morin
Capt. LeRoy	Maurice Marsac
Capt. Darbley	Louis Mercier

The dramatic stand of the French at Dienbienphu in Indo-China has been transferred to the screen in a singularly uninspired potboiler that will best serve in the programmer market as the lowercase half of the dual bills. Real and reel scenes are intermixed to depict the defense of the French fortress but it fails to come off as a graphic or exciting account of warfare.

The original screenplay by Irving Wallace, as directed by David Butler, doesn't give the affair much credibility so the viewer is never caught up in what's transpiring on the screen. The human problems posed and the dialog the players are given to speak are strictly formula. So is the production supervision by David Weisbart and the technical support, from lensing on down.

Picture gets into its story when the beleaguered fort commander sends word to France for four volunteer officers to help him defend Dienbienphu. The volunteers are Jack Sernas, Kurt Kasznar, Peter Van Eyck and Norman Dupont. Before they arrive via parachute, footage is devoted to their reasons for attempting the dangerous and abortive mission, thus permitting the display of two femmes, Pat Blake and Irene Montwill, in the flashback scenes. Otherwise, femmes mean nothing to the plot, which shows how the Communists breached the French defenses after **56 days of battling. At the windup, only Sernas and Dupont of the volunteers escape, taking with them dispatches on the defense.**

Arnold Moss plays the fort commander, but he, and such others as Marcel Dalio, Lawrence Dobkin, Alberto Morin, Maurice Marsac and Louis Mercier, fare no better at making this believeable than do the leads.

The footage is long at 92 minutes. *Brog.*

Cult of the Cobra

Well-done horror chiller with good b.o. potential in exploitation dates.

Hollywood, March 22.

Universal release of Howard Pine production. Stars Faith Domergue, Richard Long, Marshall Thompson, Kathleen Hughes; features William Reynolds, Jack Kelly, Myrna Hansen, David Janssen. Directed by Francis D. Lyon. Screenplay, Jerry Davis, Cecil Maiden, Richard Collins; story by Davis; camera, Russell Metty; editor, Milton Carruth. Previewed March 16, '55. Running time, **81 MINS.**

Lisa	Faith Domergue
Paul Able	Richard Long
Tom Markel	Marshall Thompson
Julia	Kathleen Hughes
Carl Turner	Jack Kelly
Marian	Myrna Hansen
Rico Nardi	David Janssen
Pete Norton	William Reynolds
Daru	Leonard Strong
Nick Hommel	James Dobson
Inspector	Walter Coy
Dance Team	The Carlssons
Major Martin Fielding	Olan Soule
Mrs. Weber	Helen Wallace
Army Nurse	Mary Alan Hokanson
High Lamian Priest	John Halloran
Captain Williams	Alan Reynolds

(*Aspect ratio:* 1.85-1)

This Universal release is one of those offbeat chillers that can be promoted to good returns in the exploitation market. Additionally, it is a strong entry for double bills elsewhere. Story premise is sufficiently imaginative and novel enough to build better than usual suspense and, while some may quarrel with the topic, the dramatic license taken is well done and served up for the entertainment of the horror fan.

Plot gimmick here is fashioned around an Asiatic cult of snake worshippers who believe humans can change into snakes and back again. When six American GI's disrupt a secret ceremony, the high priest places a curse on them, vowing the Snake Goddess will kill them all.

As developed in this Howard Pine production, the story line immediately knocks off one of the six and then goes after the others upon their return to New York upon Army discharge. After the violent deaths of two of the lads, each with snake venom discovered in the autopsy, the police begin to believe the theory propounded by Richard Long, one of the GI's, that a strange young woman, Faith Domergue, with whom his roommate, Marshall Thompson, has fallen in love, actually is the Snake Goddess come to exact vengeance. Windup shows Thompson pushing a cobra about to attack Kathleen Hughes, Long's fiancee, in her theatre dressingroom out of the window, and the snake transforming into Miss Domergue as she dies on the street below.

Francis D. Lyon's direction is responsible for plenty of eerie moments, further heightened by interesting optical effects as the camera becomes the eye of the striking cobra whenever Miss Domergue changes into the snake. Script by Jerry Davis, Cecil Maiden and Richard Collins realistically develops the plot, in which the femme star is a standout in an exotic role. Thompson lends conviction to his part in a well-enacted characterization, and Long is okay as the man interested in the transformation theory. Miss Hughes delivers as his fiancee, and capable support is provided by William Reynolds, Jack Kelly, David Janssen and others.

Russell Metty's photography is firstrate. *Whit.*

This Island Earth
(COLOR)

Socko science-fiction thriller, one of best outer-space film entries to date. Plenty of ballyhoo angles and large b.o. prospects.

Hollywood, March 29.

Universal release of William Alland production. Stars Jeff Morrow, Faith Domergue, Rex Reason f;eatures Lance Fuller, Russell Johnson, Douglas Spencer, Robert Nichols, Karl L. Lindt. Directed by Joseph Newman. Screenplay, Franklin Coen, Edward G. O'Callaghan; based on the novel by Raymond F. Jones; camera (Technicolor), Clifford Stine; editor, Virgil Vogel; special photography, David S. Horsley and Stine; music supervision, Joseph Gershenson. Previewed March 22, '55. Running time, **87 MINS.**

Exeter .... Jeff Morrow
Ruth Adams .... Faith Domergue
Cal Meacham .... Rex Reason
Brack .... Lance Fuller
Steve Carlson .... Russell Johnson
The Monitor .... Douglas Spencer
Joe Wilson .... Robert Nichols
Dr. Adolph Engelborg ... Karl L. Lindt

(*Aspect ratio:* 2-1)

Special effects of the most realistic type rival the story and characterizations in capturing the interest in this exciting science-fiction chiller, one of the most imaginative, fantastic and cleverly-conceived entries to date in the outer-space film field. It may be exploited for boffo returns both in the general and exploitation markets.

Impressive use is made of Technicolor in catching the full values of these effects, which give off sometimes frightening qualities in the William Alland production, which receives vigorous direction by Joseph Newman. Also, film is a particular achivement for David S. Horsley and Clifford Stine, who handled the special photography assignment, as well as for the entire list of studio technical departments who collabbed on all its eerie ingredients.

Plot motivation in the Franklin Coen - Edward G. O'Callaghan screenplay, based on the novel by Raymond F. Jones, is derived from the frantic efforts of the men of the interstellar planet, Metaluna, to find on Earth a new source of atomic energy. This is needed to set up an isolation layer completely around Metaluna to protect it from the continuous attack by forces of the more powerful planet, Zagon, both lying beyond the constellations known to earth scientists. For the accomplishment of this goal, the outstanding scientists in the field have been recruited by a character named Exeter, who has set up a completely-equipped laboratory in Georgia.

Two of these scientists are Rex Reason and Faith Domergue, experts in nuclear fission. Becoming suspicious of the true motives of Exeter they try to escape in a small plane, but the craft is drawn up into Exeter's giant space ship (a flying saucer) and they are flown to Metaluna to complete their experiments. They arrive too late, the enemy having nearly destroyed this planet, and they barely make their escape back to earth in the space ship.

One of the most thrilling sequences occurs as huge meteors attack the space ship as it is working its way to Metaluna. Ingeniously-constructed props and equipment, together with strange sound effects, also are responsible for furthering interest, which is of the edge-of-the-seat variety during the latter half of the film. For an added fillip, there's a Mutant, half human, half insect, which boards the ship as it escapes from Metaluna.

Jeff Morrow enacts the role of Exeter in a most credible fashion, and Miss Domergue and Reason likewise are excellent. Newman handles his characters very persuasively to make them convincing, never missing a trick in the building up of his subject. Strong delineations also are registered by Lance Fuller and Douglas Spencer, both Metalueans, Russell Johnson, as a scientist, and Robert Bichols as Reason's assistant.

Technical credits are tops and meriting high mention are: Alexander Golitzen and Richard H. Riedel, art direction; Russell A. Gausman and Julia Heron, set decoration; Joseph Gershenson for a particularly atmospheric score; Virgil Vogel's fast editing; the sound by Leslie I. Carey and Robert Pritchard. Stine also handled the film's regular lensing. *Whit.*

Jungle Moon Men

Routine Johnny Weissmuller jungle entry for program situations.

Hollywood, March 25.

Columbia release of a Sam Katzman production. Stars Johnny Weissmuller; features Jean Byron, Helene Stanton, Bill Henry, Myron Healey, Kimba. Directed by Charles S. Gould. Screenplay, Dwight V. Babcock, Jo Pagano, from story by Pagano; camera, Henry Freulich; editor, Henry Batista. Previewed March 23, '55. Running time, **69 MINS.**

Johnny Weissmuller
Johnny Weissmuller
Ellen Marston .... Jean Byron
Oma .... Helene Stanton
Bob Prentice .... Bill Henry
Mark Santo .... Myron Healey
Damu .... Billy Curtis
Nolimo .... Michael Granger
Max .... Frank Sully
Marro.........Benjamin F. Chapman Jr.
Link .... Kenneth L. Smith
Regan .... Ed Hinton

(*Aspect ratio:* 1.85-1)

Writers of this Johnny Weissmuller jungle starrer borrow generously from H. Rider Haggard for plot material, but film fits into the groove of past offerings in the Sam Katzman series and should do the same type of biz in program situations.

Weissmuller this time becomes involved with a high priestess who discoverd the secret of eternal life during her existence with the ancient Egyptians and has lived down through the ages. Now she's queen of a tribe of Pygmies known as the Moon Men. Johnny meets her when he and a femme writer doing research on a white civilization supposed to have flourished in the region centuries before, force their way into the temple to rescue a white man taken to be her high priest.

Star is up to the usual demands of his title role, and Helene Stanton attractively portrays the priestess, afraid to leave the temple for fear that Ra, the Sun God, will destroy her the same as he killed all her people in ancient times. Finale shows her emergence into the open and crumbling to dust when Ra beams his rays upon her. Jean Byron does a good job with the writer role, and Bill Henry is the kidnapped victim. Myron Healy is in as a heavy out to get the diamonds from the temple, killed by guardian lions, and Billy Curtis handles his Pygmy leader role in okay fashion. Kimba, of course, appears for usual amusing footage as the star's chimp companion.

Charles S. Gould had his work cut out for him to bring any realism in his direction to the Dwight V. Babcock-Jo Pagano screenplay, but manages occasionally in between unintentional laughs. *Whit.*

The Night My Number Came Up
(BRITISH)

Tense Ealing production of aircraft passengers who've been warned, via a dream, that their plane is doomed to crash. Sturdy b.o.

London, March 22.

General Film Distributors release of Ealing Studios-Michael Balcon production. Stars Michael Redgrave, Sheila Sim, Alexander Knox, Denholm Elliott. Directed by Leslie Norman; screenplay by R. C. Sherriff; camera, Lionel Banes; editor, Peter Tanner; music, Malcolm Arnold. At Odeon, Leicester Square, London, March 22, '55. Running time, **94 MINS.**

Air Marshal Hardie....Michael Redgrave
Mary Campbell .... Sheila Sim
Owen Robertson ...... Alexander Knox
F/Lt. McKenzie..........Denham Elliott
Mrs. Robertson .... Ursula Jeans
Wainwright .... Ralph Truman
Lindsay .... Michael Hordern
Pilot .... Nigel Stock
Soldier .... Bill Kerr
Soldier .... Alfie Bass
Bennett .... George Rose
Engineer .... Victor Maddern
Co-Pilot .... David Orr
Navigator .... Dave Yates
Miss Robertson .... Doreen Aris
Wireless Operator .... Richard Davies

A variation of the time theory, this Ealing production poses the question: can the future be foretold? A highly competent piece of filmmaking, it is packed with suspense and excitement and looks geared for hefty grosses in most situations.

The plot is based on a dream in which a naval officer sees a Dakota aircraft crashing at a remote point off the coast of Japan. In the dream there are eight passengers, one of whom is a girl and another a VIP. The story is told to an air marshal who is due to fly the next day to Tokyo with his personal assistant, but there's no real similarity, as their plane will be a Liberator carrying only two passengers.

By takeoff time, however, the situation is radically changed. A Dakota is substituted for the flight, and there are eight passengers, including one VIP and one female secretary. And from the moment the plane becomes airborne, the yarn unspools with almost unrelieved tension as all the events anticipated in the dream come to pass.

R. C. Sherriff has fashioned a taut screenplay which allows for mounting tension as the plane runs into an electric storm, has a radio blackout and then gets lost high above the clouds while the passengers are gasping for breath because of the lack of oxygen. Leslie Norman's incisive direction sustains the tension and Liones Banes has lensed the production with commendable skill.

With the yarn keyed to suspense, the cast refrain from overemphasis. The standard is set by Michael Redgrave's impressively quiet portrayal of the air marshal who cannot alter course to suit a dreamer, yet remains uneasy. Sheila Sim has only a modest role as the secretary but fills it with her usual competence, and Alexander Knox gives a standout performance as a civil servant scared out of his wits as he sees the dream pattern taking shape. Denholm Elliott impresses as the air marshal's aide, and there is sterling support from a fine team of British performers. *Myro.*

That Lady
(BRITISH-COLOR)

Olivia De Havilland and Gilbert Roland starred in historical Spanish romantic drama; spotty returns likely.

London, March 15.

20th-Fox release of Atalanta production. Stars Olivia de Havilland, Gilbert Roland; features, Paul Scofield, Francoise Rosay, Dennis Price. Directed by Terence Young. Screenplay by Anthony Veiller, Sy Bartlett from novel by Kate O'Brien; camera (Eastmancolor), Robert Krasker; editor, Raymond Poulton; music, John Addison. At Carlton Theatre, London, March 15, '55. Running time, **100 MINS.**

Ana de Mendoza......Olivia de Havilland
Antonio Perez ....Gilbert Roland
Philip of Spain .... Paul Scofield
Bernadina .... Francoise Rosay
Mateo Vasquez .... Dennis Price
Don Inigo ....Anthony Dawson
Cardinal .... Robert Harris
Diego .... Peter Illing
Don Escovedo .... Jose Nieto
Captain of King's Guard Christopher Lee
Fernando .... Andy Shine

(*Aspect ratio:* 2.55-1)

"That Lady," the film that ran into trouble with the Spanish censorship, is quite an innocuous entertainment. It follows the convention established for historical romantic dramas. Its lavish mounting, picturesque settings and high acting standards are the pic's main assets. Strong marquee values should give it b.o. emphasis, although spotty results seem likely in most situations. Its British quota tag will be a valuable asset for local theatre owners who are wired for CinemaScope.

Filmed on location in Spain, with studio work at Elstree, the film is notable for the screen debut of Paul Scofield, a British legit actor of repute, whose per-

formance as King Philip is one of the acting highspots. He brings a dignity and sincerity to the characterization and succeeds in surmounting the ineptness of the dialog.

Adapted from the novel by Kate O'Brien, the plot describes the intrigue at the court of King Philip as two private secretaries jostle for power to become first minister. Centrepiece of the story is the one-eyed princess (Olivia de Havilland) whose late husband was the unofficial ruler of the country. At the behest of her king, she extends a welcome to one of the contenders (Roland Young) but the scandal which ensues lands them both in jail.

Although handsomely lensed in Eastmancolor, this anamorphic entry moves only at a leisurely pace and the dramatic incident is frequently marred by banal conversational passages. The direction rarely gets to grips with the subject, and the editing looks all too casual.

Nevertheless, there is a consistently high standard of performance. Miss de Havilland's interpretation of the widowed princess combines vitality and charm. Gilbert Roland looks right for the role of the great lover but doesn't quite act up to it. Dennis Price gives a sterling portrayal as his rival for power. Francoise Rosay contributes a touching cameo as the princess's faithful servant while Robert Harris displays a full measure of dignity as the cardinal.

Myro.

The Impostor
(JAPANESE)

Lightweight Nipponese import with below par art house b.o. values.

Brandon Films release of Shochiku (Shigeki Sugiyama and Koichi Takagi) production. Stars Utaemon Ichikawa. Directed by Tatsuo Osone. Screenplay, Hyogo Suzuki, based on original story by Mitsuzo Sasaki; camera, Aaaruo Takeno; music, Seiichi Suzuki. Previewed N.Y., March 3, '55. Running time, **90 MINS.**

Baron Mondonosuke Sotome .... Utaemon Ichikawa
Kyoya .... Chikako Miyagi
Kikuji .... Keiko Kishi
Jokai-Bo .... Kokichi Takata
Naizen .... Fijiro Yanagi
Matsudaira .... Kodayu Ichikawa
Hagino .... Kuniko Ikawa
Kojiro .... Minoru Oki
Nanae .... Ayuko Saijo
Tokugawa .... Jogi Kaieda

(In Japanese; English Titles)

While a few Japanese pictures have won a niche of late on the American entertainment scene due to their charm and pageantry, "The Imposter" fails to measure up to the quality of its predecessors. Hampered by a rambling and often confusing story, this Shochiku Film production appears destined for a lukewarm reception in the art houses.

Moreover, the picture contains little on which an exhibitor can draw for exploitation material. Cast is peopled with several stars of the Kabuki, Japan's native theatre, but it's questionable whether their presence will impress the average art house patron.

Based on a story by Mitsuzo Sasaki, the film unreels a 17th century tale of rivalry for the throne of Japan. Two aspirants claim to be sons of the ruling Shogun. One is a genuine heir while the other is a pretender. There's much swordplay, chicanery and comic opera touches before the phony is exposed and the rightful claimant installed in the palace.

Under Tatsuo Osone's direction, the players make an earnest attempt to bring realism and movement into 90 minutes of footage. But possibly they were trying too hard for serious scenes frequently verge on the satirical and heavy drama takes on comedy proportions.

Star of this Brandon Films import is Utaemon Ichikawa. A Kabuki theatre veteran, he portrays a shrewd samurai of the imperial guard. Although believable when wielding a sword, there are times when his thesping, by Yank criteria, borders on the droll rather than dramatic.

Miss Chikako Miyagi, however, is effective as a spy and Keiko Kishi is sweet and demure as a kidnapped sister of Ichikawa. Other performances are best described as routine including those of Kokichi Takata and Minoru Oki, as the pair who aspire to the Shogun's mantle.

Black-and-white photography of Aaruo Takeno is fair. Seiichi Suzuki's music is adequate and physical values supplied by producers Shigeki Sugiyama and Koichi Takagi are on par with the average Japanese picture. Judicious editing could have safely trimmed at least 10 minutes from this import in the interest of getting to the point faster.

Gilb.

Contraband Spain
(BRITISH—COLOR)

Modest British actioner of U.S. Federal agent unmasking smuggling and conterfeiting gang. Okay dualler.

London, March 16.

Associated British Pathe release of Diadem Films (Philip Gartside) production. Stars Richard Greene, Anouk, Michael Denison; features Jose Nieto, John Warwick, Philip Saville. Directed by Lawrence Huntngton; screenplay, Lawrence Huntngton; camera, Harry Waxman; editor, Tom Simpson. At Pavilion, London, March 15, '55. Running time, **82 MINS.**

Lee .... Richard Greene
Elena .... Anouk
Ricky .... Michael Denison
Pierre .... Jose Nieto
Bryan .... John Warwick
Martin .... Philip Saville
Marcos .... Alfonso Estella
Lucien .... Antonio Almoros
Juan .... Conrado San Martin
Preventive Officer .... Arnold Bell
Colonel Ingleby ...... George Mulcaster
Mrs. Ingleby .... Olive Milbourne
U. S. Embassy Official .... Robert Ayres

Although lavishly staged and expertly filmed in Eastmancolor, this British pic rates only as a modest entry, but should serve as a good action dualler in most situations. It's quota tag is a prime asset for the local market.

Set on the Franco-Spanish border, the plot describes the methods of an American Federal agent (Richard Greene) in rounding up a gang of smugglers and counterfeiters after his own brother, himself one of the smugglers, is murdered. Aided by a nitery thrush (Anouk) and a British customs official (Michael Denison), his inquiries take him through France on to a cross-channel ferry, leading to the final roundup in Dover harbor.

Action moves vigorously against attractive continental backgrounds, compensating largely for weaknesses in plot structure and for slight confusion in story development. Direction is bogged down by overplus of dialog in opening sequences, but is otherwise standard. Greene gives an energetic performance as the agent and Anouk contributes a dash of glamor as the enigmatic singer. Denison portrays the Englishman abroad in the style of a caricature. Subsidiary parts are adequately filled and technical credits are up to average.

Myro.

Napoleon Bonaparte
(FRENCH)

Paris, March 22.

Cinelde production and release. Stars Albert Dieudonne. Directed and written by Abel Gance. Comera, Kruger, Hubert; editor, Marguerite Beauge; music, Henri Verdun. At Studio 28, Paris. Running time, **135 MINS.**

Napoleon .... Albert Dieudonne
Danton .... Samson Feinsillber
Marat .... Antonin Artaud
Charlotte .... Damia
Josephine .... Annabella
Saint Just .... Abel Gance

Although this pic was made in 1927, as a silent vehicle and revamped in 1934, it is reviewed again for it has just been reissued here before the recently completed Sacha Guitry panoramic of the life of Napoleon and "Desiree." Film also has a 15 minute segment which utilizes the tryptych, three screens akin to presentday Cinerama, for massive effects. Thomas Brandon has this for the U.S., and may also give it a special reissue in the arties. There is no doubt that it packs a load of curio value in its resources, treatment and technique. Film may well turn out to be a grosser in the offbeat arty spots here and in the U.S.

Original pic ran for eight hours, but this has been hacked down to 135 minutes by director Abel Gance himself. Except for a few scenes, photo quality is fine. Story is told by a group of Bonapartists during Napoleon's imprisonment on Elbe.

As sprawling and gigantic as is the subject, Gance was able to transfer its feel of grandeur and sweep to the screen plus the essence of the greatness of Napoleon. Even in its cutdown version, this transcribes the intensity of the young Napoleon, the tumbling tumbril terror of revolution, and the men who worked and tried to transform it into a meaning.

Although this beats patriotic drums blatantly, it is interesting in story and aim. Such morsels as intercutting between Napoleon trapped in a small boat, after his escape from Corsica, with the seething unrest of the Assembly by having the camera swooping over the crowds, the rapid cutting of crowd scenes and orgies, and the final use of the triple screen with its intercutting in each section for a rousing finale, makes this of interest for film patrons looking for the unusual.

Here it also marks the belated recognition of one of the great film pioneers—Abel Gance—now making pix again after a 15-year hiatus. Acting in pic is surprisingly acceptable today. Albert Dieudonne's snarp, commanding Napoleon hits sterling heights despite a few tendencies to exaggeration.

Mosk.

Escape to Burma
(SUPERSCOPE-COLOR)

Familiar names in pulp fiction-type jungle adventure; for top-of-bill dual-dating in regular program market.

Hollywood, April 4.

RKO release of Benedict Bogeaus production. Stars Barbara Stanwyck, Robert Ryan, David Farrar; features Murvyn Vye, Lisa Montell, Robert Warwick, Reginald Denny, Robert Cabal, Peter Coe, Alex Montoya, Anthony Numkena. Directed by Allan Dwan. Screenplay, Talbot Jennings, Hobart Donavan; story, Kenneth Perkins; camera (Technicolor), John Alton; editor, James Leicester; score, Louis Forbes. Previewed March 31, '55. Running time, **86 MINS.**

Gwen Moore .... Barbara Stanwyck
Jim Brecan .... Robert Ryan
Cardigan .... David Farrar
Makesh .... Murvyn Vye
Andora .... Lisa Montell
Sawbwa .... Robert Warwick
Commissioner .... Reginald Denny
Captain of the Guard ...... Peter Coe
Dacoit .... Alex Montoya
Kumat .... Robert Cabal
Kasha .... Anthony Numkena
Poo Kan .... Lal Chand Mehra
Sergeant .... John Mansfield
Astrologer .... Gavin Muir

(Aspect ratio: 2-1)

A rather stock type of jungle adventure feature is offered in this pulp fiction actioner, and in the regular program market, where the demands are not too discriminating, it will serve its purpose as a top-of-the-bill dualer. It has a photographic advantage in using the SuperScope process and Technicolor, giving visual impact to what is otherwise a routine playoff.

While equipping his production with expert technical assists, producer Benedict Bogeaus has been less show-wise in overseeing the writing and direction. The latter, by Allan Dwan, lacks the kind of drive that could have put some excitement into the footage, and the scripting by Talbot Jennings and Hobart Donavan is unimaginative, particularly in the formula dialog and situations with which stars Barbara Stanwyck, Robert Ryan and David Farrar have to wrestle. As a consequence, the performances, while adequate enough, are routine.

Ryan, a man wanted for murder, takes refuge on the estate of Miss Stanwyck, who operates in the teak forests of Burma. Hot on his trail is Farrar, British officer, and the minions of Robert Warwick, Sawbwa of Sakar, whose son Ryan is supposed to have murdered. Nothing takes place to indicate Ryan's innocence, because he's pretty ready with his luger and continually acts like a guilty man. Despite all this, Miss Stanwyck falls in love with him, they go through all kinds of escapades, including a tiger hunt, jungle bandits and attack from the Sawbwa's men before a last-minute witness turns up to clear him of the charge.

Like the three stars, the remainder of the cast goes through the formula demands of script and direction without making the action believeable. Where picture scores is in the SuperScoping of good sets and other physical furbishings under the camera guidance of John Alton, and in the musical backing given it by Louis Forbes.

Brog.

A Bullet for Joey

Robinson and Raft in fair crime meller for program dating.

Hollywood, April 5.

United Artists release of Samuel Bischoff and David Diamond. Stars Edward

G. Robinson, George Raft, features Audrey Totter, Peter Van Eyck, George Dolenz. Directed by Lewis Allen. Screenplay, Geoffrey Homes and A. I. Bezerids, from Story by James Benson Nablo; camera, Harry Neuman; editor, Leon Barsha; music, Harry Sukman. Previewed in Hollywood, April 4, '55. Running time, **86 MINS.**

Leduc ....Edward G. Robinson
Victor ....George Raft
Joyce ....Audrey Totter
Macklin ....George Dolenz
Fred ....Peter Hanson
Hartman ....Peter Van Eyck
Mrs. Hartman ....Karen Verne
Paola ....Ralph Smiley
DuBois ....Henir Letondal
Morrie ....John Cliff
Nick ....Joseph Vitale
Jack Allen ....Bill Bryant
Paul ....Stan Malotte
Yvonne ....Toni Gerry
Marie ....Sally Blaine
Garcia ....Steven Geray
Percy ....John Alvin
Artist ....Bill Henry
Benson ....Carlyle Mitchell
U Drive Clerk ....Rory Mallinson
Sergeant ....Bill Neff
Phone Man ....Sandy Sanders
Captain ....Peter Mamakos
1st officer ....Frank Richard
Truck Driver ....Roy Engel
Cuban Girl ....Carmelita Gibbs
Rosie ....Sandra Stone
Counter Girl ....Tina Carver
Bartender ....Frank Hagney
Portuguese Waiter ....Carlos Rivero
Armand ....Alan Welles
Driver-Police Car ....John Goddard
Sgt. Booking officer............Fred Libby
Policeman-car ....John Merrick
Rene ....Joel Smith
10-year-old-boy ....Paul Toffel
Gardener ....Paul Marion
1st Tail ....Barry Regan
2nd Tail ....Mal Alberts

Rousing crime melodramatics unfold slowly in this UA release and effect is just fair entertainment for program market, where the names of E. G. Robinson and George Raft should help bookings.

Against a Montreal story setting, this Bischoff-Diamond production tells the efforts of supposedly Commie agent Peter Van Eyck to kidnap atomic physicist George Dolenz, spirit him out of country. Script by Geoffrey Homes and A. T. Bezzerides, from original by James Nelson Neblo, talks but too much of the action in formula dialog, and Lewis Allen's direction unforceful in dealing with meller values, so that pace is extremely slow.

Raft is a deported ex-gangster, smuggled to Canada from Lisbon by Van Eyck to carry out the snatch and Robinson is the RCMP inspector heading the minions of the law to prevent crime. Kidnap plot seems too elaborate and unbelievable. Several seemingly senseless killings dot the footage before the denouement aboard a freighter where all principals have gathered and Raft dies saving Robinson and Dolenz after he learns the world-domination plans of Van Eyck's masters.

Concentration on detail of the snatch plot and police work becomes tedious after a while, although some ingeniousness in the RCMP scheme to trap criminals is interesting, even though it misfires in actually bringing crooks to bay. Performances follow generally acceptable pattern, but are not outstanding. Audrey Totter appears as the former Raft moll forced to use her femme wiles on Dolenz. Only other distaffer with much footage is Toni Gerry, homely secretary to Dolenz, whom gangster Bryant romances and then kills.

Technical departments all give competent support. *Brog.*

The Eternal Sea

Good film account of naval career of Admiral John M. Hoskins, with okay prospects although poorly titled and overlong.

Hollywood, April 4.

Republic release of John H. Auer production. Stars Sterling Hayden, Alexis Smith, Dean Jagger; features Ben Cooper, Virginia Grey, Hayden Rorke, Douglas Kennedy, Louis Jean Heydt, Richard Crane, Morris Ankrum, Frank Ferguson, John Maxwell. Directed by Auer. Screenplay, Allen Rivkin; story, William Wister Haines; camera, John L. Russell Jr.; editor, Fred Allen; score, Elmer Bernstein; technical advisors, Lt. Joseph D. Adkins, USN, Lt. Col. Edward R. Kandel, USAF. Previewed April 1, '55. Running time, **103 MINS.**

Admiral John M. Hoskins ....Sterling Hayden
Sue Hoskins ....Alexis Smith
Adm. Thomas L. Semple....Dean Jagger
Zuggy ....Ben Cooper
Dorothy Buracker............Virginia Grey
Capt. William Buracker...Hayden Rorke
Capt. Walter Riley.....Douglas Kennedy
Capt. Walter F. Rodee..Louis Jean Heydt
Lt. Johnson ....Richard Crane
Adm. Arthur Dewey Struble ....MorrisAnkrum
Adm. "L.D." ....Frank Ferguson
Adm. William F. Halsey John Maxwell

(*Aspect ratio*: 1:66-1)

The heroic naval career of Admiral John M. Hoskins rates a good accounting in this Republic release, which bears the singularly flat title of "The Eternal Sea." However, even with that handicap and the fact the footage is considerably overlength at 103 minutes, b.o. prospects appear okay.

Familiar names of Sterling Hayden, playing the admiral, Alexis Smith, as his wife, and Dean Jagger, as Vice Admiral Thomas L. Semple, are used to head the cast under the producer - direction helming of John H. Auer. Working from a well-balanced screenplay by Allen Rivkin, based on a story by William Wister Haines, Auer manages a good blend of sentiment and heroics that keeps the unfoldment generally interesting. However, he would have a better show if upwards of 20 minutes were trimmed from the footage.

Hayden does an excellent job of portraying the dedicated admiral, a man who lost a leg during the sinking of the Carrier Princeton early in the Pacific phase of World War II, fought to continue on an active status to command the new Princeton and then paved the way for carrier-borne jet aircraft, which proved its values in the Korean conflict. Now dedicated to rehabilitating other war - disabled men, Admiral Hoskins is currently Commander of Air Fleet, Quonset, Rhode Island. That Hayden doesn't seem to age too perceptibly during all this doesn't matter so much because he catches the spirit of the man.

Sea footage filmed aboard carriers has excitement, particularly in the later, jet phases of the story. This action angle of the pic is balanced with the heart tugs of worrying women sweating out the absence of their men and the tearful reunions. Distaffer Alexis Smith does well here, as does Virginia Grey, seen as the wife of Hayden Rorke, who plays Captain William Buracker, commander of the first Princeton. Jagger warms up the character of Admiral Semple, as does Morris Ankrum doing Vice Admiral Arthur Dewey Struble, and John Maxwell as Admiral William F. Halsey. Others giving good accounts of themselves include Ben Cooper, a gob; Douglas Kennedy, Louis Jean Heydt, Richard Crane and Frank Ferguson.

John L. Russell Jr.'s cameras are handled in firstrate fashion and the Elmer Bernstein score carries through the nautical theme well. *Brog.*

Heartbreak Ridge
(FRENCH-COLOR)

Semi-documentary of strong visual values and emotional tug. Well suited to dual bills in U. S.

Tudor Pictures release of Rene Risacher production. Directed by Jacques Dupont. Camera (Gevacolor), Henry Decat; chief cameraman, Jean Rabier; sound engineer, Claude Arrieu; editor, Pitrre Guillette; production manager, Roger LeRoch. Previewed in N.Y., March 31, '51. Running time, **86 MINS.**

(*English narration and titles*)

The heroism of a French Battalion during the Korean War is graphically depicted in this French - made semi-documentary It was filmed under the auspices of the French Ministry of Defense with the cooperation of the surviving officers of the French forces of the United Nations in Korea.

With an English narration and English titles where French is spoken, the picture is a sock contribution to the unsung heroes of the United Nations who defended the free world in the rugged terrain of Korea. Picked up by Loew's International for distribution in the foreign market, it's being handled domestically by Tudor Pictures. Why Loew's saw fit not to handle the picture in the U.S. is a mystery, for it's an excellent film, well suited for co-feature billing in general situations in the U.S. With the first opening scheduled for the Paris Theatre, N.Y., it seems to be headed for art house booking. It deserves wider circulation, for it will give many citizens a realization for the first time the difficulties faced by the UN forces in Korea.

It's not all documentary, for a story-line has been introduced. The war in Korea is seen through the eyes of a young lieutenant just out of France's West Point. To his disappointment, he is made a liaison officer in comparatively safe Seoul. This gives the camera a chance to roam about the embattled city, capturing poignantly the faces of the Korean people and especially the children, the real victims of a devasting war.

Moving up to the front, the young looey is faced with the problem of overcoming the resentment of hardened professional soldiers who have already been through numerous combat adventures. Under battle conditions, the hardly-dry-behind-the-ears officer proves his mettle and finally wins the acceptance of his men.

The battle footage is amazing, being taken under actual combat conditions. (Two of the photographers assigned to the task met their death). The battalion's assault of Heartbreak Ridge (Crevecour) is as tense and exciting as any dreamed up piece of fiction. The audience will live with the French soldiers through every step of the dangerous assault.

A large share of the credit goes to the cameramen for the exceptional color photography. The realism is breathtaking. They have filmed the Korean terrain, the battle sequences, the rest camps, the leaves in Japan, the scenes in the dugouts and aid stations with a touch that can't be beat. This is a fine tribute to the French troops who fought in Korea as well as to all soldiers who have been in combat. *Holl.*

As Long as They're Happy
(Songs)
(BRITISH-COLOR)

Filmization of a London legit hit; stout to fair for local market with limited overseas prospects.

London, March 15.

GFD release of J. Arthur Rank-Raymond Stross production. Stars Jack Buchanan, Janette Scott, Jean Carson, Brenda de Banzie. Directed by J. Lee-Thompson. Screenplay, Alan Melville from play by Vernon Sylvaine; camera, Gilbert Taylor; editor, John Guthridge; music, Sam Coslow. At Odeon, Leicester Square, London. Running time, **95 MINS.**

John Bentley ....Jack Buchanan
Gwen ....Janette Scott
Pat ....Jean Carson
Stella ....Brenda de Banzie
Corinne ....Susan Stephen
Bobby Denver ....Jerry Wayne
Pearl ....Diana Dors
Barnaby ....Hugh McDermott
Dr. Schneider ....David Hurst
Mrs. Arbuthnot ....Athene Seyler
Linda ....Joan Sims
Peter ....Nigel Green
Mavis ....Dora Bryan
Gilbert Harding ....Gilbert Harding
Barmaid ....Joan Hickson
1st Bobbysoxer ....Susan Lyall-Grant
2nd Bobbysoxer ....Jean Aubrey
French Sargeant ....Peter Illing
Woman ....Edie Martin
Ship's Purser ....Arnold Bell
Miss Prendergast ....Pauline Winter
Party Girl ....Hattie Jacques

Generously adapted from the West End stage hit of a couple of seasons back, "As Long As They're Happy" has been embellished with high quality production values to give it broader and more popular appeal. Its main farcical theme, however, remains unchanged. While it may be expected to register in the home market, this has restricted prospects overseas, particularly in the U.S. Marquee values are limited.

In transferring the original Vernon Sylvaine piece to the screen, Alan Melville's screenplay takes full advantage of the opportunities of a wider canvas. In the original much of the impact made by a Hollywood cry crooner on a middleclass London family was suggested. Here, it is told with full force in scenes which are reminiscent of the bobbysox demonstrations witnessed here in the past few years.

Jack Buchanan repeats his original stage role as the stockbroker head of the family whose wife and three daughters are overwhelmed by the arrival of the crooner at their suburban home. The youngest (Janette Scott) is full of adoration; her elder sister (Jean Carson), a Parisienne existentialiest, is full of admiration, while their mother (Brenda de Banzie) sees the chance of some honest fun at the expense of her staid husband. Around these characters, the plot develops into a hearty and good-humored romp, without much attention to storyline.

Nine songs by Sam Coslow get full treatment and although production values are toned down, they strike an effective note. Jerry Wayne, who has the dominant role of the crooner, does four of the numbers, one of which is shared by Jack Buchanan. He is a positive asset and sells the tunes with a striking combination of vocal prowess and personal charm. Fortunately he doesn't try too seriously to emulate more famous lachrymose warblers. Buchanan's performance hits a breezy note.

Jean Carson, who does a couple of numbers with great effect, always looks attractive, but Janette Scott is too repetitive as the adoring teenager. Susan Stephens has a negative part as a third sister, but there is a delightful guest bit by Diana Dors. Joan Sims is the epitome of the stock screen maid.

J. Lee-Thompson has directed the farce vigorously, with excellent color lensing by Gilbert Taylor. Other technical credits attain good average standard.
Myro.

L'Arte di Arrangiarsi
(The Art of Getting Along)
(ITALIAN)

Rome, March 15.
Cei-Incom Film release of a Documento production. Stars Alberto Sordi. Directed by Luigi Zampa. Story and screenplay, Vitagliano Brancati; camera, Marco Scappelli; editor. Eraldo Da Roma; music, Aleesandro Cicognini. At Europa, Rome. Running time, **91 MINS.**

Sasa Scimoni	Alberto Sordi
Lilli de Angelis	Armenia Balducci
Baron Mazzei	Gino Buzzanca
Mayor	Franco Coop
Paola di Grazia	Luisa della Noce
Toscano	Gianni di Benedetto

Director Luigi Zampa and the late writer-scripter Vitagliano Brancati complete their trilogy on Italian foibles through-the-years with this item, somewhere between straight comedy and bitter satire. It looks like fair b.o. on the home grounds. While some of its more obvious humor will get across, the bulk translates with more difficulty, and its export chances are therefore slimmer than its two series predecessors.

Episodic story, told in one flashback, concerns the ways in which a clever Sicilian, Alberto Sordi, adapts himself to the various regimes of Italy (monarchy, socialism, fascism, clericalism) at the right time and in the proper manner, on his rise to riches. Pic ends with Sasa's demise caused by an incautious film financing deal.

Along the way, the authors have poked occasionally very bitter fun at Italian "adaptability" to one and all situations. Lack of distinct line between the amusing and the serious makes for audience confusion, with result that pic disappoints part of the time.

Sordi does a fine, restrained job under Zampa's meticulous guidance, which shows as well in the carefully reflected period atmospheres, the sharp notations on the passing historical scene, etc. Characters throughout are colorfully brought to life by a cast of lesser-known Italo thespers, all doing creditably. Other credits, both flight.
Hawk.

Les Fruits de L'Ete
(Summer Fruit)
(FRANCO-GERMAN)

Paris March 15.

CCFC production and release. Stars Edwige Feuillere. Directed by Raymond Bernard. Screenplay, Jean Marsan, Bernard; camera, Robert Le Febvre; editor, Elkind. At Colisee, Paris. Running time, **105 MINS.**

Sabine	Edwige Feuillere
Juliette	Etchika Choureau
Edouard	Henri Guisol
Claude	Claude Nicot
Melanie	Pauline Carton
Teacher	Jeanne Fusier-Gir

"Summer Fruit," a situation comedy of manners, is a bit overripe. It is a questionable U.S. entry due to lagging pacing, trite dialog and bedroom antics which lack the underlying quality of observation and point to make this arresting or appealing. This seems limited only to possible special spots.

Lack of snap and sparkle is the main -fault of this pic, its farfetched premise never getting the pace it needs. Edwige Feuillere vacillates between drama and high comedy to make the emphasis uneven, but remains an accomplished thesp and one who commands screen attention during every appearance. Etchika Choureau is a bit colorless as the daughter while Claude Nicot has the proper stance as the amorous young swain. Lensing and editing are fine as is production gloss.
Mosk.

Above Us the Waves
(BRITISH)
Dramatic filmization of sinking of the Tirpitz during last World War; documentary-like treatment, but sturdy b.o. hopes.

London, March 29.
General Film Distributors release of J. Arthur Rank production. Stars John Mills, John Gregson, Donald Sinden. Directed by Ralph Thomas. Screenplay, Robin Estridge from a story by C. E. T. Warren and James Benson; camera, Ernest Steward; editor, Gerald Thomas; music, Arthur Benjamin. At Odeon, Leicester Square, London, March 29, '55. Running time, **99 MINS.**

Frazer	John Mills
Duffy	John Gregson
Corbett	Donald Sinden
Admiral Ryder	James Robertson Justice
Smart	Michael Medwin
Abercrombie	James Kenney
Tirpitz Captain	O. E. Hasse
Cox	Lee Patterson
X2 Diver Navigator	Lyndon Brook
Ramsey	William Russell
German Patrol Boat Officer	Theo. Bikel
Hutchins	Thomas Heathcote
McCleery	Harry Towb
X2 Engineer	Anthony Newley
Chubb	Cyril Chamberlain
Andersen	John Horsley
George	Anthony Wager
X2 No. 1	William Franklyn
Winley	Leslie Weston
Officer Interpreter	Guido Lorraine

A factual, dramatic record of the sinking of the ace German battleship, the Tirpitz, during the last war, "Above Us The Waves" has that near-documentary quality which has been the hallmark of this type of British film. From a boxoffice standpoint, it could be rated a satisfactory film with strong marquee support for the domestic market. In the U.S., it has no names which will help at the b.o.

Told entirely without femme influence, "Waves" relates an epic feat by the Royal Navy which first attempted to blow up the Tirpitz with human torpedoes and then made the successful assault with midget submarines. Although lying in the shelter of the Norwegian fjords, the Tirpitz had kept half the British Home Fleet bottled up in case it came out of hiding to strike against the island's life-line. And with so many ships kept out of action, other vessels were inadequately guarded and were being sunk by Nazi destroyers.

The problem was how to reach the Tirpitz in its hideout. Aircraft had attempted bombing attacks but this had proved useless. John Mills, as a naval commander, suggested the use of human torpedoes and to prove that this is possible sticks some dummy explosives on his admiral's flagship. The actual attempt, however, proved a failure, but by the time the crew returned to England via Sweden the midget submarines were already in service.

The dramatic strength of the picture is in the two bids to reach the German battleship and these aspects strongly play up the suspense angles. There is tension and excitement, even though there is no element of doubt as to the outcome. Ralph Thomas has directed these scenes particularly well and has made a worthwhile film from Robin Estridge's expert script.

Acting maintains a high all-round standard and the roles of the three skippers of the midget subs are realistically filled by John Mills, John Gregson and Donald Sinden. James Robertson Justice is admirable in a minor part as the admiral, Michael Medwin gives a standout performance as a ranking member of the crew and James Kenney has a youthful charm as a junior officer. Minor parts are intelligently played.
Myro.

Violent Saturday
(COLOR-CINEMASCOPE)

Taut and vivid meller looks to be a sleeper; good b.o. prospects.

20th-Fox release of Buddy Adler production. Stars Victor Mature, Richard Egan, Stephen McNally; also stars Virginia Leith, Tommy Noonan, Lee Marvin. Features Margaret Hayes, J. Carroll Naish. Sylvia Sidney, Ernest Borgnine, Dorothy Patrick, Billy Chapin, Brad Dexter. Directed by Richard Fleischer. Screenplay, Sydney Boehm, from novel by William L. Heath; camera (color), Charles G. Clarke; editor, Louis Loeffler; music, Hugo Friedhofer (Lionel Newman conducting). Tradeshown in New York April 8, '55. Running time, **90 MINS.**

Shelley Martin	Victor Mature
Boyd Fairchild	Richard Egan
Harper	Stephen McNally
Linda	Virginia Leith
Harry Reeves	Tommy Noonan
Dill	Lee Marvin
Emily	Margaret Hayes
Chapman	J. Carroll Naish
Elsie	Sylvia Sidney
Stadt	Ernest Borgnine
Helen	Dorothy Patrick
Steve Martin	Billy Chapin
Gil Clayton	Brad Dexter
Mr. Fairchild	Raymond Greenleaf
Bobby	Donald Gamble
Georgie	Rickey Murray
Stan	Robert Adler
Bart	Harry Carter
Mrs. Stadt	Ann Morrison
David Stadt	Kevin Corcoran
Anna Start	Donna Corcoran
Mary Stadt	Noreen Corcoran
Slick	Boyd Morgan
Mr. Braden	Richard Garrick
Miss Shirley	Florence Ravenel
Bank Teller	Ellene Rowers
Bank Customer	Dorothy Phillips
Marion, Secretary	Virginia Carroll
Sydney	Ralph Dumke
Roy, Bartender	Robert Osterloh
Dorothy	Joyce Newhard
Mrs. Pilkas	Helen Mayon
Drug Clerk	Mack Williams
Conductor	Harry Seymour
Amish Farmer	John Alderson
Signalman	Fred Shellac

20th-Fox has what looks like a sleeper in "Violent Saturday," a complex but taut melodrama about a bank robbery in a small mining town in the southwest. Producer Buddy Adler, in his first try for Fox, has turned out an ambitious and somewhat pretentious film in color and CinemaScope, but despite the encumbrances of some contrived subplots, the main action of the story stands out as a masterly piece of filmmaking in the meller department. Film should catch on to a good b.o. return.

Lensed on location in Arizona in a modern day setting, the film concerns the bank robbery planned by a cool trio played by Stephen McNally, Lee Marvin and J. Carroll Naish. As their preparations for the holdup unfold, the several subplots are set up—Richard Egan's unhappy marriage to Margaret Hayes; Victor Mature's trouble with Billy Chapin, his son, who's disillusioned because the old man fought the war as supervisor of the mine; Tommy Noonan as the married and moralistic bank manager who can't resist being a peeping-tom when it comes to Virginia Leith, a sexy nurse; and Sylvia Sidney, a librarian who resorts to purse-snatching to pay a longstanding debt.

Purpose of all the subplots is to set the stage for the holdup, where they all fall into place and are solved by the events of the holdup and what follows. They're highly contrived and unconvincing, but they do serve the purpose of giving the film a greater sense of scope and power, and they maintain interest for the most part while leading into the powerful climax of the pic.

Climax comes with the robbery itself and the getaway, which is foiled by Mature and Ernest Borgnine, an Amish farmer whose home is used as the getaway point. It's here that Sydney Boehm's screen version of the William L. Heath novel and Richard Fleischer's direction strip the action of the nonessentials and turn on the heat in a powerful windup that's worth the waiting. Fleischer's direction in these scenes is compelling, both from the staging and the camerawork viewpoints. And, paradoxically enough, the use of color and CinemaScope enhances the pic rather than detracting from it by giving the action sweep and vigor, confined though it is.

There's no one standout acting job here, unless it be Noonan's as the drooling bank manager. But McNally, Marvin and Naish are excellent and even sympathetic as the hoods, Miss Hayes convincing as the unfaithful wife, and Miss Leith full of s.a. as the nurse. Egan and Mature turn in okay performances, as does young Chapin, Borgnine and Miss Sidney, the latter in an abbreviated role. Color by De Luxe is excellent in quality, and Charles G. Clarke's camerawork is topnotch. Lionel Newman batoned an excellent score by Hugo Friedhofer.

Incidentally, the novel is being published simulatneously with the picture, something of a rarity.

Chan.

Strange Lady in Town
(C'SCOPE-SONG-COLOR)

Greer Garson as an 1880's femme medico from Boston who tames the wild west. Generally satisfactory prospects.

Hollywood, April 12.

Warner Bros. release of Mervyn LeRoy production. Stars Greer Garson, Dana Andrews, Cameron Mitchell, Lois Smith; features Walter Hampden, Gonzales Gonzalez, Joan Camden, Anthony Numkena, Jose Torvay. Directed by LeRoy. Story and screenplay, Frank Butler; camera (Warner-Color), Harold Rosson; editor, Folmar Blangsted; music composed and conducted by Dimitri Tiomkin; song, Tiomkin and Ned Washington; sung by Frankie Laine with Mitch Miller and his orch. Previewed April 5, '55. Running time, **112 MINS.**

Julia	Greer Garson
O'Brien	Dana Andrews
David	Cameron Mitchell
Spurs	Lois Smith
Father Gabriel	Walter Hampden
Martinez Martinez	Gonzales Gonzalez
Norah	Joan Camden
Tomasito	Anthony Numkena
Bartolo	Jose Torvay
Bella Brown	Adele Jergens
Karg	Bob Wilke
Hatlo	Frank de Kova
Shadduck	Russell Johnson
Scanlon	Gregory Walcott
Wickstrom	Douglas Kennedy
Gen. Lew Wallace	Ralph Moody
Billy the Kid	Nick Adams
Rebstock	Jack Williams
Dance Specialty	The Trianas

Conventionalism was the same in the early west as it was in Boston, but the 1880 land of cowboys and Indians also had a free-wheeling informality that made it an easier target for a femme medico, newly come to Santa Fe, New Mexico, from Beantown, complete with bag, pills and suffragette ideas. That's the setup for "Strange Lady In Town," and, with Greer Garson in the title role, the entertainment comes off in a generally satisfactory manner.

Producer - director Mervyn LeRoy chose CinemaScope and WarnerColor to insure full pictorial display of the outdoor backgrounds for the Frank Butler screen story. The visual values resulting from the Harold Rosson photography are among the several assets the film has to please ticket buyers. To be liked also is the title tune, sung by Frankie Laine, and the Dimitri Tiomkin score, which is robust when required and, elsewhere, full of melodic themes that linger.

To some extent, the deliberate pacing LeRoy uses in the initial half of the film to establish plot and characters lessens the overall entertainment impact, and this seeming slowness will get a mixed reaction from audiences who, aware of where the story is going, will want less delay in getting there. However, when LeRoy does cut loose with action, it is well established and all that the more avid fan could ask.

In this action category is the fight Dana Andrews, rival doc and suitor for Miss Garson's hand, has with Bob Wilke, itinerant teamster, who has come to drag away his unwilling ex-girl friend, Joan Camden, a mental patient of the femme medico. There's a high suspense in the sequence when an Apache band comes on Andrews and Miss Garson while they are riding in the desert. Action climaxes in the fight between a posse and a gang of bank robbers, among whom is Cameron Mitchell, Miss Garson's wayward brother, who listens to the pleas of his sister, against the intuition of Lois Smith, the young girl who loves him, and surrenders, only to be riddled by mob bullets.

Plot, simply, deals with a woman, unable to break down haughty Boston indifference to a femme who practices medicine, and goes west to Santa Fe where her younger brother is a cavalry officer. There, she finds prejudice, too, but is gradually breaking it down, even winning over an established, and opinionated, male doctor, until her brother goes completely bad. The townspeople tar her with the same brush of wickedness, but the male doctor and the unprejudiced Mexicans and Indians among whom she has worked defy public opinion and keep her with them.

Miss Garson does a job that will satisfy her following in portraying the title role. She maintains a ladylike dignity, a sort of grand dame quality, even in the more hail - fellow - well - met sequences, without necessarily seeming stiff or assuming a looking-down-the-nose attitude. The other characters are more free-wheeling, lending themselves to the flamboyance supplied by Andrews, Mitchell and Miss Smith. The two male stars are good, and Miss Smith, who lifted a small spot in Warner's "East of Eden," gives a virtually perfect portrayal of a young girl, merging into womanhood but who has not yet shaken off the ties to adolescence.

Walter Hampden, desert priest and operator of a small hospital in which Miss Garson works, is capable, and Gonzales Gonzales supplies some Latin chuckles as an aide to Mitchell. Miss Camden does well as the mentally unbalanced patient, as do Anthony Numkena, blind Mexican boy healed by Miss Garson, and Jose Torvay as his grateful father. Others supply the necessary color to character parts. Numkena, and several other juves raise sweet voices in religious music and there's a fiesta dance specialty by the Trianas that has color.

Brog.

The Looters

Modern-day outdoor thriller, modestly entertaining filmfare for programmer playdates.

Hollywood, April 11.

Universal release of Howard Christie production. Stars Rory Calhoun, Julie Adams, Ray Danton; co-stars Thomas Gomez, Frank Faylen; features Russ Conway, John Stephenson, Rod Williams. Directed by Abner Biberman. Screenplay, Richard Alan Simmons; story, Paul Schneider; camera, Lloyd Ahern; editor, Russell Schoengarth; music supervision, Joseph Gershenson. Previewed April 6, '55. Running time, **87 MINS.**

Jesse Hill	Rory Calhoun
Sheryl Gregory	Julie Adams
Pete Corder	Ray Danton
George Parkinson	Thomas Gomez
Stan Leppich	Frank Faylen
Major Knowles	Russ Conway
Lieutenant Stevenson	John Stephenson
Co-Pilot	Rod Williams

(*Aspect ratio*: 1.85-1)

Plane robbers replace train robbers in this modestly entertaining thriller and the way it goes about its melodramatics will see it through programmer bookings in the general situations.

A plane crash in the Pike's Peak region of the Colorado Rockies, where pic was filmed, sets off the story to be told in the Howard Christie production, and Abner Biberman's direction paces the plot as advantageously as possible, even though there is a lack of plausibility, keeping it from being an entirely okay show.

The script by Richard Alan Simmons, from a story by Paul Schneider sends out mountaineer Rory Calhoun and his old Army buddy, Ray Danton, now an adventurer, as a rescue team to find the plane and possible survivors. There are four, Julie Adams, model for risque art; Thomas Gomez, brokerage clerk; Frank Faylen, retiring Navy petty officer, and Rod Williams, badly injured co-pilot.

Melodramatics get into the tale through $250,000 in cash which was on the plane and which Gomez has found. Danton scents the money, too, and partners with Gomez to force Calhoun to lead them out of the wilderness, scheming to kill them all when civilization is within sight. It's a long and arduous trek, up mountain and down dale, that Calhoun leads the party, aiming via circuitous route to land the little group in an area where an Army artillery battalion will be staging target practice. Amidst salvos from the mountain battery, Calhoun and Danton have it out, leaving the mountaineer free to continue a life in his beloved hills with Miss Adams.

Satisfactory performances are turned in by the cast. Miss Adams rates special attention by virtue of a revealing getup she wears—the costuming going with her previous modelling profession being, fetching, but hardly adequate, garb for the big woods. Technical assists come over expertly, from Lloyd Ahern's lensing on down. Score supervision by Joseph Gershenson includes a melodic French tune, "Aupres de ma Blonde." *Brog.*

Bedevilled
(C'SCOPE-COLOR)

Fair chase meller with religious overtones; moderately okay for general program market.

Hollywood, April 8.

Metro release of Henry Berman production. Stars Anne Baxter, Steve Forrest; features Simone Renant, Maurice Teynac, Robert Christopher, Joseph Tomelty, Victor Francen. Directed by Mitchell Leisen. Story and screenplay, Jo Eisenger; camera (Eastman Color), F. A. Young; editor, Frank Clarke; music composed by William Alwyn, conducted by Muir Mathieson; song, Paul Durand, English lyrics by Richard Driscoll. Previewed April 4, '55. Running time, **85 MINS.**

Monica Johnson	Anne Baxter
Gregory Fitzgerald	Steve Forrest
Francesca	Simone Renant
Trevelle	Maurice Teynac
Tony Lugacetti	Robert Christopher
Mama Lugacetti	Ina De La Haye
Father Cunningham	Joseph Tomelty
Remy Hotel Manager	Olivier Hussenot
Priest, in Seminary	Jean Ozenne
Taxi Driver	Jacques Hilling
Concierge	Raymond Bussieres
Father du Rocher	Victor Francen

A chase melodrama, with religious overtones, played off against the streets and rooftops of Paris, is offered in this Metro release. Aside from the striking CinemaScope tour of the French capital, beautifully tinted in Eastman Color, the feature is in the medium entertainment class best suited for the regular program market.

Plot premise involves a young man, en route to a seminary to prepare for priesthood, with a shady lady of songs and, as the story opens, wanted for the killing of her married lover. Such a setup presents awkward problems in avoiding offense, but producer Henry Berman and director Mitchell Leisen bring it off acceptably, even though a sizeable share of the pic's audience may still get an uncomfortable feeling from the situation.

Anne Baxter is the nitery chirp, no better than she has to be to get by in life, and Steve Forrest is the young man who undertakes to protect her. The story and script by Jo Eisinger makes it rather clear that Forrest is not moved by any lure of the flesh to aid the girl. Soon the legit beginning from a simple act of kindliness boils into flight as Forrest seeks to keep Miss Baxter away from the police and the killers hired by the dead man's brother until she can be spirited out of France. During the chase sequences considerable suspense and tension develops, along with the complication of Miss Baxter falling in love with the embryo priest. He falters a bit, too, but pulls up in time to remain steadfast to a life of the cloth. Picture ends with the girl going out to face the killers and die so Forrest will be completely free of her.

Miss Baxter does her character excellently. Forrest continues to show considerable promise and his natural talent keeps his character human and believeable without stuffiness. A bit of French spice, very welcome, is Simone Renant, fashion designer attracted to the young man's good looks. Robert Christopher, with the same religious destiny as Forrest, and Victor Francen, crusty priest who attempts to keep Forrest in line during the Paris stay, are the only other important casters, although a number of smaller parts add color.

F. A. Young did the excellent C'Scope lensing, taking advantage of historic sights in Paris to dress up the footage. William Alwyn's score, conducted by Muir Mathieson, and the song, "Embrasse-Moi Bien," cleffed by Paul Durand with English lyrics by Richard Driscoll, are good. So are the Helen Rose and the Jean Desses fashions.

Brog.

Napoleon
(FRENCH; COLOR)

Paris, April 5.

Cinedis release of Filmsonor-CLM-Francinex production. Stars, Daniel Gelin, Raymond Pellegrin, Michele Morgan, Sacha Guitry; features, Henri Vidal, Daniele Darrieux, Lana Marconi, Jean Gabin, Orson Welles, Eric Von Stroheim, Dany Robin. Written and directed by Sacha Guitry. Camera (Eastmancolor), Pierre Montazel; editor, Raymond Lamy; music, Jean Francaix. At Berlitz Paris. Running time, **190 MINS.**

Bonaparte .... Daniel Gelin
Napoleon .... Raymond Pellegrin
Talleyrand .... Sacha Guitry
Josephine .... Michele Morgan
Walewska .... Lana Marconi
Murat .... Henri Vidal
Eleonore .... Daniele Darrieux
Desiree .... Dany Tobin
Hudson-Lowe .... Orson Welles
Beethoven .... Eric Von Stroheim
Marie-Louise .... Maria Schell

If Sacha Guitry's previous historical opus, "Versailles," made the French audiences cry with pride for the "glory that was once France," his new pic, "Napoleon," will only lead to a few throat tightenings and scalp tickling by the music crescendos and patriotic fanfare. Otherwise, this may tire many, not looking like the phenom grosser its predecessor was. There is no doubt that the Napoleon name and grandiose bundle of star names in the film will make for solid b.o. here and it will probably make money despite its record $1,800,000 nut. Coming soon after "Desiree," this is more problematical for the U.S. An axe, not scissors, would have to be taken to this longwinded expose of the Emperor's life.

Guitry has reduced him to the status of a figure in a parlor charade game. As the wily, statesman, Talleyrand, Guitry takes the lion's share of the wit and lines as he tells a few friends about the life of Napoleon. This allows him to dip at will into the various episodes of great man's rise to power. But this also robs the Napoleon figure of its epic spirit and very rarely does an idea about the true genius of Napoleon come through. Guitry dwells on anecdotage rather than trying to reconstruct and instill the reasons and drive that made him the greatest figure of dictatorial will.

There is only a brief shot of the Revolution as Napoleon sees Louis XVII being humiliated. Then it takes him through his rise to command, various campaigns, his elevation to Emperor, and then his final defeat by the Allies, the return from Elbe, Waterloo and his last exile to Saint Helena where he dies. It ends with Napoleon's cinders being returned to France in a symbolical shot of the Emperor on his white horse coming down the Champs-Elysees under the Arch of Triumph.

Napoleon's love life is not spared including his fervent courtship of Desiree, his wooing and marriage to Josephine, and his various extra-curricular attempts to create an heir. Marie Walewska is importantly featured as well as the family and friends of the great man.

Daniel Gelin is the young Bonaparte but only has flashes of the dynamic will needed. In a ludicrous changeover, Bonaparte becomes Napoleon during a haircutting sequence. Although Guitry has taken full license, the change from the full-nosed Gelin to the blunt-nosed, brooding Raymond Pellegrin gets titters. Pellegrin manages to make a sober if not overwhelming figure of Napoleon.

Michele Morgan is a properly enticing Josephine. Lana Marconi is a flaccid Walewska and the other roles are a grab-bag of stars. There is Orson Welles as the beady eyed Hudson-Lowe; Eric Von Stroheim doing a bit as Beethoven; Jean Gabin dying and shrieking as he points at some wounded men, etc.

Color is rich and well balanced. Costumes and ensembles are well dressed giving the film nice production. Guitry has a field day as Talleyrand. Battle scenes were staged by Hollywood director-art director Eugene Lourie who has gotten some nice movement into the vacillations of the Napoleonic wars. These are kept at picturesque, stylized length. Music has the right heroic and parody aspects but is too loud at times. Editing helps keep the span and sprawling content coherent.

The bevy of star names and Napoleon theme gives this a chance in America if well plugged and cut. *Mosk.*

Conquest of Space
(COLOR)

Science-fiction entry, exploitable but most appeal to youngsters; just medium possibilities overall.

Hollywood, April 7.

Paramount release of George Pal production. Features Walter Brooks, Eric Fleming, Mickey Shaughnessy, Phil Foster, William Redfield, William Hopper, Benson Fong, Ross Martin. Directed by Byron Haskin. Screenplay, James O'Hanlon; adaptation, Philip Yordan, Barre Lyndon, George Worthington Yates; based on the book by Chesley Bonestell and Willy Ley; camera (Technicolor), Lionel Lindon; editor, Everett Douglas; process photography, Farciot Edouart; astronomical art, Chesley Bonestell; special photographic effects, John P. Fulton, Irmin Roberts, Paul Lerpae, Ivyl Burks, Jan Domela; score, Van Cleave. Previewed April 4, '55. Running time, **80 MINS.**

Samuel Merritt .... Walter Brooke
Barney Merritt .... Eric Fleming
Mahoney .... Mickey Shaughnessy
Siegle .... Phil Foster
Cooper .... William Redfield
Fenton .... William Hopper
Imoto .... Benson Fong
Fodor .... Ross Martin
Sanella .... Vito Scotti
Donkersgoed .... John Dennis
Elsbach .... Michael Fox
Rosie .... Joan Shawlee
Mrs. Fodor .... Iphigenie Castiglioni
(*Aspect ratio*: 1.85-1)

As a jet age film entry, this science-fiction feature has enough exploitation values to steer it through the general market without a crash landing. It needs the ballyhoo help because otherwise the grossing prospects are not big. Regular dual bill patrons will find it acceptable enough, but the kiddies should provide the strongest trade.

As in most pix of this type, it's the technical stuff, such as models, special photographic effects and process lensing, that scores the best. Here, these assets support a rather stodgily developed screenplay and an unknown cast, both of which handicap the George Pal production in putting its best foot forward. When Byron Haskin's direction has a chance at action and thrills they come over well, but most of the time the pacing is slowed by the talky script that James O'Hanlon fashioned from the adaptation of the Chesley Bonestell-Willy Ley book by Philip Yordan, Barre Lyndon and George Worthington Yates.

Plot time is the future, with the setting divided between a space station wheeling some 1,000 miles above earth and a flight from this floating base to the planet Mars. Some suspense enters into the footage here and there, but a feeling of expectancy isn't sufficiently maintained to keep the entire 80 minutes commanding attention. Best moments deal with a meteor hitting the space station and spilling everything before the wheel is righted, the near crash of the rocket ship with a meteor on the trip to Mars. The latter planet is a sort of red dust affair, sere and forbidding, and from which those who have survived are able to blast off for the return trip after some curiously unexciting adventures.

The rocket ship is manned by a stereotype crew. There's Walter Brooks, the commanding officer who loses his screws because he figures God didn't want man jetting off to new planets; Eric Fleming, his son, who didn't want to make the trip anyway, but who turns out to be the ship's salvation; Mickey Shaughnessy, tough old master sergeant, devoted to the c.o.; Phil Foster, a wise-cracking Brooklynite, and Benson Fong and Ross Martin, UN personnel. These and others in the cast are acceptable in undemanding roles.

The real stars are the props and lensing, supplied in the latter instance by Lionel Lindon on the regular Technicolor photography, Farciot Edouart on process, John P. Fulton, Irmin Roberts, Paul Lerpae, Ivyl Burks and Jan Domela on special photographic effects, and Chesley Bonestell's astronomical art. The art direction by Hal Pereira and Joseph MacMillan; set decorations by Sam Comer and Frank McKelvy; sound by Harold Lewis and Gene Garvin, and the score by Van Cleave are among other top assets. *Brog.*

Cell 2455, Death Row

Film version of Caryl Chessman book with good b.o. potential in program and action markets.

Columbia release of Wallace MacDonald production. Stars William Campbell, Robert Campbell; features Marian Carr, Kathryn Grant, Harvey Stephens. Directed by Fred F. Sears. Screenplay, Jack De Witt, based upon book by Caryl Chessman; camera, Fred Jackman Jr.; editor, Henry Batista; music, Mischa Bakaleinikoff. Tradeshown N.Y., March 17, '55. Running time, **77 MINS.**

Whit .... William Campbell
Whit, as a boy .... Robert Campbell
Doll .... Marian Carr
Jo-Anne .... Kathryn Grant
Warden .... Harvey Stephens
Hamilton .... Vince Edwards
Serl .... Allen Nourse
Hallie .... Diane De Laire
Whit, as a young boy ...... Bart Bradley
Al .... Paul Dubov
Nugent .... Tyler Mac Duff
Monk .... Buck Kartalian
Blanche .... Eleanor Audley
Hatcheck Charlie .... Thom Carney
Lawyer .... Joe Forte
Judge .... Howard Wright
Superior Guard .... Glenn Gordon
Sonny .... Jimmy Murphy
Tom .... Jerry Mickelsen
Bud .... Bruce Sharpe
Skipper Adams .... Wayne Taylor

"Cell 2455, Death Row," story of condemned rapist Caryl Chessman, comes to the screen as a depressing case history of a youth who went wrong. Obviously it has strong exploitation possibilities which exhibitors will find useful, and these will tend to offset the film's lack of marquee values. But for the most part this Columbia release will find its b.o. potential confined to the program and action markets.

For although Chessman's attempts to escape the gas chamber for the last six years have been well publicized in the press and in his own book, the drama surrounding his circumstances falls far short of being a gripping human documentary in this Wallace MacDonald production. The Jack De Witt screenplay fails to probe the inner reasons for Chessman's life of crime and resorts to a long flashback of incidents which brought him to San Quentin's death row.

To De Witt's credit he never makes the character a sympathetic one. As portrayed by William Campbell (as Chessman over 18) and Robert Campbell (Chessman as a teenager), the role first comes off as a study of an incorrigible kid—and later of a youth defiant of society's laws. Much of the background and story is explained through the device of narration as William Campbell reflects while pacing his cell.

However, the criminal career of cell 2455's occupant proves to be such a senseless round of car thefts, stickups and hijacking that one wonders what mental quirk was behind all this. Little is done to establish the motivation especially in view of the elder Campbell's comment that the individual has himself to blame and not environment or other factors.

The Campbells, who head a long cast, are effective as the tough kid who couldn't go straight but wised up in death row. Okay support is provided by Marian Carr, as a blowzy moll; Kathryn Grant, teenage version of a moll, and Harvey Stephens as the San Quentin warden. Among those who register in lesser roles are Allen Nourse, Diane De Laire and Vince Edwards.

Direction of Fred F. Sears, although minimizing the psychological aspects, handles the many action sequences with finesse. Fred Jackman Jr.'s black-and-white photography is a plus as is the tight editing of Henry Batista. Music conducted by Mischa Bakaleinikoff is in keeping with the grim mood of the subject, and other technical credits measure up. Producer MacDonald's physical trappings bespeak a modest budget. *Gilb.*

Dial Red O

Program meller with Bill Elliott out of buckskins and into civvies in lightweight lowercase offering.

Hollywood, April 11.

Allied Artists release of Vincent M. Fennelly production. Stars Bill Elliott; features Keith Larsen, Helene Stanley, Paul Picerni. Written and directed by Daniel B. Ullman. Camera, Ellsworth Fredricks; editor, William Austin; music, Marlin Skiles; jazz sequences by Shorty Rogers and His Giants. Previewed April 7, '55. Running time, **63 MINS.**

Lieut. Flynn .... Bill Elliott
Wyatt .... Keith Larsen
Connie .... Helene Stanley
Roper .... Paul Picerni
Lavalle .... Jack Kruschen
Gloria .... Elaine Riley
Sgt. Colombo .... Robert Bice
Deputy Clark .... Rick Vallin
Major .... George Eldredge
Deputy Morgan .... John Phillips
Mrs. Roper .... Regina Gleason
Doctor .... Rankin Mansfield
Reporter .... William J. Tannen
Photographer .... Mort Mills
(*Aspect ratio*: 1.85-1)

Bill Elliott, stalwart of the plains, doffs his buckskins for civies in this modern-day melodrama. Results are lightweight but passable for lowercase bookings in the programmer market.

The "Dial Red O" title on the meller might indicate there are some Communists lurking in the screen story fashioned by director Daniel B. Ullman, but all it means is call the operator when you need the sheriff's office. In this case,

Elliott portrays a lieutenant in the sheriff's department who is called in when an ex-serviceman from the psychiatric ward of a veterans' hospital goes looking for the wife who has divorced him.

Keith Larsen is the young man who goes over the fence, but all he wants to do is to talk to Helene Stanley, the ex-spouse, not kill her as the authorities fear. She does get bumped off, though, by Paul Picerni, her married boyfriend who resents the idea that she has become pregnant. This leaves Larsen in a bad spot, he's jailed and then escapes, having figured out who the real killer is almost before Elliott can arrive at the same conclusion. Elliott manages to arrest Picerni in time to prevent Larsen from really becoming a murderer.

Elliott is his customary taciturn self as the sheriff, doing okay without his horse and chaps. Larsen, Miss Stanley, Picerni, Jack Kruschen, a gabby writer; Elaine Riley, femme deputy, and others in the cast do what is expected of them adequately.

Lensing by Ellsworth Fredricks and the other technical contributions are satisfactory, as is the score by Marlin Skiles and the jazz backgrounds done by Shorty Rogers and His Giants. *Brog.*

The Land
(Zemlya)
(RUSSIAN-COLOR)

Artkino release of Kiev Studios production. Stars N. Uzhvy, V. Sokirko. Directed by A. Buchma, A. Shvachko. Screenplay by Shvachko from the novel by Olga Kobylianskaya; camera, N. Slutsky; music, B. Krizhanovsky, V. Gomolyaka. At the Stanley, N.Y., starting April 9, '55. Running time, 82 MINS.

Marla	N. Uzyvy
Ivan	V. Sokirko
Savva	P. Grubnik
Anna	T. Alexeyeva
Raklura	V. Bespolyotova
Dokia	E. Kiselyova
Onufri	P. Mikhnevich
Parasya	N. Naum

(In Ukraine; English Titles)

This is a better-type Russian screen production. Like so many of those pix turned out at the Kiev Studios, "The Land" goes in more for story, fine direction and above-par acting. And this vehicle boasts U-Color, better known as Ukraine-color. It is perhaps the best tinting to come from the Soviets, and is easily stronger than the more familiar Sovcolor. Film looks geared for top grosses in Russo language theatres.

Story of two brothers' struggle for the favored spot in a typical farmer-land owner's home culminates in the death of the older one when he returns from a three-year tour of Army duty. This is laid in Ukrainian country, with its wheat fields, hard-working peasants and familiar resentment against serving in the army because of its brutal discipline. Plot has the older brother's bride-to-be quarrelling with his young brother's sweetheart, this hassel hatching the scheme whereby the villainous youngster slays his kin in order to get a bigger share of land.

While the story, which in some respects resembles "East of Eden," in its rough detail does not represent much, Director A. Shvachko and A. M. Buchma have contrived to make it a surprisingly gripping pic. Shvachko also did the screenplay from the novel by Olga Kobylianskaya, managing to get considerable action into a somewhat methodical plot. Although much detailed, graphic description is given the sequences in the army barracks, the actual slaying of the older brother never is shown. **Rather, the director has the body found in the woods and concentrates in depicting the family grief over his murder.**

Best performances are turned in by N. Zzhvy and V. Sokirko, as the sweetheart and the other brother, respectively; P. Grubnik, and T. Alexeyeva. But even the smallest bit role is well taken.

Camerawork of N. Slutsky is superb, some of his color landscape shots being almost like a painter's masterpiece. B. Krizhanovsky and V. Gomolyaka have provided a splendid, stirring musical score. *Wear.*

Les Chiffonniers D'Emmaus
(The Ragpickers of Emmaus)
(FRENCH)

Paris, April 5.

Cocinor release of Cocinor-Abeille-Nordia Films production. Stars Gaby Morlay. Directed by Robert Darene. Screenplay, Rene Barjavel, Francois Patrice, Marie D'Hyvert from novel by Boris Simon; camera, Jean Bourgoin; editor, Raymond Lamy. At Balzac, Paris. Running time, 110 MINS.

Abbe Pierre	Andre Reybaz
Mademoiselle	Gaby Morlay
Pierre	Bernard Lajarrige
Thomas	Pierre Mondy
Djibouti	Yves Deniaud
Philippe	Pierre Trabaud
Mother	Madeleine Robinson

This pic is a timely narrative based on the career of the Abbe Pierre (Andre Reybaz) whose work in saving dispossessed people and families, during the cold winter of '53, resulted in worldwide pride and interest in his cause. Film concerns only the Abbe's work in setting up a center for the homeless and derelict. Film is more for the few specialized spots, and church showing rather than elsewhere due to its documentary and surface treatment.

Film shows the Abbe taking over an old mansion for tramps. Here a colorful crew gathers with a punchy fighter, an ex-convict, an ex-soldier, a suicidal old man and other lowlife figures. How the Abbe carries on his work and close-ups of the internal conflicts of some ex-tramps forms the main part of the yarn.

Director Robert Darene has avoided the mawkish, and turned a tearjerker story into a well-made film. It lacks the drama and tug it would have had if one character were treated thoroughly. Most of the large, expert cast worked at special scale, and most of the proceeds will go the Abbe's foundation.

Lensing and editing are firstrate and acting is fine as a whole. Andre Reybaz is properly restrained and luminous as the Abbe. Nice portraits also are etched by Pierre Trabaud, as the hot headed ex-con; Charles Moulin, the violent but generous boxer, and Gaby Morlay, as the imperious assistant of the Abbe. *Mosk.*

The Safety Match
(RUSSIAN—COLOR)

Artkino presentation of Sovexportfilm production. Stars A. Gribov and A. Popov. Directed by K. Yudin. Screenplay, N. Erdman, based on a story by Anton Chekhov; camera (Sovcolor), I. Gelein and V. Zakharov; music, V. Shirnsky. Previewed at Stanley Theatre, N.Y., March 25. Running time, 55 MINS.

Shubikov	A. Gribov
Dyukovsky	A. Popov
Police Captain	M. Yanshin
His Wife	M. Kuznetsova
Klauzov	M. Nazvanov
His Sister	K. Tarasova
Psekov	N. Gritsenko
Yefrem	N. Kurochkin
Nicholas	V. Kolchin
Akulina	T. Nosova
The Doctor	V. Pokrovsky
Chief of Police	G. Georgiu

(In Russian, English Titles)

Bumbling provincial officials get the going-over in the Soviet import based on Chekhov's "The Safety Match." The satirical short story has been transferred to the screen with a light touch. This, in itself, is a departure from the usual heavy-handed Russian films extolling the virtues of cooperative farm living. In Chekhov, the Soviet film industry has apparently found a source of material that doesn't run counter to the country's propaganda line and yet can be chalked up as entertainment fare.

"The Safety Match," the principal clue in this comedy with murder overtones, relates the efforts of a farm community magistrate and his eager-beaver assistant to uncover the murderer of a missing landowner. Although the corpus delicti is not uncovered, the "detectives" lose no time in concocting fantastic motives and accusations based on an analysis of some meager clues. The "victim" is found very much alive, holed up with the wife of a police official.

The performances, especially that of A. Gribov, as the magistrate, and A. Popov, as his aide, are in keeping with the flavor of the story. The rest of the cast also carries out the assignments well. K. Yudin's direction has the right touch and the technical aspects, including the Sovcolor, come over satisfactorily. *Holl.*

Ingrid—Die Geschichte Eines Fotomodells
(Ingrid—Story of a Model)
(GERMAN)

Berlin, April 5.

Schorcht release of Filmaufbau production. Stars Johanna Matz and Paul Hubschmid. Directed by Geza Radvanyi. Screenplay, Geza Radvanyi, Gerda Corbett and Joachim Wedekind; camera, Richard Angst; music, Hans Martin Majewski. At the Kiki, Berlin. Running time, 112 MINS.

Ingrid	Johanna Matz
Robert	Paul Hubschmid
Walter	Paul Edwin Roth
Hanne, Ingrid's Sister	Erni Mangold
D'Arrigo	Louis de Funes
Directrice	Alice Treff
Herr Moga	Josef Offenbach
Ingrid's uncle	Franz Schafheitlin
Ingrid's Aunt	Elly Burgmer

The title is slightly misleading. This is not a film in the usual "boy meets girl" tradition but one that tells about a young girl in postwar Germany—and more or less the story of thousands of them. Unconventionally directed by Hungarian-born Geza Radvanyi (his first German venture), pic is remarkably realistic. Partly very impressive, occasionally it is rather confusing. Cast and title will guarantee good returns here and this may also have some chance in the foreign market. The names of Paul Hubschmid (in Hollywood: Paul Christian) and Johanna Matz (who recently marked her U.S. film debut in "They Were So Young") may help.

Johanna Matz, after having lived in a German postwar refugee camp, comes to the big city and finds a job as seamstress. She eventually becomes a successful mannequin. Her affair with a man finally ends happily after a split. However, it is not the conventional finis as she more or less decides to live with him without illusions.

Geza Radvanyi avoids also any cliche stuff in his direction, not sticking too much to the script. The results are not always convincing, but certainly interesting. Scenically, his film is very impressive.

Acting is good. Comely Miss Matz gives a warm performance as the disillusioned girl. Hubschmid, her lover, is convincing although a bit too irresistible. Paul Edwin Roth is sympathetic as the other man in her life. Very good support is given by others.

Technical contributions are firstrate, especially the brilliant camerawork by Richard Angst. Hans Martin Majewski's score is also noteworthy. Pic easily could stand some cutting. *Hans.*

Escuela de Vagabundos
(School for Tramps)
(MEXICAN)
(Songs)

Mexico City, April 5.

Distribuidora Mexicana de Peliculas release of a Diana Films production. Stars Pedro Infante and Miroslava; features Oscar Pulido, Blanca de Castejon, Anabel Gutierrez. Directed by Rogelio Gonzalez. Cameraman, Rosalio Solan; screenplay, Fernando de Fuentes, Paulino Masip; music, Manuel Esperon. At Cine Mexico, Mexico City. Running time, 100 MINS.

This pic drew 245,700 cash customers (very big here for any film) during its first six solid weeks on opening playdate here. Production achieves its sole goal in order to entertain with the maximum amount of laughter. Film is carried by Pedro Infante almost by himself. He is in top voice and handily sells his vocal wares. He has a great co-star in the late Mirosalva. She's exceptional in traditional femme wear.

The full technical staff delivers well, without anybody taxing their mental capacities. Scripters Fernando de Fuentes and Paolino Masip, readily admit that the story is not much more than a modern Mexicanization of that U.S. oldie, "His Excellency, The Tramp." Infante and Miroslava delight as well as songs and music serve well in the presentation of family life in wealthy Mexican home of today. All this makes "Tramps" worth seeing. *Grah.*

Die Stadt Ist Voller Geheimnisse
(The Town Is Full Of Secrets)
(GERMAN)

Berlin, April 5.

Europa release of Real production. Stars Carl Ludwig Diehl, Annemarie Dueringer, Paul Hoerbiger. Directed by Fritz Kortner. Screenplay, Fritz Kortner and Curt J. Braun, adapted from same-titled stageplay by Curt J. Braun; camera, Albert Benitz; music, Michael Jary. At Studio, Berlin. Running time, 100 MINS.

Professor Siebrecht	Carl Ludwig Diehl
Ernie Lauer	Annemarie Dueringer
Dr. Guenther	Werner Fuetterer
Herbert Klein	Paul Hoerbiger
Gerhard Scholz	Adrian Hoven
Susi Ecker	Bruni Loebel
Karina	Lucie Mannheim
Boehnke	Walther Suessenguth
Paula	Margot Trooger
Frida Binder	Grete Weiser

Fritz Kortner's first directorial job of a German postwar pic turns out to be a remarkably good one. Admittedly, there are several deficiencies along the line but it has refreshing individuality which will even keep the interest of many patrons. The marquee value of an all-star cast will be a good selling asset here. Elsewhere, chances for some arty spots are rated okay.

Screenplay by Kortner and Curt J. Braun, based on latter's same-titled stageplay of the same name, takes its action from a medium-sized German factory which suddenly has to shut down because of financial troubles. It then centers around a dozen factory employees, each one's private life being unfolded in episodic manner. The end sees the factory owner, persuaded by his daughter, resuming operations after one of his employees has committed suicide, indirectly because of the factory shutdown.

There are quite a number of realistic and humanly interesting sequences in this film. Unfortunately, the pic attempts to cover too much, occasionally resulting in jerkiness. Despite this, Kortner's film must be regarded as above the German average.

The acting is unusually convincing, Kortner's handling of the players being excellent. Curiously, the most remarkable performance is given by the story's most uninteresting person, Grete Weiser, whose portrayal of a self-talking charwoman is virtually a little masterpiece. Also the others come off well, including Paul Hoerbiger, Erich Schellow, Annemarie Dueringer and the late Wilfried Seyferth.

Technical aspects are only fair. Editing could have been tighter. Although the atmosphere is in general realistical, camerawork is not imaginative enough. The score is average, and production dress adequate. *Hans.*

Le Ragazze Di Sanfrediano
(The Girls of San Frediano) (ITALIAN)

Rome, April 5.
Lux Film production and release. Stars Antonio Ciffariello, Rossano Podesta, Corinne Calvet. Directed by Valerio Zurlini. Screenplay, Leonardo Benvenuti, Piero DeBernardi from novel by Vasco Pratolini; camera, Gianni di Venanzo; music, Mario Zafred; editors, Mario Benotti, Elena Zanoli. Previewed in Rome. Running time, 102 MINS.
Bob .... Antonio Ciffariello
Tosca .... Rossano Podesta
Ivce .... Corinne Calvet
Mafalda .... Giovanna Ralli
Gina .... Marcella Mariani
Silvana .... Giulia Robini
Loretta .... Luciana Liberati

Valerio Zurlini has turned out a sleeper of sorts with "Sanfrediano," his first feature megging effort. Pic is a lightweight, well-paced comedy based on a w.k. novel by Vasco Pratolini. Combo of title, names, and especially word-of-mouth should rate this one pleasing returns. It has U.S. chances.

Story is fragmentary, though generally well-knit, and concerns the adventures, with various gals of various types, of a Florentine Don Juan—a mechanic. The lure of the opposite sex is irresistible, and he goes from his fiery, melodramatic steady, Tosca (Rossana Podesta), to a chorus girl, then to a schoolteacher and finally to a chic dress designer (Corinne Calvet), with nary a thought to the gal downstairs (Marcella Mariani). Last femme is the only one to really love him.

Tale is played for laughs and forms a good combo of real-life setting with popular general audience entertainment. Youthful spirit of performers, and able direction of Zurlini, as well as a solid script, camerawork and outstanding musical backing by Mario Zafred follow through in the lighthearted vein to top results.

Gals are all lookers of varied types, and act out roles capably, but top honors go to Antonio Ciffariello, who socks across his lady-killer part to become one of Italy's most promising young performers. Lux has given the pic, entirely shot on location in Florence, solid production backing, and deserves credit for its encouragement of the young talent so favorably showcased here. *Hawk.*

Lady and the Tramp
(C'SCOPE-COLOR-SONGS)

Walt Disney returns to his cartoon homegrounds via a dog story with a sturdy boxoffice punch line.

Buena Vista release of Walt Disney production. Associate producer, Erdman Penner; directors, Hamilton Luske, Clyde Geronimi, Wilfred Jackson. Directing animators, Milt Kahl, Frank Thomas, Ollie Johnston, John Lounsbery, Wolfgang Reitherman, Eric Larson, Hal King, Les Clark. Story, Penner, Joe Rinaldi, Ralph Wright, Don DaGradi; based on an original by Ward Greene; songs, Peggy Lee and Sonny Burke; musical score, Oliver Wallace; editor, Don Halliday. Previewed at Beekman Theatre, N.Y., April 15, '55. Running time, 75 MINS.
VOICES
Darling, Peg, Si and Am ..... Peggy Lee
Lady .... Barbara Luddy
Tramp .... Larry Roberts
Jock, Bull, Dachsie .... Bill Thompson
Trusty .... Bill Baucom
Beaver .... Stan Freberg
Aunt Sarah .... Verna Felton
Boris .... Alan Reed
Tony .... George Givot
Toughy, Professor ..... Dallas McKennon
Jim Dear .... Lee Millar
The Mello Men
(Aspect ratio: 2.55-1)

A delight for the juveniles, lots of fun for adults and a good money-maker for most situations, "Lady and the Tramp" marks Walt Disney's return to the cartoon arena where he's scored many previous conquests. This is the first animated feature in Cinema-Scope and the wider canvas and extra detail work reportedly meant an additional 30% in negative cost. It was a sound investment; the pictorial values thus achieved give the entry greater stature production-wise and more entertainment impact.

Disney's stable of imaginative characters is well enhanced with "Lady & Tramp." This time out the producer turns to members of the canine world and each of these hounds of Disneyville reflects astute drawing-board knowhow and richly-humorous invention. This, of course, paves the way for merchandising tieups which make for an additional boxoffice bolstering factor. The songs by Peggy Lee and Sonny Burke figure importantly, too, in the salability.

"Lady & Tramp" is suggestive in story line of soap opera, with a pedigree, and with the comedy touches, which are characteristic of Disney product, in abundance. The early reels tend to slowness but these are forgotten once the film reaches, and maintains, its merry pace short of the halfway mark.

Characters of the title are a cutie-pie faced and ultra ladylike spaniel and the raffish mutt from the other side of the tracks. In "featured" roles are Trusty, the bloodhound who's lost his sense of smell, and Jock, a Scottie with a sense of thrift. Both have a crush on Lady but her on-and-off romance with Tramp finally leads to a mating of the minds, etc., and a litter basket.

Other characters, each with its own colorful "personality," include Boris, Russian wolfhound; Pedro, Mexican chihuahua; Peg, a Pekingese with a show business background, and Bull, gruff English bulldog.

Curiously, in making a hero out of the jaunty Tramp, the writers worked in a fight with a rat that recalls to mind the terror of the bat episode in "Lost Weekend." This is for kids?

A few "humans" are sketched in for purposes of the story telling. Among them are the folks in Lady's household who are referred to by the canines as Jim Dear and Darling. This is the way they address themselves and it comes off as amusing billing. Also, there are Tony and Joe, proprietor and cook at a pizza bistro, who engage in one of the hilarious highlights of the film. In this they serve Lady and Tramp with a backyard meal replete with candle light and a serenade. Another standout item is a vocal of the tune, "He's a Tramp," by the showgirl-like Peg. It's Miss Lee's voice and she torches it with great effect.

"Tramp" and "Bella Notte" are rated here as the best numbers and figure to cop attention on their own. "The Siamese Cat Song" goes over fine in the film because of the cleverly-etched visual accompaniment. Other songs are "La-la-'u," a lullaby; "Peace on Earth," Christmas entry, and "Home Sweet Home," which is the only non-original item in the score.

"Lady & Tramp" is excellently tinted by Technicolor. *Gene.*

The Man From Bitter Ridge
(COLOR)

Good western feature, stressing story and action, for general outdoor market.

Hollywood, April 19.
Universal release of Howard Pine production. Stars Lex Barker, Mara Corday, Stephen McNally; features John Dehner, Trevor Bardette, Ray Teal, Warren Stevens. Directed by Jack Arnold. Screenplay, Lawrence Roman; adaptation, Teddi Sherman; based on a novel by William MacLeod Raine; camera (Eastman Color), Russell Metty; editor, Milton Carruth; music supervision, Joseph Gershenson. Previewed April 12, '55. Running time, 80 MINS.
Jeff Carr .... Lex Barker
Holly Kenton .... Mara Corday
Alec Black .... Stephen McNally
Ranse Jackman .... John Dehner
Walter Dunham .... Trevor Bardette
Shep Bascom .... Ray Teal
Linc Jackman .... Warren Stevens
Clem Jackman .... Myron Healey
Norman Roberts .... John Harmon
Wolf Landers .... John Cliff
Jace Gordon .... Richard Garland
(Aspect ratio: 1.85-1)

Good, albeit familiar, story values and plenty of action shape "The Man From Bitter Ridge" for a favorable reception in the general outdoor market. The framing is expert all down the line and the running time is a handy 80 minutes, giving it a booking advantage for release intentions.

Cast toppers Lex Barker, Mara Corday and Stephen McNally go about the outdoor business in the Howard Pine production with assurance under the snappy-action direction by Jack Arnold. There's no pace lag anywhere in getting onto film the William MacLeod Raine story, adapted by Teddi Sherman and scripted by Lawrence Roman. It's apt writing to meet the demands of the action fan.

Barker is quite at ease in his role as a special investigator come to Tomahawk to get the facts on stage holdups and killings that have been blamed on a group of sheepmen headed by McNally. After some run-ins with the gun-handy brothers of aspiring politician John Dehner, Barker correctly figures who's behind the looting. So does sheriff Trevor Bardette, but it remains a question of getting the goods on Dehner and brothers, Warren Stevens and Myron Healey. Some ready gun justice at the finale leaves the heavies dead and Barker ready to settle down with Miss Corday, attractive sheepherder. She gives the role zip and McNally is colorful and excellent as the sheepman who fights with and for the hero. The Dehner trio, plus henchmen Ray Teal and John Harmon, are capable at the skullduggery.

Production and direction get in quite a bit of mass motion in the outdoor scenes of battles between Dehner hirelings and the sheepmen, and Russell Metty's camera gets it all on film in Eastman Color effectively. The editing is good, the background score fair. *Brog.*

Kiss Me Deadly
(SONG)

Hardboiled private eye meller from the Mickey Spillane pen, featuring blood, action and sex for exploitable b.o.

Hollywood, April 19.

United Artists release of Robert Aldrich (Parklane Pictures) production. Stars Ralph Meeker; features Albert Dekker, Paul Stewart, Juano Hernandez, Wesley Addy. Directed by Aldrich. Screenplay, A. I. Bezzerides; from the Mickey Spillane novel; camera, Ernest Laszlo; editor, Mike Luciani; music composed and conducted by Frank Devol. Previewed April 15, '55. Running time, **105 MINS.**

Mike Hammer	Ralph Meeker
Dr. Soberin	Albert Dekker
Carl Evello	Paul Stewart
Eddie Yeager	Juano Hernandez
Pat	Wesley Addy
Friday	Marian Carr
Velda	Maxine Cooper
Christina	Cloris Leachman
Lily Carver	Gaby Rodgers
Nick	Nick Dennis
Sugar	Jack Lambert
Charlie Max	Jack Elam
Sammy	Jerry Zinneman
Girl at Pool	Leigh Snowden
Morgue Doctor	Parcy Helton
Night Club Singer	Madi Comfort
Trivaco	Fortunio Bonanova
Super	James McCallian
Old Man	Silvio Minciotti
FBI Man	Robert Cornthwaite
FBI Man	James Seay
Nurse	Mara McAfee
Diker	Mort Marshall
Mrs. Super	Jesslyn Fax

(*Aspect ratio:* 1.85-1)

The ingredients that sell Mickey Spillane's novels about Mike Hammer, the hardboiled private eye, are thoroughly worked over in this latest Parklane Pictures presentation built around the rock-and-sock character. The combo of blood, action and sex which has attracted exploitation b.o. in previous entries should repeat here for the situations that find this type of filmfare sells tickets.

Ralph Meeker takes on the Hammer character this time around under the producer-director wing of Robert Aldrich and as the surly, hit first, ask questions later, shamus turns in a job that is acceptable, even if he seems to go soft in a few sequences. Aldrich's handling is acceptable, too, although he prolongs the footage to an unnecesssary hour and 45 minutes by his deliberate pacing of many individual scenes.

Subject of the chase in the Spillane yarn, scripted by A. I. Bezzerides, is some kind of fissionable material which a gang is trying to get out of the country. At least, that appears to be what all the shooting and shouting is about because the viewer isn't taken into guarded confidence until near the footage windup and even then the subject remains rather obscure.

From the time Hammer picks up a half-naked blonde on a lonely highway he's in for trouble. Before much footage has passed, the girl is killed and he nearly so in an arranged accident. This gets his curiosity aroused and he sets about trying to unravel the puzzle. The trail leads to a series of amorous dames, murder-minded plug-uglies and dangerous adventures that offer excitement but have little clarity to let the viewer know what's going on. Finish takes place at a beach house, where a curious blonde opens the Pandora box protecting the fissionable substance and everything goes up in flames, except Hammer and his warm brunette secretary, who manage to escape.

Albert Dekker is the top heavy, seen through all but a few closing scenes as no more than a pair of suede shoes and striped britches, while Paul Stewart is more out in the open as the boss of the gang carrying out Dekker's orders. Wesley Addy is an FBI man. For femme companions, Meeker is supplied with, in order, Cloris Leachman, the first blonde; Maxine Cooper, the secretary; Gaby Rodgers, a blonde menace, and Marian Carr, a blonde who wants to be loved. For good measure, pic has Leigh Snowden standing around as a spare blonde in case she's needed. The femmes are well equipped for the s.a. demands of their parts.

Not "King" Cole sings "Rather Have the Blues," a Frank Devol tune, as a plug piece behind the titles, and later in the film Madi Comfort does right by a piece to be known as "The Blues From Kiss Me Deadly." Devol's score elsewhere furnishes the proper kind of backing to the love and mayhem. Also fitting to the meller mood is the lowkey, artfully angled and lighted lensing by Ernest Laszlo. *Brog.*

The Marauders
(COLOR)

Minor entertainment entry in the outdoor action league for programmer bookings.

Hollywood, April 15.

Metro release of Arthur M. Loew Jr. production. Stars Dan Duryea, Jeff Richards, Keenan Wynn, Jarma Lewis; features John Hudson, Harry Shannon, David Kasday. Directed by Gerald Mayer. Screenplay, Jack Leonard, Earl Felton; from the novel by Alan Marcus; camera (Eastman Color), Harold Marzorati; editor, Russell Selwyn; music, Paul Sawtell. Previewed April 11, '55. Running time, **80 MINS.**

Mr. Avery	Dan Duryea
Corey Everett	Jeff Richards
Hook	Keenan Wynn
Hannah Ferber	Jarma Lewis
Roy Rutherford	John Hudson
John Rutherford	Harry Shannon
Albie Ferber	David Kasday
Louis Ferber	James Anderson
Perc Kettering	Richard Lupino
Ramos	Peter Mamakos
Carmack	Mort Mills
Cooper	John Damler
Sal	Michael Dugan
Thumbo	Ken Carlton

(*Aspect ratio:* 1.75-1)

The outdoor action league has a minor entertainment entry in "The Marauders" and the picture will depend mostly on programmer bookings. Although in the actioner class, it's shy of enough to get by as satisfactory outdoor fare, and the scripting fails to make the motives plausible or the characters interesting.

The Arthur M. Loew Jr., production comes equipped with standard ingredients for the market, such as rugged settings, widescreen and color, that backstop for Gerald Mayer's direction of the Alan Marcus story, screenplayed by Jack Leonard and Earl Felton. The cast isn't provided with much opportunity to show to advantage, and the direction sometimes permits ludicrous overplaying among several members.

Basic plot is the one about big ranch interests trying to keep the range free of homesteaders. Why any big rancher would worry about a lone settler on the arid piece of range chosen is a question, except the homesteader has brought in a deep water well and it's just naturally against the principles of western plotting to let small farmers alone.

Jeff Richards is the homesteader and the story opens with him doing a lone stand against the gunmen of big rancher Harry Shannon. When the latter is killed, Dan Duryea, ranch bookkeeper who fancies himself a battle tactician, takes command and soon goes completely crazy. He's no match for Richards and dies along with nearly everyone else by the time the homesteader proves he intends to hold his land.

A few in the cast manage to make their performances acceptable within the limits of the material. They are Richards, Jarma Lewis, interesting newcomer, and James Anderson, her weak husband who is killed by the crazy Duryea. The latter and Keenan Wynn, gunman, are handicapped by the overdrawn characters they are called upon to portray.

Harold Marzorati's lensing in Eastman Color (Print by Technicolor) and the editing by Russell Selwyn head up the okay technical credits. *Brog.*

Five Guns West
(COLOR)

Fair bill-filler for the general outdoor action market with John Lund, Dorothy Malone as familiar cast names.

Hollywood, April 18.

American Releasing Corp., release of Roger Corman production. Stars John Lund, Dorothy Malone; features Touch Connors. Directed by Corman. Screenplay, R. Wright Campbell; camera (Pathecolor), Floyd Crosby; editor, Ronald Sinclair; music, Buddy Bregman. Previewed April 14, '55. Running time, **78 MINS.**

Govern Sturges	John Lund
Shalee	Dorothy Malone
Hale Clinton	Touch Connors
John Candy	Bob Campbell
Billy Candy	Jonothon Haze
J. C. Haggard	Paul Birch
Uncle Mime	James Stone
Jethro	Jack Ingram
Confederate Captain	Larry Thor

(*Aspect ratio:* 2-1)

Familiar names of John Lund and Dorothy Malone, plus good color lensing for widescreen, make this second offering from the indie American Releasing Corp., acceptable fare for the smaller outdoor action situation. The entertainment values aren't all they should be for the action trade, but pic should prove out for release intentions as a bill-filler.

Story concerns five convicted murderers, pardoned into the Confederate Army to catch a deserter and retrieve the gold and a list of Southern undercover agents he is carrying. The assignment is to waylay a stage on which he is travelling under Union cavalry escort when it reaches a lonely western way station. The quintet figures to best serve its own purposes by taking the gold after the deserter is caught and killed, plus doing some double-crossing among the group so the swag won't be cut so many ways.

Scripter R. Wright Campbell's plotting is acceptable but he permits his characters to talk too much. The result is that the pacing by producer Roger Corman, on his first directorial assignment, lags often enough to make the unspooling seem slow. Too, Corman doesn't supply as much drive to the action as this type subject requires so the elements of suspense and tension present in the story aren't fully realized. On the production side, film's assets include good outdoor locations and very expert photography in Pathecolor by Floyd Crosby.

Lund portrays a member of the quintet, in reality a Confederate officer posing as a killer to make sure the job's done right. When he makes his identity known at the finale, he has to take on the gang to save himself, his prisoner and Miss Malone and her uncle, James Stone, keepers of the stage station. The two stars are satisfactory and okay support is turned in by Touch Connors, Bob Campbell, Jonothon Haze and Paul Birch, members of the murderer gang. *Brog.*

Oase
(Oasis)
(GERMAN-COLOR-C'SCOPE)

Berlin, April 12.

20th-Fox release of Roxy production. Stars Michele Morgan, Cornell Borchers and Carl Raddatz. Directed by Yves Allegret. Screenplay, Joseph and Georg Kessel; camera (Eastmancolor), Adolphe Charlet; music, Paul Misraki. At Delphi Palast, Berlin. Running time **95 MINS.**

Francoise	Michele Morgan
Karin	Cornell Borchers
Antoine	Carl Raddatz
Perez	Gregoire Aslan
Doctor	Pierre Brasseur
Juan	Gil Galion
Salem	Salem
Bechara	Bechara
Hassan	Nico
Van Grouten	Charles Regnier
Gentleman	Helmut Weiss
Barber	Ulrich Beiger

"Oasis" commands special attention because it is Germany's first CinemaScope feature. Mostly shot against actual backgrounds of French-Morocco and dealing with a gold-smuggling caravan, this might have been an ideal C'Scope action vehicle had it not been based on such an unconvincing and unimaginative script. This just doesn't give French director Allegret much chance. Pic, however, has sufficient exploitation angles to make it a healthy b.o. contender here. Although it falls short of similar Hollywood items, this also may have international chances, helped by the names of Michele Morgan and director Allegret.

Story sees Carl Raddatz, a former airline pilot and now owner of an oasis, commanding a gold-smuggling caravan through the desert. Another gang takes counter-action and sets two female agents, Michele Morgan and Cornell Borchers, against him. Eventually Miss Morgan falls in love with Raddatz and confesses her intentions. The finish sees him emerge as the victor while the two women die in a camel stampede.

The script doesn't give the players much chance to show up well. That particularly concerns the performances turned in by the two femme leads, Miss Morgan and Miss Borchers. It certainly would have been a wise idea to let Miss Morgan speak her broken German in a film like this but, instead of that, she has been synchronized with a German voice which considerably robbed her individual appeal. In all, this able actress seems to have been badly miscast. Miss Borchers, who won attention for her recent British films, has a thankless part, and is not even easy on the eye. Raddatz is generally okay as is the supporting cast including several natives.

Taking into account this is Germany's first C'Scoper, the technical standards are satisfactory. The

Eastmancolor is used to advantage. Camerawork by Adolphe Charlet is mostly very good. The scenery is often eye-filling. Actually, the scenes which have no action and deal with French-Morocco alone are the best in this. *Hans.*

Foreign Films

Paris, April 12.

Le Fils de Caroline Cherie (The Son of Caroline Cherie) (FRENCH-COLOR). Gaumont release of Gaumont-Francois Chavane production. Stars Jean-Claude Pascal; features Brigitte Bardot, Sophie Desmarets, Jacques Dacqmine, Magali Noel, Micheline Gary. Directed by Jean Devalvre. Screenplay, Cecil Saint Laurent; camera (Technicolor), Maurice Barry; editor, Germaine Artus. At Berlitz, Paris. Running time, **105 MINS.**

Film is the third in a series devoted to swashbuckling and sedate sensuality during the Napoleonic wars is Spain in the 19th Century. This concerns the son, Juan, of the easy and feminine Caroline who has been brought up in a Spanish family and does not know of his heritage. However, it shows up in his easy conquest of a bevy of beauteous females on both sides. This looks in for fair b.o. here.

But for the U.S., pic is too naive and languid to make for any possible arty fare, and with its torrid love scenes snipped, there is nothing in this to make for general U.S. chances. Jean-Claude Pascal is vapid as the young ladykiller while color is properly pastel. Editing helps get some movement in the better scenes. Shadow of Martine Carol, the previous Caroline, hangs over this and is sorely missed. *Mosk.*

Paris, April 12.

Serie Noire (Black Edition) (FRENCH). Pathe release of PAC-Pathe production. Stars Henri Vidal; features Erich Von Stroheim, Monique Van Vooren, Robert Hossein, Jacqueline Pierreux. Directed by Pierre Foucaud. Screenplay, Jean Gaspard-Huit; camera, Paul Cotteret; editor, Jean Feyte; music, Sidney Bechet. At Raimu, Paris. Running time, **90 MINS.**

"Serie Noire" is the tag of a special pop edition of detective and tough guy books here. With the cycle in full steam, the title was bought for a film, but the pubs washed their hands of it, and rightly so. This is enough to give the final black mark to this type gangster films. Derivative and imitative, at best, of its superior U.S. counterpart, this might have a fair run locally. But it emerges amateurish and too draggy for the American market except for lower casing. Erich Von Stroheim brings his talent to a lesser role and credits are ordinary in this violent affair. *Mosk.*

Paris, April 12.

Les Clandestines (FRENCH). Vascos production and release. Stars Maria Mauban, Philpe Lemaire; features Alexandre Darcy, Michele Philippe, Nicole Courcel, Dominique Willms. Directed by Raoul Andre. Screenplay, Raymond Caillava; camera, Roger Fellous; editor, Barbenchon. At Monte Carlo, Paris. Running time, **9 MINS.**

This falls into the quickie exploitation genre. Gimmick of "call girls" is used to make this primarily for the baldheaded row trade. Trite scripting, lacklustre acting and direction, and the obvious cheap technical aspects make this only possible for grind spot-

ting or maybe dualers in the U.S. For the local scene, it has some fair marquee value. A taut subject is treated with many cliches. Result is a familiar potpourri of film bits with the heroine managing to keep out of bed and be saved from "fate worse than death" by the inquisitive young hero. *Mosk.*

Paris, April 12.

Les Impures (FRENCH). Fernand Rivers release of S. B. Film production. Stars Micheline Presle, Raymond Pellegrin; features Bill Marshall, Dora Doll, Daniel Cauchy, Jacqueline Noelle. Directed by Pierre Chevalier; Screenplay, Juliette Saint-Ginez; camera, Henri Alekan; editor, Monique Kirsanoff. At Balzac, Paris. Running time, **85 MINS.**

This is obviously made for exploitation purposes in treating white slavery. But it defeats its purpose by an overly familiar story which plods its way to its foregone conclusion. The virtue of the girl, sold down the river, is saved and the soiled procurer dies for the woman he has come to love.

Ordinary direction and wasting of two talented actors, Micheline Presle and Raymond Pellegrin, make this of dubious chances in America. It has a special pegging possibilities on the theme. Locally it has enough names for a fair run. For his first pic, Pierre Chevalier has given this fair mounting, but lacked the imagination to make something of this old theme. *Mosk.*

The Big Tip Off

So-so meller entertainment with Richard Conte as columnist taken in by hoodlum pals. A programmer.

Hollywood, April 26.

Allied Artists release of William F. Broidy production. Stars Richard Conte; co-stars Constance Smith, Bruce Bennett, Cathy Downs; features James Millican, Dick Benedict. Directed by Frank McDonald. Written by Steve Fisher; camera, John Martin; editor, Chandler House; music composed and conducted by Edward J. Kay. Previewed April 22, '55. Running time, **79 MINS.**

Johnny Denton	Richard Conte
Penny Conroy	Constance Smith
Bob Gilmore	Bruce Bennett
Sister Joan	Cathy Downs
Lieutenant East	James Millican
First Hood	Dick Benedict
Father Kearney	Sam Flint
Sister Superior	Mary Carroll
Hal Trenton	Murray Alper
Mrs. Marshall	Lela Bliss
Bartender	G. Pat Collins
Orator	George Sanders
Scoop	Frank Hanley
Second Hood	Harry Guardino
Mrs. Trenton	Virginia Carroll
Noah Trenton	Robert Carraher
Cleaning Woman	Cecil Elliott
Ed	Pete Kellett
Jail Guard	Tony Rock
First Reporter	Allen Wells
Re-write Man	Tony DiMario

(Aspect ratio: 1.85-1)

The routine melodramatic complications in "The Big Tip Off" make for only so-so entertainment of the programmer variety and, while some familiar names headline the cast, general prospects are mild.

Richard Conte plays a newspaper columnist taken in by a hoodlum friend, Bruce Bennett, who makes his big coin via operating a professional fund-raising organization for charity drives. The Steve Fisher screen story might have had more dramatic punch if it had not used the weakening device of flashback. However, even without that technique it is illogically plotted with formula characters and performances that get nowhere under Frank McDonald's direction. Production backing by William F. Broidy also fails to impress, even though a telethon sequence attempts to dress the footage up with some uncredited musical bits that use April Stevens, Chuy Reyes, Spade Cooley and Ginny Jackson.

Conte, a small-timer at the columning trade, gains public notice when he refuses to reveal the source of underworld tips on killings. He couldn't have, anyway, because they are anonymous phone calls planted by Bennett, who's softening the writer up for the funds to be raised via the telethon. Plenty of confusion exists as to motivations all around, and no effort is made to explain a number of angles that develop and are left dangling at the finale. Latter sees Bennett apparently knocking off Constance Smith, his social secretary who has gone soft for Conte and is ready to spill the beans, and framing the writer with some of the telethon coin. The hero muddles through, though, and so does Miss Smith for a clinch fadeout by the pair.

Cathy Downs occupies a co-star spot as a nun for whom Bennett stages a legit charity event at Conte's urging. Just how the religious angle figures here is vague although it's present throughout the footage. James Millican, police lieutenant whose lack of savvy is matched only by Conte's, and Dick Benedict, Bennett's henchman, are featured and, like the rest of the cast, contribute little.

John Martin's lensing, the editing by Chandler House and other technical credits are standard. *Brog.*

Madame Butterfly
(Italo-Japanese)
(COLOR)

Tokyo, April 19.

An Italian-Japanese co-production by Toho Motion Picture Co., Rizzoli Film and Gallone Productions. Stars Kaoru Yachigusa and Nicola Filacuridi; features Michiko Tanaka and Ferdinando Lidonni, voices of members of Teatro dell'Opera di Roma and dancers of Takarazuka Girls Opera Co. Directed by Carmine Gallone. Based on opera by Puccini. Camera, Claude Renoir; editor, Nicolo Lazzari. Tradeshown at the Italian Film Festival in Tokyo, April 13, '55. Running time, **100 MINS.**

Chocho-san	Kaoru Yachigusa
Pinkerton	Nicola Filacuridi
Suzuki	Michiko Tanaka
Sharpless	Ferdinando Lidonni
Yamadori	Satoshi Nakamura
Goro	Kiyoshi Takagi
Priest	Yoshio Kosugi
Geishas	Takarazuka Girls Opera Co.

To date this is the first definitive filmed version of Puccini's famous opera, "Madame Butterfly." Combining the talents of Japanese actors and actresses with Italian voices, Japanese art directors and set designers (with the music of Puccini played by an Italian orchestra under an Italian director) could only result in a filmed "Butterfly" which will probably never be equalled until it is made in Japan with natural sets.

But this is still a filmed opera, and one can't forget viewing it. This is no realistic motion picture, telling a plausible story. There are anachronisms throughout and librettist J. L. Long's original literary licenses with reality have been retained in the film. Still it is a far more effective presentation of the opera than could be done in an opera house. For these reasons, and because it has not the spectacle of the pic, "Aida," nor the b.o. pull of Sophia Loren, "Butterfly's" success in the U. S. will depend on the number of opera patrons who will want to see it on the screen.

A prologue sets the scene, and then the opera follows Puccini's score faithfully with few if any sets. Only one set is used, the home and garden of Butterfly overlooking Nagasaki harbor, a poorly contrived canvas backdrop. Art director Ryotaro Mitsubayashi has built beautiful interiors which follow faithfully the best in Japanese architecture. But when he steps outside to create a Japanese garden, he lets his enthusiasm for color and decoration run wild.

Greatest praise must go to Kaoru Yachigusa in the title role. An actress with little experience (she played supporting dramatic roles in the Takarazuka Girls Opera Co. prior to the pic), she turns in a stirring tour de force in her first film. Her task was triply difficult. She had to understand the western interpretation of a Japanese woman called for by the story, then mouth the lyrics dubbed in by another's voice, and all the time portray the emotions which go with the words. She is completely believable in every scene.

This opera belongs to the principal singer, and this is also a one-role vehicle in main. Nevertheless, Miss Yachigusa receives sterling support from her Italian and Japanese co-workers. If Nicola Filacuridi fails to become a true Yank, he is at least as American as most Pinkerton's seen on opera stages. He is handsome and successfully portrays a man in love with a foreign woman.

Michiko Tanaka, as Butterfly's faithful maid, makes the most of her role, perhaps the most histrionically meaty in the opera. Kiyoshi Takagi, as Goro, the go-between in the international romance, is clever. Ferdinando Lidonni, as the American consul, is a suave diplomat throughout.

Lidonni is also the only member of the cast who sings his own lines. Butterfly is sung by Orietta Moscucci, Pinkerton by Guiseppe Camporo and Suzuki by Anna Maria Canali. All have superb voices.

Claude Renoir uses his camera effectively, especially on the splendid Italian sunset in the second act. His lensing of the geisha procession is done with restraint where it might have been made into a Ziegfeld extravaganza.

Lars.

I Cover the Underworld

Minor meller for lowercase dual-dating in the programmer market.

Hollywood, April 21.

Republic release of William J. O'Sullivan production. Stars Sean McClory, Joanne Jordan, Ray Middleton, Jaclynne Greene; features Lee Van Cleef, James Griffith, Hugh Sanders, Roy Roberts, Peter Mamakos, Robert Crosson, Frank Gerstle, Willis Bouchey, Philip Van Zandt. Directed by R. G. Springsteen. Screenplay, John K. Butler; camera, Reggie Lanning; editor, Tony Martinelli; music, R. Dale Butts. Previewed April 20, '55. Running time, **70 MINS.**

Gunner O'Hara, John O'Hara	Sean McClory
Joan Marlowe	Joanne Jordan
Police Chief	Ray Middleton
Gilda	Jaclynne Greene
Flash Logan	Lee Van Cleef
Smiley Di Angelo	James Griffith
Tim Donovan	Hugh Sanders
District Attorney	Roy Roberts
Charlie Green	Peter Mamakos
Danny Marlowe	Robert Crosson
Dum-Dum Wilson	Frank Gerstle
Warden Lewis L. Johnson	Willis Bouchey
Jake Freeman	Philip Van Zandt

(*Aspect ratio:* 1.66-1)

The current shortage of secondary pix for lowercase dualer dates will be a help to "I Cover the Underworld." The Republic offering is a minor meller for fillin bookings in the programmer market, but with little entertainment even in this classification.

The budget production makes standard use of a stock story, with nothing to distinguish it from the mine-run potboiler, under the associate producer guidance of William J. O'Sullivan. The script by John K. Butler tells how a divinity student busts up some bigcity gangs by posing as his criminal twin brother. Neither the gangs nor the racket coin appear important enough and as a consequence nothing herein seems worth the effort. The pace is draggy as directed by R. G. Springsteen.

Sean McClory, who has been seen to much better advantage, does the dual role. The divinity student gets into the act when he connives with the authorities to hold the bad brother in jail beyond his parole date so the good one can talk waterfront gangs into merging into one big outfit with written records of operations. Just as this is being accomplished, the bad boy busts jail and arrives on the scene, only to die from a bullet fired in mistake by one of his own henchmen. The gangs are wiped out in one fell swoop and McClory departs to finish his cleric studies, even though Joanne Jordan, nitery chirp, indicates she's willing.

The players have little chance to do more than run through their characters. Seen with McClory, besides Miss Jordan, are Ray Middleton, police chief; Jaclynne Greene, the bad brother's moll; Lee Van Cleef, James Griffith, Hugh Sanders and others as assorted pluguglies.

Lensing and other technical credits are standard. *Brog.*

Siluri Umani
(Human Torpedoes)
(ITALIAN)

Rome, April 19.

Paramount release of a Ponti-DeLaurentiis production. Stars Raf Vallone, Franco Fabrizi: features Andrea Checchi, Enrico Salerno, Christinan Marquand, Carlo Pederzoli, Nario Bernardi, Emilio Cigoli, Franco Chianese, Elena Varzi. Directed by Leonviola. Screenplay and story, MarcAntonio Bragadin, Franco Brusati Ennio DeConcini, Carlo Lizzani; camera, Riccardo Pallottini; editor, Renato Cinquini. At Imperiale, Rome. Running time, **87 MINS.**

Competent reenactment of some Italian naval exploits of World War II follows other recent pix on wartime heroics of the Italo Army and Navy. Okay for the Italian market and a possibility for export as a straight actioner.

Action follows the familiar pattern for these pix, from early training to preparation for the big event to this big event itself. This is perhaps more straightlaced than others in the almost total exclusion of love interest and barracks humor. Interesting is the method employed by the special Italian Navy unit, spotlighted in pic, in attacking a British convoy in Suda Bay with a specially trained shock force of motorboats war-headed with an explosive charge. Aimed at ships at full speed, pilot is given last-minute escape chance only by jumping out of the speeding boat. Actual attack, on which pic is based, took place March 26, 1941.

Acting is consistently good, with all the cast underplaying. Direction and cutting could have made for a tighter, slicker effort, but manages nevertheless. Lensing, when seen here, was marred by considerable murkiness. *Hawk.*

Seminole Uprising
(COLOR)

Fair western for the program market.

Columbia release of Sam Katzman production. Stars George Montgomery; features Karin Booth. Directed by Earl Bellamy. Screenplay, Robert E. Kent, based on novel, "Bugle's Wake," by Curt Brandon; camera (Technicolor), Henry Freulich; editor, Jerome Thoms: music conducted by Mischa Bakaleinikoff. Previewed N.Y., April 14, '55. Running time, **74 MINS.**

Lieut. Cam Elliott	George Montgomery
Susan Hannah	Karin Booth
Cubby Crouch	William Fawcett
Black Cat	Steve Ritch
Captain Phillip Dudley	Ed Hinton
Sergeant Chris Zanoba	John Pickard
Tony Zanoba	Jim Moloney
Toby Wilson	Rory Mallinson
Collnel Hannah	Howard Wright
High Cloud	Russ Conklin
Malawa	Jonni Paris
Tasson Li	Joanne Rio
Colonel Robert E. Lee	Richard Cutting
Spence	Paul McGuire
Dinker	Kenneth MacDonald
Wood	Rube Schaffer
Marsh	Edward Coch

(*Aspect ratio:* 1.85-1)

"Seminole Uprising" is a fairish western for the programmer market. While this Sam Katzman production has ample action and Technicolor to heighten its visual assets, the cast is relatively unknown save for George Montgomery, who is starred. Story draws upon familiar material and exhibs will find it difficult to find a new exploitation dress for an old subject.

Screenplayed by Robert E. Kent from a novel by Curt Brandon, the film concerns some restless Seminoles who escape from a Florida reservation circa 1855 and head for wild and woolly Texas. Montgomery, an Army lieutenant is ordered to the area to round up the tribesmen, who are headed by wily Steve Ritch.

Of course, some romantic complications develop when Karin Booth appears on the scene. Daughter of post commander Howard Wright, she previously had been smitten by Montgomery but later rejected him for another since she believed him part Indian. Much footage unreels before Montgomery rescues his onetime love from the Seminoles, bags Ritch and exposes rival officer Ed Hinton as unworthy of either his uniform or Miss Booth's affections.

Director Earl Bellamy is unable to get much plausibility into the proceedings via performances of most of the players. Battle scenes, too, come off as strictly contrived in instances where producer Katzman has elected to keep down the nut by inserting old color clips of braves on the warpath. Quality of this library stuff can't compare with the fresh Technicolor lensing of Henry Freulich.

Among those who manage to give some degree of credibility to their roles are Montgomery as an intrepid Indian fighter, Ritch as the notorious Seminole chieftain and William Fawcett as Montgomery's scout. Miss Booth, a shapely blonde, isn't too convincing in the major femme role. Wright is adequate as commander of the Army post. Rory Mallinson is amply surly as a vindictive rancher and Hinton makes himself suitably unpleasant as an officer sans scruples.

Music conducted by Mischa Bakaleinikoff is a plus contribution, editing of Jerome Thoms is competent with exception of the inexpert substitution of library shots, while sound and other technical credits shape up as okay.

Gilb.

Fortune Carree
(Square Fortune)
(FRANCO-ITALIAN)
(C'Scope—Color)

Paris, April 19.

Filmsonor release of CICC-Pathe Cinema-SGC-Noria Films-Titanus production. Stars Pedro Armendariz, Paul Meurisse. Directed by Bernard Borderie. Screenplay, Joseph Kessel, Borderie from a novel by Kessel; dialog, Kessel; camera (Eastmancolor), Nicolas Hayer; editor, Mouleart. At Normandie, Paris. Running time, **120 MINS.**

Igricheff	Pedro Armendariz
Mordham	Paul Meurisse
Caid	Fernard Ledoux
Servant	Folco Lulli
Girl	Anna-Maria Sandri

Main appeal of this here is as the first Gallic Cinemascope production. It has a colorful background in the desert with the intertribal warrings and career of a soldier of fortune as actionful figures. However, its sprawling adventures and false hair-on-chest writing, makes this primarily for local and European markets. It is hard to see where this can make the grade in U.S. spots. It has the Pedro Armendariz name and might serve for secondary spots with C'Scope, locale and adventure exploitable items.

Armendariz is a hotheaded soldier who quits his training for the other side after an adventurous trek across the desert. He has time to buy a woman on the way and makes a deal with a French smuggler to get arms. However, the smuggler fails to come through, the fight is lost and Armendariz is captured.

C'Scope lensing is colorful and lush except for badly-done night for day shots. Armendariz overacts his role and bad dubbing exaggerates his play into posturing. Paul Meurisse fares better as the Frenchman while Anna - Maria Sandri, as the battered woman, does nicely. Battle scenes are well staged. Editing and general production dress is fine. But this overdone, adventure opus is too naive to be anything but a general secondary entry in the U. S.

Mosk.

The Prisoner
(BRITISH)

Alec Guinness in grim drama of Cardinal held on treason charge; star's appeal main selling factor in U. S. and likely strong enough to beat stark theme.

London, April 19.

Columbia production and release. Stars Alec Guinness and Jack Hawkins: features Wilfred Lawson and Raymond Huntley. Directed by Peter Glenville. Screenplay, Bridget Boland: camera, Reg Wyer; editor, Freddie Wilson: music, Benjamin Frankel. At Plaza Theatre, London April 19, '55. Running time, **94 MINS.**

The Cardinal	Alec Guinness
The Interrogator	Jack Hawkins
The Cell Warden	Wilfred Lawson
The Secretary	Kenneth Griffin
The Girl	Jeanette Sterke
The Warder	Ronald Lewis
The General	Raymond Huntley
The Governor	Mark Dignam
The Doctor	Gerard Heinz

Adapted and closely following the Bridget Boland play, produced in the West End last season, this British filmization retains the essentials of this stark and dramatic narrative. With Alec Guinness repeating his original role of the Cardinal held on a phoney charge of treason, the picture has potent marquee values, particularly in the U. S. His name will need to be a major selling factor as the subject-matter is too grim for general and popular consumption.

While the usual screen credits observe that the characters in the film have no resemblance to any persons living or dead, the general theme bears a striking similarity to a comparatively recent trial of a Cardinal behind the Iron Curtain. The setting of this story is not stated; there is, however, little doubt that the action takes place somewhere in Eastern Europe.

In her own adaptation, Miss Boland has broadened the canvas of her subject, particularly to include background atmosphere of unrest in the capital while the Cardinal is held without charge. Inside the jail, the pic adheres to the stage original, illustrating the Cardinal's resistance to the persuasive charms of the Inquisitor (Jack Hawkins), but eventually weakening after a long and tortuous spell of solitary confinement. Another addition is the trial sequence in which there is a full confession to charges of petty theft, blackmail, betrayal to the Nazis and treason.

Peter Greenville's studied direction is a technical achievement, although the film just fails to achieve the anticipated emotional impact. The climactic sequence in which the Cardinal is reprieved within minutes of his execution to face a bigger punishment by going back into the world after his admission is less moving on film than on the stage. The acting, however, is exceptionally high. The flawless performance by Guinness is matched by a superb portrayal by Jack Hawkins, as the Public Prosecutor. But both of these stars find their equal in Wilfred Lawson's interpretation of the jailor. It is one of the rich performances of the screen. *Myro.*

Gran Varieta
(ITALIAN—COLOR)

Italian musical vaude cavalcade with an appeal largely limited to those familiar with the language.

Continental release of Excelsa-Roma (Carlo Infescelli) production. Stars Vittorio De Sica, Lea Padovani, Delia Scala, Maria Fiore. Directed by Dominico Paolella. Screenplay, Dino Falconi, Oreste Biancoli, Vinicio Marinucci, Michele Galdieri, Domenico Paolella; camera (Ferraniacolor), Carlo Carlini; editor, Raniero Mangione; music, M. Rustichelli. At Cinema Verdi, N.Y., beginning April 9, '55. Running time 103 MINS.
Mariantonia .... Maria Fiore
Fregoli .... Alberto Sordi
Beautiful Girl .... Lauretta Masiero
Battaglia .... Carlo Croccolo
Luciano .... Vittorio De Sica
Anna .... Lea Padovani
Mizzy .... Delia Scala
The Comic .... Renato Rascel

"Gran Varieta," an Italian import, is a cavalcade of vaudeville as seen in Italy from the turn of the century to the end of World War II. Picture occasionally has interesting production values, has Vittorio De Sica and Lea Padovani as marquee lures and contains a lively score. But the general flavor of this Excelsa-Roma production is more attuned to Italian tastes than American.

Some five writers, who toiled on the script, chose to divide their subject into five episodes. Initial chapter, "A Star Is Born," offers Maria Fiore some amusing material and she portrays the role of a singer with verve and sauciness. Alberto Sordi, in the following sketch, is cast as a quick change artist who successfully woos and wins Lauretta Masiero. Its effectiveness, however, is somewhat marred by its length.

A note of pathos crops up in a bit tagged "Military Affair." Here Carlo Croccolo is seen as a performer who troupes in vaude doing a soldier characterization. Later, he's drafted and dies in an enemy attack. The point to this scene is somewhat obscure. Perhaps best of the five sequences is "The Fading Actor," which De Sica, Miss Padovani and Delia Scala brighten with some fine acting.

Story of an actor, once a star but now rapidly declining in popularity, is a familiar one. However, De Sica gets it across nicely with an excellent portrayal of the one-time matinee idol. Miss Padovani contributes a touching performance as his rejected partner who ultimately returns to comfort him. Miss Scala, whom De Sica "discoveis" as a line girl, is a cute trick who terps a snappy Charleston.

Final episode, entitled "The Censor," purports to show the difficulties producers and writers were up against during the Fascist era when entire scripts frequently were rejected due to their wrong political significance. Renato Rascel, as the comic, does as best he can with this one. He's helped on the visual side by a chorus which looks good in scanty attire.

Direction of Domenico Paolella is competent especially in the musical sequences. Camerawork of Carlo Carlini is only fair. Although Ferraniacolor, in which this was lensed, looks very good in closeups it frequently appeared out of focus on medium shots. Raniero Mangione's editing could have been tighter. The English titles are adequate. *Gilb.*

Daddy Long Legs
(C'SCOPE—COLOR—SONGS)

This musical hath charm, Fred Astaire, Leslie Caron and good business prospects.

Twentieth-Fox release of Samuel G. Engel production. Stars Fred Astaire, Leslie Caron; features Terry Moore, Thelma Ritter, Fred Clark, Charlotte Austin, Larry Keating, Kathryn Givney, Kelly Brown. Directed by Jean Negulesco; dances staged by Astaire and David Robel; ballets, Roland Petit; songs (words and music), Johnny Mercer. Screenplay, Phoebe and Harry Ephron, from the Jean Webster novel; camera (De Luxe color), Leon Shamroy; editor, William Reynolds; music, Alfred Newman; ballet music by Alex North. Previewed in N.Y., April 28, '55. Running time, 126 MINS.
Jervis Pendleton .... Fred Astaire
June .... Leslie Caron
Linda .... Terry Moore
Miss Pritchard .... Thelma Ritter
Griggs .... Fred Clark
Sally .... Charlotte Austin
Alexander Williamson .... Larry Keating
Gertrude .... Kathryn Givney
Jimmy McBride .... Kelly Brown
Ray Anthony (Orchestra).. Themselves
Pat .... Sara Shane
Jean .... Numa Lapeyre
Madame Sevanne .... Ann Codee
Emile .... Steven Geray
Professor .... Percival Vivian
Guide .... Joseph Kearns
Butler .... Larry Kent
Hotel Manager.. Charles Anthony Hughes
Mr. Bronson .... Ralph Dumke
Larry Hamilton .... Damian O'Flynn
Mrs. Carrington .... Kathryn Card
Bellhop .... Tim Johnson
Cab Driver .... Harry Seymour
Asst. Hotel Manager..... Olan Soule
College Dean .... Helen Van Tuyl
Deliversman .... J. Anthony Hughes
Chauffeur .... George Dunn
(Aspect ratio: 2.55-1)

Mary Pickford ought to get a bang out of this one. For she was the American sweetheart of an actress who suffered the orphanage hardships when First National made "Daddy Long Legs" in 1919. And look at it now: CinemaScope sound and screen, multi-hued pictures, songs and dances, all very modern design, and no one's doing a drudgery bit. (The old Fox company brought "Daddy" to life again in 1931 as a "talker" with Janet Gaynor and Warner Baxter.)

With Leslie Caron and Fred Astaire in the leads, the property has been completely rewritten and fashioned into an appealing musical. Fair-enough amounts of sparkle, bright dialog, engaging terpery, winning performances and handsome production trappings bring the entry into the good-money class.

Astaire was a good choice and works well as the undisciplined and friendly moneybags who develops a wanna-get-married crush on the girl he sends through college, this despite the acknowledged difference in age. And he's still the agile hoofer, although the choreography he and David Robel blueprinted doesn't require too robust a work-out.

Miss Caron, as shepherdess of the kids at an orphanage in France, later to become beneficiary of "Daddy Long Legs," and, too, to return his love, is beguiling all the way. This Gallic import is a pixie charmer who gives the film much of its warmth and delightful merriment, somewhat similarly as she endowed Metro's "Lili."

Thelma Ritter and Fred Clark, as social and business aides to Astaire, team up for laughs—the Phoebe and Harry Ephron screenplay has some crackling dialog—and achieve said aim in such click fashion as to suggest more combo work. Terry Moore is attractive as Miss Caron's roommate and deports suitably, as do Charlotte Austin, Larry Keating, Kathryn Givney and Kelly Brown in featured spots.

"Daddy" is real long, exceeding two hours. First few reels where-

in plot foundation is laid are slow. But even though it takes a while before full audience attention is nabbed, the editing of individual scenes is sharp and highly effective.

The dancing is imaginative and engaging, particularly Miss Caron's ballet turns which Roland Petit directed. Miss Caron does a hotsy specialty, billed "Hong Kong," that will invite wolf calls. These and Astaire's "Texas Millionaire" and "International Playboy" episodes and his teaming with Miss Caron in the "Guardian Angel" number are written in as whimsical fantasy and come off as the entertainment highlights.

Johnny Mercer's songs include "Something's Got to Give," "Sluefoot" and "Welcome Egghead," which go okay with the Astaire-Caron dance accompaniment. Standout tune is "Dream," Mercer's oldie which is given a nice reprise in the picture.

Ray Anthony's orch appears in a campus frolic scene to back Astaire and Miss Caron in the "Sluefoot" workout.

Engel's production is laid out among elaborate (but not ornate) settings and Jean Negulesco, in directing, manages to maintain interest in the story despite the many musicalized interruptions. Color by De Luxe has sharpness and brilliance. Good rating on all other credits. *Gene.*

The Shrike

Jose Ferrer and June Allyson in a mild edition of the stage hit. Good b.o. prospects with proper selling.

Universal release of Aaron Rosenberg production. Stars Jose Ferrer, June Allyson; features Joy Page, Kendall Clark, Isabel Bonner, Jay Barney, Somer Alberg, Ed Platt. Directed by Ferrer. Screenplay, Ketti Frings based on the play by Joseph Kramm; camera, William Daniels; editor, Frank Gross; music, Frank Skinner. Previewed April 28, '55. Running time, 88 MINS.
Jim Downs .... Jose Ferrer
Ann Downs .... June Allyson
Charlotte Moore .... Joy Page
Dr. Bellman .... Kendall Clark
Dr. Barrow .... Isabel Bonner
Dr. Kramer .... Jay Barney
Dr. Schlesinger .... Somer Alberg
Harry Downs .... Ed Platt
Gregory .... Dick Benedict
Ankoritis .... Will Kuliva
O'Brien .... Martin Newman
Schloss .... Billy Greene
Major .... Joe Comadore
Carlisle .... Leigh Whipper
Wingate .... Mary Bell
Miss Raymond .... Adrienne Marden
(Aspect ratio: 2-1)

Somewhere in Joseph Kramm's Pulitzer-prize winning play, "The Shrike," there is an explanation of just what sort of an animal it is. In describing the character of the femme lead, a psychiatrist, calling her a shrike, says it's "a little, soft downy bird with a long beak on which she impales her victim."

In scripter Ketti Frings' adaptation of the play for the screen, that description is still there, but the character she has etched to go with it no longer resembles it. She is now a purposeful and determined little lady, disappointed in her career or the lack of it, jealous of her husband's success in the theatre and generally more possessive than she might have a right to be—but hardly a "shrike"

This deliberate change from the original has the effect of weakening the story and softening it to the point where it at times takes on a soap-opera quality. At the same time, it removes some of the terror of the original and supplants it with a more romantic, and decidedly more pleasant, aura, complete down to a happy ending. It leaves the audience in a much happier frame of mind but at the same time knocks the pins from under author Kramm's ironic and chilling climax.

Since chances are that the vast majority of those seeing this Aaron Rosenberg production will not have seen the play, and thus will not be tempted to compare notes, suffice it to say that there is little resemblance in the spirit of the two works. "The Shrike" on the stage was taut and terrible, a man caught up in an insane web of circumstance from which he couldn't escape because of the malice of his wife.

On the screen, Jose Ferrer recreates the same character in a performance that has much understanding but rarely communicates the true terror of the predicament in which he finds himself. He's one of those virtuoso actors who fascinate with the mere lifting of an eyebrow, and his direction is full of clever touches. Yet, on the whole, "The Shrike" for the most part skims along on the surface and only in the second half reaches a couple of rocking climaxes that shake the emotions and build tension.

Opposite him, June Allyson is a wholesome charmer who somehow fails to convince. Her reactions seem barely abnormal and certainly don't even hint at a deep psychosis or the kind of mental viciousness that would be needed to give the character substance. Miss Frings, in adapting the play, has skirted the issue to a point where for the most part, she seems to defeat her own purpose.

Story has Ferrer brought to a state hospital where he is revived from a suicide attempt as his anxious wife, Miss Allyson, hovers over him. He is committed for observation. In two major flashbacks, his story emerges. He tells of meeting Miss Allyson while a struggling young stage director, of marrying her, of becoming a success and of her real, or imagined, interference with it. He details their separation and how he met another girl, played by Joy Page. In the end, refusing to return to his wife's custody, is forced to remain in the hospital. He realizes that he must pretend to give up Miss Page and show love for Miss Allyson if he is ever to be released. When he is able to leave the ward, Miss Allyson, having realized that she herself is in need of psychiatric treatment, is there waiting for him.

Miss Frings' script has reduced this material to an interesting but not overly exciting story. Even the scenes in the ward, the desperation of an intelligent man surrounded by half-sane companions, are toned down. The doctors in the hospital are shown, with one exception, in a most unsympathetic light, but here again their lack of sympathy and understanding is inadequately explained.

Miss Allyson, who wears some stunning costumes, is miscast but does what she has to do intelligently. Miss Page would appear to be a real find. Even in her small part she had a dignity that set her aside. Kendall Clark, as the sympathetic psychiatrist, comes off well and others in the cast, such as Ed Platt as Ferrer's brother, Isabel Bonner as a woman psychiatrist, Will Kuliva as a pretentious inmate of the ward and Mary Bell as the nurse all do well in the smaller roles.

Much of what's good about "The Shrike" derives from Ferrer's performance. His final bit before the doctors, when he puts across his deception of them and his wife, has the mark of great acting and holds sock impact. The scenes in the theatre, too, have merit. "The Shrike" is definitely a notch above average and a film to please many. But it could have been a lot more.

Hift.

Tight Spot

Melodramatic thriller plotted around protection of key witness against crime czar; good entry for general playdates.

Hollywood, April 25.

Columbia release of Lewis J. Rachmil production. Stars Ginger Rogers, Edward G. Robinson, Brian Keith; features Lucy Marlow, Lorne Greene, Katherine Anderson, Allen Nourse, Peter Leeds, Doye O'Dell, Eve McVeagh. Directed by Phil Karlson. Screenplay, William Bowers; based on the play "Dead Pigeon" by Lenard Kantor, produced on the stage by Harald Bromley; camera, Burnett Guffey; editor, Viola Lawrence; score, George Duning, conducted by Morris Stoloff. Previewed March 10, '55. Running time, **95 MINS.**

Sherry Conley	Ginger Rogers
Lloyd Hallett	Edward G. Robinson
Vince Striker	Brian Keith
Prison Girl	Lucy Marlow
Benjamin Costain	Lorne Greene
Mrs. Willoughby	Katherine Anderson
Marvin Rickles	Allen Nourse
Fred Packer	Peter Leeds
Mississippi Mae	Doye O'Dell
Clara Moran	Eve McVeagh
Warden	Helen Wallace
Jim Hornsby	Frank Gerstle
Miss Masters	Gloria Ann Simpson
Carlyle	Robert Shield
Arny	Norman Keats

The protection of a key witness from a crime czar's killers provides the basis for this melodramatic thriller, which shapes as a good entry for regular playdates. Topnotch trouping by such casters as Ginger Rogers, Edward G. Robinson, Brian Keith and others, an interesting plot and well-valued direction all contribute to the entertainment. Credit Phil Karlson's first class direction of the William Bowers script, taken from the play "Dead Pigeon" by Leonard Kantor.

Miss Rogers has a pip of a character and romps home with it for a huge personal success. She's the key witness, a brassy, beatup blonde snatched from a four-year stay in prison, on reluctant leave to the Federal Government to help prosecutor Robinson deport crime biggie Lorne Greene. A lot of choice lines are tossed her way, as well as to others, some with a zingy comedy cut that helps leaven the melodramatics whenever the tension is getting too tight. In fact, it's this artful balance between suspense and lightness that keeps the show rolling.

Robinson is very good as the Fed down to his last witness—the others have been bumped off by Greene's men and he's out to get Miss Rogers. Also scoring is Keith, the police lieutenant who has the double duty of guarding the witness from the killers and fighting off her breezy advances—after all, she feels like living it up a bit after four years in a manless prison. Fact that Keith also is on Greene's payroll comes as a shock midway, but it's well-established that he will turn straight at the finale to save the girl.

Producer Lewis J. Rachmil gives the picture the benefit of smart casting, from the stars on down, and generally supervises the presentation to realize on its best values. Notable in support of the three stars are Greene, the racketeer; Katherine Anderson, prison matron who dies in an attempt on Miss Rogers' life; Allen Nourse, legal mouthpiece for Greene; Lucy Marlow, a fellow prisoner; Peter Leeds, Eve McVeagh, and Doye O'Dell, the latter figuring in a stinging satire on western hillbilly video shows.

Technical support for the film is very good, from Burnett Guffey's lensing, through the George Duning score, settings, etc. *Brog.*

Top of the World

Topnotch action drama with familiar cast names and good entertainment values for regular situations.

Hollywood, April 27.

United Artists release of Michael Baird-Lewis R. Foster (Landmark) production. Stars Dale Robertson, Evelyn Keyes, Frank Lovejoy features Nancy Gates, Paul Fix, Robert Arthur. Directed by Foster. Written by John D. Klorer, N. Alaskan aerial camera, Harry J. Wild; Alaskan aerial photography, William Clothier; editor, Robert Ford; music, Albert Glasser. Previewed April 25, '55. Running time, **90 MINS.**

Major Lee Gannon	Dale Robertson
Virgie Rayne (Mrs. Gannon)	Evelyn Keyes
Major Cantrell	Frank Lovejoy
Lt. Mary Ross	Nancy Gates
Major French	Paul Fix
Lt. Skippy McGuire	Robert Arthur
Capt. Cochrane	Peter Hansen
Sgt. Cappi	Nick Dennis
Col. Nelson	Russell Conway
Capt. Harding	William Shaliert
Lt. Johnson	Peter Bourne
Brownie (The Bartender)	David McMahon
Koora	Marya Marco

(*Aspect ratio*: 1.85-1)

Regular situations will find "Top of the World" a good entry, having both the entertainment and the cast names to go top or bottom of the bill according to booking requirements. General audiences, particularly the airminded action fan, will view it as an interesting meshing of modern Air Force service in the far north with a believeable plot that does not go in for high-flung, improbable heroics.

Producers Michael Baird and Lewis R. Foster have integrated the good story and background ingredients expertly, using the budget coin smartly to get the most on the screen. Foster, as director, goes about that chore just as expertly in working from the sound script furnished by John D. Klorer, and N. Richard Nash. The cast, from toppers Dale Robertson, Evelyn Keyes, Frank Lovejoy and Nancy Gates on down, complete the excellent teamwork that made the entertainment values possible.

The service setting is the establishment of a weather post on an ice island far up towards the Arctic. Details here are handled so as to be interesting without becoming tedious, blending into and serving the personal dramatics that carry the story. Also an integral part of the plot are some survival and rescue operations that are brought off efficiently for maximum thrills, yet without unbelieveable heroics.

The personal dramatics concern a four-sided romantic problem between the principals. Robertson is a bitter pilot, divorced from Miss Keyes after a World War II marriage that ended on a tragic note. Too old for jet work, he's reassigned to Alaska to aid Lovejoy in a weather observation outfit. There he finds Lovejoy in love with Miss Keyes, now operating a Fairbanks nitery, and Miss Gates, a public relations officer at the base, in love with Lovejoy. Thanks to intelligent handling all around, a romantic plot that could easily have become a dreary soap opera never does. The problems are satisfactorily resolved during the tests the elements put the males through.

Along with the good performances of the leads there is capable support from such other players as Paul Fix, Robert Arthur, Peter Hanson, Nick Dennie, Russell Conway, William Shallert and Peter Bourne. Cameras are used effectiveyl by Harry J. Wild for the story portions and William Clothier's Alaskan aerial photography is excellent, as is the Albert Glasser score. *Brog.*

Hell's Island
(V'VISION-COLOR)

Hard - hitting melodrama with good potential for the action market.

Hollywood, April 29.

Paramount release of a William H. Pine-William C. Thomas production. Stars John Payne, Mary Murphy; features Francis L. Sullivan, Eduardo Noriega, Arnold Moss. Directed by Phil Karlson. Screenplay, Maxwell Shane; from a story by Jack Leonard, Martin M. Goldsmith; camera, Lionel Lindon; art direction, Hal Pereira, Al Y. Roelofs; editor, Archie Marshek; music supervision, Irvin Talbot. Previewed April 29, '55. Running time, **83 MINS.**

Mike Cormack	John Payne
Janet Martin	Mary Murphy
Barzland	Francis L. Sullivan
Inspector Pena	Eduardo Noriega
Paul Armand	Arnold Moss
Lawrence	Walter Reed
Lalo	Pepe Hern
Miguel	Robert Cabal
Torbig	Sandor Szabo
Eduardo Martin	Paul Picerni

(*Aspcct ratio*: 1.85-1)

This melodrama set in an exotic background carries enough interest to rate good returns in the action market. Name of John Payne should be a potent marquee draw, and use of both lush Technicolor and the fascinating scope of VistaVision, coupled with the Pine-Thomas reputation for a punchy story line, are added inducements to strong reception.

Maxwell Shane screenplay unfolds in the Caribbean port of Puerto Rosario, where the adventuring twirls around the search for a missing ruby. Phil Karlson gives narrative a hard glossing in his direction, occasionally letting down his pace but generally delivering a briskly-told tale in which capable players lend realism to colorful characters.

Payne is handed the assignment of finding the valuable jewel after it disappears following an attempt to smuggle it out of Puerto Rosario. Francis L. Sullivan, a ruthless paralytic, is his employer, who suspects that the flyer who was to have flown it to him has double-crossed the other. Payne is selected because he once was engaged to the flyer's wife, who jilted him, and it's theorized he may be able to discover the whereabouts of the gem from her.

Main events disclose that the femme actually is the heavy in the case; she engineered an attempt to kill her husband so she could acquire the gem and get his huge life insurance. Plot backfired when her husband's former partner is killed in the plane she sabotaged, and husband is sentenced to life imprisonment for his suspected crime. Payne finds himself in the center of this situation, which he finally unravels to the tune of fights and hard action.

Payne socks over a hard-hitting role in excellent fashion, and Mary Murphy is his co-star in a change of pace, taking on her first heavy role very competently. A top supporting cast is well fulfilled by Sullivan, Walter Reed, as his triggerman; Arnold Moss, seeking to help the heroine but murdered by her; Paul Picerni, her husband; and Eduardo Noriega, police inspector who helps Payne.

Top color photography is afforded by Lionel Lindon, and Hal Pereira and Al Y. Roelofs' art direction is atmospheric. *Whit.*

Murder Is My Beat

So-so melodrama with scant entertainment values, even for fill-in bookings.

Hollywood, May 3.

Allied Artists release of Aubrey Wisberg production. Stars Paul Langton, Barbara Payton; features Robert Shayne, Selena Royle, Roy Gordon, Tracey Roberts, Kate McKenna, Henry A. Harvey Sr., Jay Adler. Directed by Edgar G. Ulmer. Screenplay, Wisberg; based on a story by Wisberg and Martin Field; camera, Harold E. Wellman; editor, Fred R. Feitshans Jr.; music, Al Glasser. Previewed April 29, '55. Running time, 76 MINS.

Patrick	Paul Langton
Eden	Barbara Payton
Rawley	Robert Shayne
Mrs. Abbott	Selena Royle
Abbott	Roy Gordon
Patsy	Tracey Roberts
Landlady	Kate McKenna
Attendant	Henry A. Harvey Sr.
Bartender	Jay Adler

(Aspect ratio: 1.85-1)

The market for second features being what it is means "Murder Is My Beat" will draw more lowercase bookings than its entertainment values justify. It's a shoddily-made melodrama, scarcely meriting filling playdates or the Allied Artists releasing label.

Aubrey Wisberg produced and did the screenplay from a story he wrote with Martin Field, performing none of the chores with any distinction. Edgar G. Ulmer's direction is on the same level and, considering the assorted handicaps, it's no surprise that the cast fails to deliver. The entire affair can be chalked off as a waste of negative.

Paul Langton is a homicide detective who makes a case against Barbara Payton for the murder of her lover, found dead with his head and hands burned beyond casual identification. She's sentenced, but enroute to prison sees the man believed dead. Langton is convinced, too, and they escape the train to solve the mystery. Biggest mystery to viewers will be what all the fuss is about because the writing has no logic and motivations remain cloaked in obscurity.

Caught up in the affair with the two nominal stars are Robert Shayne, fellow officer; Roy Gordon the "dead" man; Selena Royle, his wife, and Tracey Roberts, a gal who tries blackmail and ends up dead. The technical contributions are no better than the entertainment values. *Brog.*

Moonfleet
(C'SCOPE-COLOR)

Costumed adventure feature of English rakehellies, smugglers and a small boy; plentiful action entertainment, medium b.o. prospects.

Hollywood, May 9.

Metro release of John Houseman production. Stars Stewart Granger, George Sanders, Joan Greenwood, Viveca Lindfors; features Jon Whiteley, Melville Cooper. Directed by Fritz Lang. Screenplay, Jan Lustig, Margaret Fitts; based on the novel by J. Meade Falkner; camera (Eastman Color), Robert Planck; editor, Albert Akat; music, Miklos Rozsa; flamenco music composed and played by Vicente Gomez. Previewed May 5, '55. Running time, 86 MINS.

Jeremy Fox	Stewart Granger
Lord Ashwood	George Sanders
Lady Ashwood	Joan Greenwood
Mrs. Minton	Viveca Lindfors
John Mohune	Jon Whiteley
Gypsy	Liliane Montevecchi
Felix Ratsey	Melville Cooper
Elzevir Block	Sean McClory
Parson Glennie	Alan Napier
Magistrate Maskew	John Hoyt
Grace	Donna Corcoran
Damen	Jack Elam
Hull	Dan Seymour
Tewkesbury	Ian Wolfe
Major Hennishaw	Lester Matthews
Jacob	Skelton Knaggs
Starkill	Richard Hale
Greering	John Alderson
Tomson	Ashley Cowan
Coachman	Frank Ferguson
Capt. Stanhope	Booth Colman

Costumed action, well-spiced with loose ladies and dashing rakehellies, is offered ticket buyers in "Moonfleet," and the Cinema-Scoped feature looks headed for medium returns in regular release. Film manages to be a moody thing, while at the same time ringing in enough adventure to make the unfoldment fast, and mostly interesting, daring-do escapism.

With mood and action the keynote of the John Houseman production, the direction by Fritz Lang plays both hard, developing considerable movement in several rugged action sequences without neglecting suspense. Period of the J. Meade Falkner novel is the 1750's allowing for plenty of color in settings, costuming and script development. The screenplay by Jan Lustig and Margaret Fitts, and the trouping, ply a straight course in putting the characters on screen, yet the principals in the plot are flamboyant enough to add color.

Stewart Granger was a good choice for the dubious hero of the story, a high-living dandy who heads a gang of murderous smugglers headquartering in the English coastal village of Moonfleet. Yarn opens on a Macbeth note of cold, wild-swept moors and scary, dark shadows, establishing an eerie flavor for the kickoff. Later, it reminds of "Treasure Island" a bit when Granger and a small boy, very well played by Jon Whiteley, join up in the hunt for a long-lost diamond after the youth, sent to the dandy's keeping by a woman out of his past, has ruined the smuggling racket that had proved so profitable. The two go through some highly imaginative adventures, but with Granger planning to ditch the boy. However, the finale has him, fatally wounded, using his last strength to insure the lad's safety and future well-being.

There's a racy quality to the adult romantics that may raise eyebrows here and there. Opening finds Granger making merry with a gypsy dancer, Liliane Montevecchi, and Viveca Lindfors, weirdly made up, is his moody mistress. Wanting to earn the latter status, and there is plenty of indication she has made progress, is Joan

---

Greenwood, the not-too-loving wife of George Sanders, another satin-clad crook. All of the above, plus Melville Cooper, Sean McClory, Alan Napier, John Hoyt and others add to the film's color.

Robert Planck's lensing in Eastman Color is excellent and Miklos Rozsa's score is tuned to further story mood. Art direction, settings and costumes are good. Vicente Gomez composed and played the flamenco music heard in connection with Miss Montevecchi. *Brog.*

Green Magic
(ITALIAN—DOCUMENTARY)

IFE release of Astra Cinematografica of Rome picture. Produced by Leonardo Bonzi. Directed by Gian Gaspare Napolitano. Camera (Ferraniacolor), Mario Craveri and Giovanni Raffaldi; editor, Mario Serandrei; music, F. A. Lavanino; commentary by James Agee, narrators, Brett Morrison and Carlos Montalban. Previewed in N.Y., April 28, '55. Running time, 85 MINS.

A trip across a comparatively unknown area of South America by four adventurous Italian filmmakers is graphically depicted in the footage that is offered in the documentary "Green Magic." Filmed in Ferraniacolor, which lushly captures the terrain and the natives encountered, the film is a tribute to the explorers as well as an interesting and exciting motion picture. The English commentary by James Agee and narrated by Brett Morrison and Carlos Montalban is helpful in describing the legends and the areas covered. Picture rates as a top art house attraction and as a strong second feature for general situations.

The film, photographed during a 1952 expedition, has received prizes at the Cannes Film Festival (1953), the Berlin Film Festival (1953), a special award for Mario Craveri's color photography at Cannes, and a Silver Ribbon, Italy's Oscar, for director Gian Gaspare Napolitano.

Led by Count Leonardo Bonzi, a veteran explorer and adventurer, the expedition covered 7,800 miles crossing forests, swamplands, pampas, jungles and the Andes mountains. The four men, including cameraman Giovanni Raffaldi, traveled by jeep, often along a trackless route, from Rio de Janeiro, Brazil, to Lima, Peru. It took them six months to cover the territory, being the first ones to traverse it by auto.

Wisely centering their cameras on the scenic beauty and the people of the area rather than concentrating on their own difficulties, the Italo adventurers succeeded in recording some breathless "firsts." Perhaps the most terrifying bit of photography ever to be witnessed on a screen is to see the voracious piranha fish attack and devour a large heifer in less than 30 minutes, leaving only a bare skeleton. The footage is varied, covering such incidents as the piranha bit and snakes in mortal combat to glimpses and short vignettes of the primative existence of the people of the area traversed.

The shots of the inhabitants appear unposed and captured them in their natural environment at work and play. It makes note of the fisherman of Bahia on the coast of Brazil, freelance diamond hunters in the heart of the Mato Grosso, Brazilian pioneers felling trees to make way for fields, descendents of African slaves in a wierd, ritualistic dance ridding

---

themselves of evil spirits, a "siringuero" or rubber hunter practicing his lonely profession in dangerous jungle areas, gauchos herding cattle, and Aymara Indians high in the Andes at a wedding ceremony.

The shots of the Iguassu Falls, which are higher than Niagara, and the changing scene as the expedition heads west, add to the general fascination of the picture. Bonzi and his colleagues have come with a notable contribution to the growing field of films of exploration. *Holl.*

High Society

Routine entry in the Leo Gorcey-Huntz Hall comedies; a lowercase dualer.

Hollywood, April 28.

Allied Artists release of Ben Schwalb production. Stars Leo Gorcey, Huntz Hall; features Bernard Gorcey, Amanda Blake, David Condon, Addison Richards, Paul Harvey. Directed by William Beaudine. Screenplay, Bert Lawrence, Jerome S. Gottler; story, Edward Bernds, Elwood Ullman; camera, Harry Neumann; editor, John C. Fuller. Previewed April 26, '55. Running time, 61 MINS.

Slip	Leo Gorcey
Sach	Huntz Hall
Louis	Bernard Gorcey
Clarissa	Amanda Blake
Chuck	David Condon
Cosgrove	Addison Richards
Baldwin	Paul Harvey
Stuyvesant	Dayton Lummis
Terwilliger	Ronald Keith
Frisbie	Gavin Gordon
Palumbo	Dave Barry
Butch	Bennie Bartlett
Marten	Kem Dibbs

(Aspect ratio: 1.85-1)

High jinks in high society by Leo Gorcey and Huntz Hall feature this run-of-the-mill entry in a routine, socalled bread-and-butter comedy series. Like most of its predecessors, "High Society" exhibits little pride in the profession of filmmaking, but as a flat rental offering for dualers it fulfills release intentions.

This time, Hall is used as a foil by Dayton Lummis, society crook scheming to get an inheritance away from his young nephew. Hall is passed off as the rightful heir, but the scheme eventually goes awry when he, and his buddy, Gorcey, wise up and expose the plot. Around that shell a lot of typical Gorcey-Hall nonsense has been padded in the scripting by Bert Lawrence and Jerome S. Gottler from a story by Edward Bernds and Elwood Ullman.

With Lummis on the skullduggery end are Amanda Blake and Addison Richards. Playing the rightful heir is Ronald Keith, and Gavin Gordon is seen as the butler. William Beaudine directed the antics to the broad formula used for the series and Ben Schwalb produced. Physical furbishings are modest, even for the obviously tight budget. Technical support is standard. *Brog.*

Abbott and Costello Meet the Mummy
(SONG)

Good Abbott & Costello comedy, team's best in some time with satisfactory biz prospects where these pix play best.

Hollywood, May 3.

Universal release of Howard Christie production. Stars Bud Abbott, Lou Costello; features Marie Windsor, Michael

Ansara, Peggy King. Directed by Charles Lamont. Screenplay. John Grant; story, Lee Loeb; camera, George Robinson; editor, Russell Schoengarth; music supervision, Joseph Gershenson. Previewed April 26, '55. Running time, 79 MINS.

Pete Patterson	Bud Abbott
Freddie Franklin	Lou Costello
Madame Rontru	Marie Windsor
Charlie	Michael Ansara
Josef	Dan Seymour
Semu	Richard Deacon
Dr. Zoomer	Kurt Katch
Hetsut	Richard Karlan
Iben	Mel Welles
Habid	George Khoury
Klaris	Edwin Parker
Dance Troupe	Mazzone-Abbott Dancers
Dance Troupe	Chandra Kaly Dancers
Vocalist	Peggy King

(Aspect ratio: 1.85-1)

Abbott & Costello pick up the entertainment pace in "Meet the Mummy" to make it one of their best comedies in some time. It looks like satisfactory business right down the line in those situations that have previously done well with entries from the comics.

As the title indicates, the team's funnying is laid in Egypt, where the boys; stranded and short of coin, get mixed up in murder hijinks and the hunt for a long buried treasure. Producer Howard Christie and director Charles Lamont mix up laughs and chills, plus some suspense, to keep the footage rolling at a good clip for its 79 minutes. Bats, cobras, mummies that still live after thousands of years in wrappings and other dusty accoutrements of musty ruins are gimmicks seen frequently and used for scary comedy in the John Grant screenplay, based on a story by Lee Loeb. Added fillip is Peggy King doing a first class selling job on "You Came A Long Way From St. Louis" in a single sequence laid in an Egyptian nitery.

Outside of mummies and reptiles, A&C have human nemesis, all with the same aim of obtaining the treasure and bumping off everyone else. Principal among the heavies is Marie Windsor, a gal with some killer hirelings and murderous ways who forces the comics to lead the way to the loot because Costello has swallowed the medallion on which the map is engraved. X-ray makes it easy to read. Richard Deacon is another menace, playing the leader of a religious cult that wants the medallion and the living mummy who usually wears it back in the temple. Footage rolls along with several very funny A&C routines to keep the laughs coming.

Michael Ansara and Dan Seymour are the principal doers of Miss Windsor's bidding, while Eddie Parker is the mummy who still lives. Two dance troupes are spotted through the picture, the Mazzone-Abbott Dancers and Chandra Kaly and His Dancers, latter serving the mummy god of the religious cult. Technical end of the production gets in on the amusement with its contributions, such as George Robinson's lensing, the art direction, editing and musical supervision by Joseph Gershenson.
Brog.

The Constant Husband
(BRITISH—COLOR)

Bright, frothy British comedy with Rex Harrison, Margaret Leighton and Kay Kendall providing the appeal; standout for situations catering to sophisticated audiences.

London, May 3.

British Lion release of London Films Production. Stars Rex Harrison, Margaret

Leighton, Kay Kendall; features Cecil Parker, Nicole Maurey, George Cole, Raymond Huntley, Michael Hordern. Directed by Gilliat. Screenplay by Gilliat and Val Valentine; camera. Ted Scaife; editor. G. Turney-Smith; music. Malcolm Arnold. At Pavilion, London, April 20, '55. Running time, 88 MINS.

Man with Lost Memory	Rex Harrison
Miss Chesterman	Margaret Leighton
Monica	Kay Kendall
Professor Llewellyn	Cecil Parker
Lola Sopranelli	Nicole Maurey
Luigi Sopranelli	George Cole
J. F. Hassett	Raymond Huntley
Judge	Michael Hordern
Papa Sopranelli	Eric Pohlmann
Jack Carter	Robert Coote
Moma Sopranelli	Marie Burke
Council for Prosecution	Eric Berry
Clerk of the Court	Arthur Howard
Mr. Daniels	Charles Lloyd Pack
Giorgio Sopranelli	Derek Sydney
Stromboli	Guy Deghy
Bridget	Valerie French
Miss Brewer	Jill Adams
Miss Pargiter	Ursula Howells
Sixth Wife	Roma Dumville

A frothy comedy, "The Constant Husband" is one of the best examples of sheer entertainment to come from a British studio in some time. It is handsomely mounted, briskly directed and has adequate star values to give it b.o. appeal. A safe bet for most situations where sophisticated comedy is acceptable, even in the U. S.

This is also one of the brightest efforts to emerge from the Frank Launder and Sidney Gilliat partnership. The screenplay by Gilliat and Val Valentine is light and amusing, and none of the sparkle has been lost in the translation to the screen. The pic was an unsuccessful contender for Royal Command honors last year, but it is difficult to understand why.

The story could not be more slender. The central character is played by Rex Harrison, who wakes up one morning in the remoteness of a Welsh village to realize he's an amnesia victim. Gradually, through the help of his psychiatrist, Cecil Parker, he's able to recreate his past and learns, to his horror, that he has seven wives to his credit. A bigamy charge follows, a non-guilty plea is advanced by Margaret Leighton as a present-day Portia, but rather than face seven eager ex-spouses, he reverses his plea in favor of jail.

It's a lightweight plot, admittedly, but contrived with the requisite breezy touch to keep the provocative situations on the move. The facile direction and the effervescent star portrayals sustain the flimsy storyline.

Harrison is thoroughly diverting as the amnesia victim; this is an excellent piece of casting and his performance could hardly be bettered. Miss Leighton makes a belated appearance on the screen, but her impact is nonetheless notable.

Kay Kendall, as the last of the seven wives, gives a sparkling portrayal. Cecil Parker is typically buoyant as the psychiatrist, and Nicole Maurey is sufficiently alluring as another of the ex-wives. Michael Hordern contributes a superb bit as the judge while George Cole and Raymond Huntley fill featured roles with distinction. The big cast has a hand-picked appearance.
Myro.

Tall Man Riding
(COLOR)

Randolph Scott involved with vengeance, land grabs and killer gang back when the west was young. For the outdoor trade.

Hollywood, May 10.

Warner Bros. release of David Weisbart production. Stars Randolph Scott, Dorothy Malone, Peggie Castle; features Bill Ching, John Baragrey. Robert Barrat. John Dehner, Paul Richards. Lane Chandler. Directed by Lesley Selander. Screenplay, Joseph Hoffman from the novel by Norman A. Fox camera (WarnerColor), Wilfrid M. Cline; editor, Irene Morra; music, Paul Sawtell. Previewed April 25, '55. Running time, 82 MINS.

Larry Madden	Randolph Scott
Corinna Ordway	Dorothy Malone
Reva	Peggie Castle
Rex Willard	Bill Ching
Cibo Pearlo	John Baragrey
Tucker Ordway	Robert Barrat
Ames Luddington	John Dehner
Peso Kid	Paul Richards
Hap Sutton	Lane Chandler
Jeff Barkley	Mickey Simpson
Will	Joe Bassett
Bartender	Charles Watts
Jim Feathergill	Russ Conway

(Aspect ratio: 1.66-1)

A land grab, vengeance, gunslingers and gals keep Randolph Scott pretty well occupied in this western actioner that will serve its intended purpose in the outdoor market. It's quite talky, and often slow-moving, for a Scott western, but when the action is turned on it is rugged enough to satisfy the fans.

Scott plays an adventurer who returns to a western town after years of absence to kill the man who had driven him away in the first place after burning out his small ranch home and preventing his marriage to Dorothy Malone. The intended victim is her father, Robert Barrat, cattle baron, and while Scott bides his time he has opportunity to indulge in a few fist and gun scraps with hirelings of John Baragrey. saloon operator. attract the attention of saloon singer Peggy Castle, who's Baragrey's girl, and participate in a land rush, the goal of which are the Barrat holdings, which John Dehner, Scott's lawyer, has discovered to still be public land. In the end, Scott doesn't kill Barrat and his romance is on again with Miss Malone, who has lost the husband, Bill Ching, she had acquired during Scott's long absence.

Performances by Scott, the Misses Malone and Castle, and the others involved in the overdrawn script by Joseph Hoffman are acceptable as directed by Lesley Selander. Picture has been given standard outdoor values under the production wing of David Weisbart and Wilfrid M. Cline's WarnerColor photography shows them off prettily. Other technical contributions are satisfactory.
Brog.

Angela

Program meller lensed in Italy with Dennis O'Keefe, Mara Lane; just fair lowercase feature.

Hollywood, May 9.

20th-Fox release of Steven Pallos (Patria) production. Stars Dennis O'Keefe, Mara Lane; features Rossano Brazzi, Arnoldo Foa, Galeazzo Benti, Enzo Fiermonte. Directed by Dennis O'Keefe. Screenplay, Jonathan Rix, Edoardo Anton from a story by Steve Carruthers; camera, Leonida Barboni; editor, Giancarlo Cappelli; music, Mario Nascimbene. Previewed May 5, '55. Running time, 81 MINS.

Steve Catlett	Dennis O'Keefe
Angela Towne	Mara Lane
Nino	Rossano Brazzi
Cpt. Ambrosi	Arnoldo Foa
Gustavo Venjuri	Galeazzo Benti
Sgt. Collina	Enzo Fiermonte
Bertolati	Nino Crisman
Tony	Giovanni Fostini
Doctor Robini	Francesco Tensi
Girl of Beauty Shop	Maria Teresa Paliani
Nurse	Gorella Gori
Doorkeeper	Aldo Fini

(Aspect ratio: 1.33-1)

"Angela" is a program melodrama, lensed in Italy with Dennis O'Keefe doubling as male star and director. As entertainment, it is just a fair lowercase feature aimed at the general dualer market where it should get by with non-discriminating audiences.

Mara Lane, English sexpot, plays the title role opposite O'Keefe, but she's no angel, being the chief heavy of the piece although the males involved seem to like what she puts them through. The Steve Carruthers story, scripted by Jonathan Rix and Edoardo Anton, features a familiar plot and O'Keefe directs it at a pace that makes the footage seem longer than 81 minutes. The Rome background gives an interesting frame to the Steven Pallos production as lensed by Leonida Barboni in a lowkey suited to the melodramatics.

O'Keefe is a glib ex-GI who settled in Rome to sell sports cars after the war and falls for Miss Lane, secretary to a nitery operator. O'Keefe's troubles start when he agrees to remove the body of Miss Lane's boss from her apartment, believing her story that a heart attack caused the death. The complications that ensue are highly contrived and never ring true, and it's a not-so-merry chase poor-sap O'Keefe goes through, including dodging the police, being nearly murdered by Miss Lane's husband, Rossano Brazzi, suffering a pneumonia attack, and, to climax it all, being gunned down and crippled for life by his ever-loving when he plans to expose she knifed the boss, a fact he was a little late in discovering.

Performances by the cast are not very impressive under O'Keefe's direction, including his own, but Miss Lane is easy on the eyes and wears some outfits calculated to attract the gaze. Other than Brazzi, featured roles are played by Arnoldo Foa, as the police captain; and Galeazzo Benti, as O'Keefe's partner in the auto agency.

The score by Mario Nascimbene is keyed to the pic's mood with interesting rhythmic themes threaded throughout.

The Dark Avenger
(BRITISH-C'SCOPE-COLOR)

Historical, adventure pic with juvenile appeal; Errol Flynn name may help in U.S.

London, May 3.

20th-Fox release of Allied Artists production. Stars Errol Flynn. Joanne Dru; features Peter Finch, Yvonne Furneaux, Patrick Holt, Michael Hordern. Directed by Henry Levin. Story and screen play by Daniel B. Ullman; camera (Eastmancolor), Guy Green; editor. E. B. Jarvis; music. Cedric Thorpe Davie with "Bella Marie"; lyric by Christopher Hassall. At Fox private theatre, London, April 15, '55. Running time, 85 MINS.

Prince Edward	Errol Flynn
Lady Joan Holland	Joanne Dru
de Ville	Peter Finch
Marie	Yvonne Furneaux
Sir Ellys	Patrick Holt
King Edward	Michael Hordern
Sir Bruce	Moultrie Kelsall
Sir Philip	Robert Urquhart
Du Gueselin	Noel Willman
Genevieve	Frances Howe
Libeau	Alastair Hunter
Sir John	Rupert Davis
D'Estell	Ewan Solon
John Holland	Vincent Winter
Thomas Holland	Richard O'Sullivan
Dubois	Jack Lambert
Gurd	John Welsh
Arnaul	Harold Kasket
Francois le Clerc	Leslie Linder

The period of the 100-years' war between England and France provides the setting for Allied Artists' first excursion into British anamorphic production. With Errol Flynn and Joanne Dru in the leads, this adds marquee value which should prove a valuable selling aid in the U.S. As an historical adventure, it is rather juvenile in its appeal, but lusty fight sequences and a big scale battle climax will satisfy action fans.

Under Henry Levin's robust direction and against a colorful English countryside background, the action is almost continuous. Some of the battle sequences are a little confused, but the pace and color are fair compensation. Moated castles, which are the setting for the main bits of derring-do, have authentic appeal.

The action begins after the defeat of the French by King Edward's British troops and the return of the monarch to his native country, leaving his son, Prince Edward (Errol Flynn), in charge. But although their king is held a prisoner, the French noblemen refuse to accept defeat, mobilise for war against the Prince's depleted troops and hold a British noble-woman (Joanne Dru) as hostage. The rebellious French are routed, however after Flynn disguises himself as a Black Knight, joins the enemy forces, rescues the lady and assumes his role of conqueror.

The screenplay deliberately keeps dialog down to a minimum, allowing the plot incident to take precedence and within the scope of the treatment the Anglo-American cast does well enough.

Flynn's vigorous performance as the prince, is in characteristic vein, and Joanne Dru, in a limited role, adds a measure of charm and poise. Peter Finch contributes a particularly villainous portrayal as the French count who leads the rebellion. There is a charming, but completely inappropriate bit by Yvonne Furneaux as a gal who entertains the French troops with song. Michael Hordern, a distinguished local thesp, has only a bit as the monarch, appearing in the opening scenes. Other roles are adequately played.

Eastmancolor lensing by Guy Green is a technical highspot in the production, although Terence Verity's settings call for commendation. E. B. Jarvis' editing keeps the action rolling.

Picture will be distributed in the western hemisphere by Allied Artists under the title of "The Warriors." 20th-Fox has distribution rights in the rest of the world.

Myro.

The Tiger and the Flame
(INDIA-MADE-COLOR)

Indian adventure-drama sans marquee names; lightweight for general U.S. market, fair prospects in art houses.

United Artists release of Schrab M. Modi production; associate producer Forrest Judd. Features Mehtab and Modi. Directed by Modi. Screenplay, Geza Herczeg, Pandit Sudershan, Adi F. Keeka; story and research, Pandit S. R. Dube; camera (Technicolor), Ernest Haller; editors, P. Bhalchander, D. Shridhankar; music, Vasant Desai. Previewed N.Y., May 6, '55. Running time, **97 MINS.**

Rani Lakshmibai	Mehtab
Rajguru	Schrab Modi
Raja Gangadhar Rao	Mubarak
Ghulam Ghaus Khan	Ulhas
Sadashiv Rao	Ramsingh
Gen. Sir Hugh Rose	Sapru
Manu	Baby Shika
Lt. Henry Dowker	Anil Kishore
Doris Dowker	Gloria Gasper
Moropant	Kamalakant
Major Ellis	Michael Shea
Col. Sleeman	Marconi
Panditji	Nayampalli
Kashi	Shakila

(*Aspect ratio:* 1.66-1)

"The Tiger and the Flame" is heralded as India's first Technicolor production and no doubt is luring sizable grosses in that country. But while the film contains much material of probable interest to Indian audiences, it shapes up as a lightweight entry for the general American market. However, a fair potential looms in the art house field.

Hampering b.o. prospects of this Schrab M. Modi production on which Forrest Judd acted as associate producer is its lack of familiar names in the cast. Frequently a good story, well written, acted and directed, can easily carry a picture when its thesps are unknown. But the yarn in this case fails to unreel with as much excitement and drama as its basic plot would indicate.

Minus the frills the producers have used to pad out the footage, story concerns a legendary queen of destiny who leads her small Indian state into revolt against the British a century ago. Material the quartet of scripters who labored on this venture had at their disposal could easily have been fashioned into another "Lives of a Bengal Lancer." Unfortunately, the end result is an overlong, traveloguish saga with badly staged battle sequences.

Queen-to-be was originally chosen at the age of nine by an adviser to the throne of the Indian state of Jhansi. Wed to the aging Raja, she's later schooled in fencing and general military tactics with the view that she ultimately would lead her people in a crusade against the British and the hated East India Co. Her fight, although a valiant one, is unsuccessful and the finale finds her dying at the head of her troops.

Performances are seldom convincing. Mehtab occasionally registers on the dramatic scoreboard as the warlike femme ruler but is unimpressive in a number of other scenes. Producer-director Modi portrays the court adviser with an air of dignity and reserve, Mubarak is fair as the self-effacing, senile Raja and Sapru is undistinguished as the British Army commander. Other supporting players are mediocre under Modi's wavering direction.

Title of the film, curiously, stems from a ballet sequence presented for amusement of the Raja and his entourage and doesn't even remotely suggest what this Indian import's about. Most of the technical contributors to the venture are natives of India save for associate producer Forrest Judd and cameraman Ernest Haller. Both Judd, a onetime story editor for Allied Artists, and vet Hollywood lensman Haller have been active in Indian film making for several years.

Bespeaking a generous budget, the production trappings and physical values have been expertly photographed by Haller. Dances of Madame Simkie and Vinod Chopra, lyrics of Pandit Radheshyam, Vesant Desai's music and Kanu Desai's costumes all provide an authentic atmosphere. Editing of P. Bhalchander and D. Shridhankar could have been much tighter. Other technical credits are standard.

Gilb.

The Ship That Died Of Shame
(BRITISH)

Exciting Nicholas Monserrat sea yarn of war heroes turned smugglers; rates general b.o. appeal.

London, May 3.

J. Arthur Rank General Film Distributors release of Ealing Studios-Michael Balcon production. Stars Richard Attenborough, George Baker, Bill Owen, Virginia McKenna; features Roland Culver, Bernard Lee. Directed by Michael Relph, Basil Dearden. Screenplay, John Whiting, Michael Relph, Basil Dearden from story by Nicholas Monserrat; camera, Gordon Dines; editor, Peter Benzencenet; music, William Alwyn. At Odeon, Leicester Square, London, April 19, '55. Running time, **91 MINS.**

George Hoskins	Richard Attenborough
Bill Randall	George Baker
Birdie	Bill Owen
Helen Randall	Virginia McKenna
Fordyce	Roland Culver
Customs Officer	Bernard Lee
Raines	John Chandos
Sir Richard	Ralph Truman
Second Customs Officer	Harold Goodwin
Detective	John Longden

The author's name alone on this one should attract filmgoers who flocked to "The Cruel Sea." This fact coupled with the reputation of Ealing Studios should make it a good b.o. potentiality both here and overseas. The degradation endured, and finally overthrown by a "ship with a soul," is impressively depicted while the story of three men mainly concerned in her career is unfolded with suspensive interest. Adapted skillfully from a short novel, the dramatic highlights of war and peacetime hazards are convincingly reproduced and enhanced by excellent camerawork.

The war only occupies the early part of the story, showing the speedy, little motor gunboats known as the "Beat Up Boys" dashing in and out of enemy-held ports, sabotaging, shooting up planes, etc., the smartest and luckiest of these being the 1087. Her commander finds himself out of a job after the war and is persuaded by his ex-Lieutenant to join him in a smuggling service to and from France. Desolate on the death of his wife, he is talked into the racket and they buy their old boat 1087, and sign on its former boatswain.

The cargo soon takes on a sinister element, with forged notes and later a wanted murderer involved, but the prime mover in the partnership gets more ruthless as the easy money piles in. In too deeply to pull out, the commander feels even his ship revolts, her engines misfiring and the helm unresponsive in heavy seas. The murder of a customs officer and the attempted escape of those responsible is too much for 1087 who dashes herself on the rocks, leaving her old master to scramble to safety with his boatswain.

George Baker gives a restrained, effective performance as the bereaved husband who gradually loses his integrity. Richard Attenborough is suitably brash and cocksure as his unscrupulous partner. Virginia McKenna has a briefly moving appearance as the wife killed in an air raid while Bill Owen brings an authentic traditional navy touch to the role of the boatswain. Roland Culver deserts his usual benign demeanor as a rival racketeer. Bernard Lee registers as the conscientious customs officer.

Film is well directed. Accompanying music, particularly in the opening sequences, provides a vital adjunct to the dramatic action.

Clem.

Robbers' Roost
(COLOR-SONGS)

Familiar cast names to aid draggily-paced western actioner through outdoor market.

Hollywood, May 9.

United Artists release of Robert Goldstein production. Stars George Montgomery; costars Richard Boone, Sylvia Findley, Bruce Bennett, Peter Graves; features Warren Stevens, William Hopper, Stanley Clements, Leo Gordon, Tony Romano. Directed by Sidney Salkow. Screenplay, John O'Dea, Salkow, Maurice Geraghty; from a novel by Zane Grey; camera (Eastman Color by De Luxe), Jack Draper editor, George Gittens; score, Paul Dunlap; songs, Tony Romano, John Bradford, Barbara Hayden. Previewed May 6, '55. Running time, **83 MINS.**

Tex	George Montgomery
Hays	Richard Boone
Helen	Sylvia Findley
Herrick	Bruce Bennett
Heesman	Peter Graves
Smokey	Warren Stevens
Happy Jack	Tony Romano
Robert Bell	William Hopper
Jeff	Leo Gordon
Chuck	Stanley Clements
Stud	Joe Bassett
Sparrow	Leonard Geer
Slocum	Al Wyatt
Brad	Boyd "Red" Morgan

(*Aspect ratio:* 1.85-1)

Zane Grey's novel about a crippled rancher who hires two gangs of rustlers to watchdog each other and his cattle comes off with just minor success in this United Artists presentation. Thanks to the familiar names of George Montgomery, Richard Boone and Bruce Bennett, it will get by okay in the outdoor market, but the pace is draggy and the scripting so-so. Along with the casters, the Eastman Color lensing is an asset.

Grey's outdoor action soap opera was fashioned for the screen by John O'Dea, Sidney Salkow and Maurice Geraghty, but the writing contribution features mostly cliche dialog, and a lot of it, plus motivations and situations that could have stood freshening. Salkow's direction is along formula lines, doing little to raise the entertainment or the performances to a level above the routine oater class.

Bennett is the wheel chair jockey who hires gangs headed by Boone and Peter Graves, figuring they'll be so busy watching each other they won't be able to rustle the herd. Montgomery, a loner wanted by the law, joins up with Boome, but instead of herding cattle he's put to shepherding Sylvia Findley, Bennett's sister, to keep the outlaws away from her.

Some action develops near the plot climax when Boone outsmarts Graves, sells the herd, kidnaps the girl and hides out with his men. The law wants him, Graves wants him, and so does Montgomery, who has been going along with the gang just so he can get Boone for having killed his wife. Just about everyone gets what he's after, in one way or another and Montgomery winds up with a new love, Miss Findley, and a death-bed confession by Boome clears the hero of a murder charge.

Jack Draper did the good color photography on the Robert Goldstein production. Latter equips the film with all it needs to be a good western feature except for story treatment and direction. The editing is choppy, leaving a few holes in the continuity. Tony Romano, member of the Boone gang, sings three range songs he wrote with

John Bradford **a n d** Barbara Hayden. *Brog.*

Santa Fe Passage
(COLOR)

Strong western, with star names of John Payne, Faith Domergue and Rod Cameron, indicating good returns.

Hollywood, May 4.
Republic release of a Sidney Picker production. Stars John Payne, Faith Domergue, Rod Cameron; features Slim Pickens, Irene Tedrow, George Keymas, Leo Gordon, Anthony Caruso. Directed by William Witney. Screenplay, Lillie Hayward; based on mag story by Clay Fisher; camera, Bud Thackery; art director, Frank Arrigo; music, R. Dale Butts; editor, Tony Martinelli. Previewed May 4, '55. Running time, **91 MINS.**
Kirby Randolph .... John Payne
Aurelie St. Clair .... Faith Domergue
Jess Griswold .... Rod Cameron
Sam Beekman .... Slim Pickens
Ptewaquin .... Irene Tedrow
Satank .... George Keymas
Tuss McLawery .... Leo Gordon
Chavez .... Anthony Caruso
(Aspect ratio: 1.66-1)

This soundly-produced western has the benefit of fast motion coupled with the names of three drawing stars to assure firstrate returns in the outdoor market. Fresh scenic backgrounds also give film a strong assist for realistic story unfoldment.

William Witney has managed some particularly rugged movement in his surefire direction which pays off in thrills as theme centers on John Payne, a frontier scout, leading a wagon-train bound for Santa Fe through Indian country. The Lillie Hayward script gets fresh premise through buildup of a romance between the scout and a half-breed Indian gal (Faith Domergue), with complications after Payne, who hates all Indians, learns she's part Redskin.

Payne delivers a powerful characterization of the scout who through no fault of his gained ostracism because it is believed he betrayed a wagon-train to warring Kiowas. Rod Cameron, who with Miss Domergue owns a big cargo of guns and ammunition, finally hires him to guide the train westward, but conflict is established in their rivalry for femme's affections. It's on this trek that Payne evens up matters with the Indians who massacred the earlier train he was guiding, after Cameron tries to betray the scout to the Indians.

Cameron undertakes one of his few heavy roles here, but turns softie when he stays behind so Payne and Miss Domergue may safely get away from the Redskins. Actress is appealing in her role, who hates being a breed, and has been filmed to advantage by Bud Thackery, whose lensing is superior throughout. In support, Slim Pickens scores strongly as Payne's buckskin pal, George Keymas inserts menace as the Kiowa chief out for Payne's scalp and Irene Tedrow is good as a squaw, who turns out to be femme lead's mother.

Sidney Picker's production supervision shows careful preparation and Tony Martinelli's editing is tight to heighten tempo. *Whit.*

Marianne de Ma Jeunesse
(Marianne of My Youth)
(FRANCO-GERMAN)

Paris, May 3.
Cinedis release of Filmsonor-Regina-Francinex-Royal production. Written and directed by Julian Duvivier from a novel by Peter De Mendelssohn Camera, L. H. Burel; editor, Marthe Poncin; music, Jacques Ibert. At Colisee, Paris. Running time, **110 MINS.**
Vincent .... Pierre Vaneck
Marianne .... Marianne Hold
Lise .... Isabelle Pia
Manfred .... Gil Vidal
Captain .... Jean Galland
Felix .... Claude Aragon

With this mist-filled film, Julien Duvivier has tackled an evocation of poetic first love, and created an adroit mixture of the real and unreal. It makes for an interesting offbeater that may well make an arty house entry. This emerges as a sensitive portrayal of the mystic rites of first love. This should make it big in Germany and have good chances here. It has some possibilities in the U.S. market.

Its wispy cleavage between the poetic manifestations of love and its story of youthful dignity, cruelty and comaraderie make this cry for careful exploitation. It may go in some arty offbeaters in America.

A dreamy young man whose mother has put him in a Bavarian finishing school situated in the Alps. All the Germanic splendors and misty landscapes add the touch of enchantment to this strange boy from Argentina whose stories and songs soon win the admiration of others excepting a gang of rebels. They take him to a haunted castle for his initiation. There he meets Marianne, a comely young creature who tells him she is being held by an aging lover. *Mosk.*

Hamido
(EGYPTIAN)

David Gould release of Farid Chawky production. Stars Chawky; features Hoda Soultan, Tahia Carioca, Mahmoud Meligui. Directed by Niazi Moustapha. Previewed N.Y., April 21, '55. Running time, **115 MINS.**

An Egyptian import, "Hamido" shows few possibilities for the American market. There's an intriguing belly dance here and there to brighten up the footage but for the most part the story is a humdrum tale of a fisherman turned narcotics smuggler. If the film were trimmed by at least 30 minutes it may shape up as a filler for exploitation houses. Otherwise, b.o. prospects are meagre.

Farid Chawky, who produced, also portrays the title role, that of the smuggler. It's hardly a part calculated to stir audience sympathy for he jilts his girl friend after she becomes pregnant and later attempts to drown her. Of course, these misdeeds can't go on without retribution and the police ultimately end his career with a burst of gun fire.

Performances and direction are none too convincing. Chawky, a husky six-footer, adequately handles the physical demands of the role but his thesping leaves much to be desired. Hoda Soultan likewise is unimpressive as the femme Chawky did wrong. Tahia Carioca, however, registers nicely via some fantastic belly gyrations. Niazi Moustapha's direction does little to punch up the trite yarn. Film, for which no other credits were available, is in Arabic with English titles.

Subject of narcotics insofar as film scripts go is looked upon with disfavor by Hollywood's Production Code. Hence, some difficulty presumably would be experienced by the distributor in corraling a seal for "Hamido." David Gould, who's acting as producer's rep for the venture, may distribute it himself in the U. S. A 16m print screened at the preview was of poor quality but 35m prints reportedly will be available later. *Gilb.*

Foreign Films

Cannes, May 3.
Stella (GREEK). Millas Film production and release. Stars Melina Mercouri; features, Georges Fondas, Aleko Alexandrakis, Sophia Vambo. Directed by Michael Cacoyanis. Screenplay, J. Cambanselis; camera, Costa Theodorides; editor, Yanni Tsarouchi. At Cannes Film Festival. Running time, **90 MINS.**

This is the first Greek film to make a stir among the international press and reps at a film fest. Though this remains primarily melodrama, with its techniques and workmanship obviously gleaned from study rather than being an influence and a tool of expression, it has a well constructed rhythm and uncorks a sensual, dynamic actress in Melina Mercouri. Pic looks like a good prospect for Greek language and maybe some nabe houses. It has enough appeal for secondary foreign spots. It concerns an independent cabaret singer whose aversion to marriage, which she feels is a prison, leads to her death at the hands of an enraged lover. Although technical aspects are skimpy and lensing underlit, it has a bowling narrative style which is enhanced by the sincere playing and the workmanlike direction of Michael Cacoyanis. *Mosk.*

Cannes, May 3.
Chikamatsu Monogatari (Tales of Chikamatsu) (JAPANESE). Daiei production and release. Stars Kazuo Hasegawa, Kyoko Kagawa; features Yoko Minamida, Eitaro Shindo. Directed by Kenji Mizoguchi. Screenplay, Yoshikata Yoda from tales of Chikamatsu; camera, Kazuo Miyagawa; editor, Hiroshi Mizutani. At Cannes Film Festival. Running time **116 MINS.**

Exquisitely mounted pic looks too Oriental in style and unfoldment to make for U.S. chances excepting in special situations. With the interest in Jap films now prevailing in arty circles, this might be worth a try. A cool, classical style depicts the fatal love of a worker and the wife of his employer in a strictly codified and feudal 17th Century Japan. The illicit love affair leads to their deaths, but not before they realize that it is better to die for love than live without it. Director Kenji Mizoguchi has given this an eyefilling mounting and achieved the willing suspension of disbelief and unfamiliarity with strange customs in his careful workmanship. Black and white lensing is superb in graduations and emphasis. Thesping is topflight. An offbeater which would need extremely subtle handling because of its inflexible Eastern approach and lack of concession. This would seem too slow to most Western audiences. *Mosk.*

Cannes, May 3.
Hill 24 Does Not Answer (ISRAELI). Sikor production and release. Directed by Thorold Dickinson. Screenplay, Dickinson, Peter Frye; camera, Gerald Gibbs; editor, Dickinson. With Michael Wager, Aric Lavie, Edward Mulhare, Margaret Oved, Haya Havarit. At Cannes Film Festival. Running time, **102 MINS.**

Film was made in Israel, in English, by by Anglo director Thorold Dickinson. It emerges as one of the best to come out of the young nation. Although obviously made for nationalistic purposes, it has a depth and poignance to make for U.S. interest. More for the special spots, this also could be used for fundraising functions. It depicts incidents in the life of four people guarding a hill just before the UN Truce Commission makes its division of territory. They are killed during the night and their stories are related by an Irishman in love with an Israeli girl. He joins them out of belief in a cause. There is a young American Jewish boy whose disbelief and arrogance finally turns to a fervent feeling for the nation. Acting is uneven but Dickinson's firm directing gives this a sincere tone and its numerous incidents ring true. Production interest engendered by the location shooting. Lensing, editing and other technical credits are tops. *Mosk.*

Davy Crockett— King of the Wild Frontier
(COLOR)

A fair western but with an unusual headstart toward good money in many situations. There's that Crockett craze to consider.

Buena Vista release of Bill Walsh production (under the Walt Disney aegis). Stars Fess Parker and Buddy Ebsen; features Basil Ruysdael, Hans Conreid, William Bakewell, Kenneth Tobey, Pat Hogan, Nick Cravat, Mike Mazurki, Jeff Thompson. Directed by Norman Foster. Written by Tom Blackburn (adapted from the Disneyland tv shows); camera (Technicolor), Charles Boyle; editor, Chester Schaeffer; music, George Bruns; songs, "Ballad of Davy Crockett," by Tom Blackburn (words) and Bruns (music), and "Farewell," with the words which were penned by Crockett and music by Bruns. Previewed in N. Y. May 11, '55. Running time, **90 MINS.**

Davy Crockett	Fess Parker
George Russel	Buddy Ebsen
Andrew Jackson	Basil Ruysdael
Thimblerig	Hans Conreid
Tobias Norton	William Bakewell
Col. Jim Bowie	Kenneth Tobey
Chief Red Stick	Pat Hogan
Polly Crockett	Helene Stanley
Bustedluck	Nick Cravat
Col. Billy Travis	Don Megowan
Bigfoot Mason	Mike Mazurki
Charlie Two Shirts	Jeff Thompson
Swaney	Henry Joyne
Henderson	Benjamin Hornbuckle
Opponent Political Speaker	Hal Youngblood
1st Congressman	Jim Maddux
2d Congressman	Robert Booth
Billy	Eugene Brindel
Johnny	Ray Whitetree
Bruno	Campbell Brown

(*Aspect ratio*: 1.85-1)

By theatrical standards, and appraising the picture on its own entertainment merits, exclusively, "Davy Crockett—King of the Wild Frontier" rates as a western of moderate value for the oater outlets. But the Crockett character has recently hit the nation with such phenomenal impact via the Disneyland tv airings that the entry figures to take good revenue in a much wider market groove, middle-sized firstruns included.

The film is substantially the same as seen on the three tv segments—Crockett fighting the Indians, going to Congress and finally to the Alamo. Piecing the three together has an episodic effect which, presumably, couldn't be avoided, but is nonetheless a little disconcerting for the viewer.

Disney, of course, is pulling a switch in peddling a pic to theatres after television exposure. (Perhaps, the conventional approach to the public via theatres first might not have created such a stir.) Importantly, the theatrical ticket-buyer will have much more to behold, considering widescreen presentation and fine tinting by Technicolor. On tv, "Davy Crockett" was a poor man's road company; the production values poured into the film can be seen in full measures only by theatre audiences. And there are no interruptions for commercials.

Producer Bill Walsh provided "Crockett" with more of an elaborate mounting than is usually the case with a western of this type. It was locationed in Tenessee with a numerically big cast, and costumes and settings are devoid of any artificiality. The close-up action scenes, competently directed by Norman Foster, as well as all other sequences, come through in finer detail on the bigscreen.

The added visual assets plus the great penetration of the tv programs (including the "Crockett" ballad) are the key factors that promise good returns from the theatrical excursion. *Gene.*

The Sea Chase
(C'SCOPE-COLOR)

John Wayne, Lana Turner World War II nautical drama; fairly entertaining with names for b.o.

Hollywood, May 12.

Warner Bros. release of John Farrow production. Stars John Wayne, Lana Turner, David Farrar, Lyle Bettger, Tab Hunter; features James Arness, Dick Davalos, John Qualen, Paul Fix, Lowell Gilmore, Luis Van Rooten, Alan Hale. Directed by Farrow. Screenplay, James Warner Bellah, John Twist; from the novel by Andrew Geer; camera (WarnerColor), William Clothier; editor, William Ziegler; music, Roy Webb. Previewed May 2, '55. Running time, **116 MINS.**

Karl Ehrlich	John Wayne
Elsa Keller	Lana Turner
Commander Napier	David Farrar
Kirchner	Lyle Bettger
Cadet Wesser	Tab Hunter
Schlieter	James Arness
Cadet Walter Stemme	Dick Davalos
Chief Schmitt	John Qualen
Max Heinz	Paul Fix
Capt. Evans	Lowell Gilmore
Matz	Luis Van Rooten
Wentz	Alan Hale
Hepke	Wilton Graf
Bachman	Peter Whitney
Winkler	Claude Akin
Bo'sun	John Doucette
Brounck	Alan Lee

"The Sea Chase" has the marquee lure of John Wayne and Lana Turner to cue its business prospects, and their established draw should get the picture off to good openings. Without the star combination, this nautical drama, laid during the earlier phases of World War II, likely would be just another feature entry in Cinema-Scope and WarnerColor, slated for regulation playdates and b.o. generally.

While seemingly equipped with all the elements for exciting screenfare, the picture never quite lives up to its promise, having overlooked gripping suspense, the one basic ingredient that would have made the difference. Thus, producer-director John Farrow, and scripters James Warner Bellah and John Twist, turn a rather neat trick in making a chase picture without the suspenseful excitement of a chase, albeit based on Andrew Geer's novel of the pursuit of a nondescript German freighter from Australia to the North Sea by the British Navy.

Aside from the missing basic element, the picture registers a kind of broad action against an interesting ship-and-sea background, all well photographed by William Clothier, as the rusty tub Ergenstrasse eludes its pursuers and, short of food and fuel, still manages to make its way almost to the Fatherland before being caught and sunk. The story brings out the trials and tribulations of the hard-driven crew, and the ingenuity of the skipper and his officers in keeping going when surrender would not have been too great a shame. There is a romance woven in, between Wayne, a German who despises Nazism but as captain of his ship still determines to bring it home, and Miss Turner, Nazi spy and adventuress who has been no more than the term implies.

Wayne is all that his following could ask when engaged in driving his ship and men but, as a he-man type, seems a little embarrassed in delivering some of the boy-girl talk that occurs as he, at first hating, gradually comes to love the spy aboard his freighter. Miss Turner does her character well, developing it on as believable lines as the story permits. Ending, with the Ergenstrasse sinking in the North Sea, is rather inconclusive, pic indicating there is a possibility the lovers were again able to cheat the pursuers and death.

Co-starring are David Farrar, Lyle Bettger and Tab Hunter. All three bring off their characters with the required dispatch, with Bettger showing the best as a despicable Nazi, whose brutal murder of some shipwrecked fishermen during the flight plays an important part in the reasons for British Naval officer Farrar's determination to bring the ship and its crew to justice. Another reason is the fact Wayne smashed his affair with Miss Turner. Among the others doing satisfactory are James Arness, Dick Davalos, John Qualen, Paul Fix, Lowell Gilmore, Luis Van Rooten and Alan Hale.

Roy Webb's background score, art direction and most of the other behind-camera credits are expertly handled. Picture is long at one hour and 56 minutes. *Brog.*

Magnificent Matador
(C'Scope-Color-Song)

Maureen O'Hara, Anthony Quinn give marquee value to lensed-in-Mexico romantic-action story of bullfighter; average prospects.

Hollywood, May 17.

20th-Fox release of Edward L. Alperson (National) production. Stars Maureen O'Hara, Anthony Quinn; introducing Manuel Rojas; features Richard Denning, Thomas Gomez, Lolo Albright, William Brooks Ching, Eduardo Noriega, Lorraine Chanel, Anthony Caruso. Direction and story by Budd Boetticher; screenplay, Charles Lang; camera (Eastman Color), Lucien Ballard; editor, Richard Cahoon; sound, Manuel Topete; technical advisor, Carlos Arruza; score, Raoul Kraushaar; title theme, Edward L. Alperson Jr.; song Alperson Jr., and Paul Herrick; sung by Kitty White. Previewed May 11, '55. Running time, **94 MINS.**

Karen	Maureen O'Hara
Luis	Anthony Quinn
Mark Russell	Richard Denning
Don David	Thomas Gomez
Mona Wilton	Lola Albright
Jody Wilton	William Brooks Ching
Miguel	Eduardo Noriega
Sarita Sebastian	Lorraine Chanel
Emiliano	Anthony Caruso
Rafael Reyes	Manuel Rojas

and Matadors

Jesus (Chucho) Solorzano, Rafael Rodriguez, Joaquin Rodriguez (Cagancho), Antonio Velasquez, Felix Briones, Nacho Trevino, Jorge (Ranchero) Aguilar.

Aficionades of Mexico and bullfighting should find "The Magnificent Matador" to their liking. Most others, among general audiences, also should go along with the romantic action offered, since it was lensed south-of-the-border with an authentic flavor that bolsters a regulation story, and the CinemaScope lensing in Eastman Color has a vivid beauty that makes sight values high. Names of Maureen O'Hara and Anthony Quinn should mean something in the general market and business prospects appear about average overall.

Budd Boetticher both directed and wrote the original story on which Charles Lang based his screenplay. Boetticher's direction and story move along conventional, but acceptable, lines for most of the footage with the emphasis on the romantic drama of the plot. However, when the story actually gets into the bullring during the concluding 10 or 12 minutes the picture comes stirringly alive with some of the best bullfight scenes yet captured on film and offered to regular theatre audiences. The arena sequence is strikingly photographed by Lucien Ballard and is the next-best thing to seeing the real article. Wisely, however, for general consumption, the squeamish parts of bullfights are not shown.

The Edward L. Alperson presentation through 20th-Fox, on which Carroll Case served as co-producer, was lensed in its entirety in Mexico, using that country's villages, cities, churches and huge ranches for vividly colorful backgrounds to the story of a matador faced with a great fear when it comes time for his unacknowledged son to be initiated into the role of a full-fledged matador. His reaction to the personal problem turns him from the bullring and while he is attempting to adjust himself he meets and falls in love with a rich American girl. Finale finds him acknowledging his son, born of a youthful love, and together they play the game of life and death with the bulls for the gripping climax.

Miss O'Hara, the rich girl, and Quinn, in the title role, are both good in handling the characters, providing them with a credibility not always clear in the writing. Film introduces Manuel Rojas as the unitiated matador and his personality impresses. More conventional types are done by Richard Denning, Lola Albright and William Brooks Ching as high-living friends of the rich American femme. Interesting Latin characters are played by Thomas Gomez, Eduardo Noriega, Lorraine Chanel, Anthony Caruso and several of Mexico's top matadors.

The production puts considerable stress on music, almost too much so at times when the good score by Raoul Kraushaar is permitted to dominate, instead of support, a number of sequences. There is an excellent title tune, cleffed by Edward L. Alperson Jr., and Paul Herrick, beautifully sung by Kitty White at the beginning and end of the picture. *Brog.*

A Prize of Gold
(COLOR-SONG)

Richard Widmark in European-lensed suspense meller with good prospects generally.

Hollywood, May 13.

Columbia release of Irving Allen-Albert R. Broccoli (Warwick) production. Stars Richard Widmark, Mai Zetterling, Nigel Patrich, George Cole, Donald Wilfit; features Joseph Tomelty, Andrew Ray, Karel Stepanek, Robert Ayres, Eric Pohlmann, Olive Sloane. Directed by Mark Robson. Screenplay, Robert Buckner, John Paxton; from the novel by Max Gatto; camera (Technicolor), Ted Moore; editor, William Lewthwaite; music Malcolm Arnold, played by the London Symphony Orchestra; songs, Ned Washington and Lester Lee; Tommie Conner and Gerhardt Bronner; sung by Joan Regan. Previewed May 9, '55 Running time, **96 MINS.**

Joe Lawrence	Richard Widmark
Maria	Mai Zetterling
Brian	Nigel Patrick
Roger	George Cole
Alfie Stratton	Donald Wolfit
Uncle Dan	Joseph Tomelty
Conrad	Andrew Ray
Dr. Zachmann	Karel Stepanek
Tex	Robert Ayres
Hans Fischer	Eric Pohlmann
Mavis	Olive Sloane
Major Bracken	Alan Gifford
British Major	Ivan Craig
Benny	Harry Towb
Pole	Leslie Linder
Lisa	Monika Kossmann
Girl on Plane	Edelweiss Malchin
Canal Foreman	Erich Dunskus
German Landlady	Nelly Arno
Police-Detective	Arnold Bell
British Officer	John Witty
G. I.s	Joel Riordan, Marvin Kane

(*Aspect ratio*: 1.66-1)

"A Prize of Gold" is a taut suspense thriller unfolded against vividly interesting Berlin-London backgrounds. Produced overseas by Warwick Films, pic has Richard Widmark toplining a good cast to provide domestic marquee strength and overall business prospects shape up well.

Based on Max Catto's novel of the same title, the script by Robert Buckner and John Paxton details the hijacking of gold bullion being air-transported from Berlin to London. The writing lays a good foundation for the climaxing action, switching from lightly humorous handling in the first half to tight excitement in the latter half and Mark Robson's direction projects in all strongly with the aid of the topnotch cast.

Widmark is an American sergeant stationed in the British sector of Berlin who turns larcenous when Mai Zetterling, a refugee with whom he has fallen in love, needs funds to transport a group of war-displaced children for whom she is caring to South America and a new life. Helping to force Widmark's decision is the fact Miss Zetterling is being offered the needed money by a rich lech. With a British sergeant, George Cole, and a dissolute British flyer, Nigel Patrick, the plane bearing the gold is hijacked over the Channel, landed at an abandoned airstrip before Widmark, along with Cole, begins to have a change of heart. Patrick, handy with gun and fists, is loathe to give up his share, setting up some rough and ready action before Widmark is able to give himself up to the authorities. Before surrender, however, he assures Miss Zetterings goal by exonerating Donald Wolfit and Joseph Tomelty, aiding on the British end of the heist, on their promise to supply the coin for the South American trip.

Warwick producers Irving Allen and Albert R. Broccoli do their supervision well, particularly in the use of actual foreign sites to add authentic interest to the plot. Technicolor lensing by Ted Moore is an asset, as are the other technical functions. Malcolm Arnold's score is good and the title tune, by Ned Washington and Lester Lee, has a whistleable quality. It is prettily sung by Joan Regan.

Brog.

Five Against the House

Guy Madison, Kim Novak topping thriller entertainment with prospects for generally satisfactory playdates.

Hollywood, May 13.

Columbia release of Stirling Silliphant-John Barnwell (Dayle) production. Stars Guy Madison, Kim Novak, Brian Keith, Alvy Moore, Kerwin Mathews; costars William Conrad; features Jack Dimond, Jean Willes. Directed by Phil Karlson. Screenplay, Silliphant, William Bowers, Barnwell; based on the Good Housekeeping story by Jack Finney; camera, Lester White; editor, Jerome Thoms; music, George Duning, conducted by Morris Stoloff. Previewed April 21, '55. Running time, **82 MINS.**

Al Mercer ....Guy Madison
Kay Greylek ....Kim Novak
Brick ....Brian Keith
Roy ....Alvy Moore
Eric Berg ....William Conrad
Ronnie ....Kerwin Mathews
Francis Spieglebauer ....Jack Dimond
Virginia ....Jean Willes
Robert Fenton ....John Zaremba
Jack Roper ....George Brand
Brad Lacey ....Mark Hanna
Mrs. Valent ....Carroll McComas
Pat Winters ....Hugh Sanders

(Aspect ratio: 1.66-1)

Pitching its entertainment directly at the younger element filmgoers, "Five Against the House" delivers well enough to have prospects for generally satisfactory playdates in most regular situations. Backing the youth emphasis in cast and plot are some suspenseful melodramatics that will appeal to the chief group at which the pic is slanted.

Plot of the Dayle production for Columbia is pegged on a scheme cooked up by a thrill-seeking college student to rob Harold's Club in Reno. (For those who think the pic offers a foolproof blueprint for larceny, it should be noted that security at Harold's is quite different now than what is shown.)

Actual Reno locales are used to bolster authenticity and producers Stirling Silliphant and John Barnwell, who share script credit with William Bowers, bring the show off in okay fashion. The screenplay, from the mag story by Jack Finney, takes a light turn here and there to temper the suspense, as well as introducing a romance angle, satisfactorily projected by Guy Madison and Kim Novak. Latter pair should help ticket sales, both doing their chores well, Miss Novak with considerable s.a. voltage. Performances all down the line are excellent, with other standouts being Brian Keith, Alvy Moore, and Kerwin Mathews. The direction by Phil Karlson is a large factor in making the characterizations well valued and the suspense tight.

Mathews is the rich boy who plots the Harold's robbery just to prove it can be done. By trickery he gets Madison, fellow student, and the latter's girl, Miss Novak, cafe singer, involved. Scheme first starts to go awry when Keith, psycho, ex-GI student, decides the robbery should be for real and takes charge just before the heist is to be pulled. Fifth member of the party is Moore, in on the deal for laughs. Tension sets in when Keith takes over and he plays the psycho so realistically the nerves get tight and stay that way through the actual holdup and the climax when Madison is able to trap and talk Keith into surrender.

Lester White's lensing displays the action well, and there is an excellent score by George Duning, conducted by Morris Stoloff, to back the drama. Other credits do their jobs expertly. Score contains one uncredited song, done by Miss Novak's cafe-singer character.

Brog.

Crashout

Hard-hitting prison break melodrama for expected satisfactory grosses in program market.

Hollywood, May 11.

Filmakers release of a Hal E. Chester production. Stars William Bendix, Arthur Kennedy, Luther Adler, William Talman, Marshall Thompson, Beverly Michaels. Features Gloria Talbot, Adam Williams. Directed by Lewis R. Foster. Original screenplay, Chester, Foster. Camera, Russell Metty; editor, Robert Swink; art director, Wiard Ihnen; music, Leith Stevens. Previewed May 10, '55. Running time, **88 MINS.**

Van Duff ....William Bendix
Joe Quinn ....Arthur Kennedy
Pete Mendoza ....Luther Adler
Swanee Remsen ....William Talman
Monk Collins ....Gene Evans
Billy Lang ....Marshall Thompson
Alice Mosher ....Beverly Michaels
Girl on Train ....Gloria Talbot
Fred ....Adam Williams
Doctor Barnes ....Percy Helton
Girl in Bar ....Melinda Markey
Timmy ....Chris Olsen
Mrs. Mosher ....Adele St. Maur
Conductor ....Edward Clark
Bartender ....Tom Dugan
Head Guard ....Morris Ankrum

(Aspect ratio: 1.85-1)

"Crashout" is the violent story of six convicts after a prison break, limning their desperate efforts to reach a fortune in coin cached by the leader of the break. Its 88-minutes' running time is overlong and in need of trimming to speed up draggy footage, but in the melodrama market it should meet with good reception, spurred by the names of a strong male cast.

Hal E. Chester, who scripted with director Lewis R. Foster, is responsible for hard realistic values in his production supervision, and megger also punches over the action for frequent suspense. He gets top performances right down the line. Additionally, the music score by Leith Stevens gives sock to the individual scenes. Other technical credits also are above average for a program picture.

William Bendix, turning convincingly from comedy to a ruthless killer, is the leader of the escaped cons, who cuts them in on a share of his buried swag if they'll get him medical attention to treat a bad wound and help him to the cache, some days away from where they're holed up after the break. One by one the cons meet their death as they try for their goal, until only Bendix and Arthur Kennedy are left to uncover the coin on a mountainside, where Bendix attempts to kill his partner and falls to his death. Climax is weak and indefinite.

Both actors are standouts, and their fellow cons include Luther Adler, William Talman, Gene Evans and Marshall Thompson, each registering in his individual performance. Beverly Michaels is in for distaff interest, practically dragged in by the heels for this effect. Gloria Talbot and Adam Williams head supporting cast capably.

Whit.

Kid for Two Farthings

Warm hearted Carol Reed production based on Wolf Mankowitz's tale with an East Side setting; bright prospects in U.S. market could stem from arty house dates.

London, May 10.

Independent Film Distributors Ltd. release of London Films production. Stars Celia Johnson, Diana Dors, David Kossoff. Directed by Carol Reed. Screenplay by Wolf Mankowitz from his book; camera, Edward Scaife; editor, A. S. Bates; music, Benjamin Frankel. At Plaza, London. May 10, '55. Running time, **96 MINS.**

Joanna ....Celia Johnson
Sonia ....Diana Dors
Kandinsky ....David Kossoff
"Lady" Ruby ....Brenda de Banize
Sam ....Joe Robinson
Joe ....Jonathan Ashmore
"Madam" Rita ....Sydney Tafler
Python ....Primo Carnera
Blackie Isaacs ....Lou Jacobi
Oliver ....Harold Berens
Dora ....Daphne Anderson
Bason ....Danny Green
Mimi ....Vera Day
Ice Berg ....Sidney James
Mrs. Abramowitz ....Irene Handl
Alf, the Bird Man ....Alfie Bass
Mrs. Alf ....Rosalind Boxall
Sylvester (the photographer ....Eddie Byrne

Carol Reed has extracted a great deal of charm from Wolf Mankowitz's novel. The resultant picture will need specialized exploitation to insure top b.o. results. This is strictly offbeat entertainment, rich in color and atmosphere, which should pay handsome dividends in certain situations. It may be a more difficult proposition away from the bigger cities. It has exceptional possibilities for the U.S., which may best be developed by opening with selective art house engagements.

Having adapted his own story for the screen, author Mankowitz has retained the essential East Side atmosphere although having made a few variations in the plot development. This is not a conventional story, but a series of cameos set in the Jewish quarter of London and around the famed Petticoat Lane. And the portraits as etched by Mankowitz and filmed by Carol Reed are unveiled with warmth and sincerity.

Some of the Petticoat Lane scenes were filmed on location, and the characters mainly are real enough. There's David Kossoff as the trouser-maker, whose great ambition is to own a steam press; Diane Dors, a blonde popsie, who has been waiting four long years for her engagement ring; Joe Robinson, the muscle man, who is Kossoff's assistant and Miss Dors' intended, who is induced to go into the ring to raise some coin, and finally an engaging youngster, Jonathan Ashmore, who believes he has found the answer to all his problems when he buys a one-horned kid on learning of the miracles of the unicorn.

It's about these characters that the action moves, usually at a gentle pace, but speeded up sometimes, particularly for the wrestling scenes between Robinson and Primo Carnera. There are tender incidents throughout as the moppet makes wishes to the "Unicorn" and finds they come to pass.

Reed's direction is bold and authoritative. He uses color for the first time in his career with telling effect and, within the framework of the setting, has achieved all that could have been expected. Kossoff, who received the British Oscar as most promising screen newcomer this year, gives a performance as the trouser-maker (with an unusual bent towards philosophy) that is a model of sincerity. Miss Dors plays her part with complete conviction. Celia Johnson is badly miscast as the boy's mother, and hardly ever comes to grips with the role. Robinson looks the part of the muscle man. Sydney Tafler scores again as a storekeeper; Carnera is thoroughly aggressive as the wrestler, and Lou Jacobi makes a personal hit as the promoter. Brenda de Banzie contributes another flawless performance as Tafler's principal assistant. Competent feature performers of the calibre of Harold Berens, Danny Green, Sidney James, Vera Day, Daphne Anderson, Alfie Bass and Irene Handl head a firstclass team of British artists.

Edward Scaife has handled the Eastmancolor cameras with commendable skill. Wilfred Shingleton gets credit for his impressive sets. A. S. Bates has edited the pic concisely and Benjamin Frankel's score is a plus feature.

Myro.

Der Letzte Akt
(The Last Act)
(GERMAN)

Cologne, May 10.

Columbia release of Cosmopol production. Stars Albin Skoda and Oskar Werner. Directed by G. W. Pabst. Screenplay by Fritz Habeck after script by Erich Maria Remarque and based on book, "Ten Days to Die," by M. A. Musmano; camera, Guenther Anders; music, Erwin Halletz. At Hahnentor Theatre, Cologne. Running time, **115 MINS.**

Hitler ....Albin Skoda
Eva Braun ....Lotto Tobisch
Capt. Wuest ....Oskar Werner
Goebbels ....Herman Erhardt
Himmler ....Erich Suckmann
Fagelin ....Julius Jonak
Frau Goebbels ....Helga Dohrn
Richard ....Gerd Zoehling

A gripping and terrifying picture, "Der Letzte Akt" packs a

powerful impact from start to end. Film is probably as close to the truth as any historical presentation of this sadistic, mad fanatic can be. In its portrayal of the last days of Hitler, pic spells sock drama which keeps the viewer on edge, filled with increasing horror and reliving the appalling depths of history. It makes one wonder: "Why didn't someone stop him?"

This Cosmopol production, made in Vienna, is given an art slant. Only the title appears on the screen, then the camera moves to the bunker in which much of the pic takes place. Credits which would break the mood are never intruded. And the production, from its horrible beginning to its agonizing end, is a deeply moving one.

Albin Skoda, as Hitler, plays the maniac leader who realizes that he is trapped in the bunker at Berlin as U. S. and Russian forces close in on him. He is depicted trying in his last desperate hours only to save himself—even to the extent of flooding river tunnels to delay the Russian entrance although he knows the tunnels are filled with thousands of homeless refugees.

The tragedy of the whole world is brought out in the only figure of the film which is not historically accurate. A young captain, Wuest, touchingly played by Oskar Werner, is brought in to show the ideals of those who first fought under Der Fuehrer, then realized his terrible misdeeds and tried to stop him. The picture closes with Werner on his deathbed, shot by Hitler's henchmen while trying to stop Hitler from flooding the tunnels, and pleading to keep the world free. His last words, "Sagt nie wieder Jawohl!" (Never again say yes) are a powerful anti-war message, tracing the troubles of Germany to the first time the people agreed to follow Hitler.

There are many grim accuracies portrayed in the film: the frantic devotion of Goebbels and his wife, who brought their children to the bunker to die along with their leader; the immorality and cruelties of Hitler's top officers; the rivalry between SS and the General Staff; the growing disillusionment of some Hitler Youth Organization members as they saw the wanton waste of lives; and Hitler's idiosyncracies in following horoscopes and spending his last hours in a mad conceit of dictating his "political testimony" after the rush-marriage to Eva Braun. These also show the desperate forced gaiety of the people trapped in the canteen in the bunker, nurses, wounded soldiers, remnants of Hitler's army, getting riotously drunk and dancing with an insane abandon, knowing the end of their dictatorship and probably the end of their lives is at hand.

Cosmopol has set out to accomplish the cruel realism of a newsreel set back in 1945. Acting, settings, directing, and photography all are brilliantly done with attention to minute accuracy. Occasionally the cuts seem a little abrupt and the sound not perfectly even, which is a minor handicap. But as a film, "Der Letzte Akt" may be too soon or too late—the world has partly forgotten the terrible deeds of the mad maniac, and some of the hatred has been alleviated by time. This once again brings to the fore all the cunning, cruelty and inhuman injustices of the ruler and some of his followers. This stark film may re-intensify the hatreds and bitternesses by bringing back detailed atrocities of man-against-mankind.

Guil.

Kinder, Mutter Und Ein General

(Children, Mothers and a General)
(GERMAN)

Frankfurt, May 3.

Schorchtfilm release of an Eric Pommer-Intercontinental production. Stars Hilde Krahl, Bernhard Wicki, Ewald Balser. Directed by Laslo Benedek. Screenplay, Herbert Reinecker, after his novel; camera, Werner Pohl; music, Werner Eisbrenner. At Turmpalast, Frankfurt. Running time, **120 MINS.**

Frau Asmussen	Hilde Krahl
Others mothers	Therest Giehse, Ursula Hecking, Alice Treft, Marianne Sinclair
Inge	Beate Koepnick
Hauptmann Dornberg	Bernhard Wicki
General	Ewald Balser

When a name like Erich Pommer, one of the greats of the German film industry, is associated with a film, it's bound to be an attention-getter locally. This pic, in addition, has the added directorial achievements of Laslo Benedek. The film, however, despite the efforts of the two and some excellent acting by Hilde Krahl, Ewald Balser and Bernhard Wicki, falls into the category of a problem pic, with the entertainment played down while worthy of the prestige it attains, it will probably never be a big b.o. hit.

Story takes place in the last days of the German army's battle with the Russians. Five women find that their 15-year-old sons have been taken from school and sent to the front lines. The women, plus a young sister of one student, hike to the front and try to rescue their sons from almost certain death as the battle surges around them. The rulebound German officers try to cope with the hopeless situation.

Only relief from the grim story is supplied by the lovely sensuous presence of Beate Koepnick, who plays the young girl whose brother has become a soldier. She exudes an appealing warmth in her brief love episode, and brightens every scene.

Interesting aspect is that much of the film was made in Hamburg, only 35 miles from the actual Russian zone today in north Germany, and the actors are exceptionally true to life in portraying their situation vis-a-vis the Russians. The film, while not obviously anti-Nazi, portrays the complete futility of the war, hitting hard at today's top German topic, the rearmament.

Because of its standout directing and acting, plus the serious plot, the film might have a special U. S. art house appeal. *Guil.*

Hiroshima

(JAPANESE)

Continental Distributing presentation of East-West Films production. Directed by Hideo Sekigawa. Story and screenplay, Yasutaro Yagi; camera, Nakao Urashima; editor, Mia Yamaoka; music, Akira Ifukube. Previewed in New York, May 11, '55; running time, **85 MINS.**

Endo	Yoshi Katch
Kitagawa	Eiji Okada
Mine	Tsuzu Yamada
Yukio Endo (boy)	Yasuaki Takano
Yukio Endo (young man)	Masayuki Tsukida
Michiko (child)	Hiromi Murase
Miss Yonehara	Yumeji Tsukioka

(In Japanese, English Titles)

"Hiroshima," an effort at chronoscoping the immediate and long-range effects of the A-Bomb drop on Hiroshima, defies classification with the other Japanese imports which have won art house bookings and American b.o. As a picture, it's somewhat muddled, and by no means an artie; as a propaganda weapon, and a powerful one, it's bound to attract a good deal of attention throughout the U.S.

The picture's power comes entirely from one sequence showing the immediate aftermath of the explosion, a brilliantly staged and photographed quarter-hour which ought to go down as a masterpiece of pictorialized destruction and agony. However muddled the remainder of the picture, director Hideo Sekigawa has scored a major cinematographic and propaganda triumph with these scenes, depicting torn and bloody people lifting themselves from the wreckage amidst swirls of radiated dust; a husband abandoning his helpless wife to look for his child; school children singing in the river, where they've escaped the flames, and finally drifting off in weariness; lines of bent and dazed tatters drifting they know not where. It takes a strong stomach and heart to view these scenes, but they are as powerful as any filmed.

Unfortunately, the rest of the picture (the A-Bomb scenes come at the beginning) are anticlimactic. Moreover, the film lacks a single point of view, picking up threads of lives here and there and suddenly dropping them for no apparent reason. Most of the Yasutaro Yagi script concerns itself with the life of a youngster who had escaped the bomb but lost his parents and a brother and sister. His brushes with the law, his aimlessness and a final revolt against working in his uncle's factory where cannon shells were being made, is supposed to typify the confusion of Japanese youth today. But these points are made episodically and with a lot of diversionary material in between. The English subtitles are good as far as they go, but there aren't enough of them to follow the action completely.

Yasuaki Takano and Masayuki Tsukida both deliver expert portrayals of the boy, the former at the time of the bomb and the latter some 10 years later. Yoshi Katch does a fine job as the agonized father, searching through the wreckage for his son after leaving his wife. Eiji Okada is good as a sympathetic teacher in the postwar era.

Film quality is uneven, largely because of the integration of newsreel footage at points and also because of a couple of sequences apparently separately shot with English narration. But that bomb sequence is enough to make the entire film noteworthy, despite its other faults. And Akira Ifukube has contributed a western-style dirge-like score that heightens the horror of that post-bomb sequence.

Chan.

Heidi und Peter

(SWISS—COLOR)

Zurich, May 10.

Praesens Film release of Praesens (Lazar Wechsler) production. Directed by Franz Schnyder. Screenplay, Richard Schweizer, based on Johanna Spyri story; camera (Eastmancolor), Emil Berna; music, Robert Blum; editor, Hermann Haller. At Rex Theatre, Zurich. Running time, **93 MINS.**

Alp-Oehi	Heinrich Gretler
Heidi	Elsbeth Sigmund
Peter	Thomas Klameth
Teacher	Emil Hegetschweiler
Herr Sesemann	Willy Birgel
Grandma Sesemann	Traute Carlsen
Klara Sesemann	Isa Guenther
Sebastian	Theo Lingen
Miss Rottenmeier	Anita Mey
Dr. Classen	Carl Wery
Brigitte	Margrit Rainer
Baker	Max Haufler
Pastor	Fred Tanner
1st Geometer	Schaggi Streuli
2nd Geometer	Peter W. Loosli

(In German; No English Titles)

Though not up to its predecessor, this sequel to 1952-53's successful "Heidi" will rack up hefty coin both here and abroad. It is the first Swiss tinter, and its Eastmancolor photography (print by Technicolor) can stand comparison with some of the best foreign efforts. Color is of extreme clarity and brilliance, with some shots of the Swiss mountain scenery being virtually breathtaking. Vet cameraman Emil Berna is the real star of this one.

"Heidi und Peter" is Praesens Film's first offering in over 17 months, its last one, "The Village," not doing so well. "Heidi II" will more than make up for it, coinwise. It also looks like an okay grosser in the U. S.—plus being a terrific trailer for the Swiss Tourist Office.

The story picks up where "Heidi I" left off. It concentrates mostly on Heidi's experiences with her playmate Peter and her girl-friend from Frankfurt who comes to Switzerland with her family to recuperate from a long illness. Plot moves along leisurely without any great excitement. Towards the end it picks up, approaching the near-spectacular by means of a rousing thunderstorm in the mountains with ensuing inundation of the village. A Swiss country-fair is neatly brought to life in some final scenes. Generally, however, the plot's thinness cannot be overlooked. It is not up to that of "Heidi."

The cast is the same as in the first film, but somehow does not always seem very inspired. The two moppets, Elsbeth Sigmund and Thomas Klameth, have lost some of their naturalness which has given way to a more conscious style of acting. The contingent of players from Germany includes some important marquee names over here, especially Theo Lingen and Willy Birgel. But some of their lines are at times wooden. Of the supporting cast, Emil Hegetschweiler, Isa Guenther and Heinrich Gretler fare best.

Technically, this is superior to "Heidi." Lensing by Berna is standout while editing (Herman Haller) and sound (Rolf Epstein) are okay. Lots of outdoor scenes, lensed on location, contribute importantly to the picture's visual beauty which is considerably enhanced by the skillful use of color.

Mezo.

Romeo and Juliet

(RUSSIAN—COLOR)

Cannes, May 10.

Mosfilm production and release. Stars Oulanova, Jdanov; features, Koren, Lutchilene, Erminslaiev. Direction, screenplay choreography by L. Arnchtam, L. Lavosky. From Shakespeare's play. Camera (Sovcolor), A. Chelenov, Tchen-You-Lin; music, Serge Prokofiev; editor, Lichorshin. At Cannes Film Festival. Running time, **90 MINS.**

Juliet	Oulanova
Romeo	Jdanov
Mercutio	Koren
Lorenzo	Lutchiline
Tybett	Erminislaiev
Paris	Lapouri

Primarily for balletomanes, this well-mounted full-length ballet film, based on Shakespeare's "Romeo And Juliet," might be of interest to some arty houses on its excellence of dance conception, color and renown of prima ballerina Oulanova. It is the dance firmly welded to film form. The acting is also well controlled for exciting effects.

This interesting terp pic which will need crix, word-of-mouth and delicate handling for the limited situation showings in America. However, its unusual production makes this well worth the try. It appears to have greater appeal than its predecessors, "The Big Concert" and "Stars of the Ballet Russe." Commentary is used sparingly.

Shakespeare's plot is closely followed as the raging hatred of the Montagus and Capulets is executed with a superbly mounted dueling episode to set the tone. Oulanova's beautiful dance style mixes well with her acting ability. Others also are fine. Editing, color, music and highly skilled production aspects all blend to make this a solid off-beater. *Mosk.*

Mister Roberts
(C'SCOPE-COLOR)

A hit as a book and as a play, "Mister Roberts" clicks again as a pic; socko entertainment, bright b.o. biz.

Hollywood, May 24.

Warner Bros. release of Leland Hayward (Orange) production. Stars Henry Fonda, James Cagney, William Powell, Jack Lemmon; costarring Betsy Palmer, Ward Bond. Directed by John Ford, Mervyn LeRoy. Screenplay, Frank Nugent, Joshua Logan; Logan; from the play by Thomas Heggen and Logan; from the novel by Heggen as produced on the stage by Hayward; camera (WarnerColor), Winton Hoch; editor, Jack Murray; music, Franz Waxman. Previewed May 10, '55. Running time, 120 MINS.

Lt. (J.G.) Roberts	Henry Fonda
The Captain	James Cagney
Doc	William Powell
Ensign Pulver	Jack Lemmon
Lt. Ann Girard	Betsy Palmer
C.P.O. Dowdy	Ward Bond
Mannion	Phil Carey
Reber	Nick Adams
Dolan	Ken Curtis
Stefanowski	Harry Carey Jr.
Gerhart	Frank Aletter
Lindstrom	Fritz Ford
Mason	Buck Kartalian
Lt. Billings	William Henry
Olson	William Hudson
Schlemmer	Stubby Kruger
Cookie	Harry Tenbrook
Rodrigues	Perry Lopez
Insigna	Robert Roark
Bookser	Pat Wayne
Wiley	Tiger Andrews
Kennedy	Jim Moloney
Gilbert	Denny Niles
Cochren	Francis Connor
Johnson	Shug Fisher
Jonesy	Danny Borzage
Taylor	Jim Murphy
Nurses	Kathleen O'Malley, Maura Murphy, Mimi Doyle, Jeanne Murray, Lonnie Pierce
Shore Patrol Officer	Martin Milner
Shore Patrolman	Gregory Walcott
Military Policeman	James Flavin
Marine Sergeant	Jack Pennick
Native Chief	Duke Kahanamoko

From bestseller to hit play to click pic is the boxoffice parlay for "Mister Roberts." The late Thomas Heggen's salty comedy about life aboard a Navy cargo ship had no trouble moving from the printed page to the stage. It segues just as easily to the screen, and with the kind of entertainment that means handsome grosses in the keys and elsewhere.

While the play, as produced on the stage by Leland Hayward to a resounding success, has been transplanted to the screen virtually intact, it benefits from the camera's broader technique. The breadth and scope achieved with the CinemaScope lensing in WarnerColor puts dimensions into the works not possible previously. As producer of the picture it's a socko repeat for Hayward, as well as for the original Heggen tome and the playwrighting he did with Joshua Logan. Latter teamed with Frank Nugent on the film script, and the pairing makes for an outstanding payoff in screen entertainment.

The masculine, four-letter words used in the book and play are gone, but not their flavor on inference. Nor is the way of a sailor with a maid, either in longings at sea or on liberty ashore, treated unrealistically, so the comedy is amusingly bawdy at times. It's a thoroughly masculine story about sailors from which the distaffers will get just as much of a boot as the male viewers. Figuring importantly in the sock manner with which it all comes off is the directorial credit shared by John Ford and Mervyn LeRoy, the former having had to bow out because of illness midway in production. Particularly notable in the handling, in the midst of all the rowdy comedy, are the touching moments of drama that tug at the senses, especially during the climaxing scenes when "Mister Roberts" leaves the cargo ship and its crew later learns of his death.

Henry Fonda, who scored on the stage in the title role, repeats in the picture as the cargo officer who resented not being in the thick of the fighting in the Pacific during World War II. Film is Fonda's first in some years and should make Hollywood and the public newly aware that talent such as his should be used more frequently on the screen. All down the line the casting seems perfect, so well do the players perform their chores. James Cagney is simply great as the captain of the ship, a "little" man in size and soul who makes life aboard even more tedious and unbearable for the men under him. Audiences everywhere will enter wholeheartedly into the sailors' conspiracy against Cagney and enjoy thoroughly the comedy that results.

William Powell tackles the role of ship's doctor with an easy assurance that makes it stand out and Jack Lemmon is a big hit as Ensign Pulver, the big-talking, do-nothing schemer against the captain. The scene in which Fonda, Powell and Lemmon manufacture some phoney scotch to be used by Lemmon in his planned seduction of Betsy Palmer, a nurse, is a howler. Miss Palmer provides a welcome, too-brief, femme touch, as do the other nurses on whom the girl-hungry sailors spy from shipboard while the lovelies engage in hospital shower room activities.

Ward Bond, as the CPO, is another who stands out in the fine cast, among whom are Phil Carey, Nick Adams, Ken Curtis, particularly good as Dolan; Harry Carey Jr., Perry Lopez, Robert Roark, as Insigna; Pat Wayne, and Martin Milner, latter excellent as the mush-mouthed shore patrol officer who confines the sailors to ship after an especially riotous liberty. Stubby Kruger's motorcycle plunge off of a dock is hilarious.

Among the credits that help make this a potent entertainment buy is the photography by Winton Hoch, the score by Franz Waxman, editing, art direction, and sound handling. The two-hour length seems short. *Brog.*

Love Me or Leave Me
(C'SCOPE—COLOR—MUSICAL)

Socko offbeat filmusical based on the Ruth Etting-"Col." Gimp saga that will do beaucoup b.o.

Metro release of Joe Pasternak production. Stars Doris Day and James Cagney; features Cameron Mitchell, Robert Keith, Tom Tully, Harry Bellaver, Richard Gaines, Peter Leeds. Directed by Charles Vidor. Screenplay, Daniel Fuchs & Isobel Lennart from original by Fuchs; camera (Eastmancolor), Arthur E. Arling; new songs, Nicholas Brodszky & Sammy Cahn, Chilton Price; popular standards in the cavalcade by Irving Berlin, DeSylva, Brown & Henderson, Walter Donaldson, Arthur Freed, Gus Kahn, McCarthy & Monaco, Turk & Ahlert, Rodgers & Hart and others; musical supervision, George Stoll; Miss Day's music, Percy Faith; asst. director, Ridgeway Callow; editor, Ralph E. Winters; musical adviser, Irving Aaronson; dances, Alex Romero; special effects, Warren Newcombe. Tradeshown, N. Y., May 19, '55. Running time, 122 MINS.

Ruth Etting	Doris Day
Martin Snyder	James Cagney
Johnny Alderman	Cameron Mitchell
Bernard V. Loomis	Robert Keith
Frobisher	Tom Tully
Georgie	Harry Bellaver
Paul Hunter	Richard Gaines
Fred Taylor	Peter Leeds
Eddie Fulton	Claude Stroud
Jingle Girl	Audrey Young
Greg Trent	John Harding

Metro's concept of the Ruth Etting story, under the title of "Love Me or Leave Me," embodies one of the two basic Hollywood filmusical formulae: and-then-I-wrote or and-then-I-sang. While it's not the usual songsmith cavalcade (Miss Etting was and is depicted essentially as a song delineator), it does blend so rich a medley of some of the more popular standards of the 1920s that it's virtually a salute to ASCAP. But first it should be recorded, in the traditional first-paragraph VARIETY opinion, that the film has plenty for the boxoffice. In all situations.

"Love Me or Leave Me is unique and sufficiently offbeat to enjoy a distinction all its own. The offbeat aspects of the strange real-life relationship of Miss Etting and "Col." Moe (here called Martin) Snyder has been caught with an honesty and realism that borders on creating mixed emotions. In short, Doris Day as Miss Etting, is so consumed by ambition as to blot out the nefarious antecedents of "The Gimp," so ably played by James Cagney. His personation of the clubfooted Chicago hoodlum and muscle-man is the Cagney of the Warner Bros. gangster pictures of the early 1930s—hard-bitten, cruel, sadistic and unrelenting. Well, almost unrelenting. It is this one factor—his uncouth, clumsy carving of the ambitious girl's career to fullest fruition—that creates a somewhat leavening effect.

The fact that, after he gains her the Ziegfeldian heights, his boorishness forces her out of the glamor and the glory that is Broadway and back into the nitery circuits, and that he is alternatingly her defender and her deterrent, make for the offbeat quality.

For once this isn't a routine glorification of a show biz personality. In actuality, Miss Etting might be said to be one of the lesser known greats, and certainly so to the present generation. Even in her heights in the Volsteadian era, she was a "special" type of songstress.

Therefore it's to the credit of the Joe Pasternak production, Charles Vidor's direction and basically to the trenchant Daniel Fuchs (who also did the original)-Isobel Lennart screenplay that it unspools as it does.

The flavor and the atmosphere of the muscle days of the Chicago ginmills and The Gimp's aggressive techniques (his was a laundry business racket), which motivate her from the dumps to Broadway, to radio and to Hollywood, project a facet of the predatory kill-or-get-killed machinations which give the auditor a new insight on behind-the-scenes show biz.

It becomes difficult betimes to know for whom to root. Their "marriage" is a strange thing. Her recourse to the bottle; her dull-eyed acceptance of the somewhat unholy nuptial alliance; her consuming ambition to scale the heights; her careful decorum vis-a-vis pianist-arranger Johnny Alderman (well played by Cameron Mitchell); the patience of the agent (Robert Keith, another good job); the dogged faithfulness of Harry Bellaver as the dimwit stooge-bodyguard, and the rest of it, make for an arresting chunk of celluloid. Musically there's almost too much but Miss Day does uncork a flock of socko standards, and two good new ones, "I'll Never Stop Loving You" (Brodzky-Cahn) and "Never Look Back" (by Chilton Price).

Miss Day has been given the full treatment sartorially and cinematographically. She is easy on the optics in both departments, and certainly never assaults the aural faculties, because this Columbia recording star is essentially a commercial thrush. Given a sharp Helen Rose set of costumes, a special maestro-arranger in Percy Faith (her pro batoneer at the diskery, when it's not Culver City), she rings the bell and is thoroughly convincing at least so far as her vocal prowess is concerned. She is also effective histrionically.

Besides the title song and the two originals above mentioned, the Hit Parade of the Ignoble Experiment known as the Volsteadian period embraces "Stay on the Right Side of the Road," "You Made Me Love You," "Everybody Loves My Baby," "Mean to Me," "Sam, the Old Accordion Man," "At Sundown," "Shaking the Blues Away," "It All Depends on You," and "Ten Cents a Dance," and she does 'em all with distinction.

The Etting-Gimp saga, of course, is capped with the real-life dramatic climax when Snyder took a shot at Myrl (here called Johnny) Alderman, Miss Etting's pianist and later her husband. (In real life, The Gimp has since retired to Chicago, reportedly involved in local ward politics).

Under Metro filming, in CinemaScope and color, it's a rich canvas of the Roaring 20s with gutsy and excellent performances that spell strong b.o. all the way. One authentic little touch not in the picture was The Gimp's almost reverential way of referring to his star as "the little lady." *Abel.*

Soldier of Fortune
(C'SCOPE—COLOR)

Topnotch action-adventure with Clark Gable, Susan Hayward, plus Hong Kong backgrounds and good biz outlook.

Hollywood, May 24.

20th-Fox release of Buddy Adler production. Stars Clark Gable, Susan Hayward, Michael Rennie, Gene Barry; features Alex D'Arcy, Tom Tully, Anna Sten, Russell Collins, Leo Gordon, Richard Loo, Soo Yong, Frank Tang, Jack Kruschen, Mel Welles. Directed by Edward Dmytryk. Screenplay, Ernest K. Gann, from his novel; camera (De Luxe Color), Leo Tover; editor, Dorothy Spencer; music, Hugo Friedhofer, conducted by Lionel Newman. Previewed May 20, '55. Running time, **96 MINS.**

Hank Lee .... Clark Gable
Jane Hoyt .... Susan Hayward
Inspector Marryweather..Michael Rennie
Louis Hoyt .... Gene Barry
Rene .... Alex D'Arcy
Tweedie .... Tom Tully
Mme. Dupree .... Anna Sten
Icky .... Russell Collins
Big Matt .... Leo Gordon
Po-Lin .... Richard Loo
Dak Lai .... Soo Yong
Ying Fai .... Frank Tang
Austin Stoker .... Jack Kruschen
Rocha .... Mel Welles
Major Leith Phipps .... Jack Raine
Gunner .... George Wallace
Australian Airma..n......Alex Finlayson
Luan .... Noel Toy
Chinese Clerk .... Beal Wong
Father Xavier .... Robert Burton
Frank Stewart .... Robert Quarry
Hotel Desk Clerk..........Charles Davis
Goldie .... Victor Sen Yung
Maxine .... Frances Fong
Billy Lee .... Danny Chang

Clark Gable and Susan Hayward team advantageously in this thriller of mystery and intrigue in the Orient. There's plenty of action, a lacing of romance, and some spectacular photographic effects in CinemaScope to make it a well-balance show that should attract and please the cash customers. The business outlook is good.

Hong Kong is the setting for all of the exteriors in the Buddy Adler production and the authentic backgrounds sharpen the overall topnotch values obtained under his supervision. Ernest K. Gann committed his own novel to screenplay form, and the writing, along with Edward Dmytryk's very able direction, keeps the high adventure of the plot always on a believable plane. It's this type of handling that makes the action more exciting, the suspense more gripping, and there's plenty of both.

When Miss Hayward's husband, Gene Barry, disappears on a photographic trip into Red China, she comes to Hong Kong to institute a search for him and runs the gamut of colorful types, most all of whom have their hands out for a quick buck with little intention of doing more than taking advantage of the situation. With British authorities and others no help, her path leads to Gable, soldier of fortune reaping just that with some smuggling enterprises. Developing a personal interest in the lady, he decides to rescue the husband from the Reds because he likes his competition at hand, not remote. It's a real thriller the way he brings this off, and there are plenty of rugged scenes beforehand as he seeks out needed information from reluctant characters. The payoff's all right, too, because he gets the gal, her husband deciding he'll always be off on such escapades and a wife is a hinderance.

Gable and Miss Hayward make a sock team for this type of drama and there is no strain on credence the way they go about making the characters seem like real people. The same skilled delinations are notably throughout the cast. Michael Rennie is extremely able and likeable as a Crown officer participating in the rescue and Barry shows up well in lesser footage. Colorful types that add point to the footage are played among others, by Alex D'Arcy, Tom Tully, Anna Sten, Russell Collins, Leo Gordon, Richard Loo, very good as an ex-general; Soo Yong, Frank Tang, Jack Kruschen, Mel Welles, Jack Raine, Noel Toy, Robert Quarry, Charles Davis, Frances Fong and Grace Chang.

The standout photography by Leo Tover takes the audience on an intriguing tour of Hong Kong and its points of interest, but wisely never lets the picture become a travelog that would interfer with the story-telling. In only one department does the latter slip —it skirts calling the Communist Chinese by name. Hugo Friedhofer's score, conducted by Lionel Newman, is a mood asset, the editing is tight and the street sounds of the location sites bolster authenticity. *Brog.*

The Far Horizons
(V'VISION—COLOR)

Overlong, spottily-paced, outdoor feature in VistaVision about the Lewis & Clark Expedition. Okay cast names, mild outlook.

Hollywood, May 20.

Paramount release of William H. Pine-William C. Thomas production. Stars Fred MacMurray, Charlton Heston, Donna Reed, Barbara Hale; features William Demarest, Alan Reed, Eduardo Noriega. Directed by Rudolph Mate. Written by Winston Miller, Edmund H. North; from the novel "Sacajawea of the Shoshones" by Della Gould Emmons; camera (Technicolor), Daniel L. Fapp; 2d unit photography, William Williams editor, Frank Bracht; music, Hans Salter. Previewed May 17, '55. Running time, **107 MINS.**

Merriwether Lewis......Fred MacMurray
Bill Clark .... Charlton Heston
Sacajawea .... Donna Reed
Julia Hancock .... Barbara Hale
Sergeant Cass .... William Demarest
Charboneau .... Alan Reed
Cameahwait .... Eduardo Noriega
Wild Eagle .... Larry Pennell
Le Borgne .... Ralph Moody
President Jefferson ...... Herbert Heyes

(Aspect ratio: 1:85-1)

VistaVision dresses up this outdoor feature purportedly based on the Lewis & Clark Expedition, but, entertainwise, it strikes a program level, with the running time considerably overlength for the general dual bill market. With the current kiddie interest in frontiersmen, it may attract a fair share of the juvenile trade if the ballyhoo is slanted in that direction. Even for the youngsters, though, it's a tedious tour of the Louisiana Purchase that is made, with not enough action to sustain the long 107 minutes of footage.

Scenically, the Pine-Thomas production has magnificent values, thanks to the location lensing in the Jackson Hole country of Wyoming. However, these pictorial splendors aren't sufficient to cover for cliche writing, poor direction, and acting that is, with one exception, only so-so. The screenplay by Winston Miller and Edmund H. North was taken from Della Gould Emmons' novel "Sacajawea of the Shoshones," the story of an Indian maid who helped the expedition and, according to the plot, fell in love with Clark. This copper rose of the woods is beautifully played by Donna Reed for the only believable character in the picture.

Under Rudolph Mate's direction, the film shows the assignment of Lewis and Clark, played by Fred MacMurray and Charlton Heston, respectively, to survey the Louisiana Purchase. The party survives Indian attacks, physical hardships, the barriers of nature and personal conflicts, all of which are staged and played to formula.

Sacajawea joins the party midway, quickly falls for Clark, who forgets Barbara Hale, the girl he left behind and whom he had taken from Lewis. The result of all this romantic conflict is to have the two male stars pouting through the footage like schoolboys, with little resemblance to the leaders they were supposed to be. Wrapup finds Lewis relenting on his plan to have Clark courtmartialed and Sacajawea wisely deciding city life and Clark are not for her.

Featured players include William Demarest, a sergeant; Alan Reed, evil trader; Eduardo Noriega and Larry Pennell, Indians. They fare no better than MacMurray, Heston and Miss Hale under Mate's direction. Daniel L. Fapp scores with his Technicolor lensing, as does William Williams for his second unit photography. Hans Salter's score too often is overly loud. *Brog.*

Ain't Misbehavin'
(MUSICAL—COLOR)

Musical comedy program feature in color with familiar names for general dual dating.

Hollywood, May 24.

Universal release of Samuel Marx production. Stars Rory Calhoun, Piper Laurie, Jack Carson, Mamie Van Doren; features Reginald Gardiner, Barbara Britton, Dani Crayne. Directed by Edward Buzzell. Screenplay, Buzzell, Philip Rapp, Devery Freeman; based on "Third Girl From the Right" by Robert Carson; camera (Technicolor), Wilfrid M. Cline; editor, Paul Weatherwax; musical supervision, Joseph Gershenson; vocal arrangements, Johnny Scott; choreography, Kenny Williams, Lee Scott; songs, Paul Francis Webster, Sammy Fain; Charles Henderson, Sonny Burke; Sammy Cahn, Johnnie Scott. Previewed May 13, '55. Running time, **81 MINS.**

Kenneth Post, III..........Rory Calhoun
Sarah Hatfield .... Piper Laurie
Harold North .... Jack Carson
Jackie .... Mamie Van Doren
Piermont Rogers.......Reginald Gardiner
Pat .... Barbara Britton
Millie .... Dani Crayne
Andre Banet .... Carl Post
Corbini .... Roger Etienne
Randall .... Harris Brown
Mrs. Moffit .... Isabel Randolph
Native Boatman .... George Givot
Andy .... Peter Mamakos

(Aspect ratio: 2-1)

The requirements of the general dual market will be adequately served by "Ain't Misbehavin'." It's a lightweight bit of musical comedy fluff that should prove mildly diverting escapism, and is peopled with such likeable cast toppers as Rory Calhoun, Piper Laurie, Jack Carson and Mamie Van Doren, who helps keep it going on a reasonably pleasant course for 81 minutes.

The presentation follows a stock line in the production helming by Samuel Marx, in the direction by Edward Buzzell, and in the scripting the latter did with Philip Rapp and Devery Freeman from the story, "Third Girl From the Right" by Robert Carson. Three original tunes, plus the title song, serve their purpose in identifying the picture as a musical that tells of a breezy chorus girl who marries the youthful head of a financial empire and, in the mistaken belief she should be a lady to hold her mate, tries to change the personality that made him fall in the first place. She gets back on the beam before it's too late.

As the chorine, Miss Laurie sings the title piece, as well as "A Little Love Can Go a Long Way" by Paul Francis Webster and Sammy Fain; "The Dixie Mambo," by Charles Henderson and Sonny Burke, and "I Love That Rickey Tickey Tickey" by Sammy Cahn and Johnnie Scott. The latter two and the title tune also are used for production numbers on which Miss Laurie is joined by Miss Van Doren, Dani Crayne and chorus. Songs and terps are handled acceptably by Miss Laurie and the others, but sight appeal is the stronger asset.

Calhoun gives a pleasing account of himself as the young business man suddenly fed up with all work and no play. So does Jack Carson as the financial empire's public relations director. Reginald Gardiner is in for some mild comedy as an elderly playboy who causes some temporary misunderstanding and Barbara Britton is the society gal who wanted Calhoun.

Picture has a visual advantage in the Technicolor photography by Wilfrid M. Cline. The music supervision by Joseph Gershenson is satisfactory, as are the technical credits. *Brog.*

The Seven Little Foys
(V'VISION-MUSIC-COLOR)

Bob Hope goes straight to biopic Eddie Foy, song-dance man of vaude age. Good possibilities overall.

Hollywood, May 26.

Paramount release of Jack Rose production. Stars Bob Hope, Milly Vitale; features George Tobias, Angela Clarke; guest stars James Cagney. Directed by Melville Shavelson; written by Shavelson and Rose; camera (Technicolor), John F. Warren; editor, Ellsworth Hoagland; music scored and conducted by Joseph J. Lilley; choreography, Nick Castle; narration, Eddie Foy Jr.; technical advisor, Charley Foy. Previewed May 24, '55. Running time, **92 MINS.**

Eddie Foy	Bob Hope
Madeleine Morando	Milly Vitale
Clara Morando	Angela Clarke
Barney Green	George Tobias
Bryan Foy	Billy Gray
Charley Foy	Lee Erickson
Richard Foy	Paul De Rolf
Madeleine Foy	Linda Bennett
Mary Foy	Lydia Reed
Irving Foy	Tommy Duran
Eddie Foy Jr.	Jimmy Baird
George M. Cohan	James Cagney

(*Aspect ratio*: 1.85-1)

Bob Hope abandons the buffoon to go straight actor in biopicturing Eddie Foy, song-and-dance man of the vaudeville age. It's a commendable switch of acting pace that will be applauded in the trade and liked by the ticket buyers so business prospects shape up good. While film brings in plenty of the footlights, it is more the story of a man than a career, with the color of the two-a-day era backstopping for the drama.

The team of Melville Shavelson and Jack Rose has parlayed its early radio association with Hope into a joint venture under the Paramount banner—and with a VistaVision dress in Technicolor. What gets on screen is neatly balanced entertainment, loaded with the nostalgia of a past showbiz era and "tradey" to quite a degree, but still appeal to general audiences. Shavelson and Rose collaborated on the writing, with the former directing and the latter producing. The joint guidance comes off well, with enough flourish in the physical furnishments to bespeak a well-spent budget.

The title would indicate that Foy was a professional father. That he was in the sense that his stage career was capped by the introduction of his numerous progeny into his act after the death of his wife left him with seven youngsters to watch over. How Foy reluctantly took on this responsibility puts a touching topper to the episodic tale. Fadeout of papa herding the seven little Foys into church while steeple bells all over town herald this singular event gives a warm wrench to the heart. The fact this gets over to an audience is quite an achievement in itself because the brood, up until the time it stands by dad to get him off the hook with the law for exploiting juves on stage, is seen as a rather obnoxious collection of movie-type brats.

From the opening when Foy vows he will always remain a single, professionally and maritally, even an audience unfamiliar with his life will know it won't be long. It isn't, and Milly Vitale, Italian film actress who does a fine job of portraying the Italian ballerina who marries Foy, is reason enough for him to change his mind. Their hit-and-miss life together is told with heart in the performances of Hope and Miss Vitale. He picks himself up some new thespic honors and she has warmth and appeal.

The script is loaded with one-liners that never miss a laugh, even with reprises. Such a one is "she's pregnant again" as wearily announced by Angela Clarke, very good as the elder sister of the ballerina who stayed on to watch over the bride. A standout sequence is the appearance of James Cagney as George M. Cohan, a characterization he created with 1942 Academy Award-winning success in Warners' "Yankee Doodle Dandy." He and Hope, in a Friars Club scene, toss the Shavelson-Rose lines back and forth for sock results and then turn to in some mighty slick hoofing.

The Iroquois Fire in Chicago, in which Foy averted a panic, and other highlights of his long career flash by in the episodes, colored by such songs and dances as "Mary Is a Grand Old Name," "The Greatest Father of Them All," "Smiles," "Row, Row, Row," "Chinatown," "I'm Tired," "Nobody," "Yankee Doodle Dandy" and "The Animal Act." Joseph J. Lilley did the firstrate scoring and conducting job.

George Tobias, as the agent Barney Green, gives the stars strong feature support. Playing the Foy offspring are Billy Gray, Lee Erickson, Paul De Rolf, Linda Bennett, Lydia Reed, Tommy Duran and Jimmy Baird. Behind-scene narration is done by the real-life Eddie Foy Jr., and the real Charley Foy was technical adviser. Credits supporting the production are good, from John F. Warren's lensing on down. *Brog.*

The Private War of Major Benson
(COLOR)

Heart-warming comedy-drama surefire for family trade, and good otherwise. Charlton Heston, Julie Adams for marquees, word-of-mouth for grossing possibilities.

Hollywood, May 27.

Universal release of Howard Pine production. Stars Charlton Heston, Julie Adams; features William Demarest, Tim Hovey, Nana Bryant, Tim Considine, Sal Mineo, Milburn Stone. Directed by Jerry Hopper. Screenplay, William Roberts, Richard Alan Simmons; original, Joe Connelly, Bob Mosher; camera (Technicolor); Harold Lipstein; editor, Ted J. Kent music supervision, Joseph Gershenson. Previewed May 20, '55. Running time, **105 MINS.**

Maj. Bernard R. Benson	Charlton Heston
Kay Lambert	Julie Adams
John	William Demarest
Cadet Thomas Flaherty	Tim Hovey
Mother Redempta	Nana Bryant
Cadet Serg. Hibler	Tim Considine
Cadet Col. Dusik	Sal Mineo
Major General Ramsey	Milburn Stone
Sister Mary Theresa	Mary Field
Cadet Corp. Scawalski	Donald Keeler
Cadet Lieut. Molony	Gary Pagett
Cadet Lieut. Hanratty	Mickey Little
Mr. Hibler	Don Haggerty
Young Lieutenant	David Janssen
Monsignor Collins	Richard H. Cutting
Sister Mary Thomasina	Mary Alan Hokanson
Cadet Captain Petri	Butch Jones
Mrs. Hibler	Yvonne Peattie

Aspect ratio: 2-1)

A heart-warming excursion into comedy-drama is made by "The Private War of Major Benson" and it is especially surefire for, but not necessarily limited to, the socalled family trade. A good word-to-mouth potential will be a factor in the kind of business it registers, and since Universal is behind it with a big push, grosses may hit a respectable level.

Charlton Heston, in the title role, and Julie Adams star in the Howard Pine production, both giving the kind of performances that help punch over the well-developed screenplay by William Roberts and Richard Alan Simmons. The direction by Jerry Hopper, particularly in his handling of the many moppets, is adroitly valued to make the most of the comedy, the drama, and the sentiment to be found in the original story by Joe Connelly and Bob Mosher. Pine's overall supervision achieves a handsome effect, being noteworthy in overseeing story and casting.

Plot idea offered many possibilities and none is sluffed in telling the story of a tough, hell-for-leather, career officer who gets into trouble when he shoots off his mouth about the soft treatment rookies get in the Army. For punishment he's assigned the post of commandant at a military academy about to lose its ROTC rating unless training is snapped up.

Figuring this is better than the alternate of being booted out of the Army, Heston accepts. To his horror, he finds the school is a religious institution conducted by nuns and the officer material he is to whip into shape comes from a student body ranging in age from 6 to 15. It's Benson against the pupils, with the latter almost winning before the major is taken in hand by Miss Adams, the school doctor. The private war winds up in a victory for both sides, plus which audiences will be the entertainment winners as a result of what has transpired during the 105 minutes of footage.

Heston scores as the toughie who has trouble being human, except in his yen for Miss Adams, who is warm and human in her slick performance of the medico, besides being mighty pretty. Other adults adding to the entertainment are William Demarest, school handyman; Nana Bryant, the wise Mother Superior; Milburn Stone, the general disciplining the major; Mary Field, Dom Haggerty, Richard H. Cutting and Yvonne Peattie.

Where the picture hits at the family heart is among the moppet players, and thanks to the production, scripting and direction, they're real kids, not atrocious movie brats. Audiences will take to little Tim Hovey as "Tiger" Flaherty, a six-year-old who has his troubles. Very good too are Sal Mineo, cadet colonel; Tim Considine, spoiled cadet who plots against the commandant, and the other cadets, including Donald Keeler, Gary Pagett, Mickey Little and Butch Jones.

Film is backed with some top-notch technical credits, including the Technicolor lensing by Harold Lipstein. *Brog*

The Purple Mask
(C'SCOPE—COLOR)

Costumed swashbuckler of the Scarlet Pimpernel school with Tony Curtis doing the lah-de-dah and swordplay. For the regular run of playdates.

Hollywood, May 31.

Universal release of Howard Christie production. Stars Tony Curtis, Colleen Miller; costars Gene Barry, Dan O'Herlihy, Angela Lansbury; features George Dolenz, John Hoyt, Donald Randolph, Robert Cornthwaite, Stephen Bekassy. Directed by Bruce Humberstone. Screenplay, Oscar Brodney; based on "Le Chevalier Au Masque," play by Paul Armont and Jean Manoussi, and the adaptation by Charles Latour; camera (Technicolor print), Irving Glassberg; editor, Ted J. Kent; music supervision, Joseph Gershenson. Previewed May 24, '55. Running time, **82 MINS.**

Rene	Tony Curtis
Laurette	Colleen Miller
Capt. Laverne	Gene Barry
Brisquet	Dan O'Herlihy
Madame Valentine	Angela Lansbury
Marcel Cardonal	George Dolenz
Rochet	John Hoyt
Majolin	Donald Randolph
Napoleon	Robert Cornthwaite
Baron De Morleve	Stephen Bekassy
Duc de Latour	Paul Cavanagh
Constance	Myrna Hansen
Irene	Allison Hayes
Yvonne	Betty Jane Howarth
Edouard	Carl Milletaire
De Morsanne	Gene Darcy
De Vivanne	Robert Hunter
Roger	Richard Avonde
Raoul	Glase Lohman
Sabine	Diane DuBois
Father Brochard	Everett Glass

This costumed swashbuckler is right out of the Scarlet Pimpernel school with Tony Curtis doing swordplay. Should attract attention among the regular-run situations, where it will be okay top-of-the-bill material. The setting is Paris under Napoleon, and the period takes nicely to the CinemaScope treatment.

Curtis appears as the mysterious Purple Mask, adventurer who raises coin for the Royalists by kidnapping upper-echelon execs of the Republic and ransoming them back to Napoleon. Betimes, he's a hanky up-the-sleeve young dandy, careful of the latest in dress and dance step, seemingly more interested in terpsichore than fencing. Derring-do runs high as he thwarts all the carefully-laid scheme to capture him and, when he is taken, he does the giving up to rescue lady-friend Colleen Miller and some other Royalists. Under the shadow of the guillotine, he duels to gain safe passage for the group to England and Napoleon considers himself well rid of the poseur.

The adventuring all comes off with fair results in the Howard Christie production, as directed by Bruce Humberstone from a script by Oscar Brodney. Curtis is an acceptable hero, making the best of the dual characterization, while Miss Miller is a pretty heroine. Neither role puts much of a strain on talent. Nor do the characters played by Gene Barry and Dan O'Herlihy, execs of Napoleon, who is portrayed by Robert Cornthwaite. Others seen prominently include Angela Lansbury, George Dolenz, John Hoyt, Donald Randolph, Stephen Bekassy, Paul Cavanagh and Myrna Hansen.

Script was based on "Le Chevalier Au Masque," play by Paul Armont and Jean Manoussi and the adaptation by Charles Latour entitled "The Purple Mask." The Cinema-Scope photography by Irving Glassberg, with print by Technicolor, the art direction, settings and costumes all do their part in helping the visual attractions. *Brog.*

Son of Sinbad
(SUPERSCOPE—COLOR)

Fanciful fantasy of the sex-and-sand variety; a programmer gaining undue b.o. importance through undue censorial bellwethering.

Hollywood, May 31.

RKO release of Robert Sparks production. Stars Dale Robertson, Sally Forrest, Lili St. Cyr, Vincent Price costarring Mari Blanchard; features Leon Askin, Jay Novello, Raymond Greenleaf Nejla Ates, Kalantan, Ian MacDonald, Donald Randalph. Directed by Ted Tetzlaff. Written by Aubrey Wisberg, Jack Pollexfen; camera (Technicolor), William Snyder; editors, Roland Gross, Frederic Knudtson; music, Victor Young; musical director, C. Bakaleinikoff; choreography, Olga Lunick. Previewed May 26, '55. Running time, **88 MINS.**

Sinbad	Dale Robertson
Ameer	Sally Forrest
Nerissa	Lili St. Cyr
Omar	Vincent Price
Kristina	Mari Blanchard
Khalif	Leon Askin
Jiddah	Jay Novello
Simon	Raymond Greenleaf
Dancer in Market	Nejla Ates
Dancer in Desert	Kalantan
Murad	Ian MacDonald
Councillor	Donald Randolph
Samit	Larry Blake

(*Aspect ratio*: 2-1)

Left to its own devices, "Son of Sinbad" would find its natural level in the programmer market. It's a fanciful fantasy of the sex-and-sand variety, no better and no worse than most of the almost-countless such films that have gone ahead of it. However, the

present censorship hue and cry directed against this particular film may create the paradoxical effect of turning it into a moneymaker of medium proportions.

It would seem that the RKO release rates more censure for the dull quality of its entertainment than for its moral values. Sure, it has pretty girls with free-wheeling hips and scanty costumes, and amatory chases through wellfilled harems, but this is all presented so unrealistically that it's hard to believe that morals would be broken, or even bent, for the viewing. There's s.a. in the appeal of cuties and the way they wiggle, but one will be more inclined to laugh than pant at the manner in which sex is presented in the Robert Sparks production by the writing, direction and cast.

Dale Robertson is the flowingly costumed title character who spends a good part of his time in harems, not his, wooing the inmates with words furnished him by Vincent Price, who seems to enjoy his unrestrained portrayal of Omar, the poet. Audiences, too, will get a chuckle here and there from Price's tongue-in-cheek handling of the worries his wall-climbing friend causes. A visit to Lili St. Cyr, one of the beauties in the harem of Khalif Leon Askim, results in the capture of Robertson and Price and sets up a semblance of storyline in the script by Aubrey Wisberg and Jack Pollexfen.

The plot ,as loosely developed under Ted Tetzlaff's direction, has the hero promising to bring the secret of Greek Fire to the Khalif and defeat the forces of Tamerlane in return for his freedom. This he does, with the help of Mari Blanchard, the girl who has the secret locked in her subconsicous mind, and Sally Forrest, slave girl who secretly is a member of the current Forty Thieves gang, all femme descendants of the originals.

Some modified, almost ludicrous, torso-tossing by the Misses Forrest, St. Cyr, Nejla Ates and Kalantan takes care of the footage's socalled choreography, and the costumes designed by Michael Woulfe never get in the way. The sight appeal of these femmes, as well as that supplied by Miss Blanchard, is supplemented by a well-rounded group of distaffers who decorate much of the scenery. Jay Novelle plays the Khalif's fool who is a spy for Tamerlane.

The SuperScope lensing in Technicolor by William Synder keeps the natural and manufactured beauties of the presentation well on display. Victor Young's score, supervised by C. Bakaleinikoff, editing and other contributions are all okay. *Brog*

The Dam Busters
(BRITISH)

High grade British dramatization of triumphant wartime raid on Ruhr dams; superb acting by Michael Redgrave and Richard Todd make it worthy b.o. contender.

London, May 24.

Associated British-Pathe release of Associated British production. Stars Richard Todd, Michael Redgrave; features Ursula Jeans, Basil Sydney. Directed by Michael Anderson. Screenplay by R. C. Sheriff based on Paul Brickhill's "Enemy Coast Ahead"; camera, Edwin Hillier; editor, Richard Best; music, Louis Levy. At Studio One, London. Running time, **125 MINS.**

Dr. B. N. Wallis	Michael Redgrave
Mrs. Wallis	Ursula Jeans
Sir David Pye	Stanley Van Beers
Physical Laboratory Official	Raymond Huntley
Aircraft Production Official	Hugh Manning
Capt. Joseph ..Mutt) Summers	Patrick Barr
Air Chief Marshal	Basil Sydney
Air Vice-Marshal	Ernest Clark
Capt. J. N. H. Whitworth	Derek Farr
Farmer	Laurence Naismith
Com. Guy Gibson	Richard Todd
Lit. Lt. R. D. Trevor-Rober	Brewster Mason
Flt. Lt. R. E. C. Hutchinson	Anthony Doonan
Flt. Off. F. M. Spafford	Nigel Stock
Flt. Lt. D. J. H. Maltby	George Baker

As a record of a British operational triumph during the last war, "The Dam Busters" will be hard to beat. This is a small slice of history, told with painstaking attention to detail and overflowing with the British quality of understatement. The documentary-like treatment increases its appeal and this should be no barrier to sturdy b.o. results in most situations. It has the makings of a box-office winner at home and should notch healthy returns in overseas territories.

This is the story of the successful raid on the Ruhr dams, when a small fleet of British bombers, using a new type of explosive, successfully breached the water supplies, which fed the Ruhr factories and caused desolation and havoc to the German war machine. The yarn, adapted for the screen from Paul Brickhill's novel, is a testi-

monial to two people. One, the scientist whose faith made the raid possible, the other the Wing Commander, who translated text-book theories to actual practice.

The scientist, Dr. Barnes Wallis (played by Michael Redgrave), has a theory about crushing the Ruhr dams. Because of their size and strength, they cannot be breached by conventional bombs dropped from the air. He feels, however, that a penetration could be achieved by devising a bomb, which glides along the water like a ping-pong ball, and hits the dam smack on. After experiments with marbles and golf balls, he devises a bouncing bomb; the only problem is that it must be used with mathematical precision. It has to be dropped precisely 600 yards from the target, while the plane is travelling at 240 m.p.h. at a height only 60 feet from the water.

The late Guy Gibson (Richard Todd) was given the job of training (under conditions of top secrecy) a special crew to undertake this mission. They practiced low flying and by a simple means of cross beams from theatrical spot lamps were able to gauge their height with precise accuracy. Another piece of simple apparatus was devised as a bomb sight.

For more than 90 minutes, the film is devoted to the planning and preparation, and very absorbing material this proves to be. The actual triumph is, of course, a matter of history, but the reconstruction of the raid and the pounding of the dams is done with graphic realism. The aerial photography is one of the major technical credits.

The production is a personal triumph for Michael Anderson, a young British director, given his first major assignment with "Dam Busters." He has acquitted himself with distinction. Performancewise, the film depends almost exclusively on the two stars, both of whom succeed in submerging their own personalities. Redgrave, particularly, gives a vividly human portrayal of the scientist. Todd makes a distinguished showing as Guy Gibson; all other roles are completely subsidiary, although sincerely played. Raymond Huntley, Ursula Jeans and Laurence Naismith stand out among the supporting team.

The production is one of the most impressive to come from the Associated British studios at Elstree and the technical crew has risen to the occasion. In addition to Edwin Hillier's class lensing, Gilbert Taylor has done some impressive special effects photography. Robert Jones has designed convincing settings and Richard Best contributes a highly professional piece of editing. *Myro.*

Las Vegas Shakedown

Mild melodramatics for programmer bookings, location lensed at the gambling spa.

Hollywood, May 17.

Allied Artists release of William F. Broidy production. Stars Dennis O'Keefe, Coleen Gray, Charles Winninger, Thomas Gomez; features Dorothy Patrick, Mary Beth Hughes, Elizabeth Patterson, James Millican, Robert Armstrong, Joseph Downing. Directed by Sidney Salkow. Written by Steve Fisher; camera, John Martin; editor, Chandler House; music, Edward J. Kay. Previewed May 13, '55. Running time, **79 MINS.**

Joe Barnes	Dennis O'Keefe
Julia Rae	Coleen Gray
Mr. Raff	Charles Winninger
Sirago	Thomas Gomez
Dorothy Reid	Dorothy Patrick
Mabel	Mary Beth Hughes
Mrs. Raff	Elizabeth Patterson
Wheeler Reid	James Millican
Doc	Robert Armstrong
Matty	Joseph Downing
Collins	Lewis Martin
Angela	Mara McAfee
Sheriff Woods	Charles Fredericks
Maxine Miller	Regina Gleason
House Manager	Murray Alper
Sam Costar	James Alexander
Martin	Frank Hanley
Rick	Allen Mathews

(*Aspect ratio*: 1.85-1)

The plush desert gambling town backstops for some formula melodramatics of the "Grand Hotel" style in this programmer entry, which has familiar cast names to help it serve out its release time in the regular dual market.

Cast topper in the William F. Broidy production for Allied Artists is Dennis O'Keefe, operator of a hotel-casino. Costarring with him are Coleen Gray, school teacher researching for a book showing it's impossible to win; Charles Winninger, smalltown banker taking his first gambling fling with his wife, Elizabeth Patterson, and Thomas Gomez, racketeer, out to either kill O'Keefe or buy up his casino.

These, and other types such as divorce-seeking gals and men and women to whom gambling is like drink to the alcoholic, people the cast and come off with fair results under Sidney Salkow's direction of Steve Fisher's improbable, sometimes preposterous, script. On the assumption that life is speeded up in Las Vegas, O'Keefe and Miss Gray are engaged almost before they finish meeting for the first time and she sees him through his troubles with Gomez, a man gone crazy when he's not able to buy up the gambling spot at a bargain price. After a killing spree, Gomez is killed and the hero and heroine happily plan their wedding.

Dorothy Patrick and James Millican portray a divorcing couple, while Mary Beth Hughes is a gal who is compelled to gamble. Robert Armstrong and Joseph Downing serve as Gomez' two gunmen.

Technical credits, including the lensing, score and playing by the Matty Malneck Trio are standard contributions. *Brog.*

Bride of the Atom

Bela Lugosi in a would-be horror picture sans interest or b.o. potential.

Hollywood, May 12.

Edward D. Woods Jr. production (no release). Stars Bela Lugosi, Tor Johnson co-stars Tony McCoy, Loretta King, Harvey Dunn; features George Becwar. Directed by Woods. Story-screenplay, Woods, Alex Godon; camera, William C. Thompson, Ted Allan; music, Frank Worth; editor, Warren Adams. Previewed May 11, '55. **Running time, 68 MINS.**

Dr. Eric Vornoff	Bela Lugosi
Lobo	Tor Johnson
Lt. Dick Craig	Tony McCoy
Janet Lawton	Loretta King
Capt. Robbins	Harvey Dunn
Prof. Strowski	George Becwar
Kelton	Paul Marco
Martin	Don Nagel
Mac	Bud Osborne
Jake	John Warren
Tillie	Ann Wilner
Margie	Dolores Fuller
Newsboy	William Benedict
Drunk	Ben Frommer

(*Aspect ratio*: 1.85-1)

This re-hashed version of a story that was old-hat years ago is an amateurish effort which even the least discriminating audiences will find dull. Made without a release, the only conceivable reason for production is the Bela Lugosi name in the horror market.

Theme of the Edward D. Woods Jr. production, also directed by Woods and co-scripted with Alex Gordon, builds around a mad scientist (Lugosi) who is trying to use atomic energy to develop a race of atomic supermen. He has been successful in developing monsters; now he's experimenting on human beings. Disappearance of 12 men whom he's snatched for this purpose leads to police activity. Scientist also entraps a nosy femme reporter, whom he wants as "bride of the atom."

Lugosi's histrionics are reduced to the ridiculous through overdirection, and Tor Johnson, as his mute strongarmman, is good only for laughs. Tony McCoy, a detective, Harvey Dunn, police captain, and Loretta King, as an obnoxious newshen, haven't a chance with stilted lines. *Whit.*

In the Soviet Union
(COLOR—DOCUMENTARY)

Chronicle of contemporary Soviet life may have some curiosity value.

Artkino release of five-part documentary produced by various Soviet studios. At Stanley, N.Y., beginning May 21, '55. Running time, **105 MINS.**

What the Soviets Eat
Central Documentary Film Studio production. Directed by Kirill Eggers. Camera (color), Vladimir Pridorogin; music, Vital Gevikeman.

Laboratory on Wheels
Directed by S. Reitburt. Camera (color), Y. Tolchan.

From Moscow to Sukhumi
Documentary Film Studios of Moscow production. Directed by Marianna Semyonova. Camera (color), Sergei Semyonov.

Olympic Champions
Kiev Film Studio production. Directed by M. Monskov. Screenplay, V. Ordvnsky, Y. Segel cameraman (color), V. Shumsky; music, A. Lokshin.

(In Russian; English titles and narration)

A glimpse behind the Iron Curtain is provided by "In the Soviet Union," a five-part documentary which is billed as "a review of present-day life and people and culture in the USSR." While most of the material is of an innocuous nature, nevertheless this import does throw light on how some Russians eat, work and play.

Few art houses would book Soviet product as a matter of policy. However, in the event the distributor chose to release some of the shorts contained in the film individually it would appear that they might reach larger audiences than if all five episodes had to be shown as a unit.

Of particular interest to the American motorist is "From Moscow to Sukhumi." This is a pictorial account of a motorcade of Soviet vacationists who leave Moscow with their families for a 1,600-mile trip to Sukhumi, a small port on the Black Sea. Cars used for the junket resemble the German Volkswagen or English Ford.

Russia's roads, on the basis of this film, are largely two lane macadam, gravel and worse depending upon the region where one happens to be. There are some breathtaking views of mountain lakes in the Caucasus, eyecatching vistas at Black Sea resorts and sundry other points of interest worth noting.

Curiously, no gas stations nor garage facilities were shown. For that matter neither were motels since the motorcade slept in the cars each night. When Sukhumi was ultimately reached, the narrator noted that the cars were taken aboard a ship for the journey across the Black Sea to Crimea. At this point one suspected that these travelers weren't average Soviet citizens as far as finances go.

"What the Soviets Eat" is a dullish account of how Moscow shops are supplied with bread, cakes, canned goods, etc. via mechanized plants. Frequently the color camerawork is underexposed. "Laboratory on Wheels" shows how Soviet veterinarians are going into the field with a mobile laboratory to check disease among cows, sheep and other animals.

"Olympic Champions" is a rousing clip depicting the supremacy of the Soviets in sports—whether it be ski jumping or shot put. There are some excellent exhibitions as caught by the lensman but unfortunately the studio which assembled the footage went overboard on its propaganda aspects. *Gilb.*

French Cancan
(FRENCH—COLOR—SONGS)

Cannes, May 24.
Gaumont release of Franco London production. Stars Jean Gabin, Maria Felix, Francoise Arnoul. Written and directed by Renoir. Dialog, Andre Antoine; camera (Technicolor), Michael Kelber; editor, Borys Lewin; music, Goerges Van Parys. Previewed at Cannes Film Festival. Running time, **100 MINS.**

Danglars .... Jean Gabin
Nini .... Francoise Arnoul
Lola .... Maria Felix
Casimir .... Philipe Clay
Valet .... Gaston Modot
Count .... Caussimon
Laundress .... Annick Morice m

The birth of the Moulin Rouge and the French Cancan is nostalgically caught in a splash of perfect color and affection in a pic that glows with love, charm and eyefilling movement. Although story is sketchy and almost nonexistent, it is the feeling created that makes it a stirring personal affair. Film might be just the thing for U.S. art houses.

The slim story tells the tale of the showman, Jean Gabin, whose knowhow and drive make for the final creation of the Moulin Rouge and its rousing, riotous Cancan. Complications are brought in by the beautiful, langorous Maria Felix as the belly dancer, Lola, and Francoise Arnoul as the pert, little laundress who becomes the head exponent of the Cancan. The colorful period is evoked with its dandies, lovesick princes, laundresses and heavies. Gabin gets his dream of the Moulin Rouge only after renouncing any permanent love affiliations. All comes to a head in a vibrant cascade of color, energy and sheer elegance as the Cancan bursts forth with all its ruffled and reeling effect.

Gabin is perfect as the showman whose life only reacts to the boards and audiences. Miss Felix's lush beauty is a fine trump while Miss Arnoul is a pleasing innocent. Direction has made what might have been mawkish into poignance. Renoir lets things slow down but never sag as the side stories of the amorous prince, the lovesick count and the mixture of real and theatre life are dwelled on. Many top singers show up to impersonate turn-of-the-century idols, among them being Patachou, Edith Piaf and Andre Claveau. Color is perfectly used to denote changing moods. The tinting breaks into animated beauty in the final Cancan scene, making for the finest film painting ever seen on any screen. Editing and lensing are all tops. Word-of-mouth and crix should help this pic. *Mosk.*

Foreign Films

Cannes, May 17.
Raisces (Roots) (MEXICAN). Directed by Benito Alazraki. Screenplay, Francisco Gonzalez; camera, Walter Reuter; editor, Fernando Gam. With Olympia Alazraki, Juan Hernandez, Xanth Del Lago, Carl Robles Gil. At Cannes Film Festival. Running time, **75 MINS.**

A sketch pic, made up of four stories depicting certain aspects of the Indian life which form anomolous roots in aspects of modern, bustling Mexico, this has a forthright dignity and sincerity. This overcomes partly its obvious low budget and rough edges. Pic has rugged honesty which gives this a morbid, downbeat tinge. Primarily for special situations. Running time also limits this to deliberate slotting with a good supporter.

Pic is well lensed and edited and has a simple style in keeping with its robust, earthy subject matter. Touchy stuff and needling extra special hypoing but worth a try for that offbeat spot. *Mosk.*

Muerte De Un Ciclista (Death of a Cyclist) (SPANISH). Gonzalez and release production. Written and directed by Juan Bardem. Camera, Albert Fraile; editor, Margarita Ochao. With Lucia Bose. At Cannes Film Festival. Running time, **87 MINS.**

Mannered pic employs a slick style to tell its familiar story of two illicit lovers whose love is doomed by an accident, in which they inadvertently kill a cyclist. When they flee, the crash works on their consciences and real feelings, bringing on the tragic denouement. Director Juan Barden has imbued this with a polished mounting but given too much emphasis to technique and style. Hence, the characters suffer. Acting also seems somewhat wooden.

Still a neat polished work, this might be of interest in language houses or possibly for some arty spots. Bardem emerges an interesting, individualistic director and shows technical prowess. Lucia Bose gives a competent, professional performance as the girl whose need for riches decides her way in life. Lensing and editing are fine. *Mosk.*

Le Dosier Noir (The Block File) (FRENCH). Cinedis release of Speva Film-Rizzoli Film production. Stars Bernard Blier; features Jean-Marc Bory, Nelly Borgeaud, Daniele Delorme, Paul Frankeur. Directed by Andre Cayatte. Screenplay, Charles Spaak; Cayatte; dialog, Spaak; camera, Jean Bourgoin; editor, Paul Cayatte. At Cannes Film Festival. Running time, **120 MINS.**

Andre Cayatte, champion of social and legal problem pix, now examines miscarriages of justice due to individual corruption, underpaid and inexperienced officials plus the general irony and mischance in administering justice. Though not as lusty pamphleteering as his former pix, this still is a thematic film. It rarely gets any suspense or feeling into the story of a young magistrate whose first job leads to his exhuming the remains of his predecessor when foul play is suspected. This lets off a chain of events with police brutality forcing confessions from two people but ironic denouement has whole thing a mistake with negligence leading to belief that man had been murdered.

Film is flatly told and lacks the suspense and feeling to make this intelligible. Downbeat and languishing, this is competently made but too verbose to make for much U.S. interest. Characters are sacrificed to the theme and pic is built like a lawyer's plea rather than a film. Primarily for secondary situations in the U.S. Lack of names also militates against this. Lensing and editing are fine but flat direction and obtuse story line makes this a rare possibility for American chances. Acting is generally good. *Mosk.*

Marcelino Pan Y Vino (Marcelino Bread and Wine) (SPANISH). Chamartin and release production. Stars Pablito Calvo; features Rafael Rivelles, Antonio Vico, Juan Calvo, Jose Davo, Joaquim Roa. Directed by Ladislao Vajda; camera, play, Sanchez Silva, Vajda; camera, Enrique Guerner; editor, Julio Pena; music, Pablo Sorosabal. At Cannes Film Festival. Running time, **90 MINS.**

A Catholic film from a Catholic country about a little boy who causes a miracle, this still has the treatment, taste and entertainment values which might make this a nice grosser outside of its own country. Gentle humor and pathos, coupled with some extraordinary moppet work, makes this a natural for some language spots. With some shearing, it might do in special situations of the U.S.

A group of monks find a baby on their doorstep and adopt it. When they find no parents and see that most townspeople want it for selfish reasons, they bring the infant up themselves. Pic concerns the boy at the age of six, a wide-eyed boy whose life among the monks has made him a spirited but lonely lad. The heavy is the town mayor who wants the boy because of a slight paid him by the monks. When the boy causes a riot in the town marketplace, the mayor gets signatures needed to revoke the monk's charter of their monastery. Meanwhile the curious figures in a miracle which brings all the townspeople and saves the monastery. Director Ladislao Vajda has treated this without too much austerity. Main appeal is the boy's comportment. Acting of moppet Pablito Calvo is near perfect as are the roles of the monks, with technical credits high. *Mosk.*

The Seven Year Itch
(COLOR—CINEMASCOPE)

Marilyn Monroe-Tom Ewell in a hilarious version of the long-run stage farce cleaned up for the family trade.

20th Century-Fox release of Charles K. Feldman Group Production. Stars Marilyn Monroe and Tom Ewell. Based on George Axelrod's stage play as adapted by the author and Billy Wilder. Directed by Wilder. Editor, Hugh S. Fowler; camera De Luxe Color), Milton Krasner; music, Alfred Newman. Previewed June 1, 1955, Loew's State, N. Y. Running time, 105 MINS.

The Girl .... Marilyn Monroe
Richard Sherman .... Tom Ewell
Helen Sherman .... Evelyn Keyes
Tom McKenzie .... Sonny Tufts
Kruhulik .... Robert Strauss
Dr. Brubaker .... Oscar Homolka
Misss Morris ...... Marguerite Chapman
Plumber .... Victor Moore
Elaine .... Roxanne
Mr. Brady .... Donald MacBride
Miss Finch .... Carolyn Jones
Ricky .... Butch Bernard
Waitress .... Doro Merando
Girl .... Dorothy Ford

Here is a rundown on the assets of "The Seven Year Itch": It is a funny picture and a money picture; the title and property are pre-sold values; the exploitation possibilities are above average and word-of-mouth comment is bound to be strong; the situation fits Marilyn Monroe tighter than her skirt and the picture undoubtedly restores Tom Ewell to the screen on a bigger and better basis.

Having put all that in the first paragraph, a critic must add for the record that the film version of "The Seven Year Itch" bears only a fleeting resemblance to the play of the same name on Broadway. Which is hardly a surprise since the original George Axelrod script is a comedy of adultery, not a subject for humor in the flickers. The screen adaptation prepared by Axelrod and Billy Wilder concerns only the fantasies, and omits the acts, of the summer bachelor, who remains totally, if unbelievably, chaste. Morality wins if honestly loses, but let's not get into that. Remember the gag about the boy with the Oedipus complex—what does it matter so long as he loves his mama? In this emasculation of original plot, the question will be, what does it matter so long as the film is good boxoffice?

And that it surely is. True, the coy evasion of the basic sex fact does create a certain teasing prolongation of a single note, which can have no payoff under the code and the rules of you-know-who. What counts is that laughs come thick and fast, that the general entertainment is light and gay, that the performances are first rate and that the direction of Billy Wilder and the editing of Hugh S. Fowler, and the lush Charles K. Feldman production under head cameraman Milton Krasner all unspool an easy to enjoy 105 minutes of diversion.

The Color is by Deluxe (Leonard Doss, consulting) and it all looks very opulent. Saul Bass's main title, a series of hinged and perambulatory patches on a multi-colored field attracted audience comment at the Broadway preview Wednesday (1) at Loew's State. Remarked one lady, "Credits arranged this way are interesting—and you don't have to read them." Which is the sort of crack which gives New Yorkers a bad name in Hollywood where screen credits come first before the wife and the trust fund.

The performance of Miss Monroe is baby-dollish as the dumb-but-sweet number upstairs who attracts the eye of the guy, seven years married and restless, whose wife and child have gone off for the summer. She extracts considerable giggles which may be bona fide tidbits of acting skill (a nice conversational debate for the citizenry) or may be partly tricks of the director and the editor. The acting kudos belong to Ewell, a practiced farceur and pantomimist who is able to give entire conviction to the long stretches of soliloquy. Much of the story is told in the form of a man talking to himself, which is a considerable test of Ewell's technique.

Several small roles are given gem-sharp interpretation. First, Oscar Homolka as the psychiatrist. Then Robert Strauss as the janitor, a dilly of a silly. Such comic vets as Victor Moore and Doro Merando are used for brief flashes of deadpan foolishness. Sonny Tufts has the relatively thankless assignment of crossing the path of one of the hero's fantasies and getting himself knocked cold. Taint much, but it's first run.

To reprise: the three parties most interested, public, exhibs and 20th Century-Fox, should be content with "The Seven Year Itch." This despite some self - consciously corney theatrical liberties. One is the hokey Manhattan Indian sequence at the kickoff and another a "local aside" when the question, "Who's in that bathroom?" is answered by the quip, "It might be Marilyn Monroe."

But the wrap-up fact remains that Billy Wilder and Charles K. Feldman have steered by the yok and have brought their comedy vessel safely to port. *Land.*

The Cobweb
(C'SCOPE-COLOR)

Film study of neuroses of staff, patients in psychiatric clinic; impressive cast, good performances, limited entertainment appeal.

Hollywood, June 7.

Metro release of John Houseman production. Stars Richard Widmark, Lauren Bacall, Charles Boyer, Gloria Grahame, Lilliain Gish; introduces John Kerr, Susan Strasberg; features Oscar Levant, Tommy Rettig, Paul Stewart. Directed by Vincente Minnelli. Screenplay, John Paxton; added dialog, William Gibson; from the novel by Gibson; camera (Eastman Color), George Folsey; editor, Harold F. Kress; music, Leonard Rosenman. Previewed June 2, '55. Running time, 122 MINS.

Dr. Stewart McIver....Richard Widmark
Meg Faversen Rinehart...Lauren Bacall
Dr. Douglas N. Devanal... Charles Boyer
Karen McIver ....Gloria Grahame
Victoria Inch ....Lilliain Gish
Steven W. Holte ....John Kerr
Sue Brett .... Susan Strasberg
Mr. Capp .... Oscar Levant
Mark ....Tommy Rettig
Dr. Otto Wolff .... Paul Stewart
Lois Y. Demuth ....Jarma Lewis
Miss Cobb ....Adele Jergens
Mr. Holcomb ....Edgar Stehli
Rosemary ....Sandra Descher
Abe Irwin ....Bert Freed
Regina Mitchell-Smythe..Mabel Albertson
Edna Devanal .... Fay Wray
Curly ....Oliver Blake
Mrs. O'Brien .... Olive Carey
Shirley ....Eve McVeagh
Sally ....Virginia Christine
Mr. Appleton .... Jan Arvan
Mrs. Jenkins ....Ruth Clifford
Miss Gavney .... Myra Marsh
James Petlee ....James Westerfield
Sadie ....Marorie Bennett
Mr. Wictz ....Stuart Holmes

The neuroses of the staff and patients in a psychiatric clinic serve for drama in this filmization of William Gibson's novel, "The Cobweb." It is an impressively produced, impressively cast CinemaScope feature that fails to impress as screen entertainment of wide popular appeal.

A select minority among filmgoers may find the even-keeled clinical study interesting, but there's not enough contrast between its dramatic highs and lows, nor sufficiently developed sympathy for the characters to attract the entertainment fancy of the majority, although the latter may be lured initially by the potent marquee names and the exploitability of the theme. The insertion of even one scene of shock or high violence that could be word-of-mouthed would have helped the film's general chances.

There is a mighty thin line separating patient from doctor in the piece-meal presentation of the inmates and the staff of the clinic with which Gibson's novel was concerned. It is a sort of Grand Hotel treatment that doesn't permit too detailed a study of any particular character, thus the viewer hardly has a chance to become familiar with or warm up to any individual, despite the long running time of two hours and two minutes.

Producer John Houseman used care in the casting of the characters caught up in the cobweb of controversy, plus offshoots, developed around the hanging of a new set of drapes in the clinic's library. The quality of the performances by Richard Widmark, Lauren Bacall, Charles Boyer, Cloria Grahame, Lillian Gish and others is as expected — very good — as developed under the sensitive, but not too probing, direction by Vincente Minnelli.

The screenplay by John Paxton, with added dialog by Gibson, gives a wordy account of the controversy, and the reactions of staff and patients sometime make wonder if identities should not be reversed. Miss Grahame, the neglected wife of Widmark, top doc at the clinic, wants to select the drapes. Miss Gish, waspish old maid who directs the clinic's business affairs, wants to use cheap muslin to save money. Widmark wants John Kerr, young patient with a suicide complex, to design the drapes.

From this basic springboard, the plot goes off in different angles, mostly involving romantic conflicts that come about as the principals try to press their particular points. Widmark becomes involved with Miss Bacall, activities director and a lonely woman who strikes almost the only really sane note among the characters. Boyer, clinic executive, woman-chaser and himself in great need of therapeutic help, offers a willing shoulder to Miss Grahame in another affair that goes nowhere. **Screen newcomer Kerr has no one to turn to, but begins to find himself at the end as a result of the fuss kicked up. Additionally, he and another newcomer, Susan Strasberg, fellow patient, are responsible for one of the few touching sequences in the film—the simple act of his looking after her on a trip to a film theatre has a great deal of heart, an ingredient generally lacking in the footage.**

Glimpsed as other participants in the drama, and all performing capably, are Oscar Levant, Tommy Rettig, Paul Stewart, Jarma Lewis, Edgar Stehli, Bert Freed, Adele Jergens, Sandra Descher, Mabel Albertson, Fay Wray and Oliver Blake. The supporting roles are well-filled, too.

The production, on which Jud Kinberg served as associate, is strong on physical values, all expertly lensed in Eastman Color by George Folsey. The score by Leonard-Rosenman is mood music in keeping with the mental unrest of the plot theme. At the preview the dialog was unintelligible in a number of scenes, coming out as only a mumble. *Brog.*

Summertime
(COLOR)

Venice, June 7.

United Artists release of Ilya Lopert Films production. Stars Katharine Hepburn, Rossano Brazzi; features Isa Miranda, Darren McGavin, Mari Aldon, Jane Rose, Macdonald Parke, Gaitano Audiero, Jeremy Spenser, Andre Morrel. Directed by David Lean. Screenplay, Lean, H. E. Bates from the play by Arthur Laurents "The Time of the Cuckoo"; camera (Eastman Color), Jack Hildyard; editor, Peter Taylor; art director, Vincent Korda; music, Alessandro Cicognini. Previewed in Venice May 29, 1955. Running time, 100 MINS.

Jane Hudson .... Katharine Hepburn
Renato Di Rossi .... Rossano Brazzi
Signora Fiorini .... Isa Miranda
Eddie Jaeger .... Darren McGavin
Phyl Jaeger .... Mari Aldon
Mrs. McIlhenny .... Jane Rose
Mr. McIlhenny .... Macdonald Parke
Mauro .... Gaitano Audiero
Englishman .... Andre Morell
Vito .... Jeremy Spenser
Giovanna .... Virginia Simeon

"Summertime," made in Venice during the summer of 1954, is a loose adaptation of Arthur Laurents' stage play, "Time of the Cuckoo." With Katharine Hepburn in the role originated by Shirley Booth and with the scenic beauties of the canal city, the film stacks up as promising entertainment— with some reservations. There is a lack of cohesion and some abruptness in plot transition without a too-clear buildup. Lesser characterizations, too, are on the sketchy side, shaping as mere silhouettes against Miss Hepburn's tour-de-force brand of highpowered trouping.

Covering these flaws is a rich topsoil of drama as the proud American secretary who hits Venice as a tourist falls for and is disillusioned by the middleaged Italian charmer. The fact of his being married and the sire of a brood is tactfully handled, although that angle may just skirt Legion of Decency disapproval in the States.

Rossano Brazzi, as the attractive vis-a-vis, scores a triumph of charm and reserve and looks to be heading for international stardom in mature leading man ranks. Miss Hepburn turns in a feverish acting chore of proud loneliness. Her mannered bits are quickly forgotten in the sensitivity of "laughing through tears" gamut.

Venice emerges as a great set for sheer eyeball appeal. Jack Hildyard's visual values are superb and Venice comes alive with Technicolor (from an Eastman negative) translating its lines, dignity and beauty with a precision, space and brilliance that should make this exposure a tourist bonanza for the city. Editing is excellent in welding the story and place into firm molding, and Ilya Lopert's production dress, with the pic made entirely in Venice, is tops. There are some outstanding children, notably Gaitano Audiero as a wise street urchin who senses Miss Hepburn's plight but can only react in his self-absorbed and self-reliant manner. In a scene, when Miss Hepburn is doing some home movies and topples into the Grand Canal, the boy manages to save the camera only and lets her fall.

Music has a sprightly lilt and jangle to back the shifting moods of David Lean's craftsmanship. Lean, who directed "Brief Encounter," "Oliver Twist," "Great Expectations," and "Breaking Through the Sound Barrier," again displays his skill in guiding a slight subject to impressive heights.

Brought in for $900,000, this feature ought to do well. United Artists is distributing for U.S. and rest of the Western Hemisphere and Europe with Film Distributors and London Films International handling it for England. *Mosk.*

A Big Family
(COLOR-RUSSIAN)

Artkino release of Lenfilm production. Stars Serge Lukyanov. Directed by I. Heifits. Screenplay, V. Kochetov, S. Kara; camera, S. Ivanov; music, V. Pushkov. At Stanley, N. Y., starting June 4, '55. Running time, **105 MINS.**

Old Matvei .... Serge Lukyanov
Ilya Matveyevich .... Boris Andreyev
Agafya Karpovna ...... Vera Kuznetsova
Alexei .... Andrei Batalov
Victor .... S. Kurilov
Anton .... V. Medvede
Kostya .... B. Bityukov
Tonya .... I. Arepina
Lida .... Katya Luchko
Dunyasha .... Elena Savinova
Basmanov .... N. Sergeyev
Katya Travnikova .... E. Dobronravova
Skobelev .... P. Kadochmikov
Club Manager .... N. Gritsenko

(In Russian; English Titles)

This is easily the best all-round screen production to come out of Russia in years. It has pace, a real story, slick casting and equally crisp acting plus smart direction and trim camera work. "A Big Family" (The Zhurbins) was honored at the recent Cannes Film Festival via an award for group acting. A more appropriate designation might have been for the best feature out of Russia since the war. It is a big entry boxofficewise for Russo language houses and some arty theatres.

Plot of "Family" is actually the story of Russia's ship-building industry, with the need for teamwork in shipbuilding as exemplified by the enterprise of a single but big family. Said family is packed with shipyard technicians. A sub-plot has the sweetheart of the hero (champ ship-welder) bearing a child out of wedlock. The villain in the affair is the workers' club house manager, who takes it on the lam. This is cleared up by having the gal marry her real lover later.

There is a running conflict between the older and rougher generation of ship workers and the classroom-trained, younger group of technicians. Ultimately, the latter group triumphs but it's never made a major point. Rather, director I. Heifits has chosen to stress the varied interests and activities of this large family, all living under one roof. Another offshoot of the central theme is the struggle of the head of the family (Serge Lukyanov) to remain in active work although offered a small pension. He's past 70, and finally persuaded to become sort of a night phone operator since told he will be useful in this spot.

There are the familiar plugs for the Communist government-operated state, with the statement that "the workingman is the backbone of the nation" twice emphasized. Just why its not understood because the camera and the actors already have put across this thought. Oddly enough, the idea of a top commissar having two motor cars (treated as a sin in the script) is permitted to creep in.

The director has done very well in keeping the various story themes separated most of the time although at the outset he falters a couple of times. But not so the thespians. Besides Lukyanov as the venerable family head, the entire cast comes through with flying colors. It is a unit job from Boris Andreyev down to the shipyard director, B. Kokovkin.

It is not fault of cameraman S. Sovcolor, which even in this production continues a bit wishy-washy as a tinting job. Music by V. Pushkov is firstrate. Screenplay of V. Kochetov and S. Kara contains more originality than usually found in a Russian film, with its unwieldy nature saved by director Heifits. *Wear.*

Foreign Films

(FRENCH)

Paris, May 31.

Les Amants Du Tage (The Lovers of Tage) (**FRENCH**). Mondex release of ECC-Hoche-Fides production. Directed by Henri Verneuil. Screenplay, Marcel Rivet, Jacques Companeez from novel by Joseph Kessel; camera, Roger Hubert; editor, Monique Kirsanoff; with Daniel Gelin, Francoise Arnoul, Trevor Howard; features Dalio, Amalia Rodriguez, Jacques Moulieres, Ginette Leclerc, Betty Stockfeld. At Marignan, Paris. Running time, **110 MINS.**

Mood piece of violent love, suspense and irony is wrapped up as a solid bit of filmmaking visually, but lacks the drama and telling to make this first-rate. This has name value for local appeal, but does not measure up to arty house chances in the U.S. but may get by via special spotting on torrid love scenes.

A soldier who killed his wife in a fit of anguish is acquitted and wanders to Lisbon where he meets a beautiful young widow, Lady Kathleen Dinvers. Love blossoms but this breaks up when she gives herself up as a murderess. Director Henry Verneuil has given this nice production dress. Francoise Arnoul, a pretty feminine bundle, gives no depth to the young widow role while Daniel Gelin plays the exsoldier in a rather monotonous manner. Trevor Howard fares better as the pugnacious inspector. Lensing is excellent especially in the Swedish-type beach love scenes. *Mosk.*

Paris, May 31.

Dú Rififi Chez Les Hommes (Brawl Among the Men) (**FRENCH**). Indusfilms release of Indus-Prima Film-S.N. Pathe Cinema production. Directed by Jules Dassin. Screenplay, Dassin, Rene Wheeler from novel by Auguste Le Breton; camera, Philipe Agostini; editor, Roger Dwyre; music, Georges Auric. With Jean Servais, Carl Mohner, Robert Manuel, Magali Noel, Janine Darcy, Marie Sabouret, Robert Rossein, Dassin. At Marignan, Paris. Running time, **120 MINS.**

This looks like the peak of the gangster pic series here. It took an experienced U.S. director, Jules Dassin, who has lived in France some years, to give this type of pic the proper tension, mounting and treatment. Until now this cycle hss been an imitation of America's best. This pic, however, is something intrinsically Gallic without sacrificing the rugged storytelling. For the U. S., chances are more highly problematical since it lacks star names.

Just out of jail, the hero finds his wife living with somebody else and it prompts him to return to his old racket. A big heist of a jewelry store is planned. Then there is one brilliant bit of cinema, 30 minutes of complete silence, as the gang cuts its way into the shop and carries out its mission.

Dassin has given this a sharp treatment and has not neglected the Paris streets and atmosphere. Jean Servais has the authority, under a facade of weariness, as Tony, and the remainder of the gang is well etched with Dassin himself turning in a telling bit as Cesar, whose love for femmes gives the whole thing away. Editing is firstrate as is Philipe Agostini's lensing. This is Dassin's first pic in five years and it shows he has not lost his touch. *Mosk.*

Paris, May 31.

Razzia Sur La Chnouf (Raid on the Drug Ring) (**FRENCH**). Gaumont release of Jad Films-SNEG-Paul Wagner production. Stars Jean Gabin; features Magali Noel, Dalio, Lino Ventura, Albert Remy, Lila Kedrova, Paul Frankeur, Pierre Louis. Directed by Henri Decoin. Screenplay, Decoin, Maurice Griffe from novel by Auguste Le Breton; camera, Pierre Montazel; editor, Denise Reiss. At Colisee, Paris. Running time, **105 MINS.**

This film dips deeply into the drug racket of France to come up with some excitingly, detailed aspects of the trade to make it primarily an exploitation item. Primarily for special situations in the U. S. with Jean Gabin name a help. But its draggy, prolonged detail won't help word-of-mouth.

Gabin is a bigwig in the dope ring sent from the U. S. to take the French counterpart in hand. He is given a restaurant from where he begins to delve into all areas of the racket. Topper is a sequence in a smoky, clandestine Negro nightclub where smoking the weed causes erotic dancing.

Director Henri Decoin has made this too plodding to make it really exciting. Gabin's doubling as a secret service man is soon apparent. Gabin is appealing as the sleuth impersonating a gangster. Lila Kedrova is pitiful and pathetic as the crazed addict and Magali Noel is the one light of gentleness in this hardboiled opus. *Mosk.*

Rome, May 31.

Il Segno Di Venere (The Sign of Venus) **ITALIAN**). Titanus production and release. Stars Sophia Lorin, Franca Valeri, Vittorio DeSica, Raf Vallone, Peppino DeFilippo, Alberto Sordi. Directed by Dino Risi. Screenplay, Franca Valeri, Dino Risi, Cesare Zavattini camera, Carlo Montuori; editor, Mario Serandri. At Metropolitan, Rome. Running time, **90 MINS.**

Sentimental comedy with a sprinkling of realism, "Venus" has its comic and moving moments. But it fails to come off as intended. Good for the local trade and may be worth an export try in special situations if given some re-editing. Story concerns two cousins with opposite problems: Agnese (Sophia Loren), whose exuberant femininity catches all eyes; and Cesira (Franca Valeri), a plain working gal whose unsuccessful manhunts bring on a growing fear of spinsterhood. Involved in the romantic adventure of the two gals are such types as Vittorio DeSica, a penniless poet; Peppino DeFilippo, as Cesira's bumbling last-resort "steady"; Alberto Sordi, as a frustrated, would-be car thief; and Raf Vallone, as the level-headed fireman.

Pic's principal drawback is failure to decide whether to play for laughs or tears, resulting in audience confusion. Yet the amusing moments abound. All technical credits are top. *Hawk.*

Not as a Stranger

Drama in the operating rooms with documentary detail an important value. Lots of impact but a couple of flaws which hold verdict short of "Great."

United Artists release of Stanley Kramer production. Stars Olivia de Havilland, Robert Mitchum, Frank Sinatra, Gloria Grahame, Broderick Crawford, Charles Bickford; features Myron McCormick, Lon Chaney, Jesse White, Harry Morgan, Lee Marvin, Virginia Christine, Whit Bissell, Jack Raine, Mae Clarke. Produced and directed by Kramer. Adapted by Edna and Edward Anhalt from novel by Morton Thompson; camera, Franz Planer; editor, Fred Knudtson, music, George Antheil. Previewed in N.Y., June 10, 1955. Running time, **135 MINS.**

Kristina Hedvigson . Olivia de Havilland
Lucas Marsh .... Robert Mitchum
Alfred Boone .... Frank Sinatra
Harriet Lang .... Gloria Grahame
Dr. Aarons .... Broderick Crawford
Dr. Runkleman .... Charles Bickford
Dr. Snider .... Myron McCormick
Job Marsh .... Lon Chaney
Ben Cosgrove .... Jesse White
Oley .... Harry Morgan
Brundage .... Lee Marvin
Bruni .... Virginia Christine
Dr. Dietrich .... Whit Bissell
Dr. Lettering .... Jack Raine
Miss O'Dell .... Mae Clarke

(Aspect ratio: 1.85-1)

Producer Stanley Kramer, a man with a penchant for offbeat choices, took Morton Thompson's best-selling novel of a young doctor as the occasion of his own directorial debut. Consequently, critical comment will focus upon this aspect, perhaps over-much and possibly unfairly. The question of his personal brass in doubling assumes importance precisely because the property is so hefty a vehicle upon which to "break in." If some scenes and moments are arguably improvable, and if the direction might have been surer and subtler, it is, however, only just to stress that Kramer's savez in picture-making and scene values shines forth and the net impact is strong screen diversion.

It is smart on Kramer's, and United Artists', part that plenty of advertising and promotion is being marshalled behind the picture. There are many natural tie-in angles via hospitals, nurses, doctors. Included are some peculiarly vivid operating room scenes, notably the climactic operation when the young doctor, obsessed with the drive to heal, tries vainly to save his older colleague. A human chest wall is laid bare, the ribs cut away as the cameras photograph the pulsations of the heart organ. This has, it is reasonable to assume, never before been shown in a film for laymen. It is a very dramatic thing, dramatic as are many of the other scenes in the picture because life itself is the stake.

Stories of doctors are not new to the screen but "Not as a Stranger" is especially rich in documentary detail, notably during the interneship of the young doctor (Robert Mitchum), whose desperate need of money to pay his medical school fees leads him to cold-bloodedly marry a Swedish nurse (Olivia de Havilland) because he learns she has $7,000 in savings. In a sense there are two separate narratives. When he finally completes his interneship, one story ends. Going forth to practice in a small town, an entirely new story begins. The letdown at this point is perhaps unavoidable. It means that the screen treatment of Edna and Edward Anhalt must roll up new suspense values in midstream against a completely altered background.

Three of the most interesting characterizations appear only in the second story. First is by Charles Bickford, as the hard-bitten and noble general practioner, whose own death struggle is the picture's climax. Bickford comes near to stealing the picture. Gloria Grahame, as a neurotic widow with lots of money, also stands out, though the part is much changed from the novel and never too clear in her motivations. Myron McCormick's role, that of a weakling doctor with careless medical ethics, is also arresting in its implications. In his novel, Thompson depicted a wide variety of doctor types. The blunt discussion of medical problems, including fees, among the internes and the physicians contributes a sense of "realism" not typical of medical heroics on the screen. An acid-etched pathologist at the hospital in the early action (with his knife poised to open a cadaver) uses scorn and cynicism to drive home to the student-doctors their awful responsibility. Broderick Crawford invests this dedicated teacher with a kind of icy compassion. A stunning bit of contempt for sloppy and wisecracking youngsters has him recite a whole section from memory, after flinging a textbook at Frank Sinatra. Sinatra is another of the players who comes close to doing a little picture stealing.

And what about the hero of the story, the main protagonist? He's Robert Mitchum and he's considerably over his acting depth. Though some scenes come off fairly well, Mitchum is poker-faced from start to finish. The confinements of Expression A and Expression B hardly fit the interior drive, the confusion and furious ambition implied in the script. As for his "affair" with Miss Grahame, she's all repressed moulten lava, but he could be scrubbing up.

Call Mitchum downbeat casting for Kramer and Olivia de Haviland offbeat. She comes through very impressively as a Swede, with an accent, and her usual brunet tresses traded in for a deep platinum dye job. While hardly a tour de force, Miss de Havilland's performance is of the sort which will excite some fan buzz.

Kramer credits three, two M.D.'s and one R.N., as technical advisers and in the end the documentary detail rivals the plot proper in general interest. Word-of-mouth may be considerable, for the story makes clear, however tactfully the bad is juxtaposed by the good, that doctors make blunders, are often snobs, money-grubbers and remarkably casual about the survival of elderly patients. The leit-motif running through the yarn is the importance of never giving up while life lingers, however feebly. This is planted several times in small scenes before the big climactic scene when the young doctor is almost demented with the frenzy of his one-man battle against the grim reaper.

The cinematic technicians undoubtedly rate high praise. Start with the camera work of Franz Planer. The score of George Antheil also counts as a mood factor. Production design (Rudolph Sternad) and art direction (Howard Richmond) have succeeded probably in ratio to their inobtrusiveness in making the hospital come alive.

Fred Knudtson's editing is, at a guess, close to a collaborative contribution to the over-all impact. The foregoing comments on direction and story treatment are sufficient report. (Interestingly, the dialog director is Anne Kramer). Finally, note is taken of an added song by Jimmy Van Heusen and Buddy Kaye called, reasonably enough, "Not as a Stranger."

Summing up, Kramer has turned over to United Artists a lot of picture despite the disappointment with the main characterization and some other checks on the minus side. *Land.*

You're Never Too Young
(V'VISION—MUSIC—COLOR)

Martin & Lewis in one of their funniest pictures. Sock b.o. in all situations.

Paramount release of Paul Jones production. Stars Dean Martin and Jerry Lewis with Diana Lynn and Nina Foch. Directed by Norman Taugog; screenplay, Sidney Sheldon; suggested by a play by Edward Childs Carpenter from a story by Fannie Kilbourne; camera (Technicolor), Daniel L. Fapp; special photograpcic effects, John P. Fulton; editor, Archie Marshek; songs, music by Arthur Schwartz, lyrics by Sammy Cahn; choreography, Nick Castle; music arranged and conducted by Walter Scharf. Previewed June 11, '55 at Brown's Hotel, Loch Sheldrake, N. Y. Running time, **102 MINS.**

Bob Miles	Dean Martin
Wilbur Hoolick	Jerry Lewis
Nancy Collins	Diana Lynn
Gretchen Brendin	Nina Foch
Noonan	Raymond Burr
Skeets	Mitzi McCall
Mrs. Noonan	Veda Ann Borg
Mrs. Ella Brendan	Margery Maude
Ticket Agent	Romo Vincent
Marty's Mother	Nancy Kulp
Lt. O'Malley	Milton Frome
Girl	Donna Percy
Conductor	Emory Parnell
Pullman Conductor	James Burke
Marty	Tommy Ivo
Mike Brendan	Whitey Haupt
Sergeant Brown	Mickey Finn
Agnes	Peggy Moffitt
1st Professor	Johnstone White
2nd Professor	Richard Simmons
Faculty Member	Louise Lorimer
Faculty Member	Isabel Randolph
Tailor	Robert Carson
Hotel Guard	Dick Cutting
Francois	Hans Conreid
Faculty Member	Mary Newton

In "You're Never Too Young," Martin and Lewis have come up with one of their funniest pictures. The Paramount VistaVision yok parade will slay the M&L regulars and will tickle the risibilities of more sophisticated patrons. The combo makes it sock boxoffice for all situations.

This latest entry is, in part, a throwback to the Mack Sennett days, with out-and-out slapstick predominating the action. It's cornball, unrealistic stuff, but tailor made for the family trade.

Sidney Sheldon's screenplay is inconsequential, but who cares as long as it provides Lewis with the skeleton for his madcap antics. This is Lewis' show and the zany comic is at the peak of his accomplishment with a hilarious performance. Martin does his best with his usual straight man assignment, but he is hampered by the undeveloped character provided him by the scripter. He gets the girl at the end, in this case Diana Lynn, but it's Lewis who gets the audience.

Lewis has a field day as a barber's apprentice who unknowingly obtains possession of a stolen diamond. He gets the chance to disguise himself as an 11-year-old, wears an outlandish kid's sailor suit, and shares a train bedroom, innocently of course, with Miss Lynn. He romps around a girl's school, fights off the advances of aggressive bobby soxers, leads a choral group, falls in a pool, vies with Martin for Miss Lynn's affections, runs from the jewel thief, disrupts a faculty meeting, does a takeoff of Humphrey Bogart, and upsets Martin in an unmanageable barber's chair. The climax, with Lewis on water skiis and Martin in a motor boat, is one of the funniest chase scenes ever filmed.

Veteran songsmiths Arthur Schwartz and Sammy Cahn have provided five tunes for the film, with Martin handling the vocals. Of the five, "Simpatico" appears to have the best chance of latching on. "Every Day Is a Happy Day" provides the background for an impressive production number staged by Nick Castle. It's a spectacular march and drill musical sequence which features M&L and over 100 femmes.

Nina Foch, as Miss Lynn's rival for Martin's attentions, is wasted in a curiously unresolved role. Miss Lynn is fine as the wide-eyed school teacher who accepts Lewis as an 11-year-old. Raymond Burr, as the jewel thief-murderer, Veda Ann Borg, as his accomplice, and Mitzi McCall, as a student, fulfill the demands of their parts. Norman Taurog has directed broadly in keeping with the picture's slapstick quality. Daniel L. Fapp's camera work, John P. Fulton's special effects, and other technical aspects are tops. *Holl.*

We're No Angels
(COLOR—VISTA VISION)

Breezy comedy on a macabre theme of three benevolent convicts on Devil's Island. Adapted from the Broadway stage play. Star names for b.o. attention.

Paramount release of Pat Duggan production. Stars Humphrey Bogart, Aldo Ray, Peter Ustinov, Joan Bennett and Basil Rathbone; features Leo G. Carroll, John Baer, Gloria Talbott, Lea Penman and John Smith. Directed by Michael Curtiz. Screenplay, Ranald MacDougall, based on the Albert Husson play; camera (Technicolor), Loyal Griggs; editor, Arthur Schmidt; music, Frederick Hollander; songs, "Sentimental Moments" by Hollander (music) and Ralph Freed (lyric) and "Ma France Bien-Aimee, G. Martini (music) and Roger Wagner (lyric). Previewed in Hollywood, June 13, '55. Running time, **103 MINS.**

Joseph	Humphrey Bogart
Albert	Aldo Ray
Jules	Peter Ustinov
Amelie Ducotel	Joan Bennett
Andre Trochard	Basil Rathbone
Felix Ducotel	Leo G. Carroll
Paul Trochard	John Baer
Isabelle Ducotel	Gloria Talbott
Madame Parole	Lea Penman
Arnaud	John Smith

Hollywood, June 13.

Paramount has fashioned a breezy 105-minute VistaVision feature from the French play, "La Cuisine Des Anges" (Angels Cooking) which was seen on Broadway as "My 3 Angels." It's macabre comedy that should be titillating filmfare for goodly portion ticket-buyers. Humphrey Bogart heads star trio which gives feature names for boxoffice attention and top playdates.

Light antics swing around three convicts of Devil's Island who find themselves playing Santa Claus to a family they came to rob. At times proceedings are too consciously cute and stage origin of material still clings since virtually all scenes are interiors with characters constantly entering and exiting. However, Michael Curtiz' directorial pacing and topflight performances from Bogart, Aldo Ray and Peter Ustinov point up entertainment values in Pat Duggan production and help minimize the few flaws.

Ranald MacDougall's screenplay from Albert Husson's legiter uses great deal of conversation, mostly amusingly flavored, to tell how convicts descend on store-home operated by Leo G. Carroll, his wife, Joan Bennett, planning robbery that would finance journey to France. Trio, all lifers, Bogart for forgery, others for murder, find family in difficulties unbecoming Christmas Eve spirit. They decide to use pet poisonous snake to remove Basil Rathbone, the ruthless relative who owns store, and John Baer, young cad causing heartbreak for Gloria Talbott, daughter of family.

Some viewers may get uncomfortable feeling over benevolent murders, but since neither snake nor corpses are seen, and victims hardly deserved better treatment, situation plays for laughs, particularly under skillful thesping of all concerned.

In addition to those named, added fun is supplied by Lea Penman, fat, snobbish customer, and John Smith, young doctor who's new romance for Miss Talbott.

Period settings and costumes are well photographed in Technicolor by Loyall Griggs. All technical support is excellent. Two tunes, "Sentimental Moments," by Frederick Hollander, Ralph Freed, and "Ma France Bien-Aimee," by Roger Wagner and G. Martini, make for good listening. *Brog.*

Foxfire
(COLOR—SONG)

Jane Russell, Jeff Chandler giving interest to romantic drama with modern outdoor setting. Average entertainment, average biz.

Hollywood, June 14.

Universal release of Aaron Rosenberg production. Stars Jane Russell, Jeff Chandler; costars Dan Duryea; features Mara Corday, Barton MacLane, Frieda Inescort, Celia Lovsky. Directed by Joseph Pevney. Screenplay, Ketti Frings; based on the story by Anya Seton; camera (Technicolor), William Daniels; editor, Ted J. Kent; score, Frank Skinner; song, Jeff Chandler, Henry Mencini; sung by Chandler. Previewed June 8, '55. Running time, **91 MINS.**

Amanda	Jane Russell
Jonathan Dartland	Jeff Chandler
Hugh Slater	Dan Duryea
Maria	Mara Corday
Mr. Mablett	Barton MacLane
Mrs. Lawrence	Frieda Inescort
Saba	Celia Lovsky
Old Larky	Eddy C. Waller
Ernest Tyson	Robert F. Simon
Mrs. Mablett	Charlotte Wynters
Walt Whitman	Robert Bice
Foley	Arthur Space

(*Aspect ratio*: 2-1)

The star names of Jane Russell and Jeff Chandler, plus Dan Duryea and a title song, will help "Foxfire" through the regular market to average returns. It's a romantic drama that leans a bit towards soap opera, in a modern, outdoor western dress, with perhaps more distaffer than masculine appeal.

Eastern society, represented by Miss Russell, comes up against the fascination of the west in the person of Chandler, half-breed Apache mining engineer, and almost before they can say hello they are married and she becomes a new housewife in an Arizona ghost town. That's the setup for the drama in the Aaron Rosenberg production and lays the groundwork for the problems that develop because east doesn't understand west and vice versa. It is prettily staged in Technicolor under the good direction by Joseph Pevney, and Ketti Frings' script, based on the story by Anya Seton, expertly mixes the misunderstandings into marital drama with a happy ending.

Miss Russell will earn the most

audience sympathy for the earnest way she goes about making something of her marriage despite the handicaps to happiness thrown up by her surly husband and some gossiping neighbors. By the time she finds out what makes hubby so churlish, it's almost too late, but the day is saved by a miscarriage, his discovery of gold in an abandoned Indian mine and the realization that his redskin blood actually is no barrier to a successful marriage. Miss Russell is extremely likeable in her breezy characterization, playing it with a becoming naturalness. Chandler is handicapped somewhat in the likeable department because of the surliness in the character of a halfbreed raised on a reservation who finds it hard to adapt to matrimony, but does it well and the femmes should find his bigness attractive, as they will his singing of the title tune, which he cleffed with Henry Mancini.

Duryea comes over well as the mine doctor who nurses the bottle as much as the patients, and Mara Corday is good as the lady-in-white who is more than an assistant to the doc. Barton MacLane, mine super who despises Indians; Frieda Inescort, Miss Russell's fluttery mother; Celia Lovsky, a standout as Chandler's Indian mother, and the others of the cast contribute capably.

The 2-to-1 aspect ratio shows up for full value under the color lensing by William Daniels, and the other technical credits are expert right down the line. Frank Skinner's score, supervised by Joseph Gershenson, is good. *Brog.*

Finger Man

Crime melodrama for programmer playdates with familiar names to help bookings.

Hollywood, June 8.

Allied Artists release of Lindsley Parsons production. Stars Frank Lovejoy, Forrest Tucker, Peggie Castle; features Timothy Carey, John Cliff, William Leicester, Glen Gordon, John Close, Hugh Sanders, Evelynne Eaton, Charles Maxwell, Lewis Charles. Directed by Harold Schuster. Written by Warren Douglas; based on a story by Morris Lipsius, John Lardner; camera, William Sickner; editor, Maurice Whight; music composed and conducted by Paul Dunlap. Previewed June 6, '55. Running time, **81 MINS.**

Casey Martin	Frank Lovejoy
Dutch Becker	Forrest Tucker
Gladys Baker	Peggie Castle
Lou Terpe	Timothy Carey
Cooper	John Cliff
Rogers	William Leicester
Carlos Armor	Glen Gordon
Walters	John Close
Mr. Burns	Hugh Sanders
Lucille	Evelynne Eaton
Amory	Charles Maxwell
Lefty Stern	Lewis Charles

(*Aspect ratio:* 1:85-1)

This is a crime melodrama that falls in the programmer class for general bookings. For the label it wears it does a fairly adequate, if undistinguished, job. In its favor for bookings are the familiar names of Frank Lovejoy, Forrest Tucker and Peggie Castle.

Plot, based on a story by Morris Lipsius and John Lardner, tells how a three-time-loser, picked up by the Internal Revenue Bureau, is given the alternative of life in jail or helping the Feds put the finger on a crime bigshot. While there might be parallels in real life, there's little in the Warren Douglas script that is believable on the screen so the unfoldment under Harold Schuster's direction makes for only routine cops-and-robbers melodramatics.

Lovejoy plays the crook turned finger man in the Lindsley Parsons production, and within the limitations imposed by the script does a good job. The same is true of Tucker, the bigshot whom Lovejoy nails for the Feds on a bootlegging rap, and Miss Castle, a girl who at one time worked for the mobster but now loves Lovejoy. This affection and her fear for the finger man in his undercover work results in her death and the near demise of Lovejoy before the finale roundup is staged.

Timothy Carey heads the feature cast as a psychotic henchman always with Tucker. On the side of law are John Cliff, William Leicester, Hugh Sanders and Charles Maxwell. They and the other cast members are acceptable.

William Sickner's lensing and the other behind-camera functions are adequate for the budget. *Brog.*

Jedda
(AUSTRALIAN)

Sydney, June 7.

Columbia release of Charles Chauvel production. Stars Ngarla Kunoth, Robert Tudawali. Directed by Charles Chauvel. Original screenplay, Charles and Elsa Chauvel; camera, Carl Kayser; special photographic effects, Eric Porter; editors, Alex Ezzard & Jack Gardiner; music, Isador Goodman. Previewed in Sydney at Lyceum. Running time, **101 MINS.**

Jedda	Ngarla Kunoth
Marbuck	Robert Tudawali
Douglas McCann	George Simpson-Lyttle
Sarah McCann	Betty Suttor
Joe	Paul Reynell
Peter Wallis	Tas Fitzer
Felix Romeo	Wason Byers
Shorty	Bill Harney

Charles Chauvel's ninth film does him credit in standards of production, and it will make money for exhibitors in area. E'sewhere, it's doubtful boxoffice. The Australian aborigines figure in the plot—a triangle involving a black native, a dark-skinned girl and a half-caste male. This might succeed in Britain and European countries on the exotic appeal of a remote, strange land and its primitive natives.

The film is a simple, largely unsophisticated story told against a remarkably picturesque setting. It does possess something that clicks in Australia. Australians generally have little sentiment for their native Negro people.

Basically, Chauvel uses the chase idea. His heroine is Jedda, native girl brought up in white ways on a ranch in the northern territory of Australia. She is abducted by a wild bush native, and they are pursued into the wilderness by a half-caste who loves the girl and presently by the territory's police.

Some of the native witchcraft on which the story motivation depends may not be readily understood outside of Australia. Overseas audiences may laugh at the tribal elders' sentence—that the tribe will "sing" the offending Marbuck (Robert Tudafali) to death. Yet death by "pointing the bone" and such actually occurs among Australian aborigines.

Although the Australian aborigine in general is unlovely, Robert Tudawali is a dark native male of fine physique and a natural actor. Ngarla Kunoth, as Jedda, has the characteristic splay-nosed look of her race. She is merely adequate. Paul Reynell, white man who plays the half-caste, registers well, but speaks too impeccably to be authentic.

Continuity and editing are smooth. The color (Gevacolor) varies a little, but not violently. Carl Kayser's camerawork is splendid, catching the breadth of the wild, lonely country.

Yokihi
(JAPANESE—COLOR)

Tokyo, June 7.

A Daiei-Shaw (Hong Kong) co-production (under supervision of Masaichi Nagata) and release. Stars Machiko Kyo and Masayukn Mori. Directed by Kenji Mizoguchi. Screenplay by Tao Chin, Matsutaro Kawakuchi, Yoshikata Yoda, Masahige Narusawa; camera, Kohei Sugiyama; color supervision, Tatsuyuki Yokota; music, Fumio Hoyasaka; historical research, Lu Shin-hou. Running time, **100 MINS.**

First Sino-Japanese coproduction, and one of two Japanese films accepted for entry at the 16th Venice Film Festival, "Yokiho" is the prototype of a combo of Oriental skills which may result in a new squeeze on the Western film fan's pocketbook. Combining the cinematographic nowhow of Masaichi's Daiei Studios ("Rashamon," "Gate of Hell") with the untapped reservoir of colorful Chinese legends plus utilization of a Chinesee historian for period authenticity of sets, costumes and general decor has brought out another exotic film. Unless U.S. filmgoers are sated with the Orient, "Yokiho" looms as another success in smaller arty situations.

Based on a long poem, "Period of Long Lament," this deals with the tragic romance of Chinese Emperor Genso (Mori) of the Tang Dynasty (618-906) and a commoner who eventually becomes empress Yang Kui-fei (Yokiho in Japanese).

The emperor's courtiers, seeking to curry favor, round up a bevy of native beauties to console him for the loss of his beloved wife. The ruler falls in love at first sight of Yokiho (Machiko Kyo, who is seen for the first time without the white makeup of "Rashamon" and "Gate of Hell") and marries her.

The emperor's generals and the people, resentful of her rise, petition Yokiho's banishment. When the emperor refuses, the people revolt. The emperor's wife is hanged.

Story, narrated by the emperor, and told through a series of flashbacks, ends with the death of Genso of old age.

There is a bit of confusion in the flow of the story because the flashbacks are not worked smoothly enough, but Machiko Kyo and Fasayuki Mori are confident and at ease in their roles. With the exception of a slight overacting on the part of Mori, traceable to his Kabuki training, the histrionics are as smooth as any seen in Japanese films to date.

The Eastman color, the beautiful garb, low-key lighting and a weird musical score assure "Yokiho" of undivided attention. *Lars.*

Foreign Films

Buenos Aires, June 7.

La Ciguena Dijo Si (The Stork Said Yes) (**ARGENTINA**). General Belgrano release of Enrique, Luis and Nicolas Carreras production. Stars Lola Membrives, with Tomas Blanco, Esteban Serrador, Susana Campos and Hugo Pimentel. Directed by Enrique Carreras from legit play by Carlos Llopis. Adapted by Alejandro Casona; camera, Alfredo Traverso; music, Vlady; editor, Jose Callego. At Normandie and Roca Theatres, Buenos Aires. Running time, **72 MINS.**

This has strong marquee values locally, mainly because vet legit actress Lola Membrives, who starred in one of legit bits of 1954, is star of the pic. Pic is rated an improvement over the legit show because of Alejandro Casona's sprightly dialogue. Though light and inconsequential, the picture is pleasant with a sophisticated polish unusual in local productions. If manifestly old for the character she portrays, Lola Membrives carries off the assignment with remarkable verve, extracting the most out of every situation. The remainder of the cast appears colorless beside her. Although not sensational, this should do well as a dualer in other Spanish speaking countries. *Nid.*

Paris, June 7.

Ca Va Barder (Things Will Jump) (**FRENCH**). Dispas release of Societe Nouvelle Dispas-D. A. Medioni production. Stars Eddie Constantine; features May Britt, Jean Carmot, Jean Danet, Roger Saget, Lili Rocco, Monique Von Vooren. Directed by John Berry. Screenplay, Berry, Henri-Francoise Rey, Jacques Nahum; camera, Jacques Lemare; music, Jeff Davis; editor, Marguerite Cadix. Running time, **95 MINS.**

Now that the phenomenon of Eddie Constantine, U.S. singer become pic star, is a definite staple here, he has wisely brought some U.S. flair and knowhow into his gangster pix for good effect. Since his films are primarily imitations of the U.S. counterparts, the use of American director John Berry has given this new entry in this series a bombastic mounting, surpassing the French counterpart in its tongue-in-cheek treatment, well-staged fights and chases, but still covers the tough guy adventurer amidst the usual skulduggery.

Plot vaguely has the hero fronting for a gunrunner to uncover who is hijacking his shipments. This turns up an old flame married to a knifethrowing, scar-faced cabaret owner, many homicidal thugs and enough action to keep things moving at a rapid clip. Sketchily clad gals punctuate proceedings. *Mosk.*

Berlin, June 7.

Zwischenlandung in Paris (Intermediate Landing in Paris) (**GERMAN-FRENCH**). Schorcht release of Corona, Hoche and Marina production. Stars Dany Robin and Dieter Borsche; features Heinz Ruehmann, Simone Renant, Francois Perier, Hans Nielsen. Directed by Jean Dreville. Screenplay, Jacques Companeez, Joseph Than, based on same-titled novel by Curt Riess; camera, Helmut Ashley; music, Paul Misraki. At Kiki, Berlin. Running time, **104 MINS.**

The French airport of Orly, outside Paris, furnishes the background of this unpretenious Franco-German coproduction which depicts not too convincingly some episodes dealing with love, sentiment, business and dope-smuggling. Makes it a suitable programmer for the most domestic situations. In the U.S., the chances are very limited.

Screenplay by Jacques Companeez, Joseph Than and Curt Riess, based on latter's novel, appears quite a bit overloaded with complicated situations. Jean Dreville's direction makes good use of the fresh-appearing airport location.

Love affair is provided by lovely Dany Robin and Dieter Borsche, but the latter's portrayal of an American pilot is not very genuine. Technical credits are generally good. The musical score by Paul Misraki is noteworthy. *Hans.*

Land of the Pharaohs
(C'SCOPE-COLOR)

Tremendous CinemaScope spectacle filmed in story locale, with exploitation values for sturdy b.o.

Hollywood, June 21.

Warner Bros. release of Howard Hawks (Continental Company Ltd.) production. Stars Jack Hawkins, Joan Collins, Dewey Martin, Alexis Minotis; features James R. Justice, Luisa Boni, Sydney Chaplin, James Hayter, Kerima, Piero Giagnoni. Directed by Hawks. Written by William Faulkner, Harry Kurnitz, Harold Jack Bloom; camera (Warner Color), Lee Garmes, Russell Harlan; editor, V. Sagovsky; supervising editor, Rudi Fehr; music composed and conducted by Dimitri Tiomkin. Previewed June 7, '55. Running time, 103 MINS.

Pharaoh	Jack Hawkins
Princess Nellifer	Joan Collins
Senta	Dewey Martin
Hamar	Alexis Minotis
Vashtar	James R. Justice
Kyra	Luisa Boni
Treneh	Sydney Chaplin
Vashtar's Servant	James Hayter
Queen Nailla	Kerima
Pharaoh's Son	Piero Giagnoni

Egypt of 5,000 years ago comes to life in "Land of the Pharaohs," a tremendous film spectacle in CinemaScope and WarnerColor that is concocted of the chimerical stuff that promises sturdy boxoffice. While shy of proven draw value in cast names, the Howard Hawks production for Warners makes up for the lack with romance, adventure and intrigue played against a grandiose backdrop of actual story locales populated with teeming masses of thousands upon thousands of extras. Exploitation angles abound, so it's a show that should go at the wickets.

It's a relatively simple plot line with which the screen story by William Faulkner, Harry Kurnitz and Harold Jack Bloom is concerned, but there is nothing simple about the trappings bestowed on it by Hawks in the Continental Company Ltd. presentation through Warners. From the opening shot of a great Pharaoh and his thousands of soldiers returning from successful battle laden with vast treasure, an audience is constantly overwhelmed with spectacle, either in the use of cast thousands, tremendously sized settings or the surging background score by Dimitri Tiomkin, which almost gives the picture the quality of being an operatic drama with spoken lyrics.

The story tells of a great Pharaoh, ably played by Jack Hawkins, English actor, who for 30 years drives his people to build a pyramid in which his body and treasure shall rest secure for evermore, and of a woman, portrayed by Joan Collins, a captivating bundle of s. a., who conspires to win his kingdom and riches for herself but, by a twist of superior cunning, shares only the Pharaoh's tomb.

When the viewing senses begin to dull from the tremendous load of spectacle, the script and Hawks' direction wisely switch to sex and intrigue, and one plays off against the other at a dramatic pace that, while never fast, is well-balanced for interest. Probably only in Egypt, where the exteriors were actually lensed, could Hawks have obtained such a horde of extras to enact the Pharaoh subjects who toil and die in the quarries and on the pyramid to build the memorial to their leader. A program note states that 9,787 people appear in one quarry scene and it's easy to believe when scanned through the sweeping eye of the CinemaScope

camera, outstandingly manned by Lee Garmes and Russell Harlan.

Alexis Minotis, Greek actor, lends the picture a fine performance as Hamar, the high priest who, faithful to his Pharaoh, tricks the wicked Princess Nellifer into joining the one-way funeral procession to the pyramid's burial chamber. Another who stands out is James Robertson Justice as Vashtar, bearded architect and leader of the captive Kushites, who designs the pyramid so that when the Pharaoh's remains are sealed in their crypt the entire pyramid becomes an impregnable and unescapable tomb. Dewey Martin is seen as his adopted son who marries the slave, Kyra, played by Luisa Boni, during the long stay in royal city. Sydney Chaplin shows up well as the captain of the treasure guards who succumbs to Princess Nellifer's wiles in the plot against the Pharaoh. James Hayter and Kerima, the latter as the queen, are among others in the capable feature cast.

Picture, on which Arthur Siteman was associate producer, has been given colorful trappings in the art direction by Alexandre Trauner, in the costumes designed by Mayo, in the special effects and other technical contributions. The massive editing chore was handled effectively by V. Sagovsky under the supervision of Rudi Fehr.

Brog.

The Scarlet Coat
(COLOR—CINEMASCOPE)

Well mounted, interesting study of Revolutionary War intrigue that should cop good grosses all around.

Metro release of Nicholas Nayfack production. Stars Cornel Wilde, Michael Wilding, George Sanders, Anne Francis; features Robert Douglas, John McIntire, Rhys Williams, Bobby Driscoll. Directed by John Sturges. Screenplay, Karl Tunberg; camera (Eastman Color), Paul C. Vogel; editor, Ben Lewis; music, Conrad Salinger. Previewed in N. Y. June 16, '55. Running time, 101 MINS.

Maj. John Bolton	Cornel Wilde
Maj. John Andre	Michael Wilding
Dr. Jonathan Odell	George Sanders
Sally Cameron	Anne Francis
Benedict Arnold	Robert Douglas
General Robert Howe	John McIntire
Peter	Rhys Williams
Nathanael Greene	John Dehner
Col. Jameson	James Westerfield
Mr. Brown	Ashley Cowan
Sir Henry Clinton	Paul Cavanagh
Mr. Durkin	John Alderson
Col. Winfield	John O'Malley
and	
Ben Porter	Bobby Driscoll

The Gen. Benedict Arnold-Major John Andre phase of the Revolutionary War is related in terms of human values in "The Scarlet Coat." Pyrotechnics of the conflict are put to one side for the most part and the personal relationships accented. Nicholas Nayfack's production comes off as a welcome switch from the routine in concept. It's interesting and, at times, arresting, and never static, storytelling. Adding up to a good boxoffice possibility.

Nayfack has provided appealing production mounting for the story of the intrigue behind Gen. Arnold's defection to the British. The CinemaScope and Eastman Color photography is orb-sorbing, having been given a nice headstart via accurate costuming and location lensing in N. Y.'s Hudson area. Karl Tunberg's writing is well developed, has a full share of rousing moments for punctuation. Cast names are okay for the initial draw.

Although the Arnold character

is seen limitedly on screen, his behind-the-scenes plotting with the British, and the counter-spying of the colonists' "Major John Bolton" (Cornel Wilde) form the basis of the plot. John Sturges' direction provides the always-needed pace most of the way. A flaw, though, lies in the yarn's femme angle, for Anne Francis fails to sock across the sexy explosiveness that apparently was intended (and needed) in her couple of romantic encounters with Wilde.

Wilde fares fair against tough male competition, scoring adequately as the rebel officer who pretends loyalty only to money and takes sides with the British as a device to uncover what he eventually learns is the Arnold plot. Michael Wilding, as Andre, is a vivid likeness of history's portrait of the Anglican "martyr." Supported by Tunberg's almost always sharp dialog, Wilding expertly conveys the almost effeminate officer-gentleman of high ideals who eventually comes to see, and admire, Wilde's noble motives although the two are on different sides.

George Sanders by any other costume is still George Sanders and here, as a conspirator on the British side, his knee-high-stockinged getup looks kind of ludicrous. But the acting competence nonetheless comes through as the incisively-tongued Sanders tries in vain to convince the scarlet-coated military that Wilde is an American spy.

Sturges' direction, the camera work and the lighting are particularly effective in a few of the action scenes. Curiously, though, while there's dramatic punch in these, such as Wilde's attempt to cut the river barrier for British war vessels, the hand-to-hand grappling in a couple of instances looks like so much false make-believe.

The featured players, including Bobby Driscoll, Robert Douglas, John McIntire and Rhys Williams, do standard work for a production of this caliber. The editing allows for no intolerable lulls and music by Conrad Salinger is unusually good support.

Gene.

Herr Ueber Leben Und Tod
(Master Over Life and Death)
(GERMAN)

Berlin, June 14.

Gloria release of Interwest production. Stars Maria Schell, Ivan Desny and Wilhelm Borchert. Directed by Victor Vicas. Screenplay, Frederic Grendel and Victor Vicas after a Zuckmayer story; camera, Goeran Strindberg; music, Hans-Martin Majewski. At Gloria Palast, Berlin. Running time, 98 MINS.

Barbara Bertram	Maria Schell
Prof. Georg Bertram	Wilhelm Borchert
Dr. Danel Karentis	Ivan Desny
Anna Bertram	Olga Limburg
Werner Hansen	Walter Bluhm
Dr. Peter	Fritz Tillmann

This is strong drama film based on the Zuckmayer story of the same name. Brilliant direction by Victor Vicas, outstanding camerawork by Swedish Goeran Strindberg, rather realistic treatment of a basically unconvincing plot and a topnotch cast make this an item abreast of the also-ran category. It appears to have good chances for U.S. art houses.

What may have been convincing in Zuckmayer's original story is not too plausible in the script by Frederic Grendel and Victor Vicas. Some scenes could stand more explanation, such as the one which leads to the death of Maria Schell's lover. It's not quite clear whether he drowned himself or was killed in an accident. Some patrons may

also find that film lacks some light touches and object to its sad ending.

Film is never dull. This is mainly a merit of Vicas' subtle direction. His scenes seldom lack feeling and his cooperation with cameraman Strindberg is topflight and one of the main assets about the production. There is also a strong musical score by Hans-Martin Majewski which adds to the mood.

Story revolves around Miss Schell, wife of a reputable medico, who gives birth to a mentally sick child. Her husband attempts to kill the child and his attempt drives Miss Schell to the French Bretagne where she falls in love with a more understanding medico.

Maria Schell is the ideal in the femme lead, being natural and heart-warming. Wilhelm Borchert is impressive as her husband while Ivan Desny contributes the lover role, also a lifelike portrayal.

Hans.

The Road to Denver
(COLOR)

Firstrate western action feature, credibly done, with familiar names for the outdoor market.

Hollywood, June 20.

Republic release. Stars John Payne, Mona Freeman, Lee J. Cobb, Ray Middleton, Skip Homeier; features Andy Clyde, Lee Van Cleef, Karl Davis, Glenn Strange, Buzz Henry, Daniel White, Robert Burton, Anne Carroll, Tex Terry. Directed by Joe Kane. Screenplay, Horace McCoy, Allen Rivkin; based on a Sat Eve Post story by Bill Gulick; camera (Trucolor), Reggie Lanning; editor, Richard L. Van Enger; music, R. Dale Butts. Previewed June 17, '55. Running time, 90 MINS.

Bill Mayhew	John Payne
Elizabeth Sutton	Mona Freeman
Jim Donovan	Lee J. Cobb
John Sutton	Ray Middleton
Sam Mayhew	Skip Homeier
Whipsaw	Andy Clyde
Pecos Larry	Lee Van Cleef
Hunsaker	Karl Davis
Big George	Glenn Strange
Pete	Buzz Henry
Joslyn	Daniel White
Kraft	Robert Burton
Miss Honeywell	Anne Carroll
Passenger	Tex Terry

(Aspect ratio: 1.66-1)

"The Road to Denver" is a firstrate western feature sure to please in the outdoor market, and elsewhere where soundly developed story values, good direction and credible performances count for entertainment in the action class. Familiar cast names will help it through the regular market, too.

The familiar ingredients in Bill Gulick's SatEvePost story have been whipped into topnotch filmfare in the script by Horace McCoy and Allen Rivkin, with plenty of freshening touches to minimize the fact the plot path has been trod many times before. The situations are believable and the dialog rings true as the story comes to life under Joe Kane's able direction, which gives it plenty of action without once straining credibility.

The story is the one about two brothers. John Payne is the dependable older and Skip Homeier the foolhardy younger. Tired of getting into trouble himself getting Homeier out of difficulties, Payne decides to go his own way and heads for Colorado, where he takes a job with Ray Middleton, owner of a Central City livery stable who is planning a stage line to Denver. Homeier, a short time later, shows up in town and, lured by a quick buck, joins the henchmen surrounding Lee J. Cobb, town saloon keeper and head of a hijacking gang. What then transpires helps to resolve the fraternal feud and wins for Payne the hand of Mona Freeman, who, as the daughter of Middleton, is a believable western heroine.

The casters named above each add measurably to the excellent manner with which the action drama is brought off. Other performance assists come from Andy Clyde, who adds quite a lift to his scenes as a stable hand; Lee Van Cleef, Karl Davis, Glenn Strange, Buzz Henry, all members of Cobb's gang, and supporting members of the cast.

The Trucolor hues caught by Reggie Lanning's photography contribute to the visual values. All with story freshening, the production gains background freshness by location-lensing in Utah. Editing, score and other contributions are good. *Brog.*

Bring Your Smile Along
(MUSICAL—COLOR)

Unpretentious, pleasant musical suitable as strong co-feature.

Columbia release of Jonie Taps production. Stars Frankie Laine, Keefe Brasselle, and Constance Towers. Features Lucy Marlow and William Leslie. Directed by Blake Edwards. Screenplay, Edwards, from a story by Edwards and Richard Quine; camera (Technicolor), Charles Lawton Jr.; editor, Al Clark; music supervised and conducted by Morris Stoloff; songs, Benny Davis and Carl Fischer, Bill Carey and Fischer, Paul Mason Howard and Paul Weston, Dorothy Fields and Jimmy McHugh, Harry Woods, Allan Roberts and Lester Lee, Ned Washington and Lee. Previewed in New York June 20 '55. Running time, 83 MINS.

Jerry Dennis .... Frankie Laine
Martin Adams .... Keefe Brasselle
Nancy Willows ...... Constance Towers
Marge Stevenson .... Lucy Marlow
David Parker .... William Leslie
Ricardo .... Mario Siletti
Landlady .... Ruth Warren
Jenson .... Jack Albertson
Waldo .... Bobby Clark
Dave .... Murray Leonard
Mama .... Ida Smeraldo

"Bring Your Smile Along" is an unpretentious musical in the escapist groove. With a number of ingratiating performers to help it along, it emerges as pleasant, if not overly exciting, entertainment for the family trade. It'll make a strong co-feature for top situations and may even make the grade as the number one attraction in some spots.

Its chief asset, both as a marquee lure and from the entertainment standpoint, is Frankie Laine, a pro performer in any medium. Laine has plenty of opportunity to belt across—in his unique style—a number of tunes, including several of his own disk clicks. A couple of newcomers — Constance Towers, Lucy Marlow and William Leslie—show considerable promise and rate buildups as part of the industry's development of new personalities. Miss Towers is a blonde looker with a Grace Kelly lady-like quality. As an added plus, she has a good singing voice suitable for film tuners. Miss Marlow is a pert brunet with a flair for comedy. Leslie is a handsome leading man type. Keefe Brasselle, remembered for his portrayal of Eddie Cantor in the latter's biopic, also comes across okay in this outing.

Although Blake Edwards' screenplay is a cliche boy-meets-loses-gets-girl story, complete with a fave Italian restaurant and the "mama mia" husband-and-wife proprietors, it's not too hard to take. Miss Towers is a school-teacher who leaves a New England

high school and her biology teacher-fiance to "find herself" in New York as a lyric writer. Circumstances place her in the company of Brasselle, a tunesmith who becomes her collaborator, and Laine, a crooner. As a team Miss Towers and Brasselle click, writing hit tunes which Laine records.

The inevitable happens. Brasselle falls for his lyricist. But what about the guy back home? As usually happens in these situations, the hometown boy, in this case Leslie, loses out. To the scripter's credit, however, is the fact that the former fiance is not presented as a stuffy schnook.

The songsmithing background offers opportunity for some lively musical numbers, featuring Laine and/or Miss Towers and Brasselle. Edwards' direction contributes to the general pleasantness of the film. Charles Lawton's Technicolor photography and other technical aspects are fine. *Holl.*

It Came From Beneath the Sea

Good thriller of the science-fiction variety for exploitation dates.

Hollywood, June 17.

Columbia release of Charles H. Schneer (Clover) production. Stars Kenneth Tobey, Faith Domergue; features Donald Curtis, Ian Keith, Dean Maddox Jr., Chuck Griffiths, Harry Lauter, Richard W. Peterson. Directed by Robert Gordon. Screenplay, George Worthing Yates, Hal Smith; from story by Yates; camera, Henry Freulich; technical effects, Ray Harryhausen; editor, Jerome Thoms; music conducted by Mischa Bakaleinikoff. Previewed June 3, '55. Running time, 79 MINS.

Pete Mathews .... Kenneth Tobey
Lesley Joyce .... Faith Domergue
John Carter .... Donald Curtis
Admiral Burns .... Ian Keith
Admiral Norman ...... Dean Maddox Jr.
Griff .... Lt. C. Griffiths
Bill Nash .... Harry Lauter
Captain Stacy........ Capt. R. Peterson
Robert Chase .... Del Courtney
Navy Interne .... Tol Avery
Reporter .... Ray Storey
Hall .... Rudy Puteska
Aston .... Jack Littlefield
McLeod .... Ed Fisher
King .... Jules Irving

(Aspect ratio: 1.85-1)

Experimenting with hydrogen bombs can produce some unexpected results and "It Came From Beneath the Sea" sets about proving it with sufficient novelty to rate its science-fiction thriller classification. It's a good subject for exploitation bookings in the ballyhoo market.

A new atom submarine, out on trial runs, encounters a horrible marine monster under Pacific waters and sub commander Kenneth Tobey has his hands full getting away safely. From a part of the creature's substance caught in one of the sub's diving planes, scientists are able to figure out what it is and advance the theory that H-Bomb explosions off the Marshall Islands have chased a giant squid from its natural home far below the surface in the Great Mindanao Deep.

That's the setup for the thrills in the George Worthing Yates story which he scripted with Hal Smith for Charles H. Schneer's production under Columbia's Clover unit label. Most of the time the script, Robert Gordon's direction and the trouping keep the thrills playing convincingly and horror fans should find it to their liking. The early effect is towards the documentary, since some good sea footage has been obtained and there are a number of natural cast contributions by actual naval personnel, among them Lt. C. Griffiths,

who is quite good, and Capt. R. Peterson. Towards the conclusion, some strain is put on credibility, but all in the spirit of building thrills, when the monster gets into San Francisco Bay and creates havoc before derring-do by Tobey and Donald Curtis, one of the scientists, manages to destroy it.

Faith Domergue is the attractive femme interest, playing the distaff side of the scientist team with Curtis. The romance that develops between her and Tobey isn't particularly convincing, even though his reasons for falling are. She, along with Tobey, Curtis, Ian Keith, Dean Maddox Jr., Griffiths, Harry Lauter, Peterson and the others provide the picture with satisfactory performances, while the special effects by Ray Harryhausen take care of the chiller aspects as the Navy hunts down the creature.

There is some corner-cutting in the budget that allows the use of library footage seen in another Columbia release ("Creature With The Atom Brain"). Otherwise Henry Freulich's lensing is good, as are the technical assists. *Brog.*

Creature With the Atom Brain

Horror programmer for lower-case bookings; minor entertainment values.

Hollywood, June 17.

Columbia release of a Clover production. Stars Richard Denning; features Angela Stevens, S. John Launer, Michael Granger, Gregory Gay. Directed by Edward L. Cahn. Story and screenplay, Curt Siodmak; camera, Fred Jackman Jr.; editor, Aaron Stell; music conducted by Mischa Bakaleinikoff. Previewed June 2, '55. Running time, 69 MINS.

Dr. Chet Walker .... Richard Denning
Joyce Walker .... Angela Stevens
Capt. Dave Harris ..... S. John Launer
Frank Buchanan .... Michael Granger
Prof. Steigg .... Gregory Gay
Penny Walker .... Linda Bennett
District Att'y MacGraw..Tristram Coffin
Reporter .... Harry Lauter
Reporter .... Larry Blake
Chief Camden .... Charles Evans
Mayor Bremer .... Pierre Watkin
General Saunders ..... Lane R. Chandler
Dr. Kenneth Norton...... Nelson Leigh
Lester Banning .... Don C. Harvey
Dunn .... Paul Hoffman
Jason Franchot .... Edward Coch

(Aspect ratio: 1.85-1)

Bodies charged with atom rays roam the footage in this horror programmer, doing the bidding of a revenge-seeking mobster. Up to a point, the picture plays with sufficient conviction to meet release demands adequately and will probably spend its distribution time as the lower half of exploitation science-fiction bills.

Curt Siodmak concocted the horror plot for the Clover production directed by Edward L. Cahn, and until he has the mad master of the atomic zombies turning them loose on a whole city will keep his audience with him, even if things get rather distastefully violent. Michael Granger plays the deported mobster who returns secretly to kill the men involved in his conviction. He works with a scientist who has discovered how to charge corpses with atom rays and control their activities through electrodes in their heads.

Police Laboratory head Richard Denning and his sidekick, S. John Launer, start an investigation when a gambler and the district attorney are done in, but Launer is given the zombie treatment and almost queers a successful probe. When Denning gets too close, Granger starts to terrorize the city, but atoms or no, he's no match for Denning's wits and meets a gory

end. Others involved in the chiller doings include Angela Stevens, as Denning's wife; Gregory Gay, the scientist; and sundry character players.

Generous use of library footage, such as racing police cars and motorcycles, groups listening to radio broadcasts, etc. is made to fill out the new lensing by Fred Jackman Jr., and cut budget costs. Technical assists are standard.

The Man From Laramie
(C'SCOPE—COLOR—SONG)

Rugged, C'Scoped outdoor actioner with James Stewart; substantial b.o. indications.

Hollywood, June 28.

Columbia release of William Goetz production. Stars James Stewart, Arthur Kennedy, Donald Crisp, Cathy O'Donnell, Alex Nicol, Aline MacMahon; features Wallace Ford, Jack Elam, John War Eagle, James Millican, Greg Barton, Boyd Stockman, Frank de Kowa. Directed by Anthony Mann. Screenplay, Philip Yordan, Frank Burt; based on the SatEvePost story by Thomas T. Flynn; camera (Technicolor), Charles Lang; editor, William Lyon; score, George Duning; conducted by Morris Stoloff; song, Lester Lee and Ned Washington. Previewed June 23, '55. Running time, **102 MINS.**

Will Lockhart .... James Stewart
Vic Hansbro .... Arthur Kennedy
Alec Waggoman .... Donald Crisp
Barbara Waggoman ..... Cathy O'Donnell
Dave Waggoman .... Alex Nicol
Kate Canaday .... Aline MacMahon
Charley O'Leary .... Wallace Ford
Chris Boldt .... Jack Elam
Frank Darrah .... John War Eagle
Tom Quigby .... James Millican
Fritz .... Gregg Barton
Spud Oxton .... Boyd Stockman
Padre .... Frank de Kova

An outdoor drama starring James Stewart is virtually a certainty to get a boxoffice play. "The Man From Laramie," initialer for William Goetz' Columbia releasing deal, is rugged western filmfare, using good chracterizations to make the dramatic points as a story of vengeance is unfolded with explosive violence. The latter makes it rather rough viewing for the timid, but straight action fans will like it. So will those who buy above-average outdoor features, particularly when the star is Stewart.

The CinemaScoped production in Technicolor carries a good array of marketable entertainment values as put together under Goetz' supervision, plus a cast capable of adding depth to the characters screenplayed by Philip Yordan and Frank Burt from Thomas T. Flynn's SatEvePost story. The outdoor settings obtained from the location lensing in New Mexico, actual story locale, provide picturesque backdrops for the storytelling that takes place under the expertly punched direction by Anthony Mann.

The plot has its familiar aspects, but these in nowise detract from what the viewer will see on the screen because the more standard trappings are freshened and trouped to a high gloss by the cast in reacting to Mann's guidance. Basically, the plot concerns the search by Stewart, Army captain on leave, for the man guilty of selling repeating rifles to an Apache tribe. The rifles had been used to wipe out a small cavalry patrol to which Stewart's younger brother had been attached so there is a motive of personal vengeance.

Violence gets into the act early and repeats with regularity as Stewart's trail crosses with a number of warped, sadistic characters to be found on the vast grazing lands of the huge ranch owned by Donald Crisp, a cattle king growing blind in his eyes and already blind to the weaknesses of his psychotic son, Alex Nicol, and the ambition of his foreman, Arthur Kennedy. One shocker sequence is Stewart's first meeting with Nicol when the latter, holding the captain captive, wantonly butchers his mule teams and burns the freight wagons he had used to get from Wyoming to New Mexico.

Along the way there are other scenes of brutality and violence, but all related to story and characters, before Stewart lets the Indians exact the vengeance from Kennedy that he had been unable to mete out after having caught his man. Nicol firing a bullet at close range through the captive hand of Stewart; the pushing of Crisp over a cliff by Kennedy; the hand-to-hand fight between Stewart and Nicol and then Stewart and Kennedy in the dirt and dust of a corral full of frightened cattle are among some of the rugged sequences acted out during the 102 minutes.

Stewart goes about his characterization with an easy assurance that should have audiences pulling with him at all times. Kennedy, Crisp and Nicol are firstrate in their delineations of the twisted people on the ranch. Distaff characters are done by Cathy O'Donnell, good as the girl who wants to escape from the influence of the ranch, and Aline MacMahon, who gives a socko portrayal of a tough old rancher who has successfully fought the Crisp empire. Wallace Ford stands out as Stewart's driver who aids in the search, and among others who are capable are Jack Elam and James Millican.

The photography by Charles Lang is a major asset and technical assists line up expertly. George Duning did the background score, conducted by Morris Stoloff, and there is a title tune, heard behind the credits, which Lester Lee and Ned Washington cleffed. *Brog.*

Wichita
(C'SCOPE—COLOR—SONG)

Good Joel McCrea western feature in C'Scope with profitable prospects in outdoor action market.

Hollywood, June 23.

Allied Artists release of Walter Mirisch production. Stars Joel McCrea, Vera Miles, Lloyd Bridges, Wallace Ford, Edgar Buchanan, Peter Graves; features Keith Larsen, Carl Benton Reid, John Smith, Walter Coy, Walter Sande. Directed by Jacques Tourneur. Story and screenplay, Daniel B. Ullman; camera (Technicolor), Harold Lipstein; editor, William Austin; music composed and conducted by Hans Salter; song, Salter and Ned Washington; sung by Tex Ritter. Previewed June 16, '55. Running time, **80 MINS.**

Wyatt Earp .... Joel McCrea
Laurie .... Vera Miles
Gyp .... Lloyd Bridges
Whiteside .... Wallace Ford
Doc Black .... Edgar Buchanan
Morgan .... Peter Graves
Bat Masterson .... Keith Larsen
Mayor .... Carl Benton Reid
Jim .... John Smith
McCoy .... Walter Coy
Wallace .... Walter Sande
Ben Thompson .... Robert Wilke
Hal .... Rayford Barnes
Mrs. McCoy .... Mae Clarke
1st Robber .... Gene Wesson

As an initial venture into CinemaScope production for Allied Artsist, "Wichita" is an early-west subject that should find the going profitable in the outdoor market. It is particularly suited to drive-in dates, having a good array of action values and the star name of Joel McCrea to attract attention.

All the necessary equipment for a western feature has been marshalled for the Walter Mirisch production, on which Richard Heermance served as associate producer. Under the well-paced direction by Jacques Tourneur, the Daniel B. Ullman screen story is expertly slanted towards the outdoor action fan, who should find this film version of the career of Wyatt Earp generally interesting.

McCrea plays the lawman and gives a genuine western flavor to the character that helps sustain attention. Also on the credible side is Vera Miles, who makes much more of her western heroine role than is usual in this type filmfare. Character types are well-delivered by Lloyd Bridges, Wallace Ford, the former as a gunslinging cowpoke and the latter as publisher of the Wichita newspaper; while Peter Graves and John Smith come through as Earp's brothers. Edgar Buchanan wraps up a heavy role; Keith Larsen gives an interesting account of young Bat Masterson when he was an aspiring reporter; and there the further cast assists from Carl Benton Reid, Walter Coy, Walter Sande and others.

Plot deals, purportedly, with the enlistment of Earp as marshal of Wichita to bring law and order to the cow town when it became a cattle shipping center. When he bans pistol-toting for townspeople and trail-weary cowpokes alike, and enforces his rules without discrimination, the town leaders are as upset as they were before law came to Wichita. Earp proves his point, however, after several attempts on his life and the death of Mae Clarke, wife of the town banker, during one wild rampage by vengeful cowboys and Buchanan.

Harold Lipstein's camera work puts on a good display of the scenic values to be seen in the tinted footage printed by Technicolor. Other technical credits are good, too, as is the Hans Salter score. Latter also wrote the title tune with Ned Washington which Tex Ritter sings offstage. Melodically, the number is in a familiar oater groove; lyrically, it advances story mood. *Brog.*

Chicago Syndicate
(SONGS)

Gangbusting meller for general dual bookings in regular situations.

Hollywood, June 28.

Columbia release of a Clover production. Stars Dennis O'Keefe, Abbe Lane; features Paul Stewart, Xavier Cugat and his orch, Allison Hayes, Dick Cutting, Chris Alcaide, William Challee, John Zaremba, George Brand, Hugh Sanders. Directed by Fred F. Sears. Screenplay, Joseph Hoffman; story, William Sackheim; camera, Henry Freulich, Fred Jackman Jr.; editor, Viola Lawrence; music conducted by Ross DiMaggio. Previewed June 14, '55. Running time, **84 MINS.**

Barry Amsterdam .... Dennis O'Keefe
Connie Peters .... Abbe Lane
Arnie Valent .... Paul Stewart
Benny Chico .... Xavier Cugat
Joyce Kern .... Allison Hayes
David Healey .... Dick Cutting
Nate .... Chris Alcaide
Dolan .... William Challee
Robert Fenton .... John Zaremba
Jack Roper .... George Brand
Brad Lacey .... Mark Hanna
Mrs. Valent .... Carroll McComas
Pat Winters .... Hugh Sanders

(*Aspect ratio*: 1.85-1)

This gangbusting melodrama has been put together in suitable style to meet the demands of the general action market. As such, it will rate its share of dual dates, going top or bottom of the bill according to the situation and the booking requirements.

Turned out by the Clover production unit at Columbia, with Fred F. Sears directing, the picture tells how the law finally catches up with the head of a big crime syndicate, who believes he has his illegal traffic safely hidden behind various legitimate businesses. Joseph Hoffman does a workmanlike job of fashioning the screenplay from a story by William Sackheim, and the cast performances under Sears' direction have enough restraint to keep the events plausible and interesting.

Paul Stewart is a convincing crime kingpin, and Dennis O'Keefe is just as convincing as the smart accountant working for a citizens' committee to set Stewart up for an income tax rap. O'Keefe is out to gain Stewart's confidence and find secret books that will spotlight the mobster's income sources. Action plays off with intermittent narration and similar pseudo-documentary techniques against Chicago-filmed footage before O'Keefe is clued to the evidence, a roll of microfilm taken by Stewart's former, now killed, accountant, which can put the crime chief behind bars. Stewart doesn't go to jail, though, dying in the street after a gun battle as the police close in.

Allison Hayes' good looks and natural reserve are used effectively in her role as the slain accountant's daughter who is of aid to O'Keefe in nailing Stewart. Also, her presence provides the footage with the promise of an eventual romance when O'Keefe has a chance to relax. In the other distaff corner is Abbe Lane, for some songs, including "One At A Time," and to play Stewart's jealous girl friend. She gives a satisfactory account of the role's requirements. Xavier Cugat, Dick Cutting, Chris Alcaide, William Challee, John Zaremba, George Brand, Hugh Sanders, Mark Hanna and Carroll McComas are among other acceptable cast members.

Henry Freulich and Fred Jackman Jr. share lensing credit, and the other technical assists are okay. *Brog.*

Francis In the Navy

Below standard in the talking mule cycle.

Hollywood, June 22.

Universal release of Stanley Rubin production. Stars Donald O'Connor, Martha Hyer; features Francis, Richard Erdman, Jim Backus, Clint Eastwood, David Janssen. Directed by Arthur Lubin. Story, screenplay, Devery Freeman, based on character, "Francis," created by David Stern; camera, Carl Guthrie; editors, Milton Carruth, Ray Snyder; music supervision, Joseph Gershenson. Previewed June 21, '55. Running time, **80 MINS.**

Lt. Peter Stirling .... Donald O'Connor
Slicker Donovan .... Donald O'Connor
Betsy Donovan .... Martha Hyer
Murph .... Richard Erdman
Commander Hutch .... Jim Backus
Jonesy .... Clint Eastwood
Lieutenant Anders .... David Janssen
Appleby .... Leigh Snowden
Rick .... Martin Milner
Tate .... Paul Burke
Tony .... Phil Garris
Helen .... Myrna Hansen
Standish .... Jane Howard
Miss Kittredge .... Virginia O'Brien
Admiral .... William Forrest

(*Aspect ratio*: 2-1)

Engaging screwball spirit of past "Francis" entries gives way to labored comedy in this latest about Donald O'Connor and his talking mule. Producers spent so much time trying to develop the contrived story line that they obviously forgot all about laughs, which are few. Returns will depend upon draw of the star's name and repute of series in the dual market.

Usual format of O'Connor in trouble and Francis, the loquacious hybrid, helping him out of his difficulty serves as a springboard again, but no clear-cut pattern is followed as the Devery Freeman script engages in a frantic case of mistaken identity. O'Connor, an Army lieutenant, gets a call from Francis that he's been drafted into the Navy and is about to be auctioned off as surplus. When shavetail arrives to bid on his friend, he's mistaken for a bos'n's mate whose friends think he's gone off his rocker by impersonating an officer. Picked up by the Shore Patrol, he's returned to quarters. Balance of yarn concerns his trying to break away and resume his own identity.

O'Connor in a dual role has his work cut out for him due to lack of good material, trying hard but not up to the standard of past performances in series. Martha Hyer, as the gob's sister, has only a few scenes as costar but is pretty. Richard Erdman fares well as the gob's matey looking out for his best interests, and Jim Backus is in as a commander who looks to O'Connor, the gob, to make him look well in Naval maneuvers. Francis, of course, is Francis, with the voice of Chill Wills.

Stanley Rubin as producer gives film the once-over-lightly treatment, and Arthur Lubin, who has megged all "Francis" offerings, fails to insert his usual punch, the wandering script telling against him. Camera work by Carl Guthrie is good. *Whit.*

Wakamba!
(COLOR)

Exploitation pic of East African jungle. Combines action with factual material. Box-office if given right bally.

RKO release of American Museum of Natural History (Edgar M. Queeny) production. Directed by Queeny. Screenplay, Charles L. Tedford; narrated by Paul E. Prentiss; camera, Queeny, Fort B. Guerin, Jr., with contributions from Richard E. Bishop, Fred Wardenburg, Donald I. Ker, S. B. Eckert, E. G. S. Blanckart; editor, V. C. Lewis; music, Howard Jackson. Tradeshown in N.Y., June 24, '55. Running time, **65 MINS.**

This exploitable picture combines fantasy with fact for nice results. "Wakamba!" is perhaps the most arresting screen production of its type to come along in years. Camerawork is standout, and that is the reason release differs from the usual native-and-jungle-beast opus. Edgar M. Queeny, who directed and produced the film, and Fort B. Guerin Jr., are credited as the photographers but five others are listed as contributing additional footage. All in all, material should fare well at the wickets, especially where smart exhibs bally it intelligently.

Story is a simple one. Veteran native-hunter and bachelor decides he should marry the village belle. Femmes father says okay, but first —he wants elephant tusks of certain size. These belong to the giant bull elephant who lords it over the jungle herd. Remainder of plot concerns the efforts of this hunter-bachelor and his friend to kill the bull elephant.

While, the film starts like it would be a typical goona-goona epic, with the breasts of the black native gals in the foreground, cameras quickly leave this department behind and focus on the jungle animals—from the stately giraffes and buffalo to the lions, gazelles and falcons.

The producer has used slow-motion shots on the faster-moving wild life to represent the hunter's dream. There is a shot of the infuriated wild elephant after he has been struck by a poison arrow which is a closeup imitation of a miniature hurricane.

The color job, rather obviously a combination of several types of tinted stock, comes out for the most part a vivid closeup of the jungle's denizens via a Technicolor print. Narration is irksome but Paul E. Prentiss does all he can with it as the chief spieler. *Wear.*

Vom Himmel Gefallen
(Special Delivery)
(GERMAN)

Frankfurt, June 28.
Columbia release of Trans-Rhein production. Stars Joseph Cotten, Eva Bartok. Directed by John Brahm. Screenplay, Philip Reisman Jr. and Dwight Taylor, after an idea from Geva Radvani; camera, Ted Kornowicz; music, Bernhard Kaun. At Esplanade Theatre, Frankfurt, June 28, '55. Running time, **88 MINS.**
John Adams...............Joseph Cotten
Sonja.....................Eva Bartok
Baby Sam.................Joerg Becker
Kovac....................Rene Deltgen
Lilli....................Bruni Loebel
Sidney...................Niall MacGinnis
Wayne....................Lexford Richards
Coppenbarger.............Don Hamner
Capt. Heinikan...........Robert Cunningham
Olaf.....................Gert Froebe

This light little comedy, produced by Trans-Rhein-Films (Peter Rathvon's German-French production company) has been made in both German and English versions. Latter will be released in the U. S. by Columbia which also is handling the German counterpart.
The end result is pleasant entertainment.

It is concerned with a baby left in the garden of the U.S. embassy in an eastern dictatorship. Joseph Cotten, who heads the U.S. group, is faced with a cold war led by the propaganda chief of the dictatorship (Rene Deltgen), who wants the baby back.

The major comedy stems from the antics of the all-male embassy personnel in coping with the baby until beautiful Eva Bartok is hired as nurse. Even with old professionals like Cotten and Miss Bartok, real scene-stealer is the baby, Joerg Becker, who wins the most yocks and giggles from the audience.

The development of the plot is fairly predictable, but under director John Brahm's light hand these are amusingly handled. Hollywood director Brahm returned to his native Germany to make a pair of films last year. This one particularly is a nice showcase of his directorial ease.
Music by Bernhard Kaun provides a nice backing, especially during a well-staged ballroom scene. All credits are ably handled. *Haze.*

Foreign Films

Paris, June 21.
Le Printemps, L'Automne Et L'Amour (Spring, Autumn and Love) (FRANCO-ITALIAN). Cita Films production and release. Stars Fernandel; features, Nicole Berger, Philippe Nicaud, Claude Nollier, Georges Chamarat, Gaston Rey, Jacqueline Noel. Directed by Gilles Grangier. Screenplay, Jean Manse from idea by Raymond Joso; camera, Armand Thirard; editor, Christian Gaudin; Claude Vlery. At the Paris, Paris. Running time, **100 MINS.**

When Fernandel plays in a straight comedy there may be a chance, in secondary situations, for his pix in the U. S. But they are highly problematical when he essays his dramatico roles. This one is a hybrid with some of his comedy routines of over-expressive monologs and grimacing not jiving with his character of a restful, peaceful bachelor, in his fifties, whose life is completely changed when he rescues a pretty 18-year-old girl from drowning and falls in love with her and marries.
Director Gilles Grangler has not been able to get a dramatic floor under this theme of youth and age and the pic flounders. Chances are limited even for secondary spots

in America. Technical credits are good but acting is as uneven as the cardboard characters they are called on to do. Fernandel lends his usual expressive mug to the proceedings but is inadequate in the dramatic scenes. Nicole Berger and Philippe Nicaud are lifeless. There is nice musical background by Claude Valery. *Mosk.*

Le Port De Desir (Port of Desire) (FRENCH) Elysee Film production and release. Stars Jean Gabin, Henri Vidal, Andree Debar; features, Causimon, Edith Georges, Mireille Ozy. Directed by Edmond Greville Screenplay, Jacques Vlot; camera, Henri Alekan; editor, Aguettand. At the Broadway, Paris. Running time, **90 MINS.**

Adventure pic about sordid doings in a port town follows the usual pattern without enough unusual treatment or subject matter to make this more than an ordinary entry. It has the Jean Gabin moniker and some underwater exploitation gambits for limited lesser bookings in the U. S. It concerns a gang, led by an aging pervert, who has hidden a murdered girl in the hold of a sunken ship. Gabin etches one of his usually fine performances as an aging diver who finds the body. Henri Vidal and Andree Debar are conventional as the young lovers. Director Edmond Greville's treatment is ordinary, with the pic never achieving more than passing interest in some well-lensed underwater work. This is weak for both home and foreign markets. Lensing and editing are god. *Mosk.*

Cheri-Bibi (FRANCO-ITALIAN; COLOR). Ariel Film release of UGC-Taurus-Memnon-Ariel production. Stars Jean Richard; features, Lea Padovani, Danielle Godet, Albert Prejean, Raymond Bussieres. Directed by Marcello Pagliero. Screenplay, Paul Mesnier from novel by Gaston LeRoux; camera (Ferraniacolor), Mario Montuori; editor, Gaitena Arteni. Running time, **95 MINS.**

A famous turn-of-century novel (recently a popular comic strip, "Cheri-Bibi", now gets his second screening (one before the war). Wisely held in the comic strip tradition with its outrageous coincidence, colorful characters and melodramatic aspects, this makes a pleasing entry here. But director Marcello Pagliero has not been able to give it the verve which would have made this worthwhile in the U. S. Obvious budget limitations show but Jean Richard's solid craftsmanship, as the pugnacious Cheri-Bibi who gets a face-lifting to take the place of his rival, gives the pic a firstrate mumming job.
Color is indecisive in changing hues and flesh tones. Lensing and editing are nice. Georges Auric has given this a proper tongue-in-cheek musical background. *Mosk.*

House of Bamboo
(C'SCOPE-COLOR)

Okay gangster thriller against modern-day Tokyo setting with strong b.o. potential.

Hollywood, July 1.
20th-Fox release of Buddy Adler production. Stars Robert Ryan, Robert Stack, Shirley Yamaguchi, Cameron Mitchell; features Brad Dexter, Sessue Hayakawa, Biff Elliot, Sandro Giglio, Elko Hanahusa. Directed by Samuel Fuller. Written by Harry Kleiner; added dialog, Fuller; camera (De Luxe Color), Joe MacDonald; editor, James B. Clark; music, Leigh Harline; conducted by Lionel Newman. Previewed June 28, '55. Running time, **102 MINS.**

Sandy Dawson .... Robert Ryan
Eddie Spanier .... Robert Stack
Mariko .... Shirley Yamaguchi
Griff .... Cameron Mitchell
Captain Hanson .... Brad Dexter
Inspector Kita .... Sessue Hayakawa
Webber .... Biff Elliot
Ceram .... Sandro Giglio
Screaming Woman........Elko Hanahusa
John .... Harry Carey
Willy .... Peter Gray
Phil .... Robert Quarry
Charlie .... De Forest Kelley
Skipper .... John Doucette
Nagaya .... Teru Shimada
Doctor .... Robert Hosol
Bath Attendant .... May Takasugi
Mr. Hommaru .... Robert Okazaki

The actioner market should find "House of Bamboo" an okay thriller for general bookings. It's a regulation gangster story played against a modern-day Tokyo setting, thus gaining a novelty from location which it lacks in basic plot. Running time of 102 minutes is rather lengthy for the release destination. Good b.o. potential.

Novelty of scene and a warm, believable performance by Japanese star Shirley Yamaguchi are two of the better values in the Buddy Adler production. Had story treatment and direction been on the same level of excellence, "House" would have been an all-around good show. Pictorially, the film is beautiful to see, unfolding scenes of the Japanese countryside and Tokyo with all the revealing magic of CinemaScope under Joe MacDonald's camera guidance. It's an intimate looksee that gives the footage a lift.

Samuel Fuller directed the Harry Kleiner story, as well as contributing added dialog. The talk's mostly in the terse, tough idiom of yesteryear mob pix. While plots deals with some mighty tough characters who are trying to organize Tokyo along Chicago gangland lines, the violence introduced seems hardly necessary to the melodramatic points being made. So overboard does the deliberate toughness go that these scenes fare badly in comparison with the genuineness of those in which Miss Yamaguchi appears.

Robert Stack, required to overplay surliness by the direction, is an undercover MPCID agent out to get the murderer of a GI and break up the gang of renegade Yanks controlled by Robert Ryan, suave, personable and psychotic. Along with Ryan and Stack, Cameron Mitchell is seen as the erratic No. 1 boy to the gang leader and figures as the victim in a particularly violent gangland rubout. Brad Dexter, CID officer, and Sessue Hayakawa, Tokyo police inspector, play their roles with a welcome relief from flamboyance. Sandro Giglio, informer for Ryan; Biff Elliott, Miss Yamaguchi's secret husband who is killed by the gang, Harry Carey, Peter Gray and others are more prominent in featured spots.

A good score by Leigh Harline, conducted by Lionel Newman, and some striking art direction and set

decorations, seen in De Luxe Color, are among production assets.
Brog.

One Desire
(COLOR)

Romantic drama with "four-bawl" appeal.

Hollywood, July 5.

Universal release of Ross Hunter production. Stars Anne Baxter, Rock Hudson, Julie Adams; features Carl Benton Reid, Natalie Wood, William Hopper, Betty Garde, Barry Curtis, Adrienne Marden. Directed by Jerry Hopper. Screenplay, Lawrence Roman, Robert Blees; based on the novel "Tacey Cromwell" by Conrad Richter; camera (Technicolor), Maury Gertsman; editor, Milton Carruth; music, Frank Skinner. Previewed June 29, '55. Running time, **94 MINS.**

Tacey Cromwell	Anne Baxter
Clint Saunders	Rock Hudson
Judith Watrous	Julie Adams
Senator Watrous	Carl Benton Reid
Seely	Natalie Wood
MacBain	William Hopper
Mrs. O'Dell	Betty Garde
Nugget	Barry Curtis
Marjorie Huggins	Adrienne Marden
Flo	Fay Morley
Kate	Vici Raaf
Bea	Lynne Millan
Sam	Smoki Whitfield
Judge Congin	Howard Wright
Mr. Hathaway	Edward Earle

(*Aspect ratio:* 2-1)

Universal has pulled all stops on this romantic tearjerker, apparently on the theory there's sufficient market for a well-done soap opera slanted especially to the distaff trade. "One Desire" measures up on all these counts, being presented with a sincerity that should put it over in the regulation situations, where the cast lineup of Anne Baxter, Rock Hudson and Julie Adams provides a familiar name roster for the marquees.

There's a rather good romantic uara to the way the cast troupes the script by Lawrence Roman and Robert Blees, from Conrad Richter's novel "Tacey Cromwell." In making it a "four-bawl" offering, Jerry Hopper's direction never goes maudlin or slips into bathos. The sentiment is sincere, never sticky, as overscored in the Ross Hunter production, and viewer interest is held while the dramatic problems are worked out.

The story facets dwell chiefly on the urge of a bad woman to become respectable, a battle she loses temporarily when a respectable woman fights dirty, but a happy ending is brought on logically, if a bit drastically, to send the femme viewers out contented with the resolution.

Miss Baxter delivers commendably as the gambling hall babe in love with gambler Hudson. How she goes off with him and his kid brother, Barry Curtis, to look after the lad while Hudson turns to more respectable ways of earning a living is played believably. Hudson, too, is good as the ambitious young man, and moppet Curtis also stacks up excellently. Miss Adams makes an attractive menace with her well-played, spoiled rich girl who uses the law to gain custody of Curtis and Natalie Wood, an ophan taken in by Miss Baxter and Hudson. The chicanery gets her Hudson when Miss Baxter runs away but the latter winds up with her man, anyway, at the finale when Miss Adams dies in a climactic fire.

Cast principals gets some first-rate support from Carl Benton Reid, the father of Miss Adams; Betty Garde, a friendly neighbor; William Hopper, Adrienne Marden, Fay Morley and the others. The Technicolor photography by Maury Gertsman is a major asset in showing off the players and the early 1900's settings. A good score by Frank Skinner, editing and other credits do their share in shaping this one for the femme viewers.
Brog.

Des Teufels General
(The Devil's General)
(GERMAN)

Berlin, June 28.

Europe release of Real production. Stars Curt Juergens, Victor de Kowa, Karl John. Directed by Helmut Kaeutner. Screenplay, Georg Hurdalek and Helmut Kaeutner, after stageplay of same name by Carl Zuckmayer; camera, Albert Benitz. At Gloria Palast, Berlin. Running time, **124 MINS.**

General Harras	Curt Juergens
Schmidt-Lausitz	Victor de Kowa
Oderbruch	Karl John
Fraeulein Mohrungen	Eva-Ingeborg Scholz
Dorothea Geiss	Marianne Koch
Oberst Eilers	Albert Lieven
Anne Eilers	Erica Balque
Baron Pflungk	Werner Fuetterer
Leutnant Hartman	Harry Meyen

Carl Zuckmayer's "Devil's General," possibly the biggest stage hit in postwar Germany, has been turned into a remarkable film. It's highly suspenseful entertainment and more convincing and gripping than the widely acclaimed local stage performance (with O. E. Hasse in the title role) of several years ago.

Film is helped by an unusually tight script by Georg Hurdalek and Helmut Kaeutner's direction, having been worked on for three years by the pair. To bring the familiar story to the screen without slowness Zuckmayer's original was changed quite a bit.

Kaeutner, long one of Germany's ablest pic creators, did an efficient directing job. Several sequences have strong dramatic appeal, such as the death scene of a Jewish couple and the scenes between General Harras (Curt Juergens) and Schmidt-Lausitz (Victor de Kowa), the SS leader. The dialog is, as it was on the stage, well done. Although the war has been over for 10 years, this story has not in the least lost its authenticity. Its strong anti-Nazi message is also evident in this film.

The excellent cast is headed by Juergens in the title role. Juergens is a dashing, hard-headed Luftwaffe general here, very sympathetic and believable. Yet more impressive is De Kowa as Schmidt-Lausitz, a typical, cynical SS leader, ambitious, scheming and brutal. Also the others are highly effective, including Karl John, Albert Lieven, Paul Westermeier, Carl Ludwig Diehl and Harry Meyen.
Hans.

The Kentuckian
(C'SCOPE-SONGS-COLOR)

Pioneer Felix Holt adventure-drama, actionful in spots but slow and over-long. Burt Lancaster title-roling to give b.o. importance and good chance.

Hollywood, July 12.

United Artists release of Harold Hecht (Hecht-Lancaster) production. Stars Burt Lancaster; costars Dianne Foster, Diana Lynn; features John McIntire, Una Merkel, John Carradine, John Litel, Rhys Williams, Edward Norris, Walter Matthau, Donald MacDonald. Directed by Lancaster. Screenplay, A. B. Guthrie Jr.; based on the novel "The Gabriel Horn" by Felix Holt; camera (Technicolor), Ernest Laszlo; editor, William B. Murphy; music, Bernard Herrman; songs, Irving Gordon. Previewed July 11, '55. Running time, **103 MINS.**

Big Eli	Burt Lancaster
Hannah	Dianne Foster
Susie	Diana Lynn
Zack	John McIntire
Sophie	Una Merkel
Bodine	Walter Matthau
Fletcher	John Carradine
Little Eli	Donald MacDonald
Babson	John Litel
Constable	Rhys Williams
Gambler	Edward Norris
Luke	Lee Erickson
Pilot	Clem Bevans
Woman Gambler	Lisa Ferraday

The rather simple story of a pioneer father, his son and their dream of new lands is the basis for this adventure-drama adapted by A. B. Guthrie Jr. that wears the Hecht-Lancaster label for United Artists release. It has several factors that indicate a successful box-office play, not the least of which is the presence of Burt Lancaster as "The Kentuckian," a title which certainly has significance in the current coonskin-capped trend. The fact it is in CinemaScope and Technicolor will not hurt the chances in the outdoor market, either. A medium hit seems assured.

While the grossing outlook is okay it does not follow that the H-L offering is an overall good show, either critically or entertainmentwise. For one thing the footage is long and often slow, with the really high spots of action rather scattered during the 103 minutes. The biggest action sequence, a deadly, bloody bullwhip fight with an unarmed Lancaster the target of the heavy's rawhide, is an hour and 20 minutes in coming, and a sizeable percentage of viewers are likely to grow impatient with the waiting. More concentration on the meat of the plot and less on unnecessary incidental detail could have kept the pace lively to the satisfaction of the action-minded and, at the same time, there still would have been ample opportunities for the injection of necessary plot substance for a well-rounded show.

Lancaster takes on the added chore of director for the production, filmed in Kentucky and Indiana from the novel, "The Gabriel Horn" by Felix Holt. He does a fairly competent first-job of handling most every one but himself. His title role portrayal seems a bit too self-conscious, as though the director and the actor couldn't quite agree.

Lancaster has two beauts as costars, Dianne Foster and Diana Lynn, along with a lineup of character actors portraying the assorted pioneer types. Miss Foster makes a strong impression as Hannah, the bound girl who takes up with Lancaster and his young son, Donald MacDonald, after they use their riverboat passage money to pay off her indentures to a mean tavernkeeper. She, more than anyone else in the cast, adds something other than just a surface response to the story situations. Miss Lynn is the pretty village school teacher who temporarily takes Lancaster's mind off his dream of Texas, a change that causes an estrangement with his son, but the problem is righted by Hannah's resourcefulness in meeting the issue as well as her pioneer-woman handling of other dangers that would separate the father-son-bound girl trio. Miss Lynn is competent and attractive but, unfortunately, her role doesn't count for much in the overall drama.

Young MacDonald acquits himself acceptably as the son. So do John McIntire and Una Merkel as Lancaster's elder brother and sister-in-law who want him to settle down; John Carradine, a travelling medicine man; John Litel, leader of the landrush to Texas; Rhys Williams and Edward Norris. There's too much of ten-twent-thirt flamboyance to Walter Matthau's portrayal of the whip-cracking heavy, as there is to the two uncredited actors portraying feuding backwoodsmen out to get Lancaster.

Ernest Laszlo's camera paints a beautiful picture of the southern countryside, and Edward S. Haworth's production design is an asset as are the Bernard Herrmann score and three country style tunes by Irving Gordon.
Brog.

Female On the Beach

Joan Crawford, Jeff Chandler toplining romantic melodrama on sex and murder at the beach. Good prospects.

Hollywood, July 12.

Universal release of Albert Zugsmith production. Stars Joan Crawford, Jeff Chandler; costars Jan Sterling; features Cecil Kellaway, Charles Drake, Judith Evelyn, Natalie Schafer, Stuart Randall, Marjorie Bennett. Directed by Joseph Pevney. Screenplay, Robert Hill and Richard Alan Simmons; based on the play "The Besieged Heart" by Robert Hill; camera, Charles Lang; editor, Russell Schoengarth; music supervision, Joseph Gershenson. Previewed July 6, '55. Running time, **97 MINS.**

Lynn Markham	Joan Crawford
Drummond Hall	Jeff Chandler
Amy Rawlinson	Jan Sterling
Osbert Sorenson	Cecil Kellaway
Eloise Crandall	Judith Evelyn
Lieutenant Galley	Charles Drake
Queenie Sorenson	Natalie Schafer
Frankovitch	Stuart Randall
Mrs. Murchison	Marjorie Bennett

An emphasis on sex and murder carries exploitation possibilities for this romantic melodrama, so "Female On the Beach" will get its full share of the ready coin waiting for such features. Also important to the b.o. chances is the presence of Joan Crawford and Jeff Chandler as marquee lures.

Most of the characters seen are not particularly nice people, but for all their failings are familiar enough types to carry the plot through its sometimes obscure romantic and mystery courses. Joseph Pevney's direction gets quite a bit out of the players in putting them through the paces set by the Robert Hill-Richard Alan Simmons script based on Hill's play, "The Besieged Heart."

Setting for the Albert Zugsmith production is Balboa Beach, Southern California seaside resort, and the vacation playground provides an interesting background to the dramatics that spin off during the 97 minutes of footage. Miss Crawford portrays a gal who has had a rather rugged life and is now the widow of a Las Vegas gambler, come to take over the beach home she has never seen. Chandler is a somewhat mysterious beachboy whose principal occupation seems to be the pursuit of wealthy, lonely widows.

Melodramatic phase of the story is brought to the fore immediately with the death of Judith Evelyn, one of those wealthy, lonely widows who has been romanced by Chandler so she'll be an easy pigeon for the card manipulations and borrowings of Cecil Kellaway and Natalie Schafer, a confidence couple with whom Chandler is teamed. Whether Miss Evelyn was pushed or fell in a drunken lunge from the cottage balcony to the beach below is left open to question, which detective Charles Drake pursues at intervals by mysterious appearances into the plot.

With the old cottage occupant out of the way, Chandler turns his talents to Miss Crawford and it's a rocky pursuit that ends in marriage, even though she knows his old ways. Suspense nub of the yarn builds around the circumstances on the nuptial night when the bride discovers things that indicate she's marked for death by the groom. However, climax absolves Chandler by fixing the blame for the first death and the attempts against Miss Crawford on co-star Jan Sterling, a jealous real estate woman who wants the hero for herself.

Meat of the dramatics fall to Miss Crawford and Chandler and they deliver well. Miss Sterling's character is a bit thankless, but competently portrayed. Kellaway and Miss Schafer are good as the confidence team, as is Drake in his few appearances. An aid to the mood tried for in the film is a harmonica theme in the music supervised by Joseph Gershenson, while Charles Lang's lensing is another expert assist. Other technical contributions are good. *Brog.*

Die Ratten

(The Rats)
(GERMAN)

Berlin, June 30.

Herzog release of CCC production. Stars Maria Schell, Curd Juergens, Heidemarie Hatheyer. Directed by Robert Siodmak. Screenplay, Jochen Huth, based on stage play of same title by Gerhart Hauptmann; camera, Goeran Strindberg; music, Werner Eisbrenner; sets, Rolf Zehetbauer. At Film Festival, Berlin.

Pauline Karka .... Maria Schell
Bruno Mechelke .... Curd Juergens
Anna John .... Heidemarie Hatheyer
Karl John .... Gustav Knuth
Frau Knobbe .... Ilse Steppat
Harro Hassenreuter........Fritz Remond
Selma Knobbe .... Barbara Rost

This is without doubt one of the most interesting German films in months. West Germany's entry at the recent Berlin Film Festival, it won first prize. A modern version of Gerhart Hauptmann's successful stage play of the same title, this CCC production emerges as a remarkably well-made film which, with special regard to acting, direction and camerawork, is considerably above the current German average.

However, the film may find it tough appealing to audiences. For the average patron, "The Rats" is too heavy, also too unconventional and depressing, while class audiences may object to the film's tendency to exaggerate pessimism. Everything appears sad in it, without hope. There is also some weakness as to story development, which is not quite convincing and logical, robbing the yarn of some realism.

Screenplay by Jochen Huth, one of Germany's best screenwriters, offers some brilliant dialog sequences but appears a bit too talky, resulting in occasional dullness. Actually, story hasn't much in common with Hauptmann's original version any longer. It's Berlin 1955 now and Pauline Karka, the principal figure, is a homeless, poor girl from Germany's Soviet Zone who has been deserted by her lover and is expecting. She gives the baby to another woman who for a long time has been hoping for one in vain.

This brings up various complications, all more or less centering around the motherly feelings of these two women. Also, a murder occurs. It might have been better to make a film version of the original Hauptmann—this one appears more like an experiment, a rather interesting and courageous one, though.

But the film has many good points. One is the superb acting. That particularly applies to Maria Schell, a Swiss, who here has one of the most impressive roles of her career as Pauline. Excellent performances are also contributed by Heidemarie Hatheyer, the other woman; Gustav Knuth, the latter's husband, and Curd Juergens, who plays Bruno, Miss Hatheyer's brother, who gets killed by Miss Schell in self-defense.

Robert Siodmak's direction is refreshingly unconventional. His outstanding abilities are obvious in every scene. Camera work by Swedish Goeran Strindberg is praiseworthy. The musical score is also noteworthy. In all, a highly interesting, courageous film.

Hans.

The Night Holds Terror

Taut meller based on real-life terrorizing of a family by three hoodlums. Some exploitation possibilities for ballyhoo houses.

Hollywood, July 12.

Columbia release of Andrew Stone production. Features Jack Kelly, Hildy Parks, Vince Edwards, John Cassavetes, David Cross. Written, produced and directed by Andrew Stone. Camera, Fred Jackman Jr.; editor, Virginia Stone; score, Lucien Cailliet; song, "Every Now and Then" by Virginia Stone. Previewed July 7, '55. Running time, **85 MINS.**

Gene Courtier .... Jack Kelly
Doris Courtier .... Hildy Parks
Victor Gosset .... Vince Edwards
Robert Batsford .... John Cassavetes
Luther Logan .... David Cross
Capt. Cole .... Edward Marr
Detective Pope .... Jack Kruschen
Phyllis Harrison........Joyce McCluskey
Bob Henderson .... Jonathan Hale
Stranske .... Barney Phillips
Steven .... Charles Herbert
Deborah .... Nancy Dee Zane
Reporter .... Joel Marston

Taut, wellplayed melodramatics point up "The Night Holds Terror" as a good entry for the exploitation market. Given strong selling, pic may hit a neat grossing level, particularly in the situations that go in for the full ballyhoo treatment. A young and competent cast, while offering nothing for the marquees, plays assignments to the hilt and word-of-mouth should help.

The Columbia release, written, produced and directed by Andrew Stone, uses a real-life incident in which three hoodlums terrorize a family, as the setup for melodrama. Stone's writing and direction keep theatrics subdued, letting the situation itself and how the hoods and victims react build the tight mounting expectancy that earmarks this one as a believable suspense feature. (Plot is very close to current legit on Broadway, "Desperate Hours" and the much earlier melodrama, "Blind Alley.")

Jack Kelly plays the real-life Gene Courtier who picks up a young man while returning to his desert home in Lancaster, after a trip to Los Angeles. From this good samaritan act a chain of terrorizing events result, from the time the hitchhiker, Vince Edwards, sticks a pistol in Kelly's side and is joined by two killer pals, John Cassavetes and David Cross.

The hoods move in on Kelly's family, wife Hildy Parks and two small children, holding them frightened captives overnight until his car can be sold for cash the next morning. It becomes a kidnap case the next day when the bad boys take Kelly off to hold for ransom. To apprehend the hoods and save their victim is detailed in the comprehensive use of police, FBI and telephone resources which, under Stone's handling, is an interesting balance to the never-flagging tension.

Kelly and Miss Parks act like young, frightened parents, so are always believable. Edwards, Cassavetes and Cross are equally credible as the hoodlums, so the lead quintet makes a major contribution to the meller entertainment. Others, too, play their characters with conviction.

Furthering the suspense mood is the lensing by Fred Jackman Jr., and Virginia Stone's editing, the score by Lucien Cailliet and other behind-camera contributions are worthy. *Brog.*

Air Strike

Unexciting service programmar for less discriminating markets.

Hollywood, July 7.

Lippert release of a Cy Roth production. Stars Richard Denning; costars Gloria Jean, Don Haggerty; features Bill Hudson, Alan Wells, John Kirby, William Halop, James Courtney, Stanley Clements. Director - screenplay, Roth; camera, Alan Stensvold; editor, George McGuire; music, Andre Brummer. Reviewed July 6, '55. Running time,, 63 **MINS.**

Commdr. Blair .... Richard Denning
Marg Huggins .... Gloria Jean
Lieut. Richard Huggins ....Don Haggerty
Lieut. John Smith .... Bill Hudson
Anthony Perini .... Alan Wells
David Loring .... John Kirby
Lieut. Commdr. Swanson . William Halop
Ensign James Delaney... James Courtney
G. H. Alexander ...... Stanley Clements

Efforts of a Navy commander to weld together a jet fighter attack squadron aboard the U. S. Carrier Essex is the story peg on which this Cy Roth production is hooked. Film, an unexciting and unimaginatively turned out affair, is a programmer lacking in just about every element of entertainment.

Richard Denning plays the commander, but stands small chance with material assigned him. Script, also written and directed by Roth, carries an overload of pointless dialog. Pic is further burdened with grainy stock footage. Attempted suspense fashioned around one of Denning's pilots lost in a dense fog with all his instruments out provides a tedious climax.

Don Haggerty is the pilot in a thankless role, and his costar, Gloria Jean, is in for a single scene. James Courtney, Bill Hudson and Stanley Clements try hard but had a strike on 'em before they started. Technical departments are below average. *Whit.*

Pearl of the South Pacific

(SUPERSCOPE—COLOR)

Routine South Seas adventure for general dual dating; just mildly diverting.

Hollywood, June 29.

RKO release of Benedict Bogeaus production. Stars Virginia Mayo, Dennis Morgan, David Farrar; features Murvyn Vye, Lance Fuller, Basil Ruysdael, Lisa Montell. Directed by Allan Dwan. Screenplay, Jesse Lasky Jr.; added dialog, Talbot Jennings; story, Anna Hunger; camera (Technicolor), John Alton; editor, James Leicester; score, Louis Forbes. Previewed June 28, '55. Running time, **85 MINS.**

Rita Delaine .... Virginia Mayo
Dan Merrill .... Dennis Morgan
Bully Hayes .... David Farrar
Halemano .... Murvyn Vye
George .... Lance Fuller
Michael .... Basil Ruysdael
Momu .... Lisa Montell

(Aspect ratio: variable)

Some routine South Seas adventuring is on display in this formula film, along with Virginia Mayo in a sarong, and the mild diversion offered makes for passable filmfare in the general dual situations. Only fair returns are indicated.

Lensed in SuperScope, with print by Technicolor, the well-worn plot in the Benedict Bogeaus production has to do with some bad whites, Miss Mayo, Dennis Morgan and David Farrar, who move in on a small Pacific island to steal a fortune in black pearls from some natives who have been protected from the evil influences of civilization by a kindly white patriarch, Basil Ruysdael. There's not much freshness or ingenuity to the script by Jesse Lasky Jr., the added dialog by Talbot Jennings or the story by Anna Hunger so Allan Dwan's direction is hard-put to make something of the plot-boiler setup.

Coming up against the goodness oozing from Ruysdael brings about reform in the characters of Miss Mayo and Morgan, but Farrar refuses to change and dies from a native spear for his hard-headedness, leaving the other two stars to find a new life with the happy natives under Ruysdael's benevolent guidance. Footage has few thrills, although there is an attempt to inject some via spear-throwing natives and a rubbery octupus who guards the sacred pool under which the pearls are stashed.

Murvyn Vye, a warrior chief; Lisa Montell, his daughter, and Lance Fuller, son of Ruysdael, are other cast principals who fare no better than the star trio. John Alton's lensing and the tints are good, as are most of the other technical supports. *Brog.*

The Big Bluff

Okay meller for the programmer market.

United Artists release of W. Lee Wilder production. Features John Bromfield, Martha Vickers, Robert Hutton, Rosemarie Bowe. Directed by Wilder. Screenplay, Fred Freiberger, from story by Mindred Lord; camera, Gordon Avil; editor, T. O. Morse; music, Manuel Compinsky. Tradeshown, N.Y., July 7, '55. Running time, **70 MINS.**

Ricardo De Villa .... John Bromfield
Valerie Bancroft .... Martha Vickers
Dr. Peter Kirk .... Robert Hutton
Fritzie Darvel .... Rosemarie Bowe
Marsha Jordan .... Eve Miller
Fullmer .... Max Palmer
Don Darvel .... Eddie Bee
Dr. Harrison .... Robert Bice
Winthrop .... Pierre Watkin
Art Dealer .... Beal Wong
Frank .... Rusty Wescoatt
Coroner .... Mitchell Kowal
Master of Ceremonies......... Jack Daly
Butler .... Paul McGuire
Bell Boy .... George Conrad
Waiter .... Kay Garrett

"The Big Bluff," a modest melodrama, is tailored to the demands of the program market. Its short running time of 70 minutes will be an asset in twin bill bookings and a smooth, though obvious, story offers some appeal to mystery fans. While the cast is thin on marquee dressing nevertheless it boasts familiar names in John Bromfield, Martha Vickers and Robert Hutton.

As screenplayed by Fred Freiberger from a story by Mindred Lord, the W. Lee Wilder production generally follows a routine course with exception of a twist at the finale.

Martha Vickers, a wealthy, youngish widow suffering from a heart condition, goes to Los Angeles to improve her health. She's accompanied by her secretary, Eve Miller. Miss Vickers, despite her failing health, still has an eye for romance and she weds playboy Bromfield. His designs on her are geared more to her money than true affection for he plans to hustle off with dancer Rosemarie Bowe after arranging Miss Vickers' demise. Suspicions of Miss Miller and Hutton, a doctor, eventually lead Bromfield into the arms of the law.

Characters in this meller are mostly stock but the players turn in fair portrayals under producer Wilder's adequate direction. Bromfield is well cast as a wolf who lives by his wits. Miss Vickers is pert and suitably gullible as befits the role. Hutton is forthright as her personal physician. Miss Bowe is plenty sexy as the "other woman" in the triangle while Miss Miller registers as an amateur gumshoe. Competent support is provided by Eddie Bee and Max Palmer, among others.

Camerawork of Gordon Avil is good as is T. O. Morse's editing. An okay score, composed and conducted by Manuel Compinsky, helps sustain the mood of the yarn. Production values are standard for this type programmer. *Gilb.*

The Dragonfly
(RUSSIAN—COLOR—SONGS)

Mildly amusing Soviet comedy with songs; fair b.o.

Artkino release of Grusiafilm Studio Studio production. Stars Lina Abashidze; features L. Asatian, T. Tzutzunava, R. Chekhikvadze. Directed by S. Dolidze. Screenplay, M. Baratshvili and L. Hotivari; camera (color), T. Lobova; music, S. Tzintzadze. At Stanley, N.Y., June 25, '55. Running time, **95 MINS.**

The Dragonfly .... L. Abashidze
Efrosine .... T. Tzutzunava
Elpite .... T. Abashidze
Georgi .... A. Omiadze
Marinee .... L. Asatian
Tskriala .... F. Chakhava
Shota .... R. Chekhikvadze
Bichino .... D. Abashidze
Kirile .... A. Zhorzholiani
Archil .... G. Shavgulidze
Irakli .... S. Gambashidze
Natto .... A. Toidze
Tina .... D. Chichinadze
Shota's Mother .... T. Tzitzishvili
Levan .... G' Gegechkori

(In Russian; English Titles)

Boy-meets-girl is a universal theme and Soviet Russia's version of it is displayed in "The Dragonfly," a mildly amusing comedy with songs that should do well in sites where Red films are regularly shown. This Artkino release may also have some curiosity value for art houses which seldom use Soviet product.

Produced by the Grusiafilm Studio in the Caucasus city of Tbilisi (formerly Tiflis), the import is an elaboration on the "mistaken identity" routine which has songstress Lina Abashidze confused with her girl friend, L. Asatian, since both femmes have the same names. The obvious follows, complete with effects and situations reminiscent of Laurel & Hardy and Abbott & Costello.

Miss Abashide, who prefers singing to working, finds herself in an embarrassing position after failing her studies, accepting political honors awarded her similarly-named friend and disgracing her relatives by falsely implying there were deaths in her family. Happily, she redeems herself by studiously raising chickens and ultimately weds architect R. Chekhikvadze who's been casting a romantic eye at her since the first reel.

Under S. Dolidze's breezy direction, the screenplay hardly reaches hilarious peaks according to American standards but nevertheless the broad comedy does show that the Russians aren't entirely without a sense of humor. For Miss Abashidze is a sprightly lass who portrays her role with an air of levity and her colleagues such as Miss Asatian and architect Chekhikvadze also contribute nicely to the general merriment.

Music of S. Tzintzadze is occasionally lilting. However, the color camerawork of T. Lobova is not too good. Tint process used isn't indicated. Other technical credits are fair. *Gilb.*

Es Geschah Am 20 Juli
(It Happened on July 20)
(GERMAN)

Salzburg, June 25.

NF release of Arca-Ariston production. Stars Bernhard Wicki, Karl Ludwig Diehl, Carl Wery. Directed by G. W. Pabst. Screenplay, W. P. Zibaso and Gustav Machaty; camera, Kurt Hasse; music, Joannes Weissenbach. At Mirabell Kino, Salzburg. Running time, **85 MINS.**

Graf von Stauffenberg .. Bernhard Wicki
Generaloberst Beck .... Karl Ludwig Diehl
General Olbricht .... Erik Frey
Oberst Fromm .... Carl Wery
Oberleutnant von Haeften ..... Til Kiwe
General Remer .... Albert Hehn
General Keitel ...., Jochen Hauer

This film deals with exactly the same subject and bears almost the same title (the other one is "Der 20 Juli"), as another German film released one day earlier in the same key cities. The big difference between the two is director G. W. Pabst, which should be no surprise to anybody who knows the work of this old master. The subject is the attempt on July 20, 1944, by some German officers to assassinate Hitler and bring an end to the war which was obviously already lost.

Pabst's touch is evident in the dramatic photography, where certain scenes achieve real artistry in black-and-white. Kurt Hasse's camermanship was no doubt a great help. Director Pabst sustains interest throughout the film by canny pacing, alternating slow and fast scenes, and allowing an occasional laugh to break the tension which he then takes up again, more gripping than before. The few laughs in an otherwise serious film are a welcome relief, and one sadly lacking in the rival production.

Pabst sticks close to history in treating the political and military events of the fateful day, July 20. But he looks at the situation from the human standpoint of the conflict going on inside a handful of men who know they are on the verge of changing the course of history. Far from detracting from the seriousness of the subject, this personal (rather than detached) approach enables Pabst to catch the sympathy of his audience. He thereby adds an emotional impact to what, in the rival film, is a political discussion around an exciting cops-and-robbers story.

The latter film (directed by Falk Harnack) may give one a better understanding of what was involved in the assassination attempt, in terms of the undercurrents of resistance to Hitler among certain Germans. But it remains a lesson in history (an exciting one, however), while the Pabst version is a work of dramatic art.

Star of Pabst's film is w.k. German filmactor Bernhard Wicki, giving a fine performance as Graf von Stauffenberg, the man who plants the bomb. He is decked out with a wooden hand and a patch over one eye, but Pabst has chosen to put the patch over the opposite eye from director Harnack. Which eye should get the patch? We may never know.

Other roles are sensitively handled, with Pabst's better-known cast having a slight edge all down the line over Harnack's good but unfamiliar actors. Sole exception is the role of Propaganda Minister Goebbels, played as a sniveling coward in the Pabst version. Here, Harnack comes off with the laurels, as well he should, for his actor is Goebbels himself, in a newsreel shot.

The screenplay, music and sound are all firstrate, although the haste caused by the race to get the film onto the market before the rival product is evident in some sloppy synchronization.

The interest of the theme will assure the success of both films among German-speaking audiences, i.e., mainly Germany and Austria. But the Pabst effort figures to come off somewhat better at the boxoffice, due to the added draw of his name players, plus the director's own popularity. As for the U. S. market, wise promotion could turn this one into a sleeper. This Pabst opus has the suspense, emotional pull and fine photography to make it a possible successful import, though it will never garner the big coin. *Pimm.*

Der 20 Juli

Salzburg, June 25.

Herzog release of CCC production. Stars Wolfgang Preiss, Annemarie Dueringer, Werner Hinz, Ernst Schroeder, Robert Freytag. Directed by Falk Harnack. Screenplay, Guenther Weisenborn and Werner Joerg Luddecke; camera, Karl Loeb; music, Herbert Trantow. At Elmo Kino, Salzburg. Running time, **100 MINS.**

Oberst Graf von Stauffenberg
Wolfgang Preiss
Hildegard Klee .... Annemarie Dueringer
General von Tresckow ...... Fritz Tillmann
Generaloberst Beck .... Werner Hinz
Von Witzleben .... Peter Esser
Dr. Goerdeler .... Paul Bildt
SS Obergruppenfuehrer
Ernst Schroeder
Member Kreisauer Circle
Maximilian Schell
Protestant Priest .... Erich Schellow
Dr. Adler .... Edwin Kalser
Juhnke .... Alfred Schieske

The race is over, and Berlin's CCC Studios has brought its entry in just one day ahead of G. W. Pabst's opus on the same subject (see accompanying review). Both films deal with the plot to assassinate Hitler, which was attempted on July 20, 1944, and almost succeeded. This treatment, entitled "July 20" (the other one is called "It Happened on July 20" is directed by Falk Harnack, a little-known German director, employing a strictly documentary technique. He handles this touchy political theme in a dispassionate historical manner.

The result is an excellent documentary-type film, which packs plenty of suspense, and includes a good deal of on-the-spot footage from the recent war. It treats the subject fairly and without emotion, and represents the figures in a realistic manner, with the one exception of an exaggerated SS leader (Ernst Schroder). The only trouble is that the picture lacks the emotional kick necessary for good screen fare—at least for those who did not actually live through the events depicted. The cold documentary style of the film never succeeds in establishing a rapport between the viewer and the characters portrayed.

The screenplay by Guenther Weisenborn and Werner Luddecke tries to present a panoramic view of the military, political and moral questions involved in the 1944 rebellion against Hitler. Although the plot was basically military, the film does not neglect those labor leaders, churchmen and intellectuals who were in sympathy with the anti-Hitler movement. But the whole thing does not rise above the level of a lesson in history, except for those taut scenes where we witness the tension involved in planting the bomb, waiting for it to explode, escaping from the scene, etc.

For such scenes, the documentary technique, by its very bareness, arouses plenty of excitement. But unfortunately, the people involved never become sympathetic to the audience, and neither the direction, the script, nor the performers overcome this basic flaw. The roles are all filled by good but unfamiliar actors, with not a big name in the entire cast.

Central figure is Wolfgang Preiss as Graf von Stauffenberg, who actually plants the bomb near Hitler. He sports a small black patch over his left eye, and a wooden hand, but his deadpan acting style never lets one get inside him, which is a pity. Adequate performances are obtained from the actors representing various military and political leaders, and the one girl in the film is played attractively by Annemarie Dueringer, although the role itself is extraneous. The script contains a large number of stock phrases and noble sentiments, bordering on corniness, and leaving the characters more wooden than they otherwise might be.

This film figures to do good business in Germany and Austria, because of special interest of the plot, as well as the extra publicity involved in the dual distribution of this one and its rival in the same towns at the same time. But its chances for U.S. distribution are poor, even with special promotional handling.

"July 20" is an examination of the German conscience, performed by Germans upon themselves. It's a fascinating intellectual exercise, done humorlessly in a good sober film. But it's not likely to arouse much interest among American audiences, for whom the idea of "good German soldiers" versus "bad German soldiers" is hard to conceive. *Pimm.*

Foreign Films

Paris, July 5.

Futures Vedettes (Future Stars) (FRENCH). Columbia release of Del Duca-Regie Du Film production. Stars Jean Marais; features, Brigitte Bardot, Isabelle Pia, Yves Robert, Mischa Auer, George Reith, Odile Rodin. Directed by Marc Allegret. Screenplay, Allegret, Roger Vadim from novel by Vicky Baum; camera, Robert Juillard; editor, Suzanne De Troeye; music, Jean Wiener. At Marignan, Paris. Running time, 95 MINS.

Columbia has a lightweight entry in this melodrama about the young love of two budding artists with their dashing singing teacher. Mostly for local appeal, film has a mellow nostalgic backing set in Vienna, but lacks the forthright robustness and passion needed to make this a better looksee at adolescent love among the longhairs. Mixing comedy and drama leaves this unbalanced.

Jean Marias is much too mannered and coy as the supposed heartthrob of two young students. Both mix amorously with this Don Juan of the opera circles. But he is true only to his wife. Title does not look prophetic, with Brigitte Bardot lacking any depth as yet for star stamping. Isabelle Pia has a certain intensity for specialized roles. Mischa Auer turns in neat bit as an eccentric valet. Marc Allegret has sugar coated this and given it only a bread-and-butter pacing. Technical credits are fine and exterior Viennese production dress is appealing. *Mosk.*

Paris, July 5.

Les Evades (The Fugitives) (FRENCH). Cocinor release of Cocinor-St. James production. Stars Pierre Fresnay, Francois Pirier. Michael Andre; features, Silvia Monfort. Directed by Jean-Paul Le Chanois. Screenplay, Le Chanois, Andre from novel by Andre; camera, Marc Fossard; editor, Emma Le Chanois; music, Joseph Kosma. At Paris, France. Running time, 115 MINS.

This story of the escape of three French prisoners from a prison camp during the last war may be late in reaching the screen. Many pix have been made on this topic. This has a forceful style and some moments of suspense but it neither tops the others nor escapes a certain preachiness and propaganda. Most of the main problems are past, and this has to stand on its filmic talent. This looks to have local appeal and might do for lesser situations in the U.S. if cut. Pierre Fresnay runs an intelligent acting gamut as the nature member of the prison group, but has too much "message" to carry. Francois Perier is fine as the simpler member while Michel Andre is reserved and excellent. Bit parts are well integrated with Silvia Monfort's Polish refugee a catching cameo. Location lensing is fine.

Lensing and editing are okay as is the musical score of Joseph Kosma. *Mosk.*

To Hell And Back
(C'SCOPE—COLOR)

Audie Murphy renacting his World War II for-real-hero story in gripping screen drama; plenty of b.o. values.

Hollywood, July 19.

Universal release of Aaron Rosenberg production. Stars Audie Murphy; features Marshall Thompson, Charles Drake, Gregg Palmer, Jack Kelly, Paul Picerni, Susan Kohner, Richard Castle, Art Aragon, Felix Noriego. Directed by Jesse Hibbs. Screenplay, Gil Doud; from the Audie Murphy autobiography; camera (Technicolor), Maury Gertsman; editor, Edward Curtiss; music supervision, Joseph Gershenson. Previewed July 12, '55. Running time, 106 MINS.

Audie Murphy	Himself
Johnson	Marshall Thompson
Brandon	Charles Drake
Lt. Manning	Gregg Palmer
Kerrigan	Jack Kelly
Valentino	Paul Picerni
Maria	Susan Kohner
Kovak	Richard Castle
Sanchez	Art Aragon
Swope	Felix Noriego
Lt. Lee	David Janssen
Saunders	Brett Halsey
Capt. Marks	Bruce Cowling
Col. Howe	Paul Langton
Steiner	Julian Upton
Mrs. Murphy	Mary Field
Thompson	Denver Pyle

This biopic on the World War II exploits that made Audie Murphy tne most decorated soldier in American history is gripping season drama with the original playing himself. Uppointing its chances is the fact appeal is not limited to the action-minded, as there's plenty of warm, human drama to attract family-type audiences, too.

A strong angle to the picturization of Murphy's autobiography is the way bravado has been eliminated. There are no blustering heroics for the sake of derring-do and the action shown is that of a modest, unassuming young man. It is to the credit of producer Aaron Rosenberg, director Jesse Hibbs and scripter Gil Doud that the story is kept on this level and not allowed to become another war pic crammed with unbelievable deeds. As Murphy recounted in his book, and as here shown on the screen, he represents the infantryman who does his job despite fear and the other inglorious aspects of dogfacing.

Film opens with Murphy as a youngster helping his mother eke out less than a living in Texas. Not too much time is spent on this section of the story, which serves to establish the Murphy character and show his hard beginning before he gets into the Army in 1942 at 18. In 1943, Murphy became a replacement in Company B, 15th Infantry Regiment, Third Division, 7th Army, in North Africa, and served with the unit throughout the war in Tunisia, Italy, France, Germany and Austria. During that time he rose from PFC to company commander, was wounded three times, personally killed 240 Germans, and was one of the only two soldiers left in the original company at the end of the war. His decorations total 24, from the Congressional Medal of Honor on down.

The film makes plain that if Murphy was a hero he was a scared one, as were the battle veterans he served with. The script paints an accurate picture of the types with whom Murphy grew close in the fighting and, like Murphy's self-depiction, these GI's are played with a human quality that makes them very real. Fighting or funning, they are believable. The war action shown is packed with thrills and suspense. Among some of the more outstanding sequences are the knocking out of a Nazi machinegun nest from a farmhouse near Anzio, the crazed attack on another Nazi emplacemtent in France after one of his buddies has been killed and Murphy's almost single-handed blasting of a German tank group asd the infantrymen it is supporting.

Aside from the fighting, footage works in some touching moments between battles during too-short leaves. One such is Murphy's, and his buddies', experiences for 12 hours in Naples, during which he has the quick company of a girl, beautifully played by Susan Kohner. Bolstering the show with topnotch performances of the men who fought at Murphy's side are Marshall Thompson, Charles Drake, Gregg Palmer, Jack Kelly, Paul Picerni, Richard Castle, Art Aragon, Felix Noriego and others, most of whom fall in battle. Mary Field, as Murphy's mother in the early footage, is good, too.

This story takes naturally to CinemaScope and Maury Gertsman's lensing does right by the realistic battle scenes and the cast. The martial note in the score supervised by Joseph Gershenson is just right and the other behind-camera credits are topflig' *Brog.*

The Night of the Hunter

Heavily artistic version of the Davis Grubb novel. Robert Mitchum and Shelley Winters names to help provide fair initial draw. But general audience appeal limited.

United Artists release of Paul Gregory production. Stars Robert Mitchum, Shelley Winters; features Lillian Gish, James Gleason, Evelyn Varden, Peter Graves, Don Beddoe, Gloria Cstillo, Billy Chapin, Sally Jane Bruce. Directed by Charles Laughton. Screenplay, James Agee, based on the Davis Grubb novel of same title; camera, Stanley Cortez; editor, Robert Golden; music, Walter Schumann. Previewed in N.Y. July 15. Running time, 93 MINS.

Preacher Harry Powell	Robert Mitchum
Willa Harper	Shelley Winters
Rachel	Lillian Gish
Icey	Evelyn Varden
Ben Harper	Peter Graves
John	Billy Chapin
Pearl	Sally Jane Bruce
Birdie	James Gleason
Walt	Don Beddoe
Ruby	Gloria Csstillo
Clary	Mary Ellen Clemons
Mary	Cheryl Callaway

The relentless terror of Davis Grubb's story got away from Paul Gregory and Charles Laughton in their translation of "Night of the Hunter." This first start for Gregory as screen producer and Laughton as director is rich in promise of things to come but the completed product, bewitching at times, loses sustained drive via too many offbeat touches that have a misty effect.

Cast and credits will help the sale, and the genuinely different nature of the picture is probably a plus. Initial draw should be okay but the long-distance b.o. staying power looks dubious for the general market.

Curiously, Gregory and Laughton achieved distinction in the legit field with "reading" plays that were the epitome of simplicity in the staging. "Don Juan in Hell" had exciting movement, yet the performers merely spoke their lines on bare boards.

So why all this knitting of pictorial lace in conveying "Hunter's" story of the backwoods preacher who kills in obedience to "messages from the Lord." So many scenes are productions of camera angles, symbolisms, shadows and lighting effects to the extent that story points are rendered nebulous. Straight story telling without the embellishments, it would seem, might have rammed home with frightening force the horror of this man's diabolical quest of a hanged murderer's $10,000 which he wants to use in serving his fancied Lord.

Script by the late James Agee twists and turns through the lives of a not unlikely group of Scripture-quoting inhabitants of small town a couple decades ago. It builds fine with suspense ingredients to a fitting climax. Unfortunately, the camera flourishes interferred with what may have been a competent script. One point not clear, though, is why any elderly uncle, upon discovering the preacher's murdered wife, thinks he'd be accused of the crime if he sounded an alarm.

Robert Mitchum intermittently shows some depth in his interpretation of the preacher but in instances where he's crazed with lust for the money, there's barely adequate conviction. Shelley Winters is properly inanimate as the mother of two children who is widowed at the start when her husband is hanged. A remarkably effective scene has Miss Winters, now spirited, confessing her sins and asking forgiveness at a prayer meeting after she is persuaded into marriage by Mitchum.

Lillian Gish shows great skill in a warm, sympathetic part, that of self-appointed guardian of children left adrift in the world. Billy Crapin, who's about 10, is consistently splendid as the step-son who is on to the preacher's plot from the beginning. As his younger sister, Sally Jane Bruce does about standard for a tyke. James Gleason is a capable performer in the unfortunate position of having a role which, as the story is presented, might have been done away with with no ill effect. Evelyn Varden and Don Beddoe reflect professional competence as the proprietors of the local ice cream parlor.

Spiritualistic theme music, with lyric, by Walter Schumann has a fetching quality that has definite mood value. Other credits all good. *Gene.*

To Catch A Thief
(V'Vision-Color)

Cops and - robbers comedy-drama travelogging along Riviera for scenic action; b.o.-insured by Cary Grant, Grace Kelly.

Hollywood, July 14.

Paramount release of Alfred Hitchcock production. Stars Cary Grant, Grace Kelly; features Jessie Royce Landis, John Williams. Directed by Hitchcock. Screenplay, John Michael Hayes; based on the novel by David Dodge; camera (Technicolor), Robert Burks; editor, George Tomasini; music, Lyn Murray. Previewed July 11, '55. Running time, 103 MINS.

John Robie	Cary Grant
Frances Stevens	Grace Kelly
Mrs. Stevens	Jessie Royce Landis
H. H. Hughson	John Williams
Bertani	Charles Vanel
Danielle	Brigitte Auber
Foussard	Jean Martinelli
Germaine	Georgette Anys

Since the coming of the big screen and varied scopes there has been a growing number of productions that give the stay-at-home tourist a vicarious trip to far places. "To Catch A Thief" fits rather handily into this travelog group, being the type of glib comedy-drama, with an aura of sophistication, that goes well with the scenic values of the Riviera strikingly, if a bit self-consciously, displayed here in VistaVision. It's not the suspense piece one usually associates with the Alfred Hitchcock name, but there are compensating factors, including the star teaming of Cary Grant and Grace Kelly, to indicate healthy boxoffice in most playdates.

Cannes, the Carlton Hotel, the flower market at Nice, the Cornish Road and sundry sights make up the Riviera vista captured in Technicolor to enhance the story playoff. While strong on sight and performance values, the picture has some plot weaknesses and is not as smooth in the unfolding as one would expect from an upper "A" presentation. Neater editing then in the preview footage is called for, particularly in the first third, to level off choppiness and sudden switches in story line.

Symbolism plays quite a part in the Hitchcock handling of the script by John Michael Hayes, which was based on the novel by David Dodge. Sometimes it is overdone, but again this points up need for smoother release editing. In some spots, there's quite a saucy implication to the symbolism, as in the darkened room sequence when Grant and Miss Kelly pitch romance while a firecracker display is seen in the distance through the window. That final, gigantic burst before fadeout hints that things are popping within too.

Hayes' script is a conversation piece, albeit the talk is suave and sophisticated, with a touch of raciness here and there, that should fit preconceived hinterland notions about what takes place along the Riviera. What suspense there is comes from the fact Grant is a reformed jewel thief, once known as "The Cat," but now living quietly in a Cannes hilltop villa. When burglaries occur that seem to bear his old trademark, he has to catch the thief to prove his innocence, a chore in which he is assisted by Miss Kelly, rich American girl, her mother, Jessie Royce Landis, and insurance agent John Williams. While a suspense thread is present, Hitchcock doesn't emhasize it, letting the yarn play lightly for comedy has more than thrills.

It's been several seasons since Grant has made a film and, while this is no sock vehicle for the screen return, it's not a weak one, either. Grant gives his role his assured style of acting, meaning the dialog and situations benefit. Miss Kelly, too, dresses up the sequences is more ways than one. She clothes-horses through the footage in some fetching Edith Head creations that will catch the femme eye and, at the same time does justice to her spoiled rich girl character, a gal who looks cold but ain't when romancing time with Grant comes up.

Support from Miss Landis and Williams is firstrate, both being major assets to the entertainment in their way with a line or a look. Poor dubbing on the preview print made most of the other casters difficult to understand. Also, there's considerable French mixed in with the Yank talk, adding somewhat to lack of dialog clarity. Still, seen to advantage are Charles Vanel, Brigitte Auber, Jean Martinelli and Georgette Anys. A particular help to the footage is Miss Auber, a pert French lass who would like to play house with Grant while all the time she's the "cat" burglar he's seeking.

The scenic beauty of the foreign locale is shown to advantage by Robert Burks' lensing, even though some scences appear to have been used for spectacular visual qualities and not just for straight story furtherance. Lyn Murray's score is good. *Brog.*

How To Be Very, Very Popular
(C'SCOPE-SONGS-COLOR)

Zany, rock 'n' roll comedy with music. Good escapism.

Hollywood, July 15.

20th-Fox release of Nunnally Johnson production. Stars Betty Grable, Sheree North, Bob Cummings, Charles Coburn, Tommy Noonan; features Orson Bean, Fred Clark, Charlotte Austin, Alice Pearce, Rhys Williams, Andrew Tombes, Noel Toy, Emory Parnell. Direction and screenplay by Johnson; based on "She Loves Me Not" play by Howard Lindsay from a novel by Edward Hope; camera (De Luxe Color), Milton Krasner; editor, Louis Loeffler; music, Cyril J. Mockridge; conducted by Lionel Neuman; song, Jule Styne, Sammy Cahn. Previewed July 13, '55. Running time, 89 MINS.

Stormy	Betty Grable
Curly	Sheree North
Wedgewood	Bob Cummings
Tweed	Charles Coburn
Eddie	Tommy Noonan
Toby	Orson Bean
Mr. Marshall	Fred Clark
Midge	Charlotte Austin
Miss Syl	Alice Pearce
Flagg	Rhys Williams
Moon	Andrew Tombes
Cherry Blossom Wang	Noel Toy
Chief of Police	Emory Parnel
Bus Driver	Harry Carter
Music Teacher	Jesslyn Fax
1st Policeman	Jack Mather
2d Policeman	Michael Lally
Mr. X	Milton Parsons
Teacher	Harry Seymour

A liberal dose of zany escapism, touched up here and there with music, is offered in this comedy lark titled "How To Be Very, Very Popular." That it should be with the younger filmgoing set seems probable.

The wild and wacky doings dreamed up by producer-director-writer Nunnally Johnson are dressed up considerably in eye appeal by having the Misses Betty Grable and Sheree North running through most of the footage in costumes appropriate to their strip tease profession. The CinemaScope lensing does justice to the ladies.

In his triple play chores on the show, Johnson tosses reason to the winds to emphasize nonsense. It makes no sense but stacks up as non-intellectual. The players, too, are appropriately cast to carry out Johnson's aims so, while the show is not likely to win any critical laurels, it does fulfill its aim as light diversion.

Bearing only a fleeting resemblance to the 1933 stage play, "She Loves Me Not" (and a subsequent screen version) these caperings concern two strippers who can identify the bald-headed man who guns down ecdysiast Noel Toy right in the middle of her act in a San Francisco honkytonk. He promises the two dolls the same treatment if they don't get lost. They do, and after a bus ride along the coast take refuge in a fraternity dorm at a college. There, the major action takes place when, with eager, willing assist of some male students, the gals hide out until the killer catches up and is captured. Side issues bolstering the tale are wacky as bald-heads run through the footage to cause hectic consternation before the plot can be resolved.

Quite a bit of the fun is hinged on Miss North, a vacant-headed blonde who accidentally becomes hypnotised while Tommy Noonan is experimenting with Orson Bean. Noonan doesn't know enough to release the hypnotic spell and Bean doesn't care. Miss North goes for him, and also goes into a hips-swivelling dance whenever "Salome" is mentioned. This particular gimmick climaxes during commencement day ceremonies when Miss North breaks up the event with bumps and grinds to "Shake, Rattle and Roll," staged by Sonia Shaw, while all the student "cats" join in and the killer takes pot-shots at the twitching dancer.

Only slightly less empty-headed is Miss Grable, who uses what brains she has to protect herself and strip partner while developing a romance with Robert Cummings, a middle-aged student who for 17 years has stayed in college because if he graduates an inherited income will stop. Between these two the fun-making is expert, as it is with Miss North, Noonan and Bean. More expert assists come from Charles Coburn, college prexy, who sees a big endowment from coddling Bean—and who does a little cuddling with Miss North in her hypnotic state—Fred Clark, Bean's bald father; Alice Pearce, pixilated house mother; Rhys Williams, the brainless and bald father of Miss North; Andrew Tombes, bald detective who wears his toupee backwards, and sundry others involved in the mad affair, including Charlotte Austin, Coburn's wise, and comely, secretary.

In addition to "Shake," there's a title tune by Jule Styne and Sammy Cahn, the "Bristol Bell Song" by Lionel Newman and Ken Darby, and Ray Anthony's "Bunny Hop." Camera handling by Milton Krasner, the Cyril J. Mockridge score, Louis Loeffler's editing and other credits are good. *Brog.*

Gun That Won the West
(COLOR)

Routine Cavalry-Indians melo with good Injun scenes for secondary outdoor market.

Hollywood, July 11.

Columbia release of a Sam Katzman production. Stars Dennis Morgan; features Paula Raymond, Richard Denning. Directed by William Castle. Story-screenplay, James B. Gordon; camera (Technicolor), Henry Freulich; art director, Paul Palmentola; editor, Al Clark. Music conducted by Mischa Bakaleinikoff. Previewed July 8, '55. Running time, 69 MINS.

Jim Bridger	Dennis Morgan
Maxine Gaines	Paula Raymond
Jack Gaines	Richard Denning
Sgt. Timothy Carnahan	Chris O'Brien
Chief Red Cloud	Robert Bice
Afraid of Horses	Michael Morgan
Col. Carrington	Roy Gordon
General Pope	Howard Wright
Edwin M. Stanton	Dick Cutting
General Carveth	Howard Negley
Col. E. M. Still	Kenneth Mac Donald

The Springfield rifle gets title credit here, used to subdue the Indians after they have declared war and are about to wipe out an Army detachment. Constant editing in of considerable Indian stock footage gives this Sam Katzman film a wealth of colorful action in a routine story, even though some of the tints and grain don't match up. Film should find its mark in the secondary outdoor market.

"Gun" is another story of how "we" won the West, the plot of the James B. Gordon screenplay twirling around the efforts of the War Dept. to construct a chain of forts along the Bozeman trail in Wyoming to protect crews who will be building a new railroad. For this purpose, Dennis Morgan, as Jim Bridger, the scout, and Richard Denning, another scout, are recalled from civilian life to help in the dangerous mission which will take the Army through hostile Sioux territory, with whose chief, Red Cloud, both scouts in the past have been friendly. The Springfields, new weapon of the times, are brought up in time to save the troops and assure peace.

William Castle's work was cut out for him in handling a stereotyped set of characters and he doesn't always make the grade, but generally manages a measure of conviction. Indian scenes, however, are more interesting than the characters, with Paula Raymond, as Denning's wife, topping the femme interest. Morgan and Denning are as good as parts will allow. Robert Bice is okay as Red Cloud, Michael Morgan shoves menace into his part of his wareager righthandman, and Chris O'Brien makes like an Irish sergeant.

Henry Freulich is credited as cameraman, a job well done, and Al Clark rates a hand for his editing stint. *Whit.*

The Phenix City Story

Exploitable film expose of the headlined vice situation in the Alabama town; well-made for ballyhoo b.o.

Hollywood, July 18.

Allied Artists release of Samuel Bischoff-David Diamond production. Stars John McIntire, Richard Kiley, Kathryn Grant, Edward Andrews. Directed by Phil Karlson. Screenplay, Crane Wilbur, Dan Mainwaring; camera, Harry Neumann; editor, George White; music composed and conducted by Harry Sukman; song, Harold Spina, sung by Meg Myles. Previewed July 14, '55. Running time, 87 MINS.

Albert Patterson	John McIntire
John Patterson	Richard Kiley
Ellie Rhodes	Kathryn Grant
Rhett Tanner	Edward Andrews
Mary Jo Patterson	Lenka Peterson
Fred Gage	Biff McGuire
Ed Gage	Truman Smith
Cassie	Jean Carson
Judy	Meg Myles
Mamie	Katharine Marlowe
Clem Wilson	John Larch
Jeb Bassett	Allen Nourse
Zeke Ward	James Edwards
Helen Ward	Helen Martin
Hugh Bentley	Otto Hulett
Hugh Britton	George Mitchell
Ma Beachie	By Herself
James Ed Seymour	By Himself

Vice, Southern style, gets the expose treatment in "Phenix City Story." Result is that Allied Artists has an exploitation film, well-made, that can ring the ballyhoo b.o. bell with proper handling in situations where a "strong sell" is the key.

Contemporary headlines and magazine articles have up-pointed conditions in this Alabama town, just across the Chattahoochee River from Columbus, Georgia, and the Army's Fort Benning. Proximity of the latter contributed to the label of "the wickedest city in the U.S." hung on the southern town, particularly during World War II period, but the record shows Phenix City was no newcomer to sin even then. Presently, it is basking in comparative sinlessness, a condition brought about by the murder last year of a reformer, which finally gave vice a bad name.

With such a factual background for melodrama, the production by Samuel Bischoff and David Diamond zips along a course that mostly hews to provable incident, with some coloring or re-arrangement for dramatic emphasis. There's quite a bit of violence in the footage. Maybe it didn't always happen exactly as shown in the film, but the record book shows parallel violence did occur, so there's some dramatic justification for the emphasis in the script by Crane Wilbur and Dan Mainwaring. Also, it sets up a legitimate plea for more awareness on the part of voters everywhere. Adding to the try for documentation is a 13-minute prolog featuring radio-tv's Clete Roberts doing on-the-scene interviews with actual participants in the 1954 events, including the widow of Albert Patterson, the murdered candidate. This prolog is part of the film package, stretching show's running time to 100 minutes, but it's up to the exhibitor whether or not it is used.

The downfall of Phenix City sin is woven around the return from overseas service of Richard Kiley with wife and two children to find his hometown still living up to its wicked reputation. Kiley plays John Patterson, the son of the murdered candidate, who was elected to the attorney general post by an aroused citizenry after the death of the father, ably depicted by John McIntire. Kiley and most of the other casters bring fresh faces to the film, although most have been seen around before, including tv appearances, but not enough to be familiar types.

Under the purposeful direction by Phil Karlson, the footage details activities in the city's "sin" section, where gambling, prostitution and similar vice was available for the spending. Picture was lensed almost entirely in the actual locale, with hometown talent seen to quite an extent. Edward Andrews plays Rhett Tanner, particular kingpin of the sector, and is a menacing, entirely believable crime czar. Kathryn Grant is another who scores as Ellie Rhodes, a dealer in Tanner's joint, who loses her life to the crime interests when she tries to aid the good element in town. Lenka Peterson, as Kiley's wife; Biff McGuire, Truman Smith, Jean Carson, Katharine Marlowe, James Edwards, Helen Martin, John Larch, an idiotic killer, are among others contributing good make-believe in support of McIntire and Kiley. Ma Beachie, a madam character of the town, plays herself, as does James Ed Seymour.

A title tune cleffed by Harold Spina is given a sex pitch by the incredibly busty Meg Myles, seen as an entertainer in Tanner's joy joint. Elsewhere, Harry Sukman's score backs the melodramatics and the lensing by Harry Neumann casts a revealing eye over Phenix City. *Brog.*

The King's Thief
(C'SCOPE—COLOR)

Fanciful costumed adventure in the period of Charles II. Fairly diverting.

Hollywood, July 19.

Metro release of Edwin H. Knopf production. Stars Ann Blyth, Edmund Purdom, David Niven, George Sanders; features Roger Moore, John Dehner, Sean McClory, Tudor Owen, Melville Cooper, Alan Mowbray, Rhys Williams. Directed by Robert Z. Leonard. Screenplay, Christoper Knopf; from a story by Robert Hardy Andrews; camera (Eastman Color), Robert Planck; editor, John McSweeney Jr.; music, Miklos Rozsa. Previewed July 14, '55. Running time, **78 MINS.**

Lady Mary .... Ann Blyth
Michael Dermott .... Edmund Purdom
Duke of Brampton .... David Niven
Charles II .... George Sanders
Jack .... Roger Moore
Capt. Herrick .... John Dehner
Sheldon .... Sean McClory
Simon .... Tudor Owen
Henry Wynch .... Melville Cooper
Sir Gilbert Talbot ...... Alan Mowbray
Turnkey .... Rhys Williams
Charity Fell .... Joan Elan
Apothecary .... Charles Davis
Skene .... Ashley Cowan
Fell .... Ian Wolfe
Sir Edward Scott ...... Paul Cavanagh
Mrs. Fell .... Lillian Kemble Cooper
Mrs. Bennett .... Isobel Elsom
Adam Urich .... Milton Parsons
Jacob Hall .... Lord Layton
Apothecary's wife .... Queenie Leonard
Hoskins .... Owen McGiveney
Huskies .... Bob Dix, Michael Dugan
Guard .... James Logan

As a costumed swashbuckler, "The King's Thief" proves to be a fairly diverting period piece that should exert a mild interest at the wickets. Most of its top names are familiar, but not stout enough on which to peg strong b.o. attention.

Edmund Purdom enacts the title role, while Ann Blyth is opposite as the comely heroine, in the Edwin H. Knopf production. Under Robert Z. Leonard's direction of the Christopher Knopf script, based on a story by Robert Hardy Andrews, the plot's purpose is to restore to favor some people who have been shamefully used by David Niven, the wicked Duke of Brampton who has misused his influence with Charles II for self-gain.

There's a familiar, but still fairly interesting, air about how the story works out. Leonard and the script inject chimerical action, and work the hero into and out of any number of tight situations, some of which display good ingenuity, before Purdom gets his audience with the king by attempting to steal the crown jewels (footnoted as an actual incident during Charles' reign) and thus is able to expose the duke.

There are coach holdups, duels, chases and prison breaks involved to give a more or less lively air of movement. The reaction of cast principals, including George Sanders as Charles II, is properly evaluated to court intrigue and other colorful aspects of the era. Assisting, castwise, is good support from such as Roger Moore and Sean McClory, who aid Purdom; John Dehner, henchman to Niven; Tudor Owen, Melville Cooper, Alan Mowbray, Rhys Williams, Joan Elan, a Quaker lass, and others.

The costumes, settings and other period furbishings blend nicely with the CinemaScope lensing in Eastman Color by Robert Planck. The score by Miklos Rozsa, editing and other assists are good. *Brog.*

The Virgin Queen
(C'SCOPE-COLOR)

Historical drama revolving around Queen Elizabeth and Sir Walter Raleigh with Bette Davis, Richard Todd contributing to marquee. High acting and technical levels should mean a successful b.o. in virtually all situations.

Portland, Me., July 22.

20th-Fox release of Charles Brackett production. Stars Bette Davis; features Richard Todd, Joan Collins, Herbert Marshall, Jay Robinson. Directed by Henry Koster. Screenplay, Harry Brown, Mindret Lord; camera (De Luxe Color), Charles G. Clarke; music, Franz Waxman; editor, Robert Simpson. At Strand, Portland, Me., June 22, '55. Running time, **92 MINS.**

Queen Elizabeth .... Bette Davis
Sir Walter Raleigh .... Richard Todd
Beth Throgmorton .... Joan Collins
Chadwick .... Jay Robinson
Lord Leicester .... Herbert Marshall
Lord Derry .... Dan O'Herlihy
Sir Hatton .... Robert Douglas
French Ambassador ...... Romney Brent
Anne .... Marjorie Hellen
Mary .... Lisa Daniels
Jane .... Lisa Davis
Patch Eye .... Barry Bernard
Postillion Rider .... Robert Adler
Tailer .... Noel Drayton
Gentleman .... Iain Murray
Dame Bragg .... Margery Weston
Corporal Gwilym .... Rod Taylor
Landlord .... David Thursby
Randall .... Arthur Gould-Porter
Town Crier .... John Costello

Bette Davis seems a natural for the role of Queen Elizabeth in 20th's rendition of "The Virgin Queen," having already given one reading of this role in Warner Bros.' "Elizabeth and Essex" in 1939. In this edition, Miss Davis depicts a more mature queen, who loves and loses Sir Walter Raleigh to one of her maids-in-waiting. Miss Davis gives a bitter portrayal, but one that is a bulwark of strength since it buttresses what is essentially a weak script. Some of the language used by the royal person is shocking to the more genteel ears of modern-day filmgoers, but there's little doubt that it will help the boxoffice.

This handsomely mounted CinemaScoper may cause some controversy over the choice of words used in portraying one of the lustiest periods in English history when Britain expanded her empire. However, there's sufficient historical and dramatic justification for Miss Davis' delivery of these lines.

Structurally, Miss Davis is the major strength of the film, but storywise the yarn revolves around Richard Todd's Sir Walter Raleigh who has a dream of sailing three vessels of his own design to the New World. He brawls his way into the favor of Lord Leicester who brings him to the attention of the Queen. His rise to royal favor is marred only by his affection for Joan Collins, one of the queen's maids-in-waiting. It's a gambit that brings him to the Tower of London, but a royal pardon returns him to the ship that will carry him to found a colony in the New World and to his bride.

Miss Davis gives a strong and colorful performance as the royal lady who can hold her own in court intrigue. In this picture, she doesn't allow herself the luxury of being pitied for having loved and lost. She gives the impression of having her work cut out for her in handling the expanding enterprise of the British Empire. It's only at the end of the film that she drops her reserve and reveals herself as a lonely and bitter woman.

Todd similary essays a strong role as the ambitious soldier who slows up his dreams by taking a wife. He does extremely well and carries himself off creditably whether in the boudoir or a brawl. Joan Collins is a pretty item as his bride, impressing as a capable actress, who with further experience should be one of the femme stalwarts on the 20th roster.

Herbert Marshall, per usual, displays competence as a royal aide, and Jay Robinson, fresh, from playing mad emperors in biblical **dramas, gives an offbeat characterization as Chadwick, one of the men about court, that turns out well.**

Altogether, the general level of thesping is high and the directorial pacing by Henry Koster is sometimes crisp. Although there are lots of scenic wonders and impressive sets to fill the kingsized screen, Koster has taken the view that the pace and spinning the yarn seem to be the more important elements, the De Luxe color, although in a generally sombre key as befits the era, is well done. Producer Charles Brackett has welded the various elements of "The Virgin Queen" into a picture of high technical and thespic excellence that should do well in virtually all situations. *Jose.*

The Last Command
(COLOR-SONG)

Frank Lloyd direction makes this good b.o. for the outdoor and action markets. Marquee and exploitation values.

Republic production and release associate producer, Frank Lloyd. Stars Sterling Hayden, Anna Maria Alberkhetti; features Richard Carlson, Arthur Hunnicutt, Ernest Borgnine, J. Carrol Naish, Ben Cooper. Directed by Lloyd. Screenplay, Warren Duff, from story by Sy Bartlett camera (Trucolor), Jack Marta; editor, Tony Martinelli; music, Max Steiner. Tradeshown, N.Y., July 20, '55. Running time, **110 MINS.**

James Bowie .... Sterling Hayden
Consuela ...... Anna Maria Alberghetti
William Travis .... Richard Carlson
Davy Crockett.......... Arthur Hunnicutt
Mike Radin .... Ernest Borgnine
Santa Anna .... J. Carrol Naish
Jeb Lacey .... Ben Cooper
Lt. Dickinson .... John Russell
Mrs. Dickinson .... Virginia Grey
Evans .... Jim Davis
Lorenzo de Quesada........ Eduard Franz
Stephen Austin .... Otto Kruger
The Parson .... Russell Simpson
Dr. Sutherland .... Roy Robers
Abe .... Slim Pickens
Sam Houston .... Hugh Sanders

The Battle of the Alamo is fought again in "The Last Command" to score a decisive b.o. victory for Republic in the outdoor and action markets. Story, performances, marquee and production values all combine to give that studio one of its better films of the year.

History is freely drawn upon by Warren Duff who screenplayed from a story by Sy Bartlett. For in this saga of pre-Texas independence such figures as Jim Bowie, Davy Crockett and Sam Houston as well as Mexico's Gen. Santa Anna make with the drama and derring-do throughout the 110 minutes of footage.

While the script occasionally lags via a few talky scenes, this is more than offset via a wealth of combat that associate producer-director Frank Lloyd has spread across the screen. Events preceding revolt of the Texas colonists from Mexico's tyrannical rule are interwoven with experiences of Bowie, lustily portrayed by Sterling Hayden.

Owner of considerable Texas real estate and a personal friend of Santa Anna (J. Carrol Naish), Hayden prefers to follow a course of moderation in contrast to open resistance to Mexico as espoused by such rash settlers as Richard Carlson, Ernest Borgnine and Otto

Kruger. But actions of the despotic Santa Anna ultimately place Hayden behind the walls of the Alamo as leader of a small group who withstood a siege for 12 days.

Emphasis is primarily on the struggle between the Texans and Santa Anna's legions. However, there's a brief romance between Hayden and Anna Maria Alberghetti, daughter of a Mexican landowner who tosses his lot in with the rebels. Miss Alberghetti, whose forte is singing, does surprisingly well in this dramatic role.

As written by Duff, part of Bowie calls for a fearless, strong, shrewd type and Hayden fulfills these qualities admirably whether he's besting Borgnine in a knife duel or bargaining with Naish in a battlefield truce. Carlson registers in a slick portrayal of an impetuous lawyer and Borgnine also shines, particularly in the duel bit.

Providing good support under Lloyd's firm direction are Arthur Hunnicutt as Davy Crockett, Naish as the scheming, tyrannical Santa Anna, Ben Cooper as the lone defender to escape the Alamo siege and John Russell as a Texas officer. Among others who turn in credible performances are Kruger, Virginia Grey, Eduard Franz and Russell Simpson.

Lloyd's overall production guidance endowed the Herbert J. Yates presentation with some fine battle sequences which lensman Jack Marta ably caught in Trucolor. While the footage is a mite long at 110 minutes, Tony Martinelli's editing unreels the story in a cohesive whole. Max Steiner's score is an asset as is the film's one song, "Jim Bowie," on which he collabed with Sidney Clare. It's sung by Gordon MacRae. Other technical credits measure up.

Gilb.

The Naked Dawn
(COLOR)

Mild programmer lensed in Mexico; for general dual dates.

Hollywood, July 26.

Universal release of James Q. Radford production. Stars Arthur Kennedy, Betta St. John, Eugene Iglesias; features Charlita, Roy Engel. Directed by Edgar G. Ulmer. Original screenplay, Nina and Herman Schneider; camera (Technicolor), Fredrick Gately; editor, Dan Milner; music composed and conducted by Herschel Burke Gilbert; song, "Ai Hombre," by Gilbert and William Copeland. Previewed July 19, '55. Running time, 82 MINS.

Santiago .... Arthur Kennedy
Maria .... Betta St. John
Manuel .... Eugene Iglesias
Tita .... Charlita
Guntz .... Roy Engel

Universal has taken over the release of this independently-made drama and it should prove passable as a programmer. It has a certain Latin flavor and mood from its below-the-border lensing in Mexico, but never rises above the dualer entertainment classification.

Arthur Kennedy and Betta St. John are starred and their names give the pic some stateside identification. Costar Eugene Iglesias takes care of the cast's Latin angle, though all portray Mexicans. Performances by the top trio are quite good, although Kennedy's assumed accent occasionally throws him.

Major aim of the dramatics is to show the effect that easy money has on a young Mexican farmer and his wife, with some moralizing as to the greed that can rise in most humans under certain situations. Kennedy, a roaming rogue, is the one who puts temptation in the way of Iglesias and causes Miss St.

John to rebel against her lot as the wife of a poor farmer.

Situation is brought up in the original screenplay by Nina and Herman Schneider when Kennedy hires Iglesias to help him collect on the loot from a freight train robbery. The farmer begins to covet all the money and plots Kennedy's death. Miss St. John makes plans to run off with Kennedy. All of the schemes fail because the law catches up and Kennedy is fatally wounded rescuing Iglesias, but is able to send the farmer and his wife off to find a new life together before he dies.

The direction by Edgar G. Ulmer achieves some action here and there, and a poetic feel in other spots, but the overall pacing is slow, despite only 82 minutes of running time, and interest is inclined to wander. Picture, on which James O. Radford was associate producer, has excellent scenic values caught by Fredrick Gately's lensing and the print by Technicolor.

Score by Herschel Burke Gilbert includes the tune, "Ai Hombre," which he wrote with William Copeland. Tune is delivered by Charlita as a vivacious cantina girl during the sequence in which Kennedy and Iglesias celebrate their new wealth and partnership. Only other credited caster is Roy Engel, Kennedy's pursuer, who is killed himself while fatalling wounding the robber.

Brog.

Drei Maenner Im Schnee
(Three Men In the Snow)
(AUSTRIAN)

Berlin, July 19.

Deutsche London release of Ring-Film. Stars Paul Dahlke, Guenther Lueders, Claus Biederstaedt. Directed by Kurt Hoffmann. Screenplay, Erich Kaestner based on his novel; camera, Richard Angst; music, Alexander von Slatina; sets, Werner Schlichting. At Berlin Film Festival. Running time, 93 MINS.

Geheimrat Schlueter ...... Paul Dahlke
Johann Kesselhut ..... Guenther Lueders
Dr. Fritz Hagedorn ....Claus Biederstaedt
Hilde Schlueter.......... Nicole Heesters
Frau Kungel .... Margarethe Haagen
Polter .... Fritz Imhoff

This Austrian comedy, which landed a remarkable fifth spot (as voted by the public) at the Berlin Film Festival, is in nearly every respect an improvement over most German or Austrian features of this type seen recently. Although having an unoriginal plot, film offers witty dialog and situations and also has an undeniable plus in director Kurt Hoffman who keeps the action rolling swiftly. Domestic audiences will go for this film. It may also do well in other European areas. U. S. chances appear limited.

Based on the novel of the same name by Erich Kaestner, who also wrote the well-balanced script, this is sort of a social puzzle play with a millionaire posing as a have-not and a have-not (his servant) enacting the rich man. Action is at a luxury mountain hotel.

Paul Dahlke contributes a fine performance as the millionaire while Guenther Lueders is extremely funny as his servant who, according to his employer's plan, plays the millionaire. Sympathetic Claus Biederstaedt portrays a young lover who eventually wins the millionaire's daughter. Fine support is given by others. Technical credits are good. *Hans.*

Trial

High-voltage courtroom drama. Offbeat angles, big word-of-mouth likely and strong boxoffice.

Metro release of Charles Schnee (James E. Newcom) production. Stars Glenn Ford and Dorothy McGuire. Directed by Mark Robson. Screenplay, Don M. Mankiewicz, based on his novel; camera, Robert Surtens; editor, Albert Akst. Previewed at trade showing in N.Y., July 28, '55. Running time, 105 MINS.

David .... Glenn Ford
Abbe .... Dorothy McGuire
Barney Castle .... Arthur Kennedy
Armstrong .... John Hodiak
Mrs. Chavez .... Katy Jurado
Angelo Chavez .... Rafael Campos
Judge Motley .... Juano Hernandez
Fats Sanders .... Robert Middleton

If "Trial" were just a courtroom drama it could be rated a good one. If it were only another probing of the lynching spirit at the community level, the impact would certainly be forceful. But the picture is much more. Beyond the human interest and immediacy of saving the sympathetic Mexican boy from the gallows is the broader story —a theme never before developed on the screen—of how the Communist Party seizes upon an authentic instance of local bigotry and pumps it up into a national cause celebre for the raising of funds and the making of a class war martyr. With all this (1) storytelling and (2) political insight given strong scripting, directing and acting the result is powerful entertainment. "Trial" is bound to move people and turnstiles.

It will be said, and properly, that Dore Schary's flair for offbeat story values is again evidenced. This is a word-of-mouth and editorial-getting kind of picture which says a lot of fairly grim and unpretty things about human nature and yet leaves the spectator feeling the good guys beat the bad guys.

Primary credits probably belong to the forethought which shines in Charles Schnee's production scheme, and the tight screenplay provided by novelist Don Mankiewicz, plus the detailing and pacing of Mark Robson's direction. At a guess this was one script that got lots of advance executive skull practice. There were (there are) zones of community sensitivity implicit in the story, with special references to Dixie. But while daring to be offbeat, Metro's team has encased its case in so much professional film-making know-how that Justice itself somehow emerges as the hero and the quality of mercy, unstrained, flows freely from the heart of the plot situation.

People are sure to be gripped by the scenes in New York (presumably Madison Sq. Garden) when the Commie lawyer and transmission belt (Arthur Kennedy) organizes his campaign for the Angelo Chavez Defense Fund. The phoney showmanship, the greedy cut-ins of the participating committee chairmen, the cold cynicism of the publicity machine will hit America like a body-blow against those who turn obscure victims of local injustice into party pets. There are states and towns which have had their labor and race prejudice cases given this blow-up technique and they will nod their heads appreciatively. But against that angle there's the unflinching focus of the story upon the reality and the ugliness of the local bigotry which creates such cases in the first place. That part of the picture may be less to the taste of some home town "boosters".

There is one clever emphasis quite early in the footage: Metro drives home the truism that no town which has had a lynching ever amounts to much afterwards. Neither business nor people want to live in or move to such charged communities. This threat of economic loss is shown as registering even on the otherwise closed minds of the local hatrioteers.

Perhaps the most offbeat angle in "Trial", on a par with the Commie party stuff, is having the presiding judge a Negro. This role will almost certainly go into the books as the highlight of Juano Hernandez's acting career. In the careful, temperate, judicious rulings which he is constantly making, Hernandez proves himself one of the great rhetoricians among current character players. But his performance is deeper yet. It has heart, dignity, and the actor has thought through and felt through the implications to achieve an "integration" (to use actor language) seldom encountered. While the picture has many firstrate performances, of which more in a moment, this is peculiarly Hernandez's own private coup de theatre.

If as some social scientists have written, "Birth of A Nation" was the Negro race's greatest screen misfortune, there is fair grounds to expect that "Trial" gives the Negro race its greatest break in terms of a fully-felt, many-sided, warm, human being. Again the point: the professional know-how, of the Metro team found in-plot ways to achieve this effect.

In the story, picking a Negro judge to try the Mexican boy is supposed to be a slick trick to beat the charge of an unfair trial. A mere lad of 17 he stands indicted of murder because a white girl, a lifelong victim of rheumatic fever, has died of a heart attack at a picnic where the Mexican was "out of bounds". The story traces the failure of a lynching attempt and the gradual development of the trial strategy by a university law instructor, in search of courtroom experience, who has innocently stumbled into the case, not knowing he is a Communist catspaw. Along the way the young lawyer (Glenn Ford) falls in love with the legal secretary (Dorothy McGuire) who is a disillusioned party-liner but cannot bring herself to tip him off.

"Trial" is heavy with plot. And with suspense. From beginning to end the viewer's emotions are engaged. Here and there an occasional plot touch may seem a bit too pat. It could be wondered at that the Commie-fronting lawyer had not long since been spotted in his own home city. But taking the author on his own terms, and audiences on theirs; there seems small reason to think such touches will bother most folks. Check off the elements of a high-powered screen drama and they are all present, and counting.

The photography of Robert Surtens is everywhere imaginative, keeping the courtroom action fluid and managing a fine sense of backstage at the New York rally. Some of the long and semi-long shots are of exceptional technical inspiration, a bouquet that probably should be divided among Robson, Surtens, the two art directors, Cedric Gibbons and Randall Duell and the two set men, Edwin B. Willis and Fred MacLean, plus the special effects credit of Warren Newcombe.

There is a great deal of acting

mosaic in the rally sequence and in the courtroom during the challenging of jurors and the presentation of witnesses. These performances are not screen-credited but many sturdy old pros will be recognized. The editing of Albert Askt carries the action smoothly over the many jumps.

In stepping from his recent prototyping of an idealistic schoolteacher in "Blackboard Jungle" to his prototyping of the idealistic lawyer in "Trial", Glenn Ford racks up another top credit as a star. The demands of his role are very arduous and call for much shading. He is thoroughly convincing. So, too, as regards Dorothy McGuire although her role is somewhat mute in the writing. As the arch-plotter in the Communist camp Arthur Kennedy must range from outward urbanity to conniving rascality and finally show cruel arrogance. The actor catches hold of plausibility and never lets go, though a quibble could be registered that who he is, where he came from, how he got to be a Red is glossed over. A believable prosecutor, anxious to win but not bloodthirsty about it, gets just the right amount of aggressiveness in the interpretation of John Hodiak.

As the Mexican symbols of local "race prejudice", Katy Jurado, the mother, and Rafeal Campos, her son, both give intelligent performances, a habit with Miss Jurado, a new display on the part of the young man. Much depends upon the boy being believable, more scared by than intent upon sex experience—he didn't have seduction mind because he didn't know what it was!

The sheriff who is willing to go along with the crowd against "the dirty Mex" is so oily that Robert Middleton's performance ranks as a little gem of detestability. Daniele Amfitheatrof's dramatic mood music may be described as as offbeat as the picture, tautly nervous on occasion, jangly appropriate to montage at other points.

The final comment on "Trial" must concern, and respect, the qualities of showmanship which have gone exploring afield, with the risk thereby entailed. This picture gives the public fresh information on timeless social problems, justice and tolerance, and those who falsely pose as morality's champions. It adds the touch of the Negro judge interpreting law for white attorneys and jury. Add up the points and this is a very strong, almost a great, moving picture. *Land.*

Pete Kelly's Blues
(C'SCOPE-SONGS-COLOR)

Roaring Twenties meller with a Dixieland beat. Television's Jack Webb top marquee name. Beneficiary of big pre-opening bally.

Hollywood, July 28.

Warner Bros. release of Mark VII Ltd. production. Stars Jack Webb, Janet Leigh, Edmond O'Brien, Peggy Lee, Andy Devine, Lee Marvin, Ella Fitzgerald. Directed by Webb. Screenplay, Richard L. Breen; camera (WarnerColor), Hal Rosson; editor, Robert M. Leeds; new songs, Ray Heindorf and Sammy Cahn, Arthur Hamilton; arrangements for Pete Kelly's Big Seven by Matty Matlock. Previewed July 26, '55. Running time, **95 MINS.**

Pete Kelly .... Jack Webb
Ivy Conrad .... Janet Leigh
Fran McCarg .... Edmond O'Brien
Rose Hopkins .... Peggy Lee
George Tenell .... Andy Devine
Al Gannaway .... Lee Marvin
Maggie Jackson .... Ella Fitzgerald
Joey .... Martin Milner
Rudy .... Than Wyenn
Bedido .... Herb Ellis
Bettenhauser .... John Dennis
A Cigarette Girl .... Jayne Mansfield
Cootie .... Mort Marshall
Squat Henchman .... Nesdon Booth
Dako .... William Lazerus

The loud ballyhoo accompanying the release of "Pete Kelly's Blues" makes it a contender for stout openings. Thereafter, the second theatrical film effort by Jack Webb's Mark VII production outfit has several factors to help keep the wickets playing a satisfactory b.o. tune.

Jazz addicts (usually highly opinionated) may have a special interest in the musical frame. Beyond this special-interest factor is a melodramatic story that catches the mood of the Prohibition era with sufficient entertainment to rate the attention of the general filmgoer. With Webb's prominence via "Dragnet" as a main consideration, biz ought to be okay. This is a far cry, however, from Sergeant Joe Friday. Webb enacts a cornet player in a 1927 Kansas City speakeasy. Mostly it develops as a gangster picture (without the cops) with a Dixieland accompaniment.

It has its faults. Perhaps not ones with which the paying public will quarrel too strenuously, because the majority of viewers will have early gotten into the mood and stayed with it. Critics may center on the choppiness of the footage (the result of editing, mostly), the inhibited type of performance that has been Webb's forte on tv, and the failure to spell out strong values. The latter is rather welcome, dispensing with prolonged explanatory passages on the assumption that what the makers are about, and what the ultimate end will be, is clear enough to those likely to be looking at the picture.

The key to the atmosphere of jazz is plainly set up in the before-the-title sequence of a Negro funeral in Louisiana. The picture catches this flavor often enough in subsequent sequences so the mood is never lost. The opening scene, in which the Israelite Spiritual Church choir of New Orleans does first, to a cornet solo played by Ted Buckner, "Just A Closer Walk With Thee" and then "O, Didn't He Ramble" while a river boat sends its mournful whistle and smoke echoing through the moss-draped trees of the graveyard.

From this 1917 prolog, the main story takes a few skips to focus on 1927 and a 12th Street speak in Kansas City where Pete Kelly and his Big Seven combo are blowing in a smoke-filled, frantic atmosphere of smalltime, wouldbe Capones and hasty-living people. This feeling of live today-die tomorrow hysteria is the emphasis of the screen story by Richard L. Breen, and of Webb's direction. Pinpointing it, too, is the authenticity of Harper Goff's production design, the are direction by Field Gray, the John Sturtevant set decorations, and the costuming by Howard Shoup; all of which are strikingly put on film by Hal Rosson's CinemaScope photography in WarnerColor. Technicolor did the print.

There are 14 songs, several new like the title tune by Ray Heindorf and Sammy Cahn, and "He Needs Me" and "Sing A Rainbow" by Arthur Hamilton. All are of, or bespeak, the era depicted and are tellingly used by the Big Seven combo of accomplished musicians, or repeated in the full orchestra background score under the uncredited baton of Heindorf. When Peggy Lee sings "Sugar" or "Somebody Loves Me," and Ella Fitzgerald looses her voice and feeling on "Hard-Hearted Hannah" or the title tune, the songs are as new as tomorrow. The oldie, "I Never Knew," is a romantic theme running through the footage to sharpen the flavor of the hectic courtship of Webb and Janet Leigh, a gaiety-seeking rich girl with F. Scott Fitzgerald overtones. "Smiles," "Breezing Along With the Breeze," "Bye, Bye Blackbird" and "After I Say I'm Sorry" are among others nudging nostalgia. Scoring high in the Big Seven impact are the arrangements by Matty Matlock.

Plot around which the music is woven has to do with the move-in into the band field by Edmund O'Brien, smalltime bootlegger-racketeer, and the abortive efforts at resistance made by Webb to protect his small outfit. The cornet-playing leader knuckles under, even when his drummer, strongly portrayed by Martin Milner, is killed, and the racketeer beats into insanity his singer girl-friend, Peggy Lee, because she gets drunk when he wants to show her off. The courage to fight back brings the film to a gripping climax when Webb shoots it out in a deserted ballroom with O'Brien and his hoods. Scene showing a gunman, John Dennis, crashing through the ceiling grillwork to come smashing to the floor with the huge, many-mirrored globe, of the type so long synonymous with dance halls, is a real thriller.

Webb's understatement of his character is good and Peggy Lee scores a personal hit with her portrayal of a fading singer taken to the bottle. O'Brien registers exceptionally well as the wouldbe big shot and Miss Lee prototypes, the era with her joy-seeking flapper. Lee Marvin, as the older clarinetist with the combo; Andy Devine, although in for short footage as a detective; Than Wyenn, pinch-penny operator of the speakeasy; John Dennis and others acquit themselves ably in keeping with the overall effect. *Brog.*

John and Julie
(BRITISH—COLOR)

Entertaining, lightweight story of two children's adventures while running off to London to see the Coronation; should appeal to overseas audiences.

London, July 26.

British Lion (Herbert Mason) production and release. Features Moira Lister, Noelle Middleton, Constance Cummings, Wilfrid Hyde White. Directed by William Fairchild. Screenplay, William Fairchild; camera, Arthur Grant; editor, Bernard Gribble; music, Philip Green. At Rialto, London. Running time, **82 MINS.**

John .... Colin Gibson
Julie .... Lesley Dudley
Miss Stokes .... Noelle Middleton
Dora .... Moira Lister
Sir James .... Wilfrid Hyde White
Mr. Pritchett .... Sidney James
Mrs. Pritchett .... Megs Jenkins
Mrs. Davidson .... Constance Cummings
Mr. Davidson .... Joseph Tomelty
Jim Webber .... Patric Doonan
Uncle Ben .... Andrew Cruickshank
Mr. Swayne .... Colin Gordon
Mrs. Swayne .... Winifred Shotter
Jeremy .... Peter Jones
P. C. Diamond .... Peter Sellers
Digger .... Vincent Ball
Captain .... Peter Coke

With a firstclass aggregation of legit players and two engaging youngsters, this pic is emphatically aimed more for the overseas than the home market. It deals with the Coronation from the visitors' angle, introducing authentic camera shots, including the actual crowning in Westminster Abbey. Locally it will appeal more to the femme patrons to whom the extreme youth of the main characters will prove a major draw.

Story, which is directed by its author, tells with disarming simplicity the adventures which befall two children who run away to London to see the Coronation. The snags and setbacks encountered on their 150 mile trek are amusing and credible, with the girl stealing away from her school and the boy on his father's horse, which in turn they exchange for lifts by train, coach, stolen bicycle and private auto. They are separated in the crowds, but catch up with each other, track down the boy's uncle who is one of the mounted Life Guards preceding the royal coach and get a camera's eye view of the parade from the top of Marble Arch.

Some of the stars play quite small roles, Moira Lister a soft-hearted floosie who protects the girl when she is lost; Constance Cummings and Joseph Tomelty, as a kindly American couple who give the kids a lift; Wilfrid Hyde-White as a VIP who smooths out most of the tangles, and Sidney James and Megs Jenkins, as the boy's harassed parents; Noelle Middleton as an anxious schoolteacher and Patric Doonan, owner of the bicycle suggest a prospective love affair. There is all the noise, bustle and confusion of mixed nationalities running riot in a normally staid city.

Most of the acting falls on the tender shoulders of seven-year-old Lesley Dudley and 13-year-old Colin Gibson as her reluctant, but faithful squire. Although not newcomers to the screen, this is their first big opportunity, and they have seized it with both hands.

Camerawork is excellent, superior to the real scenes interpolated which lack clarity because of rainy conditions. *Clem.*

Doctor At Sea
(BRITISH)
(V'Vision—Color)

Britain's first V.V. production, sequel to "Doctor In House," set for hefty grosses in domestic market, with bright hopes overseas.

London, July 19.

J. Arthur Rank production (Betty E. Box) and release. Stars Dirk Bogarde, Brigitte Bardot, Brenda de Banzie and James Robertson Justice. Directed by Ralph Thomas. Screenplay by Nicholas Phipps and Jack Davies; camera; Ernest Steward; editor, Frederick Wilson; music, Bruce Montgomery. At Odeon, Leicester Square, London, July 12, '55. Running time, **93 MINS.**

Simon .... Dirk Bogarde
Helene Colbert .... Brigitte Bardot
Muriel Mallet .... Brenda de Banzie
Captain Hogg .... James Robertson Justice
Easter .... Maurice Denham
Trail .... Michael Medwin
Archer .... Hubert Gregg
Fellowes .... James Kenney
Captain Beamish .... Raymond Huntley
Hornbeam .... Geoffrey Keen
Carpenter .... George Coulouris
Corble .... Noel Purcell
Jill .... Jill Adams
Wendy .... Joan Sims

As their first British venture in VistaVision, the Rank studios play safe with a sequel to "Doctor In House," one of the top grossers in the domestic market last year. Inevitably, the comparison must be made, but "Doctor At Sea" does not rise to the same laugh-provoking heights as its predecessor. It remains, however, a solid entry, destined for hefty returns in the domestic market, with healthy prospects overseas.

Technically, the production qualifies for a high rating. The VistaVision lensing in Technicolor compares favorably with Hollywood standards. Ralph Thomas directs with a confident, light touch, and maintains a steady flow of chuckles. But this time he has failed to get the uproarious bellylaughs that characterized the earlier effort.

Two of the principal members of "House" are in the new production, but only Dirk Bogarde retains continuity of character as the doctor. James Robertson Justice changes identity from a gruff surgeon to a gruff ship's captain on whose freighter the young medico has his first appointment at sea. The ship normally does not carry passengers and has an all-male crew. But they are obliged to take on board the daughter of the chairman of the line and her friend, a pert and attractive cabaret chanteuse.

Within this plot framework, the co-scripters, Nicholas Phipps and Jack Davies, have introduced a series of comedy situations with an occasional touch of pathos, which mainly revolve around the irascible skipper and which involve the doctor.

By far the most dominating performance of the cast is given by Justice. He towers above the others and is the focal point of every scene in which he appears. Bogarde plays the medico with a pleasing quiet restraint and Brigitte Bardot, a looker from Paris, has an acting talent to match her charm. She's a positive asset to the production.

Brenda de Banzie is in good form as the other woman passenger who makes a direct bid for the captain. Maurice Denham has never been better than as the medical orderly and a string of British feature players, including Michael Medwin, Raymond Huntley, Hubert Gregg and George Coulouris top a firstrate supporting cast.

Myro.

A Los Cuatro Vientos
(To the Four Winds)
(MEXICAN-SONGS)

Mexico City, July 26.

Columbia Pictures release of Internacional Cinematrografica production. Stars Rosita Quintana; features Joaquin Pardave, Miguel Acaves Mejia. Written and directed by Alfonso Fernandez Bustamante. Camera, V. Herrera; music, Francisco Ruiz. At Cine Orfeon, Mexico City. Running time, **94 MINS.**

Music and songs of true Mexican flavor bow via Miguel Aceves Mejia, noted tenor, and Rosita Quintana in this pic. Engaging folk dancing and the fact that Alfonso F. Bustamante, chief of the local city amusements department, is credited as writer-director make this offering unique.

One can easily enjoy this one because of the good music and singing. Story is the all too familiar one—the luckless troupers getting their big break by singing for their supper, with the usual complications of jealousies, sickness until they get their big break. Miss Quintana is adequate as an annoying temperamental songstress. She sings okay, but material supplied her (brisk, rollicking ranch ditties) don't quite fit her contralto.

A real natural in the pipes department is Miguel Aceves Mejia. He also gives promise of becoming a firstrate actor. Comedy and pathos are well served, as usual, by the veteran Joaquin Pardave. Lensing is good. The dances are sightly.

Doug.

Love Is a Many Splendored Thing
(C'SCOPE—COLOR)

William Holden and Jennifer Jones bring depth, beauty and emotion to a fine love story. Bright b.o. outlook.

Twentieth Century-Fox release of a Buddy Adler production. Stars William Holden, Jennifer Jones; features Torin Thatcher, Isobel Elsom, Murray Matheson, Virginia Gregg, Richard Loo, Soo Yong, Philip Ahn, Jorja Curtright, Donna Martell, Candace Lee, Kam Tong, James Hong, Herbert Heyes, Angela Loo, Marie Tsien, Eleanor Moore, Barbara Jean Wong, Hazel Shon, Kei Chung; directed by Henry King; screenplay, John Patrick, from the Han Suyin novel, "A Many Splendored Thing"; camera (color by De Luxe), Leon Shamroy; music, Alfred Newman, with Sammy Fain-Paul Francis Webster tune, "Love's a Many-Splendored Thing." Previewed in N.Y. Aug. 5, '55. Running time, **102 MINS.**

Mark Elliott	William Holden
Han Suyin	Jennifer Jones
Mr. Palmer-Jones	Torin Thatcher
Adeline Palmer-Jones	Isobel Elsom
Dr. Tam	Murray Matheson
Ann Richards	Virginia Gregg
Robert Hung	Richard Loo
Nora Hung	Soo Yong
Third Uncle	Philip Ahn
Suzanne	Jorja Curtright
Suchen	Donna Martell
Oh-No	Candace Lee
Dr. Sen	Kam Tong
Fifth Brother	James Hong
Father Low	Herbert Heyes
Mei Loo	Angela Loo
Rosie Wu	Marie Tsien
English Secretary	Eleanor Moore
Nurses	Barbara Jean Wong, Hazel Shon
Interne	Kei Chung

Love, as portrayed and dramatized in this fine and sensitive Buddy Adler production based on the Han Suyin bestseller, is indeed a many-splendored thing and, unless audiences have lost their romantic inclination, it ought to make for a plenty strong b.o. It's an unusual picture in many ways, shot against authentic Honk Kong backgrounds and offbeat in its treatment, yet as simple and moving a love story as has come along in many a moon.

To start with, William Holden as the American correspondent, and Jennifer Jones as the Eurasian doctor, make a romantic team of great appeal. Between them, each contributing a thoroughly believable and valid performance, they carry the picture and make it the gentle and frequently emotional thing that it is. This is something of a tear-jerker, to be sure, but an awfully well-made one. Nobody is likely to object on that score. On the contrary, "Love Is a Many Splendored Thing" has a special quality that makes it top effort in many respects.

Han Suyin, who wrote the book, was less concerned with drama than with tracing the mating of two kindred souls in a world strange to both. Her story didn't revolve as much around the standard theme of the Chinese Reds as the awakening of love, and its realization, between people worlds apart in background, culture and upbringing. She also dramatized the social problem of the American linked with the Eurasian in the small and petty world of British colonialism.

A lot of this—some to the good and the rest not so—has been incorporated into the generally excellent screenplay fashioned by John Patrick. It's all here—the hesitant process of getting to know one-another, the welling of love, the delight of the lovers in finding themselves and the problems of race and custom (Holden is married, she's a widow)—but not all of it is fully explored and following the pattern of the book, there is a good deal of dialog. Some of it is quite beautiful. Certainly this is one of the most erudite romances ever brought to the screen.

But it must also be said that, up to the middle of the film, things go rather slowly. Director Henry King, with a great many thoughtful and sensitive touches, has made this into a love story that allows little else to intrude. Both he and Patrick apparently thought the romantic theme, with its heartbreaking ending, should be enough. Since Elliott is married and his wife won't give him a divorce, marriage is impossible. Although compromised, and without a job at the end, Han holds fast to her love. Then she learns that Elliott has been killed covering the Korean war.

King and lenser Leon Shamroy have done a magnificent job in utilizing the Hong Kong backgrounds. There is a great feeling of authenticity and strangeness in these reels, whether it is in the opening shots panning down on the teeming city or in the charming little scene when Han returns to her Chungking home and is followed there by Elliott. Perhaps some will feel that King has wasted too much footage on meaningless patter, but it does fill out the framework of the story and brings it into its proper perspective.

Holden as the correspondent delivers a great job of acting. He's restrained and completely believable. Miss Jones is pure delight as the beautiful Han who looks European, yet feels strongly Chinese. Her transformation from efficient doctor to passionate woman has the proper hesitancy and never for one moment hints a wrong note. Miss Jones' accomplishment in a very difficult part is quite remarkable and contributes greatly to the film's success. Her love scenes with Holden sizzle without ever being cheap or awkward. In her, the spirit of the book is caught completely.

Since "Love Is a Many Splendored Thing"—title is part of a quotation from "The Kingdom of God" by religious poet Francis Thompson—shapes up as a sock women's picture, it's just as well to point out that Miss Jones' Chinese gowns (and she wears a multitude of them) are the smartest thing any dress designer ever dreamed up. In the very good color by De Luxe, the costuming is a distinct ace up the pic's sleeve. Color and CinemaScope also are a boon to the lensing of the background scenes.

Supporting cast is fine, with Isobel Elsom properly superficial as the British matron who resents Miss Jones. Torin Thatcher as the righteous British businessman and director of the hospital (on the side he takes trips with another Eurasian girl), is good. Candace Lee as the nine-year-old refugee girl who's been in an accident is a charmer and her scene, when she sings for the doctor, tears at the heartstrings. Kam Tong as the Commie doctor, who urges Miss Jones to return to Red China and "her people," is sinister yet wisely refrains from playing the heavy. Philip Ahn portrays Third Uncle with dignity. Richard Loo and Soo Yong, as Miss Jones' friends, turn in a pleasant performance.

Sets are smart and Alfred Newman's musical backgrounds fit perfectly. Song "Love's a Many-Splendored Thing" (Sammy Fain & Paul Francis Webster) carries strong "Madame Butterfly" resemblance but has the quality that should help it sell the picture.

Most of those who will see "Love Is a Many Splendored Thing" will think it a thing of beauty and will love it. A few may consider it much ado about nothing, but they should be decidedly in the minority. It's a film that, in its deliberate restraint and intelligent—at times almost poetic—dialog draws a tender and quite lovely picture of a different kind of romance. Being so different, and yet so warm and sincere, it should wow 'em.

Hift.

City of Shadows

Okay crime melo for the program market.

Hollywood, Aug. 3.

Republic release of a William J. O'Sullivan production. Stars Victor McLaglen, John Baer, Kathleen Crowley. Directed by William Witney. Screenplay, Houston Branch camera, Reggie Lanning; editor, Tony Martinelli; music, R. Dale Butts. Reviewed Aug 3, '55. Running time, **70 MINS.**

Big Tim Channing	Victor McLaglen
Dan Mason	John Baer
Fern Fellows	Kathleen Crowley
Toni Finetti	Anthony Caruso
Linda Fairaday	June Vincent
Angelo Di Bruno	Richard Reeves
Davis	Paul Maxey
District Attorney Hunt	Frank Ferguson
Phil Jergins	Richard Travis
Kink	Kay Kuter
Roy Fellows	Nicolas Coster
Waitress	Gloria Pall
Miss Hall	Fern Hall

This crime melo fits handily into the program market, where the name of Victor McLaglen still may be a draw. After a slow opening, although the plot is fairly routine, there's enough action to maintain the 70-minute running time for average interest.

McLaglen enacts a punchy old racketeer who rises to a power in a big city's underworld. He gains this estate through a young law student whom he picked up as a boy and educated, who ferrets out loopholes in the law to help him in his upward climb. Legal-beagle turns honest when he meets a gal, successful him but lethally for the racketeer. Houston Branch's screenplay is fairly well developed, directed with an eye to best values by William Witney.

John Baer as the lawyer delivers strongly and shows promise for future castings. McLaglen is okay in his customary hardboiled-softie role, and Kathleen Crowley fares well as the femme. Anthony Caruso and Richard Reeves punch over their gangster roles effectively, Paul Maxey is good as a disbarred attorney and Frank Ferguson is believable as the harrassed district attorney, whose undercover man, Richard Travis, is public relations man for Baer in a racket.

Technical credits are standards, headed by Reggie Lanning on the cameras.

Whit.

I Am a Camera

Dialog flippancies and a few plot unconventionalities deny this import a code seal. Actually not very shocking. Best playoff chances in selected showcase bookings.

Hollywood, Aug. 4.

Distributors Corp. of America release of Romulus Films production. Stars Julie Harris, Laurence Harvey, Shelley Winters, Ron Randell; features Lea Seidl, Anton Diffring. Directed by Henry Cornelius. Screenplay, John Collier; from stage play by John van Druten, based on stories written by Christopher Isherwood; camera, Guy Greene; editor, Clive Donner; music, Malcolm Arnold. Previewed July 21, '55. Running time, 98 MINS.

Sally	Julie Harris
Chris	Laurence Harvey
Natalia	Shelley Winters
Clive	Ron Randell
Fraulein Schneider	Lea Seidl
Fritz	Anton Diffring
Herr Landauer	Ina De La Haye
Pierre	Jean Gargoet
American Editor	Stanley Maxted
Proprietor (Troika)	Alexis Bobrinskoy
Head Waiter (Troika)	Andre Mikhelson

The boxoffice effectiveness of censorial frowns seems likely to be tried once again with the release of "I Am a Camera," Romolus Films production of the stage comedy which Distributors Corp. of America is handling in the Western Hemisphere. The Production Code has nixed the dialog and unconventional bedroom antics so its playoff in select, showcase bookings could be to the accompaniment of much pro and con talk and more wicket attention than the quality of the entertainment actually deserves.

John van Druten's hit play, based on "The Berlin Stories" by Christopher Isherwood, is an episodic affair dealing with a young author who gets himself involved, innocently, with a crackpot girl in pre-World War II Berlin. In transferring the play to the screen, scripter John Collier hewed close to the original in dialog and situations and the effect is always more that of a filmed stage play than a motion picture. The direction by Henry Cornelius follows the stage line, too, and the camera handling by Guy Greene does not have the flowing freedom usual to most motion pictures.

While not an all-together satisfactory film offering, "Camera" does have its moments. Most of them will probably be more appreciated by distaff viewers than male stub-holders. The femmes will find more identification in the antics, even though most unconventional, of the wacky character so broadly projected by Julie Harris, than the men will have with the Isherwood role played by Laurence Harvey. Too, while the play's prime theme is sex, it actually offers little along this line that will prove attractive to male viewers.

The already much-quoted shocker line quipped by Miss Harris when she moves in on Harvey, about which to do first, go to bed or have a drink, is an innocent piece of dialog, but the circumstances under which it is spoken make it a foregone conclusion it will be heard with a double meaning. Less innocent, however, is the abortion situation and why Miss Harris believes she needs one.

Quite amusing is the sequence in which Miss Harris gorges on caviar and champagne to the horror of purse-poor Harvey. Another chuckler is the wild party tossed by Ron Randell, the American playboy with whom the femme screwball has taken up, and the odd characters that drift in and out as the bacchanalian celebration hits its peak. Randell does a convincing job of the character. Less frequently involved in the story is Shelley Winters, seen as a subdued German girl who, with her fiance, Anton Diffring, is beginning to feel the first anti-Jewish pressure of the Hitler regime. The top players, and others, are competent in answering the rather light demands of story and direction.

The filming was done in London and, while the technical supports are adequate, the picture lacks the production polish accomplished on practically all domestic features. *Brog.*

Continente Perduto
(Lost Continent)
(ITALIAN-COLOR-C'SCOPE)

Rome, Aug. 2.

Astra Cinematografica release of an Astra-Leonardo Bonzi production. Directed by Leonardo Bonzi, Enrico Gras, Giorgia Moser; music, Francesco Lavagnino; camera (Ferraniacolor), Mario Craveri, Gianni Rafaldi, Franco Bernetti; editor, Mario Serandrei; text, Orio Vergani; at Cinema Fiammo, Rome. Running time, 95 MINS.

This feature-length documentary, filmed by an Italian expedition to the Indonesian islands, is an impressive item in its field, with sock audio-visual appeal as well for general audiences in all countries. Already outstanding in mere material collected, impact is greatly heightened via great use of sound and CinemaScope, perhaps the best use ever made of the anamorphs. With "Green Magic," made by same director-cameraman team (Bonzi and Craveri), setting the pace, this item should go well at the b.o. Though the pic doesn't need it, it contains exploitable footage involving some lightly garbed native women. Trimming would help general pacing.

First Italian picture made in C'Scope, "Lost Continent" won a special jury prize at the last Cannes Film Fete. Pic was lensed by an obviously cooperating team under extremely difficult conditions, with sound and image receiving amazing technical handling. Starting off with a Cantonese wedding in a junk-filled harbor, film progresses through various Indonesian island settings illustrating various religious customs as well as unusual aspects and ways of life. Thus the Balinese dancers, harvest-time in wheat and rice fields, an island wedding ceremony, the "feeding" of a stirring volcano with animals and food to prevent an eruption, as well as the most impressive feature, a ceremonial chariot race (with teams of wild bulls), caught in movement with telling effect, tops anything the Roman spectacles have had to offer. Lensing in Ferraniacolor and CinemaScope by Mario Craveri and his team is expert teaming of the widescreen and the subject matter, with color hues all top-drawer.

Musical score by Lavagnino, who accompanied the expedition throughout, is likewise strikingly effective. Editing doesn't always avoid a certain episodic structure but is generally expert. *Hawk.*

The Girl Rush
(V'VISION—MUSICAL—COLOR)

Rosalind Russell in lightweight musicomedy. Routine entertainment for routine bookings.

Hollywood, Aug. 8.

Paramount release of Frederick Brisson production. Stars Rosalind Russell. Fernando Lamas, Eddie Albert, Gloria De Haven; features Marion Lorne, James Gleason. Directed by Robert Pirosh. Screenplay, Pirosh and Jerome Davis; based on a story by Phoebe and Henry Ephron; camera (Technicolor), William Daniels; editor, William Hornbeck; score, M. S. I. Spencer-Hagen; songs, Hugh Martin, Ralph Blane; dances and musical numbers staged by Robert Alton. Prevewed Aug. 1, '55. Runnng tme, 84 MINS.

Kim Halliday	Rosalind Russell
Victor Monte	Fernando Lamas
Elliott Atterbury	Eddie Albert
Taffy Tremaine	Gloria De Haven
Aunt Clara	Marion Lorne
Ether Ferguson	James Gleason
Pete Tremaine	Robert Fortier

Lightweight musicomedy filmfare is served up in "The Girl Rush." Picture will get a booking push and some coin by being the lead film in the upcoming Paramount Week drive.

Rosalind Russell and her producer husband, Frederick Brisson, didn't pick a particularly good vehicle for her screen return after B'way success in "Wonderful Town." Picture is light in virtually every department and the giddy air with which it goes about its business isn't sufficiently entertaining to cloak the weak plot and scripting. (Las Vegas interests should like it, since it's a film ad for that gambling spa, giving plush viewing to Strip hotels, especially the Flamingo, via Technicolor tints and Vista-Vision.)

Eight tunes, plus the title number, are heard, either as straight songs or as production pieces. Likely for the best play is "Occasional Man," a saucy bongo-beat tune that backstops for the most attractive of the several production numbers staged by Robert Alton. Gloria De Haven, who ably carries the pulchritude load for the film, displays voice and curves in the piece advantageously. She also has another production bit titled "Champagne," working with Robert Fortier and two other male partners. Miss Russell's special production number is a cornfed affair tagged "My Hillbilly Heart" which starts amusingly enough but wears out its welcome by running too long. Also she dances and sings with Eddie Albert to "Birmin'ham"; with three male partners to "Choose Your Partner"; sings "Out of Doors" with Albert, as well as "Take a Chance," theme song. Fernando Lamas does the ballad, "We're Alone." Hugh Martin and Ralph Blane did the cleffing for all the tunes, with M. S. I. Spencer-Hagen doing the score and conducting.

Plot scripted by director Robert Pirosh and Jerome Davis from a story by Phoebe and Henry Ephron has Miss Russell and her aunt, Marion Lorne, coming to Las Vegas to enter the gambling hotel business with James Gleason, who had partnered with her late crap-shooting dad in the venture some years back. By the time the two femmes arrive, Gleason has hocked the hotel to back losses suffered at the crap tables of Lamas' Flamingo. What takes place after that is never quite clear in the writing. Miss Russell and Lamas run through some romantic misadventures before the finale clinch, and Albert winds up with Miss De De Haven, Gleason and Miss Lorne make the third pairing. While there's quite a bit of broad slapstick action, the pacing given the footage under Pirosh's direction seems slow and the acting just adequate.

Femmes will like several of the Edith Head costumes displayed on Miss Russell and the males will like the brief production outfits Miss De Haven wears for her song-dance chores. The area in and around Las Vegas has visual value as lensed by William Daniels. *Brog.*

The African Lion
(COLOR)

Good documentary, but doesn't have the fascinating qualities of other Disney "True-Life Adventures." Moderate b.o.

Buena Vista release of Walt Disney production. Photographed (Technicolor) by Alfred G. and Elma Milotte. Associate producer, Ben Sharpsteen; directed by James Algar; written by Algar, Winston Hibbler, Ted Sears, Jack Moffitt; narration, Hibbler; music, Paul Smith; editor, Norman Palmer; special process, Ub Iwerks; animation effects, Joshua Meador, Art Riley. Tradeshown in New York, Aug. 3, '55. Running time, 75 MINS.

Walt Disney has rung up a string of critical and b.o. successes in his "True-Life Adventure" series from the start, but his latest effort, "The African Lion," is bound to have less stimulating results. The fault lies not so much in the production as in the choice of subject matter. In the past, the documentaries have dealt with little-known facts of animal life. In the present case, so much footage has been shot and shown on African wildlife that even the best of the Alfred G. and Elma Milotte color footage has an all-too-familiar ring to it, rubbing off much of the fascination and consequently the b.o. draw. Teamed with a 13-minute reprise of "Peter and the Wolf," out of Disney's "Make Mine Music," the "Lion" segment seems due for only a moderate chance at the b.o.

More's the pity, too, for the Milottes have gotten some of the best wildlife footage ever to come out of Africa. Their 30-month stint in the plateau regions were rewarded with such unusual shots as a leopard pouncing out of a tree into a milling herd of wild beasts, a pride of lionesses stalking a herd of impalas, a cheetah overtaking an antelope at 75 m.p.h., a flock of vultures and groups of hyenas and jackals fighting a lioness for a share in a half-devoured carcass, and a locust swarm descending on the grasslands. Measured with the dramatic shots are the usual quota of Disney's more amusing pictorial commentaries on animal existence.

Star of the pic, of course, is the photography, but spectacular as it is, it's not enough to compensate for the "I've seen this before" feeling the subject matter engenders. Winston Hibbler, who wrote the script around the footage with director James Algar, Ted Sears and Jack Moffitt, does a fine narrating job. And the script itself leaves little to be desired. Paul Smith's score, as orchestrated by Joseph Dubin, fits the mood of the photography without undue intrusion, and Norman Palmer's editing of some 100,000 feet of 16m color footage is sharp and smooth. Color at times is inconsistent, but this is due largely to use of telephoto lenses and is hardly a disturbing factor. *Chan.*

Desert Sands

Routine Foreign Legion action film stencilled off an old pattern. Average b.o. possibilities.

United Artists release of a Bel-Air production. Stars Ralph Meeker, Marla English, J. Carrol Naish features John Carradine, Ron Randell, John Smith, Keith Larsen. Directed by Lesley Selander. Screenplay, George W. George, George F. Slavin, Danny Arnold. Producer, Howard W. Koch; exec producer, Aubrey Schenck; camera, Gordon Avil; editor, John F. Schreyer; music, Paul Dunlap. Previewed in N.Y. Aug. 3, '55. Running time, 87 MINS.

David Malcom	Ralph Meeker
Zara	Maria English
Diepel	J. Carrol Naish
Rex Tyle	John Smith
Pete Havers	Ron Randell
Jala	John Carradine
El Zanal	Keith Larsen
Gina	Carl Victor
Gabin	Otto Waldis
Lucia	Peter Mamakos
Ducco	Albert Carrier
Wolock	Mort Mills
Sandy	Philip Tonge
Kramer	Terence deMarney
Gerard	Nico Minadros
Alita	Lita Milan
Weems	Peter Bourne
Dr. Kleiner	Peter Norman
Dylak Spokesman	Joseph Waring
Tamas	Aaron Saxon
Panton	Bela Kovacs

With the screen so intent these days on dramas of juvenile delinquency and the more literate creations of the Broadway stage, "Desert Sands," fashioned after the formula action pix of yesteryear, probably will rate a welcome reception with a segment of the audience that has begun to miss these films.

Howard W. Koch and Aubrey Schenck here present one of those improbable, fast-paced little items—in Superscope and Technicolor—that certainly should find its proper niche and probably will make money for a lot of the smaller situations that have been asking for blood-and-guts action entries. Who cares about story or performances as long as there's plenty of rough-housing, the intermittent chatter of guns, plenty of daredevil acrobatics and a spark of a love story.

What is amazing is that it should have taken three scribes—George W. George, George F. Slavin and Danny Arnold—to concoct this most routine and unimaginative of screenplays. It's the kind of thing one would suspect any one of them should be able to toss off in their sleep. However, they didn't and the results are unimpressive, to say the least. They've used every cliche in the book, not even bothering to cast around for a novel twist.

Result, "Desert Sands" is mostly visual. Director Selander, again without much imagination, does create a sense of drama and excitement in his handling of the mass action scenes, when the Arabs storm the fort. Color helps and so does Gordon Avil's lensing which at least shows occasional attempts to reach for unusual angles.

Story has Ralph Meeker as a Foreign Legion captain, taking over at Fort Valeau, somewhere in the hot Sahara. (He arrives via helicopter). The relief column is annihilated by the Arabs who eventually capture the fort. Trickery and romance combine to cause the eventual destruction of the Arab marauders, but not after a good many of them—and an equal number of Legionnaires—have bitten the dust.

Meeker, in the role of the tough desert fighter, does what he has to do without great distinction but at least he can't be accused of etching his character tongue-in-cheek. As the Arab princess who falls for him, and saves him, Marla English cuts a very pretty figure, which makes up for some of the absurd lines put into her mouth. The colorful legionnaires' crew is headed by J. Carrol Naish as the sergeant and includes Ron Rondell as—believe it or not— the Englishman addicted to the bottle, who when the fighting starts, exonorates himself. His performance has a certain merit.

Zanal, the Arab leader, is played by Keith Larsen in several resplendant outfits. He's assisted by John Carradine as Jala, his advisor, who turns out to be quite a treacherous fellow. Rest of the cast keeps active most of the time.

"Desert Sands" isn't going to win any Academy Awards, but it's an actioner that doesn't pretend to be anything else. For that reason alone, it should hold its own.

Hift.

Apache Ambush

Standard western with aftermath of Civil War tossed in to give it a different angle. Names of Tex Ritter and Bill Williams okay for marquee.

Columbia release of Wallace MacDonald production. Features Bill Williams, Tex Ritter, Richard Jaeckel, Movita, Alex Montaya, Ray Corrigan, Adelle August. Directed by Fred F. Sears. Story and screenplay, David Lang; camera, Fred Jackman, Jr.; editor, Jerome Thoms; music conducted by Mischa Bakaleinikoff. Tradeshown in N. Y., Aug. 4, '55. Running time, **68 MINS.**

James Kingston .... Bill Williams
Lee Parker .... Richard Jaeckel
Joaquin Jironza .... Alex Montoya
Rosita .... Movita
Ann .... Adelle August
Trager .... Tex Ritter
Mark Calvin ...... Ray "Crash" Corrigan
Sgt. O'Roarke .... Ray Teal
Major McGuire .... Don C. Harvey
Mr. Lincoln .... James Griffith
Colonel Marshall .... James Flavin
Chandler .... George Chandler
Silas Parker .... Forrest Lewis
Tweedy .... George Keymas
Manoel .... Victor Millan
Bailey .... Harry Lauder
Bob Jennings .... Bill Hale
Red Jennings .... Robert Foulk

"Apache Ambush" follows the accepted formula for outdoor adventure features, with an attempt to get away from the pat western pattern via the Civil War aftermath. The effort to depict how the federals and defeated rebs continued bitter out in the wide open spaces soon is lost in the general shuffle of stampeding cattle, a wild hunt for the latest repeating rifles and the triumph of justice over the Mexicano outlaws and outlaw redskins. It often is confusing but generally exciting, and will do where western pix are appreciated.

David Lang, original story concocter and screenplay scrivener, gives this a grandiose beginning—showing Lincoln striving (just before his assassination) to rush cattle from Texas to the markets up north. Plot has the president feeling that this would help southern cattlemen at the same time supplying the demand for meat up north.

The three designated by Lincoln, Ray Teal, cattle driver; Bill Williams, expert Indian scout (from the Union side); and Don Harvey, a major from the Confederate Army, find their task much more difficult than outlined when they reach the Texas territory. There is much to do about a box of Henry Repeating Rifles, with a war profiteer intent on selling them to former confed renegades and a fantastic Mexican, Alex Montoya, trying to grab them for his fight to win Texas back for Mexico. All of this brings the familiar gun battle, with some baddie Apaches aligned with the Mexican bandits for any loot they can grab.

Richard Jaeckel, depicting an embittered confederate soldier who has lost an arm in the war, finally snags the coveted rifles, sells out to the Mexicans—all building to a cattle stampede, killing on all sides and final routing of the Mexican forces and injuns. One thing about this pic; it won't make the distributor very popular in Mexico or with the Indians. Both are shown up in the worst possible light.

Williams, Harvey, Teal and Jaeckel carry the acting burden in acceptable fashion. Movita is in for a secondary role as the Mexican gal sweetheart of the Mex outlaw, Montoya. Latter emotes with fervor in the villainous role. Adelle August suffices as Williams' girl friend. Forrest Lewis, Ray Corrigan and Tex Ritter are okay in supporting roles. Ritter has been relegated to a bit character although given featured billing.

Fred Jackman has done a yeoman job as cameraman, his photography being unusually highclass for a western. Fred F. Sears directed with action as keynote to his work. Jerome Thoms' editing is unusually sharp.

Wear.

Escapade
(BRITISH)

Screen adaptation of London legit hit. Sturdy b.o. chances in home market with likely attraction for art house circuit.

London, Aug. 5.

Eros production and release. Stars John Mills, Yvonne Mitchell and Alastair Sim; features Jeremy Spenser, Andrew Ray, Marie Lohr, and Colin Gordon. Produced by Daniel M. Angel; directed by Philip Leacock; screenplay by Gilbert Holland from play by Roger McDougall; camera by Eric Cross; editor, John Trumper; music, Bruce Montgomery. At Odeon Marble Arch, London. Aug. 4, '55. Running time, **88 MINS.**

John Hampden .... John Mills
Stelle Hampden .... Yvonne Mitchell
Dr. Skillingworth .... Alastair Sim
Mrs. Hampden .... Marie Lohr
Deeson .... Colin Gordon
Daventry .... Jeremy Spenser
Max Hampden .... Andrew Ray
Johnny Hampden .... Peter Asher
Paton .... Nicky Edmett
Potter .... Christopher Ridley
Warren .... Sean Barrett
Miss Betts .... Sonia Williams
Sykes .... Mark Dignam
Smith .... Kit Terrington
Young Skilly .... Colin Freear
Parsons .... Stephen Abbott
Miss Lunt .... Anne Allen
Curly .... John Rae

In its original stage form "Escapade" was a major hit in the West End a couple of seasons back, although a Broadway version flopped dismally after a run of only a few nights. The filmization of Roger McDougall's legiter should get a more universal reaction, although it loses much of its appeal in transition. In the home market it should qualify for sturdy b.o. results, with the arties as the main outlet in the U.S.

Oddly enough, the wider canvas of the screen, which allows the introduction of additional key characters and gives scope for more action, does not improve the story. The suspense achieved in the original is replaced by lashings of sentiment, particularly in the closing sequences. Nor does it add to conviction.

Basically the plot remains the same, focusing on the three young sons of a pacifist author, who put his preachings to practical purposes by stealing an airplane and flying off to Vienna with a petition, signed by the other boys, for the four occupying powers. In the play, none of the trio appeared on stage; the screen version introduces the two younger brothers, only keeping out of the picture the guiding genius of the plot, the appropriately named Icarus. The emotional conflict between the parents and the intrusion of a snooping newsman are neatly dovetailed into the main story outline.

Gilbert Holland's screenplay crams too much talk into the earlier sequences and misses the comedy impact achieved by the bickerings among writers to agree on a peace manifesto. Direction by Philip Leacock is positive and authoritative and his sequences with Alaistair Sim as the headmaster are among the best things in the production. John Mills appears too stolid, lacking much of the temperament needed for the role of the author-father, but Yvonne Mitchell does a worthwhile job as his wife. Colin Gordon gives a quality performance as the newspaperman and Jeremy Spenser and Andrew Ray play a couple of schoolboys with absolute integrity. Marie Lohr's performance as the author's mother is a plus feature. Other parts are more than adequately filled.

Myro.

Der Dunkle Stern
(The Dark Star)
(GERMAN)

Frankfurt, Aug. 2.

Constantin release of Wega Film production. Stars Toxi. Directed by Hermann Kugelstadt. Screenplay, Maria Osten Sacken and Hermann Kugelstadt after an idea by Peter Francke and Georg Hurdalek; camera, Heinz Pehike; music, Bernhard Eichnorn. At Alemannia Theatre, Frankfurt. Running time, **94 MINS.**

Moni .... 'Toxi
Manuel .... Juergen Micksch
Frl. Rieger .... Ilse Steppat
Linda .... Ingeborg Schoener
Christian .... Siegfried Breuer Jr.
Casseno .... Viktor Staal

This begins as an interesting problem film with a realistic basis, since there are hundreds of illegitimate Negro babies in Germany, and the country has as yet no solution to the problem of making a place in the world for them. Partly based on an actual story, this does not make a good pic. Chances in U.S. seem limited.

In the picture, nine-year-old Toxi is a half-Negro orphan being brought up by a foster mother in a small German village. The girl yearns to become a farmer's wife when she grows up, but the villagers and the children realize that she is different from them, and refuse to accept her.

The friendly schoolteacher arranges for Moni to be adopted by a circus family. Truth is stranger than fiction (this is based on an actual story) but this does not always necessarily make a good screen vehicle as the outcome of this one proves.

Once in the circus, the plot falls apart into the usual big top cliches. There's the girl who is afraid to go on the trapeze since seeing her mother fall from it; the hard-hearted circus owner; the dying old clown; the nasty circus brat and the excitement of knife-throwing rehearsal. Toxi eventually finds a home in the circus, where she is no longer considered an outcast. She wins the love of everybody and goes on to glory on the high trapeze.

For addicts of films with a circus background, the brightest moments are provided by the Krone Circus, one of Europe's finest. Interesting for Americans is little dark-faced Toxi singing "Swanee River" in German. The plot oozes sentiment and could well be classed as a four-handkerchief film. However, it still remains a trite if true story.

Guil.

Djevojka I Hrast
(The Girl and the Oak)
(YUGOSLAVIAN)

Berlin, Aug. 2.

Jadran Film (Zagreb-Dubrawa) production and release. Stars Tamara Mrkovic, Miodrag Popovic and Ljubivoje Tadic. Directed by Kreso Golic. Screenplay, Mirko Bozic; camera, Frano Vodopivec; music, Branimir Sakac. At Berlin Film Festival. Running time, **97 MINS.**

Smilja .... Tamara Markovic
Bojan .... Miodrag Popovic
Josip .... Ljubivoje Tadic
Ivan .... Andrej Kurent
Roko .... Josip Petricic
Marko .... Viktor Brek
Little Smilja .... Violeta Prosevska

That the still young Yugoslavian film industry remarkably has improved in recent years is evidenced by this film which was entered at the recent Berlin Festival. Pic, which includes love, jealousy, passion and murder, will hardly appeal to average western audiences, but it may prove an interesting item for some arty houses.

Beautiful Tamara Markovic portrays a poor orphan girl who is courted by three men. One of them eventually kills his strongest rival and the latter's brothers pursue the murderer high into the mountains where he has hidden himself. The oak, incidentally, is the girl's only true friend, so the story goes. This oak tree is her biggest inspiration.

Best thing about this production is the camerawork by Frano Vodopivec. There are a number of impressive shots. *Hans.*

The McConnell Story
(C'SCOPE—COLOR)

Alan Ladd, June Allyson in topflight story of America's first triple jet ace; strong entertainment, strong grosses.

Hollywood, July 26.

Warner Bros. release of Henry Blanke production. Stars Alan Ladd, June Allyson. James Whitmore; features Frank Faylen, Robert Ellis, Willie Bouchey, Sarah Selby, Gregory Walcott, Frank Ferguson. Directed by Gordon Douglas. Screenplay, Ted Sherdeman, Sam Rolfe; story by Sherdeman; camera (Warner Color), John Seitz; editor, Owen Marks; music, Max Steiner; technical advisers, William L. Orris, Col., USAF: Manuel "Pete" J. Fernandez, Capt., USAF. Previewed July 19, '55. Running time, 106 MINS.

Mac	Alan Ladd
Butch	June Allyson
Ty Whitman	James Whitmore
Sykes	Frank Faylen
Bob	Robert Ellis
Newton Bass	Willis Bouchey
Mom	Sarah Selby
1st M.P.	Gregory Walcott
A Mechanic	Frank Ferguson

The story of America's first triple jet ace, Captain Joseph McConnell Jr., has become a tasteful, thrilling motion picture under the Warner Bros. banner. Strong grosses loom. There's a contemporary flavor in the presentation to attract the attention of the country's younger picturegoers, and a lot of heart and humaness to make it figure as entertainment for all ages, male or distaffer. It has marquee importance, too, in the star names of Alan Ladd and June Allyson.

Even while the production was being prepped the hero of the story lost his life when the experimental jet aircraft he was flying at Edwards Air Force Base in California crashed. This incident, like many others in his career as a soldier and then navigator during World War II, and as a jet ace over Korea, is thrillingly depicted, as well as being used to give an inspirational note to a very moving climax. Under the production supervision of Henry Blanke and the equally good direction by Gordon Douglas, the film has humor, romance, action and convincing performances that make the footage very real.

Ladd is not called upon for the usual brand of screen heroics and does a sock job of playing a real person. With this elimination of the stock "into the wild blue yonder" type of hero, picture gains in punch. There's nothing fanciful about the McConnell exploits, thanks to good judgment in the scripting by Ted Sherdeman and Sam Rolfe. In fashioning the character of the girl who married the ace while he was still a sorry GI in the medical corps sneaking private flying lessons, the script stays on believeable grounds, too.

Considerable humor is played up in the early footage over McConnell's determination to be a flier and his meeting with Pearl Brown, a girl to henceforth be known as "Butch" and a loving helpmate to a young soldier. From medical corps to air force, but as navigator, not pilot; the piling up of 25 missions in World War II in a big hurry so he could take pilot training; the call back to war when the Korean situation arose and his rise to captain and jet ace, and then the test piloting that took his life are sequences so well blended that attention is always held. Backing theme are the few moments back home with wife and family that add to the touching humaness which is an important part of the film.

James Whitmore scores as McConnell's friend and commanding officer. A pip of a sergeant character is developed by Frank Faylen, sparking the humor of earlier sequences. Others registering well include Robert Ellis, Willis Bouchey, Sarah Selby, Gregory Walcott and Frank Ferguson. The CinemaScope photography in Warner-Color by John Seitz figures as a major credit. So does the second unit lensing by Ted McCord under the direction of Russ Saunders. A good score by Max Steiner, concise editing by Owen Marks, count towards the entertainment. *Brog.*

Case Of The Red Monkey

Routine foreign intrigue melo for program market.

Hollywood, Aug. 10.

Allied Artists release of a Tony Owen (Alec C. Snowden) production. Stars Richard Conte, Rona Anderson; features Russell Napier, Colin Gordon, Arnold Marle, Sylva Langova, Donald Bissett, John King-Kelly. Directed by Ken Hughes. Screenplay, James Eastwood, Hughes; camera, Josef Ambor; editing, Geoffrey Muller, Inman Hunter. Reviewed Aug. 10, '55. Running time, 71 MINS.

Bill Locklin	Richard Conte
Julia	Rona Anderson
Supt. Harrington	Russell Napier
Martin	Colin Gordon
Dushenko	Arnold Marle
Hilde	Sylva Langova
Editor	Donald Bissett
Andor	John King-Kelly

Efforts of Soviet agents in London to kill a top Russian scientist who has swung over to the West, as he's under the security of British police en route to the U.S., motivates this Tony Owen-Todon production, filmed entirely in England for Allied Artists release. Like many British-produced pictures, it lacks American-type pace and is a routine entry in the program market. Owen used almost a complete English setup, Richard Conte being the only other American connected with the venture.

Conte portrays a U.S. State Dept. officer detailed to escort the scientist from London back to the States, but exhibits little of the dash and ingenuity such a part calls for. James Eastwood-Ken Hughes' screenplay shows him breaking up the Communist gang out to murder the scientist, but it's strictly mechanical in tone and Hughes' direction fails to insert any hardhitting action which might have lifted interest a notch. Pic takes its tag from a little monkey seen on the scene of a rash of murders of celebrated scientists by the Reds.

Rona Anderson co-stars with Conte for faint romantic interest and Russell Napier is the Scotland Yard superintendent assigned to safeguard the scientist, portrayed by Arnold Marle, both okay. Part of a British newshawk who learns what's going on and is a thorn in the side of the police is played fairly interestingly by Colin Gordon. Sylva Langova and John King-Kelley make the most of their Communist roles. Alec C. Snowden as producer gives picture certain scenic values via London backgrounds. *Whit.*

The Naked Street

Fair program melodrama for regulation playoff in dual market.

Hollywood, Aug. 12.

United Artists release of Edward Small production. Stars Farley Granger, Anthony Quinn, Anne Bancroft, Peter Graves; features Else Neft, Sara Berner, Jerry Paris, Mario Siletti. Directed by Maxwell Shane. Screenplay, Shane and Leo Katcher; from a story by Katcher; camera, Floyd Crosby; editor, Grant Whytock; music, Emil Newman. Previewed Aug. 10, '55. Running time, 83 MINS.

Nicky Bradna	Farley Granger
Phil Regal	Anthony Quinn
Rosalie Regalzyk	Anne Bancroft
Joe McFarland	Peter Graves
Mrs. Regalzyk	Else Neft
Latzi Franks	Jerry Paris
Nutsy	Frank Sully
Big Eddie	John Dennis
Janet	Angela Stevens
Margie	Joy Terry
Mr. Hough	G. Pat Collins
Antonio Cardini	Mario Siletti
Attorney Blaker	Whit Bissell
Evelyn Shriner	Jeanne Cooper
Millie	Sara Berner
Attorney Flanders	James Flavin
Judge Roder	Harry Harvey
Alex Campbell	Judge Stanley
Francie	Jackie Loughery
Ollie	Frank Kreig
Shimmy	Joe Turkel
Barricks	Harry O. Tyler
Lennie	Sammie Weiss

Satisfactory performances and a twist to the usual crime-doesn't-pay plot give "The Naked Street" a fair rating as program entertainment. Film does a workmanlike, if not particularly inspired, job of wrapping up its story and all loose ends in 3 minutes of footage, making it an acceptable meller for general playdates.

Helping to give substance to the characters involved are Farley Granger, Anthony Quinn, Anne Bancroft and Peter Graves, the principals involved in the Leo Katcher story, which he scripted with Maxwell Shane and which the latter directed. Plot has Quinn, racketeer, saving Granger, a cheap young hood, from the electric chair so the latter can marry the gangster's sister, Miss Bancroft, who's pregnant. When the baby dies and Granger turns out to be a bad husband, Quinn frames him for a new killing, so back to the chair he goes. Not, however, without exposing Quinn's operations to Graves, newspaperman. The baddies all get their just deserts and Graves gets Miss Bancroft.

Quinn and Miss Bancroft are both excellent in handling the characters assigned them. So is Graves, the reporter who does some bridging narration as the story unfolds. Granger, away from films for some time, turns in acceptable work in a role that calls for him to be hero-heavy without any sympathy to compensate. Among supporting parts, Else Neft as the mother of Quinn and Miss Bancroft, and Jerry Paris, as Granger's friend, do best.

Shane's direction of the Edward Small production keeps the pace moving fairly fast. Lensing, background score, and other technical factors are okay. *Brog.*

Value for Money
(British)
(COLOR—VISTAVISION)

North country comedy, okay for domestic market, but Yorkshire dialect may prove obstacle to extensive U. S. exhibition.

London, Aug. 9.

Rank VistaVision (Sergei Nolbandov) production and release. Stars John Gregson, Diana Dors, Susan Stephen, Derek Farr; features Frank Pettingell, Jill Adams. Directed by Ken Annakin. Screenplay, R. F. Delderfield and William Fairchild; camera (Technicolor), Geoffrey Unsworth; editor, Geoffrey Foot; music, Malcolm Arnold; "Toys for Boys" and "Dolly Polka" music, Jhn Pritchett. At Odeon, Leicester Square, London, Aug. 9, '55. Running time, 93 MINS.

Chayley Broadbent	John Gregson
Ruthine West	Diana Dors
Ethel	Susan Stephen
Duke Popplewell	Derek Farr
Higgins	Frank Pettingell
Joy	Jill Adams
Lumm	Charles Victor
Oldroyd	James Gregson
Limpy	Donald Pleasance
Mrs. Perkins	Joan Hickson

Mr. Hall	Hal Osmond
Mrs. Hall	Sheila Raynor
Mr. Gidbrook	Charles Lloyd Pack
Walter	Ferdy Mayne
Arkwright	John Glyn Jones
Robjohns	Leslie Phillips
Mrs. Matthews	Molly Weir
Lord Drewsbury	Ernest Thesiger

For its second production in VistaVision, the Rank Studios has chosen a north-country comedy, which will give considerable amusement to unsophisticated local audiences, but which may find it tough sledding in the Overseas territory. In the U. S., particularly, the Yorkshire dialect will not be a selling aid.

This is a modestly amusing piece, staged on a bigger scale than the story would seem to warrant, and offering a touch of spectacle in a couple of song and dance numbers. The plot revolves around John Gregson, who inherits his father's fortune, rag business and meannesses, and then has the misfortune to get involved with a blonde show girl (Diana Dors). He forgets the girl he left behind (Susan Stephen). Around this basic situation, the yarn moves from one preposterous situation to another until eventually honor is satisfied, and each of the girls ends up in a bridal gown.

As a running gimmick, the voice of Gregson's dead father is heard uttering words of caution to his son, particularly urging him to exercise stronger control of the purse strings. Although amusing at first, it is done too frequently and tends to become monotonous.

The two production numbers, arranged and danced by Paddy Stone and Irving Davis, are neatly dovetailed into the story line. They are nicely staged and each provide a pleasant contrast in background. Gregson, Miss Dors and Miss Stephen fill the three main roles more than adequately. Derek Farr shares starring honors with them as the character who ends up with the other girl. Frank Pettingell and Jill Adams lead a typically British supporting team. Ken Annakin has directed sympathetically and other technical qualities are up to regular standards. *Myro.*

Night Freight
Formula action-meller for lowercase dual-dating in the general situation.

Hollywood, Aug. 15.

Allied Artists release of Ace Herman (Wm. F. Broidy Pictures Corp.) production. Stars Forrest Tucker, Barbara Britton, Keith Larsen, Thomas Gomez; features Michael Ross, Myrna Dell, Lewis Martin, G. Pat Collins. Directed by Jean Yarbrough. Written by Steve Fisher; camera, William Sickner; editor, Chandler House; score, Edward J. Kay. Previewed Aug. 11, '55. Running time, 79 MINS.

Mike Peters	Forrest Tucker
Wanda	Barbara Britton
Don Peters	Keith Larsen
Haight	Thomas Gomez
Louie	Michael Ross
Sally	Myrna Dell
Crane	Lewis Martin
Kelly	G. Pat Collins
Gordon	Sam Flint
Engineer	Ralph Sanford
Disc Jockey	George Sanders
Bartender	Joe Kirk
First Newsman	Jim Alexander
Workman	Charles Fredericks
Fireman	Guy Rennie
Detective	Michael Dale

Formula action entertainment of lightweight values is strung together in this mild programmer. It will get by as filler material in the general dual situation. Stereotyped handling all down the line keeps it from qualifying as an okay entry in its lowercase class.

The Steve Fisher screen story deals with a feud between Forrest Tucker, operator of a shortline railroad, and Thomas Gomez, truck line owner who sees Tucker's railway putting him out of business. To further complicate matters, the plot stirs up bad blood between Tucker and his kid brother, Keith Larsen, through the medium of Barbara Britton, g.nmill B-girl for whom both the brothers yen.

A modicum of meller values are stirred up for the climax when the brothers join forces to save a munitions train which Gomez schemes to blow up. The heavy gets his and Tucker gets the girl, with Larsen's blessing.

Ace Herman's production makes repetitious use of train and track shots, as well as some other scenes that are not too well cut into the footage. There's little the players or director Jean Yarbrough can do with the script, which requires the principals to talk out, as well as act out, the plot action. The footage runs overtime at 79 minutes and the technical assist are standard for budget. *Brog.*

Maddalena
(ITALIAN-COLOR)

Stunning performance by Marta Toren in Italian village tale of uneven quality. Piety, bigotry and cruelty of the peasantry. Needs careful booking.

IFE release of Titanus Films Italo-French co-production. Stars Marta Toren. Features Gino Cervi, Charles Vanel, and Jacques Sernas. Directed by Augusto Genina. Screenplay, Genina, Alianello, Stefani and Prosperi; from the play "Servant of God" by Madeleine de Balavalla. Camera (Technicolor), Claude Renoir; music, Antonio Veretti. Previewed in N.Y. Aug. 10, '53. Running time, 90 MINS.

Maddalena	Marta Toren
Don Vincenzo	Gino Cervi
Giovanni Lamberti	Charles Vanel
Giovanni Belloni	Jacques Sernas
Farmer	Folco Lulli
Farmer's Daughter	Angiola Faranda

(Italian; English Titles)

The desire to produce a picture that will win popular appeal both in Italy and the U. S. often results in product with the stamp of compromise on it. "Maddalena," IFE's latest import with English-language subtitles, is in that category.

It has many of the qualities of the pictures produced during the Italian industry's great post-war comeback. However, it deteriorates into a soap operaish tearjerker that far outweighs its many good points. It's a polished, well-produced Titanus production, heightened by excellent Technicolor lensing. Nonetheless, its story deficiencies mark it only as a moderate art house entry.

On the credit side is an excellent portrayal of backward villagers, their devotion to the church, their bigoted resentment of outsiders,

their petty jealousies, their willingness to accept miracles, and their susceptibility to mass crowd hysteria. Director Augusto Genina has done a remarkable job in capturing on film the natives of an Italian mountain village. It's hard to believe that many of the types that come within camera range are not professional actors. As a study of an Italian village, "Maddalena" rates highly, but the flashback story of the motivations of a prostie detracts from an almost sociological probe of unenlightened townspeople.

The film opens with an interesting premise. A local bigwig who feels that the priest has overshadowed him as the town's leader decides to show up the clergyman. An annual village event is a Good Friday pageant in which a local beauty portrays the Virgin Mary. The local beauty who has had the honor for many years is ineligible because of pregnancy. Confusion reigns as the parishoners refuse to agree on a new choice, each pushing his own daughter. Fed up with the bickering, the priest decides to seek an outsider for the role. This gives the bigwig an opportunity to sneak in a prostitute for the part.

Although the villagers are unaware of the girl's background, they resent the intruder, displaying open hostility to the girl and registering their protests with the priest. The priest, however, is adamant. She remains to play the role. She wins the town's acceptance when it is thought that she is involved in a miracle relating to the recovery of a boy given up for dead. At this point, the villagers refuse to let her leave although she is tortured by the deception.

She breaks down and confesses to the priest. She undertook the assignment, she explains, because of a desire to mock the Madonna who she blames for the death of her child. Circumstances make it necessary for her to continue her pageant role. At the last moment, she is denounced by the bigwig. The townspeople turn again. They become an angry mob, eventually stoning her to death.

Marta Toren, an exceptional good looker, has a tour de force as the prostie and turns in a top performance. Gino Cervi, as the priest, Charles Vanel, as the lecherous bigwig, and Jacques Sernas, as a love-sick admirer, are convincing in their roles, with Cervi's thesping rating a special nod.

Film has exploitable possibilities for theatres which want to play up the sex angle. There are numerous scantily clad gals around in many scenes devoted to the prostitute's place of employment. *Holl.*

Foreign Films

Paris, Aug. 9.
La Castiglione (FRANCO-ITALIAN; COLOR). Warner Bros. release of Radius-Taurus production. Stars Yvonne De Carlo, Georges Marchal, Rossano Brazzi, Paul Meurisse, Lea Padovani; features Claude Boissol, Lucienne Legrand, Lisette Lebon, Tamara Lees. Directed by Georges Combret. Screenplay, Combret, Claude Boissol, Pierre Maudru; camera (Eastmancolor), Pierre Petit; editor, Germaine Fouquet. At Marignon, Paris. Running time, 90 MINS.

Stinting production values show up to make this costumer of the Napoleon III era lacking in big appeal visually. Meandering story, lacklustre direction and uneven thesping are also a detriment towards making this of much value locally. For the U.S., the only possibility is for secondary billing on the Yvonne De Carlo and Rossano Brazzi names. Otherwise this drearily told tale will militate against any real bookings.

This was held back from distrib over a year here, and is now making the summer circuit. Detailing the attempts of 19th Century Italy to unite, this is about the beauteous La Castiglione whose appeal to Napoleon is used to help save her revolutionary lover who is killed anyway.

Miss De Carlo looks out of place in court and is called upon to portray a winsome lass which is not her forte. Georges Marchal is uneven and Brazzi manages to etch some character into that of the wily Italian statesman Cavour. Color appears uneven and washed out. Sets obviously are low grade and direction is too sedentary. *Mosk.*

Berlin, Aug. 9.
The Doll Merchant (FINNISH). Oy Suomen Filmiteollisuus (SF) production and release. Stars Meriti Krtajisto and Hillevi Lagerstam; features Heikki Savolainen and Leena Kaprio. Directed by Jack Witikka. Screenplay, Walentin Chorell; camera, Marius Raichi; editor, Aarro Koivisto. At Film Buhne Wien, Berlin. Running time, 75 MINS.

Finland, with its modest resources, deserves credit for turning out this offbeat pic. It has a refreshing charm, lively treatment and an unusual theme. If well dubbed, it should merit a place in American and British arty houses.

The theme, which satirizes dictatorships, has been developed with a fine sense of restrained humor; action takes precedence over dialog and the principal players respond to the sensitive touch of the director. It's a simple yarn of a rather pathetic doll peddler who is suspected of being an anarchist. Flung into jail, he eventually is freed by a revolt of all the children in the city. Alongside the main story line, runs a gentle little romance between the peddler and the mistress of the dictator, a lush blond with a passion for dolls.

Film has okay technical qualities, but would benefit by slight scissoring in western territories. *Myro.*

The Left Hand of God
(C'SCOPE—COLOR)

Strong b.o. entry for general market; Humphrey Bogart-Gene Tierney as marquee lures.

20th-Fox release of Buddy Adler production. Stars Humphrey Bogart, Gene Tierney, Lee J. Cobb; features Agnes Moorehead, E. G. Marshall, Jean Porter, Carl Benton Reid, Victor Sen Yung, Philip Ahn, Benson Fong. Directed by Edward Dmytryk. Screenplay, Alfred Hayes, based on novel by William E. Barrett; camera (De Luxe Color), Franz Planer; editor, Dorothy Spencer; music, Victor Young. Previewed in N.Y. Aug. 19, '55. Running time, 87 MINS.

Jim Carmody	Humphrey Bogart
Ann Scott	Gene Tierney
Mieh Yang	Lee J. Cobb
Beryl Sigman	Agnes Moorehead
Dr. Sigman	E. G. Marshall
Mary Yin	Jean Porter
Rev. Cornelius	Carl Benton Reid
John Wong	Victor Sen Yung
Jan Teng	Philip Ahn
Chun Tien	Benson Fong
Father O'Shea	Richard Cutting
Pao-Ching	Leon Lentok
Father Keller	Don Forbes
Woman in Sarong	Noel Toy
Feng-Merchant	Peter Chong
Woman in Kimona	Marie Tsien
The Boy	Stephen Wong
Celeste	Sophie Chin
Li Kwan	George Chan
Orderly	Walter Soo Hoo
Orderly	Henry S. Quan
Nurse	Doris Chung
Old Man	Moy Ming
Mi Lu	Georgee Lee
Father	Beal Wong
Pao Chu	Stella Lynn
Rev. Marvin	Robert Burton
Midwife	Soo Yong

20th-Fox, which has made notable excursions into the field of religion with such pictures as "A Man Called Peter," again taps that story material fount with "The Left Hand of God." With a cast topped by Humphrey Bogart, Gene Tierney and Lee J. Cobb, this opulent production is headed for solid boxoffice in the general market.

Based on the novel by William E. Barrett and screenplayed by Alfred Hayes, the film is somewhat provocative, in that its central character is a man who masquerades as a priest. Carrying on this deception is Yank flier Bogart, who believes it to be the sole way he can escape as prisoner of Chinese warlord Cobb.

What transpires in a remote Chinese province after Bogart dons the ecclesiastical robes in 1947 largely adds up to character studies of the fake priest and his immediate colleagues at a Catholic mission, where all are stationed. For the drama and suspense aren't to be found in whether the flier escapes from China but in the soul-searching he subjects himself in continuing the masquerade.

Besides Bogart, others who have their own mental conflicts are Gene Tierney, a nurse searching for her husband lost in the war and believed dead; E. G. Marshall, a doctor who fears for the safety of the mission's staff in light of menacing gestures of warlord Cobb, and Agnes Moorehead, the physician's wife whose shrewdness in appraising the true thoughts of her associates appears to have been sharpened by her long stay at the lonely mission.

Not only does Bogart wrestle with the problem of how to avoid carrying out functions of a priest, such as hearing confessions, but he's also faced with tactfully resisting the obvious romantic interests of Miss Tierney. But on the whole he endears himself to the villagers, especially in vanquishing Cobb via a parley when the latter is bent upon laying waste the town and mission.

To sticklers of logic and realism, there are a number of scenes and incidents that strain the imagination. Particularly the tense sequence in which Bogart actually wins the village's freedom by casting dice with Cobb. As a gesture, the warlord announces publicly that he's been converted to Catholicism and is sparing the village as a modern miracle.

Entire picture has been given top-budget values by producer Buddy Adler. Notable of these are the physical backgrounds, such as the Chinese village set, the native vistas, costumes and general Oriental atmosphere. Use of many Chinese extras gives an authentic touch and a group of native children is outstanding in a community sing at the mission.

While at first glance it's difficult to picture Bogart as a priest, his smooth portrayal of a spurious man-of-the-cloth is a compliment to his acting. Nature of Miss Tierney's role somewhat dampens her glamor, but she's honest and sincere in eventually winning Bogart. Cobb scores handily as the cruel, bitingly arrogant Chinese general.

With director Edward Dmytryk's sure hand to guide them, Marshall contributes a fine characterization of the doctor who struggles with his multifold problems. Miss Moorehead registers nicely as his spouse, and Carl Benton Reid is forceful as a bonafide priest who is sent by a bishop to investigate the circumstances of Bogart's sacrilege.

Among others in the long cast who provide firm support are Jean Porter, as a Chinese concubine; Victor Sen Yung as Bogart's general helper at the mission; Philip Ahn, Richard Cutting and Robert Burton. CinemaScope lensing of Franz Planer, who photographed the film in De Luxe Color, is topnotch, as are Victor Young's music, Dorothy Spencer's editing and art direction of Lyle R. Wheeler and Maurice Ransford. Other technical credits measure up. *Gilb.*

It's Always Fair Weather
(C'SCOPE—MUSICAL—COLOR)

Topnotch musical satire of television, advertising agencies, and commercials. Sock entertainment value for family trade with excellent b.o. outlook.

Metro release of Arthur Freed production. Stars Gene Kelly, Dan Dailey, Cyd Charisse, Dolores Gray, Michael Kidd; features David Burns, Jay C. Flippen. Screenplay, Betty Comden & Adolph Green; camera (color by Eastman), Robert Bronner; editor, Adrienne Fazan; dances, Kelly & Donen; music, Andre Previn; lyrics, Comden and Green. Tradeshown in N.Y., Aug. 11, '55. Running time, 102 MINS.

Ted Riley	Gene Kelly
Doug Hallerton	Dan Dailey
Jackie Leighton	Cyd Charisse
Madeline Bradville	Dolores Gray
Angie Valentine	Michael Kidd
Tim	David Burns
Charles Z. Culloran	Jay C. Flippen

The film companies may be embracing television, but you wouldn't know it from Metro's sparkling spoof of the medium in "It's Always Fair Weather." For good measure, the Arthur Freed production also takes on advertising agencies and tv commercials, and what emerges is a delightful musical satire that should help empty living rooms and fill up theatres. The entertainment values are enhanced by a group of friendly performers, including Gene Kelly, Dan Dailey, Cyd Charisse, Lelores Gray, David Burns, and Michael Kidd. And Kelly and Stanley Domen, who share the directorial chores, give the proceedings the right tongue-in-cheek touch for sock results.

Betty Comden and Adolph Green, vet scripters of both Broadway and film tuners, have provided a number of hilarious sketches that fit neatly into the framework of the story. Like most musicals, the overall yarn is inconsequential. It is the individual production numbers and whacky bits that carry the bite in running down the film industry's great competitor.

Miss Comden and Green present Kelly, Dailey, and Kidd as a trio of former GI buddies who meet 10 years after World War II. Somehow the warm friendship that existed during the war years has deteriorated into a sour reunion as different interests has driven the buddies apart.

Kelly, bitter about a busted romance, is a cynical fight manager; Dailey has given up a promising art career to become a stuffy, ulcer-ridden advertising executive, and Kidd's dreams of becoming a famous chef end at a hambuger stand. Their luncheon at a swank restaurant, with the CinemaScope camera condensing to focus on each of the three separately to register each one's thoughts about the others, is one of the highlights of the film.

Through the efforts of Miss Charisse, coordinator of "Midnight With Madeline," femceed by Miss Gray, the three former friends unwittingly find themselves on a program similar to "This Is Your Life." It is at this point that the darts are sharpest. It's one of the funniest bits in recent films. Miss Gray, as the temperamental, syrupy hostess, registers excellently in appearance, emoting, and warbling. Kidd, better known as a choreographer, emerges as a seasoned musicomedy performer.

Kelly, Dailey and Kidd score in group routines and Kelly and Dailey have a field day in solo outings. Kelly's roller skating routine and Dailey's drunk act at a chi-chi party are standouts. A Stillman's gym production number involving assorted busted beak characters singing the pug's alma mater is a laugh riot. Miss Charisse, as lovely as ever, has only one terp routine, but she carries it off to perfection in the company of the Stillman's gym crowd. David Burns, as a Third Ave. bartender, also comes off fine.

At first hearing, Andre Previn's music doesn't appear of "Hit Parade" calibre, but in combination with the Comden and Green lyrics, it is geared perfectly for integration into the film. The picture has one objective—to provide entertainment, and it accomplishes its purpose admirably. Technical aspects are all first-rate. *Holl.*

Footsteps In the Fog
(C'SCOPE—COLOR)

Stewart Granger, Jean Simmons in a limp melodrama. Could stand up for single dating in the smaller situations.

Columbia release of M. J. Frankovich-Maxwell Setton production. Stars Stewart Granger, Jean Simmons; features Bill Travers, Finlay Currie, Ronald Squire, Belinda Lee, William Hartnell. Directed by Arthur Lubin. Screenplay, Dorothy Reid and Lenore Coffee; camera (Technicolor), Christopher Challis; editor, Alan Osbiston; music, Benjamin Frankel. Previewed in N. Y. Aug. 19, '55. Running time, 90 MINS.

Stephen Lowry	Stewart Granger
Lily Watkins	Jean Simmons
David Macdonald	Bill Travers
Inspector Peters	Finlay Currie
Alfred Travers	Ronald Squire
Elizabeth Travers	Belinda Lee
Herbert Moresby	William Hartnell
Dr. Simpson	Frederick Leister
Magistrate	Percy Marmont
Mrs. Park	Margery Rhodes
Brasher	Peter Bull
Constable Burke	Barry Keegan
Rose Moresby	Sheila Manahan
Grimes	Norman Macowan
Corcoran	Cameron Hall
Jones	Victor Maddern
Constable Farrow	Peter Williams
Vicar	Arthur Howard

Considering how much producers M. J. Frankovich and Maxwell Setton put into "Footsteps in the Fog"—color, CinemaScope and the romantic team of Stewart Granger and Jean Simmons (Mr. & Mrs. in real life)—it's surprising and somewhat disconcerting how little they managed to get out of it. Film is a humdrum, rarely exciting melodrama about a gentleman-murderer and a blackmailing maid who falls in love with him.

From the exhibitors' point of view, this made-in-Britain item should have a certain name merit, since both Granger and Miss Simmons have appeared in a good many American films. Their being together in "Footsteps" also may be an exploitable angle. Certainly, their screen teaming hasn't in any way improved their acting. Miss Simmons does have charm and looks as beautiful as ever. But Granger just walks through what is essentially an unexciting part anyway. There is a bit of heavy mugging at the end, but on the whole he just concentrates on looking evil and elegant.

Screenplay, concocted by Dorothy Reid and Lenore Coffee, is routine in every respect. Not even the dialog—and there is plenty of it—shows any attempt at originality. It's curious to think that the British, when making the same kind of films on their own, usually manage to come up with good, solid thriller fare; each character is etched out sharply and contributes importantly. Now Columbia's Frankovich comes along, with the same general story, also made in Britain, and it misses.

Rambling story tells about Stewart, who has poisoned his wife and is blackmailed by a maid who eventually becomes his housekeeper. He tries to murder her, too, but kills the wrong woman in the fog. Her false testimony wins him an acquittal in the trial. In the end, in one of his fantastic schemes, Granger poisons himself and the truth comes out.

Supporting cast goes through its paces in somewhat uninspired fashion. Bill Travers is handsome and nothing more as the fellow who loves the girl (Belinda Lee) whom Granger wants to marry but can't as long as Miss Simmons is around. Finlay Currie is okay as the inspector and Ronald Squire contributes an amusing bit as Miss Lee's stuffy father.

Arthur Lubin's direction shows some imaginative touches, but doesn't try too hard to overcome the natural obstacles put into his way by the script. At the least, the climax could have had more punch. And the way Lubin used CinemaScope, he might as well have worked on a standard-size screen.

Music composed and conducted by Benjamin Frankel has an appealing and fitting quality that goes with the turn-of-the-century atmosphere of the film. Alan Osbiston's editing is okay. Color by Technicolor is very good in what are mostly interior settings. *Hift.*

The Bar Sinister
(C'SCOPE—COLOR)

Fine dog story for family trade; less b.o. prospects in other markets.

Metro release of Henry Berman production. Features Jeff Richards, Jarma Lewis, Edmund Gwenn, Dean Jagger. Directed by Herman Hoffman. Screenplay, John Michael Hayes, from story by Richard Harding Davis; camera (Eastman Color), Paul C. Vogel; editor, John Dunning; music, Elmer Bernstein. Previewed in N.Y. Aug. 17, '55. Running time, 88 MINS.

Patch McGill	Jeff Richards
Mabel Maycroft	Jarma Lewis
Jeremiah Nolan	Edmund Gwenn
Mr. Wyndham	Dean Jagger
Tom Tattle	Willard Sage
Dorothy Wyndham	Sally Fraser
George Oakley	Richard Anderson
Paddy Corbin	J. M. Kerrigan

"The Bar Sinister," a whimsical tale of a bull terrier of uncertain parentage who rises from the Bowery to blue ribbons, adds up to good entertainment for the family trade. Situations, such as drive-ins, which rely considerably upon that market, will find this Henry Berman production a comfortable grosser. In most other spots, however, it will rate only as a de luxe programmer.

Hayes' script and Berman's production not only capture the saga of a dog but also faithfully recreate the nostalgic flavor and lusty atmosphere of the turn-of-the-century era in which the yarn takes place. In this gas-lit setting, Wildfire (the dog) takes on all canine comers in J. M. Kerrigan's Bowery saloon for his master, Jeff Richards, who's "adopted" him off the streets.

But when Richards abandons him, Wildfire is taken in by Edmund Gwenn, a groom upon the estate of crotchety Dean Jagger. Of course, there are hazards in this sudden life of luxury and they're surmounted by the pooch as they develop. For a touching finale the terrier not only wins the esteem of Jagger, who originally disliked him, but has a reconciliation with his father (a champion prize winner) whom he had sworn to kill for deserting his mother.

Under Herman Hoffman's knowing direction, the difficult story material comes off as believable and realistic. Wildfire, who relates his varied experiences in the first person, handles his role to perfection while Richards is well cast as a youthful saloon hanger-on with an aversion to work and an eye for fast women. Tops on his list is Jarma Lewis, a cafe entertainer, whose alluring figure nicely sets off yesteryear's femme fashions.

Gwenn turns in a thesping gem as the groom whose loyalty to the dog he's befriended almost costs him his job. Willard Sage makes himself suitably unpleasant as a groom who has it in for Wildfire. Sally Fraser, Jagger's daughter, is pert and attractive. Others who acquit themselves favorably are Richard Anderson, a dog judge and Miss Fraser's beau, and Kerrigan as the saloonkeeper.

Particularly noteworthy are the overall production values that have been excellently lensed in CinemaScope and Eastman Color by Paul C. Vogel. Art direction of Cedric Gibbons and Daniel B. Cathcart is an asset as are the set decorations of Edwin B. Willis and Keogh Gleason. The Elmer Bernstein score adds to the nostalgic touches, while John Dunning edited to a breezy 88 minutes. *Gilb.*

The Teckman Mystery
(BRITISH)

Average British whodunit; okay for art houses.

Associated Artists Productions release of Joseph Somlo production. Stars Margaret Leighton, John Justin. Directed by Wendy Toye. Screenplay, Francis Durbridge, James Matthews, from original story by Durbridge; camera, Jack Hildyard; editor, Albert Rule. Tradeshown in N.Y., Aug. 18, '55. Running time, 90 MINS.

Helen	Margaret Leighton
Philip	John Justin
John Rice	Meier Tzelniker
Martin Teckman	Michael Medwin
Harris	Roland Culver
Gavin	George Coulouris
Ruth	Jane Wenham
Hilton	Duncan Lamont
Miller	Raymond Huntley
Leonard	Harry Locke
Eileen Miller	Frances Rowe
Sergeant Blair	Warwick Ashton

This innocuous little British meller will have to find most of its American playdates in small art theatres. Francis Durbridge, who did the original story, also helped on the screenplay with James Matthews, which probably accounts for the plot sagging near the end. It's only in the final few reels that producer Josef Somlo and director Wendy Toye have the yarn rolling along in best British melodramatic tradition. Prior to Scotland Yard really swinging into action, the mystery is so baffling that the audience is only confused. Often it does not care what happened to Martin Teckman (Michael Medwin), an airplane test pilot, who is supposed to have crashed while testing out a new F-109.

Scripters have injected a successful author (John Justin) into the plot, since he has been commissioned to write a biography of Teckman. He meets Teckman's sister (Margaret Leighton) and falls for her. Then things start happening to him. His apartment is ransacked and wrecked. Teckman's co-worker, who helped design the fatal plane, is murdered, and a mysterious Mr. Rice (Meier Tzelniker) tries to bribe Justin to go to Berlin. Then Rice is slain.

When the Scotland Yard inspector (Duncan Lamont) and his superior, Roland Culver, decide to take drastic steps, the whole mystery is solved. The supposedly dead test pilot turns up alive just when the international gang wants him dead, and the romance between Miss Leighton and Justin comes to a strange end.

Justin suffices as the author turned amateur sleuth while Miss Leighton often appears fetching, at other times too highly dramatic. The missing Teckman is nicely played by Medwin, if only for two or three late sequences. Tzelniker proves sufficiently villainous and scheming to satisfy British melodrama addicts. Culver does an excellent job as the major, attached to a special division of Scotland Yard, while Lamont is okay as the inspector. Jane Wenham does well enough in a lesser supporting role.

Wendy Toye directed with more skill than would be expected from this screenplay and original story. Jack Hildyard's photography is standard. *Wear.*

Der Pfarrer Von Kirchfeld
(The Parson of Kirchfeld)
(GERMAN)

Frankfurt, Aug. 16.

Constantin release of HD production. Stars Ulla Jacobsson and Claus Holm. Directed by Hans Deppe. Screenplay, Ilse Lotz-Dupont and Tibor Yost after folk play of name title by Ludwig Anzengruber; camera (Eastmancolor), Willy Winterstein; music, Heinrich Riethmueller. At Alemannia Theatre, Frankfurt. Running time, 94 MINS.

The Pfarrer	Claus Holm
Anna Birkmaier	Ulla Jacobsson
Michl	Kurt Heintel
Brigitte	Annie Rosar
Sepp	Heinrich Gretler
Zenzl	Helen Vita
Frau Stricker	Hansi Knoteck
Franz	Fritz Genschow

This film, in standout color, is the old German folk play whose plot is known by other names in other lands—the story of the minister torn between love of a woman and love of God. In this modern version of the old meller, Ilse Lotz-Dupont and Tibor Yost have worked loosely with the original German plot, to base the story in a particularly scenic part of Bavaria. They also toned down the melodramatic overtones in producing a believable contemporary drama. It may do for some American arty theatres.

The picture was first made 25 years ago, but this new version is modernized and improved. It is in for some local competition because an Austrian producer is filming the same play, but titled "Das Maedchen von Pfarrhof" (The Girl From Pfarrhof), adhering much more closely to the original legiter. It is due for release at a slightly later date, similarity being considered somewhat of a handicap in booking either one.

Ulla Jacobsson plays the girl who comes to work for the parson of Kirchfeld (Claus Holm) because she has a young illegitimate son living in the nearby town. She and the minister are compromised when they attend a concert at the other town and miss the last train home. Inevitably, the minister renounces his love, and performs the marriage uniting her with the village blacksmith, Kurt Heintel. Despite the melodramatic theme and the heavy bid for emotional tugs throughout, the pic comes through as an entertaining production.

The Eastmancolor gives splendid treatment to the charm of the tiny Bavarian town and captures the colorful highlights of the church ceremonies and the picturesque village wedding. And the parson, brought up to date, becomes a believable creature as he tips an occasional mug of beer or bowls with the boys.

The film just won two awards at the San Sebastian Festival, with Ulla Jacobsson being selected as the best actress and Constantin winning an award for releasing the film. Willy Winterstein deserves special plaudits for his color camera work. The direction of Hans Deppe is standout in underplaying an otherwise heavy plot. Music by the Berlin Philharmonic Orchestra is a big plus factor.

In the heavily Catholic countries of West Germany, pic is sure to be a solid booker. As an art house piece because of the colorful portrayal of life in Bavaria and its fine acting, it could do U.S. business. *Haze.*

Illegal

Run-of-the-mill courtroom meller for programmer bookings.

Hollywood, Aug. 20.

Warner Bros. release of Frank P. Rosenberg production. Stars Edward G. Robinson; costars Nina Foch, Hugh Marlowe, Jayne Mansfield; features Albert Dekker, Howard St. John, Ellen Corby, Edward Platt, Jan Merlin. Directed by Lewis Allen. Screenplay, W. R. Burnett, James R. Webb; from a story by Frank J. Collins; camera, J. Peverell Marley; editor, Thomas Reilly; music, Max Steiner. Running time, 87 MINS.

Victor Scott	Edward G. Robinson
Ellen Miles	Nina Foch
Ray Borden	Hugh Marlowe
Angel O'Hara	Jayne Mansfield
Frank Garland	Albert Dekker
E. A. Smith	Howard St. John
Miss Hinkel	Ellen Corby
Ralph Ford	Edward Platt
Andy Garth	Jan Merlin
Joe Knight	Robert Ellenstein
Joseph Carter	Jay Adler
Taylor	Henry Kulky
Allen Parker	James McCallion
Steve Harper	Addison Richards
Al Carol	Lawrence Dobkin
Clary	DeForest Kelly
George Graves	Clark Howat
Phillips	Stuart Nedd

The courtroom melodramatics in "Illegal" seem rather dated and well-used, so there's little to this Warner Bros. release beyond its classification as a programmer. Name of Edward G. Robinson should provide some help, but in general this is lacklustre entertainment.

Original story is credited to Frank J. Collins, with screenplay by W. R. Burnett and James R. Webb, but there is not enough newness or freshness to the material to keep the dramatics from reminding of similiar features. Result is an oldfashioned look, abetted by routine settings and photography.

Robinson plays a district attorney who breaks up after sending the wrong man to the chair. After a session with the bottle, he sobers up and becomes a mouthpiece for a crime syndicate. His courtroom antics include slugging a complaining witness who says a little man can't knock him out, and at another time drinking the poison being used as evidence in a murder case to get his client off before rushing for stomach pump.

There's not much Robinson can do to make his character real and Lewis Allen's direction is slow in veering from comedy to drama. Latter indecision is one of the more readily apparent flaws in the Frank P. Rosenberg presentation. Picture never seems to decide whether it should play itself for straight melodramatics or for hokum laughs. Nina Foch, Hugh Marlowe, Jayne Mansfield, Albert Dekker and the others also suffer from the general indecision. Even the climactic scene when Robinson, fatally wounded, manages to save Miss Foch from the charge of murdering her husband, Marlowe, lacks conviction.

The overall technical contributions are no more than stock. *Brog.*

The Deep Blue Sea
(BRITISH-C'SCOPE-COLOR)

London, Aug. 23.

20th-Fox release of a London Film (Anatole Litvak) production. Stars Vivien Leigh, Kenneth More, Eric Portman, Emlyn Williams; features Moira Lister, Arthur Hill, Dandy Nichols, Jimmy Hanley, Miriam Karlin. Directed by Anatole Litvak. Screenplay by Terence Rattigan from his stageplay; camera, Jack Hildyard; editor, A. S. Bates; music, Malcolm Arnold; "Deep Blue Sea" by Francis Chagrin and Roy Bradford. At Carlton.

London, Aug. 23, '55. Running time, **99 MINS.**

Hester	Vivien Leigh
Freddie Page	Kenneth More
Miller	Eric Portman
Sir William Collyer	Emlyn Williams
Dawn Maxwell	Moira Lister
Jackie Jackson	Arthur Hill
Mrs. Elton	Dandy Nichols
Dicer Durston	Jimmy Hanley
Barmaid	Miriam Karlin
Lady Dawson	Heather Thatcher
Golfer	Bill Shine
Drunk	Brian Oulton
Man in Street	Sidney James
Ken Thompson	Tlec McCowen
Collyer's Clerk	Gibb McLaughlin

A legit hit on either side of the Atlantic, "The Deep Blue Sea" is brought to the screen in slightly embellished form, but Terence Rattigan, who has written the script from his own play, has not altered the plot in any of its essentials.

It remains, therefore, a high-grade dramatic entertainment which should do best in class situations. It may encounter spotty results in run-of-mill theatres.

Produced and directed by Anatole Litvak, with a top drawer British cast, the Rattigan play is an intelligent commentary on human emotions. The dialog sustains a high, even quality and the author makes few concessions to convention. The impeccable acting by the four principals is a highlight of the production.

Although the basic plot calls for exceptional use of interiors, Litvak has employed his CinemaScope cameras to advantage, introducing fascinating shots of the embankment and Soho, as well as an exciting sequence from an air display plus some colorful scenes of winter sports. The overall effect is to achieve a healthy balance and to relieve the main dramatic tension.

As the story opens, Vivien Leigh is frustrated in a suicide attempt. She's the former wife of a judge who left him for a young, gay and irresponsible test pilot. But his irresponsibility gets the better of her emotions and she attempts to end her life. The realization that their association has been a failure leads him firstly to take liquor to excess and then to resolve to end it all, ignoring her please to try again.

The plot emphasizes the conflicting emotions and the contrasting interpretations of love and loyalty, giving superb opportunities both to Miss Leigh and Kenneth More. The former, in the role originally created by Peggy Ashcroft in the West End, rises to emotional and dramatic heights. It is a faultless, prize-winning portrayal. More, repeating his stage role, has never done better. His is a thoroughly believable performance, rich, warm and sympathetic. Emlyn Williams makes a distinguished showing as the judge, who would happily give his ex-wife a second chance, and Eric Portman contributes a flawless portrayal as the ex-doctor in the apartment upstairs, who offers medical help as well as sound advice.

A fascinating cameo is contributed by Moira Lister as an interfering floozy in an adjoining flat. Arthur Hill, Dandy Nichols, Jimmy Hanley and Miriam Karlin lead a fine cast of supporting players. Technical credits reach the expected standard. *Myro.*

Lay That Rifle Down
(SONGS)

Lightweight Judy Canova starrer for the duals.

Republic production and release (associate producer, Sidney Picker). Stars Judy Canova; features Robert Lowery, Jil Jarmyn, Jacqueline de Wit, Tweeny Canova. Directed by Charles Lamont. Screenplay, Barry Shipman; camera, John L. Russell Jr.; editor, Arthur E. Roberts; songs, Donald Kahn, Jack Elliott; music, R. Dale Butts. Previewed in N.Y., Aug. 25, '55. Running time, **71 MINS.**

Judy	Judy Canova
Nick Stokes	Robert Lowery
Betty	Jil Jarmyn
Aunt Sarah	Jacqueline de Wit
Glover Speckleton	Richard Deacon
Professor	Robert Burton
Mr. Fetcher	James Bell
Horace Speckleton	Leon Tyler
Tweeny	Tweeny Canova

"Lay That Rifle Down," Judy Canova's latest starrer for Republic, is an unpretentious comedy whose b.o. prospects will be confined to the duals. Rustic humor and bucolic touches for which she's noted may help biz in the hinterland. But on the whole, this is a weak entry with meagre exploitational assets and scant marquee appeal.

The Barry Shipman screenplay represents little improvement over previous Canova vehicles, because the same stock situations, characters and format are again utilized for mediocre results. This time the star is seen as a girl-of-all-work at a tanktown hotel run by an avaricious aunt. Aside from her multitudinous chores, she finds time to take a correspondence school "charm" course which develops into the obvious possibilities.

Indirectly, the course brings confidence men Robert Lowery and Robert Burton on the scene. They proceed to swindle bank president Richard Deacon and the aunt, Jacqueline de Wit, with Miss Canova being used as a foil. Before the plot is exposed and the culprits nabbed, the footage unreels generous slices of slapstick and sentiment that ultimately culminate in Judy handed a fortune for oil rights on the old homestead.

Miss Canova, with a vehicle tailor-made to her talents, handles the material in her own inimitable style. Robert Lowery is suitably dashing as one of the con men who does a last-minute balk at fleecing Miss Canova. Miss de Wit as the greedy aunt does as best she can with the limited opportunities presented by the script, and under similar handicaps are Jil Jarmyn as her daughter, as well as Burton, Deacon and Tweeny Canova.

Director Charles Lamont stressed the humor whenever possible and associate producer Sidney Picker provided the film with standard physical values. Camerawork of John L. Russell Jr. is good and Arthur E. Roberts edited to a slow 71 minutes. Songsmiths Donald Kahn and Jack Elliott cleffed three fairish tunes ("I'm Glad I Was Born on My Birthday," "Sleepy Serenade" and "The Continental Correspondence Charm School") which Miss Canova warbles with a country beat. Score of R. Dale Butts is par for the course. *Gilb.*

Kiss of Fire
(COLOR)

Weak entry for the action market, with Jack Palance as marquee lure.

Hollywood, Aug. 26.
U-I release of Samuel Marx production. Stars Jack Palance, Barbara Rush, Rex Reason, Martha Hyer; features Leslie Bradley, Alan Reed, Lawrence Dobkin. Directed by Joseph M. Newman. Screenplay, Franklin Coen, Richard Collins, based on novel, "The Rose and the

Flame," by Jonreed Lauritzen; camera (Technicolor), Carl Guthrie; editor, Arthur H. Nadel; musical supervision, Joseph Gershenson. Previewed Aug. 23, '55. Running time, **89 MINS.**

El Tigre	Jack Palance
Princess Lucia	Barbara Rush
Duke of Montera	Rex Reason
Felicia	Martha Hyer
Vega	Leslie Bradley
Diego	Alan Reed
Padre Domingo	Lawrence Dobkin
Victor	Joseph Waring
Pahvant	Pat Hogan
Shining Moon	Karen Kadler
Ship Captain	Steven Geray
Acosta	Henry Rowland

A poorly-motivated story that at times becomes completely unbelievable, "Kiss of Fire" is a combination of period swashbuckler and western. It gets off to a promising start, but the promise is never realized, soon bogging down into a plodder that fails to keep the interest. Characters are poorly delineated, with no explanations offered as to how they got into their situations.

The Franklin Coen and Richard Collins screenplay is based on Jonreed Lauritzen's novel, "The Rose and the Flame," purportedly having something to do with the scramble for the throne of Spain after word gets out that Charles V is dying. The heir apparent is Barbara Rush, who seems to be in demand by all of Spain. But for some unexplained reason she is living in Santa Fe, N.M., her problem being to get back to Spain in a hurry so she can be crowned queen before any of the many pretenders to the throne grab the job first.

So Jack Palance, an ex-nobleman of Spain known throughout the west as El Tigre, is engaged to lead the royal party from Santa Fe to Monterey where a ship is waiting.

From here on the film becomes a tired western dealing with the trek toward the ocean, with Spanish conspirators and local redskins doing their best to exterminate the party. As expected, they reach the ship but by that time the rattling influence of love has gotten in its work and the princess renounces the throne and the Old World for Palance and the freedom of the New World.

Palance is thoroughly wasted in a role that calls for little more than posturing and some rough-and-tumble action. Story suffers because nothing is ever revealed about El Tigre's true identity, although there are veiled hints about a colorful past. Miss Rush decorates the film, which is about all she gets a chance to do. Ditto for Martha Hyer.

Rex Reason shows good leading man possibilities despite an ambiguous role that has him a sympathetic character up until the last few minutes, when he suddenly turns heavy. Leslie Bradley, Alan Reed and Lawrence Dobkin give okay support.

Joseph M. Newman megs the Samuel Marx production in routine style. Carl Guthrie's Technicolor lensing is one of the bright spots of the film. Settings by Alexander Golitzen and Robert Boyle and the editing by Arthur H. Nadel get an okay rating. Costumes by Jay A. Morley Jr. are attractive.

Devil Goddess

Low-calibre adventure yarn with Johnny Weissmuller for the marquee; for the juve trade.

Columbia release of Sam Katzman production. Stars Johnny Weissmuller; features Angela Stevens, Selmer Jackson, William Tannen, Ed Hinton, William M. Griffith. Directed by Spencer G. Bennet. Screenplay, George Plympton, from a story by Dwight Babcock; camera, Ira Morgan; music, Mischa Bakaleinikoff. Previewed in N.P. Aug. 25, '55. Running time, **70 MINS.**

Johnny Weissmuller	Himself
Nora Blakely	Angela Stevens
Prof. Carl Blakely	Selmer Jackson
Nels Comstock	William Tannen
Joseph Leopold	Ed Hinton
Ralph Dixon	William M. Griffith
Teinusi	Abel M. Fernandez
Nkruma	Frank Lackteen
Sarab'na	Vera M. Francis
Bert	George Berkely

There was a time, long ago, when the Tarzan pix and similar adventure yarns used to be fun. But the latest Sam Katzman entry, "Devil Goddess," is a plodding, almost amateurish attempt at making a formula theme pay off. It uses a good deal of stock footage and relies beyond reason on the ability of Kimba, the chimp, to amuse by doing endless backflips.

Obviously, it must pay for Katzman and Columbia to turn out these quickies (this one's in sepia color), but it's hard to believe that there are adults around for this sort of hokum. Even on a small budget feature like this, they could have done better.

Ingredients of "Devil Goddess" are standard, although George Plympton's script with its almost incredible dialog is sub-standard. Story has Johnny Weissmuller braving the African jungles to guide a girl and her professor father to the land of the fireworshippers where, the professor thinks, an old friend has holed up and is playing "god." Simultaneously, a party of villains arrive on the scene, looking for a buried treasure.

Caught in the middle are the spear-equipped natives who ever so often break out in frantic tribal dances. Eventually, the professor finds his man; the villains meet their due, and Weissmuller and his friends return safely.

Spliced in on suitable occasions is footage involving a fight between a tiger and a hyena, which doesn't come off any too clearly; frequent eruption of the volcano with repeat shots of rocks tumbling down the mountainside, and a dance by native girls more reminiscent of Hawaii than Africa.

Weissmuller plays his role wooden-faced and without much enthusiasm. Angela Stevens, handed some embarrassingly naive lines, looks pretty and immaculate throughout; Selmer Jackson, Vera M. Francis, William Tannen, Ed Hinton and William M. Griffith all go through their paces with only an occasional show of conviction.

Spencer G. Bennet's direction—perhaps wisely—concentrates on Kimba and on the fire effects. Moppets probably will get a kick out of the long opening sequence when Kimba and his pals have a go at the bottle and show it. There are also some good occasional moments when the fake "god" appears to the natives and demands a human sacrifice. (It's actually the professor's friend trying to save the girls from being sacrificed). Incidentally Miss Francis, who plays the maiden to be offered up to the fire god, rates future attention. *Hift.*

Eine Frau Genuegt Nicht?
(One Woman Is Not Enough?)
(GERMAN)

Berlin, Aug. 23.

Deutsche London release of Apollo production. Stars Hilde Krahl, Hans Soehnker, Heliane Bey. Directed by Ulrich Erfurth. Screenplay, Dr. Erich Ebermayer and Frank Dimen, after a novel by Michael Graf Soltikow; camera, Werner Krien; music, Peter Igelhoff. At Marmorhaus, Berlin. Running time, 98 MINS.

Maria Vossberg	Hilde Krahl
Ernst Vossberg	Hans Soehnker
Renate Reinhard	Heliane Bei
Dr. Stefan Mertens	Hans Reiser
Dr. Kern	Rudolf Forster
Dr. Koerfer	Walter Suesseguth
Frau Huber, housekeeper	Annie Rosar
Dr. Dickreiter	Ernst Stahl-Nachbaur
Court Director	Ralph Lothar
Herr Oppert	Herbert Huebner
Frau Oppert	Lola Muethel
Schratt	Paul Hoerbiger
Wenzler, Barber	Stanislav Ledinek

This is not a comedy or light entertainment but a modern love drama centering around a man and two women. The problem posed for him concerns a pregnant young girl he has fallen for and his estranged wife, who is not willing to give him up. In the main, this is a woman's picture but it also may appeal to general audiences here. International chances, however, appear hardly better than average.

Artistically speaking, film is better than most local pix of this well-known type. Although often rather conventional and centering around a familiar triangle, there is some refreshing authenticity and seriousness about this film. Here, sympathy rests on both women, both have their justified arguments to get the man. Even the man's unfaithfulness meets human sympathy in view of his childless and unhappy marriage.

Unfortunately, film solves the problem the easy and banal way: the wife shoots her rival in sort of a not intended rage.

The acting is mostly very good. This particularly applies to Hilde Krahl, as the estranged wife. Hans Soehnker, as her husband, also turns in a lifelike portrayal. Heliane Bei plays the young girl with much conviction but is overshadowed by Miss Krahl. Good supporting roles are supplied by Paul Hoerbiger and Stanislav Ledinek.

Direction by Ulrich Erfurth is not even all the way but generally adequate in view of the complicated script furnished by Erich Ebermayer and Frank Dimen. Werner Krien's lensing is okay as are other technical contributions. *Hans.*

The Quartermass Experiment
(BRITISH)

Typical science fiction meller with good production and Brian Donlevy to provide U.S. marquee appeal; attractive dualer.

London, Aug. 30.

Exclusive release of Hammer production (U.S. distribution by Columbia). Stars Brian Donlevy and Jack Warner; features Margie Dean, Richard Wordsworth. Directed by Val Guest. Screenplay by Richard Landau and Guest from BBC television play by Nigel Kneale; camera, J. Elder Willis; editor, James Needs; music, James Bernard. At London Pavilion, Aug. 22, '55. Running time, 81 MINS.

Quartermass	Brian Donlevy
Lomax	Jack Warner
Judith Carroon	Margie Dean
Victor Carroon	Richard Wordsworth
Briscoe	David King Wood
Rosie	Thora Hird
TV Producer	Gordon Jackson
Christie	Harold Lang
Marsh	Lionel Jeffries
Green	Maurice Kaufman

Taken from a BBC television play, "The Quartermass Experiment" is an extravagant piece of science fiction, based on the after effects of an assault on space by a rocket ship. Despite its obvious horror angles, production is crammed with incident and suspense. It merits rating as a reliable dualer on either side of the Atlantic.

Production qualities are better than average for this type of picture while the star billing for Brian Donlevy (in the title role), provides useful exploitation for the U.S. He is the scientist, who designs the new rocket that is sent hurtling into space with three men on board. It crash lands in a small English village, with only one survivor. The mystery is what happened to the other two who have disappeared without trace although the rocket ship remained air sealed. The plot is mainly concerned with attempts to restore the one survivor to health. His well-meaning wife has him smuggled out of a clinic, but he breaks loose, causing death, destruction and terror as he changes from man to monster.

This is unrelieved melodrama without any femme interest. It draws its entertainment from a series of wildly improbable happenings. There is an occasional over-plus if horror closeups of the victims. There is a big climax when the monster is trapped in Westminster Abbey while a mobile tv unit is beaming a program.

Donlevy plays the scientist with a grim and ruthless conviction. Jack Warner gives a realistic interpretation of a Scotland Yard detective. Richard Wordsworth, with only one word of dialog, makes a valuable contribution as the survivor. Margie Dean is completely colorless as his wife. Val Guest's vigorous direction is matched by other competent technical credits. *Myro.*

The Woman For Joe
(BRITISH)
(Color—VistaVision)

Stereotyped fairground meller, moderately acted; moderate b.o. hopes.

London, Aug. 30.

Rank Vista Vision production and release. Stars Diane Cilento, George Baker; features David Kossoff, Jimmy Karoubi. Directed by George More O'Ferrall. Screenplay, Neil Paterson; camera (Technicolor), Georges Perinal; editor, Alfred Roome; music, Malcolm Arnold; "A Fool and His Heart" by Jack Fishman. At

Gaumont, London, Aug. 25, '55. Running time, 91 MINS.

Mary	Diane Cilento
Joe Harrap	George Baker
George Wilson	Jimmy Karoubi
Max	David Kossoff
Ma Gollatz	Violet Farebrother
Lemmie	Earl Cameron
Butch	Sydney Tafler
Vendini	A. J. Dean
Freddie the Kid	Patrick Westwood
Harry the Spice	Derek Sydney
Princess Circassy	Verna Gilmore
Iggy Pulitzer	Martin Miller
Sol Goldstein	Meler Tzelniker
Gladys	Miriam Karlin
Sullivan	Philip Stainton
Jack Evans	David Gabriel
Franz	Dennis Rosaire
Stephan	Frank Paulo
Doctor (Hospital)	Douglas Hurn
Landlady	Amy Veness
Manager	Edwin Ellis
Manager's Wife	Joan Hickson
Saleswoman	Majorie Stewart
Doctor (Circus)	Terence Longdon

"The Woman for Joe" is a fairground story which breaks little new ground. The melodrama follows a conventional pattern, is devoid of any surprise twist, and limps rather lamely to its inevitable climax. At best it can only be classed as a moderate b.o. candidate.

The high quality lensing, with the VistaVision cameras, captures the atmosphere of the fairground, but the carousels and other sideshows never emerge as an integral part of the yarn. The production suffers from an inadequate script and too leisurely direction. Director George More O'Ferrall rarely takes up the slack in the narrative.

The yarn centres on a traveling fairground showman (George Baker), whose luck changes when he buys an educated midget (Jimmy Karoubi) as a special attraction. The dwarf's own brand of authority putus him in a commanding position and all is fine until he persuades the showman to recruit Diane Cilento to the show. Inevitably, he falls for her and she falls for Baker. A conveniently timed fatal accident provides the solution.

Apart from the personal charm engendered by Miss Cilento (she is going to Broadway this fall in "Tiger At the Gates"), there is little if particular note in the acting side. Baker hardly comes to grips with his role while Karoubi rarely convinces with his apparent authority. Experienced performers of the calibre of David Kossoff, Violet Farebrother, Earl Cameron and Sydney Tafler are restricted by the limitations of their roles. Technical standards are adequate. *Myro.*

Tiger Girl
(Russian)
(COLOR—SONGS)

Artkino release of Leninfilm production. Stars Lena Kasatkina, Peter Kadochnikov; features L. Bykov, P. Sukhanov, K. Sorokin, G. Bodganova-Chestnokova, N. Urgant, Boris Eder. Screenplay, K. Mints, E. Pomeshchikov. Directed by A. Ivanovsky, N. Kosheverova; camera (Sovcolor), A. Dudko; music, M. Weinberg. At Stanley Theatre, N.Y., Sept. 3, '55. Running time, 98 MINS.

Lena	Lena Kasatkina
Fyodor Yermolayev	Peter Kadochnikov
Petya Mokin	L. Bykov
Circus Manager	P. Sukhanov
Bookkeeper	K. Sorokin
His Wife	G. Bogdanova-Chestnokova
His Daughter	N. Urgant
Telegin	Boris Eder
Lena's Mother	T. Peltser
Lena's Father	A. Orlov
Almazov	S. Filippov
Magician	V. Korolkevich

Since Russian films are notoriously lacking in a sense of humor, "Tiger Girl," with a circus locale, comes as a pleasant surprise. It's the Soviet version of a romantic comedy enhanced by fairly good Sovcolor tints. Where they play

Russian pix, this ought to be a popular entry.

For those who don't often get to see Soviet productions, "Tiger Girl" should come as something of a revelation. If the Russian claim. they invented the film camera (as they probably do), they certainly have far to go in learning how to use it. Apart from the acting, which is quite good, A. Dudko's lensing is stiff and extremely inhibited. Once or twice there are angle shots, but on the whole the camera is a stoic observer of a rather commonplace little story.

In the main it's all about the daughter of a circus vet who gets along well with the tigers. The sailor who loves her wants her to quit circus life. The daredevil rider, who also loves her, just wants her to stay put. In the end, the daredevil boy wins her hand and they embrace, briefly and rather self-consciously, as if kissing just wasn't something for the camera to watch.

Lena Kasatkina is probably the heftiest romantic lead the screen has seen for some time, but she has a dimply smile and is great at displaying flashes of anger. Peter Kadochnikov as the daredevil motorcyclist looks handsome and occasionally emotes. L. Bykov as the rejected sailor has a genuine sense of comedy, and writers K. Mints and E. Pomeshchikov reserve for him their best lines. N. Urgant as the vain Olya is okay and P. Sukhanov does a good job with the part of the fatherly circus manager.

Soviet circuses, at least the one one shown in the film, aren't likely to put Ringling Bros. out of business. Yet there are some exciting scenes involving the girl and the tigers. and there are a couple of pleasant songs woven into the story. Sovcolor, billed as "magnificent," is hardly that except in some of the outdoor scenes when it comes to life. *Hift.*

Foreign Films

Venice, Sept. 6.

Shuzenji Monogatari (The Mask and Destiny) (JAPANESE-COLOR). Shochiku production and release. Directed by Noboru Nakamura. Screenplay, Kido Okamoto; camera (Eastmancolor), Toshio Yasumi; editor, Toshio Ogata. With Teiji Takaahhasi, Minosuke Bando, Chikage Awashima. At Venice Film Festival. Running time, 100 MINS.

This is another Japanese film in color and evolving in the 12th Century, with royal intrigue backed by a theme of fate and tragedy as sword fights and thwarted romance culminate in a final wholesale series of deaths. All these types of pix should be compared to their forerunner, "Gate of Hell," and this does not stack up too well enough to succeed it. Too much gratuitous exoticism and swordplay mar the attempted poetics about a monarch who would rather have been a humble man and a maskmaker.

Too Eastern and slow for most Western patrons, this could only have possible U.S. specialized spotting to cash in on the "Gate" appeal; otherwise it is of little value for U.S. situations. Color is lush and lavish; costuming exquisite with technical values tops. However, direction and acting have not been fused well, to the film's detriment. *Mosk.*

Venice, Sept. 6.

Ordet (The Word) **(DANISH)**. A/S Film Centralen Palladium production and release. Directed by Carl T. Dreyer. Screenplay by Dreyer from play by Kaj Munk. Camera, Henning Bendtser; editor, Dreyer; music, Paul Schierbeck. With Henrik Malberg, Emil Hass Christensen, Preben Lerdorff, Cav Christiansen, Brigitte Federspiel. At Venice Film Festival. Running time, **120 MINS.**

Here is that arty house paradox, a brilliant, almost monumental film, yet with a stigma of anti-b.o. on it because of its uncompromising, heavygoing style and a touchy religioso theme of faith and miracle involving a conflict between Catholic and Protestant views towards life and religion. Carl Dreyer, responsible for the silent masterpiece, "The Passion of Joan of Arc" and a more recent film, "Day of Wrath," is just as unsparing in this film.

Style is sombre and intelligent, with a shocking scene of a caesarean operation sequence. Acting is perfect as is the direction which makes this a profound study of faith and belief. This is essentially talky. It is definitely a prestige item and may well become a critical gambit for a more daring U.S. exhib. It might be worth the effort in a few special situations. Technical credits are tops. *Mosk.*

La Cicala (The Grasshopper) **(RUSSIAN-COLOR)**. Mosfilm production and release. Directed by S. Samsonov. Screenplay, Samsonov from story by Anton Tchecov; camera (Sovcolor), V. Monakhov; editor, F. Dobronvarov. At Venice Film Festival. Running time, **90 MINS.**

For a change this Russo film dips back into the rich soil of its turn-of-century writers. A short story of Anton Tchecov is rendered unerringly with its warm interpretation of a pathetic group of flighty, arty butterflys and the too resigned men of science who fritter away their lives in blind pursuits. There is a well paced dramatic feeling in this film. Its acting, mood and technical aspects are tops. Pic looks like a good bet for Russo film situations and might have interest and word-of-mouth potential for some special U.S. spots on its well adapted dramatics, topnotch acting and fine rendition of a nostalgic period.

The director has kept this between satire and drama. Color is fine, with music an asset as is the editing. A mood piece of limited U.S. chances but denoting a change of pace in Russo filmmaking. *Mosk.*

Desperate Hours
(VISTAVISION)

Exciting on many counts, including dollars in the till outlook.

Paramount release of William Wyler production. Stars Humphrey Bogart, Fredric March; features Arthur Kennedy, Martha Scott, Dewey Martin, Gig Young, Mary Murphy. Directed by Wyler. Screenplay, Joseph Hayes, based on his own novel; camera (VistaVision), Lee Garmes; editor, Robert Swink; music, Gail Kubic. Previewed Criterion Theatre, N.Y., Sept. 8, '55. Running time, **112 MINS.**

Glenn	Humphrey Bogart
Dan Hilliard	Fredric March
Jesse Bard	Arthur Kennedy
Eleanor Hilliard	Martha Scott
Hal	Dewey Martin
Chuck	Gig Young
Cindy	Mary Murphy
Ralphie	Richard Eyer
Kobish	Robert Middleton
Detective	Alan Reed
Winston	Bert Freed
Masters	Ray Collins
Carson	Whit Bissell
Fredericks	Ray Teal
Detective	Michael Moore
Detective	Don Haggerty
Sal	Ric Roman
Dutch	Pat Flaherty
Miss Swift	Beverly Garland
Bucky Walling	Louis Lettieri
Mrs. Walling	Ann Doran

A click pic all the way, "Desperate Hours" is an expert adaptation of the novel about three escaped desperadoes who gunpoint their way to temporary refuge in the suburban Indianapolis home of a respectable middleclass family.

The story is variation on a theme; similar situations have been cropping up in recent fact and fiction. But producer-director William Wyler has made "Hours" fresh and exciting through astute use of the screen medium. His penetrating character development and intense construction of the yarn have given "Hours" special values.

This is a first for VistaVision in black and white. Wise, too, for color might have rendered less effective the strong fact-like appearance of "Hours." In other words, the film looks genuine—a vivid account of the terror that was visited upon the usually uneventful lives of "nice" people.

Important point favoring the film's sale involves the reaction of these innocuous folks. They emerge as real heroes, showing substance and strength of which they themselves were unaware and which doubtless will inspire gratifying audience identification.

Wyler worker with major-league performers, particularly stars Humphrey Bogart and Fredric March. This is Bogart in the type of role that cues comics to caricature takeoffs. Here he's at his best, a tough gunman capable of murder, snarling delight with the way his captives must abide by his orders, and wise in the ways of self-preservation strategy.

March is powerful as head of the family, never before cited for bravery but now bent on protecting his family from the three intruders. March conveys with remarkable effect his initial fright and bewilderment and subsequently the cool-minded courage and wisdom that lead to Bogart's defeat.

The others prominent in the pic are uniformly fine, each just right for the role and drawing from it its full potential. Arthur Kennedy, registers without error as the local deputy sheriff, clearly confused by Bogart's elusiveness and logical in trying to nab the convicts but without the risk of endangering their captives.

Martha Scott, as March's wife, gets across with careful restraint the role of a woman who's frightened but not hysterical. Mary Murphy is spirited and a little rebellious as the nifty-looking daughter. Richard Eyer, the kid brother, is a completely likely youngster who's unable to understand, at first, why his father doesn't rid his home of the strongarm visitors.

Dewey Martin is fitting as Bogart's younger brother who makes it apparent he's regretful of his crime career and allegiance to Bogart. Gig Young is right as Miss Murphy's boyfriend, confused by her family's strange behavior and unaware of what's going on at her home.

Third member of the Bogart trio is Robert Middleton, an oversized heavy who, correctly, will stir audience revulsion with his despicable manner.

Under Wyler's probing direction, closeups and fleetingly-caught gestures of the players do much in the way of subtly establishing story points and explaining the characters.

Joseph Hayes' script, adapted from his own novel (he also did the legit dramatization), is a story completely told, melodramatic but always plausible and peopled with extreme but nonetheless logical characters. The writing is taut, and in interpreting it for the screen, Wyler apparently added a few touches of his own that add to the color and excitement.

Gail Kubik's score is heard during only a couple of scenes; absence of music for the most part of the film is another factor contributing to the this-is-for-real effect. Editing is tight and other credits all are topnotch. *Gene.*

Seven Cities of Gold
(C'SCOPE—COLOR)

Good action-drama programmer around founding of Early California missions; for general dual bill market.

20th-Fox release of Robert D. Webb-Barbara McLean production. Stars Richard Egan, Anthony Quinn, Michael Rennie, Jeffrey Hunter, Rita Moreno; features Eduardo Noriega, Leslie Bradley, John Doucette, Victor Juncos, Julio Villareal. Directed by Webb. Screenplay, Richard L. Breen, John C. Higgins; added dialog, Joseph Petracca; from a novel by Isabelle Gibson Ziegler; camera (De Luxe Color), Lucien Ballard; editor, Hugh S. Fowler; music, Hugo Friedhofer; conducted by Lionel Newman. Previewed Sept. 7, '55. Running time, **103 MINS.**

Jose	Richard Egan
Captain Portola	Anthony Quinn
Father Serra	Michael Rennie
Matuwir	Jeffrey Hunter
Ula	Rita Moreno
Sergeant	Eduardo Noriega
Galvez	Leslie Bradley
Juan Coronel	John Doucette
Lt. Faces	Victor Juncos
Pilot Vila	Julio Villareal
Schrichak	Miguel Inclan
Dr. Pratt	Carlos Musquiz
Father Vizcaino	Pedro Galvan
Capt. Rivera	Angelo De Stiffney
Pilot Perez	Ricardo Adalid Black
Blacksmith	Fernando Wagner
Miscomi	Guillermo Calles
Axajui	Eduardo Gonzales Pliego
Atanuk	Yerye Deirute
Kukura	Anna Maria Gomez
Indian Boy	Jaime Ganzalez Quinones
Rano	Lucile Nieto
Dira	Olga Kutierrez
Guitar Player	Juan Jose Hurtado
Father	Jack Mower
Mother	Kathleen Crowley

The story of how Father Junipero Serra started the establishment of a string of missions in early California is interestingly, if at times leisurely, unfolded in "Seven Cities of Gold." The trouping is excellent, and there is action and drama to go with the period setting, all helping to shape it as a satisfactory entry for top-of-the-bill bookings in the general program market. Film should have a special-interest factor for Catholic Church backing. The religious connotation blends well with the entertainment.

Where "Seven Cities" scores best is in the believable development of the part both the Church and the military played in the establishment of California under early Spanish rule. The script by Richard L. Breen and John C. Higgins does its job well in framing the Isabelle Gibson Ziegler novel for the screen. No single side or factor is made the heavy for the sake of drama. Rather, circumstance and necessity are used to expedite plot, so that conflict between the Church and the military comes about logically.

Two notably good performances are turned in by Michael Rennie, as Father Serra, and Anthony Quinn, as Captain Portola, the Spanish soldier who led the expedition from Mexico City to the California coast back in the 1700's. Both are entirely believable. Satisfactory, too, are Richard Egan, another officer in the expedition; Jeffrey Hunter, leader of the Indians who oppose the settlement of the San Diego Mission, and Rita Moreno, his sister, whose romance with Egan ends tragically.

Robert D. Webb and Barbara McLean, husband-wife producing team, staged the picture in Mexico, and the junket lensing by Lucien Ballard in CinemaScope and De Luxe Color provides the picture with some strikingly rugged backgrounds that help express the period. Action is centered entirely on the trip overland to the Bay of San Diego and the hardships the group goes through as Father Serra circumvents military necessity to establish his first mission. The dialog is good, and there's some humor mixed in to keep things from getting too heavy. There's a "miracle" staged when Rennie and Egan are saved from perishing in a sandstorm that needs more explanation or elimination from the footage.

Technical credits are used advantageously under Webb's direction of the story. *Brog.*

My Sister Eileen
(C'SCOPE MUSICAL-COLOR)

Gay musical remake of former legit-pic clicks, not to be confused with B'way musical version, "Wonderful Town"; good b.o. prospects.

Hollywood, Sept. 9.

Columbia release of Fred Kohlmar production. Stars Janet Leigh, Jack Lemmon, Betty Garrett; features Robert Fosse, Kurt Kasznar, Richard York, Lucy Marlow, Tommy Rall, Barbara Brown, Horace McMahon, Henry Slate, Hal March. Directed by Richard Quine. Screenplay, Blake Edwards and Quine; based on play by Joseph Fields and Jerome Chodorov, adapted from stories by Ruth McKenney and produced on the stage by Max Gordon; camera (Technicolor), Charles Lawton Jr.; editor, Charles Nelson; songs, Jule Styne, Leo Robin; music supervised and conducted by Morris Stoloff, assisted by Fred Karger; musical numbers and dances by Robert Fosse. Previewed Sept. 7, '55. Running time, **106 MINS.**

Eileen Sherwood	Janet Leigh
Ruth Sherwood	Betty Garrett
Bob Baker	Jack Lemmon
Frank Lippencott	Robert Fosse
Appopolous	Kurt Kasznar
Wreck	Richard York
Helen	Lucy Marlow
Chick Clark	Tommy Rall
Helen's Mother	Barbara Brown
Lonigan	Horace McMahon
Drunk	Henry Slate
Drunk	Hal March
Brazilian Consul	Alberto Morin
Alice	Queenie Smith
George	Richard Deacon
Police Sergeant	Ken Christy

This latest version of "My Sister Eileen" is another demonstration of the durability of the material from Ruth McKenny's original New Yorker articles. First successfully put on film by Columbia in 1942, after the material had clicked as a stageplay by Joseph Fields and Jerome Chodorov, studio is now back with its own musical version, which has good possibilities generally.

What Columbia will be selling this time is not to be confused with yet another musical version, "Wonderful Town," which was the Broadway tuner from the original stage comedy. That, too, was a success. Where familiarity normally is supposed to breed contempt, or at least boredom, the filmtuner is an exception. Even those well acquainted with all of the material will find a freshness here that assures acceptance. It could have used stronger names and songs, but should do excellently with what it has, since the entertainment is there to please.

Scripters Blake Edwards and Richard Quine have turned out a simplified filmusical, in that the tunes and dances come naturally to situations and are not overly staged. Thus, the problems that befall two sisters from Ohio, come to New York to seek fame as a writer and actress, respectively, play naturally, even with some broadening for comedy. Quine's direction keeps things gay and mostly moving at a spirited pace. Latter helps when some of the situations tend to be repetitious.

Producer Fred Kohlmar chose a cast of good talents to carry off the show and the performer response to script and direction is topnotch. Two major assets in the trouping and funnying are Betty Garrett, the Ruth Sherwood who pens her sister's romantic adventures and Jack Lemmon, as Bob Baker, the young publisher and wouldbe wolf who successfully romances Ruth. Seconding this pair are Janet Leigh, very attractive as the little sister, and Robert Fosse, the shy soda jerk. Others adding to the fun include Kurt Kasznar as the landlord of the basement apartment in which the girls live; Richard York, as the Wreck, the football nut; and Tommy Rall, the flashy reporter.

None of the songs is from the stage tuner, having been cleffed by Jule Styne and Leo Robin especially for the picture. While not particularly standout, the numbers are mostly pleasant and fit aptly into the sequences in which they are used.

"There's Nothing Like Love," first heard as a sister duet, is reprised later by Fosse. Lemmon, while short on voice, makes a laugh-getter out of "It's Bigger Than Both of Us" while romancing Miss Garrett. She is heard on "As Soon As They See Eileen," then on "I'm Great" with Miss Leigh, York and Kasznar; the spritely "Give Me A Hand And My Baby," sung and terped with Miss Leigh, Fosse and Rall. Still a howler is the finale conga line with the Brazilian Navy students to "What Happened To The Conga." Fosse, who staged the dances, and Rall click strongly with a challenge dance tagged "Mr. Gloom."

Charles Lawton Jr.'s CinemaScope lensing in Technicolor is very good, favoring the players, costuming and settings so that there is plenty of eye appeal throughout. Other behind-camera functions are brought off expertly.

Brog.

Gentlemen Marry Brunettes
(C'SCOPE MUSICAL—COLOR)

Musicomedy about two gals in Paris; title, cast names and travelog backgrounding might help b.o. chances, but entertainment values are disappointing.

Hollywood, Sept. 13.

United Artists release of Richard Sale-Robert Waterfield (Russ-Field Voyager) production. Stars Jane Russell, Jeanne Crain, Alan Young, Scott Brady, Rudy Vallee; features Guy Middleton. Directed by Sale. Screenplay, Mary Loos & Sale; camera (Technicolor), Desmond Dickinson; editor, G. Turney-Smith; dances, Jack Cole; music supervision and title tune, Herbert Spencer & Earle Hagen, with lyrics by Sale; incidental music composed and conducted by Robert Farnon. Previewed Sept. 9, '55. Running time, **97 MINS.**

Bonnie Jones	
Mimi Jones (1926)	Jane Russell
Connie Jones	
Mitzi Jones (1926)	Jeanne Crain
Charles Biddle	
Mrs. Biddle	
Mr. Biddle Senior	Alan Young
David Action	Scott Brady
Rudy Vallee	Rudy Vallee
Earl of Wickenware	Guy Middleton
Monsieur Ballard	Eric Pohlmann
Monsieur Dufond	Ferdy Mayne
Monsieur Dufy	Leonard Sachs
Monsieur Marcel	Guido Lorraine
State Manager	Derek Sydney
Pilot	Boyd Cabeen
Hotel Manager	Robert Favart
Couturier	Duncan Elliot
Two Blondes	Gini Young, Carmen Nesbitt
Messenger	Maurice Lane
Wardrobe Woman	Penny Dane
Stage Doorman	Michael Balfour
Chauffeur	Edward Tracy

Herewith, another entry in the cycle of CinemaScope tours of Europe. "Gentlemen Marry Brunettes," a musicomedy about two show gals in Paris, has neither the sparkle nor wit that might have rated it more than routine bookings. B.o. prospects are disappointing.

While the idea of two girls from the States clicking in the Paris show world might have suggested good possibilities for a comedy with music, the development fails to jell completely. It gives Russ-Field (Jane Russell, Robert Waterfield), which produced in association with Voyager Films (Mary Loos, Richard Sale), an unimpressive start as a new indie outfit.

With the exception of the title tune by Herbert Spencer, Earle Hagen and Richard Sale, the numbers are all oldies such as "You, You're Driving Me Crazy," "Ain't Misbehavin'," "Daddy," "I Wanna Be Loved By You" and others. They serve as assorted solo and production number backing to the unimaginatively-conceived musical side of the film and, if not already standards, would hardly grow in stature from this treatment.

Miss Loos and Sale contributed an uneven screen story from which it is difficult to pick a clear plot line. Unlike most of the films offering vicarious tours of European spots, this one might have trouble engendering audience participation or particular sympathy with the characters.

Misses Russell and Jeanne Crain are a sister act offered an engagement in Paris by promoter Scott Brady and his friend, Alan Young. (Latter plays three parts). In the long ago, the gals' mother was a Paris hit with a string of suiters, so flashbacks are mixed in to show the past era as contrast to the present. Around as old suiters are Rudy Vallee and Guy Middleton, but they, like the other principals, are handicapped by the material.

There's an apparent lack of inspiration in executive producer guidance by Robert Bassler, in Sale's direction and in the latter's producer function with Waterfield. Miss Loos is listed as associate producer. Desmond Dickinson's cameras frame Paris in Technicolor for fair effect and there are some showy femme gowns on display.

Der Hauptmann und Sein Held

Berlin, Sept. 6.

(GERMAN)
(The Captain and His Hero)

Eden release of CCC production. Stars Ernst Schroeder and Jo Herbst. Directed by Max Nosseck. Screenplay, Karl-Wilhelm Vivier after stageplay of same title by Claus Hubaleck; camera, Georg Bruckbauer; music, Martin Boettcher. At Kiki, Berlin. Running time, **82 MINS.**

Hauptmann Eisenhecker	Ernst Schroeder
Paul Kellermann	Jo Herbst
Frau Kellermann	Fita Benkhoff
Ilse	Ingeborg Schoener
Yvonne	Ilse Steppat
Hauptmann Peppmoeller	Fritz Wagner
General	Ernst Stahl-Nachbaur
Master-Sergeant Kuhnke	Bruno Fritz

Claus Hubaleck's prize-winning (Gerhart Hauptmann award and Dramatists' Award). play has been brought to the screen with remarkably positive results. Having a strong anti-militaristic message, film is enjoyable and partly very witty entertainment with some sharp satirical touches. Its b.o. prospects are a bit doubtful since "Captain" is rather unconventional film fare and has no strong marquee names. Yet the film has enough ingredients to please a majority of domestic audiences. It also appears to have a chance in U.S. arty houses.

This is the story of 18-year-old Paul Kellermann who becomes a German soldier in the last war. Barrack life is rather tough for him—he's pushed around by superiors and involuntarily soon is behind the company eight-ball. However, when he manipulates things to get himself the Iron Cross, he becomes the favorite of his captain and the idol of his company. Film attempts to explain that in the army a man's medal rather than his character is a vital factor.

This film may be compared with the German pic, "08/15," but unlike that and other Teutonic pix of same category, "Captain" is much clearer in its message since it is a heavy attack against German barrack life and militarism in general. With such a good story as the basis, Karl-Wilhelm Vivier had little difficulty in framing a suitable script. This has many fine gags and the dialog, often harsh if genuine, is convincing.

Max Nosseck, recently returned from Hollywood and doing his first German pic in 20 years, has done a creditable directing job.

Two actors are worthy of mention—Ernst Schroeder, as the ambitious and medal-conscious captain, and Jo Herbst, of the local cabaret group "Die Stachelschweine" (Porcupines), as the young recruit who becomes his Captain's "hero." Among the good supporting roles are Bruno Fritz, who gives a lovable study of a master-sergeant; Fita Benkhoff, as Herbst's mother; Ingeborg Schoener, as his girl-friend; Ilse Steppat, Clemens Hasse and Werner Mueller.

Technical credits are adequate. Camerawork by Georg Bruckbauer is often excellent. A special word of praise goes to the comparatively unknown Martin Boettcher whose score perfectly adds to the mood.

Hans.

Foreign Films

Venice, Sept. 13.

Les Mauvaises Rencontres (The Bad Liaisons) (**FRENCH**). Marceau producton and release. Stars Anouk Aimee, Jean-Claude Pascal; features, Claude Dauphin, Gaby Silvia, Philipe LeMaire, Yves Robert. Directed by Alexandre Astruc. Screenplay, Astruc, Roland Laudenbach from novel by Cecil St. Laurent; camera, Robert Le Febvre; editor, Maurice Serein. At Venice Film Festival. Running time, **90 MINS.**

Film shapes as a posey, arty entry which traces the adventures of a young girl from the provinces to the gilded, upper class segments of Paris. Flashback is utilized as the girl is questioned about whether a certain doctor was to give her an abortion. Extremely static quality and forced rhythm of the pic rob this of movement. Director Alexandre Astruc has not been able to give this a feel of humanity and passion needed in this tale of a young girl's slow analysis of her emotional life.

Very stilted dialog and wooden acting also keep this in the arty group, and for the U. S. is primarily for special situations and limited engagements. Lensing is slick but overdoes some of the effects. Acting is too one-keyed to ever get a semblance of complexity into the characters. This is a first full length pic by Astruc, and is too much of the textbook type.

Mosk.

Venice, Sept. 13.

Despues De La Tormenta (After the Storm) (**MEXICAN**). Filmdora release and production. Directed by Roberto Gavaldon. Screenplay, Gavaldon; camera, Matinez Solares; editor, Gonzalo Curiel. With Marga Lopez, Lilia Prado, Ramon Gay, J. L. Jimenez. At Venice Film Festival. Running time, **90 MINS.**

The usual lush lensing and melodramatics are abundantly present in this film. It is well mounted and acted with melodramatic flourishes. Concerning two twins, who live in a lighthouse with their respective wives, main complication is when one of the brothers becomes enamored of the other's wife. In a storm one of the twins is lost and the remaining one passes himself as the other twin to get the other man's wife he had desired all along. His real wife suspects and when the other twin returns, it makes for a stormy climax.

Acting makes the most of the histrionic opportunities while location shooting provides nice backing. This is primarily for foreign lingo situations in the U. S. since it lacks the more solid footing and storytelling values for arty houses. Direction is slick and keeps the narrative rolling along, with lensing and editing an asset. *Mosk.*

Venice, Sept. 13.

Maos Sangrentas (The Bloody Hands) (**BRAZILIAN**). Artisti Associati release of Maristola production. Directed by Carlos Hugo Christensen. Screenplay, Pedro Vignale, Christensen; camera, Mario Pages; editor, Christensen. With Arturo De Cordova, Tonia Carrero, Sadi Cabral. At Venice Film Festival. Running time, **90 MINS.**

This is a gory film which relates the fate of a group of convicts who escape from an island prison and are relentlessly tracked down by the authorities until all are wiped out. Under this is the theme of a man who has killed his wife for infidelity, but then begins to question the deed, and the hardened leader of the band finally succumbs to remorse and eventual madness. This might be a good item for nabe spots or the action market. It may be too brutal for the average runs. *Mosk.*

The Big Knife

Skullduggery behind scenes in Hollywood. Uneven story values but promising b.o.

United Artists release of Robert Aldrich production, directed by Aldrich. Features Jack Palance, Ida Lupino, Wendell Corey, Rod Steiger, Everett Sloane, Shelley Winters. Screenplay by James Poe, from Clifford Odets' stage play; camera, Ernest Laszlo; editor, Michael Luciano; music, Frank DeVol. Tradeshown N.Y. Sept. 15, '55. Running time, 111 MINS.
Charles Castle .... Jack Palance
Marion Castle .... Ida Lupino
Smiley Coy .... Wendell Corey
Dixie Evans .... Shelley Winters
Connie Bliss .... Jean Hagen
Stanley Hoff .... Rod Steiger
Patty Benedict .... Ilka Chase
Nat Danziger .... Everett Sloane
Hank Teagle .... Wesley Addy
Buddy Bliss .... Paul Langton
Nick .... Nick Dennis
Russell .... Bill Walker
Billy Castle .... Mike Winkelman
Bearded Man .... Mel Wells
Bongo Player .... Robert Sherman
Stillman .... Strother Martin
Referee .... Ralph Volke
Announcer (Prize Fight)... Michael Fox

"The Big Knife" differs from the Dwight Deere Wiman-Lee Strasberg-Clifford Odets stage production of 1949, when John Garfield starred. The legiter was something of a bore; this is one of the more interesting new entries which, despite its tight budget along with some phoney story angles and other shortcomings, is a possible sleeper of wideawake boxoffice proportion. It's a natural exploitation picture.

Film is of the "Sunset Boulevard" and "Star Is Born" genre, an inside Hollywood story. It's sometimes so brittle and brutal as to prove disturbing. Some segments in the picture business, from an intra-trade public relations viewpoint, will definitely not like it.

It mirrors the ruthlessness of talent-studio relations and overall "company town" operations. It may be seized upon as being "typical" of the industry and is fraught with the possibility of a "kickback" from some unforeseen sources and forces in future. On the other hand, although an indie-made production, it is to the credit of the industry that a major distributor is handling its release.

It's an anomaly, of course, that when Hollywood spoofs or exposes another industry it is circumspect to have a titular explanation that this is not "typical," nor is the expose or exposition as frank and forthright as is the job director-producer Robert Aldrich did on a certain phase of Hollywood.

Rod Steiger too vividly interprets the Janus aspects of the studio head who knows when to con and cajole Jack Palance into a 14-year deal, and perhaps too convincingly depicts the ruthlessness of his operations when the elements are against him. He has no compunction about staging an "accidental death" of one of those "casting couch contractees" (Shelly Winters plays it with "guest star" billing in this picture), foiled by his laconic and resourceful publicity director. Wendell Corey is properly "the cynical Celt," Steiger's resourceful hatchet-man in the clinches. Ida Lupino scores as the realistic wife who wants Palance to forget the Hollywood loot and return to his "ideals." Jean Hagen fits well as the amorous two-timing wife of a publicity staffer. Everett Sloane is effectively sympathetic as the agent with a heart of gold and a neo-Lindy's brogue. Ilka Chase is the columnist. Miss Winters, on a bender ("a woman with six martinis can ruin a town," warns Steiger) is

convincing as is Wesley Addy, the writer willing to marry Miss Lupino, who foils Corey's attempt to "cover up" Palance's suicide by making sure that this is the one time the star will be honest with the world.

Peg for all plot ins and out is the longtermer for Palance and this is one of the faultier aspects of the writing and c a s t i n g. Palance doesn't look the part of a smash b.o. lure, so all the business about the studio's desperate need of him is tough to understand. And his resistance to the deal, on grounds it would made him a "slave" to Steiger, is just inconsistent with present relationships between the big lots and the top names. Furthermore, there ain't no such animal, legally or professionally, as a "14-year contract"; California law limits any deal to seven annums.

What may disturb is the film's complete leverage on the contemporaneous, or an attempt to mirror studio operations with matter-of-fact, almost documentary authority. Mankiewicz, Stevens, Kazan, Wilder, Wyler are name-dropped with the casualness of a Romanoff's conversation. There are other occasions, however, then the dialog is as phoney as a fan mag "interview."

Another shortcoming is the editing; the cuts are ofttimes irritatingly curt. But in toto it's done with proper pace and tempo. *Abel.*

Blood Alley
(C'SCOPE-COLOR)

John Wayne, Lauren Bacall in actionful adventure drama located in Red China; good b.o.

Hollywood, Sept. 20.
Warners release of Batjac production. Stars John Wayne, Lauren Bacall; features Paul Fix, Joy Kim, Berry Kroger, Mike Mazurki, Anita Ekberg, Henry Nakamura. Directed by William A. Wellman. Screenplay, A. S. Fleischman; from his novel; camera (WarnerColor), William H. Clothier; editor, Fred MacDowell; music, Roy Webb. Previewed Sept. 8, '55. Running time 115 MINS.
Wilder .... John Wayne
Cathy .... Lauren Bacall
Mr. Tso .... Paul Fix
Susu .... Joy Kim
Old Feng .... Berry Kroger
Big Han .... Mike Mazurki
Wei Long .... Anita Ekberg
Tack .... Henry Nakamura
Mr. Han .... W. T. Chang
Mr. Sing .... George Chan

The Orient is having its day in films and herewith is another entry in the cycle. Contemporary Red China backgrounds the action-adventure drama, dressed up in CinemaScope and WarnerColor and flaunting the names of John Wayne and Lauren Bacall to point it for a profitable run through the market.

The Batjac production for Warner Bros. release, unlike the majority of foreign-located entries, went no further than the San Francisco Bay area to duplicate the China-Formosa Straits settings. From the ticket buyer's viewpoint the effect should be about the same as though an overseas junket had been made, since William A. Wellman's direction achieves considerable Oriental flavor through use of Chinese extras and ingenious set decorations and production design.

On an entertainment count, "Blood Alley" holds up rather well in a pulp fiction vein, mixing action, romance and suspense in about equal measure to draw and hold viewer interest, even over the lengthy running time of 115 minutes. The drama in A. S. Fleischman's script, based on his novel of the same title, is concerned with a small village's determination to

escape from Red China to Hong Kong. To achieve this, they manage the escape of Wayne, American sea captain, from the Reds, so he can skipper a stolen sternwheel ferryboat and all the villagers to the refuge. The boat, its motley crew and passengers make it to safety and freedom after a series of fanciful adventures that Wellman crams with action, suspense, and not a little heart.

Wayne was a perfect choice to play the rugged skipper with a gal in every port, until Miss Bacall, daughter of an American doctor who had been killed by the Communists, turns loose her wiles during the flight through Blood Alley (the Straits). Good for chuckles is Miss Bacall's i m a g i n a r y rival "Baby," with whom Wayne intermittently carries on conversations. Miss Bacall, too, contributes importantly to making the drama acceptable.

Paul Fix, as one of the village elders; Berry Kroger, head of the only Red family in the village; Mike Mazurki, burly strong man of the expedition, and Henry Nakamura, the ferryboat's Americanized engineer, are among the excellent featured players. Anita Ekberg's femme charms are hidden under Chinese rags and she has no individual dialog. A standout among the featured cast is Joy Kim, playing Miss Bacall's maid. She sings two Chinese airs cleffed by Roy Webb, who did the background scoring, too. Latter is frequently permitted to attack the ears during high action sequences. Otherwise, it is good, and the two Oriental songs melodic.

Presentation strike an incongruous note in the use of sub-titles during early C h i n e s e dialect scenes. They should be dropped entirely or continued throughout the picture whenever the dialog is all Chinese. William H. Clothier gets some beautiful C'Scope scenes on film with his WarnerColor photography. *Brog.*

Hold Back Tomorrow

Program melodrama with offbeat plot; exploitable for some situations.

Hollywood, Sept. 20.
Universal release of Hugo Haas production. Stars Cleo Moore, John Agar; features Frank de Kova, Dallas Boyd, Steffi Sidney. Directed and written by Hugo Haas. Camera, Paul Ivano; editor, Henry De Mond; score, Sidney B. Cutner; song, Franz Steininger, Johnny Rotella. Previewed Sept. 15, '55. Running time, 75 MINS.
Dora .... Cleo Moore
Joe .... John Agar
Priest .... Frank de Kova
Warden .... Dallas Boyd
Clara .... Steffi Sidney
1st Guard .... Mel Welles
Detective .... Harry Guardino
Escort Girl .... Mona Knox
Proprietress .... Arlene Harris
Warden's Wife .... Kay Riehl
Girl .... Jan England
Dancing Comedienne....... Pat Goldin

A variation on a condemned man's last request gives "Hold Back Tomorrow" an exploitation twist that may get it ballyhoo coin in some situations. As usual with the independent offerings turned out by Hugo Haas, this one tackles a subject not likely to be tried by larger companies. Results are fairly okay, but other than the exploitation angle, it's a program entry.

John Agar plays a convicted killer who, on the eve of his execution, askes for a woman—any woman—to amuse him during his final night on earth. In the small, international seaport town where

Haas has laid his story, the police find Cleo Moore, a wouldbe suicide sick of her life of easy virtue. Not caring any more, she takes on the dubious chore of making Agar's last hours interesting, and does such a good job he marries her at dawn and goes off to the gallows in a regenerated mood. Fadeout finds Miss Moore, herself willing to live again, praying that a miracle, as in a dream Agar had of the rope breaking, will happen and save her new love.

Picture, which Haas wrote, produced and directed, and which Universal is releasing, centers virtually all of the action on Miss Moore and Agar. Sometimes they get in over their dramatic depth, but generally acquit themselves quite well in putting over the offbeat plot. Frank de Kova is good as a priest and among others more prominently involved are Dallas Boyd, the warden; Steffi Sidney, the killer's young sister, and Mel Welles, a guard.

Technical assists, from camera on down, pass muster and there is a title tune by Franz Steininger and Johnny Rotella heard twice during the footage. *Brog.*

Bengazi
(SUPERSCOPE)

So-so meller for the duals but names of Richard Conte, Victor McLaglen may help.

RKO release of Panamint Pictures production (producers Sam Wiesenthal and Eugene Tevlin). Stars Richard Conte, Victor McLaglen, Richard Carlson, Mala Powers; features Richard Erdman, Hillary Brooke. Directed by John Brahm. Screenplay, Endre Bohem and Louis Vittes from story by Jeff Bailey; camera, Josef Biroc; editor, Robert Golden; music, Roy Webb. Tradeshown N.Y., Sept. 16, '55. Running time, **79 MINS.**

Gilmore .... Richard Conte
Donovan .... Victor McLaglen
Levering .... Richard Carlson
Aileen .... Mala Powers
Selby .... Richard Erdman
Nora .... Hillary Brooke
Peters .... Maury Hill
Basim .... Jay Novello
Kamal .... Gonzales Gonzales

"Bengazi" is a mild meller for the twin bill market. While this RKO release offers some marquee dressing in the names of Richard Conte, Victor McLaglen, Richard Carlson and Mala Powers, the story has an artificial flavor and never takes on the aura of a hard-hitting saga of postwar North Africa's underworld.

The Endre Bohem-Louis Vittes script as screenplayed from Jeff Bailey's story may have looked good on paper, but in it's transition to the screen the characters seldom become believable. Yarn has McLaglen, an aging gun runner turned saloonkeeper, joining with shifty Conte and paroled convict Richard Erdman in an attempt to heist gold reportedly stached away in a desert mosque.

Their plans aren't interrupted by the sudden arrival of Miss Powers who's come from Ireland for her first visit with father McLaglen in 15 years. Although reaching the mosque in a stolen British army lorry, the treasure-hunting trio ran afoul of native tribesmen. Later, sleuth Carlson who's been tracing the thieves by plane, and Miss Powers also become entrapped at the same place.

In perhaps the weakest scene of the picture Conte defies the besiegers' gunfire and buys safe conduct for those still alive in the mosque by returning the gold to the natives. It was a thankless role for Conte not only in this sequence but in most of the other footage. Also giving their assignments the old college try were McLaglen as a mellowing thief, Miss Powers as a disillusioned colleen, Carlson as a relentless police officer and Erdman as the ex-convict. Okay support is provided by Hillary Brooke and Maury Hill, among others.

John Brahm directed the Panamint Pictures production, which Sam Wiesenthal and Eugene Tevlin produced, but its obvious that the script was too much for him. Sets and general backgrounds reflect a low budget. Nevertheless, economy in physical values is partially minimized by Joseph Biroc's competent SuperScope lensing in black-and-white. Robert Golden edited to a slow 79 minutes and Roy Webb's music was adequate. *Gilb.*

Duel On the Mississippi
(Color)

Costumed romantic actioner located in early Louisiana; okay programmer.

Hollywood, Sept. 20.

Columbia release of a Clover production. Stars Lex Barker, Patricia Medina; features Warren Stevens, Craig Stevens, John Dehner, Ian Keith, Chris Alcaide, John Mansfield, Celia Lovsky, Lou Merrill, Mel Welles. Directed by William Castle. Story and screenplay, Gerald Drayson Adams; camera (Technicolor), Henry Freulich; editor, Edwin Bryant; music conducted by Mischa Bakaleinikoff. Previewed Sept. 16, '55. Running time, **72 MINS.**

Andre Tulane .... Les Barker
Lili Scarlet .... Patricia Medina
Hugo Marat .... Warren Stevens
Rene LaFarge .... Craig Stevens
Jules Tulane .... John Dehner
Jacques Scarlet .... Ian Keith
Anton .... Chris Alcaide
Louie .... John Mansfield
Celeste Tulane .... Celia Lovsky
Georges Gabriel .... Lou Merrill
Sheriff .... Mel Welles
Bidault .... Jean Del Val
Gaspard .... Baynes Barron
Benedict .... Vince M. Townsend Jr.

The demands of the general dual bill market are adequately met in this costumed actioner. Made at a price to fill the requirements of programmer bookings, it does all of these things, and, at the same time, deals out a fairly acceptable brand of pulp fiction in a Technicolor dress. Lex Barker and Patricia Medina, familiar names, topline.

The screen story by Gerald Drayson Adams, which is kept on the move under William Castle's direction, is plotted in Louisiana in 1820 and deals with raids on the sugar planatations of oldline families by a gang of bayou cutthroats. Revenge on southern aristocracy plays a part, too, since the gal promoting the raids, a lowborn Creole girl and owner of a gambling ship, resents that she hasn't been accepted as an equal.

A number of plot offshoots are juggled around with a mixture of dueling and fisticuff action to the 72 minutes spin off at an okay pace. One twist has Barker, son of aristocratic John Dehner, put under bondage to Miss Medina to keep his father from going to debtors jail after she had bought up a note. By film's end, however, she's willing to switch the relationship and he's removed Warren Stevens, leader of the bayou raiders, via a duel with machettes.

The two stars go through their assignments easily and, in addition, Miss Medina looks mighty good in Technicolor and the period costumes. Stevens is excellent as the menace and among the others who prove out are Craig Stevens, Dehner, Ian Keith, ex-pirate and Miss Medina's father, and Celia Lovsky, mother of Barker.

Henry Freulich did the lensing. Footage is intermixed with stock bayou-river boat clips. Other technical supports are okay. *Brog.*

Killer's Kiss

Low budget meller for lower half of the duals.

United Artists release of Minotaur (Stanley Kubrick and Morris Bousel) production. Features Frank Silvera, Jamie Smith, Irene Kane, Ruth Sobotka. Directed, written, photographed and edited by Kubrick. Music, Gerald Fried. Tradeshown N.Y. Sept. 19, '55. Running time, **67 MINS.**

Vincent Rapallo .... Frank Silvera
Davy Gordon .... Jamie Smith
Gloria Price .... Irene Kane
Albert (Fight Manager)...... Jerry Jarret
Hoodlums. Mike Dana, Felice Orlandi, Ralph Roberts, Phil Stevenson
Owner of Mannequin Factory Julius Adelman
Conventioneers .... David Vaughan, Alec Rubin

Although the "big picture" era is here, there are still small ones kicking around as evidenced by "Killer's Kiss" which ex-Look photographer Stanley Kubrick turned out on the proverbial shoestring for United Artists release. It may eke out some bookings as a filler on the lower half of the duals.

There's no marquee strength in the non-name cast but of some help may be a few lurid scenes that could rate special attention in exploitation houses. "Kiss," incidentally, was more than a warm-up for Kubrick's talents for not only did he co-produce but he directed, photographed and edited the venture from his own screenplay and original story.

Familiar plot of boy-meets-girl finds smalltime fighter Jamie Smith striking up a romance with taxi dancer Irene Kane who lives across the court from his modest furnished room. How he saves her from her lecherous boss, Frank Silvera, takes up most of the film's 67 minutes of running time.

Kubrick's low key lensing occasionally catches the flavor of the seamy side of Gotham life. His scenes of tawdry Broadway, gloomy tenements and grotesque brick-and-stone structures that make up Manhattan's downtown eastside loft district help offset the script's deficiencies.

In fact the yarn too frequently is reminiscent of old fashioned mellers which had the hero dashing up in the nick to save his beloved from the villain. Kubrick's direction is no better while his editing is fair. His was a nice try at taking on most of the major chores, but this picture attests anew the hazards of such an attempt.

Cast also gets "A" for effort. Despite the quality of the script and direction, Silvera is suitably sinister as the heavy. Likewise, Smith strives valiantly as the lovelorn fighter and Miss Kane is wistful as the taxi dancer who's felt a lot of life's hard knocks. Ruth Sobotka is adequate in a ballet sequence. Gerald Fried's score is okay. Production values are negligible. Much of the footage consists of city street and rooftop exteriors. *Gilb.*

A Man Alone
(COLOR)

Ray Milland goes western in outdoor suspense actioner; medium entertainment and prospects.

Hollywood, Sept. 15.

Republic release. Stars Ray Milland; costars Mary Murphy, Ward Bond; features Raymond Burr, Arthur Space, Lee Van Cleef, Alan Hale, Douglas Spencer, Thomas B. Henry, Grandon Rhodes. Directed by Milland. Screenplay, John Tucker Battle; story by Mort Briskin; camera (TruColor), Lionel Lindon; editor, Richard L. Van Enger; music, Victor Young. Previewed Sept. 14, '55. Running time, **95 MINS.**

Wes Steele .... Ray Milland
Nadine Corrigan .... Mary Murphy
Gil Corrigan .... Ward Bond
Stanley .... Raymond Burr
Dr. Mason .... Arthur Space
Clantin .... Lee Van Cleef
Anderson .... Alan Hale
Slocum .... Douglas Spencer
Maybanks .... Thomas B. Henry
Luke Joyner .... Grandon Rhodes
Ortega .... Martin Garralaga
Sam Hall .... Kim Spalding
Wilson .... Howard J. Negley

Western suspense, combined with action and drama, shape "A Man Alone" as an okay offering for the general outdoor market. Ray Milland's name in connection with the Republic release gives it marquee value and also will help the bookings.

Milland turns director with "Man" and acquits himself fairly well in the new chore. He's a mite too deliberate with his pacing, particularly in handling the character he plays, but shows plenty of promise in his guidance of the other players and in an ability to develop dramatics beyond the level of the usual outdoor feature. He had a well-written script by John Tucker Battle to start with and the plot, from a story by Mort Briskin, holds together until the climax, when things return to formula and keep the picture from being more than medium entertainment.

An asset to the film is Mary Murphy, a young lady who continues to mature as an actress and a beauty. Quarantined in her Arizona desert town home where her father, the sheriff, is ill with yellow fever, she suddenly finds the house has become sanctuary for a notorious gunman, Milland, who is being hunted by a lynch mob for several brutal murders. In this isolation, a drama of love and regeneration is developed, leading eventually to the clearance of Milland of the murder charges and the exposure of the guilty parties as Raymond Burr, local banker, and his gunmen, who had been allowed to do their dirty work with the connivance of the sick sheriff, Ward Bond.

Bond is quite good as the sheriff turned crook, but regenerated at the finale. Another scoring is Arthur Space, excellent as the town doctor. Abetting Burr's skullduggery is Lee Van Cleef, while Alan Hale is seen as the hapless deputy and Douglas Spencer as the town undertaker.

Production rounds up a good array of sight values to backstop for the action and drama, with Lionel Lindon's TruColor photography doing its share to insure visual attractiveness. Victor Young provides the story with a firstrate background score. *Brog.*

The Tall Men
(C'SCOPE—COLOR)

Clark Gable and Jane Russell in a big-scale western made to order for the wide screen. Shapes as a sock b.o. contender.

20th-Fox release of a William A. Bacher-William B. Hawks production. Stars Clark Gable, Jane Russell, Robert Ryan, Cameron Mitchell; features Juan Garcia, Harry Shannon, Emile Meyer, Stevan Darrell. Directed by Raoul Walsh. Screenplay, Sydney Boehm and Frank Nugert from the Clay Fisher novel; camera (De Luxe Color), Leo Tover; editor, Louis Loeffler; songs by Ken Darby and Jose Lopez Alaves; music, Victor Young; special effects, Ray Kellogg. Previewed in N.Y., Sept. 21, '55. Running time, **122 MINS.**

Ben Allison	Clark Gable
Nella Turner	Jane Russell
Nathan Stark	Robert Ryan
Clint Allison	Cameron Mitchell
Luis	Juan Garcia
Sam	Harry Shannon
Chickasaw	Emile Meyer
Colonel	Stevan Darrell
Gus	Will Wright
Wrangler	Robert Adler
Cowboy	J. Lewis Smith
Emigrant Man	Russell Simpson
Emigrant Women	Mae Marsh, Gertrude Graner
Miner	Tom Wilson
Stable Owner	Tom Fadden
Hotel Clerk	Dan White
Maria	Argentina Brunetti
Mrs. Robbins	Doris Kemper
Salesman	Carl Harbaugh
Stagecoach Driver	Post Park

They must have had "The Tall Men" in mind when they invented CinemaScope. It's a big, robust western that fills the wide screen with a succession of panoramic scenes of often incredible beauty. And Clark Gable and Jane Russell make on attractive team as well as a hot combo for the marquees.

Although the accent on visual values is at times allowed to come in the way of the none-too-solid story taken from the Clay Fisher novel, "Tall Men" nevertheless has just about everything the boxoffice could expect from a western. Action flares at regular intervals; there's romance and there are songs; there's a huge cattle drive and a thundering stampede, and—last but by no means least—there's the personality of Gable.

This is the Gable of old in a role that's straight up his alley—rough, tough, quick on the draw and yet with all the "right" instincts. The vet actor seems to enjoy himself thoroughly and he is equally at ease in the saddle as in his swap-a-quip dialog with Miss Russell which comes off well, frequently with the desired rib-tickling effects.

There's probably no use quibbling about Miss Russell. Teaming her with Gable assured producers William A. Bacher and William B. Hawks of combustion almost regardless of what she does or how she does it. She goes through most of the film taunting both Gable and Robert Ryan, showing off what's she got in some very provocative dresses, singing a couple of pleasant songs and rolling and unrolling her stockings. Since this pre-occupation with dressing and undressing is easy on the eyes, and may well be what the customers expect, it's probably only fair to assume that her pancake-flat acting is a secondary consideration. She does show a sense of comedy in a couple of scenes and the pic benefits from it.

Star of this show is the camera, and here lenser Leo Tover and director Raoul Walsh have outdone themselves. Never his CinemaScope looked so lovely before. In scene after scene, whether in the great shots of the men riding through a blinding blizzard, or the cattle crossing a stream, or the thunderous stampede, the camera captures the full beauty of the western country and captures the action in pulse-quickening excitement. De Luxe color is perfect and adds immeasurably to the film's value. If "Tall Men" rates among the top westerns, Tover's contribution is largely responsible for putting it there.

Story has brothers Gable and Cameron Mitchell, vets of Quantrell's Guerillas, riding into Montana where they hold up Ryan. He talks them into working for him and they become partners in a venture that calls for them to drive a large herd of cattle from Texas to Montana. On the way south, the trio runs into Miss Russell, and Gable saves her from an Indian attack. Romance blooms, but they quarrel and Miss Russell attaches herself to the wealthy Ryan. Eventually, she accompanies the trio on the cattle drive, survives another Indian attack and finds her way back to Gable.

There are many exciting scenes for the action fans, including an unusual shootin' "duel" between Gable and Mitchell. Director Walsh is an old hand at this sort of thing and "Tall Men" carries all the earmarks of a b.o. smasheroo. Certainly, they can't make the westerns any bigger than this. Stampede, started deliberately by Gable to foil the Indians, makes for breathtaking effects.

Supporting cast is fine down the line. Ryan as the pompous financier etches a convincing portrait down to the climax when he tries to outwit Gable but is in turn outwitted himself. Mitchell as the hot-headed brother has plenty of spunk and turns in a solid performance even though his character isn't satisfactorily explained; Juan Garcia as Luis, Gable's loyal Mexican friend, is colorful as the leader of the crew recruited by Gable for the drive.

Ken Darby wrote "Tall Men" for the film, and it's the kind of folksy ditty that could catch on. Miss Russell does nicely by it, too. Other song is "Cancion Mixteca," penned by Jose Lopez Alaves. Script by Sydney Boehm and Frank Nugent is tailor-made for Gable even though the dialog is like an echo from a hundred other westerns and only occasionally takes on stature of its own. Miss Russell's lines particularly are at times hard to take. Still, this isn't going to bother the western fans. They're sure to get their money's worth and more out of this ambitious and well-produced film. *Hift.*

Count Three and Pray
(C'SCOPE—COLOR)

Post-Civil War yarn rates as fair entry for general situations. Moderate b.o. outlook.

Columbia release of Copa production (produced by Ted Richmond). Stars Van Heflin. Features Joanne Woodward, Raymond Burr, Phil Carey, Allison Hayes. Directed by George Sherman, Screenplay, Herb Meadow; camera, Burnett Guffey; editor, William A. Lyon; music, George Duning. Previewed in N. Y., Sept. 15, '55. Running time, **102 MINS.**

Luke Fargo	Van Heflin
Lissy	Joanne Woodward
Albert Loomis	Phil Carey
Yancey Huggins	Raymond Burr
Georgina Decrais	Alison Hayes
Floyd Miller	Myron Healey
Matty	Nancy Kulp
Swallow	James Griffith
Big	Richard Webb
Mrs. Decrais	Kathryn Civney
Bishop	Robert Burton
Colossus	Vince Townsend
Charlie Vancouver	John Cason
Selma	Jean Willes
Mrs. Swallow	Adrienne Marden
Jake	Steve Raines
Corey	Jimmy Hawkins
Lilly Mae	Juney Ellis

The post-Civil War South serves as the setting for this uneven Copa production (Ted Richmond and Tyrone Power). Herb Meadow's rambling script attempts to accomplish too much in detailing the conflicts of the post-war rehabilitation of a devastated town. It notes the decay of the southern aristocracy, the rise of the "white trash" in the changing social order, and the bittnerness toward a fellow townsman who fought for the "North "because he saw things the other way." These are only side issues to the basic yarn of a hell-raiser turned parson's effort to rebuild the town's church—in the face of strong opposition.

Since these situations lend themselves to violent differences, there's sufficient fisticuffs in the 102-minute CinemaScope-Technicolor film to satisfy the demands of the action market. Picture shapes as a fair entry for general situations. Van Heflin is the only name that will mean anything on the marquee.

Romance is introduced via Joanne Woodward, seen as a ragged, hill girl who has survived like a wild animal in the wake of the war. This bit borders on the cliche, since it's obvious that this unkempt, unwashed femme, thought to be a 14-year-old, would turn out to be an attractive 18-year-old once she cleaned up and donned woman's clothes. And there's the prostie with the heart of gold who comes to the help of her former client in his new role of a parson.

Heflin is the post-Civil War Don Camillo. Like the doughty priest, in the recent Italo import played by Fernandel, he is also handy with his fists, weapons he reluctantly uses in his efforts to be "a sure-enough preacher of the Gospel." He returns from the war, during which he fought for the North, a thoroughly reformed individual determined to make up for his years of woman-chasing, horse-racing, and liquor-drinking. He succeeds in rebulding the church—overcomes the bitterness toward his defection to the North, defeats his enemies, wins acceptance as the parson, and walks off with Miss Woodward as his bride.

There's enough material in Meadow's screenplay for several pictures about the post-Civil War South. Thrown together, however, into one effort has diluted the overall effect. The story of the changing social order might have served as a theme by itself. Raymond Burr is appropriately villainous as the storekeeper who represents the new power of the town. Allison Hayes is seen in the familiar portrayal of a high-spirited gal who cannot accept the end of her aristocratic position.

Performances, on the whole, meet the demands of the film. Heflin is tough, fearless, and pious. Miss Woodward is defensively ornery. Phil Carey, as a horse fancier; Jean Willes, as the prostie, and Myron Healey, Nancy Kulp, James Griffith, Richard Webb, Kathryn Givny, and Robert Burton as assorted friends, enemies, and townspeople are seen in stereotyped roles.

George Sherman's direction is best in the action moments which are excitingly presented. Burnett Guffey's CinemaScope lensing as well as the other technical aspects are on the plus side. *Holl.*

Tennessee's Partner
(SUPERSCOPE—COLOR)

Good frontier meller with John Payne-Ronald Reagan-Rhonda Fleming.

RKO release of Benedict Bogeaus production. Stars John Payne, Ronald Reagan, Rhonda Fleming, Coleen Gray; features Anthony Caruso, Morris Ankrum. Directed by Allan Dwan. Screenplay, Milton Krims and D. D. Beauchamp from story by Bret Harte; camera (Eastman Color), John Alton; editor, James Leicester; music, Louis Forbes. Tradeshown N.Y. Sept. 23, '55. Running time, **87 MINS.**

Tennessee	John Payne
Cowpoke	Ronald Reagan
The Duchess	Rhonda Fleming
Goldie	Coleen Gray
Turner	Anthony Caruso
The Judge	Morris Ankrum
Grubstake	Chubby Johnson
The Sheriff	Leo Gordon

Bret Harte stories have provided a veritable fount of material for westerns and mellers dealing with America's pioneering days. This source is again tapped by producer Benedict Bogeaus for "Tennessee's Partner" which emerges as one of his better films. He has marquee insurance in John Payne-Ronald Reagan-Rhonda Fleming, and there's a generous mixture of sex, suspense and six guns, all of which should add up to comfortable grosses in the general market.

The Milton Krims-D. D. Beauchamp screenplay from a Harte story, localed in a California gold rush boomtown, nicely captures the lusty flavor and atmosphere of the era. Characters and situations are familiar but director Allan Dwan moves things along at a brisk pace. Of further assistance are the authentic appearing frontier sets and period costumes which cameraman John Alton ably catches in Eastman Color via Tushinsky widescreen Superscope. (Print is by Technicolor).

Payne, an old hand at such roles, is partnered with Miss Fleming in operating the town's top entertainment emporium. A gambler, he's a slick man not only with cards but with Colts. His proficiency with the latter is frequently put to use in quieting disgruntled players who've fallen victim to his playing skill. Likewise, Miss Fleming is equally adept at guiding her femme entertainers who romp about the rococo spot in eyefilling dress.

There's ample drama in what transpires within the funmaking establishment but the action gets an extra lift via arrival of cowpuncher Ronald Reagan. He aims to wed Miss Gray, known to Payne as a scheming trollop. Before Reagan is aware of the true situation, he cuffs the gambler about unmercifully. However, a Damon & Pythias relationship arises out of this. It ends when Reagan is shot down by a claim jumper who has attempted to frame Payne for the murder of a prospector. It goes without saying that Payne wins Miss Fleming at the finale.

Payne registers handily as the gambler, Reagan scores as his two-fisted, hard fighting friend while Miss Fleming is more than decorative as proprietress of a frontier pleasure palace. Miss Gray is well cast as an unscrupulous gal who tried to shake down Reagan. Anthony Caruso etches a solid portrayal as the heavy, Chubby Johnson rates mention as the slain prospector and Leo Gordon is good as the sheriff. Art direction of Van Nest Polglase is impressive as is the Louis Forbes musical score. Gilb.

The Treasure of Pancho Villa
(COLOR)

Outdoor actioner localed and lensed in Mexico; fair entertainment, moderate b.o. prospects.

Hollywood, Sept. 27.

RKO release of Edmund Grainger production. Stars Rory Calhoun, Shelley Winters, Gilbert Roland; features Joseph Calleia, Fanny Schiller, Carlos Mosquiz, Tony Carvajal, Pasquel Pena'. Directed by George Sherman. Screenplay, Niven Busch; story, J. Robert Bren, Gladys Atwater; camera (Technicolor), William Snyder; editor, Harry Marker; music, Leith Stevens. Previewed Sept. 23, '55. Running time, **96 MINS.**

Tom Bryan	Rory Calhoun
Ruth Harris	Shelley Winters
Juan Castro	Gilbert Roland
Pablo Morales	Joseph Calleia
Commandant	Carlos Mosquiz
Laria Morales	Fanny Schiller
Farolito	Tony Carvajal
Ricardo	Pasquel Pena'

Mexico and its revolutionary days background this action-adventure entry. Localed and lensed below the border, "The Treasure of Pancho Villa" comes off with a fair amount of success as an outdoor subject. It should hit a moderate b.o. pace as a bill-topper in the regular dual market.

Famliar names of Rory Calhoun, Shelley Winters and Gilbert Roland carry the star spots in the Edmund Grainger production. The two males handle their action chores well, but Miss Winters seems miscast. Neither does her role have as much definition in the writing as those of her co-stars. Grainger's helming gets a good Latin flavor into the picture, but he allows some story pretentions to embellish the plot unnecessarily, resulting in the footage running overlong for the release bracket into which the film falls.

After George Sherman's direction gets by the story and talk-slowed first portion of the footage, he whips up some rugged action, a number of the scenes having enough exciting punch to compensate somewhat for the literary lags in the script by Niven Busch from a story by J. Robert Bren and Gladys Atwater.

Plot opens with Calhoun and Roland making a last stand against Federal troops that have followed them to recover a treasure in gold being taken to Villa to refinance the revolution. As the pair awaits the end, story flashes back to show the events leading up to the climax, detailing how Calhoun, a mercenary, joined the venture because he wanted the gold. First portion of the flashback, showing a prior gold-for-Villa raid pulled by Calhoun, only slows the actual story start and spills unnecessary blood. As the Federals close in, Roland is killed and Calhun dynamites the mountain, burying gold and troops, and then heads off for further adventure.

Miss Winters is in the story as the daughter of an American mining engineer whom the Villistas are trying to get to Tampico and safety. Joseph Calleia is good as a greedy Villista who tries to take the gold for himself. Fanny Schiller, as his wife, also is excellent, as are Carlos Mosquiz, Federal commandant, Tony Carvajal and Pasquel Pena. The SuperScope lensing by William Snyder gives pictorial values to the footage and Leith Stevens' score has the proper Latin mood. *Brog.*

Strangers

Ingrid Bergman and George Sanders for the marquee. But otherwise a plodding feature from Italy.

Fine Arts Films release of a Roberto Rosselini production. Stars Ingrid Bergman, George Sanders. Features Mario Mauhan, Ann Proctemer, Paul Muller, Leslie Daniela, Natalia Rai, Jackie Frost Director, screenplay, Rosselini; original story, Vitaliano Brancati, Rosselini; camera, Enro Sarafin; editor, Jolanda Bonvenriti; music, Renro Rosselini. Reviewed at Egyptian Theatre, Hollywood, Calif., Sept. 1, 1955. Running time, **80 MINS.**

Hollywood, Sept. 20.

This Roberto Rosselini production starring Ingrid Bergman is the story of two people no longer in love who have become strangers to one another after eight years of marriage. Without any particular plot other than to have them fall in love again in the fadeout, Italian import is dull and plodding fare and will have little appeal here, although the name of Miss Bergman, who co-stars with George Sanders, should have exploitational lure.

Rosselini achieves a feeling of reality in the relationship of the couple, but otherwise his direction shows little distinction and he's faced with hackneyed dialog badly dubbed. Lensed partly in Naples, some of the street scenes are interesting, but these are only flashes. Spectator must wait for the femme star, for no apparent reason, to wander through four museums and ruins, which tends to slow even the meandering pace previously established.

Story thread picks up the couple, English, arriving in Naples to see about selling a villa left Sanders by an uncle. The tension that's been mounting between them biulds here to a climax, when they decide to get a divorce, but during a street religious ceremony which halts their passage en route back from visiting Pompeii they find each other.

Sanders is suavely restrained and Miss Bergman, although poorly photographed nonetheless lends charm to an indefinite role. Good support is lent by Marie Mauhan, Anna Proctemer and Paul Muller. Rosselini used an entirely Italian crew of technicians. *Whit.*

Lady Godiva
(COLOR)

Maureen O'Hara in a mild, costumed actioner. For general dual market.

Hollywood, Sept. 13.

Universal release of Robert Arthur production. Stars Maureen O'Hara, George Nader, Victor McLaglen, Rex Reason; features Torin Thatcher, Eduard Franz, Leslie Bradley, Henry Brandon, Arthur Shields, Robert Warwick. Directed by Arthur Lubin. Screenplay, Oscar Brodney, Harry Ruskin; story by Brodney; camera (Technicolor), Carl Guthrie; editor, Paul Weatherwax; music supervision, Joseph Gershenson. Previewed Sept. 1, '55. Running time, **89 MINS.**

Godiva	Maureen O'Hara
Leofric	George Nader
Grinald	Victor McLaglen
Harold	Rex Reason
Godwin	Torin Thatcher
Edward	Eduard Franz
Eustace	Leslie Bradley
Bejac	Henry Brandon
Innkeeper	Arthur Shields
Humbert	Robert Warwick
Thorold	A. E. Gould-Porter
Pendar	Grant Withers
Prior	Antony Eustrel
Abbess	Kathryn Givney
Oswin	Sim Iness
William	Thayer Roberts

This program swashbuckler is pegged on the celebrated ride of the Coventry gentlewoman. That's excuse enough for the costumer, but its release purpose in the general dual market would have been better served with more action than is found in the 89 minutes of footage. However, Universal has found this type of film subject usually profitable. So, with Maureen O'Hara gracing the title role, "Lady Godiva" should garner a fair amount of trade in the situations at which it is aimed.

Slow direction by Arthur Lubin and a wordy script with characters that never quite come alive are the chief drawbacks to the Robert Arthur production. Otherwise, it has the look of a period piece, localled in early England when the Normans were scheming to take over from the Saxons.

That bareback ride by the lady is a titillating tidbit held out until near the end of the footage. Before it's offered she becomes the bride of Saxon nobleman George Nader, who thus thwarts a plan for him to make a Norman marriage of state, and finds herself caught up in court intrigue and personal ambitions of the Norman advisors to King Edward. In the end, with the ride making the point of Saxon loyalty, she, as much as her husband, is responsible for opening the eyes of the king to the poor advice he is being given.

The trouping demanded by the Oscar Brodney and Harry Ruskin script is more or less stock, but Miss O'Hara manages to put enough extra into her character to stir interest. Nader has few opportunities to show to advantage. Others more prominently involved in the playoff are Victor McLaglen, one of a trio of pluguglies on Lady Godiva's side; Rex Reason, up for a bid to the throne; Torin Thatcher, his father; Eduard Franz, the king, and Leslie Bradley and Henry Brandon, chief schemers.

The Technicolor tints are well handled in the lensing by Carl Guthrie, while editing, art direction, settings and costumes come off okay in the overall setup. *Brog.*

King Dinosaur

Science - fiction exploitationer for smaller houses only.

Hollywood, Sept. 23.

Lippert release of an Al Zimbalist-Bert I. Gordon production. Stars Bill Bryant, Wanda Curtis; features Douglas Henderson, Patti Gallagher. Directed by Gordon. Screenplay, Tom Gries; camera, Gordon Avil; editors, John Bushelman, Jack Cornall; music, Mischa Terr. Reviewed Sept. 21, '55. Running time, **59 MINS.**

Dr. Ralph Martin	Bill Bryant
Dr. Patricia Bennett	Wanda Curtis
Richard Gordon	Douglas Henderson
Nora Pierce	Patti Gallagher

"King Dinosaur" is a mild science-fiction yarn okay for smaller double billing. Lacking any known names, it must depend for draw on exploitational value accruing to a King Dinosaur which scientists find on a planet they reach via rocket ship and which very nearly destroys them.

Produced by Al Zimbalist and Bert I. Gordon, the Tom Gries screenplay has little new to offer. A full 15 minutes is devoted to a slow preparation of the flight to a new planet which has moved into the earth's galaxy, and it's not until the ship lands in terrain very similar to the earth that there's any action. Interest here dwells mostly on the scientists' efforts to escape from monsters. (Process work is well done.) Film draws heavily on stock footage, ending with an atomic explosion set off by scientists to save them from the dinosaur.

Acting demands are few, with Bill Bryant and Wanda Curtis okay as stars and Douglas Henderson and Patti Gallagher handling featured roles adequatically. Gordon, who also directs, helms as well as script will permit. Music by Mischa Terr strikes the proper mood for a film of this sort. *Whit.*

Fort Yuma
(COLOR)

Another cavalry versus Indians programmer.

Hollywood, Sept. 27.

United Artists release of Aubrey Schenck-Howard W. Koch (Bel-Air) production. Stars Peter Graves, Joan Vohs, John Hudson, Joan Taylor; features Addison Richards, William (Bill) Phillips, James Lilburn, Abel Fernandez. Directed by Lesley Selander. Story and screenplay, Danny Arnold; camera (Technicolor), Gordon Avil; editor, John F. Schreyer; music, Paul Dunlap. Previewed Sept. 23, '55. Running time, **78 MINS.**

Lt. Ben Keegan	Peter Graves
Melanie Crowne	Joan Vohs
Sgt. Jonas	John Hudson
Francesca	Joan Taylor
General Crooke	Addison Richards
Sgt. Halleck	Wm. Phillips
Corp. Taylor	James Lilburn
Mangas	Abel Fernandez

The cavalry and the Indians fight it out for fair entertainment results in "Fort Yuma," an actioner that will serve the requirements of the general outdoor market.

Turned out by Aubrey Schenck and Howard W. Koch for United Artists release, the Bel-Air production was lensed in Technicolor on location in Utah, resulting in scenic values that help dress up the routine screen story scripted by Danny Arnold. Film is developed along regulation lines under Lesley Selander's direction, with the pacing in the first half on the slow side, but gathering momentum in the latter portion.

Story kicks off with an Apache chief being killed as he comes to Fort Yuma to sign a peace treaty. His son, the new chief, vows to wipe out the fort. Planning to dress his braves as soldiers, the chief starts attacking a supply column, enroute to the fort, to steal uniforms and equipment. The scheme nearly comes off, but three survivors get a warning through in time and it's the Indians who are wiped out at the finale.

Script puts a lot of embroidery on the basic plot line but the characters never develop into real people, although competently performed within the limits of the writing. Peter Graves plays an Indian-hating officer in charge of the supply column. Despite his contempt of the redskins, he's in love with Joan Taylor, Indian beauty whose Apache brother, John Hudson, is scout for the detachment. Joan Vohs is the fourth star, seen as a missionary accompanying the column to Fort Yuma where she plans to teach. William Phillips and James Lilburn are troopers, and Abel Fernandez is the warring young Apache chief.

Gordon Avil's photography, the score by Paul Dunlap and editing by John F. Schreyer top the list of the behind-camera credits. *Brog.*

Les Heros Sont Fatigues
(Heroes Are Tired)
(FRENCH)

Venice, Sept. 20.

Pathe release of Cila-Terra Films production. Stars Yves Montand, Maria Felix; features Curt Jurgens. Directed by Yves Ciampi. Screenplay, J. L. Bost, Ciampi from novel by Christine Garnier; camera, Henri Alekan; editor, Roger Dwyre;

music, Louiguy. At Venice Film Festival. Running time, **105 MINS.**

Michel .... Yves Montand
Manuella .... Maria Felix
Francois .... Jean Servais
Villeterre .... Gerard Coury
Nina .... Elizabeth Manet
Wolf .... Curt Jurgens
Herman .... Gert Froebe
Pepe .... Manolo Mantez
Rudi .... Rudi Castell

Film concerns a group oi white derelicts planted in the Negro republic of Liberia in Africa. To the seething movement and tomtoms is reenacted a melodramatic opus about an ex-pilot who tries to unload a bundle of hot diamonds he has picked up after his plane crashed. Atmosphere is rarely convincing in this, and the few moments of jolting brutality are gratuitous. Main attraction of this pic for U. S. market is its locale, and even so mostly for art houses. Name value is Maria Felix.

Assorted characters are a French collaborator and his sensual wife, now the mistress of a local Negro; a German refugee, a Frenchman married to the daughter of a leading politico, the pilot hero and the man, also an ex-pilot, who is charged with recovering the diamonds.

Acting of the stars, Yves Montand and Miss Felix, is primarily expressionless and wooden although the latter scores via her pulchritude. Main acting laurels are thefted by German actor Curt Jurgens, who impresses as the agent who decides to go straight. It is primarily an exploitation pic which will have to stand on that plus some volatile sex scenes. Lensing is fine as is editing and general production aspects. *Mosk.*

Amici Per la Pelle
(Friends for Life)
(ITALIAN)

Venice, Sept. 20.

Unset release of a CINES Production. Stars Geronimo Meynier, Andrea Scire, Luigi Tosi, Vera Carmi. Directed by Franco Rossi. Screenplay, Benvenuti, De Bernardi, Giagni, Guerra, Rossi, from story by Rossi, Guerra, DeBernardi, Ottavio Alesai; camera, Gabor Pogany; music, Nino Rota: editor, Otello Colangeli. At Venice Film Festival. Running time, 95 MINS.

Mario .... Geronimo Meynier
Franco .... Andrea Scire
Mario's Father .... Luigi Tosi
Mario's Mother .... Vera Carmi
Franco's Father .... Carlo Tamberlani
Prof. Martinelli .... Paolo Ferrara
English Prof. .... Marcella Rovena

Made for children, but thoroughly enjoyable to adults as well, "Amici" is one of the best moppet items to come along in some time. It should do very well locally and in Europe, especially via word-of-mouth. It has U.S. possibilities.

Pic is practically a two-man show as it sketches the increasing friendship of two schoolboys, Franco and Mario, through various youthful adventures. This friendship is interrupted when Mario lets the whole class in on one of those vital childhood secrets, but in one of two filmed endings to pic, kids wake up and the ending is happy. Version shown here at festival has one kid leaving by plane before his friend can make up with him for downbeat effect. Moppet psychology is unerringly accurate and one of film's many strong points. Acting by Geronimo Meynier and Andrea Scire is standout, with both registering winning performances in their first screen roles.

Technically, the production is high quality. Gabor Pogany's lensing is up to his usual high standard, and other credits assist in making this a success. *Hawk.*

Geordie
(BRITISH—COLOR)

Scottish highlands provide magnificent backgrounds for simple yarn of frail boy who grows up to be Olympics champion; geared for hefty grosses here and should appeal to U.S. arty theatre trade.

London, Sept. 20.

British Lion release of Launder and Gilliat production. Stars Alastair Sim, Bill Travers; features Brian Reece, Raymond Huntley, Miles Malleson, Jack Radcliffe, Francis de Wolff, Norah Gorsen. Directed by Frank Launder. Screenplay by Sidney Gilliat and Launder from novel by David Walker; camera, Wilkie Cooper; editor, Thelma Connell; music, William Alwyn. At Plaza Theatre, London. Running time, 99 MINS.

The Laird .... Alastair Sim
Geordie .... Bill Travers
Jean Donaldson .... Norah Gorsen
Geordie's Mother .... Molly Urquhart
Henry Samson .... Francis de Wolff
Reverend McNab .... Jack Radcliffe
Harley .... Brian Reece
Rawlins .... Raymond Huntley
Lord Paunceton .... Miles Malleson
Geordie's Father .... Jameson Clarke
Helga .... Doris Goddard
Postman .... Stanley Baxter
Schoolmaster .... Duncan Macrae
Young Geordie .... Paul Young
Young Jean .... Anna Ferguson
Laird's Housekeeper .... Margaret Boyd
Guard .... Alex McCrindle

With its rich, colorful Scottish Highlands background and the simple charm of its story, "Geordie" is essentially a British picture in content and treatment. Yet it has that quality which will give it its wider appeal, making it a sock attraction for the domestic market and possibly a lively entry for the U.S. art houses despite its inadequate marquee values.

Picture is another fine example of the teamwork of Launder and Gilliat. Admittedly, the film has its weaknesses and judicious scissoring would heighten the tempo. But the very naivete of the principal characters gives the subject the necessary warm human values and right degree of sentiment. The duo share most of the technical credits (as always) this time Launder gets billing for the direction. Their experienced touch is clearly in evidence.

The "Geordie" of the title is the wee son of a Scottish gamekeeper who is always being kidded by the other youngsters because of his size. He might have stayed that way, too, had he not seen an ad for a physical culture course, promising added inches and powerful muscle development. Geordie, a conscientious pupil, grows into strapping manhood, making himself a bit of a bore with his boyhood sweetheart, but developing in strength to be the champion hammer thrower at the Highland Games and being selected to represent Britain in the Olympic Games at Melbourne.

A foreword to the film explains that the story is set in the "past and present, with a wee glimpse into the future." The past and present, of course, refer to the development of Geordie from boyhood to manhood, and the peep into the future are the scenes at next year's Olympics, when the hero sets a new world record.

The appealing performance of Paul Young as young Geordie is in sharp contrast to the dour, obsessed character, as played by Bill Travers, an impressive newcomer to stardom. Alastair Sim turns in a characteristically rich study as the laird white Norah Gorsen, in her screen debut, is a radiant looker with a natural aptitude for acting although occasionally beaten by the Scottish accent. She plays the long suffering girl friend with feeling.

There's nothing subtle about the overtures made by Doris Goddard, a fellow competitor in the Olympics, who starts her big pitch as soon as the liner sails for Australia. Brian Reece, Raymond Huntley and Miles Malleson are prominent in the supporting cast who fill minor parts with distinction.

All-round technical stanards are commendable. Wilkie Cooper handles his Technicolor cameras with skill; Norman Arnold's set designs match the natural Scottish scenery; and William Alwyn's background music is attractive. *Myro.*

Man of the Moment
(BRITISH)

Norman Wisdom stars in slapstick British comedy; smash b.o. potentialities in home market, but negligible export appeal.

London, Sept. 20.

J. Arthur Rank production and release. Stars Norman Wisdom; features Lana Morris, Belinda Lee, Jerry Desmonde. Directed by John Paddy Carstairs. Screenplay, Vernon Sylvaine, John Paddy Carstairs; camera, Jack Cox; editor, John Shirley; music, Philip Green; with "Dream For Sale" by Arthur Groves, Peter Carroll; "Beware" by Norman Wisdom, "Yodelee Yodelay" and 'Man of the Moment" by Jack Fishman (sung by the Beverley Sisters). At Odeon, Leicester Square, London. Running time, 95 MINS.

Norman .... Norman Wisdom
Penny .... Lana Morris
Sonia .... Belinda Lee
Jackson .... Jerry Desmonde
Lom .... Karel Stepanek
British Delegate .... Garry Marsh
Toki .... Inia te Wiata
Sir Horace .... Evelyn Roberts
Queen of Tawaki .... Violet Farebrother
Swiss Tailor .... Martin Miller
Day Lift Man .... Eugene Deckers
Mitchell .... Hugh Morton
British Delegate .... Cyril Chamberlain
Chambermaid .... Lisa Castoni
Enrico .... Harold Kasket
Air Hostess .... Beverly Brook

Anything goes with Norman Wisdom. He is the b.o. phenomenon of the era as far as British audiences are concerned. He fills the London Palladium for months on end and his films are record grossers. "Man of Moment" does nothing to enhance his reputation but will coin money wherever it plays locally. It is, however, of little export value and would hardly stand a chance in the U. S.

Instead of giving the star a chance to show his ability as a talented artist, the producers are content to let him indulge in crude, broad slapstick and to dress him in either tight-fitting clothes or baggy pants. The comedy derives from old-fashioned knockabout situations and as an extra gimmick there's a wild chase through television studios, interrupting programs of screen personalities.

Wisdom plays a clerk in a British ministry who gets sent to a Geneva conference and has to sit in for an injured delegate. Without realizing what he's doing, he exercises his veto in favor of a small Pacific power and the queen of that island thereupon steadfastly refuses to act until he's given his approval. The British give him a knighthood, foreign powers confer decorations and a few more ruthless ones try to bump him off. But his loyalty to the queen is unaffected.

Although the entire action is centered about the star, he has strong femme support. Lana Morris is nicely demure as the girl who befriends him in Geneva and Belinda Lee is a lush, but unsuccessful seductress. Jerry Desmonde again plays the straight man to the comic with his usual skill. An average supporting cast includes Karel Stepanek, Garry Marsh, Violet Farebrother and Hugh Morton. The title song and other numbers are neatly staged and warmly delivered. John Paddy Carstairs' lively direction concentrates on keeping the ball rolling. *Myro.*

Cast a Dark Shadow
(BRITISH)

Workmanlike adaptation of stage thriller making good vehicle for Dirk Bogarde and Margaret Lockwood; should have universal appeal.

London, Sept. 20.

Eros Films' release of Daniel M. Angel production. Stars Dirk Bogarde, Margaret Lockwood, Kathleen Harrison, Kay Walsh. Directed by Lewis Gilbert. Screenplay by John Cresswell from play "Murder Mistakes," by Janet Green; camera, Jack Asher; editor, Gordon Pilkington; music by Antony Hopkins. At Odeon, Marble Arch, London. Running time, 85 MINS.

Edward Bare .... Dirk Bogarde
Monica Bare .... Monica Washbourne
Freda Jeffries .... Margaret Lockwood
Charlotte Young .... Kay Walsh
Emmie .... Kathleen Harrison
Phillip Mortimer .... Robert Flemyng
Coroner .... Walter Hudd
Charlie Mann .... Philip Stainton
Waitress .... Myrtle Reed
Singer .... Lita Roza

A good stage drama does not automatically become a good screen subject, but, in this instance, what was a gripping, well-knit play has suffered nothing in the transition. It retains all the suspense of a young murderer marrying and plotting death to elderly wealthy women. The linkup exteriors and change of scene bring more realism and scope to the story than the original cramped stage setting. With firstrate camera work and skillful casting, this should prove a sound b.o. pic.

There is no attempt to delude shots, showing the artificial loving attention bestowed by the young husband on his aged, befuddled wife. Hearing she is about to make a will, he plans an "accidental" gasfire death for her knowing the law will adjudge him sole heir if she dies intestate. The proposed will would have left him her fortune but an earlier unsuspected will bequeaths him only the house while the money goes to her sister in Australia.

Having got away with murder the frustrated fortune hunter soon finds a new victim, a jovial saloonkeeper's widow, who is more than a match for him until she discovers the truth when he plots the death of his sister-in-law, over from Australia, who has snooped around anonymously to probe her sister's untimely end. The thwarted husband rushes out to escape but gets into his projected victim's car and is hurled to his death.

The role of the scheming young killer gives Dirk Bogarde one of the best opportunities in his career and he never makes a wrong move. Monica Washbourne is excellent as the pathetic, maudlin soak who dies in vain and Margaret Lockwood gives a vivid characterization of brash hard-headness as the second wife. Kathleen Harrison scores as a faithful old servant with Robert Flemyng and Mona Washbourne convincing as the lawyer and Australian whose suspicions result in the final showdown. Film owes much to the fine direction of Lewis Gilbert. *Clem.*

Lovers and Lollipops

Venice, Sept. 20.
Spires production and release. Features Cathy Dunn. Written and directed by Morris Engel, Ruth Orkin. Camera, Engel; editor, Orkin; music, Eddy Manson. At Venice Film Festival. Running time, **85 MINS.**

Ann	Lori March
Larry	Gerald O'Loughlin
Peggy	Cathy Dunn
Peter	William Ward

Made by Morris Engel and Ruth Orkin, who were responsible for "Little Fugitive," this has many of the fine qualities of its predecessor, naturalness and color, but the emphasis on the adult amorous activities but not with the same spontaneity. It is full of fine observation and telling use of New York sites, but shapes as a specialized film for arty theatres. It may not do as much biz as "Fugitive." It has a tendency to be sketchy and uses the child, Cathy Dunn, for charm purposes rather than entering more completely into her attitudes and world.

It concerns a young widow, Lori March, who is ready for the marital plunge again. She has a six-year old daughter (Cathy Dunn), whose outspokenness both hastens and retards the new marriage to her steady beau, Gerald O'Loughlin. Sightseeing scenes around New York, and especially the visit to the Statue of Liberty and Chinatown, will open the eyes of blase New Yorkers. Moppet Dunn has an engaging quality that makes her dominate her scenes with the adults by her curiosity and unique naturalness. Miss March and O'Loughlin do well but remain shadowy figures.

Direction has a flair for bits of business and telling vignettes of the external child world. Editing by Miss Orkin helps give this tempo. Musical background, via harmonica, is a perfect counterpoint to the imagery. This got its world preem at the recent Venice Fest, being shown out of competition. *Mosk.*

Foreign Films

Venice, Sept. 20.
Le Amiche (The Girl Friends) (ITAL-IAN). Titanus release of Trionfalcine production. Stars Eleonora Rossi Drago, Valentina Cortese, Gabriele Ferzetti, Franco Fabrizi, Yvonne Fourneaux, Madeleine Fischer, Anna Maria Pancani. Directed by Michelangelo Antonioni. Screenplay, Suso Cecchi D'Amico, Alba De Cespedes, Antonioni; camera, Gianni di Venanzio; music, Giovanni Fusco. At Film Festival. Running time, **105 MINS.**

Pic, a social document done in semi-clinical analytical style, is one of those major but common paradoxes—a major prizewinner which has only modest b.o. potentialities. In this case, much of the limitations are in the intimately local dialogue and styling of the action, which hamper its export possibilities. Names will help, along with offbeat aspects and the fest kudo.

Film weaves the tales of several women and their men, generally spun about the framework of the opening of a dress shop in Turin. Marital and extra-marital relationships are revealed as the assorted groups of males and females are formed. Frustrated love drives one girl to suicide, another back to her hometown while another returns to her husband. Dialogue is sharp and action picks up after a slow, introductory series of sequences.

Thesping is fine, with newcomers Madeleine Fischer and Anna

Maria Pancani often stealing the show from such vets as Eleanora Rossi Drago and Valentina Caortese. Maria Gambarelli, ex-Met prima ballerina, does a fine job as head of the dressmaking establishment in her first serious thesping assignment. Technical credits are fine, topped by a truly standout musical accompaniment by Giovanni Fusco. *Hawk.*

Venice, Sept. 20.
Gil Sbandati (The Disbanded) (ITAL-IAN). Titanus release of C.V.C. production. Stars Lucia Bose, Jean Pierre Mocky, Isa Miranda, Goliarda Sapienza, Leonardo Botta, Giulio Paradisi, Yvy Nicholson, Marco Guglielmi, Franco Lantieri. Directed by Francesco Maselli. Screenplay, Francesco Maselli, Prando Visconti, Aggeo Savoli; camera, Gianni di Venanzio; music, Giovanni Fusco. At Film Festival. Running time, **90 MINS.**

Wartime resistance story and downbeat handling are against this item, which nevertheless should appeal to lovers of Italo film realism. Good possibilities in some European countries although this is more of a prestige item than a moneymaker. Story, which involves some city boys in countryside partisan warfare as well as young love, is well told by young director Francesco Maselli. It's his first directorial job on features.

Lucia Bose is standout in her role of a poor girl, bombed out of her city dwelling, who falls for the adolescent owner of the country house in which she's put up during hostilities. It's her best performance to date. Jean Pierre Mocky, Antonio De Teffe, Goliarda Sapienza and Isa Miranda are all fine in their character drawings while the script, after a slow start, picks up pace until it ends in a gripping finale unequaled since the days of "Open City." Most of all, this shows that Italians are still able to experiment with film, and that their artistically, realistic strain has not yet exhausted itself. *Hawk.*

The Second Greatest Sex
(C'SCOPE-COLOR-SONGS)

Attractive cast in a gay musical with a western setting. Sturdy b.o. prospects.

Universal release of an Albert J. Cohen production. Stars Jeanne Crain, George Nader, Kitty Kallen, Bert Lahr; features Mamie Van Doren, Keith Andes, Kathleen Case, Paul Gilbert, Tommy Rall, Edna Skinner, Jimmy Boyd. Directed by George Marshall. Screenplay, Charles Hoffman; camera (Eastman), Wilfrid M. Cline; editor, Frank Gross; songs by Pony Sherrell and Phil Moody, Jay Livingston & Ray Evans and Joan Whitney & Alex Kramer; choreography, Lee Scott. Previewed in N.Y. Sept. 22, '55. Running time, **87 MINS.**

Liza McClure	Jeanne Crain
Matt Davis	George Nader
Katy Connors	Kitty Kallen
Job McClure	Bert Lahr
Birdie Snyder	Mamie Van Doren
Rev. Peter Maxwell	Keith Andes
Tilda Bean	Kathleen Case
Roscoe Dobbs	Paul Gilbert
Alf Connors	Tommy Rall
Cassie Slater	Edna Skinner
Newt McClure	Jimmy Boyd
Cousin Emmy	Cynthia May Carver
The Midwesterners	The Midwesterners
Zach Bean	Ward Ellis
Sarah McClure	Mary Marlo

What Aristophanes started 2,400 odd years ago with "Lysistrata," Universal has now finished in grand style in its "The Second Greatest Sex," a gay, carefree musical with all 'round appeal. In color and CinemaScope, it's an ambitious production that looks good for a hefty payoff.

Film is actually a western operetta, with the accent on songs, dancing and the kind of homespun humor that should go over big particularly in the smaller situations. Production by Albert J. Cohen benefits from a budget splurge (this is one of U's most expensive undertakings) and a well-kept balance of action vs. music which keeps things rolling along at a merry clip.

Western scenes, including a bit of roughhousing but without the sound of gunfire, come off quite well and provide the picture with an additional sell. One of the film's highlights is the dancing, choreographed by Lee Scott. It's plenty lively and the production numbers come through with strong impact even though, once again, the folksy approach is accentuated via folk dancing, etc.

Cast is headed by Jeanne Crain and George Nader, a pleasant team, whether they're feudin' or lovin'. Pic serves to introduce thrush Kitty Kallen who does a standout solo, "How Lonely Can I Get." If Miss Kallen had been given more to do, she might easily have run away with the picture. She's got the looks and a plenty good delivery.

Story, scripted by Charles Hoffman, uses the Lysistrata theme as a base. The men of Osawkie, Kansas, are feuding with two other townships over possession of a small iron safe containing the official Kanaba County records. Wherever the safe ends up, Kanaba will have its county seat. While the men fight, their women wait. Eventually, the girls get disgusted and barricade themselves in an old Indian fort just as the women of Athens went on a love strike to bring their men away from war. The safe disappears in quicksand and the women have their way.

Woven into this are a couple slight love stories and plenty of homespun dialog. Miss Crain is a charmer with plenty of appeal who plays her part with just a touch of tongue-in-cheek. Nader's standing with the bobbysoxers should be further enhanced by this film. He's fine for the part and has a feel for comedy that comes in handy even in some of the broad comedy sit-

uations he's asked to cope with. Mamie Van Doren as the blonde who has her sights set on the Rev. Peter Maxwell, played by Keith Andes, is cute and attractive. Period costumes don't exactly hide her figure.

Andes is okay in a small part and he does nicely by his solo, "Send Us a Miracle," in which he's backed up by the chorus. Bert Lahr as the sheriff has himself a lot of fun with a tailormade part. His delivery of "The Second Greatest Sex," after a session in the local pub, ought to bring the house down. Lahr is a great comedian and he hasn't lost his touch in this one.

Minor parts are all well cast. Jimmy Boyd as the youngster waking up to the facts of life, rates some solid laughs; Edna Skinner and Paul Gilbert made a good comedy team, she as the town spinster and he as the traveling salesman. Direction by George Marshall aims at making this a rich entertainment package, and he succeeds for the most part and in the spirit of the thing.

Songs by Pony Sherrell and Phil Moody—there are eight of them—are an important contribution and some have a catchy quality that could bounce them into the popular field. Best ones are "My Love Is Yours" and "What Good Is a Woman Without a Man." Title tune, "The Second Greatest Sex," was penned by Jay Livingston & Ray Evans, and the Kitty Kallen number, "How Lonely Can I Get," was written by Joan Whitney & Alex Kramer. It's got all the earmarks of a hit even though, in the picture, the staging helped a lot. Print by Technicolor delivers rich hues in the Techni tradition. *Hift.*

08/15—Zweiter Teil
(08/15—Part II)
(GERMAN)

Berlin, Sept. 27.
Gloria release of Divina production. Stars O. E. Hasse; features Armin Dahlen, Rudolf Kutschera, Rainer Penkert, Emmerich Schrenk, Joachim Fuchsberger, Hans-Christian Blech, Paul Boesiger, Peter Carsten, Helen Vita, Gitta Lind, Ellen Schwiers, Gundula Korte, Eva-Ingeborg Scholz, Erica Beer, Erro Wacker, Ulla Melchinger, Manfred Schuster, Hans Elwenspoek, Walter Klock, Otto Bolesch, Klaus Pohl. Directed by Paul May. Screenplay, Ernst von Salomon, after same-titled novel by Hans Hellmut Kirst; camera, Georg Krause; music, Rolf Wilhelm. At Gloria Palast, Berlin. Running time, **110 MINS.**

This is the sequel to "08/15", one of Germany's biggest boxoffice successes since the war. While the first part dealt with German pre-war army barrack life in 1939, this one is localed during the war (1941/42) in Russia.

Quite a few patrons will find that this hasn't the sharpness and roundness of its predecessor. They also may feel a sense of unreality because of the laughter inserted here as part of the war on the German East front. It remains, however, a strong production, destined for big returns in the domestic market. Most of the cast is the same, as in the first "08/15." In addition, Divina has O. E. Hasse in the starring role of a German front officer which gives the pic additional exploitation value. Hasse reached big popularity here via his recent "Canaris." Film's prospects look healthy in the world market.

Knowing that domestic audience is not keen on seeing war pix, at least not the realistic ones, scriptor Ernst von Salomon wisely avoided much of the grim bitterness of the war in Russia. Actually, the war plays only a secondary role in this. Most of the film concentrates on the more or less hilarious episodes of the well-known "08/15" characters. Also love plays an essential part in this film. There is also an anti-war message, albeit a rather tame one, chiefly via the dialog.

Although not quite reaching the standard of his first "08/15" pic, Paul May's direction is still very good. Special mention goes to Hasse, whose portrayal of a German front officer is an impressive one. Also standout performances are turned in by Peter Carsten, as soldier Kowalski; Paul Boesinger as Vierbein, and Hans-Christian Blech. Not so convincing, however, are the several femme players.

Camerawork by Georg Krause is firstrate. Score also is very good.
Hans.

Heimatland
(Homeland)
(AUSTRIAN)

Vienna, Sept. 27.

Sascha-Lux Film production and release. Stars Rudolf Prack. Directed by Franz Antel. Story after Maria von Ebner-Eschenbachs novel "Krambambuli" by Josef Friedrich Perkonig, Hans Holt, Kurt Nachmann; camera, Hans Theyer; music, Willy Schmidt-Gentner, Nico Dostal; lyrics, Hermann Hermecke. At Apollo Kino, Vienna. Running time, 90 MINS.
Thomas Heimberg .... Rudolf Prack
Hans Bachinger .... Adrian Hoven
Helga Sonnleithner.......Marianne Hold
Inge Sonnleithner...Hannelore Bollmann
Vater Bachinger............ Oskar Sima
Frau Korbinian .... Annie Rosar
Apotheker .... Ernst Waldbrunn

A sentimental drama of two love triangles between human beings and the same theme, as lived by a dog, is the story of "Homeland." For the family trade, it should do well in almost any market. Maria von Ebner - Eschenbach's novel "Krambambuli" (name of the dog) is well dramatized here.

Rudolf Prack makes a convincing forester, the symbolic hero, while Adrian Hoven is suitably cast as his opponent in love and life. Marianne Hold brightens the proceedings as the girl they both love. Smaller roles are all nicely filled, especially by Hannelore Bollmann, Oskar Sima, Annie Rosar and Ernst Waldbrunn. The dog (it has the aristocratic name of Hatti von Fernstein) also fits into the plot nicely.

Director Franz Antel has fashioned an intriguing film although it is slowed down by scenes of animal life in the forest. However, this has enough exciting moments to satisfy. Music is passable. Nico Dostal's pre-war hit "Heimatland" is quite excellent. Hans Theyer's Agfacolor camera work is good, but sometimes not too dear. Exterior lensing shows Dachstein, a beauty spot of the Salzkammergut. Other technical credits are also o'.
Maas.

Lucy Gallant
(V'VISION-SONG-COLOR)

Jane Wyman, Charlton Heston in romantic drama aimed at distaff trade. Medium outlook.

Hollywood, Oct. 4.

Paramount release of William H. Pine-William C. Thomas production. Stars Jane Wyman, Charlton Heston; costars Claire Trevor, Thelma Ritter; features William Demarest, Wallace Ford, Tom Helmore. Directed by Robert Parrish. Screenplay, John Lee Mahin, Winston Miller; from the novel, "The Life of Lucy

Gallant" by Margaret Cousins; camera (Technicolor), Lionel Lindon; editor, Howard Smith; score, Van Cleave; song, Jay Livingston, Ray Evans; costumes, Edith Head. Previewed Sept. 19, '55. Running time, 104 MINS.
Lucy Gallant .... Jane Wyman
Casey Cole .... Charleton Heston
Lady MacBeth :........... Claire Trevor
Molly Basserman .... Thelma Ritter
Charlie Madden ...... William Demarest
Gus Basserman .... Wallace Ford
Jim Wardman .... Tom Helmore
Laura Wilson .... Gloria Talbott
Irma Wilson .... Mary Field
Harry Wilson .... James Westerfield
Summertime .... Joel Fluellen
Sal .... Louise Arthur
Anderson .... Roscoe Ates
Governor Allan Shivers..........Himself
Designer Edith Head .... Herself

This is a romantic drama slanted towards distaff viewers, among whom it will have the most appeal. With the names of Jane Wyman and Charlton Heston to help general market prospects, it shapes to fairly comfortable, but not outstanding, returns.

The ladies are provided with an Edith Head fashion show as a topper to the story of a gal who sidesteps love for a career and winds up with both. In line with the femme aim, the late William H. Pine and William C. Thomas frame their production in big-screen VistaVision and Technicolor to make it, the ladies and the costumes visually attractive. On these points the film scores, but is prevented from being entirely good entertainment by prolonging the footage to an overtime 104 minutes. The stretching exposes the more formula aspects of the story so that interest in how the heroine meets her problems is not sustained.

Robert Parrish's direction keeps a restraining hand on the players and, as a consequence, the performances come off quite well. The two stars appear to advantage. There are several assists to entertainment from costars Claire Trevor, again playing a madam with a heart-of-gold, and Thelma Ritter, one of the suddenly oil-rich residents of a small Texas city. Also helping considerably are other town characters such as William Demarest, Wallace Ford, Gloria Talbott, Mary Field, James Westerfield and Joel Fluellen. Finale fashion show has designer Edith Head and Texas Governor Allan Shivers appearing as themselves while eye-catching gowns and models are displayed.

Scripters John Lee Mahin and Winston Miller based their screenplay on Margaret Cousin's novel, "The Life of Lucy Gallant." It tells how Miss Wyman, running away from heartbreak and being left at the altar, comes to an oil-boom Texas town, opens an expensive, fashionable gown shop. The career stalls romantic overtures by rancher Heston, but she gives in to love at the finale when she discovers that Heston, even though opposing working wives, has worked undercover to see her through several financial upsets.

Lionel Lindon rates credit for the excellent color lensing, and the art direction by Hal Pereira and Henry Bumstead gives him something to focus on. Howard Smith edited. Film has an appropriate score by Van Cleave and a tune, "How Can I Tell Her," by Jay Livingston and Ray Evans. *Brog.*

Nana
(FRANCO-ITALIAN; COLOR)

Paris, Sept. 27.

Roitfeld release of Roitfeld-Cigno Film production. Stars Martine Carol, Charles Boyer. Directed by Christian-Jaque. Screenplay, Henri Jeanson, Jean Ferry, Albert Valentin, Jaque; dialog, Jeanson; camera (Eastmancolor), Christian Matras;

editor, Jacques Desagneaux. At Colisee, Paris. Running time, 100 MINS.
Nana .... Martine Carol
Count Muffat .... Charles Boyer
Vandeuvres .... Jacques Castelot
Sabine .... Elisa Cegani
Steiner .... Noel Roquevert
Fontan .... Walter Chiari
Napoleon III .... Jean Debucourt

This makes the fourth time around, on film, for this tome of Emile Zola. Most of the harshness of the original is jettisoned here, leaving a lush crosssection of life under the Second Empire. Pic relates how a brash courtesan leads to the fall of a high government official and her own demise at his hands. Production primarily seems to be one to unveil the natural assets of Martine Carol as she sports dresses cut practically to the navel. If this alone does not pose a censorship problem, the story and insouciant treatment probably will. However, aside from epoch locale and the Miss Carol and Charles Boyer names, this seems to have small dramatic worth for art houses. It is fundamentally good for exploitation spots.

There's the Count Muffat's (Boyer) infatuation for the flighty, looseliving Nana (Miss Carol). When she decides to run off with his rival, he strangles her as the camera looks on the dead girl before the fadeout. Color is an asset to the film in adequately capturing the frivolous costuming and action of the period. Editing and production values are tops. While director Christian-Jaque has given this only a sumptuous mounting, he rarely provides the dramatic essence of character and period needed.

Miss Carol plays this with too many brassy mannerisms. As a result it is hard to imagine why two men are ready to destroy their lives for her. Boyer tries hard to give credence to his role of the infatuated man of affairs. Remainder of the cast is good but never overcomes the handicap of the main roles.

Obiously, this could be of interest for the U.S. on its name values and sexy slant. *Mosk.*

Russian Holiday
(Russian)

Artkino release of Central Documentary Film Studios (of Moscow) production. Directed by V. Boitov (Sovcolor). M. Oshirov and 30 assistants. At Stanley, N.Y., starting Sept. 16, '55. Running time, 80 MINS.

(In Russian; English Narration)

"Russian Holiday" is a documentary covering the Soviet's Physical Culture Day in Moscow last year. It is a combination of a day-long gymnastic exhibition and a fair-sized Russian imitation of how American college students march, manipulate cheer cards and form fantastic figures during the football season. It further incorporates the maneuvers of a Boy Scout jamboree, outdoor classical dancing, a lukewarm imitation of the Saturday parades at West Point and a touch of track events. But with it all, this becomes overpoweringly dull after the first 30 minutes. With 80 minutes of documentary, it hardly suffices as a first-rate feature pic even in a Russian-language house.

'Course, there is the usual colorful parade with the gymnastics garbed in their native dress and a prolonged march of contestants garbed for the exercises, around the arena. All of them lift their

legs and swing their arms—perhaps for better effect to the cameramen. And all them grin when they pass the camera. With 16 Soviet republics determined to strut the most, swing their arms the widest and grin the greatest, this can become irksome. And it does, despite the efforts of some 30 lensmen to break up the monotony.

V. Boitov directed this documentary effort while M. Oshirov headed the huge camera crew. One gathers from the running English narration that several of the gymnastic performers are world champions. The Sovcolor, however, is not championship stock although improved over the old tinters turned out by Moscow. *Wear.*

Oklahoma
(TODD-AO—COLOR—SONGS)

Rodgers & Hammerstein stage classic is given a rousing wide-widescreen treatment that captures the tuneful delight of the stage original. Excellent cast, big b.o. prospects despite some flaws in Todd-AO system.

Magna release of Rodgers & Hammerstein presentation produced by Arthur Hornblow Jr. Stars Gordon MacRae, Gloria Grahame, Gene Nelson, Charlotte Greenwood and Shirley Jones; features Eddie Albert, James Whitmore, Rod Steiger, Barbara Lawrence, J. C. Flippen, Roy Barcroft, James Mitchell, Bambi Linn. Directed by Fred Zinnemann. Screenplay by Sonya Levien and William Ludwig; adapted from the Rodgers & Hammerstein musical play based on Lynn Riggs' dramatic play; originally produced by The Theatre Guild; camera (Eastman Color), Robert Surtees; music by Richard Rodgers; book and lyrics by Oscar Hammerstein 2d; dances staged by Agnes De Mille; production designed by Oliver Smith; music conducted and supervised by Jay Blackton; editor, Gene Ruggiero; costumes, Orry-Kelly and Motley. Previewed in N.Y. at the Rivoli Theatre, Oct. 10, '55. Running time, **145 MINS.**

Curly .... Gordon MacRae
Ado Annie .... Gloria Grahame
Will Parker .... Gene Nelson
Aunt Eller .... Charlotte Greenwood
Laurey .... Shirley Jones
Ali Hakim .... Eddie Albert
Carnes .... James Whitmore
Jud Fry .... Rod Steiger
Gertie .... Barbara Lawrence
Skidmore .... J. C. Flippen
Marshal .... Roy Barcroft
Dream Curly .... James Mitchell
Dream Laurey .... Bambi Linn
Dancers: James Mitchell, Jennie Workman, Kelly Brown, Lizanne Truex, Bambi Linn, Virginia Bosler, Evelyn Taylor, Jane Fischer, Marc Platt.

The innovating musical comedy magic that Richard Rodgers and Oscar Hammerstein 2d first created when The Theatre Guild produced their "Oklahoma!" on the stage has been captured and, in some details, expanded in the film version which Arthur Hornblow Jr. produced and Fred Zinnemann directed in the new Todd-American Optical Co. widescreen process. There must be reservations registered on the technical end, but otherwise the screen version of this peculiarly American work emerges as a fresh, crispy acted and beautifully sung concoction. It's an outstanding b.o. attraction, of course.

Actually, "Oklahoma" could have been made for a screen of any size. Score and book still couldn't have missed. The tunes, familiar to millions, ring out with undiminished delight. The characters pulsate with spirit. The Agnes De Mille choreography makes the play literally leap.

But the wide screen used for the Todd-AO process (the image measures 50x25 feet at the Rivoli) adds production scope and visual grandeur capturing a vista of blue sky and green prairie that can be breathtaking, even though director Zinneman has made comparatively sparing use of this particular aspect.

Todd-AO process decidedly is not out of the woods yet. In some respects, the image attained at the preview showing was disappointing, a letdown that some attribute to an over-expectancy. The screen was surely wide, but the print seen had a tendency to provide an occasionally unsteady and foggy picture and there were moments when disturbing scratches suggested "rain." Color, too, wasn't all it might have been, even though it seemed to improve in the second half of the film, following the intermission.

Best feature of the Todd-AO system appears to be the sound. It is truly magnificent, reproducing music and voices with a clarity and tonal fullness that fairly engulf the audience. Curiously enough, the depth of sound wasn't duplicated on the screen. While Robert Surtees' lensing for the most part is top-notch, the image frequently lacks depth and there is no great feeling of audience participation, at least not at the Rivoli.

Taken by itself, uncomplicated by the separate story of Todd-AO, "Oklahoma!" is a richly entertaining, beautifully designed and costumed production. Heading the cast, Gordon MacRae as Curly, and Shirley Jones as Laurey make a bright, romantic pair.

Each is in top vocal form and, whether singing, feudin' or lovin', they'll capture the heart of America in their roles. This is Miss Jones' first picture, and it is sure to make her a much sought-after star almost overnight.

The entire cast goes through its paces with verve and spirit. If the singing is good, the acting just fine, top honors go to Miss De Mille and her dancers. Ballet sequences, from beginning to end, are highlights, rich in imagination and artistry. (Miss De Mille's concepts started a whole new trend in modern dance in the original Broadway version).

These dance and ballet scenes, with the haunting musical background, are spaced just right. There's the delightful one when Miss Jones sings "Many a New Day" and the robust and catchy rounds of "The Farmer and the Cowman." In Laurey's big dream sequences, admirably danced by Bambi Linn and James Mitchell, with Rod Steiger as the heavy, Miss De Mille's lets her imagination soar and the result, greatly aided by Oliver Smith's distinctive sets, is socko.

Just like its stage predecessor, the film has something for everyone. Charlotte Greenwood is standout in the role of the sympathetic Aunt Eller; Rod Steiger as Jud Fry brings to the part all the dark menace it requires. He delivers a sock performance. As the addle-brained Ado Annie, Gloria Grahame comes through with a broadly humorous bit. Her delivery of "I Cain't Say No" and again of "All Er Nuthin'," with Gene Nelson, is socko all 'round. Nelson, as a lanky, love-sick cowhand, proves his competence as hoofer in the railroad station scene when he and Miss Greenwood lead the "boys" in the rhythmic and expressive "Kansas City" number.

Eddie Albert plays Al Hakim the Armenian peddler with high good humor; James Whitmore gets laughs as the gun-totin' farmer; Barbara Lawrence looks good as Gertie and J. C. Flippen does his usual reliable job as Skidmore.

After all's said and done, the main burden still falls on MacRae and Miss Jones. MacRae not only looks the part of Curly, he acts it out with a modicum of theatrics. He cuts a clean-cut figure and he delivers his songs in grand style, from his impressive entrance when, riding through the field where the corn grows "tall as an elephant's ear", he sings "Oh What a Beautiful Mornin'!," to "The Surrey With the Fringe On Top" (with Miss Jones and Miss Greenwood), "People Will Say We are in Love," which he does charmingly with Miss Jones, and the great "Pore Jud" (with Steiger). Latter number is a real winner.

In "Oklahoma!," Zinnemann was handed a director's dream, even though working with a brand new medium must have been an inhibiting handicap. All in all, Zinnemann's staging is tasteful and manages to imbue the production with a fresh outdoor feeling that grows from a fine feel for composition and the occasional clear-eyed views of sky and land. Probably playing it safe, Zinnemann has stuck to rather routine angles. Clocking 145 minutes even so rich a film as this evidences audience restlessness towards the end just before the rousing "Oklahoma" echoes from the walls.

There are many moments when Zinnemann utilizes his wide screen to perfection and makes it speak eloquently, such as those startlingly panoramic shots against the skyline, the fine angles caught for the "Surrey" number, and the exciting scene when Steiger and Miss Jones hold on for dear life as their buggy smashes through the countryside behind a pair of runaway horses. Singing sequences are integrated into the action with great skill and a perfect sense of balance.

Apart from the technical end, particularly the distortions that appear in the film when viewed from side locations, Rodgers & Hammerstein can take great, and prideful satisfaction from their picture. All things weighed in the scale, "Oklahoma" rates with the industry's best. *Hift.*

The Trouble With Harry
(V'Vision—COLOR—SONG)

Whimsical comedy about a corpse. Alfred Hitchcock, but no suspense. A feature needing slow buildup.

Hollywood, Oct. 7.

Paramount release of Alfred Hitchcock production. Stars Edmund Gwenn, John Forsythe; introducing Shirley MacLaine; features Mildred Natwick, Mildred Dunnock, Jerry Mathers, Royal Dano. Directed by Hitchcock. Screenplay, John Michael Hayes; based on the novel by Jack Trevor Story; camera (Technicolor), Robert Burks; editor, Alma Macrorie; score, Bernard Herrmann; song, Mack David, Raymond Scott. Previewed Oct. 3, '55. Running time, **99 MINS.**

Capt. Albert Wiles ...... Edmund Gwenn
Sam Marlowe .... John Forsythe
Miss Graveley .... Mildred Natwick
Mrs. Wiggs .... Mildred Dunnock
Arnie Rogers .... Jerry Mathers
Calvin Wiggs .... Royal Dano
Millionaire .... Parker Fennelly
Tramp .... Barry Macollum
Dr. Greenbow .... Dwight Marfield
Jennifer Rogers .... Shirley MacLaine

This is a blithe little comedy, produced and directed with affection by Alfred Hitchcock, about a bothersome corpse that just can't stay buried. It's not a catch-on-quick picture that can be given the usual selling, and is likely to be as leisurely in making its mark as Hitchcock is in pacing it. At any rate, "The Trouble With Harry" offers Paramount some trouble in the merchandising, and just how well it will go at the boxoffice is moot. Once carefully established for what it is—a charming comedy, despite the ghoulish subject—the response may be satisfactory.

The picture proves, if nothing else, that the American rural scene can be as inspiring as the foreign locales that have drawn so much bigscreen attention of late. Vermont in the autumn is a thing of beauty, dazzling in its many-hued splendor, and the VistaVision cameras are tellingly used by Robert Burks to show off every tinted vista with an almost in-person effect. If the plot and slick playing aren't enough, then the beauty of the locale, done in Technicolor, gives the ticket buyer an edge for his money.

Edmund Gwenn is a delight as a retired "sea" captain who stumbles on Harry's corpse while rabbit hunting. In the belief he did the killing, he decides to bury the cadaver on the spot. Harry goes in and out of the ground three or four times, is responsible for two romances and not a little consternation and physical exercise before he's finally exhumed for proper discovery, to the relief of Gwenn and the other principals who have become involved in the amateur undertaking.

During the course of events Gwenn and Mildred Natwick, middleaged spinster who thinks she did Harry in, find love, as do John Forsythe, local artist, and Shirley MacLaine, young widow of the in-and-out Harry. Miss Natwick pairs perfectly with Gwenn, and the John Michael Hayes script from the novel by Jack Trevor story provides them with dialog and situations that click. Writing is exceptionally good in the words it gives the entire cast to say. That "I have a short fuse" line uttered by Miss MacLaine as she asks Forsythe to kiss her gently is a real howler. There's a lot of other saucy talk, too.

Forsythe registers with a confident, breezy portrayal of the village artist. Miss MacLaine impresses despite the handicap of some highschool, amateur mannerisms, which manage to get by here but will need correction for the future. Others doing notable work in carrying out the whimsically fey, slightly wacky, intent of the film are Mildred Dunnock, village storekeeper; Jerry Mathers, a small boy, Royal Dano, country officer of the law; Parker Fennelly, eccentric millionaire; Dwight Marfield, screwy doctor, and Barry Macollum, a tramp. Harry is unidentified.

Vermont supplied its own art direction, but what it didn't is excellently handled by Hal Pereira and John Goodman, with set decorations by Sam Comer and Emile Kuri. Alma Macrorie did the editing and Bernard Herrmann backs the fun with a score in keeping. "Flaggin' the Train to Tuscaloosa," by Mack David and Raymond Scott, a catchy melody. *Neal.*

The Girl In the Red Velvet Swing
(C'SCOPE—COLOR—SONGS)

Slow-paced version of the 1906 murder case involving Evelyn Nesbit, Harry Thaw, and Stanford White. Marquee value in Ray Milland, Farley Granger, and well-publicized newcomer, Joan Collins. Moderate b.o. outlook.

20th-Fox release of Charles Brackett production. Stars Ray Milland, Joan Collins, and Farley Granger. Features Luther Adler, Cornelia Otis Skinner, Glenda Farrell, Frances Fuller, Philip Reed, Gale Robbins, James Lorimer, John Hoyt, Robert Simon, Harvey Stephens, Emile Meyer. Directed by Richard Fleischer. Screenplay, Walter Reisch and Brackett; camera (De Luxe), Milton Krasner; editor, William Mace; music, Leigh Harline. Previewed in N.Y. Oct. 10, '55. Running time, **109 MINS.**

Stanford White .... Ray Milland
Evelyn Nesbit Thaw .... Joan Collins
Harry K. Thaw .... Farley Granger
Delphin Delmas .... Luther Adler
Mrs. Thaw .... Cornelia Otis Skinner
Mrs. Nesbit .... Glenda Farrell
Mrs. White .... Frances Fuller
Robert Collier .... Philip Reed
Gwen Arden .... Gale Robbins
McCaleb .... James Lorimer
William Travers Jerome...... John Hoyt
Stage Manager .... Robert Simon
Dr. Hollingshead........Harvey Stephens
Greenbacher .... Emile Meyer
Charles Dana Gibson..... Richard Travis
Arthur .... Harry Seymour

Sport Donnally .... Ainslie Pryor
Nellie .... Kay Hammond
Alice .... Betty Caulfield
Margaret .... Karolee Kelly
Mr. Finley .... Jack Raine
Mrs. Jennings .... Hellen Van Tuyl
Asst. Stage Manager .... Paul Glass
Van Ness .... Paul Power
Leopold Boerner .... Fred Essler
Maitre D' .... Ivan Triesault
Judge Fitzgerald .... Raymond Bailey
Court Clerk .... Charles Tannen
Judy Foreman .... Edmund Cobb
Rev. McEwen .... James Conaty
Flora Dora Girls .Marjorie Hellen-Diane
    Du Bois, Suzanne Alexander,
    Peggy Connelly-Rosemary Ace,
    Jean McCallen

For 50 years, man and boy, the newspapers of America, and especially the Sunday Supps, have kept ever-green the sexsational murder trial of 1906 involving a devil-may-care chorus girl, Evelyn Nesbit, her brooding and not very bright millionaire husband, Harry K. Thaw, and his victim, one of the most brilliant men of his generation, Stanford White. During the half-century that has passed Miss Nesbit herself in her zig-zag career, partly in show biz, has done plenty in real-life exploitation to keep the case alive.

(The side of the story never told is that of the family of Stanford White who feel that a wealthy moron got away with the cold-blooded gunning of a genius.)

20th-Fox's version of the life and loves of Evelyn Nesbit now emerges as a rather pedestrian motion picture. However, the lingering echoes of the famous case, plus the marquee value of Ray Milland and Farley Granger should make "The Girl in the Red Velvet Swing" moderate boxoffice. Joan Collins, the English "new face" who has been publicized along sexy lines, is a plus to the selling effort.

Of the trio involved in the turn-of-the-century triangle, only Miss Nesbit is alive today. Since she is being used extensively by 20th for exploitation purposes, she has apparently given the Walter Reisch-Charles Brackett script her blessing. The story, too, is obviously her version of what transpired in her relationships with White and Thaw prior to the shooting and the trial.

Miss Nesbit, as portrayed by Miss Collins, is seen as a shy beauty carefully shepherded by her seamstress-mother, Glenda Farrell. Her facial charms and figure land her on the cover of Collier's as a Gibson girl and on the stage as a member of the Floradora girls. Her new-found position gives her an opportunity to meet White, played by Milland. In addition to being the name architect of his day (Pennsylvania Station, Madison Square Garden, the Washington Square Arch), White is a bon vivant. With his wife away in Europe, White takes up with Miss Nesbit.

Enter Harry K. Thaw, a young, a pouting Pittsburgh millionaire who usually gets what he wants. He gets Miss Nesbit when White refuses to divorce his wife. Thaw, however, is tortured by jealousy. His resentment ends with the shooting of White in full view of the cabaret audience. At the trial, Thaw cops an I'm-looney plea and is shipped off to asylum. Miss Nesbit resents a payoff attempt by Thaw's family and "reluctantly" takes to the burlesque circuit to capitalize on her notoriety.

The basic fault of the Charles Brackett production is that the audience is unable to build up sympathy for any of the characters involved. Thaw is uninterruptedly obnoxious. White, despite his polish and schizoid good inten-

tions, is not exactly the family hearthstone hero type. Perhaps a film can be made without a hero and heroine, but "The Girl in the Red Velvet Swing" is not it. It's overlong at 109 minutes and many of the stretches leading up to the climax are dull.

Milland comes out the best, capturing the right quality as the suave architect torn between the love of his wife and Miss Nesbit. Granger is unconvincing as the boisterous, hot-headed Thaw. Miss Collins has the looks. She's an exquisite, well-endowed beauty. But her performance is vacuous and fails to suggest inner emotion, if any, of Miss Nesbit. Glenda Farrell scores as the mother and Cornelia Otis Skinner, a real-life neighbor of the White family, is icy as Thaw's socially-prominent mother.

On the whole, the large cast acquits itself well, including Luther Adler, as the defense attorney; Frances Fuller, as White's wife; Philip Reed, as a publisher; Gale Robbins, as a Floradora girl; John Hoyt, as the district attorney; James Lorimer, as Thaw's sidekick; Robert Simon, as a stage manager; Harvey Stephens, as a dentist, and Emile Meyer, as the burlesque booker.

The production captures some of the flavor of the 1900 era, although occasional scenes have an obvious studio backdrop atmosphere. The picture fails to convey any dramatic impact which might be partly attributed to Richard Fleischer's slow-paced direction. The viewer never seems to become part of the film, remaining always a distinterested observer. *Holl.*

Teen-Age Crime Wave

Modest budget meller with exploitable values.

Columbia release of Clover production. Stars Tommy Cook, Mollie McCart; features Sue England, Frank Griffin, James Bell, Kay Riehl. Directed by Fred F. Sears. Screenplay, Harry Essex, Ray Buffum from story by Buffum; camera, Henry Freulich; editor, Jerome Thoms; music, Mischa Bakaleinikoff. Tradeshown N.Y. Oct. 6, '55. Running time, 77 MINS.
Mike Denton .... Tommy Cook
Terry Marsh .... Mollie McCart
Jane Koberly .... Sue England
Ben Grant .... Frank Griffin
Tom Grant .... James Bell
Sarah Grant .... Kay Riehl
Mr. Koberly .... Guy Kingsford
Sgt. Connors .... Larry Blake
Al .... James Ogg
Patrolman Smith .... Robert Bice
Matron .... Kathleen Mulqueen
Mrs. Koberly .... Helen Brown
Bill Salisbury .... Sydney Mason
Man .... George Cisar

With juvenile delinquency a hot topic these days, "Teen-Age Crime Wave" shapes as exploitable fare for the secondary market. Cast has no names to dress up the marquee. However, this deficiency can be overcome to some extent by the promotional angles contained in the story.

Title for this Clover production is somewhat a misnomer. For the Harry Essex-Ray Buffum screenplay based on the latter's story doesn't concern a "crime wave" but focusses attention on one stickup and how it affected the lives of the participants.

Script pursues the obvious possibilities with trigger-happy teener Tommy Cook and tough moll Mollie McCart arrogantly defying the law in a series of shootings while on the lam from a prison rap. Compelled to join them through no fault of her own is Sue England, a pert brunette with a good family background.

After Cook kills a sheriff in springing Miss McCart and Miss England from a reformatory station wagon, all three hide out in James Bell's farmhouse. Bell and Kay Riehl, his wife, are cowed by the teeners' guns but the police eventually close in to bag the fugitives in a chase that winds up in a mountain observatory.

Although replete with familiar situations, story manages to dish out a fair amount of suspense and action under Fred F. Sears' breezy direction. Cook carries off his role as the gun-crazed kid with a snarling proficiency while Miss McCart, a trim blonde, etches a neat portrait of a girl who went wrong. Miss England impresses as the "nice girl" who became a victim of circumstances.

Among others who provide good support are Bell, Miss Riehl and Frank Griffin as their son. Latter, incidentally, seizes Cook in the observatory tower at the climax of the chase. Black-and-white lensing of Henry Freulich gives this Columbia release a lift as does the Mischa Bakaleinikoff score. Editing of Jerome Thoms, Paul Palmentola's art direction and physical values are standard. The Clover (in which Sam Katzman is partnered with Col) production lists no producer credit. *Gilb.*

Man With the Gun

Excellent western suspense melodrama with Robert Mitchum to aid action market returns.

Hollywood, Oct. 7.
United Artists release of Samuel Goldwyn Jr. production. Stars Robert Mitchum, Jan Sterling; features Karen Sharpe, Henry Hull, Emile Meyer, John Lupton, Barbara Lawrence, Ted De Corsia, Leo Gordon, James Westerfield. Directed by Richard Wilson. Screenplay by N. B. Stone Jr. and Wilson; camera, Lee Garmes; editor, Gene Milford; score, Alex North; conducted by Emil Newman. Previewed Oct. 6, '55. Running time, 83 MINS.
Clint Tollinger .... Robert Mitchum
Nelly Bain .... Jan Sterling
Stella Atkins .... Karen Sharpe
Marshal Sims .... Henry Hull
Saul Atkins .... Emile Meyer
Jeff Castle .... John Lupton
Ann Wakefield .... Barbara Lawrence
Rex Stang .... Ted De Corsia
Ed Pinchot .... Leo Gordon
Drummer .... James Westerfield
Doc Hughes .... Florenz Ames
Virg Trotter .... Robert Osterloh
Cal .... Jay Adler
Mary Atkins .... Amzie Strickland
Arthur Jackson .... Stafford Repp
Bill Emory .... Thom Conroy
Mrs. Elderhorn .... Maudie Prickett
Mable .... Mara McAfee
Kitty .... Angie Dickinson
Luz .... Norma Calderon
Dade Holman .... Joe Barry

Westerns that capture the strong-silent-deadly hero flavor are not often come by in the present market, but "Man With the Gun" takes care of any lack in this classification. It is a humdinger of an outdoor actioner, sure to find favor with the shoot-'em-up fans, but offering sufficient otherwise to strike the fancy of many who do not usually take to bang-bang, sagebrush feature film entertainment. It should be a winner in its classification, especially as it has the name of Robert Mitchum to bolster bookings.

The foregoing doesn't mean that "Man" is an epic in its field, but the story is good, excepting a few pretentions, the acting is exactly right to lift it considerably above the oater level, and Richard Wilson's direction of the screen story he wrote with N. B. Stone Jr. for Samuel Goldwyn Jr.'s production keeps tension mounting right up to the climax. In the film's favor is the tight 83 minutes of footage, which concentrates on the story at hand and developing it so that an

audience will continue interested. There are some loquacious moments, but the talk makes good story points, so does not slow proceedings. It's a promising first-feature credit for Goldwyn Jr.

Mitchum plays the title role, a man whose profession is "town-tamer," willing to hire out to take care of any prairie village needing to rid itself of lawless elements. He's also a man with a personal cross — his father was killed by land-grabbers because he believed in a gunless existence, and his wife, Jan Sterling, has left him because of his cold-blooded ways in cleaning up western baddies.

The character is of the type that is stock with Mitchum. Plot nub has him riding into Sheridan City, small cattle town, in search of the wife who had left him. He finds the village in need of his special services, hires out to take care of a ruthless rancher and the latter's gunmen, and at the same time presses to have Miss Sterling return to him. She is now the mistress of a group of dancing (sic) girls in a saloon. He accomplishes both aims, to the satisfaction of the majority of viewers.

While it is mainly a male show, the femmes get their opportunities aplenty and do very well by them. A deglamorized Miss Sterling comes over excellently and Karen Sharpe scores in standout fashion as a town girl engaged to hothead John Lupton. Barbara Lawrence, as one of Miss Sterling's dance girls, counts attractively as the pigeon who abortively sets up Mitchum for a kill. There are a number of other lovelies well-seen in the footage. Henry Hull, sheriff who needs a strong gun backing him; Lupton, the young man who wants to tackle the heavies unaided; Emile Meyer, topnotch as village councilman-blacksmith; Ted De Corsia, Leo Gordon and James Westerfield are among others impressing. The rancher-heavy, Joe Barry, is seen only in the finale and would be completely ludicrous except for his deadly intent.

Lee Garmes' lowkey lensing and Gene Milford's tight editing contribute importantly to the entertainment, as does Alex North's score, which knows when not to intrude on the action as conducted by Emil Newman. *Brog.*

Apache Woman

Okay program western feature for the outdoor action situations.

Hollywood, Oct. 6.
American Releasing Corp. release of Roger Corman (Golden State) production. Stars Lloyd Bridges, Joan Taylor, Lance Fuller; features Morgan Jones, Paul Birch, Jonathan Haze, Paul Dubov. Directed by Corman. Story and screenplay, Lou Rusoff; camera (PatheColor), Floyd Crosby; editor, Ronald Sinclair; music composed and conducted by Ronald Stein. Previewed Oct. 4, '55. Running time, 82 MINS.
Rex Moffet .... Lloyd Bridges
Anne Libeau .... Joan Taylor
Armand .... Lance Fuller
Macey .... Morgan Jones
Sheriff .... Paul Birch
Tom Chandler .... Jonathan Haze
Ben .... Paul Dubov
Carrom .... Lou Place
White Star .... Gene Marlowe
Tall Tree .... Dick Miller
Mooney .... Chester Conklin
Mrs. Chandler .... Jean Howell

Fresh mantling is provided a familiar plot in this rugged western yarn, which is sparked by excellent performances and a generally driving treatment. Action tempo is occasionally slowed by an over-abundance of dialog, but this is compensated for by situations that will hold up in the outdoor market.

Roger Corman, as producer-director for the independent distributing outfit, American Releasing Corp., handles the Lou Rusoff story-screenplay with imagination and draws top performances from his three stars, Lloyd Bridges, Joan Taylor and Lance Fuller.

Motivation is cued by a series of raids and murders which appear to have been committed by reservation Apaches. Bridges, a Government agent, arrives in the small Arizona town as a troubleshooter to settle what appears like the outbreak of a new Indian war. Actually, the crimes have been perpetrated by Fuller, half-crazy, college-educated half-breed at the head of a small band which leaves Apache traces behind. Miss Taylor is his half-breed sister.

Working on the theory of this ruse, Bridges is able to stave off repeated threats of reprisals against the innocent Apaches. Suggestion of a romance between Bridges and Miss Taylor crops up during the times he contacts her for information and aid, and yarn is climaxed by a fast finish.

Bridges registers definitely, and Miss Taylor, who now can play an Indian without a feather, is particularly outstanding in a fiery portrayal. Fuller's characterization also is of high calibre. Paul Birch lends sturdy support as the sheriff, and Morgan Jones fills the bill as Fuller's white henchman.

On the technical end, Floyd Crosby's PatheColor lensing provides picturesque mounting and Ronald Stein's score catches the spirit of the story. *Whit.*

I Died a Thousand Times
(C'SCOPE-COLOR)

Remake of 1941 "High Sierra." Good, although overlong, melodrama for regular market bookings.

Hollywood, Oct. 11.

Warner Bros. release of Willis Goldback production. Stars Jack Palance, Shelley Winters, Lori Nelson, Lee Marvin, Gonzalez Gonzalez; features Lon Chaney, Earl Holliman, Perry Lopez, Howard St. John. Directed by Stuart Heisler. Written by W. R. Burnett; camera (Warnercolor), Ted McCord; editor, Clarence Kolster; music, David Buttolph. Previewed Oct. 5, '55. Running time, **108 MINS.**

Roy Earle .... Jack Palance
Marie .... Shelley Winters
Velma .... Lori Nelson
Babe .... Lee Marvin
Chico .... Gonzalez Gonzalez
Big Mac .... Lon Chaney
Red .... Earl Holliman
Mendoza .... Perry Lopez
Lon Priesser .... Richard Davalos
Ma .... Olive Carey
Pa .... Ralph Moody
Jack Kranmer .... James Millican
The Sheriff .... Bill Kennedy
Joe .... Dennis Hopper
Mrs. Baughman .... Mae Clarke
Mr. Baughman .... Hugh Sanders
Ed .... Dub Taylor

Despite a title that is lengthy and footage ditto "I Died A Thousand Times" averages out as an okay entry for the regular market. It's a remake of the successful "High Sierra," released by Warner Bros. in 1941 and, to some extent, duplicates the thriller aspects of that b.o. job. Names of the cast toppers, Jack Palance and Shelley Winters, are familiar and their performances are excellent, but they add no marquee importance to help the selling. Returns will be middling. A footage trim would make it a handier entry for the general situation, since 108 minutes is unwieldy for the market in which it will get its best response.

The Willis Goldbeck production attempts a new dress for the John Huston-W. R. Burnett 1941 feature and does rather well with the updating. However, running time has been added to the original and this offering can't sustain the extra length, so it veers between hot and cold in viewer interest. Outside of this flaw, though, it comes off as a cops-and-robbers, from the latter's viewpoint, thriller that should do an overall satisfactory job of entertaining the casual ticket buyer.

Palance's physical appearance and considerable skill as an actor is a major asset to the character of Roy Earle, bank-robber just released after a number of years in prison and ready to tackle a new holdup job. It's a tough man he portrays, but he gains a certain amount of audience sympathy in the doing under the direction by Stuart Heisler. Miss Winters, as the dime-a-dance girl who attaches herself to him, also comes off well, even though the character doesn't have the viewer-pull in the same measure as that played by Palance.

A simple outline of the plot has to do with Earle, a headliner in his bank-robbing trade, who is sprung from prison by a crime mastermind who has a resort holdup plotted. He rendevouzes in Los Angeles, gets his instructions and finds his confederates are untried young punks, Lee Marvin, Earl Holliman and Perry Lopez. From then on, from the waiting days in a mountain motel, through the crime, and such side issues as his friendship offered and accepted by a down-and-out family that includes a crippled girl, story builds to the big chase that has the gangster-killer defying the law in the High Sierra, only to go to his inevitable doom.

The big chase sequence near the finale is thrillingly told in CinemaScope and WarnerColor, and is so effective it makes the plot wrapup seem anti-climatic. It is an edge-of-the-seat hackle-raiser, extremely well-done for audience participation. The mountain backdrop, snow-banked highways and speeding cars and motorcycles are tellingly captured by Ted McCord's lensing. David Buttolph's score also helps the melodramatic punch.

Lori Nelson is quite good as the crippled girl made right by the operation bankrolled by Palance, and the character's decision not to love the hood out of gratefulness is rather true to life. Gonzalez Gonzalez portrays a talkative Mexican, handyman at the mountain motel, with an excellent sense of comedy. However, director Heisler, and producer Goldbeck, let that little dog angle get way out of hand until it becomes just too precious in scenes of the canine, a harbinger of doom, gazing from behind bushes at Palance, to whom the pooch had been introduced by Gonzalez. Marvin, Holliman and Lopez are very effective, as are Lon Chaney, the mastermind; Howard St. John, the doctor; James Millican, Olive Carey, Ralph Moody and others. *Brog.*

Twinkle in God's Eye

Mickey Rooney as a parson determined to bring religion to a frontier community. Strictly for program and second feature market.

Republic release of Mickey Rooney production. Stars Rooney and Coleen Gray. Features Hugh O'Brian, Joey Forman, Don Barry, Touch Connors, Jil Jarmyn, Kem Dibbs, Tony Gareen, Raymond Hatton, and Ruta Lee. Associate producer, Maurice Duke. Directed by George Blair. Screenplay, P. J. Wolfson; camera, Bud Thackary; editor, Tony Martinelli; music, Van Alexander; song, "A Twinkle in God's Eye," by Rooney. Previewed in N.Y. Oct. 5, '55. Running time, **73 MINS.**

Rev. Macklin .... Mickey Rooney
Laura .... Coleen Gray
Marty .... Hugh O'Brian
Ted .... Joey Forman
Dawson .... Don Barry
Lou .... Touch Connors
Millie .... Jil Jarmyn
Johnny .... Kem Dibbs
Babe .... Tony Garcen
Yahoo Man .... Raymond Hatton
3rd Girl .... Ruta Lee

Clerical garb appears to be the new fashion for Hollywood's leading men. In recent entries Humphrey Bogart donned the cloth for "Left Hand of God" and Van Heflin for "Count Three and Pray." Now Republic has placed the normally rambunctious Mickey Rooney in white collar and black suit for "The Twinkle in God's Eye," a low budget offering with a western background. Picture is strictly for the second feature and program market.

Rooney fans will no doubt be surprised by his portrayal of a young recently-ordained parson who attempts to bring religion to a tough frontier community. As the Rev. Macklin, determined to rebuild the church destroyed by an Indian raid, Rooney is quiet and courageous, achieving his aims with wide-eyed innocence rather than his fists. It goes without saying that he achieves his purpose and succeeds in rebuilding the church and gathering a flock of faithful worshippers.

There is an artificial, cliche flavor in P. J. Wolfson's screenplay that'll convince only the naive filmgoer. The young parson, after considerable footage, wins to his side a money-grabbing gambling hall owner and succeeds in reforming a hardened holdup man. Also he has no difficulty in gaining the support, almost immediately, of a sextet of typical western "dancing" girls.

Rooney is shut out of the romance department this time, leaving the fadeout clinch to Hugh O'Brian, the gambling hall owner who finally sees the light, and Coleen Gray, one of the church-going dancing girls.

Picture was produced under Rooney's own banner. He also contributes an original song, "The Twinkle in God's Eye," which is sung by Eddie Howard. Miss Gray is also given an opportunity to warble a number in the saloon.

Production values are typical of the lower case oaters, featuring the standard backlot western set. *Holl.*

Queen Bee

Study of a woman powerhouse. Joan Crawford fans and distaffers generally may like it but outlook spotty.

Hollywood, Oct. 18.

Columbia release of Jerry Wald production. Stars Joan Crawford; costars Barry Sullivan, Betsy Palmer, John Ireland, Lucy Marlow; features William Leslie, Fay Wray, Katherine Anderson, Tim Hovey, Linda Bennett. Direction and screenplay, Ranald MacDougall. Based on a novel by Edna Lee; camera, Charles Lang; editor, Viola Lawrence; score, George Duning; conducted by Morris Stoloff. Previewed Oct. 13, '55. Running time, **94 MINS.**

Eva Phillips .... Joan Crawford
Avery Phillips .... Barry Sullivan
Carol Lee Phillips .... Betsy Palmer
Judson Prentiss .... John Ireland
Jennifer Stewart .... Lucy Marlow
Ty McKinnon .... William Leslie
Sue McKinnon .... Fay Wray
Miss Breen .... Katherine Anderson
Ted .... Tim Hovey
Trissa .... Linda Bennett
Miss George .... Willa Pearl Curtis
Sam .... Bill Walker
Dr. Pearson .... Olan Soule

As a stinging, but non-apiarian, drama about a thoroughly selfish woman, "Queen Bee" can be figured to get its best response from among the Joan Crawford fans and distaff ticketbuyers generally. In basics it is a rather anguished soap opera, plus the brittle polish expected of a Crawford vehicle. It provides the lady with full emotional gamut. But business may be spotty.

The Jerry Wald production, scripted and directed by Ranald MacDougall from a novel by Edna Lee, tells of an outwardly charming and beautiful woman who uses any means to the end that she may have security and dominations over all those who surround her. Along in the story she is likened to a queen bee in a hive who stings to death any rivals who might challenge her position. She could also be likened to a female hound.

Miss Crawford, working well under MacDougall's direction, gives slickly styled trouping to the title character's emotional range as she insures the unhappiness of the other principals. MacDougall's script is a bit slow in starting and contains quite a bit of small talk, but once underway manages to develop sufficient expectancy as to how the queen bee will get her comeuppance. A lot of the dialog has bite and the performances are all quite good, even where the characters carry little or no sympathy.

Plot unfolks through the eyes of Lucy Marlow, kin of the rich and futile family that lives in a southern mansion, who has come to Atlanta from the north for a visit. Miss Marlow is warm and engaging as the young lady who at first sides with the restless and wordly Miss Crawford against Barry Sullivan, excellent as the bitter, drunken husband who escapes his dominating wife in the bottle. It is not until Miss Crawford maneuvers to prevent the marriage of Betsy Palmer, Sullivan's sister, and John Ireland, estate manager and ex-lover of the queen bee, that the girl's eyes are opened. Miss Palmer, who shows up exceptionally well, commits suicide and Ireland kills Miss Crawford in a deliberately arranged auto accident to free Sullivan and Miss Marlowe for the love they have found. Ireland is good, and among those providing acceptable support are William Leslie, Fay Wray, Katherine Anderson, and two juves Tim Hovey and Linda Bennett.

The southern mansion setting and the players are rewardingly photographed by Charles Lang.

The score by George Duning, conducted by Morris Stoloff and other behind-camera credits are excellent. *Brog.*

Quentin Durward
(C'SCOPE—COLOR)

Lively version of the Sir Walter Scott minor classic, with Robert Taylor name to help bookings and returns.

Hollywood, Oct. 14.
MGM release of Pandro S. Berman production. Stars Robert Taylor, Kay Kendall, Robert Morley; features George Cole, Alec Clunes, Duncan Lamont, Laya Raki, Marius Goring, Wilfred Hyde White, Eric Pohlmann, Harcourt Williams. Directed by Richard Thorpe. Screenplay, Robert Ardrey; adaptation, George Froeschel; from the novel by Sir Walter Scott; camera (Eastman Color), Christopher Challis; editor, Ernest Walter; music, Bronislau Kaper. Previewed Oct. 10, '55. Running time, 101 MINS.

Quentin Durward	Robert Taylor
Isabell, Countess of Marcroy	
	Kay Kendall
King Louis XI	Robert Morley
Hayraddin	George Cole
Charles, Duke of Burgundy	Alex Clunes
Count William De la Marck	
	Duncan Lamont
Gypsy Dancer	Laya Raki
Count Philip De Creville	Marius Goring
Master Oliver	Wilfrid Hyde White
Gluckmeister	Eric Pohlmann
Bishop of Liege	Harcourt Williams
Count De Dunois	Michael Goodliffe
Duke of Orleans	John Carson
John, Cardinal Balue	Nicholas Hannen
Lord Malcolm	Moultrie Kelsall
Petit-Andre	Frank Tickle
Trois-Echelles	Bill Shine
Lord Crawford	Ernest Thesiger

This lively film version of Sir Walter Scott's "Quentin Durward," a minor and not too well known classic in the States, finds knighthood again in bloom with enough dash and costumer derring-do to make fans of swashbucklers happy. Add the name of Robert Taylor for marquee importance and outlook is good for satisfactory returns.

Pic could have used a familiar femme name to team with Taylor and strengthen its overall prospects. Neither does the title mean much for the U.S. market.

Excellent photographic use of English castles, French chateaus and broad sweeps of fields and forests in actual overseas settings is made in the Pandro S. Berman production to give the romantic adventuring another-worldly background. Imagination and action are well mixed in Richard Thorpe's direction to keep the unfoldment of the Robert Ardrey script, from an adaptation by George Froeschel, interesting. Among several action high spots is a thrilling hero-heavy duel ingeniously staged high in a burning bell tower, with the opponents having at each other with dagger and axe and they swing back and forth on the bell ropes while the clappers bang out a many-toned clamor.

Taylor dons armor to fight for fair lady and honor though gun powder is replacing lance and he finds it difficult to maintain his ideals among the treachery and court intrigue into which the plot plunges him. He's been dispatched to France from Scotland to look over a prospective bride for his aged uncle. He falls in love with the lady himself, but nobly remembers his mission. By thus remaining steadfast of purpose he is rewarded at the finale by winning the beautiful, and very wealthy, countess after foiling the political scheming of King Louis XI and Charles, Duke of Burgundy, and downing Count William De la Marck, renegade nobleman, in the belfry brawl.

Knighthood becomes Taylor and he carries off the heroics with the proper postures. Opposite him romantically is Kay Kendall and, while her name doesn't add any selling power domestically, the payees should like her cameo beauty and considerable acting ability. Robert Morley stands out as the scheming Louis who will resort to any unscrupulous act to keep peace in France. Alec Clunes is good as the Duke of Burgundy as is Duncan Lamont as the renegade nobleman. Scoring strongly for comedy is George Cole, gypsy henchman of the last knight. Others in the predominantly British cast do well.

Christopher Challis' Eastman Color lensing is good, as are the art direction, costuming and editing. Bronislau Kaper provides a background score that is very effective because it never intrudes in an obvious manner on the action. *Brot.*

Return of Jack Slade
(SUPERSCOPE)

Good actioner and fits well into intended market; sequel to "Jack Slade" should find same good b.o. response.

Hollywood, Oct. 5.
Allied Artists release of Lindsley Parsons production. Stars John Ericson, Mari Blanchard, Neville Brand; features Casey Adams, John Shepodd, Howard Petrie. Directed by Harold Schuster. Screenplay, Warren Douglas; camera, William Sickner; editor, Maurice Wright; music, Paul Dunlap. Previewed Allied Artists Studio, Los Angeles, Calif., Oct. 3, '55. Running time, 79 MINS.

Jack Slade	John Ericson
Texas Rose	Mari Blanchard
Harry Sutton	Neville Brand
Billy Wilcox	Casey Adams
Johnny Turner	John Shepodd
Ryan	Howard Petrie
Kid Stanley	John Dennis
Polly Logan	Angie Dickinson
Laughing Sam	Donna Drew
Little Blue	Mike Ross
Abilene	Lyla Graham
George Hagen	Alan Wells
Professor	Raymond Bailey

"The Return of Jack Slade," containing popular shoot-'em-up action ingredients, should find the same patron response as did "Jack Slade," the boxoffice success of two years ago that cued this follow-up by Allied Artists.

Actually, it's Slade Jr. (John Ericson), around whom the action pivots in this Warren Douglas screenplay, the original Slade (Mark Stevens) having been killed off in the first film. Employed as a Pinkerton, Ericson's out to gain information on a large band of Wyoming outlaws. He manages to become one of the mixed gang, and before the wind-up has seen the outlaws all but wiped out, but not until he finds romance with a gal from the gang (Mari Blanchard), who really was too decent to have been connected with the baddies in the first place.

Ericson is well cast as Slade, turning in neat portrayal in a role which dominates the footage throughout. Miss Blanchard, in femme lead, is mainly called upon to display her charms. This she does in spades and comes across with a good performance, too. Neville Brand, third co-star, is okay as lead heavy who's killed by Ericson in the final reel. Supporting the principals, among others, and turning in okay stints, are Casey Adams, head of the outlaw gang; John Shepodd, a friend of Ericson's who's killed by Brand; and Howard Petrie, Pinkerton official.

Producer Lindsley Parsons came through with a film that will fit well into the intended market. Direction by Harold Schuster concentrates well on the action elements, while Maurice Wright's editing is smooth. Camera work of William Sickner and other technical contributions are standard.

Score by Paul Dunlap features "Yellow Rose of Texas," a current hit and an exploitable item. *Neal.*

Outlaw Treasure

Dull, confused low-budget outdoor action pic for fill-ins.

Hollywood, Oct. 14.
Favorite Films release of an Edyth L. Wheeler presentation produced by John Carpenter. Stars John Forbes. Co-stars Frank Carpenter, Adele Jergens, Glenn Langan, Hal Baylor, Michael Whalen. Directed by Oliver Drake; screenplay, John Carpenter; camera, Clark Ramsey; music, Darrell Calker. Reviewed Oct. 12, '55. Running time, 65 MINS.

This independent effort, made a few years ago, is a dull and confused tale of post-Civil War California that has little to recommend it. Lacking in name value and appeal its only chance is as a quick fill-in for small situations.

Produced and written by John Carpenter, it plods through 65 minutes of gunshots and horseback chases to spin something of a story about an army troubleshooter trying to clear up the mystery of missing gold shipments. The James Brothers are dragged in to lend some semblance of reality, but nothing helps much.

Oliver Drake's direction is mostly concerned with directing equine traffic and giving the actors a chance to fire as many rounds of blanks as they wish. There are adequate performances from John Forbes as the troubleshooter, Glenn Langan as an army lieutenant and Michael Whalen as a major. Adele Jergens gets co-star billing but is on screen for approximately six minutes, just long enough so the audience will know who she is when Forbes kisses her at the fadeout. *Kap.*

The View From Pompey's Head
(C'SCOPE—COLOR)

Slow-paced but highly articulate and frequently moving translation of the Hamilton Basso bestseller. Shapes for okay b.o.

20th-Fox release of Philip Dunne production. Stars Richard Egan, Dana Wynter, Cameron Mitchell. Features Sidney Blackmer, Marjorie Rambeau, Dorothy Patrick Davis, Rosemarie Bowe, Jerry Paris, Ruby Goodwin. Directed by Dunne; screenplay, Dunne, from Hamilton Basso novel; camera (De Luxe), Joe MacDonald; editor, Robert Simpson; music, Elmer Bernstein. Previewed in N.Y., Oct. 21, '55. Running time, 97 MINS.

Anson Page	Richard Egan
Dinah	Dana Wynter
Mickey Higgins	Cameron Mitchell
Garvin Wales	Sidney Blackmer
Lucy Wales	Marjorie Rambeau
Meg	Dorothy Patrick Davis
Kit	Rosemarie Bowe
Ian Garrick	Jerry Paris
Esther	Ruby Goodwin
Julia	Pamela Stufflebeam
Cecily	Evelyn Rudie
Duncan	Howard Wendell
Barlowe	Dayton Lummis
Miss Mabry	Bess Flowers
Debbie	Cheryl Calloway
Pat	Charles Herbert
Hotel Clerk	De Forrest Kelly
Garrick's Secretary	Florence Mitchell
Bellhop	Robert Johnson
Maid	Ann Mabry
Betty Jo Ann	Wilma Jacobs
Pullman Porter	Bill Walker
Servant	Frances Driver
Policeman	Jack Mather
Police Sergeant	Charles Watts
Groom	Wade Duman
Trainman	Tom Wilson

When he drew the assignment of bringing Hamilton Basso's "The View From Pompey's Head" to the screen, Philip Dunne automatically inherited a 409-page headache. Considering the verbose and intricately emotional nature of the book, along with its undercurrents of southern nostalgia, pride and prejudice, Dunne and his cast do a remarkable job in recreating an atmosphere without losing sight of what makes a film click at the b.o.

"Pompey's Head" is, on many counts, a very fine picture that respects the audience's intelligence. It's done with good taste, a sense of deep passion and a pronounced flair for pictorial beauty. In his triple capacity of producer-director-writer, Dunne shows both imagination and an earnest desire to communicate as much as possible of what Basso meant when he called this "The View From Pompey's Head."

Unfortunately, in adopting the book, Dunne didn't quite lick what is probably an unsurmountable obstacle. Like the book, which is really a study of a small Southern town, the script tends to amble and get lost in conversation. The action in the book comes in its dissection of personalities and personal relationships. In the film, traces of this remain, but they are hinted at in sentences where the book took pages and the result is at times confusing and unsatisfactory. Furthermore, retention of the book's title is apt to hurt the pic since non-literary people are apt to think of it as a story of Roman times, and decisive selling will be necessary to overcome this impression. "View From Pompey's Head" introes Dana Wynter in the part of the willful and possessive Dinah, a modern Southern belle holding on to tradition, and Richard Egan as the Southern boy who has gone north, has become a successful lawyer, and now returns home for a few days to solve a mysterious case.

Like the rest of the cast, Miss Wynter and Egan do their roles justice. Miss Wynter, who is British, does wonders with a Southern accent, but doesn't always catch the vivaciousness and hot spirit that part requires. She is an outstanding beauty and a pleasure to look at. Egan is good and properly underplays a difficult part. The two make an attractive team, and Dunne has seen to it that they're both given plenty of time to indulge in their romantic inclinations, another selling point for the film.

With them is Cameron Mitchell as Mickey Higgins, the boy from across the tracks, whom Dinah married in order to be able to keep her beloved Mulberry home. Mitchell gives the role a vivid interpretation. Marjorie Rambeau is excellent as the personification of Southern gentility and Sidney Blackmer nicely realizes Garvin Wales, the central figure in the mystery Egan is trying to solve. Dorothy Patrick Davis, Rosemarie Bowe and Jerry Paris all give strong support.

Story, in brief, has Egan coming to Pompey's Head, his home town, to look into an embezzlement charge brought against a publishing executive by the wife of a famous—now blind—author. He meets up with Miss Wynter, his youthful love, and nostalgia takes over. Eventually, it turns out that the author knew about the missing money, but wouldn't talk about it to his wife since the coin went to support his mother, who was colored. The Code obviously gets into the way of the love story and some of the southern angles are quite determinedly toned down.

When scripter Dunne found the film too short to profitably follow up the story's many threads, Dunne the director handles his performers with skill and his cameras with a well-developed sense for visual dramatics. Some of the Southern shots (lenser Joe MacDonald must get the credit, too) are stunning and show a lively awareness of the possibilities of the CinemaScope medium. Dunne the producer is responsible for some of the most magnificently elegant sets seen in a long time. Mulberry interiors are classy and serve as a perfect backdrop for part of the story. De Luxe color is of topnotch quality.

As he proved in "Prince of Players," Dunne has a knack for turning out screenfare that's above the average in quality. "Pompey's Head" has many superficial qualities and a rather pat and unsatisfying ending, but it tackles a provocative subject without sacrificing too many of the essentials and its romance carries the stamp of realism. In the long run, that's a paying combo. *Hift.*

All That Heaven Allows
(COLOR)

Handsomely produced women's picture with Jane Wyman and Rock Hudson for the marquee. Shapes as an exploitation natural.

Universal release of Ross Hunter production. Stars Jane Wyman, Rock Hudson. Features Agnes Moorehead, Conrad Nagel, Virginia Grey, Gloria Talbott, William Reynolds. Directed by Douglas Sirk. Screenplay, Peg Fenwick; camera (Technicolor), Russell Metty; editor, Frank Gross; music, Frank Skinner. Previewed in N.Y., Oct. 19, '55. Running time, 89 MINS.

Cary Scott .... Jane Wyman
Ron Kirby .... Rock Hudson
Sara Warren .... Agnes Moorehead
Harvey .... Conrad Nagel
Alida Anderson .... Virginia Grey
Kay Scott .... Gloria Talbott
Ned Scott .... William Reynolds
Mona Flash .... Jacqueline De Wit
Mick Anderson .... Charles Drake
Jo-Ann .... Leigh Snowden
Mary Ann .... Merry Anders
Howard Hoffer .... Donald Curtis
George Warren .... Alex Gerry

With "Magnificent Obsession" one of its top grossers, Universal could be fairly expected to find another vehicle for the team of Jane Wyman and Rock Hudson. In "All That Heaven Allows," Ross Hunter has produced and Douglas Sirk directed a sentimental, glossy soap opera for the screen. It's got femme appeal written all over it and, with plenty of exploitation angles to play around with, U has a picture that should click, particularly in the smaller towns.

Although this story of a long-suffering woman who, at 40 or so, finds romance with a man between ten and 15 years her junior, is hardly designed to ignite prairie fires, scripter Peg Fenwick nevertheless has managed to turn the Edna L. and Harry Lee story into a slightly offbeat yarn with some interesting overtones that accent the social prejudices of a small town. All that's been worked skillfully but without undue emphasis into a film guaranteed to touch the heartstrings of all middle-aged women, who, occasionally, must think of the possibility of such a romance.

There is little quarrelling with the b.o. appeal of the Wyman-Hudson combo. Miss Wyman, as the widow who falls hopelessly in love with her young gardener and then temporarily abandons him to conventional prejudices—only to be reunited with him at the end—is appealing and properly long-suffering. Even taking into account the selfish pressure brought on her by her children, who don't approve of Hudson as a stepfather, the script makes her into a rather weak character and it's difficult, after a while, to rouse much sympathy for her plight.

Hudson is handsome and somewhat wooden. Laconic of speech, and imbued with an angel's patience and understanding, it's at times hard to understand his passion for the widow, what with pretty girls just spoiling for his attention.

Standout performance is delivered by a young newcomer, Gloria Talbott, playing Miss Wyman's teenage daughter. As a brat given to quoting Freud, and later in her sudden understanding of her mother's position, she's delightfully fresh and cute. In Miss Talbott, U has come up with a real find and she registers very strongly. As her brother, William Reynolds is too arrogant to be believable. Agnes Moorehead, Conrad Nagel, Virginia Grey, Leigh Snowden and Charles Drake are fine in support parts.

Director Sirk keeps things rolling along and manages to get his actors to make trite dialog sound less so. Russell Metty's camerawork is routine and Frank Skinner's music has the proper "schmaltz." *Hift.*

Rebel Without a Cause

Strong action picture. Probes problem of unhappy, angry teenagers.

Warner Bros. release of David Weisbart production. Stars James Dean. Directed by Nicholas Ray. Based on Ray's story; screenplay by Stewart Stern; adaption by Irving Shulman; camera, Ernest Haller; music, Leonard Rosenman; editor, William Ziegler. Tradeshown in N.Y., Oct. 14, '55. Running time, 111 MINS.

Jim .... James Dean
Dad .... Jim Backus
Mother .... Ann Doran
Grandmother .... Virginia Brissac
Judy .... Natalie Wood
Judy's Dad .... William Hopper
Judy's Mother .... Rochelle Hudson
Buzz .... Corey Allen
Plato .... Sal Mineo
Goon .... Dennis Hopper
Servant .... Marietta Canty
Psychiatrist .... Edward Platt
Lecturer .... Ian Wolfe
Moose .... Nick Adams
Chick .... Jack Grinnage
Mil .... Steffi Sidney
Harry .... Tom Bernard
Cliff .... Clifford Morris

Here is a fairly exciting, suspenseful and provocative, if also occasionally far-fetched, melodrama of unhappy youth on another delinquency kick. The plot bears no resemblance to the content of a book of the same title published a few years ago. The book was a clinical study of a withdrawn boy. The film presents a boy whose rebellion against a weakling father and a shrewish mother expresses itself in boozing, knife-fighting and other forms of physical combat and testing of his own manhood.

"Rebel Without a Cause" cannot escape comparison with Metro's recent "Blackboard Jungle." Each film depicts modern highschool student bodies as ruled by sadistic elements given to switch-blade knives, bullying and generally unpleasant notions of fun. There is in each a suggestion of pitiable waste of human material and promise. Finally "Rebel" may draw upon itself, as did the earlier release, outcries from academic, ecclesiastic and civic bodies.

The shock impact in "Rebel" is perhaps greater because this is a pleasant middleclass community. The boys and girls attend a modern highschool. They are well fed and dressed and drive their own automobiles. Does the contrast between their healthy-seeming exteriors and their restlessly cruel natures occasionally strain credulity? The debate could go on long into the night with newspaper clippings and police court statistics arrayed on one side and belief in goodness on the other.

Although essentially intent upon action, director Nicholas Ray, who sketched the basic story developed by Stewart Stern and Irving Shulman, does bring out redeeming touches of human warmth. There is as regards the hero, if not as regards the highschool body generally, a better-than-average-for-a-psychological thriller explanation of the core of confusion in the child. And that is paying the typewriter craftsmen a considerable compliment. The police court psychiatrist (Edward Platt) also helps balance things for humanity.

The performance of the star, James Dean, will excite discussion, especially in connection with the irony of his own recent crash death under real-life conditions of recklessness which form a macabre pressagent frame as the picture goes into release. In "East of Eden," under Elia Kazan's direction, the 24-year-old actor was widely thought to be doing a Marlon Brando. But freed from Kazan's evaluations of character, this resemblance vanishes. Almost free of mannerisms under Ray's pacing, Dean is very effective as a boy groping for adjustment to people. As a "farewell" performance he leaves behind, with this film, genuine artistic regret, for here was a talent which might have touched the heights. His actor's capacity to get inside the skin of youthful pain, torment and bewilderment is not often encountered.

There are a number of other arresting performances. Jim Backus for one. His mealy-mouthed, wishy-washy, self-deprecating parent is the soft pillow against which the boy beats his fists, demanding manhood, leadership and a father he can respect. There is one powerful scene on a staircase. The boy stands between his mother (Ann Doran), who confronts him from above, and the father who is behind him. Never turning to look at his dad, the youth repeats several times, "Stand up for me, dad. Tell her off." This bit delineates the whole background of man-and-wife failure which has been the emotional ripsaw in the son's growing up.

Natalie Wood as the girl next door should add professional prestige. Here, too, there is teenage maladjustment. She, too, asks more of her father than he can give. The father (William Hopper) is seen as embarrassed by the girl's becoming a woman. Unable himself to relate to this new creature of bosoms, lipstick and sex feelings, he tries to whip away the embraces she wants to go on giving him as she has from babyhood. This time the mother (Rochelle Hudson) is not a shrew but pinhead who understands neither the daughter nor the husband.

Sal Mineo is one of two essentially love-worthy youths to lose their lives in the story. He is the abandoned child of a big Greek tycoon. The boy lives alone in a large villa with only a Negro servant (Marietta Canty) for mother, father and family. Young Mineo stands out on performance and is an important value in the film.

The various highschool "menaces" are briefly and surfacely depicted, often hardly more than a cardboard cutout. Which is not to deny that they serve well as the symbol of hostility against which the suspense develops. They and their gals form the automobile alley of death down which the two feuding youths, Dean and Corey Allen, drive the two old jalopies in a contest to prove who will lose nerve and jump first before the cars go over the bluff. This "Chicken Run" sequence comes early in the picture and results in the death of Dean's antagonist. It is a punch scene, a novelty, an insight into madcap youth. It also drives home the insanity of frightened youth lest the stigma of being called "chicken" go uncontradicted.

As with the delinquency kick generally, the switch-blade stuff and the unhappiness of kids (typically the fault of their parents in such screen fiction) there are newspaper clippings and other evidence in support of the "Chicken Run" phobia. The sequence is rooted in ghastly reality.

Adults may well come away from "Rebel Without a Cause" as from "Blackboard Jungle" and "The Wild One" and other films which spotlight the compulsive cruelties of youth, with a need to believe the facts hideously exaggerated and a silent prayer that they never meet such youths except upon the motion picture screen. *Land.*

Naked Sea
(COLOR)

Feature-length documentary on tuna-fishing. Beautifully color-lensed, over-narrated. Okay supporter.

Hollywood, Oct. 25.

RKO release of Theatre Productions Inc. presentation, produced and directed by Allen H. Miner. Written by Gerald Schnitzer; voice, William Conrad; camera (PatheColor), Miner; music composed and scored by Laurindo Almeida and George Fields. Previewed Oct. 21, '55. Running time, **69 MINS.**

There's more to a tuna than just what's in the can, and Allen H. Miner, with camera and recorder, sets about giving the full story in "Naked Sea." The result is an interesting documentary, beautifully color-lensed, albeit somewhat repetitious and vastly over-narrated. It's an okay supporter.

The piscatorial pic depicts a 16-week voyage out of San Diego by a tuna clipper, seeking the wily deep-sea game in the waters off Panama, the Galapagos Islands and the coast of Peru. Doing his lensing in 16m, Miner has come up with any number of striking seascapes, as well as capturing on film the hard work, the disappointments, and the dangers involved in getting the tuna to market. The payoff's big, if the catch is. So is the investment in time, money and work.

Provisioning the clipper and saying goodbyes take up the first eight minutes of the film, before the 12-man crew goes to sea to fill the bait tanks and look for the elusive fish. It takes 300 tons to fill the holds and it's not until the ship hits Peruvian waters that a school of big ones is found that will load the clipper. Footage is most interesting off the volcanic Galapagos during a bait-hunt.

Associate producer Gerald Schnitzer wrote the narration which is spoken by William Conrad. It is here that film falters because the talk is florid, unnecessarily theatrical, and never ceases. Some of the quiet of the sea would be welcome and many of the incidents lensed needed only an occasional, brief word of explanation to hold viewers attention.

Other than the outstanding lensing by Miner, which has been blown up to 35m in PatheColor, a big asset is the background music composed and scored by Laurindo Almeida and George Fields. Latter's harmonica and Almeida's guitar provide the beautiful accompaniment, which could almost tell the tuna saga without assistance. *Brog.*

The Tender Trap
(C'SCOPE-SONG-COLOR)

Frank Sinatra, Debbie Reynolds in fairly diverting film version of the legit comedy; for general situations.

Hollywood, Oct. 25.

MGM release of Lawrence Weingarten production. Stars Frank Sinatra, Debbie Reynolds, David Wayne, Celeste Holm; features Jarma Lewis, Lois Albright, Carolyn Jones. Directed by Charles Walters. Screenplay, Julius Epstein; based on the play by Max Shulman and Robert Paul Smith, presented on the NY stage by Clinton Wilder; camera (Eastman Color), Paul C. Vogel, editor, Jack Dunning; score composed and conducted by Jeff Alexander; song, by Sammy Cahn and James Van Heusen. Previewed Oct. 21, '55. Running time, **110 MINS.**

Charlie Y. Reader .... Frank Sinatra
Julie Gillis .... Debbie Reynolds
Joe McCall .... David Wayne
Sylvia Crewes .... Celeste Holm
Jessica .... Jarma Lewis
Poppy .... Lola Albright
Helen .... Carolyn Jones
Mr. Sayers .... Howard St. John
Sol Z. Steiner .... Joey Faye
Mr. Loughran .... Tom Helmore
Director .... Willard Sage
Ballet-Actor .... Marc Wilder
Audition Dancer .... Jack Boyle
Eddie .... James Drury

This film version of the legit comedy is a fairly diverting, but considerably overlong, takeoff on the romantic didoes of bachelors and gals. With the names of Frank Sinatra and Debbie Reynolds heading the star list, indications are that returns can hit a satisfactory level in the regular runs.

Picture has been given a plushy look in the Lawrence Weingarten production through slick settings and the CinemaScope-Eastman Color lensing, but to some extent the entertainment purpose is defeated by stretching the light plot in the Max Shulman-Robert Paul Smith to 110 minutes. Glib dialog and amusing situations in the script by Julius Epstein plug some of the holes, but there isn't enough substance in the material to keep interest from wavering over the long haul.

Charles Walters' direction is able in drawing smooth performances from Sinatra, Miss Reynolds, David Wayne and Celeste Holm. Foursome quite often hits the laugh mark and Sinatra must have liked the parade of gals through his carefree bachelor existence before he fell victim to love—the tender trap here exampled by Miss Reynolds. Making up the s.a. parade, in addition to Miss Holm, are Jarma Lewis, Lola Albright and Carolyn Jones. There's quite a bit of sizzle in that opening couch scene between Sinatra and Miss Albright.

Into the lives of Sinatra, bachelor theatrical agent, and Wayne, his married friend from Indiana. Visiting Manhattan sans spouse enters Miss Reynolds, a determined girl who already has set the date for her wedding even without having found the right man. After some preliminaries she decides Sinatra is it. Remainder of the footage details his capture, but not before he finds himself engaged both to her and Miss Holm, an impossible situation that rights itself following a humdinger of a drunken party that segues into the morning-after comedy highlight of the footage.

The title tune gets some consistent plugging in the film, being heard at both the opening and closing as well as in between, with all the principals working it over at different times. It's good cleffing by Sammy Cahn and James Van Heusen. Score by Jeff Alexander also listens easy. Paul C. Vogel's color lensing and the good settings head the list of expert technical credits.

Three Stripes in the Sun

Romantic drama in occupied Japan needs strong selling to achieve its b.o. potential.

Columbia release of Fred Kohlmar production Stars Aldo Ray, Phil Carey, Dick York, Mitsuko Kimura; features Chuck Connors, Camille Janclaire, Henry Okawa, Tatsuo Saito. Directed by Richard Murphy. Screenplay, Murphy; adaptation, Albert Duffy, based on E. J. Kahn Jr.'s New Yorker mag article, "The Gentle Wolfhound"; camera, Burnett Guffey; editor, Charles Nelson; music composed by George Duning, conducted by Morris Stoloff. Tradeshown, N.Y., Oct. 14, '55. Running time, **93 MINS.**

Hugh O'Reilly .... Aldo Ray
Colonel .... Phil Carey
Cpl. Neeby Muhlendorf .... Dick York
Yuko .... Mitsuko Kimura
Idaho .... Chuck Connors
Sister Genevieve .... Camille Janclaire
Father Yoshida .... Henry Okawa
Konoya .... Tatsuo Saito
Chiyaki .... Chivaki
Sgt. Demetrios .... Sgt. Demetrios
Sgt. Romaniello .... Sgt. Romaniello
Mr. Ohta .... I Tamaki
Major Rochelle .... Lt. Col. Mike Davis
Lt. Brazil .... Lt. Thomas Brazil
Kanno .... Takeshi Kamikubo
Satsumi .... Tamao Nakamura
Yuko's Mother .... Teruko Omi
Yuko's Sister .... Kamiko Tachibana

How life in postwar, occupied Japan affected the destiny of a battle-hardened American sergeant is interestingly related in "Three Stripes in the Sun." But with light marquee values in its trio of stars—Aldo Ray, Phil Carey and Dick York—this Columbia release will require strong selling to enhance its b.o. prospects.

Exploitation angles are difficult to figure for this one. At first glance a romance between Sgt. Ray and Mitsuko Kimura, a cute interpreter for Yank Col. Phil Carey, would appear to supply ample promotional material. Actually, however, the rich sentiment that's involved in Ray's attempts to improve the lot of some Japanese orphans tends to outweigh the romantic aspects.

Title, too, will be vague to those who aren't hep with things military and the Far East theatre. The Richard Murphy screenplay, as adapted by Albert Duffy from E. J. Kahn Jr.'s New Yorker mag piece, "The Gentle Wolfhound," meticulously shows how Jap-hating Ray ultimately softens up via exposure to the needy Nipponese kids.

A professional soldier and epitome of the G.I. expression, "20-year man," Ray curiously has a tender side. This is leisurely outlined in numerous scenes depicting him rustling G.I. chow for the orphans, contributing his own pay for the cause and even starting a fund to erect a modern building to house the moppets. Throughout all these activities he's usually accompanied by Miss Kimura, as interpreter. That they would eventually wed is telegraphed long before the finale.

As portrayed by Ray the sergeant isn't a particularly sympathetic type. On the other hand this isn't entirely his fault as the sarge's mental processes in the face of the obvious are incredibly slow. Carey turns in a slick, precise characterization of the Colonel. Miss Kimura's performance as Ray's vis-a-vis is a sparkling piece of thesping on a level with Oscar stature. York adequately fulfills demands of a stint as Ray's corporal buddy.

Among others who register nicely in supporting roles are Camille Janclaire as a Roman Catholic sister at the orphanage, Henry Okawa as a priest and Tatsuo Saito as Miss Kimura's father. Richard Murphy, who directed from his own script, extracted full value from the story's sentimental overtones. Producer Fred Kohlmar provides the film with excellent physical backgrounds that Burnett Guffey lensed to advantage in black-and-white.

Music composed by George Duning and conducted by Morris Stoloff is an asset as is Carl Anderson's art direction and Charles Nelson's editing. M/Sgt. Hugh O'Reilly, whose true story is the basis of the film's plot, acted as technical adviser. *Gilb.*

Guys and Dolls
(MUSICAL—C'SCOPE—COLOR)

Lush, marquee-loaded filmusical for socko b.o. A Goldwyn gold mine.

Metro release of Samuel Goldwyn's production. Stars Marlon Brando, Jean Simmons, Frank Sinatra, Vivian Blaine; features Robert Keith, Stubby Kaye, B. S. Pully, Johnny Silver. Directed and screenplay by Joseph L. Mankiewicz. Based on Feuer & Martin legit musical, book by Jo Swerling & Abe Burrows, from a Damon Runyon story; songs, Frank Loesser; dances, Michael Kidd; music, Jay Blackton and Cyril Mockridge; camera (Eastmancolor), Harry Stradling; special effects, Warren Newcombe; asst. director, Arthur S. Black Jr.; orchestrations, Skip Martin, Nelson Riddle, Alexander Courage, Al Sendrey; editor, Daniel Mandell. Previewed at Loew's 72d St. Theatre, N.Y., Oct. 25, 1955. Running time, **150 MINS.**

Sky Masterson .... Marlon Brando
Sarah Brown .... Jean Simmons
Nathan Detroit .... Frank Sinatra
Miss Adelaide .... Vivian Blaine
Lt. Brannigan .... Robert Keith
Nicely-Nicely Johnson .... Stubby Kaye
Big Jule .... B. S. Pully
Benny Southstreet .... Johnny Silver
Harry the Horse .... Sheldon Leonard
Rusty Charlie .... Dan Dayton
Society Max .... George E. Stone
Arvid Abernathy .... Regis Toomey
General Cartwright .... Kathryn Givney
Laverne .... Veda Ann Borg
Agatha .... Mary Alan Hokanson
Angie the Ox .... Joe McTurk
Calvin .... Kay Kuter
Mission Member .... Stapleton Kent
Cuban Singer .... Renee Renor
Louis .... John Indrisano
Pitch Man .... Earle Hodgins
Waiter .... Barry Tyler
Goldwyn Girls
Reuben De Fuentes Orch.

"Guys and Dolls" is a bangup filmusical, made-to-order for the young dolls & guys out front, and for the general family trade as well. It is in the modern idiom; insured by a strong marquee quartet in Marlon Brando, Jean Simmons, Frank Sinatra and Vivian Blaine; and fortified by a good set of songs, old and new.

As a showmanship picture it is well endowed. Besides the cast, the good-penetration job on the $1,000,000 property buy for pictures, plus the Runyonesque values, there is the overall impact of this being a lush musical in the topdrawer Goldwyn manner, including a resurrection of the Goldwyn Girls, another okay item for the ballyhoo.

Film has some minor shortcomings, even now correctable if the producer-distributor will it. One is the obvious overlength and the latitude for cutting, especially in the forepart. The other is indigenous to the basic production, not as readily corrected although there, too, if cutting is desired, some of the closeups of the drab Times Square street scenes might be elided. Apart from the fact that perhaps only the Broadway denizens might be sensitive to the lack of realism, especially where the locale is in the immediate proximity of Runyon's favored "Mindy's," anybody at all familiar with the environs of the Lindy's restaurants (whether the "old" or the "new" Lindy's, diagonally across Broadway) may wax captious on that score. If the street scenes were primed for fantasy they look what they are fundamentally—studio sets.

But filmusical license permits for a lot of things. As soon as the auditor permits himself to get lost in the "nicely-nicely" Runyon world and its "characters" it is always palatable entertainment.

The casting is good all the way. Much interest will focus, of course, around Marlon Brando in the Robert Alda original and Jean Simmons as the Salvation Army sergeant (created by Isabel Bigley), and they deport themselves in inspired manner. They're as competent song-and-dance people as in their past straight romantic credits. They make believable the offbeat romance between the gambler and the spirited servant of the gospel.

Vivian Blaine is capital in her original stage role which is well-nigh performance-proof considering her longruns both on Broadway and in the West End. Sinatra is an effective vis-a-vis in the Sam Levene original of "Nathan Detroit" and among the four they handle the burden of the score. However, Stubby Kaye (also of the Broadway original) whams 'em again with "Sit Down, You're Rockin' the Boat" and he and Johnny Silver are vocal assists in a couple of other opportunities.

The Frank Loesser songs constitute one of those durable scores which were not singularly boffo even in the original, despite the long runs, but have the plus value of being pleasantly lilting without being overly familiar. What's more, his new songs will probably eclipse the stage originals for substance and general popularity. Among these are "Pet Me, Poppa," "Adelaide" and "A Woman In Love." Of the basic legit score, there are still reprises of "Fugue for Tin Horns," "The Oldest Established," the title song, "I'll Know," "If I Were a Bell," "Take Back Your Mink," "Luck Be a Lady" and "Sue Me."

The action shifts from the Times Square street scenes to the Havana idyll, where Brando had taken the mission doll ("on a bet"); to the sundry floating crap games (with Robert Keith, as the Nemesis of a police lieutenant always on their tail); in and out of the mission; and finaleing with the double-wedding block party.

In addition to the able thesping of Robert Keith, as the harassed police lieutenant; B. S. Pully as the gravel-voiced "Big Jule," Sheldon Leonard as "Harry the Horse" and other Runyon-type characters, depicted by Dan Dayton, George E. Stone and Joe McTurk, register, Regis Toomey and Kathryn Givney, as fellow soul-savers at the mission, plus Veda Ann Borg, Mary Alan Hokanson, Kay Kuter and Stapleton Kent are others adding flavor.

The general proceedings have pace and bounce in the modern idiom yet adhering to the now somewhat historical Runyon "period." Director-scripter Mankiewicz has paced the production with verve and imagination, giving it the proper tongue-in-cheek when needed and playing it straight as the situation warranted. In this he is most ably assisted by the knowledgeable cast of seasoned troupers.

The pacing is such that the integration of the musical numbers and the noteworthy Michael Kidd dances generally constitute a smooth segue in the general overall unspooling of the footage. Kidd's terp staging is a highlight credit.

Functioning importantly in getting this plushy pic on film are any number of technical credits. Harry Stradling's CinemaScope lensing in Eastmancolor is one of them, as is the Oliver Smith production design, the art direction by Joseph Wright and Irene Sharaff's costumes. Tuneup of the pic under the baton of Jay Blackton, the fourway contribution to orchestrations by Skip Martin, Nelson Riddle, Alexander Courage and Al Sendrey, and the background music adaptation by Cyril J. Mockridge all help take care of the tune quality.

The Havana scenes give "Guys and Dolls" a nice atmospheric fillip, not to mention (1), Renee Renor, an effective Cubanola-palooza, backed by the Ruben De Fuentes rhumband, and (2), Kidd's unique staging, with a somewhat daring terp staging. Also in the ultramodern spirit is the mission belle's frank pitch to Brando to "miss the plane back to Havana" and his noble decision not to play with what he calls "loaded dice."

It is not amiss, too, as part of a trade review to accent the return to the Metro-Goldwyn-Mayer fold of the producer whose name was lent to the original setup, although he bowed out almost at the very start to remain the independent that Sam Goldwyn has been all these years. However, in this instance Metro, instead of RKO as for many years, is handling the physical distribution of "Guys and Dolls." It will be a highly lucrative reunion for both. *Abel.*

Sincerely Yours
(MUSIC—COLOR)

Sentimental and over-long but promising film star debut for Liberace. Ties in plot of the 1932 "Man Who Played God," with pianist's regular keyboard catalog.

Hollywood, Oct. 28.

Warner Bros. release of Henry Blanke (International Artist Ltd.) production. Stars Liberace, Joanne Dru, Dorothy Malone, Alex Nicol; features William Demarest, Lori Nelson, Lurene Tuttle, Richard Eyer, James Bell. Directed by Gordon Douglas. Screenplay, Irving Wallace; camera (WarnerColor), William H. Clothier; editor, Owen Marks; music advisor, George Liberace; song, Liberace and Paul Francis Webster. Previewed Oct. 18, '55. Running time, 114 MINS.

Anthony Warrin	Liberace
Marion Moore	Joanne Dru
Linda Curtis	Dorothy Malone
Howard Ferguson	Alex Nicol
Sam Dunne	William Demarest
Sarah Cosgrove	Lori Nelson
Mrs. McGinley	Lurene Tuttle
Alvie Hunt	Richard Eyer
Grandfather Hunt	James Bell
J. R. Aldrich	Herbert Heyes
Dr. Eubank	Edward Platt
Dick Cosgrove	Guy Williams
Mr. Rojeck	Ian Wolfe
Zwolinski	Otto Waldis
Mrs. Cosgrove	Barbara Brown

Liberace makes his starring debut in films in a handily handled pic. The "Sincerely Yours" tag aptly expresses his personality and what he puts into his performances, be they television, concert personals or film. Release looks like a winner at the boxoffice, thanks in part to a readymade following in other media which should carry over to celluloid.

While it's not set forth that the pianist-performer is playing himself, that's what happens. Footage can be divided into two parts. Initially, it's a re-run of Liberace's standard act—a go at the piano with classics, semi-classics, pop and boogie, mixed with patter—but tied to the story. The latter half is a remake of the 1932 George Arliss starrer, "The Man Who Played God," and the two parts segue neatly as scripted by Irving Wallace.

The Henry Blanke production for Warners tells a sentimental tale of a popular pianist who dreams of a longhair concert at Carnegie Hall. He goes deaf the night of the big date and hides away in his penthouse overlooking Central Park. Learning lip-reading, he spies on, and discovers the problems of, various people in the park and helps them. By so doing he gains the courage to go through with the operation that will save his hearing and finale finds him filling the delayed Carnegie Hall date.

Gordon Douglas' direction does a good job of keeping the sentimental hokum from becoming too sticky and in drawing a credible performane from Liberace. Same is true of his work with the two femmes who figure in the pianist's life—Joanne Dru, excellent as the secretary who loves the boss but doesn't press the point, and Dorothy Malone, also splendid as the rich girl wo becomes his fiancee but who is released by him so she can marry a young composer, well-played by Alex Nicol.

William Demarest contributes good trouping as Liberace's manager, while others seen to advantage include Lori Nelson, very good; Lurene Tuttle, moppet Richard Eyer, James Bell, Herbert Heyes and Edward Platt.

Footage is considerably longer than necessary at 114 minutes. The Liberace keyboarding that gets the show rolling in the first half is extremely good, but there's just too much of it—an observation likely to be disputed by true Liberaceans. Film could stand trimming throughout, especially some closeups of the star in the mental-torment scenes, during which the camera remains uncomfortably long on his face.

Picture contains the new title tune cleffed by Liberace and Paul Francis Webster, which the star vocals acceptably. Musical advice by George Liberace and arrangements by Gordon Robinson are assets. Also adding polish are William H. Clothier's WarnerColor lensing, the smart art direction by Edward Carrere, set decorations by George James Hopkins, and the femme costuming by Howard Shoup. *Brog.*

The Rose Tattoo
(VISTAVISION)

Selling Tennessee Williams to the masses can be a problem.

Paramount release of Hal Wallis production. Stars Anna Magnani, Burt Lancaster; features Marisa Pavan, Ben Cooper. Directed by Daniel Mann. Screenplay, Tennessee Williams, based on Williams' play and adaptation by Hal Kanter; camera, James Wong Howe; editor, Warren Low; music, Alex North. Previewed Oct. 27, '55. Running time, 117 MINS.

Serafina Delle Rose	Anna Magnani
Alvaro Margiacavallo	Burt Lancaster
Rosa Delle Rose	Marisa Pavan
Jack Hunter	Ben Cooper
Estelle Hohengarten	Virginia Grey
Bessie	Jo Van Fleet
Father De Leo	Sandro Giglio
Assunta	Mimi Aguglia
Flora	Florence Sundstrom
Schoolteacher	Dorrit Kelton
Peppina	Rossana San Marco
Guiseppina	Augusta Merighi
Mariella	Rosa Rey
Strega	Georgia Simmons
Miss Mangiacavallo	Zolya Talma
Pop Mangiacavallo	Margherita Pasquero
Mamma Shigura	Mary Lee
Taxi Driver	Lewis Charles
Rosario Delle Rose	Larry Chance
Violetta	Jean Hart
Doctor	Roger Gunderson
Salvatore	Roland Vildo
Taxi Driver	Virgil Osborne
Cashier	Fred Taylor

"The Rose Tattoo" creates a realistic Italiano atmosphere in the bayou country of the south, establishes vivid characters with one glaring exception and dwells upon a story that is important only because it gives its key character a jumping-off point for fascinating histrionics.

Anna Magnani gives "Tattoo" its substance; she's spellbinding as the signora content with the memory of the fidelity of her husband until she discovers he had a blonde on the side before his banana truck carried him to death.

With Burt Lancaster established as a boxoffice name, and Tennessee Williams credit line possibly another "sell" point plus, and the sensuality of Williams' "Tattoo" people probably provocative of word-of-mouth, this is an offbeat "A" that must be sold hard.

Hal Wallis' production is American cousin to exports from the boot country circa post-World War II. It's "earthy." Miss Magnani and her associates on screen concern themselves with sex without blanching. She impels the young sailor to swear he won't "violate the innocence" of her daughter. The latter, at 15, declares to her suitor she's ready for marriage and motherhood. Such situations are handled as a matter of natural course; there's no reaching for shock values.

But the story and its characters are not particularly appealing. Don't charge Williams with dishonesty in his script, nor Wallis with any compromise with integrity in his production. The mother and daughter, Miss Magnani and Marisa Pavan, perhaps behave consistent with Sicilian tradition. It's the very appearance of authenticity that renders "Tattoo" foreign.

The characters inspire little sympathy. Miss Magnani has animalistic drive and no beauty. She moans the loss of her husband solely because he was a robust, virile mate and she thought he was hers alone. Lancaster, as the village idiot by inheritance, is called upon to take on a role bordering on the absurdity. In the case of Miss Magnani lavish displays of emotionality convince, show no exaggeration. Lancaster, on the other hand, is over his head and overboard as a moron whose brawn attracts Miss Magnani to him. It's difficult to accept Lancaster in the part.

Otherwise Daniel Mann does fine in the directing. He provides pace where some situations might have been static. And the subtleties and shadings in the staging establish motivation without undue emphasis. (Can't tell to what extent he directed Miss Magnani or how much free rein she had in chewing up the scenery in this, her first English-speaking assignment).

Williams' screenplay, from his own legiter, sets the plot foundation with the death of Miss Magnani's husband. She has him cremated, in violation of her Catholic religion, so that she may keep his ashes. The locale seems to be a remote parish not far from where Williams' "Streetcar Named Desire" rode the rails.

Miss Pavan takes up with a Nordic-type young sailor, Ben Cooper, who himself looks the picture of innocence. Ever mindful of wordliness Miss Magnani, in a richly humorous scene, makes the bewildered Cooper go through the ritual of his hands-off vow.

Lancaster enters late. He's a banana hauler, as was Magnani's husband. And in making his crude play for Miss Magnani, he has a rose tattooed on his chest, just as the husband had. Superstition reinforces sex but it's only at the final fade, after coming face to face with her husband's extra-marital blonde, Virginia Grey, that Miss Magnani invites Lancaster to the romance that he had been seeking.

Much of this is gotten across with amusing effect. Miss Magnani's frank mutterings, vocal outbursts, sometimes falling back on Italian dialog, and uninhibited gesticulations often make for rare good fun. Miss Pavan is delicate and attractive as the youngster who craves adult carressing. Miss Grey, Sando Giglio as the Catholic priest and others in the lesser spots are competent.

Alex North's score fittingly backs up the dramatics, Warren Low's editing is sharp for the most part and all other technical assignments have been handled well.

Gene.

King's Rhapsody
(BRITISH—C'SCOPE—COLOR)

Filmization of Ivor Novello's last Ruritanian musical, with Errol Flynn, Patrice Wymore, Anna Neagle starred; strong marquee values give exploitation possibilities.

London, Nov. 1.

United Artists release of Herbert Wilcox production. Stars Anna Neagle, Errol Flynn, and Patrice Wymore; features Martita Hunt, Finlay Currie, Francis de Wolff, Jean Benham, Reginald Tate, Miles Malleson. Directed by Herbert Wilcox. Screenplay, Pamela Bower, and Christopher Hassall; additional dialogue, A. P. Herbert; original book and music by Ivor Novello; camera (Eastmancolor), Max Greene; editor, Reginald Beck; music, arranged and conducted, Robert Farnon. At Warner Theatre, London, starting Oct. 26, '55. Running time, **93 MINS.**

Marta Karillos .... Anna Neagle
Richard, King of Laurentia Errol Flynn
Princess Christiane ..... Patrice Wymore
Queen Mother .... Martita Hunt
King Paul .... Finlay Currie
The Prime Minister... Francis de Wolff
Countess Astrid .... Joan Benham
King Peter .... Reginald Tate
Jules .... Miles Malleson

Herbert Wilcox is the first British independent producer to film in CinemaScope and he has endeavored to play safe by choosing Ivor Novello's last musical which was also one of his greatest successes. The Novello tag and music will be a major ticket-selling factor for the home market. Overseas, the picture will have to rely mainly on marquee strength found in Errol Flynn, Patrice Wymore and Anna Neagle names.

The production was filmed largely on location in Spain and the handsome natural backgrounds are matched by lush decor and opulent costuming. The picture is expensively mounted. Big crowd scenes are freely used to give point to the pomp and pageantry which are part of this Ruritanian story.

Wilcox, who also directed, has kept to the style and tone of the original, using prolonged flashbacks to illustrate the events which led to Errol Flynn's banishment from his own country, his eventual return to sit on the throne, his forced marriage with Patrice Wymore and his eventual exile. The king is always more concerned with his illicit affair with Anna Neagle and has her on hand in a convenient love nest even after the birth of a son and heir.

Novello's music has a saccharine charm and a hummable quality. The tunes are pleasantly sung by Anna Neagle. Surprisingly Miss Wymore has quite an acceptable pair of pipes, too. Edmund Hockridge (now starring in "Pajama Game") also adds his vocal skill although he does not appear. Miss Wymore is also quite a graceful terper who does adequately in a dream sequence. This number is boldly staged with simple decor and is designed to emphasize her frustration at being deserted on her wedding night.

Technically, the film is of varying quality. Max Greene's Eastmancolor lensing is occasionally uneven and there are signs of fringing. Robert Farnon, however, has skillfully arranged the score and reproduction is improved by the bold use of directional sound. The three principals dominate the cast. While the femme stars radiate a measure of charm, Flynn appears to lack the enthusiasm his role demands. Supporting roles are well filled, notably by Martita Hunt and Finlay Currie as the king and queen; Miles Malleson as a faithful servant and Francis de Wolff as a bearded, intriguing Prime Minister.

Myro.

Running Wild

Meller around some not-so-juvenile car thieves. Okay secondary actioner.

Hollywood, Nov. 1.

Universal release of Howard Pine production. Stars William Campbell, Mamie Van Doren, Keenan Wynn, Kathleen Case; features Jan Merlin, John Saxon, Walter Coy, Grace Mills, Chris Randall, Michael Fox. Directed by Abner Biberman. Screenplay, Leo Townsend; from a novel by Ben Benson; camera, Ellis W. Carter; editors, Edward Curtiss, Ray Snyder; music supervision, Joseph Gershenson. Previewed Oct. 25, '55. Running time, **81 MINS.**

Ralph .... William Campbell
Irma .... Mamie Van Doren
Ken Osanger .... Keenan Wynn
Leta Novak .... Kathleen Case
Scotty Cluett .... Jan Merlin
Vince Pomeroy .... John Saxon
Lt. Newpole .... Walter Coy
Osanger's Mother .... Grace Mills
Arkie Nodecker .... Chris Randall
Delmar Graves .... Michael Fox
State Trooper .... Will J. White
Herbie .... Richard Castle
Leta's Father .... Otto Waldis

Not-so-juvenile delinquents are involved in this actioner about a rookie cop assigned to get the goods on a car-stealing gang. It figures as an okay entry for the general situations.

Howard Pine production makes use of a rock-'n'-roll type of musical background to further emphasize juve appeal. Several jukebox hot spot scenes also are in keeping. Cast capably performs what is asked of it by Abner Biberman's direction.

William Campbell is excellent as the rookie cop who poses as a 19-year-old tough to get into the car-stealing gang masterminded by Keenan Wynn, who draws a menacing portrait. Kathleen Case shows up well as Wynn's girl, forced into that unchaste role because he threatens to expose the fact her father, Otto Waldis, a Nazi persecution victim, is in the country illegally. By the time the Ben Benson story, scripted by Leo Townsend, is over, Wynn has his just desserts and Campbell has Miss Case.

Abetting the overall youthful tone are Mamie Van Doren, tough blonde girl friend of equally tough Jan Merlin, Wynn's right-hand man; John Saxon, Walter Coy, Grace Mills, Chris Randall and others in the cast.

Technical credits, including Ellis W. Carter's lensing, the music supervision by Joseph Gershenson, editing and art direction are competent.

Brog.

Adventure in Warsaw
(COLOR—SONGS)

Best feature from Poland since before war. Good foreign language prospects.

Artkino release of Film Polski production. Stars Lidia Korsak, Tadeusz Schmidt. Directed by Leonard Buczkowski. Screenplay, Ludwik Starski; camera, Seweryn Kruszynki, Franciszek Fuks; music, Tadeusz Sygietynski. At Stanley, N. Y., starting Oct. 22, '55. Running time, **98 MINS.**

Hanka Ruczaj .... Lidia Korsak
Jan Starlinski .... Tadeusz Schmidt
Leon Ciepielewski ...Adam Mikolajewski
Wladyslaw Dobrzyniec Tadeusz Kondrat

(In Polish; English Titles)

"Adventure in Warsaw," which is intended to show how Poland's capital city has risen from the ashes of the second World War, also marks a big rise in the Polish film production effort. It is probably the best feature from that country since before the war. It is ready-made for any theatre which can attract Polish patronage and is potentially a grosser for U.S. foreign-language houses.

This has pace, a well-conceived script, excellent casting and intelligent, deft directing. Even when depicting the agonies of a regimented visitors' tour of Warsaw, this moves swiftly, always striving (and usually attaining) for the lighter touch. When the Soviet "work competition drive" is dragged into the plot, it is not with the usual propaganda hammering. Rather, it is kicked around and often kidded for laughs.

Starting out with the usual "boy meets girl" plot formula, this comedy soon develops into a "man versus woman" on the labor front story. It pits a dogmatic foreman against a femme unit working on a city building project—with the women eventually winning out. Lidia Korsak is the girl of "Warsaw" who masterminds the femme triumph in building while her sweetheart, Tadeusz Schmidt, is the unwilling competitor working under the woman-hating foreman, Adam Mikolajewski. Tadeusz Kondrat gets top billing as the blundering plumber, who is Mikolajewski's buddy. But there are some 12 to 15 other types who go far in putting over an obviously not highly original story.

Miss Korsak, while not a raving beauty, goes far in making this yarn jell. She is ably assisted by Schmidt, a husky individual, who caught her eye because he has a rep as a champ bricklayer and skilled worker. Mikolajewski is excellent as an obstinate, femme-hating foreman who thinks a woman's place is in the home. Kendrat suffices in his droll comic way.

The music is tuneful with several unbilled songs and a single solo dance enlivening proceedings. Leonard Buczkowski's direction is about the best thing to come from behind the Iron Curtain in many months. Lensing by Seweryn Kruszynski and Franciszek Fuks is topflight. This is done in Polcolor, the tinting process whipped up in Poland. It shapes as an improvement over Sovcolor and ranks alongside of Eastmancolor in many respects.

Wear.

Joe Macbeth

Modern gangster story loosely based on "Macbeth." Tough entertainment, with adequate marquee appeal and distinct b.o. prospects.

London, Oct. 19.

Columbia (Mike Frankovich) production and release. Stars Paul Douglas, Ruth Roman; features Bonar Colleano, Gregoire Aslan, Sidney James. Directed by Ken Hughes. Screenplay, Philip Yordan; camera, Basil Emmott; editor, Peter Rolfe Johnson; music, Richard Taylor. At Leicester Square Theatre, London, Oct. 18, '55. Running time, **90 MINS.**

Joe Macbeth .... Paul Douglas
Lily .... Ruth Roman
Lennie .... Bonar Colleano
Duce .... Gregoire Aslan
Banky .... Sidney James
Duffy .... Nicholas Stuart
Ross .... Robert Arden
Rosie .... Minerva Pious
Dutch .... Harry Green
Marty .... Bill Nagy
Ruth .... Kay Callard
Angus .... Walter Crisham
Benny .... Mark Baker
1st Assassin .... Alfred Mulock
2nd Assassin .... George Margo

"Joe Macbeth" is far removed from the famous Shakespearean character, but there is an analogy between this modern gangster story and the bard's classic play. The purists may be taken aback by the approach in Mike Frankovich's production, but, as sheer drama, it has the elementary box-office requirements. Paul Douglas and Ruth Roman provide the front-of-house appeal.

Having stuck his neck out thus far in attempting to modernize "Macbeth," Frankovich has gone most of the way in his treatment. There are obvious flaws in the story line, which oddly enough, appear comparitively unimportant; the emphasis all the way along the line is on tough unrelenting melodrama, using the struggle for power as the main theme.

Although made in Britain, the film has an American setting. It is expensively mounted, expertly staged and directed with a keen sense of tension. The plot is basically a battle for supremacy, waged by Paul Douglas, in the title role, and egged on by his determined bride, Ruth Roman. She's not content for him to be just No. 1 man to the king-pin of the underworld; it is all or nothing so far as she's concerned. As the story unfolds, he lacks the stamina which her campaign demands for the top role and, finally, it is nothing for either of them.

The lead role makes substantial demands on Douglas but he emerges with honorable distinction. His characterization changes naturally from the confident henchman to the domineering and frightened bully. Miss Roman has the looks and talent to give a genuine veneer to her performance as his wife. Bonar Colleano, an oversentimentalized character, is one of the mob who eventually brings about Macbeth's downfall after his father (Sidney James) and his wife (Kay Callard), have been eliminated by the gangster.

Harry Green stands out as a rival gang leader, who is poisoned out of existence, and Minerva Pious gives a colorful interpretation of a flower seller who dabbles in fortune telling. Walter Crisham, as a butler, and Robert Arden, Bill Nagy and Nicholas Stuart are among the tough looking gangsters in prominent support. Most technical credits are above average standards.

Myro.

Chiens Perdus Sans Colliers
(Lost Dogs Without Collars)
(FRENCH)

Venice, Oct. 4.

Cocinor release of Franco London Film production. Stars Jean Gabin. Directed by Jean Delannoy. Screenplay, Francois Boyer, Pierre Bost, Jean Aurenche, from novel by Gilbert Cesbron; camera, Pierre Montazel; editor, Borys Lewin; music, Paul Misraki. At Venice Film Festival. Running time, **90 MINS.**

Lamy .... Jean Gabin
Sylvette .... Anne Doat
Francis .... Serge Lecointe
Gerard .... Jacques Mouliere
Alain Robert .... Jimmy Urbain
Mother .... Dora Doll
Grandmother .... Renee S. Passeur

Juvenile delinquency is the theme of this rather conventional film. All pivots around a humane children's judge whose homespun feelings and interest in the children help some in this, but lead to tragedy in other cases. Film is soberly recounted, but never really ignites much drama in this story of three delinquents and how they grew up. It is primarily for special slotting in the U.S. Much in the public eye now, the theme may be a good exploitation peg.

Judge, played by Jean Gabin, feels that the main problems are the adults plus the need of children to love as well as be loved. There is the hardboiled, wiseguyish youth from a bad home, an unloved youth who burns down a farm because mistreated, and the son of a lady of easy virtue. Tragedy ensues with the toughguy who escapes to see his girl, who is pregnant.

Gabin plays his judge too "off the cuff," and seems bored with the role rather than a tender man who is interested more in children than adults. Moppets are somewhat self-conscious. Director Jean Delannoy has given this a slick mounting but rarely the fervor and feeling it needs. Lensing is properly stark and editing is fine.

Mosk.

Touch and Go
(BRITISH—COLOR)

Brightly scripted domestic comedy with Jack Hawkins starring in light role; average prospects in home market but limited hopes in U.S.

London, Oct. 4.

J. Arthur Rank release of Michael Balcon-Ealing production. Stars Jack Hawkins, Margaret Johnston, Roland Culver. Directed by Michael Truman. Screenplay, William Rose; camera (Technicolor), Douglas Slocombe; editor, Peter Tanner; music, John Addison; "The Very Thought of You," Ray Noble. At Odeon, Marble Arch, London, Oct. 3, '55. Running time, **85 MINS.**

Fletcher	Jack Hawkins
Helen	Margaret Johnston
Peggy	June Thorburn
Richard	John Fraser
Fairbright	Roland Culver
Alice Fairbright	Alison Leggatt
Mrs. Pritchett	Margaret Halstan
Mr. Pritchett	Henry Longhurst
Kimball	James Hayter
Stevens	Basil Dignam
Mrs. Baxter	Bessie Love
Waitress	Gabrielle Brune
Policeman	Warwick Ashton

William Rose, whose screenplay of "Genevieve" resulted in one of Britain's most successful productions, has fashioned a lightweight script as a comedy vehicle for Jack Hawkins. This represents a major policy switch for the star, who is normally cast in highly dramatic roles. The result is a pleasant enough entertainment, which should do steady biz in the home market, but has limited chances in the U.S.

"Touch and Go" is also a break from the traditional comedy associated with Ealing Studios. Instead of the characteristic charm of productions like "Passport to Pimlico" and "Tight Little Island," this is downright comedy with a lashing of sentiment and occasionally bordering on farce. It is a well-knit yarn, with bright dialog passages, good all round performances and a reasonable quota of laugh situations.

In this domestic comedy, Hawkins is cast as a furniture designer who quits his job as a protest against his firm's old-fashioned ideas and decides to emigrate with his family to Australia. Two days before their departure, his daughter (charmingly played by June Thorburn), falls in love with a young engineering student, and the wife (Margaret Johnston), has serious misgivings. Almost the entire incident is devoted to their last 48 hours.

Michael Truman has handled his first directorial assignment with confidence. He keeps the action moving and maintains a vigorous pace. Hawkins gives a thoroughly pleasing performance in the main role and his parental handling of his daughter's romantic complications is one of the acting highlights. Miss Johnston is admirably cast as his wife while John Fraser gives a satisfying study as the shy youth who falls in love with Miss Thorburn. Roland Culver, one of Britain's most reliable performers, justifies his rating with a smooth and suave performance. Subsidiary parts are expertly played by a handpicked team.

Myro.

Il Bidone
(The Swindler)
(FRANCO-ITALIAN)

Rome, Oct. 18.

Titanus production and release. Stars Broderick Crawford, Guilietta Masina, Richard Basehart, Franco Fabrizi; features Irene Cefaro, Sue Ellen Blake, Xenia Valdieri, Lorella DeLuca, Giocomo Gabrielli, Mario Passante, Lucietta Muratori. Directed by Federico Fellini. Screenplay, Fellini, Ennio Flaiano, Tullio' Pinelli; from story by Fellini and Flaiano; camera, Otello Martielli. At Barberini, Rome. Running time, **100 MINS.**

Augusto	Broderick Crawford
Picasso	Richard Basehart
Roberto	Franco Fabrizi
Guilietta	Guilietta Masina

Controversial pic has been considerably trimmed since its recent Venice Film Festival showing. It now runs smoother while packing a bigger punch. Strictly an arty or special item abroad, where the Broderick Crawford name will add marquee values. Its home market appeal is problematical. May rate some U.S. spots on cast weight. But it may have to overcome handicaps, mainly its downbeat character.

Story tells of three smalltime swindlers and some of their exploits in fleecing gullible Romans of their hard-earned coin. But more than in the telling these tales, some of them amusing, pic centers on the sad loneliness which characterizes the lives of these men, and especially that of Augusto (Crawford). For while Roberto (Franco Fabrizi), the youngest, progresses in the "trade" and moves on to bigger exploits in Milan, and Picasso (Richard Basehart) gives it up while he still can, Augusto is killed by his own men in his first serious attempt to go straight.

Film is full of symbolisms and contains some powerful moments, as well as some bitingly satirical sequences such as the cocktail party brawl in the rich swindler's apartment. Yet despite the arty slant, general audiences are bound to note a general tediousness, only here and there relieved by a humorous or human touch. It is a bitter pic on a bitter subject.

Acting is good, with Crawford turning in a somber performance as Augusto, though his choice for the role is debatable. Basehart's Picasso is unclearly defined in the script while Fabrizi comes off best as the carefree member of the group. There is a fine bit by Sue Ellen Blake as the crippled girl who triggers Crawfords final decision to go straight. Giacomo Gabrielli turns in a competent performance as the rich, highclass swindler. Technical credits are excellent.

Hawk.

Artists and Models
(MUSIC-V'VISION-COLOR)

Slap-happy Martin & .Lewis comedy with girls and gags. Overdone but okay b.o. prospects.

Hollywood, Nov. 8.

Paramount release of Hal Wallis production. Stars Dean Martin, Jerry Lewis, Shirley MacLaine, Dorothy Malone, Eddie Mayeroff; features Eva Gabor, Anita Ekberg, George "Foghorn" Winslow. Directed by Frank Tashlin. Screenplay, Tashlin, Hal Kanter and Herbert Baker; adaptation by Don McGuire; based on a play by Michael Davidson, Norman Lessing; camera (Technicolor), Daniel L. Fapp; editor, Warren Low; music, Walter Scharf; new songs, Harry Warren, Jack Brooks; vocal arrangements, Norman Luboff; musical numbers created and staged by Charles O'Curran. Previewed Oct. 28, '55. Running time, **108 MINS.**

Rick Todd	Dean Martin
Eugene Fullstack	Jerry Lewis
Bessie Sparrowbush	Shirley MacLaine
Abigail Parker	Dorothy Malone
Mr. Murdock	Eddie Mayehoff
Sonia	Eva Gabor
Anita	Anita Ekberg
Richard Stilton	George "Foghorn" Winslow
Ivan	Jack Elam
Secret Service Chief Samuels	Herbert Rudley
Secret Service Agent Rogers	Richard Shannon
Secret Service Agent Peters	Richard Webb
Otto	Alan Lee
Kurt	Otto Waldis

Comedic diversion in the Martin & Lewis manner has been put together in this overdone, slaphappy, melange of gags and gals. It is the kind of nonsense, plushed out in VistaVision and Technicolor, that fans of the team like and usually buy.

Six writers figured in the Hal Wallis production for Paramount and, while giving the comics a story line to follow, also worked in e v e r y t h i n g but the proverbial kitchen sink. Picture overdoes special situation material almost to the point of no laugh return. These situations start out sock are funny, even hilarious, but invariably milked too long. Overdoing stretches to 108 minutes.

The tuning fell to Harry Warren and Jack Brooks and there are five numbers, mostly pleasantly tuneful except the title song. "When You Pretend," done by Martin & Lewis as a background for the food they do not have in their NY artist's garret. "Inamorata," romantic piece first sung straight by Martin and then used to backstop a staircase comedy dance between Lewis and Shirley MacLaine, "You Look So Familiar" and "The Lucky Song," both well-sung by Martin, are heard. Norman Luboff did the good vocal arrangements, while Walter Scharf batoned his own excellent background score. Other than the staircase terping done for chuckles, the Charles O'Curran musical numbers include a flashy, climactic artists and models number.

Costarring with the comedy team are Miss MacLaine and Dorothy Malone. The former tackles her role of model with a bridling cuteness (however, less so than in "Trouble With Harry," her other pic for Paramount), but has a figure to take the viewer's mind off her facial expression. Ditto Miss Malone, her artist roommate. These two, plus such other femmes as Eva Gabor, a femme fatale spy, and Anita Ekberg, a model, put plenty of omph into the footage in the bare Edith Head costumes. Other casters rating attention include Eddie Mayehoff, publisher of gory comic books, a character good for laughs.

Direction of Frank Tashlin, who also scripted with Hal Kanter and Herbert Baker from Don McGuire's adaptation of a play by Michael Davidson and Norman Lessing, serves hilarity with the critic's reservations already stressed. Martin is an artist and Lewis is a wouldbe writer of kiddie stories, both starving in NY. There are any number of tangents to the plot as it develops. One has to do with the comic book-wrecked mind of Lewis, who spends most of his waking time reading the lurid fiction and, at night, dreaming aloud of even more gruesome stuff. Martin steals this material to create a gory science-fiction strip, in which is the stuff that approaches a national security secret and gets both the Feds and spies on the boys' trail. Washup finds the spy ring wiped out and the boys taking up a maybe less dangerous, but just as exciting pursuit with Miss MacLaine and Miss Malone.

Daniel L. Fapp uses the Technicolor cameras to advantage in catching the beauties of the presentation, both live and those furnished by the art direction by Hal Pereira and Tambi Larsen, the set decorations by Sam Comer and Arthur Krams, the aforementioned Edith Head costumes and other physical polish.

Brog.

Tarantula

Excellent science-fiction-horror feature for the exploitation market.

Hollywood, Nov. 4.

Universal release of William Alland production. Stars John Agar, Mara Corday, Leo G. Carroll; features Nestor Paiva, Ross Elliott, Edwin Rand, Raymond Bailey. Directed by Jack Arnold. Screenplay, Robert M. Fresco, Martin Berkeley; story by Jack Arnold and Fresco; camera, George Robinson; special photography, Clifford Stine; editor, William M. Morgan; music supervision, Joseph Gershenson. Previewed Oct. 25, '55. Running time, **80 MINS.**

Dr. Matt Hastings	John Agar
Stephanie Clayton	Mara Corday
Prof. Deemer	Leo G. Carroll
Sheriff Andrews	Nestor Paiva
Joe Burch	Ross Elliott
Lt. John Nolan	Edwin Rand
Townsend	Raymond Bailey
Josh	Hank Patterson
Barney Russell	Bert Holland
Andy Anderson	Steve Darrell

A tarantula as big as a barn puts the horror into this well-made program science-fictioner and it shapes as a good entry for the exploitation market. The programmer is quite credibly staged and played, bringing off the far-fetched premise with a maximum of believability.

Producer William Alland and director Jack Arnold, old hands at Universal horror pix, work some neat "size" tricks through the special photography of Clifford Stine to give the spider dimensions that dwarf the human actors and sharpen thriller aspects of the tale which Robert M. Fresco and Martin Berkeley scripted from a story by Arnold and Fresco.

Some scientists, stationed near Desert Rock, Ariz., are working on an automatically stabilized nutritional formula that will feed the world's ever-increasing population when the natural food supply becomes too small. Through variously staged circumstances, a tarantula that has been injected with the as yet unstabilized formula escapes and, while continuously increasing in size, starts living off cattle and humans. He seems immune to attack and it's not until the Air Force moves in at the finale and sets him afire with napalm bombs that the horror is put down.

Added horror, via some slick makeup by Bud Westmore, is supplied when humans injected with the nutrient swell abnormally and take on grotesque features. That's a fate suffered by the three male scientists, although the dying Leo G. Carroll, trio leader, actually gets his when the giant insect attacks the two-story house-lab where the group has been working.

Carroll is excellent in his scientist role, while John Agar, young town medico, and Mara Corday, science student employed by Carroll, carry off the romantic demands very well. Others providing capable playing include Nestor Paiva, sheriff; Ross Elliott, town editor; and Hank Patterson, loquacious hotel clerk.

Regular lensing by George Robinson, the sound treatment by Leslie I. Carey and Frank Wilkinson, the score supervised by Joseph Gershenson, and the editing by William M. Morgan are among the factors that combine to make this a good spook show for those that like to have a scarey treatment in their films. *Brog.*

'Toughest Man Alive
(SONGS)

Actionful programmer around munitions-runners for general lowercase bookings.

Hollywood, Nov. 2.
Allied Artists release of William F. Broidy production. Stars Dane Clark, Lita Milan, Anthony Caruso; features Ross Elliott, Myrna Dell, Thomas B. Henry. Directed by Sidney Salkow. Written by Steve Fisher; camera, John Martin; editor, Chandler House; music, Edward J. Kay; songs, George Fragos, Jack Baker and Dick Gasparre; Ben Raleigh and Bernie Wayne. Previewed Oct. 31, '55. Running time, **70 MINS.**

Lee .... Dane Clark
Lida .... Lita Milan
Gore .... Anthony Caruso
York .... Ross Elliott
Nancy .... Myrna Dell
Dolphin .... Thomas B. Henry
Don .... Paul Levitt
Ingo Widmer .... John Eldredge
Salvador .... Dehl Berti
Morgan .... Richard Karlan
Proprietor .... Syd Saylor
Agency Chief .... Jonathan Seymour
Bank Manager .... Don Mathers

The rough-and-ready melodramatics in this actional programmer should meet with an okay reception in the general dual bill market, where it will fit handily as the lowercase subject.

Dane Clark gives the title role in the William F. Broidy production a tight-lipped, ready-fisted type of reading that keeps the Steve Fisher story moving along acceptably. He's an undercover U.S. agent posing as a notorious gun-runner to smoke out the stateside source of munitions that are finding their way into Central American revolutions. The direction by Sidney Salkow makes good use of dockside and other authentic outdoor location sites to get some pseudo-documentary value into the production, while handling the players the formula plot setup capably.

Lita Milan makes a good impression as a naive revolutionary, passing herself off as a cafe singer while trying to secure arms for a new uprising in her country. Chief menace is Anthony Caruso, the gun-runner Clark is impersonating, who shows up at the finale to nearly spoil the well-laid plans to nab the illegal munition magnates, Thomas B. Henry and John Eldredge. Working ably with Clark is fellow-agent Ross Elliott, while

Myrna Dell fills a small spot as the latter's wife.

Story action gets a bit bloodthirsty at times as the pat treatment unfolds, and John Martin's lensing catches it all. Besides the background score by Edward J. Kay, two tunes are introduced through Miss Milan's cafe singer character. They are "I Hear A Rhapsody" by George Fragos, Jack Baker and Dick Gasparre; and "You Walk By" by Ben Raleigh and Bernie Wayne. *Brog.*

Good Morning, Miss Dove
(C'SCOPE-COLOR)

Jennifer Jones in moving, sentimental version of the bestseller. B.o. prospect promising via word-of-mouth.

Hollywood, Nov. 10.
20th-Fox release of Samuel G. Engel production. Stars Jennifer Jones; costars Robert Stack; features Kipp Hamilton, Robert Douglas, Peggy Knudsen, Marshall Thompson, Chuck Connors, Biff Elliott, Jerry Paris, Mary Wickes. Directed by Henry Koster. Screenplay, Eleanore Griffin; from the novel by Frances Gray Patton; camera (De Luxe Color), Leon Shamroy; editor, William Reynolds; music, Leigh Harline; conducted by Lionel Newman. Previewed Nov. 8, '55. Running time, **107 MINS.**

Miss Dove .... Jennifer Jones
Tom Baker .... Robert Stack
Jincey Baker .... Kipp Hamilton
Mr. Porter .... Robert Douglas
Billie Jean .... Peggy Knudsen
Mr. Pendleton .... Marshall Thompson
Bill Holloway .... Chuck Connors
Alex Burnham .... Biff Elliott
Maurice .... Jerry H. Ris
Miss Ellwood .... Mary Wickes
David Burnham .... Ted Marc
Dr. Temple .... Dick Stewart
Annabel .... Cheryl Callaway
Markie .... Mark Engel
Bobsie .... Tim Cagney
Peggy .... Linda Bennett
Mrs. Meggs .... Vivian Marshall
Mr. Spivey .... Richard Deacon
Henry .... Bill Walker
Mr. Levine .... Than Wyenn
Alphonzo Dove .... Leslie Bradley
Dr. Hurley .... Robert Lynn Sr.
Fred Makepeace ...... Edward Firestone
Fred Makepiece (as a child) Tiger Fafara
Maurice (as a child) .. Alfred Caiazza
Grandma Holloway .... Martha Wentworth
Fae Patricia .... Nancy Randall
Vicki .... Patty Ann Gerrity
Mrs. Rigsbee .... Virginia Christine
Mr. Pruitt .... Junius Matthews
Polly Burnham .... Reba Tassell
Harrison .... Gary Diamond
Mrs. Aldredge .... Myna Cunard
Mr. Prouty .... A. Cameron Grant

It should be a fairly easy segue for "Good Morning, Miss Dove" from bestseller as a book to bestseller as a pic. Well cast, finely played, and produced with distinctive taste, it is a warm, human picture. Word-of-mouth should be a plus factor in shoving it along towards sizeable returns.

Gentle humor and honest sentiment are the keys that open the superior Samuel G. Engel production to audience affection. Henry Koster's understanding direction guides the cast through the Frances Gray Patton novel, beautifully scripted by Eleanore Griffin.

Jennifer Jones gives a moving, throat-catching portrait of a dedicated, no-nonsense, school teacher whose influence for good on a small New England community and its citizens has spanned two generations and looks likely to carry into a third. The role this "terrible Miss Dove" has played in molding character and civic pride is brought out effectively via flashbacks as she lies seriously ill in a hospital awaiting an operation that will determine whether she is to live or die.

The flashbacks never interfere with, nor lessen the impact of, the present in the story. Rather they help build interest by giving the spectator insight into the types that people the plot. Miss Dove's precise, prim speech and manner contrast humorously with the more easy gait and idiom of the modern generation, but either old or new, there's a quick identification of characters and situations that makes the unfoldment hit home in the heart and memory.

Costarring is Robert Stack in an extremely valid portrayal of a former student now grown into a young doctor and charged with saving the beloved town character. Stack has had showier roles, but none more honest. He gives a characterization in depth. Performance validity spreads through the

entire cast. Peggy Knudsen leads the list as the day nurse in the hospital. Others include Marshall Thompson, the young man Miss Dove gave up in her youth because she must work to pay off a large debt left by her father; Chuck Connors, a slum kid whose honesty and integrity were given a chance to develop by the teacher; Edward Firestone, excellent as a smalltime crook who breaks jail just to see how his old teacher is progressing; Kipp Hamilton, Robert Douglas, Biff Elliot, Jerry Paris, Mary Wickes and Richard Deacon.

On the juve side of the casting, there's none of the obnoxious brattiness that usually features screen kiddies. The moppets have their standouts, too, among which are Alfred Caiazza, little immigrant tyke whose racial problem is wisely resolved by Miss Dove; John Hensley and Gary Pagett, both fine in portraying the Connors character at various ages; Kenneth Osmond, Paul Engle, Tiger Fafara and others.

Behind-camera credits come off with equal distinction, from Leon Shamroy's CinemaScope-De Luxe Color lensing through the art direction by Lyle R. Wheeler and Mark-Lee Kirk, the settings by Walter M. Scott and Paul S. Fox, the Leigh Harline score conducted by Lionel Newman, the editing by William Reynolds, the costuming, etc. *Brog.*

Samurai
(JAPANESE—COLOR)

Strong sureseater entry from Japan. Outstanding color lensing, good acting, interesting story.

Hollywood, Nov. 15.
Fine Arts Films Inc. release of Kazuo Takimura (Toho Co. Ltd.) production presented by Homel Pictures Inc. Stars Toshiro Mifune, Kaoru Yachigusa; features Rentaro Mikuni, Mariko Okada, Kuroemon Onoe, Mitsuko Mito, Eiko Miyoshi. Directed by Hiroshi Inagaki. Screenplay, Tokuhel Wakao and Inagaki; adaptation, Hideji Hojo; from the novel "Miyamoto Musashi" by Eiji Yoshikawa; camera (Eastmancolor), Jun Yasumoto; editors, Robert Homel, William Holden; music, Ikuma Dan. Previewed Nov. 8, '55. Running time, **92 MINS.**

Takezo .... Toshiro Mifune
Otsu .... Kaoru Yachigusa
Matahachi .... Rentaro Mikuni
Akemi .... Mariko Okada
Takuan .... Kuroemon Onoe
Oko .... Mitsuko Mito
Osugi .... Eiko Miyoshi

This latest entry from the studios of Japan is a distinguished one likely to take its place with such other entries as "Rashomon," "Gate of Hell" and "Ugetsu" as strong sureseater filmfare. In some ways it is an easier picture to follow for stateside audiences, having a universally recognizable plot, good English sub-titles and clear narration by William Holden, under whose auspices it is being given domestic showcasing.

"Samurai" does outstanding things with color and photography. Either indoors or out, scene composition is artistry of the highest order, yet never interferes with the story-telling. The beauty of wooded sequences, several mass battle scenes and other settings is extraordinary. Responsible for this pictorial splendor are Jun Yasumoto behind the cameras, Kisaku Ito as art adviser, Makoto Sono as art director and the Eastman Color tints that are used.

Production credits loom large. Pic is a Toho Company Ltd., of Japan production on which Kazuo Takimura is named producer and Robert Homel associate. It is being presented in this country by

Homel Pictures Inc., with Fine Arts Films Inc., distributing. Holden also has an interest in the film for domestic release and appears in the trailer via which it will be sold, as well as doing the foreword and narration of the pic itself.

There's an early-day, Douglas Fairbanks-Sherwood Forest flavor to the story which is an asset for American audiences. Taken from Eiji Yoshikawa's novel, "Miyamoto Musashi," it tells of a Japanese Samurai, a real figure back in the 17th century, but now legendary. As a youth he leaves his poor village and goes forth to battle, seeking to elevate himself from low caste to the high ranks of Samurai, powerful warriors who are masters of the sword. Hiroshi Inagaki's direction is clear and makes its dramatic points with validity, as does the script he wrote with Tokuhei Wakao from the dramatization by Hideji Hojo.

The trouping is on a par with the other values in the film, being uniformly good and stressing a certain naturalness instead of the highly stylized portrayals usually associated with Japanese drama. Toshiro Mifune makes a splendid hero, who is steadfast in moving towards his Samurai goal, despite the temptations and dangers he is put through. Equally fine is Kaoru Yachigusa, a Dresden-doll type of beauty who is left sorrowing at the end when her hero puts her behind him. Rentaro Mikuni, a weakling; Mariko Okada and Mitsuko Mito, daughter and mother, respectively, who each try to tempt the hero; Kuroemon Onoe, a priest, and Eiko Miyoshi, a treacherous old woman, are other cast standouts.

The 92-minute pic has a background score in keeping with the class assets, with composer Ikuma Dan adapting ancient Japanese themes to more modern symphonic scoring. *Brog.*

American Farmers Visit Russia and Indonesia Today

(Russian Documentaries)

Artkino release of Central Documentary Film Studio of Moscow productions. "American Farmers Visit Russia" directed by Z. Tuzova; scenario, E. Kriger; "Indonesia Today" directed by V. Nikosa; scenario, Nikosa. At Stanley Theatre, N.Y., Nov. 2, '55. Running time, "American Farmers," 51 MINS.; "Indonesia," 40 MINS.

Two documentaries, produced by the Central Documentary Film Studios of Moscow, have been combined by Artkino for release in the United States. Best bet may be in U.S. farm belt, otherwise limited appeal, despite the non-political subject matter.

"American Farmers Visit Russia" is a 51-minute black & white account of the recent visit to Russia of the 12-member American agricultural delegation. It's hardly more than newsreel clips showing the U.S. representatives visiting and inspecting various collective farms. Although the U.S. farmers travelled extensively in Russia, the visits are repetitious in depicting similar flower-laden welcomes, dinners, and farm inspections. Would have been more effective cut to a tight 15 or 20 minutes.

Americans received full vodka treatment everywhere they went. They inspected the Ukrainian wheat belt, visited agricultural exhibitions, and sang "Old McDonald Had a Farm."

"Indonesia Today" in Sovcolor, is in the travelog vein. It captures the scenic beauty of the archipelago as well as bustling city scenes. It records Balinese dancers and Buddhist temples. In general, the cameramen have done a good job although the color does not live up to the standards of previous Russian tinters. Both films have an English narration. *Holl.*

Gli Ultimi Cinque Minuti

(The Last Five Minutes)
(FRANCO—ITALIAN)

Rome, Nov. 8.

Columbia release of a G. Amato-Excelsa-Omnium international co-production. Stars Linda Darnell, Vittorio DeSica. Directed by Giuseppe Amato. Screenplay, Aldo De Benedetti from his play of same name; camera, Carlo Monuori; editor, Eraldo Da Roma; music, Alessandro Cicognini. At Cinema Archimede. Running time, 101 MINS.

Renata .... Linda Darnell
Carlo Reani .... Vittorio DeSica
Isabella .... Sophie Desmarets
Dino Moriani .... Rossano Brazzi
Filippo .... Peppino DeFilippo
Valeria .... Nadia Gray
Dago .... Pierre Cressoy

Comedy based on a locally popular play should gross well here with the aid of a strong cast. Names will also aid it towards good reception on other markets, especially the Darnell - DeSica - Brazzi teaming. Heavy dialogue, on which pic depends to great extent, makes U.S. chances problematical and dependent on a top dubbing job.

Theatrical story is about a man and a woman who both want the same ideally located apartment. Situation is solved by a marriage pact, which leaves the wife free to act should an eventual "prince charming" come along.

Pic is ably dialogued by its original author Aldo de Benedetti, and played with charm and humor by Vittorio DeSica, Linda Darnell, Rossano Brazzi (in an offbeat takeoff on his usual charmer roles), Pierre Cressoy, Peppino DeFilippo and others. Direction has done little to make strong picture out of the stage play. Film seems to lack action. Technical credits are good. *Hawk.*

La Donna Del Fiume

(The River Girl)
(FRANCO-ITALIAN)
(Color)

Rome, Nov. 1.

Minerva release of a Ponti-DeLaurentiis-Elcelsa Production. Stars Sophia Loren. Directed by Mario Soldati. Screenplay, Soldati, Basilio Franchina, Giorgio Bassani, Pierpaolo Pasolini, Florestano Vancini, Antonio Atloviti; from story by Alberto Moravia and Ennio Flajano; camera (Eastmancolor), Otello Martelli; music, Francesco Lavagnino, Armando Trovajoli; editor, Mario Serandrei. At Cinema Barberini, Rome. Running time 105 MINS.

Nives .... Sophia Loren
Gino Lodi .... Rik Battaglia
Tosca .... Lise Bourdin
Enzo Cinti .... Gerald Oury

Lusty exploitation item, which combines elements of such past successes as "Bitter Rice" and "Anna," is a natural starrer for Sophia Loren, whose currently prominent name should help this one to healthy grosses, perhaps in subsequent-runs. Setting, star, and story will put it across in Europe while the U. S. market offers good possibilities if pic is dubbed. Censors may use their shears.

Earthy plot, conceived by writer Alberto Moravia in collab with Ennio Flajano and elaborated on by six scripters, is mostly about a girl, Nives (Miss Loren), who falls for a flighty cigaret smuggler. He runs off, she has a child and brushes off the attentions of a warm-hearted guard.

Oversudsy story actually splits pic in two, first half spotlighting a sexy Loren on the make while the second stanza overdoes the tearful aspects. Top values are obtained from Miss Loren's physique, the swampland and eel-cannery settings of the lower Po Valley, and some of the less obvious story elements.

Miss Loren shows acting talent in this one. Lise Bourdin has little to do while Gerard Oury is okay as the silent lover. Rik Battaglia will please distaffers as the hero-villain. Although direction by Mario Soldati is uneven, he has obtained some top visual values from his project, aided by Otello Martelli's able lensing. A special mambo sung by Miss Loren (for RCA records), as well as danced in one sequence (this reminds one of Mangano in "Rice"), will prove a sales aid. Other technical credits are fine. *Hawk.*

Les Grandes Manoeuvres

(The Big Maneuvers)
(FRENCH—COLOR)

Paris, Nov. 8.

Cinedis release of Filmsonor-Rizzoli production. Stars Gerard Philipe, Michele Morgan. Written and directed by Rene Clair. Camera (Eastmancolor), Robert Le Febvre; editor, Louisette Hautecoeur; music, Georges Van Parys. At Colisee, Paris. Running time, 110 MINS.

Armand .... Gerard Philipe
Marie-Louise .... Michele Morgan
Lucie .... Brigitte Bardot
Felix .... Yves Robert
Gisele .... Simone Valere
Duverger .... Jean Desailly
Rodolphe .... Jacques Francois
Orderly .... Jacques Fabbri
Colonel .... Pierre Dux
Bride .... Catherine Anouilh

Rene Clair brings his filmic finesse, elegance and topnotch technical savvy to this comedy-drama of life in a provincial garrison town in the early 1900's. Eye-catching pastel color schemes, bright costuming and setting plus a tinsely background score, adequately unite to capture the feel of the times. Clair's clever notations on the era give the film its main appeal. The names of Gerard Philipe and Michele Morgan should help to make a lucrative run here. For the U.S., these names are also potent for arty theatres, with its charm and suave theme about a military Don Juan caught in his own trap being added help.

In dividing his film into a comedy of manners and a bittersweet drama of lost love, Clair has not quite achieved the perfect wedding of the two forms. Film lets down after the bright and brilliant beginning.

Nevertheless, this has smart performances and plumage. There are many moments of high film comedy such as a clarion military trumpet call backgrounding a series of reactions of the townsfolk to the soldiers whose sole occupation, it seems, is the seducing of the townswomen, both married and unmarried. Story concerns the top heart-toppler, Philipe, who makes a bet that he can seduce any woman in a week. Victim turns out to be a divorcee of great beauty, Miss Morgan.

Production dress is opulent and technical credits perfect. Philipe portrays the ladykiller to perfection. Miss Morgan is a fine foil as his victim *Mosk.*

La Piu Bella Donna Del Mondo

(World's Most Beautiful Woman)
(ITALIAN—COLOR—SONGS)

Rome, Nov. 8.

Malenotti release of a Maleno Malenotti production. Stars Gina Lollobrigida, Vittorio Gassmann; features Robert Alda. Directed by Robert Z. Leonard. Screenplay, Malenotti, Cavagna, Ferri, Gervasi, Monicelli, Martino, Pierotti, Solinas, Soria; camera (Eastmancolor), Mario Bava; music, Renzo Rossellini. At Cinema Adriano, Rome. Running time, 115 MINS.

Lina Cavalieri .... Gina Lollobrigida
Sergio Bariatine .... Vittorio Gassmann
Doria .... Robert Alda
Manolita .... Tamara Lees
Mario Silvani .... Gino Sinimberghi
Companion .... Anne Vernon

Pic is headed for top seasonal rankings in the home market, and should gross well in most European countries. In the U.S., a dubbed version should help to okay coin in general release via marquee names and production values.

This is somewhat of a one-woman show for Gina Lollobrigida, and she makes the most of it, putting across a semi-biographical segment in the life of the famed beauty, Lina Cavalieri, in fine style. As a sample of Miss Lollobrigida's versatility, talent, and beauty, it's a top effort. She never showed to better advantage—she fights, fences, sings and dances. Use of her own voice for the operatic sequences (Tosca) provide an added gimmick, besides proving surprisingly pleasant.

Soaped-up bio script follows up the Lina Cavalieri career from her music hall debut to some unhappy love affairs, notably with a Russian prince (Vittorio Gassmann) and an Italian voice teacher (Robert Alda).

Script, which passed through at least nine credited hands, is the film's weakest element. Production values and smooth direction by Robert Z. Leonard manage to make one forget this until near the end. Second stanza of the long picture could use some trimming for pace. Opener contains one of film's highlights, the seriocomic duel between the tights-garbed Lina Cavalieri and Manolita (Tamara Lees). With exception of one sequence, lensing is of the top color quality, catching the splendid robes and sets.

Gassmann is good as the Russo prince while Robert Alda draws a less grateful part as the jealous suitor. Anne Vernon makes a sympathetic companion to the pic's star. Others in a large cast provide able support. Mario del Monaco's voice is heard dubbed into the role played by Gino Sinimberghi, in arias from "Tosca." Sound recording is of good quality, and other technical credits are fine. *Hawk.*

Cockleshell Heroes
(BRITISH—C'SCOPE—COLOR)

Gripping dramatization of epic war exploit, with warm human values and potent suspense; sturdy b.o. prospects on both sides of Atlantic.

London, Nov. 15.

Columbia release of Warwick (Irving Allen-Albert R. Broccoli) production. Stars Jose Ferrer, Trevor Howard. Directed by Jose Ferrer. Screenplay, Bryan Forbes, Richard Maibaum from story by George Kent; camera, John Wilcox, Ted Moore; editor, Alan Osbiston; music, John Addison, with "Cockleshell Heroes" march by Lt. Colonel F. Vivian Dunn. At Empire Theatre, London, Nov. 15, '55. Running time, **97 MINS.**

Major Stringer	Jose Ferrer
Captain Thompson	Trevor Howard
Sergeant Craig	Victor Maddern
Marine Clarke	Anthony Newley
Marine Ruddock	David Lodge
Marine Stevens	Peter Arne
Marine Lomas	Percy Herbert
Marine Booth	Graham Stewart
Marine Cooney	John Fabian
Marine Bradley	John Van Eyssen
Marine Todd	Robert Desmond
Gestapo Commandant	Walter Fitzgerald
Gestapo Officer	Karel Stepanek
Myrtle	Dora Bryan
Mrs. Ruddock	Beatrice Campbell
Policeman	Sydney Tafler
Barmaid	Gladys Henson
French Fisherman	Jacques Brunius
French Fisherman	Andrea Malendrinos
Submarine Commander	Christopher Lee

"Cockleshell Heroes" is an important addition to the ranks of British-made pictures to dramatize a single incident from the last war. In this reconstruction of an epic and heroic exploit, exec producers Irving Allen and Albert R. (Cubby) Broccoli have made the best film since they launched their British unit a few years ago. With full exploitation and planned selling, it may also prove to be their most successful. The two stars give the production marquee stature on either side of the Atlantic, but the picture scores by uncanny accuracy in the feature casting. The subsidiary characters frequently dominate the action and never let the side down. They're aided by a taut script and by having some of the best dialog passages.

Operation "Cockleshell" was a campaign in miniature against a concentration of German shipping in Bordeaux Harbor, employing only eight men of the Royal Marines who paddled four canoes into enemy waters and stuck limpet mines on the Nazi boats. Only one crew of two men survived; two lost their lives in attempting a getaway and the other four were executed as saboteurs when they refused to answer the Gestapo questions.

Actual assault is, of course, the suspense highlight of the yarn, but there's a wealth of admirably exploited incident in the buildup situations showing the volunteers in special training for this hazardous adventure. The script develops a forceful, if conventional, personal conflict between Jose Ferrer, as the skipper in charge of the operation, and Trevor Howard, his non-combatant administration officer. Latter eventually volunteers as a last-minute replacement and is among those to face the firing squad. Both in the preparatory training sequences and in the actual attempt, the broad expanse of the C'Scope screen is used to advantage, especially in the final shots depicting the success of the raid as ship after ship bursts into flames.

Ferrer has caught the traditional British touch of understatements in his direction and performance, and has completely avoided the pitfall of false heroics. Trevor Howard's study of an embittered officer who has been passed up for promotion is a model of restraint, and the members of the crews never falter in their portrayals. Minor femme roles are filled by Dora Bryan, Beatrice Campbell and Judith Furse with distinction. *Myro.*

The Crooked Web

Far - fetched melodrama. Brings a murderer to book.

Hollywood, Nov. 22.

Columbia release of a Clover production. Stars Frank Lovejoy, Mari Blanchard, Richard Denning; features John Mylong, Harry Lauter, Steven Ritch, Louis Merrill. Directed by Nathan Hertz Juran. Story and screenplay, Lou Breslow; camera, Henry Freulich; editor, Edwin Bryant; score conducted by Mischa Bakaleinikoff. Previewed Nov. 16, '55. Running time, **77 MINS.**

Stan Fabian	Frank Lovejoy
Joanie Daniel	Mari Blanchard
Frank Daniel	Richard Denning
Herr Koenig	John Mylong
Jancoweizc	Harry Lauter
Ray Torres	Steven Ritch
Herr Schmitt	Louis Merrill
Richard Atherton	Roy Gordon
Tom Jackson	Van Des Autels
Don Gillen	George Cezar
Charlie Holt	John Hart
Doc Mason	Richard Emory
German Guard	Harold Dyrenforth
Singer	Judy Clark

Some rather complicated melodramatics are unfurled in this detailing of an elaborate scheme to bring a G.I. killer to justice. It comes off passably well.

Frank Lovejoy, Mari Blanchard and Richard Denning are the familiar names heading the cast of the Clover production for Columbia, paced by the direction of Nathan Hertz Juran and the screenplay of Lou Breslow.

Lovejoy, now the operator of a drive-in restaurant and a horseplayer, is the man wanted for killing an M.P. in Berlin some eight years back. Before the killing had been traced to him he was out of uniform, thus has to be lured back to Germany and tricked into a confession to make prosecution for the crime stick. Miss Blanchard and Denning, as undercover agents for the dead officer's rich father, go to no end of trouble to get Lovejoy to Berlin. First, she works for him as a carhop for a year, gets him to the point of marriage, before Denning, her fiance, appears on the scene posing as her wayward brother who has a scheme to go to Berlin and dig up $200,000 in gold knicknacks he buried there during the war. Lovejoy is eventually boobytrapped in the cause of justice.

The two males seize every opportunity, and there are many, to grab and kiss Miss Blanchard. These bits are among the points that make the yarn impossible to believe. John Mylong, Harry Lauter, Steven Ritch, Louis Merrill and Roy Gordon are among those more prominently involved, and Judy Clark has a background singing chore in a Berlin cafe.

Technical credits are average, from Henry Freulich's lensing on down. *Brog.*

The Vanishing American

Standard western action feature with familiar names for the regular outdoor market.

Hollywood, Nov. 17.

Republic production and release. Stars Scott Brady, Audrey Totter, Forrest Tucker, Gene Lockhart; features Jim Davis, John Dierkes, Gloria Castillo, Julian Rivero, Lee Van Cleef, George Keymas, Charles Stevens, Jay Silverheels, James Millican, Glenn Strange. Directed by Joe Kane. Screenplay, Alan LeMay; based on the novel by Zane Grey; camera, John L. Russell Jr.; editor, Richard L. Van Enger; music, R. Dale Butts. Previewed Nov. 16, '55. Running time, **90 MINS.**

Blandy	Scott Brady
Marian Warner	Audrey Totter
Morgan	Forrest Tucker
Blucher	Gene Lockhart
Glendon	Jim Davis
Friel	John Dierkes
Yashi	Gloria Castillo
Etenia	Julian Rivero
Jay Lord	Lee Van Cleef
Coshonta	George Keymas
Quah-Tain	Charles Stevens
Beeteia	Jay Silverheels
Walker	James Millican
Beleanth	Glenn Strange

Zane Grey's old novel about the extinction that threatened the Navajos gets a new screen treatment in this Republic western feature. The cast names are familiar; so is the action. Should fare satisfactorily in the general outdoor market.

There's a curious updated quality to the Alan LeMay screenplay, although the setting remains late 19th century. Dialog is more modern than must have been uttered back in those days and Audrey Totter tackles the role of white girl come west to claim an inheritance with a modern zip and emancipated forthrightness slightly incongruous to the period. Opposite her is Scott Brady as Blandy, Grey's Navajo hero who refused to knuckle under to the renegade whites and treacherous Apaches who were decimating his people. Both are acceptable in answering the demands of script and Joe Kane's direction. And in this version there is ample evidence he gets the gal at the finale, not standing silent while she rides off into the distance.

Brady and Miss Totter join forces to put down Forrest Tucker, Indian trader who is scheming to take over all the water holes and lands controlled by the Navajos, and Gene Lockhart, crooked Indian agent in cahoots with Tucker. Key to their move-in on the baddies is the range left Miss Totter by her late uncle. Events move along a familiar course, with spots of action here and there to enliven the footage before the heavies get their just desserts.

Assisting the villains are Jim Davis, John Dierkes and some Apache types, while Gloria Castillo is seen as an Indian maid who is saved from the lechrous designs of Tucker by Miss Totter. Other casters perform okay.

Picture was lensed on Utah location and the rugged backgrounds could have used color for pictorial beauty. Otherwise, John L. Russell Jr.'s photography is good, as are the other technical contributions. *Brog.*

Target Zero

Regulation war-action programmer for general supporting bookings.

Hollywood, Nov. 15.

Warner Bros. release of David Weisbart production. Stars Richard Conte, Peggie Castle; features Charles Bronson, Richard Stapley, L. Q. Jones, Chuck Connors, John Alderson, Terence de Marney, John Dennis, Angela Loo. Directed by Harmon Jones. Screenplay, Sam Rolfe; story, James Warner Bellah; camera, Edwin DuPar; editor, Clarence Kolster; music, David Buttolph. Previewed Nov. 14, '55. Running time, **91 MINS.**

Lt. Flagler	Richard Conte
Ann Galloway	Peggie Castle
Sgt. Vince Gaspari	Charles Bronson
Sgt. David Kensemmit	Richard Stapley
Pvt. Feliz Zimbalist	L. Q. Jones
Pvt. Moose	Chuck Connors
Cpl. Devon Enoch	John Alderson
Pvt. Harry Fontenoy	Terence de Marney
P.F.C. George	John Dennis
Sue	Angela Loo
Pvt. Geronimo	Abel Fernandez
Pvt. Ma Koo Sung	Richard Park
Pvt. Stacey Zorbados	Don Oreck
Dan O'Hirons	Strother Martin

This war-actioner should prove acceptable in the general market as a regulation supporting feature. The action is rather sporadic, but good, serving to break up a situation plot about human relationships on the Korean battlefield. Yarn has the familiarity of most war pix, but plays down heroics so there is some credence to what transpires.

Richard Conte, as the lieutenant trying to lead his small patrol back to safety, and Peggie Castle, as a United Nations worker trapped behind Red lines, head the cast in the David Weisbart production. Under Harmon Jones' direction of the Sam Rolfe script from a story by James Warner Bellah, the stars and other cast members answer capably the not too taxing demands of the plot.

The small patrol, working its way to a Korean ridge where the full company is supposed to be waiting, picks up an American tank manned by three British soldiers and their passenger, Miss Castle. There's some Anglo-American friction between Conte and Richard Stapley, tank sergeant, but rank is rank, regardless of uniform, so the motley outfit arrives safely on the ridge, only to find the company wiped out. Ordered to hold the post for a big Allied advance, the patrol does, with jets and a Navy bombardment from offshore taking care of what North Koreans the group can't manage itself. In the fighting, British and Yank become friends and Miss Castle decides she's just what's needed to humanize professional soldier Conte.

Charles Bronson is good as a Yang sarg and Stapley does okay as the prejudiced Britisher (he hates all Americans because his sister cooperated too much with a G.I. from the states during World War II). Others doing their parts include L. Q. Jones, Chuck Connors, John Alderson, Terence de Marney, John Dennis, Abel Fernandez and Richard Park.

Staging of the battle skirmishes between the small patrol and Red detachments injects action excitement here and there and Edwin DuPar's camera shows it up well. Editing by Clarence Kolster, score by David Buttolph and other behind-camera credits are acceptable. *Brog.*

A Lawless Street
(COLOR)

Good Randolph Scott outdoor action feature for the western fan.

Hollywood, Nov. 18.

Columbia release of Harry Joe Brown (Scott-Brown) production. Stars Randolph Scott; costars Angela Lansbury; features Warner Anderson, Jean Parker, Wallace Ford, John Emery; James Bell, Ruth Donnelly, Michael Pate, Don Megowan, Jeannette Nolan. Directed by Joseph H. Lewis. Screenplay, Kenneth Gamet; story, Brad Ward; camera (Technicolor), Ray Rennahan; editor, Gene Havlick; score, Paul Sawtell. Previewed Nov. 10, '55. Running time.. **78 MINS.**

Calem Ware	Randolph Scott
Tally Dickinson	Angela Lansbury
Hamer Thorne	Warner Anderson
Cora Dean	Jean Parker
Dr. Amos Wynn	Wallace Ford
Cody Clark	John Emery
Asaph Dean	James Bell
Molly Higgins	Ruth Donnelly
Harley Baskam	Michael Pate
Dooley Brion	Don Megowan
Mrs. Dingo Brion	Jeanette Nolan
Hiram Hayes	Peter Ortiz
Juan Tobrez	Don Carlos
Dingo Brion	Frank Hagney
Willis	Charles Williams
Abe Deland	Frank Ferguson
Tony Cabrillo	Harry Tyler
Mayor Kent	Harry Antrim

Randolph Scott is still taming the west as a forthright marshal and this entry plays out along a generally acceptable course to make it an okay offering in the outdoor action market.

The Scott-Brown production, produced by Harry Joe Brown for Columbia release, and directed by Joseph H. Lewis with beaucoup action presents the hero as a steely-eyed, quick-draw terror of lawbreakers who goes from town to town in the Colorado Territory cleaning up the baddies so the territory can eventually become a state.

The reputation he has acquired over the years keeps him almost constantly on the defense and has cost him his wife, Angela Lansbury, who has rebelled against his killer role in life. With these personal troubles always plaguing him, the marshal still remains resolutely on the job in Medicine Bend, not willing to give up until law takes over. It does eventually, but not before the marshal almost gets his at the hands of Michael Pate, an efficient gunman hired by town crooks Warner Anderson and John Emery, who want the territory to remain as is. Finale finds Scott hanging up his gun and badge for keeps so he can make a new life with Miss Landsbury.

Scott gives a robust account of himself in a role that has become familiar to stereotyping although getting some shading in the script of Kenneth Gamet from a story by Brad Ward. Miss Lansbury also pleases as his wife who has turned to the stage during the long separation. Heavy work of Anderson and Emery fits the plot, while good feature support is turned in by Jean Parker, playful wife of rancher James Bell, Wallace Ford, town doctor; Ruth Donnelly, Don Megowan and Jeanette Nolan.

Ray Rennahan's Technicolor lensing does right by the western setting. Paul Sawtell's score is inclined to be intrusive at times.
Brog.

Storm Over the Nile
(BRITISH—C'SCOPE—COLOR)

Lavish remake of "Four Feathers" derives main entertainment from opulent C'Scope treatment which places full emphasis on spectacular action.

Independent Film Distributors-British Lion Films release of London Films production. Stars Anthony Steel, Laurence Harvey, James Robertson Justice. Directed by Terence Young, Zoltan Korda. Screenplay, R. C. Sherriff from A. E. W. Mason's novel, "The Four Feathers"; camera (Technicolor). Ted Scaife. Osmond Borradaile; editor, Raymond Poulton; music, Benjamin Frankel. At Odeon Marble Arch, London. Running time, 107 MINS.

Harry Faversham ....Anthony Steel
John Durrance ....Laurence Harvey
Peter Burroughs .... Ronald Lewis
Tom Willoughby .... Ian Carmichael
Gen. Burroughs ....James Robertson Justice
Mary Burroughs .... Mary Ure
Doc. Sutton ....Geoffrey Keen
Colonel ....Jack Lambert
Doc. Harraz ....Ferdy Mayne
Gen. Faversham ....Michael Hordern
Karaga Pasha ....Christopher Lee
Instructor .... Sam Kydd
Colonel's Aide ......Raymond Francis
Sergeant ....John Wynne
Sergeant's wife ....Avis Scott

"The Four Feathers" ranked high among Alexander Korda's pre-war successes and in this remake of the A. E. W. Mason story, his brother Zoltan assumes some producer credit as well as sharing the directorial chore with Terence Young. The new version is up-to-date inasmuch as it is filmed in CinemaScope and color, with directional sound, but in most other respects adheres to the main plot of the original story.

Use of the widescreen process is probably the main justification for the remake, particularly as it enhances the vivid battle scenes in which Kitchener's troops rout the native armies at Khartoum, while imprisoned British officers capture the enemy arsenal. These spectacular sequences are the main highlight of the picture, which in other ways is outmoded in spirit and story content.

R. C. Sherriff, who has scripted the new version, develops his screenplay from the basic incident of the young officer who resigns his commission on the eve of a foreign expedition, to allow for maximum action. Battle sequences filmed in the Sudan have a convincing look. The same can hardly be said of the disguise effected by Anthony Steel in posing as a native to purge his cowardice and return the four feathers he received on his resignation from brother officers and his fiancee.

A. E. W. Mason's story is good old-fashioned hokum, and the co-directors have played up that aspect for all they are worth, exploiting all the melodramatic incident of the hardships faced by British troops in the desert campaign.

Generally, the acting hardly matches the lavish and spectacular qualities of the production. Steel is more believable in the earlier sequences when he admits to cowardice, but is less acceptable when he decides he hasn't the guts to be a coward and joins his old regiment in the desert. Laurence Harvey as a fellow officer who gets blinded by an overdose of sun, appears miscast. Only James Robertson Justice, as a veteran of the Crimea and father of Steel's fiancee, fits happily into the story. Mary Ure, who makes her screen debut, cannot fairly be judged on this performance as her part is too limited. Principal supporting roles are adequately played. Technical qualities, notably the Technicolor lensing, are above average.
Myro.

Hell's Horizon

Poor quality Korean bomber melodrama.

Hollywood, Nov. 17.
Columbia release of a Wray Davis production. Stars John Ireland, Marla English, Bill Williams, Hugh Beaumont; features Larry Pennell, William Schallert, Paul Levitt, Wray Davis, Keene Duncan, Jerry Paris, John Murphy, Mark Scott, Don Burnett, Stanley Adams, Chet Baker. Directed by Tom Gries. Screenplay, Gries; camera, Floyd Crosby; editor, Aaron Stell; music, Heinz Roemheld. Previewed Nov. 15, '55. Running time, 78 MINS.

Indie-produced and purchased outright by Columbia, 'Hell's Horizon" is a slow-moving, over-talkative story of a bombing mission in the Korean War. Little novelty or freshness. Just a rehash of better films of the past.

John Ireland, as skipper of the bomber, and Bill Williams, his co-pilot, head cast of Wray Davis production. Written and directed by Tom Gries with a minimum of imagination. Yarn concerns a one-plane mission dispatched from its Okinawa base to bomb a strategic bridge over the Yalu River, using the cover of bad weather. It turns clear so Red fighter planes can attack. Touch and go whether plane will get back. It does, crash-landing with an empty tank.

Performances are static, characters lack force. Players do what they can to make roles credible. Ireland has task of maintaining the strong dislike of his crew and Williams is there as his counterfoil, admired by crew. Marla English as a half-caste is dragged in for romance with one of the crewmen. Larry Pennell.

Floyd Crosby's camera work highlights the technical credits, and Heinz Roemheld's music score is firstrate.
Whit.

Les Aristocrates
(FRENCH)

Paris, Nov. 15.
Gaumont production and release. Stars Pierre Fresnay. Directed by Denys de la Patelliere. Screenplay, Roland Laudenbach. Patelliere from a novel by Michel De Saint Pierre; camera, Pierre Petit; editor, Robert Isnardon. At Biarritz, Paris. Running time, 105 MINS.
Marquis ....Pierre Fresnay
Daisy .... Brigitte Auber
Artus ....Jacques Dacqmine
Pierre ....Francois Guerin
Prince ....Leo Joannon

Adapted from a bestseller, pic maintains its literary detailing of the conflict between an aging, dignified aristocrat, content to stay with his crumbling homestead in an era that has bypassed him, and his brood of children who have modernized and want him to do so along with them. Film is a first for director Denys de la Patelliere and shows it in its rambling style and lack of true dramatic heights, when the clash almost drives two of the youngsters into killing themselves. Pic remains too talky and sketchy.

It has the Pierre Fresnay name here. For the U.S., this is primarily for special spots, with overseas returns limited.

Fresnay gives one of his steely but tempered acting chores. He makes an almost moving, pathetic figure of this anachronistic nobleman living in past dreams and fading dignity. His children are all well handled, with lensing passable. Editing is somewhat choppy.
Mosk.

Les Hommes en Blanc
(Men In White)
(FRENCH)

Paris, Nov. 15.
Columbia release of Paul Graetz production. Stars Raymond Pellegrin, Jeanne Moreau. Directed by Ralph Habib. Screenplay, Maurice Auberge from novel by Andre Soubrion; camera, Pierre Petit; editor, Francosie Javet. At Marignan, Paris. Running time, 102 MINS.
Nerac ....Raymond Pellegrin
Marianne ....Jeanne Moreau
Delpeuch ....Fernand Ledoux
Surgeon ....Jean Chevrier
Director ....Jean Debucourt
Interne ....Christian Marquand

Based on a bestseller here on the medical profession, this is sincere if episodic picturization of a young doctor's life. It has the usual approach of following him through the hospital and then as a country doctor before he realizes exactly what he wants to do. Though detailing some interesting aspects of the medical life, this adds nothing in extracting a dramatic essence from the plodding decisions of the hero, Raymond Pellegrin. Lack of names slates this primarily for arty theatres. It will need plenty of delicate handling for it has nothing that was not said before, and usually more dramatically, in U.S. films.

Director Ralph Habib has given this an honest mounting but rarely gets the dramatic edge into it. Pellegrin has a fine presence but rarely gives insight into the doctor's character. Fernand Ledoux etches a fine portrait of a weary but dignified country practitioner. Lensing and editing are fine. Hospital scenes were made on the spot and have a fine documentary feel to them.
Mosk.

The Square Jungle

Prizefight action-thriller with Tony Curtis, Ernest Borgnine. Okay general market prospects.

Hollywood, Nov. 29.

Universal release of Albert Zugsmith production. Stars Tony Curtis, Pat Crowley, Ernest Borgnine; features Paul Kelly, Jim Backus, Leigh Snowden, John Day, Joe Louis, David Janssen. Directed by Jerry Hopper. Story and screenplay George Zuckerman; camera, George Robinson; editor, Paul Weatherwax; music, Heinz Roemheld. Previewed Nov. 23, '55. Running time, **86 MINS.**

Eddie Quaid (Packy Glennon)	Tony Curtis
Julie Walsh	Pat Crowley
Bernie Browne	Ernest Borgnine
Jim McBride	Paul Kelly
Pat Quaid	Jim Backus
Lorraine Evans	Leigh Snowden
Al Gorski	John Day
Joe Louis	Himself
Jack Lindsay	David Janssen
Singer	Carmen McRae
Tommy Dillon	John Marley
Dan Selby	Barney Phillips
Tony Adamson	Joseph Vitale
Mrs. Gorski	Kay Stewart

The action of the prize ring tailored into this Tony Curtis vehicle comes off with average results and the film overall shapes to generally okay prospects. Sharpening the grossing outlook overall and providing added marquee weight is the costarring of Ernest Borgnine in his first role since his "Marty" click.

With the emphasis on the squared jungle and the males that slug it out therein, there's not much room for the femmes, but costar Pat Crowley takes advantage of the small footage allotted to her in the screen story by George Zuckerman. Curtis responds well to the directorial demands of Jerry Hopper as a young man who turns to the ring to raise bail money for his drunken father and goes on to become middleweight champion. Plot has its fresh angles, but not enough of them to lift it above a generally pat pattern. However, this won't bother those who will turn out for the pic.

Borgnine gives a quiet, able performance as the trainer who readies Curtis for his ring career. Character is that of a philosophical, introverted bookworm, but Borgnine keeps it from being colorless. Under his tutelage, the young pro advances quickly to win his crown from John Day, loses it in a rematch when the referee stops the fight and then wins it back in a third, brutal meeting in which the same ref, warned to think twice before halting the action, does just that and Day is seriously injured. Thereafter, it's a question of Day recovering and Curtis getting over the horrors caused by the merciless beating he had administered.

Day, film stunt man turned actor for his first role, shows up exceptionally well, and John Marley makes his referee character count. Paul Kelly is his usual competent self as the police lieutenant who sponsors Curtis' ring career and Jim Backus does right by his role of the fighter's bottle-loving father. Leigh Snowden, whose part in the proceedings is more nebulously established than Miss Crowley's, is a blonde who comforts Curtis during his remorse binge, even though it is Miss Crowley who gets him in the end.

Albert Zugsmith's production makes good use of ring scenes to stir up excitement, and the fighters simulate the fisticuffs ably enough for a picture, although the action won't pass muster in a real squared circle. Lensing by George Robinson and the special photography by Clifford Stine are expertly handled and the score is good.

Brog.

Oh Rosalinda
(BRITISH-C'SCOPE-COLOR) (With Songs)

Modernized version of Strauss opera, "Die Fledermaus," starring ballerina Ludmilla Tcherina, Anton Walbrook, Michael Redgrave, Mel Ferrer in storybook setting; offbeat light entertainment.

London, Nov. 22.

Associated British-Pathe release of Michael Powell-Emeric Pressburger production Stars Michael Redgrave, Mel Ferrer, Anthony Quayle, Ludmilla Tcherina, Anton Walbrook (singers Sari Barabas, Alexander Young, Dennis Dowling, Walter Berry); features Dennis Price, Anneliese Rothenberger. Written, produced and directed by Michael Powell, Emeric Pressburger modernized the Johann Strauss opera, "Die Fledermaus"; camera, Christopher Challis; editor, Reginald Mills; music, Johann Strauss; new lyrics, Dennis Arundell. At Studio One, London, Nov. 16, '55. Running time, **101 MINS.**

Dr. Falke	Anton Walbrook
Colonel Eisenstein	Michael Redgrave
Rosalinda Eisenstein	Ludmilla Tcherina
Capt. Alfred Westerman	Mel Ferrer
General Orlofsky	Anton Quayle
Adele	Anneliese Rothenberger
Major Frank	Dennis Price
Frosh	Oska Sima

An opera converted to the screen inevitably loses much in transit the result being, of necessity, half fantasy, half screen reality. In this instance, the story of "Die Fledermaus" is brought up-to-date and set in Vienna on the eve of her restoration as a sovereign state, **still under the control of the four occupying powers. It is a lavish production, highly diverting and spectacular. This should make for offbeat, light entertainment anywhere.**

Anton Walbrook, as a malignant compere (Dr. Falke), takes the audience into his confidence preceding the opening of the story, explaining the progress of a malicious practical joke he is perpetrating out of revenge, at snatched intervals between arias. To accentuate the staginess and improbability of the story, the sets are exaggerated in sugarcake dressing and the famous songs given new lyrics to fit the modern sphere. Retaining the best known songs spins out the action which retards the plot halfway and supplies anti-climaxes at the end. Deft pruning could keep the action rolling to better effect.

The captivating Rosalinda (Ludmilla Tcherina), married to a French officer, is pursued by an old flame, a U. S. officer, and is caught in compromising conditions by an escort guard who mistakes him for her husband, due for barrack detention. To save her reputation, her lover allows himself to be jailed while she goes to a masked ball given by the Russian commandant and flirts outrageously with her husband. While the Frenchman explodes with jealous rage at her conduct, she rounds on him in retaliation revealing her identity as his amorous partner at the ball. The machiavellian Dr. Falke, revelling in the mischief he has engendered, brings in the whole party of Allied servicemen and dancers to laugh at his successful conniving.

Michael Redgrave has an adequate lightness of touch as the Gallic philanderer with his own pleasing voice and personality to carry the unaccustomed role. Miss Tcherina shows more of her person than personality as his gay wife, with her singing role attractively sung by Sari Barabas.

Mel Ferrer is dashing as the persistent American wooer, and Anthony Quayle supplies the requisite sombre touch to the character of the Russian officer who mellows under the influence of champagne and dames. Dennis Price makes a striking contrast as his British counterpart. Anneliese Rothenberger sings and acts vivaciously as the truant lady's maid and the other singing roles are competently handled. Camerawork is artistic and the direction is suitably adjusted to the picturebook atmosphere and satirical vein.

Clem.

El Gran Circo Chamorro
(The Big Chamorro Circus) (CHILE)

Santiago, Nov. 22.

Columbia release of Jose Bohr production. With Eugenio Retes, Doris Guerrero, Pepe Guixe, Malu Gatica, Rafael Frontaura, Gerardo Grez, Juan Leal, Eduardo Gamboa, Iris del Valle, Elsa Villa, Rolando Caicedo, Xiomara Alfaro. Directed by Jose Bohr. Written by Eugenio Retes; camera, Andres Martorell; music by Bohr; musical director, Donato Roman Heitmann. Previewed in Santiago, Chile, Nov. 21, '55. Running time, **105 MINS.**

Chile's frozen peso situation, long overlooked by the Hollywood independent producers, has been taken advantage of by Jose Bohr, Spanish language film vet on the Coast many years ago. This overlong plotless production with the circus background should do okay within Chilean borders since the cast includes the well-known local names of Eugenio Retes, Malu Gatica and Rafael Frontaura. But the colloquialisms may limit its draw outside Chile.

This runs the gamut from flag-waving to tears but it has its entertaining moments with plenty of laughs ground out by Peruvian comic, Eugenio Retes, who has a name for himself in vaudeville here. Comedian is also responsible for the rambling script which, at times, has crackling dialogue. This covers the adventures of Chamorro (himself), a provincial circus owner who does about everything in the small travelling show. Retes' script suffers from happy coincidences and is short on ingenuity but Retes makes up for it with his nonchalance and sympathetic gab.

Miss Malu Gatica and Rafael Frontaura have limited roles in the threadbare yarn. Pepe Guixe carries off the romantic lead effectively. Bohr gives the pic good pace which more effective editing would have benefitted.

Eadie.

Texas Lady
(SUPERSCOPE-COLOR-SONG)

Claudette Colbert goes west. Far-fetched plot. Outlook spotty.

Hollywood, Nov. 29.

RKO release of Nat Holt production. Stars Claudette Colbert, Barry Sullivan; features Ray Collins, James Bell, Horace McMahon, Gregory Walcott, John Litel, Douglas Fowley, Don Haggerty, Walter Sande, Alexander Campbell. Directed by Tim Whelan. Story and screenplay, Horace McCoy; camera (Techicolor), Ray Rennahan; editor, Richard Farrell; score, Paul Sawtell; song "Texas Lady" by Sawtell and Johnnie Mann; sung and played by Les Paul and Mary Ford. Previewed Nov. 22, '55. Running time, **85 MINS.**

Prudence Webb	Claudette Colbert
Chris Mooney	Barry Sullivan
Ralston	Ray Collins
Cass Gower	James Bell
Stringy Winfield	Horace McMahon
Jess Foley	Gregory Walcott
Mead Moore	John Litel
Clay Ballard	Douglas Fowley
Sheriff Herndon	Don Haggerty
Sturdy	Walter Sande
Judge Herzog	Alexander Campbell
Wilson	Florenz Ames
Nanny Winfield	Kathleen Mulqueen
Rev. Collander	Robert Lynn

Claudette Colbert and Barry Sullivan will have to carry this one since the story is improbable throughout. Horace McCoy's script sends Miss Colbert, a New Orleans gentlewoman, west to run a Texas cowtown newspaper and to encounter Sullivan, supposedly a professional gambler but always the loser at whatever game of chance he tackles in the film. Tim Whelan's direction, and the performers, never compensate for the silly plotting.

Producer Nat Holt, and his associate, Lewis P. Rosen, provide the film with good character types in such as Collins, James Bell, Horace McMahon, John Litel, Douglas Fowley, Don Haggerty, Sande and Alexander Campbell. Had the scripting been as good as the casting effective entertainment would have resulted.

An exploitation peg is hung on the title tune by Paul Sawtell, who did the background score, and Johnnie Mann. It is played and sung behind the credits by Les Paul and Mary Ford, who also have recorded it. Outdoor values are good as lensed by Ray Rennahan in SuperScope, with print in Technicolor.

Brog.

Top Gun

Sterling Hayden title-roling in regulation western filmfare for outdoor action market.

Hollywood, Nov. 29.

United Artists release of Fame Pictures Inc. production. Stars Sterling Hayden; features William Bishop, Karen Booth, James Millican, Regis Toomey, Hugh Sanders, John Dehner. Directed by Ray Nazarro. Screenplay, Richard Schayer, Steve Fisher; from story by Fisher; camera, Lester White; editors, Dwight Caldwell, Henry Adams; music, Irving Gertz. Previewed Nov. 23, '55. Running time, **74 MINS.**

Rick Martin	Sterling Hayden
Canby Judd	William Bishop
Laura	Karen Booth
Bat Davis	James Millican
O'Hara	Regis Toomey
Marsh	Hugh Sanders
Quentin	John Dehner
Sutter	Rod Taylor
Hank	Wm. Phillips
Willetts	Dick Reeves

This is stock western action, staged and played satisfactorily enough to fill the demands of the outdoor program market. Sterling Hayden toplines to give it some marquee push in that field.

The Fame Pictures presentation through United Artists bears the brand of a number of western features of recent years, but this plucking of the best from such pix hasn't necessarily paid off here with anything of special interest. There's some of "High Noon" and similar outdoor goodies in the story by Steve Fisher, which he scripted with Richard Schayer, so Ray Nazarro's direction and the players have a familiar course to tread, but all hands tackle the chores in acceptable fashion.

Hayden is the top gun of the title, a man with a reputation who of necessity must always be defending it against those who think they are faster on the draw. Plot here has him returning to his old hometown to warn of a raid planned by hoodlums led by John Dehner. The town's hostile, wanting no part in the hired killer, and he's thrown in jail after being framed by William Bishop, a sharpie who has won over Hayden's girl friend, Karen Booth. However, **at the end, it's Hayden's guns and wits that put down the Dehner** mob, with an assist from Miss Booth, who saves Hayden from a trap by gunning Dehner herself.

Other than those mentioned, there's able cast work from the late James Millican, as an understanding sheriff; Regis Toomey, Hayden's sole friend in the unfriendly town, and Hugh Sanders, a cowardly citizen. The scoring by Irving Gertz and the lensing by Lester White come off satisfactorily. *Brog.*

Shack Out on 101

Dull melodrama for lowercase bookings in program market.

Hollywood, Nov. 22.

Allied Artists release of William F. Broidy (Mort Millman) production. Stars Terry Moore, Frank Lovejoy, Keenan Wynn, Lee Marvin. Directed by Edward Dain. Story and screenplay, Edward and Mildred Dain; camera, Floyd Crosby; editor, George White; music, Paul Dunlap; song, "A Sunday Kind of Love" by Barbara Belle, Louis Prima, Anita Leonard and Stan Rhodes. Previewed Nov. 21, '55. Running time, **79 MINS.**

Kotty .... Terry Moore
Professor .... Frank Lovejoy
George .... Keenan Wynn
Slob .... Lee Marvin
Eddie .... Whit Bissell
Artie .... Jess Barker
Pepe .... Donald Murphy
Dillon .... Frank De Kova
Perch .... Len Lesser
Lookout .... Fred Gabourie

Because of some familiar cast names, "Shack" will get by as a supporting programmer, but it's a dull, confused melodrama.

Edward Dein directed from a story and screenplay he wrote with Mildred Dein, but plot moves along like it was developed as the cameras turned rather than being thought out in advance. Result is such normally good male actors as Frank Lovejoy, Keenan Wynn, Lee Marvin and Whit Bissell fail to show to advantage. Scripting and direction continually veer between comedy and melodrama and don't do well with either, adding to confusion.

Title comes from a Coast highway eatery operated by Wynn, where Lee Marvin is the cook and Terry Moore the waitress. Lovejoy, scientist at a nearby electronics lab, haunts the place, both to make love to Miss Moore and trade secrets with Marvin, who's an enemy agent. It comes out later, after many stand and talk scenes, that Lovejoy's really working with our Government to trap Marvin and see that Miss Moore's love for him isn't misplaced.

Marvin gets his at the finale via a skindiver's harpoon, fired by Wynn's friend, Bissell, who up to this point is a coward, afraid of blood and violence.

Technical support behind the Mort Millman production, for William F. Broidy Corp., is just average. *Brog.*

Proibito
(Forbidden)
(FRANCO-ITALIAN-COLOR)

Rome, Nov. 15.

Diana Cinematografica release of a Documento Production. Stars Mel Ferrer, Amedeo Nazzari. Directed by Mario Monicelli. Screenplay, Monicelli and Suso Cecchi D'Amico, from novel, "The Mother," by Grazia Deledda; camera (Technicolor), Aldo Tonti; music, excerpts from Brahm's 4th Symphony played by Santa Cecilia Orch; editor, Adriana Novelli. At Capitol, Rome. Running time, **90 MINS.**

Don Paolo .... Mel Ferrer
Corraine .... Amedeo Nazzari
Agnese Barras .... Lea Massari
Nicodemo Barras .... Henri Vilbert
Maddalena .... Germaine Kerjean
Bishop .... Eduardo Cianelli

Color locationer looks like a good grosser in the Italian market, with the Amedeo Nazzari and Mel Ferrer names aiding marquee-wise. Abroad, the rarely seen Sardinian setting, beautifully lensed by Aldo Tonti, should interest as well, and pic should get a fair play. U.S. chances rely mainly on the Ferrer name, with chances rated spotty.

Story, based on Nobel prizewinner Grazia Deledda's w.k. book, "The Mother," concerns a priest who returns to his home village in Sardegna, where inhabitants are split by an old and violent family rivalry. Don Paolo (Mel Ferrer) struggles to bring peace to the countryside. After several setbacks, he accomplishes his mission.

Ferrer is effective as the priest, giving the role an underplayed, highly sympathetic reading. Nazzari, Germaine Kerjean and others portray strong village characters. Paolo Ferrara, as the gendarme sergeant, thefts many scenes by his easy-going playing. Lea Massari is good in her first film role as the priests childhood friend.

Principal bow should go, however, to the magnificent Technicolor lensing by Aldo Tonti. It is one of the best color jobs seen here in some time. Sets and island locations are well designed and chosen. Top technical values prevail. *Hawk.*

Josephine and Men
(BRITISH—COLOR)

Lightweight British comedy with topweight local cast for Marquee appeal. Slim b.o. prospects in U.S.

London, Nov. 15.

British Lion Films release of Charter Film-Boulting Bros. production. Stars Glynis Johns, Jack Buchanan, Donald Sinden, Peter Finch. Directed by Roy Boulting. Screenplay and original story by Nigel Balchin; script and additional scenes by Frank Harvey, Roy Boulting; camera, Gilbert Taylor; editor, Maxwell Benedict; music, John Addison. At Plaza, London, Nov. 9, '55. Running time, **98 MINS.**

Josephine .... Glynis Johns
Uncle Charles .... Jack Buchanan
Alan Hartley .... Donald Sinden
David Hewer .... Peter Finch
Aunt May .... Heather Thatcher
Frederick Luton .... Ronald Squire
1st Detective .... William Hartnell
2nd Detective .... Gerald Sim
Police Inspector .... Hugh Moxey
Police Sergeant .... Sam Kydd
Mrs. McFee .... Tonie McMillan
Landlord "Five Bells" .... Wally Patch
Landlady .... Peggy Ann Clifford

There's not a great deal of substance in this British comedy made by the Boulting Bros., but a topweight local cast gives it considerable marquee strength here. Boxoffice prospects must be regarded as limited, however, and it has only slender chances in the U.S.

Nigel Balchin's screenplay from his own original develops the theme of a girl with an overpowering desire to help the underdog. For that reason she jettisons her wealthy fiancee on the eve of their wedding to marry his poverty-stricken friend, a struggling playwright living in a tenement room. Time passes, the writer prospers, and suddenly the other man turns up late in the night on the run from the police. The wife is about to switch her affections again, but comes to her senses when her ex-fiancee is cleared.

The story is related in a series of continuous flashbacks by Jack Buchanan, the girl's bachelor uncle who is forever on the run from amorous ladies. He puts a lot of charm in the character, as do the other three principal characters—Glynis Johns, Peter Finch (the husband) and Donald Sinden. But there are too many irrelevancies to the story.

Roy Boulting's direction (his brother, John, gets producer credit) is on the leisurely side. Supporting roles are neatly played. *Myro.*

Solange du Lebst
(As Long as You Live)
(GERMAN)

Frankfurt, Nov. 15.

RKO release of Eva Film. Stars Marianne Koch, Adrian Hoven. Directed by Dr. Harald Reinl. Screenplay, Joachim Bartsch and Dr. Harald Reinl; camera, Walter Riml; music, Jose Munios Molleda and City of Wiesbaden Symphony. Previewed in Frankfurt. Running time, **100 MINS.**

Theresa .... Marianne Koch
Michael .... Adrian Hoven
Escosura .... Luis Arroyo
Kommisar Malek .... Kurt Heintel
Torquito .... Willy Roesner
Maria .... Karen Dor

Theme of the Spanish Civil War is a familiar one in the U.S. but is less often used in Germany. This film, photographed in Spain and in Germany, is an exceptionally fine one, and stacks up as one of the country's best this year in production, acting, camera, music and plot.

A dusty sleepy Spanish town is caught in the impact of the war. Main plot concerns a young nurse who refuses to escape with her captain fiance, but stays to work in the tiny town which the Communists take over. She finds a German pilot, who has been fighting the Commies, and has been shot down, and risks her life to save his. Mixed emotions of townspeople, forced to turn Communist, bring the political and personal problems to the fore.

Top credit goes to Marianne Koch, recently awarded the highest prize as best actress of the year at the Berlin Film Festival. One of the prettiest German actresses, she plays with warmth and feeling. Adrian Hoven, as the wounded pilot, turns in a moving performance. Bavarian character actor Willy Roesner does one of his typically fine jobs as the Communist mayor. Karen Dor, apparently headed for German stardom, is a dark-eyed looker whose sex appeal is evident in every scene. She is the mayor's spoiled daughter. Some credit for her acting probably goes to husband, Dr. Harald Reinl, the film's director and co-writer.

Special music by Spanish composer Jose Munios Molleda deserves praise, with fine backing from the City of Wiesbaden Symphony.

With the growing prestige of Marianne Koch, and the packed action, this could do business in the U.S. *Haze.*

Picnic
(C'SCOPE-COLOR)

A solid boxoffice-sender.

Columbia release of Fred Kohlmar production. Stars William Holden; features Kim Novak, Betty Field, Susan Strasberg, Cliff Robertson, Arthur O'Connell, Verna Felton. Directed by Joshua Logan. Screenplay, Daniel Taradash, based on the William Inge play; camera (Technicolor), James Wong Howe; editors, Charles Nelson and William A. Lyon; music, George Duning, conducted by Morris Stoloff. Previewed at Loew's 72d Street Theatre, Nov. 22, '55. Running time, **115 MINS.**

Hal Carter .... William Holden
Rosemary Sydney .... Rosalind Russell
Madge Owens .... Kim Novak
Flo Owens .... Betty Field
Millie Owens .... Susan Strasberg
Alan .... Cliff Robertson
Howard Devans ...... Arthur O'Connell
Mrs. Helen Potts .... Verna Felton
Linda Sue Breckenridge ..... Reta Shaw
Bomber .... Nick Adams
Mr. Benson .... Raymond Bailey
Christine Schoenwalder
Elizabeth W. Wilson
Juanita Badger .... Phyllis Newman
1st Policeman .... Don C. Harvey
2nd Policeman .... Steve Benton

This is a considerably enlarged "Picnic," introducing new scope and style in flow of presentation without dissipating the mood and substance of the legiter by William Inge. Screenscripter Daniel Taradash and director Joshua Logan, adding the cinematic brick and mortar to the original structure, have developed a potent art and commerce property.

The boards-to-screen transplanters correctly refrained from making any basic changes with Inge's characters and the circumstances in which they're involved. It's the story of a robust and shiftless showoff who, looking up an old college chum in a small town in Kansas, sets off various emotional responses among the small group of local inhabitants he encounters.

William Holden (Ralph Meeker originated the part) is the drifter, sometimes ribald, partly sympathetic and colorful and giving a forceful interpretation all the way. And like Meeker, Holden, a broad-shouldered Atlas, stripped to the waist in some scenes, swaggers and sways for whatever effect this might arouse.

The Fred Kohlmar production expands the setting from the backyard of the prototype to include an actual picnic where considerable action now takes place. It's with this device that the film takes on its "bigness," for the Labor Day outing is an elaborate pictorial display that intertwines the familiar round of fun and games for all with development of key points in the intimate story.

Logan, who directed the play, appears to have had a field day in calling the turns in the picture, particularly the picnic spree. Along with the three-legged races, he's brought in extra bits of business like tots howling, another one Bronx cheering an off-key vocalist and a little dog at play in a basket. All as amusing, tiny asides.

Looking and acting remarkably like a facsimile of Janice Rule of the original, Kim Novak is the town's No. One looker, and an emotional blank until muscle-man (and, to her, downtrodden) Holden proves an awakening force. Miss Novak does right well.

Rosalind Russell, the spinster school teacher boarding with Miss Novak's family, is standout, moving in her plea for marriage, amusing as she pretends indifference to men and pitiable in her whiskey-inspired outburst against Holden. Matched with Miss Russell is Arthur O'Connell, a repeat from the stage, who contributes the humorous hightpoint when, utterly dazed, he finds himself on the way to the justice of the peace with Miss Russell.

Betty Field, Susan Strasberg, Cliff Robertson, Reta Shaw, Nick Adams, Raymond Bailey and Elizabeth W. Wilson all are to be credited as first-rate thesps in roles that have varying degrees of prominence. Miss Strasberg as Miss Novak's hoyden sister is a victim of her own looks, though. She's supposed to be the unpretty sister (Kim Stanley wore dental braces on the stage to help convey this illusion). But Miss Strasberg is an ingenue who can't be accepted as unpretty; she's a cutie pie.

This is Logan's first film and it's a big beginning. His picnic scenes are dazzling, rapidly paced and abounding in color. The dramatic material has strength and sting, as adapted by Taradash and staged by Logan.

"Picnic" runs 115 minutes but though sharply edited, this is excessive. Music and all technical work are in keeping with the top quality of Kohlmar's production.

Wrapping it up, the romance and sex, the exciting and the tender elements, the identifiable "real" people and the insight on human values—these must mean long runs and lotsa loot. *Gene.*

Kismet
(C'SCOPE—MUSICAL—COLOR)

Arabian Nights-type stage musical gets opulent film treatment for fair entertainment, medium prospects.

Hollywood, Dec. 6.

Metro release of Arthur Freed production. Stars Howard Keel, Ann Blyth, Dolores Gray, Vic Damone; features Monty Woolley, Sebastian Cabot, Jay C. Flippen, Mike Mazurki, Jack Elam, Ted de Corsia. Directed by Vincente Minnelli. Screenplay, Charles Lederer and Luther Davis; adapted from the musical play by Lederer and Davis, founded on "Kismet" by Edward Knoblock; music and lyrics by Robert Wright and George Forrest; music adapted from themes of Alexander Borodin; camera (Eastman Color), Joseph Ruttenberg; editor, Adrienne Fazan; musical numbers and dances staged by Jack Cole; music supervised and conducted by Andre Previn and Jeff Alexander; orchestral arrangements by Conrad Salinger, Alexander Courage and Arthur Morton. Previewed Dec. 2, '55. Running time, **112 MINS.**

The Poet .... Howard Keel
Marsinah .... Ann Blyth
Lalume .... Dolores Gray
Caliph .... Vic Damone
Omar .... Monty Woolley
Wazir .... Sebastian Cabot
Jawan .... Jay C. Flippen
Chief Policeman .... Mike Mazurki
Hassan-Ben .... Jack Elam
Police Subaltern .... Ted de Corsia
Princesses of Abubu .... Reiko Sato, Patricia Dunn, Wonci Lui
Fevvol .... Ross Bagdasarian
Zubbediya .... Julie Robinson

Opulent escapism is what "Kismet" has to sell. It will have to sell it hard because the stage musical comes to the screen with just fair entertainment results. Lushly decorated Arabian Nights fantasy in CinemaScope and Eastman Color; good, but not sock marquee names; 11 songs and several lavish production numbers are the assets; medium are the boxoffice prospects.

Howard Keel is the big entertainment factor and, in somewhat lesser degree, so is Dolores Gray. Without these two there would be very few minutes in the footage's 112 that could be counted as really good fun. Robust in voice and physique, Keel injects just the right amount of tongue-in-cheek into his role of Bagdad rogue

Miss Gray's numbers are "Not Since Ninevah" and "Bored." Keel's reaction to the latter gives it its point, while the first is assisted by the segue into a dance by Reiko Sato, Patricia Dunn and Wonci Lui as the three Princesses of Ababu, Miss Gray scores best with her response to story situations, particularly in her free-wheeling yen for the Bagdad rogue, slickly expressed in the gay Rahadlakum number, in which Keel is given the run of the scheming wazir's harem, of which she is the number-one wife.

The other two stars of this Arthur Freed production, which is guided through its escapism courses by Vincente Minnelli's direction, are Ann Blyth and Vic Damone. Vocally, as Keel's daughter, Miss Blyth does the proper thing with "Baubles, Bangles and Beads," "And This Is My Beloved" and "Stranger in Paradise." So does Damone, as the young caliph who loves the poet's daughter, on "Beloved," "Stranger" and "Night of My Nights," but otherwise their romantic pairing does not come off

Those aforementioned three princesses from Ababu, come to Bagdad at the scheming of the wazir, Sebastian Cabot, as possible brides for the caliph, have a second chance to score with their terping in the production portions and again click as they show their qualifications as prospective mates. Other than these two dance spots, Jack Cole's staging depends mostly on eye-filling spectacle that is plushy to the extreme in costuming by Tony Duquette and colorful furbishings, such as the "Night of My Nights" piece.

Charles Lederer and Luther Davis screenplayed from their stage musical book, with music and lyrics by Robert Wright and George Forrest. Founded on Edward Knoblock's "Kismet," the Bagdad fable tells of how the supposedly magical powers of street poet Keel are commandered by the scheming wazir to advance his own power. The poet's an opportunist willing to go along with a gag and so finds himself in the palace fixing things at the finale so his daughter can wed the caliph and he can be sentenced to some far-off, romantic oasis spending the rest of his life comforting Miss Gray for the loss of her wazir husband.

Monty Woolley, as the caliph's poet laureate, has practically nothing to do, but Cabot has more footage and gets his chuckles as the palace schemer. Other players do not have much chance at scene-grabbing. On the technical side, Joseph Ruttenberg's lensing provides pictorial splendor. Musically, the supervision and conducting by Andre Previn and Jeff Alexander leaves something to be desired. So does the recording of dialog, as at least a third of it is hard to understand. *Brog.*

Unternehmen Schlafsack
(Operation Sleeping-Bag)
(GERMAN

Berlin, Nov. 29.

Rank release of Real production. Stars Paul Elinger and Eva-Ingeborg Scholz. Directed by Arthur Maria Rabenalt. Screenplay, Kurt E. Walter, after novel by Hans Nogly; camera, Albert Benitz, Jost Graf Hardenberg; music, Bert Grund. At Capitol, Berlin. Running time, **104 MINS.**

Farces centering around German soldiers of the last war are currently much in vogue here. Latest along this line is "Sleeping-Bag," a type of farce since there is enough seriousness to go along with the tongue-in-cheek and comedy material. Pic benefits from outstanding direction of Arthur Maria Rabenalt, a fine cast and an amusing story. Pic is beyond the German average, and an outstanding draw here. Foreign prospects also seem better than usual.

Plot, which seems implausible, is said to have been based on actual happenings. It deals with a German front officer on a duty trip to his army headquarters in Berlin (1944). Over-complicated red tape gets him involuntarily mixed up in a "secret mission" which holds him back for "special order." Cashing in on this mixup, he manages to get his men from the East front to Berlin and establishes a phony military outfit in order to escape with his soldiers from the last murderous phase of the lost war. The truth about his fictitious outfit is discovered and faces death as punishment. The war's end, however, prevents him from being executed.

Rabenalt's brilliant direction has created a fast-moving, imaginative and enjoyable pic. Almost the entire action is centered on Paul Klinger, who as a sympathetic Hauptmann (Captain) Brack who, realizing war's senselessness, manages to save the lives of his soldiers. Topnotch performances are also turned by Karl-Heinz Boehm, Bum Krueger, Willi Rose and Kurt Meisel. Most important femme role, the secretary at army headquarters, is impressively portrayed by Eva-Ingeborg Scholz. Renate Mannhardt and newcomer Gisela Tantau also do well in lesser roles.

Technically, this film rates highly. Camerawork by Albert Benitz and Jost Graf Hardenberg is imaginative. Bert Grund's score is also an advantage. *Hans.*

The Spoilers
(COLOR)

Fifth remake for this Rex Beach adventure yarn. Good prospecting still.

Hollywood, Dec. 6.

Universal release of Ross Hunter production. Stars Anne Baxter, Jeff Chandler, Rory Calhoun; costars Ray Danton, Barbara Britton, John McIntire; features Wallace Ford, Forrest Lewis, Carl Benton Reid, Raymond Walburn. Directed by Jesse Hibbs. Screenplay, Oscar Brodney, Charles Hoffman; based on the novel by Rex Beach; camera (Technicolor), Maury Gertsman; editor, Paul Weatherwax; music supervision, Joseph Gershenson. Previewed Nov. 29, '55. Running time, **84 MINS.**

Cherry Malotte .... Anne Baxter
Roy Glennister .... Jeff Chandler
Alex McNamara .... Rory Colhoun
Blackie .... Ray Danton
Helen Chester .... Barbara Britton
Dextry .... John McIntire
Flapjack Simms .... Wallace Ford
Banty Jones .... Forrest Lewis
Judge Stillman .... Carl Benton Reid
Mr. Skinner .... Raymond Walburn
Duchess .... Ruth Donnelly
Wheaton .... Dayton Lummis
Jonathan Struve .... Willis Bouchey
The Marshal .... Roy Barcroft
Montrose .... Byron Foulger
Bartender .... Robert Foulk
Bank Manager .... Arthur Space
Piano Player .... Harry Seymour
Miner .... Bob Steele
Berry .... Edwin Parker
Deputy .... Lee Roberts
Deputy .... John Close

The outdoor action penned in early 1900's by Rex Beach in his "The Spoilers" novel has paid off big for Hollywood—either in the story itself, or in its infinite variations. This is the fifth time around for the original and Universal's second version. There's still b.o. coin to be panned, although not any longer in goldrush quantity. This 1955 entry is a general market, frozen north actioner that should find the prospecting satisfactory.

Anne Baxter, Jeff Chandler and Rory Calhoun are the principals lending familiar marquee names to the Ross Hunter production. In enacting, respectively, Cherry Malotte, femme saloonkeeper; Roy Glennister, stalwart hero, and Alex McNamara, suave heavy, the trio brings off the show in suitable fashion for those who like their action spelled out in a-b-c- terms. Jesse Hibbs' direction of the script by Oscar Brodney and Charles Hoffman is breezy most of the way, but actionfully rugged, such as in the climaxing fisticuffs between hero and heavy, when the plot demands roughness.

Beach's novel dealt with organized claim-jumping in Alaskan gold mines around Nome at the turn of the century. Calhoun is the organizer, posing as a gold commissioner, who has designs on the richest of the mines, co-owned by Chandler with John McIntire. With a phony judge, the latter's attractive socalled niece, and a crooked Attorney, Calhoun's doing okay until a hero who doesn't give up easily uncovers evidence of the illegal takeover. That epic fist fight (a label first handed out to the brawn between William Farnum and Tom Santschi in the 1914 Selig Polyscope Co., version) sprawls from Miss Baxter's plush above-saloon apartment, through the northern bistro, out the window and winds up in the mud of the Nome streets. Such punishment you won't believe but it's fun to watch, and well-staged.

Abetting the star trio are co-stars Ray Danton, faro-dealer who yens for his comely boss; Barbara Britton, the phony niece, and McIntire, Chandler's crusty old mining partner. Others contributing ably include Wallace Ford and Forrest Lewis, mine owners; Carl Benton Reid, the phony judge; Raymond Walburn, town drunk, and Ruth Donnelly, Miss Baxter's maid.

Technicolor camera handling by Maury Gertsman is expert, so are the editing and other technical factors. Background score is apt to the action and there's even a song about careless love for Miss Baxter's character, but not with the impact "See What the Boys In the Back Room Will Have" as done by Marlene Dietrich in the 1942 U version. *Brog.*

Don Camillo E L'on. Peppone
(Don Camillo and Hon. Peppone)
(ITALIAN—FRENCH)

Rome, Nov. 29.

Dear Film release of a Rizzoli production. Stars Fernandel, Gino Cervi; features Leda Gloria, Claude Silvain, Mamino Carotenuto, Saro Urzi, Marco Tulli, Carlo Duse, Umberto Spadaro. Directed by Carmine Gallone. Screenplay, Giovanni Guareschi from story by Guareschi; camera, Anchise Brizzi; music, Alessandro Cicognini. At Ariston, Rome. Running time, **100 MINS.**

No. 3 in this picture series perhaps inevitably shows up a shade under its predecessors in general values. However, the great European popularity of the first pix assures a good proportionate gross for this one. American chances appear problematical but Fernandel's popularity currently at the U.S. boxoffice may help.

Fernandel and Gino Cervi again battle it out for village honors as the cleric and the Commie mayor.

There is a good comic sequence on a war-relic tank which runs away with them. Other bits of their repartee include an election battle which neither one really wants to lose or win, and grade school exam which the Commie would fail except for the aid of the priest, who thus blackmails the mayor into approving a church project previously blocked by his assembly.

Direction by Carmine Gallone lacks the lighter touch imparted by the previous director, Julien Duvivier. Pace is resultingly slower and less subtle. Technical credits are okay, but budget seems to have been kept down. *Hawk.*

At Gunpoint
(C'SCOPE-COLOR)

Familiarly - cast, well - played western in C'Scope with satisfactory playoff indicated.

Hollywood, Dec. 2.

Allied Artists release of Vincent M. Fennelly production. Stars Fred MacMurray, Dorothy Malone, Walter Brennan; features Tommy Rettig, Skip Homeier, John Qualen, Whit Bissell, Irving Bacon. Directed by Alfred Werker. Story and screenplay, Daniel B. Ullman; camera (Technicolor), Ellsworth Fredricks; editor, Eda Warren; score, Carmen Dragon. Previewed Dec. 1, '55. Running time, 80 MINS.

Jack Wright	Fred MacMurray
Martha Wright	Dorothy Malone
Doc Lacy	Walter Brennan
Billy	Tommy Rettig
Bob Dennis	Skip Homeier
Livingstone	John Qualen
Clark	Whit Bissell
Ferguson	Irving Bacon
Kirk	Jack Lambert
Alvin	John Pickard
The Stranger	James Griffith
Marshal	Harry Shannon
Henderson	Frank Ferguson
Wally	James Lilburn
Federal Marshal	Harry Lauter

Allied Artists has a handy entry in "At Gunpoint." It's a Cinema-Scoped western equipped with cast names not heretofore common under the AA label and which should help it to a satisfactory playoff in the outdoor field.

Plotwise, the Vincent M. Fennelly production is on the same "civic consciousness" kick noticed in a number of recent westerns, but veers slightly from pattern by using a different hero type—a man who knows virtually nothing about guns. There's no quarrel with the civic responsibility reprise, but Daniel B. Ullman's screen story overworks it a bit, almost to a platform pitch. There is some overwriting elsewhere, causing occasional slowdowns but, generally, the plot shapes up to a good average for western story-telling.

A number of action moments are linked with some suspense-building expectancy, without ever rushing the story along at a regulation oater pace, under the direction by Alfred Werker. An outlaw gang rides into a peaceful Texas town and robs the bank. One of the gang is downed during the escape by a lucky shot from Fred MacMurray, owner of the general store who can't remember having ever fired a sixgun before. He's acclaimed a hero by the citizens, but they turn against him when the outlaws, led by Skip Homeier, return for revenge and endanger others in the town. MacMurray is asked to leave but stands his ground, climax finding him going it alone against the outlaws, an act that shames the citizens into helping him.

Performances are very good all down the line, with MacMurray's gun-shy hero his best in some time. Dorothy Malone registers as his wife, as do Tommy Rettig, as their young son and Walter Brennan, as

the old doctor who stands by his friend. Homeier's killer has menace and town types such as John Qualen, Whit Bissell, Irving Bacon, James Griffith, Harry Shannon and Frank Ferguson show up excellently. James Lilburn is good as Miss Malone's brother who is accidentally killed by the outlaws and Harry Lauter capably fills a visiting marshal spot. Okay as outlaws are Jack Lambert, John Pickard and others.

Ellsworth Fredrick's lensing is unusually good, with the Technicolor print doing right by the western values. Other technical credits measure up, with the exception of the Carmen Dragon score, which is constantly overused. *Brog.*

The Man With the Golden Arm

Case history of a drug addict, mercilessly and expertly detailed. Should be helped, not hindered, in exhibition.

United Artists release of Otto Preminger production. Stars Frank Sinatra, Eleanor Parker, Kim Novak; features Arnold Stang, Darren McGavin, Robert Strauss, John Conte, Doro Merande. Directed by Preminger. Screenplay, Walter Newman and Lewis Meltzer, from the novel by Nelson Algren; camera, Sam Leavitt; editor, Louis R. Loeffler; music, Elmer Bernstein. Previewed at Victoria Theatre, New York, Dec. 7, '55. Running time, 119 MINS.

Frankie	Frank Sinatra
Zosh	Eleanor Parker
Molly	Kim Novak
Sparrow	Arnold Stang
Louie	Darren McGavin
Schwiefka	Robert Strauss
Drunky	John Conte
Vi	Doro Merande
Markette	George E. Stone
Williams	George Mathews
Dominowski	Leonid Kinskey
Bednar	Emile Meyer
Shorty Rogers	Himself
Shelly Manne	Himself
Piggy	Frank Richards
Lane	Will Wright
Kvorka	Tommy Hart
Antek	Frank Marlowe
Meter Reader	Joe McTurk
Chester	Ralph Neff
Bird Dog	Ernest Raboff
Vangie	Martha Wentworth
Junkie	Jerry Barclay
Taxi Driver	Leonard Bremen
Suspenders	Paul Burns
Landlord	Charles Seel

Otto Preminger's second open defiance of the Production Code is expressed in "The Man With the Golden Arm," a feature that focusses on addiction to narcotics. Clinical in its probing of the agonies, subject matter will seem forbidding to sensitive elements of the populace. Fortunately this is a gripping, fascinating film, expertly produced and directed by Preminger and performed with marked conviction by Frank Sinatra as the drug slave.

Many of the usual boxoffice plusses are missing. But "Arm" is not the usual kind of picture. It has its power in the strangeness of its story and this has been fashioned into absorbing drama. It is bound to stir talk and controversy, assuring good "A" business initially, at least. There being no precedental guideposts, the commercial fate of the production after the first showcasing—after those with special interests in the picture have been checked in—is a toughie to figure. But—crystal ball in hand—it looks like a fair bet all around.

Does "Arm" depress an audience? This reviewer suggests the screen characters are too remote to make such personal identification with the spectators. It is perhaps this very same factor that militates against the boxoffice prospects. The dope kick is beyond the ken of the general public and as a result there can be little sense of participation in the story and not much sympathy with the characters.

Sinatra, as the picture opens, returns to his squalid Chicago haunts after six months in the federal hospital in Lexington, Ky., where he was "cured" of his addiction. Thwarted in his attempt to land a job as a musician, he resumes as the dealer in a smalltime professional poker game. The appellation, "Man With the Golden Arm," stems from this.

Eleanor Parker is a pathetic figure as his wife, pretending to be chair-ridden for the sole purpose of making Sinatra stay by her side. A downstairs neighbor is Kim Novak, and the s.a. angles are not overlooked by the camera. Arnold Stang is "Sparrow," Sinatra's subservient sidekick with the

larcenous inclinations. Darren McGavin is the peddler, insidious in his ways of luring Sinatra back to the first "fix" that leads to many others.

Robert Strauss, John Conte, Doro Merande, George E. Stone, George Matthews and Leonid Kinskey round out the cast. And in all cases, stars, featured and semi-featured players, the thesp talent is to be credited with a first-rate job.

It's the story that counts most, however. Screenplay by Walter Newman and Lewis Meltzer, from the Nelson Algren novel, analyzes the drug addict with strong conviction. What goes on looks for real. And terrifying effect is achieved in one situation wherein Sinatra experiences the pain of denial when he so desperately needs heroin.

There is nothing pretty or happy in the play. After much torment Sinatra walks away believing he again is cured but it is obvious that his future is uncertain. It makes for a powerful condemnation of the use of narcotics, merciless in its display of the cruelties of the habit. This is the kind of message that should be spread, not suppressed.

Novel titles have been designed by Saul Bass, the music by Elmer Bernstein deftly sets the moods and technical credits all around are good. *Gene.*

The Court-Martial of Billy Mitchell
(C'SCOPE—WARNERCOLOR)

Gary Cooper in the excitable, exploitable, and after 30 years perhaps still controversial, story of the fight for a separate U.S. Air Force.

Warner release of Milton Sperling production. Stars Gary Cooper; features Charles Bickford, Ralph Bellamy, Rod Steiger, Elizabeth Montgomery. Directed by Otto Preminger. Story and Screenplay by Sperling and Emmett Lavery; camera, Sam Leavitt; editor, Folmar Blangsted; music, Dimitri Tiomkin. Previewed in N.Y. Dec. 2, '55. Running time, 100 MINS.

Billy Mitchell	Gary Cooper
Gen. Guthrie	Charles Bickford
Frank Reid	Ralph Bellamy
Maj. Allan Guillion	Rod Steiger
Margaret Lansdowne	Elizabeth Montgomery
Col. Moreland	Fred Clark
Col. Herbert White	James Daly
Comdr. Z. Lansdowne	Jack Lord
Captain Elliott	Peter Graves
Russ Peters	Darren McGavin
Admiral Gage	Robert Simon
Senator Fullerton	Charles Dingle
Gen. Douglas MacArthur	Dayton Lummis
Capt. Eddie Rickenbacker	Tom McKee
Major Carl Spaatz	Steve Roberts
Gen. John J. Pershing	Herbert Heyes
Major H. H. Arnold	Robert Brubaker
Fiorello LaGuardia	Phil Arnold
President Calvin Coolidge	Ian Wolfe
Admiral William S. Sims	Will Wright
Stu Stewart	Steve Holland
Yip Ryan	Adam Kennedy
Ted Adams	Manning Ross
Pershing's Aide	Carleton Young

Mankind's inherent interest in justice, and the methods of justice, and in political controversy, and its motivating forces, should be served and satisfied by this well written, produced and directed Warner release. Here is authentic high drama though wholly free of he-she vibrations. Dealing with real-life events of 30 years ago, the subject-matter is astonishingly topical probably because it spotlights something which never dates and is always present tense, namely, official rigidity, redtape and intellectual hardening of the arteries in the brains of aging bureaucrats.

"The Court-Martial of Billy

Mitchell" seems certain to stir much word-of-mouth. It may be taken for granted that the Warner exploiteers already are lining up school, patriotic society and other umpteen natural tie-ups, including the aviation industry, the historians, military editors and so on. Of special interest is the identity of one member of the court-martial of 1925, General Douglas MacArthur. He has been cleverly cast to type and is imaginatively enacted by Dayton Lummis.

Americans of the present day are sure to be struck by the array of witnesses who finally were allowed to take the stand for Mitchell, men who were to loom large in later American politics and aviation, Eddie Rickenbacker, Carl Spaatz, Hap Arnold and Fiorello LaGuardia. The latter is a young wasp on the stand and as deftly impersonated by Phil Arnold is good for quite a few giggles. There's a flash of Cal Coolidge in the White House and several scenes with General John J. Pershing who emerges, in this treatment, as a military traditionalist with his mind locked and bolted against new ideas. By contrast Admiral William Sims is pictured as receptive to the claims of aviation and saltily aware of the Navy's own tendency to complacency.

Whether this film will be attacked as one-sided remains to be noted; suffice that the point of view is frankly Mitchell's. Those who opposed his visions and hounded him out of the army, after preliminarily breaking him from brigadier to colonel, naturally stand exposed as real dopes. For all the tactful omissions as to the moral climate of the 1920s (normalcy spelled out in Prohibition, flaming youth and stock market boom) the picture is a real kick in the shins for the cult of blind military obedience and the lesson which is laid on the line relates to Pearl Harbor. The picture shows Mitchell predicting the Japanese sneak attack on Pearl Harbor, and describing American vulnerability, all this 16 years before that catastrophic Sunday and in the presence of Douglas MacArthur.

In short, Mitchell is the prophet without honor in his own land, the early advocate of a separate air force under a unified defense department and of an academy for air officers a la West Point which at this moment is under construction at Colorado Springs.

The film is straightline storytelling with a minimum of big scenes, only a sprinkling of humor and no romance. Its appeal derives, as stated at the outset, from inherent human interest in justice. It should be remarked that since the war many magazine articles and books and the smash "Caine Mutiny" have made the public aware of the military approach to evidence, guilt and the tempering factor of mercy.

His problem being to make an exciting "documentary" feature, Otto Preminger astutely kept all performances in check. The quiet, holding-onto-himself Mitchell played by Gary Cooper may well be considerably less the firebrand than the Mitchell of real life. Plainly there was a conscientious scripting effort to show him intensely loyal to the army, unwilling to cast aspersions on offices and gentlemen, though some of them were asses, and intent upon fighting his case on the broad lines of national defense. He was, of course, crying in a wilderness of post-Wilsonian pacifism. In the end he retained a congressman as counsel, a fellow with yellow journalistic instincts, highly plausible as brought to life by Ralph Bellamy.

The main trouping is by Cooper, Bellamy, Charles Bickford, Fred Clark and Rod Steiger. All are standout in professionalism though this is a writer's, not an actor's picture. Steiger alone has a bit of a field day as a hatchet man for the adjutant-general's department who joins the prosecution late. An alumnus of New York's Actors Studio and therefore trained to be thoroughly detestable, Steiger sneers, jeers and figuratively knees the defendant with fine you'll-love-to-hate me zestiness. The one woman in the cast, and on the witness stand, the widow of a naval hero, is appealingly presented by Elizabeth Montgomery.

Sam Leavitt's photography, Folmar Blangsted's editing, Dimitri Tiomkin's scoring represent savez craftsmanship subordinated to the service of uncomplicated narration.

Land.

The Last Frontier
(C'SCOPE-SONG-COLOR)

Regulation cavalry-versus-Indians actioner.

Hollywood, Dec. 7.

Columbia release of William Fadiman production. Stars Victor Mature, Guy Madison, Robert Preston, James Whitmore, Anne Bancroft; features Russell Collins, Peter Whitney, Pat Hogan. Directed by Anthony Mann. Screenplay, Philip Yordan, Russell S. Hughes; based on the novel "The Gilded Rooster" by Richard Emery Roberts; camera (Technicolor), William Mellor: editor, Al Clark: score, Leigh Harline, conducted by Morris Stoloff; song, Lester Lee and Ned Washington, sung by Rusty Draper. Previewed Dec. 5, '55. Running time, **97 MINS.**

Jed	Victor Mature
Captain Riordan	Guy Madison
Col. Frank Marston	Robert Preston
Gus	James Whitmore
Corinna	Anne Bancroft
Captain Clark	Russell Collins
Sgt. Major Decker	Peter Whitney
Mungo	Pat Hogan
Red Cloud	Manuel Donde
Lt. Benton	Guy Williams
Luke	Mickey Kuhn
Spotted Elk	William Calles

The cavalry-Indians action offered in "The Last Frontier" never rises above a routine entertainment level. It has cast names for the outdoor market plus the benefit of Technicolor and CinemaScoped Mexican location sites, but these values are not matched by story values in the William Fadiman production under Anthony Mann's direction.

Some tentative moves towards firm establishment of character occur but they never jell into substantial people faced with the problem of hewing civilization out of a frontier.

Mexico was substituted for the northwest of the 1860's. Based on Richard Emery Roberts' novel, "The Gilded Rooster," script brings three primitive frontiersmen, Victor Mature, James Whitmore and their Indian companion, Pat Hogan, into a fort commanded by Guy Madison. Already relieved of the pelts from a year's hunting by hostile Indians, the trio decides to accept Madison's offer to become scouts for the fort.

From the on, it's a conflict in human relationships, with the threat of Indian attack always present. Not making for polite society didoes are: Mature's urge to make Anne Bancroft, the colonel's lady, his woman; everyone's hatred for the colonel, Robert Preston, harsh disciplinarian slightly off his rocker who has usurped command of the fort from Madison, and the brutish training tactics used by tough sergeant Peter Whitney to ready the men for the colonel's planned attack on the redskins. It all leads up to the big scrap in which Preston is killed and Mature can legitimately take Miss Bancroft and stay on to become a soldier.

Generally, the cast performances measure up in okay fashion to the demands asked by scripting and direction, with none being particularly outstanding. The color lensing by William Mellor is satisfactory, as are the other technical assists. A title tune, by Lester Lee and Ned Washington and sung by Rusty Draper, is heard at the beginning and end of the footage.

Brog.

Inside Detroit

Fair melodrama for the dual bill market.

Hollywood, Dec. 9.

Columbia release of a Clover production. Stars Dennis O'Keefe, Pat O'Brien; costars Tina Carver, Margaret Field; features Mark Damon, Larry Blake, Ken Christy, Joseph Turkel, Paul Bryar, Robert E. Griffin. Directed by Fred F. Sears. Written by Robert E. Kent and James B. Gordon; camera, Henry Freulich; editor, Gene Havlick; music conducted by Mischa Bakaleinikoff. Previewed Dec. 6, '55. Running time, **80 MINS.**

Blair Vickers	Dennis O'Keefe
Gus Linden	Pat O'Brien
Joni Calvin	Tina Carver
Barbara Linden	Margaret Field
Gregg Linden	Mark Damon
Max Harkness	Larry Blake
Ben Macauley	Ken Christy
Pete Link	Joseph Turkel
Sam Foran	Paul Bryar
Hoagy Mitchell	Robert E. Griffin
Jenkins	Guy Kingsford
Toby Gordon	Dick Rich
Preacher	Norman Leavitt
Ethel Linden	Katherine Warren

"Inside Detroit" is another in Clover's pseudo-factual series of program dramas for Columbia. It's a familiar good-versus-racketeer type of actioner, using the house-cleaning by the United Auto Workers local in Detroit to springboard a documentary-styled treatment. Names of Dennis O'Keefe and Pat O'Brien will help its chances in the dualer situations.

Robert E. Kent and James B. Gordon obviously peg their screen story on the real-life bombing attempt on the Reuther brothers some years ago. Yarn opens with an attempt on the life of O'Keefe, honest union leader, with a bombing in the local's headquarters. The explosion kills O'Keefe's younger brother and he immediately suspects that O'Brien, former unionite about to be freed after a five-year sentence for racketeering, is readying to move in again. His suspicions are correct and before O'Brien again learns crooks can't buck honest unions there have been some killings and people hurt, including O'Brien's own daughter, Margaret Field, and son, Mark Damon, who all along had refused to believe their father was bad.

Performances are mostly straight-line and competently handled with a couple of the cast members impressing slightly more. One is Tina Carver, who plays O'Brien's blonde mistress and his partner in a call girl operation that passes as a model agency. The other is young Damon as O'Brien's troubled, disillusioned son. Larry Blake also does okay as the plainclothesman assigned to protect O'Keefe.

Fred F. Sears' direction of the Clover unit film is competent, as are the photography by Henry Freulich, editing, and other contributions.

Brog.

The Beast With 1,000,000 Eyes

Tedious science-fictioner for less discriminating program spots.

Hollywood, Dec. 1.

American Releasing Corp. release of a David Kramarsky production. Features Paul Birch, Lorna Thayer, Dona Cole. Directed by Kramarsky. Screenplay, Tom Filer; camera, Everett Baker; editor, Jack Killeser; music, John Bickford. Reviewed Nov. 30, '55. Running time, **78 MINS.**

Allen Kelly	Paul Birch
Carol Kelly	Lorna Thayer
Sandy Kelly	Dona Cole
Larry	Dick Sargant
Him	Leonard Tarver
Old Man Webber	Chester Conklin

Whatever slight science-fiction premise this entry might hold is lost in a maze of drawout situations and tiresome dialog which leads to a confusing windup not likely to be readily understood by general audiences.

Marking his first motion picture effort, producer-director David Kramarsky hangs his theme on what happens to a small family living in the desert when a creature from another planet sets down nearby in an attempt to take over the Earth by projecting its mind into all living things. Birds attack humans, and normally gentle animals turn vicious. The family finds a strange and evil force closing in on them, until through the sheer force of love they are finally able to throw off the shackles. The interplanetary craft which brought the creature flies away, with or without the strange visitor, and it's up to the audience to figure this out, if they're still with the picture.

Paul Birch and Lorna Thayer, as the parents, and Dona Cole in daughter role play their characters as well as possible but stand small chance with the contrived Tom Filer script. Leonard Tarver is in for considerable unnecessary footage, and Chester Conklin is called upon for out-of-place comedy.

Whit.

The Rains of Ranchipur
(C'SCOPE—COLOR)

Updated version of Louis Bromfield yarn with Lana Turner for marquee. Spectacular but not outstanding.

20th-Fox release of Frank Ross production. Stars Lana Turner, Richard Burton, Fred MacMurray, Joan Caulfield, Michael Rennie; features Eugenie Leontovich, Gladys Hurlbut, Madge Kennedy, Carlo Rizzo, Beatrice Kraft. Directed by Jean Negulesco. Screenplay, Merle Miller, based on Louis Bromfield's "The Rains Came"; camera (De Luxe Color), Milton Krasner; editor, Dorothy Spencer; music, Hugo Friedhofer, conducted by Lionel Newman. Previewed in N.Y. Dec. 9, '55. Running time, **104 MINS.**

Edwina	Lana Turner
Dr. Safi	Richard Burton
Tom Ransome	Fred MacMurray
Fern	Joan Caulfield
Lord Esketh	Michael Rennie
Maharani	Eugenie Leontovich
Mrs. Simon	Gladys Hurlbut
Mrs. Smiley	Madge Kennedy
Mr. Adoni	Carlo Rizzo
Oriental Dancer	Beatrice Kraft
Mr. Smiley	King Calder

Louis Bromfield's "The Rains Came," brought to the screen once before by 20th-Fox in 1939, has been filmed again, this time with Lana Turner as the titled trollop. Somehow, the Orient (Pakistan) comes off better than the cast, thanks in part to CinemaScope although considering the wordiness of the book, which scripter Merle Miller reflected in some rather lengthy passages of dialog, "Rains of Ranchipur" fares okay.

Director Jean Negulesco's earthquake and flood sequences alone make the picture worthwhile as b.o. The earth rocks and debris comes crashing down on panicked multitudes. This is followed by equally exciting and terrifying shots as the dam bursts and the waters come rushing through the town, destroying everything and drowning thousands as torrential rains keep beating down.

Negulesco, with an obvious eye to action (there's also a fine tiger hunt scene), may have felt the story itself was least important or perhaps knew he needed such props for a mediocre script. At any rate, the cast itself hardly comes alive. Only sturdy performances are turned in by Richard Burton and Eugenie Leontovich.

Miss Turner, as Edwina (Lady Esketh) has the role of a temptress down pat, perhaps too much so. She's good in a couple of scenes, indifferent in most of them and almost embarrassing in some. Climactic bit, when she reveals the changes that have come over her, required superior acting, and it wasn't there.

Burton's portrayal of Dr. Safti, the dedicated Indian doctor who falls in love with Miss Turner, has strength and conviction and is underplayed intelligently. He registers strongly. As the Maharrani, Miss Leontovich has dignity, and the scenes between her and Burton are definite assets to the picture.

Fred MacMurray is just plain miscast as the disillusioned drunkard who grows up during the flood emergency. Joan Caulfield is cute in a part that seems to have been written for a younger girl, and Michael Rennie, always a capable performer is relegated to a minor role as the weak husband of the flirtatious Miss Turner.

Lenser Milton Krasner knows his job and the De Luxe color in this film is excellent. Producer Frank Ross hasn't spared the dollars in aiming for lavish sets and costumes which are eye-arresting.

Story, in case someone doesn't remember, has the Eskeths arriving in Ranchipur where Miss Turner loses no time trying to seduce Burton. Latter falls for her and, for the first time, she experiences real love. In the end, Miss Turner gives up her Indian and returns to her husband, while Burton devotes himself to his mission as a doctor. In between all this, there are some torrid love scenes and a great deal of conversation. *Hift.*

Helen of Troy
(C'SCOPE-COLOR)

Spectacular and lavish retelling of Homeric legend. Strong boxoffice entry.

Warner Bros. release (no producer credit). Features Rossana Podesta, Jacques Sernas, Sir Cedric Hardwicke, Stanley Baker, Niall MacGuinnis, Nora Swinburne, Robert Douglas, Torin Thatcher, Harry Andrews, and Janette Scott. Directed by Robert Wise. Screenplay, John Twist and Hugh Gray from adaptation by Gray and N. Richard Nash; camera (WarnerColor), Harry Stradling; editor, Thomas Reilly; music, Max Steiner. Previewed in N.Y. Dec. 9, '55. Running time, **118 MINS.**

Helen	Rossana Podesta
Paris	Jack Sernas
Priam	Sir Cedric Hardwicke
Achilles	Stanley Baker
Menelaus	Niall MacGinnis
Hecuba	Nora Swinburne
Agamemnon	Robert Douglas
Ulysses	Torin Thatcher
Hector	Harry Andrews
Cassandra	Janette Scott
Aeneas	Ronald Lewis
Andraste	Brigitte Bardot
Andros	Eduardo Ciannelli
Diomedes	Marc Lawrence
Ajax	Maxwell Reed
Polydrous	Robert Brown
Cora	Barbara Cavan
Patroclus	Terence Longdon
Andromache	Patricia Marmont
Nestor	Guido Notari
Alephous	Tonio Selwart
Dance Specialty	Georges Zoritch
The High Priest	Edmond Knight

The word "spectacular" achieves its true meaning when applied to Warner Bros.' "Helen of Troy." The retelling of the Homeric legend, filmed in its entirety in Italy, makes lavish use of the CinemaScope screen. The storming of the ancient city of Troy by a revenge-seeking Greek army is a breathtaking eyeful. Action sequences alone should stir word-of-mouth. All in all, looks good for sock boxoffice results.

WB and director Robert Wise piled on the extras in Greek and Trojan armies. Results rival Cecil B. DeMille. Production values ride over shortcomings in John Twist and Hugh Gray's script and dialog. Like many tales of antiquity, the story is occassionally stilted. Educators may quarrel with the liberties taken by the adaptors—Gray and N. Richard Nash—with Homer's account of the famous battle and the events leading up to it. Greeks are made 100% villainous warmongers out for spoils rather than the recovery of their abducted Queen.

As Helen, "the face that launched a thousand ships," and Paris, the love-smitten Trojan prince, Warners has cast two unknowns—Rossana Podesta, an exquisite Italian beauty, and Jacques Sernas, a brawny and handsome Frenchman. Visually both meet the demands of the roles and are probably destined for future Hollywood prominence. An appraisal of their ability as performers will have to wait until both use their own voices. In the current outing, English-speaking voices have been dubbed. (The effect is perfect and will not be recognized.)

Sir Cedric Hardwicke is seen as the kindly, peace-loving Priam, king of Troy. Niall McGuinnis, as King Menelaus whose wife has been kidnapped by Paris, and Robert Douglas as King Agamemnon, are typical heavies. The Ulysses of Torin Thatcher is shrewd and crafty as compared with the stalwart and upright Ulysses of Kirk Douglas in Paramount's "Ulysses." Stanley Baker portrays Achilles as a jealous hothead and Harry Andrews' Hector is sober and brave.

Nora Swineburne is seen as Queen Hecuba, Janette Scott as Cassandra, Ronald Lewis as Aeneas, Brigitte Bardot as Andraste, Eduardo Cianelli as Andros, and Marc Lawrence as Diomedes. The unnamed extras deserve special mention, for their efforts contribute considerably to the overall effect.

The story opens with Paris' journey to Sparta to effect a peace treaty between the Greeks and Troy. He falls in love with Helen not knowing she is the Queen of Sparta. His peace mission fails, and in making his escape from Sparta, takes Helen with him. The "abduction" unites the Greeks and sends them off on a war against Troy. It's a long war of battles and attrition and does not end until the Greeks devise the ruse of the giant wooden horse. The men concealed in the horse open the gates of Troy and the Greek army is able to enter and destroy the city.

There are many exciting side incidents—Paris' test of strength in King Menelaus court, Hector's meeting with Achilles, the downfall of Achilles with an arrow in his heel, the carousing and celebrations, the raids on the Greek camps, and the fights among the Greek generals. The staging of these events has been done masterfully and combined with the technical quality of the WarnerColor lensing, it results in top-notch action footage. *Holl.*

Benny Goodman Story
(MUSICAL—COLOR)

OK filmusical in the same idiom as "Glenn Miller Story" and will do comparable big b.o.

Universal release of Aaron Rosenberg production. Stars Steve Allen and Donna Reed. Written and directed by Valentine Davies. Camera (Technicolor), William Daniels; editor, Russell Schoengarth; asst. directors, Phil Bowles & Terry Nelson; music, Joseph Gershenson, Henry Mancini, Sol Yaged, Alan Harding, Harold Brown; dialog director, Leon Charles. Previewed Dec. 13, 1955, at RKO 86th St., N. Y. Running time, **116 MINS.**

Benny Goodman	Steve Allen
Alice Hammond	Donna Reed
Mom Goodman	Berta Gersten
John Hammond	Herbert Anderson
Pop Goodman	Robert F. Simon
Willard Alexander	Hy Averback
Harry Goodman	Shep Menken
Fletcher Henderson	Sammy Davis Sr.
Gil Rodin	Dick Winslow
Benny Goodman (16 years)	Barry Treux
Benny Goodman (10 years)	David Kasday
Mr. Hammond	Wilton Graff
Harry James	Harry James
Gene Krupa	Gene Krupa
Martha Tilton	Martha Tilton
Lionel Hampton	Lionel Hampton
Ziggy Elman	Ziggy E'man
Ben Pollock	Ben Pollock
Teddy Wilson	Teddy Wilson
Kid Ory	Edward "Kid" Ory

"The Benny Goodman Story" is of the same stripe as Universal's previously socko bandleader saga, "The Glenn Miller Story," and should achieve similar boxoffice potency. The degree may be measured perhaps by the difference in the marquee values of James Stewart (Capt. Glenn Miller) versus Steve Allen (Goodman) and June Allyson versus current femme lead, Donna Reed. Both have bespectacled bandleaders with titles, both are Aaron Rosenberg productions. "Miller" has passed $7,000,000 domestic gross, peak take in U's history.

Fundamentally both pix are insured by (1), vibrant diskology medleys; (2), strong kid appeal, because of the jukebox equation; and (3), a reasonable amount of heart interest.

If the romantics of Valentine Davies' script and the stellar pair's interpretations lack a bit, they are sufficiently glossed over because the major canvas is the saga of the Chicago youth with the licorice stick and his dedication to the cause of a new exciting tempo, later interpreted as "swing."

It's a reverse Cinderella in that Alice Hammond (now Mrs. Benny Goodman) is the one "gone" on the jazzist, aided and abetted by her jazz-buff brother, John Hammond Jr. (a real-life expert on the "beat" idiom) and a tolerant father and aunt. Allen, of course, is remarkably faithful in style and appearance to the original but the romance values, while fundamentally steeped in fact, are celluloid-aggrandized.

Screenplay follows the BG story with more or less faithful chronology, pitching to the frenzied shagging-in-the-aisles at the N.Y. Paramount (which, with Frank Sinatra's impact, remains a memorable event in the history of that Broadway flagship), and the Carnegie Hall jazz concert which culminates with the stellar pair's reunion after a previously established series of romantic hurdles.

The unfolding is uncompromising on several fronts. Apart from the parallelism of both Miller and Goodman being idols of the juvenile hot-licks aficiandos, the closeups on the very poor Jewish family and Goodman's humble environments are not glossed over.

In the same idiom there is no fanfare about the interracial mixing, socially or professionally. The common denominator of music, in its basic American unrefinements, brooks no color line, and Goodman's respect and affection of such jazz greats as Teddy Wilson, Fletcher Henderson, Lionel Hampton, Edward (Kid) Orry is played with ease and casualness. All play themselves, excepting Sammy Davis Sr.'s impersonation of the late Henderson. In similar vein Harry James, Gene Krupa, Ziggy Elman, Martha Tilton and Ben Pollack are themselves in the film. Goodman's longtime agent Willard Alexander is played by Hy Averback and his brother Harry is personated by Shep Menken who, in contrast to Allen's proper English, plays BG's frere with a Bronx brogue.

On the band medleys, which are done in sundry styles—one-nighters, jam sessions, dancehalls, speakeasies, radio broadcasts, Paramount and Carnegie, rehearsals, rooftop "clarinet blues" (good running device to set the peaks and valleys of different moods)—the basic Goodman all-stars were reassembled.

Gil Rodin, like Alexander, is another real-life character who is potent in the motivation, well played by Dick Winslow. Rodin was a name saxer but here plays it more like the road manager. David Kasday is BG at 10; Ernest Truex's son Barry Truex is Goodman at 16; and Allen does a competent job in the matured period.

He and Donna Reed are believable in most of the romantic vis-a-vis scenes, and the lapses are easily overlooked. Berta Gersten is the typical Jewish mama; Robert F. Simon plays Goodman pere; Herbert Anderson's John Hammond Jr. is crew-cut, gray-flannel-suit standard type; and the rest are more or less their real-and-reel-life selves.

The music under Joseph Gershenson's organization is top Petrillo in every respect, and the editing from "Let's Dance" to the "One O'Clock Jump" to the Dixieland jam projects to all types of audiences the values that made for the Goodman impact musically.

The contrived dialog ("can't mix caviar with bagels") and the build-up catchphrase, "Don't Be That Way" (which became the title of a Goodman jazzique standard) are among the minor lapses in a good solid entertainment which achieves its purpose—projecting 20 years of jazz in broad entertainment values. But in the main, the Davies' script is durable. He also did the "Miller" screenplay but here marks his debut as a writer-director.

Production standard is big league but not overboard budget-wise considering the kaleidoscopic ballroom, radio studio and kindred scenes. The Par and Carnegie shots did call for an unusual groupings of extras. As with Stewart's deal, Goodman has a percentage of his biopic. *Abel.*

The Littlest Outlaw
(COLOR)

Colorful made - in - Mexico. Heartwarming boy-horse. Strong family appeal.

Hollywood, Dec. 17.

Buena Vista release of a Walt Disney-Larry Lansburgh production. Features Pedro Armendariz, Joseph Calleia, Rodolfo Acosta, Andres Velasquez. Directed by Roberto Gavaldon. Screenplay, Bill Walsh, from original by Lansburgh; camera (Technicolor), Alex Phillips, J. Carlos Carbajal; music, William Lava; orchestrations, Charles Maxwell; editor, Carlos Savage. Previewed Dec. 16, '55. Running time, **73 MINS.**

General Torres	Pedro Armendariz
Padre	Joseph Calleia
Chato	Rodolfo Acosta
Pablito	Andres Velasquez
Pepe Ortiz (Matador)	Himself
Celita	Laila Maley
Tiger	Gilberto Gonzales
Vulture	Jose Torvay
Senor Garcia	"Ferrusquilla"
Senora Garcia	Enriqueta Zazueta
Gypsy	Senor Lee
Doctor	Carlos Ortigoza
Silvestre	Margarito Luna
Marcos	Rocardo Gonzales
The Bride	Maria Eugenia

This latest Walt Disney live-action feature is a moving story of a boy and a horse, which by its very simplicity smacks over a heart-warming experience of particular appeal to the family trade. There are some startling effects both pictorially and off-the-beaten path dramatically during film's Technicolor unfoldment, lensed entirely in rural Mexico and with nearly all-Mexican cast.

Producer Larry Lansburgh takes his crew to the hinterlands of the southern republic seldom photographed and the result is completely Mexican in feeling as the Bill Walsh screenplay, from Lansburgh's own original, follows the attempts of a little stableboy to save the life of a general's jumper by running away with the nag after it's been ordered destroyed.

Director Roberto Gavaldon takes this basic situation and weaves skillful action, centering his story on Andres Velasquez, whose performance has seldom been equaled by a child thesp in point of appeal. His scenes never descend to maudlin sentimentality as he limns his narrative, and he punches over both suspense and grim reality in the bullring, where the boy finds the horse after he lost it to a Gypsy. Thrills are inserted in this arena sequence, showing the goring of a matador and the boy leaping on the back of his horse after a picador has been thrown. Native color, background and folk manners of Old Mexico embellish the story.

Pedro Armendariz vividly portrays the general, whose order to do away with the horse stems from its refusal to take a certain jump during an international meet. As the padre, in whose church the boy takes refuge with the horse from the revenge of the trainer, Joseph Calleia is both rollicking and compassionate. Rodolfo Acosta in trainer role, whose cruelty is responsible for steed's refusal to jump, also is a standout. Strong support is offered by Laila Maley as the general's daughter, Pepe Ortiz, the matador playing himself, and Gilberto Gonzales, an outlaw.

Technically, film is benefitted by Alex Phillips' expert color photography and J. Carlos Carbajal's second unit lensing. William Lava's musical score is first-rate and Carlos Savage's editing tight and fast. *Whit.*

Richard III
(BRITISH-V'VISION-COLOR)

Outstanding filmization of Shakespeare's classic play.

London, Dec. 20.

Independent Film Distributors release of London Film (Laurence Olivier) production. Stars John Gielgud, Ralph Richardson, Claire Bloom, Alec Clunes, Cedric Hardwicke, Stanley Baker, Laurence Naismith, Norman Woolland, Mary Kerridge, Pamela Brown, Helen Haye, John Laurie, Esmond Knight and Laurence Olivier. Directed by Laurence Olivier. Text advisor, Alan Dent; camera (Technicolor), Otto Heller; editor, Helga Cranston; music, William Walton. At Leicester Square Theatre, London, Dec. 13, '55. Running time, **160 MINS.**

King Edward IV	Cedric Hardwicke
Archbishop of Canterbury	Nicholas Hannen
Richard III	Laurence Olivier
Buckingham	Ralph Richardson
Clarence	John Gielgud
Queen Elizabeth	Mary Kerridge
Jane Shore	Pamela Brown
Prince of Wales	Paul Huson
Page to Richard III	Stewart Allen
Lady Anne	Claire Bloom
1st Priest	Russell Thorndike
1st Monk	Wally Bascoe
2nd Monk	Norman Fisher
Brakenbury	Andrew Cruickshank
Rivers	Clive Morton
Scrivener	Terence Greenidge
Catesby	Normand Woolland
Hastings	Alec Clunes
Grey	Dan Cunningham
Dorset	Douglas Wilmer
Stanley	Laurence Naismith
Dighton	Michael Gough
Forrest	Michael Ripper
Duchess of York	Helen Haye
Young Duke of York	Andy Shine
Abbot	Roy Russell
Lord Mayor	George Woodbridge
Ratcliffe	Esmond Knight
Lovel	John Laurie
Messenger	Peter Williams
Hastings' Ostler	Timothy Bateson
2nd Priest	Willoughby Gray
Scrubwoman	Anne Wilton
Beadle	Bill Shine
1st Clergyman	Derek Prentice
2nd Clergyman	Deering Wells
George Stanley	Richard Bennet
Tyrrell	Patrick Troughton
1st Messenger	Brian Nissen
2nd Messenger	Alexander Davion
3rd Messenger	Lane Meddick
4th Messenger	Robert Bishop
Norfolk	John Phillips
Henry Tudor	Stanley Baker

The cream of British acting talent has combined to translate this great Shakespearean drama into one of the major classics of the screen. Laurence Olivier's production of "Richard III" is, with reservations, a major contribution to motion pictures, ranking with his memorable interpretations of "Henry V" and "Hamlet."

The Bard pulled no punches in his dramatization of "Richard III," and Olivier's filmization likewise portrays him as a ruthless and unscrupulous character, who stops at nothing to obtain the throne. The murder of his brother Clarence (Gielgud), the betrayal of his cousin, Buckingham (Richardson), the suffocation of the princes in the Tower are among the unscrupulous steps in the path of Richard's crowning, which are staged with lurid, melodramatic conviction. At all times Shakespeare's poetry, impeccably spoken by this outstanding cast, heightens the dramatic atmosphere.

The production, and notably Roger Furse's decor, is consistently spectacular. The climactic battle sequences rival the pageantry of "Henry V." This is, at no time, an ostentatious production. Although the use of VistaVision puts it into a more modern idiom, the film never loses its sense of intimacy. It is notably a performer's picture, with the major credit going to Olivier for his classic, subtle playing of the deformed Richard. This is a portrayal full of subtlety and understanding. The occasional asides have a fascination of their own.

Running Olivier's performance a very close second is Richardson's scheming Buckingham.

Another distinguished performance is contributed by Gielgud as Clarence. Eliminated early in the pic, his characterization is not readily forgotten. The scene in which he is drowned in wine is one of the more lurid incidents. Hardwicke as Edward IV, Michael Gough as one of the hired murderers, Clunes as Hastings, Hannen as the Archbishop of Canterbury, and Stanley Baker as the Earl of Richmond, also add to the long line of distinguished male portrayals.

Miss Brown contributes a vivid portrayal as the sensuous Jane Shore while Miss Kerridge makes a colorful Elizabeth. Miss Bloom fails to rise to the heights demanded in the role of Lady Anne. Helen Haye shines in a smaller role as the Duchess of York.

Almost as much as the cast, the technical crew commands special praise. Otto Heller's color (Technicolor) lensing is a firstgrade quality job. Anthony Bushell distinguishes himself as associate director. Helga Cranston has done a yeoman job of editing, but a little more ruthlessness in cutting earlier scenes would have quickened the tempo. Alan Dent, w.k. drama critic, admirably acquitted himself as text advisor.

"Richard III" is more than just a prestige picture. It is a screen achievement of the highest order. *Myro.*

The Indian Fighter
(C'SCOPE-COLOR)

Kirk Douglas bests the redskins in derring-do actioner. Plus sexy Elsa Martinelli from Italy.

Hollywood, Dec. 19.

United Artists release of William Schorr (Bryna) production. Stars Kirk Douglas, Walter Matthau, Diana Douglas, Walter Abel; features Lon Chaney, Eduard Franz, Alan Hale; introduces Elsa Martinelli. Directed by Anore de Toth. Screenplay, Frank Davis, Ben Hecht; original, story, Ben Kadish; camera (Technicolor), Wilfrid M. Cline; editor, Richard Cahoon; score, Franz Waxman; songs, Irving Gordon. Previewed Dec. 12, '55. Running time, **88 MINS.**

Johnny Hawks	Kirk Douglas
Onahti	Elsa Martinelli
Captain Trask	Walter Abel
Wes Todd	Walter Matthau
Susan Rogers	Diana Douglas
Red Cloud	Eduard Franz
Chivington	Lon Chaney
Will Crabtree	Alan Hale
Briggs	Elisha Cook
Tommy Rogers	Michael Winkelman
Grey Wolf	Harry Landers
Lt. Blake	William Phipps
Lt. Shaeffer	Buzz Henry
Morgan	Ray Teal
Trader Joe	Frank Cady
Crazy Bear	Hank Worden
Head Settler	Lane Chandler

This frontier actioner, more derring-do than dramatic, spins off 88 minutes of entertainment that will satisfy the demands of the outdoor fan, hence its prospects look okay in that market, especially as it has the name of Kirk Douglas, plus CinemaScope and Technicolor, to brighten the marquees.

United Artists release, produced by William Schorr for Douglas' indie Bryna company, is strong on visual values to bolster the regulation script and playing. Location lensing in Oregon by Wilfrid M. Cline is most effective, insuring scenic interest even when the story falters. Andre de Toth's direction reaches its high points in a refreshingly novel Indian attack on a frontier fort and in the death duel, Sioux-style, between Douglas and Harry Landers. Otherwise, footage is inclined to get monotonous at times.

Sex in the person of Elsa Martinelli, Italian actress introduced here, and the relationship of her Indian maid character with Douglas is a story factor and ballyhoo point. That nude bathing scene won't be overlooked in the plugging, nor will her pine-bowered romancing with the hero. She's up to all the demands of the role.

Douglas dashes about as a grinning, virile hero in the title role. His job here is to lead a wagon train through Indian country into Oregon but he gets sidetracked from duty in wooing Miss Martinelli long enough for some crooks to stir up trouble over Indian gold. It's not until he delivers the culprits to Eduard Franz, Indian chief, for justice that the redskins call off their war against the whites. Script by Frank Davis and Ben Hecht, from an original by Ben Kadish, follows a pat pattern mostly.

Walter Abel, fort commander, can't make much of his formula role, and Walter Matthau fares no better as the principal heavy. Diana Douglas has her moments as a marriage-minded young widow. Franz, Lon Chaney, Alan Hale, Elisha Cook and the others are okay in what is asked of them.

Technical credits, a couple of campfire songs by Irving Gordon and the score by Franz Waxman are capable. *Brog.*

I'll Cry Tomorrow
(SONGS)

Susan Hayward in smash dramatization of Lillian Roth's bottle bout and comeback. High b.o. potential.

Hollywood, Dec. 16.

Metro release of Lawrence Weingarten production. Stars Susan Hayward, Richard Conte, Eddie Albert, Jo Van Fleet, Don Taylor, Ray Danton; features Margo, Virginia Gregg, Don Barry, David Kasday. Directed by Daniel Mann. Screenplay, Helen Deutsch, Jay Richard Kennedy; based on the book by Lillian Roth, Mike Connolly, Gerold Frank; camera, Arthur E. Arling; editor, Harold F. Kress; score, Alex North; songs arranged and conducted by Charles Henderson. Previewed Dec. 9, '55. Running time, **117 MINS.**

Lillian Roth	Susan Hayward
Tony Bardeman	Richard Conte
Burt McGuire	Eddie Albert
Katie Roth	Jo Van Fleet
Wallie	Don Taylor
David Tredman	Ray Danton
Selma	Margo
Ellen	Virginia Gregg
Jerry	Don Barry
David (as a child)	David Kasday
Lillian (as a child)	Carole Ann Campbell
Richard	Peter Leeds
Fat Man	Tol Avery

For the second time within the year Metro has come up with a biopic that deals in realities, not story-book success values. In not backing away from facts, no matter how shabby, in telling the Lillian Roth story, it has in "I'll Cry Tomorrow" a tremendously moving picture of high b.o. potential.

Also, there will be professional and critical acclaim for Susan Hayward's smash portrayal of the alcoholic who came back—a performance that can't miss being a major Academy contender.

As it did so successfully in "Love Me Or Leave Me," Metro again approaches a biography with as near honest a viewpoint as is possible. It's no pretty, rags-to-riches fable that is told in the showmanly Lawrence Weingarten production. Instead, it pulls no punches in showing a rising star's fall into alcoholic degradation that plumbs Skid Row sewers before Alcoholics Anonymous provides the faith and guidance to help her up again.

No particular person or circumstance is blamed for Miss Roth's downfall, but the viewer will be able to fasten on any one of several possible causes. The first is the stingingly cruel portrayal of the stage mother, played with great trouping skill by Jo Van Fleet, as she pushes her daughter towards the career she never had. The death of Miss Roth's first love, effectively realized by Ray Danton, is a blow of fate and the start of the crackup. Another incident is the first drink given her by a kindly nurse, a neat credit for Virginia Gregg, which led to years of heavier and heavier drinking. Other contributing causes could have been her marriages to a playboy (Don Taylor) and later to a sadist (Richard Conte). The latter is particularly outstanding in characterization and Taylor also gives his role importance.

Audiences will experience emotional torment in depth under the sustained dramatic mood created by Daniel Mann's direction, but should walk out greatly heartened by the moving uplift ending. The upbeat starts when Miss Roth accepts the guidance of AA and finds the good and comforting love of a man, touchingly come alive in the performance of Eddie Albert, who had already himself put the bottle in its place. The final shot of Miss Roth walking up the aisle to tell her story over the nationally televised "This Is Your Life" program is full of heart and hope and current history.

In "Leave Me," Metro made a dramatic actress of a singer (Doris Day). Here the process is reversed, creating a singer of an actress known only for her dramatics. And Miss Hayward, along with the sock of her sustained character creation, reveals pleasant pipes and song-belting ability on "Sing You Sinners," "When the Red, Red, Robin Comes Bob, Bob, Bobbin' Along" and "Happiness Is a Thing Called Joe." Hers is a great performance all around.

Helen Deutsch and Jay Richard Kennedy fashioned the tremendously effective screenplay from the Roth autobiography which she wrote with Mike Connolly and Gerold Frank. The scripting always gives director Mann and his fine cast solid dramatics with which to work and they deliver flawlessly. Carole Ann Campbell's chore as Lillian Roth as a child stands out. Also good are David Kasday, doing Danton as a boy; Margo, Don Barry, Peter Leeds and Tol Avery.

The black-and-white values of Arthur E. Arling's lensing figure importantly in the dramatic development, as does Alex North's topnotch score. Charles Henderson arranged and conducted the songs capably and the other credits are expert. *Brog.*

Diane

Handsome but uneven costume drama with Lana Turner for marquee dressing.

Hollywood, Dec. 16.

Metro release of an Edwin H. Knopf production. Stars Lana Turner, Pedro Armandariz, Roger Moore, Marisa Pavan, Sir Cedric Hardwicke; features Torin Thatcher, Sean McClory, Henry Daniell, John Lupton, Taina Elg. Directed by David Miller. Screenplay, Christopher Isherwood, based on John Erskine story, "Diane de Poitiers;" camera (Eastman Color), Robert Planck; music, Miklos Rozsa; editor, John McSweeney Jr. Previewed Dec. 15, '55. Running time 110 MINS.

Diane	Lana Turner
King Francis I	Pedro Armenariz
Prince Henri	Roger Moore
Catherine de Medici	Marisa Pavan
Ruggieri	Sir Cedric Hardwicke
Count de Breze	Torin Thatcher
Alys	Taina Elg
Regnault	John Lupton
Gondi	Henry Daniell
The Dauphin	Ronald Green
Count Montgomery	Sean McClory
Duke of Savoy	Geoffrey Toone
Count Ridolfi	Michael Ansara
Lord Bonnivet	Paul Cavanagh
Court Physician	Melville Cooper
Lord Tremouille	Ian Wolfe
Chamberlain	Basil Ruysdael
Gian-Carlo	Christopher Dark
Piero	Mark Cavell
Montecuculli	Gene Reynolds
Marechal de Chabannes	John O'Malley
Sardini	Peter Gray
Charles	Mickey Maga
Francis	Ronald Anton

Metro digs back into 16th Century France for this yarn about the Countess Diane de Breze, who became the most powerful woman at the court of King Henry II. Splendidly caparisonned productionwise in the stunning effects of CinemaScope and Eastman Color, the first half is such old-fashioned costume drama as to draw laughs at unintended places, but picks up in interest during the later phases. Lana Turner star name is a plus but indications point to spotty business.

Overlength footage is highlighted by a tournament sequence in which the crossing of lances provides some exciting moments. Pageantry plays a large part in the unfoldment of the Edwin H. Knopf production, with such well known historic figures as King Francis I and Catherine de Medici appearing to motivate action which revolves around Henry II and his mistress.

John Erskine source story is given wordy treatment by Christopher Isherwood screenplay, which David Miller's often deft direction finds difficult to bridge into actionful narrative despite romantic implications.

Miss Turner is sympathetic in her role, and Roger Moore delivers a good account of himself as Henry, uncertain first as the callow youth and gaining in stature after he becomes king. As Francis, Pedro Armendariz is strongly romantic and Marisa Pavan impresses as the unhappy Catherine. Sir Cedric Hardwicke is the astrologer who foresees the death of Henry by a lance. In hardy support are Sean McClory, Torin Thatcher, Geoffrey Toone, Henry Daniell and Michael Ansara.

Fine production values accrue right down the line. Outstanding are Robert Planck's color photography, art direction by Cedric Gibbons and Hans Peters, Walter Plunkett's showy costumes and Miklos Rozsa's music score. *Whit.*

Ghost Town

Minor western entertainment, short of action, long on talk.

Hollywood, Dec. 12.

United Artists release of Howard W. Koch (Bel-Air) production. Stars Kent Taylor, John Smith, Marian Carr; features John Doucette, Wm. (Bill) Phillips, Serena Sande, Joel Ashley, Gilman H. Rankin, Ed Hashim, Gary Murray. Directed by Allen Miner. Story and screenplay, Jameson Brewer; camera, Joseph F. Biroc; editor, Mike Pozen; music, Paul Dunlap. Previewed Dec. 8, '55. Running time, 77 MINS.

Anse Conroy	Kent Taylor
Duff Dailey	John Smith
Barbara Leighton	Marian Carr
Doc Clawson	John Doucette
Kerry McCabe	Wm. Phillips
Maureen	Serena Sande
Sgt. Dockery	Joel Ashley
Simon Peter Wheedle	Gilman H. Rankin
Dull Knife	Ed Hashim
Alex	Gary Murray

Minor western entertainment is offered in "Ghost Town." Script talks out most of the action and direction meanders at a plodding pace. There are no cast names to help the prospects.

The Bel-Air (Aubrey Schenck, Howard W. Koch) production for United Artists had an okay basis for an outdoor subject in the basic story by Jameson Brewer, but his treatment fails to develop good action screen values. Better direction might still have injected some interest into the proceedings, but Allen Miner's guidance is exceptionally slack and the cast of competent players never has a chance to appear to advantage.

The plot is laid in Indian country and brings together an odd assortment of characters in an old, deserted western town, where refuge is sought from a band of drunks, marauding Cheyenne. As the redskins close in and the group's ammunition gives out, the true colors of the whites are revealed in obvious fashion. When the shooting is over, good has been separated from bad and right looks like it will triumph.

Handicapped by the many script and directorial inconsistencies are Kent Taylor, a smoothie revealed as a seller of guns to the Indians; John Smith, brave, resourceful exnewspaperman from the east who has struck gold with his partner, William Phillips, and has sent for his fiancee, Marian Carr. She's more interested in the gold than in Smith so at the fadeout he's switched to Serena Sande, Irish-Indian maid. Among others are John Doucette, Joel Ashley, Gilman H. Rankin, Ed Hashin and Gary Murray.

Film was lensed on desert locations near Kanab, Utah, by Joseph F. Biroc. The scenic values come out okay, as do most of the technical assists. Paul Dunlap's score features an old mechanical piano sound that is good. *Brog.*

Hell On Frisco Bay

(C'SCOPE-COLOR)

Routine action thriller with Alan Ladd, Edward G. Robinson to bolster general market prospects.

Hollywood, Dec. 22.

Warner Bros. release of Jaguar (Ladd-George C. Bertholon) production. Stars Alan Ladd, Edward G. Robinson, Joanne Dru; features William Demarest, Paul Stewart, Perry Lopez, Fay Wray. Directedby Frank Tuttle. Screenplay, Sydney Boehm, Martin Rackin; from the William P. McGivern Collier's mag serial; camera (Warner-Color), John Seitz; editor, Folmar Blangsted; music, Max Steiner. Previewed Dec. 14, 55. Running time, 98 MINS.

Steve Rollins	Alan Ladd
Victor Amato	Edward G. Robinson
Marcia Rollins	Joanne Dru
Dan Bianco	William Demarest
Joe Lye	Paul Stewart
Mario Amato	Perry Lopez
Kay Stanley	Fay Wray
Anna Amato	Renata Vanni
Lou Fiaschetti	Nestor Paiva
Hammy	Stanley Adams
Lieut. Neville	Willis Bouchey
Detective Connors	Peter Hanson
Sebastian Pasmonic	Anthony Caruso
Msgr. La Rocca	George J. Lewis
Bessie	Tina Carver
Brody	Rodney Taylor
George Pasmonick	Peter Votrian

Routine and contradictory melodramatics feature this action thriller produced by Alan Ladd's Jaguar unit for Warner Bros. release. However, Ladd's star teaming with Edward G. Robinson gives it okay chances in the general action field.

Pic's not without its good points, one being Robinson's masterful handling of the chief menace, character being of the type at which he shines particularly. Visual values are another factor, the CinemaScope lensing in Warner-Color getting some beautiful vistas of San Francisco under the camera-handling by John Seitz.

Sydney Boehm and Martin Rackin, scripting from a story by William F. McGivern, load the screenplay with contradictions. Lack of logic for much that transpires makes it difficult for Frank Tuttle's direction to keep interest going with the plot unfoldment. Story finds Ladd, ex-cop, released from prison after a five-year manslaughter rap and intent on bringing to justice the man responsible for railroading him on a phony rap. He pushes off friend wife, Joanne Dru, using the excuse she had strayed during his prison time, but really wanting to keep her from danger while he gets his man. He does, and it's Robinson, who has a king-sized racket working on the docks—what it is is never explained. Climax comes aboard a speeding motorboat on the bay, with Ladd checkmating Robinson's escape run and justice is done.

Ladd doesn't give himself the best of it, as far as material goes, and comes off with a performance that stresses strongarm action rather than acting. As noted, Robinson stands out. Miss Dru is good as the long-suffering wife and her nitery singer character has two oldies, "The Very Thought of You" and "It Had To Be You," to vocalize. Paul Stewart, Robinson's scarfaced killer, is good, as are Fay Wray, as his sweetie; Perry Lopez, the racketeer's weakling nephew; Renata Vanni, Nestor Paiva and Stanley Adams. As Ladd's old friend, William Demarest never has much chance to get going in the plot.

George C. Bertholon served as Ladd's associate producer on the pic. Editing, score and other behind-camera functions are standard. *Brog.*

The Ladykillers
(BRITISH—COLOR)

Alec Guinness as gang leader in holdup serio-comedy; good hokum should rate for average patron's taste.

London, Dec. 20.

Rank Organization (Ealing Studios) production and release. Continental Film Distributors release in U.S. Stars Alec Guinness; features Cecil Parker, Herbert Lom, Peter Sellers, Danny Green. Produced by Michael Balcon. Directed by Alexander Mackendrick. Screenplay by William Rose; camera, Otto Heller; editor, Jack Harris; music, Tristram Cary. At Odeon, Leicester Square, London. Running time, **96 MINS.**

The Professor	Alec Guinness
The Major	Cecil Parker
Louis	Herbert Lom
Harry	Peter Sellers
One-Round	Danny Green
Mrs. Wilberforce	Katie Johnson
Police Superintendent	Jack Warner
Barrow Boy	Frankie Howerd
Police Sergeant	Philip Stainton
Junkman	Fred Griffiths
Cab Driver	Kenneth Connor

This is an amusing piece of hokum, being a parody of American gangsterdom interwoven with whimsy and exaggeration that makes it more of a macabre farce. Alec Guinness, internationally popular, will prove a strong b.o. attraction although in this instance he sinks his personality almost to the level of anonymity. Basic idea of thieves making a frail old lady an unwitting accomplice in their schemes is carried out in ludicrous and often tense situations. The whole is a disconcerting mixture, but should be surefire for laughs and make for universal appeal.

A bunch of crooks planning a currency haul call on their leader, who has temporarily boarded with a genteel widow near a big London rail terminal. They pass as musicians gathering for rehearsals, but wouldn't deceive a baby. Hiring a truck similar to one transporting cases of banknotes to the station, they pull off the job, stowing the steel boxes in a wardrobe trunk leaving it among baggage on the platform. Under the noses of the searching police, and innocent of the nature of her errand, the old lady collects it for her lodger. The gang, sweating blood in a following car, see her taxi involved in trouble with a junkcart, and finally see their loot deposited on their doorstep by a helpful squad car.

After the shareout, one of their instrument cases bursts open disgorging not a cello but bills, and to prevent the old dame from betraying them, they draw lots to kill her. Each ducks the job and attempts a getaway until all five die. When the landlady reports the whole affair to the precinct, where she is known for her fanciful yarns, they dismiss her with tolerant smiles and tell her to keep the money.

Guinness tends to overact the sinister leader while Cecil Parker strikes just the right note as a con man posing as an army officer. Herbert Lom broods gloomily as the most ruthless of the plotters, with Peter Sellers contrasting well as the dumb muscleman. Danny Green completes the quintet. Katie Johnson in every motion and expression is the guileless old widow. Jack Warner exudes his usual genial personality as the understanding police superintendent.

Camera angles bring out the highlights of suspense. Direction stresses more evenly than the players the balance between jest and reality. *Clem.*

Paris Follies of 1956
(MUSICAL—COLOR)

Mediocre film improvised around floor show at Hollywood's real-life Moulin Rouge cafe.

Hollywood, Dec. 21.

Allied Artists release of Bernard Tabakin (Mercury-International) production. Stars Forrest Tucker, Margaret Whiting, Dick Wesson, Martha Hyer, Barbara Whiting; features Lloyd Corrigan, Wally Cassell, Fluff Charlton, James Ferris, William Henry, the Sportsmen, Frank Parker. Directed by Leslie Goodwins. Story and screenplay, Milton Lazarus; camera (De Luxe), Ed DuPar; editor, Gene Fowler Jr.; music conducted by Frank DeVol; songs, Pony Sherrell, Phil Moody, Sid Kuller; dances, Donn Arden. Previewed Dec. 19, '55. Running time, **72 MINS.**

Dan Bradley	Forrest Tucker
Margaret Walton	Margaret Whiting
Chuck Russell	Dick Wesson
Ruth Harmon	Martha Hyer
Barbara Walton	Barbara Whiting
Alfred Gaylord	Lloyd Corrigan
Harry	Wally Cassell
Taffy	Fluff Charlton
Jim	James Ferris
Wendell	William Henry
The Sportsmen	Themselves
Frank Parker	Himself

Frank Sennes' Moulin Rouge theatre-restaurant in Hollywood is showcased in this minor program effort. While pic gives viewer an idea of the elaborate floor show featured at the nitery, the packaging with a formula backstage story doesn't make for satisfactory screen entertainment.

The Bernard Tabakin production is a real quickie, turned out in five days, around a script that must have been written in less. Production numbers seen are last season's and have all the flash necessary to dress up the footage. Unfortunately, it's static beauty, however, because the numbers are patched together with a plot that tells of a producer's difficulties in getting a show together with a bankroller who's a nut and not the millionaire he makes out to be.

Margaret Whiting does a temperamental singer to pipe several Pony Sherrell-Phil Moody songs, and Frank Parker lends his tenor to others. Score includes "Can This Be Love," "I Love a Circus," "Have You Ever Been in Paris," "I'm All Aglow Again" and "I'm In a Mood Tonight." Additionally, the Sportsmen sing Sid Kuller's "The Hum Song."

Forrest Tucker is seen as the producer, with Lloyd Corrigan the nut with a false front. Martha Hyer, show's designer; Dick Wesson, comic aide to the producer; Barbara Whiting, a stagestruck chick, are some of the others who get nowhere with the material in Milton Lazarus' script. Leslie Goodwins' direction also is defeated by the plotting.

De Luxe Color was used in the Ed DuPar lensing and the hues are not always consistent. Editing, scoring and other credits are adequate.

Sudden Danger

Bill Elliott proves suicide was really murder in good meller.

Hollywood, Dec. 13.

Allied Artists release of Ben Schwalb production. Stars Bill Elliott, Tom Drake, Beverly Garland; features Dayton Lummis, Helene Stanton, Lucien Littlefield, Minerva Urecal. Directed by Hubert Cornfield. Screenplay, Daniel B. and Elwood Ullman; story by Daniel B. Ullman; camera, Ellsworth Fredericks; editor, William Austin; music, Marlin Skiles. Previewed Dec. 9, '55. Running time, **65 MINS.**

Doyle	Bill Elliott
Curits	Tom Drake
Phyllis	Beverly Garland
Wilkins	Dayton Lummis
Vera	Helene Stanton
Dave	Lucien Littlefield
Mrs. Kelly	Minerva Urecal
Woodruff	Lyle Talbot
Kenny	Frank Jenks
Caldwell	Pierre Watkin
Duncan	John Close
Dr. Hastings	Ralph Gamble

Good performances, direction and writing do a better job of meeting entertainment demands than the average supporting filmfare. In 65 minutes of footage, scripters Daniel B. Ullman and Elwood Ullman establish the characters rather well for the time limitations. Hubert Cornfield's direction is tight and soundly valued to make the most of the material within the budget range.

Film is one of Bill Elliott's series as a sheriff's office detective lieutenant. Here he's investigating the suicide of sportswear manufacturer whose son, Tom Drake, is blind. Elliott doesn't readily accept the suicide theory and uncovers facts that put the finger of suspicion on the son, who was accidentally blinded by his mother several years previously. Insurance money from the mother's death pays for an operation that cures Drake and he turns amateur sleuth. Windup finds the mother's crooked business partner, Dayton Lummis, who had been using his ill-gotten gains to support blonde Helene Stanton, nailed as the real culprit.

Performances are well above par for the usual hurried programmer, with Drake's blind-man-made-well-again, and Beverly Garland's portrayal of the fiancee who aids him, being the standouts. Others providing capable support to the stars include Lucien Littlefield, Minerva Urecal and Lyle Talbot.

Ellsworth Fredericks' photography plays an important part in plot mood and developments. Editing, background score and other credits do their parts, too. *Brog.*

Alligator Named Daisy
(With Songs)
(BRITISH—V'VISION—COLOR)

Boisterous fantastic comedy. Castings should boost appeal of this laugh-getter.

London, Dec. 13.

J. Arthur Rank (Raymond Stross) production and release. Stars Donald Sinden, Diana Dors, Jean Carson, James Robertson Justice; features Stanley Holloway, Roland Culver. Directed by J. Lee Thompson. Screenplay by Jack Davies from book by Charles Terret; camera, Reginald Wyer; editor, John D. Guthridge; songs by Sam Coslow, Paddy Roberts. At Odeon, Leicester Square, London. Running time, **88 MINS.**

Peter Weston	Donald Sinden
Vanessa Colebrook	Diana Dors
Sir James Colebrook	James Robertson Justice
Moira	Jean Carson
General Weston	Stanley Holloway
Colonel Weston	Roland Culver
Mrs. Weston	Avice Landone
Prudence Croquet	Margaret Rutherford
Albert	Stephen Boyd
Valet	Henry Kendall
Hoskins	Richard Wattis
Irishman	Wilfrid Lawson
Music Publisher	Harry Green
Band Leader	Ken Macintosh

A nonsensical but very funny picture, adapted from a novel, giving not only leading players but also other popular stars opportunities to score in very small roles. Each gives his own individual humorous touch to elaborate the basically ridiculous theme. It should have universal appeal on the stars' drawing power and the originality of the story and its treatment.

On returning from Ireland on vacation, a young piano salesman finds himself the unwilling owner of a pet alligator. He can neither sell it, give it away nor find it possible to destroy it. On the steamer he encounters a spirited colleen who pursues him by the reverse method of evading his advances and finally accepts him when he has broken away from his rich fiancee. Her father, a famed tycoon, takes exception to his palatial country home being overrun by the ubiquitous Daisy. The reptile creates havoc but the millionaire, who also owns newspapers, decides to turn the publicity to good account and organizes an alligator competition.

Camerawork and crisp direction give all possible aid to the preposterous story.

Donald Sinden plays the harassed custodian of Daisy with easy conviction, hovering between the two girls, each with contrasted sex appeal from Jean Carson with her red crewcut and tomboyish garb to Diana Dors with long platinum hair and revealing gowns, rounded off with an exotic bubble bath. Miss Carson scores on acting points, and carries off two song and dance numbers with a verve.

James Robertson Justice stampedes forcefully as the dominating financier while Roland Culver and Avice Landone play the boy's parents in subdued tones. Stanley Holloway makes the most of amusing situations as a peppery old grandpop. Wilfrid Lawson registers impishly as a drunken old salt. Harry Green contributes a jovial character study. Margaret Rutherford supplies a cameo gem as a petshop owner. All minor roles are in excellent hands. *Clem.*

The Dancing Heart
(GERMAN—MUSIC—COLOR)

United German Film Enterprises release of Capitol Films production. Stars Herta Staal, Paul Hoerbiger. Directed by Wolfgang Liebeneiner. Adapted from novel by W. F. Fichelscher; camera (color), Igor Oberberg; music, Norbert Schultze. Previewed in N.Y., Dec. 16, '55. Running time, **91 MINS.**

Susanne	Gertrud Kueckelmann
Viktor	Gunnar Moeller
The Sovereign	Paul Hoerbiger
Annchen	Herta Staal
Haberling	Paul Henckels
Leopold	Wilfried Seyferth
The Doll	Maria Fris
Julius	Harald Juhnke
Roberti	Heinz Rosen
Therese	Charlotte Ander
Innkeeper	Herbert Kiper
Applinger	Erwin Biegel

(In German; English Titles)

"The Dancing Heart," a Teutonic musical fantasy, should appeal in the world market, though story's often implausible and difficult to digest. However, it has splendid performances, particularly those of the two stars, Herta Staal and Paul Hoerbiger which may roll some arty dates and is a sure bet for German language houses.

Story technique and direction indicates this film was made some time back because German production has since improved. Main flow is that a musical comedy fantasy is dished outright without explanations. Main idea—that a skilled toymaker has perfected a life-like doll—because easily wilted. The doll goes into ballet sequences, the highlight of the pic and staged with skill and intelligence.

Miss Staal, as the daughter who attempts to save his father from losing his property, is excellent despite being called on to do outlandish things. She imitates the mechanical doll until the money-lender catches on to the switch.

The doll, itself, is played with skill by Maria Fris. Hoerbiger portrays the duke, with his usual suave mannerisms. Charlotte Ander, Gertrud Kueckelmann, Gunnar Moeller, Paul Henckels and Wilfried Seyferth serve well in top supporting roles.

Wolfgang Liebeneiner does a routine job but okay in view of the story. His ballet scenes are topflight. Igor Oberberg does nicely with his color camera although no tinter process is credited. Music of Norbert Schultze is topflight for the most part. *Wear.*

Abajo el Telon
(Drop the Curtain)
(MEXICAN)

Mexico City, Dec. 13.

Columbia Pictures release of Posa Films, S.A. production. Stars "Cantinflas" (Mario Moreno); features Christiane Martell, Beatriz Saavedra, Alejandro Chiangerotti. Directed by Miguel M. Delgado; camera, Victor Herrera; story and screenplay, Jaime Salvador; music, Federica Ruiz. At Cine Roble, Mexico City. Running time, **106 MINS.**

This is another illustration of the maxim of Mexican pictures as regards the No. 1 moneymaking comic that it's not so much the pic as the star. "Cantinflas," the big grossing comedian, more than carries this conglomeration about a window cleaner, a gang of jewel thieves, clandestine gambling, and a chase in and out of a vaude-revue theatre. This last enables him to play various parts on the stage while being avoiding his pursuers.

"Cantinflas" continues being a natural comic and a master of pantomime. He still causes gales of laughter here. He is equally good at more or less polite double-meaning material and cracks at politicos. Though genuinely Mexican, albeit in the sophisticated metropolitan manner, "Curtain" has more or less universal appeal.

Christiané Martell is statuesque, uttering clear if stilted Spanish. She seems a bit stiff. Beatriz Saavedra, comely brunette is more animated. The cancan sequence is marred by ordinary costuming. Femmes are pretty and can dance but the garb is a big handicap.

Direction is good. Production and camera work also is fine. *Grah.*

Picasso

A Van Wolf-API Productions release of Sergio Amidei (Rizzoli Film) production. Directed by Luciano Emmer. Scenario, Pablo Picasso and Amidei; camera (Ferraniacolor), Giulio Giannini and Berto Vanni; music, Roman Vlad; English commentary, Rolf Tasna; adaptation, Antonelli Trombadori and Renato Gattusa. Previewed in N.Y., Dec. 7, '55. Running time, **50 MINS.**

AND

Dementia

A Van Wolf-API Productions release of John Parker production. Written and directed by Parker. Camera, William Thompson; editor, Joseph Gluck; music, George Antheil. Previewed in N.Y., Dec. 7, '55. Running time, **55 MINS.**

The Gamin .... Adrienne Barrett
Rich Man .... Bruno Ve Sota
Father-Law Enforcer ...... Ben Roseman
Evil One .... Richard Barron
Butler .... Ed Hinkle
Mother .... Lucille Howland
Flower Girl .... Jebbie Ve Sota
Nightclub Girl .... Faith Parker
Wino .... Gayne Sullivan

Two short films, representing a total running time of 105 minutes, have been packaged by Van Wolf—API Productions for art house distribution. "Picasso," filmed in Ferraniacolor and directed by Luciano Emmer, a specialist in depicting the life and works of painters via the motion picture medium, offers an excellent survey of the contributions of the Spanish-born artist.

In addition to presenting more than 450 of Pablo Picasso's paintings, the master himself is shown in his workshop and at work painting a mural. It's all done in an interesting manner, aided by flamenco music composed by Roman Vlad and an English commentary spoken by Rolf Tasna.

"Dementia" may be the strangest film ever offered for theatrical release. It's the type of picture usually confined to showings at film societies. Filled with Freudian concepts, it aims at a depiction of the dreams of a troubled femme. Picture has no dialogue or narration. A wierd effect, however, is achieved via a frightening musical score by George Antheil and sound effects.

The film leaves the viewer confused, as it seems to shift from dream to actuality. There are some gruesome sequences. The girl murders her father, kills a lecherous suitor, cuts off his hand in attempt to retrieve her necklace. (The N.Y. Board of Censors, approved the film only after a two-year battle).

"Dementia" is more clinical study than entertainment. Definitely not for popular consumption. John Parker, who wrote, directed and produced, has done an arresting one-man job. The technical aspects and photograpy are first-rate. *Holl.*

Storm Fear

Routine outlook. Cornel Wilde in producer-director-star role

United Artists release of Theodora (Cornel Wilde) production. Stars Wilde, Jean Wallace, Dan Duryea, Lee Grant, David Stollery, Dennis Weaver, Steven Hill. Directed by Wilde. Screenplay, Horton Foote, based on novel, "Storm Fear," by Clinton Seeley; camera, Joseph La Shelle; editor, Otto Ludwig; music, Elmer Bernstein. Previewed in N.Y., Dec. 8, '55. Running time, **88 MINS.**

Charlie .... Cornel Wilde
Elizabeth .... Jean Wallace
Fred .... Dan Duryea
Edna .... Lee Grant
David .... David Stollery
Hank .... Dennis Weaver
Benjie .... Steven Hill
Doctor .... Keith Britton

There's a fair amount of action and suspense in "Storm Fear" plus a trio of familiar names—Cornel Wilde, Jean Wallace and Dan Duryea. But the script is too weak and direction too slow for this meller to generate much b.o. heat.

Based on a novel by Clinton Seeley, the Horton Foote screenplay laboriously moves around a motley collection of characters, most of whom are unsympathetic and have a mutual disregard for one another. Chief villain is Wilde who hides out in the farmhouse of brother Duryea and latter's wife, Miss Wallace, while on the lam from a bank heist.

Also fugitives in the rural retreat are Wilde's accomplices, gun moll Lee Grant and Steven Hill, a crazed killer. When a snow storm extends the thieves' stay in their unwilling hosts' home, tension increases as the law closes in. Moreover, tempers flare as it develops that Wilde is father of David Stollery, Miss Wallace's young son, and not Duryea.

Script goes the "eternal triangle" one better by having Miss Wallace eventually marrying the attentive hired man (Dennis Weaver) after Duryea is frozen to death in a snowbank. Meantime, Miss Grant, Hill and Wilde all meet death in one way or another as they trek over a snowclad mountain with young Stollery as their reluctant guide.

Wilde, who produced and directed this entry for his Theodora Productions, manages to attain a grim atmosphere and an overall morbid flavor. But this is largely wasted since not one of the characters, with exception of young Stollery, excite audience sympathy. Wilde's portrayal of the bankrobber is seldom believable, principally because of the dull story.

Also victims of the script are Miss Wallace, who makes a valiant thesping try with demands of her role; Duryea, who's cast as a man weak in mind and body, and Miss Grant as a gun girl. Stollery does nicely as a boy who's hep on the outdoors and Hill makes himself irritatingly unpleasant as the trigger-happy killer. Okay support is provided by Weaver as the hired hand and Keith Britton as a doctor.

Production values tend to reflect a modest budget. Black-and-white lensing of Joseph La Shelle shows to advantage especially in winter snow scenes, and the Elmer Bernstein score is in keeping with the film's melodramatic vein. Running time of 88 minutes is overlong for most situations in which this United Artists release will find bookings. *Gilb.*

Die Sennerin von St. Kathrein
(Cow Girl of St. Catherine)
(AUSTRIAN)

Vienna, Dec. 13.

Sascha Film release of OEfa-Schoenbrunn production. Stars Anita Gutwell, Rudolf Lenz and Rudolf Carl; features Hans Putz, Lotte Ledl, Albert Rueprecht, Heinz Rohn, Ludwig Geiger. Directed by Herbert B. Fredersdorf. Screenplay, Dr. Theodor Ottawa; camera, Walter Tuch; music, Carl Loube. At Flieger Kino, Vienna. Running time, **90 MINS.**

This is the first time that a picture was produced here based on a pop tune hit, "The Cowgirl of St. Catherine," bestseller here this year. The action occurs in the beautiful countryside of St. Catherine, Vorarlberg, which is a plus factor. This looks good boxoffice in the world market.

Theodor Ottawa has written a fetching love story while director Herbert B. Fredersdorf has provided plenty of action.

Film also has a cultural side. Scenes from famous Haflinger horse-breeding farms are excellent. Anita Gutwell, Rudolf Lenz and Rudolf Carl, provide standard acting jobs. Anton Karas makes sort of a film comeback by contributing some zither music for zither. *Maas.*

House of Ricordi
(Operatic-Technicolor)
(FRENCH—ITALIAN)

Hollywood, Dec. 16.

Manson Distributing Co. release of a joint Documento Film (Rome) and Cormoran Films (Paris) production. Producer, Franco Riganti; director, Carmine Gallone; screenplay, Leo Benvenuti, Furio Scarpelli, Age, Nino Novarese, from original by Benvenuti, Noverese, Scarpelli, Age, Ivo Perilli and Ennio De Concini; camera, Marco Scarpelli; art director, Mario Chiari; editor, Niccolo Lazzari; sound, Ennio Sensi; music of Rossini, Donizetti, Verdi, Puccini, Bellini. Previewed at Beverly Canon Theatre, Dec. 15, '55. Running time, **112 MINS.**

Rossini .... Roland Alexandre
Luisa Lewis .... Miriam Bru
Strepponi .... Elisa Cegani
Ricordi .... Andrea Checchi
Maria .... Danielle Delorme
Puccini .... Gabriele Ferzetti
Verdi .... Fosco Giachetti
Tito Ricordi .... Enzo Givampietro
Giulia Gristi .... Nadia Gray
Domenico Barbaja .... Roldano Lupi
Donizetti .... Mataroianni
Virginia Marchii .... Micheline Prelle
Bellini .... Maurice Ronet
G. Ricordi .... Paolo Stoppa
Isabella Colbran .... Marta Toren
Arrigo Boito .... Fausto Tozzi

(English Titles)

Opera lovers, a notoriously hardy breed, may give this 112 minute rundown of Italian opera a good play in the sure-seater circuit. In other situations, despite the obviously lavish scope of this color production, the lack of prominent marquee names (outside of opera field) and extreme length may prove a rough handicap to oversome.

"Ricordi" comes off best as a filmed music festival, with numerous arias and orchestral interludes, featuring such vocalists as Mario Del Monaco, Renata Tebaldi, Tito Gobbi, Italo Tajo, Nelly Corradi and Gino Mattera. Operas thus spotlighted include "The Barber of Seville," "Elixer of Love," "Masked Ball," "Othello," "La Boheme," "The Puritans" and "The Sleepwalker."

Musically, the presentation is in the lushly Italianite manner and exceptionally well done; dramatically, the story or stories, a variation of the "House of Rothschild" format, is less successful. Essentially, it is the history of the House of Ricordi, a prominent family of Milanese music publishers and impresarios and the famed composers with whom the Ricordis worked. Necessarily episodic, since it covers a period from Rossini to Puccini, the noted figures depicted are rarely given much chance in the highly romanticized biographical sketches to become more than melodramatic puppets. Among the episodes, the renowned names of Rossini, Verdi, Bellini, Donizetta, Puccini and Boito are to be found.

Given starring billing are three names somewhat familiar to American audiences; Marta Toren, Danielle Delorme and Micheline Prelle, as amours of the various composers. Other thesps worthy of note are Andre Checchi, Enzo Givampietro and Paolo Stoppa, as members of the Ricordi clan; and Fosco Ciachetti as Verdi, Roland Alexandre as Rossini, Gabriele Ferzetti as Puccini, Mataroianni as Donizetti, Maurice Ronet as Bellini and Fausto Tozzi as the libretist Boito.

Carmine Gallone's direction is in keeping with the melodramatics supplied by a host of six scripters. Technicolor filming by Marco Scarpelli, especially of operatic sequences, are lushly effective. *Kove.*

Banditen Der Autobahn
(Bandits of Highway)
(GERMAN)

Berlin, Dec. 13.

Columbia release of Arion production. With Eva-Ingeborg Scholz, Hans Christian Blech, Paul Hoerbiger, Karl-Ludwig Diehl, Charles Regnier, Hermann Speelmanns, Wolfgang Wahl, Hans Schwarz, Ellen Schwiers, Ursula Justin, Klaus Kammer, Wolf Ackva, Josef Offenbach, Wolfgang Neuss, Armin Schweizer, Wolfgang Mueller, Gert Schaefer, Earl Fleischer, Earl Walter Diess, Erich Scholz. Directed by Geza von Cziffre. Screenplay, Robert T. Theeren, Geza von Cziffra, Wolfgang Neuss; camera, Albert Benitz; music, Michael Jary. At Bonbonniere, Berlin. Running time, **101 MINS.**

In several instances this German Arion production, which sees release here through Columbia, obviously follows the familiar Hollywood pattern. Film has got the pat plot and the cop and gangster types, but all similarity with strong U.S. productions stops there. In particular, film lacks documentary sharpness and conviction. Nevertheless, it appears still okay to satisfy the greater part of the domestic action trade. Foreign chances are moderate.

Based on actual highway robberies in Germany, this airs the question as to when the police be allowed to shoot. Too frequently realism is sacrificed for convenience. What suspense remains stems mainly from good performances, particularly the evil-doers, represented by Charles Regnier, Klaus Kammer and Hans Schwarz among others.

Direction by Geza von Cziffra. better known here as a maker of musicals, is generally okay. Some car chases are nicely staged. Besides the acting, best thing about this pic is the fine camerawork by Albert Benitz and the catchy music by Michael Jary. *Hans.*

Simon and Laura
(BRITISH—V'VISION—COLOR)

London, Dec. 13.

J. Arthur Rank (Teddy Baird) production and release. Stars Peter Finch, Kay Kendall; features Muriel Pavlow, Hubert Gregg, Maurice Denham, Ian Carmichael. Directed by Muriel Box. Screenplay, Peter Blackmore from stage comedy by Alan Melville; camera, Ernest Steward; editor, Jean Berker; music, Benjamin Frankel. At Odeon, Leicester Square, London, Nov. 22, '55. Running time, **91 MINS.**

Simon	Peter Finch
Laura	Kay Kendall
Janet	Muriel Pavlow
David	Ian Carmichael
Wilson	Maurice Denham
Burton	Hubert Gregg
Jessie	Thora Hird
Timothy	Clive Parritt
Adrian Lee	Alan Wheatley
Controller of Television	Richard Wattis
Barney	Terence Longden
Television Producers	Tom Gill, David Morrell, Nicholas Parsons

A modest success as a play, this Alan Melville comedy converts to better advantage in screen technique, being a skit on corny family tv serials and the artificially ringing in top name personalities in in show biz. Slickly adapted, it makes good laugh material, unveiling backstage problems and all the tricks of the trade. There is a good deal of slapstick rough and tumble which will please the kids and enough satirical digs at the infant of the entertainment medium to amuse the more technically minded. Likely to prove more of a local attraction than in the U.S.

TV program organizers looking for a novelty angle decide on a day-by-day domestic series set in home surroundings of top ranking married stars. Peter Finch and Kay Kendall are picked, quoted as ideally happy. But in private they bicker and rage to the verge of divorce. Some lean months and heavy debts bring them to sink their differences and accept the new offer, which registers favorably from the start. After some weeks, jealousy and an alcoholic loosening of inhibitions in the Christmas session leads to a general free-for-all. Instead of the anticipated fury of the powers that be and fadeout of the serial, it is hailed as the tops.

Peter Finch conveys just the requisite touch of vanity and pomposity as the silvering matinee idol while Kay Kendall is the wildcat with enthusiasm in the "Taming of Shrew" tradition. Supporting love interest comes from Ian Carmichael as the author of the feature and Muriel Pavlow, as a script girl, each of whom gets unintentionally involved in the stars' tangled emotions. Maurice Denham and Thora Hird give good characterizations as the servants who gain reflected glory through the household's blaze of publicity. The numerous technical assistants are all neatly near-caricatured. Clive Parritt is cute as the blase moppet interpolated to intensify the family atmosphere, knowing he will steal every scene and enjoying the adults' discomfiture. Real life British radio personalities are introduced giving an emphasized authenticity. *Clem.*

Hotel Adlon
(GERMAN)

Berlin, Dec. 20.

Herzog release of CCC production. Stars Claude Farell, Werner Hinz and Rene Deltgen; features Nelly Borgeaud, Sebastian Fischer, Nadja Tiller, Erich Schellow, Karl John, Peter Mosbacher, Lola Muethel, Hans Caninenberg, Helmut Lohner, Arno Paulsen, Kurt Buecheler, Paul Wagner, Arthur Schroeder, Walter Bluhm, Werner Peters, Franz Weber, Ewald Wenck, Erich Poremski, Ernst Albert Schaah, Albert Bessler, Werner Schott. Directed by Josef von Baky. Screenplay, Dr. Emil Burri, Johannes Mario Simmel; camera, F. A. Wagner; music, Georg Haentzschel. At Gloria Palast, Berlin. Running time, **100 MINS.**

This is a biopic of Hotel Adlon, Berlin's foremost hotel until its destruction in 1945 when the Red Army invaded the city. Adapted from the memoirs by Hedda Adlon, Herzog has in "Adlon" an interesting and well made semi-documentary pic that should click at the local b.o. Because of the wide international rep this hotel once had, pic also may stir some interest abroad.

Based on a fine script by Emil Burri and J. M. Simmel, film retells some of the most vivid and characteristic dates of this famous hotel palace, starting out with its establishment in 1907 up to its destruction 38 years later, thereby covering a substantial part of German history. It contains the period under Emperor Wilhelm, the revolution in 1918, the roaring 20's, the unholy Hitler time and the war years. Neatly woven in the running throughout is the life and love story of the hotel director who started out as a bellhop.

Director Josef von Baky has done a remarkable job in recreating an atmosphere deserving the genuine label. The most outstanding performances are contributed by Nelly Borgeaud and Sebastian Fischer who play the principal couple. Whole cast is extremely well chosen.

Georg Haentzschel's score enhances the pic and F. A. Wagner's lensing is impressive. *Hans.*

Flame of the Islands
(SONGS—COLOR)

Hollywood, Dec. 9.

Republic release of Edward Ludwig production. Stars Yvonne De Carlo, Howard Duff, Zachary Scott; features Kurt Kasznar, Barbara O'Neil, James Arness, Frieda Inescort. Directed by Ludwig. Screenplay, Bruce Manning; story, Adele Comandini; camera (TruColor), Bud Thackery; editor, Richard L. Van Enger; score, Nelson Riddle; songs, Jack Elliott, Sonny Burke. Previewed Dec. 6, '55. Running time, **90 MINS.**

Rosalind Dee	Yvonne De Carlo
Doug Duryea	Howard Duff
Wade Evans	Zachary Scott
Cyril Mace	Kurt Kasznar
Mrs. Duryea	Barbara O'Neil
Kelly Rand	James Arness
Mrs. Hammond	Frieda Inescort
Gus	Lester Matthews
Johnny	Donald Curtis
Willie	Nick Stewart

A Bahamas setting provides "Flame of the Islands" with background for romantic drama, but neither the screenplay nor the direction make good use of it. The names are okay for the marquees in the program market.

Motivations behind character actions are hard to grasp in the Bruce Manning script, based on a story by Adele Comandini, and they play off in pot-boiler fashion under the guidance of associate producer-director Edward Ludwig.

Yvonne De Carlo is the chief star and is given a colorful wardrobe, as well as two tunes by Sonny Burke and Jack Elliott, "Bahama Mama" and "Take It Or Leave It," to sing. She wears her clothes well and puts the songs across but has less success with her character of a girl mixed up with bigtime gambling and upper-crust society. Same character trouble is encountered by Howard Duff, playboy Virginian with whom she almost revives a long-dead romance; Zachary Scott, old faithful who stands by to catch her on the rebound; James Arness, reformed drunk, turned preacher, who proves to be her fadeout partner, and Kurt Kasznar, gambler who sevens-out on his passes at her.

In the plot, Miss De Carlo, NY working girl, acquires a cash windfall in dubious style, uses it to partner with Kasznar and Scott in a Bahamas gambling club as hostess-singer, renews an old love, that had ended tragically, with Duff, becomes involved in some social intrigues that climax with gangsters moving in on the club and is saved at the finale by Arness.

Competent lensing is contributed by Bud Thackery and the other technical credits, except some highly improbable special effects, are okay. *Brog.*

Frou-Frou

Paris, Dec. 20.

Gamma Film release of Film Cine-Italgamma production. Stars Dany Robin; features Philipe Lemaire, Gino Cervi, Jean Wall, Louis De Funes, Melnati, Yvan Desny, Marie Sabouret, Mischa Auer. Directed by Augusto Genina. Screenplay, A. E. Carr, Cecil Saint-Laurent; camera (Eastmancolor), Henri Alekan; editor, Leonide Azar; music, Louiguy. At Marignan, Paris. Running time, **115 MINS.**

Frou-Frou	Dany Robin
Artus	Philipe Lemaire
Vladimir	Gino Cervi
Sabatier	Jean Wall
Major	Louis De Funes
Archduke	Mischa Auer
Grand Duchess	Marie Sabouret

Film is a sudsy odyssey of the life of a pre-World War I fluff who is found working as a cigarette girl by four rich, and bored middleaged men and turned into a lady. Obvious contour of this sprawling affair, plus C'Scope dimensions, makes it of little interest for arty houses. For more general situations the evident entertainment qualities, and some pleasant period recreation might make pic palatable in some secondary situations. Dubbing could help this. Dany Robin, known in U.S. for her work in "Act of Love," and Mischa Auer should provide some marquee lustre.

Frou-Frou (Dany Robin) delights the magnanimous four men when she insults their courteous companions in a nightclub. They build her into a lady and she emerges as a singer, with some catchy early '20's ditties worked in. Also unfolded is her first love deception by a gigolo, her living with her Russian benefactor and her final marrying one of her rich benefactors for security.

Director Augusto Genina has given this slick treatment. Gino Cervi and Mischa Auer hand the story good polish. Miss Robin is somewhat arch as the ingenue. C'Scope is well utilized and colors are properly overripe. Editing and production are good. *Mosk.*

L'Affaire Des Poisons

Paris, Dec. 13.

Gaumont release of Franco-London Film production. Stars Danielle Darrieux, Viviane Romance, Paul Meurisse. Directed by Henri Decoin. Screenplay, Georges Neveux, Albert Valentin, Decoin; camera (Technicolor), Pierre Montazel; editor, Borys Lewin; music, Rene Cloerec. At Berlitz, Paris. Running time, **110 MINS.**

Mme. De Montespan	Danielle Darrieux
La Voisin	Viviane Romance
Desoeillets	Anne Vernon
Fontanges	Christine Carrera
Guibourg	Paul Meurisse
De La Renie	Maurice Teynac
Desgrez	Pierre Mondy
M. De Montespan	Renaud-Mary
Hangman	Albert Remy

This pic relates the story of a much - treated French historical mystery, the wave of poisonings under the reign of Louis XIV in 17th Century France. Specifically, it concerns one of the king's ex-favorites whose anguish at being dropped by his majesty leads her to using the poisons of a professional clairvoyant. This is treated with painstaking care but the film seems to lack a definite pattern of character. Including a Black Mass, scenes of torture and some court bits, this has exploitation value for the U.S. if it does not run into censorship difficulty. It also has the names of Danielle Darrieux and Viviane Romance for the marquee.

France is shown as being in the grip of hysteria, with sickness rampant. This is capitalized on by a half-mad unfrocked priest and a fortune teller (supplier of poisons). When the king's ex-favorite (Miss Darrieux) walks in to get something to bring the king back to her bed or discredit her rival, this wily duo decide to take advantage of the situation. They poison the rival themselves and suspicion falls on the lady's maid. The police, meanwhile, are cracking down on this ring of poisoners and finally captures them all. Miss Darrieux is only banished but the others are burned at the stake.

Henri Decoin has given this a clever mounting and achieves some eerie moments during the Black Mass and executions. He is aided by the knowing acting of Paul Meurisse who makes the mad priest almost a credible character. Danielle Darrieux is somewhat flat as the great court lady. Viviane Romance is good as the poisoner who gets her comeuppance.

The Technicolor is fine in depicting the various sombre moods while production dress is excellent. In short, this is a potent recreation of past times with enough offbeat aspects. Made for widescreen, the film takes well to the bigger dimensions. *Mosk.*

La Bella Mugnaia
(The Beautiful Miller's Wife)
(ITALIAN-COLOR—C'SCOPE)

Titanus release of a Titanus-Ponti-DeLaurentiis production. Stars Sophia Loren, Vittorio De Sica, Marcella Mastroianni; features Paolo Stoppa, Ivonne Sanson, Carletto Sposito, Emilio Petacci, Elss Vazzoler, Virgilio Riento. Directed by Mario Camerini. Screenplay, Camerini, Perilli, Continenza, DeConcini; camera (Eastmancolor), Enzo Serafin; music, Angelo Lavagnino. At Cinema Metropolitan, Rome. Running time, **110 MINS.**

Titanus has a good pic in this anamorphic comedy based on Alarcon's "Three Cornered Hat." Production values and, above all, a strong cast should see this to healthy boxoffice on the Italian scene. It has plenty of export elements as well, not last the physical endowments of Sophia Loren and Ivonne Sanson. Dubbed version is indicated to catch full dialogue.

After a slowish start, action unspins at an ever-increasing pace until the fast windup. Story concerns the long-frustrated designs of fuddy-duddy governor, Vittorio DeSica, on the beautiful miller's wife, Sophia Loren. On his sidekick's suggestion, he has the miller incarcerated, then makes for the mill. Meanwhile, the miller succeeds in escaping, and a carousel of mistaken identities, involving all hands, begins to spin around the mill. Frankly rowdyish goings-on are handled with an eye to humor by director Mario Camerini, and are acted with gusto by De Sica, Miss Loren and Mastraoanni.

Lensing on print seen was uneven in color values but made good use of C'Scope. Elaborate production bases the action with much of pic made on locations around Italy. *Hawk.*

El Seductor
(The Seductor)
(MEXICAN; SONGS)
Mexico City, Dec. 20.
Peliculas Nacionales release of Producciones Guillermo Calderon production. Stars Ramon Gay, Amanda del Llano, Ana Luisa Peluffo: features Jose Luis Jimenez, Emma Roldan, Miguel Manzano, Mercedes Soler, Antonio Raxel, Roy Fletcher, Rebecca San Roman, "Los Bribones." Directed by Chano Urueta. Story and screenplay by Rafael Garcia Travesi; camera, Augustin Jimenez; music, Antonio Diaz Conde. At Cine Olimpia, Mexico City. Running time, 95 MINS.

Apart from being credited with sparking the pic-stage moralization drive of the city, this has a special interest in beauty of its femme stars, dressed and undressed (there's plenty of this) and lensing. Sprightly music, sold with unique effect by one of the top femmes here, Ana Luisa Peluffo, and "Los Bribones," two men.

Story spots Ramon Gay, painter genius, as becoming involved with the daughter of the couple whose tragic deaths he provoked.

Several sequences pose the question of censorship on this production. Minor shocker is a bevy of more or less beauteous femmes almost naked in an ad agency with the models lensed several times.

Major jolters are Ana Luisa Peluffo posing for the artist (Gay) in the nude, then Amanda del Llano, as she appears first with a flimsy shawl and then 100% sans clothes. This nudity is laid on with a trowel. *Doug.*

Despues de la Tormenta
Mexico City, Dec. 20.
Columbia Pictures release of Filmadora Argel (Emilo Tuero) production. Stars Ramon Gay, Marga Lopez, Lilia Prado. Directed by Roberto Gavaldon. Based on novel, "The Other Brother," by Julio Alejandro; adapted by Roberto Gavaldon, Julio Alejandro; camera, Raul Martinez Solares. At Cine Metropolitan, Mexico City. Running time, 85 MINS.

Strong drama is wrapped up in this physical triangle big in all departments so as to much mitigate despite the defect of badly handled flashback. This film looks like a highly salable product in the U. S. and elsewhere in the world market. Theme, setting, lensing and direction all help. Locale is on the Isla de Lobos (Wolf Island) which is in the top target zone of the devastating hurricanes of this year.

Ramon Gay, playing twin brothers, one a regular guy and the other a rotter; Marga Lopez and Lilia Prado are all big marqueers down here. They competently handle this tale of a pair of married couples, living together in the lighthouse on Wolf Island. A Gulf of Mexico hurricane that drowns the good brother and allows the heel to pass himself off as his brother-in-law, with obvious results in an affair with Miss Prado, curvy blonde looker, who is his sister-in-law. Miss Lopez ultimately finds just what her husband has been doing, and kills him.
Doug.

1956

The Lieutenant Wore Skirts
(C'SCOPE—COLOR)

Light escapist filmfare, with Tom Ewell, Sheree North, others sparking pleasant comedy.

Hollywood, Dec. 30.

20th-Fox release of Buddy Adler production. Stars Tom Ewell, Sheree North; features Rita Moreno, Rick Jason, Les Tremayne, Alice Reinheart. Directed by Frank Tashlin. Screenplay, Albert Beich, Tashlin; story, Beich; camera (De Luxe Color), Leo Tover; editor, James B. Clark; music, Cyril J. Mockridge; song, "Rock Around the Island," Ken Darby; sung by the Lancers. Previewed Dec. 28, '55. Running time, **98 MINS.**

Gregory Whitcomb .... Tom Ewell
Katy Whitcomb .... Sheree North
Sandra .... Rita Moreno
Capt. Barney Sloan .... Rick Jason
Henry Gaxton .... Les Tremayne
Capt. Briggs .... Alice Reinheart
Lt. Sweeney .... Gregory Walcott
Joan Sweeney .... Joan Willes
Takitoff .... Sylvia Lewis
Major Dunning .... Edward Platt
Buxom Date .... Jacqueline Fontaine
Mr. Curtis .... Arthur Q. Bryan
Sam .... Paul Glass
Delivery Boy .... Keith Vincent
Gloria .... Kathy Marlowe
Roger Wilkins .... Joe Locke
WAF Officer .... Bette Arlen
Sentry .... Franklin James
Officer at Gate .... Maury Hill
WAF Sergeant .... Janice Carroll
WAF .... Dorothy Gordon
Gateman .... Ralph Sanford
Chorus Girl .... Pat Marshall
Comedian .... Sam Bagley
Mildred Wilkins .... Helene Marshall
Mother in Laundromat .. Marjorie Stapp
M. P. .... Michael Ross
Girl .... Marianne Candace Kelly
WAF .... Pat McMahon

This amusing comedy affair whiles away a pleasant 93 minutes of screen time and should prove generally popular. Tom Ewell, following his click in "The Seven Year Itch," costars with Sheree North, and the teaming should supply enough initial lure to get the picture off to an okay start.

Buddy Adler's production supervision does quite well by the light escapist filmfare, as does Frank Tashlin's direction of the screenplay he wrote with Albert Beich from the latter's original. Sassy dialogue and situations predominate and make for sly fun. Footage occasionally strains into slapstick with the frenetics forcing chuckles, but the plot idea is enough to carry the show along at an amusing pace.

Story pits Ewell against the Air Force, and he wins, with an assist from nature. He's an aging World War II hero now a tv writer, and Miss North, his wife, is an ex-WAC considerably younger. The comedy of errors tees off when she rejoins the service because he is recalled. However, he's rejected, and then dejected because she likes her uniform. From then on comedy hinges on his efforts to get her discharged. He becomes the male equivalent of a servicemen's wife and upsets the base on which he lives with her. Main laugh nub spins around his efforts to trick his wife into thinking she's going nuts and thus taking a psycho discharge. Nature takes care of the battle, though, when she becomes pregnant.

Ewell makes with the facial expressions for some solid comedy scoring. Miss North mostly acts her role with her legs and hips. It's a performance with which no one should quarrel as she's equipped for such physical thesping. Rita Moreno captures the fancy in a girl-upstairs takeoff from "Itch." Rick Jason, handsome young officer with his eye on Miss North; Les Tremayne, as Ewell's literary agent, and Alice Reinheart, AF captain, are among the featured cast contributing importantly.

Beverly Hills and Honolulu serve as backgrounds for the story and, along with the cast, art direction and other settings, are shown off to advantage by Leo Tover's CinemaScope lensing in De Luxe Color. Cyril J. Mockridge's score, conducted by Lionel Newman, and the Ken Darby song, "Rock Around the Island," are good. *Brog.*

Ransom!

Television script thins when stretched double length for screen but Glenn Ford's name to help b.o. prospects.

Hollywood, Jan. 3.

Metro release of Nicholas Nayfack production. Stars Glenn Ford, Donna Reed; features Leslie Nielsen, Juano Hernandez, Robert Keith. Directed by Alex Segal. Screenplay, Cyril Hume, Richard Maibaum; camera, Arthur E. Arling; editor, Ferris Webster; music, Jeff Alexander. Previewed Dec. 27, '55. Running time, **101 MINS.**

David G. Stannard .... Glenn Ford
Edith Stannard .... Donna Reed
Charlie Telfer .... Leslie Nielsen
Jesse Chapman .... Juano Hernandez
Chief Jim Backett .... Robert Keith
Langly .... Richard Gaines
Mrs. Partridge .... Mabel Albertson
Dr. Paul Y. Gorman .. Alexander Scourby
Andy Stannard .... Bobby Clark
Al Stannard .... Ainslie Pryor
Elizabeth Stannard .... Lori March
Sheriff Jake Kessing .... Robert Burton
Shirley Lorraine .... Juanita Moore
Nurse .... Mary Alan Hokanson
Fred Benson .... Robert Forrest
Sgt. Wenzel .... Dick Rich

After twice being staged live on television as "Fearful Decision," this kidnap melodrama has made its way to theatrical films as "Ransom!" The bigscreen impact's not as sharp as was the televersion's. Still, it has a quota of tension-arousing scenes—a couple of which are really potent—plus the names of Glenn Ford and Donna Reed to dress up the marquees. Business prospects can hit a good level overall because the lure's here for that sizeable number of filmgoers who like to be rendered apart emotionally.

Principal problem faced, and one that likely will prevail for most all properties making the jump from tv to pix, was filling out the plot to meet a nearly doubled running time. The dramatic meat that was good for 54 minutes on tv gets ground mighty thin during the film's hour and 41 minutes. Alex Segal, who did the tv directorial chore, repeats here, but he and scripters (also tv) Cyril Hume and Richard Maibaum provide weak filler material, injecting a feeling of phoniness in spots and straining unnecessarily for suspense in others. That long footage could stand tightening, too.

The Nicholas Nayfack production shows what happens to a happy family and, in some respects, to a town, when the family's small son is kidnapped and held for $500,000 ransom. The father can and does raise the money as he's a prosperous industrialist, but the switch comes when he decides not to pay the ransom and goes on television to tell the watching kidnapper why. This is one of the film's big scenes, and could have been bigger if it had not run past its climax. The ransom is to become blood money for the kidnapper's capture, dead or alive, if the child's not returned unharmed. What the father's decision does to his wife, his relatives and to the town curious makes up the rest of the drama before the boy comes back.

Ford is splendid as the father, a role that takes full advantage of his talent for projection. The direction fails to get much out of Miss Reed that can be felt and most of the other players, too, seem at odds with the characters they play, leaving it to Ford to carry off the show. One exception is Juano Hernandez' understanding butler. His big scene is when he comforts the father while the latter wonders if his decision was the right one after it is believed the boy is dead.

A score by Jeff Alexander that never intrudes, and clear, sharp lensing by Arthur E. Arling, head up the generally good technical credits. *Brog.*

The Phantom From 10,000 Leagues

Confused science fiction entry

Hollywood, Dec. 30.

American Releasing Corp. release of Jack and Dan Milner production. Stars Kent Taylor, Cathy Downs, Michael Whalen; features Helene Stanton, Philip Pine, Rodney Bell, Pierce Lyden, Vivi Janiss, Michael Garth. Directed by Dan Milner. Screenplay, Lou Rusoff; original story, Dorys Lukather; camera, Bryden Baker; editors, Milner brothers; music, Ronald Stein. Previewed Dec. 29, '55. Running time, **80 MINS.**

Ted .... Kent Taylor
Lois .... Cathy Downs
King .... Michael Whalen
Wanda .... Helene Stanton
George .... Philip Pine
Bill .... Rodney Bell
Andy .... Pierce Lyden
Ethel .... Vivi Janiss
Sheriff .... Michael Garth

"The Phantom From 10,000 Leagues" is strictly a busher, but will serve its purpose in rounding out a dual ballyhoo bill because of a fairly effective title.

The science-fiction feature, turned out by Jack and Dan Milner, is a confused offering that makes little attempt at seeking thrills with sufficient logic to hold a plot together. Nor is there a clear windup explanation to cue how and why the events took place.

In the Lou Rusoff script from an original by Dorys Lukather, a mutant resulting from radiation exposure guards an underwater atomic light off the shores of California. After several swimmers and fishermen are killed by the monster, the Defense Department and others start an investigation. At the windup, it turns out that a professor at the Pacific College of Oceanography let his experiments get out of hand, but he rights things by destroying the mutant, the light source and himself.

Playing the investigators are Kent Taylor and Rodney Bell, while Cathy Downs is the daughter of prof Michael Whalen. Helene Stanton and Philip Pine appear as spies who want the professor's secret. These and others in the cast have no chance with the material. Dan Milner's direction is slow. Underwater shots of skin divers and the general lensing is handled professionally by Bryden Baker. *Brog.*

The Lone Ranger
(COLOR)

Good western feature, with the longtime radio-video character in typical derring-do.

Hollywood, Jan. 3.

Warner Bros. release of Willis Goldbeck (Jack Wrather) production. Stars Clayton Moore, Jay Silverheels, Lyle Bettger, Bonita Granville; features Perry Lopez, Robert Wilke, John Pickard, Beverly Washburn, Michael Ansara, Frank deKova. Directed by Stuart Heisler. Screenplay, Herb Meadow; based on "The Lone Ranger" legend; camera (WarnerColor), Edwin DuPar; editor, Clarence Kolster; music, David Buttolph. Previewed Dec. 29, '55. Running time, **86 MINS.**

The Lone Ranger .... Clayton Moore
Tonto .... Jay Silverheels
Reece Kilgore .... Lyle Bettger
Welcome .... Bonita Granville
Ramirez .... Perry Lopez
Cassidy .... Robert Wilke
Sheriff Kimberley .... John Pickard
Lila .... Beverly Washburn
Angry Horse .... Michael Ansara
Red Hawk .... Frank de Kova
The Governor .... Charles Meredith
Powder .... Mickey Simpson
Goss .... Zon Murray
Whitebeard .... Lane Chandler

Those who remember the quarter-century ride on radio hill and television vale of the Detroit-produced "Lone Ranger" will find the Warner feature (Jack Wrather) crammed with action and avoiding far-fetched heroics.

Willis Goldbeck produced for Wrather, using the scenic splendor of Southern Utah to provide beautiful backdrop for the Herb Meadow script. Stuart Heisler's direction is actionful and excellent. Some of the fight sequences he stages are thrillingly rugged.

Clayton Moore, in the title role, and Jay Silverheels, as his faithful Tonto, swing over from video and take easily to the big screen size. This time, it's their job to find out what is threatening a peace treaty with the Indians, who, through the machinations of heavy Lyle Bettger, greedy rancher who dreams of an empire, are being made to appear treaty-breakers. The Lone Ranger gets at the truth—Bettger has his eye on a mountain on the reservation which is sacred to the Indians and full of rich silver veins—and in so doing stalls a real Indian uprising. As peace settles on the range he's off to more good deeds to the cry of "Hi Ho, Silver."

Bettger, despite a familiar heavy character to play, gives it a believable touch by never chewing scenery. This ability to make even unbelieveable characters credible has been noticed before in Bettger's performances. Bonita Granville does well as his suffering wife, as does Perry Lopez, cowboy who is killed for trying to help the Lone Ranger. Robert Wilke, Bettger's gunman; John Pickard, Beverly Washburn, Michael Ansara and Frank de Kova are among other cast worthies.

Edwin DuPar's color photography is good and the other technical credits are on a par. *Brog.*

Glory
(SONGS—COLOR)

Sentimental film saga of Kentucky thoroughbreds and people; okay family trade entry.

Hollywood, Jan. 10.

RKO release of David Butler production. Stars Margaret O'Brien, Walter Brennan, Charlotte Greenwood; features John Lupton, Byron Palmer, Lisa Davis, Gus Schilling. Directed by Butler. Screenplay, Peter Milne; story, Gene Markey; camera (Technicolor), Wilfrid M. Cline; editor, Irene Morra; score, Frank Perkins; songs, M. K. Jerome, Ted Koehler. Previewed Jan. 5, '56. Running time, **99 MINS.**

Clarabel Tilbee .... Margaret O'Brien
Ned Otis .... Walter Brennan
Miz Tilbee .... Charlotte Greenwood
Chad Chadburn .... John Lupton
Hoppy Hollis .... Byron Palmer
Candy Trent .... Lisa Davis
Joe Page .... Gus Schilling
Sobbing Sam Cooney .... Hugh Sanders
Doc Brock .... Walter Baldwin
Beed Wickwire .... Harry Tyler
Vasily .... Leonid Kinskey
Squeaky Bob .... Paul E. Burns
Alexander .... Theron Jackson

The Kentucky bluegrass country and its thoroughbreds backstop for this sentimental saga about a filly that wins the Derby. That win puts an exciting climax on the homey little drama being offered through RKO. (Also changes the record for until this pic only one filly had crossed the Derby wire first.) Other than being overlength at 99 minutes, "Glory" is an acceptable family trade entry.

David Butler produced and directed with skill, realizing the most from the material in the Peter Milne script. Based on a story by Gene Markey, the plot offers no surprises but wends a pleasant course through long-familiar situations and the players react in kind. A more grownup, but still not grown, Margaret O'Brien, stars with Walter Brennan and Charlotte Greenwood. Trio pleases in the homey, hokey, doings. So do such other casters as John Lupton, Byron Palmer, in male romantic spots, Lisa Davis, Gus Schilling and Hugh Sanders.

Miss Greenwood and her granddaughter, Miss O'Brien, are shoestring stable operators with a filly named Glory that can't win enough to pay for her feed. That is, until the Derby is run, an event in which she is entered after Brennan, trainer for Lupton's big thoroughbred farm, and sundry stable characters raise the necessary entry fee. Before the big win, though, Miss O'Brien is put through the emotional wringer thinking Lupton is engaged to snippy society Miss Davis and has taken a fling at singing with Palmer's orchestra. Just as Glory grabs the Derby floral horseshoe, so does Miss OBrien get her man in the winners circle.

For the actual worth of the story, picture takes a long time telling it. Some history of racing is narrated throughout and pic has some good scenes of the rich bluegrass region and the equine beauties that roam it. Songwise, there are three M. K. Jerome-Ted Koehler tunes, "Glory," "Gettin' Nowhere Road" and "Kentucky (Means Paradise)." Palmer's good voice gives them something extra, as does the offstage voice (Norma Zimmer) who does the chirping for Miss O'Brien's character.

Technical assists are mostly good, from Wilfrid M. Cline's SuperScope lensing in Technicolor and Frank Perkins' score on down the list. *Brog.*

The Houston Story

Brisk meller for the secondary market; okay b.o. prospects.

Columbia release of Clover (Sam Katzman) production. Stars Gene Barry, Barbara Hale, Edward Arnold; features Paul Richards, Jeanne Cooper, Frank Jenks, John Zaremba, Chris Alcaide, Jack V. Littlefield, Paul Levitt, Fred Krone, Pete Kellett. Directed by William Castle. Screenplay and story, James B. Gordon; camera, Henry Freulich; editor, Edwin Bryant; music, Mischa Bakaleinikoff. Tradeshown, N. Y., Dec. 22, '55. Running time, **79 MINS.**

Frank Duncan .... Gene Barry
Zoe Crane .... Barbara Hale
Paul Atlas .... Edward Arnold
Gordie Shay .... Paul Richards
Madge .... Jeanne Cooper
Louie .... Frank Jenks
Emile Constant .... John Zaremba
Chris Barker .... Chris Alcaide
Willie .... Jack V. Littlefield
Duke .... Paul Levitt
Marsh .... Fred Krone
Kalo .... Pete Kellett
Inspector Gregg .... Leslie Hunt
Clara .... Claudia Bryar
Talbot .... Larry W. Fultz
Stokes .... Charles Gray

Producer Sam Katzman, who turned out a hard hitting meller a couple of seasons ago in "The Miami Story," follows a similar pattern in "The Houston Story." While the former concerned the Florida "mob," this fresh entry is built around a smalltime oil driller with "business" aspirations in a crime syndicate. It adds up to good action fare in the programmer market.

Despite the absence of stout marquee dressing, film nevertheless has some familiar names in Gene Barry, Barbara Hale and Edward Arnold. Moreover, the James B. Gordon story and screenplay contain some exploitable twists that enterprising exhibs can turn to advantage. Another asset is realistic backgrounds indigenous to Houston and the Texas oil country.

Under William Castle's crisp direction Barry contribs a smooth portrayal of a shrewd oil worker who applies his knowledge of the industry to the wrong channels. Conceiving a plan to swipe oil and gasoline from companies in the Houston area, he approaches the syndicate through mob chief Arnold.

Naturally, when the scheme is adopted by Arnold and top man John Zaremba such syndicate underlings as cafe owner Paul Richards and torpedo Chris Alcaide become jealous. Eventually Barry disposes of his adversaries but he himself is seized at the finale when his waitress-girl friend tips off the police. Also turning informer at the windup is his longtime friend, Frank Jenks, whom he had installed as front man in a dummy oil corporation.

Throughout the proceedings is a strong romantic angle via Barry's crush on cafe singer Barbara Hale who's his intermediary with the syndicate bigwigs. While the yarn isn't particularly original, it manages to provide ample opportunity for Barry to convincingly make with the strong arm stuff.

Likewise, Miss Hale's performance helps heighten the general suspense, Arnold, however, is too pat as a syndicate lieutenant. Richards impresses as a suspicious hood, Jenks breezily handles his role as an innocent dupe and Jeanne Cooper is pert as the waitress. Lending good support are Zaremba, Alcaide, Jack V. Littlefield and Paul Levitt, among others.

Camerawork of Henry Freulich is good as is the editing of Edwin Bryant who trimmed the footage to a fast 79 minutes. Producer Katzman provided adequate physical values in keeping with the budget while art direction of Palmentola and the Mischa Bakaleinikoff score are creditable. *Gilb.*

Three Bad Sisters

Formula sex thriller, not too well fashioned, for programmer bookings.

Hollywood, Jan. 6.

United Artists release of Howard W. Koch (Bel-Air) production. Stars Marla English, Kathleen Hughes, Sara Shane, John Bromfield; features Jean Barker, Madge Kennedy. Directed by Gilbert L. Kay. Screenplay, Gerald Dryson Adams; camera, Lester Shorr; editor, John F. Schreyer; music, Paul Dunlap. Previewed Jan. 4, '56. Running time, 76 **MINS.**

Vicki .... Marla English
Valerie .... Kathleen Hughes
Lorna .... Sara Shane
Jim Norton .... John Bromfield
George Gurney .... Jess Barker
Aunt Martha .... Madge Kennedy
Tony Cadiz .... Tony George
Mary .... Patsy Nayfack
Wilson .... Eric Wilton
Carlos .... Brett Halsey
Nadine .... Marlene Felton

The promise of being a passable little sex thriller is held out by "Three Bad Sisters" but it doesn't always deliver. As it is, there is cheesecake and melodrama to sell—the former having value for lobby and ballyhoo ad display—so it should command enough programmer bookings to get by.

Gerald Drayson Adams' story of three sisters, two bad and all neurotic, and the freelance plane pilot who gets mixed up with them unfolds slowly and not too credibly under Gilbert L. Kay's direction. The idea seems okay for the intended release, but the overall execution of it falters so often the customers will be hard to work up a steam over what's transpiring.

Kathleen Hughes is the murderous one of the cutie trio, while Marla English is an amoral sexpot and Sara Shane, the good one, is just as neurotic but without the offbeat tendencies of the others. John Bromfield is the pilot who enters their lives after the plane he is flying crashes and kills their rich father. None of the gals seem particularly upset by dad's death. Miss Hughes schemes to get her two sisters to do away with themselves so she'll control the family wealth, and brings in Bromfield on the plot. He likes the idea of making a dollar, until he ganders Miss Shane, falls in love and marries her. First Miss English takes a suicide out, and then Miss Hughes, when she sees her scheme being wrecked, gets herself killed trying to put Bromfield out of the way. In all those highly meller goingson, Miss Shane shakes off her complexes and the two lovers look forward to a healthy, wealthy life together.

The girls have the curves their roles demand, but Kay's direction and the Adams scripting don't draw the best performances from them. Bromfield is okay under the same handicaps, as are Jess Parker, lawyer who loses Miss Shane to the pilot, and Madge Kennedy, tippling, psycho aunt of the sister trio. Others have small footage.

The Bel-Air production for United Artists release, produced by Howard W. Koch under the executive helming of Aubrey Schenck, obtains good physical values for the budget by assorted location lensing in L. A. environs. Lester Shorr did the good photography and other credits come off okay. *Brog.*

Day the World Ended

Atom bomb obliterates most of humanity in this one. Better of two-film science fiction package.

Hollywood, Dec. 29.

American Releasing Corp. release of Roger Corman (Golden State) production. Stars Richard Denning, Lori Nelson, Adele Jergens; features Touch Connors, Paul Birch, Raymond Hatton, Paul Dubov, Jonathan Haze, Paul Blaisdell. Directed by Corman. Story and screenplay, Lou Rusoff; camera, Jock Feindel; editor, Ronald Sinclair; music, Ronald Stein. Previewed Dec. 28, '55. Running time, **78 MINS.**

Rick .... Richard Denning
Louise .... Lori Nelson
Ruby .... Adele Jergens
Tony .... Touch Connors
Maddison .... Paul Birch
Pete .... Raymond Hatton
Radek .... Paul Dubov
Contaminated Man .... Jonathan Haze
Mutant .... Paul Blaisdell

American Releasing Corp. is packaging this science-fiction melodrama with another thriller, "Phantom From 10,000 Leagues," for exploitation playdates. "Day the World Ended" is the better of the two, packs enough novelty in its plot theme to carry off its horror chores satisfactorily, even though imagination runs away with the subject at times and the dialog is inclined to be static and direction slow-paced. Roger Corman produced and directed from a screen story by Lou Rusoff.

An atomic blast touches off almost total destruction of the world, but seven people, presumably the only survivors, are brought together in a western valley where a former sea captain had prepared a hideway from just such a nuclear explosion. Intended only to shelter three people, the captain and his daughter are joined by a gangster and his ex-striptease girl friend, a young geologist carrying a badly radiation-burned victim of the blast, and an old prospector.

The threat of mutants created by the blast, and the conflict over the captain's daughter between the geologist and gangster, are joined by the shortage of food and water for such a large party. Eventually, all die but Richard Denning, the geologist, and Lori Nelson, the daughter, and at the end they go out into the world to see if there is anything else still living. Thriller angle to the climax has Denning saving her from the clutches of a deformed, three-eyed mutant, apparently created by the nuclear explosion.

Denning, Miss Nelson, Adele Jergens, the stripteaser; Touch Connors, the gangster; Paul Birch, the captain; Raymond Hatton, the prospector; Paul Dubov, the burned man, and others handle the portrayals adequately in the view of the fact no great demands are made by script and direction. The score by Ronald Stein provides an eerie musical background fitting to the subject and Jock Fiendel's camera work is okay. *Brog.*

Fun at St. Fanny's
(BRITISH—CINEMASCOPE)

London, Jan. 3.

Grand Alliance release of British Lion (David Deal) production. Stars Fred Emney, Cardew Robinson. Directed by Maurice Elvey. Screenplay, Antony Verney from story by Peter Noble and Denis Waldock, with additional dialog by Fred Emney; camera, Eric Cross; editor, Robert Hill; music, Edwin Astley. At private Hammer Theatre, London. Running time, **80 MINS.**

Dr. Septimus Jankers .... Fred Emney
Cardew Robinson .... Cardew Robinson
Maisie .... Vera Day
Ferdy .... Davy Kaye
Harry the Scar .... Freddie Mills
Mildred Mainforce .... Miriam Karlin
Mr. Winkle .... Claude Hulbert
McTavish .... Kynaston Reeves
Matron .... Gabrielle Brune
Fudge .... Paul Daneman
Horsetrough .... Roger Avon
Chumleigh .... Ronald Corbett
Praline .... Aud Johansen
Constable .... Tom Gill

Broad, slapstick comedy describes this latest British offering which should have particular appeal for the kids during the vacation period, but only for local consumption. Its main attraction in the West End is its quota ticket.

A straggling story, set in a boy's college, shows a harassed headmaster dodging pressing creditors. Humor is labored and the stock situations handed out with an edge of vulgarity showing nothing new in idea or treatment, utilizing all the immature antics of uncontrollable youngsters.

Fred Emney's massive bulk dominates the scene as the presiding tutor who for years has fattened on a now adult pupil whose trustees give a large annual donation until he gets his passing out certificate, which, of course, the wily head withholds. A plot is hatched to get the "boy" expelled, by planting a stolen painting on him, in which event the school would inherit his fortune. This is thwarted by a snooping private eye employed by the suspicious trustees, and so the elderly scholar finally gets his diploma.

Cardew Robinson, vaude-tv comic, plays himself in the role of protracted adolescent, making a play for the femme staff and extracting many laughs. Miriam Karlin handles the tough female teacher assignment realistically while Gabrielle Brune is the school matron. Vera Day swings a pretty hip as the bookie's chiselling sister. Claude Hulbert contributes his customary fatuous pose as a junior master. Freddie Mills, ex-boxing champ, and Davy Kaye represent the seamy side of the racetrack with conviction. *Clem.*

Wiretapper

Fair meller for the exploitation market.

Embassy Distributors release of Great Commission Films production presented by Continental Pictures; produced by Jim Vaus. Stars Bill Williams, Georgia Lee; features Richard Benedict, Douglas Kennedy, Stanley Clements, Ric Roman, Paul Picerni. Directed by Dick Ross. Screenplay, John O'Day, based on book, "Why I Quit Syndicated Crime," by Jim Vaus; camera, Ralph Woolsey; editor, Eugene Pendleton; music, Ralph Carmichael. Previewed N.Y., Jan. 5, 1953. Running time, 80 MINS. CAST TO COME

"Wiretapper," which also is billed as "The Jim Vaus Story" apparently in an explanatory gesture, is a curious blend of gangsterism and evangelism. Much of the yarn concerns wiretapping and since that field has been in newspaper headlines of late the film obviously is exploitable merchandise.

Strong radio-tv and newspaper campaigns may generate business at the wicket despite the picture's lack of marquee names. However, there will be scant word-of-mouth once audiences have seen this Great Commission Films production. For the John O'Day screenplay as adapted from Vaus' book, "Why I Quit Syndicated Crime," is replete with the usual cliches found in most gangster films. Moreover, Vaus' conversion to Christ "as my personal saviour" comes much too abruptly for conviction in the final reel.

Vaus, who's portrayed in the picture by Bill Williams (tv's Kit Carson), was the black sheep son of a minister according to his autobiography. He stole from a theological school, did time in an Army prison, was an electronics wizard for gambler Mickey Cohen and even devised a system of tapping track results before the bookies got 'em. Converted by evangelist Billy Graham, he renounced his sins and made restitution to those from whom he stole.

His book is an interesting one and in more talented hands might well have emerged into a forceful and compelling story of a man who saw the waste of a chiseler's' life. Instead, for the most part, the film studiously follows the formula used by countless low-budget cops-'n'-robbers pix in the past. Despite the evangelistic overtones in this one, the gangsters don't even atone for their sins. Which, of course, is a cardinal requirement of the Production Code.

Under the circumstances Williams does a fairly good job as Vaus. Georgia Lee has little difficulty in portraying his loyal and understandably distraught wife. Fair support is provided by Rich-

ard Benedict, Douglas Kennedy, Stanley Clements, Ric Roman and Paul Picerni, among others, under Dick Ross' uneven direction. Camerawork of Ralph Woolsey is so-so as is Ralph Carmichael's score and other technical credits. *Gilb.*

Les Carnets Du Major Thompson
(Notebooks of Major Thompson) (FRENCH)

Paris, Jan. 3.

Gaumont release of Gaumont-Paul Wagner production. Stars Martine Carol, Noel-Noel, Jack Buchanan; features Totti Truman Taylor, Andre Luguet. Genevieve Brunet. Catherine Boll. Directed by Preston Sturges. Screenplay, Sturges from book by Pierre Daninos; camera, Maurice Barry, Christian Matras; editor, Raymond Lanny. At Berlitz, Paris. Running time, 105 MINS.

Major Thompson	Jack Buchanan
Martine	Martine Carol
Taupin	Noel-Noel
Nurse	Totti Truman Taylor
Editor	Andre Luguet
Secretary	Genevieve Brunet
First Wife	Catherine Boil

Preston Sturges has made his first French film from a bestseller here which was primarily a series of essays supposedly written by a retired English major. These gave his reactions to French life after settling down in Paris with a lovely, frivolous French woman he had married. Pic puts the transcription on two levels, tying in the major's writing of his analysis of French life to his own marital difficulties caused by his and the wife's divergent views on bringing up their child. As a result, it offers sketchy aspects of both sides, and is somewhat lightweight. Film does have some excellent moments and satirical gambits, but a thin story plus primarily French and Anglo humor peg this for special spots in the U.S. It might also have arty prospects.

An English version also has been made, which is not to be released in the U.S. before January of 1957 because of an agreement between Gaumont and 20th-Fox which has star Martine Carol under contract for her first U.S. pic. If she scores in this American film, this production might slide in for general situations on her name. Otherwise, its humor and slight story, plus its barely outlined characters, make this dubious for regular runs and best for dualers.

Stereotyped battle over the upbringing of their child and argument over the English and French viewpoints of history are somewhat telegraphed in effects, though disarming candor makes for some yocks. The major's (Jack Buchanan) chronicling of his attitudes towards France engender the funniest scenes, with Noel-Noel scoring as the average Frenchman type.

Sturges has used slow and fast motion, commentary over some clever scenes on French eating habits and bureaucracy plus some slapstick scenes of the major's courtship of his horsefaced English first wife. These are the best parts of the pic. Martine Carol, one of the top film stars here, now has her own lenser for her scenes. As the Gallic wife, she sometimes simpers, but her luscious qualities, unveiled by daring necklines, makes it evident why the major preferred her to his first wife. Buchanan is properly the reserved major while Noel-Noel gets the lion's share of the footage as the little Frenchman. Lensing is good and editing adroitly coordinates

this patchwork film. Film looks to do well here. *Mosk.*

All For Mary
(BRITISH-COLOR)

London, Dec. 27.
Moderately entertaining British farce set in winter sports resort; okay for home trade, but restricted overseas appeal.

J. Arthur Rank production and release. Stars Nigel Patrick, Kathleen Harrison, David Tomlinson, Jill Day. Directed by Wendy Toye. Screenplay, Peter Blackmore and Paul Soskin; camera, Reginald Wyer; editor, Frederick Wilson; music, Robert Farnon. At Gaumont Theatre, London, Dec. 21, '55. Running time, 79 MINS.

Clive Morton	Nigel Patrick
Nannie Cartwright	Kathleen Harrison
Humpy Miller	David Tomlinson
Mary	Jill Day
M. Victor	David Hurst
Gaston Mikopopoulos	Leo McKern
Mrs. Hackenfleuger	Joan Young
Maitre d'Hotel	Lionel Jeffries
Alphonse	Neil Hallett
General	Nicholas Phipps
Porter	Paul Hardtmuth
Opulent Lady	Fabia Drake
Doctor	Charles Lloyd Pack
Ski Instructor	Guy Deghy
W.R.A.C. Orderly	Dorothy Gordon
American Boy	Robin Brown
Bruiser	Tommy Farr

A modest stage success in the West End last season, "All For Mary" has been brought to the screen with a cast of local players who will give the pic a reasonable marquee quality for home consumption. It is a film which will appeal mainly in the domestic market and has only limited prospects overseas.

Treated along conventional farce lines, the screenplay allows a broader canvas by embracing the scenic potentialities of a winter sports resort in Switzerland. This is the only background material, however, and the plot keeps rigidly to its basic clash of personalities in which two English tourists are rivals for the hotel keeper's daughter, in opposition to a wealthy but impossible Greek tourist.

This is all very immature comedy stuff, making no pretension toward sophistication and relying for reaction on broad farce situations.

The performers are in the right key, and apart from the two male stars, David Tomlinson and Nigel Patrick, Kathleen Harrison collars top honors as the woman who can only converse in nursery rhymes. Jill Day is a lush newcomer, who sings adequately and looks attractive enough. David Hurst as a voluble hotel proprietor and Leo McKern as the defeated suitor are at the head of an average supporting cast. Wendy Toye's direction displays an adequate vigor while Peter Blackmore and Paul Soskin with their screenplay have kept the basic laughs in their screenplay. *Myro.*

There's Always Tomorrow

Father - praising lightweight domestic triangle with tension omitted. Outlook so-so.

Hollywood, Jan. 12.
Universal release of Ross Hunter production. Stars Barbara Stanwyck, Fred MacMurray. Joan Bennett; costars William Reynolds, Pat Crowley, Gigi Perreau; features Jane Darwell, Race Gentry, Myrna Hansen, Judy Nugent, Paul Smith, Helen Kleeb. Directed by Douglas Sirk. Screenplay, Bernard C. Schoenfeld; story, Ursula Parrott; camera, Russell Metty; editor, William M. Morgan; music, Herman Stein, Heinz Roemheld. Previewed Jan. 9, '56. Running time, 88 MINS.

Norma	Barbara Stanwyck
Clifford Groves	Fred MacMurray
Marion Groves	Joan Bennett
Vinnie	William Reynolds
Ann	Pat Crowley
Ellen	Gigi Perreau
Mrs. Rogers	Jane Darwell
Bob	Race Gentry
Ruth	Myrna Hansen
Frankie	Judy Nugent
Bellboy	Paul Smith
Miss Walker	Helen Kleeb
Flower Girl	Jane Howard
Ruth Doren	Frances Mercer
Woman From Pasadena	Sheila Bromley
Sales Manager	Dorothy Bruce
Tourist's Wife	Hermine Sterler
Tourist	Fred Nurney
Bartender	Hal Smith

Neglected kids, mothers and wives have been variously explored in films. Now "There's Always Tomorrow" gives dad his turn at bat, but during his rebellion against playing second-fiddle to family this pop never gets into any real trouble, nor do his wife and kids learn any lasting lesson. That's the key to the pic's general lack of dramatic excitement. Prospects are spotty.

Fred MacMurray, successful toy manufacturer, is the father who rates a secondary spot in the activities of his wife, Joan Bennett, and their offspring, William Reynolds, Gigi Perreau and Judy Nugent. Along comes Barbara Stanwyck, an old flame of 20 years back, and pop begins to feel younger. The tepid renewal of old feelings reaches the point where MacMurray is willing to throw everything over for Miss Stanwyck. In the nick of time, she has a visit from pop's teenage children and decides to leave dad with his family. Through it all, Miss Bennett is serenely unaware of pop's problem, so things take up again just as they were without anything ever having happened.

The even-paced, almost placid scripting of the Ursual Parrott story by Bernard C. Schoenfeld gives the Douglas Sirk direction very little on which to hang some dramatic punch. Nearest thing to conflict is the wrong interpretation placed on early meetings between the wouldbe middleaged lovers by dad's teenage son, Reynolds. In casting and general supervision, Ross Hunter's production capitalizes on the basic soap opera values, without adding any distinctive thing to help put the show over. The three older stars perform smoothly, if unexcitingly, while the costarring younger trio of Reynolds, Pat Crowley, his friend, and Miss Perreau, along with little Miss Nugent, are competent in pointing up youth's tendency to dramatize trifles. Others have little footage.

Russell Metty's lensing is good, as are the art direction and settings. Score is of the hearts-and-flowers variety as cleffed by Herman Stein and Heinz Roemheld. *Brog.*

Fury at Gunsight Pass

Good western drama for program action market.

Hollywood, Jan. 13.

Columbia release of Wallace MacDonald production. Stars David Brian, Neville Brand, Richard Long; features Lisa Davis, Katharine Warren, Percy Helton, Morris Ankrum, Addison Richards, Joe Forte, Wally Vernon. Directed by Fred F. Sears. Story and screenplay, David Lang; camera, Fred Jackman Jr.; editor, Saul Goodkind; music, Mischa Bakaleinikoff. Previewed Jan. 9, '56. Running time, **66 MINS.**

Whitey Turner .... David Brian
Dirk Hogan .... Neville Brand
Roy Hanford .... Richard Long
Kathy Phillips .... Lina Davis
Mrs. Boggs .... Katharine Warren
Boggs .... Percy Helton
Doc Phillips .... Morris Ankrum
Charles Hanford ...... Addison Richards
Andrew Ferguson .... Joe Forte
Okay, Okay .... Wally Vernon
Squint .... Paul E. Burns
Sheriff Meeker .... Frank Fenton
O'Neil .... James Anderson
Daley .... George Keymas
Sam Morris .... Robert Anderson
Spencer .... Fred Coby
Forrest .... John Lehmann
Hammond .... Guy Teague

As a character study of what happens to a small town when some bank holdup loot gets misplaced, "Fury At Gunsight Pass" attempts rather too much for its budget and the 66-minute running time. However, amidst all the complex plot lines and characterizations, it still achieves a good pace and shapes up as acceptable western drama for the program action market.

Director Fred F. Sears does a rather satisfactory job of handling the varied ramifications in the David Lang screen story, leaving few angles dangling at the windup. Pic starts off as a robber double-cross, with David Brian out to hold up a bank before the time set by gang leader Neville Brand. In the shuffle the loot gets lost, having been purloined by Percy Helton, town undertaker. When he's killed by a stray bullet, his widow, Katharine Warren, recovers the money, planning to sneak off with it in the excitement of a town search being conducted by the outlaws. There are quite a few other plot angles, too, before the money finds its way back to the bank and the robbers and town crooks meet justice.

The above named players do right well at their chores, with performance assists coming from Richard Long, banker's son who aids the roundup of the killers of his dad. Addison Richards; Lisa Davis, his fiancee; Joe Forte, partner in the bank; Wally Vernon, doing well as a comedy robber, and others. Casting and thesping in the Wallace MacDonald production is above average for this type budget film.

Fred Jackman Jr.'s camera work also is above average and the other technical contributions good.

Brog.

Adorable Creatures
(FRENCH)

Continental Distributing release of Roitfeld-Sirius-C. V. C. production. Stars Martine Carol, Edwige Feuillere, Danielle Darrieux, Antonella Lualdi, Daniel Gelin; features Renee Faure, Marilyn Bufferd, Daniel Lecourtois, Louis Seigner. Directed by Christian-Jaque; screenplay and adaptation, Christian-Jaque, Charles Spaak, Jacques Companeez; camera, Christian Matras; music, de Van Parys. Previewed Jan. 5, '55. Running time, **108 MINS.**

Andre .... Daniel Gelin
Catherine .... Antonella Lualdi
Christiane .... Danielle Darrieux
Minouche .... Martine Carol
Denise .... Edwige Feuillere
Alice .... Renee Faure
Evelyn .... Marilyn Bufferd
Jacques .... Daniel Lecourtois
M. Dubreuil .... Louis Seigner
Catherine's Mother .... Marie Glory
Catherine's Father .... Georges Chamarat
Pianist .... Jean-Marc Tennberg

(In French; English Titles)

"Adorable Creatures" is probably the kind of French film Americans hope to see when they go to see a French film. This is not to say that it's particularly good, that it will win any prizes or, for that matter, that it is done in good taste. But the fact remains that it is one of the sexiest concoctions dished up by the French in quite some time and director Christian-Jaque has imbued it with a light touch that, at points, is thoroughly diverting.

Its satirical tone makes (or saves) this lightweight import. It isn't something to be taken serious and consequently its grave lapses of taste are less likely to attract harsh criticism. Vaguely suggesting Clare Boothe Luce's "The Women," except that there is at least one prominent male involved — Daniel Gelin — and there literally isn't one ordinary female on the premises. They're all either nutty, or scheming, or sex crazy. And this again, regardless of what the critics and the censors are going to say, smells suspiciously of box-office.

Story of "Adorable Creatures" is really not much more than an excuse for Gelin to engage in some sexy shenanigans, including one undressing scene with Danielle Darrieux which comes close to being vulgar and offensive. Gelin tells his bride, Antonella Lualdi, that he's never loved anyone but her, and in turn is called a liar by the offscreen commentator who proceeds to recreate Gelin's life and his women.

Latter include Miss Darrieux as the married woman enjoying an affair; Martine Carol as a shapely golddigger; the tomboyish Miss Lualdi; Edwige Feuillere as a flirtatious widow who is a patron of the arts and makes proteges of artists (who become her "houseguests"); Renee Faure, as a reformed thief and Marilyn Bufferd as a tramp. One of the characters plays a cigar-smoking lesbian and Continental Distributing would be well advised to trim these scenes to the absolute minimum as they are offensive and completely unnecessary.

Gelin is perfect as the brooding young man with the active love life and director Christian-Jaque kids the character enough to take him out of the feeling of reality. Miss Carol goes into her usual undressing act, but looks good; Miss Faure is outstanding as Alice, the petty thief; Miss Feuillere overplays badly as the widow; Louis Seigner is excellent as the sugar-daddy character and Georges Chamarat excels in a character part.

Script by Chrstian-Jaque, Charles Spaak and Jacques Companeez doggedly makes the point that sex and its byplays can be taken lightly. Most of the time, they succeed.

Hift.

Two-Gun Lady

Okay filler fare predominated by heroine heroics.

Hollywood, Jan. 2.

Associated Film Releasing Corporation release of a Richard H. Bartlett production. Stars Peggy Castle, William Talman, Marie Windsor; features Earle Lyon, Joe Besser, Robert Lowery. Directed by Bartlett. Screenplay, Norman Jolley; from story by Jolley and Bartlett; camera, Guy Roe; editor, Carl Pierson; music, Leon Klatzkin. Reviewed Jan. 11, '56. Running time, **74 MINS.**

Kate Masters .... Peggy Castle
Dan Corbin .... William Talman
Bess .... Marie Windsor
Ben Ivers .... Earle Lyon
Doc M'Ginnis .... Joe Besser
"Big Mike" Dougherty.... Robert Lowery
Jenny Ivers .... Barbara Turner
Jud Ivers .... Ian MacDonald
Gruber .... Norman Jolley

"Two-Gun Lady" stacks up as adequate outdoor program fare, mixing up heroine heroics and standard western action gimmicks in such a way as probably to please the not-too-demanding devotee of this type of picture.

Screenplay by Norman Jolley, from an original he wrote in collaboration with Richard Bartlett, brings Peggy Castle, the lady of the title, back to a one-hoss town to revenge the death of her parents, murdered years previous by the outlaw son of the town's crooked boss. With help from William Talman, a U.S. Marshal posing as a drifter, the baddies are all rounded up and headed for justice at the wind-up, while Miss Castle and Talman are headed for the preacher.

Miss Castle totes her guns in good fashion and manages to be convincing in the title role. Talman is okay as male lead and Marie Windsor, also starred, gets by as a barroom hussy. The heavies are played adequately by Earle Lyon (who's also exec producer of the film), Ian MacDonald (the associate producer), and Norman Jolley (who co-authored the original and wrote the screenplay). Turning in a noticeable stint is young and personable Barbara Turner.

Richard H. Bartlett functions capably as both producer and director. The musical score by Leon Klatzkin is good, the other technical contributions stock.

Neal.

I Killed Wild Bill Hickok
(COLOR)

Weak western for least discriminating market.

Hollywood, Jan. 12.

Wheeler Co. presentation of John Carpenter production. Stars John Forbes, Helen Westcott; features Tom Brown, Virginia Gibson, Denver Pyle, Frank "Red" Carpenter, Stan Jolley, R. J. Thomas, Ray Canada, Harvey Dunn. Directed by Richard Talmadge. Screenplay, John Carpenter; camera, Virgil Miller; editor, Marvin Wright. Reviewed Jan. 11, '56. Running time, **63 MINS.**

Johnny Rebel .... John Forbes
Bell Longtree .... Helen Westcott
Wild Bill Hickok .... Tom Brown
Ann James .... Virginia Gibson
Jim Bailey .... Denver Pyle
Ring Pardo ..... Frank "Red" Carpenter
Henry Longtree .... Stan Jolley
Tommy .... R. J. Thomas
Nato .... Ray Canade
Doc Reid .... Harvey Dunn
Tex .... Bill Chaney
Arizona Kid .... Bron Delar
Poncho .... Phil Barton
Dan .... Bill Mims
Bronco .... Billy Dean
Kate .... Lee Sheldon

Good exploitation title but otherwise misses on every count. Picture is handicapped by lack of story substance and continuity, unrealistic performances and unusually poor technical work.

Wild Bill Hickok is the heavy hero, in on cheating the U.S. Government in a horse deal for the cavalry, while sporting his sheriff's star. Hero is a former gunman, who rounds up wild horses for cavalry and who shoots it out with Wild Bill on the street in an unexciting climax.

John Carpenter, who both wrote and produced, draws heavily on unmatched color stock footage for number of sequences, while starring under name of John Forbes as man who killed Hickok. Tom Brown plays Hickok like an old-fashioned villain, and director Richard Talmadge has an impossible task with script, which he never assists.

Whit.

Guitars of Love
(GERMAN-MUSIC-COLOR)

United German Film Enterprises release of Willy Zeyn production. Stars Vico Torriani, Elma Karlowa, Topsy Kuppers. Directed by Werner Jacobs. Camera (Eastmancolor), Oskar Schnirch; music, Willy Mattes. Tradeshown in N.Y., Jan. 12, '56. Running time, **92 MINS.**

Roberto Trenti .... Vico Torriani
Enrico Mantovani.... Annunzio Montavani
Ilona Mirko .... Elma Karlowa
Gisa .... Topsy Kuppers
Fred Jaques .... Ralph Lothar
Walter .... Harald Juhnke
Tom .... Gerd Vespermann
Paul .... Horst Uhse
Bernardo .... Hermann Pfeiffer
and
Mantovani and his orchestra

(In German; English titles)

"Guitars of Love" is one of the better German musicals to come over to the U.S. since the war. With Vico Torriani, Elma Karlowa and Topsy Kuppers in the principal roles and Ralph Lothar and Hermann Pfeiffer as strong support, this one plays a lot more smoothly than its innocuous plot might indicate. Pic is strong enough to get American bookings outside of German-language houses, and is surefire for Teutonic lingo spots.

Basically, this is a yarn about an aspiring young male singer (Torriani, Italian tenor), who finds that his skill as a mechanic does not pay much. Finally he takes the plunge and heads for Rome to make a vocal career. Oddly, the plot has a name orch of the Italian capital seeking him at about the time he has decided to cast his lot with a "Hot Four" a musical combo of traveling musicians. However, the femme warbler with w.k. Mantovani orchestra, who is leaving her job, persuades him to step into her shoes. But, she falls in love with him before Torriani, as the unknown singer, finally quits his instrumental foursome for the name orch.

Topflight direction by Werner Jacobs, excellent camera work (Eastmancolor) by Oscar Schnirch and uniformly fine performances make this familiar story jell.

Torriani not only has a fine voice but also adds a sparkling personality to his performance as the aspiring young vocalist Miss Karlowa, as the name-band warbler, makes her characterization fit admirably into the context of the story, and fitting into the love story with realism. Miss Kuppers, the femme instrumentalist and clown with the "Hot Four," is excellent. Photographed properly, she looms as a Hollywood bet.

Lothar makes the band tour manager sufficiently villainous to make him thoroughly detested. Annunzio Mantovani, maestro of the Mantovani orch, portrays himself, and does amazingly well. Pfeiffer as a manager is a likeable character, easily topping the support.

Music by Willy Mattes is worth remembering with the several numbers by the Mantovani band neatly interwoven into the story for superb returns. Harald Juhnke, Gerd Vespermann and Horst Uhse are the other three members of the "Hot Four," and better instrumentalists than actors.

Wear.

Anything Goes
(MUSICAL—COLOR)

Sock Crosby-O'Connor tintuner with bright b.o. looming.

Hollywood, Jan. 23.

Paramount release of Robert Emmett Dolan production. Stars Bing Crosby Donald O'Conner, Jeanmaire, Mitzi Gaynor, Phil Harris. Directed by Robert Lewis. Screenplay, Sidney Sheldon; from the play by Guy Bolton, P. G. Wodehouse; revised by Howard Lindsay, Russell Crouse; music and lyrics by Cole Porter; camera (Technicolor), John F. Warren; editor, Frank Bracht; music arranged and conducted by Joseph J. Lilley; special orchestral arrangements. Van Cleave; new songs, Sammy Cahn, James Van Heusen; choreography, Nick Castle; Jeanmaire ballet staged by Roland Petit; title dance number staged by Ernie Platt. Previewed Jan. 13, '56. Running time, **106 MINS.**

Bill Benson	Bing Crosby
Ted Adams	Donald O'Connor
Gaby Duval	Jeanmaire
Patsy Blair	Mitzi Gaynor
Steve Blair	Phil Harris
Victor Lawrence	Kurt Kasznar
Ed Brent	Richard Erdman
Alex Todd	Walter Sande
Otto	Archer MacDonald
Suzanne	Argentina Brunetti
French Baroness	Alma Macrorie
German Woman	Dorothy Neumann
Paul Holiday	James Griffith

Paramount starts the new year off with a sock musical package, borrowing the title and songs from that yesteryear stage hit, "Anything Goes." It's a bright offering for Easter release, geared to play an engaging tune at the wickets.

Male topliners Bing Crosby and Donald OConnor go together as though born to give the zip to what scripter Sidney Sheldon has concocted here under the stage title. While there are Cole Porter songs and the legit handle is still carried, that's about all that remains of what went on behind the footlights, and there's scant resemblance to Paramount's 1936 film version, in which Crosby also starred with Ethel Merman.

Refurbishing and general freshening is pulled off with great aplomb and Robert Lewis direction keeps every one of the 106 minutes of footage rolling at a merry pace. The art direction and staging of the musical numbers are notable in more ways in one for eye and ear pleasure. Choice of the two femme stars, Jeanmaire and Mitzi Gaynor, both leggy and appealing, is a click factor. Neither has had better opportunity in pix and each delivers in a manner that should bolster future film chances. Those scant Edith Head costumes in which each displays the terp spots are a big plus, too.

Script provides Crosby with plenty of those sotto voce, throwaway cracks he and his fans dote on, as well as an overall comedic setup against which to bounce the musical numbers. Plot, simply, has Crosby and O'Connor agreeing to do a B'way musical together after European vacations. Abroad, each signs a femme star and the remainder concerns fitting the gals in with previous plans.

Jeanmaire has two ballets that are clicks. First is "I Get a Kick Out of You,' staged by Roland Petit, and for which she wears an incredibly tight, closer-than-skin, black outfit. Second is the "Dream Ballet," with a Times Square setting staged by Nick Castle, that segues from the Crosby crooning of "All Through the Night" to the dancer. In addition to the terp work, Jeanmaire unleashes a piquant personality that catches on big.

Miss Gaynor, in brief dance attire that will almost cause gasps—certainly second looks—belts the title tune staged by Ernie Platt to score solidly in her solo showcasing. She's back later with O'Connor to give punch to the singing and dancing to "It's Delovely." Off this pic, Miss Gaynor looks on her way up. Finale production number uses the four principals in an imaginatively staged "Blow, Gabriel, Blow" directed by Castle.

Musical humor gets an early start when Crosby and O'Connor pop all the corn possible on "Ya Gotta Give the People Hoke," one of the new Sammy Cahn-James Van Heusen tunes. It's a howler, as is "A Second-Hand Turban & A Crystal Ball," also new, which the two males work over later in the footage. O'Connor has a good solo song-dance in "You Can Bounce Right Back," working with rubber balls and moppets. A clever tuneterp sequence is the rehearsal aboardship to "You're the Top," in which Crosby and Miss Gaynor, O'Connor and Jeanmaire work out without being aware of the other team.

Phil Harris has a top billing as Miss Gaynor's father, who has long exiled himself abroad to avoid an income tax rap. The way the story lines up he has little chance. Kurt Kasznar, Walter Sande, Argentina Brunetti and uncredited Marcel Dalio, as ship's captain, have their moments in the general funning.

The production responsibility carried by Robert Emmett Dolan is executed with showmanship to put this one among the top musical pix. Technical assists are topflight, from John F. Warren's striking VistaVision lensing in Technicolon on down. Aiding the musical side is the arranging and conducting by Joseph J. Lilley and the special orchestral arrangements by Van Cleave. Tom Keogh shares costuming credit for his ballet designs. *Brog.*

Der Major und Die Stiere
(The Major and the Steers) (GERMAN)

Berlin, Jan. 17.

Allianz release of Allianz and Buchne-und-Film production. Stars Attila Hoerbiger, Fritz Tillmann, Christel Wessely-Hoerbiger and Hans von Borsody. Directed by Eduard von Borsody. Screenplay, Per Schwenzen and Eduard von Borsody after novel of same title by Hans Venatier; camera, Walter Riml; music, Bert Grund. At Capitol, Berlin. Running time, **96 MINS.**

Kolterner	Atilla Hoerbiger
Major Sunlet	Fritz Tillmann
Marie	Christel Wessely-Hoerbiger
Schorsch	Hans von Borsody
Segt. Bobby	Chris Howland
Frau Wendland	Eva Probst
Sigrid	Ingrid Lutz
Midwife	Carsta Loeck
Landrat Spiegel	Alexander Golling
Lieut. Houseman	Ulrich Beiger
Saeusepp	Karl Meixner

Another Teutonic film centering around American occupation forces in postwar Germany. Basically, theme appears original and could have furnished the basis for a witty farce. This one, however, is neither fish nor fowl. In most instances, it's corny slapstick, often lacking any plausibility and conviction. The fun that is poked at fraternization, American democracy and education is too amateurish. Nevertheless, pic contains a good number of substantial laughs for domestic audiences. Internationally, film will hardly contribute to prestige for German films.

"Major and Steers" opens in 1945 when U. S. troops occupy a Bavarian village, and then centers around Americans and Germans and the new problems posed on them living side by side. The Americans in this are mostly nice people, it's true, but mostly acting stupid as well. By all means, the better cleverness is on the part of these Bavarian peasants, and one almost gets the impression that it's them who teach the Americans what real democracy is. One also may ask: How did those fellows get through the 12 Nazi years?

Film cannot be called anti-American because the principal figure is an American major, who is greatly honored finally by the Bavarian villagers and he leaves them as a truly great friend. Yet film is not beneficial to the U. S. since American methods are executed stupidly.

Fritz Tillmann, wk stage actor, as the U. S. Major displays great skill while Attila Hoerbiger, the headstrong Bavarian peasant, is very good. Film also has two new faces: Hans von Borsody (son of this film's director, Eduard von Borsody) and Christel Wessely-Hoerbiger, daughter of Paula Wessely. Both supply the romantic interest. Englishman Chris Howland, who achieved some popularity here as disk jockey, portrays a good-natured American sergeant, Alexander Golling shows up as the bad German. Ulrich Belger contributes an unconvincing study of an American CIC officer.

Direction by Eduard von Borsody is only of provincial standards. A nice standard shows up in Walter Riml's lensing while Bert Grund's score is often fine. *Hans.*

Postmark for Danger

Fair British-lensed whodunit for secondary bookings.

Hollywood, Jan. 18.

RKO release of Frank Godwin (Todon) production. Stars Terry Moore, Robert Beatty, William Sylvester; features Geoffrey Keen, Josephine Griffin. Directed by Guy Green. Screenplay, Ken Hughes, Guy Green; original, Francis Durbridge; camera, Wilkie Cooper; editor, Peter Taylor; score, John Veale. Previewed Jan. 16, '56. Running time, **77 MINS.**

Alison Ford	Terry Moore
Tim Forrester	Robert Beatty
Dave Forrester	William Sylvester
Jill Stewart	Josephine Griffin
Inspector Colby	Geoffrey Keen
Henry Carmichael	Alan Cuthbertson
John Smith	Henry Oscar
Reg Dorking	William Lucas
Fenby	Terence Alexander

As a British-lensed whodunit thriller, "Postmark for Danger" averages out as a fair offering for the programmer market. Only familiar name is that of Terry Moore, so bookings will be mostly lowercase.

The Todon (Tony Owen) production being released through RKO spins a murder mystery from the pen of Francis Durbridge, which Ken Hughes and Guy Green scripted for the latter's direction. Its main line concerns a diamond-smuggling ring bringing gems into England from Europe. Before the ring is busted, there are six bodies and a flowering romance between Robert Beatty, artist, and Miss Moore, a gal who is innocent but involved because her dad's one of the crooks.

Frank Godwin's production supervision gains from the overseas locales for the melodramatics and, considering release aims, generally comes off with an average score. Miss Moore, while contributing to the chances for domestic bookings, adds nothing to the performances. However, the thesping is well taken care of by the British casters, all of whom do their work excellently considering the light demands of script and direction.

Beatty shows up nicely as the artist for a time suspected by inspector Geoffrey Keen from Scotland Yard. William Sylvester plays Beatty's brother who is mixed up with the ring and among the other crooks are Alan Cuthbertson, Henry Oscar and William Lucas. Femme honors go to Josephine Griffin, a British looker who gives a decided lift to the role of artist's model and who is killed off too soon in the footage.

Technical assists, including the lensing by Wilkie Cooper, are satisfactory for budget. *Brog.*

Last of the Desperados

Vengeance-seeking admirers of Billy the Kid get theirs in okay western.

Hollywood, June 19.

Associated Film Releasing Corporation release of a Sigmund Neufeld production. Stars James Craig, Jim Davis, Barton MacLane, Margia Dean; features Dona Martal, Myrna Dell, Bob Steele, Stanley Clements. Directed by Sam Newfield. Story and screenplay, Orville Hampton; camera, Eddie Linden.; editor, Holbrook Todd; sound, Ben Winkler; music, Paul Dunlap. Reviewed Jan. 18, '56. Running time, **70 MINS.**

Pat Garrett	James Craig
John W. Poe	Jim Davis
Mosby	Barton MacLane
Sarita	Marcia Dean
Paulita	Dona Martel
Clara	Myrna Dell
Bowdre	Bob Steele
Bert	Stanley Clements

There will, of course, continue to be many desperados in many features yet unmade, but "Last of the Desperados" wipes out five of 'em, including Billy the Kid—again. Overall, release shapes as a good programmer, with story line sustaining interest and James Craig coming through with a good performance in the lead role.

Craig takes the part of Pat Garrett, the sheriff who ends Billy's career, in this Orville Hampton story, which the author has also screenplayed. It appears, though, that Billy was a hero to half the people in his area, not to mention four gunslingers who remain from his gang, and who, to settle the score, plan to get Craig. After several innocent persons are killed by the gang, Craig, with no backing from the townspeople, resigns and moves to another town under an alias, believing this will save lives. It doesnt work, so back goes his sheriff's badge again and the four baddies, who'd traced him, are soon sprawled in the dust—dead.

Craig dominates the footage with a strong credible job. Others in the cast, all subordinated, are Jim Davis, okay as a deputy sheriff; Barton MacLane and Bob Steele, fair as gang members; and Margia Dean, Dona Martel and Myrna Dell, all routine as feminine dressing.

As produced by Sigmund Neufeld, pic shows its modest budget physically, but other departments shape up adequately. Sam Newfield's direction is good, highlighting the action values without sacrificing plot. *Neal.*

Boris Godunov
(RUSSIAN-COLOR)

Sovexportfilm release of Mosfilm production. Directed by V. Stroyeva. Screenplay, N. Golovanov, Stroyeva, based on Moussorgsky-Pushkin opera; camera, V. Nikolayev; sets, V. Kiselyov, E. Serganov. At Cameo, N.Y., Jan. 21, '56. Running time, **105 MINS.**

Boris Godunov	A. Pirogov
False Dmitri	G. Nellep
Varlaam	A. Krivchenya
Fool	I. Kozlovsky
Marina	L. Avdeyeva

The Russians, with all the people and funds needed at their disposal, have come up with a noteworthy opera picture in "Boris Godunov." Done in gaudy color, the film is a faithful recreation of the Moussorgsky-Pushkin stagework, in a lavish, sprawling music-piece full of pageantry, pomp and spectacle. Massive sets, huge crowds, rich costumes, heightened color, all contribute to the splendor. Crowds are handled artfully (both camera and director-wise); leads have been chosen carefully, and result is a rich musical masterpiece of medieval Russia.

The episodic quality of the opera libretto is eased somewhat here; the story-line is simpler and flows more intelligibly. True, the pic is still an opera, and "Boris" is a somewhat static, slow-paced one. Musically, it lacks set arias in the main, the music instead advancing the action dramatically. But the rich, undisciplined melodies flow steadily throughout the film (as in the opera), and longhairs will get their money's-worth here.

Telling the story of a conscience-stricken, murderous Czar and the revolt against him of a false pretender, and going off into tangents with scenes at country inns, in the Polish as well as the Russian court, in public squares; the film paints a rich picture of a rebellious, downtrodden people, full of drama, emotion and religious fervor. And this permits for some striking scenes—the crowds before the palace, the Coronation scene, the mad scene. Handling of the crowds catches the eye; so do some of the lavish costumes of the courts.

As to the leads, A. Pirogov is an impressive Boris, visually, thespically and vocally, with a deep, stirring bass that conveys all the pathos and drama of his role. The monolog about his guilt is high-grade art. A. Krivchenya is an imposing-looking and rich-bassoed Varlaam, whose earthy drinking song in the inn scene is also one of the film's great moments. G. Nellep sings resonantly and acts convincingly as the false Dmitri, and L. Avdeyeva is an ample though attractive Marina opposite him. Their duet in the garden of the Polish court is very appealing.

Bron.

Lola Montes
(FRANCO-GERMAN)
(C'Scope-Color)

Paris, Jan. 17.

Gamma Film release of Gamma-Florida-Union Film production. Stars Martine Carol, Peter Ustinov, Anton Walbrook; features Oskar Werner. Directed by Max Ophuls. Screenplay, Ophuls, Annette Wademant from novel by Ceceil Saint-Laurent; camera (Eastmancolor), Christian Matras; music, Georges Auric; editor, Madeleine Gug. At Marignan, Paris. Running time, **110 MINS.**

Lola Montes	Martine Carol
Ringmaster	Peter Ustinov
King of Bavaria	Anton Walbrook
Student	Oscar Werner
James	Ivan Desny
Liszt	Will Quadfleig
Maurice	Henri Guisol
Mrs. Craig	Lise Delamare

Max Ophuls brought this three-version film (English, French and German), in for a whopping negative cost of over $2,000,000. A lush color vehicle, relating the life story of a 19th Century courtesan, this has marquee names for Gallic and Germano markets in Martine Carol, Anton Walbrook and Oskar Werner, but lacks the same appeal in the U.S. Its arty treatment slants this primarily for arty houses but it is limited there because of its widescreen C'Scope. If Miss Carol ever gets around to her slated debut with 20th-Fox, and makes it, this pic could slide in on her name. Otherwise its treatment and offbeat qualities make this production problematical, at best in the general U.S. mart.

Treatment of the lady of easy virtue's life is done via flashbacks while she is being exhibited in a strangely stylized circus somewhere in America. Sketchy method of handling the subject rarely allows sympathy to be built for the much manhandled heroine or to adequately formulate the essential of the eternal woman the film is striving for. Miss Carol, as Lola Montes, lacks the depth needed. She looks good but never seems to display the temperament required.

Ophuls has given this elegant mounting and the C'Scope has lush and knowing framing. He used iris-type blacking out of the corners of the screen for more intimate scenes, and even the old fashioned iris-out at times plus fancy camera movements. Clever associations tie together the flashback episodes with the weird circus settings. However, most of film fashioning is gratuitous and little meat remains on this clever, dashing treatment.

Some fetching period observation appears from time to time, but life is rarely breathed into this frilly opus which is graced by Ophuls' usual filmic finesse. Peter Ustinov has little acting to do but registers as the ringmaster who narrates the round of Lola's life. Antón Walbrook is fine as the king.

Mosk.

Mozart
(AUSTRIAN)
(Color)

Vienna, Jan. 17.

Cosmopolfilm production and release world distribution by Columbia Film, Vienna. Stars Oskar Werner; features, Johanna Matz. Directed by Karl Hartl. Screenplay, Hartl; camera, Oskar Schnirch. Philharmonic and Symphonic Orchestra under direction of Hans Swarowsky; synchronized voices by state opera singers Hilde Gueden, Erich Kunz, Anton Dermota, Gottlob Frick, Erika Koeth and Else Liebesberg. At Forum Kino, Vienna. Running time, **100 MINS.**

Mozart	Oskar Werner
Annie Gottlieb	Johanna Matz
Konstanze	Gertrud Kueckelman
Aloysia Weber	Nadja Tiller
Schikaneder	Erich Kunz
Susi Gerl	Angelika Hauff
Mother Weber	Annie Rosar
Salieri	Albin Skoda

Director and scripter Karl Hartl's "Mozart" film tells about the last love affair of Mozart and the history of his last opera, "Magic Flute" during the last year of the maestro's life. It is the kind of romantic film opera, set to his classical music, which necessarily can't be classified as longhair.

With a lavish presentation in color and a good cast, it should find the boxoffice going easy. While the historic facts on music are authentic, the romance with Nannina, who first sang the role of "Pamina," is reputedly purely invented.

Oskar Werner in the title role is magnificent. He completely dominates the picture. Johanna Matz as Gottlieb is emotionally and sweetly understanding. Mozart's wife, Konstanze, is played by Gertrud Kueckelman in reserved style. Minor roles are done well by Nadja Tiller and Erich Kunz.

That the best melodies of Mozart were selected adds to the production's sales possibilities. Under Hans Swarowsky's direction, the Vienna Philharmonics and Symphonics alternate in either dominating the scenes or merely underscoring the never tiresome action.

Outstanding direction by Karl Hartl is helped by his work on the script. He deserves credit for adroit handling. Oskar Schnirch's lensing helps to hold interest throughout.

Maas.

Foreign Films

Paris, Jan. 17.

La Madelon (FRENCH) SONGS. Filmsonor release of Ariane-Gallus production. Stars Line Renaud, Jean Richard, Roger Pierre; features Pierre Larquey, Noel Roquevert, Georges Chamarat. Directed by Jean Boyer. Screenplay, Jacques Robert, adaption, Serge Veber, Boyer; dialog, Marc-Gilbert Sauvajon; camera, Charles Suin; music, Loulou Gaste; editor, Fanchette Mazi. At Monte Carlo, Paris. Running time, **90 MINS.**

Story is built around a first World War song about a young girl who became the mascot of the French Army. Obvious story and simple treatment still allow this a measure of sprightliness and rhythm, and it goes its familiar course with some comic gusto. Film concerns the girl's (Madelon's) search for her soldier sweetheart through the front lines when an overzealous civilian suitor writes a false letter informing her that he is going to marry another girl.

Jean Boyer has fused this into a concrete story and singer Line Renaud has a chance to belt out a batch of catchy patriotic numbers. Jean Richard is funny as the cunning yet sympathetic character of the lovesick suitor. For the U.S., this lightweight affair is primarily for dualer or some arty spots. Lensing and editing are an asset in keeping this sprawling pic moving, and some old newsreel shots are deftly cut into this trifle.

Mosk.

Paris, Jan. 17.

Un Missionnaire (A Missionary) **(FRENCH; COLOR).** UCEP release of Maurice Cloche-UGC production. Directed by Maurice Cloche. Screenplay, Paul Bernier, camera (Eastmancolor), Claude Renoir; editor, Christian Gaudin.. With Charles Vanel, Yves Massard, Albert Prejean, Jacques Berthier, Marie-France Planeze, Rene Blancard. At Biarritz, Paris. Running time, **100 MINS.**

Film concerns a young missionary to Africa whose zeal for adventure in the wilds of Africa leads to disappointment when he finds his work is primarily that of a parish priest. Pic treats subject in a stilted way, resulting rarely in any dramatic progression. Film may rate for offbeat and religioso spots for the U.S. Made by the man who did "Monsieur Vincent," Maurice Cloche, this lacks the simplicity and dramatic line of the former. Color is somewhat uneven but editing is good, Charles Vanel and Yves Massard, as the mission founder and exalted young newcomer, respectively, are more than adequate.

Mosk.

The Court Jester
(SONGS—COLOR)

Laugh-grabbing spoof on costumed swashbucklers with Danny Kaye and bright prospects.

Hollywood, Jan. 27.

Paramount release of Dena production, written, directed and produced by Norman Panama and Melvin Frank. Stars Danny Kaye, Glynis Johns, Basil Rathbone, Angela Lansbury, Cecil Parker; features Mildred Natwick, Robert Middleton, Michael Pate, Herbert Rudley. Camera (Technicolor), Ray June; Tom McAdoo; score, Victor Schoen; songs, Sylvia Fine, Sammy Cahn; choreography, James Starbuck. Previewed Jan. 20, '56. Running time, **101 MINS.**

Hawkins	Danny Kaye
Maid Jean	Glynis Johns
Sir Ravenhurst	Basil Rathbone
Princess Gwendolyn	Angela Lansbury
King Roderick	Cecil Parker
Griselda	Mildred Natwick
Sir Griswold	Robert Middleton
Sir Locksley	Michael Pate
Capt. of the Guard	Herbert Rudley
Fergus	Noel Drayton
Flack Fox	Edward Ashley
Giacomo	John Carradine
Sir Brockhurst	Alan Napier
Sir Finsdale	Lewis Martin
Sir Pertwee	Patrick Aherne
Archbishop	Richard Kean

Costumed swashbucklers undergo a happy spoofing in "The Court Jester" with Danny Kaye heading the fun-poking and making it click. The b.o. cash jingle should match the audience laugh reaction, meaning the Dena production which Paramount is releasing has bright prospects at the wickets.

While Kaye dominates, giving the film its entertainment-plus factor, there are plenty of credits to spread around for superb comedy assists. Not the least is the three-way, writing-producing-directing function fulfilled by Norman Panama and Melvin Frank. The team drags in virtually every time-honored, and timeworn, medieval drama cliche for Kaye and cast to re-play for laughs via not-so-subtle treatment.

Another major assist comes from the Sylvia Fine-Sammy Cahn songs, of which there are five all tuned to the Kaye talent. There's the quite mad "Maladjusted Jester"; a lullaby, "Loo-Loo-Loo I'll Take You Dreaming"; a ballad, "My Heart Knows A Lovely Song"; the comedic "They'll Never Outfox the Fox," and "Life Could Not Better Be." With choreography by James Starbuck, Kaye steps off several as production pieces. The big terp click is his work with the American Legion Zouaves, drill team of Post 29, Jackson, Mich. It's plot-spotted for a laugh standout. Overall, Victor Schoen's scoring falls easy on the ear.

Castwise, Kaye is surrounded by a group of players long-experienced in costumed dramas. Each contributes tellingly to the comedy spirit which puts the show over. Glynis Johns, fetched from England for the hoydenish Maid Jean role opposite Kaye, does exceedingly well. The same is true of Basil Rathbone, a many-seasoned chief heavy; Angela Lansbury, cutting a pretty picture as the Princess Gwendolyn; Cecil Parker, the not-so-bright King Roderick who has ousted the real royal family; Mildred Natwick, the princess's evil-eyed maid; Robert Middleton, Michael Pate, Herbert Rudley, Noel Drayton, Edward Ashley, John Carradine and others.

Production splendors include lavish medieval castle settings and these and other physical furbishings show up fine in VistaVision and Technicolor as lensed by Ray

June. Editing by Tom McAdoo is good. *Brog.*

The Bottom of the Bottle
(COLOR-C'SCOPE)

Meller with comfortable b.o. prospects in most situations.

20th-Fox release of Buddy Adler production. Stars Van Johnson, Joseph Cotten, Ruth Roman, Jack Carson; features Margaret Hayes, Bruce Bennett, Brad Dexter, Peggy Knudsen, Margaret Lindsay, Nancy Gates, Gonzales-Gonzales. Directed by Henry Hathaway. Screenplay, Sidney Boehm, from novel by Georges Simeon; camera (De Luxe color), Lee Garmes; music, Leigh Harline; editor, David Bretherton. Previewed N. Y. Jan. 25, '55. Running time 88 MINS.

Donald Martin .... Van Johnson
P.M. .... Joseph Cotten
Nora Martin .... Ruth Roman
Hal Breckinridge .... Jack Carson
Lil Breckinridge .... Margaret Hayes
Brand .... Bruce Bennett
Stanley Miller .... Brad Dexter
Ellen Miller .... Peggy Knudsen
George Cady .... Jim Davis
Hannah Cady .... Margaret Lindsay
Mildred .... Nancy Gates
Luis Romero .... Gonzales-Gonzales
Jenkins .... John Lee
Woman .... Shawn Smith
Rancher .... Ted Griffin
Lucy Grant .... Ernestine Barrier
Grant .... Walter Woolf King
Bit Girl .... Sandy Descher
Bit Boy .... Kim Charney
Girl .... Mimi Gibson
Man .... Carleton Young
Diaz' Wife .... Frances Dominguez
Bit Man .... Orlando Beltram
Mrs. Romero .... Maria M. Valerani
Diaz .... George Trevino
Emily .... Joanne Jordan

An escaped convict's desperate efforts to reach his wife and three children in Mexico add up to 88 minutes of melodrama in "The Bottom of the Bottle." It's a well made 20th-Fox release that should reap comfortable returns in most situations with familiar names of Van Johnson, Joseph Cotten, Ruth Roman and Jack Carson.

Based on the Georges Simenon novel, the Sydney Boehm screenplay has an emotional field day as it touches on the Cain and Abel relationship between brothers Johnson and Cotten. Former, the con who's on the lam, turns to his kin to speed his flight across the border. But Cotten, a successful lawyer-rancher who's built a flourishing practice in southern Arizona, fears for his reputation.

Conveniently, as far as CinemaScope is concerned, Cotten's hacienda is located in an area replete with scenic grandeur which cameraman Lee Garmes excellently captures in De Luxe color. It's a curious social set that fugitive Johnson stumbles in on. For the rancher fraternity, also comprising Carson, his wife Margaret Hayes, Jim Davis and Margaret Lindsay, among others, has a penchant for one party after another and the liquor flows freely.

Johnson, whose yen for alcohol was indirectly responsible for his prison stretch, turns in an earnest, sincere performance as a man spurred by a relentless desire to rejoin his family regardless of consequences. Faced by the ranchers libations, he again becomes a victim of the bottle and flees toward a rain-swollen river which separates him from his goal. At this point Cotten, under prodding of wife Ruth Roman, has softened up. Cain and Abel is a thing of the past. For in a Damon & Pythias finish he helps his brother and each looks ahead with a new slant on life.

Director Henry Hathaway, an old hand at spreading mellers on a broad CinemaScope canvas, accented the action and suspense at the right moments. For good measure there's even a scene where Johnson plunges in the surging river to save Cotten from being swept to sure death over a waterfall. Although some of the plot may tax the imagination, it's to Cotten's credit that he makes his own role relatively believable under the circumstances.

Miss Roman, unhappily married despite her husband's wealth, nicely meets the demands of her part. Carson makes a good try at being a pompous, arrogant rancher but ends up mostly as just his familiar self. The Misses Hayes, Lindsay, and Peggy Knudsen as well as Davis and Brad Dexter appear well cast as members of the saddle and bottle clique. Bruce Bennett contribs a crisp portrayal of a Border patrolman, Nancy Gates is good in a brief bit as Johnson's wife and Gonzales-Gonzales is competent as Cotten's Mexican friend. Good support is provided by a long list of other players.

Excellence of overall backgrounds and realistic sets attest to the physical values supplied by producer Buddy Adler. Art direction of Lyle R. Wheeler and Maurice Ransford is notable as are Ray Kellogg's special photographic effects and the Leigh Harline score as conducted by Lionel Newman. Editing of David Bretherton and other technical assists are on a par usually associated with top budget product. *Gilb.*

Miracle In the Rain
(SONG)

Jane Wyman, Van Johnson to bolster prospects for romantic drama, moving at times but lengthy.

Hollywood, Jan. 31.

Warner Bros. release of Frank P. Rosenberg production. Stars Jane Wyman, Van Johnson; features Peggie Castle, Fred Clark, Eileen Heckart, Josephine Hutchinson, William Gargan. Directed by Rudolph Mate. Screenplay, Ben Hecht, from his novel; camera, Russell Metty; editor, Thomas Reilly; music, Franz Waxman; song, "I'll Always Believe in You," Ray Heindorf, M. K. Jerome, Ned Washington. Previewed Jan. 10, '56. Running time, 107 MINS.

Ruth Wood .... Jane Wyman
Arthur Hugenon .... Van Johnson
Millie Kranz .... Peggie Castle
Stephen Jalonik .... Fred Clark
Grace Ullman .... Eileen Heckart
Agnes Wood .... Josephine Hutchinson
Harry Wood .... William Gargan
Waiter .... Marcel Dalio
Head Waiter .... George Givot
Arleene Witchy .... Barbara Nichols
Eli B. Windgate .... Halliwell Hobbes
Young Priest .... Paul Picerni
Sgt. Gil Parker .... Alan King
Mrs. Hamer .... Irene Seidner
Monty .... Arte Johnson
Mrs. Rickles .... Marian Holmes
Mrs. Canelli .... Minerva Urecal

As a romantic drama, "Miracle In the Rain" probably packs a certain attraction for the distaffers, but the emotionally-wearing 107 minutes of soap opera don't offer much to lure the teenage or masculine ducat buyers. Toplining names of Jane Wyman and Van Johnson give it some booking chance, but the overall prospects are not promising.

The two leads acquit themselves well in the Ben Hecht story. Script has a number of sensitive scenes for Rudolph Mate's understanding direction to develop, but otherwise is wordy and crammed with too much incident, permitting audience rapport with plot and principals to waver over the long course. The New York background for the tale is well-used in the Frank P. Rosenberg production, lending the right note of locale authenticity for the miracle of faith and love that transpires.

Theme is that love never dies, despite death or other adversity. Exponents here are a mousy NY secretary, Miss Wyman, and a soldier, Johnson, who meet in the rain, fall in love in Central Park, are first separated by war and then by the doughboy's death overseas. The miracle comes when the girl, seriously ill, staggers from her bed, and, on the rain-swept steps of St. Patrick's, her lover appears briefly, leaving with her the good-luck coin he had carried away to war and death.

Sequences concerned with the budding romance of two lonely people, the first awareness of love in a springtime Central Park scene, the few happy times they had together and the farewell on a crowded NY street corner are moving. Bathos creeps in otherwise, particularly in the girl's breakup after her lover dies and she's a long time wasting away into ill health before the finale miracle.

The inclusion of the secondary problem in the broken marriage of her parents was unnecessary and, since not very well developed, only adds to the long footage. In this side angle, Josephine Hutchinson is good as the mother in a continual state of shock over the walkout of husband William Gargan many years previously, but he doesn't have a chance to show anything. Eileen Heckart does an appealing job of the spinsterish secretary friend to Miss Wyman. Fred Clark, office boss, and Peggie Castle, his sideline romance; Marcel Dalio and George Givot, waiters in a restaurant sequence; Paul Picerni, a priest; Irene Seidner, a gabby neighbor, fill okay character spots. Barbara Nichols, as an innocent strip-teaser, and Alan King, her sergeant bridegroom, supply a welcome comedy sequence.

Technical support for the production is good, including Russell Metty's lensing (although there's an awful lot of Wyman closeups in tearful poses). The Franz Waxman background score is tuned to the romantic mood. The song, "I'll Always Believe In You," by Ray Heindorf, M. K. Jerome and Ned Washington is set up as a story point, which is left dangling at the windup. *Brog.*

World in My Corner

Exciting fisticuffs in a sketchy plot. Audie Murphy for the marquees. Prospects okay.

Hollywood, Jan. 31.

Universal release of Aaron Rosenberg production. Stars Audie Murphy, Barbara Rush, Jeff Morrow, John McIntire; features Tommy Rall, Howard St. John, Chico Vejar, Steve Ellis, Art Aragon, Dani Crayne. Directed by Jesse Hibbs. Screenplay, Jack Sher; based on a story by Sher and Joseph Stone; camera, Maury Gertsman; editor, Milton Carruth; music supervision, Joseph Gershenson. Previewed Jan. 24, '56. Running time, 81 MINS.

Tommy Shea .... Audie Murphy
Dorothy Mallinson .... Barbara Rush
Robert T. Mallinson .... Jeff Morrow
Dave Bernstein .... John McIntire
Ray Kacsmerek .... Tommy Rall
Harry Cram .... Howard St. John
Steve Carelli .... Chico Vejar
TV Announcer .... Steve Ellis
Fighter .... Art Aragon
Doris .... Dani Crayne
Ring Announcer .... James F. Lennon
Parker .... Cisco Andrade
Stretch Caplow .... H. Tommy Hart
Mrs. Mallinson .... Sheila Bromley

The prize ring action staged in "World In My Corner," coupled with Audie Murphy's name for the marquees, portends satisfactory business in the general situations for this Universal release. Murphy wears ring garb convincingly and otherwise carries off the character of a promising young welterweight in okay style to aid the pic's entertainment aims and grossing prospects.

The squared circle fisticuffs are excitingly filmed in the Aaron Rosenberg production, with Jesse Bibb's direction and the camera work by Maury Gertsman making them quite realistic. Also, use of Chico Vejar and other ring vets serves to give the sequences a welcome professional touch.

Storywise, there's something to be asked; not in the basic plot theme of a young man working himself up from the wrong side of the tracks to ring fame, but in some of the ramifications of the characters that surround him, which are only sketchily developed. Story adopts a somewhat sympathetic slant on the fight trade, without overlooking the fact there are such things as fixed scraps and other skullduggery.

Murphy, promising fighter, with a yen for money, comes under the wing of John McIntire, former manager now employed on the estate of wealthy Jeff Morrow and the latter's daughter, Barabara Rush. Through careful training, he rises in rank but still can't get the big chance because the welter champ, Vejar, is controlled by crooked promoter Howard St. John. Needing big coin fast to marry Miss Rush and take her away from an unhappy life with her dominating father, Murphy agrees to a fixed fight with Vejar, but finale finds him changing his mind, winning the match, but suffering injuries that will prevent future fights.

The neuroses plaguing Miss Rush, and her father, get a once-over-lightly in the plot, but within the inconclusive limits of the characters they do okay. McIntire is just right as the crusty trainer, while Tommy Rall, brash, buckhustling friend of Murphy's, St. John, Vejar, and the others come off acceptably. So do the technical assists on the production. *Brog.*

The Killer Is Loose

Weak story development. Average b.o. prospects for entry starring Joseph Cotten, Rhonda Fleming, Wendell Corey.

United Artists release of Crown (Robert L. Jacks) production. Stars Joseph Cotten, Rhonda Fleming, Wendell Corey; features Alan Hale, Michael Pate, John Larch, Dee J. Thompson, Virginia Christine, John Beradino, Paul Bryer. Directed by Budd Boetticher. Screenplay, Harold Medford, from story by John and Ward Hawkins; camera, Lucien Ballard; editor, George Gittens; music, Lionel Newman. Previewed N.Y. Jan. 19, '56. Running time, 73 MINS.

Sam Wagner .... Joseph Cotten
Lila Wagner .... Rhonda Fleming
Leon Poole .... Wendell Corey
Denny .... Alan Hale
Chris Gillespie .... Michael Pate
Mary Gillespie .... Virginia Christine
Otto Flanders .... John Larch
Mac .... John Beradino
Greg .... Paul Bryer
Grace Flanders .... Dee J. Thompson

"The Killer Is Loose," which Crown Productions turned out for United Artists release, falls in the suspense-thriller category. But its transition from story to screen is so poorly done that the plot is seldom convincing. Stars Joseph Cotten, Rhonda Fleming and Wendell Corey provide marquee appeal but trio is largely window dressing for their thesping efforts are generally wasted. Film has average b.o. prospects in the program market.

The John and Ward Hawkins story, as screenplayed by Harold Medford, appears to have the basic elements of a Hitchcock meller, what with a prisoner who escapes for the sole purpose of revenging himself on a detective who placed him behind bars. Suspected of being a confederate of thieves who robbed the bank where he worked, teller Corey is seized by detectives Cotten and Michael Pate at his home.

In the course of getting their man, the police accidentally slay Corey's wife. At this point his mind seems to snap and he embarks upon a crusade of retribution with the ultimate objective of escaping jail to kill Cotten's wife, Miss Fleming. Thereafter the obvious follows, what with Corey's escape, his breakthrough of a police dragnet and his own violent death as he stalks Miss Fleming on the street.

While Medford's script is no great shakes, neither is the direction of Budd Boetticher as attested by the listless performances of Cotten as the sherlock and Miss Fleming as his hunted helpmate. Former gives a mechanical interpretation to the role as does his co-star to hers. Corey fares somewhat better with the part of the psycho prisoner. John Larch, as Corey's ex-Army sergeant, gives a lift to what otherwise might have been a stock characterization. Among others lending standard support are Pate and Alan Hale as policemen.

Physical values in this entry, which Robert L. Jacks produced for Crown Productions, bespeak a modest budget. Cameraman Lucien Ballard gives the film an atmosphere of realism via his neat black-and-white lensing of Los Angeles street scenes. Other assets include Leslie Thomas' art direction, George Gittens' tight editing which kept the footage at 73 minutes, and the Lionel Newman score. *Gilb.*

Red Sundown
(SONG—COLOR)

Actionful western with good chances in regular outdoor market.

Hollywood, Jan. 30.

Universal release of Albert Zugsmith production. Stars Rory Calhoun, Martha Hyer, Dean Jagger; features Robert Middleton, Grant Williams, Lita Baron, James Millican. Directed by Jack Arnold. Screenplay, Martin Berkeley; based on "Back Trail" by Lewis B. Patten; camera (Technicolor), William Snyder; editor, Edward Curtiss; song, written and sung by Terry Gilkyson. Previewed Jan. 25, '56. Running time, **81 MINS.**

Alec Longmire	Rory Calhoun
Caroline Murphy	Martha Hyer
Jade Murphy	Dean Jagger
Rufus Henshaw	Robert Middleton
Chet Swann	Grant Williams
Maria	Lita Baron
Purvis	James Millican
Sam Baldwin	Trevor Bardette
Rod Zellman	Leo Gordon
Hughie Clore	David Kasday

Action and characterization are expertly blended in this fast-moving sagebrusher and the outdoor market will find it a handy entry for the western fan. Good cast names for release intentions and the Technicolor display of the footage are booking advantages, too.

As the story is the familiar one of a young man saddled with a gunslinger's reputation, emphasis has been wisely shifted to characterization and incident freshening, and the cast has the ability to live up to the switch. Jack Arnold's direction is an able factor in unfolding at an interesting pace the script by Martin Berkeley, based on Lewis B. Patten's "Back Trail." Production supervision by Albert Zugsmith is firstrate in bringing this one off to meet market demands.

Rory Calhoun is the cowpoke with the reputation who is trying to abandon a life with the gun. An opening sequence, of high action and plenty of punch involving the death of an old gun hand, played in topnotch style by James Millican, establishes Calhoun's search for a new life. Before it's punching cattle, rather than slinging six-shooters, though, Calhoun takes on a deputy job with sheriff Dean Jagger to prevent a range war and out of this comes the assurance he's on the right road and will find a happy life with the sheriff's daughter, attractively portrayed by Martha Hyer.

Good performances abound, from the above mentioned on down the cast list. Robert Middleton, as the greedy land owner who wants to own the entire range, is properly menacing, as is his hired killer, threateningly played by Grant Williams. Lita Baron, Trevor Bardette, Leo Gordon and David Kasday are among the others meriting mention.

A title tune, written and sung behind the credits by Terry Gilkyson, is a good mood piece that sets the scene for the action. William Snyder's color lensing is excellent, as are the other technical contributions. *Brog.*

Battle Stations

Over-stereotyped characters and situations aboard a Navy carrier, lightweight.

Hollywood, Jan. 31.

Columbia release of Bryan Foy production. Stars John Lund, William Bendix, Keefe Brasselle, Richard Boone, William Leslie; features John Craven, James Lydon, Claude Akins, George O'Hanlon, Eddie Foy 3d. Directed by Lewis Seiler. Screenplay, Crane Wilbur; based on a story by Ben Finney; camera, Burnett Guffey; editor, Jerome Thoms; music conducted by Mischa Bakaleinikoff. Previewed Jan. 27, '56. Running time, **81 MINS.**

Father Joe McIntyre	John Lund
Buck Fitzpatrick	William Bendix
Chris Jordan	Keefe Brasselle
Captain	Richard Boone
Ensign Pete Kelly	William Leslie
Commander Matthews	John Craven
"Squawk" Hewitt	James Lydon
Marty Brennan	Claude Akins
Patrick Mosher	George O'Hanlon
Tom Short	Eddie Foy III
William Halsey	Jack Dimond
Archie Golder	Chris G. Randall
John Moody	Robert Forrest
Eddie	Dick Cathcart
Lt. Hanson	Gordon Howard
Williams	James Lilburn
Bos'un No. 1	Frank Connor
Bos'un No. 2	Eric Bond

Routine life aboard an aircraft carrier occupies the major part of the footage in this service feature and doesn't sustain enough entertainment to make it figure.

Plot time is World War II and story concerns a carrier of the Essex class from the time it leaves the Alameda Naval Air Station after repairs of war damage until it returns to Brooklyn, again for repairs, after fighting in Japanese waters. Stock footage serves producer Bryan Foy well, even though the story and its stereotype characters do not. As the latter occupy most of the first hour of footage almost exclusively, it doesn't leave much time for the real battle shots.

John Lund portrays Father McIntyre, chaplain, newly assigned to the carrier, which is captained by Richard Boone, who believes in endless training to prepare his men and ship for war. William Bendix is the tough chief bos'un, Keefe Brasselle the cocky sailor always in trouble, while William Leslie plays a young pilot who wants to stay alive because he's to become a father for the first time.

Viewers will be taken on a stem-to-stern tour of the huge carrier and will then be shown how a crew is trained to man such a ship. After awhile this footage becomes monotonous and the attempts at salty, shipboard humor pay off with only minimum results. Few of the cast have a chance to show much, the principals not being supplied with enough dramatic punch in the Crane Wilbur script to come alive. Lewis Seiler's direction also is similarly handicapped.

Burnett Guffey trained the cameras on the story footage acceptably and the other technical assists come off in like fashion. *Brog.*

The Broken Star

Fair western for the program action market.

Hollywood, Jan. 31.

United Artists release of Howard W. Koch (Bel-Air) production. Stars Howard Duff, Lita Baron, Bill Williams; features Henry Calvin, Douglas Fowley, Addison Richards, Joel Ashley, John Pickard, William (Bill) Phillips, Dorothy Adams, Joe Dominguez. Directed by Lesley Selander. Screenplay, John C. Higgins; camera, William Margulies; editor, John F. Schreyer; music, Paul Dunlap. Previewed Jan. 27, '56. Running time, **81 MINS.**

Frank Smead	Howard Duff
Conchita	Lita Baron
Bill Gentry	Bill Williams
Thornton Wills	Henry Calvin
Hiram Charleton	Douglas Fowley
Wayne Forrester	Addison Richards
Messendyke	Joel Ashley
Van Horn	John Pickard
Doc Mott	Wm. Phillips
Mrs. Trail	Dorothy Adams
Nachez	Joe Dominguez

Skullduggery on the range this time concerns a deputy marshal who turns crook and how he is finally brought to justice. The Bel-Air production for United Artists release starts well, falters in the middle and then picks up pace for the finale, averaging out as a fair western for the program action market.

Howard Duff is the man who dishonors his star in the John C. Higgins screenplay. Opening finds him shooting down the agent of a big rancher and stealing the gold paid by settlers for water-use rights. Crime is made to look like a killing necessary in the line of duty, but it's such an obvious trail the lawman-gone-wrong lays out that fellow officer Bill Williams is a long time following it.

Duff handles his acting duties neatly, but Williams' reaction to character demands is too stiff. Lita Baron fares better as his girl friend, a Latin saloon singer who gets rousted about by the rancher's henchmen in the search for the loot. Just why she's put to the fist isn't explained clearly, but it does give Williams a chance to take on the plug-uglies in a barroom brawl.

Howard W. Koch produced under executive producer Aubrey Schenck, locationing the troupe near Tucson, Ariz., for the correct outdoor atmosphere, which William Margulies lenses acceptably. Considering the Higgins script, director Lesley Selander gets all that's possible out of the action setup. Assisting the three stars in feature spots are Henry Calvin as the big rancher; Douglas Fowley, a crooked Indian agent; Addison Richards, the top marshal; Joel Ashley, John Pickard, William (Bill) Phillips, Dorothy Adams and Joe Dominguez, an Indian who witnessed the original crime and gets bumped off for his trouble. *Brog.*

Betrayed Women

Sadism in a Dixie lockup for janes. Exploitation entry for program market.

Hollywood, Jan. 27.

Allied Artists release of a William F. Broidy production. Stars Carole Mathews, Beverly Michaels, Peggy Knudsen, Tom Drake; features Sara Haden, John Dierkes, Esther Dale. Directed by Edward L. Cahn. Screenplay, Steve Fisher; story, Paul L. Peil; camera, John Martin; editors, Ace Herman, Chandler House; music, Edward J. Kay; sound, Al Overton. Reviewed Jan. 25, '56. Running time, **70 MINS.**

Kate	Carole Mathews
Honey	Beverly Michaels
Nora	Peggy Knudsen
Jeff	Tom Drake
Darcy	Sara Haden
Cletus	John Dierkes
Mrs. Ballard	Esther Dale
Baby Face	Paul Savage
Mrs. Mabry	Darlene Fields
Mabry	John Damler
Hostage Guard	G. Pat Collins
First Guard	Burt Wenland
Second Guard	Pete Kellett

This melodramatic yarn about a Southern women's prison farm where old-fashioned sadistic methods still are practiced upon the inmates gets in realism, and rates okay for secondary billing in smaller situations. Performances of principals generally are persuasive enough to lend credence to story unfoldment, and subject shapes up handily for exploitation.

William F. Broidy production tees off with prison's investigation by a young attorney, Tom Drake, upon orders of the governor. He arrives simultaneously with Beverly Michaels, a gun moll whose boy friend was killed by the police, a tough cookie in her own right. Immediately, she and Carole Mathews, another toughie, clash, but throw in finally in a prison-break in which Drake, prison matron Esther Dale anh Peggy Knunsen, another inmate in love with Drake, are taken as hostages. Mathews is killed but Michaels surrenders.

Miss Michaels has the most colorful role and most footage, delivering well. Misses Knudsen and Mathews handle themselves satisfactorily, and Miss Dale enacts one of her cruel matron characters. Drake is lost in the shuffle. Edward L. Cahn's direction of Steve Fisher's screenplay hews to a fast pace. Print used at opening day's performance was unmatched. *Whit.*

Uli der Paechter
(Uli the Tenant)
(SWISS)

Zurich, Jan. 24.

Praesens-Film Zurich release of Praesens (Oscar Ducby) production. Directed by Franz Schnyder. With Hannes Schmidhauser, Liselotte Pulver, Emil Hegetschweiler, Hedda Koppe, Leopold Biberti, Marianne Matti, Alfred Rasser, Erwin Kohlund, Stephanie Glaser, Fredy Scheim, Walter Lapp, Hans Gaugler, Willy Frei, Peter Arens, Hans Kaes, Willy Fueter, Sigfrit Steiner. Screenplay, Richard Schweizer, based on novel by Jeremias Gotthelf; camera, Emil Berna; music, Robert Blum. At Scala Theatre, Zurich. Running time, **115 MINS.**

Sequel to last year's Swiss top grosser, "Uli the Servant" promises to equal its predecessor's b.o. performance. Again based on a novel by 19th Century Swiss writer Jeremias Gotthelf, widely re-popularized by a recent radio series, this is even superior to the first film in artistic merits. Direction by Franz Schnyder also is better balanced. Due to unfamiliarity of theme and lack of marquee names, U.S. chances are not too bright. Film's quality may make it worth a try in special situations.

Plot picks up where the first film left off. Young peasant Uli is now tenant of a farm, aided by his wife. After a prosperous beginning, things are going from bad to worse, with a ruined harvest, severe illness, heavy debts etc. almost smashing the young couple's existence.

Story telling is honest and straightforward. The excellent camerawork by Emil Berna is an important asset. Most of the players repeat their previous assignments. Hannes Schmidhauser and Liselotte Pulver as the young couple are excellent, and sock featured portrayals are turned in by Emil Hegetschweiler and Leopold Biberti. *Mezo.*

Cash On Delivery
(BRITISH—SONGS)

Shelley Winters toplining British-lensed comedy to help domestic market booking chances as program offering.

Hollywood, Jan. 25.

RKO release of Peter Rogers, Ben Schrift (Welbeck-Gina) production. Stars Shelley Winters, Peggy Cummins, John Gregson; features Wilfrid Hyde White. Directed by Muriel Box. Screenplay, Peter Rogers; camera, Ernest Steward; editor, Alfred Roome; score. Lambert Williamson; songs, Paddy Roberts, Jacques Abram, Fred G. Moritt, George Thorn. Previewed Jan. 23, '56. Running time, 79 MINS.

Myrtle La Mar .... Shelley Winters
Tony Rapallo .... John Gregson
Dorothy Rapallo ..... Peggy Cummins
Mr. Starke .... Wilfrid Hyde White
Nurse Appleby ..... Mona Washbourne
Livingstone Potts .... Hal Osmond
Cy Daniel .... Hartley Power
Elmer (pianist) .... M. Kaufman
Waiter .... John Warren
Furrier .... Fred Berger
Clerk .... N. Parsons
Secretary .... Dorothy Bramhall
Parsons .... Ronald Adam

This is another of RKO's British-lensed imports slanted for domestic bookings via the use of a Hollywood name on an overseas cast. In "Cash On Delivery," it's Shelley Winters headlining, with Peggy Cummins, John Gregson and Wilfrid Hyde White sharing main billing. It is a passable little program comedy with some family appeal.

Peter Rogers, who coproduced with Ben Schrift, also did the screen original, a frantic affair concerned with a $2,000,000 inheritance that hinges on the birth of a male child before a certain date and hour. It plays off in a succession of climaxes, mostly hectic, under the extremely broad direction by Muriel Box. Cast performances are in kind, and moderate chuckles result from the antics and the situations causing them.

When Miss Winters, nitery singer, is advised she stands to inherit a fortune if her former husband, Gregson, has not fathered a male offspring before a certain deadline, she's off to England to track him down. She finds him married to Peggy Cummins, who's on the brink of birth. Will it be a boy? Will it take place before or after the deadline? Time difference between New York and England, plus questions on the validity of the first marriage, the divorce and the second hitching, are among other points adding to the confusing complications. It's twins, boy and girl, but Miss Winters wins because of NY daylight savings time. However, principals generously split the dough at the finale.

Background score by Lambert Williamson plays its part in the humor, having identifying themes for characters and situations. "Give Me a Man," by Paddy Roberts, and "You're the Only One," by Jacques Abram and George Thorn, are a couple of the songs heard to no particular advantage. Lensing by Ernest Steward and other technical credits are okay. *Brog.*

Meet Me In Las Vegas
(C'SCOPE-SONGS-COLOR)

Socko tintune entertainment with potent word-of-mouth and promising prospects.

Hollywood, Feb. 3.

Metro release of Joe Pasternak production. Stars Dan Dailey, Cyd Charisse; guest stars Jerry Colonna, Paul Henreid, Lena Horne, Frankie Laine, Mitsuko Sawamura; features Agnes Moorehead, Lili Darvas, Jim Backus, Oscar Karlweis, Liliane Montevecchi, Cara Williams. Directed by Roy Rowland. Screenplay. Isobel Lennart; camera (Eastman Color), Robert Bronner; editor, Albert Akst; music supervised and conducted by George Stoll; music and lyrics, Nicholas Brodszky and Sammy Cahn; choreography, Hermes Pan; ballets, Eugene Loring; music for "Frankie & Johnny" ballet adapted by Johnny Green; Lena Horne's number arranged and conducted by Lennie Hayton. Previewed Feb. 1, '56. Running time, 111 MINS.

Chuck Rodwell .... Dan Dailey
Maria Corvier .... Cyd Charisse
Miss Hattie .... Agnes Moorehead
Sari Hatvany .... Lili Darvas
Tom Culdane .... Jim Backus
Lotsi .... Oscar Karlweis
Lilli .... Liliane Montevecchi
Kelly Donavan .... Cara Williams
Young Groom .... George Kerris
Young Bride .... Betty Lynn
Themselves .... The Slate Brothers
Conductor .... Peter Rugolo
Specialty Dancer .... John Brascia
Worried Boss .... John Harding
Croupier .... Benny Rubin
Meek Husband .... Jack Daly
Bossy Wife .... Henny Backus

Entertainment is delivered in bountiful measure in this sock Joe Pasternak production. Excellent comedy and romance, great music, songs and dances are skillfully blended into a show that merits top playing time. The boxoffice outlook is just as promising, with word-of-mouth proving a potent factor in the picture's behalf.

Dan Dailey and Cyd Charisse are great as a team, complementing each other in supplying a boff touch to the highly engaging, terrifically dialoged screen story by Isobel Lennart. Roy Rowland's direction is another big factor in the way the entertainment comes off, telling the story of a gambling cowboy who falls in love with a ballerina at a pace so engrossing it belies the 111 minutes of running time. This is one time that a musical book doesn't prove a series of stage waits between songs and production numbers.

Miss Charisse's versatility as a film dancer, ballet or modern terping, is well established. This role which brings her to life and vice versa, puts her over as an actress as well as dancer credit the metamorphosis to Rowland's skilled handling.

Pasternak's showmanly reining of the production makes the most of the entertainment ingredients. There are credited and uncredited guest stars wandering in and out for surprise visits. Agnes Moorehead, as the cowpoke's mother, and Lili Darvas, the ballerina's chaperone, brighten their scenes, as does guest star Paul Henreid, as the dancer's manager. Cara Williams scores a personal hit singing "I Refuse to Rock 'n' Roll" and playing a romantic rival. Jim Backus is delightful as the harassed club manager, and Oscar Karweis wins chuckles as a blackjack dealer who dislikes to see people lose.

Las Vegas has never had a better film showcasing or more valuable advertising, and the Sands Hotel particularly provides a glittering background for the romantic tale of how Dailey, the cowpoke (he really owns a ranch) and Miss Charisse are first brought together because when he holds her

hand he can't lose. When the association ripes into love the golden mitt loses its magic since Lady Luck's by-word is "lucky in love, unlucky at cards." A lot of amusing situations spring from the hand-holding premise and warm chuckles are constant.

The songs, with rhythmic beat by Nicholas Brodszky and catchy lyrics by Sammy Cahn; the dance numbers created and staged by Hermes Pan, and the ballets likewise by Eugene Loring, are nothing short of terrific. Tunes are "The Gal With the Yaller Shoes," first sung by Dailey and later used for a ranch production number; "If You Can't Dream," sung by Lena Horne (only person in the film not used to best advantage); the Cara Williams rock 'n' roll sequence; "My Lucky Charm," a big standout when a likkered-up Miss Charisse takes over in Vegas' Silver-Slipper from Jerry Colonna to prove something to her cowboy, and also when reprised by Dailey and little Miss Mitsuko Sawamura; "Hell Hath No Fury," strongly sold by Frankie Laine; and the smash finale version of "Frankie and Johnny," routined and arranged by Johnny Green with lyrics by Cahn. In this Miss Charisse, Liliane Montevecchi, John Brascia and company are dancing wows, with Sammy Davis Jr.'s singing narration a socko accompaniment.

The two ballets exquisitely danced by Miss Charisse are "Rhondo Brilliant," an F. Mendelssohn composition, and an adaptation of Tchaikovsky's "Sleeping Beauty Ballet," both staged by Loring. Also in the film's musical portions are an appealing Oriental piece by Mikai Minoru, "Hitori Botsuchi Wa Tsumaranai" which is sung by young Miss Sawamura, a fine personality, and the title tune, which the Four Aces do at the beginning and end.

George Stoll's supervision and conducting of the music figures most importantly in the overall excellence, as do the orchestrations by Albert Sendrey and Skip Martin, the vocal supervision by Robert Tucker, and the music coordination by Irving Aaronson.

Robert Bronner's CinemaScope lensing in Eastman Color catches the brilliance of the art direction by Cedric Gibbons and Urie McCleary, the set decorations by Edwin B. Willis and Richard Pefferle, and the fine costumes by Helen Rose. Editing by Albert Akst and the recording supervision by Dr. Wesley C. Miller are firstrate. *Brog.*

Come Next Spring
(SONG-COLOR)

Warm, simple story of Arkansas rural folk; a natural for family, farm belt trade.

Hollywood, Feb. 2.

Republic production and release. Stars Ann Sheridan, Steve Cochran, Walter Brennan, Sherry Jackson, Richard Eyer; features Edgar Buchanan, Sonny Tufts, Harry Shannon, Rad Fulton. Directed by R. G. Springsteen. Screenplay, Montgomery Pittman; camera (Trucolor), Jack Marta; editor, Tony Martinelli; music, Max Steiner; song, Steiner and Lenny Adelson; sung by Tony Bennett. Previewed Jan. 30, '5. Running time, 98 MINS.

Bess Ballot .... Ann Sheridan
Matt Ballott .... Steve Cochran
Jeff Storys .... Walter Brennan
Annie .... Sherry Jackson
Abraham .... Richard Eyer
Mr. Canary .... Edgar Buchanan
Leroy Hytower .... Sonny Tufts
Mr. Totter .... Harry Shannon
Bob Storys .... Rad Fulton

Myrtle .... Mae Clark
Shorty Wilkins .... Roscoe Ates
Delbert Meaner .... Wade Ruby
Bill Jackson .... James Best

"Come Next Spring" should be a natural for the socalled farm belt trade, and also will find high favor with family audiences anywhere. It is a warm, human drama telling with a compelling simplicity a story of an Arkansas rural community back in the late 1920's. The names of Ann Sheridan, Steve Cochran and Walter Brennan add marques flash for the Republic market.

Montgomery Pittman's screen story provides R. G. Springsteen's direction with a solid base. The script reveals a complete understanding of the people who live in such rural areas, avoids caricatures and forced situations that would have been foreign to the Arkansas folk; yet there are plenty of humorous moments, as well as exciting dramatic sequences, which the direction points up well.

Cochran is splendid as a man who comes back to his farm and wife after years of wandering have tempered his taste for liquor and wild living. He finds he's the father of a son born after his departure, as well as the mute girl who as an infant lost her ability to speak during one of her father's drinking spells. Even with this past history revealed, Cochran is not an unsympathetic character. The audience knows his wildness is behind him and is pulling for his acceptance by the wife and community. Equally fine is Miss Sheridan as the wary wife, once-burned and reluctant to release her love for Cochran until sure she won't be hurt again. Walter Brennan is very real as the sharecropper on the farm.

Two moppets, Sherry Jackson and Richard Eyer, supply juvenile appeal to the back-country drama and are two more reasons for the effective entertainment. Young Miss Jackson stands out with her sensitive portrayal of the mute. It's a touching scene at the fadeout as she screams and screams, the first sound she has been able to utter, which she joyously repeats after having been rescued by her father from an old mine pit. Eyer brings a young manliness to his part of the son who wants a dad.

Edgar Buchanan, Sonny Tufts, who wants to be a romantic rival and gets beaten up in a long brawl for his trouble, Harry Shannon, Rad Fulton, Mae Clarke, Roscoe Ates, Wade Ruby and James Best lend firstrate support as rural types. Trucolor lensing by Jack Marta, the title song by Lenny Adelson and Max Steiner which Tony Bennett sings, and the editing are among other effective credits. *Brog.*

Forever Darling
(SONG—COLOR)

Poor Lucille Ball-Desi Arnaz starrer; depends upon television names for draw.

Hollywood, Feb. 7.

Metro release of Desi Arnaz (Zanra) production. Stars Lucille Ball, Arnaz, James Mason, Louis Calhern; features John Emery, John Hoyt, Natalie Schafer. Directed by Alexander Hall. Screenplay, Helen Deutsch; camera (Eastman Color), Harold Lipstein; editors, Dann Cahn, Bud Molin; music, Bronislau Kaper; song, Kaper and Sammy Cahn; sung by the Ames Brothers (4). Previewed Jan. 25, '56. Running time, **90 MINS.**

Susan Vega .... Lucille Ball
Lorenzo Xavier Vega .... Desi Arnaz
Guardian Angel .... James Mason
Charles Y. Bewell .... Louis Calhern
Dr. Edward R. Winter...... John Emery
Bill Finlay .... John Hoyt
Millie Opdyke .... Natalie Schafer
Society Reporter .... Mabel Albertson
Henry Opdyke .... Ralph Dumke
Amy .... Nancy Kulp
Mr. Clinton .... Willis B. Bouchey
Laura .... Ruth Brady

Only modest prospects loom for "Forever Darling," the second Metro feature outing for Lucille Ball and Desi Arnaz. Their televisioned names will get playdates, but the entertainment is of a poor quality, consequently word-of-mouth will hurt.

Picture can't make up its mind whether to be comedy, drama, romance or fantasy, thus fails to score in any one department. When the Ball-Arnaz team is making with the slapstick, a la the tv marital pair, the laughs come off okay. Elsewhere there's little to keep an audience really interested, probably due to the muddled scripting by Helen Deutsch and the choppy editing. In such a setup, Alexander Hall's direction has scant chance to build a worthwhile show and the cast talents are wasted.

Film opens with the marriage of the star team, then montages through several years until boredom sets in. Arnaz is interested in his work as a chemist and she feels neglected. Under the guidance of a guardian angel who looks just like James Mason (and is), she goes off with hubby on a field trip to help him test a new bug killer. It's only in these sequences in the latter part of the footage that the comedy jells. Miss Ball involved with a sleeping bag, accidentally inflating a rubber boat in the tent and later causing it to sink in a stream are scenes good for typical antics and chuckles. The trouble is, there isn't enough of this kind of fun. Another okay comedic sequence occurs earlier when Miss Ball and Arnaz attend a theatre and she sees herself taking the place of Marilyn Maxwell in a jungle pic opposite Mason.

All that Mason and Louis Calhern have are walk-throughs, with Calhern appearing in only three scenes, which he helps. John Emery, John Hoyt, Natalie Schafer, Ralph Dumke and Nancy Kulp are among the others in the cast who have little opportunity.

Release is inauspicious start for Arnaz as a theatrical film producer. It was made through his Zanra Productions Inc., with Desilu filming. The photography shows Miss Ball to disadvantage in several scenes, but elsewhere the lensing by Harold Lipstein comes off acceptably. A title tune by Bronislau Kaper and Sammy Cahn is sung by the Ames Brothers and reprised by Arnaz, but as used in the pic doesn't impress. *Brog.*

Timetable

Insurance investigator turns crook. Well-knit script, tight direction. Above average supporting feature with letdown climax.

United Artists release of Mark Stevens production. Stars Stevens; features King Calder, Felicia Farr, Wesley Addy, Marianne Stewart. Directed by Stevens. Original story, Robert Angus; screenplay, Aben Kandel; camera, Charles Van Enger; music, Walter Scharf; story editor and dialog director, Stanley Silverman; film editor, Kenneth Crane. Previewed N.Y., Feb. 3, '56. Running time, **79 MINS.**

Charlie .... Mark Stevens
Joe .... King Calder
Linda .... Felicia Farr
Wife .... Marianne Stewart
Brucker .... Wesley Addy
Wolfe .... Alan Reed
Frankie .... Jack Klugman
Bobik .... John Marley
Lt. Castro .... Rodolfo Hoyos

It is a valid test of literary craftsmanship that the implausible is made to seem otherwise. A basic merit of "Timetable" is a professionally knowing sequencing of scenes in Aben Kandel's screenplay of an original yarn by Robert Angus. Add to this a canny ear and eye for characterization on the part of producer-director-star Mark Stevens. The result is a secondary feature which is heads up until the final five minutes when it collapses into the Hollywood platitude that a melodrama must end with an ambush and gunning down of the turpitude exponent.

The merits of the production and the overall quota of suspense show forethought and critical evaluation which makes the slapdash "climax" sorethumbishly noticeable in artificiality and contrivance. A pity Mark Stevens didn't stick to his own standards and taste. The realization, cerebrally, that he was caught in his own miscalculations would have been both psychologically more satisfying and a welcome consistency of brainpower behind action.

Considerable attention is given to the asking of the "why?" in the instance of a respected married man who breaks trust with society and a loving wife. "A job becomes a straitjacket and a home a prison to some men," explains the hero-villain. There isn't time, of course, to go into the subtleties but this is a fresh feeling for motivation in a stock release.

King Calder, as the still-honest railroad cop who finally sees the guilt of his lifetime chum, was intelligent casting and played out similarly. The weakling malpractice doctor character of Wesley Addy, the angle-shooting airport operator of Alan Reed, the Mexican police-officer (Rodolfo Hoyos) and the Mexican underworld figure (John Marley) are excellent values in the context. More suggested than written out, the two women, sex-lure Felicia Farr and sound spouse Marianne Stewart, show to advantage, both offbeat casting.

A special song, "Salud Felicidad y Amor," by musical scorer Walter Scharf and Jack Brooks is pleasant though not emphasized. Special screen credit for Stanley H. Silverman as story editor and dialog director suggests an important assist in the department of making the implausible shine with conviction. The film editing (Kenneth Crane) is presumptively a checkmark for craftsmanship and the camerawork of Charles Van Enger is sharply framed. It is scarcely his responsibility that the final closing in the sequence in the boites and streets of Tia Juana, probably intended to be colorful, doesn't overcome its essential hokey-pokey, got-to-get-this-over-with quality. *Land.*

Please Murder Me

Program meller for general lowercase bookings.

Hollywood, Feb. 6.

Distributors Corp. of America release of Donald Hyde (Gross-Krasne) production. Stars Angela Lansbury, Raymond Burr; features Dick Foran, John Dehner, Lamont Johnson. Directed by Peter Godfrey. Screenplay, Al C. Ward and Hyde; camera, Allen Stensvold; editor, Kenny Crane. Previewed Feb. 2, '56. Running time, **76 MINS.**

Myra Leeds .... Angela Lansbury
Craig Carlson .... Raymond Burr
Joe Leeds .... Dick Foran
District Attorney .... John Dehner
Carl Holt .... Lamont Johnson
Lou Kazorian .... Robert Griffin
Lt. Bradley .... Denver Pyle
Sergeant .... Alex Sharpe
Policeman .... Lee Miller
Jenny .... Madge Blake
Judge .... Russ Thorson

The melodramatics in this suspense thriller appear to spring from familiar plotting, but are brought off with enough dispatch to meet the demands of supporting bookings in the general program market. It's the initialer of several theatrical features planned by Gross-Krasne, heretofore active exclusively with telepix.

Nub of the Al C. Ward-Donald Hyde plot is not too original. It has Raymond Burr, successful attorney, scheming to have a woman, whom he had gotten off at a murder trial, murder him so justice will be done. She does, and it is, with a tape recorder nailing her for the second crime. Irony is concerned with the fact Burr loved Angela Lansbury and was to marry her, he thought, after the trial, but a delayed letter from the dead husband proved she had murdered him, not killed in self defense as she had led everyone to believe. Burr didn't have a chance from the start, because she figured to run off with an artist, a decent sort as played by Lamont Johnson, all along.

Peter Godfrey's direction of the Donald Hyde production gives satisfactory handling to the material and cast response is good. Dick Foran plays the murdered husband, John Dehner the district attorney, while others include Robert Griffin and Denver Pyle, all of whom help keep the performance score up.

Lensing by Allen Stensvold, editing by Kenny Crane and other technical assists function acceptably. *Brog.*

The Naked Night

Controversial Swedish import with stress on sex and morbidity.

Times Film Corp. release of Sandrew production. Stars Harriet Anderson and Ake Groenberg. Features Hasse Ekman, Anders Ek, Annika Tretow, and Kiki. Directed by Ingmar Bergman; screenplay, Bergman; camera, Sven Nykvist and Hilding Bladh; music, Karl-Birger Blomdahl. Previewed in N. Y. Feb. 2, '56. Running time, **82 MINS.**

Anne .... Harriet Anderson
Albert .... Ake Groenberg
Frans .... Hasse Ekman
Frost .... Anders Ek
Alma .... Annika Tretow
Agda .... Kiki

(In Swedish; English subtitles)

Sex and morbidity are served up in this strange Swedish import. Directed and written by Ingmar Bergman, whose previous efforts include "Torment" and "Frenzy," the film is a probing search of the tormented souls of a group of turn-of-the-century travelling circus performers.

It is disturbing in its presentation of the utter degradation of helpless people, apparently caught up in a life from which they cannot escape. It pulls no punches in its frank display of sex and it is often brutal in its exposure of human weakness. "The Naked Night" is not for the seeker of escapist entertainment.

It is difficult to recall another film which leaves the victims so completely without hope. The realism is stark, the web unbreakable, and the future uncertain.

Seeking the tranquillity of a normal life, Ake Groenberg, as the owner of a small, impoverished circus, fails in a reconciliation effort with his estranged wife and two sons who live quietly in a smalltown. He is betrayed by his circus performer-mistress, played by Miss Anderson. Tormented, humiliated, and severely beaten by her seducer in full view of a circus audience, he fails in a suicide attempt while in abject misery. His mistress, in turn, is betrayed and ridiculed by her seducer. At the height of their degradation, the circus owner and his mistress find comfort in each other. The circus moves on and they follow.

The outline of the story barely conveys the depressing quality of the story. There is one particularly embarrassing scene, told in flashback by a circus driver. The weak-minded wife of the circus clown goes bathing in the nude with a group of soldiers as an entire regiment looks on. The clown plunges in after her, lifts her up, and carries her in silence past the regiment and his fellow performers. His walk through the gauntlet is an emotional shocker and perhaps one of the most disturbing scenes ever put on film.

Miss Andersson and Groenberg provide excellent naturalistic performances. Hasse Ekman as the seducer, Anders Ek as the clown, Annika Tretow as the circus owner's wife, and Kiki as the clown's spouse all turn in memorable portrayals. Bergman's direction adds to the overall wierdness of the film and is especially effective in the closeups.

The photography ranges from interesting innovations to self-conscious artiness. The flashback sequence is presented as if it were footage from early silent films. The technical quality of the production is mediocre when compared with Hollywood standards.

"The Naked Night" will probably receive a divided reception. It will be condemned and denounced by many and will be championed by an enthusiastic core of devotees. *Holl.*

Lost
(BRITISH-COLOR)
London, Jan. 31.
Tense meller of police search for stolen baby; okay entry for home market with light hopes overseas.

Rank production and release. Stars David Farrar, David Knight, Julia Arnall; features Anthony Oliver, Thora Hird, Eleanor Summerfield, and Anne Paige. Directed by Guy Green. Screenplay, Janet Green; camera, Harry Waxman; editor, Anne V. Coates; music, Benjamin Frankel. At Gaumont Theatre, London. Running time, **89 MINSS.**

Craig	David Farrar
Lee	David Knight
Sue	Julia Arnall
Sergeant Lyel	Anthony Oliver
Kellys Landlady	Thora Hird
Sergeant Cook	Eleanor Summerfield
Nanny	Anne Paige
Mrs. Jeffries	Marjorie Rhodes
Mrs. Robey	Anna Turner
Viscountess	Everley Gregg
Sergeant Davies	Meredith Edwards
Mitzi	Irene Prador
Miss Gill	Anita Sharp Bolster
Pam	Beverley Brooks
Sue's Secretary	Brenda Hogan
Ice Cream Girl	Joan Sims

This is a tightly made meller based on a Scotland Yard search for a baby stolen in a London street. Almost unrelieved in its treatment, the yarn packs plenty of dramatic suspense, but lacks the quality to make it a really absorbing entertainment. As it stands, it should be a reliable attraction in the domestic market with more modest prospects overseas.

A slight Yank accent is given by the casting of David Knight in the role of the father of the missing boy. His American pronunciation seems more deliberate than natural, but the international flavor provided by this casting may help the production in the U.S.

Knight plays an official of the American Embassy in London, and his wife, Julia Arnall, is an executive in a leading fashion house. Their 18-month-old son is snatched from his baby-carriage while his nurse is making a purchase in a drugstore. There are no real clues to guide the police. They have to follow through on such slender shreds of evidence as a button off a woman's coat, a couple of empty ice cream cartons, a partly-torn page of a novel and a paper bag which had contained cakes. All these had been salvaged from the scene of the crime.

Detection work by the police, led by David Farrar, as a Detective Inspector, is good absorbing stuff, but the natural tendency of the mother towards near hysteria has a detracting influence. As it turns out, it is the torn page of the novel that leads to the final clue, and the rescue of the child from the edge of a cliff provides a tense climax. Farrar's solid performance is always believable. Knight plays in a single key which tends to become slightly monotonous while Miss Arnall, an attractive newcomer, shows promise for a bright future. Eleanor Summerfield, Anthony Oliver and Thora Hird turn in standard portrayals in support. There's a delightful cameo by Joan Sims as an icecream girl. Guy Green's direction extracts most of the suspense from Janet Green's screenplay. Benjamin Frankel's music and Harry Waxman's lensing are plus features. *Myro.*

Les Hussards
(The Cavalrymen)
(FRANCO-ITALIAN)
Paris, Jan. 31.
Cocinor release of Cocinor-Cocinex production. Stars Bernard Blier, Bourvil; features Georges Wilson, Giovanna Ralli, Louis De Funes, Gianni Esposito. Directed by Alex Joffe. Screenplay, Joffe, Gabirel Arout from play by P. A. Breal; camera, Jean Bourgoin; editor, H. Rist. At Balzac, Paris. Running time, **105 MINS.**

La Gouce	Bernard Blier
Flicot	Bourvil
Cosima	Giovanni Ralli
Luigi	Louis De Funes
Captain	Georges Wilson
Pietro	Gianni Esposito

Costumer is set during the Napoleonic invasion of Italy, and concerns the trials of two French cavalrymen whose horses are sent off by a young villager during a moment of inattention. The two men barge in on the village looking for the culprit, and must find someone to pay or otherwise they are liable to be hanged for losing their mounts. Pic vacillates between comedy, satire and a certain tragic-comic attitude towards war. However, its familiar aspects peg this primarily for special situations in the U.S. It has solid comic marquees values here in Bourvil and Bernard Blier, and has enough laughs for some chances in the U.S. marts via exploitation, with word-of-mouth a probable boost.

Alex Joffe has given this a colorful, folksy mounting and has the Italians speak in their own lingo with subtitles used. Blier and Bourvil are properly resigned, resourceful and tenderly human as the two soldiers, with ripe pulchritude supplied by Italo actress Giovanna Ralli. Lensing and editing are first rate and help point up some clever visual gags. Production dress is good and acting is fine right down the line. *Mosk.*

L'Amant De Lady Chatterly
(Lady Chatterly's Lover)
(FRENCH)
Paris, Jan. 31.
Columbia release of Regie-Orsay Film production. Stars Danielle Darrieux, Leo Genn; features Erno Crisa, Janine Crispin, Jacqueline Noelle, Jean Murat, Berthe Tissen. Directed by Marc Allegret. Screenplay, Joseph Kessel, Allegret, Gaston Bonheur, Philippe De Rothschilde from novel by D. H. Lawrence; camera, Georges Perinal; editor, Suzanne Troeye. At Normandie, Paris. Running time, **100 MINS.**

Constance	Danielle Darrieux
Clifford	Leo Genn
Mellors	Erno Crisa
Berthe	Jacqueline Noelle
Madame Bolton	Berthe Tissen
Hilda	Jeanine Crispin
Winter	Jean Murat

D. H. Lawrence's shocker novel on sex relations of the 1920's comes out a somewhat sudsy distaffer when updated to modern times. Lady Chatterly's dilemma was brought on when her husband urged her to have a child by another well-born man, he being impotent from a war accident, her sister egged her on to have a lover, and her heart and body finally went to the stolid but sensitive caretaker of her husband's estate. Though director Marc Allegret has kept this from being sensational, by subdued treatment, its frank dialog might place this in for censorship difficulties for the U.S., where, it is at best, primarily for arty situations.

In a day of freer outlooks on sex, this story of Lady Chatterly seems dated. Here she seems content to be the chaste loving companion and nurse of her invalid husband until she is awakened by her strapping caretaker. He shows her the strength of perfect physical love's height.

Danielle Darrieux is somewhat too pliant and unemotive to properly translate the sudden desires of Lady Chatterly, although director Marc Allegret has achieved a taking bit of film-making in the first seduction scene. Erno Crisa is too stiff as the lover while Leo Genn, as the husband, is handicapped in his playing by having to speak French. Lensing and editing are fine. This is primarily an exploitation item on its adulterous sex slant. Name values of Miss Darrieux and Genn also may help this in America. *Mosk.*

Der Letzte Mann
(The Last Man)
(GERMAN)
Berlin, Jan. 31.
Schorcht release of NDF production. Stars Hans Albers, Romy Schneider and Rudolf Forster. Directed by Harald Braun. Screenplay, Georg Hurdalek and Herbert Witt; camera, Richard Angst; music, Werner Eisbrenner. At Gloria Palast, Berlin. Running time, **105 MINS.**

Karl Knesebeck, headwaiter	Hans Albers
Niddy Hoevelmann	Romy Schneider
Herr Claassen	Rudolf Forster
Cousin Alwin	Joachim Fuchsberger
Helmuth Buehler	Michael Heltau
Lenchen Knesebeck	Camilla Spira
Popp, barber	Willy Stettner
Pichler	Franz Essel
Otto, waiter	Walter Gross
Eugen, waiter	Karl M. Schley
Jonas, waiter	Karl-Georg Saebisch
Enrico, waiter	Paul Bahlke
Till, bellhop	Michael Gebuehr
Uncle Ugo	Peter Luehr
Aunt Alma	Ursula v. Reibnitz

"The Last Man," one of the truly great Teutonic film classics (1924) with Émil Jannings, has been filmed again, this time with Hans Albers in the title role. As contrasted with F. W. Murnau's history-making silent pic, which was mercilessly unconventional, this one has obviously been tailored for mass appeal, with only slight off-beat ingredients and an overly happy ending. With an appealing story and the locally powerful Hans Albers name, film shapes to get outstanding domestic returns. Plot may also enjoy some foreign patronage. In the U.S., pic looks like a good bet for German language theatres.

While in the silent film version it was a hotel doorkeeper, it's now the story of a headwaiter who for many decades has been faithfully serving in a luxurious hotel. After the death of the hotel proprietress, a personal dispute with the arrogent new hotel owners' makes him lose his position of a headwaiter and he's disgraced to the job of the hotel's toilet attendant. Vaguely the film attempts to explain the tragedy of a man in need and his loneliness but then slides into a very conventional turn.

Film primarily benefits from the personality of Albers and the entertaining story although losing much of its conviction and roundness via its somewhat corny ending.

Two actors are noteworthy in this. Albers and Rudolf Forster. Albers' portrayal has always a human touch and easily wins the sympathy of the audience. Forster plays his rich friend, whom he eventually saves from committing suicide. The entire cast stands considerably in the shadow of these two actors, although some of the support, including Karl M. Schley, and little Michael Gebuehr are excellent.

Apart from a slow beginning, Harald Braun expertly directed this film. Screenplay by Georg Hurdalek and Herbert Witt concentrates largely on similar situations. Lensing by Richard Angst is fine as are other technical contributions. *Hans.*

Man Who Never Was
(C'SCOPE—COLOR)

Well-made thriller based on World War II stranger-than-fiction stunt. Here's offbeat entry which deserves playdates.

20th-Fox release of Andre Hakim production. Stars Clifton Webb, Gloria Grahame; features Robert Flemyng, Josephine Griffin, Stephen Boyd, Andre Morell, Laurence Naismith, Geoffrey Keen. Directed by Ronald Neame. Screenplay, Nigel Balchin, from Ewen Montagu novel of same title; camera (Eastman Color), Oswald Morris; music, Muir Mathieson. Previewed in N. Y. Feb. 8, 56. Running time, **103 MINS.**

Lt. Comdr. Ewen Montagu .... Clifton Webb
Lucy .... Gloria Grahame
George Acres .... Robert Flemyng
Pam .... Josephine Griffin
OReilly .... Stephen Boyd
Sir Bernard Spilsbury .... Andre Morell
Admiral Cross .... Laurence Naismith
General Nye .... Geoffrey Keen
General Coburn .... Michael Hordern
The Father .... Moultrice Kelsall
Taxi Drier .... Cyril Cusack
Landlady .... Joan Hickson
Joe .... William Russell
Shop Assistant .... Richard Wattis
Larry .... Terence Longdon
Vice-Admiral .... Allan Cuthbertson
Wills Officer .... Brian Oulton
Lt. Jewell .... William Squire
Adams .... Ronald Adams
Scientist .... Miles Malleson
Club Porter .... Gibb McLaughlin
Admiral Mountbattan .... Peter Williams
Doctor .... Michael Brill
Bank Mgr. .... John Welsh
Secretary .... Cecily Paget-Bowman
French .... Robert Brown
Club Matron .... Everley Gregg
Passport Officer .... Lloyd Lamble
Customs Officer .... Gordon Bell
Admiral Canaris .... Wolf Frees
German Colonel .... Gerhard Puritz
Laurence (Consul) .... D.A. Clarke-Smith

Of all the fantastic stories to come out of World War II, the use by British Naval Intelligence of a corpse to deceive the Germans about the planned invasion if Sicily undoubtedly out-fictions fiction. By the very nature of its intricate planning and boldness of execution, the whole subject is a natural for the screen.

In making "The Man Who Never Was," based on the Ewen Montagu novel (not Duff Cooper's), producer Andre Hakim and director Ronald Neame have turned out a suspenseful and thoroughly intriguing film with a double dose of exploitation angles. In the part of Montagu, the "master planner," they have cast Clifton Webb. The role is distinctly offbeat for him and, on the whole, he handles it competently. If shades of "Mr. Belvedere" occasionally creep into his overly-crisp characterization of a British Naval Commander, audiences will surely forgive him.

The star of this show is the corpse which, dressed up as a British marine major, is allowed to float ashore on the coast of Spain. It carries confidential letters with references to the forthcoming invasion of Greece, a ruse which actually fooled the Germans and saved many Allied lives. Much of the picture is taken up with the fascinating detail of securing the right corpse and establishing a proper identity for him.

Wisely realizing that this painstaking process, however unusual, lacks action and is bound to become tedious after a while, scripter Nigel Balchin has introduced the figure of a young Irishman sent to London by the Germans to check on the identity of Major Martin. By a combination of circumstances, some of them less credible than others, he, too, is fooled.

Paced by Webb, the cast gives thoroughly competent performances for the most part. Gloria Grahame, assigned (without her knowledge) to be the girlfriend of "Major Martin," seems an unhappy choice for the part, and she overplays it badly. Also, there is something very much amiss with her makeup in this picture. By contrast, Josephine Griffin, Miss Grahame's friend and Webb's assistant, is a British newcomer who, via the simplicity of her acting and her pleasant looks, rates attention. She's completely believable. So is legit actor Robert Flemyng as Webb's aide. Stephen Boyd as the young Irishman etches an interesting character and Moultrice Kelsall, as the father who allows Webb to use the body of his son, does well in a bit part.

Director Neame is an expert in his craft and the picture owes him many fine touches. He plays the suspense angles for all they're worth and also gets some sentiment into his film. Discovery of the body by Spanish fishermen (a scene lensed on the spot) is dramatically realistic. Brief German sequences are almost deliberately underplayed and a great deal more could have been done with them. Submarine bit, on the other hand, carries sock impact.

Lenser Oswald Morris has used CinemaScope to good advantage and the color in the film is fine. Opening shot, showing the corpse washed up on the surf, combines beauty and chills. Balchin's script fuses fiction and truth into an acceptable whole and his dialog carries conviction as well as the needed infusion of humor. Fadeout scene leaves something to wish for, as Webb returns to Spain to lay a decoration on the grave of "Major Martin." On the whole, "The Man Who Never Was" shapes as well-made and unusual entertainment. *Hift.*

Never Say Goodbye
(COLOR)

High voltage in femme appeal. Rock Hudson as marquee lure. Introduces Cornell Borchers, Universal's promising new face.

Universal release of Albert J. Cohen production. Stars Rock Hudson, Cornell Borchers, and George Sanders. Directed by Jerry Hopper. Screenplay, Charles Hoffman; based on a screenplay by Bruce Manning, John Klorer and Leonard Lee from the play "Come Prima Meglio De Prima" by Luigi Pirandello; camera (Technicolor), Maury Gertsman; editor, Paul Weatherwax; music, Frank Skinner. Previewed in N. Y. Jan. 19, '54. Running time, **96 MINS.**

Dr. Michael Carrington .... Rock Hudson
Lisa .... Cornell Borchers
Victor .... George Sanders
Dr. Bailey .... Ray Collins
Dave .... David Janssen
Suzy Carrington .... Shelley Fabares
Dr. Kelly Andrews .... Raymond Greenleaf
Dr. Barnes .... Frank Wilcox

Segments of the film industry moan about the falloff in the women's audience and exhibitor leaders in particular have called for concentrated efforts to lure the distaffers back to the theatres. "Never Say Goodbye" is apparently Universal's contribution in this direction. It's a woman's picture, pure and simple, and loaded with the ingredients of misunderstanding and mother love which classically appeal to those gals who go for soap opera and magazine romance.

In short, backfence grapevine should favor "Never Say Goodbye." As added appeal for the distaffers, there's Rock Hudson as marquee bait. The Hudson name should also serve as a draw for the teenage set.

Hudson is teamed with Cornell Borchers, the German actress who is making her American film debut in this picture. Miss Borchers, who won the British equivalent of the Academy Award for her role in "The Divided Heart," is a welcome addition to these shores. A tall, ash blonde with an Ingrid Bergman appeal, she displays a warm personality and the acting knowhow that sets her up as a performer who can become an important marquee name here. Her English is almost letter perfect, revealing only a slight, but pleasant, accent.

The story is divided into three segments and appears ideally suited for a future three-part tv serialization. Opens with Hudson as a successful Southern California physician, the father of an eight-year-old daughter whose mother is apparently dead. At a cafe following a medical convention in Chicago, he meets two people out of his past—George Sanders, a caricature artist, and Miss Borchers, Sanders' pianist-assistant. Miss Borchers turns out to be Hudson's long-lost wife. On recognizing him, she dashes out into the street where she is critically injured by a truck. Hudson performs an emergency operation. End of crisis No. 1.

While waiting for Miss Borchers to recover, Hudson's thoughts go back ten years to Vienna where, as a captain in the U.S. Medical Corps, he had met and wooed Miss Borchers. In an unjustified jealous rage, he walked out on her, taking their infant child with him. An attempt at reconciliation fails when Miss Borchers, caught in the Russian sector, is detained, arrested and sent off to an Iron Curtain camp. End of crisis two.

The shift is back to the present. Hudson convinces her to return home with him. She reluctantly agrees, mainly for the reunion with her child. She enters the house as Hudson's "new" wife and tackles the job of weaning back her daughter who refuses to accept her as her real mother. Miss Borchers finally succeeds, but not without tear-provoking and heart-tugging incidents. It's bound to bring out the handkerchiefs of the femme audience.

Hudson is satisfactory as the doctor and Sanders is convincing as the standby "good loser" in Miss Borchers' affections. Shelley Fabares, as the young daughter, manages a difficult role well. Good support is provided by Ray Collins, David Janssen, Raymond Greenleaf, and Frank Wilcox.

The Albert J. Cohen production is handsomely mounted physically and Jerry Hopper's direction meets the demands of the Charles Hoffman script, adapted from a previous screenplay by Bruce Manning, John Klorer, and Leonard Lee which, in turn, is based on a play by Luigi Pirandello. Maury Gertsman's Technicolor photography and other technical aspects are right out of the top-drawer for an overall smooth and slick production. *Holl.*

The Come On

Russell Birdwell's return to direction makes out as contrived meller unevenly valued and relying for mild prospects on Anne Baxter, Sterling Hayden names.

Hollywood, Feb. 9.

Allied Artists release of Lindsley Parsons production. Stars Anne Baxter, Sterling Hayden; features John Hoyt, Jesse White, Walter Cassell, Alex Gerry. Directed by Russell Birdwell. Screenplay, Warren Douglas, Whitman Chambers; from the novel by Chambers; camera, Ernest Haller; editor, Maurice Wright; score, Paul Dunlap. Previewed Feb. 7, '56. Running time, **82 MINS.**

Rita Kendrick .... Anne Baxter
Dave Arnold .... Sterling Hayden
Harley Kendrick .... John Hoyt
J. J. McGonigle .... Jesse White
Tony Margoli .... Walter Cassell
Joe Tinney .... Lee Turnbull
Chalmers .... Alex Gerry
Jerry Jannings .... Paul Picerni
Tony's Girl .... Karolee Kelly
Captain Getz .... Theodore Newton
Hogan .... Tyler McVey

As a melodrama equipped with some standard exploitation angles, "The Come On" may suffice for ballyhoo bookings, but the entertainment worth isn't there. Name of Anne Baxter, teamed with Sterling Hayden, can be figured for added importance in the Allied Artists market.

Feature is contrived with plot and counterplot that never quite makes it. Critically, the blame rests mostly on uneven direction plus script and characters that generate little sympathy. Russell Birdwell, better known for his publicity activities, does the direction, his first such chore in many years, and he's rusty. Direction was sans pace and punch. Warren Douglas and Whitman Chambers co-scripted from Chambers' story.

When a stolid fisherman, played by Hayden, sees a beauty, as done by Miss Baxter, on a Mexican beach, it's love and first clinch in five minutes. After that he finds the gal is money-mad and is partnered with John Hoyt in a blackmail racket. Wanting to break from Hoyt, but not willing to give up any coin, she first tries to involve Hayden in a scheme to kill Hoyt, which he doesn't go for. Double-crosser Hoyt then seemingly blows himself up so she'll be charged with murder. This fails to jell, also, thanks to a crooked private eye played by Jesse White, who's bumped off by Miss Baxter because he wants money for saving her from the police. Windup has Hoyt, already fatally wounded by the girl after she discovers him in Mexico, shooting her down and she dies in her lover's arms on the sands where they first met.

The two stars, other than the physical appearance put forth by Miss Baxter in her Edith Head costumes, fail to be very impressive. Hoyt chews up his blackmailer character in colorful fashion, as does White with his shamus part. Others have only small spots.

Picture has been well photographed in SuperScope by Ernest Haller and the Paul Dunlap score fits the melodramatics. *Brog.*

Our Miss Brooks

Eve Arden and tv cast move over to bigscreen in pleasant program comedy for general situations.

Hollywood, Feb. 10.

Warner Bros. release of David Weisbart (Lute) production. Stars Eve Arden, Gale Gordon, Don Porter, Robert Rockwell; features Jane Morgan, Richard Crenna. Directed by Al Lewis. Screenplay, Lewis and Joseph Quillan; from an idea by Robert Mann, based on CBS-TV series; camera, Joe LaShelle; editor, Fredrick Y. Smith; music, Roy Webb. Previewed Feb. 3, '56. Running time, **84 MINS.**

Miss Brooks .... Eve Arden
Osgood Conklin .... Gale Gordon
Lawrence Nolan .... Don Porter
Phillip Boynton .... Robert Rockwell
Margaret Davis .... Jane Morgan
Walter Denton .... Richard Crenna
Gary Nolan .... Nick Adams
"Stretch" Snodgrass .... Leonard Smith
Harriet Conklin .... Gloria MacMillan
Mr. Stone .... Joe Kearns
Dr. Henley .... William Newell
Mr. Webster .... Philip Van Zandt

Eve Arden and the "Our Miss Brooks" television cast move over to the big screen in a pleasant, if not outstanding, program comedy that should do an acceptable job of filling dual dates in the general situations. Negatively, it's merely an elongation of what viewers can get weekly for free on their home sets.

Al Lewis directs with a broad hand and also shares scripting credit with Joseph Quillan on this story developed from an idea by Robert Mann. Film finds Miss Brooks, the tv character delineated by Miss Arden, still chasing the stuffy biology professor, Phillip Boynton, as film and tv-played by Robert Rockwell. However, unlike that weekly living pursuit, the film brings her closer to her goal via the assistance of jealousy which sets in when she tackles the side job of tutoring poor-little-rich-boy Nick Adams and the latter's publisher-dad. Don Porter, makes a play for the heroine.

Above cast members in the David Weisbart production do their chores competently, as do such other video familiars as Gale Gordon, the pompous principal Osgood Conklin whose election race for a better post is part of the chuckles; Jane Morgan as Margaret Davis, Miss Brooks' birdbrained landlady; Richard Crenna, as squeaky-voiced Walter Denton, et al.

Camera work by Joe LaShelle and other technical supports are good. *Brog.*

The Last Hunt
(C'SCOPE—COLOR)

Nature in the rawest. Massacre of the American buffalo. Robert Taylor, Stewart Granger, Lloyd Nolan and Debra Paget for OK b.o.

Metro release of Dore Schary production. Stars Robert Taylor, Stewart Granger, Lloyd Nolan, Debrt Paget; features Russ Tamblyn, Constance Ford. Directed by Richard Brooks. Screenplay, Brooks; based on novel by Milton Lott; camera (Eastman Color), Russell Harlan; editor, Ben Lewis; music, Daniele Amfitheatrof. Previewed N. Y. Feb. 3, 56. Running time, **108 MINS.**

Charles Gilson	Robert Taylor
Sandy McKenzie	Stewart Granger
Woodfoot	Lloyd Nolan
Indian Girl	Debra Paget
Jimmy	Russ Tamblyn
Peg	Constance Ford
Ed Black	Joe DeSantis
1st Buffalo Hunter	Ainslie Pryor
Indian Agent	Ralph Moody
Bartender	Fred Graham
Spotted Hand	Ed Lonehill

Dore Schary's production of "Last Hunt" is grim, fierce, raw-boned outdoor fare. Excellently photographed in Eastman Color and CinemaScope, it's strikingly vivid in depicting the wanton mowing down of American buffalo and one man's, Robert Taylor's, lust to kill the animals, hapless Indians and even his close associates.

This is somewhat off the beaten path for wild west shows, having strong story values and well-defined characters centering on cruel conflicts that evolved toward the end of the last century. Richard Brooks' screenplay, from a novel by Milton Lott, shows marked talent for construction and organization of material that likely will stir revulsion among the sensitive and score with the "he men" of the audience.

The lead names doubtless will give it a boost and "Hunt" is arriving when action films appear going over particularly well on the market. Thus, okay overall prospects.

Film was locationed in Custer State Park, N. D., and slaying of the beasts is for real. They're shot down (annually) by Government agents to keep the herds from growing and scenes of this activity are cut and fitted into the fictional story with Taylor and Granger ostensibly at the guns.

A gallant Ivanhoe of a couple seasons back, Taylor this time hits the nadir in ruthlessness. He kills for kicks, an exhultation that's suggested as akin to, as one character puts it, "being with a woman." He takes a lethal bead on ignorant and impoverished Indians who have stolen his horses and later tries to passion up to the surviving squaw, Debra Paget, who thwarts him with the freeze of indifference.

At the start, Taylor picks up a partner in Stewart Granger, master buffalo killer of the past who would now rather settle down on his own ranch. Granger, although averse to elimination of the beasts from the American plains, joins Taylor in the association marked by the conflict in their personalities. That the differences in the makeup of these men—Granger is of gentle stock—will lead to a final blowoff is tipped at the outset. They act out the parts with believability.

Lloyd Nolan, a peg-legged, whiskey-sodden skinner, contributes a colorful, realistic performance and Russ Tamblyn registers fair enough, even though a little incongruity is sensed, as a redheaded halfbreed. Miss Paget is properly sullen as the Indian girl who teams romantically with Granger after Taylor, waiting to kill his partner, dies in a snowstorm. Constance Ford is standard as a dance-hall gal of the oater variety.

There's no dullness in "Last Hunt." Under Brooks' direction it's paced at a good clip and with alternating quiet tension and harsh action. One barroom brawl, particularly, in which Granger does a one-man cleanup job, is nifty in the true old-west sense.

Editing is sharp, Daniele Amphitheatrof's music sets up moods appropriately and other credits are good. *Gene.*

Musik Im Blut
(Music in the Blood)
(GERMAN—SONGS)

Berlin, Feb. 7.

Europa release of Central-Europa and CCC production. Stars Viktor de Kowa, Nadia Gray and Waltraut Haas. Directed by Eric Ode. Screenplay by Werner Eplinius and Janne Furch: camera, Karl Loeb; songs, Werner Mueller and Ernst Veech. At the Kiki, Berlin. Running time, **97 MINS.**

Kurt Widmann	Viktor de Kowa
Gina Martelli	Nadia Gray
Angelika Jaeger	Waltraut Haas
Cilly Mainsburg	Loni Heuser
Irma Pehlke	Ruth Stephan
Bruno Schnecke	Walter Gross
John Miller	Ed Tracy
Haeschen	Heidi Ewert

This German musical is an obvious effort to cash in on the wide popularity of Universal's "Glenn Miller Story." It even calls itself a "German Glenn Miller Story." It's a biopic of the late Kurt Widmann, Berlin's idolized bandleader. As usual with German musicals, this one can't stand comparison with American standards. There's, however, no denying the fact that this film has strong local audience appeal and should achieve above-average boxoffice. Foreign chances appear limited.

Most disappointing is the fact that the whole thing lacks quite a bit of conviction. It's hard to believe that the Widmann and latter's music in this film could achieve such stardom as depicted here. Often it's referred to jazz and the bandleader is occasionally even called a "German jazz pioneer." Yet there's hardly any jazz number in this film which would justify this distinction. The music in this, incidentally, is mostly more sweet than hot and will hardly appeal to the lovers of jazz.

Aside from being everything but a Kurt Widmann, Viktor de Kowa turns in a highly recommendable, almost masterly performance. Next to him, Walter Gross, enacting his manager, deserves mention. Gross, locally rated as a first-rate comedian, has here at last been given a substantial part and he makes the most out of it. Waltraut Haas is okay as Widmann's wife. Nadia Gray, portrays bandleader's prewar songstress (vocals by Gitta Lind), while Loni Heuser, Ruth Stephan and Ed Tracy are satisfactory in lesser roles.

Eric Ode's direction may be called good in view of the mediocre script by Werner Eplinius and Janne Furch. As more or less always the case with German-made musicals, script lacks considerable imagination. Technically, film reveals a moderate budget. *Hans.*

Das Horoskop Der Familie Hesselbach
(Horoscope of Family Hesselbach)
(GERMAN)

Frankfurt, Feb. 7.

Union Film release of Wolf Schmidt Inc. production. Stars Wolf Schmidt; features Else Knott, Irene Marhold, Joose Juergen Siedhoff, Sibylle Schindler. Directed by Wolf Schmidt. Story and screenplay by Wolf Schmidt; camera, Otto Cartharius; music, Wolf Droysen. At Zeil Theatre, Frankfurt. Running time, **95 MINS.**

Papa Hesselbach	Wolf Schmidt
Mama Hesselbach	Irene Knott
Willi Hesselbach	Joose Juergen Siedhoff
Anneliese Hesselbach	Irene Marhold
Waltrout Hesselbach	Sofie Engelke
Nina	Sibylle Schindler
Hans	Guenther Ziessler

Low budget films in Germany, just as in the U.S., are nearly a thing of the past. One man in Germany is successfully battling this trend, turning out a series of low-cost films which have meant big cash at the wickets. He is Wolf Schmidt, whose one-man direction, production, writing and starring vehicles are doing important business in this country.

Third in the "Family Hesselbach" series is "The Horoscope." Like the others, it concerns a typical lower middleclass German family with nearly stock characters —a homely daughter in search of a husband, an attractive daughter with problems about her fiance, the teenage son in search of romance, the buxom mother and the flirtatious middleaged papa. This all combines to make sort of a "Ma and Pa Kettle" of Germany.

First of the Schmidt films, shot in Schmidt's own small home in a suburb of Frankfurt, cost about $25,000. It grossed $250,000. Second and third films follow a similar pattern, mostly photographed at home.

The horoscope plot has the whole family terrified at a series of predictions that someone in the household is due to die. Superstitions lead to slapsticky comedy scenes and suspense. This is big for mass audiences but a little incredible for the sophisticated.

Schmidt plays a plausible papa. Situation is accented by some funny friends, the old spinster and the newly married, middleaged couple. Sibylle Schindler, a charmingly awkward teenager, is a real scene thefter. A 15-year-old former ballet student who is doing her first acting in this series, she seems to have a fine future in German films.

Direction and acting are excellent under Schmidt's easy handling. Music and camera are good assets.

Definitely aimed for the family trade, Family Hesselbach might convey its humor to the same sort of U.S. audience. Absence of names for America is obviously a drawback. Schmidt has proved for the third time that one doesn't need a fat bankroll to come up with a better-than-average boxoffice draw. *Haze.*

Manfish
(SONGS—COLOR)

Jamaica scenic values with Poe plots. Fair entry for second-billing.

Hollywood, Feb. 8.

United Artists release of W. Lee Wilder production. Stars John Bromfield, Lon Chaney, Victor Jory; features Barbara Nichols, Tessa Prendergast. Directed by Wilder. Screenplay, Joel Murcott; story adapted from Edgar Allan Poe's "Gold Bug" and "Telltale Heart" by Myles Wilder; camera (De Luxe Color), Charles S. Wellborn; editor, C. Turney Smith; score, Albert Elms; songs, Richard Koerner, Clyde Hoyte. Previewed Feb. 6, '56. Running time, **78 MINS.**

Brannigan	John Bromfield
"Swede"	Lon Chaney
"Professor"	Victory Jory
Mimi	Barbara Nichols
Alita	Tessa Prendergast
Chavez	Eric Coverly
Domingo	Vincent Chang
"Big Boy"	Theodore Furceli
Bianco	Vere Johns
Aleppo	Arnold Shanks
Calypso	Clyde Hoyte

W. Lee Wilder, as producer-director, has pieced together a picture from some footage shot in Jamaica and a couple of Edgar Allan Poe plots strictly for the programmer trade. Helping the film's chances are the luscious scenery and underwater sequences, tint photography by Charles S. Wellborn, and the colorful Jamaica locale.

Myles Wilder welded together Poe's "Gold Bug" and "Telltale Heart" for the story which Joel Murcott screen adapted, but unfortunately the dialog can best be described as primitive. In the first half, John Bromfield, muscular, bullyboy captain of the Manfish, turtle-fishing boat, teams with Victor Jory, a sinister professor, to find a pirate treasure, a la "Gold Bug."

Now comes the "Telltale Heart" segment, in which Jory kills Bromfield, ties the body to an oxygen cylinder and jettisons it overboard. Bubbles arising from the leaking cylinder, however, give away the crime and finale finds Lon Chaney, dimwitted crew member with a single-minded love of the boat, ending up as the owner. When he puts to sea to hunt turtles, he unwittingly lets the treasure, secured below the vessel, break loose and sink to the bottom.

Barbara Nichols and dusky Tessa Prendergast, both young ladies with spectacular topography, are on hand to lend added scenery as a hardbitten nitery thrush and a native belle, in that order. Neither is given much chance to demonstrate acting skill.

Bromfiled confines his thesping to sneering and looking menacing, Jory rolls his eyes and orates grandiloquently, Chaney mumbles and burbles, all without noticeable restraint under Wilder's loose direction. Rest of the cast is composed on native types and a few dragooned production crew members.

Included in the footage are all-too-short snips of calypso singing, but the plotting keeps getting in the way. Among numbers are "Big Fish"and "Goodbye," both by Clyde Hoyte, and "Beware the Caribbean," by Albert Elms. The sound is often out of sync and not of very good quality. *Kove.*

The River Changes
(GERMAN)

Heavy melodrama lensed in Germany with little general appeal.

Hollywood, Feb. 14.
Warner Bros. release of Owen Crump production. Stars Rossana Rory, Harald Maresch; features Renate Mannhardt, Henry Fisher, Jaspar V. Oertzen, Nick Solomatin. Written and directed by Crump; camera, Ellis W. Carter; editor, James Moore; score, Roy Webb. Previewed Jan. 31, '56. Running time, 91 MINS.
Mayram .... Rossana Rory
Kurus .... Harald Maresch
Leah .... Renate Mannhardt
The Leader .... Henry Fisher
Jonathan .... Jasper V. Oertzen
Asa .... Nick Solomatin
The Question Man .... Otto Friebel
Temen .... Rene Magron
Aaron .... Bert Brandt
Josana .... Ilse Ruth Roskam
The Little Man ...... H. Freuschtenicht
Peter .... Helge Lehmann
Tosnic .... H. C. Clemmstein
Chief Guard .... Rolf Menke

What "might" have been a tense suspense thriller comes out a heavy-handed melodrama with little general appeal for regular film-goers. Owen Crump, who wrote, produced and directed, did his lensing in Germany, using an all-foreign cast, but fails to utilize to the best advantage what started out as a story idea with suspense possibilities.

Overseas filming gives an air of authenticity to the story of a small European village that suddenly finds itself being taken over by the "people's government" (presumably Communist, although unnamed) when a boundary river changes its course overnight. From a happy farming community, the village becomes a fear-ridden place as the new leaders establish themselves. Finale finds the villagers uniting to flee to the west side of the new river course and this break does generate a measure of tension which would have been greater if the plotting had carefully built to it.

Rossana Rory suitably portrays a village beauty who, although dallying with enemy border guard Harald Maresch along the river banks, still rallies enough to help get her people through by freeing village leader Jaspar V. Oertzen, imprisoned by "Government" representative Henry Fisher as a spy. Renate Mannhardt, Nick Solomatin, Otto Friebel and Rene Magron are among others in cast who are adequate.

Ellis W. Carter's photography has a moody, artistic, flavor that goes with the presentation and the music by Roy Webb does its background supporting competently.
Brog.

Slightly Scarlet
(COLOR)

Crime-doesn't-pay meller, satisfactorily done for average prospects in regular situations.

Hollywood, Feb. 14.

RKO release of Benedict Bogeaus production. Stars John Payne, Arlene Dahl, Rhonda Fleming; features Kent Taylor, Ted de Corsia, Lance Fuller, Buddy Baer. Directed by Allan Dwan. Screenplay, Robert Blees; based on James M. Cain's novel "Love's Lovely Counterfeit"; camera (Technicolor), John Alton; editor,

James Leicester; score, Louis Forbes. Previewed Feb. 13, '56. Running time, 98 MINS.

Ben Grace .... John Payne
Dorothy Lyons .... Arlene Dahl
June Lyons .... Rhonda Fleming
Jansen .... Kent Taylor
Sol Caspar .... Ted de Corsia
Gauss .... Lance Fuller
Lenhardt .... Buddy Baer
Dietz .... Frank Gerstle
Martha .... Ellen Corby

"Slightly Scarlet," with its James M. Cain tough touches, does a fairly effective job of providing crime-doesn't-pay entertainment for the regular market. Additionally, it has the familiar names of John Payne, Arlene Dahl and Rhonda Fleming for the marquees in those playdates, as well as a Technicolor dress well-lensed in SuperScope.

Benedict Bogeaus' production draws on Cain's novel, "Love's Lovely Counterfeit" as source material for the screenplay by Robert Blees. It's the story of mobsters who fall out, reform governments and lovely ladies caught up in the melodramatic events. Overtones of s.a., along with some striking settings are values for release prospects and average returns seem likely.

Payne is seen as a bright boy on the payroll of Ted de Corsia, crime syndicate boss, who decides to switch sides and take over via supporting a reform candidate for mayor who will have a police chief willing to take orders. Payne does right well by the role's demands. Miss Fleming plays the reform mayor's secretary (who must draw a big, big salary judging by her standard of living) and decorates the role. So does Miss Dahl, her younger sister who's a confirmed kleptomaniac and an amoral neurotic as well.

A good degree of toughness is given the crime boss character by de Corsia, who has to take it on the lam, but returns at the finale to do some personal revenge work on Payne, setting being a plushy Malibu beach house. Kent Taylor, the reform candidate, comes over satisfactorily, as does Frank Gerstle as the police chief, whose sweet setup with Payne is overthrown because Miss Dahl filches a necklace, thus setting loose a train of events that reveals the power behind the office. Others are okay.

Allan Dwan's direction stirs up a good melodramatic pace, which is properly suited to the type of tale being told, and the footage unfolds with only occasional lag. John Alton handled the cameras to advantage in presenting the art direction by Van Nest Polglase and the set decorations by Alfred Spencer. Editing by James Leicester, and score by Louis Forbes are both good. *Brog.*

Liebe, Tanz Und 1000 Schlager
(Love, Dance And 1000 Songs)
(GERMAN, MUSICAL)

Berlin, Feb. 7.
Gloria release of CCC production. Stars Caterina Valente and Peter Alexander. Features Rudolf Platte, Willi A. Kleinau, Ruth Stephan, Hubert v. Meyerinck, Werner Fuetterer, Peter W. Staub, Silvio Francesco, Bruno W. Pantel, Joachim Rake, Wolf Harnisch, John Bubbles, Henry Lorenzen, Erik van Aro, Tvorek; orchestras, Kurt Edelhagen and Hazy Osterwald. Directed by Paul Martin. Screenplay, Curt Flatow and Paul Martin after story by Frederick Kohner; camera, Karl Loeb; music, Kurt Feltz and Heinz Gietz. At Gloria Palast, Berlin. Running time, 98 MINS.

This musical has been tailored primarily for Caterina Valente who in little time has managed to become Germany's No. 1 record-

ing star. Unfortunately, her debut as a big screen star cannot be regarded as a very successful one, with her material is mostly to blame.

Pic will turn out to be a top-notch moneymaker within at home. It even will appeal to provincial-minded patrons. International prospects appear rather meagre. The Valente name, however, may lure some curious patrons.

This film lacks practically everything a good musical requires—Color, pace, eye-filling scenery and imagination. However, Miss Valente's remarkable singing talents are also obvious in this film although she's not been given exactly a rewarding role. The story, a secondary factor, concerns Miss Valente who is discovered by a talent scout of a big disk company. But she has it tough to get into the act since the big boss shows an open dislike for any newcomer.

The songs featured in this musical are mostly easy on the ear.

The supporting cast is generally well chosen. Cast also includes East German Willi A. Kleinau, holder of the Commie National Prize, in the role of Miss Valente's father.

Script by Curt Flatow and Paul Martin (who also directed), based on an original story by Frederick Kohner, is not very imaginative. Technically, film represents German average. *Hans.*

Carousel
(C'SCOPE—COLOR—SONGS)

Arrival of CinemaScope 55 in bright, beautifully mounted screen version of Rodgers & Hammerstein musical. Big prospects in any situation.

20th-Fox release of Henry Ephron production. Stars Gordon MacRae, Shirley Jones, Cameron Mitchell, Barbara Ruick, Claramae Turner, Robert Rounseville; features Gene Lockhart, Audrey Christie, Susan Luckey, William Le Massena, John Dehner, Jacques D'Amboise. Directed by Henry King. Screenplay, Phoebe and Henry Ephron, from Rodgers & Hammerstein musical play based on Ferenc Molnar's "Liliom"; choreography, Rod Alexander; Louise's ballet from Agnes de Mille original; camera (Color by De Luxe,) Charles G. Clarke; editor, William Reynolds; music supervision, Alfred Newman. Previewed at the Roxy Theatre, N.Y., Feb. 16, '56. Running time, 128 MINS.
Billy .... Gordon MacRae
Julie .... Shirley Jones
Jigger .... Cameron Mitchell
Carrie .... Barbara Ruick
Cousin Nettie .... Claramae Turner
Mr. Snow .... Robert Rounseville
Starkeeper .... Gene Lockhart
Mrs. Mullin .... Audrey Christie
Louise .... Susan Luckey
Heavenly Friend ...William Le Massena
Mr. Bascombe .... John Dehner
Louise's Dancing Partner
                    Jacques D'Amboise
Captain Watson .... Frank Tweddell
Contortionist .... Sylvia Stanton
Fat Woman .... Mary Orozco
Strong Man .... Tor Johnson
Juggler .... Harry "Duke" Johnson
Sword Swallower ...... Marion Dempsey
Fire Eater .... Ed Mundy
Midget .... Angelo Rossitto
Enoch Snow Jr. .... Dee Pollock

A great score, imaginative dance sequences, and the pre-sold reputation of the work, combined with the fresh and brightly colored backgrounds of on-location Maine, make this ambitious 20th Century-Fox screen adaptation of the Richard Rodgers-Oscar Hammerstein 2d musical a major contender for important grosses.

"Carousel" was presented by the Theatre Guild in April of 1945, ran 890 performances at the Majestic Theatre. It now gets the super-treatment in the new 55m Cinema-Scope as organized by producer Henry Ephron and directed by Henry King.

There are two production numbers in the picture that are close to classic. Add the staging of the famed "Soliloquy," as sung by Gordon MacRae for strong impact. Musical numbers are all in extremely good taste. Reservations as to some scenes and a certain slowness in pace are minor.

The stars of "Carousel" remain Rodgers & Hammerstein. Their songs keep fresh and appealing in the Maine and other settings picked by King. The cast is uniformly attractive, from MacRae as the shiftless ne'er-do-well Billy Bigelow, to pretty Shirley Jones as Julie; charming Barbara Ruick as her friend, Carrie; Cameron Mitchell as the slithery Jigger; Claramae Turner as Cousin Nettie, and Robert Rounseville in great voice as the upright Mr. Snow. It may be said that Miss Jones is under-charged with facial animation and "feels" little but she is, strangely for the femme lead, subordinate on this telling.

Production number that precedes the gay clambake is a riot of color and movement and a tribute to the ingenuity of choreographer Rod Alexander who brings to the number a fresh approach on the dock and rooftop of a clam house at Boothbay Harbor, Me. Ensemble hoofing is full of movement and rates spontaneous acclaim. Sequence smacks over "June's Bustin' Out All Over" number.

If this scene is great, the finale, when Julie's daughter, Louise (danced by Susan Luckey) imagines her meeting up with a carnival and does a number with handsome Jacques D'Amboise, is even more of a rocking production success. Based on the original Agnes De Mille conception, the dance alone is of Academy Award-winning quality. Miss Luckey, incidentally, is a charmer and a gal with a great deal of talent. Graceful as an elf, with delicate beauty she deserves a lot of Hollywood attention. Cameraman, editor, director or someone should have caught the awkward bit where she lifts her head at graduation revealing dark roots beneath blondine tresses.

Some may feel film opening, a change from stage, "signals" the story. As photographed "Carousel," keeps elements of drama, humor and sentiment but starts out with MacRae already dead and in heaven, displaying some of h's stubborn traits in discussing with starkeeper Gene Lockhart whether to go back to earth for one day where, he has been told, Miss Jones (his wife) is unhappy. His courtship and marriage are then told in flashback, including his participation with Mitchell in an attempted holdup and his death when, trying to escape, he falls on his knife.

MacRae, who loves Miss Jones but is unable to tell her so until, in the end, he makes her sense it, is excellent from start to finish and again proves himself in top

voice. His performance has an appealing, masculine quality that nevertheless registers in various shades. The "Soliloquy" number, which he sings against a beautiful background of the sea pounding against surf rocks, has smash impact and is one of the highlights of the picture.

Opposite him, Miss Jones makes a quiet Julie, and registers firmly though acting is shy on expressiveness. She does her numbers in a very pleasant voice and looks just right for the part. She and MacRae (a marquee duo also in another R & H tuner, "Oklahoma") do "If I Loved You" together and the haunting beauty of that song has lost none of its appeal. Miss Jones also gives "What's the Use of Wond'rin" a moving rendition.

As Julie's friend, Miss Ruick is a real find in the part of the faithful Carrie. Miss Ruick not only has a distinct flair for comedy, but she looks good and has a voice that comes through just fine. Her rendition (with Rounseville) of "When the Children Are Asleep" is absolutely topnotch and so is her chirping of "When I Marry Mister Snow." When they talk about those "new faces" for Hollywood, Miss Ruick is high on the list.

Only one or two of the original "Carousel" numbers have been left out. Others have been cut short. But there to enjoy are "Carousel Waltz," "Blow High," "It Was a Real Nice Clambake," the soaring "Never Walk Alone," which Miss Turner does as a solo and which also brings the film to a touching finish; "You're a Queer One, Julie Jordan" (done briefly by Miss Ruick) etc.

The supporting cast is fine in every respect. Mitchell as Jigger etches a convincing portrait of a crook; Audrey Christie as the owner of the carousel does a most competent job in a brief part and she registers firmly; Miss Turner has a most enjoyable voice; Rounseville combines a fine tenor with the needed touch of comedy as Mr. Snow; Lockhart as the starkeeper, William Le Massena as the Heavenly Friend, Frank Tweddell and the rest all contribute to the mak-

ing of a fine picture. De Luxe Color deserves a distinct share of the credit.

Lensing by Charles G. Clarke is an important asset to his film and keeps coming up with visual surprises. CinemaScope 55 proves its worth in "Carousel." The images are sharp and clear and a distinct improvement over prior CinemaScope efforts. Six-channel sound at the Roxy greatly adds to the enjoyment of the music and the singing. "Carousel 'is something for the whole indusry to be proud about. *Hift.*

Dig That Uranium

So-so Bowery Boys item.

Hollywood, Feb. 16.
Allied Artists release of Ben Schwalb production. Stars Leo Gorcey, Huntz Hall; features Bernard Gorcey, Mary Beth Hughes, Raymond Hatton, Harry Lauter, Myron Healey, Richard Powers, Paul Fierro, David Condon, Bennie Bartlett, Carl Switzer. Directed by Edward Bernds. Screenplay, Elwood Ullman, Bert Lawrence; camera, Harry Neumann; editor, William Austin; music, Marlin Skiles. Reviewed Feb. 15, '56. Running time, 61 MINS.
Slip .... Leo Gorcey
Sach .... Huntz Hall
Louis .... Bernard Gorcey
Jeanette .... Mary Beth Hughes
Mac .... Raymond Hatton
Haskell .... Harry Lauter
Hody .... Myron Healey
Loomis .... Richard Powers
Indian .... Paul Pierro
Chuck .... David Condon
Butch .... Bennie Bartlett
Shifty .... Carl Switzer

The laughs come only spasmodically in "Dig That Uranium," with result that this 40th entry in Allied Artists' Bowery Boys series. At best shapes as filler fare.

In whipping up the screenplay, Elwood Ullman and Bert Lawrence seemed to have concentrated to a greater extent on Leo Gorcey's malaprops than on a story line upon which to hang some good comedic situations. Plot puts boys out in the desert, where they've purchased a uranium mine, minus uranium. They stick around to search in other spots, and when a discovery is finally made at the windup, they find it's on an Indian reservation. That's about it, save for the baddies, who are constantly on the scene to hound the boys, thinking they've come across a rich vein.

Gorcey and Huntz Hall, also starred, cavort again in the same manner which seemingly has pleased followers of this series for years, pair having long ago mastered their respective roles.

Direction by Edward Bernds of the Ben Schwalb production capitalizes as best possible on the funny moments, and really comes to life in the film's best sequence: a five-minute dream flashback which takes off on the western show-down fight, a la "High Noon." *Neal.*

The Conqueror
(C'SCOPE-COLOR)

Fanciful sex-and-sand escapism; actionful entertainment with John Wayne, Susan Hayward and good b.o. outlook.

Hollywood, Feb. 21.
RKO release of Dick Powell (Howard Hughes) production. Stars John Wayne, Susan Hayward, Pedro Armendariz; features Agnes Moorehead, Thomas Gomez, John Hoyt, William Conrad, Ted de Corsia. Directed by Powell. Screenplay, Oscar Millard; camera (Technicolor), Joseph LaShelle, Leo Tover, Harry J. Wild, William Snyder; editors, Robert Ford, Kennie Marstella; music, Victor Young, supervised by C. Bakaleinikoff;

choreography, Robert Sidney. Previewed Feb. 14, '56. Running time, 111 MINS.
Temujin .... John Wayne
Bortai .... Susan Hayward
Jamuga .... Pedro Armendariz
Hunlun .... Agnes Moorehead
Wang Kahn .... Thomas Gomez
Shaman .... John Hoyt
Kasar .... William Conrad
Kumlek .... Ted de Corsia
Targutai .... Leslie Bradley
Chepei .... Lee Van Cleef
Bogurchi .... Peter Mamakos
Tartar Captain .... Leo Gordon
Captain of Wang's Guard....Richard Loo

Just so there will be no misunderstanding about "The Conqueror," a foreword baldly states that it is fiction, although with some basis in fact. With that warning out of the way, the viewer can sit back and thoroughly enjoy a huge, brawling, sex-and-sand actioner purporting to show how a 12th Century Mongol leader started a career of conquest that led to his becoming known as Genghis Khan, It's straight escapism. Plenty of exploitation angles and points towards solid b.o. returns.

The marquee value of the John Wayne-Susan Hayward teaming more than offsets any incongruity of the casting, which has him as the Mongol leader and she as the Tartar princess he captures and forceably takes as mate. Strong point of the Howard Hughes production for RKO release is sweep of action and romantic flavor instilled by Dick Powell's vigorous direction. The latter's handling of the show demonstrates effective versatility, whether dealing with the tremendously spectacular mass clashes between mounted hordes of Mongol and Tartar, or with the more personal phases of the Oscar Millard screen story. Yarn makes no pretense of being a historical fact story. Instead, it tells a fanciful, colorful tale suggestive of the vivid period with a derring-do dash that pays off.

Costarring with Wayne and Miss Hayward is that excellent Mexican actor, Pedro Armendariz, who makes believeable his role of Wayne's blood-brother and is an important essential in the entertainment. More incongruity is found in the casting of Agnes Moorehead as the Mongol's weazened mother. Thomas Gomez is the fat, soft Chinese leader; John Hoyt an evil soothsayer; William Conrad, the Mongol's real brother, and Ted de Corsia a wicked Tartar ruler whose daughter Wayne takes for revenge. All are good in their colorful characters and have the ability not to be thrown by the archaic dialog that Oscar Millard passes for 12th Century idiom.

Four-man CinemaScope camera team consisting of Joseph LaShelle, Leo Tover, Harry J. Wild and William Snyder gets it all on film in Technicolor, along the beauties of the outdoor "oriental" locations in Utah.

Hughes presentation, on which Powell also served as producer, doesn't overlook another kind of beauty. The s.a. pitch is in a harem dance sequence choreographed by Robert Sidney, in which a covey of lookers give the appearance of being almost completely bare while gyrating to the Oriental strains of Victor Young's firstrate music. Solo dancer who catches the eye is Sylvia Lewis, and over Miss Hayward makes a few passes at terping as part of a story angle.

Albert S. D'Agostino and Carroll Clark handled the excellent art direction and Darrell Silvera and Al Orenbach the set decorations. Editing by Robert Ford and Kennie Marstella is topnotch, as is the

music supervision by C. Bakaleinikoff. Already a title tune, lifted from the theme music, with Edward Heyman supplying lyrics to the Young cleffing, is being marketed. *Brog.*

Hot Blood
(C'Scope-Songs-Color)

Offbeat comedy-drama about city-living gypsies. Played for laughs with Russell, Wilde for marquees.

Hollywood, Feb. 24.

Columbia release of Howard Welsch-Harry Tatelman production. Stars Jane Russell, Cornel Wilde, Luther Adler, Joseph Calleia; features Mikhail Rasumny, Nina Koshetz, Helen Westcott, Jamie Russell, Wally Russell, Nick Dennis, Richard Deacon. Directed by Nicholas Ray. Screenplay, Jesse Lasky Jr.; based on a story by Jean Evans; camera (Technicolor), Ray June; editor, Otto Ludwig; music, Les Baxter; lyrics, Ross Bagdasarian. Previewed Feb. 17, '56. Running time, **85 MINS.**

Annie Caldash	Jane Russell
Stephen Torino	Cornel Wilde
Marco Torino	Luther Adler
Papa Theodore	Joseph Calleia
Old Johnny	Mikhail Rasumny
Nita Johnny	Nina Koshetz
Velma	Helen Westcott
Xano	Jamie Russell
Bimbo	Wally Russell
Korka	Nick Dennis
Mr. Swift	Richard Deacon
Desk Sgt. McGrossin	Robert Foulk
Joe Randy	John Raven

Here's a tale about gypsies, the ancient breed, living in a big American city. Offbeat situations lean more to comedy than drama. Jane Russell and Cornel Wilde add some dash to the doings and familiar name adornment for the marquees. That 85-minute running time also makes it a handy entry to top a dual bill.

An occasional sociological note on the effect of city living on the free-souled gypsy is sounded in the Howard Welsch-Harry Tatelman production for Columbia. However, it's only tentative as the footage is assembled to stress a charming, carefree, somewhat roistering existence. On this score, it comes off with chuckles, even several hilarious moments, but the assemblage has left quite a few plot and sequence gaps so there's a lack of cohesion to the unfolding.

Jesse Lasky Jr.'s screenplay is based on a story by Jean Evans and, with some zippy dialog and saucy situations, concerns itself mostly with getting Miss Russell and Wilde together as a more-than-in-name-only marital team. She's the bride purchased for him by his brother, Luther Adler, king of the Los Angeles gypsies. Wilde is tricked into matrimony in a very funny sequence, but refuses to work at it, preferring to be a dancer. Windup, however, finds him more than eager and Miss Russell willing.

There are a number of other plot tangents, too, but never elucidated enough to get off the ground, so Nicholas Ray's direction concentrates on making the most fun of the marital problem and drawing some topnotch character portrayals. Miss Russell and Wilde are good in the top roles, while Adler, Joseph Calleia, a standout as the bride-selling racketeer; the late Mikhail Rasumny, Nina Koshetz and Helen Westcott contribute ably in other prominent spots.

A spirited score by Les Baxter, plus two tunes, "Tsara, Tsara," and "I Could Learn to Love You," both with lyrics by Ross Bagdasarian, help carry off the gypsy flavor. The CinemaScope lensing in Technicolor by Ray June, colorful art direction and settings and other technical contributions measure up. *Brog.*

Over-Exposed

Mild meller for the program market; average returns.

Columbia release of Lewis J. Rachmil production. Stars Cleo Moore; features Richard Crenna, Isobel Elson, Raymond Greenleaf, Shirley Thomas, James O'Rear, Donald Randolph, Dayton Lummis. Directed by Lewis Seiler. Screenplay, James Gunn, Gil Orlovitz, from story by Richard Sale and Mary Loos; camera, Henry Freulich; editor, Edwin Bryant; music, Mischa Bakaleinikoff. Previewed in N. Y., Feb. 16, '56. Running time, **80 MINS.**

Lila Crane	Cleo Moore
Russell Bassett	Richard Crenna
Mrs. Payton Grange	Isobel Elsom
Max West	Raymond Greenleaf
Shirley Thomas	Shirley Thomas
Roy Carver	James O'Rear
Coco Fields	Donald Randolph
Horace Sutherland	Dayton Lummis
Renee	Jeanne Cooper
Les Bauer	Jack Albertson
Freddie	William McLean
Mrs. Gulick	Edna M. Holland
Matt	Edwin Parker
Bud	John Cason
Jerry	Dick Crockett
Martha	Geraldine Hall
Judge Evans	Voltaire Perkins
Frank	Joan Miller
Mrs. Grannigan	Helyn Eby Rock
Steve	Frank Mitchell
Doris	Norma Brooks
Sergeant	Robert B. Williams

Cleo Moore, better known to filmgoers as Hugo Haas' leading lady, attains star status in "Over-Exposed," a mild meller for the program market. Picture may offer some femme appeal via Miss Moore's attempts to become a career girl. Star's generous proportions obviously provide exploitation angles but paradoxically have nothing to do with the title.

Screenplay by James Gunn and Gil Orlovitz from a story by Richard Sale and Mary Loos, yarn traces the ascension of Miss Moore from obscurity to a top commercial photographer. On her way up she meets such people as Raymond Greenleaf, an alcoholic lensman who teaches her the trade; Richard Crenna, handsome reporter who befriends her in the big city, and society matron Isobel Elsom who takes a fancy to her camera technique.

Scripters Gunn and Orlovitz generates a fair amount of interest when their femme photog is learning the trade and fighting her way to the top. But once she's arrived there, it's apparent that the writers were doubtful as to how to end their brainchild. For the climax, where Miss Moore is saved from clutches of racketeers by Crenna whom she presumably later weds, shapes up as strictly contrived material.

Performances generally are on par with the shaky story. While Miss Moore makes a nice try in the role of the photog who made good, she seldom is credible. For that matter, part does little to stir audience sympathy since the script depicts her as a mercenary person with few ideals. Likewise, Crenna is unconvincing as the reporter who woos and wins Miss Moore.

Lewis Seiler's direction tosses in a melodramatic punch here and there but the overall result fails to excite. Greenleaf, however, etches a neat portrayal of the aging but kindly photographer. Miss Elsom impresses as the society bigwig and effective in lesser roles are James O'Rear as a Broadway columnist, Donald Randolph as a nitery operator and Dayton Lummis as a "front man" for the mob, among others.

Henry Freulich's camerawork and art direction of Carl Anderson are good in this Lewis J. Rachmil production for Columbia release. Mischa Bakaleinikoff's score is adequate as is Edwin Bryant's editing and other technical c- -dits. *Gilb.*

Invasion of the Body Snatchers
(SUPERSCOPE)

Suspensful science-fictioner, with good grosses indicated.

Hollywood, Feb. 17.

Allied Artists release of a Walter Wanger production. Stars Kevin McCarthy, Dana Wynter; features Larry Gates, King Donovan, Carolyn Jones, Jean Willes. Directed by Don Siegel. Screenplay, Daniel Mainwaring, based on Collier's mag serial by Jack Finney; camera, Ellsworth Fredricks; music, Carmen Dragon; editor, Robert S. Eisen. Previewed Feb. 14, '56. Running time, **80 MINS.**

Miles	Kevin McCarthy
Becky	Dana Wynter
Danny	Larry Gates
Jack	King Donovan
Theodora	Carolyn Jones
Sally	Jean Willes
Nick	Ralph Dumke
Wilma	Virginia Christine
Ira	Tom Fadden
Driscoll	Kenneth Patterson
Sam	Guy Way
Mrs. Grimaldi	Eileen Stevens
Grandma	Beatrice Maude
Aunt Eleda	Jean Andren
Jimmy	Bobby Clark
Pursey	Everett Glass
Mac	Dabbs Greer
Baggage Man	Pat O'Malley
Proprietor	Guy Rennie
Martha	Marie Selland
Doctor	Whit Bissell

Walter Wanger comes up with a tense, offbeat piece of science-fiction here that looks headed for stout box-office returns, particularly in view of the present market leanings in this field. Occasionally difficult to follow due to the strangeness of its scientific premise, action nevertheless is increasingly exciting as it builds to a strong climax. With its exploitation potential, film is suitable for either top or bottom spot of double bills.

Adapted by Daniel Mainwaring from Jack Finney's Collier's serial, characterizations and situations are sharp as audience interest is enlisted from opening scene. Don Siegel's taut direction is fast-paced generally, although in his efforts to spark the climax he permits his leading character, Kevin McCarthy, to overact in several sequences. Film would have benefitted through more explanatory matter to fully illuminate the scientific premise, but all in all the topic has been developed along lines to hold the spectator.

Plotwise, narrative opens on a strange hysteria that is spreading among the populace of a small California town. Townspeople appear as strangers to their relatives and friends, while retaining their outward appearances. McCarthy, a doctor recalled from a business trip by his nurse when this epidemic starts, is confronted with solving these mysterious happenings, and helping him is Dana Wynter, with whom he's in love. Gradually they learn the explanation.

A weird form of plantlife has descended upon the town from the skies. Tiny, this ripens into great pods and opens, from each of which emerges a "blank," the form of each man, woman and child in the town. During their sleep, the blank drains them of their normal emotions, all but their impulse to survive. Windup shows the townspeople, now all but McCarthy and his girl friend afflicted, trying to halt the two from escaping to warn the rest of the world. McCarthy finally is able to get away, after femme during a sleep of sheer exhaustion becomes a "pod person," and broadcasts his fantastic story.

McCarthy delivers a persuasive account of himself, and Miss Wynter, a pretty newcomer, shows fine promise. Strong support is provided by King Donovan, Larry Gates, Carolyn Jones and Jean Willes.

Technical credits are only registered by Ellsworth Fredricks with his cameras, German Dragon for an atmospheric music score and Robert S. Eisen for tight editing. *Whit.*

Now and Forever
(BRITISH-COLOR)

Boy-girl romance, with Janette Scott in first grownup role; sturdy b.o. hopes in home market, but limited chances elsewhere.

London, Feb. 21.

Associated British-Pathe (Mario Zampi) production and release. Stars Janette Scott, Vernon Gray, Kay Walsh and Jack Warner. Directed by Mario Zampi. Screenplay, R. F. Delderfield and Michael Pertwee; camera, Erwin Hillier; editor, Richard Best; music, Stanley Black. At Ritz Theatre, London. Running time, **90 MINS.**

Janette Grant	Janette Scott
Mike Pritchard	Vernon Gray
Miss Muir	Kay Walsh
Mr. Pritchard	Jack Warner
Mrs. Grant	Pamela Brown
Farmer	Charles Victor
Farmer's Wife	Marjorie Rhodes
Waiter	Ronald Squire
Gossage	Wilfrid Lawson
Miss Fox	Sonia Dresdel
Pawnbroker	David Kossof
Doctor	Moultrie Kelsall
Hector	Guy Middleton
Reporter	Michael Pertwee
Jeweller	Henry Hewitt
Frisby	Bryan Forbes
Rachel	Jean Patterson

A saccharine-type boy and girl romance, "Now and Forever" is geared for hefty grosses in the domestic market because of the marquee value of Janette Scott in her first adult role. Outside the United Kngdom, however, and notably in the U.S., its unsophisticated treatment will not be a big help at the boxoffice.

Mario Zampi has fashioned a safe formula for Janette Scott's first grownup part—a simple story of a rich, unloved schoolgirl who falls in love with a poor garage hand. When the girl's mother intends to pack her off to Canada, the young couple decides to elope and head for Gretna Green to be wed.

First part of the story, which depicts the blossoming of young love, is told in stereotype style, using almost every known sentimental cliche. But once the two decide to head for Gretna, the plot gets moving and there is more than a modicum of interest as they make for the border with the police on their trail. These latter scenes, which allow for brief sequences with top character players, add much to the entertainment. Ronald Squire as a waiter, Wilfrid Lawson as a lodging house keeper and David Kossof as a pawn-broker standout in this connection.

Zampi's direction astutely focuses on the young couple and allows the attractive rural setting to make a fitting background. Miss Scott, a young actress of some talent, plays the schoolgirl with a persuasive charm while Vernon Gray typifies the earnest, serious-minded youth. Pamela Brown portrays the mother in an unsympathetic single key. Main sympathy comes from a warm performance by Kay Walsh as the girl's head-mistress. Jack Warner, as always, turns in a reliable study as the boy's unpretentious father. *Myro.*

Jumping for Joy
(BRITISH)

Hilarious dog racing comedy starring Frankie Howerd, with Stanley Holloway and A. E. Matthews.

London, Feb. 21.

Rank production and release. Stars Frankie Howerd, Stanley Holloway; features A. E. Matthews, Tony Wright, Susan Beaumont. Directed by John Paddy Carstairs. Screenplay, Jack Davies and Henry E. Blyth; camera, Jack Cox; editor, John D. Guthridge; music, Larry Adler. At Dominion Theatre London. Running time, **88 MINS.**

Willie	Frankie Howerd
Jack	Stanley Holloway
Lord Cranfield	A. E. Matthews
Vincent	Tony Wright
Blagg	Alfie Bass
Lady Cranfield	Joan Hickson
Bert Benton	Lionel Jeffries
Susan	Susan Beaumont
Wyndham	Terence Longdon
Max	Colin Gordon
Carruthers	Richard Wattis
Plug Ugly	Danny Green
Marlene	Barbara Archer
Blenkinsop	William Kendall
Haines	Ewen Solon
Smithers	Reginald Beckwith

This latest Rank comedy is on broad, improbable lines, catering more to the lowbrow patron and more likely to appeal to suburban and provincial audiences than the West End or the U. S. market. It has a background of dog racing, showing the triumph of a sick greyhound nursed back to health and groomed for canine stardom, against all adversities of fate and a dope gang.

Frankie Howerd, popular tv and vaude comic here, gets the maximum of laughs out of a dismissed trackboy role. Stanley Holloway in his chief support as a con man who takes in both man and beast. Vet legiter A. E. Matthews has a dry, aristocratic personality which offsets the crazy occasions in which he is involved. Joan Hickson, as his dim-witted wife, abets him with unselfconscious humor.

Tony Wright, a newcomer to the screen, registers convincingly as a gangster while Susan Beaumont brings a fleeting breath of glamor as a kennelmaid.

Pic is slickly directed by John Paddy Carstairs. *Clem.*

Si Paris Nous Etait Conte
(If Paris Were Told to Us) (FRENCH; COLOR)

Paris, Feb. 21.

Gaumont release of CLM-SNEG-Franco-London Film production. Stars Danielle Darrieux, Jean Marais, Robert Lamoureux, Francoise Arnoul, Gerard Philipe, Michele Morgan, Lana Marconi. Written and directed by Sacha Guitry. Camera (Technicolor), Philipe Agostini; music, Jean Francaix; editor, Paulette Robert. At Paris, Paris. Running time, **135 MINS.**

Agnes Sorel	Danielle Darrieux
Francois I	Jean Marais
Latude	Robert Lamoureux
Louis XI	Sacha Guitry
Gabriel Estrée	Michelle Morgan
La Trouvere	Gerard Philipe
Lady in Waiting	Francoise Arnoul

After "Versailles" and "Napoleon" Sacha Guitry now unveils his third filmic commentary on French history passing in review. Helped by a bundle of star names, this is the story of the founding, growth and meaning of Paris. The Gallic need for the past glorious will probably make this as big a grosser as its predecessors. For the U. S., this is more problematical but appears better suited than the other historical pix. The Paris monicker, plus some witty, capricious Guitry doings and comments, might make this a palatable art house morsel. Deft cutting and dubbing might make for other playdates. Drawback for general chances is lack of spectacle since Guitry keeps this an intimate exposition of Paris.

In the guise of telling the Paris story to a group of eager students, Guitry skips blandly over about 2,000 years. Though it might offend purists, his eye-view of the past is in the tradition of a master, clever vulgarizer. The kings are trotted out and commented on and the Guitry royalist feelings are evident throughout. The people are treated with grace and love, but in a patronizing manner.

Little drama emerges except for an obvious attempt to sympathize with the ordeal of Marie Antoinette. Beguiling comedy comes into its own with Robert Lamoureux who becomes a symbol of the budding revolution as the man who keeps escaping from the Bastille, by ingenious means, but is always caught within a few hours. It is his nostalgic feeling for the prison, following his final release after 35 years.

More astute is the treatment of the death of Voltaire which gets the only real period feeling. Guitry's old flair for a clever counterpoint to his sprightly commentary emerges brightly at times for its wittiest sections. Examples are the various comings and goings of bodies of great men from the Pantheon as regimes change, the reactions to Napoleon's battles via flags emerging and disappearing on a Paris street, and the general tone of this disarmingly reactonary film.

Color is uneven at times and general production is excellent although avoidance of needed spectacle sometimes gives the effect of production skimping. Acting is agreeable in all and some taking vignettes are scattered throughout with two standout in Jacques De Feraudy's dying Voltaire, and a poignant note in Guitry's ailing Louis XI because the actor-director is now confined to a wheelchair after a stroke during the film. Editing knowingly keeps this patchwork film clear, and Jean Francaix's stylish music is also an asset. *Mosk.*

Uranium Boom

Topically-titled programmer. So-so diversion.

Hollywood, Feb. 24.

Columbia release of Sam Katzman (Clover) production. Stars Dennis Morgan, Patricia Medina, William Talman; features Tina Carver, Philip Van Zandt, Bill Henry, Gregg Barton, Mel Curtis, Henry Rowland, S. John Launer, Michael Bryant. Directed by William Castle. Screenplay, George F. Slavin, George W. George, Norman Retchin; story, Slavin and George; camera, Fred Jackman Jr.; editor, Edwin Bryant; music, Mischa Bakaleinikoff. Previewed Feb. 15, '56. Running time, **66 MINS.**

Brad Collins	Dennis Morgan
Jean Williams	Patricia Medina
Grady Mathews	William Talman
Gail Windsor	Tina Carver
Navajo Charlie	Philip Van Zandt
Joe McGinnus	Bill Henry
Phil McGinnus	Gregg Barton
Chuck McGinnus	Mel Curtis
Harry	Henry Rowland
Mac	S. John Launer
Peterson	Michial Bryant
Floyd Gorman	Frank Wilcox
Old Timer	Ralph Sanford
Mr. Aldrich	Carlyle Mitchell
Reporter	Nick Tell

This is topically-titled program drama that will find its intended niche in the dual bill market. As the tag states, it deals with the overnight riches that come with the discovery of uranium, this time to Dennis Morgan and William Talman, partnered in an exploration of Colorado wastelands.

Patricia Medina supplies the femme interest in the Sam Katzman production as the gal over whom the partners fall out. Talman has her earmarked for himself, but Morgan gets her, busting up a friendship and causing Talman to seek means to trick his ex-partner into bankruptcy. He practically does, with the help of Tina Carver and her confidenceman partner, Frank Wilcox, but Miss Medina remains steadfast, so Talman bows to the inevitable and makes up with his old friend at the fadeout.

There are some other angles to the scripting by George F. Slavin, George W. George and Norman Retchin that occasionally complicate the action, but generally William Castle's direction keeps things moving along at an acceptable pace and gets okay performances from the above named, as well as from Philip Van Zandt, playing an Indian guide, Bill Henry, Gregg Barton, Mel Curtis, Henry Rowland, S. John Launer and the others.

Physical appurtenances of the production pass muster for budget and the technical assists, from Fred Jackman Jr.'s lensing on down, do their jobs satisfactory. *Brog.*

Foreign Films

Paris, Feb. 21.

Milord L'Arsouille (FRENCH; C'SCOPE; COLOR). Jeannic release of Florida production. Stars Jean-Claude Pascal; features, Lucienne Legrande, Simone Bach, Pascal Roberts, Louis Seigner, Julien Bertheau. Directed by Andre Haguet. Screenplay, Jacques De Benac, Andre Legrand, Haguet; camera, (Eastmancolor), Lucien Joulin; editor, Leonide Azar. At Marignan, Paris. Running time, **105 MINS.**

Sumptuous C-Scope production details the life of a noble rake in 19th Century Paris who becomes the friend of the downtrodden before the 1848 revolution. Though having a fine and lavish visual mounting, this lacks the dash and romantic flavor needed for the subject, and becomes a lagging, episodic story which seems slated primarily for the Continental markets.

Jean-Claude Pascal is photogenic but listless in his portrayal of the nobleman who begins to get social consciousness. Production is lavish and tasteful, but director Andre Haguet has not gotten the sweep and action of a fermenting age into it. Result, is a picturesque but uneven entry.

Paris, Feb. 21.

Marguerite De La Nuit (Marguerite of the Night) **(FRANCO-ITALIAN).** Gaumont release of SNEG-Del Duca-Gaumont production. Stars Yves Montand, Michele Morgan; features, Jean-Francois Calve, Palau, Jacques Clancy. Directed by Claude-Autant Lara. Screenplay, Ghislaine Lara, Gabriel Arout; camera (Technicolor), Jacques Natteau; music, Rene Cloerec; editor, Madeline Gug. At Colisee, Paris. Running time, **100 MINS.**

Film is another reworking of that favorite, "Faust." Here the time is 1925 and the only switch is having the Devil go soft on Marguerite and making the characters ply different vocations. Though a new dress has been put on this tale of the man who sold his soul for youth and love, its lack of dimension in characterization makes this just another entry in the field and below standards set by "All That Money Can Buy" and "Beauty and the Devil." Color does not help the mood and this is basically for arty spots with its plodding, obvious tactics limiting this even for many of these houses.

Director Claude Autant-Lara has given this an expressionistic touch, with color used garishly but is never as telling as black and white. Michele Morgan can not do much with the dreamy character of a languishing Marguerite waiting for love, and Yves Montand does okay by the Devil. Palau is a proper aging Faust while Jean-Francois Calve is much too overemphatic as the youthful Faust. *Mosk.*

Paris, Feb. 21.

Des Gens Sans Importance (People of No Importance) (French). SEDIF release of Cocinor-Chaillot-Ardennes Films production. Stars Jean Gabin, Francoise Arnoul; features Pierre Mondy, Yvette Etievant, Lella Kedrova, Dany Carrel, Paul Frankeur. Directed by Henri Verneuil. Screenplay, Francois Boyer, Verneuil from a novel by Serge Groussard; camera, Louis Page; editor, Christian Gaudin, music, Joseph Kosma. At Marignan, Paris. Running time, **105 MINS.**

A slice of life is meted out in this grim, plodding film about a truckdriver who finds romance with a maid in his stopover restaurant, and is ready to leave his family for her when fate intervenes with her death. This never gets the true spark of drama into the proceedings.

It has the Jean Gabin name for U. S. arty appeal and its theme might make this okay for exploitation, but its downbeat characteristics make it limited for U.S.

Director Henri Verneuil has given this careful mounting but has been unable to overcome the pedestrian story. Gabin is competent as usual but plays it too off-the-cuff to give much credence to the truckdriver's attitudes. Francoise Arnoul is capable as the mistreated but simple loving maid. Remainder of the cast is good. *Mosk.*

Paris, Feb. 21.

Vous Pigez! (You Get It!) **(FRANCO-ITALIAN).** Dismage-Transalpin production and release. Stars Eddie Constantine; features, Maria Frau, Yorick Royan, Francois Perrot, Roger Hanin. Directed by Pierre Chevalier. Screenplay, Victor Trivas, Jacques-Doniol-Valcroze from novel by Peter Cheney; camera, Louis Burel; editor, Francoise Javet. At Balzac, Paris. Running time, **98 MINS.**

Eddie Constantine again plays the boozing, brawling G-Man Lemmy Caution role which has made him the only American to achieve film stardom here. Pic is a lighthearted parody of the toughguy pix, and abounds in scraps, saucy wenches and a sketchy framework to allow Constantine to ease his sprightly way through. Film manages a tongue-in-cheek attitude that is saved by a series of good gags, curvaceous cuties and the aplomb and ease of Constantine who walks through his familiar antics.

Direction is unobtrusive and production credits are okay. This is the seventh pic of this series for Constantine. *Mosk.*

On the Threshold of Space
(C'SCOPE-COLOR)

Fascination here in dramatization of aero medical research work behind Air Force's ventures with speed and space. Prosperous prospects.

Hollywood, March 5.

20th-Fox release of William Bloom production. Stars Guy Madison, Virginia Leith, John Hodiak, Dean Jagger; features Warren Stevens, Martin Milner, King Calder, Walter Coy, Ken Clark, Donald Murphy, Barry Coe. Directed by Robert D. Webb. Screenplay, Simon Wincelberg, Francis Cockrell; camera (De Luxe Color), Joe MacDonald; special photographic effects, Ray Kellogg; editor, Hugh S. Fowler; music, Lyn Murray. Previewed March 1, '56. Running time, 96 MINS.

Capt. Jim Hollenbeck	Guy Madison
Pat Lange	Virginia Leith
Major Ward Thomas	John Hodiak
Dr. Hugh Thornton	Dean Jagger
Capt. Mike Bentley	Warren Stevens
Lt. Morton Glenn	Martin Milner
Lee Welch	King Calder
Lt. Col. Masters	Walter Coy
Sgt. Ike Forbes	Ken Clark
Sgt. Zack Deming	Donald Murphy
Communications Officer	Barry Coe
Medic	Richard Grant
Paramedic Officer	Donald Freed
Taxi Driver	Ben Wright
George Atkins	Carlyle Mitchell
Dawson	Robert Cornthwaite
Secretary	Jo Gilbert
Nurse	Juanita Close
Mrs. Lange	Helen Bennett

Prosperous playdates should reward this interesting dramatization of the aero medical research that lies behind Air Force experimentations with speed and space. It fits in the science-fiction classification, although is actually science-fact because of dealing with things that have advanced and will advance U. S. air might.

A satisfactory story thread is used to tie together the deeds of human guinea pigs who risk their lives so the air will be safer for the regular flyboys. There's excitement and suspense, plus thrills, as the plot puts men to the test in riding rocket sleds at break-neck speeds; being ejected from jet bombers at sky-high altitudes and daring the stratosphere in balloon-borne gondolas; all to the purpose of finding out how much the human body and equipment can take.

The William Bloom production locationed at Eglin Air Force Base in Florida and at Holloman Air Force Base in New Mexico so the footage is crammed with authenticity. Direction of the dramatization by Simon Wincelberg and Francis Cockrell is ably handled by Robert D. Webb, who keeps his cast performing naturally amidst the technicalities of real-life derring-do. Barbara McLean served as associate producer to Bloom.

Guy Madison provides a likeable, easy performance as a young medical officer who is put through some of the more daring experiments and Virginia Leith impresses as the wife who hides her fear for him behind an understanding of the worth and need for what he does. The late John Hodiak is excellent as the commanding officer who dares the rocket sled himself, as is Dean Jagger, medico-scientist working with the Air Force in the experiments. Also doing their roles well, among others, are Warren Stevens, Martin Milner, King Calder, Walter Coy, Ken Clark, Donald Murphy and Barry Coe.

The CinemaScope lensing in De Luxe Color by Joe MacDonald, plus the special photographic effects by Ray Kellogg, contribute measureably to the picture. Lyn Murray's score, conducted by Lionel Newman, is another plus factor, as are the technical contributions. *Brog.*

Comanche
(C'SCOPE-SONG-COLOR)

Actionful outdoor feature with Dana Andrews. Good prospects.

Hollywood, March 5.

United Artists release of Carl Krueger production. Stars Dana Andrews, Kent Smith; features Linda Cristal, Lowell Gilmore, Nestor Paiva, Stacy Harris, Mike Mazurki, Henry Brandon, Reed Sherman, John Litel. Directed by George Sherman. Screenplay, Carl Krueger; camera (De Luxe Color), Jorge Stahl Jr.; editor, Charles L. Kimball; score and song, Herschel Burke Gilbert; lyrics, Alfred Perry; sung by The Lancers. Previewed March 2, '56. Running time, 87 MINS.

Read	Dana Andrews
Quanah Parker	Kent Smith
Margarita	Linda Cristal
Ward	Lowell Gilmore
Puffer	Nestor Paiva
Downey	Stacy Harris
Flat Mouth	Mike Mazurki
Black Cloud	Henry Brandon
French	Reed Sherman
General Nelson A. Miles	John Litel

Good early-west actioner that should fare well in the outdoor market. The action is backed with a plot that states its case satisfactorily and the scenic values derived from the location-lensing in Mexico in CinemaScope and De Luxe Color are splendid.

Peace comes to the southwest plains in this United Artists release, but it takes some doing on the part of Dana Andrews, intrepid Indian scout, before the redskins and whites agree on a treaty. Produced and written by Carl Krueger, the film is long on pictorial beauty, but without sacrificing the kind of movement necessary to keep this type of show entertaining. George Sherman, an old hand at outdoor action, paces the plot well with his direction so the 87 minutes of footage is compact and swift-moving.

Krueger's screen story has an 1875 period and shows how an honorable peace was worked out between the maurauding Comanches that swarmed over the southwest and the whites that were moving into the country. There are very few high heroics on the part of either side, so the action dramatics play off believably as Andrews takes on the responsibility of getting Chief Quanah Parker, played well by Kent Smith, to lay down his tomahawk. Andrews comes through excellently, and there are good performance assists all down the line.

There are both white and Indian menaces to a treaty, with Lowell Gilmore, stuffed-shirt politician from Washington, and Stacy Harris, an Indian-hating white, as the paleface troublemakers. Henry Brandon, brave who defies Smith's peace orders, takes care of the other dirty work. Nestor Paiva, Andrews scouting partner; John Litel, a sensible general; Mike Mazurki and Reed Sherman are among other good casters. Film introduces Linda Cristal, Mexican actress. She's a beauty who's rescued from the Indians by Andrews.

Jorge Stahl Jr.'s camera work manages some scenes of incredible beauty and also is on top of all the mass action that generates excitement in the footage. Charles L. Kimball's editing is good. The Herschel Burke Gilbert scoring is keyed to the action demands and keeps busy through most of the film. Additionally, his tune, "A Man Is As Good As His Word," with lyrics by Alfred Perry, is sung by The Lancers as a song narrative bridging scenes. *Brog.*

Backlash
(COLOR)

Unevenly-directed but picturesque western with Richard Widmark, Donna Reed. Handy entry for outdoor action trade.

Hollywood, Feb. 28.

Universal release of Aaron Rosenberg production. Stars Richard Widmark, Donna Reed, John McIntire, William Campbell; features Barton MacLane, Harry Morgan, Robert J. Wilke, Jack Lambert, Roy Roberts. Directed by John Sturges. Screenplay, Borden Chase; based on a novel by Frank Gruber; camera (Technicolor), Irving Glassberg; editor, Sherman Todd; music, Herman Stein. Previewed Feb. 21, '56. Running time, 83 MINS.

Jim Slater	Richard Widmark
Karyl Orton	Donna Reed
Jim Bonniwell	John McIntire
Johnny Cool	William Campbell
Sergeant Lake	Barton MacLane
Tony Welker	Harry Morgan
Jeff Welker	Robert J. Wilke
Benton	Jack Lambert
Major Carson	Roy Roberts
Sheriff Marson	Edward C. Platt
Sheriff Olson	Robert Foulk
Dobbs	Phil Chambers
Sleepy	Gregg Barton
Ned McCloud	Fred Graham
Cassidy	Frank Chase

Richard Widmark and Donna Reed add name value to this regulation western drama and its prospects in the outdoor action market look satisfactory. It has Technicolor, rugged outdoor settings and other standard western feature trappings, plus a fairly tight 83-minute running time, to make it a handy entry.

Story period is early Arizona soon after the Civil War, and most of the location lensing was done in that state for picturesque visual values. When interest wanders from the story in the Aaron Rosenberg production, the eye can always pick up scenic beauty for compensation. Interest will wander, too, because John Sturges' direction is not always sure-handed and permits some characters to wander to the ludicrous side. Such a one is the young killer played by William Campbell, who does his deadly work with an overboard Liberacean grin. When Sturges is telling the Frank Gruber story, scripted by Borden Chase, with a straight toughness the guidance is good; otherwise just fair.

Identification of five white men killed in an Apache raid and of one who escaped, plus the whereabouts of $60,000 in gold the party was supposed to have had, puts the plot in gear. Widmark wants to make sure his nogood father, John McIntire, is one of the dead and not, as he secretly fears, the one who escaped with the coin. Miss Reed is in on the search for the money, believing her husband, one of the dead, had an interest in it. Widmark's fears are well-founded and Miss Reed doesn't get her gold, but they both wind up at the finale with each other after McIntire, who had used the loot to found a rustling empire, is killed by honest ranchers.

Widmark fits rather well into his outdoor character and is tough enough to please those who like him best when he's mean. Miss Reed also handles her character well, that of a girl who hasn't always been what a lady's supposed to be. McIntire is excellent, as are Barton MacLane, army sergeant who's a key figure in the search; Roy Roberts, honest rancher; Harry Morgan, Edward C. Platt, Robert Foulk, Robert J. Wilke and Jack Lambert, among others.

Irving Glassberg uses his cameras well in the action and in getting the outdoor sites on film. Other technical credits also are good. *Brog.*

Hidden Guns

Tautly suspenseful. Much beyond run-of-range melodrama.

Republic release of Gannaway-Ver Halen production. Stars Richard Arlen, Bruce Bennett, John Carradine. Directed by Al Gannaway. Original story and screenplay, Sam Rocca, Al Gannaway; camera, Clark Ramsey; editor, Leon Barsha. Music composed, directed, played by Ramez Idriss; additional songs by Gannaway, Hal Levy; choral direction, Salli Terri. Previewed in N.Y., March 2, '56. Running time, **66 MINS.**

Stragg	Bruce Bennett
Sheriff Young	Richard Arlen
Snipe Harding	John Carradine
Faron	Faron Young
Judge Wallis	Lloyd Corrigan
Becky Carter	Angie Dickinson
Kingsley	Damian O'Flynn
Doc Carter	Irving Bacon
Grandy	Tom Hubbard
Burt Miller	Ron Kennedy
Joe Miller	Bill Ward
Emmet	Raymond L. Morgan
Ben Williams	Edmund Cobb
Peabody	Ben Welden
Fiddler	Guinn Williams
Terry	Gordon Terry

This is considerably stronger and more intriguing than the run-of-mill western meller. "Hidden Guns" has new angles, an original introduction of each turn in plot and considerably more suspense than a grind-'em-out prairie opera. Film looks strong fare for western houses and okay for some others.

Basically, this is the tale of a card sharp who meets his match in a tough sheriff's son despite paid politicos and hired gunmen. Inability to find witnesses to testify in a cold-blooded killing over a card game actually starts the law on the crooked gambler's trail. Eventually this leads to slicker's arrest and downfall when the whole town turns against him.

Plot has Sheriff Arlen working with his son, Faron Young, his deputy, in a half-hearted effort to reform the bought and paid for community. Deputy Young takes charge of the sheriff's office when his dad is seriously wounded in a framed gun fight. Terrific suspense is developed by having the son go up against the same gambler in a gun duel—only that the deputy is hep to the concealed sniper and outshoots the gambler and hidden pal.

There's the usual gunplay and a whale of a fistfight between Young and one of the gambler's hirelings which carries on through a fall down hill and into a pool of water. Pic is different in that story developments are telegraphed or kept up to date via a choral group. "Hidden Guns" also has a fine original score composed and played by Ramez Idriss, the use of guitar and string instruments being reminiscent of "High Noon."

Vet Arlen is excellent as sheriff while Young, rated one of America's No. 1 western recording stars, makes a good western-type deputy serving as his father's aide. His singing is heard in the background throughout the production with fine effect.

John Carradine turns in a gripping concept of the suave but cold-blooded sniper and hired gunman. Bruce Bennett is adequately nasty as the gambler. Lloyd Corrigan makes a sharp bought-up judge while Angie Dickinson is in briefly for scenic effect. Irving Bacon makes the Doc Carter role realistic.

Al Gannaway's direction is way above par for a standard western as is his story and screenplay on which he worked with Sam Rocca. Clark Ramsey does a smart job with his camera, employing many more closeups than generally found in an oats opera. *Wear.*

Lum & Abner Abroad

Three television pilots poorly edited into a theatre feature.

Howco Productions release of James Kern production. Stars Chester Lauck, Norris Goff, Jill Alis. Directed by Kern. Screenplay, Carl Herzinger; based on stories by Herzinger and Kern; camera, Octhvian Miletich; editors, Maurice Wright and Blanche Jens. Previewed in N.Y., Feb. 24, '56. Running time, **72 MINS.**

Lum	Chester Lauck
Abner	Morris Goff
Marianne	Jill Alis
Collette	Lila Audres
Papa Possavetz	Branko Spoylar
Nicky	Gene Gary
Duchess	Vern Mesita
Mischa	Valdo Stephens
Frankenshplnin	Steven Voyt
Lisa	Nada Nuchich
Croupier	Chris Peters
Tommy Ellis	Jim Kiley
Dignitary	Joseph Batistich

There was talk some months ago of the old Ozarkian radio team doing a series of television films abroad. Apparently the project aborted and this is the net result—three hollow "pilot" films which would have run 26 minutes each for video, now edited and tied into a 72-minute theatrical release. The gyrations of the "goodwill ambassadors," as the Carl Herzinger script terms them, seem to have little marketable value as anything but a second feature in the sticks.

Lum and Abner show up first in Belgrade, getting involved in the love life of ballerina Jill Alis. Chester Lauck (Lum) and Morris Goff (Abner) get the U.S. Embassy to back a blowout campaign to find her American newspaperman—fiance, and all ends happily as a group of European hayseeds join the U.S. brand in a good old fashioned square dance. After an insufficient bridge with Gene Gary, the ballet impresario of the first part, doing a short narration and then appearing as a Gallic sportscaster, the homespun pair arrive in Paris. There they become dupes for a smuggling ring and end up being saved from the fiends (including a mace-wielding giant named Frankenshplin) by the police. Locale shifts to Monte Carlo, where they break the bank, but settle for $14.80 so that the people of Monaco won't have to pay extra taxes. Yanks take their payoff in medals from a grateful citizenry.

Boxoffice outlook of the big-hearted bumpkins isn't helped by the slapdash editing of Maurice Wright and Blanche Jens (their efforts possibly hampered by low budget). Quite often the sound fades before the visual track does, and the fade-outs are such that time is needed for reorientation. The Octhvian Miletich camera picks up nice foreign scenery, which, of everything, is the pic's best asset after whatever loyalty and following adheres to Lum and Abner. *Art.*

Wetbacks
(COLOR)

Patchwork plotting. Mediocre.

Hollywood, Feb. 24.

Banner Pictures release of a Hank McCune Production. Stars Lloyd Bridges, Nancy Gates; features Barton MacLane, John Hoyt, Harold Peary, Nacho Galindo, Robert Keys, David Colmans, Jose Gonzales Gonzales, Louis Jean Heydt, Scott Douglas, Wally Cassell, Richard Powers, Salvador Baguez. Directed by McCune. Screenplay, Pete LaRoche; camera (Eastman Color), Brydon Baker; editor, Ronald V. Ashcroft; music, Les Baxter. Reviewed Feb. 22, '56. Running time, **86 MINS.**

Jim Benson	Lloyd Bridges
Sally Parker	Nancy Gates
Karl Shanks	Barton MacLane
Steve Bodine	John Hoyt
Juan Ortega	Harold Peary
Alphonso	Nacho Galindo
Reeser	Robert Keys
Pedro	David Colmans
Wetback	Jose Gonzales Gonzales
Coast Guard Comdr.	Louis Jean Heydt
Immigration Officer	Scott Douglas
Coast Guard Lieut.	Wally Cassell
Highway Patrol Inspec.	Richard Powers
Mexican Policeman	Salvador Baguez

The most elementary sort of patchwork plotting makes this feature shoddy fodder. Some excellent scenic footage of Mexican and Catalina locales, plus a genuinely thrilling motorboat chase sequence, are its assets.

Pete LaRoche screenplay presents a financially strapped fishing boat captain, played by Lloyd Bridges, in the clutches of a wetback-smuggling gang. However, the twists and turns of the unconvincing plot finally discloses that he has been the unwitting bait set out by the U.S. Immigration Service to entrap the baddies, essayed by John Hoyt and Harold Peary. Also, a seeming femme tramp companion, portrayed by Nancy Gates, turns out to be a Government undercover agent.

The heavies pursue Bridges and Miss Gates to sea and the best footage show a ring-around-the-rosy chase around a tanker in full steam. Finally, the Coast Guard hoves into view to put the arm on the smugglers and to leave the couple time to enthusiastically intertwine.

Bridges and Miss Gates are a nice-looking couple who walk through their derring-do assignments with a certain amount of plausibility. Barton MacLane makes a convincing semi-heavy, who also turns out to be an undercover Government man.

Hoyt does his able best with the cliche-ridden role of the top heavy, but the Great Gildersleeve often shows through Peary's chore as his sidekick. In lesser parts, Nacho Galindo plays a sympathetic Mexican bar owner with commendable gusto, while Jose Gonzales Gonzales supplies a bit of welcome comic relief as a seasick wetback.

Producer-director Hank McCune is most effective when setting the earlier scenes and in staging the chase sequence. However, the weak script defeats his other efforts.

Quality of the Eastman Color footage lensed by Brydon Baker varies, from a number of beautiful picturizations to a distinctly off-key cast. Those parts of Les Baxter's score which utilize Mexican guitar themes serve well to set the tropical mood. *Kove.*

Kettles in the Ozarks

Looks like series is running out of steam after eight times at bat. Very so-so.

Hollywood, March 6.

Universal release of Richard Wilson production. Stars Marjorie Main, Arthur Hunnicutt; features Una Merkel, Ted de Corsia, Olive Sturgess, David O'Brien, Richard Eyer. Directed by Charles Lamont. Story and screenplay, Kay Lenard; camera, George Robinson; editor, Edward Curtiss; music supervision, Joseph Gernhenson. Previewed Feb. 27, '56. Running time, **81 MINS.**

Ma Kettle	Marjorie Main
Sedge Kettle	Arthur Hunnicutt
Miss Bedelia Baines	Una Merkel
Professor	Ted de Corsia
Nancy	Olive Sturgess
Conductor	David O'Brien
Billy	Richard Eyer
Susie	Cheryl Callaway
Bancroft Bainer	Joe Sawyer
Benny	Sid Tomack
Mountaineer	Louis DaPron
Joe	Harry Hines
Jack Dexter	Jim Hayward

Universal's "Kettles" series is pretty thin fun after eight times at bat. Filled with comedy antics dating back to silents, only the most loyal of smalltime fans will get much from it.

This time, Ma and the kids take off on a cornball express to the Ozarks to visit Uncle Sedge, a new character played by Arthur Hunnicut, but patterned to Percy Kilbride's Pa Kettle role. Kilbride's the smart one retiring after seven times in the series, but his presence is sorely missed. However, there's not much he could have given this one.

Aboard train enroute to Uncle Sedge's ramshackle farm, the Kettel offspring manage to keep Marjorie Main, as Ma, right busy, and, down on the farm, she straightens out Hunnicutt, a shiftless type who has kept Una Merkel on the matrimonial fence for 20 years, as well as ridding his broken-down acres of some city bootleggers who have set up in competition with traditional Ozarkian-distilled moonshine.

Whatever is possible to be made of the Kay Lenard screen story is done so by Charles Lamont's direction and the Richard Wilson production is filled with the tumbled trappings that trademark the "Kettle" pix. Miss Main does what she can to sustain the Ma Kettle character and Hunnicutt does Uncle Sedge to the point of ennui. Miss Merkel has her good moments. Ted de Corsia, head of the city crooks; Olive Sturgess, dimpled eldest daughter of the junket to the Ozarks; Richard Eyer, another offspring, and David O'Brien, harassed train conductor, are other featured players.

Lensing and other technical work is standard. *Brog.*

Dark River
(ARGENTINE)

Beatings and rape, ultimate rebellion in a labor camp. Morbid Argentine import for exploitation market.

Times Film Corp. release of Hugo del Carril production. Features del Carril, Adriana Benetti, Gloria Ferrandez, Raul del Valle. Directed by del Carril. Screenplay and story, Eduardo Borras; camera, Jose Maria Beltran; music, Tito Ribero; musical director, Prudencio Giminez; English titles, Herman Weinberg. Previewed N.Y., Feb. 23, '56. Running time, **88 MINS.**

Santos Peralta	Hugo del Carril
Rufino Peralta	Pedro Laxalt
Paraguaya	Gloria Ferrandez
Barreito	Raul del Valle
Amelia	Adriana Benetti

(In Spanish; English Titles)

Violence, rape and excessive brutality are the halmarks of

"Dark River," an Argentine import which Times Film Corp, is distributing in the U.S. This is exploitable fare for certain houses which specialize in "sensational" pix, but the film is far too morbid and sadistic to find bookings more generally.

Presumably the time of the story is of a fairly recent period, for a comparatively modern steamer takes a motley group of laborers up an Argentine river to toil at a Paraguayan tea plantation. Here the workers—both men and women—are beaten and revived by bestial overseers at the bidding of one man who proclaims, "I am the boss." This kind of slavery existed until 1911 in the hemp fields of Yucatan, Mexico, but it's hard to accept that such slavery could exist today.

Naturally there's a limit to which even the oppressed workers can be pushed. So after overseer Raul del Valle rapes defenseless Adriana Benetti, Pedro Laxalt is savagely lashed for attempting to aid Gloria Ferrandez and several laborers are slain for infractions of discipline, the workers form a union and rise up against the barbarians. It goes without saying that handsome Hugo del Carril and Miss Benedetti escape down the river, free to launch a new life elsewhere.

Producer del Carril, aside from somberly portraying a role as a key worker, directed with a heavy hand. Overall gloominess of the Eduardo Borras story and screenplay is further accented by the low key photography of Jose Maria Beltran. Sandwiched between the film's misery are two songs by Samuel Aquayo and Mauricio Cardoso Champo. Titled "Nights of Paraguay" and "Dark Enchantress," they're so-so tunes and do little to relieve the anguish generated by the yarn.

Despite the grimness of her part, Miss Benetti manages to display a wistful and appealing demeanor. Laxalt, as del Carril's brother, is suitably fatalistic in light of the circumstances he's confronted with while Miss Ferrandez registers as a pathetic prostitute in search of something better. Del Valle makes it look realistic as the rapist whose payoff is a violent death at the hands of del Carril. Herman Weinberg's English titles are adequate.
Gilb.

Serenade
(SONGS—COLOR)

Lanza sings again—to a merry b.o. tune.

Hollywood, March 13.

Warner Bros. release of Henry Blanke production. Stars Mario Lanza, Joan Fontaine, Sarita Montiel, Vincent Price; features Joseph Calleia, Harry Bellaver, Vince Edwards, Silvio Minciotti, Frank Puglia, Edward Platt. Directed by Anthony Mann. Screenplay, Ivan Goff, Ben Roberts, John Twist; based on the novel by James M. Cain; camera (WarnerColor), J. Peverell Marley; editor, William Ziegler; original songs, Nicholas Brodszky, Sammy Cahn. Previewed Feb. 29, '55. Running time, **121 MINS.**

Damon Vincenti	Mario Lanza
Kendall Hale	Joan Fontaine
Juana Montes	Carita Montiel
Charles Winthrop	Vincent Price
Maestro Marcatello	Joseph Calleia
Monte	Harry Bellaver
Marco Roselli	Vince Edwards
Lardelli	Silvio Minciotti
Manuel	Frank Puglia
Carter	Edward Platt
Giuseppe	Frank Yaconelli
Sinroma	Mario Siletti
Rosa	Maria Serrano
Felipe	Eduardo Noriega
Licia Albanese and Jean Fenn Specialties	

After some three years away from pictures—but not out of print—Mario Lanza returns in better voice than ever. "Serenade" looks like boxoffice for robust, soaring tenor and his 14 songs, two of the pop variety, which occupy approximately half of the two-hour footage. For the dramatic fan, there's a romantic triangle plot into which the music is interwoven. A satisfying show that should please the majority.

Since with a Lanza starrer, it's the music more than the story that generates the most interest, this Henry Blanke production has backed the numbers with splendid settings, all varied to fit the song and add to the colorful mood. Among the classical pieces, many will find Schubert's "Ave Maria" a tremendously moving experience as Lanza sings it in an old San Felipe, Mexico, church to the accompaniment of an organ. For setting contrast, there's the remarkably effective lighting and decor that backs his later vocalling of "Lamenti di Frederico" from "L'Arlesiana" by Cilea.

The music is skillfully interjected to help motivate the plot so there is no strain as story points are made by such arias as "La Danza," "Torna a Surriento," "O Soave Fanciulla," sung with Jean Fenn; the tenor aria from Act 1, "Rosenkavalier," "Amor Ti Vieta," "Di Quella Pira," the prayer from Act 3, Part 4, "Otello" and the Dio Ti Giocondi duet from the same opera with Licia Albanese; "Il Mio Tesoro," "O Paradiso" and "Nessun Dorma." Nicholas Brodzsky and Sammy Cahn contributed the title tune, heard twice, and "My Destiny." They, too, are used to further the story.

Ivan Goff, Ben Roberts and John Twist, in scripting from the James M. Cain novel, effectively eliminate the unnatural angle to the original triangle, and it now comes off as a basic love tussle between two girls over a man. As it stands, it's the story of a humble youth with a golden voice who gets mixed up with an amoral society girl, falls into disrepute when she finds a new romantic toy and then makes a comeback with a girl who gives him true love. As the footage is assembled, symbols rather than actual physical clinches suggest

the depth of the first affair so the point of his giving up a certain career to flee to Mexico is not as well made as it could have been.

Anthony Mann's direction is skillful in meeting the problems of blending story and music and in showing the players to the best advantage. Lanza comes off adequately in the dramatics. Joan Fontaine, the femme menace, is especially good and wears the striking Howard Shoup gowns with an outstanding clothes flare. Sarita Montiel, Mexican actress seen previously in "Vera Cruz," is warm and alive as the girl who nurses Lanza back to health at her Mexican hacienda and gives him the love that straightens him out. Vincent Price, equipped with some sharp, brittle dialog by the scripters, stands out as a caustic concert booker.

Fine support is lent the four stars by such performers as Joseph Calleia, Harry Bellaver, Vince Edwards, Silvio Minciotti, Frank Puglia, Edward Platt, Maria Serrano and Eduardo Noriega, among others. The Mexican location resulted in scenes of brilliant beauty, all well lensed in WarnerColor by J. Peverell Marley. The art direction by Edward Carrere and the set decorations by William Wallace are strikingly effective. Editing by William Ziegler and the sound by Robert B. Lee and Dolph Thomas contribute importantly.
Brog.

The Searchers
(V'VISION—COLOR)

Western in grand scale with John Wayne starring and John Ford directing. Good boxoffice potential despite deficiencies in story.

Warner Bros. release of C. V. Whitney production (Merion C. Cooper, executive producer). Stars John Wayne. Features Jeffrey Hunter, Vera Miles, Ward Bond, and Natalie Wood. Directed by John Ford. Screenplay, Frank Nugent; camera (VistaVision Technicolor), Winton C. Hoch; editor, Jack Murray; music, Max Steiner; song, "The Searchers," Stan Jones. Previewed in N.Y., March 2, '56. Running time, **119 MINS.**

Ethan Edwards	John Wayne
Martin Pawley	Jeffrey Hunter
Laurie Jorgensen	Vera Miles
Capt. Rev. S. Clayton	Ward Bond
Debbie Edwards (No. 2)	Natalie Wood
Lars Jorgensen	John Qualen
Mrs. Jorgensen	Olive Carey
Chief Scar	Henry Brandon
Charlie McCorry	Ken Curtis
Brad Jorgensen	Harry Carey Jr.
Emilio Figueroa	Antonio Moreno
Mose Harper	Hank Worden
Debbie Edwards (No. 1)	Lana Wood
Aaron Edwards	Walter Coy
Martha Edwards	Dorothy Jordan
Lucy Edwards	Pippa Scott
Lt. Greenhill	Pat Wayne
Look	Beulah Archuletta

The boxoffice appeal of John Wayne combined with the imprint of John Ford makes "The Searchers" a contender for the big money stakes. It's a western in the grand scale—handsomely mounted and in the tradition of "Shane." The VistaVision - Technicolor photographic excursion through the southwest—presenting in bold and colorful outline the arid country and areas of buttes and giant rock formations — is eyefilling and impressive.

Yet "The Searchers" is somewhat disappointing. There is a feeling that it could have been so much more. Overlong and repetitious at 119 minutes there are subtleties in the basically simple story that are not adequately explained. There are, however, some fine vignettes of frontier life in the early southwest and a realistic presentation of the difficulties faced by the settlers in carving out

a homestead in dangerous Indian country.

First C. V. Whitney picture for Warner Bros. release involves a long, arduous trek through primitive country by two men in search of nine-year-old girl kidnapped by hostile Comanche Indians. They achieve their purpose after five years of determined prowling, punctuated by privation, skirmishes with Indians, armed battles with treacherous informants, and occasional returns to their Texas home base.

Wayne, the uncle of the kidnapped girl, is a complex character. His motivations, from the time he appears out of the southwest plains at his brother's ranch to his similar exit after he accomplishes his mission, are unclear. There are vague hints of a romance with his sister-in-law, an antagonistic relationship with his brother, and a feud with Ward Bond, a combination preacher and captain of the Texas Rangers. Wayne is a bitter, taciturn individual throughout and the reasons for his attitude are left to the imagination of the viewer. All that is known about him is that he fought in the Civil War and did not return home until three years after the war ended. There are indications that he wandered endlessly and did many things before deciding to return home.

His bitterness toward the Indians is understandable. They massacred his brother's family (except for the kidnapped girl) and destroyed the ranch. However, his reaction to the girl when she is finally found seems peculiar. He feels the girl has been defiled by the Indians during her years with them and he is determined to kill her. He rides her down and as she lies helplessly on the ground he approaches menacingly with his gun drawn. At the last moment, he changes his mind, lowers his gun, picks her up tenderly and returns her to a friendly ranch family. With his task finished, he rides off.

Wayne's partner in the search is Jeffrey Hunter, who has been cared for by Wayne's brother since the young man's family was massacred by the Comanches. Hunter and a rancher's daughter (Vera Miles) provide the romantic interest and the former is also involved in labored attempts at comedy relief—such as the purchase of a squaw instead of a blanket and a knockdown fight with Ken Curtis, his rival for Miss Miles" affections.

Wayne is fine in the role of the hard-bitten, misunderstood, and mysterious searcher and the rest of the cast acquits itself notably, including Hunter and Miss Miles. Also standout are Bond as the colorful, tophatted preacher-captain; Hank Worden, as a "tetched," old Indian scout; John Qualen, as a rancher; Harry Carey Jr., as Qualen's son, Olive Carey, as Qualen's wife, and Henry Brandon, as the hostile Indian chief.

The John Ford directorial stamp **is unmistakeable. It concentrates on the characters and establishes a definite mood. It's not sufficient, however, to overcome many of the weaknesses of the story. Winton C. Hoch's VistaVision lensing and other technical aspects are of top-notch quality.** *Holl.*

Crime Against Joe

Suspenseful whodunit headed for good returns if properly exploited.

Hollywood, March 2.

United Artists release of Howard W. Koch (Bel-Air) production. Stars John Bromfield, Julie London, Henry Calvin; features Frances Morris, Addison Richards, Robert Keys, John Pickard. Directed by Lee Sholem. Screenplay, Robert C. Dennis; camera, William Margulies; music, Paul Dunlay; editor, Mike Pozen. Previewed Feb. 28, '56. Running time, **69 MINS.**

Joe Manning	John Bromfield
Slacks	Julie London
Red Waller	Henry Calvin
Christy Rowen	Patricia Blake
Philip Rowen	Joel Ashley
Detective Hollander	Robert Keyes
Irene Crescent	Alika Louis
Harry Dorn	John Pickard
Nora Manning	Frances Morris
George Niles	Rhodes Reason
Dr. Tatreau	Mauritz Hugo
Gloria Wayne	Joyce Jameson
Luther Wood	Morgan Jones
Ralph Corey	James Parnell

This well-developed whodunit hits fast stride after a prolonged opening. Story premise is sufficiently novel to peg audience interest.

Robert C. Dennis screenplay about an innocent man accused of murder gets suspenseful buildup by director Lee Sholem, who draws good performances out of a cast headed by John Bromfield, Julie London and Henry Calvin. The Howard W. Koch production never tips off the actual slayer until a surprise climax, when he's revealed naturally and sans heavy medodramatics.

Bromfield is arrested after a night of drunken roistering for the murder of a nitery singer, a high school pin of his class of 1945 clutched in her hand. He's released after Julie London, a car hop in love with him, gives him a phony alibi following the damaging statements of several others who for their own purposes have lied about him. Knowing it's only a matter of time before he'll be picked up again, since the police are suspicious of his alibi, Bromfield starts his own investigations of others in his class who might be the killer, and comes up with the answer in the school gymnasium after the murderer nearly adds him to his list of victims.

Bromfield characterizes his role well, Miss London scores as femme lead and Henry Calvin is Bromfield's taxi-driver pal, strongly cast. Alika Louis, a looker, is a standout as she chirps "I'm Looking for a Man to Love," the murder victim, and Patricia Blake, who plays a sleepwalker, also is easy on the eyes. Frances Morris is okay, too, as Bromfield's understanding mother.

Technical credits are well handled by William Margulies' camera work, Mike Pozen's editing and Paul Dunlap's music score also satisfactory. *Whit.*

Forbidden Planet
(C'SCOPE—COLOR)

Exciting science-fiction thriller with solid earning potential.

Hollywood, March 13.

Metro release of Nicholas Nayfack production. Stars Walter Pidgeon, Anne Francis, Leslie Nielsen; features Warren Stevens, Jack Kelly, Richard Anderson, Earl Holliman, George Wallace. Directed by Fred McLeod Wilcox. Screenplay, Cyril Hume; based on a story by Irving Block, Allen Adler; camera (Eastman Color), George J. Folsey; editor, Ferris Webster; special effects, A. Arnold Gillespie, Warren Newcombe, Irving G. Ries, Joshua Meador; electronic tonalities, Louis and Bebe Barron. Previewed Feb. 22, '56. Running time, **98 MINS.**

Dr. Morbius	Walter Pidgeon
Altaira Morbius	Anne Francis
Commander Adams	Leslie Nielsen
"Doc" Ostrow	Warren Stevens
Lt. Farman	Jack Kelly
Chief Quinn	Richard Anderson
Cook	Earl Holliman
Bosun	George Wallace
Grey	Bob Dix
Youngerford	Jimmy Thompson
Strong	James Drury
Randall	Harry Harvey Jr.
Lindstrom	Roger McGee
Foran	Peter Millep
Nichols	Morgan Jones
Silvers	Richard Grant

This is a "Space Patrol" for adults, but the kiddies will be there, too, and it shapes to a solid reception from science-fiction fans everywhere. Imaginative gadgets galore, plus plenty of suspense and thrills, make the Nicholas Nayfack production a top offering in the space travel category. Use of CinemaScope and Eastman Color sharpens the chimerical appeal, too, so a good boxoffice reaction looms.

Best of all the gadgets is Robby, the Robot, a mascot that should be in every home, and he's well-used in the film for some comedy touches. The conception of space cruisers, space planet terrain, the monstrous self-operating power plant, and of the terribly frightening spectre that threatens the human principals in the story are weird and wonderful. So are the electronic tonalities that provide the picture with an eerie, fitting score that heightens the suspense measureably.

With all the technical gadgetry on display and carrying the entertainment load, the players are more or less puppets with no great acting demands made. However, they still come off adequately under Fred McLeod Wilcox's direction and the 98 minutes of footage sustains a good pace as the Cyril Hume script, based on a story by Irving Block and Allen Adler is unfolded.

Leslie Nielsen, space cruiser commander, lands on Altair-4, a planet way out in outer space, to search for survivors from a previous flight to the forbidding land. He finds Walter Pidgeon, super-scientist, and the latter's daughter, Anne Francis, who, with Robby, are the planet's only inhabitants. Pidgeon, who has gained knowledge beyond usual human limits, wants the rescuers to begone, but they're stubborn. Beside, Nielsen takes to Miss Francis and she to him, so he determines to seek out the unseen menace that creates terror and death on the planet. Climax reveals the menace as a nightmare from the subconscious, unwittingly created by Pidgeon to drive the rescuers away. Mere man can't defeat the awesome thing so Pidgeon has to die to kill it.

George J. Folsey handles his cameras to the best effect. Credited for the special effects that add the punch to the show are A. Arnold Gillespie, Warren Newcombe, Irving G. Ries and Joshua Meador, latter on loanout from Walt Disney Productions, while Louis and Bebe Barron did the tonalities. *Brog.*

Twelfth Night
(RUSSIAN—COLOR)

Well-made film version of Shakespeare's comedy. Has art house possibilities.

Artkino Pictures release of Lenfilm Studio production. Directed by Y. Fried. Screenplay, Fried, from the William Shakespeare comedy; camera (Magicolor), E. Shapiro; music, A. Zhivotov. At Cameo, N.Y., March 3, '56. Running time, **56 MINS.**

Viola, Sebastian	K. Luchko
Olivia	A. Larionova
Duke Orsino	V. Medvediev
Sir Toby Beld	M. Yanshin
Sir Andrew Aguecheck	G. Vipin
Malvolio	V. Merkuriev
Antonio	S. Lukyanov
Clown	B. Freindlich
Maria	A. Lisyanskaya
Fabian	S. Filippov
Sea Captain	A. Antonov

With this film version of Shakespeare's "Twelfth Night," the Soviet picture industry shows that it's capable of handling culture as competently as studios of other lands. For the import does full credit to the Bard's comedy. It's well directed, handsomely mounted and, for the most part, excellently performed. While Russian product normally has limited distribution in the States, this entry could well be an exception.

Some art houses will find this Lenfilm Studio production a natural booking and, of course, there are always b.o. possibilities to be gained via tieups with schools, colleges, etc. "Twelfth Night" may not be too rollicking a comedy under contemporary standards. However, the use of Magicolor, the exterior scenes, and greater movement that the camera permits tend to lessen a hint of dullness that occasionally arises.

Katya Luchko, a winsome lass, vivaciously portrays the dual roles of Viola and Sebastian—twin sister and brother—who have been rescued from shipwreck at the mythical country of Illyria. From then on the Bard develops the "mistaken identity" theme in a romance that brings in the twins, a lovesick swain, a beauteous countess and assorted other characters.

Anna Larionova, a well-proportioned blonde, fetchingly plays Countess Olivia. V. Merkuriev, as Malvolio, Olivia's steward, is a trifle flamboyant at times but manages to capture the ridiculous shadings of the role. V. Medvediev is suitably regal as Duke Orsino who engages Viola as a male page to woo Olivia. M. Yanshin impresses as Sir Toby Belch, the gourmand, and G. Vipin's Sir Andrew Aguecheek is done with a flair that accents his craven qualities. Unobtrusive are the English titles and A. Zhivotov's score is an asset. *Gilb.*

The Steel Jungle

Showcaser for upcoming talents of Perry Lopez and Beverly Garland. Routine prison stuff.

Hollywood, Feb. 28.

Warner Bros. release of David Weisbart production. Features Perry Lopez, Beverly Garland, Walter Abel, Ted de Corsia, Kenneth Tobey, Allison Hayes. Written and directed by Walter Daniger; camera, J. Peverell Marley; editor, Folmar Blangsted; music, David Buttolph. Previewed Feb. 13, '56. Running time, **86 MINS.**

Ed Novak	Perry Lopez
Frances Novak	Beverly Garland
Warden Keller	Walter Abel
Steve Marlin	Ted de Corsia
Dr. Lewy	Kenneth Tobey
Mrs. Archer	Allison Hayes
Guard Weaver	Gregory Walcott
Lupo	Leo Gordon
Stringbean	Kay Kuter
Dan Bucci	Bob Steele
Andy Macklin	Ralph Moody
Beakeley	Stafford Repp
Harry	Billy Vincent

Program prison drama, showcasing newer faces of Perry Lopez and Beverly Garland. Not a strong entertainment vehicle, film does give pair, particularly Lopez, a chance to be seen in leads and test possible public acceptance. Product shortage being what it is, sufficient bookings may give newcomers a rather widespread showing.

Walter Doniger wrote and directed the David Weisbart production with a fair amount of dispatch. The melodramatics are regulation, but the freshness of the casting is a help. Lopez, married to the expectant Miss Garland, is a smalltime bookie loyal to the syndicate. This loyalty has him going to prison rather than spill what he knows, even though his wife needs him at home. Remainder of the plot deals with how he gets himself straightened out and learns the bookie combine holds no loyalties except to itself.

Some prison fight scenes develop the proper suspense feel and the 86 minutes of footage is fairly well paced through the unfoldment, even though Doniger's scripting doesn't always hold water. Walter Abel plays the warden for moderate results and Ted de Corsia is the menace as the combine head who rules his bookies from behind prison bars. Kenneth Tobey fares well as the prison psychiatrist and Allison Hayes shows up nicely in a small spot. Gregory Walcott, a crooked guard; Leo Gordon, Kay Kuter, Bob Steele and Ralph Moody are among others with formula characters to play.

Lensing, editing, scoring and other technical points are made satisfactorily for budget. *Brog.*

Singing in the Dark
(SONGS)

Moishe Oysher-Joey Adams in modest entry for big city nabes.

Budsam Distributing Co. release of A. N. O. (Joey Adams) production. Stars Moishe Oysher and Adams; features Phyllis Hill, Lawrence Tierney. Directed by Max Nosseck. Screenplay, Aben Kandel, Ann Hood, Stephen Kandel, from story by Aben Kandel based on idea by Oysher and Nosseck; camera, Boris Kaufman; editors, Leonard Anderson, Marc Sorkin. At Midtown, Ascot and St. Mark's Theatres, N.Y., week of March 7, '56. Running time, **84 MINS.**

Leo	Moishe Oysher
Joey Napoleon	Joey Adams
Ruth	Phyllis Hill
Biff	Lawrence Tierney
Luli	Kay Medford
Barry	Mickey Knox
Larry	Dave Starr
Fran	Cindy Heller
M'Sieu La Fontaine	Al Kelly
Dr. Neumann	Henry Sharpe
Stan	Stan Hoffman
Refugee	Paul Andor
Thug	Abe Simon

Rise of a onetime Nazi concentration camp inmate from wartime misery to happiness through a new life in America is haphazardly unreeled in "Singing in the Dark." A modest entry, it has little b.o. potential aside from minor prospects in metropolitan area nabe houses. In those sites name of co-star Moishe Oysher, vet of the Yiddish theatre, will help. His marquee partner, comic Joey Adams, may also generate biz at the wicket in sectors where he's known.

Although the story is credited to Aben Kandel, longtime toiler in Hollywood's script mill, it does not emerge with the clarity and polish that one would expect from such a writer. For he, along with fellow scripters Ann Hood and Stephen Kandel, has whipped up a curious screenplay that at times borders on the inane. Oysher, after surviving a Hitler camp, is troubled with amnesia but manages to succeed in the U. S. as a hotel clerk, nitery singer and eventually a cantor.

His ability as a vocalist is discovered by chance by Adams, a "Broadway chiseler" who takes him under his wing. Oysher's voice, it seems, pours forth only when stimulated by liquor, hence the phrasing of a VARIETY review of his performance as "Leo Drinko Singo Socko." Sandwiched in the footage before Oysher becomes a cantor are a number of situations and routines reminiscent of burlesque blackouts.

Oysher's thesping is much to be desired but his singing voice manages to rise above the mediocrity of the material handed him. As for Adams, he seems more at home on a nitery floor than before the cameras. Among other players involved in this low-budgeter are Phyllis Hill, who portrays Oysher's romantic interest with a wistful touch; Lawrence Tierney, tough bookie to whom Adams is in hock; Al Kelly, who does his famed doubletalk routine; Kay Medford, cast as a nitery op, and Cindy Heller, as a moll who's pleasant to look at.

Rambling script and meagre production values appear to be too much of a hurdle for Max Nosseck's direction to jump. Boris Kaufman's lensing is adequate but editing of Leonard Anderson and Marc Sorkin is rather choppy. Film, incidentally, makes liberal use of stock shots and at 84 minutes the footage is overlong.

Gilb.

The Creature Walks Among Us

Third time around for U's amphibious monster, the Gill Man. Exploiteer offering.

Hollywood, March 13.

Universal release of William Alland production. Stars Jeff Morrow, Rex Reason, Leigh Snowden; features Gregg Palmer, Maurice Manson, James Rawley. Directed by John Sherwood. Screenplay, Arthur Ross; camera, Maury Gertsman; special photography, Clifford Stine; editor, Edward Curtiss; music, Joseph Gershenson. Previewed March 1, '56. Running time, **78 MINS.**

Dr. William Barton .... Jeff Morrow
Dr. Thomas Morgan .... Rex Reason
Marcia Barton .... Leigh Snowden
Jed Grant .... Gregg Palmer
Dr. Berg .... Maurice Manson
Dr. Johnson .... James Rawley
Captain Stanley .... David McMahon
Morteno .... Paul Fierro
Mrs. Morteno .... Lillian Molieri
State Trooper .... Larry Hudson
Steward .... Frank Chase
Creature .... Don Megowan
and Rico Browning

Universal's Gill Man, an amphibious monster twice seen before (in 3-D), is back for another session of chills and thrills for the program exploitation market. To get the monster on land, the plot has him captured by a scientific expedition headed by Jeff Morrow, Rex Reason, Gregg Palmer and Leigh Snowden. During the capture the creature's scales and gills are destroyed by fire but the clever medicos discover he has a land animal's lung structure so a quick tracheotomy is performed and the sea monster is evoluted into an air-breathing thing. Things are going along fairly well until Morrow gets jealous of Palmer's attentions to his wife, Miss Snowden, and kills the rival, wounding the creature as well. The latter escapes and is last seen heading for the Pacific Ocean.

The scripting by Arthur Ross is shadowy in detailing some of the human relations and motivations but still holds together sufficiently in keeping interest centered on the main character. The trouping of the lead foursome, as well as that by Maurice Manson, James Rawley and others, comes off acceptably enough for this type of show under John Sherwood's direction. Don Megowan does the creature on land while Ricou Browning is seen in the underwater shots.

The William Alland production goes in for quite a bit of underwater footage in the earlier sequences during the hunt for the creature. Miss Snowden is the beauty among the male beasts in these. Lensing by Maury Gertsman and special photography by Clifford Stine head the competent technical credits.

Brog.

A Town Like Alice
(BRITISH)

Picturization of incident from last war when Jap conquerors forced British women and children to march across Malaya; spotty returns.

London, March 6.

Rank production and release. Stars Virginia McKenna and Peter Finch. Directed by Jack Lee. Screenplay, W. P. Lipscomb and Richard Mason; camera, Geoffrey Unsworth; editor, Sidney Hayers; music, Matyas Seiber. At Odeon Theatre, Leicester Square, London. Running time, **117 MINS.**

Jean Paget .... Virginia McKenna
Joe Harman .... Peter Finch
Japanese Sergeant .... Takagi
Captain Sugaya .... Tran Van Khe
Miss Horsefall .... Jean Anderson
Mrs. Dudley Frost .... Marie Lohr
Ellen .... Maureen Swanson
Ebbey .... Renee Houston
Mrs. Frith .... Nora Nicholson
Mrs. Holland .... John Fabian
Ben .... Vincent Ball
British Sergeant .... Tim Turner
Captain Yanata .... Vu Ngoc Tuan
Captain Takata .... Yamada
Captain Nishi .... Nakanishi
Kemptei Sergeant .... Ikeda
Solicitor .... Geoffrey Keen

A reconstruction of a true episode in the last war but using fictitious characters, "A Town Like Alice" can best be described as a worthy picture made more with an eye on prestige than the boxoffice. In good class situations, it should do fairly well, but generally speaking, can only hope for spotty returns.

Filmed largely on location in Malaya and Australia, story is based on Neville Shute's novel of the same name. Film describes how a handful of women and children were forced-marched through Malaya at the hands of the Japanese. For months on end they tramped from one camp to another, through swamp and storm, through dust and heat. Many died on the roadside, but the few survivors eventually found refuge in a village after their guard had succumbed.

During the period of their cross-country march the women and kids are befriended by a couple of Australian P.O.W.'s who have been assigned to truck driving duties for the Japs, and over a shared cigaret and an exchange of minor confidence, a bond develops between Virginia McKenna and Peter Finch. He was formerly a cattle farmer in a district known as Alice Springs and he paints a picture of his home town which captures Miss McKenna's imagination.

After one meeting he promises them chicken for the next day's lunch and when he's charged with stealing the bird, the Jap officer orders him to be crucified. The order, however, is not fully carried out and after several hours nailed to a tree he is taken away and sent to hospital. Some years later at the end of the war, Miss McKenna hears that he survived the ordeal and follows him to Alice Springs for the inevitable reunion.

The subject matter is necessarily grim, but wherever possible the script and Jack Lee's direction endeavor to infuse a touch of lighter relief. The focus, however, is almost constantly on the trials of the women and children as they fight against famine and disease. Mainly, their Japanese conquerors are portrayed unsympathetically; only the guard who escorts them is shown to have human instincts.

From a technical standpoint, the film is beyond reproach. The acting is on a consistently high level, the direction is smooth and the camerawork is firstclass. In a big cast, in addition to the stars, there are tender performances by Marie Lohr, Renee Houston, Joan Anderson and Maureen Swanson.

Myro.

Don Juan
(AUSTRIAN—COLOR)

So-so telescoping of Mozart's 'Don Giovanni' with ballet added. Okay for some U.S. arties.

Times Films release of Akkord Film production Stars Cesare Danova, Josef Meinrad, Evelyne Cormand; features Hans von Borsody, Lotte Tobisch, Jean Vinci, Marianne Schoenauer, Fred Hennings, Senta Wengraf. Directed by H. W. Kolm-Veltee. Adaptation by Veltee, Prof. Alfred Uhl, Ernest Henthaler; camera (Agfa color), Willy Sohm-Hannes Fuchs; choreography, Dia Luca. Sung by members of the Vienna State Opera. Danced by the Opera Ballet. Previewed in N.Y., Feb. 22, '56. Running time, **89 MINS.**

The Actors

Don Giovanni .... Cesare Danova
Leporello .... Josef Meinrad
Zerlina .... Evelyne Cormand
Masetto .... Hans von Borsody
Donna Elvira .... Lotte Tobisch
Don Ottavio .... Jean Vinci
Donna Anna ...... Marianne Schoenauer
Commendatore .... Fred Hennings
Elvira's maid .... Senta Wengraf

The Singers

Don Giovanni .... Alfred Poell
Leporello .... Harald Progelhof
Zerline .... Annie Felbermayer
Masetto .... Walter Berry
Donna Elvira .... Hanna Loeser
Don Ottavio .... Hugo Meyer-Welfing
Donna Anna .... Annie Felbermayer
Commendatore .... Gottlieb Frick

(In German—English Subtitles)

Somewhere along the line in "Don Juan," director H. W. Kolm-Veltee should have made up his mind whether he wanted to have Mozart in his film or not. He failed to do this, and the result is something of a handsome hodgepodge that serves as a dim reminder that once there was a charming opera called "Don Giovanni."

"Don Juan," acted out by one cast and sung by another, undoubtedly represents a considerable investment and in its more spectacular moments carries with it considerable visual impact. On the whole, it's a disappointing film that's neither here nor there and will need some concentrated selling even in the arties since it is, in a manner of speaking, neither fish nor fowl; neither opera nor action-romance. Apart from that, the sound recording isn't up to snuff.

Story of "Don Juan," essentially following the opera yarn, needs no retelling. In the lead role, Cesare Danova cuts a handsome figure, but goes in for some excessive posturing. Alfred Poell does the singing and his "Reich mir die Hand, mein Leben" is a delight.

In the smaller parts, Josef Meinrad is a comic Leporello; Evelyne Cormand a pretty Zerlina and Lotte Tobisch a commanding and sorrowful Donna Elvira.

Among the biggest assets of the picture is its Agfa color lensing. Tint effects are dramatic, particularly in the final scene when the mad Don Juan perishes in the flames. Fencing bit looks staged but has some excitement. Party sequence incuding the dancing, as well as the final ballet, are done in good taste, and here again the vivid Agfa color hues are a help.

Kolm-Veltee's direction seems handicapped by the confusion of purposes but comes up with some good effects. Costumes are handsome and some massive sets are used for scope. Film is aimed obviously below the highbrow level, but lands shy of its target. Herman Weinberg's titles keep pace with the German.

Hift.

Private's Progress
(BRITISH)

Life in the British army circa 1942, depicted in lighthearted vein.

London, March 6.

British Lion release of a Charter Film (Boulting Brothers) production. Stars Richard Attenborough, Dennis Price, Terry-Thomas and Ian Carmichael. Directed by John Boulting. Screenplay, Frank Harvey, John Boulting; camera, Eric Cross; editor, Anthony Harvey; music, John Addison. At Rialto Theatre, London. Running time, **102 MINS.**

Cox .... Richard Attenborough
Bertram Tracepurcel ...... Dennis Price
Major Hitchcock .... Terry-Thomas
Stanley Windrush .... Ian Carmichael
Egan .... Peter Jones
Sgt. Sutton .... William Hartnell
Capt. Bootle .... Thorley Walters
Prudence Greenslade .... Jill Adams
Private Horrocks .... Ian Bannen
Private George Blake .... Victor Maddern
Private Dai Jones ..... Kenneth Griffiths
Sgt.-Maj. Gradwick .... John Warren
Padre .... George Coulouris
Pat .... Derrick De Marney
Gerald .... David King-Wood
Windrush Senior .... Miles Malleson

As a lighthearted satire on British army life during the last war, "Private's Progress" has moments of sheer joy based on real authenticity. But it is not content to rest on satire alone and introduces an unreal melodramatic adventure which robs the story of much of its charm. In its present form it should get by adequately enough in the home market; overseas prospects, particularly in America, are little more than modest.

Up to the point where they confine themselves to situation comedy, the Boulting Brothers rarely miss. But they obviously felt there must be some point to the plot and they've added an adventure tail-piece in which a War Office brigadier invades enemy territory to bring back valuable art treasures to Britain.

The basic comedy, however, derives from the depiction of the typical misfit into the army way of life. Ian Carmichael is shown as the earnest University student who interrupts his studies to join the forces. He is a lamentable failure in training, fails his officer's cadet course and then is wheedled into the worst habits of the army private.

Many weaknesses of the yarn are surmounted by the allround performances of the cast. Carmichael has the biggest single role and does remarkably well. Richard Attenborough is in confident mood as a private who soon gets to know his way around. Dennis Price gives a smooth study as the brigadier and Terry-Thomas contributes an amusing cameo of an army major. Only femme role of any note is gracefully filled by Jill Adams. Expert British players take good care of the supporting parts. Technical credits are up to standard. *Myro.*

1984
(BRITISH)

George Orwell's glimpse into the future emerges as a grim, depressing picture; obvious marquee values, but subject will demand special promotion.

London, March 6.

Associated British-Pathe release of a Holiday (N. Peter Rathvon) production. Stars Michael Redgrave, Edmund O'Brien and Jan Sterling. Directed by Michael Anderson. Screenplay, William P. Templeton and Ralph Bettinson; camera, C. Pennington Richards; editor, Bill Lewthwaite; music, Malcolm Arnold. At Warner Theatre, London. Running time, **90 MINS.**

O'Connor	Michael Redgrave
Winston Smith	Edmund O'Brien
Julia	Jan Sterling
Junk Shop Owner	David Kossoff
Jones	Mervyn Johns
Parsons	Donald Pleasence
Selina Parsons	Carol Wolveridge
Outer Party Announcer	Ernest Clark
Inner Party Official	Patrick Allen
Rutherford	Ronan O'Casey
Outer Party Orators	Michael Ripper, Ewen Solon
Prisoner	Kenneth Griffiths

A sinister glimpse of the future as envisaged by George Orwell, "1984" is a grim, depressing picture. It has little entertainment value in the accepted sense of the word, but it has a distinct curiosity value which can be sparked by carefully planned promotional campaigns.

A BBC teleplay of the book a couple of seasons back provoked a horror reaction from the press, and a repeat performance effectively emptied picture theatres. There is considerable doubt, however, whether the film version will operate in a reverse trend. The production has substantial marquee strength, but the b.o. lure of the stars could be negatived by the subject-matter and word-of-mouth.

The action takes place after the first atomic war, with the world divided into three major powers. London, the setting for the story, is the capital of Oceania and is run by a ruthless regime, the heads of which are members of the inner party while their supporters are in the outer party. There are ministries of Love and Thought, anti-sex leagues and record divisions where the speeches of the great are rewritten from time to time to suit the needs of contemporary events. The story is built around the illegal romance of two members of the outer party, Edmund O'Brien and Jan Sterling; they meet furtively, join the underground headed by Michael Redgrave (a big shot of the inner party) and are eventually caught and put through a brain-washing process.

Orwell's picture of the ultimate in totalitarian ruthlessness is faithfully presented. Television "eyes" keep a day and night watch on party members in their homes and tv screens are to be found everywhere, blurting out the latest reports on the endless wars with rival powers. The city is plastered with posters warning that "Big Brother is watching you" and with slogans that "war is peace" and "freedom is slavery." The atmosphere throughout is chilling and forbidding. As Orwell saw it, there is no brave, new world ahead.

The characters are dressed in drab party uniforms and are obliged to participate in compulsory two-minute "hate" sessions, as well as in organized hate weeks. With such an atmosphere, it is a welcome relief to have the tender exchanges between O'Brien and Jan Sterling. Their eventual murder by party guards brings the picture to an inconclusive end.

Redgrave's portrayal of the top party man is in his usual polished style. David Kossoff contributes a neat twist as a junk shop man who is actually in the pay of the thought police. Mervyn Johns and Ronan O'Casey, as two party members who are purged by Big Brother, and Carol Wolveridge, as a member of a kids' espionage group, are best of the competent support. Michael Anderson has directed the piece officially and technical credits are up to standard. *Myro.*

Si Tous Les Gars Du Monde . . .
(If All The Guys In The World)
(FRENCH)

Paris, March 6.

Cinedis release of Ariane-Filmsonor-Francinex production. Directed by Christian-Jaque. Screenplay, Jacques Remy; adaptation, H. G. Clouzot, Jean Ferry, Jaque; camera, Armand Thirard; editor, Jacques Desagneaux; music, Georges Van Parys. With Andre Valmy, Jean Gaven, Marc Cassot, Georges Poujouly, Doudou-Babet, Helene Perdriere, Jean-Louis Trigntignant. At the Paris, Paris. Running time, **110 MINS.**

Captain	Andre Valmy
Joos	Jean Gaven
Mohamed	Doudou-Babet
Mate	Marc Cassot
Wife	Helene Perdiere
Jean	Jean-Louis Trignignant
Cabin boy	Georges Poujouly

Thread of this film uses the dedicated work of a group of radio hams to get needed serum to a fishing boat (off the banks of Norway) whose crew has been poisoned by bad meat. Call for help is picked up by an amateur operator in Africa who gets in touch with one in Paris. Then the serum goes through Germany, the Russian Zone, Norway and finally to the dying crew members. Suspense is whipped up, but the film is primarily sketchy and lack of characterization throws the brunt of appeal on the chase aspects. This is well maintained. Pic shapes as an offbeater of interest for special spotting in the U.S.

Shipping boat is French and the crew a rugged group of Normans who have taken on an Arab this trip. The sickness sets off feeling against the Arab. Film deftly fills out the attempts of the various hams all over the world to bring aid to people they do not know. Here the cumulative effect is cheapened somewhat by dragging in obvious effects to try to build up a suspense which should have been inherent in the very nature of the drama. Serum gets into the Russian Zone into which an American soldier, alerted by a buddy who is the boyfriend of the daughter of the German amateur radio man, goes to reclaim it from a Polish airline stewardess. He is picked up by the Russians, but on confirmation about the need for the serum, the Russians rush it to the French.

All turns out well as the Arab sailor swims out to reclaim the dropped serum and all are saved. The theme of human solidarity is commendable but needs a more

direct and sober treatment. However, director Christian-Jaque has kept this moving with the good chase melodramatic. Playing by a nameless cast is good and technical credits are fine. This shapes as a heavily exploitable pic, and will have its chances on the U.S. market via its theme and treatment. *Mosk.*

Patterns

Small-scale production but a well-told tele tale. Van Heflin stars.

United Artists release of Michael Myerberg production, presented by Jed Harris & Myerberg. Stars Van Heflin; features Everett Sloane, Ed Begley, Beatrice Straight, Elizabeth Wilson. Directed by Fielder Cook. Original television play and screen adaptation, Rod Serling; editors, Dave Kummins and Carl Lerner. Tradeshown N.Y., March 9, '56. Running time, **83 MINS.**

Fred Staples	Van Heflin
Walter Ramsey	Everett Sloane
William Briggs	Ed Begley
Nancy Staples	Beatrice Straight
Marge Fleming	Elizabeth Wilson
Miss Lanier	Joanna Roos
Sylvia Trammel	Elene Kiannos
Miss Hill	Shirley Standlee
Paul Briggs	Ronnie Welsh Jr
Ann	Sally Gracie
Billy	Michael Dreyfuss
First Secretary	Adrienne Moore
Second Secretary	Elaine Kaye

A well told tele tale, "Patterns" is themewise akin to Metro's "Executive Suite," being about big business, and productionwise akin to Hecht - Lancaster's "Marty," also derived from television.

In theatrical feature form, the Rod Serling drama first seen on Kraft TV Theatre might present selling problems at the outset because of its unelaborate presentation and lightness of weight in name value. But importantly, this is a skillfully-executed film. Once over the initial hurdles, when the word is spread about its genuine merits, it should do good business.

Substantially it's the story of a corporation boss whose only concern is the growth of his business and let the less fit of his executive personnel fall as they may. Performances are vivid; the characters are drawn with an absence of falsity. The direction keeps the audience close to the action, allows for an unusual sense of participation.

Holding the reins on the corporate octopus is Everett Sloane. He's steel-eyed, harsh and cold and every inch the ruler of an industrial empire who will not have his business judgment tempered by concern for the welfare of his colleagues. But in the Serling screenplay, as directed by Fielder Cook (also from tv), another facade of the Sloane character is deftly established. In an intensely gripping climax, he lets it be known that he'd step aside if another man could do a better job; the corporation is more important than any individual, including himself. Sloane is fascinating all the way through.

Star of the picture is Van Heflin, as an engineer from Ohio who's brought to New York and comes face to face with the impersonal top-echelon operation. He's groomed to succeed Sloane's second in command, Ed Begley, with whom he has become friendly. Thus a dilemma, for Heflin wants the title but has compunctions about seeing Begley placed in an untenable position.

Heflin shows marked understanding of the role he plays out. He's alert, eager for the more important position but infuriated with Sloane's operational patterns. Begley competently sketches a pathetic figure as the exec on the way out.

Much of this is developed in the board of directors room and other portions of Ramsey Corp.'s skyscraper office building. The cameras play on the high-domed lobby and busy people on the hop and the atmosphere of bigness is thus communicated.

Featured characters add to the story's depth. Begley's secretary, Elizabeth Wilson; Beatrice Straight as Heflin's wife and Joanne Roos as Sloane's amanuensis all, too, are part of the pattern, and contribute sensitive performances.

Michael Myerberg's production, as previously noted, reflects a "Marty"-like budget. But it's fine picture-making with major credit due Serling, Cook, the players and photographer Boris Kaufman. All technical work is good.

There's no music in the background. None was needed. *Gene.*

Tribute to a Bad Man
(C'SCOPE—COLOR)

Alternating fast and slow pacing, this scenically striking early-west action drama has so-so prospects. Stars James Cagney.

Hollywood, March 19.

Metro release of Sam Zimbalist production. Stars James Cagney; costars Don Dubbins, Stephen McNally, Vic Morrow; introduces Irene Papas. Directed by Robert Wise. Screenplay, Michael Blankfort; based on a short story by Jack Schaefer; camera (Eastman Color), Robert Surtees; editor, Ralph E. Winters; music, Miklos Rozsa. Previewed Feb. 29, '56. Running time, **95 MINS.**

Jeremy Rodock	James Cagney
Steve Miller	Don Dubbins
McNulty	Stephen McNally
Jocasta Constantine	Irene Papas
Lars Peterson	Vic Morrow
Barjak	James Griffith
Hearn	Onslow Stevens
L. A. Peterson	James Bell
Mrs. L. A. Peterson	Jeanette Nolan
Baldy	Chubby Johnson
Abe	Royal Dano
Fat Jones	Lee Van Cleef
Cooky	Peter Chong

A rugged frontier drama of the early west, played off against the scenically striking Colorado Rockies, "Tribute to a Bad Man" is somewhat spotty in entertainment impact. Thus its prospects at the boxoffice won't quite measure up to the draw worth that might be indicated by James Cagney's name and the Metro release.

Pictorially, the Sam Zimbalist production is a sight to behold, using the location sites for full visual worth—a telling CinemaScope lensing job in Eastman Color by Robert Surtees. Also, picture gets two new faces on the domestic screen and off this first look both have something to offer in the right assignments. Introduced is Irene Papas, Greek actress, and her Hollywood debut comes off well. Scoring also is Don Dubbin, late of the legit "Tea and Sympathy" national company. He's a young man with promise.

Critically, "Bad Man" is both fast and slow-paced. Latter, in part, results from a feeling of repetition in some of the story points as scripted by Michael Blankfort from a Jack Schaefer short story, and in some scene-prolonging beyond the point of good dramatic return by Robert Wise's direction. This is especially true of the cruel, barefoot march forced on some horse thieves by Cagney's title character. Elsewhere, however, the script and Wise's direction combine with good trouping to give some topflight moments of action and suspense, all of a rugged variety appropriate to the plot period.

The title is somewhat of a misnomer. The man portrayed so well by Cagney is a hard-bitten pioneer who must enforce his own law on the limitless range he controls. The picture of him is seen through the eyes of young Dubbins, eastern lad come west to make his fortune and who tarries awhile in Cagney's employe. The stay is long enough for him to fall in love with Miss Papas, strange beauty living at the horse ranch, and almost win her away from Cagney when she rebels at the latter's arrogant justice of the rope for breakers of his laws. At the end, however, Dubbins rides away alone, leaving the lovers with a bit more understanding and kindness than they had had before.

There's some notable supporting performances from Stephen McNally, James Griffith, Onslow Stevens, James Bell, Jeanette Nolan, Chubby Johnson, Royal Dano, Lee Van Cleef, Peter Chong and Vic Morrow, in about that order, as assorted types in the rough and ready drama. Miklos Rozsa's scoring is particularly good, as are most of the other credits. *Brog.*

Mohawk
(SONGS—COLOR)

Outdoor drama of the frontier days in the Mohawk Valley for regular action market.

Hollywood, March 20.

20th-Fox release of Edward L. Alperson production. Stars Scott Brady, Rita Gam, Neville Brand, Lori Nelson, Allison Hayes; features John Hoyt, Vera Vague, Rhys Williams, Ted de Corsia, Mae Clarke, John Hudson, Tommy Cook. Directed by Kurt Neumann. Screenplay, Maurice Geraghty, Milton Krims; camera (Eastman Color by Pathe), Karl Struss; editor, William B. Murphy; score, Edward L. Alperson Jr., conducted by Raoul Kraushaar; songs, Alperson Jr., and Paul Herrick. Previewed March 19, '56. Running time, **79 MINS.**

Jonathan Adams	Scott Brady
Onida	Rita Gam
Rokhawah	Neville Brand
Cynthia Stanhope	Lori Nelson
Greta	Allison Hayes
Butler	John Hoyt
Aunt Agatha	Vera Vague
Clem Jones	Rhys Williams
Kowanen	Ted De Corsia
Minikah	Mae Clarke
Captain Langley	John Hudson
Keoga	Tommy Cook
Priest	Michael Granger
Sergeant	James Lilburn
Dancer	Chabon Jadi

Outdoor market will be satisfactorily served by this Edward L. Alperson production which 20th-Fox is releasing. "Mohawk" might be termed a western that went east since it deals with a legend of the Iroquois and is laid at an American frontier outpost in New York's Mohawk Valley. With familiar cast names and color to help, pic makes for a good summer season booking generally.

The original screenplay by Maurice Geraghty and Milton Krims is inclined to lean a bit heavily on unpioneerish dialog at the start but soon settles down to business and Kurt Neumann's direction stirs up the pace over the 79-minute course so that things keep moving. Scenic values of the frontier-outdoor type are good, with a plus value in having three lookers in major femme roles. They are Rita Gam, a striking Mohawk princess; Lori Nelson, a gentle girl from Boston, and Allison Hayes, earthy barmaid in the fort tavern.

Each girl wants Scott Brady, an artist painting the valley and the Indians for the Massachusetts Society, but it's Miss Gam who gets him when an Indian-white war stirred up by John Hoyt, crazy settler who believes the entire valley belongs to him, and some trouble-seeking braves led by Neville Brand is finally out of the way. The femme trio creates a good impression and the gals' separate yens for Brady provide plenty of opportunity for clinch scenes and lobby art. Brady does his artist role with the right amount of dash, while Hoyt and Brand are properly villainous.

Vera Vague, chaperoning aunt to Miss Nelson, rates some chuckles. Ted de Corsia, wise chief who wants peace, and Mae Clarke as his equally wise wife, give dignity and good performances to their Indian characters. Rhys Williams, tavern-keeper; John Hudson, fort commander; Tommy Cook, young brave, and others perform competently, too.

Footage expertly lensed by Karl Struss is blended with some stock reelage for an overall good effect. Edward L. Alperson Jr., scored with Raoul Kraushaar conducting, as well as cleffing the title tune and "Love Plays the Strings of My Banjo," to which Paul Herrick did the lyrics. Tunes fit the pic. *Brog.*

The Price of Fear

Lacklustre telling of ingenious crime drama with Merle Oberon, Lex Barker—strictly supportive.

Hollywood, March 30.

Universal release of Howard Christie production. Stars Merle Oberon, Lex Barker; features Charles Drake, Gia Scala, Warren Stevens, Phillip Pine, Mary Field. Directed by Abner Biberman. Screenplay, Robert Tallman; story, Dick Irving Hyland; camera, Irving Glassberg; editor, Ray Snyder; music supervision, Joseph Gershenson. Previewed March 13, '56. Running time, **79 MINS.**

Jessica Warren	Merle Oberon
Dave Barrett	Lex Barker
Pete Carroll	Charles Drake
Nina Ferranti	Gia Scala
Frankie Edare	Warren Stevens
Vince Burton	Phillip Pine
Ruth McNab	Mary Field
Jim Walsh	Dan Riss
Bolasny	Konstantin Shayne
Johnny McNab	Stafford Repp
Lou Belden	Tim Sullivan

The crime dramatics in "The Price of Fear" come off with only so-so success, relegating it to programmer classification. Names of Merle Oberon and Lex Barker in the star spots will be of little help.

There's a singular lack of excitement or suspense to the footage, although the tricky plot premise should have generated some. It's the story of a man framed for two crimes, but with each alibing the other. The first is a hit-and-run killing in a car reported stolen by career woman Merle Oberon after she had done the deed. The second is the rubout of a partner in a dog track, which gangsters muscling in have framed on Barker, owner of the hounds-and-hares sports spot.

As the Robert Tallman script, from a story by Dick Irving Hyland, tells it, if Barker figured in the car accident after taking the auto in fleeing from some gangsters then he couldn't have killed his partner. The police let it lie, figuring the truth will out in the end, and it does, after Barker, who has fallen for Miss Oberon, is nearly led to his death by her. The direction by Abner Biberman is hard put to make it all believable and it never quite comes off.

The two stars in the Howard Christie production do what they can but, while delivering with a certain amount of assurance, fail to realize much that is credible or creditable. Charles Drake, homicide detective; Gia Scala, daughter of the hit-and-run victim; Warren Stevens, the gang leader; Phillip Pine, a gunman; Mary Field, wife of a taxi-driver witness, are among others who have scant success with the roles.

Photography by Irving Glassberg, editing and other technical credits are competent. *Brog.*

The Bold and the Brave
(SONG)

Okay war drama with action and comedy for program playdates.

Hollywood, March 20.

RKO release of Hal E. Chester production. Stars Wendell Corey, Mickey Rooney, Don Taylor, Nicole Maurey; features John Smith, Race Gentry. Directed by Lewis R. Foster. Screenplay, Robert Lewin; camera, Samuel Leavitt; editor, Aaron Stell; score, Herschel Burke Gilbert; song, Mickey Rooney and Ross Bagdasarian. Previewed March 15, '56. Running time, **87 MINS.**

Fairchild	Wendell Corey
Dooley	Mickey Rooney
Preacher	Don Taylor
Fiamma	Nicole Maurey
Smith	John Smith
Hendricks	Race Gentry
Wilbur	Ralph Votrian
Technician	Wright King
Master Sgt.	Stanley Adams
Bob	Bobs Watson
Tina	Tara Summers

Action and comedy mark this wartime drama as an okay entry for regular program playdates. In fact, pic has occasional touches above the standard dualer classification, but not enough to shape it for better booking treatment. The top cast names are good for the release designation and returns should reach a satisfactory level.

Hal E. Chester produced the Irving H. Levin presentation independently, with RKO taking over the distribution. Film stays away from mass war action, concentrating mostly on three infantry soldiers and how life on the front in Italy during World War II effects them. Lewis R. Foster's direction of the Robert Lewin script develops the characters with facility and scores particularly in handling Nicole Maurey, Italian girl who figures importantly in story points developed around Don Taylor, sergeant of the soldier trio.

Wendell Corey does well the role of an idealist who finds it hard to kill, even in battle. Mickey Rooney ably sells the part of an irrepressible youth and figures in an hilarious crap game sequence that makes him wealthy to the tune of $30,000 and then dies protecting his money on a patrol. Taylor is a more complex character, a religious bigot who can see no shading between right and wrong. While counterparts can be found in real life, audiences won't believe he is so pure and strong in his convictions that he would not take the love offered so appealingly and freely by Miss Maurey, a girl forced to sustain herself up to that point by selling her favors. *Brog.*

World Without End
(C'SCOPE—COLOR)

Science-fiction programmer for ballyhoo bookings.

Hollywood, March 20.

Allied Artists release of Richard Heermance production. Stars Hugh Marlowe, Nancy Gates; features Nelson Leigh, Rod Taylor, Shawn Smith, Lisa Montell, Christopher Dark, Booth Colman, Everett Glass. Direction and screenplay, Edward Bernds; camera (Technicolor), Ellsworth Fredricks; editor, Eda Warren; music, Leith Stevens. Previewed March 7, '56. Running time, **79 MINS.**

Borden	Hugh Marlowe
Garnet	Nancy Gates
Galbraithe	Nelson Leigh
Ellis	Rod Taylor
Elaine	Shawn Smith
Deena	Lisa Montell
Jaffe	Christopher Dark

Morles .... Booth Colman
Timmek .... Everett Glass
Elda .... Stanley Fraser
James .... William Vedder
Beryl .... Rankin Mansfield
Vida .... Paul Brinegar
Naga .... Mickey Simpson

This science-fiction entry, although dressed up in CinemaScope and Technicolor, doesn't figure as much of a space-spook thriller. Plenty corny. Edward Bernds' writing and direction have an ad-lib quality throughout that's reflected in slow-moving pace and performances.

Richard Heermance production has several shock sequences, fairly imaginative settings and a plot that could have been intriguing had it been put together better. Story presents Hugh Marlowe, Nelson Leigh, Rod Taylor and Christopher Dark as four scientists on a space flight to Mars in 1957.

Accidentally breaking through the time barrier, they crash on a planet which they are unable to identify at first but evidence soon labels it as this earth, and the year as 2508.

Seems that the brain men have just about run out of everything but brains and the race is dying off so the four scientists (with muscles) look good to the girls of 2508.

Nancy Gates, who pairs off with Marlowe; Shawn Smith, who doesn't quite make it with Taylor, and Lisa Montell, who does, are the three with the most to do. Booth Colman, who tries some underground dirty work as a big brain, and Everett Glass, leader of the intellectuals, complete the featured cast.

Brog.

Rock Around the Clock
(MUSIC)

Rock 'n' roll stuff. Bouncy musical drama with plenty appeal to teenagers. Special handling can lure extra b.o. coin.

Hollywood, March 16.

Columbia release of Sam Katzman (Colver) production. Stars Bill Haley and His Comets; features The Platters, Ernie Freeman Combo, Tony Martinez and His Band, Freddie Bell and His Bellboys, Alan Freed, Johnny Johnston, Alix Talton, Lisa Gaye, John Archer, Henry Slate, Earl Barton. Directed by Fred F. Sears; screenplay, Robert Kent, James B. Gordon; camera, Benjamin H. Kline; editors, Saul A. Goodkind, Jack W. Ogilvie; choreography, Earl Barton; music supervision, Fred Karger. Previewed March 12, '56. Running time, 76 MINS.

Bill Haley Comets .... Themselves
The Platters .... Themselves
Tony Martinez Band .... Themselves
Freddie Bell Bellboys........Themselves
Alan Freed .... Himself
Steve Hollis .... Johnny Johnston
Corinne Talbot .... Alix Talton
Lisa Johns .... Lisa Gaye
Mike Dennis .... John Archer
Corny LaSalle .... Henry Slate
Jimmy Johns .... Earl Barton

Speaking the teenager idiom, "Rock Around the Clock" will prove a handy entry for exhibitors packaging a show aimed by the sweater-levi trade. It takes off to a bouncy title beat and never lets up for 76 minutes of foot-patting entertainment. Regular program situations catering largely to youth should get some good boxoffice results out of this one.

Bill Haley and His Comets set the beat with nine of their record favorites, including the title tune, "Razzle Dazzle," "Happy Baby," "See You Later, Alligator," "Rudy's Rock" and others. Freddie Bell and His Bellboys are on for two solid senders, "Giddy Up, Ding Dong" and "We're Gonna Teach You to Rock." From The Platters, backed by the Ernie Freeman Combo, are heard two hits, "The Great Pretender" and "Only You," while Tony Martinez and his band slip in some cha-cha-cha with "Codfish and Potatoes," "Sad and Lonely," "Cuero" and "Mambo Capri."

The talent's not all musical in this good Sam Katzman production. Cast members around to enact the Robert Kent-James B. Gordon screen story come off well and the plot holds together satisfactorily in back-stopping for the rock and roll rhythms. Fred F. Sears' direction has excellent pace and keeps interest going with a story that tells how a band manager finds the Haley Comets in the mountains and brings dancing back to ballrooms throughout the country.

Johnny Johnston is likeable as the manager, while Alix Talton is a cool chick as a big band booker who tries unsuccessfully to get her matrimonial hooks in him. Film is a particularly strong showcasing for Lisa Gaye, who could emerge from this a teenage favorite. She plays the rock and roll dancer with the Comets. Her terping's good and that figure the dance costumes display commands added interest. Henry Slate adds some comedy, while John Archer and others do right well. Earl Barton, who choreographed, is Miss Gaye's dancing partner. Playing himself is Alan Freed as a jazz club operator.

Picture gets good technical support from Benjamin H. Kline's photography, the art direction by Paul Palmentola, the editing by Saul A. Goodkind and Jack W. Ogilvie, and Fred Karger's music supervision. *Brog.*

Emergency Hospital

Overnight happenings in a big city emergency hospital, okay for dual booking.

Hollywood, March 16.

United Artists release of a Howard W. Koch (Bel-Air) production. Stars Margaret Lindsay, Walter Reed, Byron Palmer, Rita Johnson, John Archer. Directed by Lee Sholem. Screenplay, Don Martin; camera, William Margulies; editor, John F. Schreyer; music, Paul Dunlap. Previewed March 15, '56. Running time, 62 MINS.

Janet Carey .... Margaret Lindsay
Sgt. Arnold .... Walter Reed
Ben Caldwell .... Byron Palmer
Norma Mullen .... Rita Johnson
Dr. Ellis .... John Archer
Jimmy Arnold .... Jim Stapleton
Fran Richards .... Peg LaCentra
Edward Northrop .... Frank Fenton
Mr. Fanmorn .... George Cisar
Ramon .... Tito Vuola
Ann Banks .... Cary Carver
Mitsi .... Joy Lee
Vera Winston .... Vera Francis
Sylvia Tetlow .... Maxine Gates
Flaherty .... Robert Keys
Marie Johnson .... Jan Englund
Harry Johnson .... Mark Lowell
Will Teeter .... across Wm. "Red" Murphy
Jack Larson .... George Sawaya
Earl Fanmorn .... Gary Gray
Miriam Northrup ...... Mayo Loizeaux
Ross .... Rhodes Reason
Traffic Officer .... William Boyett
Robert Wilson .... Saul Martell
Alverson .... John Merrick

Compactly-edited series of separate incidents occurring overnight in Los Angeles' Emergency Hospital, tied together by a slight story line involving two sets of principals.

Don Martin screenplay combines romance, tragedy, melodrama and some humor to season unfo'dment of the Howard W. Koch production, directed on an even keel by Lee Sholem. The individual stories of a femme doctor, Margaret Lindsay, and a detective, Walter Reed, assigned to the hospital, are interwoven in the pattern of emergency cases brought in during the night. Incidents slide naturally from one to another through the expert editing of John F. Schreyer.

Miss Lindsay persuasively undertakes her medic role, being romanced by wealthy Byron Palmer, whose marriage proposal she nixes because of his speed demon tactics on the highway. When she discovers he deliberately wrecked his expensive sport car on the Hollywood Freeway to save an injured motorcycle rider, her feelings change. Reed's story is climaxed by his 16-year-old son being brought in after latter killed a passenger in an auto accident, and the boy grabbing a gun in an attempt to get away when he thinks he's to be railroaded to prison. Rita Johnson as a nurse, the lad's godmother, and John Archer, another doctor, lend the same credence to their roles that Reed offers.

William Margulies' photography is fluid in catching the moving events of a single night, and Jack Collis' production designing creates the proper atmosphere.
Whit.

The Harder They Fall

Rousing "expose" of the fight biz; strong b.o. though not a woman's picture.

Columbia release of Philip Yordan production. Stars Humphrey Bogart; features Rod Steiger, Jan Sterling, Mike Lane, Max Baer, Jersey Joe Walcott. Directed by Mark Robson. Screenplay, Yordan; from the novel by Budd Schulberg; camera, Burnett Guffey; editor, Jerome Thoms; music, Hugo Friedhofer (directed by Lionel Newman). Previewed at Loew's 72d Street Theatre, N.Y., March 6, '56. Running time, 109 MINS.

Eddie Willis .... Humphrey Bogart
Nick Benko .... Rod Steiger
Beth Willis .... Jan Sterling
Toro Moreno .... Mike Lane
Buddy Brannen .... Max Baer
George .... Jersey Joe Walcott
Jim Weyerhause ..... Edward Andrews
Art Leavitt .... Harold J. Stone
Luis Agrandi .... Carlos Montalban
Leo .... Nehemiah Persoff
Vince Fawcett .... Felice Orlandi
Max .... Herbie Faye
Danny McKeogh .... Rusty Lane
Pop .... Jack Albertson
Frank .... Val Avery
Tommy .... Tommy Herman
Joey .... Vinnie DeCarlo
Gus Dundee .... Pat Comiskey
Sailor Rigazzo .... Matt Murphy
Chief Firebird .... Abel Fernandez
Alice .... Marion Carr

Budd Schulberg's vehement novel about the fight racket is given a strong pictorial going-over in "The Harder They Fall." It's main-event stuff.

The Schulberg story, as scripted (and produced) by Philip Yordan, deals boxing some rough blows. The vicious racket within, the promoters and managers who exploit the pugs, tank divers on the take, the pressagent who builds the hoax about the phoney ring sensation—they're under scrutiny. And all done in modern-day, the original "expose" of the Primo Carnera era having been updated by Yordan.

Today's "purified" punchingbag practitioners, as a consequence, might claim a foul. Mebbe, too, some hotsy controversy of the type that stimulates added interest could be generated.

The crowd that roars for the blood along the cauliflower ear circuit, obviously, is made up mainly of males. So, how could a picture on fighting appeal to the distaff ticket-buyer? Some limitations along these lines must be expected. The ring action is savage. Closeups of the gory canvas spectaculars are not for the sensitive.

But "Fall" is sufficiently well done, is such rousing fare, that it still rates as a strong drawing card despite the sanguine sightseeing.

Story concerns a ruthless manager-gambler who imports a behemoth from South America, discovers he's a pugilistic cream puff, but gives him the buildup via fixed fights across the country. (How much Schulberg went overboard in depicting ring violence in his tome—specifically, how close to the truth he came—well, this is not to be considered herein.) Barnum & Bailey bally for the inexpert giant from S. A. is provided by an erstwhile sports columnist who turns flack and in so doing abandons integrity because he wants a bankroll.

Humphrey Bogart is the newspaper man who goes ethically awry when his paper folds. He's glib and persuasive in promoting the boxer, cynical and defiant in his attitude toward the boss and finally reveals his courage when he breaks with the racket. Performance-wise, this is competent as-per-usual Bogart at work.

Rod Steiger rates hefty mitting as the crooked dealer in ring flesh.

He's an intriguing figure, contemptuous of the battlers, cunning in making deals and in his phoney show of sympathy for a pug who is killed, and all the while near maniacal in his determination to have his "boy" in a championship bout.

Jersey Joe Walcott is surprisingly effective in acting the part of a warm-hearted trainer. Jan Sterling fits in well as Bogart's wife; Mike Lane works well in striking a sympathetic chord as the muscle-bound captive of Steiger's who's too dumb to know his opponents are paid to fall.

Max Baer wears a goofy smirk on his face and is less than ideal, considering the calendar, as the champion eager to beat Lane to shreds. Edward Andrews, Harold J. Stone, Carlos Montalban, Herbie Faye and Pat Comiskey provide adequate support all around. Stone, as a television sportscaster, has a particularly impressive scene street-interviewing a punchy ex-fighter. Latter is Joe Greb, who for real was in the ring years ago and now, in "Fall," seems real as a financially and mentally down-and-outer.

Direction by Mark Robson gives "Fall" much of its force. In addition to the performance he drew out, the action is staged with exciting effect and the story builds nicely all the way. In a few instances, though, closer editing

could serve speed-up purposes. Music heightens the dramatics at points. Camera work by Burnett Guffey is standout; other technical credits good. *Gene.*

Gaby
(C'Scope-Song-Color)

Tender tale of wartime romance; special appeal for distaffers.

Hollywood, March 26.

Metro release of Edwin H. Knopf production. Stars Leslie Caron, John Kerr; features Sir Cedric Hardwicke, Taina Elg, Margalo Gillmore. Directed by Curtis Bernhardt. Screenplay, Albert Hackett, Frances Goodrich; based on a screenplay by S. N. Behrman, Paul H. Rameau, George Froeschel; from the play, "Waterloo Bridge" by Robert E. Sherwood; camera (Eastman Color), Robert Planck; editor, John McSweeney Jr.; score, Conrad Salinger, conducted by Charles Wolcott; choreography, Michel Panaieff. Previewed in Hollywood, March 22, '56. Running time, **96 MINS.**

Gaby .... Leslie Caron
Gregory Y. Wendell .... John Kerr
Mr. Carrington ..... Sir Cedric Hardwicke
Elsa .... Taina Elg
Mrs. Carrington ...... Margalo Gillmore
Jan .... Scott Marlowe
Registrar .... Ian Wolfe
Allen .... Joe Di Reda
Pete .... Joseph Corey
Jim .... James Best
Claire .... Lisa Montell
Denise .... Ruta Lee
Olga .... Narda Onyx
Bottle Club Singer .... Gloria Wood

This remake of the old "Waterloo Bridge" tells an updated, tender tale of World War II romance that should have special appeal for the distaffers. Its dramatics are warm and moving and, while a widespread popular draw is not indicated, the film's returns should still hit a satisfactory level.

Leslie Caron and John Kerr are aptly cast as the two young lovers in the Edwin H. Knopf production. She's particularly effective as a ballerina in wartime London and handles well the emotional stresses the story puts upon her. Kerr appeals, too, as an American paratrooper living up a 48-hour pass just before D-Day, although those bashful boy mannerisms he effects at first are too studied to appear real.

Source material for the modernized script by Albert Hackett and Frances Goodrich is the Robert E. Sherwood play and a former screenplay by S. N. Behrman, Paul H. Rameau and George Froeschel. The new scripting creates dialog and situations that play off with a becoming naturalism under the keen, understanding directorial handling by Curtis Bernhardt.

As told here, the young couple's love affair is quick and unconsummated because he's called up to the front and reported killed in action. Grief-stricken because she had not given herself to him in their last moments together, the girl turns to providing physical solace to other young soldiers who must soon face death. When the paratrooper literally returns from the dead months later she refuses to marry him because she's no longer innocent. However, his love is strong enough to forgive her erring, so there is a happy ending after all.

Others in the cast haven't much to due in the concentration on the two stars, but do their work well. Appealing is Taina Elg, ballerina who lives with Miss Caron. Sir Cedric Hardwicke is good as the friend who arranges a marriage for the young couple and Margalo Gillmore scores as his warm, sympathetic wife. Scott Marlowe, Ian Wolfe, Joe Di Reda, Joseph Corey and James Best are among others giving capable support. Gloria Wood is in as a bottle club singer vocalling the oldie, "Where or When."

Knopf's production guidance is particularly smart in handling the film's one ballet. Instead of being shown as a single big production number it is used as a graceful backdrop to the initial boy-meets-girl action. The choreography by Michel Panaieff is to Chopin's Concerto in E Minor. The music adapted and composed by Conrad Salinger, with Charles Wolcott conducting, contributes notably to the film's mood. Robert Planck's lensing in Eastman Color with print by Technicolor is outstanding, as are the art direction and set decorations. *Brog.*

The Birds and the Bees
(V'VISION—SONGS—COLOR)

Video's George Gobel in diverting comedy with music; promising prospects.

Hollywood, March 27.

Paramount release of Paul Jones (Gomalco) production. Stars George Gobel, Mitzi Gaynor, David Niven; costars Reginald Gardiner, Fred Clark; features Harry Bellaver, Hans Conreid. Directed by Norman Taurog. Screenplay, Sidney Sheldon, Preston Sturges; story, Monckton Hoffe; camera (Technicolor), Daniel L. Fapp; editor, Archie Marshek; score, Walter Scharf; songs, Mack David, Harry Warren; musical numbers staged by Nick Castle. Previewed in Hollywood, March 20, '56. Running time, **94 MINS.**

George Hamilton .... George Gobel
Jean Harris .... Mitzi Gaynor
Colonel Harris .... David Niven
Gerald .... Reginald Gardiner
Mr. Hamilton .... Fred Clark
Marty Kennedy .... Harry Bellaver
Duc Jacques de Montaigne Hans Conried
Mrs. Hamilton .... Margery Maude
Purser .... Clinton Sundberg
Assistant Butler .... Milton Frome
Burrows .... Rex Evans
Waiter .... King Donovan
Mrs. Burnside .... Mary Treen
Jenkins .... Charles Lane
Guests: Bartlett Robinson, Douglas Evans, Barry Bernard, Kathryn Card

George Gobel segues from video's small tube to VistaVision's big screen in easy style and if his fans follow him into the nation's theatres then "The Birds and the Bees" will shape to promising prospects. It's light comedy diversion, harum-scarum enough to be amusing, but not necessarily limited to risibility-tickling because it has Mitzi Gaynor around to participate in the fun and add beautly to the scene. Film, incidentally, is a remake of Paramount's 1941 "Lady Eve."

Paul Jones produced the Gomalco (Gobel and David P. O'Malley) feature for Paramount release and the antics are tailored to Gobel's wistful comedy talents. The script by Sidney Sheldon and Preston Sturges, from a story by Monckton Hoffe, is mostly sight gag stuff, with some music mixed in to balance the hoke. Norman Taurog's direction keeps a good hand on the fun's pacing and does right well in showing off Gobel and such others as Miss Gaynor, David Niven, Fred Clark, et al.

The nutty tale has Gobel as the vegetarian son of millionaire meat-packer Clark. Coming back from a snake-hunting trip to Africa he gets mixed up with some card sharps aboard ship and falls for the pretty one, Miss Gaynor. She's leveling with him, too, but before she can tell him all. Harry Bellaver, his bodyguard, spills the beans and Lonesome George renounces love. Miss Gaynor, eager to get even, then switches to a French pose and wrangles an invite to papa Clark's estate, where Gobel falls in love again and through a series of complicated complications, some funny, some not, the couple winds up married at the finale.

Gobel does his version of the title tune and Miss Gaynor wraps up "La Parisienne" for a nice score. Both tunes are by Harry Warren and Mack David and are easy listening as part of the general fun. Miss Gaynor is a striking looker in her smart Edith Head costumes. Niven clicks as her card-sharp dad and Clark makes much of the meat packer. Reginald Gardiner and Hans Conried, fellow gamblers, are okay in short footage, as is Bellaver.

The Technicolor footage rates expert lensing by Daniel L. Fapp and the other technical contributions perform their functions neatly in giving the pic a plushy look. *Brog.*

The Black Tent
(BRITISH-V'VISION-COLOR)

British war pic filmed in Libyan desert, handsomely mounted but weak on action; fair for home trade.

Rank production and release. Stars Anthony Steel, Donald Sinden, Anna Maria Sandri. Directed by Brian Desmond Hurst. Screenplay, Robin Maugham and Bryan Forbes; camera, Desmond Dickinson; editor, Alfred Roome; music, William Alwyn. At Leicester Square Theatre, London. Running time, **93 MINS.**

David Holland .... Anthony Steel
Charles Holland .... Donald Sinden
Mabrouka .... Anna Maria Sandri
Sheik Salem .... Andre Morell
Croft .... Ralph Truman
Ali .... Donald Pleasence
Baring .... Anthony Bushell
Faris .... Michael Craig
1st German Oifficer .... Anton Diffring
2nd German Officer .... Frederick Jaeger
Khalil .... Paul Homer
Interpreter .... Derek Sydney
Daoud .... Terence Sharkey

"The Black Tent" is handsomely mounted and has been superbly lensed in color, but lacks adequate incident to sustain the yarn. Marquee strength is mainly of local appeal and in the domestic market, the pic should record fair grosses.

Main plot background is the Libyan desert, and expert use of the locales adds to its visual quality. A Bedouin wedding ceremony, which is part of yarn, has a fascinating charm. In other respects, however, the story is far too

leisurely, with the action almost restricted to a few odd scenes.

Related mainly by means of a prolonged flashback, story describes the experiences of Anthony Steel as a British army captain, who receives shelter from a Bedouin tribe during the desert retreat. He marries the chieftain's daughter, but is actually killed when trying to rejoin British lines.

Main fault is to be found in the script, jointly authored by Bryan Forbes and Robin Maugham. Their story is not without merit, but falls short in dramatic values. The cast does well enough with the material. Anna Maria Sandri, an import from Italy, makes an appealing British film debut. Steel gives a standard portrayal as the captain, but Donald Sinden is severely limited by his role. Andre Morell, as the Sheikh, heads an average supporting cast. *Myro.*

Who Done It?
(BRITISH)

Stereotyped slapstick comedy of amateur sleuth on spy hunt starring revue and radio comic Benny Hill; good for star's fans.

London, March 20.

Rank release of Michael Balcon (Ealing) production. Stars Benny Hill. Directed by Michael Relph and Basil Dearden. Screenplay, T. E. B. Clarke; camera, Otto Heller; editor, Peter Tanner; music, Philip Green. At Dominion Theatre, London. Running time, **85 MINS.**

Hugo .... Benny Hill
Frankie .... Belinda Lee
Zacco .... David Kossoff
Hancock .... Garry Marsh
Barakov .... George Margo
Sir Walter .... Ernest Thesiger
Stumpf .... Denis Shaw
Gruber .... Frederick Schiller
Himself .... Jeremy Hawk
Raymond Courtney ...... Thorley Walters
Frankie's Agent .... Philip Stainton
P.C. Roberts .... Warwick Ashton
P.C. Coleman .... Stratford Johns
The Scientists .... Nicholas Phipps, Gibb McLaughlin, Ernest Jay, Harold Scott

There is plenty to please the fans of tv comic Benny Hill in this rollicking slapstick comedy, but the situations and stock ingredients are corny and unlikely to make the grade with more fastidious picturegoers. Pic will cash in with the lower bracket audiences and nabe houses.

While acting as cleaner at an ice rink, Benny wins a cash prize and a bloodhound in a sleuthing contest and sets up as a private eye. He gets involved in a spy hunt centering on a top ranking scientist from behind the Iron Curtain. From then on, in different disguises, the hunt is on with all the trimmings. A blonde tags along with him.

Opening shots provide the biggest laughs but the story tapers off in ludicrous improbabilities with the culmination of a tepid romance. Scenes at the radio exhibition and a stock car racetrack give ample scope for crashing of equipment and cars, highlights of this type of farce.

Benny Hill, for the first time, deserting the stage and mike, exploits his fatuous personality to the full, while Belinda Lee, as his casually acquired femme friend, lends fleeting glamour to an almost allmale background. David Kossof and George Margo give the most legit performances as the foreign plotters, with Garry Marsh giving an explosive interpretation of a harassed inspector. Seasoned players supply convincing support in contrasting roles, and the whole is briskly welded together by directors Michael Relph and Basil Dearden. *Clem.*

Bandidos De Rio Frio
(The Bandits of Cold River)
(MEXICAN—SONGS)

Mexico City, March 20.
Columbia Pictures release of Filmadora Argel production by Emilio Tuero. Stars Luis Aguilar, Rita Macedo; features J. M. Linares Rivas, Prudencia Grifell, Alfredo Varela Jr. Screenplay, Alfredo Varela, based on novel by Manuel Payno. Directed by Rogelio A. Gonzalez; camera, Raul Martinez Solares; music, Gonzalo Curiel. At Cine Metropolitan, Mexico City. Running time, **95 MINS.**

Remarkable part about this is that it is a case of a bad pic having several bits of brightness. Direction is wobbly, lensing is under par and acting barely misses being mediocre. As a period piece, it is dated. Presence, of the late Jose Maria Linares Rivas, who died early last year, fails to save this one entirely.

However, the film played two strong weeks at a top cinema here. And it is studded with the rich, ringing tenor of Luis Aguilar, the sleek Rita Macedo, the grandmotherly grace of Prudencia Grifell, one of Latin America's actresses; and the homespun clowning of bandits. Often it is so crude that it's funny.

A real mishmash has been made of the work of Manuel Payno, famed Mexican novelist of the 19th century, and it's served up in gobs like hash. Yet this turns out good screen fate. *Doug.*

Pane, Amore, E . . .
(Scandal In Sorrento)
(ITALIAN—COLOR—C'SCOPE)

Rome, March 20.
Titanus release of a Titanus (Marcello Girosi) production. Stars Vittorio DeSica, Sophia Loren; features Lea Padovani, Antonio Ciffariello, Tina Pica, Mario Carotenuto, Joka Berretty. Directed by Dino Risi. Screenplay, Ettore Margadonna, from story by Margadonna, Risi, Girosi, and Vincenzo Talarico; camera (Eastmancolor); Giuseppe Rotunno. At Salone Margherita, Rome. Running time, **106 MINS.**

Third in the successful "Bread, Love. . ." series, this time dressed up in color and C'Scope, it looks headed in the direction of its predecessors' top local income brackets. Subbing of Sophia Loren for Gina Lollobrigida as Vittorio DeSica's film opposite, plus the change in locale give the sequel a novelty factor within the pattern. Export returns should be strong. Pic was sold to DCA for U.S. distrib.

Plot follows the retired village marshal to his home town of Sorrento, where he's named chief of police and soon becomes involved with a saucy fish vendor (Sophia Loren), who has been living in his apartment during his long absence (with her young suitor, Antonio Ciffariello). Meanwhile, he overlooks the spinsterish landlady (Lea Padovani) in whose home he boards, until she herself unveils her beauty for the final clinch.

Although this pattern repeats those of preceding pix of series, it's brought off neatly, and the new setting offers plenty of colorful sideline and backdrop incidents to fill a smooth-paced entertainment.

DeSica is properly flamboyant as the village Don Juan, properly assisted by Miss Loren. She is given plenty of open spaces to cross in her characteristic undulating motion. Lea Padovani is fine as the part-time spinstress, ably backed by Tina Pica as DeSica's perennial sidekick maid. Mario Carotenuto, as his priest brother and Ciffariello, as Miss Loren's jealous suitor also are adequate. Ettore Margadonna's sunny dialog rings true. Cinema-Scope lensing in color captures the natural beauty of the South Italian coastline for added appeal. A lilting musical background and fine technical credits round out a sound production. *Hawk.*

Racconti Romani
(Roman Tales)
(C'SCOPE-COLOR)

Rome, March 20.
Diana release of an I.C.S. (Niccolo Theodoli)-Cormoran production. Stars Giovanna Ralli, Silvana Pampanini, Antonio Cifariello, Franco Fabrizi, Maurizio D'Arena, Maria Pia Casilio; features Toto, Vittorio DeSica. Directed by Gianni Franciolini. Screenplay, Sergio Amidei, from short stories of Alberto Moravia; camera (Eastmancolor), Mario Montuori; music, Mario Nascimbene; editor, Adriana Novelli. At Aventino, Rome. Running time, **100 MINS.**

Skillfully produced, this combines popular story ingredients with colorful Roman settings lensed in color and C'Scope for a boxoffice fillip. Combination, topped by marquee weight of Toto and Vittorio DeSica's names (both are in for bits), should make for very strong home market returns. Export chances appear good to spotty.

Plot links several short stories by Alberto Moravia. These concern the efforts of a group of Roman youths to make a fast buck. Most of the gang leader's ideas backfire, however, while the failure of a counterfeiting venture finally sets them back on the straight and narrow, and they return to their more respectful jobs. Most of the gang's activities and frustrations are played for laughs, but the humor is mainly surface quality and locally colored.

Thesping is competent by all hands, with Franco Fabrizi registering as the gang leader and Silvana Pampanini giving her role as his wife a nice reading. Musical score by Mario Nascimbene is often used creatively to highlight a scene, while lensing catches a scenically beautiful Rome in almost every shot although technically the camerawork is uneven. Soundtrack also was noisy on copy seen, with annoying audience effect and loss of dialog clarity. *Hawk.*

Escuela De Musica
(Music School)

(MEXICAN-SONGS-COLOR)

Mexico City, March 20.
Peliculas Nacionales release of Producciones Zacarias production. Stars Pedro Infante, Libertad Lamarque; features Luis Aldas, Maria Chacon, Lalo Gonzalez, Georginia Barragan. Directed by Miguel Zacarias. Screenplay, Edmundo Baez; music, Manuel Esperon. At Cine Palacio Chino, Mexico City. Running time, **95 MINS.**

Warbling of two of Latin America's toppers, Pedro Infante and Libertad Lamarque, provides a neat tabloid travelog of Mexico. The colorful national dance numbers amply sell this very light operetta. It has proved the new longrun champ of Mexico.

Whole cast helps to put across this yarn about a prim spinster (Miss Lamarque), music school proprietress who strives for the longhair type of music, and a breezy young man (Infante). Latter is a hep cat who drinks too much and sees too many girls. He features old folklore songs of Mexico, Puerto Rico, Cuba and Venezuela. The blemish is the inexpert coloring and focusing of these dance numbers. But it doesn't wreck a highly entertaining pic.

It can be said that Mexican pix are fast perfecting topdrawer tinting. That perfection is looked for long before 1956 is ended. It is the first Mexican made pic with dance numbers all in color.
Doug.

Les Salauds Vont En Enfer
(Heels Go To Hell)
(FRENCH)

Paris, March 20.
Discifilm release of Champs-Elysees Film production. Stars Marina Vlady, Serge Reggiani, Henri Vidal; features Robert Hossein, Jacques Duby, Robert Dalban, Guy Kerner, Martha Mercadier. Directed by Robert Hossein. Screenplay, Rene Wheeler, Hossein from play by Frederic Dard; camera, Michel Kelber; editor, Charles Bretoneiche; music, Andre Gosselain. At Colisee, Paris. Running time, **90 MINS.**

Film falls into the category of a Gallic prison film with the added fillip of a couple of escaped convicts killing each other over a strange, vengeful girl whose lover they have killed. Strong U.S. influences in prison scenes, plus general naivity in treatment of the female and the gangsters, limits this for art houses. It has some exploitation possibilities.

Two convicts are suspected of being informers by the rest of the inmates. Only one of them is but the two of them escape together. Their friendship and hardship weld them together. They slay a painter but keep his mistress, and both grow enamored of her. However, she stays only for revenge.

For a first film, director Robert Hossein has given this a rugged mounting. Marina Vlady is a delectable morsel and plays the mistress with photogenic appeal if lacking thespian experience. Serge Reggiani and Henri Vidal are competent as the friends. Lensing and editing are acceptable. *Mosk.*

The Man In the Gray Flannel Suit
(C'SCOPE—COLOR)

Slickly sold screen adaptation of Sloan Wilson bestseller. Cast and production values alone insure strong b.o. potential but film is overlong.

20th-Fox release of Darryl F. Zanuck production. Stars Gregory Peck, Jennifer Jones, Fredric March, Marisa Pavan; features Lee J. Cobb, Ann Harding, Keenan Wynn, Gene Lockhart, Gigi Perreau, Portland Mason, Arthur O'Connell, Henry Daniell, Joseph Sweeney. Directed by Nunnally Johnson. Screenplay, Johnson; from the novel by Sloan Wilson; camera (Color by De Luxe), Charles G. Clarke; editor, Dorothy Spencer; music, Bernard Herrmann. Previewed in N.Y., March 30, '56. Running time, **152 MINS.**

Tom Rath	Gregory Peck
Betsy	Jennifer Jones
Hopkins	Fredric March
Maria	Marisa Pavan
Judge Bernstein	Lee J. Cobb
Mrs. Hopkins	Ann Harding
Caesar Gardella	Keenan Wynn
Hawthorne	Gene Lockhart
Susan Hopkins	Gigi Perreau
Janie	Portland Mason
Walker	Arthur O'Connell
Bill Ogden	Henry Daniell
Mrs. Manter	Connie Gilchrist
Edward Schultz	Joseph Sweeney
Barbara	Sandy Descher
Pete	Mickey Maga
Mahoney	Kenneth Tobey
Florence	Ruth Clifford
Miriam	Geraldine Wall
Johnson	Alex Campbell
Freddie	Jerry Hall
Police Sergeant	Jack Mather
Dr. Pearce	Frank Wilcox
Miss Lawrence	Nan Martin
Byron Holgate	Tris Coffin
Bugala	William Phillips
Cliff	Leon Alton
Gina	Phyllis Graffeo
Mrs. Hopkins' Maid	Dorothy Adams
Maid	Dorothy Phillips
Secretary	Mary Benoit
Business Executive	King Lockwood
Elevator Starter	Lomax Study
Waiter	John Breen
Italian Farm Wife	Renata Vanni
Carriage Driver	Mario Siletti
Crew Chief	Lee Graham
Mr. Sims	Michael Jeffrey
Master Sergeant Mathews	Roy Glenn

There are at least three ways of bringing a bestselling novel to the screen. Either the basic story thread is used to tell a photographic yarn which may go way beyond the original idea; or the film is restricted to what is actually in the book, but also makes an attempt to convey the underlying idea the author may have had in mind. The third possibility would be to make a picture that carefully and conscientiously encompasses each major scene and piece of dialog in the novel, but doesn't go any further than to just visualize a story and its characters.

"The Man in the Gray Flannel Suit," which Darryl F. Zanuck has produced for 20th-Fox with an abundance of elegant sets and a solid array of marquee names, follows the latter alternative. It's big, it's long (two and a half hours), it has a wealth of visual values via CinemaScope and color, and its subject matter smacks of b.o. from start to finish. All that is missing is the spirit of the author. Some may miss it, others may not. But the lack of it doesn't enhance the value of the production.

This is the story, partly told in flashback, of a man about to go "Madison Avenue." It's the story of a young American suburbanite who gets a chance to become a big shot with a television network and turns it down—at least in the screen version—because he realizes that he's a nine-to-five man to whom family means more than success.

It's also the story of a man with a conscience, who, during the war, had a love affair in Rome which resulted in a child. When he tells his wife about it, their marriage almost breaks up. Eventually, they work things out with expected decency.

As the "Man in the Gray Flannel Suit," Gregory Peck is handsome and appealing, if not always convincing. It is only really in the romantic sequences with Marisa Pavan, who plays his Italian love, that he takes on warmth and becomes believable. These are among the best scenes in the film, and Miss Pavan, an Italian beauty, is human and delightful in the role of the girl who knows that she must make the most of the brief moments that are theirs.

Playing opposite Peck as his wife is Jennifer Jones, and her concept of the role is faulty to a serious degree. Miss Jones allows almost no feeling of any real relationship between her and Peck. She alternates between being the nagging wife and the frustrated lover, except that she rarely conveys the impression of being in love with her husband in the first place. Their scenes together, and particularly her climactic blowup when she learns about his illegitimate son, are often awkward and drawn out. They never come alive as people.

As the broadcasting tycoon, lonely in his power, Fredric March is excellent, and the scenes between him and Peck lift the picture high above the ordinary. Ann Harding as March's neglected wife has the proper air of disillusionment and turns in a topnotch performance. Gigi Perreau, on the other hand, as March's rebellious daughter, leaves much to wish for and doesn't seem right for a part that calls for more sophistication.

In smaller parts, Lee J. Cobb does nobly as Judge Bernstein; Keenan Wynn takes a straight role in his stride. Arthur O'Connell and Henry Daniell turn in precious caricatures of network execs and seem drawn from life. Connie Gilchrist is a howl as the autocratic housekeeper who keeps the children in line when Miss Jones comes down with the chickenpox.

"Man in the Gray Flannel Suit" often seems episodic and it's overlong. Where, in some spots it moves along briskly, in others it lags. Also, some parts are definitely better than others. The flashbacks to the war, when Peck as a paratrooper has to kill a German, are effective. Even better, and more exciting, is his recollection of the incident in the Pacific, when by mistake he kills his buddy with a grenade in combat and carries the dead man back to the beach, calling for a doctor.

And again in the Peck home, the incident with the boy (Mickey Maga) deciding to leave home in his Foreign Legionnaire uniform, has genuine warmth. Peck himself is an actor who seems to adapt himself to every role he takes. In this, he at times seems to lack emotion even though, on the whole, his performance will rouse few criticisms.

In adapting the screenplay from the book, Nunnally Johnson has caught the detail perfectly, and the dialog rings true. His direction is uneven, which accounts for the occasional lags. There are a good many imaginative touches in the picture, but Johnson must share the blame for Miss Jones' performance (he could at least have cut some of those closeups) and he alone is responsible for the fact that the picture so determinedly misses the point of the book which made the flannel suit a symbol rather than just a garment.

Zanuck's production has about it an opulence that automatically puts it into the big league. The sets are elegant. Cameraman Charles G. Clarke has used CinemaScope to good advantage, and the De Luxe color is better than ever, using pleasingly subtle shades. "Man in the Gray Flannel Suit" may not be Zanuck's best, but it's a cinch to please a lot of people. *Hift.*

Jubal
(C'SCOPE—COLOR)

Socko western drama with Glenn Ford, Ernest Borgnine, Rod Steiger and stout b.o. potential.

Hollywood, April 3.

Columbia release of William Fadiman production. Stars Glenn Ford, Ernest Borgnine, Rod Steiger; introducing Valerie French, Felicia Farr; features Basil Ruysdael, Noah Berry Jr., Charles Bronson, John Dierkes, Jack Elam, Robert Burton. Directed by Delmer Daves. Screenplay, Russell S. Hughes, Daves; based on "Jubal Troop," novel by Paul I. Wellman; camera (Technicolor), Charles Lawton Jr.; editor, Al Clark; score, David Raksin; conducted by Morris Stoloff. Previewed March 29, '56. Running time, **100 MINS.**

Jubal Troop .... Glenn Ford
Shep Horgan .... Ernest Borgnine
Pinky .... Rod Steiger
Mae Horgan .... Valerie French
Naomi Hoktor .... Felicia Farr
Shem Hoktor .... Basil Ruysdael
Sam .... Noah Beery Jr.
Reb Haislipp .... Charles Bronson
Carson .... John Dierkes
McCoy .... Jack Elam
Dr. Grant .... Robert Burton
Jake Slavin .... Robert Knapp
Charity Hoktor .... Juney Ellis
Jim Tolliver .... Don C. Harvey
Cookie .... Guy Wilkerson
Bayne .... Larry Hudson
Tolliver Boy .... Mike Lawrence
Tolliver Boy .... Robert Henry

A gripping dramatic story set in pioneer Wyoming and three potent male star names make "Jubal" figure as an important boxoffice entry. Decorating the marquees with the names of Glenn Ford, Ernest Borgnine and Rod Steiger gives ticket-selling impetus in most any situation and when they are tied to the type of adult, suspenseful western offered here, business prospects brighten to stout figures.

The strong point of the William Fadiman production, along with ace performances and an overall plot line that grips tightly, is a constantly mounting suspense. The expectancy never lets up once preliminaries are out of the way and the viewer sits back and tensely awaits the climactic battle between the forces of good and evil.

Delmer Daves' direction and the script he wrote with Russell S. Hughes from Paul I. Wellman's novel carefully build towards the explosion that's certain to come, taking time along the way to make sure that all characters are well-rounded and understandable. Capping all this emotional suspense is the playoff against the backdrop of the Grand Teton country in Wyoming, beautifully captured in CinemaScope and Technicolor by the lensing by Charles Lawton Jr., and the second unit photography by Ray Cory.

Ford, a drifting cowpoke, runs into trouble when he takes a job on the cattle ranch operated by Borgnine, who has befriended him. Valerie French, the rancher's amoral wife makes an open, but abortive play for him and Steiger, jealous cowpoke on the ranch who doesn't like to see himself replaced in her extra-martial activities, plots to get even with his possible rival.

The break comes when Ford is forced to kill Borgnine in self-defense after the latter has been told by his wife that she had been unfaithful. Steiger eggs on a posse to hang Ford, meantime taking time out for a brutal beating-rape scene with the new widow. However, Ford is saved by her dying words as the posse catches up with him, and turns to Felicia Farr, gentle, religious girl with whom he has found love.

Oddly enough, much of the footage is free of actual physical violence, but the nerves are stretched so taut that it's almost a relief when it does come. Ford is quietly effective in his understanding underplaying of the cowpoke who wants to settle down. Borgnine is excellent as the curiously rough but gentle man who has to die in the tragic triangle. Steiger, who has changed his accent but not his act, spews an evil venon over the footage as the drawling cowhand who wants the ranch and the rancher's wife. There hasn't been as hateful a screen heavy around in a long time.

Both femmes score strongly, particularly Miss French because of her more colorful, sexy character, but Miss Farr's sweet girl role makes just the right contrast. It's a promising introduction for both newcomers. Basil Ruysdael, as Miss Farr's kindly father; Noah Beery Jr., and John Dierkes, fellow ranch hands; Charles Bronson, Jack Elam, Robert Burton, Robert Knapp, Juney Ellis, and Guy Wilkerson are among others whose performances bolster the overall punch of the dramatics.

David Raksin's score, featuring a guitar and conducted by Morris Stoloff, is a plus factor. Al Clark's editing is topflight, as are the art direction, set decorations and other phases of the presentation. *Brog.*

Blackjack Ketchum, Desperado

Howard Duff, Victor Jory in okay western actioner.

Hollywood, April 3.

Columbia release of Sam Katzman (Clover) production. Stars Howard Duff, Victor Jory. Features Maggie Mahoney, Angela Stevens, David Orrick, William Tannen, Ken Christy, Martin Garralaga, Robert Roark, Don C. Harvey, Pat O'Malley, Jack Littlefield, Sydney Mason. Directed by Earl Bellamy. Screenplay, Luci Ward, Jack Natteford; based on the novel by Louis L'Amour; camera, Fred Jackman Jr., editor, Saul A. Goodkind. Previewed March 28, '56. Running time, **75 MINS.**

Blackjack .... Howard Duff
Jared Tetlow .... Victor Jory
Nita Riordan .... Maggie Mahoney
Laurie Webster .... Angela Stevens
Bob Early .... David Orrick
Dee Havalik .... William Tannen
Sheriff Macy .... Ken Christy
Jaime Brigo .... Martin Garralaga
Ben Tetlow .... Robert Roark
Mac Gill .... Don C. Harvey
Doc Blaine .... Pat O'Malley
Burl Tetlow .... Jack Littlefield
Matt Riordan .... Sydney Mason
Happy Harrow .... Ralph Sanford
Andy Tetlow ..... George Edward Mather
Jarry Carson .... Charles Wagenheim
Grat Barbey .... Wes Hudman

A satisfactory round of western action is dished up in this Columbia entry and it should fare okay in the outdoor market. It's another telling of the story about a gunfighter anxious to live down his reputation, but forced to fight for right when a big cattle baron tries to take over a peaceful valley.

Basic plot has some good embroidery as scripted by Luci Ward and Jack Natteford from the novel by Louis L'Amour. The playing, too, is up to all demands of script and Earl Bellamy's direction, so the playoff, although familiar, holds interest. Sam Katzman's production supervision gives the picture all it needs to merit attention in the market at which it is aimed.

Howard Duff performs easily as the gunslinger trying to shake his past and settle down with Maggie Mahoney, but when Victor Jory moves in with his brothers and a large herd of cattle to force the small ranchers out, the hero lends his special skill to down the baddies. The romantic angles are rather realistically stated for a program western; so are some of the other points the pic makes, but without detracting from the essential action.

Miss Mahoney is good opposite Duff and Jory plays his villainry to the hilt. Angela Stevens is an extra girl in the plotting but is easy to look at. Robert Roark and George Edward Mather, as Jory's two younger brothers; David Orrick, William Tannen, as Jory's chief gunman; Ken Christy, the honest sheriff; Martin Garralaga, Sydney Mason and Wes Hudman are among those providing satisfactory support.

Fred Jackman Jr.'s cameras, plus rather generous use of stock footage, help keep up the action. Editing and other behind-camera credits come off acceptably, too. *Brog.*

The Feminine Touch
(BRITISH-COLOR)

Romantic yarn of probationer nurses in London hospital; likely prospects in domestic market.

London, March 27.

Rank release of a Michael Balcon-Ealing Studios production. Stars George Baker, Belinda Lee, Delphi Lawrence, Adrienne Corri, Mandy and Diana Wynyard. Directed by Pat Jackson. Screenplay, W. P. Lipscombe and Richard Mason from novel by Sheila MacKay Russell; camera, Paul Beeson; editor, Peter Bezencenet; music, Clifton Parker. At Gaumont Theatre, London. March 27, '56. Running time, **91 MINS.**

Jim .... George Baker
Susan .... Belinda Lee
Pat .... Delphi Lawrence
Maureen .... Adrienne Corri
Anne .... Henryetta Edwards
Liz .... Barbara Archer
The Matron .... Diana Wynyard
Home Sister .... Joan Haythorne
Sister Snow .... Beatrice Varley
Theatre Sister .... Joan Carol
Assistant Matron .... Constance Fraser
Second-year Nurse ... Vivienne Drummond
Ted Russell .... Christopher Rhodes
Casualty Doctor .... Richard Leech
Lofty .... Newton Blick
The Skivvy .... Dandy Nichols
The Gardener .... Mark Daly
Jessie .... Mandy
The Suicide .... Dorothy Alison
Bateman .... Joss Ambler

As a tribute to the young women with a sense of vocation who take up nursing as a career, "The Feminine Touch" is worthwhile, and as a piece of romantic entertainment, it is more than adequate. Pic has valuable exploitation angles which should help returns in the domestic market.

Among the last of the productions to be lensed at Ealing Studios (since taken over by BBC-TV), "Touch" does not disguise the hardships and irritations endured by the trainee nurse, but does resort to a romantic veneer in its picture of hospital life. Set almost entirely in the hospital and environs, yarn has few comedy touches as well as strong dramatic angles.

Would-be nurses are shown at the hospital, main action concentrating on their probationer duties. Alongside the basic story-line, the plot focuses on the romantic aspirations of two recruits. One, Delphi Lawrence, frankly admits she has no sense of vocation, but is on the prowl for a handsome, wealthy doctor as a husband. The other, Belinda Lee, gets romantically entangled with the house physician, and has to decide whether to complete her studies or go with him to Canada.

Realistic hospital backgrounds help create a vivid atmosphere for a number of dramatic cameos, one featuring an attempted suicide victim who finds the will to live; and another depicting how the prompt action of a night nurse saves the life of a patient.

Cast is competent without being standout. Miss Lee, a handsome blonde, is rapidly improving as an actress. Miss Lawrence strikes the right note of cynicism; Adrienne Corri is a vivacious Irish trainee; and Diana Wynyard oozes sincerity as the matron. Mandy, a veteran child performer, turns in a tear-jerking study as a kid who is expecting to die of a heart ailment. George Baker gives a flawless performance of the house physician and Christopher Rhodes neatly fills the role of the pathologist. Pat Jackson's fluid direction is matched by allaround high technical standard. *Myro.*

Alexander, the Great
(C'SCOPE—COLOR)

Super-sized costumed spectacle, backed by big-scale ad-pub campaign. Shy on names, overlong and occasionally laggard entertainment but big b.o.

Hollywood, March 29.

United Artists release of Robert Rossen production. Stars Richard Burton, Fredric March, Claire Bloom, Danielle Darrieux; features Barry Jones, Harry Andrews, Stanley Baker, Niall MacGinnis. Written and directed by Rossen; camera (Technicolor), Robert Krasker; editor, Ralph Kemplen; score, Mario Nascimbene. Previewed March 27, '56. Running time, **143 MINS.**

Alexander the Great ..... Richard Burton
Philip of Macedonia ...... Fredric March
Barsine .... Claire Bloom
Olympias .... Dannielle Darrieux
Darius .... Harry Andrews
Attalus .... Stanley Baker
Parmenio .... Niall MacGinnis
Memnon .... Peter Cushing
Demosthenes .... Michael Hordern
Aristotle .... Barry Jones
Eurydice .... Marisa De Leza
Cleitus .... Gustavo Rojo
Philotas .... Ruben Rojo
Aeschines .... William Squire
Nectanebus .... Helmut Dantine
Antipater .... Friedrich Ledebur
Pausanias .... Peter Wyngarde
Ptolemy .... Virgilio Texeira
Roxane .... Teresa Del Rio
Arsites .... Julio Pena
Spithridates .... Jose Nieto
Nearchus .... Carlos Baena
Perdiccas .... Larry Taylor
Harpalus .... Jose Marco
Hephaestion .... Ricardo Valle
Stateira .... Carmen Carulla
Aristander .... Jesus Luque
Drunken Woman .... Ramsey Ames
Messenger .... Mario De Barros
Apites .... Ellen Rossen
Orchas .... Carlos Acevedo

It took "Alexander, the Great" some 10 years to conquer the known world back in the fourth century, B.C. It seems to take Robert Rossen almost as long to recreate on film this slice of history. Despite the length, however, he has fashioned a CinemaScope-Technicolor spectacle of tremendous size that bids fair to reap handsome boxoffice spoils. Helping the latter is the ad-pub campaign being used by United Artists to launch the pic. It matches in scope the spectacle itself and should be of enormous value in gaining big key city openings. Thereafter, unless the big sell has a follow-through, the film will be on its own and the usual mixed wicket reaction going to spectacles will be the rule.

Written, produced and directed by Rossen in Spain and Italy, the presentation is neither niggardly in the coin lavished on its physical makeup nor in the outlay for the talented international cast that enacts the historical saga of a man who believed both that he was a god and in his destiny to unite the world of his day—a task that is credited with starting the unification of Europe and Asia and paving the way for the spread of Christianity centuries later.

By attempting to crowd in the story of Alexander through boyhood and manhood, along with the major battles fought, the march through Persia and later India, along with the pomp and ceremony of the period, Rossen is not always able to hold interest in his story and action, resulting in some long, dull stretches. Nor do the players have much chance to be more than puppets against the giant sweep of the spectacle. There are a number of single scenes that give the individual characters a chance to grow. When they have them, artists such as Richard Burton, in the title role, and Fredric March, as his father, Philip, the Barbarian of Macedonia, give them a lifelike impact.

Alexander's romance with Barsine (Claire Bloom), recorded as the great love of his short life, is more implied than realized, but she does have some fine, expressive moments. Perhaps scoring stronger on the femme end is Danielle Darrieux (who rates special billing as "the French star") in her portrayal of Olympias, mother of Alexander, because of the intrigue she practices to fulfill her son's destiny.

Rossen reaches screen-filling heights with his battle assemblages, jamming the 2.55-1 anamorphic ratio to its very edges with scene after scene of mass warfare. Mounted and foot soldiers fight and die, and to emphasize the hand-to-hand nature of the killing, Rossen includes a number of gory shots, like the severed arm floating in blood-dyed water. He's equally able in staging his elegant court scenes, Grecian and Oriental, and, with the striking photographic work of Robert Krasker, the picture is one of pictorial splendor. However, an anamorphic flaw not yet corrected is that special effects look just that, not real.

Barry Jones, as Aristotle, who tutors and counsels Alexander during the latter's youth; Harry Andrews, as Darius, the Persian ruler; Stanley Baker, as the bloodthirsty Attalus; Niall MacGinnis, as Philip's general Parmenio; Peter Cushing, as Memnon; Gustavo Rojo, as Cleitus, whose killing by Alexander turns the conqueror away from conquest; Marisa De Leza, who replaces Miss Darrieux as Philip's queen, and Teresa Del Rio, as Roxane the Persian princess whom Alexander marries, are among cast capables.

Set design by Andre Andrejew is topflight, so is the costuming and most other technical assists except editing, which is rough in its present state. The score by Mario Nascimbene is extremely effective. *Brog...*

Madamoiselle—Age 39
(Despinia Eton 39)
(GREEK)

Hellenic Film Distributing Corp. release of Millas Film production. Stars Basil Logothetidis. Directed by Alex Sakelariou. Screenplay, Sakellariou and Chris Jianacopolou; music, Alfred Ryder. At Cameo Theatre, N.Y., March 23, '56. Running time, **92 MINS.**

Telemahos .... Basil Logothetidis
Chrisanthi .... Smaro Stephanidou
Fofo .... Ilia Livikou
Stamati .... Thano Generalis
The Widow .... Dena Stathatou
The Pensioner .... Evangelo Protos
The Argentianian ..... Stephan Stratigos
Tax Appraiser .... Michael Papadakis

(In Greek; English subtitles)

New Greek-language entry, although provided with English subtitles, is strictly for audiences who speak the lingo. Neither the story nor the subtitles will enable the film to obtain general art-house bookings.

The subtitles, flashed on the screen after five or 10 minutes of uninterrupted dialog, are poorly written as well as inadequate. They are obviously written by a foreigner not too well versed in the English language. Misspellings such as "be sitted" for "be seated" stand out obviously.

The film stars Basil Logothetidis, Greece's foremost comedian. Although played for comedy throughout — featuring pat comedy-of-errors and mistaken identity situations—the story ends on a sad note.

A bachelor brother, anxious to get married, feels obligated to find a husband first for his unattractive, spinster sister. Ads in a newspaper bring two suitors, each of whom walks off with a bride but not with the "advertised merchandise." One gets a visiting cousin and the other nabs the brother's own fiance, thus leaving the brother and sister to an unmarried life of loneliness together.

Performances, on the whole, are competent, although characterized by the usual volatile quality of European thesping. The technical aspects of the film are fair but they hardly measure up to U.S. standards. It was filmed at the Naha Studios in Cairo. *Holl.*

The Extra Day
(BRITISH-COLOR)

London, March 27.

British Lion release of William Fairchild production. Stars Richard Basehart, Simone Simon and George Baker. Written and directed by William Fairchild; camera, Arthur Grant; editor, Bernard Gribble; music, Philip Green. At Plaza Theatre, London. Running time, **83 MINS.**

Joe Blake .... Richard Basehart
Michele Blanchard .... Simone Simon
Steven Marlow .... George Baker
Toni Howard .... Josephine Griffin
Sir George Howard .... Colin Gordon
Kurt Vorn .... Laurence Naismith
Bert .... Charles Victor
Barney West .... Sidney James
Mrs. West .... Joan Hickson
Buster West .... David Hannaford
Mrs. Bliss .... Olga Lindo
Mr. Bliss .... Philip Ray
Susan .... Jill Bennett
Guy .... John Humphrey
Ronnie Baker .... Dennis Lotis
Lou Skeat .... Meier Tzelniker
Beryl .... Beryl Reid
Shirley .... Shani Wallis

A quartet of cameos fit unhappily together in "The Extra Day." The story has a film studio background and the action is focused on a search for four extras required for retakes. Richard Basehart gives the pic some marquee value in the U. S. but its b.o. chances are not very bright.

Apart from the fact that each of the cameos has an air of unreality, the story is too episodic to sustain interest. Basehart, as personal assistant to the film director, is sent to round up the extras after the can of film is lost enroute from studios to laboratories. One of them is George Baker, a struggling artist who has been doing crowd work to pay his way, and has been busy resisting the advances of Simone Simon, playing the star of the pic. Coincidence is stretched a little too far when, for a wager, he breaks into an empty house and finds himself in her bedroom. Then there is Sidney James, a tired pug, who has never won a fight and is due to meet a local champ when Basehart calls at his home. So the opponent has to be fixed not to disfigure James' face.

Josephine Griffin is a society deb turned extra to get away from the social round and is due to marry a famous crooner the next day. There is a remarkably involved and unreal stunt to stop the nuptials. Finally there are Olga Lindo and Philip Ray, two old timers who plan to retire, but find they're unwelcome in their daughter's home.

Although trimmed to a neat 83 minutes, the story drags considerably. The principal players, Richard Basehart and Miss Simon, do well enough with inadequate material. In smaller parts, Charles Victor, as a van driver, and Jill Bennett, as the daughter who refuses to have her mother stay with her, give notable portrayals. Meier Tzelniker does a fine job as the crooner's manager and Laurence Naismith is acceptable in the role of director. Dennis Lotis, a local recording star, and Shani Wallis, a pop musicomedy singer, make their screen debut as crooner and fan, respectively. *Myro.*

Abdulla the Great
(ANGLO-EGYPTIAN—COLOR)

Paris, March 27.

Sonofilm release of Misr Universal Cairo-Sphinx Film production. Stars Gregory Ratoff, Kay Kendall: features, Sidney Chaplin, Alex D'Arcy, Marina Berti. Directed by Ratoff. Screenplay, Boris Ingster, George Saint George from original story by Ismet Regeila; camera (Technicolor), Lee Garmes; editor, Maurice Rootes; music, Georges Auric. At Normandie, Paris. Running time, **105 MINS.**

Abdulla .... Gregory Ratoff
Ronnie .... Kay Kendall
Ahmed .... Sidney Chaplin
Marco .... Alex D'Arcy
Aziza .... Marina Berti

This film was made in Egypt using the regal palace and yacht for the main scenes. It points up the public disapproval of the absolute monarch Abdulla the Great. Set in an imaginary country for the screenplay, the parallel with the life of ex-King Farouk is at times apparent. Farouk's threats to sue if the film is released have made for some interest here. However, the film is heavily romanticized and melodramatic, making Abdulla's fall one caused by his obsession for a girl rather than for political causes.

Lacking much name value, this will have to be heavily sold in the U.S. Ratoff has imbued this with opulent backing and some cleverly mannered bits. As soon as his thick Russian accent can be accepted as that of the King of an obviously Arab state, the film settles down to depicting the peccadillos and whims of this degenerate potentate whose tastes run from poker, women, caviar and ostentation to American electric trains. Main dramatic thread is his love for a beauteous English model (Kay Kendall) who spurns him for one of his young revolutionary lieutenants (Sidney Chaplin).

Abdulla kidnaps Miss Kendall but she still spurns him after he offers her fabulous treasures. The people and army rise up to oust him as he cavorts with a group of belly dancers, a la Nero, while his city burns.

Platitudinous dialog and complications do not help matters as the film vacillates between the comic and serious. The obvious story line, stilted direction and routine acting relegate this for exploitation playdates. Color is passable and general production dress good. Aside from the boistering antics of Ratoff, Miss Kendall, Chaplin and D'Arcy are only adequate in their roles although Miss Kendall's looks help. A fine bit is done by Marina Berti as the only girl to ever really love the kingsize king.
Mosk.

7 Wonders of the World
(CINERAMA—TECHNICOLOR)

No. 3 Cinerama production again proves that this process is still the Big Top of the sundry big-screen processes.

Stanley Warner-Cinerama Corp. presentation of Lowell Thomas production, based on an idea by Thomas. Directed by Ted Tetzlaff, Andrew Marton, Tay Garnett, Paul Mantz, Walter Thompson. Scenario and narration contributions by Prosper Buranelli and William Lipscomb; camera (Technicolor), Harry Squire, Gayne Rescher; music, Emil Newman, David Raksin, Jerome Moross; orchestra conducted by Newman; Japanese dance, Tetsuze Shirai; editors, Harvey Manger & Jack Murray; music editors, Lovel S. Ellis & Richard C. Harris; sound, Monty Pearce, Richard J. Pietschmann Jr., Richard Vorisek, Fred Bosch, Avery Lockner; production staff, Edward R. Evans, Andre Smagghe, Henry Hartmrp, William Terry, Arthur LaSchelle, Michael Mahony, C. Thomas Conroy, Ralph M. Leo, James R. Morrison; advance arrangements, Lowell Thomas Jr., Maynard Miller, Robert W. Heussler, Eileen Salama; chorus, Apollo Club of Minneapolis; premiered April 10, 1956, Warner Theatre, N.Y.; $3.50 top. Running time, 120 **MINS.**

Until Cinerama is linked to a "plot" it would appear as if these travelogs will be more than sufficient unto the boxoffice purpose. Lowell Thomas' "7 Wonders of the World" will be as socko at the tills as his pioneer "This Is Cinerama" (1952) and Louis de Rochemont's "Cinerama Holiday" three years thereafter. All are in the same globetrotting idiom, with the wonders of the world brought almost literally into the auditor's lap, and this, like its two predecessors, bids fair to enjoy the same boxoffice bonanza.

As with Thomas' initial entry, the action opens in his Pawling (N.Y.) study and thereafter the viewer is taken by air, motor and rail into exotic farflung corners. It beats the U.S. Navy slogan because you can "join Cinerama and see the world" with less travail.

While the titular "7 Wonders of the World" might be pointed to captiously as a misnomer, it is a resourceful kickoff for a Technicolorful airlift from Manhattan through 32 countries in 120 minutes. The Sphinx and the Pyramids are pointed to as the sole remainders of the seven ancient wonders and the unfolding is a modern odyssey that starts in South America and ends back at the New York skyline.

A multiple directorial and camera crew blanketed the world. Emerging from the aerial hedgehop of local geographical closeups is a religioso pageantry which includes an exposition of Israel's renaissance; the final ceremonies of the Marian Year, culminating in the Papal blessing and a first-time lighting of Saint Peter's for motion pictures; and a curtsy to the Protestant church, back in the U.S., with a typical American countryside scene. Buddhist priests and Benares (India) temple dancers blend with scenes of African tribal dances and a glorified Japanese geisha line that looks more Leonidoff than authentic Fujiyama.

As the magic of the Cinerama glamor lenses bring strange regional, secular and tribal customs into focus there is also an awareness of the one-worldedness. Arabian-American Oil Co. relations in Saudi-Arabia, and the Israeli-Arab-Egyptian scenes cannot be wholly divorced in the present-day viewer's mind's eye from the political and economic realities of the times. However, accepted on a pure tourist perspective all these, and the other scenes in this 32-country celluloid tour, are compelling for mass audiences.

Above all, the Cinerama's audience-participation values place this process in the roadshow orbit that it is. It makes the other widescreens and scopes road companies alongside this, the Big Top of the giant-screen processes.

As to be expected there are peaks and valleys. There are inadequacies on some coverage; overextension on possibly the religioso phases. Too much accent on waterfalls and too short on, for example, the famed Rio de Janeiro mardi gras.

There are times when the music is compelling and others when the score is almost intrusive and assertive. The specially credited Jap dance "created by Tetsuzo Shirai" is more Rockette than pure Nagasaki.

The "plot," per se, is a gimmick for a many splendored cinematopographic exposition. There are times, too, when Thomas is more than a bit in awe of Nature; had he permitted the "wonders" to speak for themselves they would be even more articulate than his pear-shaped rhetorical questions.

The photography is socko and some of it borders on sheer camera portraiture. On the other hand, the theatrical intrusion above cited, and a reprise of the cobra vs. the snake fight to the death, the African tribal dancers ("the Nijinsky of Watutsi tribe") is more show business than Nature's doings. Which is not to be deprecated; showmanship is the essence of this technological globetrot.

Thomas' "7 Wonders of the World" is at its best when the old and the modern are shown in sharp juxtaposition. When it is pure Burton Holmes or James A. Fitz-Patrick it is conventional travelog; but when it contrasts ancient camel caravans in foreground to modern oildrilling machinery, air-conditioned conveniences under American technique in the Arabian oil territory, Cub Scouts playing baseball on the desert sands, and the like, it brings the world tour into sharper relief. Pan shots from the Pan-American Cinerama Clipper (which gets a generous enough cuffo commercial throughout the footage) of ancient Grecian and Roman ruins are now pretty stock stuff. But the Turkish belt, looking across the Bosporus into Russia and Asia Minor, gets short shrift. Obviously, two hours can't be everything to every facet but the feeling lingers it could have been cut elsewhere and better balance maintained.

The "chase" of a palpably staged Giovanni, Maria and their bambino, racing in their broken-down motorcycle to the Vatican ceremonies, and later on to the Castel Gandolfo—the summer palace—getting there just in time, is a bit on the Mack Sennett side.

The native American wonders—Grand Canyon, Niagara Falls, etc. —will of course remind of the No. 2 Cinerama spec, just as Tay Garnett's direction of that runaway train (in reverse-gear) on a "narrow-gauge" railway in India will remind of the first Fred Waller-Hazzard Reeves rollercoaster scene which, literally, gave some viewers mal-de-Cinerama.

On the subject of sound, while the cinematic enveloping is as effective as with the predecessor entries, the directional sound is not as vivid or dramatic in its usage in this instance.

In sum total, the third entry is a solid boxoffice commodity which fulfills its fundamental production purpose. Paul Mantz did the Bible country coverage and Ted Tetzlaff captured the grandeur of the Marian Year celebration in Rome. Andrew Marton did the African tribal dances; Garnett's Indian runaway railroad shots have been above-mentioned; and Walter Thompson covered the Orient. Harry Squire, vet lenser who helped the late Fred Waller in the development of the Cinerama process, and who was director of photography of the first two productions, repeated with able assistance from Gayne Rescher. All the other credits are ultra, and not the least must have been the pioneer missionary work done by those in charge of the "advance arrangements." Stanley Warner has another boxoffice wonder in "7 Wonders of the World."
Abel.

The Swan
(C'SCOPE—COLOR)

Graustarkian romantic comedy is surefire, aided by lead Grace Kelly's own royal romance.

Hollywood, April 10.
Metro release of Dore Schary production. Stars Grace Kelly, Alec Guinness, Louis Jourdan; features Agnes Moorehead, Brian Aherne, Jessie Royce Landis, Leo G. Carroll, Estelle Winwood, Van Dyke Parks, Robert Coote. Directed by Charles Vidor. Screenplay, John Dighton; from the Ferenc Molnar play; camera (Eastman Color), Joseph Ruttenberg, Robert Surtees; editor, John Dunning; music, Bronislau Kaper. Previewed April 4, '56. Running time, 107 **MINS.**

Princess Alexandra	Grace Kelly
Prince Albert	Alec Guinness
Dr. Nicholas Agi	Louis Jourdan
Queen Maria Dominika	Agnes Moorehead
Princess Beatrix	Jessie Royce Landis
Father Hyacinth	Brian Aherne
Caesar	Leo G. Carroll
Symphorosa	Estelle Winwood
George	Van Dyke Parks
Arsene	Christopher Cook
Capt. Wunderlich	Robert Coote
Countess Sibenstoyn	Doris Lloyd
Beatrix's Maid	Edith Barrett

Delightful make-believe of Ferenc Molnar's venerable "The Swan" makes for a welcome change of pace from the strong dramatics featured in so many current and upcoming pictures. There's a natural link to international interest in the coming royal wedding of its femme star, Grace Kelly. The entertainment worth indicates its chances would be good in any case.

Beautifully bedecked in CinemaScope and Eastman Color, the Graustarkian fable about a princess who falls in love is a genteel picture about genteel people in a never-never world of crowns, titles and luxury living as produced by Dore Schary. It's plushy, without necessarily being ostentatious, as befitting the characters with which it deals, and benefits from the tremendously effective direction by Charles Vidor from an equally good script by John Dighton. There's subtle humor and broad humor, and several scenes that reach right into the heart, including one that must be figured as belonging to the ranks of the best love scenes ever filmed.

Costarring with Miss Kelly are Alec Guinness, whose popularity in the American market is growing and who adds the correct, modified comedy touch to his role of the crown prince who, regardless of what audiences might want, must end up with the princess, and Louis Jourdan, who adds a feeling romantic flavor that is just right to his character of the commoner-tutor who dares to love the princess. Miss Kelly shines right along with her male stars as the princess who gains by knowing love before she must don the inevitable crown.

That standout romantic sequence of which Vidor's directorial insight and knowing camera work make a memorable screen love scene occurs during a ball welcoming the crown prince. The tutor, invited to make the prince believe he has a rival, and Miss Kelly, the as yet unawakened girl, fall in love right before your eyes as they dance to "The Swan Waltz," especially written by Bronislau Kaper, who also contributes a notable score otherwise. In contrast to the tenderness of this sequence are any number of humorous touches. One is a real howler when the princess, finishing a deep curtsey to the crown prince, sharply raps his chin with the top of her head.

Abetting the star trio with sock support in featured roles are Jessie Royce Landis, Miss Kelly's mother who frets and stews to get the crown prince to make her daughter the next queen; Brian Aherne, as the monk, Father Hyacinth, who rates a belly laugh with his aside to a startled butler as he dashes down a corridor with his bloomers showing: "Now you know"; Estelle Winwood, the pixilated, not-bright old maid sister of Miss Landis; Agnes Moorehead, the strident queen mother; Leo G. Carroll, the proper butler; Robert Coote, the crown prince's aide; Van Dyke Parks and Christopher, as Miss Kelly's younger brothers.

The Biltmore estate in Asheville, N. C., does an able job of standing in for the 1910, Hungarian castle in which Miss Kelly is supposed to live. Standing out here, and otherwise, is the lensing by Joseph Ruttenberg and Robert Surtees, the art direction by Cedric Gibbons and Randall Duell, set decorations by Edwin B. Willis and Henry Grace, Helen Rose's costumes, editing by John Dunning and other technical contributions. *Brog.*

Crime In the Streets

Reginald Rose's television script adapted into a dreary downbeat tale of squalor and delinquency.

Hollywood, April 9.

Allied Artists release of Vincent M. Fennelly (Lindbrook) production. Stars James Whitmore, John Cassavetes, Sal Mineo, Mark Rydell; features Denise Alexander, Virginia Gregg, Will Kuluva, Peter Votrian, Malcolm Atterbury. Directed by Donald Siegel. Story and screenplay, Reginald Rose; camera, Sam Leavitt; editor, Richard C. Meyer; music, Franz Waxman. Previewed April 2, '56. Running time, **91 MINS.**

Ben Wagner	James Whitmore
Frankie Dane	John Cassavetes
Baby Gioia	Sal Mineo
Lou Macklin	Mark Rydell
Maria Gioia	Denise Alexander
Mrs. Dane	Virginia Gregg
Mr. Gioia	Will Kuluva
Richie Dane	Peter Votrian
Mr. McAllister	Malcolm Atterbury
Blockbuster	Dan Terranova
Fighter	Peter Miller
Glasses	Steve Rowland
Benny	Ray Stricklyn
Lenny	James Ogg
Phil	Robert Alexander
Herky	Duke Mitchell
Redtop	Richard Curtis
Chuck	Doyle Baker

"Crime In the Streets," in its jump from a video origin to the theatrical screen, can be figured to scare up some ballyhoo values for Allied Artists. Otherwise, it's program filler, and mighty dreary one at that.

The Vincent M. Fennelly production sets out to be a gutsy melodrama about slum area delinquents and, within the framework of Reginald Rose's highly contrived story, succeeds in making its shock points under Donald Siegel's pat directorial handling. Plot poses the pitch that the young bums shown here need love and understanding to offset their squalid surroundings. However, as characterized by story and acting, it's likely they would be just as unpleasant and unwholesome in any setting because of the psychotic motivations.

John Cassavetes is the bitter, unlovable young tough who leads the street rat pack. It is a repeat for him, having done the same character on the Elgin Playhouse telecast of the story. When an adult, Malcolm Atterbury, slaps the young bum across the mouth for getting too uppity, the juve hood plots murder. Only two of the gang, Sal Mineo and Mark Rydell (latter repeating from tv), go along with the scheme to kill Atterbury. Climax finds Atterbury, trapped in an alley, saved at the last minute when Peter Votrian, Cassavetes' younger brother, dashes in. Faced with the switchblade, himself, little Votrian cries: "I'm your brother. I love you," and Cassavetes, now knowing someone cares, loses his taste for killing.

James Whitmore heads the cast as a settlement worker who does little more than observe and offer unheeded counsel to the juvies. In the gang are Dan Terranova, Peter Miller, Steve Rowland, Ray Stricklyn, Robert Alexander, Duke Mitchell and Doyle Baker. They, along with Denise Alexander, Virginia Gregg, Will Kuluva (repeating his tv role), and others are all cast to type and, in that category, perform well.

Sam Leavitt's lowkey lensing, Franz Waxman's brassy score, editing and other credits are keyed to the meller subject. *Brog.*

Frucht Ohne Liebe
(Fruit Without Love)
(GERMAN)

Berlin, March 27.

Columbia release of CCC (Arthur Brauner) production. Stars Gertrud Kueckelmann, Claus Holm and Bernhard Wicki. Directed by Ulrich Erfurth. Screenplay, Heinrich Oberlaender; camera, Hans Schneeberger; music, Willi Mattes. At Kiki, Berlin. Running time, **106 MINS.**

Barbara Kling	Gertrud Kueckelmann
Georg Kling	Claus Holm
Professor Schillinger	Paul Dahlke
Walter Kolb	Bernhard Wicki
Barbara's Mother	Erika von Thellmann

This German Columbia release has stirred up considerable controversy here. Domestic church circles, joined by a number of Church-influenced West German dailies, have started a boycott against the film, claiming its subject (artificial impregnation) is taboo for filmization.

Film's commercial prospects appear doubtful in some German areas. There's even the chance that "Fruit Without Love" may emerge as another German "Sinner" which some years back became a terrific moneymaker here.

However, "Fruit" is considerably below the artistic standard of "The Sinner" whose biggest exploitation angle, incidentally, was a nudie (Hildegard Neff) scene. Story centers around a couple (Gertrud Kueckelmann and Claus Holm) whose five-year old marriage is extremely happy yet psychologically handicapped by the wife's yearning for children and the man's impotency. In order to save this marriage, a doctor-friend persuades the couple to accept artificial impregnation. The wife's curiosity leads her to find the real father of her forthcoming child. This results in a conventional triangle drama as the man falls for her and she almost for him.

The big question is, of course, whether such a theme should be treated in a film at all. Such a theme requires special tact, taste and artistic delicacy. "Fruit Without Love" lacks all these.

Ulrich Erfurth's direction is inadequate even in view of the material furnished him via the inadequate script. His handling of the players is often far from being adroit. Comely Getrud Kueckelmann is hardly anything more than sweet in this one and Claus Holm (her husband) is barely sympathetic. Paul Dahlke enacts the important role of the medico. He portrays his part with competence, but so routine at times that it lacks much conviction. The most polished performance is turned in by Erika von Thellmann as Miss Kueckelmann's mother.

Hans Schneeberger's lensing deserves good classification.

Although artistically quite a disappointment, film may attract—via its "courageous" subject some curious patrons outside Germany, provided that foreign censorship regulations are not too tough. It's easily possible that Columbia's "Fruit Without Love" will cash in on this controversial topic. *Hans.*

A Day of Fury
(COLOR)

Better characterization than is typical of westerns. Offbeat action entry.

Hollywood, April 6.

Universal release of Robert Arthur production. Stars Dale Robertson, Mara Corday, Jock Mahoney; features Carl Benton Reid, Jan Merlin, John Dehner, Dee Carroll, Sheila Bromley, James Bell. Directed by Harmon Jones. Screenplay, James Edmiston, Oscar Brodney; story by Edmiston; camera (Technicolor), Ellis W. Carter; editor, Sherman Todd; music supervision, Joseph Gershenson. Previewed April 4, '56. Running time, **78 MINS.**

Jagade	Dale Robertson
Sharman Fulton	Mara Corday
Marshal Allan Burnett	Jock Mahoney
Judge John J. McLean	Carl Benton Reid
Billy Brand	Jan Merlin
Preacher Jason	John Dehner
Miss Timmons	Dee Carroll
Marie	Sheila Bromley
Doc Logan	James Bell
Claire	Dani Crayne
Vanryzin	Howard Wendell
Duggen	Charles Cane
Burson	Phil Chambers
Beemans	Sydney Mason
Mrs. McLean	Helen Kleeb

"A Day of Fury" is the story of havoc wrought by an unscrupulous gunman on a western town which has nearly become respectable. Its attempt at characterization comes off fairly well with Dale Robertson as the heavy, decidedly offbeat casting, and a sometimes realistic yarn sans usual heroics but seasoned with action should serve as okay fare in the regulation outdoor market.

Entire events in this Robert Arthur Technicolor production unfold within a single Sunday. Robertson is pictured as a tough non-conformist who is holding out against the passing of the Old West, and opposed to him is Jock Mahoney, the marshal whose life he saves from an outlaw in opening sequence. Harmon Jones' rugged direction frequently overcomes lagging moments in the James Edmiston-Oscar Brodney screenplay, and in for distaff interest is Mara Corday, a reformed dancehall femme whose marriage to the marshal is interrupted by the appearance of Robertson, whom she has known sometime in the past.

Gunman's arrival cues off a return to the town's old ways when he shoots the lock off the saloon door, opens it up for Sunday business and orders the return of the dancehall girls, who moved across the county line to a neighboring community when town tried to turn peaceful. Mahoney gets in bad when his refusal to arrest Robertson for killing a man in self-defence, and ensuing patience with gunman's tactics in payment to him, is construed as being allied with him. In final showdown, after marshal repays his debt to Robertson by saving him from Miss Corday's bullet, Mahoney kills off the gunman.

Robertson handles his role slickly, endowing it with quiet menace, and Mahoney competently essays part of the lawman who intends saving the town his way. Miss Corday lends good color, too, John Dehner as a preacher, Jan Merlin a ratty would-be desperado, Carl Benton Reid the judge and Sheila Bromley dancehall proprietress, all contribute satisfactory performances.

Ellis W. Carter's color photography leads off technical credits, and art direction by Alexander Golitzen and Robert Boyle fits the period. Joseph Gershenson's music supervision is suitable. *Whit.*

Good-Bye, My Lady
(SONG)

Warm, human story of a boy and his dog; strong for family trade.

Hollywood, April 3.

Warner Bros. of a Batjac production. Stars Walter Brennan, Phil Harris, Brandon de Wilde; features Sidney Poitier, William Hopper, Louise Beavers. Directed by William A. Wellman. Screenplay, Sid Fleischman; from the novel by James Street; camera, William H. Clothier; editor, Fred MacDowell; song, Don Powell, Moris Erby; score, Laurindo Almeida, George Field. Previewed March 16, '56. Running time, **94 MINS.**

Uncle Jesse	Walter Brennan
Cash	Phil Harris
Skeeter	Brandon de Wilde
Gates	Sidney Poitier
Grover	William Hopper
Bonnie Dew	Louise Beavers

This gentle tale of a boy and his dog is properly sentimental and thoroughly heart-warming. Besides posing a good moral lesson, it is film entertainment that can be enjoyed by all but is particularly recommendable for family audiences. The regular dual situation should find it a welcome addition to a bill and, additionally, some spots may be able to make more of it than just a companion feature because of its unpretentious quality.

The screenplay by Sid Fleischman from James Street's novel rates understanding direction by William A. Wellman, who endows the Batjac production for Warner Bros. release with an honesty of purpose that shows up strongly on the screen. The script and direction do not clutter the story with unnecessary detail or distractions, telling it with a compelling, moving simplicity. The cast answers in kind with fine performances, so that no false notes are struck at any time.

Plot finds Walter Brennan, likeable old southerner, and his young nephew, Brandon de Wilde, sharing a weather-beaten cabin on the edge of a swamp. Together they enjoy a somewhat shiftless, easy life, but despite the old man's illiteracy, he is teaching the youth the proper moral values that will make him grow into an upright, honest citizen. The dog, a barkless Basenji found in the swamp and trained by the boy as his very own, becomes the symbol for the youth's first big decision in life when the real owners of the valuable animal come for it. How the kid faces up to this puts the moral capper on a story that will have audiences going with it all the way.

The location lensing in Georgia, well-done by William H. Clothier, provides a feeling of authenticity to back Wellman's story-telling and adds an extra something to the scenes of gentle, backwoods humor, the shots of the dog working the birds in the fields and being trained by the boy, and the touching sequences in which the boy, the man and the dog share life and growing up.

Brennan is tremendous as the toothless uncle who yearns for a set of plates from Sears-Roebuck. Young de Wilde is equally splendid as the boy and Phil Harris stands out as the village storekeeper whose friendship and counsel is of aid. Sidney Poitier and Louise Beavers score as Negro friends and William Hopper is excellent as the man with the difficult task of retrieving the dog. Latter, incidentally, is a natural actor.

"When Your Boy Becomes a Man," song by Don Powell and Moris Erby, is an effective part of story mood, as is the topnotch background music composed and played by Laurindo Almeida (guitar) and George Field (harmonica). Editing and other technical aids are firstrate.

Brog.

Awara
(The Vagabond)
(INDIAN)

Mild States-side b.o. potential in art houses for this import from India.

Hoffberg Productions release of R. K. Films-Bombay production. Features Nargis, Raj Kapoor. Directed by Kapoor. Based on novel by K. A. Abbas; choreography, Mme. Simkie; music, Shankar & Jaikishan. At Cameo Theatre, N.Y., April 7, '56. Running time, **82 MINS.**

Reeta	Nargis
Raj	Raj Kapoor
Judge Raghunath	H. R. Kapoor
Raj's Mother	Leela
Criminal Court Judge	Prithvira
Jagga	A. K. Kapoor

Royal Indian Ballet and Opera

(In Hindustani; English Titles)

"Awara," an import from India, appears to be one of that country's more ambitious films. For its physical values bespeak a generous budget, and a brief sequence in which the Royal Indian Ballet and Opera participate represents an additional asset. But, unfortunately, the story is a stock soap opera yarn.

B.o. prospects for this R. K. Films-Bombay production in the U.S. market will be largely limited to curiosity seekers interested in learning something about India. It could rate attention from art houses in college towns.

Based upon a novel by K. A. Abbas, script traces a sordid tale of a poor boy dominated by a thief who exhorted him to steal. Youngster actually is the son of a noted jurist but he is unaware of this. Plot endeavors to show that if an individual is born of intelligent parents he will resist a life of wickedness even if he's subjected to an environment reeking with criminals and n'eer-do-wells.

Raj Kapoor, also director of the film, creditably portrays the boy who eventually straightens out his life after a string of bad breaks. Chiefly responsible for his rehabilitation is Nargis, a Portia who befriends Kapoor. Her performance is vitally sincere as she tells court of the circumstances which contributed to the boy's misfortunes. Of course, it's clear that she'll wait for him after he pays his debt to society.

Two heavies in the case are H. R. Kapoor, as the stern judge who ordered his expectant wife out into the street when he suspected her of being unfaithful, and A. K. Kapoor as the criminal who vowed to lead Raj Kapoor astray. Both succeed in making themselves thoroughly disliked. Leela is loyal and understanding as the falsely accused mother.

Direction of Raj Kapoor is inclined to be somewhat uncertain at times. But in view of the roaming dramatic range of the story it's quite understandable. Royal Indian Ballet and Opera impress in a "dream" scene. Score of Shankar & Jaikishan hews to typical Indian melodies. English titles are adequate.

Gilb.

The Miracle of the Reef
(COLOR)

Pictorially exciting underwater excursion featuring unique footage of marine life. Strong b.o. prospect in special situations.

Marine Studios presentation of a Butterfield and Wolf picture, produced by Alfred Butterfield. Photographed, directed and edited by Lloyd Ritter, Robert Young and Murray Lerner. Narration written by Butterfield and Ritter-Young-Lerner and spoken by Joseph Julian; music, Clinton Elliott, conducted by Simon Sadoff; color, Tri-Art. Previewed in N.Y., March 27, '56. Running time, **72 MINS.**

The bitter struggle for survival and the endless cycle of life and death below the surface of the sea provides "The Miracle of the Reef" with an abundance of colorful and exciting footage. Nature lovers, and particularly students of marine life, should find this featurelength underwater excursion a rewarding experience.

Pic, shot in excellent color and edited very intelligently with a view to maximum visual contrasts, is a documentary of more than ordinary merit. There are no people in it, yet some of the scenes—particularly the struggle between the giant moray eels and the octopus—carry a real wallop. In fact, if anything, the cruelty of the underwater world is overplayed in this Butterfield-Wolf production.

Limited as it undoubtedly is, there surely is an audience for offbeat efforts such as this. Some of the views caught by the submerged cameras of Lloyd Ritter, Robert Young and Murray Lerner are breathtaking and unusual. One might cite the wonderful bit of the seahorse giving birth to hundreds of tiny little seahorses ejecting them from his breeding pouch; or the marvellous shots of the old sea turtle wheezing her way onto the beach to lay her eggs, and the eventual breaking out of the little turtles from their shells.

There is constant, flowing movement in this strange marine world, and possibly there is too much of an accent on these large schools of fish streaking through the waters. This is made up for by the camera focusing on individual odd-looking creatures, such as the Lion's Mane Jellyfish laying its eggs while capturing little fish for food; the little crab decorating itself with bits of sponge for camouflage, and the spiny lobster jumping out of his own skin.

Narration by vet radio narrator Joseph Julian is unobtrusively poetic and yet provides much-needed explanations. Simon Sadoff's musical backgrounds are charming, particularly the gay little tune that goes with the seahorse sequence. Pictures like these have more often won prizes than customers. If properly sold, this Alfred E. Butterfield production could turn out a real pacesetter.

Hift.

The Way Out
(BRITISH)

Gene Nelson as an American husband in England. Dull entertainment.

Hollywood, April 10.

RKO release of Alec Snowden (Todon) production. Stars Gene Nelson, Mona Freeman, John Bentley; features Michael Goodliffe, Sydney Tafler, Charles Victor. Direction and screenplay by Montgomery Tully; story, Bruce Grahme; camera, Philip Grindrod; editor, Geoffrey Miller; music supervision, Richard Taylor. Previewed April 5, '56. Running time, **78 MINS.**

Greg Carradine	Gene Nelson
Terry Carradine	Mona Freeman
Detective Seagrave	John Bentley
John Moffat	Michael Goodliffe
Alf Cressett	Sydney Tafler
Tom Smithers	Charles Victor
George	Arthur Lovegrove
Anderson	Cyril Chamberlain
Vera Bellamy	Paula Byrne
Blonde	Kay Callard
Inspector Keyes	Michael Golden
Mr. Harding	Charles Mortimer
Policewoman	Margaret Harrison
Farmer	Clifford Buckton

This lensed-in-Britain melodrama is lowercase material for dual bills. It spins an unbelieveable story and is poorly directed and acted. An otherwise all-British cast is topped by Gene Nelson and Mona Freeman.

Under executive producer Tony Owen, the Todon presentation was produced by Alec Snowden for RKO release against a London setting. Montgomery Tully not only handled the inept direction, but also wrote the incredible script from a story by Bruce Graeme. Nelson's scant acting ability makes a bad role worse and Miss Freeman is never given a chance to show anything in her spot.

Nelson, an American living in England and married to Miss Freeman, comes home one night on the run, saying he has killed a man in a drunken barroom fight. His wife makes arrangements to smuggle him out of England, meantime having found out Nelson's no good and figuring this way she'll be free of him. With the bobbies closing in, it's a long, dull chase with a multitude of truck changes enroute. Windup finds Nelson run over by a bus, thus leaving Miss Freeman with a chance to get better acquainted with John Bentley, the detective masterminding the chase for Nelson.

Along with the above threesome, others in the cast include Michael Goodliffe, Sydney Tafler, Charles Victor, Arthur Lovegrove, Cyril Chamberlain, Paula Byrne and Kay Callard. They fare no better than the principals. Editing is choppy and lensing average.

Brog.

Teufel in Seide
(Devil In Silk)
(GERMAN)

Berlin, March 20.

Deutsche London release of Fono production. Stars Lilli Palmer, Curd Juergens. Features Winnie Markus, Adelheid Seeck, Hans Nielsen, Wolfgang Buettner, Hilde Koerber, Paul Bildt, Helmut Rudolph, Robert Meyn, Otto Graf, Wolfgang Martini, Else Ehser. Directed by Rolf Hansen. Screenplay by Jochen Huth from novel, "Devil Next Door," by Gina Kraus; music, Mark Lothar; camera, Franz Weihmayr. At Marmorhaus, Berlin. Running time, **105 MINS.**

This is Lilli Palmer's second German film and she again turns in a superlative performance. It's primarily her work that makes "Devil in Silk" above-average. Direction by Rolf Hansen and scripting by Jochen Huth also are top assets. This psychological society drama gives the players a chance to exhibit their abilities.

Cast includes a number of w.k. players, such as Curd Juergens, Winnie Markus, Adelheid Seeck, Hans Nielsen, Hilde Koerber and Paul Bildt.

Technically, "Devil In Silk" is also very good. Franz Weihmayr's lensing and Mark Lothar's interesting score represent nice quality. A highly recommended German film, it should have strong b.o. chances in this country and may appeal to class audiences here for whom the Lilli Palmer name means something. "Devil In Silk" looks like a good bet for overseas.

Hans.

Gri-Gri

Defense Films Corp. release of a Joelle-Yatove Films production, filmed with cooperation of UN Museum of Man; narration written by Eileen and Robert Mason Pollock; camera, Pierre Gaisseau, Jean Fichter, Andre Virel, Tony Saulnier; editors, Harry Robin, Charles Diana, Gabriel Rongier and Fernand Marralla. Reviewed at RKO Hillstreet Theatre, Apr. 4, 1956. Running time **64 MINS.**

Overdramatized commentary marks this pictorial exploration of native life and customs in French West Africa more an anthropological study than a theatrical release, market is uncertain. Material is for the strong of stomach.

Chances for wide acceptance are lessened by several fairly gruesome scenes of native sacrifice, in which a ram, a rooster and a dog have their throats cut on-screen, sparing no detail. Likewise, another sequence graphically dwells on a painfully primitive method of tattooing.

Tale deals with efforts of a quartet of French scientists to reach and film the sacred rites of the Toma tribe, wherein the maidens are "sexually mutilated' (clitoris deletion) in preparation for marriage. It should be gratefully noted that this never actually appears on the screen, although some village cronies are shown descriptively waving a ghastly set of implements in the preliminary stages of the rites. However, at the last minute and storm blows up and the natives take this as an indication that the gods are angry and stop the ceremonies. The Frenchmen return to their base without the final footage, as the tale ends.

Even if the accompanying story penned by Eileen and Robert

Mason Pollock and narrated by an unidentified commentator, seems somewhat overembroidered for complete acceptance, explanations of the native customs are well done.

Black-and-white footage is attributed equally to the four scientists—leader Pierre Gaisseau, Jean Fichter, Andre Virel and Tony Saulnier—and is of excellent quality, considering the handicaps under which it was shot. Filming was done with cooperation of UN Museum of Man. Aside from the natives, the quartet of scientists also comprises the entire cast.

Kove.

Charley's Tante
(Charley's Aunt)
(GERMAN—COLOR)

Frankfurt, March 27.

Constantin release of Berolina Film production. Stars Heinz Ruehmann; features Hertha Feiler, Claus Biederstaedt, Walter Giller. Directed by Hans Qest. Screenplay, Gustav Kampendonk after play by Brandon Thomas; camera (Eastmancolor), Kurt Schulz; music, Friedrich Schroeder. At Film Palast, Frankfurt. Running time, **90 MINS.**

Dr. Otto Dernburg .... Heinz Ruehmann
Carlotta Ramirez .... Hertha Feiler
Ralf Dernburg .... Claus Biederstaedt
Charley Sallmann .... Walter Giller
Ulla .... Elisa Loti
Britto .... Ina Peters

This enlarged joke about the helpful older brother who dresses up as Charley's aunt, so that Charley and his teen-age pal have a chaperone when they entertain two young girls has become a stage and screen classic. And the fact that it's still funny is proved because it's doing top boxoffice business in Germany and may become one of the biggest grossers since the war.

For the older audiences, who may have seen such great "aunts" as Jack Benny and Ray Bolger, a lot of spirit has gone out of the old punchlines, and the obvious disguises and ruses are strictly not for the sophisticates. But for the inexperienced audience, this up-to-date version with some fine new music, is aimed right at the b.o., and scores heavily.

Standout show tune, "Es kann heute sein" (It Can Be Today), is also a disk click via radio and tv plugging, and adds a fine plus for composer Friedrich Schroeder. Eastmancolor, too, is an asset.

Heinz Ruehmann is properly devilish as the disguised man, although anyone above the mentality of a 10-year-old would see through his falsie-fied front. For the slapsticky set, though, the pic can't miss.

Film could do same big business in the German-speaking theatre in the U.S.

Haze.

Foreign Films

La Lumiere D'En Face (The Light Across the Way) **(FRENCH).** Fernand Rivers release of Fernand Rivers-EGC-Jacques Gauthier production. Stars Raymond Pellegrin, Brigitte Bardot; features Roger Pigaut, Jean Debucourt, Claude Romain, Guy Pierraud. Directed by Georges Lacombe. Screenplay, Jean Claude Aurel, adapted by Louis Chavance, Rene Masson, Rene Lefevre; camera, Louis Page; editor, Raymond Leboursier. At Elysees, Paris. Running time, **110 MINS.**

Film concerns a truckdriver who becomes neurotic after an accident. He is counselled not to marry, for intimate relations would destroy his balance. However his luscious young fiancee insists. They buy a cafe but a virile mechanic arrives and sets off the drama. The truckdriver goes mad and tries to kill his wife and the would-be lover before being killed himself by a truck.

Though soberly recounted, this rarely gets to the core of the subject. Except for Raymond Pellegrin as the crazed driver, it is ordinarily acted. It goes in for some erotic byplay. Otherwise, it does not have the substance for art houses. Brigitte Bardot looks well but her acting does not equal her physical attributes. Direction, lensing and editing shape as only adequate with exterior settings lending some good production and documentary flavor.

Mosk.

Le Couteau Sous La Gorge (The Knife to the Throat) **(FRENCH); CINEPANORAMIC).** Filmmonde release of EGC-Film Artisque production. Stars Jean Servais, Jean Chevrier, Madeleine Robinson; features Michele Cardoux, Micheline Gary, Yves Deniaud. Directed by Jacques Severac. Screenplay, Andre Tabet, Severac; camera (Eastmancolor), Jean Isnard; editor, Monique Lacomb. At Triomphe, Paris. Running time, **90 MINS.**

Use of French anamorphoscopic process akin to C'Scope, Cinepanoramic limits this for U.S. chances because its familiar and only fairly made gangster story is of little interest for arties. For general runs, it lacks names.

Concerning a doctor whose kidnapped son is rescued by a gangster whose life he had once saved, it is too obvious to make for U.S. interest except for possible secondary dualer spots.

Cinepanoramic is only just passable, with some soft focus and lack of multiple, stereophonic sound detracting. Color is uneven as is the acting except for the principals. Jean Servais is adequate as the worried doctor with Jean Chevrier and Madeleine Robinson giving good support. Technical aspects are fair and big screen shows up skimping in set and general production dress.

Mosk.

Treize a Table (Thirteen At the Table) **(FRENCH).** Pathe release of Contact-SAFIA-Pathe production. Stars Micheline Presle, Fernand Gravey; features Mischa Auer, Jean Brochard, Germaine Montrero. Directed by Andre Hunnebelle. Screenplay by Jean Halain from play by Marc Gilbert Sauvajon; camera, Paul Coteret; editor, James Cuenet. At Balzac, Paris. Running time, **90 MINS.**

Taken from a hit play of two season's ago, this maintains the legit feel in unfoldment. It is a one joke affair about a superstitious woman who tries to avoid having 13 at her table on Christmas Eve. People come and go and the number 13 keeps up while little intrigues are unwound, such as the return of an early love of her husband, a fiery South American who claims he was a hero there and wants to take him back.

Though a few laughs are whipped up via some clever slapstick scenes, this drags in appeal and remains too talky for most U.S. spots.

It has the names of Micheline Presle and Fernand Gravey for some dualer spots; otherwise it is severely limited. Miss Presle and Gravey play easily and are surrounded by a competent cast. But director Andre Hunnebelle has rarely escaped a stagy feeling. Credits are okay.

Mosk.

Le Diciottenni (Eighteen Year-Olds) **(ITALIAN; COLOR).** Variety release of a Carlo Ponti production. Stars Marisa Allasio, Ave Ninchi; features Helen Portello, Antonio De Teffe, Virgilio Riento. Directed by Mario Mattoli. Screenplay, Mattoli, Musso, DeConcini, Aldo De Benedetti, from a play by Aldo DeBenedetti; camera (Eastmancolor - Superfilmscope), Marco Scarpelli; music, Armando Trovajoli. At Bernini, Rome. Running time, **100 MINS.**

Remake of successful pic of the '40s, with color and widescreen added, this should get plenty of dates, especially in the subsequents. Youthful cast makes up for lack of names. Might shape into fair export fare, but color and widescreen expenses might handicap it.

Story is one of those girls' finishing-school yarns in which misunderstandings, great secrets and threatened expulsions abound. It is also cast in familiar fashion—handsome young teacher, nasty directress, dynamic girl ringleader, friendly lab assistant, etc.

Format is a cliche in itself, but pic, which deals with threatened expulsion of gal whose father has a criminal background, still makes pleasant viewing. Gals are plentiful and comely, and sets and scenery are lush and colorful.

Marisa Allasio handles her troublemaker role with ease, while others contribute pleasant performances. Eastmancolor lensing is fine, though Superfilmscope process is often unclear and fuzzy over wide areas of the screen. Scripting is standard and musical score appropriate.

Hawk.

Cabo de Hornos (Cape Horn) **(MEXICAN).** Mier & Brooks and Atenea Films production. Stars Jorge Mistral, Silvia Pinal; features Myriam Thorud, Eugenio Retes, Jose Guixe, Gerardo Grez, Emilio Martinez, Agustin Orrequia, Carlos Morris. Directed by Tito Davison. Camera, Emilio Foriscot and Clemente Manzano; based on a novel by Francisco Coloane. At Cine Olimpia, Mexico City. Running time, **92 MINS.**

Scenery, atmosphere, whale gunning and lensing impart an interest to this which is different from that of many newsreels and documentaries. Story is so confused that after the finale, one expects an announcement of prizes being bestowed for solutions to the yarn. Actual local scenes (first Mexican pic to be made at the south end of the Americas) saw three producers (Mier & Brooks, Mexican; Atenea, Spanish, and Tito Davison, Chilean) turning this out, aided by the Chilean government and navy.

Jorge Mistral, Spanish actor, plays skipper of a whaler who falls for a sad femme in a pub and spends the night with her. Her interest is sparked by his indifference to her, even when she strips to black underwear. Ultimately, both go out whale hunting. Excellent shots of modern harpooning but the inexorable bleakness and coldness of the man's life is not frightened much by the plot or the sad ending.

Doug.

Autumn Leaves
(SONG)

Strong Joan Crawford vehicle. Good prospects.

Hollywood, April 13.

Columbia release of William Goetz production. Stars Joan Crawford, Vera Miles, Lorne Greene, Ruth Donnelly, Cliff Robertson; features Shepperd Strudwick, Selmer Jackson, Maxine Cooper, Marjorie Bennett, Frank Gerstle, Leonard Mudie, Maurice Manson. Directed by Robert Aldrich. Story, screenplay, Jack Jevne, Lewis Meltzer, Robert Blees; camera, Charles Lang; editor, Michael Luciano; music, Hans Salter, conducted by Morris Stoloff; song, Joseph Kosma, Jacques Prevert, with English lyrics by Johnny Mercer; sung by Nat "King" Cole. Previewed April 11, '56. Running time, **107 MINS.**

Milly .... Joan Crawford
Burt Hanson .... Cliff Robertson
Virginia .... Vera Miles
Mr. Hanson .... Lorne Greene
Liz .... Ruth Donnelly
Dr. Couzzens .... Shepperd Strudwick
Mr. Wetherby .... Selmer Jackson
Nurse Evans .... Maxine Cooper
Waitress .... Marjorie Bennett
Mr. Ramsey .... Frank Gerstle
Colonel Hillyer .... Leonard Mudie
Dr. Masterson .... Maurice Manson
Desk Clerk .... Bob Hopkins

Joan Crawford has a strong dramatic vehicle, her best in some time, in this William Goetz production for Columbia. It's the type of melodrama stressing the femme angle that has always appealed to the actress' following so they should fall in line for it.

Goetz' production helming is excellent, from story choice on through the various components. While the first half may seem a bit too long, it's not slow, and the pace thereafter is topnotch. Direction by Robert Aldrich punches every dramatic scene for its full worth, showcasing Miss Crawford, as well as comparative newcomer Cliff Robertson, to advantage. Footage contains some of the most uninhibitive bussing to come to the screen in a long time. Those scenes, alone, will get the distaffers, so enthusiastically do Miss Crawford and Robertson participate.

Jack Kevne, Lewis Meltzer and Robert Blees fashioned this good woman's story about two lonely people; a femme in the autumn of her youth and a man a number of years younger. Despite the age difference and her apprehensions, they marry. Happiness is short-lived. He turns out to be a psycho, made that way by discovering his former wife and his father in a compromising position. Risking that he might not need her if rid of his neuroses, the wife still sends him off to a sanitarium for treatment. Her happiness is complete when he returns, full of love, after the cure.

The ways of the psychotic and the methods of treatment and cure are given rather full range in the picture, making for some strong, sometimes shocking, footage. Robertson, who also appeared in Columbia's "Picnic," is a young actor of impressive promise and, because of the manner in which the story is laid out, makes a very good partner for Miss Crawford's polished way with her character. Vera Miles, the ex-wife, and Lorne Greene, the father, figure importantly, if somewhat briefly. Ruth Donnelly, a gabby landlady, lends some leavening comedy. Shepperd Strudwick is good as the psychiatrist and Maxine Cooper shows up nicely as a nurse at the sanitarium.

Charles Lang's photography does a flawless job of lensing the players and settings. The title tune, by Joseph Kosma and Jacques Prevert, with English lyrics by Johnny

Mercer, gets sterling vocal treatment by Nat "King" Cole. Hans Salter cleffed the score, with Morris Stoloff conducting. *Brog.*

Stranger at My Door

Excellent entertainment values starting with sound story (original) and religioso angle. Good family trade item.

Hollywood, April 17.

Republic release of Sidney Picker production. Stars Macdonald Carey, Patricia Medina, Skip Homeier; features Stephen Wootton, Louis Jean Heydt, Howard Wright, Slim Pickens, Malcolm Atterbury. Directed by William Witney. Screenplay, Barry Shipman; camera, Bud Thackery; editor, Howard Smith; music, R. Dale Butts. Previewed April 13, '56. Running time, 85 MINS.

Hollis Jarret .... Macdonald Carey
Peg Jarret .... Patricia Medina
Clay Anderson .... Skip Homeier
Dodie .... Stephen Wootton
John Tatum .... Louis Jean Heydt
Doc Parks .... Howard Wright
Ben Silas .... Slim Pickens
Rev. Hastings .... Malcolm Atterbury

Republic has an exceptionally well-done family trade offering in this pioneer action-drama. There's a good measure of suspense and some strong inspirational values to raise it considerably above the level of the average program entry.

The Barry Shipman screen original is filled with characters and situations entirely acceptable and believable, plus a religioso theme that does its pulpiting without soap-boxing. The writing, with very good direction by William Witney which takes the time to develop the people in the story through mood as well as characterization, puts the exceptional imprint on this release.

Sidney Picker, as associate producer, contains his overseering to values that go with what's being told, yet allows leeway for some extremely tense suspense and actionful sequences. Just one of these is the footage concerned with an "outlaw" horse and results in some of the most exciting scenes of a killer-nag on rampage against humans yet lensed. Credit Bud Thackery for fine photography here, and elsewhere.

A country preacher's faith that God can redeem those apparently lost is the theme and the people involved are completely credible in living up to the characters they play. Skip Homeier, seeking a hideout after looting a midwest town with his gang, comes to the farm worked by Macdonald Carey, man of God, and decides he'll be safe there for a few days. Carey, a widower, has a young son, Stephen Wootton, and a young second wife, Patricia Medina. He welcomes the challenge of an outlaw being close, figuring he can convert him. He, and the mysterious workings of the Lord, do, but it's the intervening portions of the story and the way they show the weaknesses and the goodness of people that provide the drama and point to the plot.

The above mentioned players earn plaudits for characters compellingly performed and right along with them are Louis Jean Heydt, as the sheriff, Howard Wright, a doctor, Slim Pickens, horse-trader and millwright, and Malcolm Atterbury, a circuit rider.

Technical support is firstrate all down the line. *Brog.*

The Rack

Another screen re-telling of a tv story. Too downbeat for pop entertainment tastes.

Hollywood, April 16.

Metro release of Arhtur M. Loew Jr. production. Stars Paul Newman, Wendell Corey, Walter Pidgeon, Edmond O'Brien, Anne Francis, Lee Marvin; features Cloris Leachman, Robert Burton, Robert Simon, Trevor Bardette. Directed by Arnold Laven. Screenplay, Stewart Stern; based on the teleplay by Rod Serling; camera, Paul C. Vogel; editors, Harold F. Kress, Marshall Neilan Jr.; music, Adolph Deutsch. Previewed April 6, '56. Running time, 99 MINS.

Capt. Edward W. Hall, Jr. Paul Newman
Maj. Sam Moulton .... Wendell Corey
Col. Edw. W. Hall, Sr. .... Walter Pidgeon
Lt. Col. Frank Wasnick .. Edmond O'Brien
Aggie Hall .... Anne Francis
Capt. John R. Miller .... Lee Marvin
Caroline .... Cloris Leachman
Col. Ira Hansen .... Robert Burton
Law Officer .... Robert Simon
Court President .... Trevor Bardette
Sgt. Otto Pahnke .... Adam Williams
Millard Chilson Cassidy ...... James Best
Col. Dudley Smith .... Fay Roope
Maj. Byron Phillips .... Barry Atwater

The court martial of a Korean War collaborationist is a topical subject but, as delivered here, poor material for an hour and 40 minutes of screen time. It's well enough done within the melodramatic category, but too depressing and dreary to be suitable for popular screen tastes.

"The Rack" is a film elongation of Rod Serling's teleplay of the same title, screen-scripted by Stewart Stern and directed by Arnold Laven under Arthur M. Loew Jr.'s production helming. They deliver expertly in the respective functions, as do the stars and featured players, so the chief quarrel is with the choice of the downbeat subject for screening.

Paul Newman is the collaborationist put on the court martial rack by Wendell Corey, prosecuting for the Army. Newman, with a hero's record before becoming a prisoner of war, is the son of Walter Pidgeon, old time Army officer. Defending him, on the grounds mental torture took the hero beyond the point where he could be responsible for his actions, is Edmond O'Brien. Also starred are Anne Francis, as the war widow of Newman's brother, and Lee Marvin, a fellow ex-prisoner of war who testifies against the collaborationist. All play their roles to the dramatic hilt.

Story is inclined to play it a bit cozy, leaning over backwards to present a full lineup of pros and cons and, actually, comes up with no solution as to what should be done or at what point a man becomes a collaborator with the enemy. Windup of the case finds Newman guilty, although certainly the verdict could have gone either way on the basis of the testimony. Clearing the hero would have added at least one upbeat note.

Supporting players do their work satisfactorily. Also in the expert class are Paul C. Vogel's lensing, the background score and editing. *Brog.*

The Scarlet Hour
(SONG)

Disappointing introduction of three new-faces as star possibilities. Stock plot spoils the pitch.

Hollywood, April 12.

Paramount release of Michael Curtiz production. Stars Carol Ohmart, Tom Tryon, Jody Lawrance; guest star Nat "King" Cole; features James Gregory, Elaine Stritch, E. G. Marshall, Edward Binns, Scott Marlowe, Billy Gray, Jacques Aubuchon, David Lewis. Directed by Curtiz. Screenplay, Rip Van Ronkel, Frank Tashlin, John Meredyth Lucas; story, Van Ronkel, Frank Tashlin. Previewed April 10, '56. Running time, 95 MINS.

Paulie .... Carol Ohmart
Marsh .... Tom Tryon
Kathy .... Jody Lawrance
Ralph .... James Gregory
Phyllis Rycker .... Elaine Stritch
Lieut. Jennings .... E. G. Marshall
Sgt. Allen .... Edward Binns
Vince .... Scott Marlowe
Tom Rycker .... Billy Gray
Fat Boy .... Jacques Aubuchon
Sam Lynbury .... David Lewis
Tom Raymond .... Johnstone White
Dean Franklin .... James F. Stone
Mrs. Lynbury .... Maureen Hurley
Inspector Paley .... James Todd

"The Scarlet Hour" is Paramount's answer to the exhibitor cry for new faces. It introduces three possibilities in the leads, as well as a number of lesser-knowns in character roles. Unfortunately, the gamble isn't backed with the kind of entertainment values that make for a strong showcasing. However, the picture will rate sufficient exposure via a programmer playoff to give some indication what public reaction will be to the newcomers.

Three writers fashioned a rather commonplace crime thriller that gains no more than casual interest as it unfolds. Producer-director Michael Curtiz is up against the hurdles of stock melodramatics and players not yet camera-wise, and doesn't always surmount them. If the script by Rip Van Ronkel, Frank Tashlin and John Meredyth, from a story by the first two, isn't realistic, the lensing is. The VistaVision process uses a new Japanese lens, the Fujinon, which permits graphic photography with much less light assistance than needed with regular lenses. Lionel Lionel handled the cameras expertly.

Carol Ohmart, Tom Tryon and Jody Lawrance are the newcomers on display. The dramatics are sometimes beyond their present ability to handle, but all show possibilities, with perhaps Tryon and Miss Lawrance registering the most promising. The plot is the one about a bad woman, Miss Ohmart, who uses Tryon's infatuation for her to plot a jewelry hijacking in which her suspicious husband, James Gregory, is accidentally killed. Tryon comes to realize what kind of a woman he is involved with and finale finds him turning to Miss Lawrance, who has indicated she will wait for him after he is through with the law.

Gregory, Elaine Stritch and Billy Gray, as friends of Miss Ohmart; E. G. Marshall and Edward Binnes, detectives; Scott Marlowe and Jacques Aubuchon, the hijacked thieves, and David Lewis, who plotted the original theft in a contrived situation that permitted Miss Ohmart and Tryon to overhear, are among character players delivering in routine fashion.

Footage makes good use of location lensing in Los Angeles environs, including the Beverly Hills' Crystal Room, where Nat "King" Cole sings "Never Let Me Go," tune by Jay Livingston and Ray Evans. Leith Stevens did the scoring to okay effect and technical credits measure up. *Brog.*

Outside the Law

Satisfactory melodramatics for general supporting playdates.

Hollywood, April 9.

Universal release of Albert J. Cohen production. Stars Ray Danton, Leigh Snowden, Grant Williams; features Onslow Stevens, Raymond Bailey, Judson Pratt, Jack Kruschen, Floyd Simmons. Directed by Jack Arnold. Screenplay, Danny Arnold; based on story by Peter R. Brooke; camera, Irving Glassberg; editor, Irving Birnbaum; music supervision, Milton Rosen. Previewed April 5, '56. Running time, 81 MINS.

Johnny Salvo .... Ray Danton
Maria Craven .... Leigh Snowden
Don Kastner .... Grant Williams
Alec Conrad .... Onslow Stevens
Philip Bormann .... Raymond Bailey
Maury Saxon .... Judson Pratt
Phil Schwartz .... Jack Kruschen
Harris .... Floyd Simmons
Milo .... Mel Welles
Warden .... Alexander Campbell
Mrs. Pulenski .... Karen Verne
Mr. Pulenski .... Maurice Doner
Bill MacReady ...... Jesse B. Kirkpatrick
Parker .... Arthur Ranson
Pomeroy .... Richard H. Cutting
Bus Station Clerk .... George Mather
Mama Gomez .... Amapola del Vando

The roundup of an international counterfeiting gang provides the melodramatics for "Outside the Law" and they are brought off in a satisfactory fashion to make the pic an acceptable programmer entry. Additionally, it gives further showcasing and experience to three of Universal's newer talents, Ray Danton, Leigh Snowden and Grant Williams, all of whom do okay by their lead assignments.

A story by Peter R. Brooke, with Danny Arnold doing the scripting, is used by Albert J. Cohen's production helming as a springboard for a thriller show. Under Jack Arnold's direction the pace holds up, as does sufficient interest in what's transpiring, over the 81-minute course. Excellent feature assists come from the playing by Onslow Stevens, Raymond Bailey, Judson Pratt, Jack Kruschen and Floyd Simmons.

Danton, paroled into the army, is an ex-prisoner called back from overseas to help round up the bogus money boys when a G.I. buddy, involved in the ring, is killed. His chore is to romance Miss Snowden, the buddy's widow, to see if she can furnish any leads. She's in the clear but the importing firm where she works isn't. Helping to tip the scales in favor of the law is Williams, in the ring and insanely jealous of Miss Snowden. He goes down in a blast of gunfire at the finale. Danton gets Miss Snowden and the events also bring about a reconciliation with his father, Stevens, chief Treasury agent, towards whom the young man is particularly bitter because he believes his father could have helped him stay out of jail for a youthful crime.

Irving Glassberg handles his cameras well and the editing by Irving Birnbaum, the music supervision by Milton Rosen and other contributions are good. *Brog.*

Star In the Dust
(COLOR)

Good suspense western with well-motivated script.

Hollywood, April 17.

Universal release of Albert Zugsmith production. Stars John Agar, Mamie Van Doren, Richard Boone, Coleen Gray, Leif Erickson; features James Gleason, Randy Stuart, Terry Gilkyson, Paul Fix, Harry Morgan. Directed by Charles Haas. Screenplay, Oscar Brodney; based on the novel, "Law Man" by Lee Leighton; camera (Technicolor), John L. Russell Jr.; editor, Ray Snyder; music, Frank Skinner. Previewed April 12, '56. Running time, 80 MINS.

Sheriff Bill Jorden .... John Agar
Ellen Ballard .... Mamie Van Doren
Sam Hall .... Richard Boone
Nellie Mason .... Coleen Gray
George Ballard .... Leif Erickson
Orval Jones .... James Gleason
Nan Hogan .... Randy Stuart
The Music Man .... Terry Gilkyson

Mike MacNamara	Paul Fix
Lew Hogan	Harry Morgan
Jess Ryman	Stuart Randall
Rigdon	Robert Osterloh
Ben Smith	Stanley Andrews
Jiggs Larribee	John Day
Leo Roos	Stafford Repp
Pastor Harris	Lewis Martin
Timothy Brown	Renny McEvoy
Ed Pardee	Jesse Kirkpatrick
Mary Tremain	James Parnell
Doc Quinn	Anthony Jochim

Action and suspense are mixed in good proportions in "Star In the Dust." As a western, it fills the bill.

Based on Lee Leighton's novel, "Law Man, the Albert Zugsmith production has a good script by Oscar Brodney that lays its action between sunup and sundown in a small western town. There's a killer to be hanged at sundown, but the young sheriff fears trouble; from the cattlemen who brought the gunman in to frighten the farmers and don't want to see him hanged, and the farmers, who are determined he shall swing.

Charles Haas' direction works up the varying angles that dress the basic plot, and time is taken to develop an assortment of divergent characters. John Agar, good as the determined sheriff, has two rough-and-ready fist fights, first with Robert Osterloh, ambitious school teacher who is stirring up the farmers, and later with Leif Erickson, town banker who ostensibly is supporting the cattlemen but actually wants killer Richard Boone to hang because he paid him to commit three murders. Both scraps come over well, contributing expertly to the action that moves the plot towards its justice-is-done conclusion.

Mamie Van Doren, the banker's naive sister and sheriff's fiancee, is okay, as is Boone in his hired gun part. Coleen Gray, the killer's lady love who is in on a plot to help him escape, and Erickson are both satisfactory. Same goes for James Gleason, doing well as jail janitor who gets deputized, Paul Fix, another deputy, and Harry Morgan, one of the cattlemen. Of the cast femmes, best is Randy Stuart, who shows up exceptionally well as a woman forced into the escape scheme to protect her husband. Terry Gilkyson portrays a sort of ne'erdowell prairie troubador with guitar, balladeering the story as it is played.

Good western town settings are expertly lensed in Technicolor by John L. Russell Jr. Editing keeps footage tight at 80 minutes and other technical contributions rate a nod. *Brog.*

The Animal World
(DOCUMENTARY—COLOR)

Engrossing study of animal world since its origin two billion years ago; for selected bookings.

Hollywood, April 13.

Warner Bros. release of an Irwin Allen production, written-directed by Allen. Camera (Technicolor), Harold Wellman, naturalist photographers throughout world; music, Paul Sawtell; are director, Bert Tuttle; editing, Gene Palmer, Robert A. Belcher; animation, Willis O'Brien, Ray Harryhausen; special effects, Arthur S. Rhoades; narrated by Theodore Von Eltz, John Storm. Previewed April 6, '56. Running time, **81 MINS.**

Irwin Allen's followup to his Academy - winning documentary, "The Sea Around Us," is marked with the same interesting and often fantastic revelations of Nature and her work. Its 81 minutes of Technicolor-printed content relates the story of struggle, survival and death in the animal world that began two billion years ago when life first feebly flickered in the primeval seas, and depicts down through the eons of time the most significant and dramatic chapters of animal history and the animal world's relationship to man. Film is particularly adaptable to special bookings, where its chances for good returns are bright.

Allen, who made documentary through his Windsor productions in association with Warners, spent two years and one-half in putting this together, and nearly two years in actual production. Special footage, in addition to his own, was turned out by scientists, zoologists and naturalist photographers in 27 countries throughout the world, on specific assignment by producer, who also wrote and directed film which combines cold scientific fact with top showmanship. In addition to startling photography, both microscopic and standard, film makes potent use of special effects and 12 minutes of animation covering the dinosaur period.

Feature has both its violent and lighter moments, all shaken together to give spectator a vivid impression of the subject. Some of the most interesting scenes are the fights between various types of dinosaurs, animated with surprising realism by Willis O'Brien and Ray Harryhousen. Real-life scenes show a lioness bringing down an impala and two lions attacking a zebra; giraffes fighting; charge of a rhino upon the camera; a ferret and cobra in combat; a giant eel and octopus locked in death embrace. Actual birth of baby starfish is caught, and there's the film vignette of a bear cub and fawn, to delight the eye. Realistic sound effects accompany various sequences.

Technical credits are topflight right down the line. Outstanding are Harold Wellman's color photography; Paul Sawtell's atmospheric music score; Gene Palmer and Robert A. Belcher's knowhow editing. Subject is narrated tellingly by Theodore Von Eltz and John Storm. *Whit.*

08/15 In Der Heimat
(08/15 At Home)
(GERMAN)

Berlin, April 10.

Gloria release of Divina production. Stars O. E. Hasse with Joachim Fuchsberger, Peter Carsten, Renate Ewert, Helen Vita, Gustav Knuth, Hans Christian Blech, Emmerich Schrenk, Mario Adorf, Edith Schulze-Westrum, Hannes Schiel, Michael Janisch, Gustav Waldau and Hertha von Hagen. Directed by Paul May. Screenplay, Ernst von Salomon, based on novel by Hans-Helmut Kirst; camera, Georg Krause; music, Rolf Wilhelm. At Gloria Palast, Berlin. Running time, **95 MINS.**

This is the third of the successful German "08/15" series. While the first pic was before and the second production during the war, this part sees the end of the warfare and Germany's early postwar period. It doesn't reach the overheights of the first "08/15" film which undoubtedly was the best of Hans-Helmut Kirst's triology. However, this film has healthy b.o. prospects here. And pic may cash in on the popularity of its predecessors elsewhere.

A substantial part of this centers around the two Germans, Joachim Fuchsberger (now a lieutenant) and Peter Carsten (a staff sergeant) who both chase two SS leaders. Latter, disguised as ordinary army officers, try to evade justice after having committed one murder after the other. Scenes which show the Germans making first contact with Americans lack conviction.

Screenplay by Ernst von Salomon is routine. Probably his main fault is that he inserted too much laughter. The last phase of the big war certainly was not as funny as depicted here.

Paul May's direction is okay. A special laurel should go to Rolf Wilhelm for his brilliant score. Georg Krause's lensing is also outstanding. *Hans.*

Toy Tiger
(COLOR)

Entertaining family comedy, with U's Tim Hovey an engaging moppet star.

Hollywood, April 17.

Universal release of Howard Christie production. Stars Jeff Chandler, Laraine Day, Tim Hovey; features Cecil Kellaway, Richard Haydn, David Jansser, Judson Pratt. Directed by Jerry Hopper. Screenplay, Ted Sherdeman; suggested by a story by Frederick Kohner, Marcella Burke; camera (Technicolor), George Robinson; editor, Milton Carruth; music supervision, Joseph Gershenson. Previewed April 9, '56. Running time, **87 MINS.**

Rick Todd	Jeff Chandler
Gwen Taylor	Laraine Day
Timmie Harkinson	Tim Hovey
James Fusenot	Cecil Kellaway
John Fusenot	Richard Hadyn
Larry Tripps	David Janssen
Mike Wyman	Judson Pratt
"Owly" Kimmel	Butch Bernard
Freddy Doobin	Brad Morrow
Etna	Jacqueline de Wit
Miss Elsie	Mary Field
State Trooper	Robert Anderson

Universal has a most entertaining family comedy in "Toy Tiger," its second screen outing with little Tim Hovey, engaging moppet initially seen in the same company's "Private War of Major Benson." While slanted mostly to strike the fancy of the family trade, the comedy is such that others will get a full share of chuckles, too. With the names of Jeff Chandler and Laraine Day on the adult end, pic shapes as a welcome bill-topper for regular dual situations.

Little Mr. Hovey, breezing through his role with a natural ability, gives the adults a run for their experience and makes this one fun for all. Of course, the way he shows up is due in sizable measure to the manner in which director Jerry Hopper stages the scenes in the amusing script by Ted Sherdeman, suggested by a story by Frederick Kohner and Marcella Burke. Adults Chandler and Miss Day, plus some choice characterizations by Cecil Kellaway, Richard Haydn, as schoolmasters, and others, do their full share to make the film well-rounded, general entertainment.

The good Howard Christie production shifts in scene between a plush New York advertising office and an upstate boarding school for kids. Chandler, art director of the firm and unaware that executive veep Miss Day is a widow with a young son (Hovey) at the school. Circumstance fixes it so that he's dispatched to nearby the chool to woo Judson Pratt, an artist gone arty, back to the advertising fold, and is conned into posing as young Hovey's fictional explorer father, a character the youngster has made up to satisfy a loneliness. Audiences might be able to figure the outcome of all this but it's fun to sit back and participate as the script and players bring it off.

George Robinson's cameras do a good tint job on the lensing, with print by Technicolor, and the art direction and set decoration dress the footage well. Editing keeps the unfoldment smooth and Joseph Gershenson's music supervision provides a fitting background score. *Brog.*

Quincannon, Frontier Scout
(COLOR—SONG)

Stilted stuff from the great outdoors with Tony Martin doffing tux for buckskins. Hard going.

Hollywood, April 17.

United Artists release of Howard W. Koch (Bel-Air) production. Stars Tony Martin, Peggie Castle, John Bromfield, John Smith, Ron Randell; features John Doucette, Morris Ankrum, Peter Mamakos, Ed Hashim. Directed by Lesley Selander. Screenplay, John C. Higgins, Don Martin; camera (De Luxe Color), Joseph F. Biroc; editor, John F. Schreyer; music, Les Baxter; song, Sammy Cahn, Hal Borne. Previewed April 13, '56. Running time, **83 MINS.**

Linus Quincannon	Tony Martin
Maylene Mason	Peggie Castle
Lt. Burke	John Bromfield
Lt. Hostedder	John Smith
Capt. Bell	Ron Randell
Sgt. Calvin	John Doucette
Col. Conover	Morris Ankrum
Blackfoot Sam	Peter Mamakos
Iron Wolf	Ed Hashim

Regulation, and stilted, frontier action is unloosed in "Quincannon, Frontier Scout," and it will work out its destiny as filler material in the mine-run outdoor market. Single gimmick attached to the United Artists presentation is Tony Martin in the title role, in which the singer doffs tux for buckskins, but since he doesn't croon even the title song, there's not much merchandising for ticket sales that will result.

Script by John C. Higgins and Don Martin is one of those affairs that accompanies every bit of action with explanatory dialog. Against a scenically beautiful background, lensed in De Luxe Color near Kanab, Utah, the Bel-Air (Aubrey Schenck-Howard W. Koch) production has a visual attraction that surpasses plot worth. However, despite story and acting deficiencies, it's a passable programmer that should take care of lowercase bill-filling needs.

Martin, who has quit his captaincy in the Army in disgust over a particularly brutal Indian massacre under Custer, is persuaded to undertake a scouting (sort of private eye) detail to find out what happened to a secret shipment of 800 repeating rifles sent to a post on the Bozeman Trail. There ensues some incredible derring-do, in which the writing never permits Lesley Selander's direction to become believable, before Martin is able to expose Ron Randall, post captain, as the traitor who sold out to the redskins.

Martin is not cut out for the type of histrionics required of the lead role. Peggie Castle lends blonde beauty as a gal who had to get to the outpost to check up on whether or not her kid brother had actually been killed in an Indian fight. John Bromfield is a stiffed-neck shavetail requisitioned by Martin for his undercover detail and Randall is a stiffed-lip, teeth-clenched heavy. John Doucette is most believable as a sergeant serving Martin.

Photography by Joseph F. Biroc was not given a good display at the preview, but the scenery came through anyway. Editing by John F. Schreyer and the score by Les Baxter are okay. The title tune, by Sammy Cahn and Hal Borne, is a lesser effort, poorly sung. *Brog.*

Safari
(C'SCOPE—SONG—COLOR)

Victor Mature, Janet Leigh in jungle thriller with Mau-Mau angles for sensationalizing. Okay prospects.

Columbia release of Adrian D. Worker (Warwick) production. Stars Victor Mature, Janet Leigh, John Justin, Roland Culver; features Liam Redmond, Earl Cameron, Orlando Martins, Juma, Lionel Ngakane, Harry Quashie, Slim Harris. Directed by Terence Young. Screenplay, Anthony Veiller; based on a story by Robert Buckner; camera (Technicolor), John Wilcox; editor, Michael Gordon; music, William Alwyn; conducted by Muir Mathieson; played by Royal Philharmonic orchestra; song, Alwyn and Paddy Roberts. Previewed April 3, '56. Running time, **90 MINS.**

Ken	Victor Mature
Linda	Janet Leigh
Brian Sinden	John Justin
Sir Vincent Brampton	Roland Culver
Roy Shaw	Liam Redmond
Jeroge	Earl Cameron
Jerusalem	Orlando Martins
Odongo	Juma
Kakora	Lionel Ngakane
O'Keefe	Harry Quashie
Renegade	Slim Harris
Chief Massai	Cy Grant
Charley	John Wynn
Blake	Arthur Lovegrove
Aunty May	Estelle Brody
Kenny	Christopher Warbey
Wambui	John Harrison
Kikuyu	Glyn Lawson
African	Frank Singuineau
Police Inspector	Charles Hayes
Special Mau Mau	Bartholomew Sketch
District Commissioner	John Cook
Henderson	Bob Isaacs

"Safari" is a jungle thriller, lensed in Africa, that promises a profitable reception in general playdates. CinemaScope and Technicolor dress up the jungle footage and animal scenes, plus giving visual point to the regulation, pulp fiction adventure. For the marquees, the Warwick production being released by Columbia has the familiar names of Victor Mature and Janet Leigh.

Adrian D. Worker produced for Irving Allen's and Albert R. Broccoli's Warwick outfit and makes good use of locales and hunt footage. So does Terence Young's direction in getting as much as possible out of the Robert Buckner story, scripted by Anthony Veiller.

Mature plays a white hunter whose young son is killed by the Mau Mau. He wants to get the leader of the particular group that did the killing but authorities stymie him by lifting his license, until a psychotic British millionaire, Roland Culver, arrives with his fiancee, Miss Leigh, and insists Mature must lead them on a lion hunt. Mature's willing, and by the time the hunt is over, he's gotten his native quarry, as well as won Miss Leigh, who really didn't love Culver, just liked him because he was rich.

The trouping follows the easy path laid out by the plotting, with Mature a stalwart hunter and Miss Leigh acceptable as a blonde in a jungle setting. Culver is properly priggish and bull-headed, faults which gets him killed in the end. John Justin, Liam Redmond, plus such notives as Earl Cameron, Orlando Martins, Juma, a toothy, grinning young lad; Lionel Ngakane, Harry Quashie, and Slim Harris go along with story demands in okay fashion.

"We're On Safari," tune by William Alwyn and Paddy Roberts, is plugged but actually sounds out of tune with the story. Alwyn also did the score, on which Muir Mathieson conducts the Royal Philharmonic orchestra at a thunderous pitch. John Wilcox's lensing, with second unit work by Ted Moore and Fred Ford, editing and other assists are good. *Brog.*

Cette Sacree Gamine
(That Darned Kid)
(FRENCH; C'SCOPE; COLOR)
(Songs; Dance)

Paris, April 10.

Sofradis release of Lutetia-SLPF-Sonodis-SELB production. Stars Brigitte Bardot; features Jean Bretonniere, Raymond Bussieres, Bernard Lancret, Francoise Fabian, Michel Serrault, Misha Auer. Directed by Michel Boisrond. Screenplay, Vadim; camera (Eastmancolor), Jo Brun; editor, Jacques Marel; choreography, George Reich; music, Hendi Crolla, Hubert Rostaing. At Paris, Paris. Running time, **90 MINS.**

Brigitte	Brigitte Bardot
Jean	Jean Bretonniere
Jerome	Raymond Bussieres
Lili	Francoise Fabian
Latour	Bernard Lancret
Inspector	Michel Serrault
Ballet Master	Misha Auer

Lighthearted comedy benefits from an unpretentious production though it is wrapped in the C'Scope dimensions. Akin to the U.S. comedies, plot is slight but it has some engaging, inventive comic bits and unfolds its 90 minutes without a lag. Songs and dances are naive but spring from plotting, rather than being dragged in, an improvement here. In short, this looks like a new trend, with U.S. influence but definite Gallic taste. It may be worth dubbing for dualer C'Scope spots on its simple entertainment values.

Familiar plot has a charm singer taking on the care of a shapely, innocent but trouble-making young girl to help out his esteemed boss, the father of this gamin. The father is sought by the police. She falls for the singer and vice versa, but complications keep them apart until the finale. Among them are a band of counterfeiters operating in the father's club, a talking parrot, the singer's psychoanalyst girl and sundry difficulties caused by the girl's candor.

Michel Boisrond uses a light touch in his direction and he gets plenty of laughs. Brigitte Bardot, now rated a star here, is the spindly but well stacked innocent. Although somewhat ingenuous, her sprightliness and naturalness manage to make her role palatable. She dances well and looks good enough to be the cause of the escapades. Jean Bretonniere is an engaging leading man and lends a pleasant voice to the ordinary songs in the pic. Misha Auer adds yocks as a zany ballet teacher taken to ramming down doors with his head while Raymond Bussieres is a proper, haughty valet. Eastmancolor and C'Scope are well utilized. This looks in for good local returns. Boisrond looms to be a new comedy-situation director to be heard from additionally. *Mosk.*

Vertigine Bianca
(White Vertigo)
(ITALIAN-COLOR)

Rome, April 10.

ENIC release of a Film Luce Istituto production. Official film of the 1956 Winter Olympic Games, under the auspices of the International Olympic Committee. Directed by Giorgio Ferroni. Screenplay, Ferroni and Giorgio Stegani; camera (Ferraniacolor), Rino Filippini, Marco Scarpelli, Enzo Serafin; music, Francesco Lavagnino; editor, Giuliana Attenni. At Metropolitan, Rome. Running time, **105 MINS.**

Italy has come up with an exciting, colorful feature-length document of this year's Winter Olympic Games. It rates a plus in almost every department, and should draw sports-lovers and others to the boxoffice in most countries. Looks good for some special situations in the U.S. though its length appears a handicap.

Director Giorgio Ferroni and his big team of color cameramen have done a top job in covering the sports festival, taking advantage of the color stock and lensing tricks, plus an obviously lavish budget, thereby capturing some of the most beautiful as well as the most exciting footage yet shot at the Games.

While one may object to technique of rapid cuts back and forth between two events, used twice in pic, and to rather inadequate coverage of the figure skating tests (with only a few quick shots of the U.S. winners), the remainder is both exciting and beautiful. Some of the highlights are the closeups of the fatigued endurance skiers struggling up a hill, the near-crash (caught in slowmotion closeup) of the U.S. 2-Bob, steered by Tyler, Toni Sailer's triple-medal descents and some of the most sensational spills seen.

Pic finales with sequence showing the ski jumping, caught from all angles. Lensing under difficult conditions is tops, with a special nod going to Giuliana Attenni, the editor, and her two collaborators for a fine job. Francesco Lavagnino has composed a musical score which strongly contributes to the combined effect. *Hawk.*

Gli Innamorati
(ITALIAN)

Rome, April 10.

Rank release of a Noria Film production. Stars Franco Interlenghi, Antonella Lualdi, Cosetta Greco, Sergio Raimondi; features Gino Cervi, Valerie Moriconi, Oscar Blando, Nino Manfredi. Directed by Mauro Bolognini. Screenplay, Bolognini, Campanile, Franciosa, from story by Campanile and Franciosa; camera, Massimo Sallusti; editor, Otello Colangeli. At Roxy, Rome. Running time, **93 MINS.**

Franco	Franco Interlenghi
Adriana	Antonella Lualdi
Nando	Sergio Raimondi
Marisa	Valeria Moriconi
Otello	Nino Manfredi
Ines	Cosetta Greco
Ines' Husband	Gino Cervi

Small-budgeter, just selected for the Cannes Film Fete, is a pleasant slice of life, cut from one of Rome's colorful popular quarters. It is neatly served up by a young group of filmmakers whose labor of love this obviously is. A word-of-mouth item, it looks a slow starter which can build in depth. Export chances are good for certain markets, but handling is important.

Story treats loves, intrigues and troubles of a Roman neighborhood and its people—mostly its youth—in realistic manner, with a nice sense for development of character notable. There's the soft drink vendor whose involvement with the tavern-keeper's sexy wife is just a means of getting his girl, while the latter accepts the barber's proposal to counter her jealousy. There's the seamstress who never realizes her love for the mechanic until his slap brings her to her senses. There's the young kid whose thievery is cured by his first love, and many other cameos of people living on a single Roman square. Dialogue rings true, action is colorful and often moving. Director Mauro Bolognini has done a fine job with both actors and pacing.

Thesping by large cast is uniformly good, effectively underplayed to suit tone of picture. Besides such vets as Gino Cervi, Antonella Lualdi, and Franco Interlenghi, other fine bits are contributed by Valeria Moriconi, Sergio Raimondi and Nino Manfredi. Location lensing in Roman streets and alleys is well handled by Massimo Sallusti while uncredited musical score is in keeping. Other credits are very good. *Hawk.*

Terror at Midnight

Lightweight programmer for the action market.

Republic production and release; associate producer, Rudy Ralston. Stars Scott Brady, Joan Vohs; features Frank Faylen, John Dehner, Virginia Gregg, Ric Roman, John Gallaudet, Kem Dibbs. Directed by Franklin Adreon. Screenplay, John K. Butler, from story by Butler and Irving Shulman; camera, Bud Thackery; editor, Tony Martinelli; music, R. Dale Butts. Tradeshown, N.Y., April 13, '56. Running time, **70 MINS.**

Neal Rickards	Scott Brady
Susan Lang	Joan Vohs
Fred Hill	Frank Faylen
Lew Hanlon	John Dehner
Helen	Virginia Gregg
Sgt. Brazzi	Ric Roman
George Flynn	John Gallaudet
Nick Mascotti	Kem Dibbs
Speegie	Percy Helton
Lt. Conway	Francis DeSales
Capt. Allyson	John Maxwell

Action and mystery fans will find "Terror at Midnight" passable entertainment. B.o. prospects generally aren't too encouraging. Weakish, too, are the marquee values of stars Scott Brady and Joan Vohs.

Yarn, screenplayed by John K. Butler from a story by himself and Irving Shulman, relates the misfortunes of a girl innocently involved in a hot car ring and a brace of murders. Plot developments offer some minor exploitation angles which exhibs can use for what they're worth.

But for the most part the script varies little from routine action material to be found in the average half-hour telefilm. Brady, a cop just upped to detective sergeant, finds himself in an embarrassing situation when girl friend Miss Vohs turns hit-and-run driver and later becomes a prime suspect in two killings.

Obviously Brady displays some fancy sherlocking to clear his fiancee and bag the real culprits, John Dehner and Kem Dibbs, who head the hot car mob. Intentionally or otherwise much of the story, dialog and performances has a tongue-in-cheek quality that provides more of a mirthful than melodramatic touch.

Prize anti-climactic line comes at the film's finale when Miss Vohs plaintively inquires of Brady: "I'm worried about you, Rick. Does this mean you've lost your sergeant's badge?" In light of that as well as similar lines they're called upon to mouth, both Brady and Miss Vohs do about as well as can be expected.

Routine support is supplied by Frank Faylen, a garage proprietor killed by wife Virginia Gregg when she suspects him of being unfaithful; Dehner and Dibbs are stock heavies and standard characterizations are also turned in by Ric Roman and John Gallaudet, among others, in lesser roles.

Franklin Adreon's direction is okay on the action sequences, camerawork of Bud Thackery is competent as is Walter Keller's art direction and the R. Dale Butts score. Tony Martinelli edited to a tight 70 minutes. Physical values of associate producer Rudy Ralston reflect a modest budget. *Gilb.*

La Meilleure Part
(The Best Part)
(FRENCH-ITALIAN)
(C'SCOPE; COLOR)

Paris, April 10.

Columbia release of Trident-Silver-Noria Films production. Stars Gerard Philipe; features Gerard Oury, Michele Cardoue, Michel Francois, Umberto Spadaro. Directed by Yves Allegret. Screenplay, Jacques Sigurd; camera (Eastmancolor), Henry Alekan; editor, Claude Nicole. At Normandie, Paris. Running time, **95 MINS.**

Perrin .... Gerard Philipe
Micheline .... Michele Cardoue
Engineer .... Gerard Oury
Doctor .... Michel Francois
Worker .... Umberto Spadaro

C'Scope, used in two French films, usually narrows its chances for the U.S. and widens it for home markets unless it is exceptional in entertainment or offbeat values to warrant dubbing. This is because C'Scope limits pix good only for arty situations. This film does not possess the necessary qualifications and Columbia has a risky pic, at best, for any U.S. possibilities.

Film has some fine visual attributes in having been photographed on a dam building site. It concerns the men involved and particularly a devoted engineer who is fighting heart disease as he strives to complete the dam. Strikes, accidents and his health are against him.

Sober pic does not get the needed injection of character to make this dramatically palatable. Director Yves Allegret has given it more documentary than moving style, and the film plods along without the needed lift. Gerard Philipe is fine as the dedicated engineer but never gets a chance to develop his role beyond the sketchy phase. Others are acceptable and technical credits are excellent. *Mosk.*

The Catered Affair

Another television script proves mild in theatre screen form. Drab story. Spotty prospects for Chayefsky story despite strong cast.

Hollywood, April 24.

Metro release of Sam Zimbalist production. Stars Bette Davis, Ernest Borgnine, Debbie Reynolds, Barry Fitzgerald; features Rod Taylor, Robert Simon, Madge Kennedy, Dorothy Stickney, Carol Veazie, Joan Camden, Dan Tobin. Directed by Richard Brooks. Screenplay, Gore Vidal; play, Parry Chayefsky; camera, John Alton; editors, Gene Ruggiero, Frank Santillo; music, Andre Previn. Previewed April 20, '56. Running time, **92 MINS.**

Mrs. Tom Hurley .... Bette Davis
Tom Hurley .... Ernest Borgnine
Jane Hurley .... Debbie Reynolds
Uncle Jack Conlon ...... Barry Fitzgerald
Ralph Halloran .... Rod Taylor
Mr. Halloran .... Robert Simon
Mrs. Halloran .... Madge Kennedy
Mrs. Rafferty .... Dorothy Stickney
Mrs. Casey .... Carol Veazie
Alice .... Joan Camden
Eddie Hurley .... Ray Stricklyn
Sam Leiter .... Jay Adler
Hotel Caterer .... Dan Tobin
Bill .... Paul Denton
Mrs. Musso .... Augusta Merighi

The Bronx bourgeoisie, represented by the Irish Hurley family, is the chief concern of this little comedy - drama originally teleplayed by Paddy Chayefsky, and now put into screen form by Gore Vidal, also from tv, for Metro production. The entertainment is mild, the prospects spotty.

Producer Sam Zimbalist has packed the star ranks of his cast with the names of Bette Davis, Ernest Borgnine, Debbie Reynolds and Barry Fitzgerald so top-of-the-bill bookings generally should be the rule. Overall, the performances are good, and there are occasionally amusing and touching moments in the otherwise talky, mostly drab, affair under Richard Brooks' direction.

The dramatic to-do set up by the plot whirls around Ma Hurley's decision to give her daughter a catered wedding, overruling the daughter's objections and overwhelming the meager savings of taxi-driving Pa Hurley. Script has a repititious quality in the spate of pros and cons unloosed but, eventually, after some unpleasant truths have been spoken, the catered affair is called off, with the mother and father winding up closer than they have ever been. Dominant emotion aroused is one of feeling sorry for everyone concerned, but principally for the daughter, Miss Reynolds, and her fiance, Rod Taylor, both of whom handle their characters very well. As the mother (played on tv by Thelma Ritter), Miss Davis is consistent in performance, if not with her dialect. and proves a strong force on the drama side of the film. Borgnine's scenes as the father have less force with the exception of the moment when he tells his side of a weary marriage to his nagging spouse. Fitzgerald, as a 12-year visiting relative, brogues most of the chuckles and Dorothy Stickney is good as his latter-day romance. Others good include Robert Simon and Madge Kennedy. as Taylor's parents; Joan Camden, a sad matron-of-honor-to-be, and Jay Adler, a cabbie.

A technical oddity created by John Alton's regular-sized, black-and-white photography of the drab Bronx setting and the projection at the preview gave the picture the look of a kinescope, instead of a motion picture. *Brog.*

Unidentified Flying Objects
(DOCUMENTARY)

Carefully documented report on the "flying saucer" investigations, including hitherto secret footage of "saucers" in flight. Interesting, informative and important.

Hollywood, April 23.

United Artists release of a Clarence Greene-Russell Rouse presentation produced by Greene. Directed by Winston Jones. Written by Francis Martin; camera, Howard A. Anderson, Ed Fitzgerald, Bert Spielvogel; editor, Chester Schaeffer; music, Ernest Gold, conducted by Emil Newman. Previewed April 23, '56. Running time, **91 MINS.**

In the wake of a rash of scientifilm subjects dealing with interplanetary travel that has stirred public imagination, producers Clarence Greene and Russell Rouse have scored an authentic beat with the first documented feature film based on the continuing governmental probe into the phenomenon officially known as "Unidentified Flying Objects" or "UFO." Based on official records, and including hitherto secret footage (in color) of "flying saucers" in flight, the film crystallizes the widely-held theory that our skies have been invaded by objects apparently controlled by an intelligent force, the nature of which is totally unknown.

In more sensational terms, "UFO" quietly proves that the "saucers" are real, but it does it without sensationalism. Rather, the producers have injected an almost studiedly documentary flavor that sometimes detracts from the presentation. For while the film is interesting, informative and important, it sometimes tends to obvious theatrics to emphasize its recreation of known events, particularly the appearance of a flight of unidentified objects over Washington, D. C.

Basically, the story is that of Albert M. Chop, onetime newspaperman who became head of the Press Section of the Air Materiel Command, who was directly involved in "Project Bluebook," the Air Force's official designation for the secret investigation of UFO. Also depicted are Captain Edward J. Ruppelt, who headed "Bluebook" and Major Dewey Fournet, Jr., Pentagon liaison officer on the project. All have attested to the accuracy and validity of the events depicted.

A bit overlong at 91 minutes, "UFO" tells the story of the project, of the careful analysis of the hundreds of reports of "sightings" and of the care and research that went into the Air Force's handling of a touchy matter. In addition to the secret footage of "saucers" in action over Utah and Montana, it tells for the first time the story of the Washington "invasion," which was tracked on radar screens but erroneously listed as caused by "air inversion." This error also is cleared up, for the first time in the film in what amounts to a gripping climax.

Unfortunately, in the careful documentation, too much time has been spent on background and almost 40 minutes elapses before the first footage of the "saucers" in action is screened. The feature moves at a quicker tempo from this point.

Born of the fact that Greene himself had seen an unidentified flying object in the sky, the film carefully presents the official findings that 15% of all "sightings" cannot be explained. And it ends

on the three important queries— "What are They? Where are They From? Who Made Them?"

Winston Jones' direction of the recreated scenes have a tendency to be stilted and the camerawork by Howard A. Anderson, Ed Fitzgerald and Bert Spielvogel occasionally has an amateur feel, a circumstance which sometimes heightens and sometimes lessens the documentary flavor.

Like its subject matter, "UFO" seems like a mystery, boxoffice-wise. The believers will hail it and the skeptics will avoid it. If there are still enough people with open minds on the subject left in the country, it should register well.

Open Government approval or disapproval would produce a definite boxoffice effect. A noncommital attitude, however, could relegate "UFO" to the ranks of a seven-day boxoffice wonder. *Kap.*

Godzilla, King of the Monsters
(JAPANESE)

Despite mediocre acting, Japanese import shapes as lusty exploitation entry for that type situation.

Embassy Pictures release of Toho (Tomoyuki Tanaka) production. Stars Raymond Burr f;eatures Takashi Shimura, Momoko Kochi, Akira Takarada. Directed by Terry Morse and Ishiro Honda. Screenplay, Takeo Murata, Ishiro Hinda from original story by Shigeru Kayama; camera, Masao Tamai, Guy Roe; special effects, Eiji Tsuburaya, Akira Watanabe, Hiroshi Mukoyama, Kuichiro Kishida; editor, Terry Morse; music, Akira Ifukube. Previewed N.Y., April 13, '56. Running time, **80 MINS.**

Steve Martin .... Raymond Burr
Dr. Yamane .... Takashi Shimura
Emiko .... Momoko Kochi
Ogata .... Akira Takarada
Dr. Serizawa .... Akihiko Hirata
Hagiwara .... Sachio Sakai
Dr. Tabata .... Fuyuki Murakami
Sieji .... Ren Yamamoto
Shinkichi .... Toyoaki Suzuki
Dr. Tabata's Assistant .. Tadashi Okabe
President of Company .. Toranosuke Ogawa
Security Officer .... Frank Iwanaga

A natural exploitation picture is "Godzilla, King of the Monsters," a Japanese import which Terry Turner and Joe Levine of Boston's Embassy Pictures Corp. picked up in association with Harry Rybnick and Ed Barison. A contemporary "King Kong," it should generate b.o. excitement in houses geared to bally product and its offbeat nature is also worth attention of deluxers harassed by the current product shortage.

Story of a prehistoric monster, who emerges from the sea to devastate Tokyo, provides a field day for special effects lensmen. There's some striking realism as the 400-foot tall "thing" lashes about the Japanese metropolis spewing flames from his mouth, trampling down skyscrapers and uprooting bridges from their foundations.

Yarn, of course, is just so much fantasy. It more than taxes the imagination. Acting, too, is unimpressive particularly thesping of Raymond Burr, one American in

an otherwise all Japanese cast. But these deficiencies are more than offset by the startling special effects which obviously lend themselves to strong promotion.

Much of the dialog has been dubbed into English. In the non-dubbed sequences an English narration handled by Burr adequately explains what's going on. The Takeo Murata-Ishiro Honda screenplay based on an original by Shigeru Kayama hints that hydrogen bomb experiments have activated a prehistoric monster, known to Japanese legend as Godzilla.

When the monster becomes a menace the Japanese government launches an investigation headed by paleontologist Takashi Shimura, his daughter and assistant, Momoko Kochi, her naval officer boy friend, Akira Takarada, and numerous scientists. They're accompanied by Burr, an American newsman. Godzilla, who's impervious to shellfire and high voltage, ultimately is finished off by a secret weapon of scientist Akihiko Hirata.

Joint direction of Terry Morse and Ishiro Honda properly accent the horror sequences which have been excellently lensed by a quartet of special effects cameramen. Balance of the camerawork, filmed by Masao Tamai and Guy Roe, is good. Physical values provided by producer Tomoyuki Tanaka reflect a high budget according to Japanese standards. Music of Akira Hukube, Morse's editing and other technical credits further assist in pointing up this import's elements.
Gilb.

Legends of Anika
(YUGOSLAVIAN)

Sexy Yugoslav import; fair art house b.o. potential.

Grand Prize Films release of Avala Film production. Stars Milena Dapcevic, Bratislav Gribic. Directed by Vladimir Pogacic. Screenplay, Vicko Rasper and Pogacic based on novel by Ivo Andric; camera, Alexander Sekulovic; editor, Milada Raisic-Levi; music, Kresimir Baranovic. At 72nd St. Playhouse, N.Y., April 18, '56. Running time, **85 MINS.**

Anika	Milena Dapcevic
Mihailo	Bratislav Gribic
Jaksa	Severin Bjelic
Khaymckam	Mata Milosevic
Lale	Nirko Milisavljevic

(In Yugoslav; English Titles)

An earthy Yugoslavian import worthy of art house attention is "Legends of Anika." There's nothing subtle about its story of lusts and passions and its production techniques are often crude. But despite the film's shortcomings, its very bluntness is enough to excite the interest of audiences in search of "something different."

Based on a novel by Ivo Andric, script concerns the amatory problems of Bratislav Gribic. A strapping, intelligent youth, he's seduced by a bosomy farmer's wife with a fixation for things carnal. When her clumsy husband intrudes upon the tryst his spouse dispatches him with a knife seized from her frightened guest.

Period is circa 1804 and its indicated that Yugoslav citizens were relatively broad minded in those days. But nevertheless Gribic develops a guilt complex. He travels far afield to think things over as a shepherd. His thoughts occupy him for eight years. But at this point he returns home to find his frustrated childhood sweetheart, Milena Dapcevic, plying the trade of a harlot.

While free with her favors, it's obvious that Miss Dapcevic cherishes only one male. Unfortunately, when this is achieved her half-wit brother slays her in a fit of rage. In this grim and frequently sensuous tale Miss Dapcevic exercises a saucy, blase demeanor that's on par with the eloquence of her flashing eyes and dark wavy hair. It's a strong contrast to Gribic's moody, almost melancholy performance.

Fair support is provided by Severin Bjelic and Mata Milosevic in lesser roles. Flavor and atmosphere of the era are further accented by scenes of several native dances. These, as well as the film's rugged types and terrains, are ably lensed in grim, low-key style by Alexander Sekulovic. Heavy-handed direction of Vladimir Pogacic is in keeping with the dark shadings of this gloomy tale. Sidney Kaufman's English narration and subtitles are adequate.
Gilb.

Jaguar

Poorly written routine jungle yarn for less discriminating playdates. Mickey Rooney as a producer.

Hollywood, April 20.

Republic release of a Mickey Rooney-Maurice Duke production. Stars Sabu; features Chiquita, Barton MacLane, Jonathan Hale, Touch Connors. Directed by George Blair. Screenplay, John Fenton Murray, Benedict Freedman; camera, Bud Thackery; music, Van Alexander; editor, Cliff Bell. Reviewed April 18, '56. Running time, **66 MINS.**

Juano	Sabu
Pita	Chiquita
Steve Bailey	Barton MacLane
Dr. Powell	Jonathan Hale
Marty Lang	Touch Connors
Tupi	Jay Novello
Francisco Servente	Fortunio Bonanova
Garcia Solimos	Nacho Galindo
First Porter	Redwing
Jorge	Pepe Hern
Motilon Boy	Raymond Rosas

This routine yarn about murderous jaguar-men in the Amazon jungle has the sole advantage of Sabu's name for the less discriminating program market. Film has little regard either for entertainment value or logical story construction, and is definitely no credit to Mickey Rooney, whose indie production company made it for Republic.

Sabu plays a young South American who was captured as a small boy in the jungle by a British doctor and raised in civilization, a far cry from his savage Indian ancestry. His great fear is that he is reverting to the jungle savagery, occasioned when he comes under suspicion of brutal murder during an expedition up river to discover oil. He thinks he may have committed three murders while under the influence of a drug without being aware of it, but finally proves his innocence to himself after he is captured by Indians.

The John Fenton Murray-Benedict Freedman screenplay permits no more than stock portrayals by the cast, and George Blair's direction never rise above script. Chiquita, the dancer, is in for romantic interest; Jonathan Hale is Sabu's foster-father and Barton MacLane and Touch Connors wildcat oil prospectors. Technical credits are standard.
Whit.

The Man Who Knew Too Much
(V'VISION—SONGS—COLOR)

Hitchcock pulling suspense strings. Good thriller with James Stewart, Doris Day. Strong b.o. prognosis.

Hollywood, May 1.

Paramount release of Alfred Hitchcock production. Stars James Stewart, Doris Day; features Brenda de Banzie, Bernard Miles, Ralph Truman, Daniel Gelin. Directed by Hitchcock. Screenplay, John Michael Hayes; based on story by Charles Bennett, D. B. Wyndham-Lewis; camera (Technicolor), Robert Burke; editor, George Tomasini; score, Bernard Herrmann; "Storm Cloud Cantata" by Arthur Benjamin and Wyndham-Lewis; songs, Jay Livingston, Ray Evans. Previewed April 23, '56. Running time **119 MINS.**

Ben McKenna	James Stewart
Jo McKenna	Doris Day
Mrs. Drayton	Brenda de Banzie
Mr. Drayton	Bernard Miles
Buchanan	Ralph Truman
Louis Bernard	Daniel Gelin
Ambassador	Mogens Wieth
Val Parnell	Alan Mowbray
Jan Peterson	Hillary Brooke
Hank McKenna	Christopher Olsen
Rien—Assassin	Reggie Nalder
Asst. Mgr.	Richard Wattis
Woburn	Noel Willman
Helen Parnell	Alix Talton
Police Inspector	Yves Brainville
Cindy Fontaine	Carolyn Jones

With Alfred Hitchcock pulling the suspense strings, "The Man Who Knew Too Much" is a good thriller of boxoffice potential. Star team of James Stewart and Doris Day means wicket business, too. Playoff should be profitable.

Hitchcock backstops his mystery in the colorful locales of Marrakesh in French Morocco and in London. While drawing the footage out a bit long at 119 minutes, he still keeps suspense working at all times and gets strong performances from the two stars and other cast members. Incidentally, Hitchcock did the same pic under the same title for Gaumont-British back in 1935. However, VistaVision, Technicolor and plot updating give it a brand spanking new look for present-day audiences.

Stewart ably carries out his title duties—he is a doctor vacationing in Marrakesh with his wife and young son. When he witnesses a murder and learns of an assassination scheduled to take place in London, the boy is kidnapped by the plotters to keep the medico's mouth shut.

Stewart's characterization is matched by the dramatic work contributed by Miss Day as his wife. Both draw vivid portraits of tortured parents when their son is kidnapped. Additionally, Miss Day has two Jay Livingston-Ray Evans tunes to sing, "Whatever Will Be" and "We'll Love Again," which are used storywise and not just dropped into the plot. Same goes for "Storm Cloud Cantata" by Arthur Benjamin and D. B. Wyndham-Lewis, conducted by Bernard Herrmann in an Albert Hall scene in which the assassination is attempted.

Young Christopher Olsen plays the son naturally and appealingly. Scoring strongly as the kidnappers and plotters are Brenda de Banzie and Bernard Miles. Ralph Truman, Scotland Yard official; Daniel Gelin, the secret agent who is murdered; Reggie Malder, the assassin; Yves Brainville and Mogens Wieth are others doing well. Alan Mowbray, Hillary Brooke, Alix Talton and Carolyn Jones contribute an amusing sequence as London friends who make things difficult for the doctor's search for his son.

John Michael Hayes's dialog stands out in the good script he fashioned from a story by Charles Bennett and D. B. Wyndham-Lewis. Color lensing by Robert Burke is another entertainment factor in the film and the background score by Bernard Herrmann abets the suspense unfoldment.
Brog.

Hilda Crane
(COLOR-C'SCOPE)

Soap opera pitched to widescreen and femme audience. Indifferent b.o. outlook marks Herbert Swope Jr. debut as film producer.

20th-Fox release of Herbert B. Swope Jr. production. Stars Jean Simmons, Guy Madison, Jean Pierre Aumont; features Judith Evelyn, Evelyn Varden, Peggy Knudsen, Gregg Palmer, Richard Garrick, Jim Hayward. Directed by Philip Dunne. Screenplay, Dunne; based on play by Samson Raphaelson; camera (Color by DeLuxe), Joe MacDonald; editor, David Bretherton; music, David Raksin. Previewed April 25, '56. Running time, **87 MINS.**

Hilda Crane	Jean Simmons
Russell Burns	Guy Madison
Jacques De Lisle	Jean Pierre Aumont
Mrs. Crane	Judith Evelyn
Mrs. Burns	Evelyn Varden
Nell Bromley	Peggy Knudsen
Dink	Gregg Palmer
Dr. Francis	Richard Garrick
Mr. Small	Jim Hayward
Cab Driver	Sandee Marriot
Caterer	Don Shelton
Maid	Helen Mayon
Clara	Blossom Rock
Minister	Jay Jostyn

Since this kind of weepy, agonized romance has paid off handsomely for powdered soap flakes over the years, there's perhaps no doubting "Hilda Crane" as an entry that'll appeal to the femme sector of the audience, though quality-wise it leaves a lot to wish for. It's initial venture of an alumnus of CBS radio and video, Herbert B. Swope Jr. serving as film producer.

In color and CinemaScope, picture has a slick veneer and an attractive cast. Samson Raphaelson's old play, offers only sporadic excitement in a sea of dialog and has been adapted and directed by Philip Dunne with a modified imagination. The so-called Dunne "touch," which has been in evidence in virtually every picture he's made, is unhappily and strangely lacking in this one.

Jean Simmons, looking attractive as a neurotic young woman with a "past" who returns to her small hometown determined to "conform," gives an okay performance that only occasionally catches a sense of realism. She's at her best when slightly tipsy. On the whole it's difficult to extend her much sympathy. Also, her costumes aren't always flattering.

As in the unsuccessful play, the treatment never comes off on the screen. Just about every trite situation in the book has been thrown into the script, and Miss Simmons suffers through a succession of melodramatic situations from being discovered by her husband in another man's hotelroom to attempting suicide. If her behavior on the whole is strange, it's all very conveniently explained by the fact that her mother didn't love her as a child.

None of the characters in "Hilda Crane" are particularly likable or believable. There's Guy Madison as the husband with guilt feeling about his late mother; Jean Pierre Aumont as a French wolf who weaves some sort of strange spell on Miss Simmons; Judith Evelyn as Mrs. Crane, who disapproves of her daughter's way of life, and Evelyn Varden as Madison's mother who wants to stop the marriage. They all try hard without being able to contribute more than just superficial portraits.

Scene where Miss Varden offers Miss Simmons $50,000 not to go through with the marriage borders on farce. Miss Varden altogether can't make up her mind whether she's there as a heavy or for comedy relief. Peggy Knudsen as Miss Simmons' friend is fresh and cute.

Even nonsophisticates may wonder why 20th bothered making "Hilda Crane." Yet, as a repeat on a long line of dated melodramas, it may be appreciated. Some may find Miss Simmons' soul-searing suffering an inducement to wet their handkerchiefs, which rates as enjoyment, too.

Dunne's script, surcharged with frustrated romance in the Helen Trent tradition, is on the soap opera level and the direction matches it. De Luxe color is good and some of the sets are impressive. Joe MacDonald's lensing keeps in mind that this is a tour-de-force for Miss Simmons whose closeups appear frequently. *Hift.*

Le Couturier De Ces Dames
(FRENCH)

Paris, May 1.

Cinedis release of Cite Film production. Stars Fernandel, Suzy Delair. Directed by Jean Boyer. Screenplay, Boyer, Gerard Carlier, Serge Veber, Jean Manse; camera, Charles Suin; editor, Christian Gaudin. At Paris, Paris. Running time **90 MINS.**

Fernand .... Fernandel
Adreienne .... Suzy Delair
Model .... Francoise Fabian
Count .... Robert Pizani
Tailor .... Berval

Since the unprecedented success of Fernandel in "The Sheep Has Five Legs," U. S. distribs have been looking for the likely followup. This does not seem to be it. Tailormade to suit the comic's talents, it casts him as a cutter who inherits an haute couture establishment and runs it without his jealous wife's knowledge. Basically a bedroom farce, this leads to squabbles as both take up with others. However, face to face in a nitery they realize it is still each other they want and ditch their respective suitors to get together again.

Fernandel and Suzy Delair burlesque their roles of husband and wife while a few comic scenes ensue. Plenty of pulchritude is trotted out during the model sequences. However, the clowning and heavyhanded swipes at Gallic insouciance and at the gayer element in couture circles are rather obvious. On the Fernandel monicker, this could be of value in the U. S. for dualer spots but it lacks the more versatile and unusual comic touches needed to make this an arty possibility. Lensing, direction, editing are just passable. *Mosk.*

Revolt of Mamie Stover
(C'SCOPE—SONGS—COLOR)

Commercial film about a commercial dame in Hawaii.

Hollywood, May 1.

20th-Fox release of Buddy Adler production. Stars Jane Russell, Richard Egan, Joan Leslie; features Agnes Moorehead, Jorja Curtright, Michael Pate, Richard Coogan, Alan Reed, Eddie Firestone, Jean Willes, Leon Lontok. Directed by Raoul Walsh. Screenplay, Sydney Boehm; from the novel by William Bradford Huie; camera (De Luxe Color), Leo Tover; editor, Louis Loeffler; music, Hugo Friedhofer, conducted by Lionel Newman; songs, Tony Todaro, Mary Johnston, and Paul Francis Webster, Sammy Fain. Previewed April 30, '56. Running time, **93 MINS.**

Mamie Stover .... Jane Russell
Jim .... Richard Egan
Annalee .... Jean Leslie
Bertha Parchman ...... Agnes Moorehead
Jackie .... Jorja Curtright
Harry Adkins .... Michael Pate
Capt. Eldon Sumac .... Richard Coogan
Capt. Gorecki .... Alan Reed
Tarzan .... Eddie Firestone
Gladys .... Joan Willes
Aki .... Leon Lontok
Zelda .... Kathy Marlowe
Peaches .... Margia Dean
Bartender .... Jack Mather
Hackett .... Boyd "Red" Morgan
Henry .... John Halloran
Hula Dancers ... Naida Lani, Anita Dano
Dance Hall Girls Dorothy Gordon, Irene Bolton, Merry Townsend, Claire James, Sally Jo Todd, Margarita Camacho
2nd Bartender .... Carl Harbaugh
Photographer .... Richard Collier
Hawaiian Cop .... Max Reid
Hawaiian Waitress.... Mary Lou Clifford
Waitress .... Eugenia Paul
Hostess .... Janan Hart

Even with a Production Code cleanup, "The Revolt of Mamie Stover" still has its naughty implications. Therein lies its prospects. Jane Russell is Mamie and customers will make of it what they will. It's a commercial pic about a commercial lady.

It was no easy matter for scripter Sydney Boehm to tone down William Bradford Huie's outspoken novel about a gal who applied assembly-line, time-card methods to the oldest profession. The story compromises that result are okay. Robust direction by Raoul Walsh keeps the Buddy Adler production on a generally entertaining road. The production is attractively glossed in De Luxe Color and CinemaScope, showing off cast and the lush island locales effectively under Leo Tover's lensing.

After Mamie's booted out of San Francisco for working a confidence game, she hies herself to Honolulu where a dance hostess job awaits. So does a fortune, because Mamie knows how to make her curves grind out dollars. She becomes the belle of the islands. She adds further to the fortune that is in the making by buying real estate unloaded cheaply in the panic that followed Pearl Harbor. That obsession for money doesn't get her love, though, and the compromise ending finds her giving the coin away to return to Mississippi, the state of her origin.

Physically and acting-wise, the Mamie character is a breeze for Miss Russell. Costar Richard Egan, socialite-writer who meets Mamie aboardship enroute to the islands and comes to love her, but not enough to forgive her money drive and the way she earns it, does his work well, too, as does Joan Leslie, in briefly as the society girl who loves him.

Agnes Moorehead is a standout as the tough dancehall proprietor who makes her girls toe the line. Also good are Jorja Curtright, Mamie's friend; Michael Pate, sadist enforcer of Miss Moorehead's rules; Richard Coogan, an officer on the make for Mamie; Eddie Firestone, pint-sized sailor in a running gag through the footage; Alan Reed, Jean Willes, Leon Lontok and others.

Hugo Friedhofer's score is excellent, and there are two good songs, "If You Wanna See Mamie Tonight" by Paul Francis Webster and Sammy Fain, and "Keep Your Eyes on the Hands" by Tony Todaro and Mary Johnston. Former number has been RCA-recorded by the Ames Brothers.

Editing, are direction and other technical assists are firstrate. *Brog.*

Star of India

Featherweight script and wooden acting, makes indifferent second feature.

United Artists release of Raymond Stross production. Stars Cornel Wilde, Jean Wallace; features Herbert Lom, Yvonne Sanson. Directed by Arthur Lubin. Screenplay, Herbert Dalmas; camera, C. Pennington Richards; editor, Russell Lloyd; music, Muir Mathieson. Previewed April 25, '56. Running time, **84 MINS.**

Pierre .... Cornel Wilde
Katrina .... Jean Wallace
Narbonne .... Herbert Lom
Madame de Montespan .... Yvonne Sanson
Emile .... John Slater
Van Horst .... Walter Rilla
Louis XIV .... Basil Sydney
Captain .... Arnold Bell

In color by Technicolor and scenery by Europe, producer Raymond Stross, via a tieup with Rome's Titanus Studios, has manufactured a swashbuckler that buckles into unintentional giggles. For awhile, "Star of India" could be mistaken for a spoof of other motion pictures about 18th century cavaliers and bosomy heroines—a la "Fan Fan the Tulip"— but at the windup there's no doubt that this Cornel Wilde-Jean Wallace costarrer has to be taken straight.

The Herbert Dalmas script doesn't have anything to say on its hackneyed theme. Wilde, hipbooted, lace-frocked, has his fortune filched and later redeemed. Miss Wallace, as the doll in the case, demonstrates neck-bending cleavage, an innocent map and a steel-trap mind. It turns out that she's a spy for Holland, living among the even-then decadent French nobility. With Wilde tightlipped and troubled in his search for an emerald known as the Star of India, and Miss Wallace perfectly wooden as the femme fatale, it's all very square.

The villain, essayed by Herbert Lom, makes the most sense. He robs Wilde of his house and fortune, with the full knowledge and consent of the self-indulgent Louis XIV, when the victim is away fighting for France. Lom has an odd love for siamese cats, preferring them to women and in a character portrayal bordering on the psychotic he manages an arch charm that contributes the picture's one characterization dimension.

Chase scenes across the countryside (it might have been either France or Italy) are beautiful and the movement of the horses and actors are nicely conceived though the color sometimes becomes a mite fuzzy. Muir Mathieson's musical score is workaday, exceeding the sentimental scenes in sentimentality and the action in its own brand of symphonic violence. *Art.*

The Maverick Queen
(NATURAMA—SONG—COLOR)

Introing Republic's anamorphic system. Acceptable Zane Grey western feature for regular outdoor playoffs.

Hollywood, April 30.

Republic release of Joe Kane production. Stars Barbara Stanwyck, Barry Sullivan, Scott Brady, Mary Murphy; features Wallace Ford, Howard Petrie, Jim Davis, Emile Meyer, Walter Sande. Directed by Kane. Screenplay, Kenneth Gamet, DeVallon Scott; based on the Zane Grey novel; camera (TruColor), Jack Marta; editor, Richard L. Van Enger; score, Victor Young; song, Ned Washington, Young; sung by Joni James. Previewed April 27, '56. Running time, **90 MINS.**

Kit Banion .... Barbara Stanwyck
Jeff .... Barry Sullivan
Sundance .... Scott Brady
Lucy Lee .... Mary Murphy
Jamie .... Wallace Ford
Butch Cassidy .... Howard Petrie
A Stranger .... Jim Davis
Malone .... Emile Meyer
Sheriff Wilson .... Walter Sande
Muncie .... George Keymas
Loudmouth .... John Doucette
Peter Callaher .... Taylor Holmes
McMillian .... Pierre Watkin

Republic introduces its anamorphic process, trade-named Naturama, effectively with this western feature. It shapes as acceptable fare for the regular outdoor market and should give a good account of itself in those playdates. As for Naturama, it's excellent, and the 2:35 to 1 aspect ratio makes it adaptable to present squeezelens projection installations in any theatre.

The familiar Zane Grey story, scripted by Kenneth Gamet and DeVallon Scott, was produced and directed on Colorado locations by Joe Kane, with the scenery coming across as a visual asset to the standard western action that ensues. Barbara Stanwyck, as the wicked lady of the title; Barry Sullivan, the Pinkerton man who poses as a baddie to break up the Wild Bunch outlaw gang; Scott Brady, as Sundance, early-west outlaw, and Mary Murphy, orphaned owner of a ranch, answer up to all requirements of the starring parts and do their work well.

The frontier drama moves along at a good action clip as directed by Kane with, as noted, the ruggedly beautiful location sites doing their share to keep up interest in the plot unfoldment. The title tune, by Ned Washington and Victor Young, is effectively sung by Joni James, first behind the title cards and later as a story bridge.

The Grey story tells of a Southern-born woman who comes to the west and makes a fortune tieing in with outlaws while operating a hotel-saloon. She's doing okay until she falls for an undercover Pinkerton man and sacrifices her life to save his so he can settle down with a pretty orphan who owns a struggling ranch. Wallace Ford, the ranch owner's double-crossing cook; Howard Petrie, leader of the Wild Bunch; Jim Davis, the real outlaw whose identity the Pinkerton man assumes; Emile Meyer, Walter Sande, John Doucette and others provide satisfactory characterizations in the outdoor plot.

Jack Marta uses his TruColor cameras expertly and the other technical support is good. *Brog.*

While the City Sleeps

Modernized "stop the press" newspaper yarn; intelligence and authenticity plus strong names spell audience favor.

Hollywood, May 1.

RKO release of a Bert Friedlob Production. Stars Dana Andrews, George Sanders, Thomas Mitchell, Sally Forrest, Rhonda Fleming, Howard Duff, Vincent Price, John Barrymore Jr., James Craig and Ida Lupino; with Robert Warwick, Ralph Peters, Larry Blake, Edward Hinton, Mae Marsh, Sandy White, Celia Lovsky, Pitt Herbert, Vladimir Sokoloff. Produced by Bert Friedlob. Directed by Fritz Lang. Screenplay, Casey Robinson from Charles Einstein novel; camera, Ernest Laszlo; editor, Gene Fowler Jr.; music, Herschel Burke Gilbert. Previewed April 26, 1956. Running time, **99 MINS.**

Mobley .... Dana Andrews
Mildred .... Ida Lupino
Dorothy .... Rhonda Fleming
Loving .... George Sanders
Walter Kyne .... Vincent Price

Griffith .... Thomas Mitchell
Nancy .... Sally Forrest
Kaufman .... Howard Duff
Kritzer .... James Craig
Manners .... John Barrymore Jr.
Amos Kyne .... Robert Warwick
Meade .... Ralph Peters
Police Sergeant .... Larry Blake
O'Leary .... Edward Hinton
Mrs. Manners .... Mae Marsh
Judith Fenton .... Sandy White
Miss Dodd .... Celia Lovsky
Bartender .... Pitt Herbert
George Pilski .... Vladimir Sokoloff

The old-fashioned "stop the presses" newspaper yarn has been updated with intelligence and considerable authenticity, and further brightened with crisp dialog from the pen of Casey Robinson. Presence of an "all-star" cast of 10 good marquee names also helps.

Robinson's screen adaptation of of Charles Einstein's novel weaves several story lines together. Among them are the murderous activities of a homicidal maniac, played by John Barrymore Jr.; a "Patterns"-like scramble for power among the top brass of a newspaper empire, after the top man dies; and a good-natured love story between the paper's Pulitzer-prize winning top reporter, played by Dana Andrews, and Sally Forrest, the secretary of one of the contestants.

When the empire's chieftain, played by Robert Warwick, dies, his insecure playboy son, enacted by Vincent Price, decides to set up a new top exec post for grabs. Contenders are three; Tom Mitchell, the canny, tough editor of the keystone paper; George Sanders, suave and ruthless head of the empire's wire service; and James Craig, dapper photo bureau chief, who's also playing extra-curricular footsie with the boss' wife, Rhonda Fleming.

Price lets it be known that the one to crack the wave of murders being committed by Barrymore gets the job. Sanders and Mitchell commence heartily to cut each other's throats, while Craig puts the pressure, literally and figuratively, on Miss Fleming.

Mitchell enlists Andrews' help and Andrews, in turn, enlists boyhood buddy Howard Duff, a shrewd police lieutenant. Andrews and Duff use Miss Forrest as bait, but Barrymore instead almost murders Miss Fleming in what used to be described as a "love nest," across the hall from Miss Forrest's apartment, before he's caught.

Mitchell sends Ida Lupino, Sanders' opportunistic g.f. and the paper's sob sister, to interview the intended victim, and she spots the real identity. With this, Price weakly gives Craig the top spot to quiet the scandal. Andrews tells him off and hies off to a honeymoon with Miss Forrest, whereupon Price reverses himself, puts Mitchell in the top spot, and sends Craig off on a worldwide "good-will" tour. At pic's end, he's paging Andrews at the honeymoon hideaway to make him managing editor, but Andrews, in a twist on "The Front Page," muffles the phone to consummate his marriage.

Plot intricacies are deftly interwoven, with director Fritz Lang doing a topflight job of balancing the ingredients without dragging the pace. Sex is treated humorously and lightly, with patches of sophisticated dialog highlighting the mutual yearnings of Miss Forrest and Andrews, as well as Miss Lupino's harder-boiled approach. Funniest scene in pic has Miss Lupino attempt to seduce a drunken and half-willing Andrews, on Sanders' behest.

Toplining cast works well together, with each in turn getting his inning. All are to be commended equally for skillful acting, but Barrymore, perhaps hampered by comparatively less footage, relies too much on eye-rolling histrionics to get his dramatic points across. In bits, Warwick, Ralph Peters, Mae Marsh, Sandy White and Vladimir Sokoloff are especially praiseworthy.

Lensing of Ernest Laszlo is of fine quality throughout and Herschel Burke Gilbert's music is a definite asset. All other technical credits show careful craftsmanship. *Kove.*

Bhowani Junction
(COLOR-C'SCOPE)

Adventure yarn with serious overtones played against realistic Pakistan setting. Action plus Ava Gardner and Stewart Granger make for solid b.o. prospects.

Metro release of Pandro S. Berman production. Stars Ava Gardner, Stewart Granger. Directed by George Cukor. Screenplay, Sonya Levien and Ivan Moffat from novel by John Masters; camera (Eastman color), F. A. Young; editors, Frank Clarke, George Boemler; music supervision, Miklos Rozsa. Previewed in New York April 25, '56. Running time, 110 MINS.
Victoria Jones .... Ava Gardner
Col. Rodney Savage ...... Stewart Granger
Patrick Taylor .... Bill Travers
Surabhai .... Abraham Sofaer
Ranjit Kasel .... Francis Matthews
Govindaswami .... Marne Maitland
Ghanshyam .... Peter Illing
Thomas Jones .... Edward Chapman
The Sadani .... Freda Jackson
Lt. Graham McDaniel .... Lionel Jeffries
Ted Dunphy .... Alan Tilvern

A lot has been said on the pros and cons of Hollywood's passion for taking its widescreen cameras to the four corners of the world in search of atmosphere. To make "Bhowani Junction," based on the John Masters novel, Metro went to Pakistan to shoot a film about India. The journey has paid rich dividends, for the sense of realism in the film is one of the best things about it.

"Bhowani Junction," starring Ava Gardner as an Anglo-Indian, and Stewart Granger as a British colonel who falls in love with her, is a horse of many colors, not the least of which is the very excellent Eastman color which reproduces the turbulent backgrounds with vivid clarity and impact. Picture goes off in quite a few directions, ranging from romance and action to a half-hearted attempt to explain the Indians and a more serious effort to dramatize the social twilight into which the British withdrawal from India tossed a small group of people who were of mixed Indian and British blood.

One may quarrel in which of these areas director George Cukor and his performers are most at home, or which will most appeal to unsophisticated American audiences. There's little doubt, however, that—with the beauteous Miss Gardner parading in a lush native and European costumes, and undergoing a variety of treatments ranging from kissing to attempted rape to being gagged and bound by the Communist villain-"Bhowani Junction" will have its following. It's uneven in pace, and at times overly melodramatic where sensitivity might be called for, but it's full of exploitable angles.

Story has Miss Gardner as the half-caste returning home to an India seething with discontent and boiling with riots prior to the departure of the British. At Bhowani Junction, a railroad center, she meets Granger who's been sent to command a security detail to guard the rail line against Communist saboteurs. Miss Gardner thinks she loves Bill Travers, the local rail superintendent, also an Anglo-Indian. She's soon torn between being European and Indian, kills a British lieutenant who's trying to rape her and is temporarily saved by the Communist boss, Peter Illing. She finds that being Indian gives her no peace-of-mind and, after a series of adventures, including an exciting chase, decides to be no more than herself. There's a romantic ending.

Scripters Sonya Levien and Ivan Moffat bit off a big piece when they tackled "Bhowani Junction." In some respects, they succeeded very well. In others, partly due to Miss Gardner's rhetorical limitations, they failed. Some of the dialog sounds more like a textbook on India and lacks conviction. Also, the character of the girl never emerges quite clearly, even though her predicament of being caught between two races is given a graphic illustration. Story, told in one long flashback, is narrated by Granger.

Director Cukor, in staging his crowd scenes, achieved some magnificent effects and F. A. Young's lensing is firstrate. The milling, sweating, shouting crowds, egged on by Red agents, are almost frighteningly real and the Cinema-Scope screen comes alive with an abundance of movement. Scene involving the train wreck is a wow and so is the half-humorous episode when the Indian Congress leader and his followers form human obstacles on the rails and are moved by Granger via a cruel device.

Miss Gardner proves once again that she's one of the screen's most attractive stars. While she's not always lensed flatteringly, she looks stunning most of the time, particularly in her Indian costumes. (And since when do Indian women run around in bare midriffs?). Miss Gardner's thesping, particularly in the emotional scenes, isn't always up to par, but she gets by with her looks.

Granger cuts a manly and restrained figure as the Britisher. Travers as the Anglo-Indian who feels more British than Indian does very well with a limited part; Francis Matthews is excellent as the Indian who wants Miss Gardner to return to his race; Peter Illing as the Red leader is properly menacing without overdoing it; Freda Jackson gives a cold fury to the role of Matthews' nationalist mother in league with the Communist boss; Lionel Jeffries as the leering lieutenant etches an oily portrayal. In other parts, Abraham Sofaer as the Congress leader, Marne Maitland, Edward Chapman and Alan Tilvern are very well cast.

Since no picture can be everything to all men, "Bhowani Junction" necessarily will disappoint some and please others. It's doubtful that it will contribute much to Americans' knowledge of India and its people. Indeed, the Indians may object to it. But it treats with a serious problem of identification and candycoats its lesson with plenty of colored (and well familiar) substance. As a contribution to Hollywood's own wide-wide world safari, it's definitely a notch above the norm. It could stand tighter editing. *Hift.*

Magic Fire
(MUSIC—COLOR)

European backgrounds, Wagner music but poor entertainment. Badly miscast male lead hampers. Prospects unpromising.

Hollywood, April 27.
Republic release of William Dieterle production. Stars Yvonne de Carlo, Car-

los Thompson, Rita Gam, Valentina Cortese, Alan Badel; features Peter Cushing, Frederick Valk, Gerhard Riedmann, Eric Schumann. Directed by Dieterle. Screenplay, Bertita Harding, E. A. DuPont, David Chantler; based on the Bertita Harding novel; camera (TruColor), Ernest Haller; editor, Stanley Johnson; musical supervision, Erich Wolfgang Korngold; conductor, Alois Melichar; opera scenes staged by Prof. Rudolf Hartmann, Munich soloists, orchestra and choir from the Bavarian State Opera. Previewed April 24, '56. Running time, **94 MINS.**

Minna .... Yvonne de Carlo
Frank Liszt .... Carlos Thompson
Cosima .... Rita Gam
Mathilde .... Valentina Cortese
Richard Wagner .... Alan Badel
Otto Wesendonk .... Peter Cushing
Minister von Moll......... Frederick Valk
King Ludwig II......Gerhard Riedmann
Hans von Buelow .... Eric Schumann
August Roeckel .... Robert Freytag
King of Saxonia.......Heinz Klingenberg
Meyerbeer .... Charles Regnier
Pfistermeister .... Fritz Rasp
Magdeburg .... Kurt Grosskurth
Robert Hubner .... Hans Quest
Michael Bakunin .... Jan Hendriks

Richard Wagner's music is the chief asset of this Republic release, but is not enough to carry the film. It's neither exceptional art house fare nor straight appeal stuff. Resultantly overall grossing potential is unpromising.

Produced and directed at actual historical locations in Europe by William Dieterle, film does have "interesting" settings against which to tell the Wagner story from the time he was 21 until his death. Music-wise, under the supervision of Erich Wofgang Korngold, soundtrack comes off well, but the scripting and acting that tie the score together fail to measure up so the entertainment is very uneven.

Alan Badel plays Wagner with an effete sneer, making it hard to believe that here was a man with the masculinity to attract women and earn himself the reputation of a great lover. (Wagner was a stormy petrel in politics, musical circles and the bedroom, a supreme egotist and genius of the 19th Century who contributed immortal music to the world.)

Yvonne de Carlo, as Wagner's first wife; Rita Gam, as his last wife, and Valentina Cortese, as a patroness who inspired "Tristan and Isolde," contribute to the romantic passages, but, other than Miss Gam, are not very effective. Carlos Thompson, as Franz Liszt, completes the star names.

A profusion of excerpts from Wagner's major works are excellently staged, from "Flying Dutchman" through "Parsifal," under the baton of Alois Melichar. Opera scenes were staged by Prof. Rudolf Hartmann, Munich soloists, orchestra and choir from the Bavarian State Opera and are colorful moments in the footage. Use of TruColor lensing by Ernest Haller sharpens scenic values of the actual location scenes that background the script by Bertita Harding, E. A. DuPont and David Chantler, which was based on Miss Harding's novel. *Brog.*

Crowded Paradise

Hume Cronyn, Nancy Kelly starred in meller of Puerto Rican problems in New York City. Well-made indie.

Tudor Pictures release of Ben Gradus production. Stars Hume Cronyn, Nancy Kelly, Frank Silvera, Enid Rudd. Directed by Fred Pressburger. Screenplay, Arthur Forrest, Marc Connelly; camera, Boris Kaufman; editor, Rita Roland; music, David Broekman; special musical numbers, Broekman, Terry Stern, William Gonzalez, Rafael Alers. Tradeshown in N.Y., May 4, 1956. Running time, **94 MINS.**

George Heath .... Hume Cronyn
Louise Heath .... Nancy Kelly
Papa Diaz .... Frank Silvera
Felicia Diaz .... Enid Rudd
Juan Figueroa .... Mario Alcalde
Big Man .... Stefan Schnabel

"Crowded Paradise," a tale of Puerto Ricans in Manhattan, has name legit people, has been nicely directed by Fred Pressburger, adequately produced in almost documentary style by Ben Gradus, apparently the latter's first screen effort. Film is a closeup of living conditions in part of New York's upper East Side and contains plenty of suspense and action.

As an arty theatre entry, the film seems ready-made if for no other reason than the superb performances contributed by Hume Cronyn and Nancy Kelly. Mario Alcade makes so much of his role of the recently-arrived Puerto Rican that he promises to be heard from in the future.

Picture naturally should attract many former P.R. residents in cities where there is a large population of such people. Added selling angle is the fact that this was photographed by Boris Kaufman, winner of an Oscar in 1954 for his work on "On The Waterfront." His lensing is a high spot of this vehicle.

Story of the young, handsome Puerto Rican boy (Alcalde) who arrives in New York City set on conquering it and marrying Felicia Diaz (Miss Rudd), follows a rather familiar cinematic pattern. Yet Fred Pressburger's direction make the yarn realistic rather than a pat screen fable.

The director has skillfully kept the two themes boiling—the effort of the boy to get a job so he can wed and the harsh existence of Mrs. Heath (Miss Kelly) as the blind wife of the sex-crazed building superintendent Cronyn. The two threads of plot collide violently when the latter decides to disrupt the wedding with a bomb. Cronyn has a despicable role and makes it one of concentrate villainy.

Miss Rudd as Puerto Rican's youth's bride-to-be does so well that she hints future screen roles of bigger stature. Frank Silvera is excellent as her father. Stefan Schnabel, Carlos Montalban and Santos Ortega head a big supporting cast. David Broekman's music is timely and supplies strong background buildup.

Rita Roland's editing is topflight. The screenplay of Arthur Forrest an Marc Connelly joints up the Puerto Rican problem in Manhattan without too much originality or attempting any clear-cut solution of the same. N.Y. City officials perhaps will be far from happy over some of the scenes or the closeups of ramshackle apartment structures. *Wear.*

The March Hare
(BRITISH-C'SCOPE-COLOR)

Colorful Irish racing yarn adapted from novel should interest horselovers but nothing original in story or treatment.

London, May 1.

British Lion release of a B.&A. production. Stars Peggy Cummins, Terence Morgan, Wilfrid Hyde White, Martita Hunt and Cyril Cusack. Directed by George More O'Ferrall. Screenplay, Gordon Wellesley, Allan MacKinnon from novel "Gamblers Sometimes Win" by Captain Field; camera, Pack Hildyard; editor, Gordon Pilkington; music, Philip Green. At Odeon Theatre, Leicester Square, London. Running time, **85 MINS.**

Pat Maguire .... Peggy Cummins
Sir Charles Hare ...... Terence Morgan
Lady Anne .... Martita Hunt
Lazy Mangan .... Cyril Cusack
Colonel Keen ...... Wilfrid Hyde White
Capt. Marlow .... Derrick De Marney
Fisher .... Charles Hawtrey
Bridget .... Maureen Delaney
Hardwick .... Ivan Samson
Maguire .... Macdonald Parke
Nils Svenson .... Peter Swanwick
Tim Doughty .... Charles Wade
Connor .... John Gilbert
Joe Duffy .... Frad Johnson
Slater .... Bernard Rook
Insurance Braker......Reginald Beckwith
Doctor .... Stringer Davis
Commissionaire .... Clem Lister

A leisurely unreeled racetrack yarn with plenty of local color and an international love story interwoven to make a conventional linking thread. It has some firstrate shots of classic race meetings, and with the usual crook plans to provide additional excitement at the winning post, runs true to pattern. It should prove attractive entertainment for the horse lover.

Most of the background is in Ireland, where a reckless young baronet gambles away his ancestral home and racing stables. Mistaken for a groom by the new owner's daughter, an American teenager, he stays on. A protracted love affair develops. It only acts as a subsidiary interest to the raising and final triumph of a young colt, bought in secret by a sympathetic aunt as a surprise for her nephew.

Pic is relieved from tedium by the rich, natural performance of Cyril Cusack, as a besotted old stablehand whose uncanny influence over the horse he has reared from a foal results in his triumph in the Derby despite a fixed jockey, and all the trimmings.

Peggy Cummins is freshly appealing as the girl almost bypassed for a nag while Terence Morgan makes her a romantic partner. Martita Hunt registers her forthright personality as the aunt while Wilfrid Hyde White displays his characteristic urbanity as her platonic aider and abetter.

In addition to the most impressive panorama of Derby Day yet seen, the Irish countryside is given full flavor through CinemaScope. Pictorially the picture ranks higher than its subject matter. *Clem.*

Charley Moon
(BRITISH-COLOR)

London, May 1.

Colin Lesslie production of a British Lion release. Stars Max Bygraves, Dennis Price and Michael Medwin. Directed by Guy Hamilton. Screenplay, Leslie Bricusse; camera, Jack Hildyard; editor, Bertie Rule; music, Francis Chagrin. At London Pavilion, London. Running time **92 MINS.**

Charley Moon ....Max Bygraves
Harold Armytage .... Dennis Price
Alf Higgins .... Michael Medwin
Mary Minton ....Florence Desmond
Angel Dream .... Shirley Eaton
Rose ....Patricia Driscoll
Miller Moon .... Charles Victor
Vicar ....Reginald Beckwith
Bill ....Cyril Raymond
Stewart .... Peter Jones
Monty Brass ....Newton Blick
Solly Silvers ....Vic Wise
Theatre Manager ....Lou Jacobi

Main interest in this modest British production centers on the introduction of Max Bygraves to the screen as a starring personality. A top local name in revue and vaudeville, who played in America a few years back with Judy Garland, he has a winning personality as well as a generous share of talent. His name value alone will give a handy b.o. lift to the pic in the domestic market. Overseas, this is something else again.

Entire subject is designed to exploit the Bygraves personality. Story built around him gives the star the opportunities he needs. And although there are prominent local actors in the cast, it is, to all intents and purposes, a one-man picture.

The story focuses on two Army recruits (Dennis Price and Max Bygraves) who link up in civilian life as a double act, starting off in thirdrate vaudeville and moving up to smalltime pantomime. Then Bygraves is picked by a manager and is soon heading for West End stardom. When his big break comes he makes the grade, but after a comparatively short while in the theatre, he runs afoul of an unruly audience, abruptly terminates his career and returns to the country village where his faithful girl friend still awaits him.

Yarn allows for a number of modest scale production numbers, particularly in scenes from their vaude and panto dates. Bygraves sings his way pleasantly through all of these, with adequate assistance from other members of the cast. Price gives an immaculate study of the pompous smalltime actor with big ideas. Michael Medwin does nicely in as an Army corporal who starts Bygraves on his professional career. Patricia Driscoll provides the modest femme interest awhile and Shirley Eaton and Florence Desmond have minor roles as actresses who appear in the Bygraves shows. *Myro.*

Zanzabuku
(Documentary-Trucolor)

Jungle documentary, with excellent action shots, weak narrative.

Republic release of Lewis Cotlow production. Narrated by Bob Danvers-Walker. Written by Ronald Davidson; camera, Fred Ford, David Mason, Fred Ford Jr., John Coquillon; editor, Eric Boyd-Perkins; music, Ivor Slaney. Previewed, May 3, '56. Running time, **64 MINS.**

Lewis Cotlow took four cameramen, much film and a couple of trucks, and, with the aid of various professional hunters, made an eight-month "Zanzabuku" (dangerous safri) through Tanganyika, Uganda, Kenya and Belgian Congo for some crack pictorial results. Trucolor was helpful in establishing the brilliance and subtlety of jungle scenery. For the average stay-homer crew of cameramen, including Cotlow himself, seem to have been daring fellows in getting as close as they did for those shots of lions, elephant herds and charging rhinos and hippos.

If photography is absorbing during most of the 64 minutes. The narration—though excellently read by resonant Britisher Bob Danvers-Walker—is written in such a way by Ronald Davidson that it's often better geared to juves than adults.

Kids should get a kick out of a captured baby lion, out of monkeys clambering up cameras and out of the primitive rites in which Hartley's son and another native boy took part. Again, however, the off-screen chatter fails to keep pace with the visual stuff. Here as elsewhere, Davidson's writing is faintly supercilious, explaining in excessive detail what the eye could readily capture on its own.

Camera was blurry during some of the shots taken from the trucks, racing over the bumpy plains, but the action more than compensated. Ivor Slaney original music is topnotch. *Art.*

Nightmare

Murder-under-hypnosis slant with Edward G. Robinson. Below par program fare.

United Artists release of Pine-Thomas-Shane production. Stars Edward G. Robinson, Kevin McCarthy, Connie Russell; features Virginia Christine, Rhys Williams, Gage Clarke, Barry Atwater, Marian Carr, Billy May and his orchestra. Directed by Maxwell Shane. Screenplay, Shane, from Cornell Woolrich novel; camera, Joe Biroc; editor, George Gittens. Previewed in New York May 9, '56. Running time, **89 MINS.**

Rene .... Edward G. Robinson
Stan .... Kevin McCarthy
Gina .... Connie Russell
Sue .... Virginia Christine
Torrence .... Rhys Williams
Belnap .... Gage Clarke
Warner .... Barry Atwater
Madge .... Marian Carr
Louie Simes .... Billy May

Name of Edward G. Robinson plus the appeal of Connie Russell for the younger set may save this routine thriller. Though it starts out with a strong promise, and throughout the film there are moments of tension, "Nightmare" rates not much more than "E" for effort.

Trouble is that picture emerges as something one has the feeling of having seen many times before. It's the old saw about the fellow who has a nightmare in which he dreams he has killed someone. When he wakes up, he finds evidence that he actually committed the crime, but he can't find anyone to believe him.

Eventually, of course, it turns out that his "dream" was reality; only he did what he did under hypnosis. With Robinson, as a sleuth, ferreting out all the dirty work, there's a happy ending.

Part of the trouble lies in the editing by George Gittens. A couple of times there are fadeouts seemingly leading into flashbacks, only they never prove to be anything but trick effects. Lensing, incidentally, by Joe Biroc, at times catches an unusual quality in creating moods and is distinctly on the plus side of the pic.

As the highstrung musician who kills under the hypnotist-criminal's spell, Kevin McCarthy is properly distraught in a part that really doesn't leave him much leeway. He's in constant emotional turmoil and even has to go through an attempted suicide routine. All things considered, McCarthy does surprisingly well with the role.

Robinson, the tough-as-nails cop with the soft heart, who's married to McCarthy's sister, etches a less than convincing portrait. He's neither at his best nor at his worst. Connie Russell is obviously more at home before a mike singing than in dramatics before the camera, but she's pretty and appealing as McCarthy's confused sweetheart. In a brief part, Marian Carr stands out and might be noted as a comer. Rhys Williams is bluff as a sheriff's deputy and Virginia Christine is adequate as Robinson's wife. Gage Clarke plays the villain.

Maxwell Shane's script and direction aren't of much help to this entry. Dialog has its crisp moments, but on the whole it fails to convince. Musical backgrounds, with a haunting jazz tune (it's connection with McCarthy is never adequately explained), help underscore the New Orleans locale. They're played effectively by Billy May and his band, with May figuring briefly in the dramatics. Miss Russell delivers her numbers in fine style. *Hift.*

Away All Boats
(V'VISION-COLOR)

Sprawling wartime Navy adventure. If strongly sold may override story deficiencies. Jeff Chandler starred.

Universal release of Howard Christie production. Stars Jeff Chandler, George Nader and Julia Adams. Directed by Joseph Pevney. Screenplay, Ted Sherdeman from the novel "Away All Boats" by Kenneth M. Dodson; camera (Technicolor), William Daniels; special photography, Clifford Stine; special action scenes directed by James C. Havens; editor, Ted J. Kent; music, Frank Skinner. Previewed in N.Y., May 1, '56. Running time, **114 MINS.**

Captain Jeb Hawks .... Jeff Chandler
Lt. Dave MacDougall ...... George Nader
Nadine MacDougall .... Julie Adams
Commander Quigley .... Lex Barker
Doctor Bell .... Keith Andes
Lt. Fraser .... Richard Boone
Ensign Kruger .... William Reynolds
Lt. Mike O'Bannion ...... Charles McGraw
Alvick .... Jock Mahoney
Old Man .... John McIntire
Chief "Pappy" Moran ...... Frank Faylen
Lt. Sherwood .... Grant Williams
Lt. Robinson .... Floyd Simmons
Ensign Twitchell .... Don Keefer
Lt. Randall .... Sam Gilman

Having clicked with the Army-themed "To Hell and Back," Universal apparently hoped the Navy-slanted "Away All Boats," would be a case of lightning striking twice. That's doubtful for "Boats" is a big, sprawling, episodic war adventure. Its action elements are tense and exciting, but as a whole the film lacks cohesion and an acceptable point of view. The introduction of an extraneous flashback romance, obviously aimed at the femme trade, hinders rather than aids the story telling.

"Boats," however, has a chance of overcoming these production handicaps via extensive and hard-selling campaign now under way. For marquee value, only Jeff Chandler's name stands out.

Perhaps "Boats" main fault is that it attempts to cover too much. Based on Kenneth M. Dodson's novel, the Howard Christie Vista-Vision production follows the World War II adventures of the U.S.S. Belinda, an attack transport. It picks it up at its shipyard mooring and follows the Belinda through its shakedown cruise, its training period in the Pacific, its landing actions, and its successful and courageous fight against Japanese Kamikaze attacks.

Combined with the ship's adventures, the Ted Sherdeman screenplay aims to give an account of the men involved in the actions. The task apparently is overwhelming, for the crew is large and all that the viewer obtains is small vignettes, some of them sharply etched; others merely sketchy and undeveloped. The primary focus is on the ship's captain, played by Jeff Chandler, and George Nader, as one of his chief aides.

Chandler's role is to convey the loneliness and responsibility of command. Mostly standoffish, he occasionally lets his guard down to reveal a sense of sensitivity but, in the main, he strains to remain emotionally detached from his officers and crew. Nader, as a former Merchant Marine captain now relegated to taking orders, is the efficient and brave officer who completely understands the captain's problems.

Other members of the crew include Lex Barker, as a socialite officer new to sea duty who eventually wins respect via battle exposure; Richard Boone, Charles McGraw, and Sam Gilman, as hardened sea officers; Don Keefer as a bumbling ensign; James Westerfield as Chief Carpenter's Mate; George Dunn as a naive enlisted man, and Kendall Clark as a finicky officer. There are also many other assorted types of officers and men, each of whom reacts differently to the various problems that confront a warship in enemy water. Julia Adams, as the wife of Nader, is the only femme in the cast.

There are many incidents—all of which take place in the regular line of duty of the crew; accidents, mistakes (firing on friendly planes), deaths in battle, boat drills, restlessness of the crew on not receiving mail and not obtaining shore leave in a populated area. The captain turns the crew's bitterness on himself by adopting certain eccentricities — acquiring a pet monkey and ordering the building of a personal sailing sloop for "yachting" when the ship is not engaged. He employs this method to set himself up as the focus of "hate" to prevent the crew from battling among themselves.

The best footage is the Kamikaze attacks. It is filmed so expertly that the audience feels that it is a member of the crew as the Japanese suicide planes plunge on the deck. William Daniels' VistaVision lensing proves helpful in the coverage and Clifford Stine's special effects are outstanding.

Performances, on the whole, meet the needs of the story. Chandler is properly taciturn and troubled as the captain and Nader is convincing as his assured assistant. There is an especially standout bit by George Dunn as a Will Stockdale ("No Time For Sergeants") type of hillbilly character oblivious to the rules of Navy discipline.

"Away All Boats" does a good public relations job for the Navy, although it occasionally lapses into cliche heroics and embarrassing sentimentality. *Holl.*

Invitation to the Dance
(COLOR)

Tardy release of offbeat but interesting all-dance (no dialog) feature with Gene Kelly and group of ballet names. Good art house entry but nervous boxoffice bet generally.

Metro release of Arthur Freed production. Stars Gene Kelly, Tamara Toumanova, Igor Youskevitch, Claire Sombert, Carol Haney, Diana Adams, Belita. Direction and choreography by Kelly. Camera (Technicolor), F. A. Young and Joseph Ruttenberg; music, Andre Previn, Jacques Ibert, and Roger Eden adaptation of Rimsky-Korsokov; cartoon sequences by Fred Quimby, William Hanna and Joseph Barbera; editors, Raymond Poulton, Robert Watts, and Adrienne Fazan; music conducted by Previn, John Hollingsworth, and Johnny Green. Previewed in N.Y., May 2, '56. Running time, **93 MINS.**

The Lover .... Igor Youskevitch
The Loved .... Claire Sombert
The Clown .... Gene Kelly

"Ring Around the Rosy"

Gene Kelly, Igor Youskevitch, Tommy Rall, David Paltenghi, Claude Bessy, Tamara Toumanova, Diana Adams, Belita, Daphne Dale, Irving Davies.

"Sinbad the Sailor"

Scheherazade .... Carol Haney
The Genie .... David Kasday
Sinbad .... Gene Kelly

"Invitation to the Dance," a full-length dance feature, is a bold and imaginative experiment in film-making. Through the medium of the dance alone, producer Arthur Freed and director-choreographer-performer Gene Kelly tell three separate stories. There is no dialog. Just ballet music, colorful costumes, and skillful photography. Admitting (1) some dull stretches and (2) that as a whole "Invitation to the Dance" is a credit to the art of motion pictures the question remains, is it boxoffice?

M-Gs waiting almost a year before placing the picture in release indicates that is a "nervous" film. It'll attract the balletomanes and other devotees of the art houses, but its chances in general situations are slim. It'll take hard selling even in the specialized houses. The word-of-mouth comment will be favorable but not ecstatic. Broken up into separate units, individual sections of "Invitation" might prove appealing to general audiences as two-reelers.

Kelly has assembled a crew of outstanding hoofers, including such experts as Tamara Toumanova, Claire Sombert, Carol Haney, Diana Adams, Igor Youskevitch, and Belita. Standout sequence is the middle entry, "Ring Around the Rosy." Using the children's song and game as the teeoff, the dance story to Andre Previn's music follows in the fashion of "La Ronde" the career of a bracelet as it changes hands from husband to wife to artist to model to crooner and to others in the perennial game of love. The bracelet finally gets back to the wife, but the interim is sparked by fascinating dancing and imaginative photography.

The opening number is similar to the Pagliacci theme as the clown, played by Kelly, is frustrated in his unrequited love for the beautiful ballerina (Miss Sombert) who only has eyes for the fearless tightrope walker, played by Youskevitch. The final sequence is a combination of live action and animations, the cartoon sequences being provided by Fred Quimby, William Hanna and Joseph Barbera. Carol Haney is seen only briefly as Scheherazade in this number, titled "Sinbad the Sailor."

It follows the adventures of an American sailor who buys a magic lantern at an exotic bazaar. The genie in the person of moppet David Kasday guides the American tar through strange experiences. There are a number of sparkling dance routines as Kelly, as the American sailor, terps away with the cartoon characters, including dragons, a fairy princess, and menacing Arabian Night guards. Although outwardly the most creative of the three numbers, "Sinbad" tends to be overlong and repetitous.

Kelly appears in all three of the dance stories and he, along with the other terpers, come off excellently in the dance-pantomime offerings. The musical accompaniments by Jacques Ibert, Previn, and Roger Eden's adaptation of Rimsky-Korsakov contribute to the overall effect of the picture. The photography by F. A. Young and Joseph Ruttenberg are especially outstanding.

"Invitation to the Dance" is offbeat and questionable boxoffice, but Metro and Messrs. Kelly and Freed deserve considerable credit for attempting something unique and challenging. *Holl.*

23 Paces to Baker Street
(C'SCOPE—COLOR)

Good suspense against colorful London background as blind playwright solves kidnapping, murder.

Hollywood, May 14.

20th-Fox release of Henry Ephron production. Stars Van Johnson, Vera Miles, Cecil Parker; features Patricia Laffan, Maurice Denham, Estelle Winwood, Liam Redmond, Isobel Elsom, Martin Benson,

Natalie Norwick, Terence de Marney. Directed by Henry Hathaway. Screenplay, Nigel Balchin; based on novel "Warrant for X" by Philip MacDonald; camera (De Luxe Color), Milton Krasner; editor, James B. Clark; music, Leigh Harline. Previewed May 9, '56. Running time, **103 MINS.**

Phillip Hannon ... Van Johnson
Jean Lennox ... Vera Miles
Matthews ... Cecil Parker
Miss Macdonald ... Patricia Laffan
Inspector Grovening ... Maurice Denham
The Barmaid ... Estelle Winwood
Mr. Murch ... Liam Redmond
Lady Syrett ... Isobel Elsom
Pilling ... Martin Benson
Janet Murch ... Natalie Norwick
Sergeant Luce ... Terence de Marney
Miss Schuyler ... Queenie Leonard
Policeman ... Charles Keane
Miss Marston ... Lucie Lancaster
Pin Ball Player ... A. Cameron Grant
Lift Operator ... Ashley Cowan
English Cop ... Les Sketchley
Hotel Porter ... Ben Wright
Spectacled Man ... Reginald Sheffield
Mrs. De Mester ... Phyllis Montiflore
Mr. De Mester ... Arthur Gomez
Invalid Child ... Janice Kane
Police Inspector ... Robert Raglan
Doorman ... Howard Lang
Demonstrator ... Margaret McGrath
Shop Assistant ... Walter Horsborough
Taxi Driver ... Fred Griffith
Photographer ... Charles Stanley
Bell Boy ... Robin Alaouf
Cabby ... Yorke Sherwood

A Sherlock Holmes flavor and a London setting blend well with the suspense and melodramatics in "23 Paces to Baker Street." Albeit a bit long at 103 minutes, the film still stands up favorably as entertainment. It's a good bill-topper for regular runs, where the name of Van Johnson, coupled with Vera Miles' upcoming one, should bolster bookings.

Philip MacDonald's novel, "Warrant for X," has been put into excellent screen form by Nigel Balchin and the writing gives Henry Hathaway's direction a solid basis from which to develop a taut, suspenseful thriller. He manages plot situations and players ably. Producer Henry Ephron uses the London setting to advantage in staging the film. The o.o. given viewers of the Thames, fog-misted streets and buildings, etc., via sterling CinemaScope lensing in De Luxe Color by Milton Krasner, is a decided asset.

Johnson appears as a blind playwright who inadvertently overhears what to his dramatist mind is a dastardly kidnap plot. When the police give him a polite brush he sets out on his own, aided by Miss Miles, ex-fiancee he has refused to marry since his blindness, and Cecil Parker, his secretary-handyman. Suspense constantly mounts in the situations that ensue, climaxing with Johnson's finale fight in a dark room with the kidnapper-murderess.

Footage isn't all jangled nerves, since considerable humor is introduced through the bumblingly efficient character done to a fare-the-well by Parker. Johnson puts plenty of conviction into his blindman role, scoring strongly, and Miss Miles adds a refreshing charm as well as some sound histrionics. Seen favorably as assorted British characters are Patricia Laffan, Maurice Denham, Estelle Winwood, Liam Redmond, Isobel Elsom, Martin Benson, Natalie Norwick, Terence de Marney and others.

One of the suspense assets is the Leigh Harline music, conducted by Lionel Newman. It complements, instead of dominating, and as a result plays a strong part in furthering the pic's mood. All the technical credits are firstrate.

Brog.

The Wedding in Monaco
(C'SCOPE—COLOR)

Metro release of Cital Monaco with cooperation of Compagnie Francaise De Films production. A motion picture documentary by Jean Masson. Music, Daniel White. Previewed in N.Y., May 10, '56. Running time, **30 MINS.**

Now that the hoopla and sideshow atmosphere has died down, Metro is offering a serious and dignified account of the "The Wedding in Monaco." The 30-minute short, produced by Cital Monaco with the cooperation of Compagnie Francaise de Films, has the blessings (and financial participation?) of Prince Rainier III and is therefore the only "official" filmed account of the Rainier-Grace Kelly nuptials.

The CinemaScope offering effectively captures the pomp of the occasion. It should make a good extra attraction for theatres which can fit the 30-minute running time into their schedules.

Film opens with an aerial tour of the tiny kingdom, focuses on the behind-the-scenes preparations for the wedding, the arrival and reception of Miss Kelly in Monaco, rehearsals and performances of stars of the Opera de Paris, the London Festival Ballet, and Tamara Toumanova and the chorus and orchestra of the Opera of Monte-Carlo, all on hand to provide special entertainment for the wedding guests. The C'Scope color lensing stands out in capturing Miss Kelly wandering about the castle and in recording the civil and religious wedding ceremonies. Camera follows the couple down to the Prince yacht as they take off on their honeymoon trip.

Jean Masson is credited with the production and Daniel White provided the music.

Holl.

Great Day in the Morning
(COLOR)

Tinted actioner around Northern-Southern sympathizers in post-Civil War Denver; okay names for average prospects in outdoor market.

Hollywood, May 15.

RKO release of Edmund Grainger production. Stars Virginia Mayo, Robert Stack, Ruth Roman, Alex Nicol; features Raymond Burr, Leo Gordon, Regis Toomey, Carlton Young, Donald MacDonald. Directed by Jacques Tourneur. Screenplay, Lesser Samuels; based on novel by Robert Hardy Andrews; camera (Technicolor), William Snyder; editor, Harry Marker; music, Leith Stevens. Previewed May 10, '56. Running time, **91 MINS.**

Ann Merry Alaine ... Virginia Mayo
Owen Pentecost ... Robert Stack
Boston Grant ... Ruth Roman
Stephen Kirby ... Alex Nicol
Jumbo Means ... Raymond Burr
Zeff Masterson ... Leo Gordon
Father Murphy ... Regis Toomey
Col. Gibson ... Carlton Young
Gary Lawford ... Donald MacDonald

A prelude to the War Between States is fought out in this tinted actioner. The entertainment that results is sufficient to fit the not-too-demanding requirements of the general outdoor market. Toplining of Virginia Mayo, Robert Stack, Ruth Roman and Alex Nicol provides the Edmund Grainger production with some familiar names.

Under Jacques Tourneur's direction, the Lesser Samuels script based on the Robert Hardy Andrews novel unfolds at a regulation, but not always fast, pace. Performancewise, Stack and Miss Roman come off the best; she with a characterization that projects plenty of s.a. and he with a portrayal that gives the hero a showy, but not too much so, derring-do flavor. Miss Mayo isn't able to best script and directional handicaps to her character. Nicol, with not as much footage, comes off okay, as do Raymond Burr, flamboyant heavy, and Leo Gordon, rabid northern sympathizer.

Northern and Southern partisans are drawing up sides in early Denver and violence flares frequently while Stack, from the deep South, is making up his mind whether or not to aid Dixie in the abortive war that is to come. Meantime, he has a couple of lovelies to provide attractive distraction, as well as a going saloon, won handily at poker from Burr. Miss Mayo is an eastern lady who has set up a gown shop in frontier Denver and Miss Roman is the saloon entertainer who went along with the chips in the poker game. Windup finds Stack losing both gals, but saving his own skin when Nicol is revealed as a Union man on a secret mission. Sidebar issues of the plot sometimes cloud the main points and slow the pace occasionally.

Exteriors have pictorial value as lensed by William Snyder in SuperScope with print by Technicolor and Leith Stevens' music plays its part well in the story-telling. Other technical effects are okay, too.

Brog.

Cannes Festival
By GENE MOSKOWITZ

Cannes, May 15.

Le Ballon Rouge (THE RED BALLOON) (French; Color). Montsouris production and release. Written and directed by Albert Lamorisse. Camera (Technicolor), Edmond Sechan; music, Maurice Le Roux; editor, Pierre Gillett. With Pascal Lamorisse. At Cannes Film Festival. Running time, **35 MINS.**

This is a whimsical short that will please almost anywhere. It got a spontaneous ovation at the recent Cannes Film Fest though only 35 minutes long. Made by the man who made "White Mane," it has excellent U. S. possibilities. This has both moppet and adult appeal.

It concerns a boy who finds a red balloon one day which follows him wherever he goes, having almost human perception and ability. It blithely makes its way through Paris on the boy's heels. Finally a gang of boys punctures the balloon, with a resulting payoff.

Director Albert Lamorisse has gotten the right feel of whimsy into this and the color touches perfection. Special effects and moppet work are all fine.

CONFIDENTIAL FILE (Anglo-Spanish). Warner Bros. release of Filmorsa production. Stars Orson Welles; features Robert Arden, Michael Redgrave, Akim Tamiroff, Patricia Medina, Suzanne Flon, Katina Paxinou, Mischa Auer, Jack Watling, Paola Mori, Peter Van Eyck. Written and directed by Welles. Camera, Jean Bourgoin; music, Paul Misraki; editor, Renzo Lucidi. At Cannes Film Fest. Running time, **95 MINS.**

WB has this for Europe and South America but not for the U.S. Orson Welles' last Continental film before heading back to renew his U.S. career, it emerges a jumbled mixture of story and effects which are striking at times but have too much flash and fantasy without enough flesh. Reminiscent of "Citizen Kane" this remains somewhat confused. Pic shapes mainly as a good programmer on its worldwide reverse chase theme as an adventurer tracks down the past of a mysterious great man to lead to his own eventual murder.

An eccentric millionaire, Orson Welles hires a nosy American, who is trying to get to his daughter, to find out about his youth. The search uncovers slowly the true shady past of the great man who dispatches all the people as they are revealed until the two are alone. His obsession in not wanting his daughter to know about his criminal past leads to the rich man's suicide.

Possessing a group of name folks in little cameo roles, these may help its chances in the U. S. Robert Arden is much too unexpressive to give credence to the young man who almost outwits the half-mad brilliance of the rich man. Lensing and editing at times carry brilliance and flash. The production dress of the Continental background also helps. But this rather confused tale will have to be sold on its splashy action quality rather than anything else. Welles, in an unusual make-up, gives it weight and power at times. Cast is good and Paola Mori emerges a taking new femme film personality. It is in English.

Mabaroshi Nouma (THE PHANTOM HORSE) (Japanese; Color). Daei production and release. Directed by Koji Shima. Screenplay, Hasegawa; camera (Eastmancolor), Michio Takahashi; editor, Omori. At Cannes Film Fest. Running time, **90 MINS.**

Sprightly and knowing colors envelop this nicely told tale of a boy and his horse. Though reminiscent of some Hollywood pix, as the horse wins the derby to save the old homestead, this has an honest unfoldment and is told with winning acting, pacing and a taking moppet understanding.

Colors are excellent and this has a general entertainment value which may make it a fine general entry or an okay item for specialized situations. Acting is nice as are technical credits.

Cela S'Appelle L'Aurore (THAT IS THE DAWN) (Franco-Italian). Marceau production and release. Stars Georges Marchal, Lucia Bose; features Nelly Bourgeoud, Gianna Esposito, Jacques Delbo, Julien Bertheau. Directed by Luis Bunuel. Screenplay, Jean Ferry, Bunuel from novel by Emmanuel Robles; camera, Robert Le Fevbre; music, Joseph Kosma; editor, Marguerite Renoir. At Cannes Film Fest. Running time, **90 MINS.**

Film unfolds on island of Corsica and concerns a man who gets involved with problems which force him to take a stand. This looks only for some special spotting in the U.S. Theme might encounter some censorship difficulties.

A young doctor feels a commitment to workers of an island who are exploited by the leading factory owner. When his wife leaves him for a trip to the mainland, he falls in love with a beautiful newcomer. The brutal eviction of the doctor's friend from his home, with his sick wife, by the owner leads to the catalyst and the doctor's decision.

Director Luis Bunuel has filled in this often banal story with clever handling. Characters are strongly etched. Georges Marchal is adequate as the humane doctor. Lucia Bose is cold but comely as the mistress while the remainder of the cast is fine. There is expert lensing by Robert Lefebvre, nice music of Joseph Kosma and knowing editing by Marguerite Renoir. This makes it an unusual film but strictly an exploitation item, with limited U. S. chances.

MARIE - ANTOINETTE (Franco - Italian-Color). Gaumont release of Franco-London Film-Glbe-Rizzoli production. Stars Michele Morgan, Richard Todd; features Jacques Morel, Aime Clariond, Jeanne Boitel, Guy Trejean, Marina Berti. Directed by Jean Delannoy. Screenplay, Bernard Zimmer, Philipe Erlanger, Delannoy; camera (Technicolor), Pierre Montazel; editor, Henri Taverna. At Cannes Film Fest. Running time, 120 MINS.

Trotted out for French edification is a retelling of the story of Marie-Antoinette and her pure love affair with Count Axel De Fersen with a background of court giddyness and eventual revolution. Its inside-Versailles intimacy and lack of real spectacle or of exciting visuals slow up this oft-told tale. It is a doubtful U.S. item. There is an Anglo version made for England which has already been insured circuit booking there. This version, with the names of Richard Todd and Michele Morgan might slant this as worthy for secondary U.S. spots, but it remains in need of bally for firstrun chances.

Director Jean Delannoy has given this a cold mounting. Michele Morgan is decorative but does not wear the regal raiment too well and rarely displays the femininity of the queen. Richard Todd is a pale figure in the unsuitable role of the queen's platonic lover. Jacques Morel manages to give a deeper note to the character of the weak king. Color is good and Versailles shooting gives it some dress and production value. Acting is sketchy in lesser roles and Revolutionary scenes have an operetta aspect while most technical credits are fine.

Les Possedees (THE POSSESSED) (French). Marceau production and release. Stars Raf Vallone, Madeleine Robinson; features, Dany Carrel, Magali Noel. Directed by Charles Brabant. Screenplay, Maurice Clavel, Andre Tabet from play, "Island of Goats," by Ugo Betti; camera, Edmond Sechan; editor, Maurice Serein. At Cannes Film Fest. Running time, 95 MINS.

The play version ran on Broadway only a week last season, and this Gallic pic rendition of the Italo piece "Island of Goats," looks to also have limited film chances except for exploitation angle on its sex drama of a goatlike man who troubles a houseful of women. It does have some torrid bits but it seems limited to offbeat spots.

Director Charles Brabant has not been able to give credence to this tale and it remains unconvincing with thesping little help. Lensing and editing are okay. It remains something for the sensational trade.

Sommarnattens Leende (SMILES OF A SUMMER NIGHT) (Swedish). Svensk Filmindustri production and release. Directed and written by Ingmar Bergman. Camera, Gunnar Fischer, Ake Njelsen; editor, Oscar Rosander. With Ulla Jacobsson, Eva Dahlbeck, Harriet Andersson, Gunnar Bjornstrand. At Cannes Film Fest. Running time, 110 MINS.

Offbeat Swedish comedy of manners and passions is limited for the U.S. due to its talky aspects. It has an unusual lusty comedy manner, and this might make this worthy of arty spots. It

---

details how a group of badly assorted couples are straightened out one summer night influenced by a strange elixir that makes people do what they want. Clever, and at times ribald, it has a too ponderous touch to really light up the comedic aspects of this slightly overlong affair. This has a topnotch acting and technical mounting, with Ingmar Bergman's direction knowing and agile.

MOZART (Austrian; Music; Color). Columbia release of Cosmopofilm production. Stars Oskar Werner; features Johanna Matz, Gertrud Kuckleman, Nadia Tiller, Angelica Hauff. Directed and written by Karl Hartl; camera, Oskar Schnirch; editor, Henriette Brunsch; music, W. A. Mozart. At Cannes Film Fest. Running time, 100 MINS.

Tinter is a rather relaxed outline of the last years of Mozart's life. Somewhat schmaltzy in detailing his love affair with a young singer who inspired his "The Magic Flute," it has the saving grace of not hoking up the process of creation and greatness. However, the real feel of Mozart's genius is absent except for his music on the soundtrack.

This has a restrained performance by Oskar Werner. Lensing gives a washedout color feel. Pic shapes as a good nabe lingo entry or for special spots on the musico appeal of Mozart with another asset in the 200th anni celebration of his birth.

Surrounding thesping is fine but music and Werner dominate this sketchily-mounted pic.

OTHELLO (Russian; Color). Mosfilm production and release by Serge Youtkevitch. Screenplay, Youtkevitch from play by Shakespeare; camera (Sovcolor), E. Andrikania; music, A. Khatchatourian; editor, K. Alleeva. With Serge Bondartchouk, I. Skotzeva, A. Popov, V. Sechalski, E. Vesnik. At Cannes Film Fest. Running time, 100 MINS.

If Shakespeare's "Romeo And Juliet" can be terped to fair U. S. box office returns by Russo filmmakers, a straight version of "Othello," shorn of its verse, might also be an offbeat arty enry. Color and playing give this a measure of taking dramatics as the Moor's jealousy grows to torture and murder of his beloved. This mounts to a fine frenzy and has a visual aspect that might make it worthy of special spotting outside the Russo houses in the U. S.

Director Serge Youtkevitch has given the Moor a stature and his depiction of the growth of jealousy, inspired by the twisted Iago, are the film's high points. One flaw is the lack of needed charm in the Iago character. However, the excellent color renditions, setting and acting make this a worthy gambit. Serge Bondartchouk gives the Moor a depth that pays off. Desdamona is played perfectly by a pulchritudinous actress, for a change, in Irini Skotzeva. Khatchatourian's robust and nuanced musical background is also an asset. This further points up the Russo switch in film policy with an adherence to the classics And a veering away from controversial matters.

LE MYSTERE PICASSO (Documentary-French-C'Scope-Color). Cinedis release of Filmsonor production. Directed by H. G. Clouzot. Camera (Eastmancolor), Claude Renoir; music, Georges Auric; editor, Hendi Colpi. At Cannes Film Fest. Running time, 87 MINS.

Black and White, color and C'Scope are used in this filmic rendition of the famed painter Pablo Picasso at work. Drawings make up the first part followed by an analysis of two paintings and how they become the finished product. Line is matched with a probing musical score and sharp film manner to produce an interesting and offbeat pic treating the creative artist.

The nature of the film makes this one for only special spotting in the U. S. since it may appeal only to those interested in Picasso's work. His genius is something taken for granted but rarely shown in the film.

However, this unusual pic creates an almost hypnotic effect and hits a cresendo when C'Scope is utilized to denote the work which goes into a painting. Color and lensing are excellent and this pic, which started out as a short and grew into a full length film, is a definite exploitable subject. However, it is limited to those interested in the work of Picasso.

To Koritsi Me Ta Mara (THE GIRL IN BLACK) (Greek). Hermes production and release. Written and directed by Michael Cacoyanis. Camera, Walter Lassally; editor, Emile Provlenglos; music, Argyris Koudanis. With Ellie Lambert, Dimitri Horn, Georges Foundas, Eleni Zafirou, Notis Pergalis. At Cannes Film Fest. Running time, 100 MINS.

Young Greek director Michael Cacoyanis is the man who gained a measure of international interest with the pic "Stella" at the Cannes Fest last year which was picked up for world distrib by Universal and won a foreign critics award in the U. S. this year. "Stella" was made for $25,000 and present entry for $35,000. It has a fine technical gloss and tells a sombre tale with marked visual talent. Coming of age of a playboy involved with the provincial, cruel lives of a group of inbred islanders, this packs some dramatic voltage which is overstated at times. It makes up for this somewhat in the playing and atmospheric handling.

The young man who comes to a Greek island to relax falls in love with a beauteous local girl who is the butt of the idle male contingent because of her loose mother. Story is extremely well played by leads Ellie Lambert and Dimtri Horn. Pic has an excellent lensing backdrop by Walter Lassally. It denotes an emerging talent in Cacoynals. Film could be a definite lingo spotter plus fodder for arty U. S. chances.

Kohrinta (LITTLE FAIRGROUND SWING) (Hungarian). Mokep production and release. Directed by Zoltan Fabri. Screenplay, Imre Sarkadi; camera, Barnabas Hegyi; editor, Fabri; music, Gyorgy Ranki. With Bela Barsi, Manyi Kiss, Mari Torocsik, Imre Sos, Adam Szirtes. At Cannes Film Fest. Running time, 100 MINS.

This shapes as the first Magyar film since the war to hint for some U. S. possibilities. Mainly the tale of two lovers separated by social and political conventions who finally assert themselves and their love, it has a human sentimental quality never descending to mawkishness. Direction shapes this into an entertaining piece with a fine flair for atmosphere, mood and drama by young director Zoltan Fabri. Shorn of some early talk of collectives versus individual farming, its tale of love can be cut into a highly offbeat pic worthy of spotting in some U. S. arty situations.

Scenes of the lovers first meeting on a fairground swing, a brilliantly mounted dance scene when the young lover makes his desires evident in a long dance with the girl (a masterful piece of cinema) and the treatment of characterization, combine to make this a fine pic. Technical credits and playing are excellent. This is of course limited for certain U. S. spots but it has the film content necessary for consideration.   *Mosk.*

Great Locomotive Chase
(C'SCOPE-COLOR)

Disney recreates Yankee railroad raid in Deep South during Civil War. Spotty entertainment but okay b.o. prospects.

Hollywood, May 22.

Buena Vista release of Lawrence Edward Watkin production. Stars Fess Parker, Jeffrey Hunter; features Jeff York, John Lupton, Eddie Firestone, Kenneth Tobey, Don Megowan, Claude Jarman Jr. Directed by Francis Lyon. Screenplay, Watkin; camera (Technicolor), Charles Boyle; editor, Ellsworth Hoagland; music, Paul Smith; song, "Sons of Old Aunt Dinah," Watkin, Stan Jones, Smith. Previewed May 18, '56. Running time, 87 MINS.

James J. Andrews	Fess Parker
William A. Fuller	Jeffrey Hunter
William Campbell	Jeff York
William Pittenger	John Lupton
Robert Buffum	Eddie Firestone
Anthony Murphy	Kenneth Tobey
Marion A. Ross	Don Megowan
Jacob Parrott	Claude Jarman Jr.
William Bensinger	Harry Carey Jr.
J. A. Wilson	Lennie Geer
William Knight	George Robotham
Wilson Brown	Stan Jones
John Wollam	Marc Hamilton
John M. Scott	John Wiley
Pete Bracken	Slim Pickens
Alex	Morgan Woodward
A Switchman	W. S. Bearden
Jess McIntyre	Harvey Hester
Henry Haney	Douglas Bleckley

Walt Disney has gone back into the historical archives for this account of a Union railroad raid into the Deep South during the War Between States. In CinemaScope and Technicolor, it varies between good and fair entertainment values, with enough exciting passages to promise okay prospects at the boxoffice.

Thrill high spots are in the chase action when a Confederate conductor takes after his stolen train, first on foot, then by push car and then by locomotive, in determined pursuit of the disguised Union soldiers led by secret agent James J. Andrews. After the chase is over, and the spies are captured, the film becomes rather anticlimactic. Overall, however, the Buena Vista release which Lawrence Edward Watkin wrote and produced, does maintain substantial period authenticity, thanks to antique rolling stock and well-chosen Georgia locations.

Fess Parker, as the Kentuckian Andrews who served the North, and Jeffrey Hunter, as the true Southerner, William A. Fuller, who frustrated the Union scheme to destroy Confederate railroad supply lines between Atlanta and Chattanooga, turn in convincing portrayals under Francis Lyon's able direction. John Lupton, too, rates credit for his work as William Pittenger, member of the raiding party who later authored an account of the actual incident. Lupton also does some bridging narration.

Jeff York, Eddie Firestone, Don Megowan, Claude Jarman Jr., Harry Carey Jr., and others enacting the raiders play their parts well, as do Kenneth Tobey, rail superintendent who joins Hunter on the chase; Slim Pickens, engineer, and the sundry other types, some native recruits on the location sites.

Paul Smith did the scoring and included are such old songs as "Roll, Jordan, Roll" and "Tenting Tonight," plus "Sons of Old Aunt Dinah" for which Smith and Stan Jones did the music and Watkin the lyrics. Charles Boyle's photography is firstrate, as are the editing by Ellsworth Hoagland, art direction by Carroll Clark, set decorations by Emile Kuri and Pat Delaney, and the other technical contributions. *Brog.*

Foreign Intrigue
(COLOR)

Television title and flavor transferred, beautifully lensed in foreign locales. Okay outlook though slow paced and overlong.

Hollywood, May 22.

United Artists release, Sheldon Reynolds production, written and directed by Reynolds. Stars Robert Mitchum. Features Genevieve Page, Ingrid Tulean, Frederick O'Brady, Eugene Deckers, John Padovano. Original story treatment, Reynolds, Harold J. Bloom, Gene Levitt; camera (Eastman Color), Bertil Palmgrem; editor, Lennart Wallen; music, Paul Durand; "Foreign Intrigue Concerto," Charles Norman. Previewed May 18, '56. Running time, 100 MINS.

Bishop	Robert Mitchum
Dominique	Genevieve Page
Brita	Ingrid Tulean
Spring	Frederick O'Brady
Sandoz	Gene Deckers
Mrs. Lindquist	Inga Tidblad
Tony	John Padovano
Mannheim	Frederick Schrecker
Jones	Lauritz Falk
Brown	Peter Copley
Smith	Ralph Brown
Dr. Thibault	George Hubert
Bistro Owner	Jim Gerald
Baum	Nil Sperber
Danemore	Jean Galland
Starky	John Starck
Dodo	Gilbert Robin
Charwoman	Valentine Camax
Charles	Robert Le Beal
Information Desk Clerk	Albert Simmons

In some aspects "Foreign Intrigue" is overdone, mostly in the deliberate directorial pacing that stretches the plot to an unnecessary 100 minutes and slows movement to a walk at times, and in the overemphasis on music. Film has a good score by Paul Durand, which includes a catchy, simple theme that attracts the ear. When the cleffing is kept simple the inherent suspense of the tale is heightened. However, the "Foreign Intrigue Concerto" by Charles Norman and other musical passages are pretentiously used, sometimes competing with dialog and story mood.

Title, overseas locales and flavor are derived by Sheldon Reynolds from his own television series. The locales are much improved in Eastman Color for theatre projection. The skullduggery of foreign spying is the same. Not that this is a literal transference from video. But the picture is a full length, and over-long, exploitation of a tv-built property.

An opening, back-dated, black-and-white scene sets the note of intrigue for the story which Reynolds wrote and directed before it moves to the present at Nice and the death of a mysterious man, whose pressagent, Mitchum, had built into a strange, romantic figure of wealth. Questions asked by odd characters lead Mitchum to back-track on the man and around that search into truth is built the suspense of the plot. The man is a blackmailer, living off of the hush-money supplied by quislings in countries that Hitler failed to invade. It's good spy stuff, and had not Reynolds spun his tale out so long would have been even more intriguing.

Mitchum gives a good account of himself in the lead role and there are any number of colorful characters to hold interest among the others in the cast. Genevieve Page, wife of the dead man, and a pretty deadly femme herself, is attractively used. Ingrid Tulean, encountered by Mitchum as the trail leads to Stockholm, has an unorthodox beauty as well as acting talent and scores soundly as the girl with whom Mitchum falls in love. Frederick O'Brady clicks as a self-seeking foreign agent, as does Gene Deckers, a bonafide government agent. Inga Tidblad is fine as Miss Tulean's mother. Frederick Schrecker and others are good types.

The production has been given exceptionally standout lensing by Bertil Palmgrem, with locales in Paris, Stockholm and Nice serving for the various international sites of the plot. Lennart Wallen's editing features those long walking shots and those quick closeup cuts seen quite often on tv dramas, and which are well suited to this story. Other technical aids are good. *Brog.*

Port Afrique
(BRITISH—COLOR)

Pier Angeli and Phil Carey in British-made melodrama with Moroccan backgrounds; fair b.o. hopes.

London, May 15.

Columbia release of David E. Rose production. Stars Pier Angeli, Phil Carey, Dennis Price. Directed by Rudolph Mate. Screenplay, Frank Partos and John Cresswell; camera, Wilkie Cooper; editor, Raymond Poulton; music, Malcolm Arnold. At Odeon Theatre, Marble Arch, London. Running time, 90 MINS.

Ynez	Pier Angeli
Rip Reardon	Phil Carey
Robert Blackton	Dennis Price
Colonel Moussac	Eugene Deckers
Nino	James Hayter
Diane Blackton	Rachel Gurney
Pedro	Anthony Newley
Abdul	Guido Lorraine
Grila	Denis Shaw
Franz Vermes	Christopher Lee
Police Driver	Guy Du Monceau

By starring Pier Angeli and Phil Carey in his color production of "Port Afrique," David E. Rose has values to help sell the picture in U.S. That's the biggest aid he has because, as an entertainment, this is lacking in suspense and tension. Little is gained from the potential exotic atmosphere of the Moroccan background.

In most respects, despite its colorful setting, this is little more than a conventional meller which tries to exploit its background. The story rarely comes to life, the dialog is mainly unspirited, and the acting never reaches accepted standards.

The story, taken from novel of the same name by Bernard Victor Dryer, has a contrived appearance in its transition from book to screen. Phil Carey plays an American airman who returns to his Moroccan home after war service to find his wife murdered. Although they know better, the police suggest it is a case of suicide, but obstinately, he refuses to accept their dictum and pursues his own inquiries. The principal suspects are a nightclub owner (James Hayter), who had been making overtures to the dead woman, and his business partner, Dennis Price, who was anxious to sell their plantation. Carey, for his part, suspects Pier Angeli, a nightclub singer, who had been a house guest with his wife. The denouement, which reveals the real killer, packs little surprises or conviction.

For the most part, the yarn is revealed in pedestrian style, the action being confined to a couple of incidents within the Casbah. Otherwise, there is no excitement or suspense. The backgrounds have a genuine look, but are hardly strong enough to sustain the main story line. The characterizations, too, lack the color and conviction to hypo the atmosphere while the total effect is disappointing.

Miss Angeli infuses a dramatic allure into her role and sings as well as she can act. Her song numbers make a romantic and dramatic impact. Carey is handicapped by a heavyhanded script, but he puts plenty of determination and sincerity into his role. Dennis Price is too obviously the suave heavy while Rachel Gurney is too clearly guilty. Eugene Deckers never convinces as the subtle police chief, but James Hayter is unfailingly polished as the tough nitery operator. Denis Shaw impresses as the latter's gorilla-like bodyguard. Rudolph Mate's direction appears to have a negative influence; other technical standards are average. *Myro.*

Murder On Approval

So-so London-localed mystery meller.

Hollywood, May 15.

RKO release of Robert S. Baker, Monty Berman production. Stars Tom Conway, Delphi Lawrence, Brian Worth, Michael Balfour; features Campbell Cotts, John Horsley. Directed by Bernard Knowles. Screenplay, Kenneth R. Hayles; camera, Monty Berman; editor, Jack Slade. Previewed May 11, '56. Running time, 70 MINS.

Tom "Duke" Martin	Tom Conway
Jean Larsen	Delphi Lawrence
Geoffrey Blake	Brian Worth
Barney	Michael Balfour
Coburn	Campbell Cotts
Inspector Taylor	John Horsley
Gordoni	Ronan O'Casey
Everleigh	Launce Maraschal
Lord Valchrist	Colin Tapley
Henry Warburg	Alan Gifford
Lady Hawksley	Grace Arnold
First Man	John Collicos
Yamina	Mayura
Sergeant Grant	John Watson
Second Man	Reg Morris
Woman Cleaner	Marianne Stone
Manager	Derrick Whittingham
Garage Attendant	Frank Pemberton
Fingerprinter	Neil Wilson
Hawksley Maid	Olive Kirby
Receptionist	Rosamund Waring
Air Stewardess	Margaret Rowe
Girl at Airport	Maureen Connell

This London-localed mystery meller is only so-so as entertainment and will just get by in lower-case programmer bookings. With possible exception of Tom Conway, the British cast is unfamiliar, so there's no help there for playdates.

Kenneth R. Hayles' plot and dialog aren't credible in telling the story of a super private investigator sent to London to find out whether a rare and expensive stamp bought by a collector is a phony. In between getting himself involved in a couple of murders and picking up unlikely clues, Conway, as a sleuth, finds time to act kittenish with all the girls that cross his path, even Delphi Lawrence, who's in on the stamp racket with Brian Worth, worthless nephew of the late, titled owner of the original rarity.

Bernard Knowles' direction is poorly paced and seldom builds to any thrills. His comedy handling is inept, too, but the script lines are no help in the chuckle department to him or to Michael Balfour, doing an ex-crook friend who helps Conway clear up the case. None of the cast can do much with the stereotype characters. Production by Robert S. Baker and Monty Berman has only fair budget values and technical assists are stock. *Brog.*

The Killing

Suspenseful melo for good showing in action market.

Hollywood, May 18.

United Artists release of a James B. Harris production. Stars Sterling Hayden; costars Coleen Gray, Vince Edwards; features Jay C. Flippen, Marie Windsor, Ted DeCorsia. Directed by Stanley Kubrick; screenplay, Kubrick, from Lionel White novel, "Clean Break"; camera, Lucien Ballard; editor, Betty Steinberg.

Previewed May 16, '56. Running time, 84 MINS.
Johnny Clay .... Sterling Hayden
Fay .... Coleen Gray
Val Cannon .... Vince Edwards
Marvin Unger .... Jay C. Flippen
Sherry Peatty .... Marie Windsor
Randy Kennan .... Ted DeCorsia
George Peatty .... Elisha Cook
Mike O'Reilly .... Joe Sawyer
Nikki Arane .... Tim Carey
Leo .... Jay Adler
Tiny .... Joseph Turkel
Kola Kwarian.........Maurice Oboukhoff

This story of a $2,000,000 race track holdup and steps leading up to the robbery is sturdy fare for the action market, where it can be exploited for better than average returns. Occasionally told in a documentary style, which at first tends to be somewhat confusing, it soon settles into a tense and suspenseful vein which carries through to an unexpected and ironic windup. Hard-hitting and colorful performances point up story values. It's first production of the new team of James B. Harris and Stanley Kubrick.

Sterling Hayden, an ex-con, masterminds the plan which includes five men. Kubrick's direction of his own script is tight and fast-paced, a quality Lucien Ballard's top photography matches to lend particular fluidity of movement, and Harris makes wise use of his budget for first-rate production results. Excellent stock footage augments outfit's own filming of racetrack scenes.

Characters involved in the crime include Elisha Cook, a colorless little cashier at the track who is hopelessly in love with his glamorous, trampish wife, Marie Windsor; Ted DeCorsia, a racketeering cop; Jay C. Flippen, a reformed drunk; and Joe Sawyer, track bartender. Each has his own job to do in the scheme that Hayden has evolved, and action follows each to the moment when Hayden dons a rubber mask and enters the track office to grab off the loot while a riot he has arranged is occupying the cops. As he's making a later getaway at the airport, a large suitcase carrying the coin falls off a baggage truck and the bills fly to the wind in the propeller wash of an arriving plane.

Hayden socks over a restrained characterization, and Cook is a particular standout as a man prodded by his wife's demands for luxury. Miss Windsor, in this role, also is particularly good, who digs the plan out of her husband and reveals it to her boyfriend, Vince Edwards, a small time hood who tries to cut himself into the deal. Both Edwards and Coleen Gray, costarred, are in only briefly, but satisfactorily. Flippen is up to his usual topgrade, and DeCorsia and Sawyer meet demands of their respective roles. Maurice Oboukhoff, a wrestler whom Hayden hires to start the riot, stages a bruising battle with the cops.

Technical credits are surefire right down the line, Betty Steinberg giving film firm editing.
Whit.

The Eddy Duchin Story
(COLOR—C'SCOPE—SONGS)

Tastefully handled film reprise of a real-life tragic show business career. Good entertainment.

Columbia release of Jerry Wald production. Stars Tyrone Power; features Kim Novak, Rex Thompson, Victoria Shaw, James Whitmore, Shepperd Strudwick, Frieda Inescort, Gloria Holden, Larry Keating. Directed by George Sidney. Screenplay, Samuel Taylor, from Leo Katcher story; camera (Technicolor), Harry Stradling; editors, Viola Lawrence and Jack W. Ogilvie; music, Morris Stoloff; piano recordings, Carmen Cavallaro. Previewed May 23, '56. Running time, 123 MINS.
Eddie Duchin .... Tyrone Power
Marjorie Oelrichs .... Kim Novak
Chiquita .... Victoria Shaw
Lou Sherwood .... James Whitmore
Peter Duchin (12) .... Rex Thompson
Peter Duchin (5) .... Mickey Maga
Mr. Wadsworth......Shepperd Strudwick
Mrs. Wadsworth .... Frieda Inescort
Mrs. Duchin .... Gloria Holden
Leo Reisman .... Larry Keating
Mr. Duchin .... John Mylong
Philip .... Gregory Gay
Native Boy .... Warren Hsieh
Piano Tuner .... Jack Albertson
Doctor .... Carlyle Mitchell
1st Boy .... Richard Sternberg
2nd Boy .... Andy Smith
Nurse .... Lois Kimbrell

The pitfalls have been averted; Jerry Wald's biopicturing of the career of "10 Magic Fingers" is not all the sorrow and woe that the story of Eddy Duchin might suggest. There's no escaping the fact that the pianist's first wife died shortly after childbirth. And that this was followed 12 years later by Duchin's own death, at the age of 41, as the result of leukemia. All sounds like "agony" material and therefor something of a "problem" entertainment-and money-wise.

But Samuel Taylor plays up humor and romance as well as the inherent hardship in his script and George Sidney's direction, sensitive for the most part, sustains a high dramatic tone with, of course, the abundance of pianistics recorded by Carmen Cavallaro) further lightening the plot matter.

"Duchin Story" falls off to schmaltziness in a few instances (as result of accent on sentimentality) but nonetheless it's a highly satisfactory offering all around.

Key asset is Tyrone Power, in the title role. Only a short memory is required to recall Duchin's affability and the high regard in which he was held by show business. The latter not only for the sympathy concerning the tragedies that befell him, but, as well, the courage he showed in War World II in insisting on combat duty in preference over the entertaining role that was offered him.

Power fits nicely. He's personable and eager as he hits Gotham from pharmaceutical school in Boston bent only on tapping out pop and pseudo-classical rhythms on the 88. He looks like he's genuinely thrilled with the splendors of New York (in color and CinemaScope) and confident that his letter of introduction will land him a job with Leo Reisman's orchestra at the old Central Park Casino.

It's through the intervention of Kim Novak, who shows more and more authority in her picture assignments, that the position in the band is his. The Novak-Power match builds tenderly—there's no hard courtin' or turbulent male-femme back and forth. Carefully established are the backgrounds, she as the high society type and he as the son of a tailor.

Sets and settings make for more plusses. Manhattan of a generation ago is colorfully reproduced and observers needn't be too vintage to go nostalgic over the Casino as it's shown here and the Waldorf's Empire Room at the time Duchin again took the spotlight upon returning from naval service.

Story is given well-rounded development. It has substance as it unreels from the passing of Miss Novak, which meant the end of an ecstatic marriage for Power, the latter's shunning of his surviving son, the war, Power's introduction to and animosity toward the British girl, incongruously named Chiquita, who cares for the boy. And then the friendship that builds between the latter, affectionately played by Rex Thompson, and Power, the second marriage, the shocking news about the leukemia affliction and, finally, Power's passing from the scene in a four-handkerchief climax.

James Whitmore, Shepperd Strudwick, Frieda Inescort, Gloria Holden and Larry Keating all register fine in subsidiary but important parts. Newcomer Victoria Shaw, Power's second wife, comes across with particular effectiveness, showing understanding of the role and executing it with proper feeling.

Sound track, as before noted, is heavy with Cavallaro and this makes for agreeable listening, plus exploitation possibilities via the obvious tieins with the album reprises already on the market. Music supervision, camera work and technical credits match the top-caliber quality of Wald's production.
Gene.

Trapeze
(C'SCOPE-COLOR)

Exciting circus drama with big earning potential, plus names of Burt Lancaster, Gina Lollobrigida, Tony Curtis.

Hollywood, May 25.

United Artists release of James Hill (Susan) production. Stars Burt Lancaster, Gina Lollobrigida, Tony Curtis, Katy Jurado, Thomas Gomez; features John Puleo, Minor Watson. Directed by Carol Reed. Screenplay, James R. Webb; adaptation, Liam O'Brien; based on "The Killing Frost" by Max Catto; camera (De Luxe Color), Robert Krasker; editor, Bert Bates; music, Malcolm Arnold, conducted by Muir Mathieson. Previewed May 23, '56. Running time, 106 MINS.
Mike Ribble .... Burt Lancaster
Tino Orsini .... Tony Curtis
Lola .... Gina Lollobrigida
Rosa .... Katy Jurado
Bouglione .... Thomas Gomez
Max .... John Puleo
John Ringling North......Minor Watson
Chikki .... Gerard Landry
Otto .... Jean-Pierre Kerien
Snake Charmer .... Sidney James
Circus Family Children.....Gimma Boys
Paul .... Gamil Batib
Stefan .... Pierre Tabard

"Trapeze" is high-flying screen entertainment equipped with everything necessary to attract a socko payoff at the boxoffice. Circus thrills and excitement, a well-handled romantic triangle, and a cast of potent marquee names make it a cinch winner. However, Hecht-Lancaster's Susan Productions and United Artists, the distributor, are insuring the wicket-whirling with a selling campaign designed to get additional dollars, so this release can be figured as one of the year's big money films.

There's an honest sawdust flavor achieved in the production by James Hill, which is exceptionally effective in heightening the entertainment. Cirque d'Hiver, Paris' famed, one-ring circus, provides the authentic, colorful, exciting setting, and nearly all scenes occur within its confines without losing any sense of bigness, so artfully does director Carol Reed stage his show and so expertly does Robert Krasker use his CinemaScope cameras for the De Luxe Color lensing.

The aerial footage literally causes the hair to stand on end as the high flyers go through their death-defying stunts. Reed's direction loads these scenes with story suspense for even more thrill effect, and male stars Burt Lancaster and Tony Curtis simulate the bigtop aristocrats so realistically the danger element reaches the nerve-snapping point.

Gina Lollobrigida, justly famed for her curves, proves she has them in the brief costumes she wears as an ambitious tumbler who tries to move in on the trapeze act being put together by the male leads. Also, she proves she can act, giving the necessary touch of flamboyance to her character without once going overboard, and yet handling the other facets of the role with a fine feel.

Lancaster and Curtis, too, register well in their acting chores. Katy Jurado, also starred, is not used to much story purpose, but lights up what scenes she has. Thomas Gomez, with the same billing, scores well as the circus proprietor, while John Puleo, from the Harmonica Rascals, clicks as a dwarfed circus handyman. Minor Watson gets off John Ringling North well.

The well-plotted James R. Webb script, from Liam O'Brien's adaptation of Max Catto's "The Killing Frost," tells how Curtis, son of an aerialist, comes to Paris to learn from Lancaster, one of the few fliers able to achieve the triple somersault, a feat which had left him crippled. Together, they start to work up an act when the tumbler moves in, using her wiles on the young man but loving the older. Ambition gives way to love at the finale after the thrill-laden climax in which Curtis achieves his "triple" goal.

The production design by Rino Mondellini, photographic effects by Walter Castle, special effects by R. J. Lannan, the sights and sounds of circus life, Faye Alexander's technical advising on the flying sequences, the Malcolm Arnold score conducted by Muir Mathieson, Colasanti's costumes and other behind-camera contributions play important parts in creating an atmosphere of high entertainment.
Brog.

The Leather Saint
(V'VISION)

Boxing and religion mix it up in okay programmer.

Hollywood, May 29.

Paramount release of Norman Retchin production. Stars Paul Douglas, John Derek, Jody Lawrance, Cesar Romero; features Ernest Truex, Richard Shannon, Ricky Vera. Directed by Alvin Ganzer. Screenplay, Retchin and Ganzer; camera, Haskell B. Boggs; editor, Floyd Knudtson; music, Irvin Talbot. Previewed May 14, '56. Running time, 86 MINS.
Gus MacAuliffe .... Paul Douglas
Father Gil Allen .... John Derek
Pearl Gorman .... Jody Lawrance
Tony Lorenzo .... Cesar Romero
Tom Kelly .... Richard Shannon
Father Ritchie .... Ernest Truex
Pepito .... Ricky Vera
Bishop Hardtke .... Thomas B. Henry
Tiger .... Lou Nova

Boxing and religion mix it up in "The Leather Saint" and the results can be scored as okay for the general runs. It has neither the quality nor the marquee names to rate top-of-the-bill playdates, but should prove an acceptable lowercase offering.

Film is a theatrical first for the production team of Norman Retchin and Alvin Ganzer, the former producing and the latter directing from their own screen story. They earn a fair rating for the dual functions, failing to go higher because of slow pacing and too much talk in the first half of the footage. However, the religioso theme is well-managed, and the trouping all it should be to get the picture by.

John Derek pleases in the title role, playing a young Episcopalian minister who, on Saturday nights, doffs his clergy robes for boxing gloves to raise money for a group of kid polio victims in his parish. Paul Douglas does well as the manager who little suspects his fighter's real profession. Scoring strongly is Jody Lawrance as a girl on the way to being a dipso who is straightened out by the leather saint. Cesar Romero, fight promoter, is okay, as are Ernest Truex, playing rather broadly a priest in Derek's parish, Richard Shannon, gymnasium director, Ricky Vera and others.

Production polish is not lavish, but values are adequate for the story and good use is made of assorted Southern California settings to help budget expenditures. Haskell B. Boggs' photography in black-and-white VistaVision didn't always show up well at the preview. Other technical assists come off acceptably. *Brog.*

D-Day, the Sixth of June
(C'SCOPE—COLOR)

Distinctive love story against a background of battle; excellent for de luxers but good mass appeal, too.

Hollywood, May 29.

20th-Fox release of Charles Brackett production. Stars Robert Taylor, Richard Todd, Dana Wynter, Edmond O'Brien; features John Williams, Jerry Paris, Robert Gist, Richard Stapley, Ross Elliott, Alex Finlayson. Directed by Henry Koster. Screenplay, Ivan Moffat, Harry Brown; from novel by Lionel Shapiro; camera (De Luxe Color), Lee Garmes; editor, William Mace; music, Lyn Murray; conducted by Lionel Newman. Previewed May 24, '56. Running time, 106 MINS.

Brad Parker .... Robert Taylor
John Wynter .... Richard Todd
Valerie .... Dana Wynter
Colonel Timmer ....Edmond O'Brien
Brigadier Russell .... John Williams
Raymond Boyce .... Jerry Paris
Dan Stenick .... Robert Gist
David Archer .... Richard Stapley
Major Mills .... Ross Elliott
Col Harkness .... Alex Finlayson
Coat Room Attendant....Cyril Delevanti
Georgina .... Marie Brown
Mala .... Rama Bai
Arkinson .... Dabbs Greer
Major McEwen .... Geoffrey Steele
Capt. Waller .... George Pelling
Lieutenant at Party ...... Conrad Feia
Sgt. Brooks .... Boyd "Red" Morgan
Grainger .... Richard Aherne
Mrs. Hamilton .... Victoria Ward
Suzette .... Patricia McMahon
Lt. Col. Cantrell............John Damler
General Bolthouse......Thomas B. Henry
General Pike .... Damien O'Flynn
General Millensbeck............ Ben Wright
Corporal .... Queenie Leonard
American War Correspondent
Howard Price
Taxi Driver .... Reggie Dvorak
Lt. Clayford Binns..........Chet Marshall
Sgt. Gerbert .... Parley Baer
Lance Corp. Bailey .... Ashley Cowan
Waitress .... June Mitchell

With the 12th anniversary of the Normandy Invasion looming, "D-Day, the Sixth of June" will serve as a strong, and grim to some, reminder of that momentous World War II date. Along with the account of the significant historical event, the picture spins an extremely moving wartime love story, distinctively done by a finely performing cast. The key de luxers should find this an excellent entry, and there's mass appeal too, if well-exploited, with star names of marquee merit to help the over/'l grossing outlook.

While the atmosphere and threat of war are always present in the topnotch Charles Brackett production, it isn't until near the end that actual fighting is shown in all of its frightening detail. Footage opens with the sailing of the forerunners of the invasion fleet, then sets its characters and tells its story through the medium of two flashbacks, skillfully handled in the firstrate scripting by Ivan Moffat and Harry Brown from the Lionel Shapiro novel, before coming back to the June 6 date and the days immediately following. These battle sequences, as well as those of war-battered England, the setting for most of the story, are full of realism as lensed in CinemaScope and De Luxe Color by Lee Garmes.

Henry Koster's direction displays extreme understanding in bringing out the moving dramatic aspects of the story and characters. There are a number of fine masculine performances by such as Robert Taylor, Richard Todd and Edmond O'Brien, the male stars, all important contributions to the story-telling, but it remains for the sensitive, tremendously compelling, work by Dana Wynter to give the real point to the drama and make the love story a valid thing.

The plot, simply, tells of an English girl, virtually committed romantically to a British soldier, who meets and falls deeply in love with a married American officer, and how this triangle is worked out in the overwhelming upset of war. There's a bitterly ironic note to the ending, beautifully done by Miss Wynter and Taylor after Todd's tragic death on the beaches of Normandy.

Taylor is especially effective as the American officer and Todd is splendid as the British officer. O'Brien creates a sock portrayal of a rank-bucking American officer who eventually cracks under the force of his own drive and the strain of war. John Williams, an embittered oldline brigadier who resents being sidetracked in this war, as well as Jerry Paris, Robert Gist, Richard Stapely, Ross Elliott, Alex Finlayson, Dabbs Greer, Thomas B. Henry, Damien O'Flynn, Queenie Leonard, Chet Marshall and others add much to the footage, whether in featured spots or bits.

Special photographic effects by Ray Kellogg, the editing by William Mace, the sounds of war and romance as recorded by Eugene Grossman and Harry M. Leonard, the Lyn Murray music, conducted by Lionel Newman, the art direction by Lyle R. Wheeler and Lewis H. Creber are among the first line technical assists helping to put over the drama. *Brog.*

Wicked as They Come
(BRITISH)

Entertaining yarn starring Arlene Dahl as ruthless adventuress, with Herbert Marshall as chief victim; average b.o.

London, May 22.

Columbia production and release. Stars Arlene Dahl, Phil Carey, Herbert Marshall. Directed by Ken Hughes. Screenplay, Ken Hughes, Robert Westerby and Sigmund Miller from novel, "Portrait in Smoke," by Bill Ballington; camera, Basil Emmott; editor, Max Benedict; music, Malcolm Arnold. At Leicester Square Theatre, London. Running time, 94 MNS.

Kathy Allen .... Arlene Dahl
Tim O'Bannion .... Phil Carey
Stephen Collins .... Herbert Marshall
Larry Buckhan..........Michael Goodliffe
Sam Lewis .... David Kossoff
Mike Lewis .... Marvin Kane
Frank Allen .... Sidney James
Chuck .... Gilbert Winfield
Willie .... Patrick Allen
John Dowling .... Ralph Truman

Good average entertainment value is provided by this Anglo-American story of a golddigger's rise to fortune. Ruthless ambition and an anti-social conscience are shown as achieving things up to a point.

Set against a background of New York, London and Paris, pic supplies sufficient variation to maintain interest, but its novelettish origin is responsible for many improbabilities, mainly the adaptability of a girl from the East Side attaining a post of importance in a big business organization despite lack of education.

Suffering from the aftermath of a sexual assault in adolescence, a factory girl hits back by making use of any male whom she can use as a ladder to improve her conditions. She immediately brushes off her first elderly victim after he has faked her winning of a beauty contest, and from then on during the ensuing prize winning European trip she exchanges one influential man after another until she weds the top executive and lands in the death cell of a Paris jail after shooting him.

Arlene Dahl looks sufficiently glamorous in an aloof manner to make her numerous conquests plausible. The stepping stones to her goal, in varying age groups, are all well depicted by Phil Carey, Herbert Marshall, David Kossoff, Ralph Truman and Michael Goodliffe. The only other femme role is played with quiet distinction by Faith Brook as the shrewd wife who bribes her rival.

Little stress is laid on the contrasting locales in the three capitals. *Clem.*

The Proud and Profane
(VISTAVISION)

Namedropping William Holden and Deborah Kerr should help but story shortcomings augur only mild returns. Shaky on long haul.

Paramount release of Perlberg-Seaton production (produced by William Perlberg). Stars William Holden, Deborah Kerr; features Thelma Ritter, Dewey Martin. Directed by George Seaton. Screenuplay, Seaton, based on novel by Lucy Herndon Crockett; camera, John F. Warren; editor, Alma Macrorie; music, Victor Young. Previewed N. Y., May 24, '56. Running time, 111 MINS.

Lt. Col. Colin Black......William Holden
Lee Ashley .... Deborah Kerr
Kate Connors .... Thelma Ritter
Eddie Wodcik .... Dewey Martin
Chaplain Holmes........William Redfield
Louis .... Ross Bagdasarian
Eustace Press .... Adam Williams
Joan .... Marion Ross
Bob Kilpatrick..........Theodore Newton
Major .... Richard Shannon
Lt. Hutchins .... Peter Hansen
Sgt. Peckinpaugh............ Ward Wood
Helen .... Geraldine Hall
Beth .... Evelyn C. Cotton
Pat .... Ann Morriss
Evvie .... Nancy Stevens
Sissy .... Lorayne Brox
Lt. Fowler .... Don Roberts
Marine .... Don House
Soldier .... Bob Kenaston
Marine .... Taylor Measom
Sailor .... Jack Richardson
Paul .... Freeman Morse
3rd Cacualty .... George Brenlin
2nd Casualty .... Robert Morse
1st Casualty .... Ray Stricklyn
Carl .... Anthony Moran

Sounds good — Deborah Kerr pitted against William Holden in romantic combat and conflict on New Calendonia Island against a background of World War II. As a Marine Corps colonel, he's arrogant and brutally forceful. It's only a matter of time before she, as a Red Cross worker, succumbs.

Holden and Miss Kerr have name weight which, together with the bally buildup, ought to assure good openings. But the story doesn't stand up. Taking spurious turns and inviting neither audience participation nor sympathy for any of its characters.

Entry is a shaky one for the long haul.

Locationed on the Virgin Islands, William Perlberg's production, as directed by Seaton, provides likely back-echelon war scenes. The hospitalized wounded, the R. C. gals at their chores, white crosses rising from the cemetery, the general activity between skirmishes with the enemy—these properly convey historical time and place.

But the script by Seaton, from the novel by Lucy Herndon Crockett, comes off as if authored by a soap opera practitioner trying for a follow-up to "From Here to Eternity." Seaton's a good man with the pen as attested by previous credits but this time out he seems to have lost some balance.

Miss Kerr, war widow, is in the fighting zone largely for the purpose of learning how her husband, who had been a lieutenant, had handled himself in battle. Comes the encounter with Holden, who's an illogical personality, and this leaves her pregnant. She figures on marriage but accidentally comes upon the news that Holden already is maritally tied up. His wife, though, who had been an alcoholic, subsequently dies. Miss Kerr loses the baby as her suicide attempt is thwarted by Holden. Latter goes off to battle, is wounded and, comatose, murmers "Forgive me, forgive me." Final fade.

In contrast with the false ring of the plot twists, some individual scenes have impact and intermittent stretches of dialog have true heart. Unfortunate that the basic structure wasn't architectured along more sincere lines.

Holden, Miss Kerr, Thelma Ritter as head of the Red Cross contingent, Dewey Martin, as a marine who is killed in action and other members of the cast can't overcome the unconvincing script. Technical credits are good and Victor Young's music is a strong contribution. VistaVision photography is in black and white, which helps in achieving the appropriately grim atmosphere. *Gene.*

The Proud Ones
(C'SCOPE—COLOR)

Good outdoor action drama.

Hollywood, May 25.

20th-Fox release of Robert L. Jacks production. Stars Robert Ryan, Virginia Mayo, Jeffrey Hunter, Robert Middleton; features Walter Brennan, Arthur O'Connell, Ken Clark, Rodolfo Acosta, George Mathews, Fay Roope, Edward Platt, Whit Bissell. Directed by Robert D. Webb. Screenplay, Edmund North, Joseph Petracca; from Verne Athanas novel; camera (De Luxe Color), Lucien Ballard; editor, Hugh S. Fowler; music, Lionel Newman. Previewed May 23, '50. Running time, 94 MNS.

Cass .... Robert Ryan
Sally .... Virginia Mayo
Thad .... Jeffrey Hunter
Honest John Barrett ...Robert Middleton
Jake .... Walter Brennan
Jim Dexter .... Arthur O'Connell
Pike .... Ken Clark
Chico .... Rodolfo Acosta
Dillon .... George Mathews
Markham .... Fay Roope
Dr. Barlow .... Edward Platt

Mr. Bolton .... Whit Bissell
Billy Smith .... Paul Burns
Barber .... Richard Deacon
Tim—Bartender .... Frank Gerstle
2nd Foreman .... Charles Tannen
Belle .... Lois Ray
Guard .... Jack Low
The Weasel .... Ken Terrell
Editor .... Harrison Lewis
Hotel Clerk .... Don Brodie
Driver .... William Fawcett
Saloon Barker .... Ed Mundy
Man on Make .... Jackie Coogan
Helen .... Juanita Close

20th-Fox has an exceptionally well-presented outdoor drama in "The Proud Ones." It's certain to hit the mark with western fans, and can prove to be an attractive entry for those who usually do not go for frontier actioners. A credible story with excellent dramatic values, direction that sharpens them and builds suspense, and strong performances by an able cast are among the entertainment assets of this well-thought-out Robert L. Jacks production.

Robert Ryan, Jeffrey Hunter and Robert Middleton are the male cast toppers. Playing a marshal who knows his business, a young man who has not yet determined where he is going, and a gambling saloon operator, respectively, the trio responds exactly right to Robert D. Webb's forceful direction. For femme interest. Virginia Mayo stars, and she gives the pic a performance asset as the girl who loves the marshal. Other acting assists come from Walter Brennan, town jailer; Arthur O'Connell, nervous deputy; Ken Clark and Rodolfo Acosta, deadly gunmen; George Mathews, Whit Bissell, Paul Burns, Richard Deacon and others.

Script by Edmund North and Joseph Petracca, from the novel by Verne Athanas, provides believable shadings to the characters and situations as the plot moves through a dramatic study of a Kansas frontier town suddenly become rich and riotous with the entry of the railroad and trail herds. How Ryan works out his personal and duty obligations, proves that sometimes the use of a gun is necessary, and wins over a young man to his side in the climaxing battle with the town's evil forces, is suspensefully and engrossingly presented. Noteworthy is the script and directorial avoidance of over-statement, resulting in a taut 94 minutes of footage.

The footage looks great in CinemaScope and De Luxe Color as photographed by Lucien Ballard. Editing, art direction and other technical credits merit mention. Picture has a good score by Lionel Newman, albeit over-emphasized in some of the more suspenseful sequences. A simple whistled, behind-scenes theme is very effective for mood. *Brog.*

Secret of Treasure Mountain

Slow, dull re-telling buried treasure.

Hollywood, May 16.
Columbia release of Wallace M. MacDonald production. Stars Valerie French, Raymond Burr, William Prince, Lance Fuller; features Susan Cummings, Pat Hogan, Reginald Sheffield, Rodolfo Hoyos. Directed by Seymour Friedman. Screenplay, David Lang; camera, Benjamin H. Kline; editor, Edwin Bryant. Previewed May 15, '56. Running time, 67 MINS.
Audrey Lancaster ....Valerie French
Cash Larsen .... Raymond Burr
Robert Kendall .... William Prince
Juan Alvarado.......... Lance Fuller
Tawana .... Susan Cummings
Vahoe .... Pat Hogan
Edward Lancaster ....Reginald Sheffield
Francisco Martinez ...... Rodolfo Hoyos
Sheriff .... Paul McGuire

Sam .... Tom Hubbard
Stub McCurdy .... Boyd Stockman

This is a poor action programmer, re-telling a familiar outdoor theme about buried gold at such a dull pace there's little to recommend it. The footage is short at 67 minutes, but the picture is long.

David Lang's screen story bears a certain basic resemblance to Columbia's 1949 "Lust For Gold," as does some of the stock footage included in this Wallace MacDonald production. Plotting and dialog are hackneyed, so there is nothing the direction by Seymour Friedman nor the thesping can do to make events even vaguely believable.

A multi-million treasure in gold is the plot lure. The early-day Fort Knox was buried by a Spaniard, who in turn was killed by Apaches and an Indian curse put on the land and cash. Apparently the Apaches didn't believe in the power of their curse, though, so some 200 years later, a redskin posing as a white stands guard. When some adventurers come along and one of them gets on the scent of the hoard, things happen and greed crops out, both for gold and gals. When the plot's all over, the gold's still cached and the bad men are dead.

William Prince, who appeared in the '49 "Lust," is again a good guy in this and his basic honesty gets him the gal, Valerie French, daughter of English remittance man Reginald Sheffield, who has sought the desert for his health. Raymond Burr is the stereotype baddie, Lance Fuller the masquerading Indian guardian. Susan Cummings, Pat Hogan and Rodolfo Hoyos are among featured players. Benjamin H. Kline's photography and the other technical credits are standard for the budget. *Brog.*

Screaming Eagles

Good war actioner.

Hollywood, May 16.
Allied Artists release of Samuel Bischoff-David Diamond production. Stars Tom Tryon, Jan Merlin, Alvy Moore, Martin Milner, Jacqueline Beer; features Joe di Reda, Mark Damon, Paul Burke, Pat Conway, Edward G. Robinson Jr., Ralph Votrian. Directed by Charles Haas. Screenplay David Lang; based Robert Presnell Jr.; story, Virginia Kellogg; camera, Harry Neumann; editor, Robert S. Eisen; score, Harry Sukman. Previewed May 14, '56. Running time, 80 MINS.
Mason .... Tom Tryon
Pauling .... Jan Merlin
Grimes .... Alvy Moore
Corliss .... Martin Milner
Marianne .... Jacqueline Beer
Dubrowski .... Joe di Reda
Lambert .... Mark Damon
Dreef .... Paul Burke
Forrest .... Pat Conway
Smith .... Edward G. Robinson Jr.
Talbot .... Ralph Votrian
Foley .... Paul Smith
Hernandez .... Bobby Blake
Torren .... Bob Roark
Peterson .... Bob Dix
Nolan .... Wayne Taylor
Hans Schacht .... Robert Boon
Gustav Bormann ...... Peter Michaels

The formula war action in "Screaming Eagles" is stirred up at an okay pace so it averages out as a good entry for regular program bills. Additionally, it nicely showcases a number of newer male faces. Younger filmgoers, particularly the action-minded male teeners, will accept this one.

Screenplay by David Lang and Robert Presnell Jr. from a story by Virginia Kellogg, rounds up a group of stereotype characters and situations for the cast to enact under Charles Haas' direction. Latter keeps the Samuel Bischoff-David Diamond production going

at a pace fast enough to hold overall interest in the familiar doings.

Tom Tryon plays a surly private replacement in the 1st Platoon, Company D, 101st Airborne Inf. Division, whose association with an understanding lieutenant, well played by Jan Merlin, and other heroes of the group brings about a change of character. The platoon's Normandy D-Day mission to take and hold a bridge. In trying to make its way to the bridge after parachuting into France, the group valiantly fights its way through all sorts of Nazi opposition, even rescues a French girl, Jacqueline Beer, and takes her along on the heroic junket.

Cast acquits itself excellently. Rating a nod, in addition to Tryon, Merlin and Miss Beer, are Alvy Moore, Martin Milner, Joe di Reda, Mark Damon, Paul Burke, Pat Conway, Edward G. Robinson, Jr. Ralph Votrian and others.

Lensing by Harry Neumann, art direction, settings, editing and other technical assists handle the physical layout expertly. Harry Sukman's music is okay. *Brog.*

That Certain Feeling
(V'VISION-SONGS-COLOR)

Bob Hope hoke, Eva Maria Saint clowning, Pearl Bailey singing make amusing comedy.

Palm Springs, June 5.
Paramount release of Norman Panama, Melvin Frank production, directed by Panama and Frank. Stars Bob Hope, Eva Marie Saint, George Sanders; features Pearl Bailey. Screenplay, Panama, Frank, I. A. L. Diamond, William Altman; based on play, "The King of Hearts" by Jean Kerr, Eleanor Brooke; camera, Loyal Griggs; editor, Tom McAdoo; score, Joseph J. Lilley; songs, George and Ira Gershwin, Johnny Mercer and Harold Arlen, James F. Hanley. Previewed at Plaza Theatre, Palm Springs, May 26, '56. Running time, 102 MINS.
Francis X. Dignan .... Bob Hope
Dunreath Henry .... Eva Marie Saint
Larry Larkin .... George Sanders
Maid (Gussie) .... Pearl Bailey
Joe Wickes .... David Lewis
Himself .... Al Capp
Norman Taylor .... Jerry Mathers
Doctor .... Herbert Rudley
Senator Winston .... Florenz Ames

Bob Hope newest hoke should mean fun for most viewers. It's backed by exceptional promotion by star and Paramount (the teeoff was a Palm Springs-datelined charity preem).

Producer-director-writer team of Norman Panama and Melvin Frank share the first two duties among themselves, but two other cooks are brought in on the script, I. A. L. Diamond and William Altman, to adapt "The King of Hearts," legiter by Jean Kerr and Eleanor Brooke, to the screen. In several scenes the material is worked beyond the point of best return, but overall what's fashioned here is amusingly frothy, with a touch of heart occasionally to add depth.

Femme costar is Eva Marie Saint in her first film start since her Academy-kudosed "On the Waterfront." Marquee-wise, her name means little, but acting-wise, what she does in the change of pace casting is all to the good, showing a versatility that will build name. She's good, both as a gal who is trying to be something she ain't, and in a tipsy scene when she's out to get her man. The producer-director team lets that scene run longer than it should, but that is no fault of hers.

A big asset is Pearl Bailey, maid in the household of renowned cartoonist George Sanders, for whom Miss Saint is secretary-fiancee and Hope is ghost "stripper." Bailey's wow personality, heretofore displayed on nitery floors, is caught by the camera and adds a most engaging comedy touch to the footage. Additionally, she gives her potent styling to "That Certain Feeling," standard by George and Ira Gershwin, "Hit the Road to Dreamland," by Johnny Mercer and Harold Arlen, and "Zing Went the Strings of My Heart," by James F. Hanley, all of which are getting a disk-jockey play at present.

Sanders has himself a free-wheeling ball as the sophisticated cartoonist who has lost the common touch and calls in ghoster Hope, a neurotic who wants to up-chuck every time he tries to stand up to the boss. Complicating his employment is the fact that Miss Saint's his ex-wife. This situation is worsened when Miss Bailey warms up the "zing" that Miss Saint still feels for Hope, but it takes a young boy, Jerry Mathers, whom Sanders is using for publicity purposes, to get the ex-marital pair back together again. Topper to the laughs is a wild takeoff on an Ed Murrow "Person To Person" telecast in which everything goes wrong for Sanders but right for Hope and Miss Saint.

David Lewis, repeating his stage role of the cartoonist's manager; Al Capp, playing himself; young Mathers, Herbert Rudley and Florenz Ames complete the ably-performing supporting cast. There's a nepotism note to the uncredited casting. One of Hope's sons does well as a playmate to young Mathers; and three other Hope offspring are in amusement park bits.

Technical credits stand up well, from Loyal Griggs' Technicolor lensing, through the fine art direction and set decorations, the editing and those fetching Edith Head costumes which Miss Saint wears. Joseph J. Lilley's score does its share in the entertainment.

Brog.

A Kiss Before Dying
(C'SCOPE-SONG-COLOR)

Series of murders by a college stude. Well done.

Hollywood, June 1.
United Artists release of Robert L. Jacks (Crown) production. Stars Robert Wagner, Jeffrey Hunter, Virginia Leith, Joanne Woodward; features Mary Astor, George Macready, Robert Quarry, Howard Petrie, Bill Walker. Directed by Gerd Oswald. Screenplay, Lawrence Roman; from novel by Ira Levin; camera (De Luxe Color), Lucien Ballard; editor, George Gittens; music, Lionel Newman; song, Newman and Carroll Coates; sung by Dolores Hawkins. Previewed May 29, '56. Running time, 94 MINS.
Bud Corliss .... Robert Wagner
Gordon Grant .... Jeffrey Hunter
Ellen Kingship .... Virginia Leith
Dorothy Kingship .... Joanne Woodward
Mrs. Corliss .... Mary Astor
Leo Kingship .... George Macready
Dwight Powell .... Robert Quarry
Chesser .... Howard Petrie
Butler .... Bill Walker
Annabelle .... Molly McCart
Medical Student .... Marlene Felton

This multiple-murder story carries enough interest and suspense to fit handily into the general market, despite a tendency to draw out situations and certain plot deficiencies. Name of Robert Wagner plus effective CinemaScope lensing and De Luxe Color, b r i g h t e n its chances at the b.o.

The Robert L. Jacks production is an offbeat sort of film, with Wagner portraying a calculating youth who intends to allow nothing to stand in his way to money. L a w r e n c e Roman's screenplay, from a novel by Ira Levin, projects the star in a role foreign to anything he's played in the past. Gerd Oswald's restrained direction suits the mood, and excellent scenic values are displayed via Lucien Ballard's color photography.

Wagner's troubles start in opening scene, when he learns that his college sweetheart, Joanne Woodward, is expecting a baby, a circumstance that means she'll be disinherited by her wealthy father and his plans to latch onto the family fortune ruined. He pushes her to her death from the top of a building where they've gone to get a wedding license, and since no one knows they've been dating (hard for the spectator to swallow), Wagner is in the clear.

The dead girl's sister, Virginia Leith, refuses, however, to believe the police report of suicide and later reopens the case on her own. Wagner now is making a play for this member of the family, who is unaware he knew her sister, and when Virginia in her investigating hits on a suspect, Wagner kills him to make it appear he was the actual murderer. He's tripped up when Virginia learns of his friendship with her sister, and Wagner is killed while trying to throw femme over a precipice.

Wagner registers in killer role, although his bobbysox followers may find this offbeat casting not to their liking. Miss Woodward is particularly good as the pregnant girl, and Miss Leith acceptable as her sister. Jeffrey Hunter is lost as a part-time university professor responsible for the final solution of the crimes. Mary Astor and George Macready are okay as Wagner's mother and the girls' father. Dolores Hawkins' offscreen chirping of title song by Lionel Newman and Carroll Coates is melodic. Technical credits are satisfactory.

Whit.

Shadow of Fear

Better than average suspense thriller.

United Artists release of Charles A. Leeds (Roxbury) production. Stars Mona Freeman, Jean Kent, and Maxwell Reed. Directed by Al Rogell. Adapted from the novel by Hal Debrett. Camera, Jack Asher; editor, Jim Connock; music Leonard Salzede. Previewed in N.Y., May 31, '56. Running time, 76 MINS.
April Haddon .... Mona Freeman
Florence Haddon .... Jean Kent
Michael Elder .... Maxwell Reed
Mr. Driscoll .... Hugh Miller
Elsie .... Gretchen Franklin
Dr. Elder .... Frederick Leister
Police Sergeant .... Alexander Gauge
Mrs. Harrison .... Josephine Middleton
Jack Storey .... Frank Forsyth
Harry .... Stanley Van Beers
Taxi Driver .... Frank Atkinson
Station Master .... Philip Ray
Parson .... Robert Sansom
Dr. Elder's Receptionist..Phyllis Cornell

Better than average suspense film by Charles Leeds and directed by Al Rogell. The premise has had a considerable workout in whodunit literature. Mona Freeman, as a college student who had studied in the United States, returns to her native English town after the death of her mother and father. Although both deaths appear normal to local authorities, Miss Freeman is suspicious of the circumstances and the part played by her stepmother who had been her mother's nurse.

Since the stepmother, played effectively by Jean Kent, is a pillar of the community, active in church, Red Cross, and other philanthropic work, Miss Freeman is unable to convey her suspicions to friends and to local authorities. As a matter of fact, Miss Freeman, who is due to receive the bulk of her father's estate on her 21st birthday, only three weeks off, finds her own life in danger.

The tension builds nicely as she uncovers bits of evidence to pinpoint the murders on her stepmother, but she is frustrated in every effort to present the facts. The stepmother's explanations seem logical, and even the viewer, until the very end, has some doubt of her guilt. A final overt act at the conclusion is the clincher.

A romantic interlude is introduced via Maxwell Reed, a childhood chum of Miss Freeman's who has become the local doctor. As most of the community, Reed is unconvinced of Miss Freeman's suspicions, but he plays a leading role in the denouement.

Miss Kent is standout as the stepmother. She neatly displays a menacing quality which overshadows the saccharine facade. Miss Freeman is fine as the troubled and confused young lady who finds herself alone in a hostile atmosphere. Reed, it appears, would be more convincing as a young English country doctor if he had his

hair cut. His thespian name doesn't fit the setting. Technical contributions are excellent.

Holl.

The Rawhide Years
(SONGS-COLOR)

Actionful western with Tony Curtis; good outdoor entry.

Hollywood, May 29.
Universal release of Stanley Rubin production. Stars Tony Curtis, Colleen Miller, Arthur Kennedy; features William Demarest, William Gargan, Peter Van Eyck, Minor Watson, Donald Randolph, Robert Wilke. Directed by Rudolph Mate. Screenplay, Earl Felton; adaptation, Robert Presnell Jr.; D. D. Beauchamp; from novel by Norman A. Fox; camera (Technicolor), Irving Glassberg; editor, Russell Schoengarth; music, Frank Skinner, Hans J. Salter; songs, Frederick Herbert and Arnold Hughes, Peggy Lee and Laurindo Almeida. Previewed May 22, '56. Running time, 85 MINS.
Ben .... Tony Curtis
Zoe .... Colleen Miller
Rick Harper .... Arthur Kennedy
Brand Comfort .... William Demarest
Marshal Sommers .... William Gargan
Andre Boucher .... Peter Van Eyck
Matt Comfort .... Minor Watson
Carrico .... Donald Randolph
Neal .... Robert Wilke
Captain .... Trevor Bardette
Deputy Wade .... James Anderson
Mate .... Robert Foulk
Gif Lessing .... Chubby Johnson
Miss Vanilla Bissell... Leigh Snowden
Frank Porter .... Don Beddoe

Plenty of rapid action and Tony Curtis' name for the marquees shape "The Rawhide Years" for a good reception in the western field. It has the ingredients required to keep the general outdoor fan happy.

Director Rudolph Mate unfolds the Stanley Rubin production at such a swift pace plot holes are passed over almost before they have a chance to show. This overall razzle-dazzle benefits the footage, playing it for fast movement so there's never a dull moment, although some customers may wonder occasionally what the shootin's all about.

Curtis plays a young adventurer, shilling for a gambler on a river boat until he is falsely accused of a killing and takes it on the lam. Some three years later he returns to the frontier town to clear his name and get his girl, Colleen Miller. The latter, by now, has taken up with gambling saloon operator Peter Van Eyck, who actually heads a gang of river boat pirates with William Demarest, supposedly respectable rancher. When the shooting is over, Curtis is cleared, the heavies are dead and Miss Miller is back where she belongs in his arms.

The above perform the characters in the Earl Felton script in acceptable fashion, even when what's motivating them isn't clear. Arthur Kennedy, who stars with Curtis and Miss Miller, puts a lot of likeable color into the character of a happy-go-lucky, larcenous opportunist who teams up with Curtis. William Gargan, the marshal; Minor Watson, murder victim; Donald Randolph, the gambler; Robert Wilke, gunman, are among others who are competent. Leigh Snowden has herself one good scene and is seen no more.

In her role of saloon entertainer, Miss Miller pleasingly sings "Give Me Your Love" and "Happy Go Lucky," by Frederick Herbert and Arnold Hughes, and "The Gypsy With the Fire In His Shoes" by Peggy Lee and Laurindo Almeida. Irving Glassberg does a good job of photographing the action in Technicolor, and the background

score by Frank Skinner and Hans J. Salter does its part well.

Brog.

Earth Vs. the Flying Saucers

Science-fictioner good for dual market exploitation dates.

Hollywood, June 1.
Columbia release of Charles H. Schneer production. Stars Hugh Marlowe, Joan Taylor; features Donald Curtis, Morris Ankrum, John Zaremba, Tom Browne Henry, Grandon Rhodes, Larry Blake. Directed by Fred F. Sears. Screenplay, George Worthing Yates, Raymond T. Marcus; story, Curt Siodmak; suggested by Major Donald E. Keyhoe's "Flying Saucers From Outer Space"; camera, Fred Jackman Jr.; technical effects, Ray Harryhausen; editor, Danny D. Landres; music, Mischa Bakaleinikoff. Previewed May 21, '56. Running time, 82 MINS.
Dr. Russell A. Marvin..... Hugh Marlowe
Carol Marvin .... Joan Taylor
Major Huglin .... Donald Curtis
General Hanley .... Morris Ankrum
Professor Kanter .... John Zaremba
Admiral Enright.......... Tom Browne Henry
General Edmunds.......... Grandon Rhodes
Motorcycle Officer........ Larry Blake
Cutting .... Harry Lauter
Dr. Alberts .... Charles Evans
Sgt. Nash .... Clark Howat
Alfred Cassidy .... Frank Wilcox
Major Kimberly .... Alan Reynolds

This exploitation programmer does a satisfactory job of entertaining in the science-fiction class. Ballyhoo playdates in the general dual bill market should show some nice b.o. returns; otherwise, it's an okay lowercase booking.

The technical effects created by Ray Harryhausen come off excellently in the Charles H. Schneer production, adding the required out-of-this-world visual touch to the screenplay by George Worthing Yates and Raymond T. Marcus. Latter was taken from the screen story by Curt Siodmak, suggested by Major Donald E. Keyhoe's "Flying Saucers From Outer Space."

Fred F. Sears' direction mixes the make-believe at a good pace, achieving a neat measure of suspense and thrills as the plot unwinds. Hugh Marlowe, space-exploration scientist, interrupts his honeymoon with Joan Taylor to find out why the free-flying, artificial satellites he has been launching for the military are being knocked down. Ancient humanoids, manning flying saucers, are the saboteurs and through communication with the hero, advise they intend to take over the earth. Yankee ingenuity comes up with a hastily devised weapon that neutralizes the saucers' magnetic, antigravity equipment. Thus, the invasion flight is destroyed and Marlowe then concentrates on unfinished honeymoon business.

Marlowe and Miss Taylor do well by their roles and other assists in the trouping department come from Donald Curtis, Army officer; Morris Ankrum, a general captured by the spacemen; John Zaremba, Tom Browne Henry, Grandon Rhodes, Larry Blake and others.

Pic, make under the executive supervision of Sam Katzman, has been given good photography by Fred Jackman Jr., with art direction, editing, special effects and sound playing their parts in putting over the thriller. *Brog.*

Massacre
(COLOR)

Trite, poorly-made, Mexico-lensed, outdoor actioner.

Hollywood, June 1.
20th-Fox release of Robert L. Lippert Jr. production. Stars Dane Clark, James

Craig, Marta Roth; features Jaime Fernandez, Ferrusquilla, Miguel Torruco, Jose Munoz, Enrique Zambrano. Directed by Louis King. Screenplay, D. D. Beauchamp; story, Fred Freiberger, William Tunberg; camera (Ansco Color), Gilbert Warrenton; editor, Carl Pierson; music, Ginzalo Curiel. Previewed May 31, '56. Running time, 75 MINS.

Ramon	Dane Clark
Ezparza	James Craig
Angelica	Marta Roth
Juan Pedro	Jaime Fernandez
Vincent	Ferrusquilla
Chavez	Miguel Torruco
Macario	Jose Munoz
Munez	Enrique Zambrano

This Mexico-lensed outdoor actioner is an extremely lightweight lowercase programmer that will have to depend mostly on a product scarcity to get playdates. Most surprising thing about the pic is that it's going out under the 20th-Fox trademark, that company having taken it over from Robert L. Lippert Jr., who produced below the border.

The story has a different ending, but the buildup to it is so routine the impact of the twist is lost. Dialog is trite and the direction formula, with playing by Dane Clark, James Craig, Marta Roth and others on the same level. Louis King directed from D. D. Beauchamp's screenplay, based on a story by Fred Freiberger and William Tunberg.

Clark is captain of a detachment of Rurales, out to run down some gun-smugglers selling weapons to the Yaqui Indians. Craig is his lieutenant, who has fallen for Miss Roth, wife of Miguel Torruco, the smuggler. Clark and his men, who have brought Miss Roth along, catch up with Torruco deep in Yaqui country. The Indians attack and kill all of the intruders. End of picture.

Clark and Craig aren't very convincing as Mexicans, and the real Latins in the cast are difficult to understand. Other than Miss Roth and Torruco, they include Jaime Fernandez, a Yaqui scout; Ferrusquilla, Jose Munoz and Enrique Zambrano. The lensing by Gilbert Warrenton gives an idea of the rugged outdoor locations where the picture was shot, but the uneven Ansco tints do not always do the photography justice. Editing, score and other technical credits are standard. *Brog.*

Cannes Festival

Le Monde Du Silence (The World of Silence) (FRENCH - DOCUMENTARY-COLOR). J. Arthur Rank-Victory Film release of Filmad production. Written and directed by Jacques-Yves Cousteau, Louis Malle. Camera (Eastmancolor), Edmond Sechan, underwater scenes, Malle Cousteau, Falco, Dumas; editor, Georges Alepee; music, Yves Baudrier. At Cannes Film Fest. Running time, 85 MINS.

Winner of the Golden Palm, the grand prize, at the recent Cannes Film Fest, this underwater documentary has a series of poetic scenes, rapturous below surface incidents and enough unusual exotic bits to make this of interest for arty spots with critics and word-of-mouth sure to help. Its high entertainment impact also slants this for general chances with a commentary easy to dub. There have been many underwater exploration pix of late, but this emerges by far the most original and the Cannes kudos should help the "sell."

Film recounts the work of Jacques-Yves Consteau's boat, the Ca-

lypso, in charting below surface aspects for world museums. Some outstanding scenes are a shark carnage on a whale being towed by the boat, undersea scooter trips, a trained fish that eats from the diver's hands, the discovery of a wreck with the poetic knell from its bell, and other savvy edited scenes which bundle this into an offbeater that pays off handsomely. Color is excellent with new hues unveiled down below, and music editing and commentary weld this into a taking documentary of high calibre. *Mosk.*

Pather Panchali (Song of the Little Road) (INDIAN). West Bengal release and production. Directed by Satyaji Roy. Screenplay, Bibhuti from a novel by Bandopa Dhyaya; camera, Subrota Mitra; editor, Roy; music, Ravi Shankar. With K. Bannerpee, Uma Dasgupta, Subir Bannerjee. At Cannes Film Fest. Running time, 90 MINS.

Film justly won the "most human document award" at the recent Cannes Film Fest. It was the fest revelation and unveiled a mature film talent, in director Satyaji Roy, now at work in India. Film poetically and lyrically unfolds a tender but penetrating tale of coming of age in India, a land of poverty but also of spiritual hope. Two adolescents, a boy and his sister, grow in this atmosphere and the film fuses all aspects of pic making into a moving whole that shows India perceptively for the first time to a Western audience.

The treatment of old age is perhaps one of the most profound ever seen on the screen. An old woman lives and dies among the budding children with a dignity and beauty that counterpoints the growth and the experiences of the children. Acting, lensing and all other aspects are masterfully orchestrated by Roy into a document on life in India that should be a natural for the art house circuit Stateside. Its high entertainment story values also give this greater distrib chances. *Mosk.*

Together (BRITISH). British Film Institute release and production. Directed by Lorenza Mazzetti. Screenplay, Denis Horn. Camera, Walter Lassally; editor, Lindsay Anderson; music, Daniele Paris. At Cannes Film Fest. Running time, 50 MINS.

Offbeater is an off-size pic on the life of two deaf mutes in the sprawling London East End. Made by the BFI as an encouragement of experimental film, this fills the bill, and the pic got a special prize nod at the Cannes Film Fest. It is a highly personalized film and this makes it more difficult to package for Stateside chances. It will have to be pegged for a special program with another outstanding medium length pic for best results. In it the daily ritual of two mutes takes on a poetic contour in their ties with life about them, with the adroit sound track and editing amply maintaining the aspect of their soundless existence. Nothing much happens for the film is an atmospheric tone poem. Somewhat repetitious at points, this might be sharpened up somewhat by some pruning. The slow pacing is suddenly broken into by a tragedy of indifference and unwitting cruelty on the part of some children whose twitting of the two ends with one falling into a river being swept off before anyone can notice him. Lensing, editing and music come into a well balanced whole in the

hands of the young 25-year-old female director Lorenza Mazzetti. *Mosk.*

The First Texan
(C'SCOPE—COLOR)

Joel McCrea, as Sam Houston, leads Texas to its independence from Mexico. For the outdoor action market.

Hollywood, June 11.
Allied Artists release of Walter Mirisch production. Stars Joe McCrea, Felicia Farr, Jeff Morrow; features Wallace Ford, Abraham Sofaer, Jody McCrea, Chubby Johnson, Dayton Lummis, Rodolfo Hoyos, William Hopper, Roy Roberts, David Silva. Directed by Byron Haskin. Screenplay, Daniel B. Ullman; camera (Technicolor), Wilfrid Cline; editor, George White; music, Roy Webb. Previewed June 4, '56. Running time, 81 MINS.

Sam Houston	Joel McCrea
Katherine	Felicia Farr
Bowie	Jeff Morrow
Delaney	Wallace Ford
Don Carlos	Abraham Sofaer
Baker	Jody McCrea
Deaf Smith	Chubby Johnson
Austin	Dayton Lummis
Cos	Rodolfo Hoyos
Travis	William Hopper
Sherman	Roy Roberts
Santa Ana	David Silva
Pepe	Frank Puglia
Veramendi	Salvador Baguez
Crockett	James Griffith
Hockley	Nelson Leigh

Texas' revolt against Mexican rule and the part Sam Houston played in leading it to independence get the CinemaScope-Technicolor treatment in this Allied Artists offering. It should be a popular pic in the Lone Star state, and Joel McCrea's name will see it through the outdoor action market elsewhere to satisfactory returns.

Film is a bit on the slow side in building to the climaxing Battle of San Jacinto, which swings the tide of revolt and establishes Texas as a Republic with Houston as first president. This historic battle, however, makes up for any previous lack of fast pacing, being exceptionally well staged under Byron Haskin's direction and excellently lensed by Wilfrid Cline.

McCrea was a good choice to top the cast-in the Walter Mirisch production. He makes the Houston character credible and handles some romantic chores with lovely Felicia Farr well. She, too, is a pleasing added attraction in the casting, and there are good assists from Jeff Morrow, as James Bowie; Wallace Ford, as Miss Farr's father; Abraham Sofaer, Chubby Johnson, Dayton Lummis, Rodolfo Hoyos, William Hopper, Roy Roberts, David Silva, as the dread Santa Ana, "Napoleon of the West," who is defeated and captured at San Jacinto by Houston; James Griffith and others portraying historical figures in the fight for independence. McCrea's son, Jody, turns in an able performance as a young soldier in the Texas forces. Others rating mention include Frank Puglia, Salvador Baguez and Nelson Leigh.

Daniel B. Ullman's carefully written screen story opens with Houston leaving Tennessee for Texas, where he at first shies away from politics and the revolt. Historical highspots are touched on, showing the prelude to the fall of the Alamo, the seeming retreat that Houston staged to lure Santa Ana deep into Texas territory before turning and fighting in the climaxing battle.

Editing by George White, the Roy Webb score, conducted by Paul Sawtell, and other behind-camera contributions are good. Score includes a title tune, with lyrics by McElbert Moore. *Brog.*

The Black Sleep

Basil Rathbone as a crazy brain surgeon. Kids should love all the gore.

Hollywood, June 7.

United Artists release of Aubrey Schenck, Howard W Koch (Bel-Air) production. Stars Basil Rathbone, Akim Tamiroff, Lon Chaney, John Carradine, Bela Lugosi; features Herbert Rudley, Patricia Blake, Phyllis Stanley. Directed by Reginald Le Borg. Screenplay, John C. Higgins; story, Gerald Drayson Adams; camera, Gordon Avil; editor, John F. Schreyer; music, Les Baxter. Previewed June 5, '56. Running time, **82 MINS.**

Sir Joel Cadman .... Basil Rathbone
Odo .... Akim Tamiroff
Mungo .... Lon Chaney
Borg .... John Carradine
Casimir .... Bela Lugosi
Dr. Gordon Ramsay....Herbert Rudley
Laurie .... Patricia Blake
Daphne .... Phyllis Stanley
Curry .... Tor Johnson
Nancy .... Sally Yarnell
K-6 .... George Sawaya
Miss Daly .... Claire Carleton
Investigative-Sergeant Steel Peter Gordon
Angelina .... Louanna Gardner
1st Bobby .... Clive Morgan
Scotland Yard Detective John Sheffield

As a straight horror pic, of the "Frankenstein's Monster" genre, "The Black Sleep" is a good entry for the special exploitation spook bills. In that market it will function adequately, having the necessary cast names and ballyhoo angles.

The Bel-Air production by Aubrey Schenck and Howard W. Koch has such masters of screen horror as Basil Rathbone, Akim Tamiroff, Lon Chaney, John Carradine and Bela Lugosi to act out the melodramatics under Reginald Le Borg's direction. Handling of the script, which John C. Higgins wrote from a story by Gerald Drayson Adams, plays the horror tale fairly straight so what's happening is not too illogical until the finale wrapup, when all restraint comes off and the melodramatics run amok.

Setting in England of the 1870's, appropriately gloomy and forbidding for spook shows of this type. Rathbone is the mad surgeon, using a drug that induces sleep resembling death to practice brain carving on unwilling subjects. He has a humane motive—his wife's in a coma from a tumor and he's merely preparing himself to carry out a delicate operation. He needs an assistant, though, so frames a young doctor, Herbert Rudley, for murder, then rescues him from the gallows via the "black sleep" drug. The grateful young medico reneges, however, when he discovers the mutilated victim of the doc still alive but hardly human. Among them is the man Rudley's supposed to have killed. These spectres get loose at the climax, storming their way through Rathbone's gaunt old abbey headquarters to the chant of "kill, kill, kill," but Scotland Yard arrives in time to rescue Rudley and Patricia Blake, daughter of Chaney, one of Rathbone's victims.

Rathbone is quite credible as the surgeon, enough so that those brain operations he performs will horrify many viewers. Rudley is good, too, as the medico and Tamiroff is excellent as the gypsy who obtains the victims for Rathbone. Chaney, Carradine and Lugosi prove okay bogeymen, along with Tor Johnson, George Sawaya, Sally Yarnell and Claire Carleton. As the stricken wife, Louanna Gardner acts out her role in a coma, Miss Blake is a nice ingenue, but femme cast honors easily go to Phyllis Stanley, convincing as Rathbone's nurse.

Music by Les Baxter, lensing by Gordon Avil and other technical contributions are keyed to the horror mood. *Brog.*

Behind the High Wall

Dull and unbelievable melodrama in stir. Script mediocrity matched by players.

Hollywood, June 12.

Universal release of Stanley Rubin production. Stars Tom Tully, Sylvia Sidney; features Betty Lynn, John Gavin, Don Beddoe, John Larch, Barney Phillips, Ed Kemmer. Directed by Abner Biberman. Screenplay, Harold Jack Bloom; story, Wallace Sullivan, Richard K. Polimer; camera, Maury Gertsman; editor, Ted J. Kent; music, Joseph Gershenson. Previewed June 5, '56. Running time, **85 MINS.**

Frank Carmichael .... Tom Tully
Hilda Carmichael .... Sylvia Sidney
Anne MacGregor .... Betty Lynn
Johnny Hutchins .... John Gavin
Todd MacGregor .... Don Beddoe
William Kiley .... John Larch
Tom Reynolds .... Barney Phillips
Charlie Rains .... Ed Kemmer
Carl Burkhardt .... John Beradino
George Miller .... Rayford Barnes
Roy Burkhardt .... Nicky Blair
Morgan .... David Garcia
First Detective .... Peter Leeds
Second Detective .... Jim Hyland

This is a routine prison melodrama with only so-so entertainment values. A supporter, although overlong at 85 minutes for that classification.

Failure to click as an acceptable thriller seems mostly due to a script that's never believable and some unconvincing acting in several of the key roles. Prison values in the Stanley Rubin production are okay as a plot setting for the Harold Jack Bloom screenplay, based on a story by Wallace Sullivan and Richard K. Polimer, as are most of the technical supports, such as the lensing by Maury Gertsman.

Tom Tully and Sylvia Sidney star to no particular advantage under Abner Biberman's direction. Of the two, she comes off best as Tully's crippled wife. Tully's characterization of a prison warden fails to register, the poor performance contrasting quite sharply with the good work he has done in previous pix. John Gavin, a new face, does well as the film's younger male lead, and Betty Lynn is good as his fiancee. There's acceptable work from such veterans as Don Beddoe, John Larch, Barney Phillips and Ed Kemmer.

Tully is an erratic warden who is kidnapped by some escaping convicts, who also force Gavin to drive the getaway truck. It's wrecked and all are killed but Tully and Gavin. Former hides $100,000 in loot the escapees had and does nothing to keep Gavin from being sentenced to death for participating in a break that resulted in the death of a policeman. Plot development is light on suspense and excitement until the climax, which does stir up a little movement as Gavin breaks from the death house, is cornered by the law, but is saved by a last-minute confession by Tully. *Brog.*

Navy Wife

American Navy wife emancipates Japanese village femmes but it makes dull entertainment.

Hollywood, June 5.

Allied Artists release of Walter Wanger production. Stars Joan Bennett, Gary Merrill, Shirley Yamaguchi; features Maurice Manson, Judy Nugent, Teru Shimada, Robert Nichols, John Craven, Tom Komuro, Shizue Nakamura. Directed by Edward L. Bernds. Screenplay, Kay Lenard; from novel by Tats Blain; camera, Wilfrid Cline; editor, Richard Cahoon; music, Hans Salter; song, "Mother Sir," by Jack Brooks and Salter. Previewed May 28, '56. Running time, **82 MINS.**

Peg Blain .... Joan Bennett
Jack Blain .... Gary Merrill
Akashi .... Shirley Yamaguchi
Capt. Arwin .... Maurice Manson
Debby Blain .... Judy Nugent
Mayor Yoshida .... Teru Shimada
Oscar .... Robert Nichols
Dr. Carter .... John Craven
Ohara .... Tom Komuro
Mitsuko .... Shizue Nakamura

The emancipation of some Japanese village femmes by an American Navy wife probably sounded like a good idea for a film comedy-drama, but it fails to click in this Allied Artists offering. It's dull entertainment mostly and just passable as a secondary programmer.

When Joan Bennett and her daughter, Judy Nugent, join husband-father Gary Merrill in the village of Sasebo, Japan, where he has been stationed for several years, trouble starts. The Japanese wives notice that American wives seem to run things and decide to try the same thing with their husbands. It's a modest pot of turmoil that's stirred up, and there is an unstated resolution of the crisis at a Christmas party attended by Americans and Japanese. This Yule shindig has about the only entertaining flavor in the footage.

The handicaps of a trite script by Kay Lenard are never surmounted by Miss Bennett, Merrill, Shirley Yamaguchi, a geisha; Maurice Manson, Merrill's commanding officer; young Miss Nugent, or the others in the cast. Edward L. Bernds' direction can't make much of the writing, either. Script was from the novel by Tats Blain, "Mother Sir," and there is a behind-credits song by that title cleffed by Jack Brooks and Hans Salter. Latter did the score, also.

The technical values backing the Walter Wanger production are strictly budget, so there is no polish to settings, etc., to divert attention from story problems. Wilfrid Cline lensed in standard fashion. *Brog.*

Congo Crossing
(COLOR)

Regulation jungle adventure thriller; a companion feature for general dual situations.

Hollywood, June 5.

Universal release of Howard Christie production. Stars Virginia Mayo, George Nader, Peter Lorre; features Michael Pate, Rex Ingram, Tonio Selwart, Kathryn Givney, Tudor Owen. Directed by Joseph Pevney. Screenplay, Richard Alan Simmons; story, Houston Branch; camera (Technicolor), Russell Metty; editor, Sherman Todd; music, Joseph Gershenson. Previewed May 29, '56. Running time, **85 MINS.**

Louise Whitman .... Virginia Mayo
David Carr .... George Nader
Colonel Arragas .... Peter Lorre
Bart O'Connell .... Michael Pate
Doctor Gorman .... Rex Ingram
Carl Rittner .... Tonio Selwart
Amelia Abbott .... Kathryn Givney
Emile Zorfus .... Tudor Owen
Peter Mannering .... Raymond Bailey
Miguel Diniz .... George Ramsey
Marquette .... Maurice Doner
Pompala .... Bernard Hamilton
Steiner .... Harold Dyrenforth

"Congo Crossing" is regulation jungle adventure. A potboiler, made on a careful budget. Familiar names top the cast. Howard Christie production and Joseph Pevney's direction sends these players through the stock situations in the Richard Alan Simmons script, based on a Houston Branch story, in a manner that is acceptable, if undistinguished.

Virginia Mayo, well outfitted and equipped, does a play-girl suspected of murder who comes to Congotanga, a piece of West Africa where fugitives gather because of a lack of extradition laws. George Nader is the stalwart hero, conducting a survey for the Belgian Congo government which will show Congotanga falls within its boundaries. Peter Lorre is the local law who keeps the fugitives in line.

This star trio handles the formula characters and situations competently, with Lorre adding his particular brand of color for an extra plus. Michael Pate, Chicago gangster hired to bump off Miss Mayo; Rex Ingram, native doctor running a jungle hospital, and Tonio Selwart, local crime bigshot who doesn't want the Congotanga boundaries changed, take care of the stock demands in okay fashion. Kathryn Givney, fugitive given to murder by poison, as well as purse-purloining, also figures in the generally acceptable performing.

Thrills of the footage mostly come from Selwart's efforts to halt the survey, and whether or not Pate will carry out the killing job for which he has been paid. The baddies all get done in, though, leaving Nader and Miss Mayo an opportunity to further a romance after it's been established she did not do the murder from which she had fled.

Russell Metty's lensing, with print by Technicolor, shows up the backlot jungle settings okay and other technical aids are satisfactory. *Brog.*

The Werewolf

Man-turned-wolf (murder not sex) in minor diversion.

Hollywood, May 24.

Columbia release of a Sam Katzman production. Features Steven Ritch, Don Megowan, Joyce Holden. Directed by Fred F. Sears. Story-screenplay, Robert E. Kent, James B. Gordon; camera, Edwin Linden; editor, Harold White; music, Mischa Bakaleinikoff. Previewed May 23, '56. Running time, **78 MINS.**

The Werewolf,
Duncan March .... Steven Ritch
Jack Haines .... Don Megowan
Amy Standish .... Joyce Holden
Helen Marsh .... Eleanore Tanin
Chris Marsh .... Kim Charney
Clovey .... Harry Lauter
Dirgus .... Larry J. Blake
Dr. James Gilchrist.......... Ken Christy
Fanning .... James Gavin
Dr. Emery Forrest .... S. John Launer
Dr. Morgan Chambers...George M. Lynn
Hoxie .... George Cisar
1st Deputy .... Don C. Harvey

It's been some years since this topic last hit the screen, and time here lends small enchantment. Once its premise of a man changing back and forth into a wolf is posed, the Sam Katzman production seldom rises above a plodding monotone and won't create much reaction in the minor program market for which it is headed.

The Robert E. Kent-James B. Oliver story-screenplay focuses on what happens after an auto accident victim is injected with wolf serum while still unconscious by a pair of experimenting doctor-scientists. Serum changes him into a wolf when he's accosted by a holdup man in a small mountain community, and he rips his assailant's throat. Action thereafter follows a sheriff as he hunts down the wolfman, who resumes normalcy after capture, and the trackdown again following wolfman's escape. No climax is reached as bullets bring down the quarry.

Steven Ritch portrays the werewolf, but characters generally lack interest and Fred F. Sears fails to insert any excitement in his directorial unfoldmen. Don Megowan is the sheriff, Joyce Holden his fiancee, and Eleanore Tanin the wife of the wolfman. Technical credits are standard. *Whit.*

Les Truands
(The Thieves)
(FRENCH)

Paris, June 5.

Gaumont release of Gaumont-Franco-London production. Stars Eddie Constantine, Jean Richard, Noel-Noel; features Yves Robert, Lucien Baroux, Julie Astor. Directed and written by Carlo Rim. Camera, Maurice Barry; editor, Monique Kirsonoff. At Paris, Paris. Running time, **105 MINS.**

Jim .... Eddie Constantine
Alexandre .... Jean Richard
Cahuzac .... Noel-Noel
Amedee .... Yves Robert
Priest .... Lucien Baroux

Three sketches, to capitalize on star names here, are worked into a tale of a dying centenarian whose rapacious relatives are already fighting over a fortune he has left in stolen goods because the old man has been a lifelong professional crook. Some clever ideas are inherent in the pic with the Gallic cynicism and insouciant treatment of crime. But the treatment is too broad to give this a high comedic polish. It can be of some interest for the U. S. on its gimmick qualities.

Amedee (Yves Robert), at 104 years of age, has a stroke while being feted by the town. However, he has been able to lift the mayor's watch just before it happens. Then his life is recounted in flashbacks and film has some measure of yocks in the mock treatment of the dedicated watch stealers through Gallic history who are finally put out of business by the wrist watch. Stars are rung in as they come to visit the old man and tell tales about themselves. Jean Richard comes out in this with Noel-Noel failing to get any savor into a skit of a burglar who finds his daughter bedded down with the owner of the house on one of his forays. Eddie Constantine plays the ladykiller with a too highly moral spirit and somewhat too deadpan. Constantine is at best in a firsticuff scene as an early U. S. western tough guy.

Robert is fine as the grouchy old crook and remainder of the cast is okay. Writer-director Carlo Rim has not fused his two jobs completely enough to get the right laughs from this gambit which sees too many good ideas going astray because of too obvious direction and writing. *Mosk.*

It's Great to Be Young
(BRITISH-COLOR)

Lively British comedy geared for hefty domestic returns and likely prospect for U.S.

London, June 5.

Associated British-Pathe production and release. Stars John Mills and Cecil Parker; features Jeremy Spenser, Dorothy Bromiley. Directed by Cyril Frankel. Screenplay, Ted Willis; camera, Gilbert Taylor; editor, Max Benedict; music, Ray Martin. At Studio One, London. Running time, **94 MINS.**

Dingle .... John Mills
Frome .... Cecil Parker
Routledge .... John Salew
Mrs. Castle .... Elizabeth Kentish
Miss Morrow .... Mona Washbourne
Miss Wyvern .... Mary Merrall
Paterson .... Derek Blomfield
Nicky .... Jeremy Spenser
Paulette .... Dorothy Bromiley
Ginger .... Brian Smith
Browning .... Wilfred Downing
Morris .... Robert Dickens
Crowther .... Dawson France
Peggy .... Carole Shelley
Lawson .... Richard O'Sullivan
Publican .... Norman Pierce
Barmaid .... Eleanor Summerfield
Organ Salesman .... Bryan Forbes
Landlady .... Marjorie Rhodes
Mrs. Morris .... Eddie Byrne
School Inspector .... Russell Waters

A lively comedy, overflowing with honest-to-goodness humor, "It's Great to be Young" has all the makings of a firstclass money spinner in the domestic market. The pic deserves to make the grade in overseas territories, too, and is worthy of serious consideration by U.S. theatres.

There is nothing sophisticated about Ted Willis's story or characters and the situations are sufficiently preposterous to insure maximum audience reaction. The action is kept at a boisterous pace, the country grammar school setting providing a handsome background.

The whole plot is little more than an uninhibited schoolboy romp in which the co-eds at grammar school take the law into their own hands to secure the reinstatement of their favorite teacher, John Mills. He had been fired for defying authority, buying musical instruments and rehearsing the kids for a national music festival.

The trouble at the school begins with the appointment of Cecil Parker as new headmaster. His reforms make him particularly unpopular with the kids but, encouraged by Mills, they plan a campaign to defeat his embargo on the purchase of new instruments. The clandestine rehearsals, which frequently turn into vigorous jam sessions, are among the best things in the production.

Mills is in top form in a role which demands a light comedy touch. He makes an impressive contribution. The co-eds are vigorously led by Jeremy Spenser, Dorothy Bromiley, Brian Smith and Carole Shelley, all of whom perform with confident expertise. Parker is almost type-cast as the headmaster and that applies also to John Salew as a senior teacher. The rest of the cast lends admirable support.

Cyril Frankel's direction keeps the pace at a lively speed and Gilbert Taylor has done a fine job with the color camera. Robert Jones has designed admirable sets and Max Benedict rates kudos for his vigorous editing. "You Are My First Love," with music and lyrics by Lester Powell and Paddy Roberts, is an attractive romantic song entry. *Myro.*

Pacific Destiny
(BRITISH-C'SCOPE-COLOR)

Strong visual appeal and genuine charm are main assets, but thin marquee values may hurt b.o. results; set for average grosses.

London, June 5.

British Lion production and release. Stars Denholm Elliott and Susan Stephen; features Michael Hordern, Gordon Jackson and Inia Te Wiata. Directed by Wold Rilla. Screenplay, Richard Mason; camera, Martin Curtis; editor, John Trumper. At Odeon Theatre, Marble Arch, London. Running time, **97 MINS.**

Arthur Grimble ....Denholm Elliott
Olivia Grimble .... Susan Stephen
Uncles......Felix Felton, Peter Bathurst, Clifford Buckton
Resident Commissioner..Michael Hordern
District Officer .... Gordon Jackson
Tauvela .... Inia Te Wiata
Lama .... Henrietta Godinet
Taloa .... Ollie Crichton
Kitiona .... Hans Kruse
Voice-of-the-Tide........Moira Macdonald
Sea-Wind .... Rosie Leavasa
King's-Bundle-of-Mats .... Sani
Grandmother .... Fiti
Tulo .... John Bryce
Tiki-Tiku .... Ezra Williams
Matangi .... Tuiletefuga
Teraloa .... Aft Kalapu
Fa' afetai .... Overlau Beruta
Movement-of-Clouds....Cecilia Fabricious
Fa'alavelave .... Polo
Prisoner .... Tusa
Warder ....Noa

James Lawrie, who first came into the industry as managing director of the National Film Finance Corp., and quit after a few years to turn indie film-maker, has come up with a creditable production in this first venture. "Pacific Destiny," based on Sir Arthur Grimble's personal experiences as a young Colonial Office cadet in the Pacific islands, has a refreshing charm and appeal. There's not much action and the suspense is almost incidental, yet the overall result is satisfying. Its b.o. rating should be around average.

This is an occasion when CinemaScope genuinely enhances the visual appeal. The widescreen captures the scenic highlights of the Samoan Islands and nice lensing touches off their natural beauties. The picture, unhappily, is thin in star values and that may ultimately affect its potential market.

Denholm Elliott plays the young Arthur Grimble, who goes out from London accompanied by his bride and encouraged by his uncles, to take up his first post in the colonial service. Within a few minutes, he has fallen foul of the Resident Commissioner (Michael Hordern) and from then onwards is perpetually in trouble. So, when he's sent to administer a smaller island where trouble is expected, the young cadet regards it as the reward for failure and quits. But his wife sparks the fire for acceptance of the challenge and paves the way for his eventual triumph.

Apart from a brief opening sequence filmed in London, the entire production was lensed on location in Samoa and director Wolf Rilla has done a competent job and made excellent use of the natural backgrounds. He's aided by an efficient technical crew and by a reliable cast. Elliott impresses with his sincerity and Susan Stephen has the requisite charm as his young wife. Hordern's interpretation of the cynical Resident Commissioner is true to type and gets the laughs. Gordon Jackson does nicely a smaller role as his assistant. Inia Te Wiata is an impressive headman and Ezra Williams is typically sinister as the sorcerer. *Myro.*

Jacqueline
(BRITISH)

Sentimental, melodramatic tear-jerker featuring new child performer; Okay for local family trade.

London, June 5.

Rank production and release. Stars John Gregson, Kathleen Ryan and Jacqueline Ryan; features Noel Purcell, Cyril Cusack, Tony Wright and Maureen Swanson. Directed by Roy Baker. Screenplay, Patrick Kirwan and Liam O'Flaherty; camera, Geoffrey Unsworth; editor, John D. Guthridge; music, Cedric Thorpe Davie. At Leicester Square Theatre, London. Running time, **93 MINS**

Mike .... John Gregson
Elizabeth .... Kathleen Ryan
Jacqueline .... Jacqueline Ryan
Mr. Owen .... Noel Purcell
Mr. Flannagan .... Cyril Cusack
Maggie .... Maureen Swanson
Jack McBride .... Tony Wright
Mr. Lord .... Liam Redmond
Mrs. McBride .... Maureen Delaney
Mrs. Flannagan .... Marie Kean
Michael .... Richard O'Sullivan
Sara Flannagan ....Rita Begley
Mrs. McMullen......Josephine Fitzgerald
Bob Quinton .... Barry Keegan
Mr. Lord's Servant........James Devlin
Schoolmaster .... Harold Goldblatt
Campbell .... Jack McGowran
Foreman .... Sam Kydd
Mr. Pike .... Christopher Steele

A saccharine, sentimental yarn, "Jacqueline" is set in Belfast and is notable for the fact that it introduces an attractive new child personality. Also that it permits most of the other characters to indulge in large doses of conventional Irish blarney. Pic is strictly for the family trade.

The story is oldfashioned in conception and presentation, and never attempts to be anything but dated melodrama. Stripped of its trimmings, it's a story of a young girl who adores her drunken father and by her good example in being picked as soloist at a church festival, gets him a job and the family a cottage on the farm of the local bigwig.

The emphasis all the way is on the tear-jerking aspects and they're frequently very contrived. There is a limited appeal in the background and the scenes of a slum neighborhood celebrating the Coronation with a street party has some interest. The picture, however, is dominated by the moppet performer who, without precociousness, and with no previous experience acts with genuine conviction and sincerity. John Gregson and Kathleen Ryan, as her parents, do well enough within the limitations of the script, but experienced feature artists of the calibre of Noel Purcell, Cyril Cusack, Maureen Swanson, Tony Wright and Liam Redmond have little opportunity to show their skill. Roy Baker's direction and the technical credits are of average standard. *Myro.*

Il Ferroviere
(The Railroad Man)
(ITALIAN)

Rome, June 5.

ENIC release of a Carlo Ponti-ENIC production. Stars Pietro Germi, Luisa della Noce, Silva, Saro Urzi; features Carlo Giuffre, Renato Speziali, Edoardo Nevola. Directed by Pietro Germi. Screenplay, Germi, Alfredo Giannetti, Luciano Vincenzpni; from story by Alfredo Giannetti; camera, Leonida Barboni; music, Carlo Rustichelli: editor, Dolores Tamburini. Previewed in Rome. Runnng time, **110 MINS.**

Andrea .... Pietro Germi
Sara .... Luisa della Noce
Silva .... Giulia
Liverani .... Saro Urzi
Sandro .... Edoardo Nevola
Renato .... Carlo Giuffre
Marcello .... Renato Speziali

Drama of life in an Italian family rates attention as one of this country's top efforts of the season. Looks a good international seller, with some possibilities for special U.S. situations. Word-of-mouth should be its forte.

Story centers around a railroad engineer and his family problems, involving his wife and three children in varied domestic conflicts, as well as his own pangs of social conscience when he is accused of being a strikebreaker. Outcast by both family and friends, he seeks solace in wine at a neighborhood tavern until his youngest son finds him and brings him back into the fold.

Plot is meant to be seen and not told, as the various bits and pieces of every day existence are mirrored with telling realism and warmth, as well as a nice eye for detail. It's practically a one-man effort by Germi, who wrote and directed, as well as handling the key role of the father (only his second pic stint) in expert fashion. Thesping is uniformly good, with moppet Edoardo Nevola stealing many scenes and Guilia registering via looks and personality in her first film role. Saro Urzi cameos a nice bit as the faithful family friend.

Pacing could be speeded somewhat for general effectiveness, but otherwise Germi's handling of his pic is concentrated and vital. Leonda Barboni's lensing is a pro job while music by Carlo Rustichelli adds much. *Hawk.*

Santiago
(COLOR)

Alan Ladd helps free Cuba in good action-adventure feature.

Hollywood, June 19.
Warner Bros. release of Martin Rackin production. Stars Alan Ladd, Rossana Podesta, Lloyd Nolan, Chill Wills; features Paul Fix, L. Q. Jones, Frank de Kova. Directed by Gordon Douglas. Screenplay, Rackin and John Twist; from novel by Rackin; camera (WarnerColor), John Seitz; editor, Owen Marks; music, David Buttolph. Previewed June 7, '56. Running time, **92 MINS.**

Cash Adams	Alan Ladd
Isabella	Rossana Podesta
Clay Pike	Lloyd Nolan
Sidewheel	Chill Wills
Trasker	Paul Fix
Digger	L. Q. Jones
Jingo	Frank de Kova
Pablo	George J. Lewis
Lobo	Royal Dano
Sam	Don Blackman
Juanito	Francisco Ruiz
Dutch	Clegg Hoyt
Josef Marti	Ernest Sarracino

"Santiago" is a good action-adventure feature of the type that generally meets with a favorable b.o. reaction in the regular runs. Alan Ladd, Lloyd Nolan and Chill Wills are among the hearties supplying muscles for the derring-do and marquees, while Rossana Podesta's striking beauty takes care of the femme values.

Martin Rackin produced and co-scripted with John Twist from his original story. Plot has plenty of regulation swashbuckling throughout to attract the action-minded, as well as some unexpected, but welcome, depth in a number of scenes. Gordon Douglas' penetrating direction of these well-written scenes commands a responsive cast reaction, adding to the overall entertainment.

Ladd and Nolan are rival gun runners, taking arms to Cuba through the Spanish blockade on an old stern-wheeler captained by Wills. Also aboard is Miss Podesta, Cuba's Joan of Arc in the fight for independence from Spain, who has the cash for the cargo—after it's delivered to the rebels. Between the personal scrapping of Ladd and Nolan, and their combined action against assorted Spanish forces, the footage fights its way along to the wrapup that sees Ladd deciding a cause and a girl are better than the money he previously worshipped. He removes Nolan when the latter tries to back out on delivery and the rebels are assured of the arms they need.

Ladd is excellent as the two-fisted gun runner and Nolan makes a rugged adversary, coloring the character properly. Wills is a particular standout, and among the several good scenes, the topper is that leading to the blowing up of his ship, along with himself and Don Blackman, very good as the Negro mate, to delay Spanish pursuit of the rebel-destined guns. Miss Podesta does quite well by the demands of her part.

Very capable support is furnished by Paul Fix, topnotch as Ladd's sidekick; Frank de Kova, as Nolan's knife-slinging aide; L. Q. Jones, George J. Lewis, Royal Dano, moppet Francisco Ruiz, Clegg Hoyt and Ernest Sarracino. Technical ends are good, including John Seitz' WarnerColor lensing, art direction by Edward Carrere, Owen Marks' editing and the score by David Buttolph. *Brog.*

Fastest Gun Alive

One more derived from television, Glenn Ford "mood" western loses its way in character obscurities. Spotty outlook.

Hollywood, June 19.
Metro release of Clarence Greene production. Stars Glenn Ford, Jeanne Crain, Broderick Crawford; features Russ Tamblyn. Directed by Russell Rouse. Screenplay, Frank D. Gilroy, Rouse; from Gilroy's teleplay "The Last Notch"; camera, George J. Folsey; editor, Ferris Webster. Harry V. Knapp; music, Andre Previn; dance number staged by Alex Romero. Previewed June 13, '56. Running time, **89 MINS.**

George Temple	Glenn Ford
Dora Temple	Jeanne Crain
Vinnie Harold	Broderick Crawford
Eric Doolittle	Russ Tamblyn
Harvey Maxwell	Allyn Joslyn
Lou Glover	Leif Erickson
Taylor Swope	John Dehner
Dink Wells	Noah Beery
Kevin McGovern	J. M. Kerrigan
Brian Tibbs	Rhys Williams
Rose Tibbs	Virginia Gregg
Frank Stringer	Chubby Johnson
Ben Buddy	John Doucette
Lars Toomy	William "Bill" Phillips
Bobby Tibbs	Chris Olsen
Sheriff Bill Toledo	Paul Birch
Joe Fenwick	Florenz Ames
Reverend	Joseph Sweeney

Starting out as a promising "mood" western, "The Fastest Gun Alive" loses its way among character and motivation obscurities, ending up as not too satisfactory entertainment. Cast has the good names of Glenn Ford, Jeanne Crain and Broderick Crawford, but the grossing prospects are spotty.

Show's origin is Frank D. Gilroy's teleplay, "The Last Notch," which he screen-scripted with director Russell Rouse under Clarence Greene's production helming at Metro. Chief flaw is the fact the audience never knows what makes the hero tick until the climax, so his moody brooding through most of the footage rates no understanding nor particular sympathy. Additionally, there's a trick ending not too readily acceptable.

Plot's about a man always on the run so he won't have to prove he can pull a six-shooter faster than any other man in the old west. Ford, the fast draw, and Miss Crain, his wife, know the secret of the running—he's afraid to test his skill in a "for-keeps" duel. Fate catches up in the little town of Cross Creek, where the couple has lived quietly for four years as a mild-mannered, peace-loving pair, when Ford gets drunk and shows off his gun skill. Word of his talent leaks to outlaw Crawford, who fancies himself the fastest, thus setting up the dusty street showdown for the title's dubious honor and the trick ending that has the graves of both gunmen side-by-side, although not both occupied.

It's about time an actor of Ford's flexible ability had even a moderately happy role for a change of pace. He handles all assignments well, including this one, but surely he's been too sorely tried emotionally in all of his recent pix. Miss Crain comes off satisfactorily as the suffering wife and Crawford is excellent as the outlaw. So are John Dehner and Noah Beery, particularly the former, as Crawford's partners in crime. Townspeople played by Allyn Joslyn, Leif Erickson, J. M. Kerrigan, Rhys Williams, Virginia Gregg, Chris Olsen and others are good.

Russ Tamblyn does a showy, acrobatic country terp number at a village square dance. It's real good, but so professional it seems out of place in the oater atmosphere. Alex Romero did the staging for it. Andre Previn's music and the lensing of the western settings by George J. Folsey are among the creditable technical assists. *Brog.*

Thunderstorm

Arty programmer produced in Spain by Binnie Barnes.

Hollywood, June 13.
Allied Artists release of Binnie Barnes (Hemisphere Films Ltd.) production. Stars Carlos Thompson, Linda Christian, Charles Korvin; features Gary Thorne, Tito Junco, Erica Vaal, Catherina Ferraz, Marco Davo. Directed by John Guillermin. Screenplay, Daniel Mainwaring; story, George St. George; camera, Manuel Berenguer; editor, Lee Doig; music, Paul Misraki. Previewed June 12, '56. Running time, **81 MINS.**

Diego Martinez	Carlos Thompson
Maria Ramon	Linda Christian
Pablo Gardia	Charles Korvin
Miguel Gardia	Gary Thorne
Toro	Tito Junco
Juana	Erica Vaal
Mrs. Martinez	Catherina Ferraz
Padre Flores	Marco Davo
Domingo Ribas	Fleixes De Pomes
Lalo	Nestor M. Neana
Pedro	Carlos Diaz Mendoza
Senora Hidalgo	Julia Caba Alba
Senora Alvarez	Isabel De Pomes
Margo	Conchita Bautista
Dolores	Amalia Iglesias
Manuel Hidego	Manuel San Roman

Produced in Spain by Binnie Barnes, "Thunderstorm" is an offbeat type of programmer to be going out domestically under the Allied Artists label. It leans to the arty and this effect, along with the overseas setting and foreign players, makes it an unusual subject for the supporting market.

Names of Carlos Thompson, Linda Christian and Charles Korvin are the only ones that might sound a familiar note for stateside audiences. Each of the star trio does very well in achieving the mood sought by John Guillermin's direction of the Daniel Mainwaring screenplay, based on a story by George St. George. That mood is a bit heavy, but goes with the story melodramatics. Photography by Manuel Berenguer is strikingly effective. The score by Paul Misraki is another good contribution.

A simple Spanish fishing village is the setting for the story, which tells of the unrest that comes when a beautiful girl is rescued from the sea by Thompson, one of the fishermen. He immediately falls in love with Miss Christian, while Korvin, town mayor, and his son, Gary Thorne, are among the other males who covet her. Resolution of the assorted troubles believed brought by the girl doesn't mean there's a happy ending. She sails away alone, convinced she would only be a jinx if she stayed with Thompson.

Miss Christian has the natural equipment to make it believeable the male villagers would all desire her and it is generously displayed in a number of scenes (which bear evidence of having been clipped somewhat for domestic viewing). Also, there's some busty shots of Erica Vaal, the mayor's amour until the castaway came along. *Brog.*

Moby Dick

John Huston's technically-absorbing re-telling of the mad captain who chased the indestructible white whale. No women and not too much excitement in this Gregory Peck starrer which will need plenty of selling.

Warner Bros. release of Moulin (John Huston) production. Stars Gregory Peck; features Richard Basehart, Leo Genn. Produced & directed by John Huston; associate producer, Lehman Katz; asst. director, Jack Martin; screenplay by Ray Bradbury & Huston based on Herman Melville's novel. Camera, Oswald Morris; editor, Russell Lloyd; music, Philip Stainton, conducted by Louis Levy. Tradeshow, N. Y. June 21, 1956. Running time, 116 MINS.

Captain Ahab	Gregory Peck
Ishmael	Richard Basehart
1st Mate Starbuck	Leo Genn
2d Mate Stubb	Harry Andrews
3d Mate Flask	Seamus Kelly
Queenqueg	Friedrich Ledebur
Father Mapple	Orson Welles
Manxman	Bernard Miles
Tavern Owner	Peter Coffin
Tashtego	Tom Clegg
Pip	Tamba Alleney
Carpenter	Noel Purcell
Blacksmith	Ted Howard
Daggoo	Edric Connor
Peleg	Mervyn Johns
Bildad	Philip Stainton
Capt. Boomer	James R. Justice
Capt. Gardiner	Francis de Wolf
Elijah	Royal Dano

Costly weather and production delays on location in Ireland and elsewhere have so enlarged the bring-home price on John Huston's "Moby Dick" that the initial question, for a tradepaper review, is whether the boxoffice returns can redeem the investment, estimated as high as $5,000,000. The answer cannot be flatly stated but this is for sure: it will be an uphill climb.

"Moby Dick" in its final 116-minute form is interesting more often than exciting, faithful to the time and text more than great theatrical entertainment. Essentially it is a "chase" picture with all the inherent interest thereby implied and yet not escaping the quality of sameness and repetitiousness which often dulls the chase formula.

The film colony and all who are respectful of cinematic technicalities will be inclined to hail the handling of the monster albino whale, in which area special effectsman Gus Lohman shares credit with the producer-director. It was astute, too, of Huston to avoid the rich calendar colors of modern film tinting and work out, with head cameraman Oswald Morris, a print combining the color and black-and-white, creating a sort of modified paraphrase of Technicolor calculated to capture the sombre beauties of New Bedford, circa 1840, and its whaling ways.

Phil Stainton's music, as conducted by Louis Levy, undoubtedly adds much to the sweep of the subject, yet never attracts attention to itself. In short, true mood music and bridging has been achieved. Together with the canny editing of Russell Lloyd, the important and unexaggerated ship and tempest sound effects of Leslie Hodgson and the formidable recording job credited to John Mitchell and Len Shilton under Harold King's supervision, the industry must surely recognize the dedicated labors of topnotch craftsmen.

As for the research, the insight, the taste and imagination of the art director, Ralph Brinton, and his two aides, Stephen and Geoffrey Drake, only the production diary could adequately trace their contributions. Cecil Ford as production manager, Jack Martin as Huston's assistant director, and Lehman Katz as associate producer, indubitably belong to the specially credit-worthy.

In the first half hour of the unspooling the viewer is struck by the quiet tone and pace of the story-telling, the slow build. This may prove a major misjudgment for the story is a long time progressing from muted orchestration to full crashing tympani.

The types in this early sequence are wondrously selected (from the natives of Ireland) and the film does exude a feeling of being refreshingly offbeat in its casting. Seldom have such sad-faced women been presented at a ship's departure.

Orson Welles appears early and briefly as a local New Bedford preacher who climbs up into a picturesque pulpit made to resemble a ship's spar and delivers a God-fearing sermon on Jonah and the whale. Present in the pews are several members of the crew the viewer is about to meet and the walls of the church are thick with memorials to men lost while whaling. Welles turns in an effective bit of brimstone exhortation, appropriate to time and place.

None of the crew of the Pequod is to return from the voyage save only he who tells the tale, Ishmael, the narrator, played with an eloquently sensitive face by Richard Basehart. The story opens and closes with his voice and Ishmael appears intermittently throughout. The ship and its odd assortment of characters are, in a sense, first seen and subsequently reported through his eyes. Yet Ishmael is only once or twice more than an observer. His initial shock upon viewing the tattooed Polynesian harpooner Queequeg and his knocking down of two sadistic sailors are about the only plot "participations" of Ishmael.

Huston has contrived arresting "business" in connection with the signing on of Ishmael and Queequeg by two pious Quaker Brethren who own, but do not sail with, the Pequod. The youth and the savage have ignored a dockside prophecy of calamity flung at them by an Elijah (Royal Dano), which is the first statement of the story's leitmotif of unswervable doom.

Something like 30 minutes elapse before the film's star is seen on screen. The patient weaving of the background tapestry is first accomplished and then Gregory Peck hovers above the crew, grim-faced and hate-obsessed. He wears a stump leg made of the jaw of a whale and he lives only to kill the greatest whale of all, the white-hided super-monster, Moby Dick, the one which had chewed off his leg.

The debate must now begin as to Peck's performance. Captain Ahab, the role played in 1932 by John Barrymore in Warners' previous version of the Herman Melville novel, is heavy with metaphysical implications. Is Ahab the incarnation of human perversity and, pride, or of hell-bent defiance of man's fate? The answer to Melville's symbology will not be found at this counter.

This is the more immediate fact: Peck's Ahab is not very "elemental." It is not that he fails in handling the rhetoric. Actually he does quite well with the stylized speech in which Melville wrote and which Ray Bradbury and Huston have preserved in their screenplay. It's just that Peck often seems understated and much too gentlemanly for a man supposedly consumed by insane fury. When Ahab is intent upon working his will upon the crew, asking them to pass up commercial kills for the sake of his grand revenge, the dramatic effects are inherent in the reactions of the crew members rather than in Peck's own inwardness.

For all that, "Moby Dick" is a technicians' picture — both its greatnesses and its shortcomings lying in that direction. There is one highly questionable detail—namely, makeup. Leaving aside the fact that the star not infrequently suggests a melancholy Abe Lincoln there is the fact that, in scene after scene, his makeup draws the eye and thereby spoils the illusion. The long white mark starting in the hair, cutting down the cheek and repeating in the chin whiskers is too frequently a put-on for the day's shooting. This becomes a serious repeated affront to believability.

Makeup also falters badly in the face and nose tattoo of Quequeg and suggests nothing so much as a decalcomania job. This characterization is inherently exotic but has been curiously miscast since Friedrich Ledebur emerges as a Polynesian with a Balkan accent!

Without a female speaking part in the film, "Moby Dick" must carry a question mark as to its appeal to women. The best selling bets lie, presumably, in the theme of adventure generally plus the mighty splashing and churning of the white whale when finally surrounded. At a guess a great amount of Moulin Production's whale-size budget went into the photographing of the feature's climactic 20 minutes.

Ahab dies roped to the back of Moby Dick after harpooning the monster again and again. The whale submerges for a time and when next surfacing the dead Ahab is pinnioned against its bulk with an obviously intended suggestion of crucifixion. The sight of the triumphant whale and the dead captain, whom he had consistently opposed as a madman, now drives the Quaker first mate (ably played by Leo Genn) himself mad with a lust to have Moby Dick's blubber. Showing an eye of calculating menace the big whale charges in one final eruption of violence. Fairly amazing scenes follow in rapid succession as the whale crunches men and long boats, whips up the ocean into a veritable maelstrom into which ship, boats and impudent mortals all go down. Only Ishmael survives, safe on the water-tight coffin which Queequeg had ordered made by the ship's carpenter.

The whale has been riddled with harpoons and tied round with ropes. But he is untouched like the dark ungraspable forces of nature and life which, runs the brooding Melville novel, are known best to those about to die.

At picture's end the viewer has a sense of a daring and imaginative producer who has, like Capt. Ahab, ventured very far indeed, only to fall short of the boxoffice kill. There is a sense of an attractive actor who cannot feel, and hence cannot project, the full convulsions of psychotic malice; and lastly it may be permissible to guess that in this age, which has looked upon the mushroom-shaped horror of the atomic explosion, the capers of Moby Dick are less awesome than of yore. *Land.*

Pardners

Martin & Lewis in amusing sagebrush antics; good prospects.

Hollywood, June 17.

Paramount release of Paul Jones production. Stars Dean Martin, Jerry Lewis, Lori Nelson, Jeff Morrow, Jackie Loughery; features John Baragrey, Agnes Moorehead. Directed by Norman Taurog. Screenplay, Sidney Sheldon; screen story, Jerry Davis; based on story by Mervin J. Houser; camera (Technicolor), Daniel Fapp; editor, Archie Marshek; music conducted by Frank De Vol; songs, James Van Heusen, Sammy Cahn; choreography, Nick Castle. Previewed June 17, '56. Running time, 86 MINS.

Wade Kingsley Jr.	Jerry Lewis
Slim Mosely Jr.	Dean Martin
Carol Kingsley	Lori Nelson
Dolly Riley	Jackie Loughery
Dan Hollis	John Baragrey
Rio	Jeff Morrow
Mrs. Kingsley	Agnes Moorehead
Whitey	Lon Chaney Jr.
Red	Mickey Finn

Dean Martin and Jerry Lewis go western with a vengeance in "Pardners," and what takes place out on the prairie is good comedy promising profitable playdates. Pic's origin (albeit extremely loose) is Paramount's 1936 "Rhythm On the Range," Bing Crosby starrer, but there have been so many switches made this can hardly be termed an actual remake.

Paul Jones helms the production, rather ironically titled in view of the upcoming Martin-Lewis divorce, in able fashion to mix up the laughs, songs and action in proportions that will strike the fancy of M&L fans. Norman Taurog, who reined "Rhythm" back in 1936, also directs "Pardners" in first class style, keeping the comedy rolling fast most of the way as the standard oater cliches are put through the risibility wringer. Sidney Sheldon gives it good scripting from a screen story by Jerry Davis, which was based on the "Rhythm" original by Mervin J. Houser.

A prolog sets the plot as a young baby is taken east by his mother while the father and his pard get themselves killed by some masked riders. A suitable number of years are jumped to have that baby now a young man who yens to return to the wide open spaces and does via buying a prize bull for the ranch run by the son of his late dad's partner, also grown up. Hilarity is mostly concerned with Lewis' comical swaggering as a wouldbe cowpoke and his cowardly reaction to the dangers of the plains and the tough hombres who inhabit it. History looks ready to repeat itself via a new gang of masked riders but Lewis, with new pardner Martin, is able to free the west of the heavies and becomes accepted.

As a team, Martin & Lewis come across strongly, with the laugh meat rightfully tossed to the latter while Martin takes care of the straighter chores and most of the vocalistics. Of the Sammy Cahn-James Van Heusen songs offered, "Buckskin Beauty," done by Lewis with some country choreography by Nick Castle, has a good square dance lilt. The title tune is fair, but better are "The Wind! The Wind!" and "Me 'N You 'N the Moon" as done by Martin.

Lori Nelson, providing the romance for Martin, and Jackie Loughery the same duties with Lewis, are the attractive femme leads, while Agnes Moorehead scores as Lewis' dominating mother. John Baragrey and Jeff Morrow are good as the principal heavies, with assists from Lon Chaney Jr., Mickey Finn and others.

The VistaVision camera work in Technicolor by Daniel Fapp is top

grade, while are direction, editing and the conducting of the score by Frank De Vol are well executed.
Brog.

Rebel In Town

Above-average entertainment in suspense, outdoor-actioner. Excellent program entry.

Hollywood, June 22.

United Artists release of Howard W. Koch (Bel-Air) production. Stars John Payne, Ruth Roman, J. Carrol Naish, Ben Cooper, John Smith; features Ben Johnson, James Griffith, Mary Adams, Bobby Clark, Mimi Gibson. Directed by Alfred Werker. Screenplay, Danny Arnold; camera, Gordon Avil; editor, John F. Schreyer; music, Les Baxter; song, Baxter and Lenny Adelson. Previewed June 20, '56. Running time, 77 MINS.

John Willoughby .... John Payne
Nora Willoughby .... Ruth Roman
Bedloe Mason .... J. Carrol Naish
Gray Mason .... Ben Cooper
Wesley Mason .... John Smith
Adam Russell .... James Griffith
Grandmaw Ackstadt .... Mary Adams
Petey Willoughby .... Bobby Clark
Lisbeth Ackstadt .... Mimi Gibson
Cain Mason .... Cain Mason
Doctor .... Joel Ashley
Frank Mason .... Ben Johnson

Occasionally, a budget picture comes along that is a great deal more worthy than its program classification would indicate. Such a one is "Rebel In Town," which shapes as an exceptionally good entry. Because of its western setting, it most likely will be an outdoor actioner, but it can also stand up to labelling as a suspense drama, thanks to a good script that is intelligently handled on the production, direction and playing ends.

The Bel-Air production, produced by Howard W. Koch and directed by Alfred Werker for executive producer Aubrey Schenck, has familiar marquee names in John Payne, Ruth Roman and J. Carrol Naish, along with the newer monickers of Ben Cooper and John Smith, to aid the bookings in its intended market.

Werker's direction keeps a fine rein on the dramatics in Danny Arnold's excellent script, unfolding the plot at a suspenseful pace and keeping audience interest high. The characters in the tale appear real and the economical dialog they speak goes well with the situations. A brief synopsizing can't take into account the various writing, directorial and performance touches that add substance.

A Confederate family of a grizzled patriarch and his four sons is on the run in the west soon after the Civil War. They stop for water in a small town. A little boy, son of an ex-Union officer, snaps a toy pistol at the back of one of the Confederates. He whirls and fires by instinct and the boy is dead. Thereafter conflict builds a mounting tension; in the town, between the little boy's parents, and among the rebel family. The ending is well-resolved after a number of actionful, and violent, sequences.

Payne and Miss Roman come over extremely well as the parents of little Bobby Clark, the boy who is killed, handling the revenge and forgiveness phases finely. Naish does another of his standout character performances as the bearded Confederate father, while Cooper scores as the sensitive younger son who wants his family to do what is right about the shooting. Smith clicks as the instinctive killer among the rebels, giving his character a suspenseful menace. Ben Johnson and Cain Mason (nee Sterling Franck) are good as the other brothers, as is James Griffith as the marshal.

Les Baxter's score is a firstrate assist in the mood-building, knowing what to let the drama play without musical competition. Gordon Avil's photography is good, having a stark effect that goes with the plot. Editing by John F. Schreyer is dramatically able. A title tune by Baxter and Lenny Adelson is heard behind the credits to mild effect.
Brog.

The Dynamiters

Slowly-paced crime detection from Britain with Wayne Morris and a bagful of plot coincidences.

Hollywood, June 21.

Astor release of a Geoffrey Goodhart-Brandon Fleming production. Stars Wayne Morris, Sandra Dorne; features Patrick Holt, Simone Silva, Eric Pohlmann. Directed by Francis Searle. Story-screenplay, Fleming; camera, Cedric Williams; editor, Douglas Myer; art director, John Elphick. Reviewed June 20, '56. Running time, 71 MINS.

This British import concerns hunt for a gang of London dynamiters. With Yankee Wayne Morris, it's a very dubious qualification for U.S.

Morris plays a private dick hired by an insurance company to track down the dynamiters who are getting away with a fortune in loot. Technique he employs would shame any second-rate investigator here, and dubiously-claimed of fiction-writer coincidenas which reduce action to a walk.

American actor, poorly directed by Francis Searle, comes in lame due to unconvincing character. Sandra Dorne, a busty blonde, costars, and Simone Silva, the curvaceous English thesp who did an alfresco strip on the French Riviera several years ago, is in for a less than enchanting song number, "Soho Mambo." Balance of cast likewise is strictly routine.

Technical credits in the Geoffrey Goodhart-Brandon Fleming production are stock.
Whit.

My Teenage Daughter
(BRITISH)

Anna Neagle starred as mother with daughter problems; stout prospect for femme audiences.

London, June 20.

British Lion release of a Herbert Wilcox production. Stars Anna Neagle and Sylvia Syms; features Norman Wooland, Wilfrid Hyde White and Kenneth Haigh. Directed by Herbert Wilcox. Screenplay, Felicity Douglas; camera, Max Greene; editor, Bunny Warren; music, Stanley Black. At Warner Theatre, London, June 20, '56. Running time, 100 MINS.

Valerie Carr .... Anna Neagle
Janet Carr .... Sylvia Syms
Hugh Manning .... Norman Wooland
Sir Joseph .... Wilfrid Hyde White
Tony Ward Black .... Kenneth Haigh
Poppet Carr .... Julia Lockwood
Aunt Louisa .... Helen Haye
Aunt Bella .... Josephine Fitzgerald
Gina .... Wanda Ventham
Don .... Murray Mayne
Sir Henry .... Michael Shepley
Barbara .... Avice Landone
Mark .... Michael Meacham
Magistrate .... Ballard Berkeley
Miss Ellis .... Edie Martin
Anne .... Myrette Morven
Miss Bennett .... Grizelda Hervey
Celia .... Betty Cooper
Senator .... Launce Maraschal

An unabashed sentimental drama, obviously conceived as unsophisticated entertainment, "My Teenage Daughter" should prove a stout b.o. proposition where the name value of Anna Neagle has potent marquee appeal. Herbert Wilcox has produced and directed with a determined eye on femme patronage and on that score he's hit the target. He has blatantly exploited the tear-jerking aspects of the plot in the clash between a devoted mother and her strong-headed daughter which ends up with the girl facing a murder rap.

Miss Neagle plays a war widow who is fiction editor of a teenagers' magazine and who is distressed over the way in which her young daughter gets caught up with a society no-good, is taken to jive sessions in a basement club and stays out till dawn. But the more the mother protests the more her daughter wilfully disobeys her until a week in a prison cell and a timely rebuke by the magistrate brings her to her senses.

There are few surprise twists in the Felicity Douglas screenplay. For the most part, the story treads a conventional and obvious path. That's of minor importance in view of the general fabric of the yarn which exclusively focusses its attention on the main issue. Miss Neagle, as attractive as ever, radiates charm and registers anguish in rotation.

Sylvia Syms, a pert newcomer, who gets star billing, does remarkably well as the teenage daughter, playing her role on a sensitive plane. Norman Wooland makes an impressive contribution as a writer who helps to settle Miss Neagle's domestic problems while Wilfrid Hyde White, as usual, turns in a polished study as a publisher. Kenneth Haigh is sincere and believable as the young man who leads the girl astray. Julia Lockwood, as the star's younger daughter, walks off with many of the scenes. Technically, the production is above average, but a jive tune, "Get With It," is repeated to the point of monotony.
Myro.

Yield to the Night
(BRITISH)

Diana Dors in dramatic de-glamorized role. Stout local b.o. with good U.S. prospects.

London, June 19.

Associated British-Pathe production and release. Stars Diana Dors and Yvonne Mitchell. Directed by J. Lee Thompson. Screenplay, John Cresswell and Joan Henry; camera, Gilbert Taylor; editor, Richard Best; music, Ray Martin. At Carlton Theatre, London. Running time, 100 MINS.

Mary Hilton .... Diana Dors
Macfarlane .... Yvonne Mitchell
Jim Lancaster .... Michael Craig
Governor .... Marie Ney
Chaplain .... Geoffrey Keen
Doctor .... Liam Redmond
Hill .... Olga Lindo
Barker .... Joan Miller
Brandon .... Marjorie Rhodes
Mason .... Molly Urquhart
Maxwell .... Mary Mackenzie
Fred .... Harry Locke
Roy .... Michael Ripper
Doris .... Joyce Blair
Bob .... Charles Clay
Miss Bligh .... Athene Seyler
Nursing Sister .... Peggy Livesley
Mrs. Thomas .... Mona Washbourne
Mr. Thomas .... Alex Finter
Richardson .... Marianne Stone
Lucy .... Mercia Shaw
Lawyer .... Charles Lloyd Pack
Mrs. Price .... Dandy Nichols
Alan .... John Charlesworth
Police Sergeant .... Frank Hawkins

Diana Dors, the glamour girl of British films (she's due to make a Hollywood picture under the RKO banner), plays a heavy dramatic role in "Yield to the Night," which calls for a drastic de-glamorizing treatment. The extremely sombre nature of the story is a complete switch from the frivolous parts she normally plays. This factor, heavily publicized locally, should yield a curiosity value which could help the boxoffice. The film rates an "X" censor's certificate in Britain, which precludes admission to juves under 16.

In view of the international press coverage which Miss Dors has garnered by her spectacular appearances at recent film fests, coupled with her upcoming Hollywood bow, the picture may merit popular showing in the U.S. But 100 minutes of celluloid, almost exclusively devoted to showing a young girl in the death cell, must be regarded as a grim form of entertainment.

The actual killing which leads the star to the death cell is depicted before the credit titles appear on the screen, but the events which led her to shoot at point blank range at the woman who forced her lover to suicide are shown in a series of flashbacks. Main footage is concentrated inside the condemned cell and the script illustrates the anguish of mind, not only of the girl under sentence of death, but of the wardresses who guard her night and day, the members of her family and the husband whom she deserted for her worthless lover.

The script succeeds in maintaining strong suspense right up to the point where the prison governor has to break the news that a reprieve has been refused.

Story bears a vivid resemblance to a recent execution in Britain and can, therefore, be said to have a topical angle as well. In the main, it must be admitted that Miss Dors rises to the occasion and shows up as a dramatic actress better than anticipated.

Yvonne Mitchell strikes the right sympathetic note as one of the wardresses, Michael Craig reveals a good presence as the lover and Marie Ney shows proper dignity and restraint as the prison governor. Athene Seyler impresses in a small scene as a prison visitor while the remainder of the cast keep up a good general standard. J. Lee Thompson has done a workmanlike job of direction and the technical crew has given him admirable support.
Myro.

The Creeping Unknown

Fairly suspenseful science fiction-monster entry for them what gets their kicks this way.

United Artists release of Anthony Hinds production. Stars Brian Donlevy and Margia Dean. Features Jack Warner and David King Wood. Directed by Val Guest. Screenplay, Richard Landau; camera, Walter Harvey; editor, James Needs. Reviewed in N. Y., June 21, '56. Running time, 78 MINS.

Quartermass .... Brian Donlevy
Judith Carroon .... Margia Dean
Lomax .... Jack Warner
Victor Carroon .... Richard Wordsworth
Briscoe .... David King Wood
Rosie .... Thora Hird
TV Producer .... Gordon Jackson
Christie .... Harold Lang
Blake .... Lionel Jeffries
Marsh .... Maurice Kauffman
Green .... Gron Davies
Reichenheim .... Stanley Van Beers

A science fiction picture involving the presentation of a weird monster seemingly has a fascination for a portion of the film-going public. So "The Creeping Unknown," which contains these ingredients, should find a groove.

It's a competently made drama, containing sufficient suspense and frightening elements. The devastation wrought by the monster and the inability of the authorities to catch up with it have the familiar overtones of similar pictures, but, as a whole, it should satisfy those fans who go for the premise.

The monster in this case is a gelatinous octupus-like mass that absorbs all plant and animal life that it touches. The monster slowly resolves from a man who has undergone a complete change of his physical structure as a result of an interplanetary expedition. Returning to earth in a state of physical shock, he is isolated in a hospital, but as he changes into the creeping, plant-like substance, he escapes and begins his reign of terror.

As the monster becomes a national menace, a state of emergency is declared in London and the Army, police, and civil defense are called out to track it down. The monster is discovered in the scaffolding in Westminster Abbey by a television camera crew shooting a documentary. It is finally destroyed by a maximum shock of electricity, with all the power in London being cut off to provide sufficient juice.

The cast in general meets the demands of Richard Landau's screenplay, with Brian Donlevy as a dedicated scientist, Richard Wordsworth as the man who turns into the monster, Margia Dean as his wife, Jack Warner as a police official, and David King Wood as an investigating scientist. Val Guest's direction brings out the maximum suspense factors. Technical aspects of the Anthony Hinds production are standard. *Holl.*

Female Jungle

Mickey Spillane-like melodramatic hoke. Includes Broadway's Jayne Mansfield among the fillies.

Hollywood, June 26.
American Releasing Corp. release of a Burt Kaiser production. Stars Kathleen Crowley, Lawrence Tierney, John Carradine, Jayne Mansfield; features James Kodl, Rex Thorsen, Jack Hill. Directed by Bruno Ve Sota (cq). No screenplay credit; camera, Elwood Bredell; editor, Carl Pingitore. Reviewed at Hawaii Theatre, Hollywood, June 20, '56. Running time, 70 MINS.
Sergeant Stevens......Lawrence Tierney
Claude Almstead........John Carradine
Candy Price.............Jayne Mansfield
Alec Voe................Burt Kaiser
Peggy Voe.............Kathleen Crowley
Joe.....................James Kodl
Sergeant Duane..............Rex Thorsen
Captain Kroger.................Jack Hill
Chuck ....Bruce Carlisle
Connie ....Connie Cezon
George ....Robert Davis
Larry Jackson..........Gordon Urquhart
Doctor Urquhart..............Alan Frost
Heckler ....Bill Layne
Frank ....Bruno Ve Sota
Monica Madison............Jean Lewis

Occasionally, the odd-bag collection of characters assembled for this effort react to the downbeat situations in a manner faintly resembling human emotion. Otherwise, this pic is an example of a Mickey Spillane-ish mood run amok.

Since there's little help from the murky plotting, most b.o. chances will have to come from the succession of chesty femmes (including Jayne Mansfield, before her current success) who strut their brief moments across the screen, and the elongated scenes of amorous fondling which leave only the ultimate to the imagination.

Briefly, the uncredited screenplay deals with the efforts of a police detective, played by Lawrence Tierney, to redeem himself with his superiors by finding the murderer of a blonde film star. It seems that Tierney had been off-duty in the vicinity, but can't remember what happened due to an overindulgence in alcoholic beverages.

So he traipses through a succession of bedrooms, back alleys and bars, first pointing the finger of suspicion at the star's mentor, a newspaper columnist, played by John Carradine, and then at the real culprit, a maniacal caricaturist, played by Burt Kaiser, (also the pic's producer). Kaiser is gunned down, but not before he also strangles his nymphomaniacal inamorata, Miss Mansfield.

Director Bruno Ve Sota (cq), who also doubles in brass with a bit role, manages a few scenes of dramatic effectiveness, but eventually the story ingredients defeat his efforts. He also overrelies on the camera trickery of Elwood Bredell, which, while fine photography, does little to advance the action.

The acting ranges over a wide variety of styles, from the stately maneuverings of Carradine, through the stolid jaw-twitchings of Tierney, the lush lisping of Miss Mansfield and the wide-eyed slinking of Kaiser. Kathleen Crowley is decorative, but little else in the ill-conceived role of Kaiser's wife.

In lesser roles, Rex Thorsen, Jack Hill, James Kodl and Robert Davis are able to do better.
Kove.

July 4, 1956

The King and I
(C'Scope—Color)
(MUSICAL)

Blockbuster of the year. One of the all-time greats among musicals. Sure to wow all classes and nations. Socko in all departments: story, performance, production, score.

20th-Fox release of Charles Brackett production. Stars Deborah Kerr and Yul Brynner. Features Rita Moreno, Martin Benson, Terry Saunders, Rex Thompson, Carlos Rivas, Patrick Adiarte, Alan Mowbray, and Geoffrey Toone. Directed by Walter Lang. Screenplay, Ernest Lehman; music by Richard Rodgers and book and lyrics by Oscar Hammerstein 2d from their musical play based on "Anna and the King of Siam" by Margaret Landon; camera (De Luxe), Leon Shamroy; choreography, Jerome Robbins; costumes, Irene Sharaff; editor, Robert Simpson; art direction, Lyle R. Wheeler and John de Clur; music supervised and conducted by Alfred Newman. Tradeshown, N. Y., June 28, '56. Running time, 133 MINS.
Anna ....Deborah Kerr
The King ....Yul Brynner
Tuptim ....Rita Moreno
Kralahome ....Martin Benson
Lady Thiang ....Terry Saunders
Louis Leonowens ....Rex Thompson
Lun Tha ....Carlos Rivas
Prince Chulalongkorn....Patrick Adiarte
British Ambassador.....Alan Mowbray
Ramsay ....Geoffrey Toone
Eliza ....Yuriko
Simon Legree ....Marion Jim
Keeper of the Dogs ....Robert Banas
Uncle Thomas ....Dusty Worrall
Specialty Dancer ......Gemze de Lappe
Twins ....Thomas, Dennis Bonilla
Angel in Ballet ....Michiko Iseri
Ship's Captain ....Charles Irwin
Interpreter ....Leonard Strong
Siamese Girl ....Irene James
Amazons ....Jadin, Jean Wong
Guards.................Fuji, Weaver Levy
High Priest ....William Yip
Messenger ....Eddie Luke
Guest at Palace ......Josephine Smith

All the ingredients that made Rodgers & Hammerstein's "The King and I" a memorable stage experience have been faithfully transferred to the screen. The result is a pictorially exquisite, musically exciting, and dramatically satisfying motion picture. It's undoubtedly the best celluloid rendition of the R&H creation. It should be the king-sized money-maker of the year, drawing audiences of both sexes, of all ages, and of all tastes.

With Deborah Kerr in the role originally created by the late Gertrude Lawrence, and Yul Brynner and Terry Saunders repeating their stage performances, the Charles Brackett production has the talent to support the opulence of this truly blockbuster presentation. Twentieth-Fox's Cinema-Scope 55, originally introduced with R&H's "Carousel," attains its full glory with "The King and I," depicting with eye-filling clarity the lush costuming and colorful and exotic backgrounds of late 19th century Siam.

To be sure, the musical score, regarded by many as Richard Rodgers' most melodic, and the original book and lyrics by Oscar Hammerstein 2d provided the filmmakers with pre-sold and pretested elements of inestimable worth. However, the film creators —including Darryl F. Zanuck, who brought the property to 20th, producer Brackett, director Walter Lang, scripter Ernest Lehman, choreographer Jerome Robbins, costumer Irene Sharaff, art directors Lyle Wheeler and John De-Cuir, and cameraman Leon Shamroy—have respected the R&H material, skillfully blending and enhancing it for its transference to the film medium. It emerges as a visual and aural triumph, with the artistic and technical contributions being meshed as perfectly as a precision-tooled gear.

As the Victorian Englishwoman who came to Siam to teach Western manners and English to the royal household, Miss Kerr gives one of her finest performances. She handles the role of Mrs. Anna, the gentle yet determined schoolteacher and part-time adviser of the gruff, education-hungry Siamese monarch, with charm and understanding and, when necessary, the right sense of comedy. The qualities that appeal to the king and endear Mrs. Anna to the king's wives, his harem, and his multitudinous offspring are skillfully conveyed by Miss Kerr to the viewing audience.

As the brusque, petulant, awkwardly-kind despot confused by the conflicts of Far Eastern and Western cultures, Yul Brynner is repeating a role for which he has already received career-establishing acclaim. The larger exposure, via the film medium, should make him an international personality. The part is an almost incredibly fat one, and Brynner gives it an effective, many-shaded reading. His incisive use of body, voice and gesture plus his elemental physical appearance give authority to his kingly-role. He will evince strong femme appeal despite the completely shaven head and may do for the bald-headed men what Pinza did for the middle-aged.

Rita Moreno, as Tuptim, the gift to the king's harem; Terry Saunders, as Lady Thiang, the head wife; Martin Benson, as the prime minister; Carlos Rivas, as Tuptim's lover; Rex Thompson, as Mrs. Anna's young son; Patrick Adiarte, as the crown prince; Alan Mowbray, as the British ambassador, and Geoffrey Toone, as an English official, all lend strong support. Miss Saunders, who played the No. 1 wife in the original stage version, is especially standout in voice and thesping, clicking especially with "Something Wonderful," a paean of praise for the king.

Twentieth-Fox's casting office deserves special praise for its selection of the oriental youngsters who play the king's children. It has come up with a group of charmers who at moments practically steal the picture. The scene in which the children are presented to Mrs. Anna—"The March of the Siamese Children"—is one of the many highlights of the film. A larger share of the credit for the socko presentation of the "March" is due director Lang.

Equally "show-stopping" is the ballet number—"The Small House of Uncle Thomas," the play-within-a-play presented by the royal household to visiting dignitaries at a state reception to prove that the king is not a "barbarian." It is beautifully narrated by Miss Moreno and danced by Yuriko, Marion Jim, Robert Banas, Dusty Worrall, and Gemze de Lappe.

Other musical highlights include Miss Kerr's and Brynner's hectic polka around the huge palace ballroom to the accompaniement of "Shall We Dance?," Brynner's "Is A Puzzlement!," Miss Kerr and Rex Thompson in "I Whistle A Happy Tune," Miss Kerr, the royal wives and children in "Getting to Know You"; Miss Moreno and Carlos Rivas in "We Kiss In A Shadow," and Miss Kerr in "Hello, Young Lovers." Although unbilled, the singing voice of Miss Kerr is Marni Nixon. It is ghosted so well that it is hard to believe that it is not Miss Kerr.

The film suggests a stronger romantic feeling between Mrs. Anna and the king than was presented in the legituner, but it is done with the utmost delicacy. It is accomplished with nothing more than the meeting of eyes and the caress of a hand at the king's deathbed scene.

Those who have seen the stage musical and even those who recall 20th's previous, non-musical "Anna and the King of Siam," with Irene Dunne and Rex Harrison, will find "The King and I" a rich and rewarding experience. It cost 20th $6,500,000 to make the new version. The film is a cinch to recover the production coin and it won't come as a surprise if it finds its way into the list of all-time moneymakers. *Holl.*

Somebody Up There Likes Me
(SONG)

Excitement and heart-tug in another of Metro's hard-hitting biopix. Superbly done. Sure of strong word-of-mouth to aid the selling.

Hollywood, July 3.

Metro release of Charles Schnee production. Stars Paul Newman, Pier Angeli; features Everett Sloane, Eileen Heckart, Sal Mineo. Directed by Robert Wise. Screenplay, Ernest Lehman; based on the Rocky Graziano autobiography written by Rowland Barber; camera, Joseph Ruttenberg; editor, Albert Akst; music, Bronislau Kaper; title song, Kaper and Sammy Cahn, sung by Perry Como. Previewed June 27, '56. Running time, **112 MINS.**

Rocky .... Paul Newman
Norma .... Pier Angeli
Irving Cohen .... Everett Sloane
Ma Barbella .... Eileen Heckart
Romolo ....Sal Mineo
Nick Barbella .... Harold J. Stone
Benny .... Joseph Buloff
Whitey Bimstein .... Sammy White
Heldon .... Arch Johnson
Questioner .... Robert Lieb
Comm. Eddie Eagan .....Theo. Newton

"Somebody Up There Likes Me" is a superbly done, frank and revealing, film probe of Rocky Graziano, the East Side punk who overcame a lawless beginning to win respect and position as middleweight champion of the world. While boxing occupies a key position in any account of Graziano's life, this is by no means a prize-fight picture. Metro has a certain sales edge in pushing it as the story of a man's redemption through a touching love story. The drama is there to back up the adjectives. Also stacks probable word-of-mouth and appeal to teenagers.

The same gutsy dramatic quality featured in Metro's "Love Me Or Leave Me" and "I'll Cry Tomorrow," studio's previous two entries in the hard-hitting biopic trend, is present here in full measure. Also, "Somebody" has the tough, real life punch of an "On the Water-Front" to grip the viewer and swell ticket sales. It isn't a pretty picture, but it's an always interesting one, with excitement and smash action, particularly in its ring phases and that finale championship bout, better than being ringside almost.

Seemingly, there's little compromising with the truth in Charles Schnee's outstanding production guidance, or in the extremely fine, dramatically—wise, screenplay Ernest Lehman did from the Graziano autobiography written by Rowland Barker. The exceptional quality to be noted in the scripting also is to be found in the direction by Robert Wise. Working on such a solid base, the direction builds a picture that, for revealing frankness, will be hard to match, as will the handling of the considerable talents of the cast.

For Paul Newman "Somebody" is a showcasing that should help remove the Brando look-alike handicap. His talent is large and flexible, revealing an approach to the Graziano character that bears no resemblance to his previous characters in "The Silver Chalice" and "The Rack.' He scores tremendously. In the first half of the footage he gets the audience near to the point of hating him as he goes through the undisciplined viciousness of a no-good young hoodlum, not yet come under the influence of the love that would guide him on the right path.

In the latter half, when Norma Unger, played with beautiful sensitivity by Pier Angeli, comes into his life the audience is back on his side, pulling for him to shake off the past, and literally cheering him on in that potently staged championship match with Tony Zale. Credit for this stirring climax and its authenticity must be shared by technical adviser Johnny Indrisano and Courtland Shepard, who fights like a true-to-life Zale.

Miss Angeli appears to have the secret of getting good roles and then knowing what to do with them. In this she must have been the agent for the guy upstairs looking after Graziano, because the swing from the sordid to the good starts with her first appearance. She gets the breath of true romance into her love scenes with Newman and generally adds an outstanding quality to the picture.

In Graziano's career from petty thief, dirty street fighter, reformatory graduate, a dishonorably discharged soldier and Leavenworth inmate to club fighter and then champion, his life is touched by a number of assorted characters, vividly and impressively played by the featured and supporting cast. Numbered among them with the kind of performances that stand large in the film's overall excellence is Everett Sloane, great as the manager Irving Cohen who guided the fighter's ring wars; Eileen Heckart, exceptionally fine as Graziano's mother; Harold J. Stone, almost uncomfortably real as the wine-sodden father whose own ring dreams had never been realized; and Sal Mineo, excellent as the street chum who shared Graziano's early, wayward ways.

Figuring importantly, too, are Joseph Buloff, sweetshop confidante and advisor; Sammy White, fight handler; Arch Johnson, Leavenworth bully; Robert Loggia, as the Frankie Peppo who tried to get Graziano to throw a fight; Judson Pratt, who played a part in getting Graziano on the right path while in prison; Robert Lieb, Theodore Newton and a number of uncredited performers.

There's a title song vocalled by Perry Como to open and close the picture that has plenty of pop value. Sammy Cahn wrote the lyrics and Bronislau Kaper, who also contributed the sock background score, did the cleffing. Sharp photography that emphasizes the East Side settings and other realistic phases of the art direction, along with strikingly actionful ring battling, was contributed by Joseph Ruttenberg. Albert Akst's editing is another top credit. *Brog.*

The Oklahoma Woman

Straight out of the oat-bin. For novelty two dames have a fight in the saloon.

Hollywood, June 26.

American Releasing Corp. release of a Roger Corman (Sunset) production. Stars Richard Denning, Peggie Castle, Cathy Downs; features Touch Connors, Tudor Owen, Martin Kingsley, Jonathan Haze, Richard Miller, Tom Dillon, Edmond Cobb. Directed by Corman. Screenplay, Lou Rusoff; camera, Fred West; editor, Ronald Sinclair; music, Ronald Stein. Reviewed at Hawaii Theatre, Hollywood. June 20, '56. Running time, **71 MINS.**

Steve Ward..............Richard Denning
Marie "Oklahoma" Saunders
Peggie Castle
Ed Grant....................Tudor Owen
Sheriff Bill Peters.......Martin Kingsley
Susan Grant................Cathy Downs
Sheriff ....Touch Connors

This western is straight out of the oat-bin, and headed for a supporting role in houses catering to less-sophisticated audiences.

Richard Denning comes out of the pen, determined to forego his gunslinging past and to settle down to some peaceable ranching. Instead, he finds himself embroiled in a political fight. His former sweetheart, Peggie Castle, proprietress of the local saloon, heads the baddie crew and his upright neighbor, Tudor Owen, and neighbor's purty dotter, Cathy Downs, head the reform ticket.

Matters are complicated by a tough sheriff, Martin Kingsley, unconvinced that Denning's really reformed, and Miss Castle's chief henchie, Touch Connors, who frames Denning several times over. As predictable, when the sheriff and Owen get killed, Denning singlehandedly cleans up the town, forces Miss Castle to flee, and settles down to the simple life with Miss Downs.

Supposed highlight, a fight between Misses Castle and Downs, turns into a ludicrous mimicry of a male saloon fight, missing few of the cliches.

Roger Corman, who bears double blame as producer-director, keeps the action appropriate to the elementary level of the Lou Rusoff script. The acting departs very little from the traditional forms laid down by William Farnum and his contemporaries. *Kove.*

Francis in the Haunted House

Mickey Rooney and Paul Frees new casting for Universal's friend-and-mule. Amusing hokum.

Hollywood, July 3.

Universal release of Robert Arthur production. Stars Mickey Rooney, Virginia Welles; features James Flavin, Paul Cavanagh, Mary Ellen Kaye, David Janssen, Ralph Dumke, Richard Gaines, Richard Deacon, Francis. Directed by Charles Lamont. Screenplay, Herbert Margolis, William Raynor; based on David Stern's "Francis" character; camera, George Robinson; editor, Milton Carruth; music supervision, Joseph Gershenson. Previewed June 25, '56. Running time, **79 MINS.**

David Prescott .... Mickey Rooney
Lorna MacLeod .... Virginia Welles
Chief Martin .... James Flavin
Neil Frazer .... Paul Cavanagh
Lorna Ann .... Mary Ellen Kaye
Lt. Hopkins .... David Janssen
Mayor Hargrove .... Ralph Dumke
Dist. Atty. Reynolds .... Richard Gaines
Jason .... Richard Deacon
Sgt. Arnold .... Dick Winslow
Malcolm .... Charles Horvath
Hugo .... Timothy Carey
Mrs. MacPherson ...... Helen Wallace
Howard Grisby .... Edward Earle
Edward Ryan .... John Maxwell
Ephraim Biddle .... Glen Kramer
FRANCIS, the Talking Mule

Universal's talking mule is introduced to a new voice and a new partner in "Francis In the Haunted House." The entertainment intent remains the same and comes close to the comedy mark most of the time for the general program dates it will play.

Mickey Rooney is the new foil for the loquacious hybrid, who is now voiced by Paul Frees, replacing Donald O'Connor and Chill Willis, respectively, who rode through the six previous starters in the series. Rooney tackles a new character, David Prescott, with the Peter Stirling played by O'Connor being dropped, and does a good job of clowning and mugging his way through the antics. Frees' mulish vocalistics are a help, too.

Picture is a rather slow-starter, and occasionally loses pace in spots thereafter, but on the whole can be figured as fulfilling its entertainment aims. Charles Lamont's direction of the Robert Arthur production points up a number of funny scenes to be found in the Herbert Margolis - William Raynor screenplay, built around the "Francis" character created by David Stern. The emphasis is on broadness and freewheeling slapstick, such as the knights-in-armor jousting between Rooney mounted on Francis and the plot heavy posing as an old Scottish ghost.

Humorous skullduggery takes place in an old castle, transported from Scotland by a now dead eccentric. The castle is loaded with old masters and other treasures and a gang of crooks, including Virginia Welles, who is being passed off as the heiress, are substituting fakes. Francis gets wind of the scheme, tells Rooney and the fun starts popping. Without Francis, Rooney would easily have been a dead hero, but the mule makes things come out okay for the right side.

Miss Welles is an attractive heavy, with Paul Cavanagh as her chief dirty-worker. James Flavin, harassed police chief; Mary Ellen Kaye, the real heiress; David Janssen, Ralph Dumke, town mayor; Richard Gaines, funny as the d.a. who just can't believe a mule can talk, even when he hears him; Richard Deacon, Charles Horvath, Timothy Carey and others do their part in the fun.

Lensing by George Robinson, a comedy-minded score supervised by Joseph Gershenson, editing and other technical credits are good. *Brog.*

The Long Arm
(BRITISH)

Conventional crook thriller showing Jack Hawkins as leading Scotland Yard sleuth tracking down almost clueless crimes; good average entertainment.

Rank release of a Michael Balcon-Ealing Studios production. Stars Jack Hawkins. Directed by Charles Frend. Screenplay, Janet Green and Robert Barr; camera, Gordon Dines; editor, Gordon Stone; music, Gerbrand Schurmann. At Gaumont, London. Running time, **96 MINS.**

Det.-Supt. Tom Halliday....Jack Hawkins
Detective Segt. Ward......John Stratton
Mary Halliday ....Dorothy Alison
Tony Halliday ....Michael Brooke
Police Constable .... Sam Kydd
Detective Segt.............Glyn Houston
Night-watchman ....Richard Leech
Deputy Commander ....Newton Blick
Supt. Malcolm ....Goffrey Keen
Stone ....Sydney Tafler
Creasey ....Peter Burton
Slob ....George Rose
Det. Inspector ....Arthur Rigby
Colonel Blenkinsop ......Ralph Truman
Young Workman .... Ian Bannen
His Wife ....Maureen Davis
Detective Inspector ......John Warwick

Cashier ....Joss Ambler
Mrs. Gilson ....Ursula Howells

Jack Hawkins dons the plain clothes of a top ranking detective in this latest Ealing Studios production, which is more conservative than earlier picture on much the same subject, "The Blue Lamp." Set almost entirely in Scotland Yard, it may have a novelty angle for the U.S. market, strengthened by the popularity of Hawkins.

Story revolves around a manhunt for a safe breaker who leaves no clues, and reaps a rich harvest, obviously having inside knowledge of when unusually large sums of money will be available. An unlucky early workman tries to stop his car after a big haul, and turns the getaway into cold blooded murder. But from the victim's dying statement faint clues emerge, and the net closes in.

After weeks of patient sifting the finest grains of evidence in a trail leading over the Welsh border, the identity of the thief is revealed and a trap set and sprung when a heavy gala night's takings at the Festival Hall in London proves a tempting bait. The tension builds up to an exciting and credible finish. There are sufficient dubious characters involved to delay the audience realization of the criminal and his confederates.

Practically an all male cast gives a straightforward, authentic insight into the inner workings of the homicide squad and the painstaking investigations. Camera work is excellent and the whole setup bears the stamp of realism.

Jack Hawkins, with an occasional glimmer of humor, brings the main character forcefully to life. He is ably supported by John Stratton as his junior sidekick. The only positive femme roles are in the hands of Dorothy Alison who conveys the resigned philosophical attitude of a neglected wife and Ursula Howells as the ruthless killer. Anonymity keeps the crook in the background during most of the time, but Richard Leech registers impressively in the closing scenes. All the minor roles are convincingly acted by seasoned players. *Clem.*

Johnny Concho

Talky western. Presents Frank Sinatra as producer of own starring vehicle.

Hollywood, July 10.

United Artists release of Kent (Frank Sinatra) production. Stars Frank Sinatra, Keenan Wynn, William Conrad, Phyllis Kirk; features Wallace Ford, Willis Bouchey. Directed by Don McGuire. Screenplay, David P. Harmon and McGuire; from story by Harmon; camera, William Mellor; editor, Eda Warren; music, Nelson Riddle. Previewed July 5, '56. Running time, **85 MINS.**

Johnny Concho .... Frank Sinatra
Barney Clark .... Keenan Wynn
Tallman .... William Conrad
Mary Dark .... Phyllis Kirk
Albert Dark .... Wallace Ford
Sarah Dark .... Dorothy Adams
Walker .... Christopher Dark
Helgeson .... Howard Petrie
Sam Green .... Harry Bartell
Judge Tyler .... Dan Russ
Sheriff Henderson ...... Willis Bouchey
Duke Lang .... Robert Osterloh
Pearl Lang .... Jean Byron
Mason .... Leo Gordon
Lem .... Claude Akins
Jake .... John Qualen
Pearson .... Wilfrid Knapp
Benson .... Ben Wright
Bartender .... Joe Bassett

Only a fair "mood" western with pace on the slow side for action fan tastes and never quite realizing on inherent story values, this one depends on Frank Sinatra whose own setup, Kent, is presenting through United Artists. He draws producer and star credits for the offering.

Passable for a first try. Could possibly have clicked strongly with surer direction and scripting. The uncertain handling is reflected in Sinatra's own work and in the performance of some other cast members, although a couple of colorful portrayals help out. Don McGuire directs, and also screenplayed with David P. Harmon from the latter's story. It's a western which inclines towards talkiness.

In the title role, Sinatra is seen as the cowardly younger brother of a dread gunslinger, whose reputation forces a small town to put up with the young man and his arrogant ways. When the brother is killed in a gun duel, the killers, colorfully portrayed by William Conrad and Christopher Dark, take over the town and chase Sinatra out. On the run, the latter finds peace nowhere and, gaining courage finally from this adversity, returns to the town to arouse the citizens to get rid of fear and oppression. He's wounded in the showdown, but his about-face inspires the townspeople and good triumphs.

Keenan Wynn makes a picturesque reformed gunman, now a preacher, who gets Sinatra started right, and Phyllis Kirk does a nice job of the girl who loves, but doesn't like, the cowardly hero. Wallace Ford, as her father, and Dorothy Adams, the mother; Howard Petrie, blacksmith; Harry Bartell, the only courageous, but foolhardy citizen; Dan Russ, conforming judge; Willis Bouchey, the sheriff; Robert Osterloh and Jean Byron are acceptable as townspeople.

Mood is stressed in the lensing by William Mellor and in the excellent background score by Nelson Riddle. Editing, art direction and other technical credits come off okay. *Brog.*

Seven Men From Now
(COLOR-SONG)

Revenge western, one of Randolph Scott's better entries, for outdoor market.

Hollywood, July 10.

Warner Bros. release of Andrew V. McLaglen, Robert E. Morrison (Batjac) production. Stars Randolph Scott, Gail Russell, Lee Marvin; features Walter Reed, John Larch, Donald Barry, Fred Graham. Directed by Budd Boetticher. Story and screenplay, Burt Kennedy; camera (WarnerColor), William H. Clothier; editor, Everett Sutherland; music, Henry Vars; songs, By Dunham and Vars. Previewed June 27, '56. Running time, 77 MINS.

Stride .... Randolph Scott
Annie .... Gail Russell
Masters .... Lee Marvin
Greer .... Walter Reed
Bodeen .... John Larch
Clete .... Donald Barry
Henchman .... Fred Graham
Clint .... John Barradino
Jed .... John Phillips
Mason .... Chuck Roberson
Fowler .... Steve Mitchell
Senorita .... Pamela Duncan
Cavalry Lieutenant .... Stuart Whitman

Revenge is the driving force cueing the action in "Seven Men From Now" and it stacks up as one of Randolph Scott's better western entries. The fans will like it and it should have a good ride through the outdoor market.

Listed as a Batjac presentation for Warner Bros., pic rates excellent production helming from Andrew V. McLaglen and Robert E. Morrison, with Budd Boetticher's direction having plenty of sinews in developing the action and suspense to be found in Burt Kennedy's well-written western screen story. Camera work by Williams H. Clothier in Warner-Color is another plus for release intentions.

Scott delivers a firstrate performance as an ex-sheriff out to get seven men who killed his wife during the holdup of a Wells Fargo office. Gail Russell, off screen for some time, has not lost her appeal and is good as a woman who becomes interested in Scott, even though she's married to Walter Reed, tenderfoot not implicated in the holdup but being used to transport the loot. Lee Marvin scores a hit as the third star, giving a menacing punch to the role of a gunman following Scott because he figures to wind up with the loot, himself, after the ex-sheriff has taken care of the robbers.

The revenge chase is played off against some rugged outdoor location sites, adding to the grimness of the mood. Showdown battling between Scott and the men he is chasing has rugged excitement, and there's real tension in the finale meeting between the wounded hero and the menacing Marvin.

Reed does well as the tenderfoot who submerges his yen for easy money to die a hero at the end. Don Barry, as Marvin's ally, does his work well, too, as do John Larch, Fred Graham, John Barradino, John Phillips, Chuck Roberson and Steve Mitchell as six of the men Scott is seeking. Pamela Duncan, dance hall girl, and Stuart Whitman, cavalry lieutenant, are other competents.

Henry Vars' score goes with the story mood, as does the title tune he wrote with By Dunham. Only a snatch of another song, "Good Love," is heard. Everett Sutherland's editing, sound and other credits are expertly handled. *Brog.*

Walk the Proud Land
(C'SCOPE—COLOR)

Misnomered early-west drama, generally unexciting but has Audie Murphy to help in outdoor market.

Hollywood, July 10.

Universal release of Aaron Rosenberg production. Stars Audie Murphy, Anne Bancroft, Pat Crowley; features Charles Drake, Tommy Rall, Robert Warwick, Jay Silverheels. Directed by Jesse Hibbs. Screenplay, Gil Doud, Jack Sher; based on a biography by Woodworth Clum; camera (Technicolor), Harold Lipstein; editor, Sherman A. Todd; music supervision, Joseph Gershenson. Previewed July 3, '56. Running time, 88 MINS.

John P. Clum .... Audie Murphy
Tianay .... Anne Bancroft
Mary Dennison .... Pat Crowley
Tom Sweeny .... Charles Drake
Taglito .... Tommy Rall
Eskiminzin .... Robert Warwick
Geronimo .... Jay Silverheels
Tono .... Eugene Mazzola
Disalin .... Anthony Caruso
Santos .... Victor Millan
Captain Larsen .... Ainslie Pryor
Chato .... Eugene Iglesias
General Wade .... Morris Ankrum
Governor Safford....... Addison Richards
Alchise .... Maurice Jara
Stone .... Frank Chase
Naylor .... Ed Hinton
Pica .... Marty Carrizosa

The rather pastel title of "Walk the Proud Land" has been hung on this early-west drama. What business it attracts in the general outdoor market will probably be sparked by Audie Murphy's name. CinemaScope and Technicolor give the footage visual attractiveness. What's lacking, however, is excitement and story action.

The true story of John Philip Clum, Indian agent at the San Carlos, Ariz., Apache Reservation back in 1874 is the basis for the Aaron Rosenberg production. Scripting by Gil Doud and Jack Sher from the biography by Woodworth Clum, makes for a leisurely unfoldment, with situations and characters that do not always ring true, although Jesse Hibbs' direction works in some flashes of action and gets good performances from most of the players.

Murphy plays the dedicated agent, who takes over from the Army at the reservation and tries to install self-government for the Apaches. He is entirely likeable as the serious young man and impressing with him is Anne Bancroft, Apache widow, a fetching rose of the desert who can't quite understand why Murphy doesn't take her for his wife along with Pat Crowley, eastern girl who comes west to be the agent's bride. Miss Crowley is capable as the new wife who has trouble adapting herself to western ways, even though the role is a bit thankless.

Clum was the first white man to force the surrender of the notorious Geronimo and the episode is brought off in the picture as the supposed story highlight with only mild tension and excitement. Jay Silverheels plays the warring Indian without much threat. Charles Drake, ex-soldier who helps Murphy; Tommy Rall, Robert Warwick, Eugene Mazzola, Anthony Caruso and Victor Millan, reservation Indians; Ainslie Pryor and Morris Ankrum, representing Army opposition to Murphy, and Addison Richards, as governor, are among okay supporting players.

Harold Lipstein's outdoor lensing is excellent. *Brog.*

The Iron Petticoat
(BRITISH—COLOR—V'VISION)

Bob Hope and Kate Hepburn for the marquee. Broad farce spoofing Russia. Some good topical quips but otherwise mediocre Ben Hecht script.

Berlin, July 1.

Independent Film Distribs release of Remus production made in association with Harry Saltzman. (Metro will distribute in the U.S.). Stars Bob Hope and Katharine Hepburn. Features James Robertson Justice and Robert Helpmann. Produced by Betty E. Box; director, Ralph Thomas; screenplay, Ben Hecht; camera, Ernest Steward; editor, Frederick Wilson; music, Ben Frankel. At Film Buehne Wen, Berlin, June 30, '56. Running time, **96 MINS.**

Chuck Lockwood	Bob Hope
Vinka Kovelonko	Katharine Hepburn
Col. Sklarnoff	James Robertson Justice
Ivan Kropotkin	Robert Helpmann
Dubratz	David Kossoff
Col. Tarbell	Alan Gifford
Lewis	Paul Carpenter
Connie	Noelle Middleton
Tony Mallard	Nicholas Phipps
Paul	Sidney James
Senator	Alexander Gauge
Sutsiyawa	Tutte Lemkow
Tityana	Sandra Dorne
Lingerie Clerk	Richard Wattis
Sklarnoff's Secretary	Maria Antippas
Grisha	Martin Boddey

Bob Hope and Katharine Hepburn were imported to Britain for starring in "The Iron Petticoat" and Ben Hecht to write the screenplay. On the performers rests the box-office burden for the script provided by Hecht is not first rate. True, some of the political quips are astonishingly pat and seemed, at the Berlin Film Festival premiere of the picture, uncannily appropriate to subsequent changes within the Soviet. Some of the dialog is so "topical" it might well have been written in hindsight rather than in anticipation of the downgrading of yesterday's saint in Russia.

To have clicked unreservedly down the line, "Petticoat" should have been a slick political satire, a la "Ninotchka." Instead, it never pretends to be any more than political farce. For Hope himself, the production outwardly represents a switch as he's supposedly not just being a funny man. That's the theory. In practice too much of his dialog resembles a Hope quipping turn extended full length into a book show; and too few of the gags, with the exceptions hinted, are sufficiently fresh to command more than casual interest.

The Remus production in Vista Vision has a lavish, professional gloss and is a credit to the producer-director team of Betty E. Box and Ralph Thomas, both of whom have collaborated on some of Britain's top b.o. winners. There's ample imagination in the settings and Benjamin Frankel has written attractive background music, which adroitly sets the mood for many of the scenes.

The basic weakness in the production is the Ben Hecht screenplay, which resorts to oldfashioned and farcial cloak and dagger, instead of coming to grips with a controversially topical issue. His story of a Soviet air heroine who flies her plane into West Berlin because she's angry at being passed over for promotion is neither believable nor realistic. But with Hope as the Yank officer assigned to brainwash the Soviet pilot, it's an easy vehicle for laughs, particularly when the Russian spies get to work to recapture the renegade red. Eventually, she surrenders to the Russians, is court-martialled and returned home for death sentence. Hope tries to seize the plane carrying her back to Moscow, but instead of a firing squad both get a heroes' welcome, complete with NBC, CBS and BBC interviewers.

Miss Hepburn makes an impressive showing as the Soviet pilot; she looks the part as well as playing it; and the gradual transition in outlook, accompanied by the change in style of her wardrobe, is accomplished with considerable sensitivity. Hope maintains the spirit of the piece at a lively pace, but never quite forgets his work habits as a gagman. Remainder of the cast was recruited in Britain, and is headed by James Robertson Justice as the principal Russian heavy, and Robert Helpmann as his mild aide. Both turn in acceptable performances. Neat cameos are provided by David Kossoff, and Richard Wattis; other members of the team are up to standard. *Myro.*

Bullfight
(DOCUMENTARY)

Beast and man face death again in the afternoon. Historic perspective and good narrative. Good bet for big city art houses.

Janus production. Written and directed by Pierre Braunberger. English narration by Bryant Haliday. Reviewed July 5, '56, at 55th St. Playhouse, N.Y. Running time, **76 MINS.**

Including some presumably new footage of bull farms and bull economics in Spain, this documentary includes much library footage, plus some maps, old etchings, diagrams and stills. It adds up into a most "educational" (that miserable word) 76 minutes on an endlessly fascinating phenomenon, the corrida, or bullfight, of the Latins—the fiesta of bravery.

At the 55th Street Playhouse the film was off Tuesday and July 4th to a record. Caught on a rainy Thursday matinee, there was a fairly full house at this sidestreet 250-seater priced at $1.25. Clientele was preponderantly male and notable for the older men. A presumption of general appeal for special selective spots is supported by such evidence plus the nature of the film

From its origins in dim antiquity (Crete about 4,000 years ago) the art (never the sports) of killing bulls with appropriate etiquette has undergone great change. Not the least arresting aspect of the present documentary is the revelation of the big-horned beasts of only 40 years ago which could not be worked "close" as contrasted with the more manageable toro of the present time, who is played cool for "domination" pas de deux and a ballet-like kill.

Manolete, who had weak legs but was otherwise a genius, matured much of present bullfighting techniques. The film wisely devotes a lion's share of its length to this true lion of courage, class and tradition. Official billing describes "the cast" as including him, Dominquin, Belmonte, Ortega and others plus Conchita Citron, the Peruvian gal who fights on horseback.

Narration of actor-exhibitor Bryant Haliday is clear and pragmatic throughout. Footage varies in quality as in age. The musical score is not always well matched to the particular scenes and there's distinctly an excess of crowd sound effect when no crowd is visible. No fortune was expended putting the film together.

But "Bullfight" readily stacks up as an offbeat triumph of the scissors, gluepot and documentary sense of Pierre Braunberger. It will find a considerable audience of those fascinated by the choreography of the Plaza del Toro. There is plenty of reminder that the matadors are not playing marbles, the gorings being more vivid than costomarily exhibited. The color of the corrida (and of Spain) makes this real "escapism"—right back to 1895, the date of some of the Madrid clips. *Land.*

Three For Jamie Dawn

Program drama about attempted jury fix; just mild entertainment.

Hollywood, July 10.

Allied Artists release of Hayes Goetz production. Stars Laraine Day, Ricardo Montalban, Richard Carlson, June Havoc; features Maria Palmer, Eduard Franz, Regis Toomey, Herb Vigran. Directed by Thomas Carr. Story and screenplay, John Klempner; camera, Duke Green; editor, Richard Cahoon; music, Walter Scharf. Previewed July 6, '56. Running time, **81 MINS.**

Sue	Laraine Day
Tom	Ricardo Montalban
Random	Richard Carlson
Lorrie	June Havoc
Julia	Maria Palmer
Karek	Eduardo Franz
Murph	Regis Toomey
Gordon	Scotty Beckett
Robbins	Herb Vigran
Jamie Dawn	Marilyn Simms
Helen March	Dorothy Adams

The attempted fix of a murder trial jury makes for a mild sort of drama in "Three For Jamie Dawn" but it will live up to the unexacting demands of the general program market. Familiar names of Laraine Day, Ricardo Montalban, Richard Carlson and June Havoc are the main assets.

When a rich and notorious girl kills her lover, shyster Carlson is called in to undertake the defense. He sets out to buy off three of the jurors—Eduard Franz, foreign-born whose son is still in Czechoslovakia; Montalban, young married man having money troubles, and Miss Havoc, faded ex-actress who would like another stage chance. They are lured by the assorted promises held out to them, but in the end, good citizenship stands triumphant and they join with the other jurors to give an unanimous guilty verdict.

Before that happens, though, some mighty unlikely situations are brought up in the John Klempner screen story, with neither Thomas Carr's direction nor the cast able to make them believeable. The four stars do what they can, with assists from Maria Palmer, wife of Franz; Regis Toomey, Carlson's fixer, and others but have only scant success.

The Hayes Goetz production is ably lensed by Duke Green to make the most of budget values and the technical and musical backing are satisfactory. *Brog.*

Loser Takes All
(BRITISH-COLOR-C'SCOPE)

Frothy Graham Greene comedy set in Monte Carlo with Rossano Brazzi and Glynis Johns starred. Bright domestic proposition, with U. S. prospects.

Berlin, July 3.

British Lion release of John Stafford production. Stars Rossano Brazzi, Glynis Johns and Robert Morley; features Tony Britton. Directed by Ken Annakin. Screenplay, Graham Greene; camera, George Perinal; editor, Jean Barker; music, Alessandro Cicognini. At Film Buehne Wien, Berlin. Running tme, **86 MINS.**

Bertrand	Rossano Brazzi
Cary	Glynis Johns
Dreuther	Robert Morley
Philip	Tony Britton
The Other	Felix Aylmer
Hotel Manager	Albert Lieven
Elderly Man	A. E. Matthews
Bird's Next	Joyce Carey
Reception Clerk	Geoffrey Keen
Stranger	Peter Illing
Arnold	Walter Hudd
Blixon	Charles Lloyd Pack
Room Waiter	Guido Lorraine
Miss Bullen	Joan Benham

As a frivolous, lightweight comedy, "Loser Takes All," with its colorful Monte Cristo setting deserves to garner steady grosses in the domestic market, where the name values of Rossano Brazzi, Glynis Johns and Robert Morley have ticket-selling appeal.

After the more serious stuff he has penned in recent years, this piece represents quite a change in style for Graham Greene. There's no message in this story nor does it have any significance. It's just featherweight entertainment, with a bright romantic story. John Stafford's production is on an expansive scale, using palatial sets where necessary, and taking full advantage of the handsome Riviera locale. Ken Annakin's breezy direction keeps the action moving and the highgrade color lensing by George Perinal gives a glossy finish to this British 'Scoper.

Appropriately for this treatment it has conceived, there's not much substance to this frothy little tale of young newlyweds who get caught up in the Riviera gambling fever. Rosanno Brazzi and Glynis Johns had intended to marry quietly and honeymoon in Bournemouth (typical English middleclass resort). But his employer will have none of that: ceremony in Monte Carlo, honeymoon aboard his yacht. Sounds fine, but the boss forgets to show up and the money runs out in a couple of days. Brazzi turns his mathematical mind to the gaming tables, while his bride turns to a young Englishman (Tony Britton) for attention.

Brazzi and Miss Johns are a pleasantly contrasting romantic team; he's the sad and earnest lover while she's the gay and sprightly bride. Robert Morley's overpowering personality fits his role of the big tycoon, while Britton impresses as the penniless Englishman who makes a pitch for the deserted bride. In a big cast, distinguished character actors of the calibre of Felix Aylmer, Walter Hudd and A. E. Matthews stand out. *Myro.*

Ic
(INDIAN)

Fair bet for U. S. art houses.

Hollywood, June 10.

United Releasing Organization release of a Raj Kapoor production. Stars Baby Naaz, Rattan Kumar, David; features Kamala Chachi, Master Kapoor, Renu, Ramseth. Directed by Prakash Arora; screenplay, Zhanu Pratap; camera, Tara Dutt; editor, G. G. Nayekar; music, Shanker and Jaikishan, lyrics, Shailender. Previewed at Vagabond Theatre, L.A., June 26, '56. Running time, **90 MINS.**

Girl	Baby Naaz
Boy	Rattan Kumar
Bootlegger	David
Aunt	Kamla Chachi
Bootblack	Master Kapoor
Mother	Renu
Father	Ramseth

From India, in Hindi dialect, comes a film which is a fair bet for the art house circuit, despite many scripting and technical faults and too specialized appeal for wider distribution.

One of the three co-stars, Baby Naaz, won a Cannes Festival award a couple of years back, which may supply an exploitation peg. Otherwise, this version ("Bootpolish" in the original, three-hour-plus release) is choppily cut and hard to follow. Inadequate subtitling cannot cope with naive script, acting and direction.

Story deals with the efforts of an orphaned pair of moppets, Baby Naaz and Rattan Kumar, to rise out of the class of street beggars, a task to which they have been set by their prostie witch of an aunt, played by Kamla Chachi. They are hampered by a bootblack, Master Kapoor, and helped by a bootlegger (sic) friend, played by the third co-star, David.

The pair manage to hold out enough gleanings from their rapacious aunt to buy a shoeshine kit, representing a step out of the begging fraternity. Their initial clumsy attempts in this field affords some humor. When the bootblack informs their aunt, they are driven, ill and hungry, out of the family hovel. They are separated. The girl is picked up and adopted by a kindly, wealthy couple. Meanwhile, much footage is occupied with the boy's search for his sister, and the reunion is accomplished by an improbably long stretch of coincidence.

Among the technical credits, the clean, sharp photography of Tara Ditt stands out in any league. Theme song, penned by Shanker and Jaikishan, with lyrics by Shailander, and sung by David, is reported to have sold 1,000,000 disks in India. While the western ear quickly becomes acclimated to the Inidan idiom, no such platter sale can be predicted here. *Kove.*

Odongo
(BRITISH-C'SCOPE-COLOR)

Stock situations in African jungle romance between Rhonda Fleming and Macdonald Carey with native boy Juma stealing honors.

London, July 3.

Columbia release of a Warwick Production. Stars Rhonda Fleming and Macdonald Carey. Directed by John Gilling. Screenplay, John Giling; camera, Ted Moore; editor, Alan Osbiston; music, George Melachrino. At Leicester Square Theatre, London. Running time, **85 MINS.**

Pamela Muir	Rhonda Fleming
Steve Stratton	Macdonald Carey
Odongo	Juma
Celia Watford	Eleanor Summerfield
George Watford	Francis De Wolff
Hassan	Earl Cameron
Walla	Dan Jackson
Lester Watford	Michael Carridia
Mr. Bawa	Errol John
Game Warden	Leonard Sachs
Mohammed	Paul Hardtmuth
Leni	Bartholomew Sketch
Leni's Brother	Lionel Ngakane

There is little new in this latest East African story, although the main events are set on an animal farm instead of in a jungle. There is the dour white hunter, his faithful aides personified in the form of a youthful African, and the customary long shots of wild animal life. Hungry crocs, charging rhinos and trumpeting elephants provide the stereotyped hazards of the jungle. Besides Juma, the scene stealing colored boy, is a mischievous chimp, whose antics are surefire for laughs. The whole makes for good allround entertainment, although supplying few novelty angles.

Macdonald Carey plays the hunter with a corral of valuable assorted animals in Kenya for sale to zoos and circuses. His most devoted help is the grinning urchin who aches for the lost freedom of his charges, but overcomes his feelings in loyalty to his master. Trouble starts when the newly arrived vet turns out to be the glamorous redhead Rhonda Fleming, and resentful antagonism flares up mutually through her foolhardiness and his obstinate refusal to accept her.

A vengeful native, fired for cruelty, lets out all the animals, resulting in a stampede the day a buyer arrives to buy the stock. The boy, accused by his master, runs off into the bush, where he is held hostage by the real culprit who, when cornered, throws him into the river.

Miss Fleming looks attractive enough to distract anyone, but her sincerity is marred by occasional coy flippancy out of character for a woman of her qualifications. Carey is consistently realistic as the exasperated hunter who is finally won over. Eleanor Summerfield gets some laughs as a fussy English visitor, and capital native support forms an authentic human background. Most of the interest focuses on the boy seen in earlier pix, and he makes the most of his increased opportunities. *Clem.*

'1905'
(RUSSIAN-COLOR)

Slow-moving tale of agitators in Czarist Russia.

Sovexportfilm release of Kiev Film Studio production presented by Artkino. Directed by Mark Donskoy. Screenplay, N. Kovarsky and Donskoy, based on Maxim Gorky's "Mother"; camera (Magicolor), A. Mishurin; music, Lev Schwartz. At Cameo, N.Y., July 7, '56. Running time, **94 MINS.**

Mother	Vera Maretskaya
Pavel Vlassov	A. Batalov
His Father	N. Kolofidin
Andrei Nakhodka	A. Petrov
Rybin	P. Usovnichenko
Nikolai Ivanovich	S. Kurilov
Sasha	T. Biletskaya
Sofya	L. Gritsenko

(In Russian; English Titles)

Sacrifices of a mother for her revolutionist son makes for grim fare in "1905," latest import from the U.S.S.R. studios. The N. Kovarsky and Mark Donskoy screenplay is based upon Maxim Gorky's "Mother." This reviewer isn't familiar with the original but the overall theme of the screen version is "workers of the world, unite!" in no unsubtle tones.

Picture has no art house appeal and its U. S. prospects will be confined to the handful of theatres screening Soviet product. It's morbid stuff. Vera Maretskaya suffers from indignities heaped upon her by a drunken husband. He's a bum because of the torture inflicted upon him by the capitalistic owner of the local steel mill. Death soon solves his problem.

Thereafter A. Batalov, son of Miss Maretskaya, picks up the cudgels to improve the worker's lot. He's aided by several other youths whose ultimate reward proves to be exile to Siberia. His mother has a rough time economically and physically. But the cause of the worker is such that she devotes herself unstintingly to surreptious distribution of books and leaflets. Of course, this can't go on. She's seized in a railway station.

Doleful atmosphere throughout the film is heightened by the heavy-handed direction of co-scripter Donskoy. Miss Maretskaya is a pathetic figure whose unhappy life automatically insures audience sympathy. Batalov, as her son, varnishes his role of the youthful agitator with a fatalistic veneer. In the same vein is the performance of P. Usovnichenko, a stoker who quits the mill only to be beaten as he preaches the cause of the masses. Color lensing of A. Mishurin is fair while Lev Schwartz's score is in keeping with the dreary yarn. *Gilb.*

Donne Sole
(Women Alone)
(ITALIAN-COLOR)

Rome, July 3.

ENIC release and production. Stars Eleanora Rossi Drago, Gianna Maria Canale Luciana Angiolilio, Antigone Costanda, Ettore Manni. Directed by Vittorio Sala. Screenplay, Sala, Adriano Baracco, Continenza, Napolitano; from story by Sala; camera (Ferraniacolor), Aldo Giordani; music, Roberto Niccolosi. At Plaza, Rome. Running time, **105 MINS.**

Pic, one of Italo entries at Berlin Film Fest has name value for the local trade in Eleanora Rossi Drago and Gianna Maria Canale, and its general format makes it acceptable export fare. Production facets, including a Monte Carlo romance and an "inside the Italian film industry" glimpse, may be plugged to help returns.

The tongue-in-cheek bits showing Italo pix at work ring true. Thesping is capably done by the three leads, with Paolo Stoppa contributing a good bit as a silent suitor. Lensing in Ferraniacolor is uneven, somewhat cutting down the effect of material at hand.

Direction by Vittorio Sala, his first effort, shows immaturity in frequent pans off into scenics as well as in loose pacing. Script too often borders soap-opera while trying to be offbeat. *Hawk.*

Satellite In The Sky
(C'SCOPE—COLOR)

Ludicrous without intention. Inept science fiction.

Hollywood, June 26.

Warner Bros. release of Edward J. and Harry Lee Danziger production. Stars Kieron Moore, Lois Maxwell, Donald Wolfit; features Bryan Forbes, Jimmy Hanley, Thea Gregory. Directed by Paul Dickson. Screenplay, John Mather, J. T. McIntosh, Edith Dell; camera (Warner - Color), Georges Perinal, Jimmy Wilson; editor, Sydney Stone; music, Albert Elms. Previewed June 21, '56. Running time, **84 MINS.**

Michael	Kieron Moore
Kim	Lois Maxwell
Merrity	Donald Wolfit
Jimmy	Bryan Forbes
Larry	Jimmy Hanley
Barbara	Thea Gregory
Lefty	Barry Keegan
Col. Galloway	Alan Gifford
Ellen	Shirley Lawrence
Blandford	Walter Hudd
Captain Ross	Donald Gray
Tony	Peter Neil
Reporter	Rick Rydon
Reporter	Ronan O'Casey
Reporter	Robert O'Neil
General Barnett	Charles Richardson
Bechstein	Carl Jaffe
Expert	Trevor Reid
Export	Alastair Hunter
Official	John Baker

Other than a good title for teaming on dual space-ship exploitation bills, "Satellite In the Sky" has nothing to recommend it. It's ineptly written and directed. Practically becomes an unconsciously funny comedy.

CinemaScope and Warner Color mean little, other than to show up the flaws in the special effects directed by Wally Veevers and to make the directorial and writing mistakes loom large on the screen. Edward J. and Harry Lee Danziger produced for Warner Bros. release but will win no stateside friends with this one.

The screenplay by John Mather, J. T. McIntosh and Edith Dell features ridiculously trite dialog and situations that are no better. Direction by Paul Dickson does nothing to relieve the ludicrous flavor; in fact, even abets it at times, as does the playing of stars Kieron Moore, Lois Maxwell and Donald Wolfit, and the other cast members.

Plot is about an experimental flight beyond the stratosphere, where a specially designed rocket plane is to explode a new Tritonium Bomb. A mishap has the bomb attaching itself to the rocket ship instead of flying off into space. When the crew finally reconciles itself to dying, two members don space suits and hustle the bomb away, dying heroically when the bomb explodes after the others are safely out of range. Viewers are asked to believe that Miss Maxwell, newshen, could slip easily through security and stow away on the ship, and then spend her time in the stratosphere plaguing the crewmen with silly questions like "are you sure you know what you're doing?"

Lensing by Georges Perinal and Jimmy Wilson, editing, art direction, music and other credits are routine. *Brog.*

Foreign Films

Paris, July 3.

Tardes De Toros (AFTERNOON OF THE BULLS) (SPANISH; COLOR). Chamartin release of Vicente Sempere production. Stars Domingo Ortega, Antonio Bienvenida, Enrique Vera; features Maruja Asquerino, Marisa Prado, Encarnita Fuentes, Jacqueline Pierruex. Directed by Ladislao Vadja. Screenplay, Manuel Tamayo, Julio Coll, Jose Santugini; camera (Eastmancolor), Enrique Guerner; editor, Julio Pena; music, Jose Molleda. Previewed in Paris. Running time, **90 MINS.**

As boxing pix are to the U.S., so bullfighting films are to Spain. However, this emerges as one of the best because of its story simplicity. Setting is that about three real bullfighters in an afternoon of their lives in the arena. Though the story is slight and audience gambits obvious, excellent camerawork and bullring aspects give this a real tang. This might have censorship trouble in the U.S. for the kills are gorily shown.

Matadors emerge as acceptable actors and all three also excel in the ring. Direction wisely plays on the bullfight and the audience interludes without dwelling too much on the lightweight story. It will have to be sold on its colorful factors, Lensing, editing and production dress are all fine. *Mosk.*

Nuit Et Brouillard (NIGHT AND FOG) (FRENCH; DOCUMENTARY; COLOR). Argos Film production and release. Directed by Alain Renais. Commentary, Jean Cayrol done by Michel Bouquet; camera (Eastmancolor), Ghislain Cloquet; editor, Anne Sarraute; music, Hans Eisler. At Studio De L'Etoile, Paris. Running time, **30 MINS.**

This is the documentary which was yanked from the recent Cannes Film Fest at the insistence of Germany. Despite a harrowing account, via old photos and film footage, of Nazi Concentration Camps, it is mounted with tact, objectivity and vision to make this a telling document of a terrible episode of human history. Film is a reminder of what can happen to humanity in its inhumanity to itself. A "lest we forget" film, this adequately demonstrates the power of the cinema.

Pic is limited to special spots, but should be shown. Editing, conception and compiling of footage of ghettos, herding of Jews into compounds plus the invidious atrocities, weld this into a searing pic. Commentary has the right emphasis and analysis to make this a vivid summation of a past infamous aspect of world history.
Mosk.

Ce Soir Les Jupons Volent (Tonight the Skirts Fly) (FRENCH; DYALISCOPE; COLOR). Imperial release of Vox Film production. Directed by Dimitri Kirsanoff. Screenplay, Jean Marsan, Claude Desailly; camera (Agfacolor), Roger Fellous; editor, Monique Kirsanoff. With Sophie Desmarets, Jean Chevrier, Brigitte Auber, Anne Vernon, Philipe Nicaud, Nadine Tellier, Ginette Pigeon. At Paris, Paris. Running time, **90 MINS.**

Film unveils a new anamorphoscope process, Dyaliscope, but it is neither completely clear in definition nor too perfect in color rendition. However, it fills the necessary screen size. The process is new but pic is familiar with the skirts in question belonging to some mannequins. The film evolves into a sketch affair as each girl's love life is looked into. Some frank gallivanting puts this primarily in the exploitation category, but screen size might limit it. It does hold a modicum of entertainment value.

Director Dimitri Kirsanoff has made a simple bread and butter pic that will pay off locally, but needs real selling for foreign situations. Thesping gives in to pulchritude, here but latter is well handled by a bevy of lookers.
Mosk.

Voici Les Temps Des Assassins (FRENCH). Agiman release of CICC-Agiman-Pathe production. Stars Jean Gabin, Danielle Delorme; features Lucienne Bogaert, Gerard Blain, Germaine Kerjean, Aime Clariond, Robert Pizani. Directed by Julien Duvivier. Screenplay, Maurice Bessy, Duvivier, Charles Dorat, P. A. Breal; camera, Armand Thirard; editor, Jean Feyte. Running time, **110 MINS.**

Julien Duvivier has served up a grim slice-of-life pic in this tale of a predatory young girl whose congenital lying leads to tragedy. Though well mounted, the lack of deeper character analysis makes this only mild melodrama. Downbeat theme limits this to arty spots for the U.S., with the Jean Gabin name a help. And it will need plenty of bally.

A simple, easygoing restaurateur gets a visit from the daughter of his ex-wife. She says her mother is dead. The result is that she is taken in for awhile by the kindly, middleaged man. It is soon evident the girl is a conniving liar, for her mother is shown alive and a drug addict.

Film had a solid structure but Duvivier's direction rarely gives dimensions to the characters. Gabin displays his usual good acting but makes the man's goodness a sort of negative quality until his sudden eruption when the enormity of the girl's actions is made clear to him. Danielle Delmore does not make the neurotic character completely plausible. Remainder of the cast is good, with Gerard Blain emerging a new find. Lensing and editing are firstrate.
Mosk.

Le Long Des Trottoirs (Along the Sidewalks) (FRENCH). Cinedis release of Speva- Francinex production. Written and directed by Leonide Moguy. Camera, Andre Bac; editor, Louisette Hautecoeur; music, Joseph Kosma. With Danik Patisson, Anne Vernon, Francois Guerin, Joelle Bernard, Pierre Promont, Rene Brancard. At Paris, Paris. Running time, **95 MINS.**

Film shapes primarily as an exploitation item for it pays lip service to certain social flaws and difficulties without translating them into recognizable film terms. Writer-director Leonide Moguy again takes his well worn theme of a young girl forced into prostitution due to social indifference. In this case, the girl is redeemed by the love of a young doctor.

Exploitation aspects are in the streetwalker sequences of the girl, but such scenes have appeared in other Gallic pix. Telegraphed proceedings relegate this to offbeat U.S. chances. Danik Patisson emerges another Moguy find. Others do as well as possible in stereotyped roles. Technical credits are fine.
Mosk.

Rencontre a Paris (Meeting in Paris) (FRENCH). Cocinex release of Lambor-Champs-Elysees production. Stars Betsy Blair, Robert Lamoureux; features Pierre Dux, Jacques Castelot, Raymond Bussieres. Directed by Georges Lampin. Screenplay, Jean-Bernard Luc, Gabriel Arout, adapted by Charles Spaak, Claude Accursi; camera, Christian Matras; editor, Gabriel Rongier; music, Georges Van Parys. At Balzac, Paris. Running time, **90 MINS.**

Film was made as a starring vehicle for Betsy Blair after her publicity splash at the Cannes Film Festival of 1955. It is easy to see why it was kept under wraps. Because this emerges a lightweight pic with more possible pull for the tourist element than the Gallic market. Yarn is about a rich U.S. girl in Paris who tries to live among the colorfully broke when father cuts off the funds.

There are some vivid visitor-eye view scenes of Paris along with the unimaginative tale. Stilted direction and simple tale rarely make for comedic breeziness or feel of character. Miss Blair does adequately in an ill-defined role as does co-star Robert Lamoureux. Technical credits are only par.
Mosk.

TORO! (MEXICAN). Producciones Barbachano Ponce production and release. Stars Luis Procuna; features Manolete, Arruza. Directed by Carlos Velo. Screenplay, Ponce, Velo; camera, H. Beimler; editor, Velo; music, R. Staffler. Previewed in Paris. Running time, **90 MINS.**

About 60% of this is newsreel footage but one would never know it. A perfect welding of fine newsreel stuff into the life of a bullfighter makes this one of the most gripping studies of the sport ever made. No cliches here but the unveiling of the "big three" in a matador's life—fear, the audience and the bull.

A real fighter, Luis Procuna, takes easily to the screen. It shows the bullfight as a part of Mexican life and even those against it can not help being taken by the drama. Kills are not shown and this should be quite palatable in the U.S. for arty spots. It is also a fine video vechicle in its present form. Editor, director, music composer and lenser have all done a good job of threading reality into their staged works.
Mosk.

La Pointe Courtel (FRENCH). Tamaris Film production and release. Written and directed by Agnes Varda. Camera, Louis Stein, Paul Soulignac; editor, Alain Renais; music, Pierre Darbaud. With Sylvia Montfort, Philipe Noiret. At Studio Parnesse, Paris. Running time, **85 MINS.**

Main aspect of this film is that it was made for $20,000 by a 25-year-old girl, a still photographer here. "La Pointe Courtel" is a little village in southwestern France where a young married couple go to try to patch up their collapsing marriage. Story of the married couple is much too stilted to ever get any feeling into the pair's predicament or action. Lensing is good and fine editing has glossed over many technical errors. It got special art house distrib here but for the U.S. it looks primarily for film club or some arty houses.
Mosk.

High Society
(MUSICAL—COLOR—V'VISION)

High finance filmusical at anybody's boxoffice. Grace Kelly-Crosby - Sinatra - Cole Porter socko parlay.

Metro release of Sol C. Siegel production. Stars Bing Crosby, Grace Kelly, Frank Sinatra; features Celeste Holm, John Lund, Louis Calhern, Sidney Blackmer. Louis Armstrong's orch Directed by Charles Walters, who also staged the dances. Screenplay, John Patrick, based on Philip Barry's unidentified (in the credits) play, "The Philadelphia Story"; songs, Cole Porter; music supervision, Johnny Green and Saul Chaplin; orchestrations, Conrad Salinger & Nelson Riddle; camera (Technicolor), Paul C. Vogel; special effects, A. Arnold Gillespie; asst. director, Arvid Griffen; editor, Ralph E. Winters. Tradeshown N. Y., July 11, '56 Running time, 107 MINS.

C. K. Dexter-Haven	Bing Crosby
Tracy Lord	Grace Kelly
Mike Connor	Frank Sinatra
Liz Imbrie	Celeste Holm
George Kittredge	John Lund
Uncle Willie	Louis Calhern
Seth Lord	Sidney Blackmer
Himself	Louis Armstrong
Mrs. Seth Lord	Margalo Gillmore
Caroline Lord	Lydia Reed
Dexter-Haven's Butler	Gordon Richards
Lords' Butler	Richard Garrick

"High Society" should spell high finance business all over. It's a solid entertainment every minute of its footage.

Fortified with a strong Cole Porter score, film is a pleasant romp for cast toppers Bing-Crosby, Grace Kelly and Frank Sinatra who, tactfully, get alphabetical top billing. Their impact is almost equally consistent. Although Sinatra has the top pop tune opportunities, the Groaner makes his specialties stand up and out on showmanship and delivery, and Miss Kelly impresses as a femme lead with pleasantly comedienne overtones. This is perhaps her most relaxed performance.

The original Philip Barry play, "The Philadelphia Story," holds up in its transmutation from the Main Line to a Newport jazz bash. Producer Sol C. Siegel's casting of Satchmo Armstrong for the jazz festivities was an inspired booking also.

The atmosphere is plush, the production and personalities lush in every respect. The unfolding of the triangle almost assumes quadrangle proportions, when Sinatra (as the Life-mag-type feature writer) sent there with Celeste Holm (a Margaret Bourke-White counterpart), almost moves in as a romantic vis-a-vis to the slightly spoiled and madcap Tracy Lord (Miss Kelly).

Crosby is her first, now ex-husband, a hip character with songsmithing predilections, hence the Louis Armstrong band booking on the local scene. Satchmo is utilized as a sort of pleasant play moderator, opening with "High Society Calypso," which sets the al fresco mood of the picture, and he's also in for the finale, after a somewhat jam Mendelssohn session when Crosby remarries Miss Kelly, whereupon Satch, in close-up, indicates "end of story."

Porter has whipped up a solid set of songs with which vocal pros like the male stars and Miss Holm do plenty. Latter and Sinatra have a neat offbeat number with "Who Wants to Be a Millionaire?"; Crosby makes "Now You Has Jazz" (aided by Armstrong) as his standout solo, although he is also effective with Miss Kelly on "True Love" and "I Love You, Samantha," and also "Little One," with the juvenile Lydia Reed (Miss Kelly's precocious kid sister in pigtails and jeans). Crosby and Sinatra milk "Well, Did You Evah?", in a sophisticated smokingroom sequence. Sinatra's impact with the already popular "You're Sensational" and "Mind If I Make Love to You?", both with Miss Kelly, have already been dwelt on for their general effectiveness.

The romantic scenes are capitally done in every sequence, whether Miss Kelly vis-a-vis Crosby, Sinatra and the stuffed-shirt fiance John Lund (who does a thankless role with professional conviction), or whether it's the laconic Miss Holm and Sinatra, who are the mag writing-lensing team sent up for the high society nuptials. The late Louis Calhern as the gay boy, Sidney Blackmer as the somewhat errant father of the bride, Margalo Gillmore as the understanding mother, right down to the bits, are topdrawer.

So is Sol C. Siegel's lush production; the effective screenplay by John Patrick; and the eyefilling, Technicolorful lensing by Paul C. Vogel, in this VistaVision and PerspectaSound production. Director Charles Walters has kept his cast in top gear and the end result is as smartly paced as the dance numbers which he also staged (Walters having started originally as a choreographer)/ *Abel.*

I've Lived Before

Reincarnation theme makes this modest-budgeter an exploitable entry for general market.

Universal release of Howard Christie production. Features Jock Mahoney, Leigh Snowden, Ann Harding. Directed by Richard Bartlett. Screenplay, Norman Jolley and William Talman; camera, Maury Gerstman; editors, Milton Carruth, Fred MacDowell; music, Herman Stein; music supervision, Joseph Gershenson. Tradeshown, N. Y., July 12, '56. Running time, **82 MINS.**

John Bolan .... Jock Mahoney
Lois Gordon .... Leigh Snowden
Jane Stone .... Ann Harding
Dr. Thomas Bryant........John McIntire
Mr. Hackett .... Raymond Bailey
Russell Smith .... Jerry Paris
Robert Allen .... Simon Scott
Stewardess .... April Kent
Mr. Anderson .... Vernon Rich
Dr. Miller .... Phil Harvey
Johnny Bolan (as a boy)....Brad Morrow

With a reincarnation cycle in the offing, Universal apparently has the first entry with "I've Lived Before." It's patently a modest-budget try to cash in on the public's current interest in old souls in new bodies, or vice versa. Film has exploitable pegs which make it a good prospect for the general market.

Despite the obvious effort of scripters Norman Jolley and William Talman to handle the subject straight, some lines and situations produce some unintended comic overtones. Screenplay amounts to a case history of commercial airline pilot Jock Mahoney. Chance meeting with Ann Harding, a middle-aged passenger on his plane, causes him to bring about a near crash as he fancies himself in a World War II dogfight.

Possibly it was a mutual exchange of "psychic" glance between the pilot and his passenger that inspired Mahoney to think that he was Miss Harding's long dead fiance—an Army pilot shot down over France in 1918. There's a fair amount of suspense in the footage as Mahoney endeavors to prove his theory of personality transference. But more logical seems to be the blunt diagnosis of John McIntire, as an investigating doctor, that institutions are full of people "who think they're Cleopatra or Alexander the Great."

For those who want to take the subject seriously Mahoney turns in a credible performance as a "reincarnated" man. His sincerity is matched by the dignified portrayal of Miss Harding who first looks upon the matter as an intrusion of her memories. Less convincing is Leigh Snowden, Mahoney's fiancee who seems uninvolved in the whole thing. McIntire is good as the disbelieving physician.

Also lending a hand in this Howard Christie production are Raymond Bailey, understandingly irascible as the airline head; Jerry Paris, quick-thinking co-pilot; Simon Scott as an attorney, and April Kent (June Havoc's daughter) in a brief scene as a plane hostess. Richard Bartlett's direction suitably accents the mystic angles and producer Christie supplies adequate physical values. Camerawork of Maury Gertsman is an asset as is the sharp editing of Milton Carruth and Fred MacDowell. Herman Stein's music, supervised by Joseph Gershenson, helps sustain the occasionally weird atmosphere. *Gilb.*

Vor Sonnenuntergang
(Before Sundown)
(GERMAN)

Won the German Public Poll at Berlin Film Festival but reeks. of American soap opera. Directed by Gottfried Reinhardt with little taste.

Berlin, July 3.

Schorcht release of CCC (Arthur Brauner) production. Stars Hans Albers, Annemarie Dueringer, Martin Held. Directed by Gottfried Reinhardt. Screenplay, Jochem Huth, adapted from the same-titled stage play by Gerhart Hauptmann. Camera, Kurt Hasse; music, Werner Eisbrenner. Preemed at Berlin Film Festival, Gloria Palast, June 28, '56. Running time, **98 MINS.**

Mathias Clausen .... Hans Albers
Inken Peters.......Annemarie Dueringer
Erich Klamroth .... Martin Held
Ottilie Klamroth ..... Hannelore Schroth
Egert Clausen.........Claus Biederstaedt
Bettina Clausen .... Maria Becker
Wolfgang Clausen ...... Erich Schellow
Paula Clausen .... Inge Langen
Dr. Hahnefeld .... Wolfgang Preiss
Dr. Steynity .... Hans Nielsen
Frau Peters .... Johanna Hofer

· This was the only German entry at the Berlin film festival and, possibly because of this, won the prize based on the popular voting. Being sentimental in the extreme, and starring an old German favorite—Hans Albers—it's an example of the type of picture that stands to make money in the German market.

It is, unfortunately, also an example of what happens when an American director gets his hands on a foreign subject, determined—one supposes — to give it "the American touch." Gottfried Reinhardt handled the chores on this one, and much of what is wrong with the film is directly traceable to him.

"Vor Sonnenuntergang," based on the Gerhart Hauptmann play, which treats with the love between a young girl and an aging industrialist and the effects of the romance on his family, could have been a tender, believable picture. Instead, Reinhardt, using a minimum of taste and a maximum of obvious cliches, turns it into a soapoperaish, unconvincing opus that has practically no chances in the U.S. where such melodramas were popular in the thirties.

He had a capable cast to work with, including Annemarie Dueringer, who looms as one of the most promising young actresses in Germany and does an excellent job within the limitations set for her. Albers, making the transition from screen playboy to character actor, turns in a creditable performance which, unfortunately, needed tighter directorial reins to avoid over-emphasis, Martin Held, Hannelore Schroth, Maria Becker and Claus Biederstaedt also are impressive in their roles.

The subject of May-December romance isn't new but, to be effective, requires a maximum of good taste. Reinhardt's conception of the theme, including the incredible kissing scene between Albers and Miss Dueringer, which is out-and-out embarassing, is heavyhanded and never really allows the characters to be themselves. It proves that there is no magic in the "Hollywood touch" unless it's cleverly applied.

Kurt Hasse's lensing is okay, but Werner Eisbrenner's music is melodramatic almost to the point of comedy. All in all, "Vor Sonnenuntergang" is a waste of a good cast and a potentially strong story. *Hift.*

Davy Crockett and the River Pirates

Transmigration from television to theatrical bigscreen and color. Actionful and surefire for kiddies. Will adults pay to see what once showed free?

Hollywood, July 16.

Buena Vista (Walt Disney) release of Bill Walsh production. Stars Fess Parker, Buddy Ebsen, Jeff York; features Kenneth Tobey, Clem Bevans, Irvin Ashkenazy, Mort Mills, Paul Newlan, Frank Richards, Walter Catlett. Directed by Norman Foster. Written by Tom B. Blackburn and Foster; camera (Technicolor), Bert Glennon; editor, Stanley Johnson; score, George Bruns; songs, Blackburn and Bruns. Previewed July 11, '56. Running time, **81 MINS.**

Davy Crockett .... Fess Parker
George Russel .... Buddy Ebsen
Mike Fink .... Jeff York
Jocko .... Kenneth Tobey
Cap'n Cobb .... Clem Bevans
Moose .... Irvin Ashkenazy
Sam Mason .... Mort Mills
Big Harpe .... Paul Newlan
Little Harpe .... Frank Richards
Colonel Plug .... Walter Catlett

The further television adventures of Davy Crockett have been put into theatrical form as an 81-minute bigscreen feature and the results look surefire for the kiddies. Adults that like their action and humor broad will accept. Question: How much resistance will there be to paying for something already seen for free on video? Against that, big screen and Technicolor give the two "Disneyland" segments a freshness and scope that the small home tubes can't match.

First half of the feature film has Fess Parker, as Crockett, and his sidekick, Buddy Ebsen, coming to terms with the hulking, self-styled King of the River, Mike Fink, boisterously played by Jeff York, and downing him in a river race to New Orleans. This portion is colorful with action and a rollicking humor that gets a broad, adventurous treatment under Norman Foster's direction of the screenplay he did with Tom B. Blackburn. On tv the portion was labelled "Davy Crockett's Keel Boat Race."

Second half, previously on video as "Davy Crockett and the River Pirates," finds the pioneer hero and the river king teaming to wipe out a gang of pirates that had been carrying on its raids disguised as Indians.

Parker strides through the title role with ease and Ebsen is an able sidekick. York's blustering Mike Fink is good for chuckles and captures the fancy. Kenneth Tobey, hardly recognizable behind a beard, collects his laughs too as Fink's scrappy boatman. Others deliver capably.

Production helming by Bill Walsh and the lensing by Bert Glennon on Ohio River locales provide strong values. Stanley Johnson's editing is good.

Disney's Buena Vista is packaging the feature with "Man In Space," live action-animation subject full of interesting footage on man's space dreams. It was a Disneyland" tv offering, also. *Brog.*

Reach for the Sky
(BRITISH)

Engrossing life story of Douglas Bader, legless ace pilot of the last war, defying disability to continue his career; good pic for Kenneth More and should have popular appeal.

London, July 10.

Rank production (Daniel M. Angel) and release. Stars Kenneth More. Directed by Lewis Gilbert. Screenplay, Lewis Gilbert from Paul Brickhill book, "Story of Douglas Bader"; camera, Jack Asher; editor, John Shirley; music, John Addison. At Odeon Theatre, Leicester Square, London. Running time, **136 MINS.**

Douglas Bader .... Kenneth More
Thelma Bader .... Muriel Pavlow
Johnny Sanderson ...... Lyndon Brook
Turner .... Lee Patterson
Mr. Joyce .... Alexander Knox
Nurse Brace .... Dorothy Alison
Harry Day .... Michael Warre
Robert Desoutter .... Sydney Tafler
"Woody" Woodhall..Howard M. Crawford
Peel .... Jack Watling
Streatfield .... Nigel Green
Sister Thornhill .... Anne Leon
Sir Hugh Dowding .... Ronald Adam
Vice-Marshal ....Charles Carson
Crowley-Milling .... Basil Appleby
Sergeant Mills .... Eddie Byrne
Sally .... Beverly Brooks
Warrant Officer .... Michael Ripper
Civilian Pilot .... Derek Blomfield
Mrs. Bader .... Avice Landone
Adjutant of Prison Camp. Eric Pohlmann
Flying Instructor ....Michael Gough

First and foremost, this is a story of courage, showing a man's triumph over physical disability and every obstacle raised to curtail his normal activities. Adapted from his biography by his fellow pilot, Paul Brickhill, it covers the career of Douglas Bader who, after losing both legs in a plane crash while stunting, succeeds in rejoining the RAF to become a Wing Commander in the last World War and one of the aces in the Battle of Britain. Pic runs over two hours and would be more impressive with pruning in the early stages which, though interesting from a life history angle, condense the later, more exciting war sequences. Camera work gives excellent background effects, and the film should have a strong universal appeal.

From the cocky young recruit's first day at the training station through all the gay comradeship and hazards of flying, Kenneth More (Bader) depicts with unerring skill the humor, friendliness and supreme fortitude of one of the war's most honored heroes. The scenes in hospital where the stricken man endures agonies in his frenzied attempts to master his tin legs are the most moving part of this. His determination to take up life where it nearly left off and return to the only job he knows, is shown without heroics. And this enhances its dramatic value. Every Air Force taboo on his disability is finally overcome and he gets airborne again with the outbreak of war.

Bearing a charmed life, the reinstated pilot inspires confidence all round, winning the respect of a bunch of tough Canadian veterans who constitute his first command. Overhearing a reference to his infirmity he proves to them, by an inspired dynamic display of aerobatics, that he is no passenger.

Many factual air battle shots are woven in, until Bader is seen to bale out after collision with the enemy, and is taken prisoner. After three attempts to escape, he gets transferred to the impregnable Colditz Castle, where he stays until the place is recaptured by the Yanks.

Lyndon Brook plays the staunch friend who has to break the news to Bader of his affliction and handles his distasteful task with sympathetic understanding. Alexander Knox is quietly effective as the surgeon whose prompt amputation saves the pilot's life. The two main femme roles of wife and nurse are sensitively played by Muriel Pavlow and Dorothy Alison. The supporting characters are in seasoned hands and the authentic personnel convincingly portrayed.
Clem.

The Naked Hills

California's goldrush days set the scene for this routine program feature. It's lowercase entertainment and will fill out that end of regular dual bills.

Hollywood, July 17.
Allied Artists release of La Salle Production. Stars David Wayne; Keenan Wynn; James Barton, Marcia Henderson. Produced and directed by Josef Shaftel; asst. director, Raoul Pagel; screenplay by Josef Shaftel based on a story by Helen S. Bilkie. Camera, Frederick Gately; editor, Gene Fowler; music, composed and conducted by Herschel Burke Gilbert. Previewed July 16, '56. Running time, 72 MINS.
Tracy Powell .... David Wayne
Sam Wilkins .... Keenan Wynn
Jimmo McCann .... James Barton
Julie .... Marcia Henderson
Willis Haver .... Jim Backus
Bert Killan .... Denver Pyle
Aggie .... Myrna Dell
Baxter .... Lewis Russell
Harold .... Frank Fenton
Pitch Man .... Fuzzy Knight
Counter Man .... Jim Hayward
Billy (as a boy) ...... Chris Olsen
Billy (as a young man)....Steven Terrell

Joseph Saftel produced, directed, scripted this release from Helen S.

Bilkie story as a La Salle Production for Allied Artists release. While occasionally handling an individual scene well, Saftel's guidance generally makes for repetitious footage in unfoldment of unreal characters. Viewer interest constantly wavers.

Cast talents are well-seasoned, but fail to inject more than regulation thesping into 1849 characters hit by gold fever. David Wayne is pivotal character, man who never shakes lust for gold, story following him on innumerable prospecting junkets into hills, back to town, where sharpies Keenan Wynn and Jim Backus always take over rich claims. Wayne came west young man, ages to 60 as episodic plot runs course, finding him still planning another trip into hills for elusive gold.

James Barton is colorful old partner during one of Wayne's expeditions, while Marcia Henderson is his not so patient wife who waits home, raising their son, during

Wayne's long absences. Denver Pyle is the goldbug's first partner, turned merchant, who waits to catch Miss Henderson on rebound but never does. Other roles are of minor importance.

Photography in Pathecolor by Frederick Gately is good, other technical credits okay. Bob Russell, Herschel Burke Gilbert song, "Four Seasons" ineffectively done behind titles by Barton vocals, but as background score theme comes off satisfactorily.
Brog.

Lo Scapolo
(The Bachelor)
(SPANISH-ITALIAN)

Rome, July 10.
CIE-INCOM release of a Film Costelazione-Aquila Film co-production. Stars Alberto Sordi; features Madeleine Fisher, Sandra Milo, Anna Marie Pancani, Fernando Fernan Gomez, Abbe Lane, Xavier Cugat. Directed by Antonio Pietrangeli. Screenplay, Pietrangeli, Continenza, Maccari, Scala, from story by Pietrangeli; camera, Ciannindi Venanzo; music, Francesco Lavagnino; editor, Ersado Da Roma. At Corso Cinema, Rome. Running time, 105 MINS.

Entertaining and intelligent comedy, Berlin Fete entry, ranks well above the many others seen here this season. Alberto Sordi name and especially word-of-mouth should help this to very strong grosses in Italian runs. Local flavor somewhat hampers its export chances, and outlook abroad must be rated spotty.

Sordi has rarely been better or funnier than in this portrayal of the eternal bachelor whose exploits with the opposite sex are mostly imaginative and exaggerated by a mental defense mechanism. After several unhappy yet humorous adventures, he not too reluctantly succumbs to marriage as a promising institution. Tight scripting keeps tongue in cheek all the way, with only one slight letup in pace near closing. Direction by Antonio Pietrangeli holds Sordi down to a well-modulated performance; and gets top results from Madeleine Fischer, Sandra Milo, Anna Maria Pancani and Pina Bottin, the women in the bachelor's life. Abbe Lane, backed by Xavier Cugat and his orch, is tied nicely into the story via a series of nitery cha-cha numbers with Sordi, adding to marquee value.

Music by Francesco Lavagnino is a further plus value as is Gianni di Venanzo's lensing. Cutting by Eraldo Da Roma is unusually adroit, adding comic effects by fine timing. Other production values are good.
Hawk.

Don Juan
(FRANCO-SPANISH; COLOR)

Paris, July 10.
Pathe release of Cyclope, DAMA production. Stars Fernandel; features, Carmen Sevilla, Erno Crisa, Jose Sepulveda, Armontel, Chrtisiane Carere. Directed by John Berry. Screenplay, Maurice Clavel, Juan Bardem, Jean Manse, Jacques Bost, John Berry; camera, (Technicolor), Nicholas Hayer; editor, Marinette Cadix. At Normandie, Paris. Running time, 95 MINS.

Well-mounted Fernandel opus looks to be the pic to follow on the heels of the successful "The Sheep With Five Legs." Given a slick color cover and possessing some good comedy and adventures, it shows the rubberfaced comedian to good advantage. This should shape well in special spots and is worth dubbing for secondary usage on the general market.

Fernandel plays the servant of Don Juan in this costumer and dons the mantel of the great lover to save him from a trap engineered

by a plotting politician. Then follows the many yocks as he slowly becomes the magnetic lover in the name and boots of the Don Juan myth.

John Berry has given this a good actioner mounting to make this an engaging film. Fernandel milks this for laughs and also puts a note of solidity in it during his metmorphosis by the true love of a gypsy dancer played engagingly by the beauteous Carmen Sevilla. Technicolor is fine and general production values bolster this new takeoff on Don Juan.
Mosk.

The Bad Seed

Study of a homicidal child, from the book and play, with controversial heredity theory. Best possibilities probably in morbid fascination for femmes.

Hollywood, July 24.
Warner Bros. release of Mervyn LeRoy production; directed by LeRoy. Stars Nancy Kelly, Patty McCormack; features Henry Jones, Eileen Heckart, Evelyn Varden, William Hopper. Screenplay, John Lee Mahin; based on play by Maxwell Anderson and novel by William March as produced on stage by The Playwrights Company; camera, Hal Rosson; editor, Warren Low; music, Alex North. Previewed July 17, '56. Running time, 127 MINS.
Christine .... Nancy Kelly
Rhoda .... Patty McCormack
LeRoy .... Henry Jones
Mrs. Daigle .... Eileen Heckart
Monica .... Evelyn Varden
Kenneth .... William Hopper
Bravo .... Paul Fix
Emory .... Jesse White
Tasker .... Gage Clarke
Miss Fern .... Joan Croyden
Mr. Daigle .... Frank Cady

The morbid fascination connected with this melodrama about a child with an inbred talent for homicide is the best bet for the boxoffice. Pretty unpleasant stuff on its own.

Taken from Maxwell Anderson's stage play, adapted from William March's novel, the Mervyn LeRoy film presentation remains more of the theatre than of the motion picture field. Nonetheless, it is well done within that qualification, exerting the pull of suspenseful drama that has been given powerful direction and skillful performances. LeRoy's handling weaves quite a dramatic spell and most of the time overcomes the tendency to long dialogic passages with a camera that keeps busy in simulating physical action.

With the possible exception of the new Production Code-conscious ending, John Lee Mahin's screenplay varies little from the Anderson legit piece. Some of the casting is from the stage success, too, with young Patty McCormack as the innocent-looking murderess, and Nancy Kelly as her distraught mother. Both are outstanding. Other legiters brought to the screen to add performance worth to the melodrama include Henry Jones, a definite click as the evilly-adled apartment house janitor; Evelyn Varden, the talkative landlady; Eileen Heckart, terrific as the alcoholic mother of one of the little girl's murder victims; and Joan Croydon, the spinterish schoolteacher. Scoring also is William Hopper, the father who never sees through the evil of his little girl. Other assists come from Paul Fix, as Miss Kelly's father; Jesse White, Gage Clarke and Frank Cady.

It is the story of a woman who discovers that her daughter, a sweet, innocent-faced child, is a killer. LeRoy mounts this and following sequences with shocking horror as it is brought out the girl deliberately murdered a schoolmate because she wanted the penmanship medal he had won. The mother feels the daughter has inherited a bad seed through her and becomes more convinced of this when it is disclosed the girl had caused the death of an old woman, before the story opens, and later sets a fire that fatally burns the apartment janitor. The mother is driven to an unsuccessful suicide try at the finale and the sweet child meets her own destruction by a lightning blast while trying to cover evidence of the schoolmate's murder.

To take some of the sting from the unleavened horror, LeRoy brings his cast on, stage fashion, after the final curtain to introduces them as only play actors who have done an outstanding job of their assignments. It helps, but the memory of the wickedness of the little girl lingers on malignantly.

Hal Rosson uses his cameras effectively in abetting the melodramatics and art director John Beckman furnishes realistic settings that are well decorated by Ralph Hurst. Warren Low's editing is good, as is the music by Alex North. *Brog.*

Pepote
(SPANISH)

Berlin, July 10.

Charmatin (Madrid) production and release. Stars Pablito Calvo, Antonio Vico. Directed by Ladislao Vajda; screenplay, Andres Laszlo, Jose Santugini, Max Korner, Gian Luigi Rondi, Ladislao Vajda; camera, Enrique Guerner; music, Roman Vlad; sets, Antonio Simont. At Berlin Film Festival. Running time, **96 MINS.**

Pepote .... Pablito Calvo
Jacinto .... Antonio Vico
Inspector .... Jose Marco Davo
Second-hand dealer .... Juan Calvo
Match dealer .... Mariano Azana
Stamp dealer .... Pastora Pena
Morgan-man .... Julio Sanjuan
Paco .... Gila

That the Spanish film industry is well able to turn out highly recommendable screen entertainment is evidenced by this film which landed a more than remarkable second spot (as voted by the public) at the recent Berlin Film Festival. Yet it's not too big a surprise since also last year a Spanish film, "The Secret of Marcelino," was chosen second best item by the audience. Both films, incidentally, see the same actor playing the lead, little Pablito Calvo, who's already become a special favorite with Berliners.

"Pepote" has the ingredients to appeal to both fastidious and average patrons, so it all looks like a good bet for a number of special situations. It also has the quality to enjoy considerable U. S. art patronage.

In brief, it's the story of an aging bullfighter who's given the last chance to appear in an arena. Along with his seven-year-old nephew, Pepote, he tries all angles to borrow a torero costume and it is the little boy who manages this. The end sees the torero being laughed at by the spectators and he who's most disappointed is Pepote, who's been his uncle's most ardent admirer.

In the main, film benefits from the superb acting of the two principal players, Antonio Vico and Pablito Calvo. While Vico's performance of an old torero is certainly worth winning an award, little Calvo steals half of the show via his amazing naturalness. The other players, although a number of them come along with impressive performances, remain considerably in the shadow of Vico and Calvo. Direction by Ladislao Vajda, who also worked on the script, is very sensitive and without cheap sentimentalities. *Hans.*

Miami Expose

Okay actioner marred by over-rigid format a la Katzman

Columbia release of Clover (Sam Katzman) production. Stars Lee J. Cobb, Patricia Medina, Edward Arnold; features Michael Granger, Eleanore Tanin, Alan Napier, Harry Lauter, Chris Alcaide, Hugh Sanders, Barry L. Connors. Directed by Fred F. Sears. Story and screenplay, James B. Gordon; camera, Benjamin H. Kline; editor, Al Clark; music, Mischa Bakaleinikoff. Tradeshown N. Y., July 19, '56. Running time, **73 MINS.**

Bart Scott .... Lee J. Cobb
Lila Hodges .... Patricia Medina
Oliver Tubbs .... Edward Arnold
Louis Ascot .... Michael Granger
Anne Easton .... Eleanore Tanin
Raymond Sheridan .... Alan Napier
Tim Grogan .... Harry Lauter
Morrie Pell .... Chris Alcaide
Chief Charlie Landon ...... Hugh Sanders
Stevie .... Barry L. Connors

Producer Sam Katzman, an experienced hand at turning out modest-budget actioners, has another one in "Miami Expose." It's in the same familiar "mob" pattern as his recent "The Houston Story" and the earlier "The Miami Story." Format is observed too religiously and dialog and situations resultantly are often trite and telegraphed.

While cast toppers Lee J. Cobb, Patricia Medina and Edward Arnold aren't top b.o. draws, nevertheless they're partly known to filmgoers and may have some marquee value. For the most part, however, this Columbia release shapes up primarily as an entry for the dualers.

After a slow start to establish the Miami flavor, the James B. Gordon script which he screenplayed from his own story, picks up speed as it shows rival mobs locked in battle for the Florida gambling "franchise." Major participants in the subsequent events include police lieutenant Cobb, opposing racketeers Michael Granger and Alan Napier, as well as lobbyist Arnold and Miss Medina, a moll on the lam.

Bulk of the action stems from Napier's attempt to bring about legalized gambling in Florida which would place him in control and throw out Granger. When a colleague of Cobb's is slain investigating a mob killing, he smokes out the culprits by hiding witness Miss Medina in an Everglades retreat. It goes without saying that the syndicate toppers fall for the bait and are rounded up at the finale in a hail of lead.

No role is a taxing stint for any of the cast. Cobb is thorough and methodical as the cop-in-charge, Miss Medina is suitably hysterical as a woman who fears for her safety and Edward Arnold provides an adequate portrayal of a lobbyist who stoops to blackmail. (Parenthetic aside, too bad that Arnold, who was fatally stricken while making this venture, didn't have a better memorial as his last film.)

Among other cast members, Granger is good as a tough mob leader, Napier is okay as his rival and Eleanore Tanin is pert and winsome as Cobb's loyal fiancee. Fred F. Sears' direction accents the action scenes, Benjamin H. Kline's black-and-white camerawork is an asset, especially his outdoor vistas; Al Clark's editing is competent save for the padded initial reel, while Mischa Bakaleinikoff's score is par for the course as are other technical credits. *Gilb.*

Tuntematon Sotilas
(The Unknown Soldier)
(FINNISH)

Berlin, July 10.

Suomen Filmiteollisuus (SF) release of T. J. Sarkka production. Directed by Edvin Laine; screenplay, Juha Nevalainen, based on novel by Vaino Linna; camera, Pentti Unho, Osmo Harkimo, Olavi Tuomi, Antero Ruuhonen; music, Jean Sibelius, Ahti Sonninen; sets, Aarre Koivisto; editor, Armas Vallasvuo. At Berlin Film Festival. Running time, **133 MINS.**

Lieutenant Koskela .... Kosti Klemela
First Lieut. Lammio .... Jussi Jurkka
Lieutenant Kariluoto .... Matti Ranin
Corporal Hietanen ...... Heikki Savolainen
Corporal Lahtinen .... Veikko Sinisalo
Corporal Rokka .... Reino Tolvanen
Major Sarastie .... Tauno Palo
Solder Rahikainen ...... Kaarlo Halttunen
Soudier Maatta .... Pentti Simes
Soldier Riitaoja .... Olavi Ahonen
Corporal Lehto .... Ake Lindman
Corporal Makila .... Vilho Siivola

This entry by Finland at the Berlin Film Fest has built-in exploitation angles on which it can cash in. Hailed as one of the biggest money-makers in all Scandinavian countries, it received above-average citicism wherever shown so far, and it made big headlines when it ran into trouble at the recent Cannes film festival, from which it then was withdrawn.

Unknown Soldier" proved in Berlin an outstanding draw as it already long in advance was considered one of the most important (due to the controversy in Cannes) films of the whole festival. Although there are a number of flaws along the line, film must be regarded as a remarkable venture which benefits from its honest and never cheap attitude and accusation against the war, and highly impressive camerawork. In Germany, film quickly found a distributor in Pallas and may at least be good enough for satisfactory returns. Chances in the U. S. appear rather weak but may be better when the same-titled bestseller by Vaino Linna, on which the film is based, will be on sale here.

Film, which has actually no plot and may be better classified as a documentary report, is a recklessly open and hard-hitting production about victory and defeat and life and death of Finnish soldiers during the last war. The camera follows a group of soldiers and shows via very impressive scenes how they go through the murderous phase of modern warfare.

Film has been cut down from a more than three-hour running time to 133 minutes, which might have made it a more suitable item for general western release, but as result it seems to have become somewhat uneven in its action development. Moreover, there is perhaps a bit too much of war battling in this. The constant battling becomes monotonous and even dull towards the end. The acting is honest and often very powerful although some of the players tend to exaggeration.

Direction by Edvin Laine is very good and praiseworthy, particularly in view of the fact that he never sought the exterior effect which easily might have cheapened the good overall impression. Technical credits are of amazingly high quality. This particularly applies to the camerawork by Unho, Harkimo, Tuomi and Ruuhonen, who also utilized newsreel footage with remarkable skill. The fine score by Jean Sibelius and Ahti Sonninen greatly adds to the mood.

In all, "Unknown Soldier" contributes much to prestige for Finnish filmmaking. Incidentally, it will also be shown at the Karlsbad (CSR) Film Festival and at the Finnish Film Week in Moscow this fall. *Hans.*

These Wilder Years

Moving and outstandingly played drama of a man's search for his illegitimate son; static title to be overcome, but James Cagney, Barbara Stanwyck names to help.

Hollywood, July 23.

Metro release of Jules Schermer production. Stars James Cagney, Barbara Stanwyck, Walter Pidgeon; features Betty Lou Keim, Don Dubbins, Edward Andrews. Directed by Roy Rowland. Screenplay, Frank Fenton; story, Ralph Wheelwright; camera, George J. Folsey; editor, Ben Lewis; music, Jeff Alexander. Previewed July 18, '56. Running time, **91 MINS.**

Steve Bradford .... James Cagney
Ann Dempster .... Barbara Stanwyck
James Rayburn .... Walter Pidgeon
Suzie .... Betty Lou Keim
Mark .... Don Dubbins
Mr. Spottsford .... Edward Andrews
Judge .... Basil Ruysdael
Roy Oliphant .... Grandon Rhodes
Old Cab Driver .... Will Wright
Dr. Miller .... Lewis Martin
Aunt Martha .... Dorothy Adams
Hardware Clerk .... Dean Jones
Traffic Cop .... Herb Vigran

Despite a dubious title, "These Wilder Years" is worthwhile drama meriting a good boxoffice play. Selling will have to be slanted at overcoming handle handicaps that says little when used in connection with the star values of James Cagney and Barbara Stanwyck as a team. There are sharp angels to ballyhoo that may lure the younger viewers, so, with the right kind of push, pic could come out ahead.

Jules Schermer's production supervision is thoughtful, exercising good taste in developing a story of a man's search for the illegitimate son he had abandoned 20 years previously. The scripting by Frank Fenton from a story by Ralph Wheelwright is razor sharp with human understanding and Roy Rowland's direction gives the plot and players a sensitive touch that's quality all the way. Story draws the parallel that the youth of today is very little different from the youth of yesterday in regards to wildness; a point that's probably responsible for the title.

Cagney, as the father looking for the lost son, and Miss Stanwyck as the kindly operator of an adoption home that takes care of unwed mothers, dig deep into their characters and turn in outstanding performances. As one of Miss Stanwyck's charges, young Betty Lou Keim, a teenager waiting the birth of a child, demonstrates all the depth and talent necessary to indicate a bright film future. She's representative of the younger generation that is repeating most of the mistakes that were just as common to the youth period of the previous era.

After 20 years, Cagney, now a selfmade big wheel in steel, casts off business affairs to look for the son he had denied when young. The search brings him to Miss Stanwyck's haven and what looks like a blind alley when she refuses to disclose the adopting parents. While she fights him successfully in court, the association with her and her charges, particularly Miss Keim, plus a meeting with his son now on the very edge of manhood, convinces Cagney of the futility of trying to intrude. Film ends on a high note as he adopts Miss Keim and her baby.

The dialog is natural and flows that way from the lips of the characters. There's a mighty moving punch to the scene where Cagney and the son, compellingly played by Don Dubbins, meet for the first and last time. It's handled in memorable fashion. Walter Pidgeon scores strongly in a comparatively short role as Cagney's wise attorney, as do Edward Andrews, mealy-mouthed smalltown lawyer; Basil Ruysdael, the judge; Grandon Rhodes, acting for Miss Stanwyck; Will Wright, wry, old taxi driver; Dorothy Adams. Dean Jones and Herb Vigran. Most of the parts are small but sharply etched.

Music by Jeff Alexander fits well into the mood and George J. Folsey's photography enhances players and settings. Technical aids are all good. *Brog.*

La Risaia
(The Rice Field)
(ITALIAN-C'SCOPE-COLOR)

Rome, July 10.

Minerva Film release of Excelsa-Carlo Ponti production. Stars Elsa Martinelli, Folco Lulli, Michel Auclair; features Rik Battaglia, Susanne Levesy, Liliana Gerace, Edith Jost, Gianni Santuccio, Vivi Gioi, Lilla Brignone. Directed by Raffaello Matarazzo. Screenplay, Aldo De Benedetti, Ennio DeConcini, Carlo Musso; camera (Eastmancolor), Luciano Trasatti; music, A. Francesco Lavagnino; editor, Mario Serandrei. At Splendore. Rome. Running time, 90 MINS.

Elena .... Elsa Martinelli
Foreman .... Folco Lulli
Mechanic .... Rik Battaglia
Landowner .... Michel Auclair

Meller set in the rice fields of the Po Valley made famous by "Bitter Rice" and given the wide-screen color treatment somewhat makes up visually what this lacks story-wise. Setting and a few cast names plus some exploitable footage give it some export values, notably for Germany.

Soapy story serves as poor vehicle for Elsa Martinelli's much-heralded Italo debut (though Italian, she made her first pic in the U.S.A.), and she fails to carry the pic as intended. Consequently, all the faults of a creaky tale show up as the plot unfolds, only now and then given a lift by some good panoramic footage of work in the rice cultivations. Foreman Folco Lulli discovers his illegit daughter in one of the workers in his rice field, guides her away from dissolate landowner Michel Auclair and into the wholesome arms of Rik Battaglia, two-fisted neighborhood mechanic.

Raffaello Matarazzo has kept the acting broad and obvious, in keeping with his material. Music by Francesco Lavagnino is excellent. Lensing by Luciano Trasatti,, especially on exteriors, is expert. *Hawk.*

Run For the Sun
(COLOR)

Good suspense and adventure in Mexican jungles, with Richard Widmark, Jane Greer, Trevor Howard and okay prospects.

Hollywood, July 23.

United Artists release of Harry Tatelman (Russ-Field) production. Stars Richard Widmark, Trevor Howard, Jane Greer; features Peter Van Eyck. Directed by Roy Boulting. Screenplay, Dudley Nichols and Boulting; based on "The Most Dangerous Game" by Richard Connell; camera (Eastman-print by Technicolor), Joe La Shelle; editor, Fred Knudtsen; score, Frederick Steiner; songs, Nestor Amaral and Steiner. Previewed July 16, '56. Running time, 98 MINS.

Mike Latimer .... Richard Widmark
Browne .... Trevor Howard
Katy Connors .... Jane Greer
Van Anders .... Peter Van Eyck
Jan .... Carlos Henning
Fernandez .... Juan Garcia
Hotel Proprietor .... Margarito Luna
Pedro .... Jose Chavez Trowe
Paco .... Guillermo Talles
Waiter .... Guillermo Bravo Sosa
Paco's wife .... Enedina Diaz de Leon

Russ-Field tees off its United Artists releasing deal with a suspense - adventure thriller that should encounter a good reception generally. Besides its action qualifications, it has Richard Widmark heading the cast, plus some beautiful Mexican backgrounds and telling SuperScope lensing in Eastman Color, with print by Technicolor, to enhance marketing qualities.

Harry Tatelman gives it expert production supervision, utilizing below-the-border location sites for atmospheric values that go well with the story and help maintain the suspense feel director Roy Boulting stirs up in handling the script he wrote with Dudley Nichols. Pic is based on Richard Connell's "The Most Dangerous Game," but there is virtually no resemblance to that old thriller in the final results.

A running time of 98 minutes is rather hard to sustain with this type of high adventure subject, but there is seldom any pacefaltering, except in the climaxing chase through the jungles, with heavies Trevor Howard and Peter Van Eyck conducting a death hunt of Widmark and Jane Greer. Fault here can be easily corrected by judicious scissoring since the sequence is prolonged beyond dramatic necessity and becomes quite repetitious.

Film is a chase feature in practically all phases. First Miss Greer, news mag staffer, comes to Mexico to find Widmark, writer-adventurer, to find why he's given up writing. It's a story that doesn't reach print because she falls for her news quarry and then plot goes into its main portion when the plane in which she is flying with him crashes in the jungle. The couple is rescued by Howard and Van Eyck, a mysterious pair. When Widmark undercovers their true identities as war criminals hiding out from trial and punishment, it becomes a murderous game through the jungle, ending with the villains dead and the lovers in a clinch. Some of the tricks Widmark pulls on his pursuers during the chase are hair-raising and deadly.

The four principals enact their roles exceptionally well. Also, it should be noted that Miss Greer should do more films; she has the needed looks and ability. It's her first in three years. Juan Garcia, as a native taxi driver, adds some good comedy and other Latin types are capable. Joe La Shelle did the fine lensing and Al Y'Barra the excellent art direction. Frederick Steiner's score is a major asset and he did two tunes, "Taco" and "Triste Ranchero" with Nestor Amaral that are good. *Brog.*

Viele Kamen Vorbei
(Many Passed By)
(GERMAN)

Berlin, July 10.

RKO release of Occident production. With Harald Maresch, Francis Martin, Christian Doermer, Heinz Schimmelpfennig, Hans-Hermann Schaufuss, Jane Tilden, Alf Marholm, Rudolf Rhomberg, Herbert von Boxberger, Heinz Schacht, Ellinor Jensen, Kai S. Seefeld. Directed by Peter Pewas; screenplay, Gerhard T. Buchholz; camera, Klaus von Rautenfeld; music, Peter Sandloff; sets, Alfred Buetow, Paul Michaelis. At Capitol, Berlin. Running time, 85 MINS.

This German Occident production, released here by RKO, centers around the notorious killings of young women along the German highways which made big headlines here some years ago. Film tells in documentary style how the murderer sets out to approach young women, waiting for a hitch-hike along the highway, and then strangle them after a short lovemaking scene.

Film doesn't follow the usual cliche but leaves much to the camera to explain the situation. The results are often a bit confusing and unconvincing but, in all, quite interesting. Pic will be hard to sell as it has little appeal for general customers. It has, however, some offbeat ingredients to please those who don't go for conventional film fare.

Peter Pewas, who directed, may be given some word of praise as he obviously tried to achieve something different. There are some scenes which are truly interesting and impressive. The biggest plus is Klaus von Rautenfeld's camerawork which has always an artistic flavor.

Harald Maresch is convincing as the psychopathic killer whose good-looks makes it easy to win the women's confidence. He's, of course, tracked down in the film's ending. Francis Martin and Christian Doermer, two newcomers playing a young couple, do their parts very realistically. Most of the others give strong support. *Hans.*

He Laughed Last
(SONGS-COLOR)

Amusing comedy treatment of gangster pic; good programmer.

Hollywood, July 20.

Columbia release of Jonie Taps production. Stars Frankie Laine, Lucy Marlow, Anthony Dexter, Dick Long; features Alan Reed, Jesse White, Florenz Ames, Henry Slate. Directed by Blake Edwards. Screenplay, Edwards; from story by Quine and Edwards; camera (Technicolor), Henry Freulich; editor, Jack W. Ogilvie; music, Arthur Morton; supervised by Fred Karger. Previewed July 10, '56. Running time, 76 MINS.

Gino Lupo .... Frankie Laine
Rosemary Lebeau .... Lucy Marlow
Dominic .... Anthony Dexter
Jimmy Murphy .... Dick Long
Big Dan Hennessy .... Alan Reed
Max Lassiter .... Jesse White
George Eagle .... Florenz Ames
Ziggy .... Henry Slate
Billy Boy Barnes .... Paul Dubov
Al Fusary .... Peter Brocco
Dave Hoffman .... Joe Forte
Two-Gun Tommy .... Robin Morse
Harry .... Dale Van Sickel
Nurse Rafferty .... Mara McAfee
Hood No. 1 .... David Tomack
Hood No. 2 .... John Truax
Hood No. 3 .... John Cason
Hood No. 4 .... Richard Benedict

Gangster pic cliches get a comedic working over in this amusing spoof, making it a rather happy offering for the general dual bill market. There's Technicolor for production flash and Frankie Laine singing two numbers to keep up the tune end of the entertainment.

Real click of the picture is Lucy Marlow, exhibiting a chassis that goes with her dumb chorine role and a good sense of comedy that gets the most out of the lines and situations handed the character in the script by Blake Edwards from a story he wrote with Richard Quine. Edwards also serves well as director on the Jonie Taps production. The pacing is good and the laugh handling productive.

Plot is a light affair, told via a long flashback, about what happens when a singer-dancer in a 1920's night club inherits the fortune and enterprises of an underworld czar. What happens doesn't please her policeman boyfriend, Richard Long, but she revels in the sudden luxury her new position affords long enough for the 76 minutes of footage to spin off mostly pleasantly, before getting back into the good graces of the fiance.

Laine sings "Save Your Sorrows" and "Danny Boy" in his role of plot narrator and nitery operator for Alan Reed, the czar and practical joker, and does okay. Reed is amusing as the bigshot, whose last practical joke is to leave his coin to Miss Marlow to spite Jesse White, the gang's number two man who arranged Reed's demise thinking he would take over. White is very able. Also good are Anthony Dexter, dancing gigolo who is no match for Miss Marlow; Florenz Ames, Henry Slate and the others involved in keeping the fun going.

Footage has a third tune, "Strike Me Pink," that serves as a small production number with Miss Marlow and other femmes. Lensing by Henry Freulich, editing by Jack W. Ogilvie, score by Arthur Morton, which Fred Karger supervised, and other technical functions are expert. *Brog.*

Akasen Chitai
(Red Light District)
(JAPANESE)

Tokyo, July 10.

Daiei release of Masaichi Nagata production. Stars Machiko Kyo, Kenji Sugawara; features Michiyo Kogore, Aiko Mimasu, Hiroko Machida. Directed by Kenji Mizoguchi; screenplay, Masahige Narusawa; sets and photography, Katsuo Miyagawa; music, Toshio Mayuzumi. Previewed July 2, '56, Tokyo. Running time, 96 MINS.

Micky .... Machiko Kyo
Hanae .... Michiyo Kogore
Yumeko .... Aiko Mimasu
Yorie .... Hiroko Machida
Eiko .... Kenji Sugawaru

Another artful triumph by the director of "Ugestu Monogatari," this film represents Kenji Mizoguchi's first efforts in a story with a modern background. Made under the personal supervision of Daiei's president Masaichi Nagata, film also presents Machiko Kyo, star of "Rashamon," who is currently making "Teahouse of the August Moon" for Metro here, in the role of a rollicking, unscrupulous prostitute. Offbeat casting also teams up four other top Daiei stars in unsavory roles for a film which, with good English translation of the excellent, realistic dialog, could ride in high in arties on basis of Kyo name pull.

Story line follows lives of four girls working in house of ill-fame in Tokyo's gay quarter of Asakusa, the Ysohiwara. Cameraman Katsuo Miyagawa's sets are such faithful reproductions of the area that only a very frequent visitor to the Yoshiwara could spot the fact that they are sets.

Micky (Machiko Kyo) defies the centuries-old tradition of the district when she takes as a customer a man who has been a steady patron of another girl in the house. Former mistress of a Negro soldier, Micky flaunts her independence throughout until a powerful scene her father comes to the house to appeal to her to give up her life of sin. Infuriated when she learns that her mother has died and her father has remarried, Micky, in a moment of harrowing spite, challenges her father to buy her for $4 an hour.

Yumeko (Aiko Mimasu) is a widow of 40 who sells herself to support her aged parents-in-law and her young son. The son gets a job which will pay him enough for his mother to give up her life of sin and go live with him. But the boy, ashamed of what his mother is doing, disowns her and she commits suicide.

Hanae (Michiyo Kogure), unlike the other girls, does not live in the house but comes there to work from her rented room where she cares for a tubercular husband and a baby. The husband attempts to kill himself to remove one burden from Hanae, but she stops his attempt and scolds him for his weakness. In this sequence there is a touch of social criticism as Hanae vows to live on to spite "this cultural state which does nothing for us." Later on, the proprietor of the house gets in a plug for his business when he asks where the girls would earn tomorrow's rice if the government outlawed prostitution. Bili is now before Diet which would do just this.

In a departure which shocks her teenage admirers, Hiroko Machida, the perennial ingenue, plays a cherubic vamp who works all her customers for all she can collect. When she spurns the attentions of one of them who has stolen from his employer to pay her debts in the hope of marrying her, the man nearly strangles her to death.

All of this, while melodramatic in the telling, is presented with excellent taste and with a unique feeling of realism, almost documentary in parts. It makes its stand clear — that trampled humanity, without losing its dignity, can somehow find its way into a better way of living than now exists in some areas. *Lars.*

Hold Back the Night

A fateful bottle of Scotch and a small Marine company fight the Korean war; fills the bill in regular situations.

Hollywood, July 24.

Allied Artists release of Hayes Goetz production. Stars John Payne, Mona Freeman; features Peter Graves, Chuck Connors, Audrey Dalton, Bob Nichols, John Wilder, Bob Easton. Directed by Allan Dawn. Screenplay, John C. Higgins, Walter Doniger; from the novel by Pat Frank; camera, Ellsworth Fredricks; editor, Robert S. Eisen: music, Hans Salter. Previewed July 20, '56. Running time, 80 MINS.

Mackenzie	John Payne
Anne	Mona Freeman
Couzens	Peter Graves
Ekland	Chuck Connors
Kitty	Audrey Dalton
Beany	Bob Nichols
Tinker	John Wilder
Ackerman	Bob Easton
Kato	Stanley Cha
Papiro	Nicky Blair
Major MacKay	John Craven
Lt. Col. Toomey	Nelson Leigh

This is the story of a bottle of Scotch, as well as a small Marine company that figured in the "fighting withdrawal" ordered in the late Korean war. While bearing a certain resemblance (except for the fateful fifth) to a number of previous Korean war action features, it is still a good entry for the regular situations. (Allied Artists is giving it a Camp Pendleton preem sendoff as a ballyhoo measure).

Pat Frank's novel, on which John C. Higgins and Walter Doniger based the screenplay, tells of a Marine officer who carried with him a bottle of Scotch through World War II, and now has it in Korea waiting for that certain "special" occasion that will justify its consumption. The fifth becomes a symbol of a goal not yet achieved to the company under his command as it fights its way back through almost constant Red attack.

John Payne is the Marine officer, giving the character a good performance under Allan Dwan's direction. Mona Freeman is the wife back home who had gifted him with the packaged goods. She, too, pleases, getting into the story via Payne's mental flashbacks to the girl he left behind. Audrey Dalton is another femme who comes into the plot the same way, representing, and very well, a World War II temptation he encountered in Australia. Peter Graves and Chuck Connors carry off main roles in the small company of fighting heroes with honor and there's some excellent support from Bob Nichols, John Wilder, Bob Easton, Stanley Cha and others.

Action gets rather violent at times in the Hayes Goetz production, simulating the dangers of warfare ably, and Dwan's directorial handling makes a number of these stand out sharply. Ellsworth Fredricks' lensing is battle-wise in catching the fighting action and the Hans Salter score does its background chore with the proper martial air. *Brog.*

El Camino De La Vida
(The Road of Life)
(MEXICAN)

Mexico City, July 11.

Peliculas Nacionales release of a Cinematografica Latino Americana presentation. Produced by Angel de la Fuente. Features Rogelio and Humberto Jimenez Pons, Ignacio G. Torres, Mario M. Navarro, Miguel Manzano. Directed by Alfonso Carona Blake; screenplay, Mathilde Landeta, from a story by Eduardo and Mathilde Landeta; camera, Jose Ortiz Ramos; editor, Carlos Savage; music Gustave C. Carreon. At Cine Arcadia, Mexico City. Running time, 110 MINS.

Chinampina	Rogelio Jimenez Pons
Frijolito	Humberto Jimenez Pons
Pedro Gangoso	Ignacio G. Torres
Luis	Mario N. Navarro
Juvenile Court Director	Rafael Estrada
Rancher	Miguel Manzano
Lawyer	Enrique Lucero
Nico	Manuel Vergara Mamber
Cancudo	Ismael Perez
Beggarwoman	Eufrosina Garcia

The Mexican industry's efforts to move in on the international market get a forward push with this low-budget realistic entry which marks the megging debut of exthesp Alfonso Carona Blake. In no sense as hard-hitting as Luis Bunuels' "Los Olvidados" (The Young and the Damned), it still should get favorable comparison as its humorous sequences make up for the lack of brutality.

Story points out the humanitarian qualities of Mexico's Juvenile Court in its efforts to aid disorientated youngsters. Without placing the blame of why kids go bad, Blake and producer Angel de la Fuente have taken Mathilde Landetas' somewhat saccharine screenplay out of the studies and into the squalid barrios and neon-lit streets and squares of modern day Mexico City. Aided by the excellent editing of Carlos Savage, the film slices well below the surface of what makes maladjusted youngsters tick, talk and behave as they do, without sledgehammering the point.

Story line follows in flashback three youngsters and their reasons for being incarcerated with their probable rehabilitation. First kills his drunken stepfather to protect his mother's life; second, whose peculiar vocal defect has caused his schoolmates' derision, blinds their vicious ringleader; third, an orphan, steals a purse in order to feed his younger brother and himself. Latter sequence is remarkably well handled and has two real-life brothers, Rogelie and Humberto Jimenez Pons, who are a surefire future series bet. Latter, no more than six years old, is an amazingly Coogan-like kid who can't fail to click.

Among the other outstanding subteeners is Ignacio G. Torres, whose sympathetic handling of the friendless frog voice makes for a surprisingly mature characterization. Standout adults are Enrique Lucero as a sympathetic lawyer, Miguel Manzano as the second boy's rancher father and Eufrosina Garcia, whose one-minute bit as a wild-looking baby-hiring beggar comes across as a terrifying piece of pathos. Tyro megger at times lets his grownups go hammy, but his handling of the kids and their personalized vernacular is a real delight. Film's most hilarious sequence, showing nude pre-adolescents getting a morning cold shower in a detention home will probably get heavy clipping by stateside censors. Realistic black-and-white regular screen photography by Jose Ortiz Ramos is top-flight throughout, with night scenes outstanding. Only the trite musical background by Gustavo C. Carreon and an embarrassing sop to officialdom as a final fadeout fail to live up to the high standards set by the rest of the film. *Pete.*

Smiley
(BRITISH-C'SCOPE-COLOR)

Unsophisticated and unusually charming yarn set in Australian backwoods with refreshing moppet characterization. Universal appeal.

London, July 11.

20th-Fox release of an Anthony Kimmins production. Stars Ralph Richardson, John McCallum and "Chips" Rafferty. Produced and directed by Anthony Kimmins; screenplay, Moore Raymond and Anthony Kimmins; camera, Ted Scaife; editor, G. Turney-Smith; music, William Alwyn. At Carlton Theatre, London. July 11, '56. Running time, 97 MINS.

Reverend Lambeth	Ralph Richardson
Rankin	John McCallum
Sergeant Flaxman	Chips Rafferty
Smiley	Colin Petersen
Miss Workman	Jocelyn Hernfield
Joey	Bruce Archer
"Ma" Greevins	Margaret Christensen
"Pa" Greevins	Reg Lye
Mr. Stevens	Charles Tingwell
Mrs. Stevens	Marion Johns
Boundary Rider	Guy Doleman
Johnson	William Rees
Fred Stevens	Gavin Davies
Ah Foo	Chow Sing
King Billy	Bob Simm
Jackie	Reggie Weigand

With its rare quality of unsophisticated charm "Smiley," filmed entirely on location in Australia—but still qualifying for British quota—deserves serious exhibitor attention, not only in the British Commonwealth, where it should be a b.o. natural, but in other markets too. It will need careful selling, but the results should give ample compensation.

The original story, on which the film is based, was written by show-columnist Moore Raymond, who collaborated on the screenplay with producer-director Anthony Kimmins. Raymond, a native of Australia, obviously knows the backwoods intimately, but this yarn also reveals a shrewd insight to characterization, as well as an unfailing sense of humor. The film gives a colorful glimpse of the Australian bush country, which is appreciably enhanced by top quality CinemaScope lensing by Ted Scaife.

The "Smiley" of the title is a young boy of poor parents whose great ambition in life is to save enough money to buy himself a bicycle which he has seen advertised in a catalog. To rake in the money he does all sorts of odd jobs from bellringer at the local church to unwitting dope peddling on behalf of the local heavy. But just as he's saved enough to make the deal, his father—just back from a long spell of cattle droving—loses his own money on gambling and steals the kid's money in a vain bid to recoup his losses.

The bare plot outline does little justice to the story itself and although the incident is always trivial it is treated in refreshing style. The youngster has a romantic and imaginative turn of mind, a genuine sense of adventure and the spirit to see only the brighter side of life. These qualities are inherent in the exceptional interpretation of the role by Colin Petersen. It's a generous part and he does extremely well with it, but never dwarfing the adult contributions by distinguished performers of the calibre of Ralph Richardson, John McCallum and Chips Rafferty. His playmate is characteristically etched by Bruce Archer and Jocelyn Hernfield has appeal as the village teacher. His parents are sincerely portrayed by Margaret Christensen and Reg Lye and the rest of the team, locally recruited, give valuable support.

Shirley Abicair, also a native Australian, puts plenty of charm into her recorded rendition of the title song. Anthony Kimmins keeps the action in top gear with his sensitive direction and the technical qualities are well up to standard. *Myro.*

Raw Edge
(COLOR)

Taming of the Oregon frontier, where any woman belonged to the first man to claim her; standard outdoor action fare.

Hollywood, July 24.

Universal release of Albert Zugsmith production. Stars Rory Calhoun, Yvonne De Carlo, Mara Corday, Neville Brand, Rex Reason; features Emile Meyer, Herbert Rudley, Robert J. Wilke. Directed by John Sherwood. Screenplay, Harry Essex, Robert Hill; story, William Kozlenko, James Benson Nablo; camera (Technicolor), Maury Gertsman; editor, Russell Schoengarth; music supervision, Joseph Gershenson. Previewed July 17, '56. Running time, 76 MINS.

Tex Kirby	Rory Calhoun
Hannah Montgomery	Yvonne De Carlo
Paca	Mara Corday
Tarp Penny	Neville Brand
John Randolph	Rex Reason
Pop Penny	Emile Meyer
Gerald Montgomery	Herbert Rudley
Sile Doty	Robert J. Wilke
Dan Kirby	John Gilmore
McKay	Gregg Barton
Whitey	Ed Fury
Missionary	William Schallert

Universal tames the Oregon frontier in "Raw Edge" with a catch line about any woman belonging to the first man to claim her. It didn't give a girl much choice, but it does lead to some rivalry action and adds up to a standard entry that will show a profit from its general dual bill bookings.

Around that first come, first served, theme scripters Harry Essex and Robert Hill have concocted a frontier drama that has the requisite values to satisfy the demands of the market at which it is aimed. John Sherwood's direction of the Albert Zugsmith production keeps it moving along for 76 minutes and the cast response is all that's required to make it come off.

Rory Calhoun does his usual, acceptable work as the male star, a young man bent on vengeance for the death of his younger brother, falsely accused of attempted attack on Yvonne De Carlo, a gal already claimed by Herbert Rudley, the self-styled Oregon frontier baron who enforces the law as it concerns the ladies. Miss De Carlo takes easily to the requirements of her spot, as does Mara Corday, the Indian widow of the younger brother who exacts her own tribal vengeance on Rudley before the plot runs out. Besides, her settlement of the affair leaves the way clear for Calhoun to claim Miss De Carlo at the finale.

Neville Brand enacts a lustful henchman of Rudley's who can't keep his hands off the boss's wife, and Rex Reason is a calm gambler who sits back waiting for the same femme stakes. Emile Meyer, as Brand's dad, wants Miss De Carlo, too, so there is a like father, like son, motivation included. Robert J. Wilke, who successfully claims the unwilling Indian widow, John Gilmore, Gregg Barton, Ed Fury and William Schall_rt deliver acceptably.

Maury Gertsman's Technicolor photography does justice to the outdoor settings and other technical support is ably handled.
Brog.

Dakota Incident
(COLOR)

Well-cast western actioner for the outdoor trade.

Hollywood, July 24.

Republic release of Michael Baird production. Stars Linda Darnell, Dale Robertson, John Lund, Ward Bond; features Regis Toomey, Skip Homeier, Irving Bacon, John Doucette, Whit Bissell. Directed by Lewis R. Foster. Screenplay, Frederic Louis Fox; camera (Trucolor), Ernest Haller; editor, Howard Smith; music, R. Dale Butts. Previewed July 42, '56. Running time, 88 MINS.

Amy Clarke .... Linda Darnell
John Banner .... Dale Robertson
Carter Hamilton .... John Lund
Senator Blakely .... Ward Bond
Minstrel .... Regis Toomey
Brank Banner .... Skip Homeier
Tully Morgan .... Irving Bacon
Rick Largo .... John Doucette
Mark Chester .... Whit Bissell
Matthew Barnes ...... William Fawcett
Bartender-Desk Clerk..Malcolm Atterbury
Giselle .... Diane Du Bois
Indian Leader .... Charles Horvath

Early-west action, familiar names and a Trucolor dressing are satisfactorily combined in this Republic offering to meet the demands of the outdoor market generally. Lewis R. Foster's direction keeps the action pace high, the characters are interestingly developed in Frederic Louis Fox's plot and the performances come off well.

It's a motley group of strangers that finds itself pinned down in a Dakota gully by a small band of marauding Indians. Dale Robertson is a bank robber, bold and dashing. Linda Darnell is an easy lady of the west, pretty and desirable. John Lund is a quietish ex-bank clerk, fleeing the charge he pulled the robbery committed by Robertson. Ward Bond is a loud-mouth politican who wants brotherhood with the redskins. Regis Toomey is a whiskey-soaked minstrel man, and Whit Bissell is a timid easterner who believes he has found gold.

The Michael Baird production tells the story against a rugged outdoor setting, with Ernest Haller's photography up-pointing scenic values most effectively. Between thirst and the Indians, the small group is gradually decimated until only Miss Darnell and Robertson are left to come out of the violent adventure alive — and regenerated.

The principal characters each has a chance to sell the role and honors are about equally divided, with all good. Also aiding the generally excellent manner in which the picture is brought off are Skip Homeier and John Doucette, in and out early in the footage as Robertson's robbery partners. Irving Bacon, William Fawcett, Malcolm Atterbury Diane Du Bois and Charles Horvath.

R. Dale Butts' background score features a tinkling mandolin that's good for the film's mood. Editing and other technical credits are expertly handled, too. *Brog.*

The Ambassador's Daughter
(C'SCOPE-COLOR)

Frothy, Paris-lensed, romantic comedy with Olivia de Havilland, others, accounting for pleasant round of fun.

Hollywood, July 26.

United Artists release of Norman Krasna production, written and directed by Krasna. Stars Olivia de Havilland, John Forsythe, Myrna Loy, Adolphe Menjou, costars Tommy Noonan, Francis Lederer, Edward Arnold, Minor Watson. Camera (Technicolor), Michael Kelber; editor, Roger Dwyre; music, Jacques Metehen. Previewed July 24, '56. Running time, **102 MINS.**

Joan .... Olivia de Havilland
Danny .... John Forsythe
Mrs. Cartwright .... Myrna Loy
Senator Cartwright ..... Adolphe Menjou
Al .... Tommy Noonan
Prince Nicholas Obelski . Francis Lederer
Ambassador Fiske .... Edward Arnold
General Harvey .... Minor Watson

This is one of those lightweight, romantic comedy affairs usually designated as good summer filmfare. It is engaging enough in spinning its familiarly-plotted antics to earn a fair share of titters. The frothy diversion whipped together by producer-director-writer Norman Krasna plays pleasantly against a Paris setting, thanks to an able cast of funsters flipping through the lines and situations, while CinemaScope and Technicolor make it visibly worthwhile.

Olivia de Havilland heads the cast and obviously enjoys her first venture into light comedy in some time. The good time she has gets through to the audience and she looks terrific in the Christian Dior outfits. John Forsythe also appears to enjoy his romantic chores opposite her, and they are an expert team in foiling for each other and in lifting a story that basically has very few surprise twists and turns.

Myrna Loy, long absent from the screen, is back in the type of breezy thing she does very well, pairing with Adolphe Menjou as his wife and the duo account for chuckles. Tommy Noonan scores strongly on the laugh end as Forsythe's G. I. buddy, while Francis Lederer. Edward Arnold and Minor Watson go along easily with the light plotting.

Krasna draws out his story for an unnecessary hour and 42 minutes, but mostly manages to keep the quips coming often enough to pick up the pace when material thinness starts slowing things down. Idea behind the fun is for Miss de Havilland, daughter of Ambassador Arnold, to test the good manners of American military personnel in Paris and prove that Senator Menjou is not justified in having the city declared off-limits. Forsythe is the chosen G. I., who believes Miss de Havilland is just a working girl. The ending is easily foreseeable, but most won't mind watching while Krasna and cast work it out.

Michel Kelber's lensing is excellent, capturing some intriguing vistas of Paris. Art direction, settings and background score are expert. Footage has an occasional flaw in the sound with some dubbed dialog effects coming through.
Brog.

Lisbon
(NATURAMA-SONG-COLOR)

Ray Milland, Maureen O'Hara in Lisbon-localed nefarious adventure meller with okay prospects.

Hollywood, July 31.

Republic release of Ray Milland production, directed by Milland. Stars Milland, Maureen O'Hara, Claude Rains, Yvonne Furneaux; features Francis Lederer, Percy Marmont, Jay Novello, Edward Chapman, Harold Jamieson, Humberto Madeira. Screenplay, John Tucker Battle; story, Martin Rackin; camera (Trucolor), Jack Marta; editor, Richard L. Van Enger; music, Nelson Riddle; filmed through the facilities of Amateau, Lda, Tobis Studios, Lisbon, Portugal. Previewed July 26, '56. Running time, 90 MINS.

Capt. Robert John Evans . Ray Milland
Sylvia Merrill .... Maureen O'Hara
Aristides Mavros ..... Claude Rains
Maria Maddalena Masanet
Yvonne Furneaux
Serafim .... Francis Lederer
Lloyd Merrill .... Percy Marmont
Joao Casimiro Fonseca . Jay Novello
Edgar Selwyn .... Edward Chapman
Phillip Norworth ...... Harold Jamieson
Tio Rabio .... Humberto Madeira

Lisbon makes a colorful setting for this tale of nefarious adventure among the international intrigue set. It's an interesting plot that, while not always well done from a writing or directing standpoint, has the melodramatic ingredients to carry it through to okay prospects generally. Republic's anamorphic Naturama process and Trucolor go a long way towards visual impressiveness, particularly in showing off the Lisbon scene.

Ray Milland stars, produces and directs. As a smooth, romantically-inclined American amusing himself with smuggling operations in the Lisbon area, his trouping comes off very well. As a production, the picture is rich in pictorial effects, but could have used a little sharper overseeing of story material, particularly that opening sequence in which sadistic Claude Rains, international crook, smashes a song bird with a tennis racket so his hungry cat can have breakfast. That's hard to take and completely unnecessary to set the Rains character. As director, Milland lets the suspense-building intrigue falter on occasion, with some staginess and obvious action to lessen tension.

Maureen O'Hara advantageously plays the young wife of a rich, old man who has been prisoner behind the Iron Curtain for two years. She wants him back, but dead so she can claim his fortune, and Rains is the big operator who arranges the details, including hiring Milland and his boat for the pickup. Miss O'Hara makes the mistake of revealing her intensions to Milland during some amatory byplay and he switches romantic interest to Yvonne Furneaux, a very interesting young lady who is one of the beauties Rains keeps around to satisfy his esthetic tastes. Climax has its thrills as Milland upsets the plans of Miss O'Hara and Rains and takes off with Miss Furneaux.

The starring foursome are quite glib and pleasing at the principal roles, and giving performance assists are Francis Lederer, Rains' killer; Percy Marmont, the old man; Jay Novello, Lisbon official; Edward Chapman, Rains' butler, and other characters in the script by John Tucker Battle from a story by Martin Rackin.

Jack Marta's color lensing is a major asset, and Nelson Riddle's music makes a strong point, too. Score includes "Lisbon Antigua" sung behind the titles by a chorus and Roby Charmandy in English, and again in Portuguese during a cafe sequence. Art direction, settings, costumes and other physical assists are excellent. *Brog.*

Gunslinger
(COLOR)

Sharpshooting Beverly Garland enforcing law a la Annie Oakly. An oater with corn mixed in liberally.

Hollywood, July 30.

American Releasing Corp. release of Roger Corman production, directed by Corman. Stars John Ireland, Beverly Garland, Allison Hayes; features Martin Kingsley, Jonathan Haze, Chris Alcaide. Screenplay, Charles B. Griffith, Mark Hanna; camera (Pathe Color), Fred West; editor, Charles Gross; music, Ronald Stein. Previewed July 27, '56. Running time, **77 MINS.**

Cane Miro .... John Ireland
Rose Hood .... Beverly Garland
Erica Page .... Allison Hayes
Gideon Polk .... Martin Kingsley
Jack Hays .... Jonathan Haze
Joshua Tate .... Chris Alcaide
Jimmy Tonto .... Richard Miller
Zebelon Tabb .... Bruno Ve Sota
Felicity Polk .... Margaret Campbell
Scott Hood .... William Schallert
Nate Signo .... Aaron Saxon
Tessie-Belle .... Chris Miller

It's a gal wearing the marshal's badge in "Gunslinger" and Beverly Garland is a right pretty enforcer of law and order, as well as being a sharpshooter whose gun doesn't miss in the line of duty, even when she's beading down on the man she loves at the finale. With this twist to the conventional western plot, the Roger Corman production should get its share of playing time attention in the program market.

John Ireland and Allison Hayes also star with Miss Garland and represent the heavies of the Charles B. Griffith-Mark Hanna plot. He's a killer imported by Miss Hayes to bump off the marshal, and she's the town saloon operator who has been buying up property in the hope the railroad's coming through. Miss Garland has that badge because Miss Hayes' men have bumped off her husband, William Schallert, at the film's opening and she is determined to clean up Oracle, Tex., not knowing that Ireland has been paid to get her if the railroad goes elsewhere. What that has to do with events is never clear but, while they wait, she and Ireland fall in love and indulge in heavy smooching when he's not busy doing the same thing with Miss Hayes. When the truth comes out, though, duty is strong and she guns down Ireland, just like any other crook.

The script and Corman's direction lean heavily on sex, sometimes justifiably in view of the story twist, and sometimes ludicrously, and the Garland-Hayes combo backs up whatever is asked in the s.a. department. Since the material isn't very believable, the star performances are on the same level, although individual personalities help some. Martin Kingsley is seen as the town mayor and Jonathan Haze as Miss Hayes' handyman who loves her.

Corman unwisely tries to dress up values with a chorus line in Miss Hayes' saloon, but since there are only three femmes doing poor routines it adds up to nothing.

Storm Center

"Principle" rendered dull. Much ado about civil liberties angle. Spotty boxoffice prospects.

Hollywood, July 31.

Columbia release of Julian Blaustein (Phoenix) production. Stars Bette Davis; features Brian Keith, Kim Hunter, Paul Kelly. Directed by Daniel Taradash. Story, screenplay, Taradash and Elick Moll; camera, Burnett Guffey; editor, William A. Lyon; music, George Dunning. Previewed July 11, '56. Running time, 86 MINS.

Alice Hull .... Bette Davis
Paul Duncan .... Brian Keith
Martha Lockridge .... Kim Hunter
Judge Robert Ellerbe .... Paul Kelly
Freddie Slater .... Kevin Coughlin
George Slater .... Joe Mantell
Laura Slater .... Sallie Brophy
Mayor Levering .... Howard Wierum
Stacey Martin .... Curtis Cooksey
Edgar Greenbaum .... Michael Raffetto
Reverend Wilson .... Edward Platt
Hazel .... Kathryn Grant
Senator Bascomb .... Howard Wendell
Carl .... Burt Mustin
Mrs. Simmons .... Edith Evanson
Mr. Morrisey .... Joseph Kearns
Bert .... Ted Marc
Charlie .... Rudy Lee
Joe .... Phillip Crampton

Failure of "Storm Center" to dress its civil liberties theme in attractive attire nullifies the controversy to be anticipated from its release. The pro and con, already being fanned in some quarters, may result in some initial wicket interest, but the pic will short change those buying it as entertainment. Overall prospects are spotty at best.

The Phoenix presentation, produced by Julian Blaustein for Columbia distribution, never gets the grip of reality on the viewer as it weaves through a wordy, slowly-paced account of the storm that develops when a smalltown librarian defies her employer, the City Council, after being instructed to remove a piece of Communist propaganda from her book shelves. The storm is a dull one, despite the contrived efforts to make it tempestuous, and never generates the kind of believable dramatic impact that might have put the show over and made the civil liberties message effective.

Director Daniel Taradash, who also did the story and script with Elick Moll, has a cast of able performers to work with and they deliver what is asked of them competently, even if the characters and situations rarely get below the surface. Bette Davis stars as the librarian, so long entrenched in her job she has come to look on the library almost as her own. Fired from her post, she decides not to fight back even though some bigotry and gossip put a Red label on her and the town's children she loves turn against her. The townspeople see the error of their ways when a child burns the library and she's promised her old job when a new building is completed.

Brian Keith plays a young politician who seizes on Miss Davis' defiance to make himself some headlines. In doing so, he loses his fiancee, Kim Hunter, who had taken over the librarian post. Paul Kelly does the City Council member who tries to back Miss Davis. Joe Mantell, an unimaginative boor who fosters the gossip against the librarian; Kevin Coughlin, his too-imaginative young son who fires the library; Sallie Brophy, his intelligent wife, are among others who take sides in the controversy.

George Dunning's score provides the footage with a rousing background, and Burnett Guffey's photography is good. Technical credits measure up to standard. *Brog.*

The Baby and the Battleship
(BRITISH-COLOR)

Wholesome British comedy of baby smuggled aboard a battleship during exercises. Spoof at Naval brass and traditions. Good fun anywhere.

London, July 10.

British Lion release of Jay Lewis production. Stars John Mills and Richard Attenborough. Produced by Anthony Darnborough; directed by Jay Lewis; screenplay, Jay Lewis and Gilbert Hackforth Jones based on novel by Anthony Thorne; camera, Harry Waxman; editor, Manuel del Campo; music, James Stevens and Humphrey Searle. At Warner Theatre, London, July 10, '56. Running time, 96 MINS.

Puncher Roberts .... John Mills
Knocker White .... Richard Attenborough
Professor .... Bryan Forbes
Whiskers .... Harold Siddons
Sails .... Clifford Mollison
George .... Lionel Jeffries
Harry .... Gordon Jackson
Joe .... Michael Howard
Captain .... Michael Hordern
Commander Digby .... Ernest Clark
Gunnery Officer ... John Forbes-Robertson
Master-At-Arms .... Duncan Lamont
C.P.O. Blades .... Harry Locke
P.M.O. .... Cyril Raymond
Marshal .... Andre Morell
Aide .... John Le Mesurier
Interpreter .... Ferdy Mayne
Maria .... Lisa Gastoni
Paolo .... Martin Miller
The Admiral .... D. A. Clarke-Smith
The Baby .... Martyn Garrett

As an example of good wholesome British fun, "The Baby and the Battleship" should be hard to beat, but as always when there's a moppet around on the screen, the adult actors are too frequently left in the shade. Nonetheless, release should garner steady results overseas.

Jay Lewis and Gilbert Hackforth Jones have shrewdly exploited the laugh angles in their screenplay, which is taken from Anthony Thorne's novel. It's no more than a frolic which frequently makes good-humored fun at the expense of naval traditions. Most of the action takes place on a battleship but location shots of Naples are shown to good advantage in handsome Eastman Color lensing.

There's not much to the basic plot, but the incident which it develops provides for hilarious situations. John Mills, a veteran of the British navy, while ashore at Naples, accidently finds himself with a baby boy in his care. Not wanting to leave the infant he takes it aboard, then suddenly finds that the ship is sailing ahead of schedule and the child cannot be returned to his family. From then he and his messmates of the lower deck are involved in a game of hide and seek, trying to conceal the child from their superior officers. Their adventures become more involved when a distinguished marshal from a foreign power makes a tour of inspection of the ship.

Richard Attenborough, now consistently type cast as a ranker in the British services, is the lower deck hand, mainly responsible for all the trouble. It was he who took John Mills along on a date to meet the baker's daughter in Naples, but the girl (Lisa Gastoni) was not allowed out unless she took care of her infant brother. While the other couple are dancing and Mills is literally left holding the baby, he becomes involved in a free-for-all, and when the roughhouse is over he finds himself alone with the child. Attenborough and the girl return to find the ship has sailed.

John Mills, one of the most dependable of British screen actors, more than adequately succeeds in standing up to the infant's inevitable scene stealing, while Attenborough makes the best of his role of a lower deck racketeer. Too *Myro.*

Czech Film Festival

Karlovy Vary, July 24.

Egy Pikolo Vilagos (A Half Pint of Beer) (HUNGARIAN). Enterprise Magyar release and production. Directed by Felix Maariassy. Screenplay, J. Maryassy; camera, I. Eiben; editor, I. Vincze. With Eva Ruttkay, T. Bitskey, E. Bull, M. Sulyok, E. Schubert. At Karlovy Vary Film Fest. Running time, **95 MINS.**

Hungarian film shapes as a pleasant comedy about two young lovers, held apart by moral differences, who finally come of age for a happy ending. Cleverly mounted, with telling notations of character and place, this is an entertaining film in the neo-realist vein and might matter enough for U.S. lingo marts. Some curio values in its closeup of daily life there in Red Hungary and its looksee at the delinquent element. Acting is excellent especially in the case of Eva Ruttkay as the wife-like fun loving girl who finds chastening in love. Direction is subtle and knowing and if this is not a lyrical pic it makes up for a familiar denouement in its progression, types and well fashioned screenplay.

Mahiru No Ankoku (Darkness at Midday) (JAPANESE). Gendai release and production. Directed by Tadashi Imai. Screenplay, Shinobu Hashimoto; camera, Shunichiro Nakao; editor, Akira Ifukube. With Kajiro Kusanagi, S. Uemura, Terno Matsuyama, T. Kojima. At Karlovy Vary Film Fest. Running time, **120 MINS.**

Hardboiled film journalism makes this an offbeat negative. Based on a real case still going on in Japan this details how police brutality breaks down a confessed murderer, of two old people, into saying that he had accomplices. Film follows through the confessions extracted from these men and their trial, also weaving in the effect on their relations. Somewhat long this is still stark, telling and actionful and might be of U.S. interest for specialized theatres though somber theme is limiting. Direction is sharp and incisive and technical credits and acting all combine to make this a staccato absorbing pic.

Hemsoborna (The People of Hesmo) (SWEDISH; COLOR). Nordisk Tonefilm release and production. Directed by Arne Mattsson. Screenplay, Rune Lindstrom from the novel by Auguste Strindberg; camera (EastmanColor), Max Wilan; editor, Lennart Lindgren. With Erik Strandmark, Hjordis Petterson, Nils Hallberg, John Norrmann, Curt Lowgren. At Karlovy Vary Film Fest. Running time, **100 MINS.**

Rustic and rugged pic deals with a group of islanders during the late 19th century. It concerns an opportunist who marries an older woman to get her estate, but meets his comeuppance at the hands of her son and the elements. Somewhat literary and sprawling, with violent bucolic and bawdy overtones, it spins a rabelasian looksee at the earthy actions of these people. Acting is somewhat too theatrical and direction sometimes tasteless, but color and story combine to make this an offbeater that may be of value for special theatres in the U.S. on its rawboned drama and humor. It spills its tale of an uncouth, insular people well.

THE WEDDING OF THE FAIRY PRINCESS (RED CHINESE; OPERA). Chinese State release and production. Directed by Sh'Chuey. Screenplay from opera by Sang Chu; camera, Lo Tsung Chou; editor, Feng; music and songs, Shts'Lin. With Yen Feng-Ying, Wang Shao Fung, Chang Yun Feng. At Karlovy Vary Film Festival. Running time, **100 MINS.**

The very conception of this film, a Chinese opera, limits this for the U.S. However, its delicate and lyrical charm might make this an unusual offbeater though it is primarily for those familiar with the sing song chanted Chinese opera. It concerns a fairy princess living in Heaven who descends to earth and marries a mortal. She helps out of bonded servitude and they are at the height of happiness, with an expected child, when she is called back by her father. Simply told in song and gesture it reaches a poetic level and moving ending. Rare chances for the U.S., but unusual enough for extremely specialized placing. Technical credits and special effects all blend into making this a successful folk opera, with actors and actresses properly stylized, and their high keyed singing is soon acceptable via the well done visuals.

DEVDAS (INDIAN). Mohan release and production. Directed by Bimal Roy. Screenplay, Nabendu Ghosh; camera, Kamal Bose; editor, Singh Bedi; music, S. D. Burman. With Dilip Kumar, Vyjayantimala, Suchitra Sen. At Karlovy Vary Film Fest. Running time, **95 MINS.**

Film is slowly outlined and played in native fashion, but has the technique and storytelling manner of the west. It emerges a lyrical love story of a rich, weak boy separated from his poorer sweetheart by convention and social differences. The seemingly mawkish story line never gets sentimental or dreary, and the deft visuals, acting and direction strike a poigant note that slant this for possible chances in specialized theatre setups in the U.S.

THREE IN ONE (AUSTRALIAN). Tradition Film release and production. Directed by Cecil Holmes. Screenplay, Rex Reinit from stories by Henry Lawson, Frank Hardy, Ralph Peterson; camera, Ross Wood; editor, Raymond Hanson. With John McCallum, Edmund Allison, Jerome Levy, Leonard Thiele, Joan Landor, Brian Viary. At Karlovy Vary Film Fest. Running time, **90 MINS.**

Film ties together three stories and is the first neo-realist film from Australia. Tales are offbeat, and though direction does not give them an original air it has a flair that might make this an okay filler for secondary U.S. spots. One concerns the burial of an unknown visitor who gets a fancy sendoff by a group of miners, another is about depression days which lead a burly, individualistic worker to steal wood for his friends, on a cold night, from a hoarding landowner, and third concerns how a young boy and girl decide to overcome financial fears and marry after a fight one night and their individual self realization of their love. Though sketchy, this is a looksee at another aspect of Australian life. Direction is fair with the story lines making for the most interest. Technical credits are good.

La Gata (The Cat) (SPANISH: COLOR; C'SCOPE). Hispano-Fox release and production. Directed by Marguerite Alexandre, Rafael Torrecilla. Screenplay, Cesar Ardavin; camera, (Eastmancolor), Juan Marine; editor, Mecedes Alonzo. With Aurora Bautista, Jorge Mistral, Nani Fernandez, Jose Nieto, Felipe Simon. At Karlovy Vary Film Fest. Running time, **100 MINS.**

First Hispano C'Scoper is a familiar tune played with fiery passions, bull fighting and flamenco. For the U.S. its simple tale and mounting limit this for the lingo circuits where its action and color might make this of interest. Direction, acting and general aspects are ordinary, but C'Scope does well by the landscapes. *Mosk.*

The Burning Hills
(C'Scope-Color)

Tab Hunter, Natalie Wood team in standard western for accent on youthful appeal.

Hollywood, July 27.
Warner Bros. release of Richard Whorf production. Stars Tab Hunter, Natalie Wood; features Skip Homeier, Natalie Franz, Earl Holliman, Claude Akins. Directed by Stuart Heisler. Screenplay, Irving Wallace; from novel by Louis L'Amour; camera (WarnerColor), Ted McCord; editor, Clarence Kolster; music, David Buttolph. Previewed July 23, '56. Running time, **93 MINS.**

Trace Jordan .... Tab Hunter
Maria Colton .... Natalie Wood
Jack Sutton .... Skip Homeier
Jacob Lantz .... Eduard Franz
Mort Bayliss .... Earl Holliman
Ben Hindeman .... Claude Akins
Joe Sutton .... Ray Teal
Tio Perico .... Frank Puglia
Braun .... Hal Baylor
Wes Parker .... Tyler MacDuff
Veach .... Rayford Barnes
Vicente Colton .... Tony Terry

With the youthful filmgoer in mind, the combo of Tab Hunter and Natalie Wood in "The Burning Hills" could prove to be a profitable one. They form a team of somewhat younger stars than is customarily found in sagebrush

Scandal Incorporated

A dull "expose" of current scandal periodicals. A film star falsely accused of murdering scandalmonger. Exploitation angles but little else.

Hollywood, Aug. 4.
Milton Mann production (no release). Stars Robert Hutton; features Paul Richards, Claire Kelly, Patricia Wright, Robert Knapp, Havis Davenport, Reid Hammond, Nestor Paiva, Gordon Wynn. Directed and edited by Edward Mann; screenplay, Milton Mann; camera, Brydon Baker; music, Paul Sawtell, Bert Shefter. Previewed Aug. 3, '56. Running time, **92 MINS.**

Brad Cameron .... Robert Hutton
Marty Ellis .... Paul Richards
June Trapping .... Claire Kelly
Marge Cameron .... Patricia Wright
Jess Blancher .... Robert Knapp
Billie Wayne .... Havis Davenport
Jerry Dexter .... Reid Hammond
Leland Miller .... Nestor Paiva
Herman Todd .... Gordon Wynn
Mr. James .... Guy Prescott
Sidney Woods .... Donald Kirke
Alice Yoland .... Marjorie Stapp
Martha Collum .... Enid Baine
Lewis Adams .... Mauritz Hugo
Champ Winter .... Joe Breen
Bob Hamilton .... Allen O'Locklin
Willie Anderson .... George Cisar
Gracie .... Tracey Morgan
Marie Ryan .... Mimi Simpson

Designed to cash in on the current controversy over scandal mags and resultant million-dollar law suits, "Scandal incorporated" is first of a series of such films planned by both majors and indies to hit the screen. This one is far over-length, ineptly turned out an lacks interest, but has some exploitation potential.

Milton Mann's production of his own screenplay is burdened with superfluous characters and tedious dialog, action seldom quickens beyond a slow walk. Plottage purporting to be an expose of the mud-slinging scandal sheets. A film star is the victim and his name linked with an ambitious starlet.

Robert Hutton has star role, but whatever acting honors are garnered go to Paul Richards, who plays his attorney when the actor is accused of murdering the writer of the scurrilous article which causes studio to drop his contract. Claire Kelly, Patricia Wright and Havis Davenport supply distaff interest, Robert Knapp portrays the mag writer, Nestor Paiva the mag publisher, all as good as parts permit—and under Edward Mann's loose direction. *Whit.*

Huk
(COLOR)

Action programmer lensed in Philippines with George Montgomery, Mona Freeman.

Hollywood, July 24.
United Artists release of Collier Young production. Stars George Montgomery, Mona Freeman; features John Baer. Novel and screenplay, Stirling Silliphant; camera (Eastman Color), William Snyder; editor, Helene Turner; music, Albert Glasser. Previewed July 23, '56. Running time, **84 MINS.**

Greg Dickson .... George Montgomery
Cindy Rogers .... Mona Freeman
Bart Rogers .... John Baer
Steven Rogers .... James Bell
Major Balatbat .... Teddy Benivedes
Kalak .... Mario Barri
Pinote .... Ben Perez

A Philippine Island setting backstops this action-adventure feature. It's programmer entertainment, with the names of George Montgomery and Mona Freeman to see it through that market to suitable returns.

Most striking part of the Collier Young production for United Artists release is the pictorial impact the location backgrounds gain from William Snyder's Eastman Color lensing. Script by Stirling Silliphant from his novel is a formula affair despite the difference in settings and villains, and John Barnwell gives it stock direction. Within the script and directorial limitations, the laying by Montgomery, Miss Freeman, John Baer. James Bell, Teddy Benivedes and others comes off satisfactorily, with a scene or two given some depth by the performers.

Huks, onetime guerilla fighters now given over to a not-clearly-expressed fanaticism, are the heavies of the plot and Montgomery is the hero who puts them down on the island where he has inherited a plantation. There are some nuances that don't come off very well about cynicism and the Philippine struggle to establish itself after World War II, but the makers keep tossing plenty of action at the customers as compensation for general viewers. *Brog.*

Magnificent Roughnecks

Jack Carson, Mickey Rooney as comedic rough-n-ready oil workers in South America; for programmer bookings.

Allied Artists release of Herman Cohen production. Stars Jack Carson, Mickey Rooney, Nancy Gates, Jeff Donnell; features Myron Healey, Willis Bouchey. Directed by Sherman A. Rose. Screenplay, Stephen Kandel; camera, Charles Van Enger; editor, Rose; music, Paul Dunlap. Previewed July 24, '56. Running time, **72 MINS.**

Bix Decker .... Jack Carson
Frank Sommers .... Mickey Rooney
Jane Rivers .... Nancy Gates
Julie .... Jeff Donnell
Werner Jackson .... Myron Healey
Ernie Biggers .... Willis Bouchey
Senor Ramon Serrano..... Eric Feldary
Danny .... Alan Wells
Chuck Evans .... Frank Gerstle
Guard .... Larry Carr
Pepi .... Matty Fain
Driver .... Joe Locke

Jack Carson and Mickey Rooney enact a couple of roughneck oilmen in South America in this programmer offering. Emphasis is on chuckles with the action, and delivers enough to take care of the light demands of companion bookings in the general dual situations.

Femme interest is divided between Nancy Gates, oil expert who comes to South America to take over Carson's job, but winds up with him, instead, and Jeff Donnell, hash-slinger who has a half-developed yen for the big braggard but gets Rooney for the finale clinch.

Story and physical values are pretty much formula throughout the Herman Cohen production, with Stephen Kandel's script using stereotype characters and situations to carry the plot load which Sherman A. Rose's direction brings off in stock fashion. When Carson feuds with his big boss, Willis Bouchey, the latter sends Miss Gates to take over. His masculine pride hurt, Carson stays on to help bring in the first gusher after some handicapping skullduggery by Myron Healey, wildcatter who is after the government lease that goes to the driller of the first producing well.

Charles Van Enger handles the photography satisfactorily in view of budget restrictions and other technical contributions fall in the same class. *Brog.*

Pillars of the Sky
(C'SCOPE-COLOR)

Good cavalry - versus - Indians feature.

Hollywood, Aug. 7.
Universal release of Robert Arthur production. Stars Jeff Chandler, Dorothy Malone, Ward Bond, Keith Andes, Lee Marvin; features Sydney Chaplin, Willis Bouchey, Michael Ansara, Olive Carey, Charles Horvath, Orlando Rodriguez, Glen Kramer, Floyd Simmons. Directed by

---

sagas and do an okay job of the outdoor assignment. The accent on youth in a western plot at least has its novelty value and the teenage fans should like their favorites in this prairie drama.

Richard Whorf's production uses CinemaScope and Warner-Color to enhance the scenic settings of the Louis L'Amour novel. Latter, and the screenplay by Irving Wallace, pretty much follows a familiar pattern in basic ingredients and dialog, so western followers are not likely to get off the story trail as director Stuart Heisler unwinds the plot at an actionful pace.

Story has to do with Hunter's efforts to avenge the death of his brother, murdered by henchmen of a big cattle baron who doesn't want small operators on his range. From avenger he becomes the chased, taking off through the hills in the company of Miss Wood, Anglo-Mexican girl, with the baron's gunslingers in hot pursuit. The young stars run the gamut of fanciful adventure in dodging the chasers, but it all makes for good action stuff, even that climax on the rocks high above a raging river during which the hero does in the last pursuing gunman.

As previously noted, Hunter and Miss Wood came off satisfactorily in the western derring-do, although there was no necessity for the actress being required to affect that Latin accent. Skip Homeier gets in his deadly licks as the son of cattle baron Ray Teal. He's just as blood-thirsty as his old man. Eduard Franz, Indian tracker reluctantly leading the gunslingers on the trail, is good, as are Earl Holliman, Claude Akins, latter good as the foreman; Hal Baylor, Tyler MacDuff and Rayford Barnes. Other acceptable support comes from Frank Puglia, as Miss Wood's drunken uncle, and Tony Terry, as her timid young brother.

Ted McCord contributes good lensing for the outdoor action. David Buttolph's music is appropriate and other production assists okay. *Brog.*

George Marshall. Screenplay, Sam Rolfe; from the novel "Frontier Fury" by Will Henry; camera (Technicolor), Harold Lipstein; editor, Milton Carruth; music supervision, Joseph Gershenson. Previewed July 30, '56. Running time, 95 MINS.

Sergt. Emmett Bell	Jeff Chandler
Calla Gaxton	Dorothy Malone
Dr. Joseph Holden	Ward Bond
Capt. Tom Gaxton	Keith Andes
Sergt. Lloyd Carracart	Lee Marvin
Timothy	Sydney Chaplin
Col. Edson Stedlow	Willis Bouchey
Kamiakin	Michael Ansara
Mrs. Anne Avery	Olive Carey
Sergt. Dutch Williams	Charles Horvath
Malachi	Orlando Rodriguez
Winston	Glen Kramer
Hammond	Floyd Simmons
Jacob	Pat Hogan
Lucas	Felix Noriego
Morgan	Paul Smith
Waco	Martin Milner
Albie	Robert Ellis
Music	Ralph J. Votrian
Major Donahue	Walter Coy
Sgt. Major Desmonde	Alberto Morin
Isaiah	Richard Hale
Zachariah	Frank de Kova
Capt. Fanning	Terry Wilson
Major Randall	Philip Kieffer
Elijah	Gilbert Conner

Plenty of action makes this cavalry-versus-Indians thriller sturdy fare for the general outdoor market. Name of Jeff Chandler and other familiar cast faces and the CinemaScope-Technicolor treatment of the East Oregon outdoor locations are assets for release intentions.

Plot is based on the uprising of Christianized Indians led by Chief Kamiakin when the cavalry starts to open a road and build a fort on lands given the redskins by treaty. George Marshall's direction is wise in outdoor action lure and he maintains the development at a fast pace. Script by Sam Rolfe, from Will Henry's novel, "Frontier Fury," is cut to order for handling the main theme and also does a good job of injecting some side plot issues having to do with the characters involved in the Robert Arthur production.

Chandler plays a rugged cavalry scout who warns the colonel, Willis Bouchey, the uprising will come if the road plans are carried out. It's the type of outdoor character he is thoroughly familiar with so he delivers with expected ease. Dorothy Malone is the vacillating wife of Keith Andes, cavalry officer, who thinks she loves Chandler but switches back to her husband at the finale. She adds a nice femme touch to the action doings, and Andes is acceptable. Ward Bond does well as the medical missionary whose Indians uprise, and it's his death at the end that brings the redskins back into line. Lee Marvin, a tough sergeant; Sydney Chaplin, Indian scout; Michael Ansara, the rebelling chief; Olive Carey, Charles Norvath and others are able in carrying out plot requirements.

Arthur's production supervision is an all-around able job and the technical assists fall in that classification, too. Harold Lipstein did the good lensing.   Brog.

Hot Cars

Melodrama of stolen car racket. Fast hour's fare for duals.

Hollywood, Aug. 3.
United Artists release of Howard W. Koch (Bel-Air) production. Stars John Bromfield, Joi Lansing, Mark Dana; features Carol Shannon, Ralph Clanton, Robert Osterloh, Dabbs Greer, Charles Keane. Directed by Donald McDougall. Screenplay, Don Martin, Richard Landau; story, H. Haile Chace; camera, William Margulies; editor, George Gittens; music, Les Baxter. Previewed Aug. 1, '56. Running time, 60 MINS.

Nick Dunn	John Bromfield
Karen Winter	Joi Lansing
Smiley Ward	Mark Dana
Jane Dunn	Carol Shannon
Arthur Markel	Ralph Clanton
George Hayman	Robert Osterloh
Detective Davenport	Dabbs Greer
Lieutenant Jefferson	Charles Keane
Otto Krantz	Kurt Katch
Lieutenant Holmes	George Sawaya
Hutton	John Merrick
Miss Rogers	Joan Sinclair
Paul (the bartender)	Maurice Marks
Betty Carson	Marilee Earle
Bret Carson	Vic Cutrier
Mrs. Davenport	Paula Hill

"Hot Cars" is a good title for this little programmer aimed at the supporting slot on regular dual bills. A crisp 60-minute running time and a fair amount of melodramatics in the plot make it acceptable for that release designation.

John Bromfield, Joi Lansing and Mark Dana make up the star trio in the Bel-Air presentation, produced by Howard W. Koch under executive producer Aubrey Schenck. They, along with featured players Carol Shannon, Ralph Clanton, Robert Osterloh, Dabbs Greer and Charles Keane, handle the characters with the desired impact under Donald McDougall's direction.

Script by Don Martin and Richard Landau, from a novel by H. Haile Chace, is no shattering expose of the stolen car racket, but there's enough indication of how hot autos are merchandised to the unsuspecting public to carry off the title. Bromfield appears as a salesman who starts selling stolen cars because he needs cash to take care of medical and surgical demands for his ailing baby son. He gets out of the racket just about as abruptly as he went into it. A police investigator gets too close to the truth and is bumped off, with Bromfield framed for the job. Windup gets him off the hook, and rather melodramatically, when he fights the killer on a rocketing roller-coaster at Ocean Park.

Les Baxter contributes the jazzy background score that lends emphasis to the plot, and William Margulies' camera work is good. Other technical credits are well handled.   Brog.

Dimanche
(Sunday's Killers)
(FRENCH-FRANSCOPE)

Paris, July 31.
Filmonde release of EDIC production. Directed by Alex Joffe. Screenplay, Gabriel Arout, Joffe; camera, Jean Bourgoin; editor, Jean Feyte. With Jean-Marc Thibault, Barbara Laage, Georges Poujouly, Dominique Willms, Paul Frankeur, Rosy Varte. At Marignan, Paris. Running time, 110 MINS.

Robert	Jean-Marc Thibault
Simone	Barbara Laage
Marie	Rosy Varte
Uncle	Paul Frankeur
Mechanic	Georges Poujouly
Janine	Dominique Willms

This one won the all-nation prize, CIDALC, at Cannes and the top kudos at the recent Cork Film Festival. Unlike the title it is not a whodunit, but a moral-suspense tale of the complications in a series of lives on a Sunday afternoon when a garage mechanic lets a car unwittingly go out on which he has not yet tightened the steering mechanism. Film hinges on the conscience state of the mechanic, and involves a group of people as he finally alerts the police, and the dragnet to stop the car and save the occupants.

Neatly made and acted by comparatively little known players, this has a fresh aspect, but plot is too fabricated to make this really outstanding. It also has the aura of a film made to warn against road excesses. However its clever notations make this entertaining and offbeat enough for possibilities in Stateside special spots. Not profound enough in treatment for the arties, it will have to be handled as an exploitation gambit to pay off accordingly on its engaging qualities.

A simple, goodhearted mechanic becomes an agonized man on discovering the car has left without the needed repairs. A frightened brother and wife talk him out of acting, but his conscience and his son galvanize him, and film builds as roadblocks and citizens try to stop a speeding car with some hitchikers and a honeymooning German couple.

Director Alex Joffe has used an anamorphoscope process in black and white, called Franscope, and it neither heightens or perceptibly lessens the impact of the film. Acting is subdued and real with technical aspects fine and location small town shooting also giving it a good natural flavor.   Mosk.

Thrillarama Adventure

Still another widescreen technique. Can be theatre-installed in 17 hours. But first film marred by seam and fade. Device inferior to photography, narration and music.

Houston, Aug. 9.
New wide screen depth perception process presented by Thillarama Production Inc. of Dallas (Albert H. Reynolds, Dowlen Russell). Photographed under contract by Raphael G. Wolff Studios Inc. of Hollywood. Presented at Metropolitan Theatre, Houston, Aug. 9, 1956. Running time, 96 MINS.

The latest of the widescreen techniques is far from being a perfected device. Thrillarama's biggest advantage to the theatre operator is its relative simplicity. It utilizes two standard cameras to produce a three-times-the-usual size picture on a curved screen.

But a disconcerting and annoying seam results when the two films are brought together on the screen. The synchronization of the two strips of film is not nearly perfect and the result is a great deal of split-level imagery.

The places and events filmed for the inaugural footage are interesting and well chosen. They vary from underwater ballet in Weeki Wachee Springs in Florida to a precision drill team of cowgirl clad coeds to a Marine training maneuver.

The color photography is often good but has a tendency in spots to wash out. This doesn't happen to the whole curved screen but mainly in an area close to the seam.

The segment on the Leathernecks was very well received and in light of the recent McKeon courts martial might lend itself to the best exploitation possibilities.   Forst.

The Solid Gold Cadillac

Comedy caper from the stage hit. Judy Holliday, Paul Douglas and bright b.o.

Hollywood, Aug. 14.
Columbia release of Fred Kohlmar production. Stars Judy Holliday, Paul Douglas; features Fred Clark, John Williams, Hiram Sherman, Neva Patterson, Ralphe Dumke, Ray Collins, Arthur O'Connell. Directed by Richard Quine. Screenplay, Abe Burrows; from play by George S. Kaufman, Howard Teichmann, produced on stage by Max Gordon; camera, Charles Lang; editor, Charles Nelson; music, Cyril J. Mockridge, conducted by Lionel Newman. Previewed July 26, '56. Running time, 99 MINS.

Laura Partridge	Judy Holliday
Edward L. McKeever	Paul Douglas
Clifford Snell	Fred Clark
John T. Blessington	John Williams
Harry Harkness	Hiram Sherman
Amelia Shotgraven	Neva Patterson
Warren Gillie	Ralph Dumke
Alfred Metcalfe	Ray Collins
Jenkins	Arthur O'Connell
Williams	Richard Deacon
Miss L'Arriere	Marilyn Hanold
Blessington's Secretary	Anne Loos
Snell's Secretary	Audrey Swanson
Chauffeur	Larry Hudson
Receptionist	Sandra White
Senator Simpkins	Harry Antrim

Original Broadway script was changed to fit an older stage actress, Josephine Hull, and is now changed back in the Columbia film version as a vehicle for a younger comedienne, Judy Holliday. The satire on minority stockholder gadfly treatment of vested interests and pompous executives makes for hilarity and the boxoffice prospects are bright.

In this version, the heroine of George S. Kaufman-Howard Teichmann play gets not only the Cadillac, but a man.

Script is by Abe Burrows. As the dizzy blonde with some native, and naive, common sense, Miss Holliday is a delight. The man's Paul Douglas, who does much to make the comedy click under Richard Quine's direction, even against such competition as a femme role tailored to Miss Holliday's particular talent.

Fred Kohlmar's production achieves a plushy look without the use of color or bigscreen assists. There is a flash of color at the tale's wrapup to show off that creampuff auto of the title, but the comedy is such that no one will miss a dye job elsewhere. Charles Lang's photography, the gowns by Jean Louis, and the art direction and set decorations do their share in contributing to the physical polish.

Laugh springboard is in playing the little against the big and making the small dog the winner. In this case, it's a broad treatment of big corporation board members who get their comeuppance from a femme who owns only 10 shares of common in the company. Slickly caricaturing the stuffed shirts are Fred Clark, John Williams, Hiram Sherman, Ralph Dumke and Ray Collins, each of whom registers strongly in the laugh line.

Along with slicing up big business, plot takes a poke at government, too, through the character done so well by Douglas. He's the company's ex-prexy, resigned to take a dollar-a-year post in Washington, but who ends up carrying the ball for Miss Holliday in her campaign to represent the small stockholders of the corporation in question.

Abetting the laughs are Arthur O'Connell, mild-manner office manager, and Neva Patterson, the shy secretary to the mischief-creating Miss Holliday. Others in the cast are able, too.

Film has a narration by George Burns, although it serves no particular purpose as far as the comedy is concerned. In the stage original the late Fred Allen officiated similarly.

Score was cleffed by Cyril J. Mockridge, with Lionel Newman conducting, and is an aid. There'll probably be some sales help from the often-spun Pearl Bailey disk of a tune wearing the picture's title, although it's not in the actual footage. *Brog.*

Bus Stop
(C'SCOPE-COLOR)

Marilyn Monroe in rowdy film treatment of the stage comedy; surefire b.o.

Hollywood, Aug. 14.

20th-Fox release of Buddy Adler production. Stars Marilyn Monroe; introduces Don Murray; features Arthur O'Connell, Betty Field, Eileen Heckart, Robert Bray, Hope Lange, Hans Conried, Casey Adams. Directed by Joshua Logan. Screenplay, George Axelrod; based on play by William Inge; camera (De Luxe Color), Milton Krasner; editor, William Reynolds; music, Alfred Newman, Cyril Mockridge; song, Ken Darby, sung by The Four Lads. Previewed Aug. 10, '56. Running time, **94 MINS.**

Cherie	Marilyn Monroe
Bo	Don Murray
Virgil	Arthur O'Connell
Grace	Betty Field
Vera	Eileen Heckart
Carl	Robert Bray
Elma	Hope Lange
Life Photog	Hans Conreid
Life Reporter	Casey Adams
Manager of Night Club	Henry Slate
Gerald	Terry Kelman
Evelyn	Linda Brace
Cover Girl	Greta Thyssen
Landlady	Helen Mayon
Blonde	Lucille Knox

William Inge's rowdy play about a cowboy and a lady (sic) gets a raucous screen treatment in this Buddy Adler production for 20th-Fox. The results, and particularly from the casting of Marilyn Monroe after her long film holdout, look like surefire boxoffice.

Pic is Miss Monroe's first since "Seven Year Itch," a b.o. success, and this return shot is headed in the same general direction at the wickets. Both the scripter and director, George Axelrod and Joshua Logan, respectively, were brought from the legit field to get the Inge comedy on film and, with a few minor exceptions, bring the chore off resoundingly.

The production, besides returning Miss Monroe, also serves to introduce a fresh new male face to film audiences in the person of Don Murray. He is the exuberant young cowhand who comes to the city to win some rodeo money and learn about women. Audiences will like him and should await his next film start, possibly in role that doesn't require quite as much broadness of playing, with interest.

The Monroe fans will find her s.a. not so positive, but still potent, in her "Bus Stop" character, but this goes with the type of well-used saloon singer and wouldbe actress she portrays. The glamour has been bleached out with extremely light, and not too becoming, makeup, but the personality is still there. Performancewise, Miss Monroe comes off acceptably, even though failing to maintain any kind of consistency in the Southern accent required of the role.

Murray is a 21-year-old Montana rancher who comes to Phoenix for the rodeo, meets and kisses his first girl and literally kidnaps her. The girl, a "chantoosie" in a cheap restaurant patronized by rodeo, performers, is reluctant about marriage, but by the time Murray ropes her, shouts at her, and gets beat up for her, she gives in, both because love has set in, as well as physical exhaustion.

Adler has given the two top players some terrific support. Arthur O'Connell milks everything from his spot as Murray's friend and watchdog and Betty Field clicks big as the amorous operator of the roadside bus stop. Another scoring strongly is Eileen Heckart, Miss Monroe's friend. Particularly good is Robert Bray, driver of the bus who likes to eye a shapely leg or pat a friendly dame. It's his character that keys the plot wrapup when he whips Murray during an enforced stop as the bus stop. Among others seen to advantage are Hope Lange, Hans Conried, Casey Adams and Henry Slate.

Phoenix footage includes quite a bit of rodeo contesting, giving an action note to the plot very effectively. Scenes in the restaurant where Miss Monroe works and further color, as do those rolling bus shots caught by the CinemaScope cameras of Milton Krasner in De Luxe Color. *Brog.*

Bigger Than Life
(C'SCOPE-COLOR)

James Mason in dramatic study of dangers of wonder drug, cortisone. Well-done.

Hollywood, Aug. 14.

20th-Fox release of James Mason production. Stars Mason, Barbara Rush, Walter Matthau; features Robert Simon, Christopher Olsen, Roland Winters, Rusty Lane, Rachel Stephens, Kipp Hamilton. Directed by Nicholas Ray. Story and screenplay, Cyril Hume, Richard Maibaum; based on a New Yorker article by Berton Rouche; camera (De Luxe Color), Joe MacDonald; editor, Louis Loeffler; music, David Raksin. Previewed Aug. 1, '56. Running time, **95 MINS.**

Ed Avery	James Mason
Lou	Barbara Rush
Wally	Walter Matthau
Dr. Norton	Robert Simon
Richie Avery	Christopher Olsen
Dr. Ruric	Roland Winters
La Porte	Rusty Lane
Nurse	Rachel Stephens
Pat Wade	Kipp Hamilton
Mrs. La Porte	Betty Caulfield
Mrs. Jones	Virginia Carroll
Mr. Jones	Henry McEvoy
Mr. Byron	Bill Jones
Joe	Dee Aaker
Freddie	Jerry Mather
Nancy	Portland Mason
Mrs. Tyndal	Natalie Masters
Milkman	Richard Collier
Dr. McLennan	Lewis Charles
Cabby	John Monoghan
Druggist	Gus Schilling
Clergyman	Alex Frazer
Mrs. Edwards	Mary-McAdoo
Salesladies	Mary Carver, Eugenia Paul
Lab Nurse	Gladys Richards
X-Ray Doctor	David Bedell
Nurse	Ann Spencer
Dr. Norton's Nurse	Nan Dolan

James Mason has picked a powerful subject for his first 20th-Fox production and delivers it with quite a bit of dramatic distinction in carrying out the supervisory duties and as the male lead subjected to a miracle drug experiment. "Bigger Than Life" exposes the good and bad in cortisone, showing it to have the potential to work great curative wonders, or to destroy physically and mentally a wrongful user. There's a certain amount of controversial material in such a subject and any pro and con that develops might be helpful at the boxoffice.

A great deal of care is taken in the forceful, realistically drafted screenplay by Cyril Hume and Richard Mailbaum to give both sides of the case, while at the same time telling a gripping, dramatic story of people that become very real under Nicholas Ray's wonder-working direction. The performances are standout under his guidance, with Barbara Rush earning particular praise for her work as Mason's troubled wife. It's an extremely moving portrayal of great depth and shading.

Mason is exceptionally fine as the modestly-circumstanced grade school teacher who undergoes a series of experiments with cortisone in the hope he can be cured of a usually fatal disease. At first the experiments progress promisingly, but he begins to overdose himself and some startling personality changes occur, building a morbid kind of suspense to the smashingly dramatic climax in which the teacher is prevented from carrying out his intention of killing his son, his wife and himself. A hopefully happy ending put a believable tag on the absorbing 95 minutes.

Christopher Olsen scores with his tremendously effective study of Mason's young son. There's no touch of moppet precociousness in his playing. Walter Matthau registers strongly as the family friend who prevents a tragic end to the story, while Robert Simon and Roland Winters are good as doctors. Rusty Lane, school principal; Kipp Hamilton, a flirty teacher; Rachel Stephens, a nurse; Lewis Charles, Gus Schilling and others lend the melodrama very good support.

The CinemaScope lensing in De Luxe Color by Joe MacDonald leads the list of a number of standout assists, which include editing by Louis Loeffler, sound by W. D. Flick and Harry M. Leonard, art direction and set decorations by Lyle R. Wheeler and Jack Martin Smith, and Walter M. Scott and Stuart A. Reiss, respectively. David Raksin's score, conducted by Lionel Newman, figures importantly. *Brog.*

The Queen of Babylon
(ITALIAN-COLOR)

Sexy spectacle starring Rhonda Fleming, Ricardo Montalban; good exploitation entry.

20th-Fox release of Pantheon Film (Nat Wachsberger) production. Stars Rhonda Fleming, Ricardo Montalban. Directed by Carlo Ludovico Bragalia. Screenplay Ennio de Concini, Giuseppe Mangione, Bragaglia from story by Maria Bory; camera (Ferraniacolor), Gabor Pogany; music, Renzo Rossellini. Tradeshown N.Y., Aug. 9, '56. Running time, **109 MINS.**

Semiramis	Rhonda Fleming
Amal	Ricardo Montalban
Assur	Roldano Lupi
Sibari	Carlo Ninchi
Lysia	Tamara Lees

Sex, scanty costumes and action are the prime ingredients of this Italian-made spectacle of pre-Biblical times. There are minor faults in the lavish Pantheon Film production but these can be overcome by an aggressive campaign for the story abounds with exploitable angles. Also an asset marqueewise are stars Rhonda Fleming and Ricardo Montalban.

Picture isn't sufficiently polished to merit much attention in the downtown deluxers, but it should mop up in subsequent runs and drive-ins if effectively sold. Dubbing of the original Italian is but fair and the dialog is occasionally stilted. While a film of this nature would have registered better pictorially in widescreen, nevertheless the movement and lusty atmosphere of ancient Babylon are adequately captured by use of the standard aspect ratio.

The Maria Bory yarn, which three scripters adapted for the screen, affords Miss Fleming a field day as far as displaying her ample proportions is concerned. For this is the legend of the Queen of Babylon to whom history attributes "every kind of extravagance and vice." Before her ascension to the throne, she was a lowly goatherder whose wants were few and tastes were simple.

But rapid changes came about when Ricardo Montalban, a dashing Chaldean warrior, took refuge in her hut from the pursuing legions of Roldano Lupi who portrays the tyrranical King of Assyria. Initially, the flaming-tressed Miss Fleming is conscripted into the ranks of the royal concubines. But she disdains both Lupi and his nefarious prime minister, Carlo Ninchi. It goes without saying that eventually Montalban overcomes adversity to install her upon the throne.

Most of Miss Fleming's contribution is confined to demonstrating her charms with a minimum of attire. To lensman Gabor Pogany's credit his Ferraniacolor camera hardly misses a contour. Montalban's performance is reminiscent of Douglas Fairbanks Sr. in his heyday for he vanquishes "hunger-crazed" crocodiles and assumes proportions of a one-man army as he swings on chandeliers, etc.

Less impressive is the thesping of Lupi and Ninchi. Former is rather colorless as the wicked king while Ninchi tends to overplay his role of the scheming royal henchman. Tamara Lees has her points as a jealous concubine who first informs upon Miss Fleming but aids her at the denouement. While things are a bit unwieldly at times, direction of Carlo Ludovico Bragaglia manages to cram copious action, femininity and suspense in the 109 minutes of footage. Score of Renzo Rossellini sets the proper mood and producer Nat Wachsberger has supplied topdrawer physical values. Print is by Technicolor.

20th-Fox, incidentally, is distributing only in the U.S. and Canada. Elsewhere in the world the film by local franchise holders. Made a couple of years ago, it originally was tagged "La Cortigiana di Babilonia" (The Courtesan of Babylon). It was also known as "Semiramis." Reportedly, the version released abroad has femme cast members wearing less than they do in the U.S. print. *Gilb.*

The First Traveling Saleslady
(COLOR—SONGS)

Ginger Rogers in hokey feminist period comedy, aided by Carol Channing and supporting tv names. Requires heavy selling.

RKO release of Arthur Lubin production, directed by Lubin. Stars Ginger Rogers, Barry Nelson, Carol Channing, David Brian, James Arness; features Clint Eastwood Robert Simon, Frank Wilcox, Daniel M. White, Harry Cheshire, John Eldredge. Screenplay, Stephen Longstreet and Devery Freeman; camera (Technicolor), William Snyder; song, Irving Gertz and Hal Levy. Tradeshown N.Y. Aug. 13, '56. Running time, **92 MINS.**

Rose Gillray	Ginger Rogers
Charles Masters	Barry Nelson
Molly Wade	Carol Channing
James Carter	David Brian
Joel Kingdom	James Arness
Jack Rice	Clint Eastwood
Cal	Robert Simon
Marshall Duncan	Frank Wilcox
Sheriff	Daniel M. White
Judge Benson	Harry Cheshire
Creavy	John Eldredge
Pete	Robert Hinkle
Dowling	Jack Rice
Annie Peachpit	Kate Drain Lawson
Theodore Roosevelt	Edward Cassidy
Schlessinger	Fred Essler

The Lancers

The first production to roll off the RKO lot under the O'Neil-O'Shea-Dozier banner is a lightweight affair that will require hard selling. It brings back Ginger Rogers in a comedy role and a host of familiar faces from tv, as well as Carol Channing essaying her first picture role. Results are disappointing, for the period comedy is cliche-ridden and the plot lines artificial and telegraphed.

The femnist angle may win some of the distaff side of the audience, but it is hard to see how this Arthur Lubin production can lift itself above the routine programmer niche.

Miss Rogers, who remains a pretty dish, does not help matters in her projection of the first-saleslady role, adopting a nasal twang as a voice characteristic. The comedy, dealing with Miss Rogers' tribulations in selling what ordinarily would be incongruous items —corsets and barbed wire—veers close to out-and-out burlesque. Scenes are replete with stock Injuns, stock western characters and situations, and numerous visual gags. Even "Teddy Roosevelt," played by Edward Cassidy, and the Prince of Wales are brought in out of left field. Producer-director Arthur Lubin, who did the "Francis" series, adopted the same bald strokes for this one, with similar hokey effects.

The broad story lines finds Miss Rogers in the period of the Gay Nineties trying to retrieve her bankrupt corset business by branching out into barbed wire selling down Texas way. Every man who tried before had been strung up by the free range advocates. She's aided by her sidekick legiter Carol Channing who, during the course of the events, belts out one number, "A Corset Can Do a Lot for a Lady," for moderate results. Irving Gertz did the music, with lyrics by Hal Levy.

The featured males are associated with tv: Barry Nelson, of "My Favorite Husband" telefilm series, plays a transcontinental autoist who finally wins Miss Rogers; David Brian, of "Mr. District Attorney," is the steel tycoon; and James Arness, of "Gunsmoke," is the Texas baron, a heavy with a heart. The players acquit themselves competently, considering the vehicle, scripted by Stephen Longstreet and Devery Freeman.

The Technicolor enriches the Gay Nineties sets and throws life on the screen, when the locale moves to Texas. The production budget appears on the modest side. The title song, "The First Traveling Saleslady," sung by The Lancers at the intro and curtain adequately sets the mood. *Horo.*

Bandido
(C'SCOPE-COLOR)

Far-fetching tale of 1916 gunrunning in Mexico. But divertingly treated and actionful. Good outlook.

Hollywood, Aug. 14.

United Artists release of Robert L. Jacks (Bandido) production. Stars Robert Mitchum, Ursula Thiess, Gilbert Roland, Zachary Scott; features Rodolfo Acosta, Henry Brandon, Douglas Fowley. Directed by Richard Fleischer. Screenplay, Earl Felton; camera (De Luxe Color), Ernest Laszlo; editor, Robert Golden; music, Max Steiner. Previewed Aug. 6, '56. Running ime, **91 MINS.**

Wilson	Robert Mitchum
Lisa	Ursula Thiess
Escobar	Gilbert Roland
Kennedy	Zachary Scott
Sebastion	Rodolfo Acosta
Gonzalez	Jose I. Torvay
Gunther	Henry Brandon
McGhee	Douglas Fowley
Lorenzo	Victor Junco
G. Brucero	Alfonso Sanchez Tello
Adolfo	Arturo Manrique
Driver	Jose A. Espinosa
Santos	Margarito Luna
Priest	Miguel Inclan
Man in Wagon	Jose Munoz
Manager	Manuel Sanchez Navarro
Indian Boy	Antonio Sandoval
Scout	Alberto Pedret

Gun-running in Mexico back in 1916 sets up a round of adventurous action for this United Artists release. It has the kind of fanciful movement, lush settings via its on-the-spot lensing below the border in CinemaScope and De Luxe Color, and marquee names that mean a good playoff in the regular market.

Robert Mitchum is a likeable not always understandable, sort of hero-heavy in the Earl Felton plot who likes war because it gives him a chance to make some money gunrunning, besides finding amusement in his profession. While the yarn is a dime thriller, it also presented with some above-average touches here and there, plus some extremely frank birds-and-bees byplay between Mitchum and the heroine, Ursula Thiess, that adds spice to the action. Film has its slow spots, mostly due to occasionally draggy direction by Richard Fleischer and a need of tighter editing. For its market, though, the flaws are minor.

In addition to Mitchum, the male end of the cast draws notable help from the presence of Gilbert Roland, leader of the rebels for whom the gun-runner is trying to obtain arms, for money naturally, by hijacking a shipment being brought in by Zachary Scott for the Regulares. It takes some doing, and quite a bit of bloodshed, before the rebels get the arms. Windup finds Mitchum taking, insterd of the money he likes, Miss Thiess, the unhappy wife of Scott who becomes a w'dow before the shooting is over.

Below-the-border locationing was a wise move on the part of producer Robert L. Jacks, giving the picture any number of strikingly beautiful scenes as lensed by Ernest Laszlo. In addition to the foursome already named, acting assists come from Douglas Fowley, in a good bit; Henry Brandon, aide to a well-played Mexican officer; Rodolfo Acosta and Jose I. Torvay, two colorful Mexican rebel-rogues. Other native players react well, too. Max Steiner's background score inject a Latin flavor and there's a snatch of a title tune heard here and there. *Brog.*

Showdown At Abilene
(COLOR)

Well-made, well-played western.

Hollywood, Aug. 14.

Universal release of Howard Christie production. Stars Jock Mahoney, Martha Hyer, Lyle Bettger; features David Janssen, Grant Williams, Ted de Corsia, Harry Harvey Sr. Directed by Charles Haas. Screenplay, Berne Giler; story, Clarence Upson Young; camera, Irving Glassberg; editor, Ray Snyder; music supervision, Joseph Gershenson. Previewed Aug. 7, '56. Running time, **80 MINS.**

Jim Trask	Jock Mahoney
Peggy Bigelow	Martha Hyer
Dave Mosely	Lyle Bettger
Verne Ward	David Janssen
Chip Tomlin	Grant Williams
Dan Claudius	Ted de Corsia
Ross Bigelow	Harry Harvey Sr.
Jack Bedford	Dayton Lummis
Nelson	Richard H. Cutting
Sprague	Robert G. Anderson
Frank Scovie	John Maxwell
Loop	Lane Bradford

A standard western plot undergoes a good polishing job in "Showdown at Abilene," making it an interesting actioner. Via excellent playing, sound direction and a script that makes its characters believable, film comes off as good entertainment for the playdates at which it is aimed.

Jock Mahoney, former sheriff of Abilene, returns from the Civil War gunshy and with a troubled conscience to find an old friend has won his girl and is taking over the range from the farmers. On that plot from the Clarence Upson Young story, Berne Giler builds a logical series of events for principals Mahoney, Martha Hyer and Lyle Bettger to enact under Charles Haas' firstrate direction.

By the time the climax comes around, Mahoney has righted his troubled conscience (he'd accidentally killed Bettger's young brother in the war) gets back his gun hand and rewins his girl, all to the tune of an actionful pace that moves along but still finds the time to make things believable.

Cast in the good Howard Christie production is an excellent one. Mahoney comes over well as the hero, giving the character a bit more than just the usual strong man handling. Miss Hyer is a gracious heroine with ability above the level into which most sagebrush femmes fall. Bettger is a topnotch heavy, underplaying it for additional menace. Among the others who help keep the footage entertaining are David Janssen, Grant Williams, two improving young male actors; Ted de Corsia and Harry Harvey Sr.

Technicolor lensing by Irving Glassberg achieves some smart pictorial values, while editing, background music and other work is good. *Brog.*

A Cry In the Night

Poorly - done meller about young girl kidnapped by psychopath; familiar names to offset production mediocrity.

Hollywood, Aug. 14.

Warner Bros. release of George C. Bertholon (Jaguar) production. Stars Edmond O'Brien, Brian Donlevy, Natalie Wood; features Raymond Burr, Richard Anderson, Irene Hervey, Carol Veazie. Directed by Frank Tuttle. Screenplay, David Dortort; based on a novel by Whit Masterson; camera, John Seitz; editor, Folmar Blangsted; music, David Buttolph. Previewed July 31, '56. Running time, **75 MINS.**

Taggart	Edmond O'Brien
Bates	Brian Donlevy
Liz	Natalie Wood
Loftus	Raymond Burr
Owen	Richard Anderson
Helen	Irene Hervey
Mrs. Loftus	Carol Veazie
Madge	Mary Lawrence
Chavez	Anthony Caruso
Gerrity	George J. Lewis
Dr. Frazee	Peter Hanson
Marie Holzapple	Tina Carver
Jensen	Herb Vigran

It will have to be the familiar cast names that carry "A Cry in the Night" through its programmer playdates because there's little in the way of entertainment to recommend.

The Jaguar production supervised by George C. Bertholon is a poorly-executed melodrama involving the kidnapping of a young girl by a psychopathic mama's boy. David Dortort's scripting fails to develop the suspense and excitement needed to carry such a plot, and Frank Tuttle's direction can make very little of the unbelievable characters and situations. The cast is similarly handicapped.

Natalie Wood is the teenager who's kidnapped by peeping-tom Raymond Burr after the latter knocks out her fiance, Richard Anderson, in a lover's lane incident. She's the daughter of Edmond O'Brien, too-stern father, but first-class police captain, and the forces of law and order are turned loose under the direction of another police officer, Brian Donlevy, to run down the kidnapper before he can harm the girl. They catch up with Burr and his victim in an abandoned brick yard and a few blows to the chin reduces the kidnapper to a blubbering hulk, crying pitifully for his mama.

Seen as O'Brien's wife is Irene Hervey, while Mary Lawrence plays his old-maid sister. Carol Veazie appears as Burr's mother. One fairly bright spot in an otherwise dull show is the jail house scene involving the booking of Tina Carver, a lady of easy virtue. Photography by John Seitz and the other technical credits are standard.

The Amazon Trader
(COLOR)

Documentary-type featurette, enacting tales of the Amazon. Well done. Replacement for regular lowercase features.

Hollywood, Aug. 14.

Warner Bros. release of Cedric Francis production. Stars John Sutton: features Maria Fernanda, Zygmunt Sulistrowski, Anthony Ryan, Guido Wolff, Janet Albuquerque, Yves Manciet, Maitland Stewart, Therenzena Prates da Costa, Padre Agostinho Liebst. Directed by Tom McGowan. Written by Owen Crump; camera (WarnerColor), Anthony J. Ryan, Maitland Stewart; editor, Leo Shreve; music, Howard Jackson. Previewed Aug. 8, '56. Running time, **42 MINS.**

The Amazon Trader .... John Sutton
Ex-Wife .... Maria Fernanda
Fairing .... Zygmunt Sulistrowski
Explorer .... Anthony Ryan
Fat Man .... Guido Wolff
Wife .... Janet Albuquerque
Laban .... Yves Manciet
Mr. Dollson .... Maitland Stewart
Mrs. Dollson
Therenzena Prates da Costa
Missionary ...... Padre Agostinho Liebst

Warner Bros. launches a new series of featurettes of approximately 42 minutes for bookings as a replacement for the usual lowercase feature. In the instance of "The Amazon Trader," the novelty is such that viewers will find it an interesting account of several tales native to that jungle region. It's a good, and different, supporter for regular dual bills.

Four such tales are strung together in this Cedric Francis production under Tom McGowan's direction, with John Sutton, in the title role doing the narration while assorted players, mostly non-pro recruits, enact the Owen Crump script. Locales are authentic, with the WarnerColor lensing by Anthony J. Ryan and Maitland Stewart being responsible for many vivid scenes of jungle life, waterways, even some half-nude natives of both sexes.

First tale finds Zgymunt Sulistrowski, medical student, getting himself lost in the jungle and then being rescued and miraculously cured of fever by native witch doctors. The second, the trek of Anthony Ryan and Maria Fernanda into the jungle in search of a mysterious tribe, never gets anywhere, because the couple is forced back before ending the search. Third has Maitland Stewart and Therezena Prates da Costa playing a man and wife, he a naturalist and she a game hunter. Sequence in which she saves a native boy from the deadly Piranha has its excitement. Fourth tells the most story, dealing with Yves Manciet, a thief and murderer escaped from Devil's Island who doublecrosses the Indians who take him in and has his head shrunk for the dirty work.

Footage was shot entirely in the South American Amazon region, with Sulistrowski handling the production supervision in that country. Editing by Leo Shreve and the music by Howard Jackson are okay. *Brog.*

War and Peace
(Italian-U. S.)
(COLOR-V'VISION)

A blockbuster destined to be a perennial cinematic classic.

Paramount release of Ponti-DeLaurentiis production, produced by Dino DeLaurentiis. Stars Audrey Hepburn, Henry Fonda, Mel Ferrer; costars Vittorio Gassman; features Herbert Lom, Oscar Homolka, Anita Ekberg, Helmut Dantine, Barry Jones, Anna Maria Ferrero, Milly Vitale, Jeremy Brett, John Mills. Directed by King Vidor. Based on Leo Tolstoy's novel. Screenplay, Bridget Boland, Robert Westerby, King Vidor, Mario Camerini, Ennio DeConcini, Ivo Perilli; camera (Technicolor), Jack Cardiff; 2d unit camera, Aldo Tonti; art direction, Mario Chari, Fraz Bachelin, Giani Polidori; editors, Stuart Gilmore, Leo Catozzo; sound editor, Leslie Hodgson; music, Nino Rota; music conductor, Franco Ferrara; costumes, Maria DeMatteis; sets, Piero Cherardi; production mgr. Bruno Todini; prod. asst. N. Y., Ralphe Serpe; dialog, Guy Thomajan; asst. to Vidor, Arthur Fellows; asst. directors, Piero Musetta, Guidarino Guidi. World premiere Aug. 21, '56, Capitol Theatre, N. Y. Running time, **3 Hours 28 MINS.**

Natasha .... Audrey Hepburn
Pierre .... Henry Fonda
Andrey .... Mel Ferrer
Anatole .... Vittorio Gassman
Helene .... Anita Ekberg
General Kutuzov .... Oscar Homolka
Napoleon .... Herbert Lam
Platon .... John Mills
Dolokhov .... Helmut Dantine
Lise .... Milly Vitale
Count Rostov .... Barry Jones
Prince Bolkonsky ..... Wilfred Lawson
Countess Rostov .... Lea Seidel
Nicholas Rostov .... Jeremy Brett
Petya Rostov .... Sean Barrett
Mary Bolkonsky.....Anna Maria Ferrero
Sonya .... May Britt
Kuragin .... Tullio Carminati
Denisov ....Patrick Crean
Peronskava ....Gertrude Flynn

The classic Leo Nicholas Tolstoy novel, "War and Peace," said by many to be the greatest ever written, took six years to create its more than 600,000 words in 1869. Long after the historic Russo-French military campaigns of 1805-1812, millions the world over have been afforded an insight on Napoleon Bonaparte of France versus Czar Nicholas I of Russia, perhaps as no history books have done. A century and half after the event, Hollywood and Italian know-how, some $6,000,000 capital investment, and an overwhelming production personnel which, in the recreated battle scenes utilized between 5,000 and 6,000 Italian troops doubling as celluloid soldiers, have produced a visual epic that is assured of permanent stature in the annals of the motion picture industry.

"War and Peace" is a real blockbuster. This is not a celluloid entry for once or even twice around. It is a rich contribution to the art form of the picture business in the best tradition. It is an entertainment and educational force and a production powerhouse on size and stature values alone. It is big in the biggest sense of the cinematurgical art and, in this alone, there is a payoff.

"War and Peace," the novel, was timely at all times and timeless throughout epochs and eras. This was never truer than now. Because, as at no time before has the world known the fast-moving means of communication as exists today, the meaning of world strife takes on new values. The graphic Dino DeLaurentiis production and King Vidor direction of this Italian-made Paramount release reduces the meaning of war—and peace—to the most common denominator of everyday understanding.

The classic Tolstoy novel which requires weeks and, more often, months to read has been digested into three and a half hours of vivid cinematic magic in the topmost scientific advances (Technicolor and VistaVision).

These factors are garnished with a marquee that reads like a benefit and a production investiture that looks like Fort Knox. For once it's a production that looks more than its $6,000,000 investment.

"War and Peace" may not be the perfect motion picture. What is? There are opportunities for the captious to become caustic. Some of the opportunities are perhaps DeLaurentiis' and Vidor's own faults, such as that heavily-cockneyed John Mills personation, quite a discordant dialog note in the general unfolding.

There may be some who will want to know what or, at the very least, profess confusion as to whom he or she can identify themselves with. There may be some who will concede the power and the artistry of the pictorial Technicolorful vignettes, some of which hold compelling beauty (both in splendor and simplicity), and yet wonder if it isn't too episodic. Some also may find their interest lagging in the long dialog stretches and the genteel pleasantries of the period.

The greater wonder is that such a monumental work could be condensed to three and a half hours. It may not be long before it penetrates to the public that almost as much footage had to be scrapped, and to this the carpingly captious may testily add then why not a few more feet if it creates a discordancy? In short order and with **relative simplicity this can be fully ascertained and, if needs be, corrected.**

Paramount has a merchandising problem which may compel revision or modification of original plan. Wisely, it is selling "War and Peace" with a forthright accent that this is a long picture—three hours and 28 minutes long. That it is being shown on a grind in a Broadway deluxer, instead of reserved-seat roadshowing, may or may not be concomitant to the fact that Par's DeMillepic, "10 Commandments," is somewheres in the offing. Public reaction can well shift "War and Peace" into an advanced-priced, two-a-dayer because it has all the attributes of a roadshow.

The wonder of the DeLaurentiis-Vidor production is that it has maintained cohesiveness and fluidity of story and also has given fullest accent to the size and sweep of Bonaparte's armies at Austerlitz and Borodino. Life among the Russian aristocracy with its passion for the good living and innate respect for the church in time of stress is brought into sharp focus in a pyramiding sequence of grand balls, gay life, debauchery, titled officers' shenanigans, the riding to the hounds in pastoral terrains, and with it all a not complete disregard for their serfs.

Audrey Hepburn is the epitome of wholesome young love under benevolent aristocratic rearing. Henry Fonda, the confused young liberal who aped the French as so many Russians did until Napoleon forced the czar's armies to resort to a scorched earth campaign, is perhaps sometimes too literally the confused character. The scenes where he, a civilian, wanders and weaves in and out of the crude battery of bombardiers manning the buttress make one wonder if a little pruning here would not be to advantage.

The ranking members of the proud Count Rostov and Prince Bolkonsky clans and their lineage have all been accorded capital histrionic investiture to match the many-splendored life, love and trappings under the imperial czaristic regime until Napoleon's would-be conquerors invaded the Russian steppes.

Other than the above and the moody but compelling performance by Mel Ferrer, the rest are lesser roles but almost wholly effective. The assorted in-laws, kin, friends, aristocracy, along with Napoleon (Herbert Lom), the opportunistic Anita Ekberg, the predatory Vittorio Gassman, Oscar Homolka as the Russian commander-in-chief and Barry Jones are done with more or less conviction. True, sometimes the English dialects make for a curious infidelity of speech. Homolka is very Akim Tamiroff as the Russian general but some of his aides speak in clipped British English. That is true also of Napoleon, as played by Herbert Lom. Some of the lesser principals, of native Italian lineage, also found themselves dubbed into British English. But these are among the relatively minor footnotes in this major production of size and realism and grandeur which easily qualifies it for the cinema hall of fame.

The majesty of Jack Cardiff's masterful lensing is not the least of the credits. Whether in the soft pastels of the pastoral scenes or in the brilliant hues of the grand ball; whether in the eye-filling sweep of gallant, fresh troops on battle plains or the bleak despair of footsore, retreating Frenchmen slogging in the mire of defeat; whether in the rich and colorful palace interiors or those arresting shots of snow-covered trees against the scorched earth, the American director, King Vidor, the Italian producer, DeLaurentiis, and the peerless British cinematographer Cardiff have restored to the Italian film industry a long forgotten tradition. It is the tradition of size and spectacle and splendor. It is Technicolor at its artistic peak.

So vivid has been the postwar Italian school of drab realism that the world has almost forgotten the epochal sweep of the once Italian standard of motion picture production which has still not completely removed the memory of a "Cabiria." With "War and Peace" the artisans have recaptured the epic canvas which was indigenous to the Italian school.

The film's scripting credits are a strangely multiple thing in light of Irwin Shaw's request to remove his billing when director Vidor reportedly rewrote so many scenes on his own. But to whomever true billing belongs, the screenwriting chore was a yeoman job for a battery of scriveners. The celluloid transmutation of Tolstoy is nothing from which anybody need hide identity. In fact, "War and Peace" has credits in plenty for all concerned. *Abel.*

The Unguarded Moment
(COLOR)

Esther Williams, sans bathing suit, in psychological sex melodrama. Slickly-produced, generally satisfactory entry.

Universal release of Gordon Kay production. Stars Esther Williams & George Nader; features John Saxon, Edward Andrews, Les Tremayne. Directed by Harry Keller. Screenplay, Herb Meadows and Larry Marcus; based on story by Rosalind Russell and Marcus; camera (Technicolor), William Daniels; editor, Edward Curtiss; music, Herman Stein. Previewed in N.Y. Aug. 16, '56. Running time, **95 MINS.**

Lois Conway .... Esther Williams
Harry Graham .... George Nader

Having severed with Metro, Esther Williams, in her first freelance outing, essays a straight dramatic role without jumping into a pool, going near the water, or even donning a bathing suit. The result is on the plus side, for the bathing suit-less and dry Miss Williams emerges as a competent and appealing performer without the aquatic accoutrements.

In the slickly-filmed Gordon Kay production, having the typical Universal polish (as identifiable with the film company as popular magazine fiction), Miss Williams portrays a high school teacher involved in a psychological sex melodrama. The story is also out of the pop magazine hopper, but it is agreeably presented and sufficiently suspenseful to place it a notch above the norm. Theatres that play Universal product will find "The Unguarded Moment" a generally satisfactory entry.

In addition to presenting a grounded Miss Williams, the film marks Rosalind Russell's debut as an author, the actress having written the original story in collaboration with Larry Marcus who, in turn, co-scripted the screenplay with Herb Meadows.

Universal, as most film companies, is seeking a performer to assume the mantle of the late James Dean. As its contender, it is offering John Saxon, a young graduate of its talent development school who is receiving the "introducing" treatment in "Unguarded Moment."

Saxon is seen as a handsome, brawny and brainy football hero who despite his many assets is outwardly girl shy. He turns out, however, to be the writer of mash notes and a night prowler criminally inclined to assault woman. Miss Williams, as a shapely, attractive music teacher, is a victim. Her efforts to protect the school and the mixed-up youth backfire and she finds herself charged with encouraging the boy, resulting in her suspension from the school.

Her attempts at clearance and reinstatement are aided by George Nader, young police lieutenant who also eyes Miss Williams romantically. The boy's sexual problem is traced to his demented father whose values are twisted by his wife's desertion.

Saxon no doubt, will have a degree of appeal among femme teenagers, but he has a long way to go before he can be compared to Dean. Nader is smoothly efficient as the police lieutenant. Edward Andrews, as the unctuous, overprotecting father, and Les Tremayne, as the confused high school principal expertly put across their roles.

Harry Keller's direction succeeds in eliciting the maximum suspense elements. William Daniels' camera work and the technical aspects of the production, as stated previously, are slick and polished. *Holl.*

The Boss

Strong exploitation picture headed for hefty returns during the election period.

Hollywood, Aug. 18.
United Artists release of Frank Seltzer (Walter Seltzer associate) production. Stars John Payne; costars William Bishop, Gloria McGhee, Doe Avedon. Directed by Byron Haskin. Screenplay, Ben Perry; camera, Hal Mohr; editor, Ralph Dawson; music, Albert Glasser. Previewed Aug. 17, '56. Running time, **88 MINS.**

"The Boss" is a hard-hitting melo of the rise and fall of an unscrupulous political boss, with controversial overtones to give it a particularly strong exploitation hook. Film's subject and release during the current political consciousness step up its chances to pay off heftily in the general market as well as program situations.

Producer Frank Seltzer has thinly veiled the Tom Pendergast regime of Kansas City infamy to backdrop his narrative, which Byron Haskin directs for punchy effect. Yarn unfolds in what is subtitled "a middle-class city," but enough of the Kansas City story and its political boss are there to lend honesty of purpose, including the so-called Union Station "massacre" of G-men. Even the entry into politics of a counterpart of Harry S. Truman is inserted, for those who would recognize him. In the title role, John Payne departs from his customary heroics to undertake an unsympathetic characterization, and comes off realistically.

The Ben Perry screenplay opens with Payne returning from World War I to the town where his elder brother is the boss. Upon latter's sudden death, Payne, hard and ambitious, takes over, and the years see his rise to such power that he virtually controls the entire state. Aiding him in his upward stride is William Bishop, a boyhood pal who becomes his legal arm. His high-handed and roughshod methods bring on a wave of reform, which gets nowhere, apparently, until Payne's tie-in with a mob in the rackets leads to his final downfall and he's put away on an income tax-evasion rap.

Payne registers impressively, particularly in the later phases of the picture, when he begins to age, and gets smooth assistance from Bishop as the man finally responsible for his conviction. Gloria McGhee is excellent as Payne's wife, whom he marries while on a drunk after the girl he loves, Doe Avedon, refuses to see him when he stands her up. Miss Avedon in her brief appearances also is good, as is Roy Roberts, Payne's brother. Robin Morse, the gang leader whose men get trigger-happy while trying to rescue a pal from Government men at the Union Station, is a particular standout. Joe Flynn enacts the Truman character.

Technical credits are first class, including photography by Hal Mohr, Albert Glasser's score and Ralph Dawson's tight editing. Walter Seltzer functions as associate producer. *Whit.*

Canyon River
(C'SCOPE—COLOR)

George Montgomery in okay western for general outdoor trade.

Hollywood, Aug. 10.
Allied Artists release of Richard Heermance production. Stars George Montgomery, Marcia Henderson, Peter Graves, Richard Eyer; features Walter Sande, Robert Wilke, Alan Hale, John Harmon, Jack Lambert, William Fawcett. Directed by Harmon Jones. Story and screenplay, Daniel B. Ullman; camera (De Luxe Color), Ellsworth Fredricks; editor, George White; music, Marlin Skiles. Previewed Aug. 3, '56. Running time, **79 MINS.**

This is about a cattle drive in reverse—the herd's being taken from Oregon back to Wyoming. To further upset western tradition, there's a gal along as trial cook. Not much else has a twist, though, so it comes out as an okay outdoor feature toplining George Montgomery for attention in the action market.

The Scott R. Dunlap presentation, produced by Richard Heermance, keeps a close eye on the budget in spots by using some trail herd stock shots that don't match at all well with the newer footage that is ably lensed in CinemaScope and De Luxe Color by Ellsworth Fredricks. Other than this incongruous touch, though, Harmon Jones' direction of the Daniel B. Ullman screen story, keeps the picture playing at an interesting pace with generally good performances to help.

Montgomery is the rancher. Longhorns are a drug on the market in Wyoming so he schemes to import some Herefords from Oregon and crossbreed a tough, new stock. His forman, Peter Graves, apparently goes along with the plan, but plots to take over himself at trail's end via joining forces with Walter Sande in a rustling deal that will eliminate Montgomery—fatally. During the rugged trail trek, though, his boss proves such a good Joe that Graves has a change of heart and gets himself killed breaking up the rustling job, leaving Montgomery to start his new herd with the help of the pretty, widowed cook, warmly played by Marcia Henderson, and her small son. Richard Eyer.

Montgomery capably goes about the hero chores and Graves is excellent as his scheming partner. Eyer is an engaging youngster, while Walter Sande and Robert Wilke are forthright heavies. Alan Hale, John Harmon, Jack Lambert and William Fawcett are colorful as the cut-throat crew Montgomery corrals for the trail drive.

Marlin Skiles' score, editing and other technical assists are okay. *Brog.*

Child in the House
(BRITISH)

Tearjerker about unhappy child loyally withholding information about her father, hunted by police.

London, Aug. 14.
Eros release of a Golden Era production. Stars Phyllis Calvert, Eric Portman, Stanley Baker, with Mandy Miller. Directed by C. Raker Endfield. Screenplay by C. Raker Endfield from novel by Janet McNeill; camera, Otto Heller; editor, Charles Hasse; music, Mario Nascimbene. At Leicester Square Theatre, London. Running time, **90 MINS.**

It is rare that the filming of a novel captures the same atmosphere of a book, unless in expert hands regarding scripting, direction and casting. In this case it is most likely the adaptors who are at fault, the result being somewhat slipshod. Modest entertainment is suited to a double bill here. It is a conventional tearjerker of a child's loyalty to a worthless father, ending in his final conversion.

Mandy Miller, who won immediate fame as the dumb child in "Mandy" some years back, has an emotional, frustrating role as an 11-year-old niece in the temporary care of her aunt and uncle. Her mother is hospitalized and her father is away on some mysterious Continental errand.

The aunt never reaches first base with the child, her barrister husband drawing together the only threads of understanding between them. The warmhearted housemaid provides the simplest human contact for the lonely girl, fretting for her mother and dimly aware of her father's criminal activities. He meets her secretly, exacting a promise she will not disclose his presence in London. Thereafter, the girl is torn between lying subterfuge and the desperate need to meet her father.

In the early stages the dialog is scrappy, and does little to impress the basic facts. The barrister accuses his wife of hating the child because of their own loveless and fruitless union. His brother-in-law had robbed him while working in his firm, but there seems no logical reason for his crookedness, except a love of luxury, travel and an aptitude to form phoney companies.

With a minimum of dialog, Mandy arouses sympathy for the forlorn, defiant child. Phyllis Calvert subtly conveys the underlying malice behind the aunt's apparent solicitude. Eric Portman is wasted as her husband, with little to do but offer frigid politeness to his wife, and mute alliance with the youngster. Stanley Baker makes a mixed personality of the crooked father, his characterization being more realistic in the later reels when he is on the run. Dora Bryan brings a breath of cockney joyousness to the role of the sympathetic housemaid, livening the otherwise stilted atmosphere. *Clem.*

Eyewitness
(BRITISH)

Compact, standard thriller of a murderer's attempt to get at an injured witness to prevent identification; Donald Sinden, turned crook, lacks conviction.

London, Aug. 14.

Rank production (Sydney Box) and release. Stars Donald Sinden, Muriel Pavlow, Belinda Lee. Directed by Muriel Box. Screenplay, Janet Green; camera, Reginald Wyer; editor, Jean Barker; music, Bruce Montgomery. At Dominion Theatre, London. Running time, **82 MINS.**

Wade .... Donald Sinden
Lucy .... Muriel Pavlow
Penny .... Belinda Lee
Jay .... Michael Craig
Barney .... Nigel Stock
Probationer Nurse ......Susan Beaumont
Mike .... David Knight
Mrs. Hudson .... Aida Reeve
Night Sister .... Avis Landone
Anaesthetist .... Richard Wattis
Patrolman .... George Woodridge
Molly .... Gillian Harrison
House Surgeon .... Nicholas Parsons
Henry Cammon .... Leslie Dwyer
Mrs. Hays .... Anna Turner
Podge .... Anthony Oliver
Chief Constable .... John Stuart
Det. Inspector .... Alan Cuthbertson
Sugdon .... Harry Towb

A neatly made, unpretentious thriller that should do well for the home market. A murderer's attempt to kill a woman who witnessed his crime makes for suspenseful action, although the story is improbable in some of its twists. Pic is well acted and well served by its director and camera crew.

Following a fight with her newlywed husband, a young woman leaves home with the threat she won't return. While at the cinema, she sees the manager struck down by his opened safe, and is chased by one of the thieves. The terrified girl dashes into the street and is knocked down by a bus. From then on the two haunt the hospital grounds in an attempt to silence her before she can gain consciousness and identify them. The various efforts to gain admittance to the building arouse both tension and humor.

The husband's frantic search for his wife ends in the police arrival at the hospital just as the second thief, jibbing at another murder, kills his partner to save the girl's life.

Donald Sinden doesn't sit too happily in the unusual badman role but Nigel Stock, as his reluctant accomplice, gives the best performance of all. Muriel Pavlow has little to do but register terror as the eyewitness. Belinda Lee spills over with appealing glamor as her nurse. Vet legiter Ada Reeve injects some down-to-earth humor as an inquisitive patient whose claim to having seen the prowler is ignored by everyone until his mission is almost accomplished.

Clem.

The Young Guns

Mild oater based on juve delinquency theme.

Hollywood, Aug. 17.
Allied Artists release of Richard Heermance production. Stars Russ Tamblyn, Gloria Talbott. Directed by Albert Band. Screenplay, Louis Garfinkle; camera, Ellsworth Fredricks; editor, George White; song, Marlin Skiles; music, Lenny Adelson & Imogen Carpenter, sung by Guy Mitchell. Previewed Aug. 17, '56. Running time, 84 MINS.

Tully .... Russ Tamblyn
Nora .... Gloria Talbott
San Antone .... Perry Lopez
Knox Cutler .... Scott Marlowe
Jonesy .... Wright King
Peyton .... Walter Coy
Grandpa .... Chubby Johnson
Deputy Nix .... Myron Healey
Georgie .... James Goodwin
Kid Cutler .... Rayford Barnes
Felix Briggs .... Stanford Jolley

"The Young Guns" is a story of juvenile delinquency on the range. As a straight out-and-out western it lacks the shoot-'em-up elements the title suggests, and leans more on the character side of a young man trying to live down the reputation of his vicious gunman-father. As a consequence there are long intervals of dialog sans action, the footage occasionally inserting a fight. Sum total adds up to a mild entry for the oater market.

Richard Heermance production picks up Russ Tamblyn as he leaves a small Wyoming settlement, outlaw hangout, where a group of young would-be gunslingers are eager to follow in the footsteps of their fugitive elders. After he beats a couple of the leaders, Tamblyn is regarded their leader but can't make up his mind whether to become active. Climax has him breaking up a band robbery performed by gang without his knowledge.

Tamblyn is rather lightweight for his role but manages a more or less persuasive performance. Gloria Talbott, his co-star, provides the romantic interest as daughter of an outlaw. In support, standouts include Walter Coy, a kindly sheriff who tries to befriend Tamblyn; Scott Marlowe and Perry Lopez, young gunmen; and Chubby Johnson, former outlaw still dwelling in the glory of the past.

Albert Band makes the most of the overlength Louis Garfinkle screenplay in his direction, and technical credits are standard. Guy Mitchell warbles "Song of the Young Guns" over title credits.

Whit.

The Last Wagon
(C'SCOPE-COLOR)

Suspenseful class western, good indications for general market.

Hollywood, Aug. 23.
20th-Fox release of William B. Hawks production. Stars Richard Widmark; features Felicia Farr, Susan Kohner, Tommy Rettig. Directed by Delmer Daves. Screenplay, James Edward Grant, Daves, Gwen Bagni Gielgud; story, Gielgud; camera (De Luxe Color), Wilfrid Cline; editor, Hugh S. Fowler; music, Lionel Newman. Tradeshown Aug. 23, '56. Running time, 98 MINS.

Todd .... Richard Widmark
Jenny .... Felicia Farr
Jolie .... Susan Kohner
Billy .... Tommy Rettig
Valinda .... Stephanie Griffin
Clint .... Ray Stricklyn
Ridge .... Nick Adams
General Howard........Carl Benton Reid
Col. Normand .... Douglas Kennedy
Bull Harper .... George Mathews
Lt. Kelly .... James Drury
Sergeant .... Ken Clark
Cole Harper .... Timothy Carey
Sarge .... George Ross
Mrs. Clinton .... Juney Ellis
Apache Medicine Man....Abel Fernandez

The mounting menace of Indian attack as the survivors of a wagon train massacre make their way through hostile Apache country provides stirring motivation for this excellent William B. Hawks production. Its suspenseful plot and rugged characterization by Richard Widmark as a Comanche-reared white man are admirably backdropped by the magnificent Northern Arizona scenery caught via CinemaScope and DeLuxe Color, and film should find sturdy payoff in the general market.

Pic tees off studio's new policy of presenting fresh young talent. Widmark is only marquee name in cast, but feature benefits by the new faces, each of whom turns in a capital job. Under Delmer Daves' shrewd direction, film comes off as an interesting enterprise far off the beaten path of routine westerns and emerges a class affair which 20th expects to exploit as a blockbuster.

Story gets under way when Widmark, who has killed three men, is captured by a brutal sheriff and pair join a wagon train. After the Apaches wipe out all but the occupants of one wagon and leave Widmark for dead, he takes on the task of leading these survivors, all in their teens, to safety, the chain of events making for exciting unfoldment as they try to elude the lurking redskins.

Widmark is seen in a forceful role, a man who killed to avenge the murder of his Comanche wife and two sons, and has none of the refinements of civilization until he meets Felicia Farr, who with her young brother, Tommy Rettig, is one of the survivors. One of film's highlights is his knife fight with two Apaches, done realistically and in keeping with Widmark's character throughout the film.

Miss Farr leads off the lineup of new talent and makes an engaging impression, as does young Rettig in his hero-worship of Widmark. Susan Kohner scores as the half-breed sister of Stephanie Griffin, an interesting newcomer, and Nick Adams and Ray Stricklyn both show promise. George Mathews is standout as the sheriff, finally killed by Widmark for his cruelty, and Douglas Kennedy is good in his brief appearance as head of the wagon train, father of Susan and Stephanie.

Technical end of the picture is above average in every department, as is the screenplay by James Edward Grant, Delmer Daves and Gwen Bagni Gielgud, adapted from latter's original. Wilfrid Cline's color photography is striking as he trains his lens for fine effect upon the Sedona background; Lionel Newman's music helps maintain mood and suspense; Hugh S. Fowler's editing is sharp.

Whit.

Back From Eternity

Jungle crash mello okay for general trade.

Hollywood, Aug. 25.
RKO release of John Farrow production, directed by Farrow. Stars Robert Ryan, Anita Ekberg, Rod Steiger; co-stars Phyllis Kirk, Keith Andes, Gene Barry; features Fred Clark, Beulah Bondi, Cameron Prud'homme, Jesse White, Adele Mara, Jon Provost. Screenplay, Jonathan Latimer; story, Richard Carroll; camera, William Mellor; editor, Eda Warren; music, Franz Waxman. Previewed Aug. 24, '56. Running time, 97 MINS.

Bill .... Robert Ryan
Rena .... Anita Ekberg
Vasquel .... Rod Steiger
Louise ,................ Phyllis Kirk
Joe .... Keith Andes
Ellis .... Gene Barry
Crimp .... Fred Clark
Martha .... Beulah Bondi
Henry .... Cameron Prud'homme
Pete .... Jesse White
Maria .... Adele Mara
Tommy .... Jon Provost

This remake of RKO's 1939 release, "Five Came Back," generates good melodrama as plottage follows what happens when a plane is forced down in the South American jungle. Film's familiar yarn is sparked by strong handling of situations and persuasively-enacted characters, sum total leading to hefty chances in the general market, where Robert Ryan and Rod Steiger's names hold meaning.

Picture is first of three which John Farrow, who also directed, will turn out for RKO as producer-director. Farrow inserts plenty of realism both in the crash sequence, when Ryan, vet pilot, is unable to weather a storm, and later when it comes time to choose who will be saved and who will be left behind, since the repaired plane can only carry half its original load. Expert technical knowhow also provides solid production values for a setting.

The Jonathan Latimer screenplay, based on Richard Carroll's story, twirls around the behavior of the assorted passengers and how they take their fate as plane lies in the midst of head-hunter country. Romance is pointed up between Ryan and Anita Ekberg, a hooker on her way to a South American city resort; and also between Keith Andes, co-pilot, and Phyllis Kirk, affianced to Gene Barry, a bullying coward. Steiger is a murderer being returned to the scene of his crime for execution, in whose hands lie the final choice of passengers.

Both Ryan and Steiger deliver highly restrained performances, and get top support right down the line. Miss Ekberg is an interesting personality, and in their triangle Andes, Miss Kirk and Barry are convincing. Fred Clark is sharp as a South American detective escorting Steiger, Cameron Prud'homme and Beulah Bondi score as an elderly couple, Jesse White is okay as a racketeer and Joe Provost appealing in a moppet role. Adele Mara makes a pretty hostess.

On technical side, William Mellor makes interesting use of his cameras. Eda Warren's editing hits a good pace and Franz Waxman's music score fits into the story.

Whit.

The Beast of Hollow Mountain
(C'SCOPE-COLOR)

Science-fiction western which can be exploited for strong returns.

Hollywood, Aug. 24
United Artists release of William & Edward Nassour production. Stars Guy Madison, Patricia Medina; features Eduardo Noriega, Carlos Rivas, Mario Carlos Rivas, Mario Navarro, Pascual Garcia Pena, Julio Villareal. Directed by Edward Nassour, Ismael Rodriguez. Screenplay, Robert Hill; additional dialog, Jack DeWitt; based on idea by Willis O'Brien; camera (De Luxe Color), Jorge Stahl Jr.; special effects, Henry Sharpe; music, Raul La Vista; editors, Holbrook Todd, Maury Wright. Tradeshown Aug. 20, '56. Running time, 81 MINS.

Jimmy Ryan	Guy Madison
Sarita	Patricia Medina
Enrique Rios	Eduardo Noriega
Felipe Sanchez	Carlos Rivas
Panchito	Mario Navarro
Pancho	Pascual Garcia Pena
Don Pedro	Julio Villareal
Margarita	Lupe Carriles
Martinez	Manuel Arvide
Manuel	Jose Chavez
Jose	Magarito Luna
Carlos	Roberto Contreras
Jorge	Lobo Negro (Guillermo Hernandez)
Shopkeeper	Jorge Trevino
Employee	Armando Guitierrez

"The Beast of Hollow Mountain" is an exploitation natural. It's hokey, but as a first in its field, a science-fiction western (as well as initial process film in Cinema-Scope), it should rack up handsome returns for its producers and provides moppet audiences particularly with edge-of-the-seat entertainment during its fantasy sequences. Name of Guy Madison in star role is a further draw for the juves, playing an American rancher in Mexico up against the menace of a pre-historic Tyrannosaurus Rex.

Filmed in De Luxe Color against the natural beauties of a heretofore Hollywood-unexplored part of Mexico, picture makes first use of the Regiscope animation process, developed after years of experimentation by co-producer Edward Nassour, who makes his bow as a feature director. An electronic process which is a definite contribution to film-making, it allows natural movement by a beast towering here over 30 feet. Story is based upon an original idea by Willis O'Brien, special effects expert known for his work on such past films as "The Lost World" and "King Kong."

The Robert Hill screenplay builds its narrative upon events leading up to the thrill sequences featuring the monster. Madison is partnered with Mexican Carlos Rivas on a ranch near Hollow Mountain, surrounded by an impenetrable swamp, where stories have it a mysterious and fearful beast dwells. Plottage twirls around the efforts of a wealthy Mexican cattleman, Eduardo Noriega, the extremely jealous fiance of Patricia Medina, daughter of the local mayor, to drive Madison out of the country. Their differences are resolved in the swamp, where the monster appears to create terror and finally meets its doom through Madison's efforts.

Nassour inserts outstanding production qualities in this film he coproduces with William Nassour, his choice of backgrounds lending further interest to its unfoldment. Special effects photography by Henry Sharpe is a strong assist to Jorge Stahl, Jr.'s principal color camera work, a potent asset, and Raul LaVista's music score helps with the suspense.

Madison delivers in his expected style and Miss Medina makes a pretty heroine, whose friendship with the American is violently resented by Noriega, heavy whose street brawl with Madison is well staged. Rivas as Madison's partner is good, and specially appealing is Mario Navarro, young son of Pascual Garcia Pena, in for semi-comical characterization. *Whit.*

The Vagabond King
(MUSICAL-COLOR-V'VISION)

Lavish remake of venerable Rudolf Friml operetta a Technicolorful spectacular.

Paramount release of Pat Duggan production. Stars Kathryn Grayson, Oreste, Rita Moreno, Sir Cedric Hardwicke, Walter Hampden. Directed by Michael Curtiz. Screenplay, Ken Englund & Noel Langley, from the operetta by Rudolf Friml (music) and William H. Post & Brian Hooker (book and lyrics); additional songs by Friml and Johnny Burke; camera (Technicolor), Robert Burks; special effects, John P. Fulton; asst. director, William McGarry; costumes, Mary Grant; score, Victor Young; arrangements, Charles Henderson, Leo Shuken, Gus Levene, Albert Sendrey; dances, Hanya Holm. Tradeshown N.Y., Aug. 30, '56. Running time, 88 MINS.

Catherine De Vaucelles	Kathryn Grayson
Francois Villon	Oreste
Huguette	Rita Moreno
Tristan	Sir Cedric Hardwicke
King Louis XI	Walter Hampden
Thibault	Leslie Nielsen
Rene	William Prince
Ferrebouc	Jack Lord
Jacques	Billy Vine
Colin	Harry McNaughton
Laughing Margot	Florence Sundstrom
Margaret	Lucie Lancaster
The Scar	Raymond Bramley
Gen. Antoine De Chabannes	Gregory Morton
Quicksilver	Richard Tone
Bishop of Paris & Turin	Ralph Sumpter
Burgundy	G. Thomas Duggan
Majordomo	Gavin Gordon
Sergeant	Richard Shannon
1st Soldier	Larry Pennell
Ladies in Waiting	Frances Lansing, Jeanette Miller
Duke of Normandy	Joel Ashley
Duke of Anjou	Ralph Clanton
Duke of Bourbon	Gordon Mills
One Eye	Sam Schwartz
Lulu	Phyllis Newman
Blanche	Nancy Bajer
Belle	Rita Maria Tanno
Jehan 'The Hook'	David Nillo
Jeannie	Albie Gaye
Lady in Waiting	Laura Raynair
Specialty Dancers	David Nillo, Dolores Starr
Jehan (The Wolf)	Slim Gaut

"The Vagabond King" is a hardy perennial whose basic production goes back to 1902 when Justin McCarthy's "If I Were King" bowed in London (with George Alexander as Francois Villon) but it was not until 1925 that the William H. Post-Brian Hooker libretto to Rudolf Friml's durable score debuted on Broadway. It has been remade a couple of times but the latest version—"in Technicolor and VistaVision"—is the lushest recreation yet. It's an eyefilling bluechip investiture which, if the customers take it in proper stride, should acquit itself profitably at the boxoffice. There are spots, however, where in this sardonic age and idiom the gusto of Villon's derring-do may strike a disturbing note.

By and large, however, the 15th century French romance, with its pageantry, splendor, royal intrigue, ducal treachery, regal wisdom, courtly graciousness and vox pop vagabondia, adds up to excellent escapist fare.

A tiptop cast is on a par with the ultra production. Its arresting, richly landscaped exteriors and palatial court appointments contrast to the fluid mob scenes as director Mike Curtiz has handled them. These include the rowdy tavern scenes, the military onslaught, not to mention Hanya Holm's skillful integration of her ballets. This marks her Hollywood debut.

Only "Someday," "Huguette's Waltz," "Only A Rose" and "Song of the Vagabonds" have been retained from the original score—durable standards all—and Friml reaffirms his skill as a composer with a set of excellent new songs, lyrics by Johnny Burke. Titles are "This Same Heart," "Bon Jour," "Viva La You," "Comparisons" and "Watch Out for the Devil," the latter incidentally keying one of the more imaginative ballets by Miss Holm. There is also an interpolation titled 'Lord, I'm Glad I Know Thee" "by V. Giovane and K. C. Rogan," both probably phoney bylines; "Rogan" is one of Burke's noms-de-plume.

Victor Young did the okay musical score.

Kathryn Grayson and Oreste have the romantic leads. Miss Grayson is too wellknown for extraneous encomiums; she is a looker and a soprano of fine calibre, ideal for the role of Lady Catherine. The mono-billed Oreste is a European import, an opera tenor of exceeding skill and trained voice and, matching Miss Grayson's pulchritudinous endowments, also a highly personable gent. He takes his place with Dennis King, who created the Broadway role at the old Casino on Broadway and who also sang it in Par's first filmusical version in 1930. (The basic story was remade once more in 1938 with Ronald Colman in the title role, Frances Dee in the Grayson part, and Basil Rathbone as the canny, not unkindly King Louis XI, well played here by Walter Hampden. Preston Sturges wrote that version, directed by Frank Lloyd).

Rita Moreno is capital as Huguette, loyal tavern wench who regards herself as Villon's "girl," playing the part with the necessary verve and spirit in the dramatic scenes, and also contributing an okay song-and-dance stint (the now standard "Huguette's Waltz") in this rogues' hangout where the ex-nitery performer is cast as dual-duty entertainer and barmaid. This was the role Lillian Roth played in the first Par version (Jane Carroll created it on Broadway) when Jeanette MacDonald had the femme lead of Catherine De Vaucelles. Miss Moreno endows her characterization with greater spitfire values.

Sir Cedric Hardwicke contributes another good personation as the crusty but loyal Tristan Chevalier, councillor to the King. Leslie Nielsen is effective as the traitorous provost marshal; Billy Vine and Harry McNaughton, from the niteries and the varieties, make their roguish roles hold up as pals of Oreste's Francois Villon; Gregory Morton is the disloyal general; G. Thomas Duggan is the Burgundian rebel duke; Florence Sundstrom is standout in her robust role. David Nillo and Dolores Starr are the terp specialists whom Miss Holm gives their opportunities in the court banquet "theatre." Jack Lord, from legit, also makes his bit stand up as a loyal king's officer.

Ken Englund and Noel Langley fashioned a colorful script, replete with the flowery dialog to match the "poet of the streets" characteriaztion of Francois Villon. The turns of phraseology are frequently barbed with metaphors of compelling flights of language. Oreste gives credence in these literary ripostes to match his basic characterization as "the king of the vagabonds." It is in these prose passages that the now dated derring-do story-line treads a fine line in its possible miscued audience reaction.

Director Michael Curtiz and producer Pat Duggan handled their charges well, with no cheating on the bankroll. It's lavish in every sense. The corps of extras, not to mention the rolling livestock for the "invasion," along with the costly costuming—undoubtedly authentic to the 15th century of Paris and Burgundy to the last degree—gives this latest remake of "The

Vagabond King" beaucoup size and stature, gilt and glamour—ingredients that defy any television road company cinematic entertainment. This is another biggie for the new selling season. *Abel.*

Strange Intruder
(SONG)

Familiar cast in fair meller for program bookings.

Hollywood, Sept. 4.

Allied Artists release of Lindsley Parsons production. Stars Edmund Purdom, Ida Lupino, Ann Harding, Jacques Bergerac. Directed by Irving Rapper. Screenplay, David Evans, Warren Douglas; from novel by Helen Fowler; editor, Maurice Wright; music, Paul Dunlap; song, Carroll Coates. Previewed Aug. 28, '56. Running time, **82 MINS.**

Paul Quentin .... Edmund Purdom
Alice .... Ida Lupino
Mary Carmichael .... Ann Harding
Howard .... Jacques Bergerac
Meg .... Gloria Talbott
James Carmichael......Carl Benton Reid
Parry .... Douglas Kennedy
Adrian .... Donald Murphy
Violet .... Ruby Goodwin
Libby .... Mimi Gibson
Johnny .... Eric Anderson
Joady .... Marjorie Bennett

A familiar cast will do its part in carrying "Strange Intruder" through its program bookings. Playing is generally competent, but a story that doesn't project much conviction results in only fair entertainment for release purposes.

Edmund Purdom plays a battle-fatigued G. I. with a strange mission. He had promised a now-dead war buddy to kill the latter's two kids so that an unfaithful wife and her lover cannot have them. The script by David Evans and Warren Douglas, from the novel by Helen Fowler, isn't too convincing in working out the problem and Irving Rapper's direction unfolds the plot at a pace too slow for much suspense.

The mission is never accomplished because in meeting the wife, Ida Lupino, and the dead buddy's family, Purdom finds mitigating circumstances, as well as affection, and manages to recover from his psychiatric trouble that had sent him on the strange errand. Purdom and Miss Lupino handle their roles acceptably, as do Ann Harding, the mother; Carl Benton Reid, the father, and Gloria Talbott, the sister. Jacques Bergerac appears as the blackmailing ex-lover who had tempted Miss Lupino in her loneliness. Douglas Kennedy, family attorney; Donald Murphy, the war buddy who exacts the crazy promise from Purdom, and others are okay.

Lindsley Parsons' production has good technical assists from Ernest Haller's lensing, editing and settings. Paul Dunlap contributes a sentimentally themed score and Carroll Coates cleffed the tune. "Bad for Each Other" heard via a record. *Brog.*

Lust for Life
(C'SCOPE—COLOR)

Class production, interesting, but long and wordy. Properly set for art theatre showcasing.

Metro release of John Houseman production. Stars Kirk Douglas; features Anthony Quinn, James Donald, Pamela Brown, Everett Sloane, Niall MacGinnis, Noel Purcell, Henry Daniell, Madge Kennedy. Directed by Vincente Minelli. Screenplay, Norman Corwin from the novel by Irving Stone. Camera (Metrocolor), F. A. Young and Russell Harlan; editor, Adrienne Fazan; music, Miklos Rozsa. Tradeshown N.Y., Aug. 30, '56. Running time, **122 MINS.**

Vincent Van Gogh........ Kirk Douglas
Paul Gauguin .... Anthony Quinn
Theo Van Gogh .... James Donald
Christine .... Pamela Brown
Dr. Gachet .... Everett Sloane
Roulin .... Niall MacGinnis
Anton Mauve .... Noel Purcell
Theodorus Van Gogh .... Henry Daniell
Anna Cornelia Van Gogh . Madge Kennedy
Willemien .... Jill Bennett
Dr. Peyron .... Lionel Jeffries
Dr. Bosman .... Laurence Naismith
Colbert .... Eric Pohlmann
Kay .... Jeanette Sterke
Johanna .... Toni Gerry
Rev. Stricker .... Wilton Graff
Mrs. Stricker .... Isobel Elson
Rev. Peters .... David Horne
Commissioner Van Den Berghe
                          Noel Howlett
Commissioner De Smet.... Ronald Adam
Ducrucq .... John Ruddock
Rachel .... Julie Robinson
Camille Pissarro......... David Leonard
Emile Bernard .... William Phipps
Seurat .... David Bond
Pere Tanguy .... Frank Perls
Waiter .... Jay Adler
Adeline Ravoux .... Laurence Badie

Metro's decision to launch "Lust for Life" in specialty, or art, theatres is an immediately understandable one. For this study of Vincent Van Gogh will need time to catch on, being without the elements of action and pace that can attract an audience right off.

John Houseman has provided a top-calibre production setting and Norman Corwin contributed a highly literate script. But this is a slow-moving picture whose only action is in the dialog itself. Basically a faithful portrait of Van Gogh, "Lust for Life" is nonetheless unexciting. It misses out in conveying the color and entertainment of the original Irving Stone novel. It's a tragic recap that Stone penned, of course, but still there was no absence of amusing incidents.

Lensed in Holland and France, "Lust for Life" will have its appeal, initially at least, for the sophisticates. It's largely conversation plus expert tint photography, and both on a high level. Manning the cameras under Vincent Minelli's direction, F. A. Young and Russell Harlan devote liberal amounts of footage to Van Gogh's originals, these being interworked with story points as they are registered.

Kirk Douglas plays the title role with undeniable understanding of the artist. He's a competent performer all the way, conveying the frustrations which beset Van Gogh in his quest for knowledge of life and the approach to putting this on canvas.

But somehow the measure of sympathy that should be engendered for the genius who was to turn insane is not realized. To draw a comparison, Jose Ferrer in "Moulin Rouge" made Toulouse-Lautrec "closer" to the audience.

Anthony Quinn as Paul Gauchin, James Donald as Theo Van Gogh, and Pamela Brown, Everett Sloane, Niall MacGinnis, Noel Purcell, Henry Daniell and Madge Kennedy contribute uniformly competent performances.

The color, billed as Metrocolor, is outstanding throughout. This, along with the CinemaScope photography, and the vivid settings place the stamp of quality on the Houseman production. Music and technical work are fine too. But this telling of the story of Vincent Van Gogh—of his struggles in Holland and southern France, of his impoverishment and handouts from a kindly brother, of the mental distress that impels him to cut off an ear and, finally his death, is not the stimulating picture it should have been. Cutting is unusually sharp but even this doesn't give it sufficient pace. *Gene.*

Hot Rod Girl

Well-knit programmer with juve interest.

Hollywood, Sept. 4.

American-International release of Norman Herman (Nacirema) production. Stars Lori Nelson, John Smith, Chuck Connors; features Frank J. Gorshin, Roxanne Arlen, Mark Andrews, Carolyn Kearney. Directed by Leslie Martinson. Screenplay, John McGreevey; camera, Sam Leavitt; editor, Leon Barsha. Previewed Aug. 29, '56. Running time, **79 MINS.**

Lisa .... Lori Nelson
Jeff .... John Smith
Ben .... Chuck Connors
Flat-Top .... Frank J. Gorshin
L. P. .... Roxanne Arlen
Bronc .... Mark Andrews
Judy .... Carolyn Kearney
Two Tanks .... Ed Reider
Steve .... Del Erickson
Yo-Yo .... Fred Essler
Logan .... Russ Thorson
Pat .... Charles Keane
Henry .... Dabbs Greer

Hot rodders provide a topical theme for this well-knit programmer which may be exploited for satisfactory returns, particularly with the juve trade. Film covers the subject thoroughly, simultaneously offering a few thrills and a story that holds water.

The John McGreevey script focuses on a cop who has been waging a one-man crusade to stop teenage speed violations by promotion of a patrolled drag strip where hot rodders may let off steam. After an older driver withdraws his support from the project, as a consequence of his kid brother's death in a street race, the cop begins to lose ground. Appearance of a troublesome newcomer who tries to take over leadership of the hot rod element further complicates matters, which finally resolve themselves following a fatal road accident and the rodders return to the drag strip.

Leslie Martinson maintains a fast pace in his direction of the Norman-Herman production, building good suspense in staging a chicken race, which consists of two cars racing head-on towards each other. Cast is generally okay, good typing all the way. Chuck Connors registers as the cop, John Smith plays the elder brother, and Lori Nelson is pretty as his girl friend. Mark Andrews impresses in the trouble-maker role. Frank J. Gorshin and Ed Reider rate as a couple of young drivers, and Roxanne Arlen and Carolyn Kearney as their sweeties.

Sam Leavitt's photography and Leon Barsha's editing lead off the standard technical credits. *Whit.*

The She-Creature

Mixed salad of the Bridey Murphy, Monster-From-The-Past and Svengali themes, aimed at unpretentious billings.

Hollywood, Aug. 29.

American-International Pictures release of Golden State (Samuel Z. Arkoff-Alex Gordon) production. Stars Chester Morris, Marla English, Tom Conway; features Cathy Downs, Lance Fuller, Ron Randell, Frieda Inescourt, Frank Jenks, El Brendel. Directed by Edward L. Cahn. Screenplay and story by Lou Rusoff; camera, Frederick E. West; editor, Ronald Sinclair; music, Ronald Stein. Reviewed at Iris Theatre, Hollywood, Aug. 29, '56. Running time, **76 MINS.**

Carlo Lombardi .... Chester Morris
Andrea .... Marla English
Timothy Chappel .... Tom Conway
Dorothy .... Cathy Downs
Ted Erickson .... Lance Fuller
Lieut. James .... Ron Randell
Mrs. Chappel .... Frieda Inescort
Police Sergeant .... Frank Jenks
Olaf .... El Brendel
Johnny .... Paul Dubov
Bob .... Bill Hudson
Marta .... Flo Bert
Mrs. Brown .... Jeanne Evans

Prof. Anderson......Kenneth MacDonald
Creature .... Paul Blaisdell

A tossed green salad of the Bridey Murphy theme, mixed with helping of monster-from-the-past, and served up with a dash of Svengali, this pic is aimed at unpretentious billings, in keeping with its very modest budget, and should serve well in these situations.

Chester Morris portrays a sideshow hypnotist who can call up a prehistoric monster from the past with the aid of his assistant, looker Marla English. But upright psychic researcher Lance Fuller becomes interested in her, and helps her fight off Morris' malevolent influence.

During the struggle over Miss English' psyche, ambitious promoter Tom Conway latches on to Morris and builds him into a nationwide craze, to gain a fast buck. In the end, Morris beckons the creature and unlooses it on the cast, depopulating most of his coplayers before Miss English gains the upper hand and turns the creature on Morris himself. With this, the creature shambles back to the sea, presumably forever.

All this is related in a disjointed, haphazard manner in the Lou Rusoff script, which utilizes a fair share of this genre's cliches before the final reel. However, director Edward L. Cahn manages to mix in a good quota of chills, especially for impressionable small fry.

Chester Morris is too able an actor to be entirely submerged in this shoddy material, and manages a capable performance, although he relies much on the baleful glare and the muttered threat for effect. Miss English, with eloquent physical attributes, doesn't have much more to register than horror and a a catatonic state. Fuller overuses a wide-eyed stare of astonishment as the skeptical scientist, while Ron Randell turns in a capable job as a tough cop. Tom Conway is properly suave as the money-hungry promoter. Cathy Downs makes an attractive ingenue, but El Brendel's comedic contribution lacks sharp material.

Technical credits are adequate, except that the monster becomes ridiculous when viewed in the strong light of the kliegs. *Kove.*

It's a Wonderful World
(SONGS)
(British-SpectaScope-Color)

Brightly spun Tin Pan Alley romance featuring Ted Heath Orch with Terence Morgan, George Cole and attractive Parisienne newcomer Mylene Nicole. Good for swing music fans.

London, Aug. 28.

Renown release of George Minter production. Stars Terence Morgan, George Cole, Kathleen Harrison and Ted Heath & His Music. Direction and screenplay by Val Guest. Camera, Wilkie Cooper; editor, John Pomeroy; music, Ted Heath & Robert Farnon. At Leicester Square Theatre, London, Aug. 28, '56. Running time, **89 MINS.**

Ray Thompson .... Terence Morgan
Ken Miller .... George Cole
Miss Gilly .... Kathleen Harrison
Ted Heath .... Himself
Bert Fielding .... James Hayter
Georgie .... Mylene Nicole
Mervyn Wade .... Harold Lang
Professional Manager ..Reginald Beckwith
Dennis Lotis .... Himself
Paul Taylor .... Maurice Kaufman
Sir Thomas van Broughton .Charles Clay
Arranger .... Derek Blomfield

Starting off through the blare of Ted Heath's orchestra, and the crazy gyrations of screaming swing-mad teenagers, this comedy develops into a gay satirical yarn. The maestro's recent U.S. trip places him among the known quantities in the U.S., and from this angle it should prove suitable there also. His personality dominates the lively story of a composer's search for a niche in Tin Pan Alley, with a diverting script and good direction to speed it along. Its prospects in the home market are surefire for the type of audience it was obviously intended.

Terence Morgan and George Cole play a couple of back room starvelings with one shirt between them, a near-unshakable faith in their future, and a charmless rooming-housekeeper bent on their eviction. Morgan gets an accompanist's job in a publishing house which tides them over until Cole pulls off a harebrained scheme that sets them skyrocketing. He foists on a gullible public a new composition by a supposedly famed foreign highbrow now living in seclusion. In reality it is a playback in reverse of Ted Heath's band recording of "D'ye Ken John Peel."

The facial expression of the audience during the first performance at Albert Hall, and the frenzied despair of the titled musical director make for some of the funniest shots seen in years. The snob critics won't admit they don't understand the appalling cacophony and sheeplike follow the crowd of longhairs in acclaiming it as a masterpiece.

Intruding gracefully into all this hokum is Mylene Nicole. a delightfully fresh young French blonde, making her debut in British pix who plays the gal across the street, with resulting jealous friction. Eventually she brings fame to the composer by singing his unpublished song with Ted Heath at the Royal Command Performance, having gatecrashed an audition and won a place with his band.

Morgan is satisfying as the plodding musician, gaining equal amounts of sympathy and laughs, but it is to George Cole, with his dry humor and expressive face that most of the best lines fall. Kathleen Harrison is her sturdy cockney self as the adamant housekeeper and James Hayter and Reginald Beckwith give sterling characterizations of the music publishing boss and his chief aide. Harold Lang injects the right amount of opportunism as a snooping columnist, and Dennis Lotis croons soulfully in his own personality. Band grouping and good lighting effects form a colorful, melodious background to what is, first and last, for the lowbrow appetite. *Clem.*

Gun Brothers

Standard outdoor feature done in okay style for action market.

Hollywood, Sept. 4.
United Artists release of Grand production. Stars Buster Crabbe. Ann Robinson. Neville Brand; features Michael Ansara, Walter Sande, Lita Milan. Directed by Sidney Salkow. Screenplay, Gerald Drayson Adams, Richard Schayer, from story by Adams; camera, Kenneth Peach; editor, Arthur Hilton; music, Irving Gertz. Previewed Aug. 30, '56. Running time, **79 MINS.**
Chad .... Buster Crabbe
Rose Fargo .... Ann Robinson
Jubal .... Neville Brand
Shawnee .... Michael Ansara
Yellowstone .... Walter Sande
Meeteetse .... Lita Milan
Blackjack Silk .... James Seay
Sheriff Jergen .... Roy Barcroft
Moose MacLain .... Slim Pickens
Molly .... Dorothy Ford

A Cain and Abel plot themes this western actioner and it's wrapped up in okay style to satisfy the demands of the general outdoor market. Buster Crabbe and Neville Brand carry off the good and bad brother characters with all-around good performances, while Ann Robinson and Lita Milan prettily fulfill the demands of the femme assignments in the Grand production for United Artists release.

Plot period of the Gerald Drayson Adams-Richard Schayer script is 1877, laid in the Jackson Hole country, where Crabbe comes after mustering out of the cavalry to join his brother, who he believes is a big rancher. Instead, he's a rustler and stage robber, bossing a band of toughies with Michael Ansara, good as the chief henchman. It's brother against brother for awhile when Brand thinks Crabbe tips off the sheriff, but at the end they fight side-by-side against a new gang mustered by Ansara, with Brand squaring his accounts with the law by dying in battle.

Sidney Salkow's direction lays the proper stress on action to keep the story moving along, but still gives the cast time to work at characterizations. Crabbe and Brand make a good brother team. Miss Robinson pleases as the dancehall singer who teams romantically with Crabbe. Miss Milan attracts attention as a comely Indian maid who is misused by Ansara and other gang members. Walter Sande, James Seay, Roy Barcroft, Slim Pickens and Dorothy Ford round out the competent cast.

Kenneth Peach's lensing, editing by Arthur Hilton, Irving Gertz's music and other behind-camera assists prove satisfactory. *Brog.*

The Power and the Prize
(C'SCOPE)

Love and big business ethics packaged in a slick production. Metro's first b&w C'Scoper.

Metro release of Nicholas Nayfack production. Stars Robert Taylor, Elisabeth Mueller, Burl Ives; features Charles Coburn, Sir Cedric Hardwicke, Mary Astor, Nicola Michaels, Cameron Prud'homme. Directed by Henry Koster. Screenplay, Robert Ardrey, from novel by Howard Swiggett; camera, George J. Folsey; editor, George Boemler; music, Bronislau Kaper. Tradeshown in N.Y., Aug. 29, '56. Running time, **98 MINS.**
Cliff Barton .... Robert Taylor
Miriam Linka .... Elisabeth Mueller
George Salt .... Burl Ives
Guy Eliot .... Charles Coburn
Mr. Carew .... Sir Cedric Hardwicke
Mrs. George Salt .... Mary Astor
Joan Salt .... Nicola Michaels
Rev. John Barton ..Cameron Prud'homme
Lester Everett .... Richard Erdman
Mr. Chutwell .... Ben Wright
Mr. Pitt-Semphill .... Jack Raine
Paul F. Farragut ....Tom Browne Henry
Howard Carruthers ..... Richard Deacon

A great many truths—possibly too many for a single picture—are dramatized in this handsomely mounted and slickly executed production. It's a drama about people and their dignity, about ethics, about love and about the thirst for power that shapes some men into a race apart. It also has international overtones and undertones and manages to squeeze in some pertinent cracks about current American attitudes.

All of which adds up to an interesting if not always plausible film that gives the outer appearance of probing to considerable depth while, to the minds of some, it'll probably only add up to little more than a somewhat hectic love story with a lot of unnecessary conversation. It's well acted for the most part and it has its tender moments so that the overall batting average looks promising.

"Power and the Prize" is primarily about an American industrial tycoon, a ruthless man who has picked a young executive as his successor and wants him to develop in his own image. He sends him to London to negotiate an unethical deal that would give the American firm control over a British mining outfit. In London, the young man can't go through with it, and he falls in love with a pretty German refugee girl who is suspected—and later cleared—of Red sympathies. In the end, the older man tries to destroy the younger one, only to have to yield to the forces of decency.

With Robert Taylor, who does his usual competent job in a role that might have looked better in the hands of a slightly younger man, Burl Ives and Elisabeth Mueller make their appearances in major parts. Ives is powerful and plenty convincing as the tycoon who chooses to live for his industrial empire and lets no one and nothing get into his way.

Miss Mueller is a newcomer from Germany. She has a fresh, appealing personality and obvious talent. However, her performance seems overly tense and charged with the kind of explosive energy that can spoil a scene. Still, she contributes much to the film and should be rated as a "comer."

In the smaller parts, Charles Coburn registers with a well-defined characterization; Sir Cedric Hardwicke is excellent as the British industrialist; Mary Astor is plausible in a small part, and Richard Erdman, Ben Wright, Cameron Prud'homme and the rest are all up to par. Single disappointment is Nicola Michaels, another new face, who doesn't ring true at all as Taylor's fiancee. Admittedly, her lines lack credulity.

This is Metro's first in black & white CinemaScope, and while some of the scenes lend themselves to the widescreen treatment, others—particularly in the elegant offices—cry out either for color, or for a smaller screen. This film will raise some questions whether, if there are no tint effects, it's worth while using CinemaScope. In this case, it certainly didn't add muh to the picture

Henry Koster's direction is without great distinction, but reveals some nice touches and keeps things moving as much as possible. Scripting by Robert Ardrey keeps the dialog bouncing along nicely and encompasses some surprising line. Sample: Ives, speaking of the British, tells Taylor they're "a nation of swindlers. They invented swindling. They . . . made it socially acceptable." That's going to go over great in Britain! Script, except when it starts philosophizing, keeps in mind a healthy sense of humor that adds to the film's enjoyment.

"Power and the Prize" is something of a message picture, and there are those who may resent the sugarcoating. On the other hand, it says what it has to say well and the romantic angle gets the proper play, so maybe Metro has hit on a formula for speaking of pride and prejudice—and making 'em like it. *Hift.*

Attack

Hard-hitting, realistic film study of men in battle; controversial angle of murder of cowardly officer to fan pro-con. Prosperous b.o. prospects.

Hollywood, Sept. 11.
United Artists release of Robert Aldrich (Associates & Aldrich Co.) production. directed by Aldrich. Stars Jack Palance, Eddie Albert, Lee Marvin, Robert Strauss, Richard Jaekel, Buddy Ebsen, William Smithers; features Jon Shepodd, James Goodwin, Peter Van Eyck, Steven Geray. Screenplay, James Poe; from stage play by Norman Brooks. produced on stage by Paul Vroom; camera, Joseph Biroc; editor, Michael Luciano; music, Frank DeVol. Previewed Aug. 28, '56. Running time, **107 MINS.**
Lt. Costa .... Jack Palance
Capt. Cooney .... Eddie Albert
Col. Bartlett .... Lee Marvin
Pfc. Bernstein .... Robert Strauss
Pfc. Snowden .... Richard Jaekel
Sgt. Tolliver .... Buddy Ebsen
Lt. Woodruff .... William Smithers
Cpl. Jackson .... Jon Shepodd
Pfc. Ricks .... James Goodwin
Tall German .... Peter Van Eyck
Short German .... Steven Geray
Pfc. Abramowitz .... Judson Taylor
Old Frenchman .... Louis Mercier
Sgt. Ingersol .... Strother Martin

Independent unit of Associates & Aldrich Co. is back with another controversial picture as its second production for United Artists release. Just as "The Big Knife" fanned some pro and con in Hollywood, so will "Attack" stir up its talk in the Pentagon since it presents a cowardly officer who's murdered by his men. Entire film is treated with a hard realism that pays off in gutsy entertainment and the b.o. prospects look prosperous.

Producer-director Robert Aldrich, also responsible for "Knife," expands Norman Brooks' stage play, "Fragile Fox," into screen form under the new title. Footage runs 107 minutes, but Aldrich's handling of the excellent James Poe screenplay maintains a tight grip on spectators. It's a grim, extremely tough account of an infantry company during the Battle of the Bulge in World War II, brightly projected by the fine characterizations contributed by the cast.

Battle phases have a stark reality, with action and suspense that shakes the nerves at times. Some typical G. I. male humor lightens the tension here and there, but the main theme of war's deadliness is never skipped over. Eddie Albert is the cowardly captain who's too yellow to back the actions attempted by his lieutenants, Jack Palance and William Smithers. Disastrous missions follow each other until Palance threatens to kill Albert if he fails on the next one. He does, but Palance dies before he can make good his threat, leaving it up to Smithers to enact justice for all the men who have fallen because of the captain.

Pic gains realism through depicting Army brass and G. I.s as humans with different reactions to the reality of combat. It's an effective psychological study, picking up impact from the performances. Palance stands out in his portrayal of the gaunt, enraged lieutenant. Albert makes an unpleasant character quite real and understandable. Scoring exceptionally strong is Lee Marvin, the opportunistic colonel who keeps the coward in command because he will be useful after the war in politics. Robert Strauss, Richard Jaeckel and Buddy Ebsen command attention with exceptional work as G.I.s in the company. William Smithers, from legit, makes a fine impression with his talented work as the lieutenant who guns down his superior officer.

Firstrate supporting work is supplied by Jon Shepodd, James Goodwin, Peter Van Eyck, Steven Geray and other members of the cast. Joseph Biroc's photography plays a major part in bringing off the action as well as the tense mood of the picture. So does Frank DeVol's martial background score. Editing, art direction and other technical points are excellent. *Brog.*

Beyond a Reasonable Doubt
(SONG)

Tricky meller about man who nearly gets away with murder; only mildly entertaining programmer.

Hollywood, Sept. 11.

RKO release of Bert Friedlob production. Stars Dana Andrews, Joan Fontaine; features Sidney Blackmer, Philip Bourneuf, Shepperd Strudwick, Arthur Franz, Edward Binns, Robin Raymond, Barbara Nichols. Directed by Fritz Lang. Story and screenplay, Douglas Morrow; camera, William Snyder; editor, Gene Fowler Jr.; music, Herschel Burke Gilbert; song, Gilbert and Alfred Perry; sung by The Hi-Los. Previewed Sept. 7, '56. Running time, **80 MINS.**

Tom Garrett	Dana Andrews
Susan Spencer	Joan Fontaine
Austin Spencer	Sidney Blackmer
Thompson	Philip Bourneuf
Wilson	Shepperd Strudwick
Hale	Arthur Franz
Lieut. Kennedy	Edward Binns
Terry	Robin Raymond
Sally	Barbara Nichols
Charlie Miller	William Leicester
Greco	Dan Seymour
Judge	Rusty Lane
Joan	Joyce Taylor
Kirk	Carleton Young
Hat Check Girl	Trudy Wroe
Clerk	Joe Kirk
Governor	Charles Evans
Announcer	Wendell Niles

A trick ending wraps up the melodrama in "Beyond a Reasonable Doubt" but comes a little too late to revive interest in a tale that will lose many of its viewers early in the footage. Result is only fair entertainment for the regular dual market, where this one will take the upper spot because of familiar cast names.

The Bert Friedlob production is about a man who nearly gets away with murder. The tricky plotting by Douglas Morrow runs to dialog and thin material that relies too often on pat contrivance rather than logical development, mitigating the value of an intriguing story idea. Fritz Lang's direction does what it can to inject suspense and interest but the melodrama never really jells.

Dana Andrews is a writer engaged to Joan Fontaine, daughter of newspaper publisher Sidney Blackmer. The latter talks Andrews into going along with his scheme for showing up the fallacy of circumstantial evidence that has given ambiticus district attorney Philip Bourneuf a long string of convictions. In brief, Blackmer plans to plant evidence that will get Andrews arrested, tried and convicted for the murder of a burlesque stripper, recently found dead without any clues to indicate the killer. Scheme works as planned, except at the crucial moment Blackmer gets himself killed and the proof of the evidence-planting is destroyed. On the night of the execution, new proof of the plot is found, absolving Andrews. Before he can be pardoned, though, the trick ending establishes he actually had committed the murder and justice is done.

Neither the above-mentioned players nor others in the cast add much to make the events credible, seemingly performing with an almost casual air. Shepperd Strudwick, defense attorney; Arthur Franz, the d.a.'s aide; Edward Binns, police lieutenant, and Robin Raymond and Barbara Nichols, a couple of burley cuties, have feature roles.

William Snyder's black-and-white photography is keyed to the melodrama, as is Herschel Burke Gilbert's background score. Gilbert and Alfred Perry contributed a title tune, heard via a recording by The Hi-Los. Technical assists are all standard. *Brog.*

It Conquered the World

Low-budget flying saucer epic, should pull its weight at b.o.

Hollywood, Sept. 11.

American-International Pictures release of Sunset (James H. Nicholson-Roger Corman) production. Produced-directed by Corman. Stars Peter Graves, Beverly Garland, Lee Van Cleef. Screenplay and story, Lou Rusoff; camera, Frederick West; editor, Charles Gross; music, Ronald Stein. Reviewed at Iris Theatre, Hollywood, Aug. 29, '56. Running time, **68 MINS.**

Paul Nelson	Peter Graves
Claire Anderson	Beverly Garland
Tom Anderson	Lee Van Cleef
Joan Nelson	Sally Fraser
Pete Shelton	Charles B. Griffith
General Pattick	Russ Bender
Pvt. Manuel Ortiz	Jonathan Haze
Sergeant Neil	Richard Miller
Ellen Peters	Karen Kadler
Visitor from Venus	Paul Blaisdell

This flying saucer pic is a definite cut above normal, and should help pull its weight at b.o., despite modest budget.

However, militating against this are a number of fairly gruesome sequences which producer-director Roger Corman has injected, and which may call down the wrath of groups who oversee kiddie pix fare. But it must be admitted that the packed house of moppets at the show caught loved the gore, and continually shrieked avid appreciation.

The Lou Rusoff screenplay poses some remarkably adult questions amidst the derring-do. Lee Van Cleef portrays a scientist who has been collaborating with an outer-space expeditionary force on earth. The force consists of one super-Venusian creature of the bug-eyed monster variety who Van Cleef feels can bring the millennium of peace on earth. Instead, the creature imposes its sinister will on an isolated American community, including the nearby space satellite installation.

Van Cleef is opposed by Peter Graves, another electronics genius, who tries to open his eyes to the true situation. But it takes the heroic self-sacrifice of Beverly Garland, as Van Cleef's wife, to move him to action. He dies destroying the creature by blow-torching out its eyes.

Director Corman does a generally good job of mingling the necessary background-setting with fast-paced dialog, to achieve the strongest impact. Only a few patches of abstract discussion fail to hold audience attention.

As the confused scientific type, Van Cleef turns in an impressive character-acting chore, while Graves, a steadily-improving young actor, makes his properly dashing anti-Venusian resistance hero a man of some intellectual position as well. Miss Garland continues to show increasing stature as a promising young actress, as well as a looker, while Sally Fraser, as Graves' doomed wife, another victim of the creature, also turns in a strong performance. Jonathan Haze does well with a Spanish-accent bit as a Mexican-American GI.

Producer Corman would have been wiser to merely suggest the creature, rather than construct the awesome-looking and mechanically clumsy rubberized horror. It inspired more titters than terror.

Ronald Stein's dissonent music is effectively keyed to the out-of-this-world mood. *Kove.*

Girls In Prison
(SONG)

Routine meller for lowercase bookings in program runs.

Hollywood, Sept. 11.

American-International release of Alex Gordon (Golden State) production. Stars Richard Denning, Joan Taylor, Adele Jergens, Helen Gilbert, Lance Fuller; features Jane Darwell, Raymond Hatton, Phyllis Coates, Diana Darrin, Mae Marsh, Laurie Mitchell. Directed by Edward L. Cahn. Screenplay, Lou Rusoff; camera, Frederick E. West; editor, Ronald Sinclair; score and song, Ronald Stein. Previewed Aug. 30, '56. Running time, **86 MINS.**

Rev. Fulton	Richard Denning
Anne Carson	Joan Taylor
Jenny	Adele Jergens
Melanee	Helen Gilbert
Paul Anderson	Lance Fuller
Matron Jamieson	Jane Darwell
Pop Cadson	Raymond Hatton
Dorothy	Phyllis Coates
Meg	Diana Darrin
Grandma	Mae Marsh
Phyllis	Laurie Mitchell
Night Club Singer	Diane Richards
Female Guard	Luana Walters
Female Guard	Riza Royce

"Girls In Prison" is as routine as its title, an overlength jail yarn with telegraphic situations which reduce movement to a walk. Characters occasionally get over well enough for casual interest, however, and film is okay for lowercase bookings in program runs.

Producer Alex Gordon has lined up a competent cast for the Lou Rusoff screenplay, headed by Joan Taylor as a girl sent up on what she claims is a bum rap. Richard Denning, prison chaplain, believes her story and goes to bat for her, but her cellmates, convinced she's stashed the $38,000 in bank loot for which she was imprisoned, conspire to make a break and take her with them to get the coin. Lance Fuller, in on the robbery, also is after the hidden dough. Showdown comes at the femme's home after an earthquake wrecks the prison and the girls escape.

Miss Taylor shows to advantage and turns in a performance better than her material. Adele Jergens and Helen Gilbert are properly hardboiled as her cellmates, and both Denning and Fuller meet the demands of their respective roles. Jane Darwell as the prison warden; Raymond Hatton, Joan's ex-con father, and Phyllis Coates, a deranged prisoner, lend capable support. Diane Richards, in prolog, warbles "Tom's Beat," a torch number by Ronald Stein, for okay effect.

Edward L. Cahn's adequate direction is backed by acceptable technical assistance headed by Frederick E. West's camera work, Don Ament's art direction and the score by Stein. *Whit.*

Heroes of Shipka
(RUSSIAN—COLOR)

Artkino release of Lenfilm and Bulgarfilm Studios Production. Features S. Papov, B. Samoilov, I. Pereverzev, K. Kasimov, V. Leonov, P. Karlukovsky. Directed by S. Vasiliev. Screenplay, A. Perventsev; camera (Magicolor), M. Kirillov; music, N. Kryukov and F. Kutev. At Cameo, N.Y., Sept. 7, '56. Running time, **90 MINS.**

Katorgin	I. Pereyerzev
Oznobishin	V. Avdushko
Sashko Kozir	G. Yumatov
Makar Lizyuta	K. Sorokin
Timofei	A. Alexeyev
Borimechka	P. Karlukovsky
Petko	A. Karamitev
Panaiot	S. Peichev
Mitko	N. Genov
Boyana	E. Bozhinova
Ionka	K. Chukova
Gurko	S. Papov
Skobelev	B. Samoilov
Vereschagin, artist	V. Leonov
Alexander II	I. Kononenko
Major Lyapunov	A. Kholodkov
Sultan Abdul-Hamid II	D. Dakovsky
Suleiman Pasha	K. Kasimov

In view of trade concern about possible film dealings with Russia and the satellites, this Soviet import warrants more spotlighting than its obviously limited U.S. release normally would suggest. It could be an example of the type of product with which USSR filmmakers hope to break through U.S. exhibition's iron curtain.

"Heroes of Shipka," which is being showcased in New York's Cameo, is not to be brushed off lightly. It's a big production, boasting of thousands of players (actually soldiers) engaged in mammoth battle scenes. These are staged excitingly and held in astute control by director S. Vasiliev.

The sweep of the 1887 fight at Shipka Pass against the Turk oppressors is caught in expertly-framed, vivid cinematography. But the 1.33-to-1 aspect ratio looks very oldfashioned in these days of Todd-AO, CinemaScope, VistaVision, etc.

Had the production been lensed in one of the "scopes," the impact would have been greater. The subject matter, suggestive of the war in "War and Peace," demands the widescreen treatment to which American and many foreign audiences have grown accustomed.

Tinting process, billed Magicolor, is fair enough but short of U.S. standards. There's some fade in the hues, due to either inherent imperfection in the dyeworks system or flaws in the print which was used.

However, presentation of the battle scenes is impressive despite the technical shortcomings. With men of the "People's Army" of Bulgaria serving as "extras," the open-country maneuvering and firing of weapons bear semblance to authenticity. This looks like genuine combat—the staging is that good.

But detracting from these values is the lack of story development and characterizations with depth. The Russian soldiers and generals and the Bulgarian volunteers in the foreground, grim and determined in their struggle against the Ottoman Turks, simply lack any personalized communication with the audience. They express no feeling and their occasional dropping of Soviet propagandized dialog renders them even less simpatico.

"Shipka" demonstrates nicely disciplined handling of a spectacular. But within its framework are people who seem mechanical. Yank ticket-buyers won't hold still for it. *Gene.*

The Gamma People

Clumsy scripting. No suspense. Mediocre horror fantasy.

Hollywood, Sept. 11.

Columbia release of John Gossage (Warwick) production. Stars Paul Douglas, Eva Bartok; features Leslie Phillips, Walter Rilla, Martin Miller, Philip Leaver. Directed by John Gilling. Screenplay, Gilling and Gossage; original, Louis Pollock; camera, Ted Moore; editor, Jack Slade; music, George Melachrino. Running time, **78 MINS.**

Mike Wilson	Paul Douglas
Paula Wendt	Eva Bartok
Howard Meade	Leslie Phillips
Boronski	Walter Rilla
Koerner	Philip Leaver
Lochner	Martin Miller
Hugo	Michael Caridia
Hedda	Pauline Drewett
Anna	Jackie Lane
Bikstein	Olaf Pooley
Frau Bikstein	Rosalie Crutchley
Telegraph Clerk	Leonard Sachs
Hans	Paul Hardmuth
Graf	Cyril Chamberlain
First Goon	St. John Stuart

Exhibs packaging a twin horror show might find "The Gamma People" a passable subject, but it has little merit otherwise. Produced in England by Warwick Films for Columbia release, picture has only the name of Paul Douglas as a familiar ring for U. S. dating.

John Gossage produced and John Gilling directed from their screenplay based on an original story by Louis Pollock. Their respective dual functions come off poorly. The characters and situations are clumsily handled, as is the comedy injected in an attempt to lighten the proceedings. The dialog is trite and there is virtually no suspense. Unspools a very draggy 78 minutes.

Douglas and Leslie Phillips, reporters enroute to Salzburg on assignment, accidentally get into the closed state of Gudavia (mythical). A mad scientist, Walter Rilla, holds the state in terror as he experiments to convert children into geniuses under his control via bombardments of gamma rays. He reckons without the press, however, and in a few days the people are saved (those not already mentally ruined) and Douglas has acquired a romantic interest in Eva Bartok, unwilling assistant to the scientist.

The performances are on a par with the script treatment and inept direction. A couple of kids, Pauline Drewett, on her way to being a musical genius under Rilla's treatment, and Michael Caridia, on his way to being a juvenile Hitler, play the principal moppet spots. Among adults in featured roles are Martin Miller, Philip Leaver, Rosalie Crutchley and Jackie Lane. Lensing by Ted Moore and editing by Jack Slade are stock, and the score by George Melachrino overdone. *Brog.*

Der Hauptmann Von Koepenick
(The Captain of Koepenick) (GERMAN—COLOR)

Berlin, Sept. 2.

Europa release of Real production. Stars Heinz Ruehmann, Hannelore Schroth, Martin Held, Erich Schellow. Directed by Helmut Kaeutner; screenplay, Carl Zuckmayer and Kaeutner, based on the play by Zuckmayer; camera (Eastmancolor), Albert Benitz; music, Bernhard Eichhorn; editor, Klaus Dudenhoefer; sets, Herbert Kirchhoff, Albrecht Becker. At Gloria Palast, Berlin. Runningtime, **93 MINS.**

Wilhelm Voigt	Heins Ruehmann
Mathilde Obermueller	Hannelore Schroth
Dr. Obermueller	Martin Held
Captain von Schlettow	Erich Schellow
Friedrich Hoprecht	Willy A. Kleinau
Marie Hoprecht	Ilse Fuerstenberg
Adolph Mormser, tailor	Leonard Steckel
Willi Wormser, his son	Walter Giller
Auguste Viktoria, his daughter	Maria Sebaldt
Prison director	Friedrich Domin
Kallenberg	Wolfgang Neuss
Drunk soldier	Reinhard Kolldehoff
Police Sergeant	Willi Rose

There have been comparatively few German postwar pix which surpassed the highest local expectations. "Koepenick" is such a film, and possibly the best domestic production of the year. Helmut Kaeutner, undoubtedly this country's top film director, made it, and he had in Heinz Ruehmann the ideal actor to play the title role. Moreover, the script by Carl Zuckmayer (which latter wrote together with Kaeutner's, based on Zuckmayer's same-titled stage play, is unusually tight and imaginative. So it looks like a standout bargain.

Film has been declared "particularly valuable" by the W-German film classification board and should have strong international (also American) possibilities. The witty and intelligent plot and the names of Zuckmayer and Kaeutner, now under Universal contract, may help in the exploitation. It's a film that should earn the German industry plenty kudos abroad.

"Koepenick" is a remake of the Richard Oswald pic made in 1931 with the late Max Adalbert in the title role. Oswald's film remained unforgotten all through the years and, despite a later British remake, still registers as one of the best pix of the early '30s. This 1956 version, now in (Eastman) color, is hardly less impressive than its predecessor and certainly more outspoken in its tendency: a heavy attack against Prussian militarism. It ridicules the power of the uniform in such an intelligent and irresistible way that even the most narrow-minded among the uniform-conscious bourgeoisie should be convinced. It's the tragicomic story of the famed Wilhelm Voigt (Heinz Ruehmann), a Berlin shoemaker, who in 1906 got hold of the uniform of a Prussian captain. Disguised as an officer, he held up some soldiers and marched them to the Town Hall of Berlin-Koepenick where he not only arrested the Burgomaster but got away with the municipal cashbox. His escapade then made headlines all over the world.

Kaeutner, who also makes a short appearance (as an organ-grinder in the film), deserves highest acclaim, for he made this feature as courageous as possible (in view of the controversial topic) and followed his aim, "to smuggle art into the movies," most successfully. With "Koepenick," Kaeutner has maintained his reputation as one of the few German directors on whom one can truly depend.

Acting is exceptionally good. Top honors undoubtedly go to Ruehmann, whose portrayal of Voigt is not only an acting masterpiece but a thing which will force people to some meditation. Excellent also are Martin Held as burgomaster, Erich Schellow as a stiff Prussian officer, Willy A. Kleinau as Voigt's brother-in-law, Friedrich Domin as prison director, Wolfgang Neuss as Voigt's friend and ex-convict and —in a brief study—Reinhard Kolldehoff as drunk soldier. Film, incidentally, has an unusually large cast consisting of nearly 45 players.

Technically, pic is way above the domestic average. That particularly applies to Klaus Dudenhoefer's skillful editing and Albert Benitz' firstrate lensing. Sets and costumes rate as strong assets. Only flaw: the frequent closeups in Eastmancolor don't treat the players' faces kindly.

"Captain" should have no trouble garnering artie dates in the U.S. The Real Film (Walter Koppel) production has the stature and the punch to break through and could be an important factor in helping to reestablish the German film with American audiences. This is class product down the line and those values can never fail to pay off. *Hans.*

Sailor Beware!
(COLOR—BRITISH)

Filmization of current West End stage hit with Peggy Mount repeating starring role. Strictly for domestic market.

London, Sept. 5.

Independent Film Distributors (in association with British Lion) release of Romulus (Jack Clayton) production. Stars Peggy Mount; features Shirley Eaton, Ronald Lewis. Directed by Gordon Parry. Screenplay, Philip King and Falkland L. Cary; music, Peter Akister. At Rialto, London, Sept. 4, '56. Running time, **81 MINS.**

Emma Hornett	Peggy Mount
Henry Hornett	Cyril Smith
Shirley	Shirley Eaton
Albert	Ronald Lewis
Edie Hornett	Esma Cannon
Daphne	Joy Webster
Carnoustie Bligh	Gordon Jackson
Mrs. Lack	Thora Hird
Rev. Mr. Purefoy	Geoffrey Keen
Toddy	Jack MacGowran
Verger	Peter Collingwood

The film version of "Sailor Beware!" is virtually a carbon copy of the original legit presentation which is still a big West End hit after a run of more than 18 months. For local tastes that will be in its favor, particularly as Peggy Mount recreates the role in which she made a name for herself as the loud, overpowering and domineering mother of the bride. Pic will garner the bulk of its income in the domestic market and will have little chances in foreign territories. It should on form, however, prove a profitable undertaking.

In its transition from stage to screen the comedy loses much of its racy good humor, but remains a tour-de-force proposition for Miss Mount. Her portrayal of the loud-mouthed and calculating wife and mother provides as much of a strain for the audience as it does for the star herself. The soundtrack is deliberately played up to accent her personal domination and that puts quite a test on the eardrums.

Apart from the fact that the film takes in a few exteriors there's no substantial difference in the plot development. It is, in fact, the same story of the young sailor who fails to turn up at church for his wedding, mainly because his bride has concealed the fact that her mother has bought them a house only three doors away.

Oddly enough, Miss Mount's performance doesn't overshadow the rest of the cast. Cyril Smith repeats his stage role of the henpecked husband with considerable effect. Shirley Eaton is pleasingly attractive as the bride and Ronald Lewis shows plenty of sincerity as the reluctant groom. Gordon Jackson, as his best man, Joy Webster, as a provocative bridesmaid, Esma Cannon and Thora Hird round off a good featured cast. [This play has no relationship to the American stage and film comedy of similar title—Ed.] *Myro.*

Venice Films

Calabuch
(SPANISH-ITALIAN)

Venice, Sept. 3.

CIFTESA release of Aguila-Costellazione Films production. Stars Edmund Gwenn; features Franco Fabrizi, Valentina Cortese, Juan Calvo, Jose Isbert, Feliz Fernandez, Jose Luis Ozores. Directed by Luis G. Berlanga; screenplay, Berlanga, Ennio Flajano, Leonardo Martin, Florentino Soria, Guerrini; editor, Pepita Orduna. At Film Festival, Venice. Running time, **98 MINS.**

Jorge	Edmund Gwenn
Teacher	Valentina Cortese
Langosta	Franco Fabrizi

One of the surprise hits of the Venice Film Festival, pic has all the elements of a crowd-pleaser. Looms big in Spain and Italy and, with proper handling, in many other markets as well. It's a special item for the U. S., needing the word-to-mouth buildup, but could pay off proportionately.

Somewhat reminiscent of the pre-war Pagnol films of Southern French village life, but sharper and deeper in its spoof and comment on humanity, as well being a consistent laugh-getter, "Calabuch" in brief tells of the happy days spent in that Spanish seaside village by a world-famed atomic scientist who has tried to escape from his world of formulas and destruction. The villagers soon embrace him as one of their own, and, until he is finally located in his hideaway, he gets a fresh breath of life, as it were uncontaminated by thoughts and fears of the atomic-crazed world he himself has contributed to. The well-written script also allows for plenty of satiric observation of village life and types, also permitting some sharp barbs at such hallowed Spanish institutions as the government, the bullfight, the police, etc.

Humor is sustained and intelligent. Thesping is likewise consistently good, from Edmund Gwenn's fine and sympathetic rendering of the scientist on a breather to Franco Fabrizi's delineation of his adopted sidekick, Valentino Cortese's schoolmarm, and the many village types. Director Luis Berlanga's sly, often semi-surrealistic humor, is noted all through the picture. Lensing by Francisco Sempere catches local flavor, and other credits are in keeping. *Hawk.*

On the Bowery
(AMERICAN)

Venice, Aug. 29.
Lionel Rogosin production, directed by Rogosin; camera, Richard Bagley; screenplay, Rogosin, Bagley and Mark Suffrin; music, C. Mills. At Film Festival, Venice. Running time, **55 MINS.**

This year's Grand Prix in the Venice Documentary Festival should help this impressive item get a booking slot despite its in-between footage and subject material. Could make a good partner to a medium-lengther in some selected bookings.

Rogosin and his collaborators have done an amazing job of capturing the life and thoughts of the denizens of the Bowery, as seen principally via three main characters, Ray Salyer, Gorman Hendricks and Frank Mathews. Slight plot skein ties pic together, with Salyer the youngish man caught up in the Skid Row whirlpool and struggling, but not too hard, to set himself free once more.

What makes pic outstanding, apart from its material and handling, is the topnotch skill with which it has been treated technically. Lensing, both hidden-camera or staged, is expert, and fine on-the-spot sound recording likewise plays a vital part in the total effect of this offbeat item. *Hawk.*

Calle Mayor
(Main Street)
(FRANCO—SPANISH)

Venice, Sept. 6.
Suevia Films release of a Suevia-Cesareo Gonzalez-Play Art-Iberia Films co-production. Stars Betsy Blair, Jose Suarez; features Dora Doll, Yves Massard, Luis Pena, Alfonso Goda, Jose Calvo, Manuel Alexandre. Directed by J. A. Bardem from screenplay by Bardem; camera, Michel Kelber; music, Joseph Kosma; editor, Margarita Ochoa. At Film Festival, Venice. Running time, **97 MINS.**
Isabel .... Betsy Blair
Juan .... Jose Suarez
Tonia .... Dora Doll
Federico .... Yves Massard

Pic looks headed for good grosses in European markets, where word-of-mouth will help it build, in addition to needed strong drumbeating. Top reviews will also help all along the line on the Continent. Stateside, pic could make headway via an arty start followed by general release. Betsy Blair name following her "Marty" stint could be an aid.

Though it gives a graphic and keenly observed picture of Spanish smalltown life, "Main Street" is principally concerned with the town wallflower (Miss Blair) on whom a group of men play what turns out to be a tragic practical joke. One of them is chosen to make her fall for him and to ask her to marry him. Sadistic joke is milked as she falls for the man (Jose Suarez), until she is told the truth and goes back to her impending spinsterhood.

Film is expertly directed by J. A. Bardem, who also wrote the tight script, and neatly acted by Miss Blair in the key role. Yves Massard stands out in a minor role, while others in cast, from Jose Suarez on down the list, back ably. Lensing by Michel Kelber and music by Joseph Kosma are both of top quality in a quality production which rates international attention. *Hawk.*

Emil to Tantei Tachi
(The Boy Detectives)
(JAPANESE)

Venice, Aug. 30.
Educational Film Exchange release of Seishi Matsamuru production. Features Ryo Iwashita, Keiko Yuri, Hisaji Komine, Miwa Saito, Kojiro Kusanagi, and others. Directed by Mitsuo Wakasugi. Screenplay, Kaoru Kataoka; from novel "Emil und die Detective" by Erich Kaestner; camera, Kiyomi Kurod; music, Hiroshi Kusakawa; editor, Fumiko Kishi. At Film Festival, Venice. Running time, **56 MINS.**

Though primarily intended for moppet eyes, this Jap version of the popular German story, "Emil and the Detectives," makes pleasant and amusing adult fare as well, while giving the original story an unusual setting. Might do for some specialized bookings in the USA., or for video use.

W.k. tale details the adventures of a youngster who is robbed of his mother's cash on his way into town. With the help of a gang of kids, he chases the thief, who is distinguished by his bowler hat, through which he finally gets him to capitulate. Pic is well acted and amusingly scripted and directed, so that laughs register beyond the lingual barrier. Technical credits are all good. *Hawk.*

Manoever Zwilling
(Twin Maneuver)
(AUSTRIAN)

Vienna, Sept. 1.
Sascha Film Co. release of Herbert Gruber production. Stars Gunther Philipp; features Doris Kirchner, Richard Romanowsky, Joachim Fuchsberger, Rudolf Carl, Helli Servi. Directed by Hans Quest; screenplay, Gunther Philipp; camera, Sepp Ketterer; settings, Friedrich Jueptner; costumes, Edith Almoslino; music, Hans Lang. At Flieger Kino, Vienna, Sept. 1, '56. Running time, **95 MINS.**
Poldi (Franz) ....Gunther Philipp
Liesl .... Doris Kirchner
Thomas ....Joachim Fuchsberger
Military physician..Richard Romanowsky
Krummbein .... Rudolf Carl
Berta .... Luise Martini
Rosl .... Helli Servi
Colonel .... Hans Olden
Stadler sen.............. Paul Lowinger
Haberl .... Ernst Waldbrunn
Doctor .... Peter Brand
Lieutenant Vogel ......Joerg Liebenfels

Fair entertainment in this pic. Though the flood of pictures with stories based on pre-World War I Austrian army affairs lessens the chances of b.o., this one cannot be overlooked for it has one point more to the good: this story actually happened almost as written by Gunther Philipp.

It concerns, as the title reveals, a double role. Scriptor-actor Gunther Philipp measures up to all demands, when called to military service and substituting for the brother. Hans Olden shows up best among the featured players as the colonel. There is much laugh value in the parts of Richard Romanowsky, Ernst Waldbrunn and Rudolf Carl. Doris Kirchner's part stresses the romance angle.

Hans Quest's direction emphasizes action and points up the old Austrian royal army. Tinted camerawork by Sepp Kettener is good, though the Agfa colors are not "smooth" enough. Settings by Friedrich Jueptner are okay, as are all other technical details. The original score, cleffed by Hans Lang, is so-so. *Maas.*

L'Impero del Sole
(Empire of the Sun)
(ITALIAN—COLOR—C'SCOPE)

Venice, Aug. 30..
Lux production and release. Written and directed by Enrico Gras and Mario Craveri; camera (Ferraniacolor) Mario Craveri; music, Francesco Lavagnino; editor, Mario Serandrei. At Film Festival, Venice. Running time, **85 MINS.**

Another impressive feature documentary from the team which made the prizewinning "Lost Continent." Top color lensing, unusual material, excellent editing and scoring form a whole which should make for strong grosses in most markets.

This time Enrico Gras and Mario Craveri have taken their cameras to Peru and returned with material which pleases all the senses while stimulating and interesting in its depiction of far-away peoples and customs. The Uru tribes of the Andes, the inhabitants of the Amazon basin, the guano bird islands, the fight between a bull and a condor, Peruvian variation of the Spanish bullfight, civilization's sweep into the South American jungle, are some of the topics treated with unusual taste and skill. Craveri's pictorial sense and expert C'Scope lensing in a beautiful Ferraniacolor as exemplified here slot him as one of the finest lensers in the world today.

But what impresses in this pic is the composite contribution of Craveri and Gras, of musician Francesco Lavagnino, of the uncredited sound technician, and of editor Mario Serandrei, all of whom have combined to produce a colorful, beautiful, always interesting and never lagging documentary. Commentary is intelligent and to the point. All technical credits are top-drawer. *Hawk.*

The Opposite Sex
(C'SCOPE-SONGS-COLOR)

High-powered remake, with music, of "The Women," 1939 pic hit; strong cast names, strong b.o. biz.

Hollywood, Sept. 18.
Metro release of Joe Pasternak production. Stars June Allyson. Joan Collins, Dolores Gray, Ann Sheridan, Ann Miller; costars Leslie Nielsen, Jeff Richards, Agnes Moorehead, Charlotte Greenwood, Joan Blondell, Sam Levene; guest stars, Harry James, Art Mooney, Dick Shawn, Jim Backus; features Bill Goodwin. Directed by David Miller. Screenplay, Fay and Michael Kanin; adapted from play by Clare Boothe; camera (MetroColor), Robert Bronner; editor, John McSweeney Jr.; musical supervision, George Stoll; new songs, Nicholas Brodzky, Sammy Cahn; musical numbers staged by Robert Sidney. Previewed Sept. 11, '56. Running time, **115 MINS.**

Kay .... June Allyson
Crystal .... Joan Collins
Sylvia .... Dolores Gray
Amanda .... Ann Sheridan
Gloria .... Ann Miller
Steve Hilliard .... Leslie Nielsen
Buck Winston .... Jeff Richards
Countess .... Agnes Moorehead
Lucy .... Charlotte Greenwood
Edith .... Joan Blondell
Mike Pearl .... Sam Levene
Howard Fowler .... Bill Goodwin
Olga .... Alice Pearce
Dolly .... Barbara Jo Allen
Debbie .... Sandy Descher
Pat .... Carolyn Jones
Leading Man Dancer ..... Jerry Antes
Ted .... Alan Marshal
Phelps Potter .... Jonathan Hole
Himself .... Harry James
Himself .... Art Mooney
Singer .... Dick Shawn
Psychiatrist .... Jim Backus

The female of the species is more deadly than the male, a fact that "The Opposite Sex" again emphasizes for the awed amusement of the male viewer and the discomfort of some distaff lookers. As a remake with music of Clare Boothe's feline comedy, "The Women," first screened by Metro in 1939, it's high-powered entertainment with a name cast and a strong boxoffice potential.

The mixture of marriage and morals, songs and satire, under Joe Pasternak's topnotch production supervision plays with a pleasing frothy glibness as the femmes test their claws on each other and on their men. Scripting by Fay and Michael Kanin is a slick surface analysis of gals who are consistently inconsistent, made entertaining viewing by plenty of spicy dialog, beautiful settings and costumes, good tunes and firstrate directorial pacing by David Miller.

June Allyson, who hasn't sung in pix for quite a few years, turns on the vocalistics pleasantly as the girl who almost loses her man to a sexpot enacted by Joan Collins before she decides to become a feline femme herself. "Young Man With a Horn," done with Harry James, and "A Perfect Love" both treat the ear via her slightly hoarse voice. For a spectacular production number, she appears with a male group in "Now! Baby, Now!" A calypso note is sounded in another production piece, "Dere's Yellow Gold On Da Trees," featuring Miss Collins and dancers. Guest stars Dick Shawn and Jim Backus act out the comedic title tune about a psychiatrist's couch cluttered with dames for a good laugh spot. The big musical scorer, though, is "Rock and Roll Tumbleweed," put over with a bang by Jeff Richards backed by Art Mooney. New tunes are by Nicholas Brodszky and Sammy Cahn, with Robert Sidney staging the production numbers.

In addition to the tune duties, Miss Allyson clicks as the ever-loving wife who runs off to Reno when hubby Leslie Nielsen gets trapped by Miss Collins, and then learns that if she wants her man back she must adopt the predatory methods of her Park Avenue sisters-under-the-skin. She gets him in an expose of feline tricks-of-the-trade that gain in mirth under such instructors as Dolores Gray, a dame who loses Bill Goodwin to the non-dancing but potent Ann Miller; Ann Sheridan, writer who doesn't have a man but knows all about them; Agnes Moorehead, a joy as the much-married, and unmarried, Reno vistor; Charlotte Greenwood, a click as the proprietor of a haven for twixt-and-between women; and Joan Blondell, delightful as a girl who thinks marriage consists of babies and proves it almost every year. Miss Collins makes a man wonder why Nielsen took so long to get caught in her web.

While it's a femme show, males are still a necessary part if the wheels of love are to go round. Ably furnishing reason for their presence are Nielsen, Jeff Richards and such others trapped in the battle-of-the-sexes as Sam Levene, Bill Goodwin and Jonathan Hole. Picture is a particularly happy vehicle for Richards, playing the bashfully amorous cowpoke at Miss Greenwood's divorcee haven. He wraps up the character in solid style. Sandy Descher does well as a moppet and there's a biting satire of a composite femme columnist by Barbara Jo Allen. Alice Pearce, a gossipping manicurist, Carolyn Jones and others contribute to the fun.

The CinemaScope photography in MetroColor by Robert Bronner is one of the technical pluses, as is the art direction, set decorations, costuming by Helen Rose and special effects. George Stoll gives the music excellent supervision.

Brog.

The Brave One
(C'SCOPE—COLOR)

Movingly sentimental tale of a little boy and his fighting bull pet, lensed in Mexico. Good special-interest feature, but with okay overall appeal.

Hollywood, Sept. 18.

RKO release of Maurice King, Frank King production. Introduces Michel Ray; features Rodolfo Hoyos, Elsa Cardenas, Carlos Navarro, Joi Lansing, Fermin Rivera, George Trevino, Carlos Fernandez. Directed by Irving Rapper. Screenplay, Harry Franklin, Merrill G. White; story, Robert Rich; camera (Technicolor), Jack Cardiff; editor, Merrill G. White; music, Victor Young. Previewed Sept. 13, '56. Running time, **100 MINS.**

Leonardo	Michel Ray
Rafael Rosillo	Rodolfo Hoyos
Maria	Elsa Cardenas
Don Alejandro	Carlos Navarro
Marion Randall	Joi Lansing
Fermin Rivera	Fermin Rivera
Salvador	George Trevino
Manuel	Carlos Fernandez

A kid's love for his pet themes this sentimentally moving story of a small Mexican boy who raises a fighting bull. Told against some magnificent CinemaScope photography of the below-the-border setting, it's a picture of overall appeal, yet with particular special-interest values. The kind of selling it receives, along with a favorable word-of-mouth, will shape its grossing prospects, which could be good over the long pull.

Maurice and Frank King produced for RKO release, using the sensitive script by Harry Franklin and Merrill G. White which, in turn, was taken from a Robert Rich story based on an actual bullring incident that occurred in the Plaza del Toros in Barcelona in 1936 when a bull of much bravery and heart was pardoned to his young master. There's some near schmaltz, along with the sensitivity, in the screenplay, but because of the warm, tender aspects, the touches of human comedy and the exciting bullring finale, most viewers won't find the tendency to over-sentimentality objectionable. Irving Rapper's direction is surehanded in handling the assorted aspects of the plot. The dramatic wallop achieved at the finale through his guidance and the standout lensing by Jack Cardiff makes for good theatre.

"The Brave One" has a few other minor flaws. One is that it tends to run longer than actually necessary at 100 minutes. Another is the tentative introduction of a sideline romantic item that never develops. About the only cash value here is the possibility of ad and lobby art using Joi Lansing, a well-filled-out blonde. Film has a fine score by Victor Young, musically meritorious, but it and the rest of the sound track was played so loudly at the preview that some of the value was lost in the noise.

Audiences won't find it much of a problem to accept young Michel Ray as the human hero of the plot once they have gotten by the fact he's a blue-eyed Mexican boy with an English accent. He soon makes you forget this, as well as the fact he doesn't grow although his pet bull spans a growth from just-born calf to a tremendous, four-year-old fighting animal.

Plot is the touching account of a young Mexican farm boy who raises a pet bull, only to have it taken away from him when the ranch owner is accidentally killed and the stock sold off. The bull is shipped to the Plaza de Mexico to face Fermin Rivera, matador playing himself, and the little boy arrives too late with a pardon for the bull from the President. However, the display of valor by the bull and the matador so influences the crowd that the animal is granted the right to live. The plaza footage is a dramatic spectacle of an ages-old Latin art and just about the best yet to reach the screen.

Performing with realistic touches are Rodolfo Hoyos, the boy's father; Elsa Cardenas, his sister; Rivera, and Carlos Navarro, the ranch owner. George Trevino adds a light touch as a truck driver, and Carlos Fernandez as Miss Cardenas' intended is good.

White, in addition to co-scripting with Franklin, also acted as supervising editor on the film and could have been tighter with his cutting.

Brog.

Passport to Treason

Routine British whodunit, with only Rod Cameron's name to recommend it.

Hollywood, Sept. 14.

Astor release of a Robert S. Baker-Monty Berman production. Stars Rod Cameron, Lois Maxwell, Clifford Evans; features Douglas Wilmer, Andrew Fau, John Collicos, Derek Sydney. Directed by Baker. Screenplay, Kenneth Hayles; novel by Manning O'Brine; camera, Berman; editor, Henry Richardson; music, Stanley Black; art director, John Stoll. Reviewed Sept. 12, '56. Running time, **70 MINS.**

"Passport to Treason" is a run-of-the-mill British whodunit with little to recommend it for the American market. Name of Rod Cameron may be certain attraction in program situations, but story line is blurry and frequently burdened by incomprehensible English dialog which automatically drops it into lowercase billing.

The Robert S. Baker-Monty Berman production focuses on Cameron as a private eye in London. When an associate is murdered, he takes over where latter left off in the investigation of a league for world peace. What he's searching for and ramifications which arise for him to hurdle aren't explained and spectator is left as confused as Cameron as he slugs his way to his unknown objective. Baker's direction doesn't help.

Cameron is sturdy in his role and Lois Maxwell is his femme lead, appearing as an undercover girl working for British government. Clifford Evans co-stars as head of the league, and Douglas Wilmer and John Collicos offer stock heavy characterizations. Technical credits also are stock.

Whit.

Venice Films

Gervaise
(FRENCH)

Venice, Sept. 11.

Corona release of Agnes Delahaye-Silver Films-CICC production. Stars Maria Schell, Francois Perier, Suzy Delair; features Armand Mestral, Mathilde Casadesus, Jacques Hilling, Jany Holt, Florelle, Jacques Arden. Directed by Rene Clement. Screenplay, Jean Aurenche, Pierre Bost from novel by Emile Zola, "L'Assomoir" (The Trap); camera, Rene Juillard; editor, Henri Rust; music, Georges Auric. At Venice Film Festival. Running time, **120 MINS.**

Gervaise	Maria Schell
Coupeau	Francis Perier
Virginie	Suzy Delair
Madame Boche	Mathilde Casadesus
Lantier	Armand Mestral
Goujet	Jacques Arden
Lorilleux	Jany Holt
Boche	Jacques Hilling
Madame Coupeau	Florelle

Rene Clement's craftsmanship, already known in U.S. art house circles via "Forbidden Games," "Walls of Malapaga" and "Monsieur Ripois," again shows his talent in this two hour naturalistic study of the life and hard times of a lowerclass woman under the Second French Empire. Technique and thesping combine for fine visual and period effects, but a downbeat, overlong tale remains primarily for special U.S. chances. Femme aspects may slant this for distaff exploitation values for more general chances, but it will need hardsell to overcome its grim manner.

An Emile Zola novel, on which this film is based, has been switched to emphasize the story of the woman Gervaise rather than sticking to its main theme of the ravages of alcoholism among the poor. Her first lover leaves her, at the age of 18, with two children. She manages to marry a gentle but weak roofer and things are fine until a fall makes him afraid and leads him into alcoholism. She then opens a store via a loan from an admirer, but a vindictive enemy brings back her first love who moves in on them to supposedly overlook the bringing up of his children.

A delerium tremens attack and death of her husband leads to the loss of her store and her final degeneration. Meantime, the camera dwells on the budding courtesan quality of Gervaise's daughter Nana, who was to become a heroine of another Zola novel.

Recreation of period is deft and expert via decors and costumes. There's also a daguerreotype feel to the lensing that underlines the closeness and downtrodden elements of slum life. They come through nicely but a lyric and more epic quality escapes the director. Maria Schell, cast in the title role, gives out with an intellectualized, mannered performance that is penetratingly effective at times and overtechnical at others. She evokes some pathos, but the twisting facets of temperament and play rarely lead to a complete character emergence in Gervaise.

Francoise Perier provides an intelligent and sympathetic portrait of the downfall of an alcoholic. Suzy Delair contributes a tightly etched addition as the narrow enemy whose pose as a friend allows her to insidiously undermine the life of Gervaise.

Director Clement shines in flashy scenes such as a violent femme fight in a public wash house. His observations and notations on the lowlife, also give the film chances for good word-of-mouth and critical acclaim.

Withal, this has enough technical and thesp brilliance to overcome its episodic and almost melodramatic qualities. It's replete with stature and gloss for art spots, and has prospects for wide appeal to the distaff element. The name of Miss Schell may also be a plus factor.

Mosk.

Biruma No Tategoto (The Harp of Burma) (Japanese). Nikkatsu release and production. Directed by Kan Ichikawa. Screenplay, Michio Takeyama, Natto Wada; camera, Minoru Yokoyama; editor, Masanori Tsujii; music, Akira Ifukube. With Rentaro Mikumi, Shoji Yasui, Tatsuya Mihashi. At Venice Film Fest. Running time, **115 MINS.**

Offbeater concerns the last days of the war in Burma and is about a Japanese private who decides to stay on to bury all the Japanese dead strewn over the land. He is wounded and saved by a holy man whose robes he steals to get back to his troop. However, he runs on a whole battalion of his dead, with vultures settling, and makes his vow to stay on. Film concerns how his captive mates learn of his resolve and try to talk him into going back with them. Film has a good narrative style, but its over-simplified storytelling, and intermittently taking action, relegate this for only lingo chances in the U. S. It is too downbeat and lacking the appeal necessary for any art house chances. Technical credits and acting are good and direction is restrained but lacks the power to make this an unusual plea. It remains a fair tale, but too morbid for any untoward U. S. interest.

Mosk.

Dracos (GREEK). Ste. Cinematographie Athens release and production. Directed by Nikos Koundouros. Screenplay, Jacobo Kambanelis; camera, Kostas Theodorides; editor, Manos Hadjidakis. With Dinos Iliopoulos, Margarita Papageorkiou, Yannis Argiris. At Venice Film Fest. Running time, **110 MINS.**

Film gives insight into the Greek underworld and the strange rituals among the men, but, overall, is too confused and amateurish technically to make for any U. S. chances, except for a possible dualer value on its tale of a timid clerk who gets mistaken for a famous crook. Though theme is familiar it gets a satirical-serio treatment here and ends with the clerk trying to return to the dangerous life, after the police find he is not the real one, only to find death at the hands of the mob.

Mixing various styles, with uneven acting, this is a curio bet, at best, and is limited for any U. S. opportunities of unusual calibre. Though somewhat unique it is hard to see why this was chosen to be a Venice entry, when a selection committee tried for a high and mighty choice level. Technical aspects are ordinary but some feverish editing and directorial flashes, such as a mass, spontaneous dance among the gangsters in a nitery, give this some distinction and point to the fact that Director Nikos Koundouros may grow into a name to be watched when he develops discipline. *Mosk.*

Enjeu De La Vie (Life at Stake) (CZECHOSLOVAKIAN). Czech State Film release and production. Directed by Jiri Weiss. Screenplay, K. J. Benes, Weiss; camera, Vladimir Novotny; editor, Miroslav. At Venice Film Festival. Running time, **95 MINS.**

Well made Czech film on the resistance movement in Prague during the last war develops thriller aspects without overstating them. Shapes U.S. lingo entry for specialized spotting.

Plot centres on woman married to a rather cowardly man who, though not a collaborator, plays into Gestapo hands by his refusal to take sides. His wife does and hides an underground leader. Her older son finds out and it's his coming of age, as well as the weakling's downfall and the mother's heroism, that make up the brunt of the pic. Directed with feeling by Jiri Weiss and poignantly and intelligently played by Vlasta Chramostova as the woman and Karel Hoger as the husband, it is a superior war feature pic. Technical credits are good and underscored to play up the character and action of the film. An ironic excerpt from Nazi newsreels claiming no resistance operates and Czechs love their conquerors, precedes the segue into this deftly conceived pic. *Mosk.*

La Traversee De Paris
(The Trip Across Paris)
(FRENCH—ITALIAN)

Venice, Sept. 11.

Franco-London release of Franco-London-Continentale production. Stars Jean Gabin, Bourvil; features Louis De Funes, Jeannette Batti, Anouk Ferjac, Georgette Anys. Directed by Claude Autant-Lara. Screenplay, Jean Aurenche, Pierre Bost from novel by Marcel Tyme; camera, Jacques Natteau; editor, Madeleine Gug; music, Rene Cloerec. At Venice Film Festival. Running time, **90 MINS.**

Grandgil	Jean Gabin
Martin	Bourvil
Mariette	Jeannette Batti
Jambier	Louis De Funes
Young Girl	Anouk Ferjac
Waitress	Georgette Anys

Offbeater treats a period of recent French history that rarely has appeared in film backgrounds here, namely the Occupation of France during the last war. A serious subject is handled in a comic manner with an attempt at irony and insouciance in this farcical fable. Smooth technique and thespian spin out this slightly overstretched anecdote which garners enough yocks to make this in for pop value locally, but it remains primarily for art house and specialized categories in the U.S.

It does not have the broader entertainment qualities for more general chances, and its intensely national humor and allusions also slant this for specialized art house trade. Producer Henry Deutschmeister says that the foreign version will have a foreword explaining the physical aspects of the Occupation seriously before segueing into the comic carryings-on of the film. This should help.

Two characters, who have never met, get thrown into a black market delivery of four valises full of meat together. One is a narrow, conventional blacketeer who is honest in his work while the other is a stranger brought into it when the regular partner is pinched. He turns out to be an artist involved for the curiosity interests.

The mission means crossing Paris and the adventures happen in the street as they are plagued by hungry dogs, inquisitive policemen, Germans and the mistrust the simpler member has for his new helper. A series of run-ins and adventures give a sardonic-eye view of the Occupation and make for some excellent vignettes, statements and moments (i.e. a streetwalker of fading looks whose reactions to Germans and French make a point on human nature; the pettiness and fright of a group of self-interested barkeepers, and the separation of a gigolo and his mistress after the usual nighttime arrests).

Main flaw is an episode quality which, though making its statement on war and human nature, rarely gets the ironic edge into it to make for complete final emphasis on the serio-comic denouement. A tacked-on ending is also somewhat patronizing and could be dispensed with to tighten up the film. End shows a meeting of the two some years later.

Jean Gabin, as the subtler member, turns in some good scenes when he is venting his spleen at the crassness and stupidity he meets on the journey, but storyline makes his character somewhat uneven. Bourvil, a Gallic comedian, turns in a finely nuanced turn as the other and less resourceful member. Support is fine and technical credits and production aspects excellent. Director Claude Autant-Lara has handed this a glossy backing and gotten savor into the high points, but not quite the ironic statement it called for. The subject is unique and its unusual qualities give this the looks of two films with a U.S. art house future with subsequents chancey. *Mosk.*

The Gadfly
(RUSSIAN—COLOR)

A Soviet import with possible U.S. art house potential.

Sovexportfilm release of Lenfilm production presented by Artkino. Directed by A. Feinzimmer. Screenplay, E. Gabrilovich, based on novel by Ethel L. Voynich; camera (Magicolor), A. Moskvin; music, Dimitri Shostakovich. At Cameo, N. Y., Sept. 15, '56. Running time, **94 MINS.**

Arthur	O. Strizhenov
Gemma	M. Strizhenova
Montanelli	N. Simonov
Martini	V. Etush
Guiseppe	P. Usovnichenko
Ciovanni	V. Vedvedyev
Cardi	R. Simonov
Grassini	A. Khodursky
James	G. Shpigel
Julia	E. Yunger

(In Russian; English Titles)

One of the better Soviet imports, "The Gadfly" is a moving period drama that may rate attention from U.S. art houses which normally eschew Russian product. While this film version of the Ethel L. Voynich novel tends to drag at times, nevertheless the suspense builds nicely to bring about a stirring denouement.

As the yarn unreels, it's quite apparent that Mrs. Voynich's 60-year-old classic contains ample material for two or three films. But the screenplay of E. Gabrilovich competently condenses this mid-19th century tale of revolution in Austrian-held Italy. Key character of the script is the illegitimate son of a cardinal who strives for a free Italy.

Known as the Gadfly, the agitator is a thorn in the side of the constabulary. Along with the film's political aspects are ample romantic overtones plus some religious discord that may provoke displeasure from the Roman Catholic hierarchy. Ultimately the Gadfly meets death before an Austrian firing squad with the Cardinal overcome with remorse and an equally penitent sweetheart also mourning him.

O. Strizhenov, cast in the title role, turns in a fine characterization of a man who occasionally is a cynic but whose overall motivations stem from sincere principles. Likewise, M. Strizhenova is wistful and loyal as a woman who once rejected her admirer and carries it on her conscience. N. Simonov's portrayal of the Cardinal accents the dignity of such a prelate, but at the same time his performance seems to hint at the danger when church and state are virtually the same. Able support is provided by V. Etush and P. Usovnichenko, among others.

Controversial theme is nicely delineated by direction of A. Feinzimmer who conveniently tosses in some action scenes when the dramatic going becomes rather heavy. Also a plus are opulent production values usually not found in the average Soviet import. Magicolor camerawork of A. Moskvin is good as is the Dimitri Shostakovich score. Sole technical defect appears to be a poor soundtrack—at least on print caught—for the sound frequently faded out entirely. *Gilb.*

Der Opernball
(OPERA BALL)
(AUSTRIAN—SONGS)

Vienna, Sept. 12.

Sascha Film release of Karl Ehrlich (Sascha Film Company) production. Stars Johannes Heesters and Hertha Feiler. Features Josef Meinrad, Sonja Ziemann, Adrian Hoven, Theo Lingen and Hans Moser. Screenplay and direction by Ernst Marischka. Camera, Bruno Mondi; settings, Fritz Jueptner-Jonstorff; costumes, Gerdago and Dr. Leo Bei; masks, Rudolf Ohlschmid and Leopold Kuhnert; music, Richard Heuberger; orchestration and directing, Anton Profes. At Apollo Kino, Vienna, Sept. 12, '56. Running time, **95 MINS.**

Georg Dannhauser	Johannes Heesters
Elisabeth	Hertha Feilee
Paul Hollinger	Josef Meinrad
Helene, his wife	Songa Ziemann
Richard Stelzer	Adrian Hoven
Eduard v. Lamberg	Rudolf Vogel
Hermine, his wife	Fita Benkhoff
Philipp, servant	Theo Lingen
Hanni	Dorit Kreysler
Mizzi Schuster	Frances Martin
Waiter	Hans Moser

"Opera Ball" is—for Austria—a very high-budget filmversion of the classical Vienna operetta with the same title. Story and production have imagination. Plot revolves around Johannes Heesters as "Georg Dannhauser," whose martial fidelity is tested (a theme dear to Austrian dramatists!) by his wife. Dialog is good and, while many situations can be anticipated, pace holds up to sustain interest, when hubby in return tests the fidelity of his spouse. Hertha Feiler and Johannes Heesters in the two roles are excellent.

Josef Meinrad shows up fine in his "Hollinger role," seeking erotic adventure. Sonja Ziemann, Adrian Hoven, Rudolf Vogel, Fita Benkhoff, Theo Lingen, Dorit Kreysler and Frances Martin are all very capable in supporting roles. Hans Moser scores as "head waiter."

Ernst Marischka directed his own script of the Karl Ehrlich production at an okay pace. (What are the prospects, with English captions for the U.S. market? At a guess, nominal but better than Austrian films' average).

Camera work by Bruno Mondi is very impressive, giving this film fine visual qualities as well as old Vienna atmosphere. Colors are good. Richard Heuberger's original score was fittingly adapted by Anton Profes, who added a few numbers from other classical operettas plus his own Csardas.

Vienna locale of the story furnishes the background for Fritz Jueptner-Jonstorff's beautiful settings and Gerdago's plus Leo Bei's fitting costumes. All technical details are high standard. The ballet scenes are outstanding. *Maas.*

Suor Letizia
(When Angels Don't Fly)
(ITALIAN)

Columbia Pictures release of a Rizzoli-Pallavicini Production. Stars Anna Magnani; features Eleonora Rossi Drago, Antonino Ciffariello, Piero Boccia, Luisa Rossi. Directed by Mario Camerini; screenplay, Cesare Zavattini and Camerini from an idea by Antonio Altoviti and Giose Rimanelli; camera, Gianni di Venanzo. At Film Festival, Venice, Running time, **101 MINS.**

Suor Letizia	Anna Magnani
Assunta	Eleonora Rossi Drago
Peppino	Antonio Ciffariello
Salvatore	Piero Boccia

Offbeat subject matter boosted by a good performance by Anna Magnani looks a good possibility in general situations on the strength of her name, both statewide and elsewhere. Pic's chances could be greatly heightened via a tightening of its first half, which builds too slowly. General, rather than arty, handling is suggested.

The Oscar winner's first film since "Rose Tattoo" has an interesting central plot core, not always successfully developed in script form. A nun, forgetting her habit and dedication, has her innate maternal instincts aroused by a young child whose parents have abandoned him; she "adopts" him, but eventually realizes her faults and brings him back to his mother, who has by this time also come round to a realization of her parental duties.

The pic's first half, with its reminiscences of other pix on "modern" nuns ("Come To The Stable") as well as of the successful Spanish "Marcelino, Pan Y Vino," in the way the moppet is handled and plotted, is weak and slow-paced, with humor appearing forced and even Miss Magnani over-straining for a lightweight comic effect which does not always suit her. However, when the conflict between her duties and her maternal instinct comes to a head, pic builds rapidly to a hard-hitting, dramatic and moving finale in which the actress is able to unleash her formidable talent.

Piero Boccia, as the kid, has his winning moments, while Eleonora Rossi Drago and Antonio Ciffariello lend okay support. Mario Camerini's direction is uneven and often appears listlessly to follow the script which, as noted, often offers the thespers indifferent material to work on. Lensing by Gianni di Venanzo, both on locations on the island of Ischia and in Roman studios, is competent, and remaining credits are good. *Hawk.*

Tea and Sympathy
(C'SCOPE—COLOR)

Stirring presentation of 'sissy-boy' theme. Exceptionally well played by Deborah Kerr and John Kerr. Strong boxoffice for sure.

Metro release of Pandro S. Berman production. Stars Deborah Kerr, John Kerr; features Leif Erickson, Edward Andrews, Darryl Hickman, Norma Crane. Directed by Vincente Minnelli. Screenplay, Robert Anderson, from Anderson's play; camera (Metrocolor), John Alton; editor, Ferris Webster; music, Adolph Deutsch. Previewed in N.Y. Sept. 13. Running time, **122 MINS.**

Laura Reynolds	Deborah Kerr
Tom Robinson Lee	John Kerr
Bill Reynolds	Leif Erickson
Herb Lee	Edward Andrews
Al	Darryl Hickman
Ellie Martin	Norma Crane
Ollie	Dean Jones
Lilly Sears	Jacqueline De Wit
Ralph	Tom Laughlin
Steve	Ralph Votrain
Phil	Steven Terrell
Ted	Kip King
Henry	Jimmy Hayes
Roger	Richard Tyler
Vic	Don Burnett

First, let Metro be congratulated for not being discouraged and for going ahead with a boxoffice property that presented unique problems right from the start. This is the story of a youngster regarded by fellow students as "not regular" (i.e. not manly). The spotlight is on clearly implied homosexuality —and that was explicit to the stage play's plot.

In fashioning this story for the screen, M-G was called upon to exercise the utmost care. Any cinematic indiscretion would set off howls of protests. And, too, the values of the original play could not be abandoned because, delicate as it was, the original was moving, forceful theatre.

The Pandro S. Berman production at hand is a success on all counts. Robert Anderson's adaptation of his own legiter (which was produced on stage by the Playwrights Company and Mary K. Frank) is a fine translation. Minor changes were made in the transition and these have the effect of partially toning down a few story points.

But Anderson's rewrite job keeps the essentials in proper focus. The pivotal role of the misunderstood sensitive boy is an excellently drawn characterization. The part is played with marked credibility by John Kerr, a repeat from the original. The housemaster's wife, who offers tea and sympathy to the students, in a character study of equal sensitivity and depth, Deborah Kerr gives the role all it deserves. She's strikingly effective.

The housemaster part, played with muscle-flexing exhibitionism by Leif Frickson, has lost some of its meaning, in the tone-down. On the stage his efforts at being "manly" carried the suggestion that, indeed, he was trying to compensate a fear of a homo trend in his own makeup. The suggestion is diluted to absence in the picture.

Edward Andrews, as Kerr's father, is the brash and understanding parent who would prefer to see his son carry on with the town tart so that this would erase his "sister-boy" reputation. Norma Crane is shown briefly but registers sharply as the waitress with whom Kerr tries but fails to establish his masculinity.

Rounding out the roster of principals is Darryl Hickman as the only students who refuses to believe the "sister boy" cracks about his roommate, Kerr. Hickman measures up to the part nicely.

"Tea and Sympathy," to wrap it up, is the story of a youth tortured by cruel, outspoken rumor-mongers. Lacking the knowledge that his home background influenced his un-athletic behavior, they brand him "sister boy," because of his artistic tastes—books, art, highbrow music. He can find no sympathy for his aesthetics from his father or his housemaster, but only from the latter's wife. It is only she, Miss Kerr, who reaches out to him, and eases his own self-doubts by offering herself in romantic embrace. This scene was an electrifying climax to the play, incidentally. It is followed in the film by another shot of Kerr returning to the school 10 years later with the dialog getting across the point that he's married and the father of three children.

Berman's production mounting has given the story additional scope, taking advantage of the flexibility of the cameras. It's a high-level production throughout, laid against impressive Cinema-Scoped and Metrocolored settings. Director Vincente Minnelli has drawn from his players expert work, somehow balancing one against the other and thus wringing out from the story its full impact. The casting, with the key roles being from the original play, is ideal. Music by Adolph Deutsch provides effective background and all technical assists are fine.
Gene.

The Friendly Persuasion
(SONGS-COLOR)

Sock comedy-drama, rich in human values, with Gary Cooper, potent word-of-mouth to launch Allied Artists in class keys.

Hollywood, Sept. 25.

Allied Artists release of William Wyler production, directed by Wyler. Stars Gary Cooper; costars Dorothy McGuire, Marjorie Main; introduces Anthony Perkins; features Richard Eyer, Robert Middleton, Phyllis Love, Mark Richman, Walter Catlett. Associate producer, Robert Wyler. From book by Jessamyn West; camera (De Luxe Color), Ellsworth Fredricks; editors, Robert Swink, Edward Biery Jr., Robert Belcher; music, Dimitri Tiomkin; songs, Tiomkin and Paul Francis Webster; title song sung by Pat Boone. Previewed Sept. 10, '56. Running time, **137 MINS.**

Jess Birdwell	Gary Cooper
Eliza Birdwell	Dorothy McGuire
Widow Hudspeth	Marjorie Main
Josh Birdwell	Anthony Perkins
Little Jess	Richard Eyer
Sam Jordan	Robert Middleton
Mattie Birdwell	Phyllis Love
Gard Jordan	Mark Richman
Professor Quigley	Walter Catlett
Purdy	Richard Hale
Enoch	Joel Fluellen
Army Major	Theodore Newton
Caleb	John Smith
Quaker Woman	Mary Carr
Widow Hudspeth's Daughters	Edna Skinner, Marjorie Durant, Frances Farwell
Elders	Russell Simpson, Charles Halton, Everett Glass
The Goose	Samantha

Allied Artists makes a bid for de luxe playing time in the top key situations with "The Friendly Persuasion" and should find the doors opening easily with this one. It's a sock comedy-drama, rich in human values under William Wyler's producer-director guidance, and offers rewarding entertainment for most all ages and classes of audience. Indications are that the word-of-mouth will be potent which, with Gary Cooper's name on the marquees, can make the boxoffice returns substantial. They will have to be if Allied Artists is to come out on its most costly production (reportedly over $3,000,-

000), but the entertainment values are there to lure the customers.

Wyler has had the project in mind for some eight years and brought the property over to Allied Artists from Paramount. The time and effort he has put into it results in a top show that will mean much to viewers. While it is the simple story of a Quaker family in Indiana back in the 1860's and carries the family and its friends through an assortment of episodes, the footage contains just about everything in the way of comedy and drama, suspense and action. Since it runs for two hours and 17 minutes there's no crowding, and the simplicity of treatment also keeps it with an uncluttered look.

Film goes into release without a screenplay credit, merely stating it is from the book by Jessamyn West, although the novelist, associate producer Robert Wyler and Harry Kleiner all worked with the producer-director at various times on the AA feature.

The episodes alternately jiggle the risibilities, warm the heart and squeeze a tear as the likeable cast enacts the Quaker and other characters. After many warm, beguiling vignettes of family life, story works into its key dramatic point tieing onto the Quaker feeling against bearing arms against a fellow man. This climaxes when the son of the family goes out to fight against a Confederate invasion, is wounded and the father, too, ventures forth to help, but without killing.

Role of the Quaker father, a man touched with gentle humor and inward strength, is glove-fit for Cooper and he carries it off to an immense success. So does Dorothy McGuire in playing the mother of the family, a preacher in her faith and not always able to understand the pixie quality that sometimes bedevils her husband. Marjorie Main tops an extremely broad comedy episode involving Cooper's yen for a faster horse so he can beat a friend to church each Sunday, and three out-sized daughters who go on the make for Cooper's unworldly son, Anthony Perkins.

Perkins scores resoundingly as the son who goes off to fight. The scene of his leave-taking of his mother and father will not leave a dry eye. Young Richard Eyer, smallest member of the family, stands out and his running feud with his mother's pet goose, Samantha, springs some tremendous laughs. Phyllis Love displays a lot of talent as the daughter, and Mark Richman also registers well as the young soldier she loves. Robert Middleton is fine as the Sunday race rival. Walter Catlett, amusing as an organ seller; Joel Fluellen, excellent as the hired hand; Richard Hale, John Smith and others help keep the acting quality high.

Figuring importantly in the way the picture plays is Dimitri Tiomkin's conducting of his own score. Also playing their part in the entertainment are the songs he did with Paul Francis Webster, such as the title number sung by Pat Boone, "Marry Me, Marry Me" and others. All have a nostalgic folktune rhythm that fits the era. Among some outstanding technical contributions is Ellsworth Fredricks' De Luxe Color photography. Edward S. Haworth's art direction, the set decorations by Joe Kish are among other valuable assists. *Brog.*

Toward the Unknown
(COLOR)

Topflight action drama around exploits of jet and rocket pilots in the Air Force. William Holden and solid b.o. biz.

Hollywood, Sept. 25.

Warner Bros. release of Mervyn LeRoy (Toluca) productions, directed by LeRoy. Stars William Holden; costars Lloyd Nolan, Virginia Leith, Charles McGraw; features Murray Hamilton, Paul Fix, James Garner, L. Q. Jones, Karen Steele. Screenplay and associate producer, Beirne Lay Jr.; camera (WarnerColor), Hal Rosson; editor, William Ziegler; music, Paul Baron; special ariobatics by the USAF Thunderbirds. Previewed Sept. 18, '56. Running time, **114 MINS.**

Maj. Lincoln Bond	William Holden
Brig. Genl. Banner	Lloyd Nolan
Connie Mitchell	Virginia Leith
Col. Mickey McKee	Charles McGraw
Maj. Bromo Lee	Murray Hamilton
Lt. Genl. Bryan Shelby	Paul Fix
Maj. Joe Craven	James Garner
Lieut. Sweeney	L. Q. Jones
Polly Craven	Karen Steele
Senator Black	Bartlett Robinson
Hank	Malcolm Atterbury
H. G. Gilbert	Ralph Moody
Mrs. Sarah McKee	Maura Murphy
Debby	Carol Kelly

The exploits of the Air Force pilots who fly experimental jet and rocket planes at Edwards Air Force Base in California are used here for an exciting action drama that should zoom to good results in regular playdates. A good cast, headed by William Holden; a story that mostly avoids the "into the wild blue yonder" service pic cliches, and some thrilling aerial photography in WarnerColor are points in favor of a profitable wicket reaction.

Film is the first for Mervyn LeRoy's Toluca production unit and under his producer-director guidance it comes off exceptionally well. His cast is topnotch and his story handling keeps an excitement pitch going throughout the 114 minutes of footage. Sharp scripting by associate producer Beirne Lay Jr.,, with dialog that contains many punch lines, effective editing by William Ziegler, and some standout lensing by Hal Rosson and second-unit photographer Harold E. Wellman all add to the entertainment wallop.

Plot ties in with, but doesn't unnecessarily pursue, the brain washing undergone by some Red prisoners in Korea to set up a drama of a war hero who must again prove himself after a harrowing experience at the hands of Red captors. He comes to Edwards looking for another chance, is given it by the general in charge, against the latter's instincts, and regains self-confidence and his old girl.

Against a pattern of incredible deeds by the experimenting pilots in testing man and machine, the plot hits a human note that adds to the interest and to the action suspense. Of a topical note is the new-as-today headline describing a rocket flight into space by the new X-2 ship, suspensefully created in the film as a story point. Footage kudoes the work going on at Edwards with a base tour, and then settles down to its fictional entertainment without further todo.

Holden is a forthright hero, troubled by his Korean experiences and seeking a renewed faith in himself. He sells the role exceptionally well. Lloyd Nolan bites into his character of base commander with just the right flavor to keep it from being the usual screen, rule-book martinet. Virginia Leith is the girl, ably fulfilling the demands of the part. Charles McGraw does an honest performance of the colonel who does what he can to help Holden.

Of special note are a number of featured and supporting roles as done by Murray Hamilton, a pilot who resents Holden; Paul Fix, the big brass who wants Nolan at a desk job; L. Q. Jones, a left-footed second lieutenant aide to Nolan, who accounts for considerable comedy; Karen Steele, Air Force wife who loses her husband, James Garner, in a crash; Bartlett Robinson, Malcolm Atterbury, Ralph Moody, and Maura Murphy.

Technical departments line up well and there's a good score by Paul Baron that points up the martial flavor. The special ariobatics by the USAF Thunderbirds are thrilling. *Brog.*

Written On the Wind
(SONG-COLOR)

Adultly treated, probing drama of morals in a multi-million Texas oil family. Good cast and b.o. possibilities.

Hollywood, Sept. 25.

Universal release of Albert Zugsmith production. Stars Rock Hudson, Lauren Bacall, Robert Stack, Dorothy Malone; features Robert Keith, Grant Williams, Robert J. Wilke, Edward C. Platt, Harry Shannon, John Larch. Directed by Douglas Sirk. Screenplay, George Zuckerman; based on Robert Wilder novel; camera (Technicolor), Russell Metty; editor, Russell F. Schoengarth; music, Frank Skinner; song, Victor Young, Sammy Cahn; sung by The Four Aces. Previewed Aug. 28, '56. Running time, **99 MINS.**

Mitch Wayne	Rock Hudson
Lucy Moore Hadley	Lauren Bacall
Kyle Hadley	Robert Stack
Marylee Hadley	Dorothy Malone
Jasper Hadley	Robert Keith
Biff Miley	Grant Williams
Dan Willis	Robert J. Wilke
Doctor Paul Cochrane	Edward C. Platt
Hoak Wayne	Harry Shannon
Roy Carter	John Larch
R. J. Courtney	Joseph Granby
Sam	Roy Glenn
Bertha	Maide Norman
Reporter	William Schallert
Brunette	Joanne Jordan
Blonde	Dani Crayne
Secretary	Dorothy Porter

This outspoken, modern drama probes rather startlingly into the morals and passions of an upper-crust Texas oil family. On shock value alone it would attract b.o. attention, but additionally, it is well done with an excellent cast so the grossing outlook is good.

Producer Albert Zugsmith makes intelligent use of the flashback technique before and during the titles credits runoff to build immediate interest and expectancy without diminishing plot punch. Tiptop scripting by George Zuckerman from the Robert Wilder novel, dramatically deft direction by Douglas Sirk and sock performances by the cast give the story development a follow-through that maintains a strong hold on the viewer.

Rock Hudson, Lauren Bacall, Robert Stack and Dorothy Malone, aptly cast in the star roles, add a zing to the characters that pays off in audience interest. Hudson scores as the normal, lifelong friend of profligate Stack. The latter, in one of his best performances, draws a compelling portrait of a psychotic man ruined by wealth and character weaknesses. Miss Bacall registers strongly as a sensible girl swept into the madness of the oil family when she marries Stack, while Miss Malone hits a career high as the completely immoral sister. Both femmes are attractively gowned by Bill Thomas in costumes that emphasis the characters they play.

Robert Keith, head of the family; Grant Williams, one of Miss Malone's many motel mates; Robert J. Wilke, Edward C. Platt, Harry Shannon, John Larch and others in the cast supply worthwhile support. Art direction and set decorations put a beautiful physical gloss on the production and Russell Metty's Technicolor lensing shows it off to advantage. Frank Skinner's score is good, as is the title tune by Victor Young and Sammy Cahn, sung by The Four Aces behind the titles. *Brog.*

Mio Figlio Nerone
(Nero's Big Weekend)
(ITALIAN-FRENCH)
(C'Scope-Color)

Rome, Sept. 18.

Titanus release of a Titanus-Vides-Les Films Merceau co-production. Stars Alberto Sordi, Gloria Swanson, Vittorio DeSica, Brigitte Bardot. Directed by Steno. From story by Rodolfo Sonego; camera (Eastmancolor), Mario Bava. Previewed in Rome. Running time, **104 MINS.**

Nero	Alberto Sordi
Agrippina	Gloria Swanson
Seneca	Vittorio DeSica
Poppea	Brigitte Bardot

Lavishly mounted ancient Rome costumer should go for fairly big money in France and Italy, where star value alone can sell it. Elsewhere, returns appear spotty, with names and some exploitation angles helping, but will need plenty of both to sell it.

Comedy plot is mainly constructed as a showcase to exhibit Alberto Sordi's considerable comic talents. That it does not quite come off as consistently amusing is mostly due to the fact that the authors never seem to have made up their minds as to whether they wanted to play their comedy broad or subtle. Rhythm wavers, therefore, alternating amusing, sometimes riotous but with some boring stretches.

Sordi is also permitted to overact a basically hammy part. There's just too much of a good thing, even for Sordi fans. On the plus side are good performances by Gloria Swanson, as Nero's mother; Vittorio DeSica, as Seneca, and Brigitte Bardot, as a beauteous Peppea, in and out of the inevitable milkbath. Other thinly veiled young ladies will aid the film's sales points, and there are a number of good sideline characterizations. *Hawk.*

The Best Things in Life Are Free
(C'SCOPE—SONGS—COLOR)

Nostalgic, slickly-produced reprise of the works of Tin Pan Alley's De Sylva, Brown and Henderson. Good cast, rosy b.o. outlook.

20th-Fox release of Henry Ephron production. Stars Gordon MacRae, Dan Dailey, Ernest Borgnine, Sheree North; features Tommy Noonan, Murvyn Vye, Phyllis Avery, Larry Keating, Tony Galento, Norman Brooks, Jacques d'Amboise, Roxanne Arlen. Directed by Michael Curtiz. Screenplay, William Bowers and Phoebe Ephron from John O'Hara story; camera (Color by DeLuxe), Leon Shamroy; editor, Dorothy Spencer; music supervised and conducted by Lionel Newman; production numbers staged by Rod Alexander. Previewed Sept. 20, '56. Running time, **104 MINS.**

B. G. De Sylva	Gordon MacRae
Ray Henderson	Dan Dailey
Lew Brown	Ernest Borgnine
Kitty	Sheree North
Carl	Tommy Noonan
Manny	Murvyn Vye
Maggie Henderson	Phyllis Avery
Sheehan	Larry Keating
Fingers	Tony Galento
Al Jolson	Norman Brooks
Specialty Dancer	Jacques d'Amboise
Perky Nichols	Roxanne Arlen
Hollywood Star	Byron Palmer
Jeannie Henderson	Linda Brace
Susie Henderson	Patty Loo Hudson
Miss Van Seckland	Julie Van Zandt
Brewer	Larry Kerr
Andrews	Charles Victor
Louis	Eugene Borden
Percy, Reporter	Harold Miller
Photographer	Emily Belser
Piano Player	Paull Glass
Dance Director	Bill Foster

In "The Best Things in Life Are Free" producer Henry Ephron and director Michael Curtiz have gone on the reasonably sound theory that, in telling the story of Tin Pan Alley's fabulous team of Buddy De Sylva, Lew Brown and Ray Henderson, all that was necessary was to fill the widescreen with a huge potpourri of their works. The formula, dressed up with some punchy laugh lines and a bit of romantic goings-on, is effective and easily rates this as one of the year's best musicals.

Considering that John O'Hara wrote the story, this CinemaScope tinter leaves a few things to wish for in that department. It catches little of the Jazz Age feeling, except in its costumes and the frantic shimmy and Black Bottom numbers, and the songwriting trio barely come to life as real people.

But the shortcoming is minor. "Best Things in Life" is a gay, tuneful romp, beautifully staged, expertly lensed by vet Leon Shamroy and directed with an eye to maximum visual values. Its dialog, written by William Bower and Phoebe Ephron, is for the most part bright and doesn't get into the way of the film's primary air, i.e. to give out with as many as possible of the catchy De Sylva, Brown & Henderson musical concoctions.

It's a sparkling string of hits that's presented here with all the nostalgic attention they deserve. Performances are top calibre, from Gordon MacRae's and Dan Dailey's pleasant crooning, to Ernest Borgnine's clowning and Sheree North's strenuously agile terp routines. Perhaps, when it's all over and done with, some will feel they've been handed too much of a good thing, for nary a minute goes by without a song or dance number. But, on the whole, it all adds up to a bundle of good entertainment with appeal to young and old.

There are no fewer than 20 numbers in this opus, decked out in the bright hues of DeLuxe color. Outstanding are the big production numbers—"Birth of the Blues" and "Black Bottom"—choreographed by Rod Alexander. Both are from the George White "Scandals of 1926" and are given the kind of super-treatment that registers doubly on the widescreen. Miss North, who has trouble with her diction in the speaking parts, is standout in the dance numbers, particularly the "Birth of the Blues" splurger in which she's teamed with Jacques d'Amboise.

Song is piled on song, making one realize the great combined talent of the trio that wrote 'em. Settings for the various renditions are tasteful and well integrated. Theme song comes from the 1927 "Good News" and is done by Miss North and the rest as a closer. Some of the other songs in this tuner read like an All-American Hit Parade.

MacRae's rendition of "Blues" is in the grand style and rates kudos. Miss North also reveals a nice vocal talent when she does "It All Depends on You" and "Sunny Side Up." In the smaller parts, Murvyn Vye registers strongly as the gangster who wants "in" on the DeSylva, Brown & Henderson shows; Roxanne Arlen is surefire as the gangster's no-talent doll who gets the lead in the show; Phyllis Avery is fine as Mrs. Henderson, and Tony Galento is the right type as Fingers, the emissary of Kansas City Jake who is sent to protect Brown from the mob.

While the story itself is corny, many of the setups are grand. Norman Brooks as Al Jolson offers a nice impersonation and the scene when the three friends watch him do "Sonny Boy" on the (black & white) screen is a howl. Also sure to bring a hearty laugh is the line handed to Borgnine: "What are we supposed to do? Sit around here on our ASCAP!"

Borgnine is obviously at home in playing the rough-at-the-edges Brown. It's a part that needs an actor to convey the warmth underneath, and Borgnine finds just the right notes. His scene with Vye, a satire on the gangster of the '20s, is a gem.

Dailey has a tendency to go through life smiling, but is here perfecely cast. MacRae, as the late Buddy DeSylva, isn't overly convincing in his easy-going manner, but he knows how to put over a song and in this picture that's what counts.

"Best Things" draws on the top-rate material of another era and comes up with a tuneful revue that's dressed up for current tastes. It may not do justice to its people as people, but it's certainly sock tribute to their genius and ingenuity. At the wickets, that's what is going to count.

Hift.

Cha-Cha-Cha Boom
(Musical)

Lively cha-cha-cha beat by Perez Prado and other mambo specialists. Music-with-a-little plot.

Hollywood, Sept. 21.

Columbia release of Sam Katzman (Clover) production. Stars Perez Prado and orch, Mary Kaye Trio, Helen Grayco, Luis Arcaraz and orch, Manny Lopez and orch; features Steve Dunne, Alix Talton, Jose Gonzales Gonzales, Sylvia Lewis, Dante De Paulo, Charles Evans, Howard Wright. Directed by Fred F. Sears. Written by James B. Gordon; camera, Benjamin H. Kline; editor, Jerome Thoms; music supervision, Fred Karger; dances created and staged by Earl Barton. Previewed Sept. 13, '56. Running time, 78 **MINS.**

Perez Prado .... Himself
Mary Kaye Trio .... Themselves
Helen Grayco .... Herself
Luis Arcaraz .... Himself
Manny Lopez .... Himself
Bill Haven .... Steve Dunne
Debbie Farmer .... Alix Talton
Pablo .... Jose Gonzales Gonzales
Nita Munay .... Sylvia Lewis
Elvarez .... Dante De Paulo
George Evans .... Charles Evans
Teasdale .... Howard Wright

The music of Perez Prado, mambo specialist, and other Latin American orchs, plus the singing of the Mary Kaye Trio and Helen Grayco, should assure okay audience reception for this rhythmic Sam Katzman production. Film has been given good mounting and should be a contender for both juve appeal and the broader musical market.

Katzman showcases the 16 numbers against a suitable story background which unfolds at a fast pace under Fred F. Sears' fluid direction. To his hot melodies producer adds an equally hot Latin dance combo, Sylvia Lewis and Dante De Paulo, femme member is a sexy dish who also is a key character in the story. In addition to Prado, other bands are Luis Arcaraz and Manny Lopez, the three groups providing plenty of toe-tapping beat.

Light plottage in James B. Gordon's screenplay follows the efforts of a diskery talent scout, Steve Dunne, to find some hot unknowns and use them as the basis for a recording company of his own. He goes to Cuba on a hunch, and brings back both Prado and his orch and the dance team, with some exciting cha-cha-cha tunes. Story theme is given enough complications, both romantic and otherwise, to carry through to an okay finale.

Pic is filled with melodic numbers, the Mary Kaye group warbling "Get Happy," "Lonesome Road" and "Save Your Sorrow," all outstanding, and Miss Grayco socking over a pair, "Lilly's Lament" and "Year Round Love," backed by Hal Mooney orch. Prado delivers strongly with six, including such tunes as "Cuban Rock and Roll," "Voodoo Suite," "Crazy Crazy," and "Mambo No. 8." Lopez offers three and Arcaraz two numbers, all in Latin tempo.

Dunne is well cast as the scout and Alix Talton supplies the romantic interest as scout for a rival waxery who helps him with his project of presenting the new type of music. Jose Gonzales Gonzales handles comedy relief well, and Miss Lewis displays an arresting personality as well as being a snappy dancer.

Benjamin H. Kline's photography is first class; ditto art direction by Paul Palmentolam and editing by Jerome Thoms. Earl Barton also rates credit for his choreography, as does Fred Karger for his music supervision.

Whit.

The Green Man
(BRITISH)

Briskly-made comedy thriller, starring Alistair Sim as genial assassin run to earth by George Cole and Jill Adams; good general appeal.

London, Sept. 18.

British Lion release of a Frank Launder and Sidney Gilliat production. Stars Alastair Sim, George Cole and Terry-Thomas; features Jill Adams. Directed by Robert Day. Screenplay by Sidney Gilliat and Frank Launder from their play, "Meet a Body"; camera, Gerald Gibbs; editor, Bernard Gribble; music, Cedric Thorpe Davie. At Gaumont Theatre, London. Running time, 80 **MINS.**

Hawkins .... Alastair Sim
William Blake .... George Cole
Boughtflower .... Terry Thomas
Ann Vincent .... Jill Adams
Marigold .... Avril Angers
McKecknie .... John Chandos
Lily .... Dora Bryan
Reginald .... Colin Gordon
Joan Wood .... Eileen Moore
Sir Gregory .... Raymond Huntley
Sgt. Bassett .... Cyril Chamberlain
Mrs. Bostock .... Doris Yorke
Landlord .... Arthur Brough
Felicity .... Maria Burke
Annabel .... Vivienne Wood

As a film, this rates higher than its stage original, which only had a modest run some years ago. Opening has some briskly projected shots showing a man's gradual rise as a time-bomb experimenter, from his college days to manhood as a hired assassin. It is an amusing mixture of farce and drama that should do for most audiences here, where the chief players are known favorites.

Alistair Sim exploits his rich, genial personality while outwardly operating as a clockmaker, and secretly flitting from victim to victim as necessity arises, obviously enjoying phase of his task. His career ends in a masterly scheme to blow up a famous public figure spending an off-the-cuff weekend before leaving for an important Far East trade mission. George Cole plays a vacuum salesman who stumbles on the body of the VIP's secretary whose suspicions proved her undoing. She recovers sufficiently to give a clue to her employer's hideout and the hunt is on to beat the clock. Cole nearly wrecks the joint looking for the deadly contraption, finds it is in the radio and hurls it through the window at zero hour.

Most of the laughs arise from Sim's unctuous villainy and his arch expression of humility when coping with any femmes in his way. Cole, who is unfailingly good in whatever role he takes, veers from timidity as a new salesman, to near panic when involved in imminent murder. Jill Adams is a pleasant eyeful as the girl caught up with him in the tangle of investigation, who transfers her affections from a stuffed shirt BBC announcer to the vacuum vendor.

Clem.

Spin a Dark Web

Melodrama of fairly entertaining quality.

Hollywood, Sept. 21.

Columbia release of George Maynard production. Stars Faith Domergue, Lee Patterson, Rona Anderson, Martin Benson; features Robert Arden, Joss Ambler, Peter Burton, Sam Kydd, Peter Hammond, Patricia Ryan, Bernard Fox. Directed by Vernon Sewell. Screenplay, Ian Stuart Black; based on novel "Wide Boys Never Work" by Robert Westerby; camera, Basil Emmott; editor, Peter Rolfe Johnson; music, Richard Taylor; song, "Love Me, Love Me Now" by Mark Paul and Paddy Roberts; sung by Julie Dawn. Previewed Sept. 14, '56. Running time, **75 MINS.**

Bella Francesi .... Faith Domergue
Jim Bankley .... Lee Patterson
Betty Walker .... Rona Anderson
Rico Francesi .... Martin Benson
Buddy .... Robert Arden
Tom Walker .... Joss Ambler
Bill Walker .... Peter Hammond
Inspector Collis .... Peter Burton
Sam .... Sam Kydd
Mick .... Russell Westwood
Audrey .... Patricia Ryan
McLeod .... Bernard Fox

There's nary a Yank around in this London racketeering feature, supplying a bit of a twist to the British-lensed melodrama which Columbia is distributing stateside. As a gangster pic, it stirs up sufficient thriller entertainment for lowercase dates in the dual market. Faith Domergue heads the otherwise all British cast in the George Maynard production, playing a Sicilian beauty with a streak of homicide with enough conviction to hold interest. Opposite her, as a dubious hero who strays towards easy money until it involves murder, Lee Patterson gives a good account of himself. Other performance assists are provided by Rona Anderson, the good girl who winds up with Patterson; Martin Benson, Miss Domergue's brother and London mobster; Robert Arden, gang member, and most of the other cast members.

Vernon Sewell's direction of the Ian Stuart Black screenplay, based on Robert Westerby's novel, "Wide Boys Never Work" (a colloquialism that'll be missed in the states) moves the plot unfoldment along at a satisfactory gait, while Basil Emmott's camera looks over the London settings for interesting framing of the action. Other technical assists function adequately and there's a Mark Paul-Paddy Roberts tune, "Love Me, Love Me Now," fetchingly sung by Julie Dawn.

Brog.

You Can't Run Away From It
(C'SCOPE—COLOR—SONGS)

Good fun although uneven is this remake of "It Happened One Night." Music values and comedy characterizations help June Allyson-Jack Lemmon costarrer.

Columbia release of Dick Powell production. Stars June Allyson, Jack Lemmon; features Charles Bickford, Paul Gilbert, Jim Backus, Stubby Kaye, Allyn Joslyn, Henny Youngman, Jacques Scott, Walter Baldwin. Directed by Powell. Screenplay, Claude Binyon and Robert Riskin, based on short story by Samuel Hopkins Adams; camera (Technicolor), Charles Lawton Jr.; editor, Al Clark; songs, Johnny Mercer (lyrics) and Gene de Paul (composer); music supervised and conducted by Morris Stoloff; choreography, Robert Sidney. Previewed at Loew's Sheridan Theatre, N.Y., Sept. 25, '56. Running time, **95 MINS.**

Ellie Andrews .... June Allyson
Peter Warne .... Jack Lemmon
A. A. Andrews .... Charles Bickford
George Shapely .... Paul Gilbert
Danker .... Jim Backus
Fred Toten .... Stubby Kaye
1st Driver .... Henny Youngman
Gordon .... Allyn Joslyn
Ballarino .... Jacques Scott
No. 1 Proprietor .... Walter Baldwin
Billings .... Byron Foulger
Hotel Manager .... Richard Cutting
No. 2 Proprietor .... Howard McNear
No. 2 Proprietor's Wife .... Elvia Allman
Maid .... Louise Beavers
Minister .... Raymond Greenleaf
TV Announcer .... Edwin Chandler
No. 3 Proprietor .... Jack Albertson
Elderly Lady .... Queenie Smith
Captain .... William Forrest
Red .... Frank Sully
Joe .... Dub Taylor
2nd Driver .... Steve Benton
Norville .... Bill Walker
1st Detective .... Herb Vigran
2nd Detective .... Larry Blake

After more than 20 years "It Happened One Night" is back, but newly titled and in the modern dress of CinemaScope and Technicolor and with some musicalization added. As when Clark Gable and Claudette Colbert performed it under director Frank Capra, it's still the tale of the rich and headstrong young miss who, in seeking to be with her fortune-hunting husband against her father's wishes, meets, loves and wins a newspaperman.

June Allyson is the girl, Jack Lemmon the reporter and "You Can't Run Away From It" makes for some good fun some of the time. The plot is not much on its own; comic incidents and humorous characterizations must be relied upon. This is the approach to the laughs, this development of story asides that score well enough to carry the load. At least, well enough to make on the overall an all right, not outstanding, diversion.

With Dick Powell calling the turns as both producer and director, the entry hits some delightful highpoints of jocularity but there also are some slow spots. It's the unevenness of pace that keeps the comedy from top-rung.

Foundation is laid as Miss Allyson skips Pappy's yacht, boards a Greyhound incognito and heads for the husband she had been forced to leave immediately after the nuptials.

Picture takes a sprightly turn as Stubby Kaye, fat and jolly sailor boy on the bus, engages fellow passengers in a spirited amusingly-worded "Howdy, Howdy, Howdy Friends and Neighbors." This is one of the colorful musical items that dot the comedy, the color derived from Johnny Mercer's lyrics. On the other hand, the tune of the title has a fetching quality, as penned by Gene de Paul, but it's done in the background and Mercer's lyrics are indistinguishable.

Miss Allyson and Lemmon, who's riding the same vehicle, are an affable combo in the leads, she looking chic and playing it straight as the rich chick and he handling comic bits of business with provocative brazeness.

Other "incidental" people in the scripe such as Kaye, who contribute sparkle along the route, include Paul Gilbert, as a fast jive-talking "buswolf"; Jim Backus, as the jalopy owner who tries to swipe Lemmon's suitcase; Henny Youngman, in for a bit as a bus driver, and Walter Baldwin and Howard McNear as motel operators.

Charles Bickword measures up as Miss Allyson's gruff millionaire father, as do Allyn Joslyn, editor driven to near distraction by Lemmon's promises of a "big story," i.e., anent the location of the missing heiress, and Jacques Scott as Miss Allyson's short-lived husband.

The hitch-hiking sequence from the original is reprised here, set to a ditty, as are the scenes of the two principals sharing the same cabin with a blanket, billed the Wall of Jericho, suspended between their beds in the interest of propriety. This motel business is given a nice pickup with Miss Allyson's and Lemmon's counter-pointing on the Mercer-de Paul "Temporarily" tune.

On a less bright side is a novelty dance number performed by Miss Allyson in a barnyard as she dons the garb of a scarecrow. Doesn't come off.

Script by Claude Binyon and Robert Riskin (only Riskin had the credit line in the original) tends to run long even though, paradoxically, the editing of some scenes appears too sharp. No intelligence available on how much footage was left in the cutting room.

Morris Stoloff rates a major nod for supervising and conducting the music, except for the barely audible dubbing of the theme. Other technical credits all good. *Gene.*

The Mountain
(V'VISION—COLOR)

Mostly ineffective entertainment but with terrificly exciting mountain - climbing sequences and names of Spencer Tracy, Robert Wagner to help.

Hollywood, Oct. 2.

Paramount release of Edward Dmytryk production, directed by Dmytryk. Stars Spencer Tracy, Robert Wagner, Claire Trevor. Screenplay, Ranald MacDougall; novel, Henri Troyat; camera (Technicolor), Franz F. Planer; editor, Frank Bracht; score, Daniele Amfitheatrof; song, Amfitheatrof and Mack David. Previewed Sept. 24, '56. Running time, 104 MINS.

Zachary Teller........... Spencer Tracy
Chris Teller.............. Robert Wagner
Marie .... Claire Trevor
Father Belacchi....... William Demarest
Simone .... Barbara Darrow
Rivial .... Richard Arlen
Hindu Girl.............. Anna Kashfi
Solange .... E. G. Marshall
Coloz .... Richard Garrick
Joseph .... Harry Townes
Servoz .... Stacy Harris
Andre .... Yves Brainville

Tremendously thrilling cliff-hanging (literally) sequences and good marquee names are the major assets of "The Mountain." Otherwise, it is an uneven piece of entertainment, with story, performance, directorial and technical flaws that lessen the impact.

The established monicker of Spencer Tracy means something at the ticket windows, while Robert Wagner should pull a share of the younger filmgoers. Thus, prospects are perhaps not too gloomy for this production-direction effort by Edward Dmytryk. Other familiar names to help include Claire Trevor, William Demarest and Richard Arlen.

Ranald MacDougall's screenplay from the Henri Troyat novel centers virtually all action on Tracy and Wagner, leaving the other cast members with what amounts to no more than walkons. Story development and the character establishment is not too good; nor is the dialog. The Tracy-Wagner characters of brothers of widely different ages never exert a strong audience pull, so interest is inclined to wander often except when the terrifying mountain climb is on the screen.

Except for his big finale scene, in which he abortively tries to lie the dead brother into heroic stature, Tracy's performance is no more than adequate. Wagner is hardly that in his portrayal of the spoiled kid brother, but Dmytryk's direction, uneven throughout, must share some of the blame. The other players are competent in the little they have to do, with Barbara Darrow and Anna Kashfi spotting brief bits of femme interest in minor spots.

Plot peg that brings on that harrowing trip up the mountain, almost realistic enough to cause acrophobia, is built around Wagner's urge the mountain valley and his too-kindly, simple-minded elder brother. He tricks his brother into guiding him to an Alpine peak on which a Calcutta-to-Paris plane has crashed so he can rob the dead. They find Miss Kashfi, Hindu girl, the only survivor and Tracy brings her down against the violent opposition of Wagner, now mad with lust for the money and jewels he has found on the dead. During the descent, Wagner falls to his death and Tracy tries to tell the villagers the robbery plot was his and the rescue idea that of his brother. Story ends as they express quiet disbelief.

On-location scenes in the Alps have been beautiful lensed in VistaVision and Technicolor by Franz F. Planer. The special photographic effects by John P. Fulton and the process photography by Farciot Edouart are both good and bad. Some studio-staged scenes in the mountain-climbing are too obviously faked, while others have a frightening reality. Editing is not smooth, maybe accounting for some of the pic's unevenness. Daniele Amfitheatrof's score is effective. He also did the title tune with Mack David.
Brog.

Reprisal
(COLOR)

'Adult theme' oater in programmer vein; average returns in secondary markets.

Columbia release of Lewis J. Rachmil production; associate producer, Helen Ainsworth. Stars Guy Madison, Felicia Farr, Kathryn Grant; features Michael Pate, Edward Platt, Otto Hulett, Wayne Mallory, Robert Burton, Ralph Moody, Frank de Kova. Directed by George Sherman. Screenplay, David P. Harmon, Raphael Hayes, David Dortort, from Harmon's screen story based on novel by Arthur Gordon; camera, (Technicolor), Henry Freulich; editor, Jerome Thoms; music, Mischa Bakaleinikoff. Tradeshown N. Y. Sept. 20, '56. Running time, 74 MINS.

Frank Madden.............. Guy Madison
Catherine Cantrell........ Felicia Farr
Taini .... Kathryn Grant
Bert Shipley.............. Michael Pate
Neil Shipley.............. Edward Platt
Sheriff Jim Dixon......... Otto Hulett
Tom Shipley............... Wayne Mallory
Jeb Cantrell.............. Robert Burton
Matara .... Ralph Moody
Charlie Washackie........ Frank de Kova
Whitey .... Paul McGuire
Buck .... Don Rhodes
Takola .... Phillip Breedlove
Luther Creel.............. Malcolm Atterbury
Nora Shipley............. Eve McVeagh
Keleni .... Victor Zamudio
Foreman .... Pete Kellett
Bartender .... Jack Lomas
Judge .... Addison Richards
Mister Willard........... John Zaremba

An Indian problem of adjusting himself to the white man's prejudices in Oklahoma a couple of generations ago gets the "adult theme" treatment in "Reprisal." There's suspense and action in this Columbia release but lack of names may restrict its grossing potential.

Title's brevity could also be a handicap. For while the tag will obviously fit nicely on a marquee, at the same time it conveys little to prospective patrons as to the nature of the story. Trio of scripters, David P. Harmon, Raphael Hayes and David Dortort, fashioned the screenplay from Harmon's story based on a novel by Arthur Gordon. They avoid the cliches of the average western in tracing the troubles of part-Indian Guy Madison who poses as a white man.

Madison, a quiet type who keeps to himself, buys a tract of range land to raise prime beef. But bordering on the property is the ranch of three brothers—Michael Pate, Edward Platt and Wayne Mallory. Freshly acquitted of lynching two Indians for trespassing, they look upon Madison as an intruder. Feud arises between the factions and is resolved only when Madison wipes out the remaining brothers after one was slain earlier by a vengeful Indian.

Strong romantic interest in the footage has Felicia Farr, daughter of land agent Robert Burton, taking a fancy to Madison. She's jealous of Kathryn Grant, an Indian gal who falsely swears Madison "spent the night with me" to save him from lynching. Windup finds the part-Indian, disillusioned with the white man's customs, returning to the fold along with Miss Farr who's cast her lot with him.

Madison does well as the strong silent type, professing to be indifferent to the white man's slurs on his race. Miss Farr likewise is impressive as a courageous frontier femme who knows the Indians are victims of injustice. Miss Grant is amply sultry and sexy as an Injun maiden with no lack of suitors. Pate, Platt and Mallory, as the three feudin' brothers, are okay as the menaces. Good support is provided by Burton and Otto Hulett, as a sheriff, among others.

George Sherman's direction paces the plot nicely in the Lewis J. Rachmil production. Both the sweeping outdoor vistas and interiors are ably captured by the Technicolor camera of Henry Freulich. Jerome Thoms edited to a tight 74 minutes and the Mischa Bakaleinikoff score adequately back the films overall mood.
Gilb.

La Escondida
(The Hidden One)
(MEXICAN—COLOR)

Mexico City, Sept. 25..
Columbia Pictures release of ALFA Films production. Stars Maria Felix, Pedro Armandariz; features Andres Soler, Arturo Martinez, Domingo Soler, Jorge M. de Hoyos. Directed by Roberto Gaveldon. Screenplay, Jose Revueltas, Roberto Gaveldon and Gunther Gerzo, from original of Miguel N. Lira; camera, Gabriel Figeroa; editor, Jorge Bustos; music, Raul Lavista. At Cine Mexico, Mexico City. Running time, 117 MINS.

Gabriela .... Maria Felix
Felipe .... Pedro Armandariz
Col. Montero.............. Carlos Agoste
Tata Agustino............. Domingo Soler
Garza .... Andres Soler
Maximo .... Jorge M. de Hoyos
Don Cosme................. Arturo Martinez

With color and wide screen as a major asset, this high budget, top Latin namer takes a backward glance at Mexico's revolutionary past, but does little to advance its filmic future. A sure fire b.o. topper in Spanish-language situations, it seems to fall short of the producer's evident hopes that the pic will have the impact of some of its historical predecessors.

Superbly, if sometimes unevenly, photoed by top lenser Gabriel Figeroa, the pictorial values of the wild and turbulent 1900's are faithfully and imaginatively captured in Eastmancolor. Major failing is the evident maturity of the two stars, whose faces, and sometimes figures, are unsuited storywise to the honest hot eye of Figeroa's color lens. Nevertheless, local audiences seem to accept this sort of thing and go for Maria Felix and Pedro Armandariz.

Going back to the period when gangs of poverty stricken peons worked, in slavery, on the rich haciendas of Mexico, film unfolds a tale of love and revolution against a background of cactus fields, immense panoramas and alternating peasant and plush interiors. Basically, it is the story of a peasant leader's fight for his principles and his eventual return to his people. Interwoven with this theme is his love for a poor girl, who has become a demi-mondaine, and who later joins him and the revolution, only to die unwittingly at his hands. Armandariz performs with his usual force and conviction but Miss Felix walks through her role, holding back fairly well on the theatrics.

Others in the cast carry their serapes and epaulets in a realistic fashion, with the Soler brothers, Andres and Domingo, outstanding. Latter playing Armandariz' father, gives a top performance as a grizzled peasant fighter. The former comes across well in the role of a tough regular Army officer.

Director Roberto Gaveldon, who also gets partial scripting credit, has played the obvious propaganda for all its worth, grouping and moving his characters, at times, somewhat stiffly. Battles between the peons and regulars are well staged, particularly the night scenes. A major assist is given by Raul Lavista's musical score, which punches hard alongside the dramatic sweep of the photography. *Pete.*

Julie

Some suspense values but Doris Day-Louis Jourdan co-starrer is overplotted Perils of Pauline stuff. Fair boxoffice in view.

Metro release of Martin Melcher production. Stars Doris Day, Louis Jourdan; features Barry Sullivan, Frank Lovejoy.

Directed by Andrew L. Stone. Screenplay, Stone; camera, Fred; Jackson Jr.; editor, uncredited but Virginia Stone has billing as assistant to both the producer and film editor; music, Leith Stevens, with title song by Stevens and Tom Adair, and piano composition "Midnight on the Cliffs" composed and performed by Leonard Pennario. Previewed in N. Y. Sept. 27, '56. Running time, 109 MINS.

Julie Benton	Doris Day
Lyle Benton	Louis Jourdan
Cliff Henderson	Barry Sullivan
Detective Captain Pringle	Frank Lovejoy
Detective Cole	John Gallaudet
Detective Pope	Harlan Warde
Detective Mace	Jack Kruschen
Ellis	Hank Patterson
Denice Martin	Aline Towne
Valerie	Ann Robinson
Pilot	Ed Hinton
Co-Pilot	Jack Kelly
Doctor	Barney Phillips
Field Man	Carleton Young
Peggy	Pamela Duncan
Hysterical Passenger	Mae Marsh
Company Official	Edward Marsh

Suspense ingredients are piled up well enough but "Julie" goes overboard both on plot and length. Story of an attractive young lady, Doris Day, who discovers her second husband, Louis Jourdan, is a murderer and aims to kill her, is paced at a good clip under Andrew L. Stone's direction. But too much story is crowded in; plausibility runs thin and some portions of the audience might grow weary.

Stone's story is of the old school—the chase, with heavy melodramatic punctuation marks. It has Miss Day coming upon the realization that Jourdan had killed her first mate and is insane with jealously so much so that he'd murder her rather than lose her. She takes off under the protection of a country club associate, Barry Sullivans, and Jourdan undertakes to track them down.

Neither the writing nor the directing is particularly imaginative, both departments falling back upon standardization. As the San Francisco police, headed by Frank Lovejoy, become convinced that Miss Day is in danger, as she had insisted, they move in to guard her but she unintentionally eludes them. She takes the elevator down from the apartment just as they take the stairs up, etc.

The climax, or rather anti-climax, has Miss Day in her former job as airlines hostess, with Jourdan boarding the plane undetected. The flareup comes as he kills the pilot, seriously wounds the co-pilot and is killed himself. Miss Day is called upon to take over the four-motor job and after a protracted session lands safely under the direction of the control tower. Say that this bit is not for sophisticates.

Martin Melcher's production is authentically backgrounded, the settings making it clear that this is a relatively substantial offering, budget-wise. No apparent stinting, in other words. Performances are adequate all around, although Miss Day has a time of it trying to behave convincingly in landing that big airplane.

"Midnight on the Cliffs," piano piece composed and performed (while Jourdan appears fingering the ivories) by Leonard Pennario, is consistent with the story, being full of fearful and furious sounds but no great shakes aesthetically. Song of the title, by Leith Stevens and Tom Adair, as vocalled by Miss Day behind the opening titles, sounds like the cleffers were trying for another "Laura" but didn't quite make it. *Gene.*

The White Squaw

Pretty half-breed, but Ugh!

Hollywood, Oct. 2.

Columbia release of a Wallace MacDonald production. Stars David Brian, May Winn, William Bishop; features Nancy Hale, William Leslie, Myron Healey, Robert C. Ross, Frank de Kova, George Keymas, Roy Roberts, Grant Withers, Wally Vernon. Directed by Ray Nazarro. Screenplay, Les Savage Jr., based on novel by Larabie Sutter; camera, Henry Freulich; editor, Edwin Bryant; music, Mischa Bakaleinikoff. Previewed Sept. 26, '56. Running time, 73 MINS.

Sigrod Swanson	David Brian
Eetay-O-Wahnee	May Wynn
Bob Garth	William Bishop
Kerry Arnold	Nancy Hale
Thor Swanson	William Leslie
Eric Swanson	Myron Healey
Knute Swanson	Robert C. Ross
Yellow Elk	Frank de Kova
Yotah	George Keymas
Purvis	Roy Roberts
Sheriff	Grant Withers
Faro Bill	Wally Vernon
Thad Arnold	Paul Birch
Swift Arrow	Neyle Morrow
Joe Hide	Guy Teague

Columbia dug deep into the grab-bag for this one, a cliche-filled story of Indian persecution and a femme halfbreed. Film is strictly for the least discriminating oater market.

May Wynn is the white squaw, living on a Sioux reservation in Wyoming, whose people are the victims of early settler David Brian's wrath. Trying to drive them off what he regards his land, he poisons water the Indians use for their cattle. Redskins start a gun battle, during which another white, Paul Birch, a friend of the Indians and femme's real father (although unknown to her), is killed. Appearance of William Bishop, young cattleman driving a herd of cattle the Indians try to buy, adds further to Brian's fury when Bishop tries to help half-white gal, and windup shows Brian burning to death in a teepee he has set on fire.

Miss Wynn is a pretty breed and Bishop a noble young man, Brian the heavy with a Swedish accent. Characters under Ray Nazarro's direction are stereotyped. Technical credits are stock in the Wallace MacDonald production. *Whit.*

Flight to Hong Kong

Routine programmer backdropped by authentic foreign locales.

Hollywood, Oct. 3.

United Artists release of a Joseph M. Newman production. Stars Rory Calhoun, Barbara Rush; costars Dolores Donlon; features Soo Yong, Pat Conway, Werner Klemperer, Mel Welles, Paul Picerni, Aram Katcher. Directed by Newman. Screenplay, Leo Townsend, Edward G. O'Callaghan; story, O'Callaghan, Gustave Field, Newman; camera, Ellis W. Carter; music Albert Glasser; editor, Ralph Dawson. Previewed Sept. 25, '56. Running time, 88 MINS.

Tony Dumont	Rory Calhoun
Pamela Vincent	Barbara Rush
Jean Blake	Dolores Donlon
Mama Lin	Soo Yong
Nicco	Pat Conway
Bendesh	Werner Klemperer
Boris	Mel Welles
Quisto	Paul Picerni
Lobero	Aram Katcher
Bob Denham	Rhodes Reason
Cappy	Bob Hopkins
Lagarto	Timothy Carey
Commander Larabee	Carleton Young
Sargas	Aaron Saxon
Gantz	Noel Cravat
Pondry	Guy Prescott
Andaras	Barry Brook
Janvoort	George Barrows
Maxler	Booth Coleman
Boussard	Ralph Smiley
Carstairs	Paul Brinegar

"Flight to Hong Kong" is given a lift by backdropping its unfoldment against actual locations in China and other foreign parts, but episodic treatment of a routine story necessarily slows film's pace. Characters are colorful, however, and with the name of Rory Calhoun to spark its chances feature should stack up okay for the action trade.

The Joseph M. Newman-Vic Orsatti production twirls around an international crime syndicate, which lends justification for the constant hopping about the globe. In addition to Hong Kong, camera picks up scenes in Macao, Tokyo, Honolulu, Tangiers and Lisbon, as well as San Francisco, all interestingly lensed by Ellis W. Carter's fluid photography. Newman, producer-director, utilizes these locales to advantage for good atmosphere.

Calhoun, who has his own import-export business in Macao, is the syndicate's chief in the Hong Kong area, where he and two henchmen secretly operate. Leo Townsend-Edward G. O'Callaghan screenplay opens with Calhoun masterminding the hijacking of a fortune in industrial diamonds on a flight from Tokyo to Hong Kong, subsequent action showing how syndicate works in an immediate disposal of the loot.

Ensuing sequences dwell on attempts to hijack a syndicate freighter and Calhoun breaking it up; the syndicate's measures in avenging itself on a member responsible for this double cross; Calhoun trying to get away from the syndicate by pulling his own job of hijacking $1,000,000 in jewels stolen by crime ring from an Indian maharajah. Yarn finales on an indefinite note when Hong Kong police move in as syndicate seizes Calhoun.

Calhoun registers well and Barbara Rush and Dolores Donlon both are effective in romance department, former as a novelist for whom Calhoun goes overboard and Miss Donlon as his devoted Macao showgirl sweetheart. Soo Yong is excellent as Mama Lin, operator of a Macao nitery; and strongly cast as various members of syndicate are Pat Conway, Mel Welles, Werner Klemperer and Paul Picerni. Aram Katcher stands out as a non-member of ring who wants Calhoun to join him in the rajah jewel deal.

Musical score by Albert Glasser and art direction by Serge Krizman lend the proper background flavor. *Whit.*

Tension at Table Rock
(SONG-COLOR)

Slow but fair "mood" western for regular outdoor situations.

Hollywood, Oct. 2.

RKO release of Sam Wiesenthal production. Stars Richard Egan, Dorothy Malone, Cameron Mitchell; features Billy Chapin, Royal Dano, Edward Andrews, John Dehner, DeForest Kelley, Joe DeSantis, Angie Dickinson. Directed by Charles Marquis Warren. Screenplay, Winston Miller; from novel "Bitter Sage" by Frank Gruber; camera (Technicolor), Joseph Biroc; editors, Harry Marker, Dean Harrison; music, Dimitri Tiomkin; song, Josef Myrow, Robert Wells. Previewed Sept. 28, '56. Running time, 93 MINS.

Wes Tancred	Richard Egan
Lorna Miller	Dorothy Malone
Sheriff Miller	Cameron Mitchell
Jody	Billy Chapin
Jameson	Royal Dano
Kirk	Edward Andrews
Hampton	John Dehner
Breck	DeForest Kelley
Burrows	Joe DeSantis
Cathy	Angie Dickinson

There's more "mood" than pace in this western entry, but it comes off with a fair classification for the regular outdoor situation because of a number of good action scenes. The familiar names of Richard Egan, Dorothy Malone and Cameron Mitchell add something for the program marquees.

Charles Marquis Warren's directorial guidance of the Sam Wiesenthal production has a deliberate pace aimed at building a brooding tension over the film. This sometimes succeeds, and when it does it usually leads into the above-noted action scenes. Elsewhere, it tends to slowness, making the 93 minutes seem long. Winston Miller's script from the Frank Gruber novel, "Bitter Sage," abets the slow moodiness and takes quite awhile to set the characters.

Richard Egan is on the run in the plot after having killed in self defense the leader of a robber gang he is riding with. The leader was falsely known as a sort of Robin Hood so all the scorn of the west is turned on Egan, even to having a ballad written branding the deed cowardly and reward-seeking. Main action takes place in Table Rock, where Egan brings a small boy, Billy Chapin, after the latter's dad has been killed by some holdup men. He finds the town prepping for the arrival of rough-and-ready Texas trailherders and the sheriff, Cameron Mitchell, frightened. Miss Malone, the sheriff's wife, could go for Egan, but he rides off alone after helping straighten out the town.

Performances are all competent, but the pacing keeps them from being as colorful as they might have been. The three stars are helped by young Chapin, Royal Dano, town publisher; Edward Andrews, effete bigshot who likes the money the trail herds bring; John Dehner, DeForest Kelley, Joe DeSantis and Angie Dickinson, plus some uncredited players

The Techoicolor lensing by Joseph Biroc handles the western settings excellently and Dimitri Tiomkin provides an okay background score. Joseph Myrow and Robert Wells did "The Ballad of Wes Tancred" heard throughout. The Misses Malone and Dickinson seem a bit too well-dressed for the prairie femmes they play. *Brog.*

Rockin' the Blues

Low-budget vaude-styled rock 'n' roll show okay for selected situations.

Austin Production release of Fritz Pollard Associates release. Features Flournoy Miller & Mantan Moreland, Harptones, Wanderers, Hurricanes, Miller Sisters, Linda Hayes, Pearl Woods, Connie Carroll, Cuban Dancers, Hal Jackson, Reese La Rue, Anita Turner. Directed by Arthur Rosenblum; camera, Jack Etra. Previewed in N. Y. Sept. 24, '56. Running time, 70 MINS.

Here's a quickie, cheapie 70-minute catch-all designed to exploit the current rock 'n' roll music craze. With the disks rolling hot and the kids jumping, this all-Negro "Rockin' the Blues" has some special status in the current market. It may be compared to a filmed version of the talent roster at, say, the Apollo Theatre in Harlem.

The musical acts come on and off without any story line and with just a few interruptions coming from some comedic scenes supplied by Flournoy Miller and Manton Moreland and emcee intros by Hal Jackson, deejay on New York indie WLIB.

It all adds up to an r&r overload that gets a bit wearisome. Neither the performers nor their musical repertoire have sustaining power. The producers should get the pic into the market fast to get any value from its marquee names.

The songstering lineup includes Honey Carroll, The Wanderers, The Miller Sisters, Linda Hayes, The Hurricanes, Pearl Woods, Connie Carroll, Reese La Rue and The Harptones. There's also a dance interlude offered by The Cuban Dancers. Teacho Wiltshire's combo lays down a noisy beat for the singers.

Pic was produced by Fritz Pollard Associates (a public relations firm) and directed by Arthur Rosenblum. The photography was handled by Jack Etra.

The producers obviously skimped on the budget outlay. Film is shot mostly as a stage presentation and when the camera wanders off it hits only stock sets. The sync job, too, leaves plenty to be desired. However, rock 'n' roll fans are notoriously easy to please. *Gros.*

Man From Del Rio

Suspenseful story of a gunfighter, good prospects for western market.

Hollywood, Oct. 2.

United Artists release of a Robert L. Jacks production. Stars Anthony Quinn; costars Katy Jurado; features Peter Whitney, Douglas Fowley, John Larch, Whit Bissell, Douglas Spencer, Guinn "Big Boy" Williams. Directed by Harry Horner. Story-screenplay, Richard Carr; camera, Stanley Cortez; music, Frederick Steiner; editor, Robert Golden. Previewed Sept. 27, '56. Running time, **82 MINS.**

Dave Robles	Anthony Quinn
Estella	Katy Jurado
Ed. Bannister	Peter Whitney
Doc Adams	Douglas Fowley
Bill Dawson	John Larch
Breezy Morgan	Whit Bissell
Jack Tillman	Douglas Spencer
Fred Jasper	Guinn "Big Boy" Williams
George Dawson	Marc Hamilton
Mrs. Tillman	Adrienne Marden
Dan Ritchy	Barry Atwater
"The Kid"	Carl Thayler
Roy Higgens	William Erwin
Tom Jordan	Otto Waldis
Mr. Brown	Paul Harber
Boy	Jack Hogan
Stableman	Frank Richards

This mostly well-plotted western packs a dramatic wallop with its surprise climax to compensate for occasional actionless sequences during story buildup. Film's offbeat flavor is conducive to good audience reception, by adults as well as moppet trade, and Anthony Quinn's character study of a gunfighter should attract attention in the market for which pic is tailored.

Under Harry Horner's restrained direction, of the Richard Carr screenplay, the Robert L. Jacks production manages frequent suspense. Interest centers almost wholly upon Quinn, as a Mexican gunman "driven" to killing by four men five years before story opens. He's already slaughtered three of these men, and as film opens outdraws the fourth, a feat believed impossible by Peter Whitney, exgunman who runs the town's only saloon.

Narrative follows Quinn's brief stay in the town, whose populace resent gunplay and finally hire gunman to be the sheriff, so order will be restored. In a fist fight with Whitney, Quinn comes out the winner but a broken wrist spells finis to his days as a gun. Learning of this turn of events, Whitney, who wants to control the town for his own purposes, challenges Quinn to meet him on the street in a duel. Finale disposes of the situation unexpectedly.

Quinn's fine thesping gives polish to picture which also has Katy Jurado in for romantic interest, fine casting for this capable actress. Whitney socks over his characterization of a man who is trying to return the town to its former cattle-town glory, so he may be a real power; Douglas Fowley ably portrays the doctor; and Whit Bissell as the town drunk makes the part count. Guinn (Big Boy) Williams also is outstanding as a gunman whom Quinn cuts down.

Film benefits by generally above-standard technical departments, including Stanley Cortez' photography, Frederick Steiner's music score and Robert Golden's editing. *Whit.*

Spy Chasers

Another (No. 40) BB (Bowery Boys) programmer.

Hollywood, Oct. 2.

Allied Artists release of Ben Schwalb production. Stars Leo Gorcey, Huntz Hall; features Bernard Gorcey, Leon Askin, Sig Ruman, Veola Vonn, Lisa Davis, David Condon, Bennie Bartlett, Richard Benedict, Frank Richards, Linda Bennett. Directed by Edward Bernds. Screenplay, Bert Lawrence, Jerome S. Gottler; camera, Harry Neumann; editor, John C. Fuller; music, Marlin Skiles. Reviewed Sept. 26, '56. Running time, **61 MINS.**

Slip	Leo Gorcey
Sach	Huntz Hall
Louie	Bernard Gorcey
Col. Baxis	Leon Askin
King Rako	Sig Ruman
Lady Zelda	Veola Vonn
Princess Ann	Lisa Davis
Chuck	David Condon
Butch	Bennie Bartlett
Boris	Richard Benedict
George	Frank Richards
Little Girl	Linda Bennett

The Bowery Boys are "Spy Chasers" in this latest entry, dishing out their usual slapstick comedy in par for the course. Screenplay by Bert Lawrence and Jerome S. Gottler provides Leo Gorcey and Huntz Hall, stars of the series, the ingredients for their favorite pastimes—hitting each other over the head or making with the malaprops.

Action is located in N. Y., where Boys become entangled with the exiled king of mythical Truania, who is incognito and awaiting just the right time to return to his country. Heavies plotting against the king stoop so low as to kidnap his pretty daughter, but the Boys are there for the rescue. Plotters are exposed, and Boys are decorated for bravery by the grateful king.

With 39 previous "BB" features under their belt, Gorcey and Hall have long been masters of their respective roles in manner pleasing to followers of the series. Supporting roles are played in animated style, with Sig Ruman, as the king, showing up best.

Under Ben Schwalb's production supervision, "Chasers" emerges neither better nor worse, than majority of the series' predecessors. There's little physical mantling, but then little is needed. Edward Bernds' direction allows the cast free rein and keeps things on the move, while technical contributions are all stock. *Neal.*

Windfall in Athens
(GREEK)

Arista Films Inc. release of a Millas Film production. Stars Elli Lambetti, Georges Pappas, Dimitri Horn; features Margarita Georgiou, Tasso Kavadia, Sapho Notara, Chris Pateraki. Directed by Michael Cacoyanis. Screenplay, Cacoyanis, from his original story; camera, Alvize Orphanelli; music, Andre Ryder. At Cameo, N. Y., Sept. 29, '56. Running time, **112 MINS.**

Mina	Elli Lambetti
George	Georges Pappas
Alexis	Dimitri Horn
Lisa	Tasso Kavadia
Ketty	Sapho Notara
Mother	Chris Pateraki
Irene	Margarita Georgiou

(In Greek; English Titles)

A Greek import, "Windfall in Athens" is an overlong comedy drama about a lost lottery ticket. There's an occasional amusing moment, but the almost interminable footage is particularly irritating since the denouement is more or less telegraphed anyway. Picture may offer some appeal to Greek audiences. However, its prospects are negligible as far as general U.S. art house clientele is concerned.

Original story of Michael Cacoyanis, which he directed from his own screenplay, centers on a millinery salesgirl, a middle-aged lawyer and a handsome-though penniless musician. Femme, whose lottery ticket has been stolen, is befriended by the attorney. Though the latter is married, he takes a romantic interest in the girl.

It develops later that the missing ticket has hit the jackpot. Naturally, the salesgirl is heartbroken. Thereafter the script takes an obvious course as the musician, who's purchased the ticket from some youthful thieves, presents it for redemption. Lawyer attempts to protect the original holder's interest, but gallantly steps aside when the boy and girl decide they're made for each other.

With better acting and direction, such a story could have emerged as a fairly good light comedy with romantic overtones. Unfortunately, there's nothing subtle about Cacoyanis' direction. Moreover, an unbilled editor was lax in failing to scissor the extraneous footage. Performances are fair. Elli Lambetti, a wistful brunette, manages to excite audience sympathy as the lost ticket victim.

Georges Pappas turns in a standard portrayal of a mature professional man who reforms before becoming a roue. Dimitri Horn is okay as the musician who's indifferent to his economic straits. Tasso Kavadis is realistic as Pappas' jealous wife and Margarita Georgiou is pert and winsome as Miss Lambetti's sister.

Physical values in this Athens-localed tale are rather meagre. Alvize Orphanelli's camerawork is so-so as is Andre Ryder's score. While the English titles are adequate, frequently they contain misspelled words and grammatical errors. The Millas Films production was turned out at the Naha studio in Cairo. *Gilb.*

Difendo Il Mio Amore
(To Defend My Love)
(FRANCO—ITALIAN)

Rome, Sept. 25.

Titanus release of a Titanus-Les Films Marceau production. Stars Martine Carol, Vittorio Gassmann, Charles Vanel, Gabriele Ferzetti; features Georgia Moll, Alan Furlan. Directed by Vincent Sherman. Italian version by Giulio Macchi. Screenplay, Suso Cecchi D'Amico, Ettore Giannini; from story by D'Amico and Giorgio Prosperi; camera, Gianni Di Venanzo; editor, Mario Serandrei. At Metropolitan, Rome. Running time, **90 MINS.**

Elisa	Martine Carol
Pietro	Gabriele Ferzetti
Giovanni	Vittorio Gassmann
Verdision	Charles Vanel

Soapy tale, smoothly handled and acted, should appeal to general and subsequent audiences in France and Italy. Outside the two countries of origin, outlook is spotty.

Plot details the effect on a family of a newspaper series in which famous court cases of the past are dug up. Martine Carol bears the brunt of the inquest when her past is delved into via her involvement in a famed murder case. To sell himself and his paper, newshawk Vittorio Gassmann oversteps professional dignity and bounds, finally being called down, but not before he's caused untold suffering among members of cast. Pic for a while wavers between straight criticism of certain newspaper practices and the soapier trail to femme tears, finally choosing the latter and letting out all stops. It has definite distaff appeal.

Acting is often convincing, thanks to Miss Carol in an unglamorous offbeat role for her, and Gabriele Ferzetti, who thesps her husband. Gassmann is typed as the villainous newshound while Charles Vanel lends assurance to the role of the editor. Georgia Moll has little to do as Gassmann's leg-girl. Alan Furlan as the publisher, and others round out a competent cast. Lensing by Gianni Di Venanzo, which includes north Italian locations, is expert. Renzo Rossellini's musical score is stirring. Physical dress is in keeping with good production. *Hawk.*

Calle Mayor
(Main Street)
(FRENCH—SPANISH)

Venice, Sept. 25.

Play-Art release of Play-Art, Iberia, Cesareo Gonzalez production. Stars Betsy Blair, Jose Suarez; features Yves Massard, Dora Doll, Lila Kedrova. Written and directed by Juan Antonio Bardem. Camera, Michel Kelber; editor, Marguerite De Ochoa; music, Joseph Kosma. At Venice Film Festival. Running time, **95 MINS.**

Isabelle	Betsy Blair
Juan	Jose Suarez
Jean	Yves Massard
Antonia	Dora Doll
Madame Pepita	Lila Kedrova

A popular subject, of late, in U.S. films has been the dilemma of the middle-aged man or woman ("Marty," "Autumn Leaves") whose chances for marriage are dimming and who face loneliness except for a last chance which makes for the central theme. This film gives a more grim view, laced with an intellectual appraisal of the situation. Downbeat aspects plus adroit technique and thesping slant this for arty spotting in the U.S. Crix and word-of-mouth might be plus factors.

In a provincial town, a group of dissatisfied, aging men carry on a battle against boredom via practical jokes. They decide to make a 35-year-old, sensitive spinster (Miss Blair) the butt of one joke by having one of their members, a weak but handsome big towner, court her.

She falls desperately in love and he becomes conscience stricken when he realizes the enormity of the situation. He wants out without hurting her too badly, but finally tells her. A friend urges the girl to leave so as to avoid the jeering but she decides to stay on in hopeless solitude.

Film has psychological overtones which, however, do not interfere too much with the drama.

Miss Blair gives her luminous quality to the role of the spinster who realizes this is love, and more than a desperate, last ditch clutching at normality. Jose Suarez is competent as the handsome weakling who cannot face any real sort of implication in emotions. As writer-director Juan Antonio Bardem confirms his technical ability but has to overcome the too rigid barriers of technique.

Bardem has helped put the Hispano cinema on the map via kudos at film festivals, with his "Death of a Cyclist," and his recent arrest, for political reasons, while filming this making him internationally known among pix people. Lensing and technical aspects are excellent and dubbing and supporting players are sound. Pic needs selling and is subtle personal handling.
Mosk.

Elena Et Les Hommes
(Elena and the Men)
(FRENCH—ITALIAN)
(Color; Songs)

Paris, Sept. 25.

Cinedis release of Franco-London-Gibe Films production. Stars Ingrid Bergman, Mel Ferrer, Jean Marais, Jean Richard. Directed by Jean Renoir. Screenplay, Renoir, Jean Ferry; camera (Technicolor), Claude Renoir; editor, Borys Lewin; music, Joseph Kosma. At Colisee, Paris. Running time, **95 MINS.**

Elena .... Ingrid Bergman
Henri .... Mel Ferrer
Rollan .... Jean Marais
Hector .... Jean Richard
Lolotte .... Magali Noel
Eugene .... Jacques Johanneau
Gypsy .... Juliette Greco
Paulette .... Elina Labordette

Jean Renoir has tagged this a musical fantasy and it was written by him expressly for Ingrid Bergman to give her a fling at comedy. Done in operetta fashion, with not enough songs, its lack of plot makes this more a series of clever notations on a period, love, politics etc. However, it has a tendency to ramble. It has excellent color, some funny and tender scenes, but its lack of clarified direction makes this primarily for special spotting in the U.S., with a chance for general appeal on the names of Ingrid Bergman and Mel Ferrer.

An English version was made which will be released in the U.S. by Warner Bros. U.S. screenwriter Cy Howard worked on the English scripting with Renoir. Exploitation is the keyword for this fragile film. It occurs in the late 19th Century and concerns a Polish princess (Miss Bergman) whose destiny is bringing talented men to fruition; after which she leaves them. She gets entangled in the fate of General Rollan (Jean Marais) who is being railroaded into dictatorship by his entourage.

However, a rather ambitionless secretary of the general (Mel Ferrer) is the one who finally wins the princess when both admit they are sincere. Film abounds in wit and color, but no clear storyline emerges.

Juliette Greco and Marjane are rung in to give out with a couple of passable period songs by Joseph Kosma. A host of fine actors disport in a cavalier manner during the adventures of the Princess.

Miss Bergman looks well and is elegantly costumed. Some torrid bussing scenes with Ferrer and Marais, as the general, come off, but she does not quite fit in with the various comedy levels. Ferrer and Marais both are primarily foils for the heroine and the mobs. A group of other characters add a slapstick note. Color is correct and production aspects are kept operettish with obvious painted backdrops.

This film has charm and class but a general lack of clearcut direction. It is a fine trailer for Miss Bergman's return to the U.S. film scene. *Mosk.*

The Ten Commandments
(VISTAVISION-COLOR)

Three hours and 39 minutes of epic from the epic-master, Cecil B. DeMille. Pictorially stupendous. Boxoffice prognosis: strong. Chief flaw: length. Secondary objection: conventional story treatment.

Paramount release of Cecil B. De Mille production. Stars Charlton Heston, Yul Brynner, Anne Baxter, Edward G. Robinson, Yvonne De Carlo, Deborah Paget, John Derek; features Sir Cedric Hardwicke, Nina Foch, Martha Scott, Judith Anderson, Vincent Price. Directed by De Mille; associate producer, Henry Wilcoxon; written for the screen by Aeneas MacKenzie, Jesse L. Lasky Jr., Jack Gariss, Fredric M. Frank; camera, Loyal Griggs; additional photography, J. Peverell Marley, John Warren, Wallace Kelley; art direction, Hal Pereira, Walter Tyler, Albert Nozaki; set decorations, Sam Comer, Ray Moyer; choreography, LeRoy Prinz; makeup, Wally Westmore, Frank Westmore, Frank McCoy; hair stylist, Nellie Manley; sound, Louis H. Mesenkop, Harry Lindgren, Gene Garvin; special photographic effects, John P. Fulton; special photography, Paul Lerpae; process photography, Farciot Edouart; costumes, Edith Head, Ralph Jester, John Jensen, Dorothy Jenkins, Arnold Friberg; editor, Anne Bauchens; unit director, Arthur Rosson; music, Elmer Bernstein. Previewed at Criterion Theatre, N. Y., Oct. 3. Running time, **219 MINS.**

Moses .... Charlton Heston
Rameses .... Yul Brynner
Nefretiri .... Anne Baxter
Dathan .... Edward G. Robinson
Sephora .... Yvonne De Carlo
Lilia .... Debra Paget
Joshua .... John Derek
Bithiah .... Nina Foch
Sethi .... Sir Cedric Hardwicke
Yochabel .... Martha Scott
Memnet .... Judith Anderson
Baka .... Vincent Price
Aaron .... John Carradine
Miriam .... Olive Deering
Jannes .... Douglass Dumbrille
Abiram .... Frank DeKova
Pentaur .... Henry Wilcoxon
Jethro .... Eduard Franz
Mered .... Donald Curtis
Hur Ben Caleb .... Lawrence Dobkin
Amminadab .... H. B. Warner
Elisheba .... Julia Faye
The Blind One .... John Miljan
Simon .... Francis J. McDonald
Rameses I .... Ian Keith
The Infant Moses ..... Fraser Heston
Eleazar .... Paul DeRolf
Gershom .... Tommy Duran
Rameses' Son .... Eugene Mazzola
Korah's Wife .... Joan Woodbury
King of Ethiopia ..... Woodrow Strode
Korah .... Ramsay Hill
Princess Tharbis ..... Esther Brown

Here at last is the epic, Cecil B. De Mille's super-spectacular about the Children of Israel held in brutal bondage until Moses, prodded by the God of Abraham, delivers them from Egyptian tyranny. It's a statistically intimidating production; the negative cost is $13,500,000 and 25,000 extras were employed, according to the producer's count.

This new version of De Mille's silent (1927) saga, "The Ten Commandments," overwhelms its audience—it's that big. Pictorially it is greatly impressive, dwarfing all cinematic things that have gone before it. It's unlikely that any producer other than De Mille would have attempted such a mammoth project and it's to be doubted that many others could have held the extraordinary production under control. He has placed legions of men before the cameras, constructed sets that establish precedent in size and against the tremendous backdrop tells the great story of the collapse of the idolators through divine intervention.

That the boxoffice returns will be mountainous seems assured. Biblical entries of the past have won marked public endorsement and this one tops them all. Its theme, its photographic magnificence and the truly powerful publicity campaign must mean that "Ten Commandments" will run on and on.

But this department shall refrain from predicting any specific gross, or the extent to which Paramount will or will not make beaucoup profit. In the enthusiastic language of the trade, a blockbuster is, currently, a tall revenue feature. When a picture grosses $10,000,000 or near it's blockbusting. But look how tall "Commandments" must grow before it's out of the red! In line with this, though, Par executives have unabashedly asserted that they have an economically supreme property.

No critical appraisal can be pure rave. While De Mille has broken new ground in terms of size, he has remained conventional with the motion picture as an art form. Emphasis on physical dimension has rendered neither awesome nor profound the story of Moses. The eyes of the onlooker are filled with spectacle. Emotional tug is sometimes lacking.

"Commandments" is too long. More than two hours' pass before the intermission and the break is desperately welcome. Scenes of the greatness that was Egypt, and Hebrews by the thousands under the whip of the taskmasters, are striking. The construction of a gigantic new city to please the pharaoh is extremely impressive. But bigness wearies. There's simply too much. Then, intermission.

"Commandments" hits the peak of beauty with a sequence that is unelaborate, this being the Passover supper wherein Moses is shown with his family while the shadow of death falls on Egyptian first-borns. This is stirring and, in contrast with production generally, marked by simplicity and deep feeling.

Curiously, the miracles of God's vengeance against the Egyptians, as detailed in the Bible, are not shown in their entirety. Instead, DeMille's film devotes much footage to the events prior to the plagues and then the exodus, beginning, of course, with the finding of the infant Moses in the bullrushes by pharaoh's daughter, his original role as Egyptian prince and the discovery that he is a Hebrew.

The Bible left a 30-year hiatus in its recounting of Moses' life—from birth to manhood. DeMille states he tapped ancient historian sources and the discoveries of modern archeologists to improvise the story of the noble Egyptian prince who, upon learning the circumstances of his birth, elects to join his true people and, commissioned by a blazing message on Mount Sinai, sets out to "set my people free."

The miracles of the Bible naturally necessitated camera trickery if they were to be depicted. The creeping shadow of darkness that destroyed the Egyptian first-borns, the trans-composition of Moses' staff into a serpent, the changeover of the life-giving water into blood, flames to engulf the land and the parting of the Red Sea—these are shown. The effect of all these special camera devices is varying, however, and does not escape a certain theatricality. Against which stands the fact that DeMille's endeavors with the optical process effects set a new high in grandeur and photographic enterprise. Perfect realism and conviction are not achieved, but the finished product still is impressive.

Script by Aeneas MacKenzie, Jesse L. Lasky Jr., Jack Gariss and Frederic M. Frank is a tremendous job of organization. One scene segues into the next and characters in large number come on stage in fine continuity. The major flaw is that too much unmeaningful material is crowded into the first two hours of running time and the more uplifting excitement is left to the final passages.

In addition to serving as producer and director of the production, De Mille is sporadically heard as narrator to provide explanatory notes and appears in a two-minute prolog to comment on his source material.

Performances meet requirements all the way but exception must be made anent Anne Baxter as the Egyptian princess Nefretiri. In expressing her intense love for Moses, even after discovering his background, Miss Baxter leans close to old-school siren histrionics and in instances this is out of sync with the spiritual nature of "Commandments."

Charlton Heston is an adaptable performer as Moses, registering as the conquering hero at the start and, later, revealing inner glow as he is called by God to remove the chains of slavery that holds his people. Yvonne De Carlo is Sephora, the warm and understanding wife of Moses. Yul Brynner is expert as Rameses, who inherits the Egyptian throne and seeks to battle Moses and his God until he's forced to acknowledge that "Moses' God is the real God."

Competent work is done, too, by Edward G. Robinson, as the evil Hebrew; John Derek as Joshua; Debra Paget as Lilia, upon whom Robinson's covetous eyes fall; Sir Cedric Hardwicke, the pharoah who favors Moses until he learns of his birth; Nina Foch as the princess who finds the infant Moses and declares him as her own; Martha Scott as Moses' real mother who sets him afloat in a basket to escape the pharoah's edict demanding death for all Hebrew male infants; Judith Anderson as the servant in the pharoah's household who witnessed the finding of Moses. Also offering contributions among the mighty cast are Vincent Price, John Carradine, Olive Deering, Henry Wilcoxon, H. B. Warner and Ian Keith.

Elmer Bernstein has provided a sensitive musical score. Rating nods for the overpowering photography, splendid in VistaVision and Technicolor except for some instances of obvious hocus pocus, are Loyal Griggs, as the top man behind the camera; assists by J. Peverell Marley, John Warren and Wallace Kelly; John P. Fulton, special effects; Paul Lerpae, optical photography, and Farciot Edouart, process photography.

Set decoration and construction, costumes and art direction are other important credits. *Gene.*

Giant
(COLOR)

Top cast does full justice to Edna Ferber's powerful Texas saga of cattle, oil and race bias. Despite over-length, it's excellent entertainment and rates as b.o. dynamite.

Warner Bros. release of George Stevens production. Stars Elizabeth Taylor, Rock Hudson, James Dean; features Carroll Baker, Jane Withers, Chill Wills, Mercedes McCambridge, Sal Mineo, Dennis Hopper. Directed by George Stevens. Screenplay, Fred Guiol and Ivan Moffat from Edna Ferber novel of same title; camera (Warner-Color), William C. Mellor; editor, William Hornbeck; songs, Paul Francis Webster and Dimitri Tiomkin; music composed and conducted by Tiomkin; production design, Boris Leven. Previewed at the Criterion Theatre, N.Y., Oct. 4, '56. Running time, **198 MINS.**

Leslie Lynnton	Elizabeth Taylor
Bick Benedict	Rock Hudson
Jett Rink	James Dean
Luz Benedict II	Carroll Baker
Vashti Snythe	Jane Withers
Uncle Bawley	Chill Wills
Luz Benedict	Mercedes McCambridge
Angel Obregon III	Sal Mineo
Jordan Benedict III	Dennis Hopper
Mrs. Horace Lynnton	Judith Evelyn
Dr. Horace Lynnton	Paul Fix
Sir David Karfrey	Rodney Taylor
Bob Dace	Earl Holliman
Pinky Snythe	Robert Nichols
Old Polo	Alexander Scourby
Judy Benedict	Fran Bennett
Whiteside	Charles Watts
Juana	Elsa Cardenas
Lacey Lynnton	Carolyn Craig
Bale Clinch	Monte Hale
Adarene Clinch	Mary Ann Edwards
Gabe Target	Sheb Wolley
Angel Obregon I	Victor Millan
Sarge	Mickey Simpson
Mrs. Obregon	Pilar del Rey
Dr. Guerra	Maurice Jara
Lona Lane	Noreen Nash
Swazey	Napoleon Whiting
Watts	Ray Whitley
Lupe	Tina Menard

There is a sound theory about story-telling. "Alice in Wonderland" stated it a long time ago. Start at the beginning and go on to the end and then stop. "Giant," with a running time of fully three hours and 18 minutes, violates that concept, but it is also, for the most part, an excellent film which registers strongly on all levels, whether it's in its breathtaking panoramic shots of the dusty Texas plains; the personal, dramatic impact of the story itself, or the resounding message it has to impart.

One immediately wonders what sort of reception "Giant" will be accorded in Texas, where the Edna Ferber novel was not popular. For the picture stands squarely on the book, and the Texans on the screen are presented with penetrating realism in a story that pulls no punches. Texas apart, "Giant" rates as sock boxoffice.

Many elements have been fused to make "Giant" click. Producers George Stevens and Henry Ginsberg have spent freely to capture the mood of the Ferber novel and the picture is fairly saturated with the feeling of the vastness and the mental narrowness, the wealth and the poverty, the pride and the prejudice that make up the Texas of today and yesterday. Here is an unflattering vivid portrayal of this rugged state where cattle raising was in part supplanted by oil derricks, and where people scaled the economic ladder from rancher to millionaire almost overnight.

But if production values are almost overpowering, the performances in this film match them under Stevens' direction. Trio of Elizabeth Taylor, Rock Hudson and James Dean turns in excellent portrayals, with each character moulded in a strongly individual vein. Carroll Baker, here introduced in her first important part, proves herself a most competent actress.

It's one of the troubles with such super-long pix that there is a tendency to lose identification with the characters. Yet, in "Giant," the personal relationships aren't subdued by the temptation to concentrate on pictorial values. These people are alive, they have warmth and dimension, and they become real in their inter-related problems.

Story starts when Hudson, as Bick Benedict, comes to Maryland to buy a black stallion and finds and marries Miss Taylor, a beautiful and strongwilled girl, who is now to be transplanted from the gentle green of her state to the dusty gray of Texas in the early twenties. In her new home she clashes with Bick's sister, Mercedes McCambridge, who is killed riding the stallion. The years pass, and as Miss Taylor gets to like her new home state, she also rebels against its prejudice against the Mexican laborers. The marriage almost breaks up, but Hudson persuades her to return to the ranch.

Jett, a ranchhand, played by James Dean, antagonistic to Hudson, finds oil on his little plot and realizes an ambition to become rich. At the start of World War II, he convinces Hudson to allow oil drilling also on Hudson's ranch and the millions come flowing in. But money only intensifies Dean's bad characteristics. Now nicknamed Mr. Texas, he is a heavy drinker and continues to play his ruthless game. Hudson's son, Dennis Hopper, marries a Mexican girl and the prejudice issue comes to a head even as there is a final showdown between Hudson and Dean. Pic ends on the racial note, with the camera closing in on the eyes of Hudson's two grandsons—one a Nordic child, the other half Mexican.

Stevens and scripters Fred Guiol and Ivan Moffat did not flinch the discrimination angle. "Giant" isn't preachy—although in the end it comes close to it—but it's a powerful indictment of the Texas superiority complex. Not since Darryl F. Zanuck found the courage to make "Pinky" and "Gentlemen's Agreement" has the screen spoken out with such a clear voice against group snobbery. In fact, the picture makes that point even stronger than it's in the book. Film at the end has a crashing fight in which Hudson stands up with his fists for the right of a Mexican couple to eat in a diner. This leads to a poignant and moving scene in which Miss Taylor, now middle-aged, tells Hudson (who has prejudices himself) of her admiration for him.

In the light of the current death cult starring the late James Dean it's probably safe to assume that he'll be the strongest draw on the "Giant" marquee. No one should be disappointed, and the film only proves what a promising talent has been lost. As the shiftless, envious, bitter ranchhand who hates society, Dean delivers an outstanding portrayal. Plenty of screentime is devoted to him, and he makes the most of the juicy role. Whether in his scenes with Miss Taylor, whom he admires, or as the oil tycoon who shows up at a banquet in his honor in a drunken stupor, Dean is believable. It's a sock performance.

Miss Taylor, whose talent and emotional ranges have usually seemed limited, turns in a surprisingly clever performance that registers up and down the line. She is tender and yet stubborn. Curiously enough, she's far better in the second half of the film, when her hair begins to show some gray, than in the earlier sequences. Portraying a woman of maturity, who has learned to adjust to a different social pattern, Miss Taylor is both engaging and beautiful. Her costumes, incidentally, are most attractive throughout.

Hudson achieves real stature as Bick Benedict. A good deal of understanding goes into his performance as a man who sees a ranching tradition destroyed by oil and whose son prefers medicine. He is excellent in adjusting to, but never seemingly comprehending, the changes going on around him. With "Giant," Hudson enters real star status.

Large cast features many fine characterizations. Miss Baker is charming as the highspirited Luz Benedict attracted by Dean; Mercedes McCambridge as Hudson's rawboned sister gives a tight, down-to-earth performance, but is occasionally stylized and hard to understand; Jane Withers, Chill Wills, Alexander Scourby, Robert Nichols, Charles Watts are all in perfect tune as Texans who live around the Reata ranch; Sal Mineo registers as the Mexican boy; Dennis Hopper is good as Jordan, Hudson's son and Elsa Cardenas is attractive and subdued as the girl he marries. Earl Holliman contributes importantly as Bob Dace, the laconic ranch youngster who marries Fran Bennett, Hudson's daughter.

Good also in smaller parts are Judith Evelyn, Paul Fix and Rodney Taylor.

"Giant" is not one but many stories; too many perhaps. And director Stevens has possibly allowed himself too much freedom in taking his time to pull all the strands together and weave them into a proper whole. The pace of the picture is frequently leisurely and some scenes, such as the burial sequence, are not only unnecessary but also impede the proper flow of the story. A good half hour could be cut from the film without hurting it.

Yet, Stevens' direction on the whole is topnotch and distinctive. In his hands, "Giant" makes the transition from the old Texas to the new with vivid intensity, catching not only the changes wrought by time and money, but also focusing on the contrasts of modern Texas, where social graces are but skindeep and distances are covered by the oil-rich ranchers in their private planes. Final banquet scene, and the raucous behavior of the people in the ballroom, is a testament to Stevenson's astuteness. Fight footage catches some of the raw power of the brawl in "Shane."

Lenser William C. Mellor deserves some sort of award for his work. He has achieved stunning effects and "Giant" benefits immeasurably from his realism. His camera has captured here some of the most impressive vistas seen on the screen to date.

Unfortunately, the WarnerColor isn't all it should be, particularly in the earlier sequences. Fleshtones show up very dark and the performers' makeup becomes obvious. Some of the closeups, particularly of Miss Taylor, are hurt by the vascillating tint effects. Color improves later in the pic and is stunning in the outdoor shots.

Dimitri Tiomkin has written the music and Paul Francis Webster the lyrics to two songs in the film, "Giant" and "There's Never Been Anyone Else But You." They're melodious, but Tiomkin's background score doesn't measure up to the overall quality of the picture. It's rousing in parts and unnecessarily emotional in others.

William Hornbeck's editing is a craftsman-like job although there are a few choppy sequences. On the whole, "Giant" fully measures up to its expectations. At the b.o., it can't do anything but collect Texas-size chunks of coin.

Hift.

No Place To Hide
(COLOR)

Close to zero as entertainment.

Hollywood, Oct. 9.

Allied Artists release of a Josef Shaftel production. Stars David Brian, Marsha Hunt; features Hugh Corcoran, Ike Jarlego Jr., Celia Flor, Eddie Infante. Directed by Shaftel. Screenplay, Norman Corwin, based on story by Shaftel; camera (De Luxe Color), Gilbert Warrenton; editor, Arthur H. Nadel; music, Herschel Burke Gilbert. Previewed Sept. 28, '56. Running time, **70 MINS.**

Dr. Dobson	David Brian
Anne Dobson	Marsha Hunt
Greg Dobson	Hugh Corcoran
Ramon	Ike Jarlego Jr.
Miss Diaz	Celia Flor
Colonel Moreno	Eddie Infante
Manuel	Manuel Silos
Priest	Lou Salvador
Dr. Lorenzo	Pianing Vidal
Dr. Mateo	Alfonzo Carvajal
Consuel	Vicenta Advincula

This Josef Shaftel production, lensed entirely in the Philippines, is unbelievably poor, its sole asset the interesting backgrounds of Manila. Due to its motivating moppet character, one of the most thoroughly obnoxious ever dreamed up, the story during its full unfoldment hits a single chord: audience irritation. Allied Artists will have a tough time selling this one, even to the least discriminating situations.

The Shaftel yarn, also written and directed by producer, deals with an American doctor, accompanied by his wife and young son, going to the Philippines to continue experiments on a drug to be used as an antidote for the most deadly germ ever discovered. These germs are isolated in a number of bright-colored round capsules, which the doctor's son, thinking they're marbles, takes from the lab. Action thereafter follows the attempts by the father, the police, the army, to locate the boy before the capsules melt and loose their fearsome load. Boy and his Tagalog pal elude them, thinking American lad's dog which came into contact with the germ is to be killed. The mad chase takes spectator through the streets of Manila, for a good look-see of the city.

David Brian is the doctor and Marsha Hunt his wife, both lost in the maze of ridiculous story development. Hugh Corcoran enacts the son, almost impossible to understand, and balance of cast is composed of Filipino talent.

Gilbert Warrenton is responsible for the fine color photography. Other technical credits are stock.

Whit.

The Search for Bridey Murphy

Just another programmer; breaks too late to benefit from retrogression ballyhoo.

Hollywood, Oct. 4.

Paramount release of Pat Duggan production. Features Teresa Wright, Louis Hayward, Nancy Gates, Kenneth Tobey, Richard Anderson. Direction and screenplay, Noel Langley. From the book by Morey Bernstein; camera, John F. Warren; special photographic effects, John P. Fulton; editor, Floyd Knudtson; music supervision, Irvin Talbot. Previewed Oct. 2, '56. Running time, **84 MINS.**

Ruth	Teresa Wright
Morey Bernstein	Louis Hayward
Hazel Bernstein	Nancy Gates
Rex Simmons	Henneth Tobey
Dr. Deering	Richard Anderson
Catlett	Tom McKee
Lois Morgan	Janet Riley
Jerry Thomas	Charles Boaz
Cranmer	Lawrence Fletcher
Father Bernard	Charles Maxwell
Professor	Walter Kingsford
Edgar Cayce	Noel Leslie
William J. Barker	William J. Barker
Bridey (15)	Eilene Janssen
Brian (17)	Bradford Jackson
Brian (68)	James Kirkwood
Bridey (66)	Hallene Hill
Bridey (8)	Denise Freeborn
Bridey (4)	Ruth Robinson

Paramount's "The Search for Bridey Murphy" is presumably breaking too late to reap any particular benefit from the retrogression hypnosis craze sparkplugged a year and more back by publication of Morey Bernstein's book. Like yesterday's headline, it's just another picture, lacking the timely bollyhoo punch that might have made the difference.

There's too much case history and not enough entertainment in the Pat Duggan production. There may be same special interest value for the staunch fan of hypnosis, but others will find it dull and talky as scripted and directed by Noel Langley. The methodical development of the story of how Bernstein age-regressed Ruth Simmons, Colorado housewife, back to another time and another life, hasn't enough suspense or excitement to hold attention. It's only near the end of the experimenting, when Mrs. Simmons almost doesn't come back to her real self, that tension is felt.

With static characters to bring off, it's surprising the cast does as well as it does. Teresa Wright plays the deep-trance subject, while Louis Hayward is the amateur hypnotist, Bernstein. Nancy Gates as the latter's wife; Kenneth Tobey, as Mr. Simmons; and Richard Anderson, doctor friend, are the other principals and all are satisfactory.

In the "astral world" searching for Bridey, Eilene Janssen engagingly plays the Irish maid in her late teens. The elderly, and dead, Bridey is played by Hallene Hill. Two other age periods are represented by Denise Freeborn and Ruth Robinson. Playing Bridey's husband at various ages are Bradford Jackson and James Kirkwood.

Special effects in the "astral world" sequences are quite good as lensed by John P. Fulton. Otherwise, the physical values have a budget look that does not permit much polishing by John F. Warren's straight photography. Background score strikes an eerie note that is just right under the music supervision of Irvin Talbot.

Brog.

Stagecoach to Fury
(REGALSCOPE)

Okay western for program bills; in RegalScope anamorphic, black-and-white.

Hollywood, Oct. 9.

20th-Fox release of Earle Lyon (Regal Films) production. Stars Forrest Tucker, Mari Blanchard, Wally Ford, Margia Dean; features Rudolfo Hoyos, Paul Fix, Rico Alaniz, Wright King, Ian MacDonald. Directed by William Claxton. Screenplay, Eric Norden; story, Norden and Earle Lyon; camera, Walter Strenge; editor, Carl Pierson; music, Paul Dunlap. Previewed Oct. 4, '56. Running time, **75 MINS.**

Frank Townsend	Forrest Tucker
Barbara Duval	Mari Blanchard
Lester Farrell	Wally Ford
Ruth	Margia Dean
Lorenzo Gracia	Rudolfo Hoyos
Tim O'Connors	Paul Fix
Miquel Torres	Rico Alaniz
Ralph Slader	Wright King
Sheriff Ross	Ian MacDonald
Bartender	William Phillips
Sarah	Ellen Corby
oro	Alex Montoya
Zick	Rayford Barnes
Customer	Norman Leavitt
Ann Stewart	Leslie Banning
Nichols	Steven Geray
Pedro	Paul Fierro
Talbot	Robert Karnes

Acceptable supporter has some added interest via being lensed in black-and-white RegalScope (Actually CinemaScope since it was that anamorphic equipment that was used) and the photographic values are a definite plus.

Picture is one of several Regal Films will make for 20th-Fox release. Earle Lyon produced from a story he wrote with Eric Norden, with the latter scripting. While the budget was small and tight, good effects have been achieved and had the story been a bit better developed the overall entertainment avereage would have been excellent for release intentions. For action purposes the tempo could have been speeded up, but otherwise William Claxton's direction unfolds the plot well and handles the cast ably.

The stagecoach to Fury is held up at a relay station by a band of Mexican outlaws led by Rudolfo Hoyos and the passengers kept prisoners while the gang waits for the gold shipment that is to be put on the stage. The strain brings out the true characters of the assorted prisoners and flashbacks on several are used to establish why they were aboard the stage. The flashbacks slow the pace somewhat, but eventually Forrest Tucker, stage guard; Paul Fix, the driver, and Wally Ford, a cowardly judge who turns brave at the end, get the best of Hoyos and save the gold.

The above trio performs well. Mari Blanchard takes care of the s.a. demands of the plot as an amoral dame fleeing with the fortune of the husband she had had killed. Margia Dean is okay as the other femme stage passenger, as is Wright King, gunslinger who is no match for the bandits. Hoyos is excellent and there are assists from Rico Alaniz, Ian MacDonald (also associate producer on pic), William Phillips, Ellen Corby (seen in a flashback), Alex Montoya, and others.

Walter Strenge was responsible for the topnotch lensing, the outdoor location shots being especially good. Paul Dunlap's score handily accents the mood and the editing by Carl Pierson keeps the footage down to 75 minutes.

Brog.

X the Unknown
(BRITISH)

Fanciful meller, with strong suspense angles, should make sturdy dualer in U.S. as well as in Britain.

London, Oct. 2.

Exclusive Films' release of Hammer Film (Anthony Hinds) Production. Stars DeanJ Jagger, Edward Chapman, Leo McKern. Directed by Leslie Norman. Screenplay, Jimmy Sangster; camera, Gerald Gibbs; edtor, James Needs; music, James Bernard. At Pavilion, London. Running time, **78 MINS.**

Dr. Adam Royston	Dean Jagger
Elliot	Edward Chapman
McGill	Leo McKern
Zena	Marianne Brauns
Peter Elliot	William Lucas
Major Cartwright	John Harvey
Lieut. Bannerman	Peter Hammond
Sergeant Grimsdyke	Michael Ripper
Private Spider Webb	Anthony Newley
Haggis	Ian MacNaughton
Private Lancing	Kenneth Cope
Old Soldier	Edwin Richfield
Jack Harding	Jameson Clark
Vi Harding	Jane Aird
Willie Harding	Michael Brook
Ian	Fraser Hines
Unwin	Neil Hallet
Old Tom	Norman Macowan
Russell	Neil Wilson
Gerry	John Stone
Sergeant Yeardye	Archie Duncan

"X the Unknown" is a highly imaginative and fanciful meller, with tense dramatic overtones which will help it along at the boxoffice. As in Britain, film needs shrewd and careful coupling for a double bill, but with suitable contrasting selection should register sturdy biz in the U.S., too.

Made with creditable slickness, it tells a story which is completely absorbing, though totally unbelievable. There's little letup in the action, and suspense angles are kept constantly to the forefront. Laboratory experiments in an atomic research station have an impressive, but familiar appeal, though ultimately they play a key role in the plot. War Office cooperated in the production, and its seal on a story of this kind should have some value.

The "unknown" of the title is a quantity of radio-active mud discovered on the Scottish moors during a military exercise, which causes the death of a soldier, proves fatal to a boy playing in the vicinity and penetrates the radiation room of a hospital, killing a doctor and sending a nurse out of her mind. Dean Jagger, as a scientist at a local atomic research station, has no logical explanation but comes to the conclusion that the eruption is attracted to all forms of radio-active energy and that it will doubtless head for their atomic pile. There's no immediate solution and their only hope is to try out their atomic neutralizer which is still in the experimental stage.

The scenes on the desolate moor, the sight of the grim atomic mass moving relentlessly towards its main target, the closeups of the radio-active victims, and the ultimate efficacy of the neutralizer combine in achieving a tense, almost horrific atmosphere. The acting, though mainly stereotype in style, is in the same vein, with Jagger, Edward Chapman and Leo McKern leading a vigorous cast. Marianne Brauns does a standout bit as the nurse, revealing a warm pert personality. Technical credits are standard.

Myro.

Between Heaven and Hell
(C'SCOPE—COLOR)

Well done action picture based on the Francis Gwaltney (Pacific) war novel. Shapes as sturdy b.o. entry.

20th-Fox release of David Weisbart production. Stars Robert Wagner, Terry Moore, Broderick Crawford, Buddy Ebsen; features Robert Keith, Brad Dexter, Mark Damon, Ken Clark, Harvey Lembeck, Skip Homeier, L. Q. Jones, Tod Andrews, Biff Elliot, Bart Burns. Directed by Richard Fleischer. Screenplay, Harry Brown, from Francis Gwaltney novel; camera (Color by DeLuxe), Leo Tover; editor, James B. Clark; music, Hugo Friedhofer. Previewed in N. Y., Oct. 8, '56. Running time, **94 MINS.**

Sam Gifford	Robert Wagner
Jenny	Terry Moore
Waco	Broderick Crawford
Willie	Buddy Ebsen
Col. Gozzens	Robert Keith
Joe Johnson	Brad Dexter
Terry	Mark Damon
Morgan	Ken Clark
Bernard Meleski	Harvey Lembeck
Swanson	Skip Homeier
Kenny	L. Q. Jones
Ray Mosby	Tod Andrews
Tom Thumb	Biff Elliot
Raker	Bart Burns
Col. Miles	Frank Gerstle
Savage	Carl Switzer
Sellers	Gregg Martell
Millard	Frank Gorshin
Mrs. Raker	Darlene Fields
Raker Girl	Ilene Brown
Raker Boy	Scotty Morrow
Oldest Raker Girl	Pixie Parkhurst
Oldest Raker Boy	Brad Morrow
George	Scat Man Crothers
Soames	Tom Edwards

As the memory of the last war recedes, the stories to come out of that war are getting a sharper and more critical perspective. "Between Heaven and Hell," produced with vivid realism by David Weisbart, serves as a pertinent example. It's a good, hard-hitting action film, replete with the usual heroics but also full with the ugly realization that the men who fought the war were far from perfect.

There is little question this isn't a picture of which the Pentagon can be expected to approve. One of the officers in it is a coward. Another is a vicious brute who struts around covered by bodyguards with automatic rifles. Only at the end, recognized as a psycho, is he relieved of command. The hero, played by Robert Wagner, is a moody Southerner in whom the camaraderie of danger awakens a social consciousness.

The Francis Gwaltney novel, adapted by Harry Brown for the screen, painted a vivid picture of battle. The film, directed by Richard Fleischer with a view to achieving maximum realism, captures the sights and sounds of the Pacific fighting and generates a good deal of tension and excitement. Not all of it is believable, and Wagner's final rushing down the Jap-infested mountain is almost ludicrous as he sideswipes one Jap party after the other. Yet many of the other battle scenes explode on the CinemaScope screen with appropriate sound and fury.

Terry Moore is the only girl in the pic and she's adequate—but no more—in a brief role. Wagner gives a good, low-key performance as the boy who gets busted to private after he hits an officer who has killed the men in his patrol. Broderick Crawford is loud and overbearing as the psycho colonel. His role is made harder since the picture fails to point out that the colonel is in charge of a group of misfits.

Buddy Ebsen stands out with a skillfull characterization as Wagner's buddy; Robert Keith is sympathetic as the colonel, and Harvey Lembeck contributes some humor as the Chicago boy in a Southern outfit.

Adapter Brown has concentrated on the war parts of the book, retaining only enough of Wagner's earlier background to establish his later realization that sharecroppers are also people. The philosophizing is, at times, a little hard to take and out of place. Director Fleischman has drawn the most out of the action scenes. Some of the jungle props look phony on the big screen. The LeDuxe tint effects are topnotch as per usual. Leo Tover handled the camera on this one with skill. Story is told partly in flashback, but remains fluid. Editing by James B. Clark has merit and so has Hugo Friedhofer's music.   *Hift.*

The Grand Maneuver
(FRENCH—COLOR)

Rene Clair tinter seasoned with plenty Gallic charm. A boon for the arties.

United Motion Picture Organization release of a Filmsonor production. Stars Michele Morgan, Gerard Philipe; features Brigitte Bardot, Yves Robert, Jean Desailly, Pierre Dux, Jacques Francois, Lise Delamare, Jacqueline Maillan, Magalie Noel. Directed by Rene Clair. Screenplay, Clair; camera (Eastman color), Robert Le Febvre; music, Georges van Parys. Previewed Oct. 1, '56, at the Sutton Theatre, N. Y. Running time, **104 MINS.**

Marie Louise Riviere ..... Michele Morgan
Lieut. Armand de la Verne
.... Gerard Philipe
Lucie .... Brigitte Bardot
Felix .... Yves Robert
Victor Duverger......... Jean Desailly
Colonel .... Pierre Dux
Rudolph .... Jacques Francois

Jeanne .... Lise Delamare
Juliette ....Jacqueline Maillan
Therese .... Magalie Noel
Gisele .... Simone Valere
Alice .... Catherine Anouilh
Armand's Batman........ Jacques Fabbri
Photographer .... Raymond Cordy
Prefect .... Olivier Hussenot

Those who expect only "great things" from Rene Clair probably will be disappointed in "The Grand Maneuver." Those who come merely to be entertained will find this bittersweet comedy-romance a thoroughly diverting, light-hearted and yet frequently thoughtful bit of Gallic fluff, done up in excellent color and acted out by an engaging company.

"Grand Maneuver" is set in a little French garrison town prior to World War I. It has as its main theme a bet made by cavalry officers that one of their numbers will conquer a lady prior to the start of summer maneuvers. He executes this bit of trickery, but falls in love while doing it, and in the end loses the lady of his heart.

Clair's sense of humor, expressed both in the dialog and somehow also in the exaggerated wooing engaged in by the colorfully costumed officers, gives the picture a value that should pay off in regular carriage trade. Add to that the performances of Michele Morgan and Gerard Philipe which come close to perfection. Philipe particularly turns in a highly animated characterization and he registers soundly in every mood. Miss Morgan has not much more to do but look lovely as the smitten divorcee. Her quiet dignity is appealing.

In other parts, Brigitte Bardot is charming as the flirtatious Lucie; Yves Robert is excellent as Felix and Jean Desailly hits it on the nose as Miss Morgan's stuffy suitor.

Clair has an uncanny eye for composition and he works with gentle pastel colors that at times take on the quality of paintings. Some of the scenes are grandly staged and very effective. This isn't Clair at his best, but his merger of fun and seriousness: Philipe's desperate predicament at the end; his staging of little intimate scenes, are all effective and blend into a most enjoyable film.

There are moments of overplay, which don't ring true, and the story itself is given a rather leisurely treatment. Robert Le Febvre's lensing is top-notch.   *Hift.*

A Hill in Korea
(BRITISH)

Well-made war episode showing British minor skirmish in Korea; exciting but unpretentious.

London, Oct. 2.
British Lion release of Ian Dalrymple Wessex Film Production. Stars George Baker, Stanley Baker, Harry Andrews, Michael Medwin. Directed by Julian Amyes. Screenplay by Ian Dalrymple from novel by Max Catto; camera, Freddie Francis; editor, Peter Hunt; music, Malcolm Arnold. At Odeon, Marble Arch, London, Sept. 18, '56. Running time, **81 MINS.**

Lieutenant Butler .... George Baker
Sergeant Payne .... Harry Andrews
Corporal Ryker .... Stanley Baker
Private Docker .... Michael Medwin
Private Wyatt .... Ronald Lewis
Private Sims .... Stephen Boyd
Private Lindop .... Victor Maddern
Private Rabin .... Harry Landis
Private O'Brien .... Robert Brown
Private Neill .... Barry Lowe
Lance-Corporal Hodge .... Robert Shaw
Private Kim .... Charles Laurence
Private Matthews .... Eric Corrie
Private Henson .... David Morrell
Private Lockyer .... Michael Caine
Private Moon .... Percy Herbert

Although British film producers have covered ground in most theatres of war, this is the first instance where Korea has been used to dramatize an actual incident in the campaign. It is little more than an incident, depicting the adventures of a small patrol sent to find out if a village is inhabited by the enemy. Its dedication is a tribute to the young drafted soldiers who, on this occasion, constitute 82% of the force.

Story is based on a book, but records actual events. There are no base camp sets, nor home scenes before the inducted boys join the army. All the action, humor and pathos centers on the mixed bunch from every walk of life, wisecracking, beefing and just plain scared, comprising one rookie officer, three regular soldiers, including one sergeant. The remainder are untried civilians.

From the silhouetted patrolmen setting out on a thankless, dangerous task, story grows through their efforts to dodge, or overpower, the lurking Chinese, reach their objective, and find a way back although blocked on all sides.

With the subdued lighting used throughout most of the shots, owing to night marches, and the indistinguishable drab jungle outfit, anonymity swamps most of the characters. Only the closeups of their sweaty faces, and calling each other's names brings individuality to the actors. All the cast has equal opportunities to score, George Baker as the conscientious officer, Harry Andrews as the tough sergeant and Ronald Lewis as the outsider, disliked by his buddies.

The director has handled the story with simplicity, there being no mock heroics, no jealous motives, nor major private issues to be settled, each man fulfilling his distasteful job to the best of his inexperienced capacity.   *Clem.*

Blonde Bait

Below-average British import with American principals; poor prospects indicated.

Hollywood, Oct. 9.
Associated Film Distributing Corp. release of an Anthony Hinds production. Stars Beverly Michaels, Jim Davis, Joan Rice, Richard Travis, Paul Cavanagh. Features Thora Hird, Avril Angers, Gordon Jackson, Valeria White, April Olrich, Ralph Michael. Directed by Elmo Williams. Camera, Walter Harvey; William Whitley; music, Leonard Salzedo; editor, James Needs. Reviewed Oct. 3, '56. Running time, **70 MINS.**

Angela Booth .... Beverly Michaels
Nick Randall .... Jim Davis
Cleo .... Joan Rice
Kent Foster .... Richard Travis
Inspector Hedges .... Paul Cavanagh
Granny .... Thora Hird
Bessie .... Avril Angers
Percy .... Gordon Jackson
Prison Governor .... Valeria White
Marguerite .... April Olrich
Julian Lord .... Ralph Michael

"Blonde Bait" offers an exploitation title but nothing more, an over-length below-par British entry strictly for lower-casing in the minor market. Hollywood names of Beverly Michaels and Jim Davis may help, but not much.

Produced by Anthony Hinds, picture was directed by American editor Elmo Williams. The non-credited screenplay follows the attempt by the U.S. State Dept., working in conjunction with Scotland Yard, to catch up to a traitor and murderer by using Miss Michaels as bait. To do this, it's arranged that she shall escape from a London prison, where she's serving six months for assault, and

unknowningly lead the way to the quarry.

Miss Michaels is as good as role will permit, and Davis, as the traitor, has no chance at all. Richard Travis and Paul Cavanagh enact State Dept. and Scotland Yard officials, respectively, and Thora Hird an old prison inmate who helps Beverly to escape and accompanies her. Part of the picture appears to have been filmed in the U.S.   *Whit.*

Teahouse of the August Moon
(C'SCOPE-COLOR)

Topnotch screen adaptation of novel and stage play. Fine cast and boxoffice prospects. Added value: Marlon Brando doing whimsy.

Metro release of a Jack Cummings production. Stars Marlon Brando, Glenn Ford, Machiko Kyo, Eddie Albert; features Paul Ford, Jun Negami, Nijiko Kiyokawa, Mitsuko Sawamura, Henry (Harry) Morgan. Directed by Daniel Mann. Screenplay, John Patrick from Patrick's play and Vern J. Sneider's book; camera (Metrocolor), John Alton; editor, Harold F. Kress; music, Saul Chaplin with Okinawan songs composed or arranged by Kikuko Kanai. Previewed Sept. 28, '56. Running time, **123 MINS.**

Sakini .... Marlon Brando
Capt. Fisby .... Glenn Ford
Lotus Blossom .... Machiko Kyo
Capt. McLean .... Eddie Albert
Col. Purdy .... Paul Ford
Mr. Seiko .... Jun Negami
Miss Higa Jiga .... Nijiko Kiyokawa
Little Japanese Girl .. Mitsuko Sawamura
Sgt. Gregovich ..... Henry (Harry) Morgan
Mr. Sumata ...... Minoru Nishida
Mr. Hokaida ...... Kichizaemon Sarumaru
Mr. Omura ...... Frank Tokunaga
Mr. Oshira .... Raynum K. Tsukamoto

Skilful use of the celluloid medium has added to the humor and charm of the original novel and subsequent play "Teahouse of the August Moon" should delight picture audiences. Tastefully and colorfully produced by Jack Cummings, directed by Daniel Mann with a fine flair for its inherent humor and enhanced by excellent tint work in the Metrocolor process, "Teahouse" retains the basic appeal that made it a unique war novel and a legit hit. There is some added slapstick for those who prefer their comedy broader. Adding to its prospects are some top comedy characterizations, notably from Glenn Ford, plus the offbeat casting of Marlon Brando in a comedy role.

In transferring his play based on the Vern Sneider novel to the screen, Patrick has provided a subtle shift in the focal interest. The result is that it becomes Ford's picture and Brando's characterization of the interpreter, though strong, becomes of secondary consideration. Other good performances and the unusual Oriental background maintain constant interest.

Deft screenplay provides an interesting fillip in retaining the stage device of a narrative prolog and epilog by Brando and the warmly-humorous verbiage has been left intact. Story line also is unsullied as the film unspools the tribulations of Ford, the young Army officer assigned to bring the benefits of democracy and free enterprise to the little Okinawan town of Tobiki. Washington's monumental Plan B, however, conflicts with native life and tradition and Ford's decision to achieve true democracy by letting the Okinawans lead their own lives gets him in trouble with his immediate superior, Paul Ford. The happy ending is achieved when news of Ford's experiment in self-determination is lauded by an American congressman and the national magazines elicit interest in extensive coverage.

The role of Capt. Fisby represents a romp for Glenn Ford, who gives it an unrestrained portrayal that adds mightily to the laughs. He's always real and appropriately boyish and he parlays the combination into one of his best efforts to date. Brando is excellent as the interpreter, limning the rogueish character perfectly. Physically, he seems a bit too heavy for the role and lacking in the suppleness expected of an Okinawan native, but he makes up for it in a performance that establishes his thespic versatility. Japanese actress Machiko Kyo is easy on the eyes as the geisha girl and there is excellent support from Eddie Albert, who sparkles as the psychiatrist who yearns to be an agricultural expert. Paul Ford is fine as the stuffed-shirt commanding officer and Henry (Harry) Morgan turns in another effective stint as an orderly. There are also good minor role jobs by some top Japanese actors, notably Nijiko Kiyokawa, Raynum K. Tsukamoto and Jun Negami.

Production is a top credit for Cummings and for Daniel Mann's skilled direction which makes the most of the contrast between two ways of life. John Alton's Metrocolor lensing is very good and the process itself lends a fine background, particularly in its reproduction of pastel colors in the teahouse sequences. Art direction by William A. Horning and Eddie Imazu rates a special nod in the skilful manner in which the location scenes were duplicated on the backlot. *Kap.*

Secrets of Life
(PARTIAL C'SCOPE-COLOR)

Highly interesting naturalist-photographer report on nature's mysteries; Disney True-Life Adventure with good family prospects.

Hollywood, Oct. 16.

Buena Vista release of Ben Sharpsteen production. Written and directed by James Algar; narrated by Winston Hibler; music, Paul Smith; editor, Anthony Gerard; camera (Technicolor), Stuart V. Jewell, Robert H. Crandall, Murl Deusing, George and Nettie MacGinitie; Tilden W. Robers, William A. Anderson; time lapse photography, John Nash Ott Jr., Stuart V. Jewell, William M. Harlow, Rex R. Elliott, Vincent J. Schaefer. Previewed Oct. 12, '56. Running time, **70 MINS.**

Walt Disney's True-Life Adventure series takes another intriguing look at the mysteries of nature in "Secrets of Life." The 70-minute documentary is scholastic only in that it is factual, as the editorial arrangements of the subjects and the background score keep it on a highly entertaining level. It should go over well, maintaining the average for the series.

Eighteen naturalist-photographers are credited with the extensive, painstaking lensing that was necessary to bring the varied stories of the assorted life shown to the screen. Practically all of it is weird and wonderful, and all of it is small, some even to the extent of requiring microscopic and time-lapse photography. Subjects range from sea to land, and under both, and climax with nature's big show—a raging volcano that is a part of the constant replenishing of earth. The volcano is impressively unveiled in CinemaScope at the finale, whereas the preceeding portion of the picture is in standard ratio.

Bees, ants and the curious workings of the plant and microcosm worlds are engrossingly depicted under the respective lensing of Stuart Jewell, Robert Crandall, John Nash Ott Jr., William M. Harlow, Rex Elliott, Fran William Hall and Roman Vishniac. Equally fascinating are the sights of the Decorator Crab, Leibe shellfish, walking Kelp Fish, jellyfish, barnacles, etc., photographed by George and Nettie MacGinitie; the hapless Stickleback fish by Murl Deusing; the comical Angle fish by William A. Anderson; the Archer fish by Tilden W. Roberts; Jack Couffer's shots of the Fiddler Crab courting. The C'Scoped volcano scenes were contributed by Claude Jendrusch and Arthur Carter. Another outstanding photographic feature is the cloud scapes by Vincent J. Schaefer.

Ben Sharpsteen's production, it was ably written and directed by James Algar, with Winston Hibler doing the narration. Paul Smith's score is fine, as is Anthony Gerard's editing. *Brog.*

Beyond Mombasa
(BRITISH-COLOR)

Donna Reed spurning Cornel Wilde in wilds of Africa. Good stereotyped action picture for general appeal, with Leo Genn supplying thrills.

London, Oct. 9.

Columbia production and release. Stars Cornel Wilde, Donna Reed, Leo Genn, Ron Randell. Directed by George Marshall. Screenplay, Richard English and Gene Levitt, based on story, "Mark of Leopard" by James Eastwood; camera, Frederick A. Young; editor, Ernest Walter; music, Humphrey Searle. At Leicester Square Theatre, London. Running time, **90 MINS.**

Matt Campbell .... Cornel Wilde
Ann Wilson .... Donna Reed
Ralph Hoyt .... Leo Genn
Elliott Hastings .... Ron Randell
Gil Rossi .... Christopher Lee
Ketimi .... Dan Jackson
Trumpet Player .... Eddie Calvert
Native Boss .... Bartholomew Sketch
Irate Englishman .... Clive Morton
Tourist .... Macdonald Parke
Tourist's wife .... Virginia Bedard
Desk Clerk .... Julian Sherrier
Dacall Chief .... Ed Johnson
George Campbell .... Roy Purcell

To add to the flock of East African safari yarns comes this one based on a story about Leopard Men. It varies little from most of these tales of hazard in the bush, following the conventional pattern, but depends less on the shots of herds of wild animals than usually pad out these pix. It should prove a satisfactory b.o. proposition from the star angle, unless the public is sated with the repetitious subject matter.

Cornel Wilde plays a rolling stone, jack-of-all-trades who arrives in Kenya to join his brother, whom he believes to have discovered uranium in a deserted gold mine. He is met by a sympathetic missionary with the news his brother has just been murdered by the leopardmen, a dormant semi-religious sect apparently active once more against the white man. The brother's two partners both profess ignorance of the mine's existence, and arouse suspicion by their behavior on a trek to unearth it, until one of them is mysteriously wounded.

The missionary and his niece also tag along, and after two native bearers are killed by blowpipe darts, most of the servants fade out. After abortive attempts to kill the newcomer, who disbelieves the leopardmen theory, the crimes are pinned down to the missionary whose niece sees him use the blowpipe on the other partner when they find the mine. His reason for the murders, and imitation leopard claw marks on his victims, is to prevent the mine being reopened.

Wilde overdoes the flippant callousness when faced with the news of his brother's death, more than justifying the girl's belief his only interest is in how he will gain financially. Leo Genn balances nicely the sincerity and fanaticism demanded for the role of the missionary turned killer. The two partners are realistically played by Ron Randell and Christopher Lee. Donna Reed almost douses her Hollywood grooming to roam the wilds and find romance with the man she at first despises.

Eddie Calvert blasts efficiently on his trumpt in a brief night club scene, and supporting Negro actors give excellent performances. The background exteriors are made the most of and the direction is on a par with the firstrate camerawork. *Clem.*

Calling Homicide

Well-motivated detective yarn.

Hollywood, Oct. 16.

Allied Artists release of a Ben Schwalb production. Stars Bill Elliott; features Don Haggerty, Kathleen Case, Myron Healey, Jeanne Cooper, Thomas B. Henry, Lyle Talbot, Almira Sessions, Herb Vigran, James Best, John Dennis. Directed by Edward Bernds. Screenplay, Bernds; camera, Harry Neumann; editor, William Austin; music, Marlin Skiles. Previewed Oct. 9, '56. Running time, **60 MINS.**

Lt. Doyle .... Bill Elliott
Sgt. Duncan .... Don Haggerty
Donna .... Kathleen Case
Haddix .... Myron Healey
Darlene .... Jeanne Cooper
Gilmore .... Thomas B. Henry
Tony Fuller .... Lyle Talbot
Mrs. Dunstetter .... Almira Sessions
Ray Engel .... Herb Vigran
Arnholf .... James Best
Benny .... John Dennis

"Calling Homicide" kindles enough whodunit action to make it acceptable for lower program market. Name of Bill Elliott will carry it through as a follow-up to past entries in the same character, and the plot, while sometimes shaky and confusing, is well motivated.

Script by Edward Bernds, who also directs, focuses on Elliott as a lieutenant of the Los Angeles Sheriff's homicide department. While investigating the mysterious dynamiting death of a young policeman, he discovers the strangle-murder of operator of a model school is linked with the first killing. Footage follows his unraveling of the case, which is tied in with an adoption racket.

Elliott shows to good advantage in this Ben Schwalb production, given satisfactory values. Don Haggerty as his side lends a rugged note, and distaff end is well handled by Jeanne Cooper, manager of the school, and Kathleen Case, in for romance with Myron Healey, former Hollywood stuntman who is a suspect. Lyle Talbot and John Dennis also are okay in key characters.

Technical departments are standard, Harry Neuman photographing and William Austin credited as editor. *Whit.*

Mesa of Lost Women

Misbegotten answer to all the product 'shortage' reports

A. J. Frances White-Joy Houck production. Producers, G. William Perkins, Melvin Gale; directors, Herbert Tevos, Ron Ormond; screenplay, Tevos; camera, Earl Struss, Gilbert Warrenton; editors, Hugh Winn, Ray Lockert. Stars Jackie Coogan, Allan Nixon, Richard Travis; co-stars Mary Hill, Robert Knapp, Tandra Quinn. Reviewed at State Theatre, Los Angeles, Calif., Oct. 10, '56. Running time, **70 MINS.**

Its exploitation tag won't help this maze of confusion. Picture obviously was made on the premise that product-hungry theatres would be forced to book anything.

Yarn in flashback recounts the story of a man and woman found wandering in the Mexican desert. It has to do with a plane forced down on a high mesa, where tarantulas have been transformed by a mad scientist into giants, and women infused with their savagery. The man, who was the pilot of plane, and femme, engaged to plane's owner, are the only ones left of the party who managed to escape. It's for laughs only.

Robert Knapp is the pilot and is the only convincing character. Mary Hill is the femme, Jackie Coogan the scientist. Herbert Tevos and Ron Ormond's direction is as bad as the Tevos' script, which must have been purchased sight-unseen by producers J. Frances White and Joy Houck. *Whit.*

The Tahitian
(COLOR)

Medical science and a Tahitian tabu; inexpertly done with dubious b.o. even for art houses.

Hollywood, Oct. 9.
Cornelius Crane-James Knott-Lotus Long production. Director, Knott; story, Knott, Miss Long; camera (Eastmancolor), Knott; editor, Otto Meyer; narration, Annabel Ross, directed by William R. Anderson. Music, Eddie Lund. Reviewed at Vagabond Theatre, Los Angeles, Oct. 8, '56. Running time, 79 MINS.

Ana .... herself
Vahio .... himself
Medicine Man .... Tala Tepava
Chief Morro .... Tehapaitua Salmon
Dr. De Motte .... Dr. George Thooris
Dr. Stuart .... Dr. Henry K. Beve
Ben .... Ben Bambridge
Robinson .... William A. Robinson
Tetoa .... Tetoa Mauu
Singer .... Denise Pottier
Narrator .... Miri Rei

Despite its interesting locale and fine Eastman color, this indie effort will have tough sledding, even on the art circuit for which it has obviously been beamed. Story is dull and slow, the unprofessional performances of the natives unconvincing and the use of narration to bridge long silent stretches frequently annoying.

Shot in 16m and blown up to 35 (and screened in 1.85 to 1 at a preview where some quality was lost), this 79-minute entry spins a story of the resistance to scientific advancement on the part of the natives spurred by a diehard medicine man. The district chief refuses to cooperate with scientists seeking to eliminate mosquitoes, and thus end filariasis, on the island until his own son is stricken with a second attack and the scientists prove the dread disease is transmitted by mosquitoes.

Footage incorporates some interesting dances and native music but has an amateurish quality that hampers its chances. There is nothing exploitable here, the producers having the good taste to bypass the obvious lure for sensation seekers, and tho' Ana, as the romantic interest, is an appealing femme she serves as no draw. *Kap.*

The Deadliest Sin
(BRITISH)

Okay meller import for lowercase bookings.

Hollywood, Oct. 11.
Allied Artists release of Alec C. Snowden production. Stars Sydney Chaplin, Audrey Dalton, John Bentley; features Peter Hammond, John Welsh, Jefferson

Clifford. Directed by Ken Hughes. Screenplay, Don Martin and Hughes; camera, Philip Grindrod; editor, Geoffrey Muller; music, Richard Taylor. Previewed Oct. 4, '56. Running time, 74 MINS.

Mike .... Sydney Chaplin
Louise .... Audrey Dalton
Kessler .... John Bentley
Alan .... Peter Hammond
Father Neil .... John Welsh
Pop .... Jefferson Clifford
Corey .... Patrick Allen
Williams .... Pat McGrath
Beckman .... Robert Raglan
Mrs. Poole .... Betty Wolfe
Young Priest .... Richard Huggett
Photographer .... Eddie Stafford

British-lensed melodrama should please though cast names are virtually unknown in the States, but all perform competently. Femme star Audrey Dalton has been seen in Hollywood-produced pix, as has Sydney Chaplin, but the others are all Britishers.

The Allied Artists release was produced by Alec C. Snowden in association with Nat Cohen and Stuart Levy, and uses the tight little isle locations effectively to up-point melodramatic angles in the script by Don Martin and Ken Hughes. The latter directs, sometimes with a little too much deliberateness for stateside meller fans, but there's enough violence in the plot to compensate.

Chaplin returns to his English home after a series of misadventures in the U. S. and is welcomed by his sister, Miss Dalton, Pop, played by Jefferson Clifford, is a hit less cordial because he senses something is wrong—and he's right. Chaplin has skipped the states with a bundle of cash, leaving his partner in a holdup without his just share. The partner follows to England and gets himself killed by Peter Hammond, Miss Dalton's boyfriend, when the latter tries to help Chaplin during a fight with the ex-partner. A devout Catholic, Hammond goes to a priest to confess and Chaplin kills him. The heavy gets his in the church later, when he's trying to murder the priest, figuring the latter may have heard enough of Hammond's confession to make him dangerous.

Miss Dalton is extremely attractive in appearance, and able in carrying out her part of the plot. Chaplin does a good job of his character and Hammond is acceptable, too. John Bentley registers as the police inspector who sets the trap for Chaplin in the church. Others lend the proper support.

Lensing by Philip Grindrod and the other technical assists are up to standard. *Brog.*

The Silken Affair
(BRITISH)

David Niven starred in farcical comedy, with average b.o. prospects.

London, Oct. 2.
RKO release of Dragon Films' (Fred Feldkamp) production. Stars David Niven; features Genevieve Page, Ronald Squire, Beatrice Straight, Wilfrid Hyde White. Directed by Roy Kellino; screenplay, Robert Lewis Taylor; camera, Gilbert Taylor; editor, Richard Best; music, Peggy Stuart. At Plaza, London. Running time, 96 MINS.

Roger Tweakham.......... David Niven
Ilsa .... Genevieve Page
Marberry .... Ronald Squire
Theora .... Beatrice Straight
Sir Horace Hogg..... Wilfrid Hyde White
Baggott ..... Howard Marion Crawford
Mrs. Tweakham........... Dorothy Alison
Mr. Blucher........... Miles Malleson
Worthington .... Richard Wattis
Lady Barber.............. Joan Sims
Receptionist .... Irene Handl
Judge .... Charles Carson
Tobacconist .... Harry Locke
Detective .... Martin Boddey
Detective .... Colin Morris

Lift Operator............. Leonard Sharp
Henry .... John Carroll

As an essay in farcical comedy, "The Silken Affair" is a near miss. Pic is Fred Feldkamp's first excursion into British production. Although he has fashioned a yarn with many amusing situations, it's a long way from hitting the jackpot, with b.o. prospects around average. Robert Lewis Taylor's screenplay never pretends to be more than a lightweight, frothy trifle, in which individual laughlines appear to take precedence over story construction. The plot itself makes little sense, and much of the incident falls flat. Occasionally, however, there's a smart dialog passage to give it a shot in the arm.

David Niven plays a bowlerhatted, hide-bound chartered accountant who has an "uncontrollable urge" to inflate the accounts of a firm of silk stocking manufacturers and to deflate the results of a rival firm of nylon manufacturers. There follows a chain of preposterous incidents, including a trial scene, until he finds himself in control of both companies.

The cause of Niven's urge is a chance meeting with Genevieve Page, who encourages him to strike a blow for freedom. As it happens, there's another chance meeting a couple of days later, and it just happens that she's a model for the nylon firm he's almost ruined. A particularly ridiculous aspect of the story concerns the daughter of the silk stocking boss: she outdoes the most ardent suffragette by heading a down-withmen organization and using her father's headquarters as a shooting gallery.

Although the film is obviously weak in story values, it's been given a polished production and is smoothly acted by a cast which includes some top local talent. Niven acquits himself with customary suavity. Genevieve Page, a scintillating Parisienne, makes a personal hit in her British film bow. Ronald Squire, Beatrice Straight and Wilfrid Hyde White put the necessary gloss into their respective performances. Impressive cameos also are provided by Richard Wattis and Miles Malleson. *Myro.*

The Flaming Teen-Age

Cheapie and icky stuff about alcohol and dope set.

A Truman Enterprises presentation of an Ervin S. Yeaworth-Charles Edwards production. Directors, Yeaworth, Edwards; screenplay, Jean Yeaworth, Ethel Barrett; camera, John Ayling; are director, Bill Jersey. Stars Noel Reyburn, Ethel Barrett, Jerry Frank, Shirley Holmes. Reviewed at State Theatre, Los Angeles, Calif., Oct. 10, '56. Running time, 67 MINS.

This ineptly-turned-out film attempts to base its unfoldment on teen-age indulgence in alcohol and dope, but misses on every count. Bookings must depend on minor exploitation situations, where its title may attract but returns must be extremely spotty.

A pitch is made to give feature a documentary flavor by use of a commentator spieling on modern youth and responsibility of the parent, resulting in so much wasted footage. Film is episodic, the first part dealing with a young chap whose dad takes him out on the town to show him the evils of drink. The second part, claimed to be the true story of a dope ad-

dict who finally became an evangelist, consumes the greater portion of picture, an unconvincing narrative throughout. Entire 67 minutes is plagued with miserable photography and sound.

Principals include Noel Reyburn, Ethel Barrett, Jerry Frank and Shirley Holmes. Ervin S. Yeaworth and Charles Edwards coproduced and directed, from script by Jean Yeaworth and Ethel Barrett. John Ayling is credited with camera work. *Whit.*

Around The World In 80 Days
(TODD-AO—COLOR)

All-star cast and socko values make this standout all 'round. Top b.o. prospects.

United Artists release of Michael Todd production. Stars David Niven, Cantinflas, Robert Newton, Shirley MacLaine; features long list of name players in bit parts. Directed by Michael Anderson. Associate producer, William Cameron Menzies. Screenplay, S. J. Perelman, based on Jules Verne novel of same title; camera (Eastmancolor), Lionel Lindon; foreign locations, Kevin McClory; editors, Gene Ruggiero, Paul Weatherwax; music, Victor Young; costumes, Miles White; art, James Sullivan. Previewed at the Rivoli Theatre, N. Y., Oct. 16, '56. Running time, **175 MINS.**

Phileas Fogg	David Niven
Passepartout	Cantinflas
Mr. Fix	Robert Newton
Aouda	Shirley MacLaine
Mon. Gasse	Charles Boyer
Stationmaster	Joe E. Brown
Tourist	Martin Carol
Colonel Proctor	John Carradine
Clerk	Charles Coburn
Official	Ronald Colman
Steward	Melville Cooper
Hesketh-Baggott	Noel Coward
Whist Partner	Finlay Currie
Police Chief	Reginald Denny
First Mate	Andy Devine
Hostess	Marlene Dietrich
Bullfighter	Louis Miguel Dominguin
Coachman	Fernandel
Foster	Sir John Gielgud
Sportin' Lady	Hermione Gingold
Dancer	Jose Greco
Sir Francis Gromarty	Sir Cedric Hardwicke
Fallentin	Trevor Howard
Companion	Glynis Johns
Conductor	Buster Keaton
Flirt	Evelyn Keyes
Revivalist	Beatrice Lillie
Steward	Peter Lorre
Engineer	Edmund Lowe
Helmsman	Victor McLaglen
Commander	Col. Tim McCoy
Club Member	A. E. Matthews
Character	Mike Mazurki
Cabby	John Mills
Consul	Alan Mowbray
Ralph	Robert Morley
Narrator	Edward R. Murrow
Captain	Jack Oakie
Bouncer	George Raft
Achmed Abdullah	Gilbert Roland
Henchman	Cesar Romero
Pianist	Frank Sinatra
Drunk	Red Skelton
Member	Ronald Squires
Member	Basil Sydney
Hinshaw	Harcourt Williams

Mike Todd's gone and done it! His first production, "Around the World in 80 Days," lensed in the Todd-AO process, is a smasheroo from start to finish. He has brought the vintage Jules Verne novel to the wide screen with a roll and a flourish, embellishing the story with big and colorful visual values and a healthy sense of humor that shapes it into perhaps the most entertaining global story-travelog ever made.

With a smash lineup of stars in major and minor parts, Todd has turned out a surefire hit.

What American hasn't, at one time or another, delighted in the fantastic adventures of that intrepid Englishman, Phileas Fogg, who, to win a bet, journeyed 'round the world in the "record time" of 80 days, using every mode of transportation, from train and boat to elephant and balloon. Well, it's all here on the screen, every penny of the $5,000,000 to $6,000,000 that went into the making of the production.

The cast, led by David Niven as Fogg, the Mexican Cantinflas as Passepartout, Robert Newton as Mr. Fix and Shirley MacLaine as Aouda, the Indian Maharanee, has been shrewdly chosen and, with a witty and clever script by S. J. Perelman (at least he's the only one getting screen credit; others who worked on it are John Farrow and James Poe), they act out the piece against some of the most impressively lensed backgrounds on view in a long time. It all adds up to a mixture of spectacle and comedy that should capture audiences young and old, and without reservation.

This is another long picture—two hours and 55 minutes plus intermission. But this time there'll be few complaints. Little time has been wasted and the story races on as Fogg and company proceed from London to Paris, thence via balloon to Spain and the bullfights; from there to Marseilles and India, where Fogg and Passepartout rescue beautiful Miss MacLaine from death on a funeral pyre; to Hong-Kong, Japan, San Francisco, across the country by train to New York (notwithstanding an Indian attack) and thence back to England where Fogg thinks he has lost his bet, but discovers in the last minute that, by traveling East, he has gained a day and is the winner yet.

Credit Todd with going all-out in giving the customers their money's worth. "80 Days," lensed by Lionel Lindon with Kevin McCrory doing the foreign locales, is a bouncy, riotous, action-packed picture that still stakes time out for hearty laughs and the magnificent scenery. The Todd "touch" is rich in evidence throughout. This picture was made with showmanship in mind and the customers are guaranteed to eat it up.

Script and director (Michael Anderson) have balanced the story cleverly, weaving in the mass of top names without ever losing trek of the main line. It's a neat trick, **and it comes off socko. There is never scenery just for scenery's sake, and never story without the rich backgrounds. Todd-AO system here, for the first time, has been properly used and fills the screen with wondrous effects. Images are extraordinarily sharp and depth of focus, aided by Lindon's lensing, is striking in many scenes. Eastman color, processed by Technicolor, helps compound the rich effects of landscape and costumes.**

Niven, as Fogg, is the perfect stereotype of the unruffled English gentleman and quite intentionally, a caricature of 19th Century British propriety. Matching him in a standout performance, is Mexican star Cantinflas (Mario Moreno) as Passepartout. He has a Chaplinesque quality that endears him immediately, and his antics provide many laughs along with the amused chuckles. A master mimic, Cantinflas makes a big contribution to the success of the film. His bullfight solo is a classic. Robert Newton in the role of Mr. Fix, the detective who trails Fogg whom he suspects of having robbed the Bank of London, is broad comic all the way through, and Miss MacLaine is appealing as the princess.

There's rarely been a picture that can boast of so many star names in bit parts. Just to name a few in the more important roles: John Carradine as the pompous Col. Proctor; Finlay Currie, Ronald Squires, Basil Sydney, A. E. Matthews and Trevor Howard as members of the Reform Club who bet against Fogg; Fernandel as a Paris coachman; Robert Morley as the stodgy governor of the Bank of England; Sir Cedric Hardwicke as a Colonial militarist; Red Skelton, as a drunk; Marlene Dietrich and George Raft. There are many others, including Frank Sinatra in a flash shot as a piano player. Jose Greco, early in the footage, wows with a heel fandango.

Todd, wisely, hasn't relied on just names. They're all well integrated. And the names must compete with the effects—from the breathtaking balloon launching in Paris, to the hilarious bullfight sequence, to the funeral parade in the Indian jungle, to the collapse of the railroad bridge, to the attacking Indian hordes and the riotus street scene in San Francisco. The combination of talents has turned these scenes into eye-filling and exciting spectacle that roars, then segues into placid, perfectly composed shots of kaleidoscopic beauty.

"80 Days" could have been just a travelog. Instead, thanks to a large part to the Perelman-Todd humor, it chuckles along tongue-in-cheek, without ever a dull moment. Asks Miss MacLaine of Cantinflas (about Niven): "Have there been women in his life?" Says he: "I assume he must have had a mother." Another time, when Cantinflas tips a waiter in San Francisco, Niven fixes a stern eye on him with "I told you before—don't spoil the natives."

The humor is subtle at times, broad elsewhere. The Indian attack bit, with the Redskins invading the train and the cavalry riding to the rescue is reminiscent of Mack Sennett; the scene of Fogg and party sailing past the broken-down train in a wind-driven cart is hokum and pure joy. So is the dismantling of the steamer to provide fuel for the boilers. The whole, crazy, wonderful story is faithfully produced. Pic's sound is extraordinarily vivid and effective and a major asset.

Introducing the picture, Edward R. Murrow, in a prologue, is a bit stuffy and too long, but he serves to set "time." Included is the 1901 Melies version of Jules Verne's "A Journey to the Moon." Saul Bass' final titles are a tribute to the kind of taste and imagination, the ingenuity and the splendor that mark this entire Todd production. Victor Young's musical backgrounds are firstrate and strongly underscore the various moods of the film. His mock use of "Rule Britannia" makes a telling point.

As for Todd himself, "80 Days" is his answer to his many critics. If anyone bet against him on this one, they might as well start paying up right now. *Hift.*

Teenage Rebel
(C'SCOPE—SONGS)

Well made comedy-drama with Ginger Rogers-Michael Rennie as marquee lures; tidy grosses.

20th-Fox release of Charles Brackett production. Stars Ginger Rogers, Michael Rennie; features Betty Lou Keim, Warren Berlinger, Diane Jergens, Mildred Natwick, Rusty Swope, Lili Gentle, Louise Beavers, Irene Hervey, John Stephenson. Directed by Edmund Goulding. Screenplay, Walter Reisch and Brackett, from play, "Roomful of Roses," by Edith Sommer; camera, Joe MacDonald; editor, William Mace; music, Leigh Harline; songs, Lionel Newman, Carroll Coates, Ralph Freed, Edmund Goulding. Tradeshown N. Y., Oct. 18, '56. Running time, **94 MINS.**

Nancy Fallon	Ginger Rogers
Jay Fallon	Michael Rennie
Grace Hewitt	Mildred Natwick
Larry Fallon	Rusty Swope
Teenager at races	Lili Gentle
Willamay	Louise Beavers
Helen McGowan	Irene Hervey
Eric McGowan	John Stephenson
Dodie	Betty Lou Keim
Dick Hewitt	Warren Berlinger
Jane Hewitt	Diane Jergens
Madeleine Johnson	Susan Luckey
Mr. Heffernan	James O'Rear
Freddie	Gary Gray
Erna	Pattee Chapman
Airport Porter	Wade Dumas
Cab Driver	Richard Collier

Edith Sommer's story of an adolescent girl in search of love was a last season Broadway flop as "A Roomful of Roses." But the film version is a well made adaptation that should ring up tidy grosses from both younger patrons as well as their elders. For the Walter Reisch-Charles Brackett screenplay has ably caught the flavor, atmosphere and problems of the contemporary teenage scene, and most audiences will have scant trouble in identifying themselves with it.

Basically the yarn is a comedy drama with an emotional tug here and there. In light of that "Teenage Rebel" is a misleading title for this tag seems to imply the picture is an excursion into the whys and wherefores of juvenile delinquency. Technically the term, "rebel," is correct since the girl for a time rebels from a normal mother-daughter relationship. But 20th-Fox' use of the title in its ad-pub campaign carries a broad connotation that here we have an exploitation special a la "Blackboard Jungle."

Obviously there are ample exploitation values in this Charles Brackett production. But these are of a wholesome nature and bear little resemblance to the veiled inferences in the title. Also a b.o. plus is a cast headed by Ginger Rogers and Michael Rennie as marquee lures. In addition the familiar exhibs' plea for new faces is answered to some extent via a trio of youngsters whom the studio hopefully introduces as "three stars of the future."

One of the "future stars" is Betty Lou Keim who reprises her original Broadway role of a 15-year-old daughter of divorced parents. Long in custody of father John Stephenson, she's shipped back to mother Miss Rogers when her sire decides to re-marry. It's a pleasant slice of suburban life the girl's confronted with when she at long last rejoins her parent. Unfortunately, the daughter has been confined to such a sheltered, motherless existence in the past that she now resents any maternal attention.

What ultimately brings her around from a sullen, unpleasant teenager is her association with next door highschoolers Warren Berlinger and his sister, Diané Jergens. They help thaw her out, aided by a bribe from stepfather Michael Rennie. Coup de grace comes when a hasty return visit to her father shows her that his interest in daughter is most superficial—his marriage to Irene Hervey is much more important. From this insight-giving discovery obviously comes the return to the maternal fold.

Miss Rogers adeptly portrays the temporarily rejected mother and shines in the frequent emotional conflicts that arise between herself and daughter. Rennie turns in a slick performance as the stepfather—a swell guy who's willing to pal along with the teenagers whether its a financial assist on a hot rod or a demonstration of some rock 'n' roll dance steps. Miss Keim is irritatingly real as the resentful daughter and she excites little audience sympathy until her reformation.

Well cast is Berlinger (from the original B'way play) as the teenager who helps Miss Keim in seeing the light . . . at least romantically. Miss Jergens, plumpish and vivacious, fits in with the typical conception of the "girl next door." Fine support is contribbed by Mildred Natwick, as a nosy, solicitous neighbor and mother of Berlinger and Miss Jergens; Rusty Swope, as a lively seven-year-old offspring of the Rennie-Rogers couple, along with Stephenson, Miss Hervey, Lili Gentle and Louise Beavers in lesser roles.

It's a fast 94 minutes under Edmund Goulding's deft direction.

His touch is particularly evident in the teenage sequences and emotional scenes. An added lift is provided by a couple of songs that blend in nicely with the yarn's overtones. Lionel Newman, who conducted Leigh Harline's unobtrusive score, authored "Cool, It, Baby" in collaboration with Carroll Coates. Other number is "Dodie" by Ralph Freed and Goulding. Both ditties have possibilities in the pop market.

Brackett, who produced aside from his chores as co-scripter, supplied tasteful physical mantling that's been more than adequately captured by the CinemaScope camerawork of Joe MacDonald. As a matter of fact since much of the black-and-white footage is interiors the widescreen frequently gilds the lily. Art direction of Lyle R. Wheeler and Jack Martin Smith, William Mace's editing as well as other technical credits all measure up to high standards one expects of a major lot. *Gilb.*

7th Cavalry
(COLOR)

Randolph Scott's name should provide okay draw for this U.S. Cavalry-Indian programmer.

Hollywood, Oct. 23.

Columbia release of a Harry Joe Brown production. Stars Randolph Scott. Features Barbara Hale, Jay C. Flippen, Frank Faylen, Jeanette Nolan. Directed by Joseph H. Lewis. Screenplay, Peter Packer, based on story by Glendon F. Swarthout; camera (Technicolor), Ray Rennahan; editor, Gene Havlick; music, Mischa Bakaleinikoff. Previewed Oct. 17, '56. Running time, **76 MINS.**

Capt. Tom Benson ...... Randolph Scott
Martha Kellogg .... Barbara Hale
Sgt. Bates .... Jay C. Flippen
Mrs. Reynolds .... Jeanette Nolan
Kruger .... Frank Faylen
Vogel .... Leo Gordon
Dixon .... Denver Pyle
Corp. Morrison.......... Harry Carey Jr.
Capt. Benteen .... Michael Pate
Lt. Bob Fitch .... Donald Curtis
Major Reno .... Frank Wilcox
Young Hawk .... Pat Hogan
Col. Kellogg .... Russell Hicks
Pollock .... Peter Ortiz

A switch in the story of Custer's last stand lends a touch of novelty to this latest Randolph Scott starrer, which unfolds directly after the battle of Little Big Horn. Film is burdened with an overage of dialog and carries little exciting action until the closing reels, but Scott's marquee draw should see it satisfactorily through the dual runs.

Scott portrays an officer in Custer's famed 7th Cavalry who is branded as a coward for being away from the post at the time of the battle, from which not a man returned. The Peter Packer screenplay builds upon this premise, main action centering upon Scott later volunteering to head a burial detail that is to go to the scene of the battle, bury the enlisted men and return with bodies of the officers. Joseph H. Lewis' direction keeps the movement as lively as writing will allow, but too much extraneous action dragged in by the heels seriously slows the tempo.

Scott is none too happily cast in role, suffering through contrived plottage ineptly developed. *Whit.*

Thunder Over Arizona
(NATURAMA—COLOR)

Uninteresting minor-league western.

Hollywood, Oct. 23.

Republic release of a Joe Kane production, directed by Kane. Stars Skip Homeier, Kristine Miller, George Macready, Wallace Ford; features Nacho Galindo, Gregory Walcott, Jack Elam, George Keymas, John Doucette, John Compton, Bob Swan, Julian Rivero, Francis McDonald. Screenplay, Sloan Nibley; camera (Trucolor), Bul Thackery; editor, Tony Martinelli; music, R. Dale Butts. Reviewed Oct. 17, '56. Running time, **75 MINS.**

Tim Mallory .... Skip Homeier
Fay Warren .... Kristine Miller
Ervin Plummer .... George Macready
Hal Styles .... Wallace Ford
Pancho .... Nacho Galindo
Mark .... Gregory Walcott
Slats .... Jack Elam
Shotgun Kelly .... George Keymas
Rand .... John Doucette
Tab .... John Compton
Jud .... Bob Swan
Padre Artega .... Julian Rivero
Pliny Warren .... Francis McDonald

To this era of the "long" picture now comes "Thunder Over Arizona." Film's 75 minutes passes like an eternity.

Central character in the Sloan Nibley screenplay is Skip Homeier, honest cowboy who, upon arrival in Tombstone, is mistaken for a professional gunman. But that enables him to get in cahoots with the baddies, who are trying to gain illegal possession of a mine belonging to an orphaned beauty (Kristine Miller) and her three hardworking brothers. Homeier actually is working to help the rightful owners and he accomplishes his aim. At fadeout, Homeier is turning full attention to Miss Miller.

Despite the handicaps, Homeier manages to turn in a generally good performance. Miss Miller is okay thespically and, further, lends the film pictorial asset. George Macready and Wallace Ford are routine heavies. *Neal.*

Man of Africa
(BRITISH—COLOR)

Eden Picture Co. release of a Group Three picture produced by John Grierson. Written and directed by Cyril Frankel. Music, Malcolm Arnold. At Embassy, N.Y., Oct. 10, '56. Running time, **75 MINS.**

Violet .... Violet Mukabuerza
Jonathan .... Frederick Bijuerenda
And members of the Bakija and Batwa tribes

Struggle for existence insofar as a native tribe is concerned is leisurely told in "Man of Africa," a semi-documentary filmed in the more remote parts of Uganda. To the picture's credit it eschews the hoky aspects found in most films lensed in "darkest Africa," but this British import is often languorous to the point of becoming dull.

Its market potential is restricted as filler material for either art or exploitation houses. Latter may stir up some wicket activity via a lively lobby display backed by a selling campaign in other media.

Producer of the Group Three picture is noted documentarian John Grierson who for a time was Film Commissioner for Canada. It's an interesting phase of African life that he's chosen to focus upon. But one suspects that a sketchy story contributed by director Cyril Frankel detracts more than adds to the realism afforded by sweeping views of the jungle flora and fauna.

For in depicting the migration of a tribe to virgin country after the fertility of their homeland was exhausted producer Grierson has seen fit to include a romance between a clerk-turned-farmer and a native belle. Their's also much rivalry between the former and a corporal that frequently treads on monotonous ground.

On the brighter side of the ledger are scenes which show the basic kindness of pygmies who are native to the Kigezi territory. They aid an injured settler and later save his child when malaria strikes the pioneers. If anything this unassuming import shows that even among African natives prejudice thrives upon misunderstanding.

Dialog of the players is in English. Cast is headed by Violet Mukabuerza and Frederick Bijuerenda who do as best they can in portraying the romantic couple. Remaining roles are filled by members of the Bakiga and Batwa tribes. Direction of Frankel is too slow to be genuinely effective. An unbilled cameraman lensed the footage in Ferrania color. Evidently the original lighting was poor or the print has deteriorated for the hues are not sharp. Malcolm Arnold's score is adequate. *Gilb.*

Donatella
(C'Scope-Color-Songs)
(ITALIAN)

Sudfilm release of a Sudefilm-Roberto Amoroso Production. Stars Elsa Martinelli, Gabriele Ferzetti; features Walter Chiari, Abbe Lane, Xavier Cugat, Aldo Fabrizi, Lilaine Bonfatti, Giuseppe Porelli, Virgilio Riento, Giovanna Pala. Directed by Mario Monicelli. Screenplay, Monicelli, Amoroso, Tellini, Continenza, Maccari; camera (Eastmancolor) Tonino Delli Colli; music, Xavier Cugat, Gino Filippini; previewed in Rome. Running time **101 MINS.**

Donatella .... Elsa Martinelli
Maurizio .... Gabriele Ferzetti
Guido .... Walter Chiari
Abbe Lane
Xavier Cugat .... themselves
Father .... Aldo Fabrizi

Pic, with the aid of Elsa Martinelli, Xavier Cugat and Abbe Lane names, looks a good risk for general American situations in a well-dubbed version. Neatly lensed Roman setting, romantic story, general entertainment factors plus a couple of new Cugat numbers sung by Abbe Lane should combine to guarantee good returns in most markets in quest of lightweight entertainment with an Italian flavor. Thespian prize garnered by Miss Martinelli with this item at the Berlin Festival this year could help add to draw.

Updated cinderella tale starts slowly but soon gets on with the story of a poor girl (Miss Martinelli) who works in a rich household as personal secretary. A visiting lawyer falls for her, thinking she's well-to-do. She dittos until the truth comes out, but even then a happy ending is assured.

Plotting is pleasant, alternating romantic with comic touches. Dialog rings true. Miss Martinelli registers as the secretary, with both Gabriele Ferzetti and Walter Chiari doing well by their roles as suitors. Aldo Fabrizi is good as her father.

Miss Lane and Cugat are in for some dialogue and a couple of listenable musical numbers which look to be high in the popularity ratings. Slick lensing by Tonino delli Colli in Eastmancolor (C'Scope) catches a good selection of that photogenic Roman secretary, and other production credits are stature. Some careful trimming could make this a more solid production. Several U. S. majors are reported interested in handling this pic. *Hawk.*

Death of a Scoundrel

From real-to-ridiculous tale of financial wizard and lover. Reminiscent of Serge Rubinstein killing; exploitation possibilities, but needs selling.

Hollywood, Oct. 30.

RKO release of Charles Martin production, written and directed by Martin; associate producer, J. Herbert Klein. Stars George Sanders, Yvonne DeCarlo, Zsa Zsa Gabor, Victor Jory, Nancy Gates, Coleen Gray; features John Hoyt, Lisa Ferraday, Tom Conway, Celia Lovsky. Camera, James Wong Howe; editor, Conrad Nervig; music, Max Steiner. Previewed Oct. 18, '56. Running time, **119 MINS.**

Clementi Sabourin...... George Sanders
Bridget Kelly .... Yvonne DeCarlo
Mrs. Ryan .... Zsa Zsa Gabor
Leonard Wilson .... Victor Jory
Stephanie North .... Nancy Gates
Mrs. Van Renassalear....... Coleen Gray
Mr. O'Hara .... John Hoyt
Zina Monte .... Lisa Ferraday
Gerry Monte .... Tom Conway
Mrs. Sabourin (Mother) ..... Celia Lovsky
Herbert, Lawyer .... Werner Klemperer
Butler .... Justice Watson
The Actor .... John Sutton
Oswald Van Renassalear Curtis Cooksey
Max Freundlich .... Gabriel Curtis
Captain Lafarge .... Morris Ankrum

Despite the usual disclaimers, many will find "Death of a Scoundrel" echoing the career and violent end of Russian-born Serge Rubinstein, financial manipulator and Manhattan playboy. Without being a case history, there's still enough similarity to recall headlines. The melodrama has a certain appeal, albeit overlength at 119 minutes, and flamboyant exploitation may give it the selling push it needs. (Although exhibs better be careful — Rubinstein came of a reputable Russian banker family, members of which are around).

Charles Martin produced, directed and scripted, with the handling sometimes varying from the real to the ridiculous but still maintaining a pull for the viewer. The expedient of the flashback is used to skip through the career of opportunists Clementi Sabourin, well-played by George Sanders. With Zsa Zsa Gabor as one of the costars, and very good, Martin's dialog between the actress and Sanders has an "inside-tip" quality for those hep to her own headline-making ability.

Story starts with Sanders discovered dead in his Park Avenue mansion. How he came to this conclusive state is unfolded via Yvonne DeCarlo, exceptionally fine as the personal business associate of the scoundrel who has risen to wealth with him from a petty thief beginning.

Femmes play a large part in Sanders' life and money-making schemes. To get a start in America, a land to which he has come with the blood of his dead brother on his hands (he informed on Tom Conway to get passage to the States). Sanders first filches the wallet Miss DeCarol has lifted from Victor Jory, Canadian financier, uses the coin to make a killing in a new penicillin stock. Miss Gabor, a wealthy widow, figures in this and later schemes, as do Nancy Gates, excellent as the young actress he promotes into a career but isn't able to romance; Coleen Gray, good as the impressionable wife of a mail order tycoon the scoundrel is plotting to ruin, and Lisa Ferraday, splendid as his widowed sister-in-law who comes from Czechoslovakia to kill him, but kills herself.

Jory handles his financier part capably, as do John Hoyt, the partner in crime who fires the fatal shots that end the scoundrel's career; Werner Klemperer, the crook's attorney; Justice Watson, the butler; John Sutton, an actor in a play-within-a-play sequence; Curtis Cooksey, the mail order king, Gabriel Curtis and Morris Ankrum. An extremely valid performance is furnished by Celia Lovsky as the mother who disowns her scoundrel son.

The film's mood benefits from the topgrade black-and-white photography by James Wong Howe and Max Steiner's robust score. Editing, the femmes' gowns by Waldo and other technical assists are worthy. *Brog.*

Swamp Women
(COLOR)

Weak filler fare with exploitable title.

Hollywood, Oct. 30.

Favorite Films release of Bernard Woolner production. Stars Marie Windsor, Carole Mathews, Beverly Garland; features Jill Jarmyn, Touch Connors, Susan Cummings. Directed by Roger Corman. Story and screenplay, David Stern; camera (Eastman Color), Fred West; editor, Ronald Sinclair; music, Willis Holman. Reviewed Oct. 24, '56. Running time, **70 MINS.**

Only meager entertainment is dished out via "Swamp Women," Woolner Bros. production lensed entirely in Louisiana some months ago. Pic's chief asset is its exploitable tag; otherwise, it's just filler material.

Story and screenplay by David Stern has policewoman Carole Mathews getting herself jailed so as to get "in" with three femme inmates who know where a fortune in stolen diamonds is hidden. Gals escape and head for the bayou country of Louisiana, where the gems are buried. After routine hardships—alligators, rattlers, friction and fights between the femmes, etc—the party reaches its destination, the loot is uncovered and shortly thereafter the police, who's been trailing group, close in for the arrests.

Miss Mathews makes the best acting impression, with Marie Windsor, Beverly Garland and Jill Jarmyn all okay in respective roles. Touch Connors, boatman taken by the gals, is good in only male role of any importance.

Roger Corman's direction, somewhat over-melodramatic, fully utilizes the bayou area to pictorial advantage, with Fred West's Eastman Color camera work also aiding here. Technical contributions to pic, produced by Bernard Woolner, are mostly sub-standard. *Neal.*

House of Secrets
(BRITISH—V'VISION—COLOR)

Lively gangster yarn set in Paris with gold and counterfeit smugglers in international police chase.

London, Oct. 23.

Rank release of a Julian Wintle (Vivian A. Cox) production. Stars Michael Craig, Julia Arnall, Brenda De Banzie, Barbara Bates; co-stars David Kossoff, Gerard Oury, Geoffrey Keen. Directed by Guy Green. Screenplay, Robert Buckner and Bryan Forbes from book, "Storm Over Paris," by Sterling Noel; camera, Harry Waxman; editor, Sidney Hayers; music, Herbert Clifford. At Gaumont Theatre, London, Oct. 23, '56. Running time, **97 MINS.**

Larry .... Michael Craig
Diane .... Julia Arnall
Madame Ballu ...... Brenda De Banzie
Judy .... Barbara Bates
Van de Heide .... David Kossoff
Pindar .... Gerard Oury
Burleigh .... Geoffrey Keen
Lauderbach .... Anton Diffring
Gratz .... Eric Pohlmann
Vidal .... Eugene Deckers
Lessage .... Jacques Brunius
Brandelli .... Alan Tilvern
Dorffman .... Carl Jaffe
Curtice .... Gordon Tanner
Marseilles Detective ...... David Lander

There are plenty of thrills and mounting tension in this workmanlike adaptation from a novel. Like most stories taken from books, the plot tends to become over-involved. It concerns two rival gangs of crooks, being hunted down by the police, and an innocent bystander who gets caught up through mistaken identity and gets battered and half killed in sorting out the mystery. It provides exciting entertainment that nears, but never bridges the borderline of credulity. It should prove a boxoffice winner here. Lack of marquee names may dim its chances elsewhere.

Locale is France, with most of the scenes shot in Paris. This makes excellent color framing for some realistic background atmosphere, and gives it an authentic ring. A young British ship's officer gets entangled with a gang of gold smugglers in Marseilles through his resemblance to its contact man who, unknown to them, has been killed in an auto crash.

Hauled before the police, he convinces the quartet of international interrogators of his innocence and is persuaded by them to link up with smugglers to uncover their head man. The police are more interested in a gigantic counterfeiting organization. The gangs overlap, and each think the new recruit is doublecrossing the other. Result is that he lives on a razor's edge, holding the secret of his identity, getting beaten up and knifed in the process.

The race to get the phony notes off a plane results in a mid-air explosion, with the police finally solving the case.

Honors are evenly divided between the four leading male characters, Michael Craig as the adventurous young sailor, Geoffrey Keen as the British end of the international criminal investigators, David Kossoff as the traitor and Gerard Oury as one of the gang leaders.

Femme contingent plays a small part in the story, the best chance to shine being given to Brenda de Banzie as the autocratic queen of the mob. Julie Arnall registers to a lesser degree as a nightclub singer who provides the romantic touch. Barbara Bates contributes a naturalistic performance as a police operator who gets killed. The supporting roles are all in competent hands and the director has spun the yarn evenly and convincingly. *Clem.*

The Girl He Left Behind

Army trainee comedy-drama with names of Tab Hunter and Natalie Wood to draw; good indications for youth and family trade.

Hollywood, Oct. 30.

Warner Bros. release of a Frank P. Rosenberg production. Stars Tab Hunter, Natalie Wood. Features Jessie Royce Landis, Jim Backus, Henry Jones, Murray Hamilton, Alan King. Directed by David Butler. Screenplay, Guy Trosper, adapted from novel by Marion Hargrove; camera, Ted McCord; editor, Irene Morra; music, Roy Webb. Previewed Oct. 24, '56. Running time, **101 MINS.**

Andy Sheaffer .... Tab Hunter
Susan Daniels .... Natalie Wood
Madeline Sheaffer...Jessie Royce Landis
Sgt. Hanna .... Jim Backus
Hanson .... Henry Jones
Sgt. Clyde .... Murray Hamilton
Maguire .... Alan King
Preston .... James Garner
Capt. Genaro .... David Janssen
Arthur Sheaffer .... Vinton Hayworth
Congressman Hardison.... Wilfrid Knapp
Lt. Taylor .... Les Johnson
General .... Raymond Bailey
Mr. Hillaby .... Florenz Ames
Sgt. Sheridan .... Fredd Wayne
Lorna .... Ernestine Wade

Former Pfc. Marion Hargrove's appreciation of the lighter side of Army trainee life gets humorous interpretation in this rambling transference to the screen of his latest novel. Film, with sometimes serious overtones, is mainly episodic and smacks of the service comedies turned out during World War II, but provides entertaining fare for the youthful and family trade, where co-star names of Tab Hunter and Natalie Wood should assure satisfactory reception.

Under David Butler's experienced comedy direction, the Frank P. Rosenberg production unfolds at Fort Ord, Cal. The slight plot centers around Hunter, an intelligent but spoiled college student, who arrives to take his training after being drafted in the peacetime Army, his only thought how to get out and return to the girl he left behind.

The daily routine, the fortunes and misfortunes of camp life known to millions of past and present G.I.'s are played up to good effect in the Guy Trosper screenplay. A serious note is inserted when the Army, unable to make a soldier out of the rebellious trainee, offers to release him via a dishonorable discharge, which he blithely accepts. Youth redeems himself, however, during a war games maneuver, when he saves the lives of four men, and stays on a changed and useful G.I.

Hunter is well cast in his role and turns in an acceptable performance which should add to his growing popularity. As the girl who resents his immaturity and lack of responsibility, Miss Wood in a more serious role is excellent. Murray Hamilton, in part of Hunter's training sergeant continually riled by the trainee's actions, is outstanding in his characterization that blends both comedy and drama. Standout work also is contributed by Jessie Royce Landis, the doting mother; David Janssen and Jim Backus, captain and sergeant in Hunter's regiment; and Henry Jones and Alan King, his two pals.

Cameraman Ted McCord leads off well-executed technical departments, which include Irene Morra's editing and Roy Webb's music score. *Whit.*

The Sharkfighters
(C'SCOPE-COLOR)

Navy quest for a shark-repellent. Good climax but otherwise actionless. Victor Mature for marquee.

Hollywood, Oct. 30.

United Artists release of a Samuel Goldwyn Jr. production. Stars Victor Mature; costars Karen Steele. Features James Olson, Philip Coolidge, Rafael Campos, Claude Akins, George Neise. Directed by Jerry Hopper. Screenplay, Lawrence Roman, John Robinson; original story, Jo and Art Napoleon; camera (Technicolor), Lee Garmes; editor, Daniel Mandell; music, Jerome Moross. Previewed Oct. 19, '56. Running time, **74 MINS.**

Ben Staves .... Victor Mature
Martha Staves .... Karen Steele
Harold Duncan .... James Olson
Leonard Evans .... Philip Coolidge
"Gordy" Gordon .... Claude Akins
Carlos .... Rafael Campos
George Zimmer .... George Neise
Captain Ruiz .... Nathan Yates
Vincente .... Jesus Hernandez
Lorin Johns .... Himself
David Westlein .... Himself
Narration .... Charles Collingwood

The U.S. Navy's search for a repellent to save fliers forced down in shark-infested waters during World War II motivates this Samuel Goldwyn Jr., production, second on his program for United Artists. With the exception of a highly suspenseful climax running approximately five minutes and another moment of excitement at the halfway mark, film is mostly an actionless talking piece which becomes almost clinical at times. Name of Victor Mature has to carry it.

Picture was filmed entirely on its Cuban location, both on the Isle of Pines, off the coast, and in Havana, where Lee Garmes' Technicolor photography is responsible for interesting background. Director Jerry Hopper was able to get some stirring footage of sharks during the try to find a repellent, when Mature, as a commander in charge of project, uses himself as a human guinea pig in the water to test the potency against maneaters swimming nearby. This sequence, and one where a native boy falls into water and is attacked, are exceptionally well-done and may be used to exploit film.

Mature arrives at Navy's scientific base on Isle of Pines to speed up the development of shark-repellent, and begins to chafe at what to him is the slow method of experimentation. Anxious to complete the task, he insists that the latest development, following large number of tests, is a sure one, but this proves useless when a young Cuban lad falls overboard and sharks come in for the kill. Working on another tack, the staff devises a solution based on a fluid secreted by octopods in protecting themselves from sharks, which proves successful, but not before Mature is almost killed.

The Lawrence Roman-John Robinson screenplay doesn't give Mature chance for much more than a walk-through performance. Karen Steele, in for distaff interest as his wife, shows a sparkling presence in her few scenes, and Philip Coolidge, in charge of project until Mature's arrival, and James Olson, young chemist attached to base, handle their roles very competently. Rafael Campos is good as the shark victim and balance of cast is okay.

Technical credits are of excellent quality, including Jerome Moross' music score, Russell Shearman's special effects and Daniel Mandell's editing. *Whit.*

The Mole People

Science-fiction entry being packaged with a jungle-thriller as an exploitation combo for program dates.

Hollywood, Oct. 26.

Universal release of William Alland production. Stars John Agar, Cynthia Patrick, Hugh Beaumont; features Alan Napier, Nestor Paiva, Phil Chambers, Rodd Redwing, Robin Hughes. Directed by Virgil Vogel. Written by Laszlo Gorog; camera, Ellis Carter; editor, Irving Birnbaum; music, Joseph Gershenson. Previewed Oct. 23, '56. Running time, **77 MINS.**

Dr. Roger Bentley .... John Agar
Adad .... Cynthia Patrick
Dr. Jud Bellamin ...... Hugh Deaumont
Elinu .... Alan Napier
Etienne Lafarge .... Nestor Paiva
Dr. Paul Stuart .... Phil Chambers
Nazer .... Rodd Redwing
First Officer .... Robin Hughes
Sharu .... Arthur Gilmour

"The Mole People" is being distributed by Universal as one-half of a program exploitation package. As the science-fiction portion, the entry should show an okay return in relation to cost.

Entertainment-wise, this little thriller has some fanciful gimmicks, but unfolds them a bit too slowly under Virgil Vogel's direction for maximum effect. William Alland's production puts a scholastic stamp on man's search for life under the earth via a prolog using the television man-of-letters, Dr. Frank Baxter of USC. This serves as a good lead-in to Laszlo Gorog's screen story, which then settles down to the accepted pattern for budget pseudo-scientific films.

When a member of a scientific party falls into a deep cavern atop a mountain peak in Asia, a lost Sumerian city, vanished centuries previously, is discovered. Along with the city are found the descendants, now albinos because of living in semi-darkness, and their slaves, a race of mole men. The trapped party is able to control the inner-earth inhabitants as long as its flashlight holds out, but eventually is made captive. Escape comes when the mole slaves turn on the Sumerians and the scientists scamper up a shaft to the outside world.

John Agar, Hugh Beaumont, Nestor Paiva and Phil Chambers make up the entrapped scientific party, all doing what the roles demand acceptably. Cynthia Patrick is the femme interest as one of the Sumerians who looks more likely an outside earth person. She almost makes it to freedom with survivors Agar and Beaumont, but dies in an earthquake that seals off the lost city's remains forever.

The technical lineup functions okay in backing the thriller aims of the future. Ellis Carter's photography, with special photography by Clifford Stine. The weird makeup of the mole men and Sumerians was contributed by Bud Westmore. Sound and background score strike the correct eerie notes to help the mood. *Brog.*

Curucu, Beast of the Amazon

Fair jungle-thriller lensed in Brazil; one-half of exploitation package being sold for ballyhoo bookings.

Hollywood, Oct. 26.
Universal release of Richard Kay, Harry Rybnick production. Stars John Bromfield, Beverly Garland; features Larri Thomas, Tom Payne, Harvey Chalk. Directed and written by Curt Siodmak; camera (Eastman Color), Rudolf Icsey; editor, Terry Morse; music, Raoul Kraushaar. Previewed Oct. 23, '56. Running time, 75 MINS.
Rock Dean .... John Bromfield
Dr. Andrea Romar...... Beverly Garland
Tupanico .... Tom Payne
Father Flaviano .... Harvey Chalk
Captain Caceres ...... Sergio De Oliveira
Tico .... Wilson Viana
Dancer .... Larri Thomas

Universal is packaging this jungle adventure feature with a science-fictioner, "The Mole People" (reviewed this issue) and the results looks like a profitable combo for program ballyhoo bookings.

"Curucu, Beast of the Amazon," independently produced in Brazil by Richard Kay and Harry Rybnick, shows off Rio de Janeiro and the jungle locations in Eastman Color most effectively, but Curt Siodmak's screenplay and direction

make formula thriller use of the settings. Directorial pacing also is somewhat slow, with the exception of some thriller inserts that will raise the hackles. Femme star Beverly Garland attacked by a large boa constrictor, a water buffalo stampede, sights of a giant spider and the carnivorous piranha fish are some of the scenes that will mean more on the scare side than the pic's title monster.

John Bromfield, playing Rock Dean, an intrepid adventurer, takes off for Amazon headwaters to find out why the natives are deserting his plantations and returning to the jungles. Miss Garland is a femme doctor heading the same way to research a basic cure for cancer in the formula used by the natives to shrink heads. They join forces, undergo perilous adventures before it turns out that their native guide, Tom Payne, is donning the bird-headed monster suit to frighten the Indians back to the jungle so he can be their chief. Bromfield and Miss Garland are up to all demands of the script and direction. They come out of the jungle alive and in love. What happens to the cancer research is not specified.

Larri Thomas, a dancer in a Rio cafe, Harvey Chalk, Sergio De Oliveira and Wilson Viana are the other players recruited in Brazil for the adventuring. Rudolf Icsey's lensing is satisfactory, as are the other technical credits and Raoul Kraushaar's music. *Brog.*

En Effeuillant La Marguerite
(While Plucking The Daisies)
(FRENCH)

Paris, Oct. 16.
Corona release of EGE-Hoche Film production. Stars Brigitte Bardot, Daniel Gelin. Directed by Marc Allegret. Screenplay, Roger Vadim, Allegret from idea by William Benjamin; camera, Louis Page; editor, Marguerite De Troeye; music, Paul Misraki. At Marignan, Paris. Running time, 105 MINS.
Agnes .... Brigitte Bardot
Daniel .... Daniel Gelin
Roger .... Robert Hirsch
Hubert .... Darry Cowl
General .... Jacques Dumesnil
Sophia .... Luciana Paoluzzi
Magali .... Nadine Tallier

With the striptease a nitery staple here it was only a matter of time before it showed up in a pic plot point as here. Surrounding the unveiled pulchritude is a situation comedy involving a runaway young authoress, who gets mixed up with a reporter. All anybody thinks about or does in this film is mixed up with sex, and this relegates it to strictly exploitation chances in the U. S. if the nude bits can get by.

Without them, however, this telegraphed tale lacks the heavyweight acting or direction to give it a good comedy status for special spotting in the U. S. As is, it is primarily an exploitation pic.

Daughter of stuffy general, ships her off to school but she jumps train in Paris to stay with her brother, a caretaker of a Balzac Museum. She barges in to mess things up. Then comes romance with a skirtchasing newshawk and her entering in peeler contest, masked, to win enough money to cover the damages done to the museum.

Brigitte Bardot is the junior miss. Although of sound chassis and sensual mien, she still lacks glib comedy assurance. Daniel Gelin just walks through this as the reporter and one wonders why all the chicks love him so. Neat comic bits are turned in by Darry Cowl and Robert Hirsch. Production dress is good and undress is

also good except that Miss Bardot, as the star, never has to show herself in the altogether since her undraping is accompanied by cutting away to get audience reactions. *Mosk.*

Everything But The Truth
(COLOR)

Family comedy about what happens when moppet Tim Hovey insists on telling the truth. Fair.

Hollywood, Nov. 6.
Universal release of Howard Christie production. Stars Maureen O'Hara, John Forsythe, Tim Hovey; features Frank Faylen. Les Tremayne. Philip Bourneuf, Paul Birch, Addison Richards. Directed by Jerry Hopper. Screenplay, Herb Meadow; camera (Eastman Color), Maury Gertsman; editor, Sherman Todd; music supervision, Milton Rosen. Previewed Nov. 2. '56. Running time. 83 MINS.
Joan Madison .... Maureen O'Hara
Ernie Miller .... John Forsythe
Willie Taylor .... Tim Hovey
Mac .... Frank Faylen
Lawrence Everett .... Les Tremayne
Mayor Parker .... Philip Bourneuf
Senator Winter .... Paul Birch
Roger Connolly ...... Addison Richards
Arthur Taylor .... Barry Atwater
Miss Adelaide Dabney .. Jeanette Nolan
Blonde .... Roxanne Arlen
Doctor .... Ray Walker
Chairman of School Board
                        Howard Negley

This fair family comedy sets about to prove that the truth can sometimes be mighty unpleasant, especially when it's told by such an engaging youngster as Tim Hovey to his elders. The family trade will find it acceptable as a companion feature in the general dual situations.

Young Hovey's work continues to be distinguished by a complete lack of precociousness, and he more than holds his own in an adult company made up of costars Maureen O'Hara and John Forsythe, and featured players that include Frank Faylen, Les Tremayne, Philip Bourneuf, Paul Birch, Addison Richards and others. In fact, he comes off quite a bit better because the script by Herb Meadow and the direction by Jerry Hopper show an admirable restraint in playing his character straight, while the adults are required to be extremely adolescent in their portrayals.

The Howard Christie production, brightly dressed up in Eastman Color, has a small-town setting, where young Hovey, an orphan, lives with his uncle, Barry Atwater. Tutored to tell the truth at all times by his pretty schoolteacher, Miss O'Hara, the boy pops off in public that his uncle gave the mayor, Philip Bourneuf, a $10,000 kickback in a civic real estate deal. Plot becomes hodge-podge of frenetics from then on, as the politicos try to make the boy retract his statement and his schoolmarm carries the fight to the capital, even enlisting the help of bigtime columnist, Forsythe, in the battle for the truth, which eventually outs.

Color queen Miss O'Hara looks just that under Maury Gertsman's lensing, and Edward Stevenson gave her some fetching outfits to wear. Forsythe's columnist is very broad, as are his amatory pitches at Miss O'Hara. Faylen, the columnist's business manager; Tremayne, the governor's secretary; Bourneuf, Paul Birch, a Senator; Addison Richards, publisher; Atwater, and Jeanette Nolan, school principal, also play for broad comedy. Roxanne Arlen spots a good scene in a powder room, wherein she instructs Miss O'Hara in the door-knob technique for handling wolves.

Art direction, editing, set decorations and other technical factors are expert. *Brog.*

Suicide Mission

Semi-documentary of little-known phase of World War II. Often exciting.

Hollywood, Nov. 6.

Columbia release of a Michael Forlong production. Features Leif Larsen, Michael Aldridge, Atle Larsen, Per Christensen, T. W. Southam, Oscar Egede Nissen. Directed by Forlong. Screenplay, David Howarth, Sidney Cole, Forlong; based on book, "The Shetland Bus," by Howarth; comera, Per G. Jonson, Mattis Mathiesen; editor, Lee Doig; narration, Anthony Oliver. Previewed Oct. 30, '56. Running time, **69 MINS.**

"Suicide Mission" is a semi-documentary about a group of daring Norwegians in the Shetland Islands during World War II who, under direction of the British Royal Navy but in Norwegian fishing boats, regularly crossed the North Sea in mid-winter to land arms, explosives and agents in their Nazi-held homeland. Film, in which appear several of the hardy Norsemen who participated in the actual heroic exploit, is often exciting and should fit patly into the program market.

Warwick Productions picked up the finished film in England, produced and directed by Michael Forlong on the scene, for inclusion on Indie's Columbia program. Title is geared to fit the action, in which the hazards of the 500-mile crossing, often under Nazi aerial attack, are graphically depicted, occasionally through use of war stock footage. Adapted from David Howarth's book, "The Shetland Bus," Forlong has succeeded in a realistic treatment of his subject, in which the camera work of Per G. Jonson and Mattis Mathieson registers stirringly.

Leif Larsen, one of the Norwegian captains during the gruelling days of the blockade running, portrays himself as an interesting figure. Balance of pro actors include Michael Aldridge, Atle Larsen, Per Christensen, T. W. Southam and Oscar Egede Nissen, each contributing to excellence of the story development. Howarth, Sidney Cole and Forlong's script-adaptation is a slick job of adventuring.

Whit.

Die Halbstarken
(The Half-strong Ones) (GERMAN)

Berlin, Oct. 30.

Union release of Wenzel Luedecke (Interwest) production. Stars Horst Buchholz; features Karin Baal, Christian Doermer and Jo Herbst. Directed by Georg Tressler. Screenplay, Will Tremper and Georg Tressler after story by Will Tremper; camera, Heinz Fehlke; music, Martin Boettcher; editor, Wolfgang Flaum. At Delphi Palast, Berlin. Running time, **97 MINS.**

Freddy Borchert .... Horst Buchholz
Sissy Bohl .... Karin Baal
Jan Borchert .... Christian Doermer
Guenther .... Jo Herbst
Mother Borchert....Viktoria V. Ballasko
Antonio Garezzo ..... Stanislaw Ahrens
Klaus .... Manfred Hoffmann
Willi .... Hans-Joachim Ketzlin
Kudde .... Kalle Gaffkus
Woelfl .... Wolfgang Heyer
Herr Borchert .... Paul Wagner
Pepe Garezzo ....Eduard Wandrey
Theo ....Friedrich Joloff

This film won special attention long before it was even completed. It's the first German pic on juvenile delinquency, one of postwar Germany's biggest problems. It makes an obvious attempt to cash in on the wide popularity of American pix of the same sort, such as "Blackboard Jungle" and "Rebel Without Cause." It's an obvious effort to give young Horst Buchholz, idol of local bobbysox set and winner of the 1955 Federal Film Award for his role in "Sky Without Stars," the opportunity to come along.

"Halbstarken" (which means "Half-Strong Ones") has the kids, the basic problem and also the realistic approach (many roles are played by amateurs), but all similarity with its American predecessors stops there. Neither can it stand comparison with Hollywood pix on the same subject. It's little more than a mediocre documentary report concentrating on a corny, thrill story.

Nevertheless, film will appeal to mass audiences here, particularly juveniles. "Halbstarken" may do well in some limited foreign territories.

While a superficial script is mostly to blame for this film's shortcomings, there is also some considerable unconviction acting. That also applies to Buchholz and Miss Karin Baal. Buchholz, a handsome lad with talents, is overacting here most of the time. Miss Baal in this, her screen debut, is nothing more than a cute looker as seductive gangster's moll, and a complete miscast. Although handicapped by the script material, Christian Doermer as Buchholz' brother as well as Jo Herbst and Kalle Gaffkus (both of Buchholz' gang) turn in promising performances.

Georg Tresler makes this film his directorial debut. His direction in the main is rather uneven. Very good is Martin Boettcher's score and there is also a plus in Heinz Fehlke's outdoor lensing which has often sharp documentary flavor. All in all, it's deplored here that such an important theme has been wasted as in this pic. Its characters, although belonging to the young generation, are real hoodlums.

Hans.

Paris Palace Hotel
(FRENCH—ITALIAN; COLOR)

Paris, Oct. 30.

Cinedis release of Speva Film-Rizzoli production. Stars Charles Boyer, Francoise Arnoul; features Roberto Risso, Raymond Bussieres, Michele Philippe, Carette, Tilda Thamar. Directed by Henri Verneuil. Screenplay, Charles Spaak, Verneuil; dialog, Spaak; camera (Eastmancolor), Philippe Agostini; editor, J. Feyte. At Berlitz, Paris. Running time, **105 MINS.**

Francoise ....Francoise Arnoul
Delomel ....Charles Boyer
Gerard ....Roberto Risso
Bebert ....Carette
Mme. Delomel .... Tilda Thamar
Barbara ....Michele Philippe

Film is in the slick femme magzine yarn and is reminiscent of the many pre-war U.S. comedies. Situations make up a Cinderella-type yarn with the main twist having both boy and girl masquerading as rich. There even is the fairy godmother, an aging, worldy skirt-chaser. Lacking enough inventiveness and flair to dispel the well-known trappings, this remains palatable for U.S. chances mainly on the Charles Boyer name and the Paris locale.

Smart color and production envelop a manicurist and garage mechanic who meet in a posh hotel and pass themselves off as clients. She is invited out by a rich, middle-aged man (Boyer) who has gotten rid of his wife by feigning gout.

Boyer plays in a suave manner as does Francoise Arnoul as the pert, knowing manicurist. But Roberto Risso is much too wooden. Director Henri Verneuil does not manage to imbue this with the charm it needs. Color is good and production fine. It seems an okay local entry but somewhat skimpy for U.S. except mainly in special situations.

Mosk.

La Mort En Ce Jardin
(Death In This Garden) (FRENCH—MEXICAN; COLOR)

Paris, Oct. 30.

Cinedis release of Dismage-Oscar Dancigers production. Stars Simone Signoret, Charles Vanel, Georges Marchal; features Michel Piccoli, Michele Girardon. Directed by Luis Bunuel. Screenplay, Juan Alcoriza, Raymond Queneau, Bunuel from a novel by Jose-Andre Lacour; camera (Eastmancolor), Georges Stahl; editor, Marguerite Renoir. At Biarritz, Paris. Running time, **110 MINS.**

Djin .... Simone Signoret
Chark ....Georges Marchal
Castin ....Charles Vanel
Marie ....Michele Girardon
Priest ....Michel Piccoli

Adventure-actioner takes place in some Latino country where strong man tactics are still rampant. It concerns a group thrown together on the lam from the military tyrants and their adventures in a seething jungle, with only two escaping. Though familiar in outline, Luis Bunuel's direct direction gives this an offbeat dimension. It may do for offbeat arty spotting.

Early segments are neatly narrated to segue into the jungle trek. Bunuel's added intrusion of sudden surrealist touches heighten and deepen this pic.

Bunuel's unmitigated statements on the characters remove their conventional trappings. Simone Signoret has the venal quality of her joy girl. The old miner gets a brilliant portrayal from Charles Vanel while Michele Girardon emerges a new find in her intelligent, poignant mumming of the deaf and dumb girl.

This is an unusual adventure opus that bears special handling. Color is fine, technical aspects and supporting playing all being tops.

Mosk.

Foreign Films

Paris, Oct. 30.

Le Sang A La Tete (The Blood to the Head) (**FRENCH**). Fernand Rivers production and release. Stars Jean Gabin; features Monique Helinand, Paul Frankeur, Jose Quaglio. Directed by Gilles Grangier. Screenplay, Michel Audiard, Grangier from the novel, "Le Fils Cardinaud," by Georges Simenon; camera, Andre Thomas; editor, Paul Cayatte. At George V, Paris. Running time, **90 MINS.**

Stolid pic brings still another of George Simenon's sociologically themed books to the screen. It also remains literary in this tale of a self-made man whose loss of his wife to a delinquent youth brings out the latent envy and hatred of the remainder of the town. Main attribute is the solid performance by Jean Gabin who walks through this with a resoluteness and understatement that gives the film its few dramatic moments. He gives it more than director Gilles Grangier has been able to.

Somewhat inconclusive in characterization, with technical credits only par and supporting cast adequate, this shapes mainly as a possible dualer for the U.S., with theme and Gabin name exploitable. Otherwise this surface-sketched pic on smalltime Gallic pettiness lacks the depth to put it into the specialized groove for U.S. chances.

Mosk.

La Chatelaine Du Liban (FRENCH-ITALIAN; C'SCOPE; COLOR). SNOF release of Jeannie Film-CTI-Cino Del Duca production. Stars Jean-Claude Pascal, Gianna-Maria Canale; features, Jean Servais, Omar Cherif, Luciana Paolucci, Juliette Greco. Directed by Richard Pottier. Screenplay, Maurice Auberge from novel by Pierre Beniot; camera (Eastmancolor), Lucien Joulin; editor, L. M. Azar. At Normandie, Paris. Running time, **100 MINS.**

Old hat tale of adventure in the desert has served for film vehicles before, and here it's updated to concern two engineers searching for uranium. Yarn covers the skulduggery with Arabs, mysterious foreign representatives and beauteous 'femmes fatales.'

Done in C'Scope and with a well-worn adventure line, this is not for arties, of course and its lack of names makes this limited for general spots also. However, it is neatly done and has good color with some fine action bits. Offbeat locale might make this worth dubbing. Acting is okay and desert activity takes emphasis away from the rather familiar happenings.

Mosk.

Mannequins De Paris (FRENCH) (FRANSCOPE; COLOR). Pathe release of S. N. Pathe-PAC-Contact production. Stars Madeleine Robinson, Ivan Desny; features Ghislaine Arsac, Jacqueline Pierreux, Yoko Tani, Max Revol. Directed by Andre Hunebelle. Screenplay, Francois Campaux, Michel Audiard, Hunnebelle; camera (Eastmancolor), Paul Coteret; editor, Jean Feyte. At Marignan, Paris. Running time, **90 MINS.**

Anamorphoscope pic, with process still somewhat buckling in perspective and not completely clear in color rendition, this is definitely unsuitable for arty houses on its lack of story or point. Pic has little for general spots except the pulchritude of the top mannequins of Paris trotted out as often as possible in all manners of undress. More like a documentary on haute couture presentations, banal story line concerns a businesswoman who neglects her designer husband for biz. He strays but comes back to the fold. Commentary and usual model mishaps make up brunt of this pic. Director Andre Hunebelle gives lacklustre treatment and seems tied down by the screen size. Acting and other aspects are generally lowlevel, this is strictly exploitation here, with less chances in the U.S.

Mosk.

Lorsque L'Enfant Parait (When the Child Appears) (**FRENCH; COLOR**). CFF release of CFCC production. Directed by Michel Boisrond. Screenplay, Frederic Grendel, Shermann Sidery from a play by Andre Roussin; camera (Eastmancolor), Marcel Girgnon; editor, Gilbert Natot; music, Hendi Sauguet. With Andre Luguet, Gaby Morlay, Brigitte Auber, Guy Bertil, Alta Riba, Suzy Prim, Armande Navarre. At Biarritz, Paris. Running time, **90 MINS.**

Since as a hit play it ran here for four years, Andre Roussin's comedy, spoofing Ministers and pregnancy naturally was finally bought for the screen. In film form, unfortunately, the dialog is kept too intact and the telegraphed proceedings lose their impact. This type of legiter, without sprightly handling, soon bogs down on film, as this does. It lacks a definite stand on satire. This looks unlikely for arty U.S. chances. The palavering about the various would-be mothers is tasteless rather than smart. Pic also looks limited for exploitation.

A minister trying to shut down bagnios and get special allowances for large families comes home to find his over-middleaged wife is expecting a baby, with the inevitable gags about who the father may be dragged in. His daughter, ready to wed a nobleman, suspects she is pregnant, and his son,

blandly announces he is to have a child by his father's secretary.

With this setup as the foundation, the director tries to slick things up with a light touch. Color is good, but to many interiors are used. Acting is in the stage vein as are many sets. *Mosk.*

Bob Le Flambeur (FRENCH). Mondial Film release of Jenner-Cyme-Play Art Film production. Directed by Jean-Pierre Melville. Screenplay, Auguste Le Breton, Melville; camera, Henri Decae; editor, Manique Bonnot. With Roger Duchesne, Isabelle Corey, Daniel Cauchy, Howard Vernon, Guy Decomble. At Radio Cine, Paris. Running time, **95 MINS.**

Pic is in the "Rififi" classification and is even written by the same man. It concerns the last job of an aging gangster who has been devoting himself to gambling until the final heist presents itself. However, here the similarity ends, for this lacks the suspense, characterization and deft direction of the predecessor.

This plods through its tale of the underworld without adding the needed filip to make it unusual. Its only American interest would be for dualer chances on its locale and action. Otherwise lagging direction so-so thesping and usual femme and lowdown aspects of this type production make this an ordinary entry. Production values show a tight budget and technical values are below par. *Mosk.*

Ensayo De Un Crimen (Attempt at a Crime) (MEXICAN). ACSA production and release. Directed by Luis Bunuel. Screenplay, Bunuel, Rodolfo Usigli from play by Usigli; camera, Augustin Jiminez; editor, Pablo Gomez; music, Jesus Bracho. With Ernesto Alonso, Miroslava, Ariana Welter. Previewed in Paris. Running time, **90 MINS.**

A macabre comedy, loaded with shock portions and erotico symbolism, this is an offbeater slanted mainly for specialized spotting in U.S. This is a serio-comic study of a rich young man whose obsession to kill is always stymied.

Luis Bunuel's sadistic touches sometimes jolt rather than tickle, but the whole film is carried out with a successful tongue-in-cheek attitude. It may have something for specialized audiences in America. However, there may be censor trouble.

Ernesto Alonso, as a child, wished for the death of his governess while playing a musicbox which she had told him, in fancy, had the power to grant wishes. She is killed by a stray bullet. The child thinks he killed her and he confuses it with a feeling of pleasure. Later in life, as a rich, independent man, he finds the musicbox again which sets up a desire to kill. He plans some crimes but he is always thwarted and his victims killed before he can get to them.

Acting of the late Miroslava as two of the intended victims and Alonso as the would-be killer catch the right note of mock comedy and seriousness. Technical credits are all topnotch and music is exceptional. *Mosk.*

The Desperadoes Are In Town

Second of Regal Films' new low-budgeters for 20th-Fox. Fair programmer.

Hollywood, Nov. 13.

20th-Fox release of Kurt Neumann (Regal Films) production, directed by Neumann. Stars Robert Arthur, Kathy Nolan; features Rhys Williams, Rhodes Reason, Dave O'Brien, Kelly Thordsen, Mae Clarke. Screenplay, Earle Snell and Neumann; from Bennett Foster's SatEvePost story, "The Outlaws Are in Town"; camera, John Mescall; editor, Merrill White; music, Paul Sawtell, Bert Shefter. Previewed Nov. 8, '56. Running time, **72 MINS.**

Lenny Kesh	Robert Arthur
Alice Rutherford	Kathy Nolan
Jud Collins	Rhys Williams
Frank Banner	Rhodes Reason
Dock Lapman	Dave O'Brien
Tobe Lapman	Kelly Thordsen
Jane Kesh	Mae Clark
Deputy Sheriff Groome	Robert Osterloh
Tom Kesh	William Challee
Hattie	Carol Kelly
Branch	Frank Sully
Mr. Rutherford	Morris Ankrum
Hank	Richard Wessel
Woman	Dorothy Grainger
Ranger (Plainville)	Todd Griffin
Mrs. Rutherford	Nancy Evans
Girl	Ann Stebbins
Jim Day	Byron Foulger

For the second of its low-budgeters for 20th-Fox, Regal Films comes up with a sort of western-southern rural, action-drama under the title of "The Desperados Are In Town." There's not as much action as there should be for the lowercase programmer dates it will fill but, overall, it shapes as a fair entry for release intentions, considering the low cost factor.

Robert Arthur and Kathy Nolan lend a youthful note as the stars of the Kurt Neumann production, responding satisfactorily to the not too taxing demands of Neumann's direction and the script he wrote with Earle Snell. Screen plotting takes a convenient and easy path, so there are some story holes, as well as some unnecessary footage in the 72 minutes running time.

Nub of the plot finds Arthur running away from his parents' poor southern farm to Texas, where he gets mixed up with an outlaw gang temporarily before being sent back by an outlaw trying to go straight. Industrious work reclaims the farm and just as the harvest celebration is to take place, the gang leader and his brother show up, insist he help rob his banker friend. Instead, Arthur kills them both, but not before one tips the banker about the Texas escapade. Tale's moral is good, including the Christian-like plot solution that finds the banker taking it upon himself to forgive and forget Arthur's past so the young man can continue to be a good citizen and marry his sweetheart, Miss Nolan.

Most of the cast are competent, with some adding a bit more to the characterizations. These include Rhys Williams, as the banker; Rhodes Reason, the outlaw trying to go straight, and Carol Kelly, his dancehall girl friend. Dave O'Brien and Kelly Thordsen are the outlaw principals, while Mae Clarke, Robert Osterloh, Frank Sully and Morris Ankrum are among others more prominently involved.

John Mescall's black-and-white RegalScope (a budget handle for CinemaScope) lensing comes off okay, as do other technical factors. *Brog.*

Vitelloni
(ITALIAN)

API-Janus release of Mario de Vecchi presentation of Peg Film-Cite production. Stars Franco Interlenghi, Franco Fabrizi, Leonora Ruffo; features Alberto Sordi, Leopoldo Trieste, Riccardo Fellini, Lida Baarowa, Arlette Sauvage, Maja Nipora, Jean Brochard, Claude Farere. Directed by Federico Fellini. Screenplay, Fellini and Ennio Flaiano, based on story by Fellini, Flaiano and Tullio Pinelli; camera, Martelli, Trasatti, Carlini; music, Nino Rota. At 55th St. Playhouse, N.Y., Nov. 7, '56. Running time, **103 MINS.**

Moraldo	Franco Interlenghi
Fausto	Franco Fabrizi
Alberto	Alberto Sordi
Leopoldo	Leopoldo Trieste
Riccardo	Riccardo Fellini
Sandra	Leonora Ruffo
Giulia	Lida Baarowa
Woman	Arlette Sauvage
Actress	Maja Nipora
Father	Jean Brochard
Sister	Claude Farere
Michele	Carlo Romano

Those who've been wanting the Italians to return to their native style of filmmaking should welcome "Vitelloni" with open arms. With the imaginative, sharp-eyed Federico Fellini at the helm, it's the kind of film that should flourish in the U.S. arties.

Many of the elements of the early postwar Italo successes are wrapped into this picture—the simplicity, the sharp contrasts in the camera work, the whisp of a story line and the sharp delineations of mood and characters. There is some humor here and, over it all, that cast of frustration and hopelessness so prevalent in many Italian productions.

"Vitelloni" are the loafers, the boys on the streetcorners who run in packs and shun work. This bunch is a cut above the hotrodders. They think of women and they dream dreams of glory. They're all caught in a web of unemployment, but in the end one—Franco Interlenghi—takes the step that could lead into a new life.

Story has Franco Fabrizi marrying the pregnant Leonora Ruffo but going right on with his affairs. He takes a job in a store selling religious articles but is fired when he makes love to the proprietor's wife. When he spends a night with a singer from a touring company, Miss Ruffo takes her child and disappears. The shock—plus a sound thrashing from his father—brings him to his senses.

Woven into this main yarn are episodes galore, some contrived, some slices from life. Fellini knows the value of pathos and he creates it with a delicate hand. The encounter between Interlenghi and the boy going to work at the railroad station is beautifully handled; so is the brusque awakening of the aspiring playwright who is propositioned by a broken-down old actor on a stormy beach. The final scene between father (Jean Brochard) and son, ending in a reconciliation, has humor and charm.

Performances are all topnotch, with Interlenghi and Fabrizi outstanding. But it's Fellini's film from start to finish, and his imprimatur raises "Vitelloni" well above the average. It's got enough sex to make it an exploitable item, and yet it doesn't depend on that alone. At a time when the good Italian films are far and inbetween, "Vitelloni" stands out like a sore thumb. *Hift.*

... Wie Einst Lili Marleen
(GERMAN)

(... Like Once Lili Marlene)

Berlin, Nov. 6.

Constantin release of Delos production. Stars Adrian Hoven and Marianne Hold; features Lale Andersen. Directed by Paul Verhoeven. Screenplay, Ilse Lutz-Dupont and Paul Verhoeven, from story by Warner Hill; camera, Karl Schroeder; music, Norbert Schultze; editor, Ilse Voigt. At Adria, Berlin. Running time, **89 MINS.**

Franz Brugger	Adrian Hoven
Christa Schmidt	Marianne Hold
Minna Lauck	Lucie Englisch
Toni Knoll	Peter Carsten
Klaerchen Mueller	Hannelore Schroth
Frau Schmidt	Kaethe Haack
Dr. Berger	Claus Holm
Alfred Linder	Wolfgang Preiss
Fraeulein Korn	Roma Bahn
Krause	Kurt Vespermann
Sister Lene	Gudrum Schmidt
Frau Berger	Hildegard Grethe
Charwoman	Else Ehser

Only vaguely this German film has to do with "Lili Marlene," this country's top song of the last World War which, via the German soldier network in Belgrade, managed to gain worldwide popularity. This Delos production, made in Artur Brauner's West Berlin CCC studios, makes substantially use of the famous tune, partly as accompanying music and sometimes sung by Lale Andersen whose voice, incidentally, made "Lili Marlene" also famous during the war.

In the main, this pic centers around the love story between a German soldier and his girl. Reference to the title tune is that both first met when it was played and that they then made a promise to think of each other whenever they hear this melody. However, when he returns to his girl after the war, he finds her in the arms of another man. But there is a happy ending.

While the title and the still catchy tune may be regarded as a valuable exploitation angle, at least with regard to nostalgia, this German pic doesn't offer much which would make it a recommended item abroad. Here, it will appeal to the majority of average patrons for whom this production has also mainly been tailored.

As usual with a German postwar film of this category, the script is mostly to blame for the film's shortcomings. The situations are too familiar. The story development lacks conviction.

Despite the handicaps, direction by Paul Verhoeven is generally satisfactory. That also applies to the players. Young, beautiful Marianne Hold portrays the role of the girl sympathetically. Adrian Hoven enacts her beau with average results. Claus Holm plays a military surgeon who has eyes on Miss Hold, an okay performance. Same goes for vet players like Lucie Englisch, Kaethe Haack and Roma Bahn. Natural performances are contributed by Peter Carsten, Hoven's war-time buddy, Hannelore Schroth as Carsten's wife. Miss Andersen sells her "Lili Marleen" song in appealing style.

Music by Norbert Schultze is filme's main asset. His "Lili Marleen" still rates extremely popular. Editing and lensing are of mediocre calibre. *Hans.*

The Last Man to Hang
(BRITISH)

Slow murder trial meller.

Hollywood, Nov. 9.

Columbia release of John Gossage (A.C.T. Film) production. Stars Tom Conway, Elizabeth Sellars, Eunice Gayson, Freda Jackson. Directed by Terence Fisher. Screenplay, Ivor Montagu, Max Trell; from Gerald Bullett novel "The Jury" and adaptation by Bullett and Maurice Elvey; camera, Desmond Dickinson; editor, Peter Taylor; music, John Wooldridge. Previewed Nov. 7, '56. Running time, **75 MINS.**

Roderick	Tom Conway
Daphne	Elizabeth Sellars
Elizabeth	Eunice Gayson
Mrs. Tucker	Freda Jackson
Mark	Hugh Latimer
Dr. Cartwright	Ronald Simpson
Bonaker	Victor Maddern
Gaskin	Anthony Newley
Mrs. Cranshaw	Margaretta Scott
Mayfield	Leslie Weston
Underhay	Bill Shine
Lucy Prynne	Anna Turner
Major Forth	Jack Lambert
Cheed	Harold Goodwin
Mrs. Iseley	Joan Newell
Bracket	Thomas Heathcote
Nywood	Tony Quinn
Coates	Hal Osmond
Lucy's Mother	Joan Hickson
Gaskin's Girl	Gillian Lynne
Bracket's Wife	Shelagh Fraser
Bayfield's Wife	Olive Sloane
Bayfield's Son	Michael McKeag
Cheed's Doctor	Harold Siddons
Cheed's Nurse	Maya Koumani
The Judge	Walter Hudd
Attorney General	Raymond Huntley
Antony Harcombe Q.C.	David Horne
Clerk of the Court	Dan Cunningham
Det. Sgt. Bolton	Russell Napier
Det. Sgt. Horne	Martin Boddey
Dr. Goldfinger	John Schlessinger
Dr. Mason	Conrad Phillips
Senior Sister	Sheila Manahan
Nurse Tomkins	Rosamund Waring

Melodramatics in "The Last Man to Hang" manage to get awfully tedious before the 75-minute footage is over. The plot is acceptable, if far-fetched; its execution is not, so this one will serve out its playing time as a lowercase programmer.

Based on Gerald Bullett's novel, "The Jury," the film plays best when in the courtroom at a murder trial, mostly because of the wigs and studied mannerisms that British legal eagles assume for the practice of their profession. Elsewhere, the screenplay by Ivor Montagu and Max Trell, and the direction by Terence Fisher put too much emphasis on side scenes and characters to permit the plot to boil along at a good pace.

Tom Conway, only recognizable caster for stateside dates, is the man on trial for murder in the average John Gossage production. He's supposed to have done his wife in with an overdose of sedative, and the jury must decide whether it was accidental or premeditated. Title came from the fact there's a move in Parliament to outlaw capital punishment and he may be the last man, etc. There's no suspense to this angle; nor elsewhere. Actually, Conway's in jeopardy because his housekeeper, Freda Jackson, hates him and schemed to get him hanged via identifying an unknown body as his wife's, who, still alive, has been given the wrong card in a hospital.

Conway, Miss Jackson, Elizabeth Sellars, the wife; Eunice Gayson, Conway's lady love; Hugh Latimer, family friend; Walter Hudd, judge; Raymond Huntley, posecutor, and David Horne, defending counsel, all play with a studied style that's laughable at times. Victor Maddern is good as a jury member.

Technically, the meller gets okay support from the lensing by Desmond Dickinson and other contributors. *Brog.*

Battle of River Plate
(BRITISH—V'VISION—COLOR)

Technically impressive filmization of defeat of Graf Spee in first major naval encounter of second World War.

London, Nov. 6.

Rank release of a Michael Powell and Emeric Pressburger production. Stars John Gregson, Anthony Quayle and Peter Finch; features Bernard Lee and Ian Hunter. Written, produced and directed by Michael Powell and Emeric Pressburger. Camera, Christopher Challis; editor, Reginald Mills; music, Brian Easdale. At Odeon, Leicester Square, London. Running time, **119 MINS.**

Captain Bell	John Gregson
Commodore Harwood	Anthony Quayle
Captain Langsdorff	Peter Finch
Captain Parry	Jack Gwillim
Captain Dove	Bernard Lee
Mike Fowler	Lionel Murton
Mr. Millington-Drake	Anthony Bushell
Captain McCall	Michael Goodliffe
Lieut. Commander	Patrick MacNee
Dr. Oangmann	John Chandos
Mr. Desmoulins	Douglas Wilmer
Ray Martin	William Squire
Capt. Varela	Roger Delgado
Capt. Stubs	Andrew Cruickshank
Manola	Christopher Lee
Pop	Edward Atienza
Dolores	April Olrich

By its selection for the Royal Command film gala, "Battle of River Plate" has garnered top quality publicity, which should be of immense help in promotion and exploitation. That aid won't go amiss for, despite its impressive technical achievements, it's lacking in human, emotional and dramatic qualities. It will need intensive selling, both in Britain and overseas to help it make the b.o. grade.

Defeat of the Graf Spee was the first major naval victory for Britain in the last big war and, as such, takes a prominent place in history. Apart from the strategy involved, it was also an exercise in subterfuge and diplomacy. All these points are neatly and simply brought out in the Michael Powell-Emeric Pressburger filmization. What they have failed to do, however, is to achieve any degree of characterization for the three naval commanders who led the British cruisers to victory against the Germans' more powerful pocket battleship. Indeed, the only really sympathetic character emerging from the screenplay is the skipper of the enemy ship.

The battle sequences, in which the lightweight British cruisers close in on the Graf Spee and give with all their firepower until they force the enemy to take shelter in Montevideo harbor, are powerful, exciting and technically impressive. However, there is some confusion as to the identity of the individual cruisers.

Story is given a neat twist by the diplomatic exchanges which take place while the Graf Spee is sheltering. The British Minister in Montevideo deliberately allows the leakage of a report that other Allied naval vessels are hurrying to the scene. When the Nazi battleship is obliged to leave harbor, the captain chooses to scuttle, rather than be outnumbered by his enemy. The atmosphere in Montevideo is heightened by a series of on-the-spot dramatic broadcasts to the U.S., a device which is most effective.

As written, produced and directed by Powell and Pressburger, the players are almost secondary to the ships themselves. John Gregson, as the skipper of the Exeter; Anthony Quayle, commodore on the Ajax; Ian Hunter, captain of the Ajax, and Jack Gwillim on the Achilles, give forthright portrayals. Peter Finch gets the plum role as the German captain, who emerges as a warm, sincere and kindly person. This attitude is helped by Bernard Lee's interpretation of Captain Dove, skipper of a merchantman which had been sunk by the Graf Spee. Lionel Murton, as the commentator; Anthony Bushell, as the British Minister; and Peter Illing, as the Uruguayan foreign minister, lead an experienced supporting cast. *Myro.*

Finger of Guilt

Well-developed mystery with three U.S names mark this British entertainment.

Hollywood, Nov. 12.

RKO release of an Alec C. Snowden production. Stars Richard Basehart, Mary Murphy; costars Constance Cummings, Roger Livesey, Faith Brook, Mervyn Johns. Directed by Snowden. Screenplay, Peter Howard; camera, Gerald Gibbs; music, Trevor Duncan; editor, Geoffrey Muller. Reviewed Nov. 7, '56. Running time, **85 MINS.**

Reggie Wilson	Richard Basehart
Evelyn Stewart	Mary Murphy
Kay Wallace	Constance Cummings
Ben Case	Roger Livesey
Lesley Wilson	Faith Brook
Ernest Chaple	Mervyn Johns
George Mearns	Vernon Greeves
Steve Vadney	Andre Mikhelson
Police Sergeant	David Lodge
Doctor	Basil Dignam
Mrs. Lynton	Grace Denbeigh-Russell

"Finger of Guilt" provides enough mystery to keep the spectator fairly engrossed during most of a well-developed unfoldment, but film's contrived climax is weak.

It's a better-than-average English import, however, and rates okay for the program market. Pic has three Hollywood names, including Richard Basehart, Mary Murphy and Constance Cummings, former American actress.

This is one which Tony Owen turned out in England, where British backgrounds lend themselves to the story of a former Hollywood film cutter who now is a London producer and wed to the studio head's daughter. Told partially in flashback form, the Peter Howard screenplay follows Basehart, happily married, after a series of intimate letters, signed "Evelyn," start to reach him.

Insisting that he has no knowledge of the girl, the harassed producer takes his wife to Newcastle, where the girl, who infers they have been secretly meeting, lives. Unwilling at first not to believe her husband, circumstantial evidence now leads the wife to leave him, and producer is on the verge of thinking he must be a split personality, one side unaware of what the other is doing. Windup discloses that it is the studio head's former righthand man, who resents Basehart, who framed the whole thing.

Basehart delivers persuasively and Miss Murphy is convincing as the lovely impersonator. Miss Cummings, still a looker after years away from Hollywood, scores briefly as a Hollywood film star whom Basehart brings to London for a picture. As the studio chief, Roger Livesey is excellent and Faith Brook registers effectively as the wife.

Alec C. Snowden, who gives film very good production mounting, does a smooth job in his direction and camera work by Gerald Gibbs is interesting. Balance of technical credits are standard. *Whit.*

Love Me Tender
(SONGS)

Presley, that's all! B.O. mopup from teenagers.

20th-Fox release of David Weisbart production. Stars Elvis Presley, Richard Egan. Debra Paget; features Robert Middleton, William Campbell, Neville Brand, Mildred Dunnock, Bruce Bennett. Director, Robert D. Webb, screenplay, Robert Buckner from story by Maurice Geraghty; songs by Presley & Vera Matson; camera, Leo Tover. At N.Y. Paramount, Nov. 15, '56. Running time, **94 MINS.**

Vance	Richard Egan
Cathy	Debra Paget
Clint	Elvis Presley
Siringo	Robert Middleton
Brett Reno	William Campbell
Mike Gavin	Neville Brand
The Mother	Mildred Dunnock
Major Kincaid	Bruce Bennett
Ray Reno	James Drury
Ed. Galt	Russ Conway
Kelso	Ken Clark
Davis	Barry Coe
Fleming	L. Q. Jones
Jethro	Paul Burns
Train Conductor	Jerry Sheldon

For the benefit of the hordes of teenagers who've made a national figure of rock 'n' roll singer Elvis Presley and who've been buying his RCA Victor platters by the millions, 20th-Fox has whipped up a minor league oater (and oncer) in which to showcase one of the hottest show biz properties around today.

It's a b.o. natural for the screaming set and some elders may even wander in out of curiosity. It looks like a payoff for 20th-Fox which moved in fast to grab Presley while he's dominating the record field.

Appraising Presley as an actor, he ain't. Not that it makes much difference. The presence of Presley apparently is enough to satisfy the juve set. And there are four songs, the title tune already a 1,000,000 plus disk seller, and lotsa Presley wriggles thrown in for good measure.

Screenplay by Robert Buckner from a story by Maurice Geraghty is synthetic. Story line centers on Presley, the youngest of four brothers, who stayed on their Texas farm while the older three are away fighting the Yankees. The older brother (Richard Egan) left a gal (Debra Paget) and when word comes that he's been killed in battle, she weds Presley. When the three boys come home to resume their civvy ways, it's hard to keep Egan down on the farm because he's still in love with Miss Paget, now his brother's wife. Before he can head west to get away from it all, Presley is stirred by jealousy and takes a pot shot at his beloved frere. One of the heavies, responsible for whipping up Presley's frenzy, then kills the youngster. Pic ends at the grave with a superimposed shot of Presley reprising "Love Me Tender."

There's a subplot concerning stolen Federal money but it's only a thin bit used to hinge the yarn together.

Egan is properly stoic as the older brother while Miss Paget does nothing more than look pretty and wistful throughout. Mildred Dunnock gets sincerity into the part of mother of the brood, an achievement. Nobody, however, seems to be having as much fun as Presley especially when he's singing the title song, "Poor Boy," "We're Gonna Move" and "Let Me." Tunes were written by Presley and Vera Matson.

Robert D. Webb directed in routine manner and the prdouction is laid out simply in black-and-white CinemaScope. *Gros.*

The Great American Pastime

Comedy about little league baseball. Fair boxoffice possibilities with promotion angles for family trade.

Metro release of Henry Berman production. Stars Tom Ewell and Anne Francis. Directed by Herman Hoffman. Screenplay, Nathaniel Benchley; camera, Arthur E. Arling; editor, Gene Ruggiero; music, Jeff Alexander. Previewed in N.Y., Nov. 14, '56. Running time, **89 MINS.**
Bruce Hallerton .... Tom Ewell
Betty Hallerton .... Anne Francis
Mrs. Doris Patterson .... Ann Miller
Buck Rivers .... Dean Jones
Dennis Hallerton .... Rudy Lee
Ed Ryder .... Judson Pratt
George Carruthers...... Raymond Bailey
Mr. Dawson .... Wilfrid Knapp
Mr. O'Keefe .... Bob Jellison
Man Mountain O'Keefe
  .... Raymond Winston
Foster Carruthers .... Paul Engle
Mrs. George Carruthers...... Ann Morriss
Samuel J. Garway........ Gene O'Donnell

What this country needs is more family pictures with American themes. At least that's the sentiment of a segment of exhibition. Metro's "The Great American Pastime" fulfills both requirements, but its ability to meet the most essential requirement—the spark to lure patrons to the boxoffice in the first instance—is open to question.

There are, however, a number of amusing incidents in the Nathaniel Benchley comedy and the story of little league baseball will be probably close to many family groups. With the proper spotting and promotional tieups with local little leaguers, fair returns can be probably realized. For the most part, though, "The Great American Pastime" appears to be headed for double feature situations.

The story concerns the trials and tribulations of a young attorney who, in order to get closer to his son, undertakes the management of a little league team. In addition to undergoing physical punishment in attempting to condition his inept nine, he is confronted with pressure from his charges' parents, all of whom want to make certain that their sons receive favorable treatment. Hero, amusingly played by Tom Ewell, practically becomes a local outcast when his team fails to win.

The pressure from the parents is similar to that applied by alumni groups when a college football coach fails to produce a winning team. Further complications in Ewell's managerial activities develop when he mistakenly interprets the attentions of a young widow, played by Ann Miller. The widow only want to make sure that her son, Herbie, is selected to pitch, but her advances arouse the jealousy of Ewell's baseball-hating wife, played by Anne Francis, who in self-defense learns how to keep score so she can keep an eye on her husband.

The character Ewell is called upon to play is unfortunately the stereotype of an American father that television, in particular, has advanced. He's a silly, bumbling nincompoop totally unaware of the realities that surround him. Somehow, of course, he overcomes the adversities and, via basic kindness and honesty, emerges the conquering, stalwart hero. He is able to arouse his team to win the league championship.

It is difficult, however, to imagine how his wife, an intelligent and

an aware individual, could have possibly married him. Or how he could have possibly been a successful lawyer.

Herman Hoffman has directed with an eye to comedy that does not always succeed. The little league games, however, are staged to perfection and the reaction of the parents is presented with a fine touch. Sociologists have commented on the effects of little league baseball on both the boys and their parents, and "The Great American Pastime," to a degree, points up the problem.

Ewell is frequently funny in a farcical way but his character never emerges as a real person. As a matter of fact, the only character that appears genuine is the one portrayed by Miss Francis. Miss Miller is okay as the young widow and the young little leaguers, portrayed by Rudy Lee, Raymond Winston, and Todd Ferrell, are properly confused by the antics of their parents.

Arthur E. Arling has done a first-rate job in filming the baseball games and all technical aspects of the film are professionally perfect. *Holl.*

The Peacemaker

Slow-moving western with religious overtones.

Hollywood, Nov. 20.
United Artists release of a Hal R. Makelim production. Stars James Mitchell, Rosemarie Bowe; costars Jan Merlin, Jess Barker, Hugh Sanders; features Taylor Holmes, Philip Tonge, Dorothy Patrick. Directed by Ted Post. Screenplay, Hal Richards, Jay Ingram, based on novel by Richard Poole; camera, Lester Shorr; editor, William Shea; music, George Greeley; art director, Frank Smith. Previewed Nov. 13, '56. Running time, 82 MINS.
Terrall Butler .... James Mitchell
Ann Davis .... Rosemarie Bowe
Viggo Tomlin .... Jan Merlin
Ed Halcomb .... Jess Barker
Lathe Sawyer .... Hugh Sanders
Gray Arnett .... Herbert Patterson
Edith Sawyer .... Dorothy Patrick
Mr. Wren .... Taylor Holmes
Ben Scale .... Robert Armstrong
Elijah Maddox .... Philip Tonge
Sam Davis .... David McMahon
Doc Runyan .... Wheaton Chambers
Walt Kemper .... Jack Holland
Miss Smith .... Nancy Evans
Cowpuncher .... Harry Shannon

"The Peacemaker," story of a newly-arrived parson in a town torn by strife between warring rancher-farmer factions, carries semi-religious overtones which may help in certain family situations but generally will make feature hard to sell for market in which it will fall. First and only picture turned out under producer's now-abandoned Makelim plan of guaranteed exhib booking, film emerges a slow-moving, over-length western drama which must depend upon lower-bracket playdates.

James Mitchell in title role portrays a former gunslinger now dedicated to the Church, through whose wisdom, rather than a return to his guns, peace is finally restored to the community. The Hal Richards-Jay Ingram screen-

play is inclined to wordiness in the long unfoldment, which Ted Post's sometimes careless direction fails to speed up for the demands of the market.

Parson finds himself in the middle when he tries to bring the ranchers and the farmers together. Further complications enter in person of the railroad's rep, who brings in gunmen to supposedly protect the farmers, who have bought land from the railroad, from the vengeance of ranchers, but actually to fan the flame so he

can personally acquire land from both parties cheap. Parson is able to expose him before all-out warfare starts.

Mitchell acquits himself in okay fashion, and Rosemarie Bowe is in nicely for romantic interest. Jan Merlin makes his gunman role fairly believable, the hireling of Herbert Patterson, an old-fashioned heavy. Hugh Sanders as head of the ranchers and Jess Barker the farmer's leader stack up satisfactorily, and acceptable support is offered by Taylor Holmes, Dorothy Patrick and Philip Tonge.

Technical credits are standard. *Whit.*

Rock, Pretty Baby
(SONGS)

Should be a hit with the teenage set but dull if not embarrassing for adults. Loaded with 17 songs.

Universal release of Edmond Chevie production. Stars Sal Mineo, John Saxon and Luana Patten. Features Fay Wray, Edward C. Platt, and Rod McKuen. Directed by Richard Bartlett. Screenplay, Herbert Margolis and William Raynor; camera, George Robinson; editor, Frederick Y. Smith; music, Henry Mancini; additional songs and lyrics by Bill Carey, Sonny Burke, Bobby Troup, Rod McKuen, and Phil Tuminello. Previewed in N.Y., Nov. 15, '56. Running time, 89 MINS.
Angelo Barrato .... Sal Mineo
Jimmy Daley .... John Saxon
Joan Wright .... Luana Patten
Thomas Daley Sr., MD..Edward C. Platt
Beth Daley .... Fay Wray
"Ox" Bentley .... Rod McKuen
"Fingers" Porter .... John Wilder
"Sax" Lewis .... Alan Reed Jr.
"Pop" Wright .... Douglas Fowley
"Half-Note" Harris ..... Bob Courtney
Twinky Daley .... Shelley Fabares
Carol Saunders .... Susan Volkmann
Claire Saunders .... Carol Volkmann
Kay Norton .... April Kent
Lori Parker .... Sue George
Mr. Reid .... Walter Reed
Bruce Carter .... Glen Kramer
Johnny Grant .... Johnny Grant
Thomas Daley Jr. .... George Winslow

Make a picture that appeals to the teenagers and you've got a hit. That appears to be the current industry philosophy. By that standard, Universal's "Rock, Pretty Baby" should emerge a boxoffice winner. It has the ingredients that cater to the whims and fads of America's most publicized age group.

Universal has liberally sprinkled the entry with rock 'n' roll tunes, offering a total of 17 musical numbers—both vocal and instrumental. Implication; the kids will be jumpin' and stompin'. As an added appeal for the teenage set, U has cast the picture with a group of vigorous youngsters, including Sal Mineo, a semi-established teenage hero; John Saxon, an aspirant for teen laurels, and Luana Patten, an all-American type bluejeaner. These members of Hollywood's Coke brigade, in addition to Rod McKuen, John Wilder, Alan Reed Jr., Bob Courtney, Susan and Carol Volkmann, April Kent, and Sue George, ostensibly represent the teenage temper of the time.

"Rock, Pretty Baby" must be judged for the purpose it was made—to cash in on the rock 'n' roll frenzy. If considered from any other standpoint, the picture is dull and embarrassing. It'll make adults squirm and probably drive 'em out of theatres. If, as it's reported, the 15-24 age group is the prime ticket buyer, "Rock, Pretty Baby" is a hot commercial entry.

The daily newspapers have carried so much about the antics of teenagers that it might be hazardous to venture the observation that the youngsters in "Rock, Pretty Baby" are stereotypes-of-

stereotypes although no juvenile delinquency is involved this time. The youngsters come from fairly well-to-do parents and live in nice neighborhoods. It concerns parental misunderstanding and the awakening of real love as distinguished from the popular pastimes of petting and smooching.

Saxon, as an 18-year-old high-school senior, wants to follow a career in music and become a band leader. His father—a physician—can't see it that way and wants his son to follow in his footsteps. That's the basic conflict. It's spiced with a sub-conflict involving the boy-girl relationship between Saxon and Miss Patten.

As the budding leader of a combo, Saxon and his colleagues have the opportunity to break out in song and instrumentals at the drop of hat. The band has a tough time getting started, but there's the cliche contest that presents the young musicians with their golden chance. Plot even includes a wild, wind-up ride to the tv studio so that the hero can get there on time to perform.

Some amusing sidelights are provided by Shelly Fabares, as Saxon's sister who is emerging from adolescence, and George Winslow, as Saxon's young brother. Coast disk jockey Johnny Grant is on hand to play himself. Fay Wray, of "King Kong" fame, makes a charming and understanding mother, and Edward C. Platt is properly stern as the confused father. Most of the youngsters in the picture have a tendency to overact, but this may be revealing the natural exuberance of the teenage set.

The Herbert Margolis and William Raynor screenplay is secondary to the music. Richard Bartlett's direction meets the demands of the picture, and technical aspects are all on the plus side. *Holl.*

The Great Man

Tale of a popular air favorite who was a heel in private. Exceptionally good performances. Should please customers.

Hollywood, Nov. 27.

Universal release of Aaron Rosenberg production. Stars Jose Ferrer, Dean Jagger, Keenan Wynn, Julie London, Joanne Gilbert, Ed Wynn; features Jim Backus, Russ Morgan, Edward C. Platt, Robert Foulk, Lyle Talbot. Directed by Ferrer. Screenplay, Al Morgan and Ferrer; from Morgan's novel; camera, Harold Lipstein; editors, Sherman Todd, Al Joseph; music, Herman Stein; song, Bobby Troup, Leah Worth. Previewed Nov. 15, '56. Running time, **92 MINS.**

Joe Harris .... Jose Ferrer
Philip Carleton .... Dean Jagger
Sid Moore .... Keenan Wynn
Carol Larson .... Julie London
Ginny .... Joanne Gilbert
Paul Beasley .... Ed Wynn
Nick Cellantano .... Jim Backus
Eddie Brand .... Russ Morgan
Dr. O'Conner .... Edward C. Platt
Mike Jackson .... Robert Foulk
Harry Connors .... Lyle Talbot
Charley Carruthers .... Vinton Hayworth
Mrs. Rieber .... Henny Backus
Mary Browne .... Janie Alexandre
Receptionist .... Vikki Dougan
Mailboy .... Robert Schwartz

The alleged behind-the-scenes world of broadcasting took a lambasting with the publication of Al (NBC) Morgan's novel, "The Great Man," the story of a guy with a gift of gab. Novel's point of view is repeated in this Universal screen version. Several aspects give it interest for the trade and professional circles, such as the outspoken approach to some characters and situations in the novel, and exceptionally good performances.

Like the book, the film is a series of flash episodes adding into a character study as a probing reporter researches the background of a nationally-known and presumably revered air figure who has died in an auto accident. The research brings out that away from the mike the late lamented was a stinker with no scruples. At the same time, there is revealed a stinging portrait of network operations and of the men who wield the power in the electronic world. The "great man" is never seen in person, but becomes known to the viewer through the picture given of him in the interviews with people who had worked for and with him. It isn't a pretty picture of a man.

Jose Ferrer who stars as the reporter collaborated with author Morgan on the screenplay and directed. In each function he is extremely able, with particular emphasis on his direction which brings out several surprise performances. Ed Wynn need never play the buffoon again, so good is he as the pious owner of a small New England radio station who gave the "morning man" his start. It's an outstanding piece of work.

Another big surprise is Julie London, who digs into a dramatic role and socks it across with all the aplomb of an actress with many years of seasoning. She plays the singer on the personality guy's show who also must hold herself available as a part-time mistress if the Studio King is minded that way. Via record, she sings "The Meanings of the Blues," tune by Bobby Troup and Leah Worth.

Dean Jagger is fine as the network head and son Keenan Wynn scores, too, as the executive always looking out for himself. Joanne Gilbert impresses with excellent work as Ferrer's secretary. Also holding up the high performance standards are Jim Backus, the all-American heel's press agent; Russ Morgan, his studio orchestra leader; Edward C. Platt, a doctor; Robert Foulk, the engineer to whom no man was a god; Lyle Talbot, Henny Backus, Janie Alexander and others.

Photography by Harold Lipstein, the editing by Sherman Todd and Al Joseph, background music by Herman Stein and other technical contributions are all good. *Brog.*

Adan Y Eva
(Adam and Eve)
(MEXICAN-COLOR)

Bible's first chapter given a phony art treatment. "Exploitation" but little else.

Peliculas Nacionales release of a Constelacion production. Exec. producer, Francisco Olivos del Valle. Stars, Christiane Martell, Carlos Baena. Directed and produced by Alberto Gout. Screenplay and adaptation based on the Genesis by Gout. Camera, Alex Phillips; editor, Jorge Bustos; music, Gustave Cesar Carreon. At Cine Alameda, Mex. City, Nov. 16, '56. Running time **78 MINS.**

Adam .... Carlos Baena
Eve .... Christiane Martell
Biblical text spoken by
C. Portillo Acosta, P. de Cervantes

What might have been a tour de force by director Alberto Gout, two principals and a few animals, turns out to be a forced tour for all concerned, including the public. Opening days here had a heavily preponderant male audience eagerly awaiting a sexy nudie, but all they got for their pesos was a stilted unsatisfactory dullie.

Gout has attempted to transfer in pantomimic dramatic terms the awakening of man and the coming of woman. In a serious vein he opens his film with the words of Genesis, backing them up with the fine natural Eastmancolor photography of one of Mexico's best pictorial cameramen, Alex Phillips. Evidently with deep sincerity he builds a flowing documentary of desert sands, corrugated skies and limpid lagoons, promising the audience a subtle and distinguished film to follow. He then proceeds to tear down all that has gone before with a cheaply wrought, weakly interpreted and ludicrously set version of the world's oldest love story.

The film will undoubtedly be offered plenty of playing time wherever censorship allows it to be shown. It is without direct dialogue, except for one scream by Eve, and therefore its off screen religious text can be easily dubbed in all languages. However, for showmen, religiously inclined or otherwise, with any honest attitude toward their community, this film will be questioned plenty as an effort toward commercialism on a subject that calls for a thoroughly sincere and devout approach.

That Gout has gone to lengths to make it a strip teaser suggests only more that his interests in the subject matter were based on its sensationalism and its supposed sensuality. The pretensions of bad taste, combined with pseudo artyness in no way cover up the shoddy "Paradise" interior-exterior devised by Manuel Fontanales, nor the corny clerical style score of Gustavo Cesar Carreon. That Eve wears heavy eye shadow and has plucked brows, and that Adam seems a foolish buffoon may make for humor in some eyes. But a brutally sadistic scene of the death of a rabbit at the paws of a wild dog seems more typical of its authors' intent.

There are moments when Gout and the principals do come to grips with the story. There are also moments of unusual pictorial beauty when the camera becomes imaginative and when the setting of man's desert banishment takes on a quality of heat and understanding. However, over all this hangs the fact, that the difficult rendition of possibly the most sincere love story of them all, has, in its present filming taken on the trappings of a perverse and cheaply portrayed sex-stimulator, whose only point of view is a corrupt one. *Mayer.*

A Woman's Devotion
(COLOR)

Mildly interesting whodunit filmed in Acapulco; acceptable for general dual situations.

Hollywood, Nov. 27.

Republic release of a John Bash production. Stars Ralph Meeker, Janice Rule, Paul Henreid; features Rosenda Monteros, Fanny Schiller, Jose Torvay, Yerye Beiruate, Tony Carbajal, Jamie Gonzales, Carlos Riquelme. Directed by Paul Henreid. Story-screenplay, Robert Hill; camera (Trucolor), Jorge Stahl Jr.; art director, Ramon Rodriguez; editor, Richard L. Van Enger; music, Les Baxter. Previewed Nov. 23, '56. Running time, **88 MINS.**

Trevor Stevenson .... Ralph Meeker
Stella Stevenson .... Janice Rule
Capt. Henrique Monteros .. Paul Henreid
Maria .... Rosenda Monteros
Senora Reidl .... Fanny Schiller
Gomez .... Jose Torvay
Amigo Herrera .... Yerye Beirute
Sergeant .... Tony Carbajal
Roberto .... Jamie Gonzalez
Chief of Police .... Carlos Requelme

Picturesquely filmed in Mexico's Acapulco, "A Woman's Devotion," old-fashioned in title, carries enough whodunit motivation to keep the spectator mildly engrossed. The John Bash production occasionally becomes heavy. Names of Ralph Meeker, Janice Rule and Paul Henreid, who co-star, should see it through the general dual situations.

Bash makes excellent use of his location, lensed in Trucolor for good tint effect, and Henreid, doubling as director, persuasively handles his characters, particularly Meeker, who portrays a war hero still sometimes mentally disturbed due to battle shock in World War II. Story and screenplay by Robert Hill may be regarded by some as inadequately solving the mystery of two Mexican femmes' murder, but apparently it was the intention to leave it up to the viewer to clarify in his own mind from the incidents which unfold.

Plottage picks up Meeker and his bride of six months upon their arrival in Mexican resort, where they plan to spend an indefinite period. The morning after, the body of a Mexican waitress, whom Meeker, a first-rate artist, met in a bar the night before and asked to pose for him, is found in her home, where it develops painter made sketches of her. Girl's widower, a prize-fighter, finds these sketches, which Meeker, because of his mental condition, has forgotten, and tries to blackmail the artist. After going to the house to pay off and getting back the sketches, Meeker leaves, and body of a Mexican maid who has acted as go-between is discovered. The prize-fighter is believed by police, who have suspected Meeker of the first crime, to be guilty of both murders and Meeker is told he may leave. At airport, however, where police come to arrest the artist, he is killed after he believes he is back in the war and has tried to gun down the police.

Meeker delivers well in a difficult role and Miss Rule enacts his wife with understanding and charm. Henreid is well cast as the police captain assigned to the murders. Outstanding portrayal of the maid, the second victim, is offered by Mexican actress Rosenda Monteros, and good support is contributed by Yerye Beirute, widower; Fanny Schiller, pension manager, Jose Torvay, Tony Carbajal, Jaime Gonzalez and Carlos Riquelme.

Technical credits are headed by Jorge Stahl, Jr.'s clever color photography, and Les Baxter provides a melodic music score. *Whit.*

Rumble on the Docks

Actionful yarn of youthful gangs on N.Y. waterfront.

Hollywood, Nov. 27.

Columbia release of a Sam Katzman production. Stars James Darren; features Laurie Carroll, Michael Granger, Jerry Janger, Robert Blake, Edgar Barrier, Celia Lovsky, David Bond, Timothy Carey, Dan Terranova, Barry Froner. Directed by Fred F. Sears. Screenplay, Lou Morheim, Jack DeWitt; based on novel by Frank Paley; camera, Benjamin H. Kline; editor, Jerome Thoms; art director, Paul Palmentola. Previewed Nov. 19, '56. Running time, **84 MINS.**

Jimmy Smigelski .... James Darren
Della .... Laurie Carroll
Joe Brindo .... Michael Granger
Rocky .... Jerry Janger
Chuck .... Robert Blake
Pete Smigelski .... Edgar Barrier
Anna Smigelski .... Celia Lovsky
Dan Kevlin .... David Bond
Frank Mangus .... Timothy Carey
Tony Lighning .... Dan Terranova
Poochie .... Barry Froner
Wimpie .... Don Devlin
Cliffie .... Stephen H. Sears
Ferdinand Marchesi ...... Joseph Vitale
Gotham .... David Orrick
Fitz .... Larry Blake
Gil Danco .... Robert C. Ross
Sully .... Steve Warren
Bo-Bo .... Don Garrett
Fuller .... Joel Ashley
14-year-old .... Salvatore Anthony

Theme of juvenile delinquency is set down in a promising background in this gutsy Sam Katzman production which combines brawling juve street gangs with longshoremen labor trouble on the Manhattan waterfront. Film packs considerable violence, but gets in good characterizations and is an okay entry for action houses.

A "rumble" in dock parlance is a gang fight and script by Lou Morheim and Jack DeWitt proceeds to limn subject ruggedly. Film intros an interesting newcomer, James Darren, in lead role, who gives evidence of going places. Fred F. Sears' direction endows story line with credibility and movement, and pic benefits by on-the-spot lensing.

Darren, head of a juve gang, becomes involved in union trouble when he's picked up and patronized by Michael Granger, ruthless gangster head of a waterfront local. Basically a good kid with a sense of fair play, he throws in with thug as much to spite his father—who kicks him out after boy takes up with gangster, whom the father blames for being injured years before in a union brawl—as for any admiration he might hold for unionist. Plot is further motivated by the father and a handful of adherents trying to set up a rival local, leading to the murder of one of these leaders. Showdown comes when Granger and a triggerman try to kill Darren when it appears he'll testify against them for murder.

Darren displays an ingratiating talent which makes him a standout, and Granger is well cast as union chief. Laurie Carroll, a promising newcomer, is in for what romantic interest story naturally develops, and Edgar Barrier portrays the father, a bitter man who somehow attaches the infirmity he gained in the union brawl years before to his son. Timothy Carey is properly menacing as gang leader's goon and David Bond rates in role of a settlement worker. Celia Lovsky, Sammy Froner and Jerry Janger lend good support, and Freddie Bell and His Bellboys offer "Get the First Train Out of Town."

Benjamin H. Kline's realistic photography heads off okay technical credits. *Whit.*

Running Target

(COLOR)

Interesting, somewhat offbeat outdoor actioner rates as okay programmer, but could be cut.

United Artists release of Canyon Pictures (Jack C. Couffer) production. Stars Doris Dowling, Arthur Franz, Richard Reeves; features Myron Healy, James Parnell, Charles Delaney. Directed by Marvin R. Weinstein. Screenplay, Weinstein, Couffer, Conrad Hall, from original story by Steve Frazee; camera (DeLuxe Color), Hall; editor, Carlo Lodato; music, Ernest Gold. Previewed in N.Y., Nov. 14, '56. Running time, 83 MINS.

Smitty .... Doris Dowling
Scott .... Arthur Franz
Jaynes .... Richard Reeves
Kaygo .... Myron Healy
Pryor .... James Parnell
Barker .... Charles Delaney
Strothers .... James Anderson
Holesworth .... Gene Roth
Castagna .... Frank Richards
Weyerhauser .... Nicholas Rutgers

Although the logic of its character sketches and story line is sometimes elusive, "Running Target" still shapes as an acceptable entry for the programmer market. As backgrounded in the Colorado Rockies, nicely lensed in DeLuxe Color, the Jack C. Couffer production springs upon its audience a switch from the routine in outdoor material, this being a sheriff's aversion to killing escaped convicts.

Man with the badge is Arthur Franz, who sets out in pursuit of four desperadoes on the loose. Where the film goes awry is in its depiction of others in the posse with Franz. Doris Dowling is the femme member, her presence being explained by the fact that the convicts had held up her gasoline station. But at near the final fade she's shown romancing the leader of the prisoners. It's difficult to savvy her motivations.

Also, there's Richard Reeves, a bar owner who, in the name of justice, is bent on a sadistic killing of the escaped men. He and Franz are at opposite poles, the latter being a moody softie who feels those he's running down have a right to live.

Franz, Miss Dowling and Reeves handle the parts competently though of course, this type of lower-case production makes relatively small histrionic demands. Myron Healy, James Parnell and Charles Delaney, among others in subordinate roles, similarly are adequate.

Marvin R. Weinstein's direction works up a fair amount of general interest and the cinematographic values are good. But the director uses too much footage in getting the story told and tighter editing could help alleviate this.

Music and technical credits all fair enough. *Gene.*

Los Amantes
(The Lovers)
(MEXICAN)

Uneven Latin treatise on sex. Some offbeat casting. Fine for language situations but dubious otherwise.

Mexico City, Nov.. 13.
Peliculas Nacionales release of a Cinematografica Latino Americana production. produced by Eduardo Quevedo. Stars Yolanda Varela, Carlos Baena. Directed by Benito Alazraki. Screenplay, Rafael Garcia Travos from original by Francisco Rejas Gonzalez and Benito Alazraki. Camera, Rosalio Solano; editor, Gloria Schoemann; music, Raul LaVista. At Cine Arcadia, Mexico City, Nov. 10, '56. Running time, 90 MINS.

Leticia .... Yolanda Varela
Juan .... Carlos Baena
Berta .... Amanda del Llano
El Raton ...... Jorge Martinez de Hoyos
Luis .... Hector Godoy
Luisa .... Sonia Furio
Juans' Mother......Hortencia Santovena
Don Pepito .... Rafael Labra
Madam La Concha .... Carolina Barret
Bar Girl .... Cleopatra Walkup

First to draw the Mexican censors' new "D" classification with the added comment, "Strictly for adults because of its prostitution theme," this not-as-sexy-as-it-sounds release should get plenty playing time in latin language situations. Its chances at U.S. art houses, for which it was evidently aimed, however, look slim. Technical faults are numerous; with poor sound recording, uneven lighting and sloppy cutting noted.

Script is realistic and sincere but never fully realized by either the films' authors, nor the tyro director, Benito Alazraki. Nevertheless the latter, in his theatrical film debut handles his cast and camera with some insight and feeling, suggesting that he may develop as directorial talent, badly needed here. Dialogue in Spanish is good.

Slight story tells of a mom-torn student who can't make up his mind between his undemonstrative fiancee and a hotter, passionate doll of the evening. Boy eventually leaves home to live with, and be supported by the latter, only to find that mother means most and that it's better to nurture love on the hearth than in any houri's hammock. At the fade boy leaves girl for mom and — possibly— sweetheart. The bawd heads for the states to continue her "career" on a dollar basis.

Attempt by the director to be realistic in his locales and atmosphere for this simple black and white tale saves the show pictorially. There are torrid bed scenes. Best of all is his producer Eduardo Quevedo's casting of numerous comparative newcomers in both minor and major roles, who give the film a new and more candid touch without going arty. Outstanding among these is Yolanda Varela, whose sensual sexpot tramp is handled with a mature restraint well beyond her years. Carlos Baena playing her indecisive lover is physically well cast, but lacks the potential for the big leagues. As a barroom tart, Cleopatra Walkup (No kidding, it's her real moniker), gives her bit part a standout quality. Rafael Labra takes a trite comedy role as a comedy grandfather and gives it surprising freshness.

Jorge Martinez de Hoyos also gives a sensitive reading to his miming as a second rate bullfighter, saving the role from becoming just another conventional latin caricature. Only miscasting is Sonia Furio, whose colorless performance as the "hero's" betrothed gives too good cause for his dilemma, if such it is. Rest of the cast give well delineated performances with Elisa De Leon in a small bit as the floozies' mother taking top honors.

Technical credits rate no applause with Rosalio Solano photographing and Gloria Shoemann editing. Score by top local composer, Rau LaVista is far below his usual high standard. *Mayer.*

Baby Doll

Sex, hate and revenge wrapped up in a strictly offbeat yarn set vs. a white-trash Southern background. Controversial but could be b.o. dynamite.

Warner Bros. release of Elia Kazan (Newtown) production. Stars Karl Malden, Carroll Baker, Eli Wallach; features Mildred Dunnock, Lonny Chapman, Eades Hogue, Noah Williamson. Directed by Kazan; story and screenplay by Tennessee Williams; camera, Boris Kaufman; editor. Gene Milford; music, Kenyon Hopkins. Previewed in New York. Running time, 114 MINS.

Archie .... Karl Malden
Baby Doll .... Carroll Baker
Silva Vacarro .... Eli Wallach
Aunt Rose Comfort....Mildred Dunnock
Rock .... Lonny Chapman
Town Marshal .... Eades Hogue
Deputy .... Noah Williamson

There's presumably never been any doubt that another combo of Tennessee Williams and Elia Kazan would produce an explosive, provocative motion picture, distinctly out of the normal screen frame of reference and probing into emotional strata not usually touched by Hollywood. "Baby Doll" is precisely that kind of film; and if sensationalism in theme and exploitation can put a picture over the top (as it has in most instances in the past), this Kazan entry should make a barrel of dough. Moralists will perhaps fight that result.

It is not a pleasant picture. Few of Williams' stories are, and Kazan is too good a director to allow the negative qualities to be polished into positive ones by the Production Code or anyone else. What some people will be wondering after seeing "Baby Doll" is how it got by the Code office in the first place.

For this film, while certainly not visually offensive in its treatment of sex, nevertheless is probably one of the strongest to come out of Hollywood. It is a raw, shattering experience, surcharged with red-hot emotionalism and directed and acted with such skill that some of the socalled "sexy" pix of the past seem like child's play.

There will inevitably be those who will call "Baby Doll" bordering on the obscene, and it has a highly suggestive element in it. Except for moments of humor that are strictly inherent in the character of the principals, "Baby Doll" plays off against a sleazy, dirty, depressing Southern background. Over it hangs a feeling of decay, expertly nurtured by Kazan who probably here turns in his greatest directing job to date. All of the people in this film are ugly in their own way and eaten up with hate and resentment. That's true of the leading characters and it shows up in the flashes of the townspeople, their poker-faced expressions passing in an unforgettable gallery of the deep South.

Out of his actors—Karl Malden as Archie, Carroll Baker as Baby Doll and Eli Wallach as Vacarro— Kazan has drawn superb performances. None are marquee names now. All will mean more after this film. Miss Baker in particular shapes as one of the most important film finds in decades.

"Baby Doll" is based on a 15-year-old Williams vignette, dramatized on Broadway in 1955 as "27 Wagons Full of Cotton." Williams here has done his own screenplay, taking out some of the more sadistic aspects of the original story. What's left is still a gall-bitter, uncompromising yarn that churns in hate and revels in its examination of the ugliness and shallowness of man. For once, ads will not disappoint those who come expecting hardhitting screen fare. Some may consider this a huge and welcome step in the screen's road towards maturity. Others may violently object to it as thinly-disguised smut.

Whatever the point-of-view—and it is usually determined by how strong are one's moral inhibitions—"Baby Doll" ranks as a major screen achievement and deserves to be recognized as such. Whether it rates as "entertainment" in the traditional sense of the word is another question.

Story briefly has Miss Baker, an immature teenager, married to middleaged Malden who runs a cotton gin. When their on-credit furniture is carted away, Malden sets fire to the Syndicate cotton gin in town. Suspecting Malden, Wallach—owner of the gin—carts his cotton to Malden's gin for processing but then proceeds to seduce Miss Baker who signs a note confessing that Malden committed the arson. Malden, who has promised not to touch his young wife until one year after their marriage (the year is almost up as the picture starts) finds Miss Baker and Wallach together in the house, suspects their relations and goes beserk with jealousy.

Miss Baker's performance captures all the animal charm, the naivete, the vanity, contempt and rising passion of the pretty flirtatious Baby Doll. Her voice, with its Southern sing-song, her movements and her overall acting make her a top contender for this year's Academy Award. Whether spittin' fire at Malden or flirting with Wallach, she etches a startingly true-to-life figure that fairly seethes with emotion.

Wallach as the vengeful Vacarro plays it to the hilt and establishes himself as a top player. His Sicilian is tough and angry, and yet underneath tinged with compassion, particularly in the final scenes. He and Miss Baker play a love scene (without kisses, if you please) on a swing outside the house that sizzles with tension. Kazan can take credit for this as one of the most revealing emotional sequences ever to be played on the screen.

Malden, the resentful, dour, sweaty husband, is cast to perfection and turns in a sock performance. He is hateful and lecherous as he bores a hole in the wall to observe his child bride curled up in her baby crib, sucking her thumb; yet he is also pitiful in his final desperation when he suspects Baby Doll's unfaithfulness, can't prove it and then goes on a drunken prowl for Vacarro.

But regardless of how good the performances, this is still Kazan's picture. It was shot down in Benoit, Mississippi, and the realism—complete with many references to "wops" and "niggers"— stands the film in good stead. The characters look real and they sound real; there is wild, teasing madness as Vacarro frightens Baby Doll in the empty house and then plays his deadly game of hide-and-seek with her to obtain the confession; there is drama in the burning cotton gin mill; there is raw passion in the Baker-Wallach embrace.

There is a good deal of Williams' original stage dialog in this opus, and despite its action, the symbolisms and the occasional sophisticated touches may be over the audiences' heads. There may be laughs in the wrong places, for Williams' humor is not necessarily popular and his occasional straining for effects may call for guffaws where none were intended. "Baby Doll" runs on a powerful line and its ugly cruelty—and sometimes viciousness—come across with undiminished fury, glazed with the aura of decadence.

Everyone in this is good. Mildred Dunnock as the pathetic Aunt Rose Comfort, tolerated and abused by Malden, contributes very importantly. Lonny Chapman as Vacarro's assistant, Eades Hogue as the Town Marshal and Noah Williamson as his deputy, all do yeoman service.

Boris Kaufman's lensing (wisely in black-and-white) is fully in tune with the story itself. His camera never intrudes, but accentuates the action, giving it intimacy and hinting subtly at the dammed-up torrents of hate in the players. It is exceedingly fine camera work. Gene Milford's editing and Kenyon Hopkins' music contribute in equal measure.

"Baby Doll" is the kind of rare screen art (and art it is, pretty or not) that towers high as b.o. bait. It is also an excellent argument for some sort of rating system that would automatically exclude the teenage set. *Hift.*

La Tercera Palabra
(The Third Word) (MEXICAN)

Mexico City, Nov. 27.

Peliculas Nacionales release of Cinematografica Filmex production. Stars Pedro Infante, Marga Lopez; features Rodolfo Landa, Miguel Angel Ferriz, Emma Roldan, Eduardo Alcaraz, Manuel Tamez, Prudencia Grifell, Sara Garcia. Directed by Julian Soler. Screenplay by Alejandro Casona; adaptation, Antonio Matouk; cameraman, Jose Ortiz Ramos. At Cine Variedades, Mexico City. Running time, **100 MINS.**

An offbeat story, that of a grownup nature boy on a prosperous Mexican rancho and two Mexican 1955 Oscar winners make this beautifully lensed production good entertainment despite an uneven yarn. It played several big weeks at a swank first-run here.

Top player is Pedro Infante and his singing of five songs is standout. He was Oscared as Mexico's head actor last year. Almost costarring with him is Marga Lopez, the Argentinian brunette looker, who for a decade has been a big name in Mexican pix. Ace character woman of 1955, Prudenica Grifell, a big stage name before she went into pix, and Rodolfo Landa, headman of the National Actors Union, lend strong support. Sara Garcia, longtime stage-pic star, also is excellent.

Infante adroitly plays the role of a baby raised by two aunts, one a widow, the other a spinster (Misses Grifell and Garcia), far into manhood by them. At 28, he is a big strong man but a gentleman, withal. Then they decide that he should get a schooling, and hire Miss Lopez as tutoress. She wants to walk out when it looks as if she's the victim of a gag since her pupil is some years her senior. But the dear old ladies and Pedro plus a snug ranch, with horseback riding, hunting, fishing and big pay induce her to stay on. *Doug.*

Four Girls in Town
(C'SCOPE-COLOR)

Hollywood talent search background gives fair interest for general dual bookings.

Hollywood, Dec. 4.

Universal release of Aaron Rosenberg production. Stars George Nader, Julie Adams, Sydney Chaplin, Marianne Cook, Elsa Martinelli, Grant Williams, Gia Scala, John Gavin. Written and directed by Jack Sher. Camera (Technicolor), Irving Gliassberg; editor, Fredrick Y. Smith; music supervision, Joseph Gershenson; special theme "Rhapsody For Four Girls" composed by Alex North. Previewed Nov. 20, '56. Running time, **85 MINS.**

Mike Snowden .... George Nader
Kathy Sonway .... Julie Adams
Johnny Pryor .... Sydney Chaplin
Ina Schiller .... Marianne Cook
Maria Antonelli .... Elsa Martinelli
Spencer Farrington, Jr. .... Grant Williams
Vicki Dauray .... Gia Scala
Tom Grant .... John Gavin
Ted Larabee .... Herbert Anderson
Bob Trapp .... Hy Averback
James Manning .... Ainslie Pryor
William Purdy .... Judson Pratt
Walter Conway .... James Bell
Mrs. Conway .... Mabel Albertson
Vince .... Dave Barry
Henri .... Maurice Marsac
Rita Holloway .... Helene Stanton
Mildred Purdy .... Irene Corlett
Paul .... Eugene Mazzola

A talent hunt is an old Hollywood device to get publicity for an upcoming production. "Four Girls In Town" goes a bit further; it puts the hunt on film, using it as the story peg, to showcase some new faces and to further the recognition of talent that has been on the Universal lot for several seasons. The combo, while spotty entertainment, gives the picture fair interest for the regular run of dual bookings.

The Universal lot, here tagged Manning, is excellently utilized in the Aaron Rosenberg production to emphasize the backstage Hollywood angle, and the authentic setting gains in value from the CinemaScope lensing in Technicolor. Where film comes up short mostly is spreading the interest among too many characters since there is bound to be a repetitious quality in dealing with four hopefuls in the same story. Jack Sher both wrote and directed. While some scenes score strongly, largely because of the talent involved, others are flat and ordinary, so his dual function is uneven.

Out of the showcasing, Marianne Cook, German actress, emerges a definite click. Italian actress Elsa Martinelli, already seen in a Hollywood-made pic, also scores, with emphasis on an earthy, s.a. quality. Good, too, is Gia Scala, another from Italy. Holding up stateside honors are Julie Adams, at Universal for some time; George Nader, also long on the lot, and such newer faces as Sydney Chaplin, very good; Grant Williams and John Gavin. Other casters handles their chores ably.

Helene Stanton, seen mostly from the rear with a Monroe-type wiggle to her walk, will cause some chuckles as the star who refuses a big role, resulting in the talent hunt which finds the hopefuls at the studio to be tested by embryo director Nader. Plot tells bits of each's story and windup finds none getting the coveted part, Miss Stanton changed her mind, if not her walk, and there's a romantic pairing up of males and females for the finale.

Alex North composed "Rhapsody For Four Girls," theme heard through the background score and Irving Glassberg handles his cameras to advantage. Costuming by Rosemary Odell bedecks the femmes beautifully and Fredrick Y. Smith's editing is good. *Brog.*

Nightfall
(SONG)

Fair action-suspense entry for the duals.

Columbia release of Copa (Ted Richmond) production. Stars Aldo Ray, Brian Keith, Anne Bancroft; features Jocelyn Brando, James Gregory, Frank Albertson, Rudy Bond. Directed by Jacques Tourneur. Screenplay, Stirling Silliphant, from novel by David Goodis; camera, Burnett Guffey; editor, William A. Lyon; music, George Duning, conducted by Morris Stoloff. Previewed N.Y., Nov. 29, '56. Running time, **78 MINS.**

James Vanning .... Aldo Ray
John .... Brian Keith
Marie Gardner .... Anne Bancroft
Laura Fraser .... Jocelyn Brando
Ben Fraser .... James Gregory
Dr. Edward Gurston .... Frank Albertson
Red .... Rudy Bond
Bus Driver .... George Cisar
Taxi Driver .... Eddie McLean
Woman .... Lillian Culver
Woman .... Maya Van Horn
Spanish Man .... Orlando Beltran
Spanish Woman .... Maria Belmar
Shoe Shine Boy .... Walter Smith

Although there's a generous slice of mystery, action and suspense in "Nightfall," this modest budgeter adds up to only a fair entertainment for the duals. Story is too reminiscent of similar material ground out of the script mills in the past. Of some b.o. help, however, will be the familiar names of Aldo Ray, Brian Keith and Anne Bancroft.

The Stirling Silliphant screenplay, based on the novel by David Goodis, employs several flashbacks to disclose that Ray is on the lam in an attempt to prove himself innocent of murdering a hunting companion and of complicity in a bank heist. Actual culprits are Keith and Rudy Bond who unwittingly lost the loot and are convinced that Ray knows where it is.

Also involved in the proceedings are Miss Bancroft, a model who first puts the finger on Ray and later falls for his charms; and James Gregory, an insurance sleuth with a hunch that Ray is guiltless. Since murderers always return to the scene of a crime, the characters all converge by chance in the snowswept Wyoming mountains. There the money is found, the thieves killed in a scuffle and Ray revealed as innocent.

Performances of most of the players are of a mechanical nature. However, Ray is suitably laconic as a man saved from a phony rap; Keith is okay as a bank robber with an occasional redeeming quality, Miss Bancroft supplies adequate romantic interest and Bond is a typical hard guy. Gregory is quiet and methodical as the insurance investigator and Jocelyn Brando is seen briefly as the former's wife.

Jacques Tourneur's direction manages to extract the action and suspense in Silliphant's par-for-the-course screenplay. Ted Richmond, who produced the Copa production, tossed in some above average values including a fashion show by the J. W. Robinson Co. of California. Physical backgrounds and action scenes show up nicely in Burnett Guffey's black-and-white lensing. Also good is Ross Bellah's are direction.

There's a fairish title tune with lyrics by Sam M. Lewis plus music by Peter DeRose and Charles Harold. It's appealingly sung by Al Hibbler's offscreen voice. *Gilb.*

Hollywood or Bust
(SONGS—COLOR)

Martin & Lewis in cross-country comedy caper; entertainment uneven. B.o. prospects okay.

Hollywood, Dec. 4.

Paramount release of Hal Wallis production. Stars Dean Martin, Jerry Lewis; costars Pat Crowley, Maxie Rosenbloom, Anita Ekberg. Directed by Frank Tashlin. Written by Erna Lazarus; camera (Technicolor), Daniel Fapp; editor, Howard Smith; music arranged, conducted by Walter Scharf; musical numbers, Charles O'Curran; songs, Sammy Fain, Paul Francis Webster. Previewed Nov. 19, '56. Running time, **94 MINS.**

Steve Wiley .... Dean Martin
Malcolm Smith .... Jerry Lewis
Herself .... Anita Ekberg
Terry .... Pat Crowley
Bookie Benny .... Maxie Rosenbloom

Hollywood's in the label and does make a finale appearance, but most of this comedy caper takes place on a cross-country junket from New York, with way stops enroute, including Las Vegas. While the laugh pace overall is uneven, there's still enough that's very funny to keep the Martin & Lewis fans amused so the box-office prospects are good.

This one was lensed pre-separation and the boys go together like hot dogs and mustard. That Erna Lazarus plot framework is mighty light, being principally a setting for frenetics and gag situations in-between five Sammy Fain-Paul Francis Webster songs and a couple of just passable production numbers.

Hal Wallis decks the production in Vista Vision and Technicolor, with Daniel Fapp's cameras taking good care of all the scenic points of interest across the country. Direction by Frank Tashlin scores enough comedy highspots to keep the pace fairly fast, even with the slow spots that his handling and the team's talent cannot overcome. One of the film's funniest bits comes before the title with Dean Martin introducing Jerry Lewis as different types of movie-watchers. Lewis' encounter with a bull and making like a matador is another fun-filled sequence, as is his champagne binge in Vegas after hexing the gambling devices into a big payoff. Team has to split honors for laughs with a huge Great Dane, Mr. Bascom, Lewis' pet.

By way of making the latter part of the title legit, Anita Ekberg appears as guest star on whom Lewis has a crush. She doesn't have much more to do than to display what nature has wrought in the fjords of Sweden, so it's still a big part. She's the attraction that enables Martin to talk Lewis into the cross-country trip after they have won a car (Lewis legally, Martin illegally with forged tickets) in a theatre drawing. Enroute west they pick up Pat Crowley so that Martin will have someone to sing romantic songs to and all end up in the film capital where Mr. Bascom becomes the picture star.

A title tune, plus "A Day in the Country," "It Looks Like Love," "Let's Be Friendly" and "The Wild and Woolly West" all fall pleasantly on the ear when Martin is doing the vocalling. Lewis cuts a raucous vocal here and there, too, and even Miss Crowley joins in on occasion. As usual, Martin sets up most of the gags for Lewis' comedic talents to milk and they come off very well as a clowning team. Miss Crowley makes out pertly in the situations, but obviously had a false friend among the designers of her more personal garb. Maxie Rosenbloom as a bookie muscleman completes the credited cast.

Technical credits tee up excellently in supplying visual gloss to the footage, and Walter Scharf's arranging and conducting of the music scores nicely, too. *Brog.*

The Wild Party

Hard-boiled sex and sadism, backed by a crazy jive beat. For exploitation situations.

Hollywood, Nov. 28.

United Artists release of Sidney Harmon (Security Pictures) production. Stars Anthony Quinn, Carol Ohmart, Arthur Franz, Jay Robinson, Kathryn Grant, Nehemiah Persoff, features Paul Stewart, Nestor Paiva, Buddy de Franco Quartet. Directed by Harry Horner. Story and screenplay, John McPartland; camera, Sam Leavitt; editor, Richard C. Meyer; music, Buddy Bregman. Previewed Nov. 26, '56. Running time, **82 MINS.**

Tom Kupfen .... Anthony Quinn
Erica London .... Carol Ohmart
Arthur Mitchell .... Arthur Franz
Gage Freeposter .... Jay Robinson
Honey .... Kathryn Grant
Kicks Johnson ...... Nehemiah Persoff
Ben David .... Paul Stewart
Sandy .... Barbara Nichols
Singer .... Jana Mason
Wino .... William Phipps
Ellen .... Maureen Stephenson
Branson .... Nestor Paiva
Bouncer .... Michael Ross
Customer .... Carl Milletaire
Barman .... James Bronte
Fat Man .... Joe Greene

Hard-boiled sex and sadism, set to a crazy jive beat and aptly titled "The Wild Party," is the type of entertainment offered in this United Artists release. It's the kind of filmfare that, with lurid ballyhoo, attracts the more impressionable and wilder elements among the younger viewers, so exploitation dates may payoff.

A deliberate shock approach is used in the Sidney Harmon production to portray a seamy side of life filled with unwholesome characters and situations. Robbery, rape, sadistic murder, even implied dope addiction, are common parts of the film. The weird dialog used in John McPartland's screen story belongs to a peculiar sect and, if you don't dig it, its not easy to follow the plot, even though Harry Horner's direction spells everything else out in basic ABCs.

None of the cast has any particularly endearing characteristics, but within the demands of story and direction the players do what is asked of them with professional dispatch in most instances. Anthony Quinn appears as a pro football has-been with only animal desires and muscles left over from his brief fame. He hangs out in dark jive cellars and shabby sections of the city with such companions as Jay Robinson, foppish, knife-wielding sadist; Kathryn Grant, apathetic young girl hanger-on to the ex-gridiron hero, and Nehemiah Persoff, piano player who lives in a dreamy, shadow world.

The title action more-or-less refers to this combo's plan to rob Carol Ohmart, excitement-seeking society girl, and her fiance, Naval Lieutenant Arthur Franz. Through plot contrivances which have little concern with logic, the group kidnaps the engaged couple and hides out in an abandoned beach amusement building. This sets the scene for plenty of brutality and lust before the incredible ending sees Quinn dead and the victims freed.

Others in the cast have only small spots. Sam Leavitt's low-key lensing goes with the plot's mood, as does the score by Buddy Bregman. The jive beat is maintained by the Buddy de Franco Quartet, heard in a cellar dive sequence and elsewhere. *Brog.*

Tiger in the Smoke
(BRITISH)

Well adapted Margery Allingham thriller with Muriel Pavlow, Donald Sinden, Tony Wright involved in gangster's hunt for hidden treasure; medium b.o. prospects anywhere.

London, Nov. 27.

Rank production and release. Stars Donald Sinden, Murial Pavlow and Tony Wright; co-stars Bernard Miles, Alec Clunes and Laurence Naismith. Directed by Roy Baker. Screenplay by Anthony Pelissier from book by Margery Allingham; camera, Geoffrey Unsworth; editor, John D. Guthridge; music, Malcolm Arnold. At Leicester Square Theatre, London. Running time, **94 MINS.**

Geoffrey Levett .... Donald Sinden
Meg Elgin .... Muriel Pavlow
Jack Havoc .... Tony Wright
Tiddy Doll .... Bernard Miles
Assistant Commissioner .... Alec Clunes
Canon Avril .... Laurence Naismith
Chief Inspector Luke Christopher Rhodes
Will Talisman .... Charles Victor
Roly Gripper .... Thomas Heathcote
Tom Gripper .... Sam Kydd
Crutches .... Kenneth Griffith
Duds Morrison .... Gerald Harper
Detective Segt. Pickett... Wensley Pithey
Uncle .... Stanley Rose
P.C. Perkins .... Stratford Johns
Trumps .... Brian Wilde
Mrs. Talisman .... Hilda Barry
Mrs. Cash .... Beatrice Varley

An intriguing, nearly plausible screenplay has been made from a book by Margery Allingham, an ace English thriller writer. With a sterling cast, and not over complicated plot, the result is good general entertainment.

Although many loose ends are left trailing, the story details how a group of ex-soldiers and petty crooks who parade as street musicians awaiting their leader just from via a jailbreak. Through a wartime association, he knows of a French seashore mansion containing buried treasure, and plans to steal the address and directions from the widow of the man concerned. She is on the verge of remarrying and gets mysterious pictures of her husband mailed to her, with the implication he is still alive. Scenting blackmail, she goes to the police who tie it all in with the escaped convict and some subsequent murders. The killer rushes down the cliffside clutching the loot only to be trapped by French and British police. Treasure turns out to be a statue of the Madonna, priceless, but useless to a thief.

Most of the action is set in fog laden London city streets, stressing the mystery and suspense. Direction and camera work enhance the realism of the scenes.

Muriel Pavlow ably displays nerve tension and anxiety throughout the entire picture, with Donald Sinden exhibiting bulldog tenacity as her impending mate. Tony Wright is making his mark in the cold killer type of roles and this one fits him like a glove. Odd assortment of crooks are convincingly portrayed. Dignity of the law is well represented by Christopher Rhodes and Alec Clunes. Lawrence Naismith as the girl's father and Charles Victor as his cockney servant bring a mellow touch to their gentler roles. Beatrice Varley turns in a realistic bit of subdued venom as the criminal's mother. *Clem.*

Foreign Films

Paris, Nov. 20.

Toute La Ville Accuse (The Whole Town Accuses) **(FRENCH).** SN-Egyra release of Radius production. Stars Jean Marais; features Etchika Choureau, Noel Roquevert, Francois Patrice. Directed by Claude Boissol. Screenplay, Boissol, Georges Combret; camera, L. Burel; editor, Dumesnil. At Cardinet, Paris. Running time, **90 MINS.**

Pic by a new young director, Claude Boissol, has emerged as a sleeper here, and though slight, might do for U.S. special situations on its happy entertainment values. It needs hypo but has narrative force. This concerns a writer who goes to a little town to work and suddenly finds himself daily recipient of a bag of money. First, he hides it but later decides to begin to use it carefully and for charitable purposes which arouses the town.

Boissol displays fine feeling for film storytelling, with the gentle mood only dissipated by a rather gratuitous explanation of how the money was left by some juveniles who stumbled onto the cache of some dead gangsters. It is adroitly acted with good technical credits. Though tenuous and reminiscent of many American comedies, it still bears freshness. *Mosk.*

La Vie Est Belle (Life Is Beautiful) **(FRENCH).** Gamma release of Davis-Gamma Film production. Stars Roger Pierre, Jean-Marc Thibault; features Colette Ricard, Veronique Zuber, Noel Roquevert. Directed by Pierre and Thibault. Screenplay, Danielle Haik, adapted by Pierre and Thibault; camera, Gustave Raulet; editor, Paule Patier. At Triomphe, Paris. Running time, **90 MINS.**

Popular nitery and music hall comedy team, Roger Pierre and Jean-Marc Thibault, have made their first pic as composite authors, directors and thesps. Their zesty in-person appeal is used in a series of sketches loosely tied up by a story. Here two young couples win a house together but their attempt at communal living leads to much friction and enmity.

Although commonplace in film form these domestic tiffs make for some yocks via the fresh clowning of the pair aided by some solid comedy character performers. It hasn't the weight for U.S. arty spots; hence, its main appeal could only be paring down for U.S. video. Technical credits are good. *Mosk.*

Pitie Pour Les Vamps (Pity for the Vamps) **(FRENCH; DYALISCOPE; COLOR).** Fernand Rivers production and release. Stars Viviane Romance; features Gisele Pascal, Jacqueline Noelle, Yves Robert, Genevieve Kervine, Jean Meyer. Directed by Jean Josipovici. Screenplay, France Roche, Robert Chazal, Josipovici; camera (Ferranicolor), Marc Fossard; editor, Paul Cayatte. At Triomphe, Paris. Running time, **105 MINS.**

This quickie will do nothing for anamorphoscoped pix. Lagging tale of an aging film star who sacrifices her man to a younger sister gets little depth or character relief. Direction is static and technical aspects below par, with this Gallic process still off in clarity. Acting is ordinary but Viviane Romance is adequate. *Mosk.*

La Plus Belles Des Vies (The Most Beautiful Life) **(FRENCH).** UGC release of CCA production. Written and directed by Claude Vermorel. Camera, Walter Wottitz; editor, Jean Douarinou. With Claire Maffei, Jean-Pierre Kerien, Roger Pigaut, Lucien Raimbourg, Alssia Barry, Nabi Youla. At Raimu, Paris. Running time, **120 MINS.**

This concerns a French teacher's dedication to his task of enlighting the natives of French West Africa. Made under government auspices, pic details the odyssey of the teacher and his wife who finally make contact with the natives, but not before they lose their only child, the wife has a breakdown and almost runs off with a young engineer.

Too literary, this is overlong. It has an interest in its locale. For the U.S., this shapes primarily for secondary spots and even there needs pruning to make more taut. Economy of means is evident but acting is good and technical credits fair. *Mosk.*

C'Est Arrive A Oden (It Happened In Aden (FRENCH; DYALISCOPE; COLOR). Cocinor release of S. B. Films production. Stars Dany Robin, Jacques Dacqmine; features Robert Manuel, Jacques Duby, Elina Labourdette, Andre Luguet. Versini, Dominique Page, Michel Etcheverry. Directed by Michel Boisrond. Screenplay, Jean Aurel, Boisrond from novel by Pierre Benoit; dialog, Constance Colline, Jacques Emmanuel; camera (Eastmancolor), Marcel Grignon; editor, Claudine Bouche. At Biarritz, Paris. Running time, **90 MINS.**

Mock adventure tale has proper tongue-in-cheek quality to make a diverting entry. Obvious aspects of a secondrate acting troupe stranded in India, with Anglo lieutenants and princes fighting over the pert, flirty ingenue, get a clever going over. For America, it does not seem suited for art houses. Film's comic touch makes this a possibility for dualers. Its screen size is akin to C'Scope, this process having good definition.

An acting troupe is bogged down in a British possession. The leading actress becomes a pawn in politics as a native prince falls for her and will sign a treaty only if he has her. Her lover, an English lieutenant, asks her to help but they do not reckon with her Gallic temperament.

Director Michel Boisrond has given this neat style. Slapstick mixes with adventure and romance as the young girl's love affairs are depicted. Dany Robin has the proper coquettish qualities as the girl while the actors all are adequate. Production values and technical credits are good. Film lacks name values except for Dany Robin. *Mosk.*

The Rainmaker
(COLOR—V'VISION)

Burt Lancaster and Katharine Hepburn in expert adaptation of the N. Richard Nash play; strong boxoffice prospects.

Paramount release of Hal Wallis production. Stars Burt Lancaster, Katharine Hepburn; features Wendell Corey, Lloyd Bridges, Earl Holliman, Cameron Prud'homme, Wallace Ford, Yvonne Lime. Directed by Joseph Anthony. Screenplay, N. Richard Nash, adapted from his play; camera (Technicolor), Charles Lang Jr.; editor, Warren Low; music, Alex North. Previewed at Loew's 72d Street Theatre, N. Y., Dec. 6, '56. Running time, **121 MINS.**

Starbuck	Burt Lancaster
Lizzie Curry	Katharine Hepburn
File	Wendell Corey
Noah Curry	Lloyd Bridges
Jim Curry	Earl Holliman
H. C. Curry	Cameron Prud'homme
Sheriff Thomas	Wallace Ford
Snookie	Yvonne Lime
Belinda	Dottie Bee Baker
Deputy	Dan White
Sheriff	Michael Bachus
Townsman	Stan Jones
Townsman	John Benson
Townsman	James Stone
Townsman	Tony Merrill
Townsman	Joe Brown
Phil Mackey	Ken Becker

The N. Richard Nash play, which ran 124 performances on Broadway, has been fashioned into a solid screen entertainment. With Burt Lancaster turning in perhaps his most colorful performance as the ingratiating con man, and Katharine Hepburn offering a freewheeling interpretation of a spinster in search of romance, the adaptation is a click show all around. It's doubtless destined to take in tall money.

Nash's own screenplay stays close to the original, establishing the title character right at the start and then moving into the story of how the smooth-talking fraud pretends to bring rain to a drought-stricken ranch area. It's humorously and imaginatively done against unusually effective sets.

Although the unreeling takes 121 minutes, director Joseph Anthony, who called the turns on the stage original and is herewith making his film debut, does a remarkable job of maintaining pace. The play moves smoothly and engagingly all the way whereas, in less competent hands, it could have become static at several points. "Rainmaker" often is wordy but there's comic action, too, and this helps the movement.

Locale is the southwestern town of Three Point where Lancaster, arriving in his outlandish wagon, sets out to pick up $100 on his promise of bringing a vitally-needed downpour. He comes into contact with rancher Cameron Prud'homme and his family, comprising Miss Hepburn as the daughter, two sons, Lloyd Bridges, who's stern and practical, and Earl Holliman, a clumsy, likeable youngster.

In addition to the drought, they're concerned with finding a husband for Miss Hepburn and figure a likely candidate is Wendell Corey, who plays a sheriff.

That's the setup, Lancaster, although he's obviously a con artist, is permitted to live in Prud'homme's tack house and work his rain magic. He convinces Miss Hepburn that she's pretty, and not plain as Bridges insists. As matters work out, the neglected Miss Hepburn finds herself with two suitors, Lancaster and the previously-reluctant Corey. And, of course, the climax brings a beaut of a thunder storm, for which Lancaster assumes credit.

The performances are fine all around. In spellbinding his way into the rancher's home and

charming Miss Hepburn into believing she has looks, Lancaster is standout. Miss Hepburn does a winning job as the spinster, discouraged by the lack of male attention shown to her but managing to make fun of the situation.

Holliman, a relative newcomer, is a funny youngster. Whether wooing the town cutie, Yvonne Lime, or awkwardly interfering in family matters, he plays his comedy role in broad fashion for a good laugh payoff. Miss Lime, who has one of the smaller parts, scores handily.

Prud'homme as the easy-going father, Corey as the sheriff, Bridges as the elder brother and Wallace Ford in a lesser role all assist in making "Rainmaker" a delight.

The Hal Wallis production is nicely set off in Technicolor and the camera work by Charles Lang Jr. is top notch. Music and technical credits all are strictly plus. *Gene.*

Dance With Me Henry

Abbott and Costello return to screen in okay programmer.

Hollywood, Dec. 11.

United Artists release of a Bob Goldstein production. Stars Bud Abbott, Lou Costello. Features Gigi Perreau, Rusty Hamer, Mary Wicks, Ted De Corsia. Ron Hargrave. Directed by Charles Barton. Screenplay, Devery Freeman; original story, William Kozlenko, Leslie Kardos; camera; George Robinson; music, Paul Dunlap; editor, Robert Golden. Previewed Dec. 4, '56. Running time, **80 MINS.**

Lou Henry	Lou Costello
Bud Flick	Bud Abbott
Shelley	Gigi Perreau
Duffer	Rusty Hamer
Miss Mayberry	Mary Wickes
Big Frank	Ted De Corsia
Ernie	Ron Hargrave
Bootsie	Sherry Alberoni
Father Mullahy	Frank Wilcox
Mushie	Richard Reeves
Dutch	Paul Sorenson
Proctor	Robert Shayne
Knucks	John Cliff
Muckey	Phil Garris
Drake	Walter Reed
Garvey	Eddie Marr
Savoldi	David McMahon
McKay	Gil Rankin
Porter	Rod Williams

Their first screen appearance in more than 18 months and initialer since bowing out of Universal last year, Bud Abbott and Lou Costello are back with familiar clowning in this Bob Goldstein indie. Carrying more story line than in most past A-C entries, film generally is quick-tempoed and spotted with enough laughs to satisfy comic's followers, particularly moppets, in the program market.

The Devery Freeman script centers on Costello as owner of Kiddyland, a moppet carnival, and prone to adopt strays, human and otherwise. One of these is Abbott, whose huge gambling debts Costello is trying to pay off. This situation leads to all the plot complications which include Costello becoming a suspect in murder of the District Attorney and his involvement with gangsters. Charles Barton, who directed many of comics' earlier films, is back again on the job, his know-how responsible for pair's smooth routines and fast windup in which a flock of orphans help beleaguered duo out of their difficulties with baddies.

Comics are up to their usual par in impersonations, Costello snagging the sympathy as Mr. Big Heart who continually is having trouble with an old maid Welfare Department worker who would take his two adopted kids away from him. Abbott straights in okay fashion as his partner. Gigi Per-

reau and Rusty Hamer are good as Costello's youngsters, and Mary Wickes as welfare worker. Ted De Corsia the gangster chief, Ron Hargrave a bopster, Frank Wilcox the orphanage head and Sherry Alberoni a little orphan who holds the key to the murder score in hefty support.

Technical credits lead off with George Robinson's fluid cameras and Robert Golden's sharp editing. *Whit.*

Rock, Rock, Rock!
(MUSIC)

Unimpressive rock and roller quickie concocted for some fast b.o. cash.

Hollywood, Dec. 7.

Distributor Corp. of America release of Max J. Rosenberg, Milton Subotsky (Vanguard) production. Stars Alan Freed and orch; features Tuesday Weld, Teddy Randazzo, Jacqueline Kerr, Fran Manfred, Ivy Schulman, LaVern Baker, Chuck Berry, Frankie Lymon and The Teenagers. Directed by Will Price. Screenplay, Milton Subotsky; from story by Subotsky and Phyllis Coe; camera, Morris Hartzband; editor, Blandine Hafela; music direction, Subotsky; songs, Subotsky, Glen Moore, Al Weisman, Ben Weisman, Aaron Schroeder, Buddy Dufault, George Goldner, Johnny Parker, Al Sears, Charles E. Calhoun, Freddie Mitchell, Leroy Kirkland, Chuck Berry. Previewed Dec. 5, '56. Running time, **85 MINS.**

Dori	Tuesday Weld
Dori's Songs	Connie Francis
Gloria	Jacqueline Kerr
Baby	Ivy Schulman
Arabella	Fran Manfred
Father	Jack Collins
Mother	Carol Moss
Miss Silky	Eleanor Swayne
Mr. Bimble	Lester Mack
Mr. Barker	Bert Conway
Melville	David Winters

RECORDING ARTISTS:
Alan Freed (Coral)
Teddy Randazzo (Vik)
The Moonglows (Chess)
Chuck Berry (Chess)
The Flamingos (Chess)
Jimmy Cavallo House Rockers (Coral)
Johnny Burnette Trio (Coral)
LaVern Baker (Atlantic)
Cirino and The Bowties (Roost)
Frankie Lymon Teenagers (Gee)
Coney Island Kids (Josie)

With the trend to "pictures for teenagers," it follows that one emphasis would be on rock and roll subjects. That doesn't mean all will be good ones, or that teenage draw will give them a sustained market. Of lesser quality is this Vanguard production being released by DCA. It has the look of a pasted-together quickie aimed only at some fast b.o. cash.

The makers have assembled a mostly unimpressive array of rock and roll talent, although LaVern Baker knows her way around a song and proves it with "Tra La La." Good, too, is Chuck Berry

with "You Can't Catch Me." Frankie Lymon and The Teenagers get in some okay licks with two numbers, including "I'm Not a Juvenile Delinquent." Talent runs out of class after that, except for maybe Connie Francis, who does the off-screen vocaling for Tuesday Weld, teenager lead in the mediocre plot script by Milton Subotsky from a story he did with Phyllis Coe.

Subotsky also can take the rap for the poor production quality, sharing this with Max J. Rosenberg, and the musical direction. Sound recording is unusually bad, many of the numbers being completely out of sync with the actor action. There's even a phony applause track thrown in, ala many tv shows.

There's not much Will Price's direction could make of the story or talent in telling a plot about a teenager who wants to get a strapless gown to wear to the high school prom and goes through all kinds of agonies to raise the necessary coin. Interspersed are the assorted acts introduced by Alan Freed, who's starred with his orchestra for no discernible reason other than he's a rock and roll expert in a few eastern spots. Band he fronts can't even. play good r&r. Some of the turns are so incredibly bad there is even a Presley-aping, guitar-playing, sideburned country singer named Johnny Burnette. Miss Weld, Teddy Randazzo, Jacqueline Kerr, Fran Manfred and others in the story portion have a long way to go.

Lensing, editing and other technical credits are low grade.

Brog.

'Un Condamne A Mort S'Est Echappe
(A Condemned Man Escaped) (FRENCH)

Paris, Dec. 4.
Gaumont release of Gaumont-SNE production. Directed by Robert Bresson. Screenplay Bresson from a true story by Andre Devigny; camera, L. H. Burel; editor, Raymond Lamy; music, Mozart. At Gaumont-Palace, Paris. Running time, 90 MINS.
Fontaine .... Francois Leterrier
Priest .... Roland Monod

Robert Bresson has only made three films before this, but is considered one of the most individual directors in Europe. His "Diary of a Country Priest" and "Angels of Sin" played the U.S. without much success. However, his latest emerges as an offbeat film that should insure arty house interest. Its break with film convention, in detailing the escape of a French resistance fighter from a Gestapo prison, is done with relentless use of the mechanics of the getaway without any recourse to familiar suspense tactics. This actually stresses a man's innate need for liberty without any shouting.

Bresson used no professional actors and made this on the actual spot where the real incident happened to Andre Devigny in 1943. Film quietly picks up the hero on the way to prison, with an attempted flight from the car causing him to be severely beaten and thrown into a cell. He begins his study of the situation and makes his resolve to escape. He meticulously takes his door apart and can soon get into the corridor at night.

Life in the cell, and stolen talk around a wash basin with other prisoners. He builds a rope from his bedding. A hook is made from a lantern frame and honed spoons serve as tools. Another man's attempted escape gives him the knowledge of the terrain—then he is condemned to death. On the eve of his escape a boy is put in his cell, though suspicious, he takes him along. Here, all the planning, the verve and dedication of director Bresson break into an absorbing, moving segment as the men make good their try.

It is a film art house managers cry for and yet often are afraid to show. It will need plenty of hypoing and remains mainly for specialize spots. However, critics and word-of-mouth should help. Nonpros all become a living part of the pic. Lensing is stark and crisp, and editing, sound and judicious use of Mozart music all combine in keeping the mood of the film intact.

Alternate title of film is "Le Vent Souffle Ou Il Veut" (The Wind Blows Where It Wants).

The picture's conciseness and tenseness make even a rustle of the hero's shirt and hair, by a sudden wind, during the escape into a vivid or startling moment. A restricted, offbeat pic, this is worth a U.S. try. It is heartening here to see an entry of this type getting a top "tandem" popular distribution in Paris. Film was done practically all in closeups, w't'l all unnecessary detail kept r to heighten its effect.

Mosk.

The Cruel Tower

Steeplejack yarn with enough chills to exploit for okay reception in program market.

Hollywood, Dec. 11.
Allied Artists release of a Lindsley Parsons production. Stars John Ericson, Mari Blanchard Charles McGraw; costars Steve Brodie; features Peter Whitley, Alan Hale, Diana Darrin, Carol Kelly, Barbara Bel Wright. Directed by Lew Landers. Screenplay, Warren Douglas; based on novel by William B. Hartley; camera, Ernest Haller; editor, Maurice Wright; music, Paul Dunlap. Previewed Nov. 30, 56. Running time, 79 MINS.
Tom .... John Ericson
Mary Thompson .... Mari Blanchard
Stretch .... Charles McGraw
Casey .... Steve Brodie
Joss .... Peter Whitney
Rocky .... Alan Hale
Kit .... Diana Darrin
Waitress .... Carol Kelly
Rev. Claver .... Barbara Bel Wright

This steeplejack yarn gets in its share of chills—particularly for the acrophobic-minded — to rate good reception in the program market, where it may be handily exploited. Characters are believable, direction and editing taut and idea is well-developed as a fast-paced melodrama.

Lindsley Parsons fashions his production around a compact cast from whom director Lew Landers draws interesting performances. Conflict is generated between Charles McGraw, boss of an itinerant crew of steeplejacks, and John Ericson, whom McGraw picks up after younger man is thrown off a freight train, over the affections of Mari Blanchard, blonde charmer whom both want to marry.

Thrills are inserted in the Warren Douglas script via the daily work on top of a tower and a sky-'reaching chimney. Climax is reached when McGraw falls off a scaffolding atop the chimney as he attempts to settle his differences with Ericson, who, though fearful of heights, has been bullied into becoming a jack.

Ericson delivers a solid characterization and McGraw scores in a rough-and-tumble impersonation of a violent man who intends to let nothing or no one bar his ambitions. Miss Blanchard is a standout in her role, who wants security after a doubtful past, clinging to McGraw as the one who can give her protection but in love with Ericson. As steeplejacks, Steve Brodie is smooth, romancing McGraw's wife in another town on the side; and Peter Whitney is a mental case. Alan Hale also is a member of a crew in a brief but rugged role.

Technical credits are excellent, particularly Ernest Haller's aerial photography and Maurice Wright's fast editing.

Whit.

Man Beast

Exploitable, but just fair entertainment-wise.

Hollywood, Dec. 6.
States rights release of Jerry Warren (Associated Producers) production, directed by Warren. Stars Rock Madison, Virginia Maynor; features Tom Maruzzi, Lloyd Nelson, George Wells Lewis, George Skaff. Screenplay, B. Arthur Cassidy; camera, Victor Fisher; editor, James R. Sweeney; music, Josef Zimanich. Reviewed Dec. 5, '56. Running time, 67 MINS.
Lon Raynon .... Rock Madison
Connie Hayward .... Virginia Maynor
Steve Cameron .... Tom Maruzzi
Trevor Hudson .... Lloyd Nelson
Dr. Erickson .... George Wells Lewis
Varga .... George Skaff
Kheon .... Jack Haffner
Trader .... Wong Sing

"Man Beast" shapes okay for the exploitation market. Though somewhat amateurishly done, it generates some suspense because of the not-so-threatening Abominable Snowmen of the Himalayas and the built-in excitement of mountain climbing.

Story-line revolves mainly around fruitless efforts of Virginia Maynor to find her brother lost in the Himalayas. Along on journey are Tom Maruzzi, a guide who warms up to Miss Maynor; George Welles Lewis, a scientist; Lloyd Nelson, Miss Maynor's b.f. until he proves himself a coward and gets killed in the process; several incidental characters, and George Skaff, another guide, who turns out to be an educated part-Snowman (fifth generation) and is killed before he can get to Miss Maynor. Wind-up of the B: Arthur Cassidy screenplay finds Miss Maynor and Maruzzi still high in the Himalayas, she yelling to him, "Take me away, Steve, take me away."

Acting-wise, Maruzzi is good; Miss Maynor isn't, and the others are just adequate.

Film was produced and directed by Jerry Warren under his own banner, and is the first release of the newly-formed Associated Producers. Release of the pic is being handled in California by Favorite Films. In other areas, various distribution outlets will take over.

Neal.

Bundle of Joy
(SONGS—COLOR)

Topnotch comedy with teaming of Eddie Fisher and Debbie Reynolds to assure hefty payoff in all situations.

Hollywood, Dec. 11.
RKO release of an Edmund Grainger production. Stars Eddie Fisher, Debbie Reynolds; with Adolphe Menjou, Tommy Noonan; features Nita Talbot, Una Merkel, Melville Cooper, Bill Goodwin, Howard McNear, Robert H. Harris, Mary Treen, Edward S. Brophy, Gil Stratton, Scott Douglas, David and Donald Gray. Directed by Norman Taurog. Screenplay, Norman Krasna, Robert Carson, Arthur Sheekman; story, Felix Jackson; camera (Technicolor), William Snyder; editor, Harry Marker; songs, Mack Gordon, Josef Myrow. Previewed Dec. 6, '56. Running time, 100 MINS.
Dan Merlin .... Eddie Fisher
Polly Parrish .... Debbie Reynolds
J. B. Merlin .... Adolphe Menjou
Freddie Miller .... Tommy Noonan
Mary .... Nita Talbot
Mrs. Dugan .... Una Merkel
Adams .... Melville Cooper
Mr. Creely .... Bill Goodwin
Mr. Appleby........... Howard McNear
Mr. Hargraves......... Robert H. Harris
Matron .... Mary Treen
Dance Contest Judge.. Edward S. Brophy
Mike Clancy............. Gil Stratton
Bill Rand............... Scott Douglas

RKO's teaming of Eddie Fisher and Debbie Reynolds has been slickly handled in this musical re-

---

make of Ginger Rogers' 1939 hit, "Bachelor Mother." Technicolor feature is loaded with the type of values which pay off and should rack up socko grosses in all situations.

Through the skillful comedy knowledge of Norman Taurog, whose direction never misses a bet, the Edmund Grainger production emerges a clever piece of showmanship with Fisher warbling five numbers and dueting with his wife in another. Some of the songs by Mack Gordon and Josef Myrow are of hit calibre, particularly "I Never Felt This Way Before," sung by Fisher and Debbie in for one chorus, and couple's "Lullaby in Blue," a homey little thing chirped while pair is trying to get the baby to sleep. Fisher makes a favorable impression in debuting as a screen actor and has a high-talent cast to back him up.

Debbie as the eager-beaver little sales-girl in the department store owned by Fisher and his dad, Adolphe Menjou, engagingly captures the full spirit of finding herself the foster-mother of an infant not her own, whom she picks up on the steps of a foundling home. When authorities there refuse to believe child isn't her's, her troubles start, leading eventually to her romance with Fisher which, blossoms along strictly comedy lines. Menjou thinks the baby was fathered by his son, complicating matters further.

Script by Norman Krasna, Robert Carson and Arthur Sheekman allows broad characterizations laugh-studded in their development and taken full advantage of by a well-picked player lineup. Fisher is as easy in his acting as he is in his singing and Debbie has never been better. Menjou excels in a flambuoyant role, and the baby, actually played by twins, David and Donald Gray, clutches at the heartstrings. Tommy Noonan scores as a stock boy ambitious to become an assistant floor-walker.

Fine support also is offered by Nita Talbot, Debbie's wisecracking sales-girl friend; Robert H. Harris, the floor-walker responsible for Debbie getting fired for over-selling; Una Merkel, her landlady; Melville Cooper, Menjou's butler; and Howard McNear, head of the foundling home who gets Debbie her job back at the store after he informs Fisher of the child.

Additional songs by Fisher include "Worry About Tomorrow, Tomorrow," "All About Love," "Some Day Soon" and "Bundle of Joy," also written by Gordon and Myrow, arranged and conducted by Hugo Winterhalter. Film's class background score was adapted and conducted by Walter Scharf, and Nick Castle is credited for staging musical numbers and dances.

Albert S. D'Agostino and Walter Holscher's art direction is a definite asset to the picture which has been expertly lensed by William Snyder, and Harry Marker's editing is sharp.

Whit.

Anastasia
(C'SCOPE-COLOR)

Posh screen treatment of highly intriguing play about the Czar's daughter. With Ingrid Bergman and Yul Brynner, this is a winner all the way.

20th-Fox release of Buddy Adler production. Stars Ingrid Bergman, Yul Brynner, Helen Hayes; features Akim Tamiroff, Martita Hunt, Felix Aylmer, Sacha Pitoeff, Ivan Desny, Natalie Schafer, Gregoire Gromoff. Directed by Anatole Litvak; screenplay, Arthur Laurents, from the Marcelle Maurette play adapted by Guy Bolton; camera (DeLuxe Color), Jack Hildyard; music, Alfred Newman; art directors, Andrei Andrejew and Bill Andrews; editor, Bert Bates. Previewed in N.Y. Dec. 10, '56. Running time, **105 MINS.**

Anastasia	Ingrid Bergman
Bounine	Yul Brynner
Empress	Helen Hayes
Chernov	Akim Tamiroff
Baroness von Livenbaum	Martita Hunt
Russian Chamberlain	Felix Aylmer
Petrovin	Sacha Pitoeff
Prince Paul	Ivan Desny
Lissenskaia	Natalie Schafer
Stepan	Gregory Gromoff
Vlados	Karel Stepanek
Marusia	Ina de la Haye
Maxime	Catherine Kath
Blonde Lady	Hy Hazell
Countess Baranova	Olga Valery
Xenia	Tamara Shayne
Grischa	Peter Sellis
Schischkin	Polycarpe Pavlov

Now that the legit hit "Anastasia" has been transferred to the screen by 20th-Fox, it becomes painfully evident how much both Hollywood and Ingrid Bergman have missed via the severing of their relationships some seven years ago.

For "Anastasia" is a wonderfully moving and entertaining motion picture from start to finish, and the major credit inevitably must go to Miss Bergman who turns in one of the great performances of the year. Parenthetically it is fair to add that, since living in Europe, Miss Bergman hasn't done such outstanding work.

Yet the picture is by no means "all Bergman." Yul Brynner as General Bounine, the tough Russian exile, etches a strong and convincing portrait that stands up perfectly to Miss Bergman's Anastasia, and Helen Hayes has great dignity as the Empress, living both in the present and the past. These performances, under the sensitive and imaginative direction of Anatole Litvak—here also doing his best work in years—turn "Anastasia" into one of those rare films that should appeal strongly on all levels. If ever a picture had the earmarks of a boxoffice winner, this is it.

Story basically is the one from the French of Marcelle Maurette adapted by Guy Bolton. New romantic angle has been introduced, however, and it's an asset since it's handled with restraint. Brynner and a group of conspirators are working in Paris to produce an Anastasia who might help them collect the £10,000,000 deposited in England by the Czar's family. Brynner keeps the destitute Miss Bergman from suicide, then grooms her to play Anastasia's part. She bears an amazing resemblance to the Czar's youngest daughter who was supposed to have been killed by the Reds in 1918.

Desperate to forget the past, Miss Bergman first resists, then begins to recover her regal bearing—and her memories. She is presented to Russian society in Paris, and some are convinced of her identity. Only the Dowager Empress, living in Copenhagen, can make the final identification. She is finally convinced to meet Miss Bergman, and recognizes her by her nervous cough. Film ends on a note of uncertainty re the Anastasia angle, but finds Brynner and Miss Bergman pairing off. It's an effective finis, even without a clinch.

Director Litvak and producer Buddy Adler have imbued the story with realistic settings ranging from a dingy cellar to the lush, plush interiors of the palace in Copenhagen. They've also thrown in some effective location shots both in Paris and in Denmark. But the backgrounds merely help accentuate the sock story which Arthur Laurents has intelligently adapted to the screen. The whole Anastasia tale is fantastic enough. Here, the mystery is cleverly and tastefully exploited for top values.

Miss Bergman's Anastasia is one of those acting marvels that come along only once in a long, long while. She is moving and tortured as the woman struggling for an identity; delightful as, under Brynner's guidance, she regains assurance; beautiful and captivating in the final phase, when her love for Brynner outweighs the struggle for recognition. There isn't a false note in this performance and it establishes Miss Bergman as what she has always been—one of the world's most talented and personable actresses.

Her transition from a worn, desperate woman looking every bit of 60 to the well-groomed, beautiful girl that is Anastasia is completely believable. She looks stunning in a variety of attractive gowns.

Brynner, the calculating Bounine who comes to love Anastasia in the end for herself rather than her potential inheritance, is ideally cast. Miss Hayes plays her difficult role to perfection. The recognition scene between her and Miss Bergman is an emotional highpoint that deserves special mention.

Supporting performances are all tops. Martita Hunt introes well-modulated humor as a lady-in-waiting; Ivan Desny looks handsome as Prince Paul who almost marries Anastasia; Akim Tamiroff and Sacha Pitoeff as Brynner's co-conspirators overplay it to just the right extent and are good for some hearty laughs. Felix Aylmer plays the doubting Russian duke to the hilt and Natalie Schafer does well in her brief role.

Litvak has wisely concentrated on Miss Bergman and he knows how to balance his picture to keep it from becoming over-dramatic. "Anastasia" has many light touches and they are well handled. Sets and costumes are elaborate and the DeLuxe color of this CinemaScope tinter is unusually bright and clear, a definite asset.

"Anastasia" is as bright a Christmas offering as exhibs could wish for. It's also Hollywood picture-making at its best. Miss Bergman couldn't have wished a better vehicle to make her comeback. She was once one of America's most popular actresses. "Anastasia" promises to restore her to that stature. *Hift.*

Ride the High Iron

Poor soap opera originally lensed for tv; a programmer.

Hollywood, Dec. 7.

Columbia release of William Self production. Stars Don Taylor, Sally Forrest, Raymond Burr; features Lisa Golin, Otto Waldis, Nestor Paiva, Mae Clarke, Maurice Marsac, Robert Johnson. Directed by Don Weis. Screenplay, Milton Gelman; camera, Joe Novak; editor, Joseph Gluck; music, Melvyn Lenard. Previewed Nov. 29, '56. Running time, 73 MINS.

Hugo Danielchik	Don Taylor
Elise Vanders	Sally Forrest
Ziggy Moline	Raymond Burr
Mrs. Danielchik	Lisa Golm
Yanusz Danielchik	Otto Waldis
Yardboss	Nestor Paiva
Mrs. Vanders	Mae Clarke
Maurice	Maurice Marsac
Porter	Robert Johnson

Originally filmed for television, "Ride the High Iron" didn't get far along the electronic track—in fact, it never left the station. Now it turns up as a theatrical release under the Columbia banner as a programmer booking.

Screenplay by Milton Gelman follows a trite soap opera story path, but with male sufferers rather than distaff weepers. Movement doesn't have the freedom of the usual motion picture, undoubtedly due to the tv origin, and scenes are mostly stagey and talky as directed by Don Weis. The William Self production has only ordinary values in both entertainment quality and physical furbishments.

Don Taylor, Sally Forrest and Raymond Burr costar in the turgid drama and do the best possible with impossible roles. Taylor is the son of a poor immigrant railroad worker who looks down on such a grubby life and wants to travel in society. Burr is a high-powered public relations man, also a snob and bitterly hurt because society doesn't accept him as an equal. Miss Forrest is the poor little rich girl whose escapades are kept out of the papers by Burr. Taylor goes to work for Burr to wet nurse Miss Forrest and, to no one's surprise, they fall in love. Potboiler ending has Taylor admitting his poor beginning and Miss Forrest is a brick about the whole thing.

Lisa Golm and Otto Waldis play Taylor's parents with broad, heart-rending performances. Nestor Paiva, the rail yard boss; Mae Clarke, the giddy mother of Miss Forrest, Maurice Marsac, snobbish head waiter, and Robert Johnson complete the cast. Joe Novak lensed in stock style and the other technical credits are of the same order. *Brog.*

King and Four Queens
(C'SCOPE—COLOR)

Weak script makes Clark Gable and Eleanor Parker vehicle average outdoorer; for regular situations only.

United Artists release of a Russ-Field-Gabco Production. Produced by David Hempstead. Stars Clark Gable, Eleanor Parker and Jo Van Fleet. Features Jean Willes, Barbara Nichols, Sara Shane. Directed by Raoul Walsh. Screenplay, Margaret Fitts, Richard Alan Simmons from a story by Miss Fitts. Camera, Lucien Ballard; editor, David Brotherton; music, Alex North. Previewed Dec. 10, '56. Running time, **83 MINS.**

Dan Kehoe	Clark Gable
Sabina	Eleanor Parker
Ma McDade	Jo Van Fleet
Ruby	Jean Willes
Birdie	Barbara Nichols
Oralie	Sara Shane
Sheriff Larrabee	Roy Roberts
Padre	Arthur Shields
Bartender	Jay C. Flippen

A good basic idea has been maltreated in "The King and Four Queens," and the result is a feature only a cut above program fare. Presence of Clark Gable and Eleanor Parker improve box-office chances, particularly with hefty exploitation of the basic situation which finds Gable as the only man in a community with four beauties.

Margaret Fitts and Richard Alan Simmons screenplayed Miss Fitts' story about a dashing adventurer who connives his way into an abandoned town held only by five women; the mother and the wives of the McDades, a gang of four bankrobbers and thieves. Three of the gang are known to have perished in a last-ditch fight after stealing $100,000 in gold, but no one knows which of the brothers escaped. Gable makes all the expected passes until he finds the gold and departs with Eleanor Parker, who has only posed as a McDade widow in order to find the loot. A sheriff's posse prevents them from keeping anything but $5,000 as a reward but the pair of connivers eventually ride off into the sunset, apparently to live suspiciously of each other ever after.

Gable is comfortably at home in roles like this and has no difficulty with the part. However, the characterization is sometimes physically unbelievable. Eleanor Parker manages to get some conviction into a role not convincingly written. Jean Willes, Barbara Nichols and Sara Shane look good and register well as the McDade brides but the talents of Jo Van Fleet are wasted in the role of the elder McDade although she often manages to lift the stock character above the niche into which it was written.

On the technical side, there is excellent camera work by Lucien Ballard and a fitting background score by Alex North. Costumes by Renie heighten the visual impact of the girls and the editing by Louis R. Loeffler and sound work by Jack Solomon are above par. *Kap.*

Pepote
(SPANISH-ITALIAN)

Rome, Dec. 11.

UMPO release of an ENIC-Chamartin-Falco Film production. Stars Pablito Calvo, Antonio Vico; features Juan Calvo, Walter Chiari, Carlo Campanini. Directed by Ladislao Vajda. Screenplay, Vajda, Rondi, Lazlo, Korner; camera, Enrique Guerrer; music, Roman Vlad. At Alcyone, Rome. Running time, **95 MINS.**

Pepote	Pablito Calvo
Jacinto	Antonio Vico

This a fine commercial followup production for Pablito Calvo, who has zoomed to European fame on the strength of his "Marcelino, Pan y Vino," released in the U. S. as "Marcelino." Though it's an entertaining, sometimes appealing item on its own, it is not quite as strong as its predecessor. "Pepote" may have to depend largely on Calvos following for strong returns.

Story told is that of a broken-down bullfighter and his nephew, Calvo, who spend a day trying to rustle up enough money to hire a toreador's costume for a third-rate fight to be held that night. The amusing moments alternate with the pathetic ones as both work for the needed coin, until Calvo (Pepote) comes through, arranges for the costume, takes Jacinto to the fight, but is unable to see it himself.

And just as well, as it turns into a pathetic parody of a corrida, with clowns purposely taking over the fight until rain brings all to a tragic head. Final scenes give the film stature.

Thesping by the boy, Calvo, is always winning, and Antonio Vico registers strongly as the broken-down bullfihter. Others are mostly bit parts, but backing is able and colorful. Paolo Stoppa contributes a good cameo as a counterfeiter.

Direction by Ladislao Vajda is fine in individual scenes though sometimes intercutting of sequences is annoying. Enrique Guerrer's camera makes the most of its settings, with good blending of studio and location shots apparent. Technical credits are all good. *Hawk.*

Full of Life

Fresh and appealing comedy with Judy Holliday and her Italo-Catholic relations, one of them Met Opera's Baccaloni. Adult fare; good b.o.

Columbia release of Fred Kohlmar production. Stars Judy Holliday, Richard Conte; features Salvatore Baccaloni, Esther Minciotti, Joe DeSantis, Silvio Minciotti. Directed by Richard Quine. Screenplay, John Fante, based on his own novel; camera, Charles Lawton Jr.; editor, Charles Nelson; music, George Dunning. Previewed in N.Y. Dec. 6, '56. Running time, **91 MINS.**

Emily Rocco	Judy Holliday
Nick Rocco	Richard Conte
Papa Rocco	Salvatore Baccaloni
Mama Rocco	Esther Minciotti
Father Gondolfo	Joe DeSantis
Joe Muto	Silvio Minciotti
Carla	Penny Santon
Mr. Jameson	Arthur Lovejoy
Mrs. Jameson	Eleanor Audley
Nora Gregory	Trudy Marshall
John Gregory	Walter Conrad
Dr. Atchison	Sam Gilman

A wholly satisfying switch from the routine, "Full of Life" is probably the most aptly-titled picture of the year. Also, one of the most surprising. It's replete with good humor although the story situations would not ordinarily suggest comedy. Commercial sizeup: Not a big picture in terms of production scope but a good grosser; the entertainment values will see to that.

"Life" concerns a young woman in the final month of pregnancy, a real character of a father-in-law who wants her to turn Catholic, her husband's trepidations about marriage by a priest after seven years of justice of the peace-sanctioned wedlock, etc.

Beguiling is the naturalness with which these people behave, and real is the material. It all actually happened this way, or so it seems.

"Life" is refreshing, should mean a good time for anyone. It may require some heavy promotional backing because of its different approach but once the word of mouth is around about its high-humor content, there should be plenty of public response.

At the outset, Judy Holliday is married into a family of Italian Catholics. She's on the homestretch toward motherhood (which serves as the peg for much comic business) and husband, Richard Conte, is a writer running low on cash. When heavy-weight (note the maternity clothes) Miss Holliday falls through the termite-ridden kitchen floor of their L. A. home, Conte's father, Salvatore Baccaloni, a bricklayer, is called in to do the repair job.

From then on, Fred Kohlmar's unpretentiously but fittingly laid out production is a series of incidents leading up to the birth of the baby, with papa-in-law in the dominant position. New to films, Baccaloni, who is the Metropolitan Opera basso, plays the part of the earthy, domineering, vino-drinking meddler with gusto. He's a natural for the part, funny to watch and steals much of the play from Miss Holliday and Conte.

Although asked only to mend the kitchen, Baccoloni is bent on building an unneeded, oversized fireplace, wonders why the couple hasn't given him more grandchildren, can't dig at all Conte's talk about planned parenthood, navigates the way to the wedding by a priest, and tries to have Miss Holliday join the church.

Miss Holliday, much less demonstrative, is appealing as ever and her professional skill shows through all the way. She can inflect a word to give it more meaning and her smile is a message in itself. Hers is toned-down playing and it gets across with fine comedy effect. The scene in which the obviously enciente wife, dressed in a wedding gown, is rushed to the hospital after the marriage ceremony makes for a laugh-getting highlight. And it's with remarkable tenderness that Miss Holliday explains that she's never had any religious affiliation and it would be unfair to both herself and the church if she suddenly were to become a Catholic.

Conte is a likeable husband and no slouch, either, in handling humorous situations. He registers just fine in trying to put up with the boss mannerisms of his father, in gratifying the pregnancy-caused whims of his wife, and, best of all, expressing alarm about going to confession after a seven-year hiatus.

Esther Minciotti offers a colorful characterization as Baccoloni's wife, a signora typed in tradition, handling her household chores while papa gulps the vino but everyonce in a while falling into a faint in sort of a mischievous way. Joe DeSantis is Father Gondolfo and gives the role of the priest both understanding and warmth. Silvio Minciotti and Penny Santon are competent in subordinate spots.

In fashioning a screenplay from his own novel, John Fante sketched genuine characters involved in amusing, believeable situations. The talk about pregnancy, etc., is handled in fine taste but probably would not be understandable to moppets. Under Richard Kline's direction, the film unfolds so real-like that the audience is given the feeling of eavesdropping on the family nextdoor.

George Dunning's music, conducted by Morris Stoloff, is an ace contribution, accenting the Napoli flavor of the picture. Camera, editing and other credits all good. *Gene.*

Battle Hymn
(C'SCOPE-COLOR)

Heart-warming story of Col. Dean Hess, man-of-God, and Korean orphans, plus war action. Good family-type film with good b.o. outlook.

Hollywood, Dec. 18.

Universal release of Ross Hunter production. Stars Rock Hudson, Anna Kashfi, Dan Duryea, Don DeFore, Martha Hyer, Jock Mahoney; features Alan Hale, Carl Benton Reid, Richard Loo, James Edwards, Phil Ahn. Directed by Douglas Sirk. Screenplay, Charles Grayson, Vincent B. Evans; camera (Technicolor), Russell Metty; editor, Russell Schoengarth; music, Frank Skinner; technical advisor, Col. Dean Hess. Previewed Dec. 5, '56. Running time, **108 MINS.**

Dean Hess	Rock Hudson
Mary Hess	Martha Hyer
Sgt. Herman	Dan Duryea
Capt. Skidmore	Don DeFore
Miss Yang	Anna Kashfi
Major Moore	Jock Mahoney
Mess Sergeant	Alan Hale
Deacon Edwards	Carl Benton Reid
General Kim	Richard Loo
Lieut. Maples	James Edwards
Old Man	Phil Ahn
Gen. Timberidge	Bartlett Robinson
Lieut. Hollis	Simon Scott
Korean Official	Teru Shimada
Major Harrison	Carleton Young
Chu	Jung Kyoo Pyo
Capt. Reardon	Art Millan
Navy Lieutenant	William Hudson
Sentry	Paul Sorensen

The inspirational story of a young clergyman is neatly integrated with fighter pilot action in "Battle Hymn." Film is an attractive offering, with particular family audience appeal and good boxoffice chances. Rock Hudson, as Col. Dean Hess, the minister whose story is told, heads the excellent cast and his name provides extra marquee weight for the playdates.

Perhaps best known of Hess's deeds were his efforts in behalf of the Korean children left orphans and homeless in the wake of the late fighting in that country. This is well-used in the Ross Hunter production as a heart-warming phase. Additionally it serves for story suspense and as a basis for the quite good air action that finds a minister at the controls of a fighter plane.

Douglas Sirk's direction and the screenplay by Charles Grayson and Vincent B. Evans stirs compassion and sympathy for the personal cross Col. Hess had to bear after accidentally bombing a German orphanage during his fighting days in World War II. This incident comes to light via flashback to establish his need to again give up his pulpit for pilot wings and go to Korea with the Air Force. In Korea he finds himself via the 1,000 or more orphans he cares for and air-lifts to safety. On Cheju Island there is a permanent institution still caring for Korea's homeless children, a group of which were flown to Hollywood to appear in the picture. While quite a bit that gets on the screen may seem typical motion picture fiction, Hess served as technical advisor to assure that fact predominates.

Hudson does one of his better performances in capturing the Hess personality and character. Martha Hyer plays Mrs. Hess, the wife who waits and worries at home, with a gracious, winning appeal, although femme emphasis more naturally falls to Anna Kashfi, very effective as Miss Wong, a true Korean heroine who literally gave her life to aid Hess' work with the orphans.

Dan Duryea, casting off his usual heavy character, adds a neat touch of lightness as a happy-go-lucky Air Force sergeant stationed in Korea with Col. Hess' outfit. Don DeFore, Jock Mahoney, Alan Hale, James Edwards and other members of the outfit come through strongly, bolstering the entertainment all down the line. Carl Benton Reid is good as a church deacon. Phil Ahn stands out as an old Korean who works with the orphans. Jung Kyoo Pyo, one of the children brought over from Korea, captures the heart.

Russell Metty's CinemaScope photography in Technicolor and the special lensing by Clifford Stine top the lineup of good technical credits, which include Russell Schoengarth's editing, the art direction by Alexander Golitzen and Emerich Nickolson, and the set decorations by Russell Gausman and Oliver Emert, and the Frank Skinner music, supervised by Joseph Gershenson. *Brog.*

Slander

Exposure of the newsstand scandal sheet racket. Sock exploitation angles, with Van Johnson, Ann Blyth, Steve Cochran for marquee.

Metro release of Armand Deutsch production. Stars Van Johnson, Ann Blyth, Steve Cochran; features Marjorie Rambeau, Richard Eyer, Harold J. Stone, Philip Coolidge, Lurene Tuttle, Lewis Martin. Directed by Roy Rowland. Screenplay, Jerome Weidman from Harry W. Junkin story; camera, Harold J. Marzorati; editor, George Boemler; music, Jeff Alexander. Previewed in N.Y. Dec. 5, '56. Running time, **81 MINS.**

Scott Ethan Martin	Van Johnson
Connie Martin	Ann Blyth
H. R. Manley	Steve Cochran
Mrs. Manley	Marjorie Rambeau
Joey Martin	Richard Eyer
Seth Jackson	Harold J. Stone
Homer Crowley	Philip Coolidge
Mrs. Doyle	Lurene Tuttle
Charles Orrin Sterling	Lewis Martin

This film hits back against the vicious gutter mags catering to the public's thirst for sensationalism and operating just on the brink of the libel laws. Metro's "Scandal" tackles the job of exposing the "exposure racket" and in the doing achieves that difficult blend of message and entertainment that is vital if a story such as this is to be put over.

Well-endowed with b.o. names—to wit Van Johnson, Ann Byth and Steve Cochran—and not lacking in guts and the willingness to call a spade a spade, pic should prove a popular entry. Subject is certainly hot enough to rouse audience interest, and the treatment is straight-from-the shoulder.

It makes it plain that the pious search for "truth" on the part of the scandal sheets is nothing more than a thinly veiled stunt to build circulation, conducted cynically and without any regard for the lives that are ruined in the process. Pic plot also hints at the sick mentality of the people who publish the scandal mags and who go scrounging in the muck for the necessary material.

Few will be in doubt that scripter Jerome Weidman's shafts are directed at one particular publisher.

"Scandal" has performer Johnson and wife (Miss Blyth) rising the ladder to success. He's about to be signed to a tv contract when Cochran, publisher of a big scandal mag, threatens to run a layout on Johnson, telling of a prison term he served for armed robbery in his teens. There's a blackmail angle, with Cochran offering to trade the story against info on a w.k. Broadway star. Behind it all is the necessity for Cochran to put out a runaway newsstand seller, or close shop.

Johnson refuses to trade, the story runs, he's fired off his job and his kid — Richard Eyer — is killed in an accident, running away from other boys teasing him about his father. Johnson then goes on tv to tell his story and to warn the public against buying the "poison" distributed by Cochran. Latter is killed by his own mother, Marjorie Rambeau.

Director Roy Rowland has gotten convincing performances from his players and the film has some genuinely touching moments. Some of its situations are contrived, and the shooting of Cochran has slightly ludicrous overtones. Also, the message is rather plainly spelled out and might have been handled with more restraint.

Cochran as H. R. Manley, the publisher, does a competent job as an actor, but the characterization isn't always well written. It is made quite plain, however, that he's a sick man suffering from a power complex, a fellow out to fight the world, petty and spiteful under the sleek veneer of the "truth crusader."

Johnson wisely underplays in a difficult role. Miss Blyth is a weak link in the cast. Miss Rambeau as

Cochran's mother has dignity and turns in a sock performance. Harold J. Stone as Johnson's agent is a find. He etches a strong portrayal that registers. Eyer as the kid is fresh and appealing.

Rowland's megging keeps the story in movement despite a generous dose of dialog. Weidman's script is mostly intelligent and forthright, if on the preachy side. Jeff Alexander's music helps create the mood and George Boemler's editing is okay. Lensing by Harold J. Marzorati is beyond reproach and is a distinct asset.

Chances are that "Scandal" isn't going to change anything. But in exposing the ugliness of the men and the thinking that goes into the gutter mags — and in making it plain that the public must share part of the responsibility—it deserves beaucoup attention. *Hift.*

Canasta De Cuentos Mexicanos

(Basket of Mexican Tales)
(MEXICAN-C'SCOPE-COLOR)

Mexico City, Dec. 11.

Columbia release of a Jose Kohn production. Stars Maria Felix, Pedro Armandariz, Arturo de Cordoba, Lorraine Chanel, Mari Blanchard, Jack Kelly; features Jorge Martinez de Hoyos. Directed by Julio Bracho. Screenplay and adaptation, Juan de la Cabada from the book by B. Traven; camera (Pathecolor), Gabriel Figueroa; editor, Gloria Shoemann, music, Lan Adomian. At Cine Mexico, Mexico City, Mex. Running time, **99 MINS.**

Pierre Duval	Arturo de Cordoba
Lorraine Arnaud (Duval)	Lorraine Chanel
Don Alfredo	Miguel Angel Ferriz
Alberto Duval	Julio Monterde
Sr. Ochoa	Rafael Alcaede
Luisa Bravo	Maria Felix
Carlos Cosio	Pedro Armandariz
Aunt Maria	Consuelo Guerrero de Luna
Grandmother	Emma Roldan
Gladys Winthrop	Mari Blanchard
Eddie Winthrop	Jack Kelly
The Indian	Jorge Martinez de Hoyos

It will take more than a basketfull of top south-of-the-border names and the obvious heavy coin involved, to push this triple vignette compilation into the international smash class. In Latin language situations it may be one of the year's top grossers due to its heavy-draw cast. However, for U. S. consumption it is merely another triptych of tales whose only tie is their Mexican locale. Taken from a series of short stories by the author of "Sierra Madre," heavy handed direction of Julio Bracho fails to make effervescent amusement of the frothily dialogued screenplay by Juan de la Cabada. An English language version, not being shown here, was directed by the pic's producer, Jose Kohn and will be marketed in the non-Spanish speaking world.

Yarns involved are all played in a pseudo satiric vein and attempt to display the foibles of modern Mexico in its various locales and social stratum. First, starring Arturo de Cordoba and Lorraine Chanel, sketches an unhappily married couple who take a few days separation to smooth out their problems.

Second parable, starring Maria Felix and Pedro Armandariz, takes place in the northern ranching country and plays on a taming of the shrew theme. Felix is an uncorraled, U. S. educated local senorita, so modern that it hurts. Armandariz, a tough, masculine rancher, sets his sights on her and eventually marries and domesticates the spitfire. In the process, and in disturbingly brutal, but humorously intended sequence, La Felix refuses to serve him his coffee, so he shoots his cat and parrot as they also make no effort to supply his needs. He is about to knock off his horse and perhaps his wife, when she in self defense heads out to get his java and make like a frau.

Third fable stars Jack Kelly and Mari Blanchard, with Jorge Martinez de Hoyos featured. Latter steals the entire show as an artistic but lackadasical Indian basketweaver who refuses to be browbeaten by a couple of not so sharp Yankee tourist slickers.

Other thesping honors are pretty well divided between the stars, with Lorraine Chanel, though miscast agewise, coming across tops as the one error wife to Arturo de Cordoba's suavely erring and erred against spouse. La Felix and Armandariz romp through their sexful duet in a gleeful and professional manner. Jack Kelly and Mari Blanchard handle themselves with unassuming modesty and are physically attractive as the "gringo" money grubbers. Numerous minor characterizations throughout the film are also well portrayed with Consuelo Guerrero de Luna and Emma Roldan as two old pixalates giving Felix and Armandariz a real run for their money.

Sets by Edward Fitzgerald are standard and lensing by Gabriel Figueroa seems spotty with some scenes definitely below his usual high quality, possibly due to the print shown here. Score by Lan Adomian is excellent but cannot do more than accentuate the lightness that the film should have had, but didn't. *Mayer.*

The Girl Can't Help It

(C'SCOPE-MUSIC-COLOR)

Tom Ewell in engaging rock and roll comedy, certain to be a teenage success, with corresponding good b.o. prospects. "Introduces" Jayne Mansfield.

Hollywood, Dec. 18.

20th-Fox release of Frank Tashlin production; directed by Tashlin. Stars Tom Ewell, Jayne Mansfield, Edmond O'Brien; guest stars Julie London, Ray Anthony, Barry Gordon; features Henry Jones, John Emery, Juanita Moore, Fats Domino, The Platters, Little Richard and his band, Gene Vincent and His Blue Caps, The Treniers, Eddie Fontaine, The Chuckles, Abbey Lincoln, Johnny Olenn, Nino Tempo, Eddie Cochran. Screenplay, Tashlin and Herbert Baker; camera (De Luxe Color), Leon Shamroy; editor, James B. Clark; score, Lionel Newman; new songs, Bobby Troup. Previewed Dec. 14, '56. Running time, **96 MINS.**

Tim Miller	Tom Ewell
Jerri Jordan	Jayne Mansfield
Murdock	Edmond O'Brien
Julie London	Harself
Ray Anthony	Himself
Barry Gordon	Himself
Mousie	Henry Jones
Wheeler	John Emery
Hilda—Mall	Juanita Moore
Fats Domino	Himself
The Platters	Themselves
Little Richard Band	Themselves
Gene Vincent Blue Caps	Themselves
The Treniers	Themselves
Eddie Fontaine	Himself
The Chuckles	Themselves
Abbey Lincoln	Herhelf
Johnny Olenn	Himself
Nino Tempo	Himself
Eddie Cochran	Himself

While there are a number of rock and roll features currently plying the market, "The Girl Can't Help It" is the first de luxe version to make release. It is an hilarious comedy with a beat, and the younger set should take to it like a double chocolate malt with cheeseburger. Business prospects are firstrate in regular situations.

On the surface, it appears that producer - director - scripter Frank Tashlin concentrated on creating fun for the juniors; a chore that he completes to a tee. However, the suspicion lurks that he also poked some fun at the current dance beat craze and the artists who deliver it. Thus, Charleston-age oldsters can delight in the ribbing and enjoy the show, too. There are so many sight gags and physical bits of business, including Jayne Mansfield and a couple of milk bottles, that males of any age will get the entertainment message.

Herbert Baker collaborated with Tashlin on the script, and the pair delivers bountifully with dialog and situations for a big laugh payoff under Tashlin's especially sharp direction. Pilot is no more than a gag peg, although it has the necessary story value to carry through with the required support. Basically, it tells how a wealthy hasbeen gangster hires a hasbeen agent to make an entertainment name out of the former's girl friend. The fun's in the viewing, not the telling, as it's the manner in which the show has been put together that makes it entertaining.

Miss Mansfield doesn't disappoint as the sexpot who just wants to be a successful wife and mother, not a glamor queen. She's physically equipped for the role, and also is competent in sparking considerable of the fun. Nature was so much more bountiful with her than with Marilyn Monroe that it seems Miss Mansfield should have left MM with her voice. However, the vocal imitation could have been just another part of the fun-poking indulged in.

Edmond O'Brien, rarely seen in comedy, is completely delightful as the hammy ex-gangster who thinks his position demands that his girl be a star name. In totalling the assets of the film, his performance ranks right on top as a major factor in the entertainment. Tom Ewell scores mightily as the hasbeen agent who is haunted by the memory of Julie London, another girl whom he had pushed to reluctant stardom. With Miss Mansfield and O'Brien, he makes it a funny caper for the ticketbuyer.

Talent abounds elsewhere, too, in those with story roles, such as Henry Jones, very amusing as O'Brien's handyman; John Emery, a rival jukebox king, and Juanita Moore, Miss Mansfield's maid. Musical talent, mostly of the r&r variety, is tops in its field, the list reading like a special performance bash. Not r&r, but good of voice and sensational in appearance, is Abbey Lincoln singing "Spread the Word" while Benny Carter's orchestra backstops. Fats Domino and band with "Blue Monday"; Little Richard with "The Girl Can't Help It" and others; The Platters on "The Great Pretender"; Gene Vincent and the Blue Caps; The Treniers, Eddie Fontaine, The Chuckles, Johnny Olenn and band; Nino Tempo and Eddie Cochran are among the rock-and-rollers purveying the beat that qualifies the film for the teenagers.

Miss London, appearing only in spirit, is heard on her click disc, "Cry Me a River." Little Barry Gordon doesn't sing at all; he sells newspapers. Ray Anthony and band beat out a situation tune, "Rock Around the Rock Pile," cleffed by Bobby Troup, who also wrote the title number. Lionel Newman functioned firstrate on supervising and conducting the music.

Physically, the film has a quality look, with Leon Shamroy's CinemaScope lensing in De Luxe Color displaying the value for top returns. Art direction and settings, and unusually good costuming of Misses Mansfield, London and Lincoln are other strong credits. *Brog.*

Westward Ho the Wagons

(C-SCOPE—SONGS—COLOR)

Walt Disney in stride with a strong entry for the outdoor market; Fess Parker name will help.

Hollywood, Dec. 18.

Buena Vista release of a Bill Walsh production. Stars Fess Parker, Kathleen Crowley, Jeff York; features David Stollery, Sebastian Cabot, George Reeves. Directed by William Beaudine; second unit director, Yakima Canutt; screenplay, Tom Blackburn; based on Mary Jane Carr novel; camera (Technicolor), Charles Boyle; editor, Cotton Warburton; music, George Bruns. Previewed Dec. 14, '56. Running time, **86 MINS.**

John "Doc" Grayson	Fess Parker
Laura Thompson	Kathleen Crowley
Hank Breckenridge	Jeff York
Dan Thompson	David Stollery
Bissonette	Sebastian Cabot
James Stephen	George Reeves
Bobo Stephen	Doreen Tracey
Mrs. Stephen	Barbara Woodell
Wolf's Brother	John War Eagle
Jerry Stephen	Cubby O'Brien
Jim Stephen	Tommy Cole
Spencer Armitage	Leslie Bradley
"Obie" Foster	Morgan Woodward
Many Stars	Iron Eyes Cody
Little Thunder	Anthony Numkena
Myra Thompson	Karen Pendleton
Ruth Benjamin	Jane Liddell
Ed Benjamin	Jon Locke
Tom Foster	Brand Stirling

Walt Disney's latest excursion into the live-action feature realm is a story of the Oregon Trail, following a wagon train plagued by hostile Indians. CinemaScope treatment allows a vast panorama against which to limn the simple, yet stirring, narrative, and there's the marquee lure of Fess Parker for the younger trade particularly. Technicolor film should rack up good grosses as a showmanly entry for the outdoor market.

Strong emphasis is placed upon the Redskin element to give the Bill Walsh production a flavor of excitement. Specially well staged is an attack on the wagon train by a band of warlike Pawnees, and the later threat of the Sious preventing the train from leaving Fort Laramie, where it stops for a few days' respite, constitutes a major plot device. Parker warbles three numbers rich with frontier flavor, and pic includes two other songs effectively presented.

Parker co-stars with Kathleen Crowley, member of the train, and Jeff York, vet Indian scout, in the Tom Blackburn screenplay, based upon the Mary Jane Carr novel of the same title. As a prairie doctor, also a scout leading the train westward, he is instrumental in gaining the friendship of the Sioux chief, after saving his young son's life when the ministrations of the tribe's medicine man proved fruitless. Feature is accorded a homely touch by director William Beaudine, with Yakima Canutt as second unit director responsible for the fast-moving Pawnee battle.

Parker delivers his usual easy characterization, and makes the most of his three songs, best of which is "The Ballad of John Colter," followed by the novelty "Wringle Wrangle" and "I'm Lonely My Darlin'." Miss Crowley is nice in an undemanding role as the romantic interest, and York is properly rugged as the hulking scout. John War Eagle is strongly cast as the Sioux chief, Iron Eyes Cody scores as medicine man, and Sebastion Cabot is a semi-heavy.

Charles Boyle's color photography heads up the above-standard technical credits, and Cotton Warburton's editing is attuned to the subject. *Whit.*

Foreign Films

Paris, Dec. 18.

La Terreur Des Dames (The Terror With Women) (FRENCH). Gaumont release of Mediterannee Film-Eminente production. Stars Noel-Noel; features Jacqueline Pagnol, Jacqueline Gauthier, Yves Robert, Noel Roquevert, Suzet Mais. Directed by Jean Boyer. Screenplay, Rene Barjavel from story, "Ce Cochon De Morin," of Guy De Maupassant; camera, Charles Suin; editor, Christian Gaudin. At Aubert-Palace, Paris. Running time, **95 MINS.**

Lightweight tale is a natural vehicle for Noel-Noel as it details how an inoffensive, small town character is mistaken for a sex maniac after a heavy night's drinking in Paris. Remainder of pic details his try to placate the husband of the woman he was supposed to have bothered. It makes a local bet for regular consumption but lacks the bite of satire needed for U.S. arty house chances. Its risque treatment could make this an exploitation gamble.

Noel-Noel gives some fine nuances to the timid soul while Yves Robert is an asset as a cynical skirt chaser. Femmes are well done by Jacqueline Gauthier and Jacqueline Pagnol. Director Jean Boyer has given this a placid mounting that lacks the necessary pacing to make this as good as a comedy as it could have been. Technical credits are okay. Current craze of the striptease is also brought in and it is the drunken remembrance of a stripper which brings on Morin's attempt to molest a stranger and all the complications.   *Mosk.*

Le Pays D'Ou Je Viens (The Country I Come From) (FRENCH—COLOR—SONGS). Cocinor release of CLM-Clement Duhour production. Stars Gilbert Becaud, Francoise Arnoul; features Claude Brasseur, Madedeine Lebeau, Gabriello. Directed by Marcel Carne. Screenplay, Jacques Emmanuel, Marcel Achard, Carne; camera (Technicolor), Philippe Agostini; music, Becaud; editor, Paulette Robert. At Biarritz, Paris. Running time, **100 MINS.**

This tinter is a showcase for first film appearance of one of the top singing stars here, Gilbert Becaud. Diverting, fable-like pic spins a tale of a stranger who comes into a small town, Christmas Eve, to right some romantic difficulties and then exits singing. Clever hand of director Marcel Carne keeps this flimsy plot from being too sentimental. Although it lacks a

poetic quality to slant this for U.S. arties, it does have enough entertainment facets.

The man who comes from nowhere arrives in town to find he is a dead ringer for a local pianist, timid soul in love with a pert, little waitress but afraid to show it. The double proceeds to pass himself off as guardian angel and assistant of Santa Claus to the moppet brother and sister of the waitress.

Becaud acquits himself well in his dual role, his sudden forays into his bombastic songs growing in acceptance. Francoise Arnoul is pert, strong headed as the waitress while the supporting cast is adequate. Film has a fine color layout, with production values helping make this beguiling. However, this is lightweight, at best, and will have to be handled accordingly.
                                        Mosk.

Vienna, Dec. 18.

Nichts als Aerger mit der Liebe (Nothing But Trouble With Love) (GER-

AAN). Sascha Film-Omnia Munich release of Heinrich Bauer-Wiener Mundus Film Co. production. Stars Victor de Kowa; features, Winnie Markus, Walter Giller, Sonja Ziemann, Helmi Mareich, Beppo Brem, Liesl Karlstadt, Ursula Herking, Lucie Neudecker (from play, "The Concert," by Herman Bahr). Directed by Thomas Engel. Screenplay by Paul Helwig and Heinz Oskar Wuttig; camera, Johann Mutala; settings, Leo Metzenbauer; costumes, Margarethe Volters. At Flieger Kino, Vienna. Running time, **90 MINS.**

Herman Bahr's much played comedy, "The Concert," has been successfully turned into a film via this West German-Austrian coproduction.

Victor de Kowa plays the role of the music professor, who invites a married pupil to a mountain climbing party, with complications developed from jealousy of the husband. Kowa has made his role one of the best in the play.

The two femmes, Winnie Markus and Sonja Ziemann, shine in their best in the well-conceived jealous scenes. The West German comedians, Walter Giller and Beppo Brehm, add the necessary humor.

Direction by Thomas Engel is well done. Setting by Leo Metzenbauer are fine. Camerawork by Johann Matula deserves praise for the strong scenes.   *Maas.*

Don't Knock the Rock
(MUSIC)

Top rock 'n' roll artists in tune-loaded juve story, probably destined for substantial boxoffice response.

Hollywood, Dec. 12.

Columbia release of a Sam Katzman (Clover) Production. Stars Bill Haley and his comets, Alan Dale, Alan Freed, The Treniers, Little Richard, Dave Appell and his Applejacks; features Patricia Hardy, Fay Baker, Jana Lund, Gail Ganley, Pierre Watkin, George Cisar, Dick Elliott, Jovada and Jimmy Ballard. Directed by Fred F. Sears. Screenplay, Robert E. Kent, James B. Gordon; Benjamin H. Kline; editor, Edwin Bryant, Paul Borofsky; music supervisors, Fred Karger, Ross Di Maggio. Previewed at Columbia Studios, Hollywood, Dec. 10, '56. Running time, **85 MINS.**

Bill Haley	Bill Haley
Arnie Haines	Alan Dale
Alan Freed	Alan Freed
The Treniers	The Treniers
Little Richard	Little Richard
Dave Appell and His Applejacks	
Dave Appell and His Applejacks	
Francine MacLaine	Patricia Hardy
Arlene MacLaine	Fay Baker
Sunny Everett	Jana Lund
Mollie Haines	Gail Ganley
Mayor George Bagley	Pierre Watkin
Mayor Tom Everett	George Cisar
Sheriff Cagle	Dick Elliott

A collection of top rock 'n' roll artists has been assembled by producer Sam Katzman for his second musical in the after-beat vein. Produced, as was "Rock Around the Clock," for under $500,000, it is packed with talent and tunes designed to appeal strongly to the juvenile trade and its prospects are bright on that reckonin'g. The R&R influence appears to be slightly on the wane, however, indicating that "Don't Knock the Rock" may not duplicate the smash box-office of "Rock Around the Clock," but interest in the genre is still strong enough to insure a profitable return on the investment.

Script by Robert E. Kent and James B. Gordon doesn't stand too close inspection but it has been wisely written so as not to get in the way of the music. What there is of the plot concerns the efforts of Alan Dale, a top R&R artist, to win over the older generation to the acceptability of the music. He and his cohorts finally make the grade after staging a program in which the elders are given a chance to look backward and remember what they themselves acted like when the Charleston and Black Bottom dances were the craze.

Production by Katzman is on the skimpy side, but it's a deficiency that won't be minded by teen-age audiences since the producer wisely spent his money for such r&r talent as Bill Haley and his Comets (stars of "Rock Around the Clock"), The Treniers, Little Richard, Dave Appell and his Applejacks and R&R deejay-promoter-disker Alan Freed. They pour out a total of 16 tunes, including such hits as "Hook, Line & Sinker" by Haley and "Tutti Frutti" and "Long Tall Sally" by Little Richard. Fred F. Sears direction keeps the plot boiling effectively between musical numbers which boast some effective teenage dancing routines staged and created by Earl Barton. Fred Karger, who shared music supervision chores with Ross DiMaggio, teamed with Robert E. Kent to turn out the title tune, which could catch on its field.

Dale is in good voice and displays an easy personality in the key role and Freed is believable as a R&R press agent. Others who register effectively in their parts are Patricia Hardy as the love interest, Fay Baker as her columnist-mother who frowns on the beat

and Jana Lund as a spoiled teenager who causes trouble.   *Kap.*

Man In the Vault
(SONG)

Confused melodrama about an honest - but - dumb locksmith. Dim entertainment.

Hollywood, Dec. 19.

RKO release of Robert E. Morrison (Batjac) production. Stars William Campbell, Karen Sharpe, Anita Ekberg; features Berry Kroeger, Paul Fix, James Seay, Mike Mazurki, Robert Keys. Directed by Andrew V. McLaglen. Screenplay, Burt Kennedy; from Frank Gruber novel; camera, William H. Clothier; editor, Everett Sutherland; score, Henry Vars; song, Vars and By Dunham. Previewed Dec. 17, '56. Running time, **72 MINS.**

Tommy Dancer	William Campbell
Betty Turner	Karen Sharpe
Flo Randall	Anita Ekberg
Willis Trent	Berry Kroeger
Herbie	Paul Fix
Paul De Camp	James Seay
Louie	Mike Mazurki
Earl Farraday	Robert Keys
Pedro	Gonzales Gonzales
Trent's Girl Friend	Nancy Duke
Singer	Vivianne Lloyd

"Man In the Vault" is a routine melodrama for programmer playdates, where the so-so entertainment values will relegate it to the lowercase slot.

The Batjac feature, produced by Robert E. Morrison for RKO release, falls in the crime thriller bracket but doesn't have the suspense or action required for the classification. Story values in the script by Burt Kennedy from the Frank Gruber novel follow a for-

mula line and leave a lot of loose ends dangling. Andrew V. McLaglen's direction works up a fair amount of tension in a couple of sequences but otherwise doesn't rise above the script.

William Campbell, poor but honest keymaker, heads the cast as a sucker who gets mixed up with Berry Kroeger, cheap hoodlum who plans to rob the safety deposit box of James Seay, crime brains of the town. Above threesome, along with Paul Fix, Mike Mazurki, Robert Keys, Gonzales Gonzales and Nancy Duke deliver stereotype performances as the confusing melodramatics unfold slowly. Scenes of Campbell in the bank vault hastily making pass keys, and in a dark bowling alley dodging bullets and bowling balls are the only time the footage manages to be suspenseful.

Karen Sharpe has the femme lead as a mixed-up rich girl. Her romantic scenes with Campbell occasionally have some meaning, but the screenplay is too lifeless to add support. Anita Ekberg's cast presence means no more than lobby and ad art possibilities.

Lensing by William H. Clothier is extremely lowkey; in fact, preview print was so dark it looked like mostly night scenes. Henry Vars did the standard background score and also contributed a song, "Let The Chips Fall Where They May," with By Dunham. Vivianne Lloyd sings it in a party sequence, but it means nothing.   *Brog.*

The Brass Legend

Sock western for good payoff in program market. Video-built Hugh O'Brian name to help.

Hollywood, Dec. 11.

United Artists release of a Herman Cohen production, presented by Bob Goldstein Productions. Stars Hugh O'Brien Nancy Gates, Raymond Burr; costars, Reba Tassell, Donald McDonald; features Robert Burton, Eddie Firestone, Willard Sage, Robert Griffin. Directed by Gerd

Oswald. Screenplay, Don Martin; original story, George Zuckerman, Jess Arnold; camera, Charles Van Enger; music, Paul Dunlap; editor, Marj Fowler. Previewed Dec. 5, '56. Running time, **80 MINS.**

Sheriff Wade Adams .... Hugh O'Brian
Linda .... Nancy Gates
Tris Hatten .... Raymond Burr
Millie .... Reba Tassell
Clay .... Donald McDonald
Gipson .... Bob Burton
Shorty .... Eddie Firestone
Tatum .... Willard Sage
Dock Ward .... Robert Griffin
George Barlow .... Stacy Harris
Cooper .... Norman Leavitt
Carl Barlow .... Dennis Cross
Jackson .... Russell Simpson
Charlie .... Michael Garrett
Earl Barlow .... Jack Farmer

"The Brass Legend" stirs up enough excitement to be a strong entry for the oater market. It has a slickly-developed plot with better-than-average characters and an excellent cast to give them meaning, as well as deft and rugged treatment throughout. Film is one of the best program westerns to come along in some time and should be received as such.

Name of Hugh O'Brian should considerably bolster its b.o. chances, on strength of actor's high rating in the "Wyatt Earp" vidpix series. Under Gerd Oswald's driving direction of the Don Martin script, the Herman Cohen production generates legitimate suspense and a bangup climax as O'Brian, a peace officer, and Raymond Burr, badman-killer, race toward each other on horseback in a deadly sixgun duel.

Events stem from O'Brian's post of an Arizona sheriff, after he captures a notorious out law, Burr. One facet of plot hinges on his being tipped off where to find badman by young brother of sheriff's fiancee, and his attempt to keep lad's name out of case, knowing some of Burr's friends will try to gun youngster down, which actually happens when the father and town's newspaper editor oppose him. In a realistic gunfight, sheriff faces down three outlaws in a bar, killing two of them, and the third, taken to jail, is the means of Burr's making his escape. Finale is fast and unusual.

O'Brian socks over his quick-draw characterization easily and in a commanding fashion, and Burr is tops as a ruthless outlaw. Nancy Gates in fiancee role has more to do than most western heroines, all to the good; Donald McDonald, her brother who worships O'Brian, delivers a good account of himself; and Robert Burton scores as the father. Reba Tassell as Burr's Mexican dancehall sweetie is a particular standout. Good support also is offered by Willard Sage, the editor; Eddie Firestone, who shoots the boy, thinking he's doing Reba a good turn; and Stacy Harris, wounded outlaw who carries a derringer hidden in his boot heel, the means by which Burr makes his escape.

Technical credits are above par. Charles Van Enger's camera work is fast, Marj Fowler's editing tight, Paul Dunlap provides an atmospheric music score and art direction by Leslie Thomas blends well with the yarn. *Whit.*

Stars In Your Eyes
(BRITISH-CAMERASCOPE-COLOR)

Lively musical of outdated vaude acts making comeback through tv; depends for appeal on Pat Kirkwood, Bonar Colleano, Nat Jackley and Dorothy Squires.

London, Dec. 18.

British Lion release of Grand Alliance production. Stars Nat Jackley, Pat Kirkwood and Bonar Colleano; co-stars Dorothy Squires; features Jack Jackson, Hubert Gregg, Meier Tzelniker, Vera Day, Joan Sims, Jimmy Clitheroe. Directed by Maurice Elvey. Screenplay, Talbot Rothwell from story by Francis Miller; camera, S. D. Onions; editor, Robert Jordan Hill; words and music by Jack Jackson, Hubert Gregg, C. W. Murphy, Will Letters, Hilda Lynn, David Lee, Edwin Astley, Hazel Astley, Bert Elms, Malcolm Harvey, Don Pelosi, Leo Towers. At Hammer Theatre, London. Running time, **96 MINS.**

Jimmy Knowles .... Nat Jackley
Sally Bishop .... Pat Kirkwood
David Laws .... Bonar Colleano
Ann Hart .... Dorothy Squires
Rigby .... Jack Jackson
Maureen Temple .... Vera Day
Crawley Walters .... Hubert Greggg
Walter's Secretary .... Joan Sims
Ronnie .... Ernest Clark
Dicky .... Gerald Harper
Maxie Jago .... Meier Tzelniker
Effie .... Gabrielle Brune
Farrow .... Aubrey Dexter
Grimes .... Roger Avon
First Recruit .... Sammy Curtis
Second Recruit .... Dennis Murray
Sergeant .... Sonny Willis
Night Club Proprietor.. Michael Mellinger
Joey .... Jimmy Clitheroe

The plight of smalltime vaude acts, with the gradually decreasing opportunities for work, forms the subject of this robust, slapstick musical. With a collection of known artists, a reasonably feasible plot is projected, which is marred by an anti-climax which could easily be remedied. The story has been handled before from many angles, and reliance on its drawing power rests on the stars' reputations.

Pat Kirkwood and Nat Jackley play a married couple of waning topliners who find, with the shuttering of so many vaude houses, they are likely to end on the scrapheap. Their best friend, Bonar Colleano, is a songwriter who has taken to the bottle since the split-up with his wife, now a famous cabaret singer. He is on the verge of selling a derelict suburban theatre left him by his father, but is persuaded by the other two to re-open it with a revue on the co-operative system with a bunch of other out-of-work troupers.

Unknown to him, his wife finances the enterprise and the building is restored. A group of toughs kill the opening performance, and the demolition squad is all ready to take over for the new owners. A tv audition of one of the sketches has aroused interest at BBC and the whole show is telecast from the theatre, bringing fame, transfer of the entire show to the West End, and reconciliation to the estranged couple.

Many of the skits have the broad vulgarity of touring burlesque revues and circus clowning, and Pat Kirkwood's numbers savor too much of the good old days for modern appeal. Jackley's grotesque comedy should amuse and register best with provincial audiences. Colleano gives a straight, sympathetic performance as the reformed souse, with Dorothy Squires providing the glamor and torch singing as his ex-mate. Hubert Gregg scores with a satirical impression of a radio program arranger, and most of the supporting characters ring true. *Clem.*

Zarak
(C'SCOPE-SONG-COLOR)

Mild Sex-and-sand potboiler.

Hollywood, Dec. 21.

Columbia release of Irving Allen, Albert R. Broccoli (Warwick) production. Stars Victor Mature, Michael Wilding, Anita Ekberg; features Bonar Colleano, Finlay Currie, Bernard Miles, Frederick Valk, Eunice Gayson, Peter Illing, Eddie Byrne, Andre Morell. Directed by Terence Young. Screenplay, Richard Maibaum; based on a story by A. J. Bevan; camera (Technicolor), John Wilcox, Ted Moore, Cyril Knowles; editors, Alan Osbiston, Bert Rule; score, William Alwyn; played by Sinfonia of London; conducted by Muir Mathieson; song, "Climb Up the Wall," Auyar, Hosseini, Norman Gimbel; sung by Yana. Previewed Dec. 12, '56. Running time, **94 MINS.**

Zarak Khan .... Victor Mature
Major Ingram .... Michael Wilding
Salma .... Anita Ekberg
Biri .... Bonar Colleano
The Mullah .... Finlay Currie
Hassu .... Bernard Miles
Haji Khan .... Frederick Valk
Cathy .... Eunice Gayson
Ahmad .... Peter Illing
Kasim .... Eddie Byrne
Moor Larkin .... Patrick McGoohan
Sergt. Higgins .... Harold Goodwin
Akbar .... Alec Mango
Youssuff .... Oscar Quitak
Chief Jalor .... George Margo
Flower Seller .... Arnold Marle
Young Officer .... Conrad Phillips

As a regulation sex-and-sand adventure potboiler, "Zarak" will help make up a formula bill shaped for the action trade. Lensed overseas by Irving Allen and Albert R. Broccoli for their Warwick unit releasing domestically through Columbia, film is a standard entry fortified with such names as Victor Mature, Michael Wilding and Anita Ekberg.

A lot of razzle-dazzle action with horsemen dashing across vast plains and deserts, and scant costuming to emphasize the voluptuous contours of Miss Ekberg are laid on thick, but still fail to veil the fact that the story by A. J. Bevan, scripted by Richard Maibaum, is strictly formula stuff, and quite old-fashioned.

Terence Young's direction mostly emphasizes movement, with assists from associate directors Yakima Canutt and John Gilling in the mass chase footage, but still accounts for an unreasonable number of static scenes between the principals, none of whom seems to have much feel for their characters.

With virtually no character reality to portray, the three stars turn in the type of performances that are stock for such desert action plots. Bonar Colleano, Finlay Currie, Bernard Miles, Frederick Valk, Eunice Gayson and others in the cast deliver in equally routine fashion.

Visually, film achieves quite a pictorial sweep at times through the CinemaScope lensing in Technicolor by John Wilcox, Ted Moore and Cyril Knowles. Other technical credits are standard, including the booming William Alwyn score, conducted by Muir Mathieson and played by Sinfonia of London. "Climb Up the Wall," a musical invitation to amor cleffed by Auyar Hosseini and Norman Gimbel, is sung by Yana in a cafe sequence. *Brog.*

La Sorciere
(The Sorceress)
(FRENCH)

Ellis Films release of Iena Productions film. Stars Marina Vlady, Maurice Ronet, Nicole Courcel; features Michel Etcheverry, Ulf Palme, Rune Lindstrom, Erik Hell, Ulla Lagnell, Eric Hellstrom, Naima Wifstrand. Directed by Andre Michel. Screenplay, Jacques Companeez, based on Alexander Kouprine novel; camera, Marcel Grignon. Previewed in N.Y., Nov. 30, '56. Running time, **97 MINS.**

Aino .... Marina Vlady
Laurent .... Maurice Ronet
Kristina .... Nicole Courcel
Camoin .... Michel Etcheverry
Matti .... Ulf Palme
The Pastor.............. Rune Lindstrom
Pullinen .... Erik Hell
Pastor's Wife .... Ulla Lagnell
Erik .... Eric Hellstrom
Maina .... Naima Wifstrand

A standout potential for the arties, "La Sorciere" proves the French capacity for locationing abroad without either losing their own filmmaking flavor or ignoring the local atmosphere. Pic was shot in Sweden and the lensing makes the best of its opportunities, providing a perfect setting for a strange and romantic story.

Director Andre Michel takes his time in telling the offbeat yarn about a young French engineer who goes to Sweden to help build a road. He encounters and falls in love with a beautiful young girl who lives in the forest because the townspeople consider her a witch. Inevitably, the affair ends in tragedy, but not before the film has provided audiences with many charming and frequently comic sequences that blend in perfectly. Leo Lax produced.

"La Sorciere" introes Marina Vlady, a young French actress with stunning looks and plenty s.a. Her performance has the grace of a cat and her concept of the witch, which she believes herself to be, is intriguing in both its strength and its childish innocence.

Opposite Miss Vlady, Maurice Ronet plays the engineer with intensity. He is convincing in his efforts to befriend the girl and to overcome the language barrier. Their excursion into town together is hilarious. As Kristina, a Swedish landowner, Nicole Courcel combines a hard beauty with the sense of a woman running away from emotion. Smaller parts are well played by Michel Etcheverry, Ulf Palme, Rune Lindstrom as the pastor and Ulla Lagnell as his wife.

Marcel Grignon's camerawork is one of the pic's great assets. It's partly due to him that the film takes on a semi-fairytale quality and a poetry of expression of movement that resolve themselves into the more earthy moments and the haunting climax. Scene of Ronet sinking into the swamp is terrifying in its realism.

"La Sorciere" is the kind of French film that should appeal in the U.S. And it should focus sharp attention on Miss Vlady as a standout foreign star. The English titles do justice to the French dialog. *Hift.*

Three Violent People
(COLOR—VISTAVISION)

Heart-tug and characterization in an "A" western starring Charlton Heston, Anne Baxter and Gilbert Roland. An audience pleaser.

Paramount release of a Hugh Brown production. Stars Charlton Heston, Anne Baxter, Gilbert Roland. Co-stars Tom Tryon. Directed by Rudolph Mate. Screenplay by James Edward Grant based on a story by Leonard Praskins and Barney Slater; camera (Technicolor), Loyal Griggs; editor, Alma Macrorie; music, Walter Scharf. Previewed in N.Y. Dec. 14, '56. Running time, **100 MINS.**

Colt Saunders .... Charlton Heston
Lorna .... Anne Baxter
Innocencio .... Gilbert Roland
Cinch .... Tom Tryon
Cable .... Forrest Tucker
Harrison .... Bruce Bennett
Ruby LaSalle .... Elaine Stritch
Yates .... Barton MacLane
Lieut. Marr .... Peter Hansen
Massey .... John Harmon
Asuncion .... Ross Bagdasarian
Rafael .... Bobby Blake
Pedro .... Jameel Farah
Luis .... Leo Castillo
Juan .... Don Devlin
Carleton .... Raymond Greenleaf
Carpetbagger .... Roy Engel
Maria .... Argentina Brunetti
Maid .... Ernestine Wade
Carpetbagger .... Don Dunning
Bartender .... Paul Levitt
One-legged Soldier ...... Robert Arthur

Part horsey, part soapy, a kind of woman's western, "Three Violent People" should divert most audiences. It has the marquee lure of Anne Baxter, Charlton Heston and Gilbert Roland, of whom the first two are currently in Paramount's "10 Commandments."

Close scrutiny could turn up some loose ends story-wise. Miss Baxter's conversion from a scheming demimonde of the post-Civil War west into a loving wife comes with slightly remarkable rapidity. The machinations of the land grabbers come into and fade away from the story at the author's and film editor's occasionally arbitrary convenience. No matter. The general movement and characterization carry the viewer along. This one is elephant's eye high above most westerns.

The story opens trite: demobilized Confederate soldiers are being taunted and abused by Yankee soldiers and carpetbaggers in Texas. The proud-as-sin captain, now mellowed from four years of war and retreating, holds his temper and his gunfire. All this has been seen so many times before. The tangent which refreshes the proceedings has to do with the precipitate marriage of the proud-as-sin Texan to the not-too-proud-to-sin fille de nuit. Of course, he doesn't know what she was and, of course, a member of the nasty occupation army camp - followers spots the gal and spills the chili beans all over the ranch porch.

Rudolph Mate, directing for producer Hugh Brown, in VistaVision and Technicolor, has things well in hand after the somewhat stereotyped opening sequence which has Barton MacLane goading the barroom louses against the noble Rebs. Miss Baxter, trim stuff in a series of period costumes and matching millinery, has the requisite sauciness combined with essential sincerity to make the woman's part stand up. Her inter-relatedness to and with Charlton Heston, a rugged and believable characterization, gives the production its underpinning.

Westerns have surely had many a beguiling and lovable and sturdy-souled Mexican. This one comes equipped with Gilbert Roland, a highly sentimental and fancy-speaking amigo. Together with his five bashful sons, this is a very real appeal for audiences and Roland was never more beautiful Mexican. Roland it is whose loyalties and warmth build the human side which redeems "Three Violent People" from being just another giddyap.

Early in the film, legit's Elaine Stritch makes an acidy blondine madame arouse interest. Another arresting performance is that of the one-armed brother of the Texan captain as interpreted by Tom Tryon, a considerably mixed up kid. The role has a hint or two of stock caricature and yet some authentic dimension, the direction and performance in this instance possibly out-shining the script.

Such reliable meanies as Forrest Tucker, Bruce Bennett and John Harmon impress the critical eye with their know-how and there are a number of bits which throw flecks of character.

Loyal Griggs' photography seems first class, with a nod for the special effects of John P. Futon and Farciot Edouart. There is a single song credited, "Un Momento," by Mack David and Martita. Don't ask what it's like. It got lost and came out hardly a strain.

All in all, this is a well-produced entertainment as to which most customers won't quibbel. And pretty nice country out there in Texas when Anne Baxter's around.
Land.

1957

Edge of the City

Provocative, courageous film with both mass and class appeal. Good b.o. potential.

Metro presentation of David Susskind production. Stars John Cassavetes, Sidney Poitier, and Jack Warden. Features Ruby Dee, Kathleen Maguire, Robert Simon, and Ruth White. Directed by Martin Ritt. Story and screenplay by Robert Alan Aurthur. Camera, Joseph Brun; editor, Sidney Meyers; music, Leonard Rosenman. Previewed in N.Y., Dec. 20, '56. Running time, 85 MINS.

Axel North .... John Cassavetes
Tommy Tyler .... Sidney Poitier
Charles Malik .... Jack Warden
Ellen Wilson .... Kathleen Maguire
Lucy Tyler .... Ruby Dee
Mr. Nordmann .... Robert Simon
Mrs. Nordmann .... Ruth White
Davis .... William A. Lee
Brother .... Val Avery
Detective .... John Kellogg
Wallace .... David Clarke
Lucy's Mother .... Estelle Hemsley
Old Stevedore .... Charles Jordan
Nightboss .... Ralph Bell

This is the first film venture for producer David Susskind, writer Robert Alan Aurthur and director Martin Ritt and the bow is an auspicious one. Trio, whose roots are in video and legit, have come up with a courageous, thought-provoking and exciting film.

Based on its budget allotment, "Edge of the City," if properly marketed and exploited, can emerge a substantial b.o. success. It is broadly in the category of "On the Waterfront" and "The Blackboard Jungle." Like its predecessors, it packs a tremendous wallop; yet at the same time it has something important to say. This does not mean that "Edge of the City" should automatically be labeled a message picture. It has elements of action and violence that will attract mass appeal audiences. Simultaneously, it has ideas that will please many sophisticates and the more-aware segment of the population. It is, to some extent, a social document. However, it is never preachy. It makes its point subtly without employing a sledgehammer.

Based on Aurthur's teleplay, "A Man Is Ten Feet Tall," a factor that should not deter from its theatre success, "Edge" marks a milestone in the history of the screen in its presentation of an American Negro. To be sure, films have tackled the Negro "question" before, but it has always been in terms of the "problem" involved. In "Edge," the Negro is immediately accepted as a fully-integrated, first-class citizen. The friendship between a Negro and a white is presented as a normal, everyday occurrence without either man taking into consideration the other's color. The relationship appears so natural in the film that viewers soon lose sight of the difference in pigmentation.

Presenting Negroes and whites on an "equal" basis will, of course, raise the issue of how the film will be accepted in the south, and elsewhere where bias is strong. In light of the current tension over integration, some southern theatremen will probably bypass the film. While this may hurt the film's grossing potential, the controversy can also work to stimulate extra interest in other areas.

The peculiar aspect of "Edge" is that it is not a film dealing with the Negro problem. The protagonist is a guilt-ridden, psychologically mixed-up white youth, sensitively played by John Cassavetes. Plagued by the memory of his part in the accidental death of his brother and his inability to "belong" either to his family or society, he AWOLs the Army. He finds employment in a New York railroad yard where he immediately is befriended by a goodnatured, philosophical Negro lad and incurs the enmity of a vicious and tough hiring boss. In a sense, it places him between consummate good and evil as he strives to straighten out his tortured life.

Through his Negro friend, he begins to feel "acceptance"; he learns how to laugh, learns the enjoyment of simple pleasures as dating, bowling, a home life, and begins to feel like "a man who is 10 feet tall." He faces a serious setback when his friend is killed in a violent fight with the bigoted hiring boss. As the police investigate the "murder," he adheres, to the "no squealing" code of the truck-loaders, but he later regains his courage, stands up to the hiring boss and "finds himself" as the picture ends.

Filmed on location in New York, the film has a real-life flavor as it roams among New York's railroad yards and upper Manhattan's apartment house district. Ritt has elicited topnotch performances from the entire cast. Cassavetes is convincing as the troubled youth. Sidney Poitier, as his Negro friend, turns in the most distinguished of his many first-rate characterizations. Jack Warden, who gains in stature as an actor with each outing, is particularly effective as the evil hiring boss. Fine performances are also given by Ruby Dee, as Poitier's wife; Kathleen Maguire, as Cassavetes' understanding girlfriend; and Robert Simon and Ruth White, as Cassavetes' parents.

The film's two fights—one with longshoremen's bale hooks—are excitingly presented. The final battle between Cassavetes and Warden is extremely potent film footage, powerfully spotted, and will keep audiences at the edge of their seats.

Despite the film's many assets, it's not without its faults as a b.o. contender. The lack of boxoffice names may be a deterrent. The manner of presentation will not appeal to all. The exaggerated naturalism of some of the scenes may appear false to many. And the romance between Cassavetes and the attractive social worker may not ring true. However, these are minor exceptions on the basis of the film's overall effect. Ritt has displayed a mastery of the film medium and will undoubtedly rate additional assignments. The sharp camerawork of Joseph Brun contributes to the documentary feeling. Leonard Rosenman has provided a fine musical score although it is occasionally intrusive in some of the dramatic scenes. Minor technical flaws will only be noticed by the experts.
Holl.

The Wrong Man

Suspenseful true-life of Stork Club musician falsely accused of crime. Handled in forceful Alfred Hitchcock style. Strong entry for general market.

Hollywood, Dec. 31.

Warners release of an Alfred Hitchcock production. Stars Henry Fonda, Vera Miles; costars Anthony Quayle; features Harold J. Stone, Charles Cooper, John Heldabrand, Esther Minciotti, Kippy Campbell, Robert Essen, Richard Robbins. Directed by Hitchcock. Screenplay, Maxwell Anderson, Angus MacPhail; story, Anderson; camera, Robert Burks; editor, George Tomasini; music, Bernard Herrmann. Previewed Dec. 18, 1956. Running time, 110 MINS.

Manny Balestrero .... Henry Fonda
Rose Balestrero .... Vera Miles
O'Connor .... Anthony Quayle
Lt. Bowers .... Harold J. Stone
Detective Matthews ...... Charles Cooper
Tomasini .... John Heldabrand
Manny's Mother .... Esther Minciotti
Mrs. Ann James .... Doreen Lang
Constance Willis .... Laurinda Barrett
Miss Betty Todd .... Norma Connolly
Gene Conforti .... Nehemiah Persoff
Olga Conforti .... Lola d'Annunzio
Robert Balestrero .... Kippy Campbell
Gregory Balestrero ...... Robert Essen
Daniell .... Richard Robbins
Judge .... Dayton Lummis
Mrs. O'Connor .... Frances Reid
Miss Dennerly .... Peggy Webber

Alfred Hitchcock draws upon real-life drama for this gripping piece of realism. He builds the case of a N.Y. Stork Club musician falsely accused of a series of holdups to a powerful climax, the events providing director a field day in his art of characterization and suspense. With its exploitation potential and names of Henry Fonda and Vera Miles to attract, film shows sturdy promise for the general market.

Subject here is Manny Balestrero, the bass fiddle player whose story hit Gotham headlines in 1953 when he was arrested for crimes he did not commit. In a case of mistaken identity, he was not freed until the actual culprit was found during his trial. Not, however, before the musician, a family man with a wife and two young sons, went through the harrowing ordeal of being unable to prove his innocence, and seeing his wife break and become a mental case under the strain.

All this the script by Maxwell Anderson and Angus MacPhail develops in minute detail, Hitchcock drains the dramatic possibilities with often frightening overtones, as the spectator comes to realize that the very same could happen to him, if he fell into such a situation. The musician, played with a stark kind of impersonation by Fonda, is positively identified by several of the holdup victims, and other circumstances arise which seem to prove his guilt.

Hitchcock gives unfoldment an extra documentary touch through use of the actual backgrounds, ranging from the Stork Club and the Queens subway to city's police stations and courtrooms. N.Y. City authorities cooperated with director on film. Low-key photography by Robert Burks and a simple yet effective music score by Bernard Herrmann additionally help maintain the grim mood.

Fonda ably portrays the unfortunate musician and finds capital assistance in Miss Miles, who registers strongly as the wife. Anthony Quayle, screen newcomer, is impressive as Frank O'Connor, defense attorney now District Attorney of Queens County. N.Y. Harold J. Stone and Charles Cooper stand out in detective roles, Kippy Campbell and Robert Essen are okay as the young sons, and Richard Robbins scores briefly as the real culprit, bearing a remarkable resemblance to Fonda, Balance of cast are carefully selected.
Whit.

The Spanish Gardener
(BRITISH—V'VISION—COLOR)

Absorbing filmization of A. J. Cronin story with colorful Spanish background; fine for domestic market, but requiring a real bally for U.S.

London, Dec. 25.

Rank (John Bryan) production and release. Stars Dirk Bogarde, Jon Whiteley, Michael Hordern. Directed by Philip Leacock. Screenplay, Lesley Storm, John Bryan from novel by A. J. Cronin. Camera, Christopher Challis; editor, Reginald Mills; music, John Veale. At Odeon, Leicester Square, London. Running time, 97 MINS.

Jose .... Dirk Bogarde
Nicholas Brande .... Jon Whiteley
Harrington Brande ..... Michael Hordern
Garcia .... Cyril Cusack
Maria .... Maureen Swanson
Robert Burton .... Lyndon Brook
Carol Burton ...... Josephine Griffin
Leighton Bailey .... Bernard Lee
Magdalena .... Rosalie Crutchley
Jose's Mother .... Ina De La Haye
Dr. Harvey .... Geoffrey Keen
Pedro .... Harold Scott
Police Escorts.......... Jack Stewart, Richard Molinas
Maid .... Susan Lyall Grant
Taxi Driver .... John Adderley
Policeman .... David Lander

A. J. Cronin's study of a minor diplomat with considerable academic qualifications, but without human understanding, translates into absorbing screen entertainment. It is a leisurely told story with colorful Spanish backgrounds and with stout marquee values.

Filmed in VistaVision, the Technicolor hues show off the beauties of the Costa Brava, providing a handsome setting for the tale. Philip Leacock has directed with a sincere, sensitive approach. He's avoided the mistake of making this another psychological drama while giving the necessary emphasis to the unhealthy father and child relationship.

Michael Hordern is the diplomat separated from his wife, continually passed up for promotion, who insists that his son is delicate, cannot join other children in games or at school and is denied every form of companionship. Dirk Bogarde is hired as a gardener and his friendly attitude to the kid sparks a violent jealousy in the father who attempts unreasonable and preposterous measures to bring their friendship to an end. This, in turn, leads to open rebellion by the child, who shows better character judgment than his father.

The mounting conflict between son and father is neatly and logically developed, but the eventual reconciliation after the boy has run away from home hits a more obvious emotional level. By its very nature the role (the father) filled by Hordern is designed to irritate, and it's a tribute to his performance that he effectively sustains the interest.

Bogarde gives a polished, restrained study as the Spanish gardener whose motives in befriending the boy are completely misunderstood. Jon Whiteley's moppet is a keenly sensitive portrayal, and will help to give the pic wide appeal. Cyril Cusack, as a sinister valet, and Maureen Swanson, as the gardner's girl friend, top a good supporting cast which includes fine performances by Josephine Griffin, Bernard Lee and Geoffrey Keen.
Myro.

Oedipus Rex
(COLOR)

Canadian-made absorbing production of Sophocles' tragedy, but with limited b.o. prospects.

Motion Picture Distributors Inc. release of an Irving M. Lesser presentation produced by Leonard Kipnis. Directed by Tyrone Guthrie. Script, W. B. Yeats' translation of the Sophocles tragedy; camera (Eastmancolor), Roger Barlow; music, Cedric Thorpe Davie. Previewed at 55th St. Playhouse, N. Y., Dec. 27, '56. Running time, 88 MINS.

Messenger .... Douglas Rain
Oedipus .... Douglas Campbell
Priest .... Eric House
Creon .... Robert Goodier
Tiresias .... Donald Davis
Jocasta .... Eleanor Stuart
Man From Corinth...... Tony van Bridge
Old Shepherd .... Eric House
Chorus Leader .... William Hutt
Nurse .... Gertrude Tyas
Ismene and Antigone Nomi Cameron, Barbara Franklin

William Butler Yeats' version of Sophocles' famed tragedy has been brought to the screen by the Stratford, Ont., Festival Players in a moving and absorbing production. But while the film undeniably marks an intellectual milestone, at the same time it's quite apparent that this finest of ancient Greek classics has little modern mass appeal.

Boxoffice potential of the picture will be limited to art houses with a cultural following. Another lucrative sales avenue lies in the school and college market which can be tapped via 16m prints after the theatrical release scrapes bottom. From an exploitation standpoint and film also presents a problem for here erudition is being sold—not entertainment.

But in lieu of familiar cast names as sales pegs, this classical entry should benefit by intelligentsia word of mouth plus critical acclaim from the press. The story of how King Oedipus unwittingly killed his father and married his mother was lensed in widescreen Eastman Color at the Canadian Film Industries' Etobicoke studio in Toronto. A lone set is used and the camera recorded the drama as the players moved about the stage.

Under Tyrone Guthrie's brilliant direction, performances of the lengthy cast are emotionally rewarding. A particular high spot is Douglas Campbell's portrayal of the unhappy king. Fine support is provided by Eric House as the priest, Robert Goodier as Creon, Donald Davis as Tiresias, the blind prophet, and Eleanor Stuart as Jocasta, the mother, among others.

For those who may not be too familiar with Greek tragedy, it's a matter of becoming attuned to the austere set, the garish masks worn by the players, the curious speech and overall dramatic style. But once attunement is attained, then this masterpiece of the theatre becomes an emotional experience. Helping in this respect are Roger Barlow's camerawork, the Cedric Thorp Davie score as well as the masks and designs of Tanya Moiseiwitsch. *Gilb.*

Three Men In A Boat
(BRITISH—C'SCOPE—COLOR)

Screen version of dated classic; mainly for home trade.

London, Dec. 25.

Independent Film Distributors release of a Romulus (Remus) production. Stars Laurence Harvey, Jimmy Edwards, David Tomlinson; co-stars Shirley Eaton, Jill Ireland and Lisa Gastoni. Directed by Ken Annakin. Screenplay, Hubert Gregg and Vernon Harris from novel by Jerome K. Jerome; camera, Eric Cross; editor, Ralph Kemplen; music, John Addison. At Carlton Theatre, London. Running time, **94 MINS.**

George .... Laurence Harvey
Harris .... Jimmy Edwards
J .... David Tomlinson
Sophie .... Shirley Eaton
Bluebell .... Jill Ireland
Primrose .... Lisa Gastoni
Mrs. Willis .... Martita Hunt
Mr. Porterhouse .... Campbell Cotts
Mrs. Porterhouse .... Joan Haythorne
Clara .... Adrienne Corri
Ethelbertha .... Noelle Middleton
Mr. Quilp .... Charles Lloyd Pack
Photographer .... Robertson Hare
1st Old Gentleman .... A. E. Matthews
2nd Old Gentleman .... Miles Malleson
3rd Old Gentleman .... Ernest Thesiger
Woman Pianist .... Pat Lanski
Man Pianist .... Christian Duvaliex
Bowler .... Mark Hashfield
Captain .... Graham Curnow
Dad .... Stuart Saunders
Mum .... Margaret St. Barbe West

In these hectic times, this dated classic seems a strange choice for the modern cinemagoer. Whatever its draw in the home market, it is fairly certain that its main prospects will be limited to this area. Whether the oldsters will welcome it for nostalgic reasons and be sufficiently numerous to make it a paying proposition, is open to question. Story seems slow and artificial in development and background but marquee names may help put it over.

The three fugitives from a humdrum existence are depicted drifting down on the Thames in a small boat on a twoweek vacation, encountering all the hazards and discomfiture of that showoff day and age.

Jimmy Edwards, popular revue and radio comic, twirls his outsize moustaches and rolls his eyes effectively when ogling the girls, subsiding under the collapsing tent and falling overboard. While bombastically protesting his superior knowledge as to the inner workings of the maze at Hampton Court Palace, he nearly gets lynched by the pack of near hysterical folks who have trustingly followed him.

Laurence Harvey plays along on subdued lines as the bank teller who boasts of his higher status to an aristocratic young blond. Her companions and his get involved in a lot of further trouble in and out of the water and on the cricket field. David Tomlinson, as the only married member of the trio, squirms pathetically throughout, being usually the butt of the others' clumsiness or malice. The three girls are charmingly played by Shirley Eaton, Jill Ireland and Lisa Gastoni while Martita Hunt is impressive as a battleaxe aunt. A. E. Matthews, Miles Malleson and Ernest Thesiger contribute some brief amusing scenes as veteran fishermen and cricketers. The supporting players fit adeadequately into the characters of the period. Camerawork is one of the best features of the production. *Clem.*

The Black Whip
(CINEMASCOPE)

Good programmer. Third in Regal's low-budget series for 20th-Fox.

Hollywood, Dec. 18.

20th-Fox release of Robert Stabler (Regal) production. Stars Hugh Marlowe, Coleen Gray; co-stars Adele Mara, Angie Dickinson, Richard Gilden, Paul Richards. Features John Pickard, Dorothy Schuyler, Charles Gray, Sheb Wooley, Strother Martin, Harry Landers. Directed by Charles Marquis Warren. Story and screenplay, Orville Hampton; camera, Joseph Biroc; music, Raoul Kraushaar; editor, Fred W. Berger. Previewed Dec. 14, '56. Runnning time, **81 MINS.**

Lorn .... Hugh Marlowe
Jeannie .... Coleen Gray
Dewey .... Richard Gilden
Sally .... Angie Dickinson
Thorny .... Strother Martin
Murdock .... Paul Richards
Hainline .... Charles Gray
Constable .... William R. Hamel
Governor .... Patrick O'Moore
Delilah .... Dorothy Schuyler
Lasater .... Sheb Wooley
Sheriff Persons .... John Pickard
Ruthie .... Adele Mara
Fiddler .... Harry Landers
Dr. Gillette .... Howard Culver
Deputy Floyd .... Duane Thorsen
Jailer Garner .... Rush Williams
Bartender .... Sid Curtis
Red Legs ... Rick Arnold, Robert Garvey, Bill Ward

"The Black Whip" fits smoothly into the programmer classification, albeit a bit too long for such purposes at 81 minutes. Film's third in a low-budget series being produced under the Regal Films banner for 20th-Fox release.

The Orville Hampton story and screenplay, localed on the Western frontier shortly after the Civil War, tells tale of the Blacklegs, part of Quantrell's old outfit. Led by Paul Richards ("The Man With The Whip"), gang holes up at the Star Valley Inn where due shortly is the stagecoach with the Kentucky governor within. Baddies hope to kidnap him and collect a ransom before heading for Mexico, but their efforts are thwarted, mainly by Hugh Marlowe, who runs the Inn. That's about it; the basic actionful ingredients are there in the script, although so is some mighty clicheish dialog.

Acting generally is on the so-so side, with exception of Paul Richards, newcomer who makes a fine impression. Coleen Gray, Adele Mara and Angie Dickinson are around mainly for femme decoration, although the first-named does wind up with Marlowe. Richard Gilden is spotted as the latter's brother.

Charles Marquis Warren's direction of the Robert Stabler production keeps things on the move and is on the plus side, and Raoul Kraushaar has proved a good musical backing. Other technical credits are stock. *Neal.*

Checkpoint
(BRITISH-COLOR)

Evenly balanced auto-racing drama with Anthony Steel having second thoughts about helping a wanted criminal over the frontier; Odile Versois supplies tepid love interest.

London, Dec. 25.

Rank production (Betty E. Box) and release. Stars Anthony Steel, Odile Versois, Stanley Baker, James Robertson Justice; features Maurice Denham, Michael Medwin, Paul Muller, Lee Patterson. Directed by Ralph Thomas. Screenplay, Robin Estridge; camera, Ernest Steward; editor, Frederick Wilson; music, Bruce Montgomery. At Leicester Square Theatre, London. Running time, **84 MINS.**

Bill Fraser .... Anthony Steel
Francesca .... Odile Versois
O'Donovan .... Stanley Baker
Warren Ingram .. James Robertson Justice
Ted Thornhill .... Maurice Denham
Ginger .... Michael Medwin
Petersen .... Paul Muller
Johnny .... Lee Patterson
Gabriela .... Anne Heywood
Michael .... Anthony Oliver
Eddie .... Philip Gilbert
Commentator .... McDonald Hobley
Frontier Guard .... Robert Rietty
Night Watchman .... Andrea Malandrinos
Hotel Hall Porter .... Dino Galvani

Auto racing, with spills and thrills, forms the basis of this latest Rank pic. It is set in Italy, with the action almost entirely centred on one of the annual Grand Prix events which draw crack drivers from all over the world. It has a strongly dramatic opening that sets the pattern, and is exciting entertainment.

An auto multi-millionaire is desperate to get the services of a designer working for a rival Italian firm, and sends an unscrupulous envoy to negotiate within legal boundaries. Instead, he raids the works, steals the blueprint of a new model and, being caught by the night watchman, shoots him and kills policemen who give chase. To effect a diversion he fires an oil drum that destroys the building and kills the rest of his pursuers.

In hiding with their local agent, he is smuggled out of the country while acting as co-driver with their ace teamster. His co-operation is shortlived and when the Swiss frontier is crossed he makes a detour bringing the murder back on Italian soil. A fight ensues ending in the car crashing over a precipice, getting the hunted man while the other scrambles out unscathed. The debris envelops the motor manufacturer who has witnessed the fight from the lakeside, and he takes the blame for the plot in a dying statement, exonerating his driver.

Anthony Steel makes a manly figure as the driver who nearly yields to bribery and Odile Versois charmingly supplies the romantic angle. Stanley Baker is duly sinister as the ruthless killer while James Robertson Justice is effectively opulent as the tycoon who is forced into trickery. The racing team and manager are all well cast with well picked minor players. The scenery makes an impressive background for the grilling race, which takes up about two-thirds of the story. Production and camera work are exellent. *Clem.*

Tomahawk Trail

Actionful cavalry - Indians melo fitting patly into program market.

Hollywood, Dec. 24.

United Artists release of a Howard W. Koch production. Stars Chuck Connors, John Smith, Susan Cummings, Lisa Montell; features George Neise, Robert Knapp, Eddie Little, Frederick Ford, Dean Stanton. Directed by Leslie Selander. Screenplay, David Chandler; camera, William Margulies; editors, John F. Schreyer, John A. Bushelman; music, Les Baxter. Previewed Dec. 20, '56. Running time, **61 MINS.**

Sergeant Wade McCoy .... Chuck Conners
Private Reynolds .... John Smith
Ellen Carter .... Susan Cummings
Tula .... Lisa Montell
Lt. Jonathan Davenport .... George Neise
Private Barrow .... Robert Knapp
Johnny Dogwood .... Eddie Little
Private Macy .... Frederick Ford
Private Miller .... Dean Stanton

Obviously was made on short budget but carries enough realistic U.S. Cavalry-Indians action to come off well in the dual market. Producers have given it the type of treatment which appeals particularly to popcorn trade, who should receive it on edge of their seats.

The Howard W. Koch production focuses on a small troop besieged by Apaches on the warpath, forcefully scripted by David Chandler. When cavalrymen's mounts are stolen on the march by redskins, column makes its way on foot back to the fort, where it's discovered there are no survivors after an Indian attack. Dramatic aspects are motivated by Chuck Conners, hardboiled vet sergeant, taking over command from a West Point martinet after latter becomes mentally unbalanced. How troopers manage to survive another Apache attack lends excitment, with director Leslie Selander making the most of the action.

Conners acquits himself in socko fashion and George Neise is good as the officer who refuses to take the seasoned advice of his sergeant, threatening him with courtmartial for his "insubordination" after Conners assumes command. John Smith is sympathetic as sergeant's pal; Susan Cummings is in for romantic interest, as a white girl captured by Indians and later recaptured by the whites; and Lisa Montell scores as Apache chief's daughter who befriended Susan while she was with the tribe. Robert Knapp also stands out as a trooper.

Photography by William Margulies leads off topgrade technical credits and Les Baxter's music score registers. *Whit.*

Up in the World
(One Song)
(BRITISH)

Norman Wisdom as a hard luck nonentity caught up in kidnapping racket; suited for home market.

London, Dec. 18.

Rank production and release. Stars Norman Wisdom; features Maureen Swanson and Jerry Desmonde. Directed by

John Paddy Carstairs. Screenplay, Jack Davies, Henry E. Blyth and Peter Blackmore; camera, Jack Cox; editor, John Shirley; music, Philip Green. At Gaumont Theatre, London. Running time, 90 MINS.

Norman .... Norman Wisdom
Jeannie .... Maureen Swanson
Major Willoughby ...... Jerry Desmonde
Lady Banderville ...Ambrosine Phillpotts
Fletcher Hethrington ...... Colin Gordon
Sir Reginald .... Michael Caridia
Maurice .... Michael Ward
Sylvia .... Jill Dixon
Harper .... Cyril Chamberlain
Mick Bellman .... William Lucas
Max .... Eddie Leslie
Yvonne .... Hy Hazell

There are a number of stereotyped gags in this latest Norman Wisdom comedy, where the little man, as always, gets pushed around and finally comes through triumphant. He gets involved with kidnappers resulting in a jail sentence, but squirms his way doggedly through all troubles. Good direction and a firstrate supporting cast give plausibility to the obvious, well-worn situations and it should prove a good holiday attraction here for the popular market.

Losing his window cleaning job in London, Wisdom gets posted to a huge country mansion, with the largest number of panes in Britain. A kidnap scare involves the newcomer in a number of mishaps.

Norman Wisdom ambles plaintively throughout all his trials in his own pathetic fashion and manages to acquire a semblance of romance with Maureen Swanson, a comely housemaid. Jerry Desmonde makes a pompous dictatorial figure and Ambrosine Phillpotts swoons distressfully as the lady of the manor. Colin Gordon, as her brother, brings the most robust air to the cloistered household while Michael Caridia revels in his power as the mischievous teenager. House servants and thugs are all convincingly played and the atmosphere of the stately home is naturally preserved.   *Clem.*

Tel Aviv Taxi
(ISRAEL)

English language comedy from Israel. Poorly made. Limited potential.

Principal Film Exchange release of Geva-Frisch production. Stars Shy Ophir, Raphael Klatchkin, Miriam Bergstein-Cohen, Nathan Cogan, Azaria Rapoport, Gilda Doorn van Steyn, Samuel Rodensky, David Vardi, Mina Cruvi. Directed and written by Larry Frisch. Camera, Leon Nissem; editor, Nellie Bagor; music, Edmond Halpern. Previewed in N.Y. Dec. 12, '56. Running time, 70 MINS.
Players: Shy Ophir, Raphael Klatchkin, Miriam Bergstein-Cohen, Nathan Cogan, Azaria Rapoport, Gilda Doorn van Steyn, Smuel Rodensky; David Vardi, Mina Cruvi.

Larry Frisch, a 26-year-old American who has been filming documentaries in Israel, braved a task that more experienced artisans have avoided. He has assumed the triple threat assignment of producer, director and writer on "Tel Aviv Taxi," a comedy completely filmed in Israel at the cost of $60,-000. The picture was filmed in both Hebrew and English and the English version is presently available for release in the United States.

Despite the Israeli background, the picture has no political overtones and was made for the sole purpose of providing entertainment. The result, however, is disappointing. The picture is inept and amateurish. Except for a few performers, the acting is ludicrous. The technical aspects are below par and the story telling technique is familiar.

From a boxoffice standpoint, the

picture may draw some who are curious to observe scenes of modern Israel.

For his picture, Frisch borrows a method, perhaps as old as the Canterbury Tales, of stranding several travelers at an abandoned roadside house. This time an ancient taxi breaks down and as the travelers wait for it to be repaired each tells a story. In all, five flashback stories are presented, each of which has an O. Henry twist.

Although Frisch employs actors from the Habima and Cameri, Israeli national theatres, the performers appear lost in the English film version. Only Raphael Klatchkin and Miriam Bergstein-Cohen reveal any genuine thespian ability. The comedy attempts of Shy Ophir are embarrassing. Frisch's direction and the camera work are below professional standards.   *Holl.*

Top Secret Affair

Susan Hayward and Kirk Douglas in slick comedy routine. Strong b.o. values.

Warner Bros. release produced by Milton Sperling and Martin Rackin. Stars Susan Hayward, Kirk Douglas; features Paul Stewart, Jim Backus, John Cromwell, Roland Winters. Directed by H. C. Potter; written by Roland Kibbee and Allan Scott and based on characters from J. P. Marquand's "Melville Goodwin, U.S.A.;" camera, Stanley Cortez; editor, Folmar Blangsted; music, Roy Webb. Previewed in New York, Jan. 10, '56. Running time, 100 MINS.
Dottie Peale .... Susan Hayward
Maj. Gen. Melville Goodwin Kirk Douglas
Phil Bentley .... Paul Stewart
Col. Gooch .... Jim Backus
Gen. Grimshaw .... John Cromwell
Senator Burwick .... Roland Winters
Butler .... A. E. Gould-Porter
Lotzie .... Michael Fox
Sgt. Kruger .... Frank Gerstle
Bill Hadley .... Charles Lane

Since there seems to be a strong demand these days for light, escapist screen entertainment, "Top Secret Affair" should get a warm welcome from both trade and public. It's got a good basic plot, plenty of glib laugh lines and—for the marquee — two top performers who'll definitely draw 'em in.

Writers Roland Kibbee and Allan Scott have fashioned their yarn using characters from J. P. Marquand's "Melville Goodwin, U.S.A." and they've tossed in an almost bewildering variety of situations, ranging from the hilarious to the almost solemn. Upshot is a click comedy that functions on three levels—slapstick, sophisticated humor and, in spots, straight romantic drama.

Since the script is barbed with shafts of satirical wit aimed in the direction of the military, Congress and the magazine publishing field (they wouldn't be talking about Time?), "Affair" in spots suffers from a profusion of plenty and from some abrupt changes in pace. It's not always easy to tell how director H. C. Potter meant his audience to react. There's no doubt, however, that he's concocted a ribtickler that'll have wide and popular appeal.

Story is about a femme mag publisher who boosts a man for a government job. When latter goes to a general, she decides to do a cover story on him which will "expose" his character. Inevitably, she falls for "Old Ironpants." He walks out on her, and she runs the story, which brings on a Congressional investigation and threatens to ruin his career.

Finale: Girl publisher admits the yarn is a fake. The general clears his record by getting White House okay to declassify a romantic episode in which he was involved during the Korean war and during which he was required to feed false information to a spy.

Comedy roles are something different for both Susan Hayward and Kirk Douglas and the change of pace becomes them. As the publisher, Miss Hayward is amusing and attractively temperamental, but it isn't a uniformly good performance. Her drunk act is great and there are moments when, in small gestures, she catches the spirit of the part. But, more often than not, Miss Hayward doesn't appear fully at home in her part, and she's also exposed to some n.s.g. camera angles.

Douglas as the publicity-conscious general who soon sees through the trap Miss Hayward sets for him does a top job in

every respect. This is a savvy portrayal that milks the role for all it's worth, without giving in completely to what must have been a great temptation to do an all-out slapstick act. Douglas contributes to some very funny scenes as Miss Hayworth takes him slumming, with photogs hidden all over the place to catch him in compromising situations.

Paul Stewart as Miss Hayward's sarcastically resigned aid-de-camp is handed some of the best lines and he turns in a sock performance. Ditto Jim Backus in the role of Col. Gooch, the army p.r. man. John Cromwell as the general holds up his end well and ditto Michael Fox as the Russian-born lenser, Frank Gerstle as Sgt. Kruger and Charles Lane as Bill Hadley.

Producers Martin Rackin and Milton Sperling have given the production plenty of rich, visual values. The interiors of Miss Hayward's Long Island mansion and her office are plush. Director Potter keeps things moving along without letup and makes the most of a funny script. Potter's handling of the swimming pool scene, with a tipsy Miss Hayward balancing on the diving board while Douglas calmly gets ready to fish her out of the water when she falls, is uproarious.

Scripters Kibbee and Scott aren't lacking in punch lines, nor do they flinch from biting satire. Stanley Cortez's camerawork is fine; ditto Folmar Blangsted's editing. Roy Webb's music is in tune with the proceedings.

"Top Secret Affair" may not hit everyone as being the year's funniest, but it's a plenty bright entry from the Warner lot.   *Hift.*

Three Brave Men
(C'SCOPE)

Topical plot, inspired by actual security risk case, gives authenticity to see through general market to okay biz.

Hollywood, Jan. 9.
20th-Fox release of Herbert B. Swope Jr. production. Stars Ray Milland, Ernest Borgnine, Frank Lovejoy, Nina Foch, Dean Jagger; features Virginia Christine, Edward Andrews, Frank Faylen, Diane Jergens, Warren Berlinger, Andrew Duggan, Joseph Wiseman, James Westerfield. Directed and written by Philip Dunne; based on Pulitzer Prize-winning articles by Anthony Lewis; camera, Charles G. Clarke; editor, David Bretherton; music, Hans Salter. Previewed Jan. 4, '57. Running time, 85 MINS.
Joe Di Marco .... Ray Milland
Bernie Goldsmith ...... Ernest Borgnine
Captain Winfield .... Frank Lovejoy
Lieutenant McCoy .... Nina Foch
Rogers .... Dean Jagger
Helen Goldsmith ..... Virginia Christine
Major Jensen .... Edward Andrews
Enos Warren .... Frank Faylen
Shirley Goldsmith....... Diane Jergens
Harry .... Warren Berlinger
Browning .... Andrew Duggan
Jim Barron .... Joseph Wiseman
O'Reilly .... James Westerfield
Lt. Horton .... Richard Anderson
Miss Scott .... Olive Blakeney
Dietz .... Robert Burton
Perry .... Jason Wincren
Sanford .... Ray Montgomery
Alice .... Sandy Descher
Ruthie .... Patty Ann Gerrity
Gibbons .... Jonathan Hole
Susie .... Barbara Gould
Miss Howell .... Fern Barry
Gaddis .... Joseph McGuinn
Funston .... Samuel Colt

Familiar names and a topical plot, inspired by an actual "security risk" case, give an air of authenticity to "Three Brave Men" which will see it through the general market as a top-of-the-bill drama. Ray Milland and Ernest Borgnine star in the Herbert B. Swope Jr. production, while Frank

Lovejoy, Nina Foch and Dean Jagger carry off costarring roles to give it marquee weight for release intentions.

Director-scripter Philip Dunne bases the picture on Anthony Lewis' Pulitzer Prize-winning articles on the discharge of Abraham Chasanow, longtime Navy Department employe, as a security risk and his subsequent reinstatement with back pay after the charges were proved false. Borgnine enacts the Chasanow counterpart, with Milland as the attorney who fought the case through, and Dean Jagger as the Assistant Secretary of the Navy who finally acknowledged that a mistake had been made.

With its semi-documentary treatment in almost old March of Time style, film points up the jeopardy most everyone lives in when terms such as "security risk" and "commie" are thrown around loosely. Probably intentionally, security investigators are made to appear extremely lax in accepting hearsay as evidence. The laxness carries through to the Assistant Secretary, who accepts such false evidence, despite trial board recommendations to the contrary. It is not a pretty, nor confidence-inspiring, picture of security precautions, particularly since the circumstances of Chasanow's situation are faithfully depicted.

Milland and Borgnine team well. Lovejoy and Miss Foch, as trial board head and attorney, respectively, are good, as is Jagger as the Assistant Secretary. Virginia Christine obtains some touching moments as Borgnine's faithful wife. Competent, too, are Edward Andrews, Frank Faylen, Andrew Duggan, James Westerfield, Olive Blakeney and others portraying friends. Diane Jergens, Warren Berlinger, Sandy Descher and Patty Ann Garrity are adequate as the Borgnine kids.

Borgnine is stripped of job and good name when dismissed as a risk to national security. Milland takes his case, presents it successfully to the hearing board, which recommends reinstatement when it is brought out the accusations come from neighbors and associates who dislike Borgnine. Despite proof that security investigators did no deep digging in their work, the charges stand and it's not until the Assistant Secretary has a change of heart and launches a new investigation that Borgnine is finally cleared.

The documentary style is ably lensed by Charles G. Clarke and the other technical aids supply good support, as does the music supervision by Hans Salter.

Brog.

Notre-Dame de Paris

(FRENCH—C'SCOPE—COLOR)

Paris, Jan. 9.

Cocinor release of Hakim production. Stars Gina Lollobrigida, Anthony Quinn; features Jean Danet, Philipe Clay, Robert Hirsch, Alain Cluny. Directed by Jean Delannoy. Screenplay, Jacques Prevert, Jean Aurenche from novel by Victor Hugo; camera (Eastmancolor), Michel Kelber; editor, Henri Taverna. At Normandie, Paris. Running time, 110 MINS.

Esmeralda .... Gina Lollobrigida
Quasimodo .... Anthony Quinn
Frollo .... Alain Cluny
Poet .... Robert Hirsch
Clopin .... Philipe Clay
Fleur De Lys .... Daniele Dumont
Phoebus .... Jean Danet
Louis XI .... Jean Tissier
Dame .... Valentine Tessier

Already sold to most European countries, and with an English version made via an investment (reportedly $400,000) of Allied Artists, this looks to make a fine boxoffice dent for itself on the Continent. With the names of Gina Lollobrigida and Anthony Quinn, plus the spectacle and locale of the pic, this should be a good general circuit item for the U. S. on its entertainment values. With smart exploitation, its scope and name assets could also make suitable for firstrun chances, but it will need heavy selling.

Made twice before in the U. S. (as a silent pic with Lon Chaney and a talking pic with Charles Laughton), this is the first time the Victor Hugo classic gets a filmic retelling in its own country. Though this lacks the more dramatic quality of the Chaney version and the more bawdy aspects of the Laughton entry, it has a stolid recreation of period and place, with fine decors, acting and special effects to make it good spectacle. Director Jean Delannoy has not quite gotten the seething quality expected from medieval times. He has tried to gloss this over by an almost overinsistent detailing of social forms and concrete places sometimes to the detriment of the plot which seems somewhat literary. However, it still remains essentially a good story.

Quinn is excellent as the misshapen bellringer and adds stature to the character of the deformed Quasimodo who saves his beloved, only to lose her.

The obsessed priest is now an alchemist and it is his desire for Esmeralda (Miss Lollobrigida) that leads him to kill her young, royal lover and brings on her death and his own at the hands of his follower Quasimodo. The settings and recreation of the times is fine, but the excursions into the beggars' and thieves' worlds is less successful. Film picks up with Quasimodo's rescue of Esmeralda from the clutches of the hangman to give her sanctuary in Notre-Dame cathedral.

Miss Lollobrigida is properly provocative and lovely as the gypsy girl who enflames men. She has a chance to parade her pulchritude and do a good dance number plus sing some medieval songs. Quinn seconds her ably and bears the brunt of the film's interest. Alain Cluny is fine as the bedeviled alchemist. Remainder of the cast is suitable.

Special effects are good, but all is dominated by the imposing facade of Notre-Dame. Lensing is blessed with fine hues and C'Scope is well utilized in the more active scenes. In short, this retelling of the story fits into current pic spec trends and should be able to cash in on it, both in Europe and in the U. S., if properly handled.

Anglo version, of Allied Artists, is to be monickered "The Hunchback of Paris" for the other "Hunchback" title is still owned by RKO. However, the crooked back of Quasimodo, in this film, is scarcely noticeable as compared to the other interpretations. It is only bared in the episode in which the bellringer is whipped in public.

Mosk.

Mister Cory

(C'SCOPE-COLOR)

Tony Curtis as ambitious gambler in okay action-drama.

Hollywood, Jan. 3.

Universal release of Robert Arthur production. Stars Tony Curtis, Martha Hyer, Charles Bickford, Kathryn Grant; features William Reynolds, Russ Morgan, Henry Daniell, Willis Bouchey. Directed by Blake Edwards. Screenplay, Edwards, based on Leo Rosten story; camera (Eastman Color), Russell Metty; editor, Edward Curtiss; music supervision, Joseph Gershenson. Previewed Dec. 27, '56. Running time, 92 MINS.

Cory .... Tony Curtis
Abby Vollard .... Martha Hyer
Biloxi .... Charles Bickford
Jen Vollard .... Kathryn Grant
Alex Wyncott .... William Reynolds
Ruby Matrobe .... Russ Morgan
Earnshaw .... Henry Daniell
Mr. Vollard .... Willis Bouchey
Mrs. Vollard .... Louis Lorimer
Lola .... Joan Banks
Andy .... Harry Landers
Ronnie Chambers .... Glen Kramer
The Cook .... Dick Crockett

This saga of a young man's rise from the slums of Chicago to its gold coast—as a gambler—has been interestingly fashioned to please general audiences. Adding to its chances, which appear okay, in the regular market is the presence of Tony Curtis as the title character, and a couple of real cuties, Martha Hyer and Kathryn Grant, who share star billing with Curtis and Charles Bickford.

Robert Arthur's production wears a slick polish, enhanced by the use of Eastman Color and CinemaScope, and the physical values do a firstrate job of backing the dramatic action, even when the latter shows some thinness here and there. Blake Edwards' direction gets good performances from the cast and gives the story-telling a well-paced unfoldment. Edwards also scripted from a story by Leo Rosten and, while the writing leaves some plot ends dangling, the characters and situations are all they should be for this type general market filmfare.

Curtis, anxious to better himself and playing all the angles, jumps from the slums to a fashionable summer resort where a bus boy's job gives him a chance to make contacts, including the two femmes, for later use. Over a story span of several years he winds up partnered with Bickford in a swank Chicago gambling club, playing it romantically cozy with Miss Hyer, society tramp who figures he's good enough for a backdoor love affair but not for marriage. At fadeout time, it's Miss Grant, the tramp's younger sister, who gets the young man and he decides to try a more legitimate profession.

Curtis gives the title role a good personality ride and pleases. Miss Hyer should play more bad girls, judging by the s.a. and feel she gets into this character. Miss Grant is an engaging miss who'll win fans for her attractive performance as the younger sister who has no trouble making up her mind about Curtis. Bickford is very good as Curtis' gambling partner. William Reynolds, Miss Hyer's weak fiance, scores strongly, particularly in his big drunk scene. Russ Morgan, Henry Daniell, latter very amusing as a snobbish maitre d', Willis Bouchey and others lend capable support.

Russell Metty's lensing heads the list of good technical credits.

Brog.

Runaway Daughters

Juve delinquency yarn may be exploited for good returns in youthful market.

Hollywood, Jan. 15.

American-International release of an Alex Gordon production. Stars Marla English, Anna Sten, John Litel, Lance Fuller, Adele Jergens; costars Mary Ellen Kaye, Gloria Castillo; features Jay Adler, Steven Terrell. Directed by Edward L. Cahn. Story-screenplay, Lou Rusoff; camera, Frederick E. West; editor, Ronald Sinclair; music, Ronald Stein. Reviewed Jan. 9, '57. Running time, 90 MINS.

Audrey Barton .... Marla English
Ruth Barton .... Anna Sten
George Barton .... John Litel
Tony Forrest .... Lance Fuller
Dixie .... Adele Jergens
Mary Rubeck .... Mary Ellen Kaye
Angela Forrest .... Gloria Castillo
Rubeck .... Jay Adler
Bob Harris .... Steven Terrell
Joe .... Nicky Blair
Tommy .... Frank J. Gorshin
Maureen .... Maureen Cassidy
Henry .... Reed Howes
Miss Petrie .... Anne O'Neal
Detective .... Edmund Cobb

"Runaway Daughters" is a lowbudgetter based on teen-age problems and specifically aimed for this age audience where it may be exploited for strong returns. Film is in need of considerable trimming, but after a slow beginning the subject begins to take form and has been well worked out for film's particular market. American-International is packaging it for release with "Shake, Rattle and Rock!"

Topic of the Alex Gordon production focuses on youth in righteous revolt against treatment by their parents. Three young girls are spotlighted in the Lou Rusoff screenplay, who finally leave home and go to Los Angeles to seek a new life. One, Marla English, is a daughter of wealth; Mary Ellen Kaye is dominated by a father whose wife left him; and third is Gloria Castillo, left to her own devices by divorced parents who are out of the country. Yarn follows their various fortunes as they come to different ends.

Trio deliver convincingly. Miss English getting the best break through greater footage. As her parents, Anna Sten and John Litel turn in satisfactory performances. Lance Fuller is Miss Castillo's nogood brother and Adele Jergens his girl friend, both okay in hard roles. Jay Adler grimly portrays Miss Kaye's father who refuses to permit her to wed the boy she loves, Steven Terrell.

Edward L. Cahn's direction fits the pattern of the story, and has been backed by adequate technical assistance. ***Whit.***

The Barretts of Wimpole Street

(C'SCOPE-COLOR)

A healthy invalid poetess and her courting. Victorian romance revisited; for old lovers, not the young.

Hollywood, Jan. 8.

Metro release of Sam Zimbalist production. Stars Jennifer Jones, John Gielgud, Bill Travers, Virginia McKenna; features Susan Stephen, Vernon Gray, Jean Anderson, Maxine Audley, Leslie Phillips, Laurence Naismith, Moultrie Kelsall. Directed by Sidney Franklin. Screenplay, John Dighton; from play by Rudolf Besier; camera (Metrocolor), F. A. Young; editor, Frank Clarke; music, Bronislau Kaper; song, "Wilt Thou Have My Hand?"; music by Herbert Stothart. Previewed Jan. 2, '57. Running time 104 MINS.

Elizabeth .... Jennifer Jones
Barrett .... John Gielgud
Robert Browning .... Bill Travers
Henriotta .... Virginia McKenna
Bella .... Susan Stephen
Captain Surtees Cook .... Vernon Gray

Lovers of the classics, and just plain-old lovers, will find "The Barretts of Wimpole Street" a reliving of the romance between Elizabeth Barrett and Robert Browning as originally plotted in Rudolf Besier's play and in a 1934 screen version, also made by Metro. Hence, select playdates may profit from the story's lure for the more mature.

Elsewhere, the film's ability to draw is a question mark. To members of the hotrod, drag strip and youthful freedom set, the Victorian atmosphere and the paternal restrictions in the plot will likely seem no more than a quaint, old-fashioned, boy-meets-girl drama, long, talky and often tedious. Other than Jennifer Jones, the star names do not carry any marquee weight for the popular market; nor does the combination of top players suggest any pop appeal. However, in the British field the combo could mean something at the b.o.

Sidney Franklin, who directed the original film version starring Norma Shearer and Fredric March, helms this Sam Zimbalist production. For the first paragraph fans above, his direction feelingly re-creates the era. As in the first pic, he makes great use of Miss Browning's pet spaniel, Flush, and when the dog is on the scenes have appeal for any age. Under Zimbalist's guidance, the film has a quality look, perfectly picturing the era with almost museum fidelity and reflecting astuteness in virtually all phases except possibly the most important—choice of story for the current, highly competitive market.

Miss Jones, while a surprisingly healthy-looking Elizabeth, plays the invalid literary figure with great skill. There will undoubtedly be some pros and cons about Bill Travers' work as Browning, the vigorous, colorful poet who managed to court and win the delicate Elizabeth under the nose of her despotic father. He's personable and competent enough, even though some may find him not their idea of Browning.

John Gielgud, the father with an almost incestuous attachment for his daughter, repeats the film role originally done by Charles Laughton with all the stern menace it requires to give suspense to the plotting. Fortunately, he's the type of parent not around much any more, what with analysts and couches nowadays. Virginia McKenna is lively and appealing as the younger sister, Henrietta, secretly in love with Vernon Gray, good as Captain Surtees Cook. Also good is Jean Anderson as Wilson, the maid. Acceptable are Maxine Audley, Leslie Phillips, Laurence Naismith, Moultrie Kelsall and the others playing Miss Browning's six brothers.

The technical expertness of F. A. Young's lensing in CinemaScope and Metrocolor, the art direction, set decorations, editing and costuming are tellingly employed, as is the score by Bronislau Kaper. The song, "Wilt Thou Have My Hand?," cleffed by Herbert Stothart, accounts for an appealing family scene. *Brog.*

Istanbul
(C'SCOPE-COLOR-SONGS)

Conventional melodrama starring Errol Flynn, plus Nat Cole. Okay potential for general market.

Hollywood, Jan. 15.

Diamond smuggling in Istanbul cues this melodrama which returns Errol Flynn to American films. Its moderately interesting story of intrigue in an exotic setting is complemented by excellent use of backgrounds lensed in color in the Turkish capital, a combo that should prove okay fare for general situations. A further plus in Nat "King" Cole, who sings two numbers, and German actress Cornell Borchers, bearing a striking resemblance to Ingrid Bergman.

Action in the Albert J. Cohen production stems from Flynn's purchase of an Oriental bracelet, in which he discovers 13 valuable diamonds, and efforts of Turkish Customs and a gang of smugglers to recover the stones. For his suspected participation in the case, Flynn, an American pilot, adventurer, is deported. Returning five years late to get the jewels he hid in his hotel room, he immediately becomes the prey of both Customs officers and the smugglers. Romantic complications enter when he learns that Miss Borchers, who presumably was burned to death on the eve of their marriage five years before, is a victim of amnesia and now wed to another man.

Under Joseph Pevney's direction characters are kept believable. Flynn has shed his former derring-do acting for a more serious vein but makes his work count, and Miss Borchers is lovely as his former betrothed. Cole is in for a straight role as well as singing "I Was a Little Too Lonely" and "When I Fall in Love." John Bentley as the Customs' chief, Torin Thatcher as Miss Borchers' husband, Leif Erickson and Peggy Knudsen as a couple of brash American tourists and Martin Benson as smuggler head show up well.

William Daniel's color photography is above average and Clifford Stine is responsible for special camera work abroad. Seton I. Miller, Barbara Gray and Richard Alan Simmons are credited with scripting, from Miller's original. *Whit.*

L'Homme Aux Cles D'Or
(The Man With Golden Keys)
(FRENCH)

Paris, Jan. 9.

Solid storyline here is too stolid because the treatment of writer-director Leo Joannon and the frozen, over-technical acting of Pierre Fresnay. Moralistic and preachy in tone, it sacrifices movement. As a U. S. possibility, pic seems only good for secondary spots or possibly for tele.

A dedicated professor finds three students with their hands in his charity till. Instead of reporting them he makes them sign a paper to hold over them for good behavior. But the delinquents turn loose a loose young girl on him and he is framed by them on an attempted rape charge. Cashiered out of the school, it is years later before he has a chance for revenge.

Talking most of this story, instead of having action or character development, hurts this. Fresnay has some good moments but submerges the growth of the character in theatrical terms. Annie Girardot and Gil Vidal emerge as possible new film personalities here. Technical credits are fine and location shooting helps get some atmosphere into this essentially arid film. *Mosk.*

Gun For a Coward
(C'SCOPE—COLOR)

Story and characterization values make this above-average western.

Hollywood, Dec. 27.

Story and characterization values raise "Gun For a Coward" a notch above the usual oater. It's good western filmfare that action fans should like. There's something for the drama-seekers, too. Fred MacMurray, Jeffrey Hunter, Chill Wills and Dean Stockwell are the familiar masculine names providing marquee flash for regular situations.

Storywise, "Gun" is well-developed in the R. Wright Campbell original script. The action is tied together credibly via the complexities of character motivations, which give reason for events as they unfold under Abner Biberman's smartly-paced direction. Producer William Alland has cast the picture well and has obtained the right kind of backing from the technical ends, including George Robinson's firstrate C'Scope lensing in Eastman Color.

Title springs from Hunter's character as a young man with a dis-

taste for violence, although no coward even if he does wear that brand. He's the middle brother on the family ranch run by MacMurray who, as the elder, has taken the place of father to his two younger brothers. Hunter does a fine piece of work as the young man with the bad rep, being entirely believable throughout. MacMurray, too, registers strongly as the brother with too many responsibilities, a yoke that at first delays his planned marriage to Janice Rule and eventually causes him to lose her to Hunter. Miss Rule, in an offbeat type of prairie heroine, is exceptionally good.

Chill Wills strolls easily and well through his chore as ranch foreman and friend. Only off-kilter performance is that contributed by Stockwell. He plays the wild young brother as though he were the late James Dean. On his past record as a younger thespian he has no need to ape another's style. Josephine Hutchinson scores as the mother whose smothering love for Hunter is the principal source of that young man's problems. Betty Lynn, John Larch, Paul Birch and other casters provide excellent support.

Cattle drives, gun fights and other action sequences keep the pace lively as the personality conflicts of the plot are worked out to a good conclusion. Technical aids all abet the sight and sound values of the presentation. *Brog.*

Kelly and Me
(C'SCOPE—SONGS—COLOR)

A vaude ham, his dog and the early days of "talkie" pix. Good family-trade entry.

Hollywood, Jan. 15.

Family audiences will find "Kelly and Me" an entertaining story about a song-and-dance vaudevillian, his dog and the early days of sound in motion pictures. Consequently, it's a good entry for the regular dual bill market, with the names of Van Johnson, Piper Laurie and Martha Hyer to rate it either equal or top billing in its playdates.

Johnson literally leads a dog's life in the Everett Freeman script as a fairly likeable vaude ham who gets nowhere until the dog adopts him, takes over his act and sets things up so the "master" can tag along for the adventure in filmmaking. The "barkies" starring Kelly are a great b.o. success and Johnson finally comes to realize it's the dog the public likes, not him. Menace to the principals' happiness is worked in via having the dog's former owner turn up to claim him, but Kelly is faithful to

Johnson and it all comes out right in the end.

Robert Z. Leonard's direction handles the subject well and draws good performances from the cast. Johnson is excellent as the hammy, conceited entertainer, neatly impersonating the type of early-thirties song-and-dance man who helped kill vaudeville. Piper Laurie pleases as the daughter of the studio head who loves Kelly and his master, while Miss Hyer is luscious and sexy as the film queen of the lot. Onslow Stevens, studio head, is excellent, and there are performance assists from Herbert Anderson, Gregory Gay, Dan Riss, Maurice Manson, Douglas Fowley and Frank Wilcox. Kelly, a white German Shepherd, is a natural actor, providing the humans with plenty of competition as trained by Ernie Smith.

Robert Arthur uses CinemaScope and Technicolor to frame his production and the values are all good. Technical assets are topped by Maury Gertsman's lensing. *Brog.*

Public Pigeon No. 1
(SONGS-COLOR)

Red Skelton in unfunny comedy based on tv show.

Hollywood, Jan. 1.

RKO release of Harry Tugend (Val-Ritchie Corp.) production. Stars Red Skelton, Vivian Blaine, Janet Blair; features Jay C. Flippen, Allyn Joslyn, Benny Baker and Seven Ashtons. Directed by Norman Z. McLeod. Screenplay, Tugend; from teleplay by Devery Freeman; based on story by Don Quinn, Larry Berns; camera (Technicolor), Paul C. Vogel; editor, Otto Ludwig; songs, Matty Malneck, Eve Marley; choreography, Miriam Nelson; music composed, conducted by David Rose. Previewed Dec. 28, '56. Running time, **79 MINS.**

Rusty Morgan	Red Skelton
Rita DeLacey	Vivian Blaine
Edith Enders	Janet Blair
Lt. Ross Qualen	Jay C. Flippen
Harvey Baker	Allyn Joslyn
Frankie Frannis	Benny Baker
Avery	Milton Frome
Dipso Dave Rutherford	John Abbott
Warden	Howard McNear
Harrigan	James Burke
Club manager	Herb Vigran

Red Skelton as a dumb cluck conned by a couple of swindlers into thinking he's working for the FBI may have looked funny on paper—and may have had its chuckles as the video program it once was. On the theatrical big-screen it's strictly unfunny and must be counted among the comic's minor league efforts. Entertainment-wise, it is no more than a filler for program bills and it's doubtful if Skelton's name will help much.

Produced by Harry Tugend from his own screenplay under the Val-Ritchie Corp. label for RKO release, film's shortcomings start with the writing, and there is nothing that Norman Z. McLeod's direction or the other contributions do to overcome the handicap. Pic is from a teleplay by Devery Freeman that was based on a story by Don Quinn and Larry Berns. It tells how Skelton and Janet Blair have started a joint savings account so they can get married. Conmen Allyn Joslyn and Benny Baker, however, sell him some phony stock and then use him as a courier to collect from other victims, even con him into going to jail in the belief they are FBI and he's helping on a case. Windup finds Skelton $10,000 richer via an unearned reward for the swindlers.

About the only passable comedy in the entire 79 minutes is the jail break sequence, in which authorities do their utmost to help Skelton escape so he will lead them to the wanted men. Elsewhere, the comedy is of the walkout variety—which many preview patrons did. Skelton never gets going and Miss Blair has practically nothing to do.

Joslyn and Baker are no better than the material; nor is Vivian Blaine, Baker's dumb blonde companion. Additionally, she has to deliver two poor songs and production numbers as a nitery singer. Matty Malneck and Eve Marley cleffed "Don't Be Chicken, Chicken" and "Pardon Me, Got To Go Mambo," while Miriam Nelson did the awkwardly performed choreography. Jay C. Flippen, police lieutenant, Milton Frome, John Abbott and others reflect what they were given to work with.

Paul C. Vogel handled the Technicolor photography satisfactorily, and David Rose composed and conducted the background score adequately. *Brog.*

Talpa
(C'SCOPE-COLOR) (MEXICAN)

Peliculas Nacionales release of a Cinematografica Latina production, produced by Adolfo Lagos. Stars Victor Manuel Mendoza, Lilia Prado, Jaime Fernandez; features Leonor Llausas, Hortensia Santovena. Directed by Alfredo Crevenna. Screenplay by Edmundo Baez from a story by Juan Rulfo. Camera, Rosalio Solano; editor, Gloria Shoemann; music, Lan Adomian. At Cine Alameda, Mexico City. Dec. 20, '56. Running time, **87 MINS.**

Tanilo	Victor Manuel Mendoza
Juana	Lilia Prado
Esteban	Jamie Fernandez
The Brazen One	Leonor Llausas
Mother	Hortensia Santovena
Drunkards' Mother	Alicia Montoya
Drunkard	Ricardo Baez

Title of this epic-size, religiously-slanted, heavily-mooded Mexican tinter will give its U.S. exhibs little to go on. It refers to a town where pilgrims congregate in supplication for religious miracles and for this reason is untranslatable. An English language version has already been prepared which runs 73 minutes, a cut of 14, which the film badly needs if it is to get stateside play. Heavy religious quality crossed with its adultery theme will undoubtably get it mixed reactions, but in the overall it's a question whether even home-front audiences will go for the purely downbeat subject matter, no matter how excellently lensed and portrayed.

Story tells of two blacksmith brothers. One older and happily married, the other a young Lothario-type drifter. Older brother is unable to continue forging, due to a loss of muscular control. Younger takes over the work and eventually the not too unwilling wife. In an attempt to work a miracle, wife and two brothers perigrinate to the virgin shrine at Talpa, where the older dies. Returning home, the adulterers are faced with the knowledge that they may, in a moral sense, have been the cause of the death and by an avenging angel mother, who inherently knows their relationship. The girl again heads for Talpa and the forgiveness. Her lover rides off, still a wanderer.

Characterizations throughout are excellent, with Hortensia Santovena's mother role a powerfully composed dramatic entity which stands out. Jaime Fernandez comes across solidly and again proves that he is one of the few top juve talents in this area. Victor Manuel Mendoza, as his older brother, has moments of force and conviction, but is faced by a role that is tough to underplay. Leonor Llausas, as the other woman in the younger brother's life, a village tramp, is a far more believable femme fatale than Lilia Prado, whose severe makeup gives her realistic quality, but fails to place her as the logical focus for all the films' sex fuss. Her portrayal nevertheless is ably and sensitively handled.

This is basically an art film. Its moments of pictorial exterior beauty as lensed by up and coming Rosalio Solano are top flight. Interiors, however, seem at times heavily overlit. Scenes of pilgrims on the march and of typical religious observances at the Talpa shrine are unusual, but traveloggy in the hands of Alfredo Crevenna. *Pete.*

Crime of Passion

Barbara Stanwyck, Sterling Hayden in okay meller for program bookings.

Hollywood, Jan. 11.

United Artists release of Herman Cohen production. Stars Barbara Stanwyck, Sterling Hayden, Raymond Burr; features Virginia Grey, Fay Wray, Royal Dano. Directed by Gerd Oswald. Story, screenplay, Joe Eisinger; camera, Joseph La Shelle; editor, Marjorie Fowley; music, Paul Dunlap. Previewed Jan. 10, '57. Running time, **85 MINS.**

Kathy	Barbara Stanwyck
Doyle	Sterling Hayden
Inspector Pope	Raymond Burr
Alice Pope	Fay Wray
Alidos	Royal Dano
Sara	Virginia Grey
Detective Jules	Dennis Cross
Detective James	Robert Griffin
Nalence	Jay Adler
Officer Spitz	Malcolm Atterbury
Chief of Police	John S. Launer
Detective Johns	Brad Trumbull
Detective Jones	Skipper McNally
Mrs. Jules	Jean Howell
Mrs. James	Peg La Centra
Mrs. Johns	Nancy Reynolds
Mrs. Jones	Marjorie Owens
Reporter	Robert Quarry
Delivery Boy	Joe Conley
Lab Technician	Stuart Whitman

"Crime of Passion" is the story of a sob sister turned murderess, with good plot twists but regulation development. It will be an okay entry for the program market on the strength of the familiar names of Barbara Stanwyck, Sterling Hayden and Raymond Burr.

The Bob Goldstein presentation through United Artists, produced by Herman Cohen, is laid in Los Angeles, after a San Francisco plot kickoff, and obtains a note of authenticity in its newspaper and police station settings. Gerd Oswald's direction of the Joe Eisinger screenplay inclines to be deliberate in pacing many scenes, spinning out the 85-minute footage a bit too long for a thoroughly satisfactory action-meller feel.

Plot deals with a woman who gives up her career ambitions as a Frisco sobsister to marry an L.A. policeman. Soon bored with the monotony of her new life, her ambitions turn to advancing her husband on the force and she uses some feline, some dirty, tricks to do it. All her schemes collapse when the police inspector, with whom she had been playing cozy to get hubby ahead, decides that duty and the department come first. His decision gets him a bullet in the head, leaving the husband with the unwelcome duty of bringing in his wife.

Miss Stanwyck, the ambitious wife; Hayden, her husband, and Burr, the inspector, put their best into the make-believe and come off okay. Royal Dano is good as a rival officer, as is Virginia Grey as his wife. Fay Wray, wife of Burr; Dennis Cross, Robert Griffin, Jay Adler, Malcolm Atterbury, Stuart Whitman are among others giving competent support.

Joseph LaShelle's black-and-white lensing, the score by Paul Dunlap and other technical assists and acceptable. *Brog.*

The Halliday Brand

Offbeat western drama for general market; Joseph Cotten name to pull.

Hollywood, Jan. 15.

United Artists release of a Collier Young production. Stars Joseph Cotten, Viveca Lindfors, Betty Blair, Ward Bond, Bill Williams; features Jay C. Flippen, Christopher Dark. Directed by Joseph H. Lewis. Story-screenplay, George W. George, George S. Slavin; camera, Ray Rennahan; editor, Stuart O'Brien; music, Stanley Wilson. Previewed Jan. 4, '57. Running time, **79 MINS.**

Daniel	Joseph Cotten
Aleta	Viveca Lindfors
Martha	Betsy Blair
Big Dan	Ward Bond
Clay	Bill Williams
Chad Burris	Jay C. Flippen
Jivaro	Christopher Dark
Mante	Jeanette Nolan

This well-knit western drama carries enough embellishments to rate good response in the general market, where the name of Joseph Cotten particularly should be a drawing card. Film has been given the type of rugged values right down the line to make it sturdy fare in playdates for which it's beamed.

Producer Collier Young has surrounded Cotten with a top cast who acquit themselves interestingly under Joseph E. Lewis' smooth direction. The George W. George-George S. Slavin script projects a story of conflict between Cotten, a sensitive man, and Ward Bond, will not be crossed and whose actions finally drive the son to outlawry.

Cotten etches an impressive portrayal in his standup against his domineering father, who fought a winning battle against the wilderness and still employs the same methods in his treatment of people. Told mostly in flashback form, story tells of the father's fierce pride in his family name the Halliday brand, he calls it which leads to all the difficulties between father and son. The son leaves home after witnessing a long series of injustices, climaxed by sheriff refusing protection from a lynch mob of the half-breed his daughter loves, and in retaliation the father brands his son an outlaw. In a dramatic climax, showing return of the son to end the feud, the father on his deathbed tries to kill Cotten but dies before he can pull the trigger.

Bond is powerfully cast as the sheriff, who cannot understand what he terms the weak side of his son's character, and Betsy Blair is heroic as the daughter, unforgiving but loyal to her father. Viveca Lindfors is in as the half-breed's sister, with whom Cotten is in love, somewhat strangely cast but still effective. Bill Williams is okay as Cotten's brother, also in love with the breed, and Christopher Dark scores as the half-breed.

Technical credits generally are good, Ray Rennahan's camera work and Stanley Wilson's music score topping the spread. *Whit.*

The Night Runner

Downbeat programmer with dim b.o. potential.

Hollywood, Jan. 15.

UI release of an Albert J. Cohen production. Stars Ray Danton, Colleen Miller; features Merry Anders, Willis Bouchey, Harry Jackson, Robert Anderson. Directed by Abner Biberman. Screenplay, Gene Levitt; story, Owen Cameron; camera, George Robinson; editor, Al Joseph; music, Joseph Gershenson. Previewed Jan. 2, '57. Running time, **79 MINS.**

Roy Turner	Ray Danton
Susan Mayes	Colleen Miller
Amy Hansen	Merry Anders
Loren Mayes	Willis Bouchey
Hank Hansen	Harry Jackson
Ed Wallace	Robert Anderson
Miss Dodd	Jean Inness
Vernon	Eddy C. Waller
Dr. Crawford	John Stephenson
Dr. Royce	Alexander Campbell
Miss Lowell	Natalie Masters
Man Interviewer	Richard Cutting
Captain Reynolds	Steve Pendleton
Real Estate Man	Jack Lomas

"The Night Runner" is a downbeat programmer with dim booking prospects. Its story of a psycho is unpleasant, a strange subject for today's discriminating audiences, and despite satisfactory production values the going will be tough.

Plottage of the Albert J. Cohen production twirls around a young man released from a state mental hospital only half-cured and his start of a new life in a small Southern California coast community after he has bolted a try in the city. When the owner of the motel where he rooms, whose daughter chap has been romancing, kicks him out after learning his past, he kills him, trying to make it appear as a robbery. The daughter, in love with the stranger, becomes suspicious, and as these suspicions begin to point to him the murderer tries to kill her, too. He recovers his sanity in time to save her from the ocean in which he pushed her off a cliff, and calls the police to come for him.

Abner Biberman's direction is slow, but he manages persuasive performances from his cast headed by Ray Danton and Colleen Miller, both okay in their respective roles. Willis Bouchey handles the father part satisfactorily, and Merry Anders and Harry Jackson make a nice young married couple about to have a baby. The Gene Levitt script is based upon a story by Owen Cameron, but topic is against him. Technical credits are standard.
Whit.

Drango

Post-Civil War "Reconstruction Period" story with Jeff Chandler name to spark film for general trade.

Hollywood, Jan. 15.

United Artists release of a Hall Bartlett production. Stars Jeff Chandler; co-stars Joanne Dru, Julie London; features Donald Crisp, John Lupton, Ronald Howard. Directed by Bartlett, Jules Bricken; screenplay, Bartlett; camera, James Wong Howe; music, Elmer Bernstein; editor, Leon Seiditz. Previewed Jan. 8, '57. Running time, **92 MINS.**

Drango	Jeff Chandler
Marc	John Lupton
Kate	Joanne Dru
Calder	Morris Ankrum
Clay	Ronald Howard
Shelby	Julie London
Allen	Donald Crisp
Mrs. Allen	Helen Wallace
Dr. Blair	Walter Sande
Randolph	Parley Baer
Mrs. Randolph	Amzie Strickland
Ragan	Charles Horvath
Cameron	Barney Phillips
Jeb Bryant	David Stollery
Ellen Bryant	Mimi Gibson
Burke	Paul Lukather
Blackford	Damion O'Flynn
Mrs. Blackford	Edith Evanson
Luke	Phil Chambers
Tom Randolph	David Saber
Scott	Chuck Webster
Mrs. Scott	Katherine Warren
Zeb	Chubby Johnson
Col. Bracken	Milburn Stone
Stryker	Anthony Jochim
Young Woman	Maura Murphy

"Drango" deals with a subject seldom touched on the screen—the Reconstruction Period in the South after the Civil War—and as such the film lends certain novelty. It's the first picture to be turned out by Jeff Chandler's new indie outfit, and while given pedestrian treatment at times, it's fairly well plotted and star's name should carry it through the general runs.

Chandler plays a Union officer in the Hall Bartlett production, sent as military governor to a Georgia community ravished by Sherman's march-to-the-sea only a few months previously. The terror still lives fresh in the minds of the people, and the officer, who wants to build and restore, is met not only with bitterness but with open hostility.

Hall, who also scripted and codirects with Jules Bricken, uses the dramatic plot device of Chandler having been the officer in charge of Sherman's troops during their reign of terror in the valley. Hope is seen for the future when the community finally recognizes Chandler's good intentions.

Chandler delivers a convincing performance and gets good support from a well-rounded cast. Film intros Ronald Howard, son of the late Leslie Howard, excellent as secret leader of the opposition who tries to recruit townsmen to again battle the Union. Joanne Dru is daughter of a Union sympathizer, in for romance with Chandler although bitter at first when he is unable to save her father from being lynched by a Southern mob. Julie London, cast as a plantation owner, is Howard's vis-a-vis who attempts to discourage his operations. Donald Crisp, as Howard's father who kills his son rather than see him destroy his people through unwise leadership, and John Lupton, aide to Chandler, also score.

James Wong Howe's camera work is fluid, topping the technical credits.
Whit.

Shake, Rattle and Rock!

Strictly for rock 'n' roll trade; good returns indicated.

Hollywood, Jan. 15.

American-International release of a James H. Nicholson production. Stars Touch Connors, Lisa Gaye, Sterling Holloway; features Fats Domino, Joe Turner, Choker Campbell & band, Tommy Charles, Annita Ray, Raymond Hatton, Douglass Dumbrille, Paul Dubov, Clarence Kolb, Margaret Dumont. Directed by Edward L. Cahn. Story-screenplay, Lou Rusoff; camera, Frederick F. West; editor, Robert S. Eisen; music, Alexander Courage. Reviewed Jan. 9, '57. Running time, **74 MINS.**

Fats Domino	Fats Domino
Joe Turner	Joe Turner
June	Lisa Gaye
Garry	Touch Connors
Axe	Sterling Holloway
Horace	Raymond Hatton
Eustace	Douglas Dumbrille
Georgianna	Margaret Dumont
Tommy Charles	Tommy Charles
Annita Ray	Annita Ray
Bugsy	Paul Dubov
Nick	Eddie Kafafian
Judge	Clarence Kolb
Hiram	Percy Helton
Choker Campbell	Choker Campbell
Bentley	Charles Evans
Director	Frank Jenks
Armstrong	Pierre Watkin
Police Captain	Joe Devlin
Eddie	Jimmy Pickford
Nancy	Nancy Kilgas
Helen	Giovanna Fiorino
Aloysius	Leon Tyler
Pat	Patricia Gregory

For the rock 'n' roll crowd this light entry should show good response. Footage is spotted with such recording artists as Fats Domino and Joe Turner for potent exploitation, and the beat is effectively taught in half a dozen numbers well presented. Film fits handily into the current r-r craze and comes up with a story to suit.

The Lou Rusoff script centers on Touch Connors, a television personality who is trying to help underpriviliged kids by setting up a center for them, where rock 'n' roll music and dancing is their meat. A small group of reformers claim this type of music is harmful and contributes to juve delinquency. It's left to the public to decide, via a tv program in which court is set up and both sides present their case.

On the musical end, Fats, backed by his combo, warbles three songs, including "I'm in Love Again," "Ain't It a Shame" and "Honey Chile." Turner comes up with "Feelin' Happy" and "Lipstick, Powder and Paint," backed by Choker Campbell and His Band. Tommy Charles and Annita Ray sing "Sweet Love on My Mind" and "Rockin' on Saturday Night," respectively.

Edward L. Cahn keeps action lively in his direction of the James H. Nicholson production, hitting a hepcat chord right down devotees' alley. Connors makes a good impression as the deejay, Lisa Gaye is in briefly for romance and Sterling Holloway a talkative jive character. Douglass Dumbrille heads the reformer group, Raymond Hatton scores as the henpecked husband of Margaret Dumont, one of the group, and Paul Dubov and Eddie Kafafian portray a couple of comedy hoods.

Frederick E. West's camera work is fast and Alexander Courage's music direction expert.
Whit.

L'Homme et L'Enfant

(The Man and the Child)
(FRENCH—C'SCOPE—COLOR—SONG)

Paris, Jan. 9.

Corona release of Hoche-Eden-Carol production. Stars Eddie Constantine; features, Folco Lulli, Juliette Greco, Tania Constantine, Jacqueline Venutra, Michele Philippe. Directed by Raoul Andre. Screenplay, Jacques Constant, Odilon Jannings, Raymond Caillava; camera (Eastmancolor), Niçolas Hayer; editor, Gabriel Rongier; music, Jeff Davis. At Balzac, Paris. Running time, **90 MINS.**

Barker	Eddie Constantine
Nicky	Juliette Greco
Cathy	Tania Constantine
Lucienne	Jacqueline Venutra
Dancer	Michele Philippe
Carlo	Folco Lulli

Eddie Constantine's toughguy career in films here, which has made this American one of the top b.o. stars, gets widened this time via C'Scope and color. However, this seems to slow up the usual activities, thereby cutting down some of the fisticuffs. Obvious storyline and lack of more robust pacing make this seem best for U. S. dualer situations despite its colorful Riviera backgrounding. It looks to do well locally.

Here, Constantine is a perfume manufacturer pulled into adventure by the kidnapping of his adopted daughter by a dope ring. He calmly trots through a series of mishaps, with a beauteous shopkeeper fence (who covets him), a group of gangsters he quite easily tames and the final chase before he gets back the little girl.

Director Raoul Andre lacks flair for the breeziness needed for this type picture. Constantine portrays his usual tough character pitted against the unlawful element and moves easily through this simple-simon. A bevy of lookers help in supporting bits. Technical credits are good. Constantine and his daughter Tania work in a capsule rendering of their bestseller disk which happens to be the title of this pic. Film has general entertainment values for possible dual spots in America.

Les Aventures De Till L'Espiegle

(FRENCH-EAST GERMAN)
(Color)

Paris, Jan. 9.

Cinedis release of Ariane-DEFA production. Stars Gerard Philipe; features Nicole Berger, Jean Vilar, Jean Carmet, Fernand Ledoux, Robert Porte, Francoise Fabian. Directed by Philipe. Screenplay, Rene Wheeler, Rene Barjavel, Philipe from novel by Charles De Coster; camera (Technicolor), Christian Matras; editor, Claude Nicole; music, Georges Auric; art director, Barsacq. At Berlitz, Paris. Running time, **90 MINS.**

Till	Gerard Philipe
Nell	Nicole Berger
Lamme	Jean Carmet
Father	Fernand Ledoux
Albe	Jean Vilar
Castille	Robert Porte
Countess	Francoise Fabian
Cardinal	Jean Debucourt

The 16th Century Flemish folk hero Till Eulenspiegel, who helped chase the occupying Spanish from his country, is the subject of this costume adventure opus. Reminiscent of "Fanfan La Tulipe," via its naive hero who is the scourge of the oppressors, this lacks the sustained movement of the former if having color and costumes. Not for arty spots, the light tempo and entertainment values could make this a possibility for more general U. S. situations with the Philipe name a probable plus. But this needs plenty of selling.

A prankish youth takes on the task of creating a liberating force for his country when his father is burned at the stake by the Inquisition. Playing a fool, he insinuates himself into the court and joins forces with one of the unyielding Flemish noblemen. Then follow a series of adventures in fighting the Spanish with comedy values uppermost.

Filled with various situations this remains sketchy, with the vague love story just a cloak for the many adventures-making up the pic. Ice skating rebels knocking the Spanish about on the ice, chases and slapstick tactics are the film's main trumps. However, it is a pleasant film and Philipe, as star and director, gives this filmic form if still lacking something.

Supporting cast is well chosen, and heavy production values help gloss over the slow spots. Pic should pay off on the Continent. It could lend itself to dubbing for the U. S. Film has East German money in it for the Eastern rights to the pic, but there is no propaganda imbedded in this except for the church heavies. Technicolor is well hued and sets and costumes also help while technical credits are topnotch.
Mosk.

Men in War

Familiar but good Korean-localed war action; saleable to young male audiences.

Hollywood, Jan. 17.

..United Artists release of Sidney Harmon (Security Pictures) production. Stars Robert Ryan, Aldo Ray, Robert Keith; features Philip Pine, Vic Morrow, Nehemiah Persoff, James Edwards. Directed by Anthony Mann. Screenplay, Philip Yordan; based on Van Van Praag's "Combat"; camera, Ernest Haller; editor, Richard C. Meyer; music, Elmer Bernstein. Previewed Jan. 16, '57. Running time, **102 MINUTES.**

Lieutenant Benson	Robert Ryan
Montana	Aldo Ray
Colonel	Robert Keith
Riordan	Philip Pine
Zwickley	Vic Morrow
Lewis	Nehemiah Persoff
Killian	James Edwards
Sam Davis	L. Q. Jones
Maslow	Adam Kennedy
Meredith	Scott Marlowe
Ackerman	Walter Kelley
Haines	Race Gentry
Christensen	Robert Normand
Penelli	Anthony Ray
Lynch	Michael Miller
Korean Sniper	Victor Sen Yung

A two-fisted account of what happens to an infantry platoon in the late Korean battling is told in "Men In War" with a general air of excitement, tension and action. Warfare and the all-male cast would seem to slant it mostly toward male audiences.

Production handling by Sidney Harmon is excellent, holding values to a realistic level for better overall effect. Battle sequences, well-staged under Anthony Mann's direction, are all small-scale, but none the less deadly, as befits the plot and its few characters. The general topnotch treatment mentioned above and the Philip Yordan scripting from Van Van Praag's novel, "Combat," do considerable to overcome the fact that there is much that is similar in warpix and the characters that inhabit them. "Men In War" is no exception, although there are fewer stereotypes.

Robert Ryan, battle-weary lieutenant trying to get the remnants of his platoon back to battalion headquarters, and Aldo Ray, hostile, disrespectful sergeant from another company trying to get his combat-shocked colonel to safety, star in the Security Pictures presentation through United Artists. Each scores strongly in reacting with masculine vigor to Mann's direction. Robert Keith, the colonel, costars and successfully carries off a role that requires only one word of dialog but much mute projection of a man shocked into dumbness but still able to sense and feel.

When the platoon's weapons carrier is wrecked, Ryan commandeers a passing jeep occupied by Ray and Keith to carry ammo and equipment. Footage graphically depicts the horror that is war as the men fight their way back, only to find the battalion is wiped out and Red Koreans occupy the hill. For the climax, Ryan and Ray join forces to retake the hill and there, with only one other survivor, honor their fallen comrades in a touching fadeout.

Prominent among the platoon members, and each doing excellently, are Philip Pine, Vic Morrow, Nehemiah Persoff and James Edwards. All are real as frightened or fighting foot soldiers, as are the other cast members.

Where the film does stand out over the usual warpic is in its intelligent use of music. Elmer Bernstein composed and conducted the score, never trying to compete with the sounds of battle and thereby heightening the effect of many scenes. Ernest Haller's lensing is a major partner in the film's vigor, and there are other good technical assists.

Brog.

Hot Summer Night

Program meller featuring violent action; no cast name help but some appeal to teen toughs.

Hollywood, Jan. 22.

Metro release of Morton S. Fine production. Stars Leslie Nielsen, Colleen Miller; features Edward Andrews, Jay C. Flippen, James Best, Paul Richards, Robert Wilke, Claude Akins, Marianne Stewart. Directed by David Friedkin. Screenplay, Fine and Friedkin; story, Edwin P. Hicks; camera, Harold J. Marzorati; editor, Ben Lewis; music, Andre Previn. Previewed Jan. 16, '57. Running time, **85 MINS.**

William Joel Partain	Leslie Nielsen
Irene Partain	Colleen Miller
Lou Follett	Edward Andrews
Oren Kobble	Jay C. Flippen
Kermit	James Best
Elly Horn	Paul Richards
Tom Ellis	Robert Wilke
Truckdriver	Claude Akins
Ruth Childers	Marianne Stewart

The violent action in "Hot Summer Night" is the kind that attracts certain groups of teenagers, so this younger audience draw, if exploited, may give the pic above-average possibilities in some situations. It's a program meller, obviously small-budgeted and with no names to add marquee weight. Although the presentation is entirely adequate to the entertainment, film has none of the plush qualities normally associated with the Metro label.

Of interest tradewise is the fact the picture was made in the nature of an experiment to see what could be done on a small budget and a short shooting schedule. Initial results were far from satisfactory, so retakes and new scenes to plug holes, tighten melodramatics and provide audiences with more interest nullify to some extent the original cost-conscious purpose. Radio-tv team of Morton Fine and David Friedkin produced and directed, respectively, and paired on the script from an Edwin P. Hicks story as their first theatrical feature venture. The combined chores are uneven, as is the performance response to plot and guidance.

A killer gang that has robbed a bank and killed an employee as the latest of many similar exploits becomes the story target of Leslie Nielsen, unemployed reporter who figures he can get a job easily with an exclusive yarn on the gang's leader, Robert Wilke. Instead of the story, what happens is that he makes his new bride, Colleen Miller, unhappy and frightened, gets himself kidnapped and the gang leader killed and is almost killed himself before the bride leads the way to his rescue.

Opening robbery sequence has some tension and suspense, as do several later scenes involving wanton inter-gang killings and the bride's efforts to shake up a town that thrives on the reputation and generosity of its notorious chief citizen. Nielsen and Miss Miller are handicapped by characters and situations not too well explained. Edward Andrews, county law officer, and Jay C. Flippen, veteran gang member, use their acting experience to good advantage. James Best does well by his role of youthful hero-worshipper among the robbers, while Paul Richards, Wilke, and Claude Akins are acceptable in their respective spots. Marianne Stewart is good as the woman who waits for the gang leader's infrequent visits.

Harold J. Marzorati does an okay lowkey lensing chore, but Andre Previn's background score is noisy to extreme.

Brog.

Utah Blaine

Speedy western with Rory Calhoun to draw.

Hollywood, Jan. 22.

Columbia release of a Sam Katzman production. Stars Rory Calhoun; features Susan Cummings, Angela Stevens, Max Baer, Paul Langton, George Keymas, Ray Teal, Gene Roth, Norman Fredric, Ken Christy. Directed by Fred F. Sears. Screenplay, Robert E. Kent, James B. Gordon; based on novel by Louis L'Amour; camera, Benjamin H. Kline; art director, Paul Palmentola; editor, Charles Nelson; music, Ross Di Maggio. Previewed Jan. 10, '57. Running time, **75 MINS.**

Utah Blaine	Rory Colhoun
Angie Kinyon	Susan Cummings
Mary Blake	Angela Stevens
Gus Ortmann	Max Baer
Rip Coker	Paul Langton
Rink Witter	George Keymas
Russ Nevers	Ray Teal
Tom Corey	Gene Roth
Davis	Norman Fredric
Joe Neal	Ken Christy
Lud Fuller	Steve Darrell
Gavin	Terry Frost
Ferguson	Dennis Moore
Clel Miller	Jack Ingram

"Utah Blaine" is an action-packed, hard-shooting open-spacer which meets demands of its market. Name of Rory Calhoun sparks its chances for better than average returns, and unfoldment packs as much appeal for adults as for the moppets.

Sam Katzman has garmented the tense Robert E. Kent-James B. Gordon screenplay with values which blend tough characters with fast movement, capturing the spirit of the Louis L'Amour novel to keep the bell ringing. Calhoun buckles on his guns to keep a gang of ruffians who claim the law is on their side from seizing a ranch owned by a man Calhoun rescues, after heavies have strung him up and departed. When one of gang's gunmen finally kills the owner, Calhoun finds himself now half-owner of the ranch, with even more incentive to fight.

Fred F. Sears' direction is taut and gutty as he builds to a gun-blazing climax, and gets realistic portrayals from entire cast. Calhoun handles his gun-slinging character effectively, as much at home in a bruising rough-and-tumble with Max Baer as with his six-shooter. Baer, who joins him after the battle, and Paul Langton, a deadly shotgun-fighter, score as Calhoun's pals in his efforts to keep the ranch, and Susan Cummings is convincing as romantic interest, willed the other half of the ranch. Ray Teal delivers strongly as gang leader, George Keymas as his gunman and Angela Stevens adds an interesting distaff note.

Camera work by Benjamin H. Kline and tight editing by Charles Nelson are further assets, topping technical credits.

Whit.

The Man in the Sky
(BRITISH)

Ealing's first for Metro is a taut meller with a bright pay-off prospects. Jack Hawkins tops all-round British cast.

London, Jan. 9.

Metro presentation of a Michael Balcon-Ealing Films production. Stars Jack Hawkins and Elizabeth Sellars. Associate producer, Seth Holt; directed by Charles Chichton; screenplay, William Rose and John Eldridge from an original story by William Rose; camera, Douglas Slocombe; editor, Peter Tanner; music, Gerbrand Schurmann. At Metro Preview Theatre, London. Jan. 8, '57. Running time, **87 MINS.**

John Mitchell	Jack Hawkins
Mary Mitchell	Elizabeth Sellars
Nicholas Mitchell	Jeremy Bodkin
Philip Mitchell	Gerald Lohan
Conway	Walter Fitzgerald
Peter Hook	John Stratton
Ashmore	Eddie Byrne
Joe Biggs	Victor Maddern
Keith	Lionel Jeffries
Crabtree	Donald Pleasence
Mary's Mother	Catherine Lacey
Mrs. Snowden	Megs Jenkins
Maine	Ernest Clark
Jenkins	Raymond Francis
Sim	Russell Waters
Ingrams	Howard M. Crawford

Ealing's first production under the Metro banner is a tautly made thriller, geared for substantial grosses in the United Kingdom and with prospects of a handsome pay-off in the United States, too. They've made no specific concessions to the American market beyond concentrating on b.o. possibilities. The cast and crew is entirely British and the action unfolds with typical British understatement.

The screenplay is based on an original by William Rose in which suspense is the keynote. Most of the action is in the air, but there's a logical personal domestic crisis between Jack Hawkins and Elizabeth Sellars, which is neatly dovetailed into the main plot. Charles Crichton's confident direction makes the best use of the ready-made suspense angles and the finished picture has been cut to a very tight 87 minutes.

Hawkins plays a test pilot, who has to demonstrate for a potential buyer a new type transport plane with rocket propulsion. The entire future of the aircraft company by whom he's employed and, by the same token, his own future, depends on the success of the demonstration. But one engine catches fire, the other passengers and crew bale out and the pilot refuses to obey orders to jettison the aircraft in the Irish Sea. Instead, he cruises for half an hour, using up sufficient oil for safety purposes, to effect a safe landing and win the contract for his company.

The aerial scenes strike a powerful dramatic wallop with mounting tension convincingly created. The tailpiece to the plot, in which the domestic friction between the pilot and his wife is eased after a stand-up row, adds an additional note of tension.

A big marquee name locally, Jack Hawkins gives one of his most impressive performances, which should help in firmly establishing him across the Atlantic. Elizabeth Sellars has little to do in the first part of the pic, but comes into her own in the final scenes in which she stands up remarkably well to her co-star. Walter Fitzgerald, John Stratton, Eddie Byrne and Victor Maddern lead a first rate supporting cast and there are two appealing child performances by Gerald Lohan and Jeremy Bodkin. The latter is the son of an Ealing publicist.

Myro.

Five Steps to Danger

'Ruth Roman, Sterling Hayden in espionage meller; okay for program bookings.

Hollywood, Jan. 15.

United Artists release of Henry S. Kesler (Grand) production, direction and screenplay by Kesler. Stars Ruth Roman, Sterling Hayden; features Werner Klemperer, Richard Gaines, Charles Davis, Jeanne Cooper. Story, Donald Hamilton, Turnley Walker; based on SatEvePost serial by Hamilton; camera, Kenneth Peach; editor, Aaron Stell; music, Paul Sawtell, Bert Shefter. Previewed Jan. 14, '57. Running time, **80 MINS.**

Ann Nicholson .... Ruth Roman
John Emmett .... Sterling Hayden
Dr. Simmons .... Werner Klemperer
Dean Brant .... Richard Gaines
Kirk .... Charles Davis
Helen Bethke .... Jeanne Cooper
Karl Plesser .... Peter Hansen
Kissell .... Karl Lindt
Deputy .... John Mitchum
Sheriff .... John Merrick

A rather tangled web of espionage and counter-espionage is spun in "Five Steps to Danger," but there is enough of general interest in the melodramatics to carry it through the program market. Ruth Roman and Sterling Hayden head the cast of the Henry S. Kesler production and, while limited somewhat by the spotty development in Kesler's direction and scripting, handle the top assignments in okay fashion.

Kesler launches the picture with promise of a good spy-chase melodrama, but the cryptic flavor soon becomes rather confusing and the direction allows the pace to falter often during the 80-minute course. Script is from a story by Donald Hamilton and Turnley Walker, based on Hamilton's Sat-EvePost serial.

All Hayden has in mind is a fishing trip, but when his car breaks down en route, he gets embroiled in a Soviet plot concerning secret ballistic missiles after Miss Roman, a mysterious traveller hurrying to Santa Fe, picks him up to help her drive. Since neither know about the Soviet plot, the strange happenings they are put through are quite a strain, but out of it all they get each other, Central Intelligence gets the coded information she's taking to a scientist in New Mexico, and the Commies get their comeuppance.

Werner Klemperer, an oily psychiatrist, and Richard Gaines, a mild college president, are the chief Soviet spies and do their characters properly. Charles Davis, Jeanne Cooper, latter good as a nurse; Peter Hansen, also good as a Soviet victim, and Karl Lindt are among other players providing okay support.

Kenneth Peach handles the cameras well on the melodramatics, while the score by Paul Sawtell and Bert Shefter fits the mood. Other technical assists measure up to release intentions. *Brog.*

Foreign Films

Paris, Jan. 15.

Crime Et Chatinaut (Crime and Punishment) (FRENCH). Pathe release of Jules Borkon-Champs Elysees Film production. Stars Jean Gabin, Marina Vlady, Robert Hossein, Ulla Jacobsson, Bernard Blier; features, Gaby Morlay, Gerard Blain, Roland Lesaffre. Directed by Georges Lampin. Screenplay, Charles Spaak from the novel of Feodor Dostoievsky; camera, Claude Renoir; editor, Emma De La Chanois. At Marignan, Paris. Running time, **110 MINS.**

Dostoievsky's great novel has already been the basis of two costume pix and one modern retelling. This is still another updated form of this classic. Bringing it to modern terms, it lacks the deeper character analysis needed, never invoking the suspense to make it jell filmically. This plods through its grim tale of a murder which leads to the spiritual redemption of the young killer. Direction and heavyhanded playing relegates this to arty or specialized playdating for the U.S.

Film has the Raskalnikoff character, now a young Gallic student, Rene, killing for money to save his sister from marriage. Jean Gabin is the policeman who breaks down the murderer's morale, doing it in his usual laconic manner. Robert Hossein overplays the tormented killer. Marina Vlady has nothing to do but pose as an angelic streetwalker. Bernard Blier adds a fine performance as the abject suitor of the sister, simply played by Swedish actress Ulla Jacobsson.

Claude Renoir's lensing is okay but the direction of Georges Lampin makes this a weak, passe illustration of the book. *Mosk.*

La Marice Est Trop Belle (The Bride Is Too Beautiful) (FRENCH). Pathe Consortium release of Gouze Renal-SN Pathe production. Stars Brigitte Bardot, Micheline Presle, Louis Jourdan; features Jean-Francis Calve, Marcel Amont, Roger Dumas. Directed by Pierre Gaspard-Huit. Screenplay, Philipe Agostini, Odette Joyeux, Juliette Saint-Giniez from novel by Miss Joyeux; camera, Louis Page; editor, Louisette Hautcouer; music, Norbert Glanzberg. At Paris, Paris. Running time, **95 MINS.**

Perhaps for lack of anybody else, Brigitte Bardot seems to be the No. 1 star here these days since three of her films, plus some oldies, are getting simultaneous runs locally. Possessed of a pouting pigeon personality, she does not seem up to dishing out either the beauteous firebrands or the wavering virgins. She appears to have been pushed too fast for her real thespic talents.

Film is a simple-simon situation comedy which lacks the body for any arty house chance in the U.S. Fair progression, with some risque bits, could make this a possibility for some dual spots. This would need exploitation but has enough to warrant dubbing, with marquee strength in the Micheline Presle and Louis Jourdan names.

Yarn shows a highpowered magazine duo, who are engaged, pick up a shapely innocent and launch her on a cover girl career. She makes the top but falls in love with the male mag man. Miss Presle and Jourdan, in over-simplified roles, acquit themselves well though the camera overdwells on Miss Bardot. The director has not been able to breathe much life into his callow characters, but it looks a local bet.

Club De Femmes (FRENCH). Cinedis release of Ariane production. Stars, Nicole Courcel, Yvan Desny, Dany Carrel, Jean-Louis Trintignant; features Noel Roquevert, Vega Vinci, Guy Bertil. Directed by Ralph Rabib. Screenplay, Jacques Companeez, Annette Wadement, Jean Aurel from original by Jacques Deval; camera, Pierre Petit; editor, Francoise Javet. At Berlitz, Paris. Running time, **90 MINS.**

This is an anemic remake of a noted pre-war pic. Concerning a group of students, all delectable femmes, who take over an old dwelling to ease the housing shortage, it spins a sketchy tale about the various dramas of the girls and their beaus. There is a vague complication about how the squatters are expelled only to get a present of the house when public opinion turns against a big company about to build a factory on the site of the girl's self-made dormitory.

Unimaginative handling of the girls, story and complications relegate this only for possibly some dualer chances in the U.S. via the pulchritude of several starlets in the pic. Technical credits are good but acting and general film level make this a limited pic, at best, for America. *Mosk.*

Et Dieu . . . Crea La Femme (And God . . . Created Woman) (FRENCH; C'SCOPE; COLOR). Cocinor release of Raoul Levy-Iena-UCIL-Cocinor production. Stars Brigitte Bardot, Curd Jurgens, Jean-Louis Trintignant; features Christian Marcuand, Georges Poujouly. Written and directed by Roger Vadim. Camera (Eastmancolor), Armand Thirard; editor, Victoria Mercanton; music, Paul Misraki. At Normandie, Paris. Running time, **90 MINS.**

Film even ran into censorship trouble in France via its emphasis on sex. However, it was shorn of its more intime sensual aspects here, and emerges primarily an exploitation item for the U.S. Lagging, familiar storyline slant this more for chances at general markets Stateside, via exploitation. It might be worth dubbing this tale of the passion and drama which a sexy little orphan inspires in three men, a world!y casino owner and two worker brothers. However, this is just average for any U.S. possibilities.

Brigitte Bardot is the orphan who evokes male desires in a Riviera port town.

Film unfolds slowly, centering on the questionable attributes of the new star here, Miss Bardot. Though a young looker, she lacks the thespian strength to get any depth into her sensual role here. Curd Jurgens acts as a sort of outsider but manages to make his presence felt while Jean-Louis Trintignant and Christian Marquand are acceptable as the brothers. Lensing (C'Scope and Eastmancolor) is excellent, and other technical credits good. *Mosk.*

The Wings of Eagles
(COLOR)

Biopicing Cmdr. Frank W. "Spig" Wead, who helped add wings to the Navy. Good names, good b.o.

Hollywood, Jan. 29.

Metro release of Charles Schnee production. Stars John Wayne, Dan Dailey, Maureen O'Hara, Ward Bond; features Ken Curtis, Edmund Lowe, Kenneth Tobey, James Todd. Directed by John Ford. Screenplay, Frank Fenton, William Wister Haines; based on the life and writings of Cmdr. Frank W. "Spig" Wead; camera (MetroColor), Paul C. Vogel; editor, Gene Ruggiero; score, Jeff Alexander; technical adviser, Adm. John Dale Price, USN (Ret.). Previewed aboard U.S.S. Lexington off Long Beach, Calif., Jan. 24, '57. Running time, **109 MINS.**

Frank W. "Spig" Wead..... John Wayne
Carson .... Dan Dailey
Minnie Wead .... Maureen O'Hara
John Dodge .... Ward Bond
John Price .... Ken Curtis
Admiral Moffett .... Edmund Lowe
Herbert Allen Hazard....Kenneth Tobey
Jack Travis .... James Todd
Capt. Jock Clark.......... Barry Kelley
Manager .... Sig Ruman
Capt. Spear .... Henry O'Neill
Barton .... Willis Bouchey
Rose Brentmann .... Dorothy Jordan

Commander Frank W. "Spig" Wead was a figure of fact and fiction. In the former case, a holder of Naval honors, both in the early days when the sea service was just beginning to test its wings and in the carrier action that marked Pacific area fighting in World War II. In the latter case, between Naval service, as a writer of a number of aviation features that attracted sizeable audiences.

With John Wayne to play this figure of a man, director John Ford here recreates his life. If it is sometimes hard to discern where fact leaves off and fiction takes over, it is always on entertaining show, with the thrills, action, heart and comedy that trademark nearly all of Ford's pictures. The Navy thinks enough of the results to give it its blessing as an inducement to recruitment. The public will give it its backing at the box-office, where the returns will be good.

Separating fact from fiction in Wead's life isn't an easy job because apparently he lived much of it as though a storybook hero-daring and dashing, given to loving and brawling for the sake of the game. The episodes dealing with early Naval aviation at Pensacola and the part Wead played in bringing the sea eagles to the attention of the public are told with an action flare that outdoes the best that Frank Merriwell ever offered, yet are all founded on fact according to the records. Particularly entertaining are the sequences dealing with Army-Navy rivalry in air advancement.

It is also the picture of an extremely courageous man, who refused to succumb to a cripplingly injury that should have left him bed-ridden the rest of his life, learned to walk haltingly again, turned to writing and then re-entered the service when the Japs struck at Pearl Harbor to conceive the jeep carriers that supplied the big carriers with planes in the famous Marianas action.

Wayne is particularly good as the vital man of action with a lust for life, turning in one of his better performances. Dan Dailey scores particularly well as the breezy Navy mechanic who sees that his officer gets the encouragement and the drinks he needs. His bottle-station technique in the hospital and handling of the extra good lines given him by scripters Frank Fenton and William Wister Haines elsewhere help to spark the entertainment. Maureen O'Hara doesn't have the usual woman's role in a man's picture; nor does she play it that way, making real and interesting her character of Wead's wife who had her own cross to bear in the happiness and unhappiness that marked their marriage.

Kenneth Tobey stands out among the featured players as Wead's Army air rival and the pier six brawls this rivalry inspires are something to see. Among others acquitting themselves well are Ken Curtis, as a member of Wead's flying team who is now Admiral John Dale Price (Ret.); Edmund Lowe, James Todd, Barry Kelley, Sig Ruman, Henry O'Neill, Willis Bouchey, Dorothy Jordan and several uncredited players, including Janet Lake, who lightens hospital sequences as a nurse eyed by Dailey.

Producer Charles Schnee, and his associate, James E. Newcom, give the picture plenty of values to use for showmanly selling. There's also nostalgia for the oldsters in the running of a scene between Clark Gable and Wallace Beery from one of Wead's film stories, which included such pix as "Test Pilot," "Ceiling Zero," "The Citadel" and "They Were Expendable."

The MetroColor lensing by Paul C. Vogel does much to abet the action. Editing and other technical assists are firstrate and Jeff Alexander supplies a background score in keeping with entertainment intent. *Brog.*

The Happy Road
(SONG)

Enchanting comedy-drama of two kids running away from Switzerland to Paris; potent word-of-mouth will give it buildup.

Hollywood, Jan. 28.

Metro release of Gene Kelly (Kerry) production, also directed by Kelly. Stars Kelly; features Barbara Laage, Michael Redgrave, Bobby Clark, Brigitte Fossey. Screenplay, Arthur Julian, Joseph Morhaim, Harry Kurnitz; story, Julian and Morhaim; camera, Robert Juillard; editor, Borys Lewin; music, Georges Van Parys; title song sung by Maurice Chevalier. Previewed Jan. 9, '57. Running time, **99 MINS.**

Mike Andrews	Gene Kelly
Suzanne Duval	Barbara Laage
General Medworth	Michael Redgrave
Danny Andrews	Bobby Clark
Janine Duval	Brigitte Fossey
Docteur Solaise	Roger Treville
Helene	Colette Dereal
Morgan	Jess Hahn
Madame Fallere	Maryse Martin
Verbier	Roger Saget
French Motorcycle Officer	Van Doude
Patronne Hotel	Claire Gerard
Armbruster	Colin Mann
Bucheron	Alexandre Rignault

Occasionally a film comes along that, on the surface, would seem to offer very little out of the ordinary, yet contains all the entertainment necessary to win an audience. Such a feature is "The Happy Road," which will be a real treat for those viewing it and the potent word-of-mouth from initial showings can well give it a profitable buildup for following dates.

Gene Kelly produced, directed and stars in the Kerry production being released through Metro. Lensing was all overseas, with the setting a cross-country chase from Switzerland to Paris as two parents try to catch up witht their respective runaway kids. The youngsters and the situations in which they are placed as they outwit parents, police, all adults and even the very best NATO security provide a heart-warming hilarity that will have an audience with them in every scene.

The pursuing end of the chase has its extremely funny Mack Sennettish touches, and there are priceless character bits supplied by the overseas cast lined up by Kelly. The latter is very able in handling the sequences with the kids; less able, but still satisfactory, in directing himself.

Bobby Clark, small son of Kelly, widowed American businessman in Paris, decides to run away from the Swiss school he attends and join his father. Little Brigitte Fossey, daughter of divorced Barbara Laage and attending the same school, decides to accompany him. Kids along the way help them elude pursuers, needing no more of a password than that they're running away from school. Hilarious adventures occur, of which only two highspots are concerned with successfully lousing up NATO security and hitch-hiking a ride in a European goodwill bicycle race. By the time the kids make Paris they've proved their point of being self-reliant and the parents are beginning to see eye-to-eye romantically.

Kelly and Miss Laage team nicely together. Moppets Clark and Fossey are a delightful pair. Among the priceless comedy characters in the script by Arthur Julian, Joseph Morhaim and Harry Kurnitz are Michael Redgrave, Britisher in the NATO maneuvers, and his staffers; Van Doude, French motorcycle officer, and the assorted natives, less easily identified, who contribute to the fun.

Maurice Chevalier sings the title tune behind the credits for an extra plus and Georges Van Parys' score is good elsewhere. Noel Howard served as associate producer and the technical credits all pass muster. *Brog.*

The Big Land
(SONG—COLOR)

Ordinary western feature; mild entry for action market but has Alan Ladd, Virginia Mayo, Edmond O'Brien.

Hollywood, Jan. 29.

Warner Bros. release of George C. Bertholon (Jaguar) production. Stars Alan Ladd, Virginia Mayo, Edmond O'Brien; features Anthony Caruso, Julie Bishop, John Qualen, Don Castle, David Ladd, Jack Wrather Jr., George J. Lewis, James Anderson. Directed by Gordon Douglas. Screenplay, David Dortort, Martin Rackin; screen story, Dortort; from "Buffalo Grass" by Frank Gruber; camera (WarnerColor), John Seitz; editor, Thomas Reilly; music, David Buttolph; song, "I Leaned on a Man" by Wayne Shanklin, Leonard Rosenman. Previewed Jan. 18, '57. Running time, **91 MINS.**

Morgan	Alan Ladd
Helen	Virginia Mayo
Jagger	Edmond O'Brien
Brog	Anthony Caruso
Kate Johnson	Julie Bishop
Sven Johnson	John Qualen
Draper	Don Castle
David Johnson	David Ladd
Olaf Johnson	Jack Wrather Jr.
Dawson	George J. Lewis
Cole	James Anderson
Billy	Don Kelly
McCullough	Charles Watts

The familiar names of Alan Ladd, Virginia Mayo and Edmond O'Brien will give some help to "The Big Land" as it plays through the general outdoor market, but the entertainment is only ordinary for the western action trade.

Ladd's J a g u a r Productions filmed for Warners release, with George C. Bertholon handling the associate producer reins for mild results. Scripting by David Dortort and Martin Rackin, from Frank Gruber's novel "Buffalo Grass," runs a routine course, seemingly more off-the-cuff than thoroughly worked out on paper before cameras started griding. Direction, too, does little to clarify most of the principal characters, so Gordon Douglas's guidance is, at best, uneven.

After finding that Missouri prices for Texas cattle are too low, Ladd talks a railroad and some Kansas farmers into building a town in that territory for the herds he promises to bring up from the Rio Grande country. Menace to his new aims is provided by Anthony Caruso, the same cattle buyer who forced prices down in Missouri, but after too much plot hemming and hawing, Ladd triumphs with a six gun.

For a western hero, the character Ladd has to play is much too lethargic and the paying customers will have some difficulty figuring it out. The same confusion in character-drawing prevails in Miss Mayo's saloon singer part, the alcoholic architect done by O'Brien, and most of the other roles. About the only character who seems to know what his purpose is and pursues it with unwavering objectivity is the heavy, Brog, well-played by Caruso. Julie Bishop, John Qualen, Don Castle, George J. Lewis and James Anderson are among others with principal roles.

John Seitz does a good lensing job in WarnerColor and the other technical credits are satisfactory. "I Leaned On a Man," tune by Wayne Shanklin and Leonard Rosenman, sung by Miss Mayo's character, is good.

The Big Boodle

Fair whodunit with Errol Flynn. Colorful background of Havana, Cuba.

Hollywood, Jan. 29.

United Artists release of a Lewis Blumberg production. Stars Errol Flynn; co-stars Pedro Armendariz, Rossana Rory, Gia Scala; features Sandro Giglio, Jacques Aubuchon, Carlos Rivas. Directed by Richard Wilson. Screenplay, Jo Eisenger, from novel by Robert Sylvester; camera, Lee Garmes; music, Paul Lavista; editor, Charles Kimball. Previewed Jan. 23, '57. Running time, **84 MINS.**

Ned Sherwood	Errol Flynn
Colonel Mastegui	Pedro Armendariz
Fina	Rossana Rory
Anita	Gia Scala
Senor Ferrer	Sandro Giglio
Collada	Jacques Aubuchon
Rubi	Carlos Rivas
Griswold	Charles Todd
Casino Manager	Guillerme Alvaraz Guedes
Chuchu	Carlos Mas
Salcito	Rogelio Hernandez
Secretary	Velia Martinez
Sales Girl	Aurora Pita

What starts out to be an intriguing whodunit dissolves into a confused piece of unfoldment in this Lewis Blumberg production for UA release. Film, however, is materially aided by interesting utilization of Havana backgrounds, where it was lensed, and with Errol Flynn as marquee lure feature should get by.

Pic takes its title from the search by Havana police for three million counterfeit peso notes, and plates which made them. Flynn, a casino blackjack dealer, receives a 500 peso note from a blonde player, and following his arrest for its possession finds himself in the position of a sitting duck. Both the police and a Havana ring think he knows where the plates are located, as well as having some of the phoney coin, and he gets plenty roughed up before the final climax out on Morro Castle.

Director Richard Wilson manages to keep his characters moving despite the uncertaintics of the Jo Eisenger screenplay. Flynn acquits himself in okay fashion and is ably assisted on the distaff side by Rossana Rory and Gia Scala, playing sisters. Former is the blonde who innocently passed him the counterfeit note, latter an unwilling participant in the deal, who strings along because her penniless playboy boy-friend, Carlos Rivas, is a counterfeiter. Pedro Armendariz delivers the most forthright performance in cast, as Havana police chief. Jacques Aubuchon is Flynn's nemesis, after the plates.

Lee Garmes photography is topflight as he trains his lenses on both familiar and unusual Havana scenes, and he makes the most of historic Morro Castle for the pic's windup. Musical score by Paul Lavista lends flavor. *Whit.*

Accused of Murder
(SONG-COLOR)

Dull melodrama for lowercase bookings.

Hollywood, Jan. 25.

Republic release of Joe Kane production, directed by Kane. Stars David Brian, Vera Ralston, Sidney Blackmer; features Virginia Grey, Warren Stevens, Lee Van Cleef. Screenplay, Bob Williams, W. R. Burnett; from Burnett's novel, "Vanity Row"; camera (Trucolor), Bud Thackery; editor, Richard L. Ven Enger; music, R. Dale Butts; song, Herb Newman, Buddy Bregman. At Hawaii Theatre, Jan. 23, '57. Running time, **73 MINS.**

Lt. Roy Hargis	David Brian
Ilona Vance	Vera Ralston
Hobart	Sidney Blackmer
Sandra	Virginia Grey
Stan	Warren Stevens
Sgt. Lackey	Lee Van Cleef
Police Captain Smedley	Barry Kelley
Chad Bayliss	Richard Karlan
Caesar Cipriano	Frank Puglia
Whitey Pollock	Elisha Cook
Trumble	Ian MacDonald
Myra Bayliss	Greta Thyssen
Marge	Claire Carleton
Les Fuller	Hank Worden

This is a sudsy saga of a singer who gets herself involved in a killing. It plays off with a minimum of entertainment so, despite the production costs involved in the use of Trucolor and Republic's anamorphic Naturama, it falls in the flat rental, lowercase bracket for general dual bills.

W. R. Burnett and Bob Williams scripted from Burnett's novel, "Vanity Row," but the screen writing is poorly plotted and the dialog completely unrealistic. Joe Kane's production and direction never rises above the unimaginative material, nor do cast principals such as David Brian, Vera Ralston, Sidney Blackmer and Virginia Grey contribute anything that would take the curse off the cliche lines and static characters.

Blackmer, a two-timing lawyer, is found dead in his car. Among suspects is Miss Ralston, cafe chirp whom he had been trying to romance. Brian is the lieutenant from homicide who doesn't believe she's guilty, even if his sidekick, Lee Van Cleef, does. Another suspect, Warren Stevens, hired by a gangster, whom Blackmer had doublecrossed, to perform the rubout, gets into the act when he's seen near the scene of the crime by Miss Grey, taxi dancer. Weak windup finds Miss Ralston confessing she was with Blackmer at the death, but that he shot himself because she did not return his passion.

As noted, the cast leads fail to survive the poor material and the other players have the same difficulty. A couple of tunes, one being "You're In Love" by Herb Newman and Buddy Bregman, are ineffectively spotted through Miss

Ralston's singer character. Lensing and other technical values are standard. *Brog.*

Pharaoh's Curse

Lightweight "horror" entry for lower half of the duals. More tedium than terror.

United Artists release of Bel-Air (Aubrey Schenck-Howard W. Koch) production. Stars Mark Dana, Ziva Rodann, Diane Brewster; features George Neise, Alvara Guillot, Ben Wright. Directed by Lee Sholem. Original story and screenplay, Richard Landau; camera, William Margulies; editor George A. Gittens; music, Les Baxter. Previewed N.Y. Jan. 25, '57. Running time, 66 MINS.
Captain Storm .... Mark Dana
Simira .... Ziva Rodann
Sylvia Quentin .... Diane Brewster
Robert Quentin .... George Neise
Numar .... Alvaro Guillot
Walter Andrews .... Ben Wright
Dr. Michael Faraday....... Guy Prescott
Sergeant Smollett........Terence deMarney
Sergeant Gromley.........Richard Peel
Hans Brecht .... Kurt Katch
Claude Beauchamp ...... Robert Fortin

Strictly a lightweight entry, "Pharoah's Curse" is in the "horror" vein. But the story, acting and overall production are so unconvincing that patrons will be more overcome with tedium than terror. Minus any marquee values, this Bell-Air production for United Artists release appears destined to wind up in the lower half of the duals.

The Richard Landau screenplay from his original story feebly relates the difficulties of an archaeological expedition headed by George Neise. Also hampered by a "curse" imposed by Egypt's ancient kings is Mark Dana's three-man Army detail which has been assigned to bring the tomb probers back to Cairo.

There are the usual walking mummies, collapsing chambers, gasps and moans—none of which is particularly realistic. Director Lee Sholem can't do much with his material, and the cast is also up against it on this score. Dana makes with the old college try as a persevering Army captain and Ziva Rodann is an unimpressive menace as a reincarnated "cat goddess."

On hand for the traditional romantic touch is Diane Brewster. She adds little to the proceedings except to shriek in the right places. Neise and other players, when not falling victim to the pharaoh's "curse," are killed by deficiencies of the script. Camerawork of William Margulies is fair as is the Les Baxter score and other technical credits. Picture seems overlong at 66 minutes. *Gilb.*

Four Boys and a Gun

Strongly told juve delinquency meller for program situations. No names.

Hollywood, Jan. 29.
United Artists release of a William Berke production. Features Frank Sutton, Tarry Green, James Franciscus, William Hinant. Directed by Berke. Screenplay, Philip Yordan, Leo Townsend; based on novel by Willard Wiener; camera, J. Burgi Contner; music, Albert Glasser; editors, Everett Sutherland, Robert Montagne. Reviewed Jan. 23, '57. Running time, 74 MINS.
Ollie Denker.............. Frank Sutton
Eddie Richards .... Tarry Green
Johnny Doyle .... James Franciscus
Stanley Badek .... William Hinant
District Attorney .... Otto Hulett
Joe Barton .... Robert Dryden
Fight Manager .... J. Pat O'Malley
Marie .... Diana Herbert
Nita .... Patricia Sloan
Sophie .... Nancy Devlin
Elizabeth .... Patricia Bosworth
Television Man .... David Burns
Mrs. Richards .... Anne Seymour
Slim .... Frank Gero
Landlord .... Noel Glass
Mr. Badek .... Karl Swenson
Mrs. Badek .... Lisa Osten
Cab Driver .... Sid Raymond

Four boys in a jam with the law after killing a cop during a holdup cues this rather grim but wellmade juve delinquency film. Cast of unknowns offer good characterizations in a story okay for the program trade.

William Berke produces and directs the Philip Yordan-Leo Townsend screenplay, building situations to an unusual climax after the four, sitting in the District Attorney's office, are ordered to come up with which fired the shot. This one will face the electric chair, the others life imprisonment with the chance of later parole. Much of the footage is told in flashback form, limning the events leading to the holdup as each recalls the circumstances.

Frank Sutton does well by his role of bookie's runner who holds back some of his collections, then is forced to raise quick money for settlement with his boss, Robert Dryden, properly menacing. Tarry Green needs the dough because he's a spender who sees his girl turn to the boss, who can spend more on her. James Franciscus, an amateur fighter is in on the crime so he can buy a truck to go in business on his own, and William Hinant, always the patsy, goes along to gain the others' respect.

Technical credits are above average for a film of this type. Standouts here include camera work by J. Burgi Contner, music score by Albert Glasser, tight editing by Everett Sutherland and Marie Montagne. *Whit.*

Manhattan's Japanese Film Festival

Japanese Film Week in Gotham, which wound up six evenings of feature and short screenings last Friday (25), at the Museum of Modern Art provided overflow audiences with a cross-section sample of Japan's motion picture output, but left many wondering whether the festival had accomplished its obvious purpose.

Summarized opinions re the films shown run something like this: They may be the kind Japanese audiences enjoy, but—with the exception of one or possibly two—the commercial potential of the selected films in the States is nil; Japanese color is as good as ever, but it can't save a picture from being dull if other values aren't there; the "shorts" (most of which run over 30 minutes) were, in many instances, more interesting than the features.

Outstanding was a halfhour documentary in black-and-white with color inserts, "Children Who Draw." Iwanami Production of Tokyo made the picture which has standout appeal in this country.

Not Cleverly Selected

It became obvious not long after the Film Week got under way that some of the Japanese execs themselves harbored doubts respecting the quality of the films imported for the N.Y. festival. One, with remarkable frankness, criticized and blamed the selection procedure in Tokyo, where each company submitted two features, of which one had to be chosen, whether it was suitable or not. No American trade opinion was solicited. At the fest, the overall audience reaction was tinged with disappointment.

The trouble is that, unlike the French or the Italians, the Japanese have evolved a screen style that is uniquely their own, representing a reflection of their own culture. On this, Western—and particularly American—influence has been superimposed. Many of the Japanese films are excruciatingly slow. They also appear pitched to a highly emotional audience, with the leading characters—male and female—apt to break into sobs and tears quite frequently.

The stories are comparatively simple ones, the technique of telling them oldfashioned. There is a good deal of overacting. Lack of continuity and pace makes them difficult to follow. Being prepared for only a single print, the titles on the films were hard to make out visually and represented very poor translations otherwise. One film—"Bliss on Earth"—was dubbed.

Of the six features shown, "Harp of Burma," while again much too long, probably got the best reception in the feature category. It's a Venice prize-winner and recaptures some of the quality of the postwar Japanese films that have appealed in the U.S.

Valuable Experiment

Queried directly on the purposes of the fest, Shin Sakai, executive director of the Daiei Co., said they were commercial rather than cultural, but added: "Perhaps the necessary value was not there." He opined that the reaction to the Film Week, once properly gauged, would determine future policy.

Several of the Japanese officials said quite frankly that this wasn't the ideal time for a film festival, the reason being that Japan's production was up sharply in numerical terms "and as production goes up, our quality goes down."

However, American observers felt that a more careful and discriminating selection procedure might have served to give the fest greater stature inasmuch as the taste of the U.S. public would have been taken into account. Pictures also badly needed editing for length.

Marjorie Geiss, who braintrusted the promotional aspects of the festival, reported that the Japanese had garnered a lot of attention press-wise. Dailies however, carried no reviews of the films shown. Japanese delegation attended a series of trade luncheons, gave interviews, etc. Its promotional literature was slick and very well prepared.

Motion Picture Export Assn., with an eye to the vital Japanese market, gave the film week its full cooperation. Japanese government helped defray part of the costs, thought to be around $20,000.

Sakai, whose Daiei films ("Rashomon," "Gates of Hell" etc.) have been among the most successful in the U.S., said his company favored establishment in the States of a Japanese industry office, but added that chances were "uneven" that this would be done. He said most of the leading Japanese companies were repped in the U.S. in one way or another. As reported by VARIETY last week, a Japanese-government info office for the Japanese films in the U.S. is under consideration.

Reviews of films seen during the Japanese Festival follow:

Bliss on Earth. Shochiku Co. release of Mitsuzo Kubo production. Stars Ayako Wakao, Ushio Akashi, Keiji Sada, Hiroko Sugita, Akira Ishihama, Takahiro Tamura, Teruko Kishi. Directed by Yoshiro Kawazu. Screenplay, Yoshiko Kusuda; camera, Hiroyuki Kusuda; editor, Yoshi Sugihara; music, Chuji Kinoshita. At Museum of Modern Art, Jan. 21, 56. Running Time, 90 MINS.

Apparently as an experiment to see if Japanese films can obtain mass bookings in the United States, the Sochiku Co. has dubbed "Bliss on Earth" into English. The effect is disastrous. Any charm the picture might have had is lost by the stilted Amercanese that emanates from the Japanese actors.

As most films dubbed abroad, the English dialog represents a foreigner's conception of how Americans speak. The actors selected to provide the English voices also sound like caricatures of Yanks. Technically, the lip sync job is good but, as all dubbing, it reveals the limitations of the medium.

"Bliss on Earth" is about young love. Set in modern Japan, it tells the story of a troubled young girl who because of her family's background is unable to marry the boy of choice. Her aunt, with whom she lives, forces her into an unwanted marriage. However, the arranged marriage turns out to be successful as she learns to love and cherish her kindly and understanding husband.

There are some interesting aspects of modern Japan revealed in the film. The performances (sans the English dialog) appear sensitive. The young performers—Ayako Wakao, Akira Ishihama and Takahiro Tamura—are especially attractive. Production qualities are also first-rate. However, even with English sub-titles, the film does not seem one that would appeal to U.S. audiences.
Holl.

Traitors. Toei Motion Picture Co. production produced by Hiroshi Okawa. Stars Utaemon Ichikawa, Hizuru Takachiho, Eitaro Shindo. Director by Sadatsugu Matsuda; screenplay, Yushitake Hisa; camera (color), Shintaro Kawasaki; music, Shiro Fukai. At the Museum of Modern Art, N. Y. Running time, 90 MINS.

Done in frequently stunning color, "Traitors"! is best described as a Japanese classical western. It's fully of swordplay, Palace intrigues, chases etc. but lacks the qualities that would endear it to Americans. In fact, it's often reminiscent of the Hollywood action pic of the 1930's.

"Traitors" tells of a samurai who is sent by the Emperor in Tokyo to investigate conditions on Okinawa. He gets in and out of a lot of scrapes, singlehandedly defeating hordes of swordswinging attackers. The effects are, at times, unintentionally funny.

Utaemon Ichikawa as the samurai makes a stout hero. Rest of the cast overplays with gusto. Sadatsugu Matsuda's direction keeps things moving, but is not always explicit. Shintaro Kawasaki's lensing makes the most of the rich color effects. Shiro Fukai somehow manages to infuse jazz rhythms into a dancing girl sequence.

Doesn't shape as an exportable item.
Hift.

Appeal On The Cross. Shin Toho Co. production. Stars Kanjuro Arashi, Ranko Hanai; features Shoji Nakayama, Kusuo Abe, Joji Oka, Misako Uji, Umpei Yokoyama. Produced by Mitsugi Okura. Directed and written by Kunio Watanabe. Camera, Takashi Watanabe; music, Yushizo Kaji. At Museum of Modern Art, N. Y. Running time, 100 MINS.

"Appeal on the Cross" is based on a centuries-old legend in Japan, reflecting the suppression of the farmers by the feudal overlords. It's a grim and unpleasant story. Its appeal for the U.S. is dim.

There is a good deal of oldfashioned overemotionalism in this yarn of self-sacrifice of one man and his family to save the rest of the farmers. After enduring great hardships, he finally presents a petition to the Emperor himself. It is accepted, but he and his wife must die on the cross, and their children are beheaded.

These tortuous scenes are drawn out in sickening detail, and in the end the bleeding corpses are brought back as ghosts to appear to the wicked Chamberlain and his henchmen. There's plenty of agonized weeping and conversation, none of which add up to American b.o.

Performances are overdrawn. Takashi Watanabe's photography achieves some interesting effects. Kunio Watanabe's direction is stylized and slow.
Hift.

Harp of Burma. Nikkatsu Corp. production. Stars Shoji Yasui, Rentaro Mikuni; features Tatsuya Mihashi, Taniye Kitabayashi, Yunosuke Ito. Directed by Kon Ichekawa. Screenplay, Natto Wada; camera, Minoru Yokoyama; music, Akira Ifukube; editor, Masonori Tsujii. At Museum of Modern Art, N. Y. Running time, 120 MINS.

"Harp of Burma" is a Venice film fest winner which, if properly edited, should stand a chance in U.S. arties. Skillfully lensed and directed, it shapes definitely as an offbeat Japanese entry.

Film's action takes place at the end of the war, when the British round up the Japanese troops in Burma and send them to camps prior to shipping them home. Story centers around a private in one Japanese unit who has found a Burmese harp and has become an expert at playing it. A gentle man, and yet a dedicated one, he is sent to convince one holdout company to surrender.

His attempt fails. In trying to rejoin his unit, he robs a monk of his robes. During the journey he becomes convinced that he must bury the Japanese dead. He is recognized by his comrades who do everything possible to get him to return to Japan with them. However, he resists the temptation to devote himself to his task.

Some Americans may find it strange to find Japanese soldiers sentimentally singing "Home Sweet Home," but on the whole the picture captures the struggle going on in the private's mind. Kon Ichikawa's direction has definite merit as does Minoru Yokoyama's lensing. Performances ,particularly by Shoji Yasui as Private Mizushima and Rentaro Mikuni as the Captain, are realistic.

Picture is much too long for U.S. consumption right now, but could easily be trimmed down.
Hift.

Undercurrent. Daiei release of Masaichi Nagata production. Stars Fujiko Yamamoto, Ken Uehara; features Michiko Ono, Michiko Ai, Kazuko Ichikawa, Keizo Kawasaki, Eijiro Tono, Sakae Ozawa. Directed by Kimisaburo Yoshimura. Screenplay, Sumie Tanaka; camera (Daiei color), Kazuo Miyagawa; music, Nari Ikeno. Running time, 104 MINS.

"Undercurrent" proved a letdown. Photography and tinting are splendid but beyond this there's little to recommend it; it fails to measure up to United States art theatre standards.

Film is soap opera, focusing on a femme specialist in a dyeworks factory who becomes enamored of a professor at a medical university. She becomes pregnant, his wife conveniently dies, and so on. Direction by Kimisaburo Yoshimura is orderly, the performances are good and the native backdrops are interesting and colorful. But the script is an overabundance of words and the light-gold titles against the bright screen are difficult to read.
Gene.

Women In Prison. Toho Co. release of Tokyo Eiga Co. production. Stars Setsuko Hara, Kinuyo Tanaka, Michiyo Kogure, Kyoko Kagawa, Yoshiko Kuga, Mariko Okada, Kyoko Anzai, Keiko Awaji, Chieko Naniwa. Directed by Seiji Hisamatsu. Screenplay, Sumie Tanaka; camera, Joji Ohara; music, Ichiro Saito. At Museum of Modern Art, N. Y., Jan. 23, 56. Running time, 102 MINS.

"Women in Prison," billed as a semi-documentary film, is a slow-moving, cliche-ridden drama reminiscent of the outmoded American films that were popular 20 years. It purports to describe the every day life of the inmates of women's prison.

Familiar types are presented—the tough, habitual criminals, the mixed-up kids, the dope addicts, and those who become enmeshed with the law because of unusual circumstances. The conflicts of prison life, and the antagonisms between the various inmates follow a familiar pattern. The picture is perhaps different because of its outspoken demonstration of lesbianism among several of the prisoners.

The main plot has to do with a kindly chief guard, known as the "angel" of the prison, and her attempts to rehabilitate an unrepentent and recalcitrant young inmate who has been incarcerated for killing her child. The chief guard's efforts meet little success until the very end. The guard is seriously wounded by a former prisoner and the antagonistic girl is responsible for saving her life by providing blood for a transfusion. After this incident, the girl, of course, reforms and walks out to start a new life.

The picture has some interest by offering an insight into aspects of life in a women's prison. The devotion of the women to their babies (who are kept in a prison nursery) is moving. Performances follow the pattern of Japanese acting and enough tears are shed to launch a battleship. Production values are good. The commonplace story and the manner in which its told gives this film little chance of being accepted by U.S. film-goers.
Holl.

A Girl In the Mist. Toho Co. release and production. Stars Yoko Tsukasa, Hitomi Nakahara, Takashi Ito, Choko Iida, Kamatari Fujiwara, Nijiko Kiyokwa, Hiroshi Koisumi. Directed by Hideo Suzuki. Screenplay, Zenzo Matsuyama, from a story by Yojiro Ishizaka; camera, Kazua Yamasaki; music, Ichiro Sito. At Museum of Modern Art, N. Y., Jan. 23, '56. Running time, 44 MINS.

This short film, described as a pastoral comedy, emerges as an artistic triumph but not a commercial entry for the U.S. However, it might fit in neatly in art houses that are able to book a 44-minute film with their feature attraction.

It's a simple, quiet film sans an elaborate story line. It offers a commentary on modern Japanese life and demonstrates the differences in the moral values of the young people of Japan and their tradition-bound parents.

It deals with the reaction of smalltown parents to the visit to their daughter of her Tokyo University classmate and boyfriend. After a family conclave, it is decided that the boy will be permitted to stay at their home.

The reaction of the precocious young sister, the knowledgeable grandmother, and the parents provides some delightful comedy. The entire family keeps a close watch on the young couple to make certain nothing untoward occurs. The picture ends on a quiet note as the boy boards the train to return to his own home.

Especially outstanding players are Hitomi Nakahara as the young sister and Choko Iida as the grandmother. The other actors also turn in fine performances. Hideo Suzuki's direction deserves special mention.   Holl.

The Incredible Shrinking Man

Science-fiction thriller for exploitation dates.

Hollywood, Feb. 1.
Universal release of Albert Zugsmith production. Stars Grant Williams, Randy Stuart. April Kent; features Paul Langton. Raymond Bailey, William Schallert, Frank Scannell. Directed by Jack Arnold. Screenplay, Richard Matheson, from his novel; camera, Ellis W. Carter; editor, Al Joseph; music supervision, Joseph Gershenson. Previewed Jan. 23, '57. Running time, 81 MINS.

Scott Carey	Grant Williams
Louise Carey	Randy Stuart
Clarice	April Kent
Charlie Carey	Paul Langton
Dr. Thomas Silver	Raymond Bailey
Dr. Arthur Bramson	William Schallert
Barker	Frank Scannell
Nurse	Helene Marshall
Nurse	Diana Darrin
Midget	Billy Curtis

The exploitation market will find "The Incredible Shrinking Man" a handy subject for ballyhoo bills. Teamed with another science-fictioner, or with a companion feature also having appeal for the younger set, returns can be good.

While its release possibilities are obvious, film isn't a thoroughly satisfactory chiller, even though there is enough on the good side to carry it. The unfoldment is inclined to slow down on occasion, resulting in flagging interest here and there, and portions of the background score are overworked, distracting from the tale of a man who shrinks into infinity after having been exposed accidentally to a radioactive fog.

The technical staff under Albert Zugsmith's production wing has done an outstanding job of the trick stuff needed to put the story on film. Art direction by Alexander Golitzen and Robert Clatworthy, and the set decorations by Russell A. Gausman and Ruby R. Levitt help to carry out the idea of a dimishing human, while the lensing by Ellis W. Carter, special photography by Clifford Stine, and optical effects by Roswell A. Hoffmann and Everett H. Broussard made the shrinking visually effective.

Richard Matheson scripted from his novel and, while most science-fiction thrillers usually contrive a happy ending, there's no compromise here. Six-footer Grant Williams and his wife, Randy Stuart, run into a fog while boating. She's below, so is untouched, but Williams gets the full force. Soon after, he finds himself shrinking and doctors decide the radioactivity in the fog has reversed his growth processes. Finale has him fading away into nothingness after strange experiences during the diminishing stages.

Director Jack Arnold works up the chills for maximum effect by the time Williams is down to two inches and the family cat takes after him. Also harrowing are his adventures in the cellar with, to him, a giant spider, which he manages to kill using a straight pin as a lance. Williams does his role quite well and Miss Stuart registers ably as his wife. April Kent is seen as a member of a circus midget troupe. Others effectively handling their parts include Paul Langton, Raymond Bailey, William Schallert and Frank Scannell.
                                                         Brog.

Fear Strikes Out

Compelling entertainment dramatizing mental breakdown of Jim Piersall, Red Sox outfielder. Good chances but needs selling because of baseball's poor b.o. reputation.

Hollywood, Feb. 5.
Paramount release of Alan Pakula production. Stars Anthony Perkins, Karl Malden; features Norma Moore, Adam Williams, Perry Wilson, Peter J. Votrian. Directed by Robert Mulligan. Screenplay, Ted Berkman, Raphael Blau; based on story by James A. Piersall, Albert S. Hirschberg; camera, Haskell Boggs; editor, Aaron Stell; music, Elmer Bernstein. Previewed Jan. 28, '57. Running time, 100 MINS.

Jim Piersall	Anthony Perkins
John Piersall	Karl Malden
Mary Teevan	Norma Moore
Dr. Brown	Adam Williams
Mrs. John Piersall	Perry Wilson
Jim Piersall (as a boy)	Peter J. Votrian
Phil	Dennis McMullen
Alice	Gail Land
Bernie Sherwill	Brian Hutton
Joe Cronin	Bart Burns
Radio Announcer	Rand Harper
Bill Tracy	Howard Price

In the sports world, the story of Jim Piersall's mental crackup and subsequent comeback as a slugging Red Sox outfielder is well-known. Outside that sphere it means little; hence Paramount has a job on its hands in selling "Fear Strikes Out" to that sizeable portion of film audiences that are not enthusiastic about baseball. Tied to the diamond or not, the film's entertainment quality, meriting a looksee for anyone's admission dollar, makes it well worth the extra push, so it may wind up as a good grosser.

Baseball is only a means to an end in this highly effective dramatization of the tragic results that can come from a father pushing his son too hard towards a goal he, himself, was not able to achieve. In trying to be the major leaguer his father had wanted to be, Piersall so filled his life with pressure and tension that he went into a complete mental breakdown right after smashing a homerun for the Boston Red Sox. Confined to the Westborough State Hospital under restraint, Piersall gradually started to respond to electro shock treatments and the kindly administrations of an understanding psychiatrist. His mental health was eventually restored and when the 1953 season opened for the Red Sox, Piersall was back in right field.

Anthony Perkins, in the young Piersall role, delivers a remarkably sustained performance of a sensitive young man, pushed too fast to the limits of his ability to cope with life's pressures. It's an exceptional job, reflecting rapport with the character, the unusually discerning and understanding direction by Robert Mulligan, who comes from a fine record in tv to score big on his first feature film, and a probing screenplay by Ted Berkman and Raphael Blau from Piersall's own story written with Albert S. Hirshberg.

Karl Malden, who puts depth into characters, is splendid as the father who gets his own ambitions mixed up with love for his son. Neither he, nor Perkins, seem to be acting a distinctive effect that bolsters the drama and which is also achieved by the others in the fine cast marshalled by Alan Pakula, here making his initial outing as a producer and winning himself an unusually good credit.

Norma Moore, new to films, is extremely good as the young nurse whom Piersall married before his breakup. She has talent and a personality to go with it. Perry Wilson, as Piersall's mother, and Peter J. Votrian, playing Piersall as a boy, are excellent cast assets.

Adam Williams, as the Dr. Brown who helped Piersall regain his sanity, is outstanding in a character that could have lost its authority in less able hands. Bart Burns, the Red Sox's Joe Cronin; Brian Hutton, and others are very able in small spots.

Elmer Bernstein's score counterpoints the drama effectively, and is particularly important dramatically in the ball park scene when Piersall goes berserk. Among the other exceptionally good credits are Haskell Boggs' photography and the editing by Aaron Stell.

Brog.

Michel Strogoff
(FRENCH; C'SCOPE; COLOR)

Paris, Jan. 29.

Films Modernes release of Emile Natan production. Stars Curd Jurgens; features Genevieve Page, Silvia Koscina, Jean Parades. Directed by Carmine Gallone. Screenplay, Marc-Gilbert Sauvajon from novel by Jules Verne; camera (Eastmancolor), Robert Le Febvre; editor, Nicolo Lizzari; music, Norbert Glanzberg. At the Paris, Paris. Running time, **115 MINS.**

Strogoff .... Curd Jurgens
Nadia .... Genevieve Page
Sancarre .... Silvia Koscina
Natko .... Francoise Fabian
Jolivet .... Jean Parades
Blond .... Gerard Buhr
Ogareff .... Henri Nassiet
Grand Duke .... Jacques Dacqmine
Feofar Khan .... Inkijinoff

Done once in the U. S., and now in for its second filming here, this carries on the recent pix rush on the public domain works of Jules Verne. Reportedly made for $1,600,000, it is hard to see where all the coin went since action is long in coming and short in duration. There are some mob scenes, battle sequences quickly skimmed over, and plenty of rich sets and costuming, but not that much. Though essentially an actioner, this is bogged down by too much talk. On its locale, this might be worth dubbing for U. S. dualers where its exotic background could be used for bally. Lack of names also limits it.

Michel Strogoff (Curd Jurgens) becomes the Czar's special courier to take a message through invading Tartar-held lands in the 19th Century. Saddled with a headstrong girl (to avoid suspicion), they fall in love during their perilous trip. Captured by the Tartars, he is saved from being blinded by a slave girl, and manages to get his message to the Czar's troops in time to defeat the invading Mongols.

Film has okay narrative style and some comic relief in two French war correspondents. Director Carmine Gallone has relied too much on dialogue without giving it rousing visual terms. Jurgens has stature as the courrier but tends to overplay his role. Supporting cast is good. Technical credits are fine but battle scenes are too languorous. It looks a good bet locally.

Mosk.

The Women of Pitcairn Island

Low-grade celluloid. Tedious rather than exploitable.

Hollywood, Feb. 5.

Twentieth-Fox release of an Aubrey Wisberg-Jean Yarbrough production. Stars James Craig, Lynn Bari, John Smith, Arleen Whelan; features Sue England, Rico Alaniz, John Stevens. Directed by Yarbrough. Story-screenplay, Wisberg; camera, Harry Neumann; editor, William Austin; music, Paul Dunlap. Reviewed Jan. 30, '57. Running time, **68 MINS.**

Page .... James Craig
Maimiti .... Lynn Bari
Thursday .... John Smith
Hutia .... Arleen Whelan
Nanai .... Sue England
Spanisher .... Rico Alaniz
Charles Quintelle .... John Stevens
Balhadi .... Carol Thurston
Tuarua .... Sonia Sorel
Susannah .... Charlita
Mortua .... Lorna Thayer
Jenny .... Roxanne Reed
Prudence .... Millicent Patrick
Fish .... Harry Lauter
Scruggs .... Pierce Lydon
Muskie .... Henry Rowland
Allard .... Paul Sorenson
Coggins .... House Peters Jr.
Miahiti .... Richard Devin
Alfred .... Rad Fulton
Tom McCoy .... Michael Miller
Moani .... Robert Cabal
John Martin .... Robert Kendall
Robert Brown .... Joel Collin
Henry Smith .... Tim Johnson

"The Women of Pitcairn Island" is a dull programmer with little to recommend it. Pic's exploitation title carries to tedious unfoldment, suitable only for the least discriminating audiences.

The Aubrey Wisberg-Jean Yarbrough production opens on the day the last of the mutineers of the HMS Bounty is buried on Pitcairn Island, leaving only the women and children to continue life. Their peace is disturbed by the arrival of a shipwrecked crew of cutthroats, who while searching for a crewman who escaped with a bag of black pearls go on the make for the women. Peace again is restored through the men killing each other over the pearls and meeting death at the hands of the infuriated islanders.

Wisberg's tired script gets no embellishment from Yarbrough's direction, and consequently the characterizations are forced and unbelievable. James Craig is leader of the sailors, Lynn Bari, as widow of Christian Fletcher, heads up the colony of women and young people, and John Smith is her son, who leads the fight against the invaders. Arleen Whelan, one of the widows, is in as a heavy, who tries to throw in her lot with the men. Sue England, Rico Alaniz, John Stevens and Harry Lauter appear in support.

Harry Neumann's lensing qualifies for the subject, and Paul Dunlap turns in a satisfactory musical score.

Whit.

Albert Schweitzer
(COLOR)

Film biog on one of the world's great living humanitarians. Definite offbeat appeal.

Jerome Hill and Erica Anderson presentation of production by Hill. Directed by Hill; camera (Eastmancolor), Erica Anderson; narrative by Albert Schweitzer with additional commentary by Thomas Bruce Morgan; spoken by Fredric March and Burgess Meredith; Schweitzer as a boy portrayed by his grandson, Phillip Eckart; Schweitzer's mother played by his sister, Mrs. Adele Woytt; music, Alec Wilder, with orchestra under Leon Barzin's direction; editors, Julia Knowlton and Henry A. Sundquist. Seen at the Guild Theatre, N. Y., Feb. 2, '57. Running time, **80 MINS.**

The lifetime work of Albert Schweitzer—jungle doctor, intellectual philosopher and virtuoso musician—is affectionately detailed in this color documentary which Jerome Hill has produced and Erica Anderson has photographed both in Gunsbach, France, where Schweitzer was born, and at Lambarene, French Equatorial Africa, where he built his hospital. Biographical documentary is too long, and at times it becomes tedious, but on the whole it has a gentle, convincing quality that seems to capture Schweitzer's humanitarian spirit.

Film really falls into two parts—Schweitzer's youth, recreated with shots of Gunsbach, old photos and little dramatic vignettes in which the old man's grandson and his sister take part; and the work that Schweitzer is perhaps most famous for, his hospital at Lambarene.

It's to the credit of producer Hill that the documentary aspects aren't allowed to overshadow Schweitzer's human qualities. He is a magnificent old man with a great compassion for those that suffer, and the scenes showing him at work among the natives and following his routine at the hospital are touching.

Miss Anderson's lensing is uneven, but it achieves its effects without striving too consciously for them. Scene showing Schweitzer playing the organ at Gunsbach has grandeur and reveals the depth of the man. Apparently a minimum of staging has been done, and this also benefits the film.

Narrative, written by Schweitzer himself, pretty much sticks to the point. Fredric March and Burgess Meredith speak it effectively and without undue emotion. Alec Wilder's music is enjoyable although there seems to be quite a lot of it on the soundtrack.

Schweitzer, now 80, is as photogenic as some of Hollywood's best. Moreoever, he is himself—a thinking, dedicated man who comes across at times with a feeling of loneliness. Editors Julia Knowlton and Henry A. Sundquist have done a good continuity job, but the footage still could stand trimming, both at the start and, later, in the hospital sequences.

If the picture lacks the "professional" touch, it seems real and Schweitzer's name should be a draw, even though the producers might have thought of a more intriguing title for the marquee. Film shapes as a definite plus for specialized situations.

Hift.

Il Tetto
(The Roof)
(ITALO-FRENCH)

Rome, Jan. 29.

Titanus release of a Titanus-Les Films Marceau co-production. Stars Gabriella Pallotti, Giorgio Listuzzi; features Gastone Renzelli, Maria di Rollo, Giuseppe Martini, Emilia Martini, Maria Sittoro, Angelo Visentin, Maria de Fiori, Luisa Alessandri. Directed by Vittorio DeSica. Screenplay and story, Cesare Zavattini; camera, Carlo Montuori; music, Alessandro Cicognini; editor, Eraldo Da Roma. At Ariston, Rome. Running time, **101 MINS.**

Well-made production of the famed DeSica-Zavattini combination falls to come up to "Umberto D." or "Bicycle Thieves" in impact. Still it offers enough neo-realistic ingredients to satisfy lovers of the genre. Pic has done surprisingly well in Italo spots, and should follow up in kind abroad, with the DeSica name an arty theatre sales point.

Plot chronicles the search of a newly-married couple for a home of their own (at the husband's modest bricklayer salary) rather than share their relations' already overcrowded rooms. Unable to find anything within their means, they decide to do as many others have done: build a hut themselves, overnight, knowing that a city ordinance forbids anyone's being thrown out of a "house" once a roof is over their heads. Half of pic is devoted to the first frustrated, then successful efforts to erect their shack, in which to start a life of hardship, but of independence.

Gabriella Pallotti, selected by DeSica from among several hundred girls for the role, is a definite find, with a film future ahead. Her partner, Giorgio Listuzzi, is less able, but fits his part in okay fashion. Rest of cast of pros and nonpros provide the colorful background so characteristic of the writer-director's previous films. However, film is consciously more straightforward than their other product.

Perhaps because the feeling (and the ending) here are upbeat, it lacks the power and even the participation of DeSica's other top films. Opinion on this item is and looks always to be split down the middle.

Technically, the pic is fine all down the line. Alessandro Cicognini contribs his usual appealing musical backdrop while Carlo Montuori's location lensing is expert, as always. Film has been re-edited since its Cannes Film Fete showing, now running considerably smoother and faster.

Hawk.

Moglie E Buoi . . .
(Wives and Obscurities)
(ITALIAN)

Rome, Jan. 29.

Variety release of a Cines Production. Stars Gino Cervi, Walter Chiari, Nino Taranto. Directed by Leonardo De Mitri. Story by De Mitri and others. Camera, Gabor Pogany. Running time, **88 MINS.**

An American immigrant and his U. S.-born son return to their hometown in Italy after 35 years. All of the local mothers thrust their daughters at him but he prefers the pretty daughter (Sandra Milo) of the town ne'er-do-well. She seems to be the only girl in sight who works.

The boys who hang out in the piazza resent the American and his flashy convertible, deriding him at every turn. Eventually he takes them all on single-handed in a fight in the neighborhood bar and wins.

Gino Cervi is the Italian-American who has become so Americanized he forgets to remove his hat when he enters a lady's house while Walter Chiara is the young Yankee. The roles are buttered with heavily-accented American words and phrases. Sandra Milo, a comely newcomer, has been pushed to stardom in the year since this film was made.

Saml.

Town on Trial
(BRITISH)

Slickly made thriller with John Mills portraying aggressive Scotland Yard man; bright boxoffice prospects.

London, Jan. 29.

Columbia release of a Maxwell Setton production. Stars John Mills, Charles Coburn, Barbara Bates, Derek Farr; features Elizabeth Seal. Directed by John Guillermin. Screenplay, Ken Hughes and Robert Westerby; camera, Basil Emmott; editor, Max Benedict; music, Tristran Cary. At Odeon Theatre, Marble Arch, London. Jan. 22, '57. Running time, **96 MINS.**

Superintendent Mike Halloran ... John Mills
Dr. Fenner .... Charles Coburn
Elizabeth Fenner .... Barbara Bates
Mark Roper .... Derek Farr
Peter Crowley .... Alex McCowen
Fiona Dixon .... Elizabeth Seal
Mr. Dixon .... Geoffrey Keen
Mrs. Dixon .... Margaretta Scott
Mrs. Crowley .... Fay Compton
D. Sgt. Rogers .... Meredith Edwards
D. Sgt. Beale .... Harry Locke
Mary Roper .... Maureen Connell
Molly Stevens .... Magda Miller
David .... David Quitak
Mrs. Wilson .... Dandy Nichols
Dr. Reese .... Raymond Huntley

A neatly conceived thriller with a powerful suspense climax, "Town on Trial" shapes as a sturdy b.o. contender with bright prospects. The story is crisply told, with shrewd direction keeping the action rolling at ag ood pace. Writer Ken Hughes takes joint screenplay credit with Robert Westerbery. Between them, they have fashioned a creditable murder meller which director John Guillermin has expertly translated to the screen. There's a consistent tension, this being adroitly relaxed from time to time as the story unfolds.

Within a few minutes of the opening Magda Miller, playing a provocative blonde, is found strangled on the grounds of a small-town social club. There are three immediate suspects but the conclusive evidence seems to elude John Mills, as the Scotland Yard man. One of the suspects is the club secretary (Derek Farr), a man with a phony war record, who fathered the child which the dead girl was expecting. The second is the local medico, Charles Coburn, who had been forced to leave Canada in a hurry. Third is a young man with a mental record (Alex McCowen), who had been in love with her. Before the denouement, another local girl (Elizabeth Seal) is murdered in the same way and the body is concealed in the doctor's car. A neat twist is employed to trap the actual killer.

Almost the entire incident is devoted to the Scotland Yard inquiries and this is related with telling dramatic effect. The scenes between the cop and the club secretary are powerful stuff. There is, perhaps, an overdose of padding in a dance hall sequence before the second killing but that gives Miss Seal (the discovery who made overnight fame in the London production of "The Pajama Game") an opportunity to display her terpsing skill.

There's fine all-round quality in the performances, with Mills playing the aggressive sleuth with considerable skill. Coburn portrays the medico with a high degree of sincerity. Barbara Bates makes an attractive showing as the latter's niece who warms to the cop. Farr is too obviously the cad, but McCowen is quite believable as the mental case. Geoffrey Keen, Maragretta Scott, Fay Compton and Harry Locke lead a sterling supporting cast. *Myro.*

Funny Face
(MUSICAL—COLOR)

Fred Astaire, Audrey Hepburn in modish Parisian tintuner; not the B'way musical of same title. Light diversion with generally favorable prospects.

Hollywood, Feb. 12.
Paramount release of Roger Edens production. Stars Audrey Hepburn, Fred Astaire; costars Kay Thompson; features Michael Auclair, Robert Flemyng. Directed by Stanley Donen. Written by Leonard Gershe; camera (Technicolor), Ray June; editor, Frank Bracht; music and lyrics, George and Ira Gershwin; added music and lyrics, Edens and Gershe; music conducted by Adolph Deutsch; songs staged by Donen; choreography, Eugene Loring, Fred Astaire. Previewed Feb. 4, '57. Running time, 103 MINS.

Jo	Audrey Hepburn
Dick Avery	Fred Astaire
Maggie Prescott	Kay Thompson
Prof. Emile Flostre	Michel Auclair
Paul Duval	Robert Flemyng
Marion	Robert
Marion	Dovima
Babs	Virginia Gibson
Specialty Dancer	Suzy Parker
Laura	Sue England
Specialty Dancer	Sunny Harnett
Lettie	Ruta Lee
Hair Dresser	Jean Del Val
Dovitch	Alex Gerry
Armande	Iphigenie Castiglioni

While it wears the title and bears several of the songs, "Funny Face's" relationship to the Broadway musical of some seasons back stops right there. With a different book and new, added tunes, this is a lightly diverting, modish, Parisian-located tintuner aimed at a generally favorable response in its playdates.

Originally slated for production at Metro (even earlier planned as a stage musical tagged "Wedding Day"), film moved to Paramount as a package so Audrey Hepburn could have the femme lead opposite Fred Astaire. This May-November pairing gives the Roger Edens production the benefits of Astaire's debonair style and terp accomplishments, and the sensitive acting talents of Miss Hepburn, each adding to the plot's high style world of fashions and models.

Leonard Gershe's script has a deliberately giddy air at times, particularly from some of its musical numbers like the chi-chi "Think Pink" opening production piece against a New York glamor mag setting. Occasionally there are touches of warmth, mostly generated through Miss Hepburn's character of a bookish introvert who is suddenly swept from her literary existence in a Greenwich Village shop to a heady, high fashion round of Paris when she's discovered by glamor photog Astaire.

For the ladies, style runs rampant, with Hubert de Givenchy creating the Paris wardrobe worn by Miss Hepburn as a model, while Edith Head takes care of things to attract the femme eye elsewhere. Tune-wise, there are six George and Ira Gershwin numbers from the stage musical and five from producer Edens and scripter Gershe. All are either sung or used as backing for dance numbers, with director Stanley Donen handling the song staging while Astaire and Eugene Loring take care of the choreography. All have a colorful dash, coupled with either humor, such as "Clap Yo' Hands" artfully done by Astaire and Kay Thompson, or with romance, as in the Astaire-Hepburn church garden dancing to, first "He Loves and She Loves" and later "'S Wonderful," the finale.

Spotted elsewhere are "Let's Kiss and Make Up," Astaire's solo dance that stands out via imagina-

tive choreography and interwoven musical story themes; "Bon Jour, Paris," which has the Misses Hepburn and Thompson and Astaire taking a dancing tour of the capital; the title tune, heard behind the titles as well as setting up a drak room dance by Astaire; "How Long Has This Been Going On." with Miss Hepburn; "Basal Metabolism," moderne acroballet indulged in by Miss Hepburn and two males in a smoky, dimly-lite Paris cellar; "On How To Be Lovely," Misses Hepburn and Thompson. "Marche Funebre" is used in a Bohemian party scene.

Kay Thompson will be well-liked by most viewers as the driving head of the glamor mag, furnishing chuckles for all under Donen's briskly able direction of the story portions. Michel Auclair, professor of Empathicalism who also has an eye for the girls, comes over well, as does Robert Flemyng as the Parisian designer who does the gowns for the plot's big fashion display. Dovima, a model, and others are acceptable, too.

Edens' production supervision gathered together some knowing talents to provide the film with its plush look and to handle the tuneterp ends. Choreography by Loring and Astaire, Donen's song staging, the adapting of the music and conducting by Adolph Deutsch, orchestral arrangements, art direction and set decorations, and, particularly, the Technicolor lensing in VistaVision by Ray June, all have the required flash. Photographic achievements by June are unusually effective. *Brog.*

Mitsou
(FRENCH; COLOR)
Paris, Feb. 5.
Victory Films release of Ardennes Films production. Stars Daniele Delorme, Fernand Gravey; features Francis Guerin, Claude Rich, Odette Laure, Jacques Duby, Jacques Dumesnil, Gaby Morlay. Directed by Jacqueline Audry. Screenplay, Pierre Laroche from novel by Colette; camera (Eastmancolor), Marcel Grignon; editor, Yvonne Martin. At Marignan, Paris. Running time, 95 MINS.

Mitsou	Daniele Delorme
Duroy-Lelong	Fernand Gravey
Lt. Bleu	Francoise Guerin
Petite-Chose	Odette Laure
Mother	Gaby Morlay
Father	Jacques Dumesnil
Kaki	Claude Rich
Compere	Jacques Duby

Based on a Colette novel, this is one of those hothouse Gallic distaffers with a frank approach to boudoir tactics. This is the tale of a Music Hall chorine who learns about life and love when caught in the triangle of an aged admirer (who keeps her) and a young lieutenant. Somewhat talky and literary, it might be okay for special situations in the U.S.

Made by a femme director, Jacqueline Audry, this pic lacks direct verve and progression, with characterizations just glossed over. Daniele Delorme is uneven in the role of the awakening ingenue (the kept femme) until the final metamorphosis. Fernand Gravey again is his suave self as the older, knowing man while others in the cast do well. Odette Laure scores as a perky singer and confidant, and adds some coy early century songs to the ensemble.

Color is rightly pastel-hued and technical credits are fine. But direction rarely infuses this with life. But this tinsely feeling makes this pic something that looks for exploitation purposes only in the U.S. Frank in its statements and story,

there should be censorship problems especially with rather intimate bedroom scenes. *Mosk.*

No Road Back
(BRITISH)

Skip Homeier's British screen debut in typical crime meller; moderate b.o. chances.

London, Feb. 5.
RKO release of a Gibraltar Pictures (Steve Pallos) production. Stars Skip Homeier, Paul Carpenter, Patricia Dainton, Norman Wooland and Margaret Rawlings; features Eleanor Summerfield and Alfie Bass. Directed by Montgomery Tully. Screenplay, Charles A. Leeds and Montgomery Tully from play by Falkland D. Cary and Philip Weathers; camera, Lionel Banes; editor, James Connock; music, John Veale. At Odeon, Tottenham Court Road, London. Running time, 83 MINS.

John Railton	Skip Homeier
Clem Hayes	Paul Carpenter
Beth	Patricia Dainton
Inspector Harris	Norman Wooland
Mrs. Railton	Margaret Rawlings
Marguerite	Eleanor Summerfield
Rudge Harvey	Alfie Bass
Spike	Sean Connery
Sergeant Brooks	Robert Bruce
Garage Man	Philip Ray
Night Watchman	Thomas Gallagher
The dog Rummy	Romulus of Welham

Skip Homeier makes his British screen bow in this Steve Pallos production, based on a play by Falkland L. Cary and Philip Weathers. It's a typical, if unconvincing, crime meller, likely to achieve moderate returns in the domestic market.

Dominating character in "No Road Back" is Margaret Rawlings, as a blind and deaf club owner who has allowed herself to be used as a fence to send her son through medical school. The boy returns from an American appointment just as his mother is plotting her greatest and final coup. Paul Carpenter is to break into the strongroom of a jewelry firm and walk out with a packet of diamonds worth $250,000. The plan, however, goes awry, the watchman is murdered and the son, who got wind of the operation, becomes involved with the law.

Script develops a consistent degree of suspense, but the frequent use of sign language, though intriguing at times, has a delaying effect. Actual holdup achieves a note of realism.

Homeier plays the young medico in a refreshing way and his realization that his mother and his fiancee (Patricia Dainton) are involved in a crime ring is neatly portrayed. Carpenter is a typical heavy, while Miss Dainton is given little opportunity as the blind woman's eyes and ears. Eleanor Summerfield, as a girl employed in the club, has a completely negative part. Norman Wooland, although given star billing, has only a minor role as a detective. Alfie Bass gives one of the best performances in the film as a driver who's ready to squeal when he discovers he's involved in a murder rap. The technical credits are about average. *Myro.*

Voodoo Island

Boris Karloff in horror pic for ballyhoo dates in programmer situations.

Hollywood, Feb. 7.
United Artists release of Aubrey Schenck, Howard W. Koch (Bel-Air) production. Stars Boris Karloff, Beverly Tyler, Murvyn Vye; features Elisha Cook, Rhodes Reason, Jean Engstrom, Frederich Ledebur. Directed by Reginald Leborg. Screenplay, Richard Landau; camera, William Margulies; editor, John F. Schreyer; music, Les Baxter. Previewed Feb. 5, '57. Running time, 77 MINS.

Phillip Knight .... Boris Karloff
Sara Adams .... Beverly Tyler
Barney Finch .... Murvyn Vye
Martin Schuyler .... Elisha Cook
Matthew Gunn .... Rhodes Reason
Claire Winter .... Jean Engstrom
The Ruler .... Frederich Ledebur
Mitchell .... Glenn Dixon
Howard Carlton ...... Owen Cunningham
Dr. Wilding .... Herbert Patterson
Vickers .... Jerome Frank

Carnivorous plants and zombies supply the chief menace for the principals in "Voodoo Island," which will top a horror package put together by Bel-Air Productions for United Artists release. The combo, in which the previously reviewed "Pharaoh's Curse" is the companion, makes for a fairly okay spook bill for ballyhoo dates in programmer situations.

Boris Karloff, an old hand, heads the cast, this time as a debunker of the supernatural, who leads a trek to a small Pacific island to investigate voodoo rumors and the mysterious disappearance of some members of another party. By the time the plot action is over, though, he's convinced and glad to get out alive. There's no attempt at explaining how various mysterious things happen in the Richard Landau script; probably because there is no way to do it logically, but the thriller gimmicks come off with the desired impact under Reginald LeBorg's direction.

The Aubrey Schenck-Howard W. Koch production was lensed on Kauai Island, Hawaii, so backgrounds have a helpful freshness as the characters are put through plot perils. Karloff doesn't have to exert himself much to handle his standard character. Beverly Tyler is okay as his mousey secretary who becomes a woman on the junket, mostly through the efforts of Rhodes Reason, World War II derelict who is reborn in the dangers the group undergoes. Murvyn Vye, hotel chain executive looking over the island as a possible resort center, ends up a zombe after having witnessed a native child eaten by a hungry plant. Elisha Cook is turned into a zombie and then killed because of his greed for money, and Jean Engstrom, sophisticated interior decorator for the chain who likes Miss Tyler more than the men, is another victim of a carnivorous plant. None of the performances is more than stock.

William Margulies did satisfactory photography, while Les Baxter gives the melodramatics an appropriate musical backing. Other technical assists are okay. *Brog.*

Daniel Boone, Trail Blazer
(COLOR)

Acceptable actioner for the supporting market.

Hollywood, Feb. 7.

Republic release of Albert C. Gannaway production. Stars Bruce Bennett; co-stars Lon Chaney, Faron Young; features Kem Dibbs, Damian O'Flynn, Jacqueline Evans, Nancy Rodman, Freddy Fernandez, Carol Kelly, Eduordo Noriega, Fred Kohler Jr., Gordon Mills, Claude Brook, Joe Ainley, Lee Morgan. Executive producers, Ben Costanten, C. J. Ver Halen. Directed by Gannaway and Ismael Rodriguez. Screenplay, Tom Hubbard, Jack Patrick; camera (Trucolor), Jack Draper; editor, Fernando Martinez A.; music, Raul Lavista. Reviewed Feb. 6, '57. Running time, **76 MINS.**

Daniel Boone .... Bruce Bennett
Blackfish .... Lon Chaney
Faron Callaway .... Faron Young
Girty .... Kem Dibbs
Andy Callaway .... Damian O'Flynn
Rebecca Boone ...... Jacqueline Evans
Susannah Boone ...... Nancy Rodman
Israel Boone .... Freddy Fernandez
Jemima Boone .... Carol Kelly
Squire Boone .... Eduardo Noriega
Kenton .... Fred Kohler Jr.
John Holder .... Gordon Mills
James Boone .... Claude Brook
General Hamilton .... Joe Ainley
Smitty .... Lee Morgan

This tale of early Americana, filmed entirely in Mexico, emerges a stock programmer with enough action to please the young 'uns and just enough plot to generally sustain the interest of their elders. Film was made independently under the Albert C. Gannaway Productions banner, with Republic subsequently taking over its release.

The Tom Hubbard-Jack Patrick screenplay is pivoted around frontiersman Daniel Boone, with his with family and a party of settlers in 1775 from Yakin Valley, North Carolina, to Boonesborough, Kentucky, to plot hook. Heavies are the Shawnee Indians, incited to fight the whites by a French renegade and the British Redcoats. Wind-up finds peace coming to Fort Boonesborough when Boone convinces the Shawnee chieftain his (Boone's) people want peace.

Bruce Bennett comes across well in the title role, as does Lon Chaney as the Shawnee leader. Faron Young is co-starred with third billing, but has little to do as the son of the officer-in-charge of Boonesborough. Likewise, most of those featured are spotted in only minor roles.

Direction by Albert C. Gannaway (who also produced for exec producers Ben Costenten and C. J. Ver Halen) and Ismael Rodriquez is a distinct credit, especially in the way the action is worked in with the picturesque Mexican backgrounds.

The Trucolor camera work by Jack Draper is clear and on the plus side, with the other technical credits also good.

There are Dan'l Boone songs included for exploitation values. Writers: Hal Levy and Al Gannaway. Publisher: Mark Warnow Music. *Neal.*

I Girovaghi
(The Wanderers)
(ITALIAN; COLOR)

Rome, Feb. 5.

S.I.C. release of Domenico Forges Davanzati production. Directed by Hugo Fregonese. Starring Peter Ustinov, Carla Del Piggio, Abbe Lane; features Gaetano Autiero. Screenplay based on a story by Luigi Capuana. Filmed in Supercinescope and Ferraniacolor. At Adriano, Rome. Running time, **102 MINS.**

Colorful setting of small Sicilian towns and the names of Peter Ustinov and Abbe Lane may make this a good second feature for the American market although its story offers little.

Don Alfonso (Ustinov) travels from town to town with his wagon to do his live and puppet shows. His wife and boy accompany him. En route he lures Miss Lane from another show and falls in love with her. When he has run out of money, she joins her old outfit. When Ustinov tries to take her back, a group of the boys give it to him. Chastened and beaten up, he returns to bully his family.

While some sequences are well-directed by Hugo Fregonese, most of the time the yarn does not seem to know where it is going. Carla del Poggio is the patient wife while young Gaetano Autiero, a vet of 15 films including "Summertime," contributes another likeable performance.

The Spirit of St. Louis
(C'SCOPE—COLOR)

An engaging but not particularly powerful reproduction of Charles A. Lindbergh's historical flight to Paris. James Stewart backed by high-integrity production.

Warner Bros. release of Leland Hayward production. Stars James Stewart. Directed by Billy Wilder. Screenplay, Wilder and Wendell Mayes; adaptation, Charles Lederer; from the Charles A. Lindbergh autobiography; camera (Warnercolor), Robert Burks and J. Peverell Marley. Previewed in New York, Feb. 15, '57. Running time, **135 MINS.**

Charles A. Lindbergh.... James Stewart
Bud Gurney .... Murray Hamilton
Mirror Girl .... Patricia Smith
B. F. Mahoney .... Bartlett Robinson
Father Hussman .... Marc Connelly
Donald Hall .... Arthur Space
O. W. Schultz .... Charles Watts

Although lacking the elaborate production trappings that would automatically mirror a multi-million dollar budget, an extensive shooting schedule and painstaking care went into this picture. It's clear that Warner Bros. needs mammoth money to come out on top with "Spirit of St. Louis."

This is quality production. But excitement about the first solo N.Y.-to-Paris hop is quiet—and that's the prospective trouble with "Spirit"—it is quiet. It's Class A picture-making yet doesn't manage to deliver entertainment wallop out of the story about one man in a single-engine plane over a 3,610-mile route.

Under veteran director Billy Wilder, "Spirit" comes off as interesting and colorful, but not sock. Heavy "sell" is demanded, for interest and color alone are not blockbuster ingredients. Considering further that Charles A. Lindbergh is today little more than a Mr. Anonymous to youngsters, the spontaneous boxoffice appeal is perhaps short of commensurate with the scope of the production.

For the spectator, "Spirit" is a James Stewart one-man show. He portrays Lindbergh with a toned-down performance intended as consistent with the diffident (i.e. non-communicative) nature of the famed aviator. The story development tends to focus on the personal side of the 1927 hero, as much as it does on the flight itself, and Stewart comes off with sort of an appropriate, shy amiability.

Film opens in the Garden City Hotel on Long Island where Stewart, on the eve of his takeoff, gets to wondering about what lies in store for him. The scene segues to some of his experiences of the past, landing on a cow pasture and other hazards of that early-day flying.

The flashback technique is used frequently to convey some of Lindbergh's background, such as his days as a mail pilot, an amusing bit re his first encounter with the Air Force, his barnstorming stunts, etc. There are interludes also with the group of St. Louis businessmen who sponsor his trip, his near frustrating efforts to come upon an adequate plane, and a brief encounter with a girl (the film's faint suggestion of a romance) who gives him a compass mirror.

Those who remember the Lindbergh crossing are robbed of surprise. There was no mishap, so there can be no anxiety about whether he can get the plane off the mud-covered field. It's known, too, that the groggy Lindbergh will awake before the plane hits the water, as it nearly does, and that the right fuel tank will be turned on in time.

Climax of "Spirit" is the most stimulating. Here is Stewart, not quite sure of his course, recognizing the shoreline of Ireland, veering over the channel, spying Paris along the Seine, coming down on Le Bourget Airfield and, fatigued and bewildered, greeted by the frenzied crowd. Finale is the newsreel account of Lindbergh's New York reception.

Others in the cast are only minorly spotted; Stewart has the prominence all the way.

The Leland Hayword production settings and costumes look like genuine 1927 and add to the color, and the group and mob scenes are handled with particularly smooth effect. Standout contribution is the WarnerColor-CinemaScope photography by Robert Burks and J. Peverell Marley. Scenes of the sea as Lindbergh sees it from his plane, the shots of a huge iceberg, fishermen off Ireland, and Paris and the airfield at night—these have visual potency.

Writing credits begin with Lindbergh's book and include an adaptation by Charles Lederer and screenplay by Wilder and Wendell Hayes. Perhaps of necessity, the script has Stewart expressing his thoughts via his own off-screen voice as he wings over the ocean. This tends to be disconcerting at times. And in trying to communicate the "human side," the writing has Stewart in some mild humorous business, such as a conversation with a fly in his plane, that achieves fair results. The writing also fails to penetrate much below the surface. The public might have been interested in learning more of the "inner man" of this first individual to hop the Atlantic.

Editing and other technical credits splendid. *Gene.*

Duel at Apache Wells
(NATURAMA)

Well-motivated western meeting demands of the market.

Hollywood, Feb. 19.

Republic release of a Joe Kane production. Stars Anna Maria Alberghetti, Ben Cooper, Jim Davis. Features Harry Shannon, Francis J. McDonald, Bob Steele, Frank Puglia, Argentina Brunetti. Directed by Kane. Screenplay, Bob Williams; camera, Jack Marta; music, Gerald Roberts; editor, Richard L. Van Enger. Reviewed Feb. 13, '57. Running time, **69 MINS.**

Anita Valdez .. Anna Maria Alberghetti
Johnny Shattuck .... Ben Cooper
Dean Cannary .... Jim Davis
Wayne Shattuck .... Harry Shannon
Hank .... Francis J. McDonald
Joe Dunn .... Bob Steele
Senor Valdez .... Frank Puglia
Tia Maria .... Argentina Brunetti
Marcus Wolf .... Ian MacDonald
Bill Sowers .... John Dierkes
Frank .... Ric Roman

"Duel at Apache Wells" is a regulation western with advantages. Producer-director Joe Kane has given rugged treatment to a well-motivated screenplay.

Ben Cooper and Jim Davis lead off the action, with Anna Maria Alberghetti also starred for romantic interest. The Bob Williams script holds on Cooper, who returns home after a four-year absence to find his father's Arizona ranch threatened by Davis, rustler-turned-rancher. After trying to outwit Davis legitimately for having fenced off a public water hole known as Apache Wells, thus making impossible the driving of cattle to market, Cooper meets Davis in a duel, where it's revealed he's the famous gunman, Durango Kid.

Cooper acquits himself in okay fashion and Davis lends credence to his heavy characterization. Miss Alberghetti is an interesting attraction. Harry Shannon as Cooper's father, Bob Steele as Davis' chief henchman and Frank Puglia in role of femme lead's father, owner of a cantina, deliver handily in their respective parts. Also in good support are Francis J. McDonald and Argentina Brunetti.

Whit.

The Man Who Turned to Stone

Scientists who live on young women's blood. Lesser entry in current crop of horror pix.

Hollywood, Feb. 15.

Columbia release of Sam Katzman (Clover) production. Features Victor Jory, Ann Doran, Charlotte Austin, William Hudson, Paul Cavanagh, Tina Carver, Jean Willes. Directed by Leslie Kardos. Screenplay, Raymond T. Marcus; camera, Benjamin H. Kline; editor, Carles Nelson; music, Ross Di Maggio. Previewed Feb. 7, '57. Running time, **71 MINS.**

Dr. Murdock .... Victor Jory
Mrs. Ford .... Ann Doran
Carol Adams .... Charlotte Austin
Dr. Jess Rogers.......... William Hudson
Cooper .... Paul Cavanagh
Big Marge .... Tina Carver
Tracy .... Jean Willes
Myer .... Victor Varconi
Eric .... Frederick Ledebur
Freneau .... George Lynn
Anna .... Barbara Wilson

This latest in the current batch of horror films headed for programmer bookings is a lesser entry. Call it adequate to intentions as lower half of an "exploitation" bill.

Sam Katzman's Clover unit produced for Columbia, using Raymond T. Marcus' script, which never rises above the incredible in telling of an ageless group of scientists from two centuries back who have been able to sustain life over the years by occasionally tapping the life force of young women. Title comes from the fact they turn to stone unless a supply of femmes is available, so they have set themselves up as heads of a reformatory for women. An unusually high death rate among the inmates arouses the curiosity of the reformatory's young welfare worker and, aided by an inquiring young prison board psychiatrist, she starts a probing that results in the long over-due demise of the ageless ones.

Leslie Kardos' direction is all that the script demands but, while there's very little payoff in thrills, he does steer the cast by plot holes for generally okay performances. Victor Jory, Ann Doran, Paul Cavanagh and Frederick Ledebur are the principal stone people. Attractive Charlotte Austin is the not-so-naive welfare worker, while William Hudson plays the young doc. Seen as inmates, and helping to decorate the footage are Tina Carver, Jean Willes and Barbara Wilson.

Lensing by Benjamin H. Kline and the other technical credits are workmanlike in supplying budget values.

Brog.

The True Story Of Jesse James
(C'SCOPE-COLOR)

Poorly plotted with confusing flashbacks, Jesse James takes another screen ride. Routine results probable.

Hollywood, Feb. 15.

20th-Fox release of Herbert B. Swope Jr. production. Stars Robert Wagner, Jeffrey Hunter, Hope Lange; costars Agnes Moorehead. Directed by Nicholas Ray. Screenplay, Walter Newman; based on a screenplay by Nunnally Johnson; camera (De Luxe Color), Joe MacDonald; editor, Robert Simpson; music, Leigh Harline, conducted by Lionel Newman. Previewed Feb. 13, '57. Running time, **92 MINS.**

Jesse James .... Robert Wagner
Frank James .... Jeffrey Hunter
Zee .... Hope Lange
Mrs. Samuel .... Agnes Moorehead
Cole Younger .... Alan Hale
Remington .... Alan Baxter
Rev. Jethro Bailey .... John Carradine
Anne .... Rachael Stephens
Dr. Samuel .... Barney Phillips
Jim Younger .... Biff Elliott
Major Cobb .... Frank Overton
Attorney Walker .... Barry Atwater
Rowena Cobb .... Marian Seldes
Askew .... Chubby Johnson
Charley .... Frank Gorshin
Robby .... Carl Thayler
Hillstrom .... John Doucette
Sheriff Trump .... Robert Adler
Sheriff Yoe .... Clancy Cooper
Bill Stiles .... Sumner Williams
Deputy Leo .... Tom Greenway
Deputy Ed .... Mike Steen
Peter .... Jason Wingreen
Wiley .... Aaron Saxon
Bob Younger .... Anthony Ray
Tucker .... Clegg Hoyt
Hughie .... Tom Pittman
Clell Miller .... Lous Zito
Sam Wells .... Mark Hickman
Dick Liddell .... Adam Marshal
Bill Ryan .... Joseph Di Reda
Jorgenson .... J. Frederik Albeck
Archie, age 4 .... Kellogg Junge Jr.

On celluloid Jesse James has had more lives than a cat, and "The True Story of Jesse James" suggests it's time screen writers let him roll over and play dead for real and reel. In the many past film reworkings of the 19th century delinquent's shoddy career just about every angle has been covered. There's nothing new to report in this CinemaScope-De Luxe Color glorification. It's a routine offering for the outdoor market with Robert Wagner and Jeffrey Hunter in top roles.

Herbert B. Swope's production had plenty of opportunity for commercial action to bolster a formula plot, but these opportunities are mostly dissipated by slowing the film with a story told in numerous flashbacks. The attempt to view the James character through the eyes of pro and con contemporaries only makes for confusion, depriving an audience of clear-cut plot line that might keep it interested. Dialog, too, is poor, continually veering from period to modern idioms in the Walter Newman script, based on Nunnally Johnson's screenplay for 20th-Fox's 1939 "Jesse James."

Nicholas Ray directs in stock fashion, adding little of substance to the picture. Admittedly, he didn't have much to work with, but there's no apparent attempt to help build performances into meaningful portrayals—an assist all of the cast members sorely needed. As Jesse and Frank James, respectively, Wagner and Hunter go through the motions of telling why the former took up the gun when Northern sympathizers made it difficult for them to live in Missouri after the War between States. Both are adequate to the demands of script and direction, as is Hope Lange, playing Zee, the girl who married Jesse. Costar Agnes Moorehead goes way overboard in her role of the mother of Jesse and Frank.

Alan Hale, as Cole Younger; Alan Baxter, the railroad detective; John Doucette, a sheriff, John Carradine, Barney Phillips, Biff Elliot, Frank Overton, Barry Atwater, Marian Seldes and Chubby Johnson are among accepted performers in the large cast that acts out the incidents in the James career. Joe MacDonald's photography does a good action job on showing the various sorties against banks and trains by the James gang, and the period decorations come off okay.

Brog.

Oh, Men! Oh, Women!
(C'SCOPE-COLOR)

Merry spoof of psycho-analysis with Ginger Rogers, David Niven, Dan Dailey, Barbara Rush and Tony Randall. Good boxoffice potential.

20th-Fox release of Nunnally Johnson production. Stars Ginger Rogers, David Niven, Dan Dailey, Barbara Rush and Tony Randall. Directed by Johnson. Screenplay, Johnson, from the play by Edward Chodorov; camera (Cinema-Scope-DeLuxe), Charles G. Clark; editor, Majorie Fowler; music, Cyril J. Mockridge. Previewed in N.Y., Feb. 14, '57. Running time, **90 MINS.**

Arthur Turner .... Dan Dailey
Mildred Turner .... Ginger Rogers
Dr. Alan Coles .... David Niven
Myra Hagerman .... Barbara Rush
Cobbler .... Tony Randall
Mrs. Day .... Natalie Schafer
Miss Tacher .... Rachel Stephens
Dr. Kraus .... John Wengraf
Melba .... Cheryll Clarke
Steward .... Charles Davis

Having taken Freud seriously for a number of years, as evidenced by the numerous psychological dramas, Hollywood—taking its cue from a Broadway success-swerves to satire. The result is a merry and occasionally hilarious spoof of the headshrinkers and the couch-happy brigade.

Taking off from Edward Chodorov's Broadway play of a few seasons ago, Nunnally Johnson, who also served as producer and director, fashioned a generally fast-paced comedy that can be converted to boxoffice dollars. Bolstered by such marquee names as Ginger Rogers, David Niven and Dan Dailey, the film has all the earmarks of a popular hit.

It's film newcomer, Tony Randall, however, who'll probably gain most of the attention. A television and legit performer who received notice as Wally Cox's sidekick in "Mr. Peepers" and as the Menckenian character in "Inherit the Wind," Randall emerges as a new screen personality. His forte—at least in "Oh, Men! Oh, Women!"—is comedy and he handles the assignment with confidence and polish.

As a mixed-up schnook completely distracted by an equally addlebrained femme, Randall's antics succeed in upsetting the composure and life of a previously complacent and sedate psychoanalyst, portrayed by David Niven. As a matter of fact, Niven, who has succeeded in keeping his professional and private life separate, is shocked to find the two merging.

Not only does he discover, via the outpourings of his patients, that Randall has had a relationship with his fiancee, (Barbara Rush), but also that the husband (Dan Dailey) another of his problem patients (Ginger Rogers) is also acquainted with his future bride.

This situation sets the stage for numerous complications—Randall's attempt to win back (for himself) his analyst's girl and Dailey's effort to break up Niven's romance because he believes that his wife's desire to leave him has been prompted by her analyst.

The thesps, all pros, turned in excellent performances. Miss Rogers is effective as the "useless" wife determined to end her "Doll's House" existence. Dailey scores as the film star utterly confused by his wife's actions and Niven excels as the analyst who sees his own life crumbling. Miss Rush is fine as the "nutty," child-like fiancee who gets rid of problems by refusing to think of them.

There are occasional slow moments in the film which tighter editing can easily remedy. For the most part, however, it fulfills its main purpose of providing entertainment that should prove appealing to mass audiences.

The production values and the technical aspects of the film are all first-rate.

Holl.

Flesh And The Spur
(COLOR)

Unexciting western for less discriminating trade.

Hollywood, Feb. 19.

American International release of an Alex Gordon production. Stars John Agar, Marla English, Touch Connors; features Raymond Hatton. Directed by Edward L. Cahn. Story-screenplay, Charles B. Griffith, Mary Hanna; camera (Eastmancolor), Frederick E. West; editor, Ronald Sinclair; music, Ronald Stein. Previewed Feb. 15, '57. Running time, **78 MINS.**

Luke Random, Mathew Random .... John Agar
Willow .... Marla English
Stacey .... Touch Connors
Windy .... Raymond Hatton
Lola .... Maria Monay
Rena .... Joyce Meadows
Tanner .... Kenne Duncan
Indian Chief .... Frank Lackteen
Blackie .... Mel Gaines
Deputy Marshal .... Michael Harris
Bud .... Eddie Kafafian
Bartender .... Richard Alexander
Outlaws..Kermit Maynard, Bud Osborne, Buddy Roosevelt

"Flesh and the Spur" is an unexciting western, burdened with trite dialog and drawn-out situations. Film will need all the draw of "Naked Paradise," with which it is being packaged, to get by. On the credit side, however, is some fine Eastman-color photography.

The Charles B. Griffith-Mark Hanna screenplay centers on a manhunt, John Agar's search for the murderer of his twin brother. He meets Touch Connors, a fast gunman, who also is seeking a quarry — the outlaw gang with which the killer is identified. They team up on the hunt, but the windup is long and dull, only livened by the brief surprise situation of Connors being the killer.

Edward L. Cahn's direction is unable to hurdle the dull aspects of the script, with the result that none of the players shows to advantage. Faring best is Connors, whose personality rises above his part. Agar is lifeless as the avenger. Marla English, an Indian girl who joins pair when they save her from another white man, is lost in the shuffle, and Raymond Hatton barely manages to make his work count as a medicine showman.

Whit.

Ten Thousand Bedrooms
(C'SCOPE—SONGS—COLOR)

Dean Martin, on own, stars acceptably in light romantic comedy with songs. Regulation tintuner for general bill-topping playdates.

Hollywood, Feb. 18.

Metro release of Joe Pasternak production. Stars Dean Martin; costars Anna Marie Alberghetti, Eva Bartok, Dewey Martin, Walter Slezak, Paul Henreid. Directed by Richard Thorpe. Screenplay, Laslo Vadnay, Art Cohn, William Ludwig, Leonard Spigelgass; camera (Metrocolor), Robert Bronner; editor, John McSweeney Jr.; new songs, Nicholas Brodszky, Sammy Cahn; music supervision and conducted by George Stoll. Previewed Feb. 13, '57. Running time, **113 MINS.**

Ray Hunter .... Dean Martin
Nina Martelli ...Anna Maria Alberghetti
Maria Martelli .... Eva Bartok
Mike Clark .... Dewey Martin
Papa Vittorio Martelli..... Walter Slezak
Anton .... Paul Henreid
Arthur .... Jules Munshin
Vittorio Gisini .... Marcel Dalio
Countess Alzani .... Evelyn Varden
Diana Martelli .... Lisa Montell
Anna Martelli .... Lisa Gaye
Bob Dudley .... John Archer
Tom Crandall .... Steve Dunne

Dan .... Dean Jones
Girl on Main Title..Monique Van Vooren

Dean Martin goes solo in "Ten Thousand Bedrooms" and proves (a) he is an affable leading man and (b) has an easy way with a song. He will have no problem handling anything in this vein that comes his way, now that he's shorn of Jerry Lewis. Besides, the typical Joe Pasternak production provides him with a number of comely femme partners, as well as several very able hands at comedy. The end result is a pleasant, albeit regulation, romantic tintuner that will head the bill in general playdates.

In addition to the above beguilements, Pasternak insures plenty of sight values via a Rome story-site, making for lush adjuncts to the light plot froth cooked up by scripters Laslo Vadnay, Art Cohn, William Ludwig and Leonard Spigelgass. Four new tunes by Nicholas Brokszky and Sammy Cahn, all with a pop flavor, head the musical end of the presentation, with Martin and Anna Maria Alberghetti to give them listener appeal.

Miss Alberghetti, venturing into more grownup roles, just might catch teenage fancy as a result of the way she performs here. The character of a young, romantically inclined Italian miss is right for her, so she has no trouble making it register strongly. It's a good showcasing for the young lady. Vocally, too, she's good in joining with Martin on such numbers as "You I Love," possibly the score's best, and "Only Trust Your Heart," also smoothly listenable.

Martin, in somewhat of a young Conrad Hilton takeoff, is a hotel tycoon en route to Rome to set his latest—the purchase of an old, established hostelry. Hence, the title and the title song, which he sings as the credits unwind and Monique Van Vooren stretches on a satined symbol. The ancient city's highspots, such as the Colosseum, Spanish Steps and Trevi Fountain (latter better known stateside for the three coins tossed therein), are displayed while Martin gets himself romantically involved with the attractive daughters of Walter Slezak. There are four, but Martin imagines he fancies Miss Alberghetti, the youngest. Amatory didoes concern his trying to get husbands for the other three first —it's a family tradition—but wind-up finds him happily losing Miss Alberghetti to Dewey Martin, pilot of the tycoon's private plane, and marrying the eldest, Eva Bartok, who is the right one for him, anyway. Miss Bartok and Martin carry off their respective duties capably, as do sisters Lisa Montell and Lisa Gaye, also heard singing "Rock Around the Clock" and "No One But You."

Besides getting all that's possible out of the romantics and songs, director Richard Thorpe also handles the cast's several comics skillfully for rewarding laughs. Slezak, in a character of a type seen in many such pix, still gives it a freshness that tickles the risibilities. Possibly a surprise comic is Paul Henreid, who milks his part as an impoverished count who, while liking Miss Bartok, likes money and position just as much, if not more. Jules Munshin also gets his share of chuckles at the hotel tycoon's valet—even does "Money Is a Problem" with the boss in a nicely routined bit staged by Jack Baker. Bows go, too, to John Archer and Steve Dunne as a couple of

hotel managers the tycoon flies in to woo the Misses Gaye and Montell.

Robert Bronner's photography uses the CinemaScope and Metrocolor to advantage. Other assists include the music supervision and conducting by George Stoll, Helen Rose's costumes, and the lush decorations.   *Brog.*

12 Angry Men

Absorbing juryroom drama by Reginald Rose. Henry Fonda, Lee J. Cobb and Ed Begley head cast of outstanding performers. Good b.o. prospects.

United Artists release of Orion-Nova production (Henry Fonda and Reginald Rose). Stars Fonda. Features Lee J. Cobb, Ed Begley. Directed by Sidney Lumet. Story and screenplay, Rose; camera, Boris Kaufman; editor, Carl Lerner. Previewed in N.Y., Feb. 14, '57. Running time, 95 MINS.

Juror No. 8	Henry Fonda
Juror No. 3	Lee J. Cobb
Juror No. 10	Ed Begley
Juror No. 4	E. G. Marshall
Juror No. 7	Jack Warden
Juror No. 1	Martin Balsam
Juror No. 2	John Fiedler
Juror No. 5	Jack Klubman
Juror No. 6	Edward Binns
Juror No. 9	Joseph Sweeney
Juror No. 11	George Voskovec
Juror No. 12	Robert Webber
Judge	Rudy Bond
Guard	James A. Kelly
Court Clerk	Bill Nelson
Defendant	John Savoca

The "12 Angry Men" of this Henry Fonda-Reginald Rose production are a jury, a body of peers chosen to decide the guilt or innocence of a teenager accused of murdering his father. They have listened to an array of witnesses. They have heard the arguments of the district attorney and the defense lawyer. They have received instructions from the presiding judge. Now they are on their own. They are locked in the jury room and are faced with the responsibility of condemning or freeing the defendant. What will they do?

That is the theme of Rose's absorbing drama. The writer has taken the material of his own teleplay and fashioned it into a tense and exciting screenplay. By usual Hollywood standards this New York-made production is a "Little" picture. But the name of Henry Fonda as marquee bait plus an assemblage of talented film-legit-tv performers lifts the entry out of the "small" picture category and good, if not socko, returns should result.

As a matter of fact, the thesping —including that of Fonda, Lee J. Cobb, Ed Begley, E. G. Marshall, Jack Warden and the rest of the jurymen—is perhaps the best seen recently in any single film. Each individual, as he is shown wrestling with his background and revealing his conscience, has an opportunity to display his acting ability. This factor alone should generate a lot of word-of-mouth.

Rose has a lot to say about the responsibility of citizens chosen to serve on a jury. He stresses the importance of taking into account the question of "reasonable doubt." As the picture opens, the jurymen are seen filing in the courthouse conference room. It is soon evident that the majority of the men regard the assignment as a chore and the sooner the matter is disposed of, the better. To most of them, it is an open and shut case. The boy is guilty and they demand a quick vote. On the first ballot it is 11 to 1 for a conviction.

Fonda is the lone holdout. He's not quite sure of the boy's guilt. He reviews every facet of the case, questions the motives of the witnesses, breaks down the argument of the district attorney, and introduces the issue of "reasonable doubt." His persistency pays off. Slowly he wins the jurors to his side. In the process, the viewer learns a great deal about each juror. The background and motivation that contributed to each one's comment and decisions are unmasked.

There are familiar types—a racial bigot, a revengeful father, a proper stockbroker, an "organization" Madison Ave. advertising man, a wise-cracking, baseball-happy salesman, a timid soul, a wise old man, a refugee imbued with democracy, and a slum-reared citizen.

Most of the action takes place in the one room on a hot summer day. The effect, rather than being confining, serves to heighten the drama. It's not static, however, for Sidney Lumet, making his bow as a film director, has cleverly manuevered his players in the small area.

There may be some complaints that the tv-originated story is thin and has been stretched for pictures. Perhaps the motivations of each juror are introduced too quickly and are repeated too often before each changes his vote. However, the film leaves a tremendous impact and should help in arousing citizens to their responsibility as jurors.

Boris Kaufman has done a fine b&w filming stint. Technical aspects are first-rate. Mention should also be made, of the fine performances of Martin Balsam, John Fiedler, Jack Klugman, Edward Binns, Joseph Sweeney, George Voskovec and Robert Webber.
                Holl.

Lizzie
(SONGS)

The fight of a woman with three faces—good, evil, neurotic—to save the best personality. Eleanor Parker and okay femme appeal; spotty prospects.

Hollywood, Feb. 25.

Metro release of Jerry Bresler (Bryna) production. Stars Eleanor Parker; costars Richard Boone; features Joan Blondell, Hugo Haas, Ric Roman, Dorothy Arnold, John Reach, Marion Ross, Johnny Mathis. Directed by Hugo Haas. Screenplay, Mel Dinelli; based on novel "The Bird's Nest" by Shirley Jackson; camera, Paul Ivano; editor, Leon Barsha; score, Leith Stevens; songs, Albert Stillman and Robert Allen, Hal David and Burt F. Bacharach. Previewed Feb. 20, '57. Running time, 81 MINS.

Elizabeth Richmond	Eleanor Parker
Dr. Neal Wright	Richard Boone
Aunt Morgan	Joan Blondell
Walter Brenner	Hugo Haas
Johnny Valenzo	Ric Roman
Elizabeth's Mother	Dorothy Arnold
Robin	John Reach
Ruth Seaton	Marion Ross
Nightclub Singer	Johnny Mathis
Helen Jameson	Jan Englund
Elizabeth—13 years old	Carol Wells
Elizabeth—9 years old	Karen Green
Guard	Gene Walker
Man in Bar	Pat Golden
Waiter	Dick Paxton
Bartender	Michael Marks

Something akin to a sister-under-the-skin feeling should make this Bryna production for Metro release more appealing to distaffers than male filmgoers. Eleanor Parker gives it performance quality, doing a woman with three faces—good, evil, neurotic—exceptionally well, but subject matter probably faces spotty prospects generally.

Based on "The Bird's Nest," novel by Shirley Jackson, it's the story of a woman with multiple personalities, with the title drawn from the name used by the evil one, who is trying to destroy the others. Elizabeth is the drab neurotic, a colorless museum worker who believes she is losing her mind. Lizzie is a wanton who, unknown to Elizabeth, sneaks out at night to drink and make love. Beth is a quiet, normal and charming girl, still hidden in the character's mind until she is awakened by the hypnotic probing of a psychiatrist and brought to life by shock techniques that allow her to dominate in the end.

Miss Parker makes her three personalities distinctly separate and interesting—a tough job—under Hugo Haas' direction of the Jerry Bresler production. The script by Mel Dinelli seems to run to rather pat expositions at times, but overall does its work satisfactory in supplying Haas with the melodramatic ingredients. Direction generally is good in cast handling, establishing the contrasting characters and situations ably as the plot builds to the disclosure of the things that had caused Elizabeth to be mixed up.

Richard Boone is thoroughly medic as the psychiatrist who puts the girl on the right mental road. Joan Blondell, as the drunkened aunt, perks her footage and Haas is acceptable as a neighbor who gets into the act. Ric Roman, Latin type favored by Lizzie on her amatory binges; Dorothy Arnold, seen briefly in a couple of flashbacks as the mother who had caused most of the trouble; John Reach, the mother's lover who had raped the young daughter at 13; and Marion Ross, friendly museum worker, are all capable.

The Bryna production shows evidence of a tight budget, with the poor physical quality sometimes distracting from the story. Editing is unusually choppy and the photography only fair. "It's Not for Me to Say," by Albert Stillman and Robert Allen, and "Warm and Tender," by Hal David and Burt P. Bacharach, both sung by Johnny Mathis, are unnecessarily emphasized, but Leith Stevens' score is good. *Brog.*

The Undead

Modern prostitute goes back to her old lives in hypnotic retrogression theme. Minor league horror programmer.

Hollywood, Feb. 19.

American-International release of Roger Corman production; directed by Corman. Stars Pamela Duncan, Richard Garland, Allison Hayes; features Val DuFour, Mel Welles. Screenplay, Charles B. Griffith, Mark Hanna; camera, William Sickner; editor, Frank Sullivan; music, Ronald Stein. Previewed Feb. 18, '57. Running time, **71 MINS.**

Helene (Diana) .... Pamela Duncan
Pendragon .... Richard Garland
Livia .... Allison Hayes
Quintus .... Val DuFour
Smolkin .... Mel Welles
Meg Maud .... Dorothy Neuman
The Imp .... Billy Barty
Scroop .... Bruno Ve Soto
Gobbo .... Aaron Saxon
Satan .... Richard Devon

A retrogression theme and bosomy dames are used in this minor league horror subject as ballyhoo pegs for quickie playdates. Pic will be packaged with "Voodoo Woman" by American-International for fast exploitation bookings in the program market.

Charles B. Griffith and Mark Hanna scripted the Roger Corman production, which the latter directs. The pacing is slow and the thrills at a minimum. A time-experimentalist picks up a prostitute and retrogresses her back 1,000 years. He then has to hustle after her because she's about to rescue her early-day self from a beheading; a deed that would destroy all her future lives, including the prostie's. The early-day heroine decides to die, anyway, so she can live her later lives. This means the experimentalist is stuck back in the Dark Ages because he had come down on her life chain. All of which is confusing, to say the least, and only Satan, an interested bystander, seems to understand and be pleased.

Pamela Duncan plays the easy lady as well as the heroine in the past. She's capable of giving substance to better material than provided here, as is Allison Hayes, bosomy witch of the Dark Ages. Richard Garland, sweetie of the early-day femme; Val DuFour, the experimentalist; Dorothy Neuman, Mel Welles, Billy Barty and others have a hard time with the material. Lensing by William Sickner, special effects, background score and other technical aids are okay for the budget and quick shooting schedule. *Brog.*

The Tattered Dress
(C'SCOPE)

Unconvincing scripting out of the click fiction hopper, Stars Jeff Chandler, Jeanne Crain, Jack Carson. Fair b.o. prospects.

Universal release of Albert Zugsmith production. Stars Jeff Chandler, Jeanne Crain and Jack Carson. Features Elaine Stewart, Gail Russell, George Tobias and Philip Reed. Directed by Jack Arnold. Screenplay, George Zuckerman; camera, Carl E. Guthrie; editor, Edward Curtiss; music, Frank Skinner. Previewed in N.Y., Feb. 20, '57. Running time, **93 MINS.**

James Gordon Blane...... Jeff Chandler
Diane Blane .... Jeanne Crain
Nick Hoak .... Jack Carson
Carol Morrow .... Gail Russell
Charleen Reston .... Elaine Stewart
Billy Giles .... George Tobias
Lester Rawlings....... Edward Andrews
Michael Reston .... Philip Reed
Ralph Adams .... Edward C. Platt
Frank Mitchell .... Paul Birch
Paul Vernon ...... Alexander Lockwood
Judge .... Edwin Jerome
Court Clerk .... William Schallert
Girl at Slot Machine....... June McCall
Cal Morrison .... Frank Scannell
Larry Bell .... Floyd Simmons
Woman on Train............ Ziva Shapir
Girls by Pool............Marina Orschel, Ingrid Goude

"The Tattered Dress" is out of the slick fiction hopper. It's a technically well-made melodrama capable of drawing fair returns in general situations. The names of Jeff Chandler, Jeanne Crain and Jack Carson should help somewhat in overcoming the artificiality of the George Zuckerman screenplay.

The film starts out with an intriguing premise, but this is dissipated by a script that lacks credibility. The picture purports to preach the responsibility of lawyers and the sacredness of the American system of justice. But Chandler's courtroom speech on the subject turns out to be a mass of sticky cliches.

From a selling standpoint, "The Tattered Dress" is a catchy title. In addition, it has exploitation angles via its sex elements. This department is handled by Elaine Stewart who portrays a wealthy, married socialite who dispenses sex as if it were going out of season. It is her advances that set the stage for the story.

A bartender, a former smalltown football hero, makes a pass at Miss Stewart and tears her dress in the attempt. This arouses Miss Stewart's ne'er-do-well husband to kill the local boy. Into the California desert town comes a famed New York criminal lawyer (Chandler) to defend the rich outsider. Chandler meets the usual antagonisms and prejudices of the smalltown mind. By clever courtroom technique, particularly by tripping up the local sheriff (Carson), he wins an acquittal.

However, the sheriff, out for revenge, frames the N.Y. invader by getting a femme juror to swear that she had been bribed. This provides an opportunity for a reconciliation between Chandler and his estranged wife (Miss Crain). defend the underdogs.

The performances meet the demand of the script. Chandler is okay as the rehabilitated lawyer. Miss Crain is adequate as the honest wife who abhors her husband's tactics. Carson is properly unctuous as the scheming smalltown sheriff. Miss Stewart, as the sexpot; George Tobias, as a comedian saved from a murder rap by Chandler; Philip Reed, as the dissipated wealthy husband, Edward Andrews, as a rival lawyer, Gail Russell, as the femme juror, Edward C. Platt, as a N.Y. newspaperman, also turn in competent performances.

Jack Arnold's direction and the technical aspects are as slick as the script. Picture was filmed in black and white CinemaScope. *Holl.*

The Shadow On The Window

A shock-muted boy cues police to violence and murder in good man-hunt thriller for general meller patronage.

Hollywood, Feb. 26.

Columbia release of Jonie Taps production. Stars Phil Carey, Betty Garrett, John Barrymore Jr.; features Corey Allen, Gerald Sarracini, Jerry Mathers, Sam Gilman, Rusty Lane, Ainslee Pryor, Paul Picerni, William Leslie, Doreen Woodbury, Ellie Kent. Directed by William Asher. Screenplay, Leo Townsend, David P. Harmon; based on story by John and Ward Hawkins; camera, Kit Carson, editor, William A. Lyon; music, George Duning; conducted by Morris Stoloff. Previewed Feb. 21, '57. Running time, **73 MINS.**

Tony Atlas .... Phil Carey
Linda Atlas .... Betty Garrett
Jess Reber .... John Barrymore Jr.
Gil Ramsby .... Corey Allen
Joey Gomez .... Gerald Sarracini
Petey .... Jerry Mathers
Sgt. Paul Denke .... Sam Gilman
Capt. McQuade .... Rusty Lane
Doctor Hodges .... Ainslie Pryor
Bigelow .... Paul Picerni
Stuart .... William Leslie
Molly .... Doreen Woodbury
Girl .... Ellie Kent
Myra .... Angela Stevens
Husband .... Mort Mills
Sgt. Nordli .... Carl Milletaire
Bergen .... Julian Upton
Conway .... Nesdon Booth
Warren .... Jack Lomas

A manhunt cued by a small, shock-muted, boy gives a good thriller pace to this melodrama which presumably will find an okay reception. While plainly slanted for supporting bookings, it should hold up its end.

Manly little Jerry Mathers is the key character. He witnesses a murder and the capture of his mother by three delinquents and wanders off in a state of blank shock, unable to give police any clue as to what had happened or where. It beomes a matter of tedious police work to build a case to back-track the boy's mavements.

The script by Leo Townsend and David P. Harmon, from a story by John and Ward Hawkins, develops interest in the methodical police sleuthing necessary and William Asher's direction gets it on film with a mounting feel of suspense. Angle that the boy is the son of a policeman adds to the interest. Phil Carey, the boy's father, and Betty Garrett, the mother, are satisfactory. John Barrymore Jr., Corey Allen and Gerald Sarricini enact the three young hoods capably, while Sam Gilman, Rusty Lane, Ainslee Pryor and Paul Picerni are among the good police types.

Jonie Taps' production achieves a realistic flavor that helps the story over, and the technical ends under his supervision do their work well. Included are the lensing by Kit Carson, editing by William A. Lyon and George Duning's score conducted by Morris Stoloff. *Brog.*

Affair In Reno
(NATURAMA)

Public relations innocent among the gamblers. Lightly handled meller suitable for regular situations.

Hollywood, Feb. 26.

Republic release of a Sidney Picker production. Stars John Lund, Doris Singleton, John Archer; features Angela Greene, Alan Hale, Harry Bartell, Howard McNear, Richard Deacon, Thurston Hall, Billy Vincent, Eddie Foster. Directed by R. G. Springsteen. Screenplay, John K. Butler; story, Gerald Drayson Adams; camera, Jack Marta; music, R. Dale Butts; editor, Tony Martinelli. Reviewed Feb. 20, '57. Running time, **75 MINS.**

Bill Carter .... John Lund
Nora Ballard .... Doris Singleton
Tony Lamarr .... John Archer
Gloria Del Monte .... Angela Greene
Deke .... Alan Hale
Conrad Hertz .... Harry Bartell
James T. James .... Howard McNear
H. L. Denham .... Richard Deacon
J. B. Del Monte...........Thurston Hall
Pete .... Billy Vincent

"Affair in Reno" fits the requirements of the routine market, its melodramatic story seasoned with light treatment which pays off in probable spectator approval.

The Sidney Picker production, given excellent physical values, projects the story of a young public relations man sent to Reno to keep the willful daughter of a millionaire from marrying a fortune-seeking gambling house operator. He carries with him $100,000 in cash to buy off gambler if his persuasions are unsuccessful. Millionaire hires a lady dick to act as his rep's bodyguard, and together pair spent most of their time trying to keep money from being stolen, femme helping p.r. man in successful windup of his assignment.

R. G. Springsteen's direction of the John K. Butler screenplay is deft and he keeps his characters constantly on the move. John Lund scores as the rather guileless p.r. man who constantly is getting into trouble from which femme private eye is ever extracting him, and Doris Singleton in this role, a newcomer from radio-tv, livens the action considerably with a talented presence. John Archer satisfactorily handles the gambler part. *Whit.*

The Delinquents
(SONG)

Elmer Rhoden Jr.'s debut as producer. Fair quality. Bored youth looking for kicks. Exploitation possibilities.

Hollywood, Feb. 19.

United Artists release of Robert Altman (Imperial) production; directed and written by Altman. Features Tommy Laughlin, Peter Miller, Richard Bakalyn, Rosemary Howard. Camera, Harry Birch; editor, Helene Turner; background music, Bill Nolan Quintet Minus Two; song, "The Dirty Rock Boogie" by Bill Nolan and Ronnie Norman; sung by Julia Lee. Previewed Feb. 14, '57. Running time, **72 MINS.**

Scotty .... Tom Laughlin
Cholly .... Peter Miller
Eddy .... Richard Bakalyn
Janice .... Rosemary Howard
Mrs. White .... Helene Hawley
Mr. White .... Leonard Belove
Mrs. Wilson .... Lotus Corelli
Mr. Wilson .... James Lantz
Sissy .... Christine Altman
Jay .... George Kuhn
Meg .... Pat Stedman
Chizzy .... Norman Zands
Steve .... James Leria
Molly .... Jet Pingston
Bartender .... Kermit Echols
Station Attendant .... Joe Adleman

The usual exploitation possibilities loom for this latest entry in the cycle about bored youth looking for kicks. It's only a fair feature, with returns to be measured by the type of handling the individual situation gives it. There is no name value; nor is any needed particularly as this kind of ballyhoo offering normally has enough program playdates at hand to more than cover the modest cost.

Elmer C. Rhoden Jr.'s Imperial Productions, which has a five-pic commitment with United Artists, lensed the film in its entirety in Kansas City, and the neophyte type of acting indicates a number of the location citizens got into the act. Lack of professionalism is, in a way, a help since the aim apparently is to keep things on a natural "it can happen here" level. However, producer - director - writer Robert Altman and his cast must have looked at too many prior juvenile delinquency pix because plot and performances, mostly the latter, are out of the torn shirt, switch blade, mold. Additionally, as a salve for the senseless violence, film indulges in some mealy-mouthed moralizing fore and aft about the need to do something about delinquency.

Story tells how a reasonably cleancut kid gets mixed up with a gang of neighborhood toughs when his girl friend's father decides his young daughter isn't old enough to go steady. There is a drive-in theatre episode wherein one of the tough's slashes the tire on the car of another gang, resulting in a free-for-all that leaves heads bashed and limbs broken. Another episode shows the kids taking over an empty house for a beer and necking party that leads to a police raid. Other choice bits of violence include smashing a service station attendant in the head with a gas pump nozzle and forcing a kid to drink glass after glass of whisky. Finale finds all principals at the police station, but with no satisfactory resolution of events.

Peter Miller and Richard Bakalyn are the chief troublemakers, while Tom Laughlin is the teenager who gets mixed up with them, and Rosemary Howard plays his girl friend too young to go steady. Julia Lee singing "The Dirty Rock Boogie" by Bill Nolan and Ronnie Norman, while Nolan's Quintet Minus Two does the backing, is a good jazz beat scene. Charles Paddock's lensing and the other productional assists are okay. *Brog.*

Poveri Ma Belli
(Poor But Handsome)
(ITALIAN)
Rome, Feb. 19.
Titanus release of Silvio Clementelli production. Features Marisa Allasio, Maurizio Arena, Renato Salvatori, Memmo Carotenuto, Mario Carotenuto, Alessandra Panaro, Lorella DeLuca, Virgilio Riento. Directed by Dino Risi. Screenplay, Risi, Massimo Franciosi, Pasquale Festa Campanile; camera, Tonino Delli Colli; editor, Mario Serandrei; music, Piero Morgan. At Capitol, Rome. Running time, 86 MINS.

Opening gun in Geoffredo Lombardo's campaign to cut down the costs of features is bearing fruit in big way with this. Run of this feature in and about Rome looks to bring in the negative cost of $100,000.

A slight story about a fickle teenager who runs two boys of the neighborhood a merry chase before she settles on an older man is happy screen fare which should find a popular American market. Director Dino Risi has avoided the usual Italian heavy-handed problems. Surprise here is that Italian audiences have responded as well

as they have to heavier and more expensive features.

Marisa Allasio, who has been building in the Italian market through half a dozen features since her debut less than two years ago, seems headed for stardom after this pic. Veteran comedian Memmo Carotenuto contributes fine comedy bit.

The Bachelor Party

Paddy Chayefsky video characters celebrate bachelor's pre-marital fling. Needs selling but wide appeal likely.

Hollywood, March 5.
United Artists release of Harold Hecht (Hecht-Hill-Lancaster-Norma) production. Stars Don Murray; features E. G. Marshall, Jack Warden, Philip Abbott, Larry Blyden, Patricia Smith, Carolyn Jones. Directed by Delbert Mann. Screenplay, Parry Chayefsky; camera, Joseph La Shelle; editor, William B. Murphy; music conducted by C. Bakaleinikoff. Previewed Feb. 6, '57. Running time, 92 MINS.
Charlie Samson .... Don Murray
Walter .... E. G. Marshall
Eddie .... Jack Warden
Arnold .... Philip Abbott
Kenneth .... Larry Blyden
Helen Samson .... Patricia Smith
The Existentialist ...... Carolyn Jones
Julie .... Nancy Marchand
Hostess .... Karen Norris
Girl on Stoop .... Barbara Ames

Hecht-Hill-Lancaster and United Artists already are consciously marking "The Bachelor Party" as another "Marty." It isn't. Nor would a "Marty" tone necessarily mean automatic success. However, with hard sell, "Party" can be a b.o. winner.

The new entry does duplicate the earlier in certain aspects. Producer Harold Hecht, who made it for HHL's Norma unit, scripter Paddy Chayefsky and director Delbert Mann are repeaters. The cast is made up mostly of film unknowns or unprovens. The plot's characters are from the same upper lowers of New York, making them easily identifiable by a large segment of any big city population.

Unlike "Marty," which concentrated the major interest on two or three characters, "Party" spreads it around, although using a key couple as a pivot. Whether this addition of universal types and division of interest will rate the same kind of emotional response as the earlier success remains to be seen.

The title tips that the comedy will come from the international institution of giving the groom-to-be his last fling as a single man. The Chayefsky script gets it all in—the drinking dinner, the stag movies, the pub-crawling, the visit to a strip show, and finally, the calling on a professional lady. Each sequence is vividly etched.

Lacing the comedy is an unusually keen insight into human nature, which successfully expresses the monotony, the fears and the small aspirations of the little people involved, perfectly spoken in the dialog and tellingly brought to life by Mann's extremely knowing direction. Also, it must be observed that some of the drabness and monotony of the lives shown overcomes the story's pace at times, and there is an inclination to hold some scenes beyond the point of good dramatic impact.

Cast, mostly from television and stage, is headed by Don Murray, previously seen in "Bus Stop." He's good as the bookkeeper husband of Patricia Smith, who is expecting a child. As he becomes a reluctant member of the bachelor party, the round of tawdry revelry is seen through his eyes, and revealing viewing it is, even involving him temporarily with a sexpot Greenwich Village character, played with great vitality by Carolyn Jones. Miss Smith, too, is good as the wife waiting at home.

Philip Abbott scores as the frightened groom-to-be, his manly abilities as yet untried. The sequences wherein he makes an abortive attempt to go through

with the introduction to sex arranged by the boys with Barbara Ames is a standout. Miss Ames, as the unused but ready partner, capably does her share. Jack Warden shows up well as the pitifully gay office bachelor who masterminds the party for Abbott, as does Larry Blyden, married man who early departs the festivities.

E. G. Marshall does a sharply defined study of an aging, sickly office worker who tries to be a gay playboy, only to crack up in a crying jag as he pours out the frustrations of his life. Nancy Marchand provides a pitiful portrait of a desperate woman clinging to an unhappy married life, and the telling of her sorry story temporarily give Miss Smith doubts about her own marriage. Karen Norris also has her moments as the hostess of the dizzy, character-ridden Greenwich party crashed by the celebrants.

Hecht's production uses N. Y. exterior, Hollywood - created interiors, to advantage in backing the story realistically, and Joseph La Shelle's lensing furthers the realish note of the art direction and set decorations. Also in the mood is the score, conducted by C. Bakaleinikoff. *Brog.*

Paris Does Strange Things
(COLOR)

Ingrid Bergman can't save this silly farce by Jean Renoir. It may squeak by on bookings via her marquee name.

Warner Bros. release. Stars Ingrid Bergman, Mel Ferrer, Jean Marais; features Juliette Greco, Pierre Bertin, Elina Labourdette, Marjane, George Higgins, J. Richard. Directed by Jean Renoir; story and screenplay, Renoir; camera (Technicolor), Claude Renoir; music, Joseph Kosma; editor, Borys Lewin. Previewed Feb. 15, '56 in New York. Running time, 86 MINS.
Elena .... Ingrid Bergman
Henri .... Mel Ferrer
General Rolan .... Jean Marais
Martin-Michaud .... Pierre Bertin
Paulette .... Elina Labourdette
Miarka .... Juliette Greco
Street Singer .... Marjane
Fleury .... George Higgins
Hector .... J. Richard

Considering the tradition of quality that attaches to the name of Jean Renoir, "Paris Does Strange Things" comes as something of a shock. It is a silly, pointless little farce that outstays its welcome after the first half hour and becomes an outright bore before it's over.

Perhaps, in the original French version, Renoir had something to say. Perhaps he meant it to be either funny, or romantic, or possibly both. In the final version for the U. S. market, with a poor dubbing job thrown in, "Paris" (originally "Elena and the Men") is simply a waste of time and talent.

If it has one bright point—at least commercially—it is the fact that Ingrid Bergman and Mel Ferrer are starred in it, along with the Frenchman, Jean Marais. After "Anastasia," Miss Bergman again has a big following and the b.o. and this could—and should—become a factor in selling the film. She looks as radiant as ever, and she is attractively gowned in this period piece. But not even her kind of special magic can rescue this poor tale.

It is, briefly, about a Russian princess in France who lives her life with abandon and specializes in men who, she believes, have a mission. In this case this means a General Rolan, played by Marais, who's being urged by a group of dissident politicians to take over the government via a march on Paris. This creates a good deal of excitement until, in the end, the General prefers to go off with his mistress while Miss Bergman latches on to the general's friend, Ferrer.

What is most painful in this broad—yet supposedly subtle—comedy is the unimaginative, almost oldfashioned way in which its situations are handled. The inherent satire on French political life, which may strike French audiences as funny, likely will be lost on Americans. They may chuckle over some of the sequences, but Renoir's sense of humor must have temporarily deserted him in this one.

Miss Bergman retains her appealing dignity and Ferrer turns in a rather wooden performance. Marais's voice is poorly dubbed, but at least he looks the part of the lovesick militarist. Very good—though not even listed in the official credits—is Pierre Bertin as the shoe tycoon engaged to Miss Bergman.

Renoir occasionally gets a nice frantic feeling into his crowd scenes. On the whole, this is one the old master must have turned out with his left hand. His direction is without distinction and the dialog—well, 'nuff said. Claude Renoir's lensing is standard as is the color.

Borys Lewin is credited as editor, but it's not clear whether for the original or the U. S. version. In any case, it's a choppy job. Joseph Kosma did the music.

There only remains the question why Warner Bros., even though it reportedly financed the picture, bothered releasing it here. Even some of the English dialog is out of sync. And that's only one of several strange things Paris does in this picture. *Hift.*

Gun the Man Down

Strongly scripted, actionful entry for western market.

Hollywood, Feb. 19.

United Artists release of a Robert R. Morrison production. Stars James Arness; features Emile Meyer, Robert Wilke, Harry Carey Jr., Angie Dichinson, Michael Emmet, Don Megowan, Frank Fenton. Directed by Andrew V. McLaglen; screenplay, Burt Kennedy; story, Sam C. Freedle; camera, William Clothier; editor, Eddie Sutherland; music, Henry Vars. Reviewed Feb. 12, '57. Running time, **74 MINS.**

Rem Anderson	James Arness
Janice	Angie Dickinson
Matt Rankin	Robert Wilke
Sheriff Morton	Emile Meyer
Ralph Farley	Don Megowan
Billy Deal	Michael Emmet
Deputy Lee	Harry Carey Jr.

"Gun the Man Down" packs enough action and suspense to rate okay for the western market. Film generally is ingrained with the type of ingredients to keep spectator interested.

First picture to be turned out by team of Robert E. Morrison and Andrew V. McLaglen, its story of a manhunt is well sustained through good writing and fast-paced direction by McLaglen. The Burt Kennedy screenplay avoids cliches and offers an opportunity for hard characterization. The usual sugar-coating for a happy romantic windup is passed up for a more realistic climax.

Arness plays a man deserted by his two companions and girl-friend after he's been wounded in the holdup of a frontier bank. After a year in prison, he starts the search for his quarry, whom he finds in a town near the border. Instead of gunning them down, however, he plays a waiting game, tracking them when they try to escape by night. Intervening action includes his two former pals hiring a gunman to kill Arness when he arrives in town.

Star handles his role well and has the benefit of a strong supporting cast. Robert Wilke is quietly menacing as one of the heavies, and Don Megowan qualifies as the other. Angie Dickinson registers impressivly as the femme, killed finally by Wilke as she tries to warn Arness of his danger during closing sequence. Emile Meyer as the sheriff and Harry Carey Jr., his deputy show to advantage, and Michael Emmet is in as the hired gunslinger whom Arness outdraws.

Morrison gives film appropriate production values and technical credits are headed by William Clothier's camera work. *Whit.*

Folies-Bergere
(FRENCH; COLOR; SONGS; DANCE)

Paris, Feb. 26.

Sirius release of Vladimir Roitfeld production. Stars Eddie Constantine, Zizi Jeanmaire; features Yves Robert, Nadia Gray, Jacques Morel, Jacques Castelot, Pierre Mondy. Directed by Henri Decoin. Screenplay, Jacques Companeez, Decoin, Georges Tabet; dialog, Andre Tabet; camera (Technicolor), Pierre Montazel; editor, Claude Durand; music, Philippe Gerard, Jeff Davis; choreography, Roland Petit, Mary-Jo Weldon; decors, Pierre Colombier. At Balzac, Paris. Running time, **100 MINS.**

Bob	Eddie Constantine
Claudie	Zizi Jeanmaire
Joe	Yves Robert
Suzy	Nadia Gray
Director	Jacques Morel
Philipe	Jacques Castelot
Roger	Pierre Mondy

The French have rarely gone for American-type musicals except in some rare instances ("An American in Paris," "Seven Brides for Seven Brothers") and now have come up with their own version of the U.S. kind of musical. Song and dance spring from and underline the plot. Lacking the zest, production values and more robust and imaginative story lines and treatment of their models, this falls way below standard. Groomed to do well here with the Eddie Constantine name, and the bally for a first large-scale Gallic tunefilm, it appears a bit limited for the U.S. Main aspect is the exploitable title and the name of Zizi Jeanmaire. Having some fairly clever gags and the Parisian background, this could fit in for the U.S.

The boy (Constantine) is a GI who thinks a pretty Folies chorine took his wallet during an audience participation number. After a fight, caused by this, apologies are in order and a walk through Paris with love blooming. Boy stays on with the girl and marries her (Miss Jeanmaire). Then comes misunderstanding as the star covets boy and he is peeved at a film producer's attentions to his wife. All is solved when their pals stall off the star and they are reunited in a big Folies number for a happy ending.

Though cliche-ridden, there are some sprightly sight gags. However, director Henri Decoin rarely gives this the pace, lilt and timing it needs to make the familiar mixture really jell. Dance routines are primarily weak girlie imitations of the real thing.

Miss Jeanmaire has a chance to show her terp aspects in a few filmically static but viewable ballets. She also uncorks her raucous voice for good effect and displays a grasp of character in this lightweight affair. Constantine, though essaying a change of pace from his tough guy roles, manages to have a chance to engage in some rough-and-tumble fights. He displays his ease in song numbers and participates in one ballet, a rhythmed fight scene.

Color is uneven but it all adds up to an okay first try at this type of pic and may catch on here, just as Constantine's pseudo U.S. type toughguy pictures scored here. It may work into more Gallic aud interest in the U.S. musical.

Music is frilly and catchy, but the Folies-Bergere takes a back seat and is never really denoted in this pic except as a place where numbers can be worked in justifiably. Nudes are not in evidence except for serving under the titles. *Mosk.*

Voodoo Woman
(SONG)

Mad scientist makes monsters out of pretty girls; routine horror pic for programmer site.

Hollywood, Feb. 19.

American-International release of Alex Gordon (Carmel) production. Stars Maria English, Tom Conway, Touch Connors; features Lance Fuller, Mary Ellen Kaye. Directed by Edward L. Cahn. Screenplay, Russell Bender, V. I. Voss; camera, Frederick E. West; editor, Ronald Sinclair; music, Darrell Calker; song, "Black Voodoo" by Calker and John Blackburn. Previewed Feb. 18, '57. Running time, **77 MINS.**

Marilyn Blanchard	Marla English
Dr. Roland Gerard	Tom Conway
Ted Bronson	Touch Connors
Rick (Harry)	Lance Fuller
Susan	Mary Ellen Kaye
Marcel	Paul Durov
Chaka	Martin Wilkins
Harry, West	Norman Willis
Bobo	Otis Greene
Gandor	Emmett E. Smith
Monster	Paul Blaisdell
Singer	Giselle D'Arc
Native Girl	Jean Davis

This is one of those "forbidden jungle" plots with scant rhyme or reason. Release will make up a combination horror package with "The Undead" (reviewed herewith) under the American-International Pictures banner.

Producer Alex Gordon, working under exec producers Samuel Z. Arkoff and James H. Nicholson, provides "budget" backing for the script by Russell Bender and V. I. Voss. The cast goes through routinized paces under Edward L. Cahn's direction. There's little worry to make things credible.

Tom Conway plays a mad scientist, headquartered at a voodoo native village, who is working on a serum to create a monster that will do his mental bidding. He's so crazy he wants to turn pretty girls into horrible creatures.

When he can't have his way with an attractive native girl, Jean Davis, because she's pure of heart, he tries his scheme with Marla English, gold-greedy girl who's in the jungle to steal native treasures.

Others mixed up these weird if familiar doings include Lance Fuller, cowardly sweetie of Miss English; Paul Dubov, thieving innkeeper, plus sundry native types. A John Blackburn-Darrell Calker tune, "Black Voodoo," is sung by Giselle D'Arc in a cafe sequence. Elsewhere, Calker's background score emphasizes a voodoo beat. Frederick E. West's lensing is okay. *Brog.*

Uomini E Lupi
(Men and Wolves)
(ITALIAN; COLOR; C'SCOPE)

Rome, Feb. 26.

Titanus-Trionfalcine release of Giovanni Addessi production. Stars Silvana Mangano, Pedro Armendariz, Yves Montand; features Irene Cefaro, Guido Celano, Giulio Cali, Euri Teodori, Giovanni Matta. Directed by Giuseppe De Santis. Screenplay by Antonio Guerra, Eraclio Elio Petri, Gianni Peccini, Ugo Mattone, Ivo Perilli from story by Petri, Guerra and DeSantis; camera (Eastmancolor), Idelmo Simonelli; music, Guido Nardone. At Adriano Theatre, Rome. Running time, **105 MINS.**

Already pre-sold to Columbia for worldwide release outside of Italy, "Men and Wolves" should be a winner wherever shown. It has vivid color, good acting, fine photography and a credible story for the locale in which it is set. Pedro Armendariz is the best name for American audiences although Silvana Mangano is still remembered by many for her "Bitter Rice" portrayal.

Set in the Abruzzi hills, the story is a tale of the fight waged by the mountain people against raids by wolf packs on their sheep and cattle. Two lupari, wolf-hunters, turn up in the same town in the persons of Armendariz and Yves Montand. The latter loses face when the wolf he delivers turns out to be a dog. Armendariz traps his live wolf, but loses his life in trying to bag it single-handed when a whole pack appears. Thereafter, his wife (Miss Mangano) teams up with Montand who kills the wolf which killed her husband. The climax comes when a hungry pack raid a town and its cattle during a snowstorm.

Filmed during the worst snows of the century last winter, the setting is most realistic. At that time, the company was snowbound and communication was established by helicopter. Both of the men give fine performances which stand out against Miss Mangano's deadpan acting which seems to fit the part. However, it grows a bit monotonous. In general, Giuseppe DeSantis has kept his cast within control and has won good performances from Irene Cefaro as the other woman who seeks to win Montand; Guido Celano, as her wealthy father, and Euri Teodori, as an old hunter.

The Eastmancolor is good and the vast vistas of snow-covered mountains in which the wolf-packs run do credit to the cinematography of Idelmo Simonelli. Titanus, which has been seeking a winner for the American market, seems to have come up with one in this film.

The Passionate Stranger
(BRITISH—MONOCHROME—COLOR)

Margaret Leighton and Ralph Richardson co-star in British comedy, which exploits story-within-a-story idea for amusing results.

London, Feb. 26.

British Lion release of Muriel and Sydney Box production. Stars Margaret Leighton and Ralph Richardson; co-stars Patricia Dainton and Carlo Justini. Directed by Muriel Box. Screenplay, Muriel and Sydney Box; camera, Otto Heller; editor, Jean Barker; music, Humphrey Searle. At London Pavilion, London. Running time, **97 MINS.**

Roger and Clement	Ralph Richardson
Judith and Leonie	Margaret Leighton
Emily and Betty	Patricia Dainton
Carlo and Mario	Carlo Justini
Old Woman	Ada Reeve
Maria	Andree Melly
Mr. Poldy	Frederick Piper
Miles Easter	Michael Shepley
Jimmy	Thorley Walters
First Landlord	George Woodbridge
Doctor	Allan Cuthbertson
Maurice	John Arnatt
Barmaid	Barbara Archer
Mrs. Poldy	Marjorie Rhodes
Millie	Megs Jenkins
Second Landlord	Michael Trubshawe
M/C at Dance	Alexander Gauge
Secretary	Barbara Graley
Peter	C. Witty
Amos	Fred Tooze
Guard	Pat Ryan

There's nothing particularly new about the basic idea of a story within a story, but the fresh treatment in "The Passionate Stranger" is good for quite a few laughs and should make for fair boxoffice returns. Margaret Leighton and Ralph Richardson, both names of U.S. appeal, should have some marquee value to help the pic along in the United States.

Muriel and Sydney Box have collaborated on a screenplay which exploits a well-worn situation for favorable results. And the production has been given an added gimmick, inasmuch as the basic plot is unspooled in black and white, while the inner story is told in color. The same backgrounds are given a contrasting appeal by the use of the two photographic processes.

In the main plot Richardson and Miss Leighton play husband and wife, he a scientist and polio victim, she a successful novelist. They hire Carlo Justini to be their chauffeur and that appointment is the inspiration for a new novel she is about to write. The chauffeur gets hold of a copy of the manuscript and sees the romantic role he plays in his mistress's book and tries to re-enact that part in real life. The results are as disastrous in fact as they are novelettish in fiction.

Obvious failing of the script is that the earlier action is repetitious although there's a new slant and a new meaning to it. To a lesser extent, that goes for the climax too, but the twist is more pronounced and the reaction more spontaneous. Miss Box has shown a nice light touch in handling the plot and characters, and even in dealing with the corny situations which emerge from the novel.

Miss Leighton and Richardson provide a smooth gloss to the proceedings. She's as elegant as always and plays both her roles with commendable taste. Sir Ralph turns in two top-notch performances, first, as the easy-going scientist, and second, as the hard, calculating character depicted in his wife's novel. Patricia Dainton makes a particularly good showing as the family domestic and she, too, figures in each of the two stories. Justini gives a solid, but humorous portrayal of the Italian chauffeur who succeeds in talking himself out of a good job when he confuses fiction with fact. Other characters play only minor roles, but fill them adequately. *Myro.*

Designing Woman
(C'SCOPE-COLOR)

Broad farce comedy with big boxoffice potential. Gregory Peck, Lauren Bacall and Dolores Gray star in opulent production. Dore Schary's swan song for Metro.

Metro release of Dore Schary production. Stars Gregory Peck, Lauren Bacall, Dolores Gray. Features Sam Levene, Tom Helmore, Jack Cole, Mickey Shaughnessy. Directed by Vincente Minnelli. Screenplay, George Wells; from a suggestion by Helen Rose; camera (C'Scope) John Alton; editor, Adrienne Fazan; music, Andre Previn; musical numbers and dances staged by Jack Cole. Previewed in N.Y., Feb. 28. Running time, **117 MINS.**

Mike Hagen	Gregory Peck
Marilla Hagen	Lauren Bacall
Lori Shannon	Dolores Gray
Ned Hammerstein	Sam Levene
Zachary Wilde	Tom Helmore
Maxie Stulz	Mickey Shaughnessy
Charlie Arneg	Jesse White
Johnnie "O"	Chuck Connors
Martin J. Daylor	Edward Platt
Luke Coslow	Alvy Moore
Gwen	Carol Veazie
Randy Owen	Jack Cole

Metro's "Designing Woman" puts Hollywood back on the beam as a purveyor of comedy. This somewhat neglected entertainment ingredient, long a screen staple, is most creditably revived in a plush production; Dore Schary's last personal effort before exiting the Metro lot. Release looms as a big boxoffice winner and maybe the popular comedy hit of the year. Gregory Peck and Lauren Bacall provide additional b.o. insurance.

Aided and abetted by Dolores Gray, Sam Levene. Tom Helmore, Jack Cole and Mickey Shaughnessy. Peck and Miss Bacall are seen in a Runyonesque-type romp. The George Wells screenplay, based on a "suggestion" by designer Helen Rose and deftly directed by Vincente Minnelli, cleverly brings together the worlds of haut couture, sports (particularly boxing), show business, and the underworld. Literal-minded viewers may find it difficult to accept the zany characters and situations, but taken on its own terms—in the same sense as one would accept a Damon Runyon story—"Designing Woman" is full of funny lines and incidents.

The combination of high fashion, boxing, show biz and old-fashioned gangsterism provides something of interest to the widest possible mass audience. It's quite obvious why Miss Rose thought of the story idea, for it gives her an opportunity to display her latest creations. The show biz segment allows for the interpolation of several musical numbers, neatly performed by Miss Gray and Cole, with the latter also contributing the staging.

Basically the story deals with the conflicts that arise when the separate worlds of sports and fashions meet head on. Peck, a crusading sports writer, marries Miss Bacall, a prominent fashion designer, and abandons his cluttered Greenwich Village apartment for her elegant East Side abode. Her friends are the chi chi set; his cronies are fellow sports scribes and Stillman Gym characters.

The never-the-twain-shall-meet groups get together at their apartment when there's a conflict between his weekly poker game and a reading for a Broadway musical for which she is designing the costumes. Added to this mish-mash of personalities is a triangle situation brought about by the presence, as the star of the show, of Peck's former girl friend, played by Miss Gray, and Miss Bacall's former suitor—the show's producer, portrayed by Helmore. And if these situations aren't enough to complicate the couple's new-found domesticity, there's the crooked fight promoter who has his boys out "to get" Peck for his expose of the fight racket.

Shaughnessy, as a punch-drunk, off-his-rocker ex-pug, serves as Peck's bodyguard. Some of the picture's funniest moments take place when Peck and Shaughnessy are holed up in a hotel room to evade the mobsters. Shaughnessy is extremely funny and his antics are laugh-provoking. However, the comedy stems from the mental disability of the character and the propriety of employing an imbecile-like character as a foil may be open to question.

Another offbeat "character"—an amazing French poodle—practically steals the performing honors from the principals. The uncredited pooch leads to Peck's exposure as he is innocently hiding out from his wife in Miss Gray's bedroom.

The picture closes with a rousing smash in a backstage alley of a Boston tryout theatre as Cole, whose virility has been questioned by Peck, overcomes the mobsters with some intricate footwork.

Miss Bacall, turning to comedy, is excellent as the fashion designer confronted by the world of fisticuffs. Peck is fine as the confused sportswriter and Miss Gray scores solidly as the ex-girl friend. Topnotch characterizations are also turned in by Sam Levene, as the "Front Page" type sports editor; Helmore as the producer, Cole as a choreographer, Jesse White as a peddler of information, and Chuck Connors as a mobster.

Minnelli deserves a large share of the credit for the film's success, for he has staged it briskly, giving the comedy sequences and other elements the emphasis each warrants. Schary and Wells, who also served as associate-producer, have given the film opulent production values, providing elegant settings in both New York and Hollywood. All technical aspects are out of the top draw. *Holl.*

Brothers in Law
(BRITISH)

A firstrate comedy making fun of the law, which reunites the "Private's Progress" starring team; smash for domestic market.

London, March 5.
British Lion release of a (John Boulting) Tudor Production (by arrangement with Charter Film Productions). Stars Richard Attenborough, Ian Carmichael and Terry-Thomas; co-stars Jill Adams, Miles Malleson. Directed by Roy Boulting. Screenplay, Frank Harvey, Jeffrey Dell and Roy Boulting; camera, Max Greene; editor, Anthony Harvey; music, Benjamin Frankel. At Gaumont Theatre, London. Running time, **94 MINS.**

Henry Marshall	Richard Attenborough
Roger Thursby	Ian Carmichael
Alfred Green	Terry-Thomas
Sally Smith	Jill Adams
Kendall Grimes	Miles Malleson
Tatlock	Raymond Huntley
Alec Blair	Eric Barker
Mrs. Newent	Olive Sloane
Charles Poole	Nicholas Parsons
Judge Ryman	John Le Mesurier
Mrs. Potter	Irene Handl
Judge Emery	Basil Dignam
Roger's Father	Henry Longhurst
Roger's Mother	Edith Sharpe
Judge Lawson	Kynaston Reeves

The three stars who combined to provide the comedy in "Private's Progress," a top grosser locally last year, are reunited in this new Boulting comedy. This time it's making fun of the law, doing full justice to a laugh-loaded script. A smash for the domestic market, and a worthy contender for dates in the U.S.

Roy Boulting, who directed the comedy, also shares the screenplay credit with Frank Harvey and Jeffrey Dell, and they've fashioned a witty and lighthearted yarn which traces the experiences of a young lawyer from the day of his graduation until he achieves his first legal victory. Their refreshing treatment holds nothing sacred, least of all the dignity and pomposity of the law.

The raw legal recruit is Ian Carmichael, who through the good offices of his roommate and fellow attorney, is accepted as a pupil barrister by Miles Malleson, a distinguished but absent-minded Queen's Counsel. Within a few minutes of his appointment he accompanies his senior to the High Court, and is left to plead the case without even knowing which side he's on.

This unhappy start to his career affects Carmichael's confidence. Briefs are few and far between, and cash is running out. What few chances come his way are dissipated, and in desperation he goes to the Old Bailey hoping he'll pick up a brief from a prisoner without a defense counsel. He gets his chance from Terry-Thomas, a seasoned swindler with 17 appearances at the Criminal Court to his credit—and gets his first practical lesson in how to beat the law. His big chance, however, comes in his hometown Assizes, when he turns an impossible situation to victory, as his proud parents applaud the judge's decision.

The breaking-in treatment for the legal novice produces a succession of amusing situations. Attenborough advises him to participate in a legal golf tourney, and Carmichael finds he's partnered with a particular sour judge. Having driven almost every ball into the rough, he inevitably has to face the judge in court a few days later. And there's the friendly rivalry for Jill Adams, the fashion model who has the upstairs apartment, with both of them losing out to a bore who tinkers with old cars.

Led by the stars and right down through to the smallest bit roles, there's an exceptional standard of acting. Carmichael's halting, cautious study is in contrast to Richard Attenborough's confident, swaggering characterization, while Terry-Thomas's brash swindler is one of the comedy highlights. Miss Adams provides the attractive femme appeal and Miles Malleson makes a standout contribution, with perfect cameos from Olive Sloane, Irene Handl, Raymond Huntley, John le Mesurier and Kynaston Reeves. Direction, lensing, etc., are all above average. *Myro.*

Spring Reunion
(SONG)

Dull comedy-drama about class reunion and renewed romance brings Betty Hutton back to screen after four year absence

Hollywood, March 12.
United Artists release of Jerry Bresler (Bryna) production. Stars Betty Hutton, Dana Andrews; features Jean Hagen, Sara Berner, Robert Simon, Laura LaPlante, Gordon Jones. James Gleason. Directed by Robert Pirosh. Screenplay, Pirosh and Elick Moll; story, Robert Alan Aurthur; camera, Harold Lipstein; editor, Leon Barsha; music, Herbert Spencer, Earle Hagen; song, Johnny Mercer, Harry

Warren; sung by Mary Kaye Trio. Previewed March 8, '57. Running time, 79 MINS.

Fred Davis .... Dana Andrews
Maggie Brewster .... Betty Hutton
Barna Forrest .... Jean Hagen
Paula Kratz .... Sara Berner
Harry Brewster .... Robert Simon
May Brewster .... Laura LaPlante
Jack Frazer .... Gordon Jones
Mr. Collyer .... James Gleason
Miss Stapleton .... Irene Ryan
Nick .... Richard Shannon
Al .... Ken Curtis
Edward .... Herbert Anderson
Jim .... Richard Benedict
Grace .... Vivi Janiss
Mary .... Florence Sundstrom
Alice .... Mimi Doyle
Caterer .... Sid Tomack
Receptionist .... Shirley Mitchell
Zimmie .... George Chandler
Roseanne .... Dorothy Neuman
Verna .... Barbara Drew
Sidney .... Richard Deacon

Betty Hutton hasn't found a very auspicious vehicle for her return to the screen after four years absence. "Spring Reunion" is dull comedy-drama, lacking pace and impact.

Jerry Bresler, producer of the Bryna presentation through United Artists, rounded up a competent cast, but neither the direction by Robert Pirosh nor the script he did with Elick Moll from a story by television's Robert Alan Aurthur make good use of the players. The story never seems to get started and, when it does begin to move towards the climax, nothing much happens that's new or freshly treated.

The Hutton bounce that was her main stock-in-trade when clicking in films is missing, so there's little here that will appeal to the younger element among filmgoers. She does sing an old standard as part of a class reunion celebration, but not very well. What touches of light comedy there are seem strained and are mostly from the cliche situations native to a reunion gathering. Miss Hutton participates very little in these, but they go on around her as she sweats out the drama portions concerned with getting her a man; in this case Dana Andrews, ex-school chum who has floated from job to job.

Popism replaces momism in the story, showing how a doting dad keeps his daughter so close to him hasn't had a chance to play the field among eligible males. When Andrews comes back to town for the class reunion, all it takes is a moonlight sail and a few philosophical words from an old lighthouse keeper to plant romance and she breaks paternal ties to go away with her lover.

Just as Miss Hutton and Andrews are bound by plot shackles, so are the other casters, including Jean Hagen who tries a fling with Gordon Jones but the pull of hubby and kids back home are too strong; Robert Simon, Miss Hutton's father; Laura LaPlante, the understanding mother who gets more out of her role than anyone else; James Gleason, the lighthouse keeper, and Irene Ryan, schoolteacher who becomes tipsy on spiked punch.

Photography, editing and other technical credits are standard. Johnny Mercer and Harry Warren cleffed the title tune sung by the Mary Kaye Trio behind the credits. It's not this group's cup of notes. Brog.

Naked Paradise
(COLOR)

Colorful Hawaiian melodrama which may be exploited for good returns.

Hollywood, Feb. 19.
American International release of a Roger Corman production. Stars Richard Denning, Beverly Garland, Lisa Montell,
Leslie Bradley; features Dick Miller, Jonathan Haze. Directed by Corman. Story-screenplay, Charles B. Griffith, Mark Hanna; camera (Pathecolor), Floyd Crosby; editor, Charles Gross Jr.; music, Ronald Stein; Hawaiian songs, Alvin Kaleolani. Previewed Feb. 15, '57. Running time, 68 MINS.
Duke .... Richard Denning
Max .... Beverly Garland
Keena .... Lisa Montell
Zac .... Leslie Bradley
Mitch .... Richard Miller
Stony .... Jonathan Haze

Interesting action and scenery lensed in elegant Pathecolor backdrop this melodrama which carries the "names" of Richard Denning and Beverly Garland. Film should be exploited for good returns in the program market.

Produced entirely in Hawaii, producer-director Roger Corman uses the natural beauties of the Islands to excellent advantage in his unfoldment of a wellknit story scripted by Charles B. Griffith and Mark Hanna. Considerable violence crops up occasionally to give rather grim overtones to the action, but this is legitimately inserted and is a natural plot development.

Denning plays the captain of a small sailing schooner in Hawaii, chartered by Leslie Bradley, ostensibly an American toy manufacturer, to carry him and his small gang to an outlying island after he's robbed a plantation of its payroll. Miss Garland is Bradley's socalled secretary, and romantic complications arise over her affections. When she attempts to escape on Denning's boat, a hurricane forces them back to face Bradley, a brutal killer. Bradley and his two henchmen meet violent deaths in a realistic climax.

Corman helms his characters convincingly and all principals come up with above-average performances. Denning is a hardy hero, and Miss Garland in particular is a standout, often in dazzling attire. Bradley scores as the heavy, and Richard Miller and Jonathan Haze follow suit as his two triggermen. Lisa Montell also handles her native girl role in capable fashion.

Color photography by Floyd Crosby is of particular benefit to the picture. Editing by Charles Gross Jr., music score by Ronald Stein and native songs by Alvin Kaleolani also are definite assists. Whit.

The Guns Of Fort Petticoat
(COLOR)

Audie Murphy commandeers a group of women to fight off attacking Indians. Okay chances in outdoor market.

Hollywood, March 12.
Columbia release of Harry Joe Brown (Brown-Murphy) production. Stars Audie Murphy; features Kathryn Grant, Hope Emerson, Jeff Donnell. Directed by George Marshall. Screenplay, Walter Doniger; story, C. William Harrison; camera (Technicolor), Ray Rennahan; editor, Al Clark; music conducted by Mischa Bakaleinikoff. Previewed March 7, '57. Running time, 81 MINS.
Lt. Frank Hewitt .... Audie Murphy
Ann Martin .... Kathryn Grant
Hannah Lacey .... Hope Emerson
Mary Wheeler .... Jeff Donnell
Cora Melavan .... Jeanette Nolan
Kettle .... Sean McClory
Hetty .... Ernestine Wade
Lucy Conover .... Peggy Maley
Mrs. Ogden .... Isobel Elsom
Stella Leatham .... Patricia Livingston
Bax .... Kim Charney
Salt Pork .... Ray Teal
Tortilla .... Nestor Paiva
Kipper .... James Griffith
Indian Chief .... Charles Horvath
Colonel Chivington .... Ainslie Pryor
Jane Gibbons .... Dorothy Crider
Hazel McCasslin .... Madge Meredith

The sagebrush action in this western pulls a switch by having a group of Texas femmes stand off an Indian attack under the leadership of Audie Murphy. It adds up to a fairly entertaining subject with okay chances in the general outdoor market.

Picture is Murphy's first indie production, in which he teams with Harry Joe Brown, an old hand at this type of filmfare; as is director George Marshall, who has guided many such prairie chases. Footage has some lagging spots, but the action is good when it does take over so giddyap fans will find it generally acceptable.

Murphy plays a Texan serving with the Union Army. He rebels when a stupid commanding officer orders the Sand Creek massacre and returns to Texas to help the women left defenseless while their menfolk are off fighting the war against the North. He knows the Indians will be riding to avenge the massacre and, despite the fact his fellow Texans look on him as a traitor, he marshals the women into an old mission, trains them in arms and defeats the redskins. In doing so, he finds himself a girl, spitfire Kathryn Grant, and is successfully defended against court martial charges brought by the c.o., who gets charged himself for the massacre.

The script by Walter Doniger from a story by C. William Harrison does an overall adequate job of the outdoor action, as does the cast in enacting the characters. Murphy does his role likeably and Miss Grant is satisfactory. Hope Emerson does another of her big, rough, tough, pioneer women who helps Murphy man his fort. Among other femmes are Jeff Donnell, Jeanette Nolan, Ernestine Wade, Peggy Maley, Isobel Elsom, Patricia Livingston and Madge Meredith.

With the exception of Murphy, the few white males in the cast are mostly all heavies.

Ray Rennahan's Technicolor lensing is all to the good, particularly in the lighting effects in the mission and the display of the Arizona location sites. Other technical credits are okay, while the music conducted by Mischa Bakaleinikoff is formula. Brog.

Seven Waves Away
(BRITISH)

Gripping drama of Atlantic shipwreck survivors in overcrowded lifeboat; stout marquee lure should be valuable ticket selling aid.

London, March 12.
Columbia release of a Copa (John R. Sloan) production. Stars Tyrone Power, Mai Zetterling, Lloyd Nolan; co-stars Stephen Boyd, Moira Lister and James Hayter. Directed by Richard Sale. Story and screenplay, Richard Sale; camera, Wilkie Cooper; editor, Raymond Poulton; music, Arthur Bliss. At Odeon, Marble Arch, London. Running time, 98 MINS.
Alec Holmes .... Tyrone Power
Julie .... Mai Zetterling
Frank Kelly .... Lloyd Nolan
Will McKinley .... Stephen Boyd
Edith Middleton .... Moira Lister
"Cookie" Morrow .... James Hayter
Mrs. Knudsen .... Marie Lohr
Daniel Cane .... Moultrie Kelsall
Aubrey Clark .... Noel Willman
John Merritt .... Gordon Jackson
Major General Barrington .. Clive Morton
Captain Darrow .... Laurence Naismith
Sparks Clary .... John Stratton
Willy Hawkins .... Victor Maddern
Michael Faroni .... Eddie Byrne
John Hayden .... David Langton
George Kilgore .... Ralph Michael
Sam Holly .... Orlando Martins
Mrs. Kilgore .... Jill Melford
Solly Daniels .... Ferdy Mayne

For its first British film, Copa Productions has chosen a difficult subject, one in which the entire action takes place in a lifeboat in the south Atlantic. There are no sets, and the only backgrounds are the turbulent seas and the cold gray sky. Yet, within these limitations the production sustains a gripping drama even though unable to oversome the inevitable repetitive incident. The stout marquee lure (Tyrone Power, Lloyd Nolan, Mai Zetterling) will probably be a major factor in selling this on either side of the Atlantic.

Story is based on a true incident which happened in the last century. A luxury cruise liner, with more than 1,100 passengers aboard, strikes a mine in the middle of the night and there are only 27 survivors on a lifeboat which should only accommodate about nine people. The dying captain hands over command to his No. 2 man (Power), and he is faced with the unenviable task of giving the orders.

Food and water are severely rationed, irrespective of the needs of the sick and the injured. Then, with a storm brewing, he has to make a fateful decision. Either some of the passengers are jettisoned or they all go down. He decides on the former course and himself picks the passengers who are to be tossed overboard. There is no mercy for the sick or the women; indeed, they are, in the main, the first to go. Only the ablebodied, who can help to row the 1,500 miles to the African coast are kept on board.

Richard Sale, who wrote the original story and screenplay, and who also directed the picture, has shown considerable ingenuity in his treatment. But he has not given maximum attention to characterization, other than to the officer-in-command. Many of the other characters emerge largely by the force of their own portrayals. He has, however, fully harnessed the dramatic potentialities and the final rescue scene strikes an effective note of restraint. All the survivors who had, a few moments earlier, been loud in their praise of his handling of the situation, suddenly fear they may be implicated. As the rescue liner pulls alongside, the passengers, who had been tossed overboard, are seen lining the rails. But there's no comment either from Power or the other survivors.

Power (who, of course, is partnered with Ted Richmond in Copa) has an outsize role, which he handles with great authority and considerable virility. The dramatic potentialities of the part are exceptional and he rarely misses an opportunity. Mai Zetterling, a ship's nurse, has fewer chances and her role calls for little more than a one-key performance. Lloyd Nolan, on the other hand, has more scope as an injured ship's engineer, who advocates the jettisoning of other survivors before throwing himself into the sea. In the big cast, there are impressive performances by Stephen Boyd, Moira Lister, James Hayter, Clive Morton and Victor Maddern.

For the record, the story is based on the U.S. freighter William Brown, which set sail from Liverpool in 1841, headed for Philadelphia. There were 80 passengers from Ireland. The ship struck an iceberg and split in two. As the freighter did not normally carry passengers, there were only two small lifeboats available. Myro.

Heaven Knows, Mr. Allison
(COLOR-C'SCOPE)

Nun and a marine marooned on Pacific island. Offbeat exloitation slants; strong potential grosser, particularly with Catholic support and general word-of-mouth.

20th-Fox release of Buddy Adler-Eugene Frenke production. Stars Deborah Kerr, Robert Mitchum. Directed by John Huston. Screenplay, John Lee Mahin and Huston, from Charles Shaw novel; camera (color by De Luxe), Oswald Morris; music, Georges Auric, conducted by Lambert Williamson; editor, Russell Lloyd. Previewed March 9, '57, at the Roxy Theatre, N.Y. Running time, **107 MINS.**

Sister Angelica .... Deborah Kerr
Mr. Allison .... Robert Mitchum

Behind the misleading title of "Heaven Knows, Mr. Allison," which suggests anything but the story this Buddy Adler-Eugene Frenke production relates, is an intriguing yarn about two people on opposite ends of the social ladder, thrown together in a highly unusual situation. It's about a marine, marooned on a small Pacific atoll with a nun. They divide their time dodging Japs and trying to steer clear of their emotions.

For what this picture might have been like, one must read the synopsis. It contains the scenes (which the picture does not) which might have made "Mr. Allison" more believable; scenes of the marine's strong, male reaction to the nun, in whom he also sees the woman, and of the sister's tender —yet restrained—affection for the man who saves her life. What appears on the screen is a watered-down version that concentrates more on melodramatic action than on (frustrated) emotions.

The implications inherent in throwing the marine together with the nun on a lonely and dangerous island will undoubtedly attract many people. On the other hand there'll be those—primarily among Roman Catholic audiences—who will find pleasure in the nun's steadfast rejection of the marine's (verbal) advances and in the glowing description of her firm faith. The fact that the nun is attractively played by Deborah Kerr and the marine by Robert Mitchum should be a plus factor for both groups.

The film, directed by John Huston with something less than outstanding imagination, but with a good measure of humor and bravado, holds out an early premise which it doesn't keep. The parallel is drawn between the nun and her vocation and the marine with his, both subject to strong discipline, and an attempt is made to delineate the rough and direct figure of "Mr. Allison."

But—apart from a few remarks —the character and motivations of Miss Kerr remain shrouded in mystery and she reveals very little of herself. Never is there allowed more than just a slight hint that she, too, is affected by either the situation or the marine's argument, i.e., we're on a lonely island, maybe for years, so what's the use my being a marine and you a nun. Point is stressed that she hasn't taken her final vows.

Huston has tackled this story with an obvious desire not to become entangled too deeply in emotions or religion, though there are the expected questions ("Why are you a nun? You're so pretty," etc.). The high spots of the film involve Mitchum's exploits—and fantastic ones they are—in the midst of the occupying Japanese force when he raids its supply depot for food. He's perhaps the bravest, most resourceful marine the corps could ever call its own and these scenes are staged with noise, gusto and a good deal of suspense.

Since Huston and his coscripter John Lee Mahin apparently weren't allowed to penetrate surface emotions to give the film the bite and turmoil implied in its basic situation, they concentrate on humor. Many of the scenes between Miss Kerr and Mitchum are genuinely funny and it's to the credit of the performers that they carry them off so well. Scene when Mitchum tries to rope a turtle has plenty of glee and some of his repartee with the nun also should go over big with audiences. The Huston wit, both in lines and occasional staging, is evident.

Miss Kerr is lovely as Sister Angelica and she reacts as best she can to the marine's fumbling declarations of love. If the nun's figure lacks reality, it's not the fault of the actress but that of the script, which avoids so studiously even the slightest hint of anything that might offend or disturb the hierarchy. Mitchum is remarkably good as the marine who falls in love for the first time in his life and seeks to reason things out his own way.

Since this is more of an adventure than a problem story, Huston has directed with a view to getting maximum suspense. He has also achieved a number of tender and sensitive moments. Film was lensed on the island of Tobago in the West Indies and cameraman Oswald Morris has done a good job with the CinemaScope medium, achieving a good degree of intimacy in the cave scenes. DeLuxe color is sharp and fine. Georges Auric's music provides a fitting background and Russell Lloyd's editing is smooth.

Fortified with good production values and propped by an intriguing proposition, "Mr. Allison" has the elements that should establish it as an audience fave. It's certainly a picture which Catholics should like, and that's a selling point for the exhibitors. *Hift.*

8 x 8
(COLOR)

Another Hans Richter excursion into the field of surrealist story telling. Very limited possibilities.

Hans Richter production of eight-part film. Produced, written, directed and designed by Richter; camera (Eastman color), Arnold Eagle; narrator, Edgar Zang; sound, Richter. All episodes acted out by non-pros. Previewed March 1, '57, in N. Y. Running time, **98 MINS.**

This one will puzzle and probably bore the average filmgoer, Add to the mystifyingly esoteric quality of the film its over-length. Result is a special item for small special enthusiasts of Hans Richter, a presiding deity of the cinema avant garde.

What is Richter trying to say with his creepy fingers, his Freudian dream symbolism, his trick camera-for-the-sake-of-trick - camera stuff? Gather round the samovar for a bull session, for it can be argued many ways.

"8 x 8" refers to the fields on the chessboard and the film's eight parts symbolize chess moves. Picture is described as "a fairytale for grownups," with the game representing eternal conflict among men. Heavy with psychological overtones and undertones, and there's no denying Richter's vivid imagination. He frequently conveys the sense of frustration implied in chess. While a man tries to make up his mind on a move, white mice are gnawing on his shoes. Situation is resolved with the appearance of the (nude) muse. (This scene ran into some censorship problems in New York).

Potential of a film such as this, dealing in abstract terms—people against wholly unrealistic settings —is extremely limited in these States. A couple of artics here and there may find an audience for it.

Some of the chess "moves" are more obvious and require less "interpretation" than others. Picture is attractively scored and interestingly photographed to accent color and composition. There are aspects to the game of chess that can be logically equated to various phases of life, and Richter is adept in drawing the parallels.

Jacqueline Matisse appears in the first move, called "Black Schemes." Miss Matisse is pretty, which helps. Involved is the Black King's efforts to catch the White Queen. He sends (depending here on the synopsis) the Bishop, who tries to do the job by hypnotic force, the Knight (the horses has sexual connotations) by making physical love to her, and the Castle, by primitive brute force. The Queen eventually destroys the King with the same token (the magic ball) with which he planned to subjugate her.

The Sixth Move, "Queening the Pawn," was written and directed by Jean Cocteau, who also stars in the chapter. The seventh, "The Fatal Move," stars Paul Bowles and an Arab. It's about a fellow who can't answer his phone, which periodically rings under water. What this actually represents to Richter is the poet cutting himself off from reality.

Probably the most fascinating and visually interesting of the "moves" is number two, "A New Twist," which features the mobiles and other work of Alexander Calder, who appears in the stance. Here, the color is particularly striking.

Richter, creator of "Blood of a Poet," etc., uses the camera in a unique way and his concept of screen "art" certainly is a break with tradition. It's doubtful that he expects many to appreciate his radical approach to film, or that many would understand it even if they were exposed to it. "8 x 8" is frequently obscure, and sometimes pretentiously so. To the uninitiated, it many also appear a mite boring. *Hift.*

Hit and Run
(SONG)

Elderly man marries showgirl, loses her to younger lover. Poor entry for programmer sales.

Hollywood, March 8.

United Artists release of Hugo Haas production; written and directed by Haas. Stars Cleo Moore, Hugo Haas, Vince Edwards. Story, Herbert Q. Phillips; camera, Walter Strenge; editor, Stefan Arnsten; music, Frank Steininger; song, "What Good'll It Do Me?" by Steininger; sung by Ella Mae Morse. Previewed March 6, '57. Running time, **85 MINS.**

Julie .... Cleo Moore
Gus .... Hugo Haas
Frank .... Vince Edwards
Miranda .... Dolores Reed
Anita .... Mari Lea
Undertaker .... Pat Goldin
Lawyer .... Carl Milltaire
Sheriff .... Robert Cassidy
Undertaker's Wife .... Julie Mitchum
Doctor .... John Zaremba
Bartender .... Steve Mitchel
Clara .... Jan Englund
Waiter .... Dick Paxton

Paradoxically, a few more cooks might have helped the melodramatics brewed in "Hit and Run." With Hugo Haas handling a fourway chore the plottage compounds a number of faults, resulting in a poor presentation overall. It's a minor entry.

Haas wrote, produced and directed from a story by Herbert Q. Phillips, and stars with Cleo Moore and Vince Edwards. Plot is one of his favorites—an elderly man marries a young girl and loses her to a younger lover. Operator of a combo junk yard and service station, Haas takes Miss Moore, showgirl, as a bride. Then, his helper, Edwards, makes a play for the girl, even involves her in his hit-and-run murder scheme to get Haas out of the way.

The bride and the victim's twin brother, just out of prison, share the estate while Edwards marks time until things quiet down. Obvious twist, coming as no great surprise, has Haas playing the twin, latter having been the one bumped off, so he can wring a confession from the bride and her lover. Too many of the scenes written and directed by Haas have an ad lib quality and none of the performances is more than just adequate.

Pat Goldin, comic undertaker; Carl Militaire, lawyer; Robert Cassidy, sheriff; Dolores Reed, Mari Lea and Julie Mitchum are among others involved to lesser degrees in the plot. Either the lensing or the preview print caused a poor showing at the screening. Franz Steininger composed and conducted the okay background score, as well as doing "What Good'll It Do Me?," which Ella Mae Morse is heard singing via a noisy radio in a plot scene. *Brog.*

The Young Stranger

Problem of understanding between the generations. Okay entertainment suitable for general program bills.

Hollywood, March 15.

RKO-Universal release of Stuart Millar production. Stars James MacArthur, Kim Hunter, James Daly; features James Gregory, Whit Bissell, Jeff Silver, Jack Mullaney, Tom Pittman, Charles Davis, Marian Seldes, Eddie Ryder. Directed by John Frankenheimer. Written by Robert Dozier; camera, Robert Planck; editors, Robert Swink, Edward Biery Jr.; music, Leonard Rosenman. Previewed Dec. 7, '56. Running time, **83 MINS.**

Hal .... James MacArthur
Helen .... Kim Hunter
Tom Ditmar .... James Daly
Shipley .... James Gregory
Grubbs .... Whit Bissell
Jerry .... Jeff Silver
Confused Boy .... Jack Mullaney
Man in Theatre .... Eddie Ryder
Girl in Theatre .... Jean Corbett
Detective .... Charles Davis
Mrs. Morse .... Marian Seldes
Donald Morse .... Terry Kelman
Lotte .... Edith Evanson
Lynn .... Tom Pittman
Doorman .... Howard Price

RKO via Universal has a marketable picture in "The Young Stranger," a subject slanted at the teenagers and family-type audiences. Regular-run situations will find it a handy entry for twin-billing with a similarly slanted feature.

A story of conflict beween youth and parents, the plot indulges in "one note" dramatics that provide very litle shading between the black and white of the problem, yet which are effective within the entertainment aim. Juvenile delinquency is not necessarily an issue. Rather, the plot purpose is to show how a father should give more time and understanding to his son. Possibly inadvertently, it also points up that parents are not always solely guilty, as youth too often takes the attitude it should be understood (a) without the necessity of explanation or (b) understanding on its part.

Film has youthful factors other than just its entertainment appeal. It marks the feature picture breakin of several younger talents. James MacArthur, teenage son of Helen Hayes and the late Charles MacArthur, gets his first prominent picture casting as the youthful star and delivers promisingly. He is seen as the rebellious son of picture producer James Daly and Kim Hunter. Film-making keeps the father too busy to give much time to his son, but he realizes the error after the son is arrested for socking a theatre manager, and a cop, at first himself ready to judge the boy guilty, supplies the correct lecture to bring understanding to the family.

Picture is young Stuart Millar's first full producership after production aprenticeship with William Wyler, and he, too, functions promisingly. Debuting as a theatrical film director is John Frankenheimer, from tv, and he handles the switch neatly. For Robert Dozier, son of RKO production veepee William Dozier, film is his first screenplay. He's another showing ability.

Miss Hunter is good as the mother and Daly excellent as the father. James Gregory, the policeman; Whit Bissel, the harassed theatre manager; Jeff Silver, MacArthur's chum; Jack Mullaney, a funny juvenile character; Eddie Ryder and Jean Corbett, the couple that starts the trouble in the theatre, and other casters are satisfactory. Robert Planck's photography abets the mood, but Leonard Rosenman's score distracts via loud recording. ,Other assists are okay. *Brog.*

Attack of the Crab Monsters

Radiation makes crawlers think like human villains. Okay half of science-fiction bill being packaged by Allied Artists; for exploitation dating.

Hollywood, March 18.

Allied Artists release of Roger Corman production, directed by Corman. Stars Richard Garland, Pamela Duncan, Russell Johnson; features Leslie Bradley, Mel Welles, Richard Cutting, Beech Dickerson, Tony Miller. Screenplay, Charles Griffith; camera, Floyd Crosby; editor, Charles Gross; music, Ronald Stein. Previewed March 11, '57. Running time, **62 MINS.**

Dale Drewer .... Richard Garland
Martha Hunter .... Pamela Duncan
Hank Chapman .... Russell Johnson
Dr. Karl Weigand .... Leslie Bradley
Jules Deveroux .... Mel Welles
Dr. James Carson .... Richard Cutting
Ron Fellows .... Beech Dickerson
Jack Somers .... Tony Miller
Ensign Quinlan .... Ed Nelson

Allied Artists is putting together two Roger Corman productions into a science-fiction package that should get some exploitation coin generally. One-half of the bill is "Attack of the Crab Monsters," an atomic mutation subject tailored to beguile the fans of this type film entertainment. The other half will be "Not of This Earth."

"Monsters," which Corman also directs, deals with a party of scientists which comes to a remote Pacific island to study the effects of atomic radiation and to find out what happened to an earlier expedition. Before long, they find that two land crabs have been turned into thinking monsters by a nuclear fallout, and the crabs almost win the ensuing battle.

It isn't believable, but it's fun as scripted by associate producer Charles Griffith and put on film by Corman and his cast. One gimmick used effectively is that of having the monsters able to acquire the knowledge and ability of the victims they eat so that the rescuers can be lured into traps. Trick footage makes these monsters eerie creatures. Also good are the underwater scenes, lensed via Maitland Stuart at Marineland of California.

Richard Garland and Pamela Duncan, fellow scientists and sweethearts, are the only survivors among the party. They, and such other players as Russell Johnson, who gives his life to save the lovers, Leslie Bradley, Mel Welles, Richard Cutting, Beech Dickerson and Tony Miller, are up to all the demands of script and direction.

Floyd Crosby provides good lensing for the chills and Ronald Stein's background score is apt to the mood. *Brog.*

The Vintage
(C'SCOPE—COLOR)

Mixture of accents in French vineyard setting. Slow-paced entertainment faces trouble in U.S. Poorly directed.

Hollywood, March 18.

Metro release of Edwin H. Knopf production. Stars Pier Angeli, Mel Ferrer, John Kerr, Michele Morgan; features Theodore Bikel, Leif Erickson, Jack Mullaney, Joe Verdi. Directed by Jeffrey Hayden. Screenplay, Michael Blankfort; from novel by Ursula Keir; camera (Metrocolor), Joseph Ruttenberg; editor, Ben Lewis; music, David Raksin. Previewed March 13, '57. Running time, **91 MINS.**

Lucienne .... Pier Angeli
Giancarlo Barandero .... Mel Ferrer
Ernesto Barandero .... John Kerr
Leonne Morel .... Michele Morgan
Eduardo Uriburri .... Theodore Bikel
Louis Morel .... Leif Erickson
Etienne Morel .... Jack Mullaney
Uncle Ton Ton .... Joe Verdi

Probably "The Vintage" will fare better in some overseas playdates than it will in the domestic market. While the pic, lensed in the vineyards of Southern France, has a certain foreign charm, neither the story content nor the combination of cast names signifies much to the U.S. wickets.

Mainstays of the names assembled by Edwin H. Knopf for his production are Pier Angeli and Michele Morgan. Both are beguilingly feminine and actresses with the ability to project the quality of the characters they portray. Less adroit are male stars Mel Ferrer and John Kerr, both pretty deadpan, particularly the latter, whose forte seems to be a "Tea and Sympathy" type and little else. However, the fault is not all the actors', as more knowing direction by Jeffrey Hayden might have helped get them, and other cast members, through a slow-moving singularly unexciting script by Michael Blankfort, based on Ursula Keir's novel.

Ferrer and Kerr are Italians (sic) who flee to France after Kerr kills a man. They get a job harvesting grapes on the vineyard run by Leif Erickson, a Frenchman (sic) married to Miss Morgan. During the harvest, Miss Morgan's young sister, Miss Angeli, falls in love with Ferrer; ditto Kerr with Miss Morgan. At the finale, the police come, kill Kerr and Ferrer unbends enough to accept Miss Angeli. That's about all there is to it, except that the assorted accents of the cast make for a curious, and incongruous, mixture. *Brog.*

The Secret Place
(BRITISH)

Moderately entertaining crime meller; modest b.o. bet here.

London, March 12.

Rank release of a John Bryan production. Stars Belinda Lee and Ronald Lewis; features Michael Brooke. Directed by Clive Donner. Screenplay, Linette Perry; camera, Ernest Steward; editor, Peter Bezencenet; music, Clifton Parker. At Odeon Theatre, Leicester Square, London. Running time, **98 MINS.**

Molly Wilson .... Belinda Lee
Mike Wilson .... David McCallum
Mrs. Wilson .... Anne Blake
Gerry Carter .... Ronald Lewis
Stephen Waring .... Michael Gwynn
Paddy .... George Selway
Harry .... George A. Cooper
Mr. Christian .... John Welsh
Freddie Haywood .... Michael Brooke
Mrs. Haywood .... Maureen Pryor
Mr. Haywood .... Geoffrey Keen
Johnnie Haywood .... Brendon Hanley
Sergeant Paynter .... Hugh Manning
Mr. Venner .... Pi ilip Ray
Receptionist .... Wendy Craig

The East Side setting among London's bombed sites provides an intriguing background for this crime meller. But the story unspools too casually, dissipating too much of the potential tension. As it stands, it's a modest b.o. bet.

There are almost two separate stories. The first half of the pic describes how a smalltime gang plans and executes an intricate diamond robbery while the second half the yarn depicts trying to recover the gems, which have accidentally fallen into the hands of a copper's son. Up to and including the holdup sequence, the action is taut and the dialog crisp. However, from then on the pace slackens and the incident lacks sufficient credibility to sustain the atmosphere. A final chase scene over the scaffolding of a new development project commands little excitement.

Ronald Lewis, in his first starring part, shows reasonable promise although his role as a gang leader virtually calls for a one-key performance. Belinda Lee, as his girl friend, still maintains a glamor appearance despite a drab environment and simple clothes. Michael Gwynn puts a rare dignity into his interpretation of Lewis's partner-in-crime. There's an understanding study by Michael Brooke of the copper's son, who is tricked by the girl into lending his father's uniform for the robbery. Other roles maintain an even standard. Jimmy Parkinson belts out the number "But You," which is featured during the credit titles and which fits into the subsequent action. *Myro.*

Fortune Is a Woman
(BRITISH)

Involved meller with Jack Hawkins and Arlene Dahl starred; favorable b.o. possibilities.

London, March 12.

Columbia release of a Frank Launder and Sidney Gilliat production. Stars Jack Hawkins and Arlene Dahl; co-stars Dennis Price, Bernard Miles, Ian Hunter. Directed by Sidney Gilliat. Screenplay, Sidney Gilliat and Frank Launder, adapted by Val Valentine from novel by Winston Graham; camera, Gerald Gibbs; editor, Geoffrey Foot; music, William Alwyn. At Odeon, Leicester Square Theatre, London, March 12, '57. Running time, **95 MINS.**

Oliver Branwell .... Jack Hawkins
Sarah Moreton .... Arlene Dahl
Tracey Moreton .... Dennis Price
Mrs. Moreton .... Violet Farebrother
Chive Fisher .... Ian Hunter
Old Abercrombie .... Malcolm Keen
Michael Abercrombie .... Geoffrey Keen
Fred Connor .... Pa'.ick Holt
Berkeley Reckitt .... John Robinson
Sgt. Barnes .... Michael Goodliffe
Det.-Const. Watson .... Martin Lane
Mr. Jerome .... Bernard Miles
Charles Highbury .... Christopher Lee
Vere Litchen .... Greta Gynt
Willis Croft .... John Phillips
Ambrosine .... Patricia Marmont

The producer-director team of Launder and Gilliat has chosen an involved plot for its first production under the Columbia banner. In this the suspense is occasionally bogged down by intricate plot development. The starring combination of Jack Hawkins and Arlene Dahl, however, may prove to be a valuable b.o. booster and should insure favorable returns.

Hawkins plays an insurance assessor, who stumbles onto a cunning fraud. But he keeps the facts to himself when he suspects that the girl with whom he was once in love (Arlene Dahl) is implicated. She is married to Dennis Price, who has evolved a scheme whereby old masters are sold to wealthy Americans, while substitute imitations are "accidentally" destroyed by fire. Then the insurance collected. The entire manor house goes up in flames while the assessor is secretly investigating the fraud. Price loses his life in the blaze.

After a lapse of some months, Hawkins and Miss Dahl are married. They intend to return the insurance money. But before they get round to it, the police and the blackmailers are on their tails.

Screenplay shows obvious signs of its origins, but while the wealth of incident may be acceptable in a novel, it does not always stand up on transfer to the screen. The film also displays some weakness in characterization; principal characters are clearly etched, whereas others are developed too casually. The shock tactics in suspense make their mark, but don't always achieve the desired effect. Glimpses of Lloyds Insurance headquarters, the English countryside and an historic country home rate among the plus features.

Hawkins, one of Britain's most consistent performers, turns in a thoroughly convincing study of the insurance man, who keeps quiet for too long. It is an unfaltering, dependable performance. Miss Dahl looks her best in the opening scenes and reacts appropriately to the ensuing dramatic development. Price makes a typical contribution as the husband, but misses out as a sinister character, Violet Farebrother, Ian Hunter, Malcolm Keen, Geoffrey Keen and Patrick Holt head a distinctive cast, with outstanding contributions by Bernard Miles, as a blackmailer, and Greta Gynt, as a gay divorcee. *Myro.*

Zombies of Mora Tau

White zombies guard diamond treasure from fortune hunters. Incredible but good in horror classification.

Hollywood, March 5.

Columbia release of Sam Katzman (Clover) production. Features Gregg Palmer, Allison Hayes, Autumn Russell, Joel Ashley, Morris Ankrum, Marjorie Eaton, Gene Roth, Leonard Geer, Karl Davis, William Baskin. Directed by Edward Cahn. Screenplay, Raymond T. Marcus; story, George Plympton; camera, Benjamin H. Kline; editor, Jack Ogilvie; music conducted by Mischa Bakaleinikoff. Previewed Feb. 28, '57. Running time, **68 MINS.**

Jeff Clark .... Gregg Palmer
Mona .... Allison Hayes
Jan .... Autumn Russell
George Harrison .... Joel Ashley

Jonathan Eggert	Morris Ankrum
Mrs. Peters	Marjorie Eaton
Sam	Gene Roth
Johnny	Leonard Geer
Zombies	Karl Davis, William Baskin
Art	Lewis Webb
Sailor	Ray Corrigan
Johnson	Mel Curtis
Capt. Peters	Frank Hagny

As program horror features go, "Zombies of Mora Tau" is a good one, put together to handle all the demands of the spook bills.

The zombies in this Sam Katzman production are a group of sailors turned into living dead men years before when they tried to steal a diamond treasure from an ancient African idol. The treasure now lies under the sea off the coast of Africa and the zombies' eternal task is to guard it from fortune hunters. They've done a good job, too, because the grounds of an old lady who lives nearby are filled with the graves of those who tried and failed.

Gregg Palmer and Joel Ashley head a new expedition to gain the diamonds but most all along on the trip die or are changed into zombies. Palmer only escapes when he decides to scatter the treasure so it can never again be rocevered. This satisfies the zombies; in fact releases them from their assignment and they turn into dust like proper dead men should. It makes the old lady happy, too, because her husband was one of the walking dead men and she wanted him to get some rest.

Palmer goes about his heroics satisfactorily under Edward Cahn's direction of the Raymond T. Marcus script, based on a story by George Plympton. Joel Ashley is adequate as the backer of the expedition, as is Autumn Russell as the old lady's granddaughter who gets romantic with Palmer. Allison Hayes, Ashley's wife, makes a fetching zombie when she's trapped by the dead men. Marjorie Eaton puts a surprising amount of credence into her character of the old lady. Morris Ankrum, Gene Roth, Leonard Geer and others are acceptable.

Background music conducted by Mischa Bakaleinikoff, the lensing by Benjamin H. Kline and other technical credits do their share in carrying out the entertainment aims.

Brog.

Ill Met by Moonlight
(BRITISH—VISTAVISION)

Filmization of British exploit in occupied Crete; stout prospect for domestic market, but needs plenty of exploitation in U.S.

London, March 5.

Rank production and release. Stars Dirk Bogarde, Marius Goring, David Oxley, Cyril Cusack. Written and directed by Michael Powell and Emeric Pressburger, from book by W. Stanley Moss; camera, Christopher Challis; editor, Arthur Stevens; music, Mikis Theodorakis. At Odeon Theatre, Leicester Square, London. Running time, **104 MINS.**

Maj. Paddy Leigh Fermer	Dirk Bogarde
Gen. Karl Kreipe	Marius Goring
Capt. Billy Stanley Moss	David Oxley
Sandy	Cyril Cusack
Manoli	Laurence Payne
George	Wolfe Morris
Andoni Zoidakis	Michael Gough
Micky Akoumianakis	Rowland Bartrop
Stratis Saviolkis	Brian Worth
Yanni Katsias	Paul Stassino
Zahari	Adeeb Assaly
Elias	John Cairney
Charis Zographakis	George Egeniou
Nikko	Demitri Andreas
A Village Priest	Theo Moreas
Michali	Takis Frangofinos

British producers have found a profitable market in the filming of heroic war time exploits, and yarns which ridicule the German army are particularly popular. "Ill Met By Moonlight," the latest in this category, is not without its faults, but has the makings of a substantial grosses in the domestic market.

Powell and Pressburger, who had a smash local winner with "Battle of the River Plate," have taken as their subject this time an operation in occupied Crete. Two British officers, with the aid of local patriots, are given the job of kidnapping the German commander-in-chief and transporting him to Cairo. Such an operation, if successful would hurt German prestige and work wonders for the morale of the occupied Cretans.

As it happens, the job of hijacking the general is accomplished with remarkable ease and luck. His car is ambushed and he's driven through endless road blocks to a mountain hideout. Then comes the tricky part. The general has to be led to the beachhead selected by the British navy for transportation to Egypt. As soon as the Germans realize that their commander has been captured, patrols are sent through the country with airborne troops in support. When the British contingent approach its destination the beachhead is found occupied by German troops. It takes a schoolboy to clear the way and complete the operation.

Dirk Bogarde, now one of the top boxoffice names in British pix, turns in another smooth and satisfying performance as a British major, with David Oxley giving valuable aid as his No. 2 man. Marius Goring, an excellent choice as the general, is smugly confident that he'll be rescued by his own men and gallantly accepts the fact that he's been outwitted by a bunch of amateurs. Cyril Cusack, as a British agent, who had gone without a wash for more than six months to fool the enemy into believing he was a native, tops a well-chosen all-male cast. To Powell and Pressburger goes full direction and scripting credit. Christopher Challis has done a fine job of VistaVision lensing.

Myro.

High Terrace
(BRITISH)

Okay whodunit with good suspense values

Hollywood, March 12.

Allied Artists release of a Robert S. Baker production. Stars Dale Robertson, Lois Maxwell; costars Derek Bond; features Eric Pohlmann, Mary Laura Wood, Lionel Jeffries, Jameson Clark. Screenplay, Alfred Shaughnessy, Norman Hudie; adaptation, Brock Williams; story, A. T. Weisman; camera, Eric Cross; editor, Henry Richardson; music, Stanley Black. Previewed Maroh 5, '57. Running time, **69 MINS.**

Bill Lang	Dale Robertson
Stephanie Blake	Lois Maxwell
John Mansfield	Derek Bond
Otto Kellner	Eric Pohlmann
Molly Kellner	Mary Laura Wood
Monkton	Lionel Jeffries
Det. Inspector MacKay	James Clark
Jock Dunmow	Carl Bernard
Raymond White	Garard Green
Mother Superior	Olwen Brookes
Violet Gage	Benita Lydal
Mansfield's Landlady	Marianne Stone
Constable West	Frederick Treves
Theatre Critic	Jonathan Field
Mrs. Webb	Gretchen Franklin
Robert Baines	Alan Robinson
Priest	Jack Cunningham

This British import is a taut, fairly well developed whodunit which rates as an okay entry. The Dale Robertson name may help.

Audience is kept guessing until final wrapup as to identity of the murderer, and good atmosphere backdrops the Alfred Shaughnessy-Norman Hudie screenplay. Robert S. Baker production unfolds in theatrical London, where Lois Maxwell, co-starred with Robertson, registers a terrific opening-night hit in a show presented by Eric Pohlmann. The producer, in love with his new star, whom he has under contract and refuses to permit appear in a play written by Robertson, an American, is found murdered in his office. Various members of the company are suspected, but it remains until almost closing scene to reveal femme star as the killer, a clever bit of writing. Henry Cass' direction makes best use of suspenseful opportunities.

Robertson is effective as the playwright who, in his desire to have femme star for his play, helps her dispose of the body which she claims she discovered with her own scissors in his back, likely to throw suspicion upon her. Miss Maxwell delivers to advantage, never a suspect to the crime; Derek Bond scores as her former husband, who in turn comes under suspicion; and Pohlmann is forceful as the producer. Jemeson Clark has some good scenes as Scotland Yarder investigating case, and satisfactory support is offered by Mary Laura Wood, victim's widow, and Lionel Jeffries, company manager.

Eric Cross' photography heads up stock technical credits.

Whit.

The Naked Eye
(Documentary)

Excellent quality with Oscar nomination prestige. Limited but good for art spots.

Hollywood, March 18.

Film Representations, Inc. release of Camera Eye Pictures presentation. Written, produced and directed by Louis Clyde Stoumen; photographed and edited by Stoumen; scenes from "The Photographer" photographed by Benjamin Doniger, directed by Willard Van Dyke; narrated by Raymond Massey; music composed and conducted by Elmer Bernstein; features photographic life work of Edward Weston, and the photographs of Margaret Bourke-White, Alfred Eisenstaedt and Weegee.

Previewed at Screen Directors Guild Bldg., March 18, 1957. Running time, **71 MINS.**

"The Naked Eye" is aptly subtitled a film about the fun and art of photography. As to its quality, the Academy nomination in the best feature-length documentary class speaks for itself. It is recommended, and highly, for all who relish brilliant pictorial artistry. The nation's millions of shutterbugs also will find it an engrossing 71 minutes of what can be done with photography, both from the examples of the artists shown and **from the equally outstanding production-photography job done by Camera Eye Pictures' Louis Clyde Stoumen.**

While a special interest subject, and undoubtedly limited in its commercial possibilities because of that classification, "Eye" still will have appeal for any who see it. Stoumen, who wrote, produced, directed, photographed and edited, uses a unique technique he calls photographic animation, along with live action documentary filming, to impart action to stills. Abetting this feeling of movement is an extremely good narration job by Raymond Massey and a most effective background score by Elmer Bernstein.

Footage covers the history of photography, without getting uninterestingly academic, while concentrating on several notable examples of the photographic art, each with story narrative to hold the interest. The works of Alfred Eisenstaedt, Margaret Bourke-White and Weegee occupy the first part of the footage. The Weegee sequence, with this eccentric NY lenser being caught in action recording the drama of a city, is particularly interesting.

The photographic life work of Edward Weston takes up the last part of the film, viewing his works at all ages, with special attention to the national scene and the development of his special technicque in different eras, his stay in Mexico and, finally, his dedication to the natural beauties of the Northern California coast. Shown, too, are a number of Weston's beautiful nudes, display of which almost prevented the film from getting a Production Code Seal until it was ruled that the studies actually were art. The final reel turns to color, just as did Weston in his later photographic days.

Brog.

Last Of The Badmen
('SCOPE-COLOR)

Well-plotted entry for western market, with George Montgomery name to draw.

Hollywood, March 12.

Allied Artists release of a Vincent M. Fennelly production. Stars George Montgomery; features James Best, Douglas Kennedy, Keith Larsen, Robert Foulk, Willis Bouchey, John Doucette. Directed by Paul Landres. Screenplay, Daniel B. Ullman, David Chantler; story, Ullman; camera (DeLuxe Color), Ellsworth Fredricks; editor, William Austin; music, Paul Sawtell. Previewed March 4, '57. Running time, **79 MINS.**

Dan Barton	George Montgomery
Ted Hamilton	James Best
Hawkins	Douglas Kennedy
Roberts	Keith Larsen
Taylor	Robert Foulk
Marshal Parker	Willis Bouchey
Johnson	John Doucette
Lila	Meg Randall
Dallas	Tom Greenway
Dillon	Addison Richards
Kramer	Michael Ansara
Elkins	John Damler
Green	Harlan Warde

Overlooking the title which bears no relation to the picture, "Last of the Badmen" is a well-made, fairly-suspenseful offering a cut above the average western. The George Montgomery name will help it through the action and oater markets, where good response should accrue to a sustained plot.

The Vincent M. Fennelly production gains an added boost by shrewd use of CinemaScope and DeLuxe Color, and Paul Landres' direction of the Daniel B. Ullman-David Chantler screenplay sets a mood in keeping with general unfoldment. Star is backed by a cast of capable players in realistic roles who add to worth of story.

Montgomery plays a Chicago detective who joins a gang of outlaws to investigate a series of stagecoach robberies. Gang uses the gimmick of springing from jail any badman with a price on his head, so this reward may later be raised when badman is recognized during subsequent holdups. When a high enough price is established, gang then kills badman for the reward. Montgomery joins gang as such an outlaw, via a faked record, knowing it's only a question of time before his own number is called when rewards for his arrest keep mounting. He manages to round up the gang and expose a town's marshal as actual gang leader in a fast shooting finale.

Montgomery shows up well in his characterization, and Douglas Kennedy scores as leader of the gang under Willis Bouchey, who registers well as the unsuspected marshal. James Best handles himself well as a member of the gang friendly toward Montgomery. Robert Foulk is realistic as a killer and Keith Larsen, in role of an undercover man who sacrifices himself so detective's identity won't be known, also is okay.

Color camera work by Ellsworth Fredericks is excellent and other credits satisfactory. *Whit.*

The Storm Rider
(REGALSCOPE)

Characterizations and story convincing. Western headed by Scott Brady for program playdates.

Hollywood, March 19.

Twentieth-Fox release of a Bernard Glasser production. Stars Scott Brady, Mala Powers, Bill Williams; features John Goddard, William Fawcett, Roy Engel, George Keymas, Olin Howlin, James Dobson, Rocky Lundy. Directed by Edward Bernds. Screenplay, Bernds, Don Martin, from novel by L. L. Foreman; camera, Brydon Baker; editor, John F. Link; music, Les Baxter. Previewed March 11, '57. Running time, **70 MINS.**

Jones	Scott Brady
Tay Rorick	Mala Powers
Coulton	Bill Williams
Collins	Olin Howlin
Cruikshank	William Fawcett
Rorick	John Goddard
Milstead	Hank Patterson
Cooper	James Dobson
Forrest	John Close
Emery	Jim Hayward
Flood	Cortland Shepard
Fred Feylan	Rocky Shahan
Will Feylan	Frank Richards
Jack Feylan	Rick Vallin
Burns	Ronald Foster
Todd	Tom London
Jake	Britt Wood
Blackie	Al Baffert
Bud Cooper	Rocky Lundy
Jasper	John Cason
Toby	Bud Osborne
Bonnard	Roy Engel
Apache Kid	George Keymas
Doctor	Lane Chandler
Mrs. Cooper	Jean Ann Lewis
Hanks	Wayne Mallory

Scott Brady-Bernard Glasser combo comes up with a regulation western that meets the demands of the oater market for their bow with Regal. Brady is bracketed with Mala Powers and Bill Williams in the speedy Glasser production to give marquee lure, and both characters and story are convincing enough to rate as okay entertainment.

Brady, former gunman for the Cattle Assn. rides into the small town of Hartwell to find a feud ready to erupt between the small ranchers and a big rancher who is trying to squeeze them out. When he prevents fireworks, the small ranchers hire him as their leader, unaware that he is the man who killed their former leader. Under Edward Bernds' know-how direction of his and Don Martin's screenplay, Brady is able to bring peace to the community, after gunning down a fast-draw brought in by the big rancher. Despite his falling for the widow of the small ranchers' leader, who in turn falls for him, he rides away, knowing that the dead man will forever be a barrier between them.

Brady lends authority to his characterization, and Mala Powers is okay on femme lead in widow role. Williams portrays the sheriff, in love with femme. Good supporting cast is headed by William Fawcett, spokesman for the small ranchers; James Dobson, one of the ranchers shot down by George

Keymas, gunman imported by Roy Engel, big rancher.

Camera work by Brydon Baker, editing by John F. Link and music score by Les Baxter lead off standard technical credits. *Whit.*

Le Schiave Di Cartegene
(The Slave of Carthage)
(ITALIAN)

Rome, March 12.

Filmar release of Cines-Yago production (in Ferraniacolor and Cinetotalscope). Stars Ganna Maria Canale, Jorge Mistral, Marisa Allasio. Directed by Guido Brignone. At Galleria, Rome. Running time, **110 MINS.**

Take the best ingredients of "Quo Vadis," "The Robe," "Demetrius and the Slave" and other films of this ilk, mix well together, move the setting, revise the tortures and this is about what one has in "The Slave of Carthage.' Spanish star Jorge Mistral even suffers and fights in the best Victor Mature tradition.

In this yarn, the death of a Roman proconsul is blamed on the black magic of the Christians, most of whom are slaves already, and they are ordered to be put to death in spite of Rome's guarantee of religious freedom.

Marco Valerio, in the person of Mistral, falls in love with Lea, the slave, played by Marisa Allasio. She is given star billing because of her current success in "Poveri Ma Balli." Single-handed he defeats Signorina Canale and all of the malefactors in some of the best single-handed fighting since Doug Fairbanks' day.

Tarzan and the Lost Safari
(COLOR)

First Tarzan under Metro banner in 15 years." Takes easily to Technicolor hues. Good general market adventure feature.

Hollywood, March 26.

Metro release of John Croydon (Sol Lesser) production. Stars Gordon Scott, Robert Beatty, Yolande Donlan, Betta St. John, Wilfrid Hyde White; features George Coulouris, Peter Arne, Orlando Martins, Cheta. Directed by Bruce Humberstone. Screenplay, Montgomery Pittman, Lillie Hayward; based on character created by Edgar Rice Burroughs; camera (Technicolor), C. R. Pennington-Richards; African photography, Miki Carter; editor, Bill Lewthwaite; music, Clifton Parker; conducted by Louis Levy. Previewed March 20, '57. Running time, **80 MINS.**

Tarzan	Gordon Scott
"Tusker" Hawkins	Robert Beatty
Gamage Dean	Yolande Donlan
Diana Penrod	Betta St. John
"Doodles" Fletcher	Wilfrid Hyde White
Carl Kraski	George Coulouris
Dick Penrod	Peter Arne
Chief Ogonooro	Orlando Martins

Tarzan, perennial screen hero in black-and-white here takes to color, giving this entry an extra plus for b.o. coin in the series' established market. "Tarzan and the Lost Safari" should prove good fare for action houses, particularly with the moppet trade and those oldsters who decline to grow up.

Along with the tint treatment, Tarzan takes to authentic jungle backgrounds for this screenplay by Montgomery Pittman and Lillie Hayward, and the antics come off entertainingly under Bruce Humberstone's actionful direction. Listed as a British production by John Croydon for the Sol Lesser presentation banner, film is the first Tarzan to wear the Metro release label in some 15 years. The combination of African footage lensed in Technicolor by Miki Carter and the matching studio-staged sequences by C. R. Pennington-Richards adds excellent sight values to go with the standard adventuring. Future Tarzans are slated for color.

Gordon Scott has the physique for the title role and does acceptably by it. This one was lensed about a year ago. It would seem in order to unstiffen character for the new era Tarzan. Nature boy has no Jane here, but Cheta (the umpteenth such) is around to supply plenty of chuckles.

This time, the script based on the Edgar Rice Burroughs character finds the hero guiding a party of bored uppercrust socialites out of the jungle after its plane has crashed. To give the hero obstacles to overcome, plot introduces Robert Beatty, hunter who has a deal to turn over some white sacrifices to native chief Orlando Martins as payment for a vast hoard of ivory. Needless to say, Tarzan is too much for Beatty and the natives.

Distaff roles fall to Yolande Donlan and Betta St. John, members of the party, and both come through nicely. Beatty is a good heavy and Wilfrid Hyde White, George Coulouris and Peter Arne, male members of the rescued party, do their share in the entertainment. Editing by Bill Lewthwaite functions expertly in blending the scenes, while Clifton Parker's music, directed by Louis Levy, ably backs the jungle dramatics. *Brog.*

Untamed Youth
(SONGS)

Crooked lady judge, plantation Legree, sex and rock-and-roll mixed together. Musical gives it boxoffice.

Hollywood, March 22.

Warners release of Aubrey Schenck production. Stars Mamie Van Doren, Lori Nelson, John Russell, Don Burnett; features Eddie Cochran, Lurene Tuttle, Yvonne Lime, Jeanne Carmen, Robert Foulk, Wayne Taylor. Directed by Howard W. Koch. Screenplay, John C. Higgins; story, Stephen Longstreet; camera, Carl Guthrie; editor, John Schreyer; music, Les Baxter; songs, Baxter, Lenny Adelson, Eddie Cochran, Jerry Capehart. Previewed March 19, '57. Running time, **79 MINS.**

Penny	Mamie Van Doren
Jancy	Lori Nelson
Tropp	John Russell
Bob	Don Burnett
Bong	Eddie Cochran
Mrs. Steele	Lurene Tuttle
Baby	Yvonne Lime
Lillibet	Jeanne Carmen
Mitch	Robert Foulk
Duke	Wayne Taylor
Ralph	Jerry Barclay
Angelo	Keith Richards
Arkie	Valerie Reynolds
Margarita	Lucita
Landis	Glenn Dixon
Pinky	Wally Brown

A combination of melodramatics, sex and rock-and-roll gives "Untamed Youth" good commercial prospects. Deliberately aimed at exploitation playdates with full-blown selling, the Aubrey Schenck production delivers as specified. The entire setup is slanted at the younger filmgoers and they will be attracted, even if some may suppose the moral tone isn't the best for this particular group.

Driving beat of the music, four r&r pieces and one calypso, holds the footage together more so than the actual story development. Numbers are well staged within the plot framework, even though director Howard W. Koch tends to overflaunt Mamie Van Doren's more prominent physical attributes and her bodily gestures.

The script by John C. Higgins from a story by Stephen Longstreet concerns a racket being worked by a femme judge and a big cotton grower whereby young people are sentenced to work on the farm for slave wages. The racket is doing okay until Miss Van Doren and Lori Nelson, sisters and entertainers, are arrested as vagrants and the judge's son, Don Burnett, gets a job on the farm and falls for Miss Nelson. Events are contrived to wreck the scheme, get Miss Van Doren on television and Miss Nelson into Burnett's arms.

Miss Van Doren sounds real good on "Salamander" and "Go, Go, Calypso," both by Les Baxter, "Rolling Stone" by Baxter and Lenny Adelson, and "Oobala Baby," by Baxter, Adelson, Eddie Cochran and Jerry Capehart. Also a click is Eddie Cochran's Presley-type treatment of "Cottonpicker," cleffed by Baxter. Miss Van Doren does okay by her story portions and Miss Nelson is appealing in her part.

John Russell heads the villainy department as the cotton-picking Legree. Lurene Tuttle is the judge, secretly married to Russell. The characters and romantic circumstances of the association never ring true. Burnett is acceptable in his spot and other assists come from Cochran, Yvonne Lime, Jeanne Carmen, Robert Foulk, Wayne Taylor, Valerie Reynolds, Lucita and Wally Brown.

Carl Guthrie's photography tops the capably-handled technical credits and Les Baxter's background score is able. *Brog.*

The Quiet Gun
(Regal Scope)

A quiet one, for a western, but okay for outdoor programmer dates.

Hollywood, March 5.

20th-Fox release of Earle Lyon (Regal) production. Stars Forrest Tucker, Mara Corday, Jim Davis, Kathleen Crowley; features Lee Van Cleef, Tom Brown, Lewis Martin, Hank Worden, Gerald Milton. Directed by William Claxton. Screenplay, Eric Norden; camera, John Mescall; editor, Robert Fritch; music, Paul Dunlap. Previewed March 4, '57. Running time, **77 MINS.**

Carl .... Forrest Tucker
Irene .... Mara Corday
Ralph .... Jim Davis
Teresa .... Kathleen Crowley
Sadler .... Lee Van Cleef
Reilly .... Tom Brown
Hardy .... Lewis Martin
Sampson .... Hank Worden
Lesser .... Gerald Milton
Judge .... Everett Glass
Mrs. Merric .... Edith Evanson

"The Quiet Gun" is a little too quiet for a good western. It's cryptic, too, so the fans will have to work as hard as the sheriff hero to figure out what's going on during the 77 minutes running time.

The Regal presentation through 20th-Fox has a good beginning and end, but loses action steam in the mid-stretch with talky scenes and vague plotting that keeps the audience as well as the principals in the dark as to what the heavies are about. With all its flaws, though, picture has some rewarding moments and makes a definite stab at mood.

Forrest Tucker heads the cast of the Earle Lyon production as the sheriff who backs his badge with a quiet authority. He's sure there is skullduggery afoot when the town council tries to get a rancher in trouble for keeping an Indian girl, and a lynch mob takes over when the rancher kills the city attorney. Not until the end, after several deaths, does he discover that saloonkeeper Tom Brown and killer Lee Van Cleef have schemed to grab the rancher's land to use as a base for rustled cattle. He corrects matters in a good finale street showdown that leaves the two heavies dead and law once more established. The Eric Norden script also has something to say about townspeople taking the law into their own hands, but doesn't say it very well.

Performances are sometimes uneven under William Claxton's direction, although Tucker, Mara Corday, the Indian girl; Jim Davis, the rancher; Kathleen Crowley, his widow; Van Cleef, Brown, and the others are acceptable. Hank Worden, as the sheriff's deputy, and uncredited Vince Barnett, an eager undertaker, add some comedy touches.

John Mescall's black-and-white lensing in the RegalScope anamorphic process is exceptionally good, and the Paul Dunlap score also is a plus credit. *Brog.*

The River's Edge
(C'SCOPE—COLOR—SONG)

Two males fight over girl and a million dollars. Familiar names, mild melodramatics spell regular-run situations.

Hollywood, March 26.

20th-Fox release of Benedict Bogeaus production. Stars Ray Milland, Anthony Quinn, Debra Paget; features Harry Carey Jr., Chubby Johnson, Byron K. Foulger, Tom McKee, Frank Gerstle. Directed by Allan Dwan. Screenplay, Harold Jacob Smith, James Leicester; from Smith's "The Highest Mountain"; camera (De Luxe Color), Harold Lipstein; editor, James Leicester; music, Louis Forbes; song, Forbes and Bobby Troup; sung by Bob Winn. Previewed March 20, '57. Running time, **87 MINS.**

Nardo Denning .... Ray Milland
Ben Cameron .... Anthony Quinn
Meg Cameron .... Debra Paget
Chet .... Harry Carey Jr.
Whiskers .... Chubby Johnson
Barry .... Byron K. Foulger
U.S. Border Patrol Captain .... Tom McKee
U.S. Border Patrolman .... Frank Gerstle

A girl and one million dollars set up the "conflict" in "The River's Edge," an ironic outdoor story about two men who want both. The melodramatics are mild, but the names of Ray Milland, Anthony Quinn and Debra Paget supply familiar dressing for the marquees in the regular twin-bill situations so an average quota of playdates should be forthcoming.

The Benedict Bogeaus production which 20th-Fox is distributing is locationed in Mexico, resulting in attractive scenic backing for the meller tale scripted by Harold Jacob Smith and James Leicester from Smith's "The Highest Mountain." CinemaScope and De Luxe Color help the plus value of Harold Lipstein's lensing. Mild rating for the melodramatics comes from deliberate pacing and not too credible plotting. Story is grim and the violence bloodthirsty, though, as it unfolds under Allan Dwan's direction.

Milland is the man with a million, a shady sharpie who wants to get his money and himself safely over the border into Mexico. To guide him across the mountains he seeks out Quinn, smalltime rancher and expert outdoorsman now married to Miss Paget, Milland's old partner in crime. Not content with a good guide, Milland also tries to steal the guide's wife, but during the long, tedious trip, Miss Paget comes to recognize the worth of her husband and the selfishness and cruelty of her ex-partner. Windup finds Milland dead, having fallen over a cliff, his money scattered to the winds, while Quinn and Miss Paget resolve to return to face the authorities for their part in the abortive flight and the murders that resulted from it.

The two male stars answer up to the demands put upon them by story and direction and Miss Paget is acceptable. Harry Carey Jr., seen briefly as a filling station operator; Chubby Johnson, an old prospector wantonly murdered by Milland; Frank Gerstle, border patrolman who meets a violent death at the hands of the sharpie, and others in the cast do their work satisfactorily.

The title tune by Louis Forbes and Bobby Troup is sung behind the credits by Bob Winn, but is no asset to the picture. Forbes' score otherwise is okay, as are the technical contributions. *Brog.*

Revolt at Fort Laramie
(COLOR)

Cavalry vs. Indians, plus Union-Confederacy conflict. Routine actioner.

Hollywood, March 12.

United Artists release of Aubrey Schenck, Howard W. Koch (Bel-Air) production. Stars John Dehner, Gregg Palmer, Frances Helm, Don Gordon; features Robert Keys, William "Bill" Phillips, Cain Mason, Robert Knapp. Directed by Lesley Selander. Written by Robert C. Dennis; camera (De Luxe Color), William Margulies; editor, John F. Schreyer; music, Les Baxter. Previewed Feb. 28, '57. Running time, **72 MINS.**

Major Seth Bradner .... John Dehner
Captain James Tenslip .... Gregg Palmer
Melissa Bradner .... Frances Helm
Jean Salignac .... Don Gordon
Sergeant Darrach .... Robert Keys
Serrell .... William Phillips
Ezra .... Cain Mason
Lieutenant Waller .... Robert Knapp
Red Cloud .... Eddie Little
Rinty .... Dean Stanton
Hendrey .... Bill Barker
Caswell .... Clay Randolph
Captain Foley .... Kenne Duncan

The cavalry and the Indians are still at it in "Revolt At Fort Laramie," but with an added complication. Plot period is just at the time the Confederacy is established and divided loyalties among the troops within the fort made it difficult to handle the common redskin enemy. While this angle gives a somewhat different twist, the playoff is to the standard action formula.

Scenic dressing is all that could be asked in the Aubrey Schenck-Howard W. Koch Bel-Air production for United Artists. Kanabe, Utah locations take well to the De Luxe Color lensing by William Margulies, even if the hues are not always consistent in values. Lesley Selander's direction generally holds to an action pace that is only occasionally slowed by plot holes, latter seemingly caused mostly by inconsistent editing.

John Dehner plays the Virginian commanding Fort Laramie who, when war comes between the states, turns over his post to Gregg Palmer so he can join the Confederacy. Meanwhile, there is the Indian problem, with Red Cloud wanting $50,000 in gold to sign a treaty. Also wanting the gold for the south are the southern loyalists, but Dehner, an honorable man, talks them out of it and the group leaves Palmer to his Indian problem, only to run into one itself. Climax deals with Palmer's rescue of the southern party from Red Cloud's attack and Robert C. Dennis' story then comes to an abrupt close with some loose ends dangling.

Neither script nor direction makes strong demands on the players, but Dehner, Palmer and most of the others comes off okay via their performances. Frances Helm is adequate, no more, as the heroine, a southern belle in love with Yankee Palmer. Les Baxter's score and other behind-camera assists are acceptable. *Brog.*

Not of This Earth

Good science-fiction thriller being packaged with "Attack of Crab Monsters" by Allied Artists; promising ballyhoo.

Hollywood, March 21.

Allied Artists release of Roger Corman production, directed by Corman. Stars Paul Birch, Beverly Garland, Morgan Jones; features William Roerick, Jonathan Haze, Richard Miller, Anne Carroll, Pat Flynn, Roy Engel. Screenplay, Charles Griffith, Mark Hanna; camera, John Mescall; editor, Charles Gross; music, Ronald Stein. Previewed March 14, '57. Running time, **67 MINS.**

Paul Johnson .... Paul Birch
Nadine Storey .... Beverly Garland
Harry Sherbourne .... Morgan Jones
Dr. F. W. Rochelle .... William Roerick
Jeremy Perrin .... Jonathan Haze
Joe Piper .... Richard Miller
Davanna Woman .... Anne Carroll
Simmons .... Pat Flynn
Sgt. Walton .... Roy Engel
Joanne .... Tamar Cooper
Specimen .... Harold Fong
Girl .... Gail Ganley
Boy .... Ralph Reed

The out-of-this-world science-fiction flavor of "Not of This Earth" makes it a handy entry for exploitation playdates generally. The Roger Corman production is being packaged by Allied Artists with another Corman thriller, "Attack of the Crab Monster" (reviewed last issue) and the teaming has marketable possibilities.

Corman also directs the script by Charles Griffith and Mark Hanna. It plays off at a regulation pace with attention to chills and thrills in telling how an advanced human comes from another planet to scout the earth as a possible source of blood for the natives of Davanna. Things get rather gory, but science fiction fans won't mind. They should like the ending because, just as the scout has been laid to rest on earth, fadeout finds another arriving to continue the work.

Paul Birch is the super human from outer space. He, like his people, are dying of a disease in which the blood evaporates and the supply on Davanna is running out. He sets up quarters on earth, replenishing his own blood from time to time while taking specimens to transport through space to his home. Mixed up in the action are attractive and competent Beverly Garland, a nurse; Morgan Jones, her suspicious policeman friend; William Roerick, the doctor for whom she works; Jonathan Haze, Birch's handyman, and sundry victims of the experimenting. The cast does all that is required by the story and its screen development.

Helping to keep the eerie tale moving is John Mescall's photography and the score by Ronald Stein. *Brog.*

The Deadly Mantis

Unimaginatively executed science-fiction "thriller" pretty tame.

Hollywood, March 22.

Universal release of William Alland production. Stars Craig Stevens, William Hopper, Alix Talton; features Donald Randolph, Pat Conway, Florenz Ames, Paul Smith, Phil Harvey, Floyd Simmons, Paul Campbell. Directed by Nathan Juran. Screenplay, Martin Berkeley; story, Alland; camera, Ellis W. Carter; special photography, Clifford Stine; editor, Chester Schaeffer; music supervision, Joseph Gershenson. Previewed March 19, '57. Running time, **78 MINS.**

Col. Joe Parkman .... Craig Stevens
Dr. Ned Jackson .... William Hopper
Marge Blaine .... Alix Talton
General Mark Ford .... Donald Randolph
Sgt. Pete Allen .... Pat Conway
Prof. Anton Gunther .... Florenz Ames
Corporal .... Paul Smith
Lou .... Phil Harvey
Army Sergeant .... Floyd Simmons
Lt. Fred Pizar .... Paul Campbell

Universal has a record for doing right well with science-fiction thrillers, but "The Deadly Mantis" is not one of its better ones although title and story idea are good.

First quarter of the footage is extremely slow, taken up with tedious explanations and world maps, so an audience is not immediately caught up in the plot. Elsewhere, too, the scripting by Martin Berkeley is poor, being singularly unimaginative for this type of feature; thus Nathan Juran's direction has a handicap that it never quite overcomes.

The prehistoric ancestor of the insect known today as the praying mantis (inches high) escapes from the polar icecap when an earthquake breaks up his iceberg home. Gigantic in size, it takes its toll of life and Continental Air Defense equipment in the polar region before heading south, killing and destroying as it goes. Finally cornered in a Hudson River vehicular tunnel at New York, poison gas land mines finally kill the monster and the world is safe.

Craig Stevens, commander of the northern base, William Hopper, paleontologist called in to help with the elimination of the creature, and Alix Talton, museum editor-photog. handle the leads in the William Alland production acceptably, while the other players are okay in lesser parts.

Straight lensing by Ellis W. Carter and the special photography by Clifford Stine help for thrills, but the latter mostly turn out rather tame considering the subject matter. *Brog.*

The Counterfeit Plan
(BRITiSH)

Okay program melodrama with Zachary Scott, Peggie Castle for names.

Hollywood, March 22.
Warners release of Alec C. Snowden (Amalgamated) production. Stars Zachary Scott,. Peggie Castle, Mervyn Johns. Sydney Tafler, Lee Patterson; features David Lodge, Mark Bellamy, Chill Bouchier, Robert Arden. Directed by Montgomery Tully. Screenplay, James Eastwood; camera, Philip Grinrod; editor, Geoffrey Muller; music, Richard Taylor. Previewed March 19, '57. Running time, 79 MINS.
Max .... Zachary Scott
Carol .... Jeggie Castle
Louie .... Mervyn Johns
Flint .... Sydney Tafler
Duke .... Lee Patterson
Watson .... David Lodge
Vik .... Mark Bellamy
Housekeeper .... Chili Bouchier
Bob .... Robert Arden
Wandelman .... Eric Pohlmann
Lepton .... Aubrey Dexter
Police Inspector .... John Welsh

"The Counterfeit Plan" is a British-made melodrama which proves suitable fare for the lowercase spot. Zachary Scott and Peggie Castle, familiar names for the domestic market, head an otherwise all-British cast on the Alec C. Snowden production and the show comes off okay.

James Eastwood's screenplay has portraying a cold-blooded crook who escapes a murder rap in France and comes to England to set up a counterfeit ring at the country home of Mervyn Johns, who is forced to be an unwilling partner in the enterprise because he's an expert ex-forger. The unexpected arrival of Johns' daughter, Miss Castle, launches a series of circumstances that eventually bring Scott to ruin.

Montgomery Tully directs satisfactorily, although his methodical atttention to detail in showing how the ring intends to operate slows the pace occasionally. Scott handles his lead chore excellently and Miss Castle is good as the girl who gets mixed up in the scheme. Johns, Sydney Tafler, Lee Patterson, David Lodge, Mark Bellamy, Robert Arden and others are okay types.

Philip Grinrod takes care of the camera chores acceptably; in fact there are some rather good shots of the British countryside and action sequences. Other technical factors are standard. *Brog.*

The Strange One

Controversial film (homosexual angles) of military school life; needs strong selling.

Columbia release of Horizon (Sam Spiegel) production. Stars Ben Gazzara; features Julie Wilson, George Peppard, Mark Richman, Pat Hingle, Arthur Storch, Paul E. Richards, Larry Gates, Clifton James, Geoffrey Horne, James Olson. Directed by Jack Garfein. Screenplay, Calder Willingham, based on his novel and play, "End As a Man"; camera, Burnett Guffey; music, Kenyon Hopkins; editor, Sidney Katz. Previewed March 25, '57 at Astor Theatre, N. Y. Running time. 97 MINS.
Jocko de Paris .... Ben Gazzara
Harold Knoble .... Pat Hingle
Cadet Colonel Corger ....Mark Richman
Simmons .... Arthur Storch
Perrin McKee .... Paul E. Richards
Major Avery .... Larry Gates
Colonel Ramey .... Clifton James
Georgie Avery .... Geoffrey Horne
Roger Gatt .... James Olson
Rosebud .... Julie Wilson
Robert Marquales .... George Peppard

Producer Sam Spiegel, often identified with controversial pictures, has another challenging entry in "The Strange One." For this story of life at a southern military school accents the seamier side replete with numerous infractions of discipline as well as homosexual overtones.

But although the exploitable film has some excellent performances and is ably directed, it poses a sales problem. This stems largely from the lack of marquee names and the limited appeal of the yarn itself. Stories involving military schools haven't been too popular with filmgoers nor do homosexual themes figure to be either.

However, a vigorous campaign plus the controversy the picture is bound to set off should generate some b.o. action in the general market particularly among masculine audiences. Cast, incidentally, is all male save for Julie Wilson in the lone femme role.

Screenplay by Calder Willingham, based on his novel and play, "End As a Man," is a taut, suspenseful adaptation which of necessity omitted much of the book. But two characters retained are homosexuals whose experiences come into considerable focus. In fact three minutes of these scenes were deleted from the original print following a ukase of the Production Code Administration that this footage violated its rules banning *"sex perversion or any inference of it . . .".*

Elimination of the "objectionable" sequences has no noticeable effect upon the overall story in the opinion of this reviewer who saw both versions. For apparently the point of the film is that while certain unscrupulous students may mar the decorum of the school for a time, ultimately they'll be rooted out and exposed by fellow classmates with a better sense of moral values.

Several members of the cast of the Broadway original are seen in the picture edition while Jack Garfein again directs. Irritatingly realistic is the performance of Ben Gazzara who reprises his stage role of Jocko De Paris. His portrayal of the rotter who dominates his colleagues is in a nonchalant, arrogant, wise guy vein reminiscent of the Actors Studio genre of acting.

Arthur Storch, also of the Broadway play, deftly handles the part of a less virile student. He's a freshman who cringes under taunts of upper classmen, balks at washing in a community shower for obvious reasons and has no interest in the opposite sex. George Peppard is refreshingly forthright as another freshman

who's instrumental in kicking Gazzara out of the school "for the good of the institution."

Julie Wilson, whose role of a woman of easy virtue is nonexistent in either the book or play, sparkles as the seductive, southern-accented femme. Laurels also go to Pat Hingle and James Olson, as buddies of Gazzara who eventually turn on him, while Larry Gates is standout as a patient officer whom Gazzara has vowed to "get." Fine support is provided by Mark Richman, Paul E. Richards and Geoffrey Horne, among others. Incidentally, some of the more overt homo scenes in which Richards appeared in the original were scissored out.

Garfein, who's making his motion picture directorial debut with this Columbia release, guides the players with a sure hand. Burnett Guffey's camerawork competently captures the atmosphere surrounding the students. Musical score, composed and conducted by Kenyon Hopkins, ably complements the air of tension that builds throughout the film.

Art direction of Joseph C. Wright is good as are Sidney Katz's editing and other technical credits. Physical backgrounds are austere in keeping with the script's demands. Interiors on this Horizon Picture were lensed at the Shamrock Studios, Winter Park, Fla. *Gilb.*

The Big Caper

Rory Calhoun in acceptable meller for dual-bill playdates.

Hollywood, March 27.
United Artists release of William Thomas, Howard Pine production. Stars Rory Calhoun, Mary Costa, James Gregory; features Robert Harris, Roxanne Arlen, Corey Allen, Paul Picerni, Pat McVey. Directed by Robert Stevens. Screenplay, Martin Berkeley; story, Lionel Lindon; editor, George Gittens; music, Albert Glasser. Previewed March 25, '57. Running time, 84 MINS.
Frank Harber ....: Rory Calhoun
Kay .... Mary Costa
Flood .... James Gregory
Zimmer .... Robert Harris
Doll .... Roxanne Arlen
Roy .... Corey Allen
Harry .... Paul Picerni
Sam Loxley .... Pat McVey
Waldo Harrington .... James Nolan
Paulmeyer .... Florenz Ames
Alice Loxley .... Louise Arthur
Keeler .... Roscoe Ates
Bennie .... Terry Kelman
Bitsy .... Melody Gale

As a melodrama about a million dollar heist, "The Big Caper" will prove readily acceptable in the general market. Other than Rory Calhoun's, the star and feature names aren't too familiar in the regular film field, but all are satisfactorily cast to type so the meller entertainment intent of the William Thomas-Howard Pine production is maintained.

A Marine Corps payroll being held in a smalltown bank near Camp Pendleton is the target of the gang of crooks headed by James Gregory. Taken from the novel by Lionel White, plot shows how Gregory moves in his girl friend, Mary Costa, and righthandman, Calhoun, to set up housekeeping as a young married couple, case the town and lay the groundwork for the big caper. Robert Stevens' direction, while handicapped at times by Martin Berkeley's script, still develops a growing suspense as the story moves towards the not unexpected payoff.

Story characters and layout of the planned robbery put an emphasis on violence and some tough action. One of the gang is a drunken pyromaniac who is to set

a warehouse ablaze and blow up the school to divert attention from the bank. Robert Harris plays it for full effect. Another is a muscle-boy thrill killer, whose sadistic bent is used to bump off a femme hangeron in the gang. Character is effectively flamboyant as done by Corey Allen.

Calhoun and Miss Costa, while playing house, undergo a change of heart that spoils the robbery just as Gregory is ready to blow town with the loot and leave everyone else holding the sack. Calhoun is good and Miss Costa acceptable. Gregory takes care of the mastermind role ably and other assists come from Roxanne Arlen, Paul Picerni, Pat McVey, James Nolan and Florenz Ames.

Lionel Lindon's lensing, the score by Albert Glasser, editing and other contributions are well-valued for release aims. *Brog.*

Man Afraid
(C'SCOPE)

Preacher kills burglar, with consequences providing contrived but suspenseful melodrama. For program bookings.

Hollywood, April 2.
Universal release of Gordon Kay production. Stars George Nader, Phyllis Thaxter, Tim Hovey; features Eduard Franz, Harold J. Stone, Judson Pratt, Reta Shaw. Directed by Harry Keller. Screenplay, Herb Meadow; story, Dan Ullman; camera, Russell Metty; editor, Ted J. Kent; music, Henry Mancini. Previewed March 26, '57. Running time, 83 MINS.
Reverend David Collins... George Nader
Lisa Collins .... Phyllis Thaxter
Michael Collins .... Tim Hovey
Carl Simmons .... Eduard Franz
Lieutenant Marlin......Edward J. Stone
Wilbur Fletcher .... Judson Pratt
Nurse Willis .... Reta Shaw
Ronnie Fletcher .... Butch Bernard
Maggie .... Mabel Albertson
Ship Hamilton .... Martin Milner

The consequences that follow the killing of a teenage burglar by a preacher are "contrived" but suspenseful in this Universal melodrama. Entertainment quality is acceptable for the general market, being calculated to thrill the undiscriminating.

George Nader, Phyllis Thaxter and Tim Hovey, the stars, constitute the religioso family which goes through several days of fear after Nader kills a delinquent teenager attempting to rob his home. It soon becomes apparent to everyone but the police that Eduard Franz, grieve-stricken father of the dead boy, plans revenge for the killing, even though accidental. Windup finds Franz chasing young Hovey underneath a beach pier, only to be saved himself from drowning by the preacher, who converts the grieving man by asking forgiveness for having killed his son.

Moppet Hovey is as likeable as ever, while Nader and Miss Thaxter are acceptable as the frightened parents. Franz goes through his role mutely, using expression to carry it. Harold J. Stone, policeman who can't act until a crime is attempted; Judson Pratt, tv announcer, and Reta Shaw, a nurse, are among others responding adequately to Harry Keller's direction of the Gordon Kay production.

While the writing falls into a patly contrived mold for this type of material, Herb Meadow's handling of the scripting from the Dan Ullman story passes muster. Meant to abet the suspense and thrills, but having almost an opposite effect, is the Henry Mancini score.

Via extremely loud recording it loses musical value and becomes only noise. The black-and-white CinemaScope lensing by Russell Metty is good. *Brog.*

Doctor at Large
(BRITISH-V'VISION-COLOR)

Third in the "Doctor" series; not up to previous standards, but still good for healthy b.o. returns.

London, March 26.

Rank (Betty E. Box) production and release. Stars Dirk Bogarde, Muriel Pavlow, Donald Sinden, James Robestson Justice; co-stars Shirley Eaton, Derek Farr, Michael Medwin. Directed by Ralph Thomas; screenplay, Nicholas Phipps; camera, Ernest Steward; editor, Frederick Wilson; music, Bruce Montgomery. At Leicester Square Theatre, London. Running time, **104 MINS.**

Simon	Dirk Bogarde
Joy	Muriel Pavlow
Benskin	Donald Sinden
Sir Lancelot Spratt	James Robertson Justice
Nan	Shirley Eaton
Dr. Potter-Shine	Derek Farr
Bingham	Michael Medwin
Eva's Mother	Freda Bamford
Dad Ives	Abe Barker
Maharajah	Martin Benson
P.C.	Cyril Chamberlain
O'Malley	John Chandos
Wilkins	Edward Chapman
Large Woman	Peggy Ann Clifford
Butler	Campbell Cotts
Pascoe	George Coulouris
Girl on Boat	Junia Crawford
Mrs. Digby	Judith Furse
Mrs. Wilkins	Gladys Henson
Emerald	Anne Heywood
Hopcroft	Ernest Jay
Dr. Hatchett	Lionel Jeffries
Smith	Mervyn Johns
Second Examiner	Geoffrey Keen
Jasmine	Dilys Laye
Porter	Harry Locke
House Surgeon	Terence Longdon
Duke of Skye & Lewes	A. E. Matthews
Major	Guy Middleton

The first two in the "Doctor" series were among the top grossers in the domestic market and the latest episode looks set for healthy returns, even though it lacks the sustained humor of its predecessors. "Doctor At Large" is intermittently funny, but the pace is too leisurely to achieve the maximum impact.

The latest Richard Gordon story continues the adventures of the young medico, who qualified in "Doctor In House" and got his first apointment in "Doctor At Sea." This time round, he's on a job hunting spree and the film depicts his experiences and adventures while working for a mean provincial doctor and in a fashionable Park Lane practice, where a good appearance is more important than a good stethoscope. The yarn develops with a blending of light comedy and a dash of sentiment, with punch comedy lines providing timely shots in the arm. They're welcome when they come, but they're too irregular.

Role of the young doctor again is played by Dirk Bogarde in a smooth, confident way. As the story opens, he's in the casualty ward of St. Swithin's hospital (where he originally received his degree) hoping to achieve his vocational ambitions to practice surgery. But he's passed up for the job of house surgeon, after falling foul of James Robertson Justice, who is the hospital's chief consultant. To gain experience (and pay the rent), he begins his job hunting trail, eventually finding his way back to the hospital in the job he wanted from the outset.

The production-direction team of Betty E. Box and Ralph Thomas has again collaborated in this new production, retaining the main cast members of the earlier productions. This time, they use the plot as a means of introducing effective short cameos, which provide a contrast without adding much to the narrative. They've given the pic lush production values and have generously used top feature names, down to the bit parts.

Bogarde, of course, is the mainstay of the story, but Justice again emerges as the standout character, even though his role is reduced to more modest proportions.

Muriel Pavlow offers the main femme interest in an amiable if undistinguished way. Shirley Eaton, as a sexy nurse; Derek Farr, as a fashionable doctor; and Michael Medwin, as Bogarde's professional rival, head a big team which includes such prominent performers as Edward Chapman, Gladys Henson, Mervyn Johns, A. E. Matthews, Guy Middleton, Nicholas Phipps and Anne Heywood. *Myro.*

True As a Turtle
(BRITISH—COLOR)

Frail yarn has some charm, with an able cast striving hard; looks to have moderate chances.

London, March 26.

Rank production and release. Stars John Gregson, June Thorburn, Cecil Parker; co-stars Keith Michell, Elvi Hale, Avice Landone. Directed by Wendy Toye. Screenplay, Jack Davies, John Coates, Nicholas Phipps; camera, Reginald Wyer; editor, Manuel del Campo; music, Robert Farnon. At Leicester Square Theatre, London. Running time, **96 MINS.**

Tony	John Gregson
Jane	June Thorburn
Dudley	Cecil Parker
Harry	Keith Michell
Anne	Elvi Hale
Valerie	Avice Landone
Charbonnier	Jacques Brunius
Mary	Gabrielle Brune
Sir Harold Brazier	Charles Clay
Lady Brazier	Betty Stockfield
Paul	Michael Briant
Susan	Pauline Drewett
1st Officer	John Harvey

The "Turtle" of this film's title is a yacht owned by Cecil Parker, on which John Gregson forces his reluctant bride, June Thorburn, to spend their honeymoon. That very nearly sums up the entire story. Situations that develop make for mild comedy entertainment. It looks to have moderate chances in the United Kingdom.

Three writers take credit for the script, but the trio has not come up with very much substance. The frail yarn depends mainly on atmosphere and on Parker's bellicose personality. There's a minimum of suspense and only a modest amount of incident. Yet, despite these obvious weaknesses, the film generates a degree of acceptable charm.

Almost the entire action takes place at sea and the amateur crew runs into typical difficulties. The pumps fail, the engine-room gets flooded and the boat is enveloped in fog. A false note, however, is injected into the plot in the inference that one member of the crew (Keith Michell) is a crook. In fact, he's an assessor sent to investigate the use of phoney chips at a French casino.

Within the limitations of the story line, Wendy Toye does a competent job of direction, making the most of the material. An able British cast, headed by Gregson, Miss Thorburn and Parker, fill their roles smoothly. Quality color lensing is the top technical credit. *Myro.*

The Phantom Stagecoach

Skulduggery in highway freight. Routine programmer for filler dates on action bills.

Hollywood, March 19.

Columbia release of Wallace MacDonald production. Stars William Bishop, Kathleen Crowley, Richard Webb; features Hugh Sanders, John Doucette, Frank Ferguson, Ray Teal, Percy Helton, Maudie Prickett. Directed by Ray Nazarro. Screenplay, David Lang; camera, Henry Freulich; editor, Edwin Bryant; music conducted by Mischa Bakaleinikoff. Previewed March 18, '57. Running time, **69 MINS.**

Glen Hayden	William Bishop
Fran Maroon	Kathleen Crowley
Tom Bradley	Richard Webb
Martin Maroon	Hugh Sanders
Harry Farrow	John Doucette
Joe Patterson	Frank Ferguson
Ned Riorden	Ray Teal
Mr. Wiggins	Percy Helton
Mrs. Wiggins	Maudie Prickett
Langton	Lane Bradford
Williams	John Lehmann
Sam	Eddy Waller
Varney	Robert Anderson

This is the type of program western that, in pre-television days, was known as a Saturday matinee oater for the kiddie trade. There's too much of the same fare seen for free on the home sets for it to get very far today in the theatrical market, although it suffices as a filler on the action dual bills.

Efforts of a freight line owner, Hugh Sanders, to wreck the passenger-freight line of his rival, Frank Ferguson, is the plot formula used on David Lang's screenplay. Use of an armored stagecoach to attack the rival line gives excuse for the title, but everything, including the dialog, has been seen and heard for many years in this kind of filmfare. Ray Nazarro's direction of the Wallace MacDonald production does provide plenty of gunplay, chases and fisticuffs to qualify it as an actioner.

William Bishop is the secret Wells-Fargo agent come to investigate the holdups, Kathleen Crowley is the innocent heroine who is involved because she's Sanders' niece, and Richard Webb is the good boy gone wrong who is helping Sanders' scheme, but who reforms long enough at the finale to foil the plans. John Doucette, Sanders' bloodthirsty henchman, and Ray Teal, brave but dumb sheriff, are others turning in standard performances to match the leads.

Henry Freulich's lensing is okay, as are most of the other technical credits. The score conducted by Mischa Bakaleinikoff is overused. *Brog.*

War Drums
(COLOR)

The feared Apache warrior, Mangas Coloradas, rides again in the person of Lex Barker; satisfactory action fare for the outdoor market.

Hollywood, March 28.

United Artists release of Howard W. Koch (Bel-Air) production. Stars Lex Barker, Joan Taylor, Ben Johnson; features Larry Chance, Richard Cutting, John Pickard. Directed by Reginald Le Borg. Screenplay, Gerald Drayson Adams; camera (De Luxe Color), William Margulies; editor, John A. Bushelman; music, Les Baxter. Previewed March 21, '57. Running time, **75 MINS.**

Mangas Coloradas	Lex Barker
Riva	Joan Taylor
Luke Fargo	Ben Johnson
Ponce	Larry Chance
Judge Bolton	Richard Cutting
Arizona	James Parnell
Sheriff Bullard	John Pickard
Chino	John Colicos
Dutch Herman	Tom Monroe
Nona	Jil Jarmyn
Yellow Moon	Jeanne Carmen
Clay Staub	Mauritz Hugo
Delgadito	Ward Ellis
Dr. Gordon	Fred Sherman
Fiero	Paul Fierro
Manuel	Alex Montoya
Johnny Smith	Stuart Whitman
Mary Smith	Barbara Parry
Lt. Roberts	Jack Hupp
Trooper Teal	Red Morgan

Mangas Coloradas, the feared Apache warrior, is almost as durable a screen figure as Cochise. This time around, it's Lex Barker portraying the Indian leader and "War Drums" is satisfactory action fare for the outdoor market, where it can go top or bottom of the bill, according to the situation booking it. Lowercase playdates will predominate, however, because of the familiarity of this type entertainment.

Barker is an honorable Indian in the Gerald Drayson Adams script, only breaking his treaty when the whites push him too far. Then he takes to the warpath to avenge injury to his people. Riding with him is Joan Taylor, half-breed whom he has made his warrior-wife because she has the bravery of a male. Only the influence and justice-mindedness of a white friend, Ben Johnson, enables Barker to escape punishment for his affrontry of white man's law, paving the way for a happy ending when the chief and his people are allowed to lose themselves in the mountains instead of being confined to a reservation.

Reginald Le Borg handles the direction with a good action emphasis that carries the ably scripted yarn along at the proper pace. Producer Howard W. Koch, working under the executive supervision of Aubrey Schenck on the Bel-Air presentation, utilizes locations around Kanak, Utah, to advantage for the necessary scenic backing; values which William Margulies' De Luxe Color lensing display expertly.

Barker takes care of his redskin hero chores neatly and Miss Taylor is an alluring warrior distaffer. Johnson rides easily through his assignment and there are capable assists from Larry Chance, Richard Cutting, James Parnell, John Pickard, Tom Monroe, Jil Jarmyn, Jeanne Carmen, Mauritz Hugo, Ward Ellis and others.

Les Baxter's score, editing by John A. Bushelman and other behind-camera functions come off properly. *Brog.*

The Tall T
(COLOR)

Offbeat western starring Randolph Scott; good b.o. potential

Columbia release of a Scott-Brown (Randolph Scott, Harry Joe Brown) production. Stars Scott, Richard Boone, Maureen O'Sullivan, Arthur Hunnicutt; features Skip Homeier, Henry Silva, John Hubbard, Robert Burton. Directed by Budd Boetticher. Screenplay, Burt Kennedy, based on story by Elmore Leonard; camera (Technicolor), Charles Lawton, Jr.; editor, Al Clark; music, Heinz Roemheld. Previewed N. Y. March 21, '57. Running time, **78 MINS.**

Pat Brennan	Randolph Scott
Usher	Richard Boone
Doretta Mims	Maureen O'Sullivan
Ed. Rintoon	Arthur Hunnicutt
Billy Jack	Skip Homeier
Chink	Henry Silva
Willard Mims	John Hubbard
Tenvoorde	Robert Burton
Jace	Robert Anderson
Hank Parker	Fred E. Sherman
Jeff	Chris Olsen

An unconventional western, "The Tall T" passes up most oater cliches to shape up as a brisk entry for the general market. Co-producer Randolph Scott, who tops the cast, is a familiar name to outdoor fans and the lush Technicolor mantling will be another asset, particularly in drive-ins.

There's a wealth of suspense in the Burt Kennedy screenplay based on a story by Elmore Leonard. From a quiet start the yarn acquires a momentum which explodes in a sock climax. Modest and unassuming, Scott is a rancher who's been seized by a trio of killers led by Richard Boone.

Also captured are newlyweds Maureen O'Sullivan and John Hubbard. Originally the outlaws planned a stage robbery, but are urged privately by the craven Hubbard to hold his heiress-wife for ransom in the hope that this move might save his skin. For the gang has already slain a stage relay man, his small son and stage driver Arthur Hunnicutt.

Under Budd Boetticher's direction the story develops slowly, but relentlessly toward the action-packed finale. Scott impresses as the strong, silent type who ultimately vanquishes his captors. Boone is crisply proficient as the sometimes remorseful outlaw leader. His psychopathic henchmen are capably delineated by Skip Homeier and Henry Silva.

Miss O'Sullivan registers nicely as the heiress who wins Scott after the outlaws slay her traitorous husband. Hubbard is good in the latter role as is Hunnicutt as the murdered stage driver. Okay support is provided by Robert Burton, wealthy rancher, and Fred Sherman, the slain relay man, among others.

Outdoor vistas are smartly lensed by Charles Lawton Jr.'s Technicolor camera. Al Clark edited to a tight 78 minutes while Heinz Roemheld's score adds to the suspenseful atmosphere. Other plusses in this Scott-Brown production are George Brooks' art direction and the physical backgrounds. Film's title, incidentally, is rather obscure since there's nothing in the action to explain it.

Gilb.

The Good Companions
(BRITISH-C'SCOPE-COLOR)

Conventional musical version of J. B. Priestley's novel about a touring company; modest local prospects.

London, March 26.

AB-Pathe release of an Associated British production. Stars Eric Portman, Celia Johnson, Hugh Griffith, John Fraser, Janette Scott; features Joyce Grenfell, Bobby Howes. Directed by J. Lee-Thompson. Screenplay, T. J. Morrison from book by J. B. Priestley; camera, Gilbert Taylor; music, C. Alberto Rossi, Paddy Roberts, Geofrrey Parsons: lyrics, Roberts, Parsons. At Warner Theatre, London. Running time **105 MINS.**

Jess Oakroyd	Eric Portman
Miss Trant	Celia Johnson
Morton Mitcham	Hugh Griffith
Susie Dean	Janette Scott
Inigo Jollifant	John Fraser
Jimmy Nunn	Bobby Howes
Elsie & Effie Longstaff	Rachel Roberts
Mr. Joe	John Salew
Mrs. Joe	Mona Washbourne
Jerry Jerningham	Paddy Stone
Partner	Irving Davis
The Three Graces	Shirley Ann Field, Margaret Simons, Kim Parker
Principal Dancer	Beryl Kaye
Mrs. Oakroyd	Thora Hird
Mrs. Jimmy Nunn	Beatrice Varley
Albert	Alec McCowen
Leonard	Jimmy Caroll
Felton	Jeremy Burnham
Daisy	Anna Turner
Mrs. Tarvin	Fabia Drake
Fauntley	Brian Oulton
Mr. Tarvin	Lloyd Pearson
Memsford	Ralph Truman
Lady Parlitt	Joyce Grenfell

J. B. Priestley's homely, and colorful yarn of a thirdrate touring company makes a pedestrian musical, with only modest b.o. prospects in the domestic market. It hardly stands comparison with a Hollywood filmusical.

Much of the characterization and writing quality of the original is lost in T. J. Morrison's conventional screenplay. An old-fashioned story line, without surprise twists, is not aided by the moderate quality of the score. There isn't a standout song, with the closing sequence the only noteworthy production number.

Opening shows some promise. In three short cameos it depicts the way in which Eric Portman, Celia Johnson and John Fraser throw in their lot with the Dinky Doos concert party, who are out of funds and facing disbandment. Miss Johnson provides the cash to keep them in business and the rest of the film describes their unhappy experiences playing No. 3 dates to empty houses, until Janette Scott, the youthful star of the company, and Fraser get their big West End chance.

There is a repetitive quality about much of this but the story livens up when a thug (who had been refused an advertising concession) organizes a rough-house in the theatre on the night when two West End managers are taking their first look at Miss Scott. The petty jealousies among the individual members of the company are sincerely presented, but they, too, follow a stereotyped pattern. Miss Scott makes a refreshing and appealing showing as the concert party star with ambitions, but hardly suggests the top star quality which the story demands. Fraser also turns in a sincere performance as a composer-accompanist, but it's also hard to accept his music as so good the publishers would be competing for it. Bobby Howes, Hugh Griffith, Rachel Roberts, Mona Washbourne and John Salew are among the members of the concert party; Paddy Stone and Irving Davies are accomplished dancers and Joyce Grenfell makes a typical contribution as a wealthy admirer. Both Portman and Miss Johnson add dignity to the story, but are both worthy of stronger roles.

Myro.

L'Homme A L'Impermeable
(The Man in the Raincoat)
(FRENCH)

Paris, March 26.

Cocinor release of Cite-Monica production. Stars Fernandel; features Bernard Blier, Judith Magre, John McGiver, Jacques Duby. Directed by Julien Duvivier. Screenplay, Rene Barjavel, Duvivier from novel by James Hadley Chase, "Tiger by the Tail"; camera, Roger Hubert; editor, Marthe Poncin; music, Georges Van Parys. At Biarritz, Paris. Running time, **110 MINS.**

Albert	Fernandel
Raphael	Bernard Blier
Blondeau	Jean Rigaux
Maurice	Jacques Duby
O'Brien	John McGiver
Eva	Judith Magre
Florence	Claude Sylvain

Putting Fernandel, as a timid, maladroit clarinetist, into the midst of a heavily plotted gangster-murder opus, turns out to be a good idea because he singlehandedly carries this pic: He engenders enough laughs and characterization to keep the film going long after its overplotting begins to buckle. Some pruning would have stressed Fernandel, and made this into a comico-macabre pic that might make a dent in the U.S. It has good possibilities for dubbing for general situations.

Fernandel's wife leaves him for a week and a roguish friend gives him the number of an easy girl. He goes to visit her and she is murdered while he waits. A bearded character has seen him leaving and later comes to blackmail him. Then the heavy plotting starts as an international smuggling ring enters into the affairs and cadavers keep ending up in the bewildered Fernandel's arms.

Director Julien Duvivier has given this a slick coating and gotten fine performances from the cast. But the mixture of a comical, ineffectual man, caught up in a murder, does not completely jell. Bernard Blier is fine as the revolting blackmailer. Technical credits are tops. This is the type of film that, with the necessary tightening, could make a neat American entry. Some okay songs are also worked into it by Georges Van Parys.

Mosk.

The Mexican
(RUSSIAN-COLOR)

Slow moving version of the Jack London story; little U. S. appeal.

Artkino Pictures release of a Mosfilm production. Directed by V. Kaplunovsky. Screenplay, E. Braginsky, from story by Jack London; camera (Magicolor), S. Polyanov; music, M. Chulaki. Previewed at Cameo Theatre, N.Y., March 29, '57. Running time, **82 MINS.**

The Mexican	O. Strizhenov
Paulino Vara	B. Andreyev
Arellano	D. Sagal
May	N. Rumyanteva
Diego	V. Dorofeyav
Maria	T. Samoilova

(In Russian; English Titles)

With "The Mexican," a film version of a Jack London story, Soviet studios appear to be treading on Hollywood's territory. This is a turn - of - the - century melodrama which has a twofisted slugging match as a denouement. While Mosfilm rates "A" for its production effort, the import nevertheless is hopelessly outclassed when judged by American meller standards.

But students of the cinema may find this Artkino release an interesting subject to probe as to the technique and approach employed by the Soviet artisans. The screenplay of E. Braginsky, for example, is a slow moving affair that gets little help from V. Kaplunovsky's heavy handed direction.

Here we have some destitute Mexican revolutionaries who are plotting to overthrow their native government from a Los Angeles hideout. They're long on ambition, but short on funds. However, a lowly compatriot solves the problem by triumphing in a 17-round winner-take-all prize fight. At the fadeout presumably the proceeds are allotted for the avowed purpose.

As might have been imagined scripter Braginsky draws a vivid picture of how the Mexican masses are eagerly awaiting their golden opportunity to break the chains of their masters. Their emancipator in this instance is O. Strizhenov, son of a noted rebel who conceals his identity until midway in the story. His performance, particularly in the marathon bout, is reminiscent of a style favored in Hollywood's silent screen days.

Among other thesping participants are B. Andreyev, fugitive general with grandiose plans; D. Sagal, a fellow revolutionary, and V. Dorofeyav, also a plotter. Their portrayals are generally wooden. A hint of romantic interest is supplied by N. Rumyanteva, 16-year-old typist who's partial to Strizhenov, and T. Samoilova, dancer who gets him at the unrealistic finale.

Femme roles could have been expanded considerably. Fact that they are minimized apparently is in line with Russian custom to get away from the boy-meets-girl stuff as much as possible. Cameraman S. Polyanov wrapped it all up in so-so Magicolor while M. Chulaki's music makes a stab at the right background atmosphere. Art direction and sets have an artificial quality.

Gilb.

The Immortal Garrison
(RUSSIAN)

Soviet film based on Nazi Germany's invasion of Russia; may have some art house appeal.

Artkino release of a Mosfilm Studios production. Directed by Z. Agnanenko and and Edward Tisse. Screenplay, Konstantin Simonov; camera, Edward Tisse; music, V. Basner. At Cameo Theatre, N.Y., March 2, '57. Running time, **90 MINS.**

Baturin	V. Makarov
Kondreyton	V. Emelyanov
Kukharkov	N. Krychitov
Marie	V. Serova

(In Russian; English Titles)

Valor and bravery of the Russian soldier is the theme of "The Immortal Garrison," a Soviet import turned out last year by the Mosfilm Studios. Grimly told, it's a powerful film that may command some attention in art houses.

While on the surface Soviet servicemen look forward to discharge, romance and civilian pursuits, beneath this hopeful veneer at the fortress of Brest on the Polish frontier is an omnious atmosphere. The guard is doubled and the commandant uneasily scans the German-held terrain on the opposite side of the river.

Such was the situation the night before June 22, 1941 when the Nazi invasion of Russia began. The Kontantin Simonov screenplay, which moves in a relentless documentary style, resorts to long flashbacks in recounting the siege of Brest. Opening scenes of the film show the victorious Russian army liberating prisoners well inside Germany.

Among those freed was the lone survivor of Brest, an officer named Baturin. Portrayed by V. Makarov, he recalls his experiences in a vivid flashback. Directors Z. Agranenko and Edward Tisse have extracted a wealth of suspense from Simonov's script and at the same time draw moving performances from Makarov and his colleagues.

Obvious point that the film tries to establish is that the Russian soldier can be a tough adversary if he so wills. For although the Nazi invader was thrusting deep into Russia elsewhere, his timetable was interrupted by the gallant defenders of Brest who vowed resistance "to the last man."

Co-director Tisse's black-and-white photography adequately records the siege along with liberal use of wartime newsreel clips. His scenes of privation affecting Soviet women and children are particularly descriptive. V. Basner's score is in keeping with the tragic story.

Gilb.

Foreign Films

Paris, March 26.
Courte Tete (By a Nose) (FRENCH).
Rank release of Intermondia production.
Stars Fernand Gravey, Jean Richard; features Jacques Duby, Louis De Funes, Darry Cowl, Max Revol, Micheline Dax. Directed by Norbert Carbonneaux. Screenplay, Albert Simenon, Carbonneaux; dialog, Michel Audiard; camera, Roger Dormoy; editor, Jacqueline Thiedot. At Balzac, Paris. Running time, **90 MINS.**

Film tells how a couple of track grifters and touts try to bilk a country bumpkin. It is done mainly with visual gags, and emerges a neat little comedy with good local possibilities on its names and yock qualities. For the U.S. this remains primarily for duals or special situations where it may have some chance.

Pic has enough inventive content and close quarter work also to make this a good U.S. tele possibility. Fernand Gravey is the clever con man who takes the bucolic Jean Richard on a ride only to lose all while Richard cleans up via dumb luck.

Director Norbert Carbonneaux displays a filmic flair which may lead to a top comedy in the near future. Technical credits are par and a group of wellknown comedians also help keep this racy.
Mosk.

Le Septieme Commandment (The Seventh Commandment) (FRENCH). UDIF release of CCFC production. Stars Edwige Feuillere; features Jacques Dumesnil, Maurice Teynac, Jacques Morel, Jean Lefevre, Jeanne Fusier-Gir. Directed by Raymond Bernard. Screenplay, Jacques Companeez, Bernard; camera, Andre Germain; editor, Paul Botie. At Colisee, Paris. Running time, **100 MINS.**

Frothy little item is reminiscent of the pre-war Gallic pix. It concerns a femme grifter who falls for one of her victims and finally finds love in outwitting her ex-collaborators with the help of one of them. It is the annual Edwige Feuillere pic here which means biz on the local marts, but this is limited to special spotting in the U.S. where it might make for an okay exploitation item. Pic lacks art house calibre.

A woman and two associates work the Continental watering spas bilking rich types in a foolproof gimmick of the femme asking them to pawn a trinket for her while an accomplice lifts it.

Miss Feuillere gives this her usual grand dame interp and support is adequate with technical credits par. It lacks some pace and flair.
Mosk.

Le Feu Aux Poudres (The Burning Fuse) (FRENCH—ITALIAN; DYALISCOPE). EFC release of Gallus-Abbey-SGGC-Jolly Film production. Stars Raymond Pellegrin, Peter Van Eyck, Charles Vanel; features Francoise Fabian, Dadio Moreno. Directed by Henri Decoin. Screenplay, Jacques Robert, Albert Simenon, Decoin; camera, Pierre Montazel. At Normandie, Paris. Running time, **110 MINS.**

In black and white C'Scope proportions, via the Gallic anamorphoscopic process Dyaliscope, this spins a familiar tale of a policeman who insinuates himself into a den of gunrunners. He falls for the chief's girl. It all ends with a gunfight and the death of all except the hero and the girl who happily live. Done with slick technical qualities, this looks okay but offers little for the U.S. except for maybe a few dualers. Actors all cavort as well as possible under the banal scripting. Dario Moreno even manages to work in a few songs as one of the thugs. There is enough violence and gunplay for general market chances.
Mosk.

Je Reviendrai A Kandara (I'll Get Back to Kandara) (FRENCH; C'SCOPE; COLOR). Fox Europa release of Jad-Film production. Stars Francois Perier, Daniel Gelin, Bella Darvi; features Jean Brochard, Andre Valmy, Guy Trejan. Directed by Victor Vicas. Screenplay, Jacques Companeez, Alex Joffe, Vicas from a novel by Jean Hougron; camera (Eastmancolor), Pierre Montazel; editor, Jean Feyte; music, Joseph Kosma. At Biarritz, Paris. Running time, **95 MINS.**

Ths mixes a tale of a simple, ineffectual teacher's difficulties in adapting himself to his station in life with a suspense theme since the hero is unwittingly the witness of a murder. Though working up some action, with enough peripities to keep the obvious plotting going, this vacillates between the two even though picking its way neatly through. Being well mounted and with the Bella Darvi name, it might be worth dualer slotting in the U.S.

Director Victor Vicas has given this okay pictorial feel but has lagged in getting the actors into their characterizations. At times the pic loses some of the suspense punch. However Francois Perier manages to make the teacher somewhat of a character. Daniel Gelin emerges honorably from his strange role of the murderer. Miss Darvi photographs agreeably but does not have much to do. Color and C'Scope are well utilized and technical credits oke.
Mosk.

Reproduction Interdite (Copying Forbidden) (FRENCH). Corona release of Orex-Film production. Stars Michel Auclair; features Annie Girordot, Paul Frankeur, Gianni Esposito, Jacqueline Noelle, Lucien Nat. Directed by Gilles Grangier. Screenplay, Rene Wheeler, Grangier from novel by Michel Lenoir; camera, Jacques Lemare; editor, Jacqueline Sadoul. At Marignan, Paris. Running time, **105 MINS.**

Plodding production has an interesting locale via the art galleries and the gangs faking a Gaugin painting. This has enough gloss and movement to hold through its complications, murder and payment for it. Not having the substance for arty house chances, this could be a good dualer on its theme. Its closely knit treatment and explicative qualities slant this as worthy of tele-dubbed chances.

Director Gilles Grangier has given this a slick envelope but the over-extended tale rarely gets the proper suspense. Acting is fine as are technical credits.
Mosk.

Rome, March 26.
Parola Di Ladro (Honor Among Thieves) (ITALIAN). CEI-INCOM release of Panal Film production. Stars Gabriele Ferzetti, Abbe Lane, Andrea Checchi, Nadia Gray. Directed by Giovanni Loy, Gianni Puccini. At Splendore, Rome. Running time, **102 MINS.**

A flip piece with the old theme of the crook with the heart of gold comes off fairly well because it has been made tongue-in-cheek. Abbe Lane has the opportunity to sing several songs and her name may give the film value as a second-feature in American houses.

Filmed in Rome and vicinity, the settings are interesting and the story moves with good pace.

Padri E Figli (Fathers and Sons) (ITALIAN). Cineriz release of Royal Film production. Stars Vittorio DeSica, Marcello Mastroianni, Antonella Lualdi, Marisa Merlini, Franco Interlenghi. Directed by Mario Monicelli. Camera (Totalscope), Lionida Barboni. At the Corso, Rome. Running time, **110 MINS.**

This is an effort at the type of film which gave Italy a great lead in neo-realism, but it doesn't quite come off as planned. The comedy asides have somewhat dispelled the theme of the five families living through the pre-Christmas season. From the usual misunderstandings between the heads of families and their children, the yarn shows the eventual reconciliation of all differences at the holiday season.

In the past this type of film has found more favor with American crix and audiences than with the Italians.

This Could Be the Night
(C'SCOPE—SONGS—DANCE)

Solid romantic comedy recommended for all and has strong word-of-mouth to aid selling.

Hollywood, April 9.
Metro release of Joe Pasternak production. Stars Jean Simmons, Paul Douglas, Anthony Francoisa; features Julie Wilson, Neile Adams, Joan Blondell, J. Carrol Naish. Ray Anthony and orch. Directed by Robert Wise. Screenplay, Isobel Lennart; from short stories by Cordelia Baird Gross; camera, Russell Harlan; editor, George Boemler; musical supervision and song. "Hustlin' Newsgal," George Stoll; title song, Nicholas Brodszky, Sammy Cahn; musical numbers staged by Jack Baker. Previewed April 3, '57. Running time, **104 MINS.**

Anne Leeds	Jean Simmons
Rocco	Paul Douglas
Tony Armotti	Anthony Franciosa
Ivy Corlane	Julie Wilson
Patsy St. Clair	Neile Adams
Crystal	Joan Blondell
Leon	J. Carrol Naish
Hussein Mohammed	Rafael Campos
Mrs. Shea	ZaSu Pitts
Stowe Devlin	Tom Helmore
Waxie London	Murvyn Vye
Ziggy Dawlt	Vaughn Taylor
Mr. Shea	Frank Ferguson
Bruce Cameron	William Ogden Joyce
Mr. Hallerby	James Todd
Music	Ray Anthony Orchestra

As to "This Could Be the Night," once the customer is in, the word-of-mouth praise should be strong because the entertainment is most rewarding, but title and cast lineup hint at nothing out of the ordinary so Metro may have a selling job to make patrons turn out. It is a film that exhibitors can push with a money-back recommendation.

Joe Pasternak, nearing the end of his long Metro association of light, engaging filmfare touched with music, comedy and romance, is in good production form, even though this latest offering is in plain black-and-white CinemaScope without the gaudily-colored, lavish decor that usually marked his presentations. The tints are not missed; neither are big production numbers nor other eye-bedazzlements that are almost a Pasternak trademark. Actually, they are here, too, but only as backdrops sketchily seen while the uninvolved plotting unfolds under the masterly direction by Robert Wise. Socko scripting by Isobel Lennart, sharply, sometimes racily, dialoged, makes the characters easily understood and entertaining.

The plot derived from a series of short stories by Cordelia Baird Gross is a simple affair, up to a point. Jean Simmons is terrific as a clean, pure, but not necessarily naive, grade-school teacher in New York, fresh from New England and Smith College, gets a part-time job as secretary at a night club. Owners are Paul Douglas, ex-bootlegger, and Anthony Franciosa, an after-hours Casanova. The humor, and not a little heart, spring from the efforts of these and other worldly club characters to shelter her and keep the facts of life from being too bruising. When Douglas calls her a "broad" everyone understands he means "lady" and when Franciosa bawls her out, you know he's protecting her standing as a girl who has had no hits, runs or errors.

Douglas scores a success with his crude, but goodhearted, character and there is the assurance of a promising film career for Franciosa, so well does he handle his rakish role. In fact, he will make a lasting impression on femme viewers.

Performance standouts continue right down the cast lineup. Julie Wilson, on whom most of the tune chores fall, is great as a sexed-up torch singer who belts with hit quality such tunes as the title number, "I'm Gonna Live Till I Die," "Taking a Chance on Love," "Sadie Green," and "I Got It Bad" while Ray Anthony and his orch provide potent backing. Storywise, she shares, too, particularly in finding someone to do the algebra lessons for busboy Rafael Campos. Latter is very fine in his part, as are Joan Blondell, terrific as the ex-burlesque queen and mother of dancer Neile Adams; J. Carrol Naish, club cook; Tom Helmore, customer who cooks his own and eats it in the office; Murvyn Vye, gangster; Vaughn Taylor, cynical columnist; William Ogden Joyce, teacher with a yen for Miss Simmons; ZaSu Pitts, Frank Ferguson and others.

Along with Miss Wilson, particular mention goes to Neile Adams, dancer held to her terpsichore by her mother but who yearns for a stove and cook book. She's great in dancing and singing George Stoll's "Hustlin' Newsgal," a number that strips down as far as the Production Code allows to show off a round and fully-packed figure, and is good in the comedy demands of her part. Anthony and his orch put the right beat to "When the Saints Go Marching In," "Trumpet Boogie," "Now, Baby, Now" and the other tunes.

From the background bits of business contributed by the Lennart script and Wise's direction, film draws an earthy, aware-of-life, sauciness that will spark knowing chuckles and these touches abound throughout. General excellence in every department contributes to the entertainment, with mention going to Russell Harlan's topflight photography, Stoll's musical supervision, the staging of the musical numbers by Jack Baker, editing, arc direction, sound and other assists.

Brog.

Yangtse Incident
(BRITISH)

Expertly made filmization of Amethyst's break-through of Red China Blockade; a smash for home market, and possibilities for the U.S.

London, April 2.

British Lion release of a Wilcox-Neagle Production. Stars Richard Todd. Directed by Michael Anderson. Screenplay, Eric Ambler; camera, Gerry Turpin; editor, Basil Warren; music, Leighton Lucas. At Rialto Theatre, London. Running time, **113 MINS.**

Lieut. Com. Kerans	Richard Todd
Leading Seaman Frank	William Hartnell
Colonel Peng	Akim Tamiroff
Lieut. Weston	Donald Huston
Capt. Kuo Tai	Keye Luke
Miss Charlotte Dunlap	Sophie Stewart
Flight Lieut. Fearnley	Robert Urquhart
Lieut. Hett	James Kenney
Lieut. Strain	Richard Leech
Lieut. Berger	Michael Brill
Petty Officer McCarthy	Barry Foster
Commissioned Gunner	Thomas Heathcote
Seaman Walker	Sam Kydd
Williams	Ewen Solon
Seaman Martin	Brian Smith
Seaman Roberts	John Charlesworth
Surgeon Lieut. Alderton	Gordon Whiting
British Ambassador	Basil Dignam
Vice-Admiral	Ralph Truman
Commander-in-Chief Far East	Cyril Luckham

In the last few years British producers have earned a high reputation with a series of films reconstructing epic incidents of the last war. "Yangtse Incident," though a postwar story, attains the same stirring quality and has the makings of smash b.o. in the domestic market. In view of its background, the Civil War in China, it may well turn out to be a worthy contender for boxoffice honors in the U.S.

Story of "Yangtse Incident" is the story of the Amethyst, which, battered though not beaten, broke the Chinese Communist blockade and rejoined the British fleet. The hazardous nature of the event, which quickly made history, is amply demonstrated in this Herbert Wilcox-Neagle production.

The Amethyst is shown sailing up the Yangtse, headed for Nanking on a lawful mission delivering supplies to the British Embassy. Suddenly, without warning, the Red shore batteries open fire and the frigate, after a heavy engagement, is grounded in the mud with many of the crew either killed or wounded and the vessel itself badly knocked about. An attempt to bring needed aid and medical supplies is beaten off by Red artillery and the wounded, sent ashore by the ship's boats, are also a target for the Chinese guns.

Next phase describes the political stage of the negotiations between the British naval commander and the Red colonel, who tries to make propaganda capital out of the incident. But all his attempts to persuade the British to issue an apology for "unprovoked aggression" are resolutely turned down and both sides play a waiting game until the British commander decides to run for it. Under cover of darkness, it's full steam ahead down the Yangtse. Despite the barrage of artillery, the boat gets to the open sea and protection of a superior escort vessel.

Vivid battle scenes have been magnificently handled. All of them look like the real thing and are the action keynote of the production. The on-board scenes are genuine enough too, as the Amethyst was reprieved from the breaker's yard to allow Wilcox to use it in the film. Human interest angles, never the strongest point in such yarns, are carefully interpolated, but there's very little in the way of light relief.

It's a tribute to Michael Anderson's direction that he succeeds in maintaining the tension although the outcome has no suspense angle to it. There's a high standard of acting by an all-round cast, led by Richard Todd as the commander who takes over after the captain is killed in the first engagement. He makes a sturdy, impressive contribution. William Hartnell puts more shading into his part as the leading seaman.

Akim Tamiroff makes a distinguished heavy of the Chinese colonel. Donald Huston gives a sincere study. Technically the film is above average and the credit to Commander Kerans, as technical adviser, may be a clear indication of the authenticity of treatment.

Myro.

Kronos
(REGALSCOPE)

Expertly-made science-fictioner, with special emphasis upon special effects; good prospects for exploitation market.

Hollywood, April 9.

Twentieth-Fox release of a Kurt Neumann production, produced in association with Jack Rabin, Irving Block, Louis DeWitt. Stars Jeff Morrow, Barbara Lawrence, John Emery; features George O'Hanlon, Morris Ankrum, Kenneth Alton, John Parrish. Directed by Neumann. Screenplay, Lawrence Louis Goldman, from a story by Irving Block; camera, Karl Struss; special effects, Rabin, Block, DeWitt; editor, Jodie Copelan; music, Paul Sawtell, Bert Shefter. Previewed April 1, '57. Running time, **78 MINS.**

Les	Jeff Morrow
Vera	Barbara Lawrence
Eliot	John Emery
Culver	George O'Hanlon
Dr. Stern	Morris Ankrum
McCrary	Kenneth Alton
General Perry	John Parrish
Manuel	Jose Gonzales
Pilot	Richard Harrison
Nurse	Marjorie Stapp
General	Robert Shayne
Weather Operator	Donald Eitner
Sergeant	Gordon Mills
Guard	John Halloran

"Kronos" is a well-made, moderate budget science-fictioner which boasts quality special effects that would do credit to a much higher-budgetted film than this Regal production for 20th-Fox release. Feature shapes up as a strong entry for the exploitation market, where it will be packaged by 20th with another Regal output, "She Devil."

Produced and directed by Kurt Neumann in association with Jack Rabin, Irving Block and Louis DeWitt, who designed and created the special effects which give eerie overtones to pic's unfoldment, the Lawrence Louis Goldman script tells of the efforts of a people from outer space to capture Earth's energy. To do this, they send an accumulator to Earth, which is directed in its movement by the head of a great American lab, whose brain has been seized by a higher intelligence from space—and he is forced to work its will. Feature takes its title from the accumulator, a huge metal cube-shaped figure 100 feet high, which is dubbed Kronos, after the mythological god of evil, and which nothing seemingly can destroy

Jeff Morrow heads cast as a scientist who has charted the course of the asteroid which has transported the accumulator to Earth, his efforts finally responsible for its ultimate destruction. His role is convincingly played and John Emery is convincing as the lab head forced by the outer-space intelligence to direct the monster as it sucks up power and energy. Barbara Lawrence is in strictly for distaff interest, but pretty. George O'Hanlon delivers as another scientist and Morris Ankrum is a doctor killed by Emery when he learns lab head's secret.

Neumann's general handling of subject is high-class and he gets top assistance from technical departments. Outstanding here are Karl Struss' camera work, Theobold Holsopple's production design, Jodie Copelan's editing, sound by James Mobley and an effective music score by Paul Sawtell and Bert Shefter.

Whit.

International Police
(BRITISH—C'SCOPE)

Fast moving action meller, showing work of Interpol in tracking down international dope peddling gang; sturdy possibilities.

London, April 2.

Columbia release of a Warwick (Irving Allen-Albert R. Broccoli) production. Stars Victor Mature, Anita Ekberg, Trevor Howard. Directed by John Gilling. Screenplay, John Paxton; camera, Ted Moore. Stars Pavey; editor, Richard Best; music, Richard Bennett. At Odeon Theatre, Leicester Square, London. Running time, **92 MINS.**

Charles Sturgis	Victor Mature
Gina Broger	Anita Ekberg
Frank McNally	Trevor Howard
Amalio	Bonar Colleano
Breckner	Andre Morell
Varolli	Martin Benson
Helen	Dorothy Alison
Captain Baris	Peter Illing
Fayala	Eric Pohlman
Curtis	Sidney Tafler
Salko	Alec Mango
Murphy	Lionel Murton
Bartender	Danny Green
Singer	Yana
Joe	Sidney James

The worldwide ramifications of Interpol, the international policing organization, provides the background for this fast-moving action melodrama. Victor Mature, Anita Ekberg and Trevor Howard take good care of the marquee values. With its obvious exploitation angles, the pic should be a sturdy b.o. contender.

A monochrome production in CinemaScope, "International Police" offers a Cook's tour with its locales, which range from London to N.Y. and Rome to Athens. The emphasis is on movement and the storyline is deliberately geared to insure ample incident. The back alleys of Rome and Athens provide a sinister setting for the subject matter.

Mature is a member of the FBI's narcotics bureau, who's assigned to work with Interpol in tracking down a gang of dope peddlers. For him it's in the nature of a personal revenge as his sister was strangled to death by the unknown gang leader. Howard is the villain, who usually succeeds in keeping one jump ahead of the law, ruthlessly using Miss Ekberg as his courier, after she's been involved in a shooting. Mature's chase starts in London and takes him all over Europe before he eventually catches up with the wanted man on the New York docks.

A foreword to the film by Sir Ronald Howe, a former British chief of Interpol, explains the operations of the service as "the longest arm of the law." And the subsequent action describes how the forces of all nations work together and exchange information to make crime an even more hazardous operation.

Mature plays it straight as the relentless pursuer, but he doesn't go in for the kid glove treatment. Miss Ekberg also plays it straight, but on a single, sad key. Howard, for his part, admirably suggests the ruthless sinister villain with a cultural accent.

Bonar Colleano gives a lively study of the police informer turned amateur sleuth. Remainder of cast help keep the action rolling. Yana has a solo number in a night club scene in which her looks are more impressive than her vocalistics. John Gilling's direction sustains the lively pace. Other technical qualities are up to standard.

Myro.

Shoot-Out at Medicine Bend
(SONG)

A thee-and-thouing Quaker by day, Randolph Scott is a dispenser of rough justice at night in this okay actioner for the outdoor market.

Hollywood, April 9.

Warner Bros. release of Richard Whorf production. Stars Randolph Scott, James Craig, Angie Dickinson; features Dani Crayne, James Garner, Gordon Jones, Trevor Bardette, Don Beddoe, Myron Healey, John Alderson, Harry Harvey Sr., Robert Warwick. Directed by Richard L. Bare. Screenplay, John Tucker Battle, D. D. Beauchamp; camera, Carl Guthrie; editor, Clarence Kolster; music, Roy Webb; song, "Kiss Me Quick." Ray Heindorf, Wayne Shanklin. Previewed March 26, '57. Running time, **86 MINS.**

Cap Devlin	Randolph Scott
Clark	James Craig
Priscilla	Angie Dickinson
Nell	Dani Crayne

Maitland	James Garner
Clegg	Gordon Jones
Sheriff	Trevor Bardette
Mayor	Don Beddoe
Sanders	Myron Healey
Walters	John Alderson
King	Harry Harvey Sr.
Brother Abraham	Robert Warwick

Randolph Scott masquerades as a thee-and-thouing Quaker during the day, dispensing range justice at night in this okay actioner for the outdoor market. It's in austere black-and-white, as contrasted with Scott's usual tinted entries, but the western action plays off handily for release intentions.

Scott and a couple of buddies, just out of the Union Army, lose their complete outfits to some thieves, get new garments from friendly Quakers and use the peaceful garb to scout out the skullduggery being practiced in Medicine Bend by James Craig, greedy town tycoon who sells bad ammunition to settlers, gyps them in his general store and gets what's left in his saloon. However, the climactic battle finds Scott, his buddies and the surprisingly belligerent Quakers too much for Craig and his gang so law and order come to the range after some solid outdoor dramatics that will please the western fan.

Scott is good as the hero, as are James Garner and Gordon Jones as his sidekicks. A couple of distaff cuties, Angie Dickinson and Dani Crayne, beautify the western setting, pairing with Scott and Garner, respectively, for the fadeout clinch. Additionally, Miss Crayne pertly handles "Kiss Me Quick," a catchy tune by Ray Heindorf and Wayne Shanklin. Craig is okay as a typical oater heavy, aided in the dirty work by Myron Healey and John Alderson. Others working satisfactorily under Richard L. Bare's action-minded direction include Trevor Bardette, Don Beddoe, Harry Harvey Sr. and Robert Warwick.

Richard Whorf's production has all the necessary outdoor values, less color, and the screenplay by John Tucker Battle and D. D. Beauchamp manages to freshen standard material right well. Lensing by Carl Guthrie, editing and other technical factors are good assists, as is the music by Roy Webb. *Brog.*

She Devil

Fly serum cures woman but ruins her character. Modestly entertaining science - fiction thriller for exploitation packaging.

Hollywood, April 3.
20th-Fox release of Kurt Neumann (Regal) production, directed by Neumann. Stars Mari Blanchard, Jack Kelly, Albert Dekker; features John Archer, Fay Baker, Blossom Rock, Paul Cavanagh. Screenplay, Carroll Young and Neumann; from "The Adaptive Ultimate" by John Jessel; camera, Karl Struss; editor, Carl Pierson; music, Paul Sawtell, Bert Shefter. Previewed April 1, '57. Running time, 77 MINS.

Dr. Bach	Albert Dekker
Dr. Scott	Jack Kelly
Kyra	Mari Blanchard
Hannah	Blossom Rock
Kendall	John Archer
Mrs. Kendall	Fay Baker
Sugar Daddy	Paul Cavanagh
Floor Manager	George Baxter
Nurse	Helen Jay
Red Head	Joan Bradshaw
Interne	Tod Griffin

Story content qualifies "She Devil" for the science-fiction league although only a few thrill points are reached during the uneven, 77-minute unfoldment. The title and the presence of Mari Blanchard in the title role, however, provide exploitation angles that make it an okay mate for teaming with "Kronos," another Regal Films science-fictioner which 20th-Fox is releasing.

A serum derived from fruit flies, "nature's most adaptive insect," is developed by a biochemist in his search for a cure for disease. The serum is tried on a hopelessly ill TB patient, who miraculously recovers, but with some unorthodox personality and physical changes. The gal can't be injured and she can change her coloring in an instant from brunette to blonde. Miss Blanchard, the patient, uses her newly-found powers to get ahead in the world. First she kills the wife of wealthy John Archer and then marries him. Later, she removes the husband. By this time Jack Kelly, the biochemist, and his sponsor, Albert Dekker, are sick of what they have fashioned and trick her into an operation that returns her to the tubercular state and death.

Kurt Neumann, who produced and directed for Regal from the script he wrote with Carroll Young, fails to generate much of a chiller atmosphere for the melodramatics and the screenplay is rather talky. Miss Blanchard is obviously alluring, while Kelly and Dekker are adequate to the demands of their top roles. Archer, Fay Baker, Blossom Rock, Paul Cavanagh and others are up to requirements. *Brog.*

Susana y Yo
(Susanna and Me)
(SPANISH)

Madrid, April 2.
C.E.A. release of Benito Perojo production. Stars Abbe Lane and Jorge Riviere; features Juan Jose Menedez, Mary Lamar, Guadalupe Munoz Sampedro, Felix Fernandez, Lidia Alfonsi, Xavier Cugat and orch. Directed by Enrique Cahen Salaberry. Story and screenplay, Augustin Laguilhoat; camera (Eastmancolor), Alejandro Ulloa; music, Francis Lopez. Running time, 90 MINS.

Talent from three continents join together for this first Spain try at modern musical comedy. Abbe Lane and Xavier Cugat from the U.S. have never before been screened in such ungraceful musical posture. Director Salaberry and star Jorge Riviere came all the way from Argentina to no avail. Production lacks any semblance to Hollywood musicals although Miss Lane shines through clouds singing and swinging "Arrivederci Roma" and two Cha-Cha-Chas. Cugat's piano accompanies an opening chanson but otherwise he stiffly fronts a raggy-looking local combo, and the chorus that couldn't get within 1,000 kilometers of the Waldorf. Color photography is uneven and rarely favors Miss Lane.

Story has staid college prof (Riviere) in love with a belle of the boites (Miss Lane). Prof's distaff progenies spend classroom hours trying for stranglehold on his heart which complicates main love affair. Chanteuse lives with a fortune-telling aunt and gently distracted inventor uncle, replicas from "Man Who Came To Dinner." Plot lengthens and thins out as auntie's magic lotion makes the girl a man in the professor's image. Thereafter double identity uses up mucho footage in hackneyed routines. Although Riviere tries hard in difficult role, script defeats in limiting screen time of eye-filling Lane whose appearances were trimmed by censor.

Felix Fernandez is outstanding as supporting uncle. Italo Lidia Alfonsi looks good as Miss Lane's friend. Francis Lopez tunes are pleasant in primitive score. Hollywood choreography and music-scoring knowhow could have cued this production for U.S. market interest. As preemed, film is strictly for local and South American screens. *Werb.*

Boy On a Dolphin
(C'SCOPE—COLOR—MUSIC)

Highly appealing filmization of novel background in Greece and may boom Greek tourism as "Three Coins In The Fountain" did Rome's. Alan Ladd, Sophia Loren, Clifton Webb for marquee.

20th-Fox release of Samuel G. Engel production. Stars Alan Ladd, Sophia Loren, Clifton Webb. Directed by Jean Negulesco. Screenplay, Ivan Moffat & Dwight Taylor from novel by David Divine; camera (DeLuxe), Milton Krasner; special effects, Ray Kellogg; editor, William Mace; asst. directors, Eli Dunn & Carlo Lastricati; music, Hugo Friedhofer, conducted by Lionel Newman; song title song based on Tinafto music by Takes Morakis, Greek text by J. Fermanglou, American lyric by Paul Francis Webster, music adapted by Hugo Friedhofer; orchestrations, Edward B. Powell; Greek Folk Dances & Songs Society "Panegyris," Dora Stratou, director; Fivos Anoyanakis, artistic & music director; Yianni Fleur, choreographer. Tradeshown, N. Y., April 5, '57. Running time, 103 MINS.

James Calder	Alan Ladd
Victor Parmalee	Clifton Webb
Phaedra	Sophia Loren
Government Man	Alexis Munotis
Rhif	Jorge Mistral
Dr. Hawkins	Laurence Naismith
Niko	Piero Giagnoni
Miss Dill	Gertrude Flynn
William B. Baldwin	Charles Fawcett
Mrs. Baldwin	Charlotte Terrabust
Miss Baldwin	Margaret Stahl
Chief of Police	Orestes Rallis

Shot in Greece's Aegean Sea and environs, with the interiors filmed in Rome's Cinecitta Studios, "Boy On A Dolphin" presents not only an offbeat locale which should prove generally appealing, but it is coupled with a compelling story. These elements, in combination with Alan Ladd, Sophia Loren and Clifton Webb for the marquee, spell sturdy boxoffice.

Miss Loren, particularly, with that now well-identified and highly merchandiseable Italo-style "built," will be something for the boys (and girls) at the wickets.

Akin to the DeLuxe spectrum values that made 20th-Fox's "Three Coins In A Fountain" a smash tourist trailer for Rome this film will have equal values for the land of Spyros Skouras' birth. The story brings into natural focus the ancient traditions and the ultramodern tourist-catering appurtenances in line with the cinematurgy.

The quest of the titular "Boy On A Dolphin" develops into a "chase" that is a pleasant blend of archaeological research, quasi-cloak & dagger stuff (vide, Clifton Webb), and earthy, primitive acquisitiveness.

Ladd is the archaeologist who has been engaged on several occasion in besting Webb's passion for antiquities. He has been invariably successful in restoring them to their rightful owners. The "boy," in the same idiom, is historic Greek property. Miss Loren's hunger for a home, the greed of an expatriate, alcohol-sotted British medico (Laurence Naismith); and the trickery of her Albanian lover (Jorge Mistral, a strong face in a chameleon role), conspire to thwart the American archaeologist and collaborate with the aesthetic, wealthy Webb in spiriting the ancient treasure from Greek waters.

The action moves from the initial sponge-diving scenes to the cosmopolitan wharf cafes; from the 14th century monastery where ancient Greek monks' archives attest to the authenticity of "The Boy On A Dolphin" (circa 100 A.D.), to Webb's luxurious yacht, to some more aquatic hijacking of the treasure. The inevitable "chase" (this is where the Greek police and the government man who looked like still another sinister character until he identified himself) furnishes the denouement wherein Miss Loren's appealing kid brother (Piero Giagnoni) proves the unexpected hero.

The Aegean sea and its islands, the rugged native environs, the bold, sun-emblazoned beauty of the natural terrain, the traditional music and Greek folk dances against the 20th century background of counter-intrigue, along with the romantic elements, combine to make "Boy" a high voltage boxoffice entry.

The credits are many. Director Jean Negulesco has not overextended any of the values, playing it in the right tempo for the locale and likewise playing down the neo-melodramatics. The natural scenic opportunities are made to order for Milton Krasner's DeLuxe color lensing and he makes generous use of all camera angles.

Ladd is the all-American boy archaelogist; Webb the suave dastard (because of his dollars), Miss Loren a lustily appealing native Greek girl whose endowments fall automatically into character. Jorge Mistral has one of those strong he-man physogs that can be cast romantically or in "heavy" roles. Naismith gives his alky medico assignment proper minor key performance. All the other values are of like top standard. *Abel.*

The Buster Keaton Story
(VISTAVISION)

Donald O'Connor as the famed silent screen pantomimic. An on-and-off entertainment. Mild possibilities.

Paramount release of Robert Smith and Sidney Sheldon production. Stars Donald O'Connor and Ann Blyth; features Rhonda Fleming, Peter Lorre. Directed by Sheldon. Written by Sheldon and Smith; camera, Loyal Griggs; editor, Archie Marshek; music, Victor Young. Previewed at Loew's Sheridan Theatre, N. Y., April 10, '57. Running time, **91 MINS.**

Buster Keaton .... Donald O'Connor
Gloria .... Ann Blyth
Peggy Courtney .... Rhonda Fleming
Kurt Bergner .... Peter Lorre
Larry Winters .... Larry Keating
Tom McAfee .... Richard Anderson
Joe Keaton .... Dave Willock
Myrna Keaton .... Claire Carleton
Buster Keaton (7 years old) Larry White
Elmer Case .... Jackie Coogan
So. American Indian Chief Dan Seymour
Asst. So. American Indian Chief —Mike Ross
Edna (Larry's Secretary) .... Nan Martin
Nick (Bar Owner)....Robert Christopher
Franklin (Butler)........Richard Aherne
Studio Policeman .... Tim Ryan
Theatre Manager .... Joe Forte
Mr. Jennings .... Ralph Dumke
Holt .... Larry Rio
Wife .... Constance Cavendish
Duke Alexander .... Ivan Triesault
Guest .... Constance Cavendish
Leading Woman.........Pamela Jayson
Leading Man .... Keith Richards
Susan's Father (playing cards) Dick Ryan
Boarder .... Guy Wilkerson
Mrs. Anderson .... Lizz Slifer

Vintage comedy is reprised and comes off as frequently funny stuff as Donald O'Connor deadpans through the same pantomimicry that Buster Keaton projected before the screen learned to talk. But "Buster Keaton Story" too often is Keaton as a pathetic figure in this fictionalized account of his life—a pathetic figure in a story that's uninterestingly developed.

It's in this respect that the Robert Smith-Sidney Sheldon production misses out. Possibly it might have been better to have no story, per se, at all, for there's much fun watching O'Connor executing the wonderful absurdities that made Keaton a comedic favorite of yesteryear. To Monday-morning-quarterback the film, it appears that any kind at all of a continuity would have sufficed so long as it provided O'Connor with sufficient springboard for resurrection of the Keaton routines.

Sheldon and Smith, though, wrote out a script that has the deadpan artist springing to the top in the picture business, hitting the bottle, spending big, going on the downtrend as sound is introduced to the film industry and, finally, returning to vaudeville. Built in, too, is a romance angle involving Ann Blyth which is unconvincingly handled. Keaton in the picture simply is not a simpatico character and just why Miss Blyth would want to marry him when he's on the skids is difficult to accept.

Paramount release has as its highlights the identical skits which Keaton himself used to put on, and O'Connor does a splendid imitation job. With flat hat and stone face he looks the part and the talent shows through as he copies the old master in great slapsticks.

Boxoffice prospects are only mild and this because of the plotting of "Keaton Story." The full potential is not realized because of Smith's and Sheldon's insistence on building story—story which doesn't have adequate impact—around a funny man who had funny material and to boot, a clever performer in O'Connor to recreate it all.

Film has O'Connor leaving a vaude act with his mother and father, crashing Hollywood's gates, and quickly hitting the top as actor and his own director. He has a crush on Rhonda Fleming, who colorfully plays an ambitious glamor puss, and buys a palatial home where he hopes to install her as his wife. She takes to foreign royalty instead.

Miss Blyth is a casting director at "Famous Studios," takes a liking to O'Connor at the start, gives him his first break, falls hard but only to be overlooked. Miss Blyth, who turns in an appealing performance, treks abroad to forget but upon returning finds O'Connor as an alcoholic hasbeen and marries him.

Peter Lorre is properly disagreeable as a film director who scowls as O'Connor, with plenty of moxie, shows Hollywood how comedy should be done and proves it. Larry Keating plays the studio boss with full authority and Richard Anderson is effective as an attorney who seeks Miss Blyth but loses out to O'Connor. Jackie Coogan does an okay bit part and others in the cast measure up to requirements.

Score by the late Victor Young is a major asset, providing the comedy bits with added punch. Camera work and technical credits standard. *Gene.*

Smallest Show on Earth
(BRITISH)

London, April 9.

Small-time film theatre as background of diverting comedy which puts the spotlight on exhibition. Lively b.o. contender anywhere.

British Lion release of a Frank Launder and Sidney Gilliat production. Stars Virginia McKenna, Bill Travers, Peter Sellers, Margaret Rutherford and Bernard Miles. Produced by Michael Relph. Directed by Basil Dearden; screenplay, William Rose and John Eldridge, from an original story by William Rose; camera, Douglas Slocombe; editor, Oswald Hafenrichter; music, William Alwyn. At London Pavilion, London, April 9, '57. Running time, **81 MINS.**

Matt Spenser .... Bill Travers
Jean Spenser .... Virginia McKenna
Robin Carter .... Leslie Phillips
Percy Quill .... Peter Sellers
Mrs. Fazackalee.....Margaret Rutherford
Old Tom .... Bernard Miles
Hardcastle .... Francis De Wolff
Marlene Hogg .... June Cunningham
Mr. Hogg .... Sidney James

Launder and Gilliat have come up with a neat little comedy in "The Smallest Show on Earth," which should do fine all-round biz, not only in its domestic market, but in most other territories, too. It's a safe contender for the US arties and also merits wider showing.

William Rose, who scripted "Genevieve," has this time fashioned a shrewd and bright comedy around the exhibition side of motion pictures. It's not focussed on the opulent side of the theatre business, but the centre of interest is a small, derelict picture house inherited by a young struggling writer.

The theatre, in a small, smelly provincial town, is adjacent to the mainline railroad station and each time a train passes by, the entire theatre vibrates. The staff comprises three ancients — Margaret Rutherford, who played the piano in the silent days, but now sits at the cash desk; Peter Sellers, the boothman with a weakness for whisky; and Bernard Miles, a doorman and general handyman, who dreams of the day he'll be given a sparkling new uniform.

When Bill Travers and Virginia McKenna inherit the theatre, their immediate reaction is to sell out to the opposition, who had made a substantial offer to the previous owner. But the offer now forthcoming would not even be adequate to meet the inherited debts, so they set about on a big bluff, pretending to re-open in the hope that the bids will be bettered. Their plot is discovered and they're compelled to go into the exhibition business, but a series of misadventures eventually decides them to abandon the project. The old doorman, inadvertently learning of their decision, promptly sets fire to the rival theatre and the next morning the price has soared to enable the other exhibitor to keep in business until his own place can be re-opened.

The accent all the way through is on lighthearted comedy, and the William Rose-John Eldridge screenplay keeps the action rolling on a nice satirical key. The film is loaded with delightful touches, and there's one prolonged laughter sequence when the projectionist is on a drinking bout and Bill Travers takes over the booth. Everything goes wrong, from the film running out of sync, at the wrong speed, upside-down and in reverse. During the upside-down sequence some members of the audience stand on their heads to follow the action.

A small, but expert, cast make a lively contribution to the yarn. Bill Travers and Virginia McKenna are an attractive romantic team, Peter Sellers, a noted impressionist, gives an old-time air to the boothman, Margaret Rutherford forcefully portrays the sentimental cashier and Bernard Miles delivers a fine character sketch as the old doorman. Leslie Phillips, Francis De Wolff, June Cunningham and Sidney James complete the very small team of polished players. Crisp direction and editing set the style for the other technical credits. *Myro.*

Rendez-Vous a Melbourne
(FRENCH; DOCUMENTARY; COLOR)

1956 Olympic Games set up as a full-length release. A French Concession "monopoly" well done.

Paris, April 16.

Gueguen-Gergely-Freemantle release of C.S.A. production. Directed by Rene Lucot, assisted by Jean Averty, Serge Griboff, Donald Eckles, Claire Attali. Commentary, Lucot, Raymond Marcillac said by Francois Perier, Marcillac; camera (Agfacolor), Jacques Duhamel, Pierre Gueguen, Pierre Lebon, Georges Leclerc; editor, Jean Dudrumet, Monique Lacombe; music, Christian Chevallier. Previewed in Paris. Running time, **110 MINS.**

Olympic-Games in Australia last November have been given the documentary treatment. That includes glimpses of Melbourne itself, closeups of the athletes in relaxation as well as performance and views of the spectators. The immediacy has passed but it may be presumed that the subject matter will fetch this French item considarable playdates in America and round the world.

Monopoly rights were handed the French group by the Australians to the vexation of western newsreel and video interests who squawked about the three minute coverage allotted to them and more or less boycotted the Olympics.

Slow motion, zoom lenses and deft cutting weld this 15-camera treatment into a well planned and manned picture of the 15-day Olympics. *Mosk.*

Time Without Pity
(BRITISH)

Michael Redgrave as an alcoholic with 24 hours to save his son from the gallows.

London, April 2.

Eros release of a Harlequin Production. Stars Michael Redgrave, Ann Todd and Leo McKern; co-stars Peter Cushing. Directed by Joseph Losey. Screenplay, Ben Barzman; camera, Frederick Francis; editor, Alan Osbiston; music, Tristram Cary. At Astoria, London. Running time, **90 MINS.**

David Graham .... Michael Redgrave
Honor Stanford .... Ann Todd
Robert Stanford .... Leo McKern
Jeremy Clayton .... Peter Cushing
Alec Graham .... Alec McCowen
Mrs. Harker .... Renee Houston
Brian Stanford .... Paul Daneman
Vicky Harker .... Lois Maxwell
Maxwell .... Richard Wordsworth
Barnes .... George Devine
Agnes Cole .... Joan Plowright
Under Secretary .... Ernest Clarke
Padre .... Peter Copley
Espresso Bar Proprietor...Richard Leech
Prison Governor .... Hugh Moxey
1st Warder .... Julian Somers
1st Journalist .... John Chandon
Comedian .... Dickie Henderson Jr.

A highly theatrical treatment of a bid to save an innocent boy from the gallows, "Time Without Pity" is a taut, well-made meller, which can expect reasonable returns. It's a potentially acceptable dualer for the U.S.

That the boy, due to be executed the following morning, is innocent is established in the few shots which precede the credit titles. Although that device removes one element of suspense, it still leaves another: will the boy's drunken father be able to establish the fact within 24 hours?

The father, Michael Redgrave, had been having treatment as an alcoholic during his son's trial and returns to London only a day ahead of the execution. The legal evidence, as the lawyers point out, is overwhelmingly loaded against the condemned youth, but the father, in between alcoholic bouts, achieves what the police failed to do—but at the cost of his own life.

Relying largely on intuition and playing a hunch, Redgrave suspects Leo McKern of being implicated in the crime. McKern, a wealthy motor magnate, had befriended his boy and the killing actually took place in his apartment. As the evidence mounts against him, McKern is confident his alibis will hold good; but one by one they begin to crack. As time slips by, Redgrave makes the desperate sacrifice to pin the guilt on the other man and free his son.

The production also strikes a topical note in its plea against capital punishment although it never sets out to be a propaganda instrument. There are tense and harrowing death cell scenes and a wide variety of familiar London backgrounds.

Redgrave's performance carries the stamp of sincerity. It is a moving, pathetic study of a father trying to make up for his past failures. Ann Todd, as Leo McKern's wife, has a less demanding part, which she fills authoritatively. McKern's performance is noteworthy for its frequent hysterical outbursts. Peter Cushing, as the lawyer, Alec McCowen, as the condemned boy, and Renee Houston, as the mother of one of McKern's mistresses, top a fine supporting team. Joseph Losey has given the piece vigorous, yet sensitive direction. The background music is, at times, overpowering.
Myro.

Koenigin Luise
(Queen Luise)
(GERMAN—COLOR)

Berlin, April 5.

Gloria release of Divina production. Stars Ruth Leuwerik and Dieter Borsche. Features Bernhard Wicki, Rene Deltgen, Hans Nielsen. Directed by Wolfgang Liebeneiner. Screenplay, Georg Hurdalek; camera (Eastmancolor), Werner Krien; music, Franz Grothe; sets, Rolf Zehetbauer. At Gloria Palast, Berlin. Running time, 10½ MINS.

Queen Luise .... Ruth Leuwerik
King Friedrich Wilhelm III .... Dieter Borsche
Czar of Russia .... Bernhard Wicki
Napoleon .... Rene Deltgen
Hardenberg .... Hans Nielsen
Prince Louis Ferdinand .... Peter Arens
Talleyrand .... Charles Regnier
Czar's advisor .... Alexander Golling
Luise's father .... Friedrich Domin
Countess Voss .... Margaret Haagen
Country-Woman .... Lottie Brackebusch

The adult life of Luise, Prussia's most popular queen and still today, nearly 150 years after her death, a darling in many Germans' hearts is treated in this Eastmancolored Divina production in a manner calculated to please majority of German average audiences. Title and big name cast will probably give this Gloria release outstanding prospects, but its chances with more fastidious audience and outside Germany are dubious.

The basic fault of this production lies in the fact that director Wolfgang Liebeneiner aimed at giving this film a "message" which unfortunately is conventionally directed and based on a banal script. Much of the dialog sounds corny. Film lacks action and remains dull. It shows how Queen Luise persuades her peace-loving husband, King Friedrich Wilhelm III, into being a more active ruler. He gives in and abandons his neutral stand, making a defense deal with the Czar to oppose the threatening Napoleon. Latter invades Prussia, beats the Prussian and the Czar's armies, and finally signs a deal with the Czar which robs Prussia of her eastern territory. Queen Luise realizes that the fall of her husband has been partly her fault and, suffering from complexes of guilt, dies at the age of 34.

The acting is not always convincing though Ruth Leuwerik is a beautiful Queen. Her gestures and mimicry tend to be repetitious and she's often overly tense in dramatic scenes. Dieter Borsche, her king-husband, is far more at home with his role and as a calm and sensitive ruler has a number of impressive scenes.

Rene Deltgen portrays Napoleon but can hardly be taken serious: He makes nearly a farce out of his role. Bernhard Wicki comes along as the Czar, a role which also could be more polished. More prolific performances are turned in by Charles Regnier as Talleyrand, the French diplomat, and Alexander Golling as the Czar's advisor. Supporting cast also includes Hans Nielsen as Hardenberg, the Prussian foreign minister, a fine performance; and Margarete Haagen as Countess Voss, a routine portrayal.

The Eastmancolor photography is an advantage about this otherwise rather disappointing production.
Hans.

Le Cas du Dr. Laurent
(Dr. Laurent's Case)
(FRENCH)

Paris, April 16.

Cocinor release of Cocinor-Cocinex-Sedif production. Stars Jean Gabin, Nicole Courcel; features Balpetre, Sylvia Monfort, Michel Barbey, Georges Lannes, Arius. Directed by Jean-Paul Le Chanois. Screenplay, Le Chanois, Rene Barjavel; camera, Henri Alekan; editor, Emma Le Chanois. At Balzac, Paris. Running time, 110 MINS.

Dr. Laurent .... Jean Gabin
Francine .... Nicole Courcel
Wife .... Sylvia Monfort
Engineer .... Michel Barbey
Dr. Bastid .... Arius

Middleaged doctor tried to introduce hygiene and medicine in a provincial, backward village, and especially the concept of painless birth. As unreeled it's a conventional tale of a good-natured, physically ill doctor gently trying to open the minds of an inbred group, and its main angle lies in an actual painless birth scene. Handled with tact story neatly leads up to this dramatic occurrence before a sceptical medical board and the townspeople.

For the U.S. pic shapes mainly as an exploitation item on its subject and actual birth scenes. Characterizations remain "surface" but workmanship is good. Jean Gabin carries weight as the tired doctor.

Nicole Courcel shows a control and depth as an unwed mother-to-be who becomes the doctor's ally in fighting the town's small mindedness.

The births are eased via the breathing exercises that the mothers perfect before the actual happening.
Mosk.

The Garment Jungle

Realistic and intense dramatic documentary-like story of organized labor vs. "protection against the unions" in New York's garment centre. Based on Readers' Digest articles. No names and no scopes and thus needs (and deserves) heavy sell effort.

Columbia release of Harry Kleiner production. Stars Lee J. Cobb, Kerwin Mathews, Gia Scala, Richard Boone, Valerie French; features Robert Loggia, Joseph Wiseman, Harold J. Stone, Adam Williams, Wesley Addy, Willis Bouchey, Robert Ellenstein, Celia Lovsky. Directed by Vincent Sherman. Screenplay, Kleiner; from articles by Lester Velie; camera, Joseph Biroc; editor, William Lyon; music, Leith Stevens. Previewed in New York, April 18, '57. Running time, 88 MINS.

Walter Mitchell .... Lee J. Cobb
Alan Mitchell .... Kerwin Mathews
Theresa .... Gia Scala
Artie Ravidge .... Richard Boone
Lee Hackett .... Valerie French
Tulio Renata .... Robert Loggia
Kovan .... Joseph Wiseman
Tony .... Harold J. Stone
The Ox .... Adam Williams
Mr. Paul .... Wesley Addy
Dave Bronson .... Willis Bouchey
Fred Kenner .... Robert Ellenstein
Tulio's Mother .... Celia Lovsky

Lester Velie's articles in Readers Digest on labor warfare within the needle trade have been turned into forceful dramatic screen fare. Harry Kleiner has scripted hard-hitting material and his production, under Vincent Sherman's taut direction, frequently has the impact and believability of a documentary.

The story within the framework of unionists pitted against goons, that of a young man who recognizes the evil inherent in hiring "protection" while his father, a dress manufacturer, rebels at the idea of a union moving in, is developed with an intensity akin to the unreeling of "On the Waterfront." Latter concerned itself with rackets on the docks; "Garment Jungle" with like power offers an insight on the struggle of the International Ladies Garment Workers to do away with the sweat shops on New York's Seventh Avenue.

It's propaganda for union labor, perhaps, but any union adversary of the hired muscle-and-murder element, as herein depicted, must look heroic. And the Velie articles which form the basis of the picture were factual; the twists and turns of the screenplay are fictional but the basics have the appearance of authenticity.

"Garment Jungle" is a well performed production, but there isn't much marquee lure in the names. Film is within reach of "A" boxoffice but substantial selling effort will be required, along with a playoff that allows for word of mouth.

Lee J. Cobb fits just fine as the dress plant owner intent on being his own boss without union "interference." He built his own company and why shouldn't he run it as he sees fit? he reasons. Cobb plays the part to the hilt. He swaggers, he's defiant and finally he's disillusioned and repentent upon learning that the protection he's buying actually has entailed first the murder of his partner and then of a union organizer.

Robert Loggia is a union zealot who plays with fiery conviction and Gia Scala as his wife is in the familiar tradition of earthy Latino imports. She's an emotional, charged-up femme who adds zest to "Jungle."

Kerwin Mathews does well as Cobb's son although he appears bland at times in contrast with the more outgoing and forceful nature of the other characters. Richard Boone is sure footed as the heavy, Valerie French is attractive as Cobb's romantic concern and Joseph Wiseman does a highly skilled job in portraying a union weakling. Harold J. Stone, Adam Williams, Wesley Addy, Willis Bouchey, Robert Ellenstein and Celia Lovsky all are competent in less prominent assignments.

The key value in "Jungle" is its realism. In one instance a newsreel shot is used with striking effect, this showing the actual funeral of a murdered union organizer with thousands of sympathizers milling about the scene. While this is the only as-it-actually-happened sequence, the tone of the rest of the picture is one of authenticity, with the probable exception of the highly melodramatic ending in which Mathews prevents Boone's escape from the police.

Kleiner's dialog is sharp and, at times, frank. There are repeated references to Loggia as a "Spik," for example. That won't go down well in many towns. But there's no strain for shock material; even the showing of Miss Scala nursing a baby seems natural.

Film provides opportunity for modeling fancy gowns, designed by Jean Louis; Joseph Biroc's black-and-white photography is remarkably effective, Leith Stevens' music provides appropriate background-ing and other technical credits all are good.
Gene.

The Iron Sheriff

A sheriff gives evidence that will hang his son, then beats the guilty verdict. Slightly different for western market.

Hollywood, April 16.

United Artists release of Jerome C. Robinson (Grand) Production. Stars Sterling Hayden, Constance Ford, John Dehner, Kent Taylor; features Darryl Hickman, Walter Sande, Frank Ferguson, King Donovan, Mort Mills, Peter Miller. Directed by Sidney Salkow. Written by Seeleg Lester; camera, Kenneth Peach; editor, Grant Whytock; music, Emil Newman. Previewed April 12, '57. Running time, 73 MINS.

Sheriff Galt .... Sterling Hayden
Claire .... Constance Ford
Pollock .... John Dehner
Quincy .... Kent Taylor
Benjie .... Darryl Hickman
Ellison .... Walter Sande
Holloway .... Frank Ferguson
Leveret .... King Donovan
Sutherland .... Mort Mills
Jackson .... Peter Miller
Kathi .... Kathy Nolan
Walden .... I. Stanford Jolley
Judge .... Will Wright
Bilson .... Ray Walker
Tilyou .... Bob Williams

The sheriff's son is in big trouble—sentenced to hang on evidence given by his own father. That's the somewhat different plot slant in "The Iron Sheriff" and it supplies sufficient entertainment to meet the demands of the western programmer market, albeit the playoff's on the slow side.

Sterling Hayden essays the strong-jawed sheriff satisfactorily, while Darryl Hickman is okay as the son. There is several well-drawn character studies under Sidney Salkow's direction, including John Dehner's portrayal of the defense lawyer fighting the efforts of prosecutor Frank Ferguson. Positions of some of the other characters in the Seeleg Lester screenplay aren't too clear, but the types pass muster, including Constance Ford, in love with the sheriff; Kent Taylor, town publisher and romantic rival; Walter Sande, marshal; and King Donovan, telegrapher who actually did the holdup murder of which Hickman is accused.

Hickman is in jail when the plot opens and the town's buzzing with talk that he'll get an acquital because he is the sheriff's son. The trial is working that way, too, until dad tells of a death-bed confession of a witness that names the boy as the killer. The sheriff still beieves his son innocent and through some range detecting the trail eventually leads to Donovan as the only man who knew the express money shipment was coming through.

Jerome C. Robinson's Grand production for United Artists release is equipped with all the necessary outdoor values, plus a note of suspense, particularly in the mental debating about whether the sheriff will bring in Donovan dead or alive. That he does the latter, despite his original intent of cold-bloodedly shooting him down, upgrades the moral tone of the ending. Kenneth Peach's lensing and Emil Newman's background score that their jobs excellently, and other technical credits are up to standard, too.

Brog.

Joe Butterfly
(C'SCOPE—COLOR)

Armed service comedy reminiscent of "Teahouse of August Moon." Probably will find favor with general audiences for okay b.o.

Universal release of Aaron Rosenberg production. Stars Audie Murphy, George Nader, Keenan Wynn and Burgess Meredith. Features Fred Clark, John Agar and Kieko Shima. Directed by Jesse Hibbs. Screenplay, Sy Gomberg, Jack Sher and Marion Hargrove; based on a play by Evan Wylie and Jack Ruge; camera (C'Scope-Technicolor), Irving Glassberg; editor, Milton Carruth; music supervision, Joseph Gershenson. Previewed in N.Y., April 9, '57. Running time, **90 MINS.**

Pvt. John Woodley........Audie Murphy
Sgt. Ed Kennedy .... George Nader
Henry Hathaway............Keenan Wynn
Joe Butterfly .... Burgess Meredith
Cheiko .... Kieko Shima
Col. E. E. Fuller..............Fred Clark
Sgt. Dick Mason .... John Agar
Sgt. Jim McNulty........Charles McGraw
Little Boy .... Shinpei Shimazaki
False Tokyo Rose .... Reiko Higa
Father .... Tatsuo Saito
Mother .... Chizu Shimazaki
Major Ferguson......Herbert Anderson
Oscar Hulick .... Eddie Firestone
Yeoman Saul Bernheim......Frank Chase
Col. Hopper .... Herold Goodwin
Soldier .... Willard Willingham

The similarity between Universal's "Joe Butterfly" and Metro's recent "Teahouse of the August Moon" is obvious. Both pit the American Army of occupation against benevolent con men in incongruos Oriental settings. Sakini, the Mr. Fixit of "Teahouse's" Okinawa, has a spiritual kinsman in Joe Butterfly of Japan. Joe, a former house boy to American gangsters, knows all the angles. His questionable techniques, while frowned upon by the law, nevertheless prove beneficial in overcoming Army red tape and aid a group of harrassed Yank magazine correspondents in putting out their publication.

Despite the sameness in the situations and characterizations of the two pictures, "Joe Butterfly" emerges as a reasonably amusing farce that should find favor with general audiences. The incidents may appear exaggerated and impossible, but to any former GI who has lived through the confusion of an occupation, they will probably seem real in retrospect. The picture follows the general pattern of service comedies in that it places a group of supposedly well-meaning GIs against the Army system. Their ingenuity in outwitting the system through the employment non-GI methods sets the stage for the comedy.

Feature opens with a reprise of a newsreel shot of the Japanese surrender to the Yank Command on the battleship Missouri. In the first contingent of occupation troops are a group of Yank correspondents who are ordered to turn out their newspaper in time to greet the main influx of the American Army. The task is not as easy as it seems. However, with the aid of the conniving Joe Butterfly, the GI newsmen find a press and set up heaquarters in a sumptuous private home. In return, the Yank men "raid" the Army commissary to provide food for Butterfly's army of destitute relatives.

Audie Murphy, an old service hand in both real and reel life, is seen as a brash photographer who constantly gets into the hair of the Army brass. George Nader, as the sergeant in charge of the Yank reporters, is the sober and steadying influencing who goes along with the shenanigans in order to meet his deadline. Keenan Wynn is an obnoxious civilian correspondent who has his eyes on the Yank press so he can publish an edition of his magazine in Japan. Fred Clark is an easily-combustible scatterbrained colonel. Burgess Meredith, absent from the screen for some time, is the larcenous Joe Butterfly.

The Sy Gomberg-Jack Sher-Marion Hargrove screenplay, based on a play by Evan Wylie and Jack Ruge, delicately introduces a romance between Murphy and a pretty Japanese girl. But, like the romance in "Teahouse," it is handled with kid gloves and emerges as an romantic attachment rather than a love affair. A side issue in the raucous hijinks, punctuated by the "borrowing" of vehicles, high living, and various run-ins with Army brass, is the search for a prize war criminal—Tokyo Rose, the femme disk jockey familiar to GIs who served in the Pacific area during the war.

Meredith is excellent as the ingratiating Joe Butterfly. The rest of the principals also turn in good performances. Good assists are offered by Herbert Anderson as the meek officer in charge of the Yank group; Eddie Firestone as the colonel's aide; John Agar, Charles McGraw, and Frank Chase as Yank correspondents; Kieko Shima as Murphy's romantic interest, and Reiko Higa, as a phony Tokyo Rose.

Jesse Hibbs has directed the Aaron Rosenberg CinemaScope production broadly and gets the most out of the farcical situations. Since the picture was filmed on location in Japan, there is nothing in it that will offend the Japanese. The authentic backgrounds are an asset in chronicling the events. Technical aspects, including Irving Glassberg's Technicolor lensing, are first-rate.

Holl.

Behind Show-Window
(Russian)
(COLOR)

Artkino release of Mosfilm Studios production. Stars I. Dmitriev, N. Medvedeva, A. Kuznetsov, O. Anofriev. Directed by S. Samsonov. Screenplay, A. Kapler; camera (Magicolor), F. Dobranow; music, A. Isfasman. At Cameo Theatre, N.Y., April 17, '57. Running time, **84 MINS.**

Krylov ....I. Dmitriev
Andreyeva .... N. Medvedeva
The Lieutenant ....A. Kuznetsov
Sonya .... O. Anofriev

(In Russian; English titles)

It seems that the Russian film industry "goes Hollywood" in this fluffy little comedy. It's the type of picture that Hollywood turned out in abundance in the pre-television era. Despite the trite story, it marks a departure from the Soviet's usual brand of heavy-handed propaganda films. It was obviously made for entertainment only, but while it may prove amusing to Soviet citizens saddled with propaganda films for years, there is very little in it that will appeal to U.S. audiences.

The action takes place in a modern department store in Moscow. Intertwined with three different romances is the attempt by a gang of crooks to steal merchandise from the state store. This may come as a revelation to many, for it is perhaps the first time that the Russians have admitted that there are gangsters and con men in Communist Russia.

Holl.

The Girl in the Kremlin

Wildly improable fast-buck exploitation-slanted release improvises on Stalin death theme. Mediocre entertainment but considerable come-on values.

Hollywood, April 23.

Universal release of Albert Zugsmith production. Stars Lex Barker, Zsa Zsa Gabor, Jeffrey Stone; features Maurice Manson, William Schallert, Natalia Daryll, Aram Katcher, Norbert Schiller, Michael Fox. Directed by Russell Birdwell. Screenplay, Gene L. Coon, Robert Hill; based on story by Harry Ruskin, DeWitt Bodeen; camera, Carl Guthrie; editor, Sherman Todd; music supervision, Joseph Gershenson. Previewed April 11, '57. Running time, **81 MINS.**

Steve Anderson .... Lex Barker
Lili Grisenko .... Zsa Zsa Gabor
Greta Grisenko .... Zsa Zsa Gabor
Mischa Rimilkin........... Jeffrey Stone
Molda (Stalin) .... Maurice Manson
Jacob Stalin .... William Schallert
Dasha .... Natalia Daryll
Lavrenti Beria .... Aram Katcher
Ivan Brubof .... Norbert Schiller
Igor Smetka .... Michael Fox
Olga Smetka .... Elena Da Vinci
Nina .... Phillipa Fallon
Deshilov .... Charles Horvath
Commissar .... Kurt Katch
Girl at Cafe .... Vanda Dupre
Tata Brun .... Alfred Linder
Dr. Petrov .... Gabor Curtiz
Dancer .... Della Malzahn

"The Girl In the Kremlin" poses the theory that Stalin, while dead, isn't buried in Moscow's Red Square along with Lenin. It is obviously exploitation-slanted for hard-hitting ballyhoo and fast playdates to make a quick cleanup, which it could even though the entertainment is no more than ordinary.

Along with the Stalin death gimmick, the Albert Zugsmith production tosses in several others for the fast sell. Not the least of these is the head-shaving trick which could make the femmes cringe as they watch attractive Natalia Daryll bare her noggin under Red razors. Some should be encouraged, however, because she remains attractive, even with the bare pate, thanks to a feminine face and a generous supply of curves.

The screenplay by Gene L. Coon and Robert Hill from a story by Harry Ruskin and DeWitt Bodeen is more often than not illogical, with the hokum laid on thick. No trouble is taken to explain many of the situations and in such farfetched surroundings the players can't be very convincing. Russell Birdwell's direction is okay, considering the obviousness of the presentation, although the guidance tends to a deliberateness that at times becomes nothing more than slowness.

Lex Barker, ex-O.S.S. man, is cloak-and-daggering in Europe when Zsa Zsa Gabor, Lithuanian refugee, asks his help in finding her twin sister, nurse who disappeared after Stalin's reported death. The viewer knows that Stalin underwent plastic surgery and decamped with Beria and a large supply of cash to parts unknown. Working with equally intrepid Jeffrey Stone, dashing one-armed underground spy, Barker locates Stalin in Greece and, after some incredibly stupid manuevering for heroes, the quarry escapes via burning to death when his car goes off a mountain road.

As noted, the three stars can't do much with the material. Same is true of other players, including Maurice Manson, who appears as the pre and-post-plastic surgery Stalin; William Schallert, his son who hates him and is eventually responsible for the mountain death plunge; Aram Katcher, the hateful Beria; Norbert Schiller, Michael Fox and others.

Carl Guthrie's lensing includes some scenes aimed at creating suspense, sometimes successfully, and there is very busy musical backing that follows stock melodrama lines under Joseph Gershenson's supervision. Other credits are standard.

Brog.

The Living Idol
(C'SCOPE—COLOR)

Reincarnation yarn against Mexican scenery. Richly mounted but routine meller with no names. So-so b.o.

Metro release of Albert Lewin-Gregorio Walerstein production. Stars James Robertson-Justice, Steve Forrest, Liliane Montevecchi; features Sara Garcia, Eduardo Noriega. Directed by Lewin. Story and screenplay, Lewin; camera (Eastman color), Jack Hildyard; music, Manuel Esperon and Rudolof Halffter; song, "Tepo," by Isamel Diaz, arranged by Esperon; editor, Rafael Ceballos; associate Mexican director, Rene Cardona; associate Mexican cinematographer, Victor Herrera. Previewed in New York April 17, '57. Running time, **101 MINS.**

Terry Matthews .... Steve Forrest
Juanita .... Liliane Montevecchi
Dr. Alfred Stones
James Robertson-Justice
Elena .... Sara Garcia
Manuel .... Eduardo Noriega

Having produced, written and directed "The Living Idol," Albert Lewin also has unintentionally demonstrated that picure-making today has grown too complicated to be a one-man's job. He's latched on to an intriguing idea with definite exploitation values, but it gets lost in a maze of sometime obscure dialog and in the attempt to equate the scientific approach with proof of the supernatural.

Film holds out promise for a lot more than it actually delivers. It's always on the threshold of something happening, but not until the last reel does any excitement really start. It's then that Lewin and his photographer, Jack Hildyard, pull all the stops as they follow a jaguar through the empty streets of Mexico City and stage a wild struggle between man and beast.

Up to that time, Lewin tries to put across the picture's "Leitmotiv," i.e. a soul can wear out many bodies. It's a tedious process, as he establishes the fact that the jaguar god of old senses in a modern Mexican girl the reincarnation of a maiden that was once sacrificed to him.

The basic story line, backgrounded by an archeological camp in the Yucatan and later Mexico City, is valid enough. But Lewin has allowed the picture to ramble and lag, particularly in the person of archeologist James Robertson-Justice who believes in the spell cast by the mythical gods of the Aztecs, and who is obsessed with the idea of human sacrifice.

Occasionally Lewin has caught moments of tension and wild visual excitement, such as the girl spellbound by a ritual dance and the flashback when, bound to a cross, she waits to be sacrified to the jaguar. But inbetween it's mostly talk and scenery and confusion.

Performances are adequate, but not more than that. Robertson-Justice is a very capable actor and he does his best with the pedantic lines handed to him. Steve Forrest seems wooden as the reporter, and Liliane Montevecchi is a dark-eyed young lady of questionable talents. Her role is most unconvincing. Sara Garcia is good as an elderly woman and Eduardo Noriege is gentle as Miss Montevecchi's father.

Lewin's direction shows occasional flashes of imagination in specific scenes, but on the whole is routine. He's also guilty of some instances of outright bad taste, such as the scene when the girl burps loudly after eating her soup. As for the script, it makes it tough for the actors to sound real. And they don't.

One of the saving graces is Hildyard's lensing, which achieves some stunning effects and which feeds on the beauties of Mexico. Much of the excitement in the film must be credited to him. Eastman Color is a definite asset for the picture. Ismael Diaz's song, "Tepa," has good rhythm and Rafael Ceballos' editing is routine.

Subject treated in "Living Idol" is a publicity natural and exhibs should latch on to the various angles in the light of the lack of star-names. If the film is going to be sold at all, it's on its exploitation values.   *Hift.*

Something of Value

Race hatred melodrama. Story of the Mau Mau uprising, with Rock Hudson, Dana Wynter, Sidney Poitier for marquee value. Grim but effective.

Metro release of Pandro S. Berman production. Stars Rock Hudson, Dana Wynter, Wendy Hiller, Sidney Poitier; features Juano Hernandez, William Marshall, Robert Beatty, Walter Fitzgerald, Michael Pate, Ivan Dixon. Directed by Richard Brooks. Screenplay by Brooks from Robert C. Ruark's "Something of Value"; camera, Russell Harlan; music, Miklos Rozsa; editor, Ferris Webster. Previewed in New York April 24, '57. Running time, 113 MINS.

Peter McKenzie	Rock Hudson
Holly Keith	Dana Wynter
Elizabeth Newton	Wendy Hiller
Kimani	Sidney Poitier
Njogu	Juano Hernandez
Leader	William Marshall
Jeff Newton	Robert Beatty
Henry McKensie	Walter Fitzgerald
Joe Matson	Michael Pate
Lathela	Ivan Dixon
Karanja	Ken Renard
Witch Doctor	Samadu Jackson
Adam Marenga	Frederick O'Neal
Waithaka	John J. Akar

This is Hollywood's first serious attempt to get to the roots of the Mau Mau uprising in Kenya, East Africa, and the dramatization of the Robert Ruark bestsel'er comes off as potent screen entertainment. It's a grim yarn, and a violent one, but it also manages to combine the action angles with plenty of thoughtful dialog concerning the rights and wrongs of the bloody revolt.

Richard Brooks, in his dual capacity as director and writer, has fashioned the kind of picture that will mean different things to different people. To some, it'll be no more than the story of the uprising, of an incredibly cruel, to-the-death struggle between a ragged band of natives and the white settlers. There's enough menace in this one to make the blood run chill.

To others, "Something of Value" will say a lot more, for the screen here also speaks of the rights of man, of equality and human dignity, of condescending colonialism in an age of comparative enlightenment, and of the waking up of the dark Continent. With all the excitement of raids and sudden death, it is still a film that can be greatly moving as it follows the tortured course of a young Negro boy, driven into desperation and violence against his better judgment, and into his death by treachery.

Shot against the actual backgrounds, which enhances the realism of the picture, most of the figures in the film ring true and their motives are believable. Cast generally is good, with Sidney Poitier as Kimani, the intelligent Kikuyu boy, delivering an outstanding portrayal. He carries the picture and gives it power and strength as one watches his resentment grow and finally explode into an orgy of killing. The performance has depth and great understanding and rates plenty kudos.

Opposite him, Rock Hudson brings a quiet dignity to the role of Poitier's white boyhood friend. The relationship between the two men, fighting on opposite sides, each with vengeance in the eye and yet full of compassion, is the picture's symbol of faith of a better world to come.

Perhaps, in the figure of Hudson, "Something of Value" crosses that thin dividing line between entertainment and "preaching." He represents the faction that believes in the rights of the Englishmen who came to Kenya to farm, yet knows, too, that colonialism cannot sur-

vive unless it is tempered with understanding and a willingness to recognize the dignity of the individual, white or black. It is he who argues that one cannot deprive a people—primitive or not—of their customs and the things they hold sacred, without replacing them with "Something of Value."

There may be some Pixie folk whose ears may be offended by the outspoken dialog about the yearning for equality and the rights of man. For them, the picture has the blazing guns and the scenes of natives cowering before the blows of the white man, smouldering with hate, but taking it all the same. They may find some apt parallels in this film.

If there is a weak link in the proceedings it is Dana Wynter. Apart from looking lovely, she delivers very little and her lines are hand'ed without conviction. Actress has registered a lot more strongly in other films. Wendy Hiller as Elizabeth Newton, whose husband is cut down by the Mau Mau and who is severely wounded in a raid, etches a strong portrait in a brief role.

Walter Fitzgerald plays the gentle and considerate ranchowner with the proper degree of understatement, which makes his eventual furor the more believable. As the native leader, Juano Hernandez turns in a good performance that reaches its climax when, trembling before a stone God, he denounces his comrades. Michael Pate hits the right note as a sadistic farmer.

Many elements have been pulled together by director Brooks, and he has achieved a difficult balance, not only in his pacing, but also in the presentation of the points-of-view. There is no question that "Something of Value" does have a point-of-view in itself, and it is one which every decent American should applaud. Yet, in arguing the British settlers' point, and in portraying the merciless and cruel violence unleashed on them by the Mau Mau, Brooks has done justice to his subject.

He has played for realism in his scenes. He doesn't hide the ugliness of the race relations, nor that of the indiscriminate eye-for-an-eye killing. There is tension in his film, and the feeling of a primitive people aroused and fanned into action by irresponsible leaders.

"Something of Value" doesn't argue for violence. It argues for understanding. Yet it manages, in the person of Poitier, to give a glimpse of the new Africa—young, easily misled through appeal to bitter resentments, and yet conscious of new responsibilities. For Brooks' script makes it quite plain that, even as he turns killer, Poitier never abandons his doubts whether what he is doing is right. He has killed and he has plundered the house where he was brought up with kindness. And when he agrees to surrender without a final fight, it is like an act of expiation, a triumph of reason over emotion.

Russell Harlan's lensing is very effective and contributes to the film's dramatic impact, particularly in his excellent closeups. Miklos Rozsa's music catches the flavor of the country and of the proceedings. But it is Ruark's story, and it is Poitier's film. And the tagline is effectively written, when Hudson's gun-carrier muses out loud as they wait for the trapped Poitier:

"I want the same thing for us as he does. Only I think there's a different way of getting it."   *Hift.*

The Kettles on Old MacDonald's Farm

A new Pa Kettle (Parker Fennelly) joins Ma (Marjorie Main) in rural antics down on on the farm. Average example of homespun series.

Hollywood, April 30.

Universal release of Howard Christie production. Stars Marjorie Main, Parker Fennelly, Gloria Talbott, John Smith; features George Dunn, Claude Akins, Roy Barcroft, Pat Morrow, George Arglen. Directed by Virgil Vogel. Screenplay, William Raynor, Herbert Margolis; camera, Arthur E. Arling; editor, Edward Curtiss; music supervision, Joseph Gershenson. Previewed April 23, '57. Running time, 79 MINS.

Ma Kettle	Marjorie Main
Pa Kettle	Parker Fennelly
Sally Flemming	Gloria Talbott
Brad Johnson	John Smith
George	George Dunn
Pete Logan	Claude Akins
J. P. Flemming	Roy Barcroft
Bertha	Pat Morrow
Henry	George Arglen

Ma and (new) Pa Kettle handle the rural antics in this ninth of the Universal comedies and score the expected laugh results. Entry is par for the series course, meaning the market that usually finds the Kettle pix profitable will continue to do so with this one.

Parker Fennelly takes over the Pa character long done by Percy Kilbride and stays close to the type created by the latter in preceding entries, although not with as sure a comedy sense. Marjorie Main's Ma creation handles most of the laugh load, with a surefire assist from George Dunn. Latter, doing a takeoff on his garbage man role from U's "Away All Boats," is a decided help in sharpening the chuckles in the William Raynor-Herbert Margolies screenplay.

Ma, Pa, and large brood get involved this time around in setting up marriage for Gloria Talbott, spoiled rich girl, and John Smith, poor but honest lumberman. Title comes from fact the Kettles have purchased Old MacDonald's farm, leaving their former ramshackle acres deserted. Latter serves as the site for Ma and Pa to teach Miss Talbott the ins-and-outs of being a backwoodsman wife.

Mixed in with the romance is a marauding bear known as Three-Toes, and his presence accounts for quite a bit of comedy chase footage as the action plays off under Virgil Vogel's okay direction. Shots of a lumberman's rodeo, showing tree-topping, log-rolling and similar outdoor sports are included as a background for plot antics.

Cast members assembled for Howard Christie's production do their chores satisfactorily, and the technical ends, including Arthur E. Arling's lensing and the editing by Edward Curtiss, are capable.   *Brog.*

Johnny Tremain
(COLOR)

Boston Tea Party and other events in Americana make only fair entertainment.

Hollywood, April 30.

Buena Vista release of Walt Disney presentation. Stars Hal Stalmaster, Luana Patten, Jeff York; features Sebastian Cabot, Dick Beymer. Directed by Robert Stevenson. Screenplay, Tom Blackburn; based on the Esther Forbes novel; camera (Technicolor), Charles P. Boyle; editor, Stanley Johnson; music, George Bruns; songs, Bruns and Blackburn. Previewed April 26, '57. Running time, 80 MINS.

Johnny Tremain	Hal Stalmaster
Cilla Lapham	Luana Patten
James Otis	Jeff York
Jonathan Lyte	Sebastian Cabot
Rab Silsbee	Dick Beymer
Paul Revere	Walter Sande

Samuel Adams .... Rusty Lane
Josiah Quincy .... Whit Bissell
Ephraim Lapham .... Will Wright
Mrs. Lapham .... Virginia Christine
Dr. Joseph Warren .... Walter Coy
Major Pitcairn .... Geoffrey Toone
General Gage .... Ralph Clanton
Colonel Smith .... Gavin Gordon
Admiral Montagu .... Lumsden Hare
Jehu .... Anthony Ghazlo Jr.

The Boston Tea Party, the Battles of Lexington and Concord, and other events in America's War of Independence provide a historically-significant background for "Johnny Tremain." Unfortunately, the Buena Vista release doesn't have the excitement, spirit or suspense that must have featured the struggle for the principles of freedom. It is only fair entertainment at best and faces a spotty boxoffice.

The elements of dramatic action needed for this type of costume feature are sacrificed to chronological authenticity in the Tom Blackburn screenplay from the Esther Forbes novel, and Robert Stevenson's direction can do little more than let it play as written. Even the conspiracy to end taxation without representation and subsequent key parts in the Minute Men rebellion play with a tameness that arouses little interest. Same goes for the performances which, while competent, lack fire or derring-do.

Story is told through the eyes of the title character, a silversmith apprentice played by Hal Stalmaster. He becomes involved in the secret plotting of such historical names as Paul Revere, Sam Adams, James Otis, and Dr. Joseph Warren, who want to gain recognition and representation for the colonists in the New World. The dumping of the British tea into Boston harbor, while the British admiral watches and practically admires the deed, makes the event's significance dim. Maybe it happened that way, but dramatic license would not have been overboard had some suspense via threat to the boarders been injected, or even implied. Same goes for most of the other historically correct events, like Revere's midnight ride, the flashing of the signal lanterns, etc.

Along with young Stalmaster, Luana Patten is pretty as his young love. Jeff York appears as Otis; Sebastian Cabot as Stalmaster's British-minded uncle; Dick Beymer, young printer; Walter Sande as Revere; Rusty Lane as Adams; Whit Bissell as Josiah Quincy; Walter Coy as Dr. Warren. Among others are Lumsden Hare as the British admiral; Geoffrey Toone, Ralph Clanton and Gavin Gordon as British officers.

"Johnny Tremain" and "Liberty Tree" are two George Bruns-Tom Blackburn tunes heard in the film. Bruns also did the background score. Charles P. Boyle's Technicolor lensing is good, with the color adding to the costumes and period settings of early-day Boston. *Brog.*

Sierra Stranger

Howard Duff turns Good Samaritan and gets into trouble; pretty confusing plotting for the western market.

Hollywood, April 29.

Columbia release of Norman T. Herman (Acirema) production. Stars Howard Duff, Gloria McGhee, Dick Foran, John Hoyt, Barton MacLane, George E. Stone; features Ed Kemmer, Robert Foulk, Eve McVeagh, Henry "Bomber" Kulky, Byron Foulger. Directed by Lee Sholem. Story and screenplay, Richard J. Dorso; camera, Sam Leavitt; editor, Leon Barsha; music, Alexander Courage. Previewed April 26, '57. Running time, **73 MINS.**

Jess Collins .... Howard Duff
Meg Anderson .... Gloria McGhee
Bert Gaines .... Dick Foran
Sheriff .... John Hoyt
Lem Gotch .... Barton MacLane
Dan .... George E. Stone
Sonny Grover .... Ed Kemmer
Tom Simmons .... Robert Foulk
Ruth Gaines .... Eve McVeagh
Matt .... Henry "Bomber" Kulky
Claim Clerk .... Byron Foulger

The range action in "Sierra Stranger" shows the trouble a man can get into by trying to help another. Plot follows a talkative course and the action doesn't carry much conviction so the best that shapes for this Columbia entry, produced by Norman T. Herman under the Acirema Productions banner, is the program oater market.

Howard Duff plays the title role in the Richard J. Dorse story and if he is puzzled as much of what's going, so will the viewer be. By the time plot angles begin to clear up, it's established that the likeable young miner Duff saves from a beating is really a bad boy, who goes on to prove it by killing a stage guard in a holdup and trying to gun Duff. With these facts made clear, it dawns on Duff why the citizens of Colton have had no use for him when he mentioned the young man's name. Lee Sholem's direction is handicapped somewhat by the complication-laden screenplay and the multitude of characters who have no apparent reason for most of their actions. Still, he gets suitable performances from the cast, from Duff on down, and Ed Kemmer, being introduced as Sonny Grover, the bad boy, makes an okay impression. Among others are Gloria McGhee as a woman who gets tired of waiting for Kemmer to straighten out and turns to Duff for romance; Dick Foran, Kemmer's half-brother who believes the lad can do no wrong; John Hoyt, a do-little sheriff; Barton MacLane and Robert Foulk, seemingly town heavies because they resent Kemmer's claim-jumping; George E. Stone, town drunk, and Eve McVeagh, Foran's suffering wife.

Technical credits are standard for budget outlay. *Brog.*

Jews in Poland
(Yiddish)
(DOCUMENTARY)

Federation of American Polish Jews release of Simon Federmann-Polish State Film Studios Films. Directed by B. Ladowicz. Narrative by A. Tadziemec. At Cameo Theatre, N.Y., April 17, '57. Running time, **42 MINS.**

(In Yiddish; English titles)

"Jews in Poland," a documentary purporting to show the recovery of the Jewish population in Poland, appears anachronistic in the light of the recent reports of a wave of anti-semitism there. Filmed in 1946 by Simon Federman with the cooperation of the Polish State Film Studios, it retraces the destruction of the Warsaw Ghetto by Hitler's mobsters, mentions the heroes of the underground, and shows Jews of the new Poland at work and play.

Film employs a reportorial technique in that it contains interviews with Polish Jewish leaders who, of course, say that things are fine now under the Communist regime. Via the itinery of two representatives of American Jewish organizations, the viewer visits factories, synagogues, and Jewish cultural centres. Most interesting is an interview with Ida Kaminska, leading performer of the Jewish State Theatre of Warsaw, a state supported company. Miss Kaminska revealed that the troupe had presented 40 plays and had given 210 performances which were seen by 30,000 people in Poland over a seven-year period.

The narration is in Yiddish and English titles are provided. The film, although photographed poorly when compared to American standards, nevertheless effectively portrays the terrible plight of Poland's Jewish population during the German occupation. Appeal of the film is, of course, limited to Jewish organizations. *Holl.*

Stella
(GREEK)

Tale of Greek passion, starring attractive newcomer, Melina Mercouri. May please in the U. S. arties.

Joseph Burstyn Inc. release of Millas Films Production. Stars Melina Mercouri, Georges Foundas, Aleko Alexandrakis, Sophia Vembo; features Voula Zoumboulaki, Christina Calogerikou, D. Papayannopoulo, Tasso Cavvadia, Costa Caralis. Directed by Michael Cacoyannis. Screenplay, Cacoyannis from stageplay by J. Cambanelis; camera, Costa Thoedorides; music, Manos Hadlidakis. Previewed in N.Y., March 29, '57. Running time, **93 MINS.**

Stella .... Melina Mercouri
Milto .... Georges Foundas
Aleko .... Aleko Alexandrakis
Maria .... Sophia Vembo
Anneta .... Voula Zoumboulaki
Milto's Mother .... Christina Calogerikou
Mitso .... D. Papayannopoulo
Aleko's Sister .... Tasso Cavvadia
Antoni .... Costa Caralis

(In Greek; English Titles)

This is the first feature film to come from Greece with a claim to real attention, and while the picture has a strong national flavor and lacks in some technical virtues, it's nevertheless an exploitation entry with a definite potential.

"Stella" is strongly reminiscent of some of the early Italian postwar imports, though it lacks their absolute sense of drama. It's a story about a strongwilled, passionate girl who drops her lovers when they become serious and propose marriage. Whether she actually loves her men, or whether she's a nymphomaniac, is hard to make out. In any case, she drives everyone mad with desire, particularly her last lover, a burly football player whom she jilts at the altar and who finally kills her.

Film vacillates between high drama and some arid stretches. Greek music and dancing are fiery, but tend to slow up the story. The tunes, while highly rhythmic, are also strange to American ears.

Melina Mercouri plays Stella. She's attractive and properly moody in a demanding role. Georges Foundas as the lover is convincing and—in his final scenes—excellent. So is Christina Calogerikou as his mother.

Direction is by Michael Cacoyannis, touted as one of the great new talents in Europe. "Stella" benefits from his flashes of imagination and his sense of the dramatic, which at times seems overplayed. Costa Theodorides' camera work is perfectly attuned to the story.

It's questionable that "Stella" will collect many critical raves, but its raw simplicity and occasionally wild spirit stand to please many. Story is sufficiently offbeat to allow for plenty exploitation handles, which is a plus factor. *Hift.*

The Ride Back
(SONG)

Suspenseful offbeat western drama, but lightweight marquee values. Average grosses.

United Artists release of William Conrad production presented by The Associates and Aldrich. Stars Anthony Quinn, Conrad; features Lita Milan. Directed by Allen H. Miner. Screenplay, Antony Ellis; camera, Joseph Biroc; editor, Michael Luciano; music, Frank de Vol. Previewed N.Y., April 12, '57. Running time, **79 MINS.**

Kallen .... Anthony Quinn
Hamish .... William Conrad
Guard .... George Trevino
Elena .... Lita Milan
Padre .... Victor Millan
Child .... Ellen Hope Monroe
Luis .... Joe Dominguez
Boy .... Louis Towers

Replete with psychological overtones is "The Ride Back," a story of a man and his mission. While the action takes place on the Mexican border, circa 1870, this Associates and Aldrich presentation is no ordinary western but a searching study of a conflict between two men.

Script is of an exploitable nature. But boxoffice prospects are hampered by relatively unknown players save for Anthony Quinn who stars. Picture can rely upon average of playdates in the general market. Sales potential overseas will be helped by the frequently used Spanish dialog.

However, the unusual Antony Ellis yarn almost falls in the art house vein. With special handling the film conceivably could tap this field for favorable results. It's a simple story Ellis tells and under Allen H. Miner's leisurely direction it slowly unfolds in a fatalistic atmosphere.

William Conrad, who also produces, is a Texas deputy assigned to bring back Quinn from Mexico. He's a fugitive there on a couple of murder charges. Pair's personal character and mental quirks come to the surface on the long "ride back."

Quinn is well cast as the part-Mexican outlaw. He's crafty, laconic and rugged. But he has his redeeming qualities, too, as shown by his friendship to children and voluntary return to trial after Conrad is wounded by marauding Apaches.

Curiously, the general drift of the story is so downbeat and moody that neither Quinn nor Conrad excite much audience sympathy. The latter, a failure by his own admission, hopes to achieve success at last by bringing Quinn in. His restrained performance accents the disquieting aspects of the Deputy's role.

Supporting players' portrayals are in keeping with the film's sombre tone. Ellen Hope Monroe, child befriended by Quinn and Conrad after her parents were slain by the Apaches, contribs a touching performance as does Lita Milan as Quinn's Mexican girl friend. George Trevino is okay as a Spanish-speaking border guard while Victor Milan registers as a padre opposed to Quinn. Joe Dominguez and Louis Towers are seen in lesser roles.

Sepiatone lensing of Joseph Biroc apparently is intended to emphasize the story's suspenseful nature, but it's almost too low key at times. Michael Luciano's editing and William Glasgow's art direction are par for the course as are other technical credits.

Music composed and conducted by Frank de Vol is good. In addition, he cleffed the music on his fairish title song which is occasionally heard in the background. It's sung by Eddie Albert. Conrad's production mantling reflects a modest budget. *Gilb.*

Hellcats of the Navy

Naval action okay but dully plotted script. Fair dual-bill situations.

Hollywood, April 12.

Columbia release of Charles H. Schneer (Morningside) production. Stars Ronald Reagan, Nancy Davis, Arthur Franz; features Robert Arthur, William Leslie, William Phillips, Harry Lauter, Michael Garth, Joseph Turkel, Don Keefer. Directed by Nathan Juran. Screenplay, David Lang, Raymond Marcus; screen story, Lang; based on book by Charles A. Lockwood, Vice-Adm., USN, Ret., and Hans Christian Adamson, Col., USAF, Ret.; camera, Irving Lippman; editor, Jerome Thoms; music, Mischa Bakaleinikoff. Previewed April 4, '57. Running time, **81 MINS.**

Comm. Casey Abbott	Ronald Reagan
Helen Blair	Nancy Davis
Lt. Comm. Don Landon	Arthur Franz
Freddy Warren	Robert Arthur
Lt. Paul Prentice	William Leslie
Carroll	William Phillips
Wes Barton	Harry Lauter
Charlie	Michael Garth
Chick	Joseph Turkel
Jug	Don Keefer
Admiral Nimitz	Selmer Jackson
Admiral Lockwood	Maurice Manson

The 1944 submarine operation in the Tsushima Strait and Sea of Japan backgrounds "Hellcats of the Navy." The underwater fighting is laced with a formula plot which at times gets awfully trite, **but results are still okay for the general dual-bill situation.**

The action stress and a feeling of suspense generated in sequences dealing with the Navy's charting of mine fields in the Strait so that it can move on Japanese shipping carry the burden under Nathan Juran's direction of Charles H. Schneer's Morningside production for Columbia release.

Script by David Lang and Raymond Marcus plies a hackneyed course dealing with problems of command that will sacrifice one man to save many and the resentment this causes. A romantic angle is plastered to the carcass of the plot and means little.

Ronald Reagan is the sub commander around whom the Navy underseas operation pivots. He plays it sternly, without being the typical film version of a martinet. Arthur Franz is the executive officer who believes Reagan's sacrifice of Harry Lauter during a frogman operation results from personal feelings rather than regard for the safety of other personnel. Franz does what he can with the stock character. Nancy Davis is the nurse waiting on shore for Reagan to make up his mind about marriage—a thankless role.

Crew characters are "to type" and include Robert Arthur, William Leslie, William Phillips, Lauter, Michael Garth, Joseph Turkel and Don Keefer. Seen as Admiral Nimitz is Selmer Jackson while Maurice Manson plays Vice Admiral Charles A. Lockwood, real life officer who wrote the book on which the script is based with Col. Hans Christian Adamson, USAF, Ret.

A foreword by Admiral Nimitz, who supervised the actual World War II operation, is used to build-up authenticity. This succeeds as far as the fighting is concerned, but cannot make real the unoriginal screen story Lang concocted from the Lockwood-Adamson book. Irving Lippman's lensing, editing and other behind-camera functions come off okay. *Brog.*

The Oklahoman
(C'SCOPE-COLOR)

Mighty close titling but solid western, with Joel McCrea. Good reaction.

Hollywood, April 23.

Allied Artists release of a Walter Mirisch production. Stars Joel McCrea, Barbara Hale, Brad Dexter, Gloria Talbott; features Verna Felton, Douglas Dick, Michael Pate, Esther Dale, Anthony Caruso, Adam Williams, Ray Teal. Directed by Francis D. Lyon. Screenplay, Daniel B. Ullman; camera (DeLuxe color), Carl Guthrie; editor, George White; music, Hans Salter. Previewed April 12, '57. Running time, **80 MINS.**

John Brighton	Joel McCrea
Anne Barnes	Barbara Hale
Cass Dobie	Brad Dexter
Maria Smith	Gloria Talbott
Mrs. Waynebrook	Verna Felton
Mel Dobie	Douglas Dick
Charlie Smith	Michael Pate
Hawk	Anthony Caruso
Mrs. Fitzgerald	Esther Dale
Randell	Adam Williams
Stableman	Ray Teal
Little Charlie	Peter Votrian
Marshal	John Pickard

Solid western values are incorporated in this story of the Oklahoma territory of 1870, carrying hefty appeal and effectively mounted in CinemaScope and lush DeLuxe color. Names of Joel McCrea and Barbara Hale, topping a first-class cast, will help lift film to a better-than-average playoff. Only title will suggest Rodgers and Hammerstein's "Oklahoma."

The Walter Mirisch production picks up McCrea, a doctor en route to California whose wife dies at childbirth, electing to remain in the Oklahoma town where she is buried. Medico sets up practice in frontier community which is pretty well run by Brad Dexter and Douglas Dick, cattlemen-brothers who ride high over the otherwise peaceful settlement. The Daniel B. Ullman screenplay traces the growing enmity between McCrea and Dexter, out to get medico after he protects an Indian whose land Dexter is trying to take over for its oil. Fast climax is provided in a gunfight in which Dexter is killed and McCrea wounded.

Director Francis D. Lyon gets good performances from his cast and keeps action tense and moving in his unfoldment. McCrea handles his doctor character, who finally straps on a gun when the going becomes hot, with authority and Miss Hale, a widow who runs a large cattle spread, supplies the romance in interesting fashion. Dexter makes a smooth and menacing heavy; Gloria Talbott, as an Indian girl in love with McCrea, socks over the part; and Michael Pate is excellent as her father, who kills Douglas Dick in self-defense. Both Miss Dale and Verna Felton, spicy-tongued and romance-loving mother of Barbara Hale, are tops. Mimi Gibsen enacts McCrea's daughter.

Technical credits generally are above par, Carl Guthrie's color photography outstanding, George White's editing tight and Hans Salter's music score benefitting the action. *Whit.*

The Burglar

About all this jewel heist film has got is what Jayne Mansfield's got for ballyhoo. Dull entertainment.

Hollywood, April 23.

Columbia release of Louis W. Kellman production. Stars Dan Duryea, Jayne Mansfield, Martha Vickers; features Peter Capell, Mickey Shaughnessy, Wendell Phillips, Phoebe Mackay, Stewart Bradley. Directed by Paul Wendkos. Screenplay, David Goodis, from his novel; camera, Don Malkames; editor, Herta Horn; score, Sol Kaplan; bassoon solo, S. Schoenbach; song, "You Are Mine," Bob Marucchi, Pete Deangelo, sung by Vince Carson. Previewed April 19, '57. Running time, 90 MINS.

Nat Harbin	Dan Duryea
Gladden	Jayne Mansfield
Della	Martha Vickers
Baylock	Peter Capell
Dohmer	Micky Shaughnessy
Police Captain	Wendell Phillips
Sister Sara	Phoebe Mackay
Charlie	Stewart Bradley
News Commentator	John Facenda
News Reporter	Frank Hall
Newsreel Narrator	Bob Wilson
State Trooper	Steve Allison
Harbin as a child	Richard Emery
Gladden as a child	Andrea McLaughlin

and

Frank Orrison, Sam Elber, Ned Carey, John Boyd, Michael Rich, George Kane, Sam Cresson, Ruth Burnat.

Ballyhoo possibilities pegged to Jayne Mansfield inheritor of the biggest facade in Hollywood honors, may help "The Burglar's" chances in the general program market, although it falls short of being satisfactory entertainment. Poor scripting and direction, and overlong footage, are strikes against a ready popular acceptance.

Dan Duryea, Miss Mansfield and Martha Vickers star in the Columbia release which Louis W. Kellman produced independently in Philadelphia. Each manages to overcome handicaps posed by David Goodis' scripting and Paul Wendkos' direction to rate an okay for performance. The same can't be said for other casters, most of whom are permitted to overact to the point of oldtime scenery-chewing, especially radio's Peter Capell in his role as a member of Duryea's burglar gang.

Novel opening is a newsreel-type prolog, in which Duryea spots a necklace he wants. Plot then moves into the story, goes through the heist of the jewels from the mansion of a Philadelphia spiritualist, followed by the gang's holing-up in a battered old house while the police look for clues and set law-enforcement machinery into work.

Basic story idea, taken from Goodis' novel of the same title, is okay, but suspense and action are by-passed and sloughed while the assorted characters go into long soliloquizing about how they got into their various predicaments. These interruptions kill any semblance of pacing and make the 90 minutes of footage, already overlong, seem even longer. Duryea, Miss Mansfield, Capell and Mickey Shaughnessy make up the gang, while Martha Vickers and Stewart Bradley are the pair trying to hijack the jewels. Among the many unfamiliar faces are Wendell Phillips, **police captain and Phoebe Mackay, the spiritualist.**

Don Malkames' lensing pays attention to highspots of the Philadelphia-Atlantic City locales while helping story mood, and the score by Sol Kaplan passes muster. "You Are Mine," tune by Bob Marcucchi and Pete Deangelo is sung by Vince Carson as a background for a barroom sequence without too much effect. ***Brog.***

Rock All Night

Lowgrade stuff attempts to cop a fast-buck ride on music fad.

Hollywood, April 24.

American-International Pictures release of a Sunset Production. Stars Dick Miller, Russell Johnson, Abby Dalton; features The Platters, The Blockbusters, with Robin Morse, Richard Cutting, Bruno VeSota, Chris Alcaide, Mel Welles, Barboura Morris, Clegg Hoyt, Jonathan Haze, Richard Carlan, Jack De Witt, Bert Nelson, Beach Dickerson, Ed Nelson. Directed by Roger Corman. Screenplay, Charles B. Griffith; story, David P. Harmon, camera, Floyd Crosby; editor, Frank Sullivan. Previewed April 24, '57. Running time, **62 MINS.**

Shorty	Dick Miller
Julie	Abby Dalton
The Platters	The Platters
The Blockbusters	The Blockbusters
Al	Robin Morse
Steve	Richard Cutting
Charley	Bruno VeSota
Angie	Chris Alcaide
Sir Bop	Mel Welles
Syl	Barboura Morris
Marty	Clegg Hoyt
Jigger	Russell Johnson
Joey	Jonathan Haze
Jerry	Richard Carlan
Philippe	Jack De Witt
Bartender	Bert Nelson
The Kid	Beech Dickerson
Pete	Ed Nelson

Here's a weirdie—on the order of "Time of Your Life"—to the rhythm of rock 'n' roll. Extremely mediocre, and drawing unintended guffaws at its matinee bow here yesterday, "Rock All Night" is being packaged as a double-bill with "Dragstrip Girl."

Entire action in the Charles B. Griffith screenplay, based on a story by David P. Harmon, takes place inside the Cloud Nine, a small neighborhood bar into which walk the local characters to catch such r&r groups as The Platters and The Blockbusters. Most of the action (aside from the vocal interludes) centers around Dick Miller, known as "Shorty" (5' 1"), who hates all big guys and thus keeps himself continually in trouble. Such trouble comes to a climax when two murderers take refuge in the bar and are recognized. It's in the interim before Miller subdues the duo that those within the tavern reveal their true natures.

Only the performance (very good, especially considering the so-so production and direction) of Dick Miller in the lead keeps the audience's interest in the film from disintegrating. The musical break-ins are unimpressive, and of the supporting cast, only Robin Morse (as the bartender) and Mel Welles (as a smalltime hip-talking agent) manage to make any impression.

James H. Nicholson functioned as executive producer, Roger Corman as producer-director. *Neal.*

Gun Duel in Durango

Routine George Montgomery western for the action situations.

United Artists release of a Peerless Productions Inc. presentation produced by Robert E. Kent. Stars George Montgomery, co-stars Ann Robinson, Steve Brodie; features Bobby Clark, Frank Ferguson, Donald Barry, Henry Rowland, Denver Pyle, Mary Treen. Directed by Sidney Salkow. Screenplay, Louis Stevens; camera, Maury Gertsman; editor, Robert Golden; music, Paul Sawtell, Bert Shefter. Previewed N. Y. April 26, '57. Running time, 73 MINS.

Dan	George Montgomery
Judy	Ann Robinson
Dunston	Steve Brodie
Robbie	Bobby Clark
Sheriff Howard	Frank Ferguson
Larry	Donald Barry
Roy	Henry Rowland
Ranger Captain	Denver Pyle
Spinster	Mary Treen
Jones	Al Wyatt
Burt	Red Morgan
Stacey	Joe Yrigoyen

Efforts of a notorious outlaw leader to go straight are the story basis of "Gun Duel in Durango." It's a modest budget western that shapes up as a routine entry for the action situations and the Saturday matinee trade. Cast offers scant marquee values save for George Montgomery who stars.

Written by Louis Stevens, the yarn concerns experiences of Montgomery after he voluntarily steps down as head of the infamous Will Sabre gang. Naturally, his former colleagues attempt to bring him back into the fold. But despite their threats and skullduggery, he triumphs at the windup in a blaze of fancy six-shooting.

Montgomery is amply forthright as the reformed gang chief. On hand as the femme interest is Ann Robinson. A pert brunette, she has a stock role as a ranch owner who vows to wed Montgomery once he's shown himself to be an honest citizen. Steve Brodie is sufficiently sinister as the outlaw who assumes leadership of the gang following Montgomery's withdrawal.

Sidney Salkow's breezy direction is particularly evident in the action sequences of this United Artists release. Topping the supporting players is moppet Bobby Clark as an orphan whom Montgomery has befriended. He's seen in much of the footage and supplies a strong element of audience identification for pre-teen filmgoers.

Among other thespers participating in this Peerless Productions presentation are Frank Ferguson, good as a laconic sheriff; Denver Pyle, okay as a Texas Ranger captain, while Don Barry, Henry Rowland, Red Morgan and Joe Yrigogen turn in standard portrayals as outlaws.

Lensing of Maury Gertsman is good as is the editing of Robert Golden who trimmed the celluloid to a tight 73 minutes. Par for the course are the physical values of producer Robert E. Kent and William Ross' art direction. Other technical credits, including music of Paul Sawtell and Bert Shefter, are standard. *Gilb.*

Dragstrip Girl

Hotrod cars and leather jacketed youth. Pretty good programmer.

Hollywood, April 24.
American-International Pictures release of a Golden State Production. Executive producer, Samuel Z. Arkoff; producer, Alex Gordon; director, Edward L. Cahn; story and screenplay, Lou Rusoff; camera, Frederick E. West; art direction, Don Ament; film editor, Ronald Sinclair; music, Ronald Stein. Stars Fay Spain, Steve Terrell, John Ashley, Frank Gorshin. Features Russ Bender, Tommy Ivo, Gracia Narciso, Tito Vuolo, Dorothy Bruce, Don Shelton, Carla Merey, Leon Tyler, George Dockstader, Bill Welsh, Edmund Cobb, Woody Lee, Judy Bamber. Reviewed at Fox Theatre, Hollywood, Calif., April 24, '57. Running time, 69 MINS.

The inherent thrills, chills and spills of teenagers in their souped-up hotrods supply enough action to make "Dragstrip Girl" a better-than-average programmer. Aimed at the levi and leather jacket trade —where it may find reception— film is being packaged as a double-bill with the not-so-much "Rock All Night."

Fay Spain essays the title role, a blonde spitfire who digs boys and hotrods. Providing the triangle are Steve Terrell, a garage worker and the hero; and John Ashley, rich, egotistical. He's the heavy, of course. Prior to the "big dragstrip race," Ashley, racing through the streets, hits and kills a man, and sneaks off the scene. Wind-up finds Terrell winning the race and Miss Spain, and the law cuffing Ashley.

The Lou Rusoff story and screenplay neatly kneads into the yarn topical racing ingredients, including the inevitable "chicken race." Edward L. Cahn's direction wisely concentrates on the action provided by the script.

Miss Spain, a looker, also proves her thespic capability here, while Terrell and Ashley are good as the male toppers.

Samuel Z. Arkoff served as executive producer of the Alex Gordon production. *Neal.*

Foreign Films

Paris, April 2.
Sous Le Ciel De Provence (Under Skies of Provence) (FRENCH-ITALIAN; COLOR). Stars Fernandel; features, Giulia Rubini, Andrex, Tina Roca, Alberto Sordi. Directed by Mario Soldati. Screenplay, Cesare Zavattini, Aldo Benedetti, Piero Tellini; camera (Eastmancolor), Nicolas Hayer; editor, Christian Gaudin. At Normandie, Paris. Running time, 100 MINS.

Film is a remake of the 1943 Italo pic, "Four Steps in Clouds." Though made by an Italian director, this lacks the more robust aspects of the Italo character to make it plausible and taking. It emerges a hybrid with French logic conflicting with the more generous Italians. As a vehicle for Fernandel it does not give him much chance for comedy. It remains chancey for the U. S., and its color, making for expensive printing costs, also limits this to a few special situations at best.

Fernandel is a henpecked traveling salesman who, out of kindness, decides to help a girl he meets in a bus. She is going home pregnant to a stern farming family and begs him to come and say he is the husband, and then leave. He is caught up by the family affairs and then unmasked. Color and production are good, but story rarely gives the right balance of comedy and drama . *Mosk.*

Paris, April 2.
Bonsoir Paris, Bonjour L'Amour (FRENCH; COLOR; SONGS; DANCES). Sonofilm release of Boreal production. Stars Daniel Gelin, Dany Robin; features Adrian Hoven, Mara Lane, Grethe Weiser, Georges Reich. Directed by Ralph Baum. Screenplay, J. E. Jouve, Baum, Jean Ferry, Claude Accurci; camera (Eastmancolor), Michel Kelber; music, L. Glass; editor, Claudine Bouche. At Marignan, Paris. Running time, 95 MINS.

Gallic attempt at a musical does not prove much. It is in the cliche groove but okay French returns are likely. This is limited for the U. S. except for possible secondary situations on its Paris background. However, color again makes for expenses that may be a detriment for any U. S. chances.

Plot vaguely concerns a Bohemian brother and sister mixed up in dancing and jam sessions. She falls for an Austrian pianist and to keep him in Paris she farms out as a "B" girl to get him money. He finds out and misunderstands but all is righted at the clinch.

Daniel Gelin and Dany Robin are at ease in this childish musical. Gags, though familiar, are acceptable. Dance and song segments are fair and color helps. French are feeling their way in musicals and have yet to approach the level of this type U. S. pic. *Mosk.*

Vienna, April 2.
Das Hellige Erbe (Holy Heritage) (AUSTRIAN). Sascha Film release of Rondo Film production. Features Hermann Erhardt, Christl Erber, Olga von Togni, Georg Groeller, Willi Roesner, Eduard Koeck, Fred Hennings, Sepp Rist, Rudolf Walter, Kurt Buelau, Alfred Boehm, Kurt Mueller-Reltzner, Peter Goeller, Otto Loewe and Herbert Kroll. Directed by Alfred Solm. Story by Frenz Mayr-Melnhof, Norbert Kunze, Guenther Schwab, Alfred Solm; music, Harald Boehmelt. Urania Kino, Vienna. Running time, 90 MINS.

Wild animal life in the Burgenland on the Hungarian border sup-

---

plies the background for "Holy Heritage." Story of a forester, who accidentally kills a poacher and must quit until he is rehabilitated plus two romantic angles is well written and directed. Casting is good.

Camera crew Richard Angst, Fritz Olesko, Albert Hoecht and Hans Gessl deserves high credit. Direction by Alfred Solm is solid. Other technical details are nice. *Maas.*

Saint Joan

Tepid screen version of G. B. Shaw's play. Good cast but newcomer Jean Seberg beyond her depth. Will need strong selling for results.

United Artists release of Otto Preminger presentation. Stars Jean Seberg, Richard Widmark, Richard Todd, Anton Walbrook, John Gielgud, Felix Aylmer; features Harry Andrews, Barry Jones, Finlay Currie, Bernard Miles, Patrick Barr, Kenneth Haigh, Archiex Duncan, Margot Grahame. Directed by Preminger. Screenplay, Graham Greene, based on G. B. Shaw play of same title. Camera, Georges Perinal; music, Mischa Spoliansky; editor, Helga Cranston; production design, Roger Furse. Previewed in New York at Astor Theatre, April 25, '57. Running time, 110 MINS.

Joan of Arc ....Jean Seberg
The Dauphin .... Richard Widmark
Dunois .... Richard Todd
Cauchon ....Anton Walbrook
Earl of Warwick ....John Gielgud
Inquisitor ....Felix Aylmer
John de Stogumber .... Harry Andrews
de Courcelles .... Barry Jones
Archbishop of Rheims .....Finlay Currie
Master Executioner .... Bernard Miles
Captain la Hire .... Patrick Barr
Brother Martin ...... Kenneth Haigh
Robert de Beaudricourt .. Archie Duncan
Duchesse de la Tremouille Margot Grahame
La Tremouille ....Francis de Wolff
English Soldier ....Victor Maddern
Bluebeard .... David Oxley
Steward .... Sydney Bromley

Otto Preminger showed courage when he decided to make G. B. Shaw's "Saint Joan" into a film and to star an unknown of next to no theatrical experience in the role. This is the kind of daring which has supported the showman in the past. The question mark is up on the present gamble.

In "Saint Joan," Preminger doesn't deal with a novel subject Nor a "shocking" one. The story itself is well known. The play is familiar. It's performed periodically. Another version of the Joan legend, "The Lark" with Julie Harris only recently played New York and toured. Thus the Preminger picture hardly contains elements of surprise, but does invite comparison.

Young Jean Seberg of Marshalltown, Ia., makes a sincere effort, but her performance rarely rises above the level of the Iowa prairie. Her pale, somehow uninspired Joan rarely if ever communicates the dramatic intensity and the magnetic, robust leadership qualities that the author had in mind.

This is an odd "Saint Joan," complete with all the trappings and spottily alive with those Shavian barbs with which he lays bare the truth of men and minds. It is a "Saint Joan" that falters around the pivotal figure of the Maid, but draws strength from some of the supporting roles.

The picture unquestionably can exploit the church and school-age markets and exhibitors will be smart to be mindful of such tieups. Since the release can hardly sustain itself at the b.o. as a work worthy of critics' support, and as popular mass entertainment is somewhat dubious, all selling slants are musts.

Miss Seberg is helped most by her appealing looks. She has a fresh, unspoiled quality and she photographs well. But the fact remains that her Joan has no dimensions and her delivery of the lines after a while becomes monotonous. Shaw's Joan is more than just an innocent country maiden. Her faith can move mountains and the flame within her kindles the faith in other men. There is no flame in Miss Seberg, just stubbornness and the almost casually-voiced belief in God and her "voices." When she speaks of her yen for soldiering and battle, it is hard to believe she means it. And throughout the film she never matures.

In vivid contrast, Preminger has surrounded her with a supporting cast that performs brilliantly. Richard Widmark plays the idiot Dauphin with gusto and his portrayal comes across vividly though some may feel he at times overacts the part. Richard Todd as Dunois is simple and appealing; Anton Walbrook registers strongly as Cauchon, the Bishop of Beauvais, and Felix Aylmer brings the necessary dedication (and resignation) to the figure of the Inquisitor.

It is Sir John Gielgud who stands out with a brilliant performance as the politically-minded Earl of Warwick, determined to get Joan to the stake, though contemptuous of the Church's winded arguments of "heretic" vs. "witch." Finlay Currie as the worldly and callous Archbishop of Rhelms makes his proper impact and so does Kenneth Haigh as the sympathetic Brother Martin.

Graham Greene wrote the screenplay, and while it is somewhat toned down, and probably less anti-clerical than the Shaw original, it still retains the essentials of the Shaw classic. He has allowed some scenes to run very long which, in view of Miss Seberg's acting limitations, was poor judgment for which Preminger must share the blame. Idea of prefacing the film with part of the epilogue—and in fact telling the story in flashback—is a good one.

Considering Miss Seberg's lack of experience, Preminger's direction must be credited with getting from her a performance that does not, at least, strike an awkward note. Also, her interpretation may be a reflection of Preminger's concept of Joan. In any case, he keeps the action (such as it is) moving and the trial and burning scenes are cinematographically well handled. Georges Perinal was the lenser and he obtained some striking effects. Mischa Spoliansky's music is in tune with the period and Helga Cranston's editing is good. Saul Bass' title design is uniquely attractive. When caught at the Astor preview, parts of the print appeared extremely fuzzy, going in and out of focus. *Hift.*

Interlude
(C'Scope-Color)

Striking photographic tour of Munich and Salzburg; otherwise rather dreary soap opera with June Allyson, Rossano Brazzi for marquees.

Hollywood, May 7.

Universal release of Ross Hunter production. Stars June Allyson, Rossano Brazzi; costars Marianne Cook, Francoise Rosay, Keith Andes; features Frances Bergen, Lisa Helwig, Herman Schwedt, Anthony Tripoli, John Stein, Jane Wyatt. Directed by Douglas Sirk. Screenplay, Daniel Fuchs, Franklin Coen; adaptation, Inez Cocke; based on a screenplay by Dwight Taylor and a story by James Crain; camera (Technicolor), William Daniels; editor, Russell Schoengarth; music, Frank Skinner. Previewed at Academy Awards, April 30, '57. Running time, 90 MINS.

Henen Banning .... June Allyson
Tonio Fischer .... Rossano Brazzi
Reni Fischer .... Marianne Cook
Countess Reinhart ...... Francoise Rosay
Dr. Morley Dwyer .... Keith Andes
Gertrude Kirk .... Frances Bergen
Prue Stubbins .... Jane Wyatt
Housekeeper .... Lisa Helwig
Henig .... Herman Schwedt
Dr. Smith .... Anthony Tripoli
Dr. Stein .... John Stein

Munich substitutes for Long Island in this remake of Universal's 1939 "When Tomorrow Comes." Despite plot modernization and CinemaScoped Technicolor, "Interlude" remains a curiously dated soap opera with little to recommend as popular entertainment although supposedly a woman's picture, via plot and the casting of Italy's Rossano Brazzi opposite June Allyson.

Best feature of the Ross Hunter production is the striking photographic tour it provides of the high points of interests in Munich, Germany and Salzburg, Austria. The terrain, old buildings, and sights of Hercules and Congress Halls, Amerika Haus, Konigsplatz, the Bernried, Nymphenburg and Schleissheim Castles around Munich, and the Mozarteum and other other points of interest in Salzburg come to life under William Daniels' outstanding lensing.

With the Cook's tour covered, there's little else to kudos. Hunter's story choice was not very showmanly, although the physical assists mustered under his supervision give it as good a display as possible. Cast responds competently to Douglas Sirk's direction but can't make the characters believable in the old-fashioned plot. New script by Daniel Fuchs and Franklin Coen is based on the 1939 screenplay by Dwight Taylor from a story by James Cain. New plot line doesn't necessarily follow the old except in basic motivations. Story now tells how an American girl comes to Munich to work at Amerika Haus in information, falls in love with a symphony conductor, has a brief love idyll with him and then learns he is married to a demented girl. Eventually she renounces him and returns to the states with a faithful young doctor who has been standing by.

Miss Allyson is the heroine (Irene Dunne appeared opposite Charles Boyer in the original), and Brazzi is the conductor. While each is able in replying to script and direction, the pairing doesn't quite jell. Consequently, there won't be much of an emotional response to the futile love affair. Marianne Cook is quite good as the demented wife, as is Francoise Rosay as the Countess who cares for her. Keith Andes has the thankless task of being the doctor waiting for Miss Allyson to rebound. Frances Bergen and Jane Wyatt are talkative Amerika Haus workers.

On the technical side, the art direction, costuming and editing are good. Frank Skinner's score goes with the romantic soap opera plot. *Brog.*

Sea Wife
(BRITISH—C'SCOPE—COLOR)

Another nun-shipwrecked-at sea yarn. Andre Hakim's second British pic, with Joan Collins as the nun plus three men on a dinghy in the Indian ocean. Fair prospects.

London, April 30.

20th-Fox release of a Sumar Film Production. Stars Joan Collins, Richard Burton, Basil Sydney and Cy Grant. Produced by Andre Hakim; directed by Bob McNaught; screenplay, George K. Burke, from the novel "Sea-Wyf and Biscuit" by J. M. Scott; camera, Ted Scaife; editor, Peter Taylor; music, Kenneth V. Jones and Leonard Salzedo. At Carlton Theatre, London. Running time, **82 MINS.**

Sea Wife .... Joan Collins
Biscuit .... Richard Burton
Bulldog .... Basil Sydney
Number Four .... Cy Grant
Clumban .... Ronald Squire
Daily Telegraph Clerk... Harold Goodwin
Club Porter .... Gibb McLaughlin
Club Barman .... Roddy Hughes
Captain "San Felix"....... Lloyd Lamble
Army Padre .... Ronald Adam
Elderly Passenger....... Nicholas Hannen
Submarine Commander ... Otokichi Ikeda
Submarine Interpreter...... Tenji Takagi
Elderly Nun .... Beatrice Varley

For his second British production, Andre Hakim brought back to London Joan Collins, who, a little while earlier, was one of Britain's star exports to Hollywood. She's cast in the offbeat, but unconvincing, role of a nun and that factor hurts the general acceptance of the story. It looks to be just a fair grosser.

There are four principal characters in "Sea Wife"—four survivors from a ship torpedoed during the war, shortly after it had left Singapore. Richard Burton is an RAF officer, who's given the name "Biscuit" because he's in charge of the meagre rations; Joan Collins, the nun, is called "Sea Wife" because she swims like a mermaid; Basil Sydney, a ruthless businessman with a pronounced color prejudice, is tagged "Bulldog"; and Cy Grant, the Negro purser of the ship, is simply "Number Four"—just because he was the fourth and last person to get into the rubber dinghy in which they are carried aimlessly in the Indian Ocean hoping for rescue. Only Cy Grant knows of Miss Collins' vocation and he's sworn to secrecy.

Richard Burton begins to fall in love with the nun, but, because "she's promised to another," she has to stifle her personal emotions. After several days at sea they sight land, but it's only a deserted island and their dinghy is destroyed while making for the beach. The Negro, who finds a machete on the island, uses it to build a bamboo raft, but he's tricked by Basil Sydney and falls victim to a shark. Eventually, the three survivors are picked up and when, in due course, he goes back to England, Burton starts his vain search for the girl.

The story begins, in fact, with Burton's hunt for Miss Collins, via a number of small ads in the personal columns of the national press. They only bring a response, however, from Basil Sydney, now a patient in a mental home. From there on, the story goes into a prolonged and continuous flashback. The picture opens briskly with a scene in Singapore harbor, where more than a thousand refugees are crowded on to the small boat. The attack by submarine and the subsequent panic and explosion, are also boldly handled. At that point, however, the yarn focuses only on the four main characters and the ensuing incident hits a repetitive note.

Joan Collins, attired mainly in a full length shift (her nun's habit is pulled off by a child as she dives into the open sea) tries hard, but doesn't make it. She certainly doesn't stand comparison with the professional performances turned in by Burton, Sydney and Grant. Two pleasing cameos come from Ronald Squire and Harold Goodwin.

The theme song "I'll Find You" is attractively sung by David Whitfield over the credit titles. *Myro.*

The Break in the Circle

Weak English import strictly for smaller program situations.

Hollywood, May 7.

Twentieth-Fox release of a Michael Carreras production. Stars Forrest Tucker, Eva Bartok, Marius Goring; features Guy Middleton, Eric Pohlman, Arnold Marle, Fred Johnson, David King-Wood, Reginald Beckwith. Directed by Val Guest. Screenplay, Guest, based on novel by Philip Loraine: camera, Walter Harvey; editor, Bill Lenny; music Doreen Carwithen. Previewed May 3, '57. Running time, 72 MINS.

Skip Morgan .... Forrest Tucker
Lisa .... Eva Bartok
Baron Keller .... Marius Goring
Hobard .... Guy Middleton
Emile .... Eric Pohlman
Kudnic .... Arnold Marle
Farquarson .... Fred Johnson
Patchway .... David King-Wood
Dusty .... Reginald Beckwith

This British import is a weak entry for the American market, difficult to follow because of a confused story line and handicapped with thick British accents. Name of Forrest Tucker may assist in smaller program situations, but film lacks the finish even less discriminating U.S. audiences demand. A further hurdle is use of the old standard 1.33 aspect ratio.

Tucker plays an American adventurer hired by a ruthless German millionaire living in London to smuggle a refugee Polish scientist out of Hamburg and back to England. Plottage of the Val Guest script twirls around the hazards that beset him after he sails to Hamburg in his own craft and becomes involved in derring-do action in getting his quarry aboard. Back in England, Tucker is up against another menace in form of the German, who poses, but intervention of the police saves the day.

Tucker shouts his way through the Michael Carreras production which Val Guest directs unimaginatively. Eva Bartok, in for romantic interest, is lost in her hazy role, in which she works somehow with the British police. Marius Goring is the German, and Eric Pohlman is okay as a Hamburg racketeer who aids Tucker.

Walter Harvey leads off technical credits with occasional interesting photography limned against London and Hamburg backgrounds. *Whit.*

The Way to the Gold
(C'SCOPE)

Stolen treasure sets stage for mild action drama.

Hollywood, May 7.

20th-Fox release of David Weisbart production. Stars Jeffrey Hunter, Sheree North, Barry Sullivan, Walter Brennan, Neville Brand; features Jacques Aubuchon, Ruth Donnelly, Tom Pittman, Philip Ahn. Directed by Robert D. Webb. Screenplay, Wendell Mayes; based on novel by Wilbur Daniel Steele; camera, Leo Tover; editor, Hugh S. Fowler; music, Lionel Newman; songs, "Strange Weather," "Drive-In Rock," by Carroll Coates and Newman. Previewed at Village, Westwood, May 2, '57. Running time, 95 MINS.

Joe Mundy .... Jeffrey Hunter
Hank Clifford .... Sheree North
Marshall Hannibal ...... Barry Sullivan
Uncle George .... Walter Brennan
Little Brother .... Neville Brand
Clem .... Jacques Aubuchon
Mrs. Williams .... Ruth Donnelly
Sid Songster Jr. .... Tom Pittman
Mr. Ding .... Philip Ahn
Brokaw .... Geraldo Mandia
Sid Songster Sr. .... Ted Edwards
Brokaw's Driver .... Alan Jeffrey

Austere black-and-white CinemaScope takes the viewer over some rugged and interested western locales in this action drama, but the story doesn't always hold up to the backgrounds. Thus, "The Way to the Gold" looks no more than a program subject for the general dual bill situation.

The David Weisbart production, while laid in the Arizona area and including many outdoor scenes, is a modern-dress drama about a young ex-convict who tries to recover a horde of gold stolen many years before by a now dead outlaw. Also on the track of the gold is a family of eccentrics, characterizations of which inject an occasional offbeat note to the Wendell Mayes script from Wilbur Daniel Steele's story. Freshness just about stops there, however, and Robert D. Webb's direction sends it along an easily-followed course. Ending does have a twist, in that the hiding place of the gold is now many feet under the man-made Lake Mead.

Jeffrey Hunter is the sullen, exconvict hero, and handles the requirements of the character well. Sheree North also is suitable to the demands of her waitress role, a girl trying to better herself and who joins Hunter in the treasure hunt, but settles for love when it is over. Barry Sullivan is the wise chief-of-police who keeps his eye on everything while bidding his time to move in. He's good. Eccentrics are Walter Brennan, crazy uncle of a weird family consisting of Neville Brand, menacing, shabby, younger son of Ruth Donnelly, added boardinghouse keeper, whose older son, unctuous Jacques Aubuchon, is master-minding the high-jacking plan. All turn in showy performances.

Unfoldment builds an air of mystery and some suspense, when Hunter leaves prison with an old con's gold secret and the eccentrics take up his trail. Climax finds Hunter and Miss North captured on the way to the treasure and Brand turns would be killer when the gold site is discovered to be in Lake Mead. Young love gets a new chance at life, however, when Sullivan arrives in the nick of time. Among supporting players who are capable are Tom Pittman, young garage worker, and Philip Ahn, employer of Miss North.

There's a jukebox beat to two tunes, "Strange Weather" and "Drive-In Rock," both by Carroll Coates and Lionel Newman, used for background touches. The excellent C'Scope photography was handled by Leo Tover. *Brog.*

Dragoon Wells Massacre

(C'SCOPE—COLOR)

Strong entry for western market, tops right down the line.

Hollywood, May 7.

Allied Artists release of a Lindsley Parsons production. Stars Barry Sullivan, Dennis O'Keefe, Mona Freeman, Katy Jurado; features Sebastian Cabot, Casey Adams, Jack Elam, Trevor Bardette, Jon Shepodd. Directed by Harold Schuster. Screenplay, Warren Douglas; story, Oliver Drake; camera (DeLuxe color), William Clothier; editor, Maurice Wright; music, Paul Dunlap. Previewed April 26, '57. Running time **87 MINS.**

Link Ferris .... Barry Sullivan
Capt. Matt Riordan .... Dennis O'Keefe
Ann Bradley .... Mona Freeman
Mara Fay .... Katy Jurado
Jonah .... Sebastian Cabot
Phillip Scott .... Casey Adams
Tioga .... Jack Elam
Marshal Bill Haney ...... Trevor Bardette
Tom .... Jon Shepodd
Hopi Charlie .... Hank Worden
Jud .... Warren Douglas
Susan .... Judy Stranges

Allied Artists has a top entry for the western market in "Dragoon Wells Massacre," a suspenseful and exciting story of passage through Apache Indian country that carries sock treatment. With such action names as Barry Sullivan and Dennis O'Keefe, and distaffers Mona Freeman and Katy Jurado, to head up cast, indications point to better-than-average returns, further aided by use of CinemaScope and De Luxe color to dress the screen.

The Lindsley Parsons production, probably his strongest to date, is heavy on pictorial values to backdrop the Warren Douglas screenplay. Lenser William Clothier has made handsome use of the Kanab location, and Harold Schuster utilizes scenery to solid effect in reaching a high point of realism in his direction. Fast editing of Maurice Wright is a further plus for picture.

Familiar premise of efforts of a band of whites to escape from warlike redskins has been given fresh embellishment to create mounting suspense.

Performances generally are strong. Sullivan plays a killer whom Trevor Bardette, the marshal, has captured, one of his best roles in some time, and O'Keefe scores as the cavalry captain, once in love with Mona Freeman but finding himself drawn to Katy Jurado, an entertainer. Femmes stage a slugging scrap which would do justice to pair of bruisers. Sebastian Cabot handles his trader role effectively, and good support is offered by Jack Elam, Casey Adams, Jon Shepodd and John War Eagle, latter as the marauding Apache chief.

Technical departments also contribute to film's smooth unfoldment. *Whit.*

Chain of Evidence

Very routine with signals-ahead plotting.

Hollywood, May 7.

Allied Artists release of a Ben Schwalb production. Stars Bill Elliott, James Lydon, Don Haggerty, Claudia Barrett; features Tina Carver, Ross Elliott, Meg Randall, Timothy Carey. Directed by Paul Landres. Screenplay, Elwood Ullman; camera, Harry Neumann; editor, Neil Brunnenkent; music, Marlin Skiles. Reviewed May 1, '57. Running time, **62 MINS.**

Lt. Doyle .... Bill Elliott
Steve Nordstrom .... James Lydon
Sgt. Duncan .... Don Haggerty
Harriet Owens .... Claudia Barrett
Claire Ramsey .... Tina Carver
Bob Bradfield .... Ross Elliott
Polly .... Meg Randall
Fowler .... Timothy Carey
Jake .... John Bleifer
Dr. Ainsley .... Dabbs Greer
Deputy .... John Close
Ramsey .... Hugh Sanders

"Chain of Evidence" is strictly for smaller program situations, its routine yarn of a parolee framed for murder telegraphing ahead most of the unfoldment.

The Elwood Ullman screenplay opens on James Lydon, a hot-tempered young chap just released from the Los Angeles County Honor Farm, where Bill Elliott, a lieutenant in the Sheriff's Department, had him committed in the belief he's still a good guy, after a conviction for assault. An amnesia victim after being attacked on his first night of freedom, Lydon is picked up by a wealthy business man, who takes him home. Latter's wife, who has a boy friend on the side, sees in Lydon an opportunity to throw a murder his way, so she'll be a wealthy widow. Through Elliott's efforts Lydon is finally cleared.

Elliott in his comparatively brief footage handles himself with his customary authority, and Lydon does as well as role will permit. Claudia Barrett is in for romantic interest as Lydon's betrothed, Hugh Sanders is okay as the murdered man and Tina Carver as his wife, cheating with Ross Elliott. Meg Randall is a lunchstand owner and Don Haggerty a sheriff's sergeant. Paul Landres' direction is standard, same going for technical credits. *Whit.*

Desk Set

(C'SCOPE-COLOR)

Funny film version of the Broadway hit with Spencer Tracy and Katharine Hepburn re-teamed, in color; good prospects.

20th-Fox release of a Henry Ephron production. Stars Spencer Tracy, Katharine Hepburn, co-stars Gig Young, Joan Blondell; features Dina Merrill, Sue Randall, Neva Patterson, Harry Ellerbe, Nicholas Joy, Diane Jergens, Merry Anders, Ida Moore, Rachel Stephens. Directed by Walter Lang. Screenplay, Henry and Phoebe Ephron, based on the play by William Marchant. Camera, Leon Shamroy; music, Cyril Mockridge; editor, Robert Simpson; Art direction, Lyle R. Wheeler, Maurice Ransford. Previewed at Village Theatre, Westwood, Cal., May 8, '57. Running time, **102 MINS.**

Richard .... Spencer Tracy
Bunny .... Katharine Hepburn
Mike Cutler .... Gig Young
Peg Costello .... Joan Blondell
Sylvia .... Dina Merrill
Ruthie .... Sue Randall
Miss Warringer .... Neva Patterson
Smithers .... Harry Ellerbe
Azae .... Nicholas Joy
Alice .... Diane Jergens
Cathy .... Merry Anders
Old Lady .... Ida Moore
Receptionist .... Rachel Stephens

With some shifts in the basic story line, "Desk Set," the Broadway hit comedy of two seasons ago, has been transformed into a gay and sometimes uproarious film by 20th-Fox. It has the elements for good returns in all situations, aided by the marquee value of the reunion of Spencer Tracy and Katharine Hepburn in the comedy field, and can derive added exploitation results from the mounting public interest in automation.

Henry and Phoebe Ephron have switched the romantic angle in transferring the comedy to the screen, to give a better payoff to the Tracy-Hepburn teaming, but have otherwise hewed closely to the William Marchant play about the installation of an electronic brain in the research department of a tv network. Tracy is the methods engineer who supervises the job and Miss Hepburn is the department head who fears she and her staff are being replaced. Tracy's advent ends a long-standing romance between Miss Hepburn and Gig Young, a rising network executive, but only after a series of highly comedic sequences in which the human element eventually triumphs over the machine. In some cases, the comedy has been stretched a trifle thin for the 102-minute running time, particularly in some interpolated scenes, but the fun generally shines through and some of the play's basic material has been enhanced by the mobility of the camera.

Walter Lang directed with a skilled and patient hand to reap a harvest of laughs and there are a series of competent performances from a cast that is largely subsidiary to the stars. Tracy is fine, albeit a trifle elderly in appearance, as the dedicated electronic engineer who triggers the action. Miss Hepburn is good as the researcher and Young is convincing as the exec. Joan Blondell shines as Miss Hepburn's assistant and Dina Merrill, Neva Patterson and Harry Ellerbe register in the best of the smaller roles.

Film is a top production credit for Ephron, who also coscripted ably with his wife Phoebe. Camera work by Leon Shamroy is good and the DeLuxe color effectively enhances the striking art direction by Lyle R. Wheeler and Maurice Ransford, although the preview print was marred by an occasional inconsistency in shading. Robert Simpson edited it down smoothly to its final running time and Cyril Mockridge has contributed a background score that complements the production. There are also some fine special effects, particularly the electronic brain's tantrum, by Ray Kellogg. *Kap.*

The Little Hut

(SONG-COLOR)

Bedroom farce on a shipwrecked isle with Ava Gardner the lure for Stewart Granger, David Niven. Good prospects.

Hollywood, May 7.

Metro release of F. Hugh Herbert, Mark Robson (Herbson S. A.) production; directed by Robson. Stars Ava Gardner, Stewart Granger, David Niven; introduces Walter Chiari; features Finlay Currie, Jean Cadell. Screenplay, Herbert; based on play by Andre Roussin and English stage adaptation by Nancy Mitford; camera (Eastman Color), F. A. Young; editor, Ernest Walter; music, Robert Farnon; title song, Eric Maschwitz, Marcel Stellman, Peggy Cochrane. Previewed May 1, '57. Running time, **90 MINS.**

Susan (Lady Ashlow) .... Ava Gardner
Sir Philip Ashlow .... Stewart Granger
Henry Brittingham-Brett .... David Niven
Mario .... Water Chiari
The Rev. Brittingham-Brett .... Finlay Currie
Mrs. Brittingham-Brett .... Jean Cadell
Captain MacWade .... Jack Lambert
Mr. Trollope .... Henry Oscar
Miss Edwards .... Viola Lyel
Indian Gentleman .... Jaron Yaltan

Sex is incessantly hinted at in this saucy triangle which keeps husband and wife intact for the moral code. It all takes place on a South Pacific Island with Ava Gardner down to her lace BVD's and much sly innuendo about her husband's preoccupation with everything else but her gender. The basic comedy is a menage a trois with the characters all in bed with a "Code." Nonetheless, synthetic or not, and though bearing only fleeting resemblance to the original French text this is 90 minutes likely to please the run-of-mill film fans, including the teenagers.

F. Hugh Herbert and Mark Robson divide a number of chores in whipping up the basically lightweight play material. They produced under the indie Herbson S. A. banner for Metro release. It is slick and showmanly.

As the choice feminine tidbit who fires the masculine libido, Ava Gardner is ideal casting. Besides what she has to start with, she's equipped with additional fighting tools in the shape of some extremely smart Christian Dior gowns and castaway costumes. As to handling the comedy demands of her part, she's up to every requirement, doing splendidly by the change in acting pace. Equally adept and effective, and certain to exert plenty of appeal for femmes, is Granger, also in a pace-change, as Miss Gardner's too-busy-to-love husband. Matching the above two is Niven, in a very amusing take-off on a proper Englishman who wants to preempt Grangers' marital rights with Miss Gardner.

Government business has left Granger with little time to practice the arts of a husband, so Miss Gardner turns to hubby's best friend, Niven, for companionship. transfer this situation to a deserted tropical isle after a shipwreck, feed the principals a stimulating seafood diet, mostly oysters, and something has to give. That it never actually does is due to the interference of a dog (the script device to mollify the censors), who doesn't like Niven, keeps him from playing house with Miss Gardner after Granger makes a calculated relinquishment of his marriage. For the wrapup, bring in an Italian chef from the wrecked ship who, in the guise of a blood-thirsty native, almost takes over the heroine. After all, he's been on the same diet and she's the only femme around. Plot complications are neatly contrived at the finale.

Walter Chiari, Italian actor, is introduced as the phony native and sells his role amusingly. Seen briefly, but to good effect, are Finlay Currie, Jean Cadell and others. The Eastman Color lensing by F. A. Young heads the lineup of fine technical credits. Robert Farnon provides a fitting background score, and there's even a title song, heard behind the credits, by Eric Maschwitz, Marcel Stellman and Peggy Cochrane. *Brog.*

Professor Tim
(IRISH)

Lively pic version of Irish comedy, with actors Abbey Theatre Players; first of Dublin Films' Productions and good b.o. potential.

Dublin, May 7.

Dublin Film and Television Productions production and release. Features Ray MacAnally, Seamus Kavanagh, Maire Keane, Phillip Flynn. Directed by Henry Cass. Based on George Shiel's play of same name; music, Stanley Black. Running time, 60 MINS.

Hugh O'Cathan	Ray MacAnally
Mrs. Scally	Maire Keane
John Scally	Phillip Flynn
Peggy Scally	Maire O'Donnell
James Kilroy	Geoffrey Golden
Mrs. Kilroy	Eileen Furlong
Joseph Kilroy	Michael O'Brien
Professor Tim	Seamus Kavanagh
Moll Flanagan	Brid Lynch
Paddy Kinney	John Hoey
Mr. Allison	Bill Foley

A familiar Abbey comedy of farm life, greed for money and a good marriage for children is the first pic to come from a deal involving the Dublin film company with the Abbey Theatre and its players. Original aim was for tele but "Professor Tim" is also to be given theatre distribution. Direction and photography of story are first rate with good naturalistic acting from Abbey players whose names have little marquee value, except as Abbey Players, outside Ireland.

Professor Tim, an amiable rumpot, returns to his native village after world wanderings. His sister, married to a farmer, is making money if not happiness for her family, and her daughter has a broken romance with local boy of the manor who is broke and about to have his home auctioned off.

Performances are very even, with Seamus Kavanagh a standout as Professor Tim. Stage Irish characters have been avoided, but the brogue and behaviour are sufficiently clear to give piece authentic ring of Irishry. Settings are naturalistic with few studio shots, and lensing first class. Dublin Films has series of Abbey plays lined up for lensing. *Mac.*

Prince and the Showgirl
(COLOR)

Generally pleasant comedy with built-in b.o. values in casting of Marilyn Monroe opposite Laurence Olivier.

Warner Bros. release of Marilyn Monroe production produced by Laurence Olivier. Stars Marilyn Monroe and Laurence Olivier. Features Sybil Thorndyke, Richard Wattis, and Jeremy Spenser. Directed by Olivier. Screenplay, Terence Rattigan; based on his play, "The Sleeping Prince"; camera (Technicolor), Jack Cardiff; editor, Jack Harris; music, Richard Addinsell. Previewed in N.Y., May 10, '57. Running time, 117 MINS.

Elsie	Marilyn Monroe
The Regent	Laurence Olivier
Queen Dowager	Sybil Thorndyke
Northbrook	Richard Wattis
King Nicolas	Jeremy Spenser
Col. Hoffman	Esmond Knight
Major Domo	Paul Hardwick
Maud	Rosamund Greenwood
Ambassador	Aubrey Dexter
Lady Sunningdale	Maxine Audley
Call Boy	Harold Goodwin
Valet	Andrea Malandrinos
Maisie Springfield	Jean Kent
Fanny	Daphne Anderson
Maggie	Gillian Owen
Betty	Vera Day
Lottie	Margot Lister
Theatre Manager	Charles Victor
The Foreign Office	David Horne
Head Valet	Dennis Edwards
Dresser	Gladys Henson

The combination of Marilyn Monroe and Laurence Olivier plus the title, "The Prince and the Showgirl," provides a pre-sold quality for this first indie production of Miss Monroe's own company. It will draw those curious to see Miss Monroe playing opposite one of England's foremost actors as well as those intrigued by the come-on title. These values give the picture a good chance of becoming a b.o. success.

The picture, being released by Warner Bros., is a generally pleasant comedy, but whether it will appeal to all those attracted by the exploitation influence is open to question. There are moments of genuine comedy in the film, but there are also stretches of dull footage and repetition.

The pace is leisurely. Filmed in London with a predominantly British cast, it may be more of a big city picture in U.S., than a small town entry, but the lure of the Monroe name may wipe out such calculations.

The film is not a cliche Cinderella story as its title might indicate. It is much more sophisticated than that though story is a thin one and is secondary to the by-play and romantic maneuverings between Miss Monroe, a scatterbrained American showgirl in a London musical, and Olivier, the suave and worldly Regent of a Balkan kingdom.

Based on Terence Rattigan's play, "The Sleeping Prince," a London success but a Broadway disappointment, the story takes place in London in 1911 at the time of the Coronation of King George V. Olivier and his entourage, including his son, the boy king of the Balkan country, and the Queen Dowager, Olivier's mother-in-law, come to London for the Coronation ceremonies. The Regent's roving eye alights on Miss Monroe and the British Foreign Office, apprehensive of the delicate balance of power in the Balkan area, makes a determined effort to give the Regent what he wants.

As a result, Miss Monroe, the showgirl from Milwaukee, finds herself in the Regent's private quarters in the Carpethian Embassy. It is several days before Miss Monroe leaves the embassy, but during that period Miss Monroe successfully parries the Regent's seductive advances, attends the Coronation as the Dowager's lady-in-waiting, brings about a reconciliation between the Regent and his son and thus avoids a revolution in the Balkan country, attends the Coronation ball, and finally falls in love and lures the Regent to renew his advances.

To Olivier's credit as producer, director and performer, he achieves the utmost from his material. His own performance as the stuffy Regent is flawless. However, the character he portrays is not an appealing one, and some viewers may wonder what draws the showgirl to him except for the fact that he's member of royalty. The art of the seemingly naive showgirl is just right for Miss Monroe and she makes the most of it attired in a skin tight revealing dress. She shows a real sense of comedy and can command a laugh with her walk or with an expression. Dame Sybil Thorndike is excellent as the hard-of-hearing not-quite-there Dowager; Jeremy Spenser, who bears a remarkable resemblance to Sal Mineo, is appropriately serious as the young king, and Richard Wattis is properly harassed as the British Foreign office representative. The rest of the large cast lends able support.

Based on his budget allotment, Jack Cardiff has provided an adequate lensing job. However, the Coronation sequences are obviously artificial, revealing the use of rear screen superimpositions. Other technical aspects are okay. *Holl.*

Monkey on My Back

Story of Barney Ross, ring champ who becomes a hophead, intensely scripted and performed; boxoffice potential good but lack of top names must be overcome.

United Artists' Edward Small production. Stars Cameron Mitchell, Diane Foster; features Paul Richards, Jack Albertson, Kathy Garver, Lisa Golm, Barry Kelley, Dayton Lumis. Directed by Andre de Toth. Written by Crane Wilbur, Anthony Veiller, Paul Dudley; editor, Grant Whytock; camera, Maury Gertsman; music, Paul Sawtell and Bert Shefter. Previewed in New York, May 8, '57. Running time, 93 MINS.

Barney Ross	Cameron Mitchell
Cathy	Dianne Foster
Rico	Paul Richards
Sam Pian	Jack Albertson
Noreen	Kathy Garver
Barney's mother	Lisa Golm
Big Ralph	Barry Kelley
McAvoy	Dayton Lummis
Lew Surati	Lewis Charles
Latham	Raymond Greenleaf
Art Winch	Richard Benedict
Spike	Brad Harris
Dr. Sullivan	Robert Holton

Producers' propensity for taking on strong subject matter—strong in that themes of a few seasons back would be tepid in comparison—is illustrated anew, and with good dramatic effect, in Edward Small's intense filmization of the story of Barney Ross.

Ross in his limelight days was a big spender, reckless gambler and on-and-off welter and lightweight champion of the boxing world. He was decorated for heroism in combat as a Marine on Guadalcanal during World War II. He was wounded and contracted malaria and his need for morphine persisted beyond his hospital internment. He had become a drug addict and in civilian life sunk to the nadir in personal existence. He entered the United States Federal Hospital in Lexington, Ky., and four and a half months later emerged with that monkey, finally, off his back.

As realistically scripted by Crane Wilbur, Anthony Veiller and Paul Dudley, and graphically staged by Andre de Toth, the Small production looks like a fairly-close reproduction of the basic facts. There's nothing dainty or delicate about it; "Monkey on My Back" is not for the lily-livered.

It is, however, a well-rounded story that's given professional presentation. The entry figures as a good commercial prospect but demands, because of the absence of top-calibre selling names, a promotional helping-hand to get it rolling in the initial dates.

While the values of the feature at hand are under discussion, some thought is suggested about the idea of "dope addict pictures." Otto Preminger's "Man With the Golden Arm" was the first to focus on such material and have important b.o. impact. 20th-Fox is now ready with "Hatful of Rain." Producers might do well to be cautious about going overboard. The public can't be counted upon to hold still for too many variations on a story line that has as its focal point a tormented hophead.

"Monkey" is played out with uniform conviction. Cameron Mitchell handles the Ross part with commendable flexibility. He's personable as the champ, impressed with his own ideas about being a winner and living high. And it is with striking realism that, following the war, he shivers and sweats in desperate quest for a "fix." The scenes of his agony and the self-injection of a hypodermic might be repulsive to tender hearted witnesses. But they are important in getting the full story told and, indeed, ramming across the meaning of the true horror of narcotics enslavement.

Diane Foster is attractive and competent as Ross' wife, a showgirl who has a daughter, Kathy Garver, by a former husband. Also providing the required talent are featured performers Paul Richards, Jack Albertson, Lisa Golm, Barry Kelley and Dayton Lumis.

Interesting and reasonable (to the layman) are brief but sharp lines of dialog on motivation behind the morphine habit and the cure possibilities. Ross had the "roar of the crowd" to ease the physical pain of a ring cuffing and provide ego inflation. When he lost the cheering section he hit upon the needle as a substitute. And it's spelled out that as he leaves the hospital he's cured—for as long as he has the will to be cured.

Music in many sequences has a dramatic quality of its own, camera work is particularly effective in close-ups of ring battles and other technical credits all are good. *Gene.*

Fury at Showdown

Slow-motion giddyap opera. So-so outlook.

United Artists release of Robert Goldstein production. Producer John Beck; directed by Gerd Oswald. Stars John Derek, John Smith, Carolyn Craig, Nick Adams; features Gage Clarke, Robert Griffin, Malcolm Atterbury. Screenplay, Jason James, from a novel by Lucas Todd; camera, Joseph LaShelle; editor, Robert Golden; music, Henry Sukman. Previewed April 3, 1957. Running time: 75 MINS.

Brock Mitchell	John Derek
Miley Sutton	John Smith
Ginny Clay	Carolyn Craig
Tracy Mitchell	Nick Adams
Chad Deasey	Gage Clarke
Sheriff Clay	Robert E. Griffin
Norris	Malcolm Atterbury
Riley	Rusty Lane
Van Steeden	Sydney Smith
Mrs. Williams	Frances Morris
Tom Williams	Tyler McDuff
Alabam	Robert Adler
Swamper	Norman Leavitt
Mr. Phelps	Ken Christy
Sheriff of Buckhorn	Tom McKee

"Fury at Showdown" is a moody western that could have used more pacing of its action. Direction spends so much time building an atmosphere of impending doom that the plot never picks up adequate momentum.

Scripting by Jason James from a Lucas Todd novel tells the story of a young man trying to overcome a reputation for gunslinging and the enmity of his neighbors, mostly fostered by a gabby lawyer who wants revenge for the death of his brother by the hero's gun.

John Derek is okay as the gunsy kid trying to forget, as is Nick Adams as the younger brother who is trying to help him. However, both get lost at times in the heavy-handed, prairie philosophizing with which the script is loaded and aren't helped by the matching deliberateness of Gerd Oswald's direction. Same handicaps face Carolyn Craig, the hometown girl who can't make up her mind about Derek, and Gage Clarke, the oily lawyer. John Smith, Clarke's bodyguard, fares somewhat better in a part developed along more general western lines. Among others are Robert E. Griffin, Malcolm Atterbury, Rusty Lane, Sydney Smith and Frances Morris, all of whom are acceptable.

John Beck produced the United Artists release under the executive supervision of Robert Goldstein and the outdoor atmosphere obtained through Joseph LaShelle's lensing is okay. So are the Henry Sukman background music, which is not overused, and the technical assists from art direction and set decorations, editing and sound. *Brog.*

High Tide at Noon
(BRITISH)

Leisurely paced yarn of island life in Nova Scotia, modest prospects.

London, April 30.

Rank (Julian Wintle) production and release. Stars Bette St. John, William Sylvester, Michael Craig, Flora Robson, Alexander Knox; co-stars Peter Arne, Patrick McGoohan. Directed by Philip Leacock. Screenplay, Neil Paterson; camera, Eric Cross; editor, Sidney Hayers; music, John Veale. At 'Gaumont, London. Running time, **109 MINS.**

Joanna .... Betta St. John
Alev .... William Sylvester
Nils .... Michael Craig
Donna .... Flora Robson
Stephen .... Alexander Knox
Owen .... Peter Arne
Simon .... Patrick McGoohan
Charles .... Patrick Allen
Mateel .... Jill Dixon
Kristi .... Susan Beaumont
Philip .... John Haywald
Peter Grant .... Errol MacKinnon
George Breck .... Stuart Nichol
Ash Breck .... George Murcell

A long, slow-moving drama with modest marquee strength, "High Tide At Noon" shapes as a tough proposition to sell. The pic has only moderate chances in the domestic market, but its quota ticket will be a valuable selling aid.

The entire action is set on an island off Nova Scotia, where the inhabitants depend on lobster fishing for a living. It is a tale of the jealousies and loves of the islanders, unfolding at a casual pace, until economic necessity drives them to the mainland.

Betta St. John plays the daughter of Alexander Knox, a man who owns the major part of the island. She is a high-spirited, tomboy type, who falls in love and marries William Sylvester, only to find that he's a gambler and has lost all their savings.

The island setting is visually attractive, although the photography is of unequal quality. The lobster fishing sequences have a distinct appeal and a couple of brawls provide the liveliest action. St. John's starry-eyed portrayal is pleasantly agreeable while William Sylvester makes a nice showing as her husband. Easily the best performance, however, comes from Knox—his interpretation of the island leader carries the stamp of dignity. Flora Robson has little scope as his wife, but Michael Craig impresses as one of Miss St. John's suitors. Remainder of the cast turns in average acceptable performances. *Myro.*

Calypso Joe
(MUSICAL)

Not the mostest probably but the firstest in getting there with a Calypso music fad film.

Allied Artists release of William F. Broidy production. Stars Herb Jeffries, Anie Dickinson, Edward Kemmer; features Stephen Bekassy, Laurie Mitchell, Claudia Drake, Murray Alper, Linda Terrace, Charles R. Keans, Genie Stone, Robert Sherman, and Herb Jeffries' Calypsomaniacs, Lord Flea and his Calypsonians, The Easy Riders, The Lester Hordon Dancers, Duke of Iron. Directed by Edward Dein. Screenplay, Edward and Mildred Dein; camera, Stuart Thompson; editor Thor Brooks; music, Richard Hazard. Previewed May 1, '57. Running time, **76 MINS.**

With upwards of a dozen tunes and/or production numbers, "Calypso Joe" should please those who like their calypso. Film abounds in exploitation value, and is being teamed by Allied Artists as a double-bill with "Hot Rod Rumble."

Film is chiefly notable as being the first in what is shaping up as a new screen cycle (Sam Katzman's "Calypso Heat Wave" and Bel-Air's "Bop Girl Goes Calypso" due shortly). Canned only last March 27, pic hits the screens pronto.

Basically, there's but the slimmest of plots in the screenplay by Edward and Mildred Dein. At the outset, in Manhattan, Angie Dickinson, an airline hostess, and Edward Kemmer, a television star, have had a spat and are phffft. At the wind-up, in South America, they've made up. And playing Cupid through it all, mostly via song, is Herb Jeffries.

Getting the main play, of course, are the musical break-ins. Jeffries puts over seven numbers in familiar fashion, including "There's Only One Love" (In a Woman's Life), which is used more-or-less as the theme. The Easy Riders, headeds by the unbilled Terry Gilkyson, are in with their popular "Marianne," also "Sweet Sugar Cane," while the Duke Of Iron and Lord Flea are others prominently spotted. Making a particularly good impression, terp-wise, are The Lester Horton Dancers.

In lead roles, Jeffries, Miss Dickinson and Kemmer are adequate to the demands of the script, while Edward Dein's direction of the William F. Broidy production runs along routine lines. Technical credits are stock.

There is, incidentally, a striking similarity herein between real and reel life. As "Calypso Joe," Jeffries has a dancing partner known as "Lady T." The real-life Calypso Joe, who resides in Hawaii, is partnered with a femme known as Coco Te. *Neal.*

The Restless Breed
(SONGS-COLOR)

Scott Brady, Anne Bancroft in western vengeance drama; suitable to regular outdoor action market.

Hollywood, May 14.

20th-Fox release of Edward L. Alperson production. Stars Scott Brady, Anne Bancroft; features Jay C. Flippen, Jim Davis, Rhys Williams. Directed by Allan Dwan. Screenplay, Steve Fisher; camera (Eastman Color), John W. Boyle; editor, Merrill G. White; music, Edward L. Alperson Jr.; conducted by Raoul Kraushaar; songs, Dick Hughes, Richard Stapley, Alperson Jr. Previewed April 29, '57. Running Time, **81 MINS.**

Mitch Baker .... Scott Brady
Angelita .... Anne Bancroft
Marshal Steve Evans ..... Jay C. Flippen
Ed Newton .... Rhys Williams
Rev. Simmons .... Jim Davis
Cherokee .... Leo Gordon
Allan .... Scott Marlowe
Caesar .... Eddy Waller
Mayor Johnson .... Harry Cheshire
Sheriff William .... Myron Healey
Bartender ....Gerald Milton
Hotel Clerk .... Dennis King Jr.
Secret Service Chief ...... James Flavan

Gun runners along the Texas border knock off a Secret Service agent, thus priming the vengeance action in this Edward L. Alperson production for 20th-Fox release. It all adds up to a suitable entry for the outdoor action trade.

Scott Brady is the man with a mission, who comes to the border town seeking the killer of his father. Title to the Steve Fisher screen story comes from the restlessness of men who want to go outside the law for justice, and the plot fashioning, while more or less to type, establishes a good pattern for this kind of action subject. Where picture falls a bit short is in the lags permitted by Allan Dwan's direction. He could have played his scenes faster to surer purpose for plotting and characterizations.

Anne Bancroft beautifies the role of a half-bred girl, ward of Rhys Williams, unordained preacher who runs a small mission for unwanted youngsters in the border town. The heavy sought by Brady is Jim Davis, a cautious man who stays below the border most of the time while his henchman, Leo Gordon, and others keep an eye on things in Mission. Finally, Brady's well-advertised presence in the town lures Davis across the border for the climaxing gun duel, but not until the hero has been in and out of a few tight places with Davis' gunmen.

Brady and Miss Bancroft, while not called upon for any acting strain by Dwan's dowdling direction, handle themselves capably. Vaudeville's gift to giddyap, Jay C. Flippen, is around to see that Davis lets the law handle the vengeance angle, and good. Davis only has a couple of scenes but does okay by them. Williams is good as the preacher and Gordon is a firstrate heavy. Scott Marlowe, whose character remains a bit nebulous, does well, however, in enacting a young man who yens to have the gun courage of the villains but never quite makes it. Myron Healey shows up expertly as a sheriff bumped off early in the footage.

Alperson's production benefits from some effective color lensing by John W. Boyle and good editing by Merrill C. White. Also an asset, even though occasionally overused under the baton of Raoul Kraushaar, are the background score by Edward L. Alperson Jr., and the title tune, plus "Angelita" and "Never Alone" which he wrote with Dick Hughes and Richard Stapley. Border town settings and the mission are expertly conceived via Ernst Fegte's art direction and the set decorations by Howard Bristol. *Brog.*

The Lonely Man
(V'VISION)

Offbeat western with Jack Palance and Anthony Perkins. names to draw.

Hollywood, May 14.

Paramount release of a Pat Duggan production. Stars Jack Palance, Anthony Perkins, Neville Brand, Robert Middleton; features Elaine Aiken. Directed by Henry Levin. Screenplay, Harry Essex, Robert Smith; camera, Lionel Lindon; editor, William B. Murphy; music, Van Cleave. Previewed May 9, '57. Running time, **87 MINS.**

Jacob Wade .... Jack Palance
Riley Wade .... Anthony Perkins
King Fisher .... Neville Brand
Ben Ryerson .... Robert Middleton
Willie .... Elisha Cook
Blackburn .... Claude A. Akins
Faro .... Lee Van Cleef
Dr. Fisher .... Harry Shannon
Judge Hart .... James Bell
Lon .... Adam Williams
Sheriff .... Denver Pyle
Sundown Whipple .... John Doucette
Fence Green .... Paul 'Tiny' Newlan
Ada Marshall .... Elaine Tiken

"The Lonely Man" is an offbeat western, more a character study of a gunfighter who tries to reform than an out-and-out action picture. Narrative carries certain interest and winds in a gun flourish when principal character is baited into one last battle, but its success at b.o. will depend upon the draw of Jack Palance and Anthony Perkins, who co-star.

The Harry Essex-Robert Smith screenplay is predicated upon Palance's desire to retire to his ranch after years of killing and win over the son he hasn't seen for 17 years, a son who hates him because he believes his father was responsible for the death of his mother. Lurking in the background is a gambler out to kill Palance for having taken his girl from him, intent upon using the same bullet to mow down gunslinger that latter used to cripple him. Interwoven in this plot line are Palance's activities in rounding up wild horses.

Palance registers strongly as the old gunfighter who is losing his eyesight, a circumstance leading to his death after he wipes out his pursuers. Perkins' characterization is more indeterminate in his hatred of his father that in the end turns to respect, but turns in a good performance. Elaine Aiken delivers well as the girl is not a easy role, Neville Brand lends menace to part of Palance' nemesis and Robert Middleton is effective as a badman vacillating between Palance and Brand. Lee Van Cleef, too, stands out briefly as Brand's henchman who dies in gunfight.

Henry Levin's direction fits the mood of the Pat Duggan production. Technical credits are quality assets, including Lionel Lindon's camera work, William B. Murphy's editing, Van Cleave's music score. Tennessee Ernie Ford warbles Jack Brooks-Cleave title song. *Whit.*

Celui Qui Doit Mourir
(He Who Must Die)
(FRENCH—C'SCOPE)

Cannes, May 7.

Cinedis release of Indusfilms-Prima-Cinetel-Filmsonor production. Features Melina Mercouri, Jean Servais, Fernand Ledoux, Pierre Vaneck, Nicole, Berger, Maurice Ronet, Roger Hanin. Directed by Jules Dassin. Screenplay, Ben Barzman, Dassin from novel, "Christ Recrucified," by Nikos Kazantzakis; dialog, Andre Obey; camera, (C'Scope), Jacques Natteau; editor, Roger Dwyre; music, Georges Auric. At Cannes Film Fest. Running time, **120 MINS.**

Fotia .... Jean Servais
Katerina .... Melina Mercouri
Manolios .... Pierre Vaneck
Patriarheas .... Gert Froebe
Michelis .... Maurice Ronet
Mariori .... Nicole Berger
Grigoris .... Fernand Ledoux
Lukas .... Carl Mohner
Pannayatoris .... Roger Hanin
Agha .... Gregoire Aslan

Jules Dassin made this entirely in Crete. Dealing with the theme of revolt against oppression, it has a generous premise which is not quite matched by the treatment. Film is slow, loosely constructed to make this a plodding pic. Its upbeat theme is limited by patchy progression, making this chancey for the U. S. It looms mainly as a possibility in special situations where needing plenty of bally.

Plot has Crete under the occupation of the Turks. A small town lives peacefully under the local Turkish overlord who does not interfere with the townspeople and lets them have their yearly passion play. Into this comes a group from a destroyed town led by a courageous priest. They are refused help and entrance by the more selfish priest, but camp nearby

Pic then concerns itself with three of the townspeople who decide to help the refugees with food. This leads to a battle between the two, with the Turks finally taking a hand.

Director Dassin has not quite welded the two story aspects, and the development is uneven. The second half is full of action and revolt, thus taking on a more dynamic air but does not quite bring it off. Acting is somewhat theatrical and Pierre Vaneck rarely gets the dignity into the role of shepherd who becomes a liberator after he is picked to play the Christ part. Melina Mercouri is somewhat too mannered as the town joy girl, transformed by love.

Location work gives this a good production aspect but CinemaScope at times hampers the movement and emphasis. Pic has a laudable theme and some fine moments. But mainly it lacks the complete blending of emotion and character. Technical credits are good and use of non-actor natives is a plus factor. Warring priests are neatly limned by Fernand Ledoux and Jean Servais.

Mosk.

Gunfight at the O.K. Corral

Smash western with double voltage names of Burt Lancaster and Kirk Douglas.

Paramount release of a Hal Wallis production. Stars Burt Lancaster, Kirk Douglas; costars Rhonda Fleming, Jo Van Fleet, John Ireland; features Lyle Bettger, Frank Faylen, Earl Holliman. Directed by John Sturges. Screenplay, Leon Uris; camera (Technicolor), Charles Lang; music, Dimitri Tiomkin; editor, Warren Low. Previewed May 6, '57. Running time, 122 MINS.

Wyatt Earp	Burt Lancaster
Doc Holliday	Kirk Douglas
Laura Denbow	Rhonda Fleming
Kate Fisher	Jo Van Fleet
Ringo	John Ireland
Ike Clanton	Lyle Bettger
Cotton Wilson	Frank Faylen
Charles Bassett	Earl Holliman
Shanghai Pierce	Ted DeCorsia
Billy Clanton	Dennis Hopper
John P. Clum	Whit Bissell
John Shanssey	George Mathews
Virgil Earp	John Hudson
Morgan Earp	DeForest Kelley
James Earp	Martin Milner
Bat Masterson	Kenneth Toby
Ed Bailey	Lee Van Cleef
Betty Earp	Joan Camden
Mrs. Clanton	Olive Carey
Rick	Brian Hutton
Mayor Kelley	Nelson Leigh
Tom McLowery	Jack Elam
Drunken Cowboy	Don Castle

Hal Wallis has a strong money picture in this film based upon what is probably the most famous gunfight in the wild history of the Old West, and consequently a highly exploitable product. Topped with the double-barrel potency of the Burt Lancaster and Kirk Douglas names for marquee draw in both the outdoor and general markets, film is further enhanced by the pictorial values allowed by VistaVision and a haunting title song written by Ned Washington and Dimitri Tiomkin, pair who

previousy collabed on "High Noon."

Producer has taken the historic meeting of Wyatt Earp, a celebrated lawman of the west, his brothers and Doc Holliday, with the Clanton gang in the O. K. Corral of Tombstone, Ariz., and fashioned an absorbing yarn in action leading up to the gory gunfight. The Leon Uris screenplay traces the strange friendship built up between the oddly-assorted pair, Holliday a reckless gambler and killer with small respect for the law, and in its development and exciting climax John Sturges has captured the stirring spirit of the period in his sock direction.

Lancaster and Douglas enact the respective roles of Earp and Holliday, story opening in Fort Griffin, Tex., when the gun-handy Dodge City marshal saves the other from a lynch mob. Action moves then to the Kansas town, where Holliday, at first ordered to leave town but permitted to stay, helps Earp in gunning three badmen. When the marshal heeds the plea of one of his brothers, marshal of Tombstone, for aid in handling the dangerous Clanton gang, Holliday accompanies him and makes the fight his in final showdown.

Both stars are excellently cast in their respective characters. Rhonda Fleming is in briefly as a femme gambler whom Lancaster romances, beautifully effective, and Jo Van Fleet, as Holliday's constant travelling companion again demonstrates her ability in dramatic characterization. John Ireland ably portrays a hired gunman killed in the climaxing gun battle, Lyle Bettger provides proper menace as head of the Clanton gang and Earl Holliman does well by a deputy part. Colorful support is afforded by Lee Van Cleef, Ted DeCorsia, Frank Faylen, John Hudson, Martin Milner, Dennis Hopper, DeForrest Kelley.

Technical credits are above average, Charles Lang's color photography a decided assist. Warren Low's editing is sharp, Hal Pereira and Walter Tyler's art direction atmospheric and music score by Dimitri Tiomkin helps set the mood. Frankie Laine sings the title song effectively. *Whit.*

Night Passage
(TECHNIRAMA-COLOR)

James Stewart and Audie Murphy paired in sock western. Good outlook.

Hollywood, May 14.

Universal release of an Aaron Rosenberg production. Stars James Stewart, Audie Murphy; costars Dan Duryea, Dianne Foster, Elaine Stewart, Brandon deWilde; features Jay C. Flippen. Directed by James Neilson. Screenplay, Borden Chase, based on story by Norman A. Fox; camera (Technicolor), William Daniels; editor, Sherman Todd; music, Dimitri Tiomkin. Previewed May 3, '57. Running time, 90 MINS.

Grant McLaine	James Stewart
The Utica Kid	Audie Murphy
Whitey Harbin	Dan Duryea
Charlotte Drew	Dianne Foster
Verna Kimball	Elaine Stewart
Joey Adams	Brandon deWilde
Ben Kimball	Jay C. Flippen
Will Renner	Herbert Anderson
Concho	Robert J. Wilke
Jeff Kurth	Hugh Beaumont
Shotgun	Jack Elam
Howdy Sladen	Tommy Cook
Mr. Feeney	Paul Fix
Mrs. Vittles	Olive Carey
Tim Riley	James Flavin
Jubilee	Donald Curtis
Mrs. Feeney	Ellen Corby
Latigo	John Day
O'Brien	Kenny Williams
Trinidad	Frank Chase
Pick Gannon	Herold Goodwin
Shannon	Harold Tommy Hart
Dusty	Jack C. Williams
Torgenson	Boyd Stockman
Pache	Henry Wills
Roan	Chuck Roberson
Click	Willard Willingham
Rosa	Polly Burson
Linda	Patsy Novak
Leary	Ted Mapes

Universal has paired stars of its two all-time high grossers, James Stewart ("The Glenn Miller Story") and Audie Murphy ("To Hell and Back"), in this taut, well-made and sometimes fascinating western. B.O. voltage gives this one a chance of emerging as studio's top money picture of the year. First use of Technicolor's new widescreen, anamorphic process, Technirama, reveals an important photographic development which further boosts its grossing potential.

Borden Chase has fashioned his script around two brothers—Stewart, decent, upright; Murphy, wild, a deadly gunman—for the Aaron Rosenberg production which carries an excitement and magnificent pictorial beauty in its fast 90-minutes' running time. James Neilson has directed with an eye both to mounting story values and colorful performances, with Dan Duryea, leader of the outlaw band of which Murphy is a member, socking over a scene-stealing characterization. The Technirama process, too, gives new depth and definition to photography, said to combine the principals of both VistaVision and CinemaScope, that lends additional interest. Pic was lensed in the Durango-Silverton region of Colorado.

Plot carries a railroad-building backdrop. Stewart is a former railroad employee recalled to help transport the payroll to rail's-end, previous attempts to take the money through to rebelling workers having been stymied when outlaw gang conducts series of raids. He becomes involved with gang during a train holdup, losing coin temporarily when he entrusts it to a small boy to carry in a lunchbox. Later, at gang's headquarters, he dons a gun, when it's revealed he's a former gunslinger. In a speedy windup, Murphy throws in with him in a blazing battle with outlaws, and is killed saving Stewart's life.

Both stars deliver sound portrayals, Murphy making up in color Stewart's greater footage. Duryea is immense as outlaw chief who isn't quite certain whether he can outdraw Murphy, a wizard with a gun. Dianne Foster plays Murphy's girl friend appealingly, Elaine Stewart provides glamour as wife of Jay C. Flippen, railroad superintendent, and Brandon deWilde has a meaty role as boy-member of the gang who unknowingly carries payroll dough. Strong support also is offered by Robert J. Wilke, Hugh Beaumont, James Flavin and Herbert Anderson.

William Daniels leads off superior technical credits with beautiful photography, Sherman Todd's editing is tight and art direction by Alexander Golitzen and Robert Clatworthy fits story. Dimitri Tiomkin's musical score is an added plus for pic. Ned Washington collabing with him on two tuneful song numbers, "Follow the River" and "You Can't Get Far Without a Railroad." *Whit.*

Badlands of Montana

Above-average program western for supporting playoff in action market.

Hollywood, May 7.

20th-Fox release of Regal production written, produced, directed by Daniel B. Ullman. Stars Rex Reason, Margia Dean, Beverly Garland, Keith Larsen; features Emile Meyer, William Phipps, Stanley Farrar, Rankin Mansfield, John Pickard. Camera, Frederick Gately; editor, Neil Brunnenkant; music, Irving Gertz; song, "The Man with the Gallant Gun," Gertz and Hal Levy; sung by Bob Grabeau. Previewed April 30, '57. Running time, 75 MINS.

Steve	Rex Reason
Emily	Margia Dean
Susan	Beverly Garland
Rick	Keith Larsen
Hammer	Emile Meyer
George	Russ Bender
Paul	Robert Cunningham
Sammy	Ralph Peters
Ling	Lee Tung Foo
Rayburn	Stanley Farrar
Travis	Rankin Mansfield
Walt	William Phipps
Vince	John Pickard
Marshal	Paul Newlan
Bank Teller	John Lomma
Cavalry Sgt.	Jack Kruschen
First Girl	Elena Da Vinci
Bank Teller	George Taylor
Bank Manager	William Forester
First Outlaw	Larry Blake
Marshal Sloan	Ralph Sanford
Second Outlaw	William Tanner
Posseman	Roydon Clark
Second Girl	Helen Jay

A good story, well-directed and played, makes "Badlands of Montana" a better-than-average program western entry. 20th-Fox will have no trouble lining up supporting playdates for it in the outdoor market.

Daniel B. Ullman takes a three-way credit for the western entertainment, having written, produced and directed. The cast supplies good performances to help hold interest in the plot, which finds the hero forced to find shelter with an outlaw gang when a political opponent tricks him into a gun duel. He comes back from the wrong side of the law, however, to clean up his home town and win the outlaw chief's daughter at the finale.

Rex Reason is a very satisfactory hero, convincingly handling the acting and action demands of the assignment. Beverly Garland is attractively excellent as the daughter of the outlaw chief, Emile Meyer, who decides loving a lawman isn't so bad after all. Meyer also is excellent, as are Keith Larsen, trigger-happy gang member; Margia Dean, widow of John Pickard, the political opponent who meets justice in an early street duel; William Phipps, Stanley Farrar, Rankin Mansfield, Ralph Peters, Robert Cunningham, Russell Bender, Lee Tung Foo and others.

The Regal Films production for 20th-Fox release is effectively lensed in anamorphic RegalScope by Frederick Gately for a strong plus on sight values. Irving Gertz' score is well-used. Also, he contributed the tune, "Man With the Gun," lyrics by Hal Levy, which Bob Grabeau sings behind the title cards. Technical assists are all excellent. *Brog.*

The Seventh Sin
(C'SCOPE)

Heavy-handed picturization of W. Somerset Maugham's "The Painted Veil"; Eleanor Parker for marquee dressing.

Hollywood, May 14.

Metro release of a David Lewis production. Stars Eleanor Parker, Bill Travers, George Sanders, Jean Pierre Aumont, Francoise Rosay; features Ellen Corby. Directed by Ronald Neame. Screenplay, Karl Tunberg, based on W. Somerset Maugham novel, "The Painted Veil"; camera, Ray June; editor, Gene Ruggiero; music, Miklos Rozsa. Previewed May 8, '57. Running time, 92 MINS.

Carol Carwin	Eleanor Parker
Dr. Walter Carwin	Bill Travers
Tim Waddington	George Sanders
Paul Duvelle	Jean Pierre Aumont
Mother Superior	Francoise Rosay
Sister St. Joseph	Ellen Corby

This re-make of Metro's 1934 version of W. Somerset Maugham's novel, "The Painted Veil," has Eleanor Parker in the Greta Garbo role. Plot is old-fashioned by today's concept and little has been done to alleviate its heaviness, with the result pic will need all the draw of the Parker name to just break even.

David Lewis production unfolds in Hong Kong and a remote section of China where star, after cheating on her bacteriologist husband, accompanies him when he travels there to fight a cholera epidemic. Karl Tunberg screenplay attempts to show her regeneration from a shallow, loveless woman into a deeply feeling individual, but transformation doesn't come off very well, even when she asserts her love, too late, for the husband who dies of the plague when he doesn't have the resistance to throw off disease.

Ronald Neame's direction fails to arouse much interest in his characters with possible exception of George Sanders, a witty and cynical Englishman who befriends doctor and his wife in plague-infested town and who manages to rise above part.

Miss Parker is beautiful but lacks sympathy, and Bill Travers, as her husband, plays an oblique character as hard for the spectator to understand as the star professes him to be. Jean Pierre Aumont is a Hong Kong diplomat with whom femme carries on an affair, Francoise Rosay is another mother superior of a convent in stricken Chinese city and Ellen Corby one of the sisters. Judy Dan, in for a single brief sequence, is lovely as Sanders' Chinese wife.

Art direction by William A. Horning and Daniel B. Cathcart strikes an appropriate exotic note for good production values, and Ray June's camera work is artistic.
Whit.

Bailout at 43,000

Swan song from Pine-Thomas. Based on TV yarn. Theatre prospects okay.

United Artists release of a Pine-Themas-Shane production. Stars John Payne, Karen Steele, Paul Kelly. Co-stars Richard Eyer. Directed by Francis D. Lyon. Story and Screenplay, Paul Monash; editor, George Gittens; music, Albert Glasser. Previewed April 26, '57. Running time, **78 MINS.**

Major Paul Peterson	John Payne
Carol Peterson	Karen Steele
Colonel Hughes	Paul Kelly
Kit Peterson	Richard Eyer
Frances Nolan	Constance Ford
Capt. Mike Cavallero	Eddie Firestone
Lt. Simmons	Adam Kennedy
Reinach	Gregory Gay
Major Goldman	Steven Ritch
Captain Nolan	Richard Crane

"Bailout at 43,000" shapes up as a fairly suspenseful adaptation of the Paul Monash yarn first presented on "Climax" over CBS television last spring. Enough commercialism to rate it okay for the general market.

As a sidelight, "Bailout" is the 87th—and last—film to be made under the Pine-Thomas banner. The first 84 were produced for Paramount by William C. Thomas and the late William H. Pine; the last three for United Artists by Thomas and Howard Pine, William's son.)

Story, which author Monash also has screenplayed, deals with the Air Research and Development Command branch of the Air Force; more specifically, the ARDC objective to develop and test under actual flying conditions a downward ejection seat for B-47 high-altitude jet bombers.

Central character is John Payne, called back into active service and requested by Paul Kelly, head of project, to serve on the ARDC team. Kelly senses a certain nervousness in Payne, and selects two other officers to precede him in the ballout tests. Payne, meantime, takes the move by Kelly, whose judgement he respects, having flown with him in the Korean war, as a lack of confidence in his ability and thus becomes unsure of himself, uncertain as to whether he'll chicken out when his turn does arrive. Making the first bailout is Eddie Firestone, who lands with a broken neck, following which Adam Kennedy, second-in-line, is suddenly hospitalized for an emergency appendectomy. It comes Payne's turn, he goes through with the jump and the test is proven a success. It also leaves Payne with faith in himself reaffirmed and assured of future peace of mind.

Payne moves through his role with ease and assurance, while Karen Steele is okay in the rather thankless part of his wife. Film is last for the late Paul Kelly, and his performance here is a good one. Among others showing up well are Richard Eyer, as Payne's young son; Constance Ford, the wife of flyer Richard Crane; and Eddie Firestone.

Direction of Francis D. Lyon, while a little off on the pacing, is generally okay and brings out the good cast performances. Lionel Lindon's camera work tops the list of good technical contributions.
Neal.

Hot Rod Rumble

More madcap youth stuff well done. Teams with "Calypso Joe."

Allied Artists release of Nacirema production. Stars Leigh Snowden, Richard Hartunioa, Wright King; features Joey Forman, Brett Halsey, Larry Dolgin, John Brinkley, Chuck Webster, Ned Glass, Phil Adams, Joe Mell. Directed by Leslie H. Martinson. Screenplay, Meyer Dolinsky; camera, Lester Shorr; editor, Richard C. Meyer; music, Alexander Courage. Previewed May 1, '57. Running time, **79 MINS.**

Fine programmer, boasting an interest-holding storyline enhanced by good acting and direction. Stacked with juve appeal, "Hot Rod Rumble" is being teamed by Allied Artists as a double-bill with "Calypso Joe."

The Meyer Dolinsky screenplay centers around Richard Hartunian, member of the "Road Devils" hot rod club and fairly unpopular because of his eccentric mannerisms. Thus, after a verbal battle with girl friend Leigh Snowden, he draws the blame when the car in which she's being driven home by another club member is harassed by a hot rodder along a dark road, causing a wreck which injures her and kills the driver. Actually, the unseen driver was Wright King, also a club member and supposed friend of Hartunian's, who caused the wreck after being rebuffed by Miss Snowden. Naturally, by time of The Big Race (which, of course, Hartunian wins), King's guilt has been discovered and Hartunian draws apologies from all concerned.

Hartunian, newcomer from east, turns in an extremely interesting performance — most notable because of its marked similarity in voice and style to Marlon Brando. In this case, however, it fits well into the particular characterization to result in a fine overall enactment.

Miss Snowden, a bit heavier than usual, is okay in the femme lead, as is King in third starred part. Good as other club members are Joey Forman, Brett Halsey and Larry Dolgin.

Leslie H. Martinson's direction is a definite plus asset, giving film a good pacing and working especially well in conjunction with cameraman Lester Shorr to capture the various racing sequences. Also on the credit side is the background score by Alexander Courage.

Film was produced by Norman T. Herman, with David T. Yokozeki serving as executive producer. Both rate a bow.
Neal.

Curse of Frankenstein
(BRITISH-COLOR)

Remake of classic thriller should satisfy sensation-seekers. Peter Cushing top ranking in mad scientist role.

London, May 7.

Warner release of a Hammer (Anthony Hinds) production. Stars Peter Cushing, Hazel Court, Robert Urquhart, Christopher Lee. Directed by Terence Fisher. Screenplay, Jimmy Sangster, based on classic by Mary Shelley; camera, Jack Asher; editor, James Needs; music, Leonard Salzedo. At Warner Theatre, London. Running time, **82 MINS.**

Baron Victor Frankenstein	Peter Cushing
The Creature	Christopher Lee
Elizabeth	Hazel Court
Paul Krempe	Robert Urquhart
Justine	Valerie Gaunt
Aunt Sophia	Noel Hood
Mother	Marjorie Hume
The Young Victor	Melvyn Hayes
The Young Elizabeth	Sally Walsh
Professor Bernstein	Paul Hardtmuth
Grandfather	Fred Johnson
Small Boy	Claude Kingston
Schoolmaster	Henry Caine
Werner	Michael Mulcaster
Kurt	Patrick Troughton
Fritiz	Joseph Behrman
Burgomaster	Hugh Dempster
Burgomaster's Wife	Anne Blake
Father Felix	Raymond Rollett
A Priest	Alex Gallier
Undertaker	Ernest Jay
Uncle	J. Trevor Davis
A Tramp	Bartlett Mullins
Second Priest	Eugene Leahy

This British version of the classic shocker well deserves its horrific rating, and praise for its more subdued handling of the macabre story. The emphasis lies not so much on the uncontrollable blood lust of the created monster as on the gruesome, distasteful clinical details whereby the crazy scientist accumulates the odd organs with which to assemble the creature to which he finally exultantly gives life. As this is the first time the subject has been depicted in color, all the grim trappings are more vividly impressive. In its present form pic will seek its own audience level, and should prove highly profitable.

Story is unfolded to a priest while the infamous Baron Frankenstein is awaiting execution for multiple murders he vainly protests have been committed by his man-made monster. In the flashback he is seen as a young boy avid for scientific research and sharing with his tutor his determination to build up a human being through chemical hocus-pocus and graveyard snatchings. When their abominable purpose has been achieved, the tutor breaks off the unholy alliance, realizing the appalling consequences when the dreadful thing escapes.

Peter Cushing gets every inch of drama from the leading role, making almost believable the ambitious urge and diabolical accomplishment. Melvyn Hayes as the child skilfully conveys the ruthless self-possession of the embryo man. Robert Urquhart convincingly marks the change of character from the young tutor to the dedicated scientist who ultimately rebels, while Hazel Court has little to do but grace the bachelors' table and express horror on her wedding eve when she ferrets out the dread secret and gets caught in the monster's clutches.

Valerie Gaunt is more vibrantly attractive as the Baron's discarded mistress while Christopher Lee arouses more of pity than horror in his interpretation of the creature. His death as a living torch plunging into a vat of acid is one of the most realistic of the spectacular highlights.

Direction and camera work are of a high order.
Clem.

Ikaru
(To Live)
(JAPANESE)

Paris, May 7.

Toho production and release. Stars Takashi Shimura; features Miki Odagari, Nobuo Kaneko, Kyoko Seki, Makoto Kobori. Directed by Akira Kurosawa. Screenplay, Kurosawa, Shinobu Hashimoto; camera, Asaichi Nakai; editor, Hideo Oguni, Kurosawa; music, Fumio Hayasaka. Preemed in Paris. Running time, **140 MINS.**

Old Man	Takashi Shimura
Girl	Miki Odagiri
Son	Nobuo Kaneko
Son's Wife	Kyoko Seki
Writer	Makoto Kobori

Here is an intrinsically Japanese film impregnated with western techniques, making this an unusual offbeater that should be a natural for U.S. arties. Its theme of a dying man's self realization is downbeat but never grim. Story emerges a profound experience probing an ordinary man's last days and its implications on friends and co-workers. It is technically excellent with a telling Occidental-type musical score.

Its theme, length and Japanese emotional patterns may limit this, at first, to specialized U.S. spots. But crix praise and word-of-mouth could build it into a substantial grosser. U.S. indies crying for product may go for this.

Director Akira Kurosawa, known for his "Rashomon" and his "Magnificent Seven," here unspools a work of compassion. An ordinary white collar worker, an aging head of a public work's bureau, finds he has cancer and a few months to live. He tells nobody but finds that he is really alone and estranged from his son and daughter-in-law. He suddenly sees that his life has been dull and useless, wasted in an office from which he has not been absent in 30 years.

He draws out his money, which he has painstakingly saved for his son, after becoming an early widower, and goes out into the Tokyo night. He meets a deadbeat poet in whom he confides. They go out on the town, and a westernized, garish nightlife is unfolded in nightmarish profusion. Death is evident in his outlook and, at times, envelops his companion and the people they meet.

He goes home where his uncomprehending son reproaches him. Meeting one of his office girls, he finds her new job, that of making toys for children, gives him a sudden goal. He will push a needed children's playground through all the bureaucratic red tape. He does it, and dies on one of the new swings.

Half of the film is told in the third person and half is his sacrifice as seen through the eyes of guests at his funeral. Kurosawa performs a tour-de-force in keeping a dramatic thread throughout and avoiding the mawkish. It is eminently filmic in form and superlatively acted.
Mosk.

Cannes Festival

Sissi (AUSTRIAN; COLOR). Erma Film production and release. Stars Romy Schneider, Karlheinz Bohm; features, Magda Schneider, Gustav Knuth, Uta Franz. Written and directed by Ernest Marischka. Camera (Agfacolor), Bruno Mondi; editor, Fritz Jonstorff. At the Paris, Paris. Running time, **102 MINS.**

Every once in awhile a tenuous little film suddenly crosses all borders and begins to pull in heavy coinage to the general puzzlement of distribs everywhere. Such is the case with this sentimental, sudsy "Sissi." Depicting the youth of Emperor Franz Joseph, and how he finally marries the little sister of his intended love, it has the usual operetta schmaltz without the music.

Sissi is a headstrong, simple little girl who meets the Emperor and love blooms finally. Color is uneven, technical credits good and playing vacillates between low comedy and haughty seriousness. Romy Schneider, a star in Germany, is a heavyset, Teutonic looker whose main plus-factor is a gurgling innocence. Her gauche girlishness manages to be acceptable. Hollywood could well take a look at her. For the U.S. this rather hokey piece still appears limited in spite of its Continental cleanup. *Mosk.*

Kanikosen (JAPANESE). Yamada production and release. Written and directed by Satoru Yamamura from novel by Tahigi Kobayashi. Camera, Akira Ifukube; editor, Yamamura. At Vendome, Paris. Running time, **100 MINS.**

Kanikosen were the infamous crab fishing boats which roamed the Japanese seas in the 1920's. Pic has a heavy socially slated, revolutionary format reminiscent of the pre-war Soviet films. It details the sordid, oppressed lives of the crab fishermen and their final revolt which is bloodily suppressed by the Royal Navy.

Though somewhat repititious and overlong, pic has power and directness. However, the overstatement in acting and direction slant this only for specialized spotting in America. *Mosk.*

Bonjour Toubib (Hi Doc) (FRENCH). Pathe production and release. Stars Noel Noel; features Georges Descrieres, Bertha Bovy, Ginette Pigeon. Directed by Louis Cuny. Screenplay, Jean Cosmos, Cuny, Serge De Boissac, Noel; camera, P. Cottevet; editor, Jean Feyte. At Marignan, Paris. Running time, **110 MINS.**

In the best soap opera tradition, this offers a day in the life a humble doctor who turns out to be better than his haughty specialized colleagues. Complications are a son who will not become a doctor but is brought around, and his many cases and charitable tendencies. Simplified and surface is characterization, it is carried along by Noel Noel's knowing limning of the little, self-effacing doctor.

Pic seems dubious for the U.S. but might be worth dubbing for video where its simple progression and happenings could be palatable. Technical aspects are good as is the cast. *Mosk.*

Elisa (FRENCH; COLOR). Roger Richebe release of Richebe-Paris-Overseas production. Stars Dany Carrel, Serge Reggiani; features Lysiane Rey, Valentine Tessier, Marthe Mercadier. Directed by Rober Richebe. Screenplay, Francois Boyer from novel by Edomond de Goncourt; camera (Eastmancolor), Roger Hubert, editor, Yvonne Martin. At Lutetita, Paris. Running time, **105 MINS.**

This is a meaty slice of life depicting the tribulations of a prostitute of the 19th Century in Paris. Despite unfolding in the bagnio milieu, it never gets erotic or suggestive, concerning itself with the exterior aspects of the setting. Story details the love which blossoms between the joy girl Elisa and a blind organist. When he finds out what she is, he tries to rape her and is killed in the scuffle.

Film plods along and is rarely infused with a feeling for the times or the girl who drifts into things normally after being imprisoned for her mother's abortion activities. Main usage for the U.S. would have to depend on exploitation. Color is uneven but decors and costumes help.

Dany Carrel displays acting ability in her first major role while Serge Reggiani confirms his talents in as the blind lover. Director Roger Richebe rarely generates feeling for the hapless plight of the heroine. Production values are good. *Mosk.*

Kome (The Rice People) (JAPANESE; COLOR). Toei release and production. With Shinjaro Ehara, Masako Nakamura, Isao Kimura, Yuko Mochiziki. Directed by Tadashi Imai. Screenplay, Yasutaro Yagi; camera (Eastmancolor), Shunichiro Nakano; editor, Yoshiki Nagasawa; music, Yasushi Akutagawa. At Cannes Film Fest. Running time, **120 MINS.**

Film concerns the poor rice workers and particularly the younger sons who are disinherited and form a band who live by fishing and poaching rather than the rice fields. Film is too involved in its preparation and only gets into its story of the tale of two lovers and the death of a mother thru official persecution in the last half. This makes it slow and lagging in spite of excellent color and a good documentary sense.

Technically it is competently managed, but the laborious, unclear scripting militates against this in spite of good thesping. *Mosk.*

Betrogen Bis Zum Juengsten Tag (Duped Till the Last) (EAST GERMAN). DEFA production and release. With Rudolph Ulrich, Wolfgang Kieling, Hans-Joachim Martens, Renate Kuster. Directed by Kurt Jung-Alsen. Screenplay, Kurt Bortfeldt from novel "Kameraden," by Franz Fuhmann; camera, W. Sussenguth; editor, Alsen. At Cannes Film Fest. Running time, **75 MINS.**

East German pic castigates the Nazi mentality in a taut tale about three friends who kill a girl by mistake while shooting at a bird. They are on the Russian border, just before the attack on Russia, and a Gestapo general, to shield his son who is one of the men involved in the accident, blames it on the Russians which preceeds Hitler's orders to march into the Soviet territory. Film is grey but absorbing as it lays bare the men's reactions to their deed.

Though somewhat morbid, it states the cast against the Nazi creed, telling it in filmic terms. Pic still remains a specialized item, but could do for arty spots in the U.S. Direction is taut, acting exact and, overall, has a suspenseful, powerful theme to overcome its propaganda aspects. *Mosk.*

Kanal (They Loved Life) (POLISH). Film Polski production and release. With Tadeusz Janczar, Teresa Isewka, Misczyslaw Glinski. Directed by Andrej Wajda. Screenplay, Jerzy Stawinski; camera, Jerzy Lipmann; editor, Roman Mann. At Cannes Film Fest. Running time, **95 MINS.**

Hallucinating pic, depicting the last days of the Polish resistance in Warsaw, is not for the squeamish. However, film has a heartfelt reenactment of these days of terror, making a taut penetrating subject that could well make a telling specialized U.S. entry. It takes a company of partisans and deftly blocks out their characters and then follows them into their nightmarish descent into the sewers to escape the Germans. Here mass heroism and the utter horror of war are made explicit.

Direction, if theatrical at times (but the subject almost calls for this), is dynamic, acting first-rate as are technical credits. Right exploitation could well make this a worthy U.S. arty theatre entry. *Mosk.*

Dolyna Miru (The Peaceful Valley) (YUGOSLAVIAN). Trigla release and production. Stars John Kitzmiller; features, Evelyn Wohlfeiler, Tugomir Stiglic. Dircted by France Stiglic. Screenplay, Ivan Rubic; camera, Rudi Vaupotic; editor, Rodjojka Ivancevic; music, Marijan Kozina. At Cannes Film Fest. Running time, **90 MINS.**

Film is reminiscent of the French film "Forbidden Games" in its detailing of the effect of war on two young children. However, it lacks the lyric quality of the former though adroitly made and children well handled. Seems a chancy U. S. item.

Children are orphaned and run away to seek a peaceful valley. On their trek they meet a grounded Negro American aviator who cares for them. They do find a peaceful valley but the Germans come and the American is killed leaving the children still searching. Film is technically acceptable, moppet work is excellent and John Kitzmiller, an American actor, is adequate. *Mosk.*

La Casa Del Angel (The House of the Angel) (ARGENTINIAN). Sono Film rerease and production. Stars, Elsa Daniel, Lautaro Murua; features, Gullermo Battaglia, Jordana Fain, Berta Ortegosa. Directed by Leopoldo Torre Nilsson. Screenplay, Nilsson, Beatriz Guido, Martin Mentasti from a novel by Miss Guido; camera, Ricardo Agudo; editor, Jorge Garate. At Cannes Film Fest. Running time, **75 MINS.**

Well mounted Spanish language film details how a puritanical upbringing brings destruction to the budding life of a young girl. Acting, direction and a firm narrative style combine to make this engrossing pic a natural for lingo spots and of possible appeal for specialized U. S. situations.

In flashback it details how a sensitive young girl is warped by her religious mother. She is made to bathe with a slip on, and so steeped in the fear of sin that her first love turns into hatred for the man and leads to her inability to accept his love.

Direction, arty at times, keeps interest but does not fully mark the dramatic poignance inherent in the tale. Acting and technical credits are excellent. *Mosk.*

Silk Stockings
(SONGS-C'SCOPE-COLOR)

"Ninotchka" made into an updated spoof of Bolsheviki. Top musical with names of Fred Astaire and Cyd Charisse, and Cole Porter tunes. Strong returns.

Hollywood, May 21.

Metro release of an Arthur Freed production. Stars Fred Astaire, Cyd Charisse; costars Janis Paige, Peter Lorre; features George Tobias, Jules Munshin, Joseph Buloff, Wim Sonneveld. Directed by Rouben Mamoulian. Screenplay, Leonard Gershe, Leonard Spigelgass; based on musical, "Silk Stockings," with book by George S. Kaufman, Leueen McGrath, Abe Burrows, suggested by "Ninotchka"; camera (Technicolor), Robert Bronner; editor, Harold F. Kress; music supervision, Andre Previn. Previewed May 15, '57. Running time, **117 MINS.**

Steve Canfield	Fred Astaire
Ninotchka	Cyd Charisse
Peggy Dayton	Janis Paige
Brankov	Peter Lorre
Vassili Markovitch	George Tobias
Ivanov	Joseph Buloff
Bibinski	Jules Munshin

"Silk Stockings," has Fred Astaire and Cyd Charisse, the music of Cole Porter and comes off as a top-grade musical version of Metro's 1939 "Ninotchka," from which studio may expect handsome returns. Adapted from the Broadway musical adaptation of same tag, latter of course inspired by the Metro spoof aforesaid film is slickly dressed in CinemaScope and Metrocolor for sock production appeal.

Porter has added two new songs for the Arthur Freed production which has a total of 13 numbers, several on the near spectacular side. Miss Charisse has role first played by Greta Garbo and on Broadway by Hildegarde Neff. Astaire enacts an American film producer in Paris who falls for the beautiful Commie when she arrives from Moscow to check on the activities of three Russian commissars.

Tighter editing of the rather long 117 minutes' running time would have improved. Assets are Janis Paige, as a Hollywood star come to French capital for Astaire's picture, and clever clowning of Peter Lorre, Jules Munshin and Joseph Buloff, the commissar trio who succumb to the allure of gay Paree.

Rouben Mamoulian in his deft direction of the well-developed Leonard Gershe-Leonard Spigelgass screenplay maintains a flowing if over-long course. Musical numbers are bright, inserted naturally, and both Astaire and Miss Charisse shine in dancing department, together and singly. Choreography is by Hermes Pan (Astaire numbers) and Eugene Loring (others).

Film has several outstanding song numbers, including "Stereophonic Sound," comedy number pairing Astaire and Miss Paige; Miss Charisse warbling title song, in a sequence showing her transformation, via dainty femme raiment, from a Commie martinet to a lovely lady who falls in love with the American; "Satin and Silk," comedy strip-tease by Miss Paige; "Siberia," Lorre - Munshin - Buloff. "Red Blues" is one of pic's highlights, as terped by femme star and a chorus of Russians. Porter's two new tunes are the melodic "Fated To Be Mated" and closing "Ritz Roll and Rock," which Astaire swings over.

Astaire delivers with his customary style, and Miss Charisse brings a fascinating brightness to her role. Miss Paige shares top honors with the stars for a knock-'em-dead type of performance, George Tobias has a few good moments as a

Commie chief, and Lorre, Munshin and Buloff are immense. Wim Sonneveld, Dutch actor making his American film bow, handles himself well as the Russian composer whose threat not to return to Russia from Paris springboards entire action.

Technical credits are above average. Robert Bronner beautifully photographs, music supervision of Andre Previn and orchestral arrangements by Conrad Salinger are finely executed and costumes by Helen Rose particularly attractive. Harold F. Kress' editing makes the most of his footage, and Robert Tucker is credited with vocal supervision of the fine Porter numbers. Art direction by William A. Horning and Randall Duell also is effective. *Whit.*

Let's Be Happy
(BRITISH-C'SCOPE-COLOR) (SONGS)

Entertaining musical for popular tastes, with Vera-Ellen and Tony Martin sure-footed in conventional roles.

London, May 14.

Associated British-Pathe release of a Marcel Hellman Production. Stars Tony Martin, Vera-Ellen, Robert Flemyng. Directed by Henry Levin. Screenplay, Diana Morgan from play "Jeannie," by Aimee Stuart; camera, Erwin Hillier; editor, E. B. Jarvis; music by Nicholas Brodsky; lyrics, Paul Francis Webster. At Studio One, London, May 8, '57. Running time, **107 MINS.**

Jeannie MacLean	Vera-Ellen
Stanley Smith	Tony Martin
Lord James MacNairn	Robert Flemyng
Helene	Zena Marshall
Sadie Whitelaw	Helen Horton
Rev. MacDonald	Beckett Hould
French Ticket Clerk	Alfred Burke
Air Line Steward	Vernon Greeves
Bearded Man	Richard Molinas
Diner Attendant	Eugene Deckers
Hotel Clerk	Russell Waters
Page Boy	Paul Young
MacTavish	Peter Sinclair
Mrs. MacTavish	Magda Miller
Hotel Valet	Brian Oulton
Mr. Fielding	Guy Middleton
Mrs. Fielding	Katherine Kath
Mr. Ferguson	Charles Carson
Elderly Dancer	Jock McKay
Monsieur Fior	Michael Anthony
Mrs. Cathie	Jean Cadell
Dougal MacLean	Gordon Jackson

A gay, lively musical has been made from the old stage comedy, "Jeannie" giving ample opportunities for Tony Martin and Vera-Ellen to exhibit their talents. The appeal of the rags-to-riches story should satisfy the general run of audiences. For overseas patrons, there is the background of the Edinburgh Festival, showing colorful panoramas of Scottish beauty spots as added interest. In addition, there is a Worth fashion parade that will insure appeal to femme patrons.

Vera-Ellen never loses the authentic wideeyed look of the smalltown girl whose sudden wealth sends her scurrying off to see the land of her forefathers. Her ticup with a high pressure salesman, who helps her over the thorny patches of foreign travel, supplies the main love interest. This, however, gets lost enroute until re-established for the final clinch. The dancer gets her opportunity to shine when she visualizes herself in the shoes of the prima ballerina in an enchanting Ballet of Cards.

The girl soon runs through her inheritance, having spent her last cent on an elaborate hotel suite and slinky clothes. She is mistaken for a millionairess and ardently wooed by a Scottish Lord reduced to living in two rooms of his ancestral castle. The mating instinct arises in the American too late, the prize having been won by the kilt. As soon as the Scot learns the true state of the girl's fortune, he gracefully backs out of their engagement. Back home in Vermont, Cinderella snaps out of her dreams and her salesman turns up again to the inevitable happy ending.

Martin as the ubiquitous Mr. Fix-It who finally gets his mate, sails through the role with an easy assurance, and gives full value to the attractive vocal numbers. Zena Marshall is alluring as an ensnaring redhead and Robert Flemyng represents with dignity and charm the impoverished nobleman. Supporting cast gives sterling support. The pic is directed with effortless precision. *Clem.*

Hell's Crossroads
(NATURAMA)

Friends of Jesse James—again. Western strictly for the lower half of a double bill.

Hollywood, May 16.

Republic release of Rudy Ralston production. Stars Stephen McNally, Peggie Castle, Robert Vaughn. Features Barton MacLane, Harry Shannon, Henry Brandon, Douglas Kennedy, Grant Withers, Myron Healey, Frank Wilcox, Jean Howell, Morris Ankrum. Directed by Franklin Adreon. Screeneplay, John K. Butler, Barry Shipman, from story by Butler; camera, John L. Russell Jr.; music, Gerald Roberts; editor, Tony Martinelli. Reviewed May 15, 1957. Running time, 73 **MINS.**

Vic Rodell	Stephen McNally
Paula Collins	Peggie Castle
Bob Ford	Robert Vaughn
Clyde O'Connell	Barton MacLane
Clay Ford	Harry Shannon
Jesse James	Henry Brandon
Frank James	Douglas Kennedy
Sheriff Steve Oliver	Grant Withers
Cole Younger	Myron Healey
Gov. Crittenden	Frank Wilcox
Mrs. Jesse James	Jean Howell
Wheeler	Morris Ankrum

The James boys (Frank & Jesse), Bob Ford and the Younger Brothers are among the outlaws romping through "Hell's Crossroads." The basic story-line holds little interest, however, so it all shapes up as a below-par programmer.

Yarn centers about Stephen McNally, long-time friend of Jesse James and a member of his gang. After a hold-up at film's start, however, he decides to give up the crime-life so he can marry the girl of his choice, Peggie Castle. Another gang member wanting to give it all up is Miss Castle's brother, Robert Vaughn (Bob Ford). McNally and Vaughn are still criminals in the eyes of the law, however, and gain their eventual freedom only after Miss Castle makes a deal with the Governor, i.e., pardons for both if either brings in Jesse—dead or alive. Ford shoots Jesse in the back, killing him, the full pardons follow, and McNally is able to settle down with Miss Castle. To a degree that was the literal history of Bob Ford.

Acting runs along acceptable lines, newcomer Robert Vaughn making the best impression. Thesp, incidentally, is now a Hecht-Hill-Lancaster contractee, temporarily pacted by the U.S. Army. Showing up well, too, as Jesse James, is Henry Brandon.

Franklin Adreon's direction of the Rudy Ralston production is stock, as are majority of the technical contributions. *Neal.*

Tammy and Bachelor
(C'SCOPE-COLOR)

Bright romantic comedy about modern South, but without "that problem." Should please family trade.

Hollywood, May 21.

Universal production and release. Stars Debbie Reynolds, co-starring Leslie Nielsen, Walter Brennan, Mala Powers, Sidney Blackmer, Mildred Natwick; features Fay Wray, Philip Ober, Craig Hill, Louise Beavers, with April Kent. Produced by Ross Hunter, directed by Joseph Pevney. Screenplay, Oscar Brodney, from Cid Ricketts Sumner novel; camera (Technicolor), Arthur E. Arling; editor, Ted J. Kent; music, Frank Skinner; song, "Tammy," Jay Livingston and Ray Evans. Previewed at Chinese Theatre, Hollywood, May 7, '57. Running time, **87 MINS.**

Tammy	Debbie Reynolds
Peter Brent	Leslie Nielsen
Grandpa	Walter Brennan
Barbara	Mala Powers
Professor Brent	Sidney Blackmer
Aunt Renie	Milded Natwick
Mrs. Brent	Fay Wray
Alfred Bissle	Philip Ober
Ernie	Craig Hill
Osia	Louise Beavers
Tina	April Kent

This Debbie Reynolds starrer, although localed in the modern South, studiously avoids any sociological-racial problems. Rather, the emphasis of the Oscar Brodney scenario, from a Cid Ricketts Sumner novel, is on romantic comedy, and a fresh and winsome offering it is, too. Bolstered by the Reynolds name, it should prove an okay attraction, especially for the family and femme trade.

Tale is a restatement of the familiar theme of the wide-eyed innocent transported to a sophisticated world, and her candid observations, spiced with a native and ingenuous wisdom. Miss Reynolds portrays a teen-aged miss from the backwoods bayous of Louisiana, who's staying with the family of playboy bachelor Leslie Nielsen. 'Pears as how Miss Tammy and her lay-preachin' grandpaw, Walter Brennan, saved Nielsen's life after a plane crash. When grandpaw gets in trouble with some fool law over a speck of corn-likker makin', Miss Tammy takes up the Nielsen invite to come and visit a spell.

Well, sir, set a wide-eyed innocent loose on a frustrated, oversophisticated household, and in practically no time at all she's solved most of their problems. There's Nielsen, yearning to make the family plantation again self-supporting; his maiden aunt, Mildred Natwick, who wants an art career in New Orleans; his insecure mother, Fay Wray, who's trying to make the plantation a re-incarnation of the Old South; his fiancee, Mala Powers, a coldly ambitious wench; and his professorial father, Sidney Blackmer, retreating into his books. Not only does Miss Reynolds win Nielsen away from Miss Powers by the time the pic has run its course, but has set the other cast characters well on their individual ways to happier lives.

Actually, there's a lot more fun to this than the bare outline indicates. Director Joseph Pevney shrewdly underlines Miss Reynalds' indomitable artlessness, without falling into the pitfall of oversentimentality.

Miss Reynolds is refreshingly attractive in both comic and romantic sequences, and makes a fetchingly tart innocent. Nielsen, largely a foil for Miss Reynolds, handles the assignment with commendable aplomb.

Brennan, a vet at this sort of thing, knows what to do and does it well. Miss Natwick also contributes a standout support chore as the briskly sentimental aunt. Miss Powers hasn't much to do, but is definitely decorative, as is Fay Wray. Craig Hill, Philip Ober, Blackmer and Louise Beaver contribute smart bits in lesser roles.

Title song, "Tammy," sung under the opening credits by the Ames Brothers and during the pic by Miss Reynolds, has a pleasant, folksy quality that fits the pic's mood well. Tune, cleffed by Jay Livingston and Ray Evans, might go as a folk-tune entry.

All technical credits are top-rate, especially excellent Technicolor photography by Arthur E. Arling. *Kove.*

China Gate
(C'SCOPE)

Okay entry for melo market.

Hollywood, May 14.

Twentieth-Fox release of a Samuel Fuller production. Stars Gene Barry, Angie Dickinson, Nat "King" Cole; features Paul DuBov, Lee Van Cleef, George Givot, Gerald Milton, Neyle Morrow, Marcel Dalio. Director-screenplay, Fuller; camera, Joseph Biroc; music, Victor Young, Max Steiner; editor, Gene Fowler Jr. Previewed May 7, '57. Running time, **96 MINS.**

Brock	Gene Barry
Lucky Legs	Angie Dickinson
Goldie	Nat King Cole
Captain Caumont	Paul DuBov
Major Cham	Lee Van Cleef
Corporal Pigalle	George Givot
Private Andreades	Gerald Milton
Leung	Neyle Morrow
Father Paul	Marcel Dalio
Colonel De Sars	Maurice Marsac
The Boy	Warren Hsieh
Corporal Kruger	Paul Busch
Private Jaszi	Sasha Harden
Charlie	James Hong
Moi Leader	William Soo Hoo
Guard	Walter Soo Hoo
Khuan	Weaver Levy

"China Gate" is an over-long but sometimes exciting story of the battle between Vietnamese and Red Chinese, told through the efforts of a small band of French Legionnaires to reach and destroy a hidden Communist munitions dump. Realistic in its action sequences, the effect frequently is dissipated through lengthy scenes of dialog which slow movement to a walk. Given a 10 to 15-minutes' trimming, it should do okay in the melodrama market.

Samuel Fuller gives his indie good production values, early use of Oriental war footage clips establishing an interesting story setting. A novel touch is inserted through the dominating character being a beautiful Eurasian woman, who leads the Legion demolition patrol to its objective through enemy territory. An added exploitation turn is the casting of Nat King Cole in dual assignment of a straight role and warbling title song.

Gene Barry and Angie Dickinson top the cast, former an American in the Legion, in charge of dynamiting operations of the Red ammunition cache; latter the Eurasian who is trusted by the Communists but on the side of the patriots. Romantic conflict is realized through their having once been married, Barry having left her when their child was born with strictly Chinese features. A return to their former relations is beginning on the march, but before they can resume femme is blown up at the dump when she deliberately makes a dynamite connection the Reds have cut.

Miss Dickinson does yoeman service with her colorful role and should benefit in further castings. Barry also handles himself well but part sometimes is negative. Cole as the only other American in Legion patrol shows he can act as well as sing. Expert support is lent by Paul DuBow, Maurice Marsac, Sasha Harden, Gerald Milton, Legionnaires; Lee Van Cleef, Communist commander; Warren Hsieh, five-year-old son of two principals.

Technical departments are well handled by Joseph Biroc, camera; Max Steiner adding to late Victor Young's music score; John Mansbridge, art direction. *Whit.*

The Monster That Challenged the World

Routine science fiction entry geared for secondary houses on double feature.

United Artists release of Jules V. Levy and Arthur Gardner production. Stars Tim Holt and Audrey Dalton. Features Han Conried, Barbara Darrow, Casey Adams and Harlan Ware. Directed by Arnold Laven. Screenplay, Pat Fiedler; from a story by David Duncan. Camera, Maurice Vaccarino; editor, John Faure; underwater cameraman, Scotty Welborn; music, Heinz Roemheld. Previewed in N.Y., May 17, '57. Running time, 83 MINS.

Lt. Comdr. John Twillinger .... Tim Holt
Gail MacKenzie .... Audrey Dalton
Dr. Jess Rogers .... Hans Conried
Lt. Bob Clemens.......... Harlan Warde
Tad Johns .... Casey Adams
Sandy MacKenzie .... Mimi Gibson
Josh Peters .... Gordon Jones
Connie Blake .... Marjorie Stapp
George Blake .... Dennis McCarthy
Jody Sims .... Barbara Darrow
Mort Beatty .... Bob Beneveds
Clarke .... Michael Dugan
Capt. Masters .... Mack Williams
Sally .... Eileen Harley
Seaman Fred Johnson .... Jody McCrea
Seaman Howard Sanders William Swan
Wyatt .... Charles Tannen
Coroner .... Byron Kane
Mr. Davis .... Hal Taggert
Deputy Scott .... Gil Frye
Deputy Brewer .... Dan Gachman
Mr. Dobbs .... Milton Parsons
Old Gatekeeper .... Ralph Moody

"The Monster That Challenged the World" is a standard and familiar science fiction-monster entry geared for secondary houses and double feature playing time. It's a technically well-made picture, however, and neatly fits the groove for which it is obviously intended.

Producers Jules V. Levy and Arthur Gardner have assembled a competent cast that does its best to provide the most for what now seems a well-worn plot. An earthquake near a Naval research center in an isolated California desert area activates pre-historic monsters in the Salton Sea, a salt water body in the middle of the desert.

The monsters, who are amphibious, cause havoc in the area as they fan out in search of food in the form of humans. An emergency is declared in the area and naval and local police authorities combine their forces to search out and kill the monsters. The job is done under the direction of the Naval Base intelligence officer, played by Tim Holt.

The search and tracking down of the creatures has a semi-documentary flavor. In addition, a degree of suspense and excitement is built up while the job is being carried out. However, there are a number of ludicrous and cliche moments.

The cast attempts to make the whole thing believable. In addition to Holt, it includes Audrey Dalton as pretty young widow who provides the romantic interest for the dedicated lieutenant commander, Hans Conried as a research scientist, Harlan Warde as a young naval officer, Casey Adams as a scientist, Gordon Jones as the local sheriff, and Mimi Gibson as Miss Dalton's five-year-old daughter.

Arnold Laven squeezes as much suspense as possible out of the Pat Fiedler screenplay. Technical contributions are good. *Holl.*

The 27th Day

Science fiction again. This time an unknown planet supplies the means for the people of this earth to destroy themselves. For exploitation playdates.

Hollywood, May 14.

Columbia release of Helen Ainsworth (Romson) production. Stars Gene Barry, Valerie French; features George Voskovec, Arnold Moss, Stefan Schnabel, Ralph Clanton, Frederick Ledebur, Paul Birch, Azemat Janti, Marie Tsien. Directed by William Asher. Screenplay, John Mantley, from his novel; camera, Henry Freullich; editor, Jerome Thoms; music conducted by Mischa Bakaleinikoff. Previewed April 18, '57. Running time, 75 MINS.

Jonathan Clark .... Gene Barry
Eve Wingate .... Valerie French
Prof. Klaus Bechner .. George Voskovec
The Alien .... Arnold Moss
Leader .... Stefan Schnabel
Mister Ingram .... Ralph Clanton
Dr. Karl Neuhaus .... Frederick Ledebur
Admiral .... Paul Birch
Ivan Godofsky .... Azemat Janti
Su Tan .... Marie Tsien
Commander .... Ed Hinton
U. N. Officer .... Grandon Rhodes

Space ships, mysterious destructive capsules and plans for conquest are the science-fiction gimmicks used in "The 27th Day" to manufacture an okay thriller. It should team handily with a similar subject in the exploitation market.

An unknown planet, whose universe is dying, sends an emissary to earth to make plans for a new home. Since the planet's moral code forbids it to invade or destroy any form of intelligent life, the space people decide to let earth's people kill themselves off. Figuring panic will help, they snatch five nationalities, give them five small plastic boxes, each containing three capsules individually capable of destroying human life within a distance of 3,000 miles and leave the rest up to the humans.

In the John Mantley screenplay from his own novel, the Communists are used as the big menace to earth since one of the box-holders is a Red soldier. Another is an English girl, Valerie French, who promptly throws hers into the sea and then joins Gene Barry, newspaper reporter, in America, where they go in hiding to wait out the time limit of 27 days before the capsules become harmless.

William Asher's direction works up a good degree of suspense via the Reds' efforts to break the secret of the box held by the soldier so Russia can take over the world. In the U. S., Washington big brains are attempting to find Barry and Miss French and get European scientist George Voskovec to reveal the secret of his. Instead, the scientist works out the secret and turns it against all men of evil, which automatically takes core of the Communists. Ending finds earth inviting the space aliens to move in and share the new era of freedom and peace.

Barry and Miss French make a good team for the requirements of the story, while Voskovec also is convincing as the scientist. Performing satisfactorily are Azemat Janti, the Red soldier with a conscience; Marie Tsien, Chinese recipient of the capsule, who immediately renders it useless by commiting hari-kari; Stefan Schnabel, Red leader who sees world domination from the space weapon; Arnold Moss, space alien; Ralph Clanton, Frederick Ledebur, Paul Birch and others.

Helen Ainsworth, under the executive supervision of Lewis J. Rachmil, produced the Romson production for Columbia and the values are good for budget outlay. Henry Freulich's lensing, editing, background score and other technical factors are expert. *Brog.*

Guendalina
(FRANCO-ITALIAN)

Rome, May 14.

Cei-Incom release of Ponti-Incom-Les Films Marceau Production. Stars Jacqueline Sassard, Raf Mattioli. Directed by Alberto Lattuada. Screenplay, Lattuada, Blondel, Benvenuti, DeBernardi, from story by Valerio Zurlini; camera, Otello Martelli; music, Piero Morgan. Previewed in Rome. Running time, 100 MINS.

Guendalina .... Jacqueline Sassard
Oberdan .... Raf Mattioli
Francesca .... Sylvia Koscina
Father .... Raf Vallone

Sentimental story of teenage love is one of the better efforts of the year in Italy, with prestige-gaining qualities for export. If properly handled, feature may have some Stateside possibilities, either for the art trade or the dubbed general market, possibly both.

Tale focuses on the end-of-summer flirt, which blossoms into first love, of Guendalina, a spoiled girl of rich divorcing parents, and Oberdan, a working boy of middle-class family. Parental disattention leads her to create a world of her own, aided by the boy, while slowly and unwittingly they fall into puppy love. Fadeout finds them being dealt life's first cruel blow as she's forced to leave to follow her family, knowing she'll never see him again.

Tale is backdropped by some sharply observed beachside doings, with special attention to an authentic flavor of teenage life. Parental dallying is straightforwardly portrayed and dialoged in the character of the father, whose eye is ever-roving to a shapely ankle, while the boy's first experience (with a prostie) is also graphically woven into the story for maximum effect, counterpointing innocence of kids' "love affair."

Thesping is expert all along the line, with Raf Mattioli and Jacqueline Sassard standing out in their first roles. Both are finds, with latter a cross between Audrey Hepburn and Leslie Caron. While script is not always as good as the basic story, dialog rings true. Alberto Lattuada's direction, while slow in warming up, keeps action to essentials and gets good performances (besides the leads) from thespers not usually known for their innate acting ability.

Lensing by Otello Martelli is expert throughout in copping the early-fall greyness on Riviera locations, while Piero Morgan has written a very apt musical score in a modern tempo. Production credits are all tops. *Hawk.*

Carry on Admiral
(BRITISH)

Light-hearted naval romp with a land'ubber in trouble masquerading as sailor.

London, May 14.

Renown Pictures release of a George Minter production. Stars David Tomlinson, Peggy Cummins, Brian Reece and Eunice Gayson; co-stars A. E. Matthews. Directed by Val Guest. Screenplay, Val Guest, from stageplay, "Off the Record," by Ian Hay and Stephen King-Hall; camera, Arthur Grant; editor, John Pomeroy; music, Philip Green. At Rialto Theatre, London. Running time, 85 MINS.

Tom Baker .... David Tomlinson
Susan Lashwood .... Peggy Cummins
Peter Fraser .... Brian Reece
Jane Godfrey .... Eunice Gayson
Admiral Godfrey .... A. E. Matthews
Mary .... Joan Sims
Psychiatrist .... Lionel Murton
Receptionist .... Reginald Beckwith
Willy Oughton-Formby
Desmond Walter Ellis
Salty Simpson .... Ronald Shiner
Lieut. Lashwood .... Peter Coke
Lieut. Dobson .... Derek Blomfield
Petty Officer .... Tom Gill
Sub-Lieut. .... Howard Williams
Mother .... Joan Hickson
Steward .... Toke Townley
Orderly .... Arthur Lovegrove
First Sea Lord............Ronald Adam
Attendant .... Sam Kydd
First Officer .... Philip Ashley
Second Officer .... Donald Pickering

The source of this film was a successful stageplay, and although the film rights were bought at the time of its production 10 years ago, it has only now reached the screen. Most recent British b.o. winners have been in broad comedy vein, and so the time was considered ripe to dust off this one and cash in on the current trend. It is neatly made, extracting every ounce of humor from ludicrous situations, which have greater scope visually than in their former limited sphere. It should rouse healthy boxoffice reaction here with its locale and typically native brand of comedy.

The mixup of identities in a Naval Dockyard that sets the ball rolling arises from two reunited wartime buddies being switched to each other's jobs following a heavy drinking session, during which they changed clothes. One is a Navy captain about to take over a new ship, the other a press relations official to the Civil fountainhead at the Admiralty. The landsman, wearing uniform, is shanghaied to the ship, while the disguised sailor is forced to pass himself off as the press exec.

Most of the humor arises when the bogus Captain is piped aboard, where, ignoring salutes and other service etiquette while uttering stupid comments, he makes futile efforts to get ashore. His crowning folly is in pressing the torpedo switch, which fires its deadly tube across the harbor, capsizing the launch of the First Sea Lord. To save further disaster he is hastily transferred to the observation ward of the Naval Hospital, where every effort to explain his predicament is by-passed. Finally through confession to the old Admiral combined with genteel blackmail and petticoat influence, the pair are shuffled back into their respective niches.

David Tomlinson and Brian Reece handle the two leading characters with commendable zest and a fine sense of the ridiculous. Vet legiter A. E. Matthews mumbles his way with delightful inconsequence through the role of the Admiral who is coerced into cooperation while Eunice Gayson is perkily attractive as his conniving granddaughter. Peggy Cummins supplies the remainder of the glamor as sister of one of the lieutenants, crisply acted by Peter Coke with main support by Derek Blomfield, Ronald Shiner, Tom Gill and Desmond Walter Ellis. Direction is smooth and workmanlike, and the camerawork is universally excellent. *Clem.*

Foreign Films

Les Aventures D'Arsene Lupin (FRENCH-ITALIAN; COLOR). SNE-Gaumont release of Francoise Chavane-Gaumont-Lambor-Costellazione production. Stars Robert Lamoureux; features, Liselotte Pulver, Huguette Hue, Henri Rollan, Renaud Mary, Georges Chamarat, O. E. Hasse. Directed by Jacques Becker. Screenplay, Becker, Albert Simonin based on character created by Maurice Leblanc; camera (Technicolor), Edmund Sechan; editor, G. Vaury. At Colisee, Paris. Running time, 103 MINS.

Not since John Barrymore played him in Hollywood years ago has this gentleman burglar been back on the screen. Here he performs in a series of adventures dressed up in color. Despite a nice period touch, this remains sketchy in its three distinct episodes and rarely builds any drama. Its languishing movement makes this a chancey item for the U. S., but may do in some special situations.

Lupin first walks off with some priceless paintings. Then he steals a mass of jewelry only to be later recognized as the gentleman thief by a manicurist who had done his hands. However, being a known rich man-about-town, nobody believes her. His final bit is in being kidnapped by the Kaiser of Germany. Film meanders too leisurely.

Robert Lamoureux takes well to the disguises, but lacks the dash needed. Liselotte Pulver is fetching as the girl who gets him at last while O. E. Hasse gives a neat cameo as the Kaiser. Director Jacques Becker has given this fine mounting. Production credits are good. *Mosk.*

Jusqu'au ernier (Until The Last One) (FRENCH). Marceau production and release. Stars Jeanne Moreau, Raymond Pellegrin, Paul Meurisse; features Mouloudji, Jacqueline Noelle, Max Revol, Midjanou Bardot. Directed by Pierre Billon. Screenplay, Michel Audiard from novel by Andre Duquesne; camera, Pierre Petit; editor, Georges Arnstam. At Berlitz, Paris. Running time, 90 MINS.

This film details how a gang of thieves wipe themselves out after one tries to run off with the loot from a bank robbery. He hides out in a travelling carnival where most of action occurs. He is tracked down by the two remaining crooks and all die in a bloody finale. Director Pierre Billon has given this arty treatment, replete with symbols, etc., which slows down the pace and makes this a lagging actioner. It has little chance for American cinemas except for possibly some dual fare.

Jeanne Moreau gives a fine performance as a sensual dancer while Raymond Pellegrin and Paul Meurisse are adequate as two of the top thieves. Direction rarely gets the needed movement into this. The carny head keeps saying that tv is killing the circus, and this pic looks mainly slanted for video. *Mosk.*

Paris, May 14.

Action Immediate (FRENCH). Gaumont release of Francois Chavane-Gaumont-SFC production. Stars Henri Vidal, Barbara Laage, Nicole Maurey; features Jacques Dacomine, Marguetite Rung, Jess Hahn, Harald Wolf, Lino Ventura. Directed by Maurice Labro. Screenplay, Frederic Dard, Yvan Audouard, Jean Redon from novel by Paul Kenny; camera, Jean Leherissey; editor, R. and M. Isnardon. At Raimus, Paris. Running time 105 MINS.

This is a racy espionage film, obviously patterned after U. S. toughguy pix. Though story is telegraphed, it has a good amount of fisticuffs, comely dolls and violence to make this an okay actioner pic.

It looks a good bet locally, but for the U. S., due to its cliches, could only do for a few spots.

Film concerns a French secret service ma'. after some stolen rocket plans. He meets some unsavory characters but plenty of pretty damsels. Cast eases through its chores agreeably. Director Maurice Labro has given this neat pacing. *Mosk.*

Cannes Festival

Cannes, May 21.

Shiros Sammyahu (The Roof of Japan) (JAPANESE COLOR). Daei production and release. Directed by Sadao Imamura. Screenplay supervision by the Oomachi Alpine Museum; commentary, Masuji Ibuse; camera (Eastmancolor), Daei Alpine Team; editor, Ichiro Saito. At Cannes Film Fest. Running time 100 MINS.

This is the first Japanese full-length nature film. It has good color and some good animal work as it follows the seasons and depicts the struggle for survival among the denizens of the slopes of the Japanese mountain ranges.

Somewhat familiar in content and not as stylish as the Walt Disney nature films, this looks like only a program possibility for the U. S. *Mosk.*

Same Jakki (Lapland Calendar) (NORWEGIAN; DOCUMENTARY; COLOR). Kinografen Film release and production. Written, directed and lensed (Eastmancolor) by Per Host; editor, Titus Vibe-Muller; music, Christian Hartmann. At Cannes Film Fest. Running time, 90 MINS.

Eastmancolor documentary sketches the daily life and ritual of the Laplander of Norway and details the yearly trek to get their reindeer to proper grazing grounds. In these scenes it has a certain amplitude, with reindeer swimming the fjords, in battle, giving birth, etc., which could make this of interest for dual supporting fare in the U.S. or for specialized shows there.

Laps' simple lives are also well done and pic emerges sincere and ethnically interesting in spite of some sudden forced dramatic shafts. Color is uneven at times but acceptable and the Laps, the landscapes and, above all, the reindeer, make this an offbeat documentary with U.S. possibilities. *Mosk.*

Qivitoq (Evil Spirit) (DANISH; COLOR). Nordisk release and production. With Poul Reichhardt, Astrid Villaume, Niels Platou, Dorthe Reimer, Justus Larsen. Directed by Erik Balling. Screenplay, Leck Fischer; camera (Agfacolor), Poul Pedersen; editor, Carsten Dahl. At Cannes Film Fest. Running time, 105 MINS.

Film is the 50th anni pic to celebrate the existence of the Danish Nordisk company and was one of the nominations for the best foreign pic award at the recent Academy Awards. It is a tale of the people of Greenland, and simply details the relations between the Danes and the Eskimos. Story is well constructed and the colorful backgrounds make this of possible dualer fare in the U.S. and it also shapes a likely video entry.

A woman comes to see her fiance who has fallen in love with somebody else. While waiting to return home in shame she meets a rough, embittered man running a trading company. Film unfolds their budding love plus that of a proud young Eskimo hunter who is talked into turning to fishing by the trader. He feels it is necessary for these people. The Eskimo is shamed when he tries it alone and runs off to an icy section where the evil spirit Qivitoq is supposed to live. He is brought back by the hunter and the people accept him again and the hunter gets his woman.

Color is fine and the exciting landscapes of icebergs, seals, plus the dignity of the Eskimos and the verisimilitude of the people and their reactions, makes this an interesting documentary-type pic with chances on the U.S. screen scene. *Mosk.*

Faustina (SPANISH; COLOR). Chapalo release and production. Stars Maria Felix; features, Fernando Gomez, Fernando Rey, Conrado Martin. Written and directed by Jose Luis Saenz De Heredia. Camera (Eastmancolor), Alfredo Fraile; editor, Julio Pena. At Cannes Film Fest. Running time, 110 MINS.

This is another comedic takeoff on the Faust legend, but this time Faust is a woman in modern times and the old Devil's assistant is a man who loved her in her youth. He spends the pic trying to foil her attempts of youthful conquest but love finally conquers all. Pic is a slight comedy, with some good moments, and shapes mainly as a lingo entry but could pass for dualers fare on its fair entertainment values.

Maria Felix from Mexico is properly hambone as the rejuvenated woman and Fernando Gomez brings a fine comic assurance to the devil's rep. Technical values are good. *Mosk.*

Sorok Pervyi (The Forty First) (RUSSIAN; COLOR). Mosfilm release and production. With Isolda Izvitskaia, Oleg Strijenov, Nikolai Kriutchov. Directed by Grigori Tchoukhrai. Screenplay, G. Koltounov from a novel by Boris Lavrensky; camera (Sovcolor), S. Curousevski; editor, J. Lyssenkova. At Cannes Film Fest. Running time, 90 MINS.

The quality of Sovcolor is no secret but in this picture it is more striking than before. Film reveals more destalinization and emerges an extremely well made adventure-love opus which has a taking mood and story despite the propaganda line.

A female sharpshooter, taking back a White Russian prisoner during the Revolution, is marooned on a desert isle with him and they fall in love only to have it end in tragedy when she shoots him rather than be rescued by Czarist soldiers searching for him. Well acted, expertly mounted and with a slick love tale, in spite of the hefty qualities of the girl, this is entertaining and could be something for specialized U. S. situations. *Mosk.*

Ztracenci (The Lost Children) (CZECHOSLAVAKIAN). Czech State Film release and production. With Stanislav Fiser, Gustav Valach, Vladimir Hlavaty, Radovan Lukavsky. Directed by Milos Makovec. Screenplay, Jiri Brdecka, Makovec; camera, Vladimir Novotny; editor, Oldrich Bosak. At Cannes Film Fest. Running time, 90 MINS.

Pacifistic pic abounds in a stylized violence giving this an "arty" format which might make this an okay entry for specialized spots Stateside. During a mitteleuropa war of the 18th century two men meet after a battle in which they are the only survivors. They encounter another soldier and film recounts their trek hiding from the enemy, their return to the home of one of them, their renouncing of war and their final death when they try to save new friends from an enemy attack.

Film is well directed and gives the battle scenes a baroque feeling. Acting is good and director Milos Makovec gives this fine pacing and rhythm. Lensing is adroit and fits the atmosphere expertly. An offbeater worth some art attention is the tag on this one. *Mosk.*

Rose Bernd (WEST GERMAN; COLOR). Bavaria-Filmkunst release and production. Stars Maria Schell, Raf Vallone; features Kathe Gold, Hans Messemer, Leopold Beberti. Directed by Wolfgang Staudte. Screenplay, Walter Ulbrich from the play by Gerhart Hauptmann; camera (Agfacolor). Klaus von Rautenfeld; editor, Herbert Windt. At Cannes Film Fest. Running time, 110 MINS.

Film is a heavyhanded tale of a servant girl on a farm in the Germany of the 1920's who is seduced by her employer, raped by a worker and finally loses her child to be saved from despair by an old admirer who really loves her. Sombre, humorless, and without much feeling for character or time, film drags. Too Teutonic to be any real possibility for the U. S.

It has Maria Schell, a big European name, who was recently signed for a Hollywood feature. She has become a mass of mannerisms and drowns the character in tricks rather than sensitivity. Direction is stilted and slow. Technical credits par. *Mosk.*

A Face in the Crowd

Provocative and hardhitting commentary on the modern American scene as dominated by television and mass communications. Teamwork of Elia Kazan and Budd Schulberg turns out b.o. contender.

Warner Bros. release of Elia Kazan (Newtown) production. Stars Andy Griffith and Patricia Neal. Features Anthony Franciosa, Walter Matthau, Lee Remick, Percy Waram, Rod Brasfield, Charles Irving, Howard Smith, Paul McGrath, Kay Medford, Alexander Kirkland, Marshall Nielan, Big Jeff Bess and Henry Sharp. Directed by Kazan. Screenplay, Budd Schulberg, based on his short story, "The Arkansas Traveler"; camera, Harry Stradling and Gayne Rescher; editor, Gene Milford; music, Tom Glazer; songs by Glazer and Schulberg. Previewed in N.Y., May 23, '57. Running time, **125 MINS.**

Lonesome Rhodes .... Andy Griffith
Marcia Jeffries .... Patricia Neal
Joey Kiely .... Anthony Franciosa
Mel Miller .... Walter Matthau
Betty Lou Fleckum .... Lee Remick
General Haynesworth ..... Percy Waram
Beanie .... Rod Brasfield
Mr. Luffler .... Charles Irving
J. B. Jeffries .... Howard Smith
Macey .... Paul McGrath
First Mrs. Rhodes .... Kay Medford
Jim Collier .... Allexander Kirkland
Senator Fuller .... Marshall Nielan
Sheriff Hosmer .... Big Jeff Bess
Abe Steiner .... Henry Sharp
1st Printer ....Willie Feibel
2d Printer ....Larry Casazza

Elia Kazan and Budd Schulberg, who teamed to bring forth the Academy Award-winning "On the Waterfront," have come up with another provocative and hardhitting entry. Based on Schulberg's short story, "The Arkansas Traveler," "A Face in the Crowd" looms as both a commercial and artistic success.

Kazan as the director and producer, Schulberg as the writer, and Warner Bros. as the financial source have shown considerable courage in dealing with the picture's theme—a devastating commentary on hero-worship and success cults in America. A lot of what Schulberg has to say may be regarded as controversial and it is not unlikely that the picture will be condemned and maligned in some quarters. It presents a particularly unflattering insight of the television industry, Madison Avenue advertising agencies, and presidential aspirants.

Its basic story is somewhat similar to that of "The Great Man" in that it exposes a beloved television personality as an unmitigated heel. However, it probes much deeper. The hero is not the only one unmasked. The influences in America that make an unknown a national hero overnight are placed under the microscope of motivation.

Story plucks an ignorant guitar-playing hillbilly from an Arkansas jail and converts him in a short space of time to America's most popular and beloved television personality. The hero, if he can be referred to such, is in private life an unsavory character, a libertine and an opportunist with loyalty to no one but himself. On the air, he's a homespun philosopher who literally has millions of Americans eating out of his hand and who accept his word as gospel. Realizing his own sense of power in moving a commercial product, he enters the political arena, becomes aligned with an "isolationist" senator, and pitches an extreme reactionary philosophy. This gives author an opportunity to comment on the effect of television in politics and the efforts made by Madison Ave. to sell a candidate as it sells lipstick.

Some of the traits and activities of the leading character will probably start a guessing game to link him up with a real life tv performer. One popular performer perhaps fills the bill more than others, but in general the character is a composite of a number of video luminaries who have hit the big, big time.

As has been his policy in the past Kazan has again called on an unknown (to films) to essay the leading role. The plum assignment went to Andy Griffith, who became a Broadway name for his performance in "No Time for Sergeants." Making his film debut as Lonesome Rhodes, the power-mad hillbilly, Griffith turns in a performance that can easily skyrocket him to fame.

As his vis-a-vis, Petricia Neal, recently neglected by Hollywood, emerges as a new and appealing personality as the girl who guided Griffith to fame and fortune. Anthony Franciosa plays the unprincipled personal manager, Walter Matthau a cynical writer. Both excellent performances. Topnotch contributions are also given by Lee Remick, Percy Waram, Kay Medford, Rod Brasfield, Paul McGrath and Charles Irving.

The film gives reality to its television background by presenting real life personalities as themselves. These include Walter Winchell, John Cameron Swayze, Mike Wallace, Earl Wilson, Fay Emerson, Sam Levenson, and Burl Ives among others.

One glaring fault in the film is its denouement. Unfortunately, Schulberg resorts to the hackneyed device of having Lonesome Rhodes expose himself by his comments when he believes he is off the air. After the show supposedly goes off the air, Miss Neal deliberately turns on the sound switch so that the millions watching can hear themselves called "slobs" by their hero. (This is part of the old radio folklore anent you-know-who).

Filmed on location and in N.Y. by Kazan's Newtown Productions, the picture demonstrates that a large-scale production can be successfully made in Gotham. The technical aspects, including the camerawork of Harry Stradling and Gayne Rescher, the art direction of Richard and Paul Sylbert, and editing of Gene Milford are out of the top drawer. Tom Glazer has composed an appropriate score and Schulberg has contributed lyrics for a number of songs.

Kazan once again demonstrates his ability as a director and why major studios are willing to give him carte blanche in selecting his own story material and working under his own conditions. *Holl.*

The D.I.

TV's Jack Webb in a realistic yarn of Marine boot camp training. Mostly masculine appeal.

Hollywood, May 23.

Warner Bros. release of a Jack Webb production. Stars Webb; costars Don Dubbins, Jackie Loughery, Lin McCarthy, Monica Lewis, Virginia Gregg; features Jeannie Beacham, Lu Tobin, Earle Hodgins, Jeanne Baird, Barbara Pepper, Melody Gale. Directed by Webb. Screenplay, James Lee Barrett; camera, Edward Colman; editor, Robert M. Leeds; music, David Buttolph. Previewed May 14, '57. Running time, **104 MINS.**

Pvt. Owens .... Don Dubbins
Anne .... Jackie Loughery
Capt. Anderson .... Lin McCarthy
Burt .... Monica Lewis
Mrs. Owens .... Virginia Gregg
Hostess .... Jeannie Beacham
Bartender .... Lu Tobin
Guard .... Earle Hodgins
Mother .... Jeanne Baird
Customer .... Barbara Pepper
Little Girl .... Belody Gale

U. S. Marines are shown in a new light in this story of boot camp training at Parris Island. Hard hitting and realistic in its semi-documentary recital of the rugged program recruits are put through by their drill instructor—the D. I.—film though liberally spattered with comedy is strictly masculine in appeal, with indications pointing to average returns in male market where Jack Webb name will help.

Certain exploitation values accrue from headline stories out of Parris Island and the Marine training program during past couple of years, although plot-line in no wise latches onto any of these heralded incidents.

For his third Warner release, Webb, who also produces and directs, takes over the part of a tough drill instructor, completely dedicated to the Corps. Film is personalized in the story of this D. I. and his psychological problems with an emotionally mixed-up recruit. Considerable repetition blights some of the sequences when Webb harangues his men for various asserted infractions. To ensure authenticity both excitement and story-line sometimes are overlooked. Some of this authenticity is gained through use of 16 actual Marines in speaking parts.

Script by James Lee Barrett concentrates on Webb's toughness with his men, in his efforts to turn them into hardened Marines in 12 weeks. His biggest problem is the recruit, Don Dubbins, who apparently makes no attempt to fit in and whom the captain gives Webb three days to straighten out or boy will be discharged. Webb, convinced that there's Marine material in boy, is able finally to pull him through.

Webb handles his D. I. character effectively, and his direction and production handling are interesting. Dubbins sensitively plays the troubled boy, whose father and two brothers before him were Marines and killed in World War II, and Lin McCarthy gives authority to his captain's role. Jackie Loughery is in briefly for romantic interest with Webb; Monica Lewis socks over in fine fashion a rock 'n' roll number, "Somebody Else Will," by Ray Coniff and Fred Weismantel; and Virginia Gregg is good as Dubbins' mother, who understands her son's problem and begs captain not to discharge him. T/Sgt. Charles A. Love shows well as a hillbilly-speaking leatherneck recruit.

Edward Colman's capable photography leads off technical credits. Also rating mention are Robert M. Leeds' editing, Feild Gray and Gibson Holley's art direction, David Buttolph's music score. *Whit.*

The Wayward Bus
(C'SCOPE)

Wayward people in John Steinbeck's offbeat vehicle. Joan Collins, a flashy Jayne Mansfield, Dan Dailey and modest boxoffice values.

20th-Fox release of Charles Brackett production. Stars Joan Collins, Jayne Mansfield, Dan Dailey; features Rick Jason, Betty Lou Keim, Dolores Michaels, Larry Keating, Robert Bray, Kathryn Givney, Dee Pollock, Will Wright. Directed by Victor Vicas. Screenplay, Ivan Moffatt, adapted from the John Steinbeck novel; camera, Charles G. Clarke; editor, Louis Loeffler; music, Leigh Harline. Previewed in N.Y., May 24, '57. Running time, **87 MINS.**

Alice .... Joan Collins
Camille .... Jayne Mansfield
Ernest Horton .... Dan Dailey
Johnny Chicoy .... Rick Jason
Norma ....Betty Lou Keim
Mildred Pritchard.......Dolores Michaels
Pritchard .... Larry Keating
Morse .... Robert Bray
Mrs. Pritchard .... Kathryn Givney
Pimples .... Dee Pollock
Dan Brunt .... Will Wright

John Steinbeck's novel of the same title has been fashioned into a mild entertainment in "The Wayward Bus" with a fair chance at the boxoffice. The story line generates some interest and its oddly assorted characters are somewhat colorful. But they are, too, lacking in depth and are not a particularly ingratiating lot.

That's perhaps key to the fault. Passengers and driver, as pictorially sketched under Victor Vicas' direction, do not stir much audience feeling. "Bus" is not a genuinely moving screen vehicle.

The bus is one assigned to transporting passengers through 60 miles of rural California, from Rebel Corners to San Juan. There is, inevitably, the glib salesman and the girl to figure in the romance. Dan Dailey and Jayne Mansfield do these parts in close to mechanical fashion. They have an occasional humorous line to help lighten matters but the material for the most part lacks sparkle. The onlooker is not likely to be concerned whether or not Miss Mansfield, as a bubble dancer, and the drummer of cheap novelties get together romantically.

Given the thickest role and wringing out its full potential is Rick Jason. He's pilot of the rundown vehicle and has a full quota of problems. Storm conditions make the trek to San Juan a hazardous one, his wife, Joan Collins, hits the bottle, and one of his passengers, Dolores Michaels, tempts him into a hayloft episode that almost breaks up his marriage.

Kathryn Givney is the girl's righteous, nagging mother, and Larry Keating her obsequious father. Miss Michaels is bent on a form of Freudian escape and this she finds in the temporary encounter with Jason.

Steinbeck's book has been around for 10 years, a fact which suggests that producers were not immediately high on its film possibilities. This Charles Brackett production of "Bus" in turn suggests that it might have had a splendid outcome; the picture does come close to being exciting.

But the writing is not right. In the screenplay by Ivan Moffat and the general handling of "Bus" the opportunities are muffed. More skillfully drawn characters are called for. On view is only the surface of the personalities.

Vicas' direction is fair enough, and other performances are adequate, all in light of the nature of the script they had to work with. Camera work (CinemaScope black & white) is a notable asset, achieving some particularly striking effects in night scenes in the bus and in coverage of a bridge washout. Other credits all right.

The up-front boxoffice evaluation of "fair" takes into account the marquee importance of the Steinbeck and principal-player names and the obvious exploitation angles that can be put to use. *Gene.*

Don Quixote
(RUSSIAN; SCOPE; COLOR)

Cannes, May 21.

Lenfilm release and production. Stars N. Tcherkassov, Y. Tolubeiv; features S. Birman, L. Kassianova, T. Agamirova. Directed by G. Kozintsev. Screenplay, E. Schwaetz from the noval by Cervantes; camera (Scope, Sovcolor), A. Moskvine, A. Doudko; editor, M. Makhanrova. At Cannes Film Fest. Running time, **100 MINS.**

Don Quixote .... N. Tcherkassov
Sancho Panza .... Y. Toloubeiv
Aldonza .... L. Kassianova
Altisidora .... T. Agamirova
Querasco .... G. Vitzine

Russians have beaten Mike Todd, Federico Fellini and Jacques Tati to the draw and come out with their version of the famed Spanish classic "Don Quixate." It is done in a process akin to CinemaScope and is a sprawling, faithful account of the book. It may make a social point, at times, but is basically the tale of the erratic knight whose purity and faith are a comic, even pathetic thing in a 17th world already fed up with chivalry and virtue. It has enough color, action, feeling that may make this palatable for U.S. art house situations.

Don Quixote, full of ideas of knighthood from his books, sneaks off from his home with his faithful retainer Sancho Panza to rid the world of its enslavement by an evil ogre who hides behind windmills etc. The adventures are recounted somewhat episodically at the beginning but then gain momentum and make a telling tale of the sad, aging would-be hero tilting at the world in his own world of illusion and fantasy.

N. Tcherkassov is touching as the old knight and makes him pathetic, brave, moving but never ridiculous. Y. Toloubiev is a fine foil as Sancho Panza. Color is uneven as is the Scope process, but the images have a faithful resemblance to preconceptions of the book.

It is well directed and such scenes as Panza's meting out of justice when he is made governor of a town as a joke, Quixote's mortification by the court and his tilt with the windmill and the strange knight are excellent film morsels although this is an uneven, at times "literary" feature. *Mosk.*

The Delicate Delinquent

In and out of straight character Jerry Lewis' first solo film is uneven and undistinguished.

Palm Springs, May 26.

Paramount release of a Jerry Lewis production. Stars Jerry Lewis; costars Darren McGavin, Martha Hyer; features Robert Ivers, Horace McMahon. Director-screenplay, Don McGuire. Camera, Haskell Boggs; editor, Howard Smith; music, Buddy Bregman; art directors, Hal Pereira, Earl Hedrick. Previewed at Plaza Theatre, May 25, '57. Running time, **100 MINS.**

Sidney Pythias .... Jerry Lewis
Mike Damon .... Darren McGavin
Martha .... Martha Hyer
Monk .... Robert Ivers
Capt. Riley .... Horace McMaon
Artie .... Ricard Bakalyan
Harry .... Joseph Corey
Patricia .... Mary Webster
Mr. Herman .... Milton Frome
Mr. Crow .... Jefferson Searles

In his first single appearance on the screen sans Dean Martin, his former partner, Jerry Lewis isn't altogether successful. A sometimes-funny comedy-drama, film is neither fish nor fowl. Lewis, also functioning as producer and writer-director Don McGuire apparently were never certain of what policy line to follow. As a result, picture never hits any form of definition. Slapstick is blended with pathos and some straight melodrama tossed in. Draw of the Lewis name is bound to assure a certain b.o. response, but biz may be spotty. (Film was given a special charity-preem in Palm Springs).

Comic turns to serious acting here while also making with the grimaces. Screenplay by McGurie endeavors to play Lewis straight, in a pathetic character, but the next moment he's off on a robust comedy tangent which dissipates characterization attempt. In his comedy routines, however, Lewis is up to his past standard of clowning and material occasionally is boisterous stuff. Such business too widely spaced.

Helping star on narrative side are Darren McGavin and Martha Hyer, in for romance as well as former being Lewis' mentor, but accent is mostly on Lewis through the overlength 100-minutes running time.

A legitimate character premise is inserted through Lewis, a harassed and blundering $60-a-month janitor, wanting to be respectable and have people look up to him. His ambition is to become a policeman, after McGavin, an idealistic cop who once was a juve delinquent, selects him as his guinea pig to prove to the police captain that juve delinquents can be converted into upright citizens through the right kind of handling. Unfoldment centers on Lewis' adventures as he struggles through to win his shield.

Lewis registers as effectively as his choice of script will permit. McGavin scores as the cop with a point to prove, who wants to help all juve delinquents and fights his captain, Horace McMahon, to have his protege admitted to the Police Academy. Miss Hyer's role of a member of the City Council who has her own thoughts on juve delinquency is somewhat hazy, but she's pretty to look at. Robert Ivers capably portrays a young hood, Mary Webster is nice for suggested romance with Lewis and Milton Frome and Jefferson Searles are in for comedy bits.

Technical credits are well handled, from Haskell Boggs' camera work through music scoring by Buddy Bregman and art direction by Hal Pereira and Earl Hedrick. *Whit.*

Run of the Arrow
(COLOR)

Indian cruelty picture for the outdoor market. Okay returns indicated.

Hollywood, May 23.

Universal release of a Samuel Fuller production. Stars Rod Steiger, Sarita Montiel, Brian Keith, Ralph Meeker; features Jay C. Flippen, Charles Bronson, Olive Carey. Director-screenplay, Fuller. Camera (Technicolor), Joseph Biroc; editor, Gene Fowler Jr.; music, Victor Young. Previewed May 16, '57. Running time, **86 MINS.**

O'Meara .... Rod Steiger
Yellow Moccasin .... Sarita Montiel
Capt. Clark .... Brian Keith
Lt. Driscoll .... Ralph Meeker
Walking Coyote .... Jay C. Flippen
Blue Buffalo .... Charles Bronson
Mrs. O'Meara .... Olive Carey
Crazy Wolf .... H. M. Wynant
Lt. Stockwell .... Neyle Morrow
Red Cloud .... Frank de Kova
General Allen .... Col. Tim McCoy
Colonel Taylor .... Stuart Randall
Ballad Singer .... Frank Warner
Silent Tongue .... Billy Miller
Corporal .... Chuck Hayward
Sergeant .... Chuck Roberson

Yankee-hating Southerner goes west after the Civil War to join the Sioux in their uprising against the U.S. Slow in takeoff, action becomes pretty rough at times, particularly for the squeamish, but Technicolor film should do okay in outdoor market.

Universal release of the Samuel Fuller-RKO production is strong on visual values to bolster Fuller's sometimes meandering screenplay highlighting Rod Steiger as Southerner taken into the tribe after he survives the run-of-the-arrow torture ordeal. Forceful use is made of Indians and their attacks on the whites to give unusual color to feature which additionally has Sarita Montiel, Spanish actress in as Steiger's Indian wife, for draw in the foreign market.

On debit side, Steiger frequently lapses from Southerner into Irish dialect, difficult to understand, and footage occasionally is impeded by irrelevant sequences.

Steiger is never sympathetic and character itself is not clearly defined though actor endows his character with vigor. Brian Keith and Ralph Meeker are well cast as Army officers. Miss Montiel shows well. Jay C. Flippen, who is making a career of Indian films, is effective as a Sioux scout and Charles Bronson and H. M. Wynant score as Redskins.

Joseph Biroc's color photography is interesting, and Victor Young score lends musical color. *Whit.*

Fire Down Below
(C'SCOPE—COLOR—MUSIC)

Rita Hayworth, Robert Mitchum, Jack Lemmon in colorful meller of West Indies; geared for top grosses.

Columbia release of Warwick Film (Irving Allen, Albert R. Broccoli) production. Stars Rita Hayworth, Robert Mitchum, Jack Lemmon; features Herbert Lom, Bonar Colleano, Edric Conner, Bernard Lee. Directed by Robert Parrish. Screenplay, Irwin Shaw, from novel, "Fire Down Below," by Max Catto; camera (Technicolor), Desmond Dickinson, Cyril Knowles; editor, Jack Slade; music, Arthur Benjamin, Vivian Comma; harmonica theme, "Fire Down Below," composed by Jack Lemmon; steel band music by the Katzenjammers of Trinidad. Previewed in N.Y., May 24, '57. Running time, **116 MINS.**

Irena .... Rita Hayworth
Felix .... Robert Mitchum
Tony .... Jack Lemmon
Harbour Master .... Herbert Lom
Lt. Sellers .... Bonar Colleano
Doctor Sam .... Bernard Lee
Jimmy Jean .... Edric Conner
Captain of Ulysses .... Peter Illing
Mrs. Canaday .... Joan Miller
Miguel .... Anthony Newley
Hotel Owner .... Eric Pohlmann
The American .... Lionel Murton
Sailors..Vivian Matalon, Gordon Tanner, Maurice Kaufmann
Bartender .... Murray Kash
Waitress .... Maya Koumani
Young Man .... Phillip Baird
Drunk .... Keith Banks

With Rita Hayworth, Robert Mitchum and Jack Lemmon in the stellar roles and a stalwart supporting cast, this Warwick Film production contains plenty of sheer entertainment, both musical and melodramatic. Contains meaty sequences and provides a fitting vehicle for Miss Hayworth's reappearance in pix after about three years. Shapes as a big b.o. grosser.

Whether turned out before or subsequently to "Mr. Allison," this pic shows Robert Mitchum in much the same tough-type likeable characterization. Jack Lemmon does somewhat of a switch from his previous comedy parts since the second portion of this provides him with many highly dramatic moments. Earlier, he is the devil-may-care American spendthrift.

Cast in a rather disreputable role, Miss Hayworth is shown in an eye-filling closeup garbed in a bathing suit and later doing a dance hardly to be found in any ballroom. She furnishes the exciting love interest, and motivation for much of the yarn. Her native dance (pic was partly shot in Trinidad) is torrid. In fact, the way in which the camera pans in and out indicates that the producers figured with calculation of the Production Code.

Story: bad, bad girl meets youthful American, and finally agrees to marry him though warning him of her past—that of sort of a Mata Hari in Europe. Mitchum, as Lemmon's pal in a small fishing and smuggling boat operation, is vastly displeased with this development and tips off the Coast Guard on a smuggling trip so that Lemmon abandons the boat rather than be captured as a smuggler. This lands him on a Greek freighter which crashes into a heavier ship in the fog. Lemmon is pinned down in the hold by a steel girder. Nearly all the second half of the film is centered on efforts to rescue him.

Rescue operation is tensed up by the fact that a blaze in another part of the freighter threatens to spread and touch off some high explosives. When efforts of U.S. navy men fail to free him, the port medico asks permission to amputate his legs to save his life. But it's not until his old partner, Mitchum, arrives and tells him the facts of life that a rescue is effected. And it is Mitchum who finally swims him free of the exploding freighter to a rescue launch.

Finale is a surprise, and gives this, a different sort of picture's different ending.

Miss Hayworth is excellent as the comely femme who is always just one step ahead of the law. Lemmon shows plainly that he can handle a dramatic type role while Mitchum, as the tough man of the world, contributes one of his better portrayals. A forthright job is done by Edric Conner as the husky native who serves as third member of the fishing-boat crew. Bernard Lee is so outstanding in his role of port physician that he often thefts the last portion of this vehicle.

Bonar Colleano makes a strong U.S. Navy lieutenant while Herbert Lom chips in sterling supporting role as harbor master. Among the many others in support, standout are Peter Illing and Eric Pohlmann.

Irving Allen and Albert R. Broccoli have given this fine production, including the spectacular blowing up of the freighter and scenes of firefighters in action preceding it. "Stretch" Cox Troupe score with their amazing Limbo Dance.

Parrish has done one of his top-flight directorial jobs. Technicolor camera work of Desmond Dickinson and Cyril Knowles is a strong asset, not only in the carnival scenes but also in the closeups and sequences aboard the doomed freighter. Lemmon takes a bow for composing the harmonica theme, "Fire Down Below." Entire score was played with precision by Sinfonia of London. *Wear.*

Lure of the Swamp
(REGALSCOPE)

Greed and slow-moving melodrama, in the swamps. Dim entertainment.

Hollywood, May 23.

Twentieth-Fox release of a Sam Hersh production. Stars Marshall Thompson, Willard Parker, Joan Vohs; features Jack Elam, Leo Gordon, Joan Lora, James Maloney. Directed by Hubert Cornfield. Screenplay, William George, from noval by Gil Brewer; camera, Walter Strenge; editor, Robert Fritch; music, Paul Dunlap.

Previewed May 23, '57. Running time, 75 MINS.

Marshall Thompson .... Simon Lewt
Willard Parker .... James Lister
Joan Vohs .... Cora Payne
Jack Elam .... Bliss
Joan Lora .... Evie Dee
James Maloney .... August Dee
Leo Gordon .... Steggins

What might have been built into a fairly suspenseful story of greed in the swamps emerges as slow-moving and unexciting fare. Film would benefit by trimming to snap up action.

Sam Hersh production is based on the search for $20,000 in stolen bank money hidden in the swamp by one of the holdup men, who afterwards is killed by a pal. Partner returns to swamp with a map and tries to enlist services of a swampman who poled gangster into the interior. Two other strangers also show up, an insurance investigator and a blonde claiming to be a mag fotog, both similarly in quest of the loot, and who also try to make deals with swampman. In final windup, blonde, actually slain gangster's widow, sinks in quicksand with the money, after her husband's murderer has met a similar end.

Marshall Thompson portrays the swampman, but under Hubert Cornfield's direction of the William George screenplay character is tedious and indecisive. Willard Parker, co-starring as first gangster, apparently was cast for name value only for he appears only in opening sequence. Miss Vohs is attractive in her role, turning heavy in climax when she tries to kill Thompson so she won't have to divvy with him. Jack Elam, second gangster, and Leo Gordon, investigator, acquit themselves in okay fashion and Joan Lora plays Thompson's spitfire girl friend with a certain flair.

Technical departments are capably handled by Walter Strenge, for photography; Ernst Fegte, production design; Paul Dunlap, music score. *Whit.*

Der Sjunde Inseglet
(The Seventh Seal)
(SWEDISH)

Cannes, May 21.

AB Svensk Filmindustri release and production. Stars Nils Poppe; features Bibi Anderson, Gunnar Bjornstrand, Inga Gill, Bengt Ekerot. Directed and written by Ingmar Bergman. Camera, Gunnar Fischer; editor, Lennart Wallen; sets and costumes, P. A. Lundgren; music, Erik Nordgren. At Cannes Film Fest. Running time, **100 MINS.**

Jof .... Nils Poppe
Valet .... Gunnar Bjornstrand
Mia .... Bibi Anderson
Lisa .... Inga Gill
Wife .... Inga Landgre
Death .... Bengt Ekerot

Director-writer Ingmar Bergman has a morality play in this tale of returning crusader in the 14th century who keeps Death at bay, via a chess game, while he tries to find out the meaning of life. Superior technical narrative, impressive lensing and thesping make this a definite U.S. art house possibility. It would be chancey for more general situations.

The knight comes back to his home which is in the grip of the black plague. The re-creation of medieval times is evocative in its bawdiness, superstition, cruelty and humanity. It spreads out an awesome canvas of human cupidity and purity. Characters abound with vitality and Bergman wraps this into an absorbing film.

The chess game with Death is interspersed with his meeting with a family of itinerant mountebanks whom he feels are worth saving,

and even Death seems to coincide with this thought as all fall before his coming except them. *Mosk.*

Cannes Festival

Torano O (Walkers on the Tiger's Tail) (JAPANESE). Toho release and production. Written and directed by Akira Kurosawa. Camert, T. Ito; editor, Kurosawa. At Cannes Film Fest. Running time, **60 MINS.**

Hour long pic is a transportation of a Kabuki-Noh play and brings over its stylized aspects to film. It details an incident in 12th century Japan of a group of men trying to get their leader through enemy lines.

It has the legendary characters of the wise statesman, the delicate prince and the buffoon, but the adroit telling and mixture of theatre and film makes this a unique pic that could be good supporting fare in any arty house program with another off-beat medium length pic.

Well lensed, directed and played this is worthy of specialized Stateside interest. *Mosk.*

Ket Vallomas (Two Wishes) (HUNGARIAN). Hunnia release and production. Stars Mari Torlcsik; features, Tibor Csogor, Marianne Krencsey. Directed by Marton Keleti. Screenplay, Gyorgy Ramos, Gabor Thurzo, Keleti; camera, Istvan Pasztor; editor, Gyorgy Ranki. At Cannes Film Fest. Running time, **110 MINS.**

Magyar pic is a sentimental opus about two juve delinquents finally straightened out by an understanding police inspector. Made without political overtones, its well worn tale goes through its telegraphed proceedings amiably enough, but it remains only something for the rare U. S. lingo spots. It again denotes the freer type of filmmaking in this beat-up Russian satellite. Technical credits are fair and acting good. *Mosk.*

Love In the Afternoon

Promising Payoff likely for Cooper — Hepburn — Chevalier frolic.

Allied Artists release of Billy Wilder production. Stars Audrey Hepburn, Gary Cooper, Maurice Chevalier; features John McGiver, Van Doude, Lise Bourdin, Olga Valery & the Gypsies. Directed by Wilder. Screenplay, Wilder and I. A. L. Diamond, from the Claude Anet novel; camera, William Mellor; editor, Leonid Azar; musical adaptation, Franz Waxman; songs, "Fascination," F. D. Marchetti & Maurice de Feraudy; "C'est Si Bon," Henri Betti & Andre Hornez; "L'Ame des Poetes," Charles Trenet; "Love in the Afternoon," "Ariane" and "Hot Paprika," Matty Malneck. Previewed in N. Y. May 17, '57. Running time, **126 MINS.**

Frank Flannagan .... Gary Cooper
Ariane Chavasse ..... Audrey Hepburn
Claude Chavasse ...... Maurice Chevalier
Mr. X .... John McGiver
Michel .... Van Doude
Madame X .... Lise Bourdin
Olga Valery Gypsies .... Themselves

Title-wise, "Love in the Afternoon' is fitting, being far more communicative of the film's content, and obviously more provocative, than the original, "Ariane." It is all about romance before nightfall, in Paris, with Audrey Hepburn and Gary Cooper as the participants. Under Billy Wilder's alternately sensitive, mirthful and loving-care direction, and with Maurice Chevalier turning in a captivating performance as a private detective specializing in cases of amour, the production holds enchantment and delight in substantial quantity.

These elements speak for themselves in conversation about the commerce. The boxoffice has got to be strong, particularly in the key runs.

"Love in the Afternoon" though is long and the casting of Cooper as the eager beaver Romeo is curious. Running time, no matter how much of it there is, is never excessive where the material plays out with sustained freshness. There are instances where "Afternoon" repeats itself.

Consider this wealthy American businessman. Cooper, constantly as the woo merchant in his lavish Parisien hotel suite, first with Madame X and then Ariane (Miss Hepburn). Several scenes spill out before Cooper comes on camera, and then on it's love in the afternoon. For leavening there are the appearances of a gypsy string quartet (very funny) kept in Cooper's hire for the purpose of creating "mood," plus other episodes of humorous satire, deftly staged.

Low-key lighting and deliberate side-glance camera angles make Cooper almost an obscure figure on the screen. Perhaps, this is in deference to the fact that this veteran actor, when in full and candid view, frankly has a much longer count on the calendar than Ariane. Or, maybe this is Wilder simply trying to set forth the clinches with a finesse designed to hoodwink the onlooker into thinking things really might happen this way.

While these criticisms are to be noted, the demerits are outweighed by the overall charm of "Afternoon." Aud much charm is exuded by Chevalier. His is a winning performance, from the opening as he introduces his audience to Paris and then to his own role as auditor and record-keeper of affairs of indiscretion in the city of light.

It's in his files that his daughter, the lovely, wistful Miss Hepburn, as a 'cello student, comes upon knowledge of Cooper's international conquests, runs to him with

the warning that his current passion (Madame X) has a husband (Mr. X) bent on murder, and finds herself soon to become a candidate for one of her own father's file cards. Several songs are heard, notably (and again an appropriate title) "Fascination."

Madame X is Lise Bourdin, who is merely a veiled figure (again that camera shyness about coming face to face with people), and Mr. X is John McGiver, suitably frenzied as the husband suspecting his mate has taken to play with another. Van Doude is a handsome and likeable young whose yen for Miss Hepburn is thwarted by her attachment to Cooper.

Screenplay is by Wilder and I. A. L. Diamond, from the novel by Claude Anet. It's a floating-in-air kind of story. And being innocent of earthiness—that is, lacking labored suggestiveness and not to be taken for real—there is no offensiveness in the content although, of course, the theme is not a suitable one for moppets.

Music, as adapted by Franz Waxman, goes splendidly hand in hand with the nature of the screen material; the continuity is smooth but more decisive cutting might have provided more pace; William Mellor's camera work is sometimes puzzling but for the most part fine, and other credits fully professional. *Gene.*

Man on Fire

Bing Crosby straight dramatic film about divorce and custody of a child. Good b.o. potential.

Metro release of Sol Siegel production. Stars Bing Crosby. Features Inger Stevens, Mary Fickett, E. G. Marshall, Malcolm Brodrick, Richard Eastham, Anne Seymour and Dan Riss. Directed by Ranald MacDougall. Screenplay, MacDougall from a story by Malvin Wald and Jack Jacobs; camera, Joseph Ruttenberg; editor, Ralph E. Winters; song, "Man On Fire" by Sammy Fain and Paul Francis Webster, sung by the Ames Brothers; music score by David Raskin. Previewed in New York, May 20, '57. Running time, **95 MINS.**

Earl Carleton .... Bing Crosby
Nina Wylie .... Inger Stevens
Gwen Seward .... Mary Fickett
Sam Dunstock .... E. G. Marshall
Ted Carleton .... Malcolm Brodrick
Bryan Seward .... Richard Eastham
Judge Randolph .... Anne Seymour
Mack .... Dan Riss

Bing Crosby, who made an impact as the alcoholic actor in "The Country Girl," again demonstrates his ability as a straight dramatic performer. As a doting father embroiled in a harsh custody battle with his ex-wife, he gives an appealing and sensitive performance. Character of Earl Carleton, a successful business man embittered by a broken marriage is understandable and sympathetic.

Producer Sol Siegel appears to have come up with a film that has good, if not socko, boxoffice potential. The Ranald MacDougall screenplay, based on a story by Malvin Wald and Jack Jacobs, resembles the fiction that is popular in the better women's magazines. Since this type of fiction has a ready-made distaff audience, indications are that "Man on Fire" should be particularly appealing to women. More discerning critics may point up its slickness and the formula solution to the problem involved.

The story tackles the question of divorce and its effect on children. Crosby is stubbornly determined to maintain the custody of his young son at any cost. Not only is he motivated by a sincere love for his child, but his actions, including an effort to "kidnap" his son in the face of a court order, are based on his own hurt feelings and bitterness over the fact that his wife left him to marry another man. Complicating the situation is the son's resentment of his mother and her new husband. Eventually both Crosby and his son both "grow up" and a satisfactory solution to the custody tiff is evolved.

Except for Crosby, the picture is dominated by new faces. Siegel has selected a pair of professional actresses to surround Crosby rather than relying on the typical ingenues that are commonly put forth as new faces. Mary Fickett, from the Broadway stage, seems a real find. As Crosby's ex-wife, Miss Fickett is excellent. She attempts to win back her son's love and bring about a satisfactory understanding with her ex-husband.

Inger Stevens, as a femme lawyer, is another newcomer who should be heard from in the future. She is particularly appealing as she nurses Crosby through his vicious and embittered moods. Fine performances are also given by Anne Seymour, as a femme judge, E. G. Marshall, as Crosby's lawyer, and Malcolm Brodrick, as Crosby's young son. Richard Eastham, either through the direction or writing, emerges just a little too stuffy as Miss Fickett's new husband.

Despite the dramatic impact of the picture, it is not all sombre. MacDougall, who directed as well as wrote the film, has provided some light dialog that fits Crosby's familiar style. The tension is relieved on a number of occasions by scenes designed to provide a chuckle or a laugh.

The picture is a well-made one technically, with the production values as slick as the story itself. An over the title song, "Man on Fire," by Sammy Fain and Paul Francis Webster, is sung by the Ames Brothers. *Holl.*

Calypso Heat Wave
(SONGS)

Neat programmer stacked with appeal for the teenager.

Hollywood, May 31.

Columbia release of Sam Katzman production. Stars Johnny Desmond, Merry Anders, Meg Myles; features Paul Langton, Joel Grey, Michael Granger, George E. Stone, The Treniers, The Tarriers, The Hi-Lo's, Maya Angelou. Directed by Fred F. Sears. Screenplay, David Chandler; story, Orville H. Hampton; camera, Benjamin H. Kline; editors, Edwin Bryant, Tony DiMarco; music, Paul Mertz, Ross Di Maggio; choreography, Josephine Earl. Previewed May 23, '57. Running time, **86 MINS.**

Johnny Conroy	Johnny Desmond
Marty Collins	Merry Anders
Mona De Luce	Meg Myles
Mack Adams	Paul Langton
Alex Nash	Joel Grey
Barney Pearl	Michael Granger
Books	George E. Stone
The Tarriers	Themselves
The Hi-Lo's	Themselves
Maya Angelou	Herself
Dick Whittinghill	Himself
Girl	Darla Hood
Hi Fi Bromley	Pierce Lyden
George	Gil Perkins
Andrew	William Challee
Mac Niles and the Calypsonians	Themselves

Combined artistry of the musical talent lined up for "Calypso Heat Wave" rates this Sam Katzman (Clover) production a neat entry for the supporting market. It's none-too-subtly aimed at the teenage market, and there will have to find its greatest appeal. Against it is the fact that the calypso song craze is on the wane and some say already dead.

David Chandler screenplay, from a story by Orville H. Hampton, is merely the springboard for the musical break-ins. Nonetheless, it's well spotted with humor and thoroughly effective as directed by Fred F. Sears.

Tale centers around Disco Records, company headed by ex-musician Paul Langton, who has as his partners secretary Merry Anders and singer Johnny Desmond. Latter, it seems, has become the calypso idol of the teenagers, and this leads Michael Granger, chiseling jukebox czar, to buy his way into the firm so as to get on the gravy train. His unethical manipulations, however, cause Desmond to take off for parts unknown and Disco's biz makes a rapid decline. It all winds with Granger out of the company, Desmond returning to make more disclicks and Langton and Miss Anders about to wed. Plus, of course, the musical sign-off via a calypso carnival.

Desmond makes a personable lead and effectively puts over some half-dozen song numbers, while Miss Anders, Langton and Granger are all adequate to the demands of the script. Meg Myles is good as Granger's g.f., as is Joel Grey as Disco's errand boy and jack-of-all-trades. Grey, incidentally, is also in with a neat dance solo.

Best of the vocal interludes are the Hi-Lo's rendition of "Swing Low Sweet Chariot" and "My Sugar Is So Refined," both from their current pop Columbia Records album; The Tarriers' "Banana Boat Song"; "Day Old Bread and Canned Beans" and "Rock Joe," both done by The Treniers; and Maya Angelou's "Run Joe."

Technical contributions are okay. *Neal.*

Joe Dakota

Slow-moving western. No shots fired, no boxoffices hit.

Hollywood, May 31.

Universal release of a Howard Christie production. Stars Jock Mahoney, Luana Patten; costars Charles McGraw, Barbara Lawrence; features Claude Akins, Lee Van Cleef, Anthony Caruso, Paul Birch, George Dunn. Directed by Richard Bartlett. Screenplay, William Talman, Norman Jolley; camera (Eastmancolor), George Robinson; editor, Fred MacDowell; music, Joseph Gershenson; art directors, Alexander Golitzen, Bill Newberry. Previewed May 28, '57. Running time, **79 MINS.**

The Stranger	Jock Mahoney
Jody Weaver	Luana Patten
Cal Moore	Charles McGraw
Myrna Weaver	Barbara Lawrence
Aaron Grant	Claude Akins
Adam Grant	Lee Van Cleef
Marcus Vizzini	Anthony Caruso
Frank Weaver	Paul Birch
Jim Baldwin	George Dunn
Sam Cook	Steve Darrell
Rosa Vizzini	Rita Lynn
Tom Jensen	Gregg Barton
Claude Henderson	Anthony Jochim
Bertha Jensen	Jeane Wood
Ethel Cook	Juney Ellis

An offbeat story and meandering treatment militates against "Joe Dakota" being more than a fair entry for the program trade. Name of Jock Mahoney may give film a boost, and film has benefit of good supporting performances generally.

The Howard Christie production is a western without a single shot fired, localing in a tiny early California community where the whole populace is engaged in an oil-drilling enterprise. Script by William Talman and Norman Jolley is overleisurely in building up Mahoney's role of a stranger who arrives with questions which seemingly cannot be answered, and because of the slow pace and patent intent to keep him mysterious the interest seldom speeds up beyond a walk.

Mahoney finds himself unwelcome when he rides into town, asking whereabouts of the old Indian who once owned the property on which drilling is going on. He's to'd the Indian has gone away, after selling property to Charles McGraw, a wildcatter who is heading operations. Later, it develops that Indian was hanged by townspeople for assertedly having attacked young daughter of the storekeeper, but Mahoney, retired cavalry captain for whom Indian was once a scout, is able to prove that McGraw framed the whole thing to get the land.

Under Richard Bartlett's direction, Mahoney delivers well, albeit his true identity is too long in revealment, necessarily allowing action still further. Luana Patten, the storekeeper's daughter, appealingly portrays her role, her former friendship with the old Indian helping Mahoney clear up the case as he falls in love with her. McGraw suitably delineates the heavy, Barbara Lawrence provides distaff interest as Luana's elder sister and okay support is offered by Paul Birch, Claude Akins, Lee Van Cleef, Anthony Caruso and George Dunn.

George Robinson's Eastmancolor lensing is interesting, Fred MacDowell's editing is as tight as script will allow and art direction is in capable hands of Alexander Golitzen and Bill Newberry. *Whit.*

That Woman Opposite
(BRITISH)

An involved whodunit adapted from a novel starring Wilfrid Hyde White and Phyllis Kirk.

London, May 28.

Monarch release (in association with British Lion) of Monarch (William Gell) Production. Stars Phyllis Kirk, Dan O'Herlihy, Wilfrid Hyde White, Petula Clark. Directed by Compton Bennett. Screenplay, Compton Bennett; from the novel "The Emperor's Snuff Box" by John Dickson Carr; camera, Lionel Banes; editor, Bill Lewthwaite; music, Stanley Black. At Hammer Theatre, London. Running time, **90 MINS.**

Eve	Phyllis Kirk
Kinross	Dan O'Herlihy
Sir Maurice	Wilfrid Hyde White
Janice	Petula Clark
Toby	Jack Watling
Ned	William Franklyn
Lady Lawes	Margaret Withers
Goron	Guido Lorraine
Busson	Jacques Cey
Gaston	Andre Charisse
Bill Morris	Robert Raikes
Marie	Tita Dane
Prue	Balbina
Diana	Irene Moore
Peggy	Concepta Fennell
Gendarme	Campbell Gray
Doctor	John Serett

Story is a bit complex, and difficult to transfer to the screen in simple terms. It is set in a French coastal resort, being mainly concerned with a series of robberies. Wilfrid Hyde White plays a baronet and noted art collector, who is rebuked by his insurance assessor for insufficient protection on his treasures. From his window he recognizes the thief being tackled by a gendarme, who subsequently dies, he in turn gets murdered when one of his historical jewels is stolen. Both his son and the boy's future bride are suspected, the son, because he had systematically robbed his father to pay off a blackmailing mistress; and the fiancee because she is tangled up in circumstantial evidence engineered by her maid.

With the aid of the investigating insurance sleuth and the local police, it is revealed the fiancee's ex-husband is both thief and murderer. She had kept quiet over his presence in her bedroom at night because of the compromising implications, and her statement of what she had witnessed through the window sounded phoney. She and the insurance agent get together and switch the romantic angle to a happy finale when all the creases are straightened out.

White's dry whimsicality hits the right note as the baronet, contrasting with the feeble characterization of the son by Jack Watling. Phyllis Kirk sustains the strong emotional role as the chief suspect while William Franklyn registers convincingly as the crook. Dan O'Herlihy balances evenly as the insurance broker turned Romeo. Guido Lorraine brings an attractive Gallic flavor to the role of the local police inspector. Petula Clark is poorly served in the colorless part of the baronet's daughter. Two excellent performances are given by Tita Dane and Balbina as the scheming French sisters. *Clem.*

Bayou

Initial production effort of Southern exhibitors is strictly amateur night in Dixie.

United Artists release of an M. A. Riggs production. Stars Peter Graves and Lita Milan. Features Douglas Fowley and Tim Carey. Directed by Harold Daniels. Screenplay and story, Edward I. Fessler. Camera, Ted and Vincent Saizis; editor, Maury Wright; music, Fessler. Previewed, May 28, '57. Running time, **83 MINS.**

Martin	Peter Graves
Marie	Lita Milan
Herbert	Douglas Fowley
Ulysses	Tim Carey
Bos	Jonathan Haze
Etienne	Edwin Nelson
Jean Titho	Eugene Sondfield
Doucette	Evelyn Hendrickson
Cousine	Milton Schneider
Felician	Michael R. Romano

Importation of a troupe of pros from Hollywood, including thesps Peter Graves, Lita Milan and Douglas Fowley, plus director Harold Daniels, can't save this from being more than amateur night in Dixie. Initial effort of Southern exhibitors, M. A. Riggs and Edward I. Fessler (who produced and scripted, respectively), this obviously low-budget item is at best adequate for modest or specialized situations, with the off-beat background a possible exploitation peg.

There's a germ of a good idea in Fessler's screenplay, but inept handling largely sterilizes it. Mainly, script shows a tendency toward flowery dialog which serves to further slow an already leisurely pace.

In story, Graves, a self-effacing and insecure architect from the North, comes to the bayou country to plug his plans for a New Orleans municipal building with a vacationing politico. He falls in love with Miss Milan, attractive daughter of shiftless fisherman Douglas Fowley, and becomes embroiled in the violent affairs of the local Cajun French colony. The simple life and Miss Milan's love regenerates Graves' faith in himself, and when she's threatened by the lustful designs of the local bully, Tim Carey, Graves finds the courage to fight and beat him.

Most vivid portrayal is that of Miss Milan, who make the most of the fiery and attractive Cajun miss. Graves is competent in the rather pallid role of the architect. Fowley again demonstrates his talents as a fine character actor, and not only makes a very convincing Cajun, but doubles in an uncredited role of a contractor friend of Graves. Tim Carey's broad style of villainy is suited to his role, Jonathan Haze's contribution is confined to a speechless bit, and local talent fills other parts with mediocre results.

Director Daniels manages several strong vignettes, notably a genial shivaree and the fight scene between Graves and Carey, but otherwise he's unable to rise above the weak script.

Black-and-white lensing quality by Ted and Vincent Saizis is good, but with attractive bayou locale, colorfilming would have been more appropriate. Music background, also by Fessler and sung in local metier by an unidentified group, is stuck in here and there without much application to the plot.

Kove.

Beau James
(TECHNIRAMA-VISTA-VISION)

Subordinating the comic to the actor, Bob Hope scores in a warm, believable telling of Jimmy Walker's rise and fall. Should please the oldsters and fascinate the newer citizens.

Paramount presentation of Hope Enterprises Production. Producer, Jack Rose; director, Melville Shavelson. Stars Bob Hope, Vera Miles, Paul Douglas. Features Alexis Smith, Darren McGavin. Adapted by Shavelson and Rose from Gene Fowler's book. Camera, John F. Warren; editor, Floyd Knudtson; music, Joseph J. Lilley; choreography, Jack Baker. Previewed in N.Y., June 3, '57. Running time, 105 MINS.
Jimmy Walker .... Bob Hope
Betty Compton .... Vera Miles
Chris Nolan .... Paul Douglas
Allie Walker .... Alexis Smith
Charley Hand .... Darren McGavin
Bernie .... Joe Mantell
Prosecutor .... Horace McMahon
Dick Jackson .... Richard Shannon
Arthur Julian .... Willis Bouchey
Sid Nash .... Sid Melton
George Jessel .... Himself
Jack Benny .... Himself
Jimmy Durante .... Himself
Al Smith .... Walter Catlett

Persons now 35 years of age were 10 years old when Jimmy Walker conked out as mayor of New York in 1932. Which means that for the run of today's film fans arguments about authenticity of detail and interpretation won't seem too real. They'll pass by the question of whether "Beau James" is good history or sweeping epic and ask, is it entertaining? The answer is yes, very.

Actually the story is probably reasonably respectful of the facts, if acknowledging in that generality the failure of experts always to agree as to what the facts were. Walker was naughty all his life, and that's the right word. He may have been more careless than culpable. Humanly enough, people who were blind to his sins and enchanted by his Irish charms usually loved him beyond logic. A good deal of this paradox comes across in the 105 minutes of celluloid produced by Jack Rose and directed by Melville Shavelson from their joint screenplay.

"Based on the book by Gene Fowler" undoubtedly explains much of the underlying story strength. But the task of steering between Walker's unmarried love and the Catholic Church, between his sorry showing in Albany before Franklin D. Roosevelt, then governor, and the theory that Walker was sacrificed to open the path to the White House for FDR, took much finesse by Messrs. Shavelson and Rose. Their canny professionalism as practical story-tellers and boxoffice operators stands forth.

Still "Beau James" would not have made it as engrossing entertainment if the "risk" casting of Bob Hope had not been vindicated. Many in show biz shook their heads at the news. They may now desist from palsy. Hope is an actor here, almost completely submerging Bob Hope in Jimmy Walker.

Oldtimers will recall that the late mayor was considerably thinner but nonetheless Hope has been dressed and chapeaued (oh, those Walker hats!) to delight nostalgia. Much of the debonair, not to say rakish, dash of Walker is captured. His flippancies ring true and may indeed often be literal remembrances dug up by research.

Once or twice, as when joining Jimmy Durante at a Lambs Club Wash in a song and dance routine, the talents of Walker are surely exaggerated for the sake of cinematic scene. And that episode at the Yankee Stadium where he admits he was a chump but tells the booing mob that they were chumps, too, since they voted for him and the people in the end get the kind of government they deserve: where, many will wonder, has the line of fiction been drawn?

It follows that Hope dominates the footage but he is vastly aided by the two women, Vera Miles as Betty Compton, she of the bangs, and Alexis Smith, a highly flattering stand-in for the seldom-seen Mrs. Walker from whom no divorce was possible because of the Church. Both women give shaded and attractive performances.

There is a good deal of allusion to the Church in the dialog, Walker always making clear his devotion to it, although willing to divorce. At the height of his troubles via the Seabury investigation he's shown leading the St. Patrick's Day parade up Fifth Avenue and he in a bad way from hangover. He quips, "If I can get by the Cathedral, maybe I can go the distance."

The screenplay skirts the question of Mrs. Walker, but leaves the impression of a woman sad in her own frigidity and religious righteousness. The authors have been discreet but the Legion of Decency's "B" rating raises a dissatisfaction that the story does not disclose Walker's reconciliation with his faith (presumably after the real-life death of Betty Compton).

It's suggested at one point that Walker was a better mayor working two hours a day than half a dozen predecessors working full schedule had been. His habit of being tardy, a dead giveaway of a juvenile strain of rebelliousness against convention, is part of his sauciness. A vice in ordinary mortals, tardiness was considered amusing (well, most of the time) in this Broadway dandy.

Treatment overall catches beguiling hints of the 1920's, though this is held down. Now and again some forgotten custom, like the corny chorus line in the Greenwich Village dump, brings a chuckle. Plainly Shavelson and Rose never forgot that the bulk of their audiences will know little about Walker or his era. They play it for human values and succeed very well indeed.

Most of the roles are "supporting" but worthies include Paul Douglas, Darren McGavin, Joe Mantell and Horace McMahon and, briefly, Walter Catlett, not quite satisfying as the too-familiar Al Smith.

Technical credits are fully pro, the New York special effects rating remark. To underscore the madcap period the chief Boswell thereof, Walter Winchell, was recruited to come in now and again with remember-when narration. The Winchell offscreen ratatat vocal style is an added punch.

The author-producers, the comic turned sincere character delineator and the two femme leads rack up the real career points. This is a breezily developed tale with an offbeat character from real life. It generates great interest. Essentially its believable and never preachy. George Jessel, Jimmy Durante and Jack Benny make quickie appearances for old time's sake.

A great study of social conditions or personal motivations or history "Beau James" is not; but a good piece of diversion it definitely is.
Land.

The Weapon

Quality plus cast of familiar names makes this a good bet for the general U.S. market.

Hollywood, June 10.
Republic release of Hal E. Chester production, presented by Irving H. Levin. Stars Steve Cochran, Lizabeth Scott, Herbert Marshall, Nicole Maurey; co-stars Jon Whiteley; features George Cole, Laurence Naismit, Stanley Maxted, Denis Shaw, Fred Johnson. Directed by Val Guest. Screenplay, Fred Freiberger; story, Hal E. Chester, Fred Freiberger; camera, Reg Wyer; editor, Peter Rolfe Johnson; music, James Stevens. Previewed June 6, '57. Running time, 77 MINS.
Mark .... Steve Cochran
Elsa .... Lizabeth Scott
Mackenzie .... Herbert Marshall
Vivienne .... Nicole Maurey
Erik .... Jon Whiteley
Joshua .... George Cole
Jamison .... Laurence Naismith
Colonel .... Stanley Maxted
Groggins .... Denis Shaw
Fitzsimmons .... Fred Johnson

Republic has a good, suspenseful melodrama in "The Weapon," and, with familiar names of the cast toppers, picture should do okay in the domestic market. Filmed entirely in England by Irving H. Levin and Hal E. Chester, pic was purchased outright by Republic some months back.

Somewhat reminiscent to "The Little Fugitive" of several years ago, the "Weapon" story by Hal E. Chester and Fred Freiberger, which latter has screenplayed, deals with a child, Jon Whiteley, who accidentally shoots another and is "in hiding" until the windup. Gun involved, found by the youth in the remains of a destroyed building, turns out to be the offbeat-make weapon involved in murder of a U.S. Army officer 10 years previous. This brings inspector Herbert Marshall and C.I.D. officer Steve Cochran into search for the boy and the gun; also seeking him are his mother, Lizabeth Scott, and the murderer, George Cole. It all winds with latter meeting his death at the hands of Cochran, and Whiteley back home with Miss Scott. The shot boy, incidentally, recovers.

Acting is top-rate, with Cochran, Miss Scott, Whiteley, Marshall and Cole all turning in extremely good portrayals. Too, Nicole Maurey is fine as a saloon hostess-suspect who Cole also rubs out.

Val Guest's direction of the Hal E. Chester production, presented by Irving H. Levin, is another plus credit, keeping the suspense high and the performances entirely credible.

Technical contributions are good.
Neal.

The Midnight Story
(C'SCOPE)

Tony Curtis, Gilbert Roland and Marisa Pavan in a strongly-developed whodunit.

Hollywood, June 7.
Universal release of a Robert Arthur production. Stars Tony Curtis, Marisa Pavan, Gilbert Roland; features Jay C. Flippen, Argentina Brunetti, Ted De Corsia, Richard Monda. Directed by Joseph Pevney. Screenplay, John Robinson, Edwin Blum; camera, Russell Metty; editor, Ted J. Kent; music, Joseph Gershenson. Previewed June 4, '57. Running time, 87 MINS.
Joe Martini .... Tony Curtis
Anna Malatesta .... Marisa Pavan

Sylvio Malatesta .... Gilbert Roland
Sergeant Jack Gillen.......Jay C. Flippen
Mama Malatesta ......Argentina Brunetti
Lieutenant Kilrain......... Ted De Corsia
Peanuts Malatesta .... Richard Monda
Rosa Cuneo .... Kathleen Freeman
Charlie Cuneo .... Herbert Vigran
Veda Pinelli .... Peggy June Maley
Father Giuseppe .... John Cliff
Det. Sergeant Sommers.....Russ Conway
Frankie Pellatrini .... Chico Vejar
Grocer .... Tito Vuolo
Mother Catherine .... Helen Wallace
Frank Wilkins .... James Hyland

Trackdown of a Catholic priest's murderer cues the action of this well-worked-out whodunit which should please audiences going for this class of entertainment. Plot has been competently fashioned, and presence of Tony Curtis, who co-stars with Marisa Pavan and Gilbert Roland, should add to its prospects in general market.

Not until almost the closing scene is the identity of the killer revealed, a good piece of craftsmanship on the part of scripters John Robinson and Edwin Blum, who keep the narrative legitimately premised and unfoldment steadily building in dramatic impact. Director Joseph Pevney makes excellent use of San Francisco locations for the Robert Arthur production in limning his story, which add atmospherically to the overall scene, and feel of the Italian quarter and its people is caught in his helming.

Curtis portrays a young Frisco traffic cop who resigns from force to track the slayer of the priest, his best friend, after being refused a transfer to homicide. His suspicions rest upon Roland, owner of a seafood restaurant, whose anguish he notes at the funeral. He gets a job with Roland, whom he learns was a close friend of the murdered man, and is invited to live in his home, shared by suspect with his mother and young cousin, Miss Pavan. The first home Curtis, an orphan, has ever known, ex-cop, while falling in love with femme, still is suspicious of his benefactor. When he discovers that Roland has an alibi for night of the murder, Curtis proposes to femme, but on occasion of the announcement party he finds that Roland's alibi is false. Latter is killed by a truck before he can be brought in.

Curtis gives character a good play and Roland socks over his part with his usual excellence. Miss Pavan is dramatically appealing. Argentina Brunetti capably plays Roland's mother, Jay C. Flippen is strongly cast as vet police sergeant who upsets Roland's alibi, and Ted De Corsia is competent as homicide lieutenant.

Film gets good production mounting all the way, from Russell Metty's crisp photography to Ted J. Kent's tight editing, Alexander Colitzen and Eric Orbom's art direction and Joseph Gershenson's music. *Whit.*

Dino

Forceful juve delinquency pic for anticipated good returns in general market. With Sal Mineo.

Hollywood, June 7.

Allied Artists release of a Bernice Block production. Stars Sal Mineo; co-stars Brian Keith, Susan Kohner; features Frank Faylen, Joe Desantis, Pat DeSimone, Penny Santon, Richard Bakalyan. Directed by Thomas Carr. Screenplay, Reginald Rose, based on his teleplay; camera, Wilfrid Cline; editor, William Austin; music, Herald Fried. Previewed June 5, '57. Running time, **93 MINS.**

Dino .... Sal Mineo
Sheridan .... Brian Keith
Shirley .... Susan Kohner
Mandel .... Frank Faylen
Mr. Minetta .... Joe Desantis
Tony .... Pat DeSimone
Mrs. Minetta .... Penny Santon
Chuck .... Richard Bakalyan
Frances .... Mollie McCart
Sylvia .... Cindy Robbins
Second Boy .... Rafael Campos

In its translation from CBS-TV's "Studio One," where it played early last year, to an Allied Artists' release, "Dino" comes off as a tense and forceful juve delinquency yarn. It can be figured as a good entry for the general as well as program market, where its chances look promising.

Reginald Rose, who authored the teleplay, repeats on screenplay for the Bernice Block-David Kramarsky indie, elaborating on his original via buildup of its dramatic aspects. Sal Mineo, who did a fine job on tv, again takes over role of the 17-year-old who returns to his slum neighborhood after a term in reform school for having participated in a murder. His work here is even better, acquitting himself with distinction and turning in one of the best bits of acting during a highly emotional scene that the screen has seen this year.

Direction of Thomas Carr sensitively catches the character of the boy, his young life crammed with hate and violence, as he gradually begins to see the light under the gentle guidance of settlement worker Brian Keith. Before the promise of this conversion, however, unfolds the tale of a rebel who thinks the whole world is against him. He cannot figure the attitude of either Keith or Frank Faylen, his parole officer, who want nothing from him, being accustomed to the cruelty and misunderstanding of his father, who has beaten him as long as he can remember.

His young brother, who worships him because of his hardness, talks him into leading a gang he belongs to in a midnight holdup of a gas station, and it's only as he realizes what this will do to the brother that he refuses to go through with the crime and saves the youngster from his own planned action. Windup has him asking settlement worker for help for his brother as well as himself.

Mineo gives role both a hard finish and sympathy. Highlight sequence is his crying for the first time in his life as he finally unloads some of his frustrations to Keith, the entire several minutes' performance never for a moment becoming maudlin or overly-dramatic, as might easily have been the case. Keith, always under-playing his role, is finely effective and Susan Kohner is excellent as an ugly duckling of the neighborhood who helps in juve's reformation.

In support, Joe Desantis scores as the father who does not like the son; Pat DeSimone handles the brother part well; Faylen makes the most of his brief role; Penny Santon is drably competent as the mother; and Richard Bakalyan is okay as a settlement house lad.

Musical score by Gerald Fried is particularly decisive in creating mood, especially in the opening in setting the scene. Wilfrid Cline's low-key photography also is a definite asset, and William Austin's editing helps in the general dramatic buildup. *Whit.*

Day of Fear

Marty Gosch's Spanish-made Lightweight Mobster Tale

Madrid, June 4.

Noisy world premiere on May 27 of the Spanish-made U. S. indie "Day of Fear" (shot in English, dubbed in Spanish) proved impossibility of asking a Madrid first-night audience to go for Spanish cops and lawbreakers who sound and act like Runyonesque characters in a Hollywood low-budget quickie.

American producer Martin Gosch gave his big bi-lingual Spanish cast a lightweight flypaper script to fight with but set up picture for other markets with a briskly-paced badge and smuggler melee that chases through a selection of expertly color-photographed Madrid exteriors to make "Day of Fear" a contender in strictly smaller program situations.

Script laboriously details plot complications before hi-jackers seize a mercy shipment of precious medicine flown to Madrid to check a young but deadly epidemic. Heartless mobsters are braintrusted by hospital officials and a drug industry exec (!) who arranged crisis shipment. Dr. Valdes (Ruben Rojo) and his sweet chic nurse (Elena Barrios) team up with Madrid gangbuster (Fernando Rey) to put the hooks on heavy Dr. Bernier (Rolf Wanka) and his two-timing ex-gypsy moll (Nina Karell), inflict lightning justice and save humanity.

Humanity can survive right well without "Day of Fear" but release has some plus factors worthy of mention. Fernando Rey performance impresses and may bring talented thespian more appropriate Anglo-Saxon vehicles. Elena Barrios is distinctly agreeable on the pantalla and Rolf Wanka is well above par. Nina Karell is okay as a sinister Miss Trouble.

Berenguer's color lensing is consistently standout, especially in his pictorial coverage of Madrid tourist high spots. Leo Arnaud's long score is an ear-filling pacesetter. Hi-jacking sequence and finale shots in the deserted fair grounds of Casa del Campo, offer first-rate screen fare in an otherwise small calibre film. Despite unknown cast, film's crime and passion under Madrid skies has limited hard and soft currency value in other markets. *Werb.*

The Black Tent
(V'VISION—COLOR)

Entertaining adventure yarn lensed in North African story locale; good action trade appeal.

Hollywood, June 7.

Rank Film Distributors release of a William MacQuitty production. Stars Anthony Steel, Donald Sinden, Anna Maria Sandri; features Andre Morell. Directed by Brian Desmond Hurst. Screenplay, Robin Maugham, Bryan Forbes; camera (Tecnicolor), Desmond Dickinson; editor, Alfred Roome. Previewed June 4, '57. Running time, **84 MINS.**

David Holland .... Anthony Steel
Charles Holland .... Donald Sinden
Mabrouka .... Anna Maria Sandri
Sheik Salem .... Andre Morell
Croft .... Ralph Truman
Ali .... Donald Pleasence
Baring .... Anthony Bushell
Faris .... Michael Craig
1st German Officer...... Anton Diffring
2nd German Officer....Frederick Jaeger
Khalil .... Paul Homer
Interpreter .... Derek Sydney
Daoud .... Terrence Sharkey

"The Black Tent" is an entertaining adventure yarn of a British officer who takes refuge with a Bedouin tribe during World War II. Film is colorfully limned in story's actual Libyan Desert setting with the added pictorial advantages of Vista-Vision and Technicolor for sometimes spectacular mounting. While lacking in U.S. marques names, the feature, released in this country by Rank's newly-formed distribution arm here, should rate okay for the action market.

The William MacQuitty production is told in flashback form, script by Robin Maugham and Bryan Forbes logically starting in present and unfolding during the British-Nazi battle years in North Africa. Effective use is made of the desert and oases of the area, a desert ruins smacking of antiquity and the natives, camels and black tents of the Bedouins providing a striking backdrop for a well-worked-out narrative. Direction by Brian Desmond Hurst is swift and sure in his battle scenes and catching the spirit of the piece, and Desmond Dickinson's photograph is a definite assist to picture, which had the cooperation of the Libyan government and army during its making.

When an Englishman, who inherited the vast estates of his brother after latter was presumed dead in the African campaign, learns that an undated promissory note signed by the brother has been delivered to the British Embassy, he goes to Tripoli to solve the mystery. His travels take him to the black tents of the Bedouins, where the daughter of the sheik hands over his brother's diary, thus setting the scent for flashback action.

Brother, wounded in tank action, is taken in by the Bedouins and he falls in love with sheik's daughter, whom he weds after learning the British whom he hoped to rejoin have been beaten back and he decides to make his home with the tribe. Later, Britisher persuades the sheik to help him carry on guerrilla warfare behind the German lines, but in saving sheik's life during an ambush of a convoy he is killed.

Anthony Steel gives a good account of himself as the British officer, and Anna Maria Sandri, an Italian actress, is charming as his bride. Donald Sinden is fine as the brother and Andre Morell delivers strongly in role of sheik. Terence Sharkey is okay as the son of Steel and Anna Maria and Donald Pleasence is good as an Arab guide.

William Alwyn's music score offers melodic backing and Alfred Roome's tight editing allows fast movement. *Whit.*

Bar Mitzvah

National Film Board of Canada release of a Peter Jones production. (Exec. producer, Nick Balla). Directed by Alvin Goldman. Camera, Grant Crabtree; editor, Marion Meadows; sound, Clark DaPrato. At Linden Theatre, Ottawa, June 5. Running time, **10 MINS.**

This short documentary, produced in Ottawa with a 13-year-old Jewish boy actually becoming "Bar Mitzvah" (roughly equivalent of "confirmed" in Christian churches) is particularly timely. Recently a Toronto rabbi spoke out publicly against "the increasing tendency" to make Bar Mitzvah more of a festive occasion than one of deeply religious significance. He was widely reported.

The party side, however, is not touched on in this straightforward account of a boy preparing for and going through the ceremony of Bar Mitzvah. Seen first in Hebrew school, he then goes to his rabbi, who puts him at his ease then gets serious.

Except for brief shots of his family, the rest of the film simply shows the actual ceremony. Lad finally takes over from the cantor and chants passages of the Torah; receives à Bible; then goes down to be greeted as a man by his parents Most of it is new and fascinating to Christian moviegoers.

Over-all production job is very smooth. But perhaps, with a scant 10 minutes' footage, more time might have been devoted to the rabbi's talk with the boy—almost completely cut—and less to the ceremonial chanting. Uncredited commentary was well handled.

Gard.

20 Million Miles to Earth

Another "monster" to scare the kids the way they like to be scared. Elephant fights monster in streets of Rome. Good bet for the fantasy addicts.

Hollywood, June 7.

Columbia release of a Charles H. Schneer production. Stars William Hopper, Joan Taylor; features Frank Puglia, John Zaremba, Thomas B. Henry, Tito Vuolo. Directed by Nathan Juran. Screenplay, Bob Williams, Christopher Knopf; story, Charlott Knight, Ray Harryhausen; camera, Irving Lippman, Carlos Ventigmilia; editor, Edwin Bryant; music, Mischa Bakaleinikoff. Previewed June 6, '57. Running time, 84 MINS.

Calder	William Hopper
Marisa	Joan Taylor
Dr. Leonardo	Frank Puglia
Dr. Judson Uhl	John Zaremba
Major McIntosh	Thomas B. Henry
Commissario of Police	Tito Vuolo
Signore Contino	Jan Arvan
Sharman	Arthur Space
Pepe	Bart Bradley
Mr. Maples	George Pelling
Verrico	George Khoury
Mondello	Don Orlando
Dr. Koroku	Rollin Moriyama

This science-fictioner is another in the long line of "monster" pictures that have racked up nice biz in situations catering to this type of product. Indications point to similar playoff, realistic special effects providing strong exploitation potential.

The Charles H. Schneer production pegs its premise on return of an American rocket ship from the planet Venus, carrying a small creature which almost overnight grows into a towering monster which destroys everything in its path as it makes its way through Rome. Large portion of pic was lensed in Italy, where the Colosseum and other piles serve as interesting backdrops for regulation story. One of the cleverest bits of special effects is a battle to the death between the monster and a giant elephant on streets of Rome. Nathan Juran generally keeps a fast pace in his direction of the Bob Williams-Christopher Knopf screenplay.

William Hopper, as only survivor of the ship as it crashes into the sea off Sicily, directs efforts first to capture the monster for scientific purposes; then, to destroy it. Immune to bullets, creature is subdued temporarily when an electrically-charged net is thrown over it from a helicopter, but an accident in the Roman museum which cuts off the power returns beast to its former strength and it breaks out, to create a reign of terror throughout the city. Creature is finally killed under an avalanche of stones when it's blown by fire power off the top of the Colosseum.

Appearing with Hopper are attractive Joan Taylor, as an Italian medic; Frank Puglia, her grandfather, a zoologist; John Zaremba, American scientist working with Hopper in monster's destruction; Thomas B. Henry, U.S. Air Force officer. Good support also is afforded by Tito Vuolo, Sicilian police commissario; Bart Bradley, a Sicilian moppet.

Irving Lippman and Carlos Ventigmilia share camera credits, art director Cary Odell is responsible for good matching of sets and Edwin Bryant's editing is fast.

Whit.

The Rising of the Moon
(IRISH)

Presumptive appeal to Irish audiences in States. Three short tales directed by John Ford with lots of Gaelic nostalgia.

Warner Bros. release of Four Provinces production. Directed by John Ford. Director of photography, Robert Krasker; screenplay, Frank S. Nugent. Editor, Michael Gordon. At Metropole, Dublin. Running time, 80 MINS.

Four Provinces Films, outfit set up by John Ford, Michael (Lord) Killanin, Michael Scott and Tyrone Power to lens motion pictures in Ireland, releases its first production through Warners. Picture got good reception from Irish critics at world premiere at Dublin's Metropole and local critics, it may be remarked, are notoriously touchy with pictures concerning Ireland.

John Ford directed with Irish nostalgia uppermost, something which should endear it to Irish audiences in U. S., but choice of Frank O'Connor's short story "The Majesty of the Law" as opener was dubious. It's a subtle little story which did not translate well to film and is inclined to confuse as to main theme, and some references may well prove too "local." Top roles are by Noel Purcell as man who'd rather go to jail than pay fine for striking neighbor, and Cyril Cusack (currently in N. Y. legit's "Moon For The Misbegotten") as police inspector sent to serve the warrant.

"A Minute's Wait" is an Abbey farce featuring Ireland's top comedian Jimmy O'Dea and concerns the happenings on a rural railway station when a train is delayed. It provides opportunities for humor on a number of Irish themes—match-making, long engagements, long-winded stories and English visitors. Plenty of laughs, and some pleasant singing from tenor Michael O'Duffy.

"1921" is an updated version of Lady Gregory's Abbey play "The Rising of the Moon" and concerns escape of Irish patriot from jail in Galway. Expanded story covers jail escape sequence as well as setting of original story on a quayside and provides conflict of loyalty for police sergeant guarding the wharf—a good performance by Denis O'Dea with Abbeyite Eileen Crowe as his wife.

Film, shot entirely on location in Ireland is black and white, has Ford's confident touch and first-class camerawork by Robert Krasker.

Mac.

Die Trapp Familie
(The Trapp Family)
(GERMAN-COLOR)

Berlin, June 4.

Gloria release of Divina production. Stars Ruth Leuwerik. Features Hans Holt, Maria Holst and Josef Meinrad. Directed by Wolfgang Liebeneiner. Screenplay, Georg Hurdalek, based on memories by Baroness Maria Trapp; camera, (Eastmancolor), Werner Krien; music, Franz Grothe; editor, Margot von Schilieffen. At UFA Pavilion, Berlin. Running time, 104 MINS.

Baroness Maria Trapp	Ruth Leuwerik
Baron Trapp	Hans Holt
Countess	Maria Holst
Dr. Wasner	Josef Meinrad
Gruber, banker	Friedrich Domin
Baroness Mathilde	Hilde von Stolz
Abbess	Agnes Windeck
Raphaela	Liesl Karstadt
Samish	Alfred Balthoff
Petroff	Hans Schumm
Female cook	Gretl Theimer

There is no doubt that Gloria has in "Trapp Family" a real moneymaker. Pic has the cast, plot and right portions of sentimentality which will appeal to most domestic cinema patrons. Story is bordering on the unbelievable but a true one. Foreign prospects appear beyond the German average. Pic will be a good bet for German language theatres in the U.S. It may also have some limited chances in the regular circuits since part of this has to do with the U.S.

Ably adapted from the memoirs of Baroness Maria Trapp, George Hurdalek's script is a sentimental if slick one. It tells about a young novice (Ruth Leuwerik) who leaves her nunnery to become temporarily a teacher in the castle of rich Baron Trapp (Hans Holt), an Austrian ex-submarine commander and father of seven motherless children. Holt soon sees more than just a teacher in Miss Leuwerik and they get married. A special pride of this family is the singing qualities of the children and latter win the first prize at a choir contest. When Hitler invades Austria (1938), the anti-Nazi Trapp family has to flee the country and starts as "the singing Trapp Family," a new life in the U.S. where the kids soon become a big success.

The cast is a plus factor in this production. Miss Leuwerik in the role of a novice who becomes baroness Trapp is sympathetic. Holt registers strongly as Baron Trapp. Very good support is given by Friedrich Domin, as Holt's banker-friend, and Josef Meinrad, as priest and musical teacher who joins the Trapps on their flight to America. Maria Holst, a countess whom Holt intended to marry before he met Miss Leuwerik, has only a minor part in this.

Wolfgang Liebeneiner's direction is very sensitive and he makes the most of the story. Werner Krien handles the Eastmancolor expertly while the production dress shows good German average. Rudolph Lamy's direction of the children's choir is extremely good. Other contributions are of fine calibre.

Hans.

Souvenir D'Italie
(ITALIAN)
(Color-Technirama)

Rome, June 4.

Rank Film release of Athena-J. A. Rank (Italy) production. Stars June Laverick, Inge Schoener, Isabelle Corey; features Vittorio DeSica, Alberto Sordi, Antonio Cifariello, Massimo Girotti, Gabriele Ferzetti. Directed by Antonio Pietrangeli. Screenplay, Pietrangeli, Age, Scarpelli; camera (Technirama), Aldo Tonti. At Cinema Corso, Rome. Running time, 100 MINS.

Margaret	June Laverick
Hilde	Ingeborg Schoener
Josette	Isabelle Corey

J. Arthur Rank has a good international entry in this scenic—and comic—romp through Italy. Top production values should pay off at the boxoffice, with special help coming from the Technirama lensing of colorful Italo backdrops. Names in feature billing will help in a few countries while the gals' good looks should overcome lack of marquee lustre.

Pic spins a loosely knit tale about three girls' hitchhiking experiences on a trip through northern Italy, hitting the Riviera, Venice, Florence and Rome. Each finds romance of sorts at one of the stops, while amusing incidents involving Vittorio DeSica and Alberto Sordi are threaded through the plot. Latter is especially good in a very funny portrayal of a gigolo who finally gets his comeuppance. Pace is rapid as the gals work their way south to Rome, where the Britisher leaves her two traveling companions to fly home.

Script and director Antonio Pietrangeli's able direction successfully blend commercial and artistic angles for an enjoyable total effect. June Laverick is fine as the prim English girl. Ingeborg Schoener engagingly draws her German companion while Isabelle Corey rough-sketches their uninhibited French fellow traveler. Supporting cast does a good backing job.

Lensing is excellent throughout, getting full value from Technicolor's new process while music and other credits on this totally location-shot pic measure up. While the version seen here is Italo-dubbed, actors speak in English, and an Anglo version is being readied, with plans calling for a general Anglo-American release this fall.

Hawk.

Die Bekenntnisse Des Hochstaplers Felix Krull
(Confessions of the Swindler Felix Krull)
(GERMAN)

Berlin, June 4.

Europa release of Filmaufbau (Goettingen) production. Stars Horst Buchholz and Liselotte Pulver; features Ingrid Andree, Susi Nicoletti, Paul Dahlke. Directed by Kurt Hoffmann. Screenplay by Robert Thoeren, after same-titled novel by Thomas Mann. Camera, Friedl Behn-Grund; music, Hans-Martin Majewski; editing, Caspar van den Berg. At Gloria Palast, Berlin. Running time, 112 MINS.

Felix Krull	Horst Buchholz
Zaza	Liselotte Pulver
Zouzou	Ingrid Andree
Madame Houpfle	Susi Nicoletti
Professor Kuckuck	Paul Dahlke
Maria Pia	Ilse Steppat
Lord Kilmarnock	Walter Rilla
Marquis de Venosta	Peer Schmidt
Mama Venosta	Alice Treff
Papa Venosta	Karl Ludwig Lindt

"Felix Krull" here has been one of the most eagerly-awaited German pix. The world-famous Thomas Mann yarn, the utilization of Horst Buchholz, Germany's brightest young star, for the title role, and the name of Kurt Hoffmann, one of this country's ablest pic creators, had won this production much advance attention before it even was completed. The results of this pic are somewhat mixed—positive and negative. It's one of the better domestic products, extremely well made, and a refreshing departure from so many recent run-of-mill pix. Many patrons, however, who have read and loved the famous Thomas Mann book, may be bitterly disappointed.

Though handled with taste and tact, "Felix Krull" misses much of what the literary original made a bestseller a favorite in this country. Despite the fact that there is very good acting all along the line, the characters portrayed don't quite come up to expectations. Film also lacks some depth. Nevertheless, the pic is amusing and entertaining enough to appeal to a majority of German audiences and, undoubtedly, also will please many of those who see in pix more than only entertainment. Since the Thomas Mann name is well known the world over, pic's foreign chances also appear above the German average.

Kurt Hoffmann, who has made a number of fine German pix within the past years, does not appear to have been able to achieve an authentic Thomas Mann film. But it is doubtful if any German pic director could have done a better job.

To some, the acting will be a thing of controversy, too. But there is no doubt that most Germans will love this film's characters. In the main, this concerns Horst Buchholz, of course. His "Felix Krull" and his romantic adventures will win him many new, particularly female admirers. He has many even impressive scenes in this film. He may well call this title role another important milestone in his career.

Film has an unusually large cast but all other performers, if contrasted with Buchholz, have relatively little to say. Liselotte Pulver, this time with blonde hair, is Zaza, a Parisian dancer, Felix Krull's No. 1 girl with whom he also sails at the end. Susi Nicoletti, Ingrid Andree and Ilse Steppat competently show up as some of his other romantic partners. Too brief but very good performances are turned in by Walter Rilla in the role of Lord Kilmarnock and Heinz Reinke as Stanko. Erika Mann, daughter of the late Thomas Mann, also has a role in this film, depicting a governess. Miss Mann, incidentally, also acted as a consultant on this film.

Technically, film is very much on the plus side. Strong assets are the score by Hans-Martin Majewski and Caspar van den Berg's tight editing. Also the lensing is often splendid while the production dress surpasses the usual German standard. *Hans.*

Les Sorcieres De Salem
(The Witches of Salem)
(FRENCH)
Paris, June 4.
Pathe release of CICC-Pathe production. Stars Yves Montand, Simone Signoret; features Mylene Demongeot, Alfred Adam, Jean Debucourt, Raymond Rouleau, Jean Gaven, Jeanne Fusier-Gir. Directed by Rouleau. Screenplay, Jean-Paul Sartre from play, "The Crucible," by Arthur Miller; camera, Claude Renoir; editor, Marguerite Renoir; music, Georges Auric. At Marignan, Paris. Running time, 135 MINS.
John Proctor .... Yves Montand
Elisabeth .... Simone Signoret
Abigail .... Mylene Demongeot
Governor .... Raymond Rouleau
Parris .... Jean Debucourt
Corey .... Jean Gaven
Martha .... Jeanne Fusier-Gir

Arthur Miller's play, "The Crucible," was a successful legiter here two years ago as "Les Sorcieres De Salem." Now the legit originators, Yves Montand, Simone Signoret and director Raymond Rouleau, have made it into a pic which was filmed almost entirely in East Germany. Jean-Paul Sartre was tagged for the screenplay. Result is a cumbersome, plodding affair which remains theatrical in feeling and execution. This arty, posed pic has U. S. chances mainly on the Miller play name and the exploitation aspects of its witchhunting theme in 17th Century Sa-

lem. It would need hard selling and looks limited for the U. S., but may fare well locally.

Film's promise is never fulfilled and it shows that a too conscious attempt to parallel past events with fairly recent happenings (i. e., Salem witch-hunting and the Un-American Activities Committee) can lead to loss of dramatic feeling. What should have been a tale of hysteria and superstition, here mixes politics, confessions, etc., to cloud the theme and, at the same time, its characters, who are never more than puppets.

Despite adding many scenes to the play, it s still essentially talky and theatrical in unfoldment. Some good bits are imbedded in this, such as the black magic incantations by a negress and some young girls in the woods, and their later feigned or almost believed possession by evil spirits. Director Raymond Rouleau has not given this a feel of time and place, and its characters appear more like those of a Flemish allegory on superstition and damnation than a group of austere American colonists at grips with ignorance.

Main tale of John Proctor, whose love for a servant girl is one of the principal points of the growth of the witch hunting rarely develops feeling. His frigid, rigid wife drives off the girl who later uses the troubles for retaliation Lead characters are played on a too subdued level by Yves Montand and Simone Signoret. However, Mylene Demongeot, as the servant, emerges a likely find as soon as she sluffs off mannerisms and substitutes acting for simulation. She has a decided film presence.

Acting is generally spotty and pompous, but lensing is striking and properly stark except in some overfiltered exteriors. Technical credits are good. This would need plenty of bally in the U. S.
Mosk.

I Vampiri
Rome. June 4.
I Vampiri (The Vampires) (ITALIAN) C'SCOPE). Titanus Film release of a Donati-Carpentieri-Athena Cinematografica Production. Stars Gianna Maria Canale, Balpetre; features Paul Muller, Carlo Dangelo, Wandisa Guida. Directed by Riccardo Freda. Story and screenplay, Piero Regnoli, Rik Sjostrom; camera (Cinema-Scope), Mario Bava; music, Roman Vlad. At Ariston, Rome. Running time, 90 MINS.

Pic is attempt at a horror film which doesn't quite come off, with only a few moments succeeding in being chilling. Strictly for devotees of the genre, with its export chances limited.

Gianna Maria Canale is at the center of a complicated mad-scientist plot designed to give her eternal youth by mysterious transfusions of blood taken from kidnapped young (and pretty) girls. The usual nosey newshawk beats the usual unbelieving police inspector to the expected solution. Process lensing is visible, though sets are elaborate and technical qualities okay. Black and white C'Scoping appears a waste. Thesping is in keeping with tone of plot. *Hawk.*

Foreign Films

Les Etoiles Ne Meurent Jamais (Stars Never Die) (FRENCH). Mercure Films production and release. Directed and compiled by Max De Vaucorbell. Commentary by Henri Jeanson, Pierre Larcohe; narrated by Francois Perier; music, Jean Weiner. At Avenue, Paris. Running time, 95 MINS.

Pic is a compilation of scenes from various pix featuring nine deceased great French stars. It loops them together adroitly and appears something of interest mainly for Gallic marts where these people were known. For the U. S., it looks like an item that could be used for special university programs, but obviously it has limited commercial possibility. Stars like Louis Jouvet, Raimu, Harry Baur, Louis Salou and Marguerite Moreno flash by in scenes from such pix as "Douce," "The Baker's Wife," "Boule De Suif" and others. *Mosk.*

Les Louves (The She Wolves) (FRENCH). Fernard Rivers S.A. release of a Zodiaque production. Stars Francois Perier, Micheline Presle, Madeleine Robinson, Jeanne Moreau; features Marc Cassot, Pierre Mondy. Directed by Luis Saslavsky. Screenplay, Saslavsky, Boileau-Narcejac from novel by Boileau-Narcejac; camera, Robert Juillard; editor, Marinette Cadix; music, Joseph Kosma. At Normandie, Paris. Running time, 100 MINS.

Since the success of "Diabolique," the works of Boileau-Narcejac have been pounced on by filmmakers here. However, lightning rarely strikes twice. In this, Luis Saslavsky aims for psychological shock rather than the direct visual aspects utilized by H. G. Clouzot in "Diabolique." Result is a dense pic with an absorbing progression, but suspense is rarely heightened and too telegraphed to make the morbid ending stark and jolting like its predecessor. Its unsavory theme may make this an okay entry for U. S. arty circuits, but at best it seems a chancey item which would need plenty of bally.

A weakling pianist escapes from a prison camp during the war with his stronger, healthier friend. The friend is killed and he manages to get to his buddy's fiancee, a pen pal, but faints on her doorstep. When he awakens he has been taken for the dead man and does not deny it. Then the attempts at suspense are piled on and director Saslavsky's good eye for atmosphere and character manage to keep the coincidences to the end.

Acting is uniformly good which helps keep some interest even after the plotting has worn thin. Francois Perier is right as the weakling. Micheline Presle is effective in her self effacing role of the murderess while Jeanne Moreau, as the loving sister, shapes fine.

Lensing is properly stark and technical credits and good supporting roles help carry along this would-be shocker. *Mosk.*

Familie Schimek (Family Schimek) (AUSTRIAN). Sascha Film release of Vienna Mundus Film production. Features Theo Lingen, Oskar Sima, Fita Bankhoff, Helga Neuner, Adrienne Gessner, Ernst Waldow, Peer Schmidt, Lucie Englisch, Helga Martin, Guenther Fischer, Rudl Priefer, Josef Meinrad, Ernst Waldbrunn. Directed by Georg Jacoby. Screenplay adapted from play of same title by Gustav Kadelburg by Earl Farkas, Helmuth M. Backhaus; music, Heinz Sandauer; camera, Elio Carniel. At Apollo Kino, Vienna. Running time, 85 MINS.

This legit hit around the turn of the century was well adapted for this film and looks to show profits for the producers. It is a "silk stocking" story with no political angle. It was shocking for a young girl to show her legs in sexy manner in those days, and Helga Martin, as "Hedwig" of bourgeoise family, does so as danseuse. This in turn leads to a bitter legal fight of her stepfather. Both Oskar Sima and Theo Lingen are extremely funny. Direction of Georg Jacoby takes care that few dull moments turn up. Settings are naturally oldfashioned. Music by Heinz Sandauer is nice. Camerawork by Elio Carniel deserves praise also. *Maas.*

Island In the Sun
(C'SCOPE-COLOR)

Alec Waugh novel comes to the screen as a good commercial, but otherwise disappointing, film. Race angles make this ticklish for Dixie playdates.

20th-Fox release of Darryl F. Zanuck production. Stars Harry Belafonte, James Mason, Joan Fontaine, Dorothy Dandridge, Joan Collins, Michael Rennie; features Diana Wynyard, John Williams, Stephen Boyd, Patricia Owens, Basil Sydney, John Justin, Ronald Squire, Hartley Power. Directed by Robert Rossen; screenplay, Alfred Hayes, from Alec Waugh novel; camera (Color by De Luxe), F. A. Young; music, Malcolm Arnold, conducting the Royal Philharmonic Orch; editor, Reginald Beck. Previewed in N.Y. June 12, '57. Running time 123 **Mins.**

Maxwell Fleury .... James Mason
Mavis .... Joan Fontaine
Margot Seaton .... Dorothy Dandridge
Jocelyn .... Joan Collins
Hilary Carson .... Michael Rennie
Mrs. Fleury .... Diana Wynyard
Colonel Whittingham ..... John Williams
Euan Templeton .... Stephen Boyd
Sylvia .... Patricia Owens
Julian Fleury .... Basil Sydney
David Archer .... John Justin
The Governor .... Ronald Squire
Bradshaw .... Hartley Power
David Boyeur .... Harry Belafonte

"Island in the Sun" must be judged on two separate levels. As a commercial property it is a picture of considerable promise. It has a strong cast headed by a "hot" boxoffice star, Harry Belafonte; it has a controversial theme that has already had a good deal of advance publicity; it's based on a bestseller, and its West Indies locales have been exquisitely photographed.

These factors are sufficient to propel the film into a strong b.o., helped along by public curiosity and an expert campaign.

Unfortunately, from an artistic point-of-view, this first Darryl F. Zanuck production for 20th-Fox under his new indie status is a letdown of major proportions, and no amount of business its plus factors bring forth can obscure the fact that "Island," for the most part, is just plain inadequate.

The script by Alfred Hayes is jumbled, the acting leaves a lot to wish for, and Reginald Beck's editing is a case of letting down the story. Result is a picture that is flat and even tedious, that hints at raw sex but stops short even of a kiss for fear it might offend. Picture is peopled by characters who appear theatrical and overdrawn simply because the script offers no motivational explanation for their behavior. Even the dubbing in some scenes is mediocre, notably Belafonte's rendition of "Lead Man Holler."

Because it attempts to deal with white-black relationships on an island in the West Indies under British rule, and because the race angle has been injected so prominently (to the exclusion of other values in the book), "Island" will be thought of as a "courageous" picture by some. Actually, it barely comes to grips with its problem. It is just candid enough to offend the South and disappoint those in the North who pay expecting to see the Alec Waugh novel come to life.

Story is about Santa Marta, an imaginary island in the British West Indies, a beautiful, colorful place. It's actually not one story, but several, which scripter Hayes simply failed to get or keep in focus. Picture moves episodically from one theme to the next, often without adequate transition. There is John Justin, the governor's aide, who falls in love with attractive Dorothy Dandridge, with whom he eventually boards a plane to London; then there's Stephen Boyd, the governor's son, who romances Joan Collins of the Fleury clan. Romance almost ends in tragedy (Miss Collins becomes pregnant) when it becomes known that her father (Basil Sydney) has some colored blood in him.

The strongest, and dramatically the weakest, episode involves Belafonte as a rising young Negro labor leader, who greatly attracts Joan Fontaine, who is finally rejected by him in an almost embarrassingly conceived scene. Another dramatic incident involves plantation operator James Mason, his wife, Patricia Owens, and Michael Rennie. Mason kills Rennie in a fit of jealousy and is then hounded by his conscience, and police inspector John Williams, to confess.

Director Robert Rossen has done what he could with the script. Lacking real-life characters to work with, he let the color CinemaScope camera wander around Grenada and Barbados. Cameraman F. A. Young comes up with some remarkably vivid shots. But he can't save the picture.

Belafonte's performance is barely satisfactory and will disappoint many. The script combines two of Waugh's key characters—the ruthless, aggressive labor leader and the sensitive young Negro attorney. Belafonte seems confused by these two characterizations and, apart from his good looks, he has little to offer. Same is true of Miss Dandridge.

Mason as Maxwell Fleury has some strong moments. Miss Fontaine is badly miscast in the role of Mavis who falls in love with Belafonte. She seems to sleepwalk through the picture. Boyd, Miss Owens and Justin are okay in a stiffly British sort of way. Basil Sydney as the governor appeals. Only really outstanding performance is delivered by Williams as the police chief. He registers solidly. Miss Collins as Jocelyn has some touching moments. Diana Wynyard is saddled with embarrassing lines.

Probably aware that there is a price on "courage," Zanuck has pulled quite a few punches in this one. The picture someone doesn't hang together, and some of it is so theatrical that the audience—at the opening at least—broke out with guffaws at a dramatically critical moment. As a "major" production, "Island" must ride on the strength of its visual values, the pull of the novel on which it is based and the current tide of controversy over miscegenation and the mixing of the races. All of which is quite a disappointment, considering the basic potential of the Waugh novel as screen entertainment.

The "Island in the Sun" theme song, written by Belafonte, is ably performed by him under the titles. The Zanuck production, apart from the scenery, also features some elaborate sets to good advantage. Color by De Luxe is top grade, as per usual. *Hift.*

The Night the World Exploded

Science-fiction this time stages earthquakes. Should divert very young. Fair b.o. prospects.

Columbia release of Clover (Sam Katzman) production. Stars Kathryn Grant, William Leslie; features Tris Coffin, Raymond Greenleaf, Charles Evans, Frank Scannell, Marshall Reed. Directed by Fred F. Sears. Screenplay, Jack Natteford and Luci Ward; camera, Benjamin H. Kline; editor, Paul Borofsky; music, Ross Di Maggio. Previewed N.Y., May 17, '57. Running time, **64 MINS.**

Laura Hutchinson .... Kathryn Grant
Dr. David Conway .... William Leslie
Dr. Ellis Morton .... Tris Coffin
Governor Cheney ..... Raymond Greenleaf
General Bartes .... Charles Evans
Sheriff Quinn .... Frank Scannell
General's Aide .... Marshall Reed
Ranger Brown .... Fred Coby
Ranger Kirk .... Paul Savage
Foreman .... Terry Frost

There are plenty of quakes in "The Night the World Exploded," but it's doubtful that this Sam Katzman production for Columbia release will be earth-shaking at the boxoffice. For the film shapes up as a modest science-fiction entry with fair prospects in the exploitation market. May, however, have potential among the juvenile set.

Key menace of the Jack Natteford-Luci Ward script is a mysterious element known as E-112. When dry and exposed to the nitrogen of the air, it forms volcanoes and is capable of destroying the earth. Obviously, alert scientists William Leslie, Tris Coffin and Kathryn Grant aren't going to allow this to happen.

So after discovering existence of the element deep in the recesses of New Mexico's Carlsbad Caverns, they hit upon a solution that calls for diverting the rivers of the world into low areas. This is supposed to keep the explosive force in check. And it does in a rousing finale that has the scientific trio blowing up a dam with the treacherous element itself.

None of the performances is particularly convincing. Miss Grant, who has had sexier roles, is strictly the scientist in this one albeit she has a romantic yen for fellow brain worker. Latter, William Leslie, gives the old college try of making with the gadgets as a stagemanager of earthquakes. Also comporting himself in a plausible professional manner is Tris Coffin, the third scientificio.

Okay support is provided by Raymond Greenleaf, a governor originally skeptical of Leslie's quake-predicting abilities; Charles Evans, general who aids in fighting the holocaust; Frank Scannell, a sheriff, along with Marshall Reed and others. Fred F. Sears' direction is par for the course as is the black-and-white camerawork of Benjamin H. Kline and music conducted by Ross Di Maggio.

Editing of Paul Borofsky is good, particularly his integration of stock disaster shots of floods, fires, etc., into the film's 64 minutes running time. Paul Palmentola's art direction, and other technical credits are standard. *Gilb.*

Assassins et Voleurs
(Killers and Thieves)
(FRENCH)

Paris, June 11.

Gaumont release of CLM-SNEG production. Stars Michel Serrault, Jean Poiret; features Magali Noel, Clement Duhour, Zita Perzel. Written and directed by Sacha Guitry; camera, Paul Cotteret; editor, Paulette Robert; music, Jean Francaix. At Paramount, Paris. Running time, **85 MINS.**

Philippe .... Jean Poiret
Thief .... Michel Serrault
Madeleine .... Magali Noel
Walter .... Clement Dohour
Kelptomaniac .... Zita Perzel

Sacha Guitry returns to his prewar obsessions of ironic comedy to make for one of his most adroit pix since the conflict. This elegantly immoral pic again raises Guitry's fine commentary and story telling techniques. Though dealing with a scabrous subject, it is cloaked in telling wit and emerges a comedy that might have a good chance in special U.S. situations.

Tale is told by a smooth, middle-aged man about to commit suicide. A burglar breaks in and he makes a pact with the intruder to help him do this thing and explains his story beforehand. Then, in a series of deft scenes, the plot is unfolded. The man, rich, young and adventurous, steals the wife of a boyhood acquaintance who had always bullied him. They carry on the flirtation under his nose until the husband comes back early one night. The man hides and the husband strangles the wife and is then shot by the man. In comes the burglar, who happened to also be robbing the house, and the man slips the gun in his pocket and escapes.

It is the same burglar listening to the story. The pic smoothly racks up these varying scenes until the cleverly cynical ending, when the would-be suicide does away with the burglar and frees himself.

Guitry has bundled together many hilarious scenes such as a day in a rest home, full of zanies and the young man's criminal life. Though primarily a raconteur's pic, this packs a saucy, irreverent punch for the long hair set.

Though technical credits are ordinary, this does not impair the telling. Jean Poiret and Michel Serrault are just right as the young man-turned-thief and the pro second-story man. Remainder of cast is nearly perfect, and it adds up to a successful, adult comedy. *Mosk.*

The Monte Carlo Story
(TECHNIRAMA-COLOR-SONGS)

Camera work superior to script. Overlength story of gambling and romance in Monte Carlo. Fair returns at best indicated.

Hollywood, June 13.

United Artists release of a Marcello Girosi production. Stars Marlene Dietrich, Vittorio De Sica; features Arthur O'Connell, Natalie Trundy, Jane Rose, Clelia Matania, Alberto Rabagliati, Mischa Auer, Renato Rascel. Director-screenplay, Samuel A. Taylor; story, Girosi, Dino Risi; camera (Technicolor), Giuseppe Rotunno; art director, Gastone Medin. Previewed June 13, '57. Running time, **100 MINS.**

Marquise Maria de Crevecoeur
Marlene Dietrich
Count Dino della Fiaba .. Vittorio De Sica
Mr. Hinkley .... Arthur O'Connell
Jane Hinkley .... Natalie Trundy
Mrs. Freeman .... Jane Rose
Sophie .... Clelia Matania
Albert, the portiere .... Alberto Rabagliati
Hector, the Maitre .... Mischa Auer
Duval .... Renato Rascel
Henri, a sailor .... Carlo Rizzo
Mr. Freeman .... Truman Smith
Roland, the barman .... Mimo Billi
Francois, the chauffeur ..... Marco Tulli
Paul, the elevator boy ..... Guido Martufi
The Hotel Managing Director
Jean Combal
Caroline, the hotel maid Vera Garretto
Gabriel, Henri's son ..... Yannick Geffroy
Zizi, the cigarette girl .. Betty Philippsen
Walter, 1st American ..... Frank Colson
Harry, 2d American ..... Serge Fliegers
Ercole, Sporting Club cashier ... Himself
Jimmy, the pianist at Sporting Club
Himself
Mr. Ewing .... Frank Elliott
Mrs. Ewing .... Betty Carter
The Hotel Assistant Director .... Himself
Hotel Check-room Attendant .... Himself
Lartigau, violinist .... Himself
The German Lady ...... Gerlaine Fournier
The Lady in Magenta . Simonemarie Rose
The American Oil Heiress ... Clara Beck

This Italian-produced film, costarring Marlene Dietrich and Vittorio De Sica, is lavishly turned out in vivid Technicolor against the actual story setting, but misses fire because of old, hackneyed plotting. Certain exploitation potential accrues from the lure of the Monte Carlo location, which with the Dietrich name makes it an entry for the general market. On merit indications point to but fair returns. Film is badly in need of trimming its overlength 100-minutes' running time.

Samuel A. Taylor, the American writer, handles dual assignment of director-scripter of the Marcello Girosi-Dino Risi original, but displays scant ingenuity. Footage actually consists of two major story lines, which militate against more than passing interest. First is the romance between the two stars, each a gambler in Monte Carlo and each making a pitch to marry the other for economic reasons.

When they discover the truth about each other, both broke, the second phase tees off. Miss Dietrich then makes a play for American millionaire Arthur O'Connell, and introduces De Sica as her brother for no apparent reason. Clincher has femme changing her mind about returning to U.S. with O'Connell as his bride, and swinging back to De Sica.

Miss Dietrich warbles a couple of songs. De Sica fits his part well. O'Connell is well cast as a Babbitt making his first trip to Europe, and Natalie Trundy, as his teenage daughter, and Jane Rose and Truman Smith, as typical American tourists in O'Connell's party, are excellent. Scoring as De Sica's creditors are Mischa Auer, as a matire de, Alberto Rabagliati, Renato Rascel, Mimo Billi, Marco Tulli and Guido Martufi.

Handsome use is made of the various Monte Carlo locations, and Giuseppe Rotunno's beautiful color photography centers particularly on backgrounds, interiors as well as exteriors of the famed gambling resort. Sound frequently is off through poor dubbing, lips not synchronizing with dialog. Other technical credits are firstrate.

Whit.

The Admirable Crichton
(BRITISH—COLOR)

Kenneth More as Barrie's famous butler who takes over his master's role after shipwreck; good allround entertainment.

London, June 11.

Columbia release of (Ian Dairymple) a Modern Screen Play production. Stars Kenneth More, Diane Cilento, Cecil Parker and Sally Ann Howes. Directed by Lewis Gilbert. Screenplay, Vernon Harris, adapted by Lewis Gilbert from play by J. M. Barrie; camera, Wilkie Cooper; editor, Peter Hunt; music, Douglas Gamley. At Odeon Theatre, Leicester Square, London. Running time, **93 MINS.**

Crichton	Kenneth More
Tweeny	Diane Cilento
Lord Loam	Cecil Parker
Lady Mary	Sally Ann Howes
Lady Brocklehurst	Martita Hunt
Treherne	Jack Watling
Brocklehurst	Peter Graves
Ernest	Gerald Harper
Catherine	Mercy Haystead
Agatha	Miranda Connell
Vicar	Miles Malleson
Captain	Eddie Byrne
Mrs. Perkins	Joan Young
Fisher	Brenda Hogan
Rolleston	Peter Welch
Lovegrove	Toke Townley
Thomas	Ronald Curram

Staged many times since its original production here in 1902, and filmed in the silent days as "Male and Female," this story of a butler who becomes master on a desert island provides a sound starrer for Kenneth More. He topped the popularity poll in Britain last year which means the b.o. potential should be strong. Comedy is lightweight and obviously dated, the snob angles being kept at their period values. The story is kept in its Edwardian setting, although the cast at times has difficulty in maintaining this illusion.

A peer of one of England's stately homes takes his three daughters off on a yachting cruise with a few friends and domestic staff. They are shipwrecked and marooned on an uncharted island, and dig themselves in awaiting rescue. Crichton (More), the impeccable butler, is obliged to take complete control, because of the inefficiency of the other castaways. In reverse to his former subservient state, he now gives, not takes orders, and establishes himself as benevolent dictator.

Lady Mary (Sally Ann Howes), the haughty eldest daughter, tries to keep aloof, but finally falls for "Governor" Crichton. This causes tearful reaction from the humble between-maid who has long cherished a secret passion for the god of below-stairs. When a passing cruiser rescues the party, the butler immediately sheds his authority, instinctively reverting to his old status. Realizing his brief romance cannot now be fulfilled and that his presence would be an embarrassment to the family, he goes off with his faithful maid.

Although More lacks the accepted stature of an English butler, his personality makes a more human and sympathetic figure of the servant who has a firmer sense of snob values than his master. Cecil Parker, alternately genial and pompous as the father, is perhaps more in keeping with the period. Miss Howes as the frosty, eldest daughter melts charmingly under the influence of the island's magic while Diane Cilento scores a special hit as her rival, the underservant. Martita Hunt registers majestically as a haughty aristocrat. Supporting players all contribute firstrate performances.

Scenes shot in Bermuda supply some excellent camera studies. Film is well directed by Lewis Gilbert.

Clem.

Sweet Smell of Success

Profiles of a vicious newspaper columnist and a lackey press-agent who plays the Broadway angles. Unpleasant people but with Burt Lancaster and Tony Curtis, good boxoffice.

United Artists release of Hecht, Hill & Lancaster production (produced by James Hill). Stars Burt Lancaster, Tony Curtis. Features Susan Harrison, Marty Millner, Sam Levene, Barbara Nichols, Jeff Donneil, Chico Hamilton Quintet. Directed by Alexander Mackendrick. Screenplay, Clifford Odets and Ernest Lehman, from novelette by Lehman; camera, James Wong Howe; music, Elmer Bernstein; songs by Hamilton and Fred Katz. Previewed N.Y., June 13, '57. Running time, **96 MINS.**

J. J. Hunsecker	Burt Lancaster
Sidney Falco	Tony Curtis
Susan Hunsecker	Susan Harrison
Steve Dallas	Marty Milner
Frank D'Angelo	Sam Levene
Rita	Barbara Nichols
Sally	Jeff Donnell
Robard	Joseph Leon
Mary	Edith Atwater
Harry Kello	Emile Meyer
Herbie Temple	Joe Frisco
Otis Elwell	David White
Leo Bartha	Lawrence Dobkin
Mrs. Bartha	Lurene Tuttle
Mildred Tam	Queenie Smith
Linda	Autumn Russell
Manny Davis	Jay Adler
Al Evans	Lewis Charles

Hecht-Hill-Lancaster is at hand with a savage indictment of a powerful and unscrupulous syndicated columnist and an unconscionable, slippery pressagent. This is strong material.

"Success" is by nature a "big city" story, not alone in the Gotham locale but also in the popular bistros visited, the show business and nightlife characters encountered and the events that come to pass. It all may be pretty remote to rural area citizenry. But the dramatic wallop it packs assures good boxoffice, particularly in key burgs.

James Hill's production, locationed in Manhattan, captures the feel of Broadway and environs after dark. It's a no-holds-barred account of the sadistic fourth estater played cunningly by Burt Lancaster. It's a remarkable change of pace for Lancaster, who appears bespectacled and quiet but smouldering with malice and menace. Failure to comply with his wishes means a broken career. Breaks in his column sustain the pressagent but for the mentions there are certain favors to be granted. To the p.a., the columnist's dictates are law; if the favors include framing a young musician on a narcotics rap, that's all right, too.

Flaw in "Success" concerns the newspaperman's devotion to his sister. It's not clear why he rebels at her courtship with a guitarist, who appears to be a nice kid. Why he goes to such lengths to break up the romance is only vaguely explained, yet so much of the plot revolves around this situation. Is it incestuous or merely possessiveness.

Tony Curtis is the time-serving publicist and here again is another departure from the routine in casting. No teenagers' idol here, Curtis is a wrong guy all the way through, eager for the success that can be his only by obsequious execution of Lancaster's orders. This is the way he obtains his payoff, the columnar items that keep his paying clients happy.

Curtis comes through with an interesting performance, although, sowehow, the character he plays is not quite all the heel as written. Yet, it's interesting to watch him showing agility in latching on to the angles in winning clients, always seeking to ingratiate himself with Lancaster and, at the end, almost engendering sympathy as Lancaster wrongfully accuses him of trying to embrace his sister.

Susan Harrison is "introduced" in the picture and comes off well as the sister. She has a fetching beauty and shows easiness in handling the assignment. Sam Levene is competent as Curtis' uncle, as is Marty Milner as the young musician romancing Miss Harrison against Lancaster's wishes. Jeff Donnell and Barbara Nichols also are capable, as featured.

Screenplay by Clifford Odets and Ernest Lehman, from a novelette by Lehman, must be "accepted"—that is, the audience must assume the columnist-sadist to be very special. (He even guides Presidential aspirants). That the performances and the splendid direction of Alexander Mackendrick provide the picture with the necessary conviction says much.

And adding to the Broadway flavor is the cutting dialog in the Odets-Lehman script. An assist, too, as background color, musicwise, is the Chico Hamilton Quintet. Photography often is low key and effective for the most part but some night scenes are so dark that pictorial details are vague.

Film was previewed at Loew's State Theatre, N.Y., where complaints were heard of instances of inaudible sound.

Gene.

Two Grooms for a Bride

Contrived plotting adds up to a minor diversion.

20th-Fox release of Eros Film (Robert S. Baker and Monty Berman) production. Stars John Carroll, Virginia Bruce. Features Brian Oulton, Kay Callard, Michael Caridia, Barbara Brown, Kit Terrington. Directed by Henry Cass. Screenplay, Frederick Stephani; camera, Berman; editor, Maurice Rootes; music, Stanley Black. Previewed N.Y., June 14, '57. Running time, **73 MINS.**

Jeff Longstreet	John Carroll
Laura Weeks	Virginia Bruce
Professor Baker	Brian Oulton
Lola Sinclair	Kay Callard
Tony	Michael Caridia
Ra	Barbara Brown
Big	Kit Terrington
Humbold	Alexander Gauge
Cadwell	Donold Stewart
Mrs. Fogarty	Anita Sharp Bolster
Mr. Fogarty	Arthur Lowe
MacCarthy	Tim Gill
Minister	Earnest Jay
Boxer	Michael Balfour
Candy Sugar	Karen Greer
Claire	Tucker Maguire
Violet Blue	Ann Doran

Imagine this. A husband-and-wife team of explorers becomes missing and care of the four surviving children is left to the husband's brother and the wife's sister. He's a free-wheeling, playboy American. She's an English entymologist. Its' decreed that which ever of the two marries shall be given permanent custody.

But will he wed the flashy blonde with the phoney Dixie accent? Not likely. And will she enter the connubial state with her straitlaced fellow scientist? No, indeed. They fall for each other.

This kind of script is strictly from tritesville. One scene segues into the next with about as much surprise as Thursday following Wednesday. Dialog and individual situations likewise are lacking in imagination. And in the instance of the two principals becoming high on a few sips of brandy, it's embarrassing.

John Carroll is the Yank. He's a personable performer but can't do much with the material he has to work with. Virginia Bruce is pleasant company to have around but, again, consider the artless script which was supplied by Frederick Stephani.

Brian Oulton as Miss Bruce's colleague in the study of bug habits, Kay Callard as the American dame with a yen for Carroll and his money, and Michael Caridia, Barbara Brown and Kit Terrington, as three of the four kids (the fourth is an infant limitedly on view), similarly started out with odds against them and the results show it.

Producers Robert S. Baker and Monty Berman shot the picture in England on a modest scale and Henry Cass directed in commonplace fashion. It stacks up as a minor item, suitable mainly for filler bookings in some situtations. Technical credits undistinguished.

Gene.

El Ultimo Cuple
(The Last Torch Song)
(SPANISH)

Madrid, June 11.

Cifesa release of a Producciones Orduna film. Stars Sara Montiel; features Armando Calvo, Enrique Vera, Julita Martinez, Alfredo Mayo, Matilde M. Sampedro and Jose Moreno. Directed by Juan de Orduna. Screenplay, Antonio Mas Guindal and Jesus M. Arozamena; camera (Eastmoncolor), Jose Aguayo; Music, Solano. Running time, **108 MINS.**

Sara Montiel returns to Spain and the director who first featured her 10 years ago in this tour de force as solo star. This Iberian musical was produced and directed by Juan de Orduna. Nostalgic Spanish vaude pop song revival has Miss Montiel in almost every scene for a standout acting and singing performance.

Story flashbacks the rise and fall of a great music hall chanteuse, (Miss Montiel), at turn of the century. Plot is soapy one with a schmalzy fringe as stereotypes draw yocks when trying for tears. Her first lover steals and goes to jail which permits her to go off with the good-looking impresario (Armando Calvo) and rise to music hall heights. As she nears that certain age, she cradle-snatches a young torero (a real one, Enrique Vera), bankrolls his Madrid premiere and ruins her heart and career when the bull gets him. She hits the skids and cries until the jilted impresario stumbles into a small cafe and thrills again to her torch.

In between the generous portions of corn, Miss Montiel again shines. She sings a dozen songs, including "Madelon," "Valencia," and many old Spanish favorites. Beautifully gowned, unlike others in the cast, Miss Montiel's face and body give the robes plenty of competish. She opens new U.S. horizons with a captivating voice and delivery.

"El Ultimo Cuple" will go big in Spanish nabes of America and in the Spanish-language market. Hollywood should gander Montiel in this one. Otherwise no soap for thè U.S. *Hank.*

La Garconne

Paris, June 11.

La Garconne (FRENCH; COLOR; SONG). Corona release of Elysees Films production. Stars Fernand Gravey, Andre Debar; features Jean Danet, Colette Mars, Georges Reich, Jean Parades, Marie Daems, Suzanne Dehelly, Rene Lefebvre. Directed by Jacqueline Audry. Screenplay, Pierre Laroche from novel by Victor Marguerite; camera (Agfacolor), Marcel Grignon; editor, Yvonne Martin; music, Jean Wiener. At Paris, Paris. Running time, **100 MINS.**

This film is about the French flapper. It concerns how a girl, finding her fiance is cheating on her, rushes out and beds down with the first man she meets. Then she goes out to live her own life. Trying to live as socially free as a man (hence the title which is a feminization of the Gallic word for boy, namely garcon), she becomes a famed interior and theatrical decorator, has many affairs, but finally realizes she loves an older cousin. It all ends happily after the early suitor tries again and is once again rejected.

Based on a scandal novel of the 1920's, this is somewhat tame now. There are scenes of minor orgies and night club meanderings by an emancipated but lost crowd. Literary and talky in progression, this is limited for the U. S. market except for possible exploitation on its locale and mildly sexy proceedings. Lesbianism and homosexuality are touched on, but the heroine, well portrayed by Andree Debar, seems to live in a gilded vacuum. Fernand Gravey seems distant to the period feeling and Jean Danet is too wooden and dreary as the fiance who leads to the heroine's first heartbreak.

Jacqueline Andry has directed placidly. Color is properly garish and supporting players fit the times as does the title song worked in by Colette Mars and cleffed by Jean Wiener. *Mosk.*

A Hatful of Rain
(C'SCOPE)

Best film so far on the subject of dope addiction. Instructive as well as entertaining and bolstered by topnotch performances by Eva Marie Saint, Don Murray, Anthony Franciosa and Lloyd Nolan.

20th-Fox release of Buddy Addler prod0uction. Stars Eva Marie Saint, Don Murray, Anthony Franciosa, Lloyd Nolan. Features Henry Silva, Gerald O'Laughlin and William Hickey. Directed by Fred Zinnemann. Screenplay, Michael V. Gazzo and Alfred Hayes; from a play by Gazzo; camera (C'Scope), Joe MacDonald; editor, Dorothy Spencer; music, Bernard Hermann. Previewed in N.Y., June 14, '57. Running time, 109 MINS.

Celia Pope .... Eva Marie Saint
Johnny Pope .... Don Murray
Polo .... Anthony Franciosa
John Pope Sr. .... Lloyd Nolan
Mother .... Henry Silva
Chuch .... Gerald O'Loughlin
Apples .... William Hickey

"A Hatful of Rain" is the first film dealing with dope addiction made with the prior approval of the Production Code. And despite the necessity of having to work within the restrictions of the industry's self-governing code, it is the best of the pictures involved with this formerly taboo subject.

This one may be initially handicapped by the fact that the public already may have had its fill of the unpleasant details of the narcotics habit. However, critical reception and word-of-mouth comment can serve to overcome this resistance. As a result, "A Hatful of Rain" has an excellent chance of becoming a solid boxoffice contender.

Not the least of the attributes of this well-made Buddy Adler production is the admirable performances director Fred Zinnemann has elicited from the small cast. Except for Lloyd Nolan, a veteran pro, the cast is dominated by a group of personable youngsters relatively new to the screen. These include Eva Marie Saint, Don Murray and Anthony Franciosa, who are all developing into important b.o. names.

With an assist from Alfred Hayes, Michael V. Gazzo has converted his Broadway play into a provocative and engrossing film drama. "A Hatful of Rain" is more than a story of junkie. It touches knowingly and sensitively on a family relationship and, as such, may be more within the scope of average audiences who may find the subject of dope addiction completely foreign.

The dramatic and emotional scenes are moving and completely believable. And despite the supercharged dramatics, moments of genuine comedy are interpolated successfully to relieve the tension. As a consequence, the picture may be said to fulfill a dual purpose—that of instructing and entertaining.

The people involved in this web of narcotics are basically decent human beings. The story revolves about their reactions when one of them turns out to be a junkie. As the pregnant wife of a narcotics addict, Miss Saint lives up to previous promise. She plays the loving, troubled wife with poignancy and taste and handles the emotional peaks and tender moments with sensitive understanding. Murray scores, too, as the likeable junkie who desperately attempts to hide his secret from his wife and his obtrusely devoted father. Yet, in his agonized and confused state, he takes tremendous liberties with his doting and helpful brother.

The role of the brother who shares an apartment in a lower east side N.Y. housing project with his dope-addicted relative and his wife is compellingly played by Franciosa, who is repeating his original stage assignment. Misunderstood and rejected by his father, Franciosa is moving as "his brother's keeper" and sister-in-law's confidante. The character is perhaps the most appealing seen on the screen in recent years and will have the audience cheering for him all the way.

As the widowed father who left his sons in an orphanage at an early age, Nolan turns in another topnotch portrayal. While he considers himself a proper father, he neither knows his sons nor understands them.

Henry Silva, also repeating his stage role, is convincingly unctuous and contemptible as the dope peddler. William Hickey is standout as one of his weird cohorts and Gerald O'Loughlin is fine as another stooge.

Zinnemann's realistic direction contributes considerably to the film's success. Joe MacDonald's black and white photography has a documentary flavor and other technical contributions are excellent, including Bernard Herrmann's music and the art direction of Lyle R. Wheeler and Leland Fuller. *Holl.*

Typhon A Nagsaki
(Typhoon On Nagasaki)
(FRENCH-JAPANESE; COLOR)

Paris, June 11.

Pathe release of CICC-Terra Films-Shochiku production. Stars Jean Marais, Danielle Darrieux, Kishi Keiko; features Gert Froebe, Hitomi Nozohe, So Yamamura. Directed by Yves Ciampi. Screenplay, Jean-Charles Tacchella, Ciampi; dialog, Annette Wademant; camera (Technicolor), Henri Alekan; editor, Roger Dwyre. At Paris, Paris. Running time, 115 MINS.

Pierre .... Jean Marais
Francoise .... Danielle Darrieux
Noriko .... Kishi Keiko
Karl .... Gert Froebe
Engineer .... Hitmoi Nozohe
Saeta .... So Yanamura

First French-Japanese coproduction even has a preface stating in English that "East is East." In fact the East wins out in this. Main attribute of pic is the colorful backgrounding and color, but the western bit of a love triangle between a Frenchman and two women, one Japanese, one French, is strictly conventional. With a well-done typhoon sequence, and its exotic locale, this may be program fare for the U.S., but is not for any arty house chances. Dubbing might be in order.

A French engineer (Jean Marais) has fallen in love with a charming Japanese girl (Kishi Keiko) while working in Nagasaki. Into this comes an old flame (Danielle Darrieux) a free thinking newswoman who had ditched the hero years before. She gets the upper hand on the more demure local girl but a typhoon, resulting in the death of the Japanese girl, makes the engineer realize he must stay on and the interloper goes off to her free life alone.

Director Yves Ciampi has given this a bread and butter mounting working in a lot of eyecatching Japanese scenery, customs, theatre, etc. The characters, unfortunately, rarely match this, except for the tightly etched performance of Miss Keiko. Marais and Miss Darrieux are competent in their roles. Typhoon has exploitation aspects.

Color is finely hued while supporting cast is good. Production values look fine, but scripting has not delved deep enough. *Mosk.*

The Land Unknown
(C'SCOPE)

Hot water oasis in deepest Antarctica site of highly competent science fiction. Fulfills on its own promise.

Hollywood, June 12.

Universal release of a William Alland production. Stars Jock Mahoney, Shawn Smith, William Reynolds; features Henry Brandon, Douglas R. Kennedy, Phil Harvey. Directed by Virgil Vogel. Screenplay, Laszlo Gorog; adaptation, William N. Robson; story, Charles Palmer; camera, Ellis W. Carter; special effects, Fred Knoth, Orien Ernest, Jack Kevan; editor, Fred MacDowell; music, Joseph Gershehson. Previewed June 11, '57. Running time, 78 MINS.

Comdr. Harold Roberts Jock Mahoney
Margareth Hathaway... Shawn Smith
Lt. Jack Carmen ......William Reynolds
Hunter .... Henry Brandon
Capt. Burnham ......Douglas R. Kennedy
Steve Miller .... Phil Harvey

Discovery by Admiral Byrd's 1947 South Pole expedition of a mysterious warm-water area in the center of ice-packed Antarctica serves as basis for this imaginative science-fictioner. Film is expertly turned out as it dwells on exiting incidents of the present, the use of special effects giving narrative a tremendous boost. Added exploitation value of the Byrd find, shown briefly in opening via actual U. S. Navy reelage, paves the way for satisfactory grosses in its intended market.

Jock Mahoney, Shawn Smith and William Reynolds star in the William Alland production, which recounts adventures of a helicopter party forced down in this strange region which is the objective of a Navy expedition. Area is untouched by the Ice Age, going back to the Mesozoic era, complete with prehistoric monsters, a setting which provides thrills as party fights for existence against the preying of such creatures as a giant tyrannosaurus Rex, and a swimming elasmosaurus. Stark realism is afforded through the remarkable smooth and lifelike movement of these carnivorous monsters, special effected by Fred Knoth, Orien Ernest and Jack Kevan.

Mahoney plays a Navy scientist in charge of expedition, Miss Smith a news hen and Reynolds the helicopter pilot. Fourth member of party is Phil Harvey, mechanic, when a storm forces them into overcast and copter strikes what looks like a prehistoric flying pterodactyl. Controls jammed, eggbeater and occupants descend through heavy fog into a deep chasm, where they discover weird tropic terrain and humid temperature as well as the monsters. They hold off a tyrannosaurus Rex with copter blades until a strange sound chases creature away.

This sound, it develops, has been caused by another scientist, who creashed 10 years previously while a member of the Byrd expedition. His mind now warped to point of insanity, he has managed to live in this prehistoric world. An enemy at first, it is through parts from his wrecked plane that copter is able to be repaired, and group is able to make its way out of the "land unknown" and back to expedition.

Under Virgil Vogel's authoritative direction, cast generally gives a good account of themselves. Mahoney makes the most of opportunities, Miss Smith is a lively distaff interest, both Reynolds and Harvey fit well into their roles and Henry Brandon, the forgotten scientist, an interesting character. Douglas R. Kennedy is in briefly as a Navy captain.

The Laszlo Gorog screenplay gets benefit of top technical assistance throughout, all the way from Ellis W. Carter's camera work, special photography by Clifford Stine and R. O. Binger, to particularly atmospheric art direction by Alexander Golitzen and Richard H. Riedel, sound by Leslie I. Carey and Corson Jowett and tight editing by Fred MacDowell.
Whit.

The Pride and the Passion
(V'VISION-TECHNICOLOR)

A major entertainment with boxoffice potential measured in epic proportions. Locationed in Spain, with Cary Grant, Frank Sinatra, Sophia Loren starred.

United Artists release of Stanley Kramer production, directed by Kramer. Stars Cary Grant, Frank Sinatra, Sophia Loren; features Theodore Bikel, John Wengraf, Jay Novello, Jose Nieto, Carlos Larrange, Phillip Van Zendt, Paco el Laberinto. Screen story and screenplay, Edna and Edward Anhalt; based on C. S. Forester's novel, "The Gun"; camera (VistaVision and Technicolor), Franz Planer; editors, Frederic Knudtson and Ellsworth Hoagland; music, George Antheil. Tradeshown New York, June 20, '57. Running time, **132 MINS.**
Capt. Anthony Trumbull .... Cary Grant
Miguel .... Frank Sinatra
Juana .... Sophia Loren
General Jouvet .... Theodore Bikel
Germaine .... John Wengraf
Ballinger .... Jay Novello
Carlos .... Jose Nieto
Jose .... Carlos Larranaga
Vidal .... Phillip Van Zandt
Manolo .... Paco el Laberinto

A big one, this is Stanley Kramer's powerful production of C. S. Forester's sweeping novel about the Spanish "citizen's army" that goes to battle against the conquering legions of the French in 1810. The scope is immense, the impact forceful, the boxoffice socko.

"Pride and the Passion has been highly touted. The publicity (statistical and otherwise) came out of Spain without letup during the year and a half the picture was in preparation and production in that country. All leading to great expectations, it now can be stated, with justification, that this one is an epic that figures to be among the industry's top grossers.

"Passion" is heavyweight with those cinematic elements that stir audiences. In addition to the size and importance of the physical production, it has a story that moves with excitement and suspense, and a provocative, highly attractive cast headed by Cary Grant, Frank Sinatra and Sophia Loren.

The Forester book, titled "The Gun," has been skillfully put into script form by Edna and Edward Anhalt. A few plot angles are projected with some vagueness but the basic points and motivations are gotten across with full clarity. It is the story of the band of guerillas who come upon an oversized cannon that is abandoned by the retreating Spanish army. All things revolve around the huge weapon; it becomes symbolic of the spirit and courage of these Spanish patriots and their leader, Sinatra.

From this point on "Passion" focuses on this unlikely army seeking to make its way to the French stronghold at Avila against incredibly tall odds. Their movements must be along remote, unbeaten paths, so as not to encounter the French in the fields.

Their ally is Grant, a British naval officer assigned to retrieve the gun for use against Napoleon's forces. His knowledge of ordinance makes him a valuable asset to Sinatra and they work together although the two men are worlds apart in makeup and temperament.

Sinatra is the "Passion" vis-a-vis Grant's "Pride." One is the emotional, zealous, inarticulate Spaniard, driven by blind passion to destruction of the French bastion at Avila. The other is stiff, organized, disciplined—all Government Issue, British style.

Miss Loren is Sinatra's sultry and inflammable mistress with beaucoup accent on the decollete. At first hostile toward Grant, she

comes to recognize his pro-Spanish motives and veers to him romantically.

They make for an engaging trio, imparting depth to the characters they portray. Grant is a strong figure. He reflects authority all the way through, in accepting Sinatra's crude ways of war, in taking command of the guerilla forces in the back-breaking salvage of the gun, and finally in firing against the French.

Sinatra is more colorful, as per script. He looks and behaves like a Spanish rebel leader, earthy and cruel and skilled in handling his men in the primitive warfare. His is a splendid performance.

Top credit must go to the producer and director. Kramer, doubling as producer and director, amasses vivid pictorial values in Technicolor and the VistaVision process. The panoramic, longrange views of the marching and terribly burdened army, the painful fight to keep the gun mobile through ravine and over waterway—these are major plusses. And within the framework of the massive expedition are the good story values.

"Passion" is not overlong at two hours and 12 minutes. But the pace does tend to slow down in the final reels as the guerillas move toward the approaches of Avila after the numerous near-tragedies and escapes from the French. The **climax is rousing and stimulating, this being the fall of the French fortress under the cannon barrage and the attack of the frenzied peasants.**

Theodore Bikel as the French general and in less prominent assignments, John Wengraf, Jay Novello, Jose Nieto, Carlos Larrange, Phillip Van Zendt and Paco el Laberinto, all are likely and convincing participants.

George Antheil has contributed an imposing score that backgrounds the screen action with marked effect. Franz Planer's photography is brilliant, the editing by Frederic Knudtson and Ellsworth Hoagland provides expert continuity and other technical credits are top calibre. *Gene.*

House of Numbers
(C'SCOPE)

Jack Palance makes a far-fetched dual role plausible in bizarre prison break plot, spun out too long. Introduces Barbara Lang, a likely sexpot. Modest chances.

Hollywod, June 21.
Metro release of a Charles Schnee production. Stars Jack Palance; features Harold J. Stone, Edward Platt; introduces Barbara Lang. Directed by Russell Rouse. Screenplay, Rouse-Don M. Mankiewicz from a Cosmopolitan novel by Jack Finney. Camera, George J. Folsey; editor, John McSweeney Jr.; music, Andre Previn. Previewed June 21, 1957. Running time, **90 MINS.**
Bill Judlow } .... Jack Palance
Arne Judlow }
Ruth Judlow .... Barbara Lang
Henry Nova .... Harold J. Stone
Warden .... Edward Platt

A bizarre idea for a prison break is the peg for this slightly overlong melodrama of no special distinction. It falls into the program market for deluxers but can go either way in action or small situations and suggests moderate response. Jack Palance in a dual role and the introduction of Barbara Lang, who shows possibilities as a new screen sexpot, are among the exploitable factors for the 90-minute entry which, within its budget, has been well produced by Charles Schnee.

Russell Rouse-Don M. Mankiewicz scenario has an occasional tendency to descend to the cliche level. Story is of a devoted older brother who breaks into the State pen to prepare the details of the crashout. It comes off on schedule, but not before romance has blossomed between the "good" brother and his sister-in-law. At the fadeout, finally realizing that the con needs mental aid, they tip the police to his whereabouts so he can be returned.

Rouse's direction permits the players to indulge in some unrestrained histrionics but Palance effectively delineates the difference between the two brothers in a frequently incredible dual role. Harold J. Stone is good as a venal prison guard and Edward Platt registers in a small role as the warden. Miss Lang, who has both looks and talent, impresses with the characterization and makes the most of her screen debut.

Technical credits are good with the lensing of George J. Folsey helping create an aura sometimes lacking in the script. Music by Andre Previn is properly unobtrusive. *Kap.*

Trooper Hook

Pretentious handling mars good story possibilities. But McCrea and Stanwyck names, plus several strong action sequences, should pull in fair returns at b.o.

Hollywood, June 21.
United Artists release of a (Sol Baer) Fielding Production. Stars Joel McCrea and Barbara Stanwyck; features Earl Holliman, Edward Andrews, John Dehner, Susan Kohner. Directed by Charles Marquis Warren. Screenplay, Martin Berkley, David Victor, Herbert Little Jr., from Jack Schaefer story; camera, Ellsworth Fredericks; editor, Fred Berger; art director, Nick Remisoff; music composed and directed by Gerald Fried. Title song by Fried and Mitzi Cummings, sung by Tex Ritter. Previewed, June 20, '57. Running time, **80 MINS.**
Sgt. Hook .... Joel McCrea
Cora .... Barbara Stanwyck
Jeff Bennett .... Earl Holliman
Charlie Travers ...... Edward Andrews
Fred Sutliff .... John Dehner
Consuela .... Susan Kohner
Trude .... Royal Dano
Quito .... Terry Lawrence
Senora .... Celia Lovsky
Nanchez .... Rudolfo Acosta
Salesman .... Stanley Adams
Col. Weaver .... Pat O'Moore
Ann Weaver .... Jeanne Bates
Corp. Stoner .... Rush Williams
Ryan .... Dick Shannon
Tess .... D. J. Thompson
Cooter Brown .,....)..... Sheb Wooley
Junius .... Cyril Delivanti

This one brings up the point that there's something to be said for the old-fashioned "non-adult" western. Agreed, the story lines were often simple to the point of simplemindedness, but at least their creator told them directly, with a minimum of philosophic and psychological chatter. "Trooper Hook" with Joel McCrea as a top sergeant is basically good tale, as written by Martin Berkley, David Victor and Herbert Little Jr., from a Jack Schaefer story but the telling is all too often pretentious and unnecessarily convoluted. It spoils the overall effect.

Pull of the marquee names of Joel McCrea and Barbara Stanwyck, plus the fact that when director Charles Marquis Warren wants to, he can stage a bang-up action sequence, may partly overcome story-telling faults for fair b.o. returns. Another plus is painstaking authenticity in detail of director Warren, who knows and loves the frontier west.

When hardbitten cavalry topkick McCrea captures Apache band led by Rudolfo Acosta, he finds Miss

Stanwyck, white captive squaw of the chief. McCrea is assigned to escort Miss Stanwyck back to her real husband, John Dehner, but matters are complicated because she won't give up her half-Indian son, Terry Lawrence, born in captivity.

When Acosta breaks loose and gathers a band to regain his son, her refusal to give up the boy and McCrea's stubborn support threatens the assorted grabbag passenger list accompanying her on the stagecoach. McCrea wins safety from Acosta in a puzzling maneuver, by threatening to shoot the boy if the helpless coach is attacked. After delivering Miss Stanwyck, McCrea finds husband Dehner unwilling to accept the lad. Final, unconvincing chase has Dehner and Acosta conveniently killing each other off, leaving Miss Stanwyck and McCrea free to consummate growing affection for each other.

Subsidiary plots sketchily developed, are awkward courtship of drifting cowhand Earl Holliman and Spanish senorita Susan Kohner; craven greed of passenger Edward Andrews; and racial enmity of frontier settlers against half-Indian boy.

McCrea fits sergeant's role well, often rising above direction and story curlicues. Miss Stanwyck, with a meaty role, also delivers strongly with skill and warmth.

Holliman impresses with contagious good humor as the shy but self-reliant cowhand, while Miss Kohner, as his aristocratic vis-a-vis, •continues to show promise. Royal Dano, as the eccentric stagedriver, is a standout in support, as is Acosta as the proud, barbaric Apache. Either through directorial guidance or his own concept, Andrews overplayed the cowardly bit, but Dehner manages his required elongated sulk okay. In lesser parts, moppet Lawrence, Sheb Wooley as a town bully, Stanley Adams as a tactless travelling salesman and Celia Lovsky as Miss Kohner's duenna grandmother all did well.

Cameraman Ellsworth Fredericks did better in his black-and-white filming of scenic sweeps, but in photographing humans, he displayed an overfondness for extreme closeups. Film editing by Fred Berger was marred by a few abrupt and illfitting transitions.

Title song, in Western ballad idiom, by Gerald Fried and Mitzi Cummings and sung throughout by Tex Ritter, attempts to emulate the "High Noon" device. It's not too successful, since it intrudes more than informs, but it's a good enough tune of its style. *Kove.*

Loving You
(V'VISION-COLOR-SONGS)

Elvis Presley returns in a picture tailor-made to his talents. It's a rock 'n' roller with a good story-line that shapes as a juve trade natural.

Paramount release of Hal B. Wallis production. Stars Elvis Presley, Lizabeth Scott, Wendell Corey; features Dolores Hart, James Gleason, Ralph Dumke, Paul Smith, Ken Becker; Jana Lund. Directed by Hal Kanter; script, Herbert Baker and Kanter, from a story by Mary Agnes Thompson; camera (Technicolor), Charles Lang; numbers staged by Charles O'Curran; music arranged and conducted by Walter Scharf; vocal accompaniment, The Jordanaires; editor, Howard Smith. Previewed at the Capitol Theatre, N. Y., June 20, '57. Running time, **101 MINS.**

Deke Rivers	Elvis Presley
Glenda	Lizabeth Scott
Tex Warner	Wendell Corey
Susan Jessup	Dolores Hart
Carl	James Gleason
Tallman	Ralph Dumke
Skeeter	Paul Smith
Wayne	Ken Becker
Daisy	Jana Lund

Though the rock 'n' roll craze perhaps passed its peak, there's little question that a sizeable part of the citizenry will welcome Elvis Presley back for his second screen appearance. An easy guess that customers will be young in years appearance. An easy guess is that have to be if they're to match the rock 'n' roller's own lungpower in the picture itself.

Producer Hal B. Wallis has chosen wisely in picking "Loving You" as a vehicle for Presley. It's a simple story, in which he can be believed, which has romantic overtones and exposes the singer to the kind of thing he does best, i.e. shout out his rythms, bang away at his guitar and perform the strange, knee-bending, hipswinging contortions that are his trademark and that, for unfathomable reasons, induce squealing noises from his young fans.

Apart from this, Presley shows improvement as an actor. It's not a demanding part and, being surrounded by a capable crew of performers, he comes across as a simple but pleasant sort. Herbert Baker and Hal Kanter have fashioned an okay script spiked with folksy humor interwoven with some sentimental strains. The corny aspects probably don't matter. As a matter of fact, they'll probably help.

Wallis has given the film a plush mounting, in VistaVision and Technicolor, which adds to the values. Working with Presley are Lizabeth Scott and Wendell Corey, both delineating definite characters and doing well in the laughs department. Film introes a newcomer, Dolores Hart, in an undemanding role as Presley's girl. Even so, the young actress conveys a very pleasing personality and handles her chores with charm. She ought to be seen again.

Story has Presley picked up by Miss Scott, a publicity girl touring with a hillbilly band on a whistlestop tour. She gets Corey, the leader of the outfit, to take on Presley, and they stunt him into a rock 'n' roll personality. Of course, there are complications and Presley takes himself off just as he's supposed to go on a national video show. Miss Scott brings him back for the happy finish that sees Presley and Miss Hart and Corey and Miss Scott united.

Director Kanter exploits the

various facets that have contributed to Presley's success. He sings a lot of songs, some of 'em western ballads and the rest of the rock 'n' roll, boggie-woogie variety. Among the numbers heard are "Hot Dog," "Lonesome Cowboy," "Got a Lot of Livin' To do," "Let's Have a Party," "Detour," "Dancing on the Dare" and the theme song— "Loving You." It's all highly exploitable stuff. Film shapes as a bangup attraction for the hinterlands and should be a crowd-pleaser in the keys where Presley is still a draw with the youngsters.

Miss Scott as the ambitious publicity gal can't be taken seriously, but she does okay. Corey displays a comic talent and is very good as Tex Warner. James Gleason contributes the pro touch, as do Ralph Dumke, Paul Smith and Jana Lund. Latter scores in the role of a smitten teenager. Kanter's direction consciously pitches the proceedings to the teenage mentality. There'll always be those who'll find the whole Presley phenomenon either laughable or even disgusting, yet these probably won't be those who'll go to see the film anyhow. It's surely not a critics' picture, but, from the looks of it, it's boxoffice. And who's to quarrel with that in 1957?

Charles Lang's photography is pleasing in Technicolor. Howard Smith's editing is competent. Charles O'Curran staged the various numbers with imagination and the Jordanaires offer good backing for Presley. Col. Tom Parker, Presley's manager, gets credit as Technical Advisor, and take that literally and seriously. He's an expert property developer. *Hift.*

God Is My Partner
(REGALSCOPE)

Contrived plot with "faith" angles. Pretty slow. Only Walter Brennan name possibly to attract. Small returns indicated.

Hollywood, June 28.

Twentieth-Fox release of a Sam Hersh production. Stars Walter Brennan; co-stars Marion Ross, Jesse White; features Nelson Leigh, Charles Lane, Ellen Corby. Paul Cavanagh. Directed by William F. Claxton. Screenplay, Charles Francis Royal; camera, Walter Strenge; editor, Robert Fritch; music, Paul Dunlap. Previewed June 26, '57. Running time, **79 MINS.**

Dr. Charles Grayson	Walter Brennan
Gordon Palmer	John Hoyt
Francis Denning	Marion Ross
Louis	Jesse White
Rev. Goodwin	Nelson Leigh
Judge Warner	Charles Lane
Mrs. Dalton	Ellen Corby
Dr. Brady	Paul Cavanagh
Maxine Spelvana	Nancy Kulp
Ben Renson	John Harmon

"God Is My Partner," produced by religioso filmmaker Sam Hersh, is more apt for the church market than theatrical release. Film is short on the punch necessary for the commercial screen and goes somewhat overboard in faith sequences on the faith theme for regular audiences. Against that generality, church or evangelical patronage may be pleased.

The Charles Francis Royal screenplay is premised on a successful, elderly surgeon being brought to trial on a charge by two nephews that he is incompetent to handle money after certain so-called eccentric activities. The basic plot never quite holds water, since the "proof" offered isn't enough for any audience to credit, even though the jury seems

so inclined. Narrative unfolds via a series of flashbacks from courtroom action, where Walter Brennan is being defended by Marion Ross, as the prosecuting attorney first presents his case, then the defense by tearing down the "halftruths" offered by the prosecution's witnesses. Pic takes its title from Brennan, testifying why he donated $50,000 to his church, explaining that without the Diety he could never have become the great surgeon that he had become.

William F. Claxton's over-leisurely direction keeps film at a sometimes tedious tempo and script doesn't allow much realism in portrayals. Brennan fares best, managing to make his work count.

Technical credits are competently handled, Walter Strenge, camera; Ernst Fegte, art direction; Robert Fritch, editing; Paul Dunlap, music. *Whit.*

X the Unknown

Poor and complicated science-fictioner not for discriminating audiences.

Hollywood, June 21.

Warner Bros. release of an Anthony Hinds production. Stars Dean Jagger, Edward Chapman, Leo McKern; features William Lucas, Peter Hammond, Michael Ripper, Anthony Newley. Directed by Leslie Norman. Story-screenplay, Jimmy Sangster; camera Gerald Gibbs; editor, James Needs; music, James Bernard. Previewed June 19, '57. Running time, **79 MINS.**

This picture carries a complicated structure difficult to follow. The "unknown" that serves as the menace in science-fiction yarn is so vague that audiences may be overmystified, with result film will have hard going in even least discriminating situations. Dean Jagger is only name. Anthony Hinds production deals with a compressed force from the center of the earth which escapes via fissure on earth's crust to feed on energy found above, but subject is so nebulous as scientists admit they are meeting with an unknown phenomenon.

Jagger plays an atomic scientist in Scotland, called upon to solve the mystery of persons suffering from severe radiation burns after it's figured some unknown element has escaped through fissure. His scenes are very t[...]y, a general fault in script of Jimmy Sangster with Jagger are Edward Chapman, as director of atomic research lab, who doesn't hold to any of Jagger's theories, and Leo McKern, investigator for the British Atomic Energy Commission. Roles are strictly static and Leslie Norman's direction isn't able to rise above what was handed him. *Whit.*

Beginning of the End

Disappointing first effort by AB-PT Pictures Corp. Low-budget, exploitation entry. Grasshoppers run mad; so does mediocrity.

Republic release of AB-PT Pictures Corp. production. Stars Peggy Castle, Peter Graves and Morris Ankrum. Produced and directed by Bert I. Gordon. Screenplay, Fred Freiberger and Lester Corn. Previewed in N. Y. June 28, '57. Running time, **73 MINS.**

Audrey	Peggy Castle
Ed	Peter Graves
General Hanson	Morris Ankrum

Corporal Mathias ......Richard Benedict
Captain Barton ....James Seay
Colonel Sturgeon ......Thomas B. Henry
Frank ....Than Wyenn
Major Everett ....John Close
1st Patrolman ....Don C. Harvey
2nd Patrolman ....Larry J. Blake
No. 1 Soldier ....Steve Warren
No. 2 Soldier ....Frank Connor
No. 3 Soldier ....Don Eitner
No. 4 Soldier ....Frank Chase
Taggert ....Pierre Watkin
General Short ....Frank Wilcox

As the first release of the brand-new AB-PT Pictures Corp. (a subsidiary of the American Broadcasting-Paramount Theatres family) this release rates as a disapointment. It's not just old hat, but old scream, an echo of all the horror "monsters" sired by King Kong. Laden with mumbo-jumbo about atomic energy and radiation, this picture, on which Bert I. Gordon takes the credit-blame as producer and director is a sorry offering for openers.

Even taken on its own terms—as a low-budget exploitation picture—"Beginning of the End" hardly reflects the best showmanship of a major theatre circuit. Based on its low cost, its protected haven in the AB-PT houses, and its susceptibility to exploitation, the film can conceivably wind up a modest money-maker. Too, the backing the picture will receive from AB-PT may work to the advantage of other exhibitors. But it's still a letdown of expectations.

Summarizing the plot of "Beginning of the End" is like rehashing the story of several dozen similar films. Mysterious deaths suddenly occur in an area where there is a government scientific station. This time it is an agricultural laboratory in the midwest where, by the use of radioactive material, strawberries and similar fruits are grown to the size of footballs. Somehow grasshoppers come in contact with the radioactive material and grow into 10-feet tall monsters. These monsters immediately menace the nation. The Illinois National Guard is called up. Town and cities are destroyed as mere humans and their modern weapons cannot halt the invasion. A national emergency is declared and the Dept. of Defense takes over the defense of Chicago.

The hopped-up grasshoppers invade the Windy City and are seen ploughing through armies, lumbering down streets, frightening a panic-stricken population, and crawling up tall buildings. All this is accomplished by obviously artificial superimpositions of drawings and the employment of stock footage. A way naturally is found to halt the monsters. They are lured into Lake Michigan where they are killed by the (surprise!) cold water.

The Fred Freiberger and Lester Corn screenplay is ludicrous, bringing out every cliche in plot and dialog. Peggie Castle is unconvincing as a national magazine newshen-photographer; Peter Graves makes a gallant try as the young scientist and Morris Ankrum is artificially harassed as the commanding general. The camerawork (uncredited) and the editing (ditto) match the scenario. *Holl.*

The Unearthly

Cheap horror programmer built around the mad doctor theme. Fodder for the very unsophisticated.

Hollywood, June 29.

Republic release of an AB-PT production. Stars John Carradine; features Allison Hayes, Myron Healy; with Sally Todd, Marilyn Buford, Arthur Batanides, Tor Johnson, Harry Fleer, Roy Gordon, Guy Prescott, Paul McWilliams. Producer-director, Brooke L. Peters. Screenplay, Geoffrey Dennis-Jane Mann, from Miss Mann's original. Camera, Merle Connell; editor, Richard Currier; art director, Daniel Hall; music direction, Henry Varse, Michael Terr. Previewed, June 28, '57. Running time, **70 MINS.**

Prof. Charlos Conway ....John Carradine
Grace Thomas ....Allison Hayes
Mark Houston ....Myron Healy
Natalie ....Sally Todd
Dr. Gilchrist ....Marilyn Buferd
Danny Green ....Arthur Batanides
Lobo ....Tor Johnson
Jedrow ....Harry Fleer
Dr. Loren Wright ....Roy Gordon
Capt. Rogers ....Guy Prescott
Police Officer ....Paul MacWilliams

The mad doctor bit again. There's nothing to recommend this one beyond its cheapness. Fodder for a very unsophisticated market.

Doc John Carradine and assistant Marilyn Buford are conducting experiments on human guinea pigs in an isolated sanatorium—something to do with transplanting glands and extending the life span "forever." Among the intended victims of Allison Hayes and Myron Healy. To no one's particular surprise, Healy turns out to be a cop, who blows the whistle on the proceedings with the proper amount of derring-do. Finale has cops discover a band of Hollywood's bulkier bit players, made up as a cellarful of doc Carradine's "mistakes."

Geoffrey Dennis and Jane Mann adapted Miss Mann's original with a maximum of cliches and a minimum of originality. Brooke L. Peters produced-directed with a heavy hand and no particular distinction.

Carradine plays the doc broadly, as good a way as any. Healy is only other competant thesp in cast. Miss Hayes, Miss Buford and Sally Todd, another of doc's victims, lend some visual pleasure to the proceedings, but otherwise aren't up to unrewarding assignments. Tor Johnson, as the doc's muscle man, and Arthur Batanides and Harry Fleer, other victims, are acceptable.

Technical credits are competant, but show the effect of a short budget. *Kove.*

The Buckskin Lady

Fairish outdoor tale though scripting attempts to add "character" dimension fliv.

Hollywood, June 25.

United Artists release of a Bishop-Hittleman Pictures production. Stars Patricia Medina, Richard Denning, Gerald Mohr, Henry Hull; features Hank Warden, Robin Short, Richard Reeves, Dorothy Adams. Producer-director, Carl K. Hittleman; screenplay, David Lang, Hittleman, from Francis S. Chase Jr. story; camera, Ellsworth Fredericks; editor, Harry Coswick; music, Albert Glasser. Title song, Glasser, Maurice Keller. Previewed, June 24, '57. Running time, **66 MINS.**

Angela Medley .... Patricia Medina
Dr. Bruce Merritt.......Richard Denning
Slinger ....Gerald Mohr
Doc ....Henry Hull
Lon ....Hank Warden
Nevada ....Robin Short
Porter ....Richard Reeves
Mrs. Adams ....Dorothy Adams
Jed ....Frank Sully
Cranston ....George Cisar
Ralphie ....Louis Lettieri
Latham ....Byron Foulger
Swanson ....John Dierkes

Strictly for the program trade is this low-budget western. There's enough action to compensate for half-hearted attempts of scripters David Lang and Carl K. Hittleman (who also produced-directed) to add character dimension to F. S. Chase's story. These attempts get bogged down and serve no purpose but to slow pace.

Patricia Medina portrays femme gambler in small western town, who's supporting her drunken doctor father, Henry Hull, with her shady earnings. Also, she's lady love of local top gunman, Gerald Mohr.

Into town rides new doc, stalwart Richard Denning, and in short order she's fallen for him and tries to go straight. Naturally, complications set in and to save him, she rides off with Mohr. But when Mohr turns outlaw, she yearns for home and Denning, especially after she catches a bullet picturesquely in her attractive shoulder. When Denning catches up to rescue her, she has to plug Mohr with his own gun to save her true love. Then she and Denning can amble off toward the sunset together.

Director Hittleman manages several fairly exciting fights and one bitterly amusing chase sequence, but otherwise his helming is routine for the course. Emoting rarely rises above the elementary. Miss Medina, attractively clad in revealing gowns and tightfitting jeans, does a good job of registering sex, but otherwise rarely has a chance to change expression. Same applies to stereotyped roles of Denning and Mohr, who look perturbed and sneer throughout, respectively. Hull is appropriately weak and befuddled.

Hank Warden is good as loyal friend of Miss Medina and Denning, who gets killed for his pains. Robert Short, in as a combo barkeeper-ballad-strummin' troubador, hasn't a chance to develop his role into anything meaningful. Dorothy Adams, Bryon Foulger and Richard Reeves also turn in capable support chores.

Technical credits are competently standard, except for choppy cutting. *Kove.*

Bernardine
(C'SCOPE-COLOR)

In the groove for youngsters and teen-aged in-the-wood oldsters but Pat Boone entry is mild item for general market.

20th-Fox release of Samuel G. Engel production. Stars Pat Boone, Terry Moore, Janet Gaynor and Dean Jagger. Features Richard Sargent, James Drury, Ronnie Burns, Walter Abel, Natalie Schaefer, Isabel Jewell. Directed by Henry Levin. Screenplay, Theodore Reeves; based on the play by Mary Chase; camera (C'Scope and De Luxe Color), Paul Vogel; editor, David Bretherton; music, Lionel Newman; songs, "Bernardine" and "Technique" by Johnny Mercer, and "Love Letters in the Sand" by Nick and Charles Kenny and J. Fred Coots. Previewed in New York June 20, '57. Running time, **94 MINS.**

Beau ....Pat Boone
Jean ....Terry Moore
Mrs. Wilson ....Janet Gaynor
J. Fullerton Weldy .... Dean Jagger
Sanford Wilson ....Richard Sargent
Lt. Langley Beaumont..... James Drury
Griner ....Ronnie Burns
Mr. Beaumont ....Walter Abel
Mrs. Beaumont ....Natalie Schafer
Ruby ....Isabel Jewell
Jack Costanzo and Orchestra...Themselves
Hilda ....Edit Angold
Friedelhauser .... Val Benedict
Cleo ....Ernestine Wade
Mr. Mason ....Russ Conway
Olson ....Tom Pittman
Kinswood ....Hooper Dunbar

Pat Boone being an important figure among the younger set, it figures that his cinematic outing in "Bernardine" will receive their attention. Further, the Samuel G. Engel offering concerns itself with teenagers, and this means those at student age ought to feel the picture was made especially for them. To boot, there are several vocals by the star.

Title song is a bright paean to a young man's ideal girl and in circulation on the Dot label. The retailer action hasn't been strong yet but very well could pick up. It's backed with the oldie, "Love Letters in the Sand" (Nick and Charles Kenny and J. Fred Coots), and this has been getting top-of-the-list spins. Third number is "Technique," by Johnny Mercer (who also composed the title song) and its chances are fair enough considering the familiar Calypso beat and clever lyrics. Boone does them all in winning style, a selling factor for the picture.

Engle's production, based on the mildly-received Mary Chase play, is not in the true sense a run-of-the-audience entertainment. Those removed from teenagers and, in this case, their fancies and frolics and glib chatter likely will find only mild diversion in the entry. Indeed, it seems that the script goes overboard in depicting all the adult characters as near-morons in contrast with the very hip juveniles on view.

Boone is a member of the local high school graduating class and a numerically limited clique whose main interests are motor boat racing, cars and, mostly conversationally, girls. Terry Moore is a new-in-town telephone operator who answers to the description of their mentally-sketched ideal. Richard Sargent lays claim to her, having "discovered" her, but Boone's brother, James Drury, as an officer on leave from the Army, wins the gal and Sargent impulsively enlists in the military.

That's about it, in the broad sense. In between there's lots of big words that make but small talk as mouthed by Boone and his classmates. As directed by Henry Levin, the treatment is lighthearted except for Sargent's romantic setback.

Performances are so-so. Boone is strong with a pop vocal but he acts with a strained-for nonchalance that is not becoming. And the camera work, in De Luxe color and CinemaScope, makes him out too much of a pretty-boy. Miss Moore is attractive and fits her part well. Sargent comes off tops as the clumsy would-be Casanova, who lacks "technique." Janet Gaynor smiles and behaves pleasantly a Sargent's widowed mother (a stronger part would have been welcome on her return to the screen) and Dean Jagger, as her admirer, meets the requirement of the Theodore Reeves script.

Ronnie Burns (son of George Burns and Gracie Allen), Walter Abel. Natalie Schaefer, Isabel Jewell and others in the cast all work fair enough. Jack Costanzo and orchestra do a bongo number which provides a fair amount of color.

Set decorations by Walter M. Scott and Stuart A. Reiss appear to be from out of a House Beautiful type of women's mag. Technical credits all okay.   *Gene.*

Band of Angels
(COLOR)

Clark Gable and Yvonne De Carlo in powerful Old South drama with miscegenation theme skillfully woven into plot. Good prospects.

Hollywood, July 5.
Warner Bros. release. Stars Clark Gable, Yvonne de Carlo; costars Sidney Poitier, Efrem Zimbalist Jr.; features Patric Knowles, Rex Reason. Torin Thatcher, Andrea King. Ray Teal, Russ Evans, Carolle Drake. Directed by Raoul Walsh. Screenplay, John Twist, Ivan Goff, Ben Roberts, based on novel by Robert Penn Warren, camera (Warner-Color), Lucien Ballard; editor, Folmar Blangsted; music. Max Steiner. Previewed June 27, '57. Running time, 125 MINS.
Hamish Bond .... Clark Gable
Amantha Starr .... Yvonne De Carlo
Rau-Ru .... Sidney Poitier
Ethan Sears .... Efrem Zimbalist Jr.
Charles de Marigny......Patric Knowles
Seth Parton .... Rex Reason
Capt. Canavan .... Torin Thatcher
Miss Idell .... Andrea King
Mr. Calloway .... Ray Teal
Jimmee .... Russ Evans
Michele .... Carolle Drake
Stuart .... Raymond Bailey
Dollie .... Tommie Moore
Aaron Star .... William Forrest
Young Manty .... Noreen Corcoran

Subject of miscegenation is explored and developed in this colorful production of the Old South. WarnerColor film, shrewdly turned out along showmanship lines to make best use of an unusual story, will come in for some social reaction and accordingly may be specially "exploited." Add to this word-of-mouth fact that Clark Gable and Yvonne De Carlo, both deliver powerful performances. Feature seems cinch to do exceptionally good biz generally despite any sensitivity below Mason-Dixon Line.

Raoul Walsh is in top form in direction of the screenplay by John Twist, Ivan Goff and Ben Roberts. Derived from a Robert Penn Warren novel, screen writers have captured the mood and spirit of the Deep South narrative which deals with a young woman of quality discovering that her mother was a slave. Sold on the auction block to a former slave-trader, unfoldment dwells on the pair's relations, both in New Orleans and later on a plantation up-river when war between the North and South moves area. Beautiful and realistic backgrounds are achieved through locationing in Louisiana.

Gable's characterization is reminiscent of his Rhett Butler in "Gone With the Wind," although there is obviously no paralleling of plot. As former slave-runner turned New Orleans gentleman, with bitter memories of his earlier days, he contributes a warm, decisive portrayal that carries tremendous authority. After he buys femme, instead of relegating her to his slave quarters he treats her as a lady in his household, where romance buds and later she refuses to accept the freedom he offers.

In the best delineation of her career, Miss De Carlo is beautiful as the mulatto, who learns of her true status when she returns from a Cincinnati finishing school to attend her father's funeral. She finds herself a chattel of the heavily-mortgaged estate, due to mother having been a slave, and is dragged off to the block. Actress makes her work count heavily and is ideally cast in role.

As co-star Sidney Poitier, young Negro actor, impresses as Gable's educated protege, whom slaver picked up as an infant in Africa and reared as his son. Character is one of complexities, the young man hating his master for having

educated him beyond his station. One of the most dramatic moments occurs when Poitier, now a Union soldier after escaping from slavery, captures Gable to turn him over to Federal forces for having burned his crops against official orders; then arranges his escape with Miss De Carlo, whom he resents for actions not in keeping with her Negro blood.

Strongly cast, too, is Efrem Zimbalist Jr., as a Union officer in love with femme; Patric Knowles, a Southern planter who goes on the make for her; and Torin Thatcher, sea captain and former associate of Gable. Standout performance also is turned in by Carolle Drake, Gable's former quadroon mistress, and Rex Reason and Ray Teal offer effective bits.

Lucien Ballard's color photography leads off above-average technical credits, and Franz Bachelin's art direction is superb. Max Steiner's music score blends perfectly and editing by Folmar Blangsted maintains fast tempo.   *Whit.*

I Was a Teenage Werewolf

Tease-titled science-fictioner, okay upper half of exploitation package.

Hollywood, July 5.
American-International release of a Herman Cohen production. Stars Michael Landon, Yvonne Lime, Whit Bissell, Tony Marshall; features Dawn Richard, Barney Phillips, Ken Miller, Cindy Robbins, Michael Rougas, Robert Griffin, Joseph Mell. Directed by Gene Fowler Jr.; story-screenplay, Ralph Thornton; camera, Joseph La Shelle; editor, George Gittens; music, Paul Dunlap. Previewed July 3, '57. Running time, 76 MINS.
Tony .... Michael Landon
Arlene .... Yvonne Lime
Dr. Alfred Brandon....... Whit Bissell
Jimmy .... Tony Marshall
Theresa .... Dawn Richard
Detective Donovan ...... Barney Phillips
Vic .... Ken Miller
Pearl .... Cindy Robbins
Frank .... Michael Rougas
Police Chief Baker .... Robert Griffin
Dr. Hugo Wagner .... Joseph Mell
Charles .... Malcolm Atterbury
Doyle .... Eddie Marr
Pepi .... Vladimir Sokoloff
Miss Ferguson .... Louise Lewis
Bill .... John Launer
Chris Stanley .... Guy Williams
Mary .... Dorothy Crehan

Another in the cycle of regression themes is a combo teenager and science-fiction yarn which should do okay in the exploitation market. American-International will topbill pic with the not-so-good "Invasion of the Saucer Men" as a horror package.

Only thing new about this Herman Cohen production is a psychiatrist's use of a problem teenager who comes to him for help using the youth for an experiment in regression, but it's handled well enough to meet the requirements of this type film. There are plenty of story points which are sloughed over in the Ralph Thornton screenplay, but good performances help overcome deficiencies. Final reels, when the lad turns into a hairy-headed monster with drooling fangs, are inclined to be played too heavily.

Michael Landon delivers a first-class characterization as the high school boy constantly in trouble, and has okay support right down the line. Yvonne Lime is pretty as his girl friend who asks him to go to the psychiatrist, and Whit Bissell handles doctor part capably, although some of his lines are pretty thick. Barney Phillips is competent as a detective trying to straighten out Landon, as is Robert Griffin in role of police

chief and Dawn Richard as one of Landon's victims.

Gene Fowler Jr.'s direction is up to standards of the script and Joseph La Shelle's photography leads technical credits.   *Whit.*

Invasion of Saucer Men

Trivial science-fiction.

Hollywood, July 5.
American-International release of a James H. Nicholson-Robert J. Gurney Jr. production. Stars Steve Terrell. Gloria Castillo; features Raymond Hatton, Lyn Osborn, Russ Bender, Douglas Henderson, Sam Buffington, Jason Johnson, Don Shelton. Directed by Edward L. Cahn. Screenplay, Gurney, Al Martin; original story, Paul Fairman; camera, Frederick E. West; editors, Ronald Sinclair, Charles Gross Jr.; music, Ronald Stein. Previewed July 3, '57. Running time, 69 MINS.
Johnny .... Steve Terrell
Joan .... Gloria Castillo
Joe .... Frank Gorshin
Larkin .... Raymond Hatton
Art .... Lyn Osborn
Doctor .... Russ Bender
Lt. Wilkins .... Douglas Henderson
Colonel .... Sam Buffington
Detective .... Jason Johnson
Mr. Hayden .... Don Shelton
1st Soldier .... Scott Peters
Waitress .... Jan Englund
Sgt Bruce .... Kelly Thordsen
Soda Jerk .... Bob Einer
Irene .... Patti Lawler
Paul .... Calvin Booth
Boy .... Ed Nelson
Sgt. Gordon .... Roy Darmour
Girl .... Audrey Conti
Boy .... Jim Bridges
Boy in Soda Shop........Jimmy Pickford
Girl .... Joan Dupuis
Policeman .... Buddy Mason
Boy in Soda Shop .... Orv Mohler

"Invasion of the Saucer Men" is a minor entry for the science-fiction trade. Film suffers from poor use of attempted comedy, and is further handicapped by a haphazard sort of yarn which makes film's 69-minutes' running time seem much more. Pic will be packaged with "I Was a Teenage Werewolf" for release by American-International.

The James H. Nicholson-Robert J. Gurney Jr. production uses the device of a saucer ship from outer space landing its crew of little monsters, to build suspense. Script by Gurney and Al Martin revolves around a pair of elopers getting involved with these little green men, but so many elements are dragged in, including a U. S. Air Force unit which arrives to investigate the space ship, that interest doesn't hold.

Steve Terrell and Gloria Castillo co-star, but haven't much chance other than to look frightened under Edward L. Cahn's direction. Frank Gorshin, in for comedy relief, has no place actually in the jagged story line. Balance of cast don't count for much. Technical credits are stock.   *Whit.*

Outlaw's Son

Outdoor cops 'n' robbers entry. Better-than-average fare. Should do okay b.o.

Hollywood, July 2.
United Artists release of a Bel-Air Production. Stars Dane Clark, Ben Cooper, Lori Nelson; co-stars Ellen Drew; features Charles Watts, Cecile Rogers, Joseph "Bucko" Stafford. Producer, Howard W. Koch. Director; Lesley Selander. Screenplay, Richard Alan Simmons, from Clifton Adams novel. Camera, William Margulies; editor, John F. Schreyer; music, Les Baxter. Previewed July 1, '57. Running time, 88 MINS.
Nate Blaine .... Dane Clark
Jeff Blaine .... Ben Cooper
Lila Costain .... Lori Nelson
Ruth Sewall .... Ellen Drew
Marshal Elec Blessingham..Charles Watts
Amy Wentworth .... Cecile Rogers
Jeff Blaine as a child....Joseph Stafford
Todd Wentworth .... Eddie Foy, III
Ed Wyatt .... John Pickard
Deputy Marshal Ralph Striker
                          Robert Knapp
Bill Somerson .... Les Mitchel

Phil Costain	Guy Prescott
Paul Wentworth	George Pembroke
Ridley	Jeff Daley
Lila Costain as a child	Wendy Stuart
Amy Wentworth as a child	Ann Maria Nanasi
Jorgenson	James Parnell
Randall	Scott Peters
Todd Wentworth as a child	Buddy Hart
Ben Jorgenson	Ernie Dotson
Mac Butler	Ken Christy
Egstrom	Audley Anderson
Kessler	Leslie Kimmell

The "Outlaw's Son" has a tendency to gallop off on several plot tangents simultaneously, not all of which pan out. Still, this outdoors cops 'n' robbers entry stacks up as better-than-average fare, which should do okay at the B.O. corral. Dane Clark, Ben Cooper and Lori Nelson have certain followings which might help.

Richard Alan Simmons screenplay, from Clifton Adams novel, follows plot line laid out in title. Son of hot-tempered gunman Clark is Cooper, who tries to adjust to small cowtown society. Townsfolk aren't too friendly, especially after pop's accused of killing the local banker during a holdup.

Also, pic opens with pop's visit to his son, being reared by maiden aunt Ellen Drew. During visit, he teaches his juve boy, played by Joseph "Bucko" Stafford, how to handle a gun. When son interjects a .44 into a schoolyard beef, naturally townfolk don't cotton to that.

Grownup son Cooper becomes casehardened deputy marshal but family hot temper soon gets him in trouble and he throws in with some outlaws to rob a mine payroll. Now-elderly pop returns to scene and goes down shooting to prevent his son following in his footsteps.

Oh, yes. Along story line Aunt Ellen confesses she testified falsely about the bank holdup, to prevent Clark from taking his boy along to a life of crime (couple of other guys done it). Also, when his "respectable" town g.f., Cecile Rogers, throws Cooper over after he gets into trouble, he takes up with fiery and unconventional Miss Nelson and windup promises a permanent union.

Clark registers well as the troubled outlaw, the role fitting his brand of intense dramatics. Cooper does quite well as the muddled young rebel, western-style. Miss Nelson's role isn't fully or logically developed, but she shows considerable promise and attractiveness.

Miss Drew is fine as the fiercely maternal aunt and Charles Watts, as the tough but understanding town mashal, also turns in a strong supporting chore. Among large cast, young Stafford, Eddie Foy III, Miss Rogers, John Pickard, Robert Knapp, Les Mitchel and Guy Prescott turns in capable performances, despite roles sometimes abbreviated to little meaning.

Direction of Lesley Selander stresses action over introspection, and largely succeeds despite a tendency to wander afield. Music by Lex Baxter and camera work by William Margulies are definite assets. Other technical credits are good. *Kove.*

L'Etrange Monsieur Steve
(The Strange Mr. Stevens)
(FRENCH)

Paris, July 9.

Jeannic release of Pechefilm production. Stars Philipe Lemaire, Jeanne Moreau, Armand Mestral; features, Lino Ventura, Jacques Varennes, Anouk Ferjac. Directed by Raymond Bailly. Screenplay, Bailly, from a novel by Marcel Pretre; camera, Jacques Lemare; editor, Louis Devaivre. At Marignan, Paris. Running time, **105 MINS.**

Georges	Philipe Lemaire
Steve	Armand Mestral
Florence	Jeanne Moreau
Mireille	Anouk Ferjac
Remy	Lino Ventura

Tale has a mediocre bank clerk, about to marry a girl he works with, thrown in with some grifters who frame him with another girl and make him an unwilling accomplice. He manages to unwittingly foil the holdup and get away with it. But his taste for living dangerously has been dangerously whetted and leads to tragedy.

Some good story points but director Raymond Bailly is rarely able to develop them. Release lacks the suspense and deeper characterization which might have made this an offbeater. It's also talky.

Philipe Lemaire is superficial as the ordinary man thrown into worldly doings, and does not give the character being and life of its own, necessary to its conviction. Armand Mestral is also wooden as the enigmatic Steve who ushers the little man into a world of crime. Jeanne Moreau is the only thespic standout as she makes her sensual character meaningful and believable. Technical credits are good. *Mosk.*

Destination 60,000

Another cocky pilot taught humility. Hackneyed plot but striking aerial photography and popularized technical data may serve as draw for aviation-minded youth.

Hollywood, July 2.

Allied Artists release of a (Jack J.) Gross-(Philip N.) Krasne Production. Stars Preston Foster, Pat Conway, Jeff Donnell, Coleen Gray; features Bobby Clark, Denver Pyle, Russ Thorson, Ann Barton. Director-screenplay, George Waggner; camera, Hal McAlpin; editor, Kenneth Crane; music, Al Glasser. Previewed July 1, '57. Running time, **66 MINS.**

Col. Ed Buckley	Preston Foster
Jeff Connors	Pat Conway
Ruth Buckley	Jeff Donnell
Mary Ellen	Coleen Gray
"Skip" Buckley	Bobby Clark
Mickey Hill	Denver Pyle
Dan Maddox	Russ Thorson
Grace Hill	Ann Barton

Striking air photography serves to counteract standard cocky youngster leavened by misfortune plot updated to the jet age. Popularized technical data and jargon may attract aviation-minded youth. Otherwise, prospects are modest.

Story by George Waggner, who also directed, revolves around tests of plane manufacturer Preston Foster's latest experimental jet. His hot-shot test pilot-wartime buddy, Pat Conway, isn't too amenable to discipline, after first trial attempt fails. Alternate pilot Denver Pyle is seriously injured in second try at ironing out bugs. Foster himself takes up a third prototype and nearly blacks out, until Conway, flying escort, snaps him out by barking combat commands over intercom radio. Sketchily developed is romance between Conway and Foster's secretary, Coleen Gray, and Foster's family life with Jeff Donnell and Bobby Clark.

Waggner's direction is able and wisely stresses low-key performances. With trite plot, high-powered dramatics would have evoked unwanted hilarity.

Foster turns in a brisk, workmanlike chore. Conway impresses as a possible b.o. heartthrob, with good looks and a nice, easygoing personality, but certainly isn't a polished actor as yet. Miss Donnell ably depicts understanding domesticity, while Miss Gray, with very little to do, does it well. Others in cast, Bobby Clark (a good juve actor), Pyle, Russ Thorson and Ann Barton, fill assignments capably.

Notable aerial photography is partly stock clips supplied by Douglas Aircraft and some original shots by cameraman Hal McAlpin. *Kove.*

Les Trois Font la Paire
(Three Make a Pair)
(FRENCH)

Paris, June 25.

Gaumont production and release. Stars Michel Simon, Sophie Desmarets; features Philipe Nicaud, Clement Duhour, Darry Cowl, Christian Mery, Carette. Written and directed by Sacha Guitry. Camera, Philipe Agostini; editor, Paulette Robert. At Raimu, Paris. Running time, **85 MINS.**

Inspector	Michel Simon
Titine	Sophie Desmarets
Twins	Philipe Nicaud
Director	Darry Cowl
Gangster	Christian Mery
Chief	Clement Duhour

This shapes as a series of sketches, and too many of the allusions are either private or too intrinsically Gallic to make this an important U. S. contender. Sacha Guitry directed this from a sick-bed by proxy but it has his familiar tone which could slant this for some specialized spots in the U. S., but it is limited at best.

It concerns a young hoodlum who kills a passerby just to prove to a gang that he is daring. However, the scene had been photographed by a hidden camera for it was being filmed as part of a picture. Then it turns out that a pair of twins resemble the killer. However, the gang is annoyed by all this and knocks off the culprit to the discomfiture of an ambitious inspector who thought this would make his career.

Film is adroitly acted and plotted and is well made. But the ingenious ideas remain unformed, and rarely turn this into saucy comedy. It is well acted and has a good gloss, but it remains a dubious U. S. item. *Mosk.*

Decision Against Time

Airplane forced landing situation. Fairly suspenseful, okay for general dating.

Hollywood, June 29.

Metro release of a Michael Balcon production. Stars Jack Hawkins; costars Elizabeth Sellars; features Walter Fitzgerald, John Stratton, Lionel Jeffries, Eddie Byrne, Victor Maddern, Donald Pleasence. Directed by Charles Crichton. Screenplay, William Rose, John Eldridge, based on original story by Rose; camera, Douglas Slocombe; editor, Peter Tanner; music, Gerbrand Schurmann. Previewed June 28, '57. Running time, **87 MINS.**

John Mitchell	Jack Hawkins
Mary Mitchell	Elizabeth Sellars
Conway	Walter Fitzgerald
Ashmore	Eddie Byrne
Peter Hook	John Stratton
Joe Biggs	Victor Maddern
Keith	Lionel Jeffries
Crabtree	Donald Pleasence
Mary's Mother	Catherine Lacey
Mrs. Snowden	Megs Jenkins
Maine	Ernest Clark
Jenkins	Raymond Francis
Sim	Russell Waters
Ingrams	Howard Marion Crawford
Nicholas Mitchell	Jeremy Bodkin
Philip Mitchell	Gerard Lohan
Betty Harris	Mary MacKenzie
Launderette Assistant	Esme Easterbrook

"Decision Against Time" has its moments of suspense but lacks development of this quality that might have made British import a truly gripping melodrama. Film is okay for program situations, where it should generate mild interest.

Practically the entire action of this Michael Balcon production occurs within the 35 to 40-minute span an English test pilot is in the air over his airport with a badly crippled freighter, circumstances of which make landing particularly precarious. His boss, owner of a small plane factory whose whole capital is tied up in this one aircraft, constantly orders him to set the automatic pilot and bail out, but pilot decides to chance landing in a desperate effort to save his company from going broke.

Charles Crichton's direction of the William Rose-John Eldridge screenplay affords certain tenseness, particularly in the final moments leading up to pilot's safe landing, but not enough happens generally. Hawkins delivers a straightforward performance and has good support from players in usual matter-of-fact roles which characterize so many British films but don't appeal particularly to American audiences. Elizabeth Sellars as his wife is effective in a restrained portrayal, Walter Fitzgerald scores as the boss and John Stratton, Eddie Byrne and Donald Pleasence rate in smaller parts. *Whit.*

Spoilers of the Forest
(COLOR)

Possibly last film to be made under the Republic banner. Okay programmer.

Hollywood, June 27.

Republic release of Joe Kane production, directed by Kane. Stars Rod Cameron, Vera Ralston, Ray Collins, Hillary Brooke; features Edgar Buchanan, Carl Benton Reid, Sheila Bromley, Hank Worden, John Compton, John Alderson, Angela Greene, Paul Stader. Story and screenplay, Bruce Manning; camera (Trucolor), Jack Marta; editor, Richard L. Van Enger; music, Gerald Roberts. Reviewed June 26, '57. Running time: **68 MINS.**

Boyd Caldwell	Rod Cameron
Joan Milna	Vera Ralston
Eric Warren	Ray Collins
Phyllis Warren	Hillary Brooke
Tom Duncan	Edgar Buchanan
John Mitchell	Carl Benton Reid
Linda Mitchell	Sheila Bromley
Casey	Hank Worden
Billy Mitchell	John Compton
Big Jack Milna	John Alderson
Camille	Angela Greene
Dan	Paul Stader

With the timber area of Montana serving as a picturesque locale, "Spoilers of the Forest" stacks up okay for the program market. Film is perhaps most notable, however, in that it appears quite likely to be Republic's last production.

The Bruce Manning story-screenplay pivots around Vera Ralston, who, with her stepfather, is equal owner of 64,000 acres of Montana timber land. Into the scene come lumber big-shot Ray Collins and his foreman, Rod Cameron, who want to make a deal to cut the timber as fast as possible, despite the owners' opposition.

Cameron woos Miss Ralston, hoping only to sway her lumber conservation views, but it winds up the real thing for both. Collins tries to wreck the romance, but fails, and he's ousted from the scene.

Cameron is good as male topper, while Miss Ralston shows some thesping development as his vis-a-vis. Collins, as always, is thoroughly competent; and Hillary Brooke attractively appealing as his spouse. Featured roles are well handled by all concerned.

The Joe Kane production is enhanced considerably in physical values via neat stock footage, with Jack Marta's Trucolor photography also aiding visually. Kane also has directed capably.

Remaining technical contributions are okay. *Neal.*

An Affair to Remember
(COLOR—C'SCOPE)

Sentimental love story with comedy overtones, played to the hilt by Cary Grant and Deborah Kerr. Shapes as sock attraction.

20th-Fox release of Jerry Wald production. Stars Cary Grant, Deborrah Kerr. Features Richard Denning, Neva Patterson, Cathleen Nesbitt, Robert Q. Lewis. Directed by Leo McCarey; screenplay, Delmer Daves and McCarey from original story by Mildred Gram and McCarey; camera (Color by De Luxe), Milton Krasner; songs by Harry Warren with lyrics by Harold Adamson and McCarey; editor, James B. Clark. Previewed in N.Y. aboard the U.S.S. Constitution, July 11, '57. Running time, 115 MINS.

Nickie Ferrante	Cary Grant
Terry McKay	Deborah Kerr
Kenneth	Richard Denning
Lois	Neva Patterson
Grandmother	Cathleen Nesbitt
Announcer	Robert Q. Lewis
Hathaway	Charles Watts
Courbet	Fortunio Bonanova
Father McGrath	Matt Moore
Mario	Louis Mercier
Miss Webb	Geraldine Wall
Gladys	Nora Marlowe
Miss Lane	Sarah Selby
Bartender	Alberto Morin
Gaimielle	Genevieve Aumont

Adding comedy lines, music, color and CinemaScope, Jerry Wald and Leo McCarey have turned this remake of the 1939 "Love Affair" into a winning film that is alternately funny and tenderly sentimental. It's got all the ingredients that should make it an ideal women's picture, and theme and treatment add up to prime b.o. appeal.

"An Affair to Remember," using plenty of attractive settings (on and off the U.S.S. Constitution), is still primarily a film about two people; and since those two happen to be Cary Grant and Deborah Kerr, one of the happiest screen combos to come along in many a moon, the bitter-sweet romance sparkles and crackles with high spirits.

Picture for the most part maintains a good pace, though it's overlong for several scenes. Particularly the final song number not only could but should be cut. It slows up and interrupts the mood building to the climax, which is played and directed with great sensitivity and excellent taste.

Story has Grant and Miss Kerr fall in love aboard ship, though both are engaged to other people. They decide to meet in six months atop the Empire State Building. Meanwhile, Grant, a faintly notorious bachelor, is to change his life in a more useful direction. He shows up for the rendezvous, but she is struck by a car on her way to the meeting and may never walk again. Disappointed, he leaves, thinking she's changed her mind. Eventually he returns and the film heads for a happy ending as Grant discovers the truth.

Director McCarey, who with Delmer Daves wrote the screenplay, has done a fine job with this picture, though for some reason or other he cut short most of the romantic clinches between the principals. One lengthy shot has them kissing for the first time, but only their legs are shown on a ship's stairway. Several other times they kiss, but the director almost seems embarassed to make a point of it.

Nevertheless, McCarey has gotten the most out of his players' talents. Both are experts in restrained, sophisticated comedy. Both are able to get a laugh by waving a hand or raising an eyebrow. The Grant-Kerr romance is never maudlin, not even at the end. It's a wholly believable relationship between two attractive people who find themselves irresistibly attracted to one another.

The bit when the ship lands, and Grant and Miss Kerr critically eye their respective fiancees; the tv broadcast, when Grant is reluctantly interviewed; the scene when the two, already linked romantically by the other passengers, have their dinners separately, sitting back-to-back—all these are scenes done with a deft touch that strikes just the right note. In updating their property, McCarey and Daves have done an expert job.

Grant is in top form in a made-to-order role. He's still one of the best, and one of the most attractive of stars. Also, he's perfectly cast. Miss Kerr in the cliche "never looked lovelier" or gave a better performance. Picture will add to her stature.

Rest of the cast are all fine. Cathleen Nesbitt plays the grandmother with dignity and heart; Richard Denning is sympathetic in a somewhat improbable role; Neva Patterson is striking as the millionairess engaged to Grant; Robert Q. Lewis comes off well as the tv interviewer. Charles Watt registers as the intruding passenger.

Milton Krasner's lensing is tip-top, and so is the DeLuxe color, which is fresh and natural. Song, "An Affair to Remember," is sung by Vic Damone. It was written by Harry Warren, with lyrics by Harold Adamson and McCarey. Miss Kerr sings a couple of numbers in a nightclub and the main theme runs effectively throughout the film. It's also performed during a tender little scene (with a profusion of closeups) involving Miss Nesbitt at the piano, Grant and Miss Kerr.

This is Jerry Wald's first as an indie for 20th-Fox. Picture can't help being a hit. But, equally important, it's a production that 20th can be proud to sell. From the hilarious beginning (radio commentators in New York, Rome and London disclosing Grant's engagement in their individual styles) to the sock ending, this is the kind of tears-and-laughter film that exhibitors will call a boon for the business. *Hift.*

La Revolucion Mexicana
(THE MEXICAN REVOLUTION)
Berlin, June 26.

Clasa Films Mundiales production. Directed by Luis Spota, camera, J. Carlos Carbajal; music, G. Cesar Carrion. At Berlin Film Festival. Running time, 84 MINS.

This Mexican full-length documentary, presenting little known aspects of the big Movement of Modern Mexican painting through the medium of painters like Clemente Orozco, Diego Rivera, David Alfaro and others, became one of Berlin Film Festival disappointments. What might have been a fairly interesting short subject, proves a tiresome enterprise as a full-length film.

Photographed paintings and frescos were not particularly impressive. Worst of all the narrative text was so one-sided (politically speaking) and so hammering in its Leftist propaganda tendency that it was completely out of place at this festival. It did the Mexicans small credit. *Hans.*

Courage of Black Beauty
(COLOR)

Good for Saturday matinee crowd. For old folks horsey tale may be a yawn.

Hollywood, July 10.

20th-Fox release of an Alco (Edward L. Alperson) Pictures Corp. production. Co-stars John Crawford, Mimi Gibson, John Bryant, Diane Brewster, J. Pat O'Malley, Russell Johnson; with Ziva Rodann. Director, Harold Schuster; screenplay, Steve Fisher; camera, John W. Boyle; editor, John Ehrin; music, Edward L. Alperson Jr. Songs, "Black Beauty" by Alperson and Paul Herrick, "The Donkey Game Song" by Alperson, and Dick Hughes and Richard Stapley. Previewed, July 9, '57. Running time, 78 MINS.

Bobby Adams	John Crawford
Lily Rowden	Mimi Gibson
Sam Adams	John Bryant
Ann Rowden	Diane Brewster
Mike Green	J. Pat O'Malley
Ben Ferraday	Russell Johnson
Janet Corday	Ziva Rodann

The Saturday matinee crowd may be glued to its seats, but unless the accompanying older generation are avid animal lovers, the going will be otherwise rough. To credit of producer Edward L. Alperson, sequelling his previous "Black Beauty" feature, he's mounted a clean, wholesome tale. However, it's an infantile offering for infantile audiences.

Contrived screenplay by Steve Fisher relates conflict between difficult lad, Johnny Crawford, and his widower father, John Bryant. Father owns a San Fernardo Valley horse ranch (and is also an agent, it's indicated) and gives boy a new-born foal, who grows up to be handsome Black Beauty. Thereafter, picture wanders through a couple of minor crises, until horse is seriously injured through father's carelessness. At last moment, when it seems the animal must be destroyed, forced finale pulls him through and affects reconciliation all around.

Harold Schuster's direction is slow-paced and elementary, aimed at pic's probable clientele. Young Crawford continues to impress as a good juve actor, despite plot confusions, but Bryant can't do much with father's role. Neither can Diane Brewster, as a widowed neighbor, and Russell Johnson, as her foreman. Cuteness of Mimi Gibson, as her moppest daughter, is continually stressed, but with complete lack of acting ability she cloys easily. J. Pat O'Malley scores as the father's trainer and the boy's confidante. Ziva Rodann is okay in a bit as one of pop's clients, directly responsible for the horse's injury.

Pathe color lensing of John W. Boyle wisely uses bright, primary colors throughout, in view of eventual audience. Cutting is extremely jerky, switching back and forth innumerable times between very short snippets of film. This eventually grates.

There's too much lush background music by Edward L. Alperson Jr., with never a moment of surcease throughout. Couple of Alperson's songs, "Black Beauty" with lyrics by Paul Herrick and "The Donkey Game Song" with lyrics by Dick Hughes and Richard Stapley, also stress kiddie orientation. *Kove.*

Bop Girl Goes Calypso
(SONGS)

Mild musical badly out-guessed by events on its premise that calypso would replace rock 'n roll. Strictly filler.

United Artists release of a Bel-Air production. Stars Judy Tyler, Bobby Troup,

Margo Woode and the musical acts the Mary Kaye Trio, The Goofers, Lord Flea and his Calypsonians, Nino Tempo, The Titans; features Lucien Littlefield, George O'Hanlon, Jerry Barclay, Judy Harriet. Producer, Aubrey Schenck; director, Howard W. Koch; screenplay, Arnold Belgard from a story by Hendrik Vollaerts; camera, Carl E. Guthrie; editor, Sam Waxman; music, Les Baxter. Previewed July 8, '57. Running time, **80 MINS.**

Jo Thomas	Judy Tyler
Robert Hilton	Bobby Troup
Marion Hendricks	Margo Woode
Professor Winthrop	Lucien Littlefield
Barney	George O'Hanlon
Jerry	Jerry Barclay
Young girl singer	Judy Harriet
Drunk	Gene O'Donnell
Taxi Driver	Edward Kafafian
Record Company Reps	George Sawaya, Jerry Frank, Dick Standish
Musical Acts	Mary Kaye Trio, The Goofers, Lord Flea Calypsonians, Nino Tempo, The Titans, The Cubanos

Current trend has invalidated much of the basic premise of "Bop Girl Goes Calypso," vitiating the potential it might have had earlier as a musical programmer. Some top specialty acts give it some appeal but otherwise marquee names and exploitation pegs rate secondary position where response will be mild.

Bel-Air production was conceived during what then appeared to be a burgeoning calypso craze and is based on the theory that the Trinidado tempo would replace rock 'n roll. It didn't. In the course of attempting to prove its unprovable point, a pedestrian screenplay by Arnold Belgard gets spasmodic lifts from 14 musical numbers, some of them performed by such cafe greats as the Mary Kaye Trio or the novelty act, the Goofers. Only real Trinidado talent involved is Lord Flea and his Calypsonians, hardly well-known.

Story line is based on research conducted by psychologist Bobby Troup for a thesis entitled "Mass Hysteria and the Popular Singer." His charts show calypso coming and R&R going to singer Judy Tyler agrees to make a style switch. She gets both Troup and fame in time for the fadeout.

Major mystery of the production is why producer Aubrey Schenck cast a musician of Bobby Troup's competence in a straight dramatic role in a musical film. He's personable, but no actor. Miss Tyler, who was killed in a July 4 car crash, shows to tremendous advantage here, indicating the accident cut off what could have been a promising career. She was both pert and proficient. Sole other top billed performer is Margo Woode, back in films after a lengthy absence. She is attractive as a eugenics researcher and registers strongly in the part. Lucien Littlefield and George O'Hanlon are good in the key featured spots and young Judy Harriet scores with one song number.

Howard W. Koch directed with a light touch and Les Baxter has done a good job of integrating the music and providing an overall musical pattern. Oldie "Fools Rush In' is revived by the Mary Kaye Trio, in a sock rendition that reprises their topnotch nitery stints. Technical credits are stock.

Kap.

Pawnee
(COLOR)

Stock cowboy-and-Indian, despite efforts to add story twists. Average outlook for western bookings.

Hollywood, July 9.

Republic release of a (Jack J.) Gross-(Philip N.) Krasne Production. Stars George Montgomery; co-stars Bill Williams; Lola Albright. Director, George Waggner; screenplay, Waggner, Louis Vittes, Endre Bohem; camera, Hal McAlpin; editor, Kenneth G. Crane; art director, Nicolai Remisoff; music, Paul Sawtell. Previewed July 8, '57. Running time, **79 MINS.**

Paul	George Montgomery
Matt	Bill Williams
Meg	Lola Albright
Tip	Francis J. McDonald
Doc	Robert E. Griffin
Brewster	Dabbs Greer
Mrs. Carter	Kathleen Freeman
Dancing Fawn	Charlotte Austin
Wise Eagle	Ralph Moody
Mrs. Brewster	Anne Barton
Obie Dilks	Raymond Hatton
Crazy Fox	Charles Horvath
Carter	Robert Nash

Story twists planted in "Pawnee," in an effort to set it off from other cowboy-and-Indian epics, don't add up to anything significant. Result, despite apparent efforts of Gross-Krasne production outfit to lend class, is pretty stock. Still, there's always a market for an action western and "Pawnee" should fill this bill for moderate returns.

George Montgomery portrays paleface adopted into Pawnee tribe as a child by chief Ralph Moody. Perhaps if tale woven by George Waggner (who also directed), Louis Vittes and Endre Bohem had stressed Indian lore, impact would have been more striking.

However, most footage revolves around Montgomery's misadventures in guiding a wagon train to Oregon, in an effort to learn the ways of his real people. He gets it from both sides: Indians think he's turned against his adoptive folk and the whites, when they learn who he really is, think he's a treacherous renegade.

Hotheaded Pawnee rival Charles Horvath wrests control from Montgomery when the chief dies and puts tribe on warpath against the train. Montgomery, also driven away from the train by wagonmaster Bill Williams, brings the U.S. Cavalry in the nick of time to rescue the besieged pioneers, killing Horvath in hand-to-hand combat.

Of course, there's romance, with Montgomery winning the love of Lola Albright away from Williams, foresaking redskin beauty Charlotte Austin in the process.

Waggner stages a good action sequence, but falls into cliches with subtle-relationships. Montgomery carries off required heroics ably enough, and Williams registers well as the doughty wagonmaster. Miss Albright is pictorially effective, but shows need of considerable thespic polish. Francis J. McDonald, Robert E. Griffin, Greer, Miss Barton and Kathleen Freeman as pioneers and Miss Austin, Horvath and Moody as the redskin contingent are okay.

Perhaps print viewed wasn't properly corrected, but Trucolor tint process was variable in quality, tending toward blues and purples of palette. Other technical credits are adequate, save one sequence in which a boom shadow was noticeable.

Kove.

Hidden Fear

Senseless violence, obscure plotting. Cops 'n' robbers through Copenhagen's streets. John Payne's name and unusual Danish background only points in favor.

Hollywood, July 8.

United Artists release of a (Robert) St. Aubrey-(Howard E.) Kohn (11) Production. Stars John Payne; co-stars Alexander Knox, Conrad Nagel, Natalie Norwick, Anne Neyland; features Kjeld Jacobsen, Paul Erling. Director, Andre de Toth; screenplay, de Toth-John Ward Hawkins; camera, Wilfred M. Cline; editor, David Wages; music, Hans Schreiber. Reviewed, Iris Theatre, Hollywood, July 8, '57. Running time, **83 MINS.**

Mike Brent	John Payne
Hartman	Alexander Knox
Arthur Miller	Conrad Nagel
Susan Brent	Natalie Norwick
Virginia Kelly	Anne Neyland
Lt. Knudsen	Kjeld Jacobsen
Gibbs	Paul Erling
Lund	Mogens Brandt
Helga Hartman	Marianne Schleiss
Jacobsen	Knud Rex
Inga	Elsie Albiin
Hans Ericsen	Buster Larsen
Jensen	Kjeld Petersen
Slim man	Preben Mahrt

While searching through Copenhagen for the baddies in this crime melodrama, John Payne should have dug himself up a plot, as well. This feature has the air of an early-day two-reeler, where the story was written on the director's cuffs. Overdrastic cutting doesn't help clarify matters. Despite the Payne name and the unusual locale, (shot in Denmark last year), this UA release seems destined to bore rather than entertain.

Andre de Toth-John Ward Hawkins story, if correctly deciphered, has something to do with Payne's efforts to clear his sister, Natalie Norwick, of a murder rap. Payne a Yank cop on leave, has a penchant for doing things the hard way and soon uncovers a counterfeiting ring, headed by Alexander Knox and with Conrad Nagel and Paul Erling as chief henchies.

After a full quota of beak-bustings and noggin-crackings, Payne practically singlehandedly polishes off the gang and clears sis, in a manner never clearly explained. Wandering through the strategic moments are a succession of Nordic beauties, who cast meaningful glances at Payne. Eventually, Anne Neyland, as a Yank performer in Copenhagen, leads the pack by an inch or two of chest expansion.

DeToth directed his own script, perpetuating his own confusion. Emphasis is on heavyhanded action and largely-senseless violence. De Toth is additionally hampered by technical work not up to U.S. standards. Sound recording is especially bad, with large patches of dialogue completely unintelligible. Additionally, print viewed was badly scratched.

Cast was distinctly uneven in quality, ranging from adequate downward. In the former category are Payne, Knox, Nagel, Erling, Miss Norwick and Kjeld Jacobsen as a Danish detective. Miss Neyland is blessed with a spectacular torso, which she exhibits more than customary on U.S. screens. Elsie Albiin, as a Copenhagen demimonde, also registers solidly in the s.a. department.

Kove.

Man of Thousand Faces
(C'SCOPE)

Life of Lon Chaney translated to a tearjerker that should appeal to general audiences, particularly distaffers. Topnotch portrayal by James Cagney.

Universal release of Robert Arthur production. Stars James Cagney, Dorothy Malone and Jane Greer. Features Marjorie Rambeau, Jim Backus, Robert J. Evans, and Celia Lovsky. Directed by Joseph Pevney. Screenplay, R. Wright Campbell, Ivan Goff and Ben Robert from story by Ralph Wheelwright; camera (C'Scope), Russell Metty; editor, Ted J. Kent; music, Frank Skinner. Previewed in N.Y. July 9, '57. Running time, **122 MINS.**

Lon Chaney	James Cagney
Cleva Creighton Chaney	Dorothy Malone
Hazel Bennet	Jane Greer
Gert	Marjorie Rambeau
Clarence Locan	Jim Backus
Irving Thalbert	Robert J. Evans
Mrs. Chaney	Celia Lovsky
Carrie Chaney	Jeanne Cagney
Dr. J. Wilson Shields	Jack Albertson
Creighton Chaney (at 21)	Roger Smith
Creighton (at 13)	Robert Lyden
Creighton (at 8)	Rickie Sorensen
Creighton (at 4)	Dennis Rush
Pa Chaney	Nolan Leary
Carl Hastings	Simon Scott
Clarence Kolb	Himself
Max Dill	Danny Beck
George Loane Tucker	Phil Van Zandt
Comedy Waiter	Hank Mann
Comedy Waiter	Snub Pollard

Having opened its own strain of biography ("The Glenn Miller Story," "To Hell and Back," and "The Benny Goodman Story"), Universal is again delving into the life of a famous personality in "Man Of A Thousand Faces." The title stems from the billing given the late Universal, later Metro, star, Lon Chaney by an alert publicity man. As everyone old enough to have lived through the silent film era is well aware, Chaney was one of the stalwarts of the period and any history of the motion picture industry would be woefully incomplete if it did not include this talented, tortured man, excellently portrayed by James Cagney in the present telling.

The R. Wright Campbell-Ivan Goff-Ben Roberts screenplay based on a story by Ralph Wheelwright is mainly concerned with Chaney's complicated domestic problems. His achievements as a consummate artist, while woven into the story, are secondary to his mixed up private life. As a result, "Man of a Thousand Faces," as presented in the Robert Arthur production, emerges as an unashamed soap opera tearjerker. This is not meant in a disparaging sense, for it is this very quality which will probably find favor with general audiences.

Here is not a film for the sophisticate or the discerning critic. But as a popular entry, it stands a good chance of duplicating U's previous successes with biofilms.

It'll have to be sold carefully. The majority of current film-goers may but barely remember Chaney or his accomplishments. However, it'll draw the silent film buffs and the nostaligic oldsters. In addition, if the word gets around, it'll bring in the distaffers in droves, for it'll give 'em a chance to experience an emotional catharsis and exercise their tear ducts.

The story, in swift sequences, takes Chaney from his early boyhood to his death of throat cancer. Born of deaf and dumb parents, this an important emotional factor in Chaney's motivations. Screenplay ranges song-and-dance vaudeville days, two marriages, the birth of his son, early struggles as a Hollywood extra, eventual rise to stardom, and tragic death. He is presented as a stubborn, unforgiving man bitterly resentful of his first wife's walkout.

As Chaney, Cagney gives one of his most notable performances. He has immersed himself so completely in the role that it is difficult to spot any Cagney mannerisms. Jane Greer, as his second wife, is particuarly appealing in her devotion to her "difficult" spouse. Dorothy Malone is fine as the wife who deems her career as a singer more important than raising children. Other good performances are turned in by Jim Backus, as Chaney's loyal and understanding press-agent friend; Robert J. Evans, as Irving Thalberg who is first production chief at Universal and then at Metro; Roger Smith, as Chaney's grown son, Creighton, who later assumed the name of Lon Chaney Jr., and Marjorie Rambeau, as a film extra.

A real heart-tug is provided by Celia Lovsky as Chaney's deaf and dumb mother. The scenes in which Miss Lovsky appears will have femme viewers drying their eyes. Nolan Leary is also effective as Pa Chaney.

Director Joseph Pevney gets the most out of the heart-tugging scenes. Technical aspects are top-notch, including Russell Metty's photography and the art direction of Alexander Golitzen and Eric Orbom. Bud Westmore deserves special mention for the excellent make-up jobs on the various characters portrayed by Chaney. The music by Frank Skinner has a hearts-and-flowers tinge. *Holl.*

Jeanne Eagels

Kim Novak and Jeff Chandler in unexciting biopic. Performances let down potentially interesting yarn. Must ride on star names for b.o. recognition.

Columbia release of a George Sidney production. Stars Kim Novak, Jeff Chandler; co-stars Agnes Moorehead; features Charles Drake, Larry Gates, Virginia Grey, Gene Lockhart, Joe De Santis, Murray Hamilton. Directed by Sidney. Screenplay, Daniel Fuchs, Sonya Levien, John Fante from a story by Fuchs. Camera, Robert Planck; editors, Viola Lawrence, Jerome Thoms; music, George Duning. Previewed July 17, 1957. Running time: **108 MINS.**

Jeanne Eagels	Kim Novak
Sal Satori	Jeff Chandler
Mme. Neilson	Agnes Moorehead
John Donahue	Charles Drake
Al Brooks	Larry Gates
Elsie Desmond	Virginia Grey
Equity Board President	Gene Lockhart
Frank Satori	Joe de Santis
Chick O'Hara	Murray Hamilton

Disclaimer on "Jeanne Eagels" is one of the most unusual in picture annals. It reads: "all events in this photoplay are based on fact and fiction." It may be assumed that the fiction predominates and the character names are mostly phoney.

In real life the actress blockbusted Broadway in 1922 when Freud was new and Somerset Maugham was hot. "Rain" also had some jabs at the Protestant clergy, not then popular because of prohibition. The authors are intent upon telling a story rather than history so this background is just for the record. For the record, too, is the doubt that Jeanne Eagels was, as the Columbia press agents would have it, "the greatest" native actress of the century. Her one big smack was "Rain."

Jeanne Eagels may have been one of the great actresses and dynamic personalities of this century, but this biofilm will hardly prove it. Those who saw Eagels in her heyday will not recognize any likeness in Kim Novak; those who didn't see Miss Eagels will most certainly not recognize her as a great actress as portrayed by Miss Novak. More likely, majority of audiences will find themselves hard put to endure the overlong, highly contrived story that promises but never fulfills any dramatic high spots. If "Eagels" does business, it will do so chiefly on strength of the star names.

It's surprising that so colorful and meteoric a personality as Miss Eagels could provide such slight inspiration of scripters Daniel Fuchs, Sonya Levien and John Fante. Miss Eagels, who had more than the normal share of interesting human frailties, emerges as a dull, complacent blonde better fitted for the cook stove than Broadway stage. When attempting to portray the carny cooch dancer, or later a temperamental star, there is neither true temper nor temperament in the unbelievable screen characterization and situations.

Producer-director George Sidney mounted film very well and tried to breathe some life into the story with some directorial tricks, many of them cliche, but didn't quite succeed. Also, quite obviously, producer Sidney failed to wield his editorial shears on director Sidney, with the result the story rambles on and on. In this case, boy loses girl and vice versa not once but five different times. Also, Sidney must shoulder the blame for the most unattractive appearance of Jeff Chandler, who is hatted and photographed in such manner as to possibly affect his screen future.

Story picks up Miss Eagels as the pickup of a travelling salesman who gets his way with her by promising her the first prize in a beauty contest in a carnival operated by friend Chandler. She loses, but stays with Chandler and, as romance blooms, becomes the sideshow coocher among other things on the midway. Consumed by a burning ambition for the Broadway stage, she makes a bee-line for dramatic coach Agnes Moorehead's studio the moment she and Chandler reach New York, he to becomes partner in his brother's Coney Island operation. Things become strangely easy for Miss Eagels, after Miss Moorehead's early disinclination to coach a beginner, and she's on her way to stardom when she subs for a vacationing player. Next step is when she double-crosses a former star and gets a leading role in "Rain." This also supposedly leads her to drink and dope when the star jumps to death and Miss Eagels sees the broken body on pavement. It all looks fictional, particularly the scene showing Miss Novak playing Eagels in a scene from "Rain," and probably is fictional except for her marriage to a football player and her suspension by Actors Equity for failure to do a performance.

Miss Novak, if little else in this film, looks very good and bears well the clothes of the period. Chandler is not only not at his best pictorially, but he doesn't quite look or play the part of an Italian-American carny man. More attuned to his role is Charles Drake, as the easy-going society boy footballer. Miss Moorehead is far too dramatic and artificial in her early scenes, later settling down for more realistic and sympathetic performance. Virginia Grey, as the suicidal faded star, Larry Gates, as a legit producer, Gene Lockhart, Joe de Santis and Murray Hamilton are okay in support.

Robert Planck's camera work on the whole is excellent. Ditto Ross Bellah's art direction and George Duning's unobtrusive music score. *Hift.*

Valerie

Strong story and good cast names. Brutality and sadistic episodes may alienate some; only laid in west, not an oater.

Hollywood, July 20.

United Artists release of a Hal R. Makelim production. Stars Sterling Hayden, Anita Ekberg, Anthony Steel; features Peter Walker, Jerry Barclay, Iphigenie Castiglioni, John Wengraf, Gage Clarke, Tom McKee. Directed by Gerd Oswald. Screenplay, Leonard Heideman, Emmett Murphy. Camera, Ernest Laszlo; editor, David Bretherton; art director, Frank Smith; music, Albert Glasser. Previewed, June 19, '57. Running time. **81 MINS.**

John Garth	Sterling Hayden
Valerie	Anita Ekberg
Reverend Blake	Anthony Steel
Herb Garth	Peter Walker
Louis Horvat	John Wengraf
Mrs. Horvat	Iphigenie Castiglioni
Mingo	Jerry Barclay
Lundy	Robert Adler
Dave Carlin	Tom McKee
Lawyer Griggs	Gage Clarke
Judge Frisbee	Sidney Smith
Nurse Linsey	Juney Ellis
Dr. Jackson	Stanley Adams

Producer Hal Makelim has come up with a success d'estime, in this challenging experiment. Whether it will be a success d' box-office remains to be seen, but with strong story and good cast names, it might prove a sleeper. Drawback (or perhaps not) is the large dose of brutality and sadism depicted on the screen, which may alienate certain audience segments.

The Leonard Heideman-Emmett Murphy tale, briskly and imaginatively directed by Gerd Oswald, is laid in the west, but is by no means a western. Rather, it is a gothic and sombre psychological tale which repeats the same theme three times, each time from the viewpoint of a different character. Save for a preposterously melodramatic finale, which doesn't fit, it's a well-told tale and a work of solid craftsmanship. Plot technique is similar to the one used in the Japanese film, "Roshomon," a couple of years ago.

Story starts with bloody shooting fray, in which Sterling Hayden and his henchmen wipe out the family of his estranged wife, Anita Ekberg, and seriously wounds her. At the trial, sympathy is on his side, since he's a leading citizen, a war hero (Civil War), and Miss Ekberg supposedly was running away with handsome preacher Anthony Steel.

But Steel's testimony, related in backflash, relates another version; that he was helping an ill and neglected parishoner by taking her to her parents. Hayden's story, also told in flashback, is that she was a loose wanton, only interested in his money, who had seduced his younger brother, Peter Walker, and was carrying on an affair with Steel.

But Miss Ekberg, supposedly near death, regains consciousness and gives her testimony, later proven. Here, Hayden had married her for a substantial dowry (her European parents, John Wengraf and Iphigenie Castiglioni, had followed old-world custom of marrying her off to a local figure, to gain security). Also, Hayden had framed the supposed affair, so he'd have an excuse to kill the pair. Shooting of her family was an aftermath, when that scheme failed.

At this point his loyal henchman, Jerry Barclay, gets the drop on the court attendants and helps his boss escape. But brother Walker shoots it out with the duo and kills them, for a finale.

All three stars show up strong in wide emotional ranges required in different versions. Hayden turns in one of his best chores in years, while Miss Ekberg impresses as an actress as well as a scenic wonder. Steel, with less to do, still makes both his characters convincing.

Especially noteworthy in support are Walker, with considerable promise shown, and Tom McKee and Gage Clarke, as opposing attorneys. Wengraf and Miss Castiglioni, Stanley Adams as a compassionate doctor and Barclay all make small parts count.

Black-and-white camera work of Ernest Laszlo is cleancut and toprate. Other technical credits reflect solid professionalism. *Kove.*

Gun Glory
(C'SCOPE-COLOR)

Stewart Granger and Rhonda Fleming in a color western. Some flaws but okay boxoffice.

Metro release of a Nicholas Nayfack production. Stars Stewart Granger, Rhonda Fleming; co-stars Chill Wills. Features Steve Rowland, Jacques Aubuchon, James Gregory, Arch Johnson. Directed by Roy Rowland. Screenplay, William Ludwig from Philip Yordan's novel "Man of the West"; camera, (Metrocolor) Harold J. Marzorati; editor, Frank Santillo; music, Jeff Alexander. Previewed Culver City, Cal., July 18, '57. Running time, **88 MINS.**

Tom Early	Stewart Granger
Jo	Rhonda Fleming

Preacher	Chill Wills
Young Tom Early	Steve Rowland
Grimsell	James Gregory
Sam Wainscott	Jacques Aubuchon
Gunn	Arch Johnson

Action and starkly photogenic backgrounds, excellently lensed in Metrocolor, help sustain interest in the ordinary western story that is "Gun Glory." It has been proficiently put together by producer Nicholas Nayfack, directed with a shrewd sense of values by Roy Rowland and competently trouped by a cast headed by Stewart Granger and Rhonda Fleming, whose names will be of some marquee value. Overall boxoffice prospects are okay.

William Ludwig screenplayed from Philip Yordan's "Man of the West," the story of a man who makes the most of a second chance; Stewart Granger, returning home after a three year absence during which he acquired a reputation as a gunslinger and gambler, finds his wife has died in his absence and his 17-year-old has turned against him. He resolves to stay and work out a new life but is immediately catapulted into trouble when cattleman James Gregory threatens to run a big herd through the peaceful farming valley, ruining the property so that he can use a shortcut to the market. Townspeople, led by preacher Chill Wills and egged on by crippled storekeeper Jacques Aubuchon, pay no heed to Granger's warning that men like Gregory understand only the language of the gun. When one of the townspeople is killed en route to Laramie to get help, they finally decide to fight but Gregory's men massacre them and start the cattle through the pass. Granger dynamites the mountain to halt the drive, wins out in a showdown fight and gains the love both of his son and of Rhonda Fleming, beautiful widow who had been the only one to accept his return.

Granger is very good in the role and there's virtually no trace of a British accent to mark the careful characterization. Miss Fleming is both easy to look at and capable in her part and Wills turns in an excellent performance as the preacher. There is fine support from Aubuchon, Gregory and Arch Johnson, a gunslinger, but much of the film is thrown to Steve Rowland, son of the director, in the role of Granger's son, and he is far too inexperienced to handle the footage.

Color photography by Harold J. Marzorati is good and other technical credits are stock. Music by Jeff Alexander is unobstrusive. Song, "The Ninety and Nine," is sung by Burl Ives behind the main title credits to help set the aura of the returning prodigal. *Kap.*

The Young Don't Cry

Mediocre filler fare with only new following of Sal Mineo to help at the b.o.

Hollywood, July 16.

Columbia release of Philip A. Waxman production. Stars Sal Mineo, James Whitmore, J. Carrol Naish; features Gene Lyons. Directed by Alfred L. Werker. Screenplay, Richard Jessup, from his novel; Camera, Ernest Haller; editor, Maurice Wright; music, George Antheil. Previewed June 27, '57. Running time, **89 MINS.**

Leslie Henderson	Sal Mineo
Rudy Krist	James Whitmore
Plug	J. Carrol Naish
Max Cole	Gene Lyons
Bradley	Paul Carr
Clancy	Thomas Carlin
Doosy	Leigh Whipper
Billy	Stefan Gierasch
Whittaker	Victor Throley
Maureen Cole	Roxanne
Mr. Gwinn	James Reese
Philomena	Ruth Attaway
Allan	Leland Mayforth
Jimmy	Dick Wigginton
Stanley	Stanley Martin
Mrs. Gwinn	Josephine Smith
Solomon	Joseph Killorin
Whigs	Phillips Hamilton
Hardhead	Victor Johnson

This Philip A. Waxman production seems to have a message—something about the necessity for youth to decide on the right way of life. Film's chief asset is the fine performance turned in by Sal Mineo in the lead, and some profitable playdates might result from this lad's rising b.o. value. Basically, however, pic is no more than mediocre filler fare.

"Cry," made independently for Columbia release, was filmed in its entirety in and around the Brockton Orphanage for Boys near Savannah, Ga. As screenplayed by Richard Jessup from his own novel, footage is frequently wordy and the action often aimless. Plot concerns Mineo, one of the "older" boys at Brockton, trying to "find himself" before setting out in the world. At the windup, it appears that he has. Other main characters in the mixup are: James Whitmore, convict working near Brockton on a road gang who utilizes an unwilling Mineo to make his escape; J. Carrol Naish, brutal prison warden who eventually kills Whitmore; and Gene Lyons, Brockton alumni who's become a millionaire by ruthless methods and thus is an idol to some and the opposite to others. Naish, always a top pro, fares best of the trio. Showing up well in support are Paul Carr, a sullen nasty-tempered Brockton youth; Leigh Whipper, Negro convict who aids Whitmore's escape and is shot in the process; and Ruth Attaway, Negress living in the vicinity who has a motherly interest in the Brockton boys. There's also a notable bit from an 11-year-old youth in the role of Crispy, also of Brockton.

The Savannah exteriors are well utilized in the Waxman production, with Alfred L. Werker's direction showing up best in the individual scenes. Ernest Haller's camera work is ace high; the musical score by George Antheil, good. *Neal.*

Apache Warrior
(REGALSCOPE)

Example of intelligence and skill applied to modest budget. Well-made and scripted Indian yarn which can serve a wide variety of booking situations.

Hollywood, July 15.

20th-Fox release of a Regal Films Production. Stars Keith Larsen, Jim Davis, Rodolfo Acosta, introduces Eugenia Paul; features John Miljan, Damian O'Flynn, George Keymas, Lane Bradford, Dehl Berti. Produced by Plato Skouras. Directed by Elmo Williams; screenplay, Carroll Young, Kurt Neumann, Eric Norden, from Young-Neumann story; camera, John M. Nickolaus Jr.; editor, Jodie Copelan; music, Paul Dunlap. Previewed June 15, '57. Running time, **73 MINS.**

Apache Kid	Keith Larsen
Ben	Jim Davis
Marteen	Rodolfo Acosta
Nantan	John Miljan
Apache No. 1	Eddie Little
Apache No. 2	Michael Carr
Chato	George Keymas
Sgt. Gaunt	Lane Bradford
Liwana	Eugenia Paul
Major	Damian O'Flynn
Chikisin	Dehl Berti
Horse Trader	Nick Thompson
Bounty Man No. 1	Ray Kellogg
Bounty Man No. 2	Allan Nixon
Bounty Man No. 3	Karl Davis
Cavalry Leader	David Carlile

Slated for the program trade, nevertheless this well-made and scripted Indian yarn, out of the Regal Films schedule for 20th-Fox, stands as an example of intelligence and skill applied to a modest budget. Chances are hampered somewhat by lack of strong name values, but this offering still can fit a wide variety of situations with good results.

Scripted by Carroll Young, Kurt Neumann and Eric Norden tale underlines predicament of proud Apaches after defeat of Geronimo, without undue sentimentality. Keith Larsen portrays "Apache Kid," an Indian scout working for Army to quell last resistance of scattered war parties and to establish a firm peace. He's a close friend of white scout Jim Davis.

However, he's still Apache. When hotheaded brave George Keymas kills his brother, Larsen fulfils primitive Apache law by hunting down and slaying Keymas. Brassbound army major, Damian O'Flynn, condemns him to prison for this, but Larsen escapes with killer Rodolfo Acosta and his band. During escape, Davis is seriously wounded by Acosta, and thinks his ex-buddy, Larsen, is responsible. After his recovery, Davis goes hunting for Larsen, unjustly accused of Acosta's renewed raids, and Larsen's newly-wed squaw, Eugenia Paul. But Larsen convinces Davis he didn't do the shooting and all three successfully combine against an unsavory trio of white bounty hunters, after Larsen's scalp.

Larsen is becoming a specialist in Indian roles (he's tv's "Brave Eagle") and turns in a perceptive, well-balanced portrayal. Davis, with a strong role, impresses. Miss Paul debuts with a bright personality and engaging promise. As unreconstructed Apache menace, Acosta contribues convincing savagery.

Vet John Miljan, as elderly, crippled Apache chief, is very good in support. O'Flynn, Keymas, Lane Bradford and Dehl Berti, also rate favorable notice.

Elmo Williams' direction is deft and sensitive, cleanly outlining problems of period and place, yet leaving proceedings with plenty of well-thought-out action. Technical credits reflect favorably to behind-the-camera crew, considering short budget. *Kove.*

Amanecer en Puerta Oscura
(Whom God Forgives)
(SPANISH-COLOR)

Berlin, July 2.

Juan Kopecky production, Madrid. Stars Francisco Rabal, Luis Pena, Alberto Farnese, Isabel de Pomes. Directed by Jose M. Forque. Screenplay, Alfonso Sastre, N. Zaro, Jose M. Forque; music, Regino Sainz de la Maza; camera (Eastmancolor), Cecilio Paniagua. At Berlin Film Fest. Running time, **99 MINS.**

Spain's entry at the Berlin film fest turned out to be a thrilling tale centering around three murderers who are chased, captured and sentenced to death. One of them, however, is acquitted due to God's decision—the finger of Jesus el Rico during a religion procession points at him and, according to an old Spanish religious law, this means acquittal.

Film has impressive acting and excellent color photography on its plus side. Direction is not smooth all the way but suspense prevails throughout. Due to pic's religious ingredients, it won't have general appeal but stands a good chance in Latin territories. Reception in Berlin was split two ways—some were thrilled, others bored. *Hans.*

Felicidad
(MEXICAN-COLOR)

Berlin, July 3.

Cinematografica Nacional, S.A. production. Stars Gloria Lozano, Carlos Lopez Moctezuma and Fanny Schiller. Directed by Alfonso Corona Blake. Screenplay, Emilio Costallido; camera, Rosalio Solano; music, Raul Savista. At Berlin Film Fest. Running time, **121 MINS.**

This Spanish release centers around an aging professor who falls in love with a girl whom he pretends to marry. Since he, however, is already married, this brings the girl the biggest disillusionment of her life, while his own marriage nearly goes to the rocks. Latino plotting is hard for others to take seriously. However, "Felicidad" has positive values. One is beautiful Gloria Lozano, who sympathetically portrays the femme lead, the other one is Moctezuma who, very convincingly, enacts her aging partner.

Another plus the color photography. The shots of Acapulco are often breathtakingly beautiful. *Hans.*

El Fettowa
(Cupidity)
(EGYPTIAN)

Berlin, June 30.

Farid Chawki production. Stars Farid Chawki, Tahia Karioca, Zaki Rostom, Twefick el Dek'n. Directed and authored by Salah Abu Seif. At Berlin Film Festival. Running time, **132 MINS.**

Overlong Egyptian feature mounts an attack against "capi' talists" and demands rights and freedom for the needy. Remarkably clumsy in its techniques, often unintentionally funny, mostly just too noisy—this is (or would be if shown) a strange item for western audiences.

Farid Shawki, who also produced this one, has an interesting face as star. He claimed here picture shows an important aspect of Egypt's society. Be that as it may. *Hans.*

Freedom for Ghana
(GHANA)

Berlin, July 2.

Ghana Film Unit production. Directed by Sean Graham. Camera, Georg Noble, R. O. Fenuku, F. I. Lagden, I. Fajemisin. Editing, G. Aryeetey. At Berlin Film Fest. Running time, **88 MINS.**

Ghana, West African colony which just recently obtained its independence from the United Kingdom, has in this full-length documentary first of its own film production. Film depicts this little state's independence festivities and attempts to explain how much and how long its populace has been longing for freedom.

Colorful dances and horse races are the highlights of this presentation which, in all, emerges as a rather awkward and technically amateurish but occasionally touching message of human aspiration. *Hans.*

Nije Bilo Uzalud
(It Was Not In Vain)
(YUGOSLAVIA)

Berlin, July 2.

Jadran Film production, Zagreb-Dubrava. Stars Boris Buzancic, Mira Nickolic, Zvonimir Rogoz, Zlata Perlic. Directed by Nikola Tanhofer; screenplay, Nikola Tanhofer, after an idea by Pero Budak; camera, Slavko Zalar; music, Milo Cipra. At Berlin Film Festival. Running time, 99 MINS.

Yugoslavian film industry product has considerably improved in recent years. This pic is by no means a masterpiece but it has impressive camerawork, good acting and even an interesting plot which may give it some (limited) chances for art houses. It's the **story of a young medic who comes to a deserted village whose narrow-minded inhabitants first show a dislike for him but in the end he wins their confidence when he frees them from a notorious evildoer.**

Direction by Nikola Tanhofer deserves the compliment of being at least satisfactory. Boris Buzancic, the medico, turns in a fully believable performance. Mira Nikolic, who gives her screen debut in this, portrays Bojka, the girl he falls in love with. Miss Nikolic, a real beauty, shows promising talent.

Technically, film is not smooth all the way but that doesn't spoil much the general good overall impression. *Hans.*

Ruf Der Goetter
(Call of the Gods)

Berlin, July 3.

Schorcht release. Directed by Dietrich Wawrzyn. Camera (Eastmancolor), Klaus Schumann; music, Peter Sandloff; commentator, Ernst Schnabel; editing, Heinz Pohl; expedition and production manager, Peter H. Backhaus. At Berlin Fest. Running time, 98 MINS.

This full-length documentary, an official German entry at the Berlin Film Festival, attempts to give an insight into India, its people, landscapes and culture. Although it's been declared "particularly valuable" by W. Germany's classification board, pic emerges as a considerable disappointment. It's rather jumpy and narration is poor.

Film's only asset is very beautiful Eastmancolor shooting. *Hans.*

These Dangerous Years
(WITH SONGS)

Crooner Frankie Vaughan on the run from a murder rap in army camp. Strong dramatic values.

London, July 4.

Associated British-Pathe release of an Anna Neagle production. Stars George Baker and Frankie Vaughan. Produced by Anna Neagle. Directed by Herbert Wilcox; screenplay, Jack Trevor Story; camera, Gordon Dines; editor, Basil Warren; music, Bert Waller. At Rialto Theatre, London, July 3, '57. Running time, 110 MINS.

The Padre	George Baker
Dave Wyman	Frankie Vaughan
Dinah Brown	Carole Lesley
Maureen	Jackie Lane
Mrs. Wyman	Katherine Kath
Mrs. Larkin	Thora Hird
Danny	Eddie Byrne
Juggler	Kenneth Cope
Cream O'Casey	Robert Desmond
Smiler Larkin	Ray Jackson
Captain Brewster	Richard Leech
Commanding Officer	John Le Mesurier
Sgt. Lockwood	David Lodge
Private Simpson	Michael Ripper
Camp Hairdresser	Reginald Beckwith
Sgt. Fawcett	Martin Boddey
Badger	John Breslin

An adult type of deadend kid drama that provides a good vehicle for the radio and disk crooner Frankie Vaughan. It is overlong but presents an entertaining problem of topical interest, the absorption by the army of juvenile delinquents. Lacking discipline and hating all kind of authority some come through and make fine men —some don't.

Story is set on the coastal outskirts of Liverpool docks, where a gang of youngsters make their headquarters, and though in the main harmless, get blamed for much of the neighborhood trouble. Their leader, Frankie and his pal are called up for military service, are posted to the same regiment and immediately get involved in brawls. A malicious older recruit fakes the rookies' instructions on the initiative test and the pair set out across the minefield, after knocking out the guards. Frankie is used to mines washed up near the docks and gets through, but his buddy gets killed and he is held responsible. In a fight the hoaxer draws a gun on him and gets killed, and from then on the dockside kid is on the run. After hiding out in his old rocky caves, he is sheltered by his girl and found by the Army Chaplain, who believes his story and persuades him to return for trial. Another soldier finally testifies and saves him from the condemned cell for a conventional happy ending.

Frankie Vaughan does well in this, his first screen appearance, his main obstacle being his maturity, which is too obvious in the early stages, but matters less when he goes into uniform. George Baker gives a sincere performance as the sympathetic Padre and Ray Jackson is good as the other rookie. Carole Lesley looks attractive as the girl who is pitchforked into romance with the deserter, and Jackie Lane, sister of Joan Collins, is cute as her tough little room mate. Army types are well characterized, and a good deal of humor is extracted from what is in the main a serious subject. Camera work is effective and direction by Herbert Wilcox on a high level. *Clem.*

Footsteps In The Night

Run-of-the-mill mystery.

Hollywood, July 18.

Allied Artists release of Ben Schwalb Production. Stars Bill Elliott. Features Don Haggerty, Eleanore Tanin, Douglas Dick, James Flavin, Gregg Palmer, Harry Tyler, Ann Griffith, Robert Shayne. Directed by Jean Yarbrough. Screenplay, Albert Band, Elwood Ullman; story, Band; camera, Harry Neumann; editor, Neil Brunnenkant; music, Marlin Skiles. Reviewed July 17, '57. Running time, 62 MINS.

Lieutenant Doyle	Bill Elliott
Sergeant Duncan	Don Haggerty
Mary Raiken	Eleanore Tanin
Henry Johnson	Douglas Dick
Fred Horner	Robert Shayne
Mr. Bradbury	Jamse Flavin
Pat Orvello	Gregg Palmer
Dick Harris	Harry Tyler
June Wright	Ann Griffith

A short and routine meller, "Footsteps In The Night" has Bill Elliott as the Jack Webbish detective called in to investigate a murder. The side-kick in this case is Don Haggerty. Douglas Dick, an avid card-playing gambler, is the main suspect, having played cards with the victim shortly before his strangulation, but the murderer actually is Gregg Palmer, neighborhood gas station owner with a long police record. Seems as though he mistakenly kills the wrong man in his attempt at robbery. Eleanore Tanin portrays Dick's fiance, but has nothing whatsoever to do with the plot.

The Albert Band-Elwood Ullman screenplay, from a story by the former, provides the basic mystery ingredients to keep up the interest, and Jean Yarbrough's direction gets it all on the screen competently.

Elliott has the majority of the footage, and his underplaying goes with the role. The others all turn in stock stints, with Dick faring perhaps a bit better than the rest.

Producer Ben Schwalb used his Allied Artists bungalow as the setting for a goodly portion of the action. *Neal.*

That Night

Excellently-made N. Y. production deals with heart attack and its family consequences. Despite power to grip audiences two factors must be overcome in selling: grim theme and tv origin of story.

Universal release of Galahad Production (Himan Brown) produced for RKO. Stars John Beal and Augusta Dabney. Directed by John Newland. Screenplay and story, Robert Wallace and Jack Rowles; camera, Maurice Hartzband; editor, David Cooper; music, Mario Nascimbene. Previewed in N. Y. July 15, '57. Running time, 88 MINS.

Chris Bowden	John Beal
Maggie Bowden	Augusta Dabney
Tommy Bowden	Malcolm Brodrick
Chrissie Bowden	Dennis Kohler
Betsey Bowden	Beverly Lunsford
Dr. Bernard Fischer	Shepperd Strudwick
Nurse Chornis	Rosemary Murphy
Dr. Perroni	Bill Darrid
Mr. Rosalie	Joe Julian

"That Night," one of the RKO pictures taken over by Universal, falls into an unusual category. It is a well-made, excellently performed and compelling film. Yet its very effectiveness may hamper its chances at the boxoffice. Many viewers may find it unpleasant just because it so successfully brings a sense of personal identification.

The Galahad production, produced by former radio packager Himan Brown at his (built with 'Inner Sanctum' profits) New York Production Center, is the story of a heart attack. It details minutely the experiences of a 41-year-old commuter who suffers his first seizure. Film is both a sociological and a clinical study.

It presents the tensions and strains of modern society that bring on the attack. The victim, a writer of tv commercials, is a "typical" suburbanite. He works in Manhattan and has a house in Connecticut. He is harrassed and badgered in his two separate worlds. In Manhattan, there is the pressure of his work, unpredictable hours and equally unpredictable demands from his bosses and clients. In Connecticut, there is the house, a wife and three children, washing machines, tv sets and all the expensive gadgetry of modern living to "keep up with the Jones."

The attack comes as the man is rushing to catch a train. Then follows in almost documentary style his trip to the hospital, his own fears of death, the treatment, notification of his family, the crisis, and his eventual recovery. The experience results in a complete reevaluation of his standards, a new sympathetic understanding between husband and wife, and a completely new outlook on life in general.

To the credit of those connected with making the film is the fact that they have done it honestly. Some of the scenes are so realistically staged that sensitive viewers could feel they are experiencing an attack of their own. There's no attempt to glamorize story or the performers.

As the heart attack victim, John Beal could easily pass for one of the myriads of commuters seen in Grand Central or Pennsylvania stations. Similarly Augusta Dabney, as the victim's wife, is a representative-surburban housewife. Both give the type of convincing and noteworthy performances that will rate important attention.

Based on a true-life incident detailed in a magazine article, the story was also presented on Robert Montgomery's tv show, a factor that may also hamper the picture's b.o. chances. Despite which as a modest-budget "small" picture, "That Night" represents an outstanding contribution in film-making. It's a picture that is worth seeing, but it'll take a lot of selling to convince the potential customers.

Robert Wallace and Jack Rowles provided the realistic and provocative story and screenplay; tv actor-director John Newland makes an auspicious bow as a theatrical film director, and producer Brown has set up production values that are right. Shepperd Strudwick, as the victim's doctor; Malcolm Brodrick, Dennis Kohler and Beverly Lunsford, as the victim's three young children; Rosemary Murphy, as a nurse; Bill Darrid, as a doctor, and Norman Corwin's old radio narrator, Joe Julian, as a patient, lend strong support.

Technical aspects are first-rate, including Maurice Hartzband's camerawork, Mel Bourne's art direction, David Cooper's editing, and Mario Nascimbene's music. *Holl.*

L'Ami De La Famille
(The Friend of the Family) (FRENCH)

Paris, July 16.

Discifilm release of Cyclope-Annery Film production. Stars Darry Cowl; features Raymond Bussieres, Annette Poivre, Micheline Dax, Pascale Audret, Jean-Claude Brialy, Beatrice Altariba. Directed by Jack Pinateau. Screenplay, Jacques Vilfrid, Jean Girault from a play by Jacques Sommet; camera, Pitrre Petit; editor, Georges Aristan. At Balzac, Paris. Running time, 85 MINS.

Pierre	Darry Cowl
Paul	Raymond Bussieres
Annette	Annette Poivre
Zozette	Micheline Dax
Monique	Pascal Audret
Sophie	Beatrice Altariba
Philippe	Jean-Claude Brialy

This is a sort of French "Man Who Came to Dinner." But here a zany character, who has been rebuffed by a girl, tries to commit suicide in a friend's home and then he moves in as they decide to cure him of his phobia. Comedy is in the havoc caused by this demanding character who upsets the life of the family. Main asset is the first starring role of comic Darry Cowl, but otherwise its humor is stilted and telegraphed ahead.

Cowl is a sort of amalgum of Harpo Marx and Jerry Lewis plus a stuttering manner of speech. He is only funny, however, when the material is strong enough to harbor his capers, and here the weak, talky plotting leaves the fun patchy.

Technical credits are good and supporting cast adequate, but director Jack Pinateau has relied too much on the shambling Cowl without making situations "logical" enough for acceptance. *Mosk.*

Miracle in Soho
(BRITISH-COLOR)

Rank Organization production and release. Stars John Gregson, Belinda Lee, with Cyril Cusack. Written and produced by Emeric Pressburger. Directed by Julian Amyes; camera, Christopher Challis; editor, Arthur Stevens; music by Brian Easdale. At Odeon, Leicester Square, London, July 9, '57. Running time, **98 MINS.**

Michael Morgan	John Gregson
Julia Gozzi	Belinda Lee
Sam Bishop	Cyril Cusack
Mafalda Gozzi	Rosalie Crutchley
Papa Gozzi	Peter Illing
Mama Gozzi	Marie Burke
Filippo Gozzi	Ian Bannen
Johnny	Brian Bedford
Gwladys	Barbara Archer
Tom	oJhn Cairney
Steve	Lane Meddick
Maggie	Billie Whitelaw
Potter	Julian Somers
Ernie	Harry Brunning
Old Bill	Douglas Ives
Foreman	George Cooper
Mr. Swoboda	Cyril Shaps
Karl	Richard Marner
Buddy Brown	Gordon Humphris
Mrs. Coleman	Betty Shale
Delia	Junia Crawford
Lorry Drive	Michael Collins
Mr. Morgan	Wilfrid Lawson

A rather slow moving sentimental yarn has been woven around the polyglot population in the foreign section in central London known as the Scho. It is a simple story that lacks punch and gives the impression that more could have been made of the colorful material. It rates as fair entertainment that should cash in on the popularity of the stars.

A small side street of shops and cafes has been shut down for road repairs and Mike, one of the working gang, proceeds to live up to his reputation as a wolf. He gets involved with an Italian family about to emigrate to Canada. The son wants to stay behind as he is in love with a barmaid, but Mike has already proved her an easy conquest, and saves him from a hopeless marriage. The elder daughter is reluctant to go as she has a chance to marry a prosperous cafe proprietor. The younger girl at first most anxious that the family shall stay together, falls for Mike's charm, and stays behind, only to find he doesn't want her.

The repairing gang moves on, after their job is complete, but after the girl is left flat she prays in the nearby church, and Saint Anthony obliges with a miracle. A broken water pipe forces up all the newly concreted street, and the workmen come back to start afresh. Mike realizes he can't get out of it this time and gets resigned to the ball and chain.

John Gregson never seems quite at home in rough clothes but makes a likeable personality of the roving Romeo, and Belinda Lee is simple and naive as the anglicized Italian girl in love with him. Her elder sister is played in more adult, alien fashion by Rosalie Crutchley, and Marie Burke and Peter Illing make an authentic, excitable Momma and Poppa.

Ian Bannen has more real opportunity to characterize as the disillusioned son, and Cyril Cusack weaves in and out like a connecting thread as a salvationist-mailman nursng a hopeless love. Supporting players provide brief nationalistic characters as a background frame, but have little impact on the story. Pic is well directed and has some excellent camera work. *Clem.*

1918—A Man and His Conscience
(FINNISH)

Berlin, June 30.

Suomen Filmiteollisuus (SF) release of T. J. Sarkka production. Stars Aake Lindman, Ann Savo, Pentti Irjala, Helge Herala, Merja Linko. Directed by Toivo Sarkka. Screenplay, Jarl Hemmer; camera, Marius Raichi; music, Heikki Aaltoila; editing, Elmer Lahti; sets, Karl Fager. At Berlin Film Fest. Running time, **105 MINS.**

This Finnish film has an unusual plot to offer: it concerns a priest who seeks to lead a prostitute back on to the right path of life. He succeeds only temporarily since the girl's former instincts awaken. The end of this film, backgrounded by the Finnish revolution, sees neither of the two principal players survive.

Although director Sarkka has maintained a certain amount of suspense, film is "remote." It's pretty limited to Finland home consumption.

A strong plus is Ann Savo who enacts the prostitute. Aside from her extremely beautiful and appealing looks, which command attention, she reveals outstanding acting abilities. Aake Lindman is very convincing as the priest and same goes for a number of supporting players. *Hans.*

Ingen Tid Til Kaertegn
(Be Dear To Me)
(DENMARK)

Berlin, July 6.

Flamingo Film Studio production. With Eva Cohn, Lily Weiding, Grethe Paaske, Hans Kurt, Joergen Reenberg, Preben Lerdorff Rye. Directed by Annelise Hovmand. Screenplay, Finn Methling and Annelise Hovmand; camera, Kjeld Arnholtz; music, Erik Fiehn. At Berlin Film Festival. Running time, **101 MINS.**

Denmark, an outstanding film producing nation in silent days, came to Berlin Festival with a feature that stands considerably above the average offerings of 1957. It's a very well made production centering around an eight-year old girl who feels neglected by her busy actress-mother and her even busier executive-father. So she goes off on a private excursion and the worried parents finally realize that it's about time to take more care of the child. This film has many advantages to offer, but its main asset is Eva Cohn, a "lovable" and highly talented moppet who pretty much steals the picture.

Direction by Annelise Hovmand, who also worked on the script, also deserves mention, the more so as Miss Hovmand succeeded in creating a film which for its poetic ingredients will also appeal to the more fastidious customers. Occasionally, there is an overdose of sentimentality but that's not anti-commercial. *Hans.*

Le Rouge Est Mis
(The Red Light Is On)
(FRENCH)

Paris, June 25.

Gaumont release of Cite Film-SNEG production. Stars Jean Gabin; features Annie Girardot, Paul Frankeur, Lino Ventura, Marcel Bozzufi. Directed by Gilles Grangier. Screenplay, Michel Audiard, Auguste Le Breton, Grangier from novel by Le Breton; camera, Louis Page; editor, Jacqueline Sadoul. At Biarritz, Paris. Running time **90 MINS.**

Louis	Jean Gabin
Helene	Annie Girardot
Freddo	Paul Frankeur
Pepito	Lino Ventura
Pierre	Marcel Bozzufi

This is an underworld pic which treats a group of aging gangsters trying to work themselves into regular bourgeois life while carrying on their payroll robberies. Plot shows most of the mob being killed. Film has some excitement but is generally plodding. Main asset is the presence of Jean Gabin who gives the pic some weight, as the gangleader. However, it telegraphs its action blows, and this limits it to dual fare for the U. S.

Gabin runs a modern garage as a cover. His kid brother has been sent up for a petty theft done for a young girl. The last gang job goes astray when it leads to a lot of killing and betrayal by one of the members. One of them thinks it is Gabin's recently released brother, but Gabin saves the boy at the cost of his own life.

Film is well played and has a rugged, crude aspect in the earthy dialog of Auguste Le Breton. An ex-gangster, he has become known for his salty gangster tales. He wrote "Rififi." However, this lacks the verve of the former. Gabin displays his usual, vigorous assurance. Annie Girardot is a saucy conniver with an attractive physique and personality.

Technical credits are good as are other actors. Pic looks good locally. *Mosk.*

Mort En Fraude
(Fraudulent Death)
(FRENCH)

Paris, May 25.

J. Arthur Rank release of Intermondia production. Stars Daniel Gelin; features Anh Mechard. Directed by Marcel Camus. Screenplay, Michel Audiard, Camus, Jean Hougron from novel by Hougron; camera, Edmond Sechan; editor, Jacqueline Thiedot. At Marignan, Paris. Running time, **105 MINS.**

Horcier	Daniel Gelin
Anh	Anh Mechard

Film starts out as a taut thriller and segues into one of the first French filmic looks at the Indochinese debacle of 1950. It has a style and pace but meanders in dramatic progression. It has some good action scenes and a solid offbeat production value in the locations of Indochina. This shapes a probable arty theatre entry and would be worth dubbing for general situations.

A Frenchman, coming to work in Indochina during the war, has agreed to smuggle in a package. It is stolen during the trip and some smugglers pursue him. Then, he realizes what the war is doing to these people and tries to help them.

For a first pic, Marcel Camus shows a firm feel for place, atmosphere and characterization. However, it advances too leisurely after a fine beginning. Daniel Gelin is excellent as the hounded Frenchman who finds a reason for living in helping the natives and Anh Mechard is telling as the Eurasian he loves. Use of natives and locals also adds a realistic element. Technical work is tops. *Mosk.*

Rose Bernd
(GERMAN—COLOR)

Berlin, June 25.

Schorcht release of Bavaria production. Stars Maria Schell and Raf Vallone; features Kaethe Gold, Leopold Biberti, Hannes Messemer, Arthur Wiesner. Directed by Wolfgang Staudte. Screenplay by Walter Ulbrich, after stageplay by Gerhart Hauptmann; camera, (Agfacolor) Klaus von Rautenfeld; music, Herbert Windt; editor, Lilian Seng. At Marmorhaus, Berlin. Running time, **98 MINS.**

Rose Bernd	Maria Schell
Arthur Streckmann	Ray Vallone
Henriette Flamm	Kaethe Gold
Christoph Flamm	Leopold Biberti
August Keil	Hannes Messemer
Vater Bernd	Arthur Wiesner
Maria Schubert	Christa Keller
Judge	Siegfried Lowitz

Gerhardt Hauptmann's "Rose Bernd" is one of the most prominent German stage plays and the kind of story German audiences love best. This is amply borne out by the boxoffice results within Germany, which have been tops. For the foreign market, and specifically for the U.S., this is a most doubtful entry, except perhaps for the German language houses. It might best be compared with a German version of an American soapopera, i.e. the bubbles are missing.

As was the case with other Hauptmann plays, such as "Die Ratten," this one, too, has been modernized. It's now the German postwar era and Rose Bernd is a refugee girl from Silesia. Although much of the original has been saved, some critical (German) filmgoers may again argue that this isn't the true Hauptman. In any case, it got the "particularly valuable" certificate from the West German film classification board.

Wolfgang Staudte, one of Germany's top directors, is responsible for this one, and while there are some flashes of imagination, his direction on the whole is pedantic and over-dramatic. Color lensing by Klaus von Rautenfeld helps the picture, but Maria Schell's performance is something to argue about. She's Germany's top actress and her name on the marquee alone assures the film stature in Germany.

But this can't detract from the fact that her portrayal of Rose Bernd is shallow and unrealistic, and that she persists in the kind of mannerisms that have become the trademark of virtually every picture in which she appears. Rose Bernd here becomes Maria Schell, instead of the other way 'round.

Story concerns Rose Bernd, a young farm girl who is in love with three men: Christoph Flamm (Leopold Biberti), the owner of an estate; Arthur Streckmann (Raf Vallone), a goodlooking but callous laborer, and August Keil (Hannes Messemer), a goodnatured printer, whom Rose has been promised by her father. When Rose realizes that she is expecting, and that Flamm is the father, everyone turns against her and she has to leave the community. Her child is born, and dies, in the snow, under a viaduct, as the train roars by overhead.

Miss Schell fails to communicate her emotional turmoil, and as a result the whole melodramatic story becomes maudlin. If Hauptmann is a difficult author for foreigners to grasp in the first place, this version of the play doesn't endear him any further. There are some good performances to compensate. Kaethe Gold has dignity and understanding as the crippled wife; Vallone has a good, masculine quality; Biberti does okay as the landowner; Hannes Messemer is good as the shy but loyal friend.

Technically, the film is firstrate. Herbert Windt's music is a plus.

Woman In A Dressing Gown
(BRITISH)

Yvonne Mitchell's prize-winning performance highlights new British domesticity problem story. Good b.o. possibilities.

Berlin, July 3.

Associated British-Pathe release of a Godwin-Willis-Lee Thompson Production. Stars Yvonne Mitchell, Anthony Quayle and Sylvia Syms. Produced by Frank Godwin and J. Lee Thompson; director, J. Lee Thompson; screenplay, Ted Willis; camera, Gilbert Taylor; music, Louis

Levy. At Zoo Palest, Berlin, July 2, '57. Running time, 98 MINS.
Amy .... Yvonne Mitchell
Jim .... Anthony Quayle
Georgie .... Sylvia Syms
Brian .... Andrew Ray
Hilda .... Carole Lesley
Pawnbroker .... Michael Ripper
Mrs. Williams .... Nora Gordon
Hairdresser .... Marianne Stone
Manageress .... Olga Lindo
Wine Merchant .... Harry Locke
Harold .... Max Butterfield
Christine .... Roberta Woolley
Newsboy .... Melvyn Hayes
Hilda's Baby .... Cordelia Mitchell

A prize winning entry at the Berlin Festival, for which Yvonne Mitchell collared the best actress award, "Woman In a Dressing Gown" is a picture with obvious b.o. potentials and distinctly geared to capture femme support. The Godwin-Willis-Lee Thompson production should be a stout home trade candidate, with brisk potentials in other territories.

The principal character in Ted Willis' screenplay is reminiscent of the Shirley Booth role in "Come Back, Little Sheba." Yvonne Mitchell plays an endearing slut on the verge of losing her husband to a younger, more attractive and more wholesome girl. The uncanny depth of her portrayal lifts the story from a conventional rut and gives it a classy stature, which will reap returns when it goes the rounds.

Miss Mitchell plays the wife who is never able to keep pace with the demands of life. Every day she tries in vain to make her home attractive for her husband and son, but the odds are always overwhelming. Dishes remain unwashed, food, such as it is, is always spoilt and she, herself, is continuously garbed in a dirty greasy dressing robe. Inevitably, her husband (Anthony Quayle) is attracted to a girl in the office (Sylvia Syms) but at the moment of crisis cannot make the break.

Astute writing and adroit direction help to retain sympathy for the leading character, although her tiresome behavior rarely justifies it. There's one moving scene in which she persuades her husband to bring the other girl to the house, so that the three of them can talk it over as adults. But Miss Mitchell gets drunk even before the other two arrive, and it develops into a highly embarrassing and emotional situation.

Miss Mitchell's performance is the walk-away highlight of the production, but Anthony Quayle does a solidly reliable job as the husband. Sylvia Syms contributes a more tender performance as the other girl and Andrew Ray makes an impressionable son. Other roles, mainly of minor importance, are adequately filled by a competent team.

J. Lee Thompson's crisp direction sets the pattern for the okay technical credits. *Myro.*

Und Die Liebe Lacht Dazu
(And Love Laughs At It)
(GERMAN-COLOR)

.Berlin, June 25.

Prisma release of Maxim production. Directed by R. A. Stemmle. Screenplay by Stemmle, after stage comedy, "Schwarzbrot and Kipferl," by Werner von der Schulenberg; camera (Eastmancolor), Heinz Schnackertz; music, Herbert Trantow; editor, Klaus Eckstein. Tradeshown at UFA Pavilion, Berlin. Running time, 98 MINS.
Count Ferdinand von Ausberg
Paul Hoerbiger
Pauline, his niece .... Gusti Wolf
Stefan, his nephew.... Gerhard Riedmann
Salvator .... Oscar Sima
Klaus Papendiek .... Gustav Knuth
Luise Papendiek .... Fita Benkhoff
Anna-Susanna Papendiek .... Eva Probst
Jan Dirksen, Captain .... Fritz Tillmann
Mizzi Fox .... Lotte Lang

This German comedy takes its fun from the natural contrasts that exist between northern Germans and Austrians. Pic has its first locality in a hotel up in the Austrian mountains where a German and an Austrian family encounter each other. After varied troubles mainly resulting from the fact that each party lays claim to the best hotel rooms, but the girl of the German and the boy of the Austrian family fall in love, and peace returns. Pic seems a natural for the German market if not in all countries.

R. A. Stemmle directed this with such speed that it makes the more familiar situations still worthwhile. He is helped by a number of experienced comics, notably Oscar Sima, Paul Hoerbiger (the Austrians) and Gustav Knuth and Fita Benkhoff (the Germans). The romantic interest is adequately supplied by Gerhard Riedmann and Eva Probst. Important supporting roles are well done by Fritz Tillmann, Gusti Wolf and Lotte Lang.

Pic has the advantage of beautiful though occasionally too bluish Eastmancolors plus a fine score by Herbert Trantow. Other technical credits are all up to par. *Hans.*

Die Liebe Familie
(Dear Family)
(AUSTRIAN)

Berlin, June 25.

Schorcht (German) release of Cosmopol production. Stars Luise Ulrich; features Hans Nielsen, Karl Schoenboeck, Ingrid Andree. Directed by Helmut Weiss. Screenplay, Helmut Weiss, Ernie Freidmann and Juliane Kay, after comedy, "It's Never Too Late," by Felicity Douglas; camera, Kurt Hasse; music, Johannes Fehring; editor, Ilse Wilken and Amalia Marschalik. Preemed at Filmbuehne Wien, Berlin. Running time, 97 MINS.
Betty Lang .... Luise Ulrich
Karl Lang .... Hans Nielsen
Stefan, publisher ..... Karl Schoenboeck
Hilde .... Doris Kirchner
Petra .... Ingrid Andree
Hans .... Peter Weck
Maria Jurancy .... Susi Nicoletti
Omi Pollinger .... Adrienne Gessner
Toni Pacher .... Michael Heltau
Fraeulein Briesnitz .... Ruth Stephan
Film Director .... Eric Frey

Felicity Douglas' comedy, "It's Never Too Late," after which this was taken, was recently a real success on the local stage. Despite a competent cast, this film is not half as good as the stageshow. There is too much concentration on slapstick while rather old-fashioned direction can be blamed. The creators of this low-budget film may be grateful to Luise Ulrich since she saves this pic via her intelligent portrayal of the femme lead. She also will guarantee this one at least saisfactory returns. "Family" will be restricted to German-language territories.

"Dear Family" shows a bunch of egoists with most of them the quarreling type. Only normal person around is Miss Ulrich. The many things occurring in her household inspire her to write a book which not only finds a publisher but also Hollywood attention. She eventually departs from her family but then returns when she realizes that everyone is basically nice.

Miss Ulrich portrays her mother role with the essential charm, being is a natural for this part. Hans Nielsen is convincing as her lawyer-husband. I–––d Andree comes off very well as her film-crazy daughter who temporarily falls for film director Erik Frey. Karl Schoenboeck contributes a routine performance of a publisher. Susi Nicoletti is cast as a nymphomaniac with a crush on Hans Nielsen, while Adrienne Gessner is a nagging but lovable grandma. Lensing editing and other technical credits are average. *Hans.*

Freedom
(NIGERIA-COLOR)

Berlin, July 9.

Moral Re-Armament presentation and production. Written by Manasseh Moerane, Ifoghate Amata and Aabayisaa Karbo. Camera (Eastmancolor), Richard Tegstroem, Aimo Jaederholm and others. Music, James W. Owens. At Berlin Film Fest. Running time, 95 MINS.

"Freedom" is based on the like titled play of the Moral Re-Armament movement and is reportedly the first African tinter. Hard to judge by artistic or other critical criteria. It's a slanted effort, financed by members of the MRA religious movement. Film shows how in Nigeria, amid colonialism and anti-colonialism, force and discord, the idea of the MRA movement is taken up and all is turned peaceful.

"Freedom" is dilettantish and contains unintended comedy but it must be regarded as well-meant and, to a certain degree, interesting enterprise.

Definite plus is the color photography, handled by Walt Disney's Swedish cameraman Richard Tegstroem and Finnish Aimo Jaederholm. The acting, mostly by inexperienced players, is occasionally moving. For its message and its sympathetic principal characters, film found a friendly reception in Berlin. *Hans.*

The Shiralee
(British)

Offbeat item locationed in Australia. Standout moppet performance by Dana Wilson main b.o. element for Ealing's second Metro release.

London, July 12.

Metro release of a Michael Balcon-Ealing Production. Stars Peter Finch and Elizabeth Sellar. Directed by Leslie Norman. Associate Producer, Jack Rix. Screenplay, Neil Paterson and Leslie Norman, from the novel by D'Arcy Niland; camera, Paul Beeson; editor, Gordon Stone; music, John Addison. At Empire Theatre, London. July 11, '57. Running time, 99 MINS.
Macauley .... Peter Finch
Marge .... Elizabeth Sellars
Buster .... Dana Wilson
Donny .... George Rose
Lily Parker .... Rosemary Harris
Parker .... Russell Napier
Beauty Kelly .... Niall MacGinnis
Bella .... Tessie O'Shea
Luke .... Sidney James
Jim Muldoon .... Charles Tingwell
Desmond .... Reg Lye
Shop Girl .... Barbara Archer
Papadoulos .... Alec Mango
Doctor .... John Phillips

Ealing's second production under the Metro banner is an outdoor adventure yarn filmed largely on location in Australia. It's a picture with a considerable amount of charm, hypoed by an outstanding moppet performance by five-year-old Dana Wilson, who acts with all the knowhow of an accomplished veteran. It's b.o. potential, however, must be considered questionable. It's the type of diversion that can be aided by word-of-mouth.

The title is also a doubtful bet as a ticket selling aid, but "Shiralee," which is an Aborigine slang word meaning burden, may arouse some customer curiosity. Peter Finch, a native Australian, can have no name value in the States.

As a native Aussie, Finch has no difficulty in affecting the local accent, which, to British ears, to start with, is akin to an unpleasant cockney dialect. It is, however, easy to follow and may be acceptable in America. In the story, he plays a roving laborer, going from town to town in search of casual work. When he eventually returns to his own home, after an absence of several years, he finds his wife (Elizabeth Sellars) living with another man. He snatches their child out of the home and, with his "shiralee" on his shoulder, he continues his trek across the country.

Apart from the opening sequences, most of the action shows Finch accompanied by his daughter, in search of work and, all too frequently, getting the brush. Also, he's clearly ill at ease with his own child, unable to show the affection and devotion for which she yearns. However, when the infant has the choice of returning to her mother, she options to rough it with the male parent. The final sequences, in which the mother tries to regain custody, the father is beaten up by a gang of thugs and the child almost killed by a truck, provides dramatic tension in a different key.

The entire plot is dominated by Finch and Dana Wilson and they carry the story with considerable force. First class players like Elizabeth Sellars, Rosemary Harris, Sidney James and Tessie O'Shea have comparatively little to do, but make impressive contributions to the overall production. Technically, the pic maintains a high standard, with particular credit to Paul Beeson's outdoor camera work. *Myro.*

De Vliegende Hollander
(The Flying Dutchman)
(NETHERLANDS)

Amsterdam, July 13.

Corona Film production and release. Directed by Gerard Rutten. Script by Ed. Hoornik and Rutten. Camera, Andor von Barsy. Music, Henk Badings. Features, Ton Kuyl. At Cineas, Plaza Cinemas, Amsterdam. Running time, 90 MINS.

First feature picture to be produced in Holland in two years has as subject early years of Dutch **aviation pioneer Anthony Fokker. Subject is apparently not popular with public; Warners' "Spirit Of St. Louis" did so-so business here, but "Flying Dutchman" was already in production then, so producers of Dutch film could not take advantage of boxoffice experience of U.S. release.**

"Flying Dutchmon" has electronic music by Henk Badings which may be in character with "the progress" the film wants to stress, but instead makes the local public laugh.

Story, depicting first years of Fokker as plane builder, is situated in Holland and Germany. No German actors were used, though, and phrasing of German dialog characters by Dutch actors proves text bookish, and may mean that whole sound track must be redubbed if or when film is released in Germany.

There is not much action in story and most of the actors show stage technique. Direction is static. Only in the German episodes is more momentum achieved.

Ton Kuyl, Dutch actor with French dramatic schooling and experience, is okay in title role. Lensing by Andor von Barsy is effective and makes most of sub-

ject, direction by Gerard Rutten is old-fashioned. "Flying Dutchman" is no box-office draw.
Saaltink.

Foreign Films

Le Grand Bluff (FRENCH). Corona release of Hoche-Ray Ventura-Belmont production. Stars Eddie Constantine, Dominique Willms; features Mireille Granelli, Moustache, Bernard Dheran, Jacques Hilling. Directed by Patrice Dally. Screenplay, Jerry Epstein, adapted by Louis Martin, Yvan Audouard, Dally; camera, Armand Thirard; editor, Gabriel Rongier. At Balzac, Paris. Running time, **95 MINS.**

Eddie Constantine, the American who became a pic star here, has been signed to do his first U.S. film for United Artists this summer. If that pic were to click, this might have a chance for dual spotting in the U.S. Otherwise, this "B" effort bodes little chance except in lowercase action spots.

Constantine plays a sympathetic grifter who gets up an oilwell combine which turns out to really have oil in it. He becomes the defender of the small stockholders against the shady group trying to buy them out. It abounds with the usual fisticuffs, which the French still have not mastered, and the usual femmes always falling into the hero's arms. Direction does not help bring out the few good ideas inherent in the script, but Constantine is his usual colorful, assured self while the girls in the pic do not fare as well. *Mosk.*

Tahati (FRENCH; FRANSCOPE; COLOR). CICC release of CICC-Discifilm-Cine Roma production. Stars, Maea Flohr, Georges De Caunes. Written and directed by Bernard Borderie. Camera (Eastmancolor), Persin, Bonneau; editor, W. R. Sivel. At Normandie, Paris. Runnng time, **95 MINS.**

This pic is anamorphoscoped and in color, being a barely dramatized documentary on Tahiti, its simple natives, terping, nude women and idyllic laziness of its existence. Done with a vague framework of a reporter supposedly doing a series of articles on the isles, but spending his time chasing beauteous natives, this is too lagging for chances as a full-length film in the U.S.

Fine lensing could make this worth documentary attention if cut down in size. Some clever takeoffs on the isle's history, the everpresent dancing girls and the nudity, if not censored, could make this an exploitable item on special bills. Otherwise, it is limited for America. Maea Flohr has a pretty spirited screen presence, but video star Georges De Caunes is too self-conscious to be telling on the big screens. *Mosk.*

Senechal Le Magnifique (FRENCH). Cinedis release of Chronos-Rizzoli-France Cinema production. Stars Fernandel; features Nadia Gray, Armontel, Jeanne Aubert, Simone Paris. Directed by Jean Boyer. Screenplay, Jean-Jacques Rouff, Serge Weber, Boyer; camera, Charles Suin; editor, Jacques Desagneaux. At Paris, Paris. Running time, **95 MINS.**

Pic is a Fernandel vehicle. It gives him a chance to play a secondrate touring actor who finds that he can never get good roles, for he is not taken seriously. But, in costume, he gets into all sorts of real adventures in life. All ends with a trial after he gets mixed up with gangsters, his first big role. His breaking up of the play and his final stardom climaxes this. Idea is good but it is rarely exploited to make this something that could have Yank chances mainly on the comic's name. He overdoes his mugging and reactions in this to lose the true comedics of the pic. However, it engenders enough laughs to make this okay locally but hard to sell in the U.S. Technical credits are standard. *Mosk.*

Gotoma The Buddha (INDIAN; DOCUMENTARY). Bimal Roy production and release. Written and directed by Rajbans Khanna; camera, Dilip Gupta; editor, H. Mukherji; music, Salil Chowdhry. Preemed in Paris. Running time, **65 MINS.**

Via sculpture, bas reliefs and paintings, this pic adroitly and feelingly tells the life of Buddha. It has a simple but telling commentary in English which gives this a legendary quality. The tale of the Buddha's quest for wisdom and faith has a natural dignity and beauty. Landscapes, sky and waters, mixed into a fluid conception of the imagery, keep this pictorially interesting throughout. Its main U.S. chances, because of length and subject, would be in pairing with another offbeat art short. At the recent Cannes Film Fest, it won a special mention.
Mosk.

Rekava (Destiny) (CEYLONESE). Chitra Lanka Ltd. production and release. With Dharma Priya, Myrtle Fernando, Iranganie Meedeniya. Written and directed by Lester James Peries. Camera, William Blake; editor, Sunil Dayaratne. Preemed in Paris. Running time, **95 MINS.**

This is the first pic from Ceylon, to be seen over here. It emerges a simple, folksy rambling tale of village life. It concerns a little boy who is thought to have healing qualities when he cures his little girl companion of blindness. But then superstition enters and the villagers try to exorcise him. Though meandering, the pic has a sincere quality and shows a firm technque. For the U.S., this has mainly curio appeal. It is limited but has exploitable qualities.
Mosk.

Elokuu (Destiny) (FINNISH). Fennada production and release. With Toivo Makela, Emma Vaanenen, Lauri Luoma. Directed by Matti Kassila. Screenplay, Kassila from novel by F. Sillapaa; camera, Esko Nevalainen; editor, Nils Holm. Preemed in Paris. Running time, **90 MINS.**

Finnish pic details the downfall of an alcoholic and the effect on his family. Pic is somewhat literary and theatrical, but has a convincing handling of the dipso's plight and shapes mainly as an exploitation item for any slim U.S. chances. Otherwise it is very limited. Acting and technical aspects are firstrate. *Mosk.*

Geliebte Corinna (Beloved Corinna) (GERMAN). NF release of Arca production. Stars Elisabeth Mueller, Hans Soehnker, Hannelore Schroth; features Inkijinoff, Alexander Kerst, Annie Rosar, Klause Kinski, Gerhard Buente, Hannes Tannert. Directed by Eduard von Borsody. Screenplay, Curt J. Braun and Ernst von Salomon, from novel of same name by Robert Pilchowski; camera, Fritz Arno Wagner; music, Lothar Bruehne. At UFA Pavilion, Berlin. Running time, **100 MINS.**

Film's only international exploitation angle is Swiss Elisabeth Mueller who last year debutted in Metro's "Power and Prize." She doesn't prove a great actress in this, but her beauty and sympathetic charm have refreshing appeal. Pic spins the tale of a young girl (Miss Mueller) who follows the "man of her life" to Malakka where she finds out that he's already married. But soon she learns that he is an honest lover and only his wife is to blame for the circumstances. Death of his wife makes the way free for both.

"Corinna" is a familiar yarn which lacks practically everything. Adapted from a novel, Curt J. Braun and Ernst von Salomon have written a morbidly, corny script. Direction by Edward von Borsody is remarkably old-fashioned. The acting remains rather unconvincing. Hans Soehnker, who gets star billing after Miss Mueller, portrays the male lead with an overemphasis. Hannelore Schroth is nearly silly as his toujours drinking wife. Vet actor Inkijinoff enacts an Asiatic nabob—also a rather odd performance. Entire film's production dress reveals a very moderate budget while technical qualities are not even average. Probably German film-making at its 1957 lowest ebb. *Hans.*

Flickan I Frack (Girl In Tails) (SWEDISH—COLOR). Sandrews release of Rune Waldekranz production. Stars Maj-Britt Nilsson, Folke Sundquist; features Lennart Lindberg, Sigge Fuerst, Anders Henrikson. Directed by Arne Mattsson. Screenplay, Herbert Grevenius, based on novel by Hjalmar Bergman; camera (Eastmansolor), Sven Nykvist; music, Hakan von Eichwald. At Film Studio, Berlin. Running time, **98 MINS.**

That Swedish comedies can be much better than their reputation was proved at the Cannes Festival last year when Ingmar Bergman's "Smile of a Summer Night" walked off with an award for the most poetic comedy. Unlike "Smiles," which was more the offbeat type of comedy, this is truly escapist entertainment. It's the kind which should also appeal to majority of sophisticated patrons. Aside from lacking names well-known in the U.S., this comedy is so familiar it likely will find it tough going in most American spots.

In brief, this is the story of a girl who goes to a ball in tails since her father refused to present her with an evening gown and so she takes her brothers' dress suit. The "girl in tails" causes a scandal in this Swedish small town at the beginning of this century.

Acting is of top calibre. Maj-Britt Nilsson enacts the title role charmingly. Folke Syndquist portrays a young count, her beau, smartly. Exceptional support helps this lightweight story. Director Arne Mattsson, creator of "Summer of Happiness," seems to have given the whole thing the right touch of slowness to catch the old-fashioned atmosphere. A fitting contribution is the music, mostly Johann Strauss waltzes. Camera and other technical credits are firstclass. *Hans.*

Sait-On Jamais (Does One Ever Know) (FRENCH; C'SCOPE; COLOR). Mondex Film release of Raoul Levy-Iena-Carol Film production. Stars Francoise Arnoul, Robert Hossein, O. E. Hasse; features Christian Marquand, Franco Fabrizi. Written and directed by Roger Vadim. Camera (Eastmancolor), Armand Thirard; editor, Victoria Mercanton; music, John Lewis. At Biarritz, Paris. Running time, **95 MINS.**

The characterizations are only emulsion-deep in this pic which makes the amorous, half-nude dallying suggestive rather than truly erotic, with flashes of violence gratuitous. However, this is wrapped in a picturesque backing via the Venice locale, and it shapes mainly as an exploitation feature for the U.S., and will take plenty of bally.

No morale fibre exists in the characters since they walk through the lush C'Scope settings rather abjectly. A Gallic reporter meats a girl one night and they are soon ensconed in her room in an esoteric looking Venetian palace inhabited by two goons and a rich, aging Baron. There is also a disquieting young hoodlum who was the girl's previous lover. Then comes complications since the Baron had hidden millions of phony but perfect Anglo pounds. Then there is the murder of the Baron by the hoodlum, all being resolved by a rooftop chase.

Director Roger Vadim rarely makes the pic exciting or plausible.

Francoise Arnoul is cute but is lost in an ill-defined role. Remainder of the cast is passable, with only Robert Hossein making a real impression as the murderer.

C'Scope and color are firstrate and the Venice backgrounding also may help in U.S. situations. Another Yank plus is the music scoring by the Modern Jazz Quartet. It's written by John Lewis.
Mosk.

Non Scherzare Con Le Donne. (Don't Trifle With Women) (ITALIAN). APICI production and release. Stars Rossana Podesta, Giorgia Moll, Marco Vicario, Armando Silvestre. Directed by Giuseppe Bennati. Story and screenplay, Bennati, Benvenuti, Stucchi, Bernardi; camera, Gabor Pogany; music, Francesco Lavagnino; editor, Franco Fraticelli. At Capranica, Rome. Running time, **95 MINS.**

Pic, which recounts the innocently amorous exploits of a summer-resort Romeo, makes for diverting entertainment in a mood similar to Fellini's "Vitelloni." However, it is lighter-veined. Could rate some U.S. attention, especially among Italo patrons.

Aided by very good dialogue, director Giuseppe Bennati keeps the pic moving at a fast episodic pace as Marco Vicario goes from one girl to the next in his never-ending search for true love. Of course, she has been right under his nose all the time. Acting, lensing, music, direction and other credits give this little pic a polish and unashamed charm not usually associated with films of its stature.
Hawk.

La Ragazza Delle Saline (Girl From Salt Fields) GERMAN-ITALIAN-COLOR). Cineriz release of a Rizzoli-Bavaria-Schorcht-Zagreb Film production. Stars Isabelle Corey, Marcello Mastroianni; features Jester Naefe, Peter Carsten. Directed by Franz Cap. Screenplay, Johannes Kay; camera, Vaclav Vich; music, Bert Grund; editor, Friedl Schier-Buchow. At Adriano, Rome. Running time, **95 MINS.**

Exploitable meller in the "Bitter Rice" vein has some chances in minor U.S. situations, but with dubbing, unless cost of color prints militates against purchase. Sexy-ingenue combo is person of star Isabelle Corey, a newcomer, is likewise a buildable sales point.

Tale is set in the fisherman and salt flat areas of the Adriatic coast, where rivalry between anglers and salt processers leads to constant tension. Further conflicts derive from the jealousy over Marina, buxom villager whose wide-eyed face belies her mature body and intentions. Nearness of water also has been handily used by makers to provide its star with an almost constantly wet, and clinging, wardrobe. Love scenes, fights, and documentaristic shots of salt field work are well blended for good general audience effects.

Stars Isabelle Corey, a definite comer, and young vet Marcello Mastroianni, make likeable topliners performing their surface chores well. Direction by Franz Cap is occasionally ponderous in the Germanic idiom, but generally keeps things moving. Color (uncredited). is uneven, though achieving some good effects. Other technical credits are average. *Hawk.*

L'Ultimo Paradiso (The Last Paradise) **(ITALIAN—COLOR—ULTRASCOPE).** Lux Film release of a Lux-Paneuropa production. Directed by Folco Quilici. Screenplay, Quilici, Golfiero Colonna, from a story by Quilici; camera. (Ultrascope Terranicolor), Marco Scarpelli; music, Francesco Lavagnino; editor, Marie Serandrei. At Capitol, Rome. Running time, **95 MINS.**

Feature documentary is a direct descendant of "Lost Continent" and similar Italo travel projects. While not nearly as successful, it has enough unusual footage, excellent lensing, plus some exploitable angles, to make it a fair investment for U.S. bookings. Trimming of overweight celluloid is suggested to avoid some repetitious material.

Episodic pic concerns itself with customs and life among the inhabitants of some central Pacific isles. Some of the tales have more plot than others, just as some show the obvious while others cite the unusual. Among these are a religious ceremony in which village males show their valor and purity by throwing themselves off a high tower headfirst, with only a vine tied to their legs to abruptly stop their fall. Likewise striking is series of shots showing unusual methods employed in combating moray eels and tiger sharks endangering fishing waters.

Of great beauty and considerable sensuality are sequences depicting marriage of two islanders, complete with fore and aftermath views of often half-naked dancing girls. Marco Scarpelli does a masterful job wth his Ferraniacolor camera (the Ultrascope process is occasionally fuzzy at the edges). A top assist comes from Francesco Lavagnino's lilting musical score which adds much to films mood. *Hawk.*

Taxichauffeur Baenz (Taxi Driver Baenz). Praesens Zurich production. Diricted by Werner Dueggelin; screenplay, Schaggi Streuli; production manager, Uors von Planta; camera, Emil Berna; music, Robert Blum. Stars Schaggi Streuli, Elisabeth Mueller, Maximillian Schell; features Emil Hegetschweiler, Elisabeth Barth, Fred Tanner, Marianne Hediger, Ruedi Walter, Fredy Scheim, Stephanie Glaser, Sigfrit Steiner, Fritz Nussbaum, Peter W. Loosli, Hans Grimm. At Urban Theatre, Zurich, June 26, '57; running time, **93 MINS.**

Latest Praesens entry, in Swiss-German, again is in the popular vein of previous Swiss b.o. winners "Policeman Waeckerli" and "Upper Town Street," telling a simple tale of simple people. Contrary to its predecessors, however, only moderate grosses, even on the local market, are in store for this one, with chances abroad questionable. "Baenz" suffers from a weak, only mildly entertaining script and unexperienced direction by newcomer-to-films Werner Dueggelin, an otherwise talented young stage director. Technical credits are fair, with choppy editing contributing to the below-par quality.

Plot is about a hackie financing his daughter's studying medicine. She is engaged to a weak young character whose emblezzling of money brings on the complications. With the father's help, all is straightened out in the end. *Mezo.*

Will Success Spoil Rock Hunter? (COLOR-C'SCOPE)

Sparkling comedy-farce, loosely based on George Axelrod stageplay. Takeoff on tv and Madison Ave., with Jayne Mansfield and Tony Randall. Shapes as hot season natural.

20th-Fox release of Frank Tashlin production. Stars Jayne Mansfield, Tony Randall, Betsy Drake, Joan Blondell; features John Williams, Henry Jones, Lili Gentle, Mickey Hargitay, Georgia Carr. Directed by Tashlin, from screenstory and screenplay by Tashlin; based on George Axelrod play, produced on stage by Jule Styne; camera (color by De Luxe), Joe MacDonald; music, Cyril J. Mockridge; song, "You Got It Made," by Bobby Troup; editor, Hugh Fowler. Previewed at the Jefferson Theatre, N.Y., July 23, '57. Running time, **94 MINS.**

Rita Marlowe .... Jayne Mansfield
Rock Hunter .... Tony Randall
Jenny .... Betsy Drake
Violet .... Joan Blondell
La Salle Jr. .... John Williams
Rufus .... Henry Jones
April 1 .... Lili Gentle
Bobo .... Mickey Hargitay
Calypso Number .... Georgia Carr
TV Interviewer .... Dick Whittinghill
Gladys .... Ann McCrea
Frenchmen...Alberto Morin, Louis Mercier

This is the kind of snappy, crackling farce that Hollywood hasn't had too much of in recent years. In converting the stageplay "Will Success Spoil Rock Hunter?" to his purposes, Frank Tashlin—who's practically a one-man band on this picture—has turned out a vastly amusing comedy that has all the earmarks of a bangup success.

There have been many in the trade who, in recent years, have deplored the lack of screen laughter. Well, this film has a bellyfull. Granted, it may strike some civilians as too much of a private joke on Madison Ave. and television, and the pace isn't even, but the whole shapes up as a well-acted, extremely funny film that doesn't shrink from slapstick in the grand tradition.

Picture bears comparatively little resemblance to the George Axelrod original, but it's to be doubted that there'll be any complaints on that grounds. Tashlin, who produced, directed, wrote the screen version and scripted it, has an ear for the gags and an eye for situation comedy. Combination clicks down the line and is helped by sock performances, notably by Jayne Mansfield and Tony Randall.

This is Randall's second excursion into the bigscreen realm (did "Oh Men, Oh Women" for 20th). His roots are in tv and the stage. "Rock Hunter" should establish him as a promising screen comedy talent. He's a fellow who knows timing, and his clowning has a slightly sophisticated touch that hits bullseye. The picture rests largely on him, and he carries it through with nary a slip. Thanks to some fine shading, he manages to make the transition from hilarity to serious moments without losing the sense of credibility.

It's not his fault that, towards the end, the whole gag is overworked and some of the sequences tend to become tedious. There the blame falls on Tashlin, who didn't know when to call a halt to a good thing.

Miss Mansfield (deliberately, or not, looks and moves and sounds like Marilyn Monroe), does a sock job as the featherbrained sex-motivated movie star. She's stunningly dressed (with all the expected exposures) and is handed some very strong laughlines which she delivers competently. Her appeal is mostly visual though.

Tashlin has fashioned a funny credit for the credits, which are introed by Randall. Trouble is that this kind of opening takes the play away from the names. Nevertheless, it sets a fine mood, and immediately establishes Randall as the boy with the laughs.

There's also an "intermission," with Randall coming out to comfort those who are used to tv commercials. Sequence lampoons the tv picture, as do the credits via a satirization of video commercials. In the end, Groucho Marx comes on for a briefy. Clowning throughout ranges from the broad to the sophisticated, so everyone should get their money's worth.

Story has Randall as a tv commercial writer about to be fired because his agency is threatened with the loss of its big lipstick account. He saves the situation by getting the endorsement from a famous movie star. In the process he almost loses his fiancee, becomes a big "success" (symbolized by his getting the keys to the executive washroom), has the screen queen fall in love with him, and ends up running a chicken farm.

Supporting roles are all very well east. Betsy Drake is cute and displays a strong sense for comedy as Randall's fiancee; Henry Jones, ad-agency v.p., coaxes from the sidelines and delivers some rather lengthy speeches; Joan Blondell is standout in a small part and Britain's John Williams is vastly amusing as the ad agency head who actually wants to be a horticulturist. Lili Gentle is appealing as Randall's teenage niece and Mickey Hargitay is properly pompous as the Tarzan he-man who triggers Randall's troubles.

Film is full of plugs for upcoming pix from 20th, and goes all-out in advertising TWA. Screen ought not to be as obvious as all that in plugging a commercial service.

Joe MacDonald's lensing is topnotch and the De Luxe color is crisp and sharp. Georgia Carr does the Bobby Troup "You Got It Made" number in calypso style. Settings of the picture are plush. Producer Tashlin obviously was determined to shoot the works for director Tashlin, who in turn knew how to handle scripter Tashlin. Combined efforts help to make "Rock Hunter" the kind of film that should pack 'em in during any weather—rain or shine. *Hift.*

Jungle Heat

Cardboard characters filmed in Hawaiian locale. Secondary bookings and results indicated.

Hollywood, July 23.

United Artists release of a Bel-Air Production. Stars Lex Barker, Mari Blanchard; features Glenn Langan, James Westerfield, Rhodes Reason, Miyoko Sasaki. Producer, Aubrey Schenck. Director, Howard W. Koch. Screenplay, Jameson Brewer; camera, William Margullies; editor, John A. Bushelman; music, Les Baxter. Previewed, Jan. 23, '57. Running time, **75 MINS.**

Dr. Jim Ransom .... Lex Barker
Ann McRae .... Mari Blanchard
Roger McRae .... Glenn Langan
Harvey Mathews ..... James Westerfield
Major Richard Grey ..... Rhodes Reason
Kimi-San Grey .... Miyoko Sasaki
Felix Agung .... Glenn Dixon
Kuji .... Bob Okazaki
Corporal .... Jerry Frank
Kaem .... Daniel Wong
Folger .... Andrew Gross
Jules .... Yun Kui Chang
Freight Agent Attendant
Kunio Fudimura
Expectant Mother .... Leo Ezell

Despite scenic opportunities of Kauai Island, in Hawaiian group, where pic was lensed, this emerges as distinctly minor-league offering. (Potboiler) can't aspire to better than secondary bookings.

Story by Jameson Brewer is notable only in invincible stupidity of all characters. Tale has to do with Japanese fifth column on eve of Pearl Harbor. Leo Barker is medico sympathetic to problems of native workers; also fighting machinations of local planter James Westerfield, head of Jap underground.

To island come Mari Blanchard and husband Glenn Langan, latter a dense troubleshooter sent out to straighten sugar plantation's labor problems. Contemptuous of natives, he's easily mislead by Westerfield. Gory finale has Westerfield and his fifth column wiped out by Barker and National Guard major Rhodes Reason. Langan perishes in the turmoil, leaving a clear romantic field for Miss Blanchard and Barker.

Barker fills bill of standard heroics ably enough and Miss Blanchard is decorative, although foolish role hampers her thesping. Westerfield plays the villain with old-fashioned, lip-smacking gusto, an effective approach to the idiotic plotting. Langan can't do much with badly-drawn part. Reason is okay as the major and Miyoko Sasaki, as his Japanese wife, impresses in short footage.

Direction of Howard W. Koch misses nary a cliche, but then, neither does the script. Technical credits are adequate. *Kove.*

Walk Into Hell (COLOR)

Exploitation entry with documentary overtones. Shot in New Guinea. Okay b.o.

Patric Pictures release of Southern International Ltd. - Discfilm production. Stars Chips Rafferty, Francoise Christophe, Reginald Lye; features Pierre Cressoy, Sgt. Major Somu, District Officer Fred Kaad. Produced by Rafferty; director, Lee Robinson; screenplay, Rex Rients; camera (Eastman Color), Carl Kayser; editor, Alex Ezard; music, Georges Auric. Previewed in N. Y. July 17, '57. Running time, **93 MINS.**

Steve McAllister .... Chips Rafferty
Dr. Dumarcet ..... Francoise Christophe
"Sharkeye" Kelly .... Reginald Lye
Jeff Clayton .... Pierre Cressoy
Towalaka .... Sgt. Major Somu
District Officer Fred Kaad ..... Himself

This goes under the heading of exploitation though actually "Walk Into Hell" is more of an adventure travelog. It's done in color, with a definite story line, and benefits from some excellent photography of the New Guinea locale.

Producer Chips Rafferty, who also stars, has brought a lot of elements together in this film, and some pan out into exciting sequences. Picture won't collect any critics awards for best performances, but it stands to please the action fans and it has, as an added plus factor, some very realistic sequences involving the natives.

There's one impressive scene where a large crowd of fierce-looking warriors performs a wild dance on a field. Actually, they've been put up to it by Rafferty who needs the area trampld down so a light plane can land.

Story has Rafferty take a French woman doctor, Francoise Christophe, and an old adventurer, Reginald Lye, into the New Guinea mountains after Lye reports he has found oil in a remote region. It's

Rafferty's job to establish an airfield and a base before the rainy season starts. On the trip they rescue Pierre Cressoy, an elephant hunter, who has killed a white bird sacred to the natives. The little expedition almost gets wiped out as a result.

Director Lee Robinson has staged some good action, and while the performances are far from believable, at least they don't get into the way of the story. Carl Kayser's camera work, with the inevitable attention to bare native bosoms, is of top quality and catches some fascinating glimpses of New Guinea and its people. There's also a spine-chilling sequence involving a snake attack on Miss Christophe.

Rafferty as the laconic leader of the troupe is good. Miss Christophe is attractive without being convincing, and Lye does okay with his part. A number of native soldiers play themselves. "Walk Into Hell" has a good title and intriguing backgrounds. It's a natural for the exploitation trade. *Hift.*

The Fuzzy Pink Nightgown

Mild comedics with Jane Russell, Ralph Meeker, Keenan Wynn; so-so boxoffice.

United Artists release of Russ-Field (Robert Waterfield) Production. Stars Jane Russell, Ralph Meeker, Keenan Wynn. Features Fred Clark, Adolphe Menjou, Una Merkel, Benay Venuta, Robert H. Harris. Directed by Norman Taurog. Screenplay, Richard Alan Simmons; based on novel by Sylvia Tate; camera, Josepn La Shelle; editor, Archie Marshek; music, Billy May. Tradeshown in N. Y. July 19, '57. Running time, **87 MINS.**

Laurel Stevens	Jane Russell
Dandy	Keenan Wynn
Mike Valla	Ralph Meeker
Sergeant McBride	Fred Clark
Arthur Martin	Adolphe Menjou
Bertha	Una Merkel
Daisy Parker	Benay Venuta
Barney Baylies	Robert H. Harris
Television Announcer	Bob Kelley
Disk Jockey	Dick Haynes
Flack	John Truax
Lieutenant Dempsey	Milton Frome

There's flimsy excuse for "Fuzzy Pink Nightown" as title for this latest from Russ-Field Productions; indeed, Jane Russell dons such a garment for no apparent reason other than to connect the title with the picture. It was the name of the original novel where presumably such attire was more important and, perhaps, this also justifies its use with the film.

Anyway, "Fuzzy Pink Nightgown' is a mild comedy that has the names of Miss Russell, Ralph Meeker and Keenan Wynn to help it collect modest returns in the general market. And to mention that title just once more, it, too, should assist.

Basic idea played around with in the Alan Simmons screenplay, based on the Sylvia Tate book, had a good deal of comedy potential. It's about a Hollywood star, Miss Russell, who is kidnapped just before her new picture, "The Kidnapped Bride," is to open. Her abductors are Meeker and Wynn and they're playing it for real, i.e., it's not the publicity stunt Miss Russell at first suspects. But they come to fall for the gal and prefer to call the whole thing off. She wants them to go through with the kidnapping for otherwise the public would suspect it actually was a shabby headline-grabbing gimmick from the start and her career would be ruined.

This kind of situation, to be gotten across with sufficient comedy effect, required a clever satirical treatment or sharp delivery of snappy dialog. But neither is the case. The amusement comes but intermittently; for the most part the writing is unimaginative and Norman Taurog's direction is routine.

Miss Russell, Meeker and Wynn are adequate under the circumstances—that is to say they're trapped with a commonplace script. Same obtains with Adolphe Menjou as film studio boss, Fred Clark, who plays a detective, and Una Merkel, Benay Venuta, Robert H. Harris and others on and off the scene.

Joseph La Shelle's camera work, Billy May's music and other credits are standard. *Gene.*

Foreign Films

Protevouslanikes Peripetles (The Girl From Korfu) **(GREEK; COLOR).** Olympus Film Corp. production. Stars Rena Vlachpoulou, Stephanos Stratigos, Anny Bol, Kulis Stolingas. Directed by Jannis Petropoulakis. Screenplay, Ilias Limberopoulos; camera (Eastmancolor), Vasilis Maros; music, Menelos Theofanides; editor, Jean Uenet. At Berlin Film Fest. Running time, **84 MINS.**

"Korfu" with a budget of about $80,000 and reportedly the most expensive Greek pic to date, comes to the screen as an item which clearly reveals the Greek producers' efforts to follow the West European pattern. It has an operatic-type plot centering around two village beauties who come to Athens where they get mixed up in all sorts of comical situations.

Only a few folk dances distinguish this film from West European run-of-mill productions. There is, however, some ease about this feature which makes it sympathetic though not very entertaining. *Hans.*

The Valley of Lost Soul (CHINESE). Cathay Film Productions Ltd., Hongkong production and release. With Yien Chuen, Lin Dai, Chen Yu Shin, Kao Chan, Yang Yih Moh, Wan Lan. Directed by Yien Chuen. Screehplay, Dick Yee; camera, Fan Jai. At Berlin Film Fest. Running time, **91 MINS.**

A rather simple boring tale centering around love, seduction and jealousy, fails to cause much excitement. Principal characters are two hostile brothers and an orphan. The latter takes the good brother home as her husband. While the film grants the curious patrons some interesting insights into Asiatic habits of love and life, this item hardly stands a chance in the world market. *Hans.*

The Wedding Day (KOREAN). Sudo Film Co. (Lee Byung Il) production. Directed by Lee Byung II. With Kim Sung Ho, Cho Mi Ryung, Kim Yoo Hi, Choi Hyun. Screenplay, Oh Yung Chin; camera, Lim Byung Ho; music, Lim Won Shik. At Berlin Film Fest. Running time, **81 MINS.**

A remarkable entry from this small nation. This is a charming tale of a man who by mistake marries his daughter's bridegroom with a sweet maid-servant. Although a far cry from western mentality, this one offers plenty of hilarious situations which really click. A refreshing outsider among the festival entries, this pic won't be forgotten so easily. Special praise goes for the camerawork which includes some impressive shots. Film garnered considerable applause in Berlin. *Hans.*

Arashi (Father Love) **(Japan).** Toho production and release. Stars Chishu Ryu, Kunio Otsuka, Akira Kubo, Izumi Yukimura, Kinuyo Tanaka. Directed by Hiroshi Inagaki. Screenplay, Ryuzo Kikushima; camera, Tadashi Limura; sets, Taeko Kita and Kan Ueda. At Berlin Film Fest. Running time, **105 MINS.**

This is a story of a high school teacher who, after the death of his wife, has to raise his four children by himself. It's a well directed and appealingly-acted film with many humorous and human touches. The only handicap for western audiences is the length. While Chihu Ryu deserves praise for his outstanding portrayal of the father, a special word goes to Izumi Yukimura, the darling of the Berlin festival who contributed a lovable portrayal of Ryu's daughter. In all, a film which doesn't reach the quality of Japanese masterpieces but nevertheless contributes to the prestige for Japan's filmmaking. With some cuts, it seems to have possibilities for situations outside Nippon. *Hans.*

Abarembo Kaido (The Horse Boy) **(JAPANESE).** Toei Motion Picture production and release. Stars Isuzu Yamada, Shuji Sano, Motoharu Ueki, Shinobu Chihara, Tamami Fujii, Kenji Susukida. Directed by Tomu Uchida. Screenplay, Yoshitaka Yoda; camera, Teiji Yoshida; music, Shiro Fukai; editor, Nobutaro Miyamoto. At Berlin Film Fest. Running time, **95 MINS.**

Japan's "Horse Boy" is another contribution to the currently popular parents' problem. It's a passionate accusation of a young boy against his mother who had to leave him for reasons of "representation."

Film borders much on sentimentality but remains entertaining and even amusing at times, thanks to the lovable acting of Motoharu Ueki who, portraying the title role, nearly steals the show. Although much about this Japanese production appears strange to western audiences, there's no doubt that its general appeal won't be limited to Japanese patrons only. *Hans.*

Bakaruhaban (In Soldier's Uniform) **(HUNGARIAN).** Hunnia Film production and release. Stars Ivan Darvas, Margit Bara; features Sandor Pecsi, Vali Korompai, Bela Barsi. Directed by Imre Feher. Screenplay, Miklos Hubay from novel by Sandor Hunyadi; camera, Janos Badal; editor, Mihaly Morell; music, Tibor Polgar. At Karlovy Vary Fest. Running time, **90 MINS.**

There is no political aspect in this, and with a U. S. distributor ready to handle an unusual pic without worrying about whether its origin will militate against it, this is it. It has the quality for American arties plus entertainment values for some regular spots.

It occurs during the first World War. A journalist, who only has to wear his uniform twice a week, meets a servant girl so garbed, and turns from a flirtation into love. She works for the family of a girl he has been linked with before. Finally it is time for the truth and the girl walks out leaving the weak hero behind.

Film has verve and is brilliantly directed by Imre Feher, who blends satire, gentle comedy and a slightly bitter denoument. Ivan Darvas and Margit Bara are excellent as the leads, turning in some of truest love scenes seen in Eastern pic. Direction, acting and technical aspects are tops to further enhance this unique pic. *Mosk.*

Lissy (EAST GERMAN). DEFA production and release. Stars Sonia Sutter; features Hans-Peter Minetti, Horst Drinda, Kurt Oligmuller. Directed by Konrad Wolf. Screenplay, Alex Wedding from novel by F. Weiskopf; camera, Werner Bergmann; editor, C. Gottchalk. At Karlovy Vary Fest. Running time, **90 MINS.**

With East German pix probably to get entry into the U.S. soon, this pic brooks interest. It examines the early growth of Naziism via a poor family during 1932-34. Ideological aspects do not swamp a growing drama of awareness, and the people remain real to give this a jolting effect. It is strictly for specialized and language spots in the U. S.

Lissy is a young girl whose weak husband turns to the Nazis—where he is unable to find work. Film details her growing hatred of it and her final desertion from her husband because of it, as it grows into a scourge. Sonia Sutter gives depth to the girl character while the rest of the cast helps make this a telling pic of troubled times. Direction is solid, if only surface at times, and technical wrap-up is fine. *Mosk.*

Donne Del Giorno (The Girl of the Day) **(ITALIAN).** Lux Film production and release. Stars Virna Lisi, Haya Hararit; features Serge Reggiani, E. Cegani, V. Sanipoli, Franco Fabrizi. Directed by Francesco Maselli. Screenplay, Cesare Zavattini, A. Sarioli, F. Bemporad, Maselli; camera, Armando Nannuzzi; editor, Mario Serandrei. At Karlovy Vary Fest. Running time, **90 MINS.**

Film digs into the harsh world of show biz success. A girl fakes an attack to get some publicity, but situation gets out of hand and she is forced to name her attackers, a group of suspicious men picked up by the police. The girl finally breaks down and tells the truth.

This is well mounted, but only rarely becomes dramatic and effective. Pic shapes mainly for specialized spots in America. Direction is careful and poised and denotes a new talent in Francesco Maselli. Haya Hararit and Virna Lisi are excellent with Miss Hararit carrying the brunt of the thesping. Production dess is fine. *Mosk.*

Bbicot (High Up) **(RUSSIAN; COLOR).** Mosfilm production and release. With Nikolai Rybnikov, Inna Makarova, Gennaid Karnovich, Vasili Makarov. Directed by Alexandre Zarkhi. Screenplay, Mikhail Papava from novel by E. Vorobiev; camera (Sovcolor), Vasili Monakhov; editor, Abram Friedin. At Karlovy Vary Fest. Running time, **95 MINS.**

This Russo film again treats work as its theme, but it has enough individual characters to attract some interest. It remains a small possibility for the U.S., however. Film concerns the building a giant blast furnace and the lives of the people working it. People fall in and out of love and one worker even falls off duty.

Characters are nicely drawn and acted while special effects and process work on the building sites are well done. Color is fine. This is another example of some better Soviet filmmaking. *Mosk.*

The Man Called Demon (JAPANESE). Nikkacu Film production and release. With Mihashi, Michiyo Aratama, Izumi Ashikawa. Directed by Eisuke Takizawa. Screenplay, Toshio Yasumi; camera, Minoru Yokayama; editor, Masuro Sato. At Karlovy Vary Fest. Running time, 100 MINS.

Film deals with a poor man who takes over a bagnio in the Japan of the 1900's only to become ruthless and obsessed by money. Pic is a journalist account of the legal prostitution setup, and this becomes the film's main interest.

Otherwise, it is well made if plodding for Western tastes. Only chance for Yank spots is via exploitation of its central theme. It is well acted and technically of high calibre. *Mosk.*

The Pajama Game
(MUSICAL—COLOR)

Socko filmusical transmutation of the click Broadway legiter with many of the original cast in the pic version. Big grosses.

Warner Bros. release of George Abbott-Stanley Donen production (Frederick Brisson, Robert E. Griffith & Harold S. Prince associate producers), directed by Abbott and Donen. Stars Doris Day and John Raitt; features Carol Haney, Eddie Foy Jr. Screenplay, Abbott and Richard Bissell from their stage libretto, adapted from Bissell's novel, "7½ Cents"; songs, Richard Adler and Jerry Ross; original stage production directed by Abbott & Jerome Robbins; camera (WarnerColor), Harry Stradling; dances, Bob Fosse; arrangements, Nelson Riddle & Buddy Bregman. Charles Henderson (vocal): asst. director, Russ Llewellyn; editor, William Ziegler; costumes, William & Jean Eckart, assisted by Frank Thompson; art director, Malcolm Bert; sets, William Kuehl; makeup, Gordon Bau; technical advisor, Weldon Pajama Co. Tradeshown N.Y. July 26, '57. Running time, 101 MINS.

Babe	Doris Day
Sid	John Raitt
Gladys	Carol Haney
Hines	Eddie Foy Jr.
Mabel	Reta Shaw
Poopsie	Barbara Nichols
Mae	Thelma Pelish
Prez	Jack Straw
Hasler	Ralph Dunn
Max	Owen Martin
1st Helper	Jackie Kelk
Charlie	Ralph Chambers
Brenda	Mary Stanton
Dancers	Buzz Miller, Kenneth LeRoy

The inherent mobility and fluidity of "Pajama Game" as a stage property apparently was such that this almost faithful transmutation into celluloid requires little physical enhancement to impress the WarnerColorful filmusical as a sock b.o. entry.

True, coproducers-codirectors George Abbott and Stanley Donen have not slighted the opportunities for size and scope when occasion warranted, such as in the picnic scenes, the labor union rallies and the pajama factory which is background for some skillful Bob Fosse-conceived choreography. Having the advantage, as did many of the back-of- and front-of-the-camera artisans and players, of longtime association with the original, the celluloid version is an extension and an enhancement of the original.

But so locked-in are the basic values that it's almost a foolproof property, and both Warners and the Brisson-Griffith & Prince original production team, which shares with the Burbank plant in the profits, are in for a hefty chunk. More important, the customers are assured of an eyeful and earful of compelling entertainment.

If the film version contains a shade more of social significance in the labor-engagement hassle, which was the springboard of the original Bissell novel, "7½ Cents," from which stems the romantic conflict between pajama factory superintendent John Raitt (who created the original stage role) and "grievance committee chairman" Doris Day (in the role created by Janis Paige) in May, 1954, it is a plus value because of the sturdy book.

Raitt, properly serious as the earnest factory executive and earnestly smitten with the blonde and beauteous Doris Day, has good antithesis in his romantic vis-a-vis. Miss Day, always authoritative with a song and now a poised picture personality as she was/is on disks, is an appealing looker. She makes her chore even a shade more believable than Raitt. Carol Haney, recreating her soubret role opposite Eddie Foy (also of the original stage cast), whams with "Steam Heat," aided by Buzz Miller (stage original) and Kenneth LeRoy (substituting for Peter Gennaro of the Broadway cast).

Reta Shaw, Thelma Pelish, Ralph Dunn and Ralph Chambers are also Broadway expatriates in the film version. Stanley Prager's factory labor president is capably done by Jack Straw and Mary Stanton has the original Marion Colby assignment.

The Dick Adler and (now the late) Jerry Ross songs are as durable as when first spawned over three years ago and it's a tribute to the Brisson-Griffith-Prince-Abbott team that they showcased and envisioned the great talent that this tunesmithing team portended. The melodies are as durable today as then and the lyrics a sizeable cut above the conventional wordage. "Small Talk," "There Once Was a Man," "I'm Not at All in Love," "Trust Her" are solid chunks of material. Some highly effective double-numbers are integrated into the libretto and, like the frothy "Once-a-Year Day" (piano number) and of course the standout ballad hit, "Hey There," prove strong contributory factors to the sum total.

There's a technical credit to the Weldon Pajama Co. which undoubtedly accounts for the authoritative factory scenes. The cinematurgical credits are consistently good on all values. Where Abbott left off and Donen began, and vice versa, on the curious co-billing as producers-directors (not to mention Abbott's multiple assists on the book) is beside the point in light of the okay sum total. Abbott and Bissell had little problem with screenplaying their stage original. Harry Stradling's WarnerColor lensing is tiptop as are all the other credits. The 101 minutes running time is just right. *Abel.*

Omar Khayyam
(VISTAVISION—COLOR)

Sometimes cumbersome and draggy but lavish and colorful romance; probably commercial.

Hollywood, July 30.
Paramount production and release. Stars Cornel Wilde, Michael Rennie, Debra Paget, John Derek, Raymond Massey; features Yma Sumac, Margaret Hayes, Joan Taylor. Producer, Frank Freeman Jr. Director, William Dieterle. Screenplay, Barre Lyndon; camera, Ernest Laszlo; technicolor consultant, Richard Mueller; editor, Everett Douglas; art directors, Hal Pereira, Joseph MacMillan Johnson; music score, Victor Young; songs, "The Loves of Omar Khayyam," by Jay Livingston and Ray Evans, "Take My Heart" by Mack David and Young, "Lament," by Moises Vivanco. Previewed at Studio, July 29, '57. Running time, 101 MINS.

Omar	Cornel Wilde
Hasani	Michael Rennie
Sharain	Debra Paget
The Shah	Raymond Massey
Malik (Young Prince)	John Derek
Karina	Yma Sumac
Zarada	Margaret Hayes
Yaffa	Joan Taylor
Nizam	Sebastian Cabot
Prince Ahmud	Perry Lopez
Imam Mowaffak	Morris Ankrum
Tutush	Abraham Sofaer
Jayhan	Edward Platt
Buzorg	James Griffith
Master Herald	Peter Adams
1st Commander	Henry Brandon
Tutush Bodyguard	Kem Dibbs
2nd Commander	Paul Picerni

Static cumbersomeness of some of the romantic love duets, pretty heavyhanded between Cornel Wilde and Debra Paget flaw this spectacular, but well-staged battle and court intrigue sequence speed up the pace and hold interest. Net of the production's lavish and colorful values is probably commercial.

Director William Dieterle impressively handles the masses of extras employed, and his staging of the big sequences score. More spotty are the personal relationships, which sometime get lost in the grandeur, and drag.

Barre Lyndon script sets forth Omar as an oriental equivalent of the later Renaissance man—poet, lover, scholar, scientist and court counsellor—all in one. Lyndon weaves romance between Omar and his wife of the ruling Shah, against intrigue in court and the machinations of the murderous and mysterious Eastern cult of Assassins (which actually existed), not to mention 11th Century warfare between Persian and Byzantine empires. Sprinkled throughout are recitations from the Rubaiyat.

Cornel Wilde, as Omar, is in love with high-born lady Debra Paget, who is bethothed to the Shah, Raymond Massey, for political reasons. Disillusioned, Omar turns to drink, verse and science to drown his sorrows, but his brilliant scholarship gains him advancement at court.

Comes now the intrigues. Noted warrior Michael Rennie, childhood friend of Omar, turns out to be the secret leader of the Assassins Cult. Margaret Hayes, as first wife of Shah, plots with Rennie to overthrow the Shah and his favorite son, John Derek, to install her son, Perry Lopez, on the throne. Meanwhile, the Assassins are knocking off other members of the Shah's personal and official family.

Wilde appeals strongly. Rennie, characteristically able, is very good as the ambition-ridden "Old Man of the Mountain," (a real historic personality). Miss Paget, however, lends little but pictorial beauty, and can't seem to catch fire.

In subordinate parts, Joan Taylor, as a devoted slave to Omar, especially impresses with fiery beauty. Margaret Hayes is good as the Queen. Yma Sumac does little along thesping lines, as slave-companion to Miss Paget, but her remarkable vocal gymnastics are a production asset. Sebastian Cabot and Abraham Sofaer are especially good in lesser parts, and Lopez, Morris Ankrum, Edward Platt, James Griffith and Peter Adams also rate mention.

Technically, production is of strikingly high order. Color photography of Ernest Laszlo, with assist from Technicolor's Richard Mueller, settings of Hal Pereira and Joseph MacMillan Johnson, special effects of John P. Fulton, and costuming of Ralph Jester all rate individual notice. Late Victor Young's musical score reflects his skill. Individual songs by Jay Livingston and Ray Evans, Mack David and Young, and Moises Vivanco are good, but none seems especially notable outside of picture setting. *Kove.*

My Gun Is Quick

Senseless blood and gore in the Spillane tradition. Only fair b.o. results indicated.

Hollywood, July 26.
United Artists release of a Victor Saville production. Stars Robert Bray; features Whitney Blake, Donald Randolph, Richard Garland, Fred Essler, Booth Colman, Pamela Duncan, Gina Core, Patricia Donahue, Jan Chaney. Produced and directed by George A. White and Phil Victor. Screenplay, Richard Powell and Richard Collins, from Mickey Spillane novel. Camera, Harry Neuman; editor, Frank Sullivan; art director, Boris Leven; music, Marlin Skiles. Previewed, July 25, '57. Running time, 91 MINS.

Mike Hammer	Robert Bray
Nancy	Whitney Blake

Dione .... Pat Donahue
Holloway .... Donald Randolph
Velda .... Pamela Duncan
Captain Pat .... Booth Colman
Red .... Jan Chaney
Maria .... Gina Core
Lou .... Richard Garland
Gangster .... Charles Boaz
La Roche .... Peter Mamakos
Proprietress .... Claire Carleton
Shorty .... Phil Arnold
Al .... John Dennis
Jean .... Terrence De Marney
Stripper .... Jackie Paul
Teller .... Leon Askin
Hotel Clerk .... Jack Holland

At the end of 91 minutes, the box score for this Mickey Spillane epic stands at seven assorted killings, two vicious beatings of the current Mike Hammer (Robert Bray) and four decorative femmes making abrupt passes at him, not to mention one strictly platonic affair. This represents a milder Spillane, fanciers of his works may insist.

Spillane has long represented a saleable commodity. However, last picturization of his novels, while still profitable, didn't do as well at the wickets as previous excursions. On this basis, senseless brutality, murky plotting and unsubtle sex seems to have diminishing appeal and prospects for this outing seem milder.

Bray, as Hammer, wends his psychopathic way through the piled-on skullduggery surrounding a batch of jewels "liberated" during World War II by Donald Randolph, an ex-army colonel. Various femmes Bray befriends en route turn up dead in picturesque ways, enraging him further.

Two separate gangs are competing for the jewels, while cops only bluster and get lost. Final shooting and stabbing match on a fishing boat wipes out one gang and it turns out that Whitney Blake, lovely femme having a torrid fling with Bray, is the ringleader of the other gang. So in the immemorial Spillane tradition, Bray turns her over to the cops with a combination of profound regret and tight-lipped scorn.

Bray has enough masculine appeal and acting ability to do better in a more sensible role. Misses Blake, Pat Donahue, Pamela Duncan and Gina Core all display attractive figures and are up to undemanding requirements. As gallant demimonde who gets killed early, Jan Chaney displays a pixieish charm. Randolph, Richard Garland, Peter Mamakos and Terrence De Marney are okay and Booth Colman is properly exasperated as a police friend of Bray's.

Scripting by Richard Powell and Richard Collins follows the original Spillane novel fairly closely, which perhaps isn't much of a recommendation. Scenario is liberally sprinkled with "hells" and "damns," lending a certain shock value.

Team of George White and Phil Victor produced and directed. They try more than the production is worth.

Technical credits are slick and able. *-Kove.*

Lady of Vengeance

Far - fetched melodramatic plotting for less discriminating bookings only.

Hollywood, Aug. 2.
United Artists release of a Burt Balaban-Bernard Donnenfeld production. Stars Dennis O'Keefe; features Ann Sears, Patrick Barr, Anton Diffring. Directed by Balaban. Story-screenplay, Irve Tunick; camera, Ian Struthers; editor, Eric Boyd-Perkins; music, Phil Cardew. Previewed Aug. 2, '57. Running time, **75 MINS.**

William T. Marshall ..... Dennis O'Keefe
Katie Whiteside .... Ann Sears
Karnak .... Anton Diffring
Inspector Madden .... Patrick Barr
Larry Shaw .... Vernon Greeves
Melissa .... Eileen Elton
Schteigel .... Frederick Schiller
Penny .... Jacqueline Curtiss
Bennett .... George Mulcaster
Hawley .... Gerald Case
Coroner .... Jack McNaughton
Bartender .... Colin Croft
Houseman .... Andy Ho
Corbey .... Humphrey Morton

Burdened with a contrived and confusing plot, import carries small appeal for American audiences. Even for the less discriminating program situations it's a dull entry, ponderously and often amateurishly produced and of a genre that went out many years ago on screen.

The revenge motive springboards the unfoldment of the Burt Balaban-Bernard Donnenfeld production, with Dennis O'Keefe the only name known to U.S. theatregoers. When his ward commits suicide, O'Keefe, a driving American publisher of a London newspaper, receives a last letter from her, asking that he wreak vengeance on the man who drove her to her death. To comply with this request, O'Keefe calls in a master criminal to plot an ingenious murder which will be mental torture before the final commitment.

O'Keefe doesn't have much chance with his character, which belongs in the silents rather than 1957, and other characters are artificial right down the line. Anton Diffring is the master mind, Ann Sears the publisher's secretary, both good enough artists but lost here, and Vernon Greeves is a London orch leader Romeo responsible for Eileen Elton, the ward, leaving home and whom audience thinks is the object of her vengeance. Patrick Barr is a police inspector.

Balaban's direction of the story-screenplay by Irve Tunick lacks finish. Technical credits are below average. *Whit.*

Tormento D'Amore
(Torment of Love)
(SPANISH-ITALIAN)

Rome, July 30.
SIDEN Release of a Romana Films-Union Films production. Stars Marta Toren, Massimo Serato; features Otello Toso, Jose Nieto. Directed by Claudio Gora. Screenplay, Gora, Leonardo Bercovici, from story by J. A. Bardem; camera (Cinepanscope), Alfredo Fraile; editor, Jolanda Benvenuti; music, Bucchi. At Supercinema, Rome. Running time, **90 MINS.**
Luigi Sanz .... Otello Toso
Sara .... Marta Toren
Pietro .... Massimo Serato

This last pic made by the late Marta Toren includes some of her best thesping in well-made, slightly overlong film. The intricate, interesting plot by J. A. Bardem is worth of remake consideration. Okay for lingual situations, this is iffy elsewhere.

Complicated plotting tells of woman's suicide for love because the crucial letter from her fiance gets stuck in letter box for three years, thus initiating a series of tragic misunderstandings. Opens slowly, and could be trimmed here, but gains power and punch towards the end where plot melds together.

Thesping is fine in all sectors, with Miss Toren moving in her portrayal of the unfortunate victim of the postal mishap. Pic was scripted by her husband, Leonardo Bercovici, who also rates co-direction credit with Claudio Gora, both handling chores creditably.

Lensing and other production credits on this Spanish-shot item are unusually expert. *Hawk.*

Woman of the River
(COLOR)

Sophia Loren in a dubbed-into-English potboiler. Doubtful b.o. potential.

Columbia presentation of Dino De Laurentiis-Carlo Ponti production. Stars Sophia Loren; features Rick Battaglia, Gerard Oury, Lise Bourdin. Directed by Mario Soldati. Screenplay, Basilio Franchina, Giorgio Bassani, Pier Paolo Pasolini, Florestano Vancini, Antonio Altoviti, Mario Soldati; from story by Alberto Morasia and Ennio Flaiano; dialog, Ben Zavin; camera (Technicolor), Otello Martelli; music, Angelo F. Lavagnino and Armando Trovaioli. Previewed in N.Y. July 31, '57. Running time, **92 MINS.**
Nives .... Sophia Loren
Gino Lodi .... Rick Battaglia
Enzo Cinti .... Gerard Oury
Tosca .... Lise Bourdin
Oscar .... Enrico Olivieri

This picture has two virtues: Sophia Loren, whose physical attributes a la Jane Russell-Jayne Mansfield, et al., are sufficient to "fill" any close-up and the outdoor lensing by Otello Martelli which is reminiscent in its effectiveness of some of the early postwar Italian neo-realist films. Apart from that, "Woman of the River" shapes as routine melodrama that is unlikely to make much of a dent on the boxoffice.

Since they didn't have much of a story, the scripters—there are six of 'em—concentrated on the part of Miss Loren, which was probably wise under the circumstances. She runs the gamut from temptress to lover to tragedienne and there's no question that, whatever she does or how she does it, the actress is a joy to behold.

Yarn involves a countrygirl who has an affair with a smuggler. He leaves her and she denounces him to the police. She moves away from her village and bears his child. Escaping from prison, he comes seeking revenge, only to arrive the day that the child has drowned. Ending brings the two together at the funeral.

With trite material to work with, director Mario Soldati has managed to come up with some interesting touches, building little scenes into impressive ones.

"Woman of the River" has been dubbed from the Italian into English, and technically it's a good job except for English dialog, which is often poor and hard to take. Rick Battaglia as Miss Loren's seducer does okay. Same is true of Gerard Oury as the policy officer in love with Miss Loren. Lise Bourdin is pretty as a friend. They all pale before Miss Loren's extrovert performance which, in its lustier moments, emerges almost as a caricature of some of her earlier roles. No question, though, that the "earthy" touch has positive exploitation values. *Hift.*

Unknown Terror
(REGALSCOPE)

Mad doctor gambit involves mold cultures and is also moldy in script and conception. For uncritical clientele. Packaged with "Back From the Dead."

Hollywood, July 31.
20th-Fox release of a Regal Films production. Stars John Howard, Mala Powers, Paul Richards, May Wynn; features Gerald Milton. Producer, Robert Stabler. Director, Charles Marquis Warren. Screenplay, Kenneth Higgins; camera, Joseph Biroc; editor, Fred W. Berger; art director, James W. Sullivan; music, Raoul Kraushaar. Previewed, July 30, '57. Runningtime, **76 MINS.**
Dan Mathews .... John Howard
Gina Mathews .... Mala Powers
Pete Morgan .... Paul Richards
Concha .... May Wynn
Dr. Ramsey .... Gerald Milton
Lino .... Duane Gray
Jim Wheatly .... Charles Gray
Butler .... Charles Postal
Dr. Willoughby .... Patrick O'Moore
Trainer .... William Hamel
Raul Kom .... Richard Gilden
Old Indian .... Martin Garralaga
Himself .... Sir Lancelot

In this variation of the mad doctor gambit, captives held in a cave are dosed with foaming, bubbling mold cultures. They wind up a mess and so does the plot.

John Howard, Mala Powers and Paul Richards portray Yanks who come down to an isolated Central American village to search for Miss Powers' brother, lost in a cave-exploring accident. They fall in with sinister doc Gerald Milton and by the end, it transpires that Milton's been using human guinea pigs in his experiments with mold cultures. Also, Howard expires heroically, leaving Miss Powers to take up again with Richards, disillusioned in a previous romantic setto.

Director Charles Marquis Warren keeps things at the necessarily elementary level. The Kenneth Higgins script is distinguished only by its moldy quality.

The Howard - Powers - Richards trio perform as capably as they could reasonably be expected to. May Wynn, in a sort of Tondelayo role as Milton's Indian wife, flares her nostrils attractively. Milton makes a completely despicable and untrustworthy knave, in a broad manner. *Kove.*

3:10 to Yuma

Superior western which bears a strong family resemblance to "High Noon." Marred by ending, but still stacks up as major b.o.

Hollywood, Aug. 7.
Columbia production and release. Stars Glenn Ford, Van Heflin, Felicia Farr; features Leora Dana, Henry Jones, Richard Jaeckel, Robert Emhardt. Producer, David Heilweil. Director, Delmer Daves. Screenplay, Halsted Welles, from Elmore Leonard story; camera, Charles Lawton Jr.; editor, Al Clark; art director, Frank Hotaling; music, composed by George Duning, conducted by Morris Stoloff. Title song by Ned Washington and Duning. Previewed, July 25, '57. Running time, 92 MINS.

Ben Wade	Glenn Ford
Dan Evans	Van Heflin
Emmy	Felicia Farr
Alice Evans	Leora Dana
Alex Potter	Henry Jones
Charlie Prince	Richard Jaeckel
Mr. Butterfield	Robert Emhardt
Bob Moons	Sheridan Comerate
Bartender	George Mitchell
Ernie Collins	Robert Ellenstein
Marshal	Ford Rainey
Mathew	Barry Curtis
Mark	Jerry Hartleben

Aside from the fact that this is an upper-drawer western, with both quality names and production, "3:10 to Yuma" will strike many for its resemblance to "High Noon." It still stacks up as a major entry, save for a contrived finale which leaves a bad taste. With starring names (especially Glenn Ford) of proven marquee value and generally high grade quality, b.o. is indicated.

Offering is carefully mounted by producer David Heilweil. Director Delmer Daves continues to justify his reputation as a rising talent in that department. That the climax fizzles must be laid on doorstep of Halsted Welles, who had adapted Elmore Leonard's story quite well until that point.

Ford portrays the deadly leader of a slickly professional outlaw gang, which holds up a stagecoach. (Keynote to Ford's character is given early, when he coldly guns down one of his band.)

Van Heflin, impoverished neighborhood rancher, helps capture Ford when the latter lags behind his gang, to dally with lovely, lonely town barmaid, Felicia Farr. But Ford's gang is too strong for local lawmen to handle. Stagecoach owner Robert Emhardt promises a large reward—which could bail out Heflin's drought-stricken ranch—to Heflin and the town drunk, Henry Jones. Idea is to hold Ford in another town, unknown to his gang, until daily train (3:10 of title) can take him to Yuma for trial.

Here, story cleaves closely to "High Noon" formula. First, Ford's henchman, Richard Jaeckel, discovers the hideout. Then, one by one, Heflin's supporters either desert him or are killed, leaving him to face the gang single-handed. Meanwhile, proud and duty-bound Heflin has threats and bribe offers from Ford to fight off.

Well-staged closing scenes has Ford's gang stalk Heflin and the gang leader through the deserted streets. But at the crucial moment, with no clear motivation, Ford himself helps Heflin carry out his mission. And then, to make Heflin's cup run over, the drought which has been ruining his ranch is suddenly broken.

Ford's switch-casting, as the quietly sinister gang leader, is authorative, impressive and successful. That the ending betrays him isn't his fault. Heflin measures up fully and convincingly to the rewarding role of the proud and troubled rancher. Miss Farr's contribution is a short one, but she registers with a touching poignancy and a delicate beauty which promises well for her future.

Supporting players, carefully cast, fully justify their choice. Leora Dana as Heflin's understanding wife, Jones as the weakling who finds momentary strength before he's brutally killed, and Emhardt as the employer who fails Heflin, are especially noteworthy. Jaeckel, as Ford's chief lieutenant, is hampered by a role a shade too simple-minded for complete acceptance, but registers well nonetheless. In lesser parts, Sheridan Comerate and Ford Rainey are especially good, as are moppets Barry Curtis and Jerry Hartleben as Heflin's sons.

Technical credits reflect painstaking and skillful care, especially the fine camera work of Charles Lawton. Title song by Ned Washington and George Duning, sung by Frankie Laine under credits and by Norma Zimmer during the picture, is a well-written tune. However, here too, it must bear the burden of likeness to "High Noon," notably in employment.
Kove.

No Time for Tears
(BRITISH-COLOR)

Leisurely, sentimental peep at life in a children's hospital. Individually smooth thesping by Anna Neagle in routine b.o. offering.

London, Aug. 13.
Associated British-Pathe release of Associated British (W. A. Whittaker) Production. Stars Anna Neagle, George Baker, Sylvia Syms, Anthony Quayle, Flora Robson. Directed by Cyril Frankel. Screenplay, Anne Burnaby; camera, Gilbert Taylor; editor, Gordon Pilkington; music, Francis Chagrin. At Rialto Theatre, London, Aug. 8, '57. Running time, 86 MINS.

The Matron	Anna Neagle
Doctor Seagrave	Anthony Quayle
Margaret	Sylvia Syms
Nigel	George Baker
Hugh	Alan White
Marian	Daphne Anderson
The Surgeon	Michael Hordern
Sister Birch	Flora Robson
Sister Duckworth	Joan Hickson
Sister Willis	Sophie Stewart
Sister Davies	Patricia Marmont
Theatre Sister	Rosalie Crutchley
Out-Patients' Sister	Joan Sims
Mr. Harris	Victor Brooks
Mrs. Harris	Angela Baddeley
Cathy	Adrienne Poster
George	Christopher Witty
Timmy	Jonathan Ley
Timmy's Mother	Josephine Stuart
The Twins	The Boulting Twins

Hospital life has long held an uncanny fascination for film producers, and staging "No Time for Tears" in a children's hospital is a shrewd move for capturing the sentimental filmgoer. In Britain, the names of such favorites as Anna Neagle, George Baker, Sylvia Syms and Anthony Quayle, plus the appeal of a dozen or more screen moppets will help this routine comedy-weepie to success. But in the U. S., the ducat-buyers will be less malleable although the Anna Neagle name means something.

Anne Burnaby's story introduces too many interwoven anecdotes. In her screenplay too many characters are only superficially developed and their personalities tend to get lost in the general scrimmage. Director Cyril Frankel has done a conscientious job in trying to weave the many threads into a pattern which fits in to the authentic, though over-jolly, hospital atmosphere. But the overall result of this uneasy blend of laughter and tears is flabby entertainment.

The various story lines include the matron's concern for two neglected children; a romance between a probationer nurse and a philandering anaesthetist; the fight to save a child from paralysis and blindness and a budding romance between a young girl and the boy next door.

The characters are mainly stock ones from the hospital files but they are all well played within the limits of a script that is ridden with cliches. Miss Neagle portrays the kindly, middle-aged matron with her usual dignity and integrity. Sylvia Syms, as a probationer nurse, gives fresh evidence that she is developing into one of Britain's best young screen actresses.

There are sound character studies by Sophie Stewart, Joan Hickson and Flora Robson as differing hospital sisters while George Baker, Alan White and Anthony Quayle are equally varied as doctors. Outstanding is an incisive cameo by Michael Hordern as a testy, cynical surgeon. Angela Baddeley also makes a distinct mark as a slatternly mother.

But the adult performances are up against stiff competition from an array of child actors. Notable are a pair of identical twins (played by the twin sons of film director Roy Boulting), Jonathan Ley, Richard O'Sullivan, and Judith Stott, who gives a touching study of a crippled girl who wants to be beautiful all over.

The laughs are too obviously planted with a view to offsetting the sentimental and pathetic moments. Although Gilbert Taylor's photography is excellent, this film would have been more effective in black and white. Color does, however, permit the climax to be a gay hospital Christmas pantomime in which Miss Syms plays Cinderella and proves that her destiny lies in straight acting, rather than as a singing star.
Rich.

Tip On a Dead Jockey
(C'Scope)

Pic takes some time to get rolling, but once it does, it stacks up as satisfactory action offering and b.o. fare.

Metro Production and Release. Stars Robert Taylor, Dorothy Malone. Co-stars Gia Scala. Features Martin Gabel, Jack Lord, Marcel Dalio, Joyce Jameson. Produced by Edwin H. Knopf. Directed by Richard Thorpe. Screenplay by Charles Lederer from an Irwin Shaw story in New Yorker magazine. Camera, George J. Folsey; editor, Ben Lewis; art directors, William A. Horning, Hans Peters; music, Miklos Rozsa. Song, "You Found Me and I Found You," Jerome Kern and P. G. Wodehouse. Previewed, Aug. 9, '57. Running time, 98 MINS.

Lloyd Tredman	Robert Taylor
Phyllis Tredman	Dorothy Malone
Paquita Heldon	Gia Scala
Bert Smith	Martin Gabel
Toto del Aro	Marcel Dalio
Jimmy Heldon	Jack Lord
Sue Fan Finley	Joyce Jameson

Once this "Jockey" spurs up momentum, film shapes as a solid, satisfactory action picture. However, plots dealing with war-weary pilots who have lost their nerve have an overfamiliar ring by now. Smart, updated dialogue by Charles Lederer, in adapting Irwin Shaw's New Yorker tale, doesn't entirely dispel the familiar.

Against foregoing, Robert Taylor still has good marquee value, and colorful background of a decadent, post-war Franco Spain should arouse some interest. With proper push, pic should do a satisfactory biz.

In brittle, cosmopolitan expatriate society of Madrid, Taylor is the ex-pilot, afraid of emotional entanglements because his war job was sending pilots to their deaths. He's now eking out a precarious existence on the fringes of Spain's precarious economy. Off-beat title reflects this, when he loses his entire bankroll on a horse-race in which his jockey is killed in a spill.

Dorothy Malone is his wife, fighting to regain his love after he requests a divorce. To help raise coin for war buddy Jack Lord, and Lord's lovely Spanish wife, Gia Scala, Taylor undertakes a currency-smuggling caper proposed by sinister Martin Gabel. Here, film picks up tempo, especially in chase sequences involving various Mediterranean police authorities. But when Taylor and acompanying friend Marcel Dalio discover that the shipment also includes narcotics, Taylor blows the whistle on the deal and sics the Spanish cops on Gabel. Meantime, Taylor's confidence is restored in himself and he resumes with both Miss Malone and his pre-war career as an airline pilot.

Taylor and direction overcome some rather overwritten soul-searching sequences to appeal with a solid, professional job of thesping. Miss Malone is a handsome addition to any cast, and sparks attractively, but should work on fidgety mannerisms which tend to detract. Miss Scala impresses as a most attractive femme and a good actress, but she still needs work on her English, which isn't always quite clear.

Among the supporting cast, Dalio is a delight as Taylor's charming, perpetual "house guest." Gabel handles his villainy with an appropriately smooth menace. Lord continues to show possibilities and Joyce Jameson, in a bit as a man-crazy Southern blonde, plays it broadly for very amusing results.

Richard Thorpe rather misses in his direction of earlier sequences, failing to lend much dimension to the exotic grabbag of characters. However, as story line simplifies, he picks up the pace.

Technical credits, especially airplane sequences well-photographed by George J. Folsey, reflects Metro's leadership in this field.
Kove.

Portland Expose

Strong exploitation entry for heavy returns; based on real-life Oregon racket setup.

Hollywood, Aug. 9.
Allied Artists release of a Lindsley Parsons production. Features Edward Binns, Carolyn Craig. Directed by Harold Schuster. Screenplay, Jack DeWitt; camera, Carl Berger; editor, Maurice Wright; music, Paul Dunlap. Previewed Aug. 7, '57. Running time, 70 MINS.

George Madison	Edward Binns
Ruth Madison	Carolyn Craig
Clara Madison	Virginia Gregg
Phillip Jacman	Russ Conway
Garnell	Larry Dobkin
Joe	Frank Gorshin
Larry	Joe Marr
Tom Cramody	Rusty Lane
Jimmy Madison	Dickie Bellis
Mrs. Stoneway	Lea Penman
Iris	Jeanne Carmen
Lennox	Stanley Farrar
Capt. Vincent	Larry Thor
Alfred Grey	Francis de Sales
Speed Bromley	Kort Falkenberg
Ted Carl	Joe Flynn

Allied Artists has a strong exploitation entry in Lindsley Parsons' "Portland Expose," based upon vice and racket setup in the Oregon city area which led to investigations by Senate McClellan Committee earlier this year involving many prominent names in Pacific Northwest. Where fact and pressagentry meet is undefined but Allied has an exploitation peg in having allegedly been cancelled out by mob-politician pressure.

Topic is of a city being taken over by organized crime, as in "respectable" Portland. The Jack DeWitt screenplay pinpoints overall situation through the experiences of a small tavern owner, an honest family man, being caught up in the webs of a syndicate trying to become overlord of Portland. Story is sharply told against actual Portland setting and developed by Parsons along showmanship lines, vigorously directed by Harold Schuster and well enacted by a capable cast.

Edward Binns captures the spirit of a man forced against his will to play along with the crowd and allow his roadhouse to be turned into a hot spot after hoods threaten to disfigure his 17-year-old daughter with acid. When daughter is attacked by one of goons, he sends his family out of town and becomes undercover man for a group of honest citizens trying to clean up the city, headed by a union labor leader. Tape recordings he's able to get finally lead to break-up of gang and restoration of order to the city, after he's nearly killed by gang.

Russ Conway ably plays the gang leader, Larry Dobkin his lieutenant and Frank Gorshin and Joe Marr a couple of hoods. Carolyn Craig is good as Binns' wife and Virginia Gregg is okay as the daughter. Balance of cast make their individual performances count.

Technical credits match general quality of film, headed by Carl Berger's camera work and Maurice Wright's tight editing. Paul Dunlap's music score also fits well.

Whit.

The Badge of Marshal Brennan

Western story ruined by inept handling. For undiscriminating houses.

Hollywood, Aug. 6.

Allied Artists release of an Albert C. Gannaway production. Stars Jim Davis, Arleen Whelan, Lee Van Cleef, Louis Jean Heydt; features Carl Smith, Harry Lauter. Producer-director, Albert C. Gannaway; screenplay, Thomas G. Hubbard; camera, Charles Straumer; editor, Asa Clark; music composed and played (guitar) by Ramez Idriss. Song, "Man On the Run," by Hal Levy, Gannaway and Idriss. Previewed, Aug. 5, '57. Running time, **74 MINS.**

Stranger .... Jim Davis
Murdock .... Arleen Whelan
Shad Donaphin .... Lee Van Cleef
Col. Donaphin .... Louis Jean Heydt
Sheriff .... Carl Smith
Felipe .... Marty Robbins
Dr. Steve Hale .... Harry Lauter
Marshal .... Douglas Fowley
Chickamon .... Lawrence Dobkin

Inept oater suitable only for anything-goes audiences. Story by Thomas Hubbard (also associate producer) roughly deals with regenerating effect of the badge lifted from a dying U.S. marshal, Douglas Fowley, mortally wounded by Apaches. Lifter is Jim Davis, itinerant gunfighter fleeing a posse.

With badge, he arrives in a cowtown dominated by ruthless cattle barons Louis Jean Heydt and Lee Van Cleef. Pair are trying to conceal diseased cattle and Davis is forced into assuming marshal's identity by local sheriff Carl Smith and doctor Harry Lauter. With his newfound virtue, Davis wins the conflict and purty hash-house proprietor Arleen Whelan.

Story itself had possibilities, but producer-director Albert Gannaway's clumsy handling fumbles the ball, relying on the tried and trite. From their past credits, there's some pretty good actors involved, but they seem justifiably discouraged here. In passing, Carl Smith, hitherto a western singer, displays a promising native acting ability.

Harve Presnell ably sings fairly interesting tune, "Man on the Run," by Hal Levy, Gannaway and Ramez Idriss, under title credits. Idriss also composed and played guitar background music which, although somewhat overused, is one of few plusses in the production.

Kove.

No Time to Be Young

Grim, downbeat drama with unclear message, cargo of unsympathetic characters. Despite good acting, direction and production, appeal very limited.

Hollywood, July 13.

Columbia Pictures production and release. Stars Robert Vaughn. Features Roger Smith, Tom Pittman, Dorothy Green, Merry Anders, Kathy Nolan, Sarah Selby. Produced by Wallace MacDonald. Directed by David Rich. Screenplay by John McPartland, Raphael Hayes, from McPartland's story; camera, Henry Freulich; editor, Jerome Thoms; art director, Carl Anderson; music, Mischa Bakaleinikoff. Previewed, July 12, '57. Running time, **81 MINS.**

Buddy Root .... Robert Vaughn
Bob Miller .... Roger Smith
Stuart Bradley .... Tom Pittman
Mrs. Doris Dexter .... Dorothy Green
Gloria Stuben .... Merry Anders
Tina Parner .... Kathy Nolan
Helen Root .... Sarah Selby
Mr. Stuben .... Fred Sherman
Mr. Parner .... Ralph Clanton
Drive-In Manager .... Don C. Harvey
Sandra .... Bonnie Bolding

In this grim, downbeat story, the protagonist is a sadistic, completely self-centered no-good who leads two weak-willed companions into a bloody hold-up. Save for an accident, they, might have gotten away with it, which is certainly not the message intended. Just what the message is, is otherwise unclear.

There's no denying that producer Wallace MacDonald and director David Rich have lavished care and skill in mounting this John McPartland-Raphael Hayes screenplay, and the assembled young cast is a highly competant crew. However, outside of the maladjusted bopster crowds it's hard to conjure who's going to buy the tickets.

Favorite expression of chief character Robert Vaughn is, "Don't bug me." Impatient of the slightest restraint, he's been flunked out of college and wants to flee the consequences, i.e., the draft. He works out a shrewd scheme to hold up a supermarket, so that he and his companions can buy a boat and sail away from responsibilities.

His buddies have picturesque troubles of their own. Roger Smith is trying to raise dough to pay hospital bills of Merry Anders, a cheap hustler injured while on a rowdy date with him. Tom Pittman, unsuccessful young writer whose marriage to Kathy Nolan has broken up because of his lies, just wants to get away from it all.

But triggerhappy Vaughn unnecessarily kills the market-manager and, one by one, the cops pick up the other two. Only Vaughn remains, and he fails to survive a spectacular runaway ride in a stolen truck, when the brakes fail.

Vaughn employs a taut brutality which may endear him to the crowd which worships rebellious youth. Both Smith and Pittman also show considerable promise as skillful young actors. Dorothy Green manages to bring some sympathy to the role of a widowed and susceptible college instructress, in love and trying to help Vaughn, despite distasteful aspects of age difference in the affair. Miss Anders is good as the mercenary chippie and Kathy Nolan registers well as Pittman's trusting wife. Sarah Selby, as Vaughn's equally self-centered career-woman mother, is properly distasteful.

All technical credits show perhaps misplaced professional skill.

Kove.

Back From the Dead
(REGALSCOPE)

Attempt, only spasmodically successful, at an "adult" horror story. Teamed with "Unknown Terror."

Hollywood, July 31.

20th-Fox release of a Regal Films production. Stars Peggie Castle, Arthur Franz, Marsha Hunt, Don Haggerty; features Marianne Stewart, Otto Reichow, Helen Wallace, James Bell. Produced by Robert Stabler. Directed by Charles Marquis Warren. Screenplay by Catherine Turney, from her novel, "The Other One." Camera, Ernest Haller; editor, Fred W. Berger; art director, James W. Sullivan; music composed and conducted by Raoul Kraushaar. Previewed, July 30, '57. Running time, **78 MINS.**

Miranda .... Peggie Castle
Dick .... Arthur Franz
Katy .... Marsha Hunt
John .... Don Haggerty
Nancy .... Marianne Stewart
Molly .... Exelyn Scott
Mrs. Bradley .... Helen Wallace
Miss Townsend .... Jeane Wood
Mr. Bradley .... James Bell
Doctor .... Ned Glass
Father Renall .... Otto Reichow
Agnes .... Jeanne Bates

This is a laudable attempt, but only spasmodically successful, at an "adult" horror story. Trouble is that when the dust settles, story gaps are too glaring for grownup acceptance and horror aspects may prove too cerebral for the moppet trade. However, pic is part of a chiller bill made for the Regal-20th-Fox lineup (see "Unknown Terror"). As such, it should serve adequately.

Catherine Turney screenplay, from her novel, deals with combination of soul transmigration and black magic. Peggie Castle is chief victim, married to Arthur Franz. She becomes possessed by malevolent spirit of Franz' departed first wife. Seems that first wife had been involved in evil-worshipping sect headed by Otto Reichow.

Sister Marsha Hunt, Franz and sympathetic neighbor Don Haggerty fight against new Miss Castle and accompanying mumbo-jumbo, finally breaking up a blood sacrifice ceremony with another neighbor as intended victim. At this point, Reichow gets plugged by a rejected disciple, Marianne Stewart, and Miss Castle returns to her former self.

Director Charles Marquis Warren shows a distinct improvement with this effort, managing several scenes of considerable promise. However, he can't make the plotting come out even.

Actors are briskly competent, if not always able to convince. With best roles, Misses Castle and Hunt are both attractive and properly disturbed, although in different ways. Franz is hampered by weak part, but Haggerty is good as the stalwart neighbor. As heavies, Miss Stewart and Reichow are okay. James Bell andy Helen Wallace, as parents of dead first wife, also register, although scripting is more than ordinarily murky here.

Ernest Haller's photography, especially locations in Laguna area, is clean and sharp. For expectant suburbanites and home-builders, James W. Sullivan's settings are most interesting.

Kove.

The Flesh Is Weak
(BRITISH)

New British pic puts spotlight on prostitution, but makes only mild impact.

London, Aug. 6.

Eros (Raymond Stross)) production and release. Stars John Derek, Milly Vitale. Directed by Don Chaffey. Screenplay, Lee Vance; camera, Stephen Dade; music, Tristram Cary. At Cameo-Royal, London. Running time, **88 MINS.**

Tony Giani .... John Derek
Marissa Cooper .... Milly Vitale
Lloyd Buxton .... William Franklyn
Angelo Giani .... Martin Benson
Trixie .... Freda Jackson
Inspector Kingcombe ... Norman Wooland
Henry .... Harold Lang
Millie .... Patricia Jessel
Sgt. Franks .... John Paul
Saradine .... Denis Shaw
Lofty .... Joe Robinson
Benny .... Roger Snowden
Doris Newman .... Patricia Plunkett
Edna .... Vera Day
Susan .... Shirley Ann Field
Salvi .... Charles Lloyd Pack

It is difficult to know what producer Raymond Stross had in mind with "The Flesh is Weak," a study of prostitution in London's sleazy West End. As a social document, it makes only the mildest impact and fails lamentably to say anything new or penetrating about an urgent problem. As entertainment, it is rather mediocre stuff which likely will bore the discerning patron and sadly disappoint those in search of cheap thrills. Stross must be relying, optimistically, on the film's "X" certificate (which bars under 16's) as a magnet for boxoffice returns.

Obviously based on the notorious Messina vice gang, whose evil activities have helped to make London's West End a cesspool, Lee Vance's stereotyped screenplay gives an authentic glimpse of London nightlife, but has nothing new or worthwhile to say about the vice racket. Never once does the treatment penetrate the mind of the streetwalkers nor is there more than a superficial insight into what makes a pimp tick.

Story tells of a decent, unsophisticated girl who comes up from the country to find a career in London. She falls in love with a young man who turns out to be one of the Giani brothers, head boys in the flesh-peddling business. She is corrupted, becomes a streetwalker and lands in jail on a framed-up assault charge before she can be persuaded by a journalist to give the evidence which puts her lover behind bars.

Milly Vitale, as the girl, and John Derek, as the unscrupulous young thug, are convincing enough. So are Martin Benson, the leader of the gang, and William Franklyn, cast as the crusading newspaper scribe.

Patricia Jessel, Patricia Plunkett, Vera Day and Shirley Ann Field are useful as assorted prostics while Harold Lang and Denis Shaw score as slimy panders. But the best performance comes from Freda Jackson, who portrays an aging harlot, still human enough to be sympathetic with the girl's plight.

"Flesh Is Weak" could have been a searing and courageous exposure of a social sore, but it merely flirts with the subject. By compromise, it ends up as a sordid, depressing little yarn which Don Chaffey directs competently, but without originality. *Rich.*

Hell Drivers
(BRITISH)

Unabashed meller with Stanley Baker as ex-convict truck driver involved in a racket. Fair prospects.

London, July 25.

Rank production and release. Directed by C. Raker Endfield; produced by S. Benjamin Fisz. Stars Stanley Baker, Herbert Lom, Peggy Cummins, Patrick McGoohan. Screenplay, John Kruse and C. Raker Endfield; camera, Geoffrey Unsworth; editor, John D. Guthridge; music, Hulbert Clifford. At Gaumont, Haymarket, London, July 23, '57. Running time, 108 MINS.

Tom ..... Stanley Baker
Gino ..... Herbert Lom
Lucy ..... Peggy Cummins
Red ..... Patrick McGoohan
Cartley ..... William Hartnell
Ed ..... Wilfrid Lawson
Dusty ..... Sidney James
Jill ..... Jill Ireland
Tinker ..... Alfie Bass
Scottie ..... Gordon Jackson
Jimmy ..... David McCallum
Johnny ..... Sean Connery
Pop ..... Wensley Pithey
Tub ..... George Murcell
Ma West ..... Marjorie Rhodes
Blonde ..... Vera Day
Mother ..... Beatrice Varley
Assistant Manager ..... Robin Bailey
Spinster ..... Jean St. Clair
Chick ..... Jerry Stovin
Doctor ..... John Horsley
Nurse ..... Marianne Stone
Barber Joe ..... Ronald Clarke

"Hell Drivers" is a slab of unabashed melodrama, which, thanks to its title and the growing popularity of Stanley Baker, could prove a useful attraction in the home market. But it lacks star b.o. appeal and is unlikely to create much of a stir elsewhere.

The story has to do with the rivalries of a gang of haulage truck drivers, operating between gravel pits and a construction site. Stanley Baker is an exconvict who gets a job as one of these drivers and immediately falls foul of Patrick McGoohan, the firm's ace driver. Baker discovers that McGoohan and William Hartnell, the manager, are running a racket. The head office pays basic salaries for five more drivers than Hartnell hires. By overworking the drivers Hartnell keeps the daily schedule of runs up to par and he and McGoohan split the extra cash. The drama comes to an uneasy head when Baker's lorry is doctored, his Italian pal is killed and the villains of the piece come to a sticky end over the edge of a convenient quarry.

Though said to be based on real happenings, it is difficult to credit that such slap-happy drivers can infest British country lanes without protest by the public or intervention by the police.

C. Raker Endfield's direction is straightforward and conventional, but some of the speed sequences provide some tingling thrills. Acting is adequate, but uninspired. Stanley Baker gives a forceful performance of restrained strength and Herbert Lom has some neat moments as his Italian buddy. Patrick McGoohan (a young actor who is potentially one of Britain's best) gives an exaggerated study as the villain. Peggy Cummins, as a village vamp, fails to spark a tepid love interest and there are a few routine cameos by Sidney James, Alfie Bass and Wilfrid Lawson. *Rich.*

Manuela
(BRITISH)

Sexy, sadistic and adult with pronounced international b.o. values. Bright prospects.

London, July 23.

British Lion release (Paramount releasing in U. S.) of an Ivan Foxwell Production. Stars Trevor Howard, Pedro Armendariz and Elsa Martinelli. Produced by Ivan Foxwell; directed by Guy Hamilton; Screenplay, William Woods, in collaboration with Guy Hamilton and Ivan Foxwell; camera, Otto Heller; editor, Alan Osbiston; music, William Alwyn. At Odeon, Marble Arch, London, July 18, '57. Running time, 95 MINS.

Prothero ..... Trevor Howard
Bleloch ..... Leslie Weston
Evans ..... Donald Pleasence
Tommy ..... Jack McGowran
Moss ..... Warren Mitchell
Wellington Jones ..... Harcourt Curacao
Murphy ..... Barry Lowe
Mario ..... Pedro Armendariz
Official ..... Juan Carolilla
Ferguson ..... John Rae
Stranger ..... Roger Delgado
Manuela ..... Elsa Martinelli
Pereira ..... Harold Kasket
Bliss ..... Max Butterfield
Cook ..... Andy Ho
Agent ..... Peter Illing
Patron ..... Armando Guinle
Coca-Cola man ..... Michael Peake

Ivan Foxwell has come up with an adult motion picture of international appeal, which chould hit sturdy results in most territories. It has already been acquired for the States by Paramount which put up an advance of $280,000—one of the highest U.S. advances ever made for a British release.

By way of a concession, Foxwell has made an alternative ending available for the American market, but the unhappy fadeout, as shown in Britain, carries more conviction and appers to be more logical. The alternative would definitely appear to be out of character.

The three principal players, Trevor Howard, Pedro Armendariz and Elsa Martinelli, are not too well known in America but their performances have the stamp of authority and sincerity. Howard plays the captain of a tramp, "43 years old and up to the ears in alcohol," who suddenly finds himself emotionally involved with Elsa Martinelli, who had been smuggled onto his freighter by his chief engineer, Pedro Armendariz. The latter, an ox of a man, had one thought in his mind when he got the waif on board ship, but the skipper thought otherwise. The scene in which the engineer is beaten up by Howard, before being placed in the cooler, is a tough piece of screen sadism.

There's also plenty of drama when the captain ignores the urgent pleas of his sanctimonious first mate and continues his lovemaking session with the girl while the ship's on fire. Eventually, they have to abandon the vessel and Howard sees that he and the girl are in separate boats — and are never reunited.

Miss Martinelli's pert and provocative personality contributes to the sex overtones of her scenes with Howard. Armendariz is completely believable as the brute of an engineer, who sees a natural affinity between his mode of life and that of his skipper's. Donald Pleasence, as the Bible-reading first mate, stands out in a highly professional supporting cast. Guy Hamilton's terse direction takes full advantage of the dramatic potentialities of the story. *Myro.*

Three Faces of Eve

Psychiatric case history of woman with three personalities, but presented half-seriously and half in comedy fashion with confusing results. Stars Joanne Woodward who shows strong potential for future. Fair b.o.

20th-Fox release of Nunnally Johnson production. Stars Joanne Woodward, Lee J. Cobb and David Wayne. Directed by Johnson. Screenplay, Johnson, from the book by Corbett H. Thigpen, M.D. and Hervey M. Cleckley, M.D.; camera, Stanley Cortez; editor, Marjorie Fowler; music, Robert Emmett Dolan; narration by Allistair Cooke. Previewed in N. Y. Aug. 12, '57. Running time, 91 MINS.

Eve ..... Joanne Woodward
Ralph White ..... David Wayne
Dr. Luther ..... Lee J. Cobb
Dr. Day ..... Edwin Jerome
Secretary ..... Alena Murray
Mrs. Black ..... Nancy Kulp
Mr. Black ..... Douglas Spencer
Bonnie ..... Terry Ann Ross
Earl ..... Ken Scott
Eve—age 8 ..... Mimi Gibson

There is a similarity between 20th's "Three Faces of Eve" and Metro's recent "Lizzie." Both deal with the psychiatric problem faced by a woman with three different and distinct personalities. "Three Faces of Eve" is based on a true life case history recored by two psychiatrists—Corbett H. Thigpen and Hervey M. Cleckley—and which received considerable attention as a popular-selling book. "Lizzie," on the other hand, was adapted from Shirley Jackson's novel, "The Bird's Nest."

"Three Faces of Eve," written, directed and produced by Nunnally Johnson, is frequently an intriguing and provocative motion picture, but Johnson's treatment of the subject matter makes the film neither fish nor foul. Curiosity and word-of-mouth may attract audience. People ought to be mildly entertained by the mental manipulations of the troubled patient.

It appears obvious that Johnson set out to make an entertaining film with comedy overtones. The propriety of this decision will be questioned by many who will feel that the subject of mental illness deserves serious and reverent treatment. Johnson shifts back and forth—striving for comedy at one point and presenting a documentary case history at another. The result is that picture does not have a specific point of view and will undoubtedly confuse many viewers who won't be quite sure what emotions are suitable.

"Three Faces of Eve," however, is notable for the performance of Joanne Woodward as the woman with the triple personality. This is Miss Woodward's first "big" appearance and gives her the once-in-a-lifetime opportunity to portray three characters in one picture. Miss Woodward, a pretty blonde, fulfills her assignment excellently and stamps herself as a performer who should be heard from. 20th's gamble in an unknown "new face" should reap rich rewards as a result of Miss Woodward's tour de force.

The three personalities Miss Woodward is called on to play are (1) a drab, colorless Georgia housewife, (2) a mischievous, irresponsible sexy dish, and (3) a sensible, intelligent and balanced woman. The emergence of a third personality is rare in splits, but under the guidance of a determined psychiatrist, played forcefully and intelligently by Lee J. Cobb, the patient is able to shed her less favorable personalities and emerges mentally sound and is able to pursue a normal healthy life once again.

The pyschiatric sessions, while possibly authentic, could readily confuse the layman. The manner in which the doctor can hypnotize and alter his patient's personality seems so easy and pat as to appear hard to believe. Some explanation of how this can be accomplished would have been helpful.

That Johnson had no intention of treating the film entirely seriously is tipped off in an opening tongue-in-cheek narration by the urbane and erudite Alistaire Cooke. Most of the comedy stems from Miss Woodward's relationship with her coarse and unsympathetic first husband, played by David Wayne. Wayne basically miscast in the role, is directed to play it for laughs.

Another oddity is Miss Woodward's speech. In her portrayal of the two personalities that eventually disappear, she speaks with a delightful southern accent. However, when she becomes the sensible and intelligent woman, she emerges as a femme who might have attended Smith or Vassar.

Edwin Jerome, as Cobb's psychiatric colleague; Terry Ann Ross, as Miss Woodward's young daughter; Ken Scott, as her second husband, Alena Murray, as the doctor's secretary, and Nancy Kulp and Douglas Spencer, as Miss Woodward's parents, lend strong support. Production values, including Stanley Cortez's black and white photography, are first class. *Holl.*

Story of Esther Costello
(BRITISH)

Strong tear-jerker based on Nicholas Monsarrat's best-seller about a pretty blind mute; powerful dramatic performances by Joan Crawford, Rossano Brazzi and Heather Sears give it top b.o. appeal.

London, Aug. 13.

Columbia release of a Romulus Production. Stars Joan Crawford, Rossano Brazzi. Directed by David Miller. Screenplay, Charles Kaufman, from novel by Nicholas Monsarrat; camera, Robert Krasker; editor, Ralph Kemplen; music, Georges Auric. At Leicester Square Theatre, London. Running time, 104 MINS.

Margaret Landi ..... Joan Crawford
Carlo Landi ..... Rossano Brazzi
Esther Costello ..... Heather Sears
Harry Grant ..... Lee Patterson
Wenzel ..... Ron Randell
Mother Superior ..... Fay Compton
Paul Marchant ..... John Loder
Father Devlin ..... Denis O'Dea
Ryan ..... Sidney James
Woman in Art Gallery ..... Bessie Love
Mr. Wilson ..... Robert Ayres
Jenny Costello ..... Maureen Delaney
Irish Publican ..... Harry Hutchinson
Irish Pub Customer ..... Tony Quinn
Esther as a child ..... Janina Faye
Tammy ..... Estelle Brody
Mrs. Forbes ..... June Clyde
Susan North ..... Sally Smith
Christine Brown ..... Diana Day
Nurse Evans ..... Megs Jenkins
Dr. Stein ..... Andrew Cruikshank
Signor Gatti ..... Victor Rietti
Mary Costello ..... Sheila Hanahan

Nicholas Monsarrat's poignant best-selling novel has been shaped by Charles Kaufman into a glossy, highly effective screenplay, with David Miller's direction affording his powerful cast every opportunity for an all-out assault on the emotions. This cast, headed by Joan Crawford, responds eagerly. The result is a pic with the strongest woman-appeal and highclass fare for world audiences.

Miller's skillful direction extracts every ounce of sentiment and pathos from a moving story, but manages to escape being maudlin. Miss Crawford is a rich American socialite who, revisiting her Irish birthplace, finds a young girl, deaf, dumb and blind as a result of an explosion when she was a child. Joan rescues the girl from her evil surroundings, takes her to the U.S. and devotes her life to the girl's recovery. This mercy campaign sparks the interest of the world, but Miss Crawford's estranged husband (played by Rossano Brazzi) and a slick exploitation guy, turn it into a giant racket. Climax to this dramatic situation comes when Brazzi seduces the innocent girl. The shock has the effect of restoring her faculties.

Apart from its gripping story, "Esther Costello" has an almost documentary quality in showing the patient way a mute can be taught to communicate with the world. So authentic are these scenes that Heather Sears, who portrays Esther, and Joan Crawford as her tutor actually learned to "hand-talk."

The acting throughout is impeccable and is noteworthy for a remarkable debut by 21-year-old Heather Sears, who stands up notably to seasoned competition though faced with the tricky chore of conveying emotion without benefit of eye-play or dialog. Miss Sears' poignant acting is of rare quality, sensitive and compelling, both as the drab waif and the blossoming young beauty.

Although Miss Crawford sacrifices many scenes to Miss Sears, she has ample opportunity for one of those intense, smooth performances which dominate the screen. She makes an effective team with Brazzi, who blends calculated charm with caddishness in just the right ratio.

Among the other performances, too, there are several that take the eye. For instance, there are Ron Randell, as the brash unscrupulous opportunist; and Lee Patterson, as an amiable young reporter who wins Miss Sears' confidence and eventually her love. These two strikingly contrasted performances fit neatly into the general setup.

There is a neat study in wily psychology by Denis O'Dea as a kindly, determined priest with more than a touch of blarney about him. Fay Compton, Maureen Delaney, Megs Jenkins, John Loder, Robert Ayres and Bessie Love take effective care of minor but significant roles. Robert Krasker's camerawork and the dramatic but unobtrusive theme music of Georges Auric, plus neat editing, all add their quota to a class [illegible]sh film. *Rich.*

Perri
(COLOR-SONGS)

Squirrels have personality. Walt Disney's newest, a "true-life fantasy" biopic of animals in the Utah-Wyoming forests; packaged with a pair of shorts. Excellent color and maximum interest. Great for moppet trade particularly.

Buena Vista release. Produced and narrated by Winston Hibler. Directed by N. Paul Kenworthy Jr., and Ralph Wright. Written by Wright and Hibler, based on a novel by Felix Salten. Camera (Technicolor), Kenworthy, Joel Colman, Walter Perkins, William Ratcliffe, James R. Simon, John P. Hermann, David Meyer, Warren E. Garst, Roy Edward Disney; music, Carl Brandt, Franklyn Marks; songs by George Bruns, Paul Smith, Gil George, Wright and Hibler; Editor, Jack L. Atwood. Reviewed in Hollywood, Aug. 16, '57. Running time, **75 MINS. (Package running time, 120 MINS.)**

The life and times of dozens of denizens of the great forests of Utah and Wyoming have been captured for the screen in "Perri," one of the most ambitious animal film undertakings of all time. Nine cameramen lived patiently through two annual cycles in the forests to capture the setting in all its stark grandeur through the changing seasons and photograph the growth process of the central character, a female pine squirrel who could easily become one of the most commercial characters Disney has ever brought to film audiences.

Excellent camera work, magnificent photography and an eavesdropping quality that permits an audience almost to imagine they know animal thought insure the broadest family appeal for the Buena Vista release. To round out a two-hour package, "Perri" is accompanied by "Niok," an engrossing study of an Indo-Chinese boy and a baby elephant, and "The Truth About Mother Goose," a one-reel color cartoon that imaginatively reconstructs the story behind a trio of nursery rhymes.

"Perri" starts shortly after the birth of the little pine squirrel and carries her adventures through her meeting with a male counterpart and their McCall's Magazine—inspired phrase, "Together Time," as the mating season is delicately described for the sex-embarrassed trade. Film is replete with interesting and unusual camera shots of forest citizens at play and at prey and includes footage of such little known animals as the flying squirrel, the snowshoe rabbit and the goshawk. There will undoubtedly be some PTA complaints that some sequences are unnecessarily nightmare-inducing, but for the most part it is a careful study of a wildwood romance that combines the charm of a love story with the entertaining antics of the animals.

Camera work by the team is always outstanding, including some terrifying forest-fire footage, views of various parts of the forest from unusual camera angles and highly imaginative composition that takes full advantage of the backgrounds and color. There has also, obviously, been a tremendous job of film editing by Jack L. Atwood to integrate the footage into a smooth-flowing story. Winston Hibler, who produced, provides the background narration which is frequently the only flaw in its insistence upon rhyme. There is a fine background score and two tunes, "Break of Day" and "Together Time," conceivably could be candidates for pop attention.

"Niok," produced by Jean Paul Guibert, was written and directed by Edmond Sechan. Simple and touching story line deals with the boy's capture of the elephant, its subsequent sale to an animal trader and the youngster's long trek to recover his pet. In the end, realizing that the elephant needs the freedom of the forests, he turns him loose.

"Goose," which opens the program, recounts the history behind "Little Jack Horner," "Mistress Mary" and "London Bridge."

Kap.

Domino Kid

Fast gun entry for the western market; Rory Calhoun name to attract.

Hollywood, Aug. 15.

Columbia release of a Rory Calhoun-Victor M. Orsatti production. Stars Rory Calhoun; features Kristine Miller, Andrew Duggan, Yvette Dugay, Peter Whitney, Eigene Iglesias, Robert Burton. Directed by Ray Nazarro. Screenplay, Kenneth Gamet, Hal Biller; camera, Irving Lippman; editor, Gene Havlick; music, Mischa Bakaleinikoff. Previewed Aug. 13, '57. Runnning time, **74 MINS.**

Domino	Rory Calhoun
Barbara Ellison	Kristine Miller
Wade Harrington	Andrew Duggan
Rosita	Yvette Dugay
Lafe Prentiss	Peter Whitney
Juan Cortez	Eugene Iglesias
Sheriff Travers	Robert Burton
Pepe Garcias	Bart Bradley
Sam Beal	James Griffith
Ed. Sandlin	Roy Barcroft
Bill Dragger	Denver Pyle
Buck	Ray Corrigan
Dobbs	Wes Christensen
Ramon	Don Orlando

First Rory Calhoun-Victor M. Orsatti indie for Columbia release is a speedy gun yarn with all the makings of a money entry for the western market. Film is given solid treatment which pays off in anticipated strong response.

Calhoun plays a man with a mission, to track down and kill the five outlaws who ran off the cattle on his ranch and murdered his father while he was away in the Confederate Army. He's already caught up to one and guns down three more in opening reel. Balance of the Kenneth Gamet-Hal Biller screenplay follows his completing his goal, plus a romance with Kristine Miller and conflict with Andrew Duggan, who finances ranches and wants Calhoun's property, to complicate matters.

Calhoun socks over his character realistically and receives good support right down the line, aided by fast direction from Ray Nazarro. Miss Miller and Duggan deliver satisfactorily, Peter Whitney as the fifth man on Calhoun's list is good in a blazing gun climax and Eugene Iglesias scores as a Mexican who identifies Whitney for Calhoun. Yvette Dugay as a cantina owner offers a fast Spanish dance and Robert Burton adds a warm note as an understanding sheriff.

Irving Lippman's fluid camera work catches film's pace, further stressed by Gene Havlick's editing. *Whit.*

Hell on Devil's Island

Confusing yarn of Devil's Island with small appeal. A mediocrity.

Hollywood, Aug. 16.

Twentieth-Fox release of a Leon Chooluck-Lawrence Stewart production. Stars Helmut Dantine, William Talman, Donna Martel, Jean Willes, Rex Ingram; features Robert Cornthwaite, Jay Adler, Peter Adams. Directed by Christian Nyby. Screenplay, Steven Ritch, based on story by Arndt and Ethel Giusti; camera, Ernest Haller; editor, Warren Adams; music, Irving Gertz. Previewed Aug. 7, '57. Running time, **00 MINS.**

Paul Rigaud	Helmut Dantine
Bayard	William Talman
Giselle Renault	Donna Martell
Suzanne	Jean Willes
Lulu	Rex Ingram
Governor Renault	Robert Cornthwaite
Toto	Jay Adler
Jacques Boucher	Peter Adams
Jean Robert	Edward Colmans
Felix Molyneaux	Mel Welles
Marcel	Charles Bohbot
Leon Philippe	Alan Lee
Guard No. 1	Henry Rowland
Gendarme	Edward Coch
Arneaux	Paul Brinegar
Bruiser No. 2	Allen Pinson
Bruiser No. 1	Roy Jenson
Gina	Elena Da Vinci
Guard No. 2	Edwin Nelson
Chauvin	Paul MacWilliams

Dealing with the efforts of a French governor to end cruelties of Devil's Island, this Regal production is long on brutality and short on entertainment.

Plottage centers on Helmut Dantine, a French journalist unjustly imprisoned for having written against French collaborators during World War II. After his release from Devil's Island, he throws in with the governor in an attempt to stop the practice of the ex-prisoners, now penniless, forced into virtual slavery by an unscrupulous plantation owner through the offices of the crooked prefect of police. Through evidence collected by Dantine, the governor succeeds in final shutdown of the French penal colony.

Script by Steven Ritch fails to give thesps any break and direction by Christian Nyby is undistinguished. Most persuasive player is Rex Ingram, a convict pal of Dantine. William Talman enacts a brutal overseer, Robert Cornthwaite is the governor, Donna Martel his daughter and Jean Willes operator of a dive where ex-cons run up bills they can't pay. Technical credits are stock.

Whit.

Action of the Tiger
(COLOR-C'SCOPE)

Van Johnson and Martine Carol in a colorful but often confusing adventure meller with Albanian background; okay for program situations.

Hollywood, Aug. 17.

Metro release of a Kenneth Harper production. Stars Van Johnson, Martine Carol, Herbert Lom; features Gustavo Rocco, Jose Nieto, Helen Haye. Directed by Terence Young. Screenplay, Robert Carson, based on book by James Wellard, adapted for screen by Peter Myers; camera (Metrocolor), Desmond Dickinson; editor, Frank Clarke; music, Humphrey Searle. Previewed Aug. 14, '57. Running time, **91 MINS.**

Carson	Van Johnson
Tracy	Martine Carol
Trifon	Herbert Lom
Henri	Gustavo Rocco
Kol Stendho	Jose Nieto
The Countess	Helen Haye
Mara	Anna Gerber
Security Officer	Anthony Dawson
Mike	Sean Connery
Katina	Yvonne Warren
Trifon's Father	Norman MacOwan
Farmer	Brian Sunners
Farmer's Wife	Helen Goss
Abdyll (Little Boy)	Richard Williams

This British adventure yarn carries, and plenty of, derring-do, but militating against its coming off as more than a program entry are a fuzzy plot and occasional opera bouffe overtones. Name of Van Johnson may be counted on for draw, and film is garbed with enough exploitation voltage—including the supercharged Mlle. Martine Carol, opposite male star—for a campaign to add to its chances.

Story of an American adventurer helping a French sexpot smuggle her blind brother out of Communist-held Albania, film gets a strong lift on several counts. Magnificent use is made of color and CinemaScope in catching the gorgeous scenery of mountainous Spain—where feature was mostly lensed—for spectacular unfoldment of the Robert Carson screenplay. Particular emphasis is placed upon the physical charms of femme star in a lusty characterization, aided by eye-filling decolletage. Potent production values also lend a picturesque quality to pic which Kenneth Harper produced for Joseph D. Blau and John W. Meyer.

Action opens in Athens, where Miss Carol hires Johnson to use his yacht and contacts to smuggle her into Albania. Once arrived at destination, Johnson decides to accompany her into the interior for her brother, risking the Red police who are out in force. They are able to finally reach safety, along with a number of Greek children who are escaping from Albania, with the aid of Albanian bandits. Story line is so vague and some of the characters so unexplainable, however, that narrative loses the force that otherwise would have made this a top action film.

Johnson never entirely convinces as the adventurous American who fights his way out of trouble with brawny fists, top interest rather resting upon Miss Carol, excellent in what is handed her. Herbert Lom makes a hardy Albanian bandit leader on the make for femme but who is responsible for party breaking through Communist lines, and Gustavo Rocco is good as the brother. Jose Nieto is in as a mysterious character, first as Johnson's contact who gets him into Albania, then as one of the Security police.

Terence Young's direction is generally vigorous, although his staging of a fight in an Athens cafe when Johnson battles his way singlehanded through a crowd of hardy souls is slightly ridiculous. On technical side, finely effective is Desmond Dickinson's color photograpy, plus Martin Curtis' second unit work, and balance of credits match up. Frank Clarke's editing is usually tight, and Scott MacGregor's art direction and Humphrey Searle's music score outstanding.

Whit.

Cyclops

Foran into the monster country. Pretty gruesome. For easily entertained.

Hollywood, Aug. 13.

Allied Artists release of an A. B. & H. production. Stars James Craig, Gloria Talbott, Lon Chaney Jr. and Tom Drake. Produced-directed-screenplay by Bert I. Gordon; camera, Ira Morgan; editor, Carlo Lodato; music, Albert Glasser. Previewed, Aug. 12, '57. Running time, **66 MINS.**

Russ Bradford	James Craig
Susan Winter	Gloria Talbott
Martin Melville	Lon Chaney Jr.
Lee Brand	Tom Drake

Elementary in conception and execution, this science-fiction entry relies heavily on the gruesome to make its point. Double-billed with "Daughter of Dr. Jekyll," it's for undiscriminating audiences.

Bert I. Gordon wrote, produced and directed, with no particular distinction in any area. His tale revolves around determined search of Gloria Talbott for her fiance, lost years before in wilds of Mexico. Motley crew accompanying her includes scientist James Craig, in love with her, shady pilot Tom Drake and shifty stock promoter Lon Chaney Jr.

Isolated area turns out highly radioactive, which stimulates growth of native creatures to tremendous sizes. Included is Miss Talbott's fiance, horribly mutilated in the crash, so that only one eye remains. Eventually, to escape his murderous attentions, Craig is forced to heave a flaming spear into his remaining eye.

With no real dimensions to work in, cast of good actors relies strongly on stereotyped patterns. Special effects, also created by Gordon, largely from stock animal footage, isn't very convincing, not even to juve audiences. *Kove.*

Chicago Confidential

Exploitation film with current Senate Committee probings into racketeering in unions probably helping grosses.

Hollywood, Aug. 16.

United Artists release of a Robert E. Kent production. Stars Brian Keith, Beverly Garland, Dick Foran; features Douglas Kennedy, Paul Langton, Elisha Cook, Gavin Gordon, Beverly Tyler, Buddy Lewis, Anthony George. Directed by Sidney Salkow. Screenplay, Raymond T. Marcus; camera, Kenneth Peach Sr.; editor, Grant Whytock; music, Emil Newman. Prev[illegible]d Aug. 12, '57. Running time, **75 MINS.**

Jim Fremont	Brian Keith
Laura	Beverly Garland
Blane	Dick Foran
Sylvia	Beverly Tyler
Candymouth	Elisha Cook
Jake Parker	Paul Langton
Duncan	Tony George
Harrison	Douglas Kennedy
Dixon	Gavin Gordon
Smitty	Jack Lambert
Partos	John Morley
Hallop	Benny Burt
Evans	Mark Scott
Milt	Henry Rowland
Tomkins	George Cisar
Heavy	Johnny Indrisano
Fingerprint Man	John Pelletti
Dispatcher	Joe McGuinn
Betty	Asa Maynor
Marion	Jean Deane
Chorus Girl	Sharon Lee
Helen	Phyllis Coates
'B' Girl	Lynne Storey
'B' Girl	Nancy Marlowe
Traynor	Harlan Warde
Morgan	John Hamilton
Martin	Jack Kenney
Customer	Joey Ray
Policeman	Tom Wade
Mitch	Ralph Volkie
Waiter	Jack Carr
Narrator	Carl Princi
'B' Girl	Helen Jay
Charing	Charles Meredith
TV Announcer	Keith Byron
Pilot	Jim Bannon
Fingerprint Man	Myron Cook
Jury Foreman	Dennis Moore
Judge	Thomas B. Henry
Patron	Frank Marlowe
'B' Girl	Linda Brent
Jordan	Bud Lewis

As an exploitation film, "Chicago Confidential" should cash in handily on the current Senate probings into racket activities in the labor unions. Pic serves its purpose for the intended market and carries enough interest for okay reception by program audiences.

Taking its title from the Jack Lait-Lee Mortimer tome but strictly an original by Raymond T. Marcus, unfoldment twirls around efforts of mobsters to take over a powerful Chicago union by framing org's prexy for murder. A politically ambitious State's Attorney innocently makes use of manufactured evidence to press the conviction, but when he learns of the frame through new evidence he throws all his energies into proving the union chief innocent, leading to ultimate cleanout of gangster element from the union.

The Robert E. Kent production carries plenty of story holes, in which both the police and State's Attorney at times are pictured as not quite bright, but generally yarn packs action and building suspense. Sidney Salkow's direction is fast and he helms characters believably through their paces. Brian Keith is acceptable as the S.A., Dick Foran, though short on footage, handles his union prexy role well and Beverly Garland provides distaff interest as his fiance who continues to fight for him after his conviction.

In featured roles, Douglas Kennedy and Gavin Gordon are persuasive as racketeer heads. Paul Langton is okay as homicide chief. Beverly Tyler scores as a victim of the mobsters after she testifies for Foran and Elisha Cook is a pivotal figure as a rummy. Buddy Lewis is in as an impersonator, whose voice was used in a recording by which Foran was framed.

Technical departments are capably executed, leading off with Kenneth Peach, Sr.'s photography and Grant Whitock's tight editing. Art direction by Albert D'Agostino is atmospheric and Emil Newman's music score fits the bill. *Whit.*

The Brothers Rico

Okay gangster yarn with good suspense for better program market.

Hollywood, Aug. 16.

Columbia release of a William Goetz-Lewis J. Rachmil production. Stars Richard Conte, Dianne Foster, Kathryn Grant; features Larry Gates, James Darren, Argentina Brunetti, Lamont Johnson. Directed by Phil Karlson. Screenplay, Lewis Meltzer, Ben Perry, from story by Georges Simenon; camera, Burnett Guffey; editor, Charles Nelson; music, George Duning. Previewed Aug. 15, '57. Running time, **90 MINS.**

Eddie Rico	Richard Conte
Alice Rico	Dianne Foster
Norah	Kathryn Grant
Sid Kubik	Larry Gates
Johnny Rico	James Darren
Mrs. Rico	Argentina Brunetti
Peter Malaks	Lamont Johnson
Mike Lamotta	Harry Bellaver
Gino Rico	Paul Picerni
Phil	Paul Dubov
Gonzales	Rudy Bond
Vic Tucci	Richard Bakalyan
Joe Wesson	William Phipps
Julia Rico	Mimi Aguglia
Mrs. Felici	Maggie O'Byrne
Dude Cowboy	George Cisar
Jean	Peggy Maley
Nellie	Jane Easton

Indie producer William Goetz has come up with an okay melodrama for his latest Columbia release, a new twist giving gangster film mounting suspense. Sans marquee names, it will require hard selling but should fare well enough on upper half of program bills.

Richard Conte, Dianne Foster and Kathryn Grant are headliners in the Lewis Meltzer-Ben Perry screenplay which follows the efforts of a crime ring to locate one of its members who bolted after participating in a murder. Missing member's elder brother, Conte, once chief accountant for the syndicate but now a reputable business man with the promise that he can go straight, is recalled to find him. Under the impression that the syndicate head is honestly trying to save his brother from being gunned down by other gangsters, Conte undertakes assignment — which amounts to an order — but learns too late that the gang merely wanted him to lead them to the wanted brother.

Phil Karlson forges hard action into unfoldment of film for which Lewis J. Rachmil has set appropriate production values. Performances are first-class right down the line, Conte a standout as a man finally disillusioned after thinking of the syndicate leader who orders his brother's execution as a close family friend. Both femmes have comparatively little to do, Miss Foster as Conte's wife and Miss Grant as the brother's, but make their work count.

Larry Gates as gang chief scores smoothly and James Darren as young brother handles character satisfactorily. Paul Picerni, as another brother whom gang also kills, is good, and Argentina Brunetti, the brothers' mother who once was crippled in saving the crime head's life, is dramatic. Other key roles are well enacted by Harry Bellaver, Lamont Johnson, Rudy Bond and Paul Dubov.

Technical departments are well executed, including Burnett Guffey's camera work, Charles Nelson's editing, art direction by Robert Boyle and music score by George Duning. *Whit.*

After the Ball
(BRITISH-COLOR)

Limp biopic of noted British vaudeville performer, Vesta Tilley; minimum appeal even on nostalgia stakes.

London, Aug. 13.

Independent Film Distributors release of a Romulus (Peter Rogers) production. Stars Laurence Harvey, Pat Kirkwood. Directed by Compton Bennett. Screenplay, Hubert Gregg, Peter Blackmore; camera, Jack Asher; editor, Peter Boita; music, Muir Mathieson. At Rialto, London. Running time, **89 MINS.**

Tilley	Pat Kirkwood
Walter	Laurence Harvey
Frank Tanhill	Jerry Stovin
Harry Ball	Jerry Verno
Henry De Frece	Clive Morton
Bessie	Marjorie Rhodes
Richard Warner	Leonard Sachs
Andrews	Ballard Berkeley
Tilley (Child)	Margaret Sawyer
Perelli	David Hurst
Tony Pastor	George Margo
Carmelita	Rita Stevens
Lottie Gilson	June Clyde

Vesta Tilley was a well-loved and talented British vaudeville performer up to and including the first World War. She specialized in male impersonations which mildly shocked the patrons, but led a singularly undramatic life. Hence, it is difficult to see how her screen story can have anything but limited appeal even for oldtimers who recall her with affection. For the younger generation and the U.S.—"After the Ball" must be rated largely a loss.

The story, which monotonously outlines her rise to fame up to her retirement in 1920, is largely an excuse for plugging the oldtime vaudeville songs with which she was associated. These are put over with verve and zest by Pat Kirkwood who also does an energetic job in trying to infuse some life into the tedious screenplay of Hubert Gregg and Peter Blackmore.

Laurence Harvey, who plays Walter de Frece, Vesta Tilley's husband, ambles through his chore with the air of a man who has not got his heart in it. Apart from Miss Kirkwood, the only performance which deserves a nod is that of veteran Jerry Verno, as her father.

Compton Bennett's direction is plodding and uninspired. But it must be admitted that there is little in this mild pic into which he could get his teeth. *Rich.*

The Time of Desire
(Swedish)

Frank sexual treatment, Swedish style, with incest overtones. Strictly limited art house offering.

Hollywood, July 23.

Janus Films distribution of a Europa Film production. Stars Barbro Larsson, Margaretha Lawler; features George Fant, Berger Malmstem, Marianne Lofgren, Nils Hallberg, Ingemar Pallin. Directed and adapted by Egil Holmsen, from Arthur Lundquist story; camera, Ingvar Borild; music, Harry Arnold. Previewed, July 22, '57. Running time, **81 MINS.**

Lilly Lilja	Barbro Larsson
Ragni Lilja	Margaretha Lawler
The Father	George Fant
Algot Wiberg	Berger Malmsten
Maid	Marianne Lofgren
Nils	Nils Hallberg
Pastor	Ingemar Pallin

Problems of a'he-ing and a'she-ing and a'she-ing and a'he-ing has long been a plot staple. More recent is a trend toward treating a'he-ing and a'he-ing themes. Comes this Swedish import in which language doesn't camouflage much, not only depicts a'she-ing and a'she-ing, but condones the practice—between sisters yet.

This is one strictly for the art houses, and in broad (no pun intended) minded communities there are the usual nude bathing scenes of Swedish delight, plus frankly sexual passage, both lesbo and more conventional. While well-made, film can't be taken too seriously as a social commentary.

Household depicted is sex-ridden, to put it mildly. Widowed papa George Fant and male help at his farm seem to play musical beds with female help most of the time. Strong indications are that love of daughters Babro Larsson and Margaretha Lawler for each other is more than sisterly. When handsome newcomer to village, Berger Malmsten arrives, Miss Lawler has an affair with him, to dismay of sister. A child results, which father accepts easily, despite lack of marriage banns. However, Miss Lawler apparently finds heterosexualism distasteful after this sample and returns to her first love, sister Barbro. Finale has fire-and-brimstone preacher, Ingemar Pallin gaze upon unconventional trio of sisters and illegitimate child ride past the church, with remarkable tolerance.

Pace of Egil Holmsen's direction is more leisurely than that Yank audiences are accustomed to, but art house devotees shouldn't mind this too much. Seduction scene between Miss Lawler and Malmsten gains powerful impact by subtle and skillful handling. Holmsen adapted script from Arthur Lundquist story, and subtitles seem adequate to non-Swedish speaker. Photography of Ingvar Borild is in solid tradition of Swedish craftsmanship, and music by Harry Arnold is delicately effective.

Cast is a very good one. Fine, cleancut looks of Misses Larsson and Lawler not only excites as counterpoint to unconventional goings-on but pair are good actresses too. Fant, as virile papa, attracts along post-middle-age lines laid out by late Ezio Pinza. Malmsten is hampered somewhat by stereotyped role of the rejected lover, despite fact that circumstances here are far from stereotyped. *Kove.*

The Joker Is Wild
(VISTAVISION—SONGS)

Good story values and top-drawer impersonation of nitery comic Joe E. Lewis by Frank Sinatra. Too long but still exploitable and saleable.

Las Vegas, Aug. 27.
Paramount release of Samuel J. Briskin production. Stars Frank Sinatra, Mitzi Gaynor, Jeanne Crain, Eddie Albert; features Beverly Garland, Jackie Coogan. Directed by Charles Vidor. Screenplay, Oscar Saul, from Joe E. Lewis biography book by Art Cohn; camera, Daniel L. Fapp; editor, Everett Douglas; music, Walter Scharf; song "All the Way" by Sammy Cahn and James Van Heusen; specialty songs and parodies, Harry Harris. Premiere at El Portal Theatre, Las Vegas, Aug. 23, '57. Running time, 126 MINS.

Joe E. Lewis	Frank Sinatra
Martha Stewart	Mitzi Gaynor
Letty Page	Jeanne Crain
Austin Mack	Eddie Albert
Cassie Mack	Beverly Garland
Swifty Morgan	Jackie Coogan
Capt. Hugh McCarthy	Harry Kelley
George Parker	Ted de Corsia
Tim Coogan	Leonard Graves
Flora	Valerie Allen
Burlesque Comedian	Hank Henry

Frank Sinatra was first to carry the ball with this one, having bought Art Cohn's story of Joe E. Lewis in galley proof form and thereafter taking a key part in the packaging. The objective was a true representation of pixie Lewis, bon vivant and nitery buffoon, and acknowledged by many in the trade as doyen of the saloon comedians. It doesn't matter much about this objective, for the fact is that the finished product is a pretty good picture.

Joe E. Lewis may not be a household word in many areas but this doesn't matter, either. Paramount is out to sell the picture, not the man, and the entertainment plusses and exploitation pegs seem sufficient to assure a fair-enough payoff.

Sinatra obviously couldn't be made to look like Lewis; any thought of a reasonable facsimile, appearance-wise, is out of the question. And Lewis' style of delivery is unique and defies accurate copying (although some of his onstage mannerisms are aped by the film's star quite well). But these are minor reservations in light of the major job Sinatra does at being an actor. He's believeable and forceful — alternately sympathetic and pathetic, funny and sad.

"Joker Is Wild" purports to be the case history of a Prohibition era entertainer who lived through a savage attack by mobsters; loved and lost a pretty, rich girl; married a dancer whom he neglected; often was a self-pitying heel; hit the bottle and gambled all the time; and meanwhile gagged his way to being a heavy favorite in the club-date sweepstakes.

Samuel J. Briskin's production tries to make contact with the inner person of this character, in addition to giving a play to the outer clown. A certain amount of success is scored and it's via this approach that the picture achieves weight. It has some good, dramatic story material.

Oscar Saul's screenplay builds splendidly and is peppered with some bright and sharp dialog along with a few old jokes, which don't rate the laughs they get by Lewis' on-screen audiences.

Eddie Albert plays Austin Mack, Lewis' longtime piano accompanist and intimate friend, with considerable feel. He's the old reliable type of buddy, sometimes confused or frustrated but ever eager to help the comic when the going gets rough. Story has it that the turn-

ing point in Lewis' career was his being jockeyed by Mack into the role of comedian when the gangland muscle men damaged his vocal chords and he could no longer be a singer.

Jeanne Crain is touching and fits in fine as the wealthy gal who falls for Lewis (and he for her) but eventually gives up on him because of his hesitancy about marriage. The leggy, shapely, cutie-pie-faced Mitzi Gaynor is colorful as a chorus dancer who marries Lewis after Miss Crain takes the powder. And she proves she can handle herself in the acting department when she despairs of the funny man as he gives his time to his cronies and the bottle.

In featured spots are Beverly Garland, who works well as Albert's wife, and Jackie Coogan, who plays the irrepressible salesman Swifty Morgan with gusto.

In lesser spots and holding their own are Barry Kelley, Ted de Corsia, Leonard Graves, Valerie Allen and Hank Henry (whose hangout continues to be Las Vegas).

Under Charles Vidor's direction, "Joker Is Wild" plays out in well organized and smooth fashion. But it goes overboard on length. Too much time and footage are taken, for example, in the buildup for the attack on Lewis. Closer editing would seem to be in order. And the business at the finish, which has Lewis talking to his own image, isn't realistic.

On the musical side, a number of old tunes are reprised by Sinatra and he introduces one new one, "All the Way," by Sammy Cahn and James Van Heusen, pleasantly okay via the Sinatra voice. Walter Scharf's scoring is a strong credit and technical work all is competent. *Gene.*

Action of the Tiger
(BRITISH-TECHNICOLOR)

Confused meller with Van Johnson as an adventurer and Martine Carol as girl in distress; will satisfy undiscriminating audiences.

London, Aug. 27.
Metro release of a Claridge (Kenneth Harper) production. Stars Van Johnson, Martine Carol, Herbert Lom. Directed by Terence Young. Screenplay, Robert Carson, adapted for screen by Peter Myers, from novel by James Wellard; camera, Edmund Dickinson; editor, Frank Clarke; music, Humphrey Searle. At Empire Theatre, London. Running time, 93 MINS.

Carson	Van Johnson
Tracy	Martine Carol
Trifon	Herbert Lom
Henri	Gustavo Rocco
Kol Stendho	Jose Nieto
The Countess	Helen Haye
Mara	Anna Gerber
Security Guard	Anthony Dawson
Mike	Sean Connery
Katina	Yvonne Warren

Somewhere along the line a good idea got lost in "Action of Tiger." Hence, what might have been an exciting thriller turns out to be confused, highly-colored stuff with casual direction and mostly routine performances. However, Van Johnson and Martine Carol have marquee value and this melodrama will satisfy the undiscriminating.

According to the credits Robert Carson's screenplay (based on James Wellard's book) was adapted for the screen by Peter Myers. Exactly how or why a screenplay has to be adapted for the screen is an intriguing point and it may be that too many writers were involved in shaping the story.

Insofar as it can be disentangled, the plot has Van Johnson as a runner in contraband — mostly Greek children, whom he rescues

from Communist Albania in his motor-launch. He meets Martine Carol who offers him considerable coin to rescue her blind brother (Gustavo Rocco), a political prisoner in Albania.

Miss Carol's charms persuade Van Johnson against his better judgment. The remainder of yarn involves the party now swollen to six children and four adults, in skirmishes with the security police and armed bandits before they ultimately find safety.

All this might have been legitimate plotting for a straight-forward drama, but director Terence Young allows too much time between his highlights, with his characters rarely emerging, as credible people. Add uninspired dialog and indifferent art-work, and it will be seen that not even excellent color and strong lensing by Edmund Dickinson (shot briefly in Athens, thence to Spain) can do much for this disappointing film.

Performances don't help a great deal. Van Johnson has the muscles for the role but plays the role with a bored scowl which hardly lifts even when grudgingly romancing comely Miss Carol. She is able to contribute little more than her good looks.

Of the leading players, only Herbert Lom impresses. He amusingly and skillfully portrays a larger-than-life bandit with curious garb and an eye-glass. Lom performs with a flourish as if he realizes that desperate measures are called for if the pic is to be saved. But Lom appears too late and is bumped off too soon for him to be of great help.

Some of the smaller roles are played competently by Helen Haye, Anna Gerber, Jose Nieto, Sean Connery and Anthony Dawson. But newcomer Gustavo Rocco, though handsome, fails to make much impact as Miss Carol's blind brother. *Rich.*

The Sun Also Rises
(COLOR-C'SCOPE)

Tyrone Power, Ava Gardner, Errol Flynn in Hemingway saga for okay b.o.

20th-Fox release of Darryl F. Zanuck production. Stars Tyrone Power, Ava Gardner, Mel Ferrer, Errol Flynn, Eddie Albert; features Gregory Ratoff, Juliette Greco, Marcel Dalio, Henry Daniell, Bob Cunningham, Danik Patisson, Robert Evans. Directed by Henry King. Screenplay, Peter Viertel, based on Ernest Hemingway novel; editor, William Mace; music, Hugo Friedhofer, conducted by Lionel Newman; camera (De Luxe color), Leo Tover. Previewed in N.Y. Aug. 20, '57. Running time, 129 MINS.

Jake Barnes	Tyrone Power
Lady Brett Ashley	Ava Gardner
Robert Cohn	Mel Ferrer
Mike Campbell	Errol Flynn
Bill Gorton	Eddie Albert
Count Mippipopolous	Gregory Ratoff
Georgette	Juliette Greco
Zizi	Marcel Dalio
Doctor	Henry Daniell
Harris	Bob Cunningham
The Girl	Danik Patisson
Romero	Robert Evans
Mr. Braddock	Eduardo Noriega
Mrs. Braddock	Jacqueline Evans
Montoya	Carlos Muzquiz
Frances	Rebecca Iturbi
Mgr. Romero	Carlos David Ortigos

In undertaking the transmutation into screen fare of the novel which first escalatored Ernest Hemingway to renown, Darryl F. Zanuck faced problems which might have given pause to a producer less intrepid, experienced, incisive. The 30-year-old book dealt with expatriates of World War I's "lost generation" careening around Europe. Since, there's been another global war much more vast, other "lost generations." Zanuck wisely surrounded "Sun" with constellations of marquee - weighty stars — Tyrone Power, Ava Gardner, Mel Ferrer, Errol Flynn, Eddie Albert — and obtained excellent locales, provided a lush production background. It remained for Peter Viertel's screenplay to bring the novel's colorful crop of characters to life as had Hemingway's book. Offsetting the film's many production plus marks is fact Viertel, while hewing to the plot line of the book, loses along the way the characterizations and the all-important mood Hemingway had conjured up. Chances of really big boxoffice are fair, and can be improved with emphasis on cast names and—particularly—on a plot hook that is provocative and certain to arouse talk and consequent b.o. reaction.

Zanuck never has been daunted by an offbeat theme, and he knows how to utilize such opportunities (witness "Pinky"). In light of the film industry's new found "freedom" of expression under the revised Production Code, Zanuck doesn't gloss over the key plot twist that Power plays an impotent newspaperman in frustrated love with Ava Gardner, who plays Lady Brett Ashley. But the script drags along their "love affair" instead of propelling it. Thus the yarn never comes off either as a love story or a definitive study of the "lost generation."

Too, performances are mixed. Power is on the wooden side, his character never wholly believable. Miss Gardner turns in a far more sympathetic and credible performance. Mel Ferrer never quite achieves the hangdog aspect required of his role, but Errol Flynn and Eddie Albert turn in topflight characterizations as drunken members of the gamoling expatriates. Flynn registers especially well, for it's an offbeat part for him. Among featured players, Robert Evans as the bullfighter, Juliette Greco as a Parisian prostie, and Gregory Ratoff as a gadabout count are standout.

Director Henry King, saddled with an overlong and never sparkling script, could instill little vital life into much of the pic, and many of the conversational scenes seemed to lag. However, when King could swerve from the script, his inventive direction is marked. The two high points of the production — for excitement, clever staging and visual delight—are a Spanish fiesta and bullfight sequences. King extracted the ultimate, deftly catching his cast in the heart of all the action, thus achieving notable results. Unfortunately, these scenes are only incidental to the plot.

Leo Tover's color photography injects much excitement, and he made maximum use of the fieldday opportunity afforded his lenses in Paris, Spain and Mexico. Other back-of-the-camera credits are excellent right down the line—Hugo Friedhofer's score, the art direction of Lyle R. Wheeler and Mark-Lee Scott, editing by William Mace.

Zanuck's overall reining of the production is obvious every frame; it is "big" in the biggest sense of the word. Too bad such general, top - tier production excellence couldn't have been extended to the more vital elements—the story—of the film. *Chan.*

Reform School Girl

Cheapie for the adolescent trade. Adequate for program situations.

Hollywood, Aug. 23.

American-International release of a Carmel Production. Stars Gloria Castillo, Ross Ford, Edward Byrnes. Producers, Robert J. Gurney Jr., Samuel Z. Arkoff. Director-Screenplay, Edward Bernds; camera, Floyd Crosby; editor, Richard C. Meyer; art director, Don Ament; music, Ronald Stein. Previewed at Warner's Hollywood, Aug. 22, '57. Running time, **71 MINS.**

Donna Price	Gloria Castillo
David Lindsay	Ross Ford
Vince	Edward Byrnes
Jackie	Ralph Reed
Ruth	Jan Englund
Roxy	Yvette Vickers
Mrs. Trimble	Helen Wallace
Cathy	Donna Jo Gribble
Josie	Luana Anders
Mona	Diana Darrin
Deetz	Nesdon Booth
Gary	Wayne Taylor
Blonde	Sharon Lee
Mr. Horvath	Jack Kruschen
Elena	Linda Rivera
Midge	Elaine Sinclair
Matron	Dorothy Crehan
Mrs. Horvath	Claire Carleton
Mrs. Patton	Lillian Powel
A Girl	Sally Kellerman

Since quality has little to do with the success of a cheapie exploitation film for a teenage audience, this should serve adequately in program situations (in this case, teamed with "Rock Around the World"). For the prurient-minded, there's mucho leg display, and for the immature audiences, there's a plaintive adolescent philosophy about non-squealing.

Edward Bernds, who also directed, wrote the screenplay and keeps things at a pretty elementary level on both counts, despite widely separated patches of refreshing adult dialog. Gloria Castillo enacts attractive youngster in bad environment, sent to reform school after involvement in a fatal car accident. Conflict with unreconstructed types at the school then revolves about whether she should name the guilty party, Edward Byrnes, an unappetizing young car thief. Sympathetic teacher Ross Ford and new b.f. Ralph Reed help her solve her problem, after considerable and none-too-convincing violence.

Pic offers employment to a large corps of local young actresses, perhaps its only real justification. Miss Castillo especially impresses, with a wholesome, fresh appeal. Ford, Byrnes and Reed haven't much chance against the plotting. *Kove.*

The Disembodied

Voodoo and mystic spells combined for a routine meller.

Hollywood, Aug. 23.

Allied Artists release of Ben Schwalb production. Stars Paul Burke, Allison Hayes; features John E. Wengraf, Eugenia Paul, Joel Marston, Robert Christopher, Norman Fredric, A. E. Ukonu, Paul Thompson, Otis Greene. Directed by Walter Grauman. Screenplay, Jack Townley; camera, Harry Neumann; editor, William Austin; music, Marlin Skiles. Previewed Aug. 16, '57. Running time, **65 MINS.**

Tom	Paul Burke
Tonda	Allison Hayes
Dr. Metz	John E. Wengraf
Lara	Eugenia Paul
Norman	Joel Marston
Joe	Robert Christopher
Suba	Norman Fredric
Voodoo Drum Leader	A. E. Ukonu
Gogi	Paul Thompson
Kabar	Otis Greene

Voodoo deep in the jungles provides the basic backdrop for this okay meller which generally sustains interest and should please the young 'uns. Film is being packaged with the sci-fi "From Hell It Came" (see review in this issue). Mesmeric spells, fatal spells and just plain spells abound in the Jack Townley screenplay, all coupled with voodoo mysticism. There are so many spells at times, one even seems to be cast over the plot. Allison Hayes, beautiful wife of a jungle doctor, is the evil one with the voodoo powers who eventually is knifed to death after trying—and sometimes succeeding—to rid the plot of several characters. Surviving the plot twists and turns are: author-lecturer Paul Burke, photog Joel Marston and Burke's assistant, Robert Christopher.

Cast members all perform adequately under the okay direction of Walter Grauman (from tv), and Ben Schwalb's production mantling and technical contributions are par for the course. *Neal.*

Rock Around the World

'The Tommy Steele Story'
(BRITISH)
(Musical)

British-filmed biopic of bigname singer over there, Tommy Steele, slightly altered for Yank consumption. Notable only in exposing Steele to Yank audiences, but it should go with rock 'n' roll, rhythm & blues crowd.

Hollywood, Aug. 23.

American-International release of an Anglo-Amalgamated Film. Stars Tommy Steele, Nancy Whiskey; features Hunter Hancock, The Steelmen, Humphrey Lyttleton band, Charles McDevitt Skiffle Group. Producer, Herbert Smith. Director, Gerard Bryant. Screenplay, Norman Hudis; camera, Peter Hennessy; editor, Ann Chegwidden; art director, Eric Saw; songs, Steele, Lionel Bart, Michael Pratt. "Freight Train," by Paul James and Fred William. Previewed at Warner's Hollywood, Aug. 22, '57. Running time, 71 **MINS.**

Tommy Steele	Tommy Steele
Brushes	Patrick Westwood
Mrs. Steele	Hilda Fenemore
Mr. Steele	Charles Lamb
John Kennedy	Peter Lewiston
Paul Lincoln	John Boxer
Junkshop Man	Mark Daly
Hospital Nurse	Lisa Daniely
Hospital Doctor	Byran Coleman
Chief Steward	Cyril Chamberlain
Busker (Guitarist)	Bernard Hunter
1st Steelman (Bass)	Alan Weighell
2nd Steelman (Pianist)	Dennis Price
3rd Steelman (Drummer)	Leo Pollini
4th Steelman (Saxophonist)	Alan Stuart
Judo Instructor	Tom Littlewood

Calypso Bands: Chris O'Brien's Caribbeans and Tommy Eytle's Calypso Band.

Teenage Party Artists: Humphrey Lyttelton's Band, Chas. McDevitt Skiffle Group and Hunter Hancock.

Aimed at rock 'n' roll and rhythm & blues aficionados, this pic should rightly be entitled "Rock Around Blighty." A British-filmed biopic of Tommy Steele, noted English rock singer (called "The Tommy Steele Story" over there), it's been crudely Americanized for local consumption by adding intro footage by Yank deejay Hunter Hancock. However, it remains emphatically British in concept and largely in locale, even if more in the Cockney than the stiff-upper-lip tradition.

Pic is most notable in exposing young Steele to Yank audiences. From this, he's got an engaging personality and a fine set of pipes, worthy of a better idiom. Otherwise, biog is a slender story thread on which to hang a multitude of rock, calypso, ballad and rhythm & blues tunes. Frankly, to the uninitiated, by the time 15 or so musical pieces (most of which young Steele helped write) go by, rock numbers have a tendency toward monotonous uniformity. However, two numbers stand out. One is "A Handful of Songs," a non-rock ballad sung by Steele; other is an interpolated sequence in which Nancy Whiskey and the Chas. McDevitt Skiffle group belt out their famed version of "Freight Train."

Technically, pic is jerry-built and reflects cheap production standards. Numbers recorded at a London teenage concert are used through pic in other contexts, but are easily recognizable by distinctive tonal quality and poor lip sync. (One notable peculiarity is that Steele speaks a strong Cockney in dramatic passages, but sings with a solid U. S. twang.) *Kove.*

Across the Bridge

(BRITISH)

Slow, contrived British drama with mounting atmosphere and sock climax. Powerful performance by Rod Steiger provides main b.o. appeal.

London, Aug. 20.

Rank production and release. Stars Rod Steiger, David Knight, Marla Landi. Directed by Ken Annakin. Screenplay, Guy Elmes, Denis Freeman, from story by Graham Greene; camera, Reginald Wyer; editor, Alfred Roome; music, James Bernard. At Odeon, Leicester Square, London. Running time, **103 MINS.**

Carl Schaffner	Rod Steiger
Johnny	David Knight
Mary	Marla Landi
Chief of Police	Noel Willman
Det.-Inspector Hadden	Bernard Lee
Paul Scarff	Bill Nagy
Police Sgt.	Eric Pohlmann
Cooper	Alan Gifford
Mrs. Scarff	Ingeborg Wells
Kay	Faith Brook
Milton	Stanley Maxted
Anna	Marianne Deeming

In marquee value, Rod Steiger is on his own in this film. Providing his name can pull in patrons on either side of the Atlantic early enough, there is sufficient quality about "Across the Bridge" to insure generous draw via word-of-mouth later on.

The screenplay by Guy Elmes and Denis Freeman, based on Graham Greene's story, unfolds slowly. At times, it needs patience to absorb. But this is strong on situation and acting stints and winds up with a sure-fire climax. In essence, it is a gripping character study of an arrogant man who, through his own crooked folly and greed, topples from power to degrading death as a gutter outcast.

Steiger is a shady international financier who is on the lam from Scotland Yard and the FBI. On the train he meets up with a gabby Mexican stranger and, by skullduggery, assumes the stranger's identity and acquires his passport, baggage and—embarrassingly—his pet spaniel, Dolores. In Mexico, he is caught between the Scotland Yard man, trying to lure him into American territory, and the Mexican police chief, who withholds Steiger's own passport in order to indulge in a spot of astute blackmail.

These complicated goings-on are background to a remarkable study of mental and physical decay by Steiger. It is the first time that the "Method" has penetrated British studios and director Ken Annakin has obviously found Steiger's acting a bit of a handful to control. At times it is irritatingly over-fussy and mannered, but he surely dominates the screen. The director has allowed him to have his head but not at the expense of the overall effect.

Aided by skillful lensing by Reginald Wyer, Annakin has excellently built up the atmosphere of a sleepy, brooding Mexican bordertown. Exteriors were shot in Spain. Although, in the acting stakes, this is very much a one-horse race, there are a number of other very good performances in what can be rated a better-than-most British production.

As the Mexican police chief, Noel Willman gives a wily, subtle performance which, because of its very restraint, contrasts admirably with the Steiger technique. The scenes between the two are filmic highlights. The juves, David Knight and Italian newcomer, Marla Landi, are a shade overwhelmed by the general proceedings. But Miss Landi is clearly an out-of-the-rut actress who should make her mark. Bernard Lee, as the Scotland Yard cop; Eric Pohlmann, as a Mexican sergeant; and Bill Nagy, as Steiger's victim, all offer useful support. There is also a touching and most promising piece of work by Ingeborg Wells, an attractive girl who will repay watching in the future. *Rich.*

Quantez
(C'SCOPE-COLOR)

Another "adult western" which creeps along at a snail-slow pace; will need plusses of Fred MacMurray and Dorothy Malone names to make much biz impression.

Hollywood, Aug. 20.
Universal-International production and release. Stars Fred MacMurray, Dorothy Malone; costars James Barton, Sydney Chaplin; with John Gavin, John Larch, Michael Ansara. Produced by Gordon Kay. Directed by Harry Keller. Screenplay by R. Wright Campbell, from Anne Edwards and Campbell story; camera, Carl E. Guthrie; editor, Fred MacDowell; art director, Alexander Golitzen, Alfred Ybarra; music, Herman Stein. Songs, "The Lonely One" and "True Love," by Frederick Herbert and Arnold Hughes. Previewed, Aug. 14, '57. Running time, **79 MINS.**

Gentry .... Fred MacMurray
Chaney .... Dorothy Malone
Minstrel .... James Barton
Gato .... Sydney Chaplin
Teach .... John Gavin
Heller .... John Larch
Delgadito .... Michael Ansara

Just to make sure the audience gets the various plot points, they are repeated about three times around. As predictable, pic emerges as a meandering and static tale which wears patience pretty thin.

There are good names involved, notably stars Fred MacMurray and Dorothy Malone, which might work to advantage in exploitation. Also, film is mounted handsomely in Eastman color and C'Scope. However, it appears offhand that these plusses are going to be sorely needed to overcome the snail-slow pace.

Anne Edwards-R. Wright Campbell original (screenplayed by Campbell) deals with an outlaw band, holed up overnight at an abandoned desert town while fleeing a posse. Town is surrounded by Apaches, who will attack at dawn.

Meanwhile, gang members endlessly bicker and fight amongst selves, until only MacMurray, Miss Malone and tenderfoot John Gavin remain. In subsequent running fight with Apaches, MacMurray, a tired and elderly gunfighter, sacrifices himself to insure escape of the young couple to a new and presumably better life.

Harry Keller's direction chews over the same dialog and situations often without advancing plot significantly, and sorely-needed bursts of action are drowned in a welter of verbiage.

MacMurray, a smooth and capable actor, delivers the competent performance to be expected. As moll of John Larch, the brutal gang leader, Miss Malone comes across very well visually and measures up well enough to plot requirements.

James Barton, in only for a bit as a wandering peddler, easily dominates every scene he's in. Sydney Chaplin, as a renegade white who tries to sell out his comrades to the Apaches, also makes his footage count. Larch is good as the heavy-handed leader and young Gavin makes promising impression as the juve. Michael Ansara solidly repeats his video role (he's Indian chief of "Broken Arrow" series) as the Apache leader.

Two songs, "the Lonely One," sung under credits by Barton; and "True Love," sung during pic by Miss Malone both by Frederick Herbert and Arnold Hughes are good period pieces, but nothing to set the jukeboxes a fire. *Kove.*

Gunsight Ridge

Routine western with Joel McCrea and Mark Stevens for marquee dressing.

Hollywood, Aug. 22.
United Artists release of a Robert Bassler production. Stars Joel McCrea, Mark Stevens; costars Joan Weldon; features Darlene Fields, Addison Richards, Carolyn Craig, Robert Griffin, Slim Pickins, Stanford Jolley, George Chandler. Directed by Francis D. Lyon. Story-screenplay, Talbot Jennings, Elisabeth Jennings; camera, Ernest Laszlo; editors, Ellsworth Hoagland, Robert Golden; music, David Raskin. Previewed Aug. 15, '57. Running time, **85 MINS.**

Mike .... Joel McCrea
Velvet .... Mark Stevens
Molly .... Joan Weldon
Rosa .... Darlene Fields
Sheriff Jones .... Addison Richards
Girl .... Carolyn Craig
Babcock .... Robert Griffin
Hank Moss .... Slim Pickens
Daggett .... Stanford Jolley
Gus Withers .... George Chandler
Justice .... Herb Vigran
Bride .... Cindy Robbins
Groom .... Jody McCrea
Ramon .... Martin Garralaga

Pairing of Joel McCrea and Mark Stevens, who ordinarily star in their own films, should assure top western market playing time for this Robert Bassler production. Likewise, it gives pic more of a draw than feature warrants. At best, it's a routine offering.

Script by Talbot Jennings and Elisabeth Jennings is oldhat, story of an Express Company undercover agent investigating a series of holdups. McCrea portrays the agent, Stevens the outlaw who ostensibly is a reputable mine owner. Unfoldment lacks excitement and imagination, and players have little chance to do more than walk through their parts. Francis D. Lyon's pat direction fails to overcome plot hurdles.

McCrea takes over as sheriff's deputy in his assignment to halt the crime wave, managing to give role certain authority. Stevens isn't particularly well cast for bandit character. Joan Weldon, in for romantic interest, plays daughter of Addison Richards, sheriff killed by Stevens when he becomes suspicious of latter's movements. Darlene Fields is okay as a dancehall girl who knows Stevens' secret.

Technical departments are well executed, leading off with Ernest Laszlo's outstanding photography. David Raksin's music score and editing by Ellsworth Hoagland and Robert Golden match up. *Whit.*

Death in Small Doses

Okay exploitation pic exposing "stay-awake" pill racket.

Hollywood, Aug. 22.
Allied Artists release of a Richard Heermance production. Stars Peter Graves, Mala Powers; features Chuck Connors, Merry Anders, Roy Engel, Robert B. Williams. Directed by Joseph Newman. Screenplay, John McGreevey, based on Satevepost article by Arthur L. Davis; camera, Carl Guthrie; editor, William Austin; music, Emil Newman, Robert Wiley Miller. Previewed Aug. 20, '57. Running time, **78 MINS.**

Tom Kayler .... Peter Graves
Val Owens .... Mala Powers
Mink Reynolds .... Chuck Connors
Amy .... Merry Anders
Wally .... Roy Engel
Dunc .... Robert B. Williams
Hummell .... Harry Leuter
Flynt .... Pete Kooy
Lennie .... Robert Christopher

Million-dollar racket of illegally supplying truck drivers with "bennys"—or "stay-awake" pills—for long hauls on the road springboards "Death in Small Doses," based upon Satevepost article which exposed the evil. Film is okay entry for smaller program situations where subject lends itself to hefty exploitation.

John McGreevey screenplay follows an investigator for U.S. Food and Drug Administration sent to Los Angeles to crack down on the drug ring. It's a straightforward narrative, as Peter Graves takes on role of undercover man, until winding reels when yarn becomes involved and some of the action inexplicable. Joseph Newman maintains a good place in his direction, however, and Richard Heermance is responsible for suitable production values in getting over the story.

Graves does a first-rate job as the investigator who becomes a truck driver and takes a room in the home of a pretty young widow whose husband met his death in a truck accident after taking too many bennys. Mala Powers, who delivers her usual capable performance, is in first for romantic interest with Graves, until it develops she's a pill pusher and is responsible for putting agent on the spot. Chuck Connors is solid as a benny-happy driver, Merry Anders acquits herself well as a pusher who helps Graves and Roy Engel and Robert B. Williams turn in okay portrayals as others involved in the racket.

Carl Guthrie's photography is fluid, William Austin's editing tight and music score by Emil Newman and Robert Wiley Miller goes with story mood. Other credits are expertly handled. *Whit.*

Daughter of Dr. Jekyll

Cheapie horror pic for the exploitation market (billed with "Cyclops").

Hollywood, Aug. 20.
Allied Artists production and release. Stars John Agar, Gloria Talbott, Arthur Shields; with John Dierkes, Martha Wentworth, Mollie McCart. Producer-screenplay, Jack Pollexfen. Directed by Edgar G. Ulmer; camera, John F. Warren; editor, Holbrook N. Todd; art director, Theobold Holsopple; music supervision, Melvyn Lenard. Previewed Aug. 12, '57. Running time, **67 MINS.**

George Hastings .... John Agar
Janet Smith .... Gloria Talbott
Dr. Lomas .... Arthur Shields
Jacob .... John Dierkes
Mrs. Merchant ...... Martha Wentworth
Maggie .... Mollie McCart

At one point, co-star John Agar declares, "This is ridiculous." That sums up cheapie horror pic for the exploitation market (billed with "Dr. Cyclops").

Gloria Talbott plays an English miss who learns from kindly guardian Arthur Shields the horrible family secret—that her late pop was the notorious Dr. Jekyll. When a number of locals in the isolated village turn up dead via vampirish goings-on, the superstitious villagers get up a stake-driving party, with Miss Talbott slated for the honors because of pop's reputation. But fiance Agar uncovers that kindly Dr. Shields is the real monster, so villager John Dierkes does the stake bit on Shields, instead.

Jack Pollexfen both wrote and produced. Cast plays it broadly under Edgar G. Ulmer's direction. Technical effects are more murky than scary. *Kove.*

Operation Mad Ball

Wacky Army comedy with big b.o. potential.

Columbia release of Jed Harris production. Stars Jack Lemmon, Kathryn Grant, Ernie Kovacs, Arthur O'Connell, Mickey Rooney. Directed by Richard Quine. Screenplay, Arthur Carter, Harris, Blake Edwards, from a play by Carter; camera, Charles Lawton; editor, Charles Nelson; music, George Duning. Previewed in N.Y., July 23, '57. Running time, **105 MINS.**

Pvt. Hogan	Jack Lemmon
Lieut. Betty Bixby	Kathryn Grant
Capt. Paul Lock	Ernie Kovacs
Colonel Rousch	Arthur O'Connell
Yancey Skibo	Mickey Rooney
Cpl. Bohun	Dick York
Pvt. Widowskas	James Darren
Cpl. Berryman	Roger Smith
Pvt. Grimes	William Leslie
Sgt. Wilson	Sheridan Comerate
Ozark	L. Q. Jones
Madame LaFour	Jeanne Manet
Lt. Johnson	Bebe Allen
Lt. Schmidt	Mary LaRoche
Sgt. McCloskey	Dick Crockett
Pvt. Bullard	Paul Picerni
Master Sgt. Pringle	David McMahon

War pictures usually fall into two categories. There are the "war is hell" and the "war is fun" films. "Operation Mad Ball," produced by Jed Harris, falls into the latter bracket and, as such, is probably one of the funniest service comedies to reach the screen since the end of World War II. Judged by the spontaneous and uninhibited laughter that ran through the audience at a sneak preview, general hilarity will be the order of the day at theatres booking the picture. It's the kind of madcap entry that will appeal to family groups and, as a result, the turnstiles should click as often as the laughs.

To the credit of producer Harris, director Richard Quine, and scripters Arthur Carter, Blake Edwards and Harris, they have geared the production strictly for farce. Like most service comedies, there is an element of truth in each of the situations, but truth presented realistically can be dull. What Harris and his associates have done is to take a series of events experienced by an Army medical unit in France shortly after the war and exaggerated them almost beyond recognition. The result is a fast-paced, slambang farce designed solely for entertainment.

Aiding the overall effect of the comedy is a group of performers who know how to go along with the joke. A less competent cast could have easily made a shambles out of the whole affair. Fortunately Jack Lemmon, Ernie Kovacs, Arthur O'Connell, Mickey Rooney, Kathryn Grant and the supporting players have completely absorbed the spirit of the picture and come through with performances that contribute greatly to the general hilarity.

The picture is indeed noteworthy for transferring Kovacs from tv to pictures. As an unctuous, busybody, promotion-bent, obnoxious officer, Kovacs makes an excellent foil for the intrigues of the enlisted men in his command. His "Mad Ball" performance, a comedy gem, will undoubtedly rate numerous calls for his services in future films.

Another standout comedy contribution is made by Rooney. Although he appears in a short scene in a part that may be termed a bit, Rooney makes such a strong impression that his limited screen time is barely noticed. He appears as a jazzed-up transportation sergeant who whisks an entire battalion out of Le Havre in no time flat.

Lemmon, the all-thumbs lieutenant of "Mr. Roberts," scores again as the Mr. Fix-it leader of the enlisted contingent in the perennial war against the officer clan. O'Connell is fine as the colonel in charge of the medical unit who seeks to avoid all difficulties that might possibly interfere with his promotion to general. Miss Grant is properly confused as the sweet commissioned nurse-dietitian caught in the enlisted man-officer conflict. Dick York, as Kovacs' clerk-corporal, is outstanding in his "counterspy" role of liaison man between the enlisted forces and headquarters.

It's probably useless to attempt to give a detailed outline of the story. Basically it has to do with a ball planned by the enlisted men and their efforts to outwit Kovacs from discovering their plans and cancelling them. The ball, to be held at a small French hotel off the base, is designed to bring the enlisted men together with their girl friends—the medical unit's nurses. Since the nurses are officers, the enlisted personnel are not permitted to fraternize with them, a situation that requires considerable intrigue.

One of the biggest laughs of the picture is garnered by William Hickey who, as Lemmon's aide on mortuary duty, does a hilarious wide-eyed "take" on seeing a supposedly dead man move.

Quine's direction is probably the moving force behind the success of the comedy. All other technical contributions, including Charles Lawton's photography, George Duning's music and Robert Boyle's art direction, are first rate.

Holl.

My Man Godfrey
(C'SCOPE—COLOR)

Amusing remake of the 1936 version with June Allyson-David Niven names to attract good grosses.

Hollywood, Aug. 30.

Universal release of a Ross Hunter production. Stars June Allyson, David Niven; costars Jessie Royce Landis, Robert Keith, Eva Gabor, Jay Robinson, Martha Hyer; features Jeff Donnell. Directed by Henry Koster. Screenplay, Everett Freeman, Peter Bermeis, William Bowers, based on script by Morrie Ryskind, Eric Hatch and novel by Hatch; camera (Eastmancolor), William Daniels; editor, Milton Carruth; music, Joseph Gershenson. Previewed Aug. 20, '57. Running time, **92 MINS.**

Irene	June Allyson
Godfrey	David Niven
Angelica	Jessie Royce Landis
Mr. Bullock	Robert Keith
Francesca	Eva Gabor
Vincent	Jay Robinson
Cordelia	Martha Hyer
Molly	Jeff Donnell
Hubert	Herbert Anderson
Brent	Eric Sinclair
Lieutenant O'Connor	Dabbs Greer
Captain	Fred Essler
Second Detective	Jack Mather
Young Man at Bar	Paul Levitt
Elliott	Harry Cheshire
George	Robert Clarke
Man With Monkey	Robert Brubaker
Investigator	Fred Coby
Man at Bar	Voltaire Perkins
Howard	William Hudson
Motor Cop	Robert Foulk
Henderson	Thomas B. Henry
Farnsworth	Richard Deacon

Updated version of "My Man Godfrey" is a pretty well turned out comedy with June Allyson and David Niven recreating the original Carole Lombard-William Powell star roles. Yarn is overly contrived at times, but generally stands up as a clever situation farce which should show heavy returns in general market.

Ross Hunter's production of the butler to an eccentric New York family of wealth who helps straighten them out, meanwhile recipient of the affections of the younger daughter, manages to pack plenty of lusty humor in the fast 92 minutes. Where film misses is in the Niven character of butler. The Everett Freeman-Peter Bermeis-William Bowers screenplay drags him in by the heels in too fabricated a character—a former Austrian diplomat in the U.S. via illegal entry. (In the original 1936 Morrie Ryskind-Eric Hatch script, Powell was a forgotten man of the depression, a more natural character.) Again, the scripters hit upon too ready a solution of the Allyson-Niven romance after Niven has been deported.

Director Henry Koster deftly handles his characters in their comedic paces and succeeds in establishing an aura of screwiness in keeping with the 1936 version. Niven is a particular standout in his helping the family back on their feet after bankruptcy faces them. Miss Allyson likewise is okay in her role but inclined to cuteness. Jessie Royce Landis as the wacky society mother registers a definite hit, Martha Hyers as the arrogant elder siser is stunning and Robert Keith ably portrays the father faced with ruin. Eva Gabor makes capital of a Continental divorcee and Jeff Donnell is in for some sparkling dialog as the weary family maid. Jay Robinson as a family leech, constantly warbling "Lovely" at the piano, also is in for capable support.

Sarah Vaughan chirps title song by Peggy Lee and Sonny Burke over the titles. William Daniels' color photography is interesting, art direction by Alexander Golitzen and Richard H. Riedel in keeping with general quality tone of picture and Milton Carruth's editing sharp. Frank Skinner's music score is fitting.

Whit.

The Long Haul
(BRITISH)

Victor Mature caught up in long distance truck racketeering with Diana Dors as the blonde menace who nearly wrecks his home. Good average entertainment.

London, Aug. 28.

Columbia release of Maxwell Setton production. Stars Victor Mature and Diana Dors. Directed by Ken Hughes. Screenplay by Ken Hughes from novel by Mervyn Mills; camera, Basil Emmott; editor, Raymond Poulton; music, Trevor Duncan. At Odeon, Marble Arch, London, Aug. 27, '57. Running time, **100 MINS.**

Harry Miller	Victor Mature
Lynn	Diana Dors
Joe Easy	Patrick Allen
Connie Miller	Gene Anderson
Frank	Peter Reynolds
Casey	Liam Redmond
Butch Miller	Michael Wade
Mutt	Dervis Ward
Jeff	Murray Kash
MacNaughton	Jameson Clark
Superintendent Macrea	John Harvey
Army Sergeant	Roland Brand
Foreman	Stanley Rose
Depot Manager	Raymond Barry

Columbia's latest British pic, starring Victor Mature and Diana Dors, proves a domestic triangle thriller, interwoven with hijackers and graft that makes good entertainment for the general run of patrons. It is a topical human problem story that should appeal to both sexes, and particularly fans of the two stars. Victor Mature plays Harry, a good-hearted GI anxious to return to the States on finshing Army service in Germany. His English wife wants to stay near her people in Liverpool, and refuses to go with him. She wins him over and her uncle fixes him up with a badly paid job as a truck driver, and from then on he's in trouble. He gets in a fight trying to stop his mate's load being robbed on the way to Scotland, not knowing the driver is getting his cut on a phony holdup. From then on it's cooperate, or else.

Out of work and desperate, Harry joins a racketeer, then gets tangled up with the boss' ritzy girl friend who has walked out on the plushy setup. The police are after him when his ex-buddy gets killed in a fake accident to collect insurance, and he plans a getaway with the gangster the girl and a load of valuable furs. After a wild dramatic journey with the heavily laden truck through narrow, stony side tracks, they get within sight of the small freighter that means freedom, when the boss gets killed, and Harry decides to go back. This nightmareish, frenzied race against time is the highlight of the film, and provides tense and exciting sequences.

Mature makes a convincing figure of the straightforward guy who turns cheat on his wife and his work, and Diana Dors gives sufficient reason as the blonde who helps him do it. Gene Anderson is quietly effective as the background wife and Michael Wade does well in the small part of her son. Liam Redmond and Patrick Allen give first-rate characterizations of the racketeer and his stooge and Peter Reynolds makes a suitably spineless yesman out of the role of the girl's brother.

Clem.

The Careless Years

Well-done entry in the teenage cycle. Moderate b.o. prospects, although name of star Dean Stockwell might help.

Hollywood, Aug. 30.

United Artists release of Edward Lewis production. Stars Dean Stockwell, Natalie Trundy; features John Larch. Directed by Arthur Hiller. Screenplay, Edward Lewis; camera, Sam Leavitt; editor, Leon Barsha; music, Leith Stevens; songs, "The Careless Years" and "Butterfingers Baby," by Joe Lubin. Previewed Aug. 26, '57. Running time, **70 MINS.**

Jerry Vernon	Dean Stockwell
Emily Meredith	Natalie Trundy
Sam Vernon	John Larch
Helen Meredith	Barbara Billingsley
Charles Meredith	John Stephenson
Harriet	Maureen Cassidy
Bob Williams	Alan Dinehart III
Mathilda Vernon	Virginia Christine
Biff Vernon	Bobby Hyatt
Uncle Harry	Hugh Sanders
Aunt Martha	Claire Carleton
Mrs. Belosi	Lizz Slifer

Whether or not to have a premarital "affar to remember" is the chief problem posed in this Dean Stockwell-Natalie Trundy costarrer. Film falls into the teenage cycle, but is several shades better than most. Lack of any marquee names dim the b.o. prospects, but rising popularity of Stockwell will help.

Screenplay by Edward Lewis, who also produced, is basically simple. Stockwell and Miss Trundy meet, fall in love, plan to marry. Respective parents reluctantly give their blessings—provided youngsters wait a while. Parents, too, are worried about couple staying within the moral code, which is practically the last thing on Stockwell's mind, although Miss Trundy has opposite views on the situation. Pair subsequently plan to elope, but a bitter argument erupts. Windup finds the pair back in love, and both agreed that they should wait before stepping up to the altar.

Stockwell herewith essays his

first starring role since his childhood thespic days at Metro. Bearing a striking resemblance to the late James Dean, it's to Stockwell's credit that he doesn't try to ape Dean's style of acting, but instead has developed his own individual personality. He's good. Miss Trundy is warm and appealing, and John Larch is fine as his father.

Edward Lewis' production mantling has class throughout. Other plus factors are Arthur Hiller's direction, the camera work of Sam Leavitt, and McClure Capps' art direction. All technical contributions, for that matter, are good.

Incidentally, there may be beefs from the American Medical Assn. over the following bit of dialog between two parents worried over their offspring:

Husband: Why don't you take a sleeping pill?

Wife: I hate sleeping pills; it's a bad habit.

Husband: One a night is NOT habit-forming. *Neal.*

Streets of Sinners

Fast police melodrama for good returns in program spots; George Montgomery to spark chances.

Hollywood, Aug. 30.

United Artists release of a William Berke production. Stars George Montgomery; costars Geraldine Brooks, Nehemiah Persoff, Marilee Earle; features William Harrigan, Stephen Joyce, Clifford David. Directed by Berke. Screenplay, John McPartland, based on story by Philip Yordan; camera, J. Burgi Contner; editor, Everett Sutherland; music, Albert Glasser. Previewed Aug. 28, '57. Running time, **76 MINS.**

John Dean .... George Montgomery
Terry .... Geraldine Brooks
Leon .... Nehemiah Persoff
Nancy .... Marilee Earle
Gus .... William Harrigan
Ricky .... Stephen Joyce
Tom .... Clifford David
Joan .... Diana Milay
Frances .... Sandra Rehn
Short Stuff .... Danny Dennis
First Sergeant .... Ted Irwin
Tiny .... Melvin Decker
Sam .... Lou Gilbert
Larry .... Barry McGuire
Boy .... Elia Clark
Fire Captain .... Jack Hartley
Joey .... Billy James
Sam's Wife .... Liza Balesca
Tiny's Mother .... Eva Gerson
Harry .... John Holland
Motor Cop .... Bob Duffy
Pete .... Joey Faye
Second Sergeant .... Fred Herrick
Customer .... Charlie Jordan
Utility Bartender .... John Barry
Tiny's Father .... Wolf Barzell
Harry .... Stephen Elliot

"Street of Sinners" is the story of a rookie cop with enough melodramatics to fit handily into the program market for good returns. George Montgomery stars, backed by plenty of top assistance from a good cast and deft writing and hard-hitting direction to maintain the interest.

The William Berke production, which he also directs, was lensed in N.Y., where atmospheric backgrounds add to film's realism. Pic takes its title from the rookie's beat, giving meaning to the street he tries to bring to some semblance of order as he's faced with an almost impossible task.

Montgomery as the rookie starts his first day on the force the hard way, by incurring the enmity of Nehemiah Persoff, operator of a bar who controls the street through his powerful connections in high places. Rookie believes in huing to the rulebook despite the fatherly advice of block's retiring patrolman: consequently, finds the going tough as neighborhood kids are stirred up against him and he's put on the spot with his superiors through sudden violence on his beat.

His position is further complicated when a pretty alcoholic jumps to her death when he's in her apartment, and he's suspended from the force. Strictly through his own actions and sans any cooperation from the police, who refuse him support, the rookie is able finally to break Persoff's hold on the community, simultaneously solving a murder.

Montgomery is okay in his role but acting honors go to his costars, leading off with Persoff, who packs his character with authority. Geraldine Brooks as the alcoholic who makes a last-chance try at happiness by proposing marriage to Montgomery before commiting suicide registers dramatically and Marilee Earle impresses as a tough neighborhood girl who falls for rookie. William Harrigan convinces as the retiring policeman and Stephen Joyce handles himself well as a punk who wants to be bigtime.

John McPartland based his screenplay on a story by Philip Yordan, and J. Burgi Contner's low-key photography and Everett Sutherland's tight editing help the mood. *Whit.*

The Unholy Wife
(COLOR)

Fairly suspenseful drama of an amoral wife, with Diana Dors' name to help program situations.

Hollywood, Aug. 30.

Universal release of a John Farrow production. Stars Diana Dors, Rod Steiger; costars Tom Tryon, Beulah Bondi; features Marie Windsor, Arthur Franz. Directed by Farrow. Screenplay, Jonathan Latimer, from story by William Durkee; camera (Technicolor), Lucien Ballard; editor, Eda Warren; music, Daniele Amfitheatrof. Previewed Aug. 21, '57. Running time, **94 MINS.**

Phyllis Hochen .... Diana Dors
Paul Hochen .... Rod Steiger
San .... Tom Tryon
Emma Hochen .... Beulah Bondi
Gwen .... Marie Windsor
Rev. Stephen Hochen..... Arthur Franz
Ezra Benton .... Luis Van Rooten
Gino Verdugo .... Joe DeSantis
Theresa .... Argentina Brunetti
Carl Kramer .... Tol Avery
Sheriff Wattling .... James Burke
Deputy Watkins .... Steve Pendleton
Michael .... Gary Hunley
Judge .... Douglas Spencer

"The Unholy Wife" is a story of poetic justice. As Diana Dors' first American release, it comes off as a fairly suspenseful drama which may be exploited for moderate returns in the regular market. Film's chances of a big payoff, however, would have been better had it been released closer to British actress' smash publicity buildup last year, when RKO staged a sex campaign around her.

The John Farrow production is a carefully developed narrative of an amoral wife who manages to escape punishment for a murder she commits but finally is convicted for a death of which she's innocent. Rich Technicolor gives splashy pictorial values to pic, lensed partially in the grape country of northern California, and offers fine mounting for femme star's dazzling personality. She displays a definite dramatic sense in her interpretation of a difficult role, and has a capable costar in Rod Steiger as her husband, who registers impressively in a semi-character role. Farrow's direction of the Jonathan Latimer screenplay maintains good pace and he keeps proceedings on a moving level.

Miss Dors plays a B-girl with a shady past who weds Steiger, wealthy California vineyard and winery owner. She becomes clandestinely involved with a rodeo rider, Tom Tryon, and resolves to kill her husband, sure she can get away with the crime on her claim she mistook him for a prowler her mother-in-law, who lives with them, has frequently mentioned. Prowler actually is Tryon, who visits the wife when her husband is away.

Conspiracy goes wrong when wife mistakenly kills her husband's best friend. She talks her husband into taking the blame, Steiger thinking he's certain of acquittal. He's convicted, however, upon her faked testimony. Mother-in-law overhears the frame, suffers a paralytic stroke and later swallows some powerful medicine which points to wife as her murderess.

Femme star turns in an excellent account of herself, and Steiger is on a par. Tryon make his work count in a smaller role, Beulah Bondi as Steiger's mother delivers dramatically and Arthur Franz as a priest, Steiger's brother, scores as another key character. Joe DeSantis and Marie Windsor lend good support.

Lucien Ballard's color photography leads off technical credits, Eda Warren keeps her editing sharp, Daniele Amfitheatrof's music score is dramatically sustaining and art direction by Albert S. D'Agostino and Frank Bachelin matches up. *Whit.*

Amazing Colossal Man

Imaginative science-fictioner which may be exploited for heavy returns.

Hollywood, Aug. 30.

American-International release of a Bert I. Gordon production. Stars Glenn Langan, Cathy Downs, William Hudson, James Seay, Larry Thor. Directed by Gordon. Screenplay, Mark Hanna, Gordon; camera, Joe Biroc; editor, Ronald Sinclair; music, Albert Glasser; special effects, Gordon. Previewed Aug. 27, '57. Running itme, **81 MINS.**

Lt.-Col. Glenn Manning.... Glenn Langan
Carol Forrest .... Cathy Downs
Dr. Paul Lindstrom......William Hudson
Colonel Hallock .... James Seay
Dr. Eric Coulter .... Larry Thor
Richard Kingman .... Russ Bender
Sgt. Taylor .... Lynn Osborn
Typist .... Diana Darrin
Control Officer .... William Hughes
Lt. in Briefing Room....... Jack Kosslyn
Girl in Bath .... Jean Moorhead
Sgt. Reception Desk ...... Jimmy Cross
Henry .... Hank Patterson
Delivery Man .... Frank Jenks
Army Guard at Gate.... Harry Raybould
Sgt. Lee Carter .... Scott Peters
Capt. Thomas .... Myron Cook
Police Lt. Keller..........Michael Harris
Lt. Peterson .... Bill Cassady
Sgt. Hanson .... Dick Nelson
Dr. McDermott .... Edmund Cobb
Robert Allen .... Judd Holdren
Attendant .... Paul Hahn
Nurse .... June Jocelyn
Lt. Kline .... Stanley Lachman

Special effects figure importantly in the unfoldment of this Bert I. Gordon production, which should lap up plenty of green stuff from the exploitation trade. With an imaginative story premise and good handling — except for over-footage which can easily be tightened — film is one of the most unusual science-fiction yarns to come along in some months. (Pic is packaged with "Cat Girl.")

Gordon, who also directs from his and Mark Hanna's screenplay and executes the special effects which lend high melodramatic potency to the suspense, has chosen the ultra-modern atomic blasts near Las Vegas as basis for his theme. When an Army colonel is frightfully burned in a plutonium explosion and against all rules of medical science overnight regrows healthy skin, he makes with the shock—he starts growing at the rate of 10 feet per day. Doctors explain the blast upset the balance of his cell growth, and unless they can halt it he will continue to soar upwards until he dies.

Pic's thrills come in the final reels when he escapes from the isolated Army sanitarium where doctors working night and day finally find a cure. Now 70 feet tall, he makes his way to Las Vegas, where he causes pandemonium as he appears in the downtown section and later on the luxury hotel Strip. He finally is killed on Boulder Dam, when it becomes clear he has become so mentally deranged there is no chance of giving him the cure. These sequences are played for fine effect.

Glenn Langan delivers persuasively in title role as the man who becomes a monstrosity, and Cathy Downs as his fiancee, who does her best to help him maintain his sanity, is likewise convincing. William Hudson and Larry Thor score as the doctors fighting to find a cure, and James Seay is good as an Army officer in charge of the case.

Technical departments are well handled throughout, leading off, apart from Gordon's special effects, with Joe Biroc's smooth photography. Ronald Sinclair's editing catches the mood and Albert Glasser's music score further enhances it. *Whit.*

Parson and the Outlaw
(COLOR)

For dyed-in-the-woolly-west fans only.

Columbia release of Charles (Buddy) Rogers production. Stars Anthony Dexter, Sonny Tufts, Marie Windsor, Rogers; features Jean Parker, Robert Lowery, Madalyn Trahey, Bob Steel. Directed by Oliver Drake. Screenplay, Drake, John Mantley; camera (Technicolor), Clark Ramsey; editor, Warren Adams; music, Joe Sodja. Previewed in N.Y., Aug. 26, '57. Running time, **71 MINS.**

Billy the Kid .... Anthony Dexter
Jack Slade .... Sonny Tufts
Tonya .... Marie Windsor
Rev. Jericho Jones .... Buddy Rogers
Mrs. Jones .... Jean Parker
Colonel Morgan .... Robert Lowery
Elly McCloud .... Madalyn Trahey

This one might have been taken from the files of a Junior Lone Ranger. An oldfashioned oater, the Charles (Buddy) Rogers production might rate a nod in undemanding sagebrush situations but otherwise rates only the brush.

Story has Billy the Kid a peaceable man no longer toting his guns and trying to forget the past when he was forced to permanently puncture 21 hombres. This was a difficult period in Billy's career; he found it hard to live with himself with the knowledge of all those defunct bodies strewn across the west.

But even in the present he can't, try as he may, remain aloof from such forms of violence as killing. His old friend, the parson, gets himself plugged in taking on the town's heavies. Billy steps in and mows them down but he, too, gets a Colt .45 clobbering.

Some familiar names are involved; Rogers as the parson, Anthony Dexter as Billy, Sonny Tufts, Marie Windsor, Jean Parker and others. They fail to put much wallop in the old west; the outdoor adventure is put together in only partially skilled fashion. Nothing special about the technical credits. *Gene.*

From Hell It Came

Amateurishly done, but stacked with horror appeal for the young.

Hollywood, Aug. 27.

Allied Artists release of Jack Milner Production. Stars Tod Andrews, Tina Carver; features Linda Watkins, John McNamara, Gregg Palmer, Robert Swan, Baynes Barron, Suzanne Ridgway, Mark Sheeler, Lee Rhodes, Grace Matthews, Tami Marsh, Chester Hayes, Lenmana Guerin. Directed by Dan Milner. Screenplay, Richard Bernstein, from story by Bernstein and Jack Milner; camera, Brydon Baker; editor, Jack Milner; music, Darrell Calker. Previewed Aug. 16, '57. Running time, **71 MINS.**

Dr. William Arnold........Tod Andrews
Dr. Terry Mason..........Tina Carver
Mrs. Kilgore.............Linda Watkins
Prof. Clark...........John McNamara
Kimo.................Gregg Palmer
Witch Doctor Tano.......Robert Swan
Chief Maranka........Baynes Barron
Korey.............Suzanne Ridgway
Eddie.................Mark Sheeler
Norgu.....................Lee Rhodes
Orchid..............Grace Matthews
Naomi.......................Tani Marsh
Maku.................Chester Hayes
Dori................Lenmana Guerin

"It," in this case, is a living monster-stump which has risen from the grave for revenge—more succinctly put, a tree man. Although somewhat amateurishly turned out, film does have the necessary horror ingredients for which teenagers are storming the b.o. just now and pic serves as a good complement to "The Disembodied" (see review in this issue). Combo is being packaged by Allied Artists.

Basic story idea of Richard Bernstein and Jack Milner is good; the former's screenplay, however, often results in cliche wordage. Locale is a Pacific isle where an atomic research group composed of Tod Andrews, Tina Carver and John McNamara is headquartered. They're there to care for natives suffering from radiation burns, but the witch doctors are blaming the Americans for deaths caused by the black plague. Meantime Gregg Palmer, son of the deceased island chief, has been put to death by the power-seeking witch doctors and cohorts because of Palmer's friendship with the Americans. Before he dies, however, he promises to return from the grave for revenge. "It" returns to stalk and kill and even kidnap the pretty femme scientist before being toppled into quicksand by a bullet. By that time the villains are also dead, the natives and the Yanks are at peace and the two leads are pitching woo.

Tina Carver, a looker with thespic competence, stands out in the femme lead, while Tod Andrews and McNamara are okay. Film "introduces" Linda Watkins, who performs satisfactorily as a white widow on the island. Gregg Palmer is good in a comparatively brief role. Miss Watkins, of course, is a vet thesp of both stage and screen; she just hasn't been in pix for some years.

Dan Milner's direction of the Jack Milner production often leaves much to be desired. Above average technical contributions are Brydon Baker's photography and the special effects of James H. Donnelly. *Neal.*

Bitter Victory
(Amere Victoire)
(U.S.—FRENCH)

Venice, Aug. 29.

Columbia release of Paul Gzaetz Transcontinental Films production. Stars Richard Burton, Curd Jurgens, Ruth Roman; features Raymond Pellegrin, Anthony Bushell, Sean Kelly, Christopher Lee, Alfred Burke. Directed by Nicholas Ray. Screenplay, Ray, Gavin Lambert, Rene Hardy, from novel by Hardy; camera, Michel Kelber; music, Maurice Le Roux. At Film Festival, Venice. Running time, **97 MINS.**

Major Brand..............Curd Jurgens
Capt. Leith............Richard Burton
Mrs. Brand...................Ruth Roman
Makron..............Raymond Pellegrin

(English Version)

Good press notices should precede this psychological actioner into most situations, with France offering the best market bet for the expansive production. Other European areas appear spotty, though the general outlook appears good. Stateside chances depend on a top bally job and on cast values in the Richard Burton and Ruth Roman names—as well as the newly "acquired" Curd Jurgens—for a better-than-average payoff; though eventual recouping of heavy costs remains problematical.

Rene Hardy's successful novel has been translated for the screen into a literary, hard-hitting screenplay which almost always manages to overcome some of the incongruities of the original story line. This sets up a deadly struggle between two British Army officers during the World War II African campaign. Conflict between Capt. Leith and Major Brand derives from fact that Leith knows of Brand's basic cowardice in action, and also from jealousy over Brand's wife, with whom Leith has had an affair. Returning from a dangerous mission in German-held Bengasi, Brand tries twice indirectly to bring about Leith's death, once by leaving him behind to guard two wounded Germans, again by deliberately letting a scorpion bite his rival. Leith finally dies and the "victorious" major brings his commando force remnants back to the post, ironically earning a medal but losing his wife's affection as well as what was left of his soldiers' respect.

Script is basically flawed by the unclearly delineated key character of the major—and Curd Jurgens' competent, straightforward performance is less successful because of it. Otherwise it includes many basic truths about the horrors of war, the relationships of man, the disintegration of character under the stresses of action, etc. It also features such strong stuff as the mercy shooting, by Burton, of a mortally wounded German soldier and the aforementioned mortal bite by the scorpion.

Fine thesping by Burton leads a series of top performances by other members of large cast. Miss Roman is good in a limited role, while Raymond Pellegrin, as an Arab guide who joins the expedition, is relegated to a comparatively minor part.

Nicholas Ray's direction is in his forceful, visually very effective manner, as witnessed by the action scenes depicting the attack on the Bengasi post, the various incidents in the desert, the shooting of the German prisoner and many others. In this he has received excellent aid from Michel Kelber's exceptional lensing effort, in which almost every image is keyed for (wide) frame-filling dramatic effect, adding to pic's audience impact. Desert scenes are of outstanding photographic beauty.

Technical credits on copy seen, which contained the original English-language soundtrack, were all outstanding, starting with the interesting initial titles, in the quality tradition of past Paul Graetz productions.

Pic was presented here at Venice without an official nationality while awaiting a decision from the appropriate French authorities. *Hawk.*

Enemy From Space

Lesser science-fiction entry for exploitation market.

Hollywood, Aug. 27.

United Artists release of an Anthony Hinds production. Stars Brian Donlevy; features Sidney James, John Longden, Bryan Forbes, Vera Day, William Franklyn. Directed by Val Guest. Screenplay, Nigel Kneale, Guest, from original by Kneale; camera, Gerald Gibbs; music, James Bernard; editor, James Needs. Previewed Aug. 21, '57. Running time, **84 MINS.**

Quatermass..............Brian Donlevy
Lomax...................John Longden
Jimmy Hall...............Sydney James
Marsh.....................Bryan Forbes
Brand................William Franklyn
Sheila..........................Vera Day
Dawson..............Charles Lloyd Pack
Broadhead...................Tom Chatto
The P.R.O.............John Van Eyssen
Gorman....................Percy Herbert
Ernie.....................Michael Ripper
McLeod........................John Rae
Secretary..............Marianne Stone
Young Man..............Ronald Wilson
Mrs. McLeod....................Jane Aird
Kelly...........................Betty Impey
Inspector....................Lloyd Lamble
Commissioner...............John Stuart
Banker........................Gilbert Davis
Woman M.P.................Joyce Adams
Peterson....................Edwin Richfield
Michaels....................Howard Williams
Laboratory Assistants.......Philip Baird, Robert Raikes
Intern.........................John Fabian
Super.......................George Marritt
Constable......................Arthur Blake
Harry......................Michael Balfour

British producers, when they turn to science-fiction, generally are vague in approach and this import does little to dispel the impression. Film is a lesser entry in its field but is adequate to release intentions as lower half of an exploitation bill.

Anthony Hinds production stars Brian Donlevy, only name in cast known to American audiences, as an English scientist engaged in interplanetary research. He suddenly stumbles upon a hush-hush government project on the moorlands where it's announced that synthetic food is being produced, but actually its operations are being directed by an enemy from space, working to take over the earth. Apparently the producers were as uncertain of their object as the audience, for yarn unfolds in fine confusion, Donlevy in some way managing to destroy the project.

Val Guest's direction is as uncertain as script on which he collabs with Nigel Kneale, with the result that all characters are stodgy. Donlevy is supported by John Longden, as a Scotland Yard inspector trying to help; Sidney James, a newspaper reporter; William Franklyn, a lab assistant, and Bryan Forbes, another assistant who comes under the out-of-this-world spell. Special effects by Bill Warrington, Henry Harris and Frank George are imaginative, and Gerald Gibbs' camera work is okay. *Whit.*

Cat Girl

Minor science-fiction entry, weakly developed; to be packaged with "Amazing Colossal Man."

Hollywood, Aug. 30.

American-International release of a Lou Rusoff-Herbert Smith production. Stars Barbara Shelley, Robert Ayres, Kay Callard; features Paddy Webster, Ernest Milton, Lilly Kann, Jack May. Directed by Alfred Shaughnessy. Screenplay, Rusoff; camera, Paddy A-Hearne; editor, Jose Jackson. Previewed Aug. 28, '57. Running time, **67 MINS.**

Leonora..................Barbara Shelley
Dr. Marlowe..............Robert Ayres
Dorothy......................Kay Callard
Cathy....................Paddy Webster
Edmund....................Ernest Milton
Anna..........................Lilly Kahn
Richard.........................Jack May
Allan............................John Lee
Cafferty....................Martin Body
Roberts....................John Watson
Nurse.................Selma Vaz Dias
Male Nurse..................John Baker
Guard....................Frank Atkinson
Caretaker..............Geoffrey Tyrrell

"Cat Girl" lacks the ingredients to rise above a very minor entry for the exploitation market, where it is being packaged with "Amazing Colossal Man" (also reviewed this week). Filmed entirely in England with an all-British cast as a joint effort with exec producer Peter Rogers, the Lou Rusoff-Herbert Smith production is weak in all departments and must depend upon its upper-bracketed companion picture for draw.

Plottage twirls around the belief of a young woman that she has inherited what is believed to be the curse of her family. She is told she must carry this curse until the day she dies, in which her soul enters the body of a leopard at times to indulge in savage bloodlust. A psychiatrist tries to help her to return to normalcy after she has had some frightening experiences, but in the end she dies at the same moment the leopard to which she thinks she's akin, is killed.

Development of the Lou Rusoff screenplay fails to fulfill the promise of his idea through blurry writing, and Alfred Shaughnessy's direction is too rambling and distorted to count for much. Barbara Shelley in title role tries hard to give some semblance of reality but doesn't stand a chance with what's handed her. Robert Ayres is the doctor and Kay Callard his wife, but roles are beyond them. Technical departments likewise are under par, much of the dialog being difficult to understand. *Whit.*

Time Lock
(BRITISH)

Compact, unambitious but gripping dualer concerning a child trapped in bank vault; better-than-average supporting pic.

London, Aug. 27.

Independent Film Distributors release of Romulus (Peter Rogers) production. Stars Robert Beatty, Lee Patterson, Betty McDowell, Vincent Winter. Directed by Gerald Thomas. Screenplay, Peter Rogers; camera, Peter Hennessy; editor, John Trumper; music, Stanley Black. At Rialto, London. Running time, **73 MINS.**

Dawson....................Robert Beatty
Lucille Walker.........Betty McDowall
Steven Walker............Vincent Winter
Colin Walker...............Lee Patterson
Evelyn Webb..............Sandra Francis
George Foster................Alan Gifford
Inspector Andrews.........Robert Ayres
Howard Zeeder...............Victor Wood
Max Jarvis..............Jack Cunningham
Dr. Foy.................Peter Mannering
Dr. Hewitson..............Gordon Tanner
Reporter.........................Larry Cross

Modestly designed as a supporting feature, "Time Lock" measures up well against more ambitious productions and will hold average audiences. Lack of starring names known there is likely to prevent this neat little suspense drama from getting much of a show in U.S. theatres, although it has already notched a success on American tele.

Story by Arthur Hailey (prominent British tv scribe operating in Canada) concerns a child inadvertently trapped in the vault of a Canadian bank. The time-lock is set for 63 hours ahead and the thrills come from the efforts of bank officials, a vault expert and a team of acetylene welders and lookers-on to cut through in a desperate race against time.

The police, a local radio station and doctors move in while the nation's attention is focused on the drama. Though the inevitable happy ending brings last minute succour to the small boy, the tension never lets up. Peter Rogers' screenplay excellently exploits the agony of the parents and the selfless efforts of the rescuers. Gerald Thomas has directed without frills and allows the slender but strong story to unfold logically and with mounting tension. More play might have been made of the child's reactions while a prisoner.

Acting is crisp and competent with the use of several Canadian thespians now working in Britain insures maximum authenticity. There are standout performances by Robert Beatty, as the tough vault expert; Alan Gifford, as the distraught bank manager; Lee Patterson and Betty McDowall, as the helpless parents; Robert Ayres, as a cop; Larry Cross, as a slick but human radio announcer; and Vincent Winter, as the kid who causes all the trouble. *Rich.*

Foreign Films

Juha (FINNISH; AGASCOPE; COLOR). Svea Film production and release. With Elina Pohjanpaa, Eino Kaipainen, Veiko Uusinmaki. Written and directed by T. J. Sarkka from novel by Juhani Aho. Camera (Eastmancolor), Osmo Harkimo, Kaumo Laine; editor, Nortia; music, Tauno Pylkkanen. At Karlovy Vary Fest. Running time, **90 MINS.**

Although based on a Finnish classic, this emerges as rather hoary melodrama. However, it has a plus factor of having excellent outdoor settings. Picture concerns an older man who has brought up a young orphan and married her. She is swept off her feet by a visiting Russian. This occurs on the Finno-Russian borders of the early 19th Century, and she is taken back by him. She finally comes back to the older man but his shame ends in his death.

AgaScope is a Swedish anamorphoscopic process that is clear with the color and a plus. Acting is heavy. Color and locale, plus its story, slant this only for certain language cinemas in America. *Mosk.*

New Year's Sacrifice (RED CHINESE; COLOR). Peking Studio production and release. With Pay Yang, Wey Cheo Ling, Li Ting-no. Directed by Sang Chu. Screenplay, Sia Yen from story by Lu Sun; camera (Agfa-color), Chien Tian; editor, Tin Chu; music, Chen Yen-Si. At Karlovy Vary Fest. Running time, **90 MINS.**

Red Chinese films are probably difficult U. S. import items at present but this deserves viewing for the record. It is a natural lingo item but remains somewhat exotic and specialized for regular American pic channels. This is a tale of the social female bondage in the China of the early 1900's, and details the odyssey of one woman sold into marriage, the death of her son and husband, and her ostracizing by a bigoted, ignorant society.

Film is neatly mounted and builds into a moving saga with color lensing, acting and subtle characterizations and techniques combining to make this a unique entry which could someday make for a good specialized U. S. entry. *Mosk.*

Die Letzten Werden Die Ersten Sein (The Last Ones Shall Be First) **(GERMAN).** Constantin release of CCC production. Stars Ulla Jacobsson, O. E. Hasse and Maximilian Schell. Directed by Rolf Hansen. Screenplay, Jochen Huth after story by John Galsworthy; camera, Franz Weihmayr, editor, Anna Hoellering. At Berlin Film Fest. Running time, **98 MINS.**

This CCC production, Germany's eagerly awaited entry at this festival, disappointed. This hardly has any big international chances. Many will find fault with the direction which is old-fashioned and unimaginative. Despite a suspenseful plot, film is a slow-paced, dull offering.

Story centers around two brothers. One is a prominent lawyer and the other a sensitive young man recently returned from a prisonship. When the latter kills a man, who has insulted his girl, the lawyer-brother takes over. Fearing a family scandal would ruin his reputation, he manages to cloak the deed of his brother and an innocent man is punished instead. The conflict of this film is "Shall I Be the Keeper of my Brother?".

While the inadequate direction by Rolf Hansen is mostly to blame, Jochen Huth, one of Germany's ablest writer, has provided unrealistic dialog passages. Even a qualified player such as O. E. Hasse (as lawyer-brother) does not come off too well. Maximilian Schell as his brother is nearly miscast although the material furnished him is not rewarding. Swedish actress Ulla Jacobsson as the girl Wanda, is very sympathetic but hardly more than that.

Technically, film is very well made. Camerawork by Weihmayr even surpasses the German average. Editing and other technical credits are good. *Hans.*

El Trueno Entre Las Hojas (Thunder Among the Leaves) **(ARGENTINE-PARAGUAYAN).** Films AM production and release. Stars Armando Bo, Isabel Sarli; features, Andres Lazlo, Felix Rivero. Written and directed by Bo. Camera, E. Baez; editor, J. France. At Karlovy Vary Fest. Running time, **105 MINS.**

This is another Latino film about a revolt in a slave labor camp of the South American wilds. This over-does its brutality but has a direct candor which, at times, gives this some action moments. It is strictly for Hispano lingo spots but also has some nude episodes and a rape scene for possible exploitation if it can be gotten through.

Armando Bo stars, directs and writes, but has not managed to combine all three successfully. Isabel Sarli has a gratuitous nude bathing scene and displays more bare skin than thespic ability. Production credits are standard. Technical aspects are ordinary but acceptable for the first Paraguayan pic try. *Mosk.*

Jagte Raho (Under Cover of Night) **(INDIAN).** Raj Kapoor production and release. Stars Kapoor; features, Rana Sahib, Pradip Kumar, Sumitra Devi. Directed and written by Shanbhu Mitre, Amit Maitra. Camera, Radhu Karmakar; editor, Irani; music, Salil Chaudhuri. At Karlovy Vary Fest. Running time, **115 MINS.**

A poor man from the villages, looking for some water in a Bombay, wanders into an apartment house. He is chased by a policeman, which awakens the outsize house occupants, and a wild chase starts after the frightened little man. This mixes slapstick, satire, social protest and allegory into an uneven but interesting pic.

This is limited to special situations in the U. S., but it is unusual enough to be worth exploiting. Raj Kapoor at times overplays the little man whose humility still do not interfere with an uncanny sense of saving his own skin. He uncovers all sorts of crimes in the house during his flight. Technical credits are okay, and acting acceptable with songs worked in for Indian tastes. In short, this is an offbeater which may rate Yank attention. *Mosk.*

Ung Leg (Youth At Play) **(DANISH).** Dansk Film production and release. With Ghita Norby, Anne Thomsen, Fritz Helmuth, Klaus Pagh. Written and directed by Johannes Allen. Camera, Karl Andersson; editor, Anker; music, Arne Lamberth. At Karlovy Vary Fest. Running time, **95 MINS.**

This Danish pic treats delinquent youth problem via various phases going from what appears to be a sex lecture to talks on divorce, parental responsibility, etc. However, it is to the film's merit that this rarely gets preachy. It shapes primarily as something for U. S. language spots. Though it talks frankly, this does not have sensational values.

Two 16-year-olds manage to fall in love despite broken homes, lack of moral values, etc. U. S. film influences are plainly manifested via its mentions of jazz, Marlon Brando and use of American slang. Technical credits are okay, acting fine but this lacks a moving point of view. It emerges an interesting pic without the deeper facets needed for international chances. *Mosk.*

Zle Pare (Cursed Money) **(YUGOSLAVIAN).** Lovcen Film production and release. With Dubravka Gal, Antun Nalis, Vaso Perisic, Petar Vojovcic, Ljuba Tadic. Directed by Velimir Stojanovic. Screenplay, Ratko Burovic; camera, Hrvoje Saric; editor, Bojan Adamic. At Karlovy Vary Fest. Running time, **110 MINS.**

A cache of money, hidden by the government in flight during the early years of war, is found by a group of peasants. Film details the effect of the money on the farm people and efforts of a trio of opportunists to get the coin and flee the country. Their efforts lead to two deaths, only to find that the money is now worthless. Story is good, and at times, witty but the tempering of irony, satire and drama is too heavyhanded. As is, this shapes a likely language house entry, and could be worth dualer attention on its imaginative story. Technical credits are excellent as is most of the acting. *Mosk.*

Kabuliwala (INDIAN). Charuchitra production and release. Written and directed by Tagrin Sinha from story by Rabindranath Tagores. Camera and editing, Sibodh Ray; music, Ravi Shankar. At Karlovy Vary Fest. Running time, **90 MINS.**

Film is handicapped by bad studio work which conflicts with the matching of exteriors plus obvious cheapie budgeting. But this has a simplicity and feeling that makes it entertaining despite these flaws. Pic is limited for the American market except for possible special situations.

It concerns a farmer who goes to the city to make some money. He misses his daughter but fills the void with the little girl of the town poet. When he gets into a fight with an avaricious landlord he is jailed and comes out 10 years later and tries to see the little girl. She is now grown and getting married. Then he realizes that the same has happened to his daughter. Film is well acted, and manages to avoid mawkishness. Music is a fitting counterpart to the emotional carryings-on. Technical credits are below par. *Mosk.*

Hang Tuah (MALAYAN; COLOR). Shaw's Malay Film production. Stars P. Ramlee, Sa Adiah, Ahmad Mahmud, Haji Mahadi. Directed by Phani Majumdar. Screenplay, M. C. Sheppard; camera, N. B. Vasudev. At Berlin Film Fest. Running time, **130 MINS.**

This Eastmancolored offering from Malaya is the story of a young merchant who does everything to serve his sultan. After numerous fights, he wins over his opponents. A love story is woven in and there are a number of colorful rhythmic dances along the line.

In many respects this is an interesting presentation despite being overlong and occasionally too sentimental. Technically, pic offers good color but a rather clumsy camera technique. However, a remarkable entry by a film nation nearly unknown to European audiences. *Hans.*

Lagoon of Desire (GREEK). Anzervo production and release. Stars Georges Fountas, Jenny Karezi, Heleni Zafiriou; features Christoforos Nezer, Sonia Zoides. Directed by Georges Zervos. Screenplay, Jacques Campanellis from play by Nicos Tsekouras; camera, Jerry Caloferatos; editor, Zervos. At Karlovy Vary Fest. Running time, **95 MINS.**

Pic nixes a neo-realistic look at poor fishermen trying to form a cooperative against the big money people and some raw sex shenanigans, which do not quite come off. It has some colorful locale work but characters are naively drawn and nudie scenes overdone.

This film shapes only as an exploitation subject for the U.S. market if the frank footage can be retained. Heleni Zafiriou is a buxom looker. General technical matter is par. *Mosk.*

Hannibal Tanur Ur (Professor Hannibal) **(HUNGARIAN).** Hungarofilm production and release. With Erno Szabo, Noemi Apor, Emmy Buttykai, Zoltan Greguss, Hilda Gobbi. Directed by Zoltan Fabri. Screenplay, Istvan Gyenes, Peter Szasz, Fabri from novel by Ferenc Moras; camera, Ferenc Szecsenyi; editor, Istvan Ambrozy; music , Zdenko Tamassey. At Karlovy Vary Film Festival. Running time, **70 MINS.**

Film concerns a Hungarian little man, during the Admiral Horthy facistic regime there in the 1930's, who becomes a victim of political oppression and expediency. Film is briskly made but makes its points over and over again.

Director Zoltan Fabri depicts a filmatic mastery in a series of bravura scenes and make a point of mob and political madness that can destroy even when it wants to help. Film is expertly mounted and acted and could make for a specialized U.S. entry on its theme. It is also a fine lingo entry. *Mosk.*

La Finestra Sul Lunapark (The Window To Luna Park) **(ITALIAN).** Noria Film production. Stars Giulia Rubini, Gastone, Renzelli, Pierre Trabaud, Giancarlo Damiani. Directed by Luigi Commencini. Screenplay, L. Commencini, Suso Cecchi D'Amico; camera, Armando Nannucci. At Berlin Film Fest. Running time, **97 MINS.**

One of the better films of the artistic type shown at the Berlin fete. Well made and never dull, pic deals with poor people. Director Luigi Commencini has created here a human and realistic film which packs emotional impact.

Taking into consideration, however, that this is actually the Italian film school of 1947, it's a little disappointing for fastidious patrons. But it's still a pic considerably above average. Commercially, it has good export possibilities.
Hans.

Pal Joey
(MUSICAL-COLOR)

Rita Hayworth, Frank Sinatra and Kim Novak in racy (not for the kids and grandma) and strictly-top-money musical.

Columbia release of Essex-George Sidney production (produced by Fred Kohlmar). Stars Rita Hayworth, Frank Sinatra, Kim Novak; features Barbara Nichols, Bobby Sherwood, Hank Henry, Elizabeth Patterson. Directed by Sidney. Screenplay, Dorothy Kingsley, from the play of same title with book by John O'Hara; music by Richard Rodgers; lyrics by Lorenz Hart; stage-produced by George Abbott; camera (Technicolor), Harold Lipstein; editors, Viola Lawrence, Jerome Thoms; choreography, Hermes Pan; music supervised and conducted by Morris Stoloff, with arrangements by Nelson Riddle and adaptation by Riddle and George Dunning. Previewed Loew's 72d Street Theatre, N. Y., Sept. 5, '57. Running time, 112 MINS.

Vera Simpson	Rita Hayworth
Joey Evans	Frank Sinatra
Linda English	Kim Novak
Gladys	Barbara Nichols
Ned Galvin	Bobby Sherwood
Mike Miggins	Hank Henry
Mrs. Casey	Elizabeth Patterson
Bartender	Robin Morse
Col. Langley	Frank Wilcox
Mr. Forsythe	Pierre Watkin
Anderson	Barry Bernard
Carol	Ellie Kent
Sabrina	Mara McAfee
Patsy	Betty Utey
Lola	Bek Nelson

"Pal Joey," to get the main point across first, is a click. It can't miss being a blockbuster, the commercial values being so stacked up.

Significant, too, is the nature of the content. "Joey" was dearly beloved in original form by many. The initial and repeat on-the-boards outings meant profitable returns. But who can deny that the play was clavicle-high in spice? Here was a guy, a real heel, who romances the dames without letup or limitation and who comes to bewitch, bother and bewilder an ex-stripper turned Nob Hill society. He gets to be her paid-for wooer.

Now it's on the screen and there are no efforts made to obscure the basics; Joey is still the constant lover. Dialog is highly seasoned and bits and story situations are uncamouflaged boudoir played for laughs. In other words, "Joey" is still another reflection of Hollywood's turn to "adult" material.

Be that as it may, this handsomely-rigged Fred Kohlmar production is a strong, funny entertainment. Dorothy Kingsley's screenplay, from John O'Hara's original book, is skillful rewriting, with colorful characters and solid story built around the Richard Rodgers and Lorenz Hart songs. Total of 14 tunes are intertwined with the plot, 10 of them (such as "Bewitched, Bothered and Bewildered," the novelty "Zip," "What Is a Man?" and "I Could Write a Book") being reprised from the original. Others by the same team of cleffers as "I Didn't Know What Time It Was," "The Lady Is a Tramp," "There's a Small Hotel" and "Funny Valentine." These are oldies penned on non-"Pal Joey" occasions but fit in well with the film's script.

Miss Kingsley pulled some switches in shaping the legiter for the screen. Given a buildup to star status is the chorine from Albuquerque who becomes Joey's prey; Rita Hayworth (in the Vivienne Segal role) does the "Zip" number that had been done by the herein-eliminated newspaper gal. there's not much terping, and the finale is happy ending stuff whereby Miss Hayworth plays Cupid in

bringing Joey and the line lass together. That finish ought to draw some complaints, for it's inconsistent with the nature of the characters.

Sinatra is potent. He's almost ideal as the irreverent, free-wheeling, glib Joey, delivering the rapidfire cracks in a fashion that wrings out the full deeper-than-pale blue comedy potentials. Point might be made, though, that it's hard to figure why all the mice fall for this rat. Kim Novak is one of the mice (term refers to the nitery gals) and rates high as ever in the looks department but her turn is pallid in contrast with the forceful job done by Sinatra.

Miss Hayworth, no longer the ingenue, moves with authority as Joey's sponsor and does the "Zip" song visuals in such fiery, amusing style as to rate an encore.

Standout of the score is "Lady Is a Tramp." It's a wham arrangement and Sinatra gives it powerhouse delivery. His "Write a Book" is another of the big plusses.

Credit Hank Henry, veteran of burlesque, with a cleverly-handled performances as the hard-exterior night club owner. And working competently, too, are Bobby Sherwood, as a bandleader with a yen for Miss Novak; Barbara Nichols as the mouse who refuses to be charmed by the rat, and Elizabeth Patterson as a rooming house operator.

The fun begins even before the credits as Joey is being booted out of town because of a hotel incident with the mayor's young daughter. It's then to San Francisco where the singer, broke, nerves his way into the emcee's job at Henry's club. He connects with both the audience and the chorus and encounters Miss Hayworth as the band does a charity date at her lavish Nob Hill residence. From then on he's giving both Miss Hayworth and Miss Novak a play.

Joey all the while is the egocentric who can tell a dame she'll cut her own throat when she realizes what it is not to have him. He's substantially the same (but no longer the dancer) as when first etched by O'Hara for George Abbott's stage entry — the self-assured, unscrupulous heel who sells himself to the rich woman in turn for his own Chez Joey fancy night club.

. George Sidney's direction makes of all this a robust, stimulating outing. He has given it sharpness and pace and eschewed subtlety. The music credits are top-drawer, ditto Harold Lipstein's Technicolor camera work and the editing by Viola Lawrence and Jerome Thoms. *Gene.*

Johnny Trouble

Human interest comedy-drama with okay prospects for general market.

Hollywood, Sept. 6.
Warner Bros. release of John H. Auer production. Stars Ethel Barrymore, Cecil Kellaway; costars Carolyn Jones, Jesse White, Rand Harper; features Stuart Whitman, Jack Larson, Edward Byrnes. Directed by Auer. Screenplay, Charles O'Neal, David Lord; story, Ben Ames Williams; camera, J. Peverell Marley; editor, Tony Martinelli; music, Frank DeVol. Previewed Aug. 27, '57. Running time, 80 MINS.

Mrs. Chandler	Ethel Barrymore
Tom McKay	Cecil Kellaway
Julie	Carolyn Jones
Parsons	Jesse White
Phil	Rand Harper
Paul	Paul Wallace
Elliott	Edward Byrnes
Tex	Edward Castagna
Charlie	Nino Tempo
Ike	Jim Bridges
Bill	Paul Lukather
Rev. Harrington	James Bell
Mr. Reichow	Samuel Colt
Boy	Kip King
Madden	Gavin Muir
Johnny	Stuart Whitman
Eddie	Jack Larson

John Carroll's Clarion Production gets off to a healthy launching with this marketable comedy-drama, long on human interest and well turned out right down the line. Film carries strong appeal for the juve and family trade especially and should do okay biz in the general market, backed by its natural exploitation potential.

The titillating situation of a wealthy widow who refuses to move and remains in her own quarters in an apartment hotel after a college purchases the building and converts it into a men's dormitory springboards the Charles O'Neal-David Lord screenplay, based on a story by Ben Ames Williams. John H. Auer as producer-director fashions the idea for sometimes rollicking unfoldment, capturing with a sure hand the entertaining possibilities of the basic situation and drawing capable portrayals from a good cast.

Ethel Barrymore heads player lineup as the widow suddenly plunged into the life of an otherwise all-masculine house where she luxuriates in the students' devotion under the nickname of "Nana." She stubbornly holds to the belief that her son, expelled from the college 27 years before and missing ever since, will one day return to her. When a recalcitrant young ex-Marine with the same name as her son checks in, she sells herself that he's her grandson, helping him in his romantic problems and even going to bat when he gets into trouble with school authorities. She dies on the eve of this boy's father arriving to see his son, never knowing that the same names are a mere coincidence.

Miss Barrymore offers a warm and penetrating characterization, a happy casting for the part, and Stuart Whitman, an interesting newcomer with showy promise, handles himself well as the former leatherneck. Cecil Kellaway as femme's faithful old retainer lends sympathy to role, and Carolyn Jones is a standout as a flip and brassy co-ed who falls for Whitman. Jesse White is amusing as a university official responsible for trying to oust the widow from the dorm, and Jack Larson and Rand Harper are okay as couple of students.

J. Peverell Marley's photography is first-class, Tony Martinelli's editing effective, James W. Sullivan's art direction fits the story and Frank DeVol's music score matches up. Title song cleffed by Peggy Lee and sung by Eddie Robertson is pleasant listening. *Whit.*

Campbell's Kingdom
(BRITISH-COLOR)

Dirk Bogarde in robust adventure yarn set in Canadian Rockies; packs a punch for all-family entertainment.

London, Sept. 3.
Rank release of a Betty E. Box production. Stars Dirk Bogarde, Stanley Baker, Michael Craig, Barbara Murray. Directed by Ralph Thomas. Screenplay by Robin Estridge from novel by Hammond Innes; camera, Ernest Steward; editor, Frederick Wilson; music, Clifton Parker. At Odeon, Leicester Square, London, Sept. 3. Running time, 100 MINS.

Bruce Campbell	Dirk Bogarde
Owen Morgan	Stanley Baker
Boy Bladen	Michael Craig

Jean Lucas .... Barbara Murray
James MacDonald
James Robertson Justice
Miss Abigail .... Athene Seyler
Creasy .... Robert Brown
Mac .... John Laurie
Timid Driver .... Sidney James
Miss Ruth .... Mary Merrall
Driver .... Roland Brand
Max .... George Murcell
Old Man .... Finley Currie
The Doctor .... Peter Illing
Fergus .... Stanley Maxted
Cliff .... Gordon Tanner
The Stranger .... Richard McNamara

"Campbell's Kingdom" is virtually a British western. It is a straightforward, virile, action-packed yarn with ample excitement and mounting drama. A popular cast, headed by Dirk Bogarde, will make it a safe bet. Bogarde's star value in U. S. may, however, be insufficient to earn this satisfying pic the support it merits.

Story is a simple clash between a stiff-lipped hero and a glowering villain. When Bogarde, with only six months to live, arrives in the township of Come Lucky in the Rockies to take up his grandfather's inheritance, a whole train of skulduggery is unleashed. Said inheritance is Campbell's Kingdom, a valley which has been a problem child for some years. The old man obstinately insisted that it held oil. The local inhabitants invested their money in his idea. His partner absconded leaving granddad to a jail sentence and the hatred of the locals. Meanwhile ruthless contractor Stanley Baker wants to flood the valley as part of a new hydro-electric scheme involving building of a new dam with inferior cement.

Bogarde, convinced that his grandfather's oil vision was genuine, decides to fight Baker and his gang and make a last attempt to prove that Campbell's Kingdom is, actually, oil-bearing. Before he proves his point, he has to plan a major military operation involving a great deal of dynamite and trickery. Bridges are blown up, landslides created and the entire dam collapsed.

The plot unfolds slowly but gathers tremendous momentum, with the dam crashing a great thrill. There is never any doubt that oil will be struck and that Bogarde will find a new lease of life so he can happily marry Barbara Murray, the nice girl from the local saloon. Yet tension is maintained. The only snag is a rather too facile finish.

Acting is solid. Bogarde leads his band of adventurers with dash and confidence. Michael Craig impresses as his surveyor-lieutenant. As the heavy, Baker proves that there is no better outdoor villain in British films. Miss Murray handles the unobtrusive romantic angle with charm. James Robertson Justic breezes through lustily as a piratic oil rig operator. Also there are a number of other neat performances, including Mary Merrall and Athene Seyler, as a brace of dear old maiden aunts. Comedy honors are stolen by Sidney James who gives 100% impact as a timid truck driver.

The alleged Rockies were lensed brilliantly in Cortina by Ernest Steward. Director Ralph Thomas wisely resists the temptation to allow his characters to indulge in personal rough stuff. As a result, the threat of coming violence broods throughout and creates a first-class edgy atmosphere.

Film keeps fairly close to the novel but it might have omitted the character of Stanley Baker's slightly crazy henchman, played well by George Murcell. *Rich.*

Satchmo The Great
(DOCUMENTARY)

Excellent documentary about Louis Armstrong with potential for special situations.

United Artists release of Edward R. Murrow-Fred W. Friendly production. Narration, Murrow; editor, Aram Avakian; camera, Charles Mack; drawings, Ben Shahn; sound, Robert Huttenloch. Previewed in N.Y., Sept. 5, '57. Running time, **63 MINS.**

"Satchmo the Great" is a swinging, colorful bouquet to America's greatest jazzman and most effective ambassador of good will—Louis Armstrong. Expanded from an Ed Murrow-Fred Friendly "See It Now" CBS videocast of a couple of years ago, this is a valuable documentary record of a standout performer and his extraordinary impact on jazz buffs here and abroad. It may do okay in specialized situations; but, in any case, there's no worry about recouping any heavy production costs on this straightforward documentary.

Most of the first half of this film originally appeared on the "See It Now" shows which covered one of the European tours made by Armstrong & His All-Stars. Here the focus is on Satchmo in Europe, mopping up with his horn and his growling vocals before capacity audiences in every country on the Continent and England.

The closeups of Armstrong at work are first-rate. Satchmo sweating through a trumpet passage or spontaneously jiving it up on planes and railroad cars between dates has been captured in a portrait that is immeasurably sharper in outline on the film screen than it was in the original video picture. Murrow, who handles the narration, is on for one visual bit in which he leads Armstrong to talk about the varieties and meaning of jazz early one morning in a Parisian spot after a jam session with the local Claude Luter dixieland combo. Armstrong, of course, is a natural performer who, even in casual conversation, "blows" some beautiful jive solo passages.

Highlight of this documentary, not shown on video, covers Armstrong's visit to the Gold Coast in Africa, his ancestral birthplace which hailed Satchmo as a national hero. The sequence included several impressive clips of Armstrong being greeted by tribal chieftains and the American jazzman returning the nod by playing for the natives. Armstrong's wife, Lucille, and Velma Middleton, his vocalist, were the heroines of this episode, both joining with the natives for a mass jitterbug hoofing display. At one of his evening concerts in the Gold Coast, Armstrong is shown in his best form, delivering one of the most touching tunes in his repertory, "Black and Blue," a number cued to the theme of racial discrimination and one which must have had special meaning for this audience, including the country's Prime Minister.

Documentary's windup scene, also not shown on video, is set in New York's Lewisohn Stadium where, together with Leonard Bernstein conducting the N. Y. Philharmonic, Armstrong and his crew performed "St. Louis Blues." Sequence is heightened by some good shots of W. C. Handy, blind composer of the tune, who was in the audience that night, and a final kudosing of Armstrong by Bernstein who tagged the jazz man "a dedicated artist."

Members of Armstrong's combo in this documentary are Edmund Hall on clarinet; Trummy Young on trombone; Arvell Shaw and Jack Lesberg on bass at different times; Billy Kyle on piano and Barrett Deems on drums. Deems and Lesberg are white and nobody in the Gold Coast Negro republic objected to Satchmo's desegregation policy towards whites.

Large line drawings by Ben Shahn, in a jazzy artistic style, illustrate some of Armstrong's early days in New Orleans. Murrow handles his narration with his usual skill. *Herm.*

The Hired Gun
(C'SCOPE)

Regulation western with Rory Calhoun and Anne Francis draw to spark chances in oater field.

Hollywood, Sept. 6.

Metro releaseof Rory Calhoun-Victor M. Orsatti production. Stars Calhoun, Anne Francis; features Vince Edwards, John Litel, Robert Burton, Guinn Williams, Chuck Connors, Salvadore Baguez, Regis Parton. Directed by Ray Nazarro. Screenplay, David Land. Buckley Angell, based on story by Angell; camera, Harold J. Marzorati; editor, Frank Santillo; music, Albert Glasser. Previewed Sept. 4, '57. Running time, **63 MINS.**

Gil McCord .... Rory Calhoun
Ellen Beldon .... Anne Francis
Kell Beldon .... Vince Edwards
Mace Beldon .... John Litel
Judd Farrow .... Chuck Connors
Nathan Conroy .... Robert Burton
Domingo Ortega ...... Salvadore Baques
Elby Kirby .... Guinn Williams
Clint .... Regis Parton

Hiring of a gunman to kidnap and return to Texas a femme convicted of murdering her husband springboards the plot of this Rory Calhoun-Victor M. Orsatti indie made for Metro release. Film is a regulations western, with somewhat short running time, which should do okay in oater field with star names of Calhoun and Anne Francis to spark it.

The David Lang-Buckley Angell screenplay is moderately interesting as it follows Calhoun on his assignment. Gun is hired by dead man's father, a wealthy Texan, after legal attempts have failed to extradite Miss Francis from New Mexico, where she returns to her father's ranch following her escape from jail a few hours before she is to hang. Enroute back to the hangman, however, femme is able to convince Calhoun that she is innocent of the murder charge, and he's able to prove that it was murdered man's brother who committed the crime.

Ray Nazarro inserts plenty of sinews in his direction and under his helming the characters emerge first class. Calhoun delivers strongly, and Miss Francis has considerably more to do than the average western heroine, acquitting herself nicely. John Litel is properly domineering as the father who has tried to hang his daughter-in-law, Vince Edwards is capable as the real murderer and Guinn Williams is in as key figure who helps Calhoun free Miss Francis. Salvadore Baguez is well cast as a Mexican friend of Calhoun.

Harold J. Marzorati's photography lends pictorial interest and Albert Glassner's music score goes with the mood. Frank Santillo's editing also is an asset. *Whit.*

Escapade in Japan
(TECHNIRAMA-COLOR)

Heartwarming story of two small boys roving in Japan; particular appeal for family market.

Hollywood, Sept. 6.

Universal release of Arthur Lubin production. Stars Teresa Wright, Cameron Mitchell; costars Jon Provost, Roger Nakagawa; features Philip Ober, Kuniko Miyake. Directed by Lubin. Screenplay, Winston Miller; camera (Technicolor), William Snyder; editor, Otto Ludwig; music, Max Steiner. Previewed Aug. 28, '57. Running time, **90 MINS.**

Mary Saunders .... Teresa Wright
Dick Saunders .... Cameron Mitchell
Tony Saunders .... Jon Provost
Hiko .... Roger Nakagawa
Lt. Colonel Hargrave..... Philip Ober
Michiko .... Kuniko Miyake
Kei Tanaka .... Susumu Fujita
Captain Hibino .... Katsuhigo Haida
Mr. Fushimi .... Tatsuo Saito
Dekko-San .... Hideko Koshikawa
Chief of Kyoto Police .... Ureo Egawa
Farmer .... Frank Tokunaga
Farmer's Wife .... Ayako Hidaka

"Escaped in Japan" is a charming and warmly human story of two small boys—one American and one Nipponese—who race through Japan under the delusion that the police are after them. Film might easily become a sleeper. Properly exploited and with the word-of-mouth bally it's sure to receive, chance are good for a satisfactory payoff, particularly in the family trade.

Arthur Lubin produced and directed pic entirely in Japan, making the most of the beautiful backgrounds afforded in the countryside, in small towns and in such cities as Kyoto, Takyo and Nara. All this is caught up for splendid pictorial effect by the Technirama process, Technicolor tones lending enchantment to the exotic locations which benefit unfoldment of narrative.

The Winston Miller screenplay creates a happy mood in following the adventures of the two frightened youngsters. On a flight from Manila to join his diplomat parents in Tokyo, six-year-old American's plane crashes at sea, and he's rescued by Jap boy's fisherman family. When small Jap overhears his mother mention the police, he thinks it's to arrest the American, and they light out together, the Jap offering to guide his new friend to his parents in Tokyo. Instead of the journey being only a few hours, as lads think, it stretches out to days, while a gigantic search in which both Jap police and U. S. Air Force participate swirls around them. They're finally rounded up atop the five-storied pagoda in Nara, second largest in Japan.

Jon Provost scores brightly as the little American and Roger Nakagawa rivals him in interest as they make their way to their destination, during which they ride freight trains, school buses, spend the night in a geisha house and are entertained by the geishas with a show all their own.

Teresa Wright and Cameron Mitchell portray the American parents, but have little to do other than act worried. As the Japanese parents, Kuniko Mitake and Susumu Jujita are excellent. Philip Ober rates okay as the Air Force colonel in charge of the boys' search and Henry Okawa handles himself well as a police officer.

Photography by William Snyder is particularly outstanding, and art direction by George W. Davis and Walter Holscher is tops. Max Steiner's music score is distinctive and Otto Ludwig's editing expert. *Whit.*

Black Patch

Attempt at psychological western, emerges an elongated mood piece, told at creeping lace.

Hollywood, Sept. 3.

Warner Bros. release of a George Montgomery production. Stars Montgomery; features Diane Brewster, Tom Pittman, Leo Gordon, Sebastian Cabot, House

Peters Jr. Producer-director, Allen H. Miner. Screenplay, Leo Gordon; camera, Edward Colman; editor, Jerry Young; art director, Nicolai Remisoff; music, Jerry Goldsmith. Previewed at Wiltern Theatre, L.A., Aug. 13, '57. Running time, **82 MINS.**

Clay Morgan .... George Montgomery
Helen Danner .... Diane Brewster
Flytrap .... Tom Pittman
Hank Danner .... Leo Gordon
Holman .... House Peters Jr.
Kitty .... Lynn Cartwright
Pedoline .... George Trevino
Harper .... Peter Brocco
Maxton .... Ted Jacques
Petey .... Struther Martin
Judge Parnell .... Gil Rankin
Frenchy De Vere ...... Sebastian Cabot
Drummer .... Stanley Adams
Colonel .... John O'Malley

The intent of this picture is praiseworthy; the execution not nearly so. Obviously, "Black Patch" was supposed to break new trails in the field of the psychological western. What emerges is an elongated mood piece, so slowly related that it abruptly ends in a resounding whimper.

Tale by Leo Gordon (who also acts in pic) presents George Montgomery as a tough cowtown marshal (title comes from patch over one eye, result of Civil War wound). Into town comes his prewar buddy Gordon, and his ex-g.f., Diane Brewster, now married. But Gordon turns out to be a bank robber, so Montgomery claps him in jail.

Villainous saloon keeper Sebastian Cabot and bully-boy assistant House Peters Jr. set a jailbreak for half Gordon's loot, but kill Gordon in the process. However, marshal finds and conceals other half. Tom Pittman, youthful butt of town's cruel jokes, first inherits Gordon's guns and turns into a superfast gunfighter, then inexplicably moves into arms of bereaved Miss Brewster. Egged on by Cabot and Peters, and eventually renounced by Miss Brewster, Pittman takes on the marshal. But incredible ending has Miss Brewster conveniently discover the Cabot plotting, just in time to get the scripter out of a bad plotting hole.

As producer-director, a double blame must fall on Allen H. Miner for allowing a weak script and for the creeping pace with which he mounted it.

This isn't one of Montgomery's better outings, and he lacks conviction as the marshal. As the gun-crazy youth, Pittman makes a strong impression with a sensative portrayal. Miss Brewster, hampered by fuzzy writing, nevertheless comes out okay. So does Gordon, and in lesser roles, Cabot and Peters are noteworthy.

Cameraman Edward Colman is a graduate of the "Dragnet" school of production and his work bears the trademark, somewhat modified, of the teleseries. However, his extreme low-key lensing in black-and-white, especially in interiors, quickly wears out its welcome. Authentic settings of art director Nicolai Remisoff is a definite plus in mood-setting. Too bad the script doesn't match. *Kove.*

Seven Thunders
(BRITISH)

Implausible, but tense, wartime thriller building up to smash race-against-time climax. Steady b.o. prospect.

London, Sept. 5.

Rank presentation and release produced by Daniel M. Angel. Directed by Hugo Fregonese. Stars Stephen Boyd, James Robertson Justice, Kathleen Harrison, Tony Wright. Screenplay, John Baines; editor, John Shirley; camera, John Wilkie Cooper; music, Anthony Hopkins. At Odeon, Leicester Square, London, Sept. 4, '57. Running time, **100 MINS.**

Dave .... Stephen Boyd
Dr. Martout....James Robertson Justice
Jim .... Tony Wright
Lise .... Anna Gaylor
Madame Abou .... Kathleen Harrison
Emile Blanchard ...... Eugene Deckers
Therese Blanchard.....Rosalie Crutchley
Madame Parfait .... Katherine Kath
Eric Triebel .... James Kenney
Colonel Trautman........Anton Diffring
Schlip .... Martin Miller
Bourdin .... George Coulouris
Salvatore .... Marcel Pagliero
Major Grautner............Carl Duering
Abou .... Edric Connor
Umschlag .... Denis Shaw
Von Kronitz .... Gerard Heinz
Ciro Piro .... Jacques Cey
Dede .... Andrea Malandrinos
Renee .... June Cowell
Priest .... Peter Augustine

Wartime Marseille, with Nazi occupation, is the setting for this competent thriller. Despite some loose ends and improbabilities it adds up to sound entertainment with a strong climax that will have patrons eagerly urging on the heroes to safety. "Seven Thunders" suggests solid home-market business, but neither the wartime setting in Europe nor the strong but far from starry cast are likely to excite U. S. patrons overmuch.

It does one useful thing for British films by introducing a refreshing newcomer, 24-year-old Anna Gaylor. This French girl, making a noteworthy bow in British pix, has a piquancy, neat sense of comedy and touch of pathos that make her a standout from some of the pleasant but uninspiring youngsters.

Rupert Croft-Cooke's novel (screenplay by John Baines) involves two husky British prisoners-of-war, Stephen Boyd and Tony Wright, smuggled from Italy into Marseille in 1943. They are befriended by Anna Gaylor, a wartime orphan waif with a winning way and a keen sense of self-preservation. Romance flowers between Boyd and Mlle. Gaylor while the POWs sweat it out in a Marseille slum awaiting the next steps of their escape to be arranged by the patriots.

Credulity is strained by the way Boyd, so obviously British, wanders hand-in-hand with Mlle. Gaylor in the Marseille streets despite the constant threat of the Nazis. Meanwhile, a suave doctor has built up a neat racket by posing as the head of an escape organization. James Robertson Justice welcomes the characters who wish to get out of Marseille with speed, dopes them with brandy, lifts their bankrolls and disposes of them in a quicklime-flooded cellar.

When the two soldiers come up against the villain it leads to a standup fight, fists and guns, and a nightmare escape when Old Marseille is blown up by the exasperated Nazis. This is nothing but sheer thick-ear hokum but it keeps the suspense rattling along till the fadeout.

Apart from Anna Gaylor's fascinating debut, Stephen Boyd and Tony Wright are appropriately tough and stiff-upper-lipped and James Robertson Justice is a benign crook. Eugene Deckers acts as Justice's unwitting catspaw and is the most satisfactorily Continental of the assorted male Frenchmen and Nazis. Comedy relief is provided by Kathleen Harrison, as a Cockney who has been living in Marseille for 20 years without any apparently sound reason. Miss Harrison gives the performance that has been garnering the yocks in British films for many years. There is also a robust performance by Denis Shaw as a fat, lecherous slob of a Nazi soldier.

Hugo Fregonese directs without frills and has brought off the evacuation before the blowing-up with care and good effect. The atmosphere of the seedy section of Marseille has been captured with great imagination by Arthur Lawson's artwork and the lensing of John Wilkie Cooper. Latter is particularly effective when Marseille is collapsing all round the trapped heroes and heroine.

"Seven Thunder" never attempts to be more than 100 minutes of straight adventure. It comes off well because it never attempts to take itself more seriously. *Rich.*

Venice Films

Cittadi Notte
(City at Night)
(ITALIAN)

Venice, Sept. 3.

Titanus release of a Trionfalcine production. Features Patrizia Bini, Henri Vilbert, Antonio DeTeffe, Rina Morelli, Corrado Pani, Luciana Lombardi. Written and directed by Leopoldo Trieste. Camera, Mario Bava; music, Nino Rota; sets, Mario Chiari; editor, Gabriele Variale. At Film Festival, Venice; shown out of competition. Running time, **90 MINS.**

Marina ....Patrizia Bini
Guido ....Henri Vilbert
Alberto ....Antonio DeTeffe
Ada ....Rina Morelli

Deliberately arty item about life in existentialist circles of Rome, pic has style and an interesting cast of young players to carry it over certain ups and downs of the script. Mild chances abroad, although it has a certain appeal among the circles whose problems it exposes.

Film is a one-man effort, his first, by young Italian Leopoldo Trieste, and as such in itself promises much for his future. While thesping of the youthful cast is sometimes hesitant, the stylized handling overcomes this handicap in most instances. Patrizia Bini and Antonio DeTeffe stand out in the large cast, the former sporting an unusual and photogenic face, while the latter looks headed up following this projection, aided by talent backed by a (locally unusual) tall physique and boyish handsomeness.

For a small-budgeter, lensing by Mario Bava and other technical credits are outstandingly good. *Hawk.*

El Gran Dia
(The Great Day)
(ITALO-SPANISH)

Venice, Sept. 3.

ASPA release of an ASPA-LUX Film production. Stars Miguelito Gil, Miguel Rodriguez; features Luis Induni, Julita Martinez, Jose Nunez. Directed by Rafael Gil. Screenplay, Vincente Escriva; camera, Cecilio Paniagua; music, Jesus Guridi. At Film Festival, Venice. Running time, **94 MINS.**

Marcos ....Miguelito Gil
Polonio ....Miguel Rodriguez
Father .... Luis Induni
Sister ....Julita Martinez
Brother ....Jose Nunez

Moppet pic with strong femme appeal should prove a big grosser in all Hispano situations as well as in its Italian run, especially in subsequent situations. While religious angle of plotting is overcome by the universality of the theme and appeal, the Catholic slant might limit the boxoffice in some situations. It's not for the arties in the U. S., but a religioso-lingual releasing sked might build into a payoff.

Based on a true happening, pic tells of the many attempts and hardships of a boy who wants to take his first communion in a white suit. His family cannot help him for reasons of economy, and a near-final gift by a dying woman is lost in a gambling bout by the boy's brother. When kid takes to gathering coal bits by night in a slag pit, he is buried and loses an arm in an accident. News hits the papers, and hundreds of suits pour in, as well as other gifts, allowing him his first communion as wished for.

A tight script by Vincente Escriva and knowing direction by Rafael Gil, both aimed at widest audience appeal, pay off in a satisfying, often moving film, in which the burden is carried by the two starred moppets who run through their paces competently and winningly. Remainder of cast is excellent, too. Pic has been given a handsome production dress by Cecilio Paniagua's lensing of Spanish village and landscapes. Other credits are likewise topdrawer. *Hawk.*

Samo Ljudi (Men Only (**YUGOSLAVIAN**). Jadran film production and release. Stars Tamara Miletic, Milorad Magetic, Niksa Stefanini, Stepan Juricevic. Directed by Branko Baure. Screenplay, Arsen Diklic; from story by Bosko Kozanovic; camera, Blanko Blazina; editor, Radojka Ivancevic. At Venice Film Festival. Running time, **105 MINS.**

Mellerish pic tells love story of blind girl for a one-legged war vet, climaxing in her seeing once more and accepting the man despite his injury. Well acted, especially by comely Tamara Miletic, film tells its story simply and, too often, obviously. Dialogue is endless and production overlong. Export chances appear nil. *Hawk.*

Uwasa No Onna (The Crucified Woman) (**JAPANESE**). Daiei production and release. Stars Kinuyo Tanaka; features Yoshiko Kuga, Tomeon Otani, Eitaro Shindo. Directed by Kenji Mizoguchi. Screenplay, Yoshikata Yoda, Mashige Narusawa; camera, Kasuo Miyagawa; etitor, T. Mayuzami. At Venice Film Fest. Running time, **90 MINS.**

Though the film takes place in a fancy bordello, there is nothing sensational about it. Pic details how the madame's daughter returns from school where her mother's profession has made things difficult. Here she falls in love with a young doctor who is also loved by her mother. She finds this out too late and drives off the young man to get reconciled with her mother again and take her place at her side. The film tellingly lays bare life in the bagnio with a compassion for the plight of the girls.

This is a subtle film which limits this to specialized playdating in the U. S. with word-of-mouth and its theme plus factors. Technically, it is perfect and acting is outstanding, especially in the sensitive portrayal of the mother by Kinuyo Tanaka. *Mosk.*

Musashino Fujin (Mrs. Musachino) (**JAPANESE**). Toho production and release. Features K. Tanaka, Masayuki Mori, So Yamamura, Yukiko Todoroki. Directed by Kenji Mizoguchi. Screenplay, Shohei Ooka, Yoshitaka Ida; camera, Masao Tamai; editor, Shoji Kameyama. At Venice Film Fest. Running time, **95 MINS.**

Delicately-woven Jap tale details how a sensitive married woman falls in love with a cousin. Her loose husband, who condones adultery, drives her into her cousin's arms but she holds back only to be betrayed by both men, and

this leads to her suicide. Film is tastefully lensed and deftly unfolds this story with a dignity that places it in a class for specialized houses of the U. S. Its Japanese pacing and mood make this less likely for any regular U. S. chances. It is technically tops with poignant acting and incisive direction.
Mosk.

Yoru No Omnatachi (Women of the Night) (**JAPANESE**). H. Itaro-E. Risaita production and release. Features K. Tanaka, Sanoo Takasugi, Tomie Sumita, Mitsugu Fujii. Directed by Kenji Mizoguchi. Screenplay, Y. Yoda; camera, M. Miki; editor, H. Ohsawa. At Venice Film Fest. Running time, **85 MINS.**

Film details how two sisters are driven to prostitution by poverty. It blocks out this nether world life via a well-developed story which gives a moving portrayal of the reasons for their lives, frought with attempts at escape.

Pic never cheapens, and it seems to have art house stature, with high exploitation values. Acting is homogeneous and a prostitute's "kangaroo" court, with the unleashing of their disdains and miseries, ends this on a high note. Technical credits are fine.
Mosk.

Ubagaruma (The Baby Carriage) (**JAPANESE**). Nikkatsu production and release. Features Jurichi Uno, H. Yamane., I. Ashikawa, Y. Sugi. Directed by Tomataka Tasaka. Screenplay, Yojiro Ishizaca; camera, Saburo Isayama; editor, I. Saito. At Venice Fest. Running time, **110 MINS.**

This film treats domestic drama with candor and manages a light, perceptive first half. Then it slows down with polite talk about adultery and illegitimacy. Pic looms as a chancey item for the U. S. except as a possible exploitation film after it has been scissored to speed up things.

An adolescent girl finds her father has a mistress and another child. She visits her and likes them both, and tries to find some way to solve the future of her half-sister. Film has some good acting and a nice feel for character, but the mixture of comedy, drama and problem approach does not jell. It is technically well made. *Mosk.*

Foreign Films

La Ciudad De Los Ninos (Boys' Town) (**MEXICAN - COLOR**). Cinematografica Filmes S. A. production. Stars Arturo de Cordova, Marga Lopez; features Sara Garcia, Carlos Rivas, Eduardo Fajardo, Oscar Pulido. Directed by Gilberto Martinez Solares. Screenplay, Julio Alejandro; camera, Agustin Martinez Solares (Eastmancolor). At San Sebastian Film Fest. Running time, **102 MINS.**

A creditable Mexican pic patterned after the Spencer Tracy opus, with a fine de Cordova performance and impressive juve thesping, "Ciudad" suffers mainly from a weighted religious slant.

Story line also fails at times to measure up to performances and technical assists. But the building of boys' town, and later the menace to it from juve dissidence, places this on solid ground. Patient understanding and humanity of Padre Farias (de Cordova) in his handling of outcast youth lends genuine dignity to this Mexican production.

Eastmancolor with kids and landscape is topflight. Mexican comic Oscar Pulido ably adds relief when pic seems about to hit skids. Technically above average in all departments, "Ciudad" should bring returns in all markets despite the heavy religioso message.
Werb.

El Abuelo Automovil (Model T or The Grandfather Automobile) (**CZECHO**). Ceskoslovensky Film production. Stars Ludek Munzar, Ginette Pigeon, Raymond Bussieres, Radovan Lukavsky, Josef Hlinomaz. Directed by Alfred Radok. Screenplay, Adolf Branold; music, J. F. Fischer. At San Sebastian Fest. Running time, **98 MINS.**

Fanciful Czeck entry is loaded with comedy, screen poetry, interesting documentation and pre-atom nostalgia to make it a definite art house candidate in the U. S. Pic opens on the runway of an airfield where a plane mechanic and an air hostess sit fingering an album of old photos. In this case the debut of the 20th century when motorcycles and cars were first being tried out starts off the plot.

Director Radok deftly weaves a simple story of a Czech mechanic's love for the daughter of a French mechanic into a documentary pattern of bygone motor races. Raymond Bussieres's comedy is somewhat like a Buster Keaton's. Ginette Pigeon has a lot of what makes French girls distinctively attractive. Czechs also help give this original tale its full measure of sentiment. *Werb.*

Pasos (Footsteps) (**SPAIN**). Rabida-Valencia Films production. Stars Lina Rosales, Alfredo Mayo; costars Marion Mitchell, Adriano Dominguez with Andres Mejuto in Spain. Directed by Clemente Pamplona. Screenplay, Clemente Pamplona, Federico Muela and Jesus Vasallo from Pamplona's story. Music, Salvador Ruiz de Luna; camera, Cesar Fraile. At San Sebastian Fest. Running time, **86 MINS.**

Unrelieved monotony of a very slow-moving, implausible psychological drama dooms screenwriter Pamplona's first effort as a director.

Esteban (Andres Mejuto) is hurt in an auto accident and hospitalized, after quarreling with his wife,. Lina Rosales. Returning home mute, he suspects Ana's infidelity. He endlessly trails his spouse for evidence with intent to kill. He finally does, but she's the wrong woman.

Cesar Fraile's off-key lighting is effective. Mejuto is good in an impossible role while writer-director Pamplona strains to hang psycho effects on a skeleton tale. Music score jars. Not for export.
Werb.

Heroes Del Aire (Air Heros) (**SPAIN-COLOR**). Arturo Gonzalez production. Stars Lina Rosales, Aldredo Mayo, Maria Piazzai, Julio Nunez, Tomas Blanco. Directed by Ramon Torrado. Story and screenplay, H. S. Valdes; camera, Ricardo Torres (Eastmancolor); music, Emilio Lemberg. At San Sebastian Fest. Running time, **95 MINS.**

Average Spanish film fare reveals tempo, humor asd youthful exuberance in early sequences. Then the plot bogs down and pic drags.

An air rescue plane crashes at Madrid's Barajas Airport and flashback to the civil war unfolds the pilot's story. Loaded with medals at the war's end, Alfredo Mayo weds the sister of a pal in the air force. Faced with scandal, he drops off a rope ladder in midair onto a civilian plane in distress to save the passengers.

Dramatic finale prompted giggles instead of bated breath. Okay cast and average technical credits but has weak miniatures and special effects. Italy's Maria Piazzai is the air hostess. For local nabes and provinces and possibly fair returns in some Latin American nations/ *Werb*

Prolog (Prologue) (**RUSSIAN; COLOR**). Mosfilm production and release. With N. Plotnikov, N. Patuchova, P. Kadocjnikov. Directed by Efim Dzigan, Screenplay, A. Shtein; camera (Sovcolor), V. Pavlov, B. Petrof; editor, D. Stolyarska; music, N. Kryukov. At Karlovy Vary Film Fest. Running time, **100 MINS.**

This is a sort of tableau-like pamphlet of romanticized revolutionary literature, which makes it unlikely for the U.S. It is worthy as a record of some new Soviet film trends. De-Stalinization had led to greater emphasis on the early revolutionary days, with Lenin played up. This has created a standardized film somewhat like the U.S. western. The good and bad guys are drawn unmistakably, giving a chance to work in fights, adventures, massacres, great names, etc.

Pic is neatly mounted with a fine use of a Soviet anamarphoscope process and stereophonic sound. It is a series of anecdotes rather than a story. Acting is in the heady, poster manner. Technical credits are fine. *Mosk.*

Urok Istorijl (In Face of the World) (**BULGARIAN-RUSSIAN; COLOR**). Bulgarofilm production and release. With S. Avov, S. Arnaud, J. Tonev, V. Line. Written and directed by Lev Arnstam. Camera (Sovcolor), A. Shelenkov, Chen Yu-Lan; editor, Kara-Karavev. At Karlovy Vary Fest. Running time, **90 MINS.**

Film is an academic recounting of the purge trials of some Communists after the Nazis set the Reichstag Fire in 1934. It mainly concerns the Bulgar Communist Dimitrov who contounded the Nazis in his brilliant defense of himself. Film is staid but still spins an interesting tale bolstered by expert color, art work and tableau-like staging.

Acting is in the grandoise manner, but manages to create character. Nazis are drawn without too much caricature. In sort, this is a propagandist but interesting historical film limited in America except for a few small spots Direction has a fine flair for mob scenes and technical credits tops. Russians again demonstrate they can get their quality into pix no matter where they are made. *Mosk.*

La Nonna Sabella (Grandma Sabella) (**ITALIAN**). Titanus production. Stars Tina Pica, Peppino De Filippo, Sylva Koschina, Renato Salvatore, Paolo Stoppa, Dolores Palumbo. Directed by Dino Risi. Screenpay, Pasquale Festa Campanile, Massimo Franciosa, Ettore Giannini, Dino Risi; camera, Tonino delli Colli. At San Sebastian Fest. Running time, **90 MINS.**

Strong casting helps pull a none too sturdy script into a palatable comedy pic. Youthful film director Dino Risi again sagely avoids stars for seasoned thesps and promising newcomers in this low-budgeter. Okay for Italian language houses in U. S.

A maverick provincial octogenarian attempts to arrange her city-wise grandson's marriage to a fat dowry. Sympatico youngster (Renato Salvatore) spoils grandma's plans, weds the childhood friend Lucie (Sylvia Koschina).

Risi employs stock-in-trade farce, but succeeds in timihg situations for solid laughs, aided by an uniformly excellent cast. Young lovers Sylva Koschina and Renato Salvatore have looks and screen stance. De Filippo, Tina Pica and Paolo Stoppa are firstrate. Music is bright and technical credits okay. This won the Golden Seashell at the festival. *Werb.*

Das Dritte Geschlecht (The Third Sex) (**GERMAN**). Constantin release of Arca production. Stars Paula Wessely, Paul Dahlke; features Ingrid Stenn, Hans Nielsen, Paul Esser, Friedrich Joloff, Hilde Koerber, Christian Wolff. Directed by Veit Harlan. Screenplay, Felix Luetzkendorf, based on a true story; camera, Kurt Grigoleit; music, Erwin Halletz. Previewed at Arca Studios, Berlin. Running time, **105 MINS.**

German postwar films centering around daring themes mostly have been financial flops and/or artistical failures. This is in the latter category, dealing largely with homosexuality, and a remarkable exception. Unlike most other Teutonic problem pix, "Third Sex" has been treated with considerable tact and taste. Commercially prospects, this appears rather doubtful. Also foreign prospects appear dubious in view of the fact that many countries consider the homo theme on the screen taboo. Others will probably demand strong cuts. (However, this pic already has been sold to a number of countries).

Screenplay centers around a well-reputed family whose 18-year-old son feels attracted to homosexual circles. In order to save her son from these surroundings, his mother makes the housemaid the proposition to win the boy for herself. The plan works but one of the queers gets even, with the mother.

Harlan's direction is frank, realistic and generally swift moving. He also deserves praise for the adroit handling of the players. For authentic atmosphere, he shot some sequences in Berlin's queer hangouts. Paul Dahlke and Paula Wessely portray the worried parents okay. An outstanding performance is turned in by Ingrid Stenn as the housemaid. Siegfried Wolff, new to the screen, is the boy who nearly goes homo. Hans Schumm, also a newcomer, is convincing as a sensitive lad. A strong plus about this pic is the score by Erwin Halletz. Lensing and other technical credits are okay. *Hans.*

Stevnemoete Met Glemte Ar (Rendezvous With Forgotten Years) (**NORWEGIAN.**), Fotorama production (Oslo). Stars Mona Hofland, Espen Skjoenberg, Henki Kolstad, Inger-Marie Andersen, Jon Lennart Mjoen, Pal Bucher Skjoenberg. Directed by Jon Lennart Mjoen. Screenplay, Bjoern Bergh-Pedersen, Olav Dalgard after Sigurd Hoel's novel; camera, Gunnar Syvertsen; music, Bjoern Woll. At Berlin Film Fest. Running time, **89 MINS.**

Norway's contribution to the Berlin junket turned out to be a big disappointment. There's nothing special about this production which centers around an old-hat plot of love and resistance plus passion and intrigue. Hope for something truly Norwegian, are sadly lacking since this is only a rather weak imitation of a mediocre Middle-European production.

Mona Hofland shows ability as the devilish woman. Same goes for some others, but it's not enough to make this film entertaining. *Hans.*

Tizoc (COLOR-C'SCOPE) (MEXICAN). Matouk Films S. A. production. Stars Pedro Infante, Maria Felix, Andres Soler, Carlos Orellano, Miguel Arenas. Directed by Ismael Rodriguez. Screenplay, I. Rodriguez, M. Ojeda and R. Parada Leon; camera, (Pathecolor), Alex Philips; music, Raul Lavista. At Berlin Film Fest. Running time, 98 MINS.

Mexico has often come along with very remarkable films. This one can't be called a top production. But it has a number of very positive assets. The (Pathe) color photography is breathtakingly beautiful at times and there is also a strong plus in the acting of the late Pedro Infante who portrays the title role.

It's the tale of an Indian and his passionate love for a white girl. Latter gets killed at the end while he commits suicide. The film's folkloristic ingredients are extremely interesting. In all, "Tizoc" is a production which will be remembered for a while. *Hans.*

O Sobrado (The Besieged House) (BRAZILIAN). Vera Cruz production and release. With Lia De Aguilar, Barbara Fazio, Marcia Real, Fernando Baleroni. Directed by Walter Durst, Gabus Mendes. Screenplay, Durst; camera, Chico Fowle; editor, Luis Paes. At Karlovy Vary Fest. Running time, 110 MINS.

Turn-of-century setting has a house beseiged by a group of revolutionaries in a small town. Though the insurgent reasons are unclear, pic has a deftly-detailed rendering of the siege and its effect on the people in the house where a group of dramas unfold until defeat of the rebels leads to freeing of the housebound group. Colorful, knowing direction makes for many dramatic scenes. This looks like a neat entry for the U.S. Latino circuits but lacks the clarity and feeling for arty spots. Lensing is excellent and acting fine. *Mosk.*

Typhoon No. 13 (JAPANESE). Yamamoto-Madoka production and release. With Keiji Sada, Kenji Sugawara, Shuji Sano, Hitomi Nozoe. Directed by Satsu Yamamoto. Screenplay, Toshio Yazumi, Yusaku Yamagata; camera, Minoru Maeda; editor, Shigetoh Yasue. At Karlovy Vary Fest. Running time, 110 MINS.

This is a Japanese satire on municipal corruption. A group of shady politicians want to make money after a typhoon by claiming the schoolhouse has been destroyed and then cashing in on building a new one. Complications have a weak schoolteacher who finally finds the strength to speak out. Though sprightly at times and reminiscent of pre-war American comedies, this vacillates between situation comedy and social comment without adequately blending the two. It is neatly acted and mounted but looks chancey, at best, for the U. S., except for some language spots. *Mosk.*

A King in New York
(BRITISH)

Half-hearted Charles Chaplin comedy with sour political undertones; Spasmodically funny show which will attract on curiosity and star value.

London, Sept. 10.

Archway release of Charles Chaplin production. Stars Charles Chaplin, Dawn Addams. Directed by Charles Chaplin. Screenplay and original story by Chaplin; camera, Georges Perinal; editor, Spencer Reeves; music, Chaplin. Previewed at Leicester Square Theatre, London. Running time, 105 MINS.

King Shadhov	Charles Chaplin
Ann Kay	Dawn Addams
The Ambassador	Oliver Johnston
Queen Irene	Maxine Audley
Lawyer Green	Harry Green
Headmaster	Phil Brown
Macabee Senior	John McLaren
School Superintendent	Allan Gifford
Night Club Vocalist	Shani Wallis
Night Club Vocalist	Jay Nichols
Rupert Macabee	Michael Chaplin
Mrs. Cromwell	John Ingram
Mr. Johnson	Sidney James
Prime Minister	Jerry Desmonde
Lift Boy	Robert Arden
Comedy Double-Act	Lauri Lupino, Lane George Truzzi

The name "Charles Chaplin" still spells stellar magic to most British cinema patrons, except perhaps the adolescents. Therefore, this his latest could attract reasonable business providing the patrons are given an adequate opportunity to view it. As of this writing, no major circuit booking has been hooked, but it will be given on the Granada chain here. Curiosity would surely stimulate active trade among U.S. patrons, but Chaplin has stoutly announced that he is not interested in an American release.

Cutting through the domestic and political hubbub surrounding Chaplin's first British offering and assessing it purely as a film, the result is a tepid disappointment. No Chaplin work can fail to have professional highlights and a fair quota of yocks, but this vet film producer has set his own high standards, and fails to measure up to them.

Few of the laugh sequences are developed with the confident zing with which the comedian is associated. He is obviously more interested in hammering home his message, which is a straightforward, unsubtle tirade against some obvious aspects of the American way of life. Cynics may well regard this as nibbling at the hand that has prosperously fed him through the well-stacked years.

Tilting against American tv is fair game and while doing this Chaplin contributes some shrewd, funny observations on a vulnerable theme. But when he sets his sights on the problem of Communism and un-American activities, the jester's mask drops. He loses objectivity and stands revealed as an embittered man who permits his tired good humor to be bogged down by personal prejudice.

The story has Chaplin as the amiable, dethroned monarch of Estrovia. He survives a revolution and, with his ambassador, seeks New York sanctuary. He arrives to find that his prime minister has decamped with the treasury and the king is financially flat. His matrimonial status is also rocky.

Dawn Addams is a winning tele personality who charmingly tricks Chaplin into guesting on her show. Overnight, he becomes a tv star. Regally he thumbs down all chances of cashing-in on this success until his dwindling bankroll forces him to advertise whiskey on television. His tv personality rockets. So far, fairly funny.

He then befriends a politically-minded 10-year-old whose parents are on the mat for not squealing on friends who are suspect by the Un-American Activities Committee. As a result, Chaplin is himself arraigned before this committee. Cleared (unconvincingly), he finds that the child has freed his parents by profferring the required information. But the child's spirit has been quelled. At this, Chaplin decides that America is no place for him and leaves for Europe to sit the matter out.

The way in which Chaplin poses his political problems through the mouth of a child is both queasy and embarrassing. He has little that is either novel or important to declare, and it has little more impact than a slightly out-of-date tract. On the funny side, there are such good moments as when Chaplin is being fingerprinted while being enthusiastically interviewed on U.S. as the land of the free; when he becomes embroiled with a hose which succeeds in dousing the probing committee; when he conducts a hotel chase because he mistakes an autograph hunter for a dick; when he advertises on tv a whiskey which practically poisons him; when a chocolate cake brings back nostalgic memories of old, near-forgotten custard-pie days. But, largely, the humor is half-hearted and jaded.

Chaplin is supported by a string of British thespians who take full advantage of the limited opportunities afforded by the star-director-producer. Miss Addams, particularly, shows fire and polished assurance as the latest in Chaplin's long list of leading ladies who, having been given a Chaplin chance, subsequently find the burden hard to bear in follow-up chores. Chaplin's own son, Michael, plays the small boy with intelligence and some pathos.

Jerry Desmonde, as the prime minister, Oliver Johnston, as the ambassador; Harry Green, as the frenetic lawyer; Sidney James, as a tv exec, and Maxine Audley, as Chaplin's estranged wife, all give standout performances.

Direction is good except where Chaplin and art director Allan Harris have been lax in permitting obvious London locations to obtrude on what is ostensibly a N.Y. scene. The ubiquitous Chaplin also composed the music which is sensitive and already has received the nod on tele and discs. Georges Perinal's lensing is okay but provides nothing noteworthy. *Rich.*

Time Limit

Well done film version of the moderately successful Broadway play examining motives for collaboration with Communists; subject matter normally would work against it, but it could be a sleeper.

Hollywood, Sept. 3.

United Artists release of Heath (Richard Widmark-William Reynolds) production. Stars Richard Widmark, Richard Basehart. Features Dolores Michaels, June Lockhart, Carl Benton Reid, Martin Balsam, Rip Torn, Kaie Deei, Yale Wexler, Alan Dexter. Directed by Karl Malden. Screenplay, Henry Denker, from the play by Denker and Ralph Berkey; camera, Sam Leavitt; editor, Aaron Stell; music, Fred Steiner. Previewed Aug. 28, '57. Running time, 96 MINS.

Col. William Edwards	Richard Widmark
Major Harry Cargill	Richard Basehart
Corporal Jean Evans	Dolores Michaels
Mrs. Cargill	June Lockhart
General Connors	Carl Benton Reid
Sergeant Baker	Martin Balsam
Lieut. George Miller	Rip Torn
Mike	Alan Dexter
Captain Joe Connors	Yale Wexler
Lieut. Harvey	Manning Ross
Colonel Kim	Kaie Deei
Poleska	Skip McNally
Gus	Joe di Reda
Boxer	Kenneth Alton
Steve	James Douglas

This could be a sleeper.

Normally, theme of "Time Limit" would force it into special booking situations where it could achieve critical acclaim but only moderate boxoffice attention. However, this initial entry from Heath Productions for United Artists release is a good, professional job of picture-making in all departments and the grim and gripping flashback sequences lend dramatic vigor to what is essentially a sobering study of a contemporary problem. The punch may provide the extra exploitation and word-of-mouth to permit good response.

Henry Denker screenplayed from his own and Ralph Berkey's play, hewing closely to the original script about an Army probe into a major's collaboration with the Reds following his capture in Korea. Flashbacks are used to give the testimony of witnesses a present-tense impact that underscores the dogged digging of a colonel determined to know the "why" of the defection before he recommends a court-martial. His painstaking investigation finally reveals that the major acted to save the lives of fellow prisoners after the murder of an informer enraged the prison camp commander who issued a cooperation-or-carnage ultimatum.

Within this basic framework, Denker tells a compelling story of a man's terrible decision as to whether the reality of saving 16 lives outweighs the abstraction of aiding enemy propagandists. It has been tautly and sympathetically directed by Karl Malden who extracts a collection of topnotch performances from the small cast. Best of the lot is that of Richard Widmark, in a strongly sympathetic role as the colonel. It's an excellent study of a man determined to find the truth despite pressure from higher brass and consistently rings the bell. Only a shade behind is the work of Richard Basehart as the soul-tortured major, a fine characterization of a man torn between humaneness and duty as exemplified by the Army code.

In lesser parts, there is another very good job by Martin Balsam, who provides comic relief as the colonel's orderly and Dolores Michaels impresses strongly as a WAC corporal in the colonel's office. Rip Torn, as the young lieutenant who finally blurts out the truth; June Lockhart, seen briefly as Baseharts' wife; Carl Benton Reid as the general; and Kaie Deei as the Korean Communist colonel, all register effectively.

Film is a good initial production job by Widmark and William Reynolds and the technical credits are uniformly good, particularly the camera work by Sam Leavitt, Aaron Stell's editing and Fred Steiner's score. *Kap.*

The Helen Morgan Story
(C'SCOPE-SONGS)

Ann Blyth, Paul Newman in another boozy biopic of a showbiz great; tuneful and nostalgic, but a phony story and the recent televersion may hurt boxoffice chances, moderate at best.

Hollywood, Sept. 3.

Warner release of Martin Rackin production. Stars Ann Blyth, Paul Newman, Richard Carlson; also stars Gene Evans, Alan King, Cara Williams; features Virginia Vincent, Walter Woolf King, Dorothy Green, Ed Platt, Warren Douglas, Sammy White. Directed by Michael Curtiz.

Screenplay, Oscar Saul, Dean Riesner, Stephen Longstreet, Nelson Gidding; camera, Ted McCord; editor, Frank Bracht; art director, John Beckman; musical numbers staged by LeRoy Prinz. Songs sung by Gogi Grant. Previewed Sept. 3, '57. Running time, **117 MINS.**

Helen Morgan .... Ann Blyth
Larry .... Paul Newman
Wado .... Richard Carlson
Whitey Krause .... Gene Evans
Ben .... Alan King
Dolly .... Cara Williams
Sue .... Virginia Vincent
Ziegfeld .... Walter Woolf King
Mrs. Wade .... Dorothy Green
Haggerty .... Ed Platt
Hellinger .... Warren Douglas
Sammy .... Sammy White
Singers........Peggy De Castro, Cheri De Castro, Babette De Castro
Jimmy McHugh .... Himself
Rudy Vallee .... Himself
Walter Winchell .... Himself

First test of any adverse box-office reaction on a feature through sudden prior production on television looms with "The Helen Morgan Story," done a few months ago as a "Playhouse 90" entry with Polly Bergen starred. Warners' feature probably would fare better in this test if it were a more potent offering; unfortunately, it is little more than a tuneful soapopera, another in what appears to be a growing series of boozy biopix of showbiz greats. Even without the added question mark of the video version, "Morgan" looks to have only moderate appeal, hampered as it is by a story as authentic as Prohibition hooch. Ann Blyth and Paul Newman will add some marquee weight.

On the studio's schedule for a long time, the Martin Rackin production finally emerges as the product of four screenwriters, Oscar Saul, Dean Reisner, Stephen Longstreet and Nelson Gidding, who have taken some of the legends and some of the realities of the Roaring '20s and loosely attributed all of them to La Morgan. The story line sometimes strains credulity and the dialog and situations occasionally give the production a cornball flavor. Overall plot of a woman in love with a heel (best exemplified by the fade-out shot on the song "Can't Help Lovin' That Man") will, however, be an asset for distaff audiences eager to use hankerchiefs.

Screenplay spans a fabulous decade, beginning in the early 1920s when Miss Morgan, played by Ann Blyth, comes to Chicago to seek a career. She gets her start, both professionally and romantically, with Paul Newman, a shady operator, and his desertion of her after one night sets the pattern for his domination of her career. When he comes back into her life to prey upon her friendship for attorney Richard Carlson, she takes to the bottle for solace, paving the way for her downfall. Eventually, she collapses in a Bowery alley and is taken to Bellevue for a cure. Her recovery conveniently coincides with Newman's release from prison and he escorts her to a party at which, for the happy windup, she discovers that she was wrong when she thought Broadway had forgotten her.

Director Michael Curtiz has done a good job with the material at hand, injecting a pacing and bits of business that help maintain interest, and the production gets added benefit from a series of hit tunes of the era, excellently sung offscreen by Gogi Grant. (Miss Blyth is prettier than Miss Morgan was and Miss Grant, from a purely technical standpoint, sings better.) In the title role, Miss Blyth turns in a sympathetic but not always convincing performance. She never seems particularly the worse for alcoholic wear. Newman is very good as the rackets guy, giving the part authority and credibility, and Carlson is convincing. There are a pair of standout supporting performances among the cast: Cara Williams is topnotch as a longtime friend of the star's and Alan King impresses powerfully as the shady guy who marries her. Gene Evans is good as a gangster menace and there is okay support from Sammy White as a waiter; Walter Woolf King and Ed Platt, both seen briefly as Ziegfeld and a Broadway detective; and Virginia Vincent as a soubret. Jimmy McHugh, Rudy Vallee and Walter Winchell appear as themselves in scenes designed to re-create the era.

Technical credits are generally good, notably the camera work of Ted McCord, highlighted by a striking shot of La Morgan at the London Palladium; art direction by John Beckman which recaptures the period; the staging of the musical numbers by LeRoy Prinz and the editing by Frank Bracht. *Kap.*

Slaughter On Tenth Avenue

Hard-hitting, realistic picture about labor racketeers on the waterfront. Good b.o. potential.

Universal release of Albert Zugsmith production. Stars Richard Egan, Jan Sterling, Dan Duryea, Julie Adams. Features Walter Matthau, Charles McGraw, Sam Levene, Mickey Shaughnessy. Directed by Arnold Laven. Screenplay, Lawrence Roman, based on the book "The Man Who Rocked the Boat," by William J. Keating and Richard Carter; camera, Fred Jackman; editor, Russell F. Schoengarth; musical arrangement, Herschel Gilbert; "Slaughter On Tenth Avenue," composed by Richard Rodgers. Previewed in N.Y., Sept. 11, '57. Running time, **103 MINS.**

William Keating .... Richard Egan
Madge Pitts .... Jan Sterling
John Jacob Masters......... Dan Duryea
Dee .... Julie Adams
Al Dahlke .... Walter Matthau
Lt. Anthony Vosnick....Charles McGraw
Howard Rysdale .... Sam Levene
Solly Pitts .... Mickey Shaughnessy
Benjy Karp .... Harry Bellaver
Midget .... Nick Dennis
Eddie "Cockeye" Cook..... Ned Weaver
"Monk" Mohler .... Billy M. Greene
Judge .... John McNamara
Mrs. Cavanaugh .... Amzie Strickland
Big John .... Mickey Hargitay

"Slaughter on Tenth Avenue," the title of Richard Rodgers' ballet music from "On Your Toes," has been effectively employed by Universal for a hard-hitting and commendable film about racketeering on the New York waterfront. The picture, adapted by Lawrence Roman from a book entitled "The Man Who Rocked the Boat," by William J. Keating and Richard Carter, is as timely as the recent headlines from Washington dealing with the Congressional probe of malpractices of labor unions.

Since Keating is a former N.Y. assistant district attorney whose true-life experiences with waterfront gangs are recorded in the book, the film has a quiet, documentary flavor and contains a minimum of the false heroics that usually appear in pictures of this type. The picture's honesty, however, does not detract from its dramatic values. As a result, the b.o. results should be highly satisfactory.

The story presents Richard Egan as Keating, a young assistant D.A. who has been assigned to a shooting case stemming from waterfront conflicts. Mickey Shaughnessy, an honest longshoreman, is shot because of his efforts to eliminate the gangster elements from the docks. Shaughnessy, his wife (played by Jan Sterling) and his supporters at first follow the underworld code of not revealing the identity of the triggermen. However, Keating is persistent. He gets them to change their minds and thus is able to corral evidence and witnesses to build his case for an indictment and a trial. Shaughnessy makes a deathbed identification which provides Keating with his most potent evidence for a murder trial.

The film is careful to point out that not all longshoremen are gangsters and racketeers and that honest workers exist who are continually attempting to bring about reforms despite the dangers of resisting the corrupt labor bosses.

Albert Zugsmith has provided good production values and has assembled a cast who make the proceedings wholly believable. Egan is convincing as the at-first-wide-eyed and then tough assistant D.A. from the Pennsylvania coal country. His college and law education have rubbed off his coal country beginnings, but he's not adverse to trading punches with the toughs when aroused. Miss Sterling is excellent as Shaughnessy's tough yet tender and understanding wife. Shaughnessy, heretofore seen mainly in comedies, shows that he can also be good in a dramatic role.

Sam Levene as Keating's hard-driving although sympathetic boss; Walter Matthau as the boss labor racketeer; Dan Duryea as the gangsters' lawyer; Julie Adams as Keating's wife; Charles McGraw as a knowledgeable and honest detective with wide experience on the waterfront; Harry Bellaver and Nick Dennis as longshoremen opposed to the gangster influences; and Ned Weaver as one of the killers, all turn in fine performances.

Arnold Laven's direction gives the picture a realistic quality which Fred Jackman's b&w photography captures effectively. The "Slaughter on Tenth Avenue" music is used expertly for some of the background. Technical credits, including Herschel Gilbert's musical arrangements under the supervision of Joseph Gershenson Russell F. Schoengarth's editing, and Phil Bowles' special photography, are all first-rate. *Holl.*

Aparajito
(Unvanquished)
(INDIAN)

Venice, Sept. 10.

Aurora release of Epic Film production. Features Pinaki Sen Gupta, Karuna Banerjee, Samaran Ghosal, Kanu Banerjee, Ramani Sen Gupta. Written and directed by Satyajit Ray, based on novel by Bibhutibhusan Bandapaddhay. Camera, Subroto Mitra; editor, Dulala Dutta; music, Ravi Shankar. At Venice Film Fest. Running time, **105 MINS.**

Apu (child) .... Pinaki Sen Gupta
Mother .... Karuna Banerjee
Apu (grown) .... Samaran Ghosal
Father .... Kanu Banerjee
Uncle .... Ramani Sen Gupta

This is the second film of a trilogy based on a leading Indian best-seller. The first, "Pather Panchali," copped "the most human document" prize at the Cannes Film Fest last year. This won the top award at this Venice festival. "Aparajito" looms mainly an art house possibility where its insight and lyricism could garner solid word-of-mouth and crix praise. Locale, slow pace and lack of story might limit this in more general U.S. runs.

Pic picks up an Indian family in the 1930's, living in poor circumstances. A 10-year-old boy, however, is enthralled by the bustling life of the river and the city, since just in from the country. The father dies, and mother and son go back to the village. However, the boy excels in school and is sent to the city on a scholarship. His mother is ill but she will not call him to interfere with his exams. When he is summoned it is too late but he resolves to go on and work harder in memory of his mother.

The film pulsates with the flow of life. If the story is slight and does not quite develop the young hero, the mother dominates it with a presence and poignance to make this a study of Indian life which rings true.

Music and imagery combine for interesting rhythmic effects. More cohesion and expansion of the characters would have given this greater possibilities for the West. As is, it remains extremely specialized. It is technically sound and the third one should round out the first real picture of India to be put on screens. Pic is also a natural for school showings.

This continues the first film but is not a sequel. It is complete in itself and is also based on the book via the proper filmic adaptation. First one opens in N.Y. shortly, and response may cue this second production's chance in America. *Mosk.*

The Deerslayer
(C'SCOPE—COLOR)

Exploitable adaptation of James Fenimore Cooper classic with sure draw in outdoor market.

Hollywood, Sept. 13.

20th-Fox release of Kurt Neumann production. Stars Lex Barker, Rita Moreno, Forrest Tucker, Cathy O'Donnell; costars Jay C. Flippen, Carlos Rivas; features John Halloran, Joseph Vitale. Directed by Neumann. Screenplay, Carroll Young, Neumann, based on novel by James Fenimore Cooper; camera (DeLuxe-Color), Karl Struss; editor, Jodie Copelan; music, Paul Sawtell, Bert Shefter. Previewed Sept. 10, '57. Running time, **76 MINS.**

The Deerslayer .... Lex Barker
Hetty .... Rita Moreno
Harry Marsh .... Forrest Tucker
Judith .... Cathy O'Donnell
Old Tom Hutter .... Jay C. Flippen
Chingachgook .... Carlos Rivas
Old Warrior .... John Halloran
Huron Chief .... Joseph Vitale
Stunt .... Rocky Shahan
Stunt .... Phil Schumacker
Stunt .... George Robotham
Stunt .... Carol Henry

This picturization of the James Fenimore Cooper classic is a well-turned-out derring-do actioner which spins off 76 minutes of entertainment slanted particularly for demands of the juve trade. Film should show good payoff in the outdoor market, where CinemaScope and DeLuxe-Color are definite assets.

Produced and directed by Kurt Neumann, pic is strong on pictorial values which bolster the Carroll Young-Neumann screenplay. Location lensing in northern California by Karl Struss is most effective in backdropping regulation action of the days of the Hurons and Mohicans of early America and which Neumann succeeds in projecting via believable characters. Twentieth is releasing film under its own production banner.

Lex Barker takes on title character, a young white man reared by the Mohicans whose blood brother is Chingachgook, Mohican chief. Together, they try to save a half-crazy hunter and his two daughters, who live on a floating fort in the river, from Huron wrath. This man, who hates Indians because they scalped his wife years before, is a bounty hunter interested only in filling his pouch with

Indian scalps. Enraged Hurons are determined to retrieve the scalps of their dead so their souls may rest in peace. Oldfashioned aspects of plot are hurdled by fast action. Barker plays his part convincingly and has okay support right down the line. Forrest Tucker is rugged as a tough frontier trader, Jay C. Flippen scores as the grizzled old hunter who hates Indians, and Rita Moreno and Cathy O'Donnell qualify as his daughters, former actually an Indian who was stolen by hunter and raised as his own. Carlos Rivas is colorful as Barker's Indian brother.

Technical credits come in for expert handling, including Jodie Copelan's fast editing, atmospheric music score by Paul Sawtell and Bert Shefter and art direction by Theobold Holsopple. *Whit.*

Copper Sky
(REGALSCOPE)

Dull western with small prospects.

Hollywood, Sept. 13.
20th-Fox release of Robert Stabler production. Stars Jeff Morrow, Coleen Gray; features Strother Martin, Paul Brinegar, John Pickard, Patrick (Pat) O'Moore, Jack Lomas, Bill Hamel, Dorothy Schuyler. Directed by Charles Marquis Warren. Screenplay, Eric Norden, from story by Stabler; camera, Brydon Baker; editor, Fred W. Berger; music. Raoul Kraushaar. Previewed Sept. 12, '57. Running time, 76 MINS.

Hack Williams	Jeff Morrow
Nora	Coleen Gray
Charlie Martin	Paul Brinegar
Trumble	William R. (Bill) Hamel
Lawson	Jack M. Lomas
Pokey	Strother Martin
Trooper Hadley	John Pickard
Col. Thurston	Patrick (Pat) O'Moore
Stunt Man	Rocky Shahan
Man No. 1	Bill McGraw
Juror	Jerry Oddo
Corporal	Rush Williams
Indian	Rod Redwing

"Copper Sky" probably sets a record high for lack of action and overage of dialog in a western. Film is so dull it will have to fight for bookings.

The Robert Stabler production opens on an Apache massacre of a town's entire populace, with Jeff Morrow, overlooked by Redskins because he's in jail, the sole survivor. Into this settlement rides a prim young Boston school-mistress the following morning. Thereafter, camera focuses on pair as they try to reach safety, following them across the range and desert.

Morrow, ex-cavalryman, is drunk and recovering from a hangover most of the trek; Coleen Gray as the teacher spends her whole time moralizing. Hating each other through most of picture, the Eric Norden script would have audiences believe they fall in love. It's one of the least interesting oaters in years, and Charles Marquis Warren's direction does nothing to alleviate the dullness.

The two principals are wasted in their respective roles. Morrow sometimes goes more than a reel without uttering a word as he stares blankly into space, but Miss Gray yackety-yacks more than any blithering stage heroine. Balance of cast in brief roles mean nothing. Brydon Baker's expert camera work is only plus for picture. *Whit.*

Forty Guns
(C'SCOPE)

Fast western with names of Barbara Stanwyck and Barry Sullivan to draw strongly in outdoor market.

Hollywood, Sept. 13.
20th-Fox release of Samuel Fuller production. Stars Barbara Stanwyck, Barry Sullivan; costars Dean Jagger, John Ericson, Gene Barry; features Robert Dix, Eve Brent, Jack "Jidge" Carroll. Director-screenplay, Fuller; camera, Joseph Biroc; editor, Gene Fowler Jr.; music, Harry Sukman. Previewed Sept. 11, '57. Running time, 76 MINS.

Jessica	Barbara Stanwyck
Griff Bonnell	Barry Sullivan
Ned Logan	Dean Jagger
Brockie Drummond	John Ericson
Wes Bonnell	Gene Barry
Chica Bonnell	Robert Dix
Louvenia Spanger	Eve Brent
Barney Cashman	Jack "Jidge" Carroll

"Forty Guns" carries enough dramatic punch to see it strongly through the outdoor market. Star team of Barbara Stanwyck and Barry Sullivan, who have paired before, means wicket business, so payoff should be profitable.

Samuel Fuller in triple capacity of producer-scripter-director has devised a solid piece of entertainment which has femme star playing a ruthless Arizona ranch owner, the boss of Cochise County. Into her realm rides Sullivan and his two brothers, former an ex-gun slinger now working for the U. S. Attorney General, his fame with a gun preceding him. He's in Tombstone on official business, which means conflict with femme, who rules her domain, including the sheriff, with an iron hand. Further complications arise between the two, even as a romance develops, over Miss Stanwyck's brother, John Ericson, a brawling, would-be killer.

Miss Stanwyck socks over her role in experienced style and Sullivan is persuasive as the marshal who loses his 10-year record for non-killing by gunning down Ericson after latter has murdered his brother, Gene Barry. Barry, also a marshal who rides as Sullivan's right hand on his official duties, handles role effectively and is in for romance with Eve Brent, excellent in her part as a gorgeous gunsmith who is widowed by Ericson's shot as she's leaving church after the wedding. Ericson impresses in a part which might have been overplayed.

Good support also is offered by Dean Jagger, sheriff completely dominated by femme ranch owner, and Robert Dix, enacting Sullivan's second brother, who wants to be a gunfighter. Jack "Jidge" Carroll delivers strongly in his rendition of two songs, the catchy "High Ridin' Woman," by Harold Adamson and Harry Sukman, and the plaintive "God Has His Arms Around Me," by Victor Young and Adamson.

Joseph Biroc uses his cameras expertly and Gene Fowler Jr.'s sharp editing gives good pace to film. *Whit.*

Search for Paradise
(CINERAMA)

Marred by doubtful touches and too much built-in promotion. But retains memorable Cineramic qualities and outlook probably okay.

Stanley Warner Cinerama Corp. release of Lowell Thomas production. Directed by Otto Lang. Scenario and narration by Thomas, Lang and Prosper Buranelli. Musical score by Dimitri Tiomkin. Lyrics by Ned Washington and Lowell Thomas. Vocals by Robert Merrill and Norman Luboff. Cameramen, Harry Squire, Jack Priestley, Harvey Manger. Film editor, Lovel S. Ellis. Sound editors, Walter Hanneman, Paul David. Air Force Major and Sergeant played by Christopher Young and James S. Parker. At Warners, N. Y., opening Sept. 24, 1957. Running time, 120 MINS.

For five years now Cinerama with the late Fred Waller's three-camera photography and three-booth projection has been a special and separate branch of show business which has piled up grosses of some $60,000,000. Each of the successive releases has appealed to the streak of wonder and awe in mankind and a good deal of this appeal should adhere and inhere in the fourth film, "Search For Paradise" though it is the least exciting and least promising of the Cineramas.

Discontent with content is less crucial here than with a storied film and invidious comparisons need not necessarily be commercially depressant though it is hardly possible not to think of Mike Todd's "Around The World In 80 Days" as the something new which has been added to the criteria by which Cinerama will be judged.

If "Search For Paradise" represents Lowell Thomas' personal search for an expanded Cinerama concept, nothing really is changed. This one sticks almost slavishly to established formulae, whatever surface pretensions there are to being "different." Once more strange lands are "seen" by two selected "tourists" this time a make-believe Air Force major and sergeant who, at the payoff, decide that they'll sign up for another hitch, the Air Force itself being the ultimate paradise.

The beginning of the picture is cornily contrived. An Associated Press newsmachine is seen ticking out a bulletin that Lowell Thomas is one of three ambassadors just appointed to represent Washington at the coronation durbar of King Mahendra of Nepal. His secretary tears off the yellow sheet and hands it to Thomas, saying, "Looks like you'll be going places again, boss." Thomas accepts the news flash as an immediacy of the present tense but then jumps at once to the past tense of "And, ladies and gentlemen, that's how it started."

Even more awkward scenario follows when Thomas is picked up aboard a U.S. Air Force Globe-Master. He comes along and seats himself beside a supposed stranger, the major, who asks, "You're Lowell Thomas, aren't you?" This time present tense jumps into future tense with Thomas "hiring" the two fliers to be his sightseers.

The Globe Master plane carrying Ambassador Thomas and presumably his Cinerama gear heads cross-Atlantic from Florida, dips in passing over Paris, the Suez Canal and Persian Gulf ports. The first letdown is to visit Ceylon, where saffron-robed Buddhist monks show the major a great shrine.

The several stops of "Search" are all way-stations en route to Nepal. The picture centres upon the approach to and environs of the Himalayas, world's greatest peaks, truthfully described as a region of mystery, age, mysticism and Communistic intrigue. One call is upon the 25,000-population pocket emirdom of Hunza, where people often live to be 100. This is fairly interesting offbeat travel.

At this point one of the film's several special songs is introduced, a sort of Himalayan Calypso number about how hale and happy you'd be in Hunza, far from jail, ulcers, hypertension and taxes. The lyrics are travel ballyhoo par excellence only the long rocky trail on saddle horses would discourage all but the bravest tourists. Lowell Thomas himself is not party to this sore derriere side-trip. Skipping Hunza, he picks up the Major and the Sarge in the Vale of Kashmir, a plausible paradise indeed, especially its Shalimar Gardens. (Kashmir is in dispute between India and Pakistan — understandably).

Another detour on the way to Nepal is a rubber boat shooting of the rapids in the Indus River. Once into the rapids in the inflated craft the net excitement and footage is only moderately memorable. Bus and Don Hatch, of Colorado River antecedents, supervised this section of the film.

The visit at Nepal is the big sequence. And a stunning display of oriental pomp it is. Here Thomas is seen in topper and cutaway on one of the royal manicured elephants. Here the Sarge, who has been played for a few giggles up to then gets a good belly laugh when almost falling off the platform of another of the ponderous pachyderms. Here, too, there is the implicit villainy of Communism in the persons of the enigmatic Chinese delegates wearing severe black proletarian garb against the crimson and gold vestments of the Nepalese court.

It is emphasized that this may well have been one of the last durbars in a changing Asia menaced by Communism. Nobody will question the uniqueness of the occasion, the insight into a faroff culture which "Search" brings to the screen. This segment is surely a genuine peep into dazzling fantasy and a true coup for Cinerama and Thomas.

Of the political importance of the Cinerama report on the Nepal coronation, it is possible only to imagine. It may well be priceless world publicity for Nepal and possibly a goodwill-by-indirection job for Uncle Sam.

Over-all, the toil and sweat of the technical crews crawling Asiatic terrain must be respected. Some of the color photography is superb, the Shalimar houseboats and the smaller craft with their after dark lanterns as a case in point. Otto Lang has captured many a beguiling native type or custom. His direction and the editing of Harvey Manger and Lovel S. Ellis are top credits.

Granting the sheer organizational fait accompli as no mean deed by itself, the film falters in some of its basic choices on what to include in. The viewer is teased by the omission of explanatory detail on the countries visited while some pretty blatant "promotion" is accommodated. Producer Thomas has overstarred himself, being in on script, narration, the song lyrics (with Ned Washington) and also credited for the basic idea. He is the principle principal, the major and sergeant remaining mostly just part of the scenery.

Thrust forward as a sort of Noel Coward of travel (without the leer) Thomas is also his own ballyhooligan. During the soft caressing lyrics which set the mood for the Shalimar water scenes and while the party is enjoying service fit for maharajahs, pre-Nehru, the offscreen singer expresses regret that there are no microphones handy for Lowell Thomas the newscaster. Quel plug!

Dimitri Tiomkin came east to score the release at Cinerama's Oyster Bay headquarters. His music is obviously intended as a dominating influence. On the whole it is probably a strong score, if occasionally too prominent and loud and now and again deliberately coy. Commercial angles have been astutely figured via four tailored songs—"Search For Paradise," "Happy Land of Hunza," "Shalimar" and "Kashmir Street Song." Vocals are by Robert Merrill of the Met.

Cinerama's bigger-than-life panorama continues to fill the curved screen to bursting optical sensation. This is the minimum net stock-in-trade. Downhill in a jeep alongside Himalayan precipices evoke nervous reaction in the spectator. Ditto the mass parachute jump which jams the sky. Orchestral and sound showmanship helps, too, as with the Islamic drums and horns of the mountain folk in Happy, Healthy Hunza. Again, as with the predecessor films, the glimpses of how the other half lives qualifies as science-updated Burton Holmes.

It is easier to be critical of this fourth Cinerama venture but it would be difficult to avoid engrossment, though the saddle-weary sequence is over-long and the song plugs over-noticeable.

The "Cineramic" values remain, in the boxoffice potency sense. True, a couple of the thrills don't quite come off and the screen is less crowded with stimuli than heretofore. These are balancing considerations. If there is too much focus on the producer, an admittedly versatile American but pretty deadpan as a personality, there is the tall wonder of the King of Nepal in bird of paradise plumage, and the party he threw for the diplomats.

At a guess "Search For Paradise" will shorten the runs chalked up by the previous three releases. As to that, time is the scorekeeper. Something else looms larger than before. The Cinerama medium shouts for that something more, that something different which tomorrow will demand. The prediction is not new. But its point jabs home more sharply this time—again because of the trip David Niven and Cantinflas recently took in another kind of widescreen medium. *Land.*

Until They Sail

New Zealand men away at war, Yank Marines take over. Powered he-she stuff based on love affairs of four sisters. Good draw.

Hollywood, Sept. 24.

Metro release of Charles Schnee production. Stars Jean Simmons, Joan Fontaine, Paul Newman. Directed by Robert Wise. Screenplay, Robert Anderson from story by James A. Michener. Editor, Harold F. Kress; music, David Raksin; songs, "Until They Sail" by Sammy Cahn. Previewed in Hollywood, Sept. 23, '57. Running time, **94 MINS.**

Barbara Leslie Forbes ...... Jean Simmons
Anne Leslie ...... Joan Fontaine
Capt. Jack Harding ...... Paul Newman
Delia Leslie ...... Piper Laurie
Capt. Richard G. Bates ...... Charles Drake
Evelyn Leslie ...... Sandra Dee
"Shinner" Phil Friskett ...... Wally Cassell
Prosecution ...... Alan Napier
Max Murphy ...... Ralph Votrian
Tommy ...... John Wilder
Marine ...... Tige Andrews
Lt. Andy ...... Adam Kennedy
Marine ...... Mickey Shaughnessy

Metro has a sharp entry for the romantic market in this compelling picturization of Michener's yarn of New Zealand during World War II. An adult love story, it seemingly carries sock appeal for distaff audiences. Particularly heavy overtones of sex also give it strong exploitation potential.

Schnee production focuses on what happens when all home men of marriageable age are away at war, U.S. Marines flood the country. Under Wise's deft and sensitive direction, Anderson's screenplay takes explosive form in following love affairs of four sisters. Clandestine romance is subtly handled. And in touching on loneliness of love-starved years plot builds dramatic punch. Top flight cast generates often poignant unfoldments which allows both lightness and tragedy.

Jean Simmons and Joan Fontaine romances lead off narrative, which includes also those of Piper Laurie and to lesser extent younger Sandra Dee. Simmons, whose husband of month is killed, pairs with Paul Newman.

Characters right down line are outstanding, Simmons and Newman as chief protagonists faring best. Fontaine gives substance to austere role. Miss Laurie scores brightly as girl who loves life while Miss Dee makes happy event of her teenage part.

Technical department effectively handled throughout. *Whit.*

High Flight
(BRITISH—COLOR)

Run-of-mill R.A.F. story with good star performance by Ray Milland and fine aerial shots; good b.o. prospects.

London, Sept. 17.

Columbia release of (Phil C. Samuel) Warwick production. Stars Ray Milland; features Anthony Newley, Bernard Lee, Helen Cherry. Directed by John Gilling. Screenplay, Joseph Landon and Kenneth Hughes, from story by Jack Davies; camera, Ted Moore; editor, Jack Slade; music, Kenneth E. Jones, Douglas Gamley. At Empire Theatre, London. Running time, **95 MINS.**

Wing Commander Rudge ...... Ray Milland
Flight Sergeant Harris ...... Bernard Lee
Tony Winchester ...... Kenneth Haigh
Roger Endicott ...... Anthony Newley
John Fletcher ...... Kenneth Fortescue
Cadet Day ...... Sean Kelly
Louise ...... Helen Cherry
Squadron Leader Blake ...... Leslie Phillips
Weapons Corporal ...... Duncan Lamont
Minister for Air ...... Kynaston Reeves
Commandant ...... John Le Mesurier
Diana ...... Jan Brooks
Parker ...... Frank Atkinson
Bishop ...... Ian Fleming
Bishop's Wife ...... Nancy Nevinson
Commandant's Wife ...... Grace Arnold
Barman ...... Hal Osmond
Publican ...... Leslie Weston
Susan ...... Anne Aubrey

Warwick, which usually specializes in high-powered adventure yarns, turns to the training in peacetime of Britain's jet-pilots for this latest pic, and it is a surprisingly gentle and uneventful affair. Nevertheless, shrewdly launched during Battle of Britain week, and with the star appeal of Ray Milland and the R.A.F., "High Flight" should have good b.o. prospects both at home and in the U.S.

Flying pix invariably do good business but rarely has one relied on a more slender story-line than that provided by ex-R.A.F. man Jack Davies. Kenneth Haigh, one of the cadets in a new intake at Cranwell Flying College, is a natural pilot but an undisciplined, hot-headed misfit. Disciplining Haigh presents a problem to Milland since his own recklessness as a young pilot in the war caused the death of Haigh's father. With this chip on his shoulder, Haigh creates a number of tense situations with his C.O. Not until the end of the film, when Milland saves the young man's life on an operational flight, does the feeling between the two ease up.

With such scanty material, director John Gilling has had to get his effect from well-balanced character-studies, an earnest peek at what goes into the training of these young giants of the modern jet-age and from some first-class aerial photography. Apart from a brace of misadventures in the air which are thrilling the aerial scenes are more academic than exhilarating. In fact, it is something of a surprise that the pic remains as airborne in its audience-grip as it does.

Milland gives a highly competent and authoritative performance as the stern, likeable Wing Commander with a conscience. Haigh shows up well as the young, mixed-up cadet. Prominent among the assorted cadets is Anthony Newley, onetime child star, who has developed into a firstclass young actor with a glib sense of comedy. Bernard Lee also provides some much-needed humor as a Flight-Sergeant assigned the job of breaking in the rookies. Helen Cherry and Jan Brooks have little to do but look decorative, a chore which neither finds difficult.

Dialog is unforced and realistic. One or two slapstick scenes are introduced to keep the pic moving when the airplanes are not mobile. Lensing of Ted Moore (and the cameramen in charge of the second unit, Stan Pavey and Cyril Knowles) is firstrate and the color is superb. The formation flying, some of which was bagged at Farnborough Air Display, will get a respectable nod from aviation fans.

Altogether, a quiet, polished film which will not raise the blood-pressure but which has a persuasive appeal. Light-music maestro Eric Coates has contributed a "High Flight" music theme which should be a natural on the airwaves. *Rich.*

Under Fire
(REGALSCOPE)

Well-done Regal production. Fine supporter.

Hollywood, Sept. 18.

20th-Fox release of Plato Skouras production. Stars Rex Reason, Henry Morgan, Steve Brodie; features Peter Walker, Robert Levin, Jon Locke, Gregory LaFayette, Karl Lukas, William Allyn, Frank Gerstle, Tom McKee. Directed by James B. Clark. Screenplay, James Landis; camera, John M. Nickolaus Jr.; editor, Jodie Copelan; art director, Rudi Feld; music, Paul Dunlap. Previewed in Beverly Hills, Cal., Sept. 16, '57. Running time, **76 MINS.**

Lt. Rogerson ...... Rex Reason
Sergeant Dusak ...... Henry Morgan
Captain Linn ...... Steve Brodie
Lt. Sarris ...... Peter Walker
Private Pope ...... Robert Levin
Cpl. Crocker ...... Jon Locke
Cpl. Quinn ...... Gregory LaFayette
Sergeant Hutchins ...... Karl Lukas
Colonel Dundee ...... Frank Gerstle
Captain O'Mar ...... Tom McKee
M. P. Sgt. ...... John Murphy
Capt. Linn's Assistant ...... Edmund Penney
1st Court Officer ...... Seymour Green
2d Court Officer ...... Dave Tomack
3rd Court Officer ...... Walter Maslow
4th Court Officer ...... David Carlile
Lt. Stagg ...... William Allyn
Singer ...... Rita Paul
Private Swanson ...... Kay Kuter
Captain Tander ...... Keith Byron
Lt. Conroy ...... Neyle Morrow
Private Finley ...... K. L. Smith
Private Barton ...... Robert Hinkle
M. P. Sentry ...... Robert Colbert
M. P. Lieutenant ...... Al Shelley
Lieutenant ...... Troy Patterson
Colonel Jason ...... Dehl Berti
Lt. D.S.C. ...... Ronald Foster
1st G.I. ...... Sid Melton
Private Steiner ...... George Chakiris
Colonel D.S.C. ...... Ed Hinton
Pvt. Tartolia ...... Nico Minardos
2nd G.I. ...... Calvin Booth
Nurse ...... Lorraine Martin
Waitress ...... Mary Townsend

This Plato Skouras production, second from the son of 20th-Fox prexy Spyros Skouras, stacks up one of the best to emerge under the Regal banner. There's thorough interest throughout yarn of an Army court martial in Germany—the result of good story combined with good direction and competent performances. It will fit well into the program market.

The James Landis screenplay revolves around four men—Henry Morgan, John Locke, Gregory LaFayette and Robert Levin—who are summoned before a U. S. Army court martial charged with desertion in combat, rather than having been lost, as they claimed. Rex Reason is the defense counsel; Steve Brodie the prosecuting attorney. Men are eventually freed when defense proves mistaken identity with Germans poising as American soldiers; that the quartet actually was lost and not merely posing as such to escape combat.

James B. Clark, former film editor (with 20th-Fox for 20 years), herewith makes his bow as a feature film director. It's an auspicious bow, Clark neatly integrating patrol sequences with the actual trial and keeping the interest high throughout.

Performances of stars Rex Reason, Henry Morgan and Steve Broidy are uniformly good, and same appraisal holds for all those featured. Among these, incidentally, and especially good, is the late Gregory LaFayette, killed along with his actress-wife, Judy Tyler, in an auto accident last July 4.

Neat technical contributions include camera work of John M. Nickolaus Jr., Rudi Feld's art direction, and the musical backing of Paul Dunlap. *Neal.*

Jet Pilot
(COLOR)

An old-fashioned Russian-spy meller with John Wayne and Janet Leigh playing an incredible spy-and-fly yarn straight. Heavy "sell" needed to put it across in initial exposures.

Universal release of RKO-Howard Hughes production. Producer, Jules Furthman. Stars John Wayne, Janet Leigh, features Jay C. Flippen, Paul Fix, Richard Rober, Roland Winters, Hans Conreid. Directed by Josef von Sternberg. Written by Furthman; camera (Technicolor), aerial photography, Philip G. Cochran, under director Winton C. Hoch; editors, Michael R. McAdam and Harry Marker; music, Bronislau Kaper. Previewed N.Y., Sept. 12, '57. Running time, **112 MINS.**

Colonel Shannon ...... John Wayne
Anna ...... Janet Leigh
Major General Black ...... Jay C. Flippen
Major Rexford ...... Paul Fix
George Rivers ...... Richard Rober
Colonel Sokolov ...... Ronald Winters
Colonel Matoff ...... Hans Conreid
General Langrad ...... Ivan Triesault
Major Lester Sinclair ...... John Bishop
Georgis Rexford ...... Perdita Chandler
Mrs. Simpson ...... Joyce Compton
Mr. Simpson ...... Denver Pyle

"Jet Pilot" was made about seven years ago and kept under wraps by indie film-maker Howard Hughes for unstated (but much speculated upon) reasons. Much of the production is a strange blend. It oscillates between light comedy-romance and melodrama, with one not complementing the other. World tensions—indeed, a cold war—render difficult immediate acceptance of a story which has a pretty, young girl as a Russian jet pilot who, on a spy mission, wings into a love match with an American airman in the United States.

Questionable is the casting of Miss Leigh. While John Wayne fits the part of a colonel in the Yank Air Force, the slick chick looks more at home in a bathing suit at Palm Springs than she does jockeying a Soviet MIG, and shooting down her own countrymen, in Russia. The incongruity would appear less glaring if "Pilot" were out to be a takeoff on secret agent stuff. But much of it is played straight. And there's nothing funny about the Russian gal dropping her colleagues out of the sky or strafing soldiers on the ground.

Film opens at a U.S. airbase in Alaska where Wayne is in charge. Miss Leigh flies in, tells skeptic Wayne that she escaped from Russia, and is taken in tow by the colonel who gets the assignment of seeking information from her. Picture moves to Palmer Field and Palm Springs, love blossoms, marriage follows (with much talk later about "that night in Yuma"). Then it's discovered that Miss Leigh is a spy.

Air Force brass fixes things so that Miss Leigh can "escape" back to Russia along with Wayne, who now becomes the spy. And when the Reds make it tough for him, Miss Leigh, now taking him in tow, fights her way through another escape—back to Palm Springs.

Aerial photography is short of expectations, which is a curious shortcoming in view of Hughes' kinship with aeronautics. The in-the-air scenes rate second to, say, the striking work done in Paramount's "Strategic Air Command."

Josef von Sternberg's direction and the writing by Jules Furthman (who also has producer credit) are reminiscent of old-fashion cops-and-robbers cinema. The appeal is for those who can sit back and relax, not too much concerned about the grim real-life background (Soviet vs. American maneuvers) from which the story is projected.

Performances are okay, including Wayne's, Miss Leigh's, and, in U.S. Air Force roles, Jay C. Flippen, Paul Fix, Richard Rober and, as Soviet officers, Roland Winters and Hans Conreid.

Editing is uneven, the color photography generally and music fair enough. *Gene.*

Short Cut to Hell
(V'VISION)

James Cagney turns director for sharp remake of 1942 "This Gun for Hire."

Hollywood, Sept. 20.

Paramount release of A. C. Lyles production. Features Robert Ivers, Georgann Johnson. Directed by James Cagney. Screenplay, Ted Berkman, Raphael Blau, based on screenplay by W. R. Burnett; from novel by Graham Greene; camera, Haskell Boggs; editor, Tom McAdoo; music, Irvin Talbot. Previewed Sept. 18, '57. Running time, **89 MINS.**

Kyle	Robert Ivers
Glory Hamilton	Georgann Johnson
Stan	William Bishop
Bahrwell	Jacques Aubuchon
Adams	Peter Baldwin
Daisy	Yvette Vickers
Nichols	Murvyn Vye
L.A. Police Capt.	Milton Frome

Updated version of the 1942 "This Gun for Hire" comes off as a crackling melodrama. Marking James Cagney's first pitch as a director and A. C. Lyle's initial full producer chore, film packs enough gutsy action to see it satisfactorily through program situations.

Cagney socks over his helming in expected style from one who has specialized in hardboiled characters, and gives parts plenty of meaning. Pair of unknowns take over the two top roles, Robert Ivers in the original Alan Ladd role and Georgann Johnson (with two eyes showing) the Veronica Lake, both doing yoeman service and handling themselves expertly. The Ted Berkman-Raphael Blau screenplay, based on original W. R. Burnett script, carries fast pace and while dented with a few soft spots holds up generally through final climax.

Yarn is motivated by the search of Ivers, a ruthless young gunman, for the man who has paid him off in stolen money for two murders. Police have the numbers of the bills, which makes it impossible for gun to pass them. He picks up Miss Johnson, girl friend of William Bishop, detective in charge of the murders, and forcibly keeps her with him during the police hunt. Killer is finally shot down by police in good climax.

Ivers does first-rate as the gunman, inserting quiet menace, and Miss Johnson's breeziness is transmitted nicely to the audience. Both players should benefit by their performances in castings for the future. Jacques Aubuchon enacts a somewhat flamboyant heavy, okay in role, and Bishop makes the most of a brief appearance. Murvyn Vye is in as his sadistic servant and Peter Baldwin also lends interest in a heavy role.

Haskell Boggs leads off firstclass technical credits with good photography, and Tom McAdoo's editing is fast. Art direction by Hal Pereira and Roland Anderson is worthy of a bigger-budgeted production. *Whit.*

The Black Scorpion

Mexican volcano belches monster what-is-it, okay entry for science-fiction market; clever special effects.

Hollywood, Sept. 20.

Warner Bros. release of Frank Melford-Jack Dietz production. Stars Richard Denning, Mara Corday, Carlos Rivas, Mario Navarro; features Carlos Muzquiz, Pascual Pena. Directed by Edward Ludwig. Screenplay, David Duncan, Robert Blees; from story by Paul Yawitz; camera, Lionel Lindon; editor, Richard Van Enger; music, Paul Sawtell. Previewed Sept. 10, '57. Running time, **85 MINS.**

Henry Scott	Richard Denning
Teresa	Mara Corday
Arturo Ramos	Carlos Rivas
Juanito	Mario Navarro
Dr. Velazco	Carlos Muzquiz
Jose de la Cruz	Pascual Pena
Florentina	Fanny Schiller
Father Delgado	Pedro Galvan
Major Cosio	Arturo Martinez

"The Black Scorpion" is a regulation science-fiction which may be exploited for returns. Somewhat haphazardly put together, it still manages some high degree of excitement and a chilling windup. Special effects are particularly well handled.

Lensed in Mexico, pic takes its tag from a mammoth death-dealing scorpion that rises from bowels of the earth when a volcano erupts. Antidiluvian monster seemingly is indestructible — large enough to snatch up automobiles and helicopters out of the air as though they were tiny toys, unharmed when an express train crashes into it—you know writers' imagination. It finally meets death in the huge coliseum in Mexico City through the devices of science.

First half of Frank Melford-Jack Dietz production is tedious and blurred by dark photography which may interfere with satisfactory projection in drive-in theatres. Yarn is personalized via Richard Denning and Carlos Rivas, American and Mexican geologist, respectively, who are investigating the eruption and consequent earthquake. Their efforts to destroy the giant scorpion takes them down into a yawning chasm where they see not one but many of the monsters. Dynamiting this opening in the belief they are bottling up the monsters, they later discover the monsters have found another outlet only 20 miles from Mexico City. One of these, the papy of them all which kills off the other giant insects and makes its way to capital city, stirs up all the excitement attending latter part of film. Edward Ludwig makes the most of his opportunities in thrill sequences of the David Duncan-Robert Blees screenplay.

Denning capably handles his role, as does Rivas, and Mara Corday as a ranch owner whose property is overrun by the giants. Mario Navarro is okay as a moppet who continually sticks up geologists and gets into trouble. Carlos Muzquiz is good as a scientist who directs the all-out attack on the scorpion in coliseum.

Special effects by Willis O'Brien and Peter Peterson lead off technical credits. Lionel Lindon's photography is too low key, and Richard Van Enger combines slow with fast editing. *Whit.*

The Wayward Girl
(NATURAMA)

Poor filler fare.

Hollywood, Sept. 24.

Republic release of William J. O'Sullivan production. Stars Marcia Henderson, Peter Walker, Katharine Barrett, Whit Bissell; features Rita Lynn, Peg Hillias, Tracey Roberts, Ray Teal, Ric Roman, Barbara Eden, Grandon Rhodes, Francis DeSales, John Maxwell. Directed by Lesley Selander. Screenplay, Houston Branch, Frederic Louis Fox; camera, Jack Marta; editor, Tony Martinelli; art direction, Ralph Oberg; music, Gerald Roberts. Previewed Sept. 20, '57. Running time, **71 MINS.**

Judy Wingate	Marcia Henderson
Tommy Gray	Peter Walker
Frances Wingate	Katharine Barrett
Ira Molson	Whit Bissell
Midge Brackett	Rita Lynn
Big Hilda	Peg Hillias
Dot Martin	Tracey Roberts
Sheriff	Ray Teal
Eddie Nolan	Ric Roman
Molly	Barbara Eden
District Attorney	Grandon Rhodes
Investigator Butler	Francis DeSales
Parole Agent	John Maxwell

Only the exhibitor in dire search of filler fare will reap any benefit from "The Wayward Girl," produced under the Variety banner for Republic release. Briefly, it's bad.

The Houston Branch-Frederic Louis Fox screenplay has Marcia Henderson imprisoned after being found guilty on a manslaughter charge. Miss Henderson, it seems, threw an iron at Ric Roman, to stop the unwelcome advances of her stepmother's drunken boyfriend. Actually, however, it was the upset stepmother, who had come in after daughter had left the scene, who finished the b.f. off. Stepmother subsequently turns alcoholic and winds up falling down a flight of stairs, in her hands a written confession of the murder.

Miss Henderson tries hard and has a few good scenes, but there's little interest in the characterization. Others around are Peter Walker, her own b.f.; and Katharine Barret, her stepmother. Also Whit Bissell, a lonely-hearts-clubs-type who—via sub-plot—manages to get Miss Henderson paroled to him for a spell.

Lesley Selander's direction of the William J. O'Sullivan production is off and the technical contributions nothing to rave about, either. *Neal.*

Lucky Jim
(BRITISH)

Cheerful lightweight comedy with Ian ("Private's Progress") Carmichael raising yocks galore as amiable misfit in a British university; a Boulting Bros. winner.

London, Sept. 17.

British Lion release of a Charter Films' (Ray Boulting) production. Stars Ian Carmichael, Terry-Thomas, Hugh Griffith. Directed by John Boulting. Screenplay, Patrick Campbell, from novel by Kingsley Amis; extra dialog, Jeffrey Dell; camera, Max Greene; editor, Max Benedict; music, John Addison. Previewed Studio One, London. Running time, **95 MINS.**

Jim Dixon	Ian Carmichael
Bertrand Welch	Terry-Thomas
Prof. Welch	Hugh Griffith
Christine Callaghan	Sharon Acker
Mrs. Welch	Jean Anderson
Margaret Peel	Maureen Connell
Sir Hector Gore-Urquhart	Clive Morton
University Porter	Reginald Beckwith
Cyril Johns	Kenneth Griffith
Bill Atkinson	Jeremy Hawk
The Principal	John Welch
Contractor	Charles Lamb
Waiter	Jeremy Longhurst
Prof. Hutchinson	Henry Longhurst
Roberts	John Cairney
Glee Singer	Ian Wilson
Miss Wilson	Penny Morrell
Registrar	Ronald Cardew
Taxi Driver	Harry Fowler

Following "Private's Progress" and "Brothers in Law" the Boulting brothers, who leap joyously upon pomposity and deflate it gleefully, can now claim three smash comedy hits in a row. "Lucky Jim," which takes a lighthearted look at British college life, will certainly rock British patrons. Judging by U.S. reception of "Private's Progress," it should register well in America.

Kingsley Amis's novel has been built up into a farcical comedy which, though slim enough in idea, provides plenty of opportunity for smiles, giggles and belly laughs. John Boulting has directed with a lively tempo and even though the comedy situations loom up with inevitable precision, they are still irresistible.

The lightweight story spotlights Ian Carmichael in the sort of predicaments that brought him plaudits in "Private's Progress" and "Brothers in Law." Once again he is the likeable fall guy. What happens to him shouldn't happen to a pooch. But, somehow, blundering amiably along he emerges on the credit side and, of course, gets the girl.

In this film he is a junior history lecturer at a British university in the sticks, who becomes disastrously involved in such serious college goings-on as a ceremonial lecture on "Merrie England" and a procession to honor the new university chancellor. There are also some minor shenanigans such as a riotous car chase, a slaphappy fist fight, a tipsy entry into a wrong bedroom containing a girl he is trying to shake off and a number of other happy-go-lucky situations.

The screenplay, written by Patrick Campbell, but clearly

boosted by the Boulting Brothers' inventiveness, veers from facetiousness to downright slapstick but never lets up on its irresistible attack on the funnybone. Ian Carmichael is a deft light-comedy performer who again proves that he also can take hold of a character and make him believable. He is supported by an array of sterling British actors of whom Terry-Thomas, as a smug high-brow novelist; Hugh Griffith, as a pompous history professor, and Clive Morton, as a University Chancellor with a twinkle in his eye, have the best chances and accept them gratefully.

The pic introduces a new Canadian youngster, Sharon Acker. Miss Acker is a comely, promising young actress but it is difficult to see why the Boulting Brothers claimed with such vigor that they could not find a British actress to play this pleasant but hardly demanding role.

American audiences may find some of the dialog a shade too British, in both writing and delivery while the lensing by Max Greene is uneven, as is the cutting. John Addison's music is appropriately gay and the theme song, sung by Al Fernhead, sets the mood of the film over the credit titles, and is then used most effectively as an occasional linking commentary. *Rich.*

Notti Bianche
(White Nights)
(ITALIAN)

Venice, Sept. 17.

Rank release of a Vides (Franco Gristaldi) production. Stars Maria Schell, Marcello Mastroianni, Jean Marais; features Clara Calamai. Directed by Luchino Visconti. Screeenplay, Visconti, Suso Cecchi D'Amico from story by Dostoiewski; camera, Giuseppe Rotuuno; music, Nino Rota; editor, Mario Searndrei. At Venice Film Festival. Running time, **105 MINS.**

Natalia .... Maria Schell
Mario .... Marcello Mastroianni
Tenant .... Jean Marais
Prostitute .... Clara Calamai

Split reactions noted here at the Venice Fest will probably characterize this film's career abroad although some markets promise well. Others must be sold via the Maria Schell name for marquee bait as well as a prestige pitch. General U. S. chances appear mild. It won second prize at this festival.

Ambitious attempt to update a Dostoiewski tale by the same name doesn't quite come off, never quite reaching necessary credibility. It remains a remarkable intellectual exercise while never really moving the spectator as it should. At times using an interesting flashback technique, this tells the tale of a woman who befriends the upstairs boarder, eventually falling in love with him. He has to leave, but promises to return in exactly a year, setting a meeting place. Meanwhile, girl is approached by another man, who likewise falls for her, offering her the advantage of presence, though she still believes and waits for her promised man. Just as she is about to give up and accept, her old flame turns up once more, and she runs off with him.

Crucial flaw in this film is the portrayal of the boarder by Jean Marais in a stiff, unappealing manner which belies her great love for him. Opposite, Marcello Mastroianni makes her occasional love into a very sympathetic, appealing role, playing it to the hilt in a fine performance. Maria Schell in the key role is very mannered, but manages her usual audience-winning moments.

Others in cast, especially an uncredited old lady playing Maria Schell's grandma, back the key trio ably. Luchino Visconti's direction wavers somewhat at the halfway mark, slowing down the action, though otherwise doing a creditable job with a near-impossible subject. There is no half-way acceptance of his picture: either one believes it, and thinks it's great, or one does not, and the whole pic suffers from it.

A special nod must go to Mario Chiari's giant stage reproduction of a town quarter, an elaborate and functional production effort which deliberately gives the pic its semi-theatrical backdrop and flavor. Giuseppe Rotunno's lensing is also extremely effective in capturing the Nordic, fogbound quality of the story. Other production credits are excellent. *Hawk.*

Un Angel Paso Sobre Brooklyn
(An Angel Passed Over Brooklyn)
(SPANISH—ITALIAN)

Venice, Sept. 17.

Falco-Chamartin production and release. Stars Peter Ustinov, Pablito Calvo; features Aroldo Tieri, Silvia Marco, Maurizio Arena. Directed by Ladislao Vajda. Screenplay, Istvan Bekeffy, G. L. Rondi, Vajda; camera, Salvador Gil; editor, Juan Penas. At Venice Film Festival. Running time, **100 MINS.**

Pozzi .... Peter Ustinov
Filipo .... Pablito Calvo
Bruno .... Aroldo Tieri
Giulia .... Silvia Marco
Alfonso .... Maurizio Arena

Probably noticing that the moppet appeal of Pablito Calvo ("Marcellino" and "Pepote") is wearing thin, director Ladislao Vajda has wisely built this fantasy around Peter Ustinov and an uncanny mongrel dog. But even this is not enough to remove the obviousness of this fable. Hence, it is primarily for lingo spots, a natural on its entertainment and sentimental aspects, but lacks the originality needed for arty house chances.

Ustinov is a harsh, greedy usurer squeezing the immigrants living in his Brooklyn house. He barks through his door at passing peddlers. One of them puts a hex on him and he is turned into a dog until he finds someone to love him. This someone is naturally child actor Pablito Calvo. A chastened Ustinov comes back from his dog days determined to live right and his timid assistant gets his girl for a happy ending in an extremely well fabricated Brooklyn set.

Ustinov gets some dimension into his before and after chores. The old adage holds half true; it is hard to surpass a dog actor in a pic, but Ustinov wins over the waning child actor Calvo.

Others in the cast are adequate in their stereotyped roles. Why the pic was set in Brooklyn is not clear. It could have had any locale. The principal house is said to have been built by a homesick Peapolitain. Actually, it was made in Naples and no house like that exists today in Brooklyn. Perhaps it did, but this pic depends on mining its sentimental qualities for best results. Technical credits are above par. *Mosk.*

Paradis Terrestre
(Paradise on Earth)
(FRANCO-ITALIAN)

Venice, Sept. 17.

NORIA Film release of a Noria-Les Films du Centaure production. Directed by Luciano Emmer. Commentary by Raymond Queneau. Screenplay, Lo-Duca, Pierre Kast; music, Roman Vlad; editor, Robert Enrico; lensed in Eastman-color by several cameramen. At Venice Fest. Shown out of competition. Running time, **85 MINS.**

Feature documentary is composite of work by several expeditions sent out to such far-removed places as the Amazon River, Central Africa, Tahiti, India, Indo-China, the Pacific, etc., coming up with much still original footage. In some cases the material has been seen in other recent documentary features (notably the Italian "Last Paradise").

Either in its present form or split into segments, this film could serve as interesting fare in specialized markets. Here the censorship problems presents itself, with pic replete with nude natives and similar censorial headaches (17 cuts have already been asked for in Italy).

Material at hand has been skillfully blended by Luciano Emmer, while top-quality lab work has resulted in fine color rendering of footage claimed to have been shot in 16m, when blown up to 35m. Pic is more in straightforward scientific vein than in the re-staged spectacular manner found in most other recent such documentary features. Script, commentary and musical backdrop, seconded by locally recorded material, are in keeping. *Hawk.*

Il Grido
(The Cry)
(ITALO-AMERICAN)

Venice, Sept. 17.

CEI-INCOM release of an SPA Cinematografica-Robert Alexander Productions coproduction. Stars Steve Cochran, Alida Valli; features Dorian Gray, Lyn Shaw, Betsy Blair, Gabriella Pallotti, Mirna Girardi. Directed by Michelangelo Antonioni. Screenplay, Antonioni, Ennio De-Concini, Elio Bartolini, from story by Antonioni; camera, Gianni Di Venanzo; music, Giovanni Fusco; editor, Eraldo Da Roma. At Venice Fest. Shown out of competition. Running time, **115 MINS.**

Aldo .... Steve Cochran
Irma .... Alida Valli
Virginia .... Dorian Gray
Elvia .... Betsy Blair

Slow-paced filmization of an interesting story, at least in its present lengthy form, is a difficult subject to appraise as a commercial entity. With considerable trimming and some re-editing to aid the jumpy continuity, pic might do as an arty entry.

Story told is of a man (Cochran) who has been living for seven years with a married woman, Alida Valli, with whom he's had a child. When she hears of her husband's death in Australia, she confesses to her lover that she's in love with another man. Cochran tries to win her back, but failing, leaves town with their child in an attempt to forget her. He has several other more and less serious affairs with other women, but Valli is still the only one he loves. After more than a year of wandering, he returns home, only to find she has had another child by her new love. Desperate, chased by Valli, he runs up a granary tower and either falls or jumps off.

Cochran is convincing in the lead, as are Lyn Shaw, Betsy Blair and others in minor roles. A standout thespic job is turned in by Dorian Gray as one of his wayside loves. Antonioni's pace is often obsessively slow in rendering the grey, depressing setting and life in his native Po Valley countryside, but it contains many telling slices of life. He has had a top-drawer assist from lenser Gianni DiVenanzio and from Giovanni Fusco, who provided the musical score in the same melancholy key. Other technical credits are excellent. Pic has had and may still encounter censor trouble. *Hawk.*

Oeil Pour Oeil
(Eye For An Eye)
(FRENCH-ITALIAN)

Venice, Sept. 17.

UGC release of UGC-Jolly Film production. Stars Curd Jurgens, Folco Lulli; features, Lea Padovani, Paul Frankeur, Pascal Audret, Dario Moreno. Directed by Andre Cayatte. Screenplay, Vahe Katcha, Cayatte from novel by Katcha; camera (Technicolor), Christian Matras; editor, Paul Cayatte; dialog, Pierre Bost; sets, Jacques Colombier; music, Louiguy. At Venice Fest. Running time, **105 MINS.**

Walter .... Curd Jurgens
Bortak .... Folco Lulli
Lola .... Lea Padovani
Sick Man .... Paul Frankeur
Sister .... Pascal Audret
Walter .... Dario Moreno

Director Andre Cayatte veers from his usual pix on justice and law, and has undertaken "case of conscience" on the screen. However, he mixes well-worn suspense tactics with a trek across the desert in which an avenger and his victim find their moments of truth. Film remains grim and downbeat, rarely making the theme and or plot plausible. Thus, it looks like mainly an art house item in the U.S. where its offbeat theme might be plus a factor. But plenty of bally will be needed.

Locale is Lebanon and a tired doctor (Curd Jurgens) goes home to relax after a weary day. Folco Lulli comes to ask him to look after his ailing wife. The doctor refuses to see him and sends him to the hospital instead. The next day he finds the wife has died on the operating table, due to the doctor's error, and it is intimated that Jurgens might have saved her. Jurgens becomes constantly aware of the presence of the husband wherever he goes. The wily Oriental finally gets him to go out to a desert outpost to prove he would help anybody and the remainder of the pic is a trek across said desert, by the two men after the doctor's auto has been put out of commission.

Hunger, thirst, fatigue, impending madness and unspoken guilts and threats make up this nightmarish trek. It finally winds with both doomed to death. Jurgens rarely imbues his character with feeling or awareness of the situation. Lulli is a definite presence and registers as the anguished husband seeking an Oriental revenge.

Cayatte has given this a good rendering of locale but the use of color detracts from the theme. Production dress is good. Jurgens has since made pix in the U.S. and if he grows into a name, this might be a plus item. Otherwise, this offbeater would need plenty of selling for any American chances. Technical credits are fine. *Mosk.*

Les Girls
(C'SCOPE-COLOR-MUSIC)

Sock musical with Cole Porter tunes, Jack Cole choreography and Mitzi Gaynor, Kay Kendall, Taina Elg and Gene Kelly in the starring roles. Another big one for producer Sol Siegel. Boffo b.o.

Metro release of Sol C. Siegel production. Stars Gene Kelly, Mitzi Gaynor, Kay Kendall, Taina Elg. Directed by George Cukor. Screenplay, John Patrick; story, Vera Caspary; camera (C'Scope), Robert Surtes; editor, Ferris Webster; songs, Cole Porter; dances, Jack Cole; musical adaptor and conducter, Adolph Deutsch; orchestrations, Alexander Courage & Skip Martin; vocal supervision, Robert Tucker. Previewed in N. Y. Sept. 5, '57. Running time, **114 MINS.**

Barry Nichols .... Gene Kelly
Joy Henderson .... Mitzi Gaynor
Lady Wren .... Kay Kendall
Angele Ducros .... Taina Elg
Pierre Ducros .... Jacques Bergerac
Sir Gerald Wren .... Leslie Phillips
Judge .... Henry Daniell
Sir Percy .... Patrick Macnee
Mr. Outward .... Stephen Vercoe
Assoc. Judge .... Philip Tonge

"Les Girls" is an exceptionally tasty musical morsel that should help to satiate the somewhat emaciated Metro lion and, at the same time, provide the necessary fodder to satisfy hungry theatre turnstiles. The tinted tuner is in the best tradition of the studio, long known and honored for its song-and-dance contributions.

It's an original and zestful entry that would have been greeted with critical handsprings if it had been originally presented on the Broadway stage. As it now stands, it represents a major effort in the art of the film musical and, as such, should rate prominent attention when the annual year-end accolades are passed around. It's almost certain to receive the approval of the film appraisers; it's sufficiently sophisticated to attract the more discerning film patrons; and it has the entertainment ingredients that will appeal to mass audiences. The parlay represents sock b.o. all the way.

First-rank creators have combined their talents to make "Les Girls" a breezy and polished film. They include producer Sol C. Siegel, scripter John Patrick, director George Cukor, composer-lyricist Cole Porter, and Vera Caspary, who provided the story. The framework they have supplied lends itself perfectly to the international cast Siegel has assembled to execute the contributions of Patrick and Porter. Gene Kelly, Mitzi Gaynor, Kay Kendall and Taina Elg whisk through the proceedings in uncommonly appealing fashion and each one contributes almost equally to the ultimate success of the picture.

The musical is set in London, Paris and Granada, Spain. It's the story of a song-and-dance team made up of Kelly and the Misses Gaynor, Kendall and Elg. Known as "Barry Nichols and Les Girls," they are a popular Continental act.

Many years after the act has broken up, Miss Kendall, now the wife of an English peer, has written a book of reminiscences about her experiences as a member of "Les Girls." Miss Kendall's version of what took place in the lives of "Les Girls" lands her in a London court, the defendant in a libel suit brought by a sister-member of the act, Miss Elg, now married to a French industrialist.

The court trial provides the setting for a series of flashbacks as three members of the "Les Girls" troupe—Kelly and the Misses Kendall and Elg—testify as to what took place in the past. Each gives a decidedly different version of what happened and it leaves the question of "what is truth?" completely up in the air. It's not a case of deliberate falsehoods on the part of any member of the trio, but on indication that the same incidents can look different to different people.

Miss Kendall, as the British member of the troupe, pictures Miss Elg as a forward, brassy, and grasping member of the act who deliberately sets out to attract Kelly, two-times her future husband, and attempts suicide when Kelly eventually turns her down. Miss Elg, as the pert French member of the act, tells the court that it was actually Miss Kendall who had carried on with Kelly and tried to commit suicide. Kelly's concept differs materially from that of both girls. He wasn't interested in either one of them, he says, and actually had his eye on Miss Gaynor, who is now his wife. Neither of the girls attempted suicide, he testifies, and that both were accidentally overcome from the gas fumes of a faulty heater.

The excursion into the past provides the setting for a number of Porter tunes and dances brightly staged by Jack Cole as "Les Girls" appear in niteries in France and Spain. Porter has created seven new songs for the picture. While they may not represent his most distinguished score, they nevertheless fit the context of the picture perfectly. "Ca C'est L'Amour," sung by Kelly and Miss Elg, has a good chance of catching on as a pop hit. Other sock routines include "Ladies in Waiting," sung and danced by the three girls; "Your Just Too, Too," sung by Kelly and Miss Kendall; "Why Am I So Gone About That Gal?" danced and sung by Kelly and Miss Gaynor; and "The Rope Song," danced by Kelly and Miss Elg. The lyrics of the song have the unmistakable Porter stamp.

Miss Kendall, heretofore known to U.S. audiences as the trumpet-blowing model in the British import "Genevieve," emerges as a delightful comedienne in her first American picture. Her performance in "Les Girls," a truly blockbuster contribution, marks her as a star of the first magnitude. Her services will be much in demand from now on by Hollywood producers.

Miss Elg, the Finnish actress-ballerina who portrays a French girl, more than lives up to Metro's hopes for her in her first important role. She has a quality that is exceedingly appealing and it will come as no surprise to see her importantly cast in future Metro productions.

Miss Gaynor, as the American member of "Les Girls," is enjoying what appears to be a rebirth of her young career. Her performance as the wholesome, uncomplicated member of the troupe contributes greatly to the new faith the industry has shown in her ability and which has been marked by her selection to play the coveted role of Nellie Forbush in "South Pacific."

"Kelly, in his first song-and-dance role since "It's Always Fair Weather" two years ago, again demonstrates why he has been for so many years one of the top performers in musical films. Jacques Bergerac, as Miss Elg's husband; Leslie Phillips, as Miss Kendall's ditto, and Henry Daniell, as the presiding judge, lend good support.

Siegel who appears to have become Metro's most potent producer, has again provided topnotch production values in assembling his tasty package. Cukor provides just the right touch in his directorial guidance of his spirited cast. The technical staff, including cameraman Robert Surtees, art directors William A. Horning and Gene Allen, musical conductor and adaptor Adolph Deutsch and vocal supervisor Robert Tucker, contributes equally to the picture's overall success. *Holl.*

Teen Age Thunder

Kid wants a hot-rod car; dad says no. Very routine.

Hollywood, Sept. 27.

Howco release of Jacques Marquette production. Stars Charles Courtney, Melinda Byron, Robert Fuller; features Tyler McVey, Paul Bryar, Helene Heigh. Directed by Paul Helmick. Screenplay, Rudy Makoul; camera, Marquette; editor, Irving Schoenberg; music, Walter Greene. Previewed Sept. 25, '57. Running time, **78 MINS.**

Johnnie Simpson........Charles Courtney
Betty Palmer .... Melinda Byron
Maurie Weston .... Robert Fuller
Frank Simpson .... Tyler McVey
Bert Morrison .... Paul Bryar
Aunt Martha .... Helene Heigh
Sgt. Benson .... Gilbert Perkins
Used Car Salesman ...... Bing Russell
Jimmy Morrison .... Gregory Marshall
Mr. Palmer .... Marshall Kent
Sis Palmer .... Mona McKinnon

This Marquette production is a run-of-the-mill addition to the seemingly endless spate of ales of teenagers and parents who don't dig them. Howco is releasing film as a combo with "Carnival Rock," also reviewed in this issue.

The Rudy Makoul screenplay centers around Charles Courtney, a hot rod enthusiast whose father, Tyler McVey, won't let him have one. This causes a breach between the two. Courtney goes to work in the local filling station, run by Paul Bryar, and while not servicing cars both of them work on a hot rod latter is building to enter in "the big race" in the name of his polio-stricken son. Wind-up, of course, finds Courtney winning the race. The father, with a new understanding of his son, then buys him road-burner of his own.

Courtney is very good in lead and future good casting could well achieve a juve following. Also starred, and okay, are Melinda Byron, as Courtney's frail, and Robert Fuller, as a cocky youth who makes his kicks needling Courtney. McVey is good as the father; ditto Bryar as the service station operator.

Paul Helmick's direction of the Jacques Marquette production runs along stock lines, and the technical contributions are average. *Neal.*

No Down Payment
(C'SCOPE)

Suburbia dissected. Good cast. Lotsa human angles. Positive b.o. outlook despite unpleasant story.

20th-Fox release of Jerry Wald production. Stars Joanne Woodward, Sheree North, Tony Randall, Jeffrey Hunter, Cameron Mitchell, Patricia Owens, Barbara Rush, Pat Hingle; features Robert Harris, Aki Aleong, Jim Hayward. Directed by Martin Ritt; screenplay, Philip Yordan from John McPartland novel; camera, Joseph La Shelle; music, Leigh Harline, conducted by Lionel Newman; editor, Louis Loeffler. Previewed in N. Y. Sept. 19, '57. Running time, **105 MINS.**

Leola Boone ....Joanne Woodward
Isabelle Flagg ....Sheree North
Jerry Flagg ....Tony Randall
David Martin ....Jeffrey Hunter
Troy Boone ....Cameron Mitchell
Jean Martin ....Patricia Owens
Betty Kreitzer ....Barbara Rush
Herman Kreitzer .... Pat Hingle
Markham ....Robert Harris
Iko .... Aki Aleong
Mr. Burnett ....Jim Hayward
Sandra Kreitzer ....Mimi Gibson
Harmon Kreitzer ....Donald Towers
Michael Flagg ....Charles Herbert

The frictions and subterranean strains and stresses of suburban living are expertly though unpleasantly explored in this slick Jerry Wald production. No question that, with the current migration to the suburbs and the boom-produced mode of modern living and buying "on credit," this film should provide the base for immediate identification on the part of many couples who find themselves in similar circumstances. And such self-identification should help the ticket sale.

Director Martin Ritt (moving over from tv) has done his best to deal realistically with the assorted characters from the John McPartland novel. The flaws of the book are, to a degree, aggravated in the picture and the revamping of the ending—almost everyone ends up going to church—adds an incongruous contrivance. Yet, the picture makes its point, and in-between the dramatics there is a glimmering of the predicament of the new mortgaged middle-class, groping for security and struggling hard to afford the luxuries and conveniences made attractive via the "No Down Payment" come-on.

If this is a social documentary, the pill has been properly sugar-coated by writer Philip Yordan. He has concentrated primarily on the problems of a number of couples, living at uncomfortably close quarters in a California housing development. Yordan can't be blamed for making this nucleus of society as diverse as possible to achieve story contrast. Unfortunately, this makes it difficult to believe the affinity of the protagonists. They are—with a single exception—unpleasant characters.

The film has been very well cast and the performances all are strongly on its credit side. Joanne Woodward as Leola Boone, wife of the cruel and tyrannical Troy, etches the film's best portrayal. She makes the childish, loyal Leola, covering up her deep hurt over having given up an illegitimate child, a moving character and she is far and away the most real of all the people in the picture. Here perhaps is one of the screen's top talents in the making.

Tony Randall also does a sock job as the shiftless, irresponsible Jerry Flagg, the used-car salesman. It's a distinct change-of-pace for him and he makes the most of a juicy role. He handles the comedy lines with deft assurance and subordinates them to the more desperate aspects of the man he portrays. Sheree North as his wife offers an agreeable surprise in a straight part.

In other lead roles, Cameron Mitchell, the man with the "leader" complex, is harsh and unpleasant as per the script. The rape scene with Patricia Owens is well handled, making for a climactic moment, though Miss Owens' reaction—she's married to the weak Jeffrey Hunter in the picture—is inadequately explained. In the book she resents the attack, but reacts positively to Mitchell). Hunter is goodlooking, but that's just about all.

Pat Hingle, the only sane, sturdy

character in the plot, is strong in the role of the anchor man, and so is his wife, Barbara Rush. It will occur to some that this is a motley crew of characters, thrown at one another's mercy by dint of their proximity to one another and the similarity of their economic circumstance. Similarity to real-life situations would be coincidental and not wholly real, since people aren't wholly dependent on their neighbors.

Ritt's direction is crisp and effective, with many endearing little human touches. Yordan's script, with some soap opera overtones, has retained the essentials of the McPartland novel. Probably due to the Code, Mitchell has to die in the end after an exciting slugfest with Hunter. Finals sees everyone going to Sunday services, except Miss Woodward, who goes off in a taxi.

There's a brief reference to the race problem, this time involving Nisei who want to move into the neighborhood. Hingle and Miss Rush end up deciding to fight for their rights.

Joseph La Shelle's lensing is helpful in establishing the mood of the setting, where people look into one another's livingrooms via the backporch. Louis Loeffler's editing is fine. Ditto the Leigh Harline musical background.

"No Down Payment" has exploitable handles as a (painful) reflection of life in America suburbia. It should ring the bell with millions of young couples. *Hift.*

Girl in Black Stockings

Good murder mystery.

Hollywood, Sept. 30.

United Artists release of Aubrey Schenck production. Stars Lex Barker, Anne Bancroft, Mamie Van Doren. Ron Randell, Marie Windsor, John Dehner; features John Holland, Diana Vandervlis, Richard Cutting, Larry Chance. Directed by Howard W. Koch. Screenplay, Richard Landau; story, "Wanton Murder," Peter Godfrey; camera, Mark Margulies; editor, John F. Schreyer; production designer, Jack T. Collis; music, Les Baxter. Previewed Sept. 24, '57. Running time, 75 MINS.
David Hewson .... Lex Barker
Beth Dixon .... Anne Bancroft
Harriet Ames ...... Mamie Van Doren
Edmund Parry .... Ron Randell
Julia Parry .... Marie Windsor
Sheriff Holmes .... John Dehner
Norman Grant .... John Holland
Louise Miles .... Diana Vandervlis
Dr. Younger .... Richard Cutting
Indian Joe .... Larry Chance
Joseph Felton .... Gene O'Donnell
Frankie Pierce .... Gerald Frank
Fred, a Deputy Sheriff..Karl MacDonald
Amos .... Norman Leavitt
Justice of the Peace Fred Walters
                         David Dwight
Brackett .... Mark Bennett
Prentiss .... Stuart Whitman
Hib, a Deputy Sheriff....Mickey Whiting

The whodunit, with final-reel exposure of the culprit, has been a film rarity as of late. Comes along now to take care of this Bel-Air's "The Girl in Black Stockings," a welcome addition to the general program market. With Lex Barker, Anne Bancroft and Mamie Van Doren—among others—film actually could top an all-suspense bill with ease.

Completed some 14 months ago, "Stockings" also shapes up as another rarity—non-western located in and around Kanab, Utah, which long has been a popular sagebrush location site. Arrival at a resort there for a rest is attorney Lex Barker, who soon turns his attention to one of its employees—Anne Bancroft. All attention, however, is soon diverted when the mutilated body of a young girl is found. Several other murders occur in the

---

course of events with these the other prime characters-suspects: Mamie Van Doren, guest at the lodge; Ron Randell, invalid proprietor of the lodge; and Marie Windsor, his sister. Sheriff John Dehner, with, of course, the help of Barker, has the guilty one (Miss Bancroft) in tow at the fade-out. She's a psycho, it seems.

Barker and Miss Bancroft are both good in top spots, while Miss Van Doren has little to do but get murdered. The other performances are average.

Richard Landau's well-developed screenplay has received good direction from Howard W. Koch, and the various technical contributions all measure up.

Deserving a nod for the overall result is exec producer Aubrey Schenck. *Neal.*

Malwa
(Color)
(RUSSIAN)

Venice, Sept. 24.
Unset release of a Kiev Film Studio production. Stars Zidra Ritenbergs, Pavel Usovicenko, Anatoli Ighnative; features Ghennady Iutkhin, Aleksei Tolbusin. Directed by Vladimir Braun. Screenplay, Nikolai Kovarski, from story by Maxim Gorki; camera (Sovolor), Vladimir Voitenko; music, Igor Sciamo. At Venice Fest. Running time, 85 MINS.
Malwa .... Zidra Ritenbergs
Vassili .... Pavel Usovicenko
Iakov .... Anatoli Ighnatiev

This pic, based on story by Maxim Gorki, looks an okay lingual entry reserved for Russo houses in the U. S. It contains no propaganda and tells its story of a woman who hates to be tied down to the love of one man. This is done in a straightforward, appealing manner.

Fishing village setting, color and good performances by all concerned add to interest value of film in which the earthy, hefty thesping of Zidra Ritenbergs as Malwa stands out. She copped the femme acting award at this fest. Vladimir Braun's last direction effort (he died recently) is faithful to the original story in feeling and mood. He makes the most of his actors and setting for an all-round pleasing effect. *Hawk.*

Hell Bound

One more in dope cycle. Okay programmer.

Hollywood, Sept. 25.
United Artists release of Howard W. Koch production. Stars John Russell, June Blair, Stuart Whitman, Margo Woode; features George Mather, Stanley Adams, Gene O'Donnell, Frank Fenton, Virginia De Lee. Exec producer, Aubrey Schenck. Director, William J. Hale Jr. Screenplay, Richard Landau, from story by Landau and Arthur Orloff; camera, Carl E. Guthrie; editor, John A. Bushelman; production designer, Jack T. Collis; music, Les Baxter. Previewed Sept. 20, '57. Running time, 69 MINS.
Jordon .... John Russell
Paula .... June Blair
Eddie Mason .... Stuart Whitman
Jan .... Margo Woode
Stanley Thomas .... George Mather
Herbert Fay Jr........... Stanley Adams
Purser .... Gene O'Donnell
Harry Quantro .... Frank Fenton
Stripteaser .... Virginia De Lee
Daddy .... Dehl Berti
Murdered Seaman .... Sammee Tong
Ship Captain .... Charles Webster
Squad Officer .... Edward DeRoo
Nurses ....Marge Evans, Ann Daro
Detective .... Frank McGrath
Quantro's Men..Kay Garrett. Bob Strong,
                         George Mayon
Accomplice "A," 16mm film   Red Morgan
Accomplice "B," 16mm film
                         Dick Standish
Purser, 16mm film .... William Flaherty
Ship Captain, 16mm film
                     George H. Whiteman
Dock Worker .... Richard Martin
Police Officer at Auto Accident
                         Jerry Frank

Doctor .... Larry Thor
Aide .... Scott Peters

Latest in cycle of features dealing with the evils of dope, "Hell Bound" will cause no special commotion due to a lack of star names and fact public interest in such type films is presumably on the wane. This one was produced under the Bel-Air banner for United Artists release.

Story by Richard Landau and Arthur Orloff, as screenplayed by the former, has a novel, interesting beginning: A brief, 16m run-off of a film turned out by master-mind criminal John Russell, partially shows an ingenious plan to steal war surplus narcotics worth over $2,000,000 from a ship in L.A. Harbor. Russell has turned out the film so as to get "backers" for his scheme, which he does via gangster Frank Fenton. Latter, to insure his investment, sends along June Blair to act as one of Russell's accomplices. Plans go according to schedule until Miss Blair falls for Stuart Whitman, ambulance driver who unknowingly becomes involved in the crime. This leads to a series of events which end with Russell's death, safe delivery of the dope and a loving Whitman at Miss Blair's side.

Russell is convincing as the brutal criminal leader; his violent "roughing-up" of some of the cast members, however, will not appeal to the squeamish. June Blair (subsequently term-pacted by 20th-Fox) is a looker with above-average dramatic ability, while Whitman makes an extremely good impression as her later vis-a-vis. Margo Woode, fourth "co-star," is good as the nurse whom Miss Blair replaces in the "plan."

The Howard W. Koch production, on which Aubrey Schenck functioned as exec producer, is well directed by William J. Hole Jr., one-time script supervisor-turned tv director who herewith makes his feature-film debut. The action is especially well staged, and makes fine use of some off-beat backgrounds.

Technical contributions are par for the course. *Neal.*

Nosotros Dos
(We Two)
(MEXICAN)

Mexico City, Sept. 24.
Cinematographica Mexicana release of Diana Films production. Stars Rossana Podesta; features Tito Junco, Marco Vicario, Jose Maria Lado, Julia C. Alba. Directed by Emilio Fernandez. Camera, Alex Philips, screenplay, M. L. Algara. At Cine Mariscala, Mexico City. Running time, 91 MINS.

Though this is between the arty and popular sectors of cinema fare, it is good boxiffce because of the beauty, vivacity and chic of the star, Rossana Podesta; excellent lensing by the veteran Alex Philips, and the mastery of one of Mexico's top directors, Emilio Fernandez. Costumer Cornejo really rates an Oscar for the fine wardrobe given Miss Podesta. Her gowns accentuate her charms.

The story is not so much. The much-done tale of lovers getting together over the long bitter feuding of their families. Miss Podesta and the work of Philips and Fernandez put this across strongly. It is typically Spanish as it stresses the dour pride of people who have lived frugally for ages and have always had to fight hard for what they get, too often very little. Humor is infrequent, and that is acrid.

The star and her chic appearance

---

even when toting a rifle and a Spanish folk dance by a sightly, sprightly mixed duo lend worthwhile relief to the solemness that is almost drab. *Doug.*

Raintree County
(COLOR—CAMERA 65)

Pictorially big Civil War Romance. Names and strong campaign best assets.

Metro release of David Lewis production. Stars Montgomery Clift, Elizabeth Taylor, Eva Marie Saint, Nigel Patrick; features Lee Marvin, Rod Taylor, Agnes Moorehead, Walter Abel. Directed by Edward Dmytryk. Screenplay, Millard Kaufman (who's also associate producer), based on novel by the late Ross Lockridge Jr.; camera (Technicolor, 65m), Robert Surtees; editor, John Dunning; music, Johnny Green; title song lyric by Paul Francis Webster. Reviewed at Brown Theatre, Louisville, Ky., Oct. 2, '57. Running time, **187 MINS.**

John Wickliff Shawnessy ... Montgomery Clift
Susanna Drake ... Elizabeth Taylor
Nell Gaither ... Eva Marie Saint
Jerusalem Webster Stiles ... Nigel Patrick
Orville "Flash" Perkins ... Lee Marvin
Garwood B. Jones ... Rod Taylor
Ellen Shawnessy ... Agnes Moorehead
T. D. Shawnessy ... Walter Abel
Barbara Drake ... Jarma Lewis
Bobby Drake ... Tom Drake
Ezra Gray ... Rhys Williams
Niles Foster ... Russell Collins
Southern Officer ... DeForest Kelley

"Raintree County" is one of the biggest and costliest (estimated at $5,000,000) productions from Metro since its release of David O. Selznick's "Gone With the Wind." Lensed via the "Camera 65" process (65m negative is used and reduced to 35m for release prints), this is a study of emotional conflicts set against the Civil War turmoil, and done with pictorial sweep. Its three-hour length and a certain vagueness in characterizations will create certain b.o. problems.

Cued by the lavishness, Metro plans call for roadshowing (as currently at the Brown Theatre, Louisville), and this suggests, immediately, an aura of importance. Cast is a strong one: Elizabeth Taylor, Montgomery Clift, Eva Marie Saint and Nigel Patrick, although not uniformly well handled. Spectacular color photography by Robert Surtees, is a real plus. All in all "Raintree" has the trappings of bigtime picture-making.

Story unfolds against a background of historic events—the war, Abraham Lincoln's election, the Northern abolition movement, Southern secession, etc. Metro shot on location near Danville, Ky., for the most part. Swamp scenes were taken at Reelfoot Lake, Tiptonville, Tenn., and ante-bellum Southern mansions were lensed in Natchez, Miss., and nearby Port Gibson.

The settings at the start is Raintree County, Indiana, where Clift and Miss Saint are blissfully in love and looking ahead to life together. Miss Taylor, whose troubled mind is later revealed, comes as a visitor from New Orleans and woos Clift away from Miss Saint and into marriage.

They take up residence in the deep south where the slavery issue is exposed to Clift, who abhors it, and the couple returns to Raintree. At first distressed by the upheaval of the times, Miss Taylor eventually becomes insane. Taking her young son with her, she runs again to her native Dixie. Clift enters the Union Army.

There's a reunion after the war as Clift discovers his son in Atlanta, which encounter leads to his finding Miss Taylor who is now in an asylum. The subsequent development, basically is logical. Miss Taylor regains soundness of mind for a period, then again cracks up, and in desperate search for the raintree (which, indeed, actually exists) she drowns. It is in pursuit of her that Miss Saint, still in love with Clift, and the latter come upon the tree.

While the production is of epic proportions, the marathon running time of more than three hours is questionable. It's a big picture in terms of pictorial size but the story doesn't always match the scope of the production. Chief story fault lies in its vagueness—the not truly specified motivations of the principals and in the conflicts involved in Clift's search for happiness alternately with Miss Saint and Miss Taylor.

Under Edward Dmytryk's direction, this adaption by Millard Kaufman of the late Ross Lockridge Jr.'s novel unfolds fairly interestingly but slowly. Picture lacks highlight material; even the war scenes don't quite have the necessary impact and the relationship between Miss Taylor and Clift could have been charged up more.

There is a fine performance by the idealist Clift, a firm portrayal of the unbalanced wife by Miss Taylor, and sensitive work by Miss Saint. Forceful are the characters rendered by Nigel Patrick, Lee Marvin, Rod Taylor, Agnes Moorehead, Walter Abel, Rhys Williams, Jarma Lewis, Tom Drake, Russell Collins, DeForrest Kelley and Myrna Hansen.

David Lewis' production is topnotch physically. Sets and backgrounds generally are an eyeful and considerable authenticity is gotten across in pictorial detail and costumes. Title song by Paul Francis Webster and Johnny Green has an engaging quality plus the additional benefit of radio and television exposure via Nat King Cole's fine rendition. Art directors William J. Horning and Urie McCleary; Edwin B. Willis and Hugh Hunt, in charge of decorations; Walter Plunkett, costumes, and editor John Dunning all rate kudos for their respective contributions.

Johnny Green's score is expert backdropping, and the Technicolor photography by Surtees is excellent. The "65" process rates as high-calibre widescreen. *Gene.*

Carnival Rock

Rock 'n' roller which Howco is packaging with "Teen Age Thunder." Satisfactory within its category.

Howco release of Roger Corman production. Stars Susan Cabot, Brian Hutton, David J. Stewart; features Dick Miller, Iris Adrian, Jonathan Haze, Ed Nelson, The Platters, David Houston, Bob Luman, The Shadows, The Blockbusters. Directed by Corman. Screenplay, Leo Lieberman; camera, Floyd Crosby; editor, Charles Gross, Jr.; production designer, Robert Kinoshita; music, Walter Greene, Buck Ram. Previewed Sept. 25, '57. Running time, **75 MINS.**

Natalie ... Susan Cabot
Stanley ... Brian Hutton
Christy ... David J. Stewart
Ben ... Dick Miller
Celia ... Iris Adrian
Max ... Jonathan Haze
Cannon ... Ed Nelson
Slug ... Chris Alcalde
M. C. ... Horace Logan
Mother ... Yvonne Peattie
Boy ... Gary Hunley
Billy ... Frankie Ray
Clara ... Dorothy Neuman
Cleaning Lady No. 1 ... Clara Andressa
Cleaning Lady No. 2 ... Terry Blake
With the music of The Platters, David Houston, Bob Luman, The Shadows, The Blockbusters.

Overtones of Pagliacci and out-and-out rock 'n' roll have been mixed together by producer-director Roger Corman for okay results in Howco's "Carnival Rock." Film is being packaged with "Teen Age Thunder," also reviewed in this issue.

Locale of the Leo Lieberman screenplay is a run-down nitery on an ocean pier operated in conjunction with a carnival. Boss-man is David J. Stewart, middle-aged former burlesque comic. He's hopelessly in love with Susan Cabot, singer at the spot, but she's in love with Brian Hutton, a gambler. Latter subsequently cuts high cards with Stewart and wins his club. Stewart, however, just to be near Miss Cabot, stays on as a burlesque tramp comedian in the rock 'n' roll show. At the wind-up, when Miss Cabot and Hutton marry, Stewart is fired and goes off to seek a new life.

Film has a couple of very good performances in Susan Cabot and Dick Miller, latter as Stewart's aide at the club. Miss Cabot also effectively puts over several song numbers. Brian Hutton does a commendable job with the male lead. In pivotal role, however, Stewart often goes far overboard in his portrayal. The okay musical break-ins come via The Platters, David Houston, Bob Luman, The Shadows and The Blockbusters.

Roger Corman did an okay job as producer, and, for the most part, as director. *Neal.*

L'Amour Est En Jeu
(Love is at Stake)
(FRENCH)

Paris, Oct. 1.

Pathe release of Gibe-Lambor-Contl-nental production. Stars Robert Lamoureux, Annie Girardot; features Yves Noel, Jeanne Aubert, Jacques Jouanneau, Jean Parades. Directed by Marc Allegret. Screenplay, Odette Joyeux from novel by Vanderene, "The Victim"; camera, Walter Wottitz; editor, Suzanne De Troye. At Marignan, Paris. Running time, **90 MINS.**

Bob ... Robert Lamoureux
Marie ... Annie Girardot
Gege ... Yves Noel
Damiano ... Jacques Jouanneau
Mme. Bremont ... Jeanne Aubert
Berlmont ... Jean Parades

A constantly spatting young couple decide to divorce and their eight-year-old son is fought over his affections. Main originality is that the boy likes this, and tries to keep his parents from getting together again. Slight pic is nicely mounted and played but lacks enough depth for art house chances. Film looks good locally but looms only for dualers in U.S.

Robert Lamoureux, as the husband, has a craggy charm while Annie Girardot is properly vinegary but appealing as the frau. Moppet Yves Noel is neither hammy nor completely taking as the child in question.

Director Marc Allegret has given this a clean mounting, but the avoidance of outright comedy or drama makes this an in-betweener for America. Technical credits and production values are good except for the street scenes which seem much too studio-like. *Mosk.*

Slim Carter
(COLOR)

Amusing satire on a western film star. Okay for family situations.

Hollywood, Sept. 26.

Universal release of Howie Horwitz production. Stars Jock Mahoney, Julie Adams, Tim Hovey; features William Hopper, Ben Johnson, Joanna Moore, Bill Williams, Barbara Hale. Directed by Richard H. Bartlett. Screenplay, Montgomery Pittman, from story by David Bramson, Mary C. McCall Jr.; camera (Eastman-color), Ellis W. Carter; editor, Fred MacDowell; music, Herman Stein. Previewed Sept. 24, '57. Running time, **80 MINS.**

Slim Carter ... Jock Mahoney
Clover Doyle ... Julie Adams
Leo Gallagher ... Tim Hovey
Joe Brewster ... William Hopper
Montana Burriss ... Ben Johnson
Charlene Carroll ... Joanna Moore
Richard L. Howard ... Walter Reed
Hat Check Girl ... Maggie Mahoney
Cigarette Girl ... Roxanne Arlen
M.C. ... Jim Healy
Frank Hanneman ... Bill Williams
Allie Hanneman ... Barbara Hale

"Slim Carter," uninspired title for this spoof on western screen heroes, is well turned out but it's a moot question whether satire will pass muster with juve trade. Moppets in their worship of oater stars may resent the implication that any fave sagebrush stalwart can be a heel. Film carries plenty of refreshing humor, however, and the heartwarming tale of an orphan responsible for humanizing the star should make it acceptable for family market, where names of Jock Mahoney, Julie Adams and Tim Hovey will spark its chances.

Hollywood background of the Howie Horwitz production provides good color for story of an egotistical smalltime western cafe entertainer who becomes a star in his first picture. Mahoney in this character is discovered by Miss Adams, femme studio publicist, who is handed the arduous chore by studio head of nursing him along in his career, since he's her baby. It's a rough assignment, because everything he does is for effect. When Tim Hovey, an orphan, arrives to spend a month in cowboy star's home as a contest winner, both femme and everyone in studio try to conceal thesp's fakery from lad, who finally converts actor into a human being and is Cupid for the romance.

Richard H. Bartlett in his direction of the Montgomery Pittman screenplay manages a light touch which spells audience interest. For Mahoney, part is a change of pace which he nevertheless handles expertly, and he capably warbles three songs. Miss Adams, though poorly photographed at times, sympathetically punches over her role. One of the outstanding bits of biz in picture is when she socks Joanna Moore, a sex-pot whom Mahoney is romancing, with a roundhouse right in the eye, good for a belly laugh. Miss Moore, a looker, comes through in fine fashion, and young Tim makes the most of every moment.

Bill Williams and Barbara Hale are in for added value for in their characters of a Hollywood couple of many years. Their footage is brief, more on the guest side. William Hopper as a director and Ben Johnson as a stunt man make their work count. Walter Reed is persuasive, too, a studio boss.

Technical credits stack up okay, leading off with Ellis W. Carter's camera work (minus a few shots of femme star). On plus side, too, are art direction by Alexander Golitzen and Eric Orbom, editing by Fred MacDowell, music by Herman Stein. *Whit.*

The Tijuana Story

Although based on real-life vice, a mild, routine meller.

Hollywood, Oct. 4.

A Columbia Pictures release of Sam Katzman production. With Rodolfo Acosta, James Darren, Robert McQueeney, Jean Willes, Joy Stoner, Paul Newlan, George E. Stone, Michael Rox, Robert Blake, William Fawcett, others. Narrator, Paul Coates. Director, Leslie Kardos. Screenplay, Lou Morheim; camera, Benjamin H. Kline; editor, Edwin Bryant; art director, Paul Palmentola; music conducted by Mischa Bakalelnikoff. Previewed in Hollywood, Oct. 3, '57. Running time, **72 MINS.**

Manuel Acosta Mesa..... Rondolfo Acosta
Mitch .... James Darren
Eddie March .... Robert McQueeney
Liz March .... Jean Willes
Linda Alvarez .... Joy Stoner
Peron Diaz .... Paul Newlan
Pino .... George E. Stone
Reuben Galindo .... Michael Fox
Enrique Acosta Mesa.... Robert Blake
Alberto Rodriquez......William Fawcett
Ricardo .... Ric Vallin
Paul Acosta Mesa........Ralph Valencia
Alma Actosta Mesa...... Susan Senforth
Miguel Fuentes..........William Tannen
Lupe .... Susan Ridgeway

Reportedly, producer Sam Katzman kept this project on the shelf a couple of years, because of threats from certain sinister underworld figures. If true, it's hard to see why, since this mild, routine melodrama couldn't step on anyone's toes. It isn't likely to raise a storm at the ticket counter either.

Screenplay by Lou Morheim is based on real-life incidents in Tijuana, including the assassination of crusading newspaperman Manuel Acosta Mesa. Mexican actor Rodolfo Acosta portrays Acosta Mesa, who falls victim here to the machinations of a vice-narcotics ring led by heavy Paul Newlan. However, the editor's fiery writing, arouses the citizenry and his astute digging turns up the names of the corrupt officials and businessmen in the ring. His son, played by Robert Blake, carries on the clean-up campaign successfully after his father's assassination (although there are certain informed quarters who remain rather doubtful about the real-life efficacy of the clean-up).

There's a few side-issues, including a tragic love affair between Joy Stoner, as the editor's secretary, and Yankee James Darren, a victim of the ring; and soul-searching of Gringo Robert McQueeney, who finds himself the more-or-less innocent front of the vicious gang. However, both these tangents are of minor importance and add little to the proceedings.

Production values and direction of Leslie Kardos rarely rise above the level of routinely competent, and more often show the evidence of a short budget and a hurried shooting schedule. Local newsman Paul Coates, who wrote a series of expose columns about Tijuana, introduces the picture and narrates a couple of plot points therein. His contribution isn't very significant, one way or another.

Acosta's fine performance is easily the outstanding thing about this picture. His dignity and force often transcends the weak scripting and makes the editor a considerable figure of courage and warmth.

Best of the rest are McQueeney, Jean Willes as his wife, and Michael Fox as Acosta's vacillating publisher. Rest of cast is okay, save for Miss Stoner. Allowing for her lack of experience, kindest thing which can be said is that she needs a tremendous amount of training.

One peculiarity is worth noting. Acosta, who is a native Mexican, speaks a comparatively accent-proof English. Other cast members portraying Mexicans speak a wide and wild variety of purported Spanish accents. *Kove.*

'I Sogni nel Cassetto
(Dreams in a Drawer)
(FRANCO-ITALIAN)
Venice, Sept. 24.

Cineriz release of a Rizzoli-Francinex production. Stars Lea Massari, Enrico Pagani; features Cosetta Greco, Sergio Tofano. Written and directed by Renato

Castellani. Camera, Leonida Barboni; music, Roman Vlad. At Venice Film Festival. Running time, **105 MINS.**

Lucia .... Lea Massari
Mario .... Enrico Pagani

One of best Italian productions of the year, this pic looks headed for a good boxoffice future both in this country, probably repeating as a crowd-pleaser abroad as well. It crackles rapid-fire dialog can be successfully translated, subtitled and / or dubbed. American chances are iffy and could be much improved by trimming some 10 minutes from the current running time. Even so, it's worth a try.

The "Dreams" are those of a young couple, both students in a North Italian University, who fall in love and marry against better advice. Both are hoping for a brilliant future, both soon reconciling themselves to a happy if brief spell of married life together. While giving birth to their first child, the bride dies, leaving the boy to take up life once more with a new, maturer, lonelier outlook, but with great gratitude for the optimistic, ever-childish girl he married. While the script sometimes falters and often repeats itself, Renato Castellani's penmanship shows in a brilliantly dialogued screenplay and a generally rapid pace in which speedy dissolves play an important dramatic (and comic) part.

Despite the downbeat ending, the film is extremely amusing in its chronicling of romance and early married life of the couple. (Another ending, in which bride does not die was shot before the current one was adopted). Lea Massari, under Castellani's painstaking direction, plays her part in high key in keeping with her screen character, while Enrico Pagani, as the boy, is somewhat in the shadows, though giving an okay reading in his first screen role. Cosetta Greco does a standout bit as a friend while Sergio Tofano and many others are sharply drawn cameos.

Added qualities of the production are found in the interesting north Italian backdrops where action is played out, as well as in Leonida Barboni's expert lensing. Other technical credits measure up. *Hawk.*

The Devil's Hairpin
(V'VISION-COLOR)

Auto racing film with exciting finish; okay for program market.

Hollywood, Oct. 3.
Paramount release of Cornel Wilde production. Stars Cornel Wilde, Jean Wallace; costars Arthur Franz, Mary Astor; features Paul Fix, Larry Pennell, Gerald Milton, Ross Bagdasarian. Directed by Wilde. Screenplay, James Edmiston, Wilde; camera (Technicolor), Daniel L. Fapp; editor, Floyd Knudtson. Previewed Sept. 30, '57. Running time, **83 MINS.**

Nick .... Cornel Wilde
Kelly .... Jean Wallace
Rhinegold .... Arthur Franz
Mrs. Jargin .... Mary Astor
Doc .... Paul Fix
Johnny .... Larry Pennell
Mike Houston .... Gerald Milton
Tani .... Ross Bagdasarian
Chico Martinez .... Jack Kosslyn
Tony Botari .... Morgan Jones

Auto road racing sparks this Cornel Wilde production for Paramount release, which benefits by exciting action in final reels but earlier is bogged down by tedious unfoldment. Subject matter, coupled with Wilde in star role, should

carry it nicely through program situations.

Feature, effectively filmed in Technicolor and with VistaVision adding to pictorial values, is a four-way effort for Wilde, who also directs and co-scripts with James Edmiston. Narrative leading up the racing sequences is confusing and often dull as it rests on a retired former racing champ who is goaded into a return to the wheel. Characters never ring quite true although entire cast tries hard, and Wilde's direction does little to hurdle this fault. From a production standpoint, however, film shows good quality.

Wilde as the egotistical ex-champ who finally dons his racing helmet after most of yarn is told in flashback form flounders occasionally in part, not one of his best. In Jean Wallace as a Martini-swilling blonde he has a beautiful costar, okay for role. Arthur Franz' character of the racing car manufacturer for whom Wilde formerly raced is never clear; it's up to audience to determine whether he's a heavy. Mary Astor plays Wilde's mother, bitter over his having nearly killed his younger brother, Larry Pennell, in a race which left latter somewhat of a mental case, but her makeup is particularly bad. Pennell in his indefinite role is good. Paul Fix lends credence to a mechanic part and Ross Bagdasarian makes the most of a piano-playing role.

Fine photography leads off technical credits, Daniel L. Fapp making his work count and Wallace Kelley handling the second unit stuff. John P. Fulton on special photographic effects and Farciot Edouart on process photography also rate strongly. Hal Pereira and Hilyard Brown created interesting sets and Floyd Knudtson's editing is good. *Whit.*

Retour De Manivelle
(The Turn of the Handle)
(FRENCH)

Paris, Oct. 1.
J. Arthur Rank release of Inermondia production. Stars Michele Morgan, Daniel Gelin; features Bernard Blier, Peter Van Eyck, Michele Mercier. Directed by Denys De La Patelliere. Screenplay, Michel Audiard, Patelliere; camera, Pierre Montazel; editor, George Alepee. At Balzac, Paris. Running time, **105 MINS.**

Helene .... Michele Morgan
Robert .... Daniel Gelin
Eric .... Peter Van Eyck
Inspector .... Bernard Blier
Girl .... Michele Mercier
Babin .... Francois Chaumette

There are shades of the "Postman Always Rings Twice" in this slick melodrama. An itinerant artist saves a drunk and takes him home with him, eventually making him his chauffeur. Artist is ruined financially and commits suicide. Then the wife enlist's the bewildered hero's aid to disguise it as a crime. All because the husband said he had cut out the suicide clause from his insurance policy.

Familiar bundle of suspense appears to limit this for art houses in the U.S. The telegraphed development may hurt some, but it should have a better fate than some dualers since its theme and some exploitable macabre bits may help.

Some twists, frank love scenes and dialogue bolster its Stateside chances. Daniel Gelin adds some weight, too, as the quizzical re-converted chauffeur who goes along with the machinations of the widow, coldly played by Michele Morgan. He even seduces a silly maid (woodenly done by Michele Mercier).

Technical credits are slick and

production dress acceptable. But director Denys De La Patelliere has rarely gotten a visual feel into this. The love and suspense scenes are usually obvious and seldom realistic. Some lesser acting roles help, especially Bernard Blier's plodding but smart police inspector. *Mosk.*

The Tin Star
(V'VISION)

Quality western with names of Henry Fonda and Anthony Perkins to send it.

Hollywood, Oct. 10.

Paramount release of William Perlberg-George Seaton production. Stars Henry Fonda, Anthony Perkins; costars Betsy Palmer, Michel Ray, Neville Ray, John McIntire. Directed by Anthony Mann. Screenplay, Dudley Nichols, from story by Barney Slater, Joel Kane; camera, Loyal Griggs; editor, Alma Macrorie; music, Elmer Bernstein. Previewed Oct. 7, '57. Running time, **92 MINS.**

Morg Hickman .... Henry Fonda
Ben Owens .... Anthony Perkins
Nona Mayfield .... Betsy Palmer
Kip Mayfield .... Michel Ray
Bogardus .... Neville Brand
Dr. McCord .... John McIntire
Millie .... Mary Webster
Zeke McGaffey .... Peter Baldwin
Buck Henderson .... Richard Shannon
Ed McGaffey .... Lee Van Cleef
Judge Thatcher .... James Bell
Harvey King .... Howard Petrie
Clem Hall .... Russell Simpson
Andy Miller .... Hal K. Dawson
Sam Hodges .... Jack Kenney
Posse (McCall) .... Mickey Finn

"The Tin Star" is a quality western with names of Henry Fonda and Anthony Perkins to give it meaning in both the sagebrush and general markets. Film has ingredients to maintain interest at a high key throughout its fast 92 minutes.

This William Perlberg-George Seaton production unfolds interestingly under the smooth direction of Anthony Mann, who draws top performances from cast also headed by Betsy Palmer, Michel Ray, Neville Brand and John McIntire. Dudley Nichols screenplay centers around Perkins' insistence upon keeping his sheriff's badge despite the pleading of his sweetheart to abandon hazards of the job, and Fonda, a former lawman turned human bounty hunter, reluctantly teaching him the tricks of the trade. A very credible story packs excellent dramatic values sharply handled throughout to lend a feeling of mounting suspense.

For Fonda, character is one of his strongest in some time and he gives it telling authority as he waits in a small western town for a reward check, then stays on to help the over-anxious young sheriff. Perkins, in this role, asserts himself forcibly, his nemesis being Neville Brand, capable as a gun-handy bully who nearly forces him to back down in his authority. Betsy Palmer is in for suggested romance with Fonda as mother of young Michel Ray (the boy in "The Brave One"), half-breed Indian lad who attaches himself to a willing Fonda, both convincing in their parts. John McIntire as the town's grizzled old doctor whose murder spurs on the eventual climax as Perkins faces a lynching mob out to get doc's killers, makes his work stand out. Good support, too, is afforded by Mary Webster, in love with Perkins, and Lee Van Cleef and Peter Baldwin as doctor's slayers.

Loyal Griggs' camera work and Alma Macrorie's tight editing head technical credits. Elmer Bernstein's music score also is effective in setting pace. *Whit.*

The Invisible Boy

Clever science-fictioner with accent on humor; strong family trade appeal.

Hollywood, Oct. 11.

Metro release of Nicholas Nayfack production. Stars Richard Eyer, Philip Abbott, Diane Brewster; features Harold J. Stone, Dennis McCarthy, Alexander Lockwood, Robert H. Harris, John O'Malley, Robby the Robot. Directed by Herman Hoffman. Screenplay, Cyril Hume, based on story by Edmund Cooper; camera, Harold Wellman; music, Les Baxter; editor, John Faure. Previewed Oct. 4, '57. Running time, **90 MINS.**

Timmie Merrinoe .... Richard Eyer
Dr. Merrinoe .... Philip Abbott
Mary Merrinoe .... Diane Brewster
General Swayne .... Harold J. Stone
Professor Allerton .... Robert H. Harris
Colonel Macklin .... Dennis McCarthy
Arthur Kelvaney .... Alexander Lockwood
Dr. Baine .... John O'Malley

"The Invisible Boy" shapes up as an imaginative entry for the science-fiction field, with type of story to extend draw to general market, particularly the family trade. Ballyhoo possibilities are heightened by story's preparations to launch sections of a space station, which though not a pertinent part of story gives strong exploitation potential in light of current Russian satellite. Overall result presages satisfactory returns.

For his initial indie production, Nicholas Nayfack lards action generously with humor, simultaneously capturing the type of scifi excitement which will appeal to moppet audiences especially. Principal character is young Richard Eyer (remembered as the boy in "Friendly Persuasion)), son of a top scientist who has invented and perfected an electronic brain so sensitive that it speaks. Nayfack, who last year as a Metro producer turned out "The Forbidden Planet," in which he intro'd Robby the Robot, makes handsome use again of this interesting mechanical man, although film in no wise is a follow-up.

The Cyril Hume screenplay, based on story by Edmund Cooper, has been directed with a ready touch by Herman Hoffman, who generates plenty of laughs with young Eyer and his robot before the chilling climax. Philip Abbott, the scientist whose super-computer is in constant use by Pentagon for solution of complex scientific problems, particularly in prepping space platform project, takes his son to the computer in an effort to further boy's education. Lad becomes hypnotized by brain, emerges a chess wizard and in a game with his father wins as a reward latter's permission to play with Robby, something of a wizard on its own. Through the robot the youngster becomes invisible so he can play sans parental objections.

Chilling aspects of narrative occur when the machine comes to life, under non-human control from outer space, and becomes a threat to national security, using scientist's son as a hostage to gain its objective.

Young Eyer plays his part skillfully and actions of Robby are nearly human. Abbott capably fulfills father role, Diane Brewster qualifies as the mother and Harold J. Stone, Dennis McCarthy, Robert H. Harris, Alexander Lockwood and John O'Malley are okay in support.

Special effects by Jack Rabin, Irving Block and Louis Dewitt are expert and lead off quality technical credits. Merrill Pye's production designing is interesting; so are Harold Wellman's photography, John Faure's editing and Les Baxter's music score. *Whit.*

Teenage Doll

Another juve delinquency cheapie. Clumsily executed. For the sex-and-sadism fanciers.

Hollywood, Oct. 4.

Allied Artists release of a Woolner Bros. production. Stars June Kenney, Fay Spain, John Brinkley; with Collette Jackson, Barbara Wilson, Ziva Rodan, Sandy Smith, Barbara Morris, Richard Devon, others. Producer-director, Roger Corman; screenplay, Charles B. Griffith; camera, Floyd Crosby; editor, Charles Gross; art director, Robert Kinoshita; music, Walter Greene. Previewed in Hollywood, Oct. 2, '57. Running time, **67 MINS.**

Barbara .... June Kenney
Hel .... Fay Spain
Eddie .... John Brinkley
May .... Collette Jackson
Betty .... Barbara Wilson
Squirrel .... Ziva Rodan
Lorrie .... Sandy Smith
Janet .... Barboura Morris
Dunston .... Richard Devon
Wally .... Jay Sayer
Phil .... Richard Cutting
Estelle .... Dorothy Neumann
Dutch Doctor .... Ed Nelson

This low-budgeter is ostensibly directed toward the fight against juve delinquency. However, only real contribution in this direction is that it offers employment to a corps of juve actors, and thus keeps them off the street, if not precisely gainfully occupied.

More and more, these delinquency pix, tailored strictly for the exploitation market despite their pious declarations, are beginning to display a deadening monotonous sameness. As a famed producer once observed, "It's time to develop some new cliches."

Unremitting and unconvincing downbeat tenor, clumsily execluted, deadens b.o. chances for any audience outside of sex-and-sadism fanciers.

Characters in Charles B. Griffith screenplay talk a stylized jargon mainly derivative of other pix of this genre; engage in continual brutality and violence; and their motivations, delinquent or otherwise, bears only the slightest resemblence of those human beings. Tale revolves around accidental killing of a hoodlum moll by a decent girl, June Kenney, running in dubious company. Dead girl's femme gang, led by Fay Spain, throws out dragnet to catch Miss Kenney. During this, backgrounds of various members are traced, but motivations remain superficial and murky.

Miss Kenney finally flees to her b.f., sneering John Brinkley, leader of another gang. Brinkley grudgingly offers her protection and brutal, sadistic gang fight follows, only to be broken up by cops, finally hep. Miss Kenney and two of Miss Spain's gang, Barbara Wilson and Ziva Rodan, give themselves up, rather than continue sordid associations.

Direction of Roger Corman, who also produced, stresses an array of facial gymnastics rarely seen since silent screen days. He sticks in several scenes of tasty young dishes in various states of dishabille, with little discernable relation to the plot. However, to Corman's credit, he does show an ability to assemble the production ingredients for a good picture, even if he doesn't know what to do with them. *Kove.*

Hear Me Good
(VISTA VISION)

Not often funny low-budget comedy, starring tv quizmaster Hal March. Routine destiny.

Paramount release of Don McGuire production. Stars Hal March and Joe E. Ross. Features Merry Anders, Jean Willes, Milton Frome, Joey Faye, Richard Bakalyan and Tom Duggan. Directed and written by McGuire. Camera (VistaVision), Haskell Boggs; editor, George Tomasini. Previewed in N.Y., Oct. 10, '57. Running time, **80 MINS.**

Marty Holland .... Hal March
Max Crane .... Joe E. Ross
Ruth Collins .... Merry Anders
Rita Hall .... Jean Willes
Mr. Ross .... Milton Frome
Charlie Cooper .... Joey Faye
Hermie .... Richard Bakalyan
TV Director .... Tom Duggan

"Hear Me Good" is an innocuous, obvious low-budget entry that aims desperately for laughs but only finds its mark occasionally. Its chief asset from a selling standpoint is the name value of Hal March, the quizmaster of tv's "$64,000 Question"—once of the radio comedy team, if anybody remembers, Sweeney and March.

Produced, written and directed by Don McGuire, the film is hardly more than a 18-minute vaude sketch stretched to 80 minutes. Talk and more talk features the proceedings and the main purpose of the film appears to be the setting up of situations for gag lines. The latter run as thick and as fast as on a Bob Hope radio or tv program, but only a handful of the gags are capable of including genuine laughter.

The picture's similarity to a radio or tv show is further demonstrated by the number of product plugs that are spotted throughout the film. The picture, however, should find its niche in double feature situations where it can provide adequate amusement to keep the customers happy before the main entry hits the screen.

The characters in "Hear Me Good" are a bunch of pleasant Manhattan conmen vaguely similar to characters created by Damon Runyon. Work is an abhorrent word to them and they live by their wits. Their lingo is strictly Runyonesque. As the chief conman, March is preparing "to fix" a beauty contest so that the moll of Irving the Hammer, a hood never seen on the screen, emerges the winner.

Complications, of course, set in when March substitutes an innocent, wide-eyed beauty who succeeds in bringing out his better instincts. It's the usual boy meets girl, loses girl, etc. stuff that works out finely when March decides to reform and employ his conning techniques for legitimate activities. Love serves as the potion that brings about his reformation.

The performances meet the demands of McGuire's screenplay. March is okay, but he's been better as a straight actor-comedian as evidenced by his performance as the punch drunk fighter in Metro's "It's Always Fair Weather" several years ago. Joe E. Ross is fine as March's trusting sidekick as is Joey Faye as a conman who outcons the master. Jean Willes is properly brash as the gangster's girl and Merry Anders displays promise as the ingenue. Richard Bakalyan's portrayal of a gangster is humorous although stereotyped.

Technical aspects, including photography and set decorations, have an obvious cost-conscious feeling. *Holl.*

Jailhouse Rock
(SONGS-C'SCOPE)

Elvis Presley starrer, which means handsome grosses when rightly booked.

Hollywood, Oct. 11.

Metro release of Pandro S. Berman production. Stars Elvis Presley; costars Judy Tyler; features Mickey Shaughnessy, Vaughn Taylor, Dean Jones, Jennifer Holden, Anne Neyland. Directed by Richard Thorpe. Screenplay, Guy Trosper, based on story by Ned Young; camera, Robert Bronner; editor, Ralph E. Winters; music, Jeff Alexander. Previewed Oct. 10, '57. Running time, **96 MINS.**

Vince Everett .... Elvis Presley
Peggy Van Alden .... Judy Tyler
Hunk Houghton .... Mickey Shaughnessy
Mr. Shores .... Vaughn Taylor

Sherry Wilson	Jennifer Holden
Teddy Talbot	Dean Jones
Laury Jackson	Anne Neyland

Continued popularity of the rock 'n' roll craze—and Elvis Presley—gives sharp outlook for this third starrer for the singer. Film is packed with type of sure-fire ingredients producers know Presley's followers go for, and its likely a considerable portion of the populace, particularly the cats, will find this Metro release in their alley.

The Pandro S. Berman production, first to be turned out under his new indie status, carries a contrived plot but under Richard Thorpe's deft direction unfolds smoothly. Director has been wise enough to allow Presley to follow his own style, and build around him, for the mannerisms which have fashioned him into the phenomenon he is with the teenagers color his character here. Presley is still no great shakes as an actor but gets by well enough, although role isn't particularly sympathetic.

Narrative as scripted by Guy Trosper intros Presley as a hot-tempered but affable youngster who goes to prison on a manslaughter rap after being involved in a bar-room fight. In stir he's cell-mated with Mickey Shaughnessy, who teaches him his dog-eat-dog philosophy, and also some singing tricks. Released, but now embittered and cynical, he claws his way to fame in the music world, riding alike over friend and foe, even Judy Tyler, a music exploitation agent who has helped in his discovery and is partnered with him in their own record company. Scene shifts between recordings, television and Hollywood, where he becomes a star.

Singer is on for six songs, top being the title production number in a prison setting. Songs are varied, from the rock 'n' roll title number and "Treat Me Nice," to the ballad, "Young and Beautiful." Also included are "I Want to Be Free," "Don't Leave Me Now" and "Baby, I Don't Care." All are stamped with singer's own brand, shouting, but some of the gyrations of the past are missing. The Jordanaires give singer melodic backing.

Star receives good support, Miss Tyler—killed in an auto accident several months ago — coming through nicely and Shaughnessy hard-hitting as the tough ex-con who becomes Presley's flunky after following youngster in release from prison. It's Shaughnessy who figures importantly in the climax. Unable to any longer take the humiliation singer keeps heaping upon him, he takes a wild swing to Presley's throat which sends him to the hospital, and some doubt he'll be able to sing again.

Following an operation, Presley finds he's ready to sing again, and also finds himself. Figuring capably also in film are Vaughn Taylor, as an attorney; Jennifer Holden as a film actress.

Technical departments are well handled. Robert Bronner's camera work shows well, Ralph E. Winters' editing sets good pace and Jeff Alexander supervises the music. *Whit.*

Melbourne Rendezvous
(COLOR-DOCUMENTARY)

Trans-Lux release of a C.S.A. production. Directed by Rene Lucot. Narration, Francois Perier; writers, Rene Lucot, Raymond Marcillac; camera (Agfacolor), Jacques Duhamel, Pierre Gueguen, Pierre Lebon, Georges Leclerc. Previewed N.Y., Oct. 3, '57. Running time, **87 MINS.**

The 16th Olympiad held last fall in Australia has been painstakingly recorded by a 15-camera crew of French technicians under an arrangement with the Olympic Committee. It will be recalled that when the committee priced its rights to the games "too high" American newsreel companies and other film outfits withdrew from the bidding.

Subsequently, the Olympic officials made a deal with a French firm which lensed highlights of the meet as "Melbourne Rendezvous." With release of the film coming almost a year after the famed contest took place, obviously the novelty and news value of such a documentary have now been largely dissipated. Thus the audience potential will for the most part be restricted to dyed-in-the-wool followers of track meets.

Overall treatment of the varied competitions in Melbourne Stadium is generally creditable. The many events such as shotput, 10,-000 meter run, high hurdles, discus throw, sculling, pole vault and 26-mile marathon have been ably lensed. Slow motion has been used to advantage, particularly in the spectacular pole vaulting.

However, it's curious why most water sports have been omitted from the footage. Missing are the fancy diving contests and the Russian-Hungarian water polo match, among other events.

To director Rene Lucot's credit, he has avoided monotony by occasionally training his cameras on scenes of Melbourne night life and other "off - the - track" vignettes. Views of Melbourne's well-groomed suburbs where champ hurdler Shirley Strickland resides, sequences depicting foreign contestants studying merchandise in department store windows and aerial clips of the Australian terrain all help in providing audiences a vicarious share in the 1956 Olympiad.

English narration occasionally resorts to cliches. But this is hardly a fault since few sports stories are free of hackneyed phrases. While Agfacolor obviously is better than black-and-white, nevertheless it often had a faded, "washed out" quality and doesn't compare with Technicolor or Eastman Color. *Gilb.*

Young and Dangerous
(REGALSCOPE)

Think screen needs 'new faces'? Here's two. 'Strong programmer with talented newcomers.

Hollywood, Oct. 11.

Twentieth-Fox release of William F. Claxton production. Stars Lili Gentle, Mark Damon; features Edward Binns, George Brenlin, Jerry Barclay, William Stevens, Dabbs Greer, Ann Doran, Frances Mercer, Connie Stevens. Directed by Claxton. Screenplay, James Landis; camera, John M. Mickolaus Jr.; editor, Frank Baldridge; music, Paul Dunlap. Previewed Oct. 9, '57. Running time, **77 MINS.**

Tommy Price	Mark Damon
Rosemary Clinton	Lili Gentle
Dr. Price	Eddie Binns
Mrs. Price	Frances Mercer
Mr. John Clinton	Dabbs Greer
Mrs. Clara Clinton	Ann Doran
Weasel Martin	George Brenlin
Stretch Grass	Jerry Barclay
Rock	William Stevens
Candy	Connie Stevens
Bones	Danny Welton
Rock's Girl	Shirley Falls
Rock's Buddy No. 1	Ronald Foster
Rock's Buddy No. 2	Bill Shannon
(LR) Girl No. 1	Marilyn Carrol
Carhop No. 1	Joan Bradshaw
Carhop No. 2	Marion Collier
Carhop No. 3	June Burt
Other Boy	James Canino
Motorcycle Cop	X Brand
Pier Cop No. 1	Bill Boyett
Tough Teenager	Don Devlin
Desk Sergeant	Paul Bryar
Station House Cop	Buddy Mason
Party Girl No. 1	Judy Bember
Party Girl No. 2	Kim Scala
Juvenile Hall Mother	Doris Kemper
Juvenile Hall Girl	Brandy Bryan
Arresting Officer	Roy Darmour
Drive-In Worker	Ron Barbanell

Exhibitor cries for fresh film talent will find ample answer in this well-made drama of youthful romance. Picture, which gets quality handling despite its modest budget, presents two promising newcomers in Lili Gentle and Mark Damon, both undoubtedly destined to make their mark. Film is being packaged with "Rockabilly Baby," another Regal production accenting youth, and indications are combo will fare very pleasantly in the general market with its particular appeal to younger generation.

William F. Clayton as producer-director, has woven a sometimes tender love story legitimately premised and carrying genuine interest. The James Landis screenplay centers on the romance between the two principals, but draws on a juve delinquency sub-plot to give meaning to its theme of regeneration. In addition to Miss Gentle and Damon, there's a pair of clever comics, George Brenlin and Jerry Barclay, for further new face lure, both the later shotwing well in several standout scenes.

Damon capably delineates his role of a rebellious, hot-headed 19-year-old who leads a gang of young toughs whose only interests are thrills, hot rods and femmes. Notorious for his successful line with girls, he finds little trouble in dating Lili Gentle, whose parents object to him. After going on the make for her on this date, which lands them both in the police station and winds with femme's parents forbidding her to see Damon, a romance buds. Damon finds himself changing through repeated dates, the common bond of feeling misunderstood by their parents strengthening their mutual attraction, for each other. Their romantic difficulties are punched over dramatically and climax is particularly strong.

Damon, who makes his work count, has an able running mate in Miss Gentle, distinctive and with a nice flair for acting. Dabbs Greer and Ann Doran as her parents, too busy to listen to their daughter's hesitant approach to adult life, are excellent ,and Eddie Binns capably fulfills role of Damon's father, who never has been able to reach his son. Connie Stevens also is a standout in her brief role of Lili's chum. William Stevens is okay as a heavy who gets into a fastly-staged brawl with Damon, and Frances Mercer good as latter's mother. Competent support is afforded down through a large cast.

John M. Micoklaus, Jr.'s photography is firstclass, and Ernst Fegte's production designing, Frank Baldridge's editing and Paul Dunlap's music score on same level. *Whit.*

Taming Sutton's Gal

Routine programmer aimed at the grassroots trade.

Hollywood, Oct. 15.

Republic release of Variety production (produced by William J. O'Sullivan). Stars John Lupton, Gloria Talbott; features Jack Kelly, May Wynn, Verna Felton. Directed by Lesley Selander; screenplay, Thames Williamson and Frederic Louis Fox, from Thames Williamson story; camera (Naturama), Jack Marta; editor, Tony Martinelli. Previewed, Sept. 18, '57. Running time, **71 MINS.**

Frank McClary	John Lupton
Lou Sutton	Gloria Talbott
Jugger Phelps	Jack Kelly
Evelyn Phelps	May Wynn
Aunty Sutton	Verna Felton

This is a lowbudget program "filler." Turned out in quickie time and looks it. Routine action and routine humor and aimed for routine small situations.

Producer William J. O'Sullivan and director Lesley Selander haven't bothered to make this one novel in any way. Two scripters—Thames Williamson and Frederic Louis Fox—come up with trite dialog that may irk even some of the non-sophisticates.

Cast is adequate, grappling with the unlikely lines and situations. Gloria Talbott is a looker with a refreshing personality that comes across even in this minor entry. John Lupton is pleasant. As the heavy, Jack Kelly is wooden and vicious without clear motive. May Wynn is supposed to personify cheap glamor and Verna Felton, as a cigar-smoking pioneer-type, takes care of the folksy wisdom and humor department.

Story has bank clerk Lupton arriving in the California back country to do some pheasant hunting. He has a run-in with Kelly and boards with Miss Talbott and her aunt, Miss Felton. He and the girl hit it off, but Miss Wynn starts making passes at him, which he rejects. Jealousy eventually makes her shoot her husband, who believes it was Lupton who did it. Inevitably, there's a showdown fight, and then a gun battle. All ends well in the end.

Selander's direction is barely adequate in this day-and-age. Jack Marta's photography has merit. Tony Martinelli's editing is okay. It's the kind of simple-minded, good vs. evil film that'll get by mostly because theatres need film. *Hift.*

The Scamp
(BRITISH)

Sentimental, unconvincing domestic drama involving excellent child actor, but offering only limited appeal to most audiences.

London, Oct. 8.

Renown release of a George Minter (James Lawrie) production. Stars Richard Attenborough, Terence Morgan, Colin (Smiley) Petersen, Dorothy Alison, Jill Adams. Directed by Wolf Rilla. Screenplay, Wolf Rilla, from play, "Uncertain Joy," by Charlotte Hastings; editor, Bernard Gribble; music, Francis Chagrin. At Odeon, Marble Arch, London, Oct. 7, '57. Running time, **88 MINS.**

Stephen Leigh	Richard Attenborough
Barbara Leigh	Dorothy Alison
Tod	Colin Petersen
Mike Dawson	Terence Morgan
Julie Dawson	Jill Adams
Mrs. Perryman	Maureen Delany
Mrs. Blundell	Margaretta Scott
Eddie	David Franks
Headmaster	Geoffrey Keen
Beamish	Charles Lloyd Pack
Annette	June Cunningham
Shopkeeper	Sam Kydd
Inspector Birch	Victor Brooks

Based on Charlotte Hasting's play, "Uncertain Joy," this emerges as a run-of-mill domestic drama which will serve as a routine booking for minor houses. It has a touch too much of sentimentality and many situations are implausible. Any draw that it may have must be chalked up to a most appealing performance by a child actor, Colin Petersen, who sprang to prominence in the film, "Smiley."

Richard Attenborough is a schoolmaster, and he and his doctor wife befriend a youngster whose father, a drunken vaudeville actor, neglects the child and leaves him to run wild. When he goes on a tour of South America, he reluctantly leaves his son with

Attenborough and his wife who try to show the kid a new way of life. But he can't live down his background and despite their kindness he continues to get into scrapes.

One of these is sufficiently serious to get him into trouble with the authorities who order that he should be returned to his father who has returned from tour with a new wife. Little Petersen is again ill-treated, and in self-defense he crowns his drunken father with an ash-tray. Thinking he has killed him, he runs in terror to Attenborough and his wife. It turns out, however, that the boy was not the guilty party. The father died in an alcoholic fall. So he is adopted by Attenborough and his wife for a happy ending.

While there is plenty of scope in such a story for a good, meaty drama, "The Scamp" suffers from unimaginative direction by Wolf Rilla and a somewhat pedestrian script. It plods along from one cliche-ridden situation to another.

But no praise can be too high for Petersen as the 10-year-old scamp. Here is a natural, if ever there was one. He has brains, humor and an urchin persuasiveness which will flutter the hearts of all femme patrons. Technically, this film is sound throughout. *Rich.*

The Story of Mankind
(COLOR)

Erratic and hokey telling of Hendrik Van Loon's serious history. Loaded with "names" but little marquee value. Prospects mild.

Warner release of Cambridge (Irwin Allen) production. Stars Ronald Colman, Hedy Lamarr, Groucho Marx, Harpo Marx, Chico Marx, Virginia Mayo, Agnes Moorehead, Vincent Price, Peter Lorre, Charles Coburn, Cedric Hardwicke, Cesar Romero, John Carradine, Dennis Hopper, Marie Wilson, Helmut Dantine, Edward Everett Horton, Reginald Gardiner, Marie Windsor, George E. Stone, Cathy O'Donnell, Franklin Pangborn, Melville Cooper, Henry Daniell, Francis X. Bushman; features Jim Ameche, David Bond, Nick Cravat, Dani Crayne, Richard Cutting, Anthony Dexter, Toni Gerry, Austin Green, Eden Hartford, Alexander Lockwood, Melinda Marx, Bart Mattson, Don Megowan, Marvin Miller, Nancy Miller, Leonard Mundi, Burt Nelson, Tudor Owen, Ziva Rodann, Harry Ruby, William Schallert, Reginald Sheffield, Abraham Sofaer, Bobby Watson. Directed by Allen. Screenplay, Allen and Charles Bennett, based on the book by Hendrik Willem Van Loon; camera (Technicolor), Nick Musuraca; editor, Roland Gross, Gene Palmer; music, Paul Sawtell; art director, Art Loel. Previewed Oct. 15, '57. Running time **99 MINS.**

Spirit of Man	Ronald Colman
Joan of Arc	Hedy Lamarr
Peter Minuit	Groucho Marx
Isaac Newton	Harpo Marx
Monk	Chico Marx
Cleopatra	Virginia Mayo
Queen Elizabeth	Agnes Moorehead
Devil	Vincent Price
Nero	Peter Lorre
Hippocrates	Charles Coburn
High Judge	Cedric Hardwicke
Spanish Envoy	Cesar Romero
Khufu	John Carradine
Napoleon	Dennis Hopper
Marie Antoinette	Marie Wilson
Anthony	Helmut Dantine
Sir Walter Raleigh	Edward Everett Horton
Shakespeare	Reginald Gardiner
Josephine	Marie Windsor
Walter	George E. Stone
Early Christian Woman	Cathy O'Donnell
Marquis de Varennes	Franklin Pangborn
Major Domo	Melville Cooper
Bishop of Beauvais	Henry Daniell
Moses	Francis X. Bushman
Alexander Graham Bell	Jim Ameche
Early Christian	David Bond
Apprentice	Nick Cravat
Helen of Troy	Dani Crayne
Court Attendant	Richard Cutting
Columbus	Anthony Dexter
Wife	Toni Gerry
Lincoln	Austin Green
Laughing Water	Eden Hartford
Promoter	Alexander Lockwood
Early Christian Child	Melinda Marx
Cleopatra's Brother	Bart Mattson
Early Man	Don Megowan
Armana	Marvin Miller
Early Woman	Nancy Miller
Chief Inquisitor	Leonard Mundi
Early 2nd Man	Burt Nelson
Court Clerk	Tudor Owen
Concubine	Ziva Rodann
Indian Brave	Harry Ruby
Earl of Warwick	William Schallert
Caesar	Reginald Sheffield
Indian Chief	Abraham Sofaer
Hitler	Bobby Watson

For more than a generation, the late Hendrik Willem Von Loon's monumental "Story of Mankind" has been a runner-up to the Bible as a steady standard. Now, it has been brought to the screen in a name-dropping production that provides a kaleidoscope of history from early Pleistocene man to today's Plutonium man. In the process, however, producer-director Irwin Allen seemed unable to decide whether to do a faithful history of man's development into a thinking being, a debate on whether man's good outweighs his evil, or a compilation of historical sagas with some humor dragged in for relief.

The possible box-office merit of the third alternative apparently won out and Allen assembled a cast of "name" performers for added impact. None, unfortunately, has real marquee value and the resultant billing problem—in which 25 names appear successively on the screen to accompanying fanfare—encompasses a 55-second span even before the title is seen.

Forgetting the effect upon the star system of billing such players

as George E. Stone, Franklin Pangborn and others above the title, the device succeeds only in getting the film off to a slow start from which it never recovers. Overall prospects seem pale since "The Story of Mankind" lacks universal appeal and the select audience that might seek it out as intelligent, adult fare will be antagonized by the handling.

As a peg on which to hang the panorama, screenplay by Allen and Charles Bennett convokes the "High Tribunal of Outer Space" upon news that man has discovered the Super-H bomb 60 years too soon. The problem is whether to halt the scheduled explosion and thereby save mankind or let it go off and exterminate the human race. To reach a decision, the tribunal permits both the Devil and the Spirit of Man to give evidence as to man's fitness to continue.

In the dreary cataloguing of man's crimes against humanity, the Devil makes a much better case. Rape and terror, banditry, greed and immorality sweep triumphantly across the screen, punctuated occasionally by the "Yes, but—" retort of the Spirit of Man. Film, however, restricts his anwers largely to narration of man's struggle upward, with enactment of his faltering success kept to a minimum. In the end, the tribunal defers a decision on man's right to continued existence but agrees to halt the bomb, at least for the time being.

Allen's nebulous conception of the property is sharply reflected in the Allen-Bennett screenplay which is ponderous and dull. There is an occasional burst of humor but, as in the case of the purchase-of-Manhattan sequence with Groucho Marx as Peter Minuit, the dialog is entirely out of keeping with the remainder of the script. Producer-director also faltered in his casting and handling of players, resulting in many uneven or stock performances. Best of the portrayals is Agnes Moorehead's handling of the role of Queen Elizabeth and Cedric Hardwicke turns in a good performance as the High Judge. Ronald Colman, as always, is a dignified personification of the Spirit of Man and Vincent Price is the sophisticated, sneering embodiment of Old Scratch. Most of the other top-billed performers have little to do, but Peter Lorre brings some conviction to the role of Nero, Dennis Hopper is moodily appropriate as Napoleon and Virginia Mayo looks the part of Cleopatra. Hedy Lamarr is miscast as Joan (yes, of Arc) in one of the few other key parts, some of the "stars" having been given roles in which they are on and off the screen so rapidly as to go unrecognized.

Technicolor lensing by Nick Musuraca is good and Paul Sawtell's music provides an appropriate background of crescendo and diminuendo. Other credits are stock. *Kap.*

Ride Out for Revenge

Haphazard and heavyhanded western, employing all the "new" cliches. Routine bookings.

Hollywood, Oct. 11.

United Artists release of a Bryna production. Stars Rory Calhoun, Gloria Grahame, Lloyd Bridges, Joanne Gilbert; with Frank DeKova, Vince Edwards, Michael Winkelman, Richard Shannon, Cyril Delevanti, John Merrick. Produced by Norman Retchin. Directed by Bernard

Girard. Screenplay, Retchin; camera, Floyd Crosby; editor, Leon Barsha; art director, McClure Capps; music, Leith Stevens. Previewed Oct. 10, '57. Running time, **77 MINS.**

Tate	Rory Calhoun
Amy Porter	Gloria Grahame
Captain George	Lloyd Bridges
Pretty Willow	Joanne Gilbert
Yellow Wolf	Frank DeKova
Little Wolf	Vince Edwards
Billy	Michael Winkelman
Garvin	Richard Shannon
Preacher	Cyril Delevanti
Lieutenant	John Merrick

The old oater cliches are turned inside out for this purported "adult" western, but the "new" cliches in the Norman Retchin script (he also produced) and laid on in a heavyhanded and haphazard manner. Results don't promise better than program bookings, since star names of Rory Calhoun, Gloria Grahame, Lloyd Bridges and Joanne Gilbert aren't potent enough to overcome the shoddy scripting and hit-and-miss production.

In this story, the cavalry, instead of being an upstanding, derring-do body of clean-cut Americans, is a drunken detachment led by a cowardly, corrupt captain, broadly played by Lloyd Bridges. The Indians are uniformly brave and honorable. In the romantic triangle among hero Calhoun, white widow Gloria Grahame and Indian girl Miss Gilbert, Miss Grahame portrays a man-crazy tramp and the Indian belle is a sweet, heroic young thing.

Tale revolves enforced move of the proud Cheyenne nation from their ancestral hunting grounds to an Oklahoma reservation. Bridges, in charge of the move, is inept as well as brutally stupid. Calhoun, town marshal and a former Indian scout, wants to see justice done, but is unsuccessful.

Discovery of gold and intolerance of townspeople inflames matters. Treacherous murders by whites, and raids by Indians in self defence, led by Vince Edwards, thicken the plot. Finally, Calhoun renounces Miss Grahame, kills the villainous Bridges and keeps Miss Gilbert behind after the Cheyennes are driven off to the reservation.

Story idea isn't bad, but it needed better treatment than it got from Retchin. Bernard Girard's loose direction, which permits a wide variety of thesping styles, isn't much help. Calhoun and Miss Gilbert come off best, while others can't be assessed too harshly for their readings of improbable lines. *Kove.*

The Sad Sack
(VISTAVISION)

Madcap fun with Jerry Lewis as the G. I. misfit. Comes off well; good grosses can be expected.

Paramount release of Hal B. Wallis production. Stars Jerry Lewis; features David Wayne, Phyllis Kirk, Peter Lorre, Joe Mantell, Gene Evans. Directed by George Marshall. Screenplay, Edmund Beloin and Nate Monaster; based on George Baker's cartoon character; camera, Loyal Griggs; editor, Archie Marshek; music, Walter Scharf; title song by Hal David and Burt F. Bacharach. Previewed at Capitol Theatre, N.Y., Oct. 16, '57. Running time, **98 MINS.**

Bixby	Jerry Lewis
Dolan	David Wayne
Major Shelton	Phyllis Kirk
Abdul	Peter Lorre
Pvt. Stan Wenaslawsky	Joe Mantell
Sgt. Pulley	Gene Evans
Ali Mustapha	George Dolenz
Zita	Liliane Montevecchi
Gen. Vanderlip	Shepperd Strudwick
Hassim	Abraham Sofaer
Sgt. Hansen	Mary Treen
Lieut. Wilson	Drew Cahill
Moki	Michael G. Ansara

Capt. Ward .... Don Haggerty
French General .... Jean Del Val
Arab Chieftain .... Dan Seymour
Hazel .... Yvette Vickers

The title, a hint of what the picture is about, and Jerry Lewis as star, communicate the message about this new Hal B. Wallis production. It's the old army game, done over. But it's fun. Not any imaginative explorations. Relying on the type of zanyism with which Lewis is readily identified. Fun for those who go for it.

Importantly, "Sad Sack" is fast in delivering its broad material. The mayhem, as when soldier boy Lewis becomes involved with native heavies in Morocco, including Peter Lorre doing a takeoff on himself, is suggestive of the wild yesteryears of the Keystone Kops.

Lewis already has proved himself a boxoffice commodity sans ex-podner Dean Martin. He'll do well with this outing, too, considering the number of his partisans and the fact that they're not likely to be disappointed.

Story has the comic as a mnemonic whiz kid but with two left feet, making him apt subject matter for a psychiatrist. Playing the part of the Army head specialist is Phyllis Kirk, making for a nifty visual plus. She undertakes to solve her problem soldier with the assistance of his squadron leader, David Wayne who, along with his comrade, Joe Mantell, takes Lewis in tow.

This, together with lightly-played romance between Miss Kirk and Wayne, represents the story from which springs the shenanigans.

Edmund Beloin and Nate Monaster fashioned a series of outlandishly humorous bits and situations in their screenplay and director George Marshall has provided the all important pace in his staging.

Lewis is, well, Lewis. Being trapped in the WAC barracks, returning the busses of a French general and eluding the sinister Moroccan figures—these add up to his cup of tea. He's at home with this type of nonsense and makes the most of it.

Producer Hall Wallis surrounded the comic with good workers for this type of an entry. Miss Kirk is a cute trick as the psychiatrist. Wayne is consistently effective as the corporal with the major migraine in Lewis. The Lorre caricature strains a bit but nonetheless provides a few laughs. Mantell and Gene Evans, latter as a rough Army sergeant, come through in the proper groove.

All in all, nothing revolutionary, but reliable. Wallis has laid it out with adequate care—meaning, the backgrounds, sets and costumes are fitting and all technical credits bespeak professionalism. Walter Scharf's musical backing is a good component although the title song, based on the one listening, figures as a so-so item, okay for the picture, but short of substantial on its own. *Gene.*

Porte Des Lilas
(FRENCH; SONGS)

Paris, Oct. 15.

Cinedis release of Filmsonor production. Stars Pierre Brasseur, Georges Brassens, Henri Vidal, Dany Carrel; features Raymond Bussieres, Amedee. Written and directed by Rene Clair. From novel by Rene Fallet with additional script by Jean Aurel. Camera, Robert Le Febvre; editor, Louisette Hautcoeur, Arlette Lalande; music, Brassens. At Colisee, Paris. Running time, 95 MINS.

Juju .... Pierre Brasseur
L'Artiste .... Georges Brassens
Barbier .... Henri Vidal
Maria .... Dany Carrel
Alphonse .... Raymond Bussieres
Paulo .... Amedee

Rene Clair returns to the lower class suburbs and milieu used for his best prewar pix. However, he has come up with a light tale which wavers between comedy and drama, making a slight, fragile pic. It is primarily for arty houses in the U. S., and it will need plenty of selling. But it has offbeat qualities for bally.

A genial neighborhood good-for-nothing, drunkard, living off his hard-working mother, and his friend, an itinerant singing troubadour, get saddled with a gangster who has just killed three people. Possessing odd ideas about hospitality the tippler, Pierre Brasseur, must hide him until the gangster can get away.

The killer stays on until he is discovered by a clever young girl. The gangster woes and wins her and tries to get her to steal money from her father. Brasseur finds out and in trying to stop him kills the gangster.

The film's mixture of styles rarely allows for the achieving the balance of irony and comedy. Its story loopholes are not quite covered by the treatment.

Brasseur gives an astute portrait of the drifter. Georges Brassens, a noted ballader here, is too unsure of his lines to do much as the troubadour. However, he is okay when he sings. Dany Carrel is a pert flirt but Henri Vidal does not infuse the gangster with enough redeeming qualities. Technical credits are fine. Clair has given this a careful finish but it remains a pic that does not quite come off. *Mosk.*

Robbery Under Arms
(BRITISH-COLOR)

Straightforward cops-and-robbers adventure yarn set in Australia. Enough virile action to keep average audiences happy.

London, Oct. 15.

Rank (Joseph Janni) production and release. Stars Peter Finch, Ronald Lewis, Maureen Swanson, David McCallum. Directed by Jack Lee. Screenplay, Alexander Baron, W. P. Lipscomb from the novel by Rolf Boldrewood; editor, Manuel Del Campo; camera, Harry Waxman; music, Matyas Seiber. At Odeon, Leicester Square, London. Running time, 99 MINS.

Starlight .... Peter Finch
Dick .... Ronald Lewis
Ben .... Laurence Naismith
Kate .... Maureen Swanson
Jim .... David McCallum
George Storefield .... Vincent Ball
Jean .... Jill Ireland
Eileen .... Dudy Nimmo
Ma .... Jean Anderson
Grace Storefield .... Ursula Finlay
Warrigal .... Johnny Cadell
Burke .... Larry Taylor
Mr. Green .... Russell Napier

Set in Australia of a 100 years ago, "Robbery Under Arms" is a well-made, straightforward drama which should click okay in British houses. As is so often the case, its American impact will depend entirely on whether its stars are sufficient magnets to attract patrons outside the British domain. The picture is part of the Rank Organization's current policy of spotlighting the Commonwealth. Its main problem is whether it does not follow a bit too soon after "The Shiralee," which also starred Peter Finch and the wide, open Aussie spaces.

The story, based on a Victorian novel, has Finch as Captain Starlight, a virile, likeable rogue whose runs a gang of bushrangers whose activities include cattle-rustling and bank holdups. In search of adventure, Ronald Lewis and David McCallum join the gang which includes their father. When the two attempt to break away and lead honest lives they find that they've lost their chance. The film ends with the gang being wiped out in an exciting gun fight with the police. There are undertones of romance but, mainly, the pic relies on action.

Jack Lee's direction splendidly captures the Australian atmosphere. He indulges in no frills. He has a story to tell and he tells it simply. Lee is admirably supported by lenser Harry Waxman. Waxman fills the screen with sweeping camera work, suggesting the vastness of the Australian canvas and the color is first-class. The scene in which 1,000 head of cattle are herded across a river is astutely contrived.

In the star role, Peter Finch has a comparatively small role but he plays it with a swagger which is highly effective. Good opportunities are given to the brothers, Lewis and McCallum. The latter, in the more subtle part, enhances his rising reputation. There is also a fine study by Laurence Naismith as the boys' father, unrepentantly caught up in the Starlight gang.

The distaff side plays second fiddle to the men in this action meller, but Maureen Swanson, in an undeveloped role as a fiery, possessive young woman who sets her amorous sights on Lewis, has her first real opportunity since "A Town Called Alice," and grabs it zestfully. Jill Ireland also makes her mark as the girl McCallum woos and wins.

But the acting is less important than the situations. With fist-fights, gunfight and a near-lynching, there is plenty of meat for good, solid thrills. *Rich.*

Zero Hour

Suspenseful action picture strong entry for regular situations.

Hollywood, Oct. 22.

Paramount release of John Champion production. Stars Dana Andrews, Linda Darnell, Sterling Hayden; costars Elroy "Crazylegs" Hirsch, Geoffrey Toone, Jerry Paris; features Peggy King, Charles Quinlivan, Carole Eden, Steve London, Raymond Ferrell. Directed by Hall Bartlett. Screenplay, Arthur Hailey, Bartlett, Champion, based on story-teleplay by Hailey; camera, John F. Warren; editor, John C. Fuller; music, Ted Dale. Previewed Oct. 17, '57. Running time, 82 MINS.

Ted Stryker .... Dana Andrews
Ellen Stryker .... Linda Darnell
Treleaven .... Sterling Hayden
Captain Wilson..Elroy "Crazylegs" Hirsch
Dr. Baird .... Geoffrey Toone
Tony Decker .... Jerry Paris
Stewardess .... Peggy King
Burdick .... Charles Quinlivan
Mrs. Wilson .... Carole Eden
Co-pilot Stewart .... Steve London
Joey Stryker .... Raymond Ferrell

"Zero Hour" should prove a handy entry for Paramount. First film to be turned out by the new Hall Bartlett-John Champion indie setup, its tightly-knit narrative carries hefty appeal and strong suspense builds to a sock climax. Feature is further sparked by draw of such names as Dana Andrews, Sterling Hayden, Elroy "Crazylegs" Hirsch and Linda Darnell for reception in the program market.

Pic is a theatrical adaptation of Arthur Hailey's original and teleplay, "Flight Into Danger," which won considerable comment when shown on "The Alcoa Hour" early in 1955. As produced by Champion and directed by Bartlett, feature, first on a two-film deal with Paramount, succeeds in keeping audience tense, and convincing performances bolster the mood of danger early established. John C. Fuller's know-how editing also potently assists the exciting pace which seldom lets up.

Basic idea dwells on what happens when the two pilots of a charter plane winging between Winnipeg and Vancouver are stricken with food poisoning, and fate of the plane depends upon a former fighter pilot who hasn't flown in 10 years taking orders via radio on how to bring the craft safely through. Andrews portrays former flyer, who gave up the air after he inadvertently led his squadron to destruction during World War II, and Hayden is the airline's chief pilot, instructing him from the ground. Unfoldment after a rather slow opening is fast and frequently stirring in dramatic impact.

Andrews gives meaning to his role of a man who cannot forget his war past, and Hayden, perhaps a little over-dramatic at times, generally comes through forcefully. Hirsch is good as plane's stricken chief pilot, Miss Darnell makes the most of her role as Andrews' wife who is leaving him but now helps him during his trial aloft, and Geoffrey Toone is excellent as a doctor trying to treat the poison victims aboard the plane. Singer Peggy King, making her film debut sans song, impresses favorably as the stewardess, and capable support is offered by Raymond Ferrell, young son of Andrews and Miss Darnell; Jerry Paris, one of the passengers; and Charles Quinlivan, an operations official.

John F. Warren's photography is fluid. Boris Leven's art direction fits the story and Ted Dale's music score enhances the dramatic unfoldment of picture. *Whit.*

Mr. Rock and Roll

Crude and quick musical pic but with appeal for the jukebox set.

Paramount release of Ralph Serpe & Howard B. Kreitsek production. Starring Alan Freed, Rocky Graziano, Teddy Randazzo, Lois O'Brien, Lionel Hampton; features Jay Barney, Al Fisher, Lou Marks. Directed by Charles Dubin. Screenplay, James Blumgarten; camera, Morris Hartzbarn; musical director, Robert Rolontz; editor, Angie Ross. Opened at N.Y. State Theatre, N.Y., Oct. 16, '57. Running time, 86 MINS.

Alan Freed .... Alan Freed
Rocky Graziano .... Rocky Graziano
Teddy Randazzo ...... Teddy Randazzo
Carol Hendricks .... Lois O'Brien
Joe Prentiss .... Jay Barney
Larry and Lou..Al Fisher and Lou Marks
Leo .... Earl George
Station Rep .... Ralph Stantly

With Lionel Hampton Band, Frankie Lymon & The Teenagers, Chuck Berry, LaVern Baker, Clyde McPhatter, Brook Benton, Little Richard, Ferlin Husky, The Moonglows, Shaye Cogan.

"Mr. Rock and Roll" has the artistic impact of an animated jukebox—but not very animated. Like the previous cinematic efforts starring Alan Freed, the WINS, N. Y., disk jockey who is chiefly responsible for the international rock 'n' roll contagion, this pic is aimed straight at the teenage disk fans. How this entry will register at the wickets will depend on whether or not the kids are tiring of this pop musical idiom. At this point, there may be enough steam left in rock 'n' roll to draw 'em in sufficient quantities to get this modest-budgeter off the nut at least.

In many respects, this pic runs off like an unadorned filmization of one of Freed's typical stage shows. For the predominant part of its running time, it consists of a series of rock 'n' roll vocalists and combos doing their routines against a simple backdrop and to the swooning tumult of canned applause. Unless one is hep to the nuances of rock 'n' roll, as most kids seem to be nowadays, the music may sound slightly monotonous and more than slightly cacaphonous.

The string of rock 'n' roll turns is pieced together by a script that's as primitive as the music. The plot revolves around some newspaper columnist's charge that rock 'n' roll generates juvenile delinquency and Freed's attempt to prove that the rocking 'n' rolling kids are the salt of the earth. The yarn is a too obvious hat-rack for the musical numbers and the pic might be more palatable as a straight revue.

The performances in the dramatic roles are on a par with a script. Freed, in the title role, does little but shout into microphones, either on a theatre stage or in a radio studio. Teddy Randazzo, as the male crooner who romances the secretary of the newspaper columnist, projects excellently as a singer, but his thesping is severely limited by a "dese, dems and dose" diction. Lois O'Brien, as the secretary, has little to do while Al Fisher and Lou Marks, as a pair of comic songpluggers, are ludicrous without being funny. Rocky Graziano, a natural performer, is utterly wasted in a silly role. Jay Barney, as the columnist, makes the most of his bit part.

Among the musical performers, Lionel Hampton has a big segment and hits with his drive even though the format is completely flat. Others who should click with the kids are Clyde McPhatter, Frankie Lymon & His Teenagers, Little Richard, and LaVern Baker. *Herm.*

Rockabilly Baby
(REGALSCOPE)

Youthful medley of songs and romance; good programmer.

Hollywood, Oct. 11.

Twentieth-Fox release of William F. Claxton production. Stars Virginia Field, Douglas Kennedy, Les Brown and Band of Renown; features Irene Ryan, Ellen Corby, Lewis Martin, Judy Busch, Marlene Willis, Gary Vinson. Directed by Claxton. Screenplay, Will George, William Driskill; camera, Walter Strenge; editor, Robert Pritch; music, Paul Dunlap. Previewed Oct. 9, '57. Running time, **81 MINS.**

Eleanor Carter .... Virginia Field
Tom Griffith .... Douglas Kennedy
Les Brown (Himself) .... Les Brown
Eunice .... Irene Ryan
Mrs. Wellington .... Ellen Corby
Mr. Hoffman .... Lewis Martin
Mr. Rogers .... Norman Leavitt
Mr. Johnson .... Gene Roth
Mrs. Rogers .... June Jocelyn
Mrs. Hoffman .... Mary Benoit
Mrs. Hill .... Hazel Shermet
Charles Leonard .... Renny McEvoy
Chuck Hoffman .... Tony Marshall
Tex .... James Goodwin
Ray Hill .... Ken Miller
Bill Haney .... Jimmy Murphy
Pete Rudd .... Barry Truex
Jackie .... Sandy Wirth
Nancy (Vougette No. 1)... Cindy Robbins
Vougette No. 2 .... Susan Easter
Vougette No. 3 .... Barbara Gayle
Vougette No. 4 .... Susan Volkmann
Vougette No. 5 .... (Caryl Volkmann
Cathy .... Judy Busch
Linda .... Marlene Willis
Jimmy Carter .... Gary Vinson
Coach Stone .... Phil Tead
The Butler .... Watson Downs
The Drunk .... Frank Marlowe
The Bum .... Frank Sully
Carnival Barker .... Ronald Foster
Singer .... Fred Darian (Luis Amando)

Bright and breezy, "Rockabilly Baby" will hit a responsive chord among teenagers especially and is refreshing fare for lower slot of program situations. Going out packaged with Regal's "Young and Dangerous," it complements the more dramatic film on light side.

The William F. Claxton production has Les Brown and his Band of Renown for name lure among the swing lovers, and film benefits strongly by six song numbers socked over for good effect. Claxton, who also directs, has tossed in several water polo sequences for novelty, since sport seldom has been glimpsed on the screen, and has lined up a flock of youthful players who generally liven up the quick-tempoed footage.

Script by Will George and William Driskill focuses on Virginia Field, a former fan dancer, and her two teenage youngsters, Gary Vinson and Judy Busch, arriving in a small town to make their home. Faced with bigotry before, they hope now to start a new life, which they do shortly by the mother becoming active in community affairs and the kids in school. Vinson, a star swimmer, leads his school to first-time victory in water polo meets, and Judy starts several clubs after refusing to join school's one exclusive club. Youngsters develop romances and the mother her own, with the school principal, Douglas Kennedy. When a jealous femme discovers family's secret, she tries to make trouble, but town's populace, headed by the social leader, insists they remain.

Cast generally turn in good accounts of themselves and Claxton has given action a high gloss of smoothness. Miss Field delivers solidly, and romance with Kennedy, capable in role, is convincing. It's the kids here who will be best received. Both Vinson and Judy display interesting talent as well as good voices, and Marlene Willis, another newcomer, comes through in top form with pair of song numbers, "Is It Love?" and "I'd Rather Be." Tony Marshall lends interest as polo captain and Sandy Wirth persuasively plays a spoiled daughter of wealth. Irene Ryan, Ellen Corby and Lewis Martin also are competent.

Technical credits add to film's worth, including Walter Strenge's photography, Ernst Fegte's production designing, Robert Pritch's editing and Paul Dunlap's music score. Dunlap also composed the song numbers. *Whit.*

L'Ultima Notte D'Amore
(The Last Night of Love)
(ITALO-SPANISH—COLOR)

Rome, Oct. 15.

Columbia-CEIAD release of a Merenfil-Hesperia production. Stars Marta Toren, Amadeo Nazzari, Rafael de Cordova, Nadia Marlowa. Directed by Luis Ardavin. Screenplay, Ardavin, Tolnay, Valeri; from story by Lahos Zilabi; camera (Ferraniacolor), Enzo Serafin. Music, Carlo Innocenzi. At Capranica, Rome. Running time, **95 MINS.**

Michele .... Amedeo Nazzari
Isabella .... Marta Toren
Marcella .... Nadia Marlowa
Alomar .... Rafael de Cordova

Professional thesping and adroit direction help make a conventional story of a mother's sacrifice to save her daughter's besmirched reputation interesting and even suspenseful. Though missing as a general situationer, pic is a good lingual entry, in either of its two versions.

A diplomat's daughter living in Madrid gets into trouble via a love affair with a dancer who lives in an upstairs apartment. When he's found murdered, clues uncovered by her father point to her mother as the mistress-killer, until the finale unveils fact that the mother was just covering up for the reckless teenager.

Marta Toren, in one of her last roles, and Amedeo Nazzari ably render their roles as the diplomats while Nadia Marlowa registers via a strange poutish beauty. Rafael de Cordova does some expert terping while others give good backing. Ferraniacolor lensing by Enzo Serafin and other technical credits are good. *Hawk.*

The One That Got Away
(BRITISH)

Well made, but often tedious, escape story based on real-life adventure; lacks star marquee appeal.

London, Oct. 15.

Rank (Julien Wiatte) production and release. Stars Hardy Kruger. Directed by Roy Baker. Screenplay, Howard Clewes, from book by Kendal Burt and Jeames Leasor; editor, Sidney Hayers; camera, Eric Cross; music, Hubert Clifford. At Odeon, Leicester Square, London. Running time, **111 MINS.**

Franz von Werra .... Hardy Kruger
Army Interrogator .... Colin Gordon
R.A.F. Interrogator .... Michael Goodliffe
R.A.F. Intelligence Officer
Terence Alexander
Commandant, Grizedale .... Jack Gwillim
Lieutenant, Grizedale ...... Andrew Faulds
Booking Clerk .... Julian Somers
Duty Officer, Hucknall.... Alec McCowen
German Prisoners ...... Harry Lockhart, Robert Crewdson, George Mikell, George Roubicek, John Van Eyssen, Frederick Jaeger, Richard Marner and Paul Hansard

Once again Britain has flipped through the war files in search of a film plot. "The One That Got Away" is a straightforward escape yarn based on a real life incident, but the switch is that the hero is a Nazi, played by German actor Hardy Kruger. The film is competently made but tends towards occasional tedium and since neither Kruger nor the supporting actors have the least marquee value either in Britain or U. S., the pic is unlikely to create more than tepid interest.

Oberleutnant Franz von Werra of the Luftwaffe was the German prisoner of war captured in Britain to escape and get back to Germany. Shot down in Britain, this brash, cocky young man made no secret of his determination to escape. He even bet the R.A.F. interrogator a bottle of champagne to a pack of cigarets that he would make his getaway within six months.

He made two audacious attempts but was recaptured. Then, with other P.O.W.'s he was sent to Canada and broke away from the train near Montreal. After an arduous trek across the frozen St. Lawrence, he got into the then-neutral America. From there he eventually broke away into Mexico and finally got back to his homeland. Fortunately, the audience is spared details of his adventures after reaching U. S.

It is not a moot point whether it was worth devoting a complete feature film to the exploits of a German making fools of the British army, air force and intelligence corps. Certainly, the screenplay and Roy Baker's direction exaggerate the British capacity for understatement in an absurd manner. The audience's sympathies will be entirely with the Nazi officer which may well be considered carrying "fair play" a bit too far.

As Von Werra, Kruger is first-class. His insolence and bravado are suggested admirably but, on the whole, he comes out of the adventure as quite a nice fellow. It is a long, exacting role and the climax where doggedly he crawls across the frozen river, dragging a boat with him to bridge the unfrozen part of the river is good cinema. But the film lacks romantic appeal and is slight on humor, the average audience likely eave the theatre as tired as Krumust have been.

The Canadian scenes—actually ot in Sweden—have been splendidly lensed by Eric Cross and director Roy Baker handles his situations well while occasionally falling down on characterization. Colin Gordon, Michael Goodliffe, Terence Alexander and Alec McCowen provide useful support. But the pic is largely a one-man show, and Kruger should be well satisfied with his own efforts. *Rich.*

Monpti
(GERMAN—COLOR)

Frankfurt, Oct. 15.

Herzog Film release of a Neue Deutsche Filmgesellschaft production. Stars Romy Schneider and Horst Buchholz; features Mara Lane, Boy Gobert. Directed by Helmut Kautner. Screenplay, after Gabor von Vaszary's novel of same name; camera, Guenther Senftleben; music, Bernhard Eichhorn; editor, Anneliese Schoennenback. At Turmpalast, Frankfurt. Running time, **97 MINS.**

Anne Claire .... Romy Schneider
Monpti .... Horst Buchholz
Nadine .... Mara Lane
Monpti II .... Boy Gobert

A sort of 20th Century "La Boheme," with words instead of opera, set in Paris. "Monpti," a shortcut version of "mon petite," my little darling, this should loom okay in U. S.

With top young German actress Romy Schneider about to be introduced to Stateside audiences with the Disney release of her last year's biggest grossing film "Sissy," this film, which co-stars her with "the James Dean of Germany," Horst Buchholz, could do real business in America once the leads become introduced there. Buchholz may win a U. S. pic pact.

This tender tragic love story, based on the novel "Montpi," concerns the two leads mainly. She's a seamstress in a dress shop, who pretends to be a wealthy girl in order to avoid the thought of a life of bleak poverty. But she falls in love with the penniless young Hungarian artist whom she calls "Montpi." With constant jealousies and misunderstandings, mostly propelled via her lies to conceal her true identity, they quarrel on the eve of their wedding. He flees in a taxi and she, pursuing on foot, runs into the street, is struck by a passing car and dies.

A double plot is the parallel love story interspersed concerning a couple of jaded sophisticates, whose paths cross with the young lovers, but without either couple being aware of the existence of the other. Sexy Mara Lane plays the about-to-be divorced playgirl, and Boy Gobert is her bored lover. They seek reality and meaning in their empty lives and never note the impoverished lovers finding it in the background. A "typical Parisian commentary" by a "typical Parisian" sitting on a park bench and philosophizing about the significance of a few moments in life opens and closes the picture. Speaker is versatile director Helmut Kautner.

Plus factors in the film are the very realistic settings of the poor artists' quarter of Paris, and the accomplished acting of the two leads, who turn the little love story into a touching one. Miss Schneider, like most leading German actresses, offers more the sweetness of a little sister than of sex appeal. Buchholz has a brooding sensitive quality that is a tremendous draw for the femmes.

In Agfacolor, this pic offers much more imagination than the usual German productions. *Haze.*

The Monolith Monsters

Another science-fiction programmer of the assembly line, although it's better made and more plausible than most.

Hollywood, Oct. 17.

Universal production and release. Stars Grant Williams and Lola Albright; features Les Tremayne, Trevor Bardette, Phil Harvey, William Flaherty. Produced by Howard Christie. Directed by John Sherwood. Screenplay by Norman Jolley and Robert M. Fresco, from story by Jack Arnold and Fresco. Camera, Ellis W. Carter; editor, Patrick McCormack; art direction, Alexander Golitzen, Robert E. Smith; music supervision, Joseph Gershenson. Previewed Oct. 16, '57. Running time, **76 MINS.**

Dave Miller .... Grant Williams
Cathy Barrett .... Lola Albright
Martin Cochrane.......... Les Tremayne
Prof. Arthur Flanders.... Trevor Bardette
Ben Gilbert .... Phil Harvey
Police Chief Dan Corey.. William Flaherty
Dr. Steve Hendricks...... Harry Jakson
Doctor Reynolds .... Richard Cutting
Ginny Simpson .... Linda Scheley
Highway Patrolman .... Dean Cromer
Joe Higgins .... Steve Darrell
Weather Man .... William Schallert

Science-fictioner off the assembly line for the program market. But better-made and more plausibly constructed than most. With recent headlines directing attention to the heavens, it has certain built-in exploitation values. However, lack of star names, plus a number of production crudities, doesn't promise too much.

Main flaws are in the screenplay of Norman Jolley and Robert M. Fresco, from a Jack Arnold-Fresco original. Story just isn't sturdy enough to be spun out to present length. Also, there's an overage of technicalities in the script, often over the heads of those who have forgotten their chemistry and geology courses. Then again, evidence of a short shooting schedule and a restricted budget are occasionally quite plain.

Tale revolves around a mysterious meteorite which falls near a remote California community. When it comes in contact with water, the meteorite material swells to huge proportions, and turns humans to stone in the process.

Scientists Grant Williams and Trevor Bardette uncover this after several deaths. By this time, it's started to rain and the community, not to mention the entire country eventually, are threatened with total destruction. However, by frantic experimentation and a lucky guess, Willams comes up with the answer, the marching rocks can be stopped by common salt.

Williams makes a capable juve and should do better in more ambitious projects. Bardette and Les Tremayne handle main support chores in an okay fashion. Role of co-star Lola Albright, as local schoolmarm and Williams' g.f., is routine in conception and gets a like performance, but she's very pretty.

Solid direction of John Sherwood extracts the maximum from script and budget. *Kove.*

Les Oeufs De L'Autruche
(The Ostrich Eggs) (FRENCH)

Paris, Oct. 15.

Jeannic release of Vauban production. Stars Pierre Fresnay; features Simone Renant, Marguerite Pierry, Georges Poujouly, Yoko Tani, Andre Roussin. Directed by Denys De La Patelliere. Screenplay, Frederic Grendel, Sherban Sidery, De La Patelliere from novel by Roussin; dialog, Roussin; camera, Pierre Petit; editor, Robert Isnardon. At Marignan, Paris. Running time, **82 MINS.**

Hippo .... Pierre Fresnay
Therese .... Simone Renant
Mother .... Marguerite Pierry
Roger .... Georges Poujouly
Henri .... Andre Roussin
Princess .... Yok Tani

This concerns a boorish, bourgeois who suddenly realizes he has been pigheadedly blind all his life. He learns that he has a homosexual son, plus another one who is being kept by a Japanese Princess. He also finds that his wife might have left him long ago for his best friend if it had not been for the sons. This all makes for comedy of a sort. Adapted from a hit stageplay, it remains much too talky. However, it looks a local entry of box-office worth but is limited for the U.S. market.

In the stage version, the pompous father suddenly emerged as almost pathetic, but a true comic figure in his blustering to hide his denseness. On screen Pierre Fresnay, who did it on stage also, remains too stagy and rarely gets any true comedics into the vehicle.

The homo son is never shown but is talked about. And when he wins a prize for the best designed dress and is to be given a business by a millionaire, the opportunistic father accepts his son's condition. However, the pic does not quite make this as sharply satirical as it was on the stage. Remainder of the cast is adequate.

Technical aspects are good, but adapters and director have not been able to erase the staginess. Here is a pic with the essential ingredients of an exploitation film but it is still not one. *Mosk.*

Foreign Films

Pied, A Cheval Et En Voiture (By Foot, By Horse and by Car) **(FRENCH).** Cinedis release of Regina-Simoja production. Stars Denise Grey, Noel-Noel, Darry Cowl; features Sophie Daumier, Gil Vidal, Noel Roquevert. Directed by Maurice Delbez. Screenplay, Serge De Boissac, Jacques Antoine, Jean-Jacques Vital; camera, Andre Germain; editor, Gilbert Natot. At the Paris, Paris. Running time, **90 MINS.**

This comedy has caught on here for solid returns. For the U.S., it measures too slight, with a dim tale utilized to get over a few skits about a bourgeois couple learning to drive and buying an auto. The car is bought so they can live up to the rich family of their daughter's beau.

Except for a few yocks this lags, and looms only for special spots in the U.S. Noel Noel overdoes his bungling pater familias. Technical credits are ordinary. *Mosk.*

Paris, Oct. 15.

Carnival Night (RUSSIAN; COLOR; SONGS; DANCE). Mosfilm production and release. With Ludmilla Gourtchenko, Igor Ilinski, Sergi Filippov, Youri Belov, Eddi Rozner Orch (15), Chmelev Sisters (3). Directed by Eldar Riazanov. Screenplay, Boris Lasskine, Vladimir Poliakov; camera (Sovcolor), Arkadi Koltzaty; editor, Oleg Grosse; music, Anatole Lepine. Preemed in Paris. Running time, **75 MINS.**

For first time since the war, at least as far as western screens are concerned, the Soviets have sent out a pert musical that also pokes fun at themselves. Reniniscent of pre-war Hollywood tuners, this details a backstage story about a group of young people staging a revue over the objections of a stuffy state cultural rep.

The latter is the butt as the show swirls around him and he is victimized by all, only to give in when the show is a hit, and tries to claim the glory. Musical numbers are modest but sprightly. Gags are clever and racy, such as a jazz band disguised with beards and going swing after faking a classic opening. Music is not unlike some Western types. Simple entertainment values could help this in European marts and perhaps for a few secondary U.S. situations. *Mosk.*

Vienna, Oct. 15.

Sieben Jahre Pech (Seven Years Hard Luck) **(AUSTRIAN).** Sascha Film release of Erma Film production. Features Edrian Hoven, Gudula Blau, Gunther Philip, Richard Romanovsky, Annie Rosar, Carla Hagen, Ellen Kessler, Chariklia Baxevanos, Helmut Qualtinger, Ernst Waldbrunn. Directed and scripted by Ernst Marischka; camera, Georg Bruckbauer; words and music, Anton Profes, Ernst Marischka. At Flieger Kino, Vienna. Running time, **90 MINS.**

This remake of one of Ernst Marischka's most successful comedies (nearly farce style) of many years ago may again catch the patrons, mainly those who like comedy. There are many comedy angles though Marischka has not forgotten the romantic angle. Two pert love stories run through the film, which deals with hard luck of a composer. Adrian Hoven plays the role of "Heinz Kersten" in excellent style.

It is an all-star cast, with Marischka giving attention to minor details in scripting and directing. The ballet of the Vienna Volksopera has several excellent choreographic scenes in the play. Camera work is fine. Anton Profes contributed a few nice songs and a fitting score while lyrics by Ernst Marischka are great. *Maas.*

Les Suspects (FRENCH). Harispuru release of CCFC-UDCF production. Stars Charles Vanel; features Jacques Morel, Yves Massard, Maurice Teynac, Anne Vernon, Robert Porte, Rene Blanchard. Directed by Jean Dreville. Screenplay, A. Dominique; camera, J. Isnard; editor, Charles Bretoneich. At Colisee, Paris. Running time, **125 MINS.**

This overlong adventure pic concerns Gallic counter espionage tactics in an affair in which a mysterious foreign power is trying to create a bloody Arab uprising in France. Timeliness has this in for okay chances here but it seems too long and obvious for any real U.S. chances except for some dualers.

Stereotyped characters get some measure of relief via the fine acting, especially in Charles Vanel's shrewd characterization of the division topper. Technical credits are good while direction gets some measure of movement into this generally plodding, telegraphed effort. *Mosk.*

Bombers B-52
(C'SCOPE-COLOR)

Exciting air footage hampered by tepid story. Moderate return in general market.

Hollywood, Oct. 25.

Warner Bros. release of Richard Whorf production. Stars Natalie Wood, Karl Malden, Marsha Hunt; features Efrem Zimbalist Jr., Don Kelly, Nelson Leigh, Robert Nichols, Ray Montgomery, Bob Hover. Directed by Gordon Douglas. Screenplay, Irving Wallace; story, Sam Rolfe; camera (WarnerColor), William Clothier; editor, Thomas Reilly; music, Leonard Rosenman. Previewed Oct. 1, '57. Running time, **106 MINS.**

Lois Brennan .... Natalie Wood
Sgt. Chuck Brennan .... Karl Malden
Edith Brennan .... Marsha Hunt
Col. Jim Herlihy ..Efrem Zimbalist Jr.
Sgt. Darren McKind .... Don Kelly
Genl. Wayne Acton .... Nelson Leigh
Stuart .... Robert Nichols
Barnes .... Ray Montgomery
Simpson .... Bob Hover

The U.S. Air Force's mighty B-52 bomber is the real star of this Warner production, which carries a human story of only middling interest. Visual insight is given for the first time on screen of the world's largest, highest and fastest-flying eight-jet intercontinental Stratofortress. Some of the footage is almost breathtaking in scope as a result of highly effective color photography. With the name of Natalie Wood to attract younger generation and exploitation beamed at more mature audiences, the film should do okay biz in general market but would have benefitted considerably by tighter editing.

Heavy focusing of the Irving Wallace screenplay upon a trifling plotline in building to the real guts of the picture, a trial run of the new B-52 from a California air base to Africa and return, militates against attention subject rates until the winding reels. A story of a feud between father and daughter, as latter insists that parent, a top ground crew chief, leave the service he's been in for 20 years and a romance between father's commanding officer and the daughter, are dragged in. Interest lies with the B-52 sequences to compensate for cluttered scripting.

In his direction of the Richard Whorf production, Gordon Douglas socks over the exciting elements and generates good suspense as the returning B-52 is threatened with fire disaster. Camera work by William Clothier and aerial photography by Harold E. Wellman lend particular interest. America's air might as displayed by B-52s in flight formation is well and stirringly pictured.

Karl Malden makes the most of his character, torn between love of duty and love of family, but is called upon for some pretty silly antics in attempted comedy sequences which paint him as an anxious father worried over his daughter staying out late on a date with Efrem Zimbalist, Jr.. Zimbalist, in his role as Malden's commanding officer, who pilots the B-52 on its African flight and safely brings the ship in despite fire, is an interesting newcomer who shows promises. Natalie Wood has little to do but be petulant as the daughter, but Marsha Hunt is warm as a service wife, who understands Malden's problems. Hefty support is afforded by Don Kelly, Nelson Leigh, Stuart Whitman and Michael Emmet in various service roles.

Technical departments are well handled generally. Leonard Rosenman's music score contributes, Leo K. Kuter's art direction registers and Thomas Reilly's editing, while prolonged in story sequences, tightens during final air reels.

Whit.

Ghost Diver
(REGALSCOPE)

Dick Einfeld as a producer. Okay entry for action market.

Hollywood, Oct. 25.

Twentieth-Fox release of Richard Einfeld production. Stars James Craig, Audrey Totter, Nico Minardos; features Lowell Brown, Rodolfo Hoyos Jr., Pira Louis. Directed by Richard Einfeld, Merrill G. White. Screenplay, Einfeld, White; camera, John M. Nickolaus Jr.; editor, White; music, Paul Sawtell, Bert Shefter. Previewed Oct. 23, '57. Running time, **76 MINS.**

Roger Bristol	James Craig
Anne Stevens	Audrey Totter
Pelu Rico	Pira Louis
Manco Capac	Nico Minardos
Bob Bristol	Lowell Brown
Rico	Rodolfo Hoyos Jr.
Bartender	George Trevino
Marguerita	Elena Da Vinci
Stunt & Actor	Paul Stader
Stunt Dble.	Diane Webber
Stunt Dble.	Robert Lorenz
Stunts	Richard Geary, Tom Garland, Michael Dugan

Search for underwater treasure cues this well-handled programmer which fits the demand of action bills. It has the type of story to maintain audience interest, and further benefits by presence of several new faces among the principals.

Film is (Charley's Son) Richard Einfeld's first solo producer effort, and he comes through for good results. He also shares screenplay and direction credit with Merrill G. White, both departments on the plus side. White additionally takes on editing chore, which is fast enough to allow satisfactory suspense, particularly in the underwater scenes when two men engage in a spear-gun duel. An authentic South American background is simulated through good selection of locations here.

James Craig, as star of a top-rating tv adventure show, and Audrey Totter, his secretary who follows him all over the globe, share star billing with Nico Minardos, an interesting new Greek actor who bows in pic as the heavy. Craig, who has come upon a Paracan idol, which is the key to the lost treasure of this forgotten South American Indian tribe, promises his audience he will find this treasure, known to be buried underwater, on his next season's program. Thereupon he heads for the locality where idol was found, accompanied by his secretary and skin-diving son, Lowell Brown.

Opposing him is Minardos, who knows the approximate location of the treasure and who cut the lifeline of the diver who found the idol. Pic takes its title from this diver whose body is found floating in the cavern housing the loot. Underwater sequences are well developed as the Americans finally are successful in their search.

Craig does a good straightforward job with his character and Miss Totter is perky as the secretary, whom he finally marries. Minardos shows favorably in a well-motivated role; Brown is persuasive as the son who stages a couple of actionful fights with Minardos; and Pira Louis, as Minardos' sweetheart, lends interest as another promising newcomer.

John M. Nickolaus Jr.'s camera work is effective and music score by Paul Sawtell and Bert Shefter atmospherically accompanies action.

Whit.

Abominable Snowman
(REGALSCOPE)

Adventure film based on Himalayan legend; handy exploitation entry.

Hollywood, Oct. 25.

Twentieth-Fox release of Aubrey Baring production. Stars Forrest Tucker, Peter Cushing; features Maureen Connell, Richard Wattis, Robert Brown, Michael Brill, Arnold Marle, Wolfe Morris. Directed by Val Guest. Story-screenplay, Nigel Kneal; camera, Arthur Grant; editor, Bill Lenny; music, Humphrey Searle. Previewed Oct. 23, '57. Running time, **83 MINS.**

Tom Friend	Forrest Tucker
Dr. Rollason	Peter Cushing
Helen Rollason	Maureen Connell
Peter Fox	Richard Wattis
Ed Shelley	Robert Brown
McNee	Michael Brill
Kusang	Wolfe Morris
Lhama	Arnold Marle
Major Domo	Anthony Chin

Based upon a legend of the Himalayas, this British import has been imaginatively produced to embrace strange elements. Subject bears good exploitation potential and is a suitable entry for the adventure market. Pic will be packaged in release with "Ghost Diver" (also reviewed here).

The Aubrey Baring production takes its theme from tales brought back by Himalayan climbing expeditions—which have received wide front-page coverage—of mysterious figures in the upper levels known as "Abominable Snowmen," whose giant footprints reportedly have been seen but never the creatures themselves. In his story and screenplay, in which he draws on Lhama philosophy, Nigel Kneal builds a plausible narrative as a small party of five men conducts a search for these Yeti—as they're called by the superstitious natives—and finds them, with tragic consequences.

Picture was lensed largely in the Pyrenees, which provides realistic backgrounds of which director Val Guest takes fine advantage. He generates plenty of suspense as the party comes under the spell of the Yetis, the premise posed here that these are a race of super-intelligent beings who will take over the world when humanity has destroyed itself. Unfoldment is logical and exciting at times.

Forrest Tucker and Peter Cushing top the cast, former as an American adventurer who heads the party, latter an English botanist with climbing experience. Both give substance to their roles, with Cushing the sole survivor of the expedition. Arnold Marle competently portrays the head of a Lhamasery possessed of occult powers, Maureen Connell scores as Cushing's wife and Richard Wattis is okay as his assistant. Michael Brill, Wolfe Morris and Robert Brown also lend capable support.

Photography by Arthur Grant is interesting and Bill Lenny's tight editing and Humphrey Searle's music score are additional assets.

Whit.

How to Murder A Rich Uncle
(C'SCOPE)

Smart comedy spoofing seedy nobility. Okay for selected situations.

Hollywood, Oct. 25.

Columbia release of John Paxton production. Stars Charles Coburn, Nigel Patrick, Wendy Hiller; features Anthony Newley, Athene Seyler, Kenneth Fortescue, Katie Johnson. Directed by Nigel Patrick. Screenplay, John Paxton; based on play, "Il Faut Tuer Julie," by Didier Daix; camera, Ted Moore; editor, Bert Rule; music, Kenneth V. Jones. Previewed Oct. 11, '57. Running time, **79 MINS.**

Henry	Nigel Patrick
Uncle George	Charles Coburn
Edith	Wendy Hiller
Alice	Katie Johnson
Edward	Anthony Newley
Grannie	Athene Seyler
Aunt Marjorie	Noel Hood
Albert	Kenneth Fortescue
Constance	Patricia Webster
Gilrony	Michael Caine
Inspector Harris	Trevor Reid
Coroner	Cyril Luckham
Radio Officer	Johnson Bayly
Police Sergeant	Martin Boddey
Bar Steward	Kevin Stoney
Colonial Type	Antony Shaw
Postman	Ian Wilson

"How to Murder a Rich Uncle," a provocative title presents dry humor in such a way that it emerges smart adult comedy. Film and subject are a trifle English but should be well received.

Produced and scripted by Hollywood writer John Paxton in England under the Warwick banner, yarn is a departure from the usual Warwick brand of product, which in the past has cleaved to action melodrama. Topic twirls around the efforts of an impoverished British nobleman, Nigel Patrick, to do away with his wealthy uncle in from Canada, as the only "honorable" way to meet his debts.

Somehow, however, these efforts seem to continually backfire, and one by one his family begins to drop off, each meeting the tragic—and violent—and meant for the uncle, played by Charles Coburn. When the always-forgetful noblemen himself is killed by a Rube Goldberg setup, a shotgun pointing straight at the uncle's bedroom door attached by a thread between trigger and door-handle, Coburn is arrested and tried for murder of his doting family but finally is cleared by an elderly cousin.

Comic aspects of the idea are richly fulfilled, the film also being a spoof on British nobility and their refusal to enter trade even as a last resort. Patrick, who also directs for subtle effect, creates a lasting impression as the stuffy and somewhat ingenious nobleman fully convinced he can get away with his plan of murder. It's his picture, rather than Coburn's, in for a good piece of work but in a more conventional role.

A highly capable cast supports, headed by Wendy Hiller as Patrick's absent-minded spouse, one of the victims. Athene Seyler is outstanding as Patrick's mother, another victim; Kenneth Fortescue caricatures the dim-witted son, who takes the uncle's place on Patrick's death calendar; and Katie Johnson is excellent as the elderly spinster responsible for Coburn's acquittal. Patricia Webster, in role of the daughter, only sane member of the family, scores brightly and Anthony Newley is a good character as her boyfriend, an amateur criminologist.

Top technical values provide further assist, including Ted Moore's photography, Bert Rule's editing, John Box' art direction and music score by Kenneth V. Jones.

Whit.

The Bolshoi Ballet
(BRITISH—COLOR)

Brilliant offering for specialized houses; ballet fans will flock to this artistic pic.

London, Oct. 22.

Rank release of a Paul Czinner-I. R. Maxwell production. Stars Galina Ulanova; features Raissa Struchkova, Nikolai Fadeyechev and Bolshoi Theatre Ballet, with Royal Opera House, Covent Garden, orchestra. Editor, Philip Hudsmith; camera, F. B. Onions. At Odeon Theatre, Leicester, London. Running time, **100 MINS.**

"The Bolshoi Ballet" is, necessarily, a specialized pic and though the pic should be assured of a hearty welcome in arty houses, it would be a bold speculator who would risk it in a broader market. Nevertheless, such is the quality of this standout ballet film that it may well appear even to those to whom ballet is either a mystery or a bore.

Paul Czinner has done a service to ballet fans in capturing for the screen the alluring Galina Ulanova, one of the top exponents to terpsichore. She is admirably supported by the Bolshoi Theatre Ballet Co. The film is in two sections. The first half consists of six short ballets while the second half is the longer ballet, "Giselle," with music by A. Adam.

Film gets away to a rousing start with the invigorating "Dance of the Tartars" from Asafiev's "Fountain of Bakhchiserai." Next comes the Spanish dance from Tschaikowsky's "Swan Lake," followed by an enchanting duet by L. Bogomalova and S. Vlasova called, "Spring Water," by Rachmaninoff. Entire ballet company does "Polonaise and Gracovienne" from Glinka's "Ivan Susanin." Ulanova makes her first appearance in Saint-Saens' "Dying Swan." Madame Ulanova dances with superb grace and artistry and this dance is a fitting prelude for the films second half which consists entirely of "Giselle."

There is no doubt that everybody connected with this film has done a great job. The Eastmancolor is magnificent and the colorful costumes and decor are well served by the lensing of F. B. Onions. The entire effect is exhilarating. L. Lavrovsky is responsible for the choreography and the screen version of "Giselle." He has been aided by the shrewd editing of Philip Hudsmith.

But the film stands or falls by the dancing of Ulanova, and even those not technically competent to judge of its quality must respond to its grace. The obvious point arises that for those who are not ballet addicts the entertainment will seem much too long. The varied music, played superbly by the Royal Opera House Covent Garden orchestra, conducted mainly by Yuri Faier, is a delight to the ear. All in all, "The Bolshoi Ballet" has come off as an artistic achievement even if it does not fare equally well at the boxoffice.

Rich.

Escape From San Quentin

Routine meller for the action market; name of Johnny Desmond may lure teenage trade.

Columbia release of Clover (Sam Katzman) production. Stars Johnny Desmond, Merry Anders; features Richard Devon, Roy Engel, William Bryant, Ken Christy, Larry Blake. Directed by Fred F. Sears. Screenplay, Raymond T. Marcus; camera, Benjamin H. Kline; editor, Saul H. Goodkind; music, Lacrindo Almedda; song, "Lonely Lament," by Johnny Desmond. Previewed N.Y., Oct. 17, '57. Running time, **81 MINS.**

Mike Gilbert	Johnny Desmond
Robbie	Merry Anders
Roy Gruber	Richard Devon
Hap Graham	Roy Engel
Richie	William Bryant
Curly Gruber	Ken Christy
Mack	Larry Blake
Piggy	Don Devlin
Mendez	Victor Millan
Sampson	John Merrick
Jerry	Norman Fredric
Georgie	Barry Brooks
Bud	Lennie Smith

With a fair quota of chases, fisticuffs and gun duels in the footage,

"Escape From San Quentin" shapes up as a routine meller for the action market. To insure teenage attention producer Sam Katzman has tossed the top role in this Columbia release to disk artist Johnny Desmond. He offers an exploitable peg of sorts.

As written by Raymond T. Marcus, the yarn recounts the escape of three cons from a San Quentin prison farm. Ringleader in the break is hardened criminal Richard Devon. His partners are Roy Engel and Desmond. Latter, an ex-Air Force man, pilots a small plane that takes him and Devon to freedom while Engel escapes on foot despite a beating from Devon.

Before the law closes in for the inevitable recapture, Desmond finds some romantic interest in Merry Anders. She's the younger sister of his wife Peggy Maley who's suing him for divorce. She's also more or less an innocent bystander in some suspenseful scenes that outline desperate attempts of Devon to arrange a rendezvous with his father who has $119,000 stashed away.

Fred Sears' direction helps point up the action and suspense, but can't get more than a passable performance out of Desmond who's making his second screen appearance with this stint. Singer appealingly warbles "Lonely Lament," a ballad of his own composition and the film's lone tune. With further experience, handsome vocalist's thesping may match the quality of his voice.

A pert blonde, Miss Anders capably handles the romantic requirements of her role. As the sadistic desperado, Devon turns in a credible characterization with the proper emotional overtones. Okay support is provided by Engel, ruthless escapee who's slain by cops; William Bryant, part-time bookie killed by Devon, and Christy, Devon's aging father, among others.

Benjamin H. Kline's camerawork is proficient, particularly in the outdoor sequences. Editing of Saul A. Goodkind is par for the course as is Paul Palmentola's art direction and the Lacrindo Almedda score. Production values bespeak a modest budget. *Gilb.*

Stopover Tokyo

Handsomely - mounted Moto-less "Mr. Moto" picture, but short on story. Outlook routine.

Hollywood, Oct. 25.

20th-Fox release of Walter Reisch production. Stars Robert Wagner, Joan Collins and Edmond O'Brien; with Ken Scott, Reiko Oyama, Larry Keating, Sarah Selby, Solly Nakamura, H. Okhawa, K. J. Seitjo, Demmie Susuki. Directed by Robert L. Breen. Screenplay by Breen and Reisch, from John P. Marquard novel; camera, Charles G. Clarke; editor, Marjorie Fowler; art director, Lyle R. Wheeler, Eddie Imazu; music, Paul Sawtell. Japanese music supervision, Tak Shindo. Previewed Oct. 22, '57. Running time, **100 MINS.**

Mark Fannon .... Robert Wagner
Tina .... Joan Collins
George Underwood .... Edmond O'Brien
Tony Barrett .... Ken Scott
Koko .... Reiko Oyama
High Commissioner .... Larry Keating
Wife of High Commissioner .... Sarah Selby
Nobika .... Solly Nakamura
Lt. Afumi .... H. Okhawa
Katsura .... K. J. Seitjo
Capt. Masao .... Demmei Susuki

What this Moto-less "Mr. Moto" tale adds up to is a handsomely-mounted feature which runs somewhat thin in story before the last reel. Visual beauty of Nipponese locales and names of Robert Wagner, Joan Collins and Edmund O'Brien help counteract plot deficiencies, but prospects seem mild.

What the innumerable heavies who have faced John P. Marquard's famed Japanese detective throughout the years could not accomplish, has been done by scripters Richard L. Breen and Walter Reisch. They have rubbed out the engaging little Oriental sleuth, substituting a clean-cut Yank counter-intelligence agent in his stead.

Wagner, as the agent, has tough assignment of protecting life of Larry Keating, American High Commissioner in Japan (a post since changed to ambassador). Since Keating refuses to recognize his danger, Wagner must accomplish his mission the hard way. Meanwhile, he's involved in an inconclusive romance with Miss Collins, with fellow-agent Ken Scott filling out the triangle.

Baddies, led by Edmond O'Brien, are Bolsheviki bent on stirring up an incident but blowing up the commissioner at a public dedication of a peace movement. O'Brien tries his ingenious best to liquidate Wagner, but succeeds with Japanese agent Solly Nakamura. In anti-climactic finale, Wagner disposes of the bomb, but gets the brush from Miss Collins, who abruptly finds him overly-dedicated to his work.

Subplot concerns joint Wagner-Collins protective custody of cute (sometimes over-cute) Japanese moppet, Reiko Oyama, as orphaned daughter of agent Nakamura. In end, she accepts up-to-then secret death of her father with a singular matter-of-factness, and goes home by herself.

Reisch and Breen also produced and directed, respectively, which is another way of saying they've only got themselves to blame. Staging is routinish in both romantic and action passages, save for colorful backdrop of Japanese scenery and folkways.

Wagner continues to grow thespically, and lends authority to role of the agent. Miss Collins, herself a lovely scenic addition, is also a good actress and handles her undemanding assignment with ease. O'Brien likewise doesn't have to extend himself, but as usual, makes a convincingly smooth heavy. Scott impresses as a find, with rugged good looks and a pleasing screen personality.

Little Miss Oyama leans rather heavily on a Pollyanna-ish note, perhaps a directorial fault, but has a nice, sunny disposition. Others in cast perform capably, including Keating, Sarah Selby as his wife, and Nakamura (especially effective), H. Okhawa and Demmei Susuki as Japanese police officials.

Technical credits are outstanding, especially the striking DeLuxe color photography by Charles G. Clarke, and art direction by Lyle R. Wheeler and Eddie Imazu. *Kove.*

The Hunchback of Notre Dame
(C'SCOPE—COLOR)

Old-fashioned picturization of Victor Hugo classic.

Hollywood, Oct. 31.

Allied Artists release of Robert and Raymond Hakim production. Stars Gina Lollobrigida, Anthony Quinn: features Jean Danet, Alain Cuny, Danielle Dumont, Jean Tissier, Maurice Sarfati, Robert Hirsch, Philippe Clay. Directed by Jean Delannoy. Screenplay, Jean Aurenche, Jacques Prevert, based on novel by Victor Hugo; camera (print by Technicolor), Michael Kelber; music, Georges Auric; editor, Henri Taverna. Previewed Oct. 25, '57. Running time, **103 MINS.**

Esmeralda .... Gina Lollobrigida
Quasimodo .... Anthony Quinn
Phoebus .... Jean Danet
Claude Frollo .... Alain Cuny
Fleur de Lys .... Danielle Dumont
Louis XI .... Jean Tissier
Jehan Frollo .... Maurice Sarfati
Gringoire .... Robert Hirsch
Clopin Trouillefou .... Philippe Clay

This version of the Victor Hugo classic, although beautifully photographed and extravagantly produced, is ponderous, often dull and far overlength. Subject as presented is old-fashioned for today's American audiences, and film will have to be strongly sold. The Gina Lollobrigida name may help in some situations.

Actress is co-starred with Anthony Quinn, who plays the Quasimodo role previously enacted by Lon Chaney (in Universal 1923 version) and Charles Laughton (RKO, 1939). Robert and Raymond Hakim as producers seem more inclined to offer spectacle than concentrate on pointing up story line with any degree of freshness, and direction by Jean Delannoy is static rather than alert to making sum total more than a pageant of color and crowds. From a production standpoint, however, film is costly mounted.

Miss Lollobrigida appears to be somewhat miscast as a naive Gypsy girl of 15th Century Paris, but occasionally displays flashes of spirit. Quinn, as the hunchbacked bell-ringer of Notre Dame who saves the Gypsy girl from hanging and hides her within the sanctuary of the Cathedral, where he becomes her devoted slave, gives a well-etched impression of the difficult role. His makeup is not as extreme as either of the two previous characterizations.

Alain Cuny, the alchemist who comes under the spell of Esmeralda, the Gypsy, and frames her for an attempted murder she did not commit, is called upon for a near-caricature of the part, scarcely convincing in today's market. Jean Danet as captain of the guard for whose stabbing Esmeralda is sentenced to the gallows, and Maurice Sarfati, a struggling poet whom Esmeralda marries to have him from execution by the Gypsies, lend capable support.

Color photography by Michel Kelber is cleverly handled and Rene Renoux' production design catches the spirit of the time of Louis XI. Music by Georges Auric provides melodic backing. *Whit.*

Kiss Them for Me
(C'SCOPE—COLOR)

Cary Grant and Jayne Mansfield in amusing comedy about war aces loving up a short leave in San Francisco; okay boxoffice.

Hollywood, Oct. 31.

Twentieth-Fox release of Jerry Wald Production. Stars Cary Grant, Jayne Mansfield, Suzy Parker, also stars Leif Erickson; features Ray Walston, Larry Blyden, Nathaniel Frey, Werner Klemperer, Jack Mullaney. Directed by Stanley Donen; screenplay, Julius Epstein from the book "Shore Leave" by Frederic Wakeman and the play version "Kiss Them for Me" by Luther Davis; camera (DeLuxe Color), Milton Krasner; editor, Robert Simpson; music, Lionel Newman. Previewed Oct. 30, 57. Running time, **102 MINS.**

Crewson .... Cary Grant
Alice .... Jayne Mansfield
Gwenneth .... Suzy Parker
Eddie Turnbill .... Leif Erickson
Mac (Lieut. McCann) .... Ray Walston
Mississip .... Larry Blyden
C.P.O. Ruddle .... Nathaniel Frey
Commander Wallace .... Werner Klemperer
Ensign Lewis .... Jack Mullaney
R.A.F. Pilot .... Ben Wright
Gunner .... Michael Ross
Roundtree .... Harry Carey Jr.
Neilson .... Frank Nelson
Debbie .... Caprice Yordan
Lucille .... Ann McCrea

It has taken a dozen years and a transition from printed page to stage to screen to lend commercial possibilities to Frederic Wakeman's first novel, "Shore Leave." It was moderately successful as a book and eked out a short run on Broadway as a play by Luther Davis, under the title of "Kiss Them For Me." Now, with virtually all of the serious material excised to hew closely to a comedy line and with Cary Grant and Jayne Mansfield as marquee bait, the film version produced by Jerry Wald for 20th-Fox release looks like okay boxoffice.

Julius Epstein's glib screenplaying of the basic material now emphasizes the comedic aspects of the beetle, four-day "informal" leave in San Francisco of Cary Grant, Ray Walston and Larry Blyden, a trio of naval air aces of the Pacific war. Grant, the reckless leader of the triumvirate, cooly circumvents red tape to get stateside after an extensive tour of duty, with the intention of loving it up for four days. He does, meeting and falling in love with Suzy Parker in the process and winning her away from stuffy tycoon Leif Erickson.

Ralston meanwhile has been victorious in a campaign to be elected a congressman and Blyden has had little luck in the quick romance department. News that their carrier has been sunk, however, sends them back to the war, ignoring the chance for extended shore leave for Grant and Blyden via speaking tours of war plants and Walston's opportunity to become a civilian as a result of his elections. There are occasional and bitter references to wartime profiteers, an angle which dominated much of the play, but the passage of time has dulled the sting and they serve now only to slow the comedy slightly. To overcome this, Epstein has come up with sharp dialog that frequently cues solid chuckles.

Stanley Donen has directed with a fine feeling for the comedy aspects and the film unspools smoothly. Grant is slick and satisfying in the key role and both Walston and Blyden register with conviction. Miss Parker is decorative but without any emotional quality in the role. And Jayne Mansfield wanders in and out to supply good humor, eye appeal and emphasis on war-weary pilots' inclinations in a good portrayal. There's also good work from Erickson and, in much smaller parts, from Nathaniel Frey as a Chief Petty officer; Werner Klemperer as a PRO officer seeking to feather a post-war nest; and Jack Mullaney as an ensign sent to check on the trio's orders and side-tracked by wine, women and song.

Wald's overall production supervision is good and the film has a professional flavor, aided by such technical assists as Milton Krasner's DeLuxe color lensing and Robert Simpson's editing. Lionel Newman did the score and teamed with Carroll Coates for the title tune which the McGuire Sisters sing over the opening and closing credits. *Kap.*

Decision at Sundown
(COLOR)

One of the better of the new-fangled westerns. Randolph Scott following, plus good staging and story values, promises okay returns.

Hollywood, Oct. 25.

Columbia Pictures release of a Scott-Brown Production. Stars Randolph Scott; co-stars John Carroll, Karen Steele, Valerie French; with Noah Beery, John Archer, Andrew Duggan, James Westerfield, John Litel, Ray Teal, Vaughn Taylor, Richard Deacon, H. M. Wynant. Produced by Harry Joe Brown. Directed by Budd Boetticher. Screenplay by Charles Lang Jr., from Vernon L. Fluherty story. Camera (Technicolor), Burnett Guffey; editor, Al Clark; art director, Robert Peterson; music, Heinz Roemheld. Previewed, Oct. 24, '57. Running time, 77 MINS.

Bart Allison	Randolph Scott
Tate Kimbrough	John Carroll
Lucy Summerton	Karen Steele
Ruby James	Valerie French
Sam	Noah Beery
Doctor Storrow	John Archer
Sheriff Swede Hansen	Andrew Duggan
Otis	James Westerfield
Charles Summerton	John Litel
Morley Chase	Ray Teal
Barber	Vaughn Taylor
Zaron	Richard Deacon
Spanish	H. M. Wynant
Abe	Guy Wilkerson

This entry stacks up as one of the better of the new-fangled westerns. Top billed Randolph Scott, with strong and loyal following, bolstered by generally high staging quality by director Budd Boetticher and strong story values, indicate a substantial return on the investment.

There are flaws, however, which should be duly noted. Occasionally, Boetticher's attempts to stretch out suspense results in lag in storytelling pace. Also, climax stoutly defies belief, aggravated by fact that similar situations have already been used in a couple of telepix this season. (With tv concentrating on the west this season, this particular problem of plot exposure promises to get worse for theatrical pix makers, before it gets any better.)

Complex screenplay by Charles Lang Jr., from Vernon L. Fluherty tale, spans a single day in cow town of Sundown. Scott, a mysterious, revengeful gunman, rides into town. He's after unsavory local wheel John Carroll, who's slated to marry local belle Karen Steele on that day. Scott breaks up the wedding and is beseiged with sidekick Noah Beery by Carroll's henchmen. Step by step, it develops that Carroll, in his none-too-scrupulous past, had stolen and later discarded Scott's wife (since dead); and that she hadn't been unwilling, a fact Scott cannot face.

But with first overt resistance to Carroll's iron control over the town, the other natives get restless. Upshot is wholesale revolt and townspeople even out odds against embattled Scott. But in showdown with Carroll, his inamorata, Valerie French, plugs Carroll in the shoulder, thus preventing a gunfight.

Pic ends in downbeat note, with town now rid of Carroll. However, Scott, who also pulls out, is still bitter over truth's he's been forced to acknowledge, plus fact that buddy Beery had been killed by treachery during the gunplay.

Role is an offbeat one for Scott, but he carries off the gunman's frustrated rage very well. Carroll makes convincingly menacing heavy in the suave tradition. Miss Steele, as his understandably confused fiance, shows much promise of things to come. Miss French's motivations aren't always convincing, but she's a good actress who exploits the role fully.

Among rest of large and good cast, Beery is outstanding as the illfated sidekick, with John Archer, Vaughn Taylor, Richard Deacon, Andrew Duggan and John Litel all contributing strong support.

Fine Technicolor lensing by Burnett Guffey and other behind-camera credits show a high degree of professional skill. *Kove.*

Baby Face Nelson

Timely (a la Anastasia hood stuff) exploitation entry with Mickey Rooney name for marquee dressing.

United Artists release of a Fryman-ZS (Al Zimbalist) production. Stars Mickey Rooney; co-stars Carolyn Jones, Sir Cedric Hardwicke, Leo Gordon, Anthony Caruso, Jack Elam, John Hoyt; features Ted De Corsia, Elisha Cook Jr., Thayer David, George Stone. Directed by Don Siegel. Screenplay, Irving Shulman and Daniel Mainwaring, from story by Shulman; camera, Hal Mohr; editor, Leon Barsche; music, Van Alexander. Tradeshown, N.Y., Oct. 25, '57. Running time 85 MINS.

Nelson	Mickey Rooney
Sue	Carolyn Jones
Doc Saunders	Sir Cedric Hardwicke
Jerry	Chrise Dark
Rocca	Ted DiCorsia
Mac	Emile Meyer
Hamilton	Tony Caruso
Dillinger	Leo Gordon
Miller	Dan Terranova
Fatso	Jack Elam
Bonner	Dabbs Greer
Johnson	Bob Osterloh
Powell	Dick Crockett
Aldridge	Paul Baxley
Connelly	Thayer David
Vickman	Ken Patterson
Preston	Sol Gorse
Duncan	Gil Perkins
Harkins	Tom Fadden
Ann Saper	Lisa Davis
Parker	John Hoyt
Van Meter	Elisha Cook
Bank Guard	Murray Alper
Mr. Hall	George Stone
Kearns	Hubie Kerns

With the barbershop murder of mobster Albert Anastasia still fresh in the headlines, United Artists has a hot exploitation picture in "Baby Face Nelson." It might even start a new gangster film cycle. Marquee dressing is provided by Mickey Rooney who essays the title role.

Nelson, in case anyone's memory may have been dimmed by the years, was a member of the notorious Dillinger gang that scourged the midwest circa 1933. Dillinger himself was biopiced by the King Bros. some 12 years ago. Now it's Nelson's turn and the Irving Shulman-Daniel Mainwaring script makes him a ruthless, trigger-happy, coldblooded killer.

Of necessity, in the interest of historical accuracy, the cast wears depression days styles and the footage is replete with chase scenes involving Model A Fords and dated "touring" cars. These aspects, incidentally, cause this Al Zimbalist production to be strongly reminiscent of oldtime action films now shown on video.

The versatile Rooney whose varying roles in his long career have ranged from Puck ("Midsummer Night's Dream") to Pinocchio is not particularly convincing as the pint-sized Nelson. True, he snarls, boils with hatred and is unrepentant. But he merely seems to be going through the motions and his performance never matches the acting found in gangster classics more than two decades ago.

More impressive is Carolyn Jones' portrayal of Rooney's loyal moll. She's a plain jane who's attracted to him by some strange affection. But with the FBI closing in on the wounded Rooney, it is she who kills him when he admits he would even shoot down small boys. This death scene in a cemetery, with which the film ends, is especially maudlin.

Sir Cedric Hardwicke, another versatile actor, turns in a fine characterization of a drunken physician who administers to the medical needs of the Dillinger mobsters. Good support is supplied by Leo Gordon as No. 1 desperado Dillinger, Anthony Caruso as henchman John Hamilton and Jack Elam as the gang's suave mastermind who devised the modus operandi of various bank jobs. *Gilb.*

The Tall Stranger
(C'SCOPE-COLOR)

Good western in an old-fashioned shoot-'em-up vein.

Hollywood, Oct. 23.

Allied Artists Production and Release. Stars Joel McCrea, Virginia Mayo; features Barry Kelley, Michael Ansara; with Whit Bissell, James Dobson, George Neise, Adam Kennedy, Michael Pate, Leo Gordon, others. Produced by Walter Mirisch. Directed by Thomas Carr. Screenplay by Christopher Knopf, from a story by Louis L'Amour; camera, Wilfred Cline; editor, William Austin; art director, David Milton; music, Hans Salter. Previewed Oct. 22, '57. Running time, 82 MINS.

Bannon	Joel McCrea
Ellen	Virginia Mayo
Bishop	Barry Kelley
Zarata	Michael Ansara
Judson	Whit Bissell
Dud	James Dobson
Harper	George Neise
Red	Adam Kennedy
Charley	Michael Pate
Stark	Leo Gordon
Cap	Ray Teal
Will	Philip Phillips
Pagones	Robert Foulk
Mary	Jenifer Lea
Chavez	George J. Lewis
Barrett	Guy Prescott
Murray	Ralph Reed
Purcell	Mauritz Hugo

This is primarily an old-fashioned shoot-'em-up, slug-it-out western, although "modernized" to include references to rape, houses of ill-fame, illegitimacy and a few "Damns" and "Hells," unheard of in the old oater format.

As such, it may offer audiences welcome relief from the current crop of "adult westerns," in which the stress is on extensive and wordy psychological probings. The heroes are quickly and cleverly established as heroes, the villains as villains, and then the plot moves on.

Also making considerable difference is that Christopher Knopf screenplay, from a Louis L'Amour story, while containing some gaps, is generally well-plotted and motivated and director Thomas Carr utilizes these advantages with a brisk skill. B.O. chances seem okay in a wide variety of situations.

Reduced to essentials, story line is the old one about the cow baron and the intruding homesteaders. In this case, homesteaders are a band of emigrating Southern veterans (time is post-Civil War), who pick up Joel McCrea, a returning Union vet, who has been brutally shot from ambush and left to die. McCrea is half-brother to heavy-handed rancher Barry Kelley, on whose land the wagon train is led through sinister machinations of scouts George Neise and Mauritz Hugo.

McCrea attempts peacemaker's role between factions, but winds up in the middle. It develops that Neise-Hugo axis is tied up with outlaw band led by Michael Ansara (who's the unknown who shot down McCrea in the opening scene), and are using the settlers in an intricate cattle-rustling scheme. Eventually, things are resolved in a bang-up gunfight, during which Kelley strangles Ansara before expiring himself, and Neise and the entire baddie crew are otherwise eliminated. Whereupon, McCrea invites the emigrants to settle on what's now his land, and takes up with Virginia Mayo, a somewhat soiled belle who's trying to turn over a new leaf.

McCrea, who knows his way around a western script, enacts the hero with customary authority and conviction. Miss Mayo does a good job as the offbeat heroine (for a western). Kelley is toprate as McCrea's blustering, but good-hearted half-brother. Leo Gordon, Michael Pate, Adam Kennedy, Whit Bissell, Ray Teal, Robert Foulk and George J. Lewis lend strong support and Ansara, Neise and Hugo are adept at their villainy.

DeLuxe color photography isn't always even in quality from shot to shot. Additionally, background music of Hans Salter, while apt enough, has a tendency to overpower in volume, perhaps a sound-editing fault. *Kove.*

All Mine to Give
(COLOR)

Old magazine-and-radio "Day They Gave Babies Away" has strong emotional appeal but very elongated.

Hollywood, Oct. 25.

Universal release of Sam Wiesenthal production. Stars Glynis Johns, Cameron Mitchell, Rex Thompson, Patty McCormack; features Ernest Truex, Hope Emerson, Alan Hale, Sylvia Field, Royal Dano, Reta Shaw. Directed by Allen Reisner. Screenplay, Dale and Katherine Eunson, based on former's Cosmo mag story, "The Day They Gave Babies Away"; camera, William Skall; editors, Alan Crosland Jr., Bettie Mosher; music, Max Steiner. Previewed Oct. 22, '57. Running time, 103 MINS.

Mamie	Glynis Johns
Robert	Cameron Mitchell
Robbie	Rex Thompson
Annabella	Patty McCormack
Dr. Delbert	Ernest Truex
Mrs. Pugmire	Hope Emerson
Tom Cullen	Alan Hale
Lelia Delbert	Sylvia Field
Howard Tyler	Royal Dano
Mrs. Runyon	Reta Shaw
Jimmie	Stephen Wootton
Kirk	Butch Bernard
Elizabeth	Yolanda White
Katie Tyler	Rita Johnson
Mrs. Raiden	Ellen Corby
Mrs. Stephens	Rosalyn Boulter
Mr. Stephens	Francis DeSales
Bobbie	Jon Provost

"All Mine To Give" is a tear-jerger. Vastly overlong in its meandering buildup to the climaxing sequences which give warmth and certain enchantment to the unfoldment, film still should be well received by both distaff and family audiences. Extreme length of 103 minutes will create certain booking difficulties.

Picturization of Dale Eunson's Cosmo mag story, "The Day They Gave Babies Away," done years ago on radio's Columbia Workshop, concerns the efforts of the eldest of six children, aged 12, to find homes on Christmas Day for his small brothers and sisters after the death the day before of their widowed mother. Present script of Eunson and his wife, Katherine, now precedes this episode with a long recital of the trials of the parents, Glynis Johns and Cameron Mitchell, when, as young, impoverished Scottish immigrants, they arrive in a small Wisconsin frontier settlement and start their family.

Allen Reisner, tv director making his bow in motion pictures, manages interesting characterizations from cast and Sam Wiesenthal comes up with suitable production values. Both Miss Johns and Mitchell are excellent, and Rex Thompson, as the youngster responsible for placing the children left in his charge, before the county can take over, delivers strongly. Stephen Wootton and Patty McCormack also score interestingly in moppet roles, and strong support is offered by Ernest Truex, Sylvia Field, Hope Emerson, Alan Hale and Royal Dano.

Technical credits are headed by William Skall's fine color photography. *Whit.*

Gun Battle at Monterey

Very minor entry for western market.

Hollywood, Nov. 1.

Allied Artists release of Carl Hittleman production. Stars Sterling Hayden, Pamela Duncan, Ted de Corsia, Mary Beth Hugh; features Lee Van Cleef, Charles Cane, Pat Comiskey, Byron Foulger, Mauritz Hugo, I. Stanford Jolley. Directed by Hittleman, Sidney A. Franklin Jr. Screenplay, Jack Leonard, Lawrence Resner; camera, Harry Neumann; editor, Harry Coswick; music, Robert Wiley Miller. Previewed Oct. 28, '57. Running time. 67 MINS.

Turner	Sterling Hayden
Maria	Pamela Duncan
Reno	Ted de Corsia
Cleo	Mary Beth Hughes
Kirby	Lee Van Cleef
Mundy	Charles Cane
Frank	Pat Comiskey
Carson	Byron Foulger
Charley	Mauritz Hugo
Idwall	I. Stanford Jolley

"Gun Battle at Monterey"—the title bearing no connection with subject matter—is a minor western entertainment. It suffers from a contrived plot and performances which neither ring true nor evoke interest. Pic's sole asset is star name of Sterling Hayden for marquee lure.

The Carl Hittleman production is premised along lines so hoary they creak, and Hittleman and Sidney A. Franklin Jr., in their dual direction add little to Jack Leonard-Lawrence Resner screenplay.

Hayden, shot in the back and left for dead by Ted de Corsia, his partner in a holdup in Monterey, seeks vengeance after his recovery.

Hayden fails to give a definite performance, with result small interest attaches to the unfoldment, and de Corsia's characterization is overplayed. Pamela Duncan, as the Mexican girl who saves his life, and Mary Beth Hughes, dealer in the casino, are as good as their few lines permit. Lee Van Cleef is heavy as de Corsia's gunman employee, and Charles Cane is a drunken sheriff.

Technical credits are standard. *Whit.*

Sayonara
(TECHNIRAMA—COLOR)

James A. Michener's tender, sometimes angry novel of love and race prejudice involving U. S. military personnel in Japan. One of year's best films. Should be b.o. smash.

Warner Bros. release of William Goetz production. Stars Marlon Brando, Ricardo Montalban, Patricia Owens, Martha Scott, James Garner, Miiko Taka, Miyoshi Umeki; presenting Red Buttons; featuring Kent Smith, Douglas Watson, Reiko Kuba, Soo Yong and Shochuku Kagekidan Girls Revue. Directed by Joshua Logan. Screenplay, Paul Osborn, from James A. Michener novel; camera (Technirama-Technicolor), Ellsworth Fredricks; editors, Arthur P. Schmidt, Philip W. Anderson; music, Franz Waxman; song ("Sayonara") words and music by Irving Berlin. Previewed Nov. 4, '57, at Criterion, N.Y. Running time, 147 MINS.

Major Gruver	Marlon Brando
Kelly	Red Buttons
Nakamura	Ricardo Montalban
Eileen Webster	Patricia Owens
Mrs. Webster	Martha Scott
Bailey	James Garner
Hana-ogi	Miiko Taka
Katsumi	Miyoshi Umeki
General Webster	Kent Smith
Colonel Craford	Douglas Watson
Fumiko-san	Reiko Kuba
Teruko-san	Soo Yong

William Goetz's "Sayonara," based on the James A. Michener novel, is a picture of beauty and sensitivity. Amidst the tenderness and the tensions of a romantic drama, it puts across the notion that human relations transcend race barriers, whether they are put up by U. S. Armed Forces in Japan or by segregationists in the American South.

Executed by a top cast and paced by Marlon Brando in an outstanding performance, "Sayonara" is, in most respects, a major screen achievement. In its long (but not too long) running time, it fuses all the vital elements of superior film drama—solid story, knowing direction, the colorful, delicately poetic backgrounds of Japan, personalities that come to life as completely believable people and—most important—a definite, unwavering point-of-view.

Joshua Logan's direction is tops. He tells his story leisurely and with a full awareness of all the values the strange locale affords his camera. Yet, action never lags, and the viewer is held from beginning to end. It's a strange story, in some respect, and certainly its "message" is an unconventional one. It may displease some racial hatrioteers. It's certainly candid in delineating the attitudes of the Army and Air Force brass towards "Asiatics."

But there are sock values in the very controversiality of the theme and the blunt manner of its execution, running side-by-side with the romantic story line. With light touches, it's the kind of many-faceted picture that should click on most audience levels.

Though strongly supported, particularly by the television refugee, Red Buttons, it's Brando who "carries" the production with one of his best performances. As Major Gruver, the Korean war air-ace, Brando affects a nonchalant Southern drawl that helps set the character from the very start. In the picture, he grows and matures, finally freeing himself of his need to conform with redneck standards. He is wholly convincing as the race-conscious Southerner whose humanity finally leads him to rebel against Army-imposed prejudice.

Story has combat-fatigued Brando transferred to Kobe for a rest and to meet his Stateside sweetheart, Patricia Owens, daughter of the commanding general of the area. They find things have changed and the sensitive, well-educated girl is no longer sure she wants to marry Brando. He in turn is upset because Airman Joe Kelly, played by Buttons, wants to marry a Japanese (Miyoshi Umeki). When Buttons goes through with the marriage, with Brando acting as best man, a Southern Army colonel goes after the boy and wants to ship him off to the States where his pregnant wife can't follow.

Brando meets a beautiful Japanese actress-dancer (Miiko Taka) and gradually falls deeply in love with her. When Buttons and his wife, in desperation, commit suicide, Brando realizes that, regardless of the consequences, he must marry Miss Taka.

There are many fine shadings in this story and Logan's direction brings them out vividly. The performance he gets out of Buttons, deeply moving in its sincerity, should raise the erstwhile air comic to entirely new stature. In this "straight" part, he's excellent and his devotion and final desperation ring completely true. He's the spunky little guy who braves the Army rules—and loses. Playing opposite him, Miss Umeki is charmingly simple. Their relationship has warmth and understanding.

Miss Taka plays the proud Hana-ogi, the dedicated dancer, who starts by hating the Americans whom she sees as robbing Japan of its culture and ends in Brando's arms. Apart from being beautiful she's also a distinctive personality and her contribution rates high. As Nakamura, the Japanese dancer, Ricardo Montalban represents Japanese refinement and intelligencia. His character allows the camera to witness several colorful Japanese classical dance sequences.

In the smaller roles, Martha Scott is properly sharp as the class and race-conscious wife of the general. It's an unsympathetic part for her, and she carries it off very well. Miss Owens plays the sensitive daughter, delighted and intrigued by Japanese culture and basically unsuited to conformist Brando. As her father, Kent Smith makes the general appear torn between personal decency and a slave to Army regulations. His little speech about the army being "father" to its "confused" boys has bite and irony.

Douglas Watson is suitably stuffy as the Dixiecrat Colonel, determined to maintain the "color line." James Garner is attractive and at ease as the marine captain, carrying on an affair with a Japanese girl, attractively portrayed by Reiko Kuba.

Lenser Ellsworth Fredricks has used the Technirama-Technicolor camera to best advantage. His landscapes are an important factor in setting the mood of the story. The colors are delicate and yet stirring, particularly in the lively music hall and other dance sequences, staged by LeRoy Prinz. The Japanese theatre scenes contribute, but could stand some cutting.

Paul Osborn's script is a model of its kind. He has adapted the story faithfully from the Michener novel, and his lines give the actors every possible chance. Scripting maintains a good balance between dialog and action. Combination of Osborn, Logan and Brando creates many poignant scenes, particularly the one where Brando finds the bodies of Buttons and his wife. Osborn also has taken the opportunity of reminding Americans that inter-marriage is frowned on as much by many Japanese as it is by some Americans.

Franz Waxman wrote the music, and Irving Berlin wrote words and music for the song, "Sayonara," which has a haunting quality. Arthur P. Schmidt and Philip W. Anderson did the editing, which maintains an even story flow. Norma Koch designed the attractive costumes which, in a story like this, are particularly important.

Producer Goetz has imbued "Sayonara" with all the values of a top production. It'll have its critics among those who claim that the screen is here simply to entertain and that the race angle is allowed to interfere with the romantic story line. But most will judge the composite to be highly effective, making this one of the year's strongest entries. *Hift.*

The Persuader

A "religious" western. Extensive verbal sermonizing. Maybe some church tie-in angles. Otherwise dull prospects.

Hollywood, Nov. 11.

Allied Artists release of a World Wide Pictures Production. Stars William Talman, James Craig; co-stars Kristine Miller, Darryl Hickman, Georgia Lee, Alvy Moore; with Gregory Walcott, Rhoda Williams, Paul Engle, Jason Johnson, Nolan Leary, John Milford, Frank Richards. Producer-director, Dick Ross. Screenplay by Curtis Kenyon; camera, Ralph A. Woolsey; editor, Eugene Pendleton; art director, Walter Keller; music, Ralph Carmichael. Title song by Carmichael, sung by James Joyce. Previewed, Nov. 5. '57. Running time, 72 MINS.

Matt Bonham,	
Mark Bonham	William Talman
Bick Justin	James Craig
Kathryn Bonham	Kristine Miller
Toby Bonham	Darryl Hickman
Cora Nicklin	Georgia Lee
Willy Williams	Alvy Moore
Jim Cleery	Gregory Walcott
Nell Landis	Rhoda Williams
Paul Bonham	Paul Engle
Morse Fowler	Jason Johnson
Dan	Nolan Leary
Clint	John Milford
Steve	Frank Richards

In recent years, the standard oater formulas have been widened to include the "adult" westerns. Comes now a new tack, "The Persuader," which is a western with a strong religious flavor.

It is not possible to report that this experiment is on par with other "adults." Stress is on "verbal" sermonizing, delivered earnestly and at great length. With staunch churchgoers the best possible audience, one exploitation possibility is a round of church dates. But as a strictly commercial venture, "The Persuader's" chances are anything but persuasive.

Story by Curtis Kenyon stresses theme that loving-kindness conquers all, even a band of hardbitten heavies. Principal opponents are preacher William Talman and gang leader James Craig. Talman arrives in a small Oklahoma town to find his brother murdered for resisting Craig and the townspeople cowed and complacent. With a powerful lot of preachifying and the example of his courage, Talman gradually stiffens the spines of the citizenry. In unconvincing climax, Craig, impressed by this new solidarity, passes a chance to burn down the new church and decides to move on.

Darryl Hickman, as the dead twin's revenge-bent son, is involved in some contrived plotting, but his role doesn't add up to anything significant.

Dick Ross produced and directed with laudable intentions, but his execution distinctly lacks professionalism. Cast falls largely into stereotype although Talman lends some stature to his double part. Kristine Miller as the dead man's widow, Hickman and Georgia Lee, as his wholesome g.f., are as good as the script will allow. Alvy Moore, as a Craig henchie who gets killed for shifting sides, is especially impressive in support. Craig himself makes a properly suave and dangerous heavy, but he can't be assessed for failure of screenplay to make sense of his role.

Title song by Ralph Carmichael and sung by James Joyce while okay in its class, was overly loud at the viewing and intrusive in overworked employment of the "High Noon" device. In several scenes, footage was very jerky and uncomfortable to watch, but this could have been a projection fault. Other technical credits are adequate. *Kove.*

Don't Go Near the Water
(C'SCOPE—COLOR)

Spoof on Navy public relations "war" in the Pacific. Broadly handled for laughs and rating a "well done" for boxoffice results; Glenn Ford and Gia Scala head cast.

Metro release of Lawrence Weingarten production. Stars Glenn Ford; features Gia Scala, Earl Holliman, Anne Francis, Keenan Wynn, Fred Clark, Eva Gabor, Russ Tamblyn, Jeff Richards, Mickey Shaughnessy. Directed by Charles Walters; screenplay, Dorothy Kingsley and George Wells; from novel of same title by William Brinkley; camera (Metrocolor), Robert Bronner; editor, Adrienne Fazan; music, Bronislau Kaper; title song lyrics, Sammy Kahn. Previewed Loew's State Theatre, N.Y., Sept. 30, '57. Running time, **107 MINS.**

Lt. Max Siegel	Glenn Ford
Melora	Gia Scala
Adam Garrett	Earl Holliman
Lt. Alice Tomlen	Anne Francis
Gordon Ripwell	Keenan Wynn
Lt. Comdr. Clinton T. Nash	Fred Clark
Deborah Aldrich	Eva Gabor
Ensign Tyson	Russ Tamblyn
Lt. Ross Pendelton	Jeff Richards
Farragut Jones	Mickey Shaughnessy
Adm. Boatwright	Howard Smith
Mr. Alba	Romney Brent
Janie	Mary Wickes
Lt. Comdr. Gladstone	Jack Straw
Lt. Comdr. Hereford	Robert Nichols
Lt. Comdr. Diplock	John Alderson
Rep. George Jansen	Jack Albertson
Rep. Arthur Smithfield	Charles Watts

Light and likeable. "Don't Go Near the Water" sets out to woo the public with impishness and comedic absurdities in describing the adventures of Madison Avenueites assigned to public relations duty with the Navy on a Pacific island during World War II. Mission is well accomplished—meaning, top bookings and boxoffice satisfaction.

Excepting Glenn Ford, who's had sea duty, the crowd of bally hooligans don't go near the water, their war heroics being in the struggle to accommodate visiting Congressmen, assuaging a correspondent bent on uncovering news they'd like to keep secret, keeping the folks at home apprised of the glories of the service, and so on.

While it comes off amusingly, due in good part to a funny slowburn performance by Fred Clark as the p.r. commandant, "Water" has one bit family trade may not fancy. Much footage is given to Mickey Shaughnessy as a brawny, ribald seaman who is addicted to constant use of a four-letter obscenity, which he mouths but everytime it's drowned out by a soundtrack boat horn. This is the glorification of a dirty joke.

Other than that, "Water" is clean fun, offering a series of humorous situations held on a light story line and backed by a handsomely laid-out Lawrence Weingarten production. Metrocolor and CinemaScope provide top visuals and sets and art work make the ocean outpost look like the real thing.

Tone of the picture is established at the outset via this foreword:- *"This is a story of some of those fearless and wonderful guys in Navy public relations. They push a perilous pencil, pound a dangerous typewriter and fire a deadly paper clip, but they' . . . 'Don't Go Near the Water'."*

Screenplay by Dorothy Kingsley and George Wells is a bright adaptation of the successful William Brinkley novel of the same title. It offers a collection of colorful characters engaged in a variety of little subplots that are meshed together in an ingratiating whole.

Among the problems the p.r. contingent also is called upon to cope with are Howard Smith who, as Admiral Boatwright, bristles and burns in his hostility toward the displaced - misplaced advertising geniuses playing war; the aforementioned correspondent (played with proper "heavy" overtones by Keenan Wynn) who insists on a regular change of linen; and, for good measure, a cleavaged, flashy Eva Gabor, who comes in late as a women's mag rep maneuvering herself aboard a cruiser that engages in actual battle. This last piece of business, which has the ship waving a pair of Miss Gabor's black panties as sort of a victory pennant after the skirmish, is comedy in its broadest sense, going overboard in the quest for laughs.

Couple of romances are woven through all this. Ford and Gia Scala, an exotic looker on hand as the European-educated daughter of a local citizen, team up nicely to the inevitable happy conclusion, including a school built for her through funds gotten out of Wynn in justified extortion. Earl Holliman makes time with Anne Francis despite regulations, he being a lowly yeoman and she a nurse lieutenant. Russ Tamblyn as an eager member of Clark's staff and Jeff Richards as the conceited wolf of the island round out the cast, all members of which are well placed for this kind of easy-to-take entertainment.

Charles Walters' direction is paced at full throttle and organized remarkably well, considering the numerous separate little adventures tucked into the overall smooth continuity. Adrienne Fazan's editing is a major credit, the rapid scene changes contributing to the picture's fast flow. Music by Bronislau Kaper is in the right kind of lighthearted mood, Robert Bronner's photography is splendid, ditto other credits. *Gene.*

The Birthday Present
(BRITISH)

Smooth, but uninspired routine offering which suffers from lack of marquee appeal; only fair b.o. prospects.

London, Nov. 5.

British Lion release of Jack Whittingham production. Stars Tony Britton, Sylvia Syms; features Jack Watling, Walter Fitzgerald, Geoffrey Keen. Directed by Pat Jackson. Story and screenplay by Jack Whittingham. Camera, Ted Scaife; editor, Jocelyn Jackson; music, Clifton Parker. Reviewed at Studio One, London. Running time, **100 MINS.**

Simon Scott	Tony Britton
Jean Scott	Sylvia Syms
Bill Thompson	Jack Watling
Sir John Dell	Walter Fitzgerald
Colonel Wilson	Geoffrey Keen
George Bates	Howard Marian Crawford
Chief Customs Officer	John Welsh
Mr. Harraclough	Lockwood West
Charlie	Harry Fowler
Careers Officer	Frederick Piper
Magistrate	Cyril Luckham
Photographer	Thorley Walters
Barrister	Ernest Clark

Jack Whittingham has produced his own story in "The Birthday Present," and it is one which, but for the grace of God, could happen to anybody. Such anecdotes, however, need more incisive approach to lift them out of the ordinary than has been granted to this yarn. Relying on reasonably well-known, but not star names, this pic will be acceptable in most British houses but seems to have little to offer the international market.

Tony Britton is a successful young salesman, who on a business jaunt for his firm to the Continent, yields to the temptation not only to buy an expensive watch (at trade terms, of course) as a birthday gift for his young wife but foolishly attempts to smuggle it through Customs. This irresponsible lapse starts a trail of events which turns his life upside down. He is nabbed by the Customs and charged in a police record. Thanks to a bungling defense, he finds himself serving a threemonth stretch in the cooler.

Attempts to keep this peccadillo under cover fall down when the office gabber gets hold of the story and spreads it round. He comes out of jail, is sacked by his firm and finds that his record prevents him getting another job. Only his young wife and his old boss keep faith in him and eventually the matter comes to a happy head, leaving Britton a wiser young man who, clearly, will never risk another brush with the law, even though his motive was stupid rather than criminal.

Directed by Pat Jackson the prison scenes have an air of authenticity which almost take on the air of a documentary and, if nothing else, "Birthday Present" will give a short, sharp jolt to anybody thinking that it's worth trying to get away with a technical evasion of the legal rules. But the whole affair lacks urgency. Events follow each other with an inevitability which causes the film to be a plodder rather than a sharp slice of everyday life.

Britton is a good-looking, pleasant young man who retains sympathy by his good humor and dignity in trouble. But audiences are never going to be overly worried about his problem. Sylvia Syms is his long-suffering young wife but, here again, audiences are never tortured by her unfortunate predicament.

Geoffrey Keen, Walter Fitzgerald and, particularly, Jack Watling, as the young man whose curiosity unwittingly aggravates an incident into an event, all contribute solid performances. Harry Fowler as a young prisoner has one brief scene which is great. Pat Jackson's direction follows the methodical but unexperimental nature of the script with technical skill. Ted Scaife's lensing is a contributary sauce to the dank, downbeat effect of the prison sequences. *Rich.*

Undersea Girl

Low-grade meller for bottom half.

Hollywood, Nov. 12.

Allied Artists release of Norman T. Herman production. Stars Mara Corday, Pat Conway, Florence Marly, Dan Seymour; features Ralph Clanton, Myron Healey. Directed by John Peyser. Screenplay, Arthur V. Jones; camera, Hal McAlpin; editor, Richard C. Meyer; art director, Nicolai Remisoff; music, Alexander Courage. Previewed Nov. 6, '57. Running time, **74 MINS.**

Val Hudson	Mara Corday
Brad Chase	Pat Conway
Leila Graham	Florence Marly
Mike Travis	Dan Seymour
Sam Marvin	Ralph Clanton
Swede Nelson	Myron Healey
Phil Barry	Lewis Charles
Dwyer	Jerry Eskow
Joe	Dehl Bertl
Susie	Sue George
Larkin	Mickey Simpson
Don Carson	Mike Mason

Filmed independently under the Nacirema banner and now being released via Allied Artists, "Undersea Girl" emerges extremely mediocre filler fare. Arthur V. Jones story-screenplay too conveniently ties events together. That many of the characters don't appear very bright in the lead doesn't help matters.

Action revolves around $2,000,000 supposedly lost when a naval ship was sunk outside of Yokohama Bay some years previous. Mixed up in the proceedings are: Mara Corday, newshen who, while skin diving, comes across murdered body of a tuna fisherman with $1,800 of the missing money on his person; Pat Conway, Navy Lt. assigned to the case, who also happens to be Miss Corday's b.f., Dan Seymour, Police Lt.; Ralph Clanton, who master-minded theft has most of the money back in the U.S. and hidden in a nearby underwater cave; Florence Marly, latter's g.f.; and Myron Healey, Clanton's accomplice who reportedly had lost his life years before when, as a frogman, he was sent on a mission to retrieve the money. Wind-up finds loot recovered and back in proper hands, the villains all done in, and Conway and Miss Corday now able to concentrate on one another.

John Peyser's direction is on the amateurish side, possibly helping to explain sub-standard performances turned in by the usually competent players.

On the plus side is Edwin Gillette's underwater photography, which includes some fairly exciting shark footage; and a tuneful song, "Daydreams," by Alexander Courage and Hal Levy, well sung in a waterfront bar by an unbilled femme.

David T. Yokozeki is credited as the executive producer, Norman T. Herman as producer. *Neal.*

Not Wanted On Voyage
(BRITISH)

Naive and corny farce which achieves its object as entertainment for undiscriminating audiences: others will find it fairly resistible.

London, Nov. 12.

Renown release of George Minter (Henry Halsted, Jack Marks) production. Stars Ronald Shiner, Brian Rix, Griffith Jones, Catherine Boyle. Directed by Maclean Rogers. Screenplay by Michael Pertwee from original by Dudley Sturrock and the play "Wanted on Volage" by Evadne Price & Ken Attiwill; camera, Arthur Grant; editor, Helen Wiggins; music, Tony Lowry. Previewed at Studio One, London. Running time, **80 MINS.**

Steward Higgins	Ronald Shiner
Steward Hollebone	Brian Rix
Guy Harding	Griffith Jones
Julie Haines	Catherine Boyle
Mrs. Brough	Fabia Drake
Chief Steward	Michael Brennan
Col. Blewton-Fawcett	Michael Shepley
Pat	Dorinda Stevens
Captain	Martin Boddey
Lady Maud Catesby	Janet Barrow
Mrs. Rose	Theresa Burton
Mr. Rose	John Chapman
Strang	Peter Prowse
Pedro	Eric Pohlman

Seriously criticizing "Not Wanted on Voyage" is like chasing a butterfly with a bazooka. It is an amiable, corny farce which is obviously devised as a money-spinning second feature and will achieve its objective with undescriminating audiences in Britain, though its future elsewhere is problematical. Ronald Shiner, one of U.K.'s top Cockney comedians, can do the sort of thing demanded by this film almost with his eyes shut. He has milked as many laughs out of this undistinguished script as possible.

He plays a smart-alecky ship's steward with a flair for extracting tips from the somewhat stupid array of passengers on a pleasure cruise to Tangiers. Supporting Shiner in this anthology of all-at-sea gags is Brian Rix, as a formless steward. The combination of Shiner and Rix is an energetic and, within its limits, highly successful one.

The plot, such as it is, involves the theft of an expensive necklace from a rich, vulgar woman with Shiner and Rix eventually finding the jewel and running the crooks to earth. The film, which is stronger on situation than on dialog, introduces a great deal of falling into swimming pools and creates the opportunity for the two main comedians to dress up as Arabs and to be disguised at a fancy dress shindig. The dialog can best be measured by a witticism when a passenger inquires of Shiner whether Gibraltar is worth visiting. He replies: "Don't miss the Rock on any account," a gag which old students of the cinema will remember from many years back.

Ronald Shiner and Brian Rix play the whole thing for far more than it is worth and they are supported by a number of equally conscientious performers in lesser roles. Griffith Jones makes a smooth crook but Catherine Boyle (once Lady Boyle, tv panelist) as his partner does little to advance her claim to be regarded as a serious actress. Dorinda Stevens, Fabia Drake, Janet Burrow, Michael Shepley, John Chapman and Therese Burton turn up as assorted passengers, of whom only Miss Stevens appears to be vaguely normal. Michael Brennan and Martin Boddey are a couple of ship's officers who give a hand to the general air of lunacy.

Rich.

Eighteen and Anxious

Routine entry on youth for program market.

Hollywood, Nov. 8.

Republic release of AB-PT production, produced by Edmond Chevie. Stars Mary Webster, William Campbell, Martha Scott; features Jackie Loughery, Jim Backus, Ron Hagerthy, Jackie Coogan. Directed by Joe Parker. Screenplay, Dale and Katherine Eunson; camera, Sam Leavitt; editor, Douglas Stewart; music. Leith Stevens. Previewed Oct. 7, '57. Running time, 93 MINS.

Judy .... Mary Webster
Pete .... William Campbell
Lottie Graham .... Martha Scott
Ava .... Jackie Loughery
Harvey Graham .... Jim Backus
Danny .... Ron Hagerthy
Eager .... Jackie Cookan
Mr. Bayne .... Damian O'Flynn
Mrs. Bayne .... Katherine Barrett
Mrs. Warren .... Charlotte Wynters
Gloria .... Yvonne Craig
1st Girl .... Joyce Andre
Morty .... Slick Slavin
Guest .... Benny Rubin

"Eighteen and Anxious" is routine. Its story of youth does not warrant 83 minutes, consequently pic may encounter certain booking difficulties. Cast of young players generally acquit themselves in okay fashion, but action is slow, often aimless.

The Edmond Chevie production, third to be turned out by AB-PT Pictures, is given satisfactory physical values and presents an interesting newcomer in Mary Webster, who undertakes leading femme role. She plays part of a girl, secretly wed to the victim of a sports-car race, who becomes a mother but can't prove she's married.

Refusing to care for her baby prior to discovery by dead boy's parents of the marriage license, she's still steadfast in her refusal to take her baby, preferring instead to "become somebody." This she attempts to do by making a play for William Campbell, a name trumpet player, in an effort to marry him. When he takes her to Las Vegas she learns he has no intention of going through with ceremony. Happy ending is rung in via Ron Hagerthy, a deejay in love with her.

Miss Webster handles herself capably and creates a favorable impression. Campbell lends conviction to his role of idol of the juke-box set, Hagerthy is good and Jackie Loughery as femme star's girlfriend adds a decorative note. Martha Scott as Miss Webster's mother and Jim Backus as the stepfather offer competent portrayals and Jackie Coogan is okay as Campbell's manager.

Joe Parker's direction of the Dale Katherine Eunson screenplay is leisurely, with technical credits standard. Phil Tuminello composed four songs, none outstanding.

Whit.

The Sceptre and the Mace
(CANADIAN—COLOR)

Finely produced documentary on what the Crown means to Canada, using Royal visit as hook. Exploitation possibilities strong, with Elizabeth II "starring."

Ottawa, Nov. 3.

Columbia (in Canada) and Rank (in United Kingdom and Europe) release of National Film Board production. Narration by John Drainie. Produced by Nicholas Balla. Directed by John Howe. Script by Ian MacNeill. Camera, Dennis Gillson; editing (film), Brian Keene and Balla; editing (music) Robert Fleming and Joan Edward; sound, Don Wellington and Kay Keene; assistant director, Richard Gilbert. Previewed at Capitol Theatre. Ottawa, Nov. 2, '57. Running time, 29 MINS.

The visit to Ottawa last month of Queen Elizabeth and Prince Philip cued this documentary on the place of the Crown and royalty in Canada. Superb color (by Eastman), editing, scripting and narration (by Canadian actor John Drainie) combine to make this a strong half-hour production. Its impact is heavier through fast release internationally, coming on the heels of the Royal visit to Canada and the United States, and the footage of the royal couple's stay in this Capital is slickly woven into the overall story that explains the history of Canada's parliament from ancient England to Her Majesty's appearance in the Senate chamber, the first reigning monarch to open Canada's parliament.

Picture was completed in 11 days, some sort of a record even for a color documentary. It shows no signs of the rush. Dramatic impact is carefully built from the opening shots of the giant BOAC carrying the Royal couple into Uplands airport, and after sync-sound has carried the track until the visual shows the Queen walk-

---

ing towards the welcoming party, the narrator asks, "Is this all nothing but pomp and show? What does the monarchy mean to Canadians?" The answer is vividly and definitely provided. It will be of interest not only in Canada but in many places where the value of and need for royalty and its status in the United Kingdom are questioned.

Use of close-ups, not only of the Queen and her Prince but of many key people in the story, add much to the film. Commentary and script by Ian MacNeill, former magazine writer and later secretary of NFB, is lucid and compact, superbly handled by Drainie. Dennis Gillson, who directed the entire NFB camera staff in this job, helped keep "The Sceptre and the Mace" from being a newsreel; it's never that. Timing of the visit in the autumn gave Eastman Color a great opportunity for sparkling backgrounds to the vivid and impressive gowns, uniforms and ceremonies.

Distribution in Canada is by Columbia, in the UK and Europe by Rank, and by various arrangements in the Middle and Far East where bookings are already largely set. United States distributor isn't set yet.

Gorm.

The Bridge On The River Kwai
(C'SCOPE—COLOR)

A smash. But no romance.

Hollywood, Nov. 3.

Columbia release of Sam Spiegel production. Stars William Holden, Alec Guinness, Jack Hawkins; features Sessue Hayakawa, James Donald, Andre Morell, Peter Williams, John Boxer, Percy Herbert, Harold Goodwin, Ann Sears, Henry Okawa, Keiichiro Katsumoto, M. R. B. Chakrabandhu (Col. Broome), Vilaiwan Seeboonreaung, Ngamta Suphaphongs, Javanart Punynchoti, Kannikar Dowklee. Introduces Geoffrey Horne. Directed by David Lean; screenplay, Pierre Boulle from his own novel; camera (Technicolor), Jack Hildyard; editor, Peter Taylor; music. Malcolm Arnold. Previewed Oct. 31, '57. Running time, 161 MINS.

Shears .... William Holden
Colonel Nicholson .... Alec Guinness
Major Warden .... Jack Hawkins
Colonel Saito .... Sessue Hayakawa
Major Clipton .... James Donald
Lieutenant Joyce .... Geoffrey Horne
Colonel Green .... Andre Morell
Captain Reeves .... Peter Williams
Major Hughes .... John Boxer
Grogan .... Percy Herbert
Baker .... Harold Goodwin
Nurse .... Ann Sears
Captain Kanematsu .... Henry Okawa
Lieutenant Miura .... K. Katsumoto
Yai .... M.R.B. Chakrabandhu
Siamese Girls Vilaiwan Seeboonreaung,
Ngamta Suphaphongs, Javanart
Punynchoti, Kannikar Wowklee

"The Bridge on the River Kwai" is a gripping drama, expertly put together and handled with skill in all departments. It's potency stems only partly from the boxoffice draw of William Holden and, to a lesser degree, Alec Guinness. What elevates "Kwai" to the rank of an artistic and financial triumph for producer Sam Spiegel is the engrossing entertainment it purveys, including some scenes which will be listed as among the best of film memorabilia.

From a technical standpoint, it reflects the care and competence that went into the $3,000,000-plus venture, filmed against the exotic background of the steaming jungles and mountains of Ceylon. It's a long picture—161 minutes of footage and without he-she angles. A story of the futility of war in general, the underlying message is never permitted to impede. The picture is loaded, but with women to be heard from.

Pierre Boulle scripted from his own novel, changing minor story points here and there to make better use of the cinematic medium. It is an excellent job of screenwriting (particularly since it marked Boulle's debut in the medium), bristling with dialog that makes the characters absorbingly real and understandable. Director David Lean picked up where the script left off, guiding his performers through a series of fine portrayals. It is a superior job with fullest use of the background.

Story is "masculine." It's about three men, Holden, Guinness and Sessue Hayakawa. Latter is the commandant of a Japanese prison camp in which Holden, a Yank sailor posing as a commander, is a prisoner. Guinness is a British colonel who commands a new group of prisoners. He's a strict rules-of-war man who clashes immediately with Hayakawa over the latter's insistence that officers as well as men must work on the railroad bridge being built over the River Kwai. Guinness wins and then proceeds to guide his men in building a superb bridge to prove the mettle of British soldiers under any conditions. Holden, meanwhile, escapes to safety but is talked into leading Jack Hawkins and British commandos back to the bridge to blow it up.

The daring mission is discovered, moments before fulfillment, by Guinness, now unbalanced by the "glory" of his bridge-building feat and he fights off the commandos until, in his death throes, he accidentally falls on the detonator and completes the mission in the climactic scene that is one of several highspots in the film.

Interspersed through the mounting suspense are some memorable scenes, particularly the one in which Guinness' defeated regiment marches into the prison compound, the men whistling their regimental song. Other standout scenes include the one in which the British troops greet Guinness' victory over Hayakawa and the quietly-dignified but potent meeting at which Guinness and his officers take over the job of building the bridge.

There are notable performances from the key characters, but the film is unquestionably Guinness'. He etches an unforgettable portrait of the typical British army officer, strict, didactic and serene in his adherence to the book. It's a performance of tremendous power and dignity. Hayakawa, once a star in American silents and long absent from the screen, also is solidly impressive as the Japanese officer, limning him as an admixture of cruelty and correctness born out of a lifetime of training and the pressing need to mollify his superiors.

Holden turns in another of his solid characterizations, easy, credible and always likeable in a role that is the pivot point of the story. Hawkins is fine as the commando chief and there is good support from Geoffrey Horne, a young commando recruit; James Donald as a British army surgeon; Ann Sears, glimpsed briefly as a British nurse; and M.R.B. Chakrabandhu, leader of the native villagers who aid the commando mission.

Spiegel's overall production suppervision is a topnotch job, from his concept of the story as a big picture, to his choice of the untried Boulle as scripter, to the deft casting and the shrewd selection of technical assistants. In the latter department, there are a succession of top credits; Jack Hildyard's exciting Technicolor lensing, Peter Taylor's editing and the music by Malcolm Arnold which is welded to the story's mood and action.

Kap.

The Violators

Soap opera quality drama for the duals; thin b.o. prospects.

Universal-International release of an RKO Teleradio picture; a Galahad Production produced by Himan Brown. Stars Arthur O'Connell; features Nancy Malone, Fred Beir, Clarice Blackburn. Directed by John Newland. Screenplay, Ernest Pendrell, based on "The Violators" by Israel Beckhardt with Wenzell Brown; camera, Morris Hartzband; editor, David Cooper; music, Elliot Lawrence. Tradeshown N.Y., Nov. 7, '57. Running time, **76 MINS.**

Solomon Baumgarden	Arthur O'Connell
Debbie Baumgarden	Nancy Malone
Jimmy Coogan	Fred Beir
Eva Baumgarden	Clarice Blackburn
David Baumgarden	Henry Sharp
Mrs. Riley	Mary Michael
Mr. Riley	Joe Julian
Anthony Calini	Bill Darrid
Sheron Riley	Sheila Copelan
Judge McKenna	Bernie Lenrow
Barnie	Martin Freed
Judge Blatz	Mercer McLeod
Jean	Eva Stern
Stephen	Norman Rose
Salesgirl	Maxine Stewart
Mollie	Margaret Draper
Sam	Frank Maxwell
Mr. Coogan	John McGovern
Ray	Norman Feld
Ralph	Tom Middleton

A quiet story of average people, "The Violators" generates little excitement dramatically. Its passiveness will likely be matched by an equal placidity at the boxoffice. Save for Arthur O'Connell who stars, the cast is relatively unknown to filmgoers.

New York-made film is the second which ex-radio producer Himan Brown's Galahad Productions has delivered to RKO Teleradio under a four-picture deal. Brown, as well as his brother, associate producer Mende Brown, and director John Newland all have had extensive air serial experience. This is clearly evident as the Ernest Pendrell screenplay, based on a story by Israel Beckhardt and Wenzell Brown, unreels.

For the script's talky soap opera overtones, modest sets and a distressing lack of movement make this Universal release look off the beltline. With the Bronx as the locale throughout, story is primarily a character study of O'Connell who supports himself, his daughter and spinster sister as a county probation officer.

His interests, like most family men, lie in his prosaic job and his close kin. The years go by and the daily routine changes little. But daughter Nancy Malone has now grown to womanhood and she plans to wed a neighborhood lad, Fred Beir. Strapped for funds, the latter permits circumstances to lead him and his girl into perpetrating a swindle on gullible friends and relatives. Naturally the law catches up with them. Windup finds O'Connell in his capacity as probation officer trying to straighten the couple out.

O'Connell manages to wring some emotional values out of his lengthy role. Father and daughter scenes at the finale are particularly touching, and may prompt some distaff audiences to reach for their handkerchiefs. Miss Malone is acceptable as the girl who temporarily rejects parental guidance. Beir is suitably callow as the suitor who turned dishonest while Clarice Blackburn does what she can with the unglamorous role of the sister who serves as family housekeeper.

With exception of the aforementioned tearful sequences, director Newland couldn't inject much sparkle and drive into the cast's performances. But admittedly the script was a formidable hazard for him. Fair support is provided by Mary Michael, Joe Julian, Henry Sharp and Bill Darrid, among others. Camerawork of Morris Hartzband at times seems too low key. The Elliot Lawrence score is adequate as is David Cooper's editing. Production values reflect a modest budget.

Gilb.

April Love
(C'SCOPE—COLOR—SONGS)

Second Pat Boone film. Story of city boy's rehabilitation in Kentucky Bluegrass region. Good returns, particularly with younger audiences.

Hollywood, Nov. 15.

Twentieth-Fox release of David Weisbart production. Stars Pat Boone, Shirley Jones. Co-stars Dolores Michaels, Arthur O'Connell. Features Matt Crowley, Jeanette Nolan, Brad Jackson. Directed by Henry Levin; screenplay, Winston Miller from novel by George Agnew Chamberlain; camera (DeLuxe color), Wilfrid Cline; editor, William B. Murphy; music adaptation, Alfred Newman, Cyril J. Mockridge; songs, Paul Francis Webster, Sammy Fain. Previewed Nov. 13, '57. Running time, **98 MINS.**

Nick Conover	Pat Boone
Liz Templeton	Shirley Jones
Fran	Dolores Michaels
Jed	Arthur O'Connell
Dan Templeton	Matt Crowley
Henrietta	Jeanette Nolan
Al Turner	Brad Jackson

For its second Pat Boone starrer, 20th has come up with a remake of "Home in Indiana," (now Kentucky) adding some tunes to take advantage of the star's chief qualification as a draw. The result is good family entertainment, with emphasis on teenage audience tastes. Returns should be okay in all situations built-in exploitation value in the title tune, a hit weeks before the picture is even released, will help.

Some minor changes have been made in the basic-story line and it has been updated by Winston Miller, who also wrote the first film version of the George Agnew Chamberlain novel. It's a bit of homespun hokum but it has been skilfully written to evoke an emotional response in the unfolding of the story of a big city boy sent to the Bluegrass region of Kentucky after a minor brush with the law. It's basically the story of his rehabilitation, his emergence as a sulky driver and the awakening of love with the girl next door. (Script slickly gets around the problem of Boone's personal aversion to public osculation; it will be more of a problem in succeeding films as the public begins to realize he's acting like a traditional film cowpoke).

Film is pro-directed by Henry Levin, with a feeling both for teenagers and the Bluegrass atmosphere. Boone is a more assured performer in this second film, turning in an easy, affable performance that registers, particularly when he's singing. Shirley Jones is fine as the girl next door, both in the song and performance department and there is a topnotch piece of character work by Arthur O'Connell as Boone's uncle. Others in the small cast, all convincing, are Dolores Michaels and Matt Crowley, as Miss Jones' sister and father respectively; Jeanette Nolan as O'Connell's wife; and Brad Jackson as Miss Michael's boy friend.

Production is a good credit for producer David Weisbart who has mounted it with an eye toward top visual appeal in addition to investing it with good components. Technical work, including Wilfrid Cline's lensing and William B. Murphy's editing, is good.

In addition to the title tune, Paul Francis Webster and Sammy Fain turned out four songs to help carry the story along. All fit effectively into the framework with "Give Me a Gentle Girl" and "Do It Yourself" both possibilities for some disk interest that will also help.

Kap.

Old Yeller
(COLOR)

Heartwarming story of boy and his dog; hefty returns indicated.

Hollywood, Nov. 15.

Buena Vista release of Walt Disney production. Stars Dorothy McGuire, Fess Parker; features Tommy Kirk, Kevin Corcoran, Jeff York, Chuck Connors, Beverly Washburn, Spike. Directed by Robert Stevenson. Screenplay, Fred Gipson, William Tunberg, from novel by Gipson; camera (Technicolor), Charles P. Boyle; music, Oliver Wallace; editor, Stanley Johnson. Previewed Nov. 8, '57. Running time, **83 MINS.**

Katie Coates	Dorothy McGuire
Jim Coates	Fess Parker
Travis Coates	Tommy Kirk
Arliss Coates	Kevin Corcoran
Bud Searcy	Jeff York
Lisbeth Searcy	Beverly Washburn
Burn Sanderson	Chuck Connors

Disney organization's flair for taking a homely subject and building a heartwarming film is again aptly demonstrated in this moving story of a Texas frontier family and an old yeller dog. Picture, caught in the lush tones of Technicolor and one of producer's better entries, carries strong family appeal which should run up good returns in the general market.

Based on Fred Gipson's novel of same tag, this is a careful blending of fun, laughter, love, adventure and tragedy. Narrative as scripted by Gipson and William Tunberg is eloquently simple, lending both charm and dramatic impact to its topic of a big, rough range dog which appears out of nowhere and proceeds to protect the family from wilderness dangers.

Emphasis is laid upon animal action, including squirrels, jackrabbits, buzzards and newborn calves as well as more rugged depictions. Packed into film's tight footage is the 115-pound dog's fight with a huge bear, its struggle with a marauding wolf and battle with a pack of wild hogs, all creating an aura of excitement which director Robert Stevenson handles expertly. Yarn is given an emotional tug when dog comes down with hydrophobia.

Dorothy McGuire and Fess Parker head up the small cast, playing the parents of two unusually promising newcomers, Tommy Kirk, 15, and Kevin Corcoran, seven.

Young Kirk is fine in his characterization and Miss McGuire gives a lasting impression in mother role. Kevin as a fiery youngster also delivers strongly, and Parker, is for footage only in the opening and ending, still manages an outstanding portrayal. Jeff York as a mooching neighbor, Beverly Washburn as his young daughter and Chuck Connors, owner of the dog who makes a present of it to the family, all are in for top support. Spike, the dog, acquits himself as a fine new canine star.

Color photography by Charles P. Boyle leads off above-average technical credits, and Oliver Wallace's music score points up the action splendidly. Editing by Stanley Johnson is a potent assist in building and holding mood. Second unit direction by Yakima Canutt is good and art direction by Carroll Clark is in keeping with pic's 1869 period.

Whit.

The Tarnished Angels
(C'SCOPE)

Poorly written and produced. Names of Rock Hudson, Robert Stack, Dorothy Malone and Jack Carson to spark its chances.

Hollywood, Nov. 8.

Universal release of Albert Zugsmith production. Stars Rock Hudson, Robert Stack, Dorothy Malone, Jack Carson; co-stars Robert Middleton; features Alan Reed, Alexander Lockwood, Chris Olsen, Robert J. Wilke, Troy Donahue, William Schallert. Directed by Douglas Sirk. Screenplay, George Zuckerman, based on novel, "Pylon," by William Faulkner; camera, Irving Glassberg; editor, Russell F. Schoengarth; music, Frank Skinner. Previewed October 29, '57. Running time, **87 MINS.**

Burke Devlin	Rock Hudson
Roger Shumann	Robert Stack

LaVerne Shumann	Dorothy Malone
Jiggs	Jack Carson
Matt Ord	Robert Middleton
Colonel Fineman	Alan Reed
Sam Hagood	Alexander Lockwood
Jack Shumann	Chris Olsen
Hank	Robert J. Wilke
Frank Burnham	Troy Donahue
Ted Baker	William Schallert
Dancing Girl	Betty Utey
Telegraph Editor	Phil Harvey
Young Man	Steve Drexel
Claude Mollet	Eugene Borden
Mechanic	Stephen Ellis

"The Tarnished Angels" is a stumbling entry, loosely produced and in need of all the draw its star power can muster. Characters are mostly colorless, given static reading in drawn-out situations, and story line is lacking in punch.

Film is designed as a follow-up to studio's last year hit, "Written On the Wind," to take advantage of the principals both before and behind the camera in that venture. Rock Hudson, Robert Stack and Dorothy Malone again co-star—this time with Jack Carson—and film is turned out by the same producer-director-scripter team. Difference, however, lies in a generally inconsequential plot reaching no particular climax, the direction by Douglas Sirk doing little to lift it above a monotone.

The Albert Zugsmith production is based on William Faulkner's novel, "Pylon," and screenplay by George Zuckerman carries an air circus setting. Hudson is intro'd as a seedy, but idealistic, New Orleans reporter covering a barnstorming show in that city. He falls for Miss Malone, trick parachutist-wife of Stack, speed flyer and World War I ace, still living in his past glory as he and his small unit cruises about the country participating in air events. Carson is third member of this combine, a hero-worshipping master mechanic in love with the wife.

Hudson appears in an unrealistic role to which he can add nothing and Stack spends most of the time with eagles in his eyes. Miss Malone devotes most of her attention to long passages of dialog, Carson to bitter reflection about Stack's treatment of his wife. Middleton comes through with an okay performance, Chris Olsen is good as the young son and Alan Reed competent as the airport manager.

Technical credits are capably undertaken, leading off with Irving Glassberg's photography. *Whit.*

Paths of Glory

Grim story of 1916 French army politics. Justice loses. Prospects dim.

Hollywood, Nov. 13.
United Artists release of James B. Harris production. Stars Kirk Douglas; costars Ralph Meeker, Adolphe Menjou; features George Macready, Wayne Morris, Richard Anderson. Directed by Stanley Kubrick. Screenplay, Kubrick, Calder Willingham, Jim Thompson, based on novel by Humphrey Cobb; camera, George Krause; editor, Eva Kroll; music, Gerald Fried. Previewed Nov. 12, '57. Running time. 87 MINS.

Colonel Dax	Kirk Douglas
Corporal Paris	Ralph Meeker
General Broulard	Adolphe Menjou
General Mireau	George Macready
Lieutenant Roget	Wayne Morris
Major Saint-Auban	Richard Anderson
Private Arnaud	Joseph Turkel
Private Ferol	Timothy Carey
Colonel Judge	Peter Capell
German Girl	Susanne Christian
Sergeant Boulanger	Bert Freed
Priest	Emile Meyer
Private Lejeune	Kem Dibbs
Cafe Owner	Jerry Hausner
Shell-Shocked Soldier	Frederic Bell
Captain Nichols	Harold Benedict
Captain Rousseau	John Stein

"Paths of Glory" is a starkly realistic recital of French army politics in 1916 during World War I. While the subject is well handled and enacted in a series of outstanding characterizations, it seems dated and makes for grim screen fare. Even with the Kirk Douglas star name to spark its chances, outlook is spotty at best and will need all the hard selling United Artists, which is distributing the Bryna production, can muster.

Produced by James B. Harris and directed by Stanley Kubrick, who lately have functioned as a team, script by Kubrick, Calder Willingham and Jim Thompson is sometimes difficult to follow and ends so abruptly audience is left with a feeling of incompletion. Purportedly an expose of the French military system, as translated from the novel by Humphrey Cobb, narrative lays bare the injustices that existed during the floweriest days of the French army, and presents one man's fight against the system.

Story nub revolves around decision of the General Staff for a military unit commanded by George Macready, a general of the old school, to take an objective held for two years by the Germans. Knowing full well the impossibility of such an assault because of lack of manpower and impregnability of the position, the general nevertheless orders Douglas, colonel in command of the regiment, to make the suicidal attempt. When his men either are driven back by enemy fire or are unable to leave the trenches, an unjust charge of cowardice against the men is lodged by the general and Douglas is ordered to arrange for three men to be selected to stand courtmartial, as an object lesson to whole army.

Douglas, previously a brilliant Paris attorney, takes upon himself the task of defending his men at the trial, but it's a hopeless case and men are executed by a firing squad. Yarn ends with Douglas presenting proof to Adolphe Menjou, corps commander repping the General Staff, of Macready having ordered his own artillery to fire on the advancing French as they attempt to storm the objective.

Kubrick in his taut direction catches the spirit of war with fine realism, and the futile advance of the French is exciting. He draws excellent performances, too, right down the line. Douglas scores heavily in his realization that his is a losing battle against the system, and Macready as the relentless general instilled with the belief that an order is an order, even if it means the death of thousands, socks over what may be regarded his most effective role to date. Menjou, in an offbeat casting, is excellent as the General Staffer who knows the weaknesses of the military system.

Ralph Meeker, one of the executed trio, gives substance to role; Wayne Morris, as the cowardly lieutenant, scores in a difficult part; and Richard Anderson is good as the prosecutor. Joseph Turkel and Timothy Carey, handle their roles well as the other two executed; Peter Capell as courtmartial judge, Bert Freed, a sergeant, and Emile Meyer, a priest, are well cast.

George Krause' photography is interesting, particularly in catching backgrounds around Munich, where pic was filmed in its entirety. Gerald Fried's music score also is effective. *Whit.*

Man in the Shadow
(C'SCOPE)

Fast modern-day western. Okay prospects.

Hollywood, Nov. 22.
Universal release of Albert Zugsmith production. Stars Jeff Chandler, Orson Welles, Colleen Miller, Ben Alexander; costars Barbara Lawrence; features John Larch, James Gleason, Royal Dano. Directed by Jack Arnold. Screenplay, Gene L. Coon; camera, Arthur E. Arling; editor, Edward Curtiss; music, Joseph Gershenson. Previewed Nov. 19, '57. Running time, 79 MINS.

Ben Sadler	Jeff Chandler
Virgil Renchler	Orson Welles
Skippy Renchler	Colleen Miller
Ab Begley	Ben Alexander
Helen Sadler	Barbara Lawrence
Ed Yates	John Larch
Hank James	James Gleason
Aiken Clay	Royal Dano
Herb Parker	Paul Fix
Chet Huneker	Leo Gordon
Jesus Cisrenos	Martin Garralaga
Tony Santoro	Mario Siletti
Len Bookman	Charles Horvath
Jim Shaney	William Schallert
Harry Youngquist	Joseph J. Greene
Jake Kelley	Forrest Lewis
Dr. Creighton	Harry Harvey Sr.
Juan Martin	Joe Schneider
Gateman	Mort Mills

Tough action and good story development combine to shape this modern-day western into an okay entry for the outdoor market. Marquee lure of Jeff Chandler and Orson Welles will help to a satisfactory payoff.

Jack Arnold has directed the Albert Zugsmith production with an eye to values which maintain interest in this tale of a domineering Texas ranch baron whose power rules a nearby town until a dedicated sheriff challenges his dictatorship. Chandler as the sheriff, new on the job, and Welles as the rancher, who governs his vast land empire with an iron hand, offer contrasting interpretations well defined, and backing them are an assortment of characters who lend color to the fast unfoldment. A sequence showing the sheriff being dragged through town behind a truck driven by two of rancher's men is somewhat over-melodramatic, but it serves to motivate film's taut climax.

Gene L. Coon screenplay gets under way when a Mexican laborer on Welles' ranch is fatally beaten and Chandler investigates the report. He immediately incurs Welles' enmity and is ordered off the ranch, but returning with a court order finds incriminating blood stain which convinces him the crime was committed. Despite the demand by town's leading citizens that he drop the cast, or they'll go broke via Welles taking his trading elsewhere, sheriff continues his quest, which nearly ends in his own murder.

Chandler in a restrained role delivers a strong characterization and Welles is powerful as the heavy. Colleen Miller as his daughter excels in a key part and Ben Alexander handily enacts a deputy who plays to Welles before transferring his loyalty back to the sheriff. Barbara Lawrence as Chandler's wife; John Larch as the ranch foreman who committed the murder; Royal Dano and Martin Garralaga all offer solid support.

On technical side, Arthur E. Arling does a good job with his cameras, Edward Curtiss' editing is tight and art direction by Alexander Golitzen and Alfred Sweeney atmospheric. *Whit.*

The Enemy Below
(COLOR—C'SCOPE)

Engrossing story about submarine warfare, which promises good b.o. Intros Curt Jurgens to Yank audiences.

Hollywood, Nov. 23.

20th-Fox production and release. Stars Robert Mitchum, Curt Jurgens; with Al Hedison, Theodore Bikel, Russell Collins, Kurt Kreuger, Frank Albertson, Biff Elliot. Produced and directed by Dick Powell. Screenplay by Wendell Mayes, from novel by Comdr. D. A. Rayner; camera, Harold Rosson; editor, Stuart Gilmore; art directors, Lyle R. Wheeler, Albert Hogsett; music, Leigh Harline. Previewed Nov. 22, '57. Running time, [illegible]8 **MINS.**

Captain Murrell .... Robert Mitchum
Von Stolberg .... Curt Jurgens
Lt. Ware .... Al Hedison
Schwaffer .... Theodore Bikel
Doctor .... Russell Collins
Von Holem .... Kurt Kreuger
C. P. O. Crain..........Frank Albertson
Quartermaster .... Biff Elliot
Mackeson .... Alan Dexter
Ensign Merry .... Doug McClure
Corky .... Jeff Daley
Ellis .... David Bair
Robbins .... Joe di Reda
Lt. Bonelli .... Ralph Manza

"The Enemy Below" is an engrossing tale of a chess-like duel of wits between the commanders of an American destroyer escort and a German U-Boat in World War II, locked in single combat and each intent on blowing the other out of this world.

Once in a while, the gallantry gets a bit thick, in the style of World War I aviation films of the '20's and '30's. However, time moves along, and perhaps World War II is now safe and remote enough so that it can be viewed through slightly rose-tinted specs.

Picture is well-made, with solid action and Robert Mitchum and Curt Jurgens to help along promising biz prospects. This is Jurgens' first American-made film exposure, but he's got a rugged, mature charm reminiscent of Gable, and is a fine actor as well. Off this entry, he promises to become a potent draw quickly.

Only discernable b.o. handicap is a lack of romantic interest, which might discourage distaff attendance. But pic is interesting enough to hold femmes, once in the theatre.

Producer-director Dick Powell has lensed two finishes, but studio publicity is carefully non commital on which will be used in final version. However, since upbeat version was used at press review, it's safe to assume that it's in the lead.

Fast-paced Wendell Mayes screenplay, from novel by British Comdr. D. A. Rayner, starts with DE's radar contact with the surfaced sub, then follows the pursuit, combat, and eventual death of both vessels. Mainly, story concentrates on maneuvers of both captains, as they try for the single mistake on their enemy's part which will end the contest.

Sub is getting the worst of it when Jurgens, in a desperation move, succeeds in sending home a crippling torpedo. But Mitchum lures the surfaced sub within range and rams it. As both ships are locked together, with a time bomb ticking off within the sub, Mitchum spots Jurgens struggling to save his mortally-wounded second-in-command, Theodore Bikel, and helps the rescue. Finale has two skippers' respectful courtesies on board a rescuing Yank destroyer, after Bikel's burial at sea.

To soft-soap the German side of the fight for American audiences, Jurgens is quickly established as an anti-Nazi old-line navy man, doing his sworn duty without too much enthusiasm.

Mitchum is established as a veteran sub hunter who takes over a new command and has to win his crew's respect, as well as whip them into shape. He does this with fine results, foregoing most of his usual screen mannerisms.

In lesser roles, Bikel and Kurt Kreuger of the sub crew, and Russell Collins and Frank Albertson of the DE, are very good. As Mitchum's exec officer, Al Hedison shows promise, but needs further seasoning.

Powell's direction is deft and show-wise, especially in handling highly technical details of present-day naval warfare clearly without intruding on the story's progress. He also does a quick, clean job of delineating the main characters, then moves on to his story telling.

Technically, professional credits reflect a high degree of craftsmanship. DeLuxe color photography by Harold Rosson is especially noteworthy. However, model shots of the destroyer-sub collision were transparently model shots. *Kove.*

Femmine Tre Volte
(Female Three Times)
(ITALIAN)

Rome, Nov. 19.

Variety Film release of a Carlo Ponti-Maxima Film production. Stars Sylva Koscina; features Alberto Bonucci, Bice Valori, German Cobos, Gianrico Tedeschi, Nino Manfredi, Gianni Agus, Gina Rovere, Brigitte Kembel, Laura Caprifoglio. Directed by Steno. Screenplay, Steno, Fulci; camera, Tonino delli Colli; music, A. F. Lavagnino. At Splendore, Rome. Running time, **85 MINS.**

Sonia .... Sylva Koscina
Vassili .... Gianrico Tedeschi
Santucci .... Alberto Bonucci
Katiuscia .... Bice Valori

Lightweight item is a takeoff on the frequent defection of Iron Curtain athletes containing some fast-paced "Ninotchka"-style doings in the broad comic manner. Should pay off handsomely in depth, though a limited item for export. Brace of lookers will aid sales anywhere.

Plot tells of several members of a world champ Russian basketball team on a visit to Rome who choose freedom while getting abundantly involved with Italian men in the proceedings. Several commissars are dispatched to bring them back at all costs—and inevitably fall victims of the wonderful capitalistic ways. Humor is often locally-slanted but pace is rapid and often spicy interludes are always brought off with taste in the able hands of director Steno ("Sins of Casanova"). Thesping is likewise the exclamatory type in keeping with plot. Sylva Koscina, rapidly rising to the top in the Italian glamor stakes, confirms her rank even though limited by her role. Rates American attention.

Technical credits are all good, especially A. F. Lavagnino's tongue-in cheek musical score. *Hawk.*

Motorcycle Gang

No-better-than average low budget pic aimed at teenage market.

Hollywood, Nov. 22.

American-International release of a Golden State Production. Stars Anne Neyland, Steve Terrell, John Ashley, Carl Switzer; features Raymond Hatton, Russ Bender, Jean Moorhead, Scott Peters, supporting players, Eddie Kalafian, Shirley Falls, Aki Aleong, Wayne Taylor, Hal Bogart, Phyllis Cole, Suzanne Sydney, Edmund Cobb, Paul Blaisdell, Zon Murray, Felice Richmond. Produced by Alex Gordon; director, Edward L. Cahn; story-screenplay, Lou Rusoff; camera, Frederick E. West; art director, Don Ament; sound, Ben Winkler; music, Albert Glasser; editor, Richard C. Meyer. Reviewed Nov. 20, '57. Running time, **78 MINS.**

Terry .... Anne Neyland
Randy .... Steve Terrell
Nick .... John Ashley
Speed .... Carl Switzer
Uncle Ed .... Raymond Hatton
Joe .... Russ Bender
Marilyn .... Jean Moorhead
Hank .... Scott Peters
Jack .... Eddie Kafafian
Darlene .... Shirley Falls
Cyrus Wong .... Aki Aleong
Phil .... Wayne Taylor
Walt .... Hal Bogart
Mary .... Phyllis Cole
Birdie .... Suzanne Sydney
Bill .... Edmund Cobb
Don .... Paul Blaisdell
Hal .... Zon Murray
Hal's Wife .... Felice Richmond

"Motorcycle Gang" kicks up a cloud of dust as soon as it hits the screen, and the haze becomes a persistent one, never letting enough story break through. Aimed for teenagers.

Lou Rusoff's screenplay borders on "The Wild One" in subject matter, but it concentrates too heavily on motorcycle action. Repetition of the action seems too much for director Edward L. Cahn to cope with, and the pic often bogs down story-wise.

Central characters are Steve Terrell and John Ashley, a couple of cycle bugs, one good and one bad. Ashley has just returned from a 15-month vacation in jail for a hit-and-run accident and tries to goad Terrell, who got probation for the same accident, into an illegal race. Conflict arises because Terrell is a member of a police-sanctioned cycle club and wants to stay in its graces to compete in regional cycle races.

Anne Neyland, a wild cyclist herself, teases the pair, trying to move the showdown a little sooner. The pretty girl succeeds, the race ensues, and Terrell winds up in a hospital.

Contrived outcome is that club refuses to disqualify Terrell from competition, making all the conflict that came before seem quite inconsequential by this time.

Cyclist quits race midstream to go fight Ashley and three cohorts who are terrorizing a small town nearby. The good guys win, the bad guys go to jail and Terrell and Miss Neyland wind up happily with their whole futures in front of them, probably on a two-seater Harley-Davidson.

Terrell and Ashley are good-looking actors, each showing he can handle more than was available here. Miss Neyland showed some spark but was handicapped by a meandering role she found difficulty in defining.

Production credits were a bit above average for low budget pix. *Ron.*

Jamboree
(SONGS)

Galaxy of singing acts strung together oldstyle production. For jukebox fans.

Hollywood, Nov. 15.

Warner Bros. release of Max J. Rosenberg-Milton Subotsky production. Directed by Roy Lockwood. Screenplay, Lenard Kantor; camera, Jack Etra; editors, Robert Broekman, Anita Posner; music, Niel Hefti. Previewed Nov. 12, '57. Running time, **85 MINS.**

Grace Shaw .... Kay Medford
Lew Arthur .... Bob Pastene
Pete Porter .... Paul Carr
Honey Wynn .... Freda Holloway
Warren Sykes .... Dave King-Wood
Cindy Styles .... Jean Martin
Stage Manager .... Tony Travis
Asst. Stage Mgr.......Leonard Schneider
Songwriter .... Aaron Schroeder
Fats Domino .... Himself
Jerry Lee Lewis .... Himself
Jimmy Bowen .... Himself
Buddy Knox .... Himself
Charlie Gracie .... Himself
Count Basie orch............Themselves
Joe Williams .... Himself
Jodie Sands .... Herself
Four Coins .... Themselves
Frankie Avalon .... Himself
Lewis Lymon Teenchords.....Themselves
Slim Whitman .... Himself
Andy Martin .... Himself
Carl Perkins .... Himself
Ron Coby .... Himself
Rocco Saints .... Themselves

"Jamboree" was filmed apparently with a single objective—to present a parade of standup singing talent. Film is old-fashioned in concept, reminiscent of the early days of talking pictures when producers slapped a group of singing acts together. Perhaps okay for program situations where younger patrons like their vocalistics stylized, and particularly the jukebox trade.

Acts in the Max J. Rosenberg-Milton Subotsky production are strung together via a loosely-contrived story line of two young singers, a boy and a girl, establishing as a romantic team and falling in love, then splitting through the machinations of boy's ambitious femme manager. Producers use the device of having 21 deejays throughout the U.S. and Canada intro various entertainers. Such artists as Fats Domino, Count Basie, Jerry Lee Lewis, Jodie Sands, Ron Coby, Slim Whitman, Charlie Gracie and The Four Coins head the entertainment section, for ensemble of rock 'n' roll, rockabilly, swing and romantic rhythms.

Paul Carr and Freda Holloway team as the youngsters beset with romantic complications, both scoring nicely. *Whit.*

Dangerous Exile
(BRITISH-V'-VISION-COLOR)

Stereotyped but competent period melodrama which should be a safe entertainment bet.

London, Nov. 19.

Rank (George H. Brown) production and release. Stars Louis Jourdan, Belinda Lee, Keith Michell. Directed by Brian Desmond Hurst. Screenplay, Robin Estridge; editor, Peter Bezencenet; camera, Geoffrey Unsworth; music, Georges Auric. At Odeon, Leicester Square, London. Running time, **100 MINS.**

Duc de Beauvais.......... Louis Jourdan
Virginia Traill .... Belinda Lee
Col. St. Gerard .... Keith Michell
Louis XVII .... Richard O'Sullivan
Aunt Fell .... Martita Hunt
Mr. Patient .... Finlay Currie
Glynis .... Anne Heywood
Chief of Police .... Jean Mercure
Director of the Republic
Raymond Gerome
De Castres .... Jean Claudio
Col. Sire Frederick Venner
Terence Longdon
Dylan Evans .... Brian Rawlinson
Ogden .... Frederick Leister
Lautrec .... Laurence Payne
William .... Derek Oldham
Petitval .... Austin Trevor

"Dangerous Exile" is a historical, cloak and dagger meller with all the typical excitements, absurdities, confusions, flashbacks, swordplay and general trimmings which invariably rear their cliche-ridden heads in such pictures. It won't stand out in the memory of patrons as one of the best pix this year, but it will provide safe entertainment at most British cinemas.

Pic is an 18th Century yarn revolving around the clash between Britain and France after the Republicans have overthrown the French throne and tumbrilled Marie Antoinette and Louis 16th to the guillotine. Richard O'Sullivan, the 10-year-old son of the dead king, is smuggled out of France by Louis Jourdan, after substituting his own son in prison. The boy lands in a Welsh island and is befriended by Belinda Lee and her rich aunt, Martita Hunt.

From then on, there is more involvement. Jourdan feels it is his duty to return the youngster to France. The boy says "No," and his protectors back him up. Meanwhile local newspaper editor Finlay Currie is acting as a spy for the French Republicans and Belinda Lee's maid, Anne Heywood, is acting as a spy for Currie. At the same time Miss Lee and Jourdan are falling in love.

The film reaches a stirring if straggling climax when Keith Michell, an idealistic Republican soldier, is ordered to go to the island to bump off the young king, and is followed by Jourdan who has discovered that his own son has been murdered. In a free-for-all sword fight Jourdan kills Michell and is free to set up home in Wales with Miss Lee and young Master O'Sullivan.

As in most films of political intrigue and counter-espionage, it is difficult for the average observer to decide who is "for" and who is "against." In the circumstances, it is perhaps fortunate that director Brian Desmond Hurst has elected to direct a pedestrian script at an equally pedestrian pace. Only towards the end does the action quicken when Miss Lee rushes around in a flimsy nightgown, her home is nearly wrecked by Michell's men and her reputation too is nearly wrecked.

Miss Lee, apart from calling the boy "Honey," has no truck with an American accent. She is comely but the script does not give either her or Jourdan much chance for histrionic fireworks. Michell is a stalwart Republican soldier. There are some neat performances in lesser roles by Finlay Currie, Anne Heywood and Terence Longdon. Little O'Sullivan, doubling as the two youngsters, shows distinct promise though he is called upon to cope with some rather dire dialog. As an eccentric but humorous invalid aunt, Miss Hunt steals most of the few amusing lines.

Geoffrey Unsworth's camera work is excellent and the color first-rate.   *Rich.*

Jonas
(GERMAN)
Frankfurt, Nov. 19.

Pallas Film release of a Dr. Ottomar Domnick production. Stars Robert Graf and Elisabeth Bohaty. Directed by Dr. Ottomar Domnick. Screenplay, Dr. Domnick; camera, Andor von Barsy; music, Duke Ellington and Winfried Zillig; commentary, H. M. Enzensberger. At Bambi Theatre, Frankfurt. Running time, **82 MINS.**
Jonas .... Robert Graf
Nanni .... Elisabeth Bohaty
M. S. .... Heinz-Dieter Eppler
The Strange Man ...... Willy Reichmann

Germany, once among the leading producers of unusual pix, has dropped behind since the last World War in creative, imaginative productions. But this is an experimental film of interest which has already received acclamation for its imaginative aspects. It has been cited for the West German Film Prize for 1957 for music and camera, and rated as "especially outstanding" by the German Film Classification Board.

"Jonas" symbolizes the biblical prophet, in presenting the problems of the modern world that beset man. Jonas is a young employee in a huge printing plant, concerned about the mechanical advances that are bringing machines forward and setting man behind, confused in the complex world. In his state of puzzlement, he goes out to lunch and buys an expensive hat from a pretty girl in a men's hat shop. While he eats lunch, his hat is stolen from the rack. And in a moment of anxiety, desperation and rage, he steals another hat from the stand.

Now a thief and panicked with the problems of his foolish act, he tries to get rid of the hat. He abandons it in another restaurant —the waiter pursues him to return it. He tosses it in front of an auto —a pedestrian risks his life to retrieve it. Spotting the monogram, "M.S.," in the hatband, he tries to find the owner. He's picked up by the police, found not guilty, but his sins oppress him. He seeks help in the church.

The problems, says the commentary, typify modern life and the complexities that beset everyone. With commentary and violent music to underline the theme, there is almost no dialog throughout the film.

The four actors and the director of this film are excellent. With the exception of Duke Ellington, whose mood music emphasizes the downbeat theme, all those associated with this production are young unknowns in the German film world.

Strictly an art house piece, this film could find a following in the U.S.   *Haze.*

Casino de Paris
(FRENCH-GERMAN)
(Musical-Color)
Paris, Nov. 19.

Pathe release of Pathe-Bavaria Filmkunst-Criterion-Elan Films production. Stars Caterina Valente, Gilbert Becaud, Vittorio De Sica; features Gregoire Aslan, Grethe Weiser, Rudolf Vogel, Vera Valmont. Directed by Andre Hunebelle. Screenplay, Hans Wilhelm, Jean Halaini; camera (Technicolor), Bruno Mondi; editor, Jean Feyte; music, Paul Durand, Becaud; sets and costumes, Rene Moulaert. At Vivienne, Paris. Running time, **100 MINS.**
Catherine .... Caterina Valente
Jacques .... Gilbert Becaud
Gordy .... Vittorio De Sica
Mario .... Gregoire Aslan
Linda .... Vera Valmont
Father .... Rudolf Vogel
Mother .... Grethe Weiser

This film, done in Franscope, an acceptable Gallic version of CinemaScope, is a Gallic musical which manages to be somewhat inventive and tries to blend story, terp scenes and song numbers. Though the big production aspects are stagebound there is an excuse supposed to take place at the Casino De Paris. Blessed with fresh stars and a name in Vittorio De Sica, this looks headed for okay local returns, but it may lack the stature for the U.S. in anything but secondary spots. With the title and marquee names it might be worth dubbing.

Tale is about a dandified, aging playwright who tries to turn a music hall star into an actress, and also endeavors to turn her head. But she comes to his villa, to rehearse, with a family, and the playwright's ghost, a young man, takes to the girl for the usual complications.

Gilbert Becaud is at ease in his role of the undercover writer and delivers some numbers in his usual manner. Caterina Valente emerges as a fine musical personality with pipes, terp ability and a good film personality. De Sica does his usual fading ladies' man routine to help package this into an obvious but fairly pleasing pic. Music is good but the dancing is in the night club vernacular to make the terp entries somewhat static. Color (Technicolor) and production are fine. Direction plays this for situation comedy rather than rapid musical comedy, which slows it down.   *Mosk.*

Witness for the Prosecution

Tyrone Power, Marlene Dietrich and Charles Laughton in click adaptation of Agatha Christie's hit play; firm business potential.

United Artists release of Arthur Hornblow production (presented by Edward Small). Stars Tyrone Power, Marlene Dietrich, Charles Laughton; features Elsa Lanchester, John Williams, Torin Thatcher, Una O'Connor, Philip Tonge, Ian Wolfe. Directed by Billy Wilder. Screenplay, Wilder and Harry Kurnitz, from story and stage play by Agatha Christie; camera, Russell Harlan; editor, Daniel Mandell; art direction, Alexandre Trauner; sound, Fred Lau; music, Matty Malneck; song, "I Never Go There Any More." Ralph Arthur Roberts and Jack Brooks. Tradeshown in N.Y., Nov. 22, '57 Running time, **114 MINS.**
Leonard Vole .... Tyrone Power
Christine Vole .... Marlene Dietrich
Sir Wilfrid Robarts... Charles Laughton
Miss Plimsoll .... Elsa Lanchester
Brogan-Moore .... John Williams
Mayhew .... Henry Daniell
Carter .... Ian Wolfe
Janet McKenzie .... Una O'Connor
Mr. Meyers .... Torin Thatcher
Judge .... Francis Compton
Mrs. French .... Norma Varden
Inspector Hearne .... Philip Tonge
Diana .... Ruta Lee
Miss McHugh .... Molly Roden
Miss Johnson .... Ottola Nesmith
Miss O'Brien .... Marjorie Eaton

A courtroom meller played engagingly and building evenly to a surprising and arousing, albeit tricked-up, climax, "Witness for the Prosecution" has been transferred to the screen with competence. Arthur Hornblow's production has dramatic and melodramatic substance, figures to do firm business all around.

"Prosecution" is the Agatha Christie play which was a click on Broadway and, earlier, in London. The West End and Times Square runs clearly establish the property's popular appeal and in this instance adept screen handling, plus the star names, adds to the values of the original.

In fashioning the screenplay, Billy Wilder and Harry Kurnitz strayed but little from the prototype, except to introduce an added character, that of a private nurse. Why re-write a hit play? In line with this, however, it's recalled that Miss Christie's multiple-barrelled, rapidly-fired ending came off as almost bewildering (at least such criticism was heard) and the picture's windup, which is substantially unchanged, likely may evoke the same comment.

But this is a minor reservation; it's an entertaining show.

Under Wilder's direction, "Prosecution" unfolds realistically, generating a quiet and steady excitement. The characters are believably participating in the Old Bailey murder trial and the few flashbacks and contemporary asides that round out the story. The plot always is in clear focus, the moods and motivations correctly established.

Cleverly worked out is the story line which has defense attorney Charles Laughton, along with the audience, wholly convinced that the likeable chap played by Tyrone Power is innocent, that he couldn't have murdered the rich widow who had taken a fancy to him. A disturbing note, however, is the unexpected attitude taken by Power's wife, Marlene Dietrich, who, as it turns out, is not legally married to him and thus is not restrained from testifying against him.

Baffling, too, are the letters which Miss Dietrich has written to her "Beloved Max." Which serve to discredit her testimony and bring about the acquittal verdict. And along with it there is the doubt that has entered Laughton's mind, plus, indeed, the admission by Power that he actually committed the crime. This is part of the multi-faceted, quickly-sprung climax that clears up everything.

As per design, the audience is given a sense of participation, seeing the case as Laughton sees it, noting the trial's developments and verdict appear too pat, sharing the same doubts and, at the denouement, surprises.

"Prosecution" reproduction of the famous London court is done with remarkable conviction and the proceedings throughout have a genuine air.

Laughton, sage of the courtroom and cardiac patient who's constantly disobeying his nurses orders about cigar-smoking and brandy-drinking, plays out the part flamboyantly and colorfully. His reputation for scenery chewing is unmarred via this outing; he's as robust as ever in making with the sarcasting cracks (the Wilder-Harry Kurnitz is well stacked with sharp dialog) and browbeating his nurse and his subordinates.

Power does a winning job as the ingratiating defendant who seems incapable of murder and Miss Dietrich is in good form, histrionically and physically, as the cause of much bafflement through the picture until the explanations are finally given. Elsa Lanchester measures up suitably as the irritating nurse.

Ian Wolfe, as Laughton's assistant; Henry Daniell, as a solicitor; John Williams, another barrister; Torin Thatcher, the probing prosecutor; Una O'Connor, the murdered woman's maid, and Philip Tonge, police inspector, all do creditbble work.

The black-&-white photography is top notch, editing contributes to the even pace, music and other credits all are commendable.

Gene.

The Hard Man
(COLOR)

Fast story of a fast gunman, with Guy Madison.

Hollywood, Nov. 29.

Columbia release of Helen Ainsworth production. Stars Guy Madison; features Valerie French, Lorne Greene, Barry Atwater, Robert Burton, Rudy Bond, Trevor Bardette, Renata Vanni. Directed by George Sherman. Screenplay, Leo Katcher, based on his novel; camera (Technicolor), Henry Freulich; editor, William Lyon; music, Mischa Bakaleinikoff. Previewed Nov. 21, '57. Running time, **80 MINS.**

Steve Burden .... Guy Madison
Fern Martin .... Valerie French
Rice Martin .... Lorne Greene
George Dennison .... Barry Atwater
Sim Hacker .... Robert Burton
John Rodman .... Rudy Bond
Mitch Willis .... Trevor Bardette
Juanita .... Renata Vanni
Larry Thompson .... Rickie Sorensen
Vince Kane .... Frank Richards
Ray Hendry .... Myron Healey
Herb Thompson .... Robert B. Williams

Plenty of hard action and Guy Madison's name for marquee lure shape "The Hard Man" for good response in the general outdoor market. Film is sparked by the type of story line to hold attention and use of Technicolor gives it plus.

Director George Sherman has taken Leo Katcher's fast-moving screenplay—based on his own novel—and come up with a study of a gunman which turns out to be one of Madison's best roles. Helen Ainsworth as producer provides suitable values, aided by Henry Freulich's fluid color cameras, and a note of authentic realism clothes the unfoldment.

Madison plays a former Texas Ranger, who resigns after his chief's objections for too often bringing back his quarry dead instead of alive. He accepts an offer made by a sheriff to be his deputy, and instantly finds himself plunged into a feud with a wealthy rancher, who means to dominate the whole country. He meets with cattle baron's further enmity through his association with latter's wife, who tries to persuade Madison to kill the husband she hates.

Madison lends authority to his character, engaging in action which includes both a bruising barroom scrap with one of cattleman's muscle men and a suspenseful six-gun battle with heavy's gunman. Lorne Greene capably portrays the rancher, shot down by his wife during a showdown with Madison, and Valerie French is okay in femme lead, doing well by her unsympathetic part. Rudy Bond as the gunman, Robert Burton the sheriff who hires Madison to do his own necessary job with the rancher and Barry Atwater, attorney romancing the wife of his employer, turn in handy performances.

Technical credits generally are good, including William Lyon's tight editing, Carl Anderson's art direction and Mischa Bakaleinikoff's music direction. *Whit.*

Just My Luck
(BRITISH)

Amiable slapstick farce with star Norman Wisdom assuring maximum acceptance from British audiences.

London, Nov. 26.

Rank (Hugh Stewart) production and release. Stars Norman Wisdom. Directed by John Paddy Carstairs. Screenplay, Alfred Shaughnessy, Peter Blackmore; camera, Jack Cox; editor, Roger Cherrill; music, Philip Green. At Leicester Square Theatre, London, Nov. 14, '57. Running time, **86 MINS.**

Norman .... Norman Wisdom
Anne .... Jill Dixon
Hon. Richard Lumb .... Leslie Phillips
Miss Daviot .... Delphi Lawrence
Mrs. Dooley .... Margaret Rutherford
Mr. Stoneway .... Edward Chapman
Mrs. Hackett .... Marjorie Rhodes
Phoebe .... Joan Sims
Weaver .... Peter Copley
Cranley .... Michael Ward
Man in Cinema .... Felix Felton
Powell .... Bill Fraser
Roberts .... Sam Kydd
Nurses ... Beth Rogan, Marigold Russell
Lord Beale .... Campbell Cotts
Sir George .... Robin Bailey
Masseur .... Michael Brennan
Man in Hole .... Eddie Leslie
Second Man in Hole .... Ian Wilson
Starter at Goodwood ... Ballard Barkeley
Eddie Diamond .... Vic Wise

Norman Wisdom, one of Britain's top stage and screen buffoons, is the amiable "Little Man" of British pix. Clad in an ill-fitting cap, jacket and pants, he sails through a series of improbable adventures with a heart of gold, ingratiating grin and a possible overdose of frenetic energy. This formula has paid off handsomely at the British foxoffice in the past. Allied again with producer Hugh Stewart and John Paddy Carstairs his latest "Just My Luck," should be equally popular even though it sometimes seems that the trio's efforts will burst at the seams.

In the U.S., Wisdom is mainly known through same casual, commuting tv appearances but since humor is international, American audiences should find enough yocks in this lively farce.

Wisdom is largely a situation comedian who has built up a rep via pratfalls, so it is unimportant that the story of "Luck" is as slim as a chorine's waist. The idea of any story line for a Wisdom film is that it should get him into sufficient incongruous situations to make people feel sorry for him, for him to get out of them with blundering ingenuity and then finish up with the girl whose role is usually so innocuous that the audience forgets all about her until the finish. In short, Wisdom is a kind of Harold Lloyd, sans spectacles.

This film follows this undemanding, but tricky formula effectively and funnily. Wisdom is a humble employee at a ritzy West End jewelery shop. Anxious to win a bank roll sufficient to buy a lush bauble for his girl friend, the little comic decides to play the horses. With a hardly-earned $2.80 stake he becomes embroiled in backing a jockey in a six-race parlay and suffers endless adventures and humiliations before landing both the cash and girl.

There are several sequences which are top screen comedy. For instance, there is Wisdom and an amorous blonde, smartly played by revue artist John Sims, making noisy nuisances of themselves in a cinema. In another sequence, Wisdom finds himself a near victim of an emergency operation through misunderstanding.

"Luck" is completely a Wisdom vehicle but some neat performances are turned in by lesser artists. The two girls, Jill Dixon and Delphi Lawrence, emerge pleasantly. Margaret Rhodes, as his nagging mother; Edward Chapman, as his boss; Vic Wise as a jockey, and Leslie Phillips and Peter Copley as two shady bookies also add their quota of fun. Margaret Rutherford is in her usual formidable form as an eccentric racehorse owner.

John Paddy Carstairs directs with his usual pace and comedy knowhow. But it often seems that he is running out of new ideas to exploit the star he knows so well. Technical problems are satisfactorily coped with, and Jack Cox handles the lensing well. *Rich.*

Love Slaves of the Amazons
(COLOR)

Green-skinned lady warriors yet! Ferocious and kittenish babes don't get their man. Borders on unintended comedy.

Universal release of Curt Siodmak production. Stars Don Taylor, Gianna Segale, Eduardo Ciannelli; features Harvey Chalk, John Herbert, Wilson Vianna, Eugenio Carlos, Anna Marie Nabuco. Directed and written by Siodmak; camera (Eastman Color), Mario Page; editor Terry Morse; song, "Song of the Amazons," composed by Radames Gnattali and sung by Jara Lex. Previewed in N.Y., Nov. 20, '57. Running time, **81 MINS.**

Dr. Peter Masters .... Don Taylor
Gina .... Gianna Segale
Crespi .... Eduardo Ciannelli
Adhemar Silva .... Harvey Chalk
Hotel Clerk .... John Herbert
Fernando .... Wilson Vianna
Fernando's Brotner .. Eugenio Carlos
Queen .... Anna Marie Nabuco
Mario .... Tom Payne
Ugly Girl .... Gilda Nery
Pilot .... Louis Serrano

"Love Slaves of the Amazons" is a simple-minded, poorly-made adventure film of which everyone says "there must be a market for them somewhere." It's being coupled by Universal with "Monolith Monsters" and, as part of such a package, probably will sneak by.

If there's anything good to be said about it it's that the Eastman color is vivid and impressive, picking up some interesting landscapes in Brazil, where this was produced by Curt Siodmak. Add that the title is "interesting" as an idea.

Story has overtones of (unintentional) comedy. Archeologist Don Taylor penetrates jungle on an expedition with eccentric Eduardo Ciannelli, who claims to once have escaped from the land of the Amazons. Taylor is finally captured by the warrior ladies and escapes with a white woman whom they've held captive. In the end, "to save this old civilization," they agree not to tell anyone about their experiences.

The "old civilization" consists of green-painted femmes creeping through the jungles, acting alternately kittenish and ferocious. Siodmak's script is so clumsy, the temptation is great to consider the whole thing a takeoff on jungle pix that have gone before. His direction isn't any much better, judging by the performances.

Photography—by Mario Page—enhanced by good use of color, is impressive. There's one prolonged scene, men battling it out in the river mud, that is well staged and lensed. Amazons' dances are harmless, though some may call them "suggestive."

Taylor stumbles through the film without half trying. Gianna Segale is attractive as the lost-and-found scientist, and Ciannelli turns in a non-pro performance that belongs in the silent flicker era. Tom Payne is okay as the scientist murdered by the Amazons.

Terry Morse's editing is routine. Considering the time and effort that must have gone into this film, Siodmak should have to answer to someone why nothing better came out. *Hift.*

Affair in Havana

Trite jealously plot. So-so entertainment but Cuban scenery and music ginger things up a bit.

Hollywood, Nov. 29.

Allied Artists release of Dudley Pictures International Corp. of Cuba production. Stars John Cassavetes, Raymond Burr, Sara Shane. Features Lilia Lazo, Sergio Pena, Celia Cruz, Jose Antonio Rivero, Miguel Angel Blanco. Producer, Richard Goldstone; director, Laslo Benedek; screenplay, Burton Lane and Maurice Zimm from original story by Janet Green; camera, Alan Stensvold; production designer, Gabriel Scognamillo; editor, Stefan Arnsten; music, Ernest Gold. Previewed Nov. 25, '57. Running time, **71 MINS.**

Nick .... John Cassavetes
Mallabee .... Raymond Burr
Lorna .... Sara Shane
Fina .... Lilia Lazo
Valdes .... Sergio Pena
Fiesta singer .... Celia Cruz
Rivero .... Jose Antonio Rivero
Police captain ...... Miguel Angel Blanco

As an oft-told tale of a jealous husband—this time with cause—"Affair In Havana" relies or the beauties of Cuba and the charm of Afro-Cuban music to take it out of the just-so class. As it is, pic is a better-than-average bet for second feature booking.

Allied Artist releases the Cuban-made film that receives some exploitation values out of John Cassavetes and Raymond Burr, both of whom benefit from good tv exposure.

Cassavetes plays an American composer who has an affair with the lovely wife (Sara Shane) of a paralytic plantation owner (Burr). When Burr learns of the recurrent trysts, he sets out to trap the lovers when trio are together on the sugar plantation. That fails and wife is about to run off with her pash when Burr tells her he has only 90 days to live and that she has $20,000,000 waiting for her. She stays.

In a subsequent argument between the marriage partners Burr is pushed into a swimming pool and drowned by his manservant who is, unencouraged, enamored with the lovely lady. Manservant's wife accuses Miss Shane of perpetrating the death; Cassavetes—who's made of stern stuff—believes her and leaves the now wealthy widow. Miss Shane chases and runs into manservant's wife who stabs her to death. Adultery costs her her life but, as if nothing had happened, Cassavetes ends up where he started—at a piano, pounding out some pretty lively tunes.

Although he previously has aroused response as an actor, Cassavetes doesn't show much more than sporadic hints in this pic, not getting much help from the Burton Lane-Maurice Zimm script or director Laslo Benedek. Burr is tyrannical enough. Miss Shane is pretty.

Rest of small cast, especially Lilia Lazo as the servant's wife, backs up nicely.

On plus side are some interesting shots of Cuba done by Alan Stensvold and some fine music by Ernest Gold and songs by Alberto Zayas Govin. Technical credits are average except sound which echoes all too frequently. *Ron.*

Plunder Road
(REGALSCOPE)

Well-made little crime melodrama.

Hollywood, Nov. 29.

20th-Fox release of a Regal Films Production. Stars Gene Raymond, Jeanne Cooper, Wayne Morris; with Elisha Cook, Stafford Repp, Steven Ritch, Nora Hayden, Helene Heigh, Harry Tyler, others; produced by Leon Chooluck and Laurence Stewart; directed by Hubert Cornfield; screenplay, Steven Ritch, from story by Ritch and Jack Charney; camera, Ernest Haller; editors, Warren Adams, Jerry S. Young; music, Irving Gertz. Previewed Nov. 25, '57. Running time, 71 MINS.

Eddie	Gene Raymond
Fran	Jeanne Cooper
Commando	Wayne Morris
Skeets	Elisha Cook
Roiy Adams	Stafford Repp
Frankie	Steven Ritch
Hazel	Nora Hayden
Society Woman	Helene Heigh
Trooper No. 1	Paul Harber
Policeman	Don Garrett
No. 1 Smog Officer and Narrator	Michael Fox
Guard No. 2	Richard Newton
Trooper No. 2	Charles Conrad
Tibbs	Jim Canino
Don	Robin Riley
Guard No. 1 and Narrator	Douglas Bank
Ernie Beach	Harry Tyler
Officer No. 1	George Keymas
Narrator	Stacy Graham

Money isn't everything, as this Regal low-budgeter for 20th-Fox release proves, both on-screen and off. A well made little crime melodrama, pic shows both skill and a keen appreciation of the value of a production buck on parts of producers Leon Chooluck and Laurence Stewart. Aside from Gene Raymond and Wayne Morris, neither current b.o. draws. name values are lacking. Otherwise, pic carries more distinction than customary for its type.

Brisk story by Steven Ritch (who also acts in pic) and Jack Charney revolves literally around a Solid Gold Cadillac. Special U. S. Mint gold train is victim of ingenious hold up, masterminded by Raymond. Bulky loot is split among three trucks for transport to L. A. and eventually out of the country. But first two trucks, one driven by Stafford Rapp and other by Elisha Cook and Wayne Morris, through various mishaps, are intercepted by cops. Additionally, en route Morris murders service station attendant Harry Tyler when his identity is accidentally uncovered.

Last load, driven by Raymond and Ritch, makes it. With help of Raymond's g.f., Jeanne Cooper, bullion is melted down and repacked about an ornate Cadillac, with gold recast as hubcaps, bumpers, grille, etc. But L. A. freeways prove too much, as car, on way to safety of harbor, gets entangled in a bumper-locking collision. When cops unwind cars, soft gold bends and reveals itself, and Raymond and Ritch are killed in escape attempt.

Action is handled tautly, with telling economy, by art direction of Hubert Cornfield. Raymond is especially convincing as the mastermind and other cast members also rate commendation for solid performances. Morris, Cook, Miss Cooper and Ritch deserve special mention, with Repp and Tyler also good.

Technical credits are polished and professional, with striking title design of Robert Gill and cleancut black-and-white photography of Ernest Haller worthy to be singled out. *Kove.*

Sorority Girl

Routine cheapie with better acting than production warrants. Teenagers may go for it. Basic story provocative though poorly scripted.

Hollywood, Nov. 22.

American-International release of Roger Corman Production (produced and directed by Roger Corman). Stars Susan Cabot, Dick Miller, Barboura O'Neill; features June Kenny, Barbara Crane, Fay Baker. Screenplay by Ed Waters and Leo Lieberman; camera, Monroe P. Askins; editor, Charles Gross, Jr.; music, Ronald Stein. Reviewed Nov. 20, '57. Running time, **60 MINS.**

Sabra Tanner	Susan Cabot
Mort	Dick Miller
Rita Joyce	Barboura O'Neill
Tina	June Kenney
Ellie Marshall	Barbara Crane
Mrs. Tanner	Fay Baker
Mrs. Fessenden	Jeane Wood

"Sorority Girl" is a sombre affair, picturing a sadistic university coed who, it is to be trusted, is an exaggerated exception. Although pic's low budget is all too apparent, film should draw curious teenagers in its bookings with "Motorcycle Gang."

Storyline is a good one — rich girl can't adjust in sorority life, so she resolves own conflict by hurting everyone else. With more care than is shown in this pic, results could have been good.

Susan Cabot displayed a few bursts of acting talent as the maladjusted student who goes in for paddlings, blackmailing and out-and-out hair-pulling. On the whole, however, her role as written is without sufficient motivation.

Entire pic revolves around her relation to other members of the Greek letter organization—a weak sister, a politicking BWOC (big woman on campus) and an-about-to-be unwed mother. She casts dirt on them all and winds up on a peaceful beach all by herself witn the entire sorority roster casting aspersions upon her.

Dick Miller, as a tavern owner who looks at college students as seekers of beer and laughs, is capable, looking like a young Mike Todd. Within the confines of what's been provided them, Barboura O'Neill and June Kenney performed well.

Outstanding part of film is background of title credits, a symbolic assortment of drawings done by Bill Martin. Lighting was too high key, and sound must have been taken in a warehouse.

Ron

Man On the Prowl

Insane killer. Prolonged anguish. For less discriminating playdates.

Hollywood, Nov. 29.

United Artists release of Jo and Art Napoleon production. Stars Mala Powers, James Best; features Ted De Corsia, Jerry Paris. Directed by Art Napoleon. Screenplay, Napoleons; camera, Nick Musuraca; editor, Paul Weatherwax; music, Ernest Gold. Previewed Nov. 27, '57. Running time, **84 MINS.**

Marian Wood	Mala Powers
Doug Gerhardt	James Best
Detective	Ted De Corsia
Woody	Jerry Paris
Mrs. Gerhardt	Vivi Jannis
Josh Wood	Josh Freeman
Jeff Wood	Jeff Freeman
Alma Doran	Peggy Maley
Dorothy Pierce	Eugenia Paul
Bob Yeakel	Bob Yeakel

"Man on the Prowl" is another story of a homicidal psycho. A picture of grim overtones, unpleasant subject militates against general acceptance. Although certain mounting suspense accompanies action, film is suitable only for lower bracketing in less discriminating program situations.

James Best in title role of the Jo and Art Napoleon production turns in a well-drawn characterization of a young killer who goes on the make for Mala Powers, mother of two small boys and wife of Jerry Paris, owner of a prosperous sports-car garage. Already wanted by the police for the murder of a girl who repulsed his advances, he's determined to have both the femme and the business, and attempts to do away with husband. Later, he holds children as hostages so the mother will come to him, but is finally killed by police who surround the house.

Art Napoleon in his direction of his and Jo Napoleon's screenplay manages convincing performances from cast. Miss Powers is convincing as the terror-stricken mother who plays up to Best to protect her young sons. Paris as the husband is okay in his brief but telling footage and Ted De Corsia is a tough homicide detective. Vivi Jannis as Best's mother knowing his condition and hanging onto him for a meal ticket, also registers.

Technical departments are adequately handled. *Whit.*

Ride a Violent Mile
(REGALSCOPE)

Oater that will even strain credulity of moppet audiences.

Hollywood, Dec. 2.

20th-Fox release of an Emirau Production. Stars John Agar, Penny Edwards; co-stars John Pickard, Bing Russell; with Richard Shannon, Charles Gray, Sheb Wooley, Rush Williams, Richard Gilden, others. Produced by Robert Stabler. Directed by Charles Marquis Warren. Screenplay by Eric Norden, from Warren story; camera, Brydon Baker; editor, Fred W. Berger; art director, James W. Sullivan; music, Raoul Kraushaar. Previewed Nov. 26, '57. Running time, **79 MINS.**

Jeff	John Agar
Susan	Penny Edwards
Marshal Thorne	John Pickard
Sam	Richard Shannon
Dory	Charles Gray
Norman	Bing Russell
Mrs. Bartold	Helen Wallace
Gomez	Richard Gilden
Jonathan Long	Sheb Wooley
Bartender	Patrick O'Moore
Edwards	Rush Williams
Abruzo	Roberto Contreras
Townswoman	Eve Novak
Dance Hall Girls	Mary Townsend, Dorothy Schuyler

Key word is incredible, which extends through original story concocted by Charles Marquis Warren, screenplay by Eric Norden, Warren's direction and the performances of the hapless thesping crew. Even moppets and dyed-in-wool western fans will have difficulty in swallowing this one.

Confused, gap-ridden story concerns Civil War espionage in Far West, with fantastic deal to trade Southern beef for Mexican ports. Innocent stranger John Agar, attracted to pretty dance-hall girl Penny Edwards, finds himself defending her from Reb agents Richard Shannon and Charles Gray, after disclosure that she's a Union agent. Sadistic U.S. Marshal John Pickard's no help, because he turns out to be the head Reb spy.

Since all the acting bears the same imprint, it's safe to assume director Warren's influence. Under the circumstances, it's the charitable thing merely to list the principal cast members, without individual comment. These unfortunates, aside from those already mentioned, include Bing Russell, Richard Gilden and Sheb Wooley.

Technically, picture is adequately mounted. *Kove.*

Der Stern Von Afrika
(The Star of Africa)
(GERMAN)

Berlin, Nov. 26.

Herzog release of Emelka-Ariel production. Stars Joachim Hansen and Marianne Koch. Directed by Alfred Weidenmann. Screenplay, Herbert Reinecker, after story by Udo Wolter; camera, Helmut Ashley; music, Hans-Martin Majewsky; editor, Carl O. Bartning. At Zoo Palast, Berlin. Running time, **98 MINS.**

Hans-Joachim Marseille	Joachim Hansen
Brigitte	Marianne Koch
Robert Franke	Hansjoerg Felmy
Albin Droste	Horst Frank
Answald Sommer	Peer Schmidt
Hauptmann Krusenberg	Karl Lange
Werner Heydenreich	Werner Bruhns
Major Niemeyer	Alexander Kerst
Major Schliemann	Albert Hehn
Unteroffizier Weiss	Johannes Grossmann
Frau Marseille	Gisela von Collande
Herr Marseille	Arno Paulsen

"Star of Africa," one of first pix financed by the new UFA, stirred up some controversy before even released by Herzog. It was rejected by the Freiwillige Selbstkontrolle, West Germany's self-censorship group, as too patriotic and had to be recut for release. Film's subject, which deals with the career of Hans-Joachim Marseille, war hero of the Nazi Luftwaffe, has found considerable objection here. All the controversy has led to substantial word-of-mouth here and latter is of the kind which will give this pic probably outstanding b.o. chances in this country. It may also do well in some foreign territories.

"Star" in its present form is neither fish nor fowl. Pic apparently wants to depict the tragedy of the German youth that became a victim of the last war, but it is far from being an honest war film. There is even quite a bit of glorification along the line. Film is supposed to show that heroism doesn't pay.

The audience must find that the war is truly a bit too "nice" in this. It must also find it rather strange that no Nazi shows up in this film and not even once is it mentioned who created this unholy war which led to the "tragedy of the German youth." The occasional criticism is too superficial.

Technically the film is of mediocre quality. The various air fignt scenes, made with the assistance by the Spanish air force, are too repetitious and basically all but exciting. In this respect, "Star" is below the quality of any American air force film of which German audiences have seen plenty through the years. Direction by Alfred Weidenmann is hardly better than average. After having seen his

"Canaris" and "Alibi," one had expected more. Part of the blame may also be put on the mediocre script by Herbert Reinecker.

Standout in the film is the acting. Most of the principal players are young unknowns. Joachim Hansen portrays the idolized German fighter pilot and pride of the German Luftwaffe. His screen debut may be called a successful one. His sympathetic blond appearance may make him a teenage idol here. Marianne Koch (Cook) supplies the romantic interest, but her role of a teacher who falls for Hansen is not very substantial. Hansjoerg Felmy and Horst Frank, Hansen's war pals and both making their screen bows, show promising talents. Same goes for Karl Lange who enacts a German captain.

Gisela von Collande and Arno Paulsen, who competently portray Hansen's parents, and Albert Hehn, who is briefly seen as a German Major, are some of the very few established players in the film.
Hans.

Pot-Bouille
(Boiling Pot)
(FRENCH)

Paris, Nov. 26.

CCFC release of Robert & Raymond Hakim production. Stars Gerard Philipe, Dany Carrel, Danielle Darrieux; features Jacques Duby, Anouk Aimee, Henri Vilbert, Jean Brochard, Claude Nollier, Jane Marken, Micheline Luccioni. Directed by Julien Duvivier. Screenplay, Henri Jeanson, Leo Joannon, Duvivier from novel by Emile Zola; camera, Michel Kelber; editor, Madeleine Gug. At Normandie, Paris. Running time, **115 MINS.**

Octave .... Gerard Philipe
Berthe .... Dany Carrel
Mme. Hedouin .... Danielle Darrieux
Vabre .... Jacques Duby
Marie .... Anouk Aimee
Narcisse .... Henri Vilbert
Varillier .... Jean Brochard
Clothilde .... Claude Nollier
Mother .... Jane Marken
Valerie .... Micheline Luccioni

After "Nana" and "Gervaise," Emile Zola's public domain properties get another raid for his naturalistic tome on the French bourgeois at the turn-of-the-century, "Pot-Bouille." Utilizing the hothouse, corrupt aspects of the era, this emerges a heavyhanded piece with chances for U.S. arty situations (if no censorship trouble) but seems too weighty for more general spots. But exploitation possibilities loom from its predominantly bedroom sequences.

A handsome, opportunistic country boy takes Paris in his stride by seducing practically every young, married or career woman in his path. The one hardheaded businesswoman, who puts him off, is the one he will marry and create a big business with. Though given handsome production mounting by Robert & Raymond Hakim, solid casting and glossy direction by Julien Duvivier, this is so absorbed in the hero's amorous activities that the dramatic punch is lost.

Gerard Philipe plays a role with which he is now familiar. Same applies to Danielle Darrieux as the woman he will marry. Dany Carrel tries hard as the young victim of a conniving mother. Remainder of big name cast is good. Technical credits are tops. Henri Jeanson script has a touch of bitter satire on a money-hungry, frantic society. Some bravura moments, such as the chorus of maids ripping apart their degenerate employers, a girl's escape from a pursuing husband and others give this an arty chance but it will need hypoing. It has the plus factor of possible censorship publicity for biz interest *Mosk.*

El Hombre Senalado
(The Marked Man)
(ARGENTINE)

Buenos Aires, Nov. 26.

Goldberg release of Cinematografica Sudamericana (Spitz-Lauric) production. Features Mario Fortuna, Antonia Herrero, Pedro Quartucci, Homero Carpena and Francisco Lopez Silva. Directed by Francis Lauric. Original story by Alberto Peyrou and Diego Santillan; camera, Enrique Ritter. Normandie Theatre. Running time, **78 MINS.**

This is a step in the right direction on the part of a new production outfit and points to a brighter future for the local film industry. Director Francis Lauric came to Argentina as a child after World War I, and has worked as a journalist and in many lines of business. But he could not interest any producer in making this picture until he received help from a Cooperative studio team.

This is a tale of dire poverty in the struggle to achieve fortune. Its theme involves the weekly lottery (run by the government with which hospitals and asylums are maintained) in which almost every Argentine has an interest. Perhaps Lauric erred in making the end too bitter, instead of giving audiences a message of hope, but the climax could not be more artistic.

A poor janitor wins a 400,000 peso prize in the weekly lottery, throws up his job and goes home to tell his wife the great news, arriving in a taxi, smoking a cigar, on which he spends his last pesos. The ticket was hidden in the hatband of an old straw hat which his wife has just sold to a peddler. The search for the hat leads him through garbage dumps, to a wake, and through a gangster murder. Finally the hat is picked up on the bridge where the murder occurred by the old driver who shares lodgings with the couple. The horse which he drives has eaten all but fragments of the hat including the prize ticket.

Suspense is painfully maintained. Mario Fortuna gives a telling performance as the despairing janitor. Antonia Herrero over-stresses the role of the wife. Pedro Quartucci as a chimneysweep, who briefly possesses the hat, stands out vigorously and sympathetically in his first role since Peron came to power. All the underworld characters are well delineated while the camera picks out that port area in a way that gives charm to a sordid quarter of Buenos Aires.

Domestically, this should overcome feeling against native product since word-of-mouth will help it. Distributor has sold European distribution rights to Export Films Associated Ltd. of London. This is the first Argentine film booked for international distribution, and the first to make foreign exchange in a decade. *Nid.*

Mefiez-Vous Fillettes
(Look Out Girls)
(FRENCH)

Paris, Nov. 26.

Corona release of Silver-Chrysaor production. Stars Robert Hossein, Antonella Lualdi; features, Michele Cardoue, Gerard Oury, Andre Luguet, Jean Gaven. Directed by Yves Allegret. Screenplay, Rene Wheeler, Jean Meckert from novel by James Hadley Chase; camera, Robert Juillard; editor, Claude Nicole. At Cine Pantheon, Paris. Running time, **90 MINS.**

Raven .... Robert Hossein
Danny .... Antonella Lualdi
Palmer .... Gerard Oury
Spad .... Andre Luguet
Fan .... Michele Cardoue
Petit Jo .... Jean Gaven

This pic had censorship trouble even here, with a few scenes axed. What is left is a plodding, poorly made gangster film which strains for sensational values via scenes in a bagnio, a club that shows porno movies and a flock of killings by a half-mad gangster. But lacking characterization and direction, to make it plausible, this looks only an exploitation item, at best, for the U.S.

An innocent girl is kidnapped when she sees a fleeing gangster following a murder. She is re-kidnapped again and again, is used as a hostage to help the murderer. He finally falls for her but it is too late because gang wars and the police are closing in. Director Yves Allegret has not given this much suspense or pacing. The violence seems gratuitous.

Robert Hossein has presence as the mad gangster while the remainder of the cast fills out the frowzy roles well, with Antonella Lualdi acceptable as the innocent doll mixed up with the underworld. Technical credits are only par and production values ordinary.
Mosk.

Foreign Films

Paris, Nov. 26.

C'Est Arrive A Trente-Six Chandelles (It Happened On The Thirty Six Candles) (**FRENCH; SONGS**). Fernand Rivers release of Panoramas-Eden-Films D'Art-Rivers production. With Jane Sourza, Jacques Riberolles, Brigitte Barbier, Guy Bertil, Jean Nohain. Directed by Henri-Diamant Berger. Screenplay, Jean Nohain, Berger; camera, Robert Juillard; editor, Helene Baste; music, Francis Lopez. At Le Raimu, Paris. Running time, **105 MINS.**

This is an excuse to present one of the top video variety programs here, "Trente-Six Chandelles," in film form. Trite story of a boy who appeals for his girl, shunted off to another by ambitious parents, over the tv program gives an excuse to work in stints by most of the top singers on the French scene.

Thus, this is of little Yank theatre interest, but might serve for video slottings of excerpts of the songs and performers. Otherwise this is oldhat stuff. Technical credits are fair, but it does show the program to any undue advantage. *Mosk.*

Marchands De Filles (Girl Merchants) (**FRENCH**). UGC release of CFPC production. Stars Georges Marchal, Agnes Laurent; features Daniele Rocca, Pascal Roberts, Roger Duchesne. Directed by Maurice Cloche. Screenplay, Cloche; camera, Jacques Mercaton; editor; Fanchette Mazin. At Avenue, Paris. Running time, **100 MINS.**

As the title implies, this deals with the white slaving racket. Setting out to be a warning to young dancers trapped by this group, it evolves as merely an exploitation pic with some spurious scenes and the usual cops-and-robbers business as one girl is saved from "a fate worse than death." Lacking the style for a true exploitation pic, this is only for possible hypoing in secondary spots of the U. S. on its theme and a few daring scenes. Technical aspects, direction and acting are all ordinary.
Mosk.

Isabelle A Peur Des Hommes (Isabelle Is Afraid of Men) (**FRENCH; DYALISCOPE**). Heraut release of SFP production. With Cathia Caro, Michel Francois, Roger Dumas, Junie Astor, Pierre Massimi. Written and directed by Jean Gourguet. Camera, Simon Hugo; editor, Jean Fevier. At Cameo, Paris. Running time, **90 MINS.**

This is an ordinary entry in those dealing with juve morals. A young girl is afraid of men because her mother likes them too much. However, she finally gets a man to love her for herself. Trite characterizations and a few scenes of youthful cutting up do not make this of much chance for either Yank specialized or exploitation chances. Done in an anamorphoscopic process, the technical aspects are routine. This is mainly for home consumption. *Mosk.*

Vienna, Nov. 26.

Die unentschuldigte Stunde (Unexcused Hour) (**AUSTRIAN**). Sascha Film production and release. With Adrian Hoven, Erika Remberg, Chariklia Baxevanos, Josef Meinrad, Alma Seidler, Erik Frey, Ursula Herking, Rudolf Forster, Hans Moser. Directed by Willi Forst. Screenplay by Kurt Nachmann, Willi Forst after comedy by Stefan Bekeffi and A. Stella; camera, Guenther Anders, Robert Hofer; music, Heinz Sandauer. At Loewen Kino, Vienna. Running time, **90 MINS.**

Sascha Film Co. has a fine comedy here. It is a quality production of the great stage success by Stefan Bekeffi and A. Stella, wherein a young school girl (Erika Remberg) marries her Professor Physician (Adrian Hoven), but continues to go to school. Naturally, the missing presence at home or the unexcused hours at school lead to hilariously funny situations. Both of these stars are competent and amusing. In supporting roles, the producing company took great care in casting such people as Chariklia Baxevanos, Josef Meinrad, Alma Seidler, Erik Frey and Hans Moser.

Willi Forst's direction has its slam-bang moments, with lots of action and play this type of comedy requires. Guenther Anders and Robert Hofer did good camera work. Heinz Sandauer's musical score is okay. *Maas.*

Paris, Nov. 26.

Ce Joli Monde (This Pretty World) (**FRENCH**). Gaumont release of Gaumont-Gray Film production. Stars Yves Deniaud, Micheline Dax, Darry Cowl; features Lila Kedrova, Jacques Charon, Noel Roquevert, Jacques Fabbri. Written and directed by Carlo Rim. Camera, Nicolas Hayer; editor, Monique Kirsanoff. At Biarritz, Paris. Running time, **95 MINS.**

This is about a gangster whose son, whom he has not seen in 25 years, comes to visit him. The gang makes up as society and takes over their chateau hideout. Lost swag, with two gangs looking for it on Christmas Eve, makes up the complications plus the rather dim son's disillusionment about his pater. Neither really comic or dramatic, and having no real satirical touch, this film lags. It looks very chancey for the U.S. except for special spots.

Darry Cowl, a comic has been pushed to stardom too fast, is the dizzy son whose purity conflicts with the underworld characters. However, the attempts at insouciance, via some gauche seduction scenes and flippancy during a church service, lack the ring of true comedy and make them tasteless. Yves Deniaud is unresolved in style as the gangleader father and the remainder of the cast vacillates.

Technical credits are good but director-writer Carlo Rim has taken a familiar theme and added nothing original to it. *Mosk.*

Wild Is the Wind
(V'VISION—SONGS)

Top performances by Anna Magnani, Anthony Quinn in a drama of passion with strong distaff appeal. Good boxoffice prospects.

Hollywood, Dec. 7.

Paramount release of Hal Wallis production. Stars Anna Magnani, Anthony Quinn, Anthony Franciosa; costars Dolores Hart, Joseph Calleia. Director, George Cukor; screenplay, Arnold Schulman from novel by Vittorio Nino Novarese; camera, Charles Lang Jr.; editor, Warren Low; music, Dimitri Tiomkin. Previewed Dec. 2, '57. Running time, **110 MINS.**

Gioia	Anna Magnani
Gino	Anthony Quinn
Bene	Anthony Franciosa
Angie	Dolores Hart
Alberto	Joseph Calleia
Teresa	Lili Valenty

Top grade performances, some unusual film sequences and expert production highlight "Wild is the Wind," a story of earthy passion. It may earn most of its attention from distaff audiences, to whom its problem of a second wife desperately seeking love will appeal strongly. In addition to its moisture content, the Hal Wallis production has some added marquee stature in the persons of Anna Magnani and Anthony Quinn, a pair of former Oscar winners who look like nominees again this year on the strength of these performances. Overall box-office prospect is good.

Screenplay by Arnold Schulman, from a story by Vittorio Nino Novarese, is a good one, particularly in its delineation of the characters. It's an unusual switch in that it starts off on a comedy level before abruptly switching to the dramatic problem and long early portions of it are almost entirely in Italian. The device, which sounds odd, effectively sets the mood of the overall family relationships involved in the story.

Quinn is a wealthy sheep rancher in Nevada and goes back to the old country to wed the sister of his long-dead wife. He brings her home to a promise of happiness, but the shadow of the first wife is constantly between them. Even when he proposes a birthday toast to his bride, he calls her by her sister's name. Her urgent need to be loved makes her mistake the growing attraction between herself and Anthony Franciosa, young Basque sheepherder who had been raised by Quinn. When their affair is discovered, Franciosa turns away from her and she's ready to return to Italy when Quinn, finally conscious of his own need for her and discovering that romance has blossomed, convinces her to try again.

George Cukor has directed with taste and imagination and his skilful handling is evident in many scenes, particularly the sequence showing a film audience how a lamb is dropped, or one in which Franciosa trains sheep dogs, and in his handling of the affair between Miss Magnani and Franciosa. Under his direction, Miss Magnani turns in another notable performance, limning expertly the problem of the seemingly unloved second wife. Characterization is particularly expert in initial scenes where, despite an almost total use of Italian, she vividly conveys her reactions.

Quinn also does a top job, capturing the domineering quality of the rancher determined to run people's lives as he does his ranch. And Franciosa also shines as the younger corner of the triangle, giving the part considerable depth. In lesser roles, Joseph Calleia does a highly effective job as Quinn's elder brother, Lili Valenty is good as Calleia's wife and Dolores Hart shows promise as Quinn's daughter whose marriage to Franciosa is taken as a foregone conclusion by the family.

Wallis has given the production top quality throughout and there are good technical credits including fine lensing by Charles Lang Jr., good art direction by Hal Pereira and Tambi Larsen, smooth editing by Warren Low and a fine underscore by Dimitri Tiomkin. Sound by Gene Merritt failed to measure up in some of the outdoor scenes. Tiomkin and Ned Washington turned out a title tune that will have some exploitation value and the Italian song "Scapricciatiello," by Fernando Albano and Pacifico Vento, sung by Miss Magnani, should also generate some interest as a noveltune entry. *Kap.*

The Dalton Girls

Gun-happy daughters of one of the Daltons. Femme outlaws make for exploitation possibilities. Well handled.

Hollywood, Dec. 5.

United Artists release of Howard W. Koch production. Stars Merry Anders, Lisa Davis, Penny Edwards, Sue George, John Russell. Directed by Reginald Le Borg. Screenplay, Maurice Tombragel; story, Herbert Purdom; camera, Carl E. Guthrie; editor, John F. Schreyer; music, Les Baxter. Previewed Nov. 29, '57. Running time, **71 MINS.**

Holly Dalton	Merry Anders
Rose Dalton	Lisa Davis
Columbine Dalton	Penny Edwards
Marigold Dalton	Sue George
W. T. "Illinois" Grey	John Russell
Detective Hiram Parsh	Ed Hinton
Mr. Slidell, the mortician	Glenn Dixon
Joe	Johnny Western
Mr. Sewell, the bank manager	Malcolm Atterbury
Bank Cashier	Douglas Henderson
George, the bartender	Kevin Enright
Sheriff St. Ives	Al Wyatt
Marshal	H. E. Willmering
Stage Driver	Red Morgan
Way Station Hostler	K. C. MacGregor
Way Station Helper	David Swapp

"The Dalton Girls" proves pretty conclusively that the female of the species can be as deadly a gunslinger as the male. Switcheroo, in which femmes play the baddies and men the good guys, is sufficiently novel as carried out in an okay story line and action to rate good acceptance in the western market, where subject allows hefty exploitation.

Plottage of the Howard W. Koch production centers on four daughters of one of the Daltons, killed by a posse, who take to outlawry after the eldest, Merry Anders, kills a man in self-defense. It being something new for women in Colorado in the '80s to be bandits, they are able to plan and execute several dandy coups. Intertwined in yarn is a gambler, who always seems to be on the spot when the Dalton dishes swoop down, in for romance with one of the girls. Windup is a blazing finish, in which the Dalton girls try to gun their way to freedom after being cornered.

Reginald Le Borg's smooth direction of the Maurice Tombragel screenplay lends credence to femmes as outlaws, and story unfolds at a fast clip. Miss Anders and Lisa Davis, as the hard members of the quartet, latter a real killer, deliver strongly and Penny Edwards and Sue George, other two sisters, carry the sympathy in wanting to live a decent, normal life, both good. John Russell socks over role of the gambler, who keeps the Dalton sisters' identity to himself and romances Penny. Ed Hinton as a detective who finally catches up to Merry also is in for a sympathetic part, as is Al Wyatt, okay as a sheriff. Balance of cast provide good color. Miss Davis, in between killings, warbles "A Gun Is My True Love," by Les and Jim Baxter, for melodic effect.

Technical credits are well handled, including Carl E. Guthrie's photography and John F. Schreyer's tight editing. *Whit.*

The Naked Truth
(BRITISH)

Good farcical attack on the funny bone. Kidding of scandal journalism provides a certain laughter-raiser for all audiences.

London, Dec. 3.

Rank (Mario Zampi) production and release. Stars Terry-Thomas, Peter Sellers, Peggy Mount, Shirley Eaton, Dennis Price. Directed by Mario Zampi. Screenplay, Michael Pertwee; editor, Bill Lewthwaite; camera, Stanley Pavey; music, Stanley Black. At Odeon, Leicester Square, London. Running time, **92 MINS.**

Lord Mayley	Terry-Thomas
Sonny MacGregor	Peter Sellers
Flora Ransom	Peggy Mount
Melissa Right	Shirley Eaton
Nigel Dennis	Dennis Price
Lady Mayley	Georgina Cookson
Ethel Ransom	Joan Sims
Rev. Bastable	Miles Malleson
Porter	Kenneth Griffith
Mactavish	Moultrie Kelsall
Paunchy Old Man	Wally Patch
Gunsmith	Henry Hewitt

Mario Zampi's well-made farce sets out to get the patrons yocks and achieves its purpose. It pokes fun at scandal journalism ruthlessly. Though relying more on the sledge hammer than the rapier for its effects, it has few dull moments, with the laughs coming thick and fast. British audiences, watching some of their favorite artists, will find this item greatly to their taste.

Coming out at a time when the to-do about the "Confidential" trial evidence is still fresh in the memory, "Truth" takes yellow journalism for an hilarious ride. Michael Pertwee's original story and screenplay always threaten to get bogged down in the tricky labyrinth of farcial complication but survive to notch the laughs steadily.

Dennis Price is a suave, unscrupulous chiseller who digs out the dirt on the private lives of people and then threatens to publish the lurid details in his magazine, "The Naked Truth," unless they pay up $28,000 within two weeks. His principal victims are a peer in the insurance racket, a star tv personality whose show has made him one of the best-loved men in the country, a pretty model and a best-seller woman novelist.

Individually, and then collectively, the four set out to bump off the blackmailer. One way and another this involves attempted bombing, drugging, drowning and other forms of ineffective mayhem. When Price is arrested his 300 victims realize that it is in their interests that he should not give evidence. They gang up, throw Scotland Yard into pandemonium and chaos, snatch the crook from jail and shanghai him by ship, helicopter and airship to mid-Atlantic.

The novelist's bungling attempts to plan a trunk murder and one of those cosy audience-participation tv shows. These are just a sample of the ludicrous situations dreamed up to keep the fun rolling.

Major acting honors must go to Peter Sellers, top UK tv and radio comedian, as the tele star. He shapes as a fine character comedian in a wide range of impersonations. Price handles the blackmailer with silky ruthlessness and Terry-Thomas extracts every ounce of meat from his role as the peer. Peggy Mount bestrides the film as a fearsome battle-axe of a woman novelist, grabbing her laughs with the subtlety of an eager battering ram. She is aided admirably by Joan Sims as her dim daughter. Smaller roles are played with success by Georgina Cookson, Shirley Eaton, Kenneth Griffiths and Miles Malleson.

Mario Zampi directs with an unerring eye for a laugh. Though the film relies on situations rather than dialog, there are some neat wisecracks. Stanley Pavey's lensing is competent. "Truth" is as good a laughter-raiser as has been released by a British studio for a long time. *Rich.*

The Green-Eyed Blonde

Neatly produced story of reform school girls. Warm approach. Should be well received.

Hollywood, Nov. 29.

Warner Bros. release of Arwin production. Stars Susan Oliver, Linda Plowman, Beverly Long, Norma Jean Nilsson, Tommie Moore, Carla Merey. Features Sallie Brophy, Jean Innes, Olive Blakeney, Anne Barton, Tom Greenway. Supporting players, Margaret Brayton, Juanita Moore, Raymond Foster, Betty Lou Gerson, Stafford Repp, Evelyn Scott, Roy Glenn. Produced by Martin Melcher; director, Bernard Girard; screenplay, Sally Stubblefield; camera, Edward Fitzgerald; art director, Art Loel; editor, Thomas Reilly; music, Leith Stevens. Previewed Nov. 26, '57. Running time, **76 MINS.**

Greeneyes	Susan Oliver
Betsy Abel	Linda Plowman
Ouisie	Beverly Long
Cuckoo	Norma Jean Nilsson
Trixie	Tommie Moore
Joyce	Carla Merey
Margaret Wilson	Sallie Brophy
Mrs. Nichols	Jean Innes
Miss Vandingham	Olive Blakeney
Sally Abel	Anne Barton
Ed	Tom Greenway
Mrs. Adams	Margaret Brayton
Miss Randall	Juanita Moore
Cliff Munster	Raymond Foster
Mrs. Ferguson	Betty Lou Gerson
Bill Prell	Stafford Repp
Helen	Evelyn Scott
Mr. Budlong	Roy Glenn

A pic aimed specifically at teenage trade but with good prospect of acceptance in general market, "The Green-Eyed Blonde" benefits from Martin Melcher's fine production values and Bernard Girard's sensitive direction. While it doesn't have enough to command top dates, it does offer more than is usually found in this type of exploitation pic.

Title song, written by Joe Lubin and sung on film by The Four Grads, also may give pic a boost, for it stands solid chance as rock 'n' roll type hit.

No stars are cast in production, but more than one of the young femme leads shows promise of star material. Susan Oliver, as Greeneyes, is especially appealing, with a down-to-earth beauty and obvious talent to go with it. Other standouts are Tommie Moore, Beverly Long and Linda Plowman.

In the young adult class, Sallie Brophy handles everything from charm to power exceptionally well.

Story is set in corrective institution for girls but doesn't delve into the hackneyed semblance of ringleaders, cigarette stealing and blackmail repeated so many times before. Rather, it depicts how morale picks up when the illigitimate baby of one of the girls is stolen and brought to the dorm. The lonely girls find family contact in the infant, and even the soured mother eventually turns to love.

When the baby is discovered and

taken to an orphanage, the girls revolt, tearing premises to shreds. Greeneyes is questioned about baby, refuses to squeal and hears her sentence extended. Already to the breaking point, she escapes to meet b.f., and the pair ride off to a police gun battle and eventual death in an auto accident.

Although the whole story isn't quite tied together, it doesn't seem to make too much difference, for in this case the characterizations are more important. Scripter Sally Stubblefield hasn't delivered much of a plotline, but she has perceptively captured an aura that shows even bad girls are good.

Director Girard has delineated his players well, making each different from the next and all a part of the well-integrated peek into the inmates' feelings. His handling of the riot scene is particularly powerful.

Technical credits are far above average. *Ron.*

This Is Russia
(DOCUMENTARY-PART COLOR)

Interesting footage, marred somewhat by dubious pre-Sputnik commentary and do-it-yourself photography. Good bet for program filler spots.

Hollywood, Dec. 6.
Universal release of a Carey Wilson-Sid Feder production. Narrated by Wilson. Written and camera by Sid Feder; editor, Leon Selditz; music supervision, Joseph Gershenson. Previewed, Dec. 3, '57. Running time, 67 MINS.

Since Russia has been a key running story in the headlines for at least two decades, this extended documentary goes into the theatres with certain built-in exploitation values. Offhand, program filler spots and newsreel houses seem to offer best possibilities.

Chances are enhanced by genuinely off-beat footage, lensed during recent trip through U.S.S.R. (by commentator-newsman Sid Feder). Counterbalancing this is fact that Feder, no pro, had to practice do-it-yourself lensing, which comes out uneven in quality. Accompanying commentary written by Feder is studded with dubious matter, including flat historical inaccuracies ("Catherine the Great had 27 lovers and had them all killed").

Commentary apparently was written before the Sputnik launchings. In view of this, certain remarks about the backwardness of Russia now seem unconvincing, to put it mildly.

Obvious, Feder took long chances to get certain shots, including an exploration of the seamier side of Soviet life. For instance, in one sequence he shows what he claims is a fight between students and police in Tiflis (actually, all that is shown is a crowd clustered around a streetcar). Feder casually winds this sequence with the remark that he was arrested during the hassle.

Unusual are the shots of slum areas and of women doing heavy physical labor (Feder makes much of this, with mysterious references to the missing males. However, perhaps he is trying to indirectly comment on the size of the Soviet war apparatus). Other shots of day-to-day Soviet life, including a State-directed fashion show, are quite interesting to the outsider.

Footage, in both Eastman Color and black-and-white, starts in Moscow, then covers other Soviet areas, including Kiev, Georgia, the Black Sea resorts, the Asiatic Soviet Republics of the Kazaks and Uzbecks, and Leningrad. This in

itself is most unusual and interesting.

Carey Wilson ably narrates the Feder commentary, with assists from several unidentified voices. *Kove.*

Herr Puntila Und Sein Knecht Matti
(Herr Puntila And His Chauffeur Matti)
(AUSTRIAN; COLOR; SONGS)
Paris, Dec. 3.
Wien Film release of Heinrich Bauer production. With Curt Bois, Heinz Engelmann, Maria Emo, Edith Prager. Directed by Alberto Cavalcanti. Screenplay by Vladimir Pozner, Ruth Wieden from play by Bertold Brecht; camera (Agfacolor), Andre Bac; editor, Josef Juvancic; music, Hanns Eisler. At Ursulines, Paris. Running time, 100 MINS.
Puntila .... Curt Bois
Matti .... Heinz Engelmann
Eva .... Maria Emo
Fina .... Edith Prager

A folksy fable has been concocted from the Bertold Brecht play about a hardbitten, mean landowner who becomes an understanding, tender man when drunk. Set in turn-of-the-century Finland, it is played in a slapstick manner, which loses it some of its savor but makes it a comedy with possible U. S. art house chances. Title is far too long.

Its use of a chorus of washerwomen, filmed in black and white while the rest is tinted, commenting on the tale, and a fast-paced directorial stint by Alberto Cavalcanti cook up plenty of yocks as Puntila zigzags between grasping penury and loving largesse.

Thus Puntila's vacillations, trying to marry his daughter off to an unctuous, fortune hunting diplomat one minute and his chauffer the next, is risible without any propaganda aspects. Curt Bois, who was at one time in Hollywood, is perceptive as Puntila as he goes from rubberlegged bonhommie to crafty cruelty with an underlying understanding of his condition to make this a sock comedy portrayal. Remainder of the cast is good as are production values.

Word-of-mouth could help plus good crix. Music has the proper folklore mood. *Mosk.*

Der 10. Mai
(The Tenth of May)
(SWISS)
Zurich, Dec. 3.
Praesens Film release of Neue Film A.G. (Frank Schnyk) production. With Linda Geiser, Heinz Reincke, Fred Tanner, Herman Wlach, Therese Giehse, Yette Perrin, Hans Gaugler, Heinrich Gretler, Max Haufler, Emil Hegetschweiler, Gustav Knuth, Koni Messikommer, Armin Schweizer, Max Werner Lenz, Margrit Rainer, Lisette Oesch, Paulette Dubost, Anneliese Egger, Walter Roderer, Max Knapp, Ellen Widmann. Directed by Franz Schnyder. Original screenplay, W. M. Treichlinger, Arnold Kuebler, Schnyder; camera, Konstantin Tschet; music, Robert Blum. At Capitol, Zurich. Running time, 95 MINS.

This first Swiss widescreen pic is the initial production effort of newly founded Neue Film A.G., bringing the number of Swiss feature-producing companies to three. The first entry takes up a by-now historic event—the critical day of May 10, 1940, when Hitler invaded Belgium, Holland and Luxemburg and the Swiss army was mobilized to the last available man to guard the frontiers. On that day, many civilians here panicked, but the majority remained calm.

Produced in 37 days, mostly on location, this film was brought in at the incredibly (for U.S.) modest budget of barely $80,000. It is a

commendable effort, but lacks statue to mean much outside this territory and, perhaps, its neighboring countries. Lack of star appeal also is a handicap.

Story focusses on a young German fugitive who is given shelter by a Swiss girl and is later persuaded to give himself up to the Swiss police instead of keeping on the run. Many episodes depicting reactions of various Swiss types to the political events are grouped around this main plot theme.

Heinz Reincke, as the German, is excellent, while Linda Geiser, as the Swiss girl, has looks, but rarely comes off as an actress. In the smaller roles, many interesting character bits register strongly, notably by Herman Wlach and Therese Giehse, as an elderly Jewish couple; Heinrich Gretler, as a police inspector and Emil Hegetschweiler, as a railroad guard. Technical credits are above par. Konstantin Tschet's widescreen black-and-white photography is a strong plus factor. Robert Blum's background score is intelligently used. *Mezo.*

Peyton Place
(C'SCOPE-COLOR)

Family version of Grace Metalious' sexy bestseller. Book's notoriety and topnotch performances should propel this into top b.o. league.

20th-Fox release of Jerry Wald production. Stars Lana Turner, Hope Lange, Lee Philips, Lloyd Nolan, Arthur Kennedy, Russ Tamblyn, Diane Varsi, Terry Moore; features Barry Coe, Betty Field, David Nelson, Mildred Dunnock, Leon Ames, Lorne Greene, Robert H. Harris, Tami Conner, Staats Cotsworth, Peg Hillias, Erin O'Brien-Moore, Scotty Morrow. Directed by Mark Robson. Screenplay, John Michael Hayes from Grace Metalious novel; camera (Color by DeLuxe), William Mellor; music, Franz Waxman; editor, David Bretherton. Previewed in New York, Dec. 6, '57. Running time, 166 MINS.
Constance .... Lana Turner
Selena Cross .... Hope Lange
Michael Rossi .... Lee Philips
Dr. Swain .... Lloyd Nolan
Lucas Cross .... Arthur Kennedy
Norman Page .... Russ Tamblyn
Allison .... Diane Varsi
Betty Anderson .... Terry Moore
Rodney Harrington .... Barry Coe
Nellie Cross .... Betty Field
Ted Carter .... David Nelson
Mrs. Thornton .... Mildred Dunnock
Harrington .... Leon Ames
Prosecutor .... Lorne Greene
Seth Bushwell .... Robert H. Harris
Margie .... Tami Conner
Charles Partridge ..... Staats Cotsworth
Marion Partridge .... Peg Hillias
Mrs. Page .... Erin O'Brien-Moore
Joey Cross .... Scotty Morrow
Paul Cross .... Bill Lundmark
Matt .... Alan Reed, Jr.
Pee Wee .... Kip King
Kathy .... Steffi Sidney
Judge .... Tom Greenway

When it was first announced that Jerry Wald would bring the sexsational "Peyton Place" to the screen a lot of people shook their heads in wonderment and asked: *"How are they going to do it?"* The question now is answered, and there is no doubt that Wald and writer John Michael Hayes have done a skillful job in stripping the unpretty novel of its objectionable material while still retaining its plot essentials. Both theme and treatment smack of boxoffice.

Rarely has there been a film with greater "presold" values. The book, though hardly a critics' favorite, was a runaway bestseller. The picture, following the novel at least as far as storyline and many characters are concerned, is bound to reap benefits, particularly since in a polite way it calls a spade a spade.

It's sure to be a topdraw for the teenage trade, which here has a unique chance for self-identification, and—due to the energetic cleanup job done on the novel—for the family audience. Apart from all this, it's ambitiously produced by Wald and impressively acted by an excellent cast.

After the foregoing, the film in its long 166 minutes running time is something of a disappointment. Though it makes the most of its several climaxes, parts of it drag, and for quite a while in the beginning, nothing happens. It has a rape scene, which is handled in good taste, and it tries hard to capture some of the "sexy" flavor of the book, but in leaning backwards not to offend, Wald and Hayes have gone acrobatic. There is, however, "mention" of miscarriage and "sleeping with a man." Hence the claim to be "daring."

On the screen is not the unpleasant sex-secret little town against which Grace Metalious set her story. These aren't the gossiping, spiteful, immoral people she portrayed. There are hints of this in the film, but only hints. The ugliness of human beings is viewed through rosecolored glasses. Where, in the book, Betty Anderson, the town tramp, is paid off (and short-changed) by Rodney's father, in the film she marries the boy. The accent throughout the production is primarily on the positive, and in being conventional, it emerges as a shocker without shock.

Under Mark Robson's direction, every one of the performers delivers a topnotch portrayal. Performance of Diane Varsi particularly is standout and in her, without question, the screen has a great new find. As the rebellious teenager, eager to learn about life and numbed by the discovery that she is an illegitimate child, she emerges as an actress of major importance and of great appeal. She gives the part of Allison a sweetness of youth that is as winning as it is believable, and she manages to put across with great skill the process of awkward maturing.

Also in top form in a difficult role is Hope Lange, stepdaughter of the school's drunken caretaker, who rapes her and is finally killed by her. Here, too, is an exciting new personality and her performance contributes greatly. As Miss Varsi's mother, Lana Turner looks elegant and registers strongly.

This being a picture in which young people figure importantly, Lee Philips is another new face as Michael Rossi, the school principal who courts the reluctant Miss Turner. Pleasant looking, and a very capable actor, Philips has a voice that is at times high and nasal. However, he does a thoroughly competent job.

Opposite Miss Varsi, Russ Tamblyn plays Norman Page, the mama's boy, with much intelligence and appealing simplicity. Their scenes together have the charm of youth and of innocence and are beautifully directed by Robson. In other roles, Arthur Kennedy personifies "lust" in the role of Lucas Cross; Lloyd Nolan has dignity as the doctor; Terry Moore is okay as the flirtatious Betty Anderson; Betty Field turns in a gem of a performance as Nellie Cross, and Barry Coe is handsome as Rodney Harrington who defies his father, millowner Leon Ames.

David Nelson registers as Ted Carter and Mildred Dunnock, Lorne Greene, Robert H. Harris, Staats Cotsworth, Peg Hillias and particularly little Scotty Morrow all do justice to their smaller roles. It's a large cast and a well-chosen one, though some of the New England accents at times take on a suspiciously Southern tinge.

Robson's direction is unhurried, though he expertly allows his climaxes to erupt periodically through the picture. His camera captures moods and faces, taking best advantage of the little town of Camden, Me., where most of the film was shot. There are scenes that are superfluous and that impede the story flow, though they're visually pleasing. William Mellor's lensing generally is excellent and there are stunning shots of the changing seasons in the New England countryside. The DeLuxe color on the wide CinemaScope screen is vivid and sufficiently subdued so as not to interfere with the dramatic story values.

Writer Hayes was confronted with a herculean job in adapting this story to the screen. He did it so well that the usually strict Legion of Decency rated the film in its A category. He preserved the vital relationships between teenagers and adults, and for once the adults aren't shown to be without faults. His dialog runs smoothly, with an almost lyrical quality at times, and he has given director

Robson plenty of contrasts to work with. As it is, he captured only enough of "Peyton Place" to satisfy those who argue that the screen must forever appeal to all audience strata, be they teenagers or adults. The "shock" in his script comes in the saying, not the doing. "Peyton Place" somehow required more than that.

On the technical side, David Bretherton's editing has quality. Charles Le Maire has designed a very appealing wardrobe for the femme leads, particularly Miss Turner, and Franz Waxman's musical background is pleasantly melodic.

Whatever its faults, "Peyton Place" shapes as a money picture and, in Miss Varsi, introes one of the bright new stars of the future. That's the combination of values the industry needs.   *Hift.*

The Girl Most Likely
(SONGS—COLOR)

Amusing, well-made musical about young love. Sold to the juve trade it should enjoy okay word-of-mouth and satisfactory returns.

Hollywood, Dec. 14.

Universal release of RKO (Stanley Rubin) production. Stars Jane Powell, Cliff Robertson, Keith Andes, Kaye Ballard, Tommy Noonan. Features Una Merkel. Director, Mitchell Leisen; screenplay, Devery Freeman; camera, Robert Planck; editors, Harry Marker, Dean Harrison; music arranged and conducted by Nelson Riddle. Songs by Bob Russell and Nelson Riddle and Hugh Martin and Ralph Blane. Previewed Dec. 10, '57. Running time, **98 MINS.**

Dodie .... Jane Powell
Pete .... Cliff Robertson
Neil .... Keith Andes
Marge .... Kay Ballard
Buzz .... Tommy Noonan
Mom .... Una Merkel
Sam .... Kelly Brown
Pauline .... Judy Nugent
Pop .... Frank Cady

In the increasing concentration on musicals aimed at the juvenile trade, "The Girl Most Likely" is a rarity in that it is a quality offering. It is light, diverting entertainment, tastefully done up in a Technicolor package that combines a Cinderella-like story of young romance with good humor. There's no strong marquee bait in either the cast names or the exploitation values of the tunes, so it will have to be specifically sold to the younger element to register better than moderate returns but word of mouth should help to make it satisfactory.

Amusing screenplay by Devery Freeman, limns the romantic aspirations of Jane Powell, a sort of musical "Dream Girl," who's convinced it's just as easy to fall in love with a rich man as with a poor one. She's in and out of love a couple of times before she lands Keith Andes, a wealthy playboy, but she bolts out of his life just before the marriage vows when she discovers that it's only Diesel mechanic Cliff Robertson's kisses that envelop her in the storied pink cloud.

Six tunes by Hugh Martin and Ralph Blane and one, the title tune, by Bob Russell and Nelson Riddle, spice the activity and there are a couple of standout dances and musical sequences staged by Gower Champion, one in and around the Balboa shore, that elicit top response. Miss Powell is eye-appealing and in fine voice in the title role and romps easily through the film. Cliff Robertson is good as the mechanic who finally wins the girl and Andes and Tommy Noonan both make the most of their roles as spurned suitors. Kaye Ballard

shines throughout as Miss Powell's best friend and could easily become a solid film comedienne. In lesser roles, Kelly Brown registers as Miss Ballard's boy-friend and Una Merkel, Judy Nugent and Frank Cady are assets in portraying Miss Powell's family.

Production is a good credit for producer Stanley Rubin, who has assembled a pleasing package. Mitchell Leisen's direction is well-paced and in the proper light vein and there are strong assists in the lensing by Robert Planck, the art direction by Albert S. D'Agostino and George W. Davis and costuming by Renie. Other credits are stock.   *Kap.*

Legend of the Lost
(TECHNIRAMA—COLOR)

Slow moving story of a search for a lost city in the Sahara, with John Wayne, Sophia Loren and Rossano Brazzi. Despite cast names, only average returns with saturation bookings needed to register strongly.

Hollywood, Dec. 14.

United Artists release of Batjac Productions Panama, Inc., production in association with Robert Haggiag, Dear Films Productions. Producer-director, Henry Hathaway. Stars John Wayne, Sophia Loren, Rossano Brazzi. Features Kurt Kasznar. Screenplay, Ben Hecht, Robert Presnell Jr.; camera, Jack Cardiff; editor, Bert Bates; music. A. F. Lavagnino. Previewed Dec. 13, '57. Running time, **107 MINS.**

Joe January .... John Wayne
Dita .... Sophia Loren
Bonnard .... Rossano Brazzi
Prefect Dukas .... Kurt Kasznar
Girls   Sonia Moser, Angela Portaluri
Galli Galli .... Ibrahim El Hadish

Slow-moving and synthetic, "Legend of the Lost" is lifted above the level of routine adventure only by the presence of John Wayne, Sophia Loren and Rossano Brazzi as cast names. Word of mouth, however, may work against these marquee values and saturation bookings will be needed to register better than average business in today's market since the entertainment, unfortunately, is meagre.

Henry Hathaway produced and directed from a screenplay by Ben Hecht and Robert Presnell Jr. that meanders aimlessly across the Sahara desert liberally employing coincidence and contrivance. Theoretically, it's the story of the degeneration of a man and the regeneration of a woman but there's little in the dialog, acting or direction to warrant classing it as anything more than an improbable adventure story about the search for a lost city in the Sahara.

Brazzi is a mysterious, apparently God-fearing man who seeks the treasure once found by his father in order to create a center that will honor his father's name. Wayne is an experienced desert guide and Miss Loren is a native girl with a bad reputation. They trudge through the desert and locate the treasure but Brazzi also discovers his father wasn't the sainted personality he thought he was. The discovery completely changes Brazzi's character and he abandons his companions to escape with the loot. They follow on foot and catch up with him for the climactic fight in which Brazzi is killed and Wayne badly wounded. But a caravan providently looms up off the horizon to give the promise of a new life to Wayne and Miss Loren. The jewels are still there in the sand where Brazzi buried them.

Hathaway's reputation as a loca-

tion director is evident in the sweeping panoramas of sand but he failed to handle his cast with any restraint. Brazzi overacts, Wayne is flat-voiced and Miss Loren alternates between petulance and subdued passion. Only really credible performance is that of Kurt Kasznar as a venal Timbuctoo police prefect.

Photography by Jack Cardiff is not up to his usual standard and the desert appears to have blunted some of the sharpness of the Technirama widescreen process. Music by A. F. Lavagnino is eerie and sometimes obtrusive and the remainder of the technical credits are stock.   *Kap.*

A Farewell to Arms
(C'SCOPE—COLOR)

Hemingway World War I novel re-done with pictorial splendor and acted by Jennifer Jones and Rock Hudson. Shapes as top earner.

20th-Fox release of David O. Selznick production. Stars Rock Hudson, Jennifer Jones, Vittorio De Sica; features Alberto Sordi, Kurt Kasznar, Mercedes McCambridge, Oscar Homolka, Elaine Stritch, Leopoldo Trieste, Franco Interlenghi, Jose Nieto, Victor Francen. Directed by Charles Vidor. Screenplay, Ben Hecht, from Ernest Hemingway novel of same title; camera (color by De Luxe), Piero Portalupi and Oswald Morris; music, Mario Nascimbene, conducted by Franco Ferrara; editors, Gerard J. Wilson, John M. Foley. Previewed at the Roxy Theatre, N.Y., Dec. 17, '57. Running time, **159 MINS.**

Lt. Frederic Henry ...... Rock Hudson
Nurse Catherine Berkley . Jennifer Jones
Maj. Alessandro Rinaldi . . Vittorio De Sica
Father Galli .... Alberto Sordi
Bonello .... Kurt Kasznar
Miss Van Campen
Mercedes McCambridge
Doctor Emerich .... Oscar Homolka
Helen Ferguson .... Elaine Stritch
Passini .... Leopoldo Trieste
Aymo .... Franco Interlenghi
Major Stampi .... Jose Nieto
Captain Bassi .... Georges Brehat
Nino, the porter ..... Memmo Carotenuto
Boy Scout .... Guido Martufi
Barber .... Umberto Spadaro
Ambulance Driver ... Umberto Sacripanti
Colonel Valentini .... Victor Francen
Blonde Nurse .... Joan Shawlee
Arrested Officer .... Alberto D'Amario
1st Carabiniere .... Giacomo Rossi Stuart
2nd Carabiniere .... Carlo Pedersoli
Carabiniere Officer .... Alex Revides
Captain at Outpost ... Franco Mancinelli
Medical Lieutenant ...... Patrick Crean
Civilian Doctor .... Guidarino Guidi
Hospital Receptionist .... Diana King
Hairdresser .... Clelia Metania
Lt. Zimmerman .... Eduard Linkers
Mrs. Zimmerman .... Johanna Hofer
Court Martial Colonel .... Luigi Barzini
Racetrack Announcer .... Carlo Licari
Firing Squad Commander . Angiolo Galassi
First Diner .... Carlo Hintermann
Second Diner .... Tiberio Mitri
Delivery Room Nurse ...... Eva Kotthaus
Nurse in Catherine's Room
Gisella Mathews
Hotel Proprietor .... Vittorio Jannitti
Milan Hotel Clerk .... Peter Illing
Swiss Sergeant .... Sam Levine

At a time when the clamor is for "big" pictures, David O. Selznick delivers "A Farewell to Arms" which, in terms of sheer magnitude and pictorial splendor, has few current rivals. New version of the Ernest Hemingway World War I story marks Selznick's return to filmmaking after an absence of eight years, and the results add up to a dazzling piece of camera workmanship.

Fact that it's also one of the boldest of love stories augurs massive public appeal. With Rock Hudson and Jennifer Jones teamed attractively in the leads, "Farewell" has the earmarks of a boxoffice winner.

There are things of great beauty in this long adaptation, and parts of it are handled sensitively, conveying some of the Hemingway spirit that speaks of the futility of war and a desperate love that grips two strangers in its midst. This is primarily a woman's picture, with all the emotional strains and stresses that go to make up such a film.

But sweep and frankness alone don't make a "great" picture; and "Farewell" suffers from an overdose of both. Selznick and director Charles Vidor, shooting all of the film in Italy and a good part of it on location in the Dolomites, have concentrated heavily on nature and war. Following Ben Hecht's script, they've also contributed some deliberate shock effects. (*"I've never felt like a whore before,"* says Miss Jones to Hudson in their hotel room). No bones are made about their extended affair, and the childbirth sequence at the climax is frightfully realistic.

All this is in the book and it's effective picture making. It's the more unfortunate that Hecht's often mature dialog is also riddled with cliches, and that the relationship between Hudson and Miss Jones never takes on real dimensions. In part this must be blamed on Miss Jones' performance, which tends to go overboard on the dramatics. In part it's the fault of the director who let scenes run too long. "Farewell" has an uneven pace, and though one can readily understand Selznick's reluctance to part with his footage, it needs tightening up. Occasionally, too, some of the Italian actors are difficult to understand.

Story, briefly, has American Red Cross ambulance driver Hudson meeting up with nurse Miss Jones and falling violently in love with her. When he's wounded on the front, he's brought back to the hospital, where she joins him. Their protracted affair ends when he's sent back to the front where he's caught up in the disastrous retreat from Caporetto. Arrested as a deserter and sentenced to die, he escapes to join Miss Jones who by then is pregnant. Together, they make their way to Switzerland, where Miss Jones dies in childbirth.

Such a tragic story requires great performances to put it across. It gets only a few of them in this picture. The real star is the color camera, guided by Piero Portalupi and Oswald Morris. Scene after scene catches the breathtaking grandeur of the Alps and of the men fighting in the deep snow. Here, Vidor's direction is superb and the film draws much of its strength from these sequences. The retreat from Caporetto is charged with excitement and expertly staged. There is doom in the air, and confusion and tragedy. By contrast, the scenes of Hudson and Miss Jones escaping across the lake to Switzerland have a calm beauty that has the quality of paintings. Ditto their moving farewell at the railroad station.

Hudson does a creditable job as Lieutenant Fredric Henry. He's ruggedly handsome and his performance has validity throughout. If his reactions are at times puzzling, that's the fault of the script more than of the actor. On the whole, Hudson is well cast and this film should enhance his already considerable draw.

Miss Jones imbues the nurse with a sense of neurosis and foreboding, but she only sporadically rises to the full challenge of this super-difficult role. Her creation of the childbirth sequence, full of screaming agony, is real, but her love scenes—and there are many of them—somehow don't ring quite true. No question, Catherine Barkley isn't supposed to be "just another girl." But as Miss Jones plays her, she frequently lacks warmth. Her resolute courage, which refuses Hudson's offers of marriage though she is already pregnant, is hard to believe.

In the supporting roles, Selznick has cast a group of very good actors. Vittorio De Sica plays the cynical Major Rinaldi with dash, and in him the Hemingway spirit comes alive with full force. He symbolizes the waste and futility of war. Alberto Sordi is moving as Father Galli and Kurt Kasznar comes through well as the ambulance driver. Mercedes McCambridge is brusque as the American nurse and Elaine Stritch registers strongly in a come vein as another American nurse. Oscar Homolka is okay as the doctor and Victor Francen has dignity as the chief surgeon.

In terms of technique, to repeat, much of "Farewell" is superb. Director Vidor, working with a thoroughly mature script and natural backgrounds, has turned out a film that makes magnificent use of the wide screen and that often rises to sharp dramatic heights. There are vignettes in this picture that are gems of their kind and contribute mightily to the story itself.

This is unquestionably one of the year's best photographed films, and the De Luxe color—often muted for excellent effect—is expertly used. Hecht's script knows where to balance drama and humor. It is forever to his credit that so much of the picture is Hemingway.

Film's emotional qualities are underscored effectively by Mario Nascimbene's music, revolving around a catchy theme.

"Farewell" occasionally runs out of breath, but Selznick has produced an important attraction that can't fail to excite the public's imagination. Picture has the mark of a master craftsman. *Hift.*

Uchujin Tokyo Ni Arawaru
(Unknown Satellite Over Tokyo)
(JAPANESE—COLOR)

Paris, Dec. 17.

Daiei production and release. With Toyomi Karita, Kaizo Kawasaki, Isao Yamagata, Shozo Nanbu, Bontaro Miake. Directed by Koji Shima. Screenplay, Gentaro Nakajima; camera (Daiei Color), Shigeo Mano; editor, Toyo Suzuki. At Studio De L'Etoile, Paris. Running time, **87 MINS.**

Ginko .... Toyomi Karita
Isobe .... Keizo Qawasaki
Matsuda .... Isao Yamagata
Komura .... Bontaro Miake

In this sputnik era a Japanese science-fiction pic is obviously timely. Though influenced by Yank efforts, it is done with a candor and simplicity which makes it a good entry of this type, and maybe something for specialized packaging in the U.S.

Flying saucers from an artificial satellite land in Tokyo. Weird people, with one eye in the center of their body, come forth. When they frighten people, they take the form of earthlings. Then they try to save the earth from a collision with another planet. They are from an unknown planet themselves.

Film plot has a scientist inventing a new bomb which can save the earth, and unscrupulous racketeers or foreign powers trying to steal it.

There is the usual love interest and good special effects plus a fine use of color during the near approach of the flaming planet which almost destroys the earth. Acting is keyed to the general actioner pace of the pic. It emerges different enough in the oriental understatement. It also has exploitation pegs. *Mosk.*

Panama Sal

Dive singer gets the Pygmalion job. Not much.

Hollywood, Dec. 14.

Republic release of a Vineland production. Stars Elena Verdugo, Edward Kemmer, Carlos Rivas. Features Harry Jackson, Joe Flynn, Christine White. Supporting players, Albert Carrier, Jose Gonzales Gonzales, Billie Bird, Ukonu and his Afro-Calypsonians. Produced by Edward J. White. Directed by William Witney. Screenplay, Arnold Belgard; camera, Jack Marta; art director, Ralph Oberg; musical director, Gerald Roberts; editor, Joseph Harrison; choreography, Roland Dupree. Reviewed Dec. 14, '57. Running time, **70 MINS.**

Sal Regan .... Elena Verdugo
Dennis P. Dennis .... Edward Kemmer
Manuel Ortego .... Carlos Rivas
Peter Van Fleet II ...... Harry Jackson
Barrington C. Ashbrook ...... Joe Flynn
Patricia Sheldon .... Christine White
Moray .... Albert Carrier
Peon .... Jose Gonzales Gonzales
Woman Manager .... Billie Bird
Ukonu Calypsonians .... Themselves

The vital personality that several tv seasons of "Meet Millie" showed Elena Verdugo to be is slowed to a near standstill in her newest pic, "Panama Sal," and the few times she's given full rein aren't enough to add up. Pic could have engendered some interest in its Calypso music had it been released when Calypso was the rage, but at this point, it's seemingly a few beats too late to cash in. Call the Vineland production filler fare.

Only infrequently does the Arnold Belgard script offer anything to work with, and producer Edward J. White and director William Witney only occasionally helped it along.

Story is "Pygmalion" set in Beverly Hills and Panama in that a kind-hearted "gentleman" takes a sexy, low-class broad and tries to make a respectable star of her. The "gentleman" actually is a playboy who crashlands his plane in the Panama jungle with two rich cohorts. They just happen upon a Panamanian waterfront dive where sexy Sal is belting 'em out under the slightly clouded spot. He talks her into going back to the States where he'll make her famous.

Sub-plot has the two friends using the relationship to break up playboy and his socialite fiance. Sal becomes a star, for some unexplained reason returns to Panama, is followed by the playboy and all ends with an indication that the future will bring more romantic things than did the past 70 minutes.

Edward Kemmer, as the playboy, and his buddies—Harry Jackson and Joe Flynn—add some amusing moments. Carlos Rivas, as a night-club owner, is sympathetic in between times he's hauling out his blood-hungry knife. Christine White is okay as the socialite.

Miss Verdugo sings in this one, and not badly either. But the dance numbers that surround her are highly unimaginative.

There are some humorous scenes—a fight that catches Sal in the middle and a rehearsal lorded over by a parrot named Oswald. Neither, however, is enough to bridge the gap.

The black-and-white print, made in Naturama process, is less than definitive around the edges, sometimes annoyingly so. *Ron.*

All At Sea
(BRITISH)

Alec Guinness stars in an amiable comedy which, though disappointing, will garner the yocks in most spots.

London, Dec. 17.

Metro release of a Michael Balcon Production. Stars Alec Guinness. Directed by Charles Frend. Screenplay, T. E. B. Clarke; editor, Jack Harris, camera, Douglas Slocombe; music, John Addison. At Empire, London. Running time, **87 MINS.**

Captain Ambrose .... Alec Guinness
Mrs. Barrington .... Irene Browne
Tommy .... Percy Herbert
Duckworth .... Harold Goodwin
Crowley .... Maurice Denham
Figg .... Victor Maddern
Bullen .... George Rose
June .... Jackie Collins
Evie .... Junia Crawford
Superintendent Browning .. Lloyd Lamble
Major Kent .... Charles Cullum
Mrs. Kent .... Joan Hickson
Adrian .... Alexander Harris
Artie White .... Warren Mitchell
Erudite Angler .... Miles Malleson
Frogman .... Sam Kydd

Harry .... Frederick Piper
Peters .... Harry Locke
Registrar of Shipping.....Richard Wattis
Liberamanian Consul......Eric Pohlmann
Bank Manager .... Newton Blick
Teller .... Donald Pleasence
Ambrose's Six Ancestors . Alec Guinness

T. E. B. Clarke has proved with such pix as "Passport to Pimlico," "The Lavender Hill Mob" and "The Titfield Thunderbolt" that he is a deft hand at dreaming up screen comedy. The combination of Clarke and Alec Guinness in "All At Sea" promised more than has been actually fulfilled. Guinness's name will undoubtedly draw plenty of film patrons. They will be rewarded with amiable light entertainment.

Clarke got the idea for "Barnacle Bill" while sunning himself on Brighton Pier. But like many other good comedy ideas it has lost much during the period between conception and execution. Instead of being borne on a wave of laughter, "Barnacle Bill" is content with mere ripples. The yarn has Guinness as the last of a long line of seafaring heroes dating back to the Stone Age. But he is a sea dog with the unfortunate knack of being sick at the very sight of a rough sea. He spent the war as a shore guinea-pig looking for a seasick remedy. Demobbed, he decides to buy an old Victorian seaside pier and run it on naval lines. At last, he has his own command, but without the distressing problem of having to go to sea.

Sandcastle Pier is a rundown choice but Guinness sets out to make the pier shipshape and aims to turn it into an entertainment centre. He is up against the local council which aims to pull down the pier for its own financial gain. From then on it's a fight between Guinness and his supporters and the mayor and his rogues, ending in the pier being wrecked. But Guinness conquers his sea-sickness and leads his forces in a "naval battle" which enables him to justify his ancestry.

The chief snag about this production is that it is never clear whether director Charles Frend is aiming at farce or satirical comedy. Star Guinness handles his chore with his usual consummate ease but never really seems to have his heart in it except during the brief opportunities he gets to impersonate his half a dozen ancestors which include a slaphappy Stone Age sailor, one of Drake's men and an officer in the First World War. These show off Guinness as a comedy actor of great versatility.

"Barnacle" is rich in supporting performances. Among those enjoying themselves in the nautical goings-on are Percy Herbert and Harold Goodwin, as members of Guinness' "crew"; Maurice Denham, Victor Maddern and George Rose, as members of the shifty Town Council; and Joan Hickson and Charles Cullum as passengers on Guinness's "H.M.S. Arabella" Miles Malleson, Eric Pohlmann, Richard Wattis, Donald Pleasence, Harry Locke and Newton Blick also appear in brief but telling cameos.

The femmes get little chance to shine except for Irene Browne, a pier hut owner, who becomes Guinness's chief ally. A young femme named Junia Crawford, however, shows up well as a local goodtime girl.

There is nothing wrong with Dorglas Slocombe's lensing, the authentic art work of Alan Withy which portrays vividly a typical middle-class British seaside resort. *Rich.*

Forbidden Desert
(COLOR)

Odd - lengthened featurette, part drama, part travelog. Interesting footage fits it for filler spots with over-long top pictures.

Hollywood, Dec. 20.
Warner Bros. production and release. Stars Rafik Shammas; with Abdallah Saleh, Ibrahim Mohammed Aly, Ahmed Abdallah, Ibrahim Abdel Hamido. Produced by Cedric Francis. Directed, screenplay and camera by Jackson Winter; editor, Robert Warwick; music, Howard Jackson. Previewed, Nov. 26, '57. Running time, 45 MINS.
John Lewis Burkhardt....Rafik Shammas
Abdel Karim .... Abdallah Saleh
Yussuf .... Ibrahim Mohamed Aly
Ayd .... Ahmed Abdallah
Hamid .... Ibrahim Adbel Hamid

Based on the journal of a daring 19th Century exploration, this odd-lengthened "featurette" adds up to a wedding of historical drama and travelog. Striking photography of locales with current interest (in view of Turkish-Syrian tensions) is strong point of this effort, although it wears somewhat thin over the course. But as drama, makeshift casting and staging proves formidable handicap. Net result is adequate filler fare for bills with extra-long features.

Ex-trumpeter Jackson Winter is a one-man band here, with script, direction and lensing credits (As well, according to studio publicity, he unearthed the source material by accident in a Hollywood Blvd. bookshop). Story is reproduction of journey by John Lewis Burkhardt, Swiss explorer who penetrated dangerous Middle East disguised as a Damascene Arab in 1812. As such, he explored the ruins of great destroyed cities, with death hovering over his head should he be uncloaked as an infidel by the ignorant, superstitous natives.

Solor footage by Winters retraces Burkhardt's trail and panorama of area's rich history, in Burkhardt's words, is narrated ably by Marvin Miller. However, to modern taste, Burkhardt's 19th Century literary style gets oevrly florid and quaint over the long run.

Cast is wholly amateur, picked up in area by Winter. *Kove.*

Night of the Demon
(BRITISH)

Clammy supernatural meller starring Dana Andrews which is too contrived to thrill overmuch; strictly for the horror trade.

London, Dec. 17.
Columbia release of a Sabre Film production. Stars Dana Andrews, Peggy Cummins, Niall MacGinnis. Directed by Jacques Tourneur. Screenplay, Charles Bannet and Hal E. Chester, based on story, "Casting the Runes," by Montague R. James; editor, Michael Gordon; camera, Ted Scaife; music, Clifton Mathieson. At Regal, Harrow Road, London. Running time, 82 MINS.
Dr. John Holden ....Dana Andrews
Joanna Harrington.......Peggy Cummins
Doctor Karswell..........Niall MacGinnis
Mrs. Karswell.......... Athene Seyler
Professor Harrington....Maurice Denham
Williamson .... Ewan Roberts
Professor Mark O'Brien....Liam Redmond
Kumar .... Peter Elliot
Mr. Meek .... Reginald Beckwith
Mrs. Meek .... Rosamund Greenwood

"Night of the Demon" has rightly had an "X" certificate slapped on it, which means that in Britain only adults over 16 can see this meller with a pronounced "horror" flavor. Technically it is a reasonably competent job, but the story and the dialog have an old fashioned ring which wavers uneasily between the melodramatic and the ludicrous.

This yarn about the supernatural dabbles in the tawdry atmosphere of modern black magic. It has Dana Andrews as an American psychologist who visits Britain to help a professor expose the alleged occult power of a rascally doctor at at special demonstration. The prof is bumped off under mysterious circumstances and the doctor threatens Andrews with a similar fate if he does not lay off his investigations.

At first sceptical, Andrews does, indeed, find himself drawn into a web of unhealthy supernatural force. With only minutes to go before the hour scheduled for his grisly doom, he and the late professor's pretty niece manage to turn the tables on the witchcraft-raising doctor, who comes to a sticky end. Andrews wanders through this trivial piece with a stiff upper lip. Niall MacGinnis is suitably oily as the spook-raising doctor while Peggy Cummins fills out decorative department charmingly. Liam Reedmond, Maurice Denham, Athene Seyler and Ewan Roberts also give a hand in support.

A major weakness is that the horror is seen from the sky instead of its presence merely being implied. Despite all the efforts of the special effects, art and musical departments this, and the other atmospheric horrors, fail to make an adequate impact. Jacques Tourneur has directed with heavy hand. Only Ted Scaife's use of heavy shadows in his lensing does anything to make this the horrific piece which the authors and producer clearly intended. *Rich.*

A Day in Moscow
(Documentary)
(RUSSIAN-COLOR)

Artkino release of All-Union Film Corp. production. Written and directed by R. Grigoryev, I. Poselsky. Cameramen . Sov-color), B. Nebilitsky. D. Kaspin, R. Halushakov, S. Medinsky; narrator, A. Adjubei; written by E. Krieger; music, A. Lepin, Tradeshown in N. Y., Dec. 19, '57. Running time, 61 MINS.

Given an interest in Moscow, its residents, street scenes, modes of living, etc., this one may pass despite almost childlike praise of the glories of the Soviet Union. Actually, the photography is excellent, and the movement for such a travelog not bad. But the amateurish script, and annoying narration by a British-toned narrator spoils chances excepting for a few Russo-language houses in this country.

When it is realized that American audiences seldom sit still for more than 25 to 30 minutes of the most exciting travelog, one gets the idea of what over 60 minutes would be like. Even if done on New York City, with some American originality, a documentary of this sort still would be a hard sell.

There is seldom any semblance of a connected line. Students at Moscow's university are introduced. each speaking his brief introduction in his own native tongue. Later on, a sequence showing the students saying farewell to classmates as they head for home is quite informal and quite osculationary.

Episode where an ambulance is called to the scene of an accident is realistic to have been for real. And the surgeon really looks exhausted when he gets through operating on the crash victim. Camera shot from the speeding ambulance is another highlight of this sequence. Mostly it's about how everybody lives happily together, how ideal the Moscow apartments are and what intensive efforts go into the schooling of Russia's youth. *Wear.*

1958

The Deep Six
(COLOR)

Routine wartime naval drama starring Alan Ladd. Average b.o.

A Jaguar Production for Warner Bros. release. Produced by Martin Rackin. Stars Alan Ladd, Dianne Foster, William Bendix and Keenan Wynn. Features James Whitmore, Efrem Zimbalist Jr. and Joey Bishop. Directed by Rudy Mate. Screenplay, John Twist, Rackin and Harry Brown, based on novel by Martin Dibner; camera (WarnerColor), John Seitz; editor, Roland Gross; music, David Buttolph. Reviewed in N. Y. Dec. 19, '57. Running time, **105 MINS.**

Alec Austen	Alan Ladd
Susan Cahill	Dianne Foster
Frenchy Shapiro	William Bendix
Lt. Comdr. Edge	Keenan Wynn
Comdr. Meredith	James Whitmore
Lieut. Blanchard	Efrem Zimbalist Jr.
Ski Krokowski	Joey Bishop
Claire Innes	Barbara Eiler
Slobodjian	Ross Bagdasarian
Mrs. Austen	Jeanette Nolan
Paul Clemson	Walter Reed
Lieut. Dooley	Peter Hansen
Lieut. (j.g.) Swanson	Richard Crane
Collins	Morris Miller
Al Mendoza	Perry Lopez
Pilot	Warren Douglas
Pappa Tatos	Nestor Paiva

Like Gary Cooper in "The Friendly Persuasion," Alan Ladd in "The Deep Six" is a Quaker who wrestles with his own conscience to overcome his pacifist training when confronted with a shooting war. Except for this plot twist, the Jaguar production for Warner Bros. release is a standard wartime naval drama. Alan Ladd's name on the marquee may prove of some value, but the picture appears destined for a fast playoff and average boxoffice results.

The screenplay by John Twist, Martin Rackin (who also produced) and Harry Brown from the novel by Martin Dibner is filled with familiar naval characters and heroic exploits. The enlisted gobs in "The Deep Six" act no differently than the sailors in hundreds of other pictures dealing with the U. S. Navy in peace and war. They're a brave (on land and on sea), aggressive, wise-cracking bunch, always chasing dames. Since this is a wartime drama, it's not too difficult for a cliche-spotter to remark early in the unfolding, "That guy is going to get killed."

It appears that the writers had some higher things in mind that just don't come off. They have teamed Ladd, as a Quaker, with William Bendix, who plays a Jewish petty officer, against Keenan Wynn, an executive officer up from the ranks who is hell bent for revenge, has a killer instinct, and gives evidence of bigotry.

The crew's reaction to Ladd's pacifism is wholly unrealistic. As the gunnery officer, he hesitates to give an order to fire on an approaching plane. At first a hero, since the plane turns out to be a friendly one, Ladd is held in disdain when word spreads around that he refused to fire because of his Quaker leanings. As a result, he is transferred to damage control. He regains his heroic stature when, with the help of Bendix, he removes an unexploded Japanese bomb from the ship. The sailors, who formerly shunned him, walk over sheepishly, extend their hands and remark: *"We had you all wrong, Sir."*

Ladd's pacifism again crops up during a voluntary mission to rescue some U. S. airmen on a Japanese-held island. This time Ladd has to prove himself to his pal, Frenchy Shapiro (Bendix). As a Japanese patrol advances, Ladd freezes at his gun. However, when the enemy riddles his pal, his trigger finger unlooses and he mows down the attackers. Bendix, with bullets in his belly and sprouting blood, smiles benignly and says, "I knew you had it in you all along, Sir."

As a result of Frenchy's death and the experience on the island, Ladd "finds" himself and determines to marry the beautiful art director (Dianne Foster) of the swank advertising agency where he had worked as an artist before donning his naval uniform. He had formerly postponed the marriage because he thought it unfair for his fiancee to risk the possibility of becoming a widow.

Performances meet the needs of the script. In addition to Ladd, Miss Foster, Bendix and Wynn, who are okay in their portrayals, James Whitmore is convincing as the dedicated ship's captain. Joey Bishop, a very funny standup night club comedian, doesn't have the material, as a fast-talking, dame-chasing gob, to match his nitery exploits. Efrem Zimbalist Jr., as the ship's doctor, and Ross Bagdasarian, as an American sailor with femme cousins in every port, come across nicely.

Rudy Mate's direction is routine. John Seitz's WarnerColor photography is topnotch as are the overall production values. *Holl.*

I Was a Teenage Frankenstein
(PART COLOR)

Sock shocker for exploitation market; good followup to "I Was a Teenage Werewolf."

Hollywood, Dec. 20.

American-International release of Herman Cohen production. Stars Whit Bissell, Phyllis Coates, Robert Burton, Gary Conway. Directed by Herbert L. Strock. Story-screenplay, Kenneth Langtry; camera (black-and-white, Pathecolor), Lothrop Worth; editor, Jerry Young; music, Paul Dunlap. Previewed Dec. 18, '57. Running time, **72 MINS.**

Professor Frankenstein	Whit Bissell
Margaret	Phyllis Coates
Dr. Karlton	Robert Burton
Teenage Monster	Gary Conway
Sergeant Burns	George Lynn
Sergeant McAffee	John Cliff
Dr. Randolph	Marshall Bradford
Arlene's Mother	Claudia Bryar
Beautiful Girl	Angela Blake
Dr. Elwood	Russ Whiteman
The Jeweler	Charles Seel
Man at Crash	Paul Keast
Woman in Corridor	Gretchen Thomas
Arlene	Joy Stoner
Young Man	Larry Carr
Police Officer	Pat Miller

This follow-up to "I Was a Teenage Werewolf," released earlier in year, is a shocker turned out on the same drill-press but of sounder fibre. Well developed to take advantage of the chill possibilities of subject, film is a sock entry for its particular market, where with its companion picture, "Blood of Dracula," package may be exploited for handsome returns.

The Herman Cohen production hits a gruesome note in certain sequences as the Kenneth Langtry screenplay limns efforts of a scientist to assemble a human body from parts of different cadavers, but it's the type of shuddery action which pays off. How this man-made monster is restored to life isn't made clear, but supposedly this spark is the result of experiments perfected by the scientist, a descendant of Dr. Frankenstein who created his own early monster, and cloudiness does not affect the mounting suspense.

Under Herbert L. Strock's knowhow direction the story line is given a legitimacy, and characters are persuasively enacted to lend sound substance to general unfoldment. Film is in Pathe-color for approximately the final minute, balance in black-and-white.

Whit Bissell plays the role of a brilliant English scientist visiting in this country whose goal is to recreate a new human body which will respond to his every wish. He enlists the unwilling assistance of an American physicist, and gradually his creation is born, firm in young body but still possessed of a hideous face. After a new face is grafted on, taken from a teenager kidnapped for purpose, Bissell plans to leave for England where he will unveil his great experiment but is killed by his monster as he is about to "disassemble" his creation for shipment to his London lab. Monster himself is electrocuted when he somes in contact with a power board as police are moving in.

Bissell delivers strongly in a sincerely-delineated characterization and has expert backing right down the line. Robert Burton portrays his unwilling assistant, shocked at the task ahead, and Phyllis Coates is good as Bissell's fiancee, acting as his secretary and left to be murdered by the monster after scientist learns she has discovered his secret. Gary Conway is the monster, with good makeup created by Philip Schneer.

Technical departments generally are well handled, including Lothrop Worth's camera work, Jerry Young's fast editing, music score by Paul Dunlap and art direction by Leslie Thomas. *Whit.*

Windom's Way
(BRITISH-COLOR)

Compact well-made drama with Peter Finch as a dedicated doctor in Far East.

London, Dec. 23.

Rank (John Bryam) production and release. Stars Peter Finch, Mary Ure. Directed by Ronald Neame. Screenplay by Jill Craigie, from novel by James Ramsay Ullman; editor, Reginald Mills; camera, Christopher Challis; music, James Bernard. At Leicester-Square Theatre, London. Running time, **108 MINS.**

Alec Windom	Peter Finch
Lee Windom	Mary Ure
Anna Vidal	Natasha Parry
George Hasbrook	Robert Flemyng
Patterson	Michael Hordern
Jan Vidal	John Cairney
Belhedron	Marne Maitland
Lollivar	Gregoire Aslan
Kasti	Kurt Siegenberg
Lansang	George Margo
Amyan	Sanny Bin Hussan
Colonel Lupat	Olaf Pooley
Rebel Commander	Martin Benson

The popularity of Peter Finch, one of Britain's top screen mummers, will insure "Windom's Way" as a safe b.o. bet in the U.K. If Finch yet has sufficient pull in America then exhibitors there might well take a chance on this slowish, but well-made, intelligent drama. There are two or three standout performances and a distinct authenticity about the Far East locale.

Finch is a dedicated doctor working in the village of Selim, a Far East island. He is loved and trusted by the villagers and finds himself involved in their political problems. Mary Ure is his estranged wife who comes out for a trial reconciliation at a time when the locality is in a state of unrest. Finch's ideals are such that he tries to prevent the villagers from getting up in arms against the local police and plantation manager.

The acting throughout this drama is first class, with Finch particularly convincing. Miss Ure has little chance in the colorless role of his wife, but Natasha Parry as a native nursing sister, in love with Finch, is warm, sensitive and technically very sound. Other excellent performances are chalked up by Marne Maitland, as commissioner for the Northern Provinces; Michael Hordern, as the fussy plantation manager, Jan Vidal, as a sort of local Trade Union leader; and little Kurt Siegenberg, as a young urchin devoted to Finch.

Jill Craigie has provided a slow moving, but literate script. Ronald Neame's direction brings out qualities of dignity and credibility. Camera work and music effects are sound throughout. "Windom's Way" adds up to a sound drama with considerable tension. *Rich.*

Count Five and Die
(BRITISH—C-SCOPE)

Reasonably gripping, but shoddily directed, meller concerning wartime espionage; will serve as adequate program filler in most houses.

London, Dec. 23.

20th-Fox release of a Zonic (Ernest Gartside) Production. Stars Jeffrey Hunter, Nigel Patrick, Annemarie Duringer, David Kossof, Rolf Lefebvre. Directed by Victor Vicas. Screenplay, Jack Seddon and David Pursall; editor, Russell Lloyd; camera, Arthur Grant; music, John Wooldridge. At Rialto Theatre, London. Running time, **92 MINS.**

Ranson	Jeffrey Hunter
Howard	Nigel Patrick
Rolande	Annemarie Duringer
Mulder	David Kossoff
Willem	Claude Kingston
Piet	Philip Bond
Faber	Rolf Lefebvre
Martins	Larry Burns
Jan	Arthur Gross
Miller	Robert Raglan
Parrish	Peter Prowse

Yet another British war film is tossed into the international market with "Count Five and Die." As a program filler, it fullfils its purpose and should click commercially in a modest way on both sides of the Atlantic. Though a tense little number, it could be so much better, being marred by casual direction by Victor Vicas, and indifferent editing.

This concerns the activities of a British intelligence unit operating in London during pre-invasion days. Its purpose was to bluff the Nazis into believing that the major invasion strike was to be through Holland. As a result of its success, when the invasion did happen, many of the German forces were waiting, in vain, in Holland.

The little unit, operating behind the facade of a fake film company in an area in Soho, is commanded by Nigel Patrick. He has with him Jeffrey Hunter as an American officer and a staff of Dutch patriots. Into this unit comes a new member. A girl, alleged to be Dutch, but rightly suspected by Patrick of being a German agent. The pic's atmosphere is built up by bluff and counter-bluff. For quite awhile the audience is steered by red herrings into not knowing quite who is to be trusted. Eventually it finishes up as a straight cloak-and-dagger meller.

The acting is competent without being inspired. For Patrick, the film is a chore which he handles suavely, without adding overmuch to his reputation. Jeffrey Hunter is also wholly adequate as the one member of the gang that not even the most naive patron could suspect. Annemarie Duringer, who plays the girl spy, is not over encumbered with good looks but has a striking personality and handles her role with persuasion. The stars are supported by a five cast of actors in which David Kossoff, Rolf Lefebvre and Philip Bond make good impressions.

The screenplay by David Pursall and Jack Seddon somehow manages to hold the tenuous line of suspense for the full 90 minutes, but Russell Lloyd's editing is untidy. The audience is often left up in the air because certain sequences are not allowed to unroll to their logical conclusion. Leslie Hodgson's sound is also suspect. It is altogether too noisy and fussy and as a result some dialog is lost in a welter of extraneous noises.

"Count Five" could have been an extremely good thriller. But it falls down, and appears to just miss. *Rich.*

The 7 Hills of Rome
(MUSICAL—COLOR)
(*Filmed in Rome*)

Lanza's back and Metro's got him for b.o. returns on songs and scenery. Plot liberties extreme but not crucial.

Metro release of LeCloud Production (coproduction by Metro-Titanus-Mario Lanza-Lester Welch), produced by Welch. Stars Mario Lanza; features Renato Rascel, Marisa Allasio, Peggie Castle. Directed by Roy Rowland. Titanus chief of production, Silvio Clementelli. Screenplay, Art Cohn and Giorgio Prosperi, from story by Giuseppi Amato. Camera (Technirama), Tonino Delli Colli & Franco Delli Colli; music composed and conducted by George Stoll; music supervisor, Irving Aaronson; editor, Gene Ruggiero; choreographer, Paul Steffen; first asst. director, Mario Russo; asst. directors, Maria Teresa Girosi, Tina Marchetti Clerici; music editor, Peter Zinner; arranger, Carlo Savina; sets, Piero Filippone & Luigi Gervasi; costumes, Maria Barony Cecchi; sound, Mario Messina; makeup, Otello Fava; hair stylist, Tina Cessetti & Marcella Cecchini. Tradeshown N.Y., Dec. 20, '57. Running time, 107 MINS.
Marc Revere .... Mario Lanza
Pepe Bonelli .... Renato Rascel
Raffaella Marini .... Marisa Allasio
Carol Ralston .... Peggie Castle
Beatrice .... Clelia Matania
Anita .... Rossella Como
Carlo .... Amos Ravoli
Luiggi .... Guido Celano
Director Ulpia Club .... Carlo Rizzo
Romoletto .... Marco Aulli
Commissario Rugarello .... Giorgio Gandos
Franco Cellis .... Carlo Guiffre
Landlady .... Adriana Hart
Mr. Fante .... Patrick Crean
Helicopter Pilot .... Pennachi
Mrs. Stone .... April Hannessy
Miller .... Stuart Hart
Street Singer .... Luisa DiMeo

"Three Coins in the Fountain" started the easy-chair, cinematic Cook's Tour of Rome in Technicolorful celluloid and Mario Lanza's "The Seven Hills of Rome" completes it. Between the Lanza voice and the eye-filling Technirama production's values Metro has a global boxoffice winner.

There is no gainsaying Lanza's compellieng voice. There is also no gainsaying that he does make impact. "The Seven Hills of Rome" marks his celluloid comeback, after four previous Metro pictures. It's also his first overseas production, jointly made by Metro with Titanus and LeCloud, the Lanza-Lester Welch unit which, while they were at it, also made an all-Italian version.

There are story lapses and towards the end there is a marked histrionic breakdown along with the script's shortcomings but, for the major portion of the film's unfolding, it is a vocal tour-de-force for the star and an arresting closeup of one of the most colorful and historic capitals of the world.

In this respect scripters Art Cohn and Giorgio Prosperi (based on Giuseppe Amato's original), director Roy Rowland and producer Lester Welch have cannily set an ultramodern plot motivation against the Eternal City's famed background.

The Italo-GI influences via the street-scene jamsession, showing the rock 'n' Roman kids very hip to the jive, segues into highly acceptable Lanza impressions of Perry Como, Dean Martin and Frankie Laine. When he did the Satchmo takeoff the dialog read, "Armstrong, no he ain't Italian, but he don't have to be; he's good too!"

A post-allnight party calls for a friendly stowaway guest, in the bohemian atelier of pianist-songsmith Renato Rascel—an excellent comedian, by the way—taking his host on an early-dawn helicopter aerial closeup of Rome and its environs. Lanza is Rascel's American cousin on his first trip to Rome. Plot motivation is a jealous chase after Peggie Castle, his socialite

American fiancee. Lanza is also on the low-flying panoramic view of the Roman scenery as is Marisa Allasio, local girl whom Lanza had met by romantic accident on the train into the Stazione Termini, Rome's central railroad station.

Thus are unfolded St. Peter's Square, the Via Campo Boari with its background of the Aurelian wall, the Casina Valadier, Ponte Palatino, Via Veneto, and the ancient Olivus Capitolinus. Similarly, some excellent street scenes unfold, in colorful Technirama authenticity, as the jobseeking Lanza doubles ad lib with winsome street urchin Luisa Dimeo in "Arriverderci Roma" (authored by the film's featured comedian, Rascel) who also composed "Ti Voglio Benne Tanto Tanto" (also with the little street singer) for that same Piazza Navena scene. The versatile Rascel has other song credits in "Na Canzone Pe Fa Ammore," done in Pepe's studio; "Venticello di Roma" (during the helicopter tour), "E' Arrivato La Bufera" (delivery boy on bike), "Ostricaro Innamorato" (fish vendor) and "Vogliamaci Tanto Bene" (laundress), a medley of the sounds and music as part of the Via della Pace street scene.

Besides the already familiar "Arriverderci Roma" and the wealth of pop standard and operatic excerpts done by Lanza, there are three other standout tunes. George Stoll, who wrote the excellent background music and so lushly batoned the musical cavalcade, also authored a "Calypso Italiano." Two other standouts are the tiptop title song, by Harold Adamson and the late Victor Young, and a fetching waltz, "Come Dance With Me."

The plot motivation of Lanza's professional and social peirerinations from the U.S. tv studio, where he opens with a snatch of "All the Things You Are," to the posh yachting party's "Aye Aye Aye" excerpt, to the Rome vaudery's amateur night where he wins with "Uesto O Quella" and clicks later again with "Lolita," to the class Ulpia nitery where he sings "Loveliest Night of the Year" (one of his own filmusical recreations), cues it all into appropriate vocal flights. The caption might observe this is a Lanza LP with Burton Holmes or James A. Fitz-Patrick visual trimmings but it is never boring. The entertainment values are there, and what fan will ask for more?

True, one major plot incongruity might have been squared away—as Peggie Castle is made to utter it too late in the plot—that a "tough business manager" for the American singing star (Lanza) keeps him conveniently broke. But until that point one will wonder how come an American tv star is so broke that he must resort to street buskin' for the groceries; rebuffed at the Ulpia and the Caballa while jobseeking; that the kids doing that rock 'n' roll session know "the singing barber" (as they call Como), Laine, Martin and Satchmo and never heard of Lanza, presumably also a big singing star in America.

The winsome Marisa Allasio is a comely film find who, when Metro brings her to the States for a builderupper (to coincide with the picture's Radio City Music Hall booking), will go places. She has the physical attributes of such other famed Italo beauts as Gina and Sophia but is a fresher and younger personality. There, too, the boy-meets-girl value are incongruous. The pseudo-social Miss

Castle so palpably telegraphs her wrongo qualifications as Lanza's romantic vis-a-vis, and Miss Allasio is so obviously the "right" femme interest, that when finally does come the clinch it is completely false. The sharp letdown does more to militate against the film's overall impression than anything else that has preceded which, in the main, has been palatable and with reasonable cinematic plausibility.

Because of the script Miss Castle is the least believable, albeit properly decorative. Rascel tops the star for personal histrionic impact although Lanza's vocalisthenics are undeniable. Incidentally, he got his weight down sufficiently to meet the standards. There are fine bit roles throughout, notably Marco Tulli as the fiacre driver; Clelia Matania, owner of the fashion salon; Guido Celano, owner of the variety house; Carlo Rizzo, director of the Ulpia nitery.

All the production credits are top-drawer, from the Rowland-Welch director-production investiture and Stoll's fine musical settings, to the excellent Technirama-glamour lensing by Tonino and Franco Delli Colli and all the other Italo aides behind the cameras and the booms. Withal "The Seven Hills of Rome" makes for a delightful "at home abroad" entertainment. *Abel.*

The Golden Age Of Comedy

Documentary on silent slapstick films. Good art house b.o. prospects.

Distributors Corp. of America release of a feature-length compilation of silent screen comedies. With Laurel & Hardy, Carole Lombard, Harry Langdon, Jean Harlow, Will Rogers, Ben Turpin, Charley Chase, others. Produced and written by Robert Youngson. Narrators, Dwight Weist, Ward Wilson; editor, Albert Helmes; music, George Steiner. At Embassy and Guild Theatres, N.Y., Dec. 26, '57. Running time, 78 MINS.

Filmgoers who may still have a yen for oldtime slapstick will find "The Golden Age of Comedy" their cup of tea. For this Distributors of America release, written and produced by Robert Youngson, is a nostalgic collection of silent screen

footage that evokes fond memories of Ben Turpin, Will Rogers and Harry Langdon, among others, in their heyday.

Nature of the picture is such that it cannot be casually thrown into the distribution hopper and left to shift for itself. It's primarily art house fare. But if the average exhibitor takes the time to contact schools, colleges and groups interested in motion picture history very likely some healthy biz can be generated.

Those with captious tendencies will have little trouble in picking flaws in Robert Youngson's production. For the comedies he's chosen to revive most bear either the Hal Roach or Mack Sennett imprint. While admittedly Roach and Sennett were kingpins of their day nevertheless they didn't have a corner on corn. Likewise, such top silent comics as Lupino Lane, Buster Keaton, W. C. Fields and Charlie Chaplin to name a few weren't included in.

At any rate within the 78 minutes running time there are a number of priceless vignettes. There are hilarious scenes of Will Rogers lampooning Douglas Fairbanks' version of Robin Hood, a myriad of Laurel & Hardy sequences and a classic Harry Langdon bit in which he portrays a clumsy groom on his honeymoon.

Youngson's commentary is not particularly objective, but it's amusingly narrated by Dwight Weist and Ward Wilson. It contains various background notes of interest to the film historian and adult layman as well. Print is in remarkably good condition. Editing of Albert Helmes and the George Steiner score are good.
Gilb.

Teenage Monster

Imbecile killer protected by mother. Stirs up little interest. For low IQ audiences only.

Hollywood.
Favorite Films release of Marquette production, presented by Howco International. Stars Anne Gwynne. Features Gloria Castillo, Stuart Wade, Gilbert Perkins. Producer-director, Jacques Marquette; screenplay, Ray Buffam; camera, Taylor Byars; sound, George Anderson; editor, Irving Schoenberg; music, Walter Greene. Reviewed Dec. 23, '57. Running time, **65 MINS.**

Ruth Cannon	Anne Gwynne
Kathy North	Gloria Castillo
Sheriff Bob	Stuart Wade
Charles Cannon	Gilbert Perkins
Charles Cannon (as boy)	Stephen Parker
Marv Howell	Charles Courtney
Deputy Ed	Norman Leavitt
Jim Cannon	Jim McCullough
Fred Fox	Gaybe Mooradian
Man with Burro	Arthur Berkeley
Man on Street	Frank Davis

This is a silly nonsense, an unworthy companion to the film with which it is being packaged ("The Brain From Planet Arous").

Ray Buffam screenplay centers around Gilbert Perkins, a huge, hairy imbecile who goes around the countryside killing people for no particular reason—the result of being struck, years before, by a weird ball of fire from the sky which also killed his father. Now, Anne Gwynne, his mother, is keeping him hidden from the world, upset about the murders but still protective of her son.

Story winds with his killing by Sheriff Stuart Wade, who also heppens to be Miss Gwynne's b.f. Gloria Castillo, top featured, plays a trollop who discovers the family's "secret," and who's paid off by mother until she (Castillo) herself is killed by Perkins.

Majority of the players way overact under the direction of Jacques Marquette, who also produced.
Neal.

The Brain From Planet Arous

Fairly good science-fiction. It carries package with mediocre "Teenage Monster."

Hollywood.
Favorite Films release of Marquette production, presented by Howco International. Stars John Agar. Features Joyce Meadows, Robert Fuller, Thomas B. Henry. Produced by Jacques Marquette. Directed by Nathan Hertz. Screenplay, Ray Buffam; camera, Jacques Marquette; sound, Philip Mitchell; editor, Irving M. Schoenberg; music, Walter Greene. Reviewed Dec. 23, '57. Running time, 70 MINS.

Steve	John Agar
Sally Fallon	Joyce Meadows
Dan	Robert Fuller
John Fallon	Thomas B. Henry
Col. Frogley	Henry Travis
Col. in Conference Room	Kenneth Terrell
Sheriff Paine	Tim Graham
General Brown	E. Leslie Thomas
Russian	Bill Giorgio

This modest-budgeter stacks up as a better-than-average entry in the seemingly endless scientific-fiction cycle, certain to attract teenage attention. Film is being packaged with a very mediocre running mate "Teenage Monster." (See separate review.)

There's good suspense worked into the familiar Ray Buffam screenplay. Yarn deals with an evil, scientifically-advanced "brain" from another planet which comes to earth, overpowers scientist John Agar, then enters his body to continue with his (the "brain's") plan to conquer the universe. Friends, especially romantic interest Joyce Meadows, notice new strange behavior, but are at a loss to understand it—until another "brain" from the same planet, a good one this time, arrives on earth and tips Miss Meadows to the one way the other "brain" can be overpowered and killed (blow to one particular part of his noggin anatomy). This subsequently happens and Agar returns to normalcy and Miss Meadows.

Agar turns in a competent performance in lead role, and Miss Meadows is okay as femme interest. Other portrayals are stock, as are majority of the technical credits.

Direction of Nathan Hertz keeps things on the move, and camera work of Jacques Marquette (who also produced for a good credit) is effective.
Neal.

Nathalie
(FRENCH)

Paris.
Gaumont release of SNEG-Internationale-Electra production. Stars Martine Carol; features Michel Piccoli, Philippe Clay, Lise Delamare, Misha Auer, Aime Clariond, Louis Seigner, Armande Navarre, Jacques Dufilho. Directed by Christian-Jaque. Screenplay, Pierre Apesteguy, Jean Ferry, Jacques Emmanuel; dialog, Henri Jeanson; camera, Robert Le Febvre; editor, Jacques Desagneaux. At Colisee, Paris. Running time, 100 MINS.

Nathalie	Martine Carol
Franck	Michel Piccoli
Coco	Philippe Clay
Cyril	Misha Auer
Count	Aime Clariond
Pippart	Louis Seigner
Friend	Armande Navarre
Valet	Jacques Dufilho

This is a light-veined whodunit with a saucy model outsmarting the coppers all the way, and finally with the model getting the young police inspector who always wanted to quit the force anyway. Direction is rapid and bowls this along for a fair entry for this type of pic. It has movement, cleverness and some name value in Martine Carol for probable good chances in Yank foreign houses as well as general entertainment values for more general possibilities.

Miss Carol is properly scatterbrained, but with enough method to her madness to confound police and crooks alike. Some of her comedy timing misses, but she is ably assisted by Philippe Clay's humorously menacing killer, Michel Piccoli's engaging policeman, and Misha Auer's shrewd playing.

Director Christian-Jacque has kept this moving to gloss over some obvious plot discrepencies which are not so important in this type of pic. Film has good technical credits and fine production values, plus a sense of style which makes it above the-run-of-the-mill entries in this genre of sophisticated cops and robbers doings.
Mosk.

Blue Murder at St. Trinian's
(BRITISH)

Zany slapstick farce with typical British appeal, unlikely to rouse other audiences to over-much enthusiasm.

London.
British Lion release of a Sidney Gilliat-Frank Launder production. Stars Terry-Thomas, George Cole, Joyce Grenfell, with Alastair Sim and Sabrina as guest stars. Directed by Frank Launder. Screenplay by Launder, Val Valentine and Sidney Gilliat; inspired by drawings of Ronald Searle; camera, Gerald Gibbs; editor, Geoffrey Foot; music, Malcolm Arnold. At Gaumont, London. Running time. **86 MINS.**

Romney	Terry-Thomas
Flash Harry	George Cole
Sgt. Gates	Joyce Grenfell
Miss Fritton	Alastair Sim
Virginia	Sabrina
Joe Mangan	Lionel Jeffries
Italian Police Inspector	Ferdy Mayne
Superintendent	Lloyd Lambie
Major	Thorley Walters
Captain	Cyril Chamberlain
Dame Maud Hackshaw	Judith Furse
Bassett	Richard Wattis
Prince Bruno	Guido Lorraine
Myrna	Lisa Gastoni
Cynthia	Jose Read
Bridget	Dilys Laye

Launder and Gilliat took a chance when, in "The Belles of St. Trinian's," they decided to try and bring the "awful schoolgirls" of Ronald Searle's cartoons to screen life. The novelty made the film a click in Britain, but in this follow-up, the gag wears a bit thin. That is not to deny that the pic packs quite a lot of yocks. But the humor now is a bit obvious and the string of slapstick situations pinned on to a thin, yet complicated, story line do not add up to a very satisfactory comedy film.

There are all the obvious gags, with the schoolgirls behaving like little fiends. But the story, if such it can be called, opens with St. Trinian's in a state of siege. The school is without a headmistress (Miss Fritton, played by Alestair Sim) is in jail and pending the arrival of a new headmistress, the police and the army have been called out to keep order.

The scene shifts to Europe. By cheating, the girls have won an Unesco essay contest with first prize a coach trip to Rome. The girls are anxious to go in order that one of them should be married off to Prince Bruno of Italy. Further complications are caused by one of the girls' fathers pulling off a diamond robbery. To get him out of the country he poses as the headmistress of St. Trinian's and goes off on the trip as chaperone.

Trip enables the girls to swing Mozart at a Vienna music festival and to become involved in a crazy water polo match with the jewels secreted in the ball. It also enables Leslie Jeffreys to pose as a woman, Joyce Grenfell to pose as an interpreter though actually a police-woman and Terry-Thomas to steal the film as a shady boss of the coach firm.

The older girls of St. Trinian's are easy on the eye but it seems stupid wasting Lisa Gastoni on this sort of tripe. There is also rather too much of George Cole as a young shyster and certainly too much of Miss Grenfell, whose coyness is fine in small doses.

There are a number of good lines and situations. But the whole affair is too contrived and lacking in subtlety to register solidly. Sabrina, Britain's much-boosted queen of the bosom cult, is dragged in as a guest artist in an unnecessary scene which fortunately does not overstrain her limited histrionic ability.
Rich.

Blood of Dracula

Okay horror film for lower-casing as packaged with "I Was a Teenage Frankenstein."

Hollywood, Dec. 20.
American-International release of Herman Cohen production. Stars Sandra Harrison, Louise Lewis, Gail Ganley, Jerry Blaine; features Heather Ames, Malcolm Atterbury, Mary Adams, Thomas B. Henry Directed by Herbert L. Strock. Story-screenplay, Ralph Thornton; camera, Monroe Askins; editor, Robert Moore; music, Paul Dunlap. Previewed Dec. 18, '57. Running time, **68 MINS.**

Nancy Perkins	Sandra Harrison
Miss Branding	Louise Lewis
Myra	Gail Ganley
Tab	Jerry Blaine
Nola	Heather Ames
Lt. Dunlap	Malcolm Atterbury
Mrs. Thorndyke	Mary Adams
Mr. Perkins	Thomas B. Henry
Eddie	Don Devlin
Mrs. Perkins	Jeanne Dean
Sgt. Stewart	Richard Devon
Mike	Paul Maxwell
Stanley Mather	Carlyle Mitchell
Terry	Shirley De Lancey
Glenn	Michael Hall

"Blood of Dracula" picks up the familiar vampire theme for a suitable offering in the horror field. Slow in takeoff, film nevertheless packs enough interest to salve its intended audience and holds to a logical climax.

Produced by Herman Cohen for lower-bracketing with his "I Was a Teenage Frankenstein," Ralph Thornton script unfolds in a girls' school, where Sandra Harrison is enrolled by her father following death of her mother. Embittered by his early marriage to another woman, Sandra comes under the influence of the chemistry teacher, Louise Lewis, who is experimenting in strange powers made possible by a centuries'-old amulet from the Carpathians, home of the vampires. Completely under teacher's spell, young femme commits a fiendish murder she does not remember, and later commits two more, when she turns into a bestial killer with flaming fangs. Realizing her condition, she begs teacher to release her, and when latter refuses chokes her to death, meeting her own violent end by impalement on a huge spike.

Herbert L. Strock directs with a sure hand and draws okay performances from his entire cast. Miss Harrison is fully up to demands of her role, Miss Lewis credibly portrays chemistry teacher willing to do anything to reach her objective and Gail Ganley does well by another student role. Jerry Blaine, one of the victims, is in for a tuneful song number, "Puppy Love," handled effectively, and other parts are satisfactorily undertaken by Heather Ames, a victim; Mary Adams, head of the school; and Malcolm Atterbury, homicide lieutenant.

Technical credits are competently executed, headed by Monroe Askins' photography and Robert Moore's editing.
Whit.

Bonjour Tristesse
(C'SCOPE—COLOR)

Loose and luxurious living on the Riviera with Deborah Kerr, David Niven, Jean Seberg. Controversy re the theme, as per Francoise Sagan original best-seller, ought to help sell provocative but basically thin fare.

Columbia release of Otto Preminger production. Stars Deborah Kerr, David Niven, Jean Seberg; features Mylene Demongeot, Geoffrey Horne, Juliette Greco, Walter Chiari. Directed by Preminger. Screenplay, Arthur Laurents, from the Francoise Sagan novel; camera (Technicolor), Georges Perinal; editor, Helga Cranston; music, Georges Auric. Previewed in New York Jan. 10, '58. Running time, **94 MINS.**

Anne	Deborah Kerr
Raymond	David Niven
Cecile	Jean Seberg
Elsa	Mylene Demongeot
Philippe	Geoffrey Horne
Herself	Juliette Greco
Pablo	Walter Chiari
Philippe's Mother	Martita Hunt
Mrs. Lombard	Jean Kent
Jacques	David Oxley
Denise	Elga Andersen
Hubert	Jeremy Burnham
Mr. Lombard	Roland Culver
Maid	Eveline Eyfel

Considerable note was taken of the tale of promiscuity on the Riviera by the then 17-year-old novelist, Francoise Sagan. It was a thin book, physically, and the characters, Bohemian manners and mores and all, were thin, too, but the fiction of the young French lass created a stir and sold like popcorn Saturday matinee.

In transplanting the work to the screen, producer - director Otto Preminger basically has stayed with Miss Sagon's first-person-told tale of the amours of a middle-aged, charming and wealthy Frenchman within both view and earshot of his daughter who, like the author at the time, is 17. It's hardly a matter of wonder that Pere's free-living escapades should prove contagious, that the girl, too, should take a fling at same.

It's a credit to Preminger's handling that a somewhat feather-light quality is effected; for any heavy-handed, all-out-for-realism treatment might have rendered the story unwholesome in family terms to the point of being repugnant to many. In its airy way, "Bonjour Tristesse" has a certain amount of charm although, of course, it seems likely that puritan circles will be heard from. If the film is to be a conversation piece, as was the book, ticket-buying interest doubtless will be provoked. To be considered in the boxoffice appraisal are the cast names, as well.

But it is not a Class "A" effort. Script deficiencies and awkward reading—some lines are spoken as though just that—they are being read—have static results. Scenario by Arthur Laurents is, indeed, shallow, though perhaps he had little choice. The characters are a surface lot, projecting little emotion.

Detracting from the make-believe also is Jean Seberg's deportment. In her second cinematic try (her first was in Preminger's unfortunate "Saint Joan"), Miss Seberg's Cecile is more suggestive of a high school senior back home than the frisky, knowing, close friend and daughter of a roue living it up in the sumptious French setting. She is, of course, a selfish and malicious character to start with.

Strangely enough, Miss Seberg, while lacking necessary expression in the early reels, appears to achieve at least some professionalism during the course of the unfoldment. Perhaps it's a matter of getting used to her. Preminger apparently insists that the public must.

David Niven is properly affable as the father who travels with a mistress and makes no attempt to disguise his pursuits. Deborah Kerr is a standout talent as the artist whom Niven proposes to marry and who speeds away to apparent suicide upon finding him in another illicit situation.

As the more conventional of the principal characters, Miss Kerr has looks and poise but there are instances where she, too, has difficulty with the stiltedness of the dialog.

Mylene Demongeot fits in well as a silly, sunburned blonde; Geoffrey Horne rates adequate as playmate for Cecile and Walter Chiari comes off as something of a caricature of a rich South American.

The Riviera villa backdrop and beach scenes are rich in eye appeal via the CinemaScope and Technicolor photography and wardrobes make for another visual plus. Effective also is the switch to monochrome for Left Bank bistro scenes. Editing is smooth and music is first-rate, particularly the title song which sets the mood of sadness as Cecile reflects on past events (it's all flashback).

Title designs by Saul Bass are colorful and clever. *Gene.*

Sing, Boy, Sing
(SONGS-C'SCOPE)

Tommy Sands in his first film. Script based on his tv click but not strong in adaptation.

Hollywood, Jan. 10.

Twentieth-Fox release of Henry Ephron production. Stars Tommy Sands, Lili Gentle; co-stars Edmond O'Brien, John McIntire; features Nick Adams, Diane Jergens, Josephine Hutchinson, Jerry Paris, Tami Conner, Regis Toomey. Directed by Ephron; screenplay, Claude Binyon, from story by Paul Monash; camera, William C. Mellor; art directors, Lyle R. Wheeler, Herman A. Blumenthal; sound, Eugene Grossman, Harold A. Root; music, Lionel Newman; editor, William Mace; musical numbers staged by Nick Castle. Previewed Jan. 8, '57; Running time, **89 MINS.**

Virgil Walker	Tommy Sands
Leora Easton	Lili Gentle
Joseph Sharkey	Edmond O'Brien
Rev. Walker	John McIntire
C. K. Judd	Nick Adams
Pat	Diane Jergens
Caroline Walker	Josephine Hutchinson
Fisher	Jerry Paris
Ginnie	Tami Conner
Rev. Easton	Regis Toomey
Disc Jockeys	Art Ford, Bill Randle, Biff Collie
Mrs. Fitzgerald	Marie Brown
Miss Keyes	Madge Cleveland
Haggarty	Tom Greenway
Hillman	Lloyd Harter
Fitzgerald	Patrick Miller

For the third time in roughly a year, 20th-Fox has come up with a screen debut of a "hot" juve vocal talent, in this case Tommy Sands. He registers as a potent new film personality who will, with proper material, become a boxoffice lure. Unfortunately, the vehicle chosen for his bow can register only moderately since the adaptation of the tv show that first catapulted him to stardom emerges as satisfactory fare for an adult video audience but not for teenage theatregoers.

Claude Binyon's screenplay contains only minor changes from the original Paul Monash telescript about a young rock 'n' roll singer and the pressures placed upon him by a somewhat unscrupulous manager on one hand and the latest pulls of his religioso background. Manager Edmond O'Brien wants to keep the kid away from the influences of his revivalist grandfather but the latter's death eventually brings Sands to a new maturity in his position as a teenage idol.

Bulk of the musical numbers are concentrated in the first half of the film; the final reels dip into the dramatics inherent in the basic story and it is in the sometimes moralizing philosophy that the picture loses its appeal for the younger generation.

Sands is excellent, both as a singer and as a performer, handling himself with an ease and naturalness that gives the part credibility. O'Brien turns in a top performance as the manager and there is prime support from Nick Adams, as an "Okie" whom Sands hires as a companion in his desperate need for companionship. In much smaller roles, Josephine Hutchinson is quietly convincing as Sands' aunt and Jerry Paris is good as the manager's press agent accomplice. Lili Gentle, as Sands hometown girl friend, has little to do except look wistful.

Henry Ephron's direction is on the slow side but sympathetically guided his tyro troupers. Musical numbers of Nick Castle help. Also Ephron has injected some solid values in the black-and-white production and surrounded himself with a good technical crew that add some assets to the film, notably in William C. Mellor's camera work and the effective art director of Lyle R. Wheeler and Herman A. Blumenthal. During the course of the film, Sands sings about a dozen numbers, including the hymn "Rock of Ages." Best is the title tune, a likely hit, and "Soda Pop Pop." *Kap.*

The Female Animal
(C'SCOPE)

Old-style slants on Hollywood. Jane Powell, Hedy Lamarr and George Nader for marquee dressing.

Hollywood, Dec. 27.

Universal release of Albert Zugsmith production. Stars Hedy Lamarr, Jane Powell, Jan Sterling, George Nader; features Jerry Paris, Gregg Palmer, Mabel Albertson, James Gleason. Directed by Harry Keller. Screenplay, Robert Hill, based on story by Zugsmith; camera, Russell Metty; editor, Milton Carruth; music, Hans J. Salter. Previewed Dec. 27, '57. Running time, **92 MINS.**

Vanessa Windsor	Hedy Lamarr
Penny Windsor	Jane Powell
Lily Frayne	Jan Sterling
Chris Farley	George Nader
Hank Lopez	Jerry Paris
Piggy	Gregg Palmer
Irma Jones	Mabel Albertson
Tom Maloney	James Gleason
Dr. John Ramsay	Richard H. Cutting
Nurse	Ann Doran
Hairdresser	Yvonne Peattie
Charlie Grant	Casey Adams
The Director	Douglas Evans

With very few exceptions, stories about Hollywood have had pretty tough sledding at the boxoffice and there's nothing in this latest try to lift it above the programmer class. Plot is old-fashioned both in concept and unfoldment and even with the Jane Powell name to brighten prospects with youthful audiences outlook is spotty.

Albert Zugsmith production, based upon his own original, centers on Hedy Lamarr, a temperamental star who falls for an extra who saves her from a falling light on the set. Robert Hill screenplay follows her setting him up as caretaker for her beach home, with mother-daughter conflict inserted when the star's daughter, Miss Powell, finds herself in love with mama's boy-friend, latter still struggling to keep his self-respect. Film opens clumsily, in what later appears to be flashback technique, and winds on an uncertain romantic note.

Miss Lamarr manages some semblance of reality as the star who seems half lit through most of the film, but George Nader as the extra suffers from lack of definitive character opportunity. Direction by Harry Keller seldom rises above the script, which generally affects various characters. Miss Powell overplays her opening drunk sequence and fares littl better later on, although she fills a bathing suit with eye-filling allure. Part of Jan Sterling, as a former star who still has a roving eye for males and goes on the make for Nader, is dragged in for no particular reason. Supporting cast headed by Jerry Paris and James Gleason are okay.

Russell Metty's camera work leads off generally competent technical credits. *Whit.*

Snowfire
(COLOR)

Neat attraction for the pre-teenage audience. Release arrangements pending.

Hollywood, Jan. 8.

A McGowan Production, written, produced and directed by Dorrell and Stuart McGowan. Stars Snowfire, Molly McGowan, Don Megowan; features John Cason, Claire Kelly, Melody McGowan, Mike Vallon, Rusty Westcott, Bill Hale, Paul Keast. Camera, Brydon Baker; editor, Arthus Nadel; music, Albert Glasser. Previewed Jan. 3, '58. Running time, **73 MINS.**

Snowfire	Himself
Molly McGowan	Herself
Mike McGowan	Don Megowan
Buff Stoner	John Cason
Carol Hampton	Claire Kelly
Melody McGowan	Herself
Poco	Mike Vallon
Luke Stoner	Rusty Westcott
Skip Stoner	Bill Hale

Patently aimed at the kiddie trade, "Snowfire" emerges a good attraction for pre-teenage audiences and a natural for Saturday matinee and schoolroom showings.

Feature, for which a release has not yet been set, was lensed a year or so ago in and around Bryce Canyon, Utah. (A tv pilot also has been edited from it, incidentally.) Action centers around the title horse and a young girl's (Molly McGowan) friendship with the nag, which had been captured earlier by dad (Don Megowan) from a wild herd. Girl lets the horse escape, then keeps pop and all the villains from capturing him by tipping off the animal as to their movements. Windup finds dad agreeing to certain concessions (no branding, and letting horse out to roam at night), and daughter bringing the equine home.

Megowan is good as the father, while Claire Kelly, in romantic lead as owner of the neighboring ranch, is a capable actress as well as a looker. Molly McGowan (daughter of Dorrell McGowan, as is other cast member, Melody McGowan) is generally okay, and her lack of experience will probably go unnoticed by the juves.

Production credits are good, most notably the Eastman Color camera work of Brydon Baker. Snowfire, by the way, is a well-trained steed that takes the title role in stride. *Neal.*

The Missouri Traveler
(COLOR)

Nostalgic piece of Americana half-century ago, aimed at family trade.

Hollywood, Jan. 10.

Buena Vista release of Patrick Ford production. Stars Brandon de Wilde, Lee Marvin, Gary Merrill, Paul Ford; co-stars Mary Hosford; features Ken Curtis, Cal Tinney, Frank Cady, Kathleen Freeman, Will Wright, Mary Field. Directed by Jerry Hopper. Screenplay, Norman Shannon Hall, from novel by John Burress; comera (Technicolor), Winton C. Hoch; editor, Tom McAdoo; music, Jack Marshall. Previewed Jan. 3, '58. Running time, **104 MINS.**

Biarn Turner	Brandon de Wilde
Tobias Brown	Lee Marvin
Doyle Magee	Gary Merrill
Finas Daugherty	Paul Ford
Anna Love Price	Mary Hosford
Fred Mueller	Ken Curtis
Clyde Hamilton	Cal Tinney
Willie Poole	Frank Cady
Nelda Hamilton	Mary Field
Serena Poole	Kathleen Freeman
Sheriff Peavy	Will Wright
Rev. Thorndyke	Tom Tiner
Henry Craig	Billy Bryant
Jimmy Price	Barry Curtis
Red Poole	Eddie Little
Herb Davis	Rodney Bell
Hattie Neely	Helen Brown
Pos Neely	Billy Newell
Simpson	Roy Jensen

C. V. Whitney comes through with an interesting piece of Americana of a half-century ago in this nostalgic followup to his first picture, "The Searchers." "The Missouri Traveler" is an often heartwarming drama of life in a small Missouri town in model-T days, richly spiced with humor and carrying a goodnatured quality about its unfoldment that communicates to the spectator. Film will have particular appeal for the family trade.

Based on the John Burress novel, this is the story of a runaway orphan whose struggle to become a farmer and earn his own way has a profound effect upon the life of a rural community. Brandon de Wilde plays the 15-year-old who becomes the center of some storm in the town where Gary Merrill, the newspaper editor, takes him under his wing, and Lee Marvin, a tough, wealthy and hardfisted neighboring farmer, seemingly appears to be taking his own bitterness out on the lad but actually is instilling in him some of the essential truths of life that he had to learn the hard way himself.

Highlighting the Patrick Ford production, which Jerry Hopper deftly directs from the Norman Shannon Hall screenplay with an eye tuned always on homely possibilities, is the windup Fourth of July celebration, including a parade and a horse-trotting race between the boy and his oppressor, with the whole town betting on young de Wilde. Clincher is a fight between Merrill and Marvin, a humor-ridden battle taking in the town's whole main street. Use is made of every cornball gag and stunt in the book in these closing reels.

Picture, which gets the benefit of exceptionally fine Technicolor lensing by Winton C. Hoch, is peppered with top performances. De Wilde captures the imagination as the courageous lad who tries to operate a farm by himself. Merrill is understanding in his relations with the boy and Marvin is brutally frank in his characterization of a man whose word is good only if it's in writing. Paul Ford, former horse trainer but now operator of the town's only chili parlor and head of town's council, makes an indelible impression in a humorously-drawn characterization. Mary Hosford as the town's leading citizen secretly in love with Marvin is okay in spinster role. Standout support also is offered by Cal Tinney, town's baker; Ken Curtis, the blacksmith, Frank Cady, school principal; Will Wright, the sheriff.

Technical credits are class, including Jack Okey's art direction, Tom McAdoo's editing and Jack Marshall's music score. *Whit.*

Day of the Badman
(COLOR)

Familiar oater material for the program market.

Universal release of Gordon Kay production. Stars Fred MacMurray, Joan Weldon, John Ericson, Robert Middleton, Marie Windsor; features Edgar Buchanan, Eduard Franz, Skip Homeier. Directed by Harry Keller. Screenplay, Lawrence Roman, from story by John M. Cunningham; camera (Eastman Color), Irving Glassberg; editor, Sherman Todd; music, Hans J. Salter. Previewed Jan. 7, '58. Running time, **81 MINS.**

Judge Jim Scott	Fred MacMurray
Myra Owens	Joan Weldon
Sheriff Barney Wiley	John Ericson
Charlie Hayes	Robert Middleton
Cora Johnson	Marie Windsor
Sam Wyckoff	Edgar Buchanan
Andrew Owens	Eduard Franz
Howard Hayes	Skip Homeier
Mrs. Quary	Peggy Converse
Silas Mordigan	Robert Foulk
Mrs. Mordigan	Ann Doran
Jake Hayes	Lee Van Cleef
Mr. Slocum	Eddy Waller
Rudy Hayes	Christopher Dark
Floyd	Don Haggerty
Monte Hayes	Chris Alcaide

A routine western for the most part, "Day of the Badman" stacks up only an average entry for the general program market, with but the size of the screen and the color to distinguish it from footage which appears constantly in the home.

Lawrence Roman screenplay, based on a story by John M. Cunningham, is pivoted around Fred MacMurray, judge in a typical hoss-opera town who's shortly to pass sentence on a convicted killer when into town ride four of the latter's kin to see that he's set free. Quartet mess up the town to such an extent that seemingly everyone but MacMurray—the sheriff included—want only "banishment" for the jailed man. MacMurray, however, sticks to his guns, announces a sentence of hanging, then returns home where, with only slight aid from side-kick Edgar Buchanan, he wipes out the four buddies who'd come to rub him out.

In MacMurray's capable playing the story-line gets some interest and substance whereas in less experienced hands the whole thing would have bordered on the ridiculous. Joan Weldon has the femme lead and is okay as the lass who's first in love with MacMurray, switches over to John Eriscon, but reverts to her first love in the end. Ericson is fine as the town sheriff who turns cowardly when the chips are down, and there's good support from, among others, Robert Middleton, leader of the baddies; Marie Windsor, town trollop and g.f. of the convicted man; and Skip Homeier, another of the four villains.

Harry Keller's direction of the Gordon Kay production wisely concentrates on the action—fights, beatings, shootings and the like—and can also be credited with helping to bring out the generally good cast work. Benefiting film, too, is the Eastman Color camera work of Irving Glassberg, the art direction of Alexander Golitzen and Alfred Sweeney, and Hana J. Salter's musical score. *Neal.*

Unter Achtzehn
(Under Age)
(AUSTRIAN)

Vienna, Jan. 8.

A Paula Wessely Film release of Otto Duerer production. Stars Paula Wessely; features Vera Tschechowa, Paul Loewinger, Peter Parak, Erik Frey, Louis Soldan, Guido Wieland, Margaret Fries, Toni Puschelik. Directed by Georg Tressler. Screenplay, Emil Burri, Johannes M. Simmel, Georg Tressler; camera, Sepp Riff; music, Carl de Groof. At Loewen Kino, Vienna. Running time, **90 MINS.**

Luise Gottschalk	Paula Wessely
Elfie Breitner	Vera Tschechowa
Herr Kutzmeier	Paul Loewinger
Stefan Maurer	Peter Parak
Walter Messmer	Erik Frey
Bauer Larsen	Louis Soldan
Dr. Janegger	Guido Wieland
Edith Messmer	Margarete Fries
Karli	Toni Puschelik

One half of this picture is a meticulous description of the activities of welfare centers. The other half is old fashioned. Nevertheless, this looks headed for a good boxoffice future, probably repeating as a crowd-pleaser abroad as well. Puritans will love it, despite several sexy and strip tease scenes.

Paula Wessely, working in a social center, sympathetically punches over her role. Scripters are to blame for such nonsense as not permitting a 18-year-old "bad girl" with a million dollar figure to become a mannequin and ordering her to work in a laundry instead. Vera Tschechowa is a looker and can act. The "bad boy" Peter Parak manages a light touch which spells audience interest. Erik Frey is the seducer and is very good.

Director Georg Tressler, grand old man of the Burgtheatre, either avoided correcting the script or added the same blunders himself in the yarn. However, he maintains a fair pace. Sepp Riff's lensing is very fine. Other technical credits measure up. *Maas.*

The Safecracker

Ray Milland starring against British Intelligence situations. Two stories tied together, okay average entertainment.

Hollywood, Jan. 10.

Metro release of John R. Sloan production. Stars Ray Milland; costars Barry Jones; features Jeannette Sterke, Ernest Clark, Melissa Stribbling, Victor Maddern, Cyril Raymond, Percy Herbert. Director, Milland. Screenplay, Paul Monash; based on story by Lt. Col. Rhys Davies, Bruce Thomas; camera, Gerald Gibbs; editor, Ernest Walter; music, Richard Rodney Bennett. Previewed Jan. 2, '58. Running time, **96 MINS.**

Colley Dawson	Ray Milland
Bennett Carfield	Barry Jones
Irene	Jeannette Sterke
Morris	Victor Maddern
Major Adbury	Ernest Clark
Inspector Frankham	Cyril Raymond
Angela	Melissa Stribling
Sergeant Harper	Percy Herbert
Mrs. Dawson	Barbara Everest
General Prior	Anthony Nicholls
Herbert Fenwright	David Horne
Dakers	Colin Gordon
Sir George Turvey	Clive Morton
Inspector Owing	John Welsh
Belgian Messenger	Pamela Stirling
Col. Charles Mercer	Colin Tapiey
Lonsen	Henry Vidon
Thomson	Ian MacNaughton
Shafter	Bernard Fox
Bailey	Richard Shaw
Lambert	Charles Lloyd Pack
Squadron Leader Hawkes	Barry Keegan
McCullers	Sam Kydd
Greek Ship Owner	Ferdy Mayne
Fenwright's Secretary	Jackie Collins

This British import consists of two separate stories, both following the experiences of a master safecracker. One serves as a prolog to the other. Each is interesting, but picture itself suffers from break in plotline. Film's melodramatic ingredients, however, should see it through the program market, where Ray Milland as star will give pic meaning.

Milland, appearing in—for him —a somewhat offbeat role, not always a pleasant character, also does a good job at direction of the David E. Rose production; produced by John R. Sloan. A lively tempo is maintained and considerable suspense accompanies the unfoldment, particularly major plot, involving British Military Intelligence in Warld War II.

First story, which runs 45 minutes, intro's Milland as an expert for a London safe manufacturer. His flair for opening safes leads to him becoming a cracksman for a seemingly respectable antique dealer who sells historical items of great value to greedy collectors who aren't interested in their origin. Second, and main story, unt-wirls two years after Milland is caught and imprisoned, when England now is at war with Germany. British MI, learning that a complete list of German spies in England is in the vault of a Belgian chateau, "borrows" safecracker from prison for the purpose of secretly opening this vault so the list may be photographed without the Germans being aware of the act. After being trained as a Commando, Milland is dropped with a British patrol into Belgium for the exciting mission.

Milland enacts his unsavory character with feeling and in his direction draws good performances from balance of principals, headed by Barry Jones, as the antique dealer, only other member of cast known to audiences here. Cyril Raymond plays a Scotland Yard inspector who jails him, then arranges for his delivery to MI for the dangerous mision, and Ernest Clark heads the mission as an Army major. Jeannette Sterke lends distaff interest as daughter of a Belgian resistance leader.

Script by Paul Monash is based on an original by Lt. Col. Rhys Davies, British Army Intelligence (Ret.) and Bruce Thomas. Gerald Gibbs' photography is fast, Ernest Walter's tight editing helps pace and Richard Rodney Bennett's music score catches the spirit.

Whit.

The World Was His Jury

Courtroom melodrama okay for program spots; names of Edmond O'Brien and Mona Freeman to help.

Hollywood, Jan. 4.

Columbia release of Sam Katzman production. Stars Edmond O'Brien, Mona Freeman; features Karin Booth, Robert McQueeney, Paul Birch, John Berardino, Dick Cutting, Harvey Stephens, Carlos Romero, Hortense Petra. Directed by Fred F. Sears. Screenplay, Herbert Abbott Spiro; camera, Benjamin H. Kline; editor, Edwin Bryant; music, Mischa Bakaleinikoff. Previewed Dec. 26, '57. Running time, **82 MINS.**

David Carson	Edmond O'Brien
Robin Carson	Mona Freeman
Polly Barrett	Karin Booth
Jerry Barrett	Robert McQueeney
Martin Ranker	Paul Birch
Tony Armand	John Berardino
D. A. Wendell	Dick Cutting
Judge Arthur Farrell	Harvey Stephens
1st Mate Johnson	Carlos Romero
Pretty Girl	Hortense Petra
Jimmy Barrett	Kelly Junge Jr.
Jane Barrett	Gay Goodwin

"The World Was His Jury" is a fairly well plotted courtroom melodrama but slow unfoldment militates against the full interest subject matter should have enjoyed.

Film is okay for programmer market, where names of Edmond O'Brien and Mona Freeman may count.

Sam Katzman production deals with the skipper of a luxury liner whose ship is burned off the New Jersey coast with loss of 162 lives and his subsequent trial for criminal negligence. O'Brien portrays his crack defense attorney, who, with nothing to go on in the way of evidence to help his client, proceeds to find this evidence via witnesses and thereby brings to justice the man responsible for the tragedy, the skipper's second in command who was out to get his superior. The Herbert Abbott Spiro screenplay skillfully builds this situation of courtroom denouement, despite a sometimes naive approach to courtroom technique, and good characterizations are provided through Fred F. Sears' direction.

O'Brien socks over his portrayal of the attorney who has never lost a case, now faced with a possible guilty verdict, and Miss Freeman persuasively plays his wife who leaves him because she's certain, as is everybody else, that he's defending a guilty man. Robert McQueeney, the accused captain, delivers well in a restrained performance, Karin Booth provides distaff allure as his wife, Paul Birch is properly rugged as second-in-command, John Berardino scores as O'Brien's private investigator and Harvey Stephens is dominant as the judge.

Katzman has lined up a full complement of capable technicians, including Benjamin H. Kline, camera; Paul Palmentola, art direction; Edwin Bryant, editing. *Whit.*

Gun Fever

Routine action meller.

Hollywood, Jan. 3.

United Artists release of Harry Jackson-Sam Weston production. Co-producer, Edward L. Rissien. Stars Mark Stevens, co-stars John Lupton, introduces Jana Davi. Features Aaron Saxon, Jerry Barclay, Norman Fredric. Directed by Stevens; screenplay, Stanley H. Silverman, Stevens from story by Harry S. Franklin, Julius Evans; camera, Charles Van Enger; editor, Lee Gilbert; music, Paul Dunlap. Previewed Jan. 3, '58. Running time, 83 MINS.

Lucas	Mark Stevens
Simon	John Lupton
Amigo	Larry Storch
Tanana	Jana Davi
Trench	Aaron Saxon
Singer	Jerry Barclay
Whitman	Norman Frederic
Kane	Clegg Hoyt
Martha	Jane Innes
Thomas	Russell Thorsen
Stableman	Michael Himm
Indian Chief	Iron Eyes Cody
2nd Indian Chief	Eddie Little
Jerry	April Delavanti
Lee	John Godard
Jack	Vic Smith
Norris	Robert Stevenson
Bartender	William Erwin
Man	David Bond
Farmer	George Selk

A drawn-out vengeance theme, "Gun Fever" shapes as acceptable program fare, particularly in action areas where patrons accept fist and gun fights as substitutes for story. It's overlong at 83 minutes but competently made within its budget boundaries and should get satisfactory returns for producers Harry Jackson and Sam Weston and co-producer Edward L. Rissien. Mark Stevens and John Lupton, both regulars on tv screens, are the only familiar cast names but little marquee value is indicated.

Stevens directed and co-scripted, in addition to starring, stretching himself thin in the process. Screenplay which Stanley H. Silverman and Stevens fashioned from a story by Harry S. Franklin and Julius Evans casts Stevens as a fast-gun miner whose parents are killed by Indians led by a white renegade and Stevens vows vengeance. Lupton is his partner and the son of the renegade from whom he has long since parted because of the father's villainy. After the required amount of violence and some incidental romance with newcomer Jana Davi, the renegade is slain and Lupton, though badly wounded, apparently will start life anew with Miss Davi while Stevens rides alone.

Dialog is sometimes incongruous for the characters and locale and Stevens' direction is much too leisurely between fights, some of which could have been staged. He's appropriately tightlipped throughout and Lupton is credible. Miss Davi has an interesting face and figure, glimpsed partially in a bathing scene (a separate, nude version was shot for foreign audiences and may engender a trifle more interest). Supporting cast work is headed by Larry Storch's work as a Mexican gunslinger but Aaron Saxon overacts as the renegade and the lesser portrayals are all stock.

Producers took full advantage of outdoor lensing, including making use of weather conditions. Camera work by Charles Van Enger is okay and the other technical credits are average. *Kap.*

The Lady Takes a Flyer
(C'SCOPE—COLOR)

Lana Turner and Jeff Chandler teamed in so-so story. Fair returns indicated.

Hollywood, Jan. 10.

Universal release of William Alland production. Stars Lana Turner, Jeff Chandler; costars Richard Denning, Andra Martin; features Chuck Connors, Reta Shaw, Alan Hale Jr., Jerry Paris. Directed by Jack Arnold. Screenplay, Danny Arnold; story, Edmund H. North; camera (Eastmancolor), Irving Glassberg; editor, Sherman Todd; music, Herman Stein. Previewed Jan. 7, '58. Running time, **93 MINS.**

Maggie Colby	Lana Turner
Mike Dandridge	Jeff Chandler
Al Reynolds	Richard Denning
Nikki Taylor	Andra Martin
Phil Donahoe	Chuck Connors
Nurse Kennedy	Reta Shaw
Frank Henshaw	Alan Hale Jr.
Willie Ridgely	Jerry Paris
Collie Minor	Lee J. Thompson
Childreth	Nestor Paiva
Tower Officer	James Doherty

Teaming of Lana Turner and Jeff Chandler figure to help the chances of this peacetime air yarn, which otherwise falls short of satisfactory entertainment. Film is burdened with plodding treatment that militates against ready acceptance, but star names—particularly femme's firepower after her performance in "Peyton Place"—coupled with a spicy bathtub sequence may be exploited for fair returns in general market.

Duo enact husband-and-wife owners of a plane ferrying service which first takes them to all parts of the world, the separates them when the husband takes his planes out alone after the birth of their baby. William Alland production is well mounted and vivid backdropping is afforded by good use of color. Dramatically, however, film seldom gets off the ground and only in the finale when femme is trying to bring in her near-gasless plane, with the airstrip shrouded by fog, does action come to life. Attempted useage of comedy sometimes results in cloying coyness.

Danny Arnold screenplay opens with Chandler, a former Air Force colonel, meeting his wartime buddy, Richard Denning, at a California airport, where latter operates a flying school and Miss Turner, former wartime ferry pilot, is an instructor. Chandler is all steamed up about starting a ferry service and trio go into partnership. In Japan, on an assignment, Chandler and distaffer fall in love and marry upon returning to States. For a honeymoon, they go on a ferrying trip through Europe. Back home, conflict rises between couple when she reveals she expects a baby and insists upon renting a house, rather than live in an apartment. Later, after infant is born, she remains at home while Chandler takes to the clouds. Film builds to a climax when wife takes one of the planes Chandler is to deliver in England and flies the Atlantic. Chandler beating her there and directing her to the ground through the fog.

Jack Arnold's direction is as smooth as script will permit and manages to get capable performances from his players. Miss Turner lends allure to her role, Chandler is properly rugged and Denning competently handles a light characterization. Andra Martin is in for romantic conflict as a femme pilot who goes on make for Chandler, and Chuck Connors and Jerry Paris are pilots and Lee J. Thompson scores as a glib secretary.

Irving Glassberg's color photography heads up good technical credits, and editing by Sherman Todd, music by Herman Stein and art direction by Alexander Golitzen and Richard H. Riedel also count. *Whit.*

Diamond Safari

Minor entertainment but filmed in Johannesburg, South Africa, for good backgrounds. Filler.

Hollywood, Jan. 6.

Twentieth-Fox release of Gerald Mayer Production, directed by Mayer. Stars Kevin McCarthy; features Andre Morell. Screenplay, Larry Marcus; camera, David Millin, Peter Lang; editors, Carl Pierson, Peter Pitt; music, Woolf Phillips. Previewed Jan. 2, '58. Running time, **67 MINS.**

Harry Jordan	Kevin McCarthy
Sgt. van der Cliffe	Joel Herholdt
Compound Manager	Gert van den Bergh
Stephen Timbu	Geoffrey Tsobe
Police Boy	Harry Mekels
Medicine Man	Thomas Buson
Williamson	Andre Morell
Petey	Joanna Douglas
Louise Saunders	Betty McDowall
Carlton	Patrick Simpson
Doc	John Clifford
Phillips	Michael McNeile
Reubens	Robert Rice
Glass Blower's Wife	Frances Driver

This indie effort, filmed for the most part in Johannesburg, South Africa, stacks up as generally uninteresting filler fare. The backgrounds provide some value, but there's little else to distinguish release.

Picture actually is the outgrowth of an idea by Edward Dukoff, **credited as exec producer, to lense a vidpix series around this foreign locale. Two "pilots" subsequently were tied together with a week's Hollywood filming to make this feature.**

Screenplay by Larry Marcus is pivoted around Kevin McCarthy, a private investigator. He first clears a native of a murder charge, then rounds up a pair of diamond smugglers. And that's about it.

McCarthy, only "name" in the cast, is authorative in star role, giving film one of its biggest assets. Betty McDowall, as one of the smugglers, eventually killed along with cohort John Clifford, also is good in the leading femme part. Top featured and okay as one of the suspects is Andre Morell.

Direction of Gerald Mayer, who also produced, is stock, as are majority of the technical contributions. Foreign filming, incidentally, was done in color, but picture is being released in black-and-white. *Neal.*

Escape From Red Rock
(REGALSCOPE)

Fast-moving oater.

Hollywood, Jan. 10.

Twentieth-Fox release of Bernard Glasser production. Stars Brian Donlevy; co-stars Eilene Janssen, Gary Murray, Jay C. Flippen; features William Phipps, Michael Healey, Nesdon Booth, Daniel White. Directed by Edward Bernds. Screenplay, Bernds; camera, Brydon Baker; editor, John F. Link; music, Les Baxter. Previewed Jan. 8, '58. Running time, 75 MINS.

Bronc Grierson	Brian Donlevy
Janie Acker	Eilene Janssen
Cal Bowman	Gary Murray
John Costaine	Jay C. Flippen
Arky Shanks	William Phipps
Joe Skinner	Michael Healey
Pete Archer	Nesdon Booth
Farris	Daniel White
Guard	Andre Adoree
Boyce	Courtland Shepard
Maria Chavez	Tina Menard
Miguel Chavez	Natividad Vacio
Krug	Zon Murray
Judd	Rick Vallin
Tarrant	Ed Hinton
Coach Driver & Double	Frosty Royse
Price	Frank Richards
Elena Chavez	Linda Dangcil
Mayor	Eumenio Blanco
Antonia Chavez	Elena Da Vinci
Grover	Hank Patterson
Mrs. Donnely	Eileene Stevens
Manager	Frank Marlowe
Clerk	Joe Becker
Krug Henchie	Dick Crockett
Double	Roydon Clark
Double	Sailor Vincent

There's enough rapid action in "Escape from Red Rock" to keep audiences occupied in the oater market. Story line is sufficiently different to warrant good suspense and star name of Brian Donlevy is good for an added boost.

Edward Bernds' direction of his own screenplay logically builds story of a young ranchman forced to take to the trail after being falsely accused of a holdup murder. Bernard Glasser tosses in the type of production values best suited to theme, which winds in an Apache attack on a shack occupied by rancher and the girl he took with him, now his bride. Donlevy apparently was cast for name value, since his role is minor, but he dominates his brief footage as an outlaw leader soft about babies.

Gary Murray is strongly set as the young rancher whose loyalty to a brother accused of being a bandit and killer is so fierce that he constantly is taking on the whole town in fights. Against his will, he's pressed into easing a holdup job planned by Donlevy, who has brought the wounded brother back to Murray, to whom it's made clear that unless he throws in on the job his brother will be left to die. After the holdup in which he doesn't participate, Murray learns he's supposed to have murdered a woman and lights out with Eilene Janssen, whose drunken stepfather constantly is beating her, and they're wed in a Mexican hamlet. Taking refuge in the cabin of a settler, they find Apaches have killed man and his wife but overlooked a tiny baby, whom the young couple proceed to care for. A sheriff's posse finally saves them from another attack.

Donlevy is his usual authoritative self, particularly in later sequences when he and his gang descend on young couple in their hideaway. Both Murray and Miss Janssen are good, although latter's dialog is brief, and Jay C. Flippen registers as a soft-hearted sheriff. William Phipps and Michael Healey also rate as outlaws, and Nesdon Booth is okay as the stepfather.

Technical departments are well executed, leading off with Brydon Baker's photography, John F. Link's editing, Les Baxter's music score and Rudi Feld's art direction. *Whit.*

Return to Warbow
(COLOR)

For minor oater market.

Hollywood, Dec. 27.

Columbia release of Wallace MacDonald production. Stars Phil Carey; features Catherine McLeod, Andrew Duggan, William Leslie, Robert J. Wilke, James Griffith, Jay Silverheels, Chris Olsen. Directed by Ray Nazarro. Screenplay, Les Savage Jr., based on his novel; camera (Technicolor), Henry Freulich; editor, Charles Nelson; music, Mischa Bakaleinikoff. Previewed Dec. 19, '57. Running time, 66 MINS.

Clay Hollister .... Phil Carey
Kathleen Fallam ...... Catherine McLeod
Murray Fallam .... Andrew Duggan
Johnny .... William Leslie
Red .... Robert J. Wilke
Frank Hollister .... James Griffith
Indian Joe .... Jay Silverheels
David Fallam .... Chris Olsen
Sheriff .... Francis de Sales
Deputy No. 1 .... Harry Lauter
Deputy No. 2 .... Paul Picerni
Doc Appleby .... Joe Forte

"Return to Warbow" is routine western entertainment. Screenplay has no highlights and direction does nothing to generate excitement. Good color pictorial values, but no cast names.

The Les Savage Jr., script starts with an okay premise but fails to develop its potential. Movement remains at a monotone. Ray Nazarro's direction is slack and the whole feeling of the Wallace MacDonald production is old-fashioned and lacking in the snap necessary to please modern-day audiences. Cast consequently suffers from lack of opportunity.

Plot follows Phil Carey, who escapes from Arizona Territorial Prison with two other cons to return to his former home to pick up $30,000 stolen in a stagecoach robbery 11 years before. Deal calls for him to share the loot with his two companions, who in turn hope to eradicate him as soon as they lay hands on the coin, supposedly held by Carey's drunken brother. It develops brother has gambled money away.

Carey tries hard to rise above role and Catherine McLeod as his former girl friend is as good as script will permit, the same said for William Leslie and Robert J. Wilke as his two pals, James Griffith in brother role. Andrew Duggan the husband of Miss McLeod and Chris Olsen as her son.

Henry Freulich's color camera work is excellent. Balance of technical credits are standard. *Whit.*

Charmants Garcons
(Charming Boys)
(FRENCH; COLOR; SONGS; DANCE)

Paris, Jan. 8.

Sirius release of Jacques Roitfeld production. Stars Zizi Jeanmaire, Henri Vidal, Francois Perier, Daniel Gelin; features Gert Froebe, Jacques Dacqmine, Marie Daems. Directed by Henri Decoin. Screenplay, Charles Spaak; camera (Eastman-color), Pierre Montazel; editor, Claude Durand; music, Guy Beart, Georges Van Parys; choreography, Roland Petit. At Marignan, Paris. Running time, 105 MINS.

Lulu .... Zizi Jeanmaire
Alain .... Daniel Gelin
Jo .... Henri Vidal
Robert .... Francois Perier
Edmond .... Gert Froebe
Charles .... Jacques Dacqmine
Max .... Gil Vidal
Germaine .... Marie Daems
Andre .... Jacques Berthier

Around Zizi Jeanmaire is built an attempted tale of a young cabaret singer-dancer besieged by a flock of men trying to win her charms, but with none having matrimony in view. Pic lays out, in sketchy fashion, her series of run-ins with all the boys who deceive her but give her plenty of attention until she meets the Mr. Right for the traditional ending.

Main flaw in the film is its traditional aspect which mainly unfolds a rather unsavory tale, saved from time to time by shafts of humor. This is primarily an exploitation item for the U.S. with a plus item in Zizi Jeanmaire. However, color print costs make this a chancey bet. Pic looks to do well here.

Miss Jeanmaire has a limp wrist manager who brings on a big, lecherous millionaire who follows her about waiting for the weak spot when he can buy in. He trails her around France when she disconsolately takes off after finding her current love is married. Follows interludes with a boxer and a gentleman thief until she finally finds the right fellow after the millionaire backs the show she has wanted to do.

Miss Jeanmaire is uneven in the character with the lowlife zest somewhat too mannered, but perks up in her song and dance bits. Some catchy tunes are involved but the dances remain stagebound. Men all impart okay aspects in their conventional roles with Gert Froebe standout as the conniving millionaire. Technical credits are good. It is a followup, from a distaff point of view to "Adorable Creatures" which did their biz in the U.S. two years ago. *Mosk.*

The Quiet American

Talky, literate version of the Graham Greene book on clashing ideologies in Indo-China. A toughie to sell the mass audience.

United Artists release of Figaro Production. Joseph L. Mankiewicz producer. Stars Audie Murphy, Michael Redgrave, Claude Dauphin, Giorgia Moll; features Kerima, Bruce Cabot, Fred Sadoff, Richard Loo, Peter Trent. Directed and written for screen by Mankiewicz, from novel by Graham Greene; camera, Robert Krasker; music, Mario Nascimbene; editor, William Hornbeck. Previewed in New York, Jan. 15, '58. Running time, 120 MINS.

The American .... Audie Murphy
Fowler .... Michael Redgrave
Inspector Vigot .... Claude Dauphin
Phuong .... Giorgia Moll
Miss Hei .... Kerima
Bill Granger .... Bruce Cabot
Dominguez .... Fred Sadoff
Mister Heng .... Richard Loo
Eliot Wilkins .... Peter Trent
Joe Morton .... Clinton Andersen
Hostess .... Yoko Tani
Yvette .... Sonia Moser
Isabelle .... Phuong Thi Nghiep
Cao-Dai Commandant ..... Vo Doan Chau
Cao-Dai Pope's Deputy .... Le Van Le
Masked Man .... Le Quynh
French Colonel .... Georges Brehat

In adapting British novelist Graham Greene's bitter and cynical "The Quiet American" into a motion picture, producer-director-adaptor Joseph L. Mankiewicz has allowed himself the luxury of turning the screen into a debating society. It's a formula that might have paid off, at least via controversy, had he retained the central character of the American in the book who, in Greene's version, represented all the determined bungling of current American foreign policy.

As it turned out, the film—shot on location in Viet Nam and at the Cinecitta Studios in Rome—is an overlong, overdialogued adaptation, concerned with the pros and cons of a Third Force in Asia and paying scant lip service to the old adage that one of the basic appeals of the motion picture is that it moves.

"The Quiet American" has its moments of fiery action, and it stars a pretty newcomer, Georgia Moll, in a comparatively small role. But it is, on the whole, still mostly a conversation, more concerned with intellectual and political problems than with dramatic entertainment. As a result, its appeal will be limited, and chances are that mass audiences will get restless.

Story follows the line of the book, but with the all-important difference that the character of the American, played without much depth by Audie Murphy, has been drained of meaning, giving the whole picture a pro-American slant. This throws rest of the characters slightly out of focus. Murphy here doesn't represent the U.S. Government, but merely works for a private U.S. aid mission. In other words, his ideas of a Third Force standing between Communism and French Colonialism are his own.

Picture actually has a couple of story strands running parallel. It's one long flashback from the moment Murphy is found murdered and Michael Redgrave, playing a British correspondent, is asked by French inspector Claude Dauphin to identify him. Redgrave, motivated by jealousy and concern over Murphy's activities, has actually been an accomplice of the Communists in the American's murder. Later it turns out that the Reds had duped Redgrave. Dauphin gradually unspools the sometimes obscure story.

Love interest in the film is Miss Moll who lives with Redgrave but leaves him for the younger Murphy. In the end she refuses to go back to Redgrave. Running throughout is the clashing views between Redgrave and Murphy. It's a consistent argument, and sometimes a violent one, and while it at times makes good listening, it doesn't help carry the narrative along.

Murphy doesn't seem very believable as a foreign affairs theorist, which may be partly the script's fault. He speaks his piece and, in his bright, untroubled way, provides a perfect counterpoint for Redgrave's moody portrayal of the neurotic aging Britisher hiding personal anxieties under a mask of cinicism. Redgrave delivers a grand performance, and in fact it's his acting that makes the whole thing at all worthwhile. The only anti-American remarks are the ones delivered by him, and they are couched in nonobjectionable terms. He represents the non-involved writer, who becomes involved up to his ears and, finally, lets the Reds betray him through his emotions.

As the inspector, Dauphin gives a strong and patient reading to his lines and registers strongly. Miss Moll is very attractive, though she hardly looks like an Indo-Chinese. As her sister, Kerima does well. Bruce Cabot, Fred Sadoff and Richard Loo have bit parts.

Mankiewicz has delivered a thoughtful script that aims primarily in contrasting political points-of-view and, sometimes, showing their application in human terms. The trouble is that, in his determination not to lose meaning, he has tended to use characters as symbols, with each mouthing a given idiology. The process is intellectually rewarding and dramatically tiresome. There are likely to be an awful lot of people who'll come out of this film saying (about Indo-Chinese problems) "Who gives a damn?" This may not be the "right" attitude, but—in terms of the mass audience—its a forgivable one.

Visually, "The Quiet American" has been photographed skillfully by Robert Krasker, though actually the number of scenes showing off Viet Nam (the story is laid in 1952, before the partition) isn't very large. There's an impressive bit of staging at the watchtower, which is collapsed by a passing tank, and the camera catches the scope of the wide plaza in Saigon after the bombing. Director Mankiewicz has staged lively crowd scenes and, considering the emphasis on conversation, he has his actors well in hand.

Mario Nascimbene's music pleasantly underscores the story. William Hornbeck's editing is smooth. Rino Mondelino has produced realistically-bare sets. "Quiet American" will require special handling. It's a picture that stimulates thought. *Hift.*

Damn Citizen

Episodic and leisurely documentary yarn of fight against crime in Louisiana.

Hollywood, Jan. 14.

Universal release of Herman Webber production. Stars Keith Andes, Maggie Hayes, Gene Evans, Lynn Bari, Jeffrey

Stone, Edward C. Platt, Ann Robinson; features Sam Buffington, Clegg Hoyt, Carolyn Kearney, Charles Horvath. Directed by Robert Gordon. Screenplay, Stirling Silliphant; camera, Ellis W. Carter; music, Henry Mancini; editor, Patrick McCormack. Previewed Dec. 30, '57. Running time, 88 MINS.

Col. Francis C. Grevemberg ...... Keith Andes
Dorothy Grevemberg ...... Maggie Hayes
Major Al Arthur ...... Gene Evans
Pat Noble ...... Lynn Bari
Paul Musso ...... Jeffrey Stone
Joseph Kosta ...... Edward C. Platt
Cleo ...... Ann Robinson
DeButts ...... Sam Buffington
Sheriff Lloyd ...... Clegg Hoyt
Col. Thomas Hastings ...... Kendall Clark
Inspector Sweeney ...... Rusty Lane
Lieut. Palmer ...... Charles Horvath
Nancy ...... Carolyn Kearney
Aaron M. Kohn ...... Himself
Rev. J. D. Grey ...... Himself
Richard R. Foster ...... Himself
Big Jim ...... Pershing Gervais
Major Sterling ...... Aaron A. Edgecombe
Captain Desmond ...... Rev. Robert H. Jamieson
Father Masters ...... Paul S. Hostetler
Thomas Gleason ...... Nathaniel F. Oddo
Fowler ...... Dudley C. Foley, Jr.
Judge ...... Charles A. Murphy
Harry ...... George M. Trussell
Reporter ...... Jack Dempsey
Reporter ...... Frank Hay
News Commentator ...... Tiger Flowers
Satchel Man ...... John Schowest

"Damn Citizen" is the true-life story of Col. Francis C. Grevemberg, World War II hero, in his one-man fight against crime and corruption in his native Louisiana and his efforts to hand state back to the people. As a piece of documentary film-making pic carries certain interest for the cops and robbers clientele, but a necessarily episodic approach, leisurely unfoldment and lack of excitement highlights hold it to the supporting feature category.

The Herman Webber production was lensed in and around New Orleans, locale of the Stirling Silliphant screenplay; consequently certain authentic values accrue. Keith Andes portrays title role, invited by the new Governor to serve as superintendent of the State Police and wage an all-out battle against every form of crime which flourished in state unabated for many years. He finds himself opposed on every side, but through the aid of his staff is able to make considerable headway in cleaning up the state.

Robert Gordon's direction is rambling but he gets convincing performances from a large cast. Andes satisfactorily handles his top role and gets expert assistance from Gene Evans as his chief aide. Edward C. Platt as the vice baron of state is smoothly realistic, Jeffrey Stone and Charles Horvath lend color to police parts, former as an undercover man and latter bouncer for bribe-taking, and Sam Buffington stands out as a gambling operator. Maggie Hayes favorable impresses as Andes' wife threatened by the gangsters.

Technical credits are sharp, including Ellis W. Carter's camera work and Henry Mancini's music score.

Whit.

Darby's Rangers

Exciting account of the true-life American Rangers of World War II. Sock entertainment for melodramatic market.

Hollywood, Jan. 17.

Warner Bros. release of Martin Rackin production. Stars James Garner, Etchika Choureau, Jack Warden; features Edward Byrnes, Venetia Stevenson, Torin Thatcher, Peter Brown, Joan Elan, Corey Allen, Stuart Whitman, Murray Hamilton, Bill Wellman Jr., Andrea King, Adam Williams, Frieda Inescort, Reginald Owen, Philip Tonge, Edward Ashley, Raymond Bailey, Willis Bouchey. Directed by William A. Wellman. Screenplay, Guy Trosper, suggested by book by Maj. James Altieri; camera, William Clothier; editor, Owen Marks; music, Max Steiner. Previewed Jan. 13, '58. Running time, 120 MINS.

Maj. Wm. Darby ...... James Garner
Angelina De Lotta ...... Etchika Choureau
M/Sgt. Saul Rosen ...... Jack Warden
Lieut. Arnold Dittman ...... Edward Byrnes
Jeggy McTavish ...... Venetia Stevenson
Sgt. McTavish ...... Torin Thatcher
Rollo Burns ...... Peter Brown
Wendy Hollister ...... Joan Elan
Tony Sutherland ...... Corey Allen
"Hank" Bishop ...... Stuart Whitman
Sims Delancey ...... Murray Hamilton
Eli Clatworthy ...... Bill Wellman Jr.
Sheilah Andrews ...... Andrea King
"Heavy" Hall ...... Aram Williams
Lady Hollister ...... Frieda Inescort
Sir Arthur ...... Reginald Owen
John Andrews ...... Philip Tonge
Lieut. Manson ...... Edward Ashley
Maj. Gen. Wise ...... Raymond Bailey
Brig. Gen. Truscott ...... Willis Bouchey

This saga of Col. William Darby, who organized the American Rangers to spearhead landings and action during World War II in North Africa and Southern Europe, strikes a high note of interest. For the melodramatic market film is a solid entry, packing mass appeal in its long but gutsy unfoldment. While cast, heavily sprinkled with fine performing talent, generally is unknown, pic should benefit from appearance in title role of James Garner, star of Warners' "Maverick" tv series and regarded as one of the top personalities of video.

Highlights in the training and subsequent war record of the Rangers are traced in hard-hitting fashion by William A. Wellman in his fine direction, and Martin Rackin as producer has given feature the proper accoutrements pertaining to subject. The Guy Trosper screenplay, suggested by the book of Maj. James Altieri, historian of the Rangers, deviates sometimes from a strict recountal of this great military body by inserting romantic episodes among its fighting personnel, but essentially it is based upon authentic material which Wellman socks over for telling effect. Occasional corn is inserted in some of the action, but it's not out of place in a film of this type, dealing with the rugged individuals who composed the Rangers.

First half of the 120-minute feature is devoted to the origin and Commando training of the Rangers, second half to the actual war exploits in North Africa, Sicily and up the Italian boot, where the corps distinguished itself. Unfoldment is crammed with exciting action as the Rangers in their smashing tactics seize coastal defenses, establish beachheads, raid behind enemy lines, make fierce lightning attacks. The straight war tale is leavened with the lighter stories of romance, some of escapades and some serious love affairs in which the Rangers engage. Two romances carry through to completion, allowing for distaff interest.

Garner is especially effective as the officer dedicated to his Rangers, lending authority and understanding to role, his initial star assignment in a theatrical feature. Starred with him is Jack Warden, his master-sergeant aide, excellent in part, and Etchika Choureau, French actress who scores as the Italian sweetheart of Edward Byres, whose delineation of a rank-conscious young West Pointer is well conceived. Stuart Whitman and Joan Elan also are teamed romantically, former a tough former gambler, latter the British daughter of titled parents, both standouts.

Also doing yoeman service as Rangers are Adam Williams, Bill Wellman, Jr., Murray Hamilton, Corey Allen, Peter Brown, latter pairing romantically with Venetia Stevenson, nicely cast as a Scotch girl. Edward Ashley contributes an outstanding bit as an English Commando who instructs Rangers in the art of killing without being killed; Torin Thatcher is his competent sergeant and Reginald Owen and Frieda Inescort are capable as Joan Elan's parents.

Technical departments are well handled, including William Clothier's photography, Owen Marks' editing, Max Steiner's music score, William Campbell's art direction and sound by Robert B. Lee.

Whit.

Man Who Wouldn't Talk
(BRITISH)

Sometimes untidy, but always absorbing legal drama; Combo of Anna Neagle and Zsa Zsa Gabor makes refreshing stellar attraction for many audiences.

London, Jan. 21.

British Lion release of Wilcox-Neagle production. Stars Anna Neagle, Anthony Quayle, Zsa Zsa Gabor. Directed by Herbert Wilcox. Screenplay by Edgar Lustgarten from story by Stanley Jackson; camera, Gordon Dines; editor, Bunny Warren; music, Stanley Black. At Ritz Theatre, London. Running time, 97 MINS.

Mary Randall Q.C. ...... Anna Neagle
Frank Smith ...... Anthony Quayle
Eve Trent ...... Zsa Zsa Gabor
Miss Delbeau ...... Katharine Kath
Telephonist ...... Dora Bryan
Kennedy ...... Patrick Allen
Bernie ...... Hugh McDermott
Professor Horvad ...... Leonard Sachs
Hobbs ...... Edward Lexy
Castle ...... John Paul
Judge ...... John Le Mesurier
Baker ...... Anthony Sharp
Jury Foreman ...... Anthony Pendrell
Liftman ...... Cyril Chamberlain

Most films or plays equipped with a good court scene invariably get away to a flying start, providing the script is intelligent and is written by someone who knows his legal onions. "The Man Who Wouldn't Talk" has this advantage. The author, Stanley Jackson, and the screenplay-writer, Edgar Lustgarten, are both professional scribes who have also had intensive legal training. Any legal slip-ups must therefore be put down to dramatic license and are not such as will cause the average filmgoer any sleepless nights.

The cast is sufficiently interesting to give the pic an even chance both in Britain and U.S. It has loose ends, but holds the interest throughout, and the court scenes are extremely well directed by Herbert Wilcox.

Anthony Quayle plays an American scientist who comes to London with Zsa Zsa Gabor. On the surface the two are on honeymoon. Actually, they are on an assignment from Washington, Miss Gabor being a secret agent. Purpose of the visit is to get information on bacteriological warfare from a Hungarian scientist. This information will only be disclosed by Quayle (on promise) only to one man in the U.S. With this solemn promise given, Quayle is in a hot spot when he finds himself arraigned on a charge of murdering Miss Gabor.

Anna Neagle plays an ace Queen's Counsel, briefed to defend him. But it's a tricky job for her since, because of his promise, he refuses to go into the box to defend himself. Miss Neagle pulls off the case but it is touch and go throughout. The drama is geared excellently to pitting the star's wits against the witnesses in an effort to win the sympathy of the jury.

Miss Neagle gives a standout performance as the Q.C. There is one sequence, when she delivers a five-minute speech which blends facts and emotionalism, which is among the finest things this versatile artist has essayed on the screen. Quayle is solidly effective as the accused and Miss Gabor shows that she can be dramatically effective as well as decorative in the role of the spy. There are also some good minor performances, particularly from Katharine Kath, as a witness with an eye to profit; Anthony Sharp, as a ballistics expert; and Dora Bryan, as a gabby telephone operator.

Some of the characters are dragged in and tossed away in an irritating fashion. But on the whole, director Wilcox has fashioned a very tense piece of drama, which shrewdly exploits a little known piece of legal versimilitude. Gordon Dines has lensed the pic smartly and the settings owe a great deal to the whole hearted co-operation of the Law Society.

Rich.

The Story of Vickie
(COLOR)

Charming story of the young Queen Victoria, beautifully produced for strong art house reception, though dubbing job not ideal.

Buena Vista release of Ernst Marischka production. Stars Romy Schneider; features Adrian Hoven, Magda Schneider, Karl Ludwig Diehl, Christl Mardayn, Paul Horbiger, Rudolf Vogel, Fred Liewehr, Otto Tressler. Directed, written by Marischka, based on letters and diaries of Victoria and comedy by Sil-vara; camera (Technicolor), Bruno Mondi; editors, Hermann Leitner, A. Wayne Smith, Manuel San Fernando; music, Anton Profes. Previewed Jan. 17, '58. Running time, 107 MINS.

Victoria ...... Romy Schneider
Prince Albert ...... Adrian Hoven
Baroness Lehzen ...... Magda Schneider
Lord Melbourne, Prime Minister ...... Karl Ludwig Diehl
Duchess of Kent ...... Christyl Mardayn
Professor Landmann ...... Paul Horbiger
George, Palace Valet ...... Rudolf Vogel
Leopold, King of the Belgians ...... Fred Liewehr
Lord Conyngham ...... Alfred Neugebauer
Archbishop of Canterbury ...... Otto Tressler
Sir John Conroy ...... Stefan Skodler
Prince Henry of Orange ...... Peter Weck
Archduke Alexander of Russia ...... Rudolf Lenz
The Dean ...... Hans Thimig
Taglione, Dance Master ...... Peter Gerhard
Lady Flora Hastings ...... Elisabeth Epp
Lady Littelton ...... Hilde Wagener
Lady Lansdowne ...... Helene Lauterbock
Johann Strauss, Senior ...... Eduard Strauss

This Viennese import is a lavishly produced story of young Queen Victoria of England, from the moments immediately preceding her ascendancy to the throne to her proposal of marriage to Prince Albert of Saxe-Coburg. Its romantic theme carries strong distaff interest particularly, and film lends itself to exploitation as a class entry for the art house circuit. Film suffers, however, from inept dubbing into English.

The Ernst Marischka production, backed by stunning Technicolor, serves to introduce Romy Schneider, young Austrian actress, who registers a vivid impression in title role. Billed as based on the letters and diaries of Victoria and a comedy by Sil-vara, unfoldment, frequently is cloaked with light humor and even the pomp and ceremony attendant upon the theme do not detract from the fact that this is the story of a very charming young woman who becomes queen overnight and goes all out to make her rule humanitarian. Marischka, who also directs from his own screenplay, strikes a masterful note in his story-telling which communicates to the spectator.

Miss Schneider is finely cast as Victoria, a young princess bored with her lessons who assumes new dignity when confronted with responsibility for affairs of state. When she discovers marriage is being planned for her, she decides to skip the birthday party arranged for her and in an amusing Dover escapade meets Albert, without either knowing the identity of the other. Their romance blooms when finally she discovers he is the man chosen for her, and she returns to her palace.

Adrian Hoven scores as Albert in a light characterization, and Magda Schneider, star's mother, engagingly portrays the queen's confidante. As Lord Melbourne, the Prime Minister, Karl Ludwig Diehl delivers strongly, and also outstanding are Christl Mardayn, Fred Liewehr, Paul Horbiger and Rudolf Vogel.

Technical credits are highly creditable, including color camera work by Bruno Mondi, editing by Hermann Leitner, A. Wayne Smith and Manuel San Fernando, art direction by Fritz Juptner-Jonstorff, costumes by Gerdago and Dr. Leo Bei, music by Anton Profes.

Whit.

Fort Dobbs

Slow Indian shoot, with tv's Clint Walker and Virginia Mayo to pep up b.o. prospects.

Hollywood, Jan. 17.

Warner Bros. release of Martin Rackin production. Stars Clint Walker, Virginia Mayo, Brian Keith. Co-stars Richard Eyer; with Russ Conway, Michael Dante. Directed by Gordon Douglas; screenplay, Burt Kennedy and George W. George; camera, William Clothier; art director, Stanley Fleischer; film editor, Clarence Kolster; sound, Francis E. Stahl; music, Max Steiner. Previewed Jan. 15, '58. Running time, **93 MINS.**

Gar Davis .... Clint Walker
Celia Gray .... Virginia Mayo
Clett .... Brian Keith
Chad Gray .... Richard Eyer
Sheriff .... Russ Conway
Billings .... Michael Dante

Well produced but slow-moving, "Fort Dobbs" is short on talk, so-so on action and long on horseback. If it edges its way out of just-better-than-average filler fare, it likely will be due to the marquee value of star Clint Walker who canters along on heavy exposure through tv's "Cheyenne" series.

Martin Rackin has assembled a cast and crew that does more with the story than scripters Burt Kennedy and George W. George did. Director Gordon Douglas let himself in for a herculean task in trying to make an interesting 90-minute production out of action that would have been about equal to a 30-minute telesegment, minus commercials. Max Steiner's musical score and William Clothier's black-and-white photography are among the better credits.

There's no telling how many Comanches were done in by Walker and his sharp-shooting friends, but after the fifth raid, there was no contest. Whatever excitement picture generates is fairly well watered down by this time, due in great measure to excessive repetition.

An accused murderer, Walker escapes his lynchers by trading coats with an arrowed-in-the-back white man. When the posse finds the dead body, they take it for Walker who, by now, is well on his way to other parts. Stumbling on a farm manned by Virginia Mayo, he eventually leads the heroine and her son (Richard Eyer) away from the war-minded Indians. On the days-long trip, Miss Mayo discovers he traded coat and realizes it belongs to her husband. Seeing the arrow hole in the back, she takes it for a bullet hole and surmises Walker killed her mate. No amount of arguing will convince her she's wrong, not until the picture's all but over, anyway.

To complicate matters, Brian Keith, a dirty scoundrel with a sackful of 15-shot repeating rifles, moves in and out of the picture with utter haste.

Several battles later, with fully 45 minutes taken up in the ride to Fort Dobbs, the trio arrives. In the next battle, the Redmen have the edge, and Walker rides for help. He finds Keith, shoots him as he must, brings the repeaters back, and the Indians are done in again. Somehow, Walker's heroism softens the hunting sheriff, and he, Miss Mayo and Eyer go off to Santa Fe with highly familiar prospects in sight.

Walker, a big, good-looking guy, is the shy stranger-type and, in that vein, comes across well. Miss Mayo has performed better, but she's still a fine-looking woman. Keith's rascally performance is the most interesting, and young Eyer, as usual, is admirable.

Ron.

Flood Tide
(C'SCOPE)

Grimly offbeat story of a crippled lad with macabre fixations. Dim prospects

Hollywood, Jan. 17.

Universal release of Robert Arthur production. Stars George Nader, Cornell Borchers, Michel Ray; features Judson Pratt, Joanna Moore, Charles E. Arnt, Russ Conway. Directed by Abner Biberman. Screenplay, Dorothy Cooper; based on story by Barry Trivers; camera, Arthur E. Trling; editor, Ted J. Kent; music, Henry Mancini, William Lava. Previewed Jan. 14, '58. Running time, **82 MINS.**

Steve Martin .... George Nader
Anne Gordon .... Cornell Borchers
David Gordon .... Michel Ray
Harvey Thornwald .... Judson Pratt
Barbara Brooks .... Joanna Moore
Mr. Appleby .... Charles E. Arnt
Bill Holleran .... Russ Conway
Detective Lieutenant ...... John Morley
John Brighton .... John Maxwell
District Attorney .... Carl Bensen
Beverly .... Della Malzarn
Charlie .... Hugh Lawrence

The havoc wrought by the warped mind of a crippled boy motivates the grim action of this offering, never conducive to entertainment. Even for the program market film is a weak entry of the also-ran category.

Robert Arthur production makes a triangle situation out of the boy, Michel Ray, insanely jealous of his long-suffering mother, Cornell Borchers, and her relations with the man next door, George Nader, who wants to marry her. Unpleasant subject is inclined to overmelodramatics, although actingwise the characterizations are well enough drawn. Direction by Abner Biberman meets the demands of the Dorothy Cooper screenplay.

Practically the entire plot revolves around the lad and efforts of Nader to swing him over to his side. Nader also is out to get boy to admit he lied in testimony which sent a man to prison for murder. He finally succeeds after nearly being killed himself by the youngster when lad swings a boom on him aboard a yacht and knocks him overboard.

Nader handles his role convincingly and Miss Borchers takes over her frustrated character in stride, but any acting honors go to young Ray, restrained in his vicious character. Joanna Moore appears briefly as Nader's blonde would-be girl-friend, and Judson Pratt plays a specialist who finally restores the boy to normalcy.

Arthur E. Arling's photography leads off competent technical credits.

Whit.

Davy
(BRITISH—COLOR)

Slim backstage comedy designed to exploit the comic and vocal talents of Harry Secombe, a No. 1 British tv and vaude comic; comes off reasonably well.

London, Jan. 14.

Metro release of a Michael Balcon (Basil Dearden) production. Stars Harry Secombe, Ron Randell and Alexander
a-n2 123456 7890$ 123456 7830
Knox. Directed by Michael Relph. Screenplay, William Rose; camera, Douglas Slocombe; editor, Peter Tanner. At Metro Private Theatre, London. Running time, **82 MINS.**

Davy .... Harry Secombe
George .... Ron Randell
Uncle Pat .... George Relph
Gwen .... Susan Shaw
Eric .... Bill Owen
Tim .... Peter Frampton
Sid Giles .... Alexander Knox
Joanna .... Adele Leigh
Miss Carstairs .... Isabel Dean
Herbie .... Kenneth Connor
Waitresses .... Gladys Henson, Joan Sins
Mrs. Magillicuddy .... Clarkson Rose
Jerry .... George Moon
Stage Doorkeeper ...... Campbell Singer

Harry Secombe, one of Britain's top tv, radio and vaude comics, makes an amiable though not sensational pic debut in "Davy," a film designed to exploit his ability as a yock-raiser but also to utilize his voice, which is of operatic class. One of Secombe's problems as an ace entertainer is that his two talents are likely to clash disconcertingly and William Rose's slim anecdote cunningly brings out this point. "Davy" is a gentle and dignified comedy that should do well in the U.K. thanks to Secombe's popularity. If his name attracts customers in the U.S., there is no doubt that he will be hailed as very promising new screen material.

Secombe is shown as the key member of a family vaude act playing the lesser halls and optimistically hoping for a break. It is a slapstick affair which seems unlikely ever to make the big time. Secombe gets the chance of an audition at Covent Garden and is offered a contract. He realizes that, without him, The Mad Morgans would fold and he turns down the operatic offer in order to keep the act together.

Script offers Secombe plenty of opportunity to put over his warm, kindly personality both with wisecracks and in an uproarious slapstick sequence on the vaude stage, involving a liberal use of paint and whitewash. It also enables him to sing a pop song in the act and an operatic aria at the Covent Garden audition, which he does splendidly. Operatic singer Adele Leigh is also pleasantly dragged in as an excuse for her singing as another auditionee and also for a slight romantic interest.

Alexander Knox gives an urbane, witty performance as a distinguished conductor and Ron Randell, Bill Owen, George Relph and Susan Shaw play the rest of "The Mad Morgans" as if they were all veteran vaude performers.

Michael Relph's direction is a shade leisurely but the atmosphere of second-class vaudeville is admirably caught. Shooting took place at both Collins Music Hall and Covent Garden Opera House so the settings are completely authentic.

Secombe can be reasonably well satisfied with his entry into British pix, but finding vehicles for him in the future is going to provide scribes with problems.

Rich.

Violent Playground
(BRITISH)

Very sound juve delinquency semi-documentary with first-rate all round acting and smooth direction; good b.o. bet for most houses.

London, Jan. 14.

Rank (Michael Ralph) production and release. Stars Stanley Baker, Peter Cushing, Anne Heywood and David McCallum. Directed by Basil Dearden. Screenplay, James Kennaway; editor, Arthur Stevens; camera, Reginald Wyer. At Odeon, Leicester Square, London. Running time, **108 MINS.**

Truman .... Stanley Baker
Cathie .... Anne Heywood
Johnny Murphy .... David McCallum
Priest .... Peter Cushing
Sgt. Walker .... John Slater
Heaven .... Clifford Evans
Superintendent .... Moultrie Kelsall
Chief Inspector ...... George A. Cooper
Mary Murphy .... Brona Boland
Patrick Murphy .... Fergal Boland
Alexander .... Michael Chow
Primrose .... Tsai Chin
Slick .... Sean Lynch

The problem of juve delinquency is no new theme for pix, but "Violent Playground" is one of the better offerings, bringing a sincere semi-documentary touch to the matter. James Kennaway has written a human and literate screenplay which is convincingly acted against authentic Liverpool backgrounds. Result is an absorbing film that works up to an overlong but tense climax. The film should do well in average houses, though for U.S. it is a bit light on star value.

Film concerns an experiment made in Liverpool in 1949, which, according to the city's chief cop, has paid off handsomely. Policemen have become Juvenile Liaison Officers whose job is to keep an eye on mischievous youngsters and steer them away from crime.

Stanley Baker gives a vigorous and sympathetic performance as a cop who is taken off the investigation of a series of unexplained fires for this work. Despite ribbing from his colleagues, he settles down in the job and finds it absorbing and rewarding. He becomes particularly involved with one family but, while helping the older brother, a teenager who runs a gang of young hoodlums, is responsible for the arson.

The young "firebug" is caught in the act but makes a getaway with a gun and hides out in a school classroom, using the kids as hostages. The police efforts to get the youngster out before he goes berserk with the gun makes a thrilling climax, with the terror of the moppets being extremely well brought out by director Basil Dearden.

Apart from Baker's work there are a number of other very creditable performances, notably David McCallum as the young delinquent, Peter Cushing as a very serious but wholehearted priest, Clifford Evans as a schoolmaster and John Slater, Moultrie Kelsall and George A. Cooper as varied cop types.

Getting her first big chance, as David McCallum's elder sister, Anne Heywood shows up as one of the most promising young actresses lately to be introduced into British pix. The girl has warmth and charm and is extremely easy on the optics. Location scenes have been splendidly planned and lensed so that the full flavor of the heart of a city is brought out.

Dearden has not forgotten story value in his direction, yet at the same time he not let occasional splashes of melodrama to cloud the fact that this is largely a film with a documentary approach. His handling of the children is particularly tactful and human.

Rich.

Une Parisienne
(FRENCH—COLOR)
Paris, Jan. 14.
Cinedis release of Ariane-Filmsonor production. Stars Brigitte Bardot, Charles Boyer, Henri Vidal, Andre Luguet. Directed by Michel Boisrond. Screenplay, Annette Wademant, Jean Aurel; camera (Technicolor), Marcel Grignon; editor, Claudine Bouche. Running time, **90 MINS.**

Brigitte	Brigitte Bardot
Michel	Henri Vidal
President	Andre Luguet
Prince Consort	Charles Boyer
Greta	Nadia Gray
Morique	Madeleine Lebeau
Caroline	Claude Maurier
Husband	Noel Roquevert

Since Brigitte Bardot, now known here in her star brackets as B.B. (which means "baby"), made it big in the U.S. in a vehicle that got few good reviews, this light, saucy comedy should also carry a real Yank potential. In the American situation comedy vein, a la Francaise, this has B.B. in several near-nude scenes fetching and insouciant but keeping her unsullied in true comedy fashion. She almost cheats on her husband but not quite. The name of Charles Boyer could also give this marquee values in the U.S. Dubbing would be in order.

Like America's Marilyn Monroe, B.B. seems to be going from a loose-jointed sex symbol to a competent actress. Her comedics in this are well timed, and a personality is emerging which should turn her into an able star asset of international scope.

In this Miss Bardot chases her father's ambitious secretary (Henri Vidal). Her father is the president of the French Council, and protocol is worked into this sex chase for some good comic asides. She gets him but is still jealous, and decides to cheat on him with a charming visiting Prince Consort (Boyer).

Director Michel Boisrond has given this crispness and a slightly bitter tang that keeps it rolling, with the undraped charms of B.B. naturally an asset. Vidal is right as the harassed secretary and Andre Luguet, as the father, has the proper note of Gallic tact and distress. Boyer is perfect in his brief role. Color is good as are production values and technical aspects. *Mosk.*

La Guerra Empieza En Cuba
(War Starts In Cuba)
(SPANISH—COLOR)
Madrid, Jan. 14.
Izaro Films release of Planeta Films production, for Cesareo Gonzalez. Directed by Manuel Mur Oti. Based on comedy by Victor Ruiz Iriarte; screenplay, Vicente Coello and Manuel Mur Oti. Camera (Eastmancolor), Manuel Berenguer; music, Salvador Ruiz de Luna. Features Emma Penella, Gustavo Rojo, Roberto Rey, Jesus Tordesilla, Matilde Munoz Sampedro. At Carlos III, Madrid. Running time, **107 MINS.**

Emma Penella stars in a double role incarnating twin sisters of inverse moral attitudes. But comedy possibilities often take a back seat while director Mur Oti holds on an overdose of double image trick effects. Script by Vincente Coello and Mur Oti, based on Ruiz Iriate's successful stage play, is also weighted by added yesteryear songs to satisfy local market fetish for cuple tunes.

The title serves to date the return from Cuba of cabaret warbler Juanita, enroute to meet the spitting-image sister Adelaida, now a matronly, domineering prude spouse of a provincial governor. Provincial mentality, deftly caricatured in secondary situations, is subjected to comic confusion by violent contrasts of sisters mistakenly identified. In the melee, first lady of Badajoz sheds self-restraint for more feminine ways.

Miss Penella is convincing, often delightful, in a taxing dual performance. She gets firstrate support from handsome Gustavo Rojo, as the dashing hussar captain, Roberto Rey, as governor, and Jesus Tordesilla, as a modernminded Marquis. Luisa de Cordoba's offstage vocals (she dubs for Penella) are easy on the ear.

Manuel Berenguer's trick photo effects hit the mark but the cameraman's usual quality color is not attained in this one. Costuming and art work are well above average. Slanted to Spanish-language taste, pic will please locally and, with pruning, could yield fair returns in the Latin American market. *Hawk.*

Le Chomeur de Clochemerle
(The Unemployed Man of Clochemerle)
(FRENCH)
Paris, Jan. 14.
FIDES production and release. Stars Fernandel; features Maria Mauban, Ginette Leclerc, Rellys, Beatrice Bretty, Georges Chamarat, Henri Vilbert. Directed by Jean Boyer. Screenplay, Jean Manse, Boyer, Gabriel Chevalier; camera, Charles Suin; editor, R. Giordoni. At Biarritz, Paris. Running time, **90 MINS.**

Tistin	Fernandel
Janette	Maria Mauban
Zozotte	Ginette Leclere
Sexton	Rellys
Priest	Georges Chamarat
Mayor	Henri Vilbert

This is a gimmicky opus for Fernandel in which the comedian is depicted as the only unemployed man in a small town. When the townspeople revolt at paying taxes for his upkeep, he ingratiates himself by becoming indispensable in doing odd jobs for all the women. After some complications he ends up with the pretty town widow as wife.

Fernandel eases through this with his usual bonhommie, but the telegraphed script as well as the bucolic, sectional humor makes this limited for Yank chances. Director Jean Boyer has kept this moving in spite of the obvious folksy aspects.

Technical credits are good. Besides the competent comedics of Fernandel, there is Ginette Leclerc in a ferocious role as the town joy girl which is much too strong for the otherwise obvious happenings. On the Fernandel name, and its general theme, this might be exploitable for secondary U.S. spots. *Mosk.*

Nachts Im Gruenen Kakadu
(At Green Cocktatoo By Night)
(GERMAN-SONGS-COLOR)
Berlin, Jan. 14.
Europa release of Real (Walter Koppel) production. Stars Marika Roekk, Dieter Borsche; features Gunnar Moeller, Renate Ewert. Directed by Georg Jacoby. Screenplay, Curt J. Braun and Helmuth M. Backhaus; camera (Eastmancolor), Willy Winterstein; music, Michael Jary; sets, Herbert Kirchhoff and Albrecht Becker; editor, Klaus Dudenhoefer. At UFA Pavillon, Berlin. Running time, **97 MINS.**

Irene Wagner	Marika Roekk
Doktor Maybach	Dieter Borsche
Hilde Wagner	Renate Ewert
Knut Peters	Gunnar Moeller
Eduard Reichmann	Hans Nielsen
Aunt Henriette	Loni Heuser
Uncle Otto	Willy Maertens
Miss Koldeway W	Trude Hesterberg

This rates a cheer for Marika Roekk. Her comeback via this Real production is more than just remarkable. Miss Roekk, idolized Hungarian-born German musical star of the 1935-1945 era, is dancing and singing in this like a vet trouper. Having been absent from the German screen for a number of years now, her comeback must be regarded as a triumph as well as a victory over her age. Film makes it obvious that none of the present German musical stars reaches the standard of Miss Roekk's dancing abilities.

Miss Roekk's experienced director-husband Georg Jacoby wisely didn't take the role she portrays too seriously. Often it seems as if she is poking fun at herself. Another plus of this film is that cheap sentimentalities are avoided. The results are undoubtedly beyond the German musical average.

Sets are quite lavish, the Eastmancolor is very good and the cast well chosen. Even the story isn't too banal if compared with other German features of the same category.

The Real company has achieved here a top hit for the domestic market. Pic also may do well in some foreign areas.

Story centers around Miss Roekk who owns an institute that teaches good manners. Yet it is way in debt. Things begin to look rosier when Miss Roekk inherits a money-spilling nightclub called "Green Cocktatoo." She starts leading a double life; In the daytime she's the good Emily Post; at night, she's dancing and singing at the Cocktatoo for money reasons. This produces some hilarious complications which see even the police and psychiatrists involved. Miss Roekk gets her man (Dieter Borsche), who shows up as an amateur musician in her night spot.

Michael Jary's melodies are easy on the ear. Film's technical standard is satisfactory. *Hans.*

Quand La Femme S'En Mele
(When the Woman Butts In)
(FRENCH)
Paris, Jan. 14.
Cinedis release of Regina production. Stars Edwige Feuillere, Bernard Blier, Jean Servais; features Pierre Mondy, Jean Debucourt, Yves Deniaud, Sophie Daumier. Directed by Yves Allegret. Screenplay, Charles Spaak, Jean Meckert from novel by Jean Amila; camera, Andre Germain; editor, Ginette Baudin. At Marignan, Paris. Running time, **90 MINS.**

Maine	Edwige Feuillere
Godot	Jean Servais
Felix	Bernard Blier
Jo	Alain Delon
Colette	Sophie Daumier
Gigi	Pascal Roberts
Inspector	Pierre Mondy
Boby	Yves Deniaud
Coudert	Jean Debucourt

This pic is another in the present gangster cycle now in full swing here. Cast has marquee value while the plot is adroitly fashioned to make this solid for local returns. It is less likely for U.S. arties, for its attempt at parody and straight violence and many shenanigans do not quite blend. This leaves the pic in the cops-and-robbers category. Its slick front could make this dualer fare however.

A classy gun moll (Edwige Feuillere) gets a visit from her first husband and her grown daughter. It is a bad time because her present lover (Jean Servais) is in the middle of a gang fight. To top this, the ex-husband is out to get revenge on a rich man who had burned down a store for insurance. All is worked out with enough corpses, gunplay and revenge assured.

Miss Feuillere, usually the "grande dame" in Gallic pix, now does a lowdown woman with class but overdoes it a bit. Servais has the right grimness while Blier is excellent as the revengeful bourgeois. A couple of youngsters, Alain Delon and Sophie Daumier, look like future film material. Director Yves Allegret keeps this moving, gives it good mounting and makes this one of the better gangland entries. Production values are fine. *Mosk.*

Oregon Passage
(C'SCOPE—COLOR)

Good Cavalry-Indians yarn for satisfaction in action market.

Hollywood, Jan. 21.

Allied Artists release of Lindsley Parsons production. Stars John Ericson, Lola Albright, Toni Gerry, Edward Platt; features Judith Ames, H. M. Wynant, John Shepodd, Walter Barnes, Paul Fierro, Harvey Stephens. Directed by Paul Landres. Screenplay, Jack DeWitt, from novel by Gordon D. Shirreffs; camera (DeLuxe-color), Ellis Carter; editor, Maury Wright; music, Paul Dunlap. Previewed Jan. 20, '58. Running time, **80 MINS.**

Lieut. Niles Ord .... John Ericson
Sylvia Dane .... Lola Albright
Little Deer .... Toni Gerry
Roland Dane .... Edward Platt
Marion .... Judith Ames
Black Eagle .... H. M. Wynant
Lieut. Baird Dobson .... Jon Shepodd
Sgt. Jed Ershick .... Walter Barnes
Nato .... Paul Fierro
Capt. Boyson .... Harvey Stephens

The U.S. Cavalry gets a run for its money in this story of the early Northwest, when peace depended upon the capture of the sole holdout against burying the hatchet. Film is an interesting actioner with the type of movement, backed by effective use of CinemaScope and color to lend spectacular pictorial values, which comes off as good entertainment for the playdates at which it's aimed.

Paul Landres' direction of the Lindsley Parsons production is fast, fitting the rugged elements of the Jack DeWitt screenplay. Picture was lensed in the Bend country of Oregon, which provides atmospheric backgrounds for this tale of the cavalry's search for Black Eagle, the Shoshone warrior who refused to smoke the peace-pipe and thus bring quiet to the Cascades region of 1871. The Shoshone character is based upon true-life incident; thus film benefits by historical overtones.

John Ericson plays a young cavalry lieutenant intent upon capture of the Shoshone chief, whose plans are constantly being opposed by his new commanding officer, a martinet insanely jealous of his wife, whom he thinks had an affair years before with Ericson. Commandant's ignorance of Indian warfare leads to several tragic incidents which wipe out patrols, despite Ericson's warning. When his wife is captured by Black Eagle's men, the commandant tries to rescue her, but both are killed. Ericson makes use of slick strategy in defending the fort against an attack by the Shoshone, and he kills Black Eagle in a savage hand-to-hand fight.

Entire cast perform in acceptable fashion, Ericson seen to advantage in a hard-hitting role. Edward Platt is properly aggressive as his superior, who allows personal feelings to color his judgment, and Lola Albright scores as his wife, willing to doublecross her husband to get away from him. As an Indian girl whom Ericson rescues from the Shoshone camp, Toni Gerry is in for romance with Ericson, well cast in character. H. M. Wynant is colorful as Black Eagle, and balance of cast are okay.

Ellis Carter's color photography is particularly outstanding, Maury Wright's editing is tight and music by Paul Dunlap well done. *Whit.*

Chase a Crooked Shadow
(BRITISH)

Smooth absorbing thriller drama with excellent star performances and more twists than a corkscrew. Good booking for most houses.

London, Jan. 21.

Associated British-Pathe release of Associated Dragon Films production. Stars Richard Todd, Anne Baxter, Herbert Lom. Directed by Michael Anderson. Screenplay by David D. Osborn and Charles Sinclair; camera, Erwin Hiller; editor, Gordon Pilkington; music, Matyas Seiber. At Warner Theatre, London. Running time, **92 MINS.**

Ward .... Richard Todd
Kimberley .... Anne Baxter
Vargas .... Herbert Lom
Chandler Brisson .... Alexander Knox
Mrs. Whitman .... Faith Brook
Carlos .... Alan Tilvern
Maria .... Thelma d'Aguiar

"Chase a Crooked Shadow" is a glossy, well-directed drama that has its fair quota of absurdities which occasionally strain credulity to the limit. Nevertheless, there are enough twists and artfully planned kicks to keep most audiences guessing. Both in Britain and U.S. "Shadow" should pay off as a safe booking.

The yarn concerns Anne Baxter as an heiress who becomes a frightened lady when Richard Todd arrives at her Costa Brava hangout and claims to be her brother, who Miss Baxter knows was killed in a car crash in South Africa a year before. What is the purpose of his visit? Is he a crook? A fortune hunter? Todd builds up as much evidence that even the local chief cop is convinced that his story is true. There begins a nightmare of terror for the star as she believes the plot is to drive her insane and then murder her over a little matter of costly diamonds missing from her late father's business. Final twist is a sock climax.

Director Michael Anderson has carefully built up the suspense and at one time or other even the most case hardened patron will be wondering about motives and who is really double crossing who. There are also the advantages of the breathtaking Costa Brava scenery and a rousing racing car sequence. Anderson, an ex-cutter, has edited the film with Gordon Pilkington very ingeniously and there is one sudden closeup which is as dramatically effective as anything that has been seen on the screen.

Erwin Hillier's lensing is top-notch and, to tie up with the title, skilful use of shadows helps to bring out the eerie atmosphere at which the director is aiming. Acting throughout by a small cast is smooth. Miss Baxter gives a convincing display as a young woman nearly off her rocker with fear. Todd is a suave villain and Faith Brook also does a useful job as his sinister female companion. Herbert Lom turns in one of his subtle studies as a Spanish chief of police and Alexander Knox fills a comparatively small part with complete competence.

"Shadow" has most of the ingredients needed to keep audiences absorbed and the combination of Todd and Miss Baxter, plus Michael Anderson's name as director will certainly give a lift to the film in British theatres. *Rich.*

The Beggar Student
('Der Bettelstudent')
(GERMAN—COLOR)
(*English Titles*)

Okay escapist entertainment with an art house potential, but lack of names may hurt.

Sam Baker Associates Inc. release of a Carlton-Film production. Stars Gerhard Riedmann, Waltraut Haas; features Elma Karlowa, Ellen Kessler, Alice Kessler. Directed by Werner Jacobs. Screenplay, Fritz Boettger, from operetta by Carl Milloecker; music, Bruno Uher; camera (Eastmancolor), Ernst W. Kalinke, Heinz Schnackerz. Previewed N.Y., Jan. 22, '58. Running time, **97 MINS.**

Symon Rymanowisz .... Gerhard Riedmann
Countess Laura .... Waltraut Haas
Countess Bronislawa .... Elma Karlowa
Katya .... Ellen Kessler
Mira .... Alice Kessler
Count Kaminsky .... Dick Price
Countess Palmatica .... Fita Benkhoff
Jan Janicki .... Gunther Philipp
Col. Ollendorff .... Gustav Knuth
Enterich .... Rudolf Vogel
Major Wangenheim .... Karl Lieffen
Lieutenant Schweinitz .... Jost Siethoff

Wine, women and song have always been a forte of German and Austrian film-makers. "The Beggar Student," based on the operetta by Carl Milloecker, falls in that tradition. For there are lilting melodies, attractive femmes and an air of fraternity throughout the 97 minutes running time of this German-made Carlton-Film production.

If it can't be denied that the book is dated and the Fritz Boettger screenplay does little to freshen the original, film, nonetheless, has an art house potential for those patrons in search of escapist entertainment. It will need strong selling since the cast is composed of unknowns for the American market.

Import, incidentally, is the second edition of the Milloecker operetta for UFA released a black and white version in 1936 with Marika Rokk in the top femme role. Current adaptation, filmed in Eastman Color, naturally takes on a lavish aura due to a wealth of hues. Print has adequate English titles for those who don't savvy German.

An 18th-century period piece, yarn is basically one of those boy-meets-girl affairs in which the lovers finally overcome a multitude of adversity to live happily ever after in the best fairy tale tradition. Villain of the piece is a colonel whose affections have been rejected by a Countess.

As a means of revenge the colonel deceives her into wedding a beggar student. But things aren't so tough since the student actually is a captain in the Polish army and the couple have found true love.

Gerhard Riedmann, who portrays the title role, dashingly interprets the part and sings in fine voice. Waltraut Haas, as the countess, pleasantly moves through the creaky plot. Elma Karlowa provides occasional comic relief as Miss Haas' always hungry sister. Of a decided visual asset are the Kessler Twins, Ellen and Alice, who dance most appealingly.

Gustav Knuth does a stock characterization of the colonel's role while Dick Price, Fita Benkhoff and Gunther Philipp, among others, provide okay support in lesser roles. Werner Jacobs' direction paces the proceedings nicely despite a lag here and there while the color lensing of Ernst W. Kalinke and Heinz Schnackerz is good. Bruno Uher's musical arrangements are highly listenable. *Gilb.*

Japanese Festival

The Sleepy Family

Toei Motion Picture Co. release of Koichi Akagawa production. Stars Naotaro Nakamura, Noriko Haruoka, Snsho Matsumoto. Directed by Hideji Tashiro. Screenplay, Nobuo Shimizu; original story, Sayolo Nakada. Presented in N.Y., at Museum of Modern Art during Japanese Film Week, Jan. 24, '58. Running time, **45 MINS.**

The Japanese apparently have a way with short films and "The Sleepy Family" is an excellent example. The 45-minute featurette is simple; yet it is amazingly appealing and touching.

It tells the story of an improverished family who through love and understanding manage to overcome economic setbacks. There's the hard-working father who likes his saki, the mother who tends house, the cute teenage daughter who is studying to be a teacher, the bright kid brother, and the mischievous baby sister.

The family's livelihood depends on a horse and when the horse, employed for the father's modest hauling business, dies, the family unites to meet the economic disaster. The father becomes a laborer, the mother goes to work making artifical flowers, the teenage daughter gets a job in a factory, and the two youngsters perform odd chores around the house.

At school, the young son submits a composition in a contest. It's about his family and their economic problems and how they're all so sleepy because of their many tasks. His entry wins first prize and is to be broadcast over the radio. At first ashamed because the son had aired the family's woes, the mother and father are proud and pleased after the broadcast when they receive the congratulations of their friends. The composition serves to point up to the family the love that exists in the group.

Naotaro Nakamura, Noriko Haruoka and Sensho Matsumoto are all excellent in their portrayals. Much of the credit for the picture's success is due Sayolo Makada for the original story, Nobuo Shimizu for the screenplay, and Hideji Tashiro for his sensitive direction. Picture might well go over as an opener in an art situation in the U.S. *Holl.*

The Lighthouse

Shochiku Co. production. Stars Hideko Takamine, Keiji Sada; features Masako Arisawa, Katsuo Nakamura, Hiroko Ito, Shizue Natsukawa. Directed and written by Keisuke Kinoshita; camera (color), Hiroyuki Kusuda; music, Chuji Kinoshita. Running time, **153 MINS.**

Though it was a top grosser in Japan (where another 2,000 feet were tacked on to the already long runningtime), "The Lighthouse" isn't much of an entry for the States. It has many things to commend it—from the performances down to the exquisite photography—but this cavalcade, telling the story of a lighthouse keeper and his wife from 1932 through 1957, moves at a tedious pace and it'd have to be drastically edited for American audiences.

Top roles are well filled by Keiji Sada and the beautiful Hideko Takamine and the production values of the film, which was shot all over Japan, are evident. Yet, the journey from one lighthouse to the other barely holds interest after a while, and there is such a profusion of climaxes that it's hard to stay with it.

Despite many emotional and weepy scenes, the plight of the characters never becomes real and director Keisuke Kinoshita tends to overdirect. For Western tastes, the love story doesn't come through, and what tenderness there is expressed mostly in the dialog which at times sounds trite. Also, the English titles don't read very well.

Lenser Hiroyuki Kusuda comes through with striking shots, in excellent Eastman color, and the passage of time is well handled in terms of the lead characters. It's an ambitious production that badly needs trimming. *Hift.*

Emperor Meiji and The Great Russo-Japanese War

Shin Toho Co. release of Mitsugi Okura production. Stars Kanjuro Arashi; features Jyun Tazaki, Kan Hayashi. Directed by Kunio Watanobe. Reviewed at Museum of Modern Art, N.Y., Jan. 23, '58. Running time, 113 MINS.

A Nipponese counterpart to "War and Peace," this account of the Russo-Japanese war of 1904-05 rates as an ambitious undertaking in terms of physical production but is primitive in motion picture technique. It could hardly be considered worthwhile for any but partisans of the film industry of the Orient. Commercial values in the states are nil, excepting, of course, regular Japanese outlets.

Feature undertakes to relate Russian aggressiveness shortly after the turn of the century, a benevolent Japanese emperor who authorizes war after extensive effort to effect peaceful settlement of differences, the great battle at Port Arthur and Japanese victory.

Kunio Watanabe, the director, has framed the battle scenes competently but the performances of his main players and the behaviour of the soldiers are so obviously staged as render the work ineffective.

Further detracting from realism is the use of an off-screen voice describing what's going on on the screen, this in lieu of the usual titles translating the dialog. In the instances where titles are used, the brightly-colored type set against the illuminated screen is difficult to read.

Numerous walkouts at the screening of "Russo-Japanese War" when shown during the Jap Film Festival at N.Y.'s Museum of Modern Art attest to the production's inadequateness. *Gene.*

The Lord Takes a Bride

Toei Motion Picture Co. release of Hiroshi Okawa production. Stars Ryutara Ohtomo, Yumiko Hasegawa, Hitomi Wakahara, Eitaro Shindo, Takshi Shimura. Directed by Sadatsugu Matsuda. Screenplay, Fumio Nakayama; camera (C'Scope), Shintaro Kawasaki; Estmn-Toei color. Presented in N.Y., at Modern Museum of Art during Japanese Film Week, Jan. 24, '58. Running time, 86 MINS.

"The Lord Takes a Bride," the first CinemaScope film produced in Japan, is apparently an example of the country's popular film fare. Viewed tongue-in-check from the American standpoint, it is a frequently amusing period piece as the hero out-Flynns Errol in feats of derring-do.

A young lord leaves his domain and travels incognito to the nearest large city to perform his filial duty—the search for a bride. A naive sort of a guy, he is fleeced by various characters. During his adventures he rescues the daughters of a rich merchant who are about to be kidnapped by renegade samurai. It's love at first sight for the bride-seeking lord, but his inexperienced, oafish wooing of

one of the girls hardly gets him to first base.

There's a smashing climax, however, when the girls again fall in the hands of the bandits. Our hero arrives in time to rescue the girls as they are tied to a stake and single-handedly knocks over several dozen villains. It has all the earmarks of an American cowboy-Indian picture.

There are good performances by Ryutaro Ohtomo, Yumiko Hasegawa and Hitomi Nakahara, all of whom have captured the spirit of the film. Miss Nakahara is a looker who exudes considerable charm.

Technically it's superb. And once again the Japanese reveal their mastery of color photography. It's not the kind of a picture that will go over in the U.S. either in general or art situations, but it has its moments as a demonstration of what the masses in Japan probably go for. *Holl.*

Lafayette Escadrille

Good young team in frank World War I drama. Plenty of romance. Good b.o. prospects.

Hollywood, Jan. 31.
Warners release of William A. Wellman Production. Stars Tab Hunter, Etchika Choureau; introduces Bill Wellman Jr.; Jody McCrea, Dennis Devine; features Marcel Dalio, David Janssen, Paul Fix, Veola Vonn, Will Hutchins, Clint Eastwood, Bob Hover, Tom Laughlin, Brett Halsey, Henry Nakamura, Maurice Marsac, Raymond Bailey, George Nardelli. Produced and directed by William A. Wellman. Screenplay, A. S. Fleischman; from a story by William A. Wellman; camera, William Clothier; music, Leonard Rosenman; editor, Owen Marks. Reviewed at the studio, Jan. 28, '58. Running time, 96 MINS.
Thad Walker .... Tab Hunter
Renee .... Etchika Choureau
Bill Wellman .... Bill Wellman Jr.
Tim Hitchcock .... Jody McCrea
Red Scanlon .... Dennis Devine
Drillmaster .... Marcel Dalio
Duke Sinclaire .... David Janssen
U. S. General .... Paul Fix
The Madam .... Veola Vonn
Dave Putnam .... Will Hutchins
George Moseley .... Clint Eastwood
Dave Judd .... Bob Hover
Arthur Bluthenthal .... Tom Laughlin
Frank Baylies .... Brett Halsey
Jimmy .... Henry Nakamura
Sgt. Parris .... Maurice Marsac
Concierge .... George Nardelli

"Lafayette Escadrille" is producer-director William A. Wellman's nostalgic and affectionate memoir of the American volunteer air squadron in France during World War I and his own yesteryears. Despite its title, it is more a love story than an action story; a very frank and personal account of one young American's romance with a French girl of the streets, ingredients that should add up to strong boxoffice.

There are some combat scenes, although not as many as might be imagined, and although the toll of war is gravely presented, the accent is on love. So, while the title, "Lafayette Escadrille" may not have the same exciting connotations for those under 35 (or 45?) as it has for an older generation, the top-starred team of Tab Hunter and newcomer Etchika Choureau will appeal strongly to younger fans. The Warner Bros. film also has many other good exploitation value, including the three young players who are "introduced," as the billing has it: Bill Wellman Pr., Jody McCrea and Dennis Devine.

A. S. Fleischman's screenplay, based on a story by Wellman, has Hunter as a bouyant youth driven from home by his father's harsh discipline, leaving mental scars that later get him in trouble. He runs away to Paris and joins the French Foreign Legion, along with Bill Wellman Jr. (playing his father), David Janssen and Jody McCrea.

Before leaving for training with the Escadrille, Hunter and Miss Choureau fall in love, although the young woman is what the French sometimes refer to as "une poule." But after falling in love with Hunter, she abandons the oldest profession to take a legitimate job.

Their romance develops as a counterpoint to Hunter's training, training which ends when a French instructor strikes him, knocks down the Frenchman and winds up with a prison term staring him in the face. His pals arrange his escape, he hides out in Paris and eventually persuades an American general (the U.S. has since entered the war) to arrange his transfer to the U.S. Air Force.

The plot structure is weakened by Hunter's reasons for being in

the Escadrille and his subsequent reason for socking the French drill instructor. This special motivation makes the plot seem unfavorably similar to those of a dozen of youth problem pictures. This is more than balanced, however, by the skill with which Wellman has captured the fresh idealism and goodwill of these young men who went so far to die.

His shot of the young fliers sleeping in their crude bunks at the French air station is a memorable vignette for which Wellman's voice the commentary as he calls their roll, many of them destined to sleep forever in France. The aerial photography by William Clothier is stunning. The planes, some of which look about as substantial as the kind kids send aloft with rubber bands for locomotive power, are caught in a way that shows why flying in those days was such an intensely personal experience. The shots as the wounded planes fall to earth like stricken sparrows are vividly done.

Most important, Wellman makes it believable that Hunter would fall in love and marry a young woman who he knows has been a prostitute. There is even symbolism in the meeting of the vigorous, idealistic young America and the weary, cynical France. Wellman also uses the language difference—Frenchmen speaking French, Americans speaking American—to work for him, for tenderness in the romantic scenes, and for conflict. It becomes not a story handicap but a propellant.

Hunter is convincing as the errant flier and Miss Choureau, her sweet, transparent face aglow, is a major factor in making her difficult role strong and believable. Young Wellman does a good job and McCrea is fine as Tommy Hitchcock, one of the real personages involved. Dennis Devine, David Janssen, Will Hutchins and Clint Eastwood are among the youthful standouts, and they get solid support from the more experienced Marcel Dalio, Veola Vonn and Maurice Marsac.

One aspect about "Escadrille" in these days of foreign locations is that it was shot entirely in California although the whole story—except for a brief introductory scene—takes place in France. The atmosphere created by art director John Beckman and set decorator Ralph Hurst shows how effectively this can be done by skilled hands, aided by a cameraman such as Clothier. Perceptive editing by Owen Marks' and first-rate sound by John Kean are also production assets, as is Leonard Rosenman's imaginative and varied musical score. *Pow.*

Summer Love

Successor to last year's successful "Rock Pretty Baby" with same characters and many of same cast and should be equally favored by teenaged audiences. Loaded with songs.

Hollywood, Jan. 31.
Universal release of William Grady Jr. production. Stars John Saxon, Molly Bee, Rod McKuen, Judy Meredith, Jill St. John; co-stars John Wilder, George Winslow; features Fay Wray, Edward C. Platt, Shelley Fabares, Gordon Gebert, Beverly Washburn, Bob Courtney, Troy Donahue, Hylton Socher, Marjorie Durant, Walter Reed. Directed by Charles Haas. Screenplay, William Raynor and Herbert Margolis; camera, Carl E. Guthrie; editor, Tony Martinelli; music, Henry Mancini; additional songs and lyrics by Rod McKuen, Bill Carey, Malvina Reynolds,

Everett Carter, Milton Rosen. Previewed in Hollywood, Jan. 24, '58. Running time, **85 MINS.**

Jim Daley .... John Saxon
Alice .... Molly Bee
Ox Bentley .... Rod McKuen
Joan Wright .... Judy Meredith
Erica Landis .... Jill St. John
Mike Howard .... John Wilder
Thomas Daley III........George Winslow
Beth Daley .... Fay Wray
Dr. Thomas Daley......Edward C. Platt
Twinkie Daley .... Shelley Fabares
Tad Powers .... Gordon Gebert
Jackie .... Beverly Washburn
Half-Note Harris .... Bob Courtney
Sax Lewis .... Troy Donahue
Fingers Porter .... Hylton Socher
Hilda .... Marjorie Durant
Mr. Reid .... Walter Reed

Universal's "Summer Love" is a sequel to last year's sucessful "Rock Pretty Baby." Although it is not as good as that earlier picture, it has some of the same stars, including John Saxon and Rod McKuen, the same writers and the same characters, all lined out directly at the same audience—tune-happy teenagers—that gave the earlier production a good ride.

Since Saxon has built as a name in the past year, his draw plus the goodwill created by "Pretty Baby," added to the other good young names in the cast should make this a profitable showing. "Summer Love" is being paired with the same studio's youth-directed musical, "The Big Beat" in some situations.

In "Rock Pretty Baby," Saxon was a music-inclined youngster whose doctor-father, Edward C. Platt, wanted the boy to concentrate on a more conventional career. This problem was resolved in that story and now Saxon has his own combo made up of McKuen, John Wilder, Bob Courtney, Troy Donahue, Hylton Socher and himself. Engaged to play at a summer camp, the boys get themselves involved in routine youthful romances and problems, none of them serious and all of which are lightly resolved at the finish.

The screenplay by William Raynor and Herbert Margolis is an expert one with good comedy setups and funny dialogue. Charles Haas' direction is capable in the romantic scenes and the musical numbers but it sometimes misses pointing up the humor in the lines, especially tag-lines.

Saxon is able as the musical entrepreneur who finds himself caught romantiically between sweet Judy Meredith and would-be temptress Jill St. John. Rod McKuen, Molly Bee and John Wilder are the other teen-agers with romantic problems, while Shelley Fabares and George Winslow supply the young, young love interest. Platt and Fay Wray are pleasant as the older generation.

Some of the seven songs used in the production will be of aid in promotion, notably the title tune, "Summer Love," and "To Know You Is To Love You," both by Bill Carey and Henry Mancini. Carl Guthrie's photography heads the good technical credits. *Pow.*

The Big Beat

Musical exploitation item in color with 18 musical groups and/or singles as guest stars and 15 musical numbers. For younger trade especially.

Hollywood, Jan. 31.

Universal release of Will Cowan production. Stars William Reynolds, Andra Martin, Gogi Grant, Jeffrey Stone; co-stars Rose Marie, Hans Conreid, Bill Goodwin, Howard Miller, Jack Straw; guest stars, Charlie Barnet, Buddy Bregman, Alan Copeland, The Del Vikings, The Diamonds, Fats Domino, Four Aces, Harry James, Lancers, Freddy Martin, Mills Brothers, Russ Morgan, George Shearing and Quintet, Jeri Southern, Bill Thompson Singers, Cal Tjader Quintet. Directed by Will Cowan. Screenplay, David P. Harmon; camera, Irving Glassberg; editor, Edward Curtiss; music, Joseph Gershenson; additional songs and lyrics, various. Previewed in Hollywood, Jan. 31, '58. Running time, **82 MINS.**

John Randall .... William Reynolds
Nikki Collins .... Andra Martin
Cindy Adams .... Gogi Grant
Danny Phillips .... Jeffrey Stone
May Gordon .... Rose Marie
Vladimir Skolsky .... Hans Conried
Joseph Randall .... Bill Goodwin
Howard Miller .... Himself
Chick .... Jack Straw
Director .... Phil Harvey
Secretary .... Ingrid Goude
Piano Player .... Steve Drexel

"The Big Beat" is not a strong beat but it is a pleasant one and with the inclusion of 18 musical groups and singles in this Will Cowan production for Universal, it should register well with younger fans. The story in David P. Harmon's screenplay is concerned with the recording business as a frame for introducing the various acts. There is some occasional humor to lighten the mood and teamed with "Summer Love," "Beat" will be an attractive package for younger fans.

Williams Reynolds is the son of successful executive Bill Goodwin. Reynolds wants to spice up the catalogue with livelier selections so when Goodwin sets up a subsidiary company for him he gets to work on that idea. He neglects distribution, however, and when dad gets home from a business trip he finds 350,000 platters piled up in his warehouse. The conflict is solved, comedy-fashion, and everyone winds up happy.

Reynolds is a handsome young actor with the light touch called for in this type of role and he teams well with Andra Martin, an exotic, green-eyed newcomer. Singer Gogi Grant shows herself a better than fair actress in her romantic teaming with personable Jeffry Stone, and Rose Marie and Hans Conreid liven things considerably with an off-beat pairing. Bill Goodwin is sympathetic and Jack Straw, Phil Harvey and Ingrid Goude give able support.

In the many musical numbers, Irving Glassberg's camera action manages to give freshness and interest to conventionally static sequences, aided by the good Eastman color by Pathe. The title song by Fats Domino and Dave Bartholomew is a standard rock and roll item. The Diamonds, a male singing quartet, score most heavily of the groups with two numbers, "Where Mary Go," by Diane Lampert and John Gluck Jr., and "Little Darlin'" by Maurice Williams. Joseph Gershenson has supervised the overall scoring with assistance from Henry Mancini. A smooth job. Edward Curtiss' editing is important and well-done and the sound by Leslie I. Carey and Corson Jowett is good. *Whit.*

Spanish Affair
(SPANISH—COLOR—VISTAVISION)

Romantic meller with good art house and drive-in prospects via color photography and gorgeous scenery.

Paramount release of a Nomad Production produced by Bruce Odlum. Stars Richard Kiley, Carmen Sevilla; costars Jose Guardiola. Directed by Donald Siegel. Written by Richard Collins; camera (Technicolor), Sam Leavitt; editor, Tom McAdoo; music, Daniele Amfitheatrof and Mack David. Tradeshown N.Y., Jan. 31, '58. Running time, **95 MINS.**

Merritt .... Richard Kiley
Mari .... Carmen Sevilla
Antonio .... Jose Guardiola
Sotelo .... Jesus Tordesillas
Fernando .... Jose Manuel Martin
Waiter .... Francisco Bernal
Flamenco Singer .... Rafael Farina
Father .... Jose Marco Davo
Purita .... Purita Vargas
Miguel .... Antonio S. Amaya

Charm and beauty of old world Spain have been used by producer Bruce Odlum as physical backgrounds for a fairish story of romance and adventure. But while the yarn may have its shortcomings, the sweep and grandeur of the exteriors are striking enough to propel "Spanish Affair" into copious art house bookings.

Strong secondary market could be developed in drive-ins since the breathtaking views of some of Spain's most celebrated scenery are a natural for ozoners' kingsize screens, especially in light of the film's Technicolor lensing in Vista-Vision. Save for Richard Kiley, the cast is composed of Spanish players who are unknown to American audiences. Hence, the picture's potential will have to be built largely upon word-of-mouth.

The Richard Collins screenplay, for the most part, is merely a device to bring the vistas of Madrid, Barcelona, El Escorial, Toledo, Segovia, the Costa Brava country and Tossa de Mars before the cameras. "Guides" on this Cook's tour are Kiley, an American architect in Spain on business, and Carmen Sevilla who accompanies him as an interpreter. A Madrid office worker of gypsy ancestry, she agrees to go along for a daily fee.

Naturally, Jose Guardiola, a gypsy to whom Miss Sevilla is engaged, feels that her business trip with Kiley is certainly no old Spanish custom. Accordingly he trails the couple for the prime purpose of killing the American. There's an element of suspense in the chase that develops. But it's more than obvious that Kiley and Miss Sevilla will soon discover a mutual affection and it's also clear that Guardiola will eventually be left at the romantic post.

Under Donald Siegel's brisk direction, cast turns in some creditable performances. Kiley is the epitome of the American businessman—quiet, taciturn, yet redblooded enough when the occasion calls for it. Miss Sevilla, a top European star, represents ideal casting in the girl's role. Her sexy carriage, plus her ability to sing and dance, are amply showcased. With suitable vehicles, she could well become the Spanish equivalent of Brigitte Bardot.

Capable support for this English-dialog release is provided by Jesus Tordesillas as a Madrid associate of Kiley's. Jose Marco Davo as Miss Sevilla's father and Rafael Farina as a flamenco singer, among others. Top asset is the physical values provided by producer Odlum who co-produced this venture with Spain's CEA Studios and indie film-maker Benito Perojo. As aforementioned the color photography of Sam Leavitt is outstanding.

Also enhancing the overall Iberian atmosphere are Daniele Amfitheatrof's score, art direction of Hal Pereira and Tambi Larsen as well as the sound recording by Harry Lindgren and Winston Leverett. Tom McAdoo's editing is good as are other technical credits. Mack David and Amfitheatrof authored "The Flaming Rose," a so-so ballad which Miss Sevilla appealingly sings. *Gilb.*

I Accuse!
(BRITISH—C'SCOPE)

Standout stellar cast in a dramatic story based on famous Dreyfus case makes this a sound b.o. prospect for thoughtful audiences.

London, Feb. 4.

Metro production (Sam Zimbalist) and release. Stars Jose Ferrer, Anton Walbrook, Viveca Lindfors, Leo Genn, Emlyn Williams, David Farrar, Donald Wolfit, Herbert Lom. Directed by Jose Ferrer. Screenplay, Gore Vidal, from book by Nicholas Halasz; editor, Frank Clarke; camera, F. A. Young; music, William Alwyn. At Metro Private Theatre, London. Running time, **99 MINS.**

Alfred Dreyfus .... Jose Ferrer
Major Esterhazy .... Anton Walbrook
Lucie Dreyfus .... Viveca Lindfors
Major Picquart .... Leo Genn
Emile Zola .... Emlyn Williams
Mathieu Dreyfus .... David Farrar
General Mercier .... Donald Wolfit
Major Du Paty De Clam Herbert Lom
Major Henry .... Harry Andrews
Edgar Demange .... Felix Aylmer
Georges Clemenceau ...... Peter Illing
Colonel Sandherr ..... George Coulouris
Colonel Van Schwarzkoppen Carl Jaffe
Bertillon .... Eric Pohlmann
Drumont .... John Chandos
Prosecutor (1st Dreyfus Trial) Ernest Clarke
Judge .... Anthony Ireland
Prosecutor (Esterhazy Trial) John Phillips
Judge .... Laurence Naismith
Prosecutor (2d Dreyfus Trial) Michael Hordern
Judge .... Keith Pyott
Capt. Avril .... Ronald Howard
Capt. Brossard .... Charles Gray
Capt. Leblanc .... Michael Anthony
Capt. Lauth .... Arthur Howard
English Publisher .. Michael Trubshawe
President of France ...... Malcolm Keen

The drama of the Dreyfus case, one of the greatest miscarriages of justice in history, has once again captured the imagination of the film producers and the latest version. "I Accuse!" makes strong, if plodding entertainment. A top stellar cast has been assembled to do justice to a story which still commands interest, even if familiarity has robbed it of much of its initial impact. Both in Britain and U.S. "I Accuse!" should prove a worthwhile booking for intelligent audiences.

Briefly, the story concerns the plight of a Jewish staff officer of the French Army who is unjustly accused of treason, found guilty through being framed to save the Army's face, and condemned to life imprisonment on Devil's Island. Friends fighting to restore his tarnished honor force a re-trial. For political reasons, he is offered a pardon and, a broken man, he accepts though it means that he is branded as a traitor. In the end, the real culprit confesses and Dreyfus returns to the Army in triumph.

Jose Ferrer has taken on the heavy task of playing both the role of Dreyfus and of directing. His performance is a wily, impeccable one, but it comes from the intellect rather than the heart and rarely causes pity. He makes Dreyfus a staid, almost fanatical patriot and, with great subtlety, suggests a mental torture of the victim.

Ferrer has directed methodically and with immense attention to detail in characterization. The action is throughout rather static, but the court scenes are pregnant with drama, thanks to a literate screenplay by Gore Vidal.

Ferrer is backed up by a top-ranking cast and critical nods must go at least to a number of distinguished players. Anton Walbrook, the real culprit, gives a splendid performance—suave, debonair and fascinating. And equally impressive is Donald Wolfit as the Army's top guy who claims that the honor of the French Army is more important than the fate of one man. Emlyn Williams, as Zola; David Farrar, as Dreyfus's brother; Leo Genn, as the officer who believes in his innocence; Harry Andrews, Herbert Lom, George Coulouris, Felix Aylmer and Peter Illing are also standouts in a large, well-balanced cast. Viveca Lindfors plays Dreyfus's wife—the only prominent woman in the cast—and she handles both the gaiety and the sadness of the role with dignity.

Technically, the film is okay. Though "Accuse" may not appeal to mass audiences, it has a strength and purpose which bring fresh lustre to a well-tried story.

Rich.

The Gypsy And The Gentleman
(BRITISH—COLOR)

Lusty costume meller which breaks no new ground but is swept along by some fine performances; should sing sweet b.o. music.

London, Jan. 28.

Rank Film Distributors release of Rank (Maurice Cowan) production. Stars Melina Mercouri, Keith Michell, Flora Robson. Directed by Joseph Losey. Screenplay by Janet Green from Nina Warner Hooke's novel, "Darkness I Leave You"; camera, Jack Hildyard; editor, Reginald Beck; music, Hans May. At Odeon, Leicester Square, London, Jan. 15, '58. Running time, **107 MINS.**

Belle	Melina Mercouri
Deverill	Keith Michell
Jess	Patrick McGoohan
Sarah	June Laverick
John	Lyndon Brook
Mrs. Haggard	Flora Robson
Vanessa	Clare Austin
Lady Ayrton	Helen Have
Ruddock	Newton Blick
Brook	Mervyn Johns
Duffin	John Salew
Hattie	Catherine Feller
Forrester	Laurence Naismith
Coco	Louis Aquilina

Harking back to the British film days of such successful pix as "The Wicked Lady" and "The Man in Grey," there is genuine reason to believe that "Gypsy" may make an equal financial sweep in Britain. Nevertheless, this is a dusty, sprawling, no-holds-barred costume melodrama which utilizes every possible cliche in the romantic "meller" book. Yet it has appeal because of its simple attack on b.o. potentiality. It gets away with it because a good cast plays it for more than it is worth. The slightest case of "tongue-in-cheek" and this old-fashioned drama would have fallen flat on its face.

Some indication of the type of film it is can perhaps be indicated by the fact that the hero is a roistering aristocratic playboy of the Regency period with the unlikely but inevitable name of Sir Paul Deverill. With a huge estate and no dough, he is embarked on a squander-lust round of pleasure which consists mainly of gambling, wenching and hitting the bottle.

About to enter into a loveless, but profitable marriage, he becomes involved with a fiery gypsy-golddigger who so intrigues him that he marries her. She is not unnaturally rightly provoked when she finds that he has no money, but many debts. From then on, the film is a disarming piece of mumbo-jumbo which involves a lot of riding and face-slapping, vandalism, forging of a will, kidnapping of an heiress and similar rollicking hokum.

This over-long film comes startingly to life when the gypsy, played by Melina Mercouri, is on the screen. Here is a flashing, personality-plus actress with blazing eyes, a wide smile and all the impudence in the world. She strides through the film like a hopped-up Lady Macbeth, spreading sex, sin and sorrow with an abandon that will leave all but the most avid fan completely exhausted. Miss Mercouri, in previous more subtle films, had proved her talent. In "The Gypsy" she has a field day, bringing a verve to a tired script for which the director and producer should be highly grateful. And apparently she inspired the remainder of the cast to similar zest.

Keith Michell plays the infatuated rake at a hell-for-leather pace while Patrick McGoohan, as the gypsy in league with him, turns in a four-star piece of villainy. By contrast, Flora Robson, as a distinguished actress; June Laverick, as the innocent girl who suffers because of her brother's infatuation for Miss Mercouri, and Lyndon Brook, as her rather dull doctor-suitor are rather in a minor key. There are also some shrewd little performances by Mervyn Johns, as a rascally lawyer; Newton Blick, as a local squire; and Catherine Feller, as a housemaid.

Since the dialogue in such frenetic items rarely reaches a distinguished level of sophistication, director Joseph Losey has sensibly played for situation and emotional violence. The atmosphere of the period has been faithfully evoked both in costume and by Ralph Brinton's art work and Jack Hildyard's color photography. Only once does the film break down technically. That is when the stars are hurled to their death in a river as their coach breaks through a bridge.

Rich.

Crash Landing

Talk overshadows action in over-plotted melodrama about a trans-atlantic plane ditching. Routine destination.

Columbia release of Clover Production. Sam Katzman producer. Stars Gary Merrill, Nancy Davis; features Irene Hervey, Roger Smith. Directed by Fred F. Sears. Screenplay, Fred Freiberger; camera, Benjamin H. Kline; music, Mischa Bakaleinikoff; editor, Jerome Thoms. Previewed Jan. 23, '58. Running time, **76 MINS.**

Steve Williams	Gary Merrill
Helen Williams	Nancy Davis
Bernice Willouby	Irene Hervey
John Smithback	Roger Smith
Nancy Arthur	Bek Nelson
Ann Thatcher	Jewell Lain
Howard Whitney	Sheridan Comerate
Jed Sutton	Richard Newton
Arthur White	Richard Keith
Mrs. Ortega	Celia Lovsky
Maurice Stanley	Lewis Martin
Calvin Havelick	Hal Torey
Phil Burton	John McNamara
Adele Burton	Dayle Rodney
Carlos Ortego	Rodolfo Hoyos
Barrie Williams	Kim Charney
Teddy Burton	Robin Warga
Red	Robert Whiteside
Mel	Ronald Green

"Crash Landing," a Clover production for Columbia, is an attempt to duplicate on a small budget the kind of story and excitement contained in "The High And The Mighty." Sam Katzman's production, directed by Fred F. Sears, does not come off, mostly because there is more talk than action with the result that the dangers inherent in a crippled plane past the point of no return in the Atlantic do not come over well to the audience. Starring Gary Merrill and Nancy Davis, it's below par for the Katzman pennant.

Fred Freiberger's script has assembled the customary contrasting characters called for in this kind of "Grand Hotel" theme. There is the pilot, Gary Merrill, a martinet in his job and his home, who pains his wife, Nancy Davis, by his insistence that his music-loving son, young Kim Charney, also be a boy of action.

The passengers include a retired businessman, Lewis Martin, who has never really lived attracted to a pretty school-teacher, Irene Hervey, who might correct that oversight. Richard Keith is the rugged tycoon up from the streets who delights in bullying his Harvard-bred associate, Hal Torrey, who in turn turns to drink. An elderly Portuguese grandmother, Celia Lovsky, is on her first flight to America to see her grandchildren; there is a Greek Orthodox priest in his imposing robes played by Frederich Ledebur and two chorus girls, Joan Bradshaw and Brandy Bryan, among others.

Nobody gets killed when the plane ditches after rendezvousing with a U.S. destroyer and nobody is hurt. The outcome is supposed to show how the experience has changed all those involved. The interest and effectiveness is premised on throwing together odd types; chorus girl and priest, businessman and teacher. But it is done with language so rich in cliches that the characters are just that, not real people. The late Fred Sears' direction is best when he is free of the script to improvise.

The cast does a capable job under the circumstances and technical credits are by and large good. There are some deficiences that detract, however. Shots of "Lisbon" air port were obviously taken at Los Angeles and no trouble has been taken to disguise this fact with background planes clearly marked "Western Air Lines," etc. Also, in the sea rescue scene, the rim of the studio tank is plainly visible in the rear of the action.

Pow.

Going Steady

Bright, funny exploitation item dealing in light-handed manner with parent-teenage problems. Good prospects.

Hollywood, Jan. 29.

Columbia release of Clover Production. Stars Molly Bee, Alan Reed Jr.; co-stars Irene Hervey, Bill Goodwin; features Ken Miller, Susan Easter, Linda Watkins, Byron Foulger, Hugh Sanders, Florence Ravenel, Ralph Moody. Produced by Sam Katzman. Directed by Fred F. Sears. Screenplay, Budd Grossman; from a story by Budd Grossman, Sumner A. Long; camera, Benjamin H. Kline; music, Mischa Bakaleinikoff; editor, Charles Nelson. Previewed at the studio, Jan. 27, '58. Running time, **82 MINS.**

Julie Ann	Molly Bee
Calvin Potter	Alan Reed Jr.
Gordon Turner	Bill Goodwin
Grace Turner	Irene Hervey
Woody Simmons	Ken Miller
Olive Nelson	Susan Easter
Aunt Lola	Linda Watkins
Mr. Potter	Byron Foulger
Mr. Ahern	Hugh Sanders
Mrs. Potter	Florence Ravenel
Justice of the Peace	Ralph Moody
Arthur Priestley	Carlyle Mitchell

Bright and breezy as the teenagers it chronicles, "Going Steady" has a sharp, attractive title for the younger set it is aimed at and should more than satisfy the kids as a presentation of their attitudes and problems. The Sam Katzman production for Columbia, directed by Fred F. Sears, actually has a rather serious story—a secret marriage between high school seniors and the situations arising out of an immediate pregnancy.

Handled as farce, the lines are pointed and funny, and the adults shown are presented with as much sympathy and intelligence as the youngsters. With Molly Bee and young Alan Reed Jr. top-starred, "Going Steady" will be a strong exploitation item. It is to be teamed with the same outfit's "Crash Landing" as a package.

If there is a weakness in Budd Grossman's screenplay, which is from an original story he co-authored with Sumner A. Long, is that it is short on plot. The story is episodic with the feel of a TV comedy series about it, proceeding from one minor crisis or laughline to another without really building to any genuine climax. But the episodes are amusing in themselves as young Miss Bee persuades her parents, Bill Goodwin and Irene Hervey, to allow her to accompany the high school basketball team on an out-of-town game then secretly marries her "steady," Alan Reed Jr., while away. The situations are routine: son-in-law moving in with father-in-law; father-in-law choking over son-in-law's gift of cigars; double meanings and misunderstandings when Miss Bee discovers she's pregnant. But Grossman has set up good laugh situations and contrived a great many funny lines. The late Fred Sear's direction paces the show so that all possible fun is extracted from both lines and situations.

Miss Bee does no singing in the picture itself but she delivers a warm interpretation of an unusually good title song (by Fred Karger and Richard Quine) behind the main titles. Her acting is natural and ingratiating. Reed, in his debut in a major role, shows himself a good-looking man with a flair for comedy who also acquits himself ably in the few serious moments. Most of the comedy rests on Bill Goodwin and Irene Hervey and the two veterans handle it with ease and charm. They also generate a pleasant mood with appealing scenes of middle-aged romance. Others in the cast who stand out include Ken Miller, Susan Easter, Linda Watkins and Hugh Sanders.

The slick technical credits include Benjamin H. Kline's camera work, editing by Charles Nelson and John Livadary's sound.

Pow.

Lost Lagoon

United Artists release of John Rawlins production. Stars Jeffrey Lynn; features Peter Donat, Lelia Barry. Directed by Rawlins. Screenplay, Milton Subotsky; camera, Harry W. Smith; editor, David Rawlins; music, Hubert Smith, Terry Brannon. Previewed Jan. 27, '58. Running time, **80 MINS.**

Charlie Walker	Jeffrey Lynn
David Burnham	Peter Donat
Elizabeth Moore	Leila Barry
Bernadine Walker	Jane Hartley
Millard Cauley	Roger Clark
Mr. Beakins	Don Gibson
Colima	Celeste Robinson
Natives	Stanley Seymour, Isabelle Jones

The Caribbean, where this John Rawlins production was filmed, provides the backdrop for this story of a man reported lost at sea who embarks upon a new life on a tropical island. Subject carries certain exploitational values, but lack of draw names and only a middling interesting plotline keep it from anything more than a routine entry for smaller program situations.

Rawlins, who also directs from the Milton Subotsky screenplay, doesn't clothe his characters with much sympathy, particularly role enacted by Jeffery Lynn, a middle-aged man harassed by an extravagant wife who goes to her hard-boiled brother for a loan to pay his big insurance premium. Out at sea, between Miami and Nassau, where pair discuss the request on brother's fishing boat, a storm comes up and craft founders. Brother gets back to mainland okay, but Lynn is washed up on a small cay where he finds Leila Barry, and he sets up a partnership in operation of a holiday resort. A romance develops, but after an insurance investigator locates missing man Lynn returns to his wife while young femme marries a former sweetheart.

Lynn appears overly stern in his role, but Miss Barry makes a nice impression. Balance of top roles, portrayed by Peter Donat as latter's boy friend, Don Gibson, Roger Clark and Jane Hartley, are stoic. Hubert Smith and His Coral Islanders dish up some rhythmic calypso tunes.

Technical credits are adequate, including Harry W. Smith's photography, editing by David Rawlins.
Whit.

Fort Bowie

Fast Cavalry-Indians actioner for good response in western market.

Hollywood, Jan. 30.
United Artists release of Aubrey Schenck production. Stars Ben Johnson, Jan Harrison, Kent Taylor, Jana Davi; features Larry Chance, J. Ian Douglas. Directed by Howard W. Koch. Screenplay, Maurice Tombragel; camera, Carl E. Guthrie; editor, John A. Bushelman; music, Les Baxter. Previewed Jan. 29, '58. Running time, **80 MINS.**
Captain Thompson..........Ben Johnson
Allison Garrett .... Jan Harrison
Colonel Garrett .... Kent Taylor
Chenzana .... Jane Davi
Victorio .... Larry Chance
Major Wharton .... J. Ian Douglas
Sergeant Kukus .... Peter Mamakos
Lt. Maywood .... Jerry Frank
Mrs. Maywood ,......... Barbara Parry
A Gentleman .... Ed Hinton
A Sergeant .... Johnny Western

Bel-Air's wrap-up release for United Artists comes through an exciting U.S. Cavalry-Indians yarn which may expect okay reception in the western market. Good situations are developed and film carries the type of fast action to keep outdoor fans engaged.

Director Howard W. Koch's unfoldment of the Aubrey Schenck production is punchy as he makes handsome use of the troopers' constant clashes with the Apaches. The Maurice Tombragel screenplay develops conflict between Kent Taylor, commandant of Fort Bowie, and Ben Johnson, one of his officers whom he wrongfully thinks has been romancing his beautiful wife, Jan Harrison. This element combined with the military action makes for a well-playing melodrama that allows good performances right down the line.

Film gets off to an unusual start when a detachment of Cavalry under an ambitious major, a political appointee on his first patrol, slaughters a band of Indians about to surrender peacefully. Johnson, a captain under this officer, is helpless to prevent the cold-blooded killing, which tees off the Apaches' campaign of revenge. After the colonel's wife falsely tells her husband, whom she no longer loves, that Johnson had tried to make love to her while bringing her back to the fort from Tucson, Johnson is sent on the suicidal mission of finding the Indian leader to demand his surrender. A switch is made from usual films of this category by having the cavalry storm their own fort after Indians have captured it.

Johnson delivers acceptably and Taylor handles his colonel role well. Miss Harrison, a blonde looker, is convincing as the wife who wants only to get away from the frontier that frightens her, but who returns to her husband's side as they face death together in the Indian attack. Jana Davi is effec-

tive as an Apache girl in love with Johnson, P. Ian Douglas creditably portrays the politically-appointed officer wiped out with his whole detachment when he misjudges Indian strategy, and Larry Chance is strongly cast as Victorio, Apache chief. Peter Mamakos also scores as a sergeant.

Technical departments are competently executed, leading off with Carl E. Guthrie's photography, Les Baxter's music score and John A. Bushelman's editing. *Whit.*

Japanese Festival

Down Town
(JAPANESE)

Toho Co. production. Stars Isuzu Yamada, Toshiro Mifune, Harunori Kametani; features Haruo Tanaka, Chieko Murata. Directed by Yasuki Chiba; from an original story by Fumiko Hayashi; camera, Rokuro Nishigaki; music, Akira Ifukube. Running time, **59 MINS.**

Though it is an awkward length for American theatres, "Down Town" is the kind of Japanese film that audiences have come to expect since "Rashomon," which paved the postwar way for Japanese pictures in the States. It's an affecting, tender little story, acted to perfection and directed in a simple, realistic style that scores.

Film tells of a poor but attractive woman who sells tea. She strikes up a friendship with a laborer which blossoms into a quiet love. The man, the woman and her little boy go downtown for an outing and spend the night in Tokyo. The next day, when she arrives at his shack, she finds he has been killed in a truck crash.

A wealth of detail has been woven into this simple story fabric, and the action is wholly believable to Western eyes. Isuzu Yamada gives a warm and many-faceted performance that implies a host of under-the-surface emotions. Toshiro Mifune plays the laborer with skill and little Harunori Kametani is enchanting as the boy.

Director Yasuki Chiba has turned out a perceptive and well-balanced film that registers down the line and his actors act and react Western-style. There is in this picture a lot of screen poetry as the two principals shed for a while their mantle of poverty and enjoy life, the boy and one another. Via understatement, and fine black-and-white lensing, this Toho production is a standout entry. *Hift.*

The Temptress
(JAPANESE—COLOR)

Nikkatsu Corp. production produced by Masayuki Takagi. Stars Yumeji Tsukioka, Ryoji Hayama; features Tadashi Kobayashi, Ichijiro Ohya, Jun Hamamura, Akitake Khono. Directed by Eisuke Takizawa; screenplay, Toshio Yazumi from original story by Kyoka Izumi; camera (Eastmancolor), Minoru Yokoyama. Running time, **87 MINS.**

There is about this Japanese legend a beauty and simplicity that makes the film unique in its appeal. Unfortunately, it falls short of the kind of enchantment that might have made it a sock entry for the art houses.

Rarely have the Japanese achieved the kind of color effects that are on display in "The Temptress." Tint tones are muted to perfectly fit the mood of the story and often achieve the quality of

paintings. Wilderness setting of the yarn gives the color camera a chance to display its potential to the fullest.

Star of the piece is the beautiful Yumeji Tsukioka who plays the temptress, married to a dwarf and free to love men but not fall in love with them. As lovers come and go, they're transformed into animals. There arrives Ryoji Hayama, a young priest, and the story deals with their mutual attraction. In the end, she sacrifices herself for his sake as her home goes up in flames.

Director Eisuke Takizawa has caught the unreal quality of the legend, though some of the performances are overdrawn. The fascination of this film is in the visual effects, from the steaming waters to Hayama's travel through the forest where leeches drop from the trees. Too much time is spent recording the mental agonies of the priest, capably portrayed by Hayama.

"The Temptress" is superior filmmaking in many respects and deserves attention on that score. With some editing, it might be a possibility for the States. *Hift.*

Story of Chikamatsu
(JAPANESE)

Daiei Co. release of Masaichi Nagata production. Stars Kazuo Hasegawa, Kyoko Kagawa, Yoko Minaminda, Eitaro Shindo. Directed by Kenji Mizoguchi. Screenplay, Yoshikata Yoda; camera, Kazuo Miyagawa. Presented in N.Y. at the Museum of Modern Art during Japanese Film Week, Jan. 30, '58. Running time, **102 MINS.**

"Story of Chikamatsu" is, evidently an example of the Japanese tearjerker. Its theme is love and the tragic ending faced by the lovers caught in an impossible situation. The tragic finale is tipped off early in the picture as two other lovers, accused of adultery, are literally crucified by the authorities.

While there are moments of tenderness in the picture, it is generally slow moving and overlong. The trials and tribulations of the lovers in 17th Century Japan will at times, seem ludicrous to U.S. audiences. Its easy to see, however, that the film could have been a big hit in its native land. It doesn't rate as an entry for U.S. consumption.

Basically, the film has to do with the undying love of a clerk and his boss' wife. Although the wife, because of economic circumstances, has been sold in marriage to a wealthy scroll-maker, there is nothing she can do, under the Japanese tradition of the time, to dissolve the union. Both the clerk and the wife are inevitably drawn into the association through circumstances they cannot control. Their love affair is a stormy and harassed one, but they cling to each other despite the complications. As they go to their death, they seem almost happy—and well they might considering what they've been through.

From the standpoint of Japanese pictures, topnotch performances are given by Kazua Hasegawa, Kyoke Kagawa, Yoko Minamida and Eitaro Shindo. *Holl.*

Untamed Woman
(JAPANESE)

Toho Co. release. Associate producer, Tomoyuki Tanaka. Stars Hideko Takamine; features Ken Uehara, Masayuki Mori, Daisuke Kato. Directed by Mikio Naruse. Screenplay, Yoko Mizuki; original story, Shusei Tokuda; camera Masao Tamai. Reviewed at Museum of Modern

Art, N.Y., Jan. 31. Running time, **121 MINS.**
Oshima .... Hideko Takamine
Tsuru-san .... Ken Uenara
Hamaya .... Masayuki Mori
Onada .... Daisuke Kato

A minor item, this is Japanese soap opera that simply fails to generate interest, certainly is devoid of dramatic impact for U.S. Further, it's far short of Hollywood standards on technical grounds.

Central figure is a young lady who looks for happiness with three men in succession but loses out on each try. Opening has her miserably married, suffering a miscarriage in the course of a row, and then divorced. Next comes a hotel owner and the promise of serenity but he turns from her in ambitious pursuit of his career. Third is a tailor who prospers with her aid but who can't bear her strong-willed personality and takes up with a mistress.

The characters of "Untamed Woman" are disagreeable to the extent of precluding audience sympathy. Story moves slowly and is loosely constructed.

Camera work is hardly professional; there's little effort to segue one scene into the next.

There's a temptation to ask why "Untamed Woman" was selected for showcasing at the Museum of Modern Art. *Gene.*

Cowboy

Out of Frank Harris classic memoirs comes rough, tough, adult story of the education of a cowboy. Hefty b.o. prospects.

Hollywood, Feb. 7.

Columbia release of a Phoenix production. Stars Glenn Ford, Jack Lemmon, Anna Kashfi, Brian Donlevy; Features Dick York, Victor Manuel Mendoza, Richard Jackel, King Donovan, Vaughn Taylor, Donald Randolph, James Westerfield, Eugene Iglesias, Frank de Kova. Produced by Julian Blaustein. Directed by Delmer Daves. Screenplay, Edmund H. North; based on a book by Frank Harris; camera, Charles Lawton Jr.; music, George Duning; editors, William A. Lyon, Al Clark. Previewed at the studio, Feb. 6, '58. Running time, **92 MINS.**

Tom Reece	Glenn Ford
Frank Harris	Jack Lemmon
Maria Vidal	Anna Kashfi
Doc Eender	Brian Donlevy
Charlie	Dick York
Mendoza	Victor Manuel Mendoza
Paul Curtis	Richard Jaeckel
Joe Capper	King Donovan
Mr. Fowler	Vaughn Taylor
Senor Vidal	Donald Randolph
Mike Adams	James Westerfield
Manuel Arriega	Eugene Iglesias
Alcaide	Frank de Kova
Slim Barrett	Buzz Henry
Aunt	Amapola Del Vando
Charlie's girl	Bek Nelson
Tucker	William Leslie
Peggy	Guy Wilkerson

"Cowboy" proves once again that there are really no old, tired stories, just old, tired story-tellers. Taking a told and re-told tale auspices comes up with one of fastest, freshest Westerns in a long time. Julian Blaustein production for Columbia, directed by Delmer Daves, is blunt and brutal. It is also loaded with salty dialogue, vigorous humor and enough romance to make it clear that if this is a man's world it is not so by choice. It has cowboys and Indians, cattle (including a stampede) and cow ponies, barroom brawls and bronco-busting, all the classic elements but seen with a fresh approach. "Cowboy," photographed in Technicolor and widescreen, should get unusual critical attention and with Glenn Ford and Jack Lemmon top-starred and giving fine portrayals, it should also be a prime box office attraction. Anna Kashfi in the single important feminine role.

The good screenplay by Edmund H. North is based on "My Reminiscences as a Cowboy" by Frank Harris and it is as forthright as the other works by that international literary know-it-all and tell-it-all of the last generation. In essence it is simply the story of a romantic young man, Jack Lemmon, who (being stuck in the East) sees the West in glowing, golden terms. He wants to mix it up with the men who are men and prove it 24 hours a day, fighting, working, loving.

He persuades Glenn Ford, easily the hardest-bitten trail boss in history, to take him on a cattle drive when Ford runs short of cash and Lemmon is able to tide him over. The story is of the education of Lemmon as a cowboy in which the romanticism is whipped out of him by the hard facts of the situation.

He discovers, as Ford warns him in a funny speech that is one of the picture's highlights, that cattle are not lovable, that horses are not necessarily a friend to man, that riding the trail is seldom as the ballad singers rhyme it, and that there is a camaraderies among the cowpokes but it is based on survival and not collegiate goodfellowship. It is, in short, a tough life, but its attraction to this peculiar breed of men is made understandable.

Delmer Daves' direction doesn't waste a minute on unessentials. The life on the trail, for instance, is shown in quick shots, some of them only seconds in length, yet the impact is to set the mood exactly without delaying the progress of the story. North's dialogue, especially his brusque comments on cowboys and cowpunching achieve the effect of stripping the false glamor and still leaving the situations attractive and fascinating.

Glenn Ford is vigorously and maturely masculine, the essence of the kind of boss who held in his horny hands the feckless lives and casual deaths of his men. His transition to a softer attitude, late in the picture, is even a little disappointing; his calculated coldness has been so intriguing. Jack Lemmon gives a performance that broadens his range greatly, completely convincing as he matures from a comical young tenderfoot—tender of feet and tender of seat—into a man and a trail boss. Anna Kashfi's role is that of the feminine side of his education as a cowboy. The romance is there, it lightens the story by its implication, but it is not allowed to drag the main story. Casting of Miss Kashfi as a daughter of Mexican aristocracy, was an inspired touch. She does a good job and her name should make an already good picture more attractive.

Brian Donlevy has a relatively small role but it is vital. He plays a disillusioned gun-slinger, an anachronism from the earlier days of the West, a man who knows his time has run out as the area changes and modifies its pattern. His suicide, briefly noted and succinctly commented upon, is a grace note to the story making clear that commercial values of the bovine gold on the hoof has doomed this kind of individualism once and for all. Others in the cast who stand out include Victor Manuel Mendoza, Donald Randolph, Dick York, Richard Jaeckel, James Westerfield, King Donovan and Vaughn Taylor.

Charles Lawton as director of photography, with second unit work by Ray Cory, has caught the ornate Chicago interiors—where the story starts and ends—and the broader outdoor areas, plus the closeups that tell what the people involved are thinking. Art direction by Cary Odell is as fresh as the story viewpoint, with equal aid from set decorators William Kiernan and James M. Crowe. George Duning's score, ably conducted by Morris Stoloff, is varied and inventive, skillfully brought out in the orchestrations by Arthur Morton. Sound by John Livadary and editing by William A. Lyon and Al Clark complete the overall excellence of the production.

Powe.

Mark of the Hawk
(SUPERSCOPE—COLOR)

Weakly scripted political yarn of Africa yearning for freedom from the white man. Eartha Kitt out of setting. Spotty outlook.

Hollywood, Feb. 7.

Universal release of Lloyd Young production. Stars Eartha Kitt, Juano Hernandez,, John McIntire, Sidney Poitier; features Patrick Allan, Earl Cameron, Gerard Heinz, Helen Horton, Clifton Macklin, Ewen Solon, Marne Maitland. Directed by Michael Audley. Screenplay, H. Kenn Carmichael; story, Young; camera (Technicolor), Edwin Hillier, Toge Fujihira; editor, Edward Jarvis; music, Matyas Seiber. Previewed Feb. 3, '58. Running time, **83 MINS.**

Renee	Eartha Kitt
Obam	Sidney Poitier
Amugu	Juano Hernandez
Craig	John McIntire
Barbara	Helen Horton
Sunday Lal	Marne Maitland
Governor General	Gerard Heinz
Gregory	Patrick Allan
Prosecutor	Earl Cameron
Kanda	Clifton Macklin
Inspector	Ewen Solon
Magistrate	Lockwood West
Overholt	Francis Matthews
Ben	Phillip Vickers
Fred	Bill Nagy
Dr. Lin	N. C. Doo
Ming Tao	David Goh
1st Officer	Harold Siddons
2nd Officer	Frederick Treves
African Doctor	Lionel Ngakane
Chinese Officer	Andy Ho
Chinese Soldier	John A. Tinn

Religious, inter-racial politics and native plotting background this melodrama of modern-day Africa, Technicolor-filmed partially on the Dark Continent and balance in England. Its theme of Africa trying to gain freedom on an equal footing with the white man who has taken over the country doesn't come off too well as story material, as here developed, so bookings necessarily will be confined to selected situations, indicating spotty returns.

With the exception of its four principals the entire cast of the Lloyd Young production is either English or native. Stars are Eartha Kitt and Sidney Poitier, latter an educated African wed to Miss Kitt, who reps the workers on legislative council of the colony, torn between his duties here and young terrorists led by his brother, John McIntire, American missionary; and Juano Hernandez, native pastor who urges the seeking of equality for his people by peaceful means.

Miss Kitt, her character of a highly educated African unexplained and seemingly out of place, warbles one song, "This Man Is Mine," in her usual sensual style but there's nothing catchy about number.

Director Michael Audley maintains good pace in the action sequences of the H. Kenn Carmichael screenplay, which deal with the menace of native attack on the white residents of the colony. However, he's up against an overage of dialog in both the political and religious sequences, in which Poitier is the principal participant. Young man comes under the influence of McIntire, who is killed by natives in an attack on a plantation, and yarn ends without any seeming solution for the Afro-white problem.

Poitier delivers strongly as the confused legislator, and Miss Kitt handles her brief footage well enough. McIntire capably portrays the missionary, Hernandez comes through okay and good support is afforded by Helen Horton, missionary's wife; Gerard Heinz, governor general; Ewen Solon, police inspector; Patrick Allan, a strong-arm colonist.

Interesting color photography by Edwin Hillier and Toge Fujihira lead off competent technical credits.

Whit.

Cattle Empire
(C'SCOPE—COLOR)

Lavish outdoor spectacle of rivalry in cattle drives. Talk overshadows action to dim interest and b.o. prospects.

Hollywood, Feb. 7.

20th-Fox release of Robert Stabler production. Stars Joel McCrea. Co-stars Gloria Talbot, Don Haggerty, Phyllis Coates. Features Bing Russell, Paul Brinegar, Hal K. Dawson, Duane Grey, Richard Shannon, Charles Gray, Patrick O'Moore, Bill McGraw, Jack Lomas. Directed by Charles Marquis Warren; screenplay, Endre Bohem and Eric Norden; camera (DeLuxe color), Brydon Baker; editor, Leslie Vidor; music, Paul Sawtell and Bert Shefter. Previewed Feb. 3, '58. Running time, **83 MINS**

John Cord	Joel McCrea
Sandy	Gloria Talbott
Ralph Hamilton	Don Haggerty
Janice Hamilton	Phyllis Coates
Douglas Hamilton	Bing Russell
Tom Jeffrey	Paul Brinegar
George Jeffrey	Hal K. Dawson
Aruzza	Duane Grey
Garth	Richard Shannon
Tom Powis	Charles Gray
Cogswell	Patrick O'Moore
Jim Whittaker	William McGraw
Sheriff Brewster	Jack Lomas
Corbo	Steve Raines
Quince	Rocky Shaham
Barkeep	Nesdon Booth
Grainger	Bill Hale
Stitch	Ronald Foster
Preacher	Howard B. Culver

"Cattle Empire," a CinemaScope picture in DeLuxe Color presented by 20th Century-Fox, is a big and often spectacular trail-driving saga highlighted by some refreshing shots of sweeping background scenery. The story in the foreground, however, is a long time getting underway, plays too lengthily at suspense and mystery, and when the "secrets" are unfolded they do not merit the build-up. Joel McCrea's name must be the prime bait on this film for the action houses.

McCrea plays a hated trail boss, who has recently been released from prison, in the screenplay by Endre Bohem and Eric Norden. He was imprisoned for complicity in a mob action by his trail drivers who burned, looted and maimed to celebrate the completion of a successful drive. McCrea is still necessary to the people of the town his men almost destroyed and he is signed to drive a herd owned by Don Haggerty, blinded in the previous melee, the sale of which will bring back the town's prosperity. Haggerty, who has married McCrea's girl, Phyllis Coates, has faith in McCrea although he does not give his reasons. McCrea meanwhile also guarantees to deliver a rival herd owned by Richard Shannon. The action develops with McCrea leading both herds, each out of sight of the other and—for a time—ignorant of the other's movements. The resolution comes when McCrea, overcoming his bitterness, brings Haggerty's cattle to safety while the other herd founders seeking water.

Some elements of the story are not well enough established to prevent audience skepticism, i.e., how two herds of about 5,000 each could move through the same territory without being aware of each other.

The good things about "Cattle Empire" are the performances. Each of the principals, McCrea, Haggerty, Miss Coates and Gloria Talbott, does a convincing job, well supported by such actors as comedians Bing Russell and Paul Brinegar, and by Hal K. Dawson, Duane Grey and Richard Shannon.

Brydon Baker's photography takes splendid advantage of the mainly outdoor settings to give a handsome, lavish feel to Robert Stabler's production. The music by Paul Sawtell and Bert Shefter is also helpful in setting the background and atmosphere, while editing by Leslie Vidor and sound by Frank McKenzie are both good.

Pow.

The Gift of Love

Tearjerker with good casting; especially attractive to femmes, with overall b.o. prospects sound.

Hollywood, Feb. 7.

20th-Fox release of Charles Brackett production. Stars Lauren Bacall, Robert Stack; with Evelyn Rudie, Lorne Greene, Anne Seymour, Edward Platt, Joseph Kearns. Directed by Jean Negulesco. Screenplay, Luther Davis; from a story by Nelia Gardner White; camera, Milton Krasner; editor, Hugh S. Fowler; music, Cyril J. Mockridge; title song by Sammy Fain and Paul Francis Webster; art direction, Lyle R. Wheeler and Mark-Lee Kirk. Previewed at studio, Feb. 5, '58. Running time, **105 MINS.**

Julie Beck .... Lauren Bacall
Bill Beck .... Robert Stack
Hitty .... Evelyn Rudie
Grant Allan .... Lorne Greene
McMasters .... Anne Seymour
Dr. Miller .... Edward Platt
Mr. Rynicker .... Joseph Kearns

A story of two kinds of love, each beautifully deep in its own way, "The Gift of Love" is one of those tear-eliciting pictures that has strong feminine appeal and therefore should do well at the boxoffice. Charles Brackett's 20th-Fox production should benefit from star names Lauren Bacall and Robert Stack plus a lilting title tune by Sammy Fain and Paul Francis Webster that should give pic an added thrust just as the pair's previous tune did for "April Love."

Director Jean Negulesco works with a poignant touch, making the loves so real, so moving, it's a cinch handkerchiefs will be in use. Scripted by Luther Davis from a Good Housekeeping magazine article that provided material for 20th's "Sentimental Journey" in 1946, "The Gift of Love" tells the story of a theoretical physicist (Stack) who's more than theoretically in love with his wife (Miss Bacall). Married for five years and childless, Miss Bacall learns she is suffering from a serious heart condition and may not be around much longer. To provide Stack with something to hold onto after she's gone, she convinces him they should adopt a child. Their choice (Evelyn Rudie) turns out to be unsuited to Stack, resulting in a conflict between the daughter who lives in fantasy and the father who's interested only in truth. To compound the irritation, Stack becomes deeply jealous over his wife's attention to the tot. Within months, Miss Bacall dies, leaving Stack a broken man. Evelyn insists she can talk to her departed mother, Stack blows his top at this last bit of nonsense, and back the girl goes to the orphanage. She takes a nasty fall and is about to be swallowed by the Pacific just as Stack lives through a bit of extra sensory perception, knowing at the precise moment that his daughter is in trouble. He knows he can't lose her, and he doesn't.

Totally proper casting keeps "Gift" above board, never falling into undue sentimentality. Miss Bacall's individual style shines brightly in this effort, her plight always reasonable and deeply rooted. Stack, whose problems are different from his wife's retains all sympathy, clearly showing how strong he can love. And Miss Rudie shows she can be as sweet as she can be precocious. Topnotch support comes from Lorne Greene, Anne Seymour and Edward Platt.

Milton Krasner's camera has captured some effective shots of northern California and the Pacific. Settings by Lyle R. Wheeler and Mark-Lee Kirk appear to have too much sameness, in decoration as well as DeLuxe Color, to other sets in recent 20th-Fox. pictures.

Cyril J. Mockridge's score marks action nicely, with the title theme used effectively and sung well by Vic Damone. Although pic seems slow in getting off the ground, with too much time and too little action before the titles, it all turns out to be quite a clever device to open five years of exposition before the body of the picture begins. *Ron.*

Los Amantes Del Desierto

(Desert Lovers)
(SPANISH-ITALIAN)
(Color-C'scope)

Madrid, Feb. 4.

CEA release of Benito Perojo-Roma Films production. Directed by Goffredo Alessandrini, Fernando Cerchio, Leon Klimovsky, Gianni Vernuccio. Stars Ricardo Montalban, Carmen Sevilla, Gino Cervi; features Jose Guardiola, Franca Bettoia. Screenplay, Alfonso Pase and Mariano Ozores; camera (Eastmancolor, Agfacolor, Ferraniacolor)) A. L. Ballesteros; art director, Sigfrido Burman and M. Garbuglia; music, Michel Michelet. At Avenida, Madrid.

Marquee names of Ricardo Montalban and Carmen Sevilla, an abundance of desert action, violence and mayhem, plus some good color lensing of sand, sphinx and pyramids lend weight to this costly Benito Perojo production, which was over a year in the making.

This cost, however, is only partially found on the screen, since it stems largely from English-French foray into Egypt which kept stars and the unit air-raid sheltered for weeks as well as the rotation of three Italian and one Spanish director, and bankruptcy of several Italo coproducers.

Montalban makes Valentino-Fairbanks nostalgia as the Arab prince who scimitars throat for throat until the usurper of his father's throne (Gino Cervi) and the traitor (Jose Guardiola) make a bloody exit. He also woos the impostor's righteous daughter and saves this desert pearl (Carmen Sevilla) in a kiss-censored romance.

Montalban, heroically unsparing of physical effort, played this one by ear. His drive is overpowering despite infantile situations and horse-opera dialogue. Other performances apparently suffer from the unusual directorial turnover. Technical credits are spotty.

Pic has exportable hip-swinging footage (scissored in Spain) and is one that lends itself to facile trimming. This looks possible for lower-case programming or late-hour tele circuits. *Hank.*

The Bride and the Beast

Gorilla-meets-girl. Sub-par adventure melodrama with African hunting and hypnotic regression an old mixture. Dim prospects.

Hollywood, Jan. 31.

Allied Artists release of Adrian Weiss Production. Stars Charlotte Austin, Lance Fuller; features Johnny Roth, Steve Calvert, William Justine, Jeanne Gerson, Gil Frye. Director, Adrian Weiss. Screenplay, Edward D. Wood Jr.; from a story by Adrian Weiss; camera, Roland Price; music, Les Baxter; editor, George Merrick. Previewed at the studio, Jan. 30, '58. Running time, **78 MINS.**

Laura .... Charlotte Austin
Dan .... Lance Fuller
Taro .... Johnny Roth
The Beast .... Steve Calvert
Dr. Reiner .... William Justine
Marka .... Jeanne Gerson
Capt. Cameron .... Gil Frye
Soldier .... Slick Slavin
Native .... Bhogwan Singh
Stewardess .... Jean Ann Lewis

A cheap quickie designed for the exploitation market, "The Bride and the Beast" will need lurid advertising to pay off. Produced and directed for Allied Artists by Adrian Weiss, the story is an odd and unconvincing mixture of hypnotic regression and big game hunting in Africa. The first element is pretty old-hat these days and the second is covered mostly by stock shots so there is little in the picture that is novel or diverting.

The story itself has unpleasant undertones. Charlotte Austin is the "Bride" of the title who discovers on her wedding day that her groom, Lance Fuller, keeps a full-grown gorilla in a cage of their home. Miss Austin finds herself attracted to the "Beast" and he displays a reciprocal tenderness. Before anything is made of this, Fuller shoots the gorilla dead.

To overcome Miss Austin's shock, hypnotic regression is brought into play and the point is made that the bride and the beast have known each other before sometime in one of Miss Austin's past lives when she was a gorilla herself. Well, this is dropped for a long sequence while Fuller and Miss Austin hunt, photograph and shoot African game.

An abrupt ending comes when Miss Austin is carried off by a male gorilla. There the story ends except for a brief tag shot where Fuller (back in America) remarks philosophically . . . *"And I never saw her again."*

The kids who make up the bulk of audiences for this kind of item are likely to be more amused than excited or fearful by the animal chase sequences. As for the girl-gorilla relationship, this is fortunately not deeply explored.

The cast does the best it can under the circumstances, with the only acting called for being variations on wide-eyed amazement or terror. Technical credits are standard although Les Baxter's music brightens up some of the sequences that otherwise would be even more tedious than they are. *Powe.*

The Beast of Budapest

Patchy, sporadic melodramatic recreation of Hungarian revolt. Selling angles despite weak script.

Hollywood, Jan. 31.

Allied Artists release of Barlene Corp. production. Features Gerald Milton, John Hoyt, Greta Thyssen, Michael Mills, Violet Rensing, John Mylong, Joseph Turkel, Booth Colman, Svea Grunfeld. Produced by Archie Mayo. Directed by Harmon C. Jones. Screenplay, John McGreevey; from a story by Louis Stevens; camera, Carl Guthrie; music, Marlin Skiles; editor, George White. Previewed at the studio, Jan. 30, '58. Running time, **72 MINS.**

Zagon .... Gerald Milton
Professor Tolnai .... John Hoyt
Christi .... Greta Thyssen
Charles Tolnai .... Michael Mills
Marissa .... Violet Rensing
General Foldessy .... John Mylong
Martin .... Joseph Turkel
Lieut. Stefko .... Booth Colman
Teresa .... Svea Grunfeld
Dr. Kovach .... John Banner
Josef .... Charles Brill
Geza .... Kurt Katch
Karolyi .... Robert Blake
Moricz .... Tommy Ivo
Elizabeth .... Colette Jackson

"The Beast of Budapest," a Barlene Corp. production for Allied Artists, is a fictionalization of the abortive Hungarian revolt of 1956. Archie Mayo's production, directed by Harmon C. Jones, is a serious effort to understand and portray the tragic episode but it still comes off as superficial comment. It is reminiscent of those early pictures about the Nazis. It is being teamed with the same studio's "The Bride And The Beast" as an exploitation package.

John Mylong plays the respected Hungarian military leader whose daughter, Violet Rensing, is a militant communist. She is attracted to Michael Mills, son of the liberal professor, John Hoyt, but politics keeps them apart. Gerald Milton is the "Beast," head of the secret police whose job is to cooperate with the Russians in maintaining a reign of terror. His lighter moments are spent with Greta Thyssen. The crux of the story is the revolt which ends, of course, with Russian tanks moving in and crushing the fighters for freedom.

Although, as noted, an attempt is made to treat this subject with the seriousness it deserves,—the script is never successful at doing more than sketch the protagonists and their motives. A good deal of stock footage is used and used well, but unfortunately its very reality undermines the other portions of the film.

The cast, occasionally injects some of the real spirit of this historical moment into the picture. Those who succeed best include John Hoyt, John Mylong, Joseph Turkel and a young actress, Svea Grunfeld.

Other credits are so-so. *Pow.*

Truth About Women

(BRITISH—COLOR)

Overlong, uneven comedy which is often witty; star cast should make this a reliable booking.

London, Feb. 4.

British Lion release of a Beaconsfield (Sydney Box) production. Stars Laurence Harvey, Julie Harris, Diane Cilento, Eva Gabor, Mai Zetterling. Directed by Muriel Box. Screenplay, Sydney and Muriel Box; editor, Anne V. Coates; camera, Otto Heller. At Studio One, London. Running time, **107 MINS.**

Humphrey Tavistock....Laurence Harvey
Helen Cooper .... Julie Harris
Ambrosine Viney .... Diane Cilento
Julie .... Mai Zetterling
Louise .... Eva Gabor
Rollo .... Michael Denison
Anthony .... Derek Farr
Comtesse .... Elina Labourdette
Charles Tavistock .... Roland Culver
Sir George Tavistock..Wilfrid Hyde White
Diana .... Catherine Boyle
Lady Tavistock......Ambrosine Philpotts
Saida .... Jackie Lane
Mary Maguire .... Lisa Gastoni
Sultan .... Robert Rietty
Marcelle .... Balbina
Francois .... Christopher Lee
Mrs. Maguire .... Aletha Orr
Otto Kerstein .... Marius Goring
Trevor .... Thorley Walters
Judge .... Ernest Thesiger
Sir Jeremy .... Griffith Jones

Sydney Box has piled a heap of stars and top class feature players into this comedy. The result is that "The Truth About Women" should make an attractive booking for houses on either side of the Atlantic. It is an over-long and rather old-fashioned comedy which effervesces quite often, but is then bogged down by flat passages. More ruthless cutting and a tighter screenplay by Sydney and Muriel Box would have been an advantage. The dialog, too, varies from the very witty to the naive.

Nevertheless, "Truth" will garner a lot of yocks from all types of audiences. There are some shrewd observations about the relationship between the two sexes. Femme patrons will particularly appreciate the manner in which the distaff side invariably comes out the victors in their clashes with the star, Laurence Harvey.

Yarn consists virtually of a number of anecdotes linked together in the reminiscences of Harvey. He is an elderly baronet, drawing on memories of the past loves to try and explain to his bewildered son-in-law that women are inexplicable. In a series of flashbacks we see the young Harvey wooing a suffragette, and then involved in a harem sequence in which he tries to abduct a slave girl with whom he has fallen in love. Posted in the Diplomatic Service in Paris he has an intrigue with a married woman which ends in a duel. In New York, he falls for a rich young American but manages to escape in time.

An encounter in a broken-down lift brings him together with a young artist to whom he is happily married for some time until her death. Then he woos a nurse whom he meets while convalescing from the first World War wounds. This romance ends up in a court suit. Finally, in his search for the truth about women he meets up with his first love and finally marries her.

Harvey, who is most convincing as the elderly raconteur, also dashes through this series of amorous interludes with considerable swagger. His comedy style tends to pall after awhile but he still performs with polish and presence. Diane Cilento, Julie Harris, Mai Zetterling, Eva Gabor and Jackie Lane are the women in his life. Each gives a pleasant, varied performance. Best sequence is the Paris episode with Elina Labourdette playing a comtesse with much subtlety. Michael Denison, Thorley Walters, Marius Goring, Roland Culver and Wilfrid Hyde White are also in excellent fettle. It is a drawback to the pic that Hyde-White and Culver disappear so soon from the scene.

Harvey is more effective in his quiet and serious moments than in his comedy playing, which is over-stylized. The Eastmancolor gives great effect to the various locales while Otto Heller's lensing, Cecil Beaton's costumes and George Provis's art work keep excellently to the early Twentieth Century period. Harvey's star value and the sympathetic playing of the Misses Harris, Cilento, Zetterling, Labourdette and Gabor help this comedy to rise above the fact that it needed to be written and directed with a more frivolous and even cynical touch. *Rich.*

Wien, Du Stadt Meiner Traeume
(Vienna, City of My Dreams)
(AUSTRIAN—COLOR)

Vienna, Feb. 4.

Sascha Film production and release. Stars Hans Holt, Erika Remberg; features Hertha Feiler, Adrian Hoven, Paul Hoerbiger, Oskar Sima, Jane Tilden, Richard Romonowsky. Directed by Willi Forst. Screenplay Paul H. Rameau and Kurt Nachmann; camera (Agfacolor), Robert Hofer; music, Alfred Uhl and Hans Lang. At Forum Kino, Vienna. Running time, 95 MINS.

Peter Lehnert	Adrian Hoven
Sandra, Princess	Erika Remberg
Elisabeth Seyboldt	Hertha Feiler
Alexander	Hans Holt
Vater Lehnert	Paul Hoerbiger
Trotum	Oscar Sima
Clara, his wife	Jane Tilden
Katzelseder	Richard Romonowsky
Mirko	Edwin Strah
Police Chief	Fred Hennings

Willi Forst has directed a class comedy so well it should win class bookings. It is one of the best Austrian productions made so far and has enough to do okay in almost any market.

Alexander, king of Alania, (Hans Holt) visits Vienna incognito. With revolution at home, the king obtains a job as chauffeur in his own embassy. This makes him so popular in Alania that the people soon seek his return, as presidential candidate. There is no doubt left about the outcome either of the election or the happy ending of two love stories, one between the former king and the future first lady, Hertha Feiler, and the other between princess Sandra (Erika Remberg) and music professor Peter Lehnert (Adrian Hoven).

Holt is fine as the king. Oscar Sima as Ambassador Trotum proves a clever comedian. Paul Hoerbiger appeals with his Viennese song, and also scores heavily in several very funny scenes.

The piano concerto by Alfred Uhl, played by Friedrich Gulda and the Vienna Symphonic under Professor Rudolf Moralt, as well as the Viennese song by Hans Lang and Kurt Nachmann may well become clicks in longhair field.

Attractive Vienna backgrounds are enhanced by the excellent Agfacolor lensing. Robert Hofer has done a fine camera job. All technical details are good. *Maas.*

A Tale of Two Cities
(BRITISH)

Obvious b.o. appeal of the title is backed up by sound acting and direction; should click with family audience.

London, Feb. 4.

Rank (Betty E. Box) production and release. Stars Dirk Bogarde, Dorothy Tutin, Cecil Parker. Directed by Ralph Thomas. Screenplay, T. E. B. Clarke, from Charles Dickens book; camera, Ernest Steward; editor, Alfred Roome; music, Richard Addinsell. At Odeon, Leicester Square, London. Running time, **117 MINS.**

Sydney Carton	Dirk Bogarde
Lucie Manette	Dorothy Tutin
Jarvis Lorry	Cecil Parker
Dr. Manette	Stephen Murray
Miss Pross	Athene Seyler
Charles Darnay	Paul Guers
Marie Gabelle	Marie Versini
Gabelle	Ian Bannen
Jerry Cruncher	Alfie Bass
Stryver	Ernest Clark
Madame Defarge	Rosalie Crutchley
Vengeance	Freda Jackson
Ernest Defarge	Duncan Lamont
Marquis St. Evremonde	Christopher Lee
Attorney General	Leo McKern
Barsad	Donald Pleasence
Sawyer	Eric Pohlmann

For the third time, Dickens' famed yarn crops up on the screen. With Dirk Bogarde in the Sydney Carton role, it will prove attractive family entertainment in British houses. If the title proves sufficient magnet for U.S. audiences, they will not be let down by a sound, rather than impaired cast. "A Tale of Two Cities" is a good adventure yarn and the French Revolution sequences offer a director lively opportunities for colorful action, which Ralph Thomas has deftly grabbed.

Set against the Storming of the Bastille, "Cities" is, of course, primarily a character study of a frustrated young lawyer who fritters his life away in drink until the moment when he makes everything worthwhile by a supreme sacrifice for the girl he loves. Bogarde brings a lazy charm and nonchalance to the Carton role but tends to play throughout in a surprisingly minor key. Hence, the pic never reaches the emotional heights that could be expected.

Leading femme is Dorothy Tutin, an accomplished young actress who has devoted her career mainly to the theatre. Her role does not strain her thesping ability. Cecil Parker, as a banker; Athene Seyler, as Miss Tutin's fussy companion; and Stephen Murray, as Dr. Manette, all have meaty portrayals which they handle with authority.

But it is among some of the other characterizations that there is most to admire, notably a new young actress, Marie Versini. Playing a young servant girl who becomes a victim of Madame Guillotine, Mlle. Versini brings a beautiful restraint and appeal to her task. She is obviously a youthful actress of talent as well as charm. Paul Guers, a French actor new to British pictures, is a handsome young man but hardly looks sufficiently like Bogarde to give real credence to the situation where Bogarde impersonates him on the guillotine.

Among other standout performances are those by Donald Pleasence, as an unctuous spy; Christopher Lee, as a sadistic aristocrat; and Duncan Lamont, as one of the leaders of the revolution. Rosalie Crutchley also makes notable impact with a brilliant study in malevolence as his vengeful wife.

Director Thomas has directed the drama with a straightforward touch. Ernest Steward's lensing takes full advantage of the opportunities provided by Carmen Dillon's first class art work. An offbeat job for script writer T. E. B. Clarke, but a commendable one. *Rich.*

Naked Earth
BRITISH—C'SCOPE)

Sultry personality of new French star, Juliette Greco, may provide b.o. potentiality for a slow-moving drama of croc hunting.

London, Feb. 4.

20th-Fox release of a Foray Production (by arrangement with Milton Holmes). Stars Richard Todd, Juliette Greco. Directed by Vincent Sherman. Screenplay, Milton Holmes; editor, Russell Lloyd; camera, Erwin Hillier. At 20th-Fox Private Theatre, London. Running time, 96 MINS.

Danny	Richard Todd
Maria	Juliette Greco
David	John Kitzmiller
Father Verity	Finlay Currie
Skin Trader	Laurence Naismith
Al	Christopher Rhodes
Tribesman	Orlando Martins

The producers of "Naked Earth" are obviously relying on the curiosity value surrounding the new import from France, Juliette Greco, to sell this. Because, apart from her interesting impact, the film is a slow-moving routine affair which rarely fulfils the promise of its screenplay. Why this should be is difficult to assess. It has a sound story, a very competent cast, much topnotch lensing by Edwin Hillier and the benefit of the fascinating and fresh locale of Uganda.

Yet it plods along conscientiously on a single level. Director Vincent Sherman seems to have lost a number of chances for pepping up the film with dramatic highlights. It is probable that many scenes landed on the cutting room floor. As a b.o. prospect both in Britain and U.S., much depends on whether Mlle. Greco can be put over as a magnet. She certainly has all the assets. She has a smouldering, sultry, earthy personality, which is lit up from time to time by glimpses of sheer beauty. The star, who has been best known as a chanteuse in ritzy cafes, reveals herself as a very promising actress with a candid, natural way of tossing off dialog.

"Earth" has Richard Todd as a young Irish farmer who comes to Uganda in 1895 to join a friend in a tobacco growing deal. His friend is dead and Todd joins up with Juliette Greco, who has been living with his buddy. They marry for convenience rather than love. With the devoted help of a native, splendidly portrayed by a new negro actor, John Kitzmiller, they begin their tobacco plantation.

The natives go off on a ceremonial junket and the crop is ruined. To raise money, Todd becomes a crocodile hunter and after a successful haul he is double-crossed by two shady traders. Disgusted by the behavior of the natives Todd decides to leave Uganda, but the yarn winds up with Todd and Mlle, Greco reconciled with the former deciding to stay in Uganda and work with the natives.

Apart from the femme star and Kitzmiller, the thesping is more competent than inspired. Laurence Naismith and Christopher Rhodes, as the traders; Finlay Currie, as a missionary; and Orlando Martins, as a native bearer, handle their chores satisfactorily. But for the hero a somewhat more commanding character than Todd would have helped.

The local atmosphere is put over well, especially in the leisurely beginning while the photography, especially in the night shots, cannot be faulted.

There is fascination, but surprisingly little to stir the pulse, in the crocodile sequences. Nevertheless, "Earth" is a pic to see because of Miss Greco. The French thrush, turned actress, is a new screen personality who is clearly going places. *Rich.*

Tamango
(FRENCH; C'SCOPE; COLOR)

Paris, Feb. 11.

Disaifilm release of Cyclops-SNEG production. Stars Curd Jurgens, Dorothy Dandridge; features Jean Servais, Alex Cressan. Directed by John Berry. Screenplay, Lee Gold, Tamara Hovey from novelette by Prosper Merimee; dialog, Georges Neveux; camera (Eastmancolor), Edmond Sechan; editor, Roger Dwyre. At Madeleine, Paris. Running time, 95 MINS.

Aiche	Dorothy Dandridge
Captain	Curd Jurgens
Corot	Jean Servais
Tamango	Alex Cressan
Bebe	Roger Hanin
Werner	Guy Mairesse
Cook	Clement Harari

This could shape as a potent box-office contender on both local and Yank screens because of its rugged subject matter, a revolt on a slave ship during the early 19th Century. There are some torrid clinches between white star Curd Jurgens and American Negro actress Dorothy Dandridge. But this is not cheapened, and film stacks up as an actioner, with plus hypo factors, that could make for a general play-off in the U. S., with perhaps the South excluded.

Director John Berry, a Yank, has given this splendid mounting and has overcome some dramatic contrivance via emphasis on a fight for freedom. Though ideologies are kept simple, the final revolt of the slaves, and Miss Dandridge's (she is the Captain's (Jurgens) mistress and slave) reversion to her own peoples, offer a stirring climax to the film.

Jurgens gives strength and some complexity to his role of a man who has accepted the injustice of slaving and lives by its code though trying for some understanding of the situation through his consuming love for the slave girl. Latter role is unevenly played by Miss Dandridge at the outset but gains depth and stature at the close. Alex Cressan, an Afro medico student, is effective as the burly, one-track minded Tamango whose need for liberty and dignity brings on the abortive revolt.

Cinemascope and color give this breadth, and it amply sets up the contrast between the ship's spacious progress and the cramped slave quarters. Cast is good while director Berry has done a melodrama with humane overtones.

Production values are excellent.

Not primarily for arty theatres, this would best be served in the U. S. via dubbing for more general playdating. It has further sell value in the names of Jurgens, who is recalled for his first Yank stint, "Enemy Below," and Miss Dandridge. An Anglo version was made alongside the French one and this could be utilized if the dubbing is of high quality. A little tightening up of the slow beginning would help give this more drive.

Mosk.

Tous Peuvent Me Tuer
(Anyone Can Kill Me)
(FRENCH—DYALISCOPE)

Paris, Feb. 4.

Sofradis release of Da-Ma Cinema production. Stars Francis Perier; features Anouk Aimee, Eleonora Rossi-Drago, Peter Van Eyck. Directed by Henri Decoin. Screenplay, Versini, Albert Simonin. Decoin; camera, Pierre Montazel; editor, Claude Durand. At Biarritz, Paris. Running time, 100 MINS.
Warden .... Francois Perier
Warden's Wife .... Eleonora Rossi-Drago
Isabelle .... Anouk Aimee
Cyril .... Peter Van Eyck
Gaston .... Pierre Louis
Karl ....Franco Fabrizi
Luigi .... Dario Moreno
Guard .... Francis Blanche
Antoine ....Andre Versini
Emile .... Piere Mondy

Pic details a holdup by five men and then their alibi which gets them a year in prison. But in the stir they start getting killed off for suspense in the film. This is slickly made but lacks the deeper characterization needed to make it anything more than a secondary feature possibility in the U.S. It has a CinemaScope size via Dyaliscope.

Director Henri Decoin has given the pic careful mounting but used visual cliches, of tilted shots, intercutting of the different actions to one plane, etc. But he has been unable to give it the necessary suspense and drama it requires.

The acting is good as are technical credits and general production values. However, this remains only a fair entry in the cycle of gangster pix here.

Mosk.

Donnez-Moi Ma Chance
(Give Me My Chance)
(FRENCH)

Paris, Feb. 4.

Sirius release of Jacques Roitfeld production. With Michele Mercier, Danick Patisson, Nadine Tallier. Directed by Leonide Moguy. Screenplay, Andre and Georges Tabet, Moguy; camera, Maurice Barry; editor, Henri Taverna. At Marignan, Paris. Running time, 95 MINS.
Nicole .... Michele Mercier
Kiki .... Nadine Tallier
Brigitte .... Danick Patisson
Gilbert .... Ivan Desny
Georges .... Francois Guerin
Father ....George Chamaret

This old-fashioned drama is about a comely girl who wins a contest and leaves her small town for Paris and a try in films. Here she languishes, even though she keeps on studying. When she is used by an unscrupulous publicist, the gal tries to commit suicide. Finally her true fiance comes to her rescue just when a big contract has come through.

This has too much coincidence and obvious characters to amount to much. This pic hints no promise of any chance in the U.S., and looks limited here too.

Director Leonide Moguy has been unable to get reality into this lagging odyssey. Michele Mercier is less wooden than usual as the harassed starlet, and may develop into a competent actress. Nadine

Tallier is a saucy, bright personality while Danick Patisson also acquits herself well.

Mosk.

Une Manche et La Belle
(Beauty Up His Sleeve)
(FRENCH)

Paris, Jan. 28.

Cinedis release of Michel Safra production. Stars Mylene Demongeot, Henri Vidal, Isa Miranda. Directed by Henri Verneuil. Screenplay, Francois Boyer, Annette Wademant, Verneuil from novel by James Hadley Chase; camera, Christian Matras; editor, L. Hautcoeur; at the Paris, Paris. Running time, 100 MINS.
Eve .... Mylene Demongeot
Philippe .... Henri Vidal
Malard .... Alfred Adam
Betty .... Isa Miranda
Bob ....Jean-Loup Philippe
Sylvette .... Simone Bach
Mayor ....Antonin Berval

This is another meaty slice of the present French film eroticosuspense cycle. Bearing resemblance to "Double Indemnity," this has enough new twists, torrid clinching and slickness to rate well here. Pic is mainly for secondary spots or as a strongly exploited subject in the U.S.

A shrewd bank clerk manages to marry an aging heiress. He falls for the conniving secretary and they decide to do away with the wife via the perfect crime which is somewhat transparent, at least for the audience. They wind up butchering each other when the secretary tries to pull a double-cross.

Henri Vidal gives some feeling to the role of weak opportunist who is dragged into murder. Isa Miranda gives this melodrama solid footing via her smart thesping as the aging rich woman. Mylene Demongeot, a rising star here, has a vinegary appeal with some dramatic ability that brings off her secretary role well.

Production values are lush. Director Henri Verneuil keeps this moving along at a nice pace if not always convincing. Technical credits are fine.

Mosk.

Scandal in Bad Ischl
(AUSTRIAN—COLOR)

Vienna, Jan. 28.

Otto Druer release of Vienna film production. Stars O. W. Fischer; features Elizabeth Mueller, Ivan Desny, Nina Sandt, Doris Kirchner, Harry Mayen, Michael Ande, Alma Seidler, Reoul Retzer, Senta Wengraf, Rudolf Forster. Directed by Rolf Thiele. Screenplay by Eberhard Keindorf and Johanna Sibelius after the stage play "The Master," by Herman Bahr; camera, Klaus von Rautenfeld. Running time, 90 MINS.

"Scandal in Bad Ischl" should spell good business in many markets, this packing solid entertainment. Fortified with a made-to-fit character role for O. W. Fischer, the Eberhard Keindorf-Johanna Sibelius screenplay (after the old stage hit, "The Master") effectively handles the story about a medico at this oldtime summer resort city of Bad Ischl. It may do for some U.S. arty houses.

Gossip in Spa Ischl is that the surgeon Fischer has committed abortion for an unmarried peasant girl. The royal family, headed by Alma Seidler the Archduchess, takes his side. This helps his rise to fame. Ultimately, it turns out the doctor actually had helped the girl get the baby.

This is a clean-cut comedy, with Fischer doing nicely as the medico. Elisabeth Mueller as his misunderstood wife, does impressive work. Remainder of the cast is excellent. Direction by Rolf Thiele is well

paced. Photography in Agfa color by Klaus von Rautenfeld is fine with other technical credits okay. Musical arrangements by Bruno Uher are okay.

Maas.

Brothers Karamazov

Lavish production of classic Russian story of love, lust and murder. Top-notch acting highlights. Strong b.o. prospects.

Hollywood, Feb. 14.

Metro release of Avon Production. Stars Yul Brynner, Maria Schell, Claire Bloom, Lee J. Cobb, Albert Salmi, Richard Basehart, William Shatner; features Judith Evelyn, Edgar Stehli, Harry Townes, Miko Oscard, David Opatoshu. Produced by Pandro S. Berman. Directed by Richard Brooks. Screenplay by Brooks from adaptation by Julius J. and Philip G. Epstein from Fyodor Dostoyevsky novel; camera, John Alton; music, Bronislau Kaper; editor, John Dunning. Previewed in Hollywood, Feb. 10, '58. Running time, 149 MINS.
Dmitri Karamazov .... Yul Brynner
Grushenka .... Maria Schell
Katya .... Claire Bloom
Fyodor Karamazov......... Lee J. Cobb
Ivan Karamazov........Richard Basehart
Smerdyakov .... Albert Salmi
Alexey Karamazov......William Shatner
Mme. Anna Hohlakov......Judith Evelyn
Grigory .... Edgar Stehli
Ippolit Kirillov .... Harry Townes
Ilusha Snegiryov .... Miko Oscard
Capt. Snegiryov ....David Opatoshu
Mavrayek ....Simon Oakland
Capt. Vrublevski .... Frank De Kova
Pawnbroker .... Jay Adler
Defense Counsel .... Gage Clarke
Marya .... Ann Morrison
Trifon Borissovitch .... Mel Welles

Bold handling of crude, unbridled passion, of violently conflicting ideas, and of earthy humor make up "The Brothers Karamazov." Sex and Salvation are the twin obsessions of the brothers and father, and they are the two themes that are hammered relentlessly home by Richard Brooks, who directed his own screenplay.

Sumptuous and sensitive MGM production by Pandro S. Berman doesn't sacrifice art to entertainment nor lose entertainment in a false conception of what constitutes art. "The Brothers Karamazov" should be one of the year's commercial successes.

Everything about the production is rich and ornate like a Byzantine basilica, yet the personalities and the story are never submerged. One of the greatest surprises about the picture is the bawdy humor that serves the double purpose of occasionally lightening the grim narrative and of deepening the depravity of some of its figures. These people, played by Yul Brynner, Maria Schell, Claire Bloom and most notably, Lee J. Cobb, are full-bodied, larger than life-size personalities who command unwavering attention. The public should take to it like vodka.

Brooks wrote his screenplay from an adaptation by Julius J. and Philip G. Epstein. Cobb is the father of the Karamazov brothers, a lecherous old buffoon who taunts, tantalizes and frustrates his sons into violence, despair and apathy. Yul Brynner is the handsome, cruel, profligate Army officer, a combination of adult power and childish pleasure. He is in conflict with his father partly because they both lust after the same woman, Maria Schell as Grushenka. Richard Basehart is in revolt because of his intellectual coldness, a rigidity brought on by revulsion at the open and untrammeled sexuality of the old rogue. The third son, William Shatner, has chosen his way of survival in contest with his father; he has retreated into the church as a monk.

The explosion that these figures ignite comes when Brynner imagines Miss Schell has gone to his father in preference to him, because he is bankrupt and his father holds the family purse. When Cobb is killed, Brynner is charged and convicted of the murder although the true killer is actually

Cobb's bastard son, Albert Salmi, warped into insanity. Claire Bloom is the alabaster beauty who saves Brynner from debtors' prison and is then deserted by him for Miss Schell. Her revenge comes at his trial when she seals his conviction by her testimony.

The picture opens in a fog of talk, of infinite detail seen dimly as the story starts in shadows from which the characters suddenly emerge sharply. The conversation runs on like a river, over-lapping, funny, disarming and confusing. Yet when the important personalities are deliberately brought into focus the viewer knows more about each than imagined.

There is difficult stuff here. There is talk about God. "Does He exist," the elder Karamazov demands of each son in turn, and each must give his reason for his answer. The next instant Cobb is baiting Brynner on Grushenka or young Shatner on his life of spiritual contemplation. These Russian mixtures make the picture constantly challenging and absorbing.

Brynner succeeds in making his Dmitri a hero despite the fact that every facet of his character is against it. Miss Schell, in her American motion picture debut, illumines her role, seemingly able to suggest innocence and depravity with the same sweet face. Miss Bloom is very moving, particularly in the court scene as her facade cracks from within, rent by bitterness and despair.

It is Lee J. Cobb, however, who walks—or rather gallops—away with the picture. The part is gargantuan and it is not a bit too big for this actor. Richard Basehart manages to glow with anger and resentment, using only his eyes and voice to suggest his great hatred, while Albert Salmi makes his role pathetic and somehow awful.

William Shatner has the difficult task of portraying youthful male goodness and he does it with such gentle candor it is effective. Those who standout in the large supporting cast include Judith Evelyn, young Miko Oscard, David Opatoshu, Harry Townes, William Vedder and Ann Morrison. Also Gage Clarke, Mel Welles, Jay Adler, Frank De Kova and Simon Oakland.

The Metrocolor used by Brooks and his cameraman, John Alton, is rich in purples, reds and blues. They also use a technique of lighting in the last, frenzied scenes, of lighting the characters with red, yellow or green that is highly effective. It fits the mood of the story and it fits the authentic settings by art directors William A. Horning and Paul Gnuesse. Walter Plunkett's costumes, the hair stylings by Sidney Guilaroff and the make-ups by William Tuttle, are particularly important in a period picture of this type. They are all done so disarmingly they seem natural and right. Set decorations by Henry Grace and Robert Priestley compliment the production; the editing by John Dunning is a masterful job and Dr. Wesley C. Miller's sound seems flawless. Bronislau Kaper's thunderous music behind the main titles sets the mood of the picture inescapably and his score throughout reflects the shifting emotions of the many and diverse characters. *Pow.*

Ambush at Cimarron Pass

Average low-budget oater for filler fare.

Hollywood, Feb. 14.

20th Century-Fox release of a Regal Production produced by Herbert E. Mendelson. Stars Scott Brady, Margia Dean; with Clint Eastwood, Irving Bacon, Frank Gerstle, Dirk London, Baynes Barron, Ken Mayer, Keith Richards, William Vaughan, John Damler, John Merrick. Directed by Jadie Copelan. Screenplay, Richard G. Taylor and John K. Butler; story, Robert A. Reeds and Robert W. Woods; camera, John M. Nickolaus Jr.; editor, Carl L. Pierson; music, Paul Sawtell and Bert Shefter. Previewed in Hollywood, Feb. 11, '58. Running time, 73 MINS.

Sgt. Matt Blake	Scott Brady
Teresa	Margia Dean
Corbin	Baynes Barron
Henry	William Vaughan
Cpl. Schwitzer	Ken Mayer
Private Zach	John Mamler
Private Lasky	Keith Richards
Private Nathan	John Merrick
Sam Prescott	Frank Gerstle
Keith Williams	Clint Eastwood
Johnny Willows	Dirk London
Stanfield	Irving Bacon
Cob	Desmond Slattery
Stunt	Joe Yrigoyen
Stunt	Bob Morgan

A westernized walk in the sun, this Regal opus creates a respectable amount of interest to fill out double feature situations. Prospects are no more than that, though a number of worthwhile performances do add a bit of spice.

As Jodie Copelan's first directorial effort, "Ambush At Cimarron Pass" moves rather well within the limitations of its low budget. The Richard G. Taylor-John K. Butler screenplay is spotty in its excitement, and Herbert E. Mendelson's production values are about average.

Topliner Scott Brady, as a Union soldier who fights Apaches now that there are no more Rebels, is sincere in his approach, quite believable in his performance. Fine portrayals also come from Margia Dean, Frank Gerstle, Clint Eastwood and Dirk London.

Things get roling with a half dozen Union soldiers transporting a prisoner to Fort Waverly. Surrounded by Apaches, the group happens upon a half dozen former Confederate soldiers. They join forces, though past animosities often get in the way, and in the next bit of excitement, the Apaches drop off a sexy Mexican dish and ride off with the white men's horses. Thus starts the seven-day walk to the fort, an experience without sufficient food or water and with the added burden of carrying a load of guns the Indians want desperately. Fact is, the Apaches say they'll give the horses back in exchange for the weapons.

Many arrows later, and with half the group killed along the way, Brady brings his charges to safety. John M. Nickolaus, Jr.'s camera shows nicely in some instances, but shifting from outdoor settings to indoor replicas is all too obvious. So is the outdoor smog. *Ron.*

The True Story of Lynn Stuart

Exciting and true, pic still may need fast promotion if boxoffice is to ring.

Hollywood, Feb. 11.

Columbia release of Bryan Foy production. Stars Betsy Palmer; with Jack Lord, Barry Atwater; also Kim Spalding, Karl Lukas, Casey Walters, Harry Jackson, Claudia Bryar, John Anderson, Rita Duncan, Lee Farr, Louis Towers. Directed by Lewis Seiler. Screenplay, John H. Kneubuhl, from newspaper articles by Pat Michaels; camera, Burnett Guffey; editor, Saul A. Goodkind. Previewed at studio, Feb. 7, '58. Running time, 76 MINS.

Phyllis Carter	Betsy Palmer
Willie Down	Jack Lord
Hagan	Barry Atwater
Ralph Carter	Kim Spalding
Hal Bruck	Karl Lukas
Eddie Dine	Casey Walters
Husband Officer	Harry Jackson
Nora Efron	Claudia Bryar
"Doc"	John Anderson
Sue	Rita Duncan
Ben	Lee Farr
Jimmy Carter	Louis Towers

Because it's constructed from California fact rather than conjured from Hollywood fiction, "The True Story of Lynn Stuart" manages to assume a semi-documentary flavor that magnifies excitement and instills deep consideration for the plight of the title character. Given a good production by Bryan Foy, pic will have to be heralded by a hearty exploitation campaign if it's going to impress b.o. watchers as anything but good second feature fare.

Topliner Betsy Palmer, who may perk up prospects with her own following of televisitors, is this Columbia film's biggest plus. As a Santa Ana, Calif., housewife who volunteers to smoke out a ring of dope pushers, she has all the good graces and well-meaning cunning needed for her role of dual identity. Director Lewis Seiler was able to garner top performances from featured players Jack Lord and Barry Atwater, but the rest of the way down the cast line, it was nip and tuck whether some performances were going to stand up. Of the nine smaller players, Harry Jackson shows the most promise.

John H. Kneubuhl's screenplay, based on newspaper articles by Santa Ana reporter Pat Michaels, is slightly heavy on talk for a picture that could benefit from additional action, but on the whole, it is a well-knit piece of work. It tells of Lynn Stuart (Miss Palmer) whose nephew is killed in an auto crash while heavily doped. With sincerity, she offers to help Orange County detectives crack the narcotics-selling mob. When desperate, the chief investigator (Atwater) accepts her offer, letting her nuzzle up to a girl-loving, dope-moving hoodlum (Lord). Actually, she helping a good deal before being carted off to Tijuana by the gentleman. Police search, ultimately find and capture the ring leaders. In a moving climax, Miss Palmer is jailed and indicted by the Grand Jury to protect her identity as the informant.

Pic gains momentum from fine night photography by Burnett Guffey. Other technical credits are well above exploitation standards. *Ron.*

Stage Struck

Unrestrained Susan Strasberg in film debut. Tyro who steps into the star's spot on a Broadway opening night. Slow. Fair prospects.

Hollywood, Feb. 21.

Buena Vista release of an RKO-Radio production. Stars Henry Fonda, Susan Strasberg, Joan Greenwood, Herbert Marshall, Christopher Plummer, also with Daniel Ocko, Pat Harrington, Frank Campanella, John Fiedler, Patricia Englund, Jack Weston, Sally Gracie, Nina Hansen, Harold Grau. Produced by Stuart Millar. Directed by Sidney Lumet. Screenplay, Ruth and Augustus Goetz; play, Zoe Akins; camera, Franz Planer, Maurice Hartzband; music, Alex North; editor, Stuart Gilmore. Previewed in Hollywood, Feb. 21, '58. Running time, 95 MINS.

Lewis Easton	Henry Fonda
Eva Lovelace	Susan Strasberg
Rita Vernon	Joan Greenwood
Robert Hedges	Herbert Marshall
Joe Sheridan	Christopher Plummer
Constantine	Daniel Ocko
Benny	Pat Harrington
Victor	Frank Campanella
Adrian	John Fiedler
Gwen Hall	Patricia Englund
Frank	Jack Weston
Elizabeth	Sally Gracie
Regina	Nina Hansen
Doorman	Harold Grau

"Stage Struck," a Buena Vista release of an RKO picture, weaves another variation on the now well-worn tale of the eager young actress who can't persuade anyone on Broadway to give her a job until the star flounces out on the eve of opening night. The tyro steps into the star's shoes, knocks the audience right out of its red plush seats; veterans backstage murmur, "that's show biz," and the camera pans slowly away from a solitary figure standing in the middle of an empty theatre; music up and out. It's a remake of "Morning Glory," a yesteryear Katherine Hepburn starrer.

Producer Stuart Millar and director Sidney Lumet have tried to mask this threadbare theme with the sheen and substance of authentic settings in Technicolor (the whole picture was shot in New York), with good actors and with touches both romantic and realistic. But the telling is not novel enough to make it freshly attractive and the result is fair box office prospects at best.

Susan Strasberg plays the would-be actress who hounds producer Henry Fonda for a chance. He is intrigued by the girl but not as an actress and turns her down. Not so his playwright, Christopher Plummer, who sees her both as actress and romantic opposite. When the star of their show, Joan Greenwood, makes a temperamental exit, Plummer has Miss Strasberg set to take over her role and she does with plot-predictable ease and success.

Miss Strasberg occupies a major portion of the footage in this Ruth and Augustus Goetz screenplay from a Zoe Akins play. She is not a conventional screen beauty but her face is expressive and lively. Her technique is formidable and her director seems to have been so bewitched by it that she receives virtually no restraint from him, and she needed some. Reactions to the young actress—here making her major motion picture debut—are likely to be highly individual and divided.

Fonda plays with his customary quiet authority and disarming command and Herbert Marshall limns a warming portrait as a stage veteran. Miss Greenwood, no mean "technician" herself, gives the rampaging star the Bankhead bit and very funny she is. Plummer has considerable depth to his playing and adds to the value of the production. Others who stand out include radio studio veteran Daniel Ocko, Patricia Englund and Pat Harrington.

The Goetz' screenplay is literate and often penetrating but it is mortally deficient on real humor. The direction is sometimes attractive, particularly in such situations as the opening sequences in Fonda's office, but it plays slow and loose when it allows such scenes as Miss Strasberg's recitation of the entire balcony scene from "Romeo and Juliet."

Camera work by Franz Planer and Maurice Hartzband is striking, notably in the Central Park scene, a setting of a Greenwich Village street, dawn in Times Square, and the interiors of the theatre (actually the National on 41st street, recently in the headlines because of its owner's death). *Powe.*

Underwater Warrior

Routine programmer of frogmen exploits.

Hollywood, Feb. 14.

Metro release of Ivan Tors production. Stars Dan Dailey, Claire Kelly; features James Gregory, Ross Martin, Raymond Bailey, Alex Gerry, Genie Coree, Charles Keane, Jon Lindbergh, Zale Parry, Alex Fane. Produced by Ivan Tors. Directed by Andrew Marton. Screenplay, Gene Levitt; camera, Joseph Biroc, Lamar Boren; music, Harry Sukman; editor, Charles Craft. Previewed at the Pantages Theatre, Hollywood, Feb. 14, '58. Running time, 90 MINS.

Comdr. David Forest .... Dan Dailey
Anne Whinmore .... Claire Kelly
Comdr. William Arnold.... James Gregory
Joe O'Brian .... Ross Martin
Adm. Ashton .... Raymond Bailey
Capt. of Battleship .... Alex Gerry
Marie .... Genie Coree
Captain .... Charles Keane
Boat Officer .... Jon Lindbergh
Girl Swimmer .... Zale Parry
Davey Jr. .... Alex Fane

Some interesting underwater photography highlights MGM's "Underwater Warrior," but the land-bound stretches in between the watery sequences bog down so that it adds up to very mild entertainment. The fault lies in the screenplay, based on the true life adventures of Navy Commander Francis D. Fane. There is no important climax to the story strong enough to justify the length of the picture. It proceeds from episode to episode without a central theme. Exploitation of the current interest in lung-diving may help to sell this Ivan Tors production to action audience. It's directed by Andrew Marton from Gene Levitt's screenplay.

Dan Dailey plays the navy officer who believes that frogmen have an important job to play in the nation's defense. He pushes his belief in the days before World War II and through that conflict and into the Korean war, often against top brass disapproval or misunderstanding. Against this action is his personal life with wife Claire Kelly, who traditionally wants her husband home for supper and not off pushing the fish around.

There is some humor in Levitt's script, and Marton's direction takes good advantage of it. The direction is also skillful in dealing at some length with the technical aspects of diving and in utilizing at length Lamar Boren's excellent underwater photography. The shark sequences, however, might better have been played for the zest of drama that the picture needs rather than the humor they are used for.

Dailey makes a believable frogman and Miss Kelly is pleasant in a standout role. James Gregory, Ross Martin and Raymond Bailey make up the other important members of the cast. Jon Lindbergh appears briefly and acceptably. His name could be an added starter in exploitation. *Powe.*

Cross-Up

Involved melodrama. Smaller program market.

Hollywood, Feb. 14.

United Artists release of Robert S. Baker-Monty Berman production. Stars Larry Parks; features Constance Smith, Lisa Daniely. Directed by John Gilling. Screenplay, Gilling, Willis Boldbeck, based on novel, "I'll Never Come Back," by John Mair; camera, Eric Cross; music, Stanley Black. Previewed Feb. 10, '58. Running time, 83 MINS.

John Desmond .... Larry Parks
Jane .... Constance Smith
Anna Ray .... Lisa Daniely

"Cross-Up" is the story of an American newspaper correspondent in London who bucks an international counterfeiting gang. Like so many British melodramas turned out on short budget it becomes involved in plottage, and emerges only a fair entry for secondary program situations. Larry Parks is only American name in cast.

Filmed in London, the Robert S. Baker-Monty Berman production suffers from a commonplace story idea and routine handling which give an old-fashioned air to unfoldment. Script by John Gilling and Willis Goldbeck has Parks becoming involved with a mystery femme who turns out to be an agent for the crime ring. She's accidentally killed while he's struggling with her for possession of a gun she pulls on him when he picks up her diary, and he makes off with diary, which turns out to be a record of the gang's agents in various countries, recorded in cipher. Major portion of action deals with efforts of the gang to retrieve this book.

John Gilling's direction lacks spark, with result the portrayals aren't particularly interesting. Parks vacillates between straight drama and out-of-place coyness, Lisa Daniely is heavy as the agent but Constance Smith manages some semblance of credibility as Parks' secretary. Cyril Chamberlain is the gang leader, Parks' nemesis, okay in part.

Technical credits are average. *Whit.*

Curse of the Demon

Unusual horror pic with good exploitable elements.

Hollywood, Feb. 21.

Columbia release of Hal E. Chester Production. Stars Dana Andrews, Peggy Cummins. With Niall MacGinnis, Maurice Denham, Athene Seyler, Liam Redmond; also Reginald Beckwith, Ewan Roberts, Peter Elliott, Rosamund Greenwood, Brian Wilde, Richard Leech, Lloyd Lamble, Peter Hobbes, Charles Lloyd-Pack, John Salew, Janet Barrow, Percy Herbert, Lynn Tracy. Director, Jacques Tourneur; screenplay, Charles Bennett and Hal E. Chester from Montague R. James story; camera, Ted Scaife; editor, Michael Gordon; music, Clifton Parker. Previewed Feb. 14, '58. Running time, 82 MINS.

John Holden .... Dana Andrews
Joanna Harrington ...... Peggy Cummins
Doctor Karswell .... Niall MacGinnis
Professor Harrington.... Maurice Denham
Mrs. Karswell .... Athene Seyler
Mark O'Brien .... Liam Redmond
Mr. Meek .... Reginald Beckwith
Lloyd Williamson......... Ewan Roberts
Kumar .... Peter Elliott
Mrs. Meek .... Rosamond Greenwood
Rand Hobart .... Brian Wilde
Inspector Mottram .... Richard Leech
Detective Simmons .... Lloyd Lamble
Superintendent .... Peter Hobbes
Chemist .... Charles Lloyd-Pack
Librarian .... John Salew
Mrs. Hobart .... Janet Barrow
Farmer .... Percy Herbert
Air Hostess .... Lynn Tracy

The only mechanical thing about "Curse of the Demon" is the fiery monster itself, the rest of the fine Hal E. Chester production flowing with eerie suspense, marking fine possibilities for b.o. exploitation. In a day when most horror pix are grasping creatures from outer space, this Columbia release, made in England, has the unique bonus of conjuring a mythical chimera-like creature from the past. Additionally, toplined Dana Andrews may perk business, with the majority of current scaries being cast with no established stars.

Scripted by Charles Bennett and producer Chester from a story by Montague R. James, "Curse" is an interesting tale, completely irrational but somehow deserving of a peculiar kind of belief. Directed with a supernatural touch by Jacques Tourneur, it abounds in magic, hypnotism, seances, strange aberations and profuse delving into the occult.

As an American psychologist who opens his mind to strange occurences, Andrews sometimes seems overly unsympathetic but he proves himself well able to hold the conflict together. Peggy Cummins is as beautiful as when she was talked of for "Forever Amber" and with a sweet British accent, she's properly and poignantly afraid. Niall MacGinnis, as the devil's desciple on earth, brings to this fearsome epic an excellent performance.

Andrews flies to England to zoom through a psychological investigation of a dealer in the black arts, MacGinnis, only to find the doctor who had started the query has been brutally mauled by some gigantic thing. That MacGinnis cast a curse becomes obvious, and though Andrews doesn't go in for this sort of tommy-rot, he eventually changes his mind when his death is set for three days hence by the magician's passing unnoticed a parchment with runic symbols. All this time, Miss Cummins, niece of the dead doctor, is prodding Andrews along the investigative path until he learns he must return the parchment to the giver in order to save his own life. He does, and the witch doctor is hauled off by the monster, all ending in a rather disastrously happy finish.

Keeping up with the frightening effects by George Blackwell and Wally Veevers, Ted Scaife's camera work is tops. Effective in its heightening of fear is the Clifton Parker score, with sound effects by Charles Crafford an added plus. *Ron.*

Man From God's Country

Routine oater in color and widescreen.

Hollywood, Feb. 14.

Allied Artists release of Scott R. Dunlap production; Stars George Montgomery, Randy Stuart; features Gregg Barton, Kim Charney, Susan Cummings, Produced by Scott R. Dunlap. Directed by Paul Landres. Screenplay, George Waggner; camera, Harry Neumann; music, Marlin Skiles; editor, George White. Previewed at the studio, Feb. 10, '58. Running time, 72 MINS.

Dan .... George Montgomery
Nancy .... Randy Stuart
Colonel .... Gregg Barton
Stony .... Kim Charney
Mary Jo .... Susan Cummings
Mark .... James Griffith
Curt .... House Peters Jr.
Sheriff .... Phillip Terry

"Man From God's Country," a Scott R. Dunlap production for Allied Artists, directed by Paul Landres, is a routine western that will have to depend upon George Montgomery's name for whatever business it is able to rustle up. The story is familiar and it is given no special treatment to make it more attractive. It contains one interesting anomaly. It had a shooting title of "New Day at Sundown," and the "title song" still has that handle.

Montgomery is a frontier sheriff who has resigned his job under fire because he kept the town clean but only by shooting down the would-be defilers. The townspeople want a quieter town even if it is less law-abiding. Montgomery drifts off to ride herd on the trail to Sundown—a frontier town—where he hopes to meet a Civil War crony, House Peters Jr. He finds Peters in the toils of the local crime boss, Frank Wilcox, who also runs Sundown. Montgomery finally rouses Peters dormant sense of justice and they pair up to gun down the lawless element. A happy and romantic ending is provided when Susan Cummings and Peters team up and Randy Stuart, the local dance hall hostess, makes a clean start with Montgomery.

The cast is equal to the demands of the script and Landres does his best to obscure its paucity by keeping things moving as briskly as possible. The CinemaScope, DeLuxe color gives the picture good physical values that are exploited by Harry Néumann's photography. *Powe.*

Amore e Chiacchere
(Love and Chatter)
(ITALO—FRANCO—SPANISH)

Rome, Feb. 18.

Cei-Incom release of an Electra Cinematografica-Ariel Film-Societe Francaise De Cinematografie co-production. Stars Vittorio DeSica, Gino Cervi; features Elisa Cegani, Isa Pola, Carla Gravina, Geronimo Meynier. Directed by Alessandro Blasetti. Screenplay, Cesare Zavattini, Isa Bartalini, Blasetti; from story by Zavattini. Camera, Gabor Pogany. Music, Mario Nascimbene. Editor, Mario Serandrei. Previewed in Rome. Running time, 105 MINS.

Father .... Vittorio DeSica
Mother .... Elisa Cegani
Son .... Geronimo Meynier

Pic is cut several notches above current local fare, and boasts an intelligent script plus some expert performances. Moreover, its often above-belt humor is handled with tongue in cheek by director Alessandro Blasetti to good effect. Pic should pay off in depth in home territory and make okay export fare.

Story comprises several tales—one about a speech-crazed town mayor (DeSica) and his attempts to keep his voters (notably a group of oldsters in a home for the aged) happy while promoting himself, and the love affair of his son (Geronimo Meynier) for the local streetcleaner's daughter (Carla Gravina). Attempts to bridge the social gap while at the same time trying to appease a rich industrialist who wants his estate's scenery kept free of buildings, make up the remainder of the pic.

Despite the split into two basic

plots, the director manages to keep a fast pace plus general unity. Performances of all are considerably better than the usual norm, another credit to direction. Vittorio DeSica is excellent in his amusing limning of the bluff-and-thunder public speaking maniac while Elisa Cegani has never been better as his underdog wife. Gino Cervi ably acts the industrialist, with Isa Pola caricaturing a nouveau riche. But the two youngsters, whose troubled puppy love affair is the better part of the picture, easily walk away with the honors. While Geronimo Meynier confirms talent noted in past pix, Carla Gravina is a definite find of her type in her first role. Music, lensing, editing, and all credits are of top order. *Hawk.*

Carve Her Name With Pride
(BRITISH)

Dignified and absorbing real-life wartime adventure with standout performance by Virginia McKenna; good biz prospects.

London, Feb. 18.

Rank (Daniel M. Angel) production and release. Stars Virginia McKenna, Paul Scofield. Directed by Lewis Gilbert. Screenplay, Vernon Harris and Lewis Gilbert from book by R. J. Minney; editor, John Shirley; camera, John Wilcox; music, William Alwyn. At Odeon, Leicester Square, London. Running time, **119 MINS.**

Violette Szabo	Virginia McKenna
Tony Fraser	Paul Scofield
Mr. Bushell	Jack Warner
Mrs. Bushell	Denise Grey
Etienne Szabo	Alain Saury
Jacques	Maurice Ronet
Lillian Rolfe	Anne Leon
Potter	Sydney Tafler
Vera Atkins	Avice Landone
Denise Bloch	Nicole Stephane
Interrogator	Noel Willman
N.C.O. Instructor	Bill Owen
Winnie	Billie Whitelaw
Colonel Buckmaster	William Mervyn
Commandant Suhren	Harold Lang

Without breaking any new ground, "Carve Her Name With Pride" nevertheless stands out as a dignified and absorbing pic. Producer Danny Angel and director Lewis Gilbert can well carve for themselves a substantial slice of the pride which their entire team can rightly enjoy for this effort. If the British public's taste for war films has not yet been sated then "Pride" should click. U.S. audiences will do themselves a good turn by examining the work of Virginia McKenna and her co-star, Paul Scofield, one of Britain's top legit artists.

The film pays tribute to the real life exploits of Violette Szabo, a beautiful young woman who became a British cloak-and-dagger agent in France and won a posthumous George Cross after, being tortured and executed in Ravensbruck Camp. Part of the pic's attraction is its lack of hysteria. It keeps resolutely to the facts and refuses to allow the espionage and torture sequences to go past the bounds of credulity. The very ordinariness of its early background heightens the impact. About 50% of the pic has unrolled before there is any hint of dramatic violence, but then these scenes have a sock effect.

Miss Szabo, an attractive 19-year-old shop assistant, lives in a humble London suburb. War had barely touched her when she fell in love and married a French officer. After two years he was killed without having seen their little daughter. Although a slim, almost fragile looking young girl, Violette was an accomplished athlete and, the daughter of a French mother, she spoke French fluently. She had all the qualifications needed to become one of the secret team working on sabotage in Europe.

Then comes active service. On the second of her assignments she is captured after a running fight against the Nazis, which ends in her capture. Then follows torturing interrogation, her incarceration in a concentration camp and her execution. Virginia McKenna, long tabbed as "The English Rose," showed signs of her ability in "A Town Like Alice." With "Carve Her Name With Pride," she is obviously topnotch. The role of Violette Szabo was not only a physical ordeal but a different emotional one. Miss McKenna runs the gamut of humor, charm and toughness. By skillful playing and equally skillful makeup, Miss McKenna's ordeal is expertly revealed.

There are other equally good performances. Paul Scofield, as the officer colleague who falls in love with his gallant young comrade, and Alain Saury, as her young husband; Jack Warner and Denise Grey, as her stolid middle-aged parents; Bill Owen, a standout as Miss McKenna's sergeant instructor, Noel Willman, Maurice Ronet, Billie Whitelaw and Sydney Tafler all contribute admirably to the thesping. There are also performances of particular interest by Anne Leon and Nicole Stephane as two girl agents who share Miss McKenna's fate.

William Alwyn's music strikes the right dramatic note. Lewis Gilbert's direction is firm and sympathetic. The air raid and concentration camp sequences are photographed admirably by John Wilcox while the screenplay by Vernon Harris and Lewis Gilbert blends humor, unmawkish sentiment and realism.

If this film can be faulted, it is that it takes a shade too long to make its early points. In an effort to establish atmosphere it lingers where its pace might have been sharpened by more dramatic cutting by John Shirley. But it is just about the best tribute yet contributed by British studios to the brand of courage which lifted an ordinary girl, with all her fears and her emotions, to the stars, and flecked her with glory. *Rich.*

The Long, Hot Summer

Violence and wild humor are well-mixed in this sex-ridden melodrama of the South. Top-notch young cast plus veterans forecasts strong b.o.

Hollywood, Feb. 28.

20th-Century Fox release of Jerry Wald production. Stars Paul Newman, Joanne Woodward, Anthony Franciosa, Orson Welles, Lee Remick, Angela Lansbury; features Richard Anderson, Sarah Marshall, Mabel Albertson, J. Pat O'Malley, William Walker. Produced by Jerry Wald. Directed by Martin Ritt. Screenplay, Irving Ravetch, Harriet Frank Jr.; based on "Barn Burning," "The Spotted Horses," and "Hamlet," by William Faulkner; camera, Joseph LaShelle; music, Alex North; editor, Louis R. Loeffler. Previewed at the Village Theatre, Westwood, Feb. 27, '58. Running time, **115 MINS.**

Ben Quick	Paul Newman
Clara Varner	Joanne Woodward
Jody	Anthony Franciosa
Varner	Orson Welles
Eula Varner	Lee Remick
Minnie	Angela Lansbury
Alan Stewart	Richard Anderson
Agnes Stewart	Sarah Marshall
Mrs. Stewart	Mabel Albertson
Ratliff	J. Pat O'Malley
Lucius	William Walker
Peabody	George Dunn
Armistead	Jess Kirkpatrick
Wilk	Val Avery
Houstin	I. Stanford Jolley
John Fisher	Nicholas King
Tom Shortly	Lee Erickson
J. V. Bookright	Ralph Reed
Pete Armistead	Terry Rango
Buddy Peabody	Steve Widders
Linus Olds	Jim Brandt
Mrs. Houstin	Helen Wallace
Harry Peabody	Brian Corcoran
Harris	Byron Foulger
Justice	Victor Rodman
Waiter	Eugene Jackson

"The Long Hot Summer" is a simmering story of life in the Deep South, steamy with sex and laced with violence and bawdy humor. Although the setting of Jerry Wald's production is Mississippi, race relations play no part in this 20th-Fox release; it is instead a kind of "Peyton Place" with the locale shifted from New England to the warmer climate and—apparently—hotter-blooded citizens.

Four of the newest and most popular young stars, Paul Newman, Joanne Woodward, Anthony Franciosa and Lee Remick are teamed with two veterans, Orson Welles and Angela Lansbury, to give "Summer" exceptionally broad marquee value. This picture, strikingly directed by Martin Ritt, will be—despite its flaws—a conversation piece.

The screenplay, by Irving Ravetch and Harriet Frank Jr., is based on two stories, "Barn Burning" and "The Spotted Horses" and a part of the novel, "The Hamlet," all by William Faulkner. It is about a young Mississippi redneck, Paul Newman, who has a reputation for settling his grudges by setting fire to the property of those he opposes. This notoriety follows him when he drifts into the town owned and operated by Orson Welles, a gargantuan character who has reduced the town to snivelling peonage; his one son, Anthony Franciosa, to the point where he seeks perpetual escape in the love of his pretty wife, Lee Remick; and, by his tactics, frozen his daughter, Joanne Woodward, into a premature old maid.

Welles senses immediately in Newman a fellow predator and they set to trying to outdo each other in villainy and connivance. Before the diverse polt elements have straightened themselves out Franciosa has attempted to kill his father and put the blame on Newman; Newman is almost lynched; the Franciosa-Remick marriage is shaken and almost shattered; and Welles is tricked or teased into marriage with his longtime mistress, Angela Lansbury.

Ravetch and Miss Frank have done a phenomenal job of putting together elements of stories that are actually connected only by their core of atmosphere, Faulkner's preoccupation with the rising redneck moneyed class and their dominance of the former aristocracy. There are still holes in the screenplay, as it is shown, but director Ritt slams over them so fast that you are not aware of any vacancies until you are past them. What makes the picture are the full-bodied, full-blown characters and their twice-as-big-as-life-size actions. It is melodrama frank and unashamed. It may be preposterous but it is never dull.

Newman slips into a cracker slouch with professional ease, never allowing a cornpone and molasses accent to completely disguise his latent energy and native intelligence. Miss Woodward is convincingly icy but you sense that the cold reserve can be melted and it is. Franciosa is pitiful and broken for much of the story, his scene with his father near the end is a memorable one.

Orson Welles plays high and handsome although he has a tendency to hit some of his lines so hard that they are completely lost, the words smashed in projecting the intent. Miss Remick is a cuddlesome object, full of meaningful squeals and wiggles. Angela Lansbury was inspired casting for Welles' romantic vis-a-vis; she gives it humor and tenderness. Richard Anderson as the washed out aristocrat give an appealing performance; Sarah Marshall makes her few scenes vivid, and among the others in the large cast, Mabel Albertson, J. Pat O'Malley and William Walker make helpful contributions.

Most of "Long Hot Summer" was shot in Louisiana and the locations pay off in the authentic flavor well captured by cameraman Joseph LaShelle. Highlighting the diverse and contrasting moods is the fine score by Alex North, conducted by Lionel Newman. North has also contributed a good title song, with lyrics by Sammy Cahn, that is sung behind the main titles by Jimmie Rodgers, that will be a plugger for the picture.

Art direction by Lyle R. Wheeler and Maurice Ransford, with set decoration by Walter M. Scott and Eli Benneche, carries through on the interiors with the rich and ornate beauty of the authentic exteriors. Sound by E. Clayton Ward and Harry M. Leonard, and editing by Louis R. Loeffler, are both first-rate. *Powe.*

Family Doctor
(BRITISH-C'SCOPE)

Little stellar or dramatic impact in this routine drama that suffers from sluggish writing and direction. Acting and lensing okay.

London, Feb. 18.

20th-Fox production and release. Stars Rick Jason, Marius Goring, Lisa Gastoni. Directed by Derek Twist. Screenplay, Derek Twist from novel, "The Deeds of Dr. Deadcert" by Joan Fleming; editor, Desmond Saunders; camera, Arthur Grant; music, John Wooldridge. At Rialto, London. Dunning time, **85 MINS.**

Jethro	Rick Jason
Kitty Mortlock	Lisa Gastoni
Doctor Dysert	Marius Goring
Stella	Sandu Scott
Miss Bettyhill	Mary Merrall
Louise	Vida Hope
Charlotte	Helen Shingler
Lady Lacy	Phyllis Neilson-Terry
Colonel	Nicholas Hannen

Mr. Sparrow .... Kynaston Reeves
Mrs. Mortlock .... Avice Landone
Dr. Alexander .... Frederick Leister
Sir George Watson ... Patrick Waddington
Mrs. Davies .... Totti Truman Taylor
Lady Watson .... Noel Hood

"Family Doctor" is a drama that never rises above the level of a cheap novelette, despite some helpful performances. It is an implausible yarn taken from Joan Fleming's novel, "The Deeds of Dr. Deadcert." Derek Twist's sluggish direction of his own uninspired screenplay helps to show up these implausibilities. "Doctor" cannot be recommended as anything but a routine program filler.

The pic has Rick Jason as a young American doctor visiting Frogmouth, a Devonshire seaside resort. He poses as a journalist on vacation. Actually he is there to probe the suspicious death of his ex-wife, who hda re-married the local medico. Played with suave assurance by Marius Goring, this doctor is a highly respected character around the district. But Jason discovers that Goring had benefitted financially from the unusual endings of his two previous wives.

Also, Goring is treating Lisa Gastoni, his secretary, for a mysterious complaint which attracts Jason's professional interest.

Putting two and two together and making it a snappy five, Jason extracts a confession of three murders from Goring who then proceeds to tr and heave Jason over a cliff. Of course, it is Goring himself himself who does the death fall in the one scene in this film that has any tension.

Jason, making his British debut, gives a pleasant, relaxed performance as the curious Yank, though he has little opportunity to do more than saunter through his stint. Goring is a debonair and sufficiently sinister crook though in the end he has to pull out all his skill to prevent his performance collapsing into absurdity. Miss Gastoni is an appealing heroine whose opportunities are a shade restricted since 50% of her performance takes place in a sick-bed. Making her first appearance in British films is Sandu Scott, a sizzling blonde cabaret singer, who plays Goring's third wife with a flashy brittleness that fails to come off. More successful are Goring's two previous wives, Vida Hope, a blowsy alcoholic, and Helen Shingler, a drab neurotic.

Mary Merrall practically steals the film with an excellent study of a good-hearted, gabby spinster. Also, there are some fair cameos from Phyllis Neilson-Terry, Nicholas Hannen, Patrick Waddington and Kynaston Reeves as visitors at the hotel. Told in an irritating series of flashbacks, "Doctor" is an aimless item. However, the Devonshire setting makes a refreshing change and Arthur Grant's lensing is very effective. *Rich.*

The Narcotics Story

Semi-documentary of unusual realism in actual mechanics of addiction. Exploitation item.

Hollywood, Feb. 21.

Harry Stern release of Police Science Production. Cast includes Sharon Strand, Darlene Hendricks, Herbert Crisp, Fred Marratto, Allen Pitt, Patricia Lynn, Bob Hopkins. Produced and directed by Robert W. Larsen. Screenplay, Roger E. Garris; camera, Jerry L. May; music, Alexander Laszlo; editor, Dave DePate. Previewed at the Four Star theatre, Feb. 19, '58. Running time: 75 MINS.

(No Character Names)

"The Narcotics Story," a semi-documentary originally produced for use by police as a training film in the habits of narcotic addicts, their arrest and imprisonment, is getting a theatrical release. It opens in the L. A. area Feb. 26 at five theatres on a bill with the British "Dance Little Lady," released some years ago.

"The Narcotics Story" should do well as an exploitation item, although there is no story to it in the conventional sense. The picture, in Eastman Color, was produced and directed by Robert W. Larsen for Police Science Productions, and uses professional actors to enact the roles of addicts, pushers and those innocently involved. It will gain its greatest interest from the wealth of intimate detail on the actual mechanics of the racket-curse.

The picture apparently was not submitted to the Production Code Administration for approval. It violates clearly one section of the Code relating to the portrayal of narcotic usage. The means of obtaining and using both marijuana and heroin—how reefers are made, how injections are performed, etc.—are showed in closeup and with clinical attention. This obviously had a special interest for the police, for whom the picture was first intended, but it also has a grisly fascination for the lay public as well.

Although the ways and means of obtaining and using these illicit drugs is blue-printed with minute detail, the overriding impact is of the deadly toll these narcotics take in human degradation.

The cast, Sharon Strand, Darlene Hendricks, Herbert Crisp, Fred Marratto, Allen Pitt and Patricia Lynn, acts mostly in pantomime with continuity supplied by narration. Larsen has kept sight of pace and tempo so the narrative does not drag despite its unprofessional nature, and the photography by Jerry L. May explores every possible angle to aid in keeping up interest. Roger E. Garris' screenplay is unemotional but effective. Other credits are adequate. *Powe.*

Saddle The Wind

Exciting old-time western with built-in teen-age appeal. Handsome color backgrounds. Good b.o.

Hollywood, Feb. 28.

Metro release of an Armand Deutsch production. Stars Robert Taylor, Julie London, John Cassavetes; co-stars Donald Crisp, Charles McGraw; features Royal Dano, Richard Erdman, Douglas Spencer, Ray Teal. Directed by Robert Parrish. Screenplay, Rod Serling; screenstory, Thomas Thompson; camera, George J. Folsey; music, Elmer Bernstein; editor, John McSweeney Jr. Previewed at the studio, Feb. 28, '58. Running time 84 MINS.

Steve Sinclair .... Robert Taylor
Joan Blake .... Julie London
Tony Sinclair .... John Cassavetes
Dr. Deneen .... Donald Crisp
Larry Venables .... Charles McGraw
Clay Ellison .... Royal Dano
Dallas Hansen .... Richard Erdman
Hamp Scribner .... Douglas Spencer
Brick Larson .... Ray Teal

The setting of Metro's "Saddle The Wind" is the frontier that was west. The basic conflict involved is the oh-so-familiar one between the farmers and the cowmen over the fencing of land, necessary to the farmers and violently opposed by the cattlemen. But actually Armand Deutsch's production is the story of a wrong kid, a real bad one, dangerous as he is charming, that is as germane to today's headlines as it was when the restless gunslingers roamed the west.

Rod Serling's screenplay is colorful and exciting and director Robert Parrish has kept it keyed high for a fast, exciting picture that will have particular appeal to younger ticket buyers. Robert Taylor, Julie London and John Cassavetes act out this tale of compulsive evil against the magnificent location backgrounds of the Colorado Rockies photographed in Metrocolor. It is a studied and effective contrast.

Taylor plays a retired gunman, sick of death and sick to death of guns. He is farming the lush valley presided over by Donald Crisp, patriarchal landowner who has given Taylor his chance to foreswear violence and bring up his orphaned, much-younger brother, John Cassavetes. But Cassavetes is one of those young men to whom a gun is more exciting than a beautiful woman, even though he does bring back saloon singer Julie London from a trip to the big city.

He also brings back a hair-triggered six-shooter and proceeds to prove his manhood, not with Miss London, but with the gun. He shoots down Charles McGraw, once a top gun himself but now on the dreary decline. This gunning whets his blood and he takes on a party of squatters next, firing their pitiful belongings. The boy is eventually shot and wounded by Donald Crisp and he crawls off to die. Taylor finds him, bleeding to death in a beautiful field of blue lupines, and before the older brother can reach him to take him in, Cassavetes shoots himself. The suicide is a bit pat but by this time; who cares? The kid is all bad and he has to go.

Taylor gives a lot of ruggedness to his role, still gentle and loving with the kid brother, understanding and attempting to be helpful even past the point where he should be. Miss London, who also sings the lyric title song by Jay Livingston and Ray Evans, gets exceptional believability into her part, somewhat hackneyed, as the dance hall girl who really wants to settle down. Cassavetes has a tendency to be rather mannered but his intensity gives great conviction and he is especially impressive in the closeups. Donald Crisp has moving dignity; Charles McGraw is tough and taciturn and others in the cast who stand out include Royal Dano, Richard Erdman, Douglas Spencer, Ray Teal and Stanley Adams.

George Folsey's photography captures the sweep of the backgrounds without slighting the humans in the foreground and John McSweeney Jr.'s editing does a slick job of matching location and interior shooting. Art directors William A. Horning and Malcolm Brown, aided by set decorators Henry Grace and Otto Siegel, have made the settings authentic and honest. Helen Rose has helped Miss London by some attractive costumes, Elmer Bernstein's music is an able component of the picture and Dr. Wesley C. Miller's recording utilizes the location sounds in maintaining the realistic, wind-swept feeling of the locale. *Powe.*

Steel Bayonet

All-male war melodrama. Filler fare. Only Leo Genn name for identification.

Hollywood, Feb. 28.

United Artists release of Hammerscope Production. Stars Leo Genn, Kieron Moore, Michael Medwin; features Robert Brown, Michael Ripper. Produced and directed by Michael Carreras. Story and screenplay, Howard Clewes; camera, John Asher; music, Leonard Salzedo; editor, Bill Lenny. Previewed at the Goldwyn studio, Feb. 27, '58. Running time, 84 MINS.

Major Gerrard .... Leo Genn
Captain Mead .... Kieron Moore
Lieutenant Vernon ...... Michael Medwin
Sgt. Major Gill .... Robert Brown
Pt. Middleditch .... Michael Ripper
Lt.-Col. Derry .... John Paul
Sgt. Gates .... Shay Gorman
Sgt. Nicholls .... Tom Bowman
Pte. Livingstone .... Bernard Horsfall
Cpl. Bean .... John Watson
Jarvis .... Arthur Lovegrove
Clark .... Percy Herbert
Ames .... Paddy Joyce
Wentworth .... Jack Stewart
Harris .... David Crowley
Ferguson .... Barry Lowe
'Tweedle' .... Michael Dear
Wilson .... Ian Whittaker

"Steel Bayonet" is a British-made war melodrama with an all-male cast that is an earnest, but inept, attempt to show the forging of character in the heat of battle. The Hammerscope production being released by United Artists was produced and directed by Michael Carreras who has not been able to extract much out of the tight-lipped, loose-drawn characters in Howard Clewes' screenplay. "Steel Bayonet" will barely fill out the lower half of a twin bill.

Leo Genn plays the British officer who must take his men on a suicidal mission to hold an African outpost against Rommel's German troops until an Allied counter-offensive in the rear can be successfully mounted. A simple, one set situation like this must be played for atmosphere and character. But in this presentation the personalities are never individual enough to be arresting, the dialogue is of the "good show," stout fellow" school and beyond that uninspired. The action is at first unbelievable and finally completely confusing, building a solid wall between the story and potential audience interest.

Leo Genn, Kieron Moore and Michael Medwin head the cast and they do what they can to make the lacklustre script seem interesting. Authentic backgrounds m ght have added some values to the picture but here tpo there is no such aid since the picture obviously was filmed in Britain amid scenery that bears little resemblance to the North African locale called for. *Powe.*

Nachts, Wenn Der Teufel Kam
(When the Devil Came By Night) (GERMAN)

Berlin, Feb. 25.

Gloria release of Divina production. Stars Mario Adorf, Claus Holm, Annemarie Dueringer. Directed by Robert Siodmak. Screenplay, Werner Joerg Lueddecke; camera, Georg Krause; music, Siegfried Franz; editor, Walter Boos. At Marmorhaus, Berlin. Running time, 105 MINS.

Bruno Luedke .... Mario Adorf
Inspector Kersten .... Claus Holm
Rossdorf, SS Leader .... Hannes Messemer
Willi Keun .... Werner Peters
Helga Hornung .. Annemarie Dueringer
Major Wollenberg .... Carl Lange
Mollwitz .... Peter Carsten
Lucy Hansen, Waitress .... Monika John
Heinrich, SS Officer ...... Wilmut Borell
Keun's Lawyer .... Lucas Amann
Anna Hohmann .... Rose Schaefer

This German Divina production is noteworthy for four reasons. It's been chosen as West Germany's only entry at the forthcoming Oscar Derby. It is Robert Siodmak's third (after "The Rats" and "My Father, the Actor") directorial job on a German postwar pic. Third is that it depicts via the incredible but true case of Bruno Luedke, mentally-deranged German mass murderer (more than 80 victims, all women), one of the darkest chapters in the history of Nazi Germany. Last but not least, "Devil" is a strong film, one of the most gripping domestic productions in years and one that looks to be a stout boxoffice contender here.

There have been several, not too many, West German films with an anti-Nazi slant in these last 13 postwar years. Although this film dedicates itself only to an individual case, with a Nazi himself even being the victim, it's perhaps the most depressing and also most convincing one. Pic depicts the brutality of the Nazi regime in a most realistic manner.

Although this has been declared "particularly valuable" (meaning considerable tax relief here) by the West German film classification board, it certainly does not look to meet everyone's taste. Word-of-mouth should help this here since two sisters of Luedke have sought court action, claiming that his guilt has never been proved. Gloria has countered that it has documentary material at its disposal which proves to the contrary.

The Luedke case was widely publicized here after 1945. It then became known that the Reich's Security Service had done everything to keep the existence of a mass murderer a secret, strictly following the Fuehrer's order. The case of Luedke, who was neither a Jew nor a foreigner, just didn't suit the "honorary era" of the then rulers. Film shows only one of Luedke's killings. An innocent man, Willy Keun (a Nazi official), is arrested as he is the logical suspect. A police inspector, however, believes in Keun's innocence and manages to track down the real murderer. The Gestapo which doesn't want this case publicized (as to Hitler's order) sacrifices the innocent Keun and Luedke is "liquidated" secretly. "A Bruno Luedke has never lived!" reads the SS order. The inspector who tried to save the innocent man is suspended from his job and sent to the battlefront.

Film benefits greatly from the tight script by W. J. Luedeke and the fast-moving direction of Siodmak. Story could have been unbearably tasteless but Siodmak's skillfully avoids all corny thriller elements. His direction is hard-hitting, open, direct and impressive, with his year-long Hollywood experience obvious in every scene.

Mario Adorf (of "08/15" fame) gives the role of Luedke depth and authenticity which borders on the sensational. One is never aware that he's acting. His portrayal of the insane killer should cause long and favorable word-of-mouth. Hannes Messemer is excellent as the cynical SS leader who takes care that the Leudke case remains a secret. Werner Peters is likewise impressive as Willi Keun, the Nazi who's sacrificed by the very regime he has been serving so obediently.

Claus Holm plays sympathetically the police inspector while Annemarie Dueringer (under contract to 20th-Fox) provides the inevitable romantic interest. Remainder of the cast helps to make this a telling pic of an unholy time. Technical credits are very good. This applies particularly to Georg Krause's camerawork which catches the whole atmosphere in superb fashion.

Hans.

Marjorie Morningstar

"Jewishness" of best-selling novel diluted. Title, good performances and Manhattan values stack up release for boxoffice.

Hollywood, March 7.

Warners release of Beachwold production. Stars Gene Kelly, Natalie Wood, Claire Trevor, Everett Sloan. Martin Milner; features Ed Wynn, Carolyn Jones, George Tobias. Martin Balsam, Jesse White, Edward Byrnes, Paul Picerni. Alan Reed Ruta Lee. Produced by Milton Sperling. Directed by Irving Rapper. Screenplay, Everett Freeman; novel, Herman Wouk; camera, Harry Stradling; music, Max Steiner; editor, Folmar Blangsted. Previewed in Hollywood, Feb. 18, '58. Running time, 125 MINS.

Noel Airman	Gene Kelly
Marjorie	Natalie Wood
Rose	Claire Trevor
Arnold	Everett Sloane
Wally	Martin Milner
Uncle Samson	Ed Wynn
Marsha	Carolyn Jones
Greech	George Tobias
Dr. David Harris	Martin Balsam
Lou Michelson	Jesse White
Sandy Lamm	Edward Byrnes
Phillip Berman	Paul Picerni
Puddles Podell	Alan Reed
Imogene	Ruta Lee

"Marjorie Morningstar" is so "switched" in the film version that admirers of the novel may be disappointed. But though dilution may have weakened the original integrity of the story, what shows on the screen is a potent combination of Manhattan stage, society and sex angles. Prospects are therefore good.

There was in the original best-seller of Herman Wouk an attempt to isolate and examine a particular segment of American life, the upper middle class Jewish stratum of Manhattan. This has been changed in the motion picture. Producer Milton Sperling has kept some aspects of the original idea, the characters are still part of their racial and religious background, but the Jewish flavor has been watered down.

Undoubtedly the film should be a box office success and Sperling played it for insurance, as a more general account with a broader base of identification.

Natalie Wood gives a glowing and touching performance as the title heroine, Gene Kelly is moving as her romantic vis-a-vis. Claire Trevor and Everett Sloane are strong in support and Martin Milner moves up as an important younger leading man. Ed Wynn is the standout as Marjorie's Uncle Samson.

The title is the clue to story. When Marjorie changes her name from "Morgenstern" to "Morningstar," she unwittingly cuts herself off from the Jewish background and plunges without support into a world of no visible connections and even less stability. She falls in love with Gene Kelly, one of those fascinating men of small talent who flourish in the theatrical fringe of Broadway. He has changed his name, too, from "Ehreman," to "Airman," and the resulting rootlessness has left him uneasy and unsatisfied—although he never truly understands why. Marjorie caroms from his rejection to a doctor, Martin Balsam. Always standing by and eventually the man with whom she finds her real love is hard-working playwright Martin Milner.

The symbolism of the name-changing is not any desire on the part of the principals to "pass" over to other racial or religious groups; it is only the common expression of youth seeking to create a character and identification of its own. Everett Freeman's screenplay has laid in some accurate and effective scenes such as the Bar Mitzvah of Marjorie's younger brother, the homely conversation between Miss Trevor and Sloane, and the casual references to Jewish custom that set the special flavor of the story. The importance of the theme—pointless rebellion by youth—is lost in the screenplay, however, is the restless thrashing about, the off-again, on-again love affair between Kelly and Miss Wood.

Kelly has a hard part since he is really a weakling, sold on his talent and brilliance so strongly that everyone else buys it too, although there is no evidence of it and he is not a young man. His characterization is a bad one for a hero because the men will feel no sympathy for him; he seems a spoiled boy, but women may take to him. Miss Wood is excellent and establishes herself more strongly than ever as an important younger star with broad capacities.

Miss Trevor and Sloane are more faithful to the original concept. They are real people and the kind you might meet in the area marked out by Wouk. They do this by subtle shadings of voice and gesture that never become grotesque. Martin Milner contributes an able performance and Carolyn Jones adds considerable dash to her scenes. Martin Balsam, Jesse White, Edward Byrnes, George Tobias, Paul Picerni, Alan Reed, Ruta Lee and young Howard Best make up the good supporting cast.

A special word should be said for Ed Wynn, not that he needs it. But his timing, his characterization, his complete empathy are so precise that he makes his minor character a major performance. Even doing a bad scene (such as the "matador" number in this) his dignity is such that he carries it off—if not completely than as fully as you know it would be possible.

Irving Rapper's direction is good at pulling together the many facets of the sprawling story and in his subtly at characterization. Harry Stradling's photography, in WarnerColor, is an important component of the production. A good theme song, already giving the picture generous exploitation, is "A Very Precious Love," by Sammy Fain and Paul Francis Webster."

Since the background is the New York theatre, there are some diverting musical numbers, staged by Jack Baker, with vocal arrangements by Lyn Murray, orchestrations by Murray Cutter and Gus Levene and musical supervision by Ray Heindorf. Max Steiner has done a score that is as good as any he has ever composed which is saying a good deal.

Art director Malcolm Bert, abetted by set decorator Ralph Hurst, has done imaginative backgrounds, particularly the West Side home of the Morgensterns and the summer camps. Sound by Stanley Jones and editing by Folmar Blangsted are both top-notch.

Powe.

Happy Is the Bride
(BRITISH)

Slightweight comedy about pre-marital complications; gay enough, but not likely to be impressive at the b.o.

London, March 4.

British Lion (Paul Soskin) production and release. Stars Ian Carmichael, Janette Scott, Cecil Parker. Directed by Roy Boulting. Screenplay, Jeffrey Dell and Roy Boulting from play, "Quiet Wedding," by Esther McCracken; editor, Anthony Harvey; camera, Ted Scaife; music, Benjamin Frankel. At Studio One, London. Running time, 84 MINS.

David Chaytor	Ian Carmichael
Janet Royd	Janette Scott
Arthur Royd	Cecil Parker
Policeman	Terry-Thomas
Aunt Florence	Joyce Grenfell
Vicar	Eric Barker
Mildred Royd	Edith Sharpe
Petula	Elvi Hale
Denys Royd	Richard Bennett
Chaytor	John Le Mesurier
John Royd	Nicholas Parsons
Marcia	Virginia Maskell
Jim	Thorley Walters
Madame Edna	Irene Handl
Miranda Royd	Sarah Drury
1st Magistrate	Miles Malleson
Aunt Harriet	Athene Seyler
George the Verger	Cardew Robinson
Shop Steward	Victor Maddern
Foreman	Sam Kydd

Adapted from Esther McCracken's successful play, "Quiet Wedding," this is Britain's second stab at this slightweight story. The result is an amiable, inconsequential comedy which will pass away an hour and a half pleasantly, but seems unlikely to cause any undue stir at the boxoffice. The screenplay by Jeffrey Dell and Roy Boulting (Boulting also directed) is a happy-go-lucky lark in which is infused a lot of fun and a certain amount of wit. But the whole thing seems altogether too slender a joke to stand up against reasonable competition.

When Ian Carmichael proposes to Janette Scott, all seems set for a quiet wedding. Not so. Relatives begin putting in their 50c worth and the harassed young couple have their first row. Bewildered by the upsets which crop up, the prospective bride and bridegroom disappear on the eve of their wedding. But on the day of the wedding they fall foul of the police on a technical driving offense and land in the cooler. After many misunderstandings and problems, they eventually arrive at the altar just in time.

The success of this flimsy premise owes much to the hand-picked cast. Carmichael seems rather subdued in this pic following his recent comedy successes, but Miss Scott is quite delightful as the young bride. Among the many supporting performances which take the eye and ear are those of Cecil Parker, as the bride's father; Elvi Hale, an exuberant rock 'n' roll girl who sparks the main trouble; John Le Mesurier, as the bridegroom's interfering father; Terry-Thomas, an officious policeman; Miles Malleson, who makes a bumbling magistrate, and Eric Barker, as a bewildered clergyman.

Benjamin Frankel's music and Ted Scaife's lensing are both okay for a production which adequately fulfils its modest ambitions.

Rich.

The Golden Disk
(BRITISH—MUSIC)

Pop music pic which aims shrewdly at the teenagers; hits mark as a useful supporting feature film.

London, March 4.

Butcher's (W. G. Chalmers) production and release. Stars Lee Patterson and Mary Steele. Directed by Don Sharp. Screenplay, Don Nicholl and Don Sharp from story by Gee Nicholl: music, Philip Green; editor, Eily Boland; camera, Geoffrey Faithfull. At Dialto, London. Running time, 77 MINS.

Harry Blair	Lee Patterson
Joan Farmer	Mary Steele
Terry Dene	Terry Dene

"The Golden Disk" shrewdly aims to attract teenagers who have helped to make pop disks big business in Britain. It is a modest, unpretentious film and will do well among patrons for whom it is intended. Older folks who can't dig this material will find the whole thing rather limp and the talent on view is unlikely to cause much of a stir in America.

"Disk" is calculated to exploit the current popularity of Terry Dene, one of the most successful young vocalists here. Dene, a youngster with a somewhat vacant expression, is no great shakes as an actor, but he sings and strums a guitar adroitly enough to please his public.

Picture has a simple enough story about two young people and their aunt who transform her cafe into an Expresso coffee bar, add a record bar to it and then start their own disk company. After a few weeks of struggle a song done by Dene sells a million disks and everything ends in a happy flurry of success. The pic would have been more acceptable had the screenplay by Don Nicholl and Don Sharp not been completely devoid of wit and suspense, and also had Sharp's direction not been so plodding.

However, the yarn is merely an excuse for putting over a dozen pop songs and for introducing a number of popular singers and instrumentalists. Philip Green, as well as acting as musical director for the film, had a hand in five of these songs and several of them stand a good chance of making the grade when plugging begins on radio and tv. "Charm," "I'm Gonna Wrap You Up" and "In Between Age" are useful ditties. "Golden Age" by Richard Dix and Michael Robbins; "Dynamo" by Tommie Connor and "C'Min and Be Loved" by Len Praverman also sound like promising entries.

Lee Patterson and Mary Steele do their best with routine roles as the young man and his girl friend. Linda Gray, as the aunt, and Ronald Adam and Peter Dyneley, as music publishers, also turn in workmanlike jobs. Dennis Lotis, Nancy Whiskey, Les Hobeaux, Sheila Buxton and the Phil Seamon Jazz Group are among the featured artists who handle the songs well.

Geoffrey Faithfull's camera work and Eily Boland's editing are technically okay but a big opportunity is lost in "Disk" by insufficient attention being paid to building up the Tin Pan Alley and disk world atmosphere.
Rich.

Escapement
(BRITISH)

Fair second feature thriller with workmanlike cast coping with implausible, but ingenious yarn.

"Escapement" is a modest thriller designed as a second feature, which can be adequately programmed in routine houses over here. But even the presence of two American artists, Rod Cameron and Mary Murphy, is unlikely to make it an acceptable entry for most U.S. houses.

Story has Cameron as an American insurance investigator sent to France to look into the mysterious death of a Hollywood film star. His probings lead him to a psychiatry hospital near Cannes and one or two similarly suspect deaths lead him to the belief that there is dirty work afoot.

There is. He discovers a scientist-doctor who is giving electronic treatment to neurotic patients, seeking a temporary escape from the rigors and cares of life. But he is the unwitting tool of the clinics owner, whose motives are far less idealistic. Peter Illing, as the big boss, is using the joint to brainwash patients so he can control their lives and money. If this capsule plot seems a shade sketchy it is because it is wrapped up in a certain amount of scientific mumbo-jumbo which may be the real McCoy or merely authentic in the scriptwriter's imagination.

The promised thrills never fully materialize, nevertheless, a bunch of very able actors manage to keep interest alive with a straightforward script that would have benefited from a few highlights. Dialog, as so often is the case with these second features, limps for much of the time. Rod Cameron, Mary Murphy, as his girl friend; Illing, as the crook; Meredith Edwards, as the duped scientist, and Kay Callard, as his wife fill their roles conscientiously. There also is a neat performance by Carl Duering as a bodyguard.

Montgomery Tully handles the direction without frills. Bert Mason's camerawork, the sets and the sound effects are effective without being outstanding. Though unfair to describe "Escapement" as a rush job, clearly the producers were disinclined to waste overmuch time on it. *Rich.*

Strange World of Planet X
(BRITISH)

Science - fiction horror film, which is not ingenious enough or sufficiently 'horrific' to add up to anything but a naive pot-boiler.

"Strange World of Planet X" is a gloomy little item which is tagged with an "X" certificate. This means that no child under the age of 16 can see it in Britain, which seems merciful for all concerned. It is yet another entry in the pseudo science-fiction horror stakes. Designed purely to cash in on a current vogue, the pic may well achieve its objective among the naive customers who thrilled to it as a tv serial. But it is a singularly uninspired pot-boiler.

Based on a novel by actress Rene Ray, it is a yarn which concerns research experiments by a slightly screwy scientist. The experiments upset cosmic rays which, in turn, affect the earth so that a mild tramp becomes a homicidal maniac and insects assume murderous instincts and man-size proportions. No layman can assess whether these shenanigans are credible or are merely figments of Miss Ray's imagination. But on the screen, they look rather daft and add up to fairly tepid entertainment.

Paul Ryder's screenplay is a plodding affair. The dialog veers between desperately dull technical jargon and coy flippancy. Under the circumstances, it is probably unfair to bludgeon the cast whose performances steer a steady course between the adequate and the dreadful. Forrest Tucker plays the stalwart assistant of the mad scientists and keeps a stiff upper lip throughout the disaster all around him. The best performance comes from Martin Benson as the invader from Planet X who tied up the out-of-hand situation. Hugh Latimer, Wyndham Goldie, Alec Mango, Geoffrey Chater and Patricia Sinclair fulfil the terms of their contracts without appearing to have much relish for the proceedings. The femme lead is taken by French actress Gaby Andre, whose showing here is routine.

Robert Sharples' music has an efficiently eerie note. Joe Amber's camera work is not sufficiently distinguished to hide the phoniness of the studio-made insects, designed to provide thrill which is more revolting than hair-raising.
Rich.

Paris Holiday
(TECHNICOLOR - TECHNIRAMA)

Pleasant diversion with Bob Hope and Fernandel.

Bob Hope's "Paris Holiday" is, as the title indicates, a pleasant spoof. It's tongue-in-cheek whodunit, with some capital Hope toppers—one-liners for the flip trade—and two solid comedy scenes for the windup. One is of the "crazyhouse" genre — it is the scene where Hope is tricked into incarceration in a mental institute outside of Paris—and the other is a funny chase, including some tiptop helicopter stuff for the getaway as the dastards are foiled.

Action is contemporaneous with a World War II flashback via spurious currency which threatens to undermine the economy of France because of the skillful counterfeiting. Preston Sturges, himself a playwright of note, is cast as the loosely disguised Sacha Guitry whose new play unmasks the villains.

Hope, on the titular Paris holiday, hungers for the American rights to the distinguished French playwright's latest effort and, because he's suspected of having one of the few manuscript copies, becomes the target for Anita Ekberg's wiles aboard the trans-Atlantic luxury liner bringing them to France and also during his hectic stay in the French capital. Fact that Hope has no concept of these machinations makes for the comedic melodramatics.

Fernandel, playing himself as a popular French favorite, is also aboard the ocean liner as is Martha Hyer, U. S. Embassy staffer whose initial rebuffing of the flip Hope eventuates into the romantic vis-a-vis, including a little international diplomatic rescue-work.

Plot is one of those things but the sturdy cast makes the most of its opportunities. The popeyed French funster, Fernandel, is given perhaps his best U. S. audience exposure for what he has to offer; after all, his excellent "Around The World In 80 Days" stint was, at best, only a bit. He is a prime comedian, excellent on the panto. He is his realistic self as a non-English-speaking funny man with a great sympatico for "Bobbee" (Hope), his fellow thespian.

Fernandel's manning of the helicopter, which he is chauffeuring from a primer on how to operate the whirlybird, makes for some strong comedy scenes. Hope is hoisted aloft on a trapeze-ladder, first making his escape from the mental institution and later eluding the quartet of free-pistoling French hoods.

Miss Ekberg is beaucoup decorative as the she menace and Miss Hyer is properly prim as the loyal Yankee lass. The other bits are very competent.

All the technical accoutrements are lush from the Technirama process to the characteristically compelling Paris and environs street scenes in lush Technicolor. Except for a phrase or two of fractured English, Fernandel either mimes or speaks his native lingo. This calls for a few English subtitles. Among the comedy titles are references to "Mr." Robert Hope as the producer and plain Robert Hope as the original story author.

Scripters Ed Beloin and Dean Riesner have supplied a barrage of toppers and nifties which read like a typical topical Hope monolog, including out-of-the-headlines references to Sputnik etc. Gerd Oswald's direction is fast paced the editing keeps it down to a tight 100 minutes; Roger Hubert's Technicolorful lensing does right by the high life atmosphere from ship to shore; the Gallic flavor, costumes and settings are in keeping for lushness and authenticity. In toto, good escapist film fare.
Abel.

Desire Under the Elms

O'Neill's shocker about lust and greed in New England. Needs plenty of selling. Best prospects as a high-grade sexploitationer.

Hollywood, March 7.

Paramount release of a Don Hartman production. Stars Sophia Loren, Anthony Perkins, Burl Ives; features Frank Overton, Pernell Roberts, Rebecca Welles, Jean Willes, Anne Seymour, Roy Fant. Directed by Delbert Mann. Screenplay, Irwin Shaw; from the play by Eugene O'Neill; camera, Daniel L. Fapp; music, Elmer Bernstein; editor, George Boemler. Previewed at the studio, March 3, '58. Running time, **111 MINS.**

Anna Cabot	Sophia Loren
Eben Cabot	Anthony Perkins
Ephriam Cabot	Burl Ives
Simeon Cabot	Frank Overton
Peter Cabot	Pernell Roberts
Lucinda	Rebecca Welles
Florence	Jean Willes
Eben's Mother	Anne Seymour
Fiddler	Roy Fant

Despite all the plus factors, "Desire Under The Elms" is not satisfactory screen entertainment. It is painfully slow in getting underway, the characters are never completely understandable or believable, and the ghastly plot climax (of infanticide) when it comes, plays with disappointingly little force. The picture is being given a double "art" house opening in New York but the commercial truth of the matter is that "Desire" will probably make its best return as a sexploitation item.

Eugene O'Neill's work has been given a "reverent" translation in Don Hartman's production for Paramount. Attempt was made, apparently, to treat the stage script with dignity. True, some elements of O'Neill have been deleted and new elements have been added. But essentially what Hartman and his director, Delbert Mann, have tried to do is remain faithful to the playwright's original design. The presentation has valuable star qualities in Sophia Loren and Anthony Perkins and it is being given a healthy exploitation campaign.

Irwin Shaw, who did the screenplay, has not improved the story. O'Neill, of course, wrote a modern version of a Greek tragedy, as raw and chilling as anything in "Oedipus" or "Medea." He chose the craggy New England of 1840 and its flinty characters with care. The casting of Sophia Loren in the role of the young (third) wife of farmer Burl Ives, is a key casting error because it injects an alien-to-the-scene element that dislocates the drama permanently.

The passion of greed and lust that takes place, in which Anthony Perkins and Miss Loren embark on a semi-incestuous love affair that ends with Miss Loren's having a child that Ives thinks is his, is strong stuff and it has been handled with discretion. Too much, perhaps.

The conflict between Ives and Perkins, son of Ives' second wife; the clash between Perkins and Miss Loren, these are powerful antagonisms but their impact has been hurt by the change from O'Neill's Greek simplicity to Hollywood gilding. O'Neill saw it as men fighting the gods and losing. Shaw apparently sees it as men understood through modern psychology, still doomed and damned, but for different reasons. In trying to understand these motivations, the straight story line has been ensnarled by Shaw in specious complications.

There are moments of great power. The scene in which Perkins in his bedroom, adjoining his father's, suffers through his imagination of Miss Loren, is skillfully done. The episode in which Ives celebrates the birth of the son he believes to be his own but which is actually not, has appalling fascination. The final, uncompromising scenes, where Miss Loren and Perkins are taken away for the murder of their infant son—killed by Miss Loren in the belief it will put things right between her and Perkins—is silently understated for tremendous effect.

Despite Miss Loren's unsuitability for the play, she does her best work in an American picture in her role. She exposes a great variety of emotion than she usually does and she manages the scenes of tenderness with special and—in view of her past roles—surprising value. Perkins is more mature in his approach than he has been in anything he has shown previously, but his character is not as exciting or vivid as it should be.

Ives is the best, a bull of a man, cold in emotion and hot in passion, his measured reading is the pace the picture should have and he keeps it as near the original intent as it ever gets. This trio plays alone for most of the long film, but in minor characterizations, there are valuable contributions.

Especially there is the two brothers, Pernell Roberts and Frank Overton, who help set the theme and do it well; Jean Willes and Rebecca Welles, as their wives; and **Anne Seymour, in a brief early scene as Perkins' mother. Greta Gransstedt as the town "widow" and young Butch Bernard as Perkins as a boy, give memorable performances, although seen briefly.**

Don Hartman has set his production against a stylized-realistic New England background that is realized beautifully in the farm settings, exteriors and interiors by art directors Hal Pereira and Joseph MacMillan Johnston, with accompanying set decoration by Sam Coner and Grace Gregory. Dorothy Jeakins' costumes are unobtrusively authentic and Wally Westmore's makeup, particularly with Burl Ives, is helpful. Editing by George Boemler and sound by Harold Lewis and Winston Leverett are good.

Powe.

The High Cost of Loving

Metro pleaser, Amusing domestic comedy about home and office problems.

Hollywood, March 7.

Metro release of Milo O. Frank Jr. production. Stars Jose Ferrer; costars Joanne Gilbert, Jim Backus; introduces Gena Rowlands; features Bobby Troup, Philip Ober, Edward Platt, Charles Watts, Werner Klemperer. Directed by Jose Ferrer. Screenplay, Rip Van Ronkel; from a story by Rip Van Ronkel and Milo O. Frank Jr.; camera, George J. Folsey; music, Jeff Alexander; editor, Ferris Webster. Previewed in Hollywood, March 5, '58. Running time, **87 MINS.**

Jim Fry	Jose Ferrer
Virginia Fry	Gena Rowlands
Syd Heyward	Joanne Gilbert
Paul Mason	Jim Backus
Steve Heyward	Bobby Troup
Herb Zorn	Philip Ober
Eli Cave	Edward Platt
Boylin	Charles Watts
Joseph Jessup	Werner Klemperer

Jose Ferrer cleverly acts and directs, and helps Gena Rowlands, from the Broadway stage hit, "Middle of the Night" achieve her film debut impressively. "High Cost of Loving" should therefor hit the adult trade, and family market, both, for good returns.

"The High Cost of Loving," includes—according to this Metro entry—the costs of installment buying, prospective parenthood and most expensive of all, the toll in man's serenity in a world of super-corporative operation where the individual is an ever increasingly minor cog. It's a world of missiles, mortgages and mechanization that Milo O. Frank Jr.'s debut production is set against.

Directed for maximum humor plus some pleasant interludes of married romance, entire action of the Rip Van Ronkel screenplay, based on a story by Frank and Van Ronkel, is centered around a few days in the life of purchasing exec Ferrer. His company has been absorbed by a bigger one and everyone is wondering who comprises the "deadwood" that is sure to be chopped off in the take-over process. To give the problem added emphasis, Ferrer's wife, is expecting a baby and the expectancy looms especially large for the couple since they have been childless for nine years. Bobby Troup plays Ferrer's close friend and business associate, and Joanne Gilbert is his daffy wife.

Sure to be commented upon is Ferrer's fine opening scene. It runs almost ten minutes, completely without dialog, and shows what is probably a basic pattern in these days of working wives and husbands. Ferrer and Miss Rowlands rise from sleep, bathe, dress, prepare breakfast and eat it like somnambulants. It is very funny, and is expert use of motion picture techniques.

The rest of the picture does not always maintain this high level but it is usually amusing and always diverting, centering mostly around the performances by Ferrer and Miss Rowlands.

Miss Gilbert only has two or three scenes and they are not strong enough to give her much to do except play a stereo silly wife. Jim Backus has only one scene, really, a tightly written satire that manages to work into it every Madison Ave. cliche, and it keeps the story bright and adds depth to the humor. The rest of the cast, Philip Ober, Edward Platt, Charles Watts and Werner Klemperer, play assorted types to be found in such business enterprises as Ferrer works for, and gives value to the over-all production.

There is a lot of frank and amusing dialog in "The High Cost of Loving," this is the trend, to deal candidly with marital sex. It is done tastefully within sensible bounds and provides a basis for adult attraction that makes the whole presentation more believable and more sensible.

The technical credits are of exceptional value because George J. Folsey's photography and Ferris Webster's editing help achieve and maintain the light, fast touches Ferrer was seeking. Jeff Alexander's music is sparing but also of aid in the picture's mood. Art direction by William A. Horning and Randall Duell, and set decorations by Henry Grace and Robert Priestley are expert.

Powe.

Le Triporteur

(The Tricyclist)
(FRENCH-COLOR)

Paris, March 4.

Pathe release of Cyclope Film production. Stars Darry Cowl; features Beatrice Altariba, Jean-Claude Brialy, Pierre Mondy, Roger Carel, Gregoire Aslan. Directed by Jack Pinoteau. Screenplay, Jacques Vilfrid, Jean Aurel, Pinoteau from novel by Rene Fallet; camera (Technicolor), Pierre Petit; editor, Georges Arnstam. At Balzac, Paris. Running time, 95 MINS.

Antoine	Darry Cowl
Popeline	Beatrice Altariba
Cop	Pierre Mondy
Peasant	Roger Carel
Jean-Claude	Jean-Claude Brialy

Darry Cowl, a stuttering, eyeglassed young comedian, looking something like a cross between Danny Kaye and Harpo Marx, is fast becoming one of the top pop film comics. Usually scoring with flash appearances, where his bumbling is funny, he finds it harder to carry a whole film. This one is no exception though it does build some old style slapstick laughs via speeded up action and general buffoonery. But it lacks the originality and pattern needed for transference to Yank scenes. It could be a passable dualer but is sans the invention for top Yank chances.

Here, Cowl follows his hometown football team on a tricycle. He has many adventures, getting into the game and winning it for his home team as well as the girl he meets.

Director Jack Pinoteau has given this a flock of running gags and some crisp movement, but rarely strikes the right comic vein. Cowl can be developed into a topflight comedian if he ever gets the right story and molds his character into a definite type. Color is rightly garish and the cast is an asset. Production values are good. Beatrice Altariba is a lush young morsel who plays this in just the right key.

Mosk.

Macabre

A graveyard tale with more death than fright. Exploitation possibilities promising.

Hollywood, March 4.

Allied Artists release of a William Castle-Robb White production. Stars William Prince, Jim Backus, Christine White, Jacqueline Scott, Susan Morrow; features Philip Tonge, Jonathan Kidd, Dorothy Morris, Howard Hoffman, Ellen Corby, Linda Guderman, Voltaire Perkins. Produced and directed by William Castle. Screenplay, Robb White, based on a novel by Theo Durant (pseudonym for Terry Adler, Anthony Boucher, Eunice Mays Boyd, Florence Ostern Faulkner, Allen Hymson, Cary Lucas, Dana Lyon, Lenore Glen Offord, Virginia Rath, Richard Shattuck, Darwin L. Teilhet, William Worley); camera, Carl E. Guthrie; music, Les Baxter; editor, John F. Schreyer; special effects and title design, Jack Rabin, Louis Dewitt, Irving Block. Previewed at the studio, March 4, '58. Running time, **73 MINS.**

Dr. Rodney Barrett	William Prince
Jim Tyloe	Jim Backus
Nancy	Christine White
Polly Baron	Jacqueline Scott
Sylvia Stevenson	Susan Morrow
Jode Wetherby	Philip Tonge
Ed Quigley	Jonathan Kidd
Alice Barrett	Dorothy Morris
Hummel	Howard Hoffman
Miss Kushins	Ellen Corby
Marge	Linda Guderman
Preacher	Voltaire Perkins

By insuring the lives of his audiences with Lloyds of London, producer William Castle inherently has insured his "Macabre" with a surefire exploitable gimmick. Each theatre patron will be asked to fill out a beneficiary agreement, and $1,000 will be forked out in the event of death by fright during any performance of the Allied Artists release. This bit of hokey-pokey should pay off, even though the picture itself isn't frightening enough to cause more than uncontrollable squirming except in the worst heart cases, and they're excluded anyway. Castle's film, however, is just as macabre as its title insinuates.

Were the film narrated and handled with the same tongue-in-cheek approach that its beginning and ending are, it could have been a witty, albeit maudlin, film to tickle the same funnybone as, say, "The Trouble With Harry," "Macabre" is a good story, fairly suspenseful and wholly unpredictable, with a gory scene or two and more death than its little funeral parlor can handle. By the time the William Castle-Robb White Production has dug its last grave, half of the dozen players have gone or will go to their last regards.

White's screenplay, adapted from a book by 12 mystery writers, moves along with the single emotion of fear, then bogs down slightly during a search through a mangey cemetery. William Prince, an affable physician, leads the way through the burial grounds, searching for his tiny daughter whom some madman supposedly has buried alive. The search is a thorough one but for two or three flashbacks which slow it to a standstill. It turns out, in the end, that Prince himself is hoaxing it all up, **trying to scare his dead wife's father to death, thus copping his riches. And, even if the moviegoer may not die of fright, the old man does, and believably so, for the thing he had just seen was a ghastly sight.** Prince finally gets his, being shot down by the mortician, a unique way to perk business.

Prince's talents are well illuminated by his changing from a socially acceptable being to a hideous deceiver capable of deathly thrusts. Jacqueline Scott, as the doctor's loving nurse, walks away, showing a good deal of promise. Susan Morrow lends a bit of class, with Christine White, Philip Tonge and Jonathan Kidd playing expertly. Jim Backus is up to more than he could display in his role as a sheriff.

Director Castle, in approaching the story with serious intentions, was unwavering in his work. Carl E. Guthrie kept the eerie plot going with his effective camera, and Les Baxter's music further moved the picture through its cloudy paces.

The most delightful part of the whole production are the closing credits, running their merry way and poking fun at the 71 minutes that preceded them. Jack Rabin, Louis Dewitt and Irving Block rate top commendation for this work.
Ron.

Ces Dames Preferent Le Mambo
(FRENCH—FRANSCOPE)

Paris, March 4.
Pathe release of CICC-GESI production. Stars Eddie Constantine; features Pascale Roberts, Veronique Zuber, Lise Bourdin, Jacques Castelot, Lino Ventura, Robert Berri. Directed and written by Bernard Borderie. Camera, Jacques Lemare; editor, Monique Kirsanoff. At Balzac, Paris. Running time, 115 MINS.
Burt .... Eddie Constantine
Constance .... Pascal Roberts
Marina .... Veronique Zuber
Claire .... Lise Bourdin
Paulo .... Lino Ventura
Lester .... Jacques Castelot
Perez .... Robert Berri

This is another Eddie Constantine mock adventure opus with plenty of girls falling into his arms, much whisky running down the hatch and plenty of brawls. But if Yank singer-actor Constantine is a big draw here on his "A" pix, they don't rate as highly on its Yank chances. As long as Constantine is still an unknown factor in the U. S., this plodding, knockabout entry seems to have little interest in America.

Here, Constantine is a Yank derelict in Mexico who gets mixed up with a yachting party. He is an ex-sea captain and takes over the ship supposedly going on a treasure

---

trip. But there is trouble, with three beauties after him plus practically everybody else on board. He finally gets things straightened out, wins one of the girls and a reinstatement in the Yank maritime service after uncovering a dope ring.

Pic has some good gags and fights, but does not quite have the sparkle, pace and feeling to blend its complicated tale and its lighthearted parody. Franscope, like C'Scope, is well utilized while technical credits are good. Cast manages to catch the film's mood part of the time. Constantine is his usual engaging, ebullient self. If he was given the right vehicle, to dovetail the satire and action, he could make something that would intro him to Yank shores. *Mosk.*

Tigre de Chamberi
(K.O. Miguel)
(SPANISH)

Madrid, March 4.
C. B. Films release of an Aspa production. Stars Jose Luis Ozores, Tony Leblanc, Helene Remy, Antonio Garisa; features Jose Marco Davo, Miguel Rodriguez, Leo Anchoriz. Directed by Pedro Ramirez. At Gran Via, Madrid. Running time, 88 MINS.

Promising young film director Pedro Ramirez bolsters this slapstick comedy takeoff on a nabe slowbrain who accidentally becomes a boxing hero with a cast drawn largely from Spain's better character actors.

Mainstay Jose Luis Ozores scores as an awed youngster with muscle who is maneuvered into the fight game by a sharp crony (Tony Leblanc) and a tough trainer (Antonio Garisa). Fumbling and flailing with good comedy effect, he wins his one pro bout and the cute Helene Remy. Then he is shown hanging up his gloves to run his dad-in-law's bistro.

There's some good-natured ribbing of rabid Madrid sport fans and city slickers. Ramirez keeps farce note within bounds and the pic moves without strain as Ozores and character comics draw loud guffaws. Technical credits are fair. Good local returns anticipated for this amusing low-budgeter.
Hank.

The Silent Enemy
(BRITISH)
Excellent real-life war adventure based on exploits of "Frogman" Crabb, starring Laurence Harvey; sturdy booking for discriminating houses

London, March 4.
Independent Film Distributors release of a Romulus (Bertram Ostrer) production. Stars Laurence Harvey, Dawn Addams, John Clements, Michael Craig. Directed by William Fairchild. Screenplay, William Fairchild from book, "Commander Crabb," by Marshall Pugh; editor, Alan Osbiston; camera, Otto Heller; music, William Alwyn. At Rialto, London. Running time 112 MINS.
Lieutenant Crabb........Laurence Harvey
Jill Masters .... Dawn Addams
Knowles .... Michael Craig
The Admiral .... John Clements
Chief Petty Officer.......Sidney James
Able Seaman Morgan......Alec McCowen
Able Seaman Fraser........ Nigel Stock
Thomas .... Ian Whittaker
Tomolino .... Arnoldo Foa
Conchita .... Gianna Maria Canale
Forzellini .... Massimo Serato
Rosati .... Giacomo Rossi-Stuart
Fellini .... Carlo Justini
Celloni .... Raymond Young
Wing Commander
                    Howard Marion Crawford
Miguel .... Cyril Shaps
Miguel's Mate .... Lee Montague
Lieutenant Bailey ...... Terence Longdon
British Consul .... Alan Webb
Driving Volunteer .... John Moffatt
Cruiser Captain .... Sydney King
Helmsman .... Peter Welch

Tattooed Sailor .... Murray Kash
Spanish Girl .... Yvonne Warren

Again Britain has plunged a hand into the real-life war adventure basket and pulled out a winner. "The Secret Enemy" tells the remarkable story of Lieutenant Crabb, a young naval bomb disposal officer, whose exploits in leading frogmen against the Italian menace earned him a George Medal. It makes smooth, impressive drama, done without heroics, but with excitement. Laurence Harvey is the stellar magnet. Pic shapes as a sturdy booking for discriminating houses in both the U.K. and the U.S.

Harvey arrives in Gibraltar in 1941 to tackle the Italian menace that is striking successfully at key shipping in the area. With courage and determination, he becomes an experienced diver. Harvey is brash, intolerant of red tape, but fired with drive. They manage to locate many charges on ships which they render harmless, but still the damage goes on. It is known that the Italian frogmen are operating from neutral Spain, but cannot locate the exact base of operations or the method with which the enemy are conducting this underwater warfare.

Without permission, Harvey and Michael Craig, one of the seamen, slip across to Spain and discover that the enemy base is in an interned Italian ship. The hull has been converted so that the frogmen can come and go underwater without being seen. Again without permission the pair sets out in a previously captured chariot and blow up the base just as the Italians are setting out to strike at the British convoy destined for the North African invasion.

Here are all the ingredients of a first-rate adventure yearn. Much of the appeal comes from gradual building up of tension. The impatience of the men as they wait to strike, the rigorous training and, above all, the feeling of men doing a thankless and arduous job with a quiet sense of duty are all admirably portrayed. The remarkable underwater scenes give this polished film a sock impact.

There is one particular sequence when Harvey and his men visit a plane at the bottom of the sea in search of a dispatch case filled with urgent documents. This is high drama. They are attacked by Italian frogmen. Silently, ruthlessly, the enemies come to grips and the cut and thrust of the struggle has all the grace and rhythm of an underwater ballet.

Egil Woxholt's underwater photography has a rare beauty which deserves top back-slapping. Otto Heller's above-water lensing has an equal quality. The art work of Bill Andrews and the special effects dreamed up by Wally Veevers all give lustre to William Fairchild's direction of his own intelligent and amusing screenplay.

Harvey has a tailor-made role and gives one of his best performances, making a thoroughly believable and human character of this energetic young buccaneer. Michael Craig and Alec McCowen, as his two rating assistants, offer fine support while John Clements gives a rounded display as an understanding Admiral.

Much of the humor comes from Sidney James as the typical chief petty-officer with a heart of gold beneath a crusty exterior. There are some useful performances, too, from a bunch of virile Italian actors, notably Arnold Foa and Giacomo Rossi-Stuart. Only the distaff side is poorly served. Dawn Addams, as a Wren, and beautiful

---

Gianna Maria Canale, as Foa's wife, have little to do but look decorative a job which they find well within their scope. *Rich.*

The Young Lions
(CINEMASCOPE)

A blockbuster.

20th Century-Fox release of Al Lichtman production. Stars Marlon Brando, Montgomery Clift, Dean Martin; features Hope Lange, Barbara Rush, May Britt, Maximilian Schell, Dora Doll, Liliane Montevecchi. Directed by Edward Dmytryk. Screenplay, Edward Anhalt from Irwin Shaw's bestselling novel. Camera, Joe MacDonald; special effects, L. B. Abbott; music, Hugo Friedhofer, conducted by Lionel Newman; editor, Dorothy Spencer; orchestrations, Edward B. Powell; asst. director, Ad Schaumer; costumes, Charles LeMaire, Adele Balkan; technical adviser, Lt. Col. Allison A. Conrad. Previewed N.Y. March 13, '58. Running time, **167 MINS.**

Christian .... Marlon Brando
Noah .... Montgomery Clift
Michael Whiteacre .... Dean Martin
Hope Plowman .... Hope Lange
Margaret Freemantle .... Barbara Rush
Gretchen Hardenberg .... May Britt
Hardenberg .... Maximilian Schell
Simone .... Dora Dell
Sgt. Rickett .... Lee Van Cleef
Francoise .... Liliane Montevecchi
Brant .... Parley Baer
Lt. Green .... Arthur Franz
Private Burnecker .... Hal Baylor
Private Cowley .... Richard Gardner
Capt. Colclough .... Herbert Rudley
Corp. Kraus .... John Alderson
Private Faber .... Sam Gilman
Private Donnelly .... L. Q. Jones
Private Brailsford .... Julian Burton

"The Young Lions" is a blockbuster. So much for the boxoffice.

It will serve as a monument to film pioneer Al Lichtman who, returning to production, made the filmization of Irwn Shaw's bestseller his first "independent" effort in his long career. So much for the sentiment.

"The Young Lions" in CinemaScope, is a canvas of World War II of scope and stature that gives accent anew to the observation that television's competition is still, fundamentally, a peepshow despite all the now familiar conveniences of at-home comfort. So much for the physical realties.

"The Young Lions" is also many more things. A few like this and the picture business' "comeback" will be here. It's a kingsized credit to all concerned, from Edward Anhalt's skillful adaptation to Edward Dmytryk's realistic direction, and not the least the highly competent portrayals of virtually everyone in the cast.

Marlon Brando's interpretation of Anhalt's modified conception of the young Nazi officer; Montgomery Clift, the drafted GI of Jewish heritage; Dean Martin as a frankly wouldbe draft-dodger until the realities of war catch up with him are standout all the way. It's inevitable that his performance as the happy-go-lucky, dame-chasing Broadway character will be likened with what "From Here To Eternity" did for Frank Sinatra.

Hope Lange gives a sensitive performance as the New England girl opposite Clift and Barbara Rush is properly more resourceful as Martin's romantic vis-a-vis. Even more vivid are the performances of Sweden's May Britt, making her U.S. film debut in the role of the cheating wife of the Nazi officer, latter capitally played by Switzerland's Maximilian (young brother of Maria) Schell, also marking his Hollywood bow. Two other debuts are Dora Doll (France) and Liliane Montevecchi (Italy) as Parisians in fraternization roles with their German conquerors.

Director Edward Dmytryk effectively highlighted the human values on both the German and American home-fronts. It gravitates from the boot-camp in the States to the fall of France, the North African campaign, the deterioration of the Third Reich, the smrking obsequiousness to the invading Yanks by the Bavarian town mayor when the GIs liberate the inhuman concentration camp, and the gradual disillusionment of the once ardent Nazi as symbolized by Brando.

There may be some dislike over the persecution of Noah Ackerman (Clift's performance is different from hs usual wont, and most convincing) by his fellow-GIs, and the countenancing thereof by the sergeant (Lee Van Cleef, okay in a thankless role) and his commanding captain (Herbert Rudley, also okay). There is some strong dialog about blacketeering, the Bronx, "is New York a part of the United States?," etc., but this may have inspired Brando's observations at a Berlin press conference: "Shaw wrote his great book while war hatreds were still white hot. We hope that they have cooled. The picture will try to show that Nazism is a matter of mind, not geography; that there are Nazis—and people of good will—in every country." A Berlin journalist is said to have observed, "Brando speaks more like a statesman than a movie actor."

It's true, also, that after one of the most realistic series of fist fights—Clift takes on his four bullies, one at a time, is badly beated by all, although he manages to knock out the fourth opponent—the dogfaces treat him with new respect; restore his James Joyce "Ulysses," and clip the $20 bill into it which they had thefted as part of the training camp persecutions.

Brando, blondined, and speaking with a German accent, underplays his role with studied deliberation and considerable conviction. His concept is not as hard-core at Shaw's original. There have been other changes, including his self-abnegation as, half-crazed by disillusionment after he stumbles into the concentration camp, he hears the functionary officer, who is in command, complain with cruel matter-of-factness that he is shorthanded and hence his schedule in the willful annihilation of his human fuel—Jews, Poles, Russians—is so retarded. "But they don't seem to understand this in Berlin," he complains.

The shocked "Christian Diestl" (Brando) staggers out of the crematory, destroys his rifle, and permits himself to become another "kraut" target for Dean Martin who accompanies Clift (Noah) into the open-air, upon an understanding officer's orders, when he observes the gas chambers and the Nazi brutalities. In Shaw's book the Brando character was unreconstructed, shoots the Jewish GI, and is ruthlessly stalked to his own death by the Dean Martin character.

The Anhalt screenplay has captured shade and nuance of role in pithy, pungent dialog. The accent on romance is as strong as the war stuff. Underplaying is the keynote of virtually all the performances. Same is true of Dmytryk's celluloid treatment of this saga which is virtually three stories in one, played almost in counterpoint to one another, and only meshing in the closing war scenes.

The bullying dogface, who was one of four whom Ackerman (Clift) had to fight for a reason that Martin doesn't seem to understand, but proves a coward when attempting to swim across a short span, is rescued by Clift, and both in turn rescued by Martin when the panicky GI almost drowns Clift in a death-grip in the water. The emaciated rabbi, who asks permission for services for the dead in the concentration camp, when the Yanks liberate the town, is a poignant touch. The romance sequences in the more or less conventional American standard are contrasted to the "golden warrior" (typified by Brando); the fanaticism of his superior officer (Schell), the two-timing by the lissome May Britt, a looker and an actress who will zoom high, the fraternization of Dora Doll with Parley Baer; and the proud French spirit of Liliane Montevecchi until she realizes that Brando is no longer the conqueror but a refugee like herself.

Credits are on the upside all the way from the authenticity of sets to the stark black-and-white lensing to the unobtrusive but effective Hugo Friedhofer score, batoned by Lionel Newman. Even the civilian men's clothes are properly period World War II, with the wide lapels and the fashionplate concept of the day (Martin as the Broadway character).

The whole kaleidoscope of war and its futilties, of the rubble and the obliteration of all human feelings ("we take no prisoners" says the Nazi office in the North African annihilation of a British company) all come vividly to life in "The Young Lions," easily one of the standout pictures of the year and one destined to remain a highlight in the annals. *Abel.*

Merry Andrew
(COLOR-C'SCOPE)

Bright, sometimes hilarious comedy - farce, with dull stretches. Not always Danny Kaye at his best but prospects good.

Hollywood, March 14.

Metro release of Sol C. Siegel production. Stars Danny Kaye; co-stars Pier Angeli, Baccaloni, Noel Purcell; features Patricia Cutts, Rex Evans, Walter Kingsford, Peter Mamakos, Rhys Williams, Tommy Rall. Directed by Michael Kidd. Screenplay, Isobel Lennart, I. A. L. Diamond; from a story by Paul Gallico; camera (Metrocolor) Robert Surtees; editor, Harold F. Kress, music adaptor-conductor, Nelson Riddle; songs, Saul Chaplin and Johnny Mercer. Previewed Mar. 14, '58. Running time, **103 MINS**

Andrew Larabee .... Danny Kaye
Selena .... Pier Angeli
Antonio Gallini .... Baccaloni
Matthw Larabee .... Noel Purcell
Dudley Larabee .... Robert Coote
Letitia Fairchild .... Patricia Cutts
Gregory Larabee .... Rex Evans
Mr. Fairchild .... Walter Kingsford
Vittorio Gallini .... Peter Mamakos
Constable .... Rhys Williams
Giacomo Gallini .... Tommy Rall

"Merry Andrew" has a happy-go-chuckley attitude and some of the smartest musical numbers in some time, set up by stand-out music and lyrics. Against this is the fact that the Sol C. Seigel production for Metro does not always maintain its own set of very high comedy values, nor the pace of its initial scenes.

The highlights of the comedy-with-music are very high, but there are low and slow stretches in between. Michael Kidd, who makes his screen debut as a director with "Andrew," still has a lot to learn about comedy set-ups and this unsureness is made the more evident by the contrast of the narrative stretches with the brisk and imaginative manner in which Kidd has choreographed the musical numbers. Here he is on experienced ground and he shows it.

Despite these reservations, however, a good cast headed by Danny Kaye in his first picture in two years, is attractive enough in the better parts of "Merry Andrew" to give it a comfortable ride at the box office.

The romance and humor of the screenplay by Isobel Lennart and I. A. L. Diamond, based on a story by Paul Gallico, are based on the fact that Andrew, played by Danny Kaye, is anything but merry in the opening sequences. He is an instructor in a stuffy British boys' school, presided over by his martinet father, Noel Purcell, and engaged to cool and detached Patricia Cutts. Via his avocation (archeology) he gets mixed up with a family circus presided over by papa Baccaloni and featuring daughter Pier Angeli. This gives Kaye an opportunity to slap on the clown makeup and do several turns with handy circus props. The free-and-easy life also so sells him on the permanent possibility of the merry life that although he returns briefly to the stuffy schoolroom corridors, he soon cuts Miss Cutts and takes off with Baccaloni, Angeli and tribe for the carefree carnival life.

Kidd has staged a fluid marvel of a number as Kaye sings one of the five Saul Chaplin-Johnny Mercer songs, "Tickety-boo," while bike-riding over what is (or seems a reasonable facsimile of) the rolling English countryside. Mercer's lyrics are exceptionally clever, rhyming "Pan," for instance with "bad Samaritan," in a number called "Pipes of Pan," is a neat trick. The other numbers, all with ingenious Chaplin melodies, are "Chin Up—Stout Fellow," "The Square of the Hypotenuse," and "You Can't Always Have What You Want."

Kaye is defeated sometimes by comedy situations that were not expertly plotted. On the songs, he is fine and on scenes where he plays alone, he shines. Pier Angeli is pretty but her accent flaws impact for punch lines. Baccaloni, too, has at times a harried look about him as if he wanted more room to expand and is defeated.

Noel Purcell, whose natural beard is one of the greatest brushes since Fuller, and Roberte Coote and Rex Evans, do stiff-upper-lip Britons to a rare turn. Miss Cutts is lovely and other cast members contribute ably.

Robert Surtees' Metrocolor photography is rich and varied, and well set off by Harold F. Kress' editing. Walter Plunkett has contributed some notable costumes—most obviously in the circus scenes—and the backgrounds of both the boys' school and the circus are imaginatively done in the art direction of William A. Horning and Gene Allen, with set decoration by Henry Grace and Richard Pfefferle. Nelson Riddle's adaptation and conducting of the musical score is memorable and ably given its truest value through Dr. Wesley C. Miller's sound. *Powe.*

High Flight
(C'SCOPE)

Fair programmer with some good aerial action; Ray Milland name to attract.

Hollywood, March 14.

Columbia release of Irving Allen-Albert R. Broccoli production. Stars Ray Milland; features Anthony Newley, Helen Cherry, Leslie Phillips, Bernard Lee, Kenneth Haigh, Kenneth Fortescue. Directed by John Gilling. Screenplay, Joseph Landon, Kenneth Hughes, based on story by Jack Davies; camera, Ted Moore; editor, Jack Slade; music, Kenneth V. Jones, Douglas Gamley. Previewed March 13, '58. Running time, **83 MINS.**

Wing Commander .... Ray Milland
Flight Sergeant Harris .... Bernard Lee
Tony Winchester ...... Kenneth Haigh
Roger Endicott ...... Anthony Newley
John Fletcher ...... Kenneth Fortescue

Cadet Day .... Sean Kelly
Louise .... Helen Cherry
Squadron Leader Blake . Leslie Phillips
Minister for Air ...... Kynaston Reeves
Commandant .... John Le Mesurier
Diana .... Jan Brooks
Jackie .... Jan Holden
Chauffeur .... Richard Wattis
Valetta Instructor .... Andrew Keir
Colonel .... Charles Clay
Tweedy Lady .... Noel Hood
Farmer .... Frank Atkinson
Policeman .... Bill Shine
Bishop .... Ian Fleming
Bishop's Wife ...... Nancy Nevinson
Commandant's Wife ...... Grace Arnold
Barman .... Hal Osmond
Publican .... Leslie Weston
Susan .... Anne Aubrey
Cadet Pringle .... John Downing
Cadet Phillips .... Richard Bennett
Cadet Wilcox .... Barry Foster
Cadet Benson .... Peter Dixon
Cadet Johnson .... Robert Raikes
Cadet Seymour .... Douglas Gibbon
Cadet Connor .... Alan Penn
Controller (Cranwell) .... William Lucas
Controller (Leuchars) .... Glyn Houston
Controller (Operations Room)
Alfred Burke
Co-Pilot .... Owen Holder
Radar Operator .... Bernard Horsfall

Some rather stirring final air sequences save this Warwick production filmed in England from utter mediocrity. It's routine story of young fliers in training—RAF cadets during a three-year course, here—has been done before and better by innumerable producers, but interest picks up during aerial footage sufficiently for film to rate as a fair program entry, where the Ray Milland name should help with bookings.

Milland enacts the wing commander in this Irving Allen-Albert R. Broccoli production, in charge of turning cadets at the Royal Air Force College into expert pilots. Story is given a certain personlization via relations between Milland and a non-conformant, Kenneth Haigh, son of Milland's former squadron leader killed during World War II in trying to save Milland.

Milland goes all out in trying to straighten out the cadet, dictated by his own conscience, but apparently can't get through. Later, in saving the boy during maneuvers in Germany when Milland leads him back to base at hedge-hopping altitude after youngster has been wounded by flak, understanding is established.

Under John Gilling's tepid direction, characterizations fail to build up interestingly for American taste. Milland is harassed in his role, and the three leading cadets, including Haigh, Anthony Newley and Kenneth Fortescue, lack spark. Bernard Lee is okay as a flight sergeant, but balance of cast are strictly English.

Second unit, responible for air scenes, functions effectively, including directors Max Varnel, Anthonk Squire and Bernard Mainwaring, and lensers Stan Pavey and Cyril Knowles. Ted Moore as first camera handle assignment well, other okay technical credits including Jack Slade, editor; John Box, are director; Kenneth V. Jones and Douglas Gamley, music. *Whit.*

The Lower Depths
(JAPANESE)

Paris, March 11.

Toho production and release. Stars Toshiro Mifune; features Isuzu Yamada, Kyoko Kagawa, Bokuzen Hidari. Directed by Akira Kurosawa. Screenplay, Hideo Oguni, Kurosawa from play by Maxim Gorki; camera, Ichio Yamaski; editor, Yoshiro Huraki. Preemed in Paris. Running time, **124 MINS.**

Sutekichi .... Toshiro Mifune
Osugi .... Isuzu Yamada
Kayo .... Kyoko Kagawa
Kahei .... Bokuzen Hidari
Rokubei .... Genjiro Nakamura

Akira Kurosawa, director of "Rashomon" and the "Magnificent Seven," now easily turns to a filmic adaptation of the Russo play, "The Lower Depths," for unique results. Pic brims with characterizations without making this grim or downbeat. It is visually taking, but its theme limits this to U.S. art house chances. There also was a French pic of the same title.

Here again an itinerant peddler comes into a hovel filled with human derelicts. Ostensibly wanted by the police, his gentleness and humanity soon win over many of the human wrecks. But he is powerless to really aid these fallen people. The drama of the thief in love with a young girl, who spurns him, and that of an aging woman in love with the thief (but spurned by him) weaves solid threads about the lower depths.

Isuzu Yamada, as the vindictive woman, gives a brilliant, vituperative turn to her character while Toshire Mifune does his cynical character of the thief nicely. Director Kurosawa has kept this moving, and his observation makes this crucible film dramatic and plausible. *Mosk.*

Teacher's Pet
(V'VISION)

Fresh approach and smart comedy lends appeal to newspaper yarn. Top stars insure strong b.o.

Hollywood, March 14.

Paramount release of Perlberg-Seaton production. Stars Clark Gable, Doris Day; co-stars Gig Young, Mamie Van Doren; features Nick Adams, Peter Baldwin, Marion Ross, Charles Lane, Jack Albertson, Florenz Ames, Harry Antrim, Vivian Nathan. Producer, William Perlberg. Director, George Seaton. Screenplay, Fay and Michael Kanin; camera, Haskell Boggs; music, Roy Webb; songs, Joe Lubin; editor, Alma Macrorie. Previewed Mar. 10, '58. Running time, **120 MINS.**

James Gannon .... Clark Gable
Erica Stone .... Doris Day
Dr. Hugo Pine .... Gig Young
Peggy Defore .... Mamie Van Doren
Barney Kovac .... Nick Adams
Harold Miller .... Peter Baldwin
Katy Fuller .... Marion Ross
Roy, Assistant .... Charles Lane
Guide .... Jack Albertson
J. L. Ballentine .... Florenz Ames
Lloyd Crowley .... Harry Antrim
Mrs. Kovac .... Vivian Nathan

The hard-boiled city editor and his devastating impact on other, more idealistic, members of his profession have become a staple of modern t h e a t r i c a l literature. "Teacher's Pet," a Perlberg-Seaton production for Paramount, might sound on hasty recap to be yet another version of "The Front Page." Actually there is rich new life and liveliness, and even a fresh approach with humor and heartiness in Fay and Michael Kanin's original screenplay. Clark Gable and Doris Day give it solid star appeal, Gable particularly turning in one of his best performances in years. It should be a winner.

The basis for humor in "Teacher's pet" is that Gable is one of these crusty, old-line newspapermen who believes that nothing good comes out of colleges, certainly not out of schools of journalism. When he is invited to lecture by journalism professor Doris Day, he replies caustically and conclusively in the negative only to discover that for what management calls "policy" he must backtrack.

When he meets Miss Day, Gable discovers his ideas about female professors were wrong, but for various reasons he must pretend he is not a city editor but a pupil. In trying to get this straightened out, his emotional relations with Miss Day become more involved and they finally arrive at the expected conclusion.

This is the straight story line, but the Kanins have decorated the framework with some hilarious comedy lines and scenes which director George Seaton has set up with skill and delivered with gusto. There is the sequence of Gable's reactions to a strip-tease by Mamie Van Doren; another between Gable and his rival for Miss Day, Gig Young, where Young is suffering from the grandfather of all hangovers, these and a dozen other bright gags spark the story. It runs long (two hours) for a comedy but it holds up.

There has been a good deal of advance exploitation about the newspaper aspects of the picture, including the fact that producer William Perlberg imported a couple dozen newsmen from around the country, using them and the local product to add authenticity to his city room scenes. Seaton does not overdo it, fortunately, or play it cute. The real newspapermen (and women) are handled naturally and at a minimum so their presence, while effective for exploitation purposes, does not matter or become an inside joke. This and other newspaper touches are authentically done although the point seems to be made that the only kind of daily newspaper possible of success these days is the "Love Nest Sex Slaying" variety, a view that seems open to debate.

Gable frankly mugs through many of his comedy scenes and it is effective ow comedy. He is also strong in his serious scenes, his relationship with his staff and its problems. Miss Day, who apparently can do almost any kind of a role is as bright and fresh as a newly set stick of type.

Gig Young gives the picture its funniest moments, milking the scenes with the expertness of a farcial master for every possible laugh. Miss Van Doren is seen briefly but importantly and others in the large cast who score include Nick Adams, Peter Baldwin, Marion Ross, Charles Lane, Jack Albertson, Florenz Ames, Harry Antrim and most particularly, Vivian Nathan.

Haskell Bogg's Vista Vision camera work in black and white is sharp and vivid for fullest comedy effect, aided by Alma Macrorie's slick editing. Joe Lubin has written two good songs, "The Girl Who Invented Rock and Roll" (a novelty) and "Teacher's Pet," both of them woven ingeniously into the musical background by Roy Webb. Art direction by Hal Pereira and Earl Hedrick, set decoration by Sam Comer and Robert Benton, and sound by Hugo Grenzbach and Winston Leverett are among the other good technical credits. *Powe.*

Touch of Evil

Orson Welles scripts, directs and stars with Janet Leigh and Charlton Heston. Confusing, somewhat "artsy" film So-so prospects.

Hollywood, March 14.

Universal release of an Albert Zugsmith production. Stars Charlton Heston, Janet Leigh, Orson Welles; costars Joseph Calleia, Akim Tamiroff; guest stars, Marlene Dietrich, Zsa Zsa Gabor. Directed by Orson Welles. Screenplay, Orson Welles, from a novel by Whit Masterson; camera, Russell Metty; music, Henry Mancini; editors, Virgil M. Vogel, Aaron Stell. Previewed at the studio, March 13, '58. Running time, **95 MINS.**

Ramon Miguel (Mike) Vargas
Charlton Heston
Susan Vargas .... Janet Leigh
Hank Quinlan .... Orson Welles
Pete Menzies .... Joseph Calleia
"Uncle Joe" Grandi......Akim Tamiroff
Marcia Linnekar .... Joanna Moore
Adair .... Ray Collins
The Night Man .... Dennis Weaver
Pancho ....Valentin de Vargas
Schwartz .... Mort Mills
Manolo Sanchez .... Victor Millan
Risto .... Lalo Rios
Pretty Boy .... Michael Sargent
Blaine .... Phil Harvey
Blonde .... Joi Lansing
Gould .... Harry Shannon
Casey .... Rusty Wescoatt
Gang Members ......Wayne Taylor, Ken
Miller, Raymond Rodriguez
Ginnie .... Arlene McQuade
Lackey .... Domenick Delgarde
Young Delinquent .... Joe Basulto
Jackie .... Jennie Dias
Bobbie .... Yolanda Bojorquez
Lia .... Eleanor Dorado

Orson Welles is back at it, playing himself as writer-director-actor and turning out a picture, "Touch of Evil," that smacks of brilliance but ultimately flounders in it. The Universal release falls in no category—it's not a "big" picture nor is it in the exploitation class—and must depend solely on star names of Welles, Charlton Heston and Janet Leigh for boxoffice lure. The added "guest" names of Marlene Dietrich and Zsa Zsa Gabor may help, but overall prospects look rather slim.

Welles establishes his creative talent with pomp, but unfortunately the circumstances of the story suffer. There is insufficient orientation and far too little exposition, with the result that much of the action is confusing and difficult to relate to the plot. Taken scene by scene, there is much to be said for this filmization of Whit Masterson's novel, "Badge of Evil." Welles' script contains some hard-hitting dialogue; his use of low key lighting with Russell is effective, and Russell Metty's photography is fluid and impressive; and Henry Mancini's music is poignant. But "Touch of Evil" proves it takes more than good scenes to make a good picture.

Within the framework of major action, Welles' direction moves with reasonable motivation, filling the picture with emotional touches that can be accepted. On the fringe, however, Welles has drawn a few eccentric characterizations that, although amusing, are disturbing to the flow of action.

In his role as actor, Welles portrays an American cop who has the keen reputation of always getting his man. Before you know it, he's hot on the trail of those scoundrels who blew to smithereens the wealthy "owner" of a small Mexican border town. Heston, a bigwig in the Mexican government, just happens to be around with his new American bride, Janet Leigh, and gets himself rather involved in the proceedings, feeling the dynamiting has something to do with a narcotics racket he's investigating. When Heston discovers Welles "always gets his man" because he plants evidence for someone else to find, he starts a good deal of trouble which results, among other things, in Miss Leigh's being accused of a murder committed by Welles, the timely death of Welles himself and a complete shakeup of the whole town.

Off his rocker since his wife was murdered years ago, Welles supposedly is deserving of a bit of sympathy. At least, there's a hint of it in dialogue, even though it isn't seen in his characterization. Aside from this, he turns in a unique and absorbing performance. Heston keeps his plight the point of major importance, combining a dynamic quality with a touch of

Latin personality. Miss Leigh, sexy as all get-out, switches from charm to fright with facility in a capable portrayal. Two of the best performances come from Joseph Calleia and Akim Tamiroff, with good work done by Joanna Moore, Ray Collins, Valentin de Vargas and Mort Mills. Dennis Weaver, as the night man, is fine though exaggerated.

Spicing up the Albert Zugsmith production are a single closeup of Zsa Zsa Gabor as a non-stripped stripper, a word or two from Joseph Cotten who's slipped in without screen credit, and a provocative few minutes with gypsy-looking Marlene Dietrich. Miss Dietrich is rather sultry and fun to watch, even though it's somewhat incongruous to see her walk into the Mexican darkness at the picture's finish, turn to wave, then wail, "Adios." *Ron.*

She Demons

Mediocre adventure yarn, lower-bracketed with 'Giant From the Unknown.'

Hollywood, March 14.

Astor release of Arthur A. Jacobs production. Stars Irish McCalla, Tod Griffin; features Victor Sen Yung, Rudolph Anders, Gene Roth, Leni Tana. Directed by Richard E. Cunha; story-screenplay, Cunha, H. E. Barrie; camera, Meredith Nicholson; editor, William Shea; music, Nicolas Carras. Reviewed March 13, '58. Running time, **76 MINS**

Jerrie Turner .... Irish McCalla
Fred Maklin .... Tod Griffin
Sammy Ching .... Victor Sen Yung
Kris Kamara .... Charlie Opuni
Egore .... Gene Roth
Herr Osler .... Rudolph Anders
Mona .... Leni Tana

"She Demons" unfolds on a volcanic island where a former high Nazi scientist, living in secrecy from the world, changes lovely maidens into snarling beasts of kill. Mediocre film is actually more straight adventure than horror, although it fits adequately into the package top-bracketed by "Giant from the Unknown."

In a hurricane, the yacht carrying Irish McCalla, spoiled rich man's daughter, and Tod Griffin, leading an expedition to find reported "animal people," is wrecked on the island and small party, including a Chinese crewman, captured by the scientist's men. The German, who years before set up a complete laboratory to find ways of developing a perfect race of men for Hitler's Reich, has been transferring the beauty of the island maidens to his wife's scarred features, result of an explosion. In the stranded newcomer he sees additional beauty for his experiments, but before he can complete them he's killed when a volcano rocks the isle.

Principals handle their roles as well as script by Richard E. Cunha, who also directs, and H. E. Barrie permits. Miss McCalla has little to do but pout, but Griffin is properly heroic. Rudolph Anders is okay as the scientist and Victor Sen Yung is in for comedy relief.

Meredith Nicholson's photography heads technical credits and special effects are expertly handled by David Koehler. *Whit.*

This Happy Feeling
(COLOR—C'SCOPE)

Part slapstick, part romantic comedy. Should get healthy return on good b.o. values.

Hollywood, March 14.

Universal release of a Ross Hunter production. Stars Debbie Reynolds, Curt Jurgens, John Saxon; co-stars Alexis Smith, Mary Astor; features Estelle Winwood, Troy Donahue, Hayden Rorke, also with Gloria Holden, Alex Gerry, Joe Flynn, Alexander Campbell, Clem Fuller. Produced by Ross Hunter. Directed by Blake Edwards. Screenplay, Blake Edwards; from the play, "For Love of Money," by F. Hugh Herbert, produced on the stage by Bernard Straus; camera, Arthur E. Arling; music, Frank Skinner; editor, Milton Carruth. Previewed in Hollywood, March 7, '58. Running time, **92 MINS.**

Janet Blake .... Debbie Reynolds
Preston Mitchell .... Curt Jurgens
Bill Tremaine .... John Saxon
Nita Holloway .... Alexis Smith
Mrs. Tremaine .... Mary Astor
Mrs. Early .... Estelle Winwood
Tony Manza .... Troy Donahue
Mr. Booth .... Hayden Rodke
Mrs. Dover .... Gloria Holden
Mr. Dover .... Alex Gerry
Dr. McCafferty .... Joe Flynn
Briggs .... Alexander Campbell
George .... Clem Fuller

Delightful comedy, strongly and happily reminiscent of the zany school of the 30's, "This Happy Feeling" should rack up strong response to its potent ingredients of humor deftly manipulated with wholesome sex.

Blake Edwards' direction of his own screenplay, from F. Hugh Herbert's play, "For Love or Money," liberally sprinkled with sight and sound gags. The lines and situations smash across in Ross Hunter's handsome production for Universal. Debbie Reynolds turns in a seemingly effortless performance in an amusing May-September-May triangle romance with Curt Jurgens and John Saxon. There's nothing wrong at Universal City that a few pictures like this can't cure.

Basically, the story is not startling. Jurgens is a retired matinee idol now breeding horses at his Connecticut farm, playing the avuncular chum of neighbor John Saxon, and fending off an acid and amorous leading lady, Alexis Smith, when Miss Reynolds shows up in all her girlish charm. Jurgens begins to feel younger than he should and Miss Reynolds is lightly torn between the glitter of his mature suavity and the glow of Saxon's fresh youth.

Estelle Winwood is the continuously sound housekeeper for Jurgens whose cooking specialty is butterscotch pancakes: principal ingredients, butter and Scotch. Troy Donahue is a heavily moody devotee of the Actors Studio school of drama. There is a demented sea gull which wanders through the proceedings for no discernible reason except to provide laughs. There has to be another reason?

Edwards' direction doesn't allow anything to go by the boards, developing line and gesture for comedy.

Jurgens does a slick and professional job and Saxon plays for full impact. Alexis Smith and Mary Astor render strong support, while Miss Winwood, Donahue and Hayden Rourke are outstanding.

Jay Livingston and Ray Evans did the adroit title song and it sounds like a disclick as Miss Reynolds does it. The Eastmancolor photography by Arthur E. Arling points up the story's moods, set against the handsome backgrounds of art directors Alexander Golitzen and Richard H. Riedel, with set decorations by Russell A Gausman and Julia Heron. Eileen Younger did Miss Reynolds' gowns, which are knockouts.

Frank Skinner's music highlights the comedy, while editing by Milton Carruth is slick and expert, with first-rate sound by Leslie I. Carey and Frank Wilkinson. *Powe.*

Giant From the Unknown

Okay horror pic for program market, packaged with "She Demons."

Hollywood, March 14.

Astor release of Arthur A. Jacobs production. Stars Edward Kemmer, Sally Fraser, Bob Steele, Morris Ankrum; features Buddy Baer, Oliver Blake, Joline Brand, Billy Dix. Directed by Richard E. Cunha. Story-screenplay, Frank Hart Taussig-Ralph Brooke, camera, Dick Cunha; music, Albert Glasser. Reviewed March 13, '58. Running time, **77 MINS.**

Wayne Brooks .... Edward Kemmer
Janet Cleveland .... Sally Fraser
Vargas, the Giant .... Buddy Baer
Professor Cleveland...... Morris Ankrum
Sheriff Parker .... Bob Steele
Ann Brown .... Joline Brand

"Giant from the Unknown" carries enough shocker treatment to make it an okay entry for the program market catering to this type of film. Subject matter is imaginative and characters are well developed. Packaged with less-meritorious "She Demons," combo has a chance of showing fair returns.

Theory of life in suspended animation is given a strong play in this Arthur A. Jacobs production, which deals with a brutal Spanish conquistador of gigantic proportions coming back to life after having "slept" for 500 years. This theory which the scientific world attributes to lower forms of life is well conceived in the Frank Hart Taussig-Ralph Brooke screenplay. Opening reels are rather slow but a fast pace later is reached by director Richard E. Cunha.

Principals are Morris Ankrum, an archaelologist searching for traces of the Spanish giant, whom his research indicates died in the California mountains; his daughter, Sally Fraser; and Edward Kemmer, a young scientist. Kemmer has already found a lizard, buried in the rocks for centuries, which is restored to life, and he and Ankrum hit upon the theory that the bygone conquistador may have repeated this process. The giant's return leads to murder before he is killed.

Kemmer delivers well and Ankrum persuasively presents the scientific theory that comes true in the case of the conquistador, realistically enacted by Buddy Baer. Miss Fraser offers attractive distaff interest, and Bob Steele effectively plays a hard-headed sheriff, investigating murders in the neighborhood. Joline Brand is the pretty murder victim.

Technical credits are well handled. Jack Pierce created Baer's interesting makeup, and Dick Cunha's photography makes the most of the subject. *Whit.*

Screaming Mimi

Psychological meller with Anita Ekberg as the femme lead; a dualler.

Columbia release of a Sage (Harry Joe Brown, Robert Fellows) production. Stars Anita Ekberg, Phil Carey, Gypsy Rose Lee; features The Red Norvo Trio, Harry Townes, Linda Cherney, Romney Brent. Directed by Gerd Oswald. Screenplay, Robert Blees, based on book by Fredrick Brown; camera, Burnett Guffey; editors, Gene Havlick, Jerome Thoms; music, Mischa Bakaleinikoff. Tradeshown N. Y. March 6, '58. Running time, **79 MINS.**

Virginia Wilson .... Anita Ekberg
Bill Sweeney .... Phil Carey
Joann Mapes .... Gypsy Rose Lee
Dr. Greenwood .... Harry Townes
Ketti .... Linda Cherney
Charlie Wilson .... Romney Brent
Capt. Bline .... Alan Gifford
Walter Krieg .... Oliver McGowan
Red Yost .... Red Norvo
Dr. Joseph Robinson.... Stephen Ellsworth
Roal Reynarde .... Vaughn Taylor
Paul .... Frank Scannell

With a nightclub background and Anita Ekberg as the femme lead, "Screaming Mimi" would appear to have a strong audience interest. But this psychological meller fails to rise above the calibre of a typical "B" programmer and its b.o. destiny lies in the duals.

Based on the book by Fredrick Brown, the Robert Blees screenplay has a pulp quality that is scarcely improved by the stock direction of Gerd Oswald and the cast's mechanical performances. Yarn concerns the hunt for the murderer of a San Francisco stripper.

As per tradition, script has a newspaper columnist who runs down all the clues long before the slow-witted police get wind of them. He's portrayed by Phil Carey who makes a good stab at going through the motions. His reportorial chores introduce him to Miss Ekberg, an exotic at a Frisco strippery run by Gypsy Rose Lee.

After Miss Ekberg is superficially wounded by an unidentified assailant, Carey is reminded of the earlier murder. Key clue is a nude statue of a frightened woman, otherwise known as "Screaming Mimi." Running down his lead, the columnist uncovers Miss Ekberg's history as a mental patient with a homicidal fixation and the rest is obvious.

There are a few scenes of Miss Ekberg in scanty garb. These may offer an exploitable touch to showmanly inclined exhibitors. Her performance, for the most part, is an uninspired one with possible exception of some romantic bits with Carey. Miss Lee has relatively little to do as the nitery proprietor. Also involved in this Columbia release, among others, are Harry Townes, suitably menacing as Miss Ekberg's doctor-manager; Romney Brent, okay as Miss Ekberg's sculptor-stepbrother; Linda Cherney, a nitery entertainer, and vibe player Red Norvo as himself.

Physical values of the Sage Production, turned out by Harry Joe Brown and Robert Fellows, bespeak a low-budget. Burnett Guffey's camerawork is good, especially in the outdoor scenes. Editing of Jerome Thoms and Gene Havlick is standard as are the music conducted by Mischa Balaleinikoff, Cary ODell's art direction and other technical credits. *Gilb.*

Juvenile Jungle
(NATURAMA)

Billed with "Young and Wild" in an effective teenage combo. Should do well in adolescent market.

Hollywood, March 14.

Republic release of a Coronado Production. Producer, Sidney Picker. Stars Corey Allen; features Rebecca Welles, Richard Bakalyan, Anne Whitfield, Joe Di Reda; with Joe Conley, Walter Coy, Taggart Casey, Hugh Lawrence, Leon Tyler, Harvey Grant, Louise Arthur. Director, William Witney; screenplay, Arthur T. Horman; editor, Joseph Harrison; music, Gerald Roberts; sound, Dick Tyler, Sr. Previewed March 11, 58. Running time: **69 MINS.**

Hal McQueen .... Corey Allen
Glory .... Rebecca Welles
Tick Tack .... Richard Bakalyan
Carolyn Elliot .... Anne Whitfield

Monte	Joe Di Reda
Duke	Joe Conley
John Elliot	Walter Coy
Lt. Milford	Taggart Casey
Officer Ellis	Hugh Lawrence
Usher	Leon Tyler
Pete	Harvey Grant
Mrs. Elliot	Louise Arthur

Republic Pictures has come up with a pair of teenage exploitation pix with the essentials to lure high school trade. Coronado's production, "Juvenile Jungle" smacks of adolescent crime, drinking and a hint of sex—all well intended to give young moviegoers what they evidently are paying to see. In its double billing with "Young and Wild" (reviewed herewith), the film should ring loudly in teenage situations.

Sidney Picker's production values frequently show the picture's low budget, but the overall effect actually in indicative of a fairly well-produced film. William Witney's direction is stable, having put his young thesps through their paces with a sure hand. Arthur T. Horman penned the script with a feeling that, at the very least, will keep young moviegoers absorbed from beginning to end.

Toplined is Corey Allen, and he does quite well, combining underplaying with highly wrought action. As a cunning hoodlum who turns good, he obviates most cliches inherent in the part he plays, turning in a good performance. The cast boasts a number of fine portrayals, with most effective jobs turned in by sexy Rebecca Welles, Richard Bakalyan, Joe Di Reda and Anne Whitfield.

All the youngsters except Allen are involved in a gang with big ideas. The teenage mobsters, in meeting Allen, realize his ideas are even bigger and are hopped up to join forces for a big payoff, all of which suits Allen just fine. He maneuvers a meeting with the daughter of a well-to-do store owner, anticipating the day he and his cohorts can fake a kidnapping to become sole owners of the merchant's safe keepings. As one might suspect, Allen falls for the girl and the respectable life she leads, ultimately trying to end the fracas and, in so doing, gets shot full of holes by his former friends. There's every indication he'll live through the ordeal and may even up with a gentle wife and a lawful life.

Ron.

La Venere di Cheronea
(The Venus of Cheronea) (FRANCO-ITALIAN)

Rome, March 11.

Euro International Films release of a Prora-Faro-Rialto Film co-production. Stars Belinda Lee, Massimo Girotti, Jacques Sernas; features Claudio Gora, E. Parv, Jean Chevrier, Camillo Pilotto. Directed by Victor Tourianski, Giorgio Rivalta. Screenplay, Federico Zardi, D. Damiani; camera, (Ferraniacolor-Totalscope), Arturo Gallea. At Cinema Galleria, Rome. Running time, 96 MINS.

Afrodite	Belinda Lee
Praxiteles	Massimo Girotti
Claudio	Jacques Sernas

Straightforward triangle tale centering around a beautiful girl who's said to have inspired Praxteles' greatest sculptures, this might make a good exploitation entry in the U.S. though color print costs may mitigate against this.

Two men are in love with Belinda Lee: the sculptor, Massimo Girotti, needs her as his model, and Jacques Sernas, a warrior whom the sculptor hides from the authorities. She tries to escape with the latter, but he's wounded. They are separated, and she winds up walking the streets of ancient Greece.

While Miss Lee's rugged suitors pine away through the picture, the camera remains focused on her attributes, displayed in various forms of garb. The censor obviously has been at work on the local copy, and trouble may be expected elsewhere.

The actress plays the role with abandon and considerable ability while her suitors haven't a chance other than to flex their muscles. Script, direction, production quality (including some impressive battle scenes), and lensing in a muted Ferraniacolor all add up to unusually high quality for this type of production.

Hawk.

Foreign Films

ECHEC AU PORTEUR (Not Delivered) **(FRENCH).** Corona release of Orex Production. Stars Jean Moreau, Serge Reggiani, Paul Meurisse; features Simone Renant, Gert Froebe, Reggie Nadler, Fernand Sardou. Directed by Gilles Grangier. Screenplay, Pierre Vary, Noel Calef from the novel by Calef; camera, Jacques Lemare; editor, Jacqueline Sadoul. At Paris, Paris. Running time 90 MINS.

Sketchy pic uses a suspense gimmick of a bomb hidden in a football that gets into the hands of kids. Director Gilles Grangier's lack of direct, telling character observation, and the telegraphed proceedings, rarely give this the chiller, ironic notations it needs.

Stars hardly get a chance to make anything of their one dimensional personnages and this emerges of little chance for the U. S. Technical credits are good and some gun fights are well staged.

Mosk.

RASCEL-FIFI (FRANCO-ITALIAN). Lux Film release of a Vides Film production. Stars Renato Rascel; features Franca Rame, Dario Fo, Annie Fratellini, Peppino DeMartino. Directed by Guido Leoni. Screenplay, Leoni, Dino Verde, Otello Colangeli; camera, Gianni di Venanzo. At Teatro Metropolitan, Rome. Running time, 91 MINS.

Modest budgeter looks to become a b.o. winner with a good payoff to its producers. Renato Rascel name is a top sales factor. If all of the pix running time was up to its first half hour, it would be a first-rate spoof of the conventional gangster meller. Early reels, though slightly derivative ("Guys and Dolls"), have a flair and style of comedy with tongue in cheek rarely seen in such obviously commercial efforts. While still remaining amusing, pic loses both pace and stature later on.

Plot tells hoary mistaken identity tale involving nitery owner Rascel and a gang of thieves. Comedian is amusing as usual, while Dario Fo makes an eccentric gang chieftain and Franca Rame plays the sexy moll.

Hawk.

RAFLES SUR LA VILLE (Raids on the City) **(FRENCH).** Corona release of Robert Woog production. Stars Charles Vanel, Bella Darvi, Michel Piccoli, Mouloudji; features Francois Guerin, Danik Patisson. Directed by Pierre Chenal. Screenplay, Jean Ferry, Paul Andreota; camera, Marcel Grignon; editor, Suzanne Rondeau. At Marignan, Paris. Running time, 85 MINS.

Gangster opus is mainly about a hardboiled police inspector out to get a shrewd, elderly gangster who has killed his best friend. Women actually best both these men and both get their comeuppance. However, film is haltingly directed and acted. It rarely gets the needed tension.

Charles Vanel gives heavyweight thesping to the old underworld character while Bella Darvi is a fine foil. However, this is a secondary gangland film way below Yank par and of little chance for American marts. It is technically well done and location shooting helps.

Mosk.

Rome, March 11.

IL COCCO DI MAMMA (Mamma's Boy) **(ITALIAN).** Warner Bros. release of a Pallavicini-Bistolfi production. Stars Inge Schoener, Maurizio Arena; features Edoardo Nevola, Enzo Fiermonte, Memmo Carotenuto, Leda Gloria, Virgilio Riento. Directed by Mauro Morassi. Screenplay, Massimo Franciosa, P. F. Campanile; camera, Guglielmo Mancori; editor, Lionello Massobria. At Capranica, Rome. Running time, 108 MINS.

One of many similar "Roman" items, principally intended to cash in on Italian run, this manages some colorful moments in telling tale of neighborhood hero who enters prizefighting game but loses out because he's afraid his face will be disfigured. His gal's advice finally wins out, and he fights and wins.

Embroidery on this plot outline furnishes pic's better moments in limning Roman life and the romance between the boy, Maurizio Arena, and the girl, Inge Schoener. Latter shows ability and looks far and away above her current material. Technical credits are standard.

Hawk.

IL MEDICO E LO STREGONE (The Doctor and the Healer) **(ITALO-FRENCH).** CINERIZ release of a Royal Film-Francinex coproduction. Stars Vittorio DeSica, Marcello Mastroianni, Marisa Merlini; features Gabriella Pallotti, Lorella De Luca. Directed by Mario Monicelli. Screenplay, Monicelli, DeConcini, Age, Scarpelli, Emmanuele; from story by Age and Scarpelli; camera (Cinescope), Luciano Trasatti; music, Nino Rota. At Capitol, Rome. Running time, 98 MINS.

Lightweight entertainment along lines already exploited in the "Bread, Love . . ." pix, film leans heavily on surefire talents of DeSica, Mastroianni and Merlini, backed by Gabriella Pallotti and Lorella DeLuca for teenage appeal. Should pay off in depth, and makes fairly acceptable export fare.

Plot has Mastroianni arriving in a backward village to start a medical practice. Here he comes face to face with a faith healer (DeSica), who has the town sewed up as far as patients are concerned. Battle ensues, with medic winning at the end. Script is often amusing though overindulging in broad, folksy humor. Direction is taut and effective in the hands of Mario Monicelli. Location lensing and technical credits are excellent.

Hawk.

BELLE MA POVERE (Poor Girl Pretty Girl) **(ITALIAN).** Titanus Films release of a Titanus Production. Stars Marisa Allasio, Renato Salvatori, Maurizio Arena; features Lorella DeLuca, Alessandra Panaro. Directed by Dino Risi. Screenplay, Risi, P. F. Campanile, Massimo Franciosa; from story by P. F. Campanile; camera, Tonino delli Colli. At Capitol, Rome. Running time, 95 MINS.

Followup of successful low-budgeter "Poor But Handsome," pic has lost some of the freshness which characterized the first. However, it looks to pay off just as lushly, especially in local release. Marisa Allasio, here given less of a chance to shine, tops an almost identical cast, and may help film's export chances.

"Belle" again chronicles the more or less legitimate doings of some Roman left-bank youth as well as their early involvements with the opposite sex. Besides Miss Allasio, both Lorella DeLuca and Alessandra Panaro brighten the scene in their attempts to win their boys, respectively Maurizio Arena and Renato Salvatori. A colorful cast of backdrop characters has been included. Script is good for plenty of laughs, albeit with the local slant. Technical credits are good.

Hawk.

TOTO, VITTORIO E LA DOTTORESSA (Toto, Vitorrio, and the Doctor) **ITALO FRANCO — SPANISH).** Jolly-Gallus-Fenix Film coproduction and release. Stars Vittorio DeSica, Toto, Abbe Lane; features German Cobos, Darry Cowl, Titina DeFilippo, Pierre Hondy. Directed by Camillo Mastrocinque. Screenplay, Metz and Marchesi; camera, Gabor Pogany. At Archimede, Rome. Running time, 94 MINS.

Amusing, mostly slapsticked comedy with good marquee values in Vittorio DeSica, Toto and Abbe Lane. Set in Naples, it lets (married) doctor Miss Lane loose on a set of eccentric patients, who soon begin chasing her, of course. Her antique in-laws suspect the worst and call in private eye Toto with predictable results.

DeSica manages an offbeat portrayal of an aging Don Juan to good effect while Miss Lane registers via a neat (and eyefilling) tongue-in-cheek rendering of the doctor. Toto acts the detective in good form, while German Cobos, Titina DeFilippo and others back colorfully. Modest-budgeted, pic should ring up a good b.o. record, especially in countries involved in the production.

Hawk.

MARITI IN CITTA (Husbands in the City) **(ITALIAN).** LUX Film release of an Oscar-Morino production. Stars Giorgia Moll, Nino Taranto, Renato Salvatori, Franco Fabrizi; features Memmo Carotenuto, Helene Remy, Irene Cefaro, Franca Valeri. Directed by Luigi Comencini. Screenplay, Anton, Verde, Maccari, Continenza, Comencini; camera, Armando Montini. At Rivoli, Rome. Running time, 101 MINS.

Amusing little item is brightened by a winning performance by Giorgia Moll, well seconded by Renato Salvatori, in one of the sketches which make up this sketchbook on the summer habits of husbands who stay behind in the city while their wives go off to the seashore. Most of the episodes are fairly obvious and overworked, such as the one about the servant girl in the opposite apartment, or another in which the husband has the tables turned on him and rushes off to the seashore to check on his wife. But the one in which a foreign painter is approached by the errant Italian husband (Salvatori), and how it's finally resolved, is handled with care and comes off best. Humor often has a decided local slant.

Direction by Luigi Comencini makes the most of his material. Technical quality is generally good.

Hawk.

LA MINA (The Mine) **(SPANISH-ITALIAN-COLOR).** Lux Film release of a Maxima Film-Aspa Cinematografica production. Stars Elsa Martinelli, Antonia Cifariello; features Giancarlo Zarfati, Luis Pena, Felix Acaso, Julia Cavas Alba. Directed by Giuseppe Bennati. Screenplay, Bennati, Benvenuti, DeBernardi, Mangione, Albani; from a story by Bennati; camera (Ferraniacolor), Marco Scarpelli; music, Carlo Rustichelli. At Imperiale, Rome. Running time, 97 MINS.

Well-made pic looks headed for only average grosses on the home market partly due to unsensational and unexploitable aspects of its telling. Conversely, it appears to have a better chance abroad in certain European countries where the Elsa Martinelli name means something. It's for the general trade, hence dubbing may be in order.

Story involves a fisherman stranded in a seaside village by a storm in a protracted fight with a local man and a love affair with a local belle. Also in the plot is a fisherman who claims he lost his arm in a wartime incident, actually was hurt while fishing with dynamite. Latter activity produces a chilling bit involving a mine caught in a fishnet and a child who tries to neutralize the explosive charge. Romance is also well handled.

Miss Martinelli is very good in her hard-to-get role as the local gal while Antonio Ciffariello makes a fine opposite number. Some good character portrayals are added by Spanish thesps Luis Pena and Felix Acaso. Direction by Giuseppe Bennati is in his usual easy-going style. Other production credits are excellent. Some trimming is suggested. *Hawk.*

Paris, March 11.

LES FANATIQUES (FRENCH). Pathe release of Cinegraph-CGC-Regent Film production. Stars Pierre Fresnay, Michel Auclair; features Gregoire Aslan, Thilda Thamar, Betty Schneider. Directed by Alex Joffe. Screenplay, Jean Levitte, Joffe; camera, L. H. Burel; editor, Raymond Lamy. At Paris, Paris. Running time, **95 MINS.**

Pic begins with some rugged newsreel footage of revolutionary terror in some unnamed South American country. Then it segues into a thriller about a revolution trying to kill the returning dictator with a time bomb on a crowded plane. Slick aftermath rarely lives up to the terse, real footage, but engenders enough suspense to make this a possible Yank dualer or good video fare. It has some name values, too, in Pierre Fresnay and Michel Auclair.

Main trouble is the lack of identifying the would-be terrorists, Fresnay and Auclair, with the revolution. Their subsequent moral dilemmas are talked out and the telegraphed suspense is effective in some spots. Film is smartly paced and directed by Alex Joffe but lacks the depth to make this a top work. Fresnay is sufficiently unyielding. Gregoire Aslan etches a fine bit as the tyrant, and Auclair is competent as the humane terrorist. *Mosk.*

South Pacific
(MUSICAL-TODD-AO-COLOR)

Boxoffice bonanza based on timeless potentials.

20th Century-Fox release of South Pacific Enterprises Inc. (Magna) production, produced by Buddy Adler. Stars Rossano Brazzi, Mitzi Gaynor; features John Kerr, Ray Walston, Juanita Hall, France Nupen, Russ Brown. Directed by Joshua Logan. Screenplay, Paul Osborn from the legit musical play by Richard Rodgers, Oscar Hammerstein 2d and Joshua Logan, originally produced by Rodgers & Hammerstein, Leland Hayward and Logan, based on James A. Michener's "Tales of the South Pacific." Songs by Rodgers & Hammerstein. Camera (Technicolor), Leon Shamroy; special effects, L. B. Abbott; Todd-AO consultant, Schuyler A. Sanford; music supervised and conducted by Alfred Newman with Ken Darby; orchestrations, Edward B. Powell, Pete King, Bernard Mayers, Robert Russell Bennett; sets, Lyle R. Wheeler, John DeCuir, Walter M. Scott, Paul S. Fox; dances, LeRoy Prinz; editor, Robert Simpson; costumes, Dorothy Jeakins; asst. director, Ben Kadish; production associate, William Reynolds; music editors, George Adams and Robert Mayer; Technicolor consultant, Leonard Doss. At Criterion, N.Y., two-a-day, $3.30 top, commencing March 19, '58. Running time, **170 MINS.** (intermission).

Emile DeBecque .... Rossano Brazzi
Nellie Forbush .... Mitzi Gaynor
Lieutenant Cable .... John Kerr
Luther Billis .... Ray Walston
Bloody Mary .... Juanita Hall
Liat ....France Nuyen
Captain Brackett .... Russ Brown
Professor .... Jack Mullaney
Stewpot .... Ken Clark
Harbison .... Floyd Simmons
Ngana .... Candace Lee
Jerome .... Warren Hsieh
Buzz Adams .... Tom Laughlin
Sub Chef .... Galvan De Leon
Co-pilot .... Ronald Ely
Communications Man......Robert Jacobs
Native Chief .... Archie Savage
Nurse (Dancer) .... Darleen Engle
Admiral Kester .... Richard Cutting

"South Pacific" is a boxoffice smash. It should mop up. It's a compelling entertainment with perhaps the peak 'pre-penetration' campaign of any stage-into-pix property in history. Between its legit impact and that undeniable Rodgers & Hammerstein score it can't miss. The songs, perennial favorites, are mated to a sturdy James A. Michener story. Combination can't be anything but boffo.

Analytical appraisal of "South Pacific" in Todd-AO and Technicolor—eventually in CinemaScope release also—must be measured only by the degree of expectancy and whatever yardstick the auditor chooses to calculate the appraisal. Nothing is perfect. "South Pacific" isn't. Sometimes there's too much to digest. Then, too, when a property has enjoyed such wide prior exposure, from Broadway to truckshows, there is the constant memory barometer.

Mitzi Gaynor is no Mary Martin but there are millions who have never seen the original Nellie Forbush. Rossano Brazzi may be no Ezio Pinza but the late, great Metropolitan Opera basso profundo hasn't the global b.o. impact of the Italian film star-gone-Hollywood. Besides, Pinza is no longer around, and Giorgio Tozzi's dubbed basso has been skillfully integrated into the Brazzi brand of romantic antics.

The histrionics are effective throughout and of high standard. John Kerr (vocally dubbed by Bill Lee) is the right romantic vis-a-vis for Eurasian beauty France Nuyen, daughter of the bawdy "Bloody Mary" which Juanita Hall recreates for the screen. She's of the Broadway original and, paradoxically, like most of the other principals she has been given a vocal stand-in (Muriel Smith, but unbilled; Tozzi alone gets screen credit as Brazzi's ghost voice). Miss Hall may have lost her vocal prowess but there's nothing wrong with her celluloid repeat of her stage creation.

Ray Walston is capital as the uninhibited seabee Luther Billis, recreating the role he did in the road company of "SP" and in London (Myron McCormick created it on Broadway).

"South Pacific" is such a cohesive and foolproof song-and-story that, for Todd-AO (and later CinemaScope) purposes the production values transcend the cast. It is here that critical captiousness is to the fore.

For one thing, the Paul Osborn "expansion" of the original Rodgers & Hammerstein & Joshua Logan libretto may give cause to ponder the values where the visualization eclipses the imaginative. The "magical island of Bali Ha'i" sequence for instance, and the scope with that Yank raiding party on a Jap armada. From the early-scene suggestion of a rather obvious miniature shot of Bali Ha'i it ultimately segues into a somewhat overwhelming LeRoy Prinz-staged ritual dance routine. The pseudo-religioso tribal custom terps, with some bumps and grinds included, borders somewhat on the Fanchon & Marco out of the yesteryear brand of Warner Bros. filmusicals.

Then there are those sepia and other colored filter shots, either director Joshia Logan's or lenser Leon Shamroy's concept of "mood music" interpretation. It has its effective moments but becomes disconcerting when the brownish-green shades clash with the full splendor of the gorgeous South Pacific backgrounds (actual locations were in Hawaii).

There is also the feeling of length. While under three hours, it is in two parts, with the intermission at the Criterion coming after the first 105 minutes.

The femme lead is a looker and while she can stand closeups, as can the personable Italian profile of Rossano Brazzi, sometimes he and Miss Gaynor, on that Todd-AO screen, loom like Gibraltars. At other times Logan, Shamroy & Co. have achieved more intimate effects, such as "framing" the closeups of the Tonkinese beauty and the American lieutenant in their love tent sequences.

Miss Gaynor is uneven in her overall impact. She is in her prime with "Honey-Bun," in that captivating misfit sailor's uniform, and she is properly gay and buoyant and believable in "Wonderful Guy." In other sequences she is conventional. No dubbee she, Miss Gaynor's song-and-dance is essentially very professional.

Brazzi is properly serious of mien and earnest in his love protestations. The seabees are forthrightly dame-hungry; and there is enough cheesecake among the nurses corps to decorate the beachhead. Their treatment of "Nothing Like A Dame" is standout. Russ Brown is effectively "iron belly" in his concept of the naval captain, and the other military are properly cast.

From "Some Enchanted Evening" through "Cockeyed Optimist," "Gonna Wash That Guy Outta My Hair" to "Younger Than Springtime," "This Nearly Was Mine," "Dites-Moi," "Happy Talk," "Balai Ha'i" to "Got To Be Taught To Hate" plus "My Girl Back Home," a new ballad, it's a sure-fire score. It's probably the greatest galaxy of popular favorites from a single show in the history of musical comedy. "Home" was originally in the legit score but eliminated for show's length but, a favorite with R&H, reinstated into the film version. Length here, too, is a factor. Also there will again arise discussion about "Got To Be Taught To Hate," a punchy Hammerstein lyric that frankly propagandizes against racial bigotry.

All the other credits are topflight—the Alfred Newman baton, the Ken Darby musical assist, the crack orchestrators, lensers, recorders, costumers, designers, makeuppers, sound mixers, technicians and all that goes with this $5,000,000 spectacle—the reported figure—which looks all of it.

For the trade, Magna (George P. Skouras) in a capital gains partnership with Rodgers & Hammerstein, Logan, Hayward & Co., under the corporate ownership of South Pacific Enterprise Inc., has the Todd-AO roadshow rights. In on the partnership also is 20th-Fox which gets the CinemaScope release rights after the two-a-day special engagements have run their course. It will be a mopup all over again in the general film runs. *Abel.*

Maigret Tend un Piege
(Maigret Lays a Trap)
(FRENCH)

Rank release of Inermondia-Jolly Film production. Stars Jean Gabin; features Annie Girardot, Jean Desailly, Gerard Sety, Lucienne Bogaert, Jeanne Boitel, Olivier Hussenot. Directed by Jean Delannoy. Screenplay, R. M. Arlaud, Michel Audiard, Delannoy from novel by Georges Simenon; editor, Henri Taverna. At Paris, Paris. Running time, **110 MINS.**

Maigret .... Jean Gabin
Yvonne .... Annie Gerardot
Michel .... Jean Desailly
Mme. Maurin .... Lucienne Bogaert
Mme. Maigret .... Jeanne Boitel
Jojo .... Gerard Sety
Inspector .... Olivier Hussenot

Georges Simenon's famed literary Police Inspector Maigret gets another turn on the screen in the person of Jean Gabin. It is Gabin who gives this whodunit some form and semblance, because otherwise this study of Maigret's capture of a psychopathic murderer lacks the drive and suspense of Yank counterparts. For the U.S., chances are slim except for possible secondary sports, but the Gabin name may help.

Four women have been knifed and their clothing ripped, but they have not been molested. Maigret slow, human and clever carefully puts the pieces together and finally narrows things down to a boy who has not even been capable of being a proper husband. Even his wife's last minute sacrificial murder, to put Maigret off the trail, does not help.

Director Jean Delannoy has given this a solid mounting but insistence on character, sans the needed observation and point, soon rubs off the edge of suspense. Cast are all competent but Gabin's presence overshadows everything. Technical credits are good but this type of psycho-police inquest remains stolid in logical French hands. *Mosk.*

Count Five and Die
(C'SCOPE)

Suspenseful meller based on "true" spy story of World War II. Good double-bill material.

Hollywood, March 21.

Twentieth-Fox release of an Ernest Gartside production. Stars Jeffrey Hunter, Nigel Patrick, Annamarie Duringer; features David Kossoff, Rolf Lefebvre, Larry Burns, Philip Bond, Beth Rogan. Directed by Victor Vicas. Screenplay, Jack Seddon and David Pursall, from a true story from O.S.S. files; camera, Arthur Grant; music, John Wooldridge; editor, Russell Lloyd. Previewed at the studio, March 18, '58. Running time, **92 MINS.**

Capt. Ranson .... Jeffrey Hunter
Major Howard .... Nigel Patrick
Rolande .... Annamarie Duringer
Prof. Mulder .... David Kossoff
Dr. Radamacher .... Rolf Lefebvre
German Agent .... Larry Burns
Dutch Radio Operator....... Philip Bond
Dutch Agent .... Beth Rogan

"Count Five and Die" was made in Britain with blocked 20th-Fox funds and is a smart spy melo-drama, well acted by a British-American cast and directed by Victor Vicas with mounting tension. The CinemaScope production is not big enough to make much of a splash on its own, but it will be a healthy addition to any double-bill.

Jeffrey Hunter is the American officer assigned to British counter-espionage to help develop a plan that will confuse the Germans on where the Allies plan to launch the European invasion of World War II. Nigel Patrick is his British superior and Annamarie Duringer a Dutch underground worker who is also part of the scheme. Double duplicity arises when the suspicion, later confirmed, comes up that Miss Duringer is actually a Nazi agent. The picture ends when she is killed, but the plan to confuse the Germans is a success.

The screenplay by Jack Seldon and David Pursall, reputedly based on O.S.S. files, is well-plotted in its early stages, but in the later events it sacrifices dramatic interest to truth. Title, incidentally, comes from the use of cyanide capsules by espionage agents to prevent their talking under torture. Take a pill, "count five and die," the saying goes.

Hunter, Patrick and Miss Duringer (latter a 20th-Fox pactee) do well in the leading roles and standouts in support include David Kossoff, Rolf Lefebvre, Larry Burns, Philip Bond and Beth Rogan. Ernest Gartside produced the 20th-Fox release. *Powe.*

Run Silent, Run Deep

Good, commercial entry with Clark Gable and Burt Lancaster.

United Artists release of Harold Hecht (Hecht-Hill-Lancaster) production. Stars Clark Gable and Burt Lancaster. Features Jack Warden, Brad Dexter, Don Rickles, and Nick Cravat. Directed by Robert Wise. Screenplay, John Gay from a novel by Capt. Edward L. Beach; camera, Russell Harlan; music, Franz Waxman. Previewed in N.Y. March 19, '58. Running time, **93 MINS.**

Comdr. Richardson............Clark Gable
Lieut. Jim Bledsoe.......Burt Lancaster
Mueller .... Jack Warden
Cartwright .... Brad Dexter
Ruby .... Don Rickles
Russo .... Nick Cravat
Kohler .... Joe Maross
Laura .... Mary LaRoche
Larto .... Eddie Foy III
Cullen .... Rudy Bond
Hendrix .... H. M. Wynant
Beckman .... John Bryant
Frank .... Ken Lynch
Bragg ....Joel Fluellen
Jessie .... Jimmie Bates
Capt. Blunt .... John Gibson

Hecht-Hill-Lancaster, which has shown the courage to tackle offbeat pictures such as "Marty" and "The Bachelor Party," is not one to neglect the good, commercial, mass appeal entry either. The b.o. clicks of "Vera Cruz" and "Trapeze" provide substantial evidence of the company's dual taste. It is further strengthened by its newest offering, "Run Silent, Run Deep," a taut, exciting drama of submarine warfare in the Pacific during World War II.

With Clark Gable and Burt Lancaster, popular prototypes of screen he-manism, heading the almost all-male cast, H-H-L appears to have assembled the ingredients for a popular b.o. film. The tense adventures of a submarine crew in Japanese-infested waters plus the marquee bait of Gable and Lancaster add up to a film that should appeal to both sexes.

Although the analogy may be far-fetched, observant viewers may recognize overtones of "Moby Dick" and "The Caine Mutiny" in the John Gay screenplay adapted from the novel by Capt. Edward L. Beach. Gable is seen as a staunch-ly-dedicated, hard-driving submarine commander with a single-minded purpose—to seek out and destroy a Japanese Akikaze destroyer which he holds responsible for sinking his previous sub. His one-track dedication leads to charges of cowardice and incompetency which results in what seems like a "mutiny" on the part of Lancaster, his tough executive officer who is resentful of Gable for taking over the command he had expected and who is in disagreement with Gable's tactics.

Since Gable has been injured, there does not seem to be much conflict about this evident "mutiny." This portion of the film, relating to the legality of Lancaster's takeover, is somewhat unclear. However, it becomes academic when Gable and Lancaster eventually see eye to eye and the sub covers itself with glory in the Japanese-held waters.

The submarine action is particularly effective and provides the audience with a sense of participation as the men sweat out depth charges and fire from enemy destroyers and planes. The miniature photography is especially good and the scenes of ships blowing up have a realistic effect. Although a good portion of the film takes place in the sub, the action is not static and in many instances the viewers will be nervously perched on the edge of their seats.

For the most part, the picture eschews the familiar cliches of war dramas, particularly in the banter of the enlisted men in their quarters. However, it departs from this commendable goal when it focuses on one naive crew member and obviously tips off early in the film that he will be killed.

Both Gable and Lancaster, who are made to order for films of this sort, give strong, convincing performances. This is the way their fans like to see them and they come through effectively. Jack Warden, as Gable's yeoman and defender, provides another standout portrayal. Brad Dexter, as a malcontent officer, is appropriately obnoxious and Don Rickles, Nick Cravat, Joe Maross, Eddie Foy III, Rudy Bond, H. M. Wynant and John Bryant are good as enlisted men and officers. Mary LaRoche, only femme in the cast, is seen only briefly as Gable's wife.

Robert Wise's tight direction, particularly in the battle scenes, heightens the appreciation of the drama. Russ Harlan's cinematography is topnotch in capturing the action in the confined area required for a submarine. Harold Hecht has seen to it that top production values have been provided and Franz Waxman has composed an appropriate musical score. *Holl.*

Jet Attack

Okay war meller for exploitation.

Hollywood, March 21.
American-International release of James H. Nicholson-Alex Gordon production. Stars John Agar, Audrey Totter, Gregory Walcott, James Dobson; features Leonard Strong, Nicky Blair, Victor Sen Yung. Directed by Edward L. Cahn; screenplay, Orville H. Hampton; based on a story by Mark Hanna; camera, Frederick E. West; music, Ronald Stein; editor, Robert S. Eisen. Previewed in Hollywood, March 19, '58. Running time, **68 MINS.**

Tom Arnett .... John Agar
Tanya .... Audrey Totter
Bill .... Gregory Walcott
Sandy .... James Dobson
Major Wan .... Leonard Strong
Chick .... Nicky Blair
Chon .... Victor Sen Yung
Olmstead .... Joe Hamilton
Major Garver .... Guy Prescott
Colonel Catlett ..../..... George Cisar
Muju .... Stella Lynn
Colonel Kuban .... Robert Carricart
Orderly .... Weaver Levy
Phillips .... Paul Power
AP Sergeant .... Hal Bogart
WAAC Corporal .... Madeline Foy
Signalman .... Bob Gilbreath

"Jet Attack," Zuma production for American-International, is a pretty good little war feature. Despite superficial characterizations in Orville H. Hampton's screenplay, Edward L. Cahn's direction stirs up some interest in a tale of U.S.-Communist fighting in Korea with the aid of a good cast. "Jet Attack" is the stronger of two features being double-billed for exploitation. With "Suicide Battalion," its companion, it should do fair to good business.

John Agar and his two buddies, Gregory Walcott and Nicky Blair, are forced to accept the help of a Russian nurse, Audrey Totter, after they are shot down behind Chinese Communist-North Korean lines. Agar's friends don't trust her, but he does, with the result that she helps all three maneuver the escape of a vital U.S. scientist who has fallen into Red hands. The wind-up sees Agar making his escape in a Communist MIG with the scientist.
Staged scenes are integrated into stock war shots exceptionally well to provide scope beyond the picture's modest budget.
Agar, Walcott, Blair and Miss Totter perform acceptably with good portrayals also from James Dobson, Leonard Strong, Victor Sen Yung and Joe Hamilton.
James H. Nicholson was the executive producer and Alex Gordon the producer on "Jet Attack." Technical credits are fair, with Frederick E. West's photography and Robert S. Eisen's editing good. *Powe.*

Dunkirk
(BRITISH-METROSCOPE)

Inspiring reconstruction of an epic war adventure, well produced, directed and acted; deserves greatest boxoffice success.

London, March 25.
Metro release of an Ealing (Michael Balcon) production. Stars John Mills. Richard Attenborough, Bernard Lee, Robert Urquhart. Directed by Leslie Norman. Screenplay, David Divine, W. F. Lipscomb; camera, Paul Beeson; editor, Gordon Stone; music, Malcolm Arnold. At National Film Theatre, London. Running time, **135 MINS.**

Binns .... John Mills
Mike .... Robert Urquhart
Barlow .... Ray Jackson
Dave Bellman .... Meredith Edwards
Military Spokesman....Anthony Nicholls
Jouvet .... Michael Shillo
Charles .... Bernard Lee
Holden .... Richard Attenborough
Frankie .... Sean Barrett
Merchant Seaman ...... Victor Maddern

Diana .... Maxine Audley
Flanagan and Allen........... Themselves
Lieutenant Lumpkin.... Kenneth Cope
Battery St Major.....Warwick Ashton
Battery Major ...... Peter Halliday
Staff Colonels..John Welsh, Lloyd Lamble
Viscount Gort .... Cyril Raymond
Vice Admiral Ramsey.. Nicholas Hannen
Commander .... Eddie Byrne
Grace .... Patricia Plunkett
Commander .... Michael Gwynn
Old Sweet .... Fred Griffiths
Sergeant on Beaches..Christopher Rhodes
Colonel .... Lionel Jeffries
Dr. Levy .... Harry Landis
Padre .... John Horsley
Sergeant .... Patrick Allen

Eighteen years after the event, Ealing Films has courageously tackled the mammoth task of committing Dunkirk to the screen. This inspiring story of a defeat which, miraculously, blossomed into ultimate victory because it stiffened Britain's resolve and solidarity, offered Sir Michael Balcon and his team many challenging problems. These have been grappled with most effectively and as a result "Dunkirk" is a splendid near-documentary which just fails to reach magnificence. The pic should prove a deserved, resounding success.

Director Leslie Norman's biggest headache was to satisfy three audiences. First, those who actually went through the hell of Dunkirk and will watch the film with an eye and ear quick to detect a false note. Second, those who, while not actually at Dunkirk, were old enough to be very aware of what was going on. Third, a new generation of cinema patrons who were either not born at the time of Dunkirk or were far too young for the name to mean anything but a French seaside town. Norman has achieved this three-prong purpose admirably. Though the youngsters may still regard "Dunkirk" as "just another war story," only the most insensitive can fail to catch something of the spirit that was to lead to "Britain's finest hour."

Norman has planned his film through the eyes of three men. John Mills, a spry Cockney corporal, who, with a few men becomes detached from his unit and leads them to the beaches without quite knowing what is happening. Bernard Lee, a newspaper correspondent who is suspicious of the red tape of the higher-ups and intolerant of the complacent attitude of many British civilians who airily dismissed the war as phoney, Richard Attenborough is one of those very civilians having an easy time in a reserved occupation. Both Lee and Attenborough take their little boats to help in the great evacuation. Lee loses his life, Attenborough gets back, but with a fresh understanding of the drama surrounding him.

The film throughout is deliberately underplayed, with no false heroics and with dialog which has an almost clinical authenticity. On the whole, it is an absorbing rather than an emotion-stirring film. Yet there are many moments to be remembered. The sound of a faint harmonica playing "A Nightingale Sang in Berkeley Square" while bombs rain on the defenseless, naked beaches. The resigned fortitude with which a gun team await certain slaughter. The neurotic wife trying to fit a gas-mask on to her month-old baby. The savage yet not over-dramatic outburst of a wounded merchant seaman as he listens to the "phoney war" talk in a comfortable British pub. The death of Lee as the beseiged soldiers join in church service. The setting out of the greatest scratch little fleet that history has ever known, though it was done with greater emotion in "Mrs. Miniver."

There are a variety of topnotch performances in "Dunkirk," but none has been allowed to dominate the greater importance of the film as a whole. In addition to the three stars, Mills, Attenborough and Lee (an excellent actor who has achieved nothing better in his film career to date), Ray Jackson, Fred Griffiths, Robert Urquhart, Kenneth Cope, Eddie Byrne, Michael Gwynn, Lionel Jeffries, Barry Landis, Warwick Ashton and Meredith Edwards all register strongly as varying servicemen in a long, well-cast string of players.

Maxine Audley and Patricia Plunkett have only limited opportunities as the wives of Lee and Attenborough, but make sure impact.

Production-wise the film is superb. Director Norman has marshalled his forces with patience and infectious enthusiasm and the beach scenes, filmed on Britain's south coast because Dunkirk is now so unlike what it was 18 years ago, are produced and directed with a masterly touch. Paul Beeson's photography is very good and the matching shots of newsreel are technically perfect. A special pat on the back must go to Fred Hellenburgh for his special effects and to Stephen Dalby and his team for the sound effects.

Balcon and the Ealing setup have spared no pains to make "Dunkirk" a film worthy of the adventure it chronicles. Congratulations are in order all round and any defects in the film can be forgiven since it is impossible in 135 minutes, to do full justice to one of the most tragic yet inspiring pages of history ever to be written in the blood and torment of war. *Rich.*

Hell's Five Hours

Moderate suspense thriller. No names. Double bill filler.

Hollywood, March 21.
Allied Artists release of Jack L. Copeland-Walter A. Hanneman production. Stars Stephen McNally, Coleen Gray, Vic Morrow; features Maurice Manson, Robert Foulk, Dan Sheridan, Will J. White, Robert Christopher, Charles J. Conrad, Ray Ferrell. Directed and written by Jack L. Copeland. Camera, Ernest Haller; music, Nicholas Carras; editor, Walter A. Hannemann. Previewed in Hollywood, March 14, '58. Running time, 73 MINS.
Mike .... Stephen McNally
Nancy .... Coleen Gray
Nash .... Vic Morrow
Dr. Culver .... Maurice Manson
Fife .... Robert Foulk
Ken .... Dan Sheridan
Al .... Will J. White
Bill .... Robert Christopher
George .... Charles J. Conrad
Eric .... Ray Ferrell

The opening ten minutes or so of "Hell's Five Hours," a suspense melodrama written, produced and directed by Jack L. Copeland for Allied Artists, is tingling action, without a word spoken. After that, as the customary dialog begins, the picture loses its momentum and never quite regains it, although it is interesting enough to make the spectator curious about the outcome. "Hell's Five Hours" is twinbill fare.

Setting of the pic is a huge plant for manufacture of a highly explosive rocket fuel, managed by Stephen McNally. When a disgruntled employe gets loose on the grounds, threatening to blow himself up, the action starts, because such a blast would set off the whole plant and surrounding residential areas. The trouble soon narrows to a personality duel between McNally and the psycho. Vic Morrow, with McNally the final winner as he pre-

vents Morrow from detonating himself until all fuel has been pumped out of the area.

"Five hours" in the title refers to the time it takes to get all the fuel out from under Morrow and his home-made bomb.

Copeland is a good director but not such a good writer, failing to provide himself with enough plot complications, character twists and fresh action to keep his story going. What he has he exploits fully. The cast does well enough with what it has to work with and technical credits are able. *Powe.*

La Ragazza Del Palio
(The Girl and the Palio)
(ITALIAN—COLOR)

Rome, March 18.
GESI release of a GESI (Maleno Malenotti)-Olimpo Production. Stars Diana Dors, Vittorio Gassmann; features Bruce Cabot, Franca Valeri, Teresa Pellati, Tina Lattanzi, Enrico Viarisio, Ronaldino. Directed by Luigi Zampa. Screenplay, Miachael Pertwee, Ennio de Concini, Liani Ferri, and Zampa; from noval by Raffaello Giannelli; camera (Technirama-Technicolor), Giuseppe Rotunno; editor, Eraldo Da Roma. At Adriano, Rome. Running time, 104 MINS.
Diana Wilson .... Diana Dors
Prince .... Vittorio Gassmann

Colorful, splendidly lensed Italian backdrops, the famed Palio horse race, and the names of Diana Dors, Vittorio Gassmann and Bruce Cabot are the principal values set forth for consideration in potential U. S. bookings for this elaborate pic. An English-language version is now being readied. This is for general release, not the arties, and with considerable pruning for pace, it rates a chance. Color print costs are an admitted problem, but the hues in this film are worth it.

Diana Dors is a Texas gal, daughter of a service station attendant, who wins a quiz show jackpot on the subject of Italian history. She uses it on a trip to Italy, where she gets entangled with an Italian prince on the make. To complicate matters, neither knows the other's family hasn't a cent. Irked by his suspicions that she's an adventuress, and learning that he's bribed a rival rider in the Palio so that his own horse will win, she talks the rivals into letting her ride instead, and eventually wins the race—and her man.

Although there are several talky stretches in which the lovers iron out their problems, the film covers plenty of territory and has some interesting digressions and subplots. The climax, the Palio race and the pageantry of Siena in all its colorful glory, has been neatly captured on film and woven into the plot.

It is probable that this will do for Siena, San Gimignano, and Tuscany in general what "Three Coins" did for Rome. Miss Dors is good as the Texan while Vittorio Gassmann is perfectly cast as the Italo nobleman. Bruce Cabot milks a brief role as an American Miss Dors meets in Siena. Franca Valeri ably outlines a particular type of Italian society gal. Teresa Pellati, Nando Bruno, Enrico Viarisio and many others are in for appropriate cameos.

Production by Maleno Malenotti and direction by Luigi Zampa have focused on the spectacular values, while keeping the plot moving, and it's here that the pic pays off in sight appeal. Lensing by Giuseppe Rotunno in splendid Technicolor hues is a top value and other credits measure up. *Hank.*

The Young and the Guilty
(BRITISH)

Sensitively told story of a young romance spoiled by the interference of parents. Excellent acting in a film which has good prospects in discriminating houses.

London, March 18.
Associated British-Pathe release of an Associated British (Warwick Ward) production. Stars Phyllis Calvert and Andrew Ray. Directed by Peter Cotes. Screenplay, Ted Willis; editor, Seymour Logie; camera, Norman Warwick; music, Sydney John Kay. At Warner Theatre, London. Running time, 65 MINS.
Mrs. Connor .... Phyllis Calvert
Eddie .... Andrew Ray
Mr. Connor .... Edward Chapman
Sue .... Janet Munro
Mr. Marshall .... Campbell Singer
Mrs. Marshall .... Hilda Fenemore
Mrs. Humbolt .... Jean St. Clair
Brenda .... Sonia Rees

Ted Willis has taken a slight but human theme for this short film. Result is that "The Young and the Guilty" emerges as a neat, often absorbing effort. Written by Willis and directed by Peter Cotes, it shows considerable sympathy and understanding of the young. Pic is a sound booking for better class houses though some of the dialog may be too sensitive for thoughtless patrons.

Thin story line concerns the problem of young love. Two children are enjoying an innocent, pure romance but their parents discover a letter, misinterpret it as the sign of a furtive affair and their suspicions take the innocence out of the affair. "The eighth deadly sin is to see evil where none exists" is Willis' contention. Fortunately, the boy's father, with an unexpected insight, persuades the girl's pop that the two youngsters should be encouraged in their friendship rather than that it should blossom as forbidden fruit.

The acting is all important in a film as slight as "The Guilty," and director Cotes is well served with his small cast. Andrew Ray brilliantly suggests the problems of a gangling, sensitive youngster who is misunderstood by his parents while Janet Munro's performance, as the girl in whom love is awakening, is equally well done. The youngsters are completely credible and enjoy several well written scenes which they play movingly and with the skill of veterans.

Phyllis Calvert, Edward Chapman, Campbell Singer and Hilda Fenemore as the parents are excellently contrasted. Chapman is particularly outstanding as the pompous father whose curiosity and lack of sensitivity sparks off the teenagers' dilemma. Tony White's camerawork plays safe and keeps the film on the note of simplicity required by Willis's straightforward but literate screenplay. *Rich.*

Le Septieme Ciel
(Seventh Heaven)
(FRENCH)

Paris, March 18.
Gaumont release of Franco London Film-Vesta production. Stars Danielle Darrieux, Noel-Noel, Paul Meurisse; features Gerard Oury. Directed by Raymond Bernard. Screenplay, Jean-Bernard Luc and Bernard from novel by Andre Lang; camera, Robert Le Febvre; editor, Charlotte Guilbert. At Colisee, Paris. Running time, 105 MINS.
Brigitte .... Danielle Darrieux
Lestrange .... Noel-Noel
Manuel .... Paul Meurisse
Xavier .... Alberto Sordi
Maurice .... Gerard Oury

This is a Gallic attempt at a suave macabre comedy which has some overtones of "Arsenic and Old Lace" but has enough switches to make this an original. However, its logic and emphasis on explanation rob this of true comic nuances. Pic emerges a slickly made affair with good possibilities here but limited to special spots in the U. S., with a plus in the Danielle Darrieux name.

A flighty rich woman, given to helping great charities, raises her money by doing away with swindlers who court her. When they bring in money to buy into her stocks, she has them electrocuted by an old friend, enamored of her. And then calmly buries them in her garden. But her 11th victim and benefactor is traced by a shrewd partner of the latter for the film's big complications. The wily woman manages to do away with him, too, but retribution is in store.

Film is deftly directed by Raymond Bernard, but he rarely imbues it with the proper feel of comedy. Result is a spotty affair. Miss Darrieux is fetching but never plausible as the killing widow. Noel-Noel is fine as her cowardly helper while the remainder of the cast is more in keeping with the aims of the pic. Technical credits are tops. *Mosk.*

Young and Wild
(NATURAMA)

Half of a teenage "package." Okay for its intended market.

Hollywood, March 14.
Republic release of an Esla Production. Producer, Sidney Picker. Stars Gene Evans, Scott Marlowe, Carolyn Kearney, Robert Arthur; with James Kevin, Tom Gilson, Ken Lynch, Emlen Davies, Morris Ankrum, Wendell Holmes, John Zaremba. Director, William Witney; screenplay, Arthur T. Horman; editor, Joseph Harrison; music, Gerald Roberts; sound, Earl Crain, Sr. Previewed March 11, '58. Running time, 69 MINS.
Detective Sgt. Fred Janusz .... Gene Evans
Rick Braden .... Scott Marlowe
Valerie Whitman .... Carolyn Kearney
Jerry Coltrin .... Robert Arthur
"Allie" Allison .... James Kevin
"Beejay" Phillips ...... Tom Gilson
David Whitman .... Ken Lynch
Mrs. Whitman .... Emlen Davies
Capt. Egan .... Morris Ankrum
Uncle Lew .... Wendell Holmes
Sgt. Larsen .... John Zaremba

"Young and Wild" is part of a Republic teenage bill. Story is one of fear, starting quickly with a trio of trouble-makers sideswiping a classy young couple. Following the incident the threesome drive off to become involved in a hit-and-run accident. The couple, the only ones who can identify the hoodlums, are threatened to the point of death. And they respond with silence until the whole mess becomes entirely too involved. They talk, lure the no-gooders to a mountain cabin and the law moves in for the grab.

Scott Marlowe's acting is effectively stylized, and the good-looking youngster shows promise of bigger things. Gene Evans, co-starred as a detective, creates a most believable picture of a law officer trying to do his duty in the face of critical and hindering parents. Robert Arthur, James Kevin and Tom Gilson turn in fine jobs, with pretty Carolyn Kearney, in her first theatrical pic, showing capable talent and ability to reflect changes of emotion with remarkable ease.

Producer Sidney Picker, director William Witney and scripter Arthur T. Horman did their work effectively, with the results equal to "Jungle."   Ron.

La Grande Strada Azzurra
(Squarcio)
(FRANCO-ITALIAN-COLOR)

G. E. S. I. release of a G. E. S. I.-Palvart (Paris) co-production in collaboration with Eichberg (Munich) and Triglav (Ljubljana). Stars Yves Montand, Alida Valli; features Francisco Rabal, Peter Carsten, Mario Girotti, Federica Ranchi, Umberto Spadaro, Ronaldino. Directed by Gillo Pontecorvo. Screenplay, Franco Solinas Pontecorvo, Ennio de Concini Maleno Malenotti from novel by Franco Solinas; camera, (Ferraniacolor - Super Scope) Mario Montuori; editor, Eraldo Da Roma. At Cinema Plaza, Rome. Running time 97 MINS.

Squarcio	Yves Montand
His wife	Alida Valli
His son	Ronaldino

Drama contained in the Franco Solinas novel is presented here in straightforward fashion by Gillo Pontecorvo. It's a remarkable achievement for a first film effort.

As entertainment, however, the pic falls somewhat short despite some very dramatic moments while the generally downbeat motif is also a negative boxoffice element. Splendid Yugoslav exteriors and the names of Alida Valli and Yves Montand are assets.

Story is about a fisherman (Montand) who illegally fishes with dynamite charges as against the majority of villagers who play it straight. When he's almost caught and has to sink his boat, he's in for hard days with no one to help. As soon as he can, he goes back to dynamiting as a last resort. Danger involved finally catches up with him, however, and he's killed by a charge. Also intertwined are subplots involving his daughter's love for a rival fisherman's son, plus some family angles.

Picture has many effective moments, thanks also to a good cast headed by an able Montand, closely followed by one of his screen sons, Ronaldino, who steals all scenes he's in, and Francisco Rabal, a vigorous fisherman type. Miss Valli has little to do as the wife while Federica Ranchi is appealing and no more as the daughter. Peter Carsten and Umberto Spadaro are differently effective as the two finance guards who chase Montand.

Mario Montuori's location lensing captures all the stark beauty of the Dalmatian coast, while Gillo Pontecorvo's direction is sober and dry, and sometimes slow. Technical credits are tops.   Hawk.

Suicide Battalion

World War II action melodrama. Fair prospects as part of exploitation package.

Hollywood, March 19.

American-International release of Samuel Z. Arkoff-Lou Rusoff production. Stars Michael Connors, John Ashley, Russ Bender, Jewell Lain, Bing Russell; features Scott Peters, Walter Maslow, John MacNamara, Clifford Kwada, Bob Tetrick. Directed by Edward L. Cahn. Screenplay, Lou Rusoff; camera, Floyd Crosby; music, Ronald Stein; editor, Robert S. Eisen. Previewed in Hollywood, March 19, '58. Running time, 79 MINS.

Major Matt McCormick	Michael Connors
Tommy Novello	John Ashley
Elizabeth Ann Mason	Jewell Lian
Harry Donovan	Russ Bender
Lt. Chet Hall	Bing Russell
Wally Skilzowski	Scott Peters
Marty Green	Walter Maslow
Colonel Craig	John McNamara
Colonel Hiosho	Clifford Kawada
Bill	Bob Tetrick
Beverly	Marjorie Stapp
Annette	Jan Englund
Julie	Isabel Cooley
Mama Lily	Hilo Hattie

Papa Lily	Sammy Tong
Peter Hendry	Gordon Barnes
Captain Hendry	Art Gilmore
Cho Cho	Jackie Joseph

"Suicide Battalion" is an American-International picture designed for the exploitation market, opening in L. A. in 11 theatres with the same company's "Jet Attack." The low budget shows at times, but "Suicide Attack" moves along and for its class is a well-produced little feature that should carry its weight in the package. The double-bill looks for fair prospects.

Michael Connors, John Ashley, Russ Bender, Scott Peters, Walter Maslow and Bing Russell make up a volunteer mission behind Japanese lines in the Philippines in the Lou Rusoff screenplay. The men are supposed to blow up secret U. S. papers left behind when headquarters was abandoned. Along with the battle scenes, some staged and some from stock footage, there are behind-the-scenes actions involving war correspondent Jewell Lian and the usual warfront cafe girls, Marjorie Stapp, Jan Englund, Isabel Cooley and their boss, Hilo Hattie.

The pic's greatest weakness is a confusion about action and motivations that is never entirely cleared up, but the cast per forms capably under Edward L. Cahn's direction. Samuel Z. Arkoff was executive producer while Rusoff acted as producer as well as scripting. Technical credits are adequate.   Powe.

Foreign Films

Paris, March 18.

AMOUR DE POCHE (Vest Pocket Love) (FRENCH) Gaumont release of Madeleine-SNEG-Contact Org production. Stars Jean Marais, Genevieve Page; features Agnes Laurent, Regine Lovi, Amedee, Jean Brialy. Directed by Pierre Kast. Screenplay, France Roche from novel by Wlademar Kaemffert; camera, Ghislain Cocquet; editor, Robert Isnardon. At Paramount, Paris. Running time. 90 MINS.

This is an attempt at a situation comedy with a scientific background. Meandering direction, telegraphed proceedings, sans the needed snap, lilt and sympathetic characterization, this does not quite come off.

A young scientist has a conniving fiancee but a succulent student walks into his life. He has invented a liquid which can transform animals and people into tiny, molecular-locked statues and he can then unfreeze them with salt water. To escape his fiancee, when he goes for the young girl, he takes the stuff. Then follows her various transformations until the wicked fiancee gets possession of the statue and uses it for blackmail.

Agnes Laurent shapes well in her first big role, but has a long way to go as an actress. Jean Marais is adequate as the scientist while Genevieve Page is the proper cold fish as the fiancee. Production and technical values are average.   Mosk.

LES VIOLENTS (FRENCH; DYALISCOPE). UA release of Oceans-Film production. Stars Paul Meurisse; features Francoise Fabian, Fernand Ledoux, Alta Riba, Jean Myer, Jean Brochard, Paul Guers. Directed by Henri Calef.

Screenplay, Andre Haguet, Andre Legrand, Jacques Chabannes, camera, Jean Isnard; editor, J. Loutre. Running time, 100 MINS.

France now deep in a suspense pic cycle, this one is a lesser entry. Use of Dyaliscope process only slows down the plodding plot even more. This lacks much for U.S. market.

The son of a man, wronged by his family, supposedly comes back from America to avenge his father. Three people are killed in his name until a taciturn inspector nabs the real murderer, one of the family using the pretext of the supposed avenger to perpetrate a crime and take over a secret gunrunning operation in which he is involved. Direction and playing are all too heavyhanded and sombre to give this much movement. Fights are poorly staged and technical credits are barely par.   Mosk.

MARISA LA CIVETTA (SPANISH-ITALIAN). Rome, March 18. CEI-INCOM release of a Carlo Ponti-Balcazar (Madrid) co-production. Stars Marisa Allasio, Renato Salvatori, Ettore Manni, Francisco Rabal; features Angel Arranca, Ennio Girolami. Directed by Mauro Bolognini. Screenplay, Bolognini. Screenplay, Bolognini, P. P. Pasolini, Titina Demby; camera, Carlo Carlini. At Archimede, Rome. Running time, 105 MINS.

Well-made item despite its somewhat repetitious plotting which finds Marisa Allasio faced with an eternal problem: which of her four serious fiances to marry? A sailor, a football player, and two station masters all try to make her decide. She fights back with all means at her disposal, but mainly promising to marry each one. Complications are predictible, and after several climaxes, she marries the sailor.

Miss Allasio plays her usual pert self in a tailor-made part while Ettore Manni, Francisco Rabal and Renato Salvatori are among the many who succumb to her looks and wiles. Mauro Bolognini rises above his material in his lightweight yet often human direction. Technical credits are good.   Hawk.

A Time to Love and a Time to Die
(C'SCOPE—EASTMANCOLOR)

Erich Maria Remarque's bigselling novel made into a sensitive love story against war background. The German side of everyday bombings and soldier love. Warm, human screen fare. Lacks names.

Universal (Robert Arthur) production and release. Stars John Gavin and Lilo Pulver; features Jock Mahoney, Don DeFore, Keenan Wynn. Directed by Douglas Sirk. Based on Erich Maria Remarque's novel. Screenplay by Orin Jannings; cameraman, Russell Metty, with special photography by Clifford Stine; music, Miklos Rozsa. Previewed in N.Y. projection room, March 19, '58. Running time, 133 MINS.

Ernest Graeber	John Gavin
Elizabeth Kruse	Lilo Pulver
Immerman	Jock Mahoney
Boettcher	Don DeFore
Reuter	Keenan Wynn
Pohlmann	Erich Maria Remarque
Captain Rahe	Dieter Borsche
Woman Guerrilla	Barbara Rutting
Oscar Binding	Thayer David
Joseph	Charles Regnier
Frau Lieser	Dorothea Wieck
Heini	Kurt Meisel
Frau Witte	Agnes Windeck
Sauer	Clancy Cooper
Political Officer	John Van Dreelen
Gestapo Lieutenant	Klaus Kinski
Frau Langer	Alice Treff
Mad R id Warden	Alexander Engel
Hirschland	Dana J. Hutton
Sgt. Muecke	Wolf Harnisch
Dr. Karl Fresenburg	Karl-Ludwig Lindt
Frau Kleinert	Lisa Helwig

At a suitable interval after World War I, Universal made and cleaned up with "All Quiet on the Western Front," presenting the German view of war. Unavoidably the question now arises, and indeed Universal's own publicity poses the thought, has the same author, Erich Maria Remarque, done as much screenwise for World War II? The answer can only be no.

"A Time to Love and a Time to Die" is not so broad a canvas. It is less a panorama of the battle horrors of war, though these are implicit, than a poignant telling of the anguish of being in love while civilian bombings rage, and decency is held hostage to vicious character traits. In unfolding the Remarque novel as a motion picture, producer Robert Arthur and director Douglas Sirk have been long on "heart" and "sentiment" and the result, in entertainment, is a bitter-sweet love story.

As a love story, Universal has an appealing entry. Along the way the film contains much that is informative about German suffering during the Hitler fiasco. There are glimpses of the lecherous life of a weakling party official and a sadistic monster who describes his techniques in operating a concentration camp. The picture informs the Americans that there were privileged V.I.P.'s who "enjoyed" the war, that illegal luxury cafes functioned in the midst of austerity, that not everybody suffered in like measure (though the luxury speakeasy is bombed and destroyed —depriving the local elite of their rendezvous).

The story is somewhat slow in development. Orin Jannings opens his screenplay with the hero (John Gavin) on the Russian front under the cloud of defeat in 1944. The wretchedness of modern war, the compassion and pity felt by the better type of German soldier in contrast to the malice and murder in the hearts of the zealots is established before the boy gets his long-delayed furlough and goes off to his native town, only to find his home in rubble and his parents disappeared—though not, it later is stated, dead.

Nearly all the action comprises the experiences of the furloughed soldier with the townspeople, the

Nazis and the Gestapo as counterpoint to his budding romance and hurry-up marriage to the girl (Lilo Pulver) and the denouement comes back at the Russian front. All of this is quite tender, very human, and makes the point that nobody escapes in modern war.

Will American audiences like this film, to be released in July? One supposes that they will. There will be a special appeal to German-Americans. Everyone will be struck by the resemblance of civilian life in Germany to the sufferings in Britain. The woman's angle has been underscored so this is a war picture with strong family and he-she angles. That may be considered a boxoffice value.

Dubious factors are the lack of names. Only the face of Keenan Wynn in a small role (a bon vivant whose stay in a military hospital is due to gout) is notably familiar to American film patrons. the two leads may well get a leg-up careerwise but neither John Gavin nor Lilo Pulver can be considered of boxoffice value in the U.S. Their performances, under Sirk's guidance, are extremely likeable.

This release stands or falls for the American public as romance. (Europe's victim nations may be something else). Its merits are basic humanity. The soldiers are plausible, most of them decent One poetic type commits suicide for very horror when forced to execute **Russian civilians,** including a cursing girl. Remarque makes clear the thesis that these Germans were guilty chiefly in not opposing the Nazis, in excusing their deeds as done under orders. The Nazi party functionary (Thayer David) has an automatic gate to close his conscience but is not a bad fellow and honestly wishes to share his black market luxuries with his old school chum, the soldier on furlough.

Orin Jannings has translated German ' character dialog into American idiom and something unconvincing lurks in many of the speeches. They sound just too Yankee on occasion. While director Sirk, born a Dane but film-educated in the old pre-war Ufa, catches much of the "Deutsch" quality he may have overplayed the gaiety - in -spite - of - all sequence which is so large a part of the footage.

Author Remarque has turned actor to play a German high school professor, released from a camp but still suspect. He does well enough as a thespian, though it adds nothing to realism to intrude this kind of stunt.

On the broad count what emerges in this film, shot mostly overseas, is touching drama of believable folk. One likes many of the characters, believes in the situations and senses the tragic, insane waste of human values. But in the end there is a certain "detachment," almost like scientific observation. This spells the difference between a good and a great "movie."

Plainly Universal has a job of hard sell facing it. At 133 minutes, without stars, the stress must fall on theme and author. It seems fair to pronounce the script inferior to the direction and the acting. Russell Metty's photography in Eastmancolor (Pathe) and the CinemaScope sweep add strong pictorial values. The spectators sense of "presence" should be strong and the technical credits rate spotlighting.

Running through the script are hints of German sensitivity and shame for the hate they have inspired in other nations and their need to explain to themselves the

rise (by public assent) of the Hitler hoodums. In the end Gavin kills a fellow-German intent upon slaughtering three Russians caught hiding in a barn. He releases the Russians who are puzzled by his quixotic generosity. One of the Russians proceeds to shoot him dead and the picture ends with the idealistic German boy dying, the letter from his bride falling from his hand and floating off in the spring thaw of a brook—reminiscent of the death scene in "All Quiet."

The film may be remembered more for types than performances. There is a mad air raid warden (Alexander Engel), a Jew hiding in a Catholic church tower (Charles Regnier) and a Teutonic hellion (Dorothy Wieck, remembered from long ago in "Maedchen in Uniform").

Historically, it is to be noted that the Germans are treated very compassionately, that the villainy of their baddies is more suggested than central. Remarque condemns the system rather than the people, their pliability rather than their culpability. This will hardly please those who have blamed the whole Prussian credo from Von Clauswitz to Bismarck to Ludendorff to Hitler. Be that as it may. "A Time to Love and a Time to Die" rejoices in the conviction that human beings differ little from uniform to uniform. The film carries a sometimes acute "shock of recognition" in its resemblance to the conditions and types on "our side." (Several recent U. S. films, including "The Young Lions" have been literal about Noel Coward's sarcastic "Let's Not Be Beastly To the Germans." In this Hollywood has gone along with John Foster and the market.)

All in all, Universal has a strong romance against war's background. The picture falls of "sensational," but has no need to apologize. This is a picture of considerable distinction. *Land.*

Robinson-Basilio Fight
United Artists release of Leslie Winik production. Narrated by Jimmy Powers. Running time, 18 MINS.

The motion pictures of Ray Robinson's victory over Carmen Basilio for the middleweight championship have been edited to a sharp 18-minute reel of exciting fisticuffs. For those who witnessed the closed-circuit telecast, with its somewhat unclear and dark images, the fight pictures will prove an eye-opener.

The telecast may have provided the overall action, but the clear films of the bout sharply outline each punch and reaction. Basilio's closed eye is unmistakingly seen in the pix.

The pix have been edited so as to include the rounds that provided the most action. These are 1, 3, 5, 9, 10, 11, 13, 15. The final round, during which both fighters were exhausted, is reprised in slow motion. Many of the actions missed in the closed-circuit telecast, such as Robinson's unintentional clout of the referee, are presented sharply in the pix.

The films were produced by Leslie Winik for the International Boxing Club. United Artists, which is releasing the films, has set an initial print order of 850 and anticipates a total of 7,000 bookings. N.Y. News sport columnist Jimmy Powers provides the narration. It's short and to the point. *Holl.*

Orders to Kill
(BRITISH)

Excellent psychological study of the mind of a wartime killer; lack of star names may make it less easy to sell to public than pic merits.

London, March 25.
British Lion release of an (Anthony Havelock-Allan) Lynx production. Stars Eddie Albert, Paul Massie, Lillian Gish, James Robertson Justice. Directed by Anthony Asquith. Screenplay, Paul Dehn from original story by Donald C. Downes; adapted by George St. George; camera, Desmond Dickinson; editor, Gordon Hales; music, Benjamin Frankel. At Studio One, London. Running time, 111 MINS.
Major MacMahon.......... Eddie Albert
Gene Summers .... Paul Massie
Mrs. Summers .... Lillian Gish
Naval Comdr.....James Robertson Justice
Leonie .... Irene Worth
Marcel Lafitte .... Leslie French
Kimbell .... John Crawford
Interrogator .... Lionel Jeffries
Blonde .... Sandra Dorne
Lecturer Lieutenant...... Nicholas Phipps
Mme. Lafitte .... Anne Blake
Louise .... Miki Iveria
Mauricette .... Lillie Bea Gifford
General Nolan .... Launce Maraschal
Colonel Snyder........Robert Henderson
Mitchell .... William Greene
Patronne .... Selma Vaz Dias
Psychiatrist .... Ralph Nossek
F.A.N.Y. .... Ann Walford
Old German Officer.....Boris Ranevsky

Yet another British film turns to war espionage as its theme. Though the subject is getting a shade threadbare, "Orders To Kill" stacks up as one of the best in the stable. A more star-studded cast might have been useful for bringing in patrons. But this is such a satisfying and intelligent picture that word-of-mouth recommendation should insure it a brisk boxoffice reception at discriminating houses in Britain and the U.S.

"Orders" gets away to a flying start because of a firstclass, adult and observantly written screenplay by Paul Dehn. It is clear that the writer, director Anthony Asquith and the players were in complete harmony. The main fault is that it slightly falls apart towards the end. More ruthless cutting in the last 20 minutes or so would have been useful.

Adapted from an original by Donald C. Downes, the yarn has Paul Massie as a grounded Yank flyer switched to espionage on a special job. The chore is to kill a small-time Paris lawyer who is suspected of double-crossing France by selling out radio operators to the Nazis.

Massie approaches the job with tremendous enthusiasm as he trains for this legalized murder. Not till he gets to Paris, meets his victim and gets to know and like him does his stomach begin to turn at the task ahead of him. But he does the job reluctantly and then goes on a mighty binge, broken up at the thought that he might have murdered an innocent man. It turns out that he has.

As the sensitive killer Massie enjoys a well-written meaty role. He is a young newcomer to films, under contract to Metro and Ealing, and looks to be a winner. His performance in this film is over-studied but he admirably suggests the transition from the carefree officer who approaches his mission almost as a lark to the uneasy, conscience-stricken killer.

There are also half a dozen other sterling jobs of acting. Eddie Albert, as an understanding officer; James Robertson Justice, as a trainer-commander who approaches the job of teaching Massie to kill with a breeziness that masks his real feelings; Irene Worth, as a French resistance agent, and Leslie French, as the victim, are all outstanding. There are neat cameos provided by veteran Lillian

Gish, as Massie's mother, and Miki Iveria, as his childhood nurse.

Desmond Dickinson's photography matches Anthony Asquith's shrewd, imaginative direction. "Orders to Kill" may have come a little too late in the British film war cycle to make full impact, but it is a production of which all concerned can be proud, despite a few loose ends which may puzzle the earnest filmgoer. *Rich.*

Gideon's Day
(BRITISH—TECHNICOLOR)

Slick combo of director, star and scripter provides satisfying Scotland Yard yarn which offers good boxoffice prospects.

London, March 25.
Columbia release of a John Ford (Michael Killanin) production. Stars Jack Hawkins, Dianne Foster. Directed by John Ford. Screenplay, T. E. B. Clarke, from novel by J. J. Marric; camera, F. A. Young; editor, Raymond Poulton; music, Douglas Gamley. At Gaumont Theatre, London. Running time, 91 MINS.
Gideon .... Jack Hawkins
Joanna Delafield..........Dianne Foster
Kate Gideon .... Anna Lee
Sally .... Anna Massey
Simon Farnsby-Green........Andrew Ray
"Birdy" Sparrow .... Cyril Cusack
Mason .... James Hayter
Paul Delafield .... Ronald Howard
The Chief ..... Howard Marion-Crawford
Sayer .... Laurence Naismith
Kirby .... Derek Bond
Mrs. Kirby .... Grizelda Hervey
Det. Sergt. Liggott....... Frank Lawton
Ponsford .... John Loder
Mrs. Saparelli .... Marjorie Rhodes
Dolly Saparelli .... Hermione Bell
Sergeant Golightly....Michael Trubshawe
Rev. Julian Small........ Jack Watling
Rev. Mr. Courtney ......Henry Longhurst
Sir Rupert Bellamy.....Michael Shepley
Inspector Cameron ...... Nigel Fitzgerald
Dawson .... Robert Raglan
Ethel Sparrow .... Maureen Potter

Screenwriter T. E. B. Clarke first earned applause for his police screenplay, "The Blue Lamp." Now, with his adaptation of J. J. Marric's novel, "Gideon's Day," Clarke returns successfully to crime, with the spotlight on Scotland Yard. Film offers nothing new, but the combo of Clarke, director John Ford and actor Jack Hawkins makes a solid team and an orthodox, but expert film, which promises satisfying boxoffice results.

This merely purports to be one busy day in the life of a C.I.D. chief inspector and it turns out to be quite a day. He accuses one of his sergeants of taking bribes. A pay snatch ties up with the killing of the sergeant in a hit-and-run car crash. A murder in Manchester has a maniac killer headed for London, and it all finishes up with a safe robbery which involves another slaying. During this time (and in between routine duties), the cop finds himself held up by a killer and shot at by a robber, pulled up for a traffic offense and "in dutch" with his family for not remembering to bring home some salmon and for being too late to attend his daughter's first concert. All in all, quite a day.

Hawkins has played this type of role so often that he could probably do it blindfolded. And it is a tribute to him that he can hold the interest with such a run-of-the-mill character. Apart from his own skill, he is greatly indebted to writer Clarke, who has made the character of Gideon a likeable one, completely credible and with many wry touches of comedy which Hawkins tackles with zest. He is also surrounded by some firstrate thesps who bring a touch of distinction to routine parts.

Among such characters are Frank Lawton, John Loder and Nigel Fitzgerald, as Scotland Yard cops; and Michael Trubshawe as a comedy sergeant. Young Andrew Ray also scores heavily as an over-zealous, young policeman who runs in a murderer in between handing out tickets for speeding offenses to Hawkins and the Chief of Scotland Yard. Cyril Cusack, Derek Bond, as the bribed dick; Jack Watling, as an ex-Commando vicar; Ronald Howard, as the pay-snatch criminal, and Laurence Naismith, as the maniac murderer, also contribute greatly to the authenticity of the goings-on.

On the femme side, Dianne Foster, Grizelda Hervey and Anna Lee also take their respective opportunities with verve. Marjorie Rhodes, as the mother of a murdered girl, gives a particularly touching cameo. Anna Massey, one of Britain's up and coming young actresses, has little chance with the small, expendable role of Hawkins' teenage daughter.

Ford, four-time Academy Award winner, is unlikely to add another to his bag with "Gideon's Day," but he has directed with a nicely blended sense of drama and comedy. F. A. Young's color lensing is top drawer. The Scotland Yard and domestic interiors and the London locations cannot be faulted. Altogether, a more than useful tribute to the work of the police and another proof that crime doesn't pay. *Rich.*

Girls On the Loose

Routine crime yarn okay for smaller program situations.

Hollywood, March 20.

Universal release of Harry Rybnick-Richard Kay production. Stars Mara Corday, Lita Milan, Barbara Bostock; costars Mark Richman; features Joyce Barker, Abby Dalton. Directed by Paul Henreid. Screenplay, Alan Friedman, Dorothy Raison, Allen Rivkin; story, Friedman, Raison, Julian Harmon; camera, Philip Lathrop; editor, Edward Curtiss. Previewed March 19, '58. Running time, 77 MINS.

Vera Parkinson	Mara Corday
Marie Williams	Lita Milan
Helen	Barbara Bostock
Lt. Bill Hanley	Mark Richman
Joyce Johanneson	Joyce Barker
Agnes Clark	Abby Dalton
Doctor	Jon Lormer
Danny	Ronald Green
Mr. Grant	Fred Kruger
Joe	Paul Lambert
Cigarette Girl	Monica Henreid

"Girls on the Loose" is the story of a $200,000 payroll robbery committed by five young women and the effect, both psychological and actual, of the crime upon them individually. An indie produced by Jewell Enterprises for Universal release, film fits into the smaller program category as a routine entry.

Action is principally devoted to distaffers, with a single major male character in for romantic overtones. Opening is reminiscent of the Brink's case, with the femme holdup artists here all dressed alike in masculine attire and rubber masks. Boodle is buried in the woods, then the various reactions set in.

Gang, led by Mara Corday, a ruthless nitery operator, consists of her sister, Barbara Bostock—innocently involved as driver of the g e t a w a y car—Lita ,Milan beauty shop worker; Joyce Barker, masseuse; and Abby Dalton, employee of the company robbed. When it's apparent latter is cracking, she's murdered by gang leader. An attempt is made by the masseuse to murder the young sister, but at finale she's the only one left alive, the others meeting violent ends by each others' hands.

Cast, mostly unknown with exception of Miss Corday, performs creditably in stock characters. Mark Richman, as a detective investigating apparent suicide of first of the five to go, is in for romance with Miss Bostock. One of the weaknesses of the Harry Rybnick-Richard Kay production, is lack of any police work on the holdup to give suspense, a quality Paul Henreid overlooks, too, in his direction. Miss Bostock also is in for one production number, warbling "How Do You Learn to Love?" She also sings "I Was a Little Too Lonely."

Technical credits are okay, headed by Philip Lathrop's camera work. *Whit.*

The Proud Rebel
(COLOR)

Fine heartwarming film for family audiences especially; Alan Ladd and Olivia de Havilland for marquee dressing.

Hollywood, March 29.

Buena Vista release of Samuel Goldwyn Jr. production. Stars Alan Ladd, Olivia de Havilland; costars Dean Jagger, Davis Ladd; features Cecil Kellaway, James Westerfield, Henry Hull, Dean Stanton, Thomas Pittman, Eli Mintz, John Carradine, King. Directed by Michael Curtiz. Screenplay, Joe Petracca, Lillie Hayward; original, James Edward Grant; camera (Technicolor), Ted McCord; editor, Aaron Stell; music, Jerome Moross. Previewed March 28, '58. Running time, 100 MINS.

John Chandler	Alan Ladd
Linnet Moore	Olivia de Havilland
Harry Burleigh	Den Jagger
David Chandler	David Ladd
Dr. Enos Davis	Cecil Kellaway
Mirm Bates	James Westerfield
Judge	Henry Hull
Jeb Burleagh	Dean Stanton
Tom Burleigh	Thomas Pittman
Gorman	Eli Mintz
Carpetbagger	John Carradine
Lance	King

Warmth of a father's love and faith, and the devotion of a boy for his dog, are the standout ingredients of this Samuel Goldwyn Jr., production, which emerges as a truly heartwarming film. With names of Alan Ladd and Olivia de Havilland for b.o. lure release seems a cinch to score strongly with public and trade, if well sold.

Goldwyn the Second establishes himself firmly as a producer of substance in this third effort of his, in which he skillfully blends the best elements of poignant drama and exciting melodrama into a suspenseful and fast-action post-Civil War yarn. Michael Curtiz, too, has achieved fine feeling in his direction of the Joe Petracca-Lillie Hayward screenplay, based on an original by James Edward Grant, and is backed by some of the finest color photography of the year, Technicolor-lensed by Ted McCord.

While an interesting story is presented, it's the characterizations that hold forth most strongly, topped, perhaps, by the very appealing performance of David Ladd, star's 11-year-old son who plays Ladd's boy in the pic. Youngster has been shocked into a mute during Union forces' sacking of Atlanta during the war, when he saw his mother killed and his home destroyed by fire, and it's Ladd's dogged wandering of the land to find a doctor who can cure his son which motivates plot.

Action unfolds in a small Southern Illinois community, where Ladd is drawn into a fight with the two sons of Dean Jagger, a big sheep-raiser; the payment of his fine after his arrest by Miss de Havilland, a lonely farm-woman whose property is coveted by Jagger; and Ladd working out this fine on the farm.

Ladd in a restrained role, the proud rebel whose whole life is devoted to his son, delivers compellingly. Miss de Havilland seems to have gained new depth and stature as a dramatic actress in her portrayal of the farm-woman whose love for Ladd and his son becomes far more important than saving for herself the farm which Jagger is trying to hornswoggle from her. Young David is a standout in a difficult part in which he tries to speak but is unable to do so until speech returns as he struggles to warn his father in a stirring gunfight climax. His devotion to his dog cues much of the action, too, and interesting highlights are reached in this dog herding sheep. Jagger scores as the heavy, with excellent assistance from Dean Stanton and Thomas Pittman as his two sons, and Cecil Kellaway also lends interest as a Quaker doctor. James Westerfield and Henry Hull are in for colorful characters, too.

Jerome Moross contributes effectively to the mood in his music score, Aaron Stell's tight editing is a valuable asset and McClure Capps' art direction colorful. *Whit.*

Cole Younger, Gunfighter
(C'SCOPE—COLOR)

Frank Lovejoy in better-than-average western; fair b.o.

Hollywood, March 28.

Allied Artists release of a Ben Schwalb production. Stars Frank Lovejoy, James Best, Abby Dalton; features Jan Merlin, Douglas Spencer, Ainslie Pryor, Frank Ferguson, Myron Healey, George Keymas, Dan Sheridan, John Mitchum. Directed by R. G. Springsteen. Scheenplay, Daniel Mainwaring, based on a story by Clifton Adams; camera (DeLuxe color), Harry Neumann; editor, William Austin; music, Marlin Skiles. Previewed March 20, '58. Running time, 78 MINS.

Younger	Frank Lovejoy
Kit	James Best
Lucy	Abby Dalton
Frank	Jan Merlin
Woodruff	Douglas Spencer
Follyard	Ainslie Pryor
Wittrock	Frank Ferguson
Bennett Twins	Myron Healey
Price	George Keymas
Phelps	Dan Sheridan
Bartender	John Mitchum

The emotional entanglements that make cigar-smoking Cole Younger a pretty fair guy stack up to make "Cole Younger, Gunfighter" a pretty fair picture. At least, it's different; it gains stature in DeLuxe Color and CinemaScope; and its capably put together. The Allied Artists western stands a chance on the open range but looms mostly as a second biller outside the zealous oater situations.

Most notable are the professional production values gleaned by producer Ben Schwalb. He boosts the picture further by using good taste in casting, coming up with a rather fine group headed by Frank Lovejoy and James Best. R. G. Springsteen directed and pulled out the action without neglecting the human and more important elements of the story. Taken from a tale by Clifton Adams, the script was tightly conceived by Daniel Mainwaring who scores for the most part with a screenplay that's easy to follow.

The setting—Texas in 1873—is spiced by the unseen presence of one Governor E. J. Davis who rules with an iron pistol through his state police force, affectionately labeled the "Bluebellies." At fade-in, Best is fed up with these carpetbaggers and leads a demonstration to prove it. Woe be it for him, he's caught and takes the first opportunity to leave the polluted town. On his journey to safer climes, he meets Cole Younger, played by Lovejoy, and a real and well depicted friendship is born. Story is complicated when Jan Merlin, in love with Best's girl, kills a couple VIP's, then tells the Bluebellies he saw Best do it. All turns out well, thank heavens, through a mighty unorthodox trial that gives one the impression it was time to wind up this opus, properly or not.

Lovejoy turns in a strong performance as the famous gunfighter, making him a little better than he was an maintaining an absorbing degree of mystery. Best makes an appealing youngster, chalking up another top performance. Good support comes from Merlin, Abby Dalton and Ainslie Pryor.

Harry Neumann caught some fine color on his film, and it is heightened by Marlin Skiles' music. Art director David Milton's indoor sets are fine, but his outdoor facsimiles and their simulated sunshine are too obviously unreal. *Ron.*

High Hell

Fair programmer about mountain mining.

Paramount release of Princess (Burt Balaban and Arthur L. Mayer) production. Stars John Derek and Elaine Stewart; features Rodney Burke, Patrick Allen, Jerold Wells. Al Mulock. Directed by Balaban. Screenplay, Irve Tunick, based on novel by Steve Frazee; editor, Eric Boyd-Perkins; music, Phil Cardew; song, "A Man's a Man," by Cardew and Sonny Miller, sung by Dick James. Previewed in N.Y. March 28, '58. Running time, 87 MINS.

Craig Rhodes	John Derek
Lenore Davidson	Elaine Stewart
Danny Rhodes	Rodney Burke
Luke Fulgham	Patrick Allen
Charlie Spence	Jerold Wells
Frank Davidson	Al Mulock
Dell Malverne	Colin Croft
Jed Thomas	Nicholas Stuart

This first production from the Burt Balaban-Arthur L. Mayer independent unit is a modest programmer that fails to wring out the full potential of basic plot ideas and physical backgrounds. Despite the obvious smalltime budget, more film-making ingenuity might have given it some distinction.

Ostensibly laid in the Canadian Rockies (and actually shot in the Swiss Alps), "High Hell" concerns a group of rugged men in quest of a gold mine high up in snow-covered craggy terrain and the romantic distractions provided by an alluring female. Explanation for the latter's presence is that she's there in an effort to rescue her faltering marriage to one of the goldseekers.

Production is reminiscent of the old-school type of meller, wherein the developments are telegraphed ahead, the principal performers eschew histrionic subtlety, the director over-emphasizes the story points. Repeated focusing on the mountain, as the mining group begins the ascent, for example, is unneeded footage, particularly since these scenes are lacking any particularly worthwhile photographic values.

Attempt at the spectacular is made in one spot where Elaine Stewart, as the lone gal in the mountain cabin, thinking she's out of sight, strips for a bath in a barrel and is rescued from a leering Patrick Allen by stalwart John Derek. It comes off a little awkwardly.

Some suspense is generated via the constant threat of an avalanche with the use of dynamite in blasting the mountain.

Song, "A Man's a Man," vocalled by Dick James has an appropriate lyric and modest tune quality. Technical credits fair. *Gene.*

Les Miserables
(FRENCH; COLOR)

Paris, March 25.

Pathe release of Pathe-PAC production. Stars Jean Gabin, Bernard Blier, Bourvil, Daniele Delorme; features Gianni Esposito, Serge Reggiani, Beatrice Altariba, Jimmy Urbain, Sylvia Montfort. Directed by Jean Paul Le Chanois. Screenplay, Rene Barjavel, Le Chancois from novel by Victor Hugo; camera (Technicolor), Jacques Natteau; editor, Emma Le Chanois. At Marignan, Paris. Running time, 240 MINS.

Jean Valjean .... Jean Gabin
Javert .... Bernard Blier
Thenardier .... Bourvil
Fantine .... Daniele Delorme
Marius .... Gianni Esposito
Enjoras .... Serge Reggiani
Cosette .... Beatrice Altariba
Eponine .... Sylvia Montfort
Gavroche .... Jimmy Urbain
Myriel .... Fernand Ledoux

The French, on the surface, have their first blockbuster in this pic. Taken from the Victor Hugo novel, with plenty of stars, production values and four hours of screen time, it should be a smash grosser. But this may not be so big in total coin because recent Yank and Italo versions date only a few years back. It will do well here but maybe not as sock as expected.

For the U. S. this is another thing. The last Yank version was released not too long ago, and this follows the monumental book too closely. All the romantic coincidence is used, with the result that the pic lags as the various threads of two generations are tied up. Much cutting of the superfluous scenes could bring this down to a more compact U. S. size for possible playoff showings, for the pic does have scope. But it would be chancey, at best, and with color and dubbing costs might not be worth it.

Main film strength is Jean Gabin's thesping of Jean Valjean, the man who served 20 years for stealing a crust of bread and then devoted himself to a lifetime of good due to a priest's kindness. The implacable policeman Javert is well played by Bernard Blier.

Made mainly in East Germany, with DEFA footing production costs and getting Eastern distrib rights in return, the film gives a good reconstruction of the 19th Century Paris barricades, with the action and derring-do well rendered. But, in all, the pic is an overdrawn, plodding odyssey, with pruning in order.

Bourvil is standout as the avaricious enemy of Valjean while the production is peppered with known names etching good smaller roles. But the main burden rests in the capable hands of Gabin.

Direction is academic if competent while the color is uneven until settling down on interiors. Technirama gives this an anamorphoscoped size. It is now playing day date on a two-a-day basis in five first-run houses here.

Mosk.

The Duke Wore Jeans
(BRITISH)

Obvious b.o. potentialities in modest but breezy vehicle for Britain's top rock-'n'-roller, Tommy Steele.

London, March 25.

Anglo Amalgamated release of a Nat Cohen and Stuart Levy (Peter Rogers) production. Stars Tommy Steele. Directed by Gerald Thomas. Screenplay, Norman Hudis from story by Lionel Bart, Michael Pratt; camera, Otto Heller; editor, Peter Boita; music, Bruce Montgomery, Lionel Bart, Michael Pratt. At Studio One, London. Running time, 90 MINS.

Tony and Tommy .... Tommy Steele
Maria .... June Laverick
Cooper .... Michael Medwin
Bastini .... Eric Pohlmann
King .... Alan Wheatley
Queen .... Mary Kerridge
Duchess .... Ambrosine Phillpotts
Lord Whitecliffe .... Clive Morton
Lady Marguerite .... Noel Hood
Bartolomeo .... Elwyn Brook-Jones
M.C. .... Arnold Diamond
Factory Manager .... Philip Leaver
Air Stewardess .... Susan Travers

Tommy Steele, Britain's No. 1 exponent of rock-'n'-roll, advances a few more paces along a new road in his short, spectacular career, with his second film, "The Duke Wore Jeans." In this, he is lured into doing a certain amount of acting, and though no great shakes as a mummer, he emerges as a likeable personality with acting potentiality. At least he must now be regarded as a full-fledged artist rather than a possible flash in a lucrative pan.

Though a higher budgeted effort than the money-spinning "Tommy Steele Story," his second pic is not an expensive affair and should return a handsome dividend in the U.K. Steele's reputation is possibly not yet secure enough overseas to make this pic a reasonable U.S. bet.

The lissom yarn has Steele playing a dual role. He is a young aristocrat who wants to evade wooing the princess of a wealthy South American oil-monarchy, as desired by his hard-up parents, mainly because he already is secretly married. When he meets a young, brash Cockney who is his exact double, he arranges for him to take his place in Ritalla. So Steele sets off for South America. After becoming involved in some political skullduggery and inevitable misunderstandings eventually woos and marries the girl.

Steele is happier when he takes over for the young peer than in the earlier stages. It would have been advantageous for a less characteristic speaking voice than Steele's to have been dubbed on to his lines as the young aristocrat. Still, Steele shows a lively sense of humor and a pleasant naturalness.

Opportunities are provided for him to sing several numbers of which "It's All Happening," "Happy Guitar" and "Thanks a Lot" are standouts. Most of the comedy is supplied via a suave performance by Michael Medwin, as a gentleman's gentleman. Alan Wheatley, as the King of Ritalla; Mary Kerridge, Clive Morton and Eric Pohlmann also turn in good support. June Laverick, as the princess, looks as pretty as a picture but is clearly not yet experienced enough for leads.

Gerald Thomas has directed Norman Hudis' lighthearted screenplay with the obvious intention of not allowing anything to take the spotlight off Steele. Photography is competent. "The Duke Wore Jeans" adds up to a modest offering by Producers Nat Cohen and Stuart Levy, who are making no secret of their plans to cash in on the current vogue for pop music. *Rich.*

Innocent Sinners
(BRITISH)

Below-average tearjerker that veers uneasily between sentiment and comedy, misfiring on both counts; with no star value this has little.

London, March 25.

Rank production and (Hugh Stewart) release. Stars Flora Robson, David Kossoff, Barbara Mullen, Catherine Lacey. Directed by Philip Leacock. Screenplay, Neil Paterson, Rumer Godden; editor, John Guthridge; camera, Harry Waxman; music, Philip Green. At Leicester Square Theatre, London. Running time, 95 MINS.

Lovejoy .... June Archer
Tip .... Christopher Hey
Sparkey .... Brian Hammond
Olivia Chesney .... Flora Robson
Vincent .... David Kossoff
Mrs. Vincent .... Barbara Mullen
Angela Chesney .... Catherine Lacey
Liz .... Susan Beaumont
Charles .... Lyndon Brook
Manley .... Edward Chapman
Mr. Isbister .... John Rae
Lovejoy's Mother .... Vanda Godsell
Cassie .... Hilda Fenemore
Mrs. Malone .... Pauline Delaney
Doctor .... Andrew Cruickshank

"Innocent Sinners" is a half-hearted stab at being a tearjerker, but it barely tugs at the emotions. With no real star value in its workmanlike cast, chances of survival in the boxoffice jungle are slim.

Based on a Rumer Godden novel, "An Episode of Sparrows," it tells of a cocky little girl who is neglected by her actress mother. She finds a packet of cornflower seeds and dreams a dream. In a bombed-out site in the streets of London she decides to build a garden, with a couple of boys from a local gang as her reluctant allies. On the whole she finds the local adults rather unsympathetic towards her ambition and she lands up in a charity home. Before then, there are some rather embarrassing moments in a church. Entire pic gets absolutely no place extremely slowly.

Main snag is that the child, as played by young June Archer, is an unsympathetic brat who would have benefitted from a spanking. Only in fleeting moments does she manage to show us the heart of an underprivileged child. Most of the kids in the film perform like puppets, though Christopher Hey makes a convincing young street Arab while little Brian Hammond deservedly registers a few yocks as the tiniest nipper in the gang.

A thoroughly competent adult cast wander through colorless roles with David Kossoff and Barbara Mullen coming off best as a kindly couple who look after young Miss Archer while trying to run an exclusive restaurant in an unfashionable area. Flora Robson plays an understanding spinster and Catherine Lacey her fussy, frigid sister. Both do as well as can be expected with carelessly written roles.

Most of the dialog in the screenplay provided by Neil Patterson and Rumer Godden is tiresomely undistinguished. Philip Leacock's solid direction is marred by John Guthridge's editing which at times lingers on a shot so long that the film becomes static. However, director Leacock has captured a certain amount of the atmosphere of London's back streets. Harry Waxman's lensing of the locations is okay. What could have been a touching idea has got lost in a welter of phoney sentimentality and banal writing. *Rich.*

Windjammer
(CINEMIRACLE—COLOR—SONGS)

First in the new Cinemiracle process, "Windjammer" spreads its adventure story on huge canvas for top effects. Looks good for big money.

National Theatres presentation of Louis de Rochemont production. Features Capt. Yngver Kjelstrup, Lasse Kolstad, Harald Tusberg, Sven Erik Liback, Kaare Terland and officers, men and boys of full-rigged Oslo Windjammer, S.S. Christian Radich. Directed by Louis de Rochemont 3d and Bill Colleran. Screenplay, Capt. Alan Villiers and James L. Shute; camera (Eastmancolor), Joseph Brun, Gayne Rescher; 35m prolog lensed by Finn Bergan, Asmund Revold; music, Morton Gould, with songs by Terry Gilkyson, Richard Dehr, Frank Miller; played by Cinemiracle Symphony under Jack Shaindlin, Arthur Fiedler and members of Boston "Pops" orch; Wilbur de Paris and his New Orleans Jazz Band, and cellist Pablo Casals; editor, Peter Katkevich; sound, Richard J. Pietschmann Jr. Associate producers, Lothar Wolff, Borden Mace, Thomas Orchard. At the Roxy Theatre, N.Y., April 5, '58. Running time, **142 MINS.** (plus intermission).

Louis de Rochemont and National Theatres have turned to adventure for "Windjammer," their first film in the new Cinemiracle wide-screen process. They've succeeded magnificently. This is a big, rousing, beautifully photographed picture, fresh and gay with the accent on youth and overwhelming in its pictorial impact on the huge screen.

Here is one of those special attractions which will gain not only via the introduction of Cinemiracle, which certainly is impressive enough, but also because it has the kind of imagination and charm that will appeal to a very wide audience. There's the smell of the sea in this, the voices of young people on a high adventure, the laughter and color-splashed gaiety of the West Indies, the towering confusion of New York and the beauty of snow-covered Norway.

"Windjammer" is a semi-documentary, relating the 18,000-mile voyage of the square-rigger Christian Radich on a training cruise from Oslo, following Columbus' route across the Atlantic, then to New York and back home. There are 14 calls at strange ports and in each the 45 Norwegian teenage sailors aboard find adventure and make friends as they explore and partake in native festivities.

"Windjammer" could have been just another travelog. Instead, partly of course due to Cinemiracle and partly due to the fact that it's set into the framework of a human interest story, it is an exciting, sometimes spectacular and sometimes quite intimate account of a group of boys on the kind of high adventure everyone has dreamed of at one time or the other.

Picture, being shown with an intermission, runs a little long, though the most impressive parts of the show have been put into the lively second part. Photographically and in terms of color effects this is probably the best film of its kind ever made. One stunning shot after the other brings audience applause and the composition on the wide screen (100 ft. x 40 ft. at the Roxy Theatre) is superb. There is a remarkable degree of audience participation in many of the scenes and the depth effect is noticeable.

Occasionally, the cameras linger too long on a given shot and there is some repetition, particularly of the ship under full sail.

Though most of the material falls into the expanded travelog category, the story itself provides sufficient variation. It switches from life aboard the beautiful, white vessel on which the boys are getting their sea legs and training to the various ports-of-call. Storms wash the deck and give way to the hot sun as the ship arrives at Madeira where the St. Sylvester festival is in progress.

No self-respecting process such as this can miss up on the roller-coaster ride, and "Windjammer" is no exception. But the variation on the theme is typical of the whole film. Here the Cinemiracle camera (actually three cameras in one) rides on one of the wooden sleds that slide down the smooth, cobble stone paths from the Madeira hills to the sea. It's enough to bring the stomach to anyone's mouth.

Musically, "Windjammer" has just about everything. Morton Gould wrote the appealing musical score and Terry Gilkyson, Richard Dehr and Frank Miller provided a number of catchy songs, including the delightful "Kari Waits for Me," "The Sea is Green," "Everybody Loves Saturday Night," a couple of calypso numbers, etc. On the more serious side, cellist Pablo Casals performs the Catalonian ballad, "Song of the Birds" in the courtyard of the Governor's Palace in Puerto Rico, and talented young Sven Erik Libaek plays the first movement of the Grieg Piano Concerto with Arthur Fiedler and the Boston Pops Orch at dockside in Boston harbor. Back on the light side, Wilbur de Paris and his New Orleans Jazz Band are heard.

Some of the most exciting scenes in the film come when the Cinemiracle cameras go underwater. The diving of a submarine is recorded with the camera lashed to the deck of the craft. Then it follows skin-divers as they regain a parctice torpedo. The New York montage, shot by "Weeggee," is outstanding and unique.

Film opens with a standard 35m prolog. Not until the windjammer is at sea and encounters its first rough weather do the curtains part and the full screen takes the pounding impact of the angry waves Transition to the wide screen naturally is breathtaking, but could be smoother. Cinemiracle, unlike Cinerama, is projected out of a single booth, with three projectors electronically synchronized and the image corrected via mirrors and a special printing process to give a continuous picture unmarred by "panels."

At the screening caught by this reviewer, the divisionary "stripes" were very much in evidence in some scenes and virtually absent in others. Also, the sections sometimes fitted perfectly and at others they "jumped." This was not serious enough to mar enjoyment of the show, but should be corrected. The seven-channel stereophonic sound setup is used intelligently.

Louis de Rochemont III and Bill Colleran have directors' credit on "Windjammer." They've done a highly skilled job, because the picture is full of human little touches (such as the recurring bit about the mascot dog) and it has genuine warmth in its treatment of the boys. Nothing ever stands still for very long, and—with the exception of the shots obviously lined up to emphasize the huge arc of the screen—few scenes appear "posed," such as the shots of the windjammer against units of the U.S. Navy.

Joseph Brun and Gayne Rescher handled the Cinemiracle cameras, and they deserve an Oscar for their work. Considering the massiveness of the camera unit, they've accomplished wonders and, even after Cinerama, Todd-AO and CinemaScope, their first Cinemiracle picture is distinctively different. The Eastman color is perfect and it should be noted that some of the scenes covered very cramped quarters, indicating that the process is fully applicable to a story-type film.

Lasse Kolstad, a w.k. Norwegian actor, is one of the few professionals in the crew and he performs nicely. Other lead parts are taken by cadets Harald Tusberg, Sven Erik Libaek and Kaare Terland. Captain Yngvar Kjelstrup, a veteran sailing master, appears throughout with great dignity.

Capt. Alan Villiers and James L. Shute wrote the book, which literally couldn't be improved on. Script has many genuinely funny touches. Much of the film is narrated by a single voice of one of the voyagers, though the boys speak English. Quite a few pretty girls show up at the various ports of call and brighten the boys' leave.

"Windjammer" doesn't have "shock" values. No wild animals attack unsuspecting travelers through the jungle. It does look and sound real though, its people are appealing and its story is told well and with compassion for those who love the sea and to sail on it. Since it also looks like a million dollars and manages to come across as the biggest ever, it should clean up at the boxoffice everywhere.

Hift.

St. Louis Blues
(SONGS—V'VISION)

Disappointing biopic of W. C. Handy. Fair b.o. prospects.

Hollywood, April 4.

Paramount release of a Robert Smith production. Stars Nat "King" Cole, Eartha Kitt, Pearl Bailey, Cab Calloway, Ella Fitzgerald, Mahalia Jackson; features Ruby Dee, Juano Hernandez. Directed by Allen Reisner. Screenplay, Robert Smith and Ted Sherdeman; based on the life of W. C. Handy; camera, Haskell Boggs; music arranged and conducted by Nelson Riddle, based on themes and songs by W. C. Handy; editor, Eda Warren. Previewed at the studio, March 31, '58. Running time, **92 MINS.**

Will Handy .... Nat 'King' Cole
Gogo .... Eartha Kitt
Blade .... Cab Calloway
Singer .... Ella Fitzgerald
Bessie May .... Mahalia Jackson
Elizabeth .... Ruby Dee
Charles Handy .... Juano Hernandez
Musicians .....Teddy Buckner, Barney Bigard, George 'Red' Callender Lee Young, George Washington
Will Handy as a boy......Billy Preston
Aunt Hagar .... Pearl Bailey

Paramount's "St. Louis Blues" purports to tell the story, or a part of it, of the life and music of the just deceased W. C. Handy. Unfortunately, in this Robert Smith production directed by Allen Reisner, the screenplay by Smith and Ted Sherdeman, is unconvincing. Worst of all—the music is seldom seen or heard to advantage.

Only occasionally does one of the principals, Nat "King" Cole, Eartha Kitt, Pearl Bailey, Ella Fitzgerald or Mahalia Jackson, cut loose and the pure music soars across. But in the end the reaction is to wonder what about the man and why was his music so great. "St. Louis Blues" may start fairly strong on the names in the cast and the name of its central character, but it is doubtful that it will hold up.

According to this story, Handy (played by Nat Cole) wanted to write a new kind of music but was deterred by his stern clergyman father (Juano Hernandez). Handy is torn between what his father terms "The devil's music," i.e., popular, and "the Lord's music," sacred music.

Handy is also torn between Eartha Kitt, a New Orleans girl, who recognizes his talent and encourages him. He is also attracted to Ruby Dee, a sweet homebody who just wants him to be happy. Handy is struck with psychosomatic blindness, recovers, takes a combo on the road to play his own music and is rewarded in the end with a concert at Aeolian Hall, New York. The recognition of Handy's music by the longhairs and socially elite brings his father around to the value of his son's compositions.

The cast is all Negro, except for very minor roles. A real effort has been made to avoid any possible charge of "Uncle Tom" in the characters. This libel seems to have been avoided. But for this reason or others, the result is such a genteel portrayal of life in Memphis in the early years of this century that you might wonder why the Negroes ever sang the blues.

A clumsy effort is made to show Handy getting inspiration from watching Negro laborers load a wagon. Handy is shown giving a rhythm beat to a spiritual. The blues certainly came in part out of the spirituals that expressed the deep and justified melancholy of the Negro, they came from laborers' folk songs, but they also came from the honky-tonks, the bordellos and the bistros, and this is barely indicated.

Beale Street was more, as Will Handy's song clearly says, than just a thoroughfare. It was a way of life but this is not shown in "St. Louis Blues." Why did Handy write "Careless Love," "Yellow Dog Blues," "Beale Street Blues," "St. Louis Blues," "Got No Mo' Home Dan A Dog" and (in a new arrangement) "Steal Away to Jesus"? You can find the answer in those titles more than in the picture "St. Louis Blues."

Cole does a sympathetic job as Handy although he is still at his best when he is allowed to caress vocally the master's inimitable melodies. Miss Kitt gets spice into her portrayal and songs, and Pearl Bailey, although neglected as to musical numbers, contributes some saving humor. Cab Calloway, Rudy Dee and the fine Juano Hernandez make some contribution, although not completely effective, while Ella Fitzgerald and Mahalia Jackson do beautifully when they simply cut loose and sing. Teddy Buckner, Barney Bigard, George "Red" Callender, Lee Young and George Washington, do just fine as musicians, which they are, and young Bill Preston is engaging as the boy Handy.

Haskell Boggs' camera work is able and other credits, such as art direction by Hal Pereira and Roland Anderson, set decoration by Sam Comer and Robert Benton, editing by Eda Warren and sound by Gene Merritt and Charles Grenzbach, are all good. Nelson Riddle has done an effective job of arranging and conducting Handy's music.

What is lacking throughout "St. Louis Blues" is not the accurate story of W. C. Handy or the correct presentation of his music. What is really lacking is the spirit of W. C. Handy and his people.

Powe.

Handle With Care

Some merit but small b.o. potential.

Metro release of Morton Fine production. Stars Dean Jones, Thomas Mitchell, Joan O'Brien, Walter Abel, and John Smith. Directed by David Friedkin. Screenplay, Fine and Friedkin from a teleplay by Samuel and Edith Grafton. Camera, Harold J. Marzorati; editor, Ben Lewis; music, Alexander Courage. Previewed in N.Y., March 27, '58. Running time, **82 MINS.**

Zachary Davis .... Dean Jones
Mary Judson .... Joan O'Brien
Mayor Dick Williston....Thomas Mitchell
Bill Reeves .... John Smith
Prof. Bowdin .... Walter Abel
Ray Crowder .... Burt Douglas
Matilda Iler .... Anne Seymour
Al Lees .... Royal Dano
Sam Lawrence............Ted De Corsia
Carter .... Peter Miller

This is probably the type of picture that teenagers "should" see, but it's doubtful that the David Friedkin-Morton Fine entry will have youngsters storming theatres. There's no rock 'n' roll, teenage monsters or Frankensteins, or any concern with juvenile delinquency. As a consequence, the film's an innocuous programmer.

By all standards, "Handle With Care" is a "little" picture that aims to teach a lesson in citizenship and, as a result, will undoubtedly be characterized as a message picture. Objective of the Friedkin and Fine screenplay, based on a teleplay by Samuel and Edith Grafton, is to make the point that justice should not be blind and that it must be tempered with compassion and understanding.

After the spate of films dealing with the unsavory aspects of teenage life, it's refreshing to come across a film that shows a group of youngsters more interested in education and the world around them than in the latest rock 'n' roll record. Unfortunately, small pictures stressing do-goodism are not often boxoffice in the present motion picture market.

"Handle With Care" has numerous faults. It is pretentious and unbelievable in parts, but as a whole it deserves an "A" for effort, which is more than can be said for the quickie exploitation pix made especially for the teenage trade.

"Handle With Care" deals with a group of law students who stage a mock trial as a classroom exercise. With the class sitting as a grand jury and certain students selected as prosecutors, it's decided to make an investigation of the local government rather than choosing a make-believe situation. During the probing, Dean Jones, the brightest student and the designated district attorney, discovers that the mayor, played by Thomas Mitchell, had deposited less money than he had collected during his tenure as city tax collector.

Since the mayor is well-loved and respected by his constituents, Jones meets considerable opposition when he determines to push his investigation. He is not deterred, however, despite warnings and ostracism. Eventually he learns that the mayor had indeed deposited less money, but had given out phoney tax receipts in order to save the homes of the townspeople caught in a depression and a severe drought. All the money was later repaid and deposited in the city's account.

All the trouble, of course, could have been prevented if Jones had been given the true facts earlier, but then there would have not been a story or a picture. Mitchell, as the mayor, and Walter Abel, as the law professor, turn in the pro performances for which they have long been noted. Except for Joan O'Brien, who plays a fellow student and Jones' romantic vis-a-vis, the young thesps involved in the proceedings are too glib and knowing. Jones, who has the potential of developing into a teenage idol, gives a cliche imitation of a tough d.a. Miss O'Brien is just right as the girl torn between her loyalty to her boy friend and her town.

Although there is an artificial slickness to Fine's production and Friedkin's direction, the young film-making team shows promise.
Holl.

Live Fast, Die Young

Average teenage crime meller. For exploitation double-bills.

Hollywood, April 4.

Universal release of a Harry Rybnick-Richard Kay production. Stars Mary Murphy, Norma Eberhardt, Sheridan Comerate, Michael Connors; features Peggy Maley, Jay Jostyn, Troy Donahue, Carol Varga. Directed by Paul Henreid. Screenplay, Allen Rivkin, Ib Melchior; based on a story by Melchior and Edwin B. Watson; camera, Philip Lathrop; music, Joseph Gershenson; editor, Edward Curtiss. Previewed at the studio, April 1, '58. Running time, **82 MINS.**

Kim .... Mary Murphy
Jill .... Norma Eberhardt
Jerry .... Sheridan Comerate
Rick .... Michael Connors
Sue .... Peggy Maley
Knox .... Jay Jostyn
Artie .... Troy Donahue
Violet .... Carol Varga
Judy Tobin .... Joan Marshall
Pop .... Gordon Jones
Mona .... Dawn Richard
Mary .... Jamie O'Hara

The title of "Live Fast, Die Young" is not literal. The teenaged characters involved make an attempt at fast living but nobody dies, young or otherwise. The Universal release, directed by Paul Henreid, was produced by Harry Rybnick and Richard Kay with Edward B. Barison (a B. R. K. production) as associate producer. It doesn't have much of a story and the names are not important but Henreid's direction manages to inject sporadic interest in the characters and their motives. "Live Fast, Die Young" can be sold as an exploitation item or will suffice as a programmer.

The screenplay by Allen Rivkin and Ib Melchior, from a story by Melchior and Edwin B. Watson, tells of two sisters, Mary Murphy and Norma Eberhardt, the good and the bad. Bad sister Eberhardt wants all the things that money can buy, but lacking the money with which to buy, she goes out to make it as a B-girl or in any other way that seems profitable. She winds up in possession of a large convertible and several thousand dollars in cash as well as a member of a gang headed by Peggy Maley. Just as the gang is about to bring off the robbery of $150,000 in diamonds, good sister Murphy shows up, blows the deal and gets everyone involved sent to prison.

It is hoped that teenaged audiences will see some moral in this other than that you don't take your older sister in on your heist jobs because she is likely to be a squealer. The picture has the merit of being a crime story without gunplay, physical violence or other sadism other than that implied in such a narrative.

Miss Eberhardt and Miss Murphy do well by their roles and others who are notable include Sheridan Comerate, Miss Maley, Down Richards and Jamie O'Hara (latter a female).

Technical credits are adequate.
Powe.

Rooney
(BRITISH)

Warmhearted, amiable little Irish comedy about a garbage man and his romantic problems; certain b.o. draw in all family houses.

London, April 1.

Rank (George H. Brown) production and release. Stars John Gregson, Murial Pavlow, Barry Fitzgerald. Directed by George Pollock. Screenplay, Patrick Kirwan from novel by Catherine Cookson; camera, Christopher Challis; editor, Peter Bezencenet; music, Philip Green. At Odeon, Leicester Square, London. March 24, '58. Running time, **88 MINS.**

James Ignatuis Rooney .... John Gregson
Marie Hogan .... Muriel Pavlow
Grandfather .... Barry Fitzgerald
Doreen O'Flynn .... June Thorburn
Tim Hennessy .... Noel Purcell
Mrs. O'Flynn .... Marie Kean
Mr. Doolan .... Liam Redmond
Joe O'Connor .... Jack MacGowran
Micky Hart .... Eddie Byrne
Paddy Ryan .... Philip O'Flynn
Mrs. Manning French ...... Irene Browne
Sheila O'Flynn .... Joan Phillips
Kathleen O'Flynn .... Maureen Toal

Without any blarney, this happy-go-lucky little Irish comedy is one of the most pleasing British candidates for the entertainment stakes yet entered this season. It will rate no Oscars, but its down-to-earth appeal cannot fail to please audiences in every family house in Britain and the U.S. Having passed, with honors, the Dublin boxoffice test, "Rooney" can face the Irish in N. Y. with equal confidence.

This cheerful jest has John Gregson as a stalwart bachelor garbage man who enjoys his daily work and spends his weekends as star of the local hurley team, hurley being an Irish sport which is a mixture of hockey, lacrosse and all-round wrestling. It appears to be the nearest approach to legalized mayhem this side of Yank football. Gregson, with no wish to wed, finds himself constantly on the move to escape the amorous attentions of widowed landladies who wish to mother him with a view to a more permanent arrangement.

Eventually, he lands up as lodger with a shrewish, snobbish widow, who despises him for his trade but thinks to be a fair catch because of his sporting accomplishments plus a poor niece who is treated as a drudge by all but her bedridden grandfather. It needs no great astuteness as a cinemagoer to guess that, after some predictable complications, which nearly land the niece in the local hoosegow, Gregson finishes up by marrying the girl.

From the first glimpse of the River Liffey, the Dublin scene is set with marked accuracy and atmosphere. Though Patrick Kirwan's screenplay and dialog are geared to good humor rather than wit or satire, the yocks are constant. Director George Pollock, handling his first major directorial stint, has set his sights at an unabashed middle-brow level and rarely misses his target.

Gregson is a thorough likeable hero while Muriel Pavlow, as the understanding niece, and June Thorburn, as the snooty cousin, fit snugly into the Irish scene though not themselves Irish. They are surrounded by a group of outstanding Irish players who enter into the romp with national zest. There's Liam Redmond, a stolid lawyer with a passion for hurley; and Marie Kean, as the widow. Noel Purcell, Eddie Byrne and Jack MacGowran are three garbage-men chums of Gregson, and they might have been handling trash all their lives. Barry Fitzgerald, as granddad, has a field day. Slyly swigging whisky, scrounging tobacco and making a thorough nuisance of himself, he dominates his scenes like a jovial leprechaun before conveniently dying and throwing a spanner in the works by the terms of his humble will.

"Rooney" hits the mark because it rarely lapses into caricature and has the absolute minimum of "Begorrahs" and "Bejabbers." Jack Maxsted's sets and decor keep the Dublin flavor, as does Christopher Challis's camerawork. There are a couple of production highlights in the exciting hurley scenes. Philip Green's music also gives a sparkle to the affair and is attuned to the mood. The patron would have to be stone deaf not to recognize this as an Irish comedy. The title song (lyric by Tommie Connor) is sung over the credit titles by Michael Holliday, British pop singer, and by the dustmen during the pic. This catchy ditty will have patrons whistling it in less time than it takes to say "shillelagh."
Rich.

Das Gab's Nur Einmal
(That Only Happened Once)
(GERMAN)

Berlin, April 1.

UFA release of Kurt Ulrich production. Stars Hans Albers; features Helga Martin, Stanislav Uedinek, Alexa von Porembsky, Karl Hellmer. Directed by Geza von Bolvary. Screenplay, Gustav Kampendonk, after magazine ("Stern") series of same name; camera, Bruno Timm. At Atelier am Zoo, Berlin. Running time, **117 MINS**

The nostalgic-conscious among German picture-goers will love this pic. Film presents, along with an uptodate story, excerpts from the most memorable German pix of past years, including history-making silents. Kurt Ulrich produced this long-prepared pic for UFA release, with at least a satisfactory b.o. click since helped by Hans Albers who stars and plays himself in it. Numerous German stars, such as Pola Negri, Conrad Veidt, Emil Jennings, Felix Bressart, Marlene Dietrich, Oskar Homolka, are seen during this film.

Pic shows a teenage girl who's crazy about pix and who finally goes on her own to Berlin in hope of landing a film role. In the Tempelhof UFA studios, she meets the idolized German vet star Hans Albers. He takes her to a party at which he shows old films to his guests. He tries to explain to her that all that glitters is not gold. The girl listens to Albers and finally goes home to reconsider a screen career.

Helga Martin, a beautiful UFA newcomer, portrays the young girl with nice results. Hans Albers is a natural but the others haven't too much to say or do. The lion's share of this belongs to such venerable pix as "Dubarry," "Nibelungen," "Student of Prague," "Metropolis" (all silents) and such talkies as "Blue Angel," "Gold," "The Congress Dances" and "Robert Koch" to name a few. Excerpts from these pix are shown during the films action.

Both an entertaining and interesting offering, it is adequately directed by ex-Hungarian Geza von Bolvary.
Hans.

Bel Ami
(FRENCH; COLOR)

Paris, April 1.

Marceau release of Kleber production. Stars Jean Danet, Renee Faure, Anne Vernon; features Rene Lefevre, Jean-Pierre Caussimon. Directed by Louis Daquin. Screenplay, Vladimir Pozner, Roger Vailland from novel by Guy De Maupassant; camera (Agfacolor), Nicolas Hayer; editor, E. Le Chanois. At Cluny, Paris. Running time, **90 MINS.**

Duroy .... Jean Danet
Madeleine .... Renee Faure
Clotilde .... Anne Vernon
Valtaire .... Rene Lefevre
Forentier .... Jean-Pierre Caussimom

Guy De Maupassant's tale of a climbing, ambitious journalist in late 19th Century France is again put on the screen with this. Pic was banned here for some time because of references to North Africa which seemed somewhat too timely even today. With these cuts made, the pic is out on release. It emerges a faithful transcription of the book and is backed up by good atmosphere. But familiarity relegates this to only a chancey status in the U. S., with special showings possible on its exploitation pegs and theme.

In this version the rising journalist is made partly a victim and product of a corrupt society. Handsome and ruthless in his ambition, he uses women on his climb to the top. He is routed a few times but the femmes make him a great success. Yet it ends with an ironic touch as the next in line for power looms threateningly on the horizon.

Color is uneven but helps in establishing the period. Acting is somewhat stiff but fits in with the general writing and direction of this widely known book. This is more of a social study than a real drama, which makes the characters somewhat sketchy rather than full-blooded.

Technical credits are good. Jean Danet is a properly cold but an almost human Bel Ami, the classic-makes it.
Mosk.

6.5 Special
(BRITISH)

Based lightly on a top BBC-TV program, this modest musical will prove a big hit with followers of up-to-minute disk artists.

Anglo Amalgamated release of a Nat Cohen and Stuart Levy (Herbert Smith) production. With Lonnie Donegan, Dickie Valentine, Jim Dale, Petula Clark, Russ Hamilton, Joan Regan, King Bros., Don Lang, Johnny Dankworth, Cleo Lane, Jackie Dennis, The Kentones, Desmond Lane, John Barry Seven, Mike and Bernie Winters, Victor Soverall, Jimmy Lloyd, Paddy Stone, Leigh Madison, Avril Leslie, Finlay Currie, Diane Todd, Jo Douglas, Pete Murray, Freddie Mills. Directed by Alfred Shaughnessy. Screenplay, Norman Hudis; choreography, Paddy Stone; camera, Leo Rogers; editor, Jocelyn Jackson. At Studio One, London. Running time, **85 MINS.**

"Six-Five Special" is a hit BBC television show which is slanted unerringly at the teenage market. It features the kind of pop singers and bands which nowadays can become overnight sensations on the strength of a disk or two. It provides lively, uninhibited entertainment for modern youth. Jumping on the current bandwagon, producers Nat Cohen and Stuart Levy (responsible for a brace of Tommy Steele pix) have used the show as a bright excuse for providing an equally cheerful and effervescent musical which, though unpretentious, will give a load of kicks to all hep youngsters and dismay only the squarest of middle-aged fuddy-duddies.

As a co-feature, this pic will ring all the boxoffice bells in the U.K. sticks. For American consumption, it could fall down as a standout case of taking coals to Newcastle. Within its modest limits, the pic achieves what it sets out to do and part of its infectious charms is that, though considerably accenting rock 'n' roll, jive and skiffle, it has the good sense to change the pace with the intro of two or three ballads and less energetic pops.

Norman Hudis' screenplay is purely an excuse to put over 16 or so locally known acts. His central figures are two provincial teenagers who set out for the bright lights of London. One of them is a "bathtub soprano," her friend, and an ambitious young woman who is determined to steer her buddy into the big-time of the tv and disk worlds. They set out on the "Six-Five Special," which turns out to be a pro train and here Hudis hits on the rather alarming idea that all the acts rehearse on board the train. This enables a number of acts to do their stuff, and also for Dianne Todd to snatch an audition with Jo Douglas and Pete Murray of the BBC's "Six Five Special" team. Result is she gets a spot on the following Saturday's program. This gives patrons an inside view of the tv program in production and enables the remaining star acts to be slotted logically into the scheme of things.

Outstanding among the many acts are Dickie Valentine giving out with "King of Dixieland" and "Come to My Arms"; The Kentones, with "The Gypsy in My Soul"; Victor Soverall, with "Say Goodbye Now"; Jimmy Lloyd, with "Ever Since I Met Lucy"; Joan Regan, the King Brothers and Desmond Lane, with his popular penny whistle version of "Midgets." Paddy Stone and Leigh Madison score heavily with a neat dance to Geoff Love's music. Mike & Bernie Winters have a comedy interlude which rates some mild laughs.

Dianne Todd has a pleasing voice but needs to trim down physically and look to her acting if she is to score as a potential new discovery. Her friend, Avril Leslie, is a cute blonde of some promise. Veteran actor Finlay Currie has a devastating few minutes as an old thespian deploring the way up-and-comers score overnight successes in this day and age.

Alfred Shaughnessy's direction is straightforward and takes the modern generation seriously. Particularly he brings out the atmosphere of the tv studio and the toe-tapping hysteria of the teenage fans. It is unfortunate that the cameras should have accented the slightly uncomfortable and moronic behavior of some of these fans.

Leo Rogers' lensing is sound. The film would have profited with a gayer opening to have set the tone of a musical but, apart from its ready-made audience due to the tv program, it could well make new friends among those seeing these pop stars for the first time.
Rich.

Foreign Films

"JENNY." Dutch-German coproduction: Standaard Films, Bittins Film Production. Directed by Willy van Hemert. Script by Fischer, Textor, Van Hemert. Camera, Otto Becker, Henk Hazelaar. Starring Elen van Hemert (Gisela Fritsch in German version), Kees Brusse, Ko van Dijk, Andrea Domburg, Maxim Hamel. 65 MINS.

This initial production of new film company, Standaard Films, proved partially a success. Made in coproduction with a German firm, "Jenny" is sold at this moment to an odd dozen countries, including France, Italy, Scandinavia; the remarkable thing is that many foreign distributors preferred the Dutch version to the German.

"Jenny" is a remake of pre-war German feature Eight Girls In A Boat," about a girls' rowing team and the romantic involvements of one of the girls, who expects a baby, while father won't accept re-

sponsibility and marry the girl. In the original film there was a slant on abortion which is eliminated in new version; doctor is transformed into a young man who helps girl face fate and be happy.

Though film has slight story, over-emphasizing what little action there is, "Jenny" has some charm, in form of name-part actress Ellen van Hemert, making her debut and proving herself to be a fresh, talented newcomer. Her father, tv. director Willy van Hemert, with his first feature film directional stint lacks imagination (he also co-scripted pic) and he obviously could not bridge gaps in story.

Film is first color pic made here (Agfacolor, with predominantly orange and blue) and has a large fragment devoted to a tour around the Amsterdam canals, inserted probably for the foreign market.

Too Much, Too Soon

Frank if incomplete account of Diana Barrymore's drinking and love life. Disappointing as biopic, may sell as sensational account of inside on well-known names.

Hollywood, April 11.

Warner Bros. release of a Henry Blanke production. Stars Dorothy Malone, Errol Flynn; co stars Efrem Zimbalist Jr.; features Ray Danton, Neva Patterson, Murray Hamilton, Martin Milner, John Dennis, Edward Kemmer, Robert Ellenstein. Directed by Art Napoleon. Screenplay. Art and Jo Napoleon; based on the book by Diana Barrymore and Gerold Frank; camera, Nick Musuraca. Carl Guthrie; music, Ernest Gold; editor. Owen Marks. Previewed at the studio. March 24, 1958. Running time, 122 MINS.

Diana Barrymore	Dorothy Malone
John Barrymore	Errol Flynn
Vincent Bryant	Efrem Zimbalist Jr.
John Howard	Ray Danton
Michael Strange	Neva Patterson
Charlie Snow	Murray Hamilton
Lincoln Forrester	Martin Milner
Walter Gerhardt	John Dennis
Robert Wilcox	Edward Kemmer
Gerold Frank	Robert Ellenstein

Diana Barrymore's as-told-to autobiography, "Too Much, Too Soon," has to be considered on two levels as a motion picture. On the first count it is a fragment of the Barrymore story, a good deal of the life of Diana and a part of the life of her father, John. As such it is more Main Street than Main Stem. The Barrymore glow is seen as something produced more by bottled firewater than by the inner fire of genius. It will probably satisfy no one who knew John Barrymore, whether they liked him or not, and it gives no indication at all of why the Barrymore name means something in the theatrical profession.

On the second count, as a melodrama of high life in social and theatrical worlds, with very frank scenes of sex and alcoholism," "Too Much, Too Soon," will probably be successful commercially. Henry Blanke's production for Warner Bros. is subtitled "The Daring Story of Diana Barrymore," and that is what it comes down to: an expose of a famous name and its sad and speedy descent to ruin and despair.

The screenplay by Art and Jo Napoleon does one important thing well. It takes the annoying whine out of the story, so that the heroine is not forever blaming everyone for her troubles and travail. If it is over-simplication it is justified, but Diana is represented as a child who sought love but was denied it by her busy parents, actor Barrymore and poet Michael Strange, pen-name for socialite Blanche Oelrichs. This loneliness is acceptable as the reason for Miss Barrymore's frantic romances and marriages, all eyed with clear-seeing candor though sordid and unappetizing. The film story ends when Diana decides to cleanse her soul by the current substitute for the confessional or the couch, the ultra-frank autobiography. This is represented as a step in her regeneration.

There are many omissions that constitute falsity as far as the full story goes. Barrymore, for instance, is represented as married only to Miss Strange; no other marriages are alluded to, undoubtedly because of the problem of legal clearances.

There are other such omissions that will be noted and that cannot

fail to detract from the impact of the story. The Napoleons undoubtedly worked with what material they could, balked from giving the complete account by the reluctance of the living to be involved. But understanding these problems does not concern an audience and an audience is going to feel that something is missing, and it is.

What is missing is the feeling that the story of this girl named Diana Barrymore is a story that should matter. The Napoleons have been skilfull in making Diana more sympathetic; her story is pitiful. But it is not important and it is not admirable. There is not the lift of Lillian Roth's "I'll Cry Tomorrow," a story of infinitely greater degradation but of eventually higher hope.

Dorothy Malone is often very moving as Diana, successfully limning the character from late adolescence to a woman mature in years if not in character. Errol Flynn makes John Barrymore an aimable drunk but not much else. Efrem Zimbalist Jr. is one of the fictionized characters, Diana's first husband, a decent actor who tries to help her. His portrayal is warm and sympathetic. Ray Danton makes the second husband, a tennis bum of nasty disposition, a properly repulsive character but one of understandable attraction. Neva Patterson as Michael Strange,

and Murray Hamilton as a picture director, Martin Milner as an old friend, all contribute ably. Others seen prominently include John Dennis, Edward Kemmer and Robert Ellenstein, latter as Gerold Frank, author of the book with Miss Barrymore.

Art Napoleon's direction is thoughtful and sharp, making the most of individual scenes and attempting a cumulative meaning beyond the book's appraisal. Two photographers, Nick Musuraca and Carl Guthrie, make the most of the narrative's dramatic possibilities. Ernest Gold's music score is a highlight of the film, and editing by Owen Marks and sound by Francis J. Stahl are both top-notch.
Powe.

Cry Terror

Highly-charged suspense meller. High-class exploitationer that lives up the sensational billing. Good names, good b.o.

Hollywood, April 11.

Metro release of a Virginia and Andrew L. Stone production. Stars James Mason. Rod Steiger, Inger Stevens; costars Neville Brand; features Angie Dickinson. Kenneth Tobey, Jack Klugman, Jack Kruschen, Terry Ann Ross. Directed and written by Andrew L. Stone; camera, Walter Strenge; music, Howard Jackson; editor, Virginia Stone. Previewed at the studio. April 11, '58. Running time, 96 MINS.

Jim Molner	James Mason
Paul Hoplin	Rod Steiger
Joan Molner	Inger Stevens
Steve	Neville Brand
Kelly	Angie Dickinson
Frank Cole	Kenneth Tobey
Vince	Jack Klugman
Charles Pope	Jack Kruschen
Pat Molner	Terry Ann Ross

For a Virginia and Andrew L. Stone production such as "Cry Terror," the opening titles represent a kind of dramatic count-down Once they are over—and the power is building even while they are on —the story is launched with dizzying speed and suspenseful pursuit that hardly relaxes until the final frame. The Stones are unashamed story-tellers. They throw anything into their narratives that give them added interest or excitement. This production for Metro is one of their best and it is a solid, satisfying picture that will have excellent box office returns.

Basic premise seems a little shaky, but before viewer has a chance to examine it, writer Andrew Stone has got the plot so chock-full of the FBI, bombs in airplanes, sexual psychopaths, female sadists, benzedrine addicts, knifings, shootings, extortion, kidnapping, murder and police detection methods that your critical faculties are completely numbed in happy anticipation of the next curve to be smashed at you, and still dazed from the last one.

In this one, James Mason is an electronic expert who constructs a small bomb for a man, Rod Steiger, who tells him it is to be submitted for approval to the U.S. government in bidding on a military contract. Instead Steiger tucks it away on an airplane, warns the officials in time where it is, but threatens to repeat the job unless $500,000 is immediately forthcoming.

Mason and his wife, Inger Stevens, are held captive by Steiger & Co., while the half a million is ponied up. The hostages also include the small daughter of Mason and Miss Stevens, Terry Ann Ross, which adds another dimension of harrowing suspense, as Steiger's colleagues are made known. They include Angie Dickinson as a shiv-wielding beauty, Neville Brand as a killer-rapist, and Jack Klugman as the third member of the evil trio.

Stone, as director, and Virginia Stone, as editor, keep several scenes boiling simultaneously, cutting sharply from one to another, heightening the effect of each by playing it off against another. The picture, as with other Stone productions, has the grimy feel of reality through their shooting in actual locations away from any studio. For the kind of story they do, it pays off.

Walter Strenge's photography is a vital element of this kind of realistic drama, with shots inside a New York subway tube, along New York's West Side Highway, inside an elevator shaft and other equally difficult but rewarding areas. Mason and Steiger play well together as the chief antagonists, but it is Miss Stevens who gives the most touching performance. Her evocation of terror and despair are shafted straight to the spectator's heart. Miss Dickinson, young Miss Ross, Brand, Klugman, Jack Kruschen and Kenneth Tobey give strong and varied support in their characterizations.

Other technical credits include the sparing but effective music by Howard Jackson and the realism of the unretouched sound, by Francis J. Scheid. *Powe.*

Hong Kong Affair

Average mystery deriving interest from Hong Kong locations. Jack Kelly may boost prospects, but overall possibilities dim.

Hollywood, April 11.

Allied Artists release of a Claremount Pictures production. Stars Jack Kelly, May Wynn; features Richard Loo, Lo Lita Shek, Gerald Young, Michael Bulmer, James Hudson. Produced by Paul F. Heard and J. Raymond Friedgen. Directed by Paul F. Heard. Screenplay by Herbert G. Luft, Paul F. Heard, J. Raymond Friedgen. Helene Turner; camera, S. T. Chow; editor, Helene Turner; score, Louis Forbes. Previewed at the studio April 9, '58. Running time, **79 MINS.**

Steve Whalen .... Jack Kelly
Chu Lan .... May Wynn
Li Noon .... Richard Loo
Sou May .... Lo Lita Shek
Louis Jordon .... Gerald Young
Inspector Stuart .... Michael Bulmer
Jim Long .... James Hudson

Not long after his plane touches ground in "Hong Kong Affair," star Jack Kelly is asked, "Why don't you see the city first?" This is a helpful suggestion, for it brings a trip through the colony that lends more intrigue and mystery to the film than the storyline itself. Kelly, whose usual mode of transportation is a horse on tv's "Maverick," will help this Claremount Pictures production along its sampan course, but the Allied Artists release is destined for program situations.

Several hands were in this Oriental pot, with the major work having fallen to Paul F. Heard who directed, co-produced (with J. Raymond Friedgen) and co-authored. With the entire production filmed in Hong Kong, Heard has co-ordinated his work to take advantage of what there is to see—crowded streets, crowded waters and crowded living. The only familiar thing is a Coca-Cola sign, and it's a case where unfamiliarity breeds interest.

Kelly is an American who owns half-interest in a Hong Kong tea plantation which has had jolly good luck with a brand called Iron Lady Budha Tea, but Kelly hasn't seen any money from this enterprise in three years. In Hong Kong to find out why, he meets May Wynn, Chinese secretary of the English attorney (Gerald Young) who handles the plantation's business affairs. She goes for him, and he goes to see why his tea isn't finding its way into hot little pots. A murder, an attempted knifing, a near drugging and two chases later, Kelly discovers Young has been hoarding all the profits himself while using the tea shipments to hide his parcels of opium. And, in the middle of Hong Kong's harbor, Kelly's supersleuthing brings him into the hands of the short-pantsed, long-socked police.

Kelly, the most believable part of the show, is genuinely concerned and quite convincing. Miss Wynn, a lovely lady who can act, isn't given much chance, for her put-on Oriental accent puts a kick into much of her portrayal. As a young Chinese femme, Lo Lita Shek adds a delightful touch.

The screenplay—which Herbert G. Luft and Helene Turner cowrote with Heard and Friedgen—basically is the average tale of hidden narcotics. Heard's direction is solid for the most part but could have been picked up slightly in the hurry-up scenes. His production values, especially considering everything was done in the Orient, are fine, with only one set appearing contrived. Photography by S. T. Chow has caught the feeling of Hong Kong, and the Louis Forbes score helps. Title song by Forbes and Paul Herrick is a pleasant lead-in, and it's given a good run by singer Ronnie Deauville. *Ron.*

Manhunt in the Jungle
(COLOR)

Semi-documentary jungle adventure filmed on the spot in South America. Good prospects for its type.

Hollywood, April 11.

Warner Bros. release of a Cedric Francis production. Stars Robin Hughes; with Luis Alvares, James Wilson, Jorge Montoro, James Ryan, Natalie Manzuelas. Directed by Tom McGowan. Screenplay, Sam Merwin Jr., Owen Crump; based on the book, "Manhunting in the Jungle" by G. M. Dyott; camera, Robert Brooker; music, Howard Jackson; editor, Robert Warwick. Previewed at the studio, April 10, '58. Running time, **82 MINS.**

Comdr. George M. Dyott ... Robin Hughes
Aloique .... Luis Alvarez
Col. P. H. Fawcett ...... James Wilson
Carissimo .... Jorge Montoro
Native Woman .... Natalie Monzuelas
Wilbur Harris .... James Ryan

"Manhunt in the Jungle" was made by the same team responsible for the featurette of a year and a half ago, "The Amazon Trader," producer Cedric Francis, director Tom McGowan and writer Owen Crump, with latter sharing writing credits this time with Sam Merwin Jr. It is localed in the same South American area as the earlier, excellent short feature and as a true story adventure, beautifully photographed and capably produced, it should have a most successful acceptance. Considering its probable cost, Warners may have a small bonanza on its hands.

The "manhunt" referred to is the actual trek into the Amazon jungles of British Commander George M. Dyott, who set out in 1928 to find Col. P. H. Fawcett, British explorer who had disappeared three years before. The Fawcett legend is still active, from time to time, lending itself naturally to exploitation, but Dyott's expedition is not so well-known. The screenplay by Crump and Merwin nicely withholds the outcome until the end so there is suspense in both adventures leading up to the climax and in the tragic conclusion itself.

The Warnercolor photography by Robert Brooker, shot entirely in the Amazon country of South America, with some background shots done in Peru, is exceptionally faithful in color reproduction. The river and the jungle are caught with clarity and imagination, although the shots are not as breath-taking as some displayed in "Amazon Trader."

McGowan is at his best as a director in handling of the real natives; some of the actors recruited in the area being unfamiliar with motion picture technique are inclined to indulge in brush-chewing. Robin Hughes, as the central figure, is restrained, however, both in his acting and his narration which is used for a major portion of the film in lieu of dialogue. It suits this kind of story and adds to the reality.

Editing by Robert Warwick and sound by Dolph Thomas, both vital in a production where no retakes and no rushes were possible, are excellent. Howard Jackson's music is also a plus factor. *Powe.*

The Return of Dracula

Francis Lederer as zombie in horror pic short on horror. Teenaged angles may overcome deficiency. Fair exploitationer.

Hollywood, April 11.

United Artists release of Jules V. Levy-Arthur Gardner production. Stars Francis Lederer, Norma Eberhardt; features Ray Stricklyn, John Wengraf, Virginia Vincent; with Jimmie Baird, Greta Granstedt, Gage Clark, John McNamara, Harry Harvey Sr., Mel Allen, Hope Summers, Dan Gachman, Robert Lynn. Directed by Paul Landres. Story and screenplay by Pat Fielder; camera, Jack MacKenzie; music, Gerald Fried; editor, Sherman Rose. Previewed in Hollywood, April 12, '58. Running time, **77 MINS.**

Bellac .... Francis Lederer
Rachel .... Norma Eberhardt
Tim .... Ray Stricklyn
Mickey .... Jimmie Baird
Cora .... Greta Granstedt
Jennie .... Virginia Vincent
Merriman .... John Wengraf
Reverend .... Gage Clark
Sheriff Bicknell .... John McNamara
Station Master .... Henry Harvey Sr.
Porter .... Mel Allen
Cornelia .... Hope Summers
County Clerk .... Dan Gachman
Doctor .... Robert Lynn

"The Return of Dracula" is a well-made little picture but it is somewhat short on its most marketable quantity—horror. Francis Lederer plays the title role with considerable restraint and it is not until the final reel that things get at all exciting. As a horror exploitation item, it could stand some juicing up. It could be, you might say, more full-blooded. Except for this deficiency, the Arthur Gardner-Jules Levy production for United Artists release is capably made and tightly directed by Paul Landres. Pat Fielder did the screenplay.

Lederer is not our old friend Count Dracula, in this one, but is a Dracula-type zombie who sets out to transplant himself from his native Balkans to sunny California. He arrives in the United States having taken the identity of a man he murdered en route. He takes his place in a household of the man's relatives. The daughter of the house, Norma Eberhardt, immediately catches his eye, although not for the usual male reasons, and after enlisting his first victim, Virginia Vincent, he starts after her. Partly through the aid of her teen-aged suitor, Ray Stricklyn, Miss Eberhardt escapes his clutches. Lederer is eventually done in by the complications of modern life when the U.S. Immigration Dept. comes around to check up on his passport.

Miss Eberhardt, Stricklyn, Greta Granstedt, Jimmie Baird, Miss Vincent and John Wengraf do nicely with their material.

It is an acceptable production but until the traditional wooden stake is driven into the zombie's heart, the screen turns color for a moment and the blood spurts forth, there is a regrettable shortage of the weird and eerie. *Powe.*

Thundering Jets
(REGAL SCOPE)

Action in the sky. Very good exploitation feature.

Hollywood, April 11.

Twentieth-Fox release of a Regal Films production. Stars Rex Reason, Dick Foran, Audrey Dalton, Barry Coe, Buck Class, Robert Dix; features Lee Farr, John Douglas, Robert Conrad, Sid Melton, Gregg Palmer, Lionel Ames, Dick Monahan, Maudie Prickett, Jimmie Smith, Bill Bradley, Robert Rothwell, Kevin Enright, Walter Kent, Tom Walton, Ronald Foster, Kenneth Edwards. Produced by Jack Leewood. Directed by Helmut Dantine. Screenplay by James Landis; camera, John Nicholaus Jr.; editor, Frank Baldridge; music, Irving Gertz. Previewed in Beverly Hills, April 10, '58. Running time, **73 MINS.**

Capt. Morley .... Rex Reason
Lt. Col. Spalding .... Dick Foran
Susan Blair .... Audrey Dalton
Lt. Erskine .... Robert Dix
Capt. Murphy .... Lee Farr
Capt. Davis .... Barry Coe
Major Geron .... Buck Class
Kurt Weber .... John Douglas
Lt. Kiley .... Robert Conrad
Sgt. Stone .... Sid Melon

Capt. Dexter .... Gregg Palmer
Capt. Anderson .... Lionel Ames
1st Mechanic .... Dick Monahan
Mrs. Blocher .... Maudie Prickett
Long .... Jimmie Smith
1st Student .... Bill Bradley
2nd Mechanic .... Robert Rothwell
Saunders .... Kevin Enright
Pianist .... Walter Kent
Vocalist .... Tom Walton
Control Tower Sgt........ Ronald Foster
2nd Student .... Kenneth Edwards

With in-flight photography that could brighten a much costlier production than this one, "Thundering Jets" will zoom through its bookings as a second feature, but it will be one with a healthy share of interest. Producer Jack Leewood has come up with a respectable little picture which showcases some promising young actors, and Helmut Dantine has directed the Regal film with taste if little fire.

The James Landis screenplay weaves three conflicts into the framework of an air force training school for test pilots, and though none of the conflicts is deeply handled, each at least is understandable. Rex Reason is the jet ace who's been forced to shake a hickory stick at a new crop of students every six months, feeling the whole time he'd rather be in the air himself. He takes out his frustrations on his pupils, has an argument with his girl (Audrey Dalton) and finally threatens to resign from the service. When one of the neophyte jetesters freezes at the dual controls and is saved by Reason, thus prompting a surprise party and some kindly words, the unhappy instructor realizes how important his job really is. Underlying this conflict is an attempted conquest of Miss Dalton by Buck Class, the "lover boy" of the school. And brought in for good measure is the conflict between Robert Dix, a student whose brother was killed over Germany during World War II, and John Douglas, a new American who flew with the German air force during that war. Both of these are solved in happy fashion.

Though there seems to be a nonchalant attitude in some of the performances, the roles are filled capably. Rex Reason is right in both looks and temperament, and Miss Dalton is pretty and capable. Class and Barry Coe, both whom are under contract to 20th-Fox which releases "Jets," are fine in evidencing sound talent. Good work also is done by Dick Foran, John Douglas, Sid Melton and especially Lee Farr as the class clown.

Cameraman John Nicholaus, Jr., added a major portion of entertainment to this film with his lensing. Sound by Don McKay and Bernard Hurlen helped as did montage work by editor Frank Baldridge. The Irving Gertz score pinpoints action effectively upbeats patriotism with its march tempo   *Ron.*

Foreign Films

Le Dos Au Mur (Back to the Wall) (FRENCH). Gaumont release of Francoise Chavane production. Stars Jeanne Moreau; features Gerard Oury, Philippe Nieaud, Claire Maurier, Colette Renard, Jean Lefebvre; Directed by Edouard Molinaro. Screenplay, J. P. Roncoroni, Jean Redon, Chavane from novel by Frederic Dard; camera, Robert Lefebvre; editor, Robert Isnardon. At Biarritz, Paris. Running time, 100 MINS.

Pic unveils another young director, Edouard Molinaro, with his first feature. He shows a sure technical grasp with a background denoting knowledge of Yank thrillers. But his insistence on a documentary unravelling of a fairly complicated murder setup makes the outcome inevitable. This emerges a slickly-made film with good local opportunities but chancy Yank possibilities. It does not measures up to its U.S. counterparts. General theme could make this an okay dualer.

A rich, young industrialist finds his wife cheating on him with a youthful, second-rate actor on coming home early from a weekend of hunting. He lays a trap to win her back via convincing her the actor is blackmailing her. She kills the actor and he covers up and all seems well again. Crime does not pay and she discovers his perfidy and kills herself but not before branding him the killer of her lover.

Director Molinaro lacks the verve to help gloss over many plot improbabilities. One - dimensional characterizations also rob this of the needed suspense. Jeanne Moreau is properly sensual as the cheating wife but Philipe Nicaud's pallid performance makes one wonder what she ever saw in the actor. Gerard Oury has weight as the husband. Technical credits are fine. Molinaro may emerge a fine technical addition to directorial ranks here.   *Mosk.*

La Bonne Tisane (Good Medicine) (FRENCH). Lux release of Contac-Cofrabel-CCF production. Stars Raymond Pellegrin, Madeleine Robinson, Bernard Blier; features Estelle Blain, Roland Lesaffre, Henri Vilbert, Jacques Fabbri. Directed by Herve Bromberger. Screenplay, Louis Duchesne, Bromberger from novel by John Amila; dialog, Jacques Sigurd; camera, Jacques Mercanton; editor, H. Sevein. At Marignan, Paris. Running time, 100 MINS.

This pic combines a story of gangsters settling scores and a tale of a young nurse's first night of duty. Split theme film rarely achieves perfect cohesion, even when the two blend. This emerges only a fair entry here with U.S. possibilities dubious except for possible dualer usage on its theme.

A homecoming gangster finds others have encroached on his territory. In a fight he is shot, but manages to crawl to a hospital where he is found by a sensitive, young nurse. She is caught up in drama as the gangster uses her in an escape try.

This ends in a gunfight with the death of the gunman and love assured for the debutant nurse.

Only rounded character is supplied by Bernard Blier, authoritative as the gangster, with a fine assist from Madeleine Robinson as an elderly gunmoll. Others are conventional as is Herve Bromberger's directorial chore. Production dress is passable, and aided by shooting in a real hospital. *Mosk.*

The Sheepman
(COLOR; C'SCOPE)

Boff western comedy. Livelier than its cryptic title. With Glenn Ford.

Hollywood, April 18.
Metro release of an Edmund Grainger production. Stars Glenn Ford, Shirley MacLaine; costars Leslie Nielsen, Mickey Snaughnessy, Edgar Buchanan; with Willis Bouchey, Pernell Roberts, Slim Pickens, Buzz Henry, Pedro Gonzalez Ganzalez. Directed by George Marshall. Screenplay, William Bowers and James Edward Grant; based on a story by Grant adapted by William Roberts; camera, Robert Bronner; music, Jeff Alexander; editor, Ralph Winters. Previewed in Hollywood, April 16, '58. Running time, 86 MINS.

Jason Sweet .... Glenn Ford
Dell Payton .... Shirley MacLaine
Johnny Bledsoe .... Leslie Nielsen
Jumbo McCall...... Mickey Shaughnessy
Milt Masters .... Edgar Buchanan
Mr. Payton .... Willis Bouchey
Choctaw .... Pernell Roberts
Marshal .... Slim Pickens
Red .... Buzz Henry
Angelo .... Pedro Gonzalez Gonzalez

The title of Metro's "The Sheepman" gives little indication of its content which is too bad, because this Edmund Grainger production is a fresh and delightful western comedy-drama. With Glenn Ford's name for solid boxoffice appeal and Shirley MacLaine's off-beat casting as a western heroine for an added starter, the picture could be a strong attraction.

The title will not work for it, however, giving no hint of the laughs and excitement, although some of this handicap may be overcome by the ad and exploitation campaign with which Metro is launching it. "The Sheepman" is a good bet in any case, a solid and satisfying production, an entertaining and absorbing show, directed by George Marshall.

The basis for conflict in "The Sheepman" is the historic one that arose between sheepmen and cattlemen in the West, late in the last century. The cattlemen thought the sheep would over-graze their land and they fought with every legal and extra-legal means to keep them out. Glenn Ford, who comes blithely into a cow town with a freight-train load full of sheep, explains his preference for the creatures briefly. He prefers them to cattle, or dislikes them less, "because they are easier to kick—woolier, you know." He fails to make a sale on this ground, however, mostly because the local big man, Leslie Nielsen, is an oldtime enemy who has the locals convinced he is the greatest gift to cattlemen since humans got a taste for roast beef. And Nielsen is intent on running Ford out of town—with his sheep—on personal grounds as well as economic.

The screenplay by William Bowers and James Edward Grant, from a story of Grant's adapted by William Roberts, does not neglect any of the action possibilities of the Colorado Rockies' background. It also fully exploits the usual gunplay and the romantic attachment Miss MacLaine forms for Ford. The comedy is both visual and in the dialoge, good, broad scenes and characters.

Ford gives a hard - bitten and sympathetic portrayal, much like the character he essayed in "Cowboy." His comic lines and cockeyed attitude do not soften his strength as a loner, determined to graze his sheep where and how he wishes. Not, as he points out at the end, because he is particularly attached to sheep, but because he is opposed—in the frontier tradition—to being ordered around and forced to conform just for conven-

tion's sake. Miss MacLaine is a mostly unlikely heroine in a sloppy felt hat and jeans, not at all dainty ginghamed darling of the plains. She is natural girl, a perfect comedy and romantic foil to Ford. Nielsen plays a good heavy, handsome and suave; Mickey Shaughnessy is another casting against type as a would-be villain but too bumbling and cowardly ever quite to make it, while Edgar Buchanan is a comedy standout as a town conniver. Others who do well with their good material are Willis Bouchey, Pernell Roberts, Slim Pickens, Buzz Henry and Pedro Gonzalez Gonzalez.

George Marshall's direction is sharp at pointing up the comedy and drama and most memorable in his composition of the sweeping outdoor scenes. There is one especially notable scene where the sheep in pasture stand out against a background of yellow aspens and snow-topped, granite-colored peaks. All these outdoor values have been realized to give the intimate story a feeling of being a big production. Robert Bronner's CinemaScope photography, in vivid Metrocolor, is a strong job. Others who contributed ably include art directors William A. Horning and Malcolm Brown, set directors Henry Grace and Hugh Hunt, editor Ralph E. Winters and soundman Wesley C. Miller. Jeff Alexander's music is sparing but important.   *Powe.*

Another Time, Another Place

Soggy saga of a wartime triangle romance with two femmes involved in struggle for dead man's memory. Fair b.o. with Lana Turner topstarred.

Hollywood, April 18.
Paramount release of a Joseph Kaufman production. Stars Lana Turner, Barry Sullivan; co-stars Glynis Johns, Sean Connery; features Sidney James, Terrence Longdon, Doris Hare, Martin Stephens. Directed by Lewis Allen. Screenplay, Stanley Mann; based on a novel by Lenore Coffee; camera, Jack Hildyard; music, Douglas Gamley; editor, Geoffrey Foot. Previewed at the studio, April 14, '58. Running time, 95 MINS.

Sara Scott .... Lana Turner
Carter Reynolds .... Barry Sullivan
Kay Trevor .... Glynis Johns
Mark Trevor .... Sean Connery
Jake Klein .... Sidney James
Alan Thompson........Terrence Longdon
Mrs. Bunker .... Doris Hare
Brian Trevor .... Martin Stephens

Paramount is rushing release of "Another Time, Another Place," the Lana Turner starrer made in Britain under Lewis Allen's direction, hoping to pick up some business on current headlines. Film will need some such stimulant, because otherwise it is a weeper without anything special to recommend it. A triangle-melodrama set in wartime Britain, "Another Time, Another Place," will have its greatest appeal to women; men are likely to wonder what all the agonizing is about.

Miss Turner plays an American correspondent in London, involved in a love affair with Sean Connery, a BBC commentator. Just before he flies off to cover a continental assignment, he tells her for the first time that he has a wife and child in his native Cornwall village.

When Connery is killed in a plane crash, Miss Turner breaks down emotionally and enters a nursing home. She emerges determined to make a sentimental pilgrimage to Connery's home, intending (she says) only to take a look and depart. But she meets Connery's widow, Glynis Johns, is invited into her home and settles down there for a lengthy visit. Miss Turner's association with Connery or even the fact that there was an association is unknown to Miss Johns.

The screenplay by Stanley Mann, which is based on a novel by Lenore Coffee (Titled "Weep No More" in Britain and published under the picture title here), gets into a conclusion that is neither satisfactory nor believable. The idea is that Miss Turner must inform Miss Johns of the love affair. This, it seems, will make everyone feel better. Miss Turner leaves with her publisher-fiance, Barry Sullivan, and Miss Johns is left with her late husband's best friend, Terrence Longdon.

Miss Turner is beautifully photographed by Britain's crack cameraman, Jack Hildyard, but she only occasionally cuts loose with the kind of dramatic fireworks the picture needs. Glynis Johns, less tenderly lensed, makes a poignant and convincing figure of the wife. Barry Sullivan is stalwart as the publisher. Sean Connery, who gets "introducing" billing, is a young Scots actor who is obviously capable but he plays somewhat pallidly for a romantic lead. Sidney James is a standout, bringing some needed humor to the otherwise soggy saga. *Powe.*

Violent Road

Production is good, but story lacks sufficient interest for universal appeal.

Hollywood, April 18.

Warner Bros. release of an Aubrey Schenck production. Stars Brian Keith, Dick Foran, Efrem Zimbalist Jr., Merry Anders; with Sean Garrison, Joanna Barnes, Perry Lopez, Arthur Batanides, Ed Prentiss, Ann Doran, John Dennis. Directed by Howard W. Koch. Screenplay by Richard Landau; from a story by Don Martin; camera, Carl Guthrie; film editor, John F. Schreyer; music, Leith Stevens. Previewed at the studio, April 11, '58. Running time, **85 MINS.**

Mitch .... Brian Keith
Sarge .... Dick Foran
George Lawrence....Efrem Zimbalist Jr.
Carrie .... Merry Anders
Ken Farley .... Sean Garrison
Peg Lawrence .... Joanna Barnes
Manuelo .... Perry Lopez
Ben .... Arthur Batanides
Nelson .... Ed Prentiss
Edith .... Ann Doran
Pat Farley .... John Dennis

If Warner Bros.' "Violent Road" seems to lead to a dead end, it may be due to a repetitious storyline that runs over a mountain in three diesel trucks. Everything else about the action drama is fine—acting, direction, photography—but the Aubrey Schenck production fails to hurdle the first roadblock and therefore looms as a second feature whose greatest impact will be on the grease monkey trade. The Richard Landau screenplay is soundly constructed, with the initial problem being that the Don Martin story simply doesn't provide enough contrasting plot situations to sustain excitement for 85 minutes.

Six characters are brought together to truck tanks of explosive rocket fuel components across rough terrain, and to compound the excitement the chemicals will blow if jarred in the slightest. The half dozen drivers brave the dangers because each has something to prove and something to gain, namely $5,000. Driving the three trucks are Brian Keith who simply wants the money; Efrem Zimbalist, Jr., who developed the fuel and who set off the rocket that went wild, landed in town and killed his wife and two children; Dick Foran, a World War II marine who's out to prove he's not too old; Sean Garrison, out to prove he's not too young, additionally wants to use the money to cure his alcoholic brother; Perry Lopez, a young Mexican who wants the money to go to college; and Arthur Batanides, a gambler who wants the money to go to Las Vegas. Now that's a motley enough crew and to make things interesting for them, the added ingredients include rockslides, a careening school bus, a brakeless truck, and leaking acid which takes Foran's life though it seems totally unnecessary. The drivers do finally make it, however, and each has proved what he set out to prove.

Howard W. Koch directed with authority, making the dangerous scenes seem even more so and building each of the six characters with haste. Keith casts the appearance of the rough, tough boss in a good performance; Foran, Lopez, Batanides and Garrison are fine, and Zimbalist tops all in a sympathetic, sincere portrayal. On the femme side, Merry Anders is capable; Joanne Barnes and Ann Doran are too, and Venetia Stevenson, in a tight-fitting, uncredited scene, lends a luscious air.

Carl Guthrie's photography has caught some effective road action, and the Leith Stevens music helps things considerably. *Ron.*

Dragstrip Riot

Hot rods and switchblades for a fair teenage melodrama.

Hollywood, April 18.

American International release of an O. Dale Ireland production. Director, David Bradley; screenplay, George Hodgins; based on a story by Ireland and Hodgins; additional story and dialog by V. J. Rheims; camera, Gil Warrenton; music, Nicholas Carras; editor, John A. Bushelman. Previewed in Hollywood, April 18, '58. Running time, **68 MINS.**

Janet Pearson .... Yvonne Lime
Rick Martin .... Gary Clarke
Mrs. Martin .... Fay Wray
Bart Thorsen .... Bob Turnbull
Marge .... Connie Stevens
Silva .... Gabe DeLutri
Cliff .... Marcus Dyrector
Gramps .... Ted Wedderspoon
Gordie .... Barry Truex
Rae .... Marilyn Carroll
Helen .... Marla Ryan
Dutch .... Steve Ihnat
Joe .... Tony Butula
Betty .... Carolyn Mitchell
Lisa .... Joan Chandler
Gary .... Marc Thompson
Mike .... Allan Carter

"Dragstrip Riot" has a novel gimmick; all its teenagers are overprivileged delinquents. All its hotrodders drive Corvettes. The interesting angle is not explored, however, and the O. Dale Ireland production being released by American International is a conventional exploitation item paired with "The Cool and the Crazy." It is well-made and will rack up satisfactory returns for its kind of booking.

The romantic interest is supplied by Gary Clarke and Yvonne Lime, leading members of the Corvette set. Clarke has a small cloud hanging over him; a jail sentence for beating up a fellow teenager, and his mother, Fay Wray, has extracted a promise he will not fight again with anyone. This pledge gets knocked about when a black leather-jacketed motorcycle gang makes trouble for Clarke and chums, culminating in the accidental death of one of the cyclists. Clarke is suspected because of his "record," but everything is eventually cleared up.

There is a tendency in George Hodgins' screenplay, based on a story by producer Ireland and Hodgins, with additional dialog and story by V. J. Rheims, to pit parent against child for dramatic incident.

The largely youthful cast does a capable job, headed by Miss Lime and Clarke, with Bob Turnbull as the teenaged heavy, Gabe DeLutri, the motorcycle chieftain, and others including Connie Stevens, Marcus Dyrector, Barry Truex, Marilyn Carroll and Marla Ryan. Fay Wray and Ted Wedderspoon handle the adult level nicely.

David Bradley's direction keeps things moving at a good clip, even for a covey of Corvettes, and some of Gil Warrenton's camera setups are especially striking. Nicholas Carras' music is tuned to the story while John A. Bushelman's editing is slick. *Powe.*

The Goddess

Semi - poetic, semi - realistic melodrama tracing the growth, degradation of a movie queen. May have exploitation values, if hurried to market.

Columbia release of a Milton Perlman production. Director John Cromwell. Stars Kim Stanley, Lloyd Bridges; features Steve Hill, Betty Lou Holland; with Burt Brinckerhoff, Gerald Hiken, Joan Copeland, Bert Freed, Elizabeth Wilson, Joyce Van Patten, Joanne Linville. Directed by John Cromwell. Screenplay, Paddy Chayefsky; camera, Arthur J. Ornitz; music, Virgil Thompson; editor, Carl Lerner. Previewed at the studio, April 10, '58. Running time, **104 MINS.**

Rita Shawn .... Kim Stanley
Dutch Seymour .... Lloyd Bridges
John Tower .... Steve Hill
Mrs. Faulkner .... Betty Lou Holland

Hollywood, April 11.

If Columbia will get this show on the road in a hurry (if it can), its natural magnetism towards current headlines may make it a good deal more profitable than it would otherwise be. "The Goddess," produced by Milton Perlman and directed by John Cromwell, is about a motion picture star, how she got where and how she is, and the effect her life has on others, including her daughter and her mother.

Pictures about Hollywood have a reputation for being slow at the boxoffice and the title of this one is not likely to be an antidote to the tradition. Despite flashes of brilliance in the acting (by Kim Stanley) and in John Cromwell's direction, "The Goddess" is not going to be the picture to break that jinx. Not unless, that is, it can be fitted neatly into the public curiosity about the tragedy and heartbreak of being a motion picture personality.

Paddy Chayefsky wrote the screenplay for "The Goddess." Kim Stanley, making her picture bow, plays the actress. Chayefsky's first script excursion into the world away from his native New York is an episodic and self-consciously artistic effort to probe the "movie star" from her days of girlhood in a Southern slum community to her finish as a pill-ridden shell who goes through her acting chores before the camera by rote.

The picture, shot much on location in the East, is divided into three parts: Portrait of a Young Girl; Portrait of a Young Woman; Portrait of a Goddess.

Kim Stanley, as the central figure, is hardly offscreen for a moment during the hour and three quarters of the picture, and although the construction of the sreenplay does not allow her to create a finished character, she does show that she is as undeniably a movie personality in the fullest sense as the character she is portraying. She is too mature in appearance to be completely convincing as a teenaged girl, but other than that qualification, she displays great variety and virtuosity, keeping the story alive even through some stretches of hackneyed scenes and pretentious dialogue.

John Cromwell's return to screen direction undoubtedly was an aid to Miss Stanley because he keeps her keyed to the shifting moods of the character exactly, while maintaining also the underlying, unchanging personality, doomed to tragedy and defeat.

Lloyd Bridges is impressive as her second husband and Steve Hill is touching as her first, but neither characterization is ever thoroughly explored and remains unsatisfactory. Betty Lou Holland creates a vivid portrayal as a Tennessee Williams-kind of Southern woman, giddy in her youthful scenes and maddeningly serene later as a religious fanatic. Elizabeth Wilson is a standout as the secretary and nurse to Miss Stanley in her final scenes.

There is too much that is cliche in "The Goddess," viz., the studio head who signs Miss Stanley to a term contract and then informs her she is expected at his house that evening. There is also too much left unexplained and unpenetrated, so that the deck seems stacked for the author and against the star. The tragic conclusion seems not only inevitable but foreseeable and this disperses some excitement and interest.

Arthur J. Ornitz' camera does a superb job of catching the seamy backgrounds and the equally seamy characters in the foreground, more revealing often than the lines. Virgil Thompson's score is almost entirely restricted to entr'act (between the "portraits") music. It is charming and original.

The basic weakness of Chayefsky's screenplay is that it is not truly a Hollywood story. He is guilty therefore of the bogus qualities with which he would charge Hollywood, since Chayefsky has attempted to use the glamor and **glory of Hollywood to give importance to an essentially ordinary and familiar story.**

If it were not for Cromwell and Miss Stanley, this would make his picture more hackneyed than it otherwise seems. It would have been a better story if Chayefsky had stuck to the Bronx instead of trying a transplant to Hollywood and Vine. *Powe.*

Uncle Vanya

Off-the-stage filming of Chekhov classic. Well done, but strictly an art circuit entry.

Presentation of "The Uncle Vanya" Co. Stars Franchot Tone, George Voskovec, Clarence Derwent, Peggy McCay; features Gerald Hiken, Mary Perry, Shirley Gale; introes Dolores Dorn-Heft. Produced by Marion Parsonnet and Tone. Directed by John Goetz, Tone; from translation of Anton Chekhov play by Stark Young; music, Werner Jannssen; art direction, Kim E. Swados. Previewed in N.Y., April 16, '58. Running time, **98 MINS.**

Marina .... Mary Perry
Astroff .... Franchot Tone
Voinitsky .... George Voskovec
Serebriakoff .... Clarence Derwent
Sonia .... Peggy McCay
Elena Andreevna.......Dolores Dorn-Heft
Telegin .... Gerald Hiken
Voinitskaya .... Shirley Gale

Franchot Tone, who had a good deal to do with the success of Chekhov's "Uncle Vanya" when it was presented at David Ross' Fourth Street Playhouse in late 1956, again is very much in evidence in this filmed version of the play. He's the star, co-producer and co-director. And, for once, the one - man - band proposition comes off, the picture being a most faithful reproduction of this witty, often cynical piece.

There is never any pretension that "Uncle Vanya" is anything but a play on film. The only concession to the camera medium comes in the profusion of closeups. Some of the performers, notably Tone, Peggy McCay and Mary Perry, take to them like ducks to water. Others seem almost handicapped by this minute attention. Dolores Dorn-Heft, for instance, though a pleasure to look at, has too immobile a face to benefit from the closeup treatment.

The picture captures the essence of the bitter-sweet Chekhov opus. It is expertly acted and very competently directed by John Goetz and Tone. Being a play in which words must carry the burden of character development, the film suffers from an overdose of dialog. Were this done for the broad audience—which assuredly it was not—"Uncle Vanya" would serve as a standout example of how the needs of the screen differ from that of the theatre, though both have many elements in common.

Yet, the technique adopted by this production has its advantages, and it does avoid the static quality of one or two similar attempts in the past. The play and its characters come alive, the movement is well worked out and the Chekhov characters interact smoothly and believavy.

This is in essence the same cast that acted in the play originally. Tone is excellent as Astroff, the sensitive country doctor who has withdrawn into his work and falls in love with the beauty of a woman he cannot have. There is authority in the way he delivers his lines and the whole portrayal has depth and understanding. It's probably the best work Tone has ever done.

Matching him is Peggy McCay as Sonia, the girl who loves him and who, finally, accepts her fate as an old maid. It's a fine, sensitive performance and Miss McCay emerges as an actress of stature. George Voskovec plays the frustrated, love-smitten Uncle Vanya, a pathetic man, fumbling in a world that has passed him by. Clarence Derwent is standout as the pompous professor, married to a young wife.

Latter role is played by Dolores Dorn-Heft. Part is that of a languid, beautiful woman, bored with herself and with life. Miss Dorn-Heft is attractive, but she doesn't come across very convincingly. In the smaller parts, Mary Perry, Gerald Hiken and Shirley Gale all are very good. It's obvious from the film that this is a cast that has worked together.

"Uncle Vanya" shapes as top material for the carriage trade. It's made to order for the eggheads and the arties should snap it up. At any rate, it's a pleasant switch from Brigitte Bardot. *Hift.*

Thunder Road

Robert Mitchum presenting himself, his son and his own script. Talky but some road action. Okay for program situations.

Hollywood, April 17.

United Artists release of DRM production (no producer credit). Stars Robert Mitchum; costars Gene Barry, Jacques Aubuchon; features Keely Smith, Trevor Bardette, Sandra Knight, Jim Mitchum. Directed by Arthur Ripley. Screenplay, James Atlee Phillips, Walter Wise; original story, Mitchum; camera, Alan Stensvold, David Ettinson; editor, Harry Marker; music, Jack Marshall. Previewed April 15, '58. Running time, **94 MINS.**

Lucas Doolin	Robert Mitchum
Troy Barrett	Gene Barry
Carl Kogan	Jacques Aubuchon
Francie Wymore	Keely Smith
Vernon Doolin	Trevor Bardette
Roxanna Ledbetter	Sandra Knight
Robin Doolin	Jim Mitchum
Mary Barrett	Betsy Holt
Sarah Doolin	Francis Koon
Singer-Guitarist	Randy Sparks
Jed Moultrie	Mitch Ryan
Stacey Gouge	Peter Breck
Lucky	Peter Hornsby
Niles Penland	Jerry Hardin
Preacher	Robert Porterfield

"Thunder Road" was turned out by Robert Mitchum's own indie company from his own original story. Burdened with an overage of dialog and an abundance of uneventful footage, film still has plenty of fast auto action and with the Mitchum name for marquee draw so may get out in the melodrama market.

Men who transport illicit whiskey to southern markets and their trackdown by tax agents of the U. S. Treasury Department set the backdrop. Mitchum plays one of these transporters, whose Kentucky mountain family has been moonshining for generations. Plot ramifications are provided by a powerful racketeer trying to muscle in on the markets held by Mitchum and neighboring hideaway distillers.

Film is mainly interesting because of a series of auto chases and spectacular accidents, since narrative is routine. Singer Keely Smith is in for romancing by Mitchum and warbles a couple of songs, including "Whippoorwill," lyrics by Don Raye, music by Mitchum, not headed for Hit Parade. Jim Mitchum, star's 16-year-old son, makes his film bow here, acquitting himself reasonably well as Mitchum's young brother and bearing striking resemblance to his father. Pic carries no producer credit and Arthur Ripley's direction leans to the leisurely.

Mitchum's performance is rather colorless, due to lack of strong situations to give him opportunity for much more than walk-on. Gene Barry and Jacques Aubuchon as Federal agent and racketeer, respectively, handle themselves in okay fashion, and Sandra Knight is a fresh newcomer, playing part of a girl in love with Mitchum. Trevor Bardette is capable, too, as Mitchum's father.

Technical credits are well executed, Jack Marshall's music score contributing an effective note, Harry Marker doing a good job with his editing and fast photography provided by Alan Stensvold and David Ettinson. *Whit.*

The Cool and the Crazy

Standard teener exploitationer. Narcotics among the highschool trade. Good b.o. for its kind.

Hollywood, April 18.

American International release of an E. C. Rhoden Jr. production. Stars Scott Marlowe, Gigi Perreau, Dick Bakalyan, Dick Jones; features Shelby Storck; Marvin J. Rosen, Caroline von Mayrhauser, Robert Hadden, Kenneth Plumb. Directed by William Witney. Screenplay, Richard C. Sarafian; camera, Harry Birch; music, Raoul Kraushaar; editor, Helene Turner. Previewed in Hollywood, April 18, '58. Running time, **78 MINS.**

Bennie Saul	Scott Marlowe
Amy	Gigi Perreau
Jackie Barzan	Dick Bakalyan
Stu. Summerville	Dick Jones
Lt. Sloan	Shelby Storck
Eddie	Marvin J. Rosen
Mrs. Ryan	Caroline von Mayrhauser
Cookie	Robert Hadden
Marty	Kenneth Plumb
Mr. Saul	Anthony Pawley
Sgt. Myers	James Newman
Police Sgt.	Joe Adelman
Amy's mother	Jackie Storck
Amy's father	Leonard Belove
Blue Note Proprietor	Jim Bysol
Drunk	John Hannahan

American International's "The Cool and the Crazy" is a low-budget exploitation item but it has the irritating itch of reality about it. In some good scenes viewer gets feeling that these are real kids with terribly real problems, despite the fact that the story of teenage exposure to narcotics has been covered before. "Cool and Crazy" is part of a dual package (with "Dragstrip Riot") that lives up to its sensational advertising campaign.

Scott Marlowe plays the highschool student who drifts into pushing marijuana through his own use of the weed. He gets his classmates, Dick Bakalyan, Dick Jones, Robert Hadden and Kenneth Plumb, to try the stuff and almost gets them hooked, except for Bakalyan, who resists. Gigi Perreau is the nice young girl in school, whose good influence helps Bakalyan stay away from the marijuana and prevent his involvement in violence and killing that eventually entraps the rest.

Richard C. Sarafian's screenplay is often very adept at recreating the kind of language with which the young communicate—or fail to. A criticism is that some of the adults seem too dense and thoughtless in their handling of their juniors. But that's the way the kids see it, fair or not.

Scott Marlowe's performance, under William Witney's direction, is exceptional. His character is never made particularly sympathetic, except for a conventional swipe at background by showing a drunken father, but he generates genuine tenderness and sympathy. Miss Perreau, Bakalyan, Jones and the others in the cast perform capably under Witney's guidance.

Harry Birch's photography has a good documentary quality about it and Raoul Kraushaar's music simulates the unreality that the story's characters operate in.

The Elmer Rhoden Jr. production is the kind of seamy story, in which the seams are laid open and exposed so that every sweaty thread is seen, that almost approaches the Italian neo-realism. It is an exploitation picture but it also has some thought content.

Powe.

The Camp on Blood Island
(BRITISH-MEGASCOPE)

Japanese prisoner of war meller with contrived situations, too much obvious brutality add too little stellar value to be a big click.

London, April 15.

Hammer (Anthony Hinds) production and release. Stars Carl Mohner, Andre Morell, Edward Underdown, Walter Fitzgerald. Directed by Val Guest. Screenplay, Jon Manchip White, Val Guest; camera, Jack Asher; editor, Bill Lenny; music, Gerard Schurmann. At London Pavilion, London. Running time, **82 MINS.**

Piet Van Elst	Carl Mohner
Colonel Lambert	Andre Morell
Major Dawes	Edward Underdown
Cyril Beattie	Walter Fitzgerald
Lt. Bellamy	Phil Brown
Kate Keiller	Barbara Shelley
Father Anjou	Michael Goodliffe
Tom Shields	Michael Gwynn
Doctor Keiller	Richard Wordsworth
Sergeant Major	Edwin Ritchfield
Colonel Yamamitsu	Ronald Radd
Captain Sakamura	Marne Maitland
Interpreter	Wolfe Morris
Jap Driver	Michael Ripper
Mrs. Beattie	Mary Merrall
Mala	LilianeSottane
Thin Woman	Grace Denbigh Russell

"Camp on Blood Island" is Hammer Films' latest and most ambitious project in a program of horror films which, currently, have been hitting the boxoffice jackpot. As usual, this Hammer film has been tagged with an "X" certificate, which means that youngsters under 16 cannot see it in Britain.

The yarn, based on a real life incident, takes place in a Japanese prisoner of war camp, ruled over by a sadistic commandant who has sworn to massacre all the British prisoners should Japan lose the war. The British officers learn on a secret radio that the war has ended but, somewhat implausibly, they manage to keep the secret from the Nips until the end of the film when they stage a highly successful revolt.

There are as many holes in the film as there are in a fishing net. Yet it holds the attention mainly because of the frightful realization that such things did actually happen in the war. It is a film which will jerk out of complacency any person who now tend to regard the Japanese as not being as bad as thought during the war.

The dialog and situations have been devised on the very simple premise that all Japs are rats. This lack of subtlety, both in writing and direction by Val Guest, mars the film and makes the prison scenes far less effective than those in "Bridge on River Kwai." Over dark and sometimes fuzzy lensing by Jack Asher does not help to lift the film out of a sombre rut.

Nevertheless, there are a number of very satisfying performances by Andre Morell, Carl Mohner, Michael Goodliffe, Michael Gwynn, Walter Fitzgerald, Marne Maitland, Wolfe Morris Edward Underwood and others as assorted British soldiers and Japs. The femme side has little opportunity to shine but Barbara Shelley, Mary Merrall and Jacqueline Curtiss grasp their limited opportunities with skill. The production side have done a convincing job in its sets and location work. Hence, it's a pity that the whole affair has the effect of being a rushed job.

Rich.

Kathy O

Good comedy with no top names to help b.o.

Hollywood, April 18.

Universal release of a Sy Gomberg production. Stars Dan Duryea, Jan Sterling, Patty McCormack, Mary Fickett; with Sam Levene, Mary Jane Croft; also Rickey Kelman, Terry Kelman, Ainslie Pryor, Barney Phillips, Mel Leonard, Casey Walters, Walter Woolf King, Alexander Campbell, Joseph Sargent, Mary Carver. Directed by Jack Sher. Screenplay by Jack Sher and Sy Gomberg; from a magazine story by Jack Sher; camera, Arthur E. Arling; music, Frank Skinner; film editor, George Gittens. Previewed April 18, '58. Running time, **99 MINS.**

Harry Johnson .... Dan Duryea
Celeste Saunders .... Jan Sterling
Kathy O'Rourke ...... Patty McCormack
Helen Johnson .... Mary Fickett
Ben Melnick .... Sam Levene
Harriet Burton .... Mary Jane Croft
Robert "Bo" Johnson .....Rickey Kelman
Lieut. Chavez .... Ainslie Pryor
Matt Williams .... Barney Phillips
Sid .... Mel Leonard
Billy Blair .... Casey Walters
Donald C. Faber .... Walter Woolf King
Bixby .... Alexander Campbell
Mike .... Joseph Sargent
Marge .... Mary Carver

For Patty McCormack, who plays "Kathy O'," this Universal comedy shows that a bad environment as well as a bad seed can concoct a brat. Evidencing the same staunch talent, Miss McCormack is not quite as mean as she was in "The Bad Seed," and this story about Hollywood turns out to be a satisfying comedy somewhat reminiscent of the farcical features of two decades ago. Because there's little top star value, however, it will take a hefty exploitation campaign before the return is commensurate with the offering. Pic's title tune, already cut for Dot Records by Miss McCormack, could possibly lend a helping hand.

Producer Sy Gomberg and director Jack Sher, both scripting from a SatEvePost story by Sher, have filmed "Kathy O'" with comedy, warmth and suspense. The comedy, especially an uproarious scene aboard a Pacific fishing boat, is delightful; the warmth may bring out a handkerchief or two; and the suspense—well, there's one scene that without question should raise as hearty a scream as Dracula could. With the tale set within the film industry, Universal has taken good advantage of Universal, using the Studio City lot for locations and adorning set walls with photographs of UI actors.

It's evident that no one connected with this picture had much faith in the Dodgers moving to Los Angeles, for a black hat marked "Angels" plays a major role in the film. It's a small point, really, but it is too bad something couldn't be done about all those references to a now non existent team.

Miss McCormack plays a little devil, uncooperative and spoiled beyond reason. As a child star "who's loved by millions and yet loved by no one," she is an orphan whose guardian aunt treats her more an as investment than a human being. Dan Duryea is a publicity man at the moppet's studio and is handed the unwanted task of keeping her in hand while she's being interviewed by Jan Sterling, a noted magazine writer who, incidentally, is Duryea's former wife.

There are two stories here—a tender relationship which develops between the young actress and the magazine writer plus a conflict between Duryea and his present wife created by the attention he pays to his former wife. The first is full and rich, the second innocent.

When the girl's aunt goes back on her word, the actress runs away to be with Miss Sterling, is intercepted by Duryea and taken to his home, and the whole affair turns into a reported kidnaping. Fear of reprisal keeps Duryea from turning the tot in, and she's not anxious to leave Duryea's two young sons anyway. Everything eventually turns out well, with the girl losing her blonde pigtails and her surly attitude.

Miss McCormack shows remarkable feeling for the many character changes she assumes in this film. Duryea and Miss Sterling do very

well and Mary Fickett is tops in a tender, sympathetic portrayal of Duryea's wife. Sam Levene adds a good deal of comedy, with Mary Jane Croft and Ainslie Pryor sobering things up in good fashion. Rickey and Terry Kelman are joyously naive as the publicist's sons.

Arthur E. Arling's color photography is alluring, with Frank Skinner's score used nicely to set mood. The title song, ably written by Charles Tobias, Ray Joseph and Jack Sher, is sung on film by The Diamonds. Other credits — sound by Leslie I. Carey and Joe Lapis, art direction by Alexander Golitzen and Bill Newberry and editing by George Gittens—are handled with taste.   *Ron.*

Ten North Frederick
(CINEMASCOPE)

John O'Hara's novel. Gary Cooper having a bitter-sweet romance. Mostly well done tale of the disintegration of a gentleman who could protect neither himself nor those he loved.

20th Century-Fox release of a Charles Brackett production. Stars Gary Cooper, Diane Varsi, Suzy Parker. Co-stars Geraldine Fitzgerald, Tom Tully. Features Ray Stricklyn, Philip Ober, John Emery, Stuart Whitman, Linda Watkins, Barbara Nichols. Directed and screenplayed by Philip Dunne after John O'Hara's novel. Camera, Joe MacDonald; music, Leigh Harline, conducted by Lionel Newman; editor, David Bretherton. Previewed in N. Y. Projection Room, April 23, '58. Running time, **102 MINS.**

Joe Chapin .... Gary Cooper
Ann Chapin .... Diane Varsi
Edith Chapin ...... Geraldine Fitzgerald
Joby Chapin .... Ray Stricklyn
Slattery .... Tom Tully
Kate Drummond .... Suzy Parker
Charley Bongiorno ...... Stuart Whitman
Lloyd Williams .... Philip Ober
Arthur McHenry .... Jess Kirkpatrick
Dr. English .... Joe McGuinn
Paul Donaldson .... John Emery
Peg Slattery .... Linda Watkins

Accenting the positive first, "Ten North Frederick" is a fairly interesting study of a man who is the victim of his own virtues. The average filmgoer ought to find this tale-with-a-thesis absorbing diversion. After that it may be stated that because of the psychological intricacies involved the screen telling sacrifices detail and explanation at some loss to audience satisfaction.

The politics section has been so foreshortened and telescoped as to be puzzling. The question of whether the protagonist actually entertains the dream of the presidency or jollies his wife on the point is never clear. And it is crucial to conviction. Joe Chapin (Gary Cooper) is a regional lawyer, rich but not apparently otherwise distinguished. Most of all he is a gentleman and from this fact flows his troubles. The fantastic unreality of a White House ambition goes unexplained save in terms of an aggrandizing wife and leaves the whole beginning of the film oddly conflicted, since the modesty characterization is fighting the vanity of the ambition, which doesn't fit as screenplayed.

Though well acted Tom Tully's party politician is a main contribution to audience wondering about motives which are not stated nor shown if occasionally hinted. Does he personally pocket the $100,000 given him to promote the hero's wish to be, like his grandfather, lieutenant-governor of the state, or does he share the money with his cronies, or divert it to party uses?

Curiosity is aroused but not satisfied on this and other important plot points. Tully seems motivated by a private malice against the "quality" and "family" of the fat cat. He may have a professional's detestation of a well-bred amateur. Only one oblique line of dialog in reference to himself as an Irish politician gives the clue. Hence the audience is not prepared adequately, does not quite get the full implication of the subsequent double-cross.

The vaguest part of the screen version is the home town attitude toward the hero although at his 50th birthday party he is twitted by a philanderer with being a dull and slow fellow. Nonetheless the story gets on and after his series of disillusionments, including his beloved daughter's forced marriage, subsequent miscarriage, annullment and leaving home, the lawyer moves to his bitter-sweet romance in New York with a

younger woman. Gradually the central figure becomes more fully dimensioned and the thesis comes across that he has suffered because he cannot take advantage of people but is himself much put upon.

Told in flashback, the story opens at the 1945 funeral of the lawyer and shows the hypocrites gathered afterwards in his home. The greatest hypocrite of all is the widow, played with iceberg selfishness by Geraldine Fitzgerald. It could open a new gamut of formidable screen females for her. At the payoff the G.I. son tells off the company, in his cups, and breaks completely with his mother. Ray Stricklyn makes this boy stand up and out.

The Charles Brackett production obviously serves a variety of purposes. First the John O'Hara book is a pre-sold value by a name author. Then the main character is sympathetic to and tailored for an aging star and a sad September romance is integral to his situation just as his being too considerate makes him send the girl away, though she wishes to stay on any terms. Finally "Ten North Frederick" suitably showcases two 20th CenturyFox actresses being upbuilt, Diane Varsi and Suzy Parker.

Few will be inclined to vote Suzy Parker a great actress, or a prospect to be, but after the wooden maiden display she gave opposite Cary Grant in "Kiss Them for Me" it is possible to report that in her present work is the difference between a breathing human body with eyes that move and a store window mannikin. Knowledgeable coaches have been busy unlearning her everything taught at Harper's Bazaar. She is actually quite likeable here.

Fans will probably be further enthused about Miss Varsi who had her big major credit recently via "Peyton Place." Here she is the daughter of an old nativist snob family who falls in love with an upstart jazz trumpeter, born a Catholic and considered a bum by the cruel men, the gentlemanly father standing by, who break up her marriage and break her heart in the process. Stuart Whitman makes the jazzbo come real in limited footage.

Leigh Harline's score, kept properly neutral by Lionel Newman, fits mood and never intrudes and the same compliment may be paid Joe MacDonald's camera work. It is hard to visualize just what kind of a town it is that has a house like Ten North Frederick but it is not to be supposed that many will notice that detail of art direction (Lyle R. Wheeler and Addison Hehr) nor wonder where the two career girls living in New York found that sumptuous flat in which they reside.

With the mental reservations on story detailing previously mentioned, "Ten North Frederick" has many points of interest and appeal. It is possibly the best job of acting Gary Cooper has done in a very long time and as an armpiece Miss Parker is far more plausible for him than Audrey Hepburn.

By the time the story is played out the thesis makes sense—Joe Chapin has indeed been hopelessly handicapped in life by being a gentleman. He could never take advantage but others could exploit him. Out of defects, born of his gentleness and basic decency, he comes to disintegration. It is convincing in the end and in Cooper's performance, and it is also sad. This perhaps is proof that Dunne has flown free of the obscurities in the emasculated political segment of the story. *Land.*

Gang War

Story has interest; production about average; should do nicely in filling out the bill.

Hollywood, April 25.

Twentieth-Fox release of a Regal Films production. Stars Charles Bronson, Kent Taylor, Jennifer Holden, John Doucette; with Gloria Henry, Gloria Grey, Barney Phillips, Ralph Manza, George Eldredge, Billy Snyder, Lyn Guild, Dan Simmons, Jack Reynolds, Jack Littlefield, Larry Gelbmann, Shirle Haven, Ed Wright. Produced by Harold E. Knox. Directed by Gene Fowler Jr. Screenplay by Louis Vittes; from the novel, "The Hoods Take Over," by Ovid Demaris; camera, John M. Nickolaus Jr.; film editor, Frank Baldridge; music, Paul Dunlap. Previewed April 25, '58. Running time, **75 MINS.**

Alan Avery	Charles Bronson
Bryce Barker	Kent Taylor
Marie	Jennifer Holden
Maxie Matthews	John Doucette
Edie Avery	Gloria Henry
Marsha Brown	Gloria Grey
Sam Johnson	Barney Phillips
Axe Duncan	Ralph Manza
Sgt. Ernie Tucker	George Eldredge
Mr. Tomkins	Billy Snyder
Joe Reno	Jack Reynolds
Bob Cross	Dan Simmons
Little Abner	Larry Gelbmann
Johnny	Jack Littlefield
Henchman No. 1	Ed Wright
Nicki	Shirle Haven

The stock characters that might take part in a gang war—the "big boss," the dumb dame, the punch-drunk fighter, the "bought" cop, and the gangland attorney—take parts in "Gang War," a Regal production that holds up as a bang-bang opus with more than enough excitement for a second-feature life.

There's another character, too, and though he's been seen before, he still perks up interest. He's a high school mathematics teacher who has the misfortune of being eye witness to a gangland murder. At first, he wants nothing to do with the affair, then is shamed into testifying. In the fracas, he's assaulted, his wife is killed, the "big boss' shrinks, the dumb dame is murdered, the punchdrunk fighter is mauled, the "bought" cop is fired, and the gangland attorney goes straight and is eradicated.

Charles Bronson, in underplaying his role of the teacher, keeps a sympathetic interest centered on himself. As the boss, John Doucette turns in an excellent performance. Kent Taylor, as the attorney, is fine, and Jennifer Holden as the dumb dame is sexy to behold. As the teacher's wife, Gloria Henry does well in a part that is too small to allow much excitement.

Gene Fowler Jr., directed, and his work seems quite capable. The Harold E. Knox production shows infrequent signs of low budget but manages to appear attractive for the most part. Screenwriter Louis Vittes, despite the stereotyped characters, penned the [illegible]pt with a proper tone. *Ron.*

This Angry Age
(TECHNIRAMA-TECHNICOLOR)

Somewhat blurry story against interesting backgrounds, and photographed with stress on scenic values. Cast names—Silvano Mangano, Anthony Perkins, Richard Conte and Jo Van Fleet—ought to help, but still only a so-so bet.

Columbia release of Dino De Laurentiis production. Stars Silvano Mangano, Anthony Perkins, Richard Conte and Jo Van Fleet; features Nehemiah Persoff, Yvonne Sanson, Chu Shao Chuan, Guido Celano, Alida Valli. Directed by Rene Clement. Screenplay, Irwin Shaw and Clement; from novel, "Sea Wall," by Marguerite Duras: camera (Technicolor) Otello Martelli; music, Nino Rota; songs, "Uh-Huh," by Leroy Kirkland and Billy Dawn, "Ya Ya Ya," by Alvy West, "One Kiss from Heaven" by A. Romeo and Sam Coslow and "Only You" by Ram-Rand. Tradeshown in N.Y. April 23 '58. Runing time **111 MINS.**

(Following cast list is incomplete, producer Dino De Laurentiis not having made the full roster available, according to Columbia in New York).

Joseph	Anthony Perkins
Suzanne	Silvano Mangano
Michael	Richard Conte
Madame Dufresne	Jo Ann Fleet
Albert Legros	Nehemiah Persoff

Yank and non-Yank interests, mainly Columbia and italian producer Dino De Laurentiis, have joined in an enterprise obviously packaged with a view to the world market. The product is an adaptation of the Marguerite Duras novel, "The Sea Wall," is set on the coast of French Indo-China, and actually was lensed in Thailand.

It's apparent that De Laurentiis went for a good-sized budget in laying the backgrounds for "This Angry Age," which, incidentally, is a title less apt than Miss Duras' original. Indeed, it's likely to be construed as having kinship with the relatively new literati mood from Britain, whereas the picture is timed at pre-war.

The reviewer (and the viewer) can only guess at what went on in the transposition of the book to the screen but it appears likely that De Laurentiis and Rene Clement, latter having called the directorial shots, placed so much stress on "character development" that the plot was largely overlooked. Film abounds in somber atmosphere and sensual situations but the story at times is out of focus.

It's a yarn about a widow, Jo Van Fleet, who has built up wastelands in the Oriental area to a productive rice field and seeks to protect this from the menacing sea with a dike made of palm logs.

Her aides are her children, daughter Silvano Magnano and son Anthony Perkins. Left uncertain is why Miss Van Fleet and her family are on this unlikely location in the first place and how Perkins, who looks strictly from Midland, U. S. A., and Miss Mangano, obviously of Latino extraction, would be paired as brother and sister.

And the behavior of these two is so suggestive of incestuous desire that "Angry Age" ought to score well in what Sindlinger calls "talk about" but as displayed herein such a situation seems reached out for, and doesn't have a rightful place in the story. A crawl dance they do, for example, has them performing like a couple on romantic hop.

Dramatic pivot is a break in the dam that comes just as Richard Conte enters. He's a government agent out to force Miss Van Fleet, her family and the natives supported by the rice field from the treacherous area, an objective which he abandons upon "discovering" Miss Mangano. A cement dike would solve everything, he decides.

Second romance is introduced as Perkins, running away from his family, encounters Alida Valli in a town film theatre. They hit the bistros along with her male companion, who's constantly on a binge.

Still another aside has Nehemiah Persoff, who while seeking to buy out Miss Van Fleet's property at the behest of his father, makes some clumsy propositions to Miss Mangano, including one request that he might see her taking a shower.

The cast, which also includes Yvonne Sanson, Chu Shao Chuan and Guido Celano, is in good cinematic company with the photographic work (filming is in Technirama and Technicolor), particularly the expert handling of the scenic detail and the exciting flood scene. But the script by Irwin Shaw and Clement seems to have been mismanaged so far as getting story on screen is concerned. Thus, performances can only be rated as fair.

"Angry Age" has its values; clear-cut plot organization might have given it distinction.

Music is good and of the four songs, "One Kiss Away from Heaven," as sung by Perkins, sounds as though having a fair-enough chance on its own. Editing should be sharper, the 111 minutes of footage being excessive. Other technical credits competent. *Gene.*

The Light In the Forest
(COLOR)

Pre-Revolutionary tale of boy raised by the Indians. Good b.o. prospects for family and general situations.

Buena Vista release of a Walt Disney production. Starring Fess Parker, Wendell Corey, Joanne Dru, James MacArthur; co-starring Jessica Tandy, John McIntire, Joseph Calleia, Rafael Campos, and introducing Carol Lynley. Directed by Herschel Daugherty. Screenplay, Lawrence Edward Watkin; from the novel by Conrad Richter; camera, Ellsworth Fredericks; music, Paul Smith; editor, Stanley Johnson. Previewed in Hollywood, April 25, '58. Running time, **93 MINS.**

Del Hardy	Fess Parker
Wilse Owens	Wendell Corey
Milly Elder	Joanne Dru
Johnny Butler	James MacArthur
Myra Butler	Jessica Tandy
John Elder	John McIntire
Cuyloga	Joseph Calleia
Shenandoe Hastings	Carol Lynley
Half Arrow	Rafael Campos
Harry Butler	Frank Ferguson
Niskatoon	Norman Fredric
Kate Owens	Marian Seldes
Col. Henry Bouquet	Stephen Bekassy
George Owens	Sam Buffington

Not for the black leather jacket trade, Walt Disney's "The Light in the Forest" is a good picture for almost anyone else, with the same wholesome adventure quanties that distinguished "Old Yeller." Like most Disney productions, it is pastoral in quality, almost fable-like in its gentle approach to some basically bitter situations, but it is well-paced, has capable acting and a brace of marquee names, plus wide screen and Technicolor.

Lawrence Edward Watkin's screenplay is based on Conrad Richter's novel, set in the pre-Revolutionary days. Apart from its conscious avoidance of violence, it has a salutary lesson in tolerance. The theme is not preached, but its meaning is inescapable, and it gives depth to a story that would otherwise seem too placid.

Disney's production, directed by Herschel Daugherty, is notable on several counts, one being that it is about the Delaware Indians, an Eastern tribe, different from the usual Indians encountered these days. Since they were a more colorful and picturesque tribe than some of the Plains Indians, it makes for good background and plot development.

James MacArthur is the white boy who has been kidnapped by the Delawares and raised as the son of chief Joseph Calleia. As part of a treaty between the Indians and the British Colonial Forces, all such hostages are to be returned, and MacArthur is reluctant and recalcitrant in making the change. He is received with understanding by Fess Parker, as the chief intermediary between Indians and white, but his new life is made harder by Indian-hater Wendell Corey. He runs away and attempts to become again the Indian he always wished to be, but he eventually comes back to live among his own people, having learned there are bad Indians as well as good, and love among the white people as well as hate.

Although Fess Parker, Wendell Corey and Joanne Dru are the leading adult players in "The Light In The Forest," and they occupy a large portion of the footage, the story is essentially one for young people. Parker is capable as the man understanding of both Indian and white life, and Corey is strong as the villain of the piece. Miss Dru is attractive as Parker's romantic opposite. The most attractive portions of the picture, though, are those in which MacArthur makes his difficult way, and particularly in the love scenes between MacArthur and Carol Lynley, a real find. Daugherty's direction is especially perceptive in handling the young lovers, awkward and touching. The supporting cast is strong with Jessica Tandy, John McIntire, Rafael Campos and Calleia. Marian Seldes and Norman Fredric also contribute notable performances.

Ellsworth Frederick's photography captures the feeling of the Arcadian land and its people, meshing the Ohio River locations and the authentic back lot scenes. Carroll Clark's art direction, with set decorations by Emile Kent and Fred McLean, is richly authentic whether in Indian teepee or settler's cabin. Music by Paul Smith, with evocative orchestration by Franklyn Marks, is first-rate as are the songs by Gil George, Lawrence Edward Watkin and Paul Smith. Editing by Stanley Johnson and sound by Robert O. Cook and Dean Thomas, are both excellent.

The Left Handed Gun

Overlong but super-charged study of Billy the Kid with special teenage appeal. Fred Coe's maiden production. Good b.o. prospects.

Hollywood, April 18.

Warner Bros. release of Fred Coe production. Stars Paul Newman; co-stars Lita Milan, John Dehner, Hurd Hatfield; features James Congdon, James Best, Colin Keith-Johnston, John Dierkes, Bob Anderson. Directed by Arthur Penn. Screenplay, Leslie Stevens; based on a teleplay, "The Death of Billy the Kid," by Gore Vidal; camera, J. Peverell Marley; music, Alexander Courage; editor, Folmar Blangsted. Previewed at the studio, March 27, '58. Running time, **105 MINS.**

Billy Bonney	Paul Newman
Celsa	Lita Milan
Moultrie	Hurd Hatfield
Charlie Boudre	James Congdon
Tom Folliard	James Best
Turnstall	Colin Keith-Johnston
McSween	John Dierkes
Hill	Bob Anderson
Moon	Wally Brown
Joe Grant	Ainslie Pryor
Saval	Martin Garralaga
Ollinger	Denver Pyle
Bell	Paul Smith
Maxwell	Hestor Paiva
Mrs. Garrett	Jo Summers
Brady	Robert Foulk
Mrs. Hill	Anne Barton

"The Left Handed Gun" is another look at Billy the Kid, probably America's most constantly celebrated juvenile delinquent. In this version from Warners he's Billy, the crazy, mixed-up Kid. It is a motion picture bow for television producer Fred Coe and director Arthur Penn, and their picture is a smart and exciting western paced by Paul Newman's intense portrayal of the Kid. There is plenty of action for western buffs and the added value of a psychological story for general appeal.

Leslie Stevens' screenplay is based on a teleplay by Gore Vidal that was called "The Death of Billy the Kid." The action is concerned with the few events that led up to the slaying of the Brooklyn boy by lawman Pat Garrett. Stevens emphasizes the youthful nature of the desperado by giving him two equally young companions, James Best and James Congdon. The three team after Newman's mentor, cattleman Colin Keith-Johnston, is shot by a crooked officer of the law. Newman is determined to avenge the cattleman's death, and the plot becomes a crazed crusade in which Newman, Best and Congdon are all killed, the death of a badman and the birth of a legend.

Stevens' screenplay makes use of Billy's affinity for Mexican girls for what love interest there is, but not much is needed, just enough to leaven his character. The best parts of the film are the moments of hysterical excitement as the three young desperados rough-house with each other as feckless as any innocent boys and in the next instant turn to deadly killing without flicking a curly eyelash.

Although this is Penn's first picture, he shows himself in command of the medium, using motion picture technique and advantages, such as in a wild house-burning, that are not available elsewhere, to their fullest value.

Newman dominates the picture but there are excellent performances from others, including Lita Milan in a dimly-seen role as his Mexican girl friend, John Dehner as the remorseless Pat Garrett, and Hurd Hatfield, a mysterious commentator on events. James Congdon and James Best stand out as Newman's deadly playmates, and others who etch smaller but important portraits include Keith-Johnston, John Dierkes, Bob Anderson, Wally Brown, Ainslie Pryor and Martin Garralaga.

J. Peverell Marley's photography is top-notch, aided by Folmar Blangsted's editing, in keeping the pace and tempo of the picture swift and varied. Alexander Courage's music is helpful as is the sound by Earl Crain Sr. *Powe.*

Fort Massacre
(COLOR; C'SCOPE)

Realistic Apache vs. Cavalry scalper. Joel McCrea toplines for good b.o. return.

Hollywood, April 25.

United Artists release of a Walter M. Mirisch production. Stars Joel McCrea; costars Forrest Tucker, Susan Cabot, John Russell, George N. Neise. Directed by Joheph Newman. Screenplay, Martin N. Goldsmith; camera, Carl Guthrie; music, Marlin Skiles; editor, Richard Heermance. Previewed in Hollywood, April 23, '58. Running time, 80 MINS.

Vinson	Joel McCrea
McGurney	Forrest Tucker
Piute Girl	Susan Cabot
Travis	John Russell
Pawnee	Anthony Caruso
Schwabacker	Bob Osterloh
Collins	Denver Pyle
Pendleton	George W. Neise
Moss	Rayford Barnes
Tucker	Guy Prescott
Moving Cloud	Larry Chance
Charlie	Irving Bacon
Adele	Claire Carleton
Piute Man	Francis J. McDonald
Chief	Walter Kray

"Fort Massacre," first production by the Mirisch Co. for United Artists, is an off-beat western that follows its unusual and honest story to a relentless conclusion. It will attract attention, and it has some spectacular visual values in CinemaScope and DeLuxe Color.

The Walter M. Mirisch production, directed by Joseph Newman, does not come off completely, however. It is one of those psychological stories in which the spectator is left with some unanswered questions when all details should have been tidied up. Apart from these reservations, it's safe to predict that "Fort Massacre" will do well as a superior program picture.

Joel McCrea is the sergeant of the U. S. Cavalry unit who takes over command when his superior officer is wounded and dies. McCrea leads the remnants of his men, against their better judgment and desire, through restricted Apache territory. He says his reason is to provide a shortcut to the nearest U. S. Army post. His real reason, as his men suspect and as proves to be the case, is that he is half-crazed with revenge because his wife and two children were killed by Indians. He is out to provoke an attack so he can kill as many Indians as possible, even if it means endangering the lives of his fellow cavalrymen. A few escape as McCrea is finally shot dead by one of his own men.

Martin N. Goldsmith's screenplay is excellent in its use of appropriate imagery in the dialog and in the creation of character, even escaping most of the cliches of such comrades-in-arms situations. His plotting is less successful. The underlying theme—McCrea's revenge—is not disclosed early enough and when it comes it is revealed more through dialog than action. Suspense and horror are lost in concealing or obscuring the motivation and it is never sufficiently clear to gain full value.

As a result, McCrea is not completely convincing as the ruthless Indian-killer, although he gives a characteristically strong performance. Forrest Tucker is interesting in a character role, and John Russell, Anthony Caruso, Bob Osterloh, Claire Carleton, Larry Chance, Walter Kray and Irving Bacon give good support. Susan Cabot, as an Indian girl, is a beaut but no Piute.

Newman's direction is skillful in limning the various characters and at taking advantage of the stunning backgrounds, excitingly photographed by Carl Guthrie. Technical credits are good, including the editing by Richard Heermance and sound by B. F. Remington. Marlin Skiles' music is also an asset. *Powe.*

The Matchmaker
(V'VISION)

Topnotch picturization of the Broadway hit.

Hollywood, May 2.

Paramount release of Don Hartman production. Stars Shirley Booth, Anthony Perkins, Shirley MacLaine, Paul Ford; features Robert Morse, Perry Wilson, Wallace Ford. Directed by Joseph Anthony. Screen, John Michael Hayes, from play by Thornton Wilder; camera, Charles Lang; editor, Howard Smith; music, Adolph Deutsch. Previewed May 1, '58. Running time, **100 MINS.**

Dolly Levi	Shirley Booth
Cornelius	Anthony Perkins
Irene Molloy	Shirley MacLaine
Horace Vandergelder	Paul Ford
Barnaby Tucker	Robert Morse
Minnie Fay	Perry Wilson
Malachi Stack	Wallace Ford
Joe Scanlon	Russell Collins
August	Rex Evans
Rudolph	Gavin Gordon
Maitre D'	Torben Meyer

The late Don Hartman's second indie comes off one of the most engaging comedies of the season, the very antithesis to the grim and moody overtones struck by his first, "Desire Under the Elms." "The Matchmaker" is sophisticated and it is gay, nostalgic and down-to-earth, enlivened by some of the liveliest performances seen on the screen in years. Adult audiences will love it, and for the juves there's Anthony Perkins. Result is a bright outlook at the boxoffice.

Based on the Thornton Wilder Broadway hit, Shirley Booth takes over the Ruth Gordon stage role of "marriage counsellor," dominating character in this yarn of 1884. Its period unfoldment permits added opportunity for laughs, some of the belly genre. The John Michael Hayes screenplay catches every nuance of the situation of the widowed Miss Booth ostensibly seeking a wife for the grasping Yonkers merchant, Paul Ford, while adroitly plotting to capture him for her own. Use of "asides" by various principals, speaking directly into the camera, lends a charming old-fashioned aspect which peppers the action. All these ingredients are handled with distinction by Joseph Anthony in his clever direction, and each cast member is a standout.

Most of the story unreels in New York, where Ford goes from nearby Yonkers to propose to Shirley MacLaine, a man-hungry milliner, and to meet a sexpot promised by Miss Booth, who against his will has taken over Ford's romantic interess. Following Ford are the two over-worked clerks in his general store, Perkins and Robert Morse, who pool their resources and determine to live it up in the big city, with ten bucks between them. The climax will be to kiss a girl in some "dangerous adventure" before they return to work. Complications arise as the two clerks try to elude their boss, Perkins falling for the prety hat shop lady and Miss Booth active in her machinations.

Miss Booth is no less than superb in her role, draining part of comedic possibilities. Perkins' switch to farce is also a bright experience. Ford is immense as the romantically-inclined but tight small-towner, and Miss MacLaine is pert and lovely. Robert Morse, from the original Broadway cast, amusingly enacts Perkins' pardner, Wallace Ford socks over his Paddy Irishman character, and Perry Wilson, Rex Evans, Gavin Gordon, Russell Collins and Torben Meyer are in for expert support.

Technical credits are highly placed, rating mention Charles Lang for photography; Hal Pereira and Roland Anderson, art direction; Howard Smith, editing; Adolph Deutsch, music; Edith Head, costumes. *Whit.*

No Time for Sergeants

Whacky comedy of service life, the peacetime Air Force this time. Enough hilarious situations to satisfy general audiences.

Warner Bros. release of Mervyn LeRoy production. Stars Andy Griffith, Myron McCormick and Nick Adams. Directed by LeRoy. Screenplay, John Lee Mahin, from the play by Ira Levin, based on the novel by Mac Hyman; camera, Harold Rosson; editor, William Ziegler; Music, Ray Heindorf. Previewed in N.Y., April 24, '58. Running time, **111 MINS.**

Will	Andy Griffith
Sgt. King	Myron McCormick
Ben	Nick Adams
Irvin	Murray Hamilton
General Bush	Howard Smith
Lieut. Bridges	Will Hutchins
General Pollard	Sydney Smith
Psychiatrist	James Milhollan
Manual Dexterity Corporal	Don Knotts
W.A.F. Captain	Jean Willes
Captain	Bartlett Robinson
Cover	Henry McCann
Draft Board Man	Dub Taylor
Pa	William Fawcett
Colonel	Raymond Bailey

This is the fourth time around for "No Time for Sergeants." Spawned as a novel by Mac Hyman and later converted to a teleplay and a Broadway play by Ira Levin, it is now being offered as a motion picture by Warner Bros. Although the material may be familiar to a segment of the public, the Mervyn LeRoy production, screenplayed by John Lee Mahin, still has a fresh appeal and should emerge as a solid boxoffice entry.

Andy Griffith, who originated the role of the naive hillbilly on tv and repeated the assignment on Broadway, is once again seen as the permanent latrine orderly whose love of humanity and unawareness of duplicity upsets the entire U.S. Air Force. The film follows the format of the play closely and depicts the experience of Will Stockdale, a Georgia backwoodsman suddenly thrust into the intricacies of Army life. Will is a naive, friendly and helpful sort of a guy unaccustomed to the rigid discipline of GI requirements. As Will meets and copes with these new situations results in frequently hilarious scenes. Griffith is perfect in the role.

"No Time for Sergeants," of course, is out and out farce, but anyone who has had some association with organizational routine will probably recognize the source of the exaggeration. Experiences in the service appear to be particularly prone to this treatment as evidenced by the spate of post-war novels and films presenting the humorous aspects and snafus connected with life in any branch of the Defense Dept.

"No Time for Sergeants" plays up these situations in spades. It's fortunate, however, that Americans can laugh at these experiences, for an Air Force operated as the one shown in the film would never be a match for the Russians.

As the barracks sergeant entrusted with the unenviable task of supervising Griffith, Myron McCormick, repeating his stage role, is excellent. He's a career enlisted man whose philosophy — that the peace-time Air Force can be a quiet life if nobody rocks the canoe —is completely destroyed by the arrival of Griffith. McCormick is a master of the slow burn and he has numerous opportunities to fret and fume as he attempts to get Griffith classified, a process that proves an unprecedented trial for the whole base.

Griffth's experience with the base psychiatrist, admirably portrayed by James Milhollan, is one of the highlights of the picture. Nick Adams, as Griffith's horn-rimmed sidekick who wants to transfer to the infantry, contributes a topnotch portrayal of a serious but completely inept soldier.

Good performances in tone with the farcial quality of the picture are given by Murray Hamilton, Howard Smith, Will Hutchins, Sydney Smith, Don Knotts and Bartlett Robbinson as assorted enlisted men and officers.

LeRoy, who also directed, has provided just the right pace for the screwy proceedings and, as producer, has seen to it that the production values are of top calibre. Harold Rosson's photography, Malcolm Brown's art direction, Robert R. Benton's sets, Louis Lichtenfield's special effects and Ray Heindorf's music contribute to the picture's appeal. *Holl.*

Edge of Fury

Clinical study of a psycho entirely lacking in entertainment or boxoffice potential.

Hollywood, May 1.

United Artists release of Robert Gurney Jr., production. Stars Michael Higgins, Lois Holmes; features Jean Allison, Doris Fesette. Directors, Gurney, Irving Lerner. Screenplay, Gurney, based on novel, "Wisteria Cottage," by Robert M. Coates; camera, Conrad Hall, Marvin Weinstein, Jack Couffer. Previewed April 29, '58. Running time, **77 MINS.**

Cast: Michael Higgins, Lois Holmes, Jean Allison, Doris Fesette, Malcom Beggs, Craig Kelly, John Harvey, Beatrice Furdau, Mary Elizabeth Boylan.

"Edge of Fury" is incredibly bad, a waste of talent and spectators' time. Even for the least demanding smaller market it will have hard sledding, and deserves it.

Story is about a psycho, a young man who becomes friendly with a mother and two daughters, and events leading up to a double murder in a lonely seaside cottage he has persuaded them to rent. The Robert Gurney Jr., production is more quasi-clinical than entertainment, the blame here resting on Gurney, who also scripted and co-directs with Irving Lerner.

Whatever talent cast might possess is lost in unreal characterization and overall poor handling. Michael Higgins portrays the psycho, and Lois Holmes the elder daughter who drives him to his maniacal fury. Jean Allison and Doris Fesette complete the family. Photography by Conrad Hall, Marvin Weinstein and Jack Couffer is okay. *Whit.*

I Married a Woman

George Gobel in old-fashioned comedy that doesn't come off; will need hard plugging in general market.

Universal release of William Bloom production. Stars George Gobel, Diana Dors; costars Adolphe Menjou; features Jessie Royce Landis, Nita Talbot, William Redfield, Steve Dunne. Director, Hal Kanter. Screenplay, Goodman Ace; camera, Lucien Ballard; editor, Kenneth Marstella; music, Cyril Mockridge. Previewed April 3, '58. Running time, **80 MINS.**

Marshal	George Gobel
Janice	Diana Dors
Sutton	Adolphe Menjou
Mother	Jessie Royce Landis
Miss Anderson	Nita Talbot
Eddie	William Redfield
Bob	Steve Dunne
Girard	John McGiver
Photographer	Steve Pendleton
Mrs. Wilkins	Cheerio Meredith
Camera Girl	Kay Buckley
Screen Wife	Angie Dickinson

Devotee of the George Gobel particular brand of humor may find mild diversion in this film made nearly two years ago, but essentially it's pretty tired stuff. One of the 11 pix RKO turned over to Universal for release, offering is an old-fashioned effort at screwball comedy which doesn't come off with much success. It should have been released while Gobel was still a top name and nearer the big glamour buildup RKO gave its femme star, British Diana Dors, now virtually forgotten.

The William Bloom production depends almost entirely for laughs on the Gobel rambling monolog in old hat situations. Wed to Miss Dors, an eyeful in many of her scenes both in evening gowns and black negligees, he plays the idea man in Adolphe Menjou's ad agency, faced with dreaming up a new campaign for a beer account about to ankle agency. Footage follows efforts to retain the account and win back his wife, who wants a divorce because she thinks he isn't as attentive as when he was courting her. There's the running business, too, of everybody knowing she's about to have a baby but Gobel, who'll never listen to her attempts at information.

The Goodman Ace screenplay keeps Gobel in his familiar character, but his type of comedy seems misspent on the theatrical screen. Hal Kanter's direction is leisurely.

Miss Dors handles herself expertly and displays an apt knowledge of comedy timing. Menjou's is loquacious as agency head who dumps his problem into Gobel's lap, Jessie Royce Landis is Gobel's mooching mother-in-law and Nita Talbot is Gobel's secretary, good for a few chortles. William Redfield as a law-studying elevator boy and Steve Dunne as a former suitor are okay as a couple of guys Miss Dors uses to make her husband jealous.

Technical credits are first-class, with art direction by Albert S. D'Agostino and Walter E. Keller outstanding. Lucien Ballard's camera work, editing by Kenneth Marstella and Howard Shoup's gowns for femme star also rate. *Whit.*

Thing That Couldn't Die

Well-made horror suspense film undermined by plot deficiency. No names, but good exploitation angles, for fair b.o.

Hollywood, May 2.

Universal release of Will Cowan production. Stars William Reynolds, Andra Martin, Jeffrey Stone, Carolyn Kearney; features Peggy Converse, Robin Hughes, James Anderson, Charles Horvath, Forrest Lewis. Directed by Will Cowan. Screenplay, David Duncan; camera, Russell Metty; music supervision, Joseph Gershenson; editor, Edward Curtiss. Previewed in Hollywood, April 30, '58. Running time, **69 MINS.**

Gordon Hawthorne	William Reynolds
Linda Madison	Andra Martin
Hank Huston	Jeffrey Stone
Jessica Burns	Carolyn Kearney
Flavia	Peggy Converse
Gideon Drew	Robin Hughes
Boyd Abercrombie	James Anderson
Mike	Charles Horvath
Ash	Forrest Lewis

"The Thing That Couldn't Die" is a well-made horror picture, capably acted and directed, but its grisly gimmick doesn't quite sustain the latter portions. Will Cowan produced and directed the David Duncan screenplay for Universal which will have to exploit it heavily for good returns. There are no names in the cast that mean anything at the box office.

Carolyn Kearney is a young woman with a gift for "dowsing," or water-tracing, by means of a willow wand and psychic reaction. Her instinct leads her to a buried chest which turns out to contain the head of an evil Britisher, beheaded and interred in the 16th Century by Sir Francis Drake and his men. The head is still active and wants to be reunited with its body. To this end it bewitches the various members of the cast until it is finally laid thoroughly to rest and reduced to a dusty—and harmless—skeleton.

Williams Reynolds supplies a pleasant love interest with Miss Kearney, and Andra Martin and Jeffrey Stone make another romantic duo. Character actors Peggy Converse, James Anderson, Charles Horvath and Forest Lewis give able support. Robin Hughes is the over-active corpse.

Cowan's direction is well-paced and thoughtfully conceived in arousing interest before the horror element is unmasked. He is not so successful when the "thing" is unveiled simply because he doesn't have strong enough material to work with. Otherwise, Duncan's script is good, in its characters and in the dialog.

Other helpful technical credits include Russell Metty's moody photography and Joseph Gershenson's eerie music. *Powe.*

Let's Rock

Slick roller-'n'-roller for the juve crowd; Julius La Rosa name should be top draw.

Hollywood, May 2.

Columbia Pictures release of Harry Foster production. Stars Julius La Rosa; costars Phyllis Newman; features Conrad Janis, Joy Harman, Paul Anka, Danny and the Juniors, Roy Hamilton and the Cues, Wink Martindale, Della Reese, Royal Teens, Tyrones. Directed by Foster. Screenplay, Hal Hackady; camera, Jack Etra; editor, S. Charles Rawson. Previewed May 1, '58. Running time, **78 MINS.**

Tommy Adano	Julius La Rosa
Kathy Abbott	Phyllis Newman
Charlie	Conrad Janis
Pickup Girl	Joy Harman
Monk	Fred Kareman
Gordo	Pete Paull
Clinch	Charles Shelander
Wink Martindale	Himself
Shep Harris	Harold Gary
Floor Manager	Jerry Hackady
Engineer	Ron McLewdon
Studio Manager	Ned Wertimer
Bartender	Tony Brande

Columbia has an exploitable piece of rock-'n'-roll merchandise here which should gladden exhibs as well as juve audiences. Name of Julius La Rosa, who makes his film bow, should be a potent draw and lineup of name recording artist guestars further embellishes musical's possibilities in the particular younger market for which it patently is aimed.

Simple story line of a ballad singer who refuses to go along with the musical tide is merely a device to present musical numbers, and here is where film scores. La Rosa, as a top recording star who believes his sweet singing style will return to popularity, warbles three of these ballads before he turns to rock-'n'-roll to save his career, all done with slickness. "Crazy, Crazy Party" is his closing r-r number, others being "Two Perfect Strangers," "Casual" and "There Are Times." Phyllis Newman is in for romantic interest, a sweet chick, and Conrad Janis scores as his long-suffering manager.

Film is kept on the lively side via the large number of guest artists. Roy Hamilton and the Cues, regularly not a r-r combo, sock over two such numbers, "Here Comes Love" and "The Secret Path of Love." Danny and the Juniors are on for their wide-selling waxing, "At the Hop," and the Royal Teens for their "Short Shorts." Della Reese torches up "Lonelyville," and other names include Paul Anka, the Tyrones and Wink Martindale.

As producer-director, Harry Foster leads off strongly as a filmmaker in the know, getting good technical backing from Jack Etra's cameras, Paul Barnes' art direction, S. Charles Rawson's editing and Peter Gennaro's choreography. Hal Hackady's screenplay also fits the bill. *Whit.*

An American Girl

Anti-Defamation League of B'nai B'rith release of 16m production by Dynamic Films (Nathan Zucker). Stars Bennye Gatteys, Frank Overton, Audra Lindley, Patty Duke and Richard Ide. Directed by Lee Bobker. Screenplay, Howard Rodman. Previewed in N.Y. at Barbizon Plaza, April 24, '58. Running time, **28½ MINS.**

"The American Girl," a 28½-minute film produced by Dynamic Films for the Anti-Defamation League of B'nai B'rith, is described as a "human relations film" which aims to entertain "with a purpose." The 16th entry, written by Howard Rodman and directed by Lee Bobker, effectively achieves its purpose in discussing prejudice among teenagers.

Theme, said to be based on an actual event, shows the awakening of a suburban community to the evils of prejudice when a young girl is mistakenly believed to be Jewish by her friends and neighbors. In a general way, the story is similar to "Gentleman's Agreement" in that an alert and intelligent non-Jew, in this case the young teenager, decides to expose the existence of the irrational prejudice in her community.

Production values, direction and the thesping of Benney Gatteys, Frank Overton, Audra Lindley, Patty Duke and Richard Ide contribute to the general excellence of the film. *Holl.*

Fraulein
(C'SCOPE-COLOR)

World War II from German femme angle; good for general market.

Hollywood, May 2.

Twentieth-Fox release of Walter Reisch production. Stars Dana Wynter, Mel Ferrer, Dolores Michaels; features Maggie Hayes, Theodore Bikel, Luis Van Rooten, Helmut Dantine, Herbert Berghof, James Edwards, Ivan Triesault, Blandine Ebinger, Jack Kruschen. Director, Henry Koster. Screenplay, Leo Townsend, from novel by James McGovern; camera (De Luxe color), Leo Tover; music, Daniele Amfitheatrof; editor, Marjorie Fowler. Previewed April 30, '58. Running time, **95 MINS.**

Erika Angermann	Dana Wynter
Foster MacLain	Mel Ferrer
Lori	Dolores Michaels
Lt. Berdie Dubbin	Maggie Hayes
Dmitri	Theodore Bikel
Fritz Graubach	Luis Van Rooten
Hugo	Helmut Dantine
Karl	Herbert Berghof
Corp. S. Hanks	James Edwards
Professor Angermann	Ivan Triesault

Berta Graubach .... Blandine Ebinger
Grischa .... Jack Kruschen

"Fraulein" continues the current war cycle. Story of a girl in war-torn Germany during the closing days of World War II and directly afterwards, it paints a vivid and sometimes moving picture of what befalls her in struggle for survival. While lacking star names of proven b.o. pull, because of its central character film carries good distaff interest and should do moderately well in general market.

Walter Reisch production benefits by having been filmed in actual plot locales of Cologne and Berlin, further aided by CinemaScope lensing and lush De Luxe color. Henry Koster's direction of the Leo Townsend screenplay, based on novel by James McGovern, is realistic and catches the feeling of both the conquered and conquerors.

Dana Wynter in title role is an appealing figure as a girl of gentle birth overcome by the storm of war, and her romance with Mel Ferrer, an American officer, is persuasively presented.

Pair meet when Ferrer, a prisoner of war, escapes during an air raid in Cologne and receives reluctant aid from femme and her professor father. They meet again in Berlin, after femme has had frightening experiences with the Russians and innocently has signed a register designating her as a prostitute. Romance at first is one-sided, since girl is intent upon finding her hospitalized fiance, but after Ferrer locates fiance for her and it becomes apparent to her that he doesn't want her, she turns to the American. Her dream of happiness is nearly ruined by the registration with the Health Department, but a friendly American corporal changes the record.

Miss Wynter lends conviction to her character and Ferrer is satisfactory. Dolores Michaels offers an interesting presence as a German entertainer who helps heroine escape from the Russians, then later helps her in the American zone. Strong support also is contributed by Theodore Bikel, as a Russian colonel on the make for femme star; Luis Van Rooten and Blandine Ebinger, operators of the house where femme signed the register; James Edwards, the colored corporal; Ivan Triesault, the professor; Helmut Dantine, the fiance; Herbert Berghof, the cousin.

Expert technical assistance is apparent right down the line: Leo Tover, for color camera work; Marjorie Fowler, editing; Daniele Amfitheatrof, music; Lyle R. Wheeler and Leland Fuller, art direction. *Whit.*

Quantrill's Raiders
(C'SCOPE-COLOR)

Fast-action yarn on guerrilla leader; good prospects in dual market.

Hollywood, April 30.

Allied Artists release of Ben Schwalb production. Stars Steve Cochran, Diane Brewster, Leo Gordon; features Gale Robbins, Will Wright, Kim Charney, Myron Healy, Lane Chandler, Guy Prescott. Directed by Edward Bernds. Screenplay, Polly James; camera (DeLuxe color), William Whitley; editor, William Austin; music, Marlin Skiles. Previewed April 24, '58. Running time, **65 MINS.**

Westcott .... Steve Cochran
Sue .... Diane Brewster
Quantrill .... Leo Gordon
Kate .... Gale Robbins
Judge .... Will Wright
Joel .... Kim Charney
Jarrett .... Myron Healey
Hager .... Robert Foulk
Todd .... Glenn Strange
Sheriff .... Lane Chandler
Major .... Guy Prescott
Fred .... Dan M. White

A tight, showmanly piece of filmmaking, "Quantrill's Raiders" packs plenty of movement in its comparatively short footage and is probably the best yet of films on this guerrilla leader turned out in recent years. Feature should fit handily in upper bracket for action market, with fine color, CinemaScope and name of Steve Cochran to draw.

The Ben Schwalb production gives an accurate portrayal of Quantrill, who terrorized the Missouri-Kansas border during the Civil War, but the Polly James screenplay misses in the climax from a historical standpoint, easily discernible. The famous Quantrill raid on Lawrence, Kansas, when more than 400 towns-people were killed by many hundreds of the guerrilla's men is reduced to a simple attack on the town by less than two dozen raiders, and instead of citizens meeting death here it's Quantrill, who actually went on to further raiding. Story leading up to this, however, is well-plotted and given proper motivation, with an excellent set of characters and fast direction by Edward Bernds.

Cochran plays a Confederate officer detailed to contact Quantrill —portrayed by Leo Gordon—and arrange for attack on union arsenal in Lawrence. Ostensibly, he's a horse supplier for the army, and he's accepted as such by the major in command at Lawrence. When officer discovers ammo depot is being transferred to another location, he calls off raid in favor of attacking the wagon train, but Quantrill wants to raid town to settle an old score and keeps Cochran under guard at his headquarters. Escaping, Confederate gets to Lawrence in time for townsmen and few remaining soldiers to set up a defense, during which guerrilla is killed.

Cochran handles his character authoritatively and Gordon is colorful as Quantrill. Diana Brewster is in for romantic interest, and good work is contributed by Gale Robbins, as Quantrill's girl friend; Guy Prescott, the major; Lane Chandler, sheriff; Kim Charney, Miss Brewster's nephew; and Will Wright, head of vigilante committee.

Technical departments are expertly handled, headed by William Whitley's color camera work, William Austin's editing and music score by Marlin Skiles. *Whit.*

Toughest Gun in Tombstone

Routine rustlers vs. rangers bush-beater. George Montgomery's name only b.o. bait.

Hollywood, May 2.

United Artists release of a Robert E. Kent production. Stars George Montgomery; costars Jim Davis, Beverly Tyler, Gerald Milton. Directed by Earl Bellamy. Screenplay, Orville H. Hampton; camera, Kenneth Peach Sr.; music, Paul Dunlap; editor, Grant Whylock. Previewed in Hollywood, April 28, '58. Running time, **72 MINS.**

Matt Sloane .... George Montomery
Della .... Beverly Tyler
Cooper .... Don Beddoe
Ringo .... Jim Davis
Terry .... Scotty Morrow
Barger .... Harry Lauter
Beasley .... Charles Waggenheim
Purdy .... Jack Kenny
Burgess .... John Merrick
Olmstead .... Al Wyatt
Hellman .... Joey Ray
Clanton .... Gerald Milton
Bill .... Lane Bradford
Leslie .... Gregg Barton
Liveryman .... Hank Worden
Stage Driver .... Tex Terry
Shot Gun .... Charles Hayes
Mrs. Oliver .... Kathleen Mulqueen
Colonel .... Rudolph Hoyas
Sergeant .... Alex Montoya
Fernandez .... Rico Alaniz
Telegraph Operator .... Jack Carr
Governor .... William Forrest
Dr. MacAvoy .... Harry Strang
Mrs. Beasley .... Mary Newton

"The Toughest Gun in Tombstone" is a routine western laid in the Arizona Territory when Tombstone was a wide-open town and secret U. S. agents sought to close it down. Although the Robert E. Kent production is sprinkled with famous names of the era, and a semi-documentary approach by Orville H. Hampton attempts to give it realism, the story is not particularly novel or exciting. Action, whether physical or cerebral, is the touchstone of the eastern, and "The Toughest Gun in Tombstone" doesn't have enough of it. George Montgomery's name will give this picture its strongest momentum.

Montgomery is U. S. Marshal Matt Sloane, working undercover to find out why local badmen Johnny Ringo, Ike Clanton and Curly Bill Broces are rustling cattle into Mexico and bringing back illegal silver bullion. His problem is complicated by the fact that on a previous assignment his wife was murdered and his son, Scotty Morrow, saw the killer. The son is now being pursued and Montgomery has to protect his boy while solving his police riddle.

Hampton's script attempts to give important and urgency to the story by supplying a narrative that gives the background and meaning of the clash between the Rangers headed by Montgomery and the rustlers headed by Gerald Milton, as the notorious Clanton. The story is not straight enough, however, and seems constantly building to action that never quite comes off.

The cast, headed by Montgomery, Milton, Beverly Tyler as Montgomery's romantic opposite, and young Scotty Morrow as the son, do capably with their assignments. Others who contribute include Don Beddoe, Harry Lauter, Charles Wagenheim, Lane Bradford and Rodolfo Hoyos. *Powe.*

Horror of Dracula
(BRITISH-COLOR)

Stout b.o. prospects for this chiller; exploitation values offset lack of names.

Universal release of a Hammer production. Stars Peter Cushing; costars Michael Gough, Melissa Stribling, Christopher Lee. Executive producer, Michael Carreras; producer, Anthony Hinds. Directed by Terence Fisher. Screenplay, Jimmy Sangster, from novel by Bram Stoker; camera (Eastman color), Jack Asher; editor, Bill Lenny; musical director, John Hollingsworth; composer, James Bernard. Previewed N.Y., May 2, '58. Running time, **82 MINS.**

Van Helsing .... Peter Cushing
Arthur Holmwood .... Michael Gough
Mina Holmwood .... Melissa Stribling
Count Dracula .... Christopher Lee
Lucy .... Carol Marsh
Jonathan Harker........John Van Eyssen
Marx, the Undertaker....Miles Malleson
Vampire Woman .... Valerie Gaunt

Universal, which was aboard the spine-chill bandwagon with "Frankenstein" and "Dracula" as early as 1931, has another "fright" picture in "Horror of Dracula" that should pay off handsomely at the b.o. despite the non-name cast. A British-made film, it's being packaged as a "horror special" with U's own Will Cowan production, "The Thing That Couldn't Die."

There's gore aplenty in this import turned out by Michael Carreras' Hammer Film Productions. Specializing in "raw heads and bloody bones" product, Hammer also has to its credit last year's "Curse of Frankenstein" which mopped up at the wicket. As was "Curse," "Dracula" too is in color —a factor that tends to heighten the exploitation values inherent in the film.

For those familar with the original "Dracula" thriller, the Jimmy Sangster screenplay has ably preserved the sanguinary aspects of the Bram Stoker novel. Here again we have Count Dracula sleeping in a coffin by day and plying his nefarious role of a blood-sucking vampire at night. Modern version has its usual quota of victims before his reign of terror is ended by a fearless doctor.

Both director Terence Fisher as well as the cast have taken a serious approach to the macabre theme that adds up to lotsa tension and suspense. Peter Cushing is impressive as the painstaking scientist-doctor who solves the mystery. Christopher Lee is thoroughly gruesome as Dracula, and Michael Gough is suitably skeptical as a bereaved relative who ultimately is persuaded to assist Cushing.

Good support is provided by three femmes—all victims of the vampire. They're Melissa Stribling, Gough's wife; Carol Marsh, the couple's daughter, and busty Valerie Gaunt, prisoner in Lee's creepy looking castle. John Van Eyssen gasps nicely as a male victim while some scant comic relief is supplied by Miles Malleson as a mortician.

Eerie atmosphere is accented by producer Anthony Hinds physical values and Bernard Robinson's art direction. These assets are aided by the Eastman color (processed by Technicolor) lensing of Jack Asher, and the ominous qualities of the James Bernard score conducted by John Hollingsworth. Bill Lenny edited to a tight 82 minutes. U is distributing only in the U.S. *Gilb.*

No Time to Die
(BRITISH-C'SCOPE-COLOR)

Wartime escape drama, ridden with cliches and with only average thrills.

London, April 22.

Columbia release of an (Irving Allen-Albert Broccoli) Warwick production. Stars Victor Mature, Leo Genn. Directed by Terence Young. Screenplay, Richard Maibaum, Terence Young; editor, Bert Rule; camera, Ted Moore; music, Kenneth V. Jones. At Odeon, Marble Arch, London. Running time, **103 MINS.**

Thatcher .... Victor Mature
Kendall .... Leo Genn
Noakes .... Anthony Newley
The Pole .... Bonar Colleano
Carola .... Luciana Paluzzi
Bartlett .... Sean Kelly
Johnson .... Kenneth Fortescue
Italian Girl .... Anne Aubrey
Camp Commandant......George Coulouris
Captain Ritter .... Alfred Burke
Patterson .... David Lodge
The Sheikh .... Maxwell Shaw
Silverio .... Alan Tilvern
2nd English Soldier.......Kenneth Cope
Alberto .... Robert Rietty
S.S. Colonel .... Martin Boddey
Italian Cook .... Andrea Malindrinos

Another war escape drama has been churned out in "No Time To Die," this time set in the Libyan desert. As a routine adventure yarn, it will probably get by with undiscriminating audiences. But the dialog, situations, artwork and acting are all unremittingly artificial, with even the presence of Victor Mature as star having little to make this piece acceptable to American audiences.

Mature, Leo Genn, Anthony Newley, Sean Kelly and Bonar Colleano escape from a prison camp in the desert. Mature is a Yank sergeant whose pre-war anti-Nazi activities have made him hot bait. Result is that the Nazis put on extreme pressure to recapture the fugitives. This they do with the help of Arabs. Mature is tortured but keeps a stiff studio upper lip and, with the help of a friendly German, the gang get away again. But one way and other they have a hard time, and the film mercifully winds up with only Mature and Newly alive. The others have been mowed down by Nazi bullets. However, the whole cast is virtually mowed down by the script, which is riddled with cliches and stereotyped characters.

Individually the actors turn in competent jobs but their roles are all over-written and fall too neatly into slots. Mature is the tough, brash American who is really a hero. Genn is the frightfully decent King's Regulation British sergeant. Colleano is a vicious Polish killer. Newly is around to handle the comic lines which are inserted into the script with stolid persistence. The tank sequences in the desert scenes, directed by Terance Young who was himself an officer in the tanks during the war, must be presumed to be authentic. But they do not come over convincingly, savoring too much of models and studio work.

Altogether, "Die" is an unsatisfying piece of work in which a great deal of effort seems to have gone astray through unimaginative writing and direction. There have been too many first-class war films for there to be room for inferior stuff. *Rich.*

Le Cerf-Volant Du Bout Du Monde

(The Kite From Across the World) (French; COLOR)

Cannes, May 6.
Cocinor release of Garance production. Directed by Roger Pigaut. Screenplay, Antoine Tudal, Pigaut; camera (Eastmancolor), Henri Alekan; editor, Marinette Cadix. With Patrick De Bardine, Sylviane, Gerard Szymanski, Souan Wou Kong. Preemed in Cannes. Running time, **90 MINS.**

Pierrot	Patrick De Bardine
Nicole	Sylviane
Bebert	Gerard Szymanski
Monkey King	Souan Wou Kong

Film blends fantasy and moppet shenanigans ably to make this a highly pleasing item for a children's film. Adults might also be beguiled by its views of Paris and Peking, China. Played without any pretense, this is simple and engaging and looms mainly for specialized bookings.

An ornate Chinese kite alights in Paris in a treetop and two rival gangs fight over it with the heavies getting off with the tail. A note is found in the kite from a Chinese boy who would like an answer from a Western friend. The leader gets the letter translated and, in a dream, is wafted to China, with his little, coquettish sister, to find his friend.

After a series of adventures, his enemy also turns up in China, he finds his friend. Next day he makes up with his rival and they send a note to their kite pal.

Color is nicely utilized as are subdued special effects. The appearance of the Chinese Monkey King, who gives magic powers to the children, also helps give this a nice fairy tale push without overdoing it.

Children are natural and taking while the Paris and Peking backdrops are colorful, though somewhat drawn out at times. Director Roger Pigaut shows sensitivity and the ability to translate warmth and sentiment short of getting maudlin or precious. *Mosk.*

Blood Arrow

(REGALSCOPE)

Dull western for filler datings.

Hollywood, April 22.
Twentieth-Fox release of Robert W. Stabler production. Stars Scott Brady; costars Paul Richards, Phyllis Coates, Don Haggerty; features Diana Darrin, Richard Gilden, Rocky Shahan, John Dierkes. Directed by Charles Marquis Warren. Screenplay, Fred Freiberger; camera, Fleet Southcott; editor, Michael Luciano; music, Raoul Kraushaar. Previewed April 22, '58. Running time, **73 MINS.**

Dan Kree	Scott Brady
Brill	Paul Richards
Bess	Phyllis Coates
Gabe	Don Haggerty
Taslatch	Rocky Shahan
Ceppi	Des Slattery
Norm	Bill McGraw
McKenzie	Patrick O'Moore
Aimee	Jeanne Bates
Little Otter	Richard Gilden
Ez	John Dierkes
Lennie	Diana Darrin

"Blood Arrow" is singularly lacking in any of the essential story elements and handling necessary for moderate response even from the less discriminating audiences. Unreeling at a dull pace, there's little to recommend film.

The Robert W. Stabler production, scripted by Fred Freiberger, follows the valiant attempt of a pretty Mormon girl, Phyllis Coates, to transport smallpox serum through hostile Blackfoot country to her valley home, where medicine is needed to save the few remaining families not already stricken. Aiding her are four men, including Scott Brady, a gunfighter. Trek, despite Indian attacks, fails to generate much excitement.

Stock performances are the best that can be offered under Charles Marquis Warren's over-leisurely direction. Paul Richards, a gambler, joins party in search of gold; Don Haggerty, a trapper, to search for his partner, found with his eyes burned out by Indians. Rocky Shahan is the fourth escort, a devoted Indian. Richard Gilden is Blackfoot chief warring against the whites.

Technical departments are competently handled by Fleet Southcott, camera; Michael Luciano, editor; Raoul Kraushaar, music. *Whit.*

Les Bijoutiers Du Clair De Lune

(The Jewelers of Moonlight) (FRENCH; C'SCOPE; COLOR)

Paris, April 29.
Columbia release of Iena-UCIL production. Stars Brigitte Bardot, Alida Valli, Stephen Boyd; features Fernando Rey, Jose Nieto. Directed by Roger Vadim. Screenplay, Jacques Remy, Vadim from novel by Albert Vidalie; camera (Eastmancolor), Armand Thirard; editor, Victoria Mercanton. At Normandie, Paris. Running time, **90 MINS.**

Ursula	Brigitte Bardot
Florentine	Alida Valli
Lambert	Stephen Boyd
Uncle	Fernando Rey
Inspector	Jose Vieto

B.B. now stands for Brigitte Bardot, but has practically become synonomous with blockbuster on a worldwide scale as far as pix in which she appears are concerned. This was produced by Raoul Levy under his Columbia deal, with an Anglo version for the U.S. called, "The Night That Heaven Fell." Whether in English or French, this combines the factors which made the team's "And God Created Woman" an international grosser. As long as the interest in B.B. continues, this should follow suit.

As in "Woman," the yarn is melodramatic in the worst sense of the word, with contrived situations and sudden passions. The technique is somewhat overdone, and there is too much strain for effect. Story is meandering and the dialog disastrous.

But there is B.B. as a perverse, pretty lass down from Paris for a supposedly quiet vacation in Spain. However, under her seeming girlishness lurks the frankly, morally free girl who takes what she wants and asks for it by her looks, demeanor and pigeon pout. She is soon involved in a hot Latin adventure. Her aunt, a well-bred woman on the surface, well played by Alida Valli, has a hopeless passion for a local hothead. Latter is portrayed okay by Stephen Boyd. He winds up by killing her husband. She does not seem to mind and is ready to go away with the fellow until B.B. beats her to the punch.

The so-called pure love in caves of picturesque Spain then follows until the law tracks them down and kills her as she shields him. But not before there has been time for some ruggedly exploitable scenes with B.B. giving her all for love. With its retribution, this might run into less censorship troubles' than its predecessors.

Film is eye-filling because CinemaScope and colors are well used. Levy has not skimped on production values and the Hispano on-the-spot lensing also helps. This might well be exploited in the U.S. arty spots (in the French version) and generally in the Anglo version. The English-language version will also help since it does away with dubbing. Prospects look bright for this everywhere as B.B. goes onwards and upwards as a growing pic star and sex symbol.

There is plenty of bare B.B. in this besides some colorful Hispano topography, bullfights, etc. But B.B.'s acting ability does not measure up to her bodily values. *Mosk.*

The Lineup

Double-bill filler; fair action meller based on characters and background of "The Lineup" teleseries.

Hollywood, April 25.
Columbia release of a Jaime Del Valle production. Stars Eli Wallach; costars Robert Keith and Warner Anderson; features Richard Jaeckel, Mary LaRoche, William Leslie and Emile Meyer. Screenplay, Stirling Silliphant; based on the teleseries created by Lawrence L. Klee; camera, Hal Mohr; music, Mischa Bakaleinikoff; editor, Al Clark. Previewed at the studio, April 17, '58. Running time, **85 MINS.**

Dancer	Eli Wallach
Julian	Robert Keith
Lt. Guthrie	Warner Anderson
Sandy McLain	Richard Jaeckel
Dorothy Bradshaw	Mary LaRoche
Larry Warner	William Leslie
Inspector Al Quine	Emile Meyer
Inspector Fred Asher	Marshall Reed
Philip Dressler	Raymond Bailey
The Man	Vaughn Taylor
Cindy	Cheryl Callaway
Porter No. 1	Bert Holland
Dr. Turkel	George Eldredge
Staples	Robert Bailey

"The Lineup" poses an interesting situation in feature picture production and distribution, since it is based on a popular teleseries and has some of the same characters. The screenplay by Stirling Silliphant is not taken from the series itself; it is original material, but this fact will be hard to get across.

The Jaime del Valle production, directed by Don Siegel, is a moderately exciting melodrama based on dope smuggling in San Francisco, but short on action until the final, well-plotted and photographed, climax. Eli Wallach, usually associated with the stage and art productions, is the surprising star of "The Lineup" and the only name of any consequence.

The action centers around the attempt by a narcotics gang to get the heroin it has planted abroad on the possession of travelers returning to this country and debarking in San Francisco. Wallach heads the gang's pickup squad, aided by brains Robert Keith and driver Richard Jaeckel. The best part of the action is its background, the Mark Hopkins motel, a Nob Hill mansion, Sutro's museum, the Opera House. There is also a good chase sequence at the end on an unfinished freeway, well staged by Siegel and excitingly photographed by Hal Mohr, who also takes splendid advantage of such picturesque interiors at Sutro's. But the early parts of the film waste too much time on police procedure and lingo, now a routine thing. The script is not up to the other production values.

Wallach is wasted in the leading role. He seems an ordinary heavy, competent but not particularly interesting. Robert Keith, Warner Anderson, Richard Jaeckel, Mary LaRoche and William Leslie go about their chores with intelligence, hampered only by the one-dimensional characters they attempt to animate.

Technical credits, including Al Clark's editing and John Livadary's sound, are both first-rate. *Powe.*

Les Espions

(The Spies) (FRENCH)

Paris, April 22.
Cinedis release of Filmsoner-Vera Film production. Stars Curd Jurgens, Peter Ustinov, Vera Clouzot; features Sam Jaffe, Gerard Sety, Martita Hunt, O. E. Hasse, Paul Carpenter. Directed by H. G. Clouzot. Screenplay, Clouzot, Jerome Jeronimi from novel, "Midnight Patient," by Egon Hostowsky; camera, Christian Matras; editor, Robert Sivel. At Paris, Paris. Running time, **120 MINS.**

Malic	Gerard Sety
Visitor	Curd Jurgens
Patient	Vera Clouzot
Russian	Peter Ustinov
American	Sam Jaffe
Nurse	Martita Hunt
Vogel	O. E. Hasse
Colonel	Paul Carpenter

After the shock-suspense values contained in "Diabolique," director H. G. Clouzot tries his hand here with an involved tale of espionage. Atmospherically successful at the beginning, pic then falls short as all is explained and tied up. It shapes as too long and talky for general Yank chances, but might do as an arty house entry on its theme, with the names of Curd Jurgens, Peter Ustinov and Sam Jaffe obvious plus factors.

An ineffectual, secondrate psychologist, operating a rundown sanatorium with two patients, is offered big money by an American military man to hide somebody. The confused doctor, Gerard Sety, accepts and the next day a stranger arrives, followed soon afterwards by a flock of spies from several countries.

Sety's staff is strangely replaced by shifty new ones, and an eerie adventure begins for him. He is supposedly hiding a German physicist who has invented something to make the Atom bomb look like a firecracker. The military man feels that no country, not even the U. S., can be trusted with it.

The hide-and-seek game starts as the man hiding out is found to be only a stand-in for the real one, with Russo and Yank forces striving for the man while scores of spies, many not really knowing who they work for anymore, arrive to complicate things. Finally, the scientist kills himself along with his secret.

Picture's main assets are the fine portraits racked up by the top-flight cast, and Clouzot's solid technical knowhow as he builds his puzzle meticulously. He almost succeeds in making a statement about world distrust. Too much explanation finally wears off the edge on this subject.

Curd Jurgens is effective as the stand-in for the scientist while Peter Ustinov and Sam Jaffe have drawn sharp portraits of the Russo and Yank espionage chiefs. Comedy appears to lie underneath everything. Sety is fine as the victimized doctor while Vera Clouzot is moving. Technical credits are tops. *Mosk.*

Montparnasse 19
(FRENCH)

Paris, April 22.

. Cocinor release of Franco London Film production. Stars Gerard Philipe, Lil Palmer; features Anouk Aimee, Lea Padovani, Bernard Sety, Lila Kedrova, Lino Ventura. Directed by Jacques Becker Screenplay, Max Ophuls, Henri Jeansson Becker; camera Christian Matras; editor Marguerite Renoir. At Colisee, Paris Running time, **120 MINS.**

Modigliani ....Gerard Philipe
Beatrice ....Lili Palmer
Jeanne ....Anouk Aimee
Rosalie ....Lea Padovani
Sborowsky ....Gerard Sety
Mrs. Sborowsky ....Lila Kedrova
Morel ....Lino Ventura

After Yank pic chronicling of the lives of turn-of-century artists in "Moulin Rouge" (UA) and "Lust For Life" (M-G), the French now take to it in dealing with the last year in the life of the tortured Italo painter (he lived in Montparnasse in 1919), Amedeo Modigliani. Unlike the others, this is not in color and does not purport to be a faithful transcription. Thus it avoids being academic and is mainly the love story of a man who happened to be a painter. This gives it its strong and weak points.

Modigliani (Philipe) is already a hapless drunk and still unrecognized for his work when the pic opens in the teeming days of Montparnasse 1919. Mixed up with a debauched Anglo writer, Miss Palmer, he seems well on his way to the d-ts when along comes beateous Anouk Aimee. But parental objections to this saving love and Philipe's alcoholic condition lead to his early demise.

Sans deeper insight into the painter's despair and addiction, the character as done here lacks force and makes him a spoiled, headstrong type. It is more a tale of ill-fated lovers than the story of a painter.

. Director Jacques Becker's flair for character, plus fine performances, cloak the refusal to go into Modigliani's life any deeper than his last days and tragic love. Philipe makes his rumpled youth effective as the childish but genial artist while Miss Palmer is effective as the Bohemian English lady. Miss Aimee is probably fresh and faithful as his sweetheart.

Technical credits are tops. It will take hard sell but word-of-mouth and critics may help plus the art tag. Making flash, but telling appearances are Yank singer-actress Cynda Glenn, as a waspish. rich American woman as well as Denise Vernac, Eric Von Stroheim's widow, as Miss Aimee's understanding mother. *Mosk.*

Foreign Films

Italienreise-Liebe Inbegriffen (Italian Journey—Love Included) (**GERMAN—COLOR**). UFA release of CCC (Arthur Brauner) production. Stars Paul Hubschmid, Susanne Cramer, Walter Giller; features Hannelore Schroth, Bum Krueger, Walter Koch, Gretl Theimer. Directed by Wolfgang Becker. Screenplay, Jochen Huth, after novel by Barbara Noack; camera (Eastmancolor), Heinz Pehlke; music, Friedrich Schroeder; editor, Walter Wischniewski. At UFA Pavillon, Berlin. Running time, **98 MINS.**

This UFA release is one of those unpretentious features that are seen and forgotten (by the crix) but whose mass appeal makes them good program fillers here. Domestically, "Journey" is already on its way to become a substantial moneymaker. International chances, if any, are only spotty. Screenplay, adapted from a best-seller by Barbara Noack and written by Jochen Huth, concerns a company of German tourists who go on a bus ride to beautiful Italy. Their various experiences, mostly of the romantic kind, are depicted in a harmless manner.

Under the conventional, and partly pace-lacking, direction by Wolfgang Becker, the cast, headed by Paul Hubschmid (in Hollywood, Paul Christian), turns in rather mechanical if satisfactory performances. Hubschmid is the guide and he's probably the handsomest and most elegant guide the tourists have ever seen. He turns his eyes on comely Susanne Cramer, one of the tourists. However, she is followed in an auto by her jealous lover, Walter Giller. Supporting cast has Hannelore Schroth, as a medium-aged maid who joins the tourists to find a hubby at last; Walter Jansen and Mita von Ahlefeld, an old couple, on their wedding-tour after 35 years, among others. The Italian scenery, which serves practically the entire film as background, is always attractive. *Hans.*

La Tour, Prends Garde! (Watch Out, La Tour) ((**FRENCH — ITALO — YUGOSLAV**) (**COLOR; DYALISCOPE**). Sirius release of Vega-Ufus- Sonorama production. Stars Jean Marais, Eleonora Rossi-Drago, Nadja Tiller; features Cathia Caro, Jean Paredes, Christian Duvalcix, Yves Massart. Directed by Georges Lampin. Screenplay, Claude Accursi, Denys De La Patelliere, Lampin; camera (Eastmancolor), Jean Bourgoin; editor, Robert Isnardan. At Paris, Paris. Running time, **90 MINS.**

Naive costumer tells of a Robin Hoodish troubador who helps his king, Louis XIV, during the lacey wars of those decades. Satire and adventure rarely combine as in "Fanfan La Tulipe." This looks okay for home marts but of scant Yank interest except maybe for dualers.

Jean Marais lacks the dash and stature to give a true breath of high adventure to the proceedings as the heroic singer. Result is that most of the derring-do falls flat. He saves his King's flag from enemy hands to avenge a beating by a nobleman and finally wins the girl and unmasks the usurpers.

Made in Yugoslavia, the production denotes a big money outlay but director Georges Lampin has not been able to make it jell into a big-scale look. C'Scope proportions and color make this even more expensive for Yank secondary chances. General cast level is good. This looms okay for moppet appeal but not for the grownups. *Mosk.*

Ascenseur Pour L'Echafaud (Elevator to the Gallows) (**FRENCH**). Lux release of NEF production. Stars Maurice Ronet, Jeanne Moreau; features Georges Poujouly, Jean Wall, Yori Bertin, Lino Ventura. Directed by Louis Malle. Screenplay, Roger Nimier, Malle from novel by Noel Calef; camera, H. Decae; editor, Leonide Azar; music, Miles Davis. At Colisee, Paris. Running time, **90 MINS.**

Made by a 25-year-old director as his first pic, this has already garnered a top film award of the year, Le Prix Delluc. It is a slickly-made suspense item which generates a taking first part but then falls off. It looks to do well here, and could have a chance in the U.S. if given plenty of hard-sell. It does not shape as much of an arty entry.

A young engineer, hero from the Indochinese debacle, kills his boss to get his wife, a younger woman madly in love with him. It is perfectly covered as a suicide but he is stuck in the elevator on the way out when the current is shut off. Meanwhile his car is stolen by two young delinquents who kill some German tourists with his gun. He finally gets out of the elevator undetected but a police inspector gets him on the other charge. Though his girl clears him of that, they are finally linked up with the murder of her husband.

For an initial pic, Louis Maile shows a fine technical assurance and builds up some suspense. But the overdose of stilted dialog, and the final denoument lets this trail off sharly at the end. Acting is fine with Jeanne Moreau intense as the woman. Technical credits are outstanding. A plus is Yank trumpeter Miles Davis' nervous, knowing musical backgrounding. *Mosk.*

"Heiratskandidaten" (Candidates for Marriage) (**AUSTRIAN**). International Film Co. release of a Rex-Schoenbrunn Film production. Features Beppo Brem, Paul Hoerbiger, Gerlinde Locker, Walter Korth. Directed by Hermann Kugelstadt. Book by Hugo Wiener and August Rieger; camera, Walter Partsch; music, Hans Lang. At Tabor Kino, Vienna. Running time, **90 MINS.**

"Candidates for Marriage" is a very humorous story of two henpecked husbands of the province, who get a chance to visit Vienna alone. Beppo Brem plays the Bavarian and Paul Hoerbiger, the Austrian type. Both telegraph their wives that they must go to jail for eight days after a traffic accident. Interwoven is a love story about Walter Korth, as veterinarian student (he composes pop music), and Serlinde Locker, as photographer of marriage institute. Cast is excellent.

Walter Partsch did a fine job with his camera. Picture has many beautiful scenes of the world famous Wachau, wine district. Hans Lang wrote a few songs for this production, which though not outstanding for other countries, proved that Austria is still in the market. *Maas.*

C'Est La Faute d'Adam (It's Adam's F... (**FRENCH; COLOR; DYALISCOPE**). Sonofilm release of Socipex production. Stars Dany Robin ...ques Sernas; features Rene Lefevre, Gaby Sylvia, Noel Roquevert, Robert Vattier, Denise Grey. Directed by Jacqueline Audry. Screenplay, Raymond Caillava, Pierre Laroche; camera (Eastmancolor), Roger Dormoy; editor, Marguerite Beague. At Balzac, Paris. Running time, **100 MINS.**

French situation comedy is quite reminiscent of Anglo and Yank laugh pix. But it lacks the genuine comedics and inventiveness to make this more than a hybrid. It looms a tossup both on home and in foreign marts, and is further hampered by color costs.

An orphan loses her memory in an accident via a car driven by a young bridegroom-to-be. His helping her loses him his bride. Then thieves use her for they think she is an accomplice sent by one of the gang. Also involved is a headstrong colonel with a batch of doddering sons to marry off. After some dragged out complications, all is happily resolved.

Dany Robin's cuteness gets cloying while Jacques Sernas is wooden as her vis-a-vis. Rene Lefevre adds some yocks as the colorful old colonel, but the remainder of the cast is only acceptable. Technical credits are good. *Mosk.*

Man Ist Nur Zweimal Jung (Youth Comes Only Twice) (**Austrian**). Sascha Film Co. release of Wiener Mundus-Excelsior Film production. Features Wolf Albach Retty, Ernst Waldbrunn, Winnie Markus, Heidi Bruehl, Margit Saad, Susi Nicoletti, Lotte Lang, Louise Martini. Directed by Helmut Weiss. Adapted from the play by Otto F. Beer and Peter Preses by Wolf Neumeister; camera, Elio Carniel; music, Hans Lang. At Cosmos Kino, Vienna. Running time, **90 MINS.**

The entertaining comedy, "Youth Comes Only Twice," ran successfully at the Vienna Kammerspiele. Scripter Wolf Neumeister did not change much and that is to his credit. It is about two men about with gossip having it that they are no longer interested in the opposite sex. But they become young again, with surprising results. Some of the cast of the Josefstadt ensemble, which also runs the Kammerspiele Theatre, play the same roles in this film. Production seems sure to show good b.o. results in this part of the world.

Helmut Weiss did an excellent directorial job. Camerawork of Elio Carniel is fine. Hans Lang contributed the music. All technical details are okay. *Maas.*

Trois Jours A VIVRE (Three Days to Live) (**FRENCH**). F. Rivers release of IMP production. Stars Daniel Gelin, Jeanne Moreau; features Lino Ventura, Aime Clariond, Evelyne Rey. Directed by Gilles Grangier. Screenplay, Guy Bertret, Michel Audiard from novel by Peter Vanett; camera, Armand Thirard; editor, Jacqueline Sadoul. At Triomphe, Paris. Running time, **85 MINS.**

Pic concerns a smalltime actor who sees a man shot. He identifies the killer for publicity even though he did not really see him. The man escapes and decides to kill the actor. Latter is saved by a young actress in love with him. However, lacklustre direction, acting and writing kill the suspense in this. It shapes a dubious pic both at home and abroad.

Too much talk stifles the movement. Jeanne Moreau and Daniel Gelin are misused as the lovers. Technical credits are par but, production values are nil. *Mosk.*

Cargaison Blanche (White Cargo) **(FRENCH).** CCFC release of Lopez-Mars production. Stars Francoise Arnoul; features Georges Rivieres, Georges Aminel, Colette Mars; Judith Magre. Directed by Georges Lacombe. Screenplay, Jean Masson, Jacques Sigurd; camera, Roger Hubert; editor, Denise Baby. At Marbeuf, Paris. Running time, **90 MINS.**

The "B" film frame and a star name may make this an okay entry here. But in spite of its suggestive title and theme of the prostie racket, this holds little exploitation value for the U. S., except for grind or dualer spots.

A stubborn young femme mag writer follows the trail of a group of white slavers. Then she becomes as a victim-to-be. But her friendship with a dope addict, a Negro bongo player, and a fellow newshound save her from a fate worse than death.

Contrived scripting and lacklustre playing do not help infuse this with the tautness and movement so necessary for an actioner with b.o. appeal. Sans direction, star Francoise Arnoul makes like a sleepwalker but the heavies register well. However, top acting honors go to colored actor Georges Aminel for his sensitive portrayal of the junkie who saves the day. Technical credits are only par. *Mosk.*

Cannes Festival

L'Uomo Di Paglia
(A Man of Straw)
(ITALIAN)

LUX FILM release of a VIDES-LUX-Cinecitta production. Stars Pietro Germi; features Franca Bettoja; Edoardo Nevola, Luisa della Noce, Saro Urzi. Directed by Pietro Germi. Screenplay, Germi, Giannetti, Benvenuti, DeBernardi; from a story by Gemi and Giannetti. Camera, Leonida Barboni. Music, Carlo Bustichelli; editor, Dolores Tamburini. At Film Festival, Cannes. Running time, **95 MINS.**

Andrea Zaccardi .... Pietro Germi
Luisa .... Luisa della Noce
Rita Fabiani .... Franca Bettoja
Giulio .... Edoardo Nevola
Beppe .... Saro Urzi

Undoubtedly one of the year's best releases by an Italian studio, "A Man of Straw" has sales points in its honest approach to an adultery tale, and in its fine performances and lensing, which should overcome the downbeat story elements especially in subsequent runs. Final returns here should prove healthy, while pic makes okay export fare. Could make an art item in the US.

Andrea Zaccadari (Germi), married father of a boy, falls in love with a young girl, begins to desert family life in fa[illegible] of the new flame. Though both know it can't last, she's hit hardest by the shock of separation, and commits suicide. His wife forgives him and he returns to his home once more, but knowing that something has changed and that things can never again be the same. Tale is soberly told and with the exception of the suicide and some of the latter half of pic rings particularly true and moving. The psychological character play as the relationship develops is also deftly turned.

Germi is excellent as the errant husband, while Franca Bettoja is a find in her first role as the focus of his extracurricular attention. Luisa della Noce and Edoardo Nevola ably round out the family picture as wife and child while Saro Urzi etches a sympathetic picture as the family confidant. Direction by Germi from his own script is hard-hitting, and confidant. Direction by Germi from his own script is hard-hitting, and only occasionally repetitious, though it loses its grip a bit towards finale. He gets top assistance from lenser Leonida Barboni and from Carlo Bustichelli, who wrote the catchy score. Other production credits are tops. *Hawk.*

Giovani Mariti
(Young Husbands)
(ITALO-FRENCH)

LUX FILM release of a Nepi-Silver Film Zodiaque (Paris) co-production. Features Sylva Koscina, Antonella Lualdi, Antonio Ciffariello, Isabelle Corey, Gerard Blain, Raf Mattioli, Anna Maria Guarnieri, Enio Girolami, Franco Interlenghi. Directed by Mauro Bolognini. Screenplay, Bolognini, Flaiano, Cureli, Pasolini, Martino; from story by P. F. Campanile and Massimo Franciosa. Camera, Armando Nannuzzi. Music, Marie Zafred. Editor, Roberto Cinquini. At Film Festival, Cannes. Running time, **101 MINS**

Mara .... Sylva Koscina
Lucia .... Antonella Lualdi
Marcello .... Gerard Blain
Antonio .... Franco Interlinghi
Ettore .... Antonio Ciffariello
Laura .... Isabelle Corey
Giulio .... Raf Mattioli

Elegantly produced and directed feature concerns young love at the threshhold of (married) life. Film has slick appeal and cast to help it to consistent payoff in depth, both in this country and on the continent. For the States, its appeal appears more limited, since players are little known.

Tale told is of several youths in a small Italian town who slowly begin drifting into marriage, almost against their wishes, enjoying their last flings, etc. One last rebellion to convention, when they all burst into town to live it up as in the good old days, ends in dismal flop, and they realize that their days of carefree youth are gone forever. Though at times inconsistently episodic, film which occasionally echoes "I Vitelloni" manages many excellent moments of human observation. Director Bolognini has guided almost all his many actors to good efforts, with Gerard Blain and Antonella Lualdi, perhaps also due to their parts, coming off a bit above the rest.

Armando Nannuzzi's lensing is outstanding in securing the grey atmosphere of the Italian town where pic locations. Other production credits are all fine. *Hawk.*

God's Little Acre

Smash b.o. prospects. Artistic but still earthy version of the longtime-selling Erskine Caldwell novel.

Hollywood, May 9.

United Artists release of a Sidney Harmon production. Stars Robert Ryan, Aldo Ray; costars Buddy Hackett; introduces Tina Louise. Directed by Anthony Mann. Screenplay, Philip Yordan; from the novel by Erskine Caldwell; camera, Ernest Haller; music, Elmer Bernstein; editor, Richard C. Meyer. Previewed in Hollywood, May 7, '58. Running time, **112 MINS.**

Ty Ty Walden .... Robert Ryan
Bill Thompson .... Aldo Ray
Griselda .... Tina Louise
Pluto .... Buddy Hackett
Buck Walden .... Jack Lord
Darlin' Jill .... Fay Spain
Shaw Walden .... Vic Morrow
Rosamund .... Helen Westcott
Jim Leslie .... Lance Fuller
Uncle Felix .... Rex Ingram
Dave Dawson .... Michael Landon

Rousing, rollicking and ribald, "God's Little Acre" is a rustic revel with the kick of a Georgia mule. The Sidney Harmon production for United Artists, directed by Anthony Mann, promises to be one of the season's smash hits. It is also a very fine picture in which Robert Ryan gives the performance of his career.

Harmon's production of Erskine Caldwell's novel is adult, sensitive and intelligent. The sex is still there, prime and juicy, but the outhouse atmosphere is gone; the sly, peeping-tomism erased. What remains is a folk comedy, sassy and forthright, but realistic enough to make the final tragic moments important and touching.

The direct, bucolic humor is virtually intact, and so is Caldwell's larger scheme, the morality play he told through the artless, sometimes disastrous behavior of his foolish and lovable characters. A changed ending gives a different meaning to the story, but the ending is sound, aethestically and popularly. Some of the changes made by Philip Yordan were dictated by necessity, but all of them work to give the story dignity and the stature it needs to offset the notion that it is just sex, sex, sex.

The story, and it is told in scene after scene of striking power, remains that of a Georgia farmer, Robert Ryan, who believes he can find gold on his farm. In the book it was a gold mine; in the picture it is buried treasure. Ryan has spent years of his life digging for it, all his energies and those of his two sons, Jack Lord and Vic Morrow, go into the search and the dream it represents. The hunt leads everywhere on their farm except on the one acre Ryan has set aside, in the olden way of tithing, for God. "God's Little Acre" is marked with a cross. Fortunately the cross is movable, because sometimes the gold seems to be underneath it. In which case, God gets a less desirable acre. The cross is moved. And what was God's little acre, becomes another of the gaping holes that pit Ryan's farm as the endless, senseless search goes on.

There is nothing irreligious or irreverent about this. It is a story of primitive people, and primitive people bargain with nature and with God. This is established dexterously and economically in Yordan's screenplay. A major factor in this is Ryan's playing under Mann's direction, because he implies an inherent nobility that saves the story from falling into the dangerous ruts left by that other Caldwell story of the south, "Tobacco Road." "God's Little Acre" takes another pathway altogether than that "Road."

The story erupts in tragedy as each of the people, childlike in his beliefs, seeks a simple solution (like finding gold) to his complex problems and those of his world. Ryan's son-in-law, Aldo Ray, is a townsman. He is convinced that he has only to turn on the power in his company town's shutdown cotton mill to have life surge back into him and his community. Ryan doesn't find his gold and Ray dies trying to start up his plant. The ending, different from the book, has Ryan and his sons planting the earth, as a farmer should, putting into the earth rather than trying to take out.

One of Mann's notable achievements is his success in getting his players to work in ensemble. They are always colloquial and related. Ryan dominates the picture, as his character should. He opens a whole vista of roles for himself by this portrayal, as remarkable, perhaps, as Walter Huston's performance in "Treasure of the Sierra Madre."

Ray creates a moving characterization as the husband torn between his wife, sensitively played by Helen Westcott, and the voluptuous barnyard Susannah, strikingly projected by newcomer, from legit, Tina Louise. Buddy Hackett, best known until now as a [illegible] club and tv comic, gives perception and depth and real acting to his role of ridicule and whimsy. Jack Lord, brooding and jealous, and Vic Morrow, a sad carbon of his brother, are both pitiful and strong as Ryan's sons.

Fay Spain, the goofy and delightful Darling Jill, makes the role less a caricature than the book; she is a human being. Rex Ingram, as the Negro farmhand, sometimes seems to be the only sensible human being of the lot, achieving a simple and moving strength. Lance Fuller and Michael Landon, with highly individual playing, complete the cast.

Elmer Bernstein's music is another important factor in increasing the story's depth. He has also contributed a delightful, bouncy title song—words by Caldwell—that has all the racy vigor of country music and sounds like a traditional spiritual. Ernest Haller's camera work is stunning.

To sum it up, the feeling one gets in evaluating the production in all its phases is one of harmony. This extends to the art direction by John S. Poplin, Jr. and set decoration by Lyle B. Reifsnider, for the authentic settings; to the sound by Jack Solomon and J. Henry Adams; editing by Richard C. Meyer, special photographic effects by Rabin and DeWitt, all under production supervisor Leon Chooluck. *Powe.*

From Hell to Texas
(C'SCOPE—COLOR)

Slick western for action and drive-in markets; lacks marquee lure for de luxe spots.

20th-Fox release of Robert Buckner production. Stars Don Murray, Diane Varsi; co-stars Chill Wills, Dennis Hopper. Directed by Henry Hathaway. Screenplay, Buckner and Wendell Mayes, based on book by Charles O. Locke; camera (De Luxe color), Wilfrid M. Cline; editor, Johnny Ehrin; music, Daniele Amfitheatrof. Previewed N.Y., April 11, '58. Running time, **100 MINS.**

Tod Lohman .... Don Murray
Juanita Bradley .... Diane Varsi
Amos Bradley .... Chill Wills
Tom Boyd .... Dennis Hopper
Hunter Boyd .... R. C. Armstrong

Jake Leffertfinger......... Jay C. Flippen
Mrs. Bradley .... Margo
Hal Carmody .... John Larch
Otis Boyd .... Ken Scott
Bayliss .... Rodolfo Acosta
Cardito .... Salvador Baguez
Trueblood .... Harry Carey Jr.
Morgan .... Jerry Oddo

Designed to showcase a couple of new faces—Don Murray and Diane Varsi— "From Hell to Texas" is a crisply made western with fine b.o. potential in the action market and drive-ins. It's been handsomely mounted in CinemaScope and De Luxe color by producer Robert Buckner but lacks sufficient marquee dressing to lure substantial biz in class first-run sites.

Reminiscent of Stanley Kramer's "High Noon," this 20th-Fox production and release is the same kind of adult fare with a similar tension that builds throughout the footage. Screenplayed by Buckner and Wendell Mayes from Charles O. Locke's book, "The Hell Bent Kid," film depicts the grim story of a hunted man.

Object of a relentless search through New Mexico badlands is Murray who has accidentally killed one of wealthy rancher R. G. Armstrong's three sons. The cattle baron, who's the law in them thar parts, vows retribution. His fury mounts when a second son is trampled to death and several members of a posse become victims either at Murray's hand or warring Indians.

Director Henry Hathaway, an old hand at these outdoor sagas, wrings suspense galore from the yarn as the sharpshooting Murray manages to keep a whisper ahead of his pursuers. There's even a dash of romance when he meets Miss Varsi in his flight. She's the daughter of another rancher, Chill Wills. They both lend him more than moral support.

What could be called "High Moon" is a sock moonlit climax when Murray breaks up a tense gun duel by suddenly dropping his rifle to save Armstrong's sole remaining son, Dennis Hopper, from a flaming death. Under Hathaway's expert guidance, Murray turns in a taut and gripping performance. Less impressive, however, is Miss Varsi who's pretty but not quite the frontier type.

Wills is thoroughly believable as the kindly rancher while Armstrong is firm and methodical in carrying out his peculiar ideas of justice. Hopper is capable for the most part as the son but occasionally over-acts. Good support is provided by Jay C. Flippen, an itinerant merchant; Margo, as Wills wife, and John Larch, a posse member slain by Murray—a man who feared being a killer.

Outdoor vistas, lushly photographed by Wilfrid M. Cline, are frequently eyefilling on the CinemaScope screen. Johnny Ehrin's editing heightens the effectiveness of the 100 minutes running time while the Daniele Amfitheatrof score and the Lyle R. Wheeler-Walter Simonds art direction are also assets. *Gilb.*

Vertigo
(V'VISION-COLOR)

Psychological murder mystery in gimmick-laden Alfred Hitchcock tradition. Starts slow and too long but top marquee names should make it b.o. click.

San Francisco, May 10.

Paramount release of Alfred Hitchcock production. Stars James Stewart, Kim Novak; costars Barbara Bel Geddes; features Tom Helmore, Henry Jones. Directed by Hitchcock. Screenplay, Alec Coppel, Samuel Taylor, based on novel, "D'Entre Les Morts," by Pierre Boileau, Thomas Narcejec; camera (Technicolor), Robert Burks; editor, George Tomasini; music, Bernard Herrmann. Previewed in San Francisco, May 9, '58. Running time, **126 MINS.**

Scottie .... James Stewart
Madeleine and Judy .... Kim Novak
Midge .... Barbara Bel Geddes
Gavin Elster .... Tom Helmore
Official .... Henry Jones
Doctor .... Raymond Bailey
Manageress .... Ellen Corby
Pop Leibel .... Konstantin Shayne
Mistaken Identity .... Lee Patrick

"Vertigo" is prime though uneven Hitchcock and with the potent marquee combination of James Stewart and Kim Novak should prove to be a highly profitable enterprise at the boxoffice.

Stewart, on camera almost constantly throughout the film's 126 minutes, comes through with a startlingly fine performance as the lawyer-cop who suffers from acrophobia—that is, vertigo or dizziness in high places.

Miss Novak, shopgirl who involves Stewart in what turns out to be a clear case of murder, is interesting under Hitchcock's direction and nearer an actress than she was in either "Pal Joey" or "Jeanne Eagles."

Unbilled, but certainly a prime factor in whatever success film may have, is the city of San Francisco, which has never been photographed so extensively and in such exquisite color as Robert Burks and his crew have here achieved.

Through all of this runs Hitchcock's directorial hand, cutting, angling and gimmicking with mastery.

Unfortunately, even that mastery is not enough to overcome one major fault, for the plain fact is that the film's first half is too slow and too long. This may be because:

(1) Hitchcock became overly enamored with the vertiginous beauty of Frisco;

(2) Or the Alec Coppel-Samuel Taylor screenplay (from the novel, "D'Entre Les Morts" by Pierre Boileau and Thomas Narcejec) just takes too long to get off the ground.

Film opens with a rackling scene in which Stewart's acrophobia is explained: he hangs from top of a building in midst of chasing a robber over rooftops and watches a police buddy plunge to his death.

But for the next hour the action is mainly psychic, with Stewart hired by a rich shipbuilder to watch the shipowner's wife (Miss Novak) as she loses her mental moorings, attempts suicide and immerses herself in the gloomy maunderings of her mad great-grandmother. Stewart, of course, falls in love with her and eventually is lured to the high belltower of an old mission, San Juan Bautista, where his acrophobia prevents him from climbing high enough to stop the girl's suicide. Or so he thinks.

Stewart goes off his rocker and winds up in a mental institution. When he comes out, still a trifle unbalanced, he keeps hunting for girl who resembles dead girl, eventually finds her and, in a rip-snorting denouement, discovers he's been tricked—that this girl is, indeed, his supposedly dead mystery woman who, with the shipbuilder, played on Stewart's fear of height to allow the shipbuilder to push wife off the mission belltower.

Film's last minute, in which Stewart fights off acrophobia to drag Miss Novak to top of belltower, finds she still loves him and and then sees her totter and fall to her death through mortal fright of an approaching nun, is a spectacular scene, gorgeously conceived.

But by then more than two hours have gone by, and it's questionable whether that much time should be devoted to what is basically only a psychological murder mystery.

Supporting players are all excellent, with Barbara Bel Geddes, in limited role of Stewart's down-to-earth girl friend, standout for providing early dashes of humor.

Tom Helmore, as rich shipbuilder, is a convincing heavy, and Henry Jones has one memorable, lifelike scene as the official presiding at a coroner's inquest. Raymond Bailey, Ellen Corby, Konstantin Shayne and Lee Patrick handle lesser roles competently.

Bernard Herrmann's music, conducted by Muir Mathieson overseas, is properly atmospheric and Hal Pereira-Henry Bumstead art direction, plus photographic effects of John P. Fulton, Farciot Edouart and Wallace Kelley, superb. Other technical credits, especially Saul Bass titles and John Ferren's special sequence, are tops, too.

Frisco location scenes—whether of Nob Hill, interior of Ernie's restaurant, Land's End, downtown, Muir Woods, Mission Dolores or San Juan Bautista—are absolutely authentic and breathtaking. But these also tend to intrude on story line too heavily, giving a travelogueish effect at times.

Despite this defect, "Vertigo" looks like a winner at the boxoffice as solid entertainment in the Hitchcock tradition. *Stef.*

Hot Spell
(VISTAVISION)

Performances top thin material. Good cast has hard going. Pale prognosis.

Hollywood, May 13.

Paramount release of Hal B. Wallis production. Stars Shirley Booth, Anthony Quinn, Shirley MacLaine, Earl Holliman; features Eileen Heckart, Clint Kimbrough, Warren Stevens, Jody Lawrance, Harlan Warde, Valerie Allen. Directed by Daniel Mann. Screenplay, James Poe, based upon a play by Lonnie Coleman; camera, Loyal Griggs; editor, Warren Low; music, Alex North. Previewed at Academy Awards Theatre May 12, '58. Running time, **88 MINS.**

Alma Duval .... Shirley Booth
Jack Duval .... Anthony Quinn
Virginia Duval .... Shirley MacLaine
Puddy Duval .... Earl Holliman
Fan .... Eileen Heckart
Billy Duval .... Clint Kimbrough
Wyatt .... Warren Stevens
Dora May .... Jody Lawrance
Harry .... Harlan Warde
Ruby .... Valerie Allen
Baggage Man .... Stafford Repp
Essie Mae .... Irene Tedrow
Attendant .... Bill Walker
Colored Woman .... Louise Franklin
Preacher .... Anthony Jochim
Colored Man .... Johnny Lee
Librarian .... Elsie Waller
Pool Player .... Len Hendry
Pool Player .... John Indrisano
Funeral Car Driver .... Watson H. Downs
Conductor .... William Duray
Bit Man .... Tony Merrill
Bit Man .... Fred Zendar

Hal Wallis' "Hot Spell" is a somewhat passive account of a violent summer in the life of a family of Deep South. Locale has no particular significance since regional problems are not explored. As drama, Paramount presentation directed by Daniel Mann is satisfactory although highpowered cast headed by Shirley Booth and Anthony Quinn plus Shirley MacLaine and Earl Holliman for younger set may mean okay boxoffice.

Miss Booth plays dreamy mother of three children, impersonated by MacLaine, Holliman and Clint Kimbrough, and is estranged wife of Quinn. She's not part of any of their loves mostly because she's living in past that never existed. Quinn's cheating with younger woman but wife won't admit she knows this. Booth exclaims at one point, "Once we all were part of each other . . . but now we're all pulling in different directions." She believes if they just return to small town where she and Quinn started life and where children were born they'll recapture.

Family goes back to small town at end, but with Quinn's body to bury it, after he's been killed in accident running away with girl friend. Only then does Booth concede you can't go back.

James Poe's screenplay based on play "Next of Kin" by Lonnie Coleman possesses moody atmospheric character study quality but lacks poetic feeling or climactic situations necessary for big impact. There's no attempt to convey Southern accent and thus orientate story regionally. There's one fine scene, mildly drunken sequence between Miss Booth and Eileen Heckart, latter neighborly adviser, which these two pros play to high point of low comedy.

Some of scenes play as if transplanted directly from stage. One long one between Quinn and Kimbrough is seen by camera from same position throughout when minimum of cutting would've livened tempo, deepened feeling and increased total impact. Mann's direction is notable on individual scenes and characters, but scenes don't add up to impressive whole.

Star gives material everything which means fine technique. She's most effective when holding camera alone and with gentle glow and incomparable deportment suffuses pedestrian lines. Quinn's handicapped in interpretation by single dimensional almost unrelievedly unsympathetic character capable of arousing no genuine concern. MacLaine, Holliman, Kimbrough and Warren Stevens do well despite insufficiently conceived roles. Miss Heckart is a standout and welcome value in her brief appearance.

Loyal Griggs' camera conveys feeling of brooding "Hot Spell" although significance of this title is never clear. Other technical credits excellent. Alex North's musical scores a haunting poignant threnody that, like some of the acting, embroiders essentially thin material with fabric and meaning. *Powe.*

Case Against Brooklyn

Well-made crime melodrama. No names, but can be good exploitation or program item.

Hollywood, May 9.

Columbia release of a Charles H. Schneer production. Stars Darren McGavin, Maggie Hayes; features Warren Stevens, Peggy McCay, Tol Avery, Emile Meyer, Nestor Paiva, Brian Hutton, Robert Osterloh, Joseph Turkel, Bobby Helms. Directed by Paul Wendkos. Screenplay, Raymond T. Marcus; screenstory, Daniel B. Ullman; based on an article in True magazine by Ed Reid; camera, Fred Jackman; music, Mischa Bakaleinikoff; editor, Edwin Bryant. Previewed at the studio, May 8, '58. Running time, **82 MINS**

Pete Harris .... Darren McGavin
Lil Polombo .... Maggie Hayes
Rudi Franklin .... Warren Stevens
Jane Harris .... Peggy McCay
Michael W. Norris .... Tol Avery
Captain P. T. Wills .... Emile Meyer
Finelli .... Nestor Paiva
Jess Johnson .... Brian Hutton
Bonney .... Robert Osterloh
Monte .... Joseph Turkel
Edmondson .... Thomas B. Henry
Mrs. Carney .... Cheerio Meredith
Bobby Helms .... Himself

A great many people in different parts of the country—perhaps the world—may have their own ideas on what "The Case Against Brooklyn" is, but the meaning of the title in the case of this Columbia Pictures presentation is a legal one. The Charles H. Schneer production, directed by Paul Wendkos, is based on the true story of the situation in the New York borough when book-makers corrupted a frightened portion of the police force. Although the ground has been covered before, this is a good melodrama, suspenseful, well-plotted and well-acted. It does not have the names to make it a top attraction but it could be exploited for good returns.

Darren McGavin plays a new graduate of the police training school who is put into under-cover work to try to ferret out the tenacles of the book-making ring that is buying off the police. Taking an apartment in a section of the city that seems particularly wide open, he meets and courts Maggie Hayes, whose husband has committed suicide because he could not pay off threatening bookies. The plot is thickened on one level because McGavin already has a wife, Peggy McCay, and on another when his rescue from thugs depends upon the precinct captain, Emile Meyer, who is on the take from the same mobsters. The conclusion pulls few punches. McGavin's friend and fellow cop, Brian Hutton is killed; his wife, Miss McCay, is blown to bits, and he winds up in the hospital.

Raymond T. Marcus' screenplay, based on a screen story by Daniel B. Ullman, which in turn came from a True magazine article by Brooklyn Eagle reporter Ed Reid, is sensible in emphasizing the mechanics of book-making and police detection. It is also strong in setting up and making recognizable characters of the many who people the story.

Darren McGavin (tv's Mike Hammer) does a capable job as the beleaguered cop, and other contribute include Miss Hayes, Warren Stevens, Miss McCay, Tol Avery and Meyer. Veteran character actress Cheerio Meredith pops on the screen in a bit that bursts with vitality and humor, the latter quality something the picture could have had more of.

Wendko's direction is well-paced and Fred Jackman's photography makes the backlot photography look like Brooklyn locations.
Powe.

Maracaibo

Cornel Wilde as producer, director and co-star (with Jean Wallace). Well-paced combination of romance and adventure revolving about the hazards of offshore (Venezuela) oil drillings; rates attention for many "A" situations.

Paramount release of Cornel Wilde production. Stars Wilde, Jean Wallace. Features Abbe Lane, Francis Lederer, Michael Landon. Directed by Wilde. Screenplay, Ted Sherdeman; from novel by Sterling Silliphant; camera, Ellsworth Fredricks; editor, Everett Douglas; music, Laurindo Almeida. Tradeshown in N.Y., April 30, '58. Running time. 88 MINS

Vic Scott .... Cornel Wilde
Laura Kingsley .... Jean Wallace
Elena Holbrook .... Abbe Lane
Miguel Orlando .... Francis Lederer
Lago .... Michael Landon

In an industry becoming accustomed to so many super efforts, "Maracaibo" would seem hardly to rate the "A" classification. Player names are short of overpowering and production values, while good, aren't blockbuster.

With what the picture isn't out of the way, on to what it is. It is a

---

well-turned tale of romance and action having to do with a treacherous offshore oilwell fire in Maracaibo, Venezuela, and the people who come together to either extinguish the oil blaze or ignite romantic ones.

Screenplay by Ted Sherdeman, from a Sterling Silliphant novel, as produced and directed by Cornel Wilde has sufficient elements of excitement, along with sharp dialog, to warrant bookings above the level of just the dual policy houses —that is, it's a fair enough bet for a good part of the "A" exhibition outlets.

Triple-threat man Wilde, considering him as director, has done a competent job of providing action in a steady flow, whether it's actor Wilde looking to elbow up to Jean Wallace for the love of it, or to that gusher of fire in the sea for the reason that there's hardly another man who can do the job of putting it out.

Producer Wilde has provided some interesting and colorful Caracas and Maracaibo settings that do, indeed, provide the necessary authenticity to the physical production.

Miss Wallace (Mrs. Wilde in real life) comes across all right as the successful novelist who, upon a Caracas encounter, tries to remain aloof to Wilde because of his reputation as femme conqueror, but then joins him in the hasty flight to Maracaibo as enchantment sets in.

Abbe Lane (now on Broadway in the "Oh, Captain" legiter) has a featured spot as a tramp. At least, that's the way Wilde describes her because of her love-'em-and-leave-'em escapades of the past, including one involving the embittered Wilde. She's on hand as the fiance of wealthy Francis Lederer, whose oil wells include the one that's ablaze and liable to explode all over Maracaibo any minute.

Miss Lane is the sexy dish, and from any perspective. Registers fair, too, with the dialog demands. Lederer plays as a mute in a story angle that doesn't have any particular meaning but it's a sympathetic role that can't be complained about too much.

Michael Landon comes through appealingly as Lederer's aide and medium of communication; Joe E. Ross provides the standardized "character" to a guy-from-Brooklyn role and lesser parts are handled well enough by Jack Kosslyn, Lillian Buyeff and George Ramsey. Martin Vargas is on view as a flamenco dancer, which is his specialty, and other hotsy but brief Latino terp calisthenics can be glimpsed in the background for color effect.

Fitting musical score came from Laurindo Almeida, Ellsworth Fredricks' camera work and the other technical credits all good, but perhaps with a special nod to Sam Comer and Grace Gregary for the set decoration in the scenes laid in Lederer's manse.
Gene.

War of the Satellites

Confusing space action melo, to go out with "Attack of the 50 Foot Woman."

Hollywood, May 8.
Allied Artists release of Roger Corman production. coproducers, Jack Rabin, Irving Block. Stars Dick Miller, Susan Cabot, Richard Devon; features Eric Sinclair. Michael Fox, Robert Shayne, Jerry Barclay. Directed by Corman. Screenplay, Lawrence Louis Goldman. from story by Block, Rabin; camera, Floyd Crosby; editor, Irene Morra; music. Walter Greene. Previewed May 6, '58. Running time 66 MINS.

Dave Boyer .... Dick Miller
Sybil Carrington .... Susan Cabot
Dr. Van Pander .... Richard Devon
Dr. Lazar .... Eric Sinclair
Akad .... Michael Fox
Hodgkiss .... Robert Shayne
John .... Jerry Barclay
Jay .... Jay Saver
Mitzi .... Mitzi McCall
Crew Members .... John Brinkley.
                         Beech Dickerson

"War of the Satellites" is a lesser entry for the exploitation market, where it will be packaged with "Attack of the 50 Foot Woman" by Allied Artists, also on weak side. Plot built around a United Nations satellite program is so contrived and confusing it misses fire completely.

Over-talkative-script by Lawrence Louis Goldman. leaving audience unenlightened through most of film's rambling unfoldment. deals with UN attempts to send human-cargoed rockets into space. and an inpenetrable barrier set up by minds from outer space to prevent this. Earth is warned it will be destroyed if it continues project, and the scientist in charge of UN plan, killed in an auto accident, is returned to life as an instrument of outer space powers. He nearly is successful in causing another rocket to crash into the barrier, but is overcome by one of the crew.

Characters are so unrea' they are are mere walk-throughs. Richard Devon plays the scientist. Dick Miller the man who ostensibly saves rocket from destruction and Susan Cabot a mathematician, in for romantic interest. Roger Corman produced and directed, utilizing fewer special effects than are normal for a subject of this type. Technical credits are stock, Jack Rabin and Irving Block handling special effects; Floyd Crosby, camera; Dan Haller, art direction; Walter Greene, music.   *Whit.*

Attack of the 50 Foot Woman

Minor science fiction, packaged with "War of the Satellites."

Hollywood, May 8.
Allied Artists release of Bernard Woolner production. Stars Allison Hayes, William Hudson, Yvette Vickers; features Roy Gordon, George Douglas, Ken Terrell, Otto Waldis, Frank Chase. Directed by Nathan Hertz. Screenplay, Mark Hanna; camera, Jacques R. Marquette; editor, Edward Mann; music, Ronald Stein. Previewed May 6, '58. Running time, 65 MINS.

Nancy Archer .... Allison Hayes
Harry Archer .... William Hudson
Honey Parker .... Yvette Vickers
Dr. Cushing .... Roy Gordon
Sheriff Dubbitt .... George Douglas
Jessup Stout .... Ken Terrell
Dr. Von Loeb .... Otto Waldis
Nurse .... Eileen Stevens
Tony .... Mike Ross
Charlie .... Frank Chase

"Attack of the 50 Foot Woman" shapes up as a minor offering for the scifi trade where demands aren't too great. Film's title should help sell package in which it's paired with "War of the Satellites."

Bernard Woolner production is the story of a femme who overnight grows into a murderous giantess, out to get husband who's cheating with another woman. Growth was caused by ray burns suffered when she's seized by huge monster, who lands in the desert near home in a satellite from outer space. Breaking the chains used to restrain her in her luxurious mansion, she makes her way to a tavern where spouse is with his lady love and literally squeezes him to death before the sheriff kills her with a riot gun.

Allison Hayes takes over title role, as a mentally-disturbed

---

woman who has been in a sanitarium, William Hudson is the husband and Yvette Vickers his girl friend, all good enough in their respective characters. Nathan Hertz' direction is routine. up against considerable corny dialog in Mark Hanna's screenplay. Technical departments are well enough executed, including Jacques R. Marquette's photography and Ronald Stein's music score.
Whit.

Gigi

(MUSICAL—C'SCOPE—COLOR)

Gay 90s Gallic "Gigi" beaucoup b.o.

Metro release of Arthur Freed production. Stars Leslie Caron, Maurice Chevalier, Louis Jourdan; features Hermione Gingold, Eva Gabor, Jacques Bergerac. Directed by Vincente Minnelli. Screenplay and lyrics, Alan Jay Lerner (based on the novel by Colette); music, Frederick Loewe. Music Supervision, Andre Previn; orchestrations, Conrad Salinger; costumes and scenery, Cecil Beaton; art, William A. Horning & Preston Ames; camera (Metrocolor), Joseph Ruttenberg; asst. directors, William McGarry & William Shanks. Premiered reserved-seat policy May 15, '58, Royale, N.Y. Running time, **116 MINS.**

Gigi .... Leslie Caron
Honore Lachaille .... Maurice Chevalier
Gaston Lachaille .... Louis Jourdan
Mme. Alvarez .... Hermione Gingold
Liane D'Exelmans .... Eva Gabor
Sandomir .... Jacques Bergerac
Aunt Alicia .... Isabel Jeans
Manuel .... John Abbott

"Gigi" is destined for a global boxoffice mopup.

It has all the ingredients. It's a naughty but nice romp of the hyper-romantic naughty 90s of Paris-in-the-spring, in the Bois, in Maxim's, and in the boudoir. How can it miss?

Despite the sex and, to the credit of all concerned including the censorial authorities who abstained, it is replete with taste from its sartorial investiture to the ultimate histrionic performances.

Alan Jay Lerner's libretto is tailor-made for an inspired casting job for all principals, and Fritz Loewe's tunes (to Lerner's lyrics) already vie with and suggest their memorable "My Fair Lady" score.

"Gigi" is a French variation, by Colette, of the "Pygmalion" legend. The analogy of this tiptop Arthur Freed film production to Herman Levin's legit production of the Shavian source becomes increasingly apparent as the film unfolds. And, of course, the Lerner-Loewe association heightens the comparison as their compelling melodies punch over with pyramiding effect in the expert hands (and voices) of the cast (or their skillful vocal doubles). Just to complete the package Cecil Beaton's imaginative costumes, scenery and production design, which figured so importantly in "Lady," repeats in "Gigi." It's Beaton's Hollywood debut and Lerner - Loewe's first score post-"Fair Lady."

"Gigi" is 100% escapist fare and is a cinch for worldwide impact, probably including those territories not overly partial to musicals because, in this instance, it's fundamentally of a "foreign" pattern. The preoccupation of the French for the amour-amour department, both sexes, is an undeniable common denominator, and as Colette's character unfolds it is apparent that the hoydenish "Gigi" has a greater preoccupation with a wedding ring than casual, albeit supercharged romance.

The sophistications of Maurice Chevalier (who well nigh steals the picture), Isabel Jeans, Hermione Gingold and Eva Gabor are in contrast to the wholesomeness of the Leslie Caron-Louis Jourdan romance. Despite his plaintive "I'm Bored," one of the several tailormade lyrics that match the plot so well, his attachment for the blossoming "Gigi" is an intangible yet vibrant romance motivation.

Miss Caron is completely captivating and convincing in the title role. She is part of the illusion of the fin-de-siecle characters of the period whose volcanic peccadilloes highlighted the spice and gossip at Maxim's. Skillful casting, performance and presentation have endowed realism to the sum total. Even Betty Wand's vocal doubling for Miss Caron appears authentic, in fact a shade more than some of the synchronization by the others, Louis Jourdan for example.

The songs are already an LP delight and, with the film's extended circulation, bound to enhance in value as the celluloid characterizations project into the popular consciousness. The Maxim's waltz ("She Is Not Thinking Of Me") is Jourdan's vocal solo; he does "Bored" as a double with Chevalier and "The Night They Invented Champagne" with Miss Caron and Miss Gingold. Latter scores in a telling double-lyric with Chevalier, a nostalgic item titled "I Remember It Well," as she corrects the lothario's faltering romantic reminiscense. Chevalier is a standout in this and two solo opportunities which he milks to the last lyrical line—"I'm Glad I'm Not Young Any More" and "Thank Heaven For Little Girls," latter a delightful opener which also serves as the fadeout finale. "Young Any More" is an old roue of an uncle's philosophic summation of life lived to the fullest. Miss Caron's (Betty Wand's) solo is a paean of love and impatience with "The Parisians" and their predilections for toujours amour, and she thrushes "Say A Prayer For Me Tonight" as she decides to accept Jourdan's romantic if not altogether honorable proposal, preparatory to meeting him at Maxim's.

Produced in France, "Gigi" is steeped in authentic backgrounds from Maxim's to the Tuilleries, from the Bois de Boulogne to the Palais de Glace which sets the scene for Eva Gabor's philandering with Jacques Bergerac, her skating instructor and establishes the pattern of playing musical boudoirs, which was par for the circa 1890s Paris course.

The performances are well nigh faultless. From Chevalier, as the sophisticated uncle, to John Abbott, his equally suave valet; from Miss Gingold's understanding role as Gigi's grandma to Isabel Jeans, the worldly aunt who would tutor Gigi in the ways of demi-mondaine love; from Jourdan's eligibility as the swain to Bergerac's casual courting of light ladies' loves; from Eva Gabor's concept of said 1.1. to Miss Caron's sincere performance —all are ideal choices for their roles.

Miss Caron's London experience in the stage version of Colette's cocotte (Audrey Hepburn did it in the U.S.) stands her in excellent stead in her cinema concept. This marks her film return since "Lili." Jourdan, of course, is capital as the unwilling philanderer opposite her.

Director Minnelli's good taste in keeping it in bounds and the general sound judgment of all concerned—with full awareness that Lerner's excellent basic libretto dictated no other choice—distinguishes this Arthur Freed independent production. The Metrocolor rates recognition for its soft pastels under Joseph Ruttenberg's lensing; the Beaton costumes, sets and general production design are vivid physical assets at first sight. The skillful integration of words-and-music with the plot motivation makes this "Gigi" a very fair lady indeed as a boxoffice entry.

Abel.

Golfo

(Girl of the Mountains) (GREEK)

Greek Motion Pictures release of Finos Films production. Stars Antigoni Valakou, Nikos Kazis, Mimi Fotopoulos. Directed by Orestis Laskos. Screenplay by Laskos from story by Spyros Peresiadi; music, Ttkis Morekis. Tradeshown in N. Y. Running time, **90 MINS.**

Golfo .... Antigoni Valakou
Tassos .... Nikos Kazis
Stavroula .... Kyveli Theochari
Kitso .... Byron Pallis
Old Thanassoula .... Yorgos Glynos
Yanos .... Mimi Fotopoulos

(In Greek; English titles)

This is perhaps the best Greek feature to be unveiled in the U. S. to date. Screen vehicle has no complicated plot—it's simply boy meets girl. Variation here is that a wealthy dame, who is left out in the cold, decides to entice said boy away from the comely, if poor village maiden. Further complication is that the rich landowner also courts the comely lass. From this, a modern-dress Greek tragedy is developed. With a longrun record already marked up in Greece, this shapes surefire for Greek and some foreign-language houses here.

While there are moments of claimed comedy in this piece, plus an interlude with two Yank tourists, film essentially wrings tears. How well it succeeds, of course, is what gives it appeal to Greek situations. An added asset is the fact that it has been filmed in the mountain area of Helmos.

The hadnsome shepherd, Nikos Kazis, finally achieves his long-sought ambition—to wed the delectable shepherdess, Antigoni Valakou. This stems from the reward money he receives for rescuing the tourists. To revenge herself from some imaginary grievance, the rich girl, Kyvenli Theochari, then conspires to wean him away from the sweetheart with surprising results. Miss Valakou finally gets her boy friend back but unfortunately she has taken poison. When she dies, Kazis kills himself.

Miss Valakou is standout member of an excellent cast. Aside from her beauty and thespian ability, she has also an excellent voice. Kazis makes a stalwart lover while Miss Theochari is sufficiently vengeful to satisfy in a distasteful role. Mimi Fotopoulos, as the clowning shepherd and matchmaker, measures up to his previous performances though his rep in Greek films as the standout comedian becomes a bit annoying at times when he tries to theft every scene.

Orestis Laskos' screenplay takes advantage of every fresh slant Spyros Peresiadi has framed in his far from original story. Camera work is remarkably excellent for a black-and-white pic but the lensman is not credited. Takis Morekis' music makes for powerful backgrounding.

Wear.

The Vikings

(TECHNIRAMA—TECHNICOLOR)

Kirk Douglas' grandscale account of the fighting Norsemen of the 8th Century. Action is fierce and plentiful, photography exquisite. Popular appeal ingredients in abundance. Good outlook.

United Artists release of Kirk Douglas production (produced by Jerry Bresler) Stars Kirk Douglas, Tony Curtis, Ernest Borgnine, Janet Leigh; features James Donald, Alexander Knox, Frank Thring. Directed by Richard Fleischer. Screenplay, Calder Willingham, adaptation by Dale Wasserman from the Edison Marshall novel; camera (Technicolor), Jack Cardiff; editor, Hugo Williams; music, Mario Mascimbene. Previewed at Victoria Theatre, N. Y., May 9, '58. Running time **114 MINS.**

Einar .... Kirk Douglas
Eric .... Tony Curtis
Ragnar .... Ernest Borgnine
Morgana .... Janet Leigh
Egbert .... James Donald
Father Godwin .... Alexander Knox
Aella .... Frank Thring
Enid .... Maxine Audley
Kitala .... Eileen Way
Sandpiper .... Edric Connor
Bridget .... Dandy Nichols
Bjorm .... Per Buckhoj
Pigtails .... Almut Berg

"The Vikings" is spectacular, rousing and colorful. Blood flows freely as swords are crossed and arrows meet their mark in barbarian combat. And there's no hesitance about throwing a victim into a wolf pit or a pool of crabs.

Under Richard Fleischer's direction, the terror of the 8th and 9th centuries is communicated and this makes for audience excitement. The faint-of-heart many wince, but no one's likely to be bored. This story of the fearless and greatly-feared Norsemen, whose god is Odin and who thrive on battle conquests, is on the move all the way.

There is some complication at the start, however, as the various characters are brought into view—as the Vikings army of 200 raids the Kingdom of Northumbria, in England, and elements of mystery and intrigue are brought into the story. But it is not too long before Calder Wallingham's screenplay and director Fleischer have their people in clear focus and the basic plot and asides are then easy to follow.

History is highly fictionalized, subtleties are eschewed. It stars with a raid on one of the small kingdoms in England, the death of the English leader, the succession to the throne of Frank Thring who's strictly the heavy. The queen tells her confidante she is with child, the father being Ernest Borgnine, head of the marauding Vikings. To escape the new king's wrath she flees to another land and with the proper passage of time the child, now a young man, Tony Curtis, turns up in the Viking village as a slave whose identity is not known.

It is at this point that Curtis encounters Douglas, latter as heir to the Viking throne. Neither is aware of the fact that the other is his brother. They clash and Curtis directs his malicious trained bird to strike Douglas. Douglas becomes a grotesque figure, with one eye clawed out, and Curtis gets the crab pool punishment from which he miraculously escapes.

Janet Leigh participates as daughter of the king of Wales who is to be taken as a bride by the sadistic English king. But the marriage never comes off, for her ship is captured, overtaken by Douglas and she's taken into custody by the Vikings.

Douglas falls for Miss Leigh in a big way but she comes to favor Curtis, and thus is established the romantic triangle.

Yarn has many twists and turns; the foregoing outline ought to suffice. It's the production that counts and producer Jerry Bresler, working with Douglas' indie outfit, has done it up big and with apparent authenticity. Lensing was in the Norse fjord area and various parts of Europe, including the Bavarian Studios wh[illegible] facilities apparently are top qua[illegible]y in view of the type of picture that was accommodated.

Photography is standout in Technicolor and the Technirama widescreen process. Jack Cardiff's camera work has filled the screen with an enchanting beauty in capturing the little fleet of Viking ships at sea. The lighting and coloring are subdued and remarkably effective. The battle scenes are striking, although some of the closeups may seem to some observers as placing too much emphasis on the gore.

Douglas, doing a bangup, freewheeling job as the ferocious and disfigured Viking fighter, fits the part splendidly. Borgnine's Viking chief is equally convincing. He's a conqueror of authority. Curtis, as the bearded slave who's to become a ruler, handles the assignment with sufficient competence, playing it out with more restraint than Douglas. Miss Leigh would have benefitted from some emotional charging-up, what with a couple of armies fighting for her. Thring, James Donald and Alexander Knox contribute good feature-role work.

All in all a rousing, adventure special. Music provides lively backstopping without being too intrusive, the editing is sufficiently sharp for the most part and other technical credits are top-notch.

Gene.

Unseen Heroes
(BRITISH)

Straightforward war adventure about the planning of flying bombs; has fair measure of thrills and sound all-round acting.

London, May 13.

Eros release of a John Bash (George Maynard) production. Stars Michael Rennie, Patricia Medina, Milly Vitale, David Knight. Directed by Vernon Sewell. Screenplay, Jack Hanley and Eryk Wlodek from book by Bernard Newell; camera, Basil Emmott; editor, Lito Carruthers; music, Robert Sharples. At Warwick Private Theatre, London. Running time, 104 MINS.
Stefan	Michael Rennie
Zofia	Patricia Medina
Anna	Milly Vitale
Tadek	David Knight
Stricker	Esmond Knight
Brunner	Christopher Lee
Fritz	John G. Heller
General	Carl Jaffe
Stanislaw	Peter Madden
Karewski	George Pravda
Margraaf	Gordon Sterne
Scientist	Carl Duering
W. Com. Searby	Harold Siddone
Eryk	George Pastell
Konim	Henry Vidom
Kubala	Stanley Zevic
Franus	Gregory Dark
Wlodek	Jan Conrad
Anton	Tom Clegg
Dakota Pilot	Robert Raikes
Forewoman	Valerie White
Min. of Defense	Geoffrey Chater
Himmler	Julian Somers

"Unseen Heroes" is the negative title chosen for the Yank presentation of "They Saved London," a true-life war adventure concerning Hitler's secret weapon, the V.1. missile. It is a straightforward account of how the Polish underground movement helped to delay the planned Nazi attacks and enable Britain to prepare to meet the menace which Hitler hoped to crush her overnight. With well-known and competent actors rather than stars, the pic must depend largely on its theme for appeal. It will have considerable curiosity attraction in the U.K. but is less likely to intrigue U.S. patrons.

The film is set in Warsaw back in 1942. Michael Rennie and David Knight are the two Poles rounded up for forced labor. They are sent to work on a large secret construction site, at Peenemunde. It is obviously a top-secret experimental station and their job is to find out what's going on and get the information to Britain via the Polish underground.

They discover the new form of missile which is being manufac-

tured. As a result the RAF plans a mass bombing raid which obliterates the factory. Rennie and Knight escape and set about the task of capturing an intact flying bomb to help British scientists in their task. The Poles try to ambush a lorry transporting one of the V.I's but are beaten off by the Nazis. Some weeks later a flying bomb crashes in a field and fails to explode. The Poles secrete the Bomb, smuggle it to Britain.

"Unseen Heroes" has several episodes of considerable tension. The bombing raid on Peenemunde is exceptionally well done with an adroit use of newsreel shots interwoven. There is also excitement as Knight and Rennie tackle the dangerous job of defusing the flying bomb's warhead. As so often happens in these underground films the heroes seem to be given overmuch and over convenient room to go about their business considering that it is being done in occupied territory. But this is a sound, absorbing adventure yarn, exceptionally well photographed by Basil Emmott and directed with a sure touch of Vernon Sewell.

Rennie and Knight are thoroughly credible as the heroes, especially in the concentration camp sequences. Patricia Medina, as Rennie's wife, joins in the adventures with an impeccable hairdo, a brave smile and a camera. Milly Vitale, as a Polish girl, has one very good scene when she is captured and tortured to death.

The director falls into the trap of allowing all his Nazis to be either exaggerated brutes or nitwits but the use of a large number of Polish actors insures that the local atmosphere is retained faithfully. The American version is shorter than that designed for U.K. consumption but even so there are a few static scenes which would have benefitted from more ruthless editing.

Rich.

The Old Man and the Sea
(COLOR)

Hemingway's Life Mag novelette tackled in offbeat style. Top lensing can't hide thinness of basic material. Should click with special handling.

Warner Bros. release of Leland Hayward production. Stars Spencer Tracy; features Felipe Pazos, Harry Bellaver. Directed by John Sturges. Script, Peter Viertel, from Ernest Hemingway novel of same title; camera (Warnercolor), James Wong Howe; additional photography by Floyd Crosby, Tom Tutwiler; music, Dimitri Tiomkin; editor, Arthur P. Schmidt. Previewed in N.Y., April 30, '58. Running time, 86 MINS.
The Old Man	Spencer Tracy
The Boy	Felipe Pazos
Martin	Harry Bellaver

Credit Warner Bros. and producer Leland Hayward with a surplus of guts for tackling Ernest Hemingway's introspective one-episode novelette, "The Old Man and the Sea." This very decidedly isn't the stuff ordinary films are made of, and the picture version of this minor classic represents a bold attempt to do what some probably would have termed "the impossible."

This is virtually a one-character film, the spotlight being almost continuously on Spencer Tracy as the old Cuban fisherman who meets his final test in his tremendous struggle with the huge marlin. The picture has power, vitality and sharp excitement as it depicts the gruelling contest between man and fish. It has been exquisitely photographed and skillfully directed. It captures the dignity and the

stubborness of the old man, and it is tender in his final defeat.

And yet "Old Man and the Sea" isn't a completely satisfying picture. There are long and arid stretches, when it seems as if producer and director were merely trying to fill time. The eye grows tired of the man and the sea, and eventually even of the fish. The sharks once too often and the recurring dream sequences lose their impact.

This being an age when "offbeat" seems to carry boxoffice value, "Old Man and the Sea" may break through, particularly if it's handled as offbeat adventure drama. Fact that it's based on the Hemingway story should carry weight with the eggheads, while the fishermen in the audience certainly will get their fill and thrill. Unquestionably, there will be those who'll be bored. And then there'll be as many who will gasp at the cinematic values of this film and enjoy it completely.

Perhaps it should be mentioned, too, that this is likely to be a "critics' picture." It has artistic integrity and it certainly captures the essence of the book, though some may argue that this film proves that the screen has a certain responsibility to itself, i.e. that it can go too far in borrowing from other media and neglecting its own requirements. Word pictures, with their intermingling of thoughts and description, are a lot easier to paint, and they tend to hold the reader's attention a lot longer, than those same images on a screen. This is the great weakness of "The Old Man and the Sea," and it is one which simply could not be overcome.

This, of course, is Tracy's picture from beginning to end. One could quarrel with his interpretation of the old man. There are moments when he is magnificent and moving, and others when he seems to move in a stupor. It is, on the whole, a distinguished and impressive performance, ranging from the old man's pursuit of the fish, to hooking him, to the long chase and the final slashing battle. And then the heartbreaking road back, when the sharks devour and destroy the prize until nothing much more than a glistening skeleton is left. This is one of those solo acts performers presumably dream about and Tracy is up to the chore. His old man is weary and heartbroken, his eyes glazed with tiredness, but he still has the strength to look to the future, even as he dreams of the past.

In a supporting part, Felipe Pazos plays the boy who loves the old man and understands him. It is a very appealing and tender performance. Harry Bellaver has a small role as the tavern owner who sympathizes with the old man and, with the rest of the village, learns to admire him for his catch.

Peter Viertel's adaptation of the Hemingway book is a very good job within the prescribed limits. He gets around one of the prime difficulties by having Tracy narrate part of the story off-screen, slipping every so often into actual dialog. The narration helps catch the Hemingway flavor, which is nourished further by the topnotch lensing of James Wong Howe. The vet cameraman outdoes himself on this one and many of the film's values must be attributed directly to his work.

Additional camerawork was done by Floyd Crosby and Tom Tutwiler. The camera generates excitement and the shots of the hooked marlin slashing on the sur-

face are cleverly integrated. Also, the underwater shots of Lamar Boren, picturing the sharks tearing away at the dead fish, add to the realism. Warnercolor adds to the magnificence of Howe's photography.

John Sturges directs with a view to keeping the essential values intact. It's not his fault that the basic material simply doesn't sustain interest throughout 86 minutes of pictures. Dimitri Tiomkin wrote and conducted the score, which is massive and at times distinctive. This is one of those pictures where the music is of more than ordinary importance.

Arthur P. Schmidt's editing cleverly integrates special footage and keeps everything moving as much as possible.

Producer Hayward, who did some pioneering in the direction of the "offbeat" via "The Spirit of St. Louis," seems to have a penchant for picking difficult themes. But he has turned out a film that, in many ways, is extraordinary. Whether the broad audience will go for Tracy on his lonely voyage, battling a huge fish with nary a female leg in sight, remains to be seen and proably depends to some extent on how the picture is sold. It certainly isn't anything the ladies are likely to flip over, unless they have learned to enjoy seeing hungry men cutting up raw fish and eating it.

But audiences have come a ways in recent years, and "Old Man and the Sea" might well shape as a strong entry. It certainly is a composite—technically and artistically —of some of the best Hollywood has to offer.

Hift.

Voice in the Mirror
(C'SCOPE)

Good but long story of an alcoholic. Richard Egan and Julie London brighten prospects.

Hollywood May 16.

Universal release of a Gordon Kay production. Stars Richard Egan, Julie London; co-stars Walter Matthau, Arthur O'Connell; with Troy Donahue, Harry Bartell, Peggy Converse, Ann Doran, Mae Clarke, Casey Adams, Hugh Sanders, Ken Lynch, Doris Singleton, Dave Barry, Alan Dexter, Richard Hale. Directed by Harry Keller. Screenplay, Larry Marcus; camera, William Daniels; editor, George Gittens; music, Henry Mancini. Previewed May 14, '58. Running time, 105 MINS.
Jim Burton	Richard Egan
Ellen Burton	Julie London
William Tobin	Arthur O'Connell
Doctor Leon Karnes	Walter Matthau
Paul Cunningham	Troy Donahue
Harry Graham	Harry Bartell
Paul's Mother	Peggy Converse
Mrs. Devlin	Ann Doran
Mrs. Robbins	Mae Clarke
Don Martin	Casey Adams
Mr. Hornsby	Hugh Sanders
Bartender	Ken Lynch
Liz	Doris Singleton
Pianist	Dave Barry
Bartender	Alan Dexter
Gaunt Man	Richard Hale

"Voice in the Mirror," a fully detailed account of what anonymously appears to be the birth of Alcoholics Anonymous, is a hard-hitting film that belabors but nonetheless makes good its point: Only a drunk can help a drunk. The names of Richard Egan and Julie London will add a spirit or two for this Universal production, and overall sales prospects loom above satisfactory.

There is no specific mention of AA in the Larry Marcus screenplay, though there can be little doubt what is being described. Egan, following the death of his infant daughter, has become an alcoholic, and no amount of understanding and help from wife Julie London has been able to set him straight. Neither have the call-to-reform harangues from his doctor (Walter Matthau). Landing in the city drunk tank, Egan meets a trumpet-playing alcoholic who once stayed sober for 20 months on spiritual help alone. Egan is unreceptive to this theory and heads straight to the nearest bar but later, finding his drinking has caused nerve damage, he is shocked into wanting out. In his search he finds Arthur O'Connell, a former arithmetic teacher on a 14-year bender, and the men find they can help each other stay away from whisky.

Egan's portrayal is a powerful one, and though he isn't given the histrionic chance to shake the DT's in all their dramatic splendor, he does paint a most convincing picture of the alcoholic who wants to stop drinking. Miss London, her sensuous beauty, keeping things alive, sings smoothly over the main titles, then concentrates on straight acting which, she proves, she can handle with talent and ease. O'Connell is touching as Egan's imbibing friend, and Matthau is exceptionally strong as hte doctor. Good support comes from Harry Bartell, Ann Doran, Troy Donahue and Doris Singleton.

This Gordon Kay production benefits from the sensation of realism grabbed in downtown Los Angeles, mostly on Main Street. Harry Keller's direction is potent, with vigorous performances the result. He carefully moves the long but good Marcus screenplay through the battle of alcoholism and to the lofty victory.

The whole story was capably photographed by William Daniels, and other assists came from composer Henry Mancini, art directors Alexander Golitzen and Richard H. Riedel, soundmen Leslie I. Carey and Robert Pritchard and film editor George Gittens.

Titie song, with words and music by Miss London and Bobby Troup, isn't likely to raise much interest. But the framed motto which ends the film is always worthy of note: "God grant the serenity to accept the things I cannot change; the courage to change the things I can; and the wisdom to know the difference." *Ron.*

Up the Creek
(BRITISH—HAMMERSCOPE)

Lively naval comedy registering excellent quota of yocks; cheerful b.o. prospects for family audiences.

London, May 13.

Warner release of a (Henry Ralsted) Byron production. Stars David Tomlinson, Peter Sellers. Directed by Val Guest. Screenplay, Val Guest; camera, Moray Grant; music, Tony Fones, Tony Lowry. At Warner Theatre, London. Running time, **86 MINS.**

Lieut. Fairweather	David Tomlinson
Bosun	Peter Sellers
Admiral Foley	Wilfrid Hyde White
Loly	Vera Day
Susanne	Liliane Sottance
Flag Lieut.	Tom Gill
Nelson	Michael Goodliffe
Publican	Reginald Beckwith
Perkins	Lionel Murton
Cooky	John Warren
Steady Barker	Lionel Jeffries
Bates	Sam Kydd
Stationmaster	Frank Pettingell
Farm Laborer	Donald Bisset

"Up The Creek" is an amiable navy farce, which rates a fair measure of guffaws, but often has its slim joke stretched to the breaking point. It makes up in good humor what it lacks in wit. But there are a sufficient number of slaphappy situations to make it a good bet for most U.K. houses. Its Yank problem is whether the stars, David Tomlinson and Peter Sellers, are sufficiently known to lure patrons. Directed by Val Guest at a swift pice, it manages to skate rather successfully over its occasional soggy patches.

The joke has David Tomlinson as a dim-witted navy officer with a passion for inventing rocket missiles which explode inconveniently. He is posted out of harm's way as commanding officer of an ancient destroyer which is sitting on a remote part of the British coast.

For two years, it has been without a boss and the bosun, played exuberantly by Peter Sellers, has set up the ship as a base for H.M.S. Berkeley Enterprises. These involve a one-day laundry service, eggs from chickens kept on the bridge, paint sold at cut prices to the village plus various other ways of supplementing his earnings. By the time Tomlinson discovers the shenanigans he is himself involved, and the pic finishes with a crazy inspection by an admiral which winds up haphazardly if hilariously.

The cast play this tiny anecdote for laughs and get them effortlessly. Tomlinson, Sellers and Wilfrid Hyde-White head a cast which is experienced in making a jest look like a full-powered joke. Tom Gill, Lilliane Sottane, Reginald Beckwith and Lionel Jeffries also land a slick hand in keeping this genial frivolity bubbling. Mostly, however, "Up the Creek" depends on a ripe and fruity performance by tv and radio comedian Peter Sellers and it is somewhat disconcerting to find that a sequel, "Further Up The Creek," has been started without Sellers, who has another engagement. **This may well press the luck of the producers a shade too far.**

Moray Grant's lensing is adequate. Technical adviser is Lieutenant-Commander J. H. Puller of the Royal Navy who, without any doubt, has cut himself off from any further diplomatic relations with the Admiralty. ***Rich.***

Cannes Festival

Letiat Jouravly
(Flying Cranes)
(RUSSIAN)

Cannes, May 13.

Mosfilm release and production. Stars Tatiana Samoilova, Alexis Batalov; features V. Merkouriev, A. Chvorine, S. Kharitonova. Directed by Mikhail Kalatozov. Screenplay, Victor Rosov; camera, Serge Ouroussevski; editor, E. Svidetelev, At Cannes Film Fest. Running time, **90 MINS.**

Veronique	Tatiana Samoilova
Boris	Alexis Batalov
Fyodor	V. Merkouriev
Marc	A. Chvorine
Irina	S. Kharitonova

Film has been taken for U.S. distrib already by Ilya Lopert and United Artists as part of a "barter" deal. For the Russians the film is a stride forward with no propaganda and evoking a moving tale of a tender love affair shattered by the war.

Technically and thespically excellent, this appears a logical release to start Russo-Yank exchanges. Its bravura is sometimes too flashy, but the sensitivity of portrayals, lift this over-contrived plot on to a poignant level.

A pair of young lovers are split by the war. He loses touch with her and she is seduced by his brother on a raging, bomb-torn night. They marry but she still keeps her feelings for her absent lover. Story details the lives on the home front, with its heroisms and shirkings, and the war front. The boy is killed but the girl finally has the courage to leave her callow husband and embrace life again.

Virile sometimes overboard direction nonetheless brings out intelligent acting by Tatiana Samoilova, and Alexis Batalov. *Mosk.*

Mon Oncle
(My Uncle)
(FRENCH; COLOR)

Cannes, May 16.

Gaumont release of Specta-Gray-Alter Film production. Written by, directed by, and starring Jacques Tati; technical assistants, Jean L'Hote, Jacques La Grange, Camera (Eastmancolor), Jean Bourgoin; editor, Suzanne Baron; music, Alain Romans, Franck Barcellini. At Cannes Film Fest. Running time, **120 MINS.**

Uncle Hulot	Jacques Tati
Arpel	Jean-Pierre Zola
Mrs. Arpel	Adrienne Servanti
Gerard	Alain Becourt

Somewhat long for a comedy, Jacques Tati's new film has inventiveness, gags, warmth and a "poetic" approach to satire. Tati has succeded in creating his own world on the screen. He is a truly original screen artist.

"My Uncle" is a definite U.S. art house bet with Tati's previous pic, "Mr. Hulot's Holiday," and his Yank video appearances, helping set it up.

Film took two years to make. Tati has built film via comic juxtaposition of two ways of life, his, as the eccentric, independent uncle, alongside a super-modern, hygienic, materialistic brother-in-law.

There are scenes that could be sheared to speed it up for more general Yank distribution. An English version has already been made which is nine minutes shorter.

Antiseptic house of Hulot's relatives operates a myriad of timesaving but noisy electronic gadgets. Tati is the catalyst who unintentionally creates havoc. He wins over his nephew whose parents have no time for him and who is only really happy during the wonderful escapades he has with his uncle. But Tati is finally sent off to be a traveling representative of the brother-in-law's firm while father and son are finally brought closer by what they have learned from the uncle.

Satire is not barbed or vicious and everybody can laugh at it and themselves. Expert blocking out of characters, the creative use of sound, and the eschewing of all useless dialog should make it a film with international utility. *Mosk.*

Nara Livet
(Brink of Life)
(SWEDISH)

Cannes, May 16.

Nordisk Tonefilm release and production. Stars Eva Dahlbeck, Ingrid Thulin, Bibi Anderson; features, Barbro Hiort Af Ornas, Erland Josephson, Max Von Sydow, Gunnar Sjouberg. Directed by Ingmar Bergman. Screenplay, Ulla Isaksson; camera, Max Wilen; editor, Carl-Olov Skeppstedt. At Cannes Film Fest. Running time, **83 MINS**

Stina	Eva Dahlbeck
Cecilia	Ingrid Thulin
Hjordis	Bibi Andersson
Brita	Barbro Hiort Af Ornas
Anders	Erland Josephson
Harry	Max Von Sydow
Doctor	Gunnar Sjoberg

Clinical tale stays in a hospital with three expectant mothers, one who wants and eventually loses her child, one who does not want it and has tried an abortion, and the other who has had a miscarriage. Emphasis on the physical aspects, with a neglecting of a humanizing influence, limit this for U.S., but it might be exploitable on its frankness and theme.

Director Ingmar Bergman has kept the film caged in the hospital with some occasional visits as the backgrounds of the protagonists are blocked out. The climax is the agony of the one woman who truly wants her baby leading to the acceptance of hers by the unwed girl. Acting is expert but characters are conventional.

Technical credits are expert and the deft observations make the lack of music a plus factor. *Mosk.*

Parash Pathar
(The Philosopher's Stone)
(INDIAN)

Cannes, May 13.

L. B. International release and production. With Tulsi Shakraverty, Ranibala, Kali Banerji, Gangapada Besu. Directed by Satyajit Ray. Screenply, Ray from the novel by Parasurum; camera, Subrata Mitra; editor, Dulal Dutta. At Cannes Film Fest. Running time, **90 MINS.**

Paresh Dutt	Tulsi Chakraverty
Mrs. Dutt	Ranibala
Biswas	Kali Banerji
Kachalu	Gangapada Basu

Director Satyajit Ray has won two major prizes at both the Cannes and Venice Festivals with first two of a trilogy on Indian life. He interrupted the trio to make this lightweight comedy. It emerges an uneven bit of whimsy which does not come off, and looks chancey for any possibilities outside of its native country.

An aging clerk finds a stone that can turn things to gold. He makes enough to live comfortably, but one day gives things away when he is snubbed at a cocktail party. Then comes a gold panic, arrest and final absolution when a lovesick clerk swallows the magic stone to commit suicide and it dissolves and turns the gold back to stone.

Ray has given story a bright beginning, but then let it flatten out. Technical credits and acting are good. A near-miss. *Mosk.*

Ni Liv
(Nine Lives)
(NORWEGIAN)

Cannes, May 13.

Nord Film release and production. Stars Jack Fjeldstad; features Henry Moan, Alf Malland, J. Holst-Jensen. Directed by Arne Skouen. Screenplay, Skouen from the book by David Howarth; camera, Ragnar Sorensen; editor, Bjorn Breigutu. At Cannes Film Fest. Running time, **97 MINS.**

Jan Baalsrud	Jack Fjeldstad
Agnes	Henry Moan
Martin	Alf Malland
Grandfather	J. Holst-Jensen

Film is based on a true, harrowing odyssey during the last war. It makes a reasonable actioner, but lacks the imagination to convert story into a great study of man's ability and endurance. It looks a chancey Yank item.

Story: When the Germans blow up a ship of Norwegian commandos on its way to Norway for a special job, only one man survives. He is helped by a series of people as he tries to make neutral Sweden. In the process he goes snowblind, cuts off his own frozen toes, is lugged over mountains by brave resistants, and lies in a snow pit for over a month until finally sent over the border in a rush of reindeer by helpful Laplanders.

Direction is too stolid to really hoist this to plane where adventure would be transcendent. Jack Fjeldstad does well as the amazingly resilient man who really seems to have nine lives.

Technical credits are good and the on-the-spot lensing gives this a needed authenticity. Still alive, the actual here was presented to the Cannes audience after the feature, to big applause. *Mosk.*

La Venganza
(The Vengeance)
(SPANISH) (COLOR)

Cannes, May 20.

Gonzalez release of Guion-Vides-Suevia production. Stars Raf Vallone, Carmen Sevilla, Jorge Mistral; features Jose Prada, Fernando Rey, Louis Seigneur. Written and directed by Juan Antonio Bardem. Camera (Eastmancolor), Mario Pacheco; editor, Margarita Ochoa. At Cannes Film Fest. Running time, 123 MINS.

Andrea .... Carmen Sevilla
Luis .... Raf Vallone
Juan .... Jorge Mistral
Bermejo .... Arnoldo Foa
Forastero .... Fernando Rey
Merlin .... Louis Seigneur

This one's about a group of agricultural migratory workers with vendetta between an unjustly prisoned man and his accuser and the labor troubles, loves and lives of these Spanish fascimiles of the pre-war dust bowl "Oakies" of U.S. Film is overlong and over-telegraphed and emerges melodrama rather than drama.

A man is released from prison and goes home. His sister makes him swear to avenge himself on the leader of a migratory work team, whom, she feels, turned in her brother. On the work trip the sister falls for the supposed squealer and love finally triumphs over vengeance.

Color is somewhat garish and the scripting glosses over too many happenings, such as strikes and scabbing, a sudden fire destroying a town's wheat crop, and a man's fight against a machine that is replacing him in the fields.

Director Juan Barde has given Spain some international acclaim at festivals via "Age of Infidelity" and "The Lovemaker," but does not quite bring this off. It is too diffused in point, dramatics and feeling. *Mosk.*

En Djungelsaga
(A Jungle Saga)
(SWEDISH; AGASCOPE; COLOR)

Cannes, May 6.

Sandrews release of Arne Sucksdorff production. Written, photographed (Technicolor), directed and edited by Sucksdorff, aided by Graeme Ferguson, Astrid Sucksdorff. Commentary, Pierre Gascar spoken by Michel Auclair, Martine Sarcey; music, Ravi Shanker. At Cannes Film Fest. Running time, 90 MINS.

This one can be termed a storied documentary. Loving care has been put into this tale of isolated tribe in India and its daily detail. The storyline is subordinate to this preoccupation, which is the film's weakness as also its strong point. It emerges a hard—to—sell exotic item for U.S.

Director Arne Sucksdorff spent two years with the Muria tribe in central India. It is a communal life passed in mutual aid, and living with its own superstitions. A young hunter marries a girl from another tribe and when a marauding leopard takes a toll on the people and their livestock a public ritual puts the blame on the hunter. He is exiled but the leopard still strikes and he is reconciled to die in a titanic struggle with the big cat.

Unable to really treat character in this film, the interest sometimes lags. But Sucksdorff's expert visual sense leads to startling work with animals and especially the leopard. *Mosk.*

Pardesi
(The Foreigner)
(RUSSIAN-INDIAN; SOVSCOPE; COLOR)

Mosfilms-N.S. International release and production. Stars Oleg Streeshenov; features Balraj Sahni, Prithviraj. Directed by D. Pronin, K. Abbas. Screenplay, Abbas, Maria Smirnova; camera (Sovcolor), A. Renkov; editor, Ronuc. At Cannes Film Fest. Running time, 110 MINS.

Here's a sort of Russo-styled Marco Polo. Tale concerns first Russian to go to India in the 15th century to set up trading. Film is well photographed but emerges a naive adventure film with colorful backgrounding in India.

Viewer (and traveller) discover a picturesque India and the dialectics are held to a minimum to make this an engaging moppet adventure pic, but with color print costs making this dubious for export. Performances and technical details firstrate. *Mosk.*

Ciulinii Baraganului
(Fools of Baragan)
(RUMANIAN)

Bucerestí release and production. With Nuta Chrilea, Ana Vladesco. Directed by Louis Daquin. Screenplay, Antoine Tudal, Daquin from the novel by Panait Istrati; camera, Andre Dumaitre; editor, Liviu Popa. At Cannes Film Festival. Running time, 116 MINS.

Though made by a French director, this Rumanian film is an old-hat bucolic melodrama about the uprising of a group of peasants in the feudal Rumania. Lacklustre quality misses humanity and action inherent in the story.

Little chance outside of the Eastern countries and denotes that Rumania is still in the stilted filmmaking era. *Mosk.*

L'Eau Vive
(The Live Water)
(FRENCH; FRANSCOPE; COLOR)

Cannes, May 13.

Carlton Film release of Caravelle production. With Pascal Audret, Charles Blavette, Andree Debar, Arlette Thomas, Milly Mathis. Directed by Francois Villiers. Screenplay, Jean Giono; camera (Eastmancolor), Paul Soulignac; editor, Edouard Berne. At Cannes Film Fest. Running time, 95 MINS.

Hortense .... Pascal Audret
Simon .... Charles Blavette
Vignerone .... Andree Debar
Dabisse .... Arlette Thomas
Maraicher .... Milly Mathis

Film has a pleasant candor in its treatment of a rapacious peasant family when the family heritage has gone to a young girl. It skirts melodrama but is helped by fine imagery, an outstanding script and a beguiling tale of innocence triumphing over greed.

A governmental dam dooms a little town alongside a river. A young girl is vividly courted by greedy relatives when her father dies and his fortune is not found. They, in turn, try to find the money and the girl finally comes on it and gives the family the air and goes off to live with her one good uncle, a sheepherder.

Film's fine anamorphosocopic lensing builds the dam construction into a parallel line with the girl's growth and final defeat of her designing family. It escapes being turgid and flows on peacefully in its simple tale full of smart notations on French provincial life.

Pascal Audret lacks the drive to really make a vital character of the persecuted but independent girl, and Francois Villiers' direction lags somewhat. But Jean Giono's script gives excellent insight into its people and the land for the film's main merit. Technical credit and supporting cast are tops. *Mosk.*

Liberte Surveille
(Provisional Liberty)
(FRENCH-CZECH; FRANSCOPE, COLOR)

Cannes, May 16.

Silver Film release of Czech State-Trident production. Stars Marina Vlady, Robert Hossein; features, Rene Lefevre. Directed by Vladimir Voltchek, Henri Aisner. Screenplay, Pierre Laroche, Colette Audry; camera (Agfacolor), H. Alekan; editor, J. L. Lacour. At Cannes Film Fest. Running time, 90 MINS.

It is easy to see why this film was finally nixed by the Czechs as their entry, and why the fest selectors finally showed it out of competition rather than as a French film. It is a cliche-ridden opus about a Western (French) fugitive who manages to escape the police to Eastern Europe (Czechoslovakia) by being mistaken for the new member of a French boating team.

Love is waiting in the East and he renounces his former life by returning a stolen museum painting and deciding to stay in the East. Turgid direction and ordinary thesping do not help.

East-West coproduction will have to do better than this to catch with either side. *Mosk.*

Rosaura A Las Diez
(Rosaura At 10 O'Clock)
(ARGENTINIAN)

Cannes, May 13.

Argentino-Sono Film release and production. Stars Juan Verdaguer, Susana Campos; features Maria Robledo, Alberto Dalbes. Directed by Mario Soffici. Screenplay, Marco Denevi, Soffici from the novel by Denevi; camera, Anibal Paz; editor, Gobi Munez. At Cannes Film Fest. Running time, 98 MINS.

Rosaura .... Susana Campos
Camilo .... Juan Verdaguer
Milagros .... Maria Robledo
Reguel .... Alberto Dalbes

Looks suitable mainly for Hispano lingo houses in States, where it could have exploitation values. Otherwise this complicated tale from Argentina of a timid painter, who invents a fantasy girlfriend who comes to life, is too slow moving and sans necessary characterization, mood or poetics.

Timid soul has invented this girl to interest his landlady's daughter in him. But he has done it from an old photograph and one day the girl stumbles in. He is whirlwinded into marrying her by his landlady and she is then killed for the film's various flashbacks and different versions of the affair before it is straightened out.

Feature is in a 1:2.5 process called Alexscope and has okay technical resources with competent thesping. *Mosk.*

To Telefteo Psemma
(No More Credit)
(GREEK)

Cannes, May 13.

Finos Film release and production. Stars Ellie Lambetti; features, Georges Pappas, Athena Michaelidou, Eleni Zafiriou. Directed and written by Michael Cacoyannis. Camera, Walter Lassally; editor, Yanni Tsarouchi. At Cannes Film Fest. Running time, 100 MINS.

Chloe .... Ellie Lambetti
Cleon .... Georges Pappas
Roxane .... Athena Michaelidou
Katerina .... Eleni Zafiriou

Director Michael Cacoyannis has impressed at other film festivals, and put the Greek feature on the international art house map, with his preceeding "Stella" and "The Girl in Black." This one is more difficult and skirts melodrama in its tale of a ruined bourgeois family fighting to keep its dignity and standing.

Actress Ellie Lambetti has some striking dramatic scenes as the daughter who finally escapes from the milieu, but she is too overindulged and given a tragic mask too early in the pic to make her final self-realization telling. Stacks as chancy art house item for the U. S.

Miss Lambeti is willing to marry a rich man for his money but relents when the family's selfishness and cowardice in the face of adversity leads to the death of their devoted maid when the mother and daughter try to stop her from telling all when she demands money for her ailing child. It is a heart attack and Miss Lambetti exits the family and life of lies with the child.

Director Michael Cacoyannis has a flair for telling notation on conventialism, but the uneven scripting obscures the present theme and makes it somewhat conventional in its own way. Technical credits are good and this was brought in for $35,000. *Mosk.*

Goha
(TUNISIAN)

Cannes, May 20.

UGC release and production. Stars Omar Cheriff; features, Zina Bouzaiane, Laurro Gazzolo, Gabriel Jabbour, Daniel Emilfark. Directed by Jacques Baratier. Screenplay, Georges Schehade; camera (Agfocolor), Jean Bourgoin; editor, Trmand Becque. At Cannes Film Fest. Running time, 85 MINS.

Film is a colorful adaptation of a Tunisian folk tale. Unreeled in the form of a yarn told by a storyteller, it has forthright folk qualities, fine technical aspects and good trouping.

Concerns a seemingly simpleminded youth who has more imagination and sense than his family, teachers and friends. When he is involved in a love affair with the beauteous second young wife of the town wiseman, the film suddenly turns from whimsy to drama. It is a tribute to director Jacques Baratier's knowhow, in his first feature, that he manages the Swerve. Color and technical credits are first-class. *Mosk.*

Vasvirag
(Iron Flower)
(HUNGARIAN)

Cannes, May 16.

Hunnia Film release and production. Stars Mari Torocsik, Zoltan Varkonyi; features, Istvan Avar. Directed by Janos Hersko. Screenplay, Miklos Kollo from the novel by Andor Gelleri; camera, Ferenc Szecsenyi; editor, Zoltan Kerenyi. At Cannes Film Fest. Running time, 90 MINS.

The recent picketing of and lukewarm reaction in the U. S. to another Magyar pic, "Merry Go Round," suggest that it is still hard for satellite pix to break into Yank marts.

This one is a tale of a love affair during the depression period of the

1930's, a little shop girl wolf-called by her rich boss leaves her poor but honest lover for luxury only to regret it.

Tale avoids banality and emerges a tender film obscured somewhat by an ambiguous ending. Direction is knowing and thesping outstanding. *Mosk.*

Indiscreet
(COLOR)

Rousing finish makes up for slow start. Cary Grant and Ingrid Bergman names promise bright b.o.

Hollywood, May 23.
Warner Bros. release of a Grandon Production. Stars Cary Grant, Ingrid Bergman; with Cecil Parker, Phyllis Calvert, David Kossoff, Megs Jenkins, Oliver Johnston, Middleton Woods. Producer-Director, Stanley Donen. Screenplay, Norman Krasna, based on his play, "Kind Sir"; camera, Frederick A. Young; editor, Jack Harris; music, Richard Bennett and Ken Jones. Previewed May 20, '58. Running time, **100 MINS.**
Philip Adams .... Cary Grant
Anna Kalman .... Ingrid Bergman
Alfred Munson .... Cecil Parker
Margaret Munson .... Phyllis Calvert
Carl Banks .... David Kossoff
Doris Banks .... Megs Jenkins
Finleigh .... Oliver Johnston
Finleigh's Clerk .... Middleton Woods

A beguiling love story delicately deranged by the complications of sophisticated comedy, "Indiscreet" is an expert film version of Norman Krasna's 1953 stage play, "Kind Sir." Though tedious in its opening reels, the Stanley Donen production warms up in direct relation to the heat of the love affair and, in the end, manages to fade out in a blaze of playful merriment. Its stars, Cary Grant and Ingrid Bergman, lift this Warner Bros. release into the "must see" class, a pickup which the boxoffice is likely to reflect.

Striking hardest is Miss Bergman, who gives what well may be the most delightful performance of her career. As the successful actress who has yet to find love, Miss Bergman is alluring, most affectionate and highly amusing. Grant makes a ripping gadabout, conniving and gracious, his performance sometimes hilarious and always smooth.

Moving from the New York of "Kind Sir," the locale of "Indiscreet" has been shipped to London where Miss Bergman lives and wants to love. Grant, a rich American who holds a NATO post, lives there too (at least on weekends, commuting as he does from Paris) and he too wants to love. But the difference is he wants nothing of marriage and, to protect all concerned, advises Miss Bergman on first meeting that he is a married man, separated and unable to obtain a divorce. Still she invites him to the ballet, and there is born a touching love. She, with her heart full, settles for an affair with no strings attached.

Eventually finding out from her nosey sister that Grant truly isn't married, Miss Bergman goes into an enchanting tirade, blasting, "How dare he make love to me when he's not a married man!" She sets a trap for him, building a fire under his jealousy and, after a rollicking set-to, he proposes . . . marriage.

Cecil Parker, as the brother-in-law, becomes funnier as he becomes more unnerved, and Phyllis Calvert is excellent as the sister. Megs Jenkins turns in a fine performance as the maid, and David Kossoff, as the chauffeur, admirably grabs the high spot of hilarity with his pseudo-lover stroll-on.

Technical credit is difficult to assess in light of the preview film being a work print. Frederick A. Young's Technicolor photography mostly stays indoors, though what little he does show of London is distinguished. Art Director Don Ashton has created a lush living room interior, loaded with paintings, pillows and color, and his recreation of the Royal Naval College's Painted Hall is artistically and skillfully accomplished. Music

by Richard Bennett and Ken Jones is particularly effective in its romantic emphasis on piano. And an engaging wrapping is provided by clever title credits designed by Maurice Binder. *Ron.*

King Creole
(V'VISION—SONGS)

Teenaged sex, teenaged violence and Elvis Presley singing. Best Presley pic so far. Strong b.o. in right situations.

Hollywood, May 23.
Paramount release of a Hal B. Wallis production. Stars Elvis Presley; costars Carolyn Jones, Dolores Hart; features Dean Jagger, Liliane Montevecchi, Walter Matthau, Jan Shepard, Paul Stewart, Vic Morrow. Directed by Michael Curtiz; screenplay, Michael V. Gazzo, Herbert Baker; based on the novel, "A Stone for Danny Fisher," by Harold Robbins; camera, Russell Harlan; music, various, arranged and conducted by Walter Scharf; Choreography, Charles O'Curran; editor, Warren Low. Previewed at the studio, May 19, '58. Running time, **116 MINS.**
Danny Fisher .... Elvis Presley
Ronnie .... Carolyn Jones
Maxie Fields .... Walter Matthau
Nellie .... Dolores Hart
Mr. Fisher .... Dean Jagger
Nina .... Liliane Montevecchi
Shark .... Vic Morrow
Charlie Le Grand .... Paul Stewart
Mimi Fisher .... Jan Shepard
Sal .... Brian Hutton
Dummy .... Jack Grinnage
Eddie Burton .... Dick Winslow
Mr. Evans .... Raymond Bailey

Hal Wallis has attempted to take the curse off Elvis Presley, for those still resistant to his charms, by giving him an extraordinary backing in "King Creole," a solid melodrama with plenty of action and color. The Paramount presentation shows the young singer this time as a better-than-fair actor. Whether the picture will pick up additional supporters for Presley is something else, but it won't, at any rate, provoke new attacks.

The picture is based on Harold Robbins novel, "A Stone For Danny Fisher," but the locale has been switched to New Orleans, to Bourbon Street and to an indigenous cafe called the King Creole. Presley is a high school youth who is prevented from graduation by his attempts to take care of his weak-willed father and the density of his school teachers. He gets involved in a minor theft but thereafter goes straight when given a chance to perform in Paul Stewart's Vieux Carre saloon. His brief fling at crime returns to haunt him when the local crime boss, Walter Matthau, decrees that Presley shall leave Stewart and come sing for him. The picture ends with a spurt of gunplay that knocks off Matthau as well as Carolyn Jones, Matthau's girl friend who has been confusing Presley's love life, and allows the hero to get back to Stewart's club and together again with his teenaged sweetheart, Dolores Hart.

Essentially a musical, since Presley sings 13 new songs, including a title number, film runs a little long and the premise that Matthau would launch a minor crime wave just to get one performer for his club is a little shaky. The byplay keeps the action lively and helps obscure this thin plotting.

Presley does not modify his performance from previous appearances while singing one of his rock-and-roll numbers, but director Michael Curtiz and cameraman Russell Harlan have worked wonders with low-key lighting and adroit camera angles. In all fairness, Presley does show himself to be a surprisingly sympathetic and believable actor on occasion. He also does some very pleasant,

soft and melodious, singing, unlike most of his better known work.

Miss Jones contributes a strong and bitter portrait of a good girl gone wrong, moving and pathetic. Miss Hart is an unusual ingenue, pretty but with character. Dean Jagger, Liliane Montevecchi, Walter Matthau, Jan Shepard, Paul Stewart and Vic Morrow give vigorous performances in important supporting roles.

The black-and-white camera work by Harlan is in the realistic vein and Warren Low's editing does a fine job of matching New Orleans-locationed exteriors with studio setups, as well as keeping the pace of the picture even and consistent.

Several teams of songwriters, Al Wood and Kay Twomey, Fred Wise and Ben Weisman, Jerry Leiber and Mike Stoller, Sid Wayne and Abner Silver, Sid Tepper and Roy C. Bennett, Aaron Schroeder and Rachel Frank, Schroeder and Martin Kalmanoff, and Claude DeMetruis, have contributed to the music, and the songs are good. *Powe.*

La Chatte
(FRENCH)

Paris, May 20.
Discifilm release of Elysees Film production. Stars Francoise Arnoul, Bernard Wicki; features Kurt Meisel, Andre Versini, Roger Hanin, Bernard Blier, Louise Roblin. Directed by Henri Decoin. Screenplay, Jacques Remy, Eugene Tucherer, Decoin; camera, Pierre Montazel; editor, Claude Durand. At Biarritz, Paris. Running time **100 MINS.**
Cora ....Francoise Arnoul
Bernard ....Bernard Wicki
Heinz .... Kurt Meisel
Captain ....Bernard Blier
Bernadette ....Louise Roblin
Pierre .... Roger Hanin
Henri ....Andre Versini

This film is an over-contrived actioner set during the occupation of France by the Germans. Though this period is rarely treated in Gallic pix, this rates as only a passable item because of its failure to bring depth to the characterizations and give the feel for the period. It shapes only as dualer or exploitation fare for the U.S.

Francoise Arnoul's husband is killed by the Gestapo, and she becomes a resistance worker. A German undercover man wins her love by posing as a Swiss journalist. He turns in her group and she is killed by the group.

Miss Arnoul sleepwalks through her role of the unwitting betrayer, but shows plenty of pulchritude in her love scenes. Bernard Wicki and Kurt Meisel become German caricatures because of the weak plot and Henri Decoin's indecisive direction. Sympathetic Germans are creeping into Gallic war films, too. Technical aspects are good while Pierre Montazel's excellent, contrasty lensing is worth a special mention. The remainder of the French cast is good. *Mosk.*

Fiend Without A Face

Horror item. Pretty gory for the tenser kiddies, otherwise good for its class.

Hollywood, May 23.
Metro release of a John Croydon production. Stars Marshall Thompson. Director, Arthur Crabtree; screenplay, Herbert J. Leder; based on a story by Amelia Reynolds Long; camera, Lionel Banes; music, Buxton Orr; editor, R. Q. McNaughton. Previewed at the studio, May 23, '58. Running time, **74 MINS.**
Jeff Cummings........Marshall Thompson
Capt. Chester .... Terence Kilburn
Sgt. Kasper .... Michael Balfour

Dr. Warren .... Gil Winfield
Nurse .... Shane Cordell
Col. Butler .... Stanley Maxted
Mayor Hawkins.........James Dyrenforth
Barbara .... Kim Parker
Atomic Engineer.......Kerrigan Prescott
Professor Walgate......Kynaston Reeves
Dr. Bradley .... Peter Madden
Ben Adams .... R. Meadows White
Amelia Adams .... Lala Lloyd
Gibbons .... Robert MacKenzie
Melville .... Launce Maraschal

"Fiend Without A Face," is an Amalgamated production, made in Britain for Metro, and will be released with "The Haunted Strangler" for an exploitation horror package. It oozes and gurgles with Grand Guignol blood and crunching bones, easily one of the goriest horror pictures in the current cycle. Story, direction and acting are primitive, but the macabre effects may satisfy the blood-thirsty. The pic was shown for review in the old 1.66 aspect ratio.

Locale of Herbert J. Leder's screenplay, based on a story by Amelia Reynolds Long, is a U. S.-Canadian air base and radar station, one of those that form part of the warning screen for North America. A scientist-philosopher living nearby has used the base's atomic power to develop a theory—one that rapidly gets out of hand—that thought can be materialized. His thoughts materialize as "beings" composed of a skull and a spine. They look like a cross between a scorpion and a spider and they spend their time attacking victims and sucking out their brains and spine. The only way to halt them is to shut off the air base's atomic power. Before this is done several of the monsters have to be shot which is shown with closeups of the blood and brains pouring out of their skulls with accompanying sound effects.

The story, which involves a romance between star Marshall Thompson and feminine lead, Kim Parker, is on shaky ground with some of its science, but none of this is too important. The only thing that seems to satisfy audiences of this type of picture is gore and there is plenty of it here.

Powe.

High School Confidential

Could be "I Was a Teenaged Undercover Federal Narcotics Agent." B.o. appeal for teeners and twenties.

Hollywood, May 23.

Metro release of an Albert Zugsmith production. Stars Russ Tamblyn, Jan Sterling, John Drew Barrymore; "guest stars" Mamie Van Doren, Ray Anthony, Jackie Coogan, Charles Chaplin Jr.; features Diane Jergens. Directed by Jack Arnold. Screenplay, Lewis Meltzer and Robert Blees; screenstory, Blees; camera, Harold J. Marzorati; editor, Ben Lewis. Previewed in Hollywood, May 21, '58. Running time, **85 MINS.**

Tony Baker .... Russ Tamblyn
Mike Wilson
Arlene Williams .... Jan Sterling
J. I. Coleridge......John Drew Barrymore
Gwen Dulaine .... Mamie Van Doren
Joan Staples .... Diane Jergens
Himself .... Jerry Lee Lewis
Bix .... Ray Anthony
Mr. A. .... Jackie Coogan
Quinn .... Charles Chaplin Jr.
Jukey Judlow .... Burt Douglas
Steve Bentley .... Michael Landon
Doris .... Jody Fair
Poetess .... Phillipa Fallon
Kitty .... Robin Raymond
Jack Staples .... James Todd
William Remington Kane .... Lyle Talbot
Wheeler-Dealer......William Wellman Jr.
Henchman .... Joe Foster
Gloria .... Diana Darrin
Petey .... Carl Thayler
Morino .... Irwin Berke

"High School Confidential," the first of Albert Zugsmith's productions for Metro since his move-over from Universal, is a sensational account of pills, marijuana and narcotics among the high school set. A good cast, headed by Russ Tamblyn and Jan Sterling, does a capable job of projecting the sad and sordid aspects of this kind of story. Although the presentation seems to "exploit" to the fullest every facet of this evil situation, it does so skillfully and with compelling effect.

Unknown to fellow students at Santa Bello high school—and to the audience for much of the film—Russ Tamblyn is in reality an undercover narcotics agent when he registers as a transfer student from Chicago.

The screenplay by Lewis Meltzer and Robert Blees, from a story by Blees, is well-constructed and faithfully told in the special language of today's juniors. The story seems to have some missing parts, however, notably the ambiguous relationship of Tamblyn towards Mamie Van Doren, who is described as his "aunt," but who all too obviously has other than a substitute maternal feeling for him. Mel Welles has contributed two pieces of special material, one of which, an existentialist poem recited by Phillip Fallon, is a standout.

Tamblyn is excellent. Miss Sterling, who must convey both adult maturity as the teacher most involved and yet be convincing as someone to stir the male students to other than scholastic efforts, is most effective.

Zugsmith has cast the picture with an array of names, John Drew Barrymore, Jackie Coogan, Charles Chaplin Jr., Jerry Lee Lewis, Mamie Van Doren and Ray Anthony, as special audience bait. Young Barrymore gives a tough performance and Coogan does a vivid job as the chief dope peddler. Chaplin is seen only briefly. Diane Jergens is attractive as a young victim of the marijuana habit and others who contribute include Burt Douglas, Michael Landon, Jody Fair, Robin Raymond, James Todd, Lyle Talbot and William Wellman Jr.

Jack Arnold's direction is well-paced and draws some believable and sharp characterizations. Harold J. Marzorati's photography, art direction by William A. Horning and Hans Peters; sound by Dr. Wesley C. Miller and editing by Ben Lewis, all contribute to the technically excellent production.

Powr.

Smiley Gets A Gun
(BRITISH—C'SCOPE—COLOR)

Simple kid story with a favorite character, "Smiley." Has open-air tang of Australia, and fine for family audiences.

London, May 20.

20th-Fox (Anthony Kimmins) production and release. Stars Sybil Thorndike, Chips Rafferty, Keith Calvert. Directed by Anthony Kimmins. Screenplay, Anthony Kimmins, Rex Rienits, from novel by Moore Raymond; editor, G. Turney-Smith; camera, Ted Scaife; music, Wilbur Sampson. At Rialto, London. Running time, **90 MINS.**

Granny McKinley .... Sybil Thorndike
Sergeant Flaxman .... Chips Rafferty
Smiley .... Keith Calvert
Joey .... Bruce Archer
Ma Greevins .... Margaret Christensen
Pa Greevins .... Reg Lye
Stiffy .... Grant Taylor
Miss McCowan .... Verena Kimmins
Mr. Stevens .... Leonard Teale
Jean Holt .... Jannice Dinnen
Fred Jackson .... Brian Farley
Jimmy Goodwin .... Richard Pusey
Elsie .... Barbara Eather
Quirk .... Guy Dolman
Mrs. Gaspen .... Ruth Cracknell
Dr. Gaspen .... Bruce Beeby
Vicar .... Charles Tasman
Mick Mooney .... Frank Ransom
Tom Graham .... John Fegan
Dave Rudge .... John Tate
Nurse .... Val Cooney
Mr. Protheroe .... William Rees
Rev. Galbraith .... Gordon Chater

After the useful boxoffice reception of "Smiley" a followup was inevitable. "Smiley Gets a Gun" does a neat job in cashing on the popularity of the previous pic. It's a simple, naive film which offers wholesome family entertainment though the average adult will have trouble in suppressing an occasional yawn. As a b.o. prospect, it represents a sound booking.

Smiley is the mischievous son of the blacksmith in Murrumbilla, an Australian hamlet. Always up to his grubby little neck in scrapes, the likeable youngster is persuaded to reform by the local cop who promises him a gun if he learns a sense of responsibility. He is to get the weapon when he has earned eight good marks. Smiley finds this tough going, especially when the locals start betting on the result. He becomes the victim of a lot of double crossing which ends up with him being suspected of theft from the eccentric oldest inhabitant. But he wins out in the end.

The somewhat pedestrian dialog is not enhanced by the twangy Aussie accents and much of the acting has a casual, almost amateurish flavor. But there is a fresh warmheartedness and an artless charm about the whole affair which will win over all but the most cynical.

A new Smiley has been found in 10-year-old Keith Calvert. He is a pleasant kid with an obvious appeal to the maternal in femme film patrons. He and his buddy, Bruce Archer, handle the juve sequences excellently and there are some pleasant if unsubtle performances by such adults as Chips Rafferty, as the cop; Reg Lye, Grant Taylor, Bruce Beeby and Margaret Christensen.

Guy Dolman is too obvious and suave a villain but veteran actress Sybil Thorndike has a field day as Granny McKinley, the eccentric old woman who is a miser.

Anthony Kimmins has brought a splendidly open air atmosphere to the screen, helped considerably by firstrate color lensing by Ted Scaife. Theme song by Clyde Collins, "A Little Boy Called Smiley," is simple enough to be a winner. There is one particularly impressive sequence of a bush fire which was the authentic thing, smartly dropped into the yarn for good effect. The virtues of "Smiley" are its complete sincerity and lack of pretentiousness.

Rich.

The Haunted Strangler

Boris Karloff's back and Metro's got him as half of a horror bill. Okay exploitation item.

Hollywood, May 23.

Metro release of an Amalgamated production. Stars Boris Karloff. Produced by John Croydon. Directed by Robert Day. Screenplay, Jan Read and John C. Cooper, from an original story by Read; camera, Lionel Banes; music, Buxton Orr; editor, Peter Mayhew. Previewed at the studio, May 23, '58. Running time, **81 MINS.**

James Rankin .... Boris Karloff
Supt. Burk .... Anthony Dawson
Hospital Supt. .... Derek Birch
Hannah .... Dorothy Gordon
Mrs. Rankin .... Elizabeth Allan
Lily .... Diane Aubrey
Dr. McColl .... Tim Turner
Cora .... Jean Kent
Pearl .... Vera Day
Turnkey .... Max Brimmell
Prison Governor .... Leslie Perrins
Young Blood .... John Fabian
Dr. Johnson .... Desmond Roberts
Asylum Maid .... Jessica Cairns

Perhaps because he's been practicing fairy tales on children, Boris Karloff has an especially kind, gentle look about him in "The Haunted Strangler." It's contrast, indeed, for his fiendish alter ego, and the Jekyll-Hyde character makes for mild horror in this British-produced Metro release. Packaged with "Fiend Without A Face," it will stand up under heavy campaigning and thus could loom as substantial exploitation fare.

Starting with a picturesque hanging in 1860, this Amalgamated Production picks up its story 20 years later with Karloff, a successful novelist, investigating that same hanging. The executed man, Karloff surmises, really wasn't the Haymarket Strangler, after all, and every clue now points to the doctor who performed autopsies on the five women he supposedly half strangled, then slashed to death.

After much sleuthing, it turns out that Karloff, having suffered a lapse of memory that score of years ago, really is the doctor. And he was right—he is the murderer. Now, retrieving the scalpel with which he did his original slashing, Karloff again twists his mouth, bites his lip, hunches over and hisses as the mad monster. He kills three more ladies, including his wife, and in his sane moments tries unsuccessfully to convince someone of his guilt. Eventually caught trying to bury the scalpel, he's shot and, blood trickling from his now calmed lips, dies over the hanged man's grave.

Karloff masters both characters and comes off well in each, with good work also turned in by Diane Aubrey, Tim Turner, Jean Kent, Vera Day, Elizabeth Allan and Anthony Dawson.

Screenplay by Jan Read and John C. Cooper, from an original story by Read, is suspenseful to some degree, and many of its holes are plugged up nicely by director Robert Day. There are, to say the least, interesting touches, full-blooded scenes and a cute little rat who nibbles contentedly at a rather handsome skull. Technically, the John Croydon production is worthy, especially considering its budget.

Ron.

The Moonraker
(BRITISH-COLOR)

Conventional costume melodrama with lots of swordplay; will satisfy average family houses.

London, May 20.

Associated British-Pathe release of an Associated British (Hamilton G. Inglis) production. Stars George Baker, Sylvia Syms, Peter Arne, Marius Goring. Directed by David Macdonald. Screenplay, Robert Hall, Wilfrid Eades, Alistair Bell based on play by Arthur Watkyn; editor, Richard Best; camera, Max Greene; music, Laurie Johnson. At Studio One, London, May 19, '58. Running time, **82 MINS.**

The Moonraker .... George Baker
Anne Wyndham .... Sylvia Syms
Edmund Tyler .... Peter Arne
Colonel Beaumont .... Marius Goring
Lord Harcourt .... Clive Morton
Charles Stuart .... Gary Raymond
Henry Strangeways........Richard Leech
Judith Strangeways...........Iris Russell
Martin Strangeways..Michael Anderson Jr.
Parfitt .... Paul Whitsun-Jones
Cromwell .... John Le Mesurier
Captain Wilcox........Patrick Troughton
Captain Foster .... Julian Somers
Lord Dorset .... Patrick Waddington
Lady Dorset .... Frances Rowe
Henrietta Dorset .... Jennifer Browne
Trooper .... Richard Warner
Captain Lowry ...... George Woodbridge
Blacksmith .... Victor Brooks

"The Moonraker" is a routine costume meller with a Civil War setting, which will hardly strain the grey matter of customers. But it contains enough hard riding and sword play to satisfy those who don't get restive at naive dialog and predictable situations. British family audiences will enjoy its simple ingredients, which have all the

earmarks of an endless commercial tv series. However, its stars do not carry enough weight to lure U. S. ducat buyers.

It is based on a play by one-time British film censor Arthur Watkyn which failed to rouse much enthusiasm in the West End. As a film it is much better, because of the extra scope for action. The pic is set in 1661. The Civil War is over, but the Royalists and the Roundheads are still at each others throats. "The Moonraker" has George Baker as a daring Cavalier with a price on his head, whose mission it is to get Charles II to the safety of France.

He arranges for a ship to pick up the king from a lonely part of the coast but Baker is discovered by one of Cromwell's agents and is betrayed by the fiancee of a Roundhead colonel. Surrounded by Roundheads, it needs all Baker's wit, daring and skill with the sword to fulfill his mission. He still has time to fall in love with the girl during the few hours he is at the inn.

The screenplay sags occasionally but there are enough clashes between the Cavaliers and Cromwellites to keep enthusiasm high. The acting, which is reliable rather than inspired, has the necessary degree of hamminess to make the proceedings amusing. Baker rides and scraps his way through the script with virility, charm and unflagging energy while Peter Arne scores as his chief protagonist. Richard Leech, Marius Goring, Clive Morton and Gary Raymond give Baker sound support. Paul Whitsun-Jones, as a fiery and portly Royalist, chips in with some unsophisticated fun. Sylvia Syms, the leading lady, looks pretty but cannot do very much with a colorless role.

David Macdonald's direction is straightforward. Max Greene's lensing is excellent. "The Moonraker" is very easy on the eye, the color being particularly good. This simple film will give a lot of innocent pleasure to many people. It has a theme song with a lyric so pathetically banal that it stands every chance of being a hit.

Rich.

Badman's Country

Fair oater, should reap good returns in action market.

Warner Bros. release of a Robert E. Kent production. Stars George Montgomery; co-stars Neville Brand, Buster Crabbe. Directed by Fred F. Sears; screenplay, Orville H. Hampton; camera, Benjamin H. Kline; music, Irving Gertz; editor, Grant Whytock. Previewed in Hollywood, May 21, '58. Running time, 85 MINS.
Pat Garrett .... George Montgomery
Butch Cassidy .... Neville Brand
Wyatt Earp .... Buster Crabbe
Lorna .... Karin Booth
Bat Masterson .... Gregory Walcott
Buffalo Bill Cody...... Malcolm Atterbury
Sundance .... Russell Johnson
Harvey Logan .... Richard Devon
Mayor Coleman .... Morris Ankrum
Marshal McAfee .... Dan Riss

"Badman's Country" assembles practically the whole roster of the frontier west's famed law officers, including Wyatt Earp, Bat Masterson, Pat Garrett and Buffalo Bill, to defend the sprouting city of Abilene, apparently on the supportable theory that if the fans go for one heroic marshal they should go four times as enthusiastically for a quartet of them.

The Robert E. Kent production for Warners doesn't have any other novelties about it, but it is a well-plotted, suspenseful western of the non-psychological, or action, type. Not much soul-wrestling or insight

about these characters, but plenty of action. George Montgomery heads the cast, which has been capably directed by the late Fred F. Sears.

The problem, in Orville H. Hampton's screenplay, is that a large collection of outlaws, headed by Neville Brand, is gathering outside Abilene to knock off a train shipment of gold worth half a million dollars. Montgomery, as Garrett, wants to suck the outlaws into town, where they can be more easily ambushed. He is supported by his fellow law officers, including Crabbe who looks remarkably like the real Earp, and Gregory Walcott as Masterson and Malcolm Atterbury as Buffalo Bill. The townspeople are shortsightedly opposed to this plan since it will involve a considerable amount of gunplay and they are chary of this even if it does mean the town will be cleaned up. They finally see the light, however, and Montgomery & Co. trap the gunmen, save the gold and free the town from the bandit's domination.

The picture does a good job of laying in the threads of the conflict so they can be knotted for a sharp, tight climax and then in prolonging the outcome until the final shoot-out. Suspense is achieved and so is excitement. In addition to those mentioned above, Karin Booth as the romantic interest, Russell Johnson, Richard Devon, Morris Ankrum and Dan Riss all contribute effectively.

Benjamin H. Kline's photography is able and there is a title song that might get some play to help in exploitation. Other technical credits are adequate. *Powe.*

Der Fuchs Von Paris
(The Fox of Paris)
(GERMAN)

Berlin, May 20.

Constantin release of Kurt Ulrich production. Stars Martin Held, Marianne Koch, Hardy Krueger, Michel Auclair; features Peter Mosbacher, Paul Hartmann, Viktor Staal. Directed by Paul May. Screenplay, Herbert Reinecker; camera, Georg Bruckbauer; music, Hans Martin Majewski; editor, Klaus Eckstein. At Marmorhaus, Berlin. Running time, 97 MINS.
General Quade .... Martin Held
Captain Euerstenwerth.. Hardy Krueger
Yvonne .... Marianne Koch
Major Wedekind ..... Peter Mosbacher
Von der Heinitz .... Paul Hartmann
Colonel Toller .... Viktor Staal
Andre .... Michel Auclair
Francois .... Jean Paul Roussillon
Yvonne's father .... Jean Murat

Some 10 years ago, Paul May directed the Austrian pic, "Duel With Death," an impressive anti-Nazi film which centered around the underground movement in Austria during the last World War. "Fox" has a similar plot but any other comparison with his "Duel" would be unfair. May's latest opus is disappointing. Commercial prospects, however, may be just the opposite. While his "Duel" was a b.o. flop, this looks good enough to get adequate returns. It even looks to have some foreign chances, helped by the names of French actor Michel Auclair, Marianne Koch alias Cook (a Universal pactee) and Hardy Krueger, who was starred in Rank's "The One That Got Away."

Story has its locale in Paris, shortly before the Allied invasion in 1944. It centers on a young German officer (Hardy Krueger) who gets involved with the French resistance and simultaneously also with a German generals' plot which is aimed at saving the lifes of German soldiers instead of sacrificing

them for (senseless) defense according to Hitler's order. The young officer becomes an innocent victim since treated like a traitor, and shot by the Germans.

Screenplay lacks the necessary conviction to make it suspenseful. Moreover, May's direction is quite wooden. Cast has a tough time making it believable.

Krueger plays the young German officer sympathetically. Martin Held enacts a German general with an overdose of noblesse. Miss Koch portrays a French resistance girl, speaking German with a Gallic accent which eventually sounds ridiculous. Hans Martin Majewski's score has quality.

Hans.

Incognito
(FRENCH; DYALISCOPE)
Paris, May 20.

Gaumont release of Odeon-Hoche Film production. Stars Eddie Constantine; features Tilda Thamar, Danick Pattisson, Gaby Andre, Dario Moreno. Directed by Patrice Dally; Screenplay, Albert Siminon, Ben Barzman, Yvan Audouard, Dally; camera, Michel Kelber; editor, Claude Nicole. At Triomphe, Paris. Running time, 100 MINS.
Stanley .... Eddie Constantine
Barbara .... Danick Patersson
Blonde .... Tilda Thamar
Redhead .... Gaby Andre
Fernando .... Dario Moreno

Yank actor Eddie Constantine again portrays an American G-man on the trail of dollar counterfeiters. It involves a fictional Latino power, plenty of good looking girls, fights and gags. This one is smoothly played and directed. Although story is familiar, it is easy to take. However, stacked up against Yank film counterparts, it rates only as a possible dual entry. Constantine has yet to make the pic to break the barrier into his home country where he is still an unknown quantity filmically.

Done in an anamorpho-scoped process, this moves lightly. It is helped by Constantine's ease in his well worn role. Fights are well staged and some clever sight gags and pretty lookers enliven the pic. Technical credits are good and this looks to do well on the Continent. *Mosk.*

The Law and Jake Wade
(COLOR; C'SCOPE)

Topnotch suspense western pursued to a relentless conclusion. Highlight performances and direction for strong b.o.

Metro release of a William Hawks Production. Stars Robert Taylor and Richard Widmark; costars Patricia Owens; features Robert Middleton, Henry Silva, De Forest Kelley, Burt Douglas, Eddie Firestone. Directed by John Sturges; screenplay, William Bowers; from a novel by Marvin H. Albert; camera, Robert Surtees; editor, Ferris Webster. Previewed in Hollywood, May 28, '58. Running time, 86 MINS.
Jake Wade .... Robert Taylor
Clint Hollister .... Richard Widmark
Peggy .... Patricia Owens
Ortero .... Robert Middleton
Rennie .... Henry Silva
Wexler .... De Forest Kelley
Lieutenant .... Burt Douglas
Burke .... Eddie Firestone

A high, wide and handsome western, "The Law and Jake Wade," has the elements to make it an unusually profitable presentation. Robert Taylor and Richard Widmark head the cast, with Patricia Owens costarred, and trio turn in crisp, exciting performances under John Sturges' direction. William Hawks' production, filmed in Metrocolor and Cinema-Scope, features spectacular backgrounds in the High Sierras and Death Valley, well worth the time and effort

Taylor and Widmark are ex-partners in crime who met again after the passage of some years. Taylor is now the marshal of a town near where Widmark has been jailed, but he turns Widmark loose in return of a favor his former associate once did him. Widmark does not let it end so easily, however, and insists Taylor accompany him—at gunpoint—to search out some swag that Taylor buried when he decided to end his career as an outlaw.

They begin their trek after Widmark's gang, Robert Middleton, Henry Silva, De Forest Kelly and Eddie Firestone, kidnap Taylor's fiancee, Miss Owens. The trail starts against the rugged background of the chilly Sierras and ends in a ghost town in the desert. The story leads inevitably to the final conflict between Taylor and Widmark and is resolved when the latter is killed.

This is simple and straightforward plotting by William Bowers in his screenplay from Marvin H. Albert's novel. But there is so much interest in the diverse characters and the dialog so good in itself, rich with irony and sardonic humor, that the individual scenes carry for their own value as well as sustaining the forward motion of the plotting and helping build suspense.

Taylor's role is relative simple one, he has made his decision for the law, and the complexities by which he must decorate his character are those of plot, that is how and where he will ambush Widmark. Widmark is the more interesting of the two men, he is thoroughly amoral, but such an engaging villain that when he is finally shot you are sorry to see him go. Despite the greater diversity of his characterization, the two actors balance nicely and the contest never seems unequal. Miss Owens, as the sole woman in the cast, has a role that must be kept to a minimum for believability, still she makes her presence gently and effectively felt. The members of Widmark's gang, Middleton, Silva, Kelley and Firestone, each create individual characters and Sturges uses them skilfully. Burt

Douglas, in a brief scene, gives a good account of himself.

Robert Surtees' photography is an ally of the director and the writer in providing interest for the eye during transitional passages and in heightening the drama during the crucial ones. Art directors William A. Horning and Daniel B. Cathcart, with set decorators Henry Grace and Otto Siegel, have done an outstanding job, notably in their creation of an eerie and poetic ghost town. Walter Plunkett's costumes deserve a mention, particularly in his single wardrobe for Miss Owens' whose disintegrating and ladylike hat is a symbol of the lady herself. Ferris Webster's editing helps set and maintain the story's tempo and Dr. Wesley C. Miller's sound, memorable on a popular level for the sinister sound of the Indian arrows and spears, is overall excellent.

One factor of "The Law and Jake Wade" is that the musical background is "canned," this is drawn from Metro's musical library. It has been chosen appropriately for mood and pace, but there is no doubt that it is inadequate for a major production such as this. The spectator has become accustomed to distinctive themes and orchestration and the picture suffers to a degree because of music that is adequate but nothing more. *Powe.*

The Bravados
(COLOR; C'SCOPE)

End weakens otherwise potent western of pursuit and revenge bitterly sought, savagely extracted. Strong b.o.

Hollywood, May 30.
20th-Fox release of a Herbert B. Swope Jr. production. Stars Gregory Peck; costars Joan Collins, Stephen Boyd, Albert Salmi; features Henry Silva, Kathleen Gallant, Barry Coe, Lee Van Cleef, George Voskovec, Herbert Rudley, Andrew Duggan, Ken Scott, Gene Evans and Los Ninos Cantores De Morelia. Directed by Henry King. Screenplay by Philip Yordan; adaptation by John O'Hara; based on the novel by Frank O'Rourke; camera, Leon Shamroy; music, Lionel Newman; editor, William Mace. Previewed in Hollywood, May 29, '58. Running time, 99 MINS.

Jim Douglas	Gregory Peck
Josefa Velarde	Joan Collins
Bill Zachary	Stephen Boyd
Ed Taylor	Albert Salmi
Lujan	Henry Silva
Emma	Kathleen Gallant
Tom	Barry Coe
Gus Steinmetz	George Voskovec
Sheriff Eloy Sanchez	Herbert Rudley
Alfonso Parral	Lee Van Cleef
Parde	Andrew Duggan
Primo	Ken Scott
Butler	Gene Evans
Quinn	Jack Mather
Simms	Joe De Rita
Tony Mirabel	Robert Adler
Nichols	Jason Wingreen
Banker Loomis	Robert Griffin
Mrs. Parral	Ada Carrasco
Pepe Martinez	Juan Garcia
Mrs. Barnes	Jacqueline Evans
Angela Lujan	Alicia del Lago
Ninos Cantores De Morelia	Choral Group

A hard and ruthless account of a revenge-maddened man's trackdown of the outlaws he believes raped and killed his wife, "The Bravados" is a western of sweeping vistas and men who held the law in the same hands as their six-shooters.

The ending, including a somewhat debatable explanation of Gregory Peck's motives by the local padre, tends to weaken the impact of the picture. Also, a romantic plot thread involving Peck and Joan Collins, never seems real or even necessary to the story. It is a drag. The characters of the outlaws should have been more individual and separate. Their deaths do not have the importance they

should because they have not become people. The dialog is not particularly novel, tending towards cliches.

The 20th-Fox production in glowing DeLuxe Color and CinemaScope, produced by Herbert B. Swope Jr. and directed by Henry King, presents Peck in one of his best performances and the whole package should make for brisk business.

Philip Yordan's screenplay opens in a town of unspecified geography, although its nationality is Spanish-American. Four men are in town waiting to be hanged and the town is anticipating the event with unpleasant zeal. The quartet, Stephen Boyd, Albert Salmi, Henry Silva and Lee Van Cleef, is freed by a confederate posing as the imported hangman and the chase begins. The townspeople want the men for holding up their bank and killing a man in the process. Gregory Peck, who wanders into town as a Mysterious Stranger, heads the posse and becomes its driving spirit. He wants to kill each man personally because of what was done to his wife.

The pursuit leads over the precipitous mountains and gorges (photographed in remote areas of the Mexican states of Michiocan and Jalisco) as Peck singles out and kills Boyd, Salmi and Van Cleef. He is about to finish off Silva when he learns the truth; it was a trusted neighbor who actually raped and killed his wife, not the outlaws. Peck's private lynch law has not only been wrong legally, it has been completely unjustified murder. This is a powerful moment and Peck gives it great value. There has been a "happy ending" given to the story, with Peck returning to the town where the hanging was to have taken place and his acclaim there by its citizens.

Despite story handicaps, King has organized and propelled his drama so effectively that the action is fast and breathless enough to minimize these deficiencies. Peck's performance is taciturn but compelling; you know what he is thinking, and his climactic scene is a powerful one. Miss Collins is sabotaged by a role that apparently was inserted only to supply "romantic interest," but she is believable and interesting. Boyd, Salmi and Van Cleef are forceful and malignant. Henry Silva, whose short career up to now has been only as a juvenile heavy, performs an outstanding job that would seem to open the possibility that he is of potentially leading man calibre in romantic roles. Others who stand out include Kathleen Gallant, Barry Coe, George Voskovec, Andrew Duggan, Ken Scott, Gene Evans, Joe De Rita and Alicia del Lago. The famed Mexican boys choir, Los Cantores de Morelia, are interestingly employed in a church sequence.

Leon Shamroy, who is up to some more of his tricks with color filters, also shows that his compositions are surpassed by no one.

His perspective in depth is especially important in these backgrounds and his color work in the pursuit scenes is especially vital in creating variation and interest. Lionel Newman's score is sparing but rich (recorded abroad). The Mexican town chosen by art directors Lyle R. Wheeler and Mark-Lee Scott, with set decoration by Walter M. Scott and Chester Bayhi, and particularly the important church interior, is striking. Editing by William Mace keeps the determinedly contrasting color moods of the photographer from seeming abrupt, and also helps give the picture its pace, while sound

by Bernard Freericks and Warren B. Delaplain is proficient. *Powe.*

Rock-a-Bye Baby
(VISTAVISION-COLOR-SONGS)

Fun and schmaltz with Jerry Lewis as star and producer. Reliable boxoffice in most Lewis situations.

Paramount release of Jerry Lewis production. Stars Lewis, Marilyn Maxwell, Connie Stevens; features Baccaloni, Reginald Gardiner. Directed by Frank Tashlin. Screenplay, Tashlin, from his own story; camera, Haskell Boggs; editor, Alma Macrorie; music, Walter Scharf; songs, Sammy Cahn and Harry Warren. Previewed at Loew's 72d Street Theatre, N.Y. Running time, 95 MINS.

Clayton Poole	Jerry Lewis
Carla Naples	Marilyn Maxwell
Sandy Naples	Connie Stevens
Salvatore Naples	Salvatore Baccaloni
Henry Herman	Reginald Gardiner
Mr. Wright	Hans Conried
Bessie Polk	Ida Moore
Young Clayton	Gary Lewis
Young Carla	Judy Franklin
Mrs. Van Cleve	Isobel Elsom
Judge Jenkins	Alex Geary

The record is not likely to be marred with "Rock-A-Bye-Baby"—the record being the consistent "A" boxoffice returns chalked up by the Jerry Lewis pictures (including Lewis as a single). This new outing combines the familiar zanyisms with lots of schmaltz centering on babies (three of them are left on the comic's doorstep). Include, too, some okay tunes by Sammy Cahn and Harry Warren and the visuals of Technicolor and VistaVision and the total looks agreeable at most anyone's boxoffice.

There's fun here, but at least one observer wonders about how long the Lewis-type picture can go on without the introduction of some originality in the humor department. Perhaps forever, on the basis of the public receptivity right along.

It's to be stressed that prediction of the commercial outcome is based on the past. This new one measures up to the average of its predecessors. It's Jerry Lewis the clown and the awkward softie. And done in the well-known fashion; fresher material would have been welcome.

"Baby" has to do with a hotcha film star, Marilyn Maxwell, who wants to keep secret the arrival of her triplets because this kind of situation doesn't go hand in hand with being a glamor puss. So she and her agent (a Mexican bullfighter is the husband) leave them with Lewis.

Complications ensue, of course. Her father is Salvatore Baccaloni, the former Met Opera basso, whose character name in the picture is Salvatore Naples, he's of fiery Italo stock and regards Lewis as a numbskull. Papa's other daughter is Connie Stevens, a cutie who has a yen for Lewis and undertakes to help him bring up the children. And then it becomes known that Miss Maxwell is the mother and Baccaloni the grandfather (and very proud of it). But because Lewis is a bachelor the court orders that the children be placed in the care of a wealthy matron, Isobel Elsom.

Lewis hides out with his trio of youngsters until Miss Maxwell turns up to take them over. Lewis marries Miss Stevens. They have quintuplets.

For a little background, Lewis brought in a couple members of his own family to appear in the picture. His father, Danny, and his son, Gary, have small parts and do well enough.

"Baby" is a series of situations,

rather than substantial story, and the focus is on Lewis for the most part. He's as ever the funny fellow and gets the comedy across. Baccaloni at times goes overboard in being the outraged Papa Naples. The Misses Stevens and Maxwell work well and look nifty and others in the cast can't be complained about.

Music is an important asset, particularly the song interludes. Camera work (there are some clever shots of the babies that stand out) is good, editing sufficiently tight and other technical credits competent. *Gene.*

The Lone Ranger and the Lost City of Gold
(COLOR)

Hearty full-length tale of the masked rider from Detroit and Tonto. Kiddies should keep b.o. high.

Hollywood, May 26.
United Artists release of a Jack Wrather production. Stars Clayton Moore, Jay Silverheels. Produced by Sherman A. Harris. Directed by Lesley Selander. Screenplay, Robert Schaefer and Eric Freiwald, based on the Lone Ranger legend; camera (Eastmancolor), Kenneth Peach; music, Les Baxter; editor, Robert S. Golden. Previewed in Hollywood May 26, '58. Running time, 80 MINS.

The Lone Ranger	Clayton Moore
Tonto	Jay Silverheels
Ross Brady	Douglas Kennedy
Oscar Matthison	Charles Watts
Frances Henderson	Noreen Nash
Paviva	Lisa Montell
Padre Vicente Esteban	Ralph Moody
Dr. James Rolfe	Norman Frederic
Tomache	John Miljan
Redbird	Maurice Jara
Travers	Bill Henry
Wilson	Lane Bradford
Caulama	Belle Mitchell

Out of the Arizona hills comes the hearty cry of "Hi Yo Silver," and away we go into a full-screened, full-colored blowup of what well may be the most sacred of all cowboy heroes. This is the Lone Ranger's 25th anniversary, that trail rider from Detroit, and the Jack Wrather production of "The Lone Ranger and the Lost City of Gold" is invitation enough to promote a profitable kiddie party at the boxoffice.

The United Artists release, produced for Wrather by Sherman A. Harris, is a respectable piece of work with enough adventure to keep the moppets from moping. With the masked stranger and Tonto constant tv companions in recent years, the feature version additionally benefits from fine Eastman Color lensing.

Story, penned by Robert Schaefer and Eric Freiwald, tells of a group of hooded riders who have been murdering friendly Indians, just to take ragged-edged medallions from them. It seems these pieces, when placed together, reveal the whereabouts of the lost city of gold. The Lone Ranger and Tonto ride into the case, tying up loose ends and discovering the connection between the dead men is that each wears one of the trinkets. They save a few lives, become involved in a rousing chase or two, then a hot gun battle, and eventually recover the stolen medallions. Finding the golden city, a glittering promise of riches for the Indians. Kemosabe and his Indian friend ride back into the Arizona hills.

Clayton Moore, as the Lone Ranger, and Jay Silverheels, as Tonto, are just the way LR fans want them—honest, strong and courageous. They're helped, too, by sturdy work from Silver and Scout, two fair hunks of horse flesh. Good performances are turned in by Douglas Kennedy,

Charles Watts, Noreen Nash, Ralph Moody, Norman Frederic and an especially charming femme, Lisa Montell.

The Schaefer-Freiwald script, bolstered by bows and arrows and even a dash of subplotted prejudice, is in keeping with the legend, and director Lesley Selander has done a fine job of keeping the story exciting and in tune. Kenneth Peach's photography beautifully catches the dry Tucson area, with assists coming from editor Robert S. Golden, are director James D. Vance and soundman Philip Mitchell. Music by Les Baxter, with a main titles song, "Hi Yo Silver," by Baxter and Lenny Adelson, keeps action at a high pitch.   *Ron.*

Le Beau Serge
(The Handsome Serge)
(FRENCH)

Cannes, May 27.
AJYM release and production. With Gerard Blain, Jean-Claude Brialy, Michele Meritz, Bernadette Lafont, Edmond Beauchamp. Written and directed by Claude Chabrol. Camera, Henri Decae; editor, Jacques Gaillard. At Cannes Film Fest. Running time, **97 MINS.**
Serge .... Gerard Blain
Francois .... Jean-Claude Brialy
Marie .... Bernadette Lafont
Yvonne .... Michel Meritz
Father .... Edmond Beauchamp

An important new French director, Claude Chabrol, is unveiled in this pic. Chabrol used his own money and made this feature entirely on location in his old home town. Brought in for $150,000, this bodes interest and biz for French situations but carries question mark for States.

Recovering from an illness a young man goes back to his home town. Here he finds an old friend has becomes a hopeless alcoholic. He at first blames it on his wife but then finds that the boy's disorientation comes from a stillborn, idiotic first child and the general provincialism and lack of moral or spiritual strength in the small, inbred town.

Technically excellent, director Chabrol should be heard from.
Mosk.

Bullwhip
(COLOR; C'SCOPE)

Guy Madison and Rhonda Fleming in lavish outdoor romantic comedy-drama. Good returns in action market.

Hollywood, May 30.
Allied Artists release of a Helen Ainsworth production. Stars Guy Madison and Rhonda Fleming. Executive producer, William F. Broidy. Director, Harmon Jones; screenplay, Adele Buffington; music, Leith Stevens; camera, John J. Martin; editor, Thor Brooks. Previewed in Hollywood, May 22, '58. Running time, 81 MINS.
Steve .... Guy Madison
Cheyenne .... Rhonda Fleming
Karp .... James Griffith
Judge .... Don Beddoe
Parnell .... Peter Adams
Podo .... Dan Sheridan
Pine Hawk .... Burt Nelson
Lem .... Al Terr
Pete .... Tim Graham
Tex .... Hank Worden
Larry .... Wayne Mallory
Mrs. Mason .... Barbara Woodell
Judd .... Rush Williams
Hotel Keeper .... Don Shelton
Sheriff .... Jack Reynolds
Keeler .... Frank Griffin
Indian Chief .... J. W. Cody
Trimble .... Jack Carr
Marshal .... Rick Vallin
Deputy Luke .... Saul Gorss

"Bullwhip" is not a picture to tax the mind, but it is a big, colorful outdoor romance designed purely and simply to be a box-office success and it has the neces-

sary and proper ingredients for that. Guy Madison and Rhonda Fleming head the cast of Helen Ainsworth's production for Allied Artists, directed by Harmon Jones, and the DeLuxe color in Cinema-Scope makes it an appealing presentation. William F. Broidy was executive producer.

The screenplay by Adele Buffington has Madison as a man about to be hanged (unfairly, of course), when his life is spared on condition he will marry Rhonda Fleming, which is an unusual and interesting variation of the special dish usually given the condemned man.

The ceremony is performed and Miss Fleming departs, warning Madison he is not to try to find out who she is. Madison, however, pursues. Miss Fleming eludes him. But they finally get together and he discovers his kissless bride is a part-Cheyenne who is ruthlessly determined to be the most successful fur trader in the west. She dominates her crew and her surroundings with a dynamic personality and a nasty bullwhip. Madison takes the whip away from her in their first setto, and then proceeds to bring her to heel on other accounts in a modified western version of "The Taming of the Squaw."

Picture allows some mildly racy humor in the situation of a man and woman who are married but have not consummated. There is also comedy in some other characters and situations, but it is not always as fully developed as it might be. The whole production lacks pace which, had it been provided, would have turned the picture into a very good one instead of what it is now, satisfactory.

Madison does a capable job, with glints of humor, as the reprieved man. Miss Fleming, spectacularly lovely, is appropriately fiery and eventually tender. James Griffith makes an amusing and unusual killer, and Peter Adams is suave as another offbeat heavy. Others in the cast who stand out include Don Beddoe, Dan Sheridan, Burt Nelson, Al Terr, Tim Graham and Hank Worden.

John J. Martin's camera work is perceptive and catches most imaginatively the soft autumn colors of what appear to be fresh location backgrounds. Leith Stevens' score highlights the action and there is a strong title song by Hal Hooper and James Griffith, sung by Frankie Laine. Other technical credits, including Thor Brooks' editing, and sound by Al Overton, are first-rate   *Powe.*

Zizkowska Romance
(A Suburban Romance)
(CZECHOSLAVAKIAN)

Czech State Film release and production. Stars Jiri Vala, Renata Olarava; features Eduard Cupak, Jana Brojchova. Directed by Zbynek Brynych. Screenplay, Vladimir Kaline, Brynych; camera, Jan Curik; editor B. Kulik. At Cannes Film Fest. Running time, 100 MINS.

Conventional romance concerns an unwed mother who hides the fact from her lover. But it ends on a note of acceptance after some fairly colorful character sketches and incidents.

Film possesses little Yank appeal but denotes an escape from propaganda-features in Eastern bloc countries. Technically it is will made and interpreted, improving on ordinary scripting. *Mosk,* are par.   *Mosk.*

The Key
(BRITISH—CINEMASCOPE)

Triple stellar magnet of Holden, Loren & Howard, plus Carol Reed's direction gives punch to this sea drama and romantic story. Terrific sea thrills in a certain b.o. winner.

London, May 28.
Columbia presentation of a Carl Foreman-Open Road production, produced by Aubrey Baring. Stars William Holden, Sophia Loren, Trevor Howard. Directed by Carol Reed. Screenplay, Carl Foreman based on Jan De Hartog's novel, "Stella"; camera, Oswald Morris; editor, Bert Bates; music, Malcolm Arnold. At Odeon, Leicester Square, London, May 28, '58. Running time, 134 MINS.
David Ross .... William Holden
Stella .... Sophia Loren
Chris Ford .... Trevor Howard
Van Dam .... Oscar Homolka
Kane .... Kieron Moore
Wadlow .... Bernard Lee
Housekeeper .... Beatrice Lehmann
Hotel Porter .... Noel Purcell
Weaver .... Bryan Forbes
Grogan .... Sydney Vivian
Baker .... Rupert Davies
Sparks .... Russell Waters
Clerk .... Irene Handl
American Captain .... John Crawford
English Captain .... Jameson Clark

Everything possible has been done to insure "The Key" being a click success. Carl Foreman's skilled, well-written screenplay, based on a popular novel, "Stella," has been given the works. Three international stars, William Holden, Sophia Loren and Trevor Howard, are supported by a topline bunch of feature players. Add to that, direction by Carol Reed, good lensing, superb sea thrills, a fascinating romantic story line and there are all the ingredients of a b.o. winner. At 134 minutes it runs over-long, and there are occasions, away from the sea, when interest flags slightly. But, all in all, "The Key" is certain to have tab-buyers queueing everywhere in Britain and the States.

It's a wartime yarn, with Holden and Howard as commanders of tugs engaged on convoy rescue duty in U-Boat Alley—the Western Approaches. This highly hazardous chore provides "The Key" with some standout thrills which alone make the pic great entertainment. But its title provides the clue to the intriguing love story which runs through the film and which will certainly interest women filmgoers even more than the fighting sequences. When Holden joins up with his old buddy, Howard, he finds him sharing an apartment with a beautiful Swiss refugee, played with dignity and sensitive understanding by Sophia Loren.

Miss Loren was to have married a tug commander who was killed on the eve of the wedding. When another skipper takes over the apartment she stays on with him. He, in turn, bequeathes the haven to Howard. She identifies both these men with her dead fiance. When Howard is killed, again just before marriage, Holden uses the spare key that Howard has given him to keep the apartment among tug men. Holden and Miss Loren fall in love and, for the first time, she ceases to see her first fiance in the owner of the key. Holden, thinking he will not return from a particularly dangerous mission, passes the key on to yet another tug skipper. Thinking this to be a betrayal the girl walks out on Holden and, refusing to bow to the conventional happy ending, the pic winds up.

This theme requires some pretty delicate handling on the part of the stars. Though Miss Loren is obviously more than a housekeeper

to the strained tug skippers it would have been fatal to the film if she had given the impression that she was just a good-time tramp. Looking serenely beautiful, she invests the role with warmth and dignity and it is not her fault if some of the apartment sequences tend to drag.

There are some outstanding scenes as, for instance, when Holden takes over command of his ship and indulges in crazy maneuvers to test its seaworthiness; a splendidly played tipsy scene between Howard and Holden; a fierce bombing and fire sequence at sea; and a tender moment when Holden and Sophia Loren fall in love. These are just a few of the highlights, but a lot of the strength of the film comes from the screenplay, Reed's direction and some cast-iron acting from all members of the cast. It is a necessary weakness of the film that Howard has to be removed from the pic all too early. Till his death he had brought a genuinely salty bite and rough good humor to his role.

Holden, too, is heroic, edgy, tender and understanding as the occasion demands and it is one of his best all round showings. Supporting players are too numerous to mention, but there are gems of characterization from Bernard Lee as a shore-based naval officer, Oscar Homolka and Kieron Moore as tug skippers, and Noel Purcell as a seedy porter at a sleazy waterside hotel.

The problem of "The Key" was to hold the balance between the sea adventure and the love story and this has been fairly capably handled by Foreman and Reed. There are occasional overtouches of symbolism and Miss Loren's relationship between the various men in her life, past and present, are sometimes glossed over a shade glibly. Oswald Morris' camerawork is realistically vivid and special effects, sound, art work and model effects are all skillfully put over.

"The Key" is very nearly a great film, and though it occasionally misfires it is still an adult entertainment which will excite and grip.   *Rich.*

Showdown at Boot Hill
(REGALSCOPE)

Well-directed, well-acted suspense western. No names for top billing but strong support on dualler.

Hollywood, June 6.
Twentieth-Fox release of a Regal production. Stars Charles Bronson. Robert Hutton. John Carradine, Carole Matthews, Fintan Meyler. Producer, Harold E. Knox; director, Gene Fowler Jr.; screenplay, Louis Vittes; camera, John M. Nickolaus Jr.; music, Albert Harris; editor, Frank Sullivan. Previewed in Hollywood, June 6, '58. Running time, 71 MINS.
Luke .... Charles Bronson
Sloane .... Robert Hutton
Doc Weber .... John Carradine
Jill .... Carol Mathews
Sally .... Fintan Meyler
Judge .... Paul Maxey
Con Maynor .... Thomas B. Henry
1st Cowhand .... William Stevens
2nd Cowhand .... Martin Smith
Mr. Creavy .... Joseph McGuinn
Charles Maynor .... George Douglas
Patton .... Michael Mason
Sheriff .... George Pembroke
Mrs. Bonventura ...... Argentina Brunetti
Brent .... Ed Wright

"Showdown on Boot Hill" is a low budget picture and does not have the production values or star names to make it a top attraction but it's a well-directed and well-acted picture done with taste and imagination. Produced by Regal, for 20th-Fox release, by Harold E. Knox, and directed by Gene Fowler Jr., it will, no doubt, be given the lower berth on a double bill but it will add strength and attraction to any booking.

Louis Vittes' screenplay is the familiar one of a stranger in a western frontier town who finds himself at odds with the community. But Vittes' dialog and his plotting make up for familiarity of situation, because the language is pungent and striking, and the frail story is given meaning and interest through characterization and lively scenes.

Charles Bronson plays the U.S. Marshal who comes to town, shoots it out with a wanted character and then has to persuade the townspeople to admit the man he killed had a price on his head. His only support comes from John Carradine as the town barber-doctor-undertaker, and from Fintan Meyler, a wistful girl trying to live down the fact that her mother, Carole Mathews, is the town madam, a point not much glossed over in the frank account. The rest of the town resents the outside interference and the fact that Bronson is what was called a bounty hunter. There is some final gunplay as Bronson is sustained in his mission but actually a minimum of shooting for a western. The ending is romantic and valid.

Fowler shows his editing background in his cohesive direction; all the picture is of one piece from the beginning of the opening titles to the final shot; he appreciates and achieves an entity. He also gets a remarkable number of camera setups, well done by cameraman John M. Nicholaus Jr., for a low budget picture. One device, using two local cowhands as a kind of Greek chorus commentary on the town, is also notable in setting the mood and nature of the community. He does it, also, with humor, the kind of grim joking typical of the time and the place.

The performances are uniformly excellent, with Bronson, Carradine, Miss Mathews, Miss Meyler and Michael Mason most important. Valuable in support are Robert Hutton, Paul Maxey, William Stevens, Martin Smith, George Pembroke and Argentina Brunetti. They are all individuals and memorable.

Fowler and Nicholaus employ the RegalScope projection for a number of interesting compositions and the rest of the staff has shown that they realized they were doing something more than a routine, program picture. These contributions include Frank Sullivan's editing, sound by David Dockendorf and Harry M. Leonard, art direction by John Mansbridge and set decoration by Walter M. Scott.
't Harris' music is a further asset.
Powe.

Kings Go Forth

Sinatra, Curtis, Wood top romantic wartime triangle with black-and-white race angle for "shock" value. Good b.o. prospects.

United Artists release of Frank Ross production. Stars Frank Sinatra, Tony Curtis, Natalie Wood; features Leora Dana, Karl Swenson. Anne Codee, Jackie Berthe. Directed by Delmer Daves; screenplay, Merle Miller, from Joe David Brown novel, "King's Go Forth"; camera, Daniel L. Fapp; music, Elmer Bernstein; editor, William Murphy. Seen at the UA screening room in N.Y., June 4, '58. Running time, 109 MINS.

Sam Loggins	Frank Sinatra
Britt Harris	Tony Curtis
Monique Blair	Natalie Wood
Mrs. Blair	Leora Dana
Colonel	Karl Swenson
Mme. Brieux	Anne Codee
Jean Francoise	Jackie Berthe

Frank Sinatra goes back to soldiering in this Merle Miller adaptation of Joe David Brown's novel, "Kings Go Forth." It's a simple, rather straightforward action-romance, laid against the attractive background of the French Riviera and the Maritime Alps. Not a very plausible item, it nevertheless has the sort of sentimental wrapping, emotional incidents and dramatic heroics that should boost the b.o.

Film's strongest exploitation asset, apart from the top names, is the race angle, which is played to the hilt. The girl, played by Natalie Wood—an American living in France—is of mixed blood, her mother being white and the (dead) father having been a Negro. This revelation is the key to Miss Wood's romantic entanglements. It leaves Sinatra stunned for a while and produces a rather cynical attitude in playboy Tony Curtis. Neither reaction rings particularly true, as the script puts it, and the gravity of the whole issue therefore appears overemphasized.

Still, the mixed-marriage question gets a thorough—and positive—going-over in the dialog, particularly on the part of Leora Dana, the mother, who movingly recounts the fullness and happiness of her marriage to her Negro husband, and the penalty of exile from the U.S. which she had to pay for it. It's in these sequences that "Kings Go Forth" takes on an adult shape and deviates from the otherwise routine pattern.

It's an odd war that is being fought in this picture. The men fight and die in the mountains during the week. On weekends, there are passes for visits to the Riviera, where the war seems but a memory. The year is late 1944, and while Allied armies push into and beyond Paris, the Amercian Seventh Army has the job of cleaning out pockets of German resistance in the south.

Among the replacements joining Sinatra's platoon is Curtis, a rich man's son, with charm to spare and an eye for all the angles. Sinatra meets Miss Wood and falls in love with her. She in turns falls in love with Curtis. When Curtis admits he won't marry the girl because she's of mixed blood, Sinatra vows to kill him. They go on a dangerous mission to help spot artillery fire on a German-held munitions depot. The mission is successful, but Curtis dies and Sinatra loses an arm. At the end of the war, he returns to Nice for another meeting with Miss Wood, who has set up a school for war orphans.

This potpourri of plots offers Daniel L. Fapp's camera a chance for some pretty lively goings-on, and he takes good advantage of the scenery. Curtis and Miss Wood go in for some pretty hot romancing and the scene when he tells her to her face that he wouldn't marry her because she isn't white has a certain brutal quality, though it's somehow out-of-character. In fact, several of the personalities in the Miller script aren't very consistent in their attitudes, and as a consequence not believable.

Sinatra, the rough-tough soldier, in action for six months and frustrated in his love for Miss Wood, turns in a capable performance. He's likable, and understandable, and creates sympathy by underplaying the role. Miss Wood looks pretty, but that's just all. She is best when the script gives her a chance to say out aloud what she feels. Curtis has had experience acting the heel, and he does a repeat, though his is a tough character to swallow. He's best when acting the charm boy. Miss Dana gives stature to the role of the mother who takes pride in what others see as her "shame." In fact, Miss Dana is standout in this difficult part and through her the picture gains a great deal.

Delmer Daves directed with more attention to formula than to logical character development. "Kings Go Forth" is, on the whole, well paced, though it runs dry in some talky stretches and there's never very much doubt about the outcome. The final action scenes, when Sinatra and Curtis manage to sneak into the German camp and set up an observation post in a tower, is a little ridiculous and on the naive side. Still, this being one of those films that tries hard to have something for everyone, it rates as a popular entry.
Hift.

Law and Disorder
(BRITISH)

Cheerful offbeat crook comedy with star value which rates plenty of laughs, potential b.o. click on both sides of Atlantic.

London, June 10.
British Lion (Paul Soskin) production and release. Stars Michael Redgrave and Robert Morley. Directed by Charles Crichton. Screenplay, T. E. B. Clarke and Patrick Campbell-Vivienne Knight, from the novel "Smuggler's Circuit," by Denys Roberts; editor, Oswald Hafenrichter; camera, Ted Scaife; music. Humphrey Searle. At Studio One, London. Running time, 76 MINS.

Percy Brand	Michael Redgrave
Judge Crichton	Robert Morley
Colonel Masters	Ronald Squire
Gina Lasalle	Elizabeth Sellars
Aunt Florence	Joan Hickson
Major Proudfoot	Lionel Jeffries
Colin Brand	Jeremy Burnham
Mary	Brenda Bruce
Blacky	Harold Goodwin
Bennie	George Coulouris
Sergeant Bolton	Meredith Edwards
Vickery	Reginald Beckwith
Freddie	David Hutcheson
Lady Crichton	Mary Kerridge
Pomfret	John Le Mesurier
Police Inspector	Allan Cuthbertson
Shorty	Sam Kydd
Police Superintendent	John Warwick

The nifty combination of Michael Redgrave, Robert Morley and director Charles Crichton makes "Law and Disorder" a highly amusing off-beat comedy which notches guffaws and giggles with disarming ease. Pic stands a solid chance of emulating the success of previous laughter-makers of similar tone, such as "Tight Little Island." The fact that Crichton is a graduate of the Ealing studios accounts for the fact that "Law and Disorder" has more than a little of the Ealing stamp. It is a potential b.o. click on both sides of the Atlantic.

There are several moments when the wheeze sags and a lot of skill has been needed to keep it floating. There is also a certain amount of confusion due to over-drastic editing. Running at 76 minutes, it lost 15 minutes in the final version and the hacking has left at least a couple of scenes in mid-air. Despite these faults, "Law and Disorder" is a slick entry in the comedy sweepstakes.

Redgrave is a con man who does rather well financially in his racket even though Robert Morley, a strict and pompous judge, is constantly sending him to the cooler. Redgrave accepts this occupational risk with good grace. His only problem is to keep his profession away from his young son, who grows up to manhood in the belief that his dad is a missionary away for long stretches in far-off lands.

All's well until the boy becomes a barrister and, worse still, marshal to Morley. So Redgrave retires to a quiet seacoast village. But old habits die hard and Redgrave becomes involved with the villagers in an ingenious brandy-smuggling racket.

This leads to a teaming up with his old gang and considerable complications when Redgrave is due, once again, to be hauled before Morley. A wild scheme is devised to involve Morley himself in a smuggling stunt to get him off the bench. This goes awry, but things eventually disentangle. And Redgrave faces another stretch with his secret still kept from his son.

The screenplay writers, T. E. B. Clarke, Patrick Campbell and Vivienne Knight, have dreamed up some neat comedy situations as well as deft dialog. And they are backed up by first-class performances all along the line. Redgrave gives charm to his plausible rogue while Morley revels in his stint as the judge whose pomposity gets badly jarred. Among others employed to whip along the yocks are some of Britain's finest character actors. Lionel Jeffries, as another astute con man; Joan Hickman, as Redgrave's card-sharping sister; Brenda Bruce, as a barmaid; Meredith Edwards, as a dim-witted village cop; Ronald Squire, as a local squire; and Elizabeth Sellars, as an attractive barrister, have the best opportunities, and grasp them firmly.

Oswald Rafenrichter's editing is suspect, but witty music by Humphrey Searle and the lensing of Ted Scaife is of a high standard. "Law and Order" is a cheerful item which is ideal fare for the summer season for which it is skedded.
Rich.

Dangerous Youth
(SONGS)

Tame tale of juvenile delinquency with some musical moments. Lower half of duals.

Hollywood, May 15.
Warner Bros. release of Anna Neagle production. Stars George Baker, Frankie Vaughan; features Sarole Lesley, Jackie Lane, Katherine Kath. Directed by Herbert Wilcox. Story-screenplay. Jack Trevor Story; camera, Gordon Dines; editor, Basil Warren; music, Stanley Black. Previewed May 13, '58. Running time, 97 MINS.

Padre	George Baker
Dave Wyman	Frankie Vaughan
Dinah Brown	Carole Lesley
Maureen	Jackie Lane
Mrs. Wyman	Katherine Kath
Mrs. Larkin	Thora Hird
Danny	Eddie Byrne
Juggler	Kenneth Cope
Cream O'Casey	Robert Desmond
Smiler Larkin	Ray Jackson
Captain Brewster	Richard Leech
Commanding Officer	John Le Mesurier
Sgt. Lockwood	David Lodge
Pvt. Simpson	Michael Ripper
Camp Barber	Reginald Beckwith

Juvenile delinquency theme lacks needed punch. While second half of pic is stronger than opening reels the characters are unbelievable. For the program market, where feature obviously is headed, its overlength footage has to be taken into reckoning.

Anna Neagle, one of Britain's

leading stars and heretofore associated strictly with dramatics, is credited as producer and hubby Herbert Wilcox, who has always produced and directed her screen efforts, handles the direction. Jack Trevor Story screenplay, unfolding in and around Liverpool, deals with the leader of a youthful gang who is drafted. His involvements during the training period comprise the plot, including his false accusation of shooting a troublemaker responsible for the death of his best friend.

Bright moments are provided by femme lead, Carole Lesley, a looker, who nicely warbles "Isn't It a Lovely Evening," and Frankie Vaughan, male lead, socks over a couple of rock 'n' rollers, "These Dangerous Years" and "Cold, Cold Shower." Mild suspense accompanies Vaughan's desertion after he's arrested at camp for the shooting.

George Baker co-stars with Vaughan as the camp padre who tries to straighten out the young gang leader but his lines are against him. Jackie Lane is pert as Miss Lesley's roommate and Katherine Kath makes her work count as Vaughan's mother.

Gordon Dines' low-key photography catches the grimness of the Liverpool waterfront, where probably most of action unfolds, and Basil Warren's editing is okay. Music score by Stanley Black is appropriate to the mood. *Whit.*

Wink of an Eye

Sub-standard comedy-mystery. Only chance, bottom half of double-bill.

Hollywood, May 30.
United Artists release of Fernando Carrere production. Features Jonathan Kidd, Doris Dowling, Barbara Turner, Irene Seidner. Director-cameraman, Winston Jones; screenplay, Robert Radnitz, Robert Presnell Jr., James Edmiston; from an original story by Chester Davis, Winston Jones; music, Ernest Gold; editor, Chester Shaeffer. Previewed in Hollywood, May 29, '58. Running time, **72 MINS.**
Mr. Atterbury .... Jonathan Kidd
Myrna Duchane .... Doris Dowling
Judy .... Barbara Turner
Mrs. Lazlow .... Irene Seidner
Mrs. Atterbury .... Jaclynne Greene
Sheriff Cantrick .... Wally Brown
Vanryzin .... Taylor Holmes
Max .... Max Rich
Ben Lazlow .... Paul Smith
Delivery Boy .... Jack Grinnage
Old Man .... Lucien Littlefield
Rand .... Rodney Bell
Butler .... Dick Nelson
Trumpet Player .... Sam Levin
Guitar Player .... Howard Roberts
Attendant .... Henry Slate
Mr. Hix .... Tom Browne Henry

An attempt at comedy-murder mystery in the tradition of "A Slight Case of Murder" and "Arsenic and Old Lace," this Fernando Carrere production, "Wink of an Eye" is too thin in plot and too weak in invention to be more than a double-bill filler item, and a dubious one at that. Fernando Carrere produced, Winston Jones directed, and Jonathan Kidd and Doris Dowling head the cast, which contains no names that will be of any help either.

The screenplay by Robert Radnitz, Robert Presnell Jr. and James Edmiston has Kidd as a Milquetoast character who supposedly is plotting and carrying out his wife's murder so he can run off to South America with his lab assistant, Doris Dowling. Although the audience is led to believe he has dissected his wife and stowed the parts in the deep-freeze, it turns out to be an elaborate misunderstanding that supplies the story with a gimmick conclusion and a few laughs in the final scenes.

When a story has a snapper like this it is hard to sustain interest along the way unless the dialog and characters are particularly interesting, which, in this case, they are not. *Powe.*

Life Begins at 17

Joys and sorrows of teenaged romance, with double-meaning sex angles for sensational exploitation. Satisfactory for teenage fans.

Hollywood, June 13.
Columbia release of a Sam Katzman production. Stars Mark Damon, Dorothy Johnson, Edward Byrnes. Directed by Arthur Dreifuss. Screenplay, Richard Baer; camera, Fred Jackman; editor, Saul A. Goodkind. Previewed in Hollywood, June 12. '58. Running time, **74 MINS.**
Russ Lippincott .... Mark Damon
Elaine Peck .... Dorothy Johnson
Jim .... Ed Byrnes
Virginia Peck .... Ann Doran
Harry Peck .... Hugh Sanders
Carol Peck .... Luana Anders
Pooky Peck .... Cathy O'Neill
Mr. Lippincott .... George Eldredge
Earl Williamson .... Tommy Ivo
Allen Sperry .... Bob Dennis
George Tewksbury ...... Robert Moechel
Mr. Tilling .... Maurice Manson

"Life Begins At 17," a Sam Katzman production for Columbia, has the virtue of being a teen-age picture aimed at teen-agers that is not about the hot rod-switch blade set. It does get into some rather sticky sex involving a false pregnancy and the villains of the piece are, as usual, dense and unsympathetic parents, but for the audience it is aimed at it will probably be popular. Particularly since it lends itself to lurid exploitation.

Luana Anders plays the ugly duckling daughter of Hugh Sanders and Ann Doran. To get a date with her beautiful older sister, Dorothy Johnson, prep school student Mark Damon dates her and pretends he finds her attractive. When Miss Anders discovers she has been a pawn in a plot, she rebels and claims she is about to have Damon's baby. It turns out by this time that he has actually been captured by her off-beat charm, the older sister is united with her longtime beau, Edward Byrnes, and the adults are put in their proper place — the background.

Richard Baer's screenplay is inventive and well-plotted and Arthur Dreifuss' direction keeps it going interestingly. The mostly youngthful cast is attractive and capable.

There is a melodic "title" song but unfortunately its title is that used while the picture was in production, "The Teen Age Story." Still, it should be a selling aid. *Powe.*

Gunman's Walk
(COLOR-C'SCOPE)

Good b.o. prospects for this action melodrama of youth-age, parent-son conflict set in the frontier west. Special teener appeal in star names.

Hollywood, June 13.
Columbia release of a Fred Kohlmar production. Stars Van Heflin, Tab Hunter; costars Kathryn Grant, James Darren. Director, Phil Karlson. Screenplay, Frank Nugent; from a story by Dic Hardman; camera, Charles Lawton Jr.; music, George Duning; editor, Jerome Thoms. Previewed at the studio, June 10, '58. Running time, **95 MINS.**
Lee Hackett .... Van Heflin
Ed Hackett .... Tab Hunter
Clee Chouard .... Kathryn Grant
Davy Hackett .... James Darren
Will Motely ...... Mickey Shaughnessy
Harry Brill .... Robert F. Simon
Purcell Avery .... Edward Platt
Jensen Sieverts .... Ray Teal
Bob Selkirk .... Paul Birch
Curly .... Michael Granger
Judge .... Will Wright
Black Horse .... Chief Blue Eagle
Paul Chouard .... Bert Convy
Cook .... Paul E. Burns
Bartender .... Paul Bryar
Rev. Arthur Stotheby..... Everett Glass
Mrs. Stotheby...........Dorothy Adams

"Gunman's Walk" shapes up as a promising box office come-on with three young stars, Tab Hunter, Kathryn Grant and James Darren, given solid backing in the age-youth conflict story by Van Heflin. The Columbia presentation, produced by Fred Kohlmar and directed by Phil Karlson, has been given a handsome production in CinemaScope and Technicolor that should mean brisk business at the box office.

Frank Nugent's screenplay, from a story by Ric Hardman, has Hunter and Darren as sons of Heflin, a western rancher in the old tradition, who brought law and order to the country with his own guns. He finds it hard to adjust to the changing order of things, towns, fences and established law, and subconsciously encourages one son, Hunter, to be the kind of rugged individual that is outmoded in the new setup. The other boy, Darren, through neglect, develops more naturally as a young man and as a person in accord with the times as they are. The situation comes to a climax when Hunter, trying to outdo the legend of his father, goes bad in a series of killings.

There is more subtlety than this simple outline in Nugent's screenplay, the personal relations between the brothers, the introduction of Miss Grant as a half Indian girl and the racial discrimination she suffers, but basically it is a story—and a good one—of men who failed to grow up with the country.

The characters are complex because Heflin, through his ignorance, is actually the heavy, although Hunter is made to seem that. It is not quite right that Heflin, in the end, should be comforted by Darren and Miss Grant, after Hunter has been shot (by the father) to prevent him prolonging his gun-slinging career. But it is realistic, and Heflin's rock-hard performance makes it believable and sympathetic. Hunter is cold and deadly, his boyishness underlining the ferocious hate that explodes from his guns.

Darren's role of the good son seems relatively mild in comparison, but he endows it with gentleness and interest so he is not submerged. Miss Grant, as the half-breed girl, is fine. Others in the cast who contribute include Mickey Shaughnessy, Robert F. Simon, Edward Platt, Ray Teal, Paul Birch, Michael Granger and Will Wright.

Although Fred Kohlmar's production is a period piece, it has contemporary pertinancy with the outspoken discussion of the racial elements, in this case, of course, involving the Indians. Phil Karlson's direction sets up the different characters and keeps each one distinct in his own development as well as in relation to the others.

Charles Lawton Jr.'s camera work is equally good in the interior and closeup shots, and in the sweeping panoramas. George Duning's effective score, well conducted by Morris Stoloff, points up the story's drama. Other technical credits, art direction by Robert Peterson, set decoration by Frank A. Tuttle sound by John Livadary and editing by Jerome Thoms, are all first-rate. *Powe.*

The Revenge of Frankenstein
(BRITISH—COLOR)

Successor to last year's successful "Curse of Frankenstein," should have same strong b.o.

Hollywood, June 13.

Columbia release of an Anthony Hinds production. Stars Peter Cushing, Francis Matthews, Eunice Gayson, Michael Gwynn. Executive producer, Michael Carreras; director, Terence Fisher; screenplay, Jimmy Sangster, with additional dialog by Hurford Janes; camera, Jack Asher; music, Leonard Salzedo; editor, Alfred Cox. Previewed in Hollywood, June 13, '58. Running time, **89 MINS**

Dr. Victor Stein .... Peter Cushing
Dr. Hans Kleve .... Francis Matthews
Margaret .... Eunice Gayson
Karl .... Michael Gwynn
Bergman .... John Welsh
Fritz .... Lionel Jeffries
Dwarf .... Oscar Quitak
Up Patient .... Richard Wordsworth
President .... Charles Lloyd Pack
Inspector .... John Stuart

"The Revenge of Frankenstein" is made by the same team, including Peter Cushing as Baron Frankenstein, that made last year's highly successful "Curse of Frankenstein." A Hammer production, released this time by Columbia, "Revenge" is also in blood-red color, as was the earlier picture, and should prove to have the same pull as its predecessor. It's a high grade horror film, gory enough to give adults a squeamish second thought and a thoroughly unpleasant one. The kids apparently are impervious.

Cushing, as the famed medical experimenter, is still determined to make a monster, although that is not how he would put it. Despite official pressure, Frankenstein is again collecting bits of bone and tissue, muscle and blood, to put together a man of his creation. Again he succeeds, but again something goes wrong and his creature—through brain damage—becomes a cannibal, slavering blood and saliva before he is destroyed. Frankenstein, surely the most indomitable medical experimenter in history, again outwits and eludes his would-be captors. As the film ends he has set up practice again, this time in London, and another juicy sequel can be expected.

Anthony Hinds' production, for which Michael Carreras was executive producer, is a rich one. The settings, the costumes and other physical aspects are on the level of any top production. The screenplay, by Jimmy Sangster, with additional dialog by Hurford Janes, is well-plotted, peopled with interesting characters, aided by good performances from Francis Matthews as his chief assistant; Eunice Gayson, Michael Gwynn, John Welsh, Lionel Jeffries, Oscar Quitak, Richard Wordworth and Charles Lloyd Pack.

Jack Asher's photography and Leonard Salzedo's music are other plus values of the production.

Powe.

Hot Car Girl

Teenage exploitation item. Satisfactory.

Hollywood, June 13.

Allied Artists release of a Gene Corman production. Stars Richard Bakalyan, June Kenney, John Brinkley. Executive producer, Roger Corman; director, Bernard L. Kowalski; screenplay, Leo Gordon; camera, John M. Nickolaus Jr.; music, Cal Tjader; editor, Irene Morra. Previewed in Hollywood, June 11, '58. Running time, **71 MINS.**

Duke .... Richard Bakalyan
Peg .... June Kenney
Fred .... John Brinkley
Ryan .... Robert Knapp
Janice .... Jana Lund
Mickey .... Sheila McKay
Joe .... Bruno Ve Soto
Mrs. Dale .... George Albertson
Older Sheriff .... Jack Lambert
Young Sheriff .... Ed Nelson
Dolman .... Hal Smith
Desk Sergeant .... Howard Culver
Mr. Wheeler .... Tyler McVey

The juvenile heroes of "Hot Car Girl" make a living by stealing auto accessories and spend their leisure hours drinking spiked soft drinks illegally peddled. In a way, the Gene Corman production for Allied Artists has its salutary effects, because this life of crime looks so depressing that it is unlikely to make many recruits. The production will probably be an okay presentation for houses playing this kind of attraction.

Richard Bakalyan is the leading delinquent in the screenplay by Leo Gordon, with his chief confederate John Brinkley. Bakalyan takes up with a nice girl, June Kenney, but gets annoyed when she suggests he give up his career of petty theft. In a pique he indulges in an impromptu race with Jana Lund, their cars collide and Miss Lund is killed. Bakalyan takes it on the lam, holes up in a remote cave and is eventually flushed out by police tear gas and killed. Chivalrously, he leaves a note exonerating Miss Kenney. The explanation for his behavior is that he was once beaten up by the cops as a kid. Unfortunately, his character makes a case in favor of police brutality.

Bernard L. Kowalski's direction does a good job of making this shaky premise seem valid. He keeps his story going at a nervous pace, his young players give believable portrayals and the story, while unsatisfactory, is absorbing. Cal Tjader's unusual musical background is adroitly utilized to accent the unhealthy mood and atmosphere.

Others in the cast besides the principals who do creditable work include Robert Knapp, Sheila McKay, Bruno Ve Soto and Grace Albertson.

John M. Nickolaus Jr.'s photography has an appropriately realistic flavor.

Powe.

The Cry-Baby Killer

Topical values and youth appeal make this a satisfactory entry for houses specializing in teen audiences.

Hollywood, June 13.

Allied Artists release of a David Kramarsky-David March production. Stars Harry Lauter, Jack Nicholson, Carolyn Mitchell. Executive producer, Roger Corman; director, Jus Addiss; screenplay, Leo Gordon, Melvin Levy; from a story by Gordon; camera, Floyd Crosby; music, Gerald Fried; editor, Irene Morra. Previewed in Hollywood, June 11, '58. Running time, **62 MINS.**

Porter .... Harry Lauter
Jimmy .... Jack Nicholson
Carole .... Carolyn Mitchell
Manny .... Brett Halsey
Julie .... Lynn Cartwright
Joey .... Ralph Reed
Gannon .... John Shay
Mrs. Maxton .... Barbara Knudson
Sam .... Jordan Whitfield
Werner .... Claude Stroud
Mrs. Wallace .... Ruth Swanson
Mr. Maxton .... William A. Forester
Reed .... John Weed
Gambelli .... Frank Richards
Mr. Wallace .... Bill Erwin
Al .... James Fillmore
Rick .... Ed Nelson
Evelyn .... Mitzi McCall

"Cry Baby Killer" adopts a semi-documentary style to exploit what happens when a teen-aged gunman holes up while police and other authorities try to persuade him to surrender. There isn't much depth to the David Kramarsky-David March production, and the screenplay by Leo Gordon and Melvin Levy runs out of plot too early, but the Allied Artists presentation will probably suffice on its name alone for the exploitation market for which it is planned.

Jack Nicholson plays the "Cry Baby Killer." In a scuffle with some other teen-agers he discharges a gun and, believing he has killed two of his opponents, barricades himself in a small storeroom on the grounds of the drive-in restaurant that is their hangout. Trapped with him is a Negro handyman and a young mother and her infant child. Police, parents and friends take turns in attempting to persuade him to surrender. He eventually does with no more bloodshed.

The Gordon-Levy screenplay, from a story by Gordon, is intended to be identified with real-life occurrences, such as have occupied the front pages from time to time. But for dramatic value there should have been more motivation than is given for the boy's action. In other aspects, the carnival atmosphere of the gathering crowd, the morbid and ghoulish approach of television in its coverage of the event, and the contrast of life continuing in the shadow of the horror, are intelligently presented.

Young Nicholson is handicapped by having a character of only one dimension to portray. Others who contribute include Harry Lauter as the cop in charge, Carolyn Mitchell as the boy's girl, Brett Halsey, Lynn Cartwright, Ralph Reed and John Shay.

Jus Addiss' direction gets the feel of reality into the production, and Floyd Crosby's photography—shot entirely, except for interiors, at night—has a newsreel flavor.

Powe.

The Wind Cannot Read
(BRITISH-COLOR)

Compelling romantic drama set in India. Fine performances, and a good b.o. prospect.

London, June 12.

Rank release of a Betty E. Box-Ralph Thomas Production. Stars Dirk Bogarde and Yoko Tani. Features John Fraser and Ronald Lewis. Producer, Betty E. Box; director, Ralph Thomas; screenplay, Richard Mason; editor, Frederick Wilson; camera, Ernest Steward; music, Angelo Lavagnino. At Odeon, Leicester Square, London, June 11, '58. Running time **115 MINS.**

Flt. Lt. Michael Quinn ..... Dirk Bogarde
Suzuki San .... Yoko Tani
Leader Fenwick .... Ronald Lewis
Officer Peter Munroe ...... John Fraser
Brigadier .... Anthony Bushnell
Lt. Nakamura .... Henry Okawa
Bahadur .... Marne Maitland
Officer Lamb .... Michael Medwin
Hobson .... Richard Leech
Moss .... Anthony Wager
Itsumi San .... Tadashi Ikeda
Corp. Mori .... Yoichi Matsue
Doctor .... Donald Pleasence
First Nurse .... Joy Michael
Second Nurse .... Avice Landone

Richard Mason's novel, "The Wind Cannot Read," has shaped up as a useful romantic drama which should attract appreciative audiences. It is overlong and the first half is a shade leisurely, but it has been written, directed and acted with polish and sincerity and the superb Asiatic locale helps a great deal. Ernest Steward has done a great job with his camera and Eastmancolor.

The pic is a love story told against a Burma war background. It's done delicately and with very good taste. Scenery pluses include the doll-like good looks of the young Japanese actress, Yoko Tani. She and Dirk Bogarde hold the acting side together in what is an almost uninterrupted Cupid duolog.

Bogarde is a grounded flyer sent to learn Japanese in order to be able to interrogate Japanese p.o.w's. He falls for Miss Tani, one of the instrutors, marries her in secret and is then sent off to the front where he is captured, tortured and humiliated before escaping. He gets back to base just in time to find his wife dying after a brain operation. It's a simple enough yarn which hardly needed 115 minutes to unfold. But director Thomas can be forgiven for falling in love with his locale as ardently as Bogarde does for the girl.

The gradual falling in love of the two stars is written with trite dialog but is directed charmingly. Then, when the action moves to the front, the prison torture scenes are put over with stark realism. Production highlights include a superb look at a Delhi bazaar, in which the color and atmosphere sizzles excitingly, and the ambushing of a convoy by Japanese soldiers which strikes suddenly and grimly.

Dirk Bogarde, not usually over happy in romantic roles, responds admirably to his attractive co-star, Miss Tani, and the two handle their many scenes skilfully, never descend to mawkishness. The final, "unhappy-ending" death bed scene is particularly well done. There are a number of other performances worth noting, too. Anthony Bushell, for instance, as an understanding brigadier, Michael Medwin as an officer with an eye for the girls and a "who gives a damn" attitude to life, and John Fraser as Bogarde's buddy.

Ronald Lewis spends the first part of the film as a stuffy rank-conscious flying officer constantly needling Bogarde and doing his best to fling a spanner into the romantic intrigue of the two stars. Here, he has little to do but scowl and register irritation. But in the more active jungle sequences he proves a powerful actor and is quite brilliant in one or two of the prison camp sequences.

The film's title provides a theme song, which is put over with smooth professionalism by one of Britain's thrushes, Vera Lynn, and should be a solid entry in the current ballad stakes.

Rich.

The Snorkel

Gimmicked suspense meller. Adequate for twin bills.

Hollywood, June 13.

Columbia release of a Michael Carreras Production. Stars Peter Van Eyck, Betta St. John, Mandy Miller. Directed by Guy Green. Screenplay, Peter Myers and Jimmy Sangster; from a novel by Anthony Dawson; camera, Jack Asher; music, Francis Chagrin; editor, James Needs. Previewed in Hollywood, June 4, '58. Running time, **73 MINS**

Jacques Duval .... Peter Van Eyck
Jean .... Betta St. John
Candy .... Mandy Miller
Inspector .... Gregorie Aslan

"The Snorkel," a British production for Columbia, has an intriguing gimmick as the clue to its murder mystery plot and some moments of suspense and horror, but lackadaisical direction and unresourceful screen writing prevent the film from being continuously engrossing. It will serve adequately on double bills.

Peter Van Eyck has devised an ingenious method of murdering his wife, according to Peter Myers-Jimmy Sangster screenplay from

Anthony Dawson's novel. He quiets her with sedatives then turns on all the gas in her sealed room, hiding himself in a cavity in the floor, and insuring his own breathing by means of a skin-diver's snorkel device. Police see the room sealed and locked from the inside and assume it must be suicide. After the body and the authorities have departed, Van Eyck emerges and passes himself off as just returned from an overnight trip away from home.

His undoing is brought about by the suspicious teenage daughter of the wife by a former marriage. Although everyone keeps telling the child she is unbalanced and will be shut up in a mental home if she doesn't stop her blathering, she persists until she brings the murderer to justice.

The director, Guy Green, has achieved two interesting scenes, the opening and the closing, but in between he allows his actors, particularly the leading ones, Peter Van Eyck, Betta St. John and young Mandy Miller, to play with too little variety. The girl, Miss Miller, particularly, who should evoke sympathy, arouses only annoyance after a time by her shrill and whiny insistence on justice for a murderer.

The French Riviera locations have some interest and give the picture authenticity. *Powe.*

The Space Children

Exploitable science - fictioner for the juvenile market; no marquee names.

Paramount release of a William Alland production. Stars Michel Ray, Adam Williams, Peggy Webber. Directed by Jack Arnold. Scheenplay, Bernard C. Schoenfeld, based on story by Tom Filer; camera, Ernest Laszlo; editor, Terry Morse; music, Van Cleave. Previewed N.Y., June 6, '58. Running time, **69 MINS.**

Dave Brewster	Adam Williams
Anne Brewster	Peggy Webber
Bud Brewster	Michel Ray
Ken Brewster	John Crawford
Hank Johnson	Jackie Coogan
Eadie Johnson	Sandy Descher
Lt. Col. Manley	Richard Shannon
Tim Gamble	John Washbrook
Joe Gamble	Russell Johnson
Dr. Wahrman	Raymond Bailey

Somewhat in vogue of late is the practice of coupling two films of a similar nature on a double bill. That's what's being done with "The Space Children" and "The Colossus of New York," both of which were produced by William Alland for Paramount release. "Children," as well as its running mate, shape up as exploitable merchandise for the juvenile trade.

While there's nothing pretentious about "Children," its science-fiction aspects have a topical slant that may serve to lure adult action fans. But basically this is a crack, suspense thriller for the Saturday matinee trade. With a flock of moppet thespers on the screen the kids in the audience will have no difficulty in achieving a sense of personal identification.

As screenplayed by Bernard C. Schoenfeld from a story by Tom Filer, yarn concerns a mysterious force from outer space that compels earth children to obey its commands. Plot follows familiar lines for its only too obvious that the mesmerized youngsters will succeed in foiling a launching of an American "six-stage rocket" that's intended to place a satellite with a hydrogen warhead far above the globe.

There's a hint that the outer space "thing," by coercing the earth's nations to abandon missile warfare, has given the world a "second chance." In any event, the bally values contained in the subject matter may offset the cast's lack of names. Handed star billing is young Michel Ray whose performance as the children's leader, ably fills the demands of the script.

Adam Williams and Peggy Webber, as Ray's parents, register as a typical couple. Okay as their other child is John Crawford while Sandy Descher is lively and inquisitive as another of the "space children." Routine support is provided by Jackie Coogan, Sandy's father; Richard Shannon, commandant at the missile base, and Raymond Bailey, scientist who ferrets out the mystery, among others.

Direction of Jack Arnold manages to get some credence in the portrayals despite the imaginative story. Ernest Laszlo's black-and-white camerawork is effective. Other visual assets include John P. Fulton's special effects and the process photography of Farciot Edouart. Art direction of Hal Pereira and Roland Anderson is good while Terry Morse edited to a tight 69 minutes. Van Cleave's eerie score adds to the sci-fiction atmosphere. *Gilb.*

The Big Money
(BRITISH—TECHNICOLOR)

Tame comedy, with thinly spaced laffs which will satisfy only easily pleased audiences.

London, June 10.

Rank Film Distributors' release of a R..nk (Joseph Yanni) production. Stars Ian Carmichael, Belinda Lee, Kathleen Harrison, Robert Helpman. Directed by John Paddy Carstairs. Story and screenplay by John Baines; camera, Jack Cardiff; editor, Alfred Roome (reedited by Hugh Stewart); music, Van Phillips. Previewed at Odeon, Leicester Square, London. Running time, **86 MINS.**

Willie Frith	Ian Carmichael
Gloria	Belinda Lee
Mrs. Frith	Kathleen Harrison
The Reverend	Robert Helpmann
Mr. Frith	James Hayter
The Colonel	George Coulouris
Doreen Frith	Jill Ireland
Bobby	Renee Houston
Receptionist	Leslie Phillips
Bookmaker	Harold Berens

Several months ago the Rank organization cashed in on comedian Ian Carmichael's soaring popularity by thrusting him into a comedy called "The Big Money." Rank topper John Davis took the unusual step of publicly announcing the shelving of the pic because, in his opinion, it wasn't very funny. That could have been the end of that. But recently producer Hugh Stewart asked for a chance to reedit the film which had been directed by his professional buddy, John Paddy Carstairs. Now the result has hit the screen and all Stewart's labors cannot disguise the fact that Davis was right in the first place.

Though sparking from an amusing idea, "The Big Money" is funny only in spots. It is bogged down by gag situations that are telegraphed, and feeble dialog. The producer's name, Joseph Yanni, has been taken off the credits. Though it may prove a modest filler in certain British houses, it will do nobody's reputation any good if it is entered for U.S. consumption.

The story has Carmichael as the misfit son of a suburban household who live prosperously as small-time crooks. But he cannot even get to first base in the larceny biz until one day when he lifts a suitcase from a clergyman which contains a fortune in banknotes. His father turns him out of the house, his professional pride outraged, when the loot is discovered to be counterfeit, each bill bearing the same number. Remainder of film has the star desperately trying to dispose of the dud cash in order to squander it on a goodtime barmaid, while the clergyman-crook tries to get it back.

There are a few cute notions which, treated with a lighter touch might have raised greater yocks. As, for instance, when Carmichael desperately changes a number of bills and enters a nightclub loaded down with small change. The scene where he interrupts the cabaret with an attack of hiccoughs and then finds a load of coins descending on the dance floor comes over rather funnier than it sounds in cold print. But, mainly, the film is tied together with some rather tired stuff.

Carmichael, handicapped by a ginger toupee and a stammer, works fiendishly to raise the merriment, but the role is played on too much of a Johnny-one-note of silly ass pathos. Belinda Lee, as a barmaid, looks a dish but turns in a formance of unrestrained mediocrity. Ballet dancer Robert Helpmann, as the crook clergyman, turns to comedy with a singular lack of success. Smaller roles played by Renee Houston, as an experienced barmaid; James Hayter, as Carmichael's pickpocket father and, notably, Leslie Phillips as a suave hotel receptionist, are standouts in a film which it is undoubtedly best to forget.

Direction, photography and artwork are adequate, but cannot lift John Baines' screenplay to any reasonable standard. *Rich.*

Girl in the Woods

Well made. Half of an exploitation package.

Hollywood, June 11.

Republic release of an AB-PT production. Stars Forrest Tucker, Maggie Hayes, Barton MacLane. Produced by Harry L. Mandell. Directed by Tom Gries. Screenplay by Oliver Crawford and Marcel Klauber, based on Crawford's novel, "Blood on the Branches"; camera, Jack Marta; editor, Doug Stewart; music, Albert Glasser. Reviewed at the Downtown Paramount, L.A., June 11, '58. Running time, **71 MINS.**

Steve Cory	Forrest Tucker
Bell Cory	Maggie Hayes
Big Jim	Barton MacLane
Sonda	Diana Francis
Whitlock	Murvyn Vye
Luke Plummer	Paul Langton
Aunt Martha	Joyce Compton
Jerry Plummer	Kim Charney
Samson	Mickey Finn
Dr. Wyndham	Bartlett Robinson
Marty	Harry Raybould
Operator	George Lynn
Bartender	Joey Ray

"Girl in the Woods," aside from its title, has none of the now-common exploitation values, no horror, no juvenile delinquency, and only average crime, violence and sex. In fact, it's a respectably produced film that benefits from stars Forrest Tucker and Maggie Hayes and a fetching young ingenue, Diana Francis. But the paucity of exploitational items will be made up for in its packaging with "Eighteen and Anxious" (reviewed Nov. 13, 1957, by VARIETY), and the AB-PT pair should garner satisfactory results.

The film actually should be called "Man in the Woods," for it centers around Paul Langton who steals trees from Murvyn Vye because he and the whole town feel Vye's ancestors stole the land. Tucker and Miss Hayes come to town, he to climb trees as a high rigger and she to keep him on his toes, and they become involved with Langton. Tucker is hoodwinked into leading Vye to Langton's hiding place and thence is framed as the cause for Langton's demise by Vye's bullets. The whole town against him, Tucker stays to prove his innocence and his intention to continue climbing trees.

Tucker and Miss Hayes are fine, and good work is turned in by Barton MacLane, Joyce Compton, Vye, Langton, Kim Charney, Bartlett Robinson and the pretty Miss Francis who looks remarkably like Liz Taylor and whose presence enlivens every frame.

Director Tom Gries has obtained a proper mood from his players, and the Oliver Crawford-Marcel Klauber screenplay, based on Crawford's novel, "Blood on the Branches," is good if somewhat spotty in interest.

Technically, the Harry L. Mandell production benefits from Jack Marta's camera and Albert Glasser's music. *Ron.*

Le Desert De Pigalle
(FRENCH)

Paris June 3.

Cinedis release of Play-Art-Speva Films production. Stars Annie Girardot, Pierre Trabaud; features Nelly Vignon, Serge Jolivet Claire Guibert, Monique Vita. Directed by Leo Joannon. Screenplay, Herve Bromberger, Jacques Robert, Jacques Sigurd, Serge Groussard, Joannon; camera, Andre Bac; editor, Jean Feyte. At the Paris, Paris. Running time, **105 MINS.**

Janin	Pierre Trabaud
Josy	Anne Girardot
Gege	Serge Jolivet
Maurice	Leo Joannon
Malou	Claire Guibert
Georgette	Nelly Vignon
Vera	Monique Vita

Film concerns a worker-priest's valiant attempt to salvage the souls of prostitutes in the underworld of Pigalle. Pic is explicit so it shapes an exploitation possibility for the U.S. But its conventional characters, heavyhanded direction and obviously studio-made exteriors limit this for arty house chances.

The young priest is fighting a rugged bunch of white slavers. A hardhearted prostie feels something for him and helps him, but not before plenty of killing and mayhem. The panderers are finally caught, the prostie killed and the priest hospitalized.

Director Leo Joannon plays the aging head of the gang with theatrical aplomb which denotes what is weak in the remainder of the pic. With its concessions it becomes another pic on the eternal French problem of prostitution, but it adds little. Pierre Trabaud is convincing as the priest while Annie Girardot has the proper metallic edge for the prostie. Others in the cast are adequate in their slim roles. *Mosk.*

Country Music Holiday
(SONGS)

Bouncy ride through Cornville—set to music in the bucolic fashion. Lightweight fare with Zsa Zsa Gabor and Rocky Graziano along with warbler Ferlin Husky to help put it in fair-enough "country" market groove.

Paramount release of Aurora Production. (Ralph Serpe and Howard B. Kreitsek). Features Ferlin Husky, Jesse White, Rod Brasfield, Rocky Graziano, Farin Young, June Carter, Al Fisher, Lou Marks. Directed by Alvin Ganzer. Story and screenplay, H. B. Cross; camera, William J. Kelly; editor, Ralph Rosenbloom; musical director, Dave Dryer.

Previewed in N. Y. June 7, '58. Running time, 80 MINS.
Verne Brand .... Ferlin Husky
Zsa Zsa .... Zsa Zsa Gabor
Rocky .... Rocky Graziano
Clyde Woods .... Faron Young
Al Fisher .... Al Fisher
Lou Marks .... Lou Marks
Marietta .... June Carter
Sonny Moon .... Jesse White
Morty Chapman .... Cliff Norton
Pappy .... Rod Brasfield
Ma .... Hope Sansberry
Sis .... Patty Duke
Donovan .... Art Ford
Lew Parker .... Lew Parker

Former I.F.E. exec Ralph Serpe and Howard B. Kreitsek have teamed in the production of an obviously low-budgeted cornball special about the music business and the practitioners who work the "country" side of the street. Comes off okay in its modest way, being a combination of farce, vocalizing and "specialities" by such acts as The Jordanaires, Drifting Johnny Miller, Lonzo & Oscar, the La Dell Sisters and Bernie Nee.

It's the type of musical for which Republic once held the franchise, being strictly in that old earthy groove. That it's a Paramount release would appear inconsistent with industry trends toward "bigness" but Par doubtless has its own ideas about costs vis-a-vis returns in the country-n-western field and not to be overlooked are the likely tieins with the film company's own Dot Records subsid. Latter is from Tennessee.

Given top billing is Ferlin Husky, who is agreeable in both voice and personality as the small-town, modest bumpkin who sings himself into the company of highly competitive managers of talent. Among the latter is Jesse White who takes Husky in tow, but only to find that Zsa Zsa Gabor, who's a flashy femme in any man's picture, has come upon 50% of his contract.

Rocky Graziano is just a little too goofy to be funny as a song biz exec but perhaps his name will count some in sale of the picture. Clyde Woods appears as the other local lad who made good, also the modest sort, and among the others on the roster are Al Fisher, Lou Marks, June Carter, Cliff Norton and Art Ford. All work well enough for the purposes although Ford, as a big television m.c., is not too at home before the theatrical cameras.

There are about 14 songs by at least twice that number of cleffers —so obviously there's not too much time for story. But Alvin Ganzer nonetheless has done an acceptable job of integration and organization in his direction and the H. B. Cross screenplay, while nothing standout, gets by, too.

Specialty numbers are so worked into the overall layout that appraisal of the individual talent just wouldn't be warranted.

Technical credits, considering the production level, all fair.
Gene.

Wonderful Things
(BRITISH)

Pleasant romantic drama against refreshingly different locale.

London, June 12.
Associated British-Pathe release of an Anna Neagle Production. Stars Frankie Vaughan and Jeremy Spenser. Features Jackie Lane and Wilfrid Hyde White. Producer, Anna Neagle; director, Herbert Wilcox; screenplay, Jack Trevor Story; editor, Basil Warren; camera,
Gordon Dines; music, Harold Rome. At Associated British Private Theatre, Elstree, June 10, '58. Running time, 88 MINS.
Carmello .... Frankie Vaughan
Mario .... Jeremy Spenser
Pepita .... Jackie Lane
Sir Bertram .... Wilfrid Hyde White
Anne .... Jean Dawnay
Harry .... Eddie Byrne
Poppa .... Harold Kasket
Codger .... Christopher Rhodes
Mamma .... Nancy Nevinson
Butler .... Cyril Chamberlain
Courtesy Appearance..... Barbara Goalen

Actor-singer Frankie Vaughan, now one of Britain's hottest show-biz bets, turns in a vigorous performance in his second dramatic role, "Wonderful Things!" (with exclamation) gives him scope in a role that blends drama, comedy and romance, as well as giving him a chance to exercise his pipes. With Vaughan's undoubted appeal, film measures up as prospect for popular audiences.

Title is not particularly relevant, except as an excuse for including a first-rate Harold Rome ditty. Story opens at Catalan Bay on the Rock of Gibraltar offering opportunities for attractive lensing and Gordon Dines has done the scenery proud.

Jack Trevor Story's simple yarn has produced a refreshing film which tingles with youth. It fits in nicely with the unsophisticated settings and characters involved. It tells of two happy-go-lucky brothers who earn a meagre living by fishing. They both love the same girl and after local adventures and a spell in London for the elder brother, the younger one gets the girl while the jilted one ends up conveniently, if implausibly, with a society girl.

Vaughan and Jeremy Spenser are convincing as the brothers, sharing the same dark good looks and charm. They handle the comedy and romantic sequences with plenty of dash. Jackie Lane, a brunette cutie, is here given her best acting chance and responds well considering her lack of experience.

Jean Dawnay, a cool blonde model makes her screen debut as the society girl—and it looks it (like a firster) as she is elegant, but unrelaxed, and the task obviously beyond her. As her father, Wilfrid Hyde White provides h's usual bland humor. The stars are supported by a troupe of surefire character artists, notably Eddie Byrne, Harold Kasket and Christopher Rhodes.

Herbert Wilcox has captured fully the flavor both of the island and British fairground sequences and Basil Warren's editing ensures the film moving at a fair pace.
Rich.

Desert Hell
(REGALSCOPE)

Routine meller featuring Arabs vs. French Foreign Legion in desert setting. Satisfactory filler material.

Twentieth-Fox release of a Regal production. Stars Brian Keith, Richard Denning, Johnny Desmond, Barbara Hale. Executive producer-director Charles Marquis Warren; producer, Robert W. Stabler; screenplay, Endre Bohem; story, Charles Marquis Warren; camera, John M. Nickolaus Jr.; editor, Fred W. Berger, Al Joseph; music, Raoul Kraushaar. Previewed in Hollywood, June 6, '58. Running time, 82 MINS.
Capt. Edward .... Brian Keith
Colie Edwards .... Barbara Hale
Sgt. Benet .... Richard Denning
Lt. Forbes .... Johnny Desmond
Corporal Parini .... Phillip Pine
Pvt. Hoffstetter ...... Richard Shannon
Private Aruzza .... Duane Grey
Pvt. Bandurski .... Charles Gray
Pvt. Knapp .... Lud Veigel
Pvt. Kabussyan .... Richard Gilden
Pvt. Bergstrom .... Ronald Foster
Pvt. Corbo .... Patrick O'Moore
Kufra .... John Verros
Pvt. Brocklin .... Bill Hamel
Pvt. Sirmay .... Roger Etienne
Marsaya .... Felix Locher

"Desert Hell," a Regal production for 20th-Fox, is a melodrama with a French Foreign legion flavor and some names for marquee value. Charles Marquis Warren directed the Robert W Stabler production which has Brian Keith, Barbara Hale, Richard Denning and Johnny Desmond starrer. It rates an adequate presentation for double-bill booking.

Keith, an officer in the Legion, discovers his wife, Barbara Hale, in the arms of fellow officer, Johnny Desmond, just before the two sold'ers are to leave for a dangerous desert mission. Their conflict takes on wider implication when a dispute arises over the necessity of the mission and the best way to carry it out. Everything turns out for the best, "Pour La Gloire," as the Legion puts it, even though both men are knocked off in the end just after seeing the final success of their mission.

The production is handicapped by a situation that appears overly familiar, but this is overcome to some extent by authentic desert locations, well photographed by John M. Nickolaus Jr.

Cast gives a good account of itself with Keith and Desmond most important. Denning creates an interesting character and in supporting roles Richard Shannon, Philip Pine, Lud Veigel, Patrick O'Moore and Duane Gray are able. Miss Hale appears only briefly.

The Regalscope pictures will be an adequate addition to a twin bill.
Powe.

The Vicious Breed
(SWEDISH)

Okay for sexploitation houses but dubious b.o. elsewhere.

Joseph Brenner Associates release of a Raymond Rohauer production. Stars Arne Ragneborn. Maj-Britt Lindholm. Directed by Ragneborn. Music. Les Baxter. (No other credits available). Previewed in N.Y., May 7, '58. Running time. 86 MINS.
Myggan .... Arne Ragneborn
Lila .... Maj-Britt Lindholm

Sweden, too, has its problem with juvenile delinquents if this import is any criterion. The crime wave that a 19-year-old boy embarks upon after he's released from reform school makes this Joseph Brenner Associates release a likely booking for exploitation houses. Its appeal elsewhere is doubtful.

Aside from the story's criminal aspects, there's sex by the shovelful and a homosexual scene apparently tossed in for good measure. No one is accorded story or screenplay credit on the print. It's understandable why the author may have wished to preserve his anonymity. For there's nothing subtle or objective about the plot. It appears to revel in characterizing unfortunate souls and hints only vaguely as to a solution.

Arne Ragneborn, who also directed, has the top role as the No. 1 delinquent. His is a bitter, sadistic performance that excites no audience sympathy. Maj-Britt Lindholm, as Ragneborn's loyal girl friend, goes through the thespic motions mechanically while sharing his bed and flight from the law. Other players are involved in lesser parts but none is identified.

Ragneborn's direction stresses a downbeat, low-key style. What with the numerous amatory scenes, boy-meets-boy sequence and excessive violence the film may run into some local censorship difficulties. Lensing of an uncredited cameraman is fair. Les Baxter's score shows some originality. English titles are adequate. *Gilb.*

White Wilderness
(COLOR)

Another fabulous entry in Walt Disney's "True-Life Adventure" program. Cinch for top grosses in its market.

Hollywood, June 21.

Buena Vista release of Ben Sharpsteen production. Director-writer, James Algar. Camera, (Technicolor), James R. Simon, Hugh A. Wilmar, Lloyd Beebe, Herb and Lois Crisler; additional photography, William Carrick, Tom McHugh, Carl Thomsen, Cecil Rhode, Dick Bird, Rickard Tegstrom; narration, Winston Hibler; music, Oliver Wallace; editor, Norman Palmer. Previewed June 20, '58. Running time, **80 MINS.**

"White Wilderness" is a fascinating screen experience. Filmed in awesome detail in the icy wastes of the Arctic, where struggle for existence is savage and cruel, feature is one of the most spectacular of Walt Disney's "True-Life Adventure" series, and as such can expect handsome returns from its particular market.

Footage is a compilation of various teams of nature photographers who scoured the Polar regions through three seasons of swift summers and bitter winters, each concentrating upon some individual phase of wild life. Due to many of the animals being familiar by name and fable, but nothing more, they offer added appeal as the expert lensers catch them in all their moments of survival. Color photography is both magnificent and amazing, there's an atmospheric music score that matches action perfectly and shrewd editing holds various sequences to one fluid movement.

Entire fauna of the Far North is pictured, after an opening showing results of the Ice Age. The walrus, polar bear, wolf and wolverine, all are limned in complete detail, often in graphic closeup, as well as innumerable smaller animals and birds. The ferocity of the wolverine is depicted as it battles two wolves for their kill and raids an osprey's nest of its young, one of the highlights of the film. Polar bear cubs provide an amusing note as they frolic, and one facing down a huge walrus, traditional enemies.

Schooling of the wolf pup is another highlight, as well as wolves going about their hunting of caribou. Migration and death march of the lemming, a small rodent, is almost incredulous. The musk ox, sole survivor of the Ice Age, is glimpsed interestingly, and white Beluga whales, resembling ghosts as they travel in formation on the ocean surface, lend another fabulous note. One of the exciting moments is a fight between a loon and two polar bear cubs. There's a new thrill every few moments to be remembered.

Principal photography is handled by James R. Simon, Hugh A. Wilmar, Lloyd Beebe and Herb and Lois Crisler, each contributing fine appreciation and knowledge of their subject. Ben Sharpsteen as producer rates a big credit and James Algar, writer-director, does a fine job, with Winston Hibler deftly handling the narration.

Oliver Wallace' music score is sock and, editing by Norman Palmer is craftmanship at its best.

Whit.

The Naked Earth

Excellent film introducing sure-to-make-talk Juliette Greco. Well above usual "second feature" quality.

Hollywood, June 17.

Twentieth-Fox release of a Foray Film. Stars Richard Todd and Juliette Greco. Produced by Adrian Worker. Directed by Vincent Sherman. Screenplay and story, Milton Holmes; camera (C'Scope), Erwin Hillier; editor, E. Jarvis; music, Arthur Benjamin. Previewed in Hollywood, June 17, '58. Running time, **96 MINS.**

Danny	Richard Todd
Maria	Juliette Greco
Father Verity	Finlay Currie
David	John Kitzmiller
Skins Trader	Laurence Naismith
Al	Christopher Rhodes
Tribesman	Orlando Martins
Arab Captain	Harold Kasket

"The Naked Earth" is a thoroughly well-made film that peeks into the heart of Africa and comes out with a captivating actress in Juliette Greco. It also presents a twinkling performance by Richard Todd and an excellent photographic record of a bird picking the teeth of a crocodile. The British-made Foray production for 20th-Fox release has an arty touch and is much too good for a second-feature life, but whether it's sturdy enough to lure a safari of filmgoers by itself is questionable.

Miss Greco, already taken over by 20th and Darryl F. Zanuck for a co-starring role in "The Roots of Heaven," has the humor and sarcasm of a Magnani, and, to top that, a totally sensuous appeal. The French actress is bound to create word-of-mouth, and the noise may help b.o. returns.

Tale is set in a forsaken section of the darkest continent at the end of the 19th century. It's a story of man's struggle against nature, a bout in which he loses every round but still wins the fight. Todd, an Irishman looking for new wealth, treks to the African hinterlands to launch a farming effort with an old friend he's to meet there. When he finds the friend has been devoured by one of the feared crocodiles, he and the dead friend's female companion get married for convenience, then plant tobacco for profit. Bad luck with his plants pushes Todd into the gloomy rivers to stalk the treacherous crocodiles for their valued skins. And, having skinned 40 of the beasts, he's set to leave Africa and send his wife back to her native France. But two white men steal the skins, and three natives, including Todd's new-found friend, are killed in retrieving them. Now feeling they owe so much to the natives, Todd and Miss Greco stay, and, having found need in each other, also find love.

To support the spirited portrayals of two stars, John Kitzmiller, as the native friend, and Finlay Currie, as a missionary, are excellent. The Milton Holmes script, from his own story, is skillfully constructed and sustains interest with a minimum of involvment. With the help of director Vincent Sherman, the film says something without preaching, and the director pulls all the truths from the screenplay, wrapping them up in well-delineated characterizations.

The Adrian Worker production is a well-knit piece of work, with particular nods going to photographer Erwin Hillier and composer Arthur Benjamin.

Ron.

Wild Heritage
(COLOR)

Mild frontier western with special teenage and family trade angles.

Hollywood, June 20.

Universal release of a John E. Horton production. Stars Will Rogers Jr., Maureen O'Sullivan, Rod McKuen, Casey Tibbs, Judy Meredith; features George Winslow, Gigi Perreau, Troy Donahue, Gary Gray, Jeanette Nolan, Paul Birch. Directed by Charles Haas. Screenplay, Paul King and Joseph Stone; based on a story by Steve Frazee; camera, Philip Lathrop; music, Joseph Gershenson; editor, Edward Mann. Previewed in Hollywood, June 19, '58. Running time, **78 MINS.**

Judge Copeland	Will Rogers Jr.
Emma Breslin	Maureen O'Sullivan
Dirk Breslin	Rod McKuen
Rusty	Casey Tibbs
Callie Bascomb	Judy Meredith
Talbot Breslin	George Winslow
Missouri Breslin	Gigi Perreau
Jesse Bascomb	Troy Donahue
Hugh	Gary Gray
Ma Bascomb	Jeanette Nolan
Jake	Paul Birch
Arn	John Beradino
Jud	Phil Harvey
Josh Burrage	Lawrence Dobkin
Bolivar Bascomb	Stephen Ellsworth
Hilda Jansen	Ingrid Goude
Brazos	Christopher Dark
Chaco	Guy Wilkerson

"Wild Heritage" is a frontier Western angled for the family trade and for younger fans. It is handicapped in its impact by a somewhat confusing story line, but the Universal production, directed by Charles Haas and produced by John E. Horton, should prove a satisfactory feature with several attractive names, plus values of CinemaScope and good Eastman color.

The Paul King-Joseph Stone screenplay is concerned with two families heading west by covered wagon. Maureen O'Sullivan is widowed early in the story but continues on with her brood, Rod McKuen, George Winslow, Gigi Perreau and Gary Gray. Their fortunes become involved with another family headed by Stephen Ellsworth and Jeanette Nolan, whose children are Troy Donahue and Judy Meredith.

These families represent the new, more solid west, who must stand up to cattle rustlers and gunslingers of the fading, more adventursome days. The picture reaches its climax when McKuen, Gray and Donahue stalk and kill two hardened gunmen, and presumably clean up the community for respectable folks.

The younger players do well enough with their chores, although none of the characters is ever developed enough to arouse much interest or sympathy. Will Rogers Jr. appears as a frontier lawyer.

Miss O'Sullivan is the only one in the cast, in addition to Miss Nolan, who is enough of a veteran to give a variety and depth to her characterization through her own playing. Miss Nolan too achieves some of this substance, although her role is less important. Rodeo champ Casey Tibbs plays a straight role without displaying any of the feats for which he is famed.

Technical aspects of the production are slickly done.

Powe.

The Last of the Fast Guns
(COLOR; C'SCOPE)

Authentic Mexican locations give added interest to this period oater for fair returns in outdoor market.

Hollywood, June 20.

Universal release of a Howard Christie production. Stars Jock Mahoney, Gilbert Roland, Linda Christal; features Eduard Franz, Lorne Greene, Carl Benton Reid, Edward C. Platt. Directed by George Sherman. Screenplay, David P. Harmon; camera, Alex Phillips; music, Joseph Gershenson; editor, Patrick McCormack. Previewed in Hollywood, June 16, '58. Running time, **82 MINS.**

Brad Ellison	Jock Mahoney
Miles Lang	Gilbert Roland
Maria O'Reilly	Linda Cristal
Padre Jose	Eduard Franz
Michael O'Reilly	Lorne Greene
John Forbes	Carl Benton Reid
Samuel Grypton	Edward C. Platt
Cordoba	Eduardo Noriega
Manuel	Jorge Trevino
Alcalde	Rafael Alcayde
Johnny Ringo	Lee Morgan
James Younger	Milton Bernstein
Ben Thompson	Stillman Segar
Garcia	Jose Chavez Trowe
Pablo	Francisco Reyguera
Sheriff	Richard Cutting
Bartender	Ralph Neff

A period Western, set in the time when the leading badmen of the West were rapidly being eliminated by occupational hazards of their trade, "The Last of the Fast Guns," is a good entry for houses specializing in the outdoor market. Howard Christie's production for Universal was shot largely in the rugged mountains of northern Mexico and George Sherman's direction makes skillfull use of the awesome background for dramatic value. Jock Mahoney, Gilbert Roland and Linda Cristal head the good cast.

Mahoney is the "last of the fast guns," and the era is apparently the early 1880's, since he notes at one point that Billy the Kid and Jesse James have lately been done in. Mahoney's job is to try to find the brother of wealthy U. S. industrialist Carl Benton Reid, who has disappeared into Mexico many years before. Working against Mahoney are gunmen hired by Reid's partner. If Reid's brother doesn't show up, the partner gets all the money. Mahoney finds the brother, Eduard Franz, and persuades him to return to civilization only after the opposing elements attempt to kidnap and kill him.

"Last of the Fast Guns" is an example of an outdoor adventure that might have seemed routine without the considerable aid of unusual and authentic backgrounds. Sherman has staged his chase and climax to take full advantage of the lush green, mist-hung Mexican mountains and give them fresh appeal. David P. Harmon's screenplay, while somewhat predictable in plot, is strong in character and offbeat dialog.

Mahoney makes a sympathetic and interesting character of his role, although his motivations seem somewhat dim, and his romance with Miss Cristal is too thinly prepared. Gilbert Roland gives dash and excitement as the smiling, double-dealing villain. Notable in support are Franz, Lorne Greene, Reid and Edward C. Platt.

Alex Phillips' photography is a valuable asset of the picture and other plus factors including Patrick McCormack's editing and sound by Leslie I. Carey and Javier Mateos.

Powe.

The Colossus Of New York

Okay horror meller for the moppet trade; less appeal for adult audiences.

Paramount release of a William Alland production. Stars John Baragrey, Mala Powers, Otto Kruger, Robert Hutton, Ross

Martin. Directed by Eugene Lourie. Screenplay, Thelma Schnee, based on story by Willis Goldbeck; camera, John F. Warren; editor, Floyd Knudtson; music, Van Cleave. Previewed N.Y., June 6, '58. Running time, **70 MINS.**

Dr. Jeremy Spensser ...... Ross Martin
Anne Spensser .... Mala Powers
Billy Spensser .... Charles Herbert
Dr. Henry Spensser ...... John Baragrey
Dr. William Spensser ...... Otto Kruger
Prof. John Carrington ... Robert Hutton
The Colossus .... Ed Wolff

A variation on the "Frankenstein" theme is "The Colossus of New York," which Paramount is pairing with "The Space Children" as a "thriller" package. While the cast of "Colossus" may be more familiar to filmgoers than thespers appearing in the companion picture, this horror meller's b.o. prospects lie primarily in its "shock" appeal.

Adults will probably find the Willis Goldbeck story, screenplayed by Thelma Schnee, pretty hokey fare. However, the new generation whose bedtime is much too early to expose it to tv's early Karloff and Lugosi pix, will likely accept this William Alland production as an exciting 70 minutes. For the piece de resistance is surgeon Otto Kruger's transplant of a dead man's brain into the body of a mechanical monster.

Script offers some contemporary touches as the monster runs amuck in New York's United Nations Bldg. Brain, incidentally, is that of Kruger's scientist-son Ross Martin who died in an accident. His father felt that Martin's death shouldn't end his services to mankind—hence the transplantation. But lacking a soul, the mechanical man refuses to follow instructions and goes on a rampage until subdued by moppet Charles Herbert who is Martin's son.

Under adult standards the story, direction and performances are just about as mechanical as the monster. Juvenile market, however, will overlook these shortcomings. Direction of Eugene Lourie gets as much suspense possible out of the hackneyed yarn. John Baragrey, as another son, is somewhat wooden as Kruger's assistant. Kruger is inclined to be too glib as the transplanter while Mala Powers, as Martin's widow, has little to do but look frightened. Martin is seen only briefly in the introductory minutes. Rounding out the cast are young Herbert, Robert Hutton, as a professor, and Ed Wolff who disports as the monster.

Occasional science-fiction overtones in this meller are enhanced by John F. Warren's lensing black-and-white along with some aid from John P. Fulton's special effects and process photography of Farciot Edouart. Producer Alland's physical values reflect a low budget. Either economy or perhaps the studio musicians' strike may have accounted for the Van Cleave novel score, played solely by a piano. It proves a lotta mood can be generated by one instrument. Other technical credits, including Floyd Knudtson's editing and the Hal Pereira-John Goodman art direction, are standard. *Gilb.*

Vynalez Zkazy
(Weapons of Destruction)
(CZECHOSLOVAKIAN)
Brussels, June 24.

Czech State Film production and release. Features Arnost Navratil, Lubor Tokos, Miloslav Holub, Jana Zatloukalova. Directed by Karel Zeman. Screenplay, Frantisek Hrubin, Zeman from several Jules Verne novels; camera, Jiri Tarantik; editor, Zdenek Stehlik; music, Zdenek Liska. At Brussels Film Fest. Running time, **85 MINS.**

Thomas .... Arnost Navratil
Simon .... Lubor Tokos
Artigas .... Miloslav Holub
Serke .... Vaclav Kyzlink
Jeanne.. .... Jana Zatloukalova

This unique trick pic uses various Jules Verne adventure novels in such a manner as to make it a possible Yank item for arty houses or specialized theatres. It definitely has moppet appeal and will divert older crowds familiar with the works of Verne.

Real actors have been put into painted decors, emulating the first illustrations for the Verne books. Result is a sort of quaint, animated imagery that details how a crooked nobleman, possessed of a submarine a la "20,000 Leagues Under Sea," captures an old scientist who has succeeded in his atomic experiments. His aide manages to escape with a young lady just before the professor bows up the secret lab hideaway, in an old extinct volcano cone, when he realizes how his invention is to be used.

Atomic analogies are not pressed and this details all the rush of Verne's imagination and the inventions of a seething 19th Century. Trick footage is exemplary while characters have the right acting to fit in with this cheery adventure tale. Pic is laced with fine visuals, humor and outstanding special effects. It looms as a difficult product to sell at general spots but word-of-mouth and crix could help. *Mosk.*

Yoru No Tsuzari
(The Adulterous Wife)
(JAPANESE)
Brussels, June 24.

Shochiku production and release. Stars Rentaro Mikuni, Ineko Arima, Keiko Yukishiro, Masayuki Mori. Screenplay, Shinobu Hashimoto, Kaneto Shindo; camera, Shunichiro Nakao; editor, Akikazu Kono. At Brussels Film Fest. Running time, **95 MINS.**

Ogura .... Rentaro Mikani
Isobe .... Ineko Arima
Tane .... Keiko Yukishiro
Miyaji .... Masayuki Mori

Unreeling in feudal days of 18th Century Japan, this elegantly details a drama of an adulterous wife in a sealed society. She is driven to unfaithfulness by her husband's enforced absences and the lies of a friend. It ends in hari-kiri and a murder as the whole family avenges itself on the seducer.

Its Eastern pacing, mores and approach make this a difficult Yank entry except for special spots. But it is exceedingly well played, sensitively directed and with top technical credits. It is a natural for the lingo circuits. *Mosk.*

Imitation General
(C'SCOPE)

Farcical Army comedy with Glenn Ford and Red Buttons. Enough laughs for okay b.o.

Metro release of William Hawks production. Stars Glenn Ford, Red Buttons and Taina Elg. Features Kent Smith, Dean Jones and Tige Andrews. Directed by George Marshall. Screenplay, William Bowers from a story by William Chamberlain; camera, (C'Scope), George J. Folsey; editor, Sydney Guilaroff. Previewed in New York June 10, '58. Running time, **88 MINS.**

M/Sgt. Murphy Savage ..... Glenn Ford
Cpl. Chan Derby .... Red Buttons
Simone .... Taina Elg
Cpl. Terry Sellers .... Dean Jones
Brig. Gen. Charles Lane ... Kent Smith
Pvt. Orville Hutchmeyer ...Tige Andrews
Lt. Jeff Clayton .... John Wilder
Pfc .... Ralph Votrian

"Imitation General" is another entry in the current cycle of comedies about the armed forces. As such, it follows the pattern of similar recent contributions in that it presents an exaggerated and farcical version of life in the service.

War, as far these comedies are concerned, is one big laugh and "Imitation General" won't let audiences down in the yok department. It is frequently a very funny film and should prove to be fairly successful at the boxoffice for general situations and the drive-in trade.

William Bowers, who wrote the screenplay from William Chamberlain's story, has cooked up some unbelieveable farcical situations and has spiced it with the appropriate dialog. However, the main success of the film is the light, tongue-in-cheek interpretations rendered by Glenn Ford, Red Buttons and Tige Andrews. Expertly guided by director George Marshall, they play the film for what it is — a screwy concoction without a semblance of reality to real life. The picture, therefore, must be judged for what it attempts to accomplish although there will undoubtedly be exceptions taken to the introduction of this type of humor on an actual battlefield.

Previous service comedies, for the most, have dealt with the humorous aspects of camp life or experiences in non-combat zones. "Imitation General" is perhaps the first of these films to inject laughs in the midst of a shooting war. Some sensitive viewers may find nothing funny about scenes where death occurs between and concurrent with the laughs.

The title of the picture tells the story. Ford, as a master sergeant, disguises himself as a one-star general to carry out the mission of his commanding officer, Kent Smith, who is killed in action. The action takes place during World War II in France in a period when a portion of the U.S. Army is disorganized and the enemy is closing in. It had been the view of Smith that the presence of a general on the actual battlefield would help boost morale and regroup the soldiers roaming the battlefield. Ford, despite the warnings of his sidekick, Buttons, about the consequences of imitating an officer, is determined to carry out the general's plan.

Donning the general's helmet and his brass, Ford regroups the forces and astonishes the GI's with his feats of derring-do as he leads the attack in knocking out a machine gun nest and destroying a couple of enemy tanks. His nemesis, however, turns up in the form of Andrews, a crude, revengeful busted non-com with whom Ford had a setto in the states. As a result of Andrews' presence, Ford has difficulty maintaining his disguise and goes through considerable pains to be a general in front of the other soldiers and "dead" when his personal enemy is around.

Ford is an old hand at this type of part, having had his training in "Teahouse of the August Moon" and "Don't Go Near the Water" and gives the role the correct shading. Buttons, who won an Academy Award for his serious portrayal as the corporal in "Sayonara," scores solidly in his second film role as Ford's buddy. This time Buttons is on home grounds as a comedian and he tosses off the one-liners and banter with aplomb. The outing adds to Buttons' stature as a film thesp. As the sloppy, leering "villain," Andrews contributes a first-rate performance. Taina Elg, Metro's Finnish ballerina, is just right as the French gal at whose farmhouse Ford sets up headquarters. Smith, as the general, and Dean Jones, as a frightened soldier, also contribute good performances.

William Hawks has provided right production values and cinematographer George J. Folsey has done a good job in capturing the comedy battle sequence. All other technical aspects are fine. *Holl.*

The Case of Dr. Laurent
(FRENCH)

Well done film on natural childbirth; strong b.o. prospects in the art house market. Available dubbed or with titles.

Trans-Lux Distributing Corp. release of a Cocinor production. Stars Jean Gabin; features Nicole Courcel. Directed by Jean-Paul Le Chanois. Screenplay, Le Chanois and Rene Barjavel; camera, Henri Alekan; music, Joseph Kosma. At Trans-Lux 52nd St. Theatre, N. Y., June 27, '58. Running time **93 MINS.**

Dr. Laurent	Jean Gabin
Francine	Nicole Courcel
Catherine Loubet	Sylvia Monfort

Advantages of natural childbirth are championed in "The Case of Dr. Laurent," a French import that looms as a solid art house boxoffice entry. It's a courageous, controversial film that will profit by word-of-mouth in addition to the marquee pull of Jean Gabin who stars in the title role. Women, obviously, will constitute the bulk of the picture's potential audience.

Such a subject automatically conjures up endless hospital scenes with white clad nurses and doctors shouting forceps, scalpel and similar commands, but the approach that the script of Jean-Paul Le Chanois and Rene Barjavel has chosen to use avoids the obvious. Instead, the story treatment accents the humor, earthiness and varied traits any country doctor finds in his patients.

Gabin, a physician who formerly practiced in Paris, moves to a small village in the French maritime Alps where he replaces a retired doctor. A firm believer in natural childbirth, he extolls its merits in a lecture at the local town hall and attempts to convert those who believe in other methods.

Of course, the region's medical society looks askance upon his campaign and some women resent his suggestions and advice as an intrusion. But Gabin's ace in the hole is an unwed mother, portrayed engagingly and wistfully by Nicole Courcel, who has faith both in him and the natural way of delivery. When she gives birth without apparent pain or discomfort it goes without saying that he has scored a personal triumph.

Throughout the footage the deft direction of Le Chanois is constantly evident. In fact his touch is so delicate and of such good taste that the more squeamish members of the audience would hardly find the actual birth scenes disturbing. Gabin, too, makes a perfect doctor what with his patient air of understanding and unruffled demeanor.

Among other scenes that add to the film's interest is a view of the town playboy, who fathered Miss Courcel's child, nonchalantly fishing while friends are hustling her to Gabin so that he may supervise the event. And he does all of that with the precision and studied technique of a conductor directing a symphony. Also impressive is the performance of Sylvia Monfort as a mother won over by the natural method.

Black-and-white camerawork of Henri Alekan is good as is the Joseph Kosma score. Particularly well done are Herman Weinberg's English titles which admirably translate the occasionally risque French dialog. *Gilb.*

Tarzan's Fight for Life
(COLOR)

Above average for this hardy series, plus unusual promotion planned, should lift this Tarzan out of the routine class for stronger-than-usual returns.

Hollywood, June 27.

Metro release of a Sol Lesser Production. Stars Gordon Scott, Eve Brent, Rickie Sorenson; features Jil Jarmyn, James Edwards, Carl Benton Reid. Directed by Bruce Humberstone. Screenplay, Thomas Hal Phillips; based on characters created by Edgar Rice Burroughs; camera, William Snyder; music, Ernest Gold; editor, Aaron Stell. Previewed in Hollywood, June 25, '58. Running time, **86 MINS.**

Tarzan	Gordon Scott
Jane	Eve Brent
Tahtu	Rickie Sorensen
Anne Sturdy	Jil Jarmyn
Futa	James Edwards
Dr. Sturdy	Carl Benton Reid
Dr. Ken Warwick	Harry Lauter
Ramo	Woody Strode

Metro is putting a big push behind "Tarzan's Fight For Life," in the belief that there is an additional market for the perennial favorite beyond its regular and dedicated fans. There should be, too, and the current Sol Lesser production has handsome color, wide screen, capable acting and able direction. If the campaign is to be carried through, however, the approach and writing will have to be lifted above the current level, which is persistently juvenile. A more realistic, adult Tarzan and better African photography would help. As it is, "Tarzan's Fight For Life" will probably do better than the usual in the series, aided by Metro's campaign. Gordon Scott again plays the title role.

This chapter in the life of the Edgar Rice Burroughs character, has him involved with a medical outpost headed by Carl Benton Reid. The natives are wary of the scientific experiments and their natural superstition is given a healthy assist by witch doctor James Edwards, eager to stir them up for reasons of his own. The climax has Tarzan thwarting the witch doctor and curing the young tribal chief to the satisfaction of natives and medical mission alike.

Scott makes a good Tarzan, in fact his natural ease as a performer make him attractive for other kinds of roles, as well. He makes the athletic stunts believable and possible and he also handles the few romantic scenes with Eve Brent with acceptable finesse. Miss Brent is attractive as Jane, and young Rickie Sorenson makes a good son for the couple. Carl Benton Reid is strong in support as are Jil Jarmyn, James Edwards, Harry Lauter and Woody Strode. Cheta, the chimp, has some charming comedy scenes.

Bruce Humberstone's direction gets all possible action and excitement out of the Thomas Hal Phillips' script, and William Snyder's camera work is effective. The African photography by Miki Carter does not contain any particularly new or exciting material, although it is visually appealing. Editor Aaron Stell has smoothly integrated this 16m stuff with the wide-screen lot shooting. *Powe.*

Sierra Baron
(C'SCOPE-COLOR)

Good early California yarn with pleasant prospects for program situations.

Hollywood, June 27.

Twentieth-Fox release of Plato A. Skouras production. Stars Brian Keith, Rick Jason; costars Rita Gam, Mala Powers, Steve Brodie; features Carlos Muzquiz, Lee Lorgan, Allan Lewis, Pedro Galvan, Frenando Wagner, Ferrusquilla (Jose Expinoza). Directed by James B. Clark. Screenplay, Houston Branch, from novel by Thomas Wakefield Blackburn; camera (Deluxe Color), Alex Phillips; editor, Frank Baldridge; music, Paul Sawtell, Bert Shefter. Previewed June 25, '58. Running time, **78 MINS.**

Jack McCracken	Brian Keith
Miguel Delmonte	Rick Jason
Felicia Delmonte	Rita Gam
Sue Russell	Mala Powers
Rufus Bynum	Steve Brodie
Andrews	Carlos Muzquiz
Frank Goheen	Lee Morgan
Hank Moe	Allan Lewis
Judson Jeffers	Pedro Galvan
Grandall	Fernando Wagner
Felipe	Jose Expinoza
Anselmo	Enrique Lucero
Lopez	Alberto Mariscal
Vicky Russell	Lynne Ehrlich
Ralph	Michael Schmidt
Ralph's father	Tommy Riste
Sheriff	Reed Howes
Baker	Robin Glattley
Assayer	Enrique Inigo
Young Sue	Faith Ferry
Young Felicia	Doris Contreras
Cart Driver	Marc Lambert
Butcher	Stillman Segar
Juanita	Alicia del Lago
Major Domo	Jose Trowe
Eduardo	Armando Saenz
Emmy	Lolla Davila
1st Playboy	Ricardo Adalid
2d Playboy	Roy Fletcher
Express Rider	John Courier
1st Miner	Mark Zachary
2d Miner	Paul Arnett
Henchman	Bob Janis

Plato A. Skouras, son of 20th-Fox prexy Spyros Skouras, produced this one as an indie and comes up with a workmanlike job which displays good production knowledge. Limned in fine Deluxe Color which sets off the beauties of the Mexican landscape where it was made, feature catches the spirit of early California before it became a state and offers an interesting plot with melodramatic ingredients. It's a good entry for the better program market.

Brian Keith as a Texas gunslinger and Rick Jason, son of a don who inherits a vast Spanish land grant near the Sierras upon the death of his father, are the chief protagonists in this 1848 story of attempts by a Yankee landgrabber to move in. Script by Houston Branch gets logical motivation and is responsible for fast action as the Californian fights to retain his empire against the ruthless advances of Steve Brodie, the American, who hires Keith to kill the landowner. Texan changes sides when he falls in love with don's beautiful sister, Rita Gam.

As a production, film is rich in pictorial effects and has been strongly directed by James B. Clark, who builds and sustains moments of excitement. Film benefits by superior acting right down the line. Jason is a commanding figure in a deft characterization and Keith powerfully underplays his role of gunman, whose romance with the sister ends in his death before it can actually begin. Miss Gam is colorful in her part, Mala Powers is in as an American member of a wagon train, romanced by Jason, and Brodie capably enacts the heavy. Large cast is filled with Mexican performers, headed by "Ferrusquilla" (Jose Expinoza).

Technical credits are outstanding, headed by Alex Phillips' expert photography, sometimes breathtaking in beauty as it delineates the Mexican scene. Editing by Frank Baldridge is fast, art direction by John Mansbridge flavorful and Paul Sawtell and Bert Shefter's music score lends impressive melodic baking. *Whit.*

I Bury the Living

Suspense murder mystery short on plot but strengthened by ingenious camera use. Satisfactory for horror and exploitation entry.

Hollywood, June 29.

United Artists release of an Albert Band-Louis Garfinkle production. Stars Richard Boone. Directed by Albert Band; screenplay, Louis Garfinkle; camera, Frederick Gately; music, Gerald Fried; editor, Frank Sullivan. Previewed in Hollywood, June 27, '58. Running time, **76 MINS.**

Robert Kraft	Richard Boone
Andy McKee	Theodore Bikel
Ann Craig	Peggy Maurer
Jess Jessup	Herb Anderson
George Kraft	Howard Smith
Lt. Clayborne	Robert Osterloh
Henry Trowbridge	Russ Bender
Charles Bates	Matt Moore
Bill Honegger	Ken Drake
Stu Drexel	Glenn Vernon
Beth Drexel	Lynn Bernay
W. Isham	Cyril Delevanti

"I Bury The Living," an Albert Band-Louis Garfinkle production for United Artists, is being promoted and sold as a horror picture, which it is not. What it is is a pretty good, low budget murder mystery or ghost story. Its plot has more holes than you would find on a busy day at a cemetery and it is often as wispy as a wraith, but to balance this there is expert direction that gets a lot more out of the material than it deserves, plus some intriguing photographic tricks. Richard Boone is the only name involved.

Boone plays a businessman who takes over chairmanship of a local cemetery as part of his civic duties. A map showing location of various burial plots immediately engages his attention and, in fact, rivets it. A white-headed pin indicates a plot is sold, a black-headed pin shows it is occupied, so to speak. When Boone inadvertently puts black pins into sections where white pins should have been, and the owners promptly die, he begins to wonder if he possesses some malevolent power. It turns out happily, except for the victims, when it develops that the deaths were murders carried out by Theodore Bikel, the elderly Scots caretaker who is trying to unhinge Boone so Boone will not retire him.

There are not enough complications in Garfinkle's screenplay to keep things going at a very satisfactory clip, but this deficit is almost compensated for by some intriguing camera tricks and art work by visual designer E. Vorkapich, photographer Frederick Gateley, and editor Frank Sullivan. Gerald Fried's eerie music is also a help.

Boone gives a good, straight performance and others in the cast who are helpful include Bikel, Peggy Maurer, Herb Anderson, Howard Smith, Robert Osterloh, Russ Bender, Matt Moore, Ken Drake, Glenn Vernon, Lynn Bernay and Cyril Delevanti. *Powe.*

Foreign Films

Paris, June 24.

Ni Vu, Ni Connu (Neither Seen Nor Recognized) **(FRENCH)**. Pathe release of Champs Elysees Film Production. Stars Louis De Funes, Noelle Adam; features Moustache, Claude Rich, Colette Richard, Duvalles, Pierre Mondy. Directed by Yves Robert. Screenplay, Jean Marsan, Jacques Celhay, Robert from book by Alphone Allais; camera, Jacques Letellier; editor, Gilberte Natot. At Marignan, Paris. Running time, **95 MINS.**

There are plenty of good comic ideas in this pic which are not quite brought to fruition because of the insistence on explaining all aspects. This makes the pic plot repetitious. It emerges a bucolic comedy of only chancey status in the U.S. Its main plus factor is the grimacing comic Louis De Funes.

De Funes, as a poacher in a small town, hounded by the local constable, brings a perfection in timing, mugging and risible reactions into this, which is otherwise submerged in a too sketch-like treatment. He is finally falsely arrested, and becomes the town hero.

Director Yves Robert has used speeded-up motion and all sorts of tricks, but flagged in playing this out too methodically. Noelle Adam is a pert, fresh actress who bodes well for future chances. Technical credits are fine. *Mosk.*

Le Temps Des Oeufs Durs (Hardboiled Egg Time) (**FRENCH**). CCFC release of Lyrica-Filmel-Mars Films production. Stars Darry Cowl, Fernand Gravey; features Beatrice Altariba, Pierre Mondy, Suzanne Dehelly, Julien Carette. Directed by Norbert Carbonnaux. Screenplay, Serge De Boissac, Carbonnaux; camera, Roger Dormoy; editor, Jacqueline Thiedot. At Balzac, Paris. Running time, **85 MINS.**

Film is a slapstick offering that goes way back to the early days of filmmaking for its visual gags. It is funny in spots, but the simplesimon story, without true satire, makes this only intermittently funny. Thus it is doubtful as an U.S. entry. A simpleminded, innocent taxi driver wins a lottery prize. He gets mixed up with a broken down painter and his lovely daughter. Complications of counterfeit money and an art show in a fish market help this loose-jointed tale.

Darry Cowl again plays the little man, but with an arrogance not usually found in comic personnages. Fernand Gravey neatly etches the posturing artist. Others in the cast are helpful. Director Norbert Carbonnaux emerges a fairly interesting comedy director, but still lacking in punching home the gags. *Mosk.*

Subotom Uvece (Saturday Night) (**YUGOSLAVIAN**). Avala Film production and release. Features Radmila Radovanovic, Zoran Stojilikovic, Milam Srdoc, Payle Vujisic. Directed by Vladimir Pogacic. Screenplay, Dragoslaw Ilic; camera, Aleksander Sekulovic; editor, Milan Slovik. At Brussels Film Fest. Running time, **80 MINS.**

Sketch film encompasses three happenings during a typical Saturday night in Belgrade. However, it is somewhat commonplace, sans the needed lift or imagination for any American chances except in foreign language situations. In one skit two secretly married young people finally get accepted by their family, in another a little fight fan gets a coveted chance alongside a champ, and the last is about a love-at-first-sight affair at a local dance. Film is brightly mounted, acted and directed, but is primarily for home consumption. *Mosk.*

Dom V A Kotorom Ia Jivou (The House I Live In) (**RUSSIAN**). Mosfilm production and release. Features V. Teleghina, N. Elisarov, V. Zemlanikine, Iura Miasnikov. Directed by L. Koulidjanov, J. Sethel. Screenplay, I. Olchanski; camera, V. Choumski; editor, V. Bogomolov. At Brussels Film Fest. Running time, **95 MINS.**

This denotes the Russo interest in more human story material. It resembles the recent Cannes Film Fest prizewinner, "Flying Cranes," in detailing the lives of a group of people quartered closely in a co-op house. Then it relates the advent of war and its toll in misery and death. Film rarely shows the war, but it is felt, and pic emerges a sincere looksee into the lives of little people sans the usual Russ propaganda. It is another Soviet pic with some good Yank possibilities. Direction is slow at times but has a feeling for people, place and time. Acting is excellent and technical credits are superior.

Mosk.

Los Jueves Milagro (Miracles of Thursday) (**SPANISH**). PCA release of Enrique Bolader production. Stars Richard Basehart; features Jose Ibert, Paolo Stoppa, June Calva. Written and directed by Luis Garcia Berlanga. Camera, Francisco Sempere; editor, Pepeta Orduna. At Brussels Film Fest. Running time, **90 MINS.**

Film deals with a group of business connivers who try to put over a miracle on the people of a small Spanish watering town and thereby get back the tourist trade. It backfires when in comes a supposed criminal, on the run, who blackmails them and then helps get the boom started and suddenly disappears. He leaves faith behind him in the plotting group for he was a real saint.

Pic has an amusing first half but bogs down a bit with the apparition of the Saint. Some pruning at the end could make this a possibility for special Yank spots. And it is definitely a good language house entry. Film has the Richard Basehart name and some sprightly acting, directing and storytelling, all of which keep this racing along until the fairly hokey end.

Mosk.

Rome, June 24.

Le Fatiche Di Ercole (The Labors of Hercules) (**ITALIAN; COLOR**). LUX FILM release of OSCAR-Galatea Film production. Stars Steve Reeves, Sylva Koscina; features Gianna Maria Canale, Fabrizio Mioni, Ivo Garrand, Gina Rovere, Arturo Dominici, Lydia Alfonsi. Directed by Pietro Francisci. Screenplay, Francisci, Ennio DeConcini, Gaio Frattini from story by Pietro Francisci based on "The Argonauts"; camera (Eastmancolor-Dyaliscope), Mario Bava; music, Enzo Masetti; editor, Mario Serandrei. At Adriano, Rome. Running time, **97 MINS.**

A good example of production savvy, this should pay off. For the U. S., attractive production, sexy garbing and physiques, should help build this into a good exploitation entry. Not for the arties, and dubbing is called for.

Mythological melange spotlights the muscular Hercules (Steve Reeves) in various adventures, most involving spectacular (trick-lensed) physical prowess based on legendary sagas of the past. There is something for all but the most demanding audiences. Much of it is done with tongue in cheek for good risible effect. Two of the femmes involved, Sylva Koscina and Gianna Maria Canale, are extremely easy on the eyes, especially the former. Their veiled costumes will make many forget plot deficiencies. Reeves, a former Mr. Universe, may have a following of his own. Others in the vast east are well-chosen for their roles.

Production values, starting with excellent lensing (Eastmancolor) by Mario Bava, which milks the utmost from the widescreen, are all good. The spectacular angles and location sequences appear well integrated for top effect. *Hawk.*

Domenica E Sempre Domineca (Sunday Is Always Sunday) (**ITALIAN**). Cineriz release of a Donati-Carpentieri Production. Stars Alberto Serdi, Vittorio DeSica; features Mario Ruva, Lorella de Luca, Dorian Gray, Achille Togliani, Ugo Tognazzi, Dolores Palumbo, Vira Silenti. Directed by Camille Mastrocinque. Screenplay, Biancoli, Sonego, Veerde, Sordi, Gianviti; inspired by RAI-TV presentation of "Il Musichiere"; camera, Alvaro Mancori. At Bernini Cinema, Rome. Running time, **90 MINS.**

This is the second pic effort here to be inspired by a popular teleshow, this time Garinei-Giovannini's "Il Musichiere." As a cash-in try, the film is remarkably successful, making for a solid 90 minutes of entertainment. Though comic Alberto Sordi here gives another sharp portrayal as a contestant in a quiz show and Vittorio DeSica has a few scenes as a family father, this is weak for export values, with most of the humor being of local vintage.

Plot concerns various contestant's efforts to prepare for the popular Italian video quiz show, leading up to their final appearance, where the winning contestant saves family from bankruptcy and dishonor. The quizzer's cast, headed by Mario Riva are all there. Remainder of the actors perform capably, aided by a well-written script and good production values for the effort involved (pic was shot in two weeks). *Hawk.*

Brussels, June 24.

Eifelkor (Before Midnight) (**HUNGARIAN**). Hunnia Film production and release. Stars Eva Ruttkay, Miklos Gabor; features Zsuzsa Bancky, Istvan Rozzos. Directed by Gyorgy Revesz. Screenplay, Laszlo Bank, Ivan Boldizzar, Revesz; camera, Barnagas Hegyi; editor, Maria Szecsenyi. At Brussels Film Fest. Running time, **92 MINS.**

This is the first Magyar pic to cover the 1956 revolution. It spins a delicate love tale about a married actor and a young dancer under a cloud because her family is against the Communist regime. They fall in love and marry after his divorce. But the idyl is cut short by the revolution. She decides to leave Hungary, and he stays on. Though the upheaval is kept in the background, pic has sound human values and some curio interest. But in the U.S., it would have to contend with possible picket lines. It might barely be worth it on its tender tale, fine acting and knowing direction.

Mosk.

The Naked and the Dead
(WARNERSCOPE-COLOR)

Norman Mailer's rough-tough World War II yarn scrubbed clean. Shapes as action entry for male patronage and should click in that sector.

Warner Bros. release of RKO Teleradio Pictures production, produced by Paul Gregory. Stars Aldo Ray, Cliff Robertson, Raymond Massey; features Lili St. Cyr, Barbara Nichols, William Campbell, Richard Jaeckel, James Best, Joey Bishop, Jerry Paris, Robert Gist, L. Q. Jones, Casey Adams, John Berardino, Edward McNally, Greg Roman, Henry Amargo. Directed by Raoul Walsh; screenplay, Denis and Terry Sanders, from Norman Mailer novel of same name; camera (Technicolor), Joseph LaShelle; editor, Arthur P. Schmidt; music, Bernard Herrmann. Previewed at Warner Bros. in N. Y., June 31, '58. Running time, **131 MINS.**

Croft	Aldo Ray
Hearn	Cliff Robertson
Genl. Cummings	Raymond Massey
Lily	Lili St. Cyr
Mildred	Barbara Nichols
Brown	William Campbell
Gallagher	Richard Jaeckel
Ridges	James Best
Roth	Joey Bishop
Goldstein	Jerry Paris
Red	Robert Gist
Wilson	L. Q. Jones
Dalleson	Casey Adams
Mantelli	John Berardino
Conn	Edward McNally
Minetta	Greg Roman
Martinez	Henry Amargo

Considering the gutsy material producer Paul Gregory, director Raoul Walsh and writers Denis and Terry Sanders had to work with, this screen version of "The Naked and the Dead" is a disappointment. The film bears little more than surface resemblance to the hard hitting (and foul-mouthed) Norman Mailer novel of the same title. It catches neither the spirit nor the intent of the original yarn and thus "The Naked and the Dead" becomes just another war picture, weighed with some tedious dialog sporadically lifted from the book, but becoming tense and exciting in extremely well-photographed action sequences.

Though the trappings are more elaborate, this is the kind of film the studios turned out soon after the war was over, when the public was being impressed with the fact that battles were fought by men, not all of them heroes and each driven, frustrated or elated by circumstances that had precious little to do with any fixed "cause."

Unfortunately, in adapting "The Naked and the Dead," the Sanders team failed to bring the novel's characters to life. Perhaps the need to emasculate the book in order to make it palatable for the Code had something to do with it. Or perhaps Walsh must carry the major share of the blame for this strange melee of action and dialog. In any case, the men of the platoon in the Pacific war, led by bully Aldo Ray as sergeant Croft, seem an unrealistic, artificial bunch, and the same holds true of Cliff Robertson as Lieutenant Hearn and Raymond Massey as General Cummings. What's worse, this is one of those films in which the acting leaves a great deal to wish for.

The characters go through the motions, hating themselves, hating each other, hating the jungle war that flares around them. Exchanges between the lieutenant and the general, dealing with the meaning of war and of power, seem so forced they're almost formal lectures.

"The Naked and the Dead" was a powerfully realistic book. It laid bare the souls of the men in the platoon and it fairly bristled with the sort of rough, pithy dialog of G.I.s in action. It was not a pleasant book, and for the most part this is not a pleasant picture. The trouble is that the novel was true to itself whereas the film is not. Such a strenuous effort is made to have each man represent a type, and to accent their differences, that the whole thing never really jells.

This could have been a special kind of war picture. As is, it's been turned into just another war film, with a couple of characters thrown in for variety's sake. The action sequences come in spurts, but when they do, lenser Joseph LaSheele has seen to it that they impress and the dangers of the jungle warfare become vividly real, underscored by the excellent color. Unfortunately, a good deal of the footage is taken up with the platoon moving up a mountain or down a mountain, crossing rivers, etc. and, after a while, these scenes begin to wear thin. Individual sequences, such as the one when a man dies of a snakebite, are very well done.

Only marquee name in this one is that of Aldo Ray who plays the frustrated, bitter and sadistic Sergeant Croft. It's not a very plausible part in the first place, and the strenuous efforts to "explain" him (his wife, Barbara Nichols, has been unfaithful) don't help. He's a man with a killer instinct and in the film, unlike in the book, he dies at the end. Ray plays this beefy character with gusto and certain raw power.

As the playboy whom the general picks as his aide, Cliff Robertson turns in a slick performance. He's good in his verbal encounters with the general, whom he eventually defies, but lacks conviction once he's assigned to lead the Croft platoon on its final and disastrous sortie. Whereas the Croft flashback is handled well, that of Robertson dreaming of the girls in his penthouse just doesn't come off. In fact, the whole Robertson character is inadequately explained, though—like everyone else in this film—he's carefully niched to "stand for something."

Massey as the general with the power complex, who believes the men under him must hate him, is hardly convincing, but then he, too, represents a fixed idea. He acts his part well within the confines of the script. Taking the men one by one, many showing only their ugliest side and suffering from various complexes and prejudices, one can't help wondering how the Pacific war was ever won. When the "good" fellows do have their day, such as the men who carry the wounded Robertson out of the jungle, they're as hard to take as the rest.

Members of the platoon are played by William Campbell, Richard Jaeckel, James Best, Joey Bishop, Jerry Paris, Robert Gist (who makes an impression as the total cynic), L. Q. Jones, John Berardino, Edward McNally and Greg Roman. Their performances vary. Henry Amargo plays an Indian who's part of the outfit and is used by Croft as an advance scout. He does well in the role.

Director Walsh turns in a curiously vascillating job. Some scenes are handled with plenty of imagination, others seem almost amateurish, such as the one in the command tent when Casey Adams as the colonel in command pounds the table and announces he's going to start a major attack. Ending also fails to convince, being "arranged" to the point of absurdity.

This is obviously an entry that'll appeal to male patrons. Lili St. Cyr has a bit part, just enough to help along in the ads. The war scenes and the massive photography are definite plus factors. Bernard Herrmann's music fits the story and Arthur P. Schmidt's editing is standard. A lot of time and effort obviously has gone into the making of this film. It's paid off in terms of creating an occasionally punchy war picture which captures the sounds of war, but not the feel of it. *Hift.*

Twilight for the Gods

(COLOR)

Sea-going version of "The High and Mighty," but lacking the excitement of the latter. Bolstered, however, by the marquee value of Rock Hudson and Cyd Charisse. Better than average b.o. anticipated.

Universal-International release of Gordon Kay production. Stars Rock Hudson and Cyd Charisse. Features Arthur Kennedy, Leif Erickson, Charles McGraw, Ernest Truex, Richard Haydn, Judith Evelyn, Wallace Ford, Celia Lovsky, Vladimir Sokoloff and Charles Horvath. Directed by Joseph Pevney. Screenplay, Ernest Gann from his own novel of the same title; camera, Irving Glassberg; editor, Tony Martinelli; music, David Raskin. Previewed in N. Y., June 25, '58. Running time, **120 MINS.**

Captain Bell	Rock Hudson
Charlotte	Cyd Charisse
Ramsay	Arthur Kennedy
Hutton	Leif Erickson
Yancey	Charles McGraw
Rev. Butterfield	Ernest Truex
Wiggins	Richard Haydn
Ethel Peacock	Judith Evelyn
Old Brown	Wallace Ford
Ida Morris	Celia Lovsky
Feodor Morris	Vladimir Sokoloff
Lott	Charles Vorvath
Keim	Robert Hoy
Shipping Clerk	Maurice Marsac
Myra Pringle	Virginia Gregg
Sweeney	William Challee
Sea Captain	Morris Ankrum
Officer	Arthur Space
Dak Sue	William Yip
Uala	Kimo Mahi

"Twilight for the Gods," by Ernest Gann, may be termed the seagoing version of the author's own successful "The High and the Mighty." The latter concerned a crippled commercial airliner's flight across the Pacific and the reactions of the diverse passengers to the dangers entailed. It was a tense and exciting entry and gave the viewers a sense of identification with the people on the plane.

"Twilight" makes an attempt to do the same thing by placing a group of passengers on a battered, leaking, old two-masted brigantine and following the ship's adventures in a sail from the South Sea islands to Honolulu. The result, however, is not the same. While there are moments of tension and excitement as the small sailing vessel combats storms and the crew plans a mutiny against the skipper, the deep sense of audience participation that "High and the Mighty" conveyed is lacking.

Consequently "Twilight for the Gods" emerges as a routine sea adventure drama, bolstered by the marquee names of Rock Hudson and Cyd Charisse. The value of the star names, particularly Hudson's, and a campaign linking the film to Gann's earlier success can, however, make the entry a better than average boxoffice draw for general audiences.

Gann, who also wrote the screenplay, has employed the familiar technique of assembling a group of passengers of different personalities and backgrounds, including several with shady pasts, and studies their reactions to the dangers encountered during the long sea voyage. The experience has an exhilarating effect on most of those involved and they emerge cleansed and better human beings.

There's Hudson, a court-martialed ship's captain fighting alcoholism, as the skipper of the battered sailing ship; Miss Charisse as a Honolulu call girl running away from the authorities; Arthur Kennedy as a bitter and treacherous second mate; Leif Erickson as a down-and-out showman; Judith Evelyn as a has-been opera singer; Vladamir Sokoloff and Celia Lovsky as an elderly refugee couple; Ernest Truex as a missionary, and Richard Haydn as a British beachcomber. In addition, there's the small crew and a number of natives who accompany the vessel on part of the trip.

The cramped quarters present an opportunity for observing various passengers and members of the crew as they face situations foreign to their previous lives. In this case, most of them come through with flying colors as they pitch in to save the sinking ship as it nears the end of its journey. Hudson overcomes his guilt feelings and Miss Charisse decides to face up to her mistakes. Hudson, of course, will be waiting when she emerges from a two-year jail term.

Filmed on location in the Hawaiian Islands, the photography of Irving Glassberg is a delight to the eyes as it captures the sailing ship in motion, a sea village, various beaches and sites on a chain of islands, the Honolulu Harbor, and Waikalulu Falls.

Performances of the leads, while serviceable, are not standout. Hudson is adequate as the ship's captain. Miss Charisse, in a rare appearance in a non-dancing role, is stiff and cold. Kennedy, Erickson, Miss Evelyn, Truex, Miss Lovsky, Sokoloff and Haydn are much more convincing and turn in excellent performances. Good portrayals are also given by Wallace Ford, as an old seaman, and Charles McGraw, as the leader of the mutinous deckhands.

Joseph Pevney's direction has failed to capture the plight and the jeopardy of the ship and its passengers. The sense of excitement the film is obviously meant to convey does not come across completely. Gordon Kay has provided outstanding production values and all other technical aspects are topnotch. *Holl.*

Never Love a Stranger

Dull, unbelievable melodrama.

Hollywood, June 27.

Allied Artists release of a Harold Robbins-Richard Day production. Stars John Drew Barrymore, Lita Milan, Robert Bray. Directed by Robert Stevens. Screenplay, Harold Robbins and Richard Day; based on a novel by Robbins; camera, Lee Garmes; music, Raymond Scott; editor, Sidney Katz. Previewed in Hollywood, June 23, '58. Running time, 91 **MINS.**

Frank Kane	John Drew Barrymore
Julie	Lita Milan
'Silk' Fennelli	Robert Bray
Martin Cabell	Steve McQueen
Moishe Moscowitz	Salem Ludwig
Flix	R. G. Armstrong
Brother Bernard	Douglas Rodgers
Bert	Felice Orlandi
Mrs. Cazzolina	Augusta Merighi
'Fats' Crown	Abe Simon
Frances Kane	Dolores Vitina
Keough	Walter Burke

"Never Love A Stranger," a New York locationed and produced melodrama for Allied Artists, may get some response within the current gangster cycle, but this is about its only chance. It is so ineptly unprofessionally done, especially in its handling of such volatile subjects as race and religion, that it has nothing else to recommend it except a vague topicality. Harold Robbins and Richard Day produced their own screenplay from Robbins' novel, and Robert Stevens directed.

John Drew Barrymore plays a young man raised in a Catholic orphanage who discovers when he is almost grown that his parents were Jewish. Under the law, he must be removed to the jurisdiction of an orphanage of his own faith. Young Barrymore is already involved with hoodlum elements and, feeling rejection by the orphanage that has been his home and parents, takes the final plunge into the gangster world. He rises swiftly to the top, becoming the boss of the entire syndicate (New York-New Jersey division), until he is finally gunned down by police.

Barrymore does an able job with his role although he is repeatedly sabotaged by a story that is persistently old hat in its approach to religion, gangsterism and unwed mothers, the three chief plot threads, where it is not old-fashioned, the attitude is so naive, as in the idea that Barrymore could become a junior Costello just by slapping up a few mob bosses, that it loses all credibility. There are other technical inconsistencies, such as the aging of some characters to indicate passage of time while others eschew the eyelines and the temple-graying completely.

Others in the cast who manage sporadically to arouse sympathy or interest include Lita Milan, Robert Bray, Steve McQueen, Salem Ludwig, Douglas Rodgers and Augusta Merighi. R. G. Armstrong is good casting as an unusual gunman.

Lee Garmes' photography is technically proficient and at times striking. Raymond Scott has contributed a melodic score and a title song that is attractively sung by Dorothy Collins. *Powe.*

Now That April's Here

(CANADIAN)

Four short stories bunched in Toronto-made feature of amateur acting standards and limited prospect.

Toronto, June 24.

International Film Distributors release of a Norman Klenman-William Davidson production. Based upon four short stories by Morley Callaghan, introduced and narrated by Raymond Massey. Director, William Davidson; screenplays, Norman Klenman; camera, William Gimmi; music, John Hubert Bath. At Towne Cinema, Toronto, June 19, '58. Running time 84 **MINS.**

SILK STOCKINGS

David Munro	Don Borisenko
Anne Greenleaf	Judy Welch
Boyfriend	Michael Mann
Mrs. Greenlear	Beth Amos
Salesgirls,	Sheila Billing, Pam D'Orsay

ROCKING CHAIR

Tom Boultbee	John Drainie
Hilda Adams	Katherine Blake
Henry	Alan Hood
Salesman	Art Jenoff

THE REJECTED ONE

Mamie	Nancy Lou Gill
Karl Henderson	Tony Grey
Helen Henderson	Paisley Maxwell
John Henderson	Fred Diehl
Mrs. Henderson	Josephine Barrington

A SICK CALL

John Williams	Walter Massey
Elsa Williams	Anne Collings
Jane Stanhope	Kathy McNeil
Father MacDowell	Georges Toupin
The Doctor	Rolf Carston

"Now That April's Here" is the first all-Canadian feature in that the producer, director and writer were all born in this country; the $75,000 bankroll was gathered here; the picture was filmed in Toronto; and it is being handled by International Film Distributors whose president, Nat Taylor, runs a chain of some 60 houses in Ontario. The cast of "April" has never been on screen before.

The film comprises four short stories written by Morley Callaghan some three decades ago but the present offering is a mediocre one that has no parallel in such omnibus films of the past as Somerset Maugham's "Trio" and "Quartet." The title-piece has never been published but two tales appeared in The New Yorker and one in The Atlantic Monthly. In their transference to the screen, these mood pieces lose most significance they might have once held for mag readers.

With a shoestring budget, the producer-director team of Norman Klenman and William Davidson has given a sad and unimaginative cinematic treatment of the four stories photographed against Toronto streets and parks. Apart from amateur quality film-acting, there is also the monotonous sameness of frustrated love in "April," with the most interesting break being the narrative intros of Raymond Massey, whose presumable presence is that he was born in Canada and that his cousin, Walter Massey, is one of the stars of the fourth episode.

As a matter of record, Walter Massey scores the acting honors in "Sick Call," this dealing with a Protestant husband battling over his Catholic wife's need of a priest for death-bed reconversion. With Georges Toupin as the priest, here are two males in conflict over theology for a highlight of acting and the Callaghan dialogue but this peters out on inconclusive results and still puzzles an audience.

The first episode, "Silk Stockings," deals with the unrequited love of a gauche, out-of-town boarder for his landlady's daughter, who is in love with a more worldly male character; "The Rejected One," in which the scion of a wealthy family falls in love with an illiterate and blousy biond from the wrong side of the tracks who unsuccessfully talks herself out of acceptance when meeting the family. "The Rocking Chair" treats of a widower who, from memories of his first wife, rejects the love of a lusty tenant in the same boarding house. Here John Drainie and Katharine Blake give some semblance to an otherwise unconvincing story, with the girl not getting the remembering man.

The technical direction shows flashes on the part of William Davidson and the scripting of Norman Klenman, plus the original writing of Morley Callaghan; but the overall result points up amateurish production and acting values.

McStay.

A Night to Remember
(BRITISH)

Expertly directed reconstruction of the Titanic disaster told with documentary authenticity; familiar yarn is given added b.o. appeal by the name of Kenneth More.

London, July 1.

Rank Organization (William MacQuitty) production and release. Directed by Roy Baker. Stars Kenneth More. Screenplay by Eric Ambler from Walter Lord's book; camera, Geoffrey Unsworth; editor, Sidney Haynes; music, William Alwyn. At Odeon, Leicester-Square, London. Running Time, **123 MINS.**

Lightoller .... Kenneth More
Mrs. Lucas .... Honor Blackman
Capt. Rostron .... Anthony Bushell
Mrs. Clarke .... Jill Dixon
Mrs. Lightoller .... Jane Downs
Col. Gracie .... James Dyrenforth
Andrews .... Michael Goodliffe
Phillips .... Kenneth Griffith
Lady Richard .... Harriette Johns
Chairman .... Frank Lawton
Murdoch .... Richard Leech
Bride .... David McCallum
Cottam .... Alec McCowen
Mrs. Brown .... Tucker McGuire
Lucas .... John Merivale
Capt. Smith .... Laurence Naismith
Capt. Lord .... Russell Napier
Joughin .... George Rose
Boxhall .... Jack Watling
Mrs. Farrell .... Bee Duffell
Sir Richard .... Patrick Waddington

Once again the tragic sinking of the "Titanic" in 1912 has intrigued filmmakers. Producer William MacQuitty and director Roy Baker have done an honest job in putting the disaster on the screen with an impressive, almost documentary flavor. With the name of Kenneth More as marquee bait, "A Night To Remember" likely will attract ticket buyers on both sides of the Atlantic. The fact that the same Titanic sinking has been done already in the U.S. will hurt.

With around 200 speaking roles in the pic, it is obvious that few of the actors have been given much chance to develop as characters. Even More, in the star role, is only part of a team. The ship itself is the star. The story tells how the "unsinkable" new ship set out for the U.S. on the night of April 14, 1912, how it struck an iceberg and sank in less than three hours with 1,302 people drowned and only 705 survivors. The film takes only 37 minutes less than the time of the actual disaster and during that time patrons will have a frightening sense of audience-participation.

The errors and confusion which played a part in the drama are brought out with no whitewashing. Allthough many of the passengers and crew come vividly to life, there has been no attempt to hang a fictional story on any of them. Technically, director Baker has done a superb job in difficult circumstances. His direction of some of the panic scenes during the manning of the lifeboats—of which there were not nearly enough to accommodate all on board—is masterly. Eric Ambler's screenplay, without skimping the nautical side of the job, has brought out excellently how some people kept their heads and others became cowards.

Dialog is natural, devoid of undue sentimentality and without needless humor dragged in for light relief. The main problem here is that the story is too familiar to most people for there to be any element of suspense. There is simply the question of waiting for quite a long while for the disaster to happen, and then watching the victims either perish or survive. That interest is held throughout is due much to acting that is worthy of Baker's shrewd direction. More, as the second officer whose job it is to man the lifeboats, comes out as a likeable and reliable fellow, not particularly brave, but just doing his job. It is not really a star role at all; hence, it is a measure of More's ability that he stands out in the crowd.

Others who manage to make impact are Laurence Naismith as the "Titanic's" skipper; Anthony Bushell, captain of the rescue ship 'Carpathia'; Kenneth Griffith and David McCallum, as a couple of radio operators; Tucker McGuire, as a hearty American woman; George Rose, as a bibulous ship's baker, Michael Goodliffe, as the designer of the ship; and Frank Lawton, as the chairman of the White Star Line.

There are a number of moving touches which stand out in the general tapestry. The ship's orchestra playing "Nearer My God to Thee" as the ship goes down; a number of farewells as husbands say goodbye to their wives and children; a rocking horse and a violin floating on the sea amid the debris; Goodliffe's emotion as he realizes that his beloved ship is doomed; the pathos of an old man calmly reading his Bible as he awaits death. And the wreck of the ship and its breaking up offer quiet excitement.

Geoffrey Unsworth's lensing is very good and a special word should be thrown in for art director Alex Vetchinsky, production manager Jack Hanbury and continuity girl Penny Daniels, all of whom must have been up to their eyebrows in intricate detail. "Night to Remember" is a sincere and conscientious reconstruction of a tragic event, which will satisfy all but those who like their entertainment glossed over with contrived fiction.

Rich.

The Littlest Hobo

Generally well-made and attractive animal-angled feature for good b.o. in certain situations.

Hollywood, July 4.

Allied Artists release of a Hugh M. Hooker production. Associate producer, Forrest L. Royse. Director, Charles R. Rondeau; screenplay, Dorrell McGowan; camera, Perry Fennerman and Walter Strenge; music, Ronald Stein; editors, Howard Epstein and Arthur H. Nadel. Previewed in Hollywood, July 3, 1958. Running time, **77 MINS.**

Tommy .... Buddy Hart
Molly .... Wendy Stuart
Governor Malloy .... Carlyle Mitchell
Captain in Mission ...... Howard Hoffman
Mike .... Robert Kline
Joe .... Pat Bradley
Attendant .... Bill Coontz
Sister Ophelia .... Dorothy Johnson
Dr. Hunt .... William Marks
Nurse .... Pauline Moore
Police Captain .... Larry Thor
Police Sergeant .... Norman Bartold

For the first two-thirds of "The Littlest Hobo," when the action is confined almost exclusively to a handsome German shepherd dog and a frisky lamb, this Allied Artists release is suspiciously close to being an uncommonly good artistic feature. When human beings take charge in the latter third, the picture gets cute and morbidly sentimental. Its sins may be forgiven for its virtues, however, because the good parts are exceptionally well done. "Littlest Hobo" is being paired by Allied with "Snowfire" (reviewed in VARIETY, Jan. 15, '58) for a double-bill that should do particularly well in less sophisticated areas.

Charles R. Rondeau directed "Hobo" and he and his patient and painstaking photographers, Perry Fennerman and Walter Strenge, are chiefly responsible for the notable portions of the picture. The story, by Dorrell McGowan, picks up the dog (trained by Charles P. Eisenmann) as he rides into town on a freight train. He gets mixed up with the lamb when he spots the animal at a slaughter house about to be turned into mutton. The pair run off and when the dog is reported "mad," a hectic and funny pursuit starts. Eventually the pair winds up on the grounds of the governor's mansion where the dog's antics and the sheep's playfulness, enables the chief executives paralyzed daughter to walk again. The lamb finds a home with the governor and the dog hops the next freight out of town.

The animal scenes are carefully and skillfully done. Trouble has been taken to get good (and mostly fresh) local locations that give authenticity to the narrative. There is also humor, sharp and bright, and some of the credit for this must go to Ronald Stein's music. Which counterpoints an astringent jazz score to some of the story's sentimentality, effectively taking the curse off what might otherwise be banal and maudlin. The music fills another function, that of commentator, because there are long stretches where there is no dialog or naration. A song with music and lyrics by Stein, sung by Randy Sparks, "Road Without End," is a good theme melody.

The humans involved on the screen do not come off well generally, no match for the two animal stars.

Powe.

The Bonnie Parker Story

Femme member of a double-bill pair that should do well on the current gangster exploitation spree. No names.

Hollywood, July 4.

Allied Artists release a James H. Nicholson-Samuel Z. Arkoff production. Producer-writer, Stanley Shpetner; director, William Witney; camera, Jack Marta; music, Ronald Stein; editor, Frank Keller. Reviewed in Hollywood, July 2, '58. Running time, **79 MINS.**

Bonnie Parker .... Dorothy Provine
Guy Darrow .... Jack Hogan
Duke Jefferson .... Richard Bakalyan
Chuck Darrow .... Joseph Turkel
Paul .... William Stevens
Manager (of restaurant) ..... Ken Lynch
Tom Steel .... Douglas Kennedy
Chuck's Girl .... Patt Huston
Bobby .... Joel Colin
Marv .... Jeff Morris
Alvin .... Jim Beck
Little Boy .... Stanley Livingston
Girl .... Carolyn Hughes
Ranger Chief .... John Halloran
Ranger's Secretary .... Madeline Foy
Scoutmaster .... Sid Lassick
Old Man .... Howard Wright
Texan .... Karl Davis

"The Bonnie Parker Story" is one-half of an American-International double-barrelled echo from the gangster era. The James. H. Nicholson-Samuel Z. Arkoff presentation is obviously an exploitation item, but it is capably constructed and intelligently carried out. Whether or not it follows the facts in the case is perhaps of academic interest, since this period—the early 1930's—is as remote to most audiences today as the era of Billy the Kid. Paired with the same unit's "Machine Gun Kelly," another of the same genre, the William Witney-directed picture should prove a good money-maker.

Dorothy Provine, a sultry blonde, plays the infamous gunwoman of the thirties, led, according to Stanley Shpetner's screenplay, into a life of crime by the crude treatment handed her by society when her husband, Richard Bakalyan, is sent up for 175 years. Bonnie swiftly becomes as tough and then tougher than the men she takes up with, smokes big black cigars and handles a tommy gun as casually as a lipstick. Her life of crime increases in savagery and depravity as she feels herself, as the script comments, on a lonesome ride on a one-way ticket. Although the production may be aimed at the young and impressionable, the way of life it depicts is never shown as anything but shabby and drab. Without glamorizing, Shpetner and Witney make this dreary existence absorbing and engrossing. Without preaching, either, they manage to point a moral.

Miss Provine gives a good performance, as do the two principal men in her life, Jack Hogan and Bakalyan. Others who are noticeable include Joseph Turkel, William Stevens, Ken Lynch, Douglas Kennedy and Patt Huston.

Ronald Stein's frantic music emphasizes the nervous and wracking life of those running and in hiding, and Jack Marta's camera work makes the inexpensive production look better, physically. Other plus credits include Frank Keller's editing and Ron Ament's purposely sleazy period settings. *Powe.*

Machine Gun Kelly

Gats and girls in the life of the thirties' infamous outlaw. Well-made low budgeter for returns in exploitation market.

Hollywood, July 4.

Allied Artists release of a James H. Nicholson-Samuel Z. Arkoff production. Producer-director, Roger Corman; screenplay, R. Wright Campbell; camera, Floyd Crosby; music, Gerald Fried; editor, Ronald Sinclair. Reviewed in Hollywood, July 2, '58. Running time, 84 MINS.

Machine Gun Kelly	Charles Bronson
Flo	Susan Cabot
Fandango	Morey Amsterdam
Howard	Jack Lambert
Maize	Wally Campo
Vito	Bob Griffin
Lynn	Barboura Morris
Apple	Richard Devon
Teddy	Ted Thorp
Harriet	Mitzi McCall
Harry	Frank de Kova
Martha	Shirley Falls
Ma	Connie Gilchrist
Clinton	Mike Fox
Drummond	Larry Thor
Frank	George Archambeault
Philip Ashton	Jay Sayer

American - International's "Machine Gun Kelly" beats out a tattoo of the thirties in its account of the criminal career of one of that decade's most notorious outlaws. Roger Corman, who produced and directed, has taken a good screenplay by R. Wright Campbell, and made a first-rate little picture out of the depressing but intriguing, account of a badman's downfall. Coupled with "The Bonnie Parker Story" (subtitled in local showings as "The Female Mobster"), "Machine Gun Kelly" and its companion piece should make one of the more profitable exploitation duos of the year.

Charles Bronson plays Kelly, shown as an undersized sadist who grows an extra foot or so as soon as he gets a submachine gun tucked under his arm. His exploits, proceeding from penny ante robbery to bigtime kidnapping, are adroitly and swiftly shown, leading inevitably to the moment when he is surrounded and captured by the police.

Campbell's script is remarkable for the crisply colorful flavor of his dialog, putting additional interest in scenes that of themselves might otherwise have been merely repetitive. Corman also takes the trouble to sketch briefly but effectively, minor characters and incidents that give weight and meaning to the otherwise sordid story.

Bronson gives a brooding, taut performance that somehow takes the curse off the character without lessening the horror of the casual slayings. Susan Cabot is good as the woman behind his deeds, and Morey Amsterdam contributes an offbeat portrayal of a squealer who has the final revenge of turning Kelly in. Others in the cast who stand out include Jack Lambert, Wally Campo, Bob Griffin, Barboura Morris, Richard Devon, Ted Thorp and Connie Gilchrist, the latter as a wonderfully disheveled "house" mother.

Gerald Fried, using piano and taps for an unusual and striking combination, has done a fine progressive jazz score, and Floyd Crosby's photography penetrates the motivations of these unlovely characters. Editing by Ronald Sinclair is good and art direction by Dan Haller is of more than background value. *Powe.*

Ice Cold In Alex
(BRITISH)

Taut offbeat drama with war background. Good stellar value with powerful performances and direction. Surefire booking.

London, July 1.

Associated-British-Pathe release of an Associated-British (W. A. Whittaker) production. Stars John Mills, Sylvia Syms, Anthony Quayle, Harry Andrews. Directed by J. Lee-Thompson. Screenplay, T. J. Morrison, Christopher Landon, based on Landon's novel; editor, Richard Best; camera, Gilbert Taylor; music, Leighton Lucas. At Warner Theatre, London, June 24, '58. Running time, 132 MINS.

Captain Anson	John Mills
Sister Diana Murdoch	Sylvia Syms
Captain Van der Poel	Anthony Quayle
M. S. M. Pugh	Harry Andrews
Sister Denise Norton	Diane Clare
Captain Crosbie	Richard Leech
Brigadier	Liam Radmond
British officer	Peter Arme

Yet another war film, but this time concerned purely with human emotions. "Ice Cold In Alex" stands up absorbingly for its 132 minutes, produces some solid acting, imaginative direction and lensing. It is a worthwhile booking on both sides of the Atlantic. Based on a slight, real-life anecdote, pic is the story of a handful of people who drive an ambulance through the mine-ridden, enemy-occupied desert after the collapse of Tobruk in 1942.

There are a nerve-strained officer who has taken to the bottle, his tough, reliable sergeant-major, a couple of nurses and a South African officer, who turns out to be a German spy. The acting of this quintet brings to vivid life a film which is, deservedly, an official entry at the Berlin Film Fest. Director J. Lee-Thompson has captured the stark, pitiless atmosphere of the desert superbly. The screenplay skilfully blends excitement, a hint of romance and a fearful sense of danger in which the audience will find full participation.

Apart from a few small cameos, the action is in the hands of five thesps and they do a valiant job. John Mills is the skipper, strained to the limit, who seeks solace in a few swift swigs. This is a credible, edgy performance which rates among the best that this capital performer has yet given the screen. Anthony Quayle, as the spy, has a suspect accent, but brings a plausible charm to the role of the heavy which helps the audience to stomach a fairly glib ending. Harry Andrews is first-rate as the sergeant-major.

The two reps of the distaff side might well have been submerged in the documentary atmosphere of this pic but, stripped of any glamor, Sylvia Syms fits snugly into the plot. It seems a pity that the director didn't allow the budding romance between her and Mills to develop a shade more. Diane Clare, a newcomer, plays a frightened nurse who gets bumped off half way through the film but does enough to warrant future, bigger chances.

The dialog is occasionally too mundane, but it is intelligent, authentic and, occasionally, surprisingly frank. Dramatic highlights are introduced skillfully to keep the tension bubbling. The toughness of the location is used to give the film full flavor.

"Ice Cold In Alex" is the story of a miserable, courageous, fearful journey and nobody watching it will be able to do so dispassionately. Every viewer will feel that they themselves are taking part in the journey. The whole audience will share the kick of that glass of cold lager which the cast enjoys when the journey's end is reached. *Rich.*

Berlin Festival

The Temptress
(JAPANESE—C'SCOPE—COLOR)

Berlin, July 1.

Nikkatsu Corp. (Tokio) production in C'Scope and color, directed by Eisuke Takizawa. Camera, Minoru Yokoyama; script, Kyoka Izumi and Toshio Yasumi; editor, Masanori Tsuji-i; music, Yutaka Makino. Stars Yumeji Tsukioka and Ryoji Hayama. At Berlin Film Festival, June 30. Running time, 88 MINS.

A quaint legendary tale, "The Temptress" may have some curiosity value, but in the main it must be regarded as unacceptable for Western tastes. It is, however, technically outstanding. The color camera work in a local anamorphic process has exceptional beauty, and many of the backgrounds offers a visual treat. The femme star, too, Yumeji Tsukioka, is quite a stunner, and plays an unenviable role with commendable polish.

"The Temptress" of the title is married to a cretin and, by ancient custom, every man who succumbs to her charms is transformed into an animal. The grounds of their home are filled with ex-lovers who now serve as bulls, horses, bats, etc. The film itself describes how a young monk who seeks shelter in her home avoids the transformation process, although he's an easy victim to her wiles. Among the provocative, scenes is a nude bathing sequence, and another in which the star bears her breast to pacify one of her ex-lovers, now a bull. *Myro.*

The Strange Gods
(ARGENTINE—CINEMASCOPE COLOR)

Berlin, June 29.

Cinematografica d'An-Fran SRL (Buenos Aires) production, directed by Roman Vinnoly Barreto; script, Hugo Moser; camera, Ricardo Younis; editor, Jose J. Serra; music, Waldo de los Rios. Stars Olga Zubarry, Enrique Fava. At Berlin Film Festival, June 28. Running time, 80 MINS.

Filmed entirely on location in the mountain region of Quebrada de Humahuaca in the northern part of the Argentine, "The Strange Gods" has only two professional performers; the rest of the cast is recruited from the local inhabitants, and their immaturity as actors is transparent. Technically, too, the pic is inadequate; direction is limp, and the editing lacks authority.

There is an ingenuous love story between an archaeologist and the local school teachr, padded out with irrelevant scenes of local customs. Only one, a ritual tribal dance at a funeral, had general appeal, but, here again, tauter editing would improve the sequence.

Pictorially, the pic is okay, but the backgrounds are by no means exceptional. *Myro.*

Fear of Power
(SWISS)

Berlin, June 28.

Neue Film (Zurich) production, directed by Franz Schnyder; script, W. M. Treichlinger, Arnold Kubler and Franz Schnyder; camera, Knonstantin Tschet; editor, Hans Heinrich Egger; music, Robert Blum. Stars Heinz Reincke and Linda Geiser. At Berlin Film Festival, June 27. Running time, 86 MINS.

An invited entry to Berlin and selected to open the festival, "Fear of Power" sets out to describe the events of May 10, 1940, when the Nazi armies began their march through Europe, and the Swiss feared invasion. The screenplay, for which three writers get credit, is ragged and uneven, and that sets the tone for the finished picture.

The plot focusses on a German who decides to cross the border when the Gestapo begins to turn on the heat for some minor indiscretions which he has committed. Once in neutral territory, he sets out for Zurich, hoping for the help of a girl he knew as a childhood friend. Continuity is at times erratic, and new characters are introduced without any attempt at establishment. Acting by the principals is on a moderately competent level. *Myro.*

Traumstrasse Der Welt
(The Dream Road of the World)

Berlin, July 3.

Deutsche Film Hansa (Hamburg) release of a Hans Dominick production. Direction, editing, camera, commentary by Dominick. At Berlin Film Festival, July 2. Running time, 85 MINS.

Hans Dominick, one of Germany's leading documentarians, with most of the technical credits for this production, makes it seem virtually a one-man-gang. It is, of its type, and extremely well-made picture, rich in its backgrounds and handsomely photographed in Eastmancolor.

The "dream road" of the title is the highway which transverses the American continent, starting from Alaska in the north and working south down to Mexico, (and theoretically beyond to Panama).

With a keen eye and a selective camera, Dominick has collected some interesting items on his continental travels, among them some offbeat footage on a rodeo in Calgary, more conventional material on Bryce Canyon and Grand Canyon, and some arresting scenes of Monument Valley. *Myro.*

Foreign Films

Paris, July 1.

Tabarin (FRENCH; COLOR). Jeannic release of STF-Florida-Nepi Film production. Stars Michel Piccoli, Sonia Ziemann, Annie Cordy, Sylvia Lopez; features Henri Vilbert, J. P. Kerien, Mischa Auer. Directed by Richard Pottier. Screenplay, Jean Ferry, Andre Legrand; camera (Eastmancolor), Lucien Joulin; editor, Maurice Serein; music, Francis Lopez. At Triomphe, Paris. Running time, 110 MINS.

Tired story about the director of nitery show whose friends get him a club so he can put on the spec he wants is segued into a musical. The numbers are worked out in the old Tabarin nitery, opened for this pic. Yank choreographer Lee Sherman has injected some spice into the usual chorus production numbers, but this can not make this oldhat musical palatable for any U.S. chances. It is strictly for the Continent. Technical credits and cast are good. *Mosk.*

Sans Famille (Nobody's Boy) **(FRENCH; COLOR).** Cocinor release of Francinex-Rizzoli-SPCE production. Stars Pierre Brasseur, Gino Cervi; features Bernard Blier, Joel Flateau, Raymond Bussieres, Jacques Moulieres, Jean-Marc Thibault, Roger Pierre, Simone Renant. Directed by Andre Michel. Screenplay, Pitrre Very, Remo Forlani from novel by Hector Malot; camera (Eastmancolor), Robert Juillard; editor, Boris Lewin. Preemed in Paris. Running time, **100 MINS.**

Based on the 19th century Gallic classic, this emerges a fairly engaging moppet pic. It manages to keep its romantic theme simple and serious. In color, this is not a U.S. art house gambit, but could emerge a sound kiddie film, with family patronage overtones.

Tale is about a little boy kidnapped by a malevolent uncle who wants to inherit the family fortune. Given to an assassin the latter does not kill him but gives him to a family to bring up. Pic follows the kid's adventures through the French countryside and to London. Good cast makes this all acceptable. Pierre Brasseur is properly sinister as the soft-hearted assassin. Gino Cervi is a colorful travelling troubador while Joel Flateau manages to be engaging as the nobody's boy. Color is an asset while direction is good. Technical credits also are okay. *Mosk.*

Le Naif Aux 40 Enfants (The Innocent With 40 Children) **(FRENCH).** Cinedis release of Regina production. Stars Michel Serrault, Jean Poiret, Silva Koscina; features Jean Rigaux, Darry Cowl, Clement Duhour. Directed by Philippa Agostini. Screenplay, Odette Joyeux, Paul Guth, Andre Tabet; camera, Andre Bac; editor, Suzanne De Bonn. At the Paris, Paris. Running time, **100 MINS.**

Film concerns a young teacher in a smalltown school who tries to intro new methods, falls for the beauteous mother of one of the students, and finally gets his just deserts. Pic remains conventional and is too stereotyped to make for any untoward Yank chances. The teacher wins his students but loses his heart to a lovely mother. Michel Serrault is made arch rather than naive. All his good timing and sincerity can not erase the banality of the character. Children are good, and the remainder of the cast competent. Technical credits are fine, but direction rarely raises this from the familiar level of school pix. *Mosk.*

Sois Belle Et Tais Toi (Look Lovely and Shut Up) **(FRENCH)** Dispa release of EGE production. Stars Mylene Demongeot, Henri Vidal; features Rene Lefevre, Roger Hanin. Directed by Marc Allegret. Screenplay, William Benjamin, Jean Mersan, Odette Joyeux, Roger Vadim, Gabriel Arout; camera, Armand Thirard; editor, Suzanne De Troeye. At Biarritz, Paris. Running time, **110 MINS.**

This film vacillates between a romantico situation comedy and an actioner. Neither are adequately mastered. Probably too many screenwriters have spoiled the broth of this. It emerges an okay programmer here and is limited for the U.S. except for possible dualer slotting on its fine technical gloss, pleasant playing and theme. Credits are good all along the line.

It is about a hairbrained girl who becomes the innocent foil for a smuggling racket. But the handsome police inspector saves her for the clinch and happy end. *Mosk.*

South Seas Adventure
(CINERAMA-TECHNICOLOR)

Latest of the Cinerama travelogs. Fairly diverting entertainment along familiar lines with special church and educational angles of boxoffice lure.

Stanley Warner presentation of Carl Dudley production (Richard Goldstone, co-producer) directed by Dudley, Goldstone, Francis D. Lyon, Walter Thompson, Basil Wrangell. Camera (Technicolor), John F. Warren, also Paul Hill. Narrated by Orson Welles, Shepherd Mencken, Walter Coy, Ted de Corsia. Score composed and conducted by Alex North, vocals by Norman Luboff Choir. Edited by Frederick Y. Smith and Walter Stern. Opened July 15 at Warners, N.Y. Running time. **120 MINS.**

If "South Seas Adventure" were not No. 5 in a sequence of travelogs its merits would no doubt seem more estimable. This trip has been well organized by a seasoned travel and documentary producer, Carl Dudley, and it must be assumed that Cinerama itself still has boxoffice mileage left although the original and sensational momentum was slowed by "Search For Paradise."

There is no evading the broader issue, important to film showmen and Cinerama shareholders alike, that with a fifth "carbon," the three-camera medium is imitating its own past and again postponing the solution of its own growth. By now something more and new was reasonably expected and urgently needed.

What was arrestingly and excitingly novel only six years ago grows a bit too familiar to meet the demands of showmanship. Here again is the airplane ride over the snow, the ocean, the endless prairie. Glacial and other geologic wonders, raging waters and smouldering volcanic mud are again glanced. There is even once again the ride in the amusement park, fairly tame this time and rendering the off-screen shreiks pretty "stagey."

Yet the voyage by liner, schooner and aircraft adds up to a fairly diverting if not very exciting journey. Cinerama still conveys its unique brand of pictorial experience, though distortion and seams persist.

Continuity is the work of three writers, Charles Kaufman, Joseph Ansen and Harold Medford. It is pretty straightforward, dotted with a few giggles but eschewing the purple prose, and especially the built-in songplugs and private exploitation which marred "Search For Paradise." There is one delicious scene, outbound on the S.S. Lurline for Honolulu showing the passengers, good middle class, middleaged Yanks, taking their daily hula-hula lesson.

Some confusion in the viewer may result from the use of a main narrator. Orson Welles, but spelled off in different sequences by three other narrators, Shepherd Mencken, Walter Coy, Ted de Corsia. The shift from one personality and point of view to another jolts attention away from the eye to the ear.

Alex North's special score, soundtracked at Cinerama's Oyster Bay plant, stays in the background, where it belongs, most of the time, but in some of the flying and Australian scenes, notably the demented steeplechase of the kangaroos the music comes forward strongly and imaginatively.

Counting producer Dudley and co-producer Richard Goldstone as two there were five directors on "South Seas." A tradester would

---

be inclined to detect some evidence of patchquilting but it's doubtful that this will bother the general public. Francis D. Lyon, Walter Thompson and Basil Wrangell have brought in competent work. Some of the tropical longshots seem sunhazed and previous Cinerama camera work, possibly because it was then years fresher in emotional impact, undoubtedly drew more audience "ohs" and "ahs" than are contained here. John F. Warren gets the top credit with Paul Hill billed on "additional photography." Whole production, of course, is in Technicolor and plenty of opulence shows, especially in the Hawaiian opener, which ought to help push the islands as America's 50th State.

Dudley has played his materials for safety and tact. This is an updated and primly respectable South Seas in which Paul Gaugin is only a name and cannibalism, beachcombing, Somerset Maughan, Robert Louis Stevenson and J. C. Furnas tales are only implied in the promotion, not on the screen.

If some viewers may look for and miss Miss Sadie Thompson the church folk will no doubt be enchanted with the abundant footage granted the work of the missionaries. This may well bring plenty of party trade into the fifth Cinerama offering. In Tonga a Wesleyan choir sings Handel and **"Onward Christian Soldiers" with Polynesian words. On another island The Lord's Prayer is rendered in Pidgin English.**

Big physical thrill among the islands is the jump off the bamboo tower by the natives of the New Hebrides, the fall being broken by vine ropes attached to the men's ankles.

In the sense that the missionary stuff will bring out the religious, Australia's radio school in the "Out-Back" country may have special professional engrossment for American educators. The brave techniques developed by the Australians to defeat the dreadful isolation of this area, including the flying doctors which speed hundreds of miles to a call on radio summons add up to an admirable demonstration of modern science linked to rugged pioneering guts.

There is the usual boy meets girl angle included in the Hawaiian segment, a great promotional stunt for the Matson Line. On the final fadeout when the cameras swing back to Honolulu an outdoor wedding between the two amateur, but amateur, actors is taking place. Apart from these corny touches and the familiar stereotypes of the medium itself Cinerama is still a success, though in need of new millinery and a story to tell.
Land.

The Fly
(COLOR; C'SCOPE)

Top budget horror-science fiction thriller. Heavy payoff if sold for its general superiority over run-of-the-mine exploitationers.

Hollywood, July 11.

Twentieth-Fox release of its own production. Stars Al Hedison, Patricia Owens, Vincent Price, Herbert Marshall; features Kathleen Freeman, Betty Lou Gerson, Charles Herbert. Produced and directed by Kurt Neumann. Screenplay, James Clavell; based on a story by George Langelaan; camera, Karl Struss; music, Paul Sawtell; editor, Merrill G. White. Previewed at the studio, July 9, '58. Running time, **94 MINS.**

Andre	Al Hedison
Helene	Patricia Owens
Francois	Vincent Price
Inspector Charas	Herbert Marshall
Emma	Kathleen Freeman
Nurse Andersone	Betty Lou Gerson
Philippe	Charles Herbert
Dr. Ejoute	Eugene Borden
Gaston	Torben Meyer

"The Fly" is a high-budget, beautifully and expensively mounted exploitation picture.

Al Hedison plays a scientist who has invented a machine that reduces matter to disintegrated atoms and another machine that reassembles the atoms. He explains to his wife, Patricia Owens, that this will enable humans to travel—disintegrated—anywhere in the world (or out of it) in the speed of light, to be "integrated" when they arrive at their destination. In experimenting on himself, however, a fly gets into the disintegration chamber with him. When Hedison arrives in the integration chamber, he discovers some of his atoms have been scrambled with the fly's. Hedison has the head and "arm" of a fly; the fly has the head and arm of the man—each, of course, in his own scale of size. The problem is to catch the fly and rescramble. But before this can happen, Hedison finds the predatory instincts of the insect taking over so he persuades Miss Owens to put him in a high pressure press and snuff out his life.

One strong factor of the picture is its unusual believability. It is told, by Clavell and Neumann, as a mystery suspense story, so that it has a compelling interest aside from its macabre effects. There is an appealing and poignant romance between Miss Owens and Hedison, which adds to the reality of the story. Although the flashback technique purposely robs the picture of any doubt about the outcome, it is justified because it prepares the audience for a somewhat unconventionally unhappy ending.

Hedison's face is not seen for too much of the picture, but he and Miss Owens give validity to the narrative. Vincent Price, as Hedison's brother, and Herbert Marshall, as the police inspector, give solid performances, well supported by Kathleen Freeman, Betty Lou Gerson, young Charles Herbert, Eugene Borden and Torben Meyer.

Karl Struss' DeLuxe color, CinemaScope photography is especially notable in capturing the vivid excitement of the scientific workshop, aided by L. B. Abbott's special effects. Art direction by Lyle R. Wheeler and Theobold Holsopple, with set decoration by Walter M. Scott and Eli Benneche, is especially important, making the laboratory a thing of wonder and dread. Sound, including the menacing buzz of a fly, by Eugene is proficient and editing by Mer-Gertsman and Harry M. Leonard, rill G. White, give momentum to the story. Ben Nye's makeup also deserves a special credit. *Powe.*

The Night Heaven Fell
(C'SCOPE—COLOR)

Fair Brigitte Bardot offering, with star name to attract in art houses. English subtitles limits.

Hollywood, July 12.

Kingsley International release of Raoul J. Levy production. Stars Brigitte Bardot; features Stephen Boyd, Alida Valli, Director, Roger Vadim. Screenplay, Vadim, Jacques Remy, based on novel, "The Moonlight Jewelers," by Albert Visalie; camera (Eastmancolor), Armand Thirard;

music, Georges Auric. Previewed July 11, '58. Running time, **91 MINS.**

Ursula Desfontaines	Brigette Bardot
Florentine	Alida Valli
Lamberto	Stephen Boyd
Count Ribera	Pepe Nieto
Conchita	Maruschi Fresno
Fernando	Adriano Dominguez
Chief Policeman	Jose Marco Davo
Count's Driver	Antonio Vico
Alfonso	Mario Moreno
The Captain	Tosi
Stableman	Jose Tasso Tena
Priest	Nicholas Perchicaut
Veterinary	Dr. Rafael Torrobo

(English Titles)

One more to the influx of Brigitte Bardot imports. Obviously intended to cash in on the sex kitten's name and depending again on epidermis. Certain censorable scenes may limit its U. S. release to arty outlets, where bare derrieres and skimpy attire are accepted. English titles of French dialog aren't particularly helpful in lightening only a fair Gallic yarn.

Turned out by same producer, Raoul J. Levy, and director, Roger Vadim, responsible for "And God Created Woman," which brought French star to attention of American audiences, pic was filmed in mountain area of Spain, with some interesting color and scenic effects. Old-fashioned story deals with Bardot arriving to visit her aunt and uncle, and helping killer of the uncle escape from the police. Action is slow in unfoldment and for American audiences holds limited meaning.

Mlle. Bardot displays little thespic ability despite reports she now receives $150,000 per picture, her appeal being confined to an inborn sensual quality. Stephen Boyd, an English actor, does his best with killer role but is up against French treatment, and Alida Valli, once under contract to David O. Selznick here, qualifies as the aunt. Pepe Nieto is heavy as the uncle, slain because he ravished a village girl, sister of the killer. Maruschi Fresno ably portrays a gypsy girl.

Technical credits are well carried, particularly Armand Thirard's fine color photography. *Whit.*

Frankenstein—1970
(C'SCOPE)

Well-made entry in the horror class, good returns probable if thoroughly exploited.

Hollywood, July 11.

Allied Artists release of an Aubrey Schenck production. Stars Boris Karloff; features Tom Duggan, Jana Lund, Donald Barry, Charlotte Austin. Directed by Howard W. Koch. Screenplay, Richard Landau and George Worthing Yates; from a story by Aubrey Schenck and Charles A. Moses; camera, Carl E. Guthrie; music, Paul A. Dunlap; editor, John A. Bushelman. Previewed at the studio, July 7, '58. Running time, **83 MINS.**

Baron Frankenstein	Boris Karloff
Mike Shaw	Tom Duggan
Carolyn Hayes	Jana Lund
Douglas Row	Donald Barry
Judy Stevens	Charlotte Austin
Inspector Raab	Irwin Berke
Wilhelm Gootfried	Rudolph Anders
Morgan Haley	John Dennis
Shuter	Norbert Schiller
Hans	Mike Lane

With Frankenstein and his heirs and assigns now in the public domain, it must be somewhat confusing to the horror addict who tries to figure out who done what and to whom. Allied Artists' "Frankenstein—1970," a title that means nothing, incidentally, puts the baron and his family in Germany, although the last previous picture on the monster-maker had him in Switzerland (Columbia's "The Revenge of Frankenstein") on his way to England. Presumably, however, these discrepancies don't bother the devoted, and this current presentation, produced by Aubrey Schenck and directed by Howard W. Koch, is a competently made production that will do well in its class.

Boris Karloff is the grandson of the original baron, and his reason for wanting to exploit the family specialty and construct a living, breathing man, is so he can place his own brain in the creation. Karloff was a victim of Nazi persecution and aged prematurely. He plans to get an atomic reactor as part of his experiment by renting his ancestral castle to a troupe of American movie-makers. To get parts for his monster it is necessary to appropriate them from various people around the castle, but Karloff achieves success. At the last minute, the monster gets damaged and has to be destroyed. Or at least seems to be. Chances are the way to a sequel has been left open.

Karloff, made up to look rather like a disfigured Hindenburg, does a careful, convincing job with his role, which is competently written by Richard Landau and George Worthing Yates, from a story by Charles A. Moses and Schenck. The professionalism of the cast is somewhat thrown by the appearance in important roles of Tom Duggan and Irwin Berke, local tv personalities, who do well enough but are hardly in a class with Karloff. Others in the cast who help contribute authenticity are Jana Lund, Donald Barry, Charlotte Austin and Norbert Schiller.

Carl E. Guthrie's CinemaScope camera work is fluid and perceptive and Jack T. Collis' sets are a major asset of believability. *Powe.*

Madchen in Uniform
(Girls in Uniform)
(GERMAN—COLOR)

Berlin, July 9.

CCC Production (Berlin), directed by Geza Radvanyi. Script, Franz Hollering; camera, Werner Krien; music, Peter Sandloff. Stars Lilli Palmer and Romy Schneider. At Berlin Film Festival, July 8, '58. Running time, **94 MINS.**

A remake of a prewar German film, "Madchen in Uniform" is a disappointment for the generation able to recall the original, but should have some appeal to those to whom the subject is fresh. Marquee values of Lilli Palmer and Romy Schneider will also be of some help in promoting the pic in overseas markets. Probably only a so-so entry for the U. S. arties.

Black and white photography would have helped in establishing the sombre discipline that prevails in the girls school to which Romy Schneider, an orphaned member of the aristocracy, is sent to finish her education; the use of color strikes a false glamour note.

Potent dramatic values lie in the emotional attraction of the young girl to her teacher, Lilli Palmer, and of the ensuing conflict with the principal of the school. Miss Palmer acts with commendable authority and restraint, but there is a lack of subtlety in Miss Schneider's interpretation of a difficult role. Therese Giehse impreshes as the head of the school. *Myro.*

Le Desordre Et La Nuit
(Disorder and Night)
(FRENCH)

Paris, July 8.

Corona Films release of Orex production. Stars Jean Gabin, Danielle Darrieux, Nadja Tiller; features Paul Frankeur, Robert Manuel, Roger Hanin, Hazel Brooks. Directed by Gilles Grangier. Screenplay, Jacques Robert, Yvan Audouard, Grangier from novel by Grangier; camera, Louis Page; editor, Jacquline Douarinou. At Paris, Paris. Running time, **95 MINS.**

Vallois	Jean Gabin
Therese	Danielle Darrieux
Lucky	Nadja Tiller
Chaville	Paul Frankeur
Blasco	Robert Manuel
Simoni	Roger Hanin
Valenine	Hazel Scott

Film deals with a vice inspector's involvement with a suspect in a murder case. The girl is a drug addict but the inspector solves the case and gets the girl whom he turns over for the cure before marrying her. Film has a telegraphed plot and a plodding pace, but its "Paris by Night" flavor could shape this for some use in the U.S. where it has obvious exploitation values. It is chancey for arty houses.

Director Gilles Grangier gets some good elements via a brawling party, the offbeat Paris boites and the general night aspects of the city. But the tale tends to drag without any penetration into character.

Jean Gabin's solid filmic presence gives the films its main trump. Nadja Tiller is good as the dope addict while Danielle Darrieux registers in a small but telling role. *Mosk.*

Story of a Pure Love
(JAPAN—C'SCOPE—COLOR)

Berlin, July 8.

Toei Motion Picture Co. (Tokyo) presentation, directed by Tadashi Imai. Script, Yoko Mizuki; editor, Kaki Nagasawa; music, Masao Oki. Stars Shinjiro Ebara and Hitomi Nakahara. At Berlin Film Festival July 7, '58. Running time, **134 MINS.**

Against a background of brutality among juvenile delinquents, "Story of a Pure Love" features a tender romance between two youngsters who are victims of society. More so than most recent Japanese productions, this film has a definite commercial look; but it is too leisurely paced and needs substantial scissoring of its two hours-plus to make it acceptable in Western markets.

The "tough" aspects include an attempted rape by five youths of one girl, realistic fights with flick knives, and a free for all among girls in a reformatory who try to break out. On the other side is a fearful reminder of the effects of the atom bomb as the heroine dies from anaemia 10 years after the Hiroshima explosion.

Hitomi Nakahara has an appealing and winning personality in the femme lead, and Shinjiro Ebara plays opposite her in earnest style. Anamorphic color lensing is first rate. *Myro.*

The Badlanders
(C'SCOPE; COLOR)

Topnotch western, highlighted by offbeat story and treatment. Good names for opening and good word-of-mouth for sustained b.o.

Hollywood, July 11.

Metro release of an Aaron Rosenberg production. Stars Alan Ladd, Ernest Borgnine, Katy Jurado, Claire Kelly. Directed by Delmer Daves; screenplay, Richard Collins; based on a novel by W. R. Burnett; camera, John Seitz; editors, William H. Webb, James Baiotto. Previewed in Hollywood, July 9, '58. Running time, **85 MINS.**

Peter Van Hoek	Alan Ladd
John McBain	Ernest Borgnine
Anita	Katy Jurado
Ada Winton	Claire Kelly
Cyril Lounsberry	Kent Smith
Vincente	Nehemiah Persoff
Sample	Robert Emhardt
Comanche	Anthony Caruso
Leslie	Adam Williams
Warden	Ford Rainey
Lee	John Day

It is possible to make an adult western without making it a psychological western. Aaron Rosenberg proves the point with his production of "The Badlanders" for Metro. This picture is a truly original frontier drama, a suspense melodrama on one level and a huge horselaugh on another, with each element playing off on the other for laughs, excitement and romance, all quite off-beat and doubly rewarding for the novelty.

The title, "The Badlanders," seems unlikely to stir much boxoffice response of itself, but good names and word-of-mouth should boost this presentation into the hit class.

The heroes of Richard Collins' screenplay, based on a novel by W. R. Burnett, are two ex-cons, released from the Nevada Territorial Prison, circa 1900, with little but revenge and larceny in their hearts. It is the plan of one of them, Alan Ladd, to do nothing less than rob a gold mine, and he enlists the other, Ernest Borgnine, in support. The problem, of course, is formidable. They must blast the ore —half a ton of it—from a spot right next to a mine full of workmen, then get the huge load away from under the noses (and shotguns) of the legal owners.

Collins' script not only avoids the usual cliches of the form— there is not one single gun duel with opponents approaching each other from opposite ends of a long, emptied street — but serves up some characters, scenes and incidents that are fresh and vital. The heroines, Katy Jurado and Claire Kelly, for instance, are ladies who are plainly of easy and saleable virtue and there is none of the usual subterfuge about dance hall girls.

Delmer Daves' direction has a facility, almost a trademark, of throwing a laugh into the midst of a suspense buildup, relieving and heightening it with flashes of humor. He sets his motivations quickly and firmly, for example, justifying his heroes' whole conduct by showing prison brutality and swiftly sketching their back grounds. His climatic scene, in which Ladd and Borgnine are aided in their escape with the gold by a huge Mexican carnival scene that overruns their pursuers, is a gaudy burlesque of the Cavalry-to-the-rescue that is both funny and thrilling.

For the top stars, Ladd, Borgnine and Miss Jurado, "The Badlanders" is the best picture in some time. Ladd is not required over-heroic, physically. His strength is emotional, and with casual grace and away with an ironic line, he creates an effective contrast to Borgnine, who has his best portrayal since "Marty," and makes a calculated uncertainty a poignant and moving thing. Miss Jurado is handsomely colorful and alternately touching as a Mexican girl. Miss Kelly, who makes her major bow in this picture, is a stunning redhead but she is not yet a strong enough actress to hold her own with this trio. Nehemiah Persoff makes an appealing character as chief aide to Ladd and Borgnine; Kent Smith is a slick and persuasive villain; while Adam Williams as a young and corrupt law officer is helpful. Others who make able contributions include Robert Emhardt, Anthony Caruso, Ford Rainey and John Day.

John Seitz' CinemaScope photography in Metrocolor heightens the action whether catching the

brawling carnival scenes or the tense moments within the mine at the uncertain rock slips and slides. Editing by William H. Webb and James Baiotto is skillful and sound by Wesley Miller top-notch.
Powe.

Intent to Kill
(BRITISH-C'SCOPE)

Well-made suspense drama, smoothly directed and competently acted; excellent program topper for most houses.

London, July 16.

20th-Fox release of Zonic (Adrian D. Worker) Production. Stars Richard Todd, Betsy Drake, Herbert Lom, Warren Stevens; features Carlo Justini, Paul Carpenier, Alexander Knox, Lisa Gastoni, Peter Arne, Catherine Boyle. Directed by Jack Cardiff. Screenplay, Jimmy Sangster from novel by Michael Bryan; editor, Tom Simpson; camera, Desmond Dickinson; music, Kenneth V. Jones. At 20th-Fox Private Theatre, London. Running time, **89 MINS.**

Bob McLaurin	Richard Todd
Nancy Ferguson	Betsy Drake
Juan Menda	Herbert Lom
Finch	Warren Stevens
Francisco Flores	Carlo Justini
O'Brien	Paul Carpenter
Dr. McNeill	Alexander Knox
Carla Menda	Lisa Gastoni
Kral	Peter Arne
Margaret McLaurin	Catherine Boyle
Boyd	John Crawford
Anaesthetist	John McLaren
Carol Freeman	Jackie Collins
Carol's Friend	Kay Callard

With "Intent to Kill," Jack Cardiff, one of Britain's ace lensers, has stepped into the directorial field and has done a smooth, workmanlike job with an unpretentious yet holding thriller. A very competent cast insures this pic as a worthwhile booking for both sides of the Atlantic. Cardiff's experience as a cameraman has had an obvious effect on camera angles and editing. He has worked shrewdly with Desmond Dickinson and Tom Simpson respectively.

Based on Michael Bryan's novel, "Kill" is a yarn set in Montreal. It concerns the efforts of a political gang to rub out the prexy of a South American republic who, incognito, is in Montreal undergoing a delicate brain operation. There is also a romantic side issue between a dedicated doctor and an attractive femme medico which really hasn't much bearing on the plot, and often bogs down the whole affair. The main point of interest is whether the killers will get their man and the tension is neatly spaced out until the end which finishes up with a socko climax of murder and mayhem.

Jimmy Sangster's screenplay meanders occasionally when he has to deal with the romantic side of the story. However, the dialog and action is taut and to the point in the assassination build-up. Cardiff has assembled a first-class bunch of actors and there are meaty roles for at least a dozen talented thesps. Richard Todd makes a credible doctor, though the role doesn't offer him much range. Betsy Drake, as the doctor for whom he falls, glows pleasantly through a routine role. Much greater opportunities are offered to Herbert Lom as the prexy and Warren Stevens, headman of the murder gang. Lom plays most of his role in bed and gives subtlety to his portrayal of a frightened man. Stevens invests his part with a cool humor which gives added weight to his menace as the heavy. He is ably supported by Peter Arne, as a discredited doctor, and John Crawford as the strong arm member of the trio. Carlo Justini, as a treacherous ambassador; Alexander Knox, a sympathetic surgeon, and Paul Carpenter, as a cop, are also usefully and skilfully employed.

Apart from Miss Drake, there are two main femme roles. Lisa Gastoni, as the dictator's wife, is a seductive dish and has several emotional moments which she handles well. Catherine Boyle

plays Todd's philandering wife effectively. The wintry atmosphere of Montreal is well sustained.
Rich.

Ride A Crooked Trail
(COLOR—C'SCOPE)

Pleasant, light treatment of reformed gunfighter. Good for family and some action situations.

Hollywood, July 18.

Universal release of a Howard Pine production. Stars Audie Murphy, Gia Scala; features Walter Matthau, Henry Silva, Joanna Moore. Directed by Jesse Hibbs. Screenplay, Borden Chase; based on a story by George Bruce; camera, Harold Lipstein; music, Joseph Gershenson; editor, Edward Curtiss. Previewed in Hollywood, July 15, '58. Running time, **87 MINS.**

Joe Maybe	Audie Murphy
Tessa Milotte	Gia Scala
Judge Kyle	Walter Matthau
Sam Teeler	Henry Silva
Little Brandy	Joanna Moore
Jimmy	Eddie Little
Mrs. Curtis	Mary Field
Sam Mason	Leo Gordon
Pecos	Mort Mills
Ben (Deputy)	Frank Chase
Jackson	Bill Walker
Attorney Clark	Ned Wever
Mr. Curtis	Richard Cutting

Howard Pine production, directed by Jesse Hibbs, is concerned with a gunman who allows himself to be reformed by a boy and a town that makes him feel at home. Film should do well in family and some action situations. A good group of names, headed by Audie Murphy and Gia Scala, provide marquee decoration.

Borden Chase's screenplay has Murphy as a gunslinger who is mistaken for a U.S. marshal and then is forced by circumstances to play the role. This means trouble because he has already made a deal with fellow outlaw Henry Silva to heist the local bank. He has to decide whether to continue his life of crime or accept his place in the community. Another complication is Gia Scala, who has been both his girl and Silva's.

Chase's screenplay leavens the sentimentality of the basic story with some salty humor, notably in the Matthau character, an amusing boozer. Some of the comic lines are not as sharply pointed up as they might be—not the writer's fault—so the production as a whole does not sparkle and snap as it should. Despite this, it is an interesting presentation, peopled with diverse characters and will satisfy the audiences it is aimed at.

Murphy gives an ingratiating performance and Miss Scala is good contrast as a vigorous Creole girl. Matthau's free-wheeling characterization sometimes borders on caricature but the broadness of his playing actually helps enliven the picture a great deal. Henry Silva etches an impressive part and youthful Eddie Little plays without saccharine. Others who contribute include Joanna Moore, Mary Field, Mort Mills, Frank Chase and Bill Walker.

Harold Lipstein's CinemaScope photography, in Eastman Color, gives rich background to the story, localed in a river-front town, while art direction by Alexander Golitzen and Bill Newberry is rich and authentic. Sound by Leslie I. Carey and Donald McKay, and editing by Edward Curtiss, are both first-rate.
Powe.

Raw Wind In Eden
(COLOR; C'SCOPE)

Mild romantic adventure melodrama, with appeal chiefly to Esther Williams and Jeff Chandler fans.

Hollywood, July 18.

Universal release of a William Alland production. Stars Esther Williams, Jeff Chandler; costars Rossana Podesta, Carlos Thompson, Rik Battaglia, Eduardo de Filippo. Director, Richard Wilson; screenplay, Elizabeth and Richard Wilson; based on a story by Dan Lundberg and Elizabeth Wilson; camera, Enzo Serafin; music, Hans J. Salter; editor, Russell F. Schoengarth. Previewed at the studio, July 17, '58. Running time, **93 MINS.**

Laura	Esther Williams
Moore	Jeff Chandler
Costanza	Rossana Podesta
Wally	Carlos Thompson
Gavino	Rik Battaglia
Urbano	Eduardo de Filippo

A worldly melodrama set in the primitive islands off Sardinia, "Raw Wind In Eden" has some striking location backgrounds, but the action in the foreground is seldom exciting or even convincing, so the strength of the Universal production will rest on the marquee value of Esther Williams and Jeff Chandler, who are starred.

Miss Williams plays a fashion model working in Rome, in the screenplay by Elizabeth and Richard Wilson from a story by Dan Lundberg and Elizabeth Wilson. She takes off by plane for a Mediterranean cruise with playboy Carlos Thompson. When their plane crashes on a remote island, they are rescued by mystery man Jeff Chandler. They are forced to remain on the island for some weeks until Thompson discovered a beached sailing yacht on the island, repairs it and takes off. By this time, Miss Williams has discovered Chandler's tragic past and they have discovered each other.

There is the setting and occasion here for an unusual and attractive story. William Alland's production is well-conceived except that the script is not strong enough and the direction by Richard Wilson, does nothing to disguise its weakness. The production seems to waver between smart comedy and a Technicolored Italian realism, with neither element successfully projected.

Miss Williams and Chandler do well enough within the limits of their roles, but it is the Italians in the cast who come off best, perhaps because they have less dialog. Rossana Podesta, as a peasant girl of the island, Rik Battaglia, as her determined suitor, and Eduardo de Filippo, as her philosophical father, at least are believable and acceptable characters.

Enzo Serafin's CinemaScope photography is well composed and visually strong, and put together for most effective use by editor Russell F. Schoengarth, particularly in his color matching. Sound, by Leslie I. Carey and Umberto Picistrelli, is natural and unobtrusive. Hans J. Salter's score is often very imaginative.
Powe.

Space Master X-7
(REGALSCOPE)

Low-budget but well-made science fiction-plus-horror.

Hollywood, July 18.

Twentieth-Fox release of a Regal production. Stars Bill Williams, Lyn Thomas, Robert Ellis. Produced by Bernard Glaser; director, Edward Bernds; screenplay, George Worthing Yates, Daniel Mainwaring; camera, Brydon Baker; music, Josef Zimanich; editor, John F. Link. Previewed in Hollywood, July 17, '58. Running time, **71 MINS.**

John Hand	Bill Williams
Lora Greeling	Lyn Thomas
Radigan	Robert Ellis
Charles Palmer	Paul Frees
Miss Meyers	Joan Barry
Professor West	Thomas B. Henry
Morse	Fred Sherman
Captain	Jesse Kirkpatrick
Cab Driver	Moe Howard
Miss Archer	Rhoda Williams
Elaine Frohman	Carol Varga
Collins	Thomas Wilde
Engineer	Gregg Martell
Chief Hendry	Court Shepard
Passenger	Al Baffert

"Space Master X-7," which 20th-Fox is packaging with its class horror pic, "The Fly," is a competent science fiction tale with horror touches. Regal production, produced by Bernard Glasser and directed by Edward Bernds, runs out of story before it runs out of film, but for the lower half of a double bill it is passable.

The screenplay by George Worthing Yates and Daniel Mainwaring has Bill Williams and Robert Ellis as U.S. security agents. They are alerted to find a menacing organism brought back from Mars by a space satellite. The "blood rust," so-called, kills the scientist, Paul Frees, who discovers it, and it escapes out into the world from his laboratory by means of his former sweetheart, Lyn Thomas. The pic then devolves into a woman-hunt for Miss Thomas, a Typhoid Mary on a colossal scale.

To give validity and added strength, the picture is told in a semi-documentary style with occasional narration, film clips and a realistic approach. The interest sustains although it wears thin towards the end when invention and situation are about exhausted.

Miss Thomas does a capable job as the hunted woman, and Williams and Ellis are convincing as the largely luckless sleuths. Frees, Joan Barry, Thomas B. Henry, Fred Sherman and Jesse Kirkpatrick contribute. Moe Howard does a brief bit that is a comedy standout.

Technical credits are satisfactory. *Powe.*

A Question of Adultery
(BRITISH)

Novelettish drama about artificial insemination; unconvincing treatment of controversial subject, which merits only mild interest.

London, July 15.
Eros release of a Raymond Stross production. Stars Julie London, Anthony Steel; features Basil Sydney, Donald Houston and Anton Diffring. Directed by Don Chaffey. Screenplay, Anne Edwards; editor, Peter Tanner; camera, Stephen Dade; music, Philip Green. At Cameo-Poly, London. Running time, **90 MINS.**

Mary	Julie London
Mark	Anthony Steel
Sir John Loring	Basil Sydney
Mr. Jacobus	Donald Houston
Carl Dieter	Anton Diffring
Dr. Cameron	Andrew Cruickshank
Mario	Conrad Phillips
Judge	Kynaston Reeves
Mr. Stanley	Frank Thring
Nurse Parsons	Mary Mackenzie
Foreman of the Jury	John Rae
Court Usher	Michael Logan
Reporter	Trevor Reid
Cub Reporter	John Charlesworth
Flamenco Dancers	Trader Faulkner, Vola Van Dere

The subject of artificial insemination is a challenging one and, if regarded as suitable material for a film, a bold, searching light should have been thrown on to the problem. But "A Question of Adultery" does no such thing. It emerges as a soggy, novelettish affair which dodges the vital issue in a contrived, happy ending. It would seem that the producers had hit on the theme and its catchpenny title with more of an eye on the boxoffice than on presenting a thoughtful social document. With an "X" certificate—which means that no child under 16 may see it—"Adultery" may well attract the curious. But those expecting to be shocked will be disappointed.

The story has Anthony Steel as the violently jealous, car-racing husband of Julie London. Miss London hopes that their forthcoming child will help to stabilize their rocky marriage. But the two are involved in a car crash, she loses her unborn baby and Steel becomes sterile. She suggests artificial insemination and Steel reluctantly agrees. When it is too late, however, he changes his mind and, egged on his father, sues his wife for divorce. The jury, faced with a unique case, can reach no decision, but a re-trial is not needed because the two are finally reconciled.

Arguments for and against artificial insemination as grounds for divorce are put forward gingerly and without much conviction by Ann Edwards, the screenplay writer, though the two counsels, Donald Houston and Frank Thring, do their best with the material at hand. Houston, in fact, gives a very convincing study as Miss London's defending counsel.

Anthony Steel has little to do except glower jealousy and suffer silently. Miss London brings grace and charm to her difficult part. Anton Diffring, who is framed as the corespondent; Basil Sydney, as Steel's father, and Andrew Cruickshank, as the doctor in charge of the case, all bring authority to their roles. Stephen Dade's camerawork is okay and Don Chaffey has directed in a straightforward manner except for one rather involved Spanish sequence devised mainly, it would seem, to introduce a couple of flamenco dancers.

But stilted dialog and a screenplay that sits firmly on the fence has resulted in a subject of some significance being wasted. *Rich.*

Es Geschah Am Hellichten Tag
(It Happened In Broad Daylight)
(SWISS)

Zurich, July 12.
Praesens Film (Lazar Wechsler) production, based on "The Promise" by Friedrich Duerrenmatt. Directed by Ladislao Vajda. Screenplay, Duerrenmatt, Hans Jacoby, Vajda; camera, Heinrich Gaertner; editor, Hermann Haller; music, Bruno Canfora. Stars Heinz Ruchmann, Michel Simon, Gert Froebe, Ewald Balser. At Rex Theatre, Zurich, July 11, '58. Running time, **102 MINS.**

Lt. Matthaei	Heinz Ruehmann
Detective Feller	Sigfrit Steiner
Lt. Henzi	Siegfrier Lowitz
Jacquier	Michel Simon
Chief of Police	Heinrich Gretler
Schrott	Gert Froebe
Frau Schrott	Berta Drews
Professor Manz	Ewald Balser
Frau Heller	Maria Rosa Salgado
Annemarie Heller	Anita von Ow
Ursula Fehlmann	Barbara Haller
President of Community	Emil Hegetschweiler

(In German)

Friedrich Duerrenmatt, author of the Lunts' recent stage play, "The Visit" has this Swiss entry, preemed at the recent Berlin Film Festival. It offers three definite assets, making it eligible for a broader-than-usual market for a locally produced pic: (1) the topical theme of child murder by sex criminals; (2) a name cast including Heinz Ruchmann who recently won plaudits for his "Captain of Koepenick" role, Swiss-French thesp Michel Simon and Spanish director Ladislao Vajda of "Marcelino" fame; (3) a logical and convincing screenplay by Friedrich Duerrenmatt whose "Visit" scored on Broadway. These, plus firstrate direction and acting, should make it pay off both in Europe and outside, with indications of U.S. arthouse possibilities. Pic is old for Europe and South America, and negotiations are underway for English-dubbed U.S. presentation.

Basically a melodrama, feature concerns a police lieutenant's personal research for a sex murderer after the wrong suspect, an old peddler, has been forced into a false confession, followed by his suicide. With a drawing of the murdered child as his only clue and aided by a psychiatrist, he succeeds in circling the killer and preventing a last-minute repeat crime.

Delicate theme is handled with taste and conviction. Leisurely (though not lagging) pace prevents its slipping into sensationalism. No attempt is made at "artie" or "clever" treatment, with naturalness and realism dominating instead. Vajda's directorial job is of high calibre, and camerawork by Heinrich Gaertner rates kudos.

The cast is uniformly excellent. Ruehmann gives a thoroughly convincing performance away from his usual comic parts. Michel Simon in a relatively short role as the peddler is topnotch, and Gert Froebe impresses as the perverted killer. Moppet Anita von Ow as the fourth victim-to-be is engagingly natural. Other important parts are well handled by Spanish actress Maria Rosa Salgado as the girl's mother, Ewald Balser as the psychiatrist and Heinrich Gretler, Siegfried Lowitz and Sigfrit Steiner as police officers. *Mezo.*

A Certain Smile
(C'SCOPE—COLOR)

Francoise Sagan's bitter-sweet romance "edited" to prove adultery doesn't pay. Stunning Paris and Riviera scenery add to saleability.

20th-Fox release of Henry Ephron production. Stars Rossano Brazzi, Joan Fontaine, Bradford Dillman, Christine Carere; features Eduard Franz, Kathryn Givney, Steven Geray, Trude Wyler, Sandy Livingston, Renate Hoy, Muzaffer Tema, Katherine Locke. Directed by Jean Negulesco; script, Frances Goodrich and Albert Hackett, from Francoise Sagan novel of same title; camera (Color by De Luxe), Milton Krasner; music, Alfred Newman; song ("A Certain Smile") performed by Johnny Mathis and written by Sammy Fain and Paul Francis Webster, editor, Louis R. Loeffler. Previewed at 20th-Fox homeoffice in N.Y., July 24, '58. Running time, **105 MINS.**

Luc	Rossanno Brazzi
Francoise Ferrand	Joan Fontaine
Bertrand	Bradford Dillman
Dominique Vallon	Christine Carere
Mons. Vallon	Eduard Franz
Mme. Griot	Kathryn Givney
Denis	Steven Geray
Mme. Denis	Trude Wyler
Catherine	Sandy Livingston
Mlle. Minot	Renate Hoy
Pierre	Muzaffer Tema
Mm. Vallon	Katherine Locke

This is the second of Francoise Sagan's novels to be filmed. Once again, the principal character is a young and attractive girl, only this time the "shocker" involves her week-long affair with an older man. When this interlude has run its course, the rest of the picture is mostly devoted to proving that old and young don't mix, that adultery inevitably exacts its punishments, and that the bonds of real love are strong.

Only the very basic elements in the slim Sagan book have been retained in the Frances Goodrich-Albert Hackett script, and they tend to make this glossy, emotional yarn into a picture that should hold considerable appeal for women. None of the moody disenchantment of the girl in the book comes through in the film, and of course the ending has been totally changed, for in Miss Sagan's original the heroine blithely continued her affairs both with regular boyfriend and older lover.

As a film "A Certain Smile" is well made, reasonably well acted and quite magnificently photographed. Having so strenuously toned down the amoral aspects of their story, producer Henry Ephron and director Jean Negulesco apparently decided to go whole hog for the visual aspects. As a result, the film abounds with mouth-watering vistas of the French Riviera, which is photographed from every possible vantage point, providing an idyllic setting for the romantic goings-on between the stars, Rossano Brazzi and Christine Carere. Scenes in the Paris streets also come alive temptingly in CinemaScope and color. The travelog aspects of the film are among its most attractive features.

Story of "A Certain Smile" is briefly this: Thwarted in her romance with boyfriend Bradford Dillman, Miss Carere takes up the invitation of Dillman's uncle (Brazzi) to spend a week on the Riviera. The girl does this despite the fact that Brazzi's wife, Joan Fontaine, has been very kind to her in Paris. When the week is up, Miss Carere follows Brazzi to Paris, but finds that (1) her romantic interlude has been discovered, and (2) Brazzi would like to forget the whole thing. This leads to a confrontation between the girl and Miss Fontaine and a forgiveness scene between Miss Fontaine and Brazzi, with final indications Miss Carere and Dillman will resume.

This is Miss Carere's first appearance in an American film. She is charming and petite, turning in a capable performance that's just a shade too much on the wholesome side. Dillman also is a newcomer, good-looking in an unconventional way. He does well in a frustrating role that doesn't really give him much leeway. Brazzi is suavely Continental as the middle-aged Don Juan, and Miss Fontaine suffers as required by script. In the smaller parts, Eduard Franz and Katherine Locke play Miss Carere's parents in a sombre mood; Kathryn Givney has just the right sharpness as Dillman's selfcentered mother.

There's a musical interlude when Johnny Mathis performs "A Certain Smile" in his unique and trembling style at a nightclub. It's a catchy tune that is used throughout the picture and makes an effective themesong.

Director Negulesco obviously had his "Three Coins in a Fountain" in mind when he shot "A Certain Smile." His Riviera and Paris scenery is stunning, though it does tend to slow up the action. There are also several scenes in a Paris boite where young people from the Sorbonne hang out and in these the direction shows real imagination.

Unfortunately, Negulesco was saddled with a most commonplace romance and a script that with only occasional flashes of humor. The affair between Brazzi and Miss Carere is implied more than anything else and the sex details played down so determinedly that their relation never really rings true.

The Hacketts' script definitely goes overboard on the penitence angle at the end, though it does produce moments of charm throughout the picture. The "forgiveness" scene between Miss Fontaine and Brazzi is just a little short of ridiculous. If there must be Code-imposed "compensation" for adultery, must it be obvious to boot?

Milton Krasner handles his color camera with skill, making the photography one of the stars of the picture. Color is generally excellent, though some of the blue suits worn by Brazzi come through rather harshly. Alfred Newman's musical score is pleasant. Louis R. Loeffler has done a smooth editing job. "A Certain Smile" handles a ticklish subject with delicacy and good tastes, though it tends to go overboard on the dramatics in a few scenes.

It shapes as (a) promising b.o. fare and (b) a boon to French tourism. *Hift.*

Harry Black
(BRITISH-COLOR-C'SCOPE)

Overlong but often exciting Yarn of a tiger hunt in India, with romantic story line; Stewart Granger and Barbara Rush in stellart roles. Promising B.O.

London, July 22.

20th-Fox release of Mersham (John Brabourne) production. Stars Stewart Granger, Barbara Rush, Anthony Steel. Directed by Hugo Fregonese. Screenplay, Sydney Boehm from David Walker's book; editor, Reginald Beck; camera, John Wilcox; music, Clifton Parker. At Rialto, London. Running time, 117 MINS.
Harry Black .... Stewart Granger
Christian Tanner .... Barbara Rush
Desmond Tanner .... Anthony Steel
Bapu .... I. S. Johar
Michael Tanner ...... Martin Stephens
Dr. Chowdhury ...... Frank Olegario
Nurse Somola .... Kamala Devi
German Sergeant .... John Helier
British Officers .... Tom Bowman,
Harold Siddons, Allan McLelland, Norman Johns
Mrs. Tanner .... Gladys Boot

Mr. Philip Tanner ...... George Curzon
Woolsey .... Archie Duncan
Fisherman .... John Rae

"Harry Black" is a good, sturdy drama of big game hunting both in Britain and U.S. in India which is a safe b.o. bet

Story has Stewart Granger as a lame, but courageous, famous hunter, who has on hand the sticky task of disposing of a man-eating tiger. He meets up with Anthony Steel whom he had known in a German prisoner of war camp and who, by losing his nerve, was responsible for Granger getting the bullet which caused his leg to be amputated. Steel joins Granger in the hunt, again loses his nerve and, as a result, Granger is savagely mauled by the tiger.

Granger is gradually nursed back to health and in Steel's absence in Calcutta the hunter falls again for Steel's wife, with whom he had been in love years earlier in Scotland. This added complication causes Granger to hit the bottle but, when Steel's son is lost in the jungle and at the mercy of the tiger, Granger pulls himself together, finishes off the man-eater and realizes that he cannot upset the married life of the girl.

The atmosphere of the film is brilliantly set in the opening sequence, with the cat stalking through the jungle, into a village and killing a native girl. From then on most of the jungle sequences are splendidly done. The climax, with Granger and his native trapper, finishing off the trapped tiger in a dark cave, carries a real wallop. It is on the romantic side that the film occasionally drags. There is one flashback, with Granger delirious, in which he recalls the trip to Scotland where he first fell for Barbara Rush. Despite knockout Scottish scenery these sequences are unnecessarily protracted.

Granger gives a manly, convincing portrait of the hunter and shows a wry sense of humor, while Steel is adequate in a colorless role. Miss Rush makes a dainty, intelligent heroine. The film owes much to an amusing and touching performance by I. S. Johar, as Granger's plucky, faithful trapper with a penchant for philosophy and frequent swigs of "whiskey-wine." Native types are well portrayed.

Hugo Fregonese has directed strongly and has excellently captured the color and menace of the jungle. The tiger sequences are handled with mounting excitment. John Wilcox' lensing aids Fregonese's stint considerably. It is just a pity that editor Reginald Beck has not been more ruthless. *Rich.*

Gunsmoke in Tucson
(C'SCOPE-COLOR)

Routine oater with names of Mark Stevens and Forrest Tucker to hypo engagements in western market.

Allied Artists release of William D. Coates production. Stars Mark Stevens, Forrest Tucker, Gale Robbins; features Vaughn Taylor, John Ward, Kevin Hagen, John Cliff, Gail Kobe, George Keymas. Directed by Thomas Carr. Screenplay, Paul Leslie Peil, Robert Joseph, from story by Peil; camera (DeLuxe-Color), William Whitley; editor, George White; music, Sid Cutner. Previewed July 21, '58. Running time, 80 MINS.
Chip Coburn .... Mark Stevens
John Brazos .... Forrest Tucker
Lou Crenshaw .... Gale Robbins
Ben Bodeen .... Vaughn Taylor
Slick Kirby .... John Ward
Clem Haney .... Kevin Hagen
Young Chip .... Paul Engle
Young Brazos .... Anthony Sydes
Cass .... John Cliff
Katy Porter .... Gail Kobe
Hondo .... George Keymas
Notches .... Richard Reeves
Sheriff Blane .... Bill Henry
Bragg .... Zon Murray

A standard western plot of two brothers on opposing sides of the law. Given moderate exposition in this Allied Artists release, backed by good use of CinemaScope and DeLuxe-Color. Film would have benefited from a punchier script and more definite character delineation, but names of Mark Stevens and Forrest Tucker will see it nicely through regular oater situations.

Stevens and Tucker as the brothers follow different paths as they mature after having seen their father strung up as a horse-thief. Stevens turns to outlawry; Tucker becomes a righteous lawman. Plottage builds following Stevens' release from the pen, centering in Tucson where a battle is on between a greedy cattleman and a group of farmers over the acquisition of rich land. Stevens, constantly referred to in dialog as leader of the Blue Chip gang, remains neutral, figuring to take the land for himself and return to honest living after it is won by one of the warring sides. He finally throws in with the farmers and kills cattleman in a gunfight climax.

Stevens is nondescript in a cloudy character, the audience never clear as to how he intends to operate. Tucker does his best with a role that doesn't always ring true, and Gale Robbins, who melodically warbles "I Need a Man," is in for distaff interest as Stevens' inamorata who weds the cattleman.

The baddies get the best breaks in acting line, Vaughn Taylor properly heavy as grasping cattleman who wants to become a land baron, and John Cliff and George Keymas as his henchmen. John Ward as Stevens' gunman meanders in and out of plot and Kevin Hagen is leader of the farmers.

Thomas Carr's direction is straightforward but is handicapped by the Paul Leslie Peil-Robert Joseph screenplay. William D. Coates is responsible for okay production values, and William Whitley's color photography is excellent. *Whit.*

Nor the Moon by Night
(BRITISH-COLOR)

Wonderful African animal photography and action marred by a novelettish yarn, limp dialog and plodding thesping; only fair prospects.

London, July 22.

Rank Organization (John Stafford) production and release. Stars Belinda Lee, Michael Craig, Patrick McGoohan, Anna Gaylor. Directed by Ken Annakin. Screenplay, Guy Elmes from novel by Joy Packer; editor, Alfred Roome; camera, Harry Waxman; music, James Bernards. At Odeon, Leicester Square, London. Running time, 92 MINS.
Alice Lang .... Belinda Lee
Rusty Miller............. Michael Craig
Andrew Miller........Patrick McGoohan
Thea Boryslawski........ Anna Gaylor
Anton Boryslawski....... Eric Pohlmann
Mrs. Boryslawski.......Pamela Stirling
Nimrod ....Lionel Ngakane
Harriet Carver .... Joan Brickhill
Sergeant Van Wyck....Ben Hydenrych
Chief .... Alfred Kumalo
Oasis .... Doreen Hlantie
Sandy.................John Withers
Jan .... Ken Oelofse
Tom .... Gordon MacPherson

The scenery and animal shots of "Nor the Moon By Night" are great. It's too bad that the cast has to get in front of it all. And the actors have a rough time of it. Apart from competing with the superb colored life of Africa, they are up against an incredibly silly story and stodgy dialog. Under the circumstances, it can be said they go down gallantly. British audiences will probably accept the result passively. American audiences, with no allegiance to a far from star-studded cast, will prove more diffident. In no way does the finished pic stand up to the undoubted effort that must have gone into production.

The hearts-and-flowers story concerns a young woman who for years has been tending her sick mother. Meanwhile she corresponds (for a reason unexplained) with a game warden in Africa who she has never met. When mother dies, she goes out to marry her pen pal. Because he is busy rounding up a herd of elephants, she is met, instead, by his brother who disapproves of the match. Yet, he manages to fall for her, in between beating off crocodiles and shooting a rogue elephant.

The complicated is all tidied up by the brother marrying the nurse from England, while the original bridegroom-to-be suddenly decides to marry a teenager who has worshipped him from afar. If this all sounds rather inane to the audience, it must have seemed equally so to the cast.

This farrago of nonsense is relieved only by some first class photography of animal life by Harry Waxman and the second unit lenser, Alex Bryce plus some stirringly-directed action scenes by Ken Annakin.

For the cast it must have been a rugged adventure. Patrick McGoohan grapples with lions, dodges elephants, turns over his jeep, struggles with a cobra and has a whip fight with Eris Pohlmann. Belinda Lee, the heroine, merely had a brush with a porcupine, looks a rogue elephant squarely in the eyes and gets involved with a wolf, nicely played by Michael Craig. It's a small wonder that, amid this game of Animal Grab or Who's Zoo, the human beings come out second best.

Nevertheless, McGoohan and Craig, as the brothers, keep stiff upper lips and Polhmann hams up the role of the villain with relish. Miss Lee swims among the crocs, tends wounded natives and veers emotionally between the two brothers with wide eyes and an air of utter surprise. Blonde Anna Gaylor mixes it for Miss Lee with a coy desperation. There is also a forest fire which seems to have been dragged in by the roots of its trees.

Ken Annakin has done a good tongue-in-cheek job of direction. But though he has coped admirably with the physical problems of Darkest Africa, he has been defeated by Guy Elmes' screenplay. *Rich.*

Spy In the Sky

Poorly and cheaply made espionage intrigue. Low-grade filler on twin-bills.

Hollywood, July 11.

Allied Artists release of a W. Lee Wilder production. Stars Steve Brodie and Sandra Francis; features Andrea Domburg and George Coulouris. Directed by W. Lee Wilder; screenplay, Myles Wilder; based on the novel, "Counterspy Express," by A. S. Fleischman; camera, Jim Harvey; music, Hugo de Groot; editor, Lien d'Oliveyra. Previewed in Hollywood, July 10, '58. Running time, **75 MINS.**

Cabot	Steve Brodie
Eva	Sandra Francis
Duvivier	Andrea Domburg
Col. Benedict	George Coulouris
Jardine	Bob De Lange
Dr. Keller	Hans Tiemeyer
Pepl	Herbert Curiel
Fritzl	Dity Oorthuis

"Spy in the Sky," a W. Lee Wilder production made in Holland with a largely Dutch staff, attempts to cash in on the satellite interest through its title and exploitation. Actually, however, it is a routine spy story of poor quality that will be adequate in U.S. only for lower case double-bill bookings. Allied Artists is releasing.

Steve Brodie is represented as an American intelligence agent attempting to locate a missing German scientist. The locale is supposed to be Vienna, where George Coulouris directs the Communist spy ring combatting Brodie. The U.S. agent finally gets the secret plans from the scientist but not before there have been chases, gun battles and plentiful sluggings.

The screenplay, by Myles Wilder, is the kind of story that will only confirm European pessimism about the capabilities of American agents to best their Russian opposites. Brodie is represented as a chuckleheaded bungler and incompetent who believes the first thing anyone tells him. He is also a great one for the ladies, including Sandra Francis and Andrea Domburg, and they present further distractions to his job.

The cast performs adequately under Wilder's direction, but not to any advantage, their own or the picture's. The continuity is confusing and finally annoying. The photography, by Jim Harvey, is often interesting, but it has a curious composition. It consists almost entirely of medium close-ups, two or three-shots, and closeups, indicating it was shot with television, not feature picture release in mind. Very little advantage is taken of the foreign location. *Powe.*

Andy Hardy Comes Home

Topnotch family entertainment, with Mickey Rooney repeating (updated) his old Andy Hardy role.

Hollywood, July 25.

Metro release of Red Doff production. Stars Mickey Rooney; costars Patricia Breslin, Fay Holden; features Cecilia Parker, Sara Haden, Joey Forman, Jerry Colonna. Directed by Howard W. Koch. Screenplay, Edward Everett Hutshing, Robert Morris Donley, based on characters created by Aurania Rouverol; camera, William W. Spencer, Harold E. Wellman; editor, John B. Rogers; music, Van Alexander. Previewed July 23, '58. Running time, **80 MINS.**

Andy Hardy	Mickey Rooney
Jane Hardy	Patricia Breslin
Mother Hardy	Fay Holden
Marian	Cecilia Parker
Aunt Milly	Sara Haden
Beezy Anderson	Joey Forman
Doc	Jerry Colonna
Thomas Chandler	Vaughn Taylor
Mayor Benson	Frank Ferguson
Jack Bailey	William Leslie
Councilman Warren	Tom Duggan
Sally Anderson	Jeanne Baird
Cricket	Gina Gillespie
Chuck	Jimmy Bates
Andy Jr.	Teddy Rooney
Jimmy	Johnny Weissmuller Jr.
Betty Wilson	Pat Cawley

Metro's plans for re-embarking upon an "Andy Hardy" series, dormant for past 12 years, is tipped off in fadeout of this Mickey Rooney starrer with the notation, "To Be Continued." It's a meritorious and showmanship idea, judging by this first entry, a heartwarming comedy-drama which nicely catches the spirit of the past and should chalk up good returns in family situations. Film presumably already has an audience from past fans of the series, and more can be created among newer customers.

It's a grown-up Andy Hardy who appears here, coming back to his small Midwest hometown from the West Coast, where he lives with his wife and two children. There's a natural change in the Hardy character from the ebullient youngster who once managed to get into constant complications, romantic and otherwise. As developed in the Edward Everett Hutshing-Robert Morris Donley screenplay, however, the same characteristics are still there, albeit more reserved, and the Hardy family is re-established despite the absence of the late Lewis Stone as Judge Hardy, with whom Andy had so many uproarous "man-to-man" talks.

Certain novel aspects are incorporated by three natural flashbacks to past "Hardy" pix, in which the adult Andy does some dreaming. Interludes in which he appears with Judy Garland, Esther Williams and Lana Turner, who figured in former films, are logically intro'd, nostalgic for those who recall the features. Brought back for this new one, too, are three family members, Fay Holden as the mother, Cecilia Parker the sister and Sara Haden the aunt. Howard W. Koch makes his direction for producer Red Doff count, a heart tug here, a laugh there, and overall maintaining an appreciation of the Hardy family screen tradition.

Plottage projects Andy, now employed as an attorney with a Pacific Coast aircraft corporation, selling his bosses on establishing a branch plant in his old hometown. He arrives to scout suitable property, but immediately runs into trouble when a double-crossing businessman, finding Andy won't buy his over-priced land, starts a campaign to keep industry out of Carvel, with most of town going along with him. After complications, Andy resolves difficulty with an appearance before the City Council. Not only that, Andy is offered a judgeship, to sit on his father's bench, perhaps not altogether logical but certainly the makings of a family finish.

Rooney is still Andy Hardy and gets top support right down the line. Patricia Breslin is lovely as his wife, Teddy Rooney, Mickey's eight-year-old, plays his son naturally, and Misses Holden, Parker and Haden as his family repeat their past excellence. Joey Forman, Jerry Colonna, Vaughn Taylor, Frank Ferguson handle town's-people roles well, and two newcomers, Johnny Weissmuller Jr., and Pat Cawley, are well cast.

Technical credits stack up well, including camera work by William W. Spencer and Harold E. Wellman, editing by John R. Rogers, music score by Van Alexander. *Whit.*

The Defiant Ones

Topnotch "case" drama with human brotherhood theme. Race and action angles merged for stunning impact. Ticklish for Dixie.

United Artists release of Stanley Kramer production. Stars Tony Curtis, Sidney Poitier; features Cara Williams, Theodore Bikel, Charles McGraw, Lon Chaney, King Donovan, Claude Akins, Lawrence Dobkin, Whit Bissell, Carl Switzer, Kevin Coughlin. Directed by Kramer; script, Nathan E. Douglas and Harold Jacob Smith; camera, Sam Leavitt; music, Ernest Gold; song "Long Gone" adapted from "Long Gone (from Bowling Green)" with music by William C. Handy, words by Chris Smith; editor, Frederic Knudtson. Previewed in N. Y. July 23, '58. Running time, **97 MINS.**

John Jackson	Tony Curtis
Noah Cullen	Sidney Poitier
Sheriff Max Muller	Theodore Bikel
Captain Frank Gibbons	Charles McGraw
Big Sam	Lon Chaney
Solly	King Donovan
Mac	Claude Akins
Editor	Lawrence Dobkin
Lou Gans	Whit Bissell
Angus	Carl Switzer
The Kid	Kevin Coughlin
The Woman	Cara Williams

Doubling in brass as producer and director, and working with a well and carefully picked cast, Stanley Kramer has turned out a raw, powerful film that is as exciting as it is moving, real and literate. It uses potential of the screen in putting across its "message" without hammering it home with a sledgehammer.

The theme of "The Defiant Ones" is as controversial as it is believably human. The picture, with its deft combination of stark drama, tenderness and a sense of humor, makes the point that what keeps men apart is their lack of knowledge of one another. With that knowledge comes respect, and with respect comradeship and even love.

Since this thesis is exercised in terms of a colored and a white men, both convicts chained together as they make their break for freedom from a Southern prison gang, it is safe to predict that the film will encounter resistance in some areas of the South. Its rather grim theme also may be something of a deterrent elsewhere, for Kramer has made no compromises. But none of this alters one iota the fact that this is one of the best motion pictures to hit the screen in many a year, and word-of-mouth alone should sock it across.

Because he has managed to keep himself from overstating his case, and because "The Defiant Ones" emerge as wholly believable human beings, capable of violence, hate and hurt, Kramer has created a film that creates complete, tense audience participation. This is the classic cinematic chase, refined to capture those exciting elements of pure action. Its principles are hunted down by a posse that combines Southerners of different types, none of them stereotypes and yet all of them clearly recognizable.

The performances by Tony Curtis and Sidney Poitier are virtually flawless. Poitier, always a capable actor, here turns in probably the best work of his career as the intelligent Negro, suddenly presented with a chance to escape to the North. He captures all of the moody violence of the convict, serving time because he assaulted a white man who had insulted him. It is a cunning, totally intelligent portrayal that rings powerfully true and establishes Poitier as one of the best actors appearing on the screen today.

As "Jocker" Jackson, the arrogant while man chained to a fellow convict whom he hates because of his skin and his need to feel himself superior, Curtis delivers a true surprise performance. He starts off as a sneering, brutal character, willing to fight it out to-the-death with his equally stubborn companion. When, in the end, he sacrifices a dash for freedom to save Poitier from certain death, he has managed the transition with such skill that audience sympathy is completely with him. This picture automatically establishes Curtis as a major acting talent, perhaps to his own surprise.

Picture has other surprises, not the least of which is Kramer's sensitive and skilled direction, this being only his third try at calling the scenes. Given an excellent script by Nathan E. Douglas and Harold Jacob Smith to work with, he manipulates the action with an instinctive feeling for the need of the audience. The scenes of Poitier and Curtis groping their way painfully out of a deep clay pit, their perilous journey down the river, as well as their clumsy attempt to break into a store and the subsequent near-lynch scene, become integral parts of the larger chase, for the posse is never far behind. But integrated into this vital action are those revealing glimpses of the two men, tied together by more than their ch[illegible] and gradually shedding their i[illegible]bred hate as they share the dangers and the knowledge of what makes the other tick.

Here is one of those films where the smaller parts rate every bit as important as the leads. Theodore Bikel as the moderate sheriff who knows his career depends on catching up with the prisoners, but who refuses to be either caught up in or intimidated by the mob psychology of the rest of the posse, is sock. Fine port royals also come from Charles McGraw as the eager statetrooper captain who enjoys the chase and the rest of the posse—Carl Switzer, Whit Bissell, Claude Akins, and King Donovan. Kenvin Coughlin is good as the boy and Lawrence Dobkin registers as the newspaper man.

Standout in her part is Cara Williams as the only woman in the film. She takes in the convicts and, being lonely, she spends the night with Curtis. When, in the morning, she sends Poitier to his death in the quicksand, Curtis abandons her and rushes after his friend to save him. Miss Williams is attractive and she is remarkably effective in the role. In leaving her, Curtis is shot and wounded by the boy. In the end, Poitier jumps from the north-bound train to help his exhausted friend and the sheriff finds them, Poitier cradling the white man in his arms and definantly shouting his "Long Gone" song.

Sam Leavitt's photography enhances the values of the film and Frederic Knudtson's editing is topnotch. This Kramer film is an artistic triumph and unquestionably will be recognized as just that. It certainly requires a special "sell," but it's also a stirring and in some of its sequences amusing picture which, for the very excellence of its production, deserves top attention. *Hift.*

The Hunters
(C'SCOPE—COLOR)

Exploits of jet pilots during the Korean War. Particularly exciting serial footage and colorful shots of Japan. Robert Mitchum as the b.o. bait. Fairly successful film for general situations.

20th-Fox release of Dick Powell production. Stars Robert Mitchum, Robert Wagner, May Britt, Richard Egan, and Lee Philips. Features John Gabriel, Stacy Harris, Victor Sen Yung and Candace Lee. Directed by Powell. Screenplay, Wendell Mayes, based on the novel by James Salter; camera (C'Scope), Charles G. Clarke; editor, Stuart Gilmore; music, Paul Sawtell. Previewed in N. Y. July 31, '58. Running time, **108 MINS.**

Major Cleve Saville	Robert Mitchum
Lt. Ed Pell	Robert Wagner
Col. "Dutch" Imil	Richard Egan
Kristina (Kris)	May Britt
Lt. Abbott	Lee Philips
Lt. Corona	John Gabriel
Col. Moncavage	Stacy Harris
Korean Farmer	Victor Sen Yung
Korean Child	Candace Lee

The exploits of U. S. jet pilots during the Korean War are presented in 20th-Fox's slick production. The entry, produced and directed by Dick Powell, is a technically well-made drama, filled with the exciting ingredients that usually appeal to general audiences. The majesty of the jet planes in flight, the aerial combat scenes, and the backgrounds of Japan and Korea are worthy pictorial contributions.

Although the story is contrived and contains elements all too familiar in war stories, "The Hunters" nevertheless has the ability to become a fairly successful boxoffice attraction for most situations. It concerns jet pilots stationed near the Yalu River in Korea in January, 1952. Their job is to pursue and knockout the Chinese "volunteers" flying Russian Migs. There is mention of the fact that the U.S. airmen are not permitted to cross the Yalu in pursuit of the invaders, but no position is taken on the subject, one of the most controversial of the Korean War.

While the film may be basically a war adventure, femme side of audiences has not been neglected. There is a romance—a triangle involving a squadron commander, one of the pilot's in his command, and the latter's wife.

Robert Mitchum is seen as a World War II ace who is assigned to the fighter group made up mainly of younger men. A professional soldier, known as the "iceman" because of his complete lack of fear, he finds himself romantically entangled with May Britt, the Swedish wife of Lee Philips, a young pilot who takes to drink and neglects his wife because of his all-consuming fear. At the urging of Miss Britt, Mitchum takes the young pilot under his wing and has him assigned to his flying unit.

In between the missions, the Wendall Mayes screenplay, based on James Salter's novel, concerns itself with the personal conflict between Mitchum and Philips, Mitchum's occasional excursions to Japan for romantic interludes with Miss Britt (including visits to picturesque Japanese scenic spots), and the growing up to maturity of a cocky young pilot, played by Robert Wagner.

During one of the missions, Philips' plane is hit and he is forced to bail out in enemy territory. Mitchum crash lands his plane to go to his aid and Wagner parachutes out to join them. The last third of the picture is concerned with their adventures behind enemy lines and the efforts of Mitchum and Wagner to bring back safely the injured Philips. The experience works wonders for Philips, who finally understands himself. It brings about a reconciliation with his wife and she bids farewell to Mitchum, who stays to fight on.

Powell has elicited good performances from his cast. Mitchum is convincing as the tough, fearless professional Air Force man; Miss Britt, an attractive blonde, is fine as the confused wife torn between two loves; Philips does a neat job as the frightened pilot determined to prove himself. Other good portrayals are turned in by Wagner, as a cigar-smoking hot-shot egotistical fly boy; Richard Egan, as commander of the fighter group; Stacy Harris, as another professional airman; and John Gabriel, as a young pilot.

Production values are topnotch, particularly the CinemaScope-Deluxe color photography of Charles G. Clarke and the aerial shots of Tom Tutwiler. Paul Sawtell has provided an approprite musical score.

Holl.

It! The Terror From Beyond Space

Half of a horror-science fiction package. Story not unique; production okay.

Hollywood, July 29.

United Artists release of a Vogue Pictures production. Stars Marshall Thompson, Shawn Smith, Kim Spalding; with Ann Doran, Dabbs Greer, Paul Langton, Robert Bice; also, Richard Benedict, Richard Hervey, Thom Carney, Ray Corrigan. Produced by Robert E. Kent. Directed by Edward L. Cahn. Screenplay by Jerome Bixby; camera, Kenneth Peach Sr.; editor, Grant Whytock; music, Paul Sawtell and Bert Shefter. Running time, 68 MINS.

Carruthers	Marshall Thompson
Ann Anderson	Shawn Smith
Van Heusen	Kim Spalding
Mary Royce	Ann Doran
Eric Royce	Dabbs Greer
Calder	Paul Langton
Purdue	Robert Bice
Bob Finelli	Richard Benedict
Gino	Richard Hervey
Kienholz	Thom Carney
'It'	Ray Corrigan

"It" is a Martian by birth, a Frankenstein by instinct and a copycat. As star of this Vogue Pictures' excursion, the monster dies hard, brushing aside grenades, bullets, gas and an atomic pile, before snorting its last snort. It's old stuff, with only a slight twist, but it shows possibilities of lending itself to heavy exploitation in its twin billing with "The Curse of the Faceless Man."

Production-wise, Robert E. Kent has endowed the United Artists release with a number of gimmicks, and Edward L. Cahn's direction stands up for the most part. As for the Jerome Bixby screenplay, there are a few pills that are hard to take and a few more that, within their horror-science fiction coating, go down easily.

Film starts some dozen years in the future with a disabled U.S. rocketship on Mars. Only one of the 10 space travellers has survived, and a second rocketship has landed to drag him back to earth where he is to face a courtmartial. It seems the U.S. government is of the opinion the spaceman murdered his nine companions so he could hoard the food and supplies for himself and, thus, stay alive until help arrived. But the accused swears the nine deaths come at the hands of a strange "It"-type monster.

Most of the film's 68 minutes are spent aboard the second rocketship on its way to earth, and, to spice up the trip, the monster has stowed away. It kills with a swat of its grisly hand, then sucks all available liquids from its victims. Nothing, but nothing, will do away with the beast until one of the cosmic scientists suggests donning space suits and letting all the air out of the ship. The monster keels over, suffocated, and, by this time, the accused murderer has been transformed into an outer space hero.

None of the performances are outstanding, though admirable work is done by Marshall Thompson, Shawn Smith, Ann Doran, Paul Langton and Richard Benedict, with okay work by Kim Spalding and Dabbs Greor. Ray (Crash) Corrigan makes a fetching monster.

Technical credits, including the special effects footage and the rocketship interior, are capable, with the William Glasgow art direction and the Paul Sawtell-Bert Shefter musical score the most notable features. *Ron.*

Me and the Colonel

Subtle comedy-drama based on Franz Werfel's "Jacobowsky And the Colonel." Stars Danny Kaye and Curt Jurgens. May rate a big-city film.

Columbia Pictures release of Court-Goetz production. Stars Danny Kaye, Curt Jurgens, Nicole Maurey; features Francoise Rosay, Akim Tamiroff, Martita Hunt, Alexander Scourby, Liliane Montevecchi, Ludwig Stossel, Gerard Buhr, Franz Roehn, Celia Harari, Alain Bouvette. Directed by Peter Glenville; script, S. N. Behrman and George Froeschel from original Franz Werfel play, "Jacobowsky and the Colonel"; American play, Behrman; produced on stage by Theatre Guild in association with Jack Skirball; camera, Burnett Guffey; music, George Duning; editors, William A. Lyon and Charles Nelson. Previewed in N. Y. at Loew's Sheridan Theatre July 29, '58. Running time, **105 MINS.**

S. L. Jacobowsky	Danny Kaye
Colonel Prokoszny	Curt Jurgens
Suzanne Roualet	Nicole Maurey
Madame Bouffier	Francoise Rosay
Szabuniewicz	Akim Tamiroff
Mother Superior	Martita Hunt
Major Von Bergen	Alexander Scourby
Cosette	Liliane Montevecchi
Dr. Szicki	Ludwig Stossel
German Captain	Gerard Buhr
Monsieur Girardin	Franz Roehn
Mme. Arle	Celia Lovsky
Man of the Gestapo	Clement Harari
Rothschild's Chauffeur	Alain Bouvette
M. Gravat	Albert Godderis
Denise	Karen Lenay
Pierre Michel	Eugene Borden
French Lieutenant	Maurice Marsac

The tragi-comic joke which Franz Werfel perpetrated in his play, "Jacobowsky and the Colonel," has been faithfully translated to the screen by producer William Goetz. It makes for an adult, often uproarious film, acted to perfection and spiked with a thousand clever little lines serving to contrast the two leading characters—the resourceful, ingratiatingly humble little Jew from Poland and the aristocratically arrogant, anti-semitic Polish colonel whose animosity gradually turns into respect and even admiration.

The fact that Jacobowsky is played with infinite skill by Danny Kaye (almost unrecognizable with a little mustache and impeccably dressed), and the colonel is vividly brought to life by German actor Curt Jurgens, contributes to shaping this opus into a gay, stimulating attraction. It's difficult to envision this as a "popular" picture, but between the sophisticates and the Kaye following it should do well.

Story, scripted by S. N. Behrman and George Froeschel from Behrman's original American version of the play, has both Kaye and Jurgens stranded in Paris in 1940, with the Germans approaching rapidly. Both must leave the city, and when Kaye turns up with a car, and with gasoline, Jurgens overcomes his prejudices and agrees to a joint escape. But first he heads in the direction of the German lines to pick up a girlfriend, Nicole Maurey. Eventually, Jacobowsky's cunning ends them in a castle, where Jurgens realizes that Miss Maurey is beginning to fall in love with the gentle Kaye. Then the whole company falls into German hands and, again, is saved by Jacobowsky who pretends Jurgens is his cousin from Galicia.

Jacobowsky is picked up by the Gestapo for questioning about Jurgens, who is to be picked up by a British submarine. He prefers death rather than give his friend away. Jurgens and Kaye dupe the Germans and escape. Story is handled in the light vein throughout, with the Nazis never represented as a serious threat. Accent is on the two opposing characters, and director Peter Glenville spends quite a lot of time allowing them to engage in their amusing interchanges. This is fun, though it also slows up the picture.

Here is hardly the Danny Kaye his fans may expect. He is immensely funny, this gently determined, philosophical Jacobowsky who somehow manages to retain his dignity even as he takes abuse from the colonel, but this is not the broad Kaye humor of old. The comedian tackles this acting challenge with a good deal of intelligence and understanding and his Jacobowsky reveals a strong fibre that, finally, outshines the rash bravado of the pompous colonel. Perhaps it should be commented that even though Kaye is in it, this is hardly a film to enchant young people.

As the colonel, Jurgens delivers a hilarious and well-paced performance that never goes overboard. His point is made, and with emphasis, but never in poor taste. There is pathos in his "courage" and yet he emerges in the end as a man of stature when he is able to finally say: "I think I like that fellow Jacobowsky." Miss Maurey is charming in a role that doesn't call for much more than good looks.

In the smaller roles, Alexander Scourby has merit as the Nazi officer; Akim Tamiroff is broadly comic as the colonel's aide; Martita Hunt is funny in a brief appearance as a nun; Liliane Montevecchi appeals as one of the colonel's girlfriends, and Francois Rosay has dignity in a brief scene. Glenville's direction maintains a delicate balance between the need for action and the necessity of conveying what the original play was trying to say. Some of the scenes, particularly the sojourn in the palace, are extremely cleverly handled.

Burnett Guffey's lensing is beyond reproach as is the editing of William A. Lyon and Charles Nelson. George Duning's music is effective. This is unquestionably a critics picture, which should boost its stock in the key cities. Whether it's grist for the broad audience mill is open to some question.

Hift.

Reluctant Debutante
(C'SCOPE-COLOR)

Entertaining f e a t h e r weight farce. Rex Harrison and Kay Kendall are alluring and should draw b.o. returns.

Hollywood, July 30.

Metro release of an Avon production. Stars Rex Harrison, Kay Kendall, John Saxon, Sandra Dee, Angela Lansbury; features Peter Myers, Diane Clare. Produced by Pandro S. Berman. Directed by Vincente Minnelli. Screenplay by William Douglas Home, from his own play; camera (color by Metrocolor), Joseph Ruttenberg; editor, Adrienne Fazan. Previewed at the Village Theatre, Westwood, July 30, '58. Running time, **96 MINS.**

Jimmy Broadbent .... Rex Harrison
Sheila Broadbent .... Kay Kendall
David Parkson .... John Saxon
Jane Broadbent .... Sandra Dee
Mabel Claremont ...... Angela Lansbury
David Fenner .... Peter Myers
Clarissa Claremont .... Diane Clare

"The Reluctant Debutante" is refreshing and prettily dressed, a colorful, saucy film version of the William Douglas Home stage trifle. With Rex Harrison and Kay Kendall for the more worldly and John Saxon and Sandra Dee for the too-young-to-have-been-very-far, there shouldn't be too many reluctant filmgoers.

There aren't enough substantial story elements to build this comedy to or sustain it on a high pitch, but its overall approach makes it a hit for producer Pandro S. Berman and Avon Productions. Director Vincente Minnelli has driven his characters, in a pleasant vehicle, to the point of exaggeration, and then, by stopping to let in a tone of underplaying, has come up with what this frothy, farcically sophisticated comedy needs.

Home, who also screenplayed, not only has allowed the spicier situations and dialog to stand, he has added to them. There are changes in plot, mostly for the better, although the main thread remains intact, and getting out of a single London flat setting unmistakably has improved the action.

"Debutante" is the story of London's social "season," a time when bright and not-so-bright 17-year-olds make their debuts in society, carrying on at one deb's ball after another. Harrison and Miss Kendall, as newly married on screen as they are off, invite his American daughter (by a former marriage) for a British visit that results in the girl's coming out socially. As played by Sandra Dee, the teenager is bored with English stiffs but falls madly for an American drummer (Saxon) who's tabbed with a most dubious reputation. Mixed-up telephone calls, embarrassing situations and advances—both wanted and unwanted—follow with rapidity until finally the lad's reputation is cleared and he inherits wealth and a title from a recently deceased Italian uncle, besides.

Harrison is suavely disturbed as the father, and he comes through most admirably in his first film role since "My Fair Lady." Miss Dee proves to be a rather good actress who maintains a lively character throughout, and Saxon lends a fine boyish charm to the proceedings. But it's really Miss Kendall's picture, and she grabs it with a single wink. She's flighty and well-meaning, snobbish and lovable. And, with certain help from director Minnelli, she has created one of the best female comedy turns in years.

Rounding out the cast, all with fine portrayals, are Angela Lansbury, Peter Myers and Diane Clare. Joseph Ruttenberg's p h o t o g-raphy catches the beautiful full-blown hues of Metrocolor, and A. J.

d'Eaubonne's art direction and Robert Christides' set decoration are rich and colorful. Film editor Adrienne Fazan builds a busy mood with fine montages, and dance music and arrangements by Eddie Warner are alternatingly smooth and jumping. Sound is at many times indistinct, with the sometimes heavy British accent barely understandable. Topping everything, as far as the female patrons will be concerned, undoubtedly will be Pierre Balmain's wardrobe creations for Miss Kendall, and the feathery frocks are sure to cause a stir. *Ron.*

Buchanan Rides Alone
(COLOR)

Well-done western action story.

Hollywood, Aug. 1.

Columbia release of a Harry Joe Brown production. Stars Randolph Scott. Director, Budd Boetticher. Screenplay, Charles Lang; based on the novel, "The Name's Buchanan," by Jonas Ward; camera, Lucien Ballard; editor, Al Clark. Previewed at the studio, July 23, '58. Running time, **89 MINS.**

Buchanan ....:... Randolph Scott
Abe Carbo .... Craig Stevens
Lew Agry .... Barry Kelley
Simon Agry .... Tol Avery
Amos Agry .... Peter Whitney
Juan .... Manuel Rojas
Pecos Hill .... L. Q. Jones
Waldo Peek .... Robert Anderson
Esteban Gomez .... Joe De Santis
Roy Agry ..,........ William Leslie
K. T. .... Jennifer Holden
Nacho .... Nacho Galindo
Hamp .... Roy Jenson
Lafe .... Don C. Harvey

"Buchanan Rides Alone" is one of those work-horses of saddle opera. Turned out on a relatively modest budget (as those things go these days), released with no special fanfare, still it is an honest picture, made with skill and craftsmanship, and if it starts no stampede to the boxoffice, it should be thoroughly satisfactory to audiences and will make money. Budd Boetticher directed the Harry Joe Brown production for Columbia which stars Randolph Scott.

Charles Lang's well-paced screenplay, based on a novel by Jonas Ward, has Scott as a man more or less innocently involved in the problems of a frontier western border town, as he is passing through to his home in Texas from making his stake in Mexico. He befriends a young Mexican, Manuel Rojas, who kills the town bully. The dead man was related by blood to the local big shots and Scott is thrown in jail with Rojas for the shooting and both are threatened with lynching. ·

The plotting is tricky, with the local First Family divided among itself by greed and lust for power. Scott plays one member off against another, until the final blow-off, marked by a good gunfight dexterously handled by Boetticher with suspense and realism. There is no romantic interest of any importance, although Rojas' defense of his wronged wife is an implied one. Lang's screenplay shows he knows the west, it is sharp with brutal, authentic frontier humor; a burial scene highlights this facet.

Scott gives an understated performance as the pivotal figure, taciturnity relieved by humor and warmth. Craig Stevens is intriguing as a man of mystery; Barry Kelley, Tol Avery and Peter Whitney, particularly the latter, make diverse and interesting villains; L. Q. Jones is picturesque as an off-beat gunman, and Rojas handles his role with finesse.

Others who contribute include Robert Anderson, Joe De Santis, William Leslie and Nacho Galindo. Lucien Ballard's photography, in Columbia color, gives added interest to the story, and other technical credits are good. *Powe.*

The Whole Truth
(BRITISH)

Glossy routine meller about the murder of a film star, with red herrings adroitly tossed around by useful cast. Reasonable prospects.

London, July 29.

Columbia release of a (Jack Clayton) Romulus production. Stars Stewart Granger, Donna Reed, George Sanders, Gianna Maria Canale. Directed by John Guillermin; screenplay, Jonathan Latimer from play by Philip Mackie; editor, Gerry Hambling; camera, Wilkie Cooper; music, Mischa Spoliansky. At Gaumont, London. Running time, **85 MINS.**

Max Poulton .... Stewart Granger
Carol Poulton .... Donna Reed
Carliss ....,...... George Sanders
Gina Bertini ...... Gianna Maria Canale
Inspector Simon .... Michael Shillo
Gilbert .... Richard Molinas
Willy Reichel .... Peter Dyneley
Archer .... John Van Eyssen
Jack Leslie .. .. Philip Vickers
First Assistant .... Jimmy Thompson

The most remarkable thing about "The Whole Truth" is that it has lured Stewart Granger away from his ranch and his open-air, hard-hitting adventure pix and persuaded him to don a tuxedo and smart lounge suits. Adapted from Philip Mackie's stage and tv play, this is a cosy little meller with some suave dialog, a slightly confused plot and some straightforward playing. The marquee names should insure it satisfactory bookings on both sides of the Atlantic. But it is a routine effort which is unlikely to create outstanding interest.

The yarn involves Granger as a film producer who two-times his wife by having an affair with his temperamental star. When he tires of the romance and wishes to return to his wife, the lady cuts up roughly. When she finishes up very dead, with a knife in her back, Granger is not unnaturally under suspicion. George Sanders, the victim's unscrupulous husband and, predictably, the murderer, is a further complication. What . with Granger's lying and Sanders' ingenuity, the police don't know whether they are coming or going. Main interest in this minor item is the cat-and-dog duel between Granger and Sanders which both carry out with polish and professional touch.

Granger and Sanders can play such roles on their heads, and Donna Reed, as Granger's long-suffering wife, has little to do but look decorative. The most interesting piece of thesping comes from an elegant Italian actress, Gianna Maria Canale, who not only looks exciting but produces fireworks in the role of temperamental, possessive film actress. Unfortunately, as the victim, Miss Canale is rubbed out a shade too early. She only makes a brief reappearance in a gimmick ending as the temperamental double.

The stars are supported by a sound group of supporting players, with Peter Dyneley, Philip Vickers and John Van Eyssen particularly on the ball.

John Guillermin's direction is brisk and brings out as much tension as the story permits. Wilkie Cooper's lensing and Tony Masters' artwork are both technically okay.

Taut editing by Gerry Hambling adds pace to a pic which owes more to conversation than to action. *Rich.*

Once Upon A Horse
(C'SCOPE)

A scatter-blast of laughs in this farce western. Introduces tv comics Dan Rowan and Dick Martin.

Hollywood, Aug. 1.

Universal release of Hal Kanter production. Stars Dan Rowan, Dick Martin, Martha Hyer, Leif Erickson, Nita Talbot; features James Gleason, John McGiver, Paul Anderson. Produced, written and directed by Hal Kanter; from a story by Henry Gregor Felsen; camera, Arthur E. Arling; music, Frank Skinner; editor, Milton Carruth. Previewed at the New Fox Theatre, Hollywood, July 22, '58. Running time, **85 MINS.**

Dan Casey .... Dan Rowan
Doc Logan .... Dick Martin
Miss Amity Babb .... Martha Hyer
Granville Dix .... Leif Erickson
Miss Dovey Barnes .... Nita Talbot
Postmaster .... James Gleason
Mr. Tharp .... John McGiver
Blacksmith .... Paul Anderson
Bruno de Gruen .... David Burns
Henry Dick Coryell .... Dick Ryan
Ben .... Max Baer
Beulah's Brother .... Buddy Baer
Milligan .... Steve Pendleton
Engineer .... Sydney Chatton
Justice of the Peace ...... Sam Hearn
Beulah .... Ingrid Goude
Small Boy .... Rickey Kelman
Fireman .... Joe Oakie
Tom Keene .... Himself
Bob Livingston .... Himself
Kermit Maynard .... Himself
Bob Steele .... Himself

A farce western that attempts to kid some of the stable-staples, "Once Upon A Horse" does not have a uniform gait, but it has some funny lines and situations. The Universal presentation, produced, directed and written by Hal Kanter, is a budget picture and in this class it will be a good bet for better than average. It is the picture bow for Dan Rowan and Dick Martin, tv and night club comedians.

The story line is not very important in this kind of production because it serves chiefly as a framework for gags, both visual and sound, with which Kanter plays for laughs. Rowan and Martin are a couple of luckless cowpokes, failing to make a living whether they go straight or attempt a crooked path.

Rowan and Martin, an original and distinctive air comedy team, prove acceptable actors and occasionally get going on some good gags. There is an episodic quality to the film, however, rather like a series of sketches, that does not allow them to build the jokes and situations as they might have with a better knit screenplay.

Kanter is one of the few directors to use trick effects these days for comedy and it pays off in laughs, although some of the lines occasionally get a little tradey.

Martha Hyer and Nita Talbot supply the feminine allure, Leif Erickson does a very consciously heavy heavy, and the large supporting cast boasts some interesting names, James Gleason, John McGiver, Paul Anderson, David Burns, Max and Buddy Baer and Dick Ryan. Kanter has also rounded up some noted film western stars, Tom Keene, Bob Livingston, Kermit Maynard and Bob Steele, for a burlesque posse chase.

Technical credits, notably Arthur E. Arling's photography, handsome art direction by Alexander Golitzen and Robert Clatworthy, and editing by Milton Carruth and sound by Leslie I. Carey and Corson Jowett, are all excellent. *Powe.*

The Fiend Who Walked The West
(C'SCOPE)

Stock Western with "horror" angles. Robert Evans as sadistic killer. Should cash in on exploitation angles.

20th-Fox release of Herbert B. Swope Jr. production. Stars Hugh O'Brien, Robert Evans; features Dolores Michaels, Linda Cristal, Stephen McNally, Edward Andrews, Ron Ely, Ken Scott, Emile Mayer, Gregory Morton, Shari Lee Bernath. Directed by Gordon Douglas; script, Harry Brown and Philip Yordan, based on screenplay by Ben Hecht and Charles Lederar; from story by Eleazar Lipsky; camera, Joe MacDonald; music, Leon Klatzkin; editor, Hugh S. Fowler. Previewed in N.Y., Aug. 4, '58. Running time, **101 MINS.**

Hardy	Hugh O'Brian
Felix Griffin	Robert Evans
May	Dolores Michaels
Ellen Hardy	Linda Cristal
Emmett	Stephen McNally
Judge Parker	Edward Andrews
Dyer	Ron Ely
Finney	Ken Scott
Ames	Emile Meyer
Gage	Gregory Morton
Janie	Shari Lee Bernath

When, back in 1947, 20th-Fox made "Kiss of Death," the role of the maniacal killer helped establish Richard Widmark. Now 20th comes along 11 years later with a remake of the same yarn in a western setting, starring Robert Evans and supported by a crafty campaign pitching the "horror Western" angle. "The Fiend Who Walked the West" (formerly "Quick Draw") isn't, in reality, as "shocking" as the campaign makes it out to be, though it does pack quite a wallop in several of its more sadistic scenes.

Picture comes pretty close to being a routine action western, which doesn't take itself or its principals very seriously. In fact, there are moments when it appears that director Gordon Douglas is striving for tongue-in-cheek effects as the mad killer leers and sneers at his intended victims. Only the very gullible or the very young will take the story at face value.

It has two distinct plus values: One is the presence of Hugh O'Brian, well established via the tv series "Wyatt Earp." The other are the exploitation values which are being pounded home by 20th and which automatically transform this into a "horror" western in which villain Evans feeds ground glass to one of his victims, breaks a girl's neck, shoots an arrow through an old lady, scares a pregnant woman into a miscarriage, mistreats his girl friend and finally meets his just deserts at the hands of O'Brian, himself a convict and cellmate of Evans.

There isn't much rhyme or reason to the whole thing, though it does allow Evans to emerge as one of the most vicious, cold-blooded killers to hit the screen for some time. He does a very creditable job within the confines of the script, this being only his third screen role. Though he's given some pretty impossible lines to say, Evans does carry off the impression of the psychopath and proves himself a capable actor.

O'Brian has a he-man quality that comes through. In the final scenes, when he provokes Evans, who hates to be touched (it's never explained how he got to be that way), the television personality overacts to the point of comedy.

Dolores Michaels is long-suffering and pretty as Evans' much-abused gal, and Linda Cristal plays O'Brian's equally long - suffering wife. Stephen McNally is quietly efficient as the sheriff. Edward Andrews is okay as Judge Parker.

Harry Brown and Philip Yordan fashioned the screenplay, which is just barely adequate. It's based on the 1946 Ben Hecht-Charles Lederer script. Douglas' direction is routine, though there are a couple of well-staged fights. Joe MacDonald's lensing in black-and-white CinemaScope has moments of imagination. Leon Klatzkin wrote the proper score for a "horror" film.

Since audiences apparently can be "shocked" into seeing films like this, "Fiend" stands to make a mint for exhibitors. It's not a good picture by any stretch of the imagination, but producer Herbert B. Swope Jr. has provided it with the "handles" that make for effective exploitation. Whether films like this contribute to the rising juvenile delinquency graph, or whether they're accepted for what they are, only time can tell. *Hift.*

Czech Festival

Karlovy Vary, July 29.

Stories About Lenin (RUSSIAN; COLOR). Mosfilm production and release. Stars M. Atrauch; features, M. Pastoukhova, A. Lissianskaia. Directed by Sergei Youtkevitch. Screenplay, M. Volpine, N. Erdman, E. Gabrilovitch; camera (Sovcolor), E. Andrekanis, A. Moskvine; editor, A. Bergare. At Karlovy Vary Film Fest. Running time, **100 MINS.**

This is part two of a duo of pix depicting some stories about Lenin. The ta'es are mostly personal data about the Soviet leader. They try to humanize him in one based on his escape into Finland in 1917 and then the story of his last days. Film mixes color as well as black and white and is well acted and mounted. Pic manages to hold interest in spite of the academic aspects of the direction, thesping and story telling. It remains very dubious for the U.S. except for possible curio interest. *Mosk.*

Vieras Mies (The Stranger) (FINNISH). Suomi-Film production and release. With Rauni Ikaheimo, Esko Vettenranta, Kaarlo Halttunen, Hannes Hayrinen. Directed by Hannu Laminen. Screenplay, Mike Waltari; camera, Erkki Imberg; editor, Einar Englund. At Karlovy Vary Film Fest. Running time, **105 MINS.**

This drama revolves around a vicious drunkard who makes his wife's life a living hell. When she falls in love with a hired hand on their farm, the husband kills him and then falls into a bog and drowns. She is left with one consolation, the child she will bear from her lover. Film is carefully made and works in some tender love scenes but rarely gives a depth. Result is this has only mild exploitation chances for the U.S. but okay lingo possibilities. Technical credits are good as is the acting. Some nude scenes also help. *Mosk.*

Dosango (No Return) (JAPANESE; COLOR; C'SCOPE). Gez production and release. With Johsio Omori, Fumio Omachi, Natsujo Kawakami. Written and directed by Seigo Kaneko. Camera (Eastmancolor), Kaichi Okodzima; editor, M. Ikeda. At Karlovy Vary Film Fest. Running time, **65 MINS.**

Moppet pic concerns a boy and a horse. The horse is the boy's pet but one day it gets ill and runs off to be killed by a bear. The boy never forgets him and salutes his grave every morning. Pic is too skimpy to make for any Yank chances. But its C'Scope and color make this expensive and doubtful. Acting is good as is the general technical aspect. But it never comes to grips with its subject and is overlong and laggard in movement. *Mosk.*

Bijutarii de Familie (The Family Jewels) (RUMANIAN). Bucaresti production and release. With Tantzi Cocea, Eliza Petrachesco, Sabine Thomas, Geo Barton. Directed by Marisu Theodoresco. Screenplay, Malvin Ursinu, Theodoresco from novel by Petru Dumitriu; camera, Alexandre Rosinau; editor, Constantin Simionesco. At Karlovy Vary Film Fest. Running time, **90 MINS.**

This costume meller takes place in 1900. It concerns a woman who cheats her aunt out of the family fortune only to lose all in a peasant uprising. Though slickly made, the dramatics are obvious and characterizations elementary. This is only for possible lingo spots. But it does show an advance in Rumanian filmmaking even if the insistence on bourgeois decay and the budding revolution are oldhat. *Mosk.*

Ikari No Koto (The Seven Forgotten Men) (JAPANSES; COLOR; C'SCOPE). Daiei production and release. With Kazuo Suzuki, Shiegeo Tezuka, Akio Shibata. Written and directed by Yoko Mizuki. Camera (Eastmancolor), Seiichi Kizuka; editor, Y. Akutagata. At Karlovy Vary Film Fest. Running time, **99 MINS.**

Based on a true incident about youthful slave labor on a fishing island in Japan back in 1930, this is too dressed up in color and C'Scope to make its harshness dramatic or plausible. It details how poor fisherman take out their misery on their own more miserable slaves. Ploddingly plotted, the main trump in this is its fine color work. Technically, this is well done but it remains only a longo possibility for the U.S. *Mosk.*

Tichy Don (Quiet Flows the Don) (RUSSIAN; COLOR). Gorki Film production and release. With Ellina Bystritskaya, Pyotr Glebov, Zinaida Kirienko. Directed by Sergei Gerasimov. Screenplay, Gerisimov from novel by Mikhail Sholokhov; camera (Sovcolor), Vladimir Rapoport; editor, N. Oslikovsky. At Karlovy Vary Film Fest. Running time, **120 MINS.**

This is part three in a trilogy based on a famous Soviet novel tracing the life of a Cossack from 1900 to 1918. Each pic is a detailed portion of his life. Present film is about the aging hero's loss of faith in the White Russian cause and his attempt to return to the land stymied by war and the death of his loved ones. It is well mounted and acted, with telling use of color. But its postured, academic qualities limit this for American chances in anything but foreign language spots. *Mosk.*

Dobro Morje (The Good Sea) (YUGOSLAVIAN). Triglav Film production and release. With Evelina Wohlfeiler, Tomaz Pesek. Directed by Mirko Grobler. Screenplay, Ernest Adamic; camera, France Cerar; editor, Bojan Adamic. At Karlovy Vary Film Fest. Running time, **90 MINS.**

Moppet pic is successful in telling a story through the eyes of a child and making it okay for grownups, too. It concerns a young boy who defeats a crooked landowner's attempt to foil a fisherman's attempt to buck his monopoly via getting his own nets. Good and bad guys are obvious as is the progression and characterization. But it is adroitly made and emerges a good lingo or moppet entry for Yank spots. Technically, it is fine and the kids act well and naturally. *Mosk.*

I Slik En Natt (It Happened One Night) (NORWEGIAN). Norsk Film production and release. With Anne-Lise Tankstad, Holst-Jensen, Lala Carlsen. Written and directed by Sigval Martmann Moe. Camera, Per Jonson; editor, L. Kraft. At Karlovy Vary Film Fest. Running time, **95 MINS.**

Still another war film, this one differs slightly in detailing how a femme doctor helps 10 Jewish children escape into Sweden. Though conventional in unfoldment, sans surprises, this is an okay actioner. It could be a neat dualer for U.S. use and a natural for lingo slotting. It is technically polished. *Mosk.*

Cesta Duga Godinu Dana (The Year Long Road) (YUGOSLAVIAN; ULTRASCOPE). Jadran Film release of Croatia production. Stars Silvana Pampanini, Eleonora Rossi-Drago, Massimo Girotti, Bert Sotlar; features Gordana Miletic, Milivoje Zivanovic, Maurizio Ferrara. Directed by Giuseppe De Santis. Screenplay, De Santis, Tonino Guerra, Elio Petri, Gianni Puccini; camera, Marco Scarpelli; editor, L. Savona. At Karlovy Vary Film Fest. Running time, **160 MINS.**

Italian director Giuseppe De Santis, responsible for "Bitter Rice" and "Rome 11 O'Clock," made this Yugoslavian entry with a mixed Italo and Yugo cast. Rambling tale transcends national aspects as it deals with the building of a road undertaken by a poor villager to create work for himself and his neighbors. Most of them think it is endorsed by the government and underwrite it only to have obstacles pop up as the truth comes out. But the road becomes a symbol and lives and loves are built around it as it looms the primary purpose of life in this town. De Santis has given this telling mounting, but it is overlong and loses its way at times. Drastic pruning is needed. Pic does not have the exploitation quality of "Bitter Rice," but it might be a worthy arty house entry for America. Its more general chances are more unpredictable. Acting is well controlled and pic builds to many emotional highpoints but then has a tendency to drag. *Mosk.*

Csampeszek (The Smugglers) (HUNGARIAN). Hunnia Film production and release. Stars Margit Bara, Gabor Agardy; features Laszlo Bahnidi, Alfred Deesy, Antal Farkas. Directed by Felix Mariassy. Screenplay, Pal Szabo, Gabor Thurzo; camera, Barnabas Hegyi; editor, Maria Szecsenyi. At Karlovy Vary Film Fest. Running time, **90 MINS**

Hungary 1930, with the Rumanian-Magyar border as locale backgrounds this tenderly told tale of a married Hungarian smuggler who meets a Rumanian widow smuggler and how they love briefly and part. Expertly acted and mounted, this also blocks in a telling looksee at the impoverished times and people's frantic groping for security, life and love. Nothing is overdone. The expert acting, mounting and atmosphere could make this a worthy U.S. art entry if the pickets don't interfere. *Mosk.*

Danse Macabre (HUNGARIAN). Hunnia Film production and release. With Andor Ajtay, Margit Bara, Gyorgy Bardy, Gyula Buss. Directed by Laszlo Ranody. Screenplay, J. Horvath; camera, Gyula Illes; editor, M. Morell. At Karlovy Vary Film Fest. Running time, **90 MINS.**

Film is a warmly-told slice-of-life affair that packs an emotional wallop. It intros a group of characters living in an apartment house and details their characters and problems via deft sketches. Then one kid finds an unexploded bomb which finally leads to tragedy. The sketchy treatment is the only drawback, but is made up for by deft progression and telling direction. This is another example of the improving Magyar film industry. It could have American possibilities in arty spots and looks to be a natural language house entry. It is technically tops. *Mosk.*

Cat on a Hot Tin Roof
(METROCOLOR)

Tennessee Williams stageplay in color. Everything in favor of this Metro film version. With Elizabeth Taylor and Paul Newman, it looks big b.o.

Metro release of an Avon Production. Stars Elizabeth Taylor, Paul Newman, Burl Ives. Co-stars Jack Carson and Judith Anderson. With Madeleine Sherwood, Larry Gates and Vaughn Taylor; also, Patty Ann Gerrity, Rusty Stevens, Hugh Corcoran, Deborah Miller, Brian Corcoran, Vince Townsend, Jr., Zelda Cleaver. Produced by Lawrence Weingarten. Directed by Richard Brooks. Screenplay by Richard Brooks and James Poe, based on play by Tennessee Williams; camera (Metrocolor), William Daniels; editor, Ferris Webster. Previewed at the studio, Aug. 6, '58. Running time, **108 MINS.**

Maggie	Elizabeth Taylor
Brick	Paul Newman
Big Daddy	Burl Ives
Cooper	Jack Carson
Big Mama	Judith Anderson
Mae	Madeleine Sherwood
Dr. Baugh	Larry Gates
Deacon Davis	Vaughn Taylor
Dixie	Patty Ann Gerrity
Sonny	Rusty Stevens
Buster	Hugh Corcoran
Trixie	Deborah Miller
Boy	Brian Corcoran
Lacey	Vince Townsend Jr.
Brightie	Zelda Cleaver

"Cat on a Hot Tin Roof" via Avon Productions' is an intense, important motion picture which, with the help of Elizabeth Taylor, Paul Newman and Burl Ives should give meaty returns to Leo the Lion.

By no means is this a watered-down version. It's a hard-hitting and pointed about sex, though "immature dependence" has replaced any hint of homosexuality. Motivations remain psychologically sound. Credit producer Lawrence Weingarten's adroit approach and Richard Brooks' direction with achieving a powerful, well-seasoned film produced within the bounds of good, if "adults only," taste.

Brooks and James Poe co-scripted an emotion-laden screenplay that gathers momentum. Deep hatred it describes is extended and belabored before getting around to causes, and that produces some rather repetitious action on the part of guzzling Paul Newman who has left his material bed for the solace of the bottle. For any man to thwart the advances of an Elizabeth Taylor, there must be a deep-rooted reason, and filmgoers are kept wondering perhaps too long. To the credit of the writers, however, is their handling of exposition—those events that "happened" before the film's opening—and Miss Taylor's explanation of prior events is both vivid and exciting. From that point on, the Brooks-Poe script is impassioned and stimulating.

"Cat," per Williams, is set in the South, but the land is not as decadent as he has so often pictured it. The earth is fertile, the plantation is large and Big Daddy's wealth now amounts to $10,000,000. Burl Ives, playing Big Daddy, unknowingly is dying of cancer, and his first son (Jack Carson) is out for more than his share of the estate. He and his obnoxious wife (Madeleine Sherwood) make capital of the problems besetting Big Daddy's favorite son (Newman) and his wife, he being a drunk and she being childless. It's an often gruesome, often amusing battle and one that is highlighted by skillfully drawn scenes. Newman's displeasure with his wife, it turns out, stems from his blaming her for the suicide of his close friend. Only when he faces the fact that it is he who must bear the blame, if anyone must, that love begins to replace the smouldering deceit and discord that is impacted in this large, unfriendly house.

Elizabeth Taylor has a major credit with her portrayal of Maggie. The frustrations and desires, both as a person and a woman, the warmth and understanding she molds, the loveliness that is more than a well-turned nose—all these are part of a fell-accented, perceptive interpretation. That she performed in this manner under the stress of recent tragedy makes her performance certain to provoke conversation.

Newman again proves to be one of the finest actors in films, playing cynical underacting against highly developed action. His command of the articulate, sensitive sequences is unmistakable, and the way he mirrors his feelings is basic to every scene. Ives, repeating his legit role, is a vibrant and convincing plantation king.

As the first son, Carson hits what probably is a dramatic high spot in his film career, and Judith Anderson, as "Big Mama" is excellent, as is Madeleine Sherwood as the sister-in-law.

"Cat on a Hot Tin Roof" is the first of Tennessee Williams' works to be transcribed to the screen in full color, and the richness of William Daniels' Metrocolor lensing spreads through the entire film as a warm change from the stark realism of black-and-white. Art directors William A. Horning and Urie McCleary have most ably created the Southern mansion, and set decorators Henry Grace and Robert Priestly have done a fine job in filling it, doing especially good work in adorning the cellar with sundry bric-a-brac and antiques. Top credit is due film editor Ferris Webster and recording supervisor Dr. Wesley C. Miller. And Helen Rose's limited wardrobe for Miss Taylor is effective, with the star's white slipe a pure delight.

"Cat on a Hot Tin Roof" is, in part, heavy stuff. It tells of many things Big Daddy can only describe as 'Bull!" Along with everything else, it's wonderful entertainment, and that's no bull. *Ron.*

A Cry From the Streets
(British)

Very good comedy-drama about child welfare. Name of Max Bygraves and some talented moppets makes this a sound booking for family houses.

London, Aug. 12.

Eros release of a Lewis Gilbert (Ian Dalrymple) production. Stars Max Bygraves, Barbara Murray, Colin "Smiley" Petersen, Dana "Shiralee" Wilson. Directed by Lewis Gilbert. Screenplay, Vernon Harris from novel by Elizabeth Coxhead; editor, Peter Hunt; camera, Harry Gillam; music, Larry Adler. At Plaza, London. Running time, **100 MINS.**

Bill Lowther	Max Bygraves
Ann Fairlie	Barbara Murray
Georgie	Colin Petersen
Barbie	Dana Wilson
Mrs. Farrer	Kathleen Harrison
Don Farrer	Sean Barrett
Gloria	Eleanor Summerfield
Mrs. Daniels	Mona Washbourne
Mr. Daniels	Toke Townley
Derek	Charles McShane
Alex	David Bushell
Tony	Tony Baker
Police Sergeant	Glyn Houston
Mrs. Jenks	Dandy Nicholls
Police Inspector	Basil Dignam
Rachael Seymour	Avice Landone
Mr. Robbins	Vi Stevens
Mr. Hodges	Fred Griffiths

Stage and tele star Max Bygraves gets his first major screen break in "A Cry From The Street," and promises to become just as big a film personality. "Cry" is an unpretentious film which comes off because it is directed with warmth and insight, because the characters are human and mainly credible and because Vernon Harris's screenplay skilfully blends laughter and pathos. Max Bygraves as its star, this will be a big draw in Britain. American, who know him mainly for song and comedy on tv, may be puzzled that he sings only once and plays a straight role.

But his relaxed and amiable personality permeates the film. This will win over the most cynical audiences. He is ably supported by his co-star, Barbara Murray, several fine features players and an engaging bunch of child actors.

Story has Bygraves as an electrical engineer who meets Barbara Murray, a children's welfare officer. She is concerned with the fate of several children, who are either orphans or have been abandoned by their parents. Notably there are three kids whose father has been hanged for the murder of his wife, another whose mother is a drunken actress and an older boy, who is anxious to find the mother abandoned him eight years before. This is a large handful for Miss Murray and, almost against his will, Bygraves finds himself becoming drawn into her activities.

Although the adults do a very sound chore, audience reaction mostly will center around the children. Lewis Gilbert has directed them with a sure touch and much sympathy. Miss Murray is a sure touch and such sympathy. Miss Murray is a sensitive, pretty heroine who blends nicely with Bygraves' light humor and throwaway technique. Outstanding among the children are Dana Wilson, a precocious, tough but endearing infant; Charles McShane also winning, and Colin (Smiley) Petersen, a cute snub-nose cherub with a sense of fun. Kathlene Harrison, Eleanor Summerfield, Mono Washbourne and Toke Townley offer useful performances among the adult thesps.

Highlights in this include a comedy act by the youngsters which nearly turns into grim drama when one of them gets hold of a loaded gun, a picnic scene in which Bygraves and the kids join in a song called "Gotta Have Rain'. Incidentally, the star wrote and composed this tune which may well click as a pop number The Welfare home and the London street sequences are realistically handled and lensed. Larry Adler's music has the polished touch expected of a musician of his standing.

In a film world where everybody is apparently trying to make an epic, "A Cry From the Streets" is a refreshing little film with the golden ingredient of heart. *Rich.*

The Big Country
(TECHNIRAMA-COLOR)

Big western with big b.o. potential.

United Artists release of Anthony-Worldwide (Gregory Peck and William Wyler) production. Stars Gregory Peck, Jean Simmons, Carroll Baker, Charlton Heston, Burl Ives and Charles Bickford. Features Chuck Connors and Alfonso Bedoya. Directed by William Wyler. Screenplay, James H. Webb, Sy Bartlett and Robert Wilder; screen adaptation, Jessamyn West and Robert Wyler from a novel by Donald Hamilton. Camera (Technirama-Technicolor) Franz F. Planer; editor, Robert Belcher and John Faure; music, Jerome Moross. Previewed in N.Y., Aug. 4, '58. Running time, **166 MINS.**

James McKay .... Gregory Peck
Julie Maragon .... Jean Simmons
Patricia Terrill .... Carroll Baker
Steve Leech .... Charlton Heston
Rufus Hannassey .... Burl Ives
Major Henry Terrill ... Charles Bickford
Ramon .... Alfonso Bedoya
Buck Hannassey .... Chuck Connors
Rafe .... Chuck Hayward
Dude .... Buff Brady
Cracker .... Jim Burk
Hannassey Woman .... Dorothy Adams
Terrill Cowboys Chuck Roberson, Bob Morgan, John McKee, Jay Slim Talbot

"The Big Country lives up to its title. The Gregory Peck-William Wyler production, starring Peck and directed by Wyler, is massive in its pictorial splendor. Technicolor-Technirama camera has captured a vast section of the southwest with such fidelity that it leaves an awe-inspiring effect on the viewer. The long stretches of dry country, in juxtaposition to tiny western settlements, and the giant canyon country in the arid area, have been recorded with almost three-dimensional effect. This is one of the best photography jobs of the year and compares favorably with anything that has been accomplished with Cinerama, Todd-AO or CineMiracle.

Although the story—based on Donald Hamilton's novel, with James R. Webb, Sy Bartlett and Robert Wilder credited with the screenplay and Jessamyn West and Robert Wyler with the screen adaptation—is dwarfed by the scenic outpourings, "The Big Country" is nonetheless armed with a serviceable, adult western yarn which should find favor with audiences of all tastes. It perhaps represents how well a carefully-conceived theatrical sagebrush drama can overwhelm and render puny anything the western telepix producers can possibly place on a 21-inch screen.

The combination of United Artists' promotional push, one of the largest in the company's history, the value of the names of Peck, Charlton Heston, Jean Simmons and Carroll Baker, the reputation of Wyler as a meticulous and creative director, and the excellent production job should help in making "The Big Country" one of the big 1958 b.o. pictures.

Deficiencies in the story have been overcome by the excellence of the production, the trouping, the numerous Wyler touches. The story carries some philosophic comments about the meaning of bravery and the value of a sane, peaceful approach to hot-headed issues.

Basically it concerns the feud between Major Henry Terrill (Charles Bickford) and Rufus Hennassey (Burl Ives), rugged individualists who covet the same watering area for their cattle. The water spot is open to both camps since it is the property of Julie Maragon (Jean Simmons) who has been willed the property by her grandfather. In their desire to destroy and drive out each other, Bickford and Ives constantly make overtures to acquire Miss Simmon's ranch. She holds, out, knowing that either Bickford or Ives will utilize her land to ruin the other.

Bickford is the "have" rancher of the area, with a fine home, a large head of cattle, a beautiful daughter (Carroll Baker), and a full crew of ranch hands. Ives is the "have not," with a brood of unruly and uncouth sons, a bunch of shacks, and an army of "white trash" relatives.

Into the atmosphere of hate and vengance comes Peck, a genteel eastern dude, to marry Miss Baker, a tempestuous girl with a strong attachment to her father and her father's mode of living. It's obvious early in the story that Peck and Miss Baker will not marry and that he will eventually wind up with Miss Simmons.

Peck arouses Miss Baker's displeasure when he refuses to ride a wild horse and backs away from a fight with Heston, Bickford's truculent foreman who's after Miss Baker himself. Peck, however, proves himself in his own way and serves as the catalyst that eventually brings an end to the feud, not until, however, blood is spilled and a number of people are killed.

As the peace-loving easterner, Peck gives one of his better performances. Ives is topnotch as the rough but fair-minded Rufus Hannassey; Bickford is fine as the ruthless, unforgiving rancher and so is Heston as the jealous foreman, Miss Simmons as the sedate schoolteacher-ranch owner, Miss Baker as Bickford's strong-minded daughter, and Alfonso Bedoys as a Mexican ranch hand. Chuck Connors, a former professional baseball player, is especially convincing as Ives' uncouth son who attempts to rape Miss Simmons.

Cinematography of Franz F. Planer and Wallace Chewning deserves special mention. Jerome Moross' musical score is also on the plus side. *Holl.*

Queen of Outer Space
(COLOR: C'SCOPE)

Girls and science-fiction blended with some humor. Lends itself to exploitation.

Hollywood, Aug. 8.

Allied Artists production and release. Stars Zsa Zsa Gabor. Producer, Ben Schwalb; director, Edward Bernds; screenplay, Charles Beaumont; based on a story, by Ben Hecht; camera, William Whitley; music, Marlin Skiles; editor, William Austin. Previewed at the studio in Hollywood, Aug. 6, '58. Running time, **80 MINS.**

Talleah .... Zsa Zsa Gabor
Capt. Patterson .... Eric Fleming
Queen Yllana .... Laurie Mitchell
Prof. Konrad .... Paul Birch
Kaeel .... Babara Darrow
Cruze .... Dave Willock
Motiya .... Lisa Davis
Larry Turner .... Patrick Waltz
Odeena .... Marilyn Buferd

Most of the female characters in Allied Artists' "Queen of Outer Space," look like they would be more at home on a Minsky runway than the Cape Canaveral launching pad, but Ben Schwalb's production is a good-natured attempt to put some honest sex into science-fiction and as such it is an attractive production. There is considerable humor, the CinemaScope, DeLuxe color photography is good, and with Zsa Zsa Gabor as the regal star, the presentation lends itself to profitable expoitation.

The year is 1985, and Eric Fleming, Patrick Waltz and Dave Willock are U.S. officers in charge of a space ship assigned to check on an American satellite space station. They are deflected from their course by mysterious energy rays from the planet Venus, where their ship is eventually wrecked. Taken prisoner by a malignant queen, Laurie Mitchell, they are about to be destroyed, when they are rescued by a pro-masculine group headed by Miss Gabor.

The cast, under Edward Bernds' direction, is predominantly feminine and attractively garbed in the brief raiment that appears to be customary on other planets than this one. Miss Gabor makes a handsome leading lady, romanced by Fleming, and the others, including Miss Mitchell, Paul Birch, Barbara Darrow, Willock, Lisa Davis and Waltz, lend the necessary ingredients to their roles.

Technical credits are adequate and the screenplay, by Charles Beaumont, occasionally contains some amsuing lines. *Powe.*

Guld Og Gronne Skove
(Golden Mountains)
(DANISH-COLOR)

Berlin, Aug. 5.

Vinod S. Pathak release of AS Nordisk Films Kompagni (Copenhagen) production. With Axel Bang, Verner Tholsgaard, Mogens Viggo Petersen, Cay Christiansen, Karl Stegger. Directed by Gabriel Axel. Screenplay, Johannes Allen; camera, Joergen Skov; music, Svend Erik Tarp; editing, Carsten Dahl; settings, Kai Rasch. At Berlin Film Festival. Running time, **89 MINS.**

This Danish comedy is quite amusing and enjoyable. Its best exploitation chance for America lies in fact that it centers much around Americans.

Story concerns two small Danish islands which have been feuding fussing and fighting with each other for years. Not even the romantic angle (three boys of island A love three girls of island B) can wipe out this dispute since their parents are against unions. Then oil is found on one of the islands and this registers an unexpected boom for one community through an American oil company. Finally it's the Americans who end the general dispute between the two islands. And they also manage that a three-couple wedding can take place.

Feature pokes some fun at youths. Its done in a cute way that should amuse American audiences, with English titles on dubbing. Adequate acting is turned in by the entire cast. Direction by Gabriel Axel is competent and Eastmancolor lensing first rate. In all, a handsomely made film that surpasses the quality of so many a comedy turned out by the big European film nations these days. *Hans.*

Cop Hater

Limited by budget and cast to double-bills, New York-locationed pic is still superior to average; imaginative and interesting.

Hollywood, Aug. 8.

United Artists release of a William Berke production. Stars Robert Loggia, Gerald O'Loughlin; features Ellen Parker, Shirley Ballard. Directed by William Berke. Screenplay, Henry Kane; based on a novel by Ed McBain; camera, Burdi Contner; editor, Ed Sutherland. Previewed at the Goldwyn studio, Hollywood, Aug. 7, '58. Running time, **75 MINS.**

Steve Carelli .... Robert Loggia
Mike Maguire .... Gerald O'Loughlin
Teddy .... Ellen Parker
Alice .... Shirley Ballard
Lt. Byrne .... Russell Hardie
Mercer .... Hal Riddle
Kling .... William Neff
Killer .... Gene Miller
Mama Lucy .... Marion Goldina
Dave Foster .... Lincoln Kilpatrick
Willis .... Ralph Stantley
Havilland .... Ted Gunther

"Cop Hater," produced and directed by William Berke for United Artists, is a compact melodrama with a touch of poetry. It is not big enough to carry marquee weight on its own, but it will be a good addition to double-bill programming. Robert Loggia and Gerald O'Loughlin are starred.

The screenplay by Henry Kane, based on a novel by Ed McBain, concerns the hunt by fellow cops Loggia and O'Loughlin through the hot and steamy streets of Manhattan for a cop-killer. It is essentially a murder mystery, but it has romantic overtones and achieves a social significance without making a point of it.

"Cop Hater," despite its exploitation title, is a good example of the New York school of film-making. It is imaginatively conceived and intelligently presented, with a detail of character that is not usual in small budget productions made in Hollywood. Manhattan backgrounds and interiors are authentic and good.

Loggia and O'Loughlin, as the cop buddies, are engaging figures, showing intelligence and sensativity without indulging in any excess dramatics. Ellen Parker is appealing as Loggia's fiancee, a deaf-mute, and Shirley Ballard is effective as O'Loughlin's wife. Others who give strength to the performance include Russell Hardie, Hal Riddle, William Neff, Gene Miller and Marion Goldina.

Burdi Contner's photography is good and so are other technical credits. *Powe.*

Saga of Hemp Brown
(COLOR; C'SCOPE)

Program oater with fair action, romance, production values.

Hollywood, Aug. 8.

Universal production and release. Stars Rory Calhoun; costars Beverly Garland, John Larch. Produced by Gordon Kay; director, Richard Carlson; screenplay, Bob Williams; based on a story by Bernard Girard; camera, Philip Lathrop; music, Joseph Gershenson; editor, Tony Martinelli. Previewed at the studio, Universal City, Aug. 5, '58. Running time, **80 MINS.**

Hemp Brown .... Rory Calhoun
Mona Langley .... Beverly Garland
Jed Givens .... John Larch
Hook .... Russell Johnson
Bolanos .... Fortunio Bonanova
Sheriff .... Allan Lane
Judge .... Trevor Bardette
Bo Slauter .... Morris Ankrum
Colonel .... Addison Richards
Chang .... Victor Sen Yung
Murphy .... Theodore Newton
Prosecutor .... Francis MacDonald

Although Universal's "Saga of Hemp Brown" contains some divertingly off-beat plot ideas, it is basically a budget western that will have to depend for its success on the strength of Rory Calhoun as the star. Gordon Kay produced and Richard Carlson directed the screenplay by Bob Williams, whose values have been ably conveyed in the Eastman Color-CinemaScope presentation.

Calhoun is a maligned U.S. cavalry officer, stripped of his uniform and sentenced to disgrace because he has been falsely accused accused of allowing an ambush in which several fellow troopers and his colonel's wife were murdered. Calhoun, out to find the real murderer, hitches a ride with a medicine show man, Fortunio Bonanova, and his lissome assistant, Beverly Garland. Miss Garland eventually saves him from lynching by an irate mob and he proves his innocence by exposing the true killer, John Larch, and then his romantic nature by joining up with Miss Garland.

Although some of the situations seem stock, the show wagon is a nice touch, and lends itself to Philip Lathrop's photography, giving the production, at times, a feeling of bigness and importance. Calhoun plays it mostly taciturn, but Miss Garland has dignity as well as allure. Larch does well as the heavy, Russell Johnson is effective as a drink-soggy villain and Bonanova is good as a double-dealing spieler. Others who give good account of themselves include Allan Lane, Trevor Bardette, Morris Ankrum and Addison Richards. *Powe.*

Wind Across the Everglades
(COLOR)

Handsome, interesting story of Audubon Society's efforts to protect Florida wild-life, but only mild response indicated.

Hollywood, Aug. 15.
Warner Bros. release of a Schulberg production. Stars Burl Ives, Christopher Plummer; features Gypsy Rose Lee, George Voskovec, Tony Galento, Howard I. Smith, Emmett Kelly, Pat Henning, Chana Eden. Produced by Stuart Schulberg. Directed by Nicholas Ray. Screenplay, Budd Schulberg; camera, Joseph Brun; editors, George Klotz, Joseph Zigman. Previewed at Warner Bros. studio, Burbank, Aug. 12, '58. Running time, **91 MINS.**

Cottonmouth .... Burl Ives
Walt Murdock......Christopher Plummer
Mrs. Bradford .... Gypsy Rose Lee
Aaron Nathanson.......George Voskovec
Beef .... Tony Galento
George .... Howard I. Smith
Bigamy Bob .... Emmett Kelly
Sawdust .... Pat Henning
Naomi .... Chana Eden
Perfesser .... Curt Conway
Writer .... Peter Falk
Slowboy .... Gred Grossinger
Loser .... Sammy Renick
One-Note .... Toch Brown
Howard Ross Morgan ... Frank Rothe
Judge Harris .... MacKinlay Kantor

"Wind Across The Everglades" is a worthy atttempt to make a picture about some original situations and material—in this case early efforts of the Audubon Society to preserve the bird wild life of Florida. But the Warner Bros. release, produced by Stuart Schulberg, written by Budd Schulberg and directed by Nicholas Ray, is not, in execution, up to its conception. It is an "interesting" picture, with some impressive backgrounds of the Everglades country (where it was shot) in Technicolor, but it is not consistently engrossing and will be most satisfactory as a double-bill attraction.

It's hard to be too hard on a picture such as this. Despite its flaws, it is honest and even carries a certain amount of passionate conviction. With a cast headed by Burl Ives and Christopher Plummer, and with the Schulbergs and Ray involved, there remains the feeling that it should have been far better.

Schulberg's screenplay fictionalizes the struggle of the Audubon Society to end the slaughter of Florida's plume birds, whose feathers were so highly prized around the turn of the century for women's hats. The action revolves around the almost singled-handed efforts of an agent, Christopher Plummer, to stop the mass killings, and in particular his battle with the leader of one band of birdhunters, Burl Ives. The ending is inconclusive, although it resolves with symbolic victory for Plummer as Ives is killed as he is taking him to justice. Presumably this means the end of this gang of plumage-pilllagers and a signaling of a general victory for the conservation forces.

There are some good shots by cameraman Joseph Brun of the egrets and other fowl, some with spectacular effect, and satisfactory simulated scenes of the birds' slaughter. But the screenplay tends to go off on diversions that have little to do with the main story and the total impact is dissipated.

Plummer does a good job as the idealistic bird warden, although not much motivation is ever given for his dedication. Ives, looking remarkably like Henry VIII in a red beard, eyebrows and hair, does a characteristically intense job, and his character, as a free-boot-

ing, civilization-hating rugged individualist, makes sense if not sympathy.

Gypsy Rose Lee has some good comedy scenes which she handles adroitly while displaying some of the most startling cleavage seen in some time. George Voskovec, Tony Galento, Howard I. Smith, Emmett Kelly, Pat Henning, Chana Eden, novelist, novelist MacKinlay Kantor, Sammy Renick, and others make up the interesting supporting cast. *Powe.*

Curse of the Faceless Man

Okay exploitation pic, to be packaged with "It! The Terror from Beyond Space."

Hollywood, July 31.
United Artists release of Robert E. Kent production. Stars Richard Anderson, Elaine Edwards, Adele Mara, Luis Van Rooten. Features Gar Moore, Jan Arvan, Felix Locher, Bob Bryant. Directed by Edward L. Cahn. Screenplay, Jerome Bixby; camera, Kenneth Peach; editor, Grant Whytock. Previewed July 31, '58. Running time, **67 MINS.**

Dr. Paul Mallon ...... Richard Anderson
Tina Enright .... Elaine Edwards
Maria Fiorillo .... Adele Mara
Dr. Fiorillo .... Luis Van Rooten
Dr. Enricco Ricci .... Gar Moore
Inspector Renaldi .... Jan Arvan
Dr. Emanuel .... Felix Locher
Quintillus .... Bob Bryant

"Curse of the Faceless Man" digs back into antiquity for motivation of plot, sufficiently novel in **theme to rate okay exploitation for its marticular market. Subject matter of a man from the past reappearing in the present is given enough substance to build a more or less imaginative scifi yarn** which will complement "It! The Terror from Beyond Space," a tale of the future with which it is being packaged.

The Robert E. Kent production unfolds in Naples, where the stone body of a man uncovered in new excavations in Pompeii is taken to a museum. There's still life in the huge form, however, which from certain inscriptions on a medallion beside body is revealed as Quintillus, the greatest gladiator of his time who was buried when Vesuvius erupted. Topic of reincarnation is inserted in story line, in person of an American artist who appear to have been a noble lady 2,000 years ago with whom gladiator was in love. Stone man as he partially returns to life is possessed with obsession of saving his sweetheart, now the artist, from the fires of the volcano, and he kidnaps her from her apartment. Into this pattern is woven several scientists who try to piece together the past and the present.

Edward L. Cahn's direction of the Jerome Bixby screen-play while over-leisurely at times catches the spirit well enough to make narrative semi-believable. Elaine Edwards as the artist is standout here, turning in a credible job. Richard Anderson as her fiance, a skin cell specialist; Luis Van Rooten, museum curator; and Adele Mara, latter's daughter, are okay, as are balance of cast. Bob Bryant as Quintillus, man from the past, moves as character requires, his makeup excellent.

Technical credits are standard, including photography by Kenneth Peach, William Glasgow's art direction and Grant Whitock's editing. *Whit.*

Terror in a Texas Town

Slow-moving western.

United Artists release of a Seltzer Films Inc. presentation produced by Frank N. Seltzer. Stars Sterling Hayden; costars Sebastian Cabot, Carol Kelly, Eugene Martin; features Marilee Earle. Directed by Joseph H. Lewis. Screenplay and story by Ben L. Perry. camera, Ray Rennahan; editors, Frank Sullivan, Stefan Arnsten; music, Gerald Fried. Previewed N.Y., Aug. 15, '58. Running time, **80 MINS.**

George Hansen .... Sterling Hayden
Ed McNeil .... Sebastian Cabot
Molly .... Carol Kelly
Pepe Mirada .... Eugene Martin
Johnny Crale .... Ned Young
Jose Mirada .... Victor Millan
Rosa Mirada .... Ann Varela
Baxter .... Sheb Wooley
Weed .... Fred Kohler
Keeno .... Steve Mitchell
Monsy .... Marilee Earle
Johnson .... Jamie Russell
Sheriff Stoner .... Tyler McVey
Sven Hansen .... Ted Stanhope
Barnaby .... Gil Lamb
Holmes .... Frank Ferguson
Brady .... Hank Patterson

Handicapped by a slow-moving story, "Terror in a Texas Town" shapes up as a routine filler for the duals. There's little that lends itself to exploitation in this Seltzer Films presentation released by United Artists. Moreover, the cast is composed of relative marquee unknowns save for Sterling Hayden who stars.

Ben L. Perry's yarn, which he also screenplayed, revives the time-honored incident where the unscrupulous land-grabber attempts to toss the squatters off their property by hook or crook. In this case Sebastian Cabot is the No. 1 heavy who carries on a campaign of intimidation with the aid of gunman Ned Young and several other cohorts.

There's oil under them thar fields and Cabot aims to get it. But he fails to reckon with Hayden, a seafaring Swede who comes on the scene after his farmer father has been shot down by Young. In due course he urges the townspeople to fight back and in a poor man's version of "High Noon" kills Young with a whaling harpoon.

Hayden isn't too convincing as the hero and either the story, Joseph H. Lewis' direction or both could be listed as the culprits. For his performance suffers by resemblance to caricatures of bumbling Swedes usually found in comic strips. Cabot's portrayal of the would-be land-grabber is of the stock variety.

Young is amply sinister as the top killer and Carol Kelly is good as the moll who eventually gives him the air. Victor Millan registers nicely as a farmer who's slain because he's a key witness. Marilee Earle has little to do as Cabot's "secretary." Sheb Wooley, of "Purple People Eater" fame, is seen briefly as a hired gunman.

Ray Rennahan's camerawork is par for the course as is Gerald Fried's music, William Ferrari's art direction, editing of Frank Sullivan and Stefan Arnsten along with other technical credits. Producer Frank N. Seltzer evidently guided **this one with an eye to economy for while there are many scenes in a hotel and on the town's street seldom is anyone seen with exception of the immediate principals.** *Gilb.*

Attack of the Puppet People

Good special effects highlight otherwise routine exploitationer.

Hollywood, Aug. 8.

American-International release of a James H. Nicholson-Samuel Z. Arkoff production. Stars John Agar, John Hoya, June Kenney. Producer-director, Bert I. Gordon. Screenplay, George Worthing Yates; from a story by Bert I. Gordon; camera, Ernest Laszlo; music, Albert Glasser; editor, Ronald Sinclair. Previewed at Warner's Hollywood Theatre projection room, Aug. 4, '58. Running time, 78 MINS.

Bob Westley .... John Agar
Mr. Franz .... John Holt
Solly Reynolds .... June Kenny
Emil .... Michael Mark
Sgt. Paterson .... Jack Kosslyn
Laurie .... Marlene Willis
Stan .... Ken Miller
Georgia .... Laurie Mitchell
Mac .... Scott Peters
Agnes .... Susan Gordon
Brownie Leader .... June Jocelyn
Janet .... Jean Moorehead
Doorman .... Hank Patterson
Mailman .... Hal Bogart
Elevator Operator .... Troy Patterson
Janitor .... Bill Giorgio
Switchboard Operator .... George Diestel
Ernie .... Jaime Forster
Salesman .... Mark Lowell

Bert I. Gordon is a master of special effects and his tricks in "The Attack of the Puppet People" are ingenious and intriguing. The remainder of the James H. Nicholson-Samuel Z. Arkoff production for American-International is not up to this technical achievement, however, and the presentation can be satisfactory, but no more, in exploitation situations.

Gordon also produced, directed and supplied the story for "Puppet People," which is, basically, a reworking of the Pygmalion legend. John Hoyt is the doll-maker who has been a puppeteer and now has invented a machine that reduces humans to about one-tenth their normal size. He uses the little people only to relieve his loneliness, but they are understandably not amused.

The screenplay, by George Worthing Yates, attempts to arouse some interest by a love story between John Agar and June Kenny, as two those who undergo reduction, and with suspense about the ability of Hoyt's victims to regain their normal size. But the story lacks punch because there is no real point to it, so the ending when it comes is inconclusive and somewhat flat.

Gordon's miniature work, his ability (with cameraman Ernest Laszlo) to show his characters apparently only a fraction of normal size, and his ingenuity at creating situations that gives these special problems interesting flavor, these are all interesting and sometimes amusing.

The cast, including Hoyt, Agar and Miss Kenny, are adequate to their tasks and other contributions, Albert Glasser's music, and editing by Ronald Sinclair, are capable.

Powe.

China Doll

Adequately done story of a romance in wartime. Victor Mature only b.o. peg.

Aug. 1.

United Artists release of a Romina Production. Stars Victor Mature; features LiLi Hua, Ward Bond, Bob Mathias, Johnny Desmond, Stu Whitman, Elaine Curtis, Ann McCrea, Danny Chang, Denver Pyle, Don Barry, Tiger Andrews, Steve Mitchell, Ken Perry, Ann Paige. Produced and directed by Frank Borzage; exec producer, Robert E. Morrison. Screenplay by Kitty Buhler; story by James Benson Nablo and Thomas F. Kelly. Camera, William Clothier; music, Henry Vars; editor, Jack Murray. Previewed at the Picwood Theatre, Westwood, Aug. 1, '58. Running time, 99 MINS.

Cliff Brandon .... Victor Mature
Shu-Jen .... LiLi Hua
Father Cairns .... Ward Bond
Phil Gates .... Bob Mathias
Steve Hill .... Johnny Desmond
Dan O'Neill .... Stu Whitman
Alice Nichols .... Elaine Curtis
Monna Perkins .... Ann McCrea
Ellington .... Danny Chang
Col. Wiley .... Denver Pyle
Hal Foster .... Don Barry
Carlo Menotti .... Tiger Andrews
Dave Reisner .... Steve Mitchell
Ernie Fleming .... Ken Perry
Sally .... Ann Paige
Shiao-Mee .... Tita Aragon

About average in its war storytelling, "China Doll" has a field day with the warmth and humor of a romance between a burly air corps captain and a fragile oriental beauty. Producer-director Frank Borzage has filmed the Romina Production with an admirable touch, but whether star Victor Mature's name is strong enough to fight the boxoffice battle by itself is something else again.

Kitty Buhler screenplayed this United Artists release from a story by James Benson Nablo and Thomas F. Kelly. The script often is highly interesting, often humorous and sometimes corny. It's a tale of China in 1943, at a time when the Japanese had cut off all supply lines and American airman took to flying the hump. Smack in the middle is Mature, a lonely leader who has dropped good books and bad women and has taken to the bottle. In one of his most alcoholic states, he unknowingly purchases a young Chinese girl as a housekeeper, and she ends up carrying his child, drawing his love and marrying him, in that order. Both are killed in a subsequent air attack, and the child lives to spend the next 13 years in Chinese orphan homes before being brought to America and her parents' friends.

Mature displays his share of love, emotion and humor. Highlight of the picture is LiLi Hua who, in playing the title role, is as sumptuous a femme as has flecked the American screen. Ward Bond is excellent as an understanding man of the cloth, and Danny Chang is fine as the barracks' boy. A good supporting cast also includes Bob Mathias, Stu Whitman, Johnny Desmond (who sings one rather nondescript tune), Elaine Curtis and Ann McCrea.

Photography by William Clothier is sharp, with stock war footage used with precision despite its tell-tale darker tones. Other technical credits, including Henry Vars' music, Jack Murray's editing and Howard Richmond's art direction are capable.

Ron.

Next to No Time
(BRITISH—COLOR)

Flimsy comedy kept alive via stylish acting by Kenneth More and Betsy Drake; boxoffice prospects depend entirely on this stellar draw.

British Lion release of a Henry Cornelius (Albert Fennell) production. Stars Kenneth More, Betsy Drake; features Roland Culver, Harry Green, Patrick Barr, Maureen Connell. Directed by Henry Cornelius. Screenplay by Cornelius from Paul Gallico's story, "The Enchanted Hour"; editor, Peter Hunt; camera, Freddie Francis; music, Georges Auric. At Studio One, London. Running time, 93 MINS.

David Webb .... Kenneth More
Georgie Brant .... Betsy Drake
Becky .... Bessie Love
Saul .... Harry Green
Jerry .... Patrick Barr
Sir Godfrey Cowan .... Roland Culver
Warren .... Reginald Beckwith
Steve .... John Walsh
Hobbs .... Howard Marion-Crawford
Wallis .... Clive Morton
Abercrombie .... John Laurie
Mrs. Crowley .... Irene Handl
Mary .... Maureen Connell
Forbes .... Raymond Huntley
Mario .... Ferdy Mayne
Clerk .... Russell Waters

Paul Gallico's stories are usually little gems of wisdom, good taste and shrewd observation, but any producer deciding to turn one into a film is usually leading with his chin. The stories are so slight and such gentle anecdotes. "Next To No Time!", based on Gallico's "Enchanted Hour," is a case in point. The story-line is as slim as a chorine's waist. That the pic turns out to be bright entertainment is because of neat direction and impeccable casting. The film will certainly be popular in British cinemas. In America, it depends on whether Kenneth More and Betsy Drake will attract the ducat-buyers.

More is a planning engineer who has hit on a way of using automatism to up production at his firm's factory. But finance is needed. So More is shipped on the Queen Elizabeth to persuade a financier to put coin into the project. He is not happy about the assignment since he tends to dry up in front of strangers. But with the help of a superstitious Irish barman an an attractive Yank film star he finds himself the life and soul of the Liz party and clinches the deal just in time for the film to wind up.

He has a number of amusing episodes and puts them over in a gay, inconsequential manner which has made him a top star in this country. Miss Drake, cast as a film star, again produces her usual brand of charm and happiness. But, despite the efforts of the two stars, it is the supporting actors who really make this jell. Roland Culver, as the stuffy financier; Sidney Jones, as a jovial cabin steward; Harry Green, as a Hollywood tycoon, Ferdy Mayne, as the ship's Casanova; Howard Marion-Crawford, as the ship's bore, John Walsh, cast as a bar-steward; and Reginald Beckworth as Culver's "yes man" are all highly useful aids.

Freddie Francis's color lensing is excellent and the dialog somehow manages to keep sufficiently effervescent to make audiences forget that a tiny little joke is being spun out incredibly. This was the last film Henry Cornelius made before his premature death. It also features Harry Green in his last screen performance before he died. They both made their final bow under pleasant circumstances.

Rich.

War of the Colossal Beast

Sequel to "The Amazing Colossal Man"; handicapped by lack of novel situations; aided by good special effects. Average return for an exploitationer.

Hollywood, Aug. 8.

American-International release of a James H. Nicholson-Samuel Z. Arkoff production. Stars Sally Fraser, Roger Pace, Dean Parkin. Producer-Director, Bert I. Gordon; screenplay, George Worthing Yates; based on a story by Bert I. Gordon; camera, Jacgk Marta; music, Albert Glasser; editor, Ronald Sinclair. Previewed at Warner's Hollywood Theatre projection room, Aug. 4, '58. Running time, 68 MINS.

Joyce .... Sally Fraser
Glen .... Dean Parkin
Major Baird .... Roger Pace
Dr. Carmichael .... Russ Bender
Capt. Harris .... Charles Stewart
Swanson .... George Becwar
Miguel .... Robert Hernandez
Sgt. Luis Murillo .... Rico Alaniz
Army Officer .... George Alexander
Mexican Doctor .... George Navarro
Neurologist .... John McNamara
Corres.—Pent .... Bob Garnet
Medical Corps Officer .... Howard Wright
Mayor .... Roy Gordon
General Nelson .... George Milan
Operator (Switchboard) .... Warren Frost
Bus Driver .... Bill Giorgio
Joan .... Loretta Nicholson
Mother .... June Jocelyn
Newscaster .... Jack Kosslyn

"The War of the Colossal Beast" is a sequel to American-International's earlier "The Amazing Colossal Man," but invention seems to have been exhausted in the first picture. Sequel will have to ride to whatever success it enjoys on that picture. Bert I. Gordon is producer and director as well as the creator of the special effects. He is most successful in the last category, largely because he doesn't have much story to work with aside from the fact that his central figure is 60 feet tall. "Beast" may be promoted into successful boxoffice, but it will take considerable exploitation and word-of-mouth will not be enthusiastic.

"Colossal Man" ended with the outsize man—whose growth had been unnaturally stimulated by plutonium radium—falling into Boulder Dam and being drowned. It turns out he escaped, however, and is captured again only to raise the problem of what is to be done with him. He escapes as he is about to be transported for permanent exile to an uninhabited Pacific isle, and is disposed of this time by walking into high tension wires.

For fans of these pictures, it might be somewhat confusing to find different actors playing roles that occurred in the first picture, and some of the same actors who were in the original playing other roles in the sequel. Gordon has also interpolated a film clip from the early film into this one, as a dream sequence, and unfortunately it is more exciting than anything in the current version.

Dean Parkin plays the "Beast" in this version, in properly horrible makeup, and others in the cast include Sally Fraser, Roger Pace, Russ Bender, Charles Stewart and George Becwar.

Jack Marta's camera work and Ronald Sinclair's editing help achieve the photographic tricks that are the Gordon specialty. But there should be more substantial basis otherwise these special effects lose considerable value.

Powe.

Yugoslav Films

Aleksa Dundic
(Color)
(RUSSIAN-YUGOSLAV)

Pula, Aug. 12.

Avala-Film (Belgrade) and Maxim Gorki Studio (Moscow) production, directed by Leonid Lukov. Stars Branko Plesa; features Dragomir Felba, Milan Puzik, Tatjana Piljeckaja. Screenplay, Antonije Isakovic and Lukov; camera (Agfa) Mihail Kirilov; music, Nikita Bogoslovski. At Pula Film Festival. Running itme, 117 MINS.

This one commands attention as it is the first big-scale Sovietic-Yugoslavian coproduction. Directed by a Russian (Lukov), with a mixed cast and shot in both countries, pic centers on Aleksa Dundic, legendary Yugoslavian-born hero of the Russian October revolution. It sees him going through numerous battles until he is killed in one of them.

It's an action film, a "Communist Western" one may say, which has its plus points in some very skillfully arranged mass and battle scenes and a fine Agfacolor photography which adds greatly to the mood. But the usual black-and-white treatment, poor dialog plus party-line plot probably make this an unsuitable item for the western market. Quite obviously, however, the creators of "Dundic" haven't thought much in commercial terms anyway. *Hans.*

H 8
(YUGOSLAVIAN)

Pula, Aug. 12.

Jadran (Zagreb) production, directed by Nicola Tanhofer. With Durda Glazer-Ivezic, Mija Oromovic, Marija Kohn. Boris Buzancic and Rudolf Kukic. Screenplay, Zvonimir Berkovic and Tomica Butorac; camera, Slavko Zalar; music, Dragutin Savin. At Pula Film Festival. Running time, 112 MINS.

This one captured nearly all the major awards, including the Grand Prize, at the Pula festival in Yugoslavia. It's an extremely well made, both artistically and humanly interesting production which contributes much to prestige of Yugoslav's film-making. It may have some art-house possibilities abroad.

Film deals with an actual traffic accident that happened last summer on the Zagreb-Belgrade highway when the driver of a never identified car (only part of latter's licence plate, H 8, were remembered by a few witnesses) caused the fatal collision of a bus and a truck. Pic starts and ends with the accident and between them tells via a flashback how the passengers of the bus spent their last hours until the collision.

Direction by 32-year old Nicola Tanhofer reveals remarkable know-how, especially (he's a former cameraman) optically. Cast is generally well chosen. Script is tight and interesting, if a bit too talky and "stretched" at times. *Hans.*

Kroz Granje Nebo
(The Sky Through The Trees)
(YUGOSLAVIAN)

Pula, Aug. 12.

UFUS (Belgrade) production, directed by Stole Jankovic. With Branko Plesa, Predrag Lakovic, Ljuba Kovacevic and Nada Skrinjar. Screenplay, Antonije Isakovic; camera, Mihajlo Popovic; at Pula Film Festival. Running time, 98 MINS.

Patriotic (Tito period) subjects still play crucial part in Yugoslav's film making. This one deals with wounded freedom fighters who are desperately trying to evade German captivity as this means death. Film offers grim realism and, partly magnificent camerawork. There are several highly impressive shots. Though not much for the export, "Sky" may be classified as an above-average item from this "independent" Red State.

Direction by Mihajlo Popovic and also the script are not smooth all the way, but there is a strong plus in the acting. Less convincing are (as often in Yugoslavian features of this type) the Germans whose language is simply impossible, although home-market audiences won't be bothered. *Hans.*

Tri Koraka U Prazno
(Three Steps Into the Emptiness)
(YUGOSLAVIAN)

Pula, Aug. 12.

Lovcen-Film (Budva) production, directed by Vojislav Nanovic. With Zlata Perlic, Pavle Vujisic and Dragan Lakovic. Screenplay by Nanovic; camera, Milorad Markovic; music, . At Pula Festival. Running time, 92 MINS.

"Emptiness" created some fuss in its native land for alleged immorality. First forbidden and only released after several cuts, film is centered on a barge and presents an eternal triangle of two men and one woman. Woman married to one of the men, accepts the love of the other one. This leads to a violent and brutal fight between the two males, considered roughest ever for a Yugoslavian film.

Director Nanovic, who wrote the script, obviously followed American (violence) and French (erotic) patterns. His result is not very convincing. *Hans.*

Crni Biseri
(Black Pearls)
(YUGOSLAVIAN)

Pula, Aug. 12.

Basna-Film (Sarajewo) production, directed by Svetomir Janic. With Severin Bijelic, Mihajlo Viktorovic, Milan Ajvaz. Screenplay, Jug Grizelj; camera, Eduard Bogdanic; music, Bojan Adamic. At Pula Festival. Running time, 90 MINS.

This one deals with juvenile delinquents, Tito version. Unjust treatment and lack of understanding on the part of reform school director and instructors lead to a revolt of the boys. A young teacher manages to find the way to their hearts. There's a happy end. It's a well made film which, subject-wise, could also have chances outside its homegrounds.

There is a definite plus in the superior camerawork by Eduard Bogdanic. Of good quality also is Bojan Adamic's score.

Some of the moppets turn in fine performances. *Hans.*

Cesta Duga Godinu Dana
(The One-Year Long Road)
(YUGOSLAVIA-TOTALSCOPE)

Pula, Aug. 12.

Jadran-Film (Zagreb) production, directed by Giuseppe de Santis. Stars Silvana Pampanini. Features Eleonora Rossi-Drago, Massimo Girotti, Bert Sotlar, Gordana Miletic, Toni Vrdoljak, Niska Stefanini. Screenplay, De Santis, Maurizio Ferrara, Tomino Guerra, Elio Petri, Gianni Puccini, Mario Socrate; camera, Pasquale de Santis; music, Vladimir Kraus. At Pula Festival. Running time, 150 MINS.

Film is noteworthy as Yugoslavia's most expensive production (300,000,000 Dinar or $750,000) of all time and one year in the making. The names of Italian director Giuseppe de Santis, who, along with five other Italians, also worked on the script, plus the European marquee names of Silvana Pampanini, Eleonora Rossi-Drago and Massimo Girotti make this undoubtedly an important Yugoslavian production with, the unusual possibility: Export!

"Road" is considerably above-the-average if compared with the bulk of Yugoslavian product. Whether it will be able to gross enough to cover production costs, is certainly another question. One commercial handicap will be pic's overlength (150 mins.).

While "Road" represents a solid technical standard, many may not fancy De Santis mixing too generously social problems with cheap commercialism.

Story concerns the poor inhabitants of Zagora, a village located high up in the mountains. One of the men gets the idea that the building of a road to the valley would solve the problem of unemployment and poverty. After some

complications, he finds support. But the whole enterprise proves only a temporary solution.

The acting comes generally up to good standards and Pasquale de Santis' camerawork catches the atmosphere. Film captured the second prize at the recent Pula festival, a matter of some controversy in the Yugoslavian press. This is a film of divided qualities. *Hans.*

Rafal U Nebo
(Shots In The Sky)
(YUGOSLAVIAN)

Pula, Aug. 12.

UFUS (Belgrade) production, directed by Vojislav Vanja Bjenjas. With Bert Sotlar, Darinka Calenic, Pavle Vujisic. Screenplay, Bogdan Jovanovic; camera, Branko Ivatovic; music, Bojan Adamic. At Pula Festival. Running time, 91 MINS.

This one deals with the theme of revenge. A partisan lieutenant returns to his home after the war and finds that all his relations have been murdered by a Chetnik, a claimed sympathizer of the Nazi regime. He sets out to seek revenge by killing latter's family. He aims his machine gun at his enemy's children and parents, but suddenly realizes that they are innocent and shoots all his munition up into the sky.

Typical of recent Yugoslavian pix, this one benefits primarily from a superb camerawork. Acting tends to exaggeration. Direction is only fair. *Hans.*

Patterson-Harris Fight
United Artists Release of TelePrompter Corp. presentation. Produced by Mel Sawelson. Narrated by Chris Schenkel.

The film footage of the recent Floyd Patterson-Roy Harris heavyweight championship fight has been edited down to 18½ minutes to cover the highlights of Patterson's one-sided victory. In general, the action segments are forcefully delineated, but in other aspects the film is found wanting.

The editing and synchronization of Chris Schenkel's commentary with the action is a case in point. In one instance, Schenkel, describing the action, says the crowd is shouting and is on its feet. However, a panning shot of Wrigley Field. Los Angeles, shows the crowd sitting quietly and unperturbed.

The ending of the fight is another example of poor editing. Schenkel merely says that Patterson has been awarded a knockout after the 12th round and all the viewers see is Patterson exiting the ring. There is no shot of the official decision or of Patterson's arm being raised in victory.

On the asset side, however, are the slow motion shots which follow immediately after a particular flurry instead of being reprised at the end of the round. The average fan should enjoy the film account, although it's hoped that the producers will include the sound of the bell to signify the end of each round. *Holl.*

Ghost of the China Sea

Little action dualer.

Hollywood, March 28.

Columbia release of a Charles B. Griffith production. Stars David Brian; with Lynn Bernay, Jonathan Haze, Norman Wright; also Harry Chang, Gene Bergman, Kam Fong Chun, Mel Prestige, Jaime Del Rosario, Dan Taba, Bud Pente. Directed by Fred F. Sears. Screenplay, Charles B. Griffith; camera, Gilbert Warrenton; music, Alexander Laszlo; editor, Charles Nelson. Previewed at the studio March 31, '58. Running time, 73 MINS.

Martin French	David Brian
Justine Woolf	Lynn Bernay
Larry Peters	Jonathan Haze
Darby Edwards	Norman Wright
Hito Matsumo	Harry Chang
Sabatio Trinidad	Gene Bergman
Pvt. Hakashima	Kam Fong Chun
Gaetano Gato	Mel Prestige
Jaime Del Rosario	Jaime Del Rosario
Capt. Zaikaku	Dan Taba
Colonel McCutcheon	Bud Pente

Reviewed last March, only now released. "Ghost of the China Sea," in its 73-minute seance, fails to materialize as anything but a laggardly and somewhat boresome trip through the Philippines. A rualer.

Producer-writer Charles B. Griffith had an interesting idea in bringing together an embittered man and enough courageous souls to effect a change of heart. But the Columbia release pounds too hard, lacks even a dash of subtlety and sports too little action to make up for it. It was one of the last efforts for director Fred F. Sears and, though he tried hard, there was little that could be done.

"Ghost" of the title is a dilapidated boat, nicknamed the "U.S.S. Frankenstein," that carries David Brian and his wards away from the invading Japanese during World War II. The problems on hand include no food, no oil, no gasoline, no weapons. But enterprising Brian is up to it all and chases immediate danger to reach eventual safety. There's an effective tag to the opus, with Brian and three friends jumping into the Pacific after setting their boat afire to attract what they think is a

Dutch cruiser but turns out to be a Japanese craft. The British save the day, however, sinking the enemy and finding the allies.

Brian is rough and tough and not at all nice. He sees nothing good in those around him. And finally, when his followers act with courage, he's ready to change his feelings, and he does it quite capably. Lynn Bernay, as the only femme, is fine, with okay support from the rest of the cast.

Filmed with the cooperation of Polynesian Productions, Ltd. "Ghost" benefits from a good score by Alexander Laszlo. *Ron.*

Der Arzt Von Stalingrad
(The Doctor of Stalingrad)
(GERMAN)

Berlin, Aug. 19.
Divina production of Gloria release. Stars O. E. Hasse, Eva Bartok and Hans Messemer; features Mario Adorf, Walther Reyer, Vera Tschechowa, Paul Boesiger, Valery Inkijinoff, Leonard Steckel, Siegfried Lowitz. Directed by Geza von Radvanyi. Screenplay, Werner Zibaso, after novel by Heinz G. Konsalik; camera, Georg Krause; music, Siegfried Franz. At Marmorhaus, Berlin. Running time, **104 MINS.**

Have makers of this film ever been to Russia? This question comes up after having seen "Stalingrad" because too much rings untrue in vehicle. Pic may stir up considerable controversy, especially among those who had to live in Russian prison camps. But the Divina production has its favorable points, too. It tries to be objective and to avoid any cliches. So there are good and bad people on both sides. Film also says (at the end) that it was the Germans who started all that unholy hatred among both nations. Commercially, "Stalingrad" seems to have at least satisfactory b o. chances here.

Action takes place in a prisoner-of-war camp in Russia and centers around a German medico who's depicted as a good soul. He operates by means of a pocket-knife and helps wherever he can. The doctor also removes the brain tumor of the camp commander's son and that wins him the human friendship of his former enemies. Woven in is the love story of a Russian woman doctor and a German surgeon which, however, ends tragically. A large part of the public may like these scenes and perhaps the entire film but, seen through more critical eyes, this is nothing more than a prison drama of mediocre calibre.

Acting is partly very good, but "Stalingrad" gives clearly evidence of the old fact that even good actors cannot substitute an ample book or clean direction. Latter was in the hands of Hungarian-born (now Austrian) Geza von Radvanyi, and it is not very convincing, often being too conventional and stands no comparison with some of his earlier pix. Lensing by George Krause surpass this film's artistic qualities. *Hans.*

High School Hellcats

Exploitable teenager with high school background; to be packaged with "Hot Rod Gang."

Hollywood, Aug. 22.
American - International release of Charles Buddy Rogers production. Stars Yvonne Lime, Bret Halsey, Jana Lund; features Suzanne Sydney, Heather Ames, Nancy Kilgas, Rhoda Williams, Don Shelton. Directed by Edward Bernds. Story-screenplay, Mark and Jan Lowel; camera, Gilbert Warrenton, editor, Edward Samp-son. Reviewed Aug. 22, '58. Running time, **69 MINS.**

Joyce	Yvonne Lime
Mike	Bret Halsey
Connie	Jana Lund
Dolly	Suzanne Sydney
Meg	Heather Ames
Laurie	Nancy Kilgas
Miss Davis	Rhoda Williams
Martin	Don Shelton
Mrs. Martin	Viola Harris
Lt. Manners	Robert Anderson
Rip	Martin Braddock
Mr. Anderson	Arthur Marshall

Aimed at the teenage set, "High School Hellcats" should run up satisfactory grosses paired with "Hot Rod Gang" in package's intended market. There are enough exploitable ingredients to attract and topic has been handled with view to playing up these elements.

Buddy Rogers' production centers on a phase of life increasingly prevalent in the nation's schools, girl gangs. The Mark and Jan Lowel screenplay personalizes this in a transfer student to a high school where femmes are dominated by the gang leader. In the belief she won't be able to get along if he doesn't join, newcomer is drawn into a troubled existence climaxed by involvement in the death of leader at a party.

A fairly good pace is hit by Edward Bernds in his direction and performances generally are okay. Yvonne Lime acquits herself well as the new student, Jana Lund suffices as the gang leader and Rhoda Williams makes the most of an understanding teacher role. Bret Halsey displays a nice personality as Miss Lime's romantic interest who tries to help her through her trouble. Balance of cast fit more or less smoothly into their respective characters.

Expert technical credits are headed by Don Ament's art direction, Gilbert Warrenton's facile camera and Edward Sampson's tight editing. *Whit.*

Miercoles De Ceniza
(Ash Wednesday)
(MEXICO)

Berlin, Aug. 19.
Cinematografica Filmex (Mexico) production, directed by Roberto Galvaldon. Stars Maria Felix, Arturo de Cordova, Victor Junco, Maria Teresa Rivas, Rodolfo Landa, Andrea Palma and Maria Rivas. Screenplay, Luis G. Basurto, Julio Alejando and Roberto Galvaldon; camera, Agustin Martinez Solares; music, Antonio Diaz Conde. At Berlin Film Festival. Running time, **112 MINS.**

The best that can be said about this film is that it has, as nearly always in Mexican features, outstanding photography. Otherwise, film is on the dull side—mainly because of its endless talkiness. It should have, however, some commercial chances, particularly in Catholic-dominated countries since this is, almost entirely, a Catholic film. The names of Maria Felix and Arturo de Cordova also spell marquee value.

Attractive Maria Felix and Arturo de Cordova as well as the other players turn in adequate performances. But subject-matter is limiting. *Hans.*

Hot Rod Gang

Combines hot rod and rock 'n' roll action. Okay for younger audiences.

Hollywood, Aug. 22.
American-International release of Lou Rusoff production. Stars John Ashley, Jody Fair, Gene Vincent; features Steve Drexel, Henry McCann, Maureen Arthur, Gloria Grant, Dorothy Newman, Lester Dorr, Doodles Weaver. Directed by Lew Landers. Story-screenplay, Rusoff; camera, Floyd Crosby; editor, Robert S.

Eisen; music, Ronald Stein. Reviewed Aug. 22, '58. Running time, **71 MINS.**

John Abernathy the Third	John Ashley
Lois Cavendish	Jody Fair
Gene Vincent	Gene Vincent
Mark	Steve Drexel
Dave	Henry McCann
Marley	Maureen Arthur
Tammy	Gloria Grant
Anastasia Abernathy	Dorothy Newman
Abigail Abernathy	Helen Spring
Dryden Philpot	Lester Dorr
Wesley Cavendish	Doodles Weaver
Bill	Russ Bender
Agatha	Claire Dubray
Al Berrywhiff	Dub Taylor
Jack	Scott Peters
Jimmy	Robert Whiteside
Johnny Red Eye	Simmy Bow
Earl McDaniels	Earl McDaniels
Specialty Dancer	Kay Wheeler

"Hot Rod Gang" offers a combo hot rod-rock 'n' roll backdrop to draw aficionados in both these fields. If narrative rambles afield at times pic more than makes up for it in youthful action which will appeal to younger audiences, sum total spelling out the type of entertainment which elicits sequels.

Film is given a rock 'n' roll shot by appearance of recording artist Gene Vincent and his Red Caps, socking over several numbers including "Dance in the Streets." Script by Lou Rusoff, who also produces, deals with a young heir who must lead a very circumspect life to come into a fortune. Unbeknownst to the two maiden aunts with whom he lives and family attorneys, he has organized a hot rod gang and also a small r-r combo. Involved plot has him donning a disguise to join the Vincent group to earn coin for a de luxe hot rodder club he wants to build to enter into a national meet.

John Ashley makes a good impression as the lead, handily warbling a couple of songs headed by swing version of "Annie Laurie." Jody Fair, in for romance as daughter of one of the family attorneys, capably fulfills role and Vincent is strongly cast in his jazzbo character. Dorothy Newman and Helen Spring as the two aunts are dragged in for comedy, Doodles Weaver as Miss Fair's father is a standout in brief role and Steve Drexel, another recording artist, is competent as the heavy.

Lew Landers' direction keeps action hopping and is backed by capable technical assistance, including Floyd Crosby's photography, Ronald Stein's musical supervision, Don Ament's art direction and Robert S. Eisen's editing. *Whit.*

Stormy Crossing
(BRITISH)

Naive, rather dull second feature enhanced only by novel theme for murder, Channel swimming; routine acting and direction.

London, Aug. 19.
Eros release of Tempean production. Stars John Ireland, Derek Bond, Leslie Dwyer. Producer, Monty Berman. Directed by C. Pennington-Richards. Screenplay, Brock Williams from original story by Sid Harris and Lou Dyer; editor, Doug Myers; camera, Geoffrey Faithfull; music, Stanley Black. Previewed at Hammer Theatre, London. Running time, **72 MINS.**

Griff Parker	John Ireland
Paul Seymour	Derek Bond
Bill Harris	Leslie Dwyer
Shelley Baxter	Maureen Connell
Danny Parker	Sheldon Lawrence
Kitty Tyndall	Joy Webster
Inspector Parry	John Horsley
Doctor	Cameron Hall
Sam Rockett	Himself

This naive, dull little number may rate second billing in minor houses. It's a pity the pic isn't better fare because it has the service of some capable performers, and also has the merit of a novel back-ground for murder, a Channel swim setting. But the film offers no surprises and flounders through old-fashioned dialog and direction plus uninspired thesping.

Joy Webster is a fashion model, attempting to swim the English channel as a publicity gimmick. Also attempting this arduous, unrewarding chore is Sheldon Lawrence, a young Yank pro swimmer. Miss Webster has been having an affair with her boss and sponsor, a smooth character ably played by Derek Bond. When he wants to break off her clinging attentions, he hits on the ungentlemanly plan of gatecrashing the Cannel swim and drowning the shapely mermaid. By script coincidence, a fog makes his task easier.

Lawrence suspects that she has been murdered and Bond has to try the same murder lark on him. By this time, everybody's suspicions are aroused, even those of the police. Since the audience has seen Bond doing his dirty work, it merely has to settle back and wait for the time when he is rounded up.

As a basic idea there's nothing wrong with this and, in the right hands, quite a lot of tension might have been worked up. But Brock Williams' screenplay plods through incredibly trite dialog and Pennington-Richards has directed with no sense of pace, urgency or imagination. Small wonder that the actors walk through their parts as if waiting merely for pay day.

John Ireland and Leslie Dwyer are wasted in their roles as swimming trainers. Though some femme glamour is supplied by Miss Webster and Maureen Connell, neither contribute much in the way of acting. Ex-Channel swimmer Sam Rockett acted as technical adviser and plays himself in the film. His main contribution is to offer a few documentary remarks advising anybody in the audience who wants to swim the Channel how to set about it. Camerawork is adequate. But the location sequences at Dover are obviously the real thing and provide some refreshing atmosphere. *Rich.*

Foreign Films

Film concerns a natural samba composer, who cannot write music, but who is exploited by a man who passes his work off as his own. The samba writer has a rugged life but finds release and happiness in his songs. He is a Negro, but this does not make it a problem pic since there is no color line in Brazil. It is simply told and is backed by some fine music. He falls from a crowded train while composing a song and dies. Pic looks like a likely U.S. lingo entry but lacks the polish for arty house use. Acting and technical credits are good. *Mosk.*

This is reminiscent in theme of "Paths of Glory." It concerns a group of Slovak soldiers during the first World War who revolt against their leaders. The mutiny is crushed and the 44 men are executed. But this lacks the essential whiplash dramatics. It is more composite in flashbacks and developing characters as well as denoting why the Slovaks revolted against their treatment by Austro-Hungarian officers.

Film is patchy with some good action segments. It is too long, but cut down might be of program interest of for U.S. foreign language spots. Acting, technical qualities and direction are all okay.
Mosk.

Ewa Chce Spac (Eva Wants to Sleep) (POLISH). Polski State Film production and release. With Barbara Kiratkowsko, Tadeusz Mikulski, I. Benoit. Written and directed by Tadeusz Chuielewski. Camera, Josef Stawiski; editor, Roman Mann; music, Henryk Boyz. At Karlovy Vary Film Fest. Running time, **95 MINS.**

This film kids the serious side of Polski pix, being a deft satire about pompous bureaucracy, silly police and prostitution in review. Woven with the underworld goings-on is a love story between a girl looking for a place to sleep (she arrives too late for her school dorm) and a young policeman. Whitty visual gags and fine pacing make this a possibility for U.S. foreign language houses. Some of the illusions might be lost for those not hep to the Polski scene, but its light and entertaining proceedings might make this possible Yank dualer fare also. Acting, technical aspects and the well sustained direction and light vein of the pic all combine to make this a nice parody. Lilting musical score is also fine.
Mosk.

Vrci Jana (The Wolf Trap) (CZECHO-SLOVAKIAN). Czech State Film production and release. Stars Jana Brejchova, Jirina Sejbalova, Miroslav Dolezal. Screenplay, Jarmila Glazarova; camera, Vaclav Hanus; editor, Miroslav Hacek. At Karlovy Vary Film Fest. Running time, **90 MINS.**

Well thought out period piece of the 1920's, this is a subtle, restrained love story with a perfection in observation and execution right down the line. It is an offbeater with good art house chances in the U.S. Pic concerns an aging woman married to a much younger man and the love that grows between her young ward and her husband. The wife's over-endulging of her spineless spouse and the growing love are neatly counterpointed. A blending of interior and surface emotions in the thesps, a controlled mood and high technical virtuosity make this an outstanding film of its type.

Lone flaw is the somewhat over-drawn aspects of the spiteful, revengeful servants, but this is made up for by the taking qualities of the pic. It will be the Czech entry at the coming Venice Film Fest. This should make a good pic gambit for Western European marts as well as for possible chances in the U.S.
Mosk.

Rita (RUSSIAN). Riga Studios production and release. With I. Gulbe, E. Pavuls, V. Zandberg. Directed by A. Neretek. Screenplay, F. Knorre; camera, M. Rudzitis; editor, A. Skulte. At Karlovy Vary Film Fest. Running time, **90 MINS.**

Latvian-made pic is a competent war story about how a little girl

helps save four escaped war prisoners by hiding them right under the German's noses. It's interesting to note that the Russkis are beginning to show good German soldiers since one helps Rita escape from a collaborator. This is nicely made and escapes sentimentality. Technically it is solid, as is the acting. But for the U.S., this has little chance except for possible language spots.
Mosk.

Sobalvany (Pillar of Salt) (HUNGARIAN). Hunnia Film production and release. Stars Antal Pager; features Eva Ruttkay, Miklos Gabor, Anna Tokes, Iren Psota. Directed by Zoltan Varkonyi. Screenplay, Gabor Thurzo; camera, Istvan Pasztor; editor, Mihaly Morell. At Karlovy Vary Film Fest. Running time, **95 MINS.**

Picture concerns the coming of political and social age of a dedicated doctor who thinks only of his work. Some knowing direction and acting manage to partly humanize this. However, its early human drama ends as a political tract. The recent picketing of a Hungarian film in the U.S. makes this a chancey item for America at best. It is technically sound.
Mosk.

Bharat Mata (Mother India) (INDIAN; SONGS; COLOR). Columbia release of Mehboob production. Stars Nargis, Sunil Dutt; features Radj Kumar, Mukri, Shila Nayak. Directed by Mah Boob. Screenplay, Vahajat Mirza, Ali Raza; camera (Technicolor), Faridun Arani; editor, Naushad. At Karlovy Vary Film Fest. Running time, **120 MINS.**

Columbia has picked up an unabashed melodrama that is a saga of a woman who led a veritable dog's life after the beginning of a happy marriage. Her husband loses his arms working their land to pay off a greedy man they are sharecropping for. Her son turns out to be a wild one and kills their exploiter only to be slain by the mother for sullying her honor.

Pic is full of songs and dances. Interior-made exteriors are blended with the real. But this has a direct action flavor that could make this of curio interest for Yank special situations or even for more general dualers. Acting, except for the mother played by Nargis, is as outlandish as the plot. Color is good and technical aspects opulent.
Mosk.

Synnove Solbakken (The Girl of Solbakken) (SWEDISH; COLOR). Sandrews production and release. With Synnove Strigen, Gunnar Hellstrom, Harriet Anderson, Edvin Adolphson. Directed by Gunnar Hellstrom. Screenplay, Olle Mattson, Hellstrom; camera (Eastmancolor), Sven Nykvist; editor, Lennart Wallen. At Karlovy Vary Film Fest. Running time, **95 MINS.**

Earthy period piece deals with dramatic events among an elemental people. Fights are frequent as are love scenes, drunken orgies, etc. Main theme concerns an embittered man, incapable of affection, who almost ruins lives around him until he finally recants at a show of affection. Too overstated, this is strictly for U.S. exploitation usage, lacking the depth for arty spots. Color and location shooting help. Acting is competent as are technical standards.
Mosk.

Inquilino (The Tenant) (SPANISH). Delta production and release. Stars Fernando Fernan-Gomez, Maria Salgado; features Jose Davo, Paco Camoiras. Directed by Jose Nieves Conde. Screenplay, Manuel Caso, Jose Lozano, Nieves Conde;

camera, Francisco Sempere; editor, Margarita Ocha. At Karlovy Vary Film Fest. Running time, **95 MINS.**

The housing problem is handled for laughs here, and pic has a plus in its underlying note of seriousness and characterization. Though conventional on the surface this emerges with good general entertainment values.

This makes the film a possibility for Yank-Latino-language chances, but not much possibility for art circuits or general runs. Direction is witty and knowing. Acting and technical values are fine.
Mosk.

Apache Territory
(COLOR)

Routine oater spiced only by Rory Calhoun.

Hollywood, Aug. 26.

Columbia release of Rorvic Production, produced by Rory Calhoun and Victor M. Orsatti. Stars Rory Calhoun. Directed by Ray Nazarro. Screenplay, Charles R. Marion and George W. George, based on Frank Moss' adaptation of Louis L'Amour novel; camera (Eastman Color), Irving Lippman; editor, Al Clark. Previewed at the studio, Aug. 26, '58. Running time, **72 MINS.**

Logan Cates	Rory Calhoun
Jennifer Fair	Barbara Bates
Grant Kimbrough	John Dehner
Junie Hatchett	Carolyn Craig
Lonnie Foreman	Thomas Pittman
Zimmerman	Leo Gordon
Webb	Myron Healey
Sgt. Sheehan	Francis De Sales
Lugo	Frank De Kova
Conley	Reg Parton
Graves	Bob Woodward
Styles	Fred Krone

Little imagination apparently was poured into the title, "Apache Territory," and the Rorvic production itself is likewise of little unique interest. Trudging through the hot desert, however, is Rory Calhoun, whose ability as an actor is on the upswing, and the Columbia release appears oke hay for the horse market and an Eastman colorful lower-half oater in other situations.

Calhoun is a drifter, a loner, a saddle tramp, a man of ideals. He's rugged and capable of leading the hunted to safety, even if it does mean the majority bite the dust first. He finds himself commanding a variously composed group of citizens who are being sought by the Apaches and have taken refuge next to a desert well. Animosities run wild, jealously runs rampant and several of the clan run to their deaths before Calhoun leads a black-powder brigade to blow up the pursuing Indians during a blinding windstorm. The whole experience has taught him one thing—he's tired of being a bachelor—and he rides off with pretty Barbara Bates who was about to marry another but who loved Calhoun all the time.

Western was produced by Calhoun and Victor M. Orsatti, with the most favorable physical asset being Irving Lippman's Eastman Color lensing. Charles R. Marion and George W. George screenplayed from Frank Moss' adaptation of a Louis L'Amour novel. It's an adequate job, but the cliches—in situation, character and dialog—are obvious. The scripters have built an exciting climax, and Ray Nazarro's direction, fairly substantial all the way around, helps it along. There's even one point when nerves are tingled as a Gila monster and Calhoun try to outstare each other.

Thesping, topped by the star's good performance, is creditable, with fine jobs turned in by Miss Bates and John Dehner and capable performances by Carolyn Craig, Thomas Pittman, Leo Gordon, Myron Healey, Francis De Sales, Frank De Kova, Reg Parton, Bob Woodward and Fred Krone.

Art director Cary Odell made the interior sets look as if they were under the sun. Film editing by Al Clark and sound by Josh Westmoreland are competently handled.
Ron.

Blood of the Vampire
(BRITISH-COLOR)

Routine horror film, indifferently acted and written, which will satisfy horror addicts; b.o. potential for certain houses.

London, Aug. 26.

Eros release of a Tempean production. Stars Donald Wolfit, Barbara Shelley, Vincent Ball. Directed by Henry Cass. Screenplay, Jimmy Sangster; camera, Geoffrey Seahorne; editor, Douglas Myers; music, Stanley Black. At London Pavilion, London. Running time, **84 MINS.**

Callistratus	Donald Wolfit
Dr. John Pierre	Vincent Ball
Madeleine	Barbara Shelley
Carl	Victor Maddern
Kurt Urach	William Devlin
Wetzler	Andrew Faulds
Herr Auron	Bryan Coleman
Small Sneakthief	Hal Osmond
Tall Sneakthief	Bernard Bresslaw
The Judge	Colin Tapley
Chief Justice	John Le Mesurier
Meinster	Henry Vidon
Madeleine's Uncle	John Stuart
Drunken Doctor	Cameron Hall
Serving Wench	Yvonne Buckingham

With the current popularity of horror pix, "Blood of the Vampire" can be expected to clean up in undiscriminating theatres. In Britain, however, it is tagged with an "X" certificate, which means that no children under 16 may see it.

Donald Wolfit is a doctor executed in 1880 as a vampire and restored to life, with little explanation, by Victor Maddern, who plays a one-eyed hunchback. Meanwhile, Maddern is sentenced to life imprisonment for murdering a patient whom he was trying to save by blood transfusion.

He finds himself in a jail for the criminally insane, run by Wolfit. He is warned by another prisoner (William Devlin) about prison atrocities and finds he is signed up by Wolfit to assist him in blood tests on other prisoners. Wolfit is trying to find a man in his own blood group, so that he can free himself of the vampire strain. These rather silly proceedings involve a certain amount of torture and a pack of ferocious dogs.

There is not much in the direction, acting or dialog in this picture. It may well be that Jimmy Sangster, who has made a corner for himself in the British film horror stakes with his "Frankenstein" screenplays, is finding the field less fertile than awhile ago. Wolfit hams the role of the mad doctor with doggedness. Ball keeps a stiff upper lip through his ordeal. William Devlin, Barbara Shelley, John Stuart and Bryan Coleman turn in professional performances under unrewarding circumstances.

The best that can be said for "Vampire" is that the color-lensing of Geoffrey Seahorne is very effective. *Rich.*

Nattens Ljus
(Lights in the Night)
(SWEDISH)

Venice, Aug. 26.

Svensk Filmindustri production. Stars Marianne Bengtsson, Lars Ekborg; features Gunnar Bjornstrand, Birger Malmsten, Gosta Cederlund. Written and directed by Lars-Eric Kjellgren. Camera, Ake Dahlkvist; music, Lars-Erik Larsson. At Film Festival, Venice. Running time, **90 MINS.**

Maria	Marianne Bengtsson
Peter	Lars Ekborg

Offbeat Swedish pic possesses limited export chances. Film wants to be a fable about an innocent small town girl's first night in the big city, but only partly succeeds in its intent.

Result is an often charming but sometimes garbled vehicle in which the humor, at least to non-Nordic observers, is at times accidental and not where its ambitious author intended it. What value the pic has lies in the winning performance by Marianne Bengtsson. She combines a radiant youthful beauty with already mature acting assurance, adding still another name to the seemingly endless list of Swedish beauties of promising talent.

Film's technical qualities and other credits are good. *Hawk.*

Appointment With A Shadow
(C'SCOPE)

Routine handling of a crime melodrama. Double-bill bookings indicated.

Hollywood, Aug. 29.

Universal production and release. Stars George Nader, Joanna Moore, Brian Keith, Virginia Field; features Frank de Kova, Stephen Chase. Produced by Howie Horwitz. Directed by Richard Carlson. Screenplay, Alec Coppel, Norman Jolley; based on an Argosy story by Hugh Pentecost; camera, William E. Snyder; music supervisor, Joseph Gershenson; editor, George Gittens. Previewed at the studio, Universal City, Aug. 26, '58. Running time, **73 MINS.**

Paul Baxter	George Nader
Penny	Joanna Moore
Lt. Spencer	Brian Keith
Florence Knapp	Virginia Field
Dutch Hayden	Frank de Kova
Sam Crewe	Stephen Chase

"Appointment With A Shadow," which mixes crime melodrama with alcoholic rehabilitation, has an unusual theme but it is not developed to obtain much excitement or interest. Lacking, as well, any important names, the Universal production will find its bookings on double-bills as a routine program picture.

George Nader plays a booze-battered newspaper reporter who is given a chance to make a comeback by being the only newsman present when a notorious criminal is captured by police. Nader is present but discovers the wrong man is gunned down; the real fugitive has arranged it to cover his own escape. Nader's problem is then to convince police of their mistake, doubly difficult because of his own reputation as an unreliable drunk.

The simple, and acceptable, plot has been unhelpfully complicated by making the story also that of Nader's rejection of alcohol. It is possible, but dubious, that a confirmed alcoholic would be cured of his drinking compulsions by a single day's experience, which is the basic premise of this story. Technically, the screenplay, by Alec Coppel and Norman Jolley, based on a magazine story by Hugh Pentecost, makes the mistake of plunging the spectator into Nader's efforts to fight off his craving for drink before his character has been established. As a result, there can be little sympathy and only cursory interest in the problem of a character as yet undelineated.

Nader and the others in the cast, Joanna Moore, Brian Keith, Virginia Field, Frank de Kova and Stephen Chase, do well with their roles, considering the limitations.

Richard Carlson's direction is good on individual scenes although it seems to lack a cohesive, overall strength. Howie Horwitz produced. Technical credits are adequate. *Powe.*

Do Ankhen Barah Haath
(Two Eyes-Twelve Hands)
(INDIA)

Berlin, Aug. 26.

Rajkamal Kalamandir Private Ltd. (Bombay) production, directed by V. Shantaram. Stars V. Shanta Ram, Baburao Pendharkar, Sandhya and Ulhas. Screenplay, G. D. Madgulkar; camera, G. Balkrishna; music, Vasant Desai; narrator, G. D. Madgulkar. At Berlin Film Festival. Running time, **160 MINS.**

Feature from India is impressive (captured the Silver Bear, the second prize, in the feature film category at this year's Berlin Film Festival). Can be recommended everywhere. It benefits greatly from a skillful mixture of optical composition and harmonious music which often creates fascinating effects. Although the mentality of India is a barrier for the general market, film may still be a bet for special selected situations. It will appeal to quite a few, and fastidious customers.

Action centers around a jailer who believes in the good of every human being. He marches with six convicts to an uncultivated place and succeeds in wringing a rich harvest from the barren soil. More important, however, is the fact that he succeeds in making out of the notorious evil-doers (all murderers) into good and valuable human beings.

Technically as well as artistically, film can very well stand comparison with many a classy or arty European production. It's a refreshing departure from so many a cliche or run-of-the-mill production seen around here. *Hans.*

Der Greifer
(The Catcher)
(GERMAN)

Berlin, Aug. 26.

Deutsche Film Hansa release of Kurt Ulrich production. Stars Hans Albers; features Hansjoerg Felmy, Susanne Cramer, Horst Frank, Mady Rahl, Werner Peters, Siegfried Lowitz. Directed by Eugen York. Screenplay, Curt J. Braun; camera, Ekkehard Kyrath; music, Hans Martin Majewski. At UFA Palast, Berlin. Running time, **96 MINS**

This one has been tailored for vet trooper Hans Albers, still one of the top names in the German film industry. Although his performance isn't overwhelming as histrionic art, the Albers name makes this film a powerful b.o. contender here. However, it's probably too German to give it better than average chances outside the home market.

Story sees Albers playing a criminal inspector who is put on the retired list even before he finishes his last case. But he still feels himself very young. So he on his own he tracks down a notorious woman-killer.

Script has a number of flaws. It appears uneven often and towards the end, rather confusing. All in all, the pic not only lacks suspense but also falls considerably short of similar noted foreign pix.

This is Albers' film, and he surely makes the most of it. Good performances are also turned in by Werner Peters as a former underworld character and Siegfried Lowitz as ambitious criminal inspector who takes over Albers' job. Horst Frank is the psychopathic killer. Hans-Martin Majewski's score is good while Ekkehard Kyrath did a trim lensing job. *Hans.*

Cerny Prador
(The Black Battalion)
(CZECH)

Karlovy Vary, Aug. 26.

Czech State Film release and production. With Jaroslav Mares, Frantisek Peterka, Gunther Simon. Directed by Vladimir Cech. Screenplay, Kamil Pixa, Miroslav Fabera; camera, Rudolf Milic; editor, Antonin Zelenka. At Karlovy Vary Film Fest. Running time, **90 MINS.**

Film is a competently made actioner concerning the French Foreign Legion fighting in Indochina. It has a big measure of war brutality interlarded with the revenge of a Czech private on a lieutenant who turns out to be the German SS man who killed his family.

Feature has some jolting scenes but general characterization and progression are conventional. *Mosk.*

The Eighth Day Of The Week
(POLISH—GERMAN)

Story of young love against grim, sordid Polish backgrounds; sensitive production would need careful specialized selling in the U. S.

Venice, Aug. 26.

CCC Films—Arthur Brauner (Berlin) release of CCC-Film Polski co-production. Stars Sonia Ziemann, Zbigniew Cybolski. Directed by Alexander Ford. Screenplay, Ford and Marek Hlasko; camera, Jerzy Dipman; music, Kazimietz Serocki. At Venice Film Festival. Running time, **90 MINS.**

Agnieska	Sonia Ziemann
Piotr	Zbigniew Cybolski
Mother	Ilse Steppat
Father	Bum Kreuger
Gregorio	Tadeuzs Lomnicki
Elisabetta	Barbara Polomska

"The Eighth Day of the Week," a German - Polish coproduction filmed in Warsaw, had originally been entered for the Cannes festival, but was yanked under pressure by the Poles. Even now there is doubt as to whether it will be shown in Poland, or in any of the other eastern European countries. That, in fact, would need to be one of the main exploitation angles in selling the film, especially in the U.S. as it is a rather sombre and depressing piece of entertainment.

The Polish reaction is quite understandable. Life in Poland is portrayed as grim and sordid. Blitzed slums and decadent cafes and bars are the main locales; drowning one's sorrows in liquor seems to be one of the main pastimes, and there is no evidence of the cultural uplift of which the East European countries always boast.

Against this sleazy background is depicted a story of young love, in which Sonia Ziemann and Zbignew Cybolski long for a home of their own, but would happily settle for the use of a room where they could be alone for just a few hours. After experiencing endless frustrations, the girl gets drunk with someone she casually picks up in a bar, and allows herself to be seduced just at the moment when the boy has succeeded in getting an apartment.

Film was originally made in the Polish language, and that, it is understood, will be the version available for export. At Venice, a dubbed German version was screened, and the synchronization was unusually bad. That weakness, however, did not conceal the merit of Alexander Ford's sensitive and sincere direction in handling (as a Polish subject) a difficult subject with considerable social significance.

The two main characters dominate the entire film and carry off the story with commendable conviction. Miss Ziemann, a favorite German actress and the only member of the cast who is at all known in the west, plays the young girl with considerable feeling while Cybolski makes the young boy a tender and earnest character. The girl's nagging invalid mother and drunken brother are neatly etched by Ilse Steppat and Tadeuzs Lomnicki. But apart from the principals, none of the characters is completely developed. Technical credits are okay. Although the film is basically in monochrome, there is one scene in color. *Myro.*

Schab Neschini Dar Djahannam
(A Night in Hell)
(IRAN)

Berlin, Aug. 26.

Mehdi Missaghieh Film Studio (Teheran) production, directed by Samuel Khotschikian. Stars Wosugh, Rufia and Arhom Sadre. Screenplay, Mehdi Missaghieh; camera, Eneujatallah Famin; music, Del Kash. At Berlin Film Festival. Running time, 110 MINS.

This film is noteworthy for one reason: It's Iran's first contribution to any international film festival. As admitted by its producer himself, it doesn't stand any chance to compete internationally. That's just it. But, nevertheless, it may lure some curio-seekers. Pic is not dull, even amusing.

Story concerns a wealthy Persian money-lender who's a miser of the meanest type. But then he has a dream, and in his delirium, which leads him into the hell, he realizes that he's been doing wrong all his life. He changes and becomes a benefactor of the most generous type. (This type of situation is of ancient oriental fable origin).

There are roars of laughter when hell gets into the picture: Quite a few "celebrities," ranging from Adam and Eve, Julius Caesar, Napoleon and Adolf Hitler, show up. Another amusing highlight when some of the hell inhabitants give out with a rock 'n' roll-type dance. As primitive (both technically and artistically) the whole thing is, one cannot say that it lacks imagination.

Pic's producer said that this one is now the Number One moneymaker in his land and has collected already five times as much as negative cost. Iran, incidentally, has currently an annual output of seven to 10 features. *Hans.*

Boot Polish
(INDIAN)

Hoffberg Productions release of Raj Kapoor production. Stars Rattan Kumar, Baby Naaz, Kapoor. Directed by Prakash Arora. Screenplay, Kapoor; music Shankar Jakishaw. At Cameo Theatre, N.Y., Aug. 20, '58. Running time, 90 MINS.

Import from Bombay has cast names and credits unknown in the United States. But this much is for sure: it's an okay art theatre entry.

India is rarely heard from with a picture to play New York commercially. "Boot Polish," which has adequate titles, rates it though and the film is small in the usual production sense.

It follows the sometimes sad, sometimes humorous antics of a couple of impoverished and browbeaten children in the big city in appealing and sympathetic fashion, and the youngsters, Baby Naaz and Rattan Kumar, are remarkably fetching.

These two orphans, boy and girl, show a genuine tenderness in their love for each other, their sharing of misery as they are forced into begging by a despicable aunt and their feeling of triumph as they find themselves in the shoe-shining business. They have a good friend in Raj Kapoor, a vagabond type, but his encounter with the police causes their separation. They finally get to each other again in a particularly touching scene.

Kapoor wrote and produced and Prakash Arora directed. They've worked out a "little" picture but a competent one and the technical credits are fair enough. *Gene.*

Chaque Jour a Son Secret
(Every Day Has Its Secret)
(FRENCH)

Paris, Aug. 26.

Sonofilm release of Gray-Socipex production. Stars Jean Marais, Danielle Delorme, Francoise Fabian; features Denise Gence, Yven Brainville, Marcelle Praince. Directed by Claude Boissol. Screenplay, Paul Andreota, Pierre Larcohe, Boissol from novel by Maria-Luisa Linares; camera, Roger Fellous; editor, Louis Devaivre; music, Eddie Barclay. At Normandie, Paris. Running time, 85 MINS.

Xavier	Jean Marais
Olga	Danielle Delorme
Helene	Francoise Fabian
Housekeeper	Denise Gence
Inspector	Yves Brainville
Mother	Marcelle Praince

Mixture of mystery and melodrama spells a hokey pic made slickly enough for okay possibilities locally but with only mild dualer chances in the U.S. With its overtones of "Rebecca," this lacks the force, originality and persuasion to give it the offbeat ring it needs.

A woman who married a French explorer in South America and was lost in the wilds after a plane crash, comes to France to find her husband dead and her relatives acting strangely. Since she had been pronounced dead, her husband had remarried. She falls for the brother-in-law and the mystery is cleared up via the advent of a crazed housekeeper who had secretly loved the dead husband.

Acting is average with Jean Marais managing to give the film some edge as the weak brother who comes of age. Direction is slick if a bit listless while technical credits are par. It is glossy material with skimpy Yank chances. *Mosk.*

La Fille de Hambourg
(The Girl From Hamburg)
(FRENCH)

Paris, Aug. 26.

Pathe release of Univers production. Stars Daniel Gelin, Hildegarde Neff; features Daniel Sorano, Jean Lefebvre, Frederic O'Brady. Directed by Yves Allegret. Screenplay, Jose Benazeraf, Frederic Dard, Maurice Auberge; camera, Armand Thirard; editor, Claude Nicole. At Berlitz, Paris. Running time, 90 MINS.

Marian	Hildegarde Neff
Pierre	Daniel Gelin
Jean	Daniel Sorano
Georges	Jean Lefebvre
Barman	Frederic O'Brady

Pic appears somewhat dated in its story of a French prisoner of war who goes back to Hamburg 10 years later to find a girl who gave him cigarettes and hope to subsist. Film fails in its attempt at poetics and symbolism, and plods through its tale without any surprises.

Via some wild Hamburg nitery scenes, and a drawn-out love scene, in bed, this could shape as an exploitation film for the U. S. But it seems to lack the direction and depth in characterization for any arty theatre chances. The man turns out to be married and is ironically knifed for his dough by a petty hoodlum, while the girl commits suicide thinking he has left her to her degrading life of wrestling in the mud of a nitery, the prey to the smalltime hoodlums who come to the nightclub.

Missing the perception in direction, writing and acting, this lags and misses the needed irony. Hildegarde Neff appears listless throughout while Daniel Gelin can not put any weight to the happenings in spite of his obvious sincerity. Technical credits are good, but too much extreme wide-angle work and camera movement make viewing difficult at times. *Mosk.*

Foreign Films

Paris, Aug. 26.

Le Piege (The Trap) (FRENCH). Globe Omnium release of Globe-Electra production. Stars Raf Vallone, Magali Noel, Charles Vanel; features Roland Lesaffre, Betty Schneider. Directed by Charles Brabant. Screenplay, Jacques Marcerou, Andre Tabet, Roland Laudenbach; camera, Edouard Shuftan; editor, J. Feyte. At Balzac, Paris. Running time, 95 MINS.

Pic is a familiar melodrama of a fugitive on the run (killed a man by mistake) who meets up with love. He becomes a truckdriver while she is a waitress in a roadside restaurant. They plot to run off when the restaurant owner, an old man who desires the girl, finds out about the man's past. He blackmails them to get the girl, and she kills him in a fight to ironically thwart their plan to start a new life together.

Pic is tautly made with some exploitation angles via its strong sex scenes. But characters remain stereotyped. Despite neat acting, technical credits and okay direction, this is strictly a hypo item for Yank chances. *Mosk.*

En Legitime Defense (FRENCH). Paul Wagner production and release. Stars Bernard Blier, Philipe Nicaud, Maria Mauban; features Jean Lefevbre, Pierre Mondy. Directed by Berthomieu. Screenplay, Frederic Dard, Berthomieu; camera, Walter Wottitz; editor, Raymond Gaugier. At Le Francais, Paris. Running time, 95 MINS

This is a fair gangster pic about a cop and his buddy. The buddy runs a bar in Pigalle and kills an extorting gangster in self defense. He panics and runs off, but his friend, the cop, gets him back to face justice and also saves him from avenging hoods. Acting and technical credits are good. But this is conventional fare and only for possible Yank exploitation possibilities on its looksee at Pigalle lowlife and nightlife. *Mosk.*

Mon Coquin De Pere (My Darned Father) (FRENCH). Delux-Ifra Film production and release. Stars Claude Dauphin, Gaby Morlay, Antonella Lualdi; features Philipe Lemaire, Jean Wall. Directed by Georges Lacombe. Screenplay, Louis Martin, Serge Veber; camera, Roger Dormoy; editor, Denise Baby. At Marignan, Paris. Running time, 95 MINS.

Main aspect of this film is an adroit flashback culled from an old film, working in an incident in the youth of three characters now stylishly aged in the film. Otherwise it is an ordinary situation comedy about a seductive father who refuses to grow old and vies with his son for the hand of a young girl. Youth wins out in this. Flashback scene, of the meeting of the father with a girl, is the most imaginative part of the film. It is from Auguste Genina's "We Are No Longer Children," made in 1938. Acting is par as is the general makeup of the film, but it is of little Yank interest. *Mosk.*

Le Passager Clandestin (FRENCH-AUSTRALIAN; COLOR). Corona release of Silver - Discifilm - Southern International production. Stars Martine Carol, Karlheinz Boehm, Serge Reggiani; features Roger Livesey, Reginald Lye, Maea Flohr, Arletty. Directed by Ralph Habib. Screenplay, Maurice Auberge, Paul Andreota, Habib from novel by Georges Simenon; camera (Eastmancolor), Desmond Dickinson; editor, Monique Kirsanoff. At Biarritz, Paris. Running time, 145 MINS.

This garishly colored pic was shot in Tahiti. That is its main trump with the easygoing island habits and its scenery. Otherwise, this fairly hackneyed adventure yarn lacks the pace, mounting and acting to make color prints worthwhile for Yank chances.

A big hearted prostie (Martine Carol) stows away on a ship with the aid of a young officer in love with her. She is trying to join an ex-love in Tahiti. After some telegraphed proceedings the two adventurers are killed off, and Miss Carol falls for her sailor. Ralph Habib's cliche-ridden direction does not help instill life into this. Miss Carol walks through this listlessly and shows some rounded anatomy at times. Serge Reggiani and Roger Livesey are fine as the fortune hunters. *Mosk.*

L'Ecole Des Cocottes (School for Coquettes) (FRENCH). Pathe release of Metropolitaines Films release. Stars Dany Robin, Fernand Gravey, Bernard Blier; features Robert Vattier, Odette Laure, Darry Cowl. Directed by Jacqueline Audry. Screenplay, Pierre Laroche from play by Paul Armont and Marcel Gerbidon; camera, Marcel Grignon. At Marignan, Paris. Running time, 110 MINS.

Turn-of-century bedroom shenanigans are handled with tact; hence, this emerges one of those naughty bedroom farces which the French can bring off without being objectionable. On this score, this could be a good specialized item for American chances.

Pygmalion theme traces the rise of a bright, little coquette from an affair with a headstrong pianist to becoming the toast of Paris. But she longs for those old carefree days and finds she can not escape her dreary destiny of being so in demand.

Director Jacqueline Audry has given this some good period atmosphere and movement to underline the fluffy aspects of the times. Though its final dramatic threads are weakened by the too sketchy rise of the girl to affluence, it has some okay acting and good production values. *Mosk.*

Cheri, Fais Moi Peur (Honey, Scare Me) (FRENCH). Pathe release of Cyclope production. Stars Darry Cowl; features Tilda Thamar, Sophie Daumier, Pierre Mondy, Jacques Dufilho. Directed by Jack Pinoteau. Screenplay, Jacques Vilfrid, Jean Aurel, Jean Girault; camera, Andre Bac; editor, Georges Arnstam. At Balzac, Paris. Running time, 90 MINS.

Pic is a slapstick cocktail piled up around a flock of proven comedy gambits. There are the Russo and Yank spies fighting over something in the hands of the madcap hero, rapacious women, the ingenue, and plenty of chases. This has a fair share of laughs but they come at the end when they lack punch due to the conventional, lacklustre beginning.

Comic Darry Cowl is now developing a definite screen presence and may yet be able to carry a pic, provided he gets more directorial and script backing than he does here. Technical credits are good but gags are overworked. For America, this is strictly for dualers.
Mosk.

La Bigorne, Caporal de France (FRENCH; DYALISCOPE; COLOR) Lux release of Edic Film production. Stars Francois Perier, Rossana Podesta; features Robert Hirsch, Henry Cogan, Jean Lefevbre, Jean Carmet. Directed by Robert Darene. Screenplay, Gabriel Arout, Darene from novel by Pierre Nord; camera (Eastmancolor), Marcel Weiss; editor, Germaine Artus. At Triomphe, Paris. Running time, 90 MINS.

In a C'Scope-like process, this is a kidding historical version of how a handful of French soldiers got France some of its island colonies in the 18th century. In this film, it was done by outwitting some pirates and marrying a convenient halfbreed daughter of a native chief.

It might not be so funny here with Algeria still touchy, but it appears primarily a local bet. Its fights and action are only so-so in the imagination department and thesping is only par. Main trump is the savvy on-the-spot lensing.
Mosk.

Ibo Kyodal (Stepbrothers) (JAPANESE). Nikkatsu production and release. With Tanaka, Kito. Directed by Mioji Iyeki. Screenplay, Y. Yoda, N. Terada; camera, Yoshio Miyajima; editor, Y. Akutagawa. At Karlovy Vary Film Fest. Running time, 95 MINS.

This problem pic castigates the military mind via a tale about a martinet career officer who marries his maid after his wife dies. Well observed and played, with a good subject and exposition, this still remains somewhat specialized for any U.S. chances except in lingo spots.
Mosk.

Houseboat

Warm comedy with good box-office appeal in Cary Grant and Sophia Loren.

Hollywood, Sept. 5.

Paramount release of Paramount-Scribe production, produced by Jack Rose, directed by Melville Shavelson. Stars Cary Grant, Sophia Loren; features Martha Hyer, Harry Guardino, Eduardo Ciannelli. Screenplay by Shavelson & Rose; camera, Ray June; editor, Frank Fracht; music, George Duning. Previewed Aug. 21, '58. Running time, 112 MINS.

Tom Winston	Cary Grant
Cinzia Zaccardi	Sophia Loren
Caroline Gibson	Martha Hyer
Angelo	Harry Guardino
Arturo Zaccardi	Eduardo Ciannelli
Alan Wilson	Murray Hamilton
Elizabeth Winston	Mimi Gibson
David Winston	Paul Petersen
Robert Winston	Charles Herbert
Mrs. Farnsworth	Madge Kennedy
Mr. Farnsworth	John Litel
Harold Messner	Werner Klemperer

The voyage of "Houseboat" is to a nearly extinct era in motion pictures when screens and hearts bubbled over with the warmth of original family humor. Wholly new and superbly lensed, it is, by all means, a welcome return trip, captained by Cary Grant who will have little trouble guiding the Paramount film to a welcome return at the boxoffice. "Houseboat" also should be the first financially successful American film excursion for Sophia Loren, strange in that it's mostly a "woman's picture."

The beauty of "Houseboat," as conceived and executed by Mel Shavelson and Jack Rose, is the beauty of a growing love and understanding, of an outsider's "intrusion" to help the emotions along and of the lightness yet importance with which the conflicts are handled.

It's a perfect role for Grant, who plays a government lawyer separated from his wife and who, upon her accidental death, is brought into contact with his three children, none of whom are very friendly toward him. The two boys and the girl, in fact, rebel against him, but the now-patient father is determined to straighten out their neuroses and gain their love at the same time. Enter Miss Loren, a full-blown lass with lovely knees who's been kept in tow by her father, a noted Italian symphony conductor, and who takes the first chance to get away from it all. Grant, though he takes her for a tramp, hires her as a maid at seeing her ability to handle his children upon first meeting. Off goes everyone to the country, and when their intended home, being moved to the Potomac, is struck by a train, the crew boards a decrepit houseboat, puts it in a state of repair, and through living together begin to understand and love each other. This, of course, also goes for the two adults (by now, he's noticed her knees) and it all ends merrily in a shipboard wedding ceremony attended en masse by the reconditioned children.

Grant mixes concern with disconcern and says more with a head tilt than most residents of situation comedy are able to say with an entire script. He may not always understand his children, but he's certain to keep filmgoers on his side while he's trying. Miss Loren continues to act better in irate Italian than in emotional English, but, despite a physical appearance that overcomes any inner talents, she is believable and sometimes downright warm as the lover of Grant and his children.

Harry Guardino is outstanding

as a fiery wolf who will take anything but a wife, and, with this role, steps up a notch in proving himself a top film actor. Martha Hyer, becoming typed as the rich "other" woman, is, as always, beautiful and skillfully competent. Eduardo Ciannelli is fine as Miss Loren's father, and Murray Hamilton is very good as Grant's military friend.

As one might expect, the moppets—Mimi Gibson, Paul Petersen and Charles Herbert—steal the show. Miss Gibson portrays a childish fear with finesse; Petersen makes his "wrong path" well traveled; and Herbert is a real hijacker of audiences' hearts.

Rose, who produced, and Shavelson, who directed, scripted "Houseboat" from their original story. It's light and happy all the way round, and it's put together with taste. There's corn, to be sure, but the bin hasn't been filled to capacity.

Technically, the film is excellent. Ray June's Technicolor-Vista-Vision photography is artistic, and there are fine shots of Washington, D.C. .

One of film's top attributes is its musical score—a colorful, frothy creation by George Duning. And the two Jay Livingston-Ray Evans tunes—"Almost in Your Arms" and "Bing, Bang, Bong"—are catchy enough to give "Houseboat" an extra shove.
Ron.

Sea Fury
(BRITISH)

Thrills and romance on sea and land. Good solid performances, a piquant heroine and hefty storm sequences add up to holding entertainment.

London, Aug. 26.

Rank release of Ben Fisz production. Stars Stanley Baker, Victor McLaglen, Luciana Paluzzi. Directed by C. Raker Endfield. Screenplay, John Kruse and C. Raker Endfield; camera, Reginald Wyer; editor, Arthur Stevens; music, Philip Green. At Odeon, Leicester Square, London, Aug. 26. Running time 97 MINS.

Abel	Stanley Baker
Bellew	Victor McLaglen
Josita	Luciana Paluzzi
Fernando	Gregoire Aslan
Mulder	Francis de Wolff
Blanco	David Oxley
Loudon	George Murcell
Walker	Percy Herbert
Bosun	Rupert Davies
Gorman	Robert Shaw
Salgado	Roger Delgado
Vincent	Barry Foster
Hendrik	Joe Robinson
Kelso	Dermot Walsh
Kershaw	Richard Pearson
Doc	Fred Johnson
onkeyman	Jack Taylor

"Sea Fury" is an entertaining blend of sea adventure and romantic intrigue on land. There are very sound performances, a fascinating Spanish background and the pic represents a worthwhile booking for most houses.

Off the Spanish coast, two tugs, one British, the other Dutch, compete for prize money gained by the dangerous job of salvaging wrecks off the Spanish coast. Stanley Baker, a first mate, gets a job as a deckhand on the "Fury," skippered by Victor McLaglen. When McLaglen's first mate dies and Baker is promoted to second officer, he antagonizes the crew of the "Fury."

Meanwhile, despite his years, McLaglen is infatuated by Luciana Paluzzi, a beautiful young Spanish girl. Her father insists on her becoming affianced to McLaglen, for his money. But she and Baker are drawn together. She is in the tricky position of having to defy

her father. He is in the even tougher spot of having to double-cross his fiery-tempered skipper.

This romantic intrigue, while entertaining, should be merely a background to the drama at sea, but it takes a long while for the sea thrills to work up and the doings on land tend to dominate too much of the film. Nevertheless, when the big sea sequence does come it fairly bursts on to the screen and will have audiences biting nails with tension. In a tremendous storm the "Fury" sets off to rescue a valuable abandoned ship. It is loaded with sodium which is likely to explode at any moment. Baker courageously leaps on to the floundering ship, makes the towline fast and then makes the sodium cargo safe. Here the storm effects are wonderfully realistic and the excitement flares.

There are some hefty fist fights, salty dialog and one very saucy scene when Miss Paluzzi visits McLaglen's ship and drives him to near desperation as, behind a screen, she changes into the undies and gown that he has given her as a present.

McLaglen's craggy personality, sometimes riproaring, sometimes engagingly kind and simple, dominates the scenes in which he appears. Baker gives a straightforward, virile performance as the hero and Luciana Paluzzi, a Continental actress, is an appealing dish. An assortment of sailors are played by a number of sound British supporting actors and Roger Delgado as Miss Paluzzi's oily father and Robert Shaw, as Baker's chief enemy, give excellent portrayals.

Reginald Wyer's lensing makes the most of the Spanish locations, and the storm sequences, and those faked in the studio, are most effective. In short, "Sea Fury" is a useful p...e of its type, which might h...n even better had the st... ...dered a shade leisurely at the beginning. *Rich.*

Villa!!
(COLOR—C'SCOPE)

Physical values highlight this handsome outdoor actioner, best aimed at oater markets.

Hollywood, Sept. 5.

20th-Fox release of Plato Skouras production. Stars Brian Keith, Cesar Romero, Margia Dean; costars Rudolfo Hoyos. Directed by James B. Clark. Screenplay, Louis Vittes; camera (De Luxe Color), Alex Phillips; music, Paul Sawtell & Bert Shefter; editor, Benjamin Laird. Previewed Sept. 5, '58. Running time, 72 MINS.

Harmon	Brian Keith
Fierro	Cesar Romero
Julie	Margia Dean
Villa	Rodolfo Hoyos
Mariana	Rosenda Monteros
Gabe	Carlos Muzquiz
Manuela	Elisa Loti
Tenorio	Enrique Lucera
Capt. Castillo	Jose Trevino
Don Alfonso	Rafael Alcayde
Pajarito	Mario Navarro
Posado	Jose Espinoza
Rancher	Lee Morgan
Don Octavio	Felix Gonzalez
Bailarina Flamenca	Gisela Martinez
Colonel	Jose Trowo
Carlos	Raphael Sevilla Jr.
Perez	Lamberto Gayou
Abraham Gonzalez	Jose Lopez
Mujer Elegante Tren	Angelina Regis
Ballarin	Carlos Guarneros
Teniente Rural	Jorge Russek
Alcalde	Eduardo Pliego

"Villa!!" is a Plato Skouras production for 20th-Fox, and although it is obviously a budget picture it has been skillfully done in some areas so that it appears a bigger presentation than the money that went into it. It is an action picture that concentrates on the more romantic aspects of the Mexican revolutionary's career. Handsomely photographed on Mexican locations in CinemaScope and DeLuxe Color, James B. Clark has directed with an eye to the outdoor market where it will find its most ready acceptance.

Louis Vittes' screenplay picks up Villa, played by Rudolfo Hoyos, when he was still a smalltime bandit. His chief lieutenant, Cesar Romero, and he are joined by an American, Brian Keith, shortly before his banditry is put to the service of Mexican patriots attempting to overthrow the feudal landowners. His final conversion comes when he meets the men intent on overthrowing the government to bring land to the peons. It is helped by the savage treatment given his family and other peasants by the hacienda owners.

Hoyos makes a sympathetic Villa, playing with intelligence as well as the unlettered vigor that apparently was characteristic of the man. His boisterous side is shown in romantic episodes, chiefly with Margia Dean, latter appealing as an American singer. Keith's role is that of a gun-runner who becomes concerted to Villa's cause, and Romero contributes some humor with his swashbuckling portrayal.

"Villa!!" does not have the impact it might if its script had been more incisive in the delineation of the title character. The romance between Keith and Miss Dean seems an intrusion and an unnecessary one that does nothing to forward the action, slowing it rather. With this diversion and the episodic nature of the screenplay, it is not always clear exactly what Villa and his fellow compatriots were up to and why.

A plus factor is the photography by Alex Phillips, especially in some stirring action shots. The Paul Sawtell-Bert Shefter music is also militant, underlining the important passage. Other technical credits, including Benjamin Laird's editing, are good. *Powe.*

The Blob
(COLOR-SONG)

Exploitable science-fiction entry for juvenile market; good prospects.

Paramount release of a Jack H. Harris production. Stars Steven McQueen; co-stars Aneta Corseaut, Earl Rowe. Directed by Irvin S. Yeaworth Jr. Screenplay, Theodore Simonson and Kate Phillips, from idea by Irvine H. Millgate; camera (DeLuxe Color), Thomas Spalding; music, Jean Yeaworth; song, Bert Bachrach, Mack David; editor, Alfred Hillmann. Tradeshown in N.Y., Sept. 4, '58. Running time, **85 MINS**
Steve .... Steven McQueen
Judy .... Aneta Corseaut
Police Lieut. .... Earl Rowe
Old Man .... Olin Howlin

With the science-fiction cycle still in orbit, "The Blob" has good good prospects of turning a profit for both its producer and distributor. Film has a cast of unknowns, but its exploitable angles will be sufficient to stir up interest among sci-fi fans and younger filmgoers.

Picture is the initial production of Jack H. Harris, a regional distrib in the Philadelphia area who plans a series of similar pix to cash in on what he believes is a strong market for such product.

with "The Blob" budget a reported $240,000 and with Paramount handling distribution, comfortable returns seem assured.

Story, which Theodore Simonson and Kaye Phillips screenplayed from an idea by Irvine H. Millgate, will tax the imagination of adult patrons. However, the dialog and most of the situations are tailored to the teenage set and they should reciprocate at the wicket.

A small Pennsylvania town has been plagued by teenage pranks. Hence, when highschoolers Steven McQueen and Aneta Corseaut report that a parasitic substance from outer space has eaten the local doctor and his nurse, no one will believe them. Especially when no bodies can be found. Of course, this menacing purple substance later makes itself apparent and the authorities take steps to halt the holocaust. ("Purple People Eater" would have been a natural for a tag).

Neither the acting nor direction of Irvin S. Yeaworth Jr. is particularly creditable. McQueen, who's handed star billing, makes with the old college try while Miss Corseaut also struggles valiantly as his girlfriend. Routine support is provided by Earl Rowe and Olin Howlin in lesser roles.

Star performers, however, are the De Luxe color camerawork of Thomas Spalding and Barton Sloane's special effects. It's apparent that much of the budget went into this area. Production values otherwise are geared to economy. Music of Jean Yeaworth helps sustain a suspenseful mood which could have been heightened if 10 or 12 minutes were sliced from the running time. Other technical credits are standard.

Intriguing is the title number, written by Bert Bachrach and Mack David. It's sung offscreen by a harmony group as the credits unreel. Novelty tune has been cut on such labels as MGM and Dot and obviously is a potential biz stimulator. Picture, incidentally was lensed at the Valley Forge, Pa., studios. *Gilb.*

To Nhei the Equeh
(The Island of Silence)
(GREEK)

Venice, Sept. 2.

Messaglos release and production. Stars Orestis Macris, Nina Sguridou, Giorgio Cabanellis; features, Giannis Sparidis, Tzanis Courcoulakos. Directed by Lila Courcoulacou. Screenplay, Vanghelis; camera, N. Gardelis; editor, G. Tsaoulis. At Venice Film Fest. Running time 80 **MINS**.

Manolis ....Orestis Macris
Angela ....Nina Sguridou
Doctor ....Giorgio Cabanellis
Anestis ....Giannis Sparidis
Sistis ....Tzanis Courcoulakos

Pic deals with a touchy background of a leper colony on an island off the Greek mainland. It is fairly primitive technically but handles its ticklish subject with taste and sometimes makes its theme ring with deep flashes of insight.

But on the whole the pic is too meandering and ordinary for other than lingo spots in the U.S. It does not have much exploitation possibilities either. It tells how a femme and male doctor manage to get needed cures into effect to help the banished peoples. Thesping, direction and technique are

all wanting but are helped by a definite note of sincerity. *Mosk.*

Otarova Vdova
(Otar's Widow)
(RUSSIAN-COLOR)

Venice, Sept. 1.

Soviet release of Grusia Film production. Stars Veriko Angiaparidze, G. Scenghelaia; features Andronikashvili, Zhorzholani. Directed by Mikail Ciaureli. Screenplay, Ciaureli and A. Belianshvili; camera, (Sovcolor) D. Kandelaki, D. Feldman; music, S. Sinzadze. At Film Festival, Venice. Running time, 75 MINS.
Otar's Widow ......Veriko Angiaparidze
Gheorgi ....G. Scenghelaia

Oldfashioned, heavyhanded handling of a similarly dated story make this Soviet item hard to take for any audience. Add the propagandistic undertones which abound throughout, and you have few if any redeeming features. No export interest whatsoever.

Nor is casting euch better, with four principals walking through their roles in energetic but empty fashion. More than a story of Otar's widow, who sees her son live and die before her, it's about the son's unhappy love for the rich princess on whose land he works, and who only realizes this infatuation after he is killed in a fall. Soviet dictums are often mouthed in soliloquy by the characters. Color is occasionally excellent, especially in Georgian exteriors, but at other times very irregular in quality. *Hawk.*

The Man Inside
(BRITISH—C'SCOPE)

Cops-and-robbers chase story with some tension, comedy and good marquee names; brisk entertainment for most audiences.

London, Sept. 1.
Columbia release of a Warwick (Harold Huth) production. Stars Jack Palance, Anita Ekberg, Nigel Patrick. Directed by John Gilling. Screenplay, John Gilling, David Shaw, from novel by M. E. Chaberi camera, Ted Moore; editor, Bert Rule; music, Richard Bennett. At New Victoria, London. Running time, 97 MINS.
Milo March .... Jack Palance
Trudie Hall .... Anita Ekberg
Sam Carter .... Nigel Patrick
Ernesto .... Anthony Newley
Martin Lomer .... Bonar Colleano
Rizzio .... Sean Kelly
Franklin .... Sidney James
Organ-grinder .... Donald Pleasence
Tristao .... Eric Pohlmann
Stone .... Gerard Heinz
Lopez .... Alec Mango
Girl on Train .... Anne Aubrey
English Husband .... Bill Shine
English Wife .... Joan Ingram
Jane Leyton .... Naomi Chance
Desk Clerk, Lisbon.......Maxwell Shaw

"The Man Inside" could have been an absorbing psychological peek into the mind of a humble little man, vain as a peacock, who aspires to riches, power and the love of beautiful women. He is ready to rob and murder to satisfy his ambitions. But any such subtlety has been tossed away in favor of a routine cops-and-robbers chase yarn. As such, it has some suspense, some comedy and two or three capable performances. It offers brisk entertainment and its stellar appeal should make it a safe booking for all audiences.

For 15 years Nigel Patrick has been a depressed clerk, coveting a famous diamond. Patiently, he waits his chance and by cunning (and a killing) steals the rock. He blossoms out as a cosmopolitan man-about-Europe. Jack Palance is a private sleuth, hired to track

down Patrick. Soon Palance, Anita Ekberg (she claims the jewel rightfully belong to her family), and Sean Kelly and the late Bonar Colleano, a coupla murderous thugs, are all hot after Patrick and the stone.

The trail begins in N. Y. and carries on endlessly through Lisbon, Madrid, Paris and London, leaving a trail of skulduggery and murder before Patrick gets his chips, Scotland Yard gets the rock and Palance gets Miss Ekberg. The screenplay is too predictable and there are too many directorial loose ends for "The Man Inside" to achieve the tension that it might have done. However, there is sufficient incident to keep an audience mildly amused.

The two best performances come from Patrick and Anthony Newley. The former gives a suave, dapper show, and it is a pity that his character has not been developed. Newley, who came to the fore in "Oliver Twist," when a kid actor, has developed into a splendid character comedian. In this pic, he plays an ingratiating Madrid cab driver, with a disarming eye for a pretty girl and a genius for avoiding trouble. This is a rich, amusing performance and mops up most of the comedy opportunities.

Palance, electing to play the dick with a vacant eye and a permanent, vapid grin, is adequate as the tough, patient pursuer while Miss Ekberg has little to do but look shapely, which she achieves with a minimum of effort. Colleano, in his last role before his death in a car crash, and Kelly provide icy menace as the thugs. Sidney James, Donald Pleasence and Eric Pohlmann are among the supporting artists who chip in with sturdy cameos.

Ted Moore and Cyril Knowles do sound work with their cameras and audiences get some tantalizing glimpses of world capitals in the chase scenes. There are a couple of songs, "The Man Inside" and "Trudie," neither of which seem destined to be hits. *Rich.*

Damn Yankees
(COLOR)

Top filmization of Broadway musical. Should do very well on popularity of original stage version alone.

Hollywood, Sept. 9.

Warner Bros. release of a George Abbott-Stanley Donen production. Produced and directed by Abbott and Donen. Stars Tab Hunter, Gwen Verdon, Ray Walston; features Russ Brown, Shannon Bolin, Nathaniel Frey, Jimmie Komack, Rae Allen, Robert Shafer, Jean Stopleton, Albert Linville. Associate producers, Frederick Brisson, Robert Griffith, Harold Prince. Screenplay, George Abbott, based on play, "Damn Yankees," with book by Abbott and Douglass Wallop, from Wallop's novel, "The Year the Yankees Lost the Pennant." Music and lyrics by Richard Adler and Jerry Ross; camera (Technicolor), Harold Lipstein; editor, Frank Bracht; production and costumes designed by William and Jean Eckart; choreography, Bob Fosse; main titles, Maurice Binder. Previewed at the studio, Sept. 9, '58. Running time, 110 MINS.

Joe Hardy .... Tab Hunter
Lola .... Gwen Verdon
Applegate .... Ray Walston
Van Buren .... Russ Brown
Meg .... Shannon Bolin
Smokey .... Nathaniel Frey
Rocky .... Jimmie Komack
Gloria .... Rae Allen
Joe Boyd .... Robert Shafer
Sister .... Jean Stapleton
Vernon .... Albert Linville

The "Damn Yankees" team, which ran the score high for three seasons in Broadway's legit ballpark, has been reassembled to go to bat in a sparkling Technicolored film version. Lack of "big name" draw could keep the George Abbott-Stanley Donen production from going into extra innings in some spots, but it does loom as a crackling musical comedy hit in the domestic markets for Warner Bros. It's also likely to project Gwen Verdon and Ray Walston into major star status on the screen.

Sole "newcomers" in the trek from Broadway to Burbank are Donen, who co-produced and co-directed the film with Abbott, and Tab Hunter, who stars. That 10 of the top 11 players, plus creators from writer to costume designer, have been transferred enmasse from Broadway just about insures a film that is at least as good as its stage counterpart.

What stands out like an inside-the-park home run is the skill and inventiveness with which the film is coated, thus making "Damn Yankees" a funny picture. Multiple-picture sequences mark high points in clever screen techniques, and Maurice Binder's bristling main titles put the hex of fun on the production, with only infrequent pauses coming in the following 110 minutes.

Story, based on the Faust legend and Douglass Wallop's novel, "The Year the Yankees Lost the Pennant," revolves around a Washington Senator fan who would give his soul for a long-ball hitter and a chance to beat the New York Yankees. Given his chance by the devil himself, the fan is wooshed into a 22-year-old who proceeds to become the national hero of the national pastime in the national capital, thus giving the Senators a pennant and the Yankees a bad name.

Gwen Verdon makes a sprightly 172-year-old witch who has been sumptuously embodied to stalk Tab Hunter. Her eccentric dancing and singing are stylishly engrossing, and her zany comedy adds to the screen one of its finest new comediennes. Walston, with exaggerated widow's peak and devilish red accessories, makes a perfect comedy Satan. Whereas much of the action is superficial, Walston does a great job of tying up loose ends and moving the satire to its logical conclusion. Hunter is sympathetic as the young baseball great, confused by all that's happening to him. His role requires less talent to pull off than do those of his costars, but the ability with which he does it is no less effective.

Rest of the cast is excellent, with fine work from Russ Brown, Shannon Bolin, Nathaniel Frey, Jimmie Komack, Rae Allen, Robert Shafer, Jean Stapleton and Albert Linville.

Still held in prominence is the Richard Adler-Jerry Ross musical score—a tuneful, storytelling assortment of gag songs and ballads. Top production goes to "Two Lost Souls" (a la "Hernando's Hideaway" from same pair's "Pajama Game") and "Shoeless Joe from Hannibal, Mo." (which proves the Washington Senators, if not always for the best in baseball, are mighty good at terping). "You've Gotta Have Heart" remains a standout, and "Those Were the Good Old Day's" in a satirical routine, scoring with a seductive "Whatever Lola Wants," a highly amusing "A Little Brains, a Little Talent, and a fast-moving "Who's Got the Pain," danced with choreographer Bob Fosse, himself a fine hoofer.

To add to the original score—which also includes "Goodbye, Old Girl," "Six Months Out of Every Year" and the strains of "The Game"—is one new tune, "The Empty Chair," a sorrowful creation that looks to make little impression.

Abbott, who co-authored the stage book, has screenplayed with pointed accuracy, and he and Donen have put together an alluring package. Legit producers Frederick Brisson, Robert Griffith and Harold Prince are credited as associate producers. William and Jean Eckart effectively designed the production and costumes for the film, as they did for the stage version, and Fosse choreographed with spirit all the way through.

To put "Damn Yankees" on film, cinematographer Harold Lipstein has made excellent use of camera, lighting and color, and art director Stanley Fleischer has created a combination of realistic and impressionistic settings that have been nicely decorated by John P. Austin. Film editing by Frank Bracht and sound by Stanley Jones and Dolph Thomas are of top quality. Makeup supervisor Gordon Bau did a magic job of turning Miss Verdon from a pert redhead to an age-old witch and then, thankfully, back again. *Ron.*

The Party Crashers

Well-made action film for the teenage market; good b.o. prospects.

Paramount release of William Alland production. Stars Connie Stevens, Bobby Driscoll, Mark Damon, Frances Farmer, Doris Dowling; features Gary Gray, Bob Padget, Skip Torgerson, Joe Sonessa, Gene Perrson, Denver Pyle, Walter Brooke, Cathy Lewis, Onslow Stevens. Directed by Bernard Girard. Story-screenplay, Girard; camera, Eddie Fitzgerald; editor, Everett Douglas. Previewed in N.Y., Sept. 12, '58. Running time, 78 MINS.

Twig Webster .... Mark Damon
Josh Buckford .... Bobby Driscoll
Barbara Nickerson .... Connie Stevens
Mrs. Bickford .... Frances Farmer
Mrs. Webster .... Doris Dowling
Don Hartlow .... Gary Gray
Mumps Thornberg .... Bob Padget
Bill Leeds .... Skip Torgerson
Larry Bronsen .... Joe Sonessa
Stan Osgood .... Gene Perrson
Mr. Bickford .... Denver Pyle
Mr. Webster .... Walter Brooke
Mrs. Nickerson .... Cathy Lewis
Mr. Nickerson .... Onslow Stevens
Sharon Lee .... Theodore Davitt

Patently primed for the teenage market is "The Party Crashers," a modest programmer which William Alland turned out for Paramount release. While life among the hot rod and pony tail set has been frequently filmed in the past, this entry comes up with some novel approaches that should pay off at the boxoffice.

Although film has no top marquee names, nevertheless the cast includes a number of players familiar to most patrons. Such younger thespers as Connie Stevens, Bobby Driscoll and Mark Damon have an identification with the highschool trade while their elders will remember Frances Farmer who's making her first screen appearance since 1942.

There's ample action and suspense in the screenplay which director Bernard Girard turned out from his own story. Subject of his cinematic canvas is the teenage offspring of the country club set. And it's far from "still life," for these kids roam the highways with expensive sports cars and their favorite pastime, it seems, is crashing parties.

Top party crasher is Mark Damon, son of alcoholic Walter Brooke and trollop Doris Dowling. While pop and mom may have their faults, both appear to have enough money to insure their son's social standing among three-car garage suburbanites. Folly of parental neglect is clear at the finale when Damon and his crowd crash an adult party at a motel.

Damon's mother turns out to be one of the "party girls." The shocked son remonstrates with mom who falls down a flight of stairs and is critically injured. Windup at the local station house finds both kids and parents discovering a new sense of values. Script's moralizing, however, is subordinate to the action and story tension which director Girard makes the most of.

Good performances help the yarn ring true. Damon easily handles his role of the wise guy who ultimately softens up. Miss Stevens sparkles as a pretty blonde pony tailer whose object in life is to have a "ball." Driscoll, a child star of yesteryear, registers nicely as Miss Stevens' conservative boyfriend. Miss Farmer does well as a distraught parent, as do Denver Pyle, Onslow Stevens and Cathy Lewis.

Particularly effective is Walter Brooke's portrayal of the drunken father. Likewise, Miss Dowling is competent in an unsympathetic role. Okay support is provided by Gene Perrson and Gary Gray, among others. Eddie Fitzgerald's black-and-white camerawork is able, as are other technical credits. Everett Douglas edited to a tight 78 minutes. *Gilb.*

Man of the West
(COLOR; C'SCOPE)

Uneven but often powerful period frontier drama. Big names, big production values for good response.

Hollywood, Sept. 12.

United Artists release of Walter M. Mirisch production. Stars Gary Cooper, Julie London, Lee J Cobb, Arthur O'Connell, Jack Lord. Directed by Anthony Mann. Screenplay, Reginald Rose, based on a novel by Will C. Brown; camera (DeLuxe Color), Ernest Haller; music, Leigh Harline; editor, Richard Heermance. Previewed at the Screen Directors Guild, Sept. 12, '58. Running time, 100 MINS.

Link Jones .... Garp Cooper
Billie Ellis .... Julie London
Dock Tobin .... Lee J. Cobb
Sam Beasley .... Arthur O'Connell
Coaley .... Jack Lord
Claude .... John Dehner
Trout .... Royal Dano
Ponch .... Robert Wilke
Alcutt .... Jack Williams
Conductor .... Guy Wilkerson
Rifleman .... Chuck Roberson
Marshal .... Frank Ferguson
Gribble .... Emory Parnell
Mexican Woman .... Tina Menard
Mexican Man .... Joe Dominquez

"Man of the West," initial production by the Mirisch Co. for United Artists, is one of the bloodiest, most brutal and unsparing portraits of the Old West in a long, long time. It is also somewhat of a puzzler. Contrary to the current stream of big budget westerns, the Walter M. Mirisch production, directed by Anthony Mann., is more a realistic story than a psychological one. The unsparing ferocity with which it strips its badmen of their glamor veneer does not skip motivation, but is concerned more with their present evil than their past reasons for being so. It is not a completely satisfactory presentation, but the combination of action and romance with a good cast, headed by Gary Cooper, assures good boxoffice return.

Reginald Rose's screenplay, from a novel by Will C. Brown, has Cooper as a reformed gunman, now a respected citizen entrusted with the savings of his community. He is on a mission to get the town a schoolteacher when he is robbed of the money by members of his old gang. The fact that he is involved in the holdup is more or less by chance, and it is also somewhat by accident that he, and two other victims, Julie London and Arthur O'Connell, wind up taking refuge in the bandits' hideout, which had once been Cooper's, too.

Superficially, the story is simply the account of Cooper's efforts to free himself, Miss London and O'Connell of the outlaws. It is given dimension by the fact that to do this he must revert to the savagery he has foresworn. Before he and Miss London escape, Cooper has killed every member of the gang, headed by Lee J. Cobb, his uncle, and O'Connell has died saving Cooper.

Mann and Rose have constructed scenes of great power. The slugging match between Cooper and Jack Lord, one of the outlaws, is superbly staged, bringing fresh value to one of the most hackneyed sequences in frontier films. Another scene, in which Lord forces Miss London to disrobe while he holds a knife at Cooper's throat, makes the spectator crawl with pity for Miss London and with revulsion for the men who make her submit to this outrage.

One reason why "Man of the West" achieves some unique values is that it shows accurately the obsession with pseudo-masculinity that was typical of these frontier characters, and produced such senseless manifestations as the gory man-to-man combats that resulted in maimings and deaths over often trivial disputes. It shows, too, in the animalistic attitude of the outlaws to Miss London; they are men incapable of any approach to a woman except rape. The projection of this mentality is used, implicitly, to give reasons seldom explored for the repugnance these legendary "heroes" of the west inspired in most of their contemporaries and for Cooper's decamping their company.

The picture is likely to be unsatisfactory to some. The opening scenes are too long for their value, and they are misleading in treatment and confusing in meaning. It is a long time before the audience can sense what is up. The ending is abrupt and seems unresolved, chiefly because Cooper's mention of his absent wife has been so casual that a romance between him and Miss London seems indicated. Cooper gives a characteristically virile performance, his dominance of the outlaws quietly believable, while Miss London achieves some touching and convincing moments in a difficult role. Lee J. Cobb, a frontier Fagan of demoniac violence and destruction, and Arthur O'Connell, with whimsical grace and gaiety, add considerably to the picture's interest. Jack Lord, his handsome face distorted by jealousy and malevolence, is fine in an offbeat casting, while John Dehner provides solid support.

Ernest Hallet's CinemaScope photography, in limpid DeLuxe color, is equally good in the rugged exteriors, where the splendid locations are advantageously used, and in the tension-charged interiors. Leigh Harline has contributed a useful score and Bobby Troup has done a title song that will be an exploitation assist. *Powe.*

Kill Her Gently

British-made melodrama for double-bill filler.

Hollywood, Sept. 11.

Columbia release of Guido Coen production. Stars Griffith Jones, Maureen Connell, Marc Lawrence; features George Mikel, Shay Gorman, Marianne Brauns, Frank Hawkins. Directed by Charles Saunders. Screenplay, Paul Erickson; camera, Walter J. Harvey; music, Edwin Astley; editor, Margery Saunders. Previewed at the studio, Sept. 11, '58. Running time, **75 MINS.**

Connors	Marc Lawrence
Sven	George Mikell
Jeff Martin	Griffith Jones
Truck Driver	John Gayford
Constable Brown	Roger Avon
Kay Martin	Maureen Connell
Doctor Landers	Shay Gorman
Raina	Marianne Brauns
Inspector Raglan	Frank Hawkins
Detective Sgt. Thompson	Patrick Connor
Bank Clerk	Jonathan Meddings
Bank Manager	Peter Stephens
Barmaid	Susan Neil
Slade	David Lawton
Mrs. Douglas	Elaine Wells

"Kill Her Gently" is a British-made melodrama that will have to do for double-bill fare, at least in this country. The plot, of a man who hires two escaped convicts to murder his wife, is over-familiar, and the treatment is not supenseful enough to give it fresh value. The names of the stars, Griffith Jones, Maureen Connell and Marc Lawrence, mean little to American audiences. Guido Coen produced and Charles Saunders directed. Columbia is releasing.

Jones is the psychopathic husband of Miss Connell, who decides he wants to do away with her because he blames her for his incarceration in a mental institution. When he encounters Lawrence and George Mikell, on the run from a prison break, he promises them money and aid in escaping if they will do the deed. They agree at first, but a series of events prevents them from carrying out the act, and in the end they and the husband are either killed or apprehended.

Paul Erickson's screenplay is strong on dialog and weak on development. The characters are interestingly drawn but there seems to be difficulty in maintaining action; complications are thin and overworked.

Jones, Lawrence, Mikell and Miss Connell are capable in their roles, Miss Connell particularly endowing her part with a terror and bewilderment that is often genuinely affecting. In a small role, as a floozy, Marianne Brauns is notable. *Powe.*

Step Down to Terror

Program meller. Budget class but competently made.

Hollywood, Sept. 5.

Universal release of Joseph Gershenson production. Stars Colleen Miller, Charles Drake and Rod Taylor. Directed by Harry Keller. Screenplay, Mel Dinelli, Czenzi Ormonde and Chris Cooper; based on story by Gordon McDonell; camera, Russell Metty; editor, Frank Gross. Preview at studio, Universal City, Aug. 28, '58. Running time, **75 MINS.**

Helen	Colleen Miller
Johnny Williams	Charles Drake
Mike Randall	Rod Taylor
Mrs. Walters	Josephine Hutchinson
Lily	Jocelyn Brando
Roy	Alan Dexter
Doug	Rickey Kelman

"Step Down To Terror" is a straight melodrama with no frills but enough thrills to make it a satisfactory package for the program market it will fill. Joseph Gershenson produced the picture for Universal-International and Harry Keller directed.

Charles Drake is the central figure of the screenplay, by Mel Dinelli, Czenzi Ormonde and Chris Cooper, based on a story by Gordon McDonell. Drake's reappearance in his home town after a six-year absence is enthusiastically welcomed by his mother, Josephine Hutchinson, his widowed sister-in-law, Colleen Miller, and his orphaned nephew, young Rickey Kelman. Miss Miller's joy becomes tempered, however, when Drake's behavior arouses her suspicions about what he has been up to during his long absence. He is a psychological killer and he very nearly does her in before a sleuthing cop, Rod Taylor, comes on the scene to bring things to a climax.

The cast responds to Keller's direction with interesting performances. In addition to the central figures, capable supporting characterizations are turned in by Jocelyn Brando and Alan Dexter. Russell Metty's photography is a plus credit and other aspects of the picture are uniformly top-notch. *Powe.*

The Horse's Mouth
(BRITISH—COLOR)

Alec Guinness comedy. Great star vehicle in so-so story.

Venice, Sept. 2.

United Artists presentation and release of a Knightsbridge Films Production. Stars Alec Guinness; features Kay Walsh, Renee Houston and Mike Morgan. Produced by John Bryan. Directed by Ronald Neame. Screenplay, Alec Guinness, from novel by Joyce Carey; camera, Arthur Ibbetson; editor, Anne V. Coates; settings, Bill Andrews; music, Kenneth V. Jones. At Venice Film Festival, Sept. 1, '58. Running time: **97 MINS.**

Gully Jimson	Alec Guinness
CoRer	Kay Walsh
Nosey	Mike Morgan
Sir William Beeder	Robert Coote
Alabaster	Arthur McRea
Lady Beeder	Veronica Turleigh
Capt. Jones	Reginald Beckwith
Abel	Michael Gough
Hickson	Ernest Thesiger
Lollie	Gillian Vaughn
Butler	Richard Caldicott

On the fairly safe assumption that the name of Alec Guinness on the marquee will bring in the customers, in the United States particularly, "The Horse's Mouth" should prove a hit. But although it provides the star with a magnificent vehicle it is an odd and uneasy blending of comedy and farce which doesn't quite come off. The Guinness angle, of course, will be the dominant selling factor.

While there is no lack of comic invention in the Guinness screenplay, the belly-laugh situations are intermittently spaced and too often are derived from a farcical treatment. The main weakness of the script, however, is in its characterization. Even the star's self-written plum part is more of a caricature, and that criticism applies, in varying degree, to the other personalities featured in the story.

Ronald Neame's slick and professional direction rightly keeps the limelight on the star. He handles the broad and improbable comedy smoothly and keeps the action rolling. Arthur Ibbetson's Technicolor lensing captures the rich and vivid hues in the John Bratby paintings, which play a vital role in the pic, while taut editing keeps the story down to a trim 97 minutes.

Guinness plays a talented but down and out artist whose home and studio is a leaky old houseboat moored on the River Thames. As the story opens he's leaving jail, having scored a short sentence for sending abusive telephone messages to a patron of the arts; within minutes of his release he's up to his old tricks again, disguising his voice and posing in turn as the president of the Royal Academy and a duchess.

The main part of the plot is devoted to Guinness's efforts, aided by cockney barmaid Kay Walsh, to retrieve a collection of paintings which he left behind when he deserted his wife. All but one had been sold to the patron he had plagued on the phone in settlement of outstanding debts; the remaining one is held by the ex-wife, but she defeats his schemings to get it back by passing off a parcel made of toilet rolls.

Although that is the chief story thread, the main comedy originates from the artist's love of murals and his inability to resist a blank and undecorated wall. There's one incident, somewhat protracted but nevertheless basically amusing, in which he visits the wealthy Sir William and Lady Beeder (Robert Coote and Veronica Turleigh) in the hope of doing a deal, notices an empty wall (a tapesry had been removed for cleaning) and tricks the housekeeper into letting him have the key when the owners leave on vacation. With Michael Gough, a penniless sculptor, whose block of masonry is lowered through the fanlight, and crashes to the apartment below, they wreck the home, but Guinness leaves his masterpiece behind.

There's another scene in which Guinness moves into a vacant church hall which is in the hands of a demolition squad and, with a corps would-be art students, undertakes his biggest-ever project, only to push a bulldozer through the whole thing the moment it is completed. But the best moment, in the true Guinness tradition, comes just before fadeout. To escape the well-meaning but hard-to-take Kay Walsh, he sets sail in his houseboat, and as he's moving down the Thames, passes alongside a newly-painted liner, the side of which could provide him with his biggest-ever canvas. The final line of dialog which follows this scene could well be erased.

Guinness, as one has come to expect, is great. Indeed, he's not apparently capable of giving anything but a first-class performance. There's an impeccable quality about his work which shines through most of the time, giving an added flavor to his mannerisms and gestures. A handpicked team supports the star, but is only given limited chances. Miss Walsh overdoes her cockney role, while Mike Morgan, as a youth who idolizes the maestro, never emerges as a positive personality. As the ex-wife, Renee Houston hardly suggests the wily character she is supposed to be; and as wealthy patrons of the arts, Robert Coote and Veronica Thurleigh, with their secretary, Arthur McRea, are little more than caricatures. Michael Gough as the sculptor, Gillian Vaughn as his nude model (only back view shown on the screen), together with Reginald Beckwith, Ernest Thesiger and Richard Caldicott, together with some distinguished players in bit parts, give useful backing.

"The Horse's Mouth" was the sole British entry at the Venice Festival. While falling far short of vintage Guinness, it didn't let the side down. *Myro.*

I Married a Monster From Outer Space

Imaginative sci-fi entry, to be lower-cased with "The Blob" as horror combo.

Hollywood, Sept. 9.

Paramount release of Gene Fowler Jr. production. Stars Tom Tryon, Gloria Talbott; features Chuck Wassil, Maxie Rosenbloom. Directed by Fowler. Story-screenplay, Louis Vittes; camera, Haskell Boggs; editor, George Tomasini. Previewed Sept. 8, '58. Running time, **78 MINS.**

Bill Farrell	Tom Tryon
Marge Farrell	Gloria Talbott
Swanson	Peter Baldwin
Harry	Robert Ivers
Ted	Chuck Wassil
B Girl	Valerie Allen
Mac	Ty Hungerford
Dr. Wayne	Ken Lynch
Collins	John Eldredge
Sam Benson	Alan Dexter
Weldon	James Anderson
Helen Rhodes	Jean Carson
Schultz	Jack Orrison
Charles Mason	Steve London
Bartender	Maxie Rosenbloom

"I Married a Monster from Outer Space" carries imaginative plottage which makes it strong fare for horror package topbilled by "The Blob" in the exploitation market. Pic has been given class production by Gene Fowler Jr., who also directs, and cast headed by Tom Tryon and Gloria Talbott is first-rate.

Premise of the Louis Vittes story-screenplay deals with a race of monsters from another galaxy who invade the earth and secretly take over the form of some of the male townspeople. Film opens with Miss Talbott marrying Tryon, unaware the man she loves is now one of these monsters. After a year of tension she follows him one night and watches him change into his original form and enter a spaceship. Through her doctor, to whom she goes in her terror, enough normal people are recruited to successfully break up the invasion by an attack on spaceship.

Fowler's direction, while sometimes slow, latches onto mounting suspense as action moves to a climax. He gets the benefit of outstanding special photographic effects from John P. Fulton, which aid in maintaining interest. Both Miss Talbott and Tryon in lead roles deliver strongly, and get top support from Ken Lynch, the doctor; John Eldridge, police chief, one of the monsters; Alan Dexter, another victim; and Jean Carson. Maxie Rosenbloom is in briefly as a barkeep.

Tchnical credits all rate highly, including Haskell Boggs' camerawork, George Tomasini's tight editing and art direction by Hal Pereira and Henry Bumstead. *Whit.*

Viva Lo Imposible

(Family Adventure)

Madrid, Sept. 1.

CEA release of a Coral production. Stars Paquita Rico, Manolo Moran, Miguel Gila, Jose Maria Rodero; features Julio Nunez, Jose Marco Davo, Julia Caba Alba. Directed by Rafael Gil. Screenplay by Rafael Gil and Miguel Mihura. Camera, Alfredo Fraile; art director, Enrique Alarcon. Filmed at CEA Studios. At Palacia de la Prensa, Madrid. Running time, **98 MINS.**

Rafael Gil, cne of Spain's better directors, has converted Mihura-Calvo Sotelo's sentimental comedy "Star-gazing Bookkeeper" to the screen, leaning heavily on stage precursor to lose film impact.

Central idea of a veteran ledger slave, kicking over traces of a humdrum existence and leaving with grownup son and daughter in search of adventure, offers comic possibilities Gil achieves in part. When offspring, and later, father find little enchantment in breadwinner's circus triumphs to discover life a routine even under the big tent, film slows as sentimental theatrics dominate.

Manolo Moran contributes a convincing performance as father. Roles assigned Paquita Rico, comic Gila and Jose Cuadro are vaguely conceived. Gil's circus sequences and satiric play on official newsreels score. Technical credits are fair. Comedy is pegged to local taste. *Hank.*

The Gun Runners

Well-done adventure yarn with average b.o. prospects.

Hollywood, Sept. 12.

United Artists release of a Seven Arts Production, produced by Clarence Greene. Stars Audie Murphy, Eddie Albert, Patricia Owens, Everett Sloane; introduces Gita Hall. Directed by Don Siegel. Screenplay, Dan Mainwaring and Paul Monash, based on an Ernest Hemingway story; camera, Hal Mohr; editor, Chester Schaeffer; music, Leith Stevens; songs, Joe Lubin. Previewed at Goldwyn Studios, Sept. 10, '58. Running time, **83 MINS.**

Sam Martin	Audie Murphy
Hanagan	Eddie Albert
Lucy Martin	Patricia Owens
Harvey	Everett Sloane
Eva	Gita Hall
Buzurki	Richard Jaeckel
Sy Phillips	Paul Birch
Arnold	Jack Elam
Peterson	John Harding
Blonde	Peggy Maley
Carlos	Carlos Romero
Juan	Edward Colmans
Pepito	Steven Peck
Pepita	Lita Leon
Commander Walsh	Ted Jacques
Pop	John Qualen
Berenguer	Freddie Roberto

Seven Arts Productions, which by reputation has become one of Hollywood's major independents before canning a single picture, has now come up with its first film in "The Gun Runners." It's not likely the company has a sleeper in this medium-budget pic, but it is a good film that has been carefully produced. Main chance at the box-office lies in star Audie Murphy's name and exploitation of the Cuban Revolt angle, with prospects looking just above run-of-the-mill for the United Artists release.

"Gun Runners" is not a very controversial film despite its background, but it does show off some highly capable talents which deserve credit, from producer Clarence Greene down. Don Siegel's direction maintains a fluidity of action and emotions, and the Daniel Mainwaring - Paul Monash screenplay, based on a story by Ernest Hemingway, is adept, particularly in its dialog.

Murphy uses a touch of underplaying and a good deal of love in his portrayal of the cabin cruiser captain who's sucked in on an illegal cruise. He's solidly supported by an excellent slap-on-the-back, tough-guy performance from Eddie Albert and a lovable portrayal from Patricia Owens, as h's wife. Everett Sloane finds a change-of-pace as Murphy's wino sidekick, and he does .vell, though the part of a dullard is not his forte. Pic introduces Gita Hall, who's put together nicely but who doesn't impress too strongly this time out.

Storyline has Murphy running his craft off Key West, Fla. He's hard-put for the next payment on the boat and, so, takes on Albert as a charter, with the smooth operator turning out to be a seller of machine-guns to the Cuban rebels. But, as Sloane says to Murphy at one point: "A man that hasn't got it in him to go bad, can't go bad. And, Sam, you haven't got it in you." Sam doesn't go bad, and, in fact, does away with the gun runners.

Technical credits, topped by Hal Mohr's photography, are fine, with the Leith Stevens score an outstanding contribution to the production. *Ron.*

Teenage Caveman

(SUPERAMA)

Good exploitation item with teenage appeal.

Hollywood, Sept. 5.

American International release of a James H. Nicholson-Samuel Z. Arkoff production. Stars Robert Vaughn, Darah Marshall, Leslie Bradley. Produced and directed by Roger Corman. Screenplay, R. Wright Campbell; camera, Floyd Crosby; music Albert Glasser; editor, Irene Morra. Reviewed at the Hawaii Theatre, Hollywood, Sept. 3, '58. Running time, **65 MINS.**

The Boy	Robert Vaughn
The Maiden	Sarah Marshall
Symbol Maker	Leslie Bradley
The Villain	Frank De Kova
Members of the Tribe	Joseph Hamilton, Marshal Bradford, Robert Shayne, Beach Dickerson, June Jocelyn, Charles P. Thompson, Jonathan Haze.

"Teenage Caveman" is, as the title states, the story of a teenager in the prehistoric world. The James H. Nicholson-Samuel Z. Arkoff production for American International, produced and directed by Roger Corman, is also, somewhat surprisingly, a plea for international cooperation in terms of the dangers of atomic radiation. This is obviously a low budget picture, and in theatrical terms it doesn't always sustain, but the "message" is handled with restraint and good taste, and gives substance to the production. "Teenage Caveman" is paired with the same studio's "How To Make A Monster" and will be a very negotiable twin bill.

Robert Vaughn is the youthful caveman whose thoughts stray beyond the limits of the isolated area inhabited by his clan. Clan law prohibits traffic beyond the area and decrees death for anyone going out or coming in. Strangers are automatically enemies and killed without discussion. The plot is based on Vaughn's belief that good things for the tribe may be had in exploring the world beyond its limited horizons and the conflict arises when the elders oppose him.

Action in the story isn't always strong enough to keep the excitement keyed very high, and the screenplay, by R. Wright Campbell, tends to get a little heavily symbolic, at times. But, at least, its symbols are fresh and thoughtful, and the ending is provocative. (It leaves unanswered the question of what "prehistoric" period this is; one caused by previous atomic devastation or one that present mishandling of the atom may bring about.)

Vaughn is satisfactory as the questing caveman although there is a tendency, on occasion, to give the role a little too much "method." Leslie Bradley, Darah Marshall and Frank De Kova, as the other three chief characters, give solid performances.

Floyd Crosby's photography is good, and technically the prehistoric beast shots are of considerable value in setting the scene and mood. *Powe.*

Im Prater Bluch'n Wieder die Baeume

(Trees Are Blooming In Vienna)
(AUSTRIAN-COLOR-MUSIC)

Vienna, Sept. 9.

Paula Wessely Film release of Otto Duerer production. Stars Johanna Matz, Gerhard Riedmann; features Nina Sandt, Marte Harell. Directed by Hans Wolff. Screenplay, Juliane Kay, based on play by Rudolf Oesterreicher and Siegfried Geyer; camera, Willi Sohm; settings, Fritz Moegle, Heinz Ockermueller; costumes, Fred Adlmueller; music, Robert Stolz. At Weinzeile Kino, Vienna, Sept. 6, '58. Running time, **95 MINS.**

Lixie Haertl	Johanna Matz
Archduke Peter	Gerhard Riedmann
Mizzi Starek	Nina Sandt
Mr. Schindler	Theo Lingen
Mrs. Sacher	Marte Harell
Isabella	Susi Nicoletti
Singer	Ljuba Welitsch
Baron Koeroezhazi	Fred Liewehr
Baroness Ilona	Elisabeth Stiepl
Jankowitz	Egon von Jordan
Stangl	Erik Frey

"Trees Are Blooming In Vienna" has two distinct plus values, the Robert Stolz score and the bitter-sweet Vienna love story of an archduke and a plain girl. Pic is loaded with nostalgic sentiment, humor and drama. The Rudolf Oesterreicher and Siegried Geyer plots are always good.

The title of the picture is after a Robert Stolz evergreen, the melody being an important feature of the film.

Johanna Matz as the plain girl shows excellent acting and has in a duet "music for Love," which is sweet and haunting, a song that will go over big. Her vis-a-vis Gerhard Riedmann is outstanding. Nina Sandt deserves high praise for acting and interpreting, especially the philosophical ditty "There is Always Hope." The supporting players, including Marte Harell, Theo Lingen, Ljuba Welitsch and others all rang among the first.

Willi Sohm's photography catches the beautiful scenery, and the settings are rich and colorful. Production by Otto Duerer is excellent. Direction by Hans Wolff is brisk and brings out much tension.

It would be regrettable if this picture should wind up "artie only" abroad. Pic is ripe for dates in any country. Highly recommendable for U.S. *Maas.*

How to Make a Monster

(SUPERAMA)

Suspense murder plot with Hollywood and horror touches. Good exploitation fare.

Hollywood, Sept. 5.

American International release of a James H. Nicholson-Samuel Z. Arkoff production. Stars Robert H. Harris, Paul Brinegar, Gary Conway, Gary Clarke. Produced by Herman Cohen. Directed by Herbert L. Strock. Story-screenplay, Kenneth Langtry and Herman Cohen; camera, Maury Gertzman; music, Paul Dunlap; editor, Jerry Young. Reviewed at the Hawaii Theatre, Hollywood, Sept. 3, '58. Running time, **75 MINS.**

Pete Drummond	Robert H. Harris
Rivero	Paul Brinegar
Tony Mantell	Gary Conway
Larry Drake	Gary Clarke
Richards	Malcolm Atterbury
Monahan	Dennis Cross

"How To Make A Monster" is actually a switch on the old and reliable Mad Scientist who, in this case, is a Mad Makeup Man. The setting is Hollywood and the "Monster" of the title is one created for a horror picture. The James H. Nicholson-Samuel Z. Arkoff production for American International, produced by Herman Cohen and directed by Herbert L. Strock, is rather mild as these exploitation pictures go. But paired with the same studio's "Teenage Caveman", it appears headed for as healthy a response as previous exploitation duos from AIP.

Robert H. Harris plays the veteran makeup man whose studio is taken over by eastern executives. Their first move is to fire him and end production on horror pix for which he has created a variety of monsters. Threatened with extinction of his artistic creations, he takes action. He compounds a new makeup for his young actors that performs externally the same function, as Harris explains it, as a surgical pre-frontal lobotomy. Memory is excised and while under Harris' hypnotic suggestion, the young thesps take on the personalities of the roles they play—a teenage Frankenstein and a teenage werewolf—and proceed to throttle the economy-minded studio heads.

"Monster," with a screenplay by Kenneth Langtry and Herman Cohen, is more a mystery-suspense picture than a horror item, and the horror effects are rather mild. The script has some sharp dialog and occasionally pungent Hollywood talk ("that's the way the footage cuts") although these aspects will be largely lost on the audiences this picture will attract.

Harris gives the chief role conviction and Paul Brinegar as his faithful assistant is a convincing aide. Gary Conway and Gary Clarke as the youthful thesps do well, although masked much of the time, and others who contribute include Malcolm Atterbury, Dennis Cross, Morris Ankrum, Paul Maxwell and Eddie Marr.

Technical credits, including Maury Gertzman's excellent photography, are helpful. The finish, a good fire scene, is in color. *Powe.*

La Sfida

(The Challenge)
(SPANISH-ITALIAN)

Lux film release of a Lux-Vides-Cinecitta-Suevia Film co-production. Stars Jose Suarez, Rosanna Schiaffino; features Nino Vingelli, Pasquale Cenanmo, Decimo Cristiani. Directed by Francesco Rosi. Screenplay, Rosi, Suso Cecchi D'Amico, Enzo Provenzale; camera, Gianni di Venanzo; music, Roman Vlad; editor, Mario Serandrei. At Film Festival, Venice. Running time, **110 MINS.**

Vito	Jose Suarez
Assunta	Rosanna Schiaffino
Gennaro	Nino Vingelli

This is an expertly directed melodrama set in the Mafia-dominated general markets of Naples. American-styled story and handling should help this find a ready market in Italy and in lingual situations abroad, including the U.S. Pic will inevitably lose in translation, and this is a problem producers have to lick in aspiring for other non-Italian releases.

Story is based on recent real-life happening. It tells of a young man who tries to break into, then double-cross, the combine which dominates supply and sales at Naples' fruit and vegetable mart. Finale finds him shot by gang boss, and his young and recent wife a desperate widow.

Director Francesco Rosi, whose first pic this is, obviously been inspired, among other things, by the American gangster film, but the assimilation is well adapted to his present item, and he brings it off in vigorous, effective style with only a few slow spots in mid-action.

Jose Suarez is good in the lead, but pic is dominated by Nino Vingelli and Pasquale Cenammo, respectively a sidekick and the gang boss, both strong characterizations. Rosanna Schiaffino projects her striking beauty to advantage, though she has relatively little to do except in the strong finale, which she brings off well. Neapolitan dialog is colorful and gives pic a strong assist, as do settings lensed in this all-locationer on and off the streets of Naples. Gianni di Venanzo's photography is of top quality throughout, and Riman Vlad has written an able musical backdrop to highlight dramatic action. Other technical credits are all fine, except for lip-sync of dubbed role by Suarez. *Hawk.*

Venice Films

Narayama Bushi-Ko
(The Legend of Narayama)
(JAPANESE—COLOR)

Venice, Sept. 9.

Shochiku production and release. Stars Kinuyo Tanaka, Teiji Takahashi; features Yuko Mochizuki, Danko Ichigawa. Written and directed by Keisuke Kinoshita, from a story by Shichiro Fukazawa; camera (Fujicolor-Grandscope), Hiroyuki Kusuda; art direction, Kisaku Ito; editor, Yoshi Sugihara. At Film Festival, Vienna. Running time, 98 MINS.

Orin .... Kinuyo Tanaka
Tatsuhei .... Teiji Takahashi
Tama-yan .... Yuko Mochisuki

An artistically important film with little or no commercial prospects. Basically distasteful story and slow pace are basic strikes against pic, despite moments of great poetry and top acting by all concerned, and especially by Kinuyo Tanaka, in the leading role.

Plot concerns a 69-year-old widow Orin (Kinuyo Tanaka), who must settle her family affairs and find a wife for her son before the law of the land forces her to the hills to die on reaching the age of 70. When all is done and her great-grandchild is on the way, her son reluctantly carries her up the mountain to her peaceful death in the snow, which has just begun to fall to speed her on her way. Theme of hunger also permeates entire pic.

To further director Keisuke Kinoshita's semi-theatrical style, speaker commentary and song, lighting effects, and stage-like scenic changes are used to span sequences. Entire pic is studio-shot to achieve this. Pace is deliberately slow, and Japanese weakness for violence is seen in a shot in which the old woman knocks out her teeth, supposedly to still her hunger.

This one is strictly for the aficionados, who should find in it a pic of great artistry and poetry of lasting universal value, in the tradition of great Japanese films of the past. Technical credits are good. *Hawk.*

Weddings and Babies

Venice, Sept. 9.

Morris Engel Associates presentation of a Morris Engel Production. Stars Viveca Lindfors, John Myhers; features Chiarina Barile, Leonard Elliott, Joanna Merlin, Chris, Gabriel Kohn, Mary Faranda. Directed by Engel. Screenplay, Engel, Mary-Madeleine Lanphier, Blanche Hanalis, Irving Sunasky, from story by Engel; music, Eddy Manson; camera, Engel; editor, Stan Russell, Michael Alexander. At Film Festival, Venice. Running time, 81 MINS.

Bea .... Viveca Lindfors
Al .... John Myhers
Mama .... Chiarina Barile
Ken .... Leonard Elliott
Josie .... Joanna Merlin
Tony .... Chris
Carl .... Gabriel Kohn
Mrs. Faranda .... Mary Faranda

Morris Engel, who some years back made "The Little Fugitive," has come up with another midget-budgeter in the same manner and concept, though here the ambitions are greater and the style more mature. Pic, with proper sendoff, should do good business in special situations, aided by word-of-mouth. A second-feature general release might develop from there and European interest has also been voiced after Venice screening. Viveca Lindfors gives it a name peg, but pic should basically be sold on its unusual values and special charm.

Basically, plot tells the love story of a photographer (John Myhers) and his assistant (Viveca Lindfors). She wants marriage (and babies), but he is hesitant, beset by financial and other worries. At finale, after many doubts, he decides to take the step. Sub-plot concerns man's mother, who is confined to a rest home for the aged but nevertheless tries to help him out financially. Plot, however, is not the important factor here: much as in the postwar tradition of the better Italian films, it's the handling and development that give "Weddings and Babies" its special quality and impact. The intimate approach, the total realism in setting, lensing, and acting by all concerned give pic a dimension rarely seen in Yank films. Result is an offbeat item which is often humorous, often moving, always real and human. The more discriminating ticket-buyer should go for this in a big way.

Film also has what some of Engel's films did not have in past: top-rate acting. Miss Lindfors has rarely been better than in this labor-of-love performance as the girl who desperately wants her man, marriage, and kids. Myhers shades his role of the hesitant suitor with just the right nuances, is just right for the part. Miss Lindfors' own child, Chris, winningly plays a friend's boy, while Leonard Elliott, Joanna Merlin, Gabriel Kohn, Mary Faranda and others give stars able backing. But it's 75-year-old Chiarina Barile who almost walks away with the picture as the mother, a superb figure of character strength fighting senility.

Engel's own all-location lensing in New York's Little Italy, with its colorful backdropping, and other Gotham locales, help give pic its special flavor, as does the realistic natural-lighting quality captured throughout. Occasionally fuzzy lensing, resulting from desire for "real" lighting, is acceptable in this context. Other technical credits are good, with Eddy Manson's music an effective assist. *Hawk.*

Les Amants
(The Lovers)
(FRENCH-DYALISCOPE)

Venice, Sept. 9.

Lux release of Nouvelles Editions De Films production. Stars Jeanne Moreau; features Alain Cuny, Jean-Marc Borry, Jose-Luis De Villalonga, Judith Magre. Directed by Louis Malle. Screenplay, Louise de Vilmorin, Malle; camera, Henri Decae; editor, Leonide Azar. At Venice Film Fest. Running time, 90 MINS.

Jeanne .... Jeanne Moreau
Henri .... Alain Cuny
Raoul .... Jose-Luis De Villalonga
Bernard .... Jean-Marc Bory
Maggy .... Judith Magre

A comedy of manners is mixed with an attempt at outright eroticism in this film. Neither is completely successful, and hence this looms a pic with only exploitation chances in the U.S. on its 20-minute love scene between a young wife and a young man in the house and grounds of the husband who happens to be at home during the tryst.

The lovers snuggle, moan and even take a bath together, but the lack of dimension in the characters dissipates its impact. The wife, married to an older man who seems to think more of his newspaper than her, spends weekends in Paris where she has taken a lover, an effeminate polo-playing playboy. She thinks she loves him but one day the husband, suspecting something, insists she invite the man for a weekend.

The wife goes to Paris to do the invites and on the way home her car breaks down. She is picked up by a simple young man who hates what her rich, smug set stands for. That night she cannot sleep and goes out for a walk where she meets the young man. Love comes quickly and after the love scenes she leaves husband, lover, child and her empty life to run off with the young man.

Fairly banal dialog, and a narration imposed over the action, diminish its needed early vitality. It limps along until the sex scenes. But since it is adultery and fairly lucid, a la "Ecstacy," by which it was obviously influenced, Legion of Decency trouble is in store. If these scenes have to be cut there isn't much left to the pic.

Direction dwells on too many unessential points and lacks the true feel for this woman's plight to make her emotional release effective drama. Jeanne Moreau displays some insight into her character, which is more than most of the men can do. Anamorphoscope process helps in the long reclining stretches of the pic, and technical credits are good with the misty lensing an atmospheric help.

Pic got a special jury award at the recent Venice Film Fest for the direction of 28-year-old newcomer Louis Malle, in his second film. His work is competent but never overcomes the stagnant stretches. Jury stipulated the prize was to encourage a promising newcomer and not for the pic. *Mosk.*

Rasskaz Moei Materi
(Stories of My Mother)
(RUSSIAN-COLOR)

Venice, Sept. 9.

Mosfilm release and production. With Eugheni Urbanski, Sofia Pavlova, E. Smirnov. Directed by Juli Raisman. Screenplay, Eugheni Gabrilovich; camera (Sovcolor), A. Scelenkov; editor, R. Scedrin. At Venice Film Fest. Running time, 110 MINS.

Vassili .... Eugheni Urbanski
Aniuta .... Sofia Pavlova
Fiodor .... E. Smirnov

The film is about the life and love of a young Communist put in charge of a warehouse in a small town during the revolution. Story is conventional, a la the oaters, but has a sweep and visual plus in the times. The White Russians replace the Indians and the pic races along and emerges an above-average actioner with an asset in the well conceived characters, the expert mounting and the right tempo in acting.

This is, of course, limited to special situations in the U.S. and entertaining enough for language showings. Tale is about the young man's conquest of a woman and his final demise, in a grandiose way, at the hands of 20 White Russians. *Mosk.*

Rosemarie
(GERMAN)

Story of Germany's most famous postwar courtesan, with obvious exploitation possibilities.

Venice, Sept. 1.

Neue Film (Munich) release of a Roxy production. Stars Nadja Tiller, Peter Van Eyck, Carl Raddatz, Gert Frobe; features Mario Adorf, Horst Frank. Directed by Rolf Thiele. Screenplay, Erich Kuby and Thiele, Klaus von Rautenfeld; music, Norbert Schultze. At Venice Film Festival, Aug. 25, '58. Running time, 104 MINS.

Rosemarie .... Nadja Tiller
Fribert .... Peter Van Eyck
Hartog .... Carl Raddatz
Bruster .... Gert Frobe
Horst .... Mario Adorf
Student .... Horst Frank
Marga .... Hanna Wieder
Walter .... Jo Herbst
Nakonski .... Werner Peters
Do .... Karin Baal
von Killenschiff .... Erich von Loewis
Schmidt .... Arno Paulsen
Kleie .... Hubert von Meyerinck
Eveline .... Helen Vita
Oelsen .... Tilo von Berlepsch
Frau Hartog .... Ruth Hausmeister

Less than a year ago, Rosemarie Nitribitt, Germany's most famous postwar courtesan, who also ran a profitable blackmailing sideline, was found strangled in her luxury Frankfurt apartment. Without wasting any time, the producers have developed a credible but fictitious yarn around this notorious character. They have turned out a picture with obvious exploitation possibilities which should do hefty business in its domestic market, and which has obvious chances in the foreign markets.

The director, Rolf Thiele, and Erich Kuby, who dreamed up the story idea, have fashioned their screenplay with some ingenuity. They have introduced some interesting ideas in the development, notably the use of the Mercedes car as a symbol of success among the top industrialists who patronized Rosemarie.

In direction and editing, too, the standard is above average for recent West German films. Several songs in cabaret style have been neatly woven into the main theme. The lyrics have a sophisticated stamp, but might conceivably not translate too effectively.

Story depicts the rapid rise of Miss Nitribitt from a street singer to highly priced, popular strumpet, who is installed in a fashionable apartment. She extracts a flashy sports car as the price of a break with one of her regulars. Her customers, all top industrialists, are encouraged to confide in her. The girl makes good use of a concealed tape recorder.

There is, however, an uneven quality about the acting. Nadja Tiller gives a provocative enough interpretation in the title role, but there is not much evidence of the sincerity needed to make the worried businessman pour out his secrets. Peter Van Eyck, as a

Frenchman who uses the recordings to get valuable info on an important secret German development, is largely expressionless. However, Carl Raddatz, and Gert Frobe, the girl's most important clients, are believable enough. Mario Adorf and Hort Frank head an average supporting cast.

The actual strangulation is not seen, but as the girl's screams penetrate the street from her apartment, a fleet of Mercedes drive away—all owned by the men she had embarrassed and blackmailed. A neat and effective ending. *Myro.*

Une Vie
(A Life)
(FRENCH-COLOR)

Venice, Sept. 9.

Corona release of Agnes Delahaie production. Stars Maria Schell; features Christian Marquand, Antonella Lualdi, Ivan Desny, Pascale Petit. Directed by Alexandre Astruc. Screenplay, Roland Laudenbach, Astruc, from the novel by Guy De Maupassant; camera (Eastmancolor), Claude Renoir; editor, Claudie Boucher. At Venice Film Fest. Running time, **105 MINS.**

Jeanne .... Maria Schell
Julien .... Christian Marquand
Gilberte .... Antonella Lualdi
Fourcheville .... Ivan Desny
Rosalie .... Pascale Petit

Maria Schell plays a valiant, long suffering, one-man woman married to the wrong man in this mannered costumer. She remains the main selling point, for the trouble with "A Life" is that it lacks it.

Film is a series of narrated sketches showing how Miss Schell is infatuated by and marries Christian Marquand who, it develops, did it for money to pay his debts. But he is soon carrying on with the maid and refusing Miss Schell's money though he tells her he only married her for this. A child is borne by the maid and a brief reconciliation takes place until, years later, he carries on with his friend's wife and is killed by him when he finds them in a tryst.

Taking place primarily in an old country house, the film lacks the necessary life a more comprehensive picture of the time and surroundings might have given it. Characters are unclear and the film hits mainly dramatic highpoints.

Miss Schell, sans her usual tics of hand play and smiling, appears too guileless in her blind love and sudden disdains, and Christian Marquand lacks the virility or drive to make his brooding husband plausible. Pascale Petit is the only one who registers well as the put-upon servant girl.

Main selling points for film in the U.S. are Miss Schell and its exquisite color rendering by Claude Renoir. Its sombre craftsmanship could make this a possible U.S. entry for big city art houses, but its meandering quality and coldness make this chancier for more general distrib. Expensively made film looks primarily a Continental bet. Production dress is opulent and technical credits tops. *Mosk.*

En Cas de Malheur
(In Case of Accident)
(FRENCH)

Venice, Sept. 9.

Columbia release of Iena-UCIL production. Stars Brigitte Bardot, Jean Gabin, Edwige Feuillere; features Franco Interlenghi, Madeleine Barbulee, Nicole Berger. Directed by Claude Autant-Lara. Screenplay, Jean Aurenche, Pierre Bost, from a novel by Georges Simenon; camera, Jacques Natteau; editor, Madeleine Gug. At Venice Film Fest. Running time, **130 MINS.**

Yvette .... Brigitte Bardot
Andre .... Jean Gabin
Wife .... Edwige Feuillere
Mazzetti .... Franco Interlenghi
Maid .... Nicole Berger
Secretary .... Madeleine Barbulee

Film fulfills most of the precepts that have made Brigitte Bardot a boxoffice here in the U.S. B.B., surrounded by top professional stars Jean Gabin and Edwige Feuillere, is (a) the required perverse accessible, precociously provocative character she developed in "And God Created Woman"; (b) she gives more evidence of trying to act, though still far from the goal, and (c) this could mean U.S. cash if tightened somewhat and cleared of the bad rating the Legion of Decency will probably give it.

It runs too long and rarely develops its characters. Pic is a May-December romance between B.B. as a delinquent who attempts a holdup in which her friend is captured, and Jean Gabin, a topflight lawyer who defends and gets her acquitted by corrupt means when he falls for her.

Pic then goes into the loves of B.B. who likes Gabin's riches and physique but also cannot resist a young student who leads the pic into ironic drama when he finally does in the ubiquitous B.B.

Director Claude Autant-Lara has given this fairly slick mounting and tried to make B.B. act. But the dragging tale and lack of true progression of the characters make this somewhat slow moving and not quite art house calibre. It has B.B. nude and shapes a probable grosser in regular and special spots as long as the Bardot appeal continues.

Gabin is his usually solid self as the lawyer and B.B. still has a long way to go to develop into an actress but displays a surer grasp of her own personality that audiences have paid to see in various countries. Pic is slickly made but will depend mainly on its sex and sensational aspects for U.S. chances. *Mosk.*

Muhomatsu No Issho
(Muhomatsu the Rickshaw Man)
(JAPANESE—COLOR)

Venice, Sept. 2.

Toho production and release. Stars Toshiro Mifune, Hideko Takamine; features Hiroshi Akutagawa, Hichiro Arishima, Jun Tanara. Directed by Hiroshi Inagaki. Screenplay, Inagaki and Mansaku Itami, from story by Shunsaku Iwashita; camera (Agfacolor-Tohoscope) Kazuo Yamada; music, Ikuma Dan. At Film Festival, Venice; Running time, **105 MINUTES.**

Muhomatsu .... Toshiro Mifune
Mrs. Yoshioka .... Hideko Takamine

This is a moving story of a man's unexpressed love for a woman, topped by a great performance by Toshiro Mifune. Combination of high commercial level and tasteful handling for dual appeal to both artist and general patrons should help this pic break through barriers for good export chances. In the U.S., film has every element for a good playoff if properly slotted and sold.

Tale told is of a rickshaw driver (Toshiro Mifune) who befriends a young boy and his parents (Hideko Takamine and Hiroshi Alutagawa). When the father dies, the driver helps out the mother in bringing up the boy but, though in love with her, never confesses it. When the boy goes away to school, Muhomatsu feels he is no longer needed and leaves. Saddened by the separation, he resumes his heavy drinking habits; when he dies, it's revealed that he has put his meagre savings in an account for mother and boy, who then realize all that he meant to them.

Japanese taste always avoids turning this into a banal tearjerker and it resultingly winds up a vigorous yet warm and moving portrait of a dedicated man, an aggressive and brawling fighter of great strength and will who keeps his greatest fight within himself in not confessing his love. It's a superb performance by Japan's greatest actor. The rip-roaring scenes in which his strength and brawling nature are established, as well as his low-key sequences showing his relations with the family and the bringing up of the boy, aptly give pic its dramatic balance for general appeal.

Pic's visual impact is topped by a scene in color negative, which follows Muhomatsu's death in a winter snowbank, in which his past is briefly flashbacked in poetic fashion. Action builds slowly, and for western tastes some pruning might be indicated in this early part. Acting, direction, music, sound and other technical credits all deserve plaudits, with a special nod to color work in Agfacolor and widescreen (2:1) Tohoscope by Kazuo Yamada, in the fine Japanese tradition. *Hawk.*

Los Clarines Del Miedo
(The Bugles of Fear)
(SPANISH-COLOR)

Venice, Sept. 2.

Procusa release of PCU production. Stars Francisco Rabal, Rogello Madrid, Silvia Solar, Manuel Luna; features Angel Ortiz, Miguel Avalle. Directed by Antonio Roman. Screenplay, Jose Maria De Lera; camera (Eastmancolor), Antonio Ballasteros; editor, Julio Pena. At Venice Film Fest. Running time, **80 MINS.**

Aceituno .... Francisco Rabal
Filigranas .... Rogelio Madrid
Fina .... Silvia Solar
Periodista .... Manuel Luna
Raposo .... Angel Ortiz
Aciclo .... Miguel Avalle

For a change bullfighting is not romanticized in this Hispano pic. It depicts the grimy, sordid side of this national pastime via scared practictioners plying their trade in little villages, battling the bulls only with capes, sans the bull-weakening picadors.

This aspect, plus well drawn village life and then the spectator brutality in the wake of this so-called art, make this an entry with good Spanish language possibilities for the U.S. Its fairly sketchy story of village intrigues hampers this for either art or general chances in the U.S.

Color is somewhat garish and the first part of the pic fairly conventional in denoting village types. But its limning of the toreador's fears, and the demystifying of the whole process, are exceedingly well done. Acting is adequate and Francisco Rabal is able to give this more depth as the man whose momentary cowardice leads to the death of his friend and then great triumph as he manages to go out and kill the bull well. It gives the film a proper ironic edge. It is technically sound. *Mosk.*

Vlci Jama
(Wolf Trap)
(CZECHOSLAVAKIAN)

Venice, Sept. 9.

Czech State Film production and release. Stars Jana Brejchova, Jirina Sojbalova, Miroslav Dolozal. Directed by Jiri Weiss. Screenplay, Jarmila Glazarova, Weiss, J. Brdecka from novel by Miss Glazarova; camera, Vaclav Janus; editor, Jiri Srnka. At Venice Film Fest. Running time, **95 MINS.**

Girl .... Jana Brejchova
Wife .... Jirina Sejbalova
Husband .... Miroslav Dolozal

Taut period drama gets the needed topflight thesping and direction to make this an arresting pic. Detailing how a weakling, married to an older rich woman, falls in love with a pretty young ward of the house, this has the sharp observation, character delineation and mounting progression to make it a possible bet for some Yank specialized showings. However, its adherence to the drama, with a telling re-creation of the times, make this chancier for more general U.S. chances. Good critical acceptance and word-of-mouth may help it.

A vulgar, overbearing woman smothers her young ambitious husband in her all-consuming love. The husband immediately falls for an innocent young ward taken on by the wife for company and work. But he will not admit his love and the girl is finally appalled by the cloying life about her and leaves the house even after the wife dies and they can be together.

Director Jiri Weiss has sagely brought out all the conflicts by telling visual pacing. Acting falls in with his control and all the characters emerge somewhat pitiable. Though sans propaganda, this does have a weak point in the overstating the servant angle. They are always giving out hints about changes to come. Technical credits are excellent on this unusual pic. *Mosk.*

Le Bourgeois Gentilhomme
(FRENCH; COLOR)

Venice, Sept. 9.

Cinedis release of LPC-Filmsonor production. With Jean Meyer, Louis Seigner, Jacques Charon, Marie Sabouret, Robert Manuel. Directed by Jean Myer. Screenplay, Meyer, based on the Moliere play; camera (Eastmancolor), Henri Alekan; editor, K. Feyte; music, Lulli. At Venice Film Fest. Running time, **90 MINS.**

The staid, nationalized film theatre, the Comedie-Francaise, has put its first rep piece on film, and it remains strictly a filmed theatre piece. The tale of the climbing, oafish, newly rich man is scrupulously adhered to, but it is static and talking and is primarily for school use in the U.S., with some possibility for special spots with exploitation gambit of the recently successful visit of the C-F to N.Y.

Acting is properly stylized but still too overdone for the films. Color is an asset and this canned Moliere should have calls from schools all over the world. *Mosk.*

Venice, Sept. 2.

El Secuestador (The Kidnapper) (**ARGENTINIAN**). Sono Film release and production. With Lautaro Murua, Maria Vaner, Leonardo Favio, Carlos Monet. Directed by Leopoldo Torre-Nilsson. Screenplay, Beatrice Guido, Torre-Nilsson; Camera, Alberto Etchebehere; editor, Jorge Garate. At Venice Film Fest. Running time, **75 MINS.**

Wanting to show the morally debilitating effects of poverty, this pic jars with the scenes of a pig eating a baby, young lovers finding only a mortuary room in a cemetery to make love, a rape etc. Director Leopoldo Torre-Nilsson has thus overloaded his argument and this loses point to deteriorate into a macabre affair. It is only for possible exploitation spots in the U.S. and its length makes this strictly secondary fare. It is technically well done, however, with thesping good. *Mosk.*

Haz A Sziklak Alatt (The House Under the Rocks) **(HUNGARIAN)**. Hunnia Films release and production. Stars Margit Bara, Janos Gorbe, Iren Psota; features Adam Szirtes, Bela Barsi. Directed by Karoly Makk. Screenplay, Sandor Tatay; camera, Gyorgy Illes; editor, Gyorgy Hintsch. At Venice Film Fest. Running time, **100 MINS.**

Well made Magyar pic tells the tale of a homecoming soldier's attempt to return to his land after the death of his wife. His sister-in-law cares for him and nurses him back to health, but he marries another, and her rancor, the overcrowding and the refusal to move to new parts lead to tragedy when the distraught man kills the intruding sister-in-law. Pic benefits from topflight acting, excellent technical assets and a knowing direction. It looms mainly for U.S. lingo or art spots on its plus factors, but its slow unfoldment and bucolic background make this a gamble. A tastefully done nude scene may help for exploitation purposes.

This is a fine pic hampered by its touchy nationality and uncomprising tale of the resistance to change and its effects. *Mosk.*

Veliki I Mali (The Big and the Small) **(YUGOSLAVIAN)**. Avala release and production. With Ljuba Tadio, Jozo Laurencic, Nikola Ivkovic, Severin Bjelic. Directed by Vladimir Pogacic. Screenplay, Miodrag Djurdjevic; camera, Alexandre Sekulovic; editor, N. Radanovic. At Venice Film Fest. Running time, **82 MINS.**

Well made suspense-chase item has a plus in more rounded characters who become more human and meaningful in having to take moral viewpoints. It concerns a partisan on the run who holes up with an old uncommitted friend who lives without taking sides under the German occupation. His children help the man, but by the time he decides it is too late and his indecision leads to tragedy.

Suspense is well sustained and this looms a possible Yank programmer or video entry or, even better, as a likely item for remake. Direction is taut, acting brisk and movement crisp to make this a good entry. Technical credits are fine. *Mosk.*

Onionhead

Promises potent b.o. in strong mixture of farce, drama, romance, with topnotch cast. Should build on "No Time For Sergeants."

Hollywood, Sept. 19.

Warner Bros. release of Jules Schermer production. Stars Andy Griffith, Felicia Farr, Walter Matthau, Erin O'Brien, Joe Mantell. Directed by Norman Taurog. Screenplay, Nelson Gidding, based on the novel by Weldon Hill; camera, Harold Rosson; music supervisor, Ray Heindorf; editor, William Ziegler. Previewed at Academy Awards Theatre, Sept. 18, '58. Running time, **110 MINS**

Al Woods	Andy Griffith
Stella	Felicia Farr
Red Wildoe	Walter Matthau
Jo Hill	Erin O'Brien
Doc O'Neal	Joe Mantell
Ensign Higgins	Ray Danton
The Skipper	James Gregory
Gutsell	Joey Bishop
Windy Woods	Roscoe Karns
Poznicki	Claude Akins
Chief Miller	Ainslie Pryor
Yoeman Kaffhamp	Sean Garrison
Ensign Fineberg	Dan Barton
Gailla	Louise Glenn
Lieut. Bennett	Mark Roberts
Clark	Peter Brown
Charlie Berger	Tige Andrews
Agnelli	Karl Lukas

"Onionhead" is a boxoffice-potent combination of service comedy, drama and romance, including some remarkably candid, but carefully handled, explorations of wartime sex problems. The Jules Schermer production for Warner Bros., directed by Norman Taurog, should duplicate or better the success of the same studio's earlier "No Time For Sergeants." Andy Griffith again heads the cast, a uniformly good one down to the smallest role, and one that is highlighted by unusual casting of Felicia Farr and by a standout comedy portrayal by Walter Matthau.

Setting of the Nelson Gidding screenplay, from the book by Weldon Hill, is World War II, and the service involved is the Coast Guard, which Griffith joins on a toss of the coin when he decides he is getting nowhere in college with his studies or extra-curricular activities, mostly dames. They love him like a brother but a sister is not what he's seeking. He leaves a nice girl, Erin O'Brien, at home, but promptly takes up with another, not-so-nice, Felicia Farr, when his ship is stationed at Boston.

Griffith is not the bumpkin in "Onionhead" that he was in "Sergeants," although there is a basic similarity in the roles. This story is essentially more serious, although the points are generally made with humor. The picture cuts deeply in its characterization of Miss Farr, who is, in fact, a nymphomanic, a delicate point made with taste and poignance. When she marries Matthau, Griffith's shipside boss, there is real tragedy in the fact that she cannot keep her hands off whatever other man is around when Matthau is at sea. The pity of it is only heightened, too, by the the fact that Matthau plays one of the most crustily cynical characterizations since the late W. C. Fields. Griffith's exposture to this experience is part of his maturity. The other comes when he rebels against chicken officer (not chicken colonel) who is shortchanging the enlisted mess to the benefit of the officers.

Norman Taurog's direction, building on the good Gidding screenplay, does a fine job of welding disparate elements, such as the romantic and tragic, with unabashed farce that uses all aspects of motion picture sight and sound in a way few directors today do. "Onionhead" is rich with lesser characterizations, each of them perfectly clear, surely set early so each can be used spontaneously for instant effect, for comedy or drama, again and again throughout the picture. It is somewhat long for comedy, nearly two hours, but it is so carefully constructed and balanced it would only suffer from further editing; and it sustains.

Griffith dominates the picture with his special quality of the shrewd rube whose hapless machinations seem always about to precipitate disaster but instead ride cheerily, if bumpily, to success. There is strong identification and sympathy for this kind of character. Miss Farr, whose fragile looks have almost always been used for roles of exceptional gentility, plays against type in the part of an unhappy girl consumed by frustration, and makes it a moving portrait. Matthau is valuable in all his scenes, and he displays a talent for comedy to provide a drunk sequence that is one of the year's funniest single sequences. Joe Mantell, as one of Griffith's sidekicks, is also valuable to the comedy; Ray Danton uses his clean-cut good looks to underscore his despicable role; James Gregory gives dignity and importance to the captain's role, and Joey Bishop scores repeatedly as a skirt-chasing gob. Among the others in the large cast who make a vivid impression are Roscoe Karns as Griffith's barber father, Claude Akins, Louise Glenn, Ainslie Pryor, Mark Roberts, Dan Barton, Peter Brown, Tige Andrews, Karl Lukas and Sean Garrison.

Harold Rosson keeps his camera-work bright and clean for the comedy and reflects the shifting moods when the picture gears for serious moments. *Powe.*

The Decks Ran Red

Realistic adventure yarn of mutiny at sea. Good enttry for action houses.

Hollywood, Sept. 19.

Metro release of Andrew and Virginia Stone production. Stars James Mason, Dorothy Dandridge, Broderick Crawford; costars Stuart Whitman, Katherine Bard. Director-writer, Andrew Stone; camera, Meredith M. Nicholson; editor, Virginia Stone. Previewed at the studio, Sept. 16, '58. Running time, **97 MINS.**

Capt. Edwin B Rumill	James Mason
Mahia	Dorothy Dandridge
Henry Scott	Broderick Crawford
Leroy Martin	Stuart Whitman
Joan Rumill	Katharine Bard
Alex Cole	Jack Kruschen
"Bull" Pringle	John Gallaudet
Karl Pope	Barney Phillips
Mace	David R. Cross
Mr. Moody	Hank Patterson
Tom Walsh	Harry Bartell
Pete	Joel Fluellen
Jim Osborne	Guy Kingsford
Mr. Adams	Jonathan Hole
Vic	Harlan Warde
Russ Henderson	Joel Marston
Mansard	Ed Hinton
Sammy	Marshall Kent
Seaman	Robert Christopher
Seaman	Art Lewis

"The Decks Ran Red" is a descriptive title for this story, presented as fact, of an attempted mutiny at sea. Before the mutineers in the Andrew and Virginia Stone production for Metro have been beaten down, they have spilled enough blood to make the decks sticky, if not running, with gore. This presentation is in the Stone genre: all location shooting, concentration on realism and suspense, a film of almost pure adventure. By the classifications of today's market, "Decks" qualifies as a superior exploitation picture, aided by some offbeat castings and star names.

The plot of the story, written as well as directed by Andrew Stone, is a plan by Broderick Crawford and Stuart Whitman, crew members of a chartered freighter, to kill off other members of the crew, rig the ship to make it look like an abandoned derelict, and then bring it in as salvage. According to maritime law, it's said, they will get half the ship's value—$1,000,000—as prize money.

James Mason, who has been first officer on a trim Matson liner, is flown to Australia to take charge of this dingy vessel when its captain mysteriously dies. It is Mason's first command. He quickly discovers he is in for trouble from a lack-lustre and sullen crew, trouble that is compounded by taking aboard a native Maori cook and his wife, latter being Dorothy Dandridge. Her obvious charms add another element of discontent to the jinxed ship. The plot is eventually foiled by Mason derring-do but not before a large part of the crew has been maimed or murdered.

The Stones, producers, writer, director, editor of the picture, make every foot of film count. The story is faintly incredible at times and there is a tendency to impose dialog on a scene when the action has already spoken for itself. But the picture moves swiftly and absorbingly. The emphasis on action inevitably leaves characterizations sketchy and sometimes indistinct. While this kind of pace insures attention, it also dilutes potential sympathy.

Story is actually the only weak element in the Stones' production values. What story they have they tell exceedingly well, utilizing all devices of the screen, sight and sound, to a degree not always explored. As always, too, they endow their film with a vivid degree of realism in shooting entirely, interiors and exteriors, on location.

The actors must rely on intensity of performance rather than rounded characterization for interest. Mason, really the only one for whom any background or motivation is provided, handles an athletic role with ease and projects strength in confusion. Miss Dandridge contributes an exotic note; Broderick Crawford is a menacing heavy, Stuart Whitman an intriguingly weak one, and Katherine Bard is effective in her brief appearance. Others in the large cast who register include Jack Kruschen, Joel Marston, David R. Cross, Hank Patterson, John Gallaudet and Barney Phillips.

Meredith M. Nicholson's photography is especially impressive in his interior compositions, such as the ship's engine room. There is virtually no music in the film, but the authentic sounds of the ship at sea—sound by Ryder Sound Service and John Kean—are skillfully captured and used for heightening dramatic effect. *Powe.*

The Fearmakers

Melodrama with Washington, D. C., setting and international complications. Satisfactory attraction for program bills.

Hollywood, Sept. 26.

United Artists release of Martin H. Lancer production. Stars Dana Andrews; costars Dick Foran, Marilee Earle, Mel Torme. Directed by Jacques Tourneur. Associate producer, Leon Chooluck. Screenplay Elliot West and Chris Appley, based on the novel by Darwin L. Teilhet; camera, Sam Leavitt; music, Irving Gertz; editor, J. R. Whittridge. Previewed at Goldwyn studio, Sept. 17, '58. Running time, **83 MINS.**

Alan Eaton	Dana Andrews
Jim McGinnis	Dick Foran

Barney Bond	Mel Torme
Lorraine Dennis	Marilee Earle
Vivian Leder	Veda Ann Borg
Harold Loder	Kelly Thorsden
Rodney Hillyer	Joel Marston

"The Fearmakers" of this title are the poll-takers, those of this modern breed who twist their polls and the reactions they get to create opinion rather than reflect it. Martin H. Lancer's production for United Artists thus deals with a pertinent, little-explored subject of contemporary interest, and it makes an absorbing melodrama when it sticks to its point. Jacques Tourneur's direction makes the most of the action involved and with Dana Andrews toplined, "The Fearmakers" will be a satisfactory attraction.

The screenplay by Elliot West and Chris Appley, from the novel by Darwin L. Teilhet, has Andrews as a returned Korean vet who is suffering from the brainwashing received as a Communist prisoner. He is further shocked on his return to his Washington, D. C., home to find his public relations-opinion sampling firm has been taken over by a stranger, Dick Foran. Andrews' partner has been killed in an accident of curious circumstance just before selling out the business. Andrews finds those in charge now using highly suspicious polls to bolster peculiar causes, to choose candidates for public office and to help write their platforms. Andrews sets out to rescue his business and winds up battling a nest of foreign agents.

Scenes dealing directly with the poll business have a fascination because they are fresh and different. The cops-and-robbers aspects of the picture make it seem less interesting, and give it a routine flavor. There are also a number of diversionary plot threads that are not particularly helpful to the central story line or its developments. It is also not helpful to identify the "villain" of the piece as a committee opposed to atomic tests without making clear that not all those against such experiments are dupes or agents of a foreign power.

Andrews has warmth and charm as the confused war vet and his strong conviction lends weight to the role. Foran is able as the chief poll-rigger. Marilee Earle is pleasant as Andrews' romantic interest, and Mel Torme is promising in a straight dramatic role. Veda Ann Borg is a standout in a character comedy part, and Kelly Thorsden and Joel Marston are valuable in supporting characterizations.

Sam Leavitt's photography is perceptive and J. R. Whittredge's editing is valuable in combining the Washington location shooting with studio work. Other technical credits, Serge Krizman's art direction, John Kean's sound, and the score by Irving Gertz, are first-rate. *Powe.*

As Young as We Are

Attractively produced school drama; b.o. chances are good.

Hollywood, Sept. 18.

Paramount release of William Alland production. Stars Robert Harland and Pippa Scott. Features Majel Barrett, Ty Hungerford, Barry Atwater, Carla Hoffman, Ellen Corby, Harald Dyrenforth, Ross Elliott, Linda Watkins, Beverly Long, Mack Williams. Directed by Bernard Girard. Screenplay, Meyer Dolinsky, from story by Dolinsky and Alland; camera, Haskell Boggs; editor, Everett Douglas. Previewed at the studio, Sept. 18, '58. Running time, 75 MINS.

Hank Moore	Robert Harland
Kim Hutchins	Pippa Scott
Joyce Goodwin	Majel Barrett
Roy Nielson	Ty Hungerford
Mr. Peterson	Barry Atwater
Nina	Carla Hoffman
Mettie McPherson	Ellen Corby
Mr. Evans	Harald Dyrenforth
Bob	Ross Elliott
Mrs. Hutchins	Linda Watkins
Marge	Beverly Long
Dr. Hutchins	Mack Williams

"As Young As We Are" is persuasive evidence that a film's values can be exploitable and artistic at the same time. Put together with taste and perception, if little money, it will be especially appealing to highschool trade and with proper packaging and promotion should bring back to Paramount considerably more than it paid out.

The problem spun by "As Young As We Are" is based in life, and it's aptly described in the Meyer Dolinsky screenplay, based on a good story by Dolinsky and producer Alland. With exceptional skill and feeling, Bernard Girard again proves his liberal talent for directing young actors and has created a schoolroom atmosphere that is natural and exciting.

Story revolves around Pippa Scott, a young highschool teacher who takes a job in a desert community when her youthful appearance prevents her from gaining employment in more desirable locales. In the week before the start of school, she meets Robert Harland and falls for him nearly as hard as he falls for her. When school gets underway and he turns up as a student, the problems begin, with the youth not wanting to give up Miss Scott, even if it means death. Everything works out relatively satisfactorily for all, with Harland returning to his former girl, Carla Hoffman, who, from the looks of her, should have been mighty tough to leave in the first place.

Miss Scott is truly a sensitive actress, and with this role should make an impression in filmdom. Harland, too, is very good as he gathers the needed sympathy. Tops in support is Majel Barrett, as another young teacher, with fine performances also turned in by Ty Hungerford as a ruffian student, Barry Atwater as the vice-principal and Harold Dryenforth as the understanding school head. Miss Hoffman proves to be as fine a thesp as she is a looker.

Haskell Boggs' camerawork is adept, as is art direction by Hal Pereira and Henry Bumstead, editing by Everett Douglas and sound by Gene Merritt and Charles Grenzbach. Harold Barlow has penned a pleasant title song which Andy Russell sings well on film. *Ron.*

Rockets Galore
(BRITISH-COLOR)

Lighthearted topical comedy with some marquee value in name of Jeannie Carson. Good bet for all houses.

London, Sept. 17.

Rank presentation and release. Stars Jeannie Carson, Donald Sinden. Producer, Basil Dearden. Director, Michael Relph. Screenplay, Monja Danischewsky, from the novel by Compton Mackenzie; camera, Reginald Wyer; editor, John Guthridge; music, Cedric Thorpe Davie. At Rank preview theatre, London, Sept. 16, '58. Running time, 94 MINS.

Janet Macleod	Jeannie Carson
Hugh Mander	Donald Sinden
Capt. Waggett	Roland Culver
Mrs. Waggett	Catherine Lacey
Father James	Noel Purcell
Air Commodore Watchorn	Ian Hunter
Duncan Ban	Duncan Macrae
Mrs. Campbell	Jean Cadell
George Campbell	Gordon Jackson
Joseph MacLeod	Alex Mackenzie
Dr. Hamburger	Carl Jaffe
Andrew Wishart	Nicholas Phipps
Constable MacRae	Jameson Clark
Drooby	Ronald Corbett
Kenny MacLeod	James Copeland
Reverend Angus	John Stevenson Lang
Kirsty	Nell Ballantyne
Mumford	Reginald Beckwith
Meeching	Arthur Howard
Capt. MacKechnie	John Laurie
Roderick	Jack Short
Catriona	Gabrielle Blunt

The rocket, which hangs so menacingly over the world, could misfire badly as a comedy subject. But "Rockets Galmore" handles the topical idea tactfully. There is satire in the film, but the treatment is warmly lighthearted and the result is a picture which is full of fun and should amuse most audiences. The presence of Jeannie Carson as the heroine will give it added interest for U.S. audiences.

"Rockets" was filmed on the remote Isle of Barra where, some time ago, "Tight Little Island" was shot. "Rockets" is not nearly as funny as that film, but has the advantage of color and superb shots of the island scenery. It is at its best when it is gagging at the expense of television and the newspapers, and it is distinguished by a number of sound performances.

The Isle of Todday is selected as the site of a rocket base and Donald Sinden, a Royal Air Force officer, is sent to explore the lay of the land. The place is a dreamy, secluded spot where the islanders want no truck with modern "civilization." When rocket experts arrive to start work on the base the islanders start to sabotage operations, even the kids joining in to thwart the experts. Then a misguided rocket from the mainland lands on Todday and the natives are more than ever determined that the rocket base must not be allowed to happen. Leader of the rebels is Jeannie Carson, the island's schoolmistress.

But despite all their efforts, work on the base proceeds and the islanders are faced with eviction. But nobody in high places gives a rap for the feelings of the natives. Then Miss Carson has an idea. How better to stir public opinion than to appeal to their sentimentality—not over people but over birds. She dyes a nesting gull pink and immediately there is a public outcry protesting against the rare birds being disturbed. It reaches Cabinet level, is splashed in the newspapers and discussed on television. And Todday gets its own way.

This is quite a slight theme, but Monja Danishcewsky's witty screenplay and Michael Relph's friendly direction create a pleasant atmosphere admirably sustained by a sound cast. Miss Carson is a fresh, appealing heroine with a nice sense of fun, and Sinden is a stalwart hero. Roland Culver, Noel Purcell, Duncan Macrae and Ian Hunter are among those who join in the fun and games to good effect.

Reginald Wyer has done some effective camerawork and Jack Maxsted's art work is good throughout. "Rockets Galore" is an inocuous comedy, but nonetheless appealing. *Rich.*

Kvinna I Leopard
(Woman In Fur Coat)
(SWEDISH)

Stockholm, Sept. 9.

Europa Film production and release. Stars Harriet Andersson, Ulf Palme; features Erik Strandmark, Sture Strom, Renee Bjoerling, Georg Funkqvist, Siv Ericks, Curt Masreliez, Mona Malm. Written and directed by Jan Molander. Camera, Ingvar Borild and Bertil Palmgren; music, Harry Arnold. At Saga, Stockholm, Sept. 8, '58. Running time, 100 MINS.

Marianne Croneman	Harriet Andersson
Arvid Croneman	Ulf Palme
Doctor Lennart Haegg	Erik Strandmark
Hans Lundin, actor	Sture Stroem
Mother-in-law	Renee Bjoerling
Lawyer	Georg Funkqvist
Eirgitta	Siv Ericks
Curt	Curt Masreliez
Young actress	Mona Malm

A Swedish thriller that tends to be too conventional, "Woman in Fur Coat" shapes as a good entry for the European trade but it looks rather doubtful for U.S. audiences. Writer-director Jan Molander has good ideas anent how to do a crime film with the right horror effects. But his psychological touches make the story improbable and slow up the action.

Harriet Andersson, wed to wealthy Ulf Palme, tires of him since she's in love with the family doctor. They murder Palme and take a honeymoon trip shortly after the funeral. Although the police fail to take action, suspicious relatives start a war of nerves against the femme culprit who becomes a victim of hysteria.

Miss Andersson turns in an acceptable performance as the murderer, well assisted by Palme, despite the short time he's on screen. Erik Strandmark is good as the doctor-lover while newcomer Sture Stroem deserved a better debut role than that of an actor involved in the proceedings.

Camerawork of Ingvar Borild and Bertil Palmgren is an asset.

Harry Arnold's score, including a catchy tune, "I Love You Forever," is tuneful. *Wing.*

Carry On, Sergeant
(BRITISH)

Corny but mostly very funny Army farce which will click in U.K. provinces, and is not designed for any other type of audience.

London, Sept. 16.

Anglo Amalgamated release of a Nat Cohen and Stuart Levy production. Stars William Hartnell, Bob Monkhouse, Shirley Eaton, Eric Barker, Dora Bryan, Bill Owen, Kenneth Connor. Producer, Peter Rogers. Director, Gerald Thomas. Screenplay, Norman Hudis; camera, Peter Hennessy; editor, Peter Boita; music, Bruce Montgomery. At Plaza, London, Sept. 15, '58. Running time, 85 MINS.

Sergeant Grimshawe	William Hartnell
Charlie Sage	Bob Monkhouse
Mary	Shirley Eaton
Captain Potts	Eric Barker
Nora	Dora Bryan
Corporal Copping	Bill Owen
Horace Strong	Kenneth Connor
Peter Golightly	Charles Hawtrey
James Bailey	Kenneth Williams
Miles Heywood	Terence Longdon
Herbert Brown	Norman Rossington
Captain Clark	Hattie Jacques
Andy Galloway	Gerald Campion
Gun Sergeant	Cyril Chamberlain
1st Specialist	Gordon Tanner
2nd Specialist	Frank Forsyth
3rd Specialist	Basil Dignam
4th Specialist	John Gatrell
5th Specialist	Arnold Diamond
6th Specialist	Martin Boddey
Medical Corporal	Ian Whittaker
Stores Sergeant	Anthony Sager

"Carry On, Sergeant" is a blatant, unashamed, all-out bid for yocks. It will make a cash-killing in the British sticks and probably die almost everywhere else. It's an Army farce exploiting practically every Army gag, but while some of the writing is careless and there is no attempt to develop a reasonable story, it is by no means a sloppily produced second feature.

Anybody who has served in the Army will recognize that, though fantastically exaggerated, the characters and the situations are based on some sort of possibility, with the exception of the miraculous ending. A bunch of talented character comedians have been handed these situations and, in their respective styles, they wring a lot more out of them and the dialog than the writers provide. Director Gerald Thomas' job has been to keep things moving merrily and at a speed that will prevent the customers thinking overmuch.

William Hartnell is a training sergeant who is about to retire from the service and has one more chance to fulfill his life ambition, which is to train the champion troop of the intake. Moreover, he has a $140 bet on the outcome. Of course, he is handed a bunch of rookies which is believable only in farce. The stock characters are there. The barrack-room attorney, the young man in love, the hypochondriac malingerer, the man always out of step . . . in fact, the repertory company of trainees. There's the sergeant with the bark, the fussy officer.

Everything goes wrong throughout training and it looks as though the sergeant's ambition and bet will go down the drain. But, by some sort of miracle which West Point would never find aceptable, they become an overnight sensation and win all the passing-out honors.

Among the situations which inevitably crop up there are some surefire yock-earners. Like the man who shows up at the sick bay so often that the medical officer finishes the examination with the casual "see you tomorrow." These hit the audience over the head with their predictable laugh-potentiality.

Kenneth Connor, a w.k. radio comic, steals most of the honors as the hypochondriac being chased by a love-starved Army waitress, played characteristically by Dora Bryan. He has a shade too much to do, but never misses a trick. Bob Monkhouse, called up on his wedding day, Shirley Eaton as his frustrated wife who crops up in camp, and Charles Hawtrey, Terence Longdon, Kenneth Williams, Norman Rossington and Gerald Campion as assorted recruits add their quota to the fun and games. Other smart performances come from Eric Barker as a fussy officer, William Hartnell as the gravelly-voiced sergeant and Bill Owen as his faithful corporal.

"Carry On, Sergeant" is a modest, unimportant film. But it keeps entirely within its terms of reference and for at least 75% of its way will have ordinary family audiences in a cheerful state. Atmosphere in the training barracks is authentic, thanks to Army cooperation. *Rich.*

Venice Films

Paris, Sept. 2.

La Moucharde (The Informer) (FRENCH). Fernand Rivers release of Poste Parisien-Films Artistiques release. Stars Dany Carrel, Pierre Vaneck; features Yves Deniaud, Dinan. Directed by Guy Lefranc. Screenplay, Georges Tabet. Andre Tabet, Lefranc; camera, Maurice Barry; editor, Armand Psenny. At Balzac, Paris. Running time, 100 MINS.

Familiar accoutrements are exhibited in this plodding pic: a nubile young girl who does all for love, including robbery; plays police stool pigeon and engages in double-crossing of men who love her; some nude scenes; and the final chase. Though having overtones on youthful discord here, it never brings any real perception or comment on the situation and thus this entry emerges as only a possible U.S. exploitation item

on its nude and love scenes. It's primarily a local bet. *Mosk.*

Mimi Pinson (FRENCH). Heuze release of Hergi production. Stars Dany Robin, Raymond Pellegrin, Andre Luguet; features, Robert Hirsch, Mireille Granelli. Directed by Robert Dareno. Screenplay, Maurice Auberge, Marie-Jose Dareno, camera, Marcel Weiss; editor, L. Barbenchon. At Marignon, Paris. Running time, 100 MINS.

Meandering situation comedy shapes strictly home fare on its unimaginative, obvious unfolding of how an innocent, too archly and annoyingly played by Dany Robin, gets her man in spite of the worldly enemies plotting to cheat her out of everything, including her virtue.

Bit of fluff lacks the breeziness and inventiveness for any Yank chances. Playing, technical aspects and production dress are fair. *Mosk.*

Venice, Sept. 9.

Smultronstallet (The End of Day) (SWEDISH). Svensk Film release and production. Stars Victor Sjostrom, Bibi Andersson, Ingrid Thulin. Written and directed by Ingmar Bergman. Camera Gunnar Fischer; editor, Erik Nordgren. At Venice Film Fest. Running time, 92 MINS.

Film copped the Grand Prix at the recent Berlin Film Fest. Grim drama deals with an old man who is on his way to get an honorary doctorate degree after 50 years as a doctor. He is accompanied by his daughter-in-law. The trip becomes a reliving of the old man's life as he realizes he led an empty life due to his stuffiness, egotism and inability to really love and feel. Nightmares, dreams and reminiscences are expertly blended as space and time are broken to work on the various levels of the man's thoughts.

Pic sometimes talks too much in philosophical asides, but it remains a searching pictorial analysis of a man's life. Expert directorial touches and notations of director Ingmar Bergman, and the dignified miming of oldtime director Victor Seastrom, as the old man, plus other fine thespic additions, make this an offbeater with good U.S. arty chances. It's too personal and profound a work for ordinary situations. Word-of-mouth and critics could help this in special Yank situations. *Mosk.*

The Barbarian And The Geisha
(COLOR; C'SCOPE)

Lavish but not very exciting period spectacle set in mid-19th Century Japan. Production will rest strongly on John Wayne's star pull.

Hollywood, Sept. 26.

20th-Fox release of Eugene Frenke production. Stars John Wayne; features Eiko Ando, Sam Jaffe, So Yaramura. Directed by John Huston. Screenplay, Charles Grayson; based on a story by Ellis St. Joseph; camera (DeLuxe Color), Charles G. Clarke; music, Hugo Friedhofer; editor, Stuart Gilmore. Previewed at the studio, Sept. 25, '58. Running time, 105 MINS.

Townsend Harris	John Wayne
Okichi	Eiko Ando
Henry Heusken	Sam Jaffe
Tamura	So Yamamura
Ship Captain	Normal Thomson
Lt. Fisher	James Robbins
Prime Minister	Morita
Daimyo	Kodaya Ichikawa
Shogun	Hiroshi Yamato
Harusha	Tokujiro Iketaniuchi
Lord Hotta	Fuji Kasai
Chamberlain	Takeshi Kumagai

"The Barbarian and the Geisha" is an Oriental pageant of primitive beauty based on the "true" story of the exploits of the first U. S. consul to establish headquarters in Japan. Eugene Frenke's production for 20th-Fox is lavish as John Huston has directed it with an eye to utilizing native backgrounds and people for exotic effect. But it is light in other departments. The John Wayne starrer, which introduces an attractive Japanese newcomer, Eiko Ando, is being released in immediate mass bookings, which seems the smart handling of this not fully satisfying presentation for maximum return.

Once opened to Christian Missionaries, then closed, Japan was a Forbidden Kingdom to outsiders in 1856 when U. S. Consul-General Townsend Harris, played by Wayne, arrived off the port of Shimoda, where the Charles Grayson screenplay, based on Ellis St. Joseph's story, begins. Prodded by Yankee gunboats Japan had signed a treaty granting diplomatic representation but the Japanese had no intention of honoring the document. Even shipwrecked U. S. mariners were murdered when they landed in Japan. Harris was under orders from his government to open the door on the hermetically-sealed country, and, armed only with his own personality and accompanied only by his European translator, Sam Jaffe, he prepared to do so.

After initial harrassing and setbacks, Wayne gains the confidence of the local noble, So Yamamura, who agrees to take him to the court of the Shogun to plead his case. Meantime, to make Wayne's isolation easier, Yamamura delivers a geisha, Eiko Ando, to the non-Nipponese barbarian. Although there is no explicit romance between Wayne and Miss Ando, an attachment is suggested, so there is pathos in the end when circumstances force them apart. Wayne is successful, however, in his diplomatic mission.

"The Barbarian and the Geisha" (originally titled "The Townsend Harris Story") is rich in atmosphere and in some stirringly-staged scenes, such as Wayne's arrival by ship at Shimoda, his presentation to the Shogun's court and an archery meet of medieval pomp. It is less exciting in its personal delineations. Huston uses a technique of having the Japanese speak Japanese throughout. It is effective initially from several points of view, but it becomes somewhat annoying as the film

progresses. The character played by Miss Ando acts as the narrator behind some of this action, but this device is only partially successful.

The excitement that is usually a hallmark of Huston's direction is surprisingly sparse. His special facility of creating strong and commanding characters seems to be submerged, perhaps deliberately, in the interests of historical accuracy. The dialog is often declamatory and does little to make the principles come alive. While the film is continuously pleasing to the eye, it too seldom stirs the mind or touches the heart.

Wayne makes a stalwart and credible hero, although handicapped by a role that seems more a figurehead of the U. S. government than a figure of a single American. Miss Ando, whose looks are only slightly Oriental, is most moving and makes a vivid film bow. Sam Jaffe creates sympathy in his role, and the Japanese actors who make up the bulk of the cast, include So Yamamura, Morita, Hiroshi Yamato and Kodaya Ichikawa in memorable portrayals.

Charles G. Clarke's photography, in glowing DeLuxe color, is adept at catching the delicate shadings typical of Japanese coloration, and captures also a sense of flow and grandeur in the action scenes. Hugo Friedhofer's score is purposely romantic, and useful in infusing a warmth into scenes otherwise lacking. Stuart Gilmore's editing and the sound by W. D. Flick and Warren B. Delaplain makes the production as slick as if it had all been done on a sound stage. Art direction by Lyle B. Wheeler and Jack Martin takes full advantage of the Japanese background. *Powe.*

Hong Kong Confidential

Program meller on Oriental espionage, but well done within its limits for strengthening double bills.

Hollywood, Sept. 26.

United Artists release of Robert E. Kent production. Stars Gene Barry; co-stars Beverly Tyler, Allison Hayes; features Edward Kemmer, Michael Pate, Rico Alaniz. Directed by Edward L. Cahn. Screenplay, Orville H. Hampton; camera, Kenneth Peach; music, Paul Sawtell and Bert Shefter; editor, Edward Mann. Previewed at Goldwyn studio, Sept. 23, '58. Running time, 67 MINS.

Casey Reed	Gene Barry
Fay Wells	Beverly Tyler
Elene Martine	Allison Hayes
Owen Howard	Noel Drayton
Frank Paige	Edward Kemmer
John Blanchard	Michael Pate
Muto	W. Beal Wong
Mao	Mel Prestige
Dan Young	King Calder
Brooks	Bryan Roper
Fernando	Rico Alaniz
Chung	Philip Ahn
Chief	Walter Woolf King
Youseff	Joe Vitale
Redhead	Asa Maynor
Inspector	Owen McGivney
Linov	Lou Krugman
Maitre D'	Jack Kenny
Jen	Bill Saito

British and American espionage agents are pitted against the Communists in "Hong Kong Confidential," a melodrama designed for program bills that will be an asset in the lower position that is its niche. Robert E. Kent's production for United Artists, directed by Edward L. Cahn, deals with some supposed behind-the-scenes action by the major powers in the Middle and Far East, but it wisely sticks to almost purely personal adventure without getting too involved in higher echelon machinations or their meanings.

Gene Barry plays a U.S. agent whose cover is that of a night club singer in Hong Kong. When the young son of a Middle East Arab potentate is kidnapped and believed held in Barry's area by Communist abductors, Barry is assigned to locate him. The climax of the story is a plan by the Communists to murder the boy and Barry so it will appear that the snatch was a U.S. trick to pressure the Arab state into a favorable alliance with the West. Action shifts from Hong Kong to neighboring Macao, with interpolated shots of world capitals—some stock and some staged—and gains substance by use of a semi-documentary, narration device.

Orville H. Hampton's screenplay avoids the pitfalls of pedantry, establishes the simple characters well, and provides plenty of plot turns which director Cahn uses to keep things boiling. Gene Barry is likable and credible as the singer-spy, and Beverly Tyler, as a good girl, and Allison Hayes, as a bad one, are capable. Edward Kemmer, Michael Pate, Rico Alaniz, Noel Drayton, King Calder and Philip Ahn are important in the supporting cast.

Kenneth Peach's photography does everything possible to make the back lot sets look like the Far East and Edward Mann's editing ties in all together for superior effect. Music by Paul Sawtell and Bert Shefter is good. *Powe.*

Passionate Summer
(BRITISH—COLOR)

Leisurely romantic drama set in Jamaica; appealing performance by Virginia McKenna and lush tropical locale.

London, Sept. 25.

Rank production (Kenneth Harper-George Willoughby) and release. Stars Virginia McKenna, Bill Travers, Yvonne Mitchell. Directed by Rudolph Cartier. Screenplay, Joan Henry; editor, Reginald Mills; camera, Ernest Steward; music, Angelo Lavagnino. At Leicester Square Theatre, London. Running time, 104 MINS.

Judy .... Virginia McKenna
Douglas Lockwood .... Bill Travers
Mrs. Pawley .... Yvonne Mitchell
Mr. Pawley .... Alexander Knox
Louis .... Carl Mohner
Silvia .... Ellen Barrie
Duffield .... Guy Middleton
Coroner .... Gordon Heath
Mrs. Morgan .... Pearl Prescod
Joe .... Harry Quashie
Cable Clerk .... Roscoe Holder
Boatman .... Danny Daniels
Air Hostess .... Jan Holden
Shopkeeper .... John Harrison
John .... Bruce Pitt
Norah .... Waveney Lee
Alan .... Martin Stephens

Despite an appealing performance by Virginia McKenna and some excellent color lensing by Ernest Steward, "Passionate Summer" remains the sort of glossy novelettish yarn that will do nothing for the reputation of the British film industry. It is a leisurely romantic drama, cluttered with cliches and uninspired dialog. Although the stars may have some marquee value in U.K., the pic cannot expect to go far in the U.S.

Set in Jamaica, "Summer" has Bill Travers as a dedicated schoolmaster teaching at Alexander Knox's progressive school. One of the pupils is a particular problem child whose confidence Travers works patiently to gain. That is one yarn. The other story line deals with Travers' chequered romance with a glamorous air-hostess, and the headmaster's frustrated wife trying to wreck the romance and capture Travers for her own amusement. Where the two stories impinge on each other is towards the end. Loaded, Travers' resistance to the schoolmarm breaks down, the child spots them smooching in his rooms and, in a fit of jealous rage, rushes out into a hurricane and falls to her death over a cliff. This brings the schoolmarm to her senses and paves the way for Travers' romance with the air-hostess to pan out satisfactorily.

Miss McKenna as the fickle air-hostess looks the complete charmer and hers is the only major performance to rate any medals. But she is not helped overmuch by her co-star, Bill Travers, who is also her real life husband. He plays the role of the schoolmaster with a stolidity that is rarely less than dull. Audiences may find it difficult to believe that Miss McKenna would have preferred him to the other string to her bow, man-about-town Carl Mohner. Yvonne Mitchell does the best that she can with the ungrateful part of the headmaster's embittered and sulky wife while Knox is his usual competent self as the stuffy headmaster. There are a couple of small cameos which are well played. Guy Middleton as a racy schoolmaster and Gordon Heath with a subtle and cultured performance as a Negro coroner.

An American child, Ellen Barrie, makes her British debut in "Passionate Summer" and shows much intelligence as the precocious moppet over whom all the fuss is about. That some sound performers fail to give very much to the film is due partly to the screenplay by Joan Henry. Miss Henry is an established and skilled writer but this stodgy tale defeated her.

Rudolph Cartier's direction does less for the actors than for the colorful backgrounds. He has caught splendidly the flavor of the Jamaican locale, the noise, the happiness and the heat. While a lot of the film was actually shot in the West Indies, a great deal was done in the studio and the matching is faultless. *Rich.*

Lek Pa Regnbagen
(The Rainbow Dilemma)
(SWEDISH)

Stockholm, Sept. 10.

Svensk Filmindustri production and release. Stars Mai Zetterling, Alf Kjellin; features Birger Malmsten, Gunlog Hagberg, Isa Quensel, Claes Thelander, Else-Marie Brandt, Inga Landgre, Gunnar Sjoberg, Lars Egge. Directed by Lars-Eric Kjellgren. Screenplay, Vilgot Sjoman; camera, Gunnar Fischer; music, Eric Nordgren. At Roda Kvarn, Stockholm, Sept. 9, '58. Running time, 92 MINS.

Vanja .... Mai Zetterling
Bjoern .... Alf Kjellin
Hasse .... Birger Malmsten
Barbro .... Gunloeg Hagberg
Bjoern's mother .... Isa Quensel
Hannes .... Claes Thelander
The Blonde .... Else-Marie Brandt
The Redhead .... Inga Landgre
District Attorney ...... Gunnar Sjoeberg
The Judge .... Lars Egge

Fine boxoffice prospects in the international market loom for "The Rainbow Dilemma," a romance drama with sexy overtones. Names of Mai Zetterling and Alf Kjellin will help dress marquees. The Svensk Filmindustri production appears to be a particularly strong entry for U. S. art houses and Swedish-language areas.

While the Vilgot Sjoman screenplay outlines the familiar story of boy-meets-girl, nevertheless its treatment is fresh and engaging. Miss Zetterling, a girl with certain complexes and a social pathos, meets Kjellin in Stockholm U. circles. A man of 30, he shuns marriage due to unpleasant recollections of his parents' experiences.

Couple become romantically attached, but a conflict arises and finally Miss Zetterling leaves Kjellin. He salves his disappointment by having affairs with new girls. However, he can't forget his true love and asks her to marry him when she's on the verge of leaving the country. As the plane leaves with her aboard at the finale, Kjellin is figuratively left up in the air as is the audience.

Miss Zetterling is convincing as a girl haunted by the feelings of a woman in love. Kjellin is impressive as her romantic vis-a-vis while other cast members headed by Birger Malmstem and Gunloeg Hagberg lend good support. Direction of Lars-Eric Kjellgren is tops as are Eric Nordgren's music and Gunnar Fischer's camerawork.

Boudoir scenes are tastefully done and shouldn't affect the film's chances in any censor's eyes. Swedish dialog, however, occasionally is a bit risque and could offend some quarters. On the whole this production has ample exploitation values since the story hints at a "sinful" Sweden. *Winq.*

Pezzo, Capopezzo, e Capitano
(ITALO-GERMAN)
(Ferraniacolor-Scope)

Rome, Sept. 17.

Atlantisfilm release of an Atlantisfilm-Bamberger co-production. Stars Vittorio DeSica; features Folco Lulli, Lianella Carell, Heinz Reincke, Nino Manfredi, Ingmar Zeisberg, Helene Remy. Directed by Wolfgang Staudte. Screenplay, Duccio Tessari, Wolfgang Staudte, Ennio De Concini; camera, Gabor Pogany; music, Francesco Lavagnino. Previewed in Rome. Running time, 97 MINS.

Ernesto DeRossi .... Vittorio DeSica
Hans Richter .... Heinz Reincke
Sciaccabratta .... Folco Lulli

Good story in the British Ealing Studio tradition, given uneven handling here for disappointing results, though opening half of pic, plus cast names, will carry it through to okay returns in its countries of origin. Has remake possibilities.

Anti-war theme pervades tale of captain of a tiny vegetable steamer plying the Italian coastline during the last war. A chance meeing with a British sub, which avoids battle with the midget prey, and subsequent interrogation by German intelligence, gives Capt. DeRossi (DeSica) a mistaken idea of his ships' battle possibilities vs. the Allied Navy. Equipped with a ridiculous cannon, he decides to let his vegetable cargo rot and steam into battle, only to sink in knee-deep water when his strained boilers explode.

Buildup is fine and often hilarious, but director Staudte lets pace slacken at halfawy mark, and pic loses style and momentum from then on. DeSica correctly hams up his role as the would-be battle commander, while able backing comes from Folco Lulli as his engineer, Heinz Reincke as a German sailor detached to the tramp steamer, and Rolf Tasna as a German officer. Others in large cast have less to work with.

Gabor Pogany's Ferraniacolor lensing captures the Riviera locations colorfully, and Francesco Lavagnino's musical score appropriately counterpoints action. Technical credits are standard. *Hawk.*

Cette Nuit La
(That Night)
(FRENCH)

Paris, Sept. 23.

Cinedis release of Soprofilm production. Stars Mylene Demongeot, Maurice Ronet, Jean Servais; features Bernard Noel, Jean Lara. Directed by Maurice Caseneuve. Screenplay, P. Guerin, H. F. Rey, from the novel by Michel Lebrun; camera, L. H. Burel; editor, Louisette Hautecoeur. At Marignan, Paris. Running time, 100 MINS.

Sylvie .... Mylene Demongeot
Jean .... Maurice Ronet
Editor .... Jean Servais
Blackmailer .... Bernard Noel
Inspector .... Jean Lara

Suspense item also mixes in glimpses of a rather decadent Parisian highlife as well as variations on pure and profane love. But suspense is somewhat obvious, and characterization not up to the amorous revelations, thus making this an okay local entry and mainly for possible dualer or program situations internationally on its well-made aspects.

A young magazine layout man has his wife, a model for the mag, coveted by his rather degenerate editor. When the wife toys around with the elder editor to get a loan, the young man tries to kill him outside his home but strikes down the wrong man. Then comes blackmail, the true love arising between husband and wife, and the final telegraphed denouement.

Acting is good but not knowing enough to give true substance to the too simply etched characters. Direction by newcomer Maurice Caseneuve is slick but too mannered. Fewer effects and more humanity would have made this a more worthwhile item. Technically, it is fine. *Mosk.*

Au Pied, Au Cheval et Par Spoutnik
(FRENCH)

Paris, Sept. 23.

Cinedis release of Regina-Filmsonor production. Stars Noel-Noel; features Denise Grey, Mischa Auer, Darry Cowl, Noel Roquevert. Directed by Jean Dreville. Screenplay, Jean-Jacques Vital, Robert Rocca, Jacques Grello; camera, Andre Bac; editor, Jean Fayte. At Paris, Paris. Running time, 94 MINS

Martin .... Noel-Noel
Marguerite .... Denise Grey
Panov .... Mischa Auer
Maire .... Noel Roquevert
Ministre .... Darry Cowl

Science fiction and French bourgeois situation comedy are fairly well mixed in this spoof. Some good comic invention goes astray when the amnesiac middle-aged hero gets mixed up in a trip in a man-carrying Russian sputnik. On its timely qualities it could rank for dualer use in offshore situations.

After losing his memory in an accident, Noel-Noel mistakes a Russo dog which lands in a sputnik in his yard for his own long lost canine. When the government cannot get the hound from him the Russians invite him to Moscow where he accidentally goes off in the new sputnik with a Russo professor, well played by Mischa Auer.

Noel-Noel's clever acting as the shrewd, distructful Frenchman, caught up in sci-fi, gets the most laughs in this easygoing pic. Others also join in to make the going quite funny at times. But so-so special effects detract from the final episodes. Russo scenes are well done and kidding hits home at times, especially in scenes where the absentminded Frenchman keeps asking about the Czar, etc. *Mosk.*

Soledad
(ITALO-SPANISH)
(Color-CinemaScope)

Rome, Sept. 17.

Lux Film release of a Lux-Aspa co-production. Stars Fernando Fernan Gomez, German Cobos, Pilar Cansino. Directed

by Enrico Gras and Mario Craveri. Screenplay, Gras, Craveri, DeConcini, Escriva, Linares, and Guerra, from a story by Vicente Escriva. Camera (C'Scope-Ferraniaclor), Mario Craveri; music, Francesco Lavagnino; editor, Mario Serandrei. Previewed in Rome. Running time, 90 MINS.

Pac .... Fernando Fernan Gomez
Manuel .... German Cobos
Soledad .... Pilar Cansino

A single plot line is the basic difference between "Soledad" and the authors' previous feature documentaries such as "Los Continent" and "Smpire of the Sun." Basically, this one is an illustration of certain Spanish folkways as the others handled other areas, yet somehow "Soledad" fails to click with the same impact. It should play o well, however, in its bracket, with okay export chances.

Some of the usual, and much unusual footage on Spain has been compiled and splendidly lensed by Mario Craveri and his team. There are the bullfights, the gypsy dances, the colorful processions and pageants which abound in that country, plus some previously unlensed facets of Iberia. Perhaps what hurts the picture most is the compromise solution adopted: it's neither a fully satisfying feature documentary (the plot takes up too much footage) nor a satisfactory feature film (too much backdrop color). Plot as such concerns unhappy wanderings of man whose girl is forced into unhappy marriage with a rival. After flashbacks and incidental adventures along his travels, rival is reported dead in gunfight, and end sees lovers reunited.

German Cobos, Fernando Fernan Gomez, and comely Pilar Cansino do their best with material, with healthy assist from music by Frencesco Lavagnino. *Hawk.*

Foreign Films

Ballarina a Buon Dio (The Ballerina and God). (ITALIAN). Lux Film release of an EBE Cinematografica production. Stars Vera Cecova, Vittorio DeSica; features Marietto, Gabriele Ferzetti, Roberto Risso. Written and directed by Leonviola; camera, Enza Serafin; music, Piero Morgan; editor, Roberto Cinquini. Previewed in Rome. Running time, 95 MINS.

Modern-day fairy tale about orphan boy who decides to pick out a mother for himself. He's aided in this by Vittorio DeSica, who plays a Divine Messenger in various disguises, and the boy (Marietto) finally winds up with his chosen one, ballerina Vera Cecova, who in turn winds up with her promised suitor.

Fable is handled with some taste and looks headed for good general audience response in Italy and other lingual situations. The Cecova name will help in Germany, plus that of DeSica. Doubtful for the U.S. *Hawk.*

The Perfect Furlough
(C'SCOPE—COLOR

Well-paced comedy with fair-enough merriment and Tony Curtis and Janet Leigh to provide sufficient boxoffice returns.

Universal release of Robert Arthur production. Stars Tony Curtis, Janet Leigh, Keenan Wynn, Linda Cristal, Elaine Stritch; features Marcel Dalio, Les Tremayne, Jay Novello. Directed by Blake Edwards. Screenplay, Stanley Shapiro; camera (Eastman Color), Philip Lathrop; editor, Milton Carruth; music, Frank Skinner. Previewed at RKO 86th Street Theatre, N.Y., Sept. 30, '58. Running time, 93 MINS.

Paul Hodges .... Tony Curtis
Vicki Loren .... Janet Leigh
Harvey Franklin .... Keenan Wynn
Sandra Roca .... Linda Cristal
Liz Baker .... Elaine Stritch
Henri .... Marcel Dalio
Col. Leland .... Les Tremayne
Rene .... Jay Novello
Major Collins .... King Donovan
M.P. No. 1 .... Gordon Jones
Pvt. Brewer .... Alvy Moore
French Nurse .... Lilyan Chauvin
Sgt. Nickles .... Troy Donahue
M.P. No. 2 .... Dick Crockett
French Doctor .... Eugene Borden
Asst. Hotel Manager.... James Lanphier

Basic story is lacking in substance and it's difficult to figure the sense behind the casting of Janet Leigh as a U.S. Army psychologist. But, then, "Perfect Furlough" is done up strictly for laughs and, for those who are on an anything-goes kind of basis, it stacks up well enough.

Writer Stanley Shapiro, in plotting the farce, followed obvious lines. Group of soldiers in an Arctic outpost are in dire need of morale uplifting. They have nothing but women on their minds and daydream about erotic opportunities.

Miss Leigh provides what's intended to be the solution. One of the group is to be given the "perfect furlough" and the others are to experience it vicariously. Tony Curtis, who's a sharp operator with a big reputation for taking a fancy to femmes, cops the leave. He chooses three weeks in Paris with nifty looker film star Linda Cristal. Miss Leigh goes along to supervise and it's only a matter of time before Miss Leigh and Curtis team up at the altar.

While the script's turns can easily be guessed in advance there are within its framework some amusing situations. Too, director Blake Edwards keeps the broad action going at a good clip and Robert Arthur has wrapped up his production handsomely in CinemaScope and Eastman Color.

The overall result is a fair-enough boxoffice contender with Curtis' name providing an extra lift.

Curtis plays comedy well, playing it broadly (there's not much subtlety in the screenplay) and agreeably. Miss Leigh, as noted, is the psychologist; this profession rarely yields such attractive practitioners.

Keenan Wynn is Miss Cristal's manager and comes off as a stereotyped zany caricature. Elaine Stritch does handily as a hard-boiled, cynical pressagent. Marcel Dalio, Les Tremayne and Jay Novello work competently in feature-billing spots and King Donovan, as the perplexed army major in charge of Curtis' expedition to Paris is an amusing all the way.

Miss Cristal as the film star who keeps her marriage a secret until she becomes pregnant (a situation for which Curtis at first is held responsible) looks and plays her part in appealing fashion.

Philip Lathrop's camera work is sharp, editing is tight enough and music, editing and technical credits all are good. *Gene.*

Joy Ride

No names, but exceptionally well-done suspense item.

Hollywood, Oct. 3.

Allied Artists release of Ben Schwalb production. Stars Rad Fulton, Ann Doran, Regis Toomey. Directed by Edward Bernds. Screenplay, Christopher Knopf; from a story by C. B. Gilford; camera, Carl Guthrie; music, Marlin Skiles; editor, William Austin. Previewed at the studio, Sept. 30, 1958. Running time, 65 MINS.

Paul .... Rad Fulton
Grace .... Ann Doran
Miles .... Regis Toomey
Arnie .... Nicholas King
Vince .... Robert Levin
Dirk .... Jim Bridges
Barrett .... Roy Engel
Taverner .... Robert Colbert
Ellensten .... Robert Anderson

"Joy Ride" is a tough and often terrifying melodrama of juveniles underpriviliged in mind only who set out to demoralize and dominate an older man for no apparent reason except "kicks." The Ben Schwalb production for Allied Artists, skillfully directed by Edward Bernds, is too modest in structure to attract much attention, but it is absorbing screen entertainment and will be no disappointment to the customers. Slated for double-bills, it will be a strong entry in this class.

The plot of Christopher Knopf's screenplay, based on a story by C. B. Gilford, is very simple. A quartet of teen-agers, Rad Fulton, Nicholas King, Jim Bridges and Robert Levin, spot a sports car owned by Regis Toomey. They want a ride in it. Sensing Toomey's uncertainty to their request, and mistaking his natural kindness as fear, they launch a campaign of systematic intimidation and mounting ferocity. The "Joy Ride" now becomes secondary to their immature desire to conquer the car's owner, symbol of authority and adulthood. Their campaign culminates when they openly invade Toomey's home while he is away and terrorize his wife, Ann Doran, into a heart attack.

Basically, of course, this kind of story is similar to "The Desperate Hours," and others of that genre. But this does not mitigate against its power to absorb the spectator. Knopf's screenplay does not neglect the reasons for the youths' behavior and it attempts an ending along contemporary sociological lines in which Toomey as shown as almost superhumanly tolerant and understanding of the situation. (He gets the charges against three of the boys reduced, conscious that prison terms may not be the answer to their problem.)

Toomey performs with dignity and authority and Miss Doran, as the wife, is a fine study in muted hysteria. The young men, Fulton, King, Bridges and Levin, are uniformly good, and other cast members, Roy Engle, Robert Colbert and Robert Anderson give solid support.

All aspects of the production respond to Bernds' incisive direction, including the photography of Carl Guthrie, Marlin Skiles' imaginatively-used music, and the expertly paced editing by William Austin. *Powe.*

The Man Upstairs
(BRITISH)

Modest, well-made little thriller; should be useful entertainment in average houses.

London, Sept. 30.

British Lion release of an ACT (Robert Dunbar) production. Stars Richard Attenborough, Bernard Lee, Donald Houston, Dorothy Alison. Directed by Don Chaffey. Screenplay, Alun Falconer; camera, Gerald Massie-Collier; editor, John Trumper. At Hammer Theatre, London. Running time, 88 MINS.

The Man .... Richard Attenborough
Inspector .... Bernard Lee
Sanderson .... Donald Houstor
Mrs. Barnes .... Dorothy Alison
Nicholas .... Charles Houston
Eunice .... Maureen Connell
Pollen .... Kenneth Griffith
Helen .... Virginia Maskell
Mrs. Lawrence .... Patricia Jessel
Miss Acres .... Amy Dalby
P. C. Stevens .... Edward Judd
Injured Sergeant.........Patrick Jordan
Mr. Barnes .... Alfred Burke
Johnny .... David Griffith
Superintendent .... Walter Hudd
Dulcie .... Polly Clark
Sgt. Morris ....Graham Stewart

"The Man Upstairs" is a competently made, often tense, little drama, which comes off well within its own modest terms. But it is doubtful if many people will be happy to pay out good money to see the kind of pic which could have been handled equally well on television. This seems no way to combat the small screen. Starring several popular British players, it should be a useful booking for most British houses, but it is not important enough to arouse much interest in the U.S.

The story has Richard Attenborough as a scientist who has been involved in a laboratory accident in which his fiancee's brother has been killed. Burdened with a sense of guilt, he has changed his name and is living in a seedy lodging house. The film concerns one night in his life. His peculiar behaviour causes one of the guests to call the police. Attenborough locks himself in his room and the story line concerns the reactions of the various guests to the situation and the clash between an intolerant police officer and a local mental welfare officer.

Don Chaffey's direction is straightforward and brings out several good performances, notably by Attenborough, in a difficult role. Kenneth Griffith is a fussy busybody, Dorothy Allison an understanding housewife and Donald Houston the welfare officer, all nice portrayals. Bernard Lee, as the cop also is good.

Virginia Maskell also shows considerable promise in a tiny part as Attenborough's girl friend. Dialog is sometimes a trifle too literary and the acting taking place in such cramped circumstances makes it difficult for the requisite tension to be unflagging. But the atmosphere of fear and suspicion has been excellently created and handled. *Rich.*

Money, Women and Guns
(COLOR; C'SCOPE)

Suspense oater of routine interest and prospect.

Hollywood, Sept. 5.

Universal release of a Howie Horwitz production. Stars Jock Mahoney, Kim Hunter, Tim Hovey; costars Gene Evans, Tom Drake, Lon Chaney, William Campbell, Jeffrey Stone, James Gleason, Judy Meredith. Directed by Richard H. Bartlett. Screenplay, Montgomery Pittman; camera (Eastman color), Philip Lathrop;

music supervisor, Joseph Gershenson; editor, Patrick McCormack. Previewed at the studio, Sept. 4, '58. Running time, **80 MINS.**

Hogan	Jock Mahoney
Mary Kingman	Kim Hunter
Davey Kingman	Tim Hovey
Sheriff Crowley	Gene Evans
Jess Ryerson	Tom Drake
Art Birdwell	Lon Chaney
Clint Gunston	William Campbell
Johnny Bee	Jeffrey Stone
Henry Devers	James Gleason
Sally Gunston	Judy Meredith
Damion Bard	Phillip Terry
Setting Sun	Richard Devon
Nibbs	Ian Mac Donald
John Briggs	Don Megowan
Job Kingman	Nolan Leary
Joe	Kelly Thordsen

"Money, Women and Guns" title doesn't have much to do with the product but is apparently dedicated to the proposition that magic in the billing will overcome the lack of it in the production. A mysterious will and the suspense involved in carrying out its terms supply the plot for the Howie Horwitz production, directed by Richard H. Bartlett. Satisfactory for double-bill booking.

Jock Mahoney is the frontier detective hired to unravel the mystery caused by the will of an old prospector, bushwacked by three guns. Mahoney must track down each name mentioned in the will and not only make sure each beneficiary is legitimate but, in the process, find the killers. In the course of his investigation he meets and falls in love with Kim Hunter, mother of Tim Hovey, one of those named in the testament. He also solves the mystery of the murder, when he discovers that Jeffrey Stone, who has been wandering through the picture as a mystery stranger, was one of the three gunmen—but a repentant one—who took part in the killing.

Montgomery Pittman's screenplay is interesting and Bartlett's direction is capable, although lacking in much tension. Mahoney does a rough-hewn job of the restless detective, but Miss Hunter's talents are wasted in a routine role. Young Hovey contributes some humor, and others in the cast who make effective contributions include Stone, Gene Evans, Lon Chaney, Tom Drake, James Gleason, William Campbell and Judy Meredith.

Philip Lathrop's Eastman-color-CinemaScope photography is a plus value. *Powe.*

Menace in the Night

Melodrama for second billing.
(BRITISH)

Hollywood, Sept. 25.
United Artists release of a Gibraltar Production. Stars Griffith Jones, Lisa Gastoni, Vincent Ball; features Eddie Byrne, Victor Maddern, Clifford Evans, Joan Miller, Leslie Dwyer, Leonard Sachs. Produced by Charles A. Leeds. Directed by Lance Comfort. Screenplay by Norman Hudis and John Sherman, from a novel, "Suspense," by Bruce Graeme; camera, Arthur Graham; editor, Peter Pitt; music, Richard Bennett. Previewed at Goldwyn Studios, Sept. 26, '58. Running time, **78 MINS.**

Rapson	Griffith Jones
Jean Francis	Lisa Gastoni
Bob Meredith	Vincent Ball
Art	Eddie Byrne
Ted	Victor Maddern
Inspector Ford	Clifford Evans
Victor's Wife	Joan Miller
Victor	Leonard Sachs
Toby	Leslie Dwyer
Postman's Widow	Jenny Laird
Betty Francis	Angela White
Mrs. Francis	Barbara Couper
Auntie	Marie Burke
Bank Manager	Andre Van Gyseghem

Instead of falling down, London Bridge draws up in "Menace in the Night," and, in so doing, allows a sleek British sedan and its robbery-prodded driver to be hurled into the murky Thames, thus producing the only real thrill this Scotland Yard epic has to offer. An English film, apparently made two years ago and just now picked up for U.S. release by United Artists, it has scarcely a peg to sell it on and likely will live its life as a somewhat off-beat filler.

Charles A. Leeds produced the Gibraltar Production on what couldn't have been a very hefty budget, but scenes of internal London will be bonuses for American audiences. Norman Hudis and John Sherman screenplayed from a Bruce Graeme novel called "Suspense," and, although too talky in the first reel or two, it's a fair script when the action rolls around. Direction by Lance Comfort, likewise, picks up in direct relation with the action.

Story is a simple one, revolving around four Britishers who plan and execute the robbery of a mail van hauling 250,000 pounds sterling worth of soiled banknotes to the furnaces. But, it seems, there's an eyewitness—a fetching blonde who co-operates with the bobbies until threatened by one of the culprits—and then there's an overzealous reporter who's out to scoop London's other dailies. The robbers bicker among themselves, resulting in one death and three remaining who steal from each other, and finally there's the big chase, at the end of which the leader drives off the bridge.

Performances, with few highlights, are nonetheless adequate. Lisa Gastoni, as the blonde, is fine to look at, and she manages to create a considerable amount of fear. It does seem strange, though, that, despite a thoroughly British family, she converses in a delightful continental accent. Griffith Jones, as the gang leader, and Vincent Ball, as the reporter, are fine, and Clifford Evans, as the inspector, Eddie Byrne, Victor Maddern and Leonard Sachs, as the other gangsters and Leslie Dwyer, as an underworld barber, are good.

Cameraman Arthur Graham's work is generally proficient in spite of frequent overexposures, with editing by Peter Pitt and art direction by John Stoll adequate. Philip Martell directed an excellent Richard Bennett musical score that turns out to be more exciting than most other aspects of the film. *Ron.*

Le Gorille Vous Salue Bien

(The Gorilla Greets You)
(FRENCH; FRANSCOPE)
Paris, Sept. 30.
Pathe release of Raoul Ploquin production. Stars Lino Ventura, Bella Darvi, Charles Vanel; features Pierre Dux, Rene Lefevre, Robert Manuel. Directed by Bernard Borderie. Screenplay, Antoine Dominique, Jacques Robert, Borderie, from the novel by Dominique; camera, Louis Page; editor, Pierre Gaudin. At Balzac, Paris. Running time, **105 MINS.**

Gorille	Lino Ventura
Moll	Bella Darvi
Colonel	Charles Vanel
Inspector	Rene Lefevre
Lawson	Pierre Dux
Kanas	Robert Manuel

Film kicks off what may turn into a long, lucrative series here. It concerns a secret service man, known as "The Gorilla," forever caught between gangsters and the police, to whom he must remain unknown. This allows for plenty of fights, dolls and intrigue. Well manned, slickly paced, it is okay entertainmentwise, but emerges for only possible dualer fare outside of its own country.

"The Gorilla" is investigating stolen missile plans which brings him into contact with counterfeiters, dope peddlers and high ranking espionage agents. He comes through via his shrewdness, great strength and wise chief who overlords it all via quiet mastery.

With top actors in the many overdrawn parts, the film is acceptable on most counts and is helped by Lino Ventura's miming of the clever, strong and pugnacious Gorilla. Bella Darvi is a fine, perverse gun moll and technical credits are helpful. This is played straight, unlike the successful Eddie Constantine parody G-Man films it seems to be emulating. *Mosk.*

She Didn't Say No!
(BRITISH-COLOR)

Naive, but warmhearted piece of Irish blarney. Fairly amusing mixture of comedy, whimsy and sentiment which lacks marquee value.

London, Sept. 30.
Associated-British release of a Sergei Nolbandov production. Features Eileen Herlie, Niall MacGinnis, Ray McAnally, Perlita Neilson, Liam Redmond, Betty McDowell, Ian Bannen. Directed by Cyril Frankel. Screenplay, T. J. Morrison and Una Troy, from Una Troy's novel, "We Are Seven"; camera, Gilbert Taylor; editor, Charles Hasse; music, Tristram Carey. At Studio One, London. Running time, **85 MINS.**

Bridget Monaghan	Eileen Herlie
Mary Monaghan	Perlita Nielson
Tommy Monaghan	Wilfred Downing
Poppy Monaghan	Ann Dickins
The Twins	Teresa & Lesley Scoble
Toughy Monaghan	Raymond Manthorpe
Jamesy Casey	Niall MacGinnis
Matthew Hogan	Patrick McAlinney
William Bates	Jack MacGowran
Mrs. Bates	Joan O'Hara
Jim Powers	Ray McAnally
Mrs. Power	Betty McDowell
Peter Howard	Ian Bannen
Miss Hogan	Eithne Dunne
The Film Director	Hilton Edwards
Miss Kelly	Maureen Halligan
The Judge	Harry Hutchinson
Darmody	Paul Farrell
Maybella Merton	Shirley Joy
Mrs. Merton	Viola Keats
Maggie Murphy	Anna Manahan
The Sergeant	Michael O'Brien
Doctor Cassidy	Liam Redmond
The Inspector	John Welsh

The story line of "She Didn't Say No!" sounds a fairly risque theme for a film, unless treated as sharp satire. But actually it is a warmhearted comedy. It's naive and loaded with Irish blarney which sometimes teeters uncomfortably to the verge of sentimentality. But the accent is mainly on comedy and a competent bunch of Irish players extract a healthy measure of yocks. There are also some attractive moppets, and it should appeal particularly to femme picturegoers. Pic will be a worthwhile proposition in British family houses, but lack of stellar names may soft-pedal its prospects further afield.

Based on Una Troy's novel, "We Are Seven," this vehicle has Eileen Herlie as an attractive, romantically-minded, indulgent woman whose lover died before they could marry, leaving her with a child. Her idealistic search for a father for the child has unfortunate results. She is mother of six born on the wrong side of the blanket.

Since the last five children have been fathered by men of the village, Miss Herlie's family is something of a local embarassment, with villagers anxious to get them out of their hair. There is a predictable, but neat pay-off leading up to a happy ending for a film which despite early misgivings, is put over without any offense.

Cyril Frankel has directed with a light touch while Gilbert Taylor's color photography makes good use of the pleasant Irish scenery. The dialog has good humor rather than wit. Sentimental sequences do not obtrude so that this disarming film seems rather better while watching it than it probably is.

Eileen Herlie gives an attractive performance as the woman who unwittingly causes all the bother. Among other adult performances which add to the film's merits are those of Betty McDowell, Jack McGowran, Ian Bannen, Perlita Neilson, Eithne Dunne, Liam Redmond, Ray McAnally and Niall MacGinnis.

But it is the children who contribute most to "She Didn't Say No!". This introduces a youngster named Raymond Manthorpe. He is a tiny kid with tremendous self-assurance and sense of comedy. Another promising newcomer is Ann Dickens, with a neat performance as a screen-struck teenager. Shirley Joy, as a precocious child film star. Tristram Carey's music leans heavily on typical Irish airs, but is well suited to the subject. *Rich.*

The Last Hurrah

Strong although somewhat overlong politico saga starring Spencer Tracy, topically attuned to the times. Will do OK b.o.

Columbia release of John Ford production, directed by Ford. Stars Spencer Tracy; features Jeffrey Hunter, Dianne Foster, Pat O'Brien, Basil Rathbone, Donald Crisp, James Gleason. Screenplay, Frank Nugent, based on novel by Edwin O'Connor. Camera, Charles Lawton Jr.; editor, Jack Murray; asst. directors, Wingate Smith & Sam Nelson. Tradeshown N.Y., Oct. 10, '58. Running time, 121 MINS.

Skeffington	Spencer Tracy
Adam Caulfield	Jeffrey Hunter
Maeve Caulfield	Dianne Foster
John Gorman	Pat O'Brien
Norman Cass St.	Basil Rathbone
The Cardinal	Donald Crisp
Cuke Gillen	James Gleason
Ditto Boland	Edward Brophy
Amos Force	John Carradine
Rober Sugrue	Willis Bouchey
Bishop Gardner	Basil Ruysdael
Sam Weinberg	Ricardo Cortez
Hennessey	Wallace Ford
Festus Garvey	Frank McHugh
Mr. Winslow	Carleton Young
Jack Mangan	Frank Albertson
Degnan	Bob Sweeney
Dan Herlihy	William Leslie
Gert	Anna Lee
Monsignor Killian	Ken Curtis
Delia	Jane Darwell
Norman Cass Jr.	O. Z. Whitehead
Frank Skeffington Jr.	Arthur Walsh
Ellen Davin	Ruth Warren
Kevin McCluskey	Charles Fitzsimmons
Mrs. McCluskey	Helen Westcott
Mamie Burns	Mimi Doyle
Pete	Dan Borzage
Police Captain	James Flavin
Doctor	William Forrest
Fire Captain	Frank Sully
Chauffeur	Charlie Sullivan

"The Last Hurrah" is the "this ain't Jim Curley" story, from Edwin O'Connor's novel, which John Ford and Spencer Tracy have transmuted to the screen in slick style destined for good grosses. The star has made the most of the meaty role of the shrewd politician of the "dominantly Irish-American" metropolis in New England (unmistakably Boston but not Boston) and producer-director Ford has likewise contributed a top professional job.

The two-hour running length is somewhat overboard but Tracy's characterization of the resourceful, old-line politician-mayor has such consummate depth that it sustains the interest practically all the way. A little editing might have helped but the canvas is rich and the political machinations replete.

The graft and coercion is made to appear chiefly as an obbligato to Tracy's do-gooding for the poor wards, and if the wardheelers (dominantly Irish although Ricardo Cortez as Sam Weinberg accounts for another segment of the votes) are crude in their delivery of the ballots, Tracy's quasi-benevolence and impatience with the too proper Bostonians, in their Plymouth Club retreats, more than vitiate the brasher aspects.

Tracy's resourcefulness in besting the stuffy bankers who nixed a loan for a much needed low-rent housing development; his foiling of the profiteering undertaker when a constituent is buried (the wake is transformed into a political rally); the passionate loyalty of his political devotees; the rivalry between the "respectable" elements in combating the direct-approach tactics of the Irish-American politicos; the pride in defeat when the "reform" candidate bests Tracy at the polls; his verve even on his deathbed, as he sends for his old cronies; the opposition men-of-the-cloth supporting the rival political candidates for the mayoralty; and Tracy's own "last hurrah" as he tells off the fatuous banker (Willis Bouchey)—with a parting "like hell I would!"—in reviewing his gaudy career, make for a series of memorable scenes.

Ford's chore wasn't easy; he has too much plot material to dovetail and correlate but the end-result is thoroughly acceptable.

The cast is a roster of stalwarts in the main. Jeffrey Hunter is first-billed, in the support. He is the shrewd mayor's favored nephew who, despite his ties to the opposition sheet, perceives the old codger's humaneness. He is a sympathetic and attractive juvenile who, however, doesn't always match up histrionically against the other prime supporting players, all old pros. These include Pat O'Brien, James Gleason, Edward Brophy and Ricardo Cortez as Tracy's faithfuls; or Basil Rathbone, John Carradine, Carleton Young as the bankers; and others like Basil Ruysdael, Donald Crisp (both as clerics), Frank Albertson, Wallace Ford, Frank McHugh and others.

This is not a "woman's picture" and the femme interest is incidental. There are a couple of missouts also as regards Tracy's playboy-son and the scenes with the babes, and that goes also for the scene of the new candidate and his wife fluffing their way through an "at-home interview" scene for benefit of the tv cameras. But it holds the interest and, coming in a political year, has a neo-topical value.

The technical credits are topnotch; Charles Lawton Jr.'s lowkey black-and-white lensing is well-attuned to the theme. But primarily its Tracy's picture. Amidst a bunch of old pros he is head-and-shoulders above them in his thespic assignment. He makes his solo marquee stardom mean something beyond the billing. *Abel.*

Grip of the Strangler
(BRITISH)

Routine Boris Karloff horror pic which will slot into unambitious bills.

London, Oct. 7.

Eros (John Croydon) production and release. Stars Boris Karloff. Directed by Robert Day. Screenplay, Jan Read and John C. Cooper from original story by Jan Read. At Hammer Theatre, London. Running time, 80 MINS.

James Rankin	Boris Karloff
Kenneth McColl	Tim Turner
Cora Seth	Jean Kent
Pearl	Vera Day
Mrs. Rankin	Elizabeth Allen
Det. Burke	Anthony Dawson
Lily	Diane Aubrey
Hannah	Dorothy Gordon
Kate	Peggy Ann Clifford
2nd Governor	Leslie Perrins
Styles	Michael Atkinson
Police Surgeon	Desmond Roberts
Maid	Jessica Cairns
Medical Superintendent	Ray Russell
Superintendent of Guys	Derek Birch
1st Governor	Arthur Hall
Can Can Troupe Leader	John Elvin

Still trying to cash in on the current horror stakes comes this routine Boris Karloff murder pic. Dialog and screenplay make this okay as an unambitious supporter, but it is all too far-fetched to provide more than moderate entertainment.

Story has Karloff as a novelist investigating the 20-year-old case of "The Haymarket Strangler," who was hanged for murders involving strangling and slashing with a knife. Karloff suspects that the murders were actually done by the surgeon who conducted the post mortems on all the victims. Following through his inquiries, he discovers that his theory is right, but the payoff is that an insane Karloff turns out to be the criminal, which most students will find predictible. Further development is that Karloff has to commit several more murders before he can convince the police of his guilt.

With suitable horror makeup whenever killing, Karloff finds no difficulty in keeping to his usual talented form. He is less successful, however, as the gentle novelist. Vera Day, Elizabeth Allan, Anthony Dawson and Jean Kent lend competent support in this old-fashioned piece which has been directed by Robert Day with more force than subtlety. Period settings are adequate. *Rich.*

Muchachita De Valladolid
(Girl From Valladolid)
(SPANISH-COLOR)

Madrid, Sept. 30.

Universal Films Espana release of a Cinematograficas DIA production. Directed by Luis Amadori. Screenplay by Luis Marquina and Luis Amadori from Calvo Sotelo's comedy of the same name. Stars Alberto Closas, Analia Gade and Lina Rosales; features Alfredo Mayo, Lopez Vazquez and Vicky Lagos. Camera (Eastmancolor), Jose Aguayo; art director, Enrique Alarcon; music by Cristobal Halffter. Filmed at Chamartin Studios. At Coliseum, Madrid. Running time, 95 MINS.

Patricio	Alberto Closas
Mercedes	Analia Gade
Alexandra Aymat	Lina Rosales
Canciller	Alfredo Mayo
Secretary	Lopez Vazquez
Erika	Vicky Lagos

Calvo Sotelo's diverting and successful stageplay, short on situations and long on character studies, topical satire and smart dialogue, resists screen adaptation. Director Luis Amadori and producer-writer Luis Marquina only partially succeed.

Added prologue footage focusses mainly on Valladolid's twin claims to fame—its Holy week procession and collection of polychromatic sculpture, but contributes little film value to basic stage material.

Naive provincial newlywed Analia Gade discovers that strait-laced virtue is not easily reconciled with the sophisticated unrestraint of her ambitious diplomatic spouse, Alberto Closas. When she fully awakens to the behind-the-scenes role of an attractive dame in foreign affairs, she shakes the straw from her hair and lands her nettled husband the oil deal he had been ardently soliciting from the chancellor's wife, Lina Rosales.

Closas is smooth but his stage performance had more ease and charm. Argentine's Gade is fine only in the deprovincialized portion of her role, because that's the way she stacked. Others are creditable, including director Amadori and technical departments.

Universal should do well with this fairly amusing comedy in Spain. Popular in South America, cast should help film in Spanish-language market. *Werb.*

The Tunnel of Love
(C'SCOPE)

Racy, risque filmization of legit hit. Top b.o. forecast.

Hollywood, Oct. 14.

Metro release of Joseph Fields production. Stars Doris Day, Richard Widmark; co-stars Gig Young, Gia Scala; features Elisabeth Fraser, Elizabeth Wilson. Produced by Fields and Martin Melcher. Directed by Gene Kelly. Screenplay, Joseph Fields; from the stage play by Fields and Peter De Vries; based on the novel by Vries; camera, Robert Bronner; McSweeney Jr. Previewed at the Westwood Village Theatre, Sept. 19, '58. Running time, 98 MINS.

Isolde Poole	Doris Day
Augie Poole	Richard Widmark
Dick Pepper	Gig Young
Estelle Novick	Gia Scala
Alice Pepper	Elisabeth Fraser
Miss MacCracken	Elizabeth Wilson
Actress	Vikki Dougan
Escort	Doodles Weaver
Day Motel Man	Charles Wagenheim
Night Motel Man	Robert Williams
Themselves	The Esquire Trio

Exurbia is the current tag for the commuter country where "The Tunnel of Love" is located. Judging by the preoccupations of the principals in this Metro comedy, it may hereafter be referred to as Sexurbia. For this Joseph Fields production is ribald treatment.

The Broadway hit on which it is based has been transferred virtually intact to the screen. The screenplay makes a brief bow to motion picture morality with a last-minute switch ending, making the basis for most of the gags an elaborate misunderstanding. But by that time it doesn't make much difference.

"Tunnel of Love" may run into some censorship problems, but this is the only possible obstacle that could prevent it from hurtling to top boxoffice. Gene Kelly's direction, plus topflight performances by the cast headed by Doris Day and Richard Widmark, make it one of the year's funniest pictures.

Although the locale and the social status of the characters in "Tunnel" are pretty special, their situations are universal. Widmark is a would-be cartoonist for a New Yorker-type magazine, whose gags are good but whose drawings are not. He and his wife, Miss Day, want a child and cannot catch. They live in a remodeled barn (naturally) adjacent to the home of their best friends, Gig Young and Elisabeth Fraser, whom they envy in many ways. Young is an editor of the magazine Widmark aspires to crack, and as a parent. Young adds to his and Miss Fraser's brood as regularly as the seasons. Widmark and Miss Day are planning to adopt a baby. Not only do they want the foster child, there is hope (and considerable accompanying comment) that its adoption may work for them as it has for other childless couples and result in natural offspring.

Meantime, back at the barn, Young, whose homework has been stimulated by extracurricular activities, urges his system on Widmark. With this suggestion in the back of his mind, Widmark is visited by an adoption home investigator, Gia Scala. When he wakes up in a motel after a night on the town with her, he assumes the thought has been father to the deed in more ways than one. Just a little over nine months later, the adoption agency presents a baby to Miss Day and Widmark, and Widmark again assumes nature has taken its course. As the baby begins to look more and more like Widmark, others, including Miss Day, begin to get the same idea.

The only important change Fields has made in the screenplay, from the play by him and Peter DeVries (based on DeVries' book), is to explain at the very end that the child is not actually Widmark's. As noted, at this point it doesn't make much difference. While some aspects of the special hot house culture indigenous to the Westport locale may be lost on the citizens of Brooklyn and Dallas, no one, anywhere, could miss the references to Dr. Spock and fever charts, visits to the family doctor, and the counting of months and the result to be expected after nine of them.

It should be emphasized that there is nothing in bad taste about any of this. It is handled with lightness and without a snickering leer at any time.

Miss Day and Widmark make a fine comedy team, working as smoothly as if they had been trading gags for years. Despite the broad nature of the comedy, they also achieve a pleasant romantic effect in which married love is made to seem exceptionally felicitous. They are ably abetted by Gig Young, one of the greatest flycatchers in current operation, and Gia Scala, who displays a nice and unexpected gift for comedy. Elisabeth Fraser, as the almost perpetually pregnant neighbor, shows a good, off-hand flair for these proceedings, and Elizabeth Wilson, as an outraged social workers, is a standout in a brief appearance.

This is the first time Gene Kelly has operated entirely behind the camera, and he emerges as an inventive and capable comedy director. The timing, emphasis and pacing achieve a maximum return on both comedy and romantic aspects.

Robert Bronner's photography is well-lit and sharp. Backgrounds are handsomely and accurately suggested in the art direction by William A. Horning and Randall Duell, and in set decoration by Henry Grace and Robert Priestley. Helen Rose makes an unobtrusive contribution with dresses for Miss Day and Miss Scala. Wesley C. Miller's sound is slick and editing by John McSweeney Jr. prevents any loss of fun or lag in the proceedings.

There are two songs used in the production, a title tune sung by Miss Day as part of the opening titles, and a novelty, "Run Away, Skidaddle Skidoo," casually introduced in a party sequence, that are not only good pop tunes but have the unusual merit of fitting the structure of a non-musical comedy. Patty Fisher and Bob Roberts did the first, and Ruth Roberts and Bill Katz the second. *Powe.*

The Trollenberg Terror
(BRITISH)

Exciting science-fiction film with genuine horror thrills; solid b.o. proposition.

London, Oct. 7.

Eros (Robert S. Baker-Monty Berman) production and release. Stars Forrest Tucker. Directed by Quentin Lawrence. Screenplay, Jimmy Sangster from television serial by Peter Key; camera, Monty Berman; music, Stanley Black; editor, Henry Richardson. At Hammer Theatre, London. Running time, 85 MINS.

Alan Brooks	Forrest Tucker
Philip Truscott	Laurence Payne
Anne Pilgrim	Janet Munro
Sarah Pilgrim	Jennifer Jayne
Crevett	Warren Mitchell
Klein	Frederick Schiller
Dewhurst	Stuart Saunders
Brett	Andrew Faulds
Hans	Colin Douglas
Wilde	Derek Sydney
Villagers	Richard Golding, George Herbert, Anne Sharp
Child	Caroline Glazer
Pilot	Garard Green

"The Trollenberg Terror" is a likely candidate for big b.o. honors in the science-fiction pic realm. Based on a successful tv serial by Peter Key, it has had an "X" certificate slapped on it by the censor. Eliminates the under-16's from seeing it, but will give a fillip to the takings. Most U.K. managers will be happy to have "Trollenberg" on a suitable bill.

Like those of most science-fiction films, the story may seem far-fetched to the layman but, as H. G. Wells proved way back, the imagination of authors is often only a few jumps ahead of actual scientific fact. The yarn concerns a creature from outer space secreted in a radio-active cloud on the mountain of Trollenberg in Switzerland. The mysterious disappearance of various climbers brings Forrest Tucker to the scene as a science investigator for UNO. He and a professor at the local observatory set out to solve the problem.

During investigations, two headless corpses are discovered and a couple of ordinary citizens go berserk and turn killer. Main object of the two is Janet Munro who is one of a sister mind-reading act and obviously presents a threat to the sinister visitor. Climax comes when the villagers are besieged in the observatory as the cloud draws nearer and nearer. It is discovered scientifically that the creature can exist only in extreme cold and it is eventually destroyed by fire bombs dropped from a plane.

The tension of this well-made and gripping thriller comes not so much from seeing the creature in the final stages, which turns out to be a huge, repellent octopus-like mass, but from the eeriness of the atmosphere and doubt about when the cloud will strike. Tucker's bewilderment and that of his henchmen accentuate the air of death and disaster.

Jimmy Sangster's taut screenplay extracts the most from the situations and is helped by strong, resourceful acting from a solid cast. Tucker tackles the problem with commendable lack of histrionics and Miss Munro adds considerably to the film's interest with an excellent portrayal of the girl whose mental telepathy threatens the creature's activities and draws her into danger. Laurence Payne, as a newspaperman; Jennifer Jayne, as Miss Munro's distraught elder sister; Warren Mitchell, the professor, and Andrew Faulds and Colin Douglas, as two of the monster's victims, also give the stars full backing.

Stanley Black's music is appropriately sinister while Monty Berman's camerawork and the special effects department's contribution are extremely effective. This is a better-than-most horror film which, despite its extravagant play upon the imagination, retains a ch[illegible]ing air of plausibility. *Rich.*

Home Before Dark

Romantic melodrama with mental illness theme. Absorbing, moving pic, highlighted by Jean Simmons' performance.

Hollywood, Oct. 3.

Warner Bros. release of Mervyn LeRoy production. Stars Jean Simmons, Dan O'Herlihy, Rhonda Fleming, Efrem Zimbalist Jr. Directed by Mervyn LeRoy. Screenplay, Eileen and Robert Bassing; from the novel by Eileen Bassing; camera, Joseph F. Biroc; music supervisor, Ray Heindorf; editor, Philip W. Anderson. Previewed at the studio, Oct. 3, '58. Running time, 137 MINS.

Charlotte Bronn	Jean Simmons
Arnold Bronn	Dan O'Herlihy
Joan Carlisle	Rhonda Fleming
Jake Diamond	Efrem Zimbalist Jr.
Inez Winthrop	Mabel Albertson
Hamilton Gregory	Steve Dunne
Frances Barrett	Joan Weldon
Cathy Bergner	Joanna Barnes
Mattie	Kathryn Card
Hazel Evans	Marjorie Bennett
Malcolm Southey	Johnstone White
Mrs. Hathaway	Eleanor Audley

"Home Before Dark" is the kind of film that once was classified—perhaps smugly—as a woman's picture, and it will certainly find its widest appeal and acceptance in female audiences. It should give the Kleenex a vigorous workout. Based on one woman's battle to regain her slipping sanity, it is a romantic melodrama of considerable power and imprint. Mervyn LeRoy's production for Warner Bros. is exceptionally well cast and staged, and his direction wisely throws the picture to Jean Simmons, who lights almost every frame with uncommon artistry.

The screenplay by Eileen and Robert Bassing, based on Mrs. Bassing's novel of the same name, sometimes seems rather skimpy in its character motivation. It is also difficult at times to understand the mental tone of the mentally ill heroine, played by Miss Simmons. But these are necessarily shadowy areas, anyway, and the test is that while the tale is unfolding it is made so gripping that factual discrepancies are relatively unimportant.

Miss Simmons is the wife of Dan O'Herlihy, who has ceased to love her before mental breakdown and has not changed his attitude on her recovery. Living in their home, to which she returns on her release from hospitalization, are her stepmother, Mabel Albertson, and her stepsister, Rhonda Fleming. They are masterful females who could drive anyone to the edge of madness with their insistence on managing even the smallest details of Miss Simmons' life. They are also allied, none too subtly, with her husband and against her. It was Miss Simmons' suspicion of a romance between O'Herlihy and Miss Fleming that helped crack her fragile grasp on sanity. Now partially cured, she wonders if her suspicion was the fragment of a disintegrating mind or a reality.

Her only real ally in the house is a stranger, Efrem Zimbalist Jr., who is also an alien in the setting of the inbred New England college community. Zimbalist is the only Jewish member of the faculty, and ostensibly a protege of O'Herlihy's. O'Herlihy is the kind of liberal who favors minority groups in principle but doesn't care much for their individual members; they're always the "wrong kind." Miss Simmons and Zimbalist are both on sufferance; she is too weak to know how to fight it, he is too smart and tough to be grateful about it. Their eventual romance ends the picture on a hopeful note.

There is meat here and pretty strong stuff. It is tastefully and soundly handled. Neither in the Bassings' screenplay nor in LeRoy's direction are the cards stacked against the odious family and the community. Miss Fleming and Miss Albertson can't be blamed; they are too shallow to expect any perception of them. O'Herlihy is not shallow, but he is weak. In refusing to acknowledge his vacillation, he shifts it to his wife and almost destroys her. By suggesting his knowledge of what he is doing, against his will, O'Herlihy avoids seeming too heavy and arouses in the end only a scornful pity.

The whole picture is seen from Miss Simmons's viewpoint, which means she is "on" virtually the whole time. It is a long picture, two hours and a quarter, and there is little to relieve the attention to individuals. Miss Simmons must display unusual versatility to maintain interest and sympathy and she does. Her voice is a vibrant instrument, used with thoughtful articulation and placement, the only vital part of her at times—her beauty effectively drabbed by a dowdy gray wig—the only thing youthful and romantic. This is no Ophelia, and Miss Simmons must register with a quiet intensity rather than more showy histrionics, which she does.

Miss Fleming uses her good looks to make her brainlessly vicious character even more effective than it would be in the hands of an ordinary actress. Zimbalist advances in stature considerably with this portrayal and becomes a consideration for more important things. Miss Albertson plays with abrasive technique and minute inflection to create a memorable character. Steve Dunne, as another weakling in Miss Simmons' life, does a good job, and others in the large cast who stand out include Joan Weldon, Joanna Barnes, Kathryn Card and Joel Marston.

Joseph Biroc's black and white photography is suited to the grim New England atmosphere. It is winter, a depressingly gray winter, and the locations in Massachusetts give the picture the authentic feel. Art direction by John Beckman is helpful in this. Technical credits include the good editing by Philip W. Anderson and proficient sound by Stanley Jones.

There is a title song by Jimmy McHugh and Sammy Cahn which will be sung behind the titles by Mary Kaye, but it had not been added to the picture at the time it was previewed. Ray Heindorf's musical score is background music, ably done. *Powe.*

Wolf Larsen

Realistic treatment of Jack London classic. Moderate grosses indicated.

Hollywood, Oct. 8.

Allied Artists release of Lindsley Parsons production. Stars Barry Sullivan, Peter Graves; features Gita Hall, Thayer David, John Alderson, Rico Alaniz. Directed by Harmon Jones. Screenplay, Jack DeWitt, Turnley Walker, based on Jack London's "The Sea Wolf"; camera, Floyd Crosby; editor, John Blunk; music, Paul Dunlap. Previewed Oct. 6, '58. Running time, 83 MINS.

Wolf Larsen	Barry Sullivan
Van Weyden	Peter Graves
Kristina	Gita Hall
Mugridge	Thayer David
Johnson	John Alderson
Louis	Rico Alaniz
Matthews	Robert Gist
Leach	Jack Grinnage
Haskins	Jack Orrison
Henderson	Henry Rowland

This sixth time around for "The Sea Wolf"—tabbed here for its lead character—catches the Jack London flavor but subject itself is inclined to be somewhat old-hat. By cleaving so closely to original, in light of modern screen melodramatic taste the sum total doesn't stack up as particularly exciting or forceful fare. Names of Barry Sullivan and Peter Graves, however, should see it through program market for moderate returns.

Sullivan, hard-hitting as the brutal sea captain in this Lindsley Parsons production, follows in part such stalwarts of the past as Hobart Bosworth—who produced, directed and starred in original 1913 version—Noah Beery, Ralph Ince, Milton Sills and Edward G. Robinson. Under Harmon Jones' vigorous direction, he gives good shadings in restrained style to wolfish character who skippers the worst hell ship afloat but attracts whatever crew he doesn't shanghai because his sealing operations in North Pacific always nets men more money than any other ship. Graves portrays the wealthy young landsman, Van Weyden, whom Sullivan picks up after a shipwreck and makes one of his crew, the only man aboard unafraid of the half-mad killer who finally meets his death at the hands of this crew.

The Jack DeWitt-Turnley Walker screenplay unfolds entirely aboard Wolf Larsen's sealing schooner—circa 1892—where plenty of interesting maritime scenes add to film's pictorial values. Limited confines of the ship doesn't prove any deterrent to the action, which in itself Jones keeps at a realistic clip, and good atmosphere is established through Floyd Crosby's facile camera work.

Sullivan and Graves, latter persuasive as the soft landsman who hardens under Larsen's tutelage without absorbing any of cruelties that result in master's death, are backed by a competent cast. Gita Hall is in briefly for pic's sole femme character, rescued from another shipwreck; Thayer David is the cookie who loses his foot to a shark; John Alderson, Rico Alaniz, Robert Gist and Jack Grinnage are crewmen.

Technical departments are well handled, including John Blunk's editing, Paul Dunlap's music score and William Ross' art direction.
Whit.

Monster on the Campus

Well-developed shocker for the scifi market.

Hollywood, Oct. 8.
Universal release of Joseph Gershenson production. Stars Arthur Franz, Joanna Moore; features Judson Pratt, Troy Donahue, Nancy Walters, Phil Harvey. Directed by Jack Arnold. Screenplay, David Duncan; camera, Russell Metty; editor, Ted J. Kent. Previewed Oct. 7, '58. Running time. 77 MINS.
Donald Blake .... Arthur Franz
Madeline Howard .... Joanna Moore
Mike Stevens .... Judson Pratt
Sylvia Lockwood .... Nancy Walters
Jimmy Flanders .... Troy Donahue
Sgt. Powell .... Phil Harvey
Molly Riordan .... Helen Westcott
Gilbert Howard ..... Alexander Lockwood
Dr. Oliver Cole .... Whit Bissell
Sgt. Eddie Daniels .... Ross Elliott

Universal comes up with a pretty fair shocker in this expertly produced story of retrogression. Its premise is logically developed without any great strain on the imagination, acting is convincing and there's a general professional air about the unfoldment. Film is a good entry for its particular market.

Plottage of the Joseph Gershenson production follows a chain of terrifying events which occur on a college campus after the carefully preserved body of a species of fish that has lasted millions of years without evolving from its original state, arrives from Madagascar. A gentle police dog suddenly becomes a raging, snarling attacker, resembling in appearance and manner a prehistoric wolf; a dragon fly feasting on the fish carcass becomes a two-foot flying killer. Two horrific murders are committed by a beast-like creature. All these gruesome happenings, it develops, are due to whatever comes in contact with fish transforming backwards to their native savage state in the evolutionary scale.

Jack Arnold's direction of the skilfull David Duncan screenplay builds constant suspense and provides a sock climax. Arthur Franz, science instructor who falls victim to the dread, deceased blood of the fish, delivers strongly as the unwitting murderer who commits his crimes while transformed into a beast. His experiments finally prove that he, himself, is the monster and in remorse he again injects himself with the blood so he is killed by the police.

As his fiancee, Joanna Moore lends fine presence and Judson Pratt also scores as the homicide lieutenant in charge of the case. Troy Donahue and Nancy Walters are good as pair of students, Alexander Lockwood as college prexy-father of heroine and Whit Bissell as college doctor also are okay. Helen Westcott is one of the murder victims.

On technical end, photography by Russell Metty and special photography by Clifford Stine are standouts and Ted J. Kent's fast editing adds to suspense. *Whit.*

The Roots of Heaven
(COLOR—C'SCOPE)

Story development does not match the magnificent backgrounds in this African-localed elephant saga. A disappointment, but will probably reap good b.o.

Hollywood. Oct. 17.
Twentieth-Fox release of Darryl F. Zanuck production. Stars Errol Flynn, Juliette Greco, Trevor Howard, Eddie Albert, Orson Welles. Directed by John Huston. Screenplay, Romain Gary and Patrick Leigh-Fermor; based on Gary's novel; camera (DeLuxe color), Oswald Morris; music, Malcolm Arnold; editor, Basil Fenton Smith. Previewed at the studio, Oct. 13, '58. Running time, 130 MINS.
Forsythe .... Errol Flynn
Minna .... Juliette Greco
Morel .... Trevor Howard
Abe Fields .... Eddie Albert
Cy Sedgewick .... Orson Welles
Saint Denis .... Paul Lukas
Orsini .... Herbert Lom
Habib .... Gregoire Aslan
Governor .... Andre Luguet
Peer Qvist............Friedrich Ledebur
Waitari .... Edric Connor
Baron .... Olivier Hussenot
Major Scholscher......... Pierre Dudan
De Vries .... Marc Doelnitz
Madjumba .... Dan Jackson
Haas .... Maurice Cannon
Cerisot .... Jacques Marin
Korotoro .... Habib Benglia
Yussef .... Bachir Toure
A.D.C. .... Alain Saury
N'Dolo .... Roscoe Stallworth
Inguele .... Assane Fall
Father Fargue .... Francis de Wolff

"The Roots of Heaven," Darryl F. Zanuck's production for 20th-Fox, has striking pictorial aspects, some exciting performances and builds to a pulsating climax of absorbing tension. Unfortunately, these plus factors almost all come in the second half of the picture. Director John Huston has let most of the first half dawdle and meander. Interest seriously suffers. The elusive theme is likely to remain obscure to many. "Roots of Heaven" will probably be good at boxoffice but not the blockbuster 20th-Fox hoped for.

The locale of the screenplay by Patrick Leigh-Fermor and Romain Gary, from Gary's novel, is French Equatorial Africa and the time is the present. Trevor Howard, whose presence is never completely explained, is launching a campaign to save the elephants of Africa. He believes they are threatened with extinction from big game hunters, ivory poachers and the encroachment of civilization.

When he tries to get signers of his petition to outlaw the killings, he is rebuffed on three fronts. The governor of the territory, Andre Luguet, points out his concern is with the health and welfare of his human charges. A missionary priest, Francis de Wolff, reminds Howard the Church is interested chiefly in men's souls. A native leader, Edric Connor, informs him the Africans don't want their continent to remain a giant zoo.

Howard gets only two signatures. One is from Errol Flynn, an alcoholic British ex-officer, and the other is from Juliette Greco, a prostitute. So Howard decides on a campaign of harassment of the hunters and his counter-attack attracts the attention of a safari-ing American tv personality, Orson Welles; a Danish scientist, Friedrich Ledebur; a German nobleman, Olivier Hussenot, and some of Connor's native followers who propose to use Howard as a symbol of their own resistance to colonial law and practice. Howard is finally joined by Eddie Albert, photographer-correspondent for an American news and picture syndicate.

Howard fails in his crusade, defeated by the inertia of public opinion and the rigidity of officialdom. In the end he marches off into the desert brush with those of his followers who survive the government's repression and attacks from the hunters. Flynn has been killed and Miss Greco is so ill she must be left behind.

Although Howard movingly describes the elephants as "the biggest and most powerful of man's company on earth" and a symbol of "all that's beautiful—all that's free," the crusade to save them does not particularly stir the spectator. It seems laudable, like a super-Audubon Society, but not the kind of effort that would impell men to fight and die.

Perhaps one reason is that while the slaughter of elephants is graphically described, it is never shown. It is hard to respond with the fervor the film attempts to elicit when the horror to be fought is never displayed. Especially when it is something so removed from the ordinary frame of reference. One single shot of an elephant being deprived of his life for evil reasons would have helped. Since such shooting goes on all the time in Africa, it would not have been difficult or inhumane to obtain such a scene. Location shots of the great herds are impressive, so much so, in fact, they make it hard to believe beasts are threatened with decimation or extinction.

Huston has staged his exterior scenes superbly. Full advantage is taken here of the arduous African locations. Howard gives a fine performance and is responsible for conveying as much as comes across of the tricky theme. His performance is undercut somewhat by an irritating tendency, apparently on Huston's part, of excessive use of reaction shots, when the story would be better served by keeping the camera rooted on Howard.

Errol Flynn plays the drunken officer competently but without suggesting any latent nobility or particular depth. Miss Greco is interesting without being very moving. Eddie Albert sparks the screen with bubbling vitality and humor in his scenes, and Orson Welles in a brief bit (reportedly done as a favor to Zanuck) is a pinwheel of flashing vigor, his exit to be lamented.

In the supporting cast, Paul Lukas has an engaging world-weariness; Friedrich Ledebur a moving dignity; Edric Connor, splendid and baffled grandeur as the native leader; Gregoire Aslan an amusing knave; and Francis de Wolff, in one scene, etches a memorable character. The rest of the cast, largely European, is competent but allowed little scope for subtleties of characterization. In principal roles are Herbert Lom, Olivier Hussenot, Marc Doelnitz, Alain Saury, Bachir Toure and Andre Luguet.

Oswald Morris was the director of photography, which is excellent, with second unit work by Skeets Kelly, Henri Persin and Gilles Bonneau. Art direction by Stephen Grimes effectively carries through the African feeling from the authentic exteriors to the French-shot interiors. Malcolm Arnold has done a notable score, one that avoids the "tom-tom" cliches. With a theme for Miss Greco, by Henri Pattison, that is going to get single-record exploitation, it is going to be a good promotion item for the film.

Editing, by Russell Lloyd, is first-rate, and the sound by Basil Fenton Smith preserves the African sounds unobtrusively but tellingly. *Powe.*

Bell, Book and Candle
(COLOR)

Strong cast and lavish production values strongest points of offbeat comedy. Good b.o. despite bad miscasting of Kim Novak.

Hollywood, Oct. 17.

Columbia release of Phoenix production. Stars James Stewart, Kim Novak; costars Jack Lemmon, Ernie Kovacs; features Hermione Gingold, Elsa Lanchester, Janice Rule. Produced by Julian Glaustein. Directed by Richard Quine. Screenplay, Daniel Taradash; based on the play by John Van Druten; camera (Technicolor), James Wong Howe; music, George Duning; editor, Charles Nelson. Previewed in Hollywood, Oct. 9, '58. Running time, **106 MINS.**

Sheperd Henderson .... James Stewart
Gillian Holroyd .... Kim Novak
Nicky Holroyd .... Jack Lemmon
Sidney Redlitch .... Ernie Kovacs
Mrs. De Pass .... Hermione Gingold
Queenie .... Else Lanchester
Merle Kittridge .... Janice Rule
French Singer .... Philippe Clay
Secretary .... Bek Nelson
Andy White .... Howard McNear
Musicians .... The Brothers Candoli
Proprietor .... Wolfe Barzell
Exterminator .... Joe Barry
Merle's Maid .... Gail Bonney
Herb Store Owner .... Monty Ash

"Bell, Book and Candle" is a good example of casting for box-office rather than story. The result, in this Julian Blaustein production for Columbia, is that story suffers at the expense of marquee value. The novelty comedy has a brace of good names, headed by James Stewart and Kim Novak, and it will depend on them for its success but it does not come off as a whole, and the chief reason is Miss Novak. This star is clearly not equipped for light comedy.

Richard Quine's direction gets everything possible out of the screenplay and the cast. But with Miss Novak the central figure, the picture lacks the spontaneity and sparkle written in by John Van Druten.

The off-beat story is concerned with witches and warlocks (male gender of the broomstick set) operating against today's world of skepticism and realism. Stewart is the straight man thrust by chance into a group of people, headed by Miss Novak, where encantations, spells and sorcery are accepted as realities as commonplace as processed foods. Miss Novak literally weaves a spell on Stewart to make him fall in love with her. But she becomes bewitched by her own magic, and loses her powers of the supernatural when she breaks witchcraft rules and falls in love with the object of her devotions. When a witch falls in love, so the theory goes, she ceases to be a witch.

There are some wonderfully wierd proceedings here, including Elsa Lanchester and Hermione Gingold as rival witches, and Jack Lemmon as a clean-cut, bongo-beating warlock. Ernie Kovacs is a comedy standout as a perpetually booze-soaked author, investigating witchcraft for a book.

The hazard of the story is that there is really only one joke. This is the humor of surprise and startled acceptance of the fact that the bizarre occupations of these witches and warlocks could exist in contemporary Manhattan.

This was sustained in the play by Van Druten's witty dialog. It is undercut in the picture by the fact that the backgrounds are too often as wierd as the situations. The contrast—and the basis for humor—is therefore softened or lost.

Biggest laugh in the picture is provided by Stewart attempting to drink a horrible mess concocted by witch Gingold, a magic potion guaranteed to free him from Miss Novak's spell. The laughter springs from Stewart as a modern man indulging in ancient mumbo-jumbo and plays superbly. Conversely, when Miss Gingold's headquarters is shown as all too obviously a house where only a witch would live, the joke is telegraphed and lost.

As if realizing this, producer Blaustein and director Quine have assembled a great comedy cast. Stewart, adept at light comedy as at drama, gives a fine performance. Lemmon is an able farceur, too, and Kovacs drapes his character with dozens of fussy, funny touches. Hermione Gingold and Elsa Lanchester are perhaps the greatest witches to brew a stew since "Macbeth." In lesser roles, Janice Rule, Philippe Clay, Bek Nelson and Howard McNear, are helpful and often laugh-getters.

James Wong Howe's Technicolor camera work is artistically creative and often, imaginative, although the tricky use of color does not always seem in the comedy mood. George Duning's music, however, helps by counter-pointing the mood and action. Art direction by Cary Odell is rich, matched by Louis Diage's set decoration. Sound by John Livadary and editing by Charles Nelson are both firstrate. *Powe.*

Party Girl
(COLOR-C'SCOPE)

Straight gangland melodrama, well done.

Hollywood, Oct. 17.

Metro release of Joe Pasternak Production. Stars Robert Taylor, Cyd Charisse, Lee J. Cobb. Directed by Nicholas Ray. Screenplay, George Wells; based on a story by Leo Katcher; camera, Robert Bronner; music, Jeff Alexander; editor, John McSweeney. Previewed at Academy Awards theatre, Oct. 17, '58. Running time, **99 MINS.**

Thomas Farrell .... Robert Taylor
Vicki Gaye .... Cyd Charisse
Rico Angelo .... Lee J. Cobb
Louis Canetto .... John Ireland
Jeffrey Stewart .... Kent Smith
Genevieve .... Claire Kelly
Cookie .... Corey Allen
Danny Rimett .... Lewis Charles
Lou Forbes .... David Opatoshu
Joey Vulner .... Dem Dibbs
O'Malley .... Patrick McVey
Tall Blonde .... Barbara Lang
Joy Hampton .... Myrna Hansen
Showgirl .... Betty Utey

"Party Girl" is a straight melodrama of gangster days in Chicago. played straight. There is none of the currently fashionable effort to understand the phenomenon or to relate it to the times. The Joe Pasternak production for Metro is apparently an attempt to duplicate on a class scale the success of lower budget pictures similarly concerned with the hey-day of the rackets. It is an interesting picture and will be satisfactory for routine playdates, but it is not going to do any extraordinary business.

Robert Taylor plays a crippled lawyer, mouthpiece for gangster boss Lee J. Cobb. Taylor uses his disability to play on the sympathies of juries to get the mobster underlings, such as John Ireland, free of murder and mayhem charges he knows they are guilty of.

He begins to be disturbed about his way of life when he meets Cyd Charisse, a dancer at a nightclub who picks up a little money occasionally at parties. Taylor sees he cannot censure Miss Charisse for making money out of the mobs when he is doing the same thing himself.

Taylor's breaking point comes when he is called on by Cobb to defend a psychopath mobster, Corey Allen. In somewhat curious philosophy, Taylor tells Cobb that the difference between Cobb and Allen is that the former is a predictable (and hence, presumably, more acceptable) outlaw, while Allen is not. Taylor breaks with Cobb, spills all he knows to the cops, and in the end escapes with Miss Charisse as the gangsters are wiped out by the police.

George Wells' screenplay, based on a story by Leo Katcher, is intelligent and convincing, and Nicholas Ray's direction is good within the limits of the action. But the production seems old hat. It seems to promise revelations about the character or nature of these period monsters that are not forthcoming. As a result its effect is rather flat, unsatisfying.

Taylor carries considerable conviction as the attorney, suave and virile. Miss Charisse's character has little background to supply her with any acting exercise, but she is interesting and, in two fine dance numbers, exciting. Lee Cobb contributes another of his somewhat flamboyant characterizations. Although it seems a sentimentalized approach to such a character—until the end—Cobb makes it vivid. The others are stock roles, well done, by Ireland, Kent Smith, Claire Kelly, Allen, Lewis Charles, David Opatoshu, Kem Dibbs and Patrick McVey. Barbara Lang, Myrna Hansen and Betty Utey are decorative additions.

Robert Bronner's CinemaScope photography, in Metrocolor, is handsome, and other technical credits are equally good. Art direction by William A. Horning and Randall Duell is especially fine in a courtroom that actually looks like one and not like a set. There is a title song by Nicholas Brodszky and Sammy Cahn sung by Tony Martin that will be a welcome exploitation assist. *Powe.*

Torpedo Run
(C'SCOPE-COLOR)

Topnotch submarine meller with Glenn Ford and Ernest Borgnine names to attract.

Hollywood, Oct. 17.

Metro release of Edmund Grainger production. Stars Glenn Ford, Ernest Borgnine; costars Diane Brewster, Dean Jones; features L. Q. Jones, Philip Ober, Richard Carlyle. Directed by Joseph Pevney. Screenplay, Richard Sale, William Wister Haines, based on stories by Sale; camera (Metrocolor), George J. Folsey; editor, Gene Ruggiero. Previewed Oct. 15, '58. Running time, **86 MINS.**

Lt. Comdr. Barney Doyle .... Glenn Ford
Lt. Archer Sloan .... Ernest Borgnine
Jane Doyle .... Diane Brewster
Lt. Jake "Fuzz" Foley .... Dean Jones
"Hash" Benson .... L. Q. Jones
Adm. Samuel Setton .... Philip Ober
Comdr. Don Adams .... Richard Carlyle
Orville "Goldy" Goldstein .... Fredd Wayne
Ens. Ron Milligan .... Don Keefer
Lt. Redley .... Robert Hardy
Lt. Burl Fisher .... Paul Picerni

U. S. Navy's submarine action in the Pacific during World War II gets further graphic enlightenment in this well-made Edmund Grainger production. Story of a commander's relentless trackdown of biggest aircraft carrier in the Japanese fleet is handled realistically through full cooperation of the Navy, with performances to match. For the general market film is an exciting entry, and names of Glenn Ford and Ernest Borgnine add to its bright chances as a coin-getter.

Director Joseph Pevney unfolds the Richard Sale-William Wister Haines screenplay at a suspenseful pace, capitalizing on an unusual story twist to draw highly dramatic portrayals from both Ford, as the commander, and Borgnine, his executive officer. Ford, who has caught up to the flattop being screened by a transport carrying 1,200 American war prisoners from Manila to Tokyo, among them his wife and daughter, misses the Japanese carrier and instead sinks the transport. Thereafter, with this tragic circumstance preying on his mind, the hunt and ultimate sinking of the carrier takes on a personal aspect for Ford.

Ford returns to straight dramatic acting after a year or more in comedy roles, for boff characterizations as a man plagued by what he was forced to do. Borgnine is very effective not only as his closest friend but his exec who helps him through his ordeal, relinquishing an offer of his own sub to remain with his commander. Diane Brewster, is briefly in flashbacks as the wife; Dean Jones, a junior officer; Philip Ober as the admiral, lend strong support.

Color photography by George J. Folsey is particularly outstanding, his lighting one of the most interesting technical achievements of the year. Standouts, too, are Gene Ruggiero's tight editing, William A. Horning and Malcolm Brown's atmospheric art direction and special effects by A. Arnold Gillespie. *Whit.*

Lost, Lonely and Vicious

Lightweight "Hollywood" drama; may have some teenage appeal.

States rights release of a Bon Aire production presented by Howco International. Produced by Charles Casinelli. Features Ken Clayton, Barbara Wilson, Lilyan Chauvin. Directed by Frank Myers. Screenplay, Norman Graham; camera, Ted and Vincent Saizis; editor, Herb Hoffman; music, Frederick David. Previewed N.Y., Oct. 17, '58. Running time, **73 MINS.**

Johnnie .... Ken Clayton
Preach .... Barbara Wilson
Tanya .... Lilyan Chauvin
Walt .... Richard Gilden
Pinkie .... Carole Nugent
Darlene .... Sandra Giles
Buddy .... Allen Fife
Father .... Frank Stallworth
Young Actor .... Johnny Erben
Reporter .... Clint Quigley
Psychiatrist .... T. Earl Johnson

Reminiscent of the career of the late James Dean is "Lost, Lonely and Vicious." A Howco International presentation, it's being sold as a package with the same company's "My World Lies Screaming." With a cast of relative unknowns, "Vicious" will have to depend upon exploitation angles purporting to expose the Hollywood "inside."

Both performances and direction are shaky in this Charles Casinelli production. Basic idea of the Norman Graham screenplay had merit, but it seldom becomes credible most due to the writer's own unimaginative treatment. Here the filmgoer is confronted with a promising actor who can't resolve an inner conflict.

His problem is a morbid one—a continual thought of death that becomes an obsession with him. Fortunately he meets a pretty drug store clerk who straightens him out before he can commit suicide in his famed sports car. Ken Clayton is fairish as the "crazy, mixed up" actor while Barbara Wilson is winsome and pert as the femme saviour.

Providing for what passes as Hollywood atmosphere are Lilyan Chauvin, Clayton's drama coach;

Carole Nugent and Sandra Giles, as a coupla busty blondes, and Richard Gilden, an aspiring actor envious of Clayton's success. None is particularly convincing. Frank Myers' direction is mechanical as are most of the technical credits. Sports car scenes and a few fisticuff sequences may stir some teenage interest. Otherwise, this is a lightweight filler at best. *Gilb.*

The Restless Years
(C'SCOPE)

Youth-angled story, well handled, for easy acceptance by younger and family audiences.

Hollywood, Oct. 17.
Universal release of Ross Hunter production. Stars John Saxon, Sandra Dee, Teresa Wright, James Whitmore; features Luana Patten, Margaret Lindsay, Virginia Grey. Directed by Helmut Kautner. Screenplay, Edward Anhalt; based on the play, "Teach Me How to Cry," by Patricia Joudry; camera, Ernest Laszlo; music, Joseph Gershenson; editor, Al Joseph. Previewed at the studio, Oct. 14, '58. Running time, **86 MINS.**

Will Henderson	John Saxon
Melinda Grant	Sandra Dee
Elizabeth Grant	Teresa Wright
Ed Henderson	James Whitmore
Polly Fisher	Luana Patten
Dorothy Henderson	Margaret Lindsay
Miss Robson	Virginia Grey
Bruce	Jody McCrea
Alex Fisher	Alan Baxter
Mr. Booth	Hayden Rorke
Laura	Dorothy Green

A touching account of adolescence and some of its problems as compounded by adult density, "The Restless Years," has strong appeal for younger audiences and will also fit into programming aimed for the family trade. Ross Hunter's production for Universal has good, young stars for marquee value, John Saxon and Sandra Dee, and plenty of strong, longer-established players, to give them solid backing. Helmut Kautner's American directorial bow shows a talented hand.

Edward Anhalt's screenplay is based on Patricia Joundry's play, "Teach Me How To Cry." In almost the first line of dialog, Miss Dee is described as an illegitimate child. Her problems arise out of this and the fact that her unwed mother, Teresa Wright, has never recovered from the desertion by the father.

Everyone in town, apparently, knows the story except Miss Dee. She believes what her mother has told her; that her father died when she was an infant. But she feels set apart, nevertheless, because her mother is obviously unstable, and by the effect this has had on her life. Miss Wright, a dressmaker, keeps her garbed in creations too frilly for today's streamlined youth, and too young for her budding womanhood.

The girl begins to grow up when a new boy in town, John Saxon, who doesn't know or doesn't care about local gossip and prejudice, meets her and falls in love. His life is complicated by his luckless father, James Whitmore, who has come back to his home town in the hopes he can use his childhood connections to achieve the success that has eluded him elsewhere.

So the normal evolution into adulthood for the two youngsters is complicated and harrassed by the machinations of their elders as they connive for financial or social achievement.

It makes a superior story in Anhalt's treatment, although the setting, of a conventional small city, somewhat lessens its believability. It is a period piece, with the dressmaker mother of an illegitimate child, and would have been more plausible if it had been played in period. It seems doubtful that today's youth would be so uniformly bigoted in visiting the sins of the fathers on the children.

But granting this, it has a feeling of poetry and sensitivity. Miss Dee, an especially appealing ingenue, gives the picture its strongest sense of reality. Saxon seems somewhat miscast as a youth of sensitivity, but he is convincing in his scenes with Miss Dee. Teresa Wright has good moments of pathos as the mother, and Whitmore is strong as Saxon's father. The picture is exceptional in its attention to lesser characters, so Margaret Lindsay is able to make an impression as Saxon's mother, Virginia Grey as the children's understanding teacher, and Alan Baxter and Dorothy Green as other parents. Luana Patten, Jody McCrea and Hayden Rorke do well with other roles.

Ernest Laszlo's photography is notably fine in the exterior sequences. Joseph Gershenson's music, using familiar tunes for time setting, plus original music for overall mood, is good. Technical credits are top-notch. *Powe.*

My World Dies Screaming

"Subliminal" angles lift this dull psychological meller into an okay exploitation entry.

States rights release of a William S. Edwards production presented by Howco International. Stars Gerald Mohr, Cathy O'Donnell; features William Ching, John Jualen. Directed by Harold Daniels. Screenplay, Robert C. Dennis; camera, Frederick West; editor, Tholen Gladden; music, Darrell Calker. Previewed N.Y. Oct. 17, '58. Running time, **81 MINS.**

Philip Tierney	Gerald Mohr
Sheila Wayne	Cathy O'Donnell
Mark Snell	William Ching
Janah Snell	John Qualen
Dr. Victor Forel	Barry Bernard

Subliminal perception provides an exploitational crutch for "My World Dies Screaming," a psychological meller which ordinarily would be a candidate for the bottom half of the duals. "Not only will the picture communicate with you visually," star Gerald Mohr tells the audience in a brief prolog, "but s u b c o n s c i o u s l y through your brain."

A Howco International presentation, it's being packaged with a companion film, "Lost, Lonely and Vicious." Distribution will be through franchised outfits in various territories. George Waldman, for example, is handling in the New York area. Both pix obviously were turned out on modest budgets, but the subliminal gimmick in "Screaming" appears sufficient to pull the curious through the wicket in less demanding situations.

Original screenplay of Robert C. Dennis concerns Mohr's efforts to free wife Cathy O'Donnell from a "horror" complex. It develops later that her nightmares stem from the fact she witnessed ax murders of Mohr's family when but a child. Crime was committed in the family's ancestral mansion. Couple returns to the scene of the killings and familiarity of the surroundings helps snap Miss O'Donnell out of her complex.

Dennis' script has lotsa dialog and little action. Hence, the 81 minutes running time seems far too long. Harold Daniels' direction occasionally comes up with some suspense but not nearly enough to overcome the deficiencies of the potboiler yarn. Mohr struggles with his role as does Miss O'Donnell. William Ching and John Qualen are so-so as "menaces" in the mansion while Barry Bernard is seen briefly as a psychiatrist.

Sock novelty is an epilog in which Mohr explains to the audience "what's been getting to them through their subconscious mind." Sequence runs off several scenes replete with superimposed symbols depicting love (fluttering hearts), hate (a crawling snake), etc.

Technical aspects are good, particularly Frederick West's camerawork. Darrell Calker's score is suitably eerie. *Gilb.*

I Want To Live

One of year's top dramas. Grim theme and treatment, but likely to be b.o. and critical bombshell. Brings Susan Hayward new stature.

Hollywood, Oct. 24.
United Artists release of Figaro, Inc., production. Stars Susan Hayward; features Simon Oakland, Virginia Vincent, Theodore Bikel, Wesley Lau, Philip Coolidge, Lou Krugman. Produced by Walter Wanger. Directed by Robert Wise. Screenplay, Nelson Gilling and Don M. Mankiewicz; based on articles by Ed Montgomery and letters of Barbara Graham; camera, Lionel Lindon; music, John Mandel; editor, William Hornbeck. Previewed at Fox Beverly Theatre, Oct. 22, '58. Running time, **120 MINS.**

Barbara Graham	Susan Hayward
Ed Montgomery	Simon Oakland
Peg	Virginia Vincent
Carl Palmberg	Theodore Bikel
Henry Graham	Wesley Lau
Emmett Perkins	Philip Coolidge
Jack Santo	Lou Krugman
Bruce King	James Philbrook
District Attorney	Bartlett Robinson
Richard G. Tibrow	Gage Clark
Al Matthews	Joe De Santis
Father Devers	John Marley
San Quentin Warden	Raymond Bailey
San Quentin Nurse	Alice Backes
San Quentin Matron	Gertrude Flynn
San Quentin Sergeant	Russell Thorson
San Quentin Captain	Dabbs Greer
Sergeant	Stafford Repp
Lieutenant	Gavin MacLeod

"I Want to Live" is a drama dealing with the last years and the execution of Barbara Graham, who was convicted at one time or another of prostitution, perjury, forgery and murder. It is not pleasant but the picture based on it is so overwhelming in its compulsion and power, that it will probably be one of the year's big boxoffice successes as well as garnering considerable critical applause. While it may be prevented by its grim honesty from being a blockbuster, nothing can stop it from being a bombshell.

Walter Wanger's explosive production for Figaro Inc., for United Artists, is superb on almost every count, most notably in the producer's insight that there was a story in this life of sordid and unappetizing crime. It becomes much more than that in the direction of Robert Wise, the screenplay by Nelson Gidding and Don M. Mankiewicz, and most particularly the performance of Susan Hayward in the central role. It is probably the most damning indictment of capital punishment ever documented in any medium.

There is no attempt to gloss the character of Barbara Graham, in the Gidding-Mankiewicz screenplay, only an effort to understand it through some fine irony and pathos. The woman apparently lived an almost completely sordid life. She had no hesitation about indulging in any form of crime or vice that promised excitement on her own, rather mean, terms. To describe her depravity, it is easier to say what she was not. She was not a narcotics addict and, according to a psychiatrist, she was incapable of physical violence.

The screenplay is based on newspaper and magazine articles by San Francisco reporter Ed Montgomery, and on letters written by the woman herself. Its premise is that she was likely innocent of the brutal and vicious murder for which she was executed in the California gas chamber. Actually, however, the picture is not too concerned with her guilt or innocence. It is more concerned with the fact that she was a fallible human being and that the state executed her.

The final 30 to 40 minutes of the

film are as harrowing as anything ever done in pictures. It is a purposely understated account of the mechanics involved in the state's legal destruction of life, and its effects is to raise serious thoughts about what constitutes "cruel and unusual punishment."

The execution is on, it is stayed. It is off, it is on. The sequence is almost unbearable, mounting unswervingly in its intensity. What might seem the greatest horror of it, actually seeing Miss Hayward die in the real gas chamber, comes finally as an anticlimax of relief. As the writers, director and producer certainly intended it should. Subtly, inferentially, the creators of the film raise the question of which is the more degraded, the object of this ordeal or the law that ordains it.

There is a splendid feeling of the might of the Law. Not one of those actually involved in preparing Miss Hayward's death is eager for it. They wait almost as breathlessly as she for the word that might come from a court or the governor that will put it off. They go about their jobs, routinely, but with ironic compassion. It is the Law, mysterious and aloof, which rules and the warden, the priest, the executioners, all are as helpless in halting it as the victim. It is horror compounded and superbly done.

It is hard to think of any other star except Miss Hayward who could bring off this complex characterization. She gives a performance that undoubtedly will return her, after her recent hiatus, to the top of pouplar and critical lists.

Simon Oakland, as Montgomery, who first crucified Barbara Graham in print and then attempted to undo what he had done, underplays his role with telling assurance. The character he plays employs a hearing aid, a fact that gives the picture a vivid symbolic ending. He and Virginia Vincent, the latter as Miss Graham's one female friend, are vital in eliciting what understanding can be gained of the woman. Oakland is a symbol of respectability and Miss Vincent, a bad girl turned good, shows by her faithfulness that there is something to be faithful to. She achieves great pathos with simplicity and conviction.

The other actors represent fine casting for character rather than for type. Theodore Bikel as a friendly pyschologist; Wesley Lau as the woman's drug-ridden husband; Philip Coolidge and Lou Krugman as the unholy pair she teamed with; Gage Clark as her vacillating lawyer, and Alice Backes, a sympathetic nurse. All are excellent. Others who stand out include James Philbrook, Bartlett Robinson, Joe De Santis, John Marley, Raymond Bailey, Gertrude Flynn, Russell Thorson, Dabbs Greer, Stafford Repp and Gavin MacLeod.

Lionel Lindon's photography has the realism and seeming spontaneity of a first-class documentary, but calculated in its staging and effect. Music is supplied by a jazz combo made up of Gerry Mulligan, Shelly Manne, Red Mitchell, Art Farmer, Frank Rosolino, Pete Jolly and Bud Shank, with music composed and conducted by John Mandel.

Edward Haworth's art direction is imaginative and accurate down to the last sleazy background, aided by set decorator Victor Gangelin. William Hornbeck's editing helps give the picture its relentless pace, and sound by Fred Lau is another factor in its complete and absorbing conviction. *Powe.*

The Mugger

Routine meller with little chance to excite.

Los Angeles, Oct. 28.

United Artists release of a Barbizon Production presented by Helprin-Crown. Producer-director, William Berke. Stars Kent Smith; features Nan Martin, James Franciscus, Stefan Schnabel, Connie Vaness, Sandra Church, Dick O'Neil, Leonard Stone, John Alexander, Arthur Storch. Screenplay, Henry Kane, based on novel by Ed McBain; camera, J. Burgi Contner; music, Albert Glasser. Previewed at Goldwyn Studio, Oct. 20, '58. Running time, **74 MINS.**

Peter Graham	Kent Smith
Claire Townsend	Nan Martin
Eddie	James Franciscus
Fats	Stefan Schnabel
Katherine	Connie Vaness
Jeannie	Sandra Church
Cassidy	Dick O'Neil
Kelly	Leonard Stone
Skippy Randolph	Arthur Storch

A contrived film that sets out to tell one story and ends up telling another, "The Mugger" is a routine melodrama that, despite a few capable performances, has nothing to pull it out of the filler class.

A Barbizon Production, presented by Helprin-Crown and released through United Artists, the cops-'n'-crooks yarn centers on the search for a mugger who leaves his female victims with a slight cheek scar, while he makes off with their black shoulder strap bags. Kent Smith, a police psychiatrist, builds a picture of the terrorist through psychological composition, and then the force sets out to find him. In the midst of the search, a girl is killed, but the crime looks like the work of the mugger. Through super sleuthing the culprit is found, and, when he dènies killing the girl, the search for the murderer continues, finally landing on the girl's brother-in-law who is a friend of the psychiatrist's. It's all too simple and very pat.

Screenplay is by Henry Kane, based on the novel by Ed McBain. Film was produced and directed by William Berke in New York City, and, although his direction is sound, he would have done well to take better advantage of the scenery.

Smith is fine as the police doctor, but top acting work is turned in by Nan Martin, as a policewoman, and James Franciscus, as the brother-in-law. Good work also comes from Arthur Storch, as a cheap hood, Connie Vaness, as a cheap blonde, Sandra Church, Dick O'Neil, Stefan Schnabel and Leonard Stone.

Technical credits are stock, with J. Burgi Contner's photography better on the outside than it is in. The Albert Glasser musical score, though sometimes melodramatic, is artistically handled for the most part. *Ron.*

Ivan Grozny

(Ivan the Terrible: Part 2)
(RUSSIAN)

Brussels, Oct. 28.

Mosfilm release and production. Stars Nikolai Sherkasov; features Seraphima Birman, Piotr Kadochnikov, A. Mgebrov. Written, directed and edited by Sergei Eisenstein. Camera, Edward Tisse, Andrei Mosvin; music, Sergei Prokofiev. At Brussels Greatest Films of All Times Film Fest. Running time, 90 MINS.

Ivan	Nikolai Cherkasov
Staritzkaya	Seraphima Birman
Vladimir	Piotr Kadochnikov
Pimen	A. Mgebrov

Though completed in 1946, this feature has only been allowed to be shown abroad (and in Russia) recently. Part two of a proposed trilogy on the life of the 16th century czar, Ivan the Terrible, director Sergei Eisenstein never lived to complete the third part. But as Part II stands, it's a full and an imposing historical opus.

Russians have never made it clear why this one was banned, but an analogy between Ivan and the defunct, now downgraded demigod, Stalin, is evident. It makes Ivan out to be both good and malevolent in his attempts to unite his country. The story also relates the intrigues within his own family for the throne, as well as his clashes with the scheming landowning peerage, some ready to sell out to foreign enemies.

Film has sheer visual elegance and splendor and amounts to arresting drama. It's "theatrical," almost "operatic" at times. Power struggle and political squabbles generate excitement.

The character of Ivan is brilliantly limned by Nikolai Cherkasov as he goes from dedicated monarch to tyrant to a man accepting the loneliness of position and power and substituting even terror to achieve his goal of a united country. The flashes of incipient madness are also there.

Feature looms as a good entry for special U.S. situations. Some critics may consider it a tour-de-force. Technically, it is superb and Sergei Prokofiev's music is just right. *Mosk.*

In Love and War

(COLOR—C'SCOPE)

Story fares better with love than war. Strong accent on youthful casting. Good b.o.

Hollywood, Oct. 24.

Twentieth-Fox release of a Jerry Wald production. Stars Robert Wagner, Dana Wynter, Jeffrey Hunter, Hope Lange, Bradford Dillman, Sheree North, France Nuyen; features Mort Sahl, Steven Gant, Harvey Stephens, Paul Comi, Joe di Reda, Buck Class. Directed by Philip Dunne. Screenplay by Edward Anhalt, based on Anton Myrer's novel, "The Big War"; camera (DeLuxe Color), Leo Tover; music, Hugo Friedhofer; editor, William Reynolds. Previewed at the Westwood Village Theatre, Oct. 23, '58. Running time, **107 MINS.**

Frankie O'Neill	Robert Wagner
Sue Trumbell	Dana Wynter
Nico Kantaylis	Jeffrey Hunter
Andrea Lenaine	Hope Lange
Alan Newcombe	Bradford Dillman
Lorraine	Sheree North
Kalai Ducanne	France Nuyen
Danny Krieger	Mort Sahl
Babe Ricarno	Steven Gant
Amory Newcombe	Harvey Stephens
Father Wallensack	Paul Comi
Capistron	Joe Di Reda
Derek	Buck Class
Mrs. Kantaylis	Lili Valenty
Mrs. Lenaine	Edith Barrett
Sidney Lenaine	James Bell
Terrence	Frank Murphy
Grace Scanlon	Mary Patton
Charlie Scanlon	Murvyn Vye
Lt. D'Allesandro	Edward "Tap" Canutt
Lt. Col. Herron	Nelson Leigh
Allie O'Neill	Veronica Cartwright
Bobby O'Neill	Brian Corcoran

"In Love and War" is a keen appraisal of the utility of love and the futility of war. Its most imposing element is honesty, and it uncompromisingly handles its sex. The film represents a gamble for producer Jerry Wald and 20th-Fox, as they are banking on the excitement values rather than the marquee values of their cast. It's a smart risk and one that should pay off.

Wald has backed up his "need for new talent" words with the casting of Robert Wagner, Dana Wynter, Jeffrey Hunter, Hope Lange, Bradford Dillman, Sheree North and France Nuyen in the starring roles. It's a fresh, enthusiastic concept in big picture making that, in these days of percentages, is one way to keep the ink from running red.

Edward Anhalt's screenplay, based on Anton Myrer's novel, "The Big War," is hard-hitting, both in action and dialog. And, through the perceptive direction of Philip Dunne, each of the relationships and all of the ideas are developed with clarity. The characterizations are built in San Francisco and the Monterey Peninsula, and the sequences are particularly effective. The Pacific war footage, however, tends to ramble with little point from scene to scene and with little or no forward movement. It may be that the filmmakers felt the lack of an objective, the neglect of a goal in the battle, would paint war as more futile—and it does—but, even **though the marines may not know** what they're doing, the audience should.

Story is one of the changing ideals and the growing maturity of three marines entrenched in the second world war. At the start, Hunter is the patriot, Wagner the coward and Dillman the intellectual who fights because he must. At the end, Hunter dies in battle, Wagner turns hero and Dillman discovers the uselessness of war. More than one of war, the tale is one of love, Wagner for Miss North, Hunter for Miss Lange and Dillman, having discarded Miss Wynter, for Miss Nuyen.

High spots are numerous, and the seven stars—plus comic Mort Sahl in his first film role—are excellent. Wagner retains sympathy even when cockeyed; with her death scene, Miss Wynter hits a high point in her career; Hunter is tops and a solid force behind the film's action; Miss Lange, most effective, is the maximum of affection, warmth and sensitivity; Dillman portrays a change in philosophy with skill; Miss North, who is used too sparingly, proves an attuned actress and well-paced comedienne; and Miss Nuyen is fine as the tender Hawaiian-French nurse.

Sahl's Jewish marine role was written especially for him, and, from the sound of it, by him. The satirist undoubtedly will gain world-wide guffaws when, in the midst of the mortars, bombs and bullets, he answers a buzzing walkie-talkie, "Good morning, World War Two." Good in support are Joe di Reda, Steven Gant, Harvey Stephens, Paul Comi, Mary Patton, Murvyn Vye and moppets Veronica Cartwright and Brian Corcoran.

Technically, the film excels in the work of photographer Leo Tover, art directors Lyle R. Wheeler and George W. Davis, set decorators Walter M. Scott and Fay Babcock, film editor William Reynolds, soundman E. Clayton Ward and Harry M. Leonard and particularly composer Hugo Friedhofer. *Ron.*

Ten Days to Tulara

Lower berth item for routine double-bills. Mexican-locationed version of cops and robbers.

Hollywood. Oct. 24.

United Artists release of George Sherman-Clarence Eurist production. Stars Sterling Hayden; costars Grace Raynor, Rodolfo Hoyos. Directed by George Sherman. Screenplay, Laurance Mascott; camera, Alex Phillips; music, Lon Adomian; editor, Carlos Savage. Previewed at Goldwyn studio, Oct. 22, '58. Running time, **77 MINS.**

Scotty	Sterling Hayden
Teresa	Grace Raynor
Cesar	Rodolfo Hoyos
Dario	Carlos Muzquiz
Francisco	Tony Caravajal
Piranha	Juan Garcia
Colonel	Rafael Alcayde
Marco	Felix Gonzales
Capitan	Jose Pulido
Co-Pilot Luis	Major M. Badager
Teniente	Milton Bornstein
Medico	Barry Grail
Chris	Paco Arenas

"Ten Days To Tulara" is only suitable for lower place on routine double-bills. Produced in Mexico by Clarence Eurist and George Sherman, and directed by Sherman, the Sterling Hayden starrer hasn't enough plot interest even to sustain its brief length. What there is exhibits small imagination in the treatment. It quickly boils down to a Latin-American version of cops and robbers but even as soldados y bandidos, this combination doesn't have enough variation to make it interesting.

Sterling Hayden plays a barnstorming U. S. pilot operating a one-man airline in Central America in Laurance Mascott's screenplay. He is forced to join a gang of desperados headed by Rodolfo Hoyos, when Hoyos kidnaps his son and holds him hostage. The gang has stolen $250,000 in gold bullion and wants to use Hayden's plane as a getaway. When the plane is shot down, they continue the trek by car and finally afoot.

There is some novelty about using a plane in this connection and Sherman wisely avoids doing the jungle bit because the background is Central America. There is an interesting attempt to use native festivals as part of the plot development, but it doesn't play with much success. The result is that the chase seems a series of repetitious episodes, and despite considerable gunfire, there isn't much jeopardy generated. There is a romance between Hayden and Grace Raynor, Hoyos' convent-bred daughter who accompanys the trek, but it, too, lacks conviction. In the end, Hoyos is killed and Hayden is united with his son.

In addition to other drawbacks, the film quality is often poor and other technical aspects, such as music and sound, are elementary. Performances are adequate although there is no more than superficial attempt at characterization. *Powe.*

Tank Battalion

Routine war entry, packaged with "Hell Squad;" okay performer in program market.

Hollywood, Oct. 23.

American International release of Richard Bernstein production. Stars Don Kelly, Marjorie Hellen, Edward G. Robinson Jr.; features Frank Gorshin, Regina Gleason, Barbara Luna, Bob Padget, Mark Sheeler. Directed by Sherman A. Rose. Screenplay, Bernstein, George W. Waters; original story, Waters; camera, Frederick Gately; editor, Rose; music, Dick La Salle. Reviewed Oct. 22, '58. Running time, 80 MINS.

Brad	Don Kelly
Alice	Marjorie Hellen
Corbett	Edward G. Robinson Jr.
Skids	Frank Gorshin
Norma	Regina Gleason
Nikko	Barbara Luna
Collins	Bob Padget
Captain Caswell	Mark Sheeler
Buck	Baynes Barrow
Egg Charlie	Tetsu Komai
Lieutenant	John Trigonis
1st Soldier	Don Devlin
2nd Soldier	Warren Crosby
Soldier	Troy Patterson

"Tank Battalion" is a routine Korea war yarn with generally good production values and performances. For the program market, where it's packaged with "Hell Squad," it should run up okay returns.

Richard Bernstein production centers on the four-man crew of a tank in enemy territory, their loves and battle action. Script by Bernstein and George W. Waters is inclined to be fragmentary at times but builds in climaxing sequences, when tank is disabled and under enemy fire.

Don Kelly heads cast as tank's commander, persuasive both in fighting scenes and in his romance with Marjorie Hellen, briefly effective as an Army nurse. Edward G. Robinson, Jr., competently undertakes role of the crewman who makes his way back to base to return with part needed to repair tank. Frank Gorshin and Bob Padget portray other two crewmen, both lending conviction, and romancing Regina Gleason and Barbara Lund, respectively, former a nurse, latter a Eurasian bar-maid, each strongly cast. Mark Sheeler handles role of a stuffy captain satisfactorily.

Frederick Gately's facile camera sets a fast pace further aided by director Rose' tight editing. Rudi Feld's art direction and music score by Dick La Salle are further assets. *Whit.*

Hell Squad

Low - budgetter for lowerbracketing with "Tank Battalion"; pedestrian appeal.

Hollywood, Oct. 23.

American International release of Burt Topper production. Stars Wally Campo, Brandon Carroll, Frederic Gavlin; features Greg Stuart, Cecil Addis, Leon Schrier, Don Chambers. Directed-screenplay-story, Topper; camera, Erik Daarstad, John Morrill; editor, Marvin Wallowitz. Reviewed Oct. 22, '58. Running time, 64 MINS.

Russo	Wally Campo
German Officer	Brandon Carroll
Clemens	Fred Galvin
Nelson	Greg Stuart
Lippy	Cecil Addis
Roth	Leon Schrier
American Captain	Don Chambers

Larry Shuttleworth, Jerry Bob Weston, Gordon Edwards, Jack Sewards, Jim Hamilton, Ben Bigelow, Jow Hearne. Jack N. Kramer, Dick Walsh, Curtis Lozer, Bob Williams.

Efforts of a small American patrol, lost in the Tunisian desert in early days of World War II, to find its way back to base triggers the events of this Burt Topper production. Interest is delayed in starting, due to repetitious action, but picks up enough later to rate as second half of a double bill. (Film goes out with "Tank Battalion.")

Topper directs as well as wrote the original story and screenplay, and manages a somewhat novel plot finale. Sole survivor of the patrol is wounded and trapped in a mine field set by the Nazis, and in his rifle sights is a German lieutenant, nearly delirious with thirst and with a map of the mine placements. Situation is well-enough developed to offer something a little different story-wise, but too much footage is wasted in leading up to it.

Wally Campo socks over his role of the wounded GI, and Brandon Carroll scores as the German. Okay performances also are contributed by Fred Gavlin, leader of the patrol; Greg Stuart, Leon Schrier and Cecil Addis, remaining members.

Technical credits are well handled by Erik Daarstad and John Morrill, photography; Marvin Wallowitz, editor. *Whit.*

Enchanted Island
(COLOR)

Visually handsome, dramatically confusing film version of Melville's cannibalistic "Typee." Prospects dim.

Hollywood, Oct. 31.

Warner Bros. release of Benedict Bogeaus production. Stars Dana Andrews, Jane Powell; costars Don Dubbins. Directed by Allan Dwan. Screenplay, James Leicester and Harold Jacob Smith; based on Herman Melville's "Typee"; camera (Technicolor), George Stahl; music, Raul LaVista; editor, James Leicester. Previewed at the studio, Oct. 28, '58. Running time, 93 MINS.

Abner Bedford	Dana Andrews
Fayaway	Jane Powell
Tom	Don Dubbins
Jimmy Dooley	Arthur Shields
Captain Vangs	Ted de Corsia
Mehevi	Friedrich Ledebur
Kory Kory	Augustin Fernandez
Medicine Man	Francisco Reiguera
First Mate Moore	Les Hellman

"Enchanted Island," a disguised version of Herman Melville's public domain "Typee," features some spectacular location scenery as background and practically nothing but confusion in the foreground. Benedict Bogeaus produced the Dana Andrews-Jane Powell starrer (originally for RKO) which Warner Bros. is releasing. Its prospects, except as a visually attractive filler, are dim. Allan Dwan directed.

The screenplay by James Leicester and Harold Jacob Smith has Andrews and Don Dubbins as disgruntled U.S. seamen who jump ship in the South Seas. The period is mid-19th Century. They escape from one part of the island to another, where they are befriended by a tribe of natives supposedly cannibalistic—the Typees.

Whether or not, they are maneating is never clear in the film, though Melville was explicit. Jane Powell, a toothsome native dish, turns up to offer romantic interest for Andrews. He teaches her English quicker than Berlitz could, and they became "we" in a native ceremony.

Marital bliss is clouded by Dubbins' disappearance. He intended to get away, but Andrews wonders how far he got, considering the reported gourmet habits of the Typees. Andrews decides something is wrong when he sees a local urchin wearing Dubbins' striped jersey, and spots the medicine man sporting Dubbins' shoes. His ardor for his native bride also cools, somewhat, when he realizes she has been covering up for the murderers. But he overcomes this feeling with the observation that customs differ the world over.

At the end, Andrews and Miss Powell must flee and they are picked up by the tyrannical ship captain Andrews originally fled. He has been threatening through much of the picture to hang Andrews for mutiny but now jovially proposes to make him first mate. Miss Powell appears to have been harpooned dead by the irate medicine man, but it isn't clear whether she is really kayoed or only nicked.

Dwan's direction is hampered by characters that are never realized and dialog that has an overly familiar ring. He doesn't help it much by scenes photographed from a fixed position, seldom using the moving camera to break or highlight them.

It isn't fair to blame the actors for the debacle. George Stahl's Technicolor photography is the one plus factor of the production. He gets some lovely compositions and they are recorded with fidelity and taste.

Editing is sloppy. In at least two cases, connecting shots don't match.

Powe.

Revolt in the Big House

Well-made low budgeter that has some b.o. value if exploited. Mostly, a good dualer.

Hollywood, Oct. 28.

Allied Artists production and release. Stars Gene Evans, Robert Blake; features Timothy Carey, John Qualen, Sam Edwards, John Dennis, Walter Barnes, Frank Richards, Emile Meyer, Arlene Hunter. Produced by David Diamond. Directed by R. G. Springsteen. Screenplay by Daniel Hyatt and Eugene Lourie; camera, William Margulies; editor, William Austin. Previewed at the studio, Oct. 28, '58. Running time, 79 MINS.

Gannon .... Gene Evans
Rudy .... Robert Blake
Kyle .... Timothy Carey
Doc .... John Qualen
Al .... Sam Edwards
Red .... John Dennis
Starkey .... Walter Barnes
Jake .... Frank Richards
Warden .... Emile Meyer
Girl .... Arlene Hunter

A well-concocted prison story, "Revolt in the Big House" is, by any standard, more impressive than its budget. Confined to cell blocks and yards, producer David Diamond doesn't have strong production values, but, especially in Folsom Prison location footage, he has drama. Although it will play well on its own in scattered situations, the Allied Artists release primarily is a strong second-feature entry for most markets.

Director R. G. Springsteen skillfully handled his actors, making the most of a good, well-planned Daniel Hyatt-Eugene Lourie screenplay. Most notable in the generally capable production is a sensitive, fiery performance from a young actor named Robert Blake. As a young Mexican boy caught in prison circumstance, Blake should earn for himself a deserved reputation as a natural, though not a "torn-shirt," actor.

Central character is a big time operator (Gene Evans) who, after many narrow escapes with the law, finally is hauled in on a rap that sticks. From the beginning, he takes over his fellow inmates, setting up a clique whose purpose it is to set up and carry out a prison break. Evans' young cellmate (Blake) is conned into the break by his con friends, and a riot is instigated so that Evans can go over the back wall while the guards are busy killing his friends at the front one. Evans knifes Blake who nevertheless manages to warn the prisoners that there are machine guns waiting for them at the front gate. And, in the end, Evans gets his in a subway.

Evans is steadfast, appearing honest, yet brandishing a hoodlum's sense. Timothy Carey is excellent in creating a caricature-like rôle, and fine support comes from John Qualen, Sam Edwards, John Dennis, Frank Richards and Emile Meyer.

Technically, the production is capably done, with cameraman William Margulies' work standing out. Art director David Milton recreated an authentic-looking cell block, and film editor William Austin, kept pace with the action.

Ron.

The Spider

Good exploitationer, helped by interesting special effects.

Hollywood, Oct. 31.

American-International release of James H. Nicholson-Samuel Z. Arkoff production. Stars Edward Kemmer, June Kenny, Gene Persson. Producer-director, Bert I. Gordon. Screenplay, Laszlo Gorog and George Worthing Yates; from a story by Gordon; camera, Jack Marta; music, Albert Glasser; editor, Ronald Sinclair. Previewed at KTTV, Oct. 24, '58. Running time, 72 MINS.

Kingman .... Ed Kemmer
Carol Flynn .... June Kenny
Mike Simpson .... Gene Persson
Sheriff Cagle .... Gene Roth
Mr. Simpson .... Hal Torey
Mrs. Flynn .... June Jocelyn
Mr. Haskel .... Mickey Finn
Helen Kingman .... Sally Fraser
Joe .... Troy Patterson
Sam .... Skip Young
Jake .... Howard Wright
Sheriff Sanders .... Bill Giorgio
Hugo .... Hank Patterson
Mr. Fraser .... Jack Kosslyn

The pattern for science-fiction-fantasy-horror pictures is usually that of the amazingly colossal or the incredibly shrinking. "The Spider," a Bert I. Gordon concoction produced by James H. Nicholson and Samuel Z. Arkoff for American International, has for its gimmick the out-sized rather than the under-sized. It is characterized by well done special effects, a reasonably credible plot, and will be a good feature for the exploitation market.

"The Spider" of the Laszlo Gorog-George Worthing Yates screenplay, from Gordon's story, is a monster that has been trapped in a cave but breaks out and starts ravaging the countryside and its inhabitants. As usual in such stories to ward off annoying audience doubts, the community it hits is described as an isolated one, so the residents are forced to handle the situation with whatever meagre resources they have at hand.

This consists of the local police force and a posse made up mostly of high school students and their parents. A high school teacher, Ed Kemmer, and two of his pupils, June Kenny and Gene Persson, lead the hunt and eventually help destroy the beast, accomplished after considerable snarlings and slaverings by the huge insect in its lair.

Gordon, who produced and directed as well as doing the special effects with Flora M. Gordon, uses Carlsbad Caverns backgrounds by means of split screen and travelling matte photography, and gets some eerie sequences. These technical aspects are particularly interesting and well done.

Acting and direction are routine in the bridge sequences not directly involving the spider. Those who contribute in the former category are Kemmer, Miss Kenny, Persson, Gene Roth, Hal Torey, June Jocelyn, Mickey Finn and Sally Fraser.

Jack Marta's photography is capable, Ronald Sinclair's editing is a plus factor, and Albert Glasser's music is good.

Powe.

Tarawa Beachhead

Well-made budget pic for programming; intelligent mixing of war, romance, tension.

Hollywood, Oct. 31.

Columbia release of Charles H. Schneer production. Stars Kerwin Mathews, Julie Adams, Ray Danton. Directed by Paul Wendkos. Screenplay, Richard Alan Simmons; camera, Henry Fraulich; editor, Jerome Thoms. Previewed at the studio, Oct. 16, '58. Running time, 77 MINS.

Sgt. Tom Sloan .... Kerwin Mathews
Ruth Campbell .... Julie Adams
Lt. Joel Brady .... Ray Danton
Paula Nelson .... Karen Sharpe
General Nathan Keller .... Onslow Stevens
Casey Nelson .... Russell Thorsen
Lt. Gideon .... Eddie Ryder
Johnny Campbell .... John Baer
Major Westerly .... Mike Garth
Col. Kempler .... Larry Thor
Brodzky .... Buddy Lewis
Sgt. Anderson .... Lee Farr
Ullman .... Bill Boyett
Greer .... Don Reardon

"Tarawa Beachhead," Charles H. Schneer production for Columbia, is a well-made program pictures that will be an asset in the double bill market for which it is intended.

It does not cover any particularly new ground in its examination of Marine combat in the Pacific in Word War II, but Richard Alan Simmons' screenplay is given well-paced direction by Paul Wendkos so it compels interest continuously.

Kerwin Mathews plays an idealistic young Marine who is witness to the murder in combat of a fellow gyrene by their commanding officer, Ray Danton. Mathews keeps his mouth shut about this for a time, believing as an enlisted man his word will be of little worth against Danton's.

Mathews and Danton are thrown together repeatedly, both as servicemen and in their private lives. On leave in New Zealand, Mathews falls in love with Julie Adams, widow of the man Danton shot, and Danton marries her sister, Karen Sharpe.

Climax of the story is the Marine attack on Tarawa. Mathews has prepared charges against Danton which he mens to file after the action is completed. Danton is killed, however, in what appears a heroic gesture. The final shot has the commanding general asking Mathews for information on Danton because he intends to recommend him for the Medal of Honor. Mathews can only answer "Nobody knows anybody . . . That's a fact."

The story is a good action picture but it also has some depth. Simmons writes good dialog and he handles his somewhat enigmatic situation with simplicity and directness. Wendkos emphasizes the action, properly so, to hold interest, but he is also adept at making the story's thought content palatable.

Mathews is both virile and thoughtful as the marine troubeld by his conflicts between justice and the Marine Corps. Miss Adams is tender as the Marine widow, and Ray Danton handles his tricky role with skill. Others who contribute include Karen Sharpe, Onslow Stevens, Russell Thorson and Eddie Ryder.

Film Editor Jerome Thoms does an exceptionally good job of integrating stock and staged battle scenes so there is no obvious disparity between film quality or lighting. Henry Freulich's photography is first-rate.

Powe.

When Hell Broke Loose

Uninspired war meller dealing with Nazi activity.

Hollywood, Oct. 31.

Paramount release of Oscar Brodney-Sol Dolgin production. Stars Charles Bronson, Richard Jaeckel, Violet Rensing. Director-film editor, Kenneth G. Crane. Screenplay, Oscar Brodney; based on articles by Ib Melchior; camera, Hal McAlpin; music, Albert Glasser. Previewed at the studio, Oct. 27, '58. Running time, 78 MINS.

Steve Boland .... Charles Bronson
Karl .... Richard Jaeckel
Ilsa .... Violet Rensing
Jonesie .... Robert Easton
Eddie Foy III .... Brooklyn
Ludwig .... Arvid Nelson
Chaplain .... John Morley

The fact that two of the characters in "When Hell Broke Loose," are named "Brooklyn" and "Jonesie," respectively, tells a great deal about the quantity of inventiveness of this war melodrama, an indie production for Paramount. Although the Oscar Brodney-Sol Dolgin film is said to be based on factual material, it fails to convince or to entertain, and it will find a niche only in double-bill filler situations.

Charles Bronson is an unwilling conscript in World War II, in the Brodney screenplay, from articles by Ib Melchior. A bookie, a sharpie and a misanthrope, be joins the army only to escape a prison sentence. He spends most of his time in the guardhouse until he gets to Germany. There he meets Violet Rensing, a German girl who kindles a spark of decency in him in addition to the usual boy-girl reactions.

Miss Rensing's brother, Richard Jaeckel, is a member of the Nazi Werewolves, underground group which plans to assassinate General Eisenhower and disrupt the Allied war effort. Miss Rensing spills the plot to U.S. officers because Bronson has been nice to her, and she gets killed in the resulting fracas.

The picture wastes too much time on what should be brief establishing shots and gives other segments only cursory attention and insufficient background. Dialog is trite.

The struggle by the cast is unequal, but its members try to give some vitality to their shapeless characterizations and occasionally succeed. Most successful are Bronson, Jaeckel, Miss Rensing, Robert Easton, Eddie Foy III, Arvid Nelson and John Morley.

Kenneth G. Crane, who edited as well as directing, succeeds in the first capacity better than the second. Use of stock footage is skillful. Hal McAlpin's photography and Albert Glasser's music are good.

Powe.

Further Up the Creek!
(BRITISH—MEGASCOPE)

Cheerful followup to a previous successful navy farce; good b.o. for family houses.

London, Oct. 28.

Columbia release of a Byron-Hammer (Henry Halsted) production. Stars David Tomlinson, Frankie Howerd, Shirley Eaton. Directed by Val Guest. Original story and screenplay, Val Guest, John Warren, Len Heath; editor, Bill Lenny; camera, Len Harris; music, Stanley Black. At New Victoria, London. Running time, 91 MINS.

Fairweather .... David Tomlinson
Bos'n .... Frankie Howerd
Jane .... Shirley Eaton
Mrs. Galloway .... Thora Hird
Barker .... Lionel Jeffries
Perkins .... Lionel Murton
Bates .... Sam Kydd
Cooky .... John Warren
Scouse .... David Lodge
Lofty .... Ian Whittaker
Edie .... Amy D'Alby
Maudie .... Esma Cannon
Phillipe .... Tom Gill
Kentoni Brothers .... Jack Le White, Max Day
First Model .... Mary Wilson
Second Model .... Katherine Byrne
President .... Eric Pohlman
Lieut. Commander .... Michael Goodliffe
Algeroccan Major .... Wolfe Morris
Despatch Rider .... John Singer
Postman .... Larry Noble
Whacker Payne .... Ballard Berkeley
Chief Wren .... Judith Furse
Ticket Collector .... Michael Ripper
Taxi Driver .... Joe Gibbon
Policeman .... Victor Brooks
Signalman .... Cavan Malone
Chief Yeoman .... Desmond Llewellyn
Flagship Comm. .... Basil Dignam
Armiral .... John Stuart
Signals .... Jean Conrad
First Lieut. .... Patrick Holt
Algeroccan Officer .... George Herbert
El Diabolo .... Charles Lloyd Pack
British Consud .... Walter Hudd
Sea Scout .... John Hall

Following the successful "Up the Creek," this comes as a whacky sequel. In "Further Up The Creek," the surprise element of the joke is wearing a shade thin. But there seems no reason why this simple formula for yocks should not continue indefinitely. This latest pic is not so consistently funny as the first, but it's still a breezy, light-hearted pic which will be a useful booking for most family houses.

David Tomlinson is still the dim-witted, dithering young naval officer who is posted to the command of the frigate "Aristotle." He comes up against virtually the same crew which caused him all his trouble in "Creek." This time, the crew is running a profitable bookmaking business when the frigate is sold to the Algeroccan government. Ordered to deliver the frigate to Algerocco they set out to make the trip lucrative. The ship is well under way when Tomlinson finds, to his horror, that the bos'n and his men have fixed up nine passengers for a one-way luxury cruise.

The humor is scrappy and often predictable, but Val Guest keeps things moving at a brisk pace and the laughs come easily. Most of the crew is on parade again, Lionel Jeffries, Lionel Murton, John Warren and Sam Kydd being among those who keep the fun bubbling over.

There is, however, a change in the bos'n. Instead of Peter Sellers, whose excellent character acting contributed largely to the humor of "Up The Creek," Frankie Howerd plays this role. Howerd's humor is very different, and does not fit quite so snugly into the plot. Howerd is far more of an individual comedian and dialog, and situations often have been tailored directly for his personality. He has a big following and brings some boisterous fun to the role.

Tomlinson does not put a wrong foot forward as the naval officer. Among the passengers there are some stalwart performances by Thora Hird, as a fussy everybody; Amy D'Alby and Esma Cannon as two old spinsters out on a spree, and Shirley Eaton, as a delectable glamor girl. "Further Up Creek" is recommended for a ch---ful night out. *Rich.*

The Sheriff of Fractured Jaw

(BRITISH-C'SCOPE-COLOR)

A click yock-gathering job; combo of Kenneth More and Jayne Mansfield looks surefire draw in both UK and the U.S. Not to be missed.

London, Oct. 28.

20th-Fox release of a Daniel M. Angel production. Stars Kenneth More, Jayne Mansfield. Directed by Raoul Walsh. Screenplay, Arthur Dales, from story by Jacob Hay; camera, Otto Heller; editor, John Shirley; music, Robert Farnon. At Rialto, London, Oct. 28, '58. Running time, **100 MINS.**

Jonathan Tibbs .... Kenneth More
Kate .... Jayne Mansfield
Uncle Lucius .... Robert Morley
Toynbee .... Ronald Squire
James .... David Horne
Mason .... Eynon Evans
Masters .... Henry Hull
Keeno .... William Campbell
Jack .... Bruce Cabot
The Drummer .... Donald Stewart
The Drunk .... Sidney James
Clayborne .... Reed de Rouen
Luke .... Charles Irwin
Wilkins .... Gordon Tanner
Luke's Wife .... Tucker McGuire
Bartender .... Charles Farrell
Running Deer .... Jonas Applegarth
Red Wolf .... Joe Buffalo

Who ever greenlighted the starring combo of Jayne Mansfield and Kenneth More in "The Sheriff of Fractured Jaw" has done themselves and filmgoers a good turn. These two effervescent personalities merge like bacon and eggs, and the result is a wave of yocks. On both sides of the Atlantic, the team of M. & M. should prove alluring marquee, and the b.o. should tinkle happily.

Raoul Walsh has directed this cheerful skit about the wild, woolly west with vigor and pace. He gives little time to remind the audience that many of the situations are predictable and that Arthur Dales' brisk screenplay occasionally needs an upward jolt from the skill of the leading thesps. It could be that "Sheriff" will give the film biz an unwittingly body blow, since many future patrons may be unable to take a "cowboys and Indians" pic with any degree of seriousness.

Yarn starts off in London at the turn of the century. More has inherited a fading gunsmith business. Reading that there is a spot of bother in the Wild West he decides that that's the place to sell his guns. So this dude salesman (walking stick, brown derby and strictly West End suiting) nonchalantly sets off with some samples, and all the confidence in the world. It's not long before he is up to his surprised eyebrows in trouble.

He becomes involved with Injuns, two warring sets of cowboys and with Miss Mansfield, who plays the pistol-packing boss of a saloon. He is conned into becoming the sheriff of the one-horse town of Fractured Jaw. Before it's all over, he has tamed the tough guys, made the Indians peaceful citizens and married Miss Mansfield. He has also sold a new automatic pistol and revived the fortunes of his firm.

More's immaculate throwaway line of comedy gets full rein in this production. With polite manners, impeccable accent and a brash line of action, which leaves the locals in doubt as to whether he is the biggest fool or the bravest man ever to hit their territory, he carries all before him and lands in and out of scrapes with amiable aplomb. Among the memorable incidents are those in which he learns to fire a pistol, the first time he rides a horse, breaks up an Indian attack by appeasement, gets tipsy in a saloon, introduces afternoon tea to the hard-drinking local citizens, becomes adopted as a blood brother of an Indian tribe and constantly escapes the local undertaker's hearse which follows him through hs adventures like a macabre vulture.

Miss Mansfield gives More hearty support, looks attractive in a big, bosomy way and sings two or three numbers very well. One of them "Valley of Love," is sufficiently simple and lilting to be a possible click. The two stars carry most of the weight of this irrepressible film on their shoulders. But there are other neat performances, notably by Henry Hull, as the local mayor, Bruce Cabot and Gordon Tanner, as two of the local baddies, Charles Irwin, as a squatter, and Jonas Applegarth and Joe Buffalo, as the two leading incredible Indian warriors.

The film was made in Spain and at Pinewood, but the locations have an authentic western air while Bernard Robinson's indoor sets are most effective. Otto Heller's color photography cannot be faulted. Anybody looking for an uninhibited laugh should not fail in their search with "Sheriff." *Rich.*

Eve Wants to Sleep

(POLISH)

San Francisco, Oct. 30.

Film Polski (Warsaw) production, directed by Tadeusz Chmielewski; script, T. Chmielewski, A. Czekalski; camera, Josef Stawiski; music, Henryk Boyz. Stars Barbara Kwiatkowska, Stanislaw Mikulski, Ludwik Benoit, Z. Zintel. At San Francisco Film Festival, Oct. 29. Running time, **97 MINS.**

This Polish farce has some amiable qualities but is rather uneven and somewhat too long.

Film centers on a naive, saucer-eyed country girl, Eve (Barbara Kwiatowska), sent to school in a provincial city. She arrives a day too early, is turned away and, though penniless, must then find a place to spend the night—thus the title.

Her nocturnal adventures involve her with a gang of young toughs, a police force reminiscent of Mack Sennett's Keystone Kops, a safecracker masquerading as a cop, a handsome policeman whom the thugs mistake for a master safecracker, a drunken undertaker, a barkeep and his wife who drop a hand grenade in a jar of pickles and all the city's horsedrawn vehicles.

Parts of film are very funny, indeed, but other sequences don't come off so well. In the end, of course, Eve gets to school and the handsome cop is making goo-goo eyes at her.

One of film's troubles is that it veers back and forth between a lovely, insane style of surrealistic farce and rather mushy realism. This gets tiresome, because it's hard to find one's bearings over and over. The surrealistic style, and its low farce, is film's greatest virtue.

Miss Kwiatowska, innocent but impudent, is excellent, and Stanislaw Mikulski is satisfactory as the good looking policeman.

The Mack Sennett types, led by Ludwik Benoit (who looks and acts like Fernandel) as the safecracker and Z. Zintel (shades of Ben Turpin) as a police commissioner, are very good.

Funniest scene involves trying to find heroine a room in a women's hotel—dozens of men hang out windows, lock themselves in bathrooms, etc., as policeman seeks an empty bed.

Film probably has some political significance, but this escapes U. S. audience completely.

Director Tadeusz Chmielewski could have tightened picture up and cut down—or out—Eve's young-love angle, but he's thrown in fine small touches, such as a well-worn doxie leaning against a lamppost and knitting while waiting for a pickup. Script, by the director and A. Czekalski, seems sly enough and Henryk Boyz's music, leaning heavily on U. S. jazz, is pleasant, as is Joseph Stawiski's camera work.

Picture may have some potential in U. S. arthouse situations. *Stef.*

I Was Monty's Double

(BRITISH)

Novel war film crisply telling story of a fantastic strategic hoax involving the impersonation of Lord Montgomery.

London, Oct. 21.

Associated British-Pathe release of an Associated British (John Guillermin) production. Stars John Mills, Cecil Parker. Directed by Maxwell Setton. Screenplay, Bryan Forbes, based on a book by M. E. Clifton James; camera, Basil Emmott; editor, Max Benedict; music, John Addison. At Warner Theatre, London. Running time, **100 MINS.**

Major Harvey .... John Mills
Col Logan .... Cecil Parker
Col. Matthers .... Patrick Allen
Col. Dawson .... Patrick Holt
Major Tennant .... Lelie Phillips
Governor of Gibraltar..Michael Hordern
Neilson .... Marius Goring
Hester .... Barbara Hicks
Wing Co. Bates..........Duncan Lamont
Guard Sgt. .... Anthony Sagar
1st Guard .... Max Butterfield
2nd Guard .... Michael Oliver
Flt. Lt. Osborne................ John Gale
F. O. Davies .... Kenneth Warren
Sgt. Adams .... James Hayter
Porter Y.M.C.A.............Sidney James
Publican .... Michael Bird
Barmaid .... Diana Beaumont
Despatch Rider .... Brian Weske
American Captain .... Bill Nagy
Orderly Sgt. .... Victor Maddern
Young Lt. .... Bryan Forbes
The Small Man .... Alfie Bass
American Driver.......... Ronald Wilson
Sgt. Driver .... David Browning
Adjutant R.A.P.C.......John Le Mesurier
German Col. .... Walter Gottell
American General ..... Macdonald Parke
Arab Proprietor .... Marne Maitland
Angela .... Vera Day
Peggy .... Maureen Connell
Go-Between .... Sam Kydd
Guards Officer .... Alan Cuthbertson
As Himself and Gen. Montgomery
M. E. Clifton James

One of the most remarkable stories of the war comes to the screen as a crisp and novel adventure yarn, excellently acted and directed. The title and presence of two such sound actors as John Mills and Cecil Parker should insure wide interest on both sides of the Atlantic.

"I Was Monty's Double" tells about a great and important wartime hoax, almost incredible in its audacity. **Clifton James, a small-time stock actor serving as a junior officer in the Royal Army Pays Corps, bore a startling resemblance to General Montgomery. This was used in a daring scheme devised by Army Intelligence to persuade the Germans that the forthcoming Allies' invasion might well take place on the North African coast.**

With Monty's full cooperation, James was trained gruellingly to impersonate the famous soldier. Secretly he studied every mannerism of the general and then, posing as Monty, set off on a tour of North African divisions, a tour which was noted by the Nazis. The deception proved so successful that the enemy moved several divisions to the North African coast, a move which helped the actual invasion tremendously. The film has several moments of real tension. Even with a somewhat fictionalized ending, there is a documentary flavor about it which is absorbing.

Plenty of news footage has been woven into the pic and it has been done with commendable ingenuity. Bryan Forbes' taut screenplay is liberally spiced with humor. James plays both himself and General Montgomery, the biggest and most arduous role he has ever had to tackle in show business. Apart from his uncanny resemblance to Monty, James shows himself to be a resourceful actor in his own right.

Mills and Parker are the two officers who hatch the plot and see it through. The former gives one of his most likeable and unselfish performances as the officer who trains James to his task and accompanies him on the eventful tour which culminates in James being kidnapped by the Germans and rescued. Parker, a master of the throwaway line, bumbles brilliantly to give one of his outstanding acting jobs.

Marius Goring makes a suave appearance as a German spy who is fooled by the hoax. In the big, talented cast, Barbara Hicks makes a hit as an M.I. 5 stenographer while Sidney James, Alfie Bass, Michael Nordern and Leslie Phillips contribute brilliant little cameos.

Though many filmgoers must think that it is time to cease fire when it comes to war films, "I Was Monty's Double" is a refreshingly different pic. An extraordinary story told convincingly and compellingly. *Rich.*

Murder Reported
(BRITISH)

Murder mystery of routine interest.

Hollywood, Oct. 24.

Columbia release of Guido Coen production. Stars Paul Carpenter, Melissa Stribling; features John Laurie, Peter Swanwick, Patrick Holt. Directed by Charles Saunders. Screenplay, Doreen Montgomery; based on the novel, "Murder for the Million," by Robert Chapman; camera, Brendan Stafford; music, Reg Owen; editor, Jerry Levy. Previewed at the studio, Oct. 23, '58. Running time, 58 MINS.

Jeff Holly .... Paul Carpenter
Amanda North .... Melissa Stribling
Mac .... Jack Laurie
Hatter .... Peter Swanwick
Bill Stevens .... Patrick Holt
Carmady .... Maurice Durant
Myra .... Georgia Brown
Betty .... Yvonne Warren
Inspector Palissy .... Trevor Reid
Miss Jack .... Anne Blake
Mrs. Vince .... Edna Kove

"Murder Reported," a British import being distributed by Columbia, works over the plot of the crusty newspaper editor, the hard-driving star reporter and the latter's early exasperation and eventual adoration of the pretty, young tyro femme reporter. It's pretty old hat in conception, and there isn't much diverting about its variations. It stacks up as just another feature for double-bill filler and mild even in that classification.

Paul Carpenter is the reporter assigned to cover a murder in a London suburb by his apoplectic Scots editor, John Laurie. He is also told to take along the boss's daughter, Melissa Stribling. He resents this, naturally, until it develops, with not very amazing revelation, that she has had sound grounding in her trade and is an asset as a newspaperwoman and a girl friend.

The screenplay, by Doreen Montgomery, is based on a novel, "Murder For the Million," by Robert Chapman, although there is hardly enough plot apparent for either book or film. A trunk murder touches off developments which finally are found to have been engineered by a small-town politician who turns to killing as the only means of disposing of his opposition.

Performances are adequate although nothing much can be done with the frequently tiresome characters. The picture is exceptionally short (less than an hour), and this, possibly, will be its greatest asset in booking. *Powe.*

Virgin Island
(COLOR—BRITISH)

Pleasant comedy romance set in the Caribbean, with sparkling performances by John Cassavetes and Sidney Poitier; stout entertainment for femme audiences.

London, Oct. 28.

British Lion release of a (Leon Close-Grahame Thorp) Countryman Film production. Stars John Cassavetes, Virginia Maskell, Sidney Poitier. Directed by Pat Jackson. Screenplay, Philip Rush and Pat Jackson, from novel, "Our Virgin Island," by Robb White; editor, Gordon Pilkington; camera, Freddie Francis; music, Clifton Parker. At Studio One, London. Running time, 94 MINS.

Evan .... John Cassavetes
Tina .... Virginia Maskell
Marcus .... Sidney Poitier
Mrs. Lomax .... Isabel Dean
The Commissioner .... Colin Gordon
Prescott ...... Howard Marion Crawford
Captain Jason .... Edric Connor
Ruth .... Ruby Dee
Mrs. Carruthers .... Gladys Boot
Band Leader .... Julian Mayfield
Doctor .... Reginald Hearne
Heath .... Arnold Bell
Grant .... Alonzo Bozan

Set in the Caribbean isles and richly photographed in exciting color by Freddie Francis, "Virgin Island" is a happy-go-lucky pic whose atmosphere compensates for a slim story, some uneven acting and sloppy editing. Basically, it is a happy, naive film which will certainly lure femme customers to the boxoffice. Two sparkling performances by John Cassavetes and Sidney Poitier will stimulate U.S. interest in this amiable entertainment.

The plot is pure woman's magazine hokum. A young woman, enjoying a luxury cruise with her mother, meets an attractive young American writer on a beach. He sweeps her off her dainty feet, sells her a bill of goods about living their own lives "away from it all." He marries her, buys a remote, deserted island for $85 and persuades her, without much difficulty, to set up home as a sort of Mr. and Mrs. Robinson Crusoe.

With somewhat too much happy laughter, which occasionally cloys, the young couple build a home, aided by a Man Friday, run into trouble with the local governor and even greater trouble when mother-in-law comes visiting. They have a baby in circumstances which are unnecessarily melodramatic.

Pat Jackson's direction is sympathetic and touches real heights in the scenes when the two young people become aware of each other. There is a love scene in the sea which is beautifully portrayed, directed and lensed.

A standout performance is given by Sidney Poitier as a gentle, comic islander who helps the couple through their problems. John Cassavetes plays the role of the young man with too much of a "Johnny One Note" style, but is a likeable character. Virginia Maskell, the girl, makes her screen debut in this film. She is a pretty young woman, obviously inexperienced, but easy on the eye and an actress worth nurturing.

Isabel Dean, playing her mother, can get little out of an undeveloped character. But there are two gems of comedy by Howard Marian Crawford, as a genial beachcomber, and Colin Gordon, the friendly governor of the islands. Two-thirds of the way through the film, the screenplay switches to satire, too briefly and too ineffectively. This should either have been more important in the film or ignored entirely.

What went wrong with the editing is difficut to pin down, but there are several moments when even dialog is interrupted irritatingly. Nevertheless, "Virgin Island" provides pleasant, leisurely entertainment. Anybody who has ever visited the Caribbean will relive the experience nostalgically. *Rich.*

Jazzgossen
(The Jazz Boy)
(SWEDISH)
(Color; Songs)

Stockholm, Oct. 28.

Svensk Filmindustri production and release. Stars Hasse Ekman, Maj-Britt Nilsson; features Elof Ahrle, Bengt Ekerot, Karl Gerhard, Sigge Furst, Georg Funkquist, Per Linqvist, Meg Westergren. Directed by Hasse Ekman. Screenplay, Ekman and Gosta Stevens; camera, Martin Bodin; dances, John Ivar Deckner; music, Charles Redland, Jules Sylvain; Evert Taube, Ernst Rolf, Kaj Stighammer, Helge Lindberg, Edvard Brinck, Earl Wehle, Georg Enders, Kai Gullmar, Nils Perne, Kaj Normann-Andersen, Karl-Gustaf Hulthe, Mark Strong. At Roda Kvarn, Stockholm. Running time, 104 MINS.

Teddy Anker .... Hasse Ekman
Karin .... Maj-Britt Nilsson
Mille .... Elof Ahrle
Erik Jonsson .... Bengt Ekerot
Karl Gerhard .... Himself
Ernst Rolf .... Sigge Furst
Theatre Manager ...... Georg Funkquist
A Young Man .... Per Lindqvist
Madeleine .... Meg Westergren
Einar Fagstad .... Himself

It has often been said that the Swedish film producers should make a historical biopic about the great showman of the 1920s. Ernst Rolf. Still this has not happened, but is at least a film **about the '20s, including portions of the '30s and start of the '40s.**

"The Jazz Boy" is the title of a popular, parody song popularized by Karl Gerhard, a famous artist who plays himself in this. The jazz boy was the sorrowless society boy from the gay '20s, living a life in evening clothes and champagne. Here he is portrayed by Hasse Ekman, a young man with millions. He makes a career as showman on big scale. He starts a nightclub, promotes prizefights, hires an operetta theatre (where he presents "The Camille"—the first fiasco of his career), launches a film company, record company, music publishing outfit, etc.

Opening scene contrasts the society of the theatre watching Gerhard present his number, "The Jazz Boy," and the socialists and syndicalists having their meeting in People's House, talking about freedom and fraternity. Success after success ends this period of 1920, then comes the Kreuger crash at the start of the '30s. Millionaire Ekman has lost his millions. But the show must go on.

Dark clouds loom on the horizon, all stemming from Adolf Hitler. People who once spoke of World War I as the last of all wars, are beginning to wonder. Gerhard, one of the world's leading anti-Nazi showmen, sings ironic songs about the new Reich. German Embassy protests and the Foreign Office stops the show. Then comes the war, Norway and Denmark are occupied, and the former playboy is seen now in uniform "somewhere in Sweden."

Undoubtedly, this is one of the best Swedish pix productions in a long time, and definitely the best musical.

The complete cast has 64 names. Outstanding is Gerhard who plays himself, Ernest Rolf, onetime Scandinavia's Ziegfeld, is brilliantly portrayed by Sigge Furst. Ekman and Maj-Britt Nilsson provide the love interests. Ekman, of course, is Anker, the playboy millionaire but not very convincingly. Because of its atmosphere, this picture is of greater value to the Swedish public than to foreigners. But undoubtedly, it will prove worth seeing.

Color by Eastmancolor is very good. All technical credits are excellent, especially the special stereo sound. Old newsreel clips are woven into the story. It brings interesting scenes from the past, showing Douglas Fairbanks and Mary Pickford in Stockholm, Greta Gustafson debuting in films as Miss Gustafson (later she became Greta Garbo), the first broadcast in Sweden, etc. *Wing.*

Terror From the Year 5,000

Confusing "science fiction" for small exploitation field.

Hollywood, Oct. 30.

American International release of Robert J. Gurney Jr., production. Stars Joyce Holden, Ward Costello, Frederic Downs; features John Stratton. Director-story-screenplay, Gurney; camera, Arthur Florman; editor, Dede Allen. Previewed Oct. 29, '58. Running time, 66 MINS.

Robert Hedges .... Ward Costello
Claire Erling .... Joyce Holden
Victor .... John Stratton
Prof. Erling .... Frederic Downs
Angelo .... Fred Herrick
Miss Blake .... Beatrice Furdeaux
1st Lab Technician ...... Jack Diamond
2nd Lab. Technician .... Fred Taylor

An experimental time machine from which emerges a creature from the future year 5,000 A.D., is the motivating element of this sci-fi repast. Overall unfoldment is so clothed in confusion, however, that it's a weakie for even the small exploitation field.

Robert J. Gurney, Jr., quadruples in brass as producer-director, author of original story and scripter. Dangerous experiments are being made by a scientist's assistant on lab head's time machine, which already has produced a statuette made not in the past but in the future, and is highly radio-active. A horribly disfigured woman from year 5,000 materializes, who seeks to take the assistant back into the future with her to provide pre-atomic genes to start a new non-contaminated race, but both are killed before change can be made.

Players are hard put to make any sense of their characters, villians here including Ward Costello, an archaeologist; Joyce Holden, scientist's daughter; Frederic Downs, the scientist; and John Stratton, his assistant. Arthur Florman's photography and Dede Allen's editing are okay. *Whit.*

The Brain Eaters

Routine science fiction-fantasy horror pic. Same plot gimmick as this producer's 'The Spider'.

Hollywood, Oct. 31.

American International release of Edwin Nelson production. Stars Edwin Nelson, Joanna Lee, Alan Frost. Directed by Bruno VeSota. Screenplay, Gordon Urquhart; camera, Larry Raimond; music, Tom Jonson; editor, Carlo Lodato. Previewed at KTTV, Oct. 24, '58. Running time, 60 MINS.

Dr. Kettering .... Edwin Nelson
Glenn .... Alan Frost
Senator Powers .... Jack Hill
Alice .... Joanna Lee
Elaine .... Jody Fair
Dr. Wyler .... David Hughes
Dan Walker .... Robert Ball
Sheriff .... Greigh Phillips
Cameron .... Orville Sherman
Protector .... Leonard Nemoy
Doctor .... Doug Banks
Telegrapher .... Henry Randolph

American International showed two pictures for review at one time, "The Spider" and "The Brain Eaters," that both rely on the same mechanism—electrocution—for disposing of their monster-horror villains. The pix will not be booked together, so the duplication of plot resolution will not be glaring, but indicates such features run short of inventive potential. It is no particular criticism of "The Brain Eaters," an Edwin Nelson production, which is well-enough done as these horror films go, but this cycle appears to have reached the point of diminishing returns.

"The Brain Eaters" of Gordon Urquhart's screenplay are visitors from another planet, blobs of matter which attach themselves to the brains of earthlings and thus control their actions. News of the inter-planetary invasion brings a U.S. Senator to investigate and a research scientist to fight it. The problem posed is how to dispose of the things and their space ship home, after ordinary means of destruction fail. Finally a live electric cable is thrown over the ship and it explodes and the creeping things shrivel and die.

This gimmick, of outer space protoplasms which attach themselves to humans' necks, has been used before. Since much of this fantasy-fiction material is the same in basis, it doesn't make too much difference, except that these pictures are supported by largely the same audiences who notice such things. There isn't much else inventive about "The Brain Eaters" except its grisly title.

Within these drawbacks, it is competently done. Bruno Ve-Sota's direction is adequate, and performances by Edwin Nelson, Joanna Lee, Alan Frost, Jack Hill, Jody Fair and David Hughes are capable.

Larry Raimond's photography is good and Tom Jonson's music is imaginative. *Powe.*

La Vie a Deux
(Life As A Couple)
(FRENCH)

Paris, Oct. 28.
Cocinor release of CLM production. Stars Pierre Brasseur, Danielle Darrieux, Fernandel, Edwige Feuillere, Louis De Funes, Robert Lamoureux, Joan Marais, Lili Palmer, Gerard Philipe and Jean Richard. Directed by Clement Duhour. Screenplay, Sacha Guitry with additions by Jean Martin; camera, Robert Lefebvre; editor, Paulette Robert. At Biarritz, Paris. Running time, 100 MINS.
Carreau .... Pierre Brasseur
Monique .... Danielle Darrieux.
Marcel .... Fernandel
Francoise ...., Edwige Feuillere
Stephane .... Louis De Funes
Thierry .... Robert Lamoureux
Teddy .... Jean Marais
Desire .... Gerard Philipe
Andre .... Jean Richard

Made from the final scenario outline of the late Sacha Guitry, which was rounded out with bits from his other writings, this is a sketch-gimmick entry reminiscent in form of the 1930 Yank comedy, "If I Had A Million" (Par). It also bundles up a batch of star names and intros them via the will of a dying old millionaire.

The millionaire in this case is patterned after Guitry. He wants to leave his coin to any of the couples, on whom he based a book years ago, who have remained happy. Investigators, hampered by the author's friends who want to prove all unhappy, show they are all cheating on one another.

Sketches are thus dragged in as one spatting couple finds the wife's escapade producing a Negro child, another broken up by a mother-in-law, and another marriage only a whim to a lady with her eyes on young men and adroit at fooling her husband. Some censors likely will leap on this with both feet.

Pic thus stirs up some racy moments but it lacks the ironic edge and shrewdness that Guitry might have given it himself. Stars all shine in their brief bits. This looks like a local bet, with possible exploitation chances abroad on some of its risque episodes and the star names. It certainly is not a fitting tribute to Guitry's memory.
Mosk.

From the Earth to the Moon
(COLOR)

Handsomely staged but dramatically confusing period science-fiction yarn based on Jules Verne's classic. Good exploitation pic.

Hollywood, Nov. 7.
Warner Bros. release of Benedict Bogeaus production. Stars Joseph Cotten, George Sanders, Debra Paget, Don Dubbins. Directed by Byron Haskin. Screenplay, Robert Blees and James Leicester; based on the story by Jules Verne; camera. (Technicolor) Edwin B. DuPar; music, Louis Forbes; editor, James Leicester. Previewed at Academy Awards Theatre, Oct. 27, '58. Running time, 100 MINS.
Victor Barbicane .... Joseph Cotten
Stuyvesant Nicholl ...... George Sanders
Virginia Nicholl .... Debra Paget
Ben Sharpe .... Don Dubbins
Josef Cartier .... Patric Knowles
J. V. .... Carl Esmond
Morgana .... Henry Daniell
Bancroft .... Melville Cooper
Aldo Von Metz .... Ludwig Stossel
U. S. Grant .... Morris Ankrum

"From Earth To The Moon" suffers from the Cape Canaveral complaint; getting off the ground. The Benedict Bogeaus production, which Warner Bros. is releasing, should be a natural exploitation item, concerned, as it is, with early attempts at a moon shoot. It is handsome, well cast and timely. Unfortunately, it is a horse-and-buggy treatment of a rocket-propelled theme and as confusing as a scientific formula for solid fuel. If played for quick returns on its promise rather than its payment, it should turn a fast buck.

Robert Blees and James Leicester did the screenplay from the Jules Verne story. The locale is Florida, three years after the end of the Civil War. Joseph Cotten has discovered a new source of energy that can be used as a fuel or an explosive. George Sanders, a rival munitions manufacturer, first ridicules Cotten's claims, then joins him to exploit them.

They raise $50,000,000 to finance a rocket ship to the moon. Problems develop, caused partially by the fact that Debra Paget, Sanders' daughter, stows away on the ship. The ending is so confusing it is difficult to say with certainty what happens, but apparently Cotten and Sanders get to the moon in a damaged portion of the rocket ship, while Miss Paget and Don Dubbins, Cotten's assistant, return safely to earth.

In addition to confusion about what is going on, the film suffers from anachronisms and factual discrepancies. Perhaps the fault lies in too stringent editing. Connective scenes may have been eliminated that perhaps explained what is now obscure. At any rate, the result is bewilderment and irritation.

Technically, it is a beautiful film. The Mexican locations result in some striking exteriors and interiors. The art work on the rocket ship is reminiscent of the submarine in that other Jules Verne story, Walt Disney's "20,000 Leagues Under The Sea."

Byron Haskin, who directed, has staged individual scenes with considerable imagination, and the cast cannot be accused of muffing their assignments. Joseph Cotten, George Sanders, Debra Paget and Don Dubbins perform with their customary competence. In lesser roles, Patric Knowles, Carl Esmond, Henry Daniell, Melville Cooper, Ludwig Stossel and Morris Ankrum give brisk and capable performances.

Edwin B. DuPar's Technicolor lensing is very good, and the spe-

cial camera effects by Albert M. Simpson and special effects by Lee Zavitz are often highlights of the picture. Hal Wilson Cox's production design is interesting, often more fascinating than the story in front of it. Leicester's editing is slick as is sound by Weldon Coe. Louis Forbes' music is helpful.
Powe.

The House Under the Rocks
(HUNGARIAN)

San Francisco, Nov. 5.
Hunnia Film Studios (Budapest) production, directed by Koroly Makk; script, Sandor Tatay; camera, Gyorky Illes; music, Istvan Sarkozi. Stars Janos Gorbe, Margit Bara, Iren Psota. At San Francisco Film Festival, Nov. 4, '58. Running time, 93 MINS.

This impressive picture is what film festivals are made for—exposure of completely unknown product of high quality.

Shot in black and white, set in the hilly vineyards around Lake Balaton, film centers on a sick soldier who has returned from war to find his wife dead and his sister-in-law caring for his little cottage and his son. The sister-in-law, a hunchback, nurses the soldier back to health and keeps him out of touch with the community, earning the soldier's gratitude if not the love she desires.

Eventually the **soldier's mother goads the soldier back to work and his sexual desires awaken.** His landlord finds him a beautiful, shapely young wife, the sister-in-law is moved out and the newlyweds are deliriously happy—until the sister-in-law first tries to hang herself and then insists on moving back in with the couple on the grounds that half the cottage is hers. Slowly the sister-in-law ruins the couple's love and in a superb climactic scene the soldier pushes the sister-in-law to death atop a high bluff, thinking he'll regain his wife's love. He tells his wife he's a murderer, she recoils and the soldier gives up to the police and will pay with his life as film ends.

As the soldier, Janos Gorbe, offers a performance of depth and mobility. The sister-in-law, played by Iren Psota, is tender and hateful by turns, and Margit Bara, as the young wife, is passionate, knowing and, incidentally, very handsome.

Koroly Makk's direction is crisp and wastes no footage—every scene contributing to unfolding the story effectively and artistically. Gyorgy Illes' camera work is impeccable and Istvan Sarkozi's score is unobtrusive.

Picture abounds with great scenes, such as one in which the hunchbacked sister-in-law, riding atop an oxcart, comes down a narrow, rutted road from the cottage as the soldier's wedding party, with bride in pristine white, struggles up the road. Climactic scene, which drives soldier to murder, shows sister-in-law's morbid, hysterical fury at a fox being run down by fellow grape growers in the woods—this touches off the essentially gentle soldier. *Stef.*

Frontier Gun
(REGALSCOPE)

Routine oater for lower berth placement.

Hollywood, Nov. 7.
Twentieth-Fox release of Regal production. Stars John Agar, Joyce Meadows,

Barton MacLane, Robert Strauss, Lyn Thomas. Produced by Richard E. Lyons. Directed by Paul Landres. Screenplay, Stephen Kandel; camera, Walter Strenge; music, Paul Dunlap; editor, Robert Fritch. Previewed at Wrather's screening room, Nov. 4, '58. Running time, 70 MINS.
Jim Crayle .... John Agar
Peg Barton .... Joyce Meadows
Simon Crayle .... Barton MacLane
Yubo .... Robert Strauss
Kate Durand .... Lyn Thomas
Andrew Barton .... Morris Ankrum
Cash Skelton .... James Griffith
Rev. Jacob Hall .... Leslie Bradley
Eph Loveman .... Doodles Weaver
Tanner .... Mike Ragan
Cowhand .... Tom Daly
Virgil Barton .... Sammy Ogg
Judge Ard Becker .... George Brand
Bess Loveman .... Claire DuBrey
Sam Kilgore .... Daniel White
Harry Corman .... Dan Simmons
Doc Studdeford .... Sydney Mason

"Frontier Gun" is yet again the story of the town terrorized by the ruthless outlaw, and the hunt for one fearless guy to restore order. The Regal production for 20th-Fox has nothing to distinguish it from too many others of the same formula. It is competently made by producer Richard E. Lyons and director Paul Landres, but the lack of originality in treatment makes it basically a dull item even for its normal placement on the lower half of twin bills.

John Agar takes on the job of city marshall dedicated to putting badman Robert Strauss out of business. The local townspeople don't give him much backing. There is a promising hint for a time that the Stephen Kandel screenplay will develop the theme that it is the fault of the people when they wind up cowed and cowering under a criminal. But this premise is blown when the climax scene turns out to be the old gun duel between lawman and badman.

There is some romance between Agar and Joyce Meadows, and a subsidiary attempt at character and depth between Lyn Thomas and James Griffith, latter abused minions of Strauss. There seems a tendency here to set some interesting characterizations and then back away from them, so no value ever develops out of them.

Walter Strenge's camera work is a highlight of the picture, making scenes more interesting in composition than they are in the writing, and Paul Dunlap's music is also a plus factor, showing once again how these so-called technical credits can give a shallow story and superficial treatment depth and importance, however transitory.

The cast is competent, including Agar, Miss Meadows, Strauss Miss Thomas, Barton MacLane, Griffith, Morris Ankrum, Leslie Bradley and Doodles Weaver. *Powe.*

The Road a Year Long
(Yugoslav-Ultrascope)

Jadran (Zagreb) production, directed by Giuseppe de Santis; script, Giuseppe de Santis, Maurizio Ferrara, Teniono Guerra, Elio Petri, Gianni Puccini, Mario Socrate; camera, Pasquale de Santis. Stars Silvana Pampanini, Elenora Rossi-Drago, Bert Sotlar, Gordana Miletic. At San Francisco Film Festival, Nov. 2. Running time, 159 MINS.

This is a long, rambling semi-documentary about one Yugoslavian village's fight against poverty embodied in its fight for a road to the sea.

One unemployed villager starts hacking away at the road, almost as a joke, and persuades the other unemployed, unhappy villagers—men and women—to join him. A dozen obstacles are thrown in their way, including government opposition, but eventually all obstacles are overcome and the road is completed, amid rejoicing.

In the course of this story, four separate love stories are told and the camera observes Lysistrata-like revolt against governmental authorities, a Gandhi-like hunger strike on the part of the village's men, an older leader's death, a triangle among a storekeeper, his wife and a good-looking young buck and the serious injury of a young boy.

Some of this is fairly absorbing, but it tends to be quite drawn out, as if there were enough material here for half a dozen pictures. The black-and-white photography is good, catching the bleakness of Yukoslavian mountain life and dollying in on many fine closeups of the rugged villagers' faces.

Some of the film's transitions seem rather rough and the Socialistic moral—"*if we all put together, we can create a brave new world*"—seems pat, but picture has considerable interest, nevertheless.

Silvana Pampanini, Eleanora Rossi-Drago and Gordana Miletic head a cast of exceedingly buxom women—sturdiness, rather than slenderness, must be the hallmark of the Yugoslavian female. The women do a good acting job, as do the men, led by Bert Sotler.

Film may have some value in U.S. art situations, and could be exploited on the strength of the leading women's curves. *Stef.*

Sea of Sand
(BRITISH)

Well directed and acted, offering several good thrills; adds up to routine war drama of which the market has been fairly saturated, but good b.o.

London, Nov. 4.
Rank release of a Robert S. Baker-Monty Berman Tempean Films production. Stars Richard Attenborough, John Gregson, Michael Craig. Directed by Guy Green. Screenplay, Robert Westerby; editor, Gordon Pilkington; camera, Wilkie Cooper; music, Clifton Parker. At Odeon, Leicester Square, London. Running time, **97 MINS.**

Trooper Brody	Richard Attenborough
Captain Williams	John Gregson
Captain Cotton	Michael Craig
Sergeant Nesbitt	Vincent Ball
Trooper White	Percy Herbert
Corporal Matheson	Barry Foster
Sergeant Parker	Andrew Faulds
Corporal Simms	George Murcell
Sergeant Hardy	Ray McAnally
1st Road Watch	Harold Goodwin
Captain Giles	Tony Thawnton
A German Sergeant	Wolf Frees
A German Officer	George Mikell

"Sea of Sand," it's claimed, is based on an original story by Sean Fielding, but there is nothing very original about it. It is a routine war adventure such as has been filmed many times before. But it stands up as a good b.o. proposition, thanks to excellent all-round acting and taut direction by Guy Green. If the public is still in the mood for war episodes then "Sea of Sand" will satisfy.

Pic deals with the Long Range Desert Group on the eve of Alamein. Y Patrol is given the arduous task of blowing up one of the Nazis' biggest petrol dumps. Mission accomplished, the nine men fight their way back to base and five survive. Shot entirely on location, director Green and cameraman Wilkie Cooper splendidly capture the remote loneliness of the vast desert, the heat, the boredom and the sense of pending danger. Robert Westerby's screenplay is predictable, but the dialog is reasonably natural and the various characters well drawn.

The characters follow the conventional lines of such films. There are the two officers who at first are at loggerheads but who come to respect each other in their mutual danger. There's the new boy fighting his fear. There's the irrepressible Cockney, the countryman who yearns to be back on his farm and the man whose only interest in the war is getting regular food and drink. In between fighting, the Nazis they indulge in some sentimental talk about home, and the usual banter between themselves.

Though audiences will feel that they've been through all this before, the acting throughout reaches a high standard. Michael Craig as the "indestructible" Desert Rat officer gives one of his best performances to date. He is well matched by John Gregson as the regular officer who cannot tolerate the Desert Rats' apparent lack of discipline. Richard Attenborough is also outstanding as an irrepressible Cockney trooper with a complete disregard for discipline. Percy Herbert and Barry Foster have the best opportunities among the remander of the cast, and turn in sound performances.

For a great deal of the time nothing very much happens, but the blowing up of the dump is spectacular. And there is considerable tension as the cut-off patrol encounters the Germans. Some excellent music by Clifton Parker occasionally is too obtrusive but the whole film has a compelling air of realism. Only once or twice is it in danger of falling into false heroics. *Rich.*

Behind the Mask
(BRITISH—COLOR)

Smooth, hospital romantic drama, with impressive performances by Michael Redgrave and Tony Britton; sound booking.

London, Nov. 4.
British Lion release of Sergi Bolbankov-Josef Somlo production. Stars Michael Redgrave, Tony Britton, Carl Mohner, Niall MacGinnis. Directed by Brian Desmond Hurst. Screenplay, John Hunter, from "The Pack," by John Rowan Wilson; camera, Robert Krasker; editor, Alan Morrison; music, Geoffrey Wright. At Studio One, London, Oct. 24, '58. Running time, **99 MINS.**

Sir Arthur Benson Gray	Michael Redgrave
Mr. Philip Selwood	Tony Britton
Dr. Carl Romek	Carl Mohner
Mr. Neil Isherwood	Niall MacGinnis
Mr. Alan Crabtree	Ian Bannen
Elizabeth Fallon	Brenda Bruce
Walter Froy	Lionel Jeffries
Sir Oswald Pettiford	Miles Malleson
Colonel Langley	John Welsh
Pamela Benson Gray	Vanessa Redgrave
Mrs. Judson	Ann Firbank
Mr. John Greenwood	John Gale
Dr. Galbraith	Jack Hedley
Examiner at Royal College	Hugh Miller
Theatre Sister	Mary Skinner
Night Sister	Margaret Tyzack

Hospital yarns invariably add up to good cinema drama and "Behind the Mask" is no exception. It shou'd reap useful b.o. rewards, for though produced on conventional lines it has a sound story, literate dialog and some impressive performances. There are several of the usual hospital film cliches, but the atmosphere is credible and Brian Desmond Hurst's directorial chore has dignity.

Film is based on John Rowan Wilson's novel, "The Pack," which title gives a better key to the plot than the one chosen for the pic. Set in a country hospital, it implies that not to run with the pack is to have the success dice loaded formidably against one. Intrigue, ambition, strained loyalties, tradition and unscrupulous saving-of-face all play a part in the goings-on at Graftondale Royal Hospital.

The principal characters involved are two senior surgeons who are deadly rivals. One favors traditional methods of running a hospital; the other wants to turn it into a research laboratory. Also concerned are the first surgeon's assistant, who is in love with his daughter, and an anaesthetist who is a Polish refugee, a drug addict, who is being blackmailed.

Michael Redgrave, smooth, urbane and highly professional, and Niall MacGinnis, bluff, blustering and envious, give rounded performances as the two senior surgeons. Tony Britton plays the assistant with charm and integrity while Carl Mohner is strong support as the anaesthetist. The film also introduces Redgrave's own daughter, Vanessa Redgrave, as his screen daughter. She is a good-looking girl, obviously short on experience but equally obviously having inherited some of her father's ability.

As so often happens in British films, its value is built up by some excellent smaller performances. Ian Bannen, as a cynical young surgeon; Brenda Bruce, as a blackmailing young woman, Miles Malleson, as chairman of the hospital's board; Lionel Jeffries, as the hospital secretary, and Ann Firbank, in a charming cameo as a patient all bring real value to their roles.

There is one tense highspot in production. It is a heart operation, seen on a close-circuit tv screen, which is uncommonly revealing. Color throughout is good. Robert Krasker's photography and William Kellner's production designs are faultless. *Rich.*

The Screaming Skull

Fair entry for horror market.

Hollywood, Oct. 30.
American International release of John Kneubuhl production. Stars John Hudson, Peggy Webber, Alex Nicol. Directed by Nicol. Screenplay, Kneubuhl; camera, Frank Crosley; editor, Betty Lane; music, Ernest Gold. Previewed Oct. 29, '58. Running time, **68 MINS.**

Eric	John Hudson
Jenni	Peggy Webber
Mrs. Snow	Toni Johnson
Rev. Snow	Russ Conway
Mickey	Alex Nicol

"The Screaming Skull" is a pitch at the horror fan who takes his entertainment as he finds it. A straight story line is embellished with weird sound and photographic effects, but misses in an overly-contrived ghost climax. For the less discriminating exploitation market, film is a fair entry.

Scripted and produced by John Kneubuhl, action follows efforts of a husband to drive his new wife to suicide for her money. He takes her to the big mansion left him by his first wife, who died mysteriously, and here strange goings-on begin to return her to the mental state for which she once was treated in an institution. Suspicion rests upon the dull-witted gardener, who worshipped his first mistress and resents others in the house, until it becomes apparent husband is the perpetrator.

John Hudson and Peggy Webber undertake their roles well enough as man and wife and Alex Nicol plays the gardner. His direction, however, isn't able to rise above static qualities of his script. Russ Conway and Toni Johnson are competent as minister neighbor and his wife.

On technical end, Ernest Gold's music score contributes to mood and Betty Lane's editing is sometimes effective. Frank Crosley's camera work is standard. *Whit.*

La Loi C'Est La Loi
(The Law Is The Law)
(FRENCH-ITALIAN)

Paris, Nov. 4.
Cinedis release of Arione-Filmsonor-Vides production. Stars Fernandel, Toto; features Noel Roquevert, Nathalie Nerval, Leda Gloria. Directed by Christian-Jaque. Screenplay, Jean Emmanuel, Jean-Charles Tachella; camera, A. Venanza; editor, Jacques Desageneaux. At Normandie, Paris. Running time, **100 MINS.**

Ferdinand	Fernandel
Giuseppe	Toto
Captain	Noel Roquevert
Helene	Nathalie Nerval
First Wife	Leda Gloria

Fernandel is Fernandel and Toto is Toto in this, with the top French and Italo comics trotting out their hep routines before the background of a little town divided by the French and Italo borders.

The former is a stolid customs guard while Toto is a wily smuggler. The byplay between the two leads to the biggest yocks as Fernandel bristles and burns with outraged pompous dignity as he is exasperated by the cowering but shrewd Toto. This rarely lets the secondary characters emerge rounded, with the result the film's more serious edge never quite jives with its folksy comedy.

This looks to have good Continental pull, and is slickly made with enough offbeat humor to slant this for arty and even general dates in the world marts. Fernandel finds he is not really French when Toto proves he was born in the kitchen of a hotel divided by the border. The kitchen is on the Italo side.

Fernandel is bluff and unsparing in his timing and facial contortions and brings more into the pic than its storyline gives it. Toto is a perfect foil as the clever smuggler. Christian-Jaque has directed smoothly and gotten some good comics bits out of it. The Fernandel name is a plus for U.S. chances. *Mosk.*

Inn of the Sixth Happiness
(BRITISH-C'SCOPE-COLOR)

Bit overlong, but colorful story, well mounted and acted. Title and star combination of Bergman, Jurgens and Donat make this a sure b.o. click.

London, Nov. 18.

20th-Fox release of Buddy Adler production. Stars Ingrid Bergman, Curt Jurgens, Robert Donat. Directed by Mark Robson. Screenplay, Isobel Lennart, from novel, "The Small Woman," by Alan Burgess; camera, F. A. Young; editor, Ernest Walter; music, Malcolm Arnold. At 20th-Fox Preview Theatre, London. Running time, **160 MINS.**

Gladys Aylward .... Ingrid Bergman
Capt. Lin Nan .... Curt Jurgens
Mandarin .... Robert Donat
Sir Francis .... Ronald Squire
Miss Thompson .... Noel Hood
Cook .... Joan Young
Dr. Robinson .... Moultrie Kelsall
Secretary .... Edith Sharpe
Mr. Murfin .... Richard Wattis
Mrs. Lawson .... Athene Seyler
Yang .... Peter Chong
Ho Ka .... Michael David
Prison Guard .... Zed Zakari
Li .... Burt Kwouk
Madman .... Frank Blaine
Young Lin .... Ronald Kyaing
Sui-Lan .... Tsai Chin
Mai-Da .... Louise Lin
Aide .... Michael Wee

The eagerly awaited "Inn of the Sixth Happiness" turns out to be an unduly lengthy job. It would have benefited from some judicious trimming, but this pic is spectacularly mounted, impressively acted and directed and, with its attractive title and glamorous stellar lineup, has all the earmarks of a boxoffice winner on both sides of the Atlantic.

Based on Alan Burgess' novel, "The Small Woman" which, in turn, was based on the adventures of a real person, the film has Ingrid Bergman as a rejected missionary in China, who gets there determinedly under her own steam. First met with hostility by the natives, she gradually wins their love and esteem. She falls in love with a Eurasian colonel, converts a powerful mandarin to Christianity and becomes involved in the Chino-Japanese war. Finally she guides 100 children to the safety of a Northern mission by leading them on an arduous journey across the rugged mountains and through enemy territory.

The inn in the film is run by Miss Bergman and an elderly missionary (Athene Seyler). Here they dispense hospitality and Bible stories to the muleteers in transit. On the surface, the casting of the lovely Miss Bergman as "the small woman" seems odd. But such is the star's warm, radiant charm and ready sense of humor that audiences soon forget any preconceived notions they may have held that "the small woman" and Miss Bergman were probably poles apart in physique and personality. Her early scenes as she strives to get to China and those in which she gradually settles down in her environment and begins the urgent task of winning the confidence of the Chinese are brilliantly done with humor and a sense of urgent dedication. The film's climax is the trek with the children and, perhaps because of its length, this sequence gives the feeling that the dangerous exploit is merely a Sunday School ramble.

Miss Bergman shows every facet of her acting craft—humor, determination, compassion, tenderness and toughness. And throughout she brings to the role that sharp intelligence which invariably distinguishes her performances. Curt Jurgens is less happily served as the Eurasian colonel. The slender love theme seems to have been dropped into the main story and Jurgens has less command of an awkward role than usual. A standout performance comes from Robert Donat as an astute yet benign mandarin. It was Donat's swansong before his untimely death and only rarely can signs of his physical collapse be detected.

Among other smaller, but well-played roles are those of Peter Chong, as Miss Bergman's faithful Chinese servant and friend; Athene Seyler, wonderfully alert as the unorthodox missionary; Ronald Squire, as the servant-girl's former employer, and Moultrie Kelsall, as the man who turned down her application to be a missionary.

The film was shot in Wales and in the Elstree studio, converted expertly into a Chinese village. The atmosphere of Old China seems to be completely authentic and Margaret Furse's costumes and the art work of John Box and Geoffrey Drake lend color and beauty to the pic, which has been well captured by F. A. Young's camerawork. Also, deserving a hand, is Cecil F. Ford who had an onerous task as production manager. Mark Robson's direction has slickly caught both the sweep of the crowd sequences and the more intimate ones.

"The Inn" has its faults, but these are outweighed by its many virtues which include an absorbing story, convincing dialog and many poignant moments that will catch the average audience by its throat.

Rich.

The Geisha Boy
(COLOR; V'VISION)

Jerry Lewis comedy. An attractive holiday entry.

Hollywood, Nov. 14.

Paramount release of Jerry Lewis production. Stars Lewis; costars Marie McDonald and Sessue Hayakawa. Director-writer, Frank Tashlin; based on a story by Rudy Makoul; camera (Technicolor), Haskell Boggs; music, Walter Scharf; editor, Alma Macrorie. Previewed at Pantages Theatre, Nov. 10, '58. Running time, **95 MINS.**

Gilbert Wooley .... Jerry Lewis
Lola Livingston .... Marie McDonald
Kim's Father .... Sessue Hayakawa
Major Ridgley .... Barton MacLane
Beatty Pearson ...... Suzanne Pleshette
Kimi Sikita .... Nobu Atsumi McCarthy
Mitsuo Watanabe
Robert Kazuyoshi Hirano
Ichiyama .... Ryuzo Demura

"The Geisha Boy" is a good Jerry Lewis comedy, one that rips along with never a backward glance at shattered remnants of plot behind it. Concentration is on just one concern, laughs, wherever and however they can be achieved.

Frank Tashlin, who wrote and directed, has loaded the Paramount presentation with wild sight and sound gags, parodies and takeoffs that relieve Lewis of some comic burden and show him in his best light. Lewis was also producer of the picture, with Ernest D. Glucksman associate producer, and it will be a popular entry, especially with Lewis fans.

Tashlin's screenplay, from a story by Rudy Makoul, has Lewis as a very low man on the show business totem pole. He is a magician who "can't even get a job on daytime television." He and his rabbit, Harry, join a USO tour of the Orient, because, as he says frankly, they couldn't get a job anywhere else.

Lewis first tangles with the troupe's headliner, Marie McDonald, who serves the picture as a kind of young Margaret Dumont; then with the army brass, represented by Barton MacLane, an officer so military he is looking forward to his own military funeral he loves the sound of "Taps," and finally with the Japanese themselves. There is a romance between Lewis and a Japanese widow, Nobu McCarthy, whose young son, Robert Hirano, "adopts" Lewis as his father. It's an interesting commentary on changing screen mores that just a year after the inter-racial romance in "Sayonara" seemed quite daring, there is a similar attachment between Lewis and Miss McCarthy in "Geisha Boy" and it hardly seems worth noting.

Tashlin is practically the only screen director these days who uses motion pictures for the kind of zany sight gags that once characterized some of the best film comedy. (When Lewis sees Fujiyama it has a circlet of stars around its peak and the Paramount theme music is heard offscreen.) He takes a few offhand cracks at contemporary social nonsense, but lightly, so it is not out of key with the farcical aspects of the picture.

Lewis is at his best when he eschews some the stock physical mannerisms that were originally his trademarks. He is more appealing and much funnier when he is playing more or less straight, using his timing and more restrained reactions for fine comedy effect. He is also effective in the few serious moments. Miss McDonald disappears after the early sequences, but she does a neat job of the scenes she dominates of a film star beset by more than ordinary bad luck, i. e., Lewis. Sessue Hayakawa's appearance is a gag; he is a Japanese who is building a bridge over his swimming pool to the off-screen whistling of the Marching Song from "Bridge on the River Kwai." It sounds fairly foolish, but it plays.

Miss McCarthy is decorative, and young Hirano is a charmer. Suzanne Pleshette, Barton MacLane and Ryuzo Demura all contribute, and the rabbit's a real trouper.

The picture is a physical pleasure to watch. Haskell Bogg's photography uses the big screen and color well for comedy, including some trick cinematics that are smoothly integrated by editor Alma Macrorie. Sound, by Gene Merritt and Charles Grenzbach, is an important comedy element. Art direction by Hal Pereira and Tambi Larsen, and set decoration by Sam Comer and Robert Benton, are imporant assets in gaining the authentic Japanese feeling to the home lot-shot picture. Walter Scharf's music is light and amusing, and has, as well, a recurrent and melodic theme that impresses. Edith Head's costumes are also a plus factor.

Powe.

Mardi Gras
(COLOR; C'SCOPE)

The one about the film star at the prom. Bright, colorful, bouncy musical. A natural for holiday trade.

Hollywood, Nov. 14.

Twentieth-Fox release of Jerry Wald production. Stars Pat Boone and Christine Carere; costars Tommy Sands, Sheree North, Gary Crosby, Fred Clark. Directed by Edmund Goulding. Screenplay, Winston Miller and Hal Kanter; based on a story by Curtis Harrington; camera (De Luxe Color), Wilfrid M. Cline; music supervision, Lionel Newman; songs, Sammy Fain, Paul Francis Webster; editor, Robert Simpson. Previewed at the studio, Nov. 12, '58. Running time, **107 MINS.**

Pat Newell .... Pat Boone
Michelle Marton .... Christine Carere
Barry Denton .... Tommy Sands
Eadie .... Sheree North
Tony Runkle .... Gary Crosby
Curtis .... Fred Clark
Dick Saglon .... Richard Sargent
Torchy .... Barrie Chase
Sylvia .... Jennifer West
Ann Harris .... Geraldine Wall
Lt. Col. Vaupell .... King Calder
and the Corps of Cadets of the Virginia Military Institute
Com. Tydings .... Robert Burton

"Mardi Gras" is a colorful carnival of songs, romance and comedy that should liven up the box-office. Seems a strong attraction for the younger trade and a natural for holiday business.

Jerry Wald uses bright, young personalities in the 20th-Fox presentation. Edmund Goulding has them performing like veterans. Songs, by Sammy Fain and Paul Francis Webster, are a major asset, contributing not only to the picture but to its promotion.

Screenplay, by Winston Miller and Hal Kanter, has a reminiscent borrowed theme, i.e., the motion picture star invited to a college prom and the complications that result. It's billed as an "original" story by Curtis Harrington, Wald's executive assistant. Makes a good enough basis for a musical comedy.

Pat Boone, Tommy Sands, Gary Crosby and Richard Sargent are the quartet of cadets at Virginia Military Institute who set up a $1-a-chance lottery. Winner is to get a date with film star Christine Carere, with total investment to pay for expenses involved.

The boys get to the Mardi Gras when the VMI band, of which they're members, goes to New Orleans for the carnival. Miss Carere is a Mardi Gras queen, accompanied by studio publicists Sheree North and Fred Clark. There is the customary confusion and clarification. Boone and Miss Carere fall in love when he doesn't know who she is. Studio publicity blows up the romance for crass commercial purposes. True love triumphs when everything is more or less straightened out. Not much plot, but enough to hang some good songs and pleasant comedy on.

The "Brother Rat" setting of VMI — cadets call each other by this nickname — also recalls another musical, "She Loves Me Not," which had a non-military college locale and somewhat the same plot, and in which another Crosby was starred just about the time this one was born. But if the general plot outlines are familiar, the Kanter-Miller screenplay has given the current script topicality and contemporary humor and freshness.

Boone plays more or less straight to his three male cohorts, but continues to show considerable growth as a song-and-dance man, particularly in the latter capacity, with a promise of broadening in his range and appeal. Miss Carere displays wholesome sex appeal and a flair for comedy. Tommy Sands gives pro treatment to his comedy role, and Gary Crosby's adult bow as an actor shows he has more than his share of the Crosby ease and insouciance. All three young men, of course, handle their vocal assignments with aplomb and charm.

Sheree North doesn't have much chance to cut loose, but when she does, as in the song, "That Man," and with some sharp comedy lines, she supplies an astringent quality to the sometimes too juvenile proceedings. Fred Clark does an amusing, high-pressure publicity man;

Richard Sargent shows again that he is one of the more distinctive character juveniles, and Barrie Chase forecasts as bright a future for herself in features as she recently showed in tv. Jennifer West, Geraldine Wall, King Calder contribute in key roles. Robert Wagner and Jeffrey Hunter make unbilled, walkon appearances.

Goulding's direction ably welds romance, comedy and musical numbers, with a strong assist on the latter score from choreographer Bill Foster. In such numbers as "Loyalty," "Stonewall Jackson" and "A Fiddle and a Rifle," Foster has his four young men move in rhythm—since they are not dancers — to create the illusion of dance without making it pretentious or clumsy. The Fain-Webster songs are diversified, jazz, ballad and country-style, with a high hit potential, which Lionel Newman gives a sparkling treatment. Charles Henderson's vocal work is notable, particularly in his use of four-part harmony, exploiting the different values of his singers.

"Mardi Gras" is confection, beautifully photographed by Wilfrid M. Cline, with New Orleans stock footage, adroitly integrated.

Powe.

Johnny Rocco

Appealing human-angled gangster meller, paired with "Revolt In The Big House." Good exploitation returns.

Hollywood, Nov. 14.

Allied Artists release of Scott R. Dunlap production. Stars Richard Eyer, Stephen McNally and Coleen Gray. Directed by Paul Landres. Screenplay, James O'Hanlon and Samuel F. Roeca; based on a story by Richard Carlson; camera, William Margulies; music, Edward J. Kay; editor, George White. Previewed at the studio, Nov. 6, '58. Running time, **84 MINS.**

Johnny	Richard Eyer
Rocco	Stephen McNally
Lois	Coleen Gray
Inspector Garron	Russ Conway
Father Regen	Leslie Bradley
Mooney	James Flavin
Dino	M. G. Fain
Stakeout Officer	John Mitchum
Mitchell Choir	Mitchell Choir
Choir Leader	Bob Mitchel
Lane	Frank Wilcox

"Johnny Rocco" is a gangster melodrama, but with an original twist. It is the story of the effect on a young boy of his mobster father's connections. The Scott R. Dunlap production for Allied Artists sometimes gets sidetracked by diversions, and it is occasionally rather sentimental, but it gets distinction and interest by trying and achieving something outside the routine. Paul Landres' direction sets the characters well and has brisk, knowledgeable pace. Pic will be billed with "Revolt in the Big House" (reviewed in VARIETY, Nov. 5) to make a well-matched, attractive dualler.

Young Richard Eyer plays the title character, son of Stephen McNally, one of the higher-ups in a crime syndicate. The boy is shocked into stuttering by exposure to some mob mayhem, and his condition arouses the sympathy and interest of his teacher, Coleen Gray. The child is pinpointed by the mob members, as well, because he has information detrimental to them, and the story develops into a chase between the law and the lawless with the boy as the aim of both.

The James O'Hanlon-Samuel F. Roeca screenplay sounds faintly incredible in summary, and in recollection it is rather difficult to justify a father who is both tender with his son and tough with his mobster cohorts. But it plays.

Young Eyer does a great deal to making the story believable with his usual competence, avoiding the overly winsome. McNally is convincing as the father and Miss Gray warm and helpful as the teacher. Other cast members who contribute ably include Russ Conway, Leslie Bradley, James Flavin and M. G. (Matty) Fain. The Mitchell Boys' Choir is effectively used.

William Margulies' camera work is an asset, as is Edward J. Kay's music.

Powe.

Kvinna Drom
(Women's Dreams)
(SWEDISH)

Paris, Nov. 11.

Lisbon Films release of Sandrew Films production. Stars Harriet Andersson, Eva Dalhbeck; features Gunnar Bjornstrand, Sven Lindberg, Ulf Paulme. Written and directed by Ingmar Bergman. Camera, Hilding Blahd; editor, Carl-Olav Skeppstedt. At Agriculteurs, Paris. Running time, **85 MINS.**

Doris	Harriet Andersson
Suzanne	Eva Dahlbeck
Palle	Sven Lindberg
Consul	Gunnar Bjornstrand
Henri	Ulf Paulme

Writer-director Ingmar Bergman's personal, offbeat Swedish pix have become regular art and general circuit fare here. Latest entry is a deft analysis of two women's lives to make for possible arty theatre chances in the U.S. as well as probable general chances abroad.

Bergman shrewdly dovetails the adventures of an older and younger woman before they come of emotional age. Though seemingly slick and melodramatic on the surface, the keen notations, solid narrative and expert blending of direction and acting make this a deep tale of emotional upheavals.

The older woman is a fashion photo expert in love with a married man while the other is a young, flighty model who has broken with her prosaic boyfriend.

Tecnical credits are tops. This digs deep into human foibles and emotions to make it an enticing art film.

Mosk.

Anna Lucasta

All-Negro cast headed by Eartha Kitt and Sammy Davis Jr. in earthy meller based on play. Shapes as okay earner on exploitation values alone.

United Artists release of Longridge Enterprise Inc. production. Stars Eartha Kitt, Sammy Davis Jr.; features Frederick O'Neal, Henry Scott, Rex Ingram, Georgia Burke, James Edwards, Rosetta Lenoire, Isabelle Cooley. Alvin Childress, Claire Leyba, John Proctor, Charles Swain. Produced by Sidney Harmon. Directed by Arnold Laven; script, Philip Yordan from his own play of same title; camera, Lucien Ballard; music, Elmer Bernstein; editor, Richard C. Meyer. Previewed in N.Y., Nov. 12, '58. Running time, **97 MINS.**

Anna Lucasta	Eartha Kitt
Danny Johnson	Sammy Davis Jr.
Frank	Frederick O'Neal
Rudolph Slocum	Henry Scott
Joe Lucasta	Rex Ingram
Theresa	Georgia Burke
Eddie	James Edwards
Stella	Rosetta Lenoire
Katie	Isabelle Cooley
Noah	Alvin Childress
Blanche	Claire Leyba
Stanley	John Proctor
Lester	Charles Swain
Cop	Isaac Jones
Secretary	Wally Earl

From Philip Yordan's play of the same title (originally a stage work of a Polish family) about a Negro prostitute who finds love but can't break with her past, Sidney Harmon has produced and Arnold Laven has directed a sincere, often compelling film. It'll unquestionably be billed as a "shocker," and to a degree it is just that. Also "Anna Lucasta" on the screen still carries the mark of a stage production, and is inhibited by it.

Picture is acted by a highly competent all-Negro cast. Individual performances, notably those of Rex Ingram as the father and of Sammy Davis Jr. as the irresponsible, tight-wound lover of Anna, stand out and give the film a unique, authentic flavor. Unfortunately, the entire story hinges on the central character of Eartha Kitt, and she gives the part little more than a superficial reading. It's hard to believe in her character.

Miss Kitt has a stunning figure and the clinging dresses she's given to wear accentuate the positive. There are some scenes when director Laven gets a good deal of emotion out of her, and then the film comes to life with crackling tension, for the story—while hardly novel—is a vehicle for any actress. In other sequences, Miss Kitt more or less goes through the required motions in an almost cliche type of acting that doesn't ring true.

Yordan wrote his own screenplay in adapting his play, and while it naturally expands on the limits of the stage, the feeling of actors being on the boards persists. This tends to rob the film of some of its mood, and pace, but gives a greater chance to individual actors. This "Anna Lucasta" is a remake; Paulette Goddard starred in the 1949 version which was in the original ofay concept.

Ingram as old Joe Lucasta is excellent from start to finish. As the story develops, it is made clear that under his pretense of detesting a daughter who has become a street-walker, he is also fighting off his own temptations, for Joe is in love with his own daughter. Fogged by age and alcohol, stubborn and torn, Ingram creates a vivid portrait of the old man, and to a large extent he steals the show.

Sammy Davis Jr. lives his role as the cocky little fellow who wants to swallow life in big gulps and almost wrecks Anna's marriage. He brings to the character a good deal of understanding and balance, so that when, in the end, he walks out and leaves Anna to her husband, it becomes a believable act. As Frank, the bullying husband of another Lucasta daughter, Rosetta Lenoire, Frederick O'Neal also delivers a sturdy performance, which at times seems overdrawn, but registers nevertheless.

Henry Scott is sympathetic as Rudolph, who marries Anna knowing her past; Georgia Burke is warm and motherly as Ingram's wife; Miss LeNoire is very attractive, and John Proctor and Isabelle Cooley do well as two more members of the Lucasta clan. Alvin Childress has stature as the barkeeper.

This isn't a pretty story, and the film speaks forcefully about human greed, and ignorance, and man's lack of compassion. With some blunt dialog for spice, and a provocative subject, theatres should have no trouble selling this film to their customers. Apart from this, both Miss Kitt and Davis are good names for the marquee.

Story, briefly, has Ingram receiving a letter from an old friend saying that his son would soon come to Los Angeles with $4,000. The Lucasta family intends to marry off the boy to Anna to get their hands on the money. He turns out to be a college graduate, and he falls in love with Anna just the same. The girl's a prostitute who gradually drops her cynical attitude and returns the boy's feelings. After the marriage, Sammy Davis Jr. drops around and the two of them go off together on a wild whirl.

Coming home to get her money, Anna finds the house empty and her father dying. There's a deathbed reunion and Davis walks out, leaving Anna to her returning husband.

Lucien Ballard did the photography and the camerawork is generally good, if a little static. Montage sequence in the end is very effective. Elmer Bernstein's music is appealing. Richard C. Meyer's editing is standard. "Anna Lucasta" may not rate as a character study, but it's blunt and it definitely rates attention as an unusual film for many situations.

Hift.

Aparajito
(INDIAN)

San Francisco, Nov. 8.

Satyajit Ray (Calcutta) production, directed by Satyajit Ray. Camera, Satyajit Ray; script, Satyajit Ray; music, Ravi Shankar. Stars Pinaki Sen Gupta, Samaran Ghosal, Karuna Banerjee, Kanu Banerjee. At San Francisco Film Festival, Nov. 7. Running time, **108 MINS.**

As the second in Satyajit Ray's trilogy of Indian life, "Aparajito" is a worthy successor to the first film, "Pather Panchali."

It doesn't have quite the tension or quite the variety of mood that the first picture had, but it has a special brooding quality and a more explicit conflict between East and West.

The story simply continues to follow the fortunes and misfortunes of one Brahman family. In "Aparajito" the family has moved to the holy city of Banares, where the father, movingly played by Kanu Banerjee, practices as a priest until he contracts a fatal illness.

The mother, played by sad-eyed Karuna Banerjee, is forced to take work as a rich family's cook until a priestly uncle takes her and her little son, played by Pinaki Sen Gupta, back to a small village, where the 10-year-old boy becomes a priest.

The little boy, however, yearns for a Western education, persuades his poor mother to send him to school, eventually wins a scholarship to a Calcutta university. The city tears the young man, played by Samaran Ghosal, from his mother, she becomes ill and dies before her son gets home. The film ends on a note of poignant affirmation: the son will hold his mother's funeral rites in Calcutta, in order to return to college.

On its face, this is not much of a story. Two of the principals die and the third is striving for an education. But it is told so stunningly well, with such deep feeling and genuine love, that it completely fascinates the audience.

It is impossible not to become involved emotionally with these people. They are flesh-and-blood, with all the frailties and virtues of ordinary people anywhere.

The relationship between mother and son is explored more fully, possibly, than it has even been on the screen—in one explosive scene, for instance, the mother slaps the lanky son who towers over her and then seeks him out, comfortingly.

Satyajit Ray's relentless camera

searches out the foibles of mankind, a half-Westernized Hindu lecher hiding a bottle of forbidden liquor, a fellow Brahman trying to put the touch on the father, a hideous railway butcher peddling religious nostrums, an Oxford-educated Calcutta don ordering the sleepy youth from class, a fat, rich, high-caste woman patronizing the mother in much the same way a Park Avenue matron might patronize the family cook.

There are moments of lightness, too, when the father offers to buy his family some special spices, when the neighbors help the mother, when the son and a schoolmate stretch out on a grassy slope and contemplate the Calcutta roadstead and even a voyage to England.

This is the India of the 1920s, an awakening India, an empire bound by stringent religious precepts which are physically debilitating and spiritually comforting, and yet uncertainly, slowly growing to realize its own strength.

The picture is well-edited and Ray's camera, direction and script are impressive. The principals are superb—indeed, they never seem to be acting—and Ravi Shankar's music, performed on native instruments, is a fitting accompaniment to a memorable film.

If "Pather Panchali" has box-office potential in U.S. art houses, so does "Aparajito." *Stef.*

I Only Arsked!
(BRITISH)

Cheerful, slapstick, army farce based on a tele series plenty of laughs provide brisk escapist fare.

London, Nov. 11.
Columbia release of a Hammer-Granada production. Stars Bernard Bresslaw, Michael Medwin, Alfie Bass, Geoffrey Sumner, Charles Hawtrey, Norman Rossington. Directed by Montgomery Tully. Screenplay, Sid Colin and Jack Davies; camera, Lionel Banes; editor, Alfred Cox; music, Benjamin Frankel. At Plaza Theatre, London. Running time, 82 MINS.
Popeye .... Bernard Bresslaw
Corporal Springer ...... Michael Medwin
Excused Boots .... Alfie Bass
Major Upshot-Bagley.... Geoffrey Sumner
The Professor .... Charles Hawtrey
Cupcake .... Norman-Rossington
Sgt. Chambers .... David Lodge
Sir Redvers .... Arthur Howard
King Fazim .... Marne Maitland
Fred .... Michael Bentine
Mahmoud .... Francis Matthews
Azim .... Michael Ripper
Salaman .... Wolf Morris
Ferrers .... Ewen McDuff

Based loosely on the successful Granada tv series, "The Army Game," this is another profitable dip into the realms of military farce. It covers little new territory and is content to reap the yocks from a well-tried anthology of army gags. It is a sound booking for most audiences who are looking for escapist entertainment.

The story line, such as it is, concerns the cockeyed adventures of a small bunch of misfit soldiers who, in error, are sent to a trouble spot in the Middle East. The crack regiment which the governor is expecting to guard against a possible revolution consists of an officer, a sergeant-major, a corporal and four privates. Much of the fun takes place in a harem and leads up to a hectic scrap with the rebels.

Scriptwriters, Sid Colin and Jack Davies, have not bothered overmuch to keep this a credible story, being content to provide dialog, gags and situations custom-made to the personalities of the tv characters. The one on whom the producers are obviously mainly pinning their faith is Private Popeye,

a tall character, played by Bernard Bresslaw. Bresslaw has sprung to national fame as Popeye, whose catch-phrase, "I Only Arsked," provides the pic's title.

Other characters who fit into the charade are Michael Medwin, as a resourceful corporal; Alfie Bass, a lugubrious character comedian whose army gag is that he is "excused boots"; Norman Rossington, Charles Hawtrey, Geoffrey Sumner, as a dithering silly ass type of officer, and David Lodge as a loud-voiced sergeant major.

Marne Maitland, Arthur Howard and Francis Matthews all give useful assistance. Michael Bentine, as a native guide, gives the best-rounded comedy performance of all. A large group of delectable damsels in the harem sequences have little to do but look shapely, a task which they find easy.

Montgomery Tully's direction is brisk while Lionel Banes has done a fine job with his lensing. "I Only Arsked!" is unabashed slapstick and fills its task admirably.
Rich.

The Rickshaw Man
(JAPANESE—C'SCOPE—COLOR)

San Francisco, Nov. 12.
Toho Corp. (Tokyo) production in C'Scope and Agfa Color, directed by Hiroshi Inagaki. Script, Mansaku Itami, Hiroshi Inagaki; camera, Kazuo Yamada; music, Ikuma Dan. Stars Toshiro Mifune, Hideko Takamine, Hiroshi Akutagawa. At San Francisco Film Festival (out of competition), Nov. 11. Running time, 98 MINS.

"The Rickshaw Man" is a most impressive film, combining superb visual imagery with humor, touching pathos and a simple story acted and directed beautifully.

It is merely the story of an uneducated rickshaw man in the early years of the 20th Century. He befriends a timid little boy, son of an Army Officer. The officer suddenly dies but the rickshaw man continues to befriend the widow and the little boy. Indeed, the rickshaw man inspires the little boy to grow up to be a strong, courageous man. In the final scenes the rickshaw man's love for the widow—a hopeless love because of their caste differences — becomes explicit, and the rickshaw man, realizing he can never marry the woman and realizing the little boy has grown up beyond him, drinks himself to death.

Central figure, as played by Toshiro Mifune, is a furious, unruly and tender fellow who dominates the whole picture. Story is told with some flashbacks which always add to audience understanding of the man's character and ugly early life. Mifune is tops, whether he is showing the little

boy how to win a footrace (hands held high, as if he were pulling his rickshaw), ignoring a customer while he straightens out the boy's kite (a magnificently funny scene), beating a big drum in the town festival or confessing his abject, pitiable love for the widow.

Hideko Takamine, as the widow, is graceful, restrained and moving in the single-minded pursuit of manliness for her only son, and Hiroshi Akutagawa is excellent in the lesser role of the husband who dies suddenly.

Hiroshi Inagaki's direction is sure and deft. *Stef.*

The Precipice
(JAPANESE—COLOR)

San Francisco, Nov. 9.
Daiei Corp. (Tokyo) production in Agfa color, directed by Yasuzo Masumura.

Camera, Hiroshi Murai; script, Kanento Shindo; music, Akira Ifukube. Stars Kenji Sugawara, Keizo Kawasaki, Fujiko Yamamoto, Hitomi Nozoe. At San Francisco Film Festival, Nov. 8. Running time, 94 MINS.

"The Precipice" is the Japanese version of a program picture, slick, well-made and somehow never very interesting because the audience isn't convinced of the illusion it is watching on the screen.

Two young mountain-climbers are involved here, one of whom is having an affair with the young wife of an aging scientist employed by a big corporation. She breaks off the affair, the two chaps climb a snowy peak and the fellow who was having the affair falls to his death because his nylon climbing rope snapped. The young wife has guilt feelings—she thinks her ex-lover committed suicide—but the remaining climber staunchly denies this and blames the rope. No one in Japan believes him and a test conducted by the aging scientist is supposed to prove a nylon rope can't break.

By that time the dead man's body is found—sure enough, the rope broke.

The dead man's sister is in love with the remaining climber and he is torn between her and his dead pal's ex-lover. He climbs the peak and gets killed in an avalanche. The two women are left grief-stricken.

All this is played in modern dress, against a background of electric kitchens, bachelor apartments, corporation offices and scurrying pedestrians. It looks like midtown Manhattan, except for the young wife, who by some quirk is still wearing a kimono.

Hiroshi Murai's color camera work, especially in the mountain snow scenes, is beautiful, and Hitomi Nozoe, as the sister of the climber who gets killed first, is one of the most strikingly handsome women gracing the screen today —she looks a bit like a Smith undergrad in her cablestitch ski sweater and ponytail.

Kenji Sugawara and Keizo Kawasaki are properly masculine as the two climbers, even though they emote somewhat like Actors' Lab grads, and Fujiko Yamamoto is a pretty, fearful young wife. Yasuzo Masumura keeps things hopping the way a competent director should, but the script and Akira Ifukube's overly Western music betray him.

Ludicrous scene: a dozen or so brawny young skiers gathered around the first dead climber's funeral pyre in a snowy forest singing Japanese words to "Clementine."

This doesn't figure to make the grade in the U.S. art circuit. *Stef.*

Two Eyes, Twelve Hands
(INDIAN)

San Francisco, Nov. 7.
Rajkamal Kalamandir Private Ltd., (Bombay production, directed by Shri V. Shantaram; script, G. D. Madgulkar; camera, G. Balkrishna; music, Vasant Desai. Stars Shri V. Shantaram, Sandhya. At San Francisco Film Festival, Nov. 6. Running time, 124 MINS.

A somewhat naive folk-tale focuses on the two eyes of an idealistic Indian jail official and the 12 hands of six Indian murderers, who play a sort of a Greek chorus to the hopes of their jailer. The jailer theorizes that all men are basically good and to prove his point persuades higher authorities to let him take the six murderers to a desolate area. The

murderers gradually come to cooperate with him and turn their barren area into a flourishing farm. When they go to a nearby village to sell their produce at what the jailer considers a fair price a villainous food broker, who enjoys a monopoly in the village, tries to wreck the jailer's plan and eventually lets loose a herd of cattle on the farm and has the crops burned. The jailer is gored to death by one of the cattle as he tries to save the lives of his murderers but his reforms are carried on by the murderers.

Film has humor, despite its macabre outcome, and Shri V. Shantaram, who also directed, is very good as the patient, idealistic jailer who becomes a demi-god to the six fat, swaggering, simple-minded cutthroats.

A marvelous addition is a swivel-hipped female toy-seller whose path leads directly by the farm and who become very fond of all the men. She is played by Sandhya, whose singing of several Indian songs throughout course of picture is a delight. Direction is excellent, camera work is satisfactory and Vasant Desai's score is terrific. Film probably has limited U.S. appeal but is very interesting.
Stef.

Taiga
(GERMAN)

San Francisco, Nov. 10.
Bavaria Filmkunst A. G. (Munich) production, directed by Wolfgang Liebeneiner. Camera, Georg Kraus; script, Herbert Reinecker. Stars Ruth Leuwerik, Hannes Messemer, Gunter Pfitzmann. At San Francisco Film Festival, Nov. 9. Running time, 99 MINS.

Ruth Leuwerik turns in a top-notch job as a woman doctor sent to a German prisoner-of-war camp in mid-Siberia because she resisted a Russian officer after World War II. She is a sensitive actress who has a considerable resemblance to the Garbo of 25 years ago and she runs away with this rather drab film.

Story concerns the hopelessness of German POW's caught in Siberia. The woman doctor inspires new hope in all of them, clouts one swaggering lout, played by Gunter Pfitzmann, who tries to molest her and then defends him against the other 299 men in the camp. She and a fellow prisoner, played by Hannes Messemer, fall in love and film ends with her going free and her lover expecting to follow her shortly.

Aside from Miss Leuwerik, none of the characters seems to come alive very much — possibly that's because they're supposed to be only half-alive. Hopelessness of their situation, however, is never made very explicit and the Russian guards and commandant are only thin caricatures.

Audience see scenes of men complaining of sickness and men griping, but to anyone who's ever lived in a barracks this seems pretty commonplace. Indeed, one of these Germans' biggest gripes is lack of mail from home over a period of years — this, of course, was not exactly unknown among nonprisoners in the late war.

George Kraus's camera goes in heavily for shadow-shrouded scenes and Wolfgang Liebeneiner has apparently directed with an eye to keeping some of a POW camp's stark horror out of this picture so that film will be acceptable to German filmgoers.

Nevertheless, Miss Leuwerik,

lovely despite her unattractive prison garb, manages to rescue picture from mediocrity and it probably has some chance in U.S. art circuit. Title, incidentally, refers to the name of the vast Siberian forests. *Stef.*

Toi Le Venom
(You Are The Venom)
(FRENCH)

Paris, Nov. 11.
Pathe release of Jules Borkon production. Stars Robert Hossein, Marina Vlady, Odile Versois; features Helena Manson, Henri Cremieux. Written and directed by Hossein from novel by Frederic Dard. Camera, Robert Juillard; editor, Gilbert Natot. Preemed in Paris. Running time, **90 MINS.**
Pierre .... Robert Hossein
Eva .... Marina Vlady
Helene .... Odile Versois
Amelie .... Helena Manson
Doctor .... Henri Cremieux

Suspense and psychology are the two main themes of this melodrama. Though slickly mounted, pic does not quite bring off enough character perception to make the involved tale plausible. As a result, this emerges an okay local bet with mainly exploitation possibilities for international markets.

A jobless young man, Robert Hossein, is picked up one night by a girl in a big motor car. She disrobes and then throws him out, subsequently trying to run him down after a love bout. He does not see her face but grabs the car license number, and locates the house where there are two sisters, both with long blonde hair. One is confined to a wheelchair.

Plot has both falling for him but he is not sure which girl was the love marauder.

Marina Vlady and Odile Versois, being sisters in real life, have the proper resemblance. But it is hard to accept the hero's not having really seen the girl in the auto. Technical credits are good and the pic has some good narrative quality. However, Hossein has taken on too much as star, writer and director. He is best in his role of the befuddled man trying to identify a venomous woman. *Mosk.*

Foreign Films

Zurich, Nov. 11.
Zum goldenen Ochsen (Golden Ox Inn) Praesens-Film Zurich release of Unitas-Film (Oscar Dueby) production. Directed by Hans Trommer; screenplay, Schaggi Streuli, Werner Wollenberger; camera, Emil Berna; music, Hans Moeckel. Stars Schaggi Streuli, Margrit Rainer; features Ursula Kopp, Paul Boesiger, Lina Carstens, Willy Ackermann, Rueli Walter, Hens Grimm, Karl Meier, Friedrich Braun, Armin Schweizer, Valerie Steinmann, Elisabeth Wenger. At Urban Theatre, Zurich. Running time, **98 MINS.**

First offering of new Swiss producing outfit, Unitas-Film, is a comedy with strictly home-market appeal, brought in at a (by U.S. standards) pint-size budget of $93,000 and filmed in 41 days mostly on location near Zurich, Basle and along the Rhine in Germany, Holland and France. Plot concerns a Swiss innkeeper who is so busy piling up money that he nearly wrecks his marriage and loses his daughter. He is brought to reason just in time to keep everyone concerned happy for the fadeout.

Best assets are some picturesque shots of the Rhine landscape and lively performances by Schaggi Streuli (who also co-authored the screenplay), Margrit Rainer, pert newcomer Ursula Kopp and especially Lina Carstens from the Munich Residenz-Theatre.

Paul Boesiger as the girl's fiance is wooden and unconvincing. Supporting roles are satisfactorily cast and technical credits average. *Mezo.*

Auntie Mame
(COLOR; TECHNIRAMA)

Smash b.o. version of the Broadway hit.

Hollywood, Nov. 21.
Warner Bros. production and release. Stars Rosalind Russell; costars Forrest Tucker, Coral Browne, Fred Clark. Directed by Morton DaCosta. Screenplay, Betty Comden and Adolph Green; based on the novel by Patrick Dennis, as adapted for the stage by Jerome Lawrence and Robert E. Lee; camera (Technicolor), Harry Stradling Sr.; music, Bronislau Kaper; editor, William Ziegler. Previewed at Academy Awards Theatre, Nov. 20, '58. Running time, **143 MINS.**
Mame Dennis .... Rosalind Russell
Beauregard Burnside ...... Forrest Tucker
Vera Charles .... Coral Browne
Mr. Babcock .... Fred Clark
Patrick Dennis .... Roger Smith
Lindsay Woolsey .... Patric Knowles
Agnes Gooch .... Peggy Cass
Patrick (as a child) ...... Jan Handzlik
Gloria Upson .... Joanna Barnes
Pegeen Ryan .... Pippa Scott
Mrs. Upson .... Lee Patrick
Mr. Upson .... Willard Waterman
Brian O'Bannion .... Robin Hughes
Norah Muldoon .... Connie Gilchrist
Ito .... Yuki Shimoda
Sally Cato .... Brook Bryon
Mrs. Burnside .... Carol Veazie
Acacius Page .... Henry Brandon

The film version of "Auntie Mame" is a faithfully funny recording of the hit play, changed only in some small details to conform to motion picture mores. Morton DaCosta, who directed the Broadway version, has restaged his smash for Warner Bros. and it looks to repeat its legit success. It is perhaps the strongest b.o. prospect of the Christmas pictures yet shown. Rosalind Russell recreates the title role for the film and reestablishes herself as a top picture personality.

Betty Comden and Adolph Green have done the screenplay, based on the play by Jerome Lawrence and Robert E. Lee, which in turn was taken from the "novel" of Patrick Dennis. There isn't too much difference in the picture's finished version (at least one original scene written for the film was dropped in final editing) from the play. Some of the gamier aspects and language have been toned down and some others suggested rather than stated. It is a top screenplay job.

Miss Russell plays the character described in the dialog as "a loving woman—odd, but loving." The odd part of her character supplies the comedy and the loving supplies the warmth and heart. The story is actually not very convincing, the characterizations of little depth, dialog is really only a series of comedy skits. But "Auntie Mame" is hilarious and human in about equal measure, and it is a surefire combination when mounted in as handsome and slick a production as this one.

Miss Russell is a high-class—or, at least, rich—Bohemian. She mixes Greek Orthodox bishops with Gertrude Stein-type females, for her own amusement, directing this chorus of mixed voices with a cigarette holder loaded with gems as phony as most of her guests. "Life is a banquet" is her philosophy. Even when the stock market crash wipes her out, the depression that follows fails to depress her for long. There is a rich husband to rescue her from clerking at R. H. Macy's, and when he falls off a mountain in Switzerland on their marathon, globe-trotting honeymoon, she bounces back to do her memoirs.

The climax of her career is saving her nephew from the stuffy life she has always fought, and then taking off for a new career with the nephew's son.

The problem for an actress with a character like "Mame" is to make her seem more full-hearted than empty-headed. Miss Russell scores because her native intelligence augments her sharp comedy sense. She can spike a line and drive it in, but she can also carry off the scenes of mother love and romance with her nephew and her husband. Miss Russell is a knockout in the series of now celebrated wigs, and in Orry-Kelly's gamut of fantastic costumes.

As in the legit version, Peggy Cass—who reprises her Broadway assignment—is a comedy standout as the helpless "Agnes Gooch." Miss Cass keeps her unwed pregnancy firmly in good taste, but sets her character so well in her early scenes that she has only to lurch through the background later to excite howls of glee.

Coral Browne, as the alcoholic actress who is Mame's best friend, and Fred Clark, as the baffled banker assigned to trustee Mame's nephew, are also strong comedy supports. Forrest Tucker, playing somewhat straighter, makes a human figure of his Southern millionaire but gets a great deal of fun out of it, too. Young Jan Handzlik (also from the stage) does a good job as Mame's nephew as a boy, and Roger Smith is sympathetic in the same part, as an adult. Joanna Barnes is another comedy figure of considerable humor as Smith's stuffy fiancee, and Lee Patrick and Willard Waterman do fine as her bigotted parents. Patric Knowles, Pippa Scott, Robin Hughes, Connie Gilchrist, Yuki Shimoda, Brook Bryon, Carol Veazie and Henry Brandon each create individual characterizations of immense value.

To an unusual degree, the art director deserves a special nod on "Auntie Mame." Malcolm Bert did the successive versions of the apartment that is the chief set, and they are not only lavish versions of "Before and After" but get fun and sympathy out of them. Robert Hanley was consultant on the interiors, and George James Hopkins was the set decorator.

Morton DaCosta's direction is lively and inventive, especially in adapting some of the techniques he used on stage. However, a few punchy closeups might have got more laughs out of some of the lines.

Harry Stradling's photography is bright and lucid, as it should be for comedy, diffusing the background only occasionally to highlight a foreground figure. He keeps the Technirama process from overwhelming his figures and his Technicolor is brilliant and true. Bronislau Kaper's score, supervised by Ray Heindorf, is discreet with only a "Mame" theme to give it emphasis. Editing by William Ziegler is fine, as is the sound by M. A. Merrick. *Powe.*

Sally's Irish Rogue
(BRITISH)

Simple, but cheerful Irish comedy, with Julie Harris and the Dublin Abbey Players, which can well blarney its way into most cinemas as a useful dualer.

London, Nov. 18.
British Lion release of an Emmet Dalton (Monty Berman-Robert S. Baker) production. Stars Julie Harris, Tim Seely, Abbey Players. Directed by George Pollock. Screenplay by Patrick Kirwan and Blanaid Irvine, from "The New Gossoon," a play by George Shields; camera, Stanley Pavey; editor, Gerry Hambling; music, Ivor Slaney. At Studio One, London. Running time, **74 MINS.**

Sally Hamil .... Julie Harris
Luke Carey .... Tim Seely
Rabit Hamil .... Harry Brogan
Ellen Carey .... Maire Kean
Mag Kehoe .... Brid Lynch
Ned Shay .... Eddie Golden
John Henly .... Philip O'Flynn
Biddy Henly .... Finola O'Shannon
Seamus Doyle .... Noel Magee
Saloon Landlord .... Paul Farrell
McKeefry .... Dermot Kelly
Postman .... John Hoey
Uncle Peter .... Geoffrey Golden
Garage Dealer .... John Cowley

Irish film comedy is in a specialized class, either leaving an audience cold or in raptures. With the Dublin Abbey Players on parade, "Sally's Irish Rogue" has an authenticity which makes its naivete and whimsey quite disarming. It emerges as a pleasant, modest joke which creates plenty of happy-go-lucky yocks and should prove a useful dualer for most houses.

The slim story line concerns an amiable, weak young man who is more interested in motorcycles than in the farm he is due to inherit. He acquires the bike, breaks off with the girl he has promised, secretly, to marry and becomes unwittingly involved with another one to such an extent that he is nearly forced to the altar. Between the threats of breach-of-promise and a shotgun wedding, he is all over the place, but everything is tidied up satisfactorily, if slightly illogically.

The screenplay by Patrick Kirwan and Blanaid Irvine has a lot of loose ends. The dialog is so determinedly "Oirish" that it is sometimes almost incomprehensible to English-speaking purists. But it is directed with such breezy blarney by George Pollock that this scarcely matters. Filmed unostentatiously at the new Ardmore Studios, near Dublin, it has the advantage of pleasant Irish village scenery. Stanley Pavey's photography captures the atmosphere of the locale admirable.

Tim Seely is the young man in question while Julie Harris was imported from the U.S. to play the role of the forthright young woman who brings him to heel. Both of these young people fit excellently into the Irish scene. But it is the Abbey Players who really matter. Harry Brogan has a field day as Miss Harris's father, a wily poacher. Brogan, overplaying riotously, gives a gem of a comedy performance. Philip O'Flynn, Brid Lynch, Dermot Kelly, Paul Farrell and Noel Magee add a cheerful quota to the fun and games. Eddie Golden and Maire Kean soundly carry the weight of the more serious roles.

Ivor Slaney's background music is relentlessly, but fittingly, Irish. The pic winds up with pictorial credits for the various characters, a service to audiences which should be a "must" for all producers.

Rich.

Unwed Mother

Routine, improbable exploitationer, for teaming with same studio's "Joy Ride."

Hollywood, Nov. 21.

Allied Artists release of Joseph Justman production. Stars Norma Moore, Robert Vaughn. Associate producer, Maurice Horn. Directed by Walter A. Doniger. Screenplay, Anson Bond and Alden Nash; based on a story by Bond; camera, Lothrop Worth; music, Emil Newman; editors, Lou Moss and Neil Brunnenkant. Previewed at the studio, Nov. 17, '58. Running time, **74 MINS.**

Betty .... Norma Moore
Dona .... Robert Vaughn
Mousie .... Diana Darrin
Gertie .... Billie Bird
Mrs. Horton .... Jeanne Cooper
Ben .... Ron Hargrave
Linda .... Kathleen Hughes
Mr. Paully .... Sam Buffington
Mrs. Miller .... Claire Carleton
Louella .... Collette Jackson
Curtis .... Ken Lynch
Mrs. Paully .... Dorothy Adams
Minister .... Ralph Gamble

The beauty of this title is its accuracy. There are no obscurities or subtleties in the Joseph Justman production for Allied Artists. "Unwed Mother" is about a girl who is not married and is pregnant. Some exploitation values may be assumed. It will be teamed by Allied with "Joy Ride," (Reviewed in VARIETY, Oct. 8, '58) which is the stronger of the two films. They make a fair pair for exploitation dualling.

The Anson Bond-Alden Nash screenplay, from a story by Bond, starts off promisingly, chiefly because of the male in the illicit romance, Robert Vaughn. He is such a thoroughly reprehensible character, but one of those fascinating heels, that he gives the otherwise routine and shabby seduction some class. When Vaughn disappears from the story, the screenplay seems to run out of invention, and winds up so lacerated by factual errors and improbable situations that it loses all realism and conviction.

Norma Moore is the title character, a country girl from Visalia, Calif. She comes to Los Angeles and promptly starts giving her paychecks to Vaughn, who presents himself as a scion of wealth temporarily strapped. His promise to marry her turns out to be no more negotiable than his I.O.U.'s, and she winds up in a home for expectant, unwed mothers.

She agrees to put the baby up for adoption but changes her mind after the child is born, providing the film with a wild and unbelievable conclusion as she pursues the foster parents by auto to reclaim her infant.

Walter K. Doniger, who directed, has done a better than routine job in dealing with these elements, although handicapped by the limits of the story and screenplay. The actors do well, particularly Vaughn, aided by Miss Moore, Diana Darrin, Billie Bird, Jeanne Cooper and Claire Carleton.

Powe.

7th Voyage of Sinbad
(COLOR)

Fairytale actioner with science-fiction and horror trimmings. Parts of it will scare under-10 small fry. Prospects good.

Columbia Pictures release of a Morningside Production. Stars Kerwin Mathews, Kathryn Grant, Richard Eyer, Torin Thatcher; features Alec Mango, Danny Green, Harold Kasket, Alfred Brown, Nana de Herrera. Produced by Charles H. Schneer. Directed by Nathan Juran. Script, Kenneth Kolb; camera (Technicolor) and using Dynamation process, Wilkie Cooper; visual effects, Ray Harryhausen; music, Bernard Harrmann. Previewed at the Roxy Theatre, N.Y., Nov. 15, '58. Running time, **89 MINS.**

Sinbad .... Kerwin Mathews
Parisa .... Kathryn Grant
The Genie .... Richard Eyer
Sokurah .... Torin Thatcher
Caliph .... Alec Mango
Karim .... Danny Green
Sultan .... Harold Kasket
Harufa .... Alfred Brown
Sadi .... Nana de Herrera
Gaunt Sailor .... Nino Falanga
Crewman .... Luis Guedes
Ali .... Virgilio Teixeira

As every alert youngster should know, Sinbad the Sailor went on some pretty exciting voyages and met with the kind of fantastic adventures that make the heart throb and the pulse race. In "The 7th Voyage of Sinbad," this world of makebelieve has been recreated in rich Technicolor and with the kind of gusto and bravado that certainly catches the spirit of the tale.

Just about every trick in the book—including a new one called Dynamation, i.e. the animation of assorted monsters, vultures, skeletons, etc.—has been used to bring a vivid sort of realism to the various and terrifying hazards which Sinbad encounters on his voyage and in his battle with Sokurah the magician. Add to this a love story (interrupted when the princess Parisa is shrunk to inch-size by the magician and must view the world around her from that vantage point) and what emerges is a bright, noisy package for youngsters and adults alike.

It should be pointed out that some of the scenes in the film are sufficiently scary to be of concern to parents of small children. Kids under 10 will be alternately delighted and horrified. Inasmuch as they obviously must have been aiming primarily for the juvenile market, it's difficult to understand why producer Charles H. Schneer and director Nathan Juran had to turn this into a quasi horror-thriller. At the Roxy Theatre preview in N.Y., quite a few parents took their youngsters out, and a good many children were heard to complain they were frightened.

Which, however, does not detract from the fact that this "Sinbad" is frequently exciting and technically imaginative and inventive. Trick photography is used effectively to create the huge, roaring cyclops, the one-eyed monster; the Genie in the magic lamp; the shrinking of the princess; the rattling duel Sinbad fights with the skeleton; the firespitting dragon; the giant Roc mother bird, etc.

Kerwin Mathews makes a pleasant Sinbad, acting the part with more restraint than bravuro; Kathryn Grant is pretty as the princess; Torin Thatcher has a fittingly evil look as the magician; Richard Eyer is cute as the Genie; Alec Mango has dignity as the Caliph.

But this isn't the sort of film in which performances matter much. It's primarily entertainment for the eye, and that end certainly is served, for the settings are a-glitter with resplendent costumes and the action moves swiftly and almost without interruption. Sinbad rescues the magician from the island of the cyclops but incurs Sokurah's wrath when he refuses to return to pick up the magic lamp which commands the Genie.

Sokurah then shrinks the princess and maintains that, to restore her to normal size, he needs a piece from the egg of the Roc bird. Sinbad fits out a vessel and goes on the voyage, armed with a huge crossbow and arrow to kill the cyclops. There follow some hair-raising adventures, climaxed with the final struggle of the magician and Sinbad, with the latter and his princess escaping from Sokurah's castle after a phantastic chase.

Director Juran keeps proceedings moving satisfactorily and somehow manages to draw that fine line between the incredible and the ridiculous. Wilkie Cooper's camera work is good and Bernard Harrmann has contributed the required turbulent musical score. Ray Harryhausen, who was responsible for visual effects, emerges as the hero of this piece. He's responsible for some striking scenes that create real magic on the screen. Robert Gill's main titles are very original and fun to watch.

Hift.

El Jefe
(The Boss)
(ARGENTINE)

Buenos Aires, Nov. 18.

AAA release of Aries production in black and white, directed by Fernando Ayala and Hector Olivera from a script by David Vinas. Cast: Alberto de Mendoza, Duilio Marzio, Orestes Caviglia, Leonardo Favio, Graciela Borges, Luis Tasca, Ana Casares, Ignacio Quiros and Violeta Antier. Camera: Ricardo Younis; sets by Mario Vanarelli; editing, Atilio Rinaldi and Ricardo Nistal. Reviewed in Buenos Aires, Oct. 23, 1958.

The thought behind David Vinas' script is condemnation of all dictators. Subtly enough drawn, and with such abundant local color as to make it domestically acceptable entertainment. (It also hits at the current "get rich quick" mania amongst juveniles). With strong, well-paced cast, film may have some Spanish market export value.

Alberto de Mendoza does well as the ruthless "boss," if unconvincing in the final dramatic sequence. A more special draw with the femmes is Duilio Marzio, as a journalist who hires out his typewriter for a mess of pottage. An intelligent actor with looks, Emilio Alfaro is responsible for an excellently humorous vignette of a Carlos Gardel fan.

The yarn describes the rise and fall of a suburban bully, who rules his gang with brutal insight, filling gaps in the lives of aimless young men, who later can't evade his clutches. He is just climbing to upper echelons of gangsterism, through help from a strong man's mistress, when he commits a stupid murder, and trying vainly to pin it on his most loyal admirer, is shown up as a rank coward.

Story is weakly developed at points. Nonetheless its merits suggest okay outlook for Latin situations.

Nid.

Passport to Shame
(BRITISH)

Yank actor-singer Eddie Constantine's first English-speaking role in an exploitation item of fair calibre on a white-slave ring theme.

Paris, Dec. 2.

British Lion release of John Clein production. Stars Diana Dors, Eddie Constantine, Odile Versois, Herbert Lom; features Brenda De Banzie, Robert Brown. Directed by Alvin Rakoff. Screenplay, Patrick Alexander; camera, Jack Asher; editor, Lee Doig; music, Ken Jones, Jeff Davis. Preemed in Paris. Running time, **95 MINS.**

Larry .... Eddie Constantine
Vicki .... Diana Dors
Malou .... Odile Versois
Nick .... Herbert Lom
Madame .... Brenda de Banzie
Mike .... Robert Brown

Purportedly brought in for about $180,000, this is worth the money. Though a familiar entry in characters and general action, it has a plus in fairly unfettered looks at prostitution in London and the workings of a white slave ring. It looks to have exploitation facets for Yank dualer chances and its "X" certificate in England should also help at the boxoffice.

Add to this the Eddie Constantine pull on the Continent, and it looks like a low budgeter with good chances all around. Constantine, in his first English-speaking role, plays a Canadian who gets mixed up with the ring when he goes through with a courtesy marriage to an intended French victim to help her get Anglo papers.

However, love blooms and, with the help of a bunch of fellow taxi-drivers, Constantine routs the gang, saves the girl, still pure, and this time is soundly beaten in various fight scenes rather than always winning as he does in his popular Yank gangster parody pix he makes in France and now Germany.

Constantine appears at ease in this part and displays a catchy screen personality that could be used more often in English speaking films. Odile Versois is the innocent and Diana Dors fits well into the part of a bighearted doxie. Supporting cast is good and, though quite routine, this pic has some strong meat in street scenes of the prosties at work.

Direction is taut and moves along in spite of a few cliches. Technical credits are good and this shapes an okay entry of its type for international chances. Constantine will make another English film before coming back to his French chores. He also warbles some catchy ditties by Jeff Davis on the soundtrack in both English and French.

Constantine is still an unknown quantity in the U.S., in spite of being an American, but displays promise for Yank pix on his European pull. *Mosk.*

The Two-Headed Spy
(BRITISH)

Well-made, offbeat spy story with Jack Hawkins posing as a Nazi general; quiet tension builds up to a sound b.o. proposition.

Columbia release of a Sabre (Bill Kirby) production. Stars Jack Hawkins and Gia Scala. Directed by Andre De Toth. Screenplay, James O'Donnell, based on story by J. Alvin Kugelmass; editor, Raymond Poulton; camera, Jack Mills; music, Gerrard Schurman. At Odeon, Marble Arch, London, Nov. 17, '58. Running time, **93 MINS.**

General Schottland	Jack Hawkins
Lili	Gia Scala
Reinisch	Erik Schumann
Gestapo Leader Mueller	Alexander Knox
Cornaz	Felix Aylmer
Admiral Canaris	Walter Hudd
Kaltenbrunner	Edward Underdown
General Hauser	Laurence Naismith
Dietz	Geoffrey Bayldon
Adolph Hitler	Kenneth Griffith
1st Gestapo Agent	Robert Crewdson
2nd Gestapo Agent	Michael Caine
Karen Croscher	Henriette Johns
General Wagner	Martin Benson
Pawnbroker	Victor Woolf
Marshal Keitel	Richard Grey
German Corporal	Ronald Hines
General Hardt	Donald Pleasance
General Opitz	Martin Boddey

Latest in the long stream of war stories is "The Two-Headed Spy," interesting offbeat spy pic with that most British of actors Jack Hawkins surprisingly cast as a Nazi general. Though almost totally devoid of humor, and with a necessarily sombre performance by Hawkins, "Spy" holds the attention admirably and is a worthwhile entry.

James O'Donnell's screenplay, which is based on a real-life story, pursues a fairly pedestrian beat but it builds its tension excellently and without too blatant use of the usual cloak-and-dagger methods. Director Andre de Toth has sought to get his effects by showing the mental strain of Hawkins in his dilemma rather than by stress on too much physical danger.

Hawkins, a British spy in both wars, and therefore an exile in Germany between the two conflicts, has built up confidence as an astute, loyal and resourceful member

of the Nazi machine. He rises to the rank of general and manages to steer his double life effectively. His job is not to sabotage the Germans but to delude them by doing his job excellently. At the same time he is feeding the Allies invaluable information through a British agent, neatly played by Felix Aylmer, disguised as an antique clock seller.

When Aylmer is arrested and murdered, suspicion falls on Hawkins through his aide, a member of the Gestapo. But he manages to brush off this suspicion and continues his espionage through his new contact, a beautiful singer. His association with her is suspected merely to be an understandable love affaire. His task completed, Hawkins escapes to Britain, but not before the singer, with whom Hawkins has genuinely fallen in love, has been killed by his aide.

Hawkins plays the role of the general with his usual reliability. Rightly not attempting to assume the suspicion of a German accent, he is thoroughly convincing as the general, with the right hint of arrogance. Gia Scala, a beautiful, cool Italian actress, has only limited opportunities but is a neat complement to the intense masculinity of the pic. Erik Schumann, as Hawkins, suspicious, suave young aide, gives a fine picture of dedicated Nazidom while Alexander Knox is a crafty Gestapo chief. Donald Pleasence, Walter Hudd, Laurence Naismith and Edward Underdown are among a long list of stalwart actors who portray German high officers effectively. Hitler is played by Kenneth Griffith. The Fuehrer is mainly heard, with just an occasional lock of hair and an outstretched beating fist to suggest his physical side. Griffith's voice has just the proper note of hysteria.

The German atmosphere is well-sustained but there is an overgenerous use of newsreel footage which too often jerks the film from fiction into a documentary mood. Apart from that, the camerawork of Jack Mills makes good employment of light and shade and creates a sinister effect which is excellent. Far too obtrusive is the persistent use of Gerrard Schurman's music. The film might have benefited by one or two more dramatic highlights such as when Hawkins, attempting to radio a message to the Allies from the German front, is surprised by a patrol and has to bump them off. But the main purpose of this well-made film is to show the essential loneliness of a man whose job has cut him off from his own country and who walks in constant danger of discovery. A man who cannot afford to make the slightest slip. This "Two-Headed Spy" (and Hawkins) does skilfully. *Rich.*

Girls at Sea
(BRITISH—COLOR)

Amiable naval comedy with farcical complications; briskly played by Ronald Shiner and three sprightly girls. Sound b.o. for family spots.

London, Nov. 18.
Associated British-Pathe release of an Associated British Vaughn Dean-Gilbert Gunn production. Stars Guy Rolfe, Alan White, Michael Hordern, Ronald Shiner. Directed by Gilbert Gunn. Screenplay, T. J. Morrison, based on play by Stephen King-Hall and Ian Hay; camera, Erwin Hiller; editor, E. B. Jarvis; music, Laurie Johnson. At Metro Private Theatre, London. Running time, **80 MINS.**

Captain	Guy Rolfe
Marine Ogg	Ronald Shiner
Commander	Alan White
Admiral Hewitt	Michael Hordern
Mary	Anne Kimbell
Antoinette	Nadine Tallier
Lady Hewitt	Fabia Drake
Jill	Mary Steele
Captain Randall	Richard Coleman
Tourist	Lionel Jeffries
Singer	Teddy Johnson
Flag Lieutenant	Daniel Massey
Corporal Duckett	David Lodge

"The Middle Watch," a comedy by Stephen King-Hall and Ian Hay, was staged in the West End back in 1929. It has been filmed before and crops up again as "Girls at Sea." Dusted down and in freshly-colored guise, the amiable little joke has not dated and gains plenty of yocks, with only occasional signs of strain. As a crisp, inoffensive piece of family entertainment it should register in most U.K. houses. American audiences may be mildly deterred by lack of star names.

The story, such as it is, can be disposed of briskly. It concerns the complications when, following a ship's party, three lovelies miss the last shore-boat. Two of them are known by the captain and a couple of other officers to be aboard, and are given the hospitality of the skipper's quarters. The third is a redheaded stowaway who is chasing a marine who has promised her marriage.

The minor complications arousing from this unusual naval situation are stirred up, when during the night, the ship is ordered to embark for Italy and the admiral makes it his flagship. He comes aboard to take over the captain's quarters and the problem is to keep the femme presence unknown to him.

This slim plot demands high spirits, rather than urgent thesping ability, from the cast which rises nobly to T. J. Morrison's screenplay and to Gilbert Gunn's smart direction. Much of the fun comes from Ronald Shiner who is a model marine aboard but a menace among the girls when in port. Shiner has made a deserved reputation for himself in this type of part and doesn't put a wrong foot forward. He can time a gag or a grimace to a second and is particularly funny as a sentry with squeaky boots, reluctant to remove them even on captain's orders because of a hole in his sock.

Michael Hordern provides his usual fussy pomposity to the role of the admiral while Guy Rolfe, as a shy captain, is most effective. Alan White, Lionel Jeffries and Richard Coleman are other useful male performers. Daniel Massey makes a gem of his facial comedy as a bewildered young officer. Of the three attractive girls, American Anne Kimbell (making her British screen debut) and Mary Steele have the major screen space. But it is Nadine Tallier, as the fiery young French redhead after Shiner's head, who makes the most impact. She is lush, alluring and full of pep.

Erwin Hiller's color lensing brings out the gaiety of blue skies, the Riviera and, particularly, the ship's dance while E. B. Jarvis's editing is technically okay. "Girls at Sea" is a neat little comedy which bubbles along at a reasonable pace. *Rich.*

Floods of Fear
(BRITISH)

Strong "meller" with convicts on the run in flooded country; U.K. film in a Yank setting with good production values, but limp dialog.

London, Nov. 18.
Rank (Sydney Box) production and release. Stars Howard Keel and Anne Heywood. Directed by Charles Crichton. Screenplay, Charles Crichton, from novel by John and Ward Hawkins; camera, Christopher Challis; editor, Peter Bezencenet; music, Alan Rawsthorne. At Gaumont, Haymarket, London. Running time, **84 MINS.**

Donavan	Howard Keel
Elizabeth	Anne Heywood
Peebles	Cyril Cusack
Sharkey	Harry H. Corbett
Murphy	John Crawford
Sheriff	Eddie Byrne
Dr. Matthews	John Phillips
Fatchman	Mark Baker
Mayor	James Dyrenforth
Businessman	Jack Lester
Banker	Peter Madden
Deputy Sheriff	Guy Kingsley Poynter
Lt.-Colonel	Gordon Tanner
Police Captain	Robert Mackenzie

"Floods of Fear" is one of Britain's most determined attempts to woo the U.S. market. Not only does it have Howard Keel as its male star, but the meller is unabashedly set in the U.S. The film has a novel setting, but an old idea, and corny dialog doesn't help the characters to develop overmuch. However, there is some sound acting and the production quality is tops. It adds up to reasonable entertainment, but it is one of those annoying pix that should—and could—have been much better. It is questionable whether its marquee value is sufficiently strong to lure Yank patrons.

Two convicts, one serving a life sentence for murder, a wounded warder and a terrified girl are stranded in a partly submerged house when the Humbolt River valley is flooded. The story focusses largely on the girl's fright as she discovers the identity of the men. The "lifer" (Howard Keel), is determined to get away to kill the man who had him framed. The girl, who gradually falls for Keel, gets away and is able to inform the police in time for them to prevent Keel from fulfilling his threatened killing.

Keel, who spends a large proportion of the film submerged in the floods, gives a robust display, combining virility with a surprising gentleness. Cyril Cusack is the mean convict who does most to terrorize the girl, played by Anne Heywood. Miss Heywood, one of Britain's most promising young actresses, has a role which offers her no glamor and very little opportunity to do more than act as chorus to the men. But she is easy on the eye and tackles a very tough role with conviction.

Harry H. Corbett, as the warder; Eddie Byrne, as a sheriff and John Crawford, as a heavy, add useful contributions. But the main interest in the film is the production and direction. Charles Crichton's direction is a rather more skillful job than his screenplay, which limps quite a lot. The American scene is well displayed, and excellent matching of newsreel shots with scenes lensed in tanks in the studio and with those done on a location near London gives the flood sequences a dramatic authenticity which is wholly gripping. Christopher Challis also has done a standout chore with his photography.

This is a film which the background is more important than either the story or the characters. The result is a downbeat film with only occasional moments of suspense leading up to a sock fight climax. It may have been the most vigorous job that Keel has ever had to tackle. It is not his most rewarding performance though it is good to see him back in the field where he started—in British pix—before becoming a musical star in Hollywood. *Rich.*

Foreign Films

Paris, Nov. 18.

Les Fils De L'Eau (The Sons of Water) (FRENCH; DOCUMENTARY; COLOR). Pleiad Films production and release. Written, directed and edited by Jean Rouch with photographic assistant Roger Rosfelder. At La Pagode, Paris. Running time, **60 MINS.**

There can be money in these travel films about native customs, especially if the makers have some filmic gifts. Jean Rouch found this out when a series of his pix on French West African native customs began to win film fest prizes. A few were put together to make this 60-minute feature which delves into some rituals among various Afro tribes living alongside great rivers. The dances of possession and an explosively exciting hippopotamous hunt are well documented. But Rouch has a sense of the vital in denoting primitive conduct, and his pic holds dramatic interest.

Another Rouch item is "Les Maitres Fou" (The Mad Masters) on a native sect which went in for weekend meetings where the colonial leaders were strangely caricatured as they gave vent to this in trance. These two might make an offbeat package for specialized bookings in the U.S. It is strong stuff but with a fine technical finish. Color is good and the progression despite being made under actual conditions and being blown up to 35m Eastmancolor from 16m originals. *Mosk.*

Lettre De Siberie (FRENCH DOCUMENTARY; COLOR). Argos Films production and release. Written and directed by Chris Marker. Camera (Eastmancolor), Sacha Vierny; commentary, Georges Rouqier; editor and special effects, Arcady. At Boneparte, Paris. Running time, **60 MINS.**

Good documentary travelogue footage is given a new feeling and tang by a witty commentary in the form of a letter from Siberia in this vehicle. Pic also has a built-in curio interest in this part of Russia which is so rarely filmed. Sudden comic interludes when the same scene is shown with propaganda aspects or inserted animation make this a medium-length pic which could be used on some specialized programs in the U.S.

Technical aspects are good. The film was yanked out of the Karlovy Film Fest in Czechoslavakia this summer when the Russians objected on the claim that they knew of no film having been authorized to be made in Siberia. However, this obviously proves there was permission, this pic validly and wittily makes this clear. *Mosk.*

Separate Tables

Topnotch version of the stage hit. Bolstered by marquee names and excellent performances.

United Artists release of Harold Hecht (Hecht-Hill-Lancaster) production. Stars Rita Hayworth, Deborah Kerr, David Niven, Wendy Hiller and Burt Lancaster. Features Gladys Cooper, Cathleen Nesbitt, Felix Aylmer, Rod Taylor and Audrey Dalton. Directed by Delbert Mann. Screenplay, Terence Rattigan and John Gay, based on a play by Rattigan; camera, Charles Lang Jr.; editor, Marjorie Fowler and Charles Ennis; music, David Raksin; song, "Separate Tables," by Harry Warren and Harold Adamson. Previewed in N.Y., Nov. 20, '58. Running time, **98 MINS.**

Ann Shankland	Rita Hayworth
Sibyl Railton-Bell	Deborah Kerr
Major Pollock	David Niven
Miss Cooper	Wendy Hiller
John Malcolm	Burt Lancaster
Mrs. Railton-Bell	Gladys Cooper
Lady Matheson	Cathleen Nesbitt
Mr. Fowler	Felix Aylmer
Charles	Rod Taylor
Jean	Audrey Dalton
Miss Meacham	May Hallatt
Doreen	Priscilla Morgan
Mabel	Hilda Plowright

On marquee value alone, "Separate Tables" has the earmarks of a boxoffice hit. The names of Rita Hayworth, Deborah Kerr, David Niven, Wendy Hiller and Burt Lancaster should satisfy any theatreowner and represent the bait to attract general audiences. But the Terence Rattigan-John Gay screenplay, based on Rattigan's hit play, is more than just a framework for a galaxy of stars. It is a provocative and intelligent film, adult in theme and execution, and bolstered by some of the best performances of the year.

Producer Harold Hecht and his colleagues in the Hecht-Hill-Lancaster organization deserve credit for undertaking a story that does not meet the conception of what is generally considered sure-fire material in today's market. More importantly, it has the ingredients to interest and draw the more discriminating filmgoer. As such, "Separate Tables" emerges as a film that can comfortably play discriminating as well as the larger general situations.

As a play, "Separate Tables" consisted of two separate vignettes set against the same English boarding house and served as an acting tour de force for Eric Portman and Margaret Leighton. Much of the appeal of the play was due to the remarkable change in characterization they were able to make as they assumed different roles in each of the segments. However, Rattigan and Gay have masterfully blended the two playlets into one literate and absorbing full-length film. Four performers selected to play the separate roles more than meet the thespian requirements. It won't come as a surprise if Niven, Miss Kerr and Miss Hiller are cited for Academy Award notice.

Basically, Rattigan's story is a character study of a group of residents at a small British seaside town of Borunemouth, described in the film as a tourist spot in the summer and a haven for the lonely and the desperate in the winter. The majority of the residents are tortured by psychological problems and unhappy pasts.

As a phoney major, with a made-up Sandhurst background, Niven gives one of the best performances of his career. His nervous mannerisms, "eh whats," "good shows" and boring lies of his World War II adventures in the desert campaign are a cover up for basic inadequacies and fears. He is finally exposed when he's caught molesting women in a theatre.

Miss Kerr is excellent as a plain, shy girl completely cowed by a domineering and strong mother, finely portrayed by Gladys Cooper. Miss Kerr, who has an attachment for the equally mixed-up major, has some of the most touching scenes in the film and her final rebellion against her mother emerges as a scene that will be remembered.

A separate but integrated story concerns Lancaster, Miss Hayworth and Miss Hiller. As a writer hurt by life and living a don't-care existence at the out-of-the-way hotel, Lancaster turns in a shaded performance. Miss Hayworth is equally good as his former wife whose narcissism and desire to dominate men leads to Lancaster's downfall. Miss Hiller is the efficient manager of the hotel who finds her romance with Lancaster shattered on the arrival of his physically attractive and fashionable ex-wife. She presents a moving and touching performance.

Topnotch portrayals are also given by other assorted residents of the hotel, including Felix Aylmer, who dwells in the past memories of his school teaching days; May Hallatt, as an outspoken, individualistic horse player; Cathleen Nesbitt, as a good-hearted but meek follower; Rod Taylor, as a medical student, and Audrey Dalton, as his girlfriend.

Delbert Mann, who guided "Marty" to an Academy Award, has again come up with a sensitive and painstaking directorial job. And producer Hecht has seen to it that the production values are first class. Technical assets, including Charles Lang Jr.'s black and white photography, Marjorie Fowler and Charles Ennis' editing, and the production design of Harry Horner are all top-draw. David Raksin has provided an appropriate musical score and Harry Warren and Harold Adamson have a good over-the-titles tune in "Separate Tables." Incidentally, the "Separate Tables" of the title refers to the hotel's policy of seating each of its guests at different tables in the dining room. *Holl.*

Nowhere to Go
(BRITISH-METROSCOPE)

Sound acting and a well-made crime yarn add up to good entertaining; pic lacks marquee value, especially for U.S.

London, Dec. 2.

Metro release of a Michael Balcon production. Stars George Nader, Maggie Smith, Bernard Lee. Directed by Seth Holt. Screenplay, Seth Holt and Kenneth Tynan, based on novel by Donald Mackenzie; camera, Paul Beeson; editor, Harry Aldous; music, Dizzy Reece. At Metro Private Theatre, London. Running time, **87 MINS.**

Greg	George Nader
Sloane	Bernard Lee
Mrs. Jefferson	Bessie Love
Bridget	Maggie Smith
Inspector Scott	Geoffrey Keen
Rosa	Andree Melly
Cameron	Howard Marion Crawford
Dodds I	Arthur Howard
Dodds II	John Welsh
Rosemary	Margaret McGrath
Sullivan	Harry Corbett
Bendel	Harry Locke
Anna Berg	Lilly Kahn
Pet Shop Man	Lionel Jeffries
Policeman	John Turner
Welsh Garageman	Lane Meddick
Man on Tractor	Charles Price

"Nowhere To Go" is a well-made, literate crime yarn with the usual polished stamp of the Ealing stable. Good acting is insured by a sound cast of established British thesps, plus Hollywood actor, George Nader. But there is precious little marquee in the cast, especially for U.S. consumption.

The pic gets away to a slick start with Nader being helped by Bernard Lee, his outside accomplice, to break jail. He is serving a 10-year sentence for swindling a wealthy widow out of the $154,000, proceeds from the sale of a rare coin collection. Following the jail break, a flashback shows the plausible manner in which Nader cons the widow and salts the cash away in a safe deposit before the police get their hooks on him. Now, away from jail, he starts his plans to recover the money and get out of the country. But everything goes wrong. His accomplice double-crosses him, his crook friends squeal on him, he is robbed of the key to the safe deposit box and the accomplice dies after Nader has roughed him up.

Thwarted on all sides and with a murder rap to face, he is a convict on the run. The lone person to lift a finger to help him is a rich, offbeat Bohemian girl who specializes in helping lost causes. But, believing that the girl is turning him into the cops, Nader makes a final desperate break in the Welsh hills and is shot by a farmer and dies.

Seth Holt, who wrote the screenplay with Kenneth Tynan, has directed tautly and the dialog is reasonably brisk. The London and Welsh locations are authentic. Paul Beeson's black-and-white lensing is sharp and well edited.

Nader's performance as the plausible, ice-cold crook who finds his plans going frustratingly astray and who gradually finds himself out on his own is an intelligent study. Bernard Lee gives solid support as his greedy accomplice. The heroine, Maggie Smith, provides an interesting new face and this, her first starring role, suggests that she has a worthwhile future in pix.

There are a number of useful performances in smaller roles. Geoffrey Keen, as a very authentic dick; Bessie Love, as the garrulous widow; Andree Melly, as a nightclub waitress, Howard Marian-Crawford, as the urbane club proprietor, and Harry Corbett as a sleazy crook all add their quota to a sound all-round cast.

The music of Dizzy Reece, played by his own quartet, adds considerably to the atmosphere. It is offbeat, staccato and exciting, and particularly helps to set the mood at the start. *Rich.*

Lonelyhearts

Disappointing film with Montgomery Clift and Robert Ryan for the marquee.

Hollywood, Nov. 28.

United Artists release of a Schary Production. Stars Montgomery Clift, Robert Ryan, Myrna Loy, Dolores Hart; introduces Maureen Stapleton; features Jackie Coogan, Mike Kellin, Frank Overton, Onslow Stevens, Frank Maxwell. Produced by Dore Schary. Directed by Vincent J. Donehue. Screenplay, Dore Schary, based on the book "Miss Lonelyhearts" by Nathanael West and the play by Howard Teichman; camera, John Alton; music, Conrad Salinger; editor, Aaron Stell. Previewed at the Academy Theatre, Nov. 21, '58. Running time, **101 MINS.**

Adam White	Montgomery Clift
William Shrike	Robert Ryan
Florence Shrike	Myrna Loy
Justy Sargent	Dolores Hart
Fay Doyle	Maureen Stapleton
Pat Doyle	Frank Maxwell
Gates	Jackie Coogan
Goldsmith	Mike Kellin
Mr. Sargent	Frank Overton
Older Brother	Don Washbrook

Younger Brother	John Washbrook
Mr. Lassiter	Onslow Stevens
Edna	Mary Alan Hokanson
Bartender	John Galludet
Jerry	Lee Zimmer

Dore Schary's first film is so-so. For the first half it's tedious, usually uneasy trip to nowhere. There is progress in much of the film's latter half, and United Artists will have to bank on this and a fine though distinctly offbeat and "tortured" performance by Montgomery Clift to help the film.

The property is cliche-ridden—the idealist who becomes disillusioned at the hands of the cynic; the cynic who, in the end, is softened by success of the idealist. Schary penned the screenplay from Nathanael West's "Miss Lonelyhearts" and Howard Teichmann's play of the same name. In its original version, the idealist is killed, but at Schary's discretion he goes off to become even more idealistic while the bitter man plucks a rose, wraps it in white paper and rushes off to forgive his wife for being an adulteress 10 years ago. The change is more elevating and certainly less sordid than the original, but it isn't sufficiently motivated and thus appears out of harmony with the rest of the film.

There are touches of warmth in Schary's script, most of them building the appealing character of young Clift. Not so with the cynical newspaper editor, as played by Robert Ryan. Here Schary's dialog—a kind of maudlin skepticism—grates heavily, and Vincent J. Donehue's direction makes something less than a man out of the character, the effect being more irritating than dramatic. Otherwise, Donehue handles the actors strongly as he deeply etches contrasts and human frailties. A good deal of the story is told in closeup.

Setting for the clash is a midwestern newspaper whose feature editor (Ryan) has minimum use for his fellow man. Clift joins the Chronicle and is assigned the "Lonelyhearts" column with which he is to answer problems and build circulation at the same time. A battle is waged between the two as Clift becomes involved with his "patients" while Ryan calls them fakers. The writer is challenged into following up one of the letters and finds Maureen Stapleton whose sad story has her husband a cripple and incapable of making love to her. Clift obliges the love-starved woman and, when he's led to believe the story was a fabrication aimed at "a little action," he falls apart. In rather contrived fashion, however, everything falls into a happy ending.

Dolores Hart, as Clift's fiancee, brings honest love from a bewildered man and, in so doing, glows with a spirited sensitivity. Myrna Loy, as Ryan's wife, handles with taste a part that offers practically nothing to do. Dramatic values gain considerably with the work of Miss Stapleton who, in her first film role, proves a powerful character actress. Excellent support comes from Frank Maxwell as the impotent husband, Jackie Coogan and Mike Kellin as two hack reporters, Frank Overton as Miss Hart's father and Onslow Stevens who, to complicate matters as Clift's father, is imprisoned for having murdered his wife and her lover.

Film fades in with a documentary flavor, and John Alton's photography remains in low-key throughout. Mood is maintained by work of art director Serge Krizman and composer Conrad Salinger, and film editor Aaron Stell appears to have put together with precision what there was to splice in the first place.

Schary's attempt at adult fare was an earnest one even if it didn't quite come out of the clouds. His mark as an independent producer will be welcome, but "Lonelyhearts" doesn't look to be the film that will make it. There is nothing quite as devastating as deliberately "adult" fare that doesn't come off. Regardless of how literate the dialog and how sincere the message, pictures like this still must tell their story in terms of the screen, with all its limitations and advantages. "Lonelyhearts" benefits from Schary's skill and integrity as a filmmaker and it's "offbeat" in an acceptable sense. It's obvious there's room today for pictures that "say something." *Ron.*

The Doctor's Dilemma
(BRITISH-COLOR)

Lush version of stagey Bernard Shaw period play. Useful arty theatre entry, with advantage of stellar names.

Metro release of a Comet production. Stars Dirk Bogarde, Leslie Caron; features Robert Morley, John Robinson, Felix Aylmer, Alastair Sim. Directed by Anthony Asquith. Screenplay, Anatole de Grunwald, from George Bernard Shaw's play; camera, Robert Kraaker; editor, Gordon Hales; music, Joseph Kosna. Previewed at Metro Private Theatre, London. Running time, **98 MINS.**

Jennifer Dudebat	Leslie Caron
Louis Dudebat	Dirk Bogarde
Cutler Walpole	Alastair Sim
Sir Ralph Bonington	Robert Morley
Sir Patrick Cullen	Felix Aylmer
Sir Colenso Ridgeon	John Robinson
Dr. Blenkinsop	Michael Gwynn
Emmy	Maureen Delaney
Redpenny	Alec McCowen
Newspaper Man	Colin Gordon
Minnie Tinwell	Gwenda Ewen
Mr. Lancaster	Terence Alexander

London, Dec. 2.

The success of "My Fair Lady" has whooped up a George Bernard Shaw vogue here; "The Doctor's Dilemma" thus was made into a pic. The magic initials "G.B.S." can surely be the only excuse for this one which takes the British motion picture biz back to the exciting, but troublesome days of Korda. In a film world which must face up grimly to the realistic economic facts of present day life, "Dilemma" looks a risky prestige venture.

It is handsomely produced, dressed and directed. It has Shaw's dialog and some good actors. But even with the names of Leslie Caron and Dirk Bogarde it still lines up merely as a worthwhile artyhouse booking. In Britain, it has been cynically suggested that its main hope of economic survival is that the run-of-the-mill ducat buyers will be confused into the belief that it is another of the highly successful "Doctor" series which has starred Bogarde in pix inspired by the humorous novels of Richard Gordon.

Shaw's stringent wit still shines in this film, but, staged in 1903, his comments on Harley Street (London's medical row) and the doctoring profession have by now lost much of their impact. "Dilemma" remains, relentlessly, an easy-on-the-eye filmed version of an out-of-date play. As a reminder of the plot, it concerns a young woman married to an artist who is a complete bounder—a sponger, a potential blackmailer and a man who can't resist other women.

But she is blinded by hero-worship. He suffers from consumption, she pleads with a doctor to save his life. He thinks that he would do better to use his limited serum on a more worthwhile case. And so the young artist dies, still a shining knight in armour to the starry-eyed young wife.

Bogarde gives a stimulating performance as the selfish young artist and is particularly convincing in his final, highly theatrical death sequence. Miss Caron is often moving in her blind belief in her man, but never suggests the strength necessary to fight the cynical doctors. These are played as caricatures.

Producer Anatole de Grunwald has spared no expense in lining up a team which gives Shaw's lusty medicinal characters the works. John Robinson is suitably stiff-upper-lipped as the bachelor specialist who knows Bogarde's reputation and prefers to save another man, despite his liking for Miss Caron. Alastair Sim, Robert Morley and Felix Aylmer play the roles of Harley Street fuddy-duddies with rich fun and vigor. There is also a good, neat performance by the ever-dependable Colin Gordon as an obtrusive journalist

Dedicated direction by Anthony Asquish and lush costumes by Cecil Beaton all add up to the richness of this film. But none of them can disguise the plain, implacable fact that "Dilemna" is an extravagant whim. **Admirers of Shaw's witty tilting at the chicanery of medicine in the early part of this century will still prefer the play. The emotional angle to the plot still stands up to modern day examination. The reason for making the film is more difficult to assess.** *Rich.*

House on Haunted Hill

From the producers of "Macabre," this well-made ghost story should build on that success.

Hollywood, Nov. 28.

Allied Artists release of William Castle-Robb White production. Stars Vincent Price, Carol Ohmart; features Richard Long, Alan Marshal, Carolyn Craig. Produced and directed by William Castle. Screenplay, Robb White; camera, Carl E. Guthrie; music, Von Dexter; editor, Roy Livingston. Previewed at Academy Awards Theatre, Nov. 24, '58. Running time, **75 MINS.**

Frederick Loren	Vincent Price
Annabelle Loren	Carol Ohmart
Lance Schroeder	Richard Long
Dr. David Trent	Alan Marshal
Nora Manning	Carolyn Craig
Watson Pritchard	Elisha Cook
Ruth Bridgers	Julie Mitchum
Mrs. Slykes	Leona Anderson
Jonas	Howard Hoffman

In the welter of grim and grisly pictures that make up the bulk of exploitation fare these days, there are few genuine ghost stories. Allied Artists did exceptionally well with one of these in "Macabre," earlier this year. Now the same producers, William Castle and Robb White, have come up with another in the same vein. The present item, "House on Haunted Hill," should build on the success of the former, to be a top exploitation grosser for its class.

White's screenplay, which Castle produced and directed, is the one about the group of people who promise to spend the night in a haunted house. In this case, it's pure monetary gain. Vincent Price, owner of the house, is offering $10,000 to anyone who lasts out the night. There is a gimmick in the plot which explains the screams, ghosts, bubbling vats of lye and perambulating skeltons, when it's finally explained that Price's wife, Carol Ohmart, has rigged the whole thing with her lover, Alan Marshal. They intended to have Price accidentally shot so she could get his money and be free to marry Marshal.

"Haunted Hill" is expertly put together. There is some good humor in the dialog which not only pays off well against the ghostly elements, but provides a release for laughter so it does not explode in the suspense sequences. The characters are interesting and not outlandish, so there is some basis of reality. Castle keeps things moving at a healthy clip.

Robb and Castle have a new gimmick on "House on Haunted Hill" called "Emergo." This device is an illuminated skeleton mounted on trolley wires, moving out from the side of the screen over the heads of the audience. It is a reasonably effective mechanism that will add to the picture's promotional qualities, without detracting from the film if theatre-owners elect to dispense with it.

Vincent Price gives a suave performance that carries suggested menace but is acceptable when it turns out the menace is coming from the other direction. Miss Ohmart is good as the wife, and others who contribute include Richard Long, Alan Marshal, Carolyn Craig and Elisha Cook.

It may seem like a small point, but it won't to exhibitors, to note that Carl Guthrie's photography is appropriately moody but not so low-key that it won't be suitable for the drive-ins. Von Dexter's music and the special effects by Herman Townsley contribute to the mood. *Powe.*

Tom Thumb
(SONGS; COLOR)

Novelty musical based on fairytale looks like a winner for holiday dates, strong on general release, and good reissue property.

Hollywood, Nov. 28.

Metro release of George Pal production. Stars Russ Tamblyn. Directed by Pal. Screenplay, Ladislas Fodor; based on the Grimm Bros. fairy tale; camera, Georges Perinal; music, Douglas Gamley and Ken Jones; editor, Frank Clarke. Previewed at the studio, Nov. 18, '58. Running time, **92 MINS.**

Tom Thumb	Russ Tamblyn
Woody	Alan Young
Ivan	Terry-Thomas
Tony	Peter Sellers
Anna	Jessie Matthews
The Forest Queen	June Thorburn
Jonathan	Bernard Miles
The Cobbler	Ian Wallace
and	
The Puppetoons	

The only thing lower case about this production is the Metro spelling of "tom thumb." Otherwise film is top-drawer, a comic fairy tale with music that stacks up alongside some of the Disney classics of similar nature. George Pal's fun-filled production for Metro will have a broader appeal than just for kids, and should be a winner for the studio on its original playdates as well as packing perennial, re-release appeal.

With the captivating special effects so ingeniously used, and likely to provide the greatest word-of-mouth on "tom thumb," it should not be obscured that this is really a musical comedy. It has five good songs, two by Peggy Lee, two by Fred Spielman and Janice Torre, and one by Spielman and Kermit Goell. There are musical production numbers, lavish and colorful. And while the basis for the picture is a children's story, its handling gives it plenty of diversion for adults.

The screenplay by Ladislas Fodor, from the Grimm Bros. fairy tale, is as pure simple as it can be. A childless couple, Bernard Miles and Jessie Matthews, are past the age when they can expect to have a child of their own. They get a miniature son, Russ Tamblyn, when wood-cutter Miles spares a special tree in the forest surrounding their home, and is rewarded by the Forest Queen, June Thorburn.

Complications in the story come from Tom's size, only five and one-half inches. There are villains, Terry-Thomas and Peter Sellers, attempting to use Tom for their own evil purposes. There is romance between Alan Young, a neighbor, and Miss Thorburn, finally un-bewitched (or whatever the technical term is) from a fairy queen to a real, live girl. Everything ends happily, unlike some fairy tales. The merry villagers are singing and dancing, the villains are put into chains and lovers and families are united.

Highlights of the production are the musical numbers and the special effects. Alex Romero staged the dance numbers, in which Tamblyn does some of the most athletic and exciting dancing he has had a chance at since "Seven Brides for Seven Brothers." Georges Perinal's photography, in color, with special effects by Tom Howard, catches all the fun and liveliness of the staging, and keeps tom's perspective firmly in hand. There is an absolute minimum of washout or wavering in the super-imposed photography.

Alan Young, as Tom's chief life-sized friend, has charm, and Miss Thorburn is a queen whether fairy or life-size. Terry-Thomas and Peter Sellers make a classic pair of comic villains, a hilarious combination of Rudolph Rassendale and Joe Weber ,complete with funny hat and Dutch low comedy accent). There is a wild parody of the adventure film fight scene between this pair and Young that is exciting in itself without any real fear or damage.

Bernard Miles is properly stolid as Tom's father, and Jessie Matthews, matronly and graying, is fine as his foster mother. Stan Freberg does the voice for one of the puppets, on "The Yawning Man" song, and Dal McKennon, for another, "Con-Fu-Shon," with humor.

The production preserves the mild horror of most fairy tales without letting it get out of hand for the youngsters. Pal's direction is equally sensitive to the difference between the gory and the gorgeously scary.

At the screening here for adults and kids, it was somewhat surprising (and heartening) to see the numbers of teen-agers who attended and obviously enjoyed the film.

Miss Lee's "tom thumb's tune" is obviously the big winner from the score, conducted with bounce by Muir Mathieson. The jingly song will probably be the winter's big novelty tune, with several recordings already out or on the way. The miniature work was done here in Hollywood, based on Pal's Puppetoon figures, and the life-size

work in London, with scoring there. In this respect, Frank Clarke's film editing is especially notable.
Powr.

Les Tricheurs
(The Cheats)
(FRENCH)

Paris, Nov. 25.
Corona release of Silver Films-Cinetel production. With Pascale Petit, Jacques Charrier, Andrea Parisy, Laurent Terzieff, Roland Lesaffre. Directed by Marcel Carne. Screenplay, Carne, Jacques Sigurd; camera, Claude Renoir; editor, Albert Jurgenson. At Marignan, Paris. Running time, **125 MINS.**
Mic .... Pascale Petit
Clo .... Andrea Parisy
Bob .... Jacques Charrier
Alain ....Laurent Terzieff
Roger .... Roland Lesaffre

This film purposts to treat a certain type of French youth whose maladjustments and antisocial behavior mainly take the form of a yen for Yank jazz, philosophizing about their free sex habits as showing their disdain of bourgeois habits, doing dangerous things, drinking and hopping in and out of bed on the Paris Left Bank.

But it is not as sexy as it sounds, for most of the shenanigans are only suggested or talked about. Pic is bogged down by too much dialog and pontificating by these youthful people who remain mostly symbols rather than real characters the audience can feel empathy for.

Story is mainly about a young man from the good side of the tracks who gets involved with this free-wheeling crowd. He falls for a girl and she for him, but their code eschews romance and her naive desire for a sports car even leads to doing a bit of blackmail.

Pic has various side issues. Shorn down to concentrate on the main theme, this could have art house possibility.

Direction of Marcel Carne is somewhat turgid and he is not helped by the fairly wooden work of a group of mostly unknown actors. The only ones giving some substance to their characters are Pascale Petit, as the doomed girl; Laurent Terzieff, as the machiavellian type; and Roland Lesaffre, as the more substantial brother of the mixed-up girl.

Technical credits are fine, but this film pussyfoots around the problem and ends up giving all sides.
Mosk.

Le Miroir a Deux Faces
(The Mirror Has Two Faces)
(FRENCH)

Paris, Nov. 25.
Gaumont release of Franco London Film production. Stars Michel Morgan, Bourvil; features Yvan Desny, Elisabeth Manet, Gerard Oury, Sandra Milo. Directed by Andre Cayatte. Screenplay, Oury, Cayatte; camera, Christian Matras; editor, Paul Cayatte. At Berlitz, Paris. Running time, **105 MINS.**
Marie-Jose .... Michele Morgan
Tardivet .... Bourvil
Gerard .... Yvan Desny
Veronique .... Elisabeth Manet
Bosc .... Gerard Oury
Ariane .... Sandra Milo

Slick melodrama has a gimmick in taking an ugly duckling wife and transforming her into the beauteous Michele Morgan. Then it studies the effects on her family, love life and the pros and cons on whether people are equipped for these sudden almost fairy tale transformations.

Though pic has some sudsy aspects, it is well made and could emerge a good arty house entry for foreign spots, or even for general bookings.

Miss Morgan plays the homely miss who loves her brother-in-law secretly, but finally marries a selfish, oafish, petty little teacher. She bears his boorishness even though the film makes out that she is sensitive, intelligent and fine underneath deserving a face to match.

Fate brings this about when her husband has an accident with the auto of a plastic surgeon who offers to remake her face as compensation. She does it on the sly and it brings on the film's complications as she finds true love. The husband ends up killing the doctor.

Pic is somewhat tiresome in giving all sides of the question verbally, but rarely transposing it filmically. Miss Morgan does well with the homely aspect but is much too well groomed and a film star to make her metamorphosis really taking. Bourvil is competent as the husband. Technical credits are fine. But ex-lawyer, now director, Andre Cayatte, has allowed too much explanation to bog the action.
Mosk.

The Lost Missile

Routine science fiction, highlighted by some fair special effects and well-used stock.

Hollywood, Nov. 28.
United Artists release of William Berke production. Stars Robert Loggia and Ellen Parker. Produced by Lee Gordon. Directed by Lester William Berke. Screenplay, John McPartland and Jerome Bixby; based on a story by Lester William Berke; camera, Kenneth Peach; music, Gerald Fried; editor, Ed Sutherland. Previewed at Goldwyn studio, Nov. 26, '58. Running time, **70 MINS.**
David Loring .... Robert Loggia
Joan Woods .... Ellen Parker
General Barr .... Larry Kerr
Joe Freed .... Philip Pine
Ella Freed .... Marilee Earle
TV Personality .... Fred Engleberg
Ella's mother .... Kitty Kelly
Secretary of State ...... Selmer Jackson
Young .... Joe Hyams
Bradley .... Bill Bradley

"The Lost Missile," last production by the late William Berke, should fit neatly into the science-fiction exploitation market. It is strong on its use of stock footage and special effects, less so in its portrayal of human elements. But it is tightly made and should be a satisfactory entry. United Artists is releasing

There is plenty left unexplained in the John McPartland-Jerome Bixby screenplay, based on a story by Lester William Berke (son of the late producer). Its plot is based on what happens when a missile from outer space gets into the earth's atmosphere, and by the heat of its velocity starts cindering cities and population. It's impervious to ordinary means of destruction, until atomic scientist Robert Loggia devises a make-shift, with a "baby" hydrogen warhead inside a Nike missile. This works and destroys the missile before it gets to New York City, although it has already crisped Ottawa and points between.

Best points of the production— a joint U.S.-Canadian effort—are the results of the research on the stock footage by Berke and producer Lee Gordon. This, with the runaway missile, provide the greatest interest and reality. Ed Sutherland, who edited, has also done a capable job, and Kenneth Peach's photography fits well.

The actors are less happily served by the screenplay, which is not always too clear on sequence and goes overboard heavily for melodrama. Dialog tends to be oratorical, particularly in high-

echelon scenes involving civilian and military officials. Of the cast, Loggia, Larry Kerr, Ellen Parker, Philip Pine and Marilee Earle come off best.
Powe.

The Tempest
(ITALIAN-YUGOSLAV-FRENCH)
(V'vision-Technicolor)

Naples, Dec. 2.

Dino DeLaurentiis release of a Dino DeLaurentiis-Bosna Film (Sarajevo) production (in partnership with Gray Films, Paris). Stars Silvana Mangano, Van Hefflin, Viveca Lindfors, Geoffrey Horne; features Vittorio Gassmann, Aldo Silvani, Fulvia Franco, Claudio Gora, Jovan Gec, Guido Celano, Cristina Gajoni, Helmut Dantine, Agnes Moorehead, Robert Keith, Finlay Currie, Lawrence Naismith, Dragutin Felba, Nevenka Mikulic, Janez Vrhovec, Milutin Jasnik, Mavid Popovic, Niksa Stefanini, Pera Obradovic, Mirko Sereckovic. Directed by Alberto Lattuada. Screenplay, Lattuada, Luis Peterson, and Ivo Perilli, from work of Alekasnder Puchkin; camera (Technicolor-Technirama), Aldo Tonti; sets, Mario Chiari; editor, Otello Colangeli, Henry Rust; music, Piero Piccioni. Previewed at San Carlo Opera House, Naples. Running time, **121 MINS.**

Masha .... Silvana Mangano
Pugacev .... Van Heflin
Catherine II .... Viveca Lindfors
Peter Griniev .... Geoffrey Horne
Capt. Mironov .... Robert Keith
Vasilisa .... Agnes Moorehead
Savelic .... Oscar Homolka
Svabrin .... Helmut Dantine
Prosecutor .... Vittorio Gassmann
Palaska .... Fulvia Franco
Count Griniev .... Finlay Currie
Major Zurin .... Lawrence Naismith
Pope Gerasim .... Aldo Silvani
Akulina .... Nevenka Mikulic
Suvorov .... Milivoi Zivanovic
Capt. Dimitri .... Javon Gec
Beloborodov .... Niksa Stefanini
Sokolov .... Janez Vrhovec
Minister .... Claudio Gora
Girl .... Maria Cristina Gajoni
Pugacev chief ... Milivoje Pepovic Mavid
Bashir prisoner .... Milutin Jasnik
Peasant .... Guido Celano
Woman on cart .... Marija Crnobori

Dino DeLaurentiis' "The Tempest" should prove just that—at the boxoffice. Despite a generally weaker marquee appeal than the producer's "War and Peace," it has the potential to top that more expensive pic, and looks headed for the top money brackets. Film's claimed $2,000,000 budget includes a minority contrbution from Paramount (which, however, has most foreign distrib rights). This Yank investment also should prove highly profitable.

Production-wise, the pic shows many times the budget spent on it in physical values while the Yugoslav-locationed footage (with its lavish use of manpower and horses) shows the tremendous possibilities of well-planned co-productions. Both the action-spectacle public as well as the more discerning patron should go for this item, thanks to an expert balance struck between film's epic qualities and the generally tasteful handling of the story line, script and dialog.

Print shown here was Italian-language, said to be identical to English one in cutting. Italo-dubbing was not top-quality, indicating a rush job. The U.S. print is considered the "original" version of the pic.

"The Tempest" not to be confused with the Shakespeare play (and this presents a major problem of titling for English-language countries, where the Bard's classic could bring about a damaging mix-up), is based on two works by Alexander Pushkin, "The Captain's Daughter" and "The Revolt of Pugacev." Splice is ably effected, with accent placed on the latter.

Plot concerns an officer of the Empress' guard who is punished by being sent to a remote post in the Russian hinterlands. On the way, he saves a Cossack from freezing. The man he's saved becomes the famed rebel leader, Pugacev, who, as self-titled Tzar Peter III leads a peasant-Cossack revolt against Catherine II. Officer, who has meanwhile fallen for the daughter of the remote fort's commandant (thus incurring jealousy of a rival, Svabrin) is captured by Pugacev when the fort falls to the latter's forces, but released when the rebel recognizes the man who saved him.

Back in St. Petersburg, the officer is suspected a friend and spy of Pugacev's. Finally he flees to join his girl, succeeding in convincing the rebel to let him marry her, despite the villainous intentions of Svabrin.

Dominant figure of this historical fresco is Van Heflin and his portrayal of the fiery rebel leader. It's an arresting effort. Silvana Mangano's interpretation of Masha is one of her better ones, while Geoffrey Horne makes an okay opposite number to her as Peter Griniev. Agnes Moorehead socks across her character of Masha's mother and wife of fort commander Robert Keith, another excellent rendering.

Oscar Homolka gives another one of his colorful and expert performances as Griniev's faithful sidekick-servant Savelic. Helmut Dantine is fully at ease as the villainous Svabrin. In for a brief but effective (and decorative) cameo is Viveca Lindfors, as the Empress of Russia. A long list of feature roles are ably set forth by such character thesps as Finlay Currie (the elder Griniev), Vittorio Gassmann (the prosecutor), Lawrence Naismith (Major Zurin) and other Italian and Yugoslav actors in the huge cast.

Alberto Lattuada's script and direction keep the story line clear and fast-paced. In a period of inflated running times, the film's concise two hours show that a tale of epic proportions after all can be told in a reasonable 120 minutes. Actually, the edited-down final print has the audience wishing for more of the top scenes such as the two main battles, the spring festival, etc. It's an effective leaf borrowed from the stage, and makes for a compact, rich, untiring diet of spectacle and plot.

Top moments of "Tempest" are undeniably the spectacular ones. Rarely if ever have such battle scenes been seen, combining bigness with color, excitement and above all a clear idea of what is going on. Topping all are the two main cavalry attacks, effectively highlighted via camera angles and a perfectly-used sound track to show the power of mass (cavalry) movement.

Other major plus factors are the spring festival sequence, a riot of color aptly used to set a mood or character. The execution of Keith by the rebels, highlighted by a powerful and chilling scene as Agnes Moorehead damns the murderous rebels and their chief; the capture of Pugacev by the Tzar's forces.

On the debit side in a certain lack of audience participation in love interest, despite a very effective initial love scene between Miss Mangano and Horne. Also, some of the characters are stereos and often lack depth—but then, that would have led to longer running time.

Producer and director have generally succeeded in their efforts at a quality spectacle kept almost throughout on a tasteful level, rarely slipping into the obvious or banal. There's no mistaking the fact that pic locationed in various parts of Yugoslavia, and nowhere before in a west-produced film (not even in DeLaurentiis' previous "War and Peace") has the genuineness of place been so striking.

Technically, the pic is a fine achievement. The sharp, rich Technicolor - Technirama - processed hues, lensed by Aldo Tonti, do full justice to the Mario Chiari-Maria de Matteis team (sets and costume design) who also worked on "War and Peace." Piero Piccioni's music is perhaps the weakest element.

Granted the relative shortage of top marquee names, but given the production expenditure, the resulting pic spells production value with a capital "V." *Hawk.*

Machete

Routine filler.

Hollywood, Dec. 5.

United Artists release of a J. Harold Odell Production. Stars Mari Blanchard, Albert Dekker; costars Juano Hernandez, Carlos Rivas, Lee Van Cleef, Ruth Cains, Produced and directed by Kurt Neumann. Screenplay by Carroll Young and Neumann; camera, Karl Struss; editor, Jodie Copelan; music, Paul Sawtell and Bert Shefter. Previewed at Goldwyn Studios, Nov. 24, '58. Running time, **75 MINS.**

Jean .... Mari Blanchard
Don Luis Montoya .... Albert Dekker
Bernardo .... Juano Hernandez
Carlos .... Carlos Rivas
Miguel .... Lee Van Cleef
Rita .... Ruth Cains

The tale of the middle-aged plantation owner whose young bride falls in love with the foreman was a hackneyed plot when screens were square.

The J. Harold Odell production for United Artists release was produced and directed by the late Kurt Neumann who obviously didn't take the time and patience he did with his last film, "The Fly." Screenplay was penned by Carroll Young and Neumann.

"Machete" takes place in Puerto Rico on a sugar cane plantation that sweeps wide and reaps heavily for owner Albert Dekker. When he brings home his new wife, Mari Blanchard, she puts on the lure for Carlos Rivas, manager of the spread, whom Dekker has raised from childhood. Both men are good and have the greatest respect for each other, so the only solution when the blonde comes between them is for the femme to die. And so she does, with death coming in the midst of a field fire.

Dekker, who mostly leers, has done a whole lot better in most previous outings. Miss Blanchard looks the part, and Rivas turns in the best all-around performance. Okay are Lee Van Cleef as a trouble-making cousin, Juano Hernandez as Dekker's close aide and Ruth Cains as a young native girl.

Karl Struss' photography catches the wind-blown effect of the islands, while the Paul Sawtell-Bert Shefter musical score is a plus. Jodie Copelan's film editing is capable, and sound by Howard Warren varies from proficient to tinny. *Ron.*

Uncle Tom's Cabin
(WITH VOICE & MUSIC TRACK)

Dixie integration crisis provides the exploitation market for this reissue. Old 'Massah' Lincoln interpreter Raymond Massey handles the updated narration.

Jules B. Weill and Carroll L. Puciato (Colorama Features) reissue of Universal silent production of 1926. New continuity by Sheldon Stark and Marian Kraft, narrated by Raymond Massey. Original director, Harry Pollard. Reviewed Dec. 2, '58, at Trans-Lux, N.Y. Running time, **93 MINS.**

Uncle Tom .... James B. Lowe
Eliza .... Margarita Fischer
Little Eva .... Virginia Grey
Topsy .... Mona Ray
Simon Legree .... George Siegmann
Cassie .... Eulalie Jensen
Aunt Ophelia .... Aileen Manning
George Harris .... Arthur Edmond Carew
Mrs. Shelby .... Vivian Oakland
Mr. Shelby .... Jack Mower
Tom Loker .... J. Gordon Russell
Marks .... Lucien Littlefield
Mrs. St. Clare .... Gertrude Astor
Mr. St. Clare .... John Roche
Phineas Fletche .... Nelson McDowell

Today's segregation tension in Dixie has brought scattered revivals and playdates for the pro-Ku Klux Klan 1915 silent, "Birth of a Nation." Now comes the Northern answer, a reissue of the 1926 silent version of "Uncle Tom's Cabin" made by Universal.

The D. W. Griffith 1915 film is, of course, an authentic work of great artistry. The Harry Pollard direction of the Harriet Beecher Stowe work was never of comparable impact or significance but both pictures have this much in common: a power to evoke emotion and to prove, not that proof is needed, that the race issue is deep-rooted in American feeling —and, showmen therefor assume plausibly, that the subject has boxoffice potential.

Via their Colorama office Jules B. Weill and Carroll L. Puciato set a Broadway showcasing at the Trans-Lux. The film opens with Raymond Massey (old Massah Lincoln!) visiting the birthplace of the authoress in Litchfield, Conn. Standing before the old carriage barn, he muses on the 100-year-old propaganda novel and prepares the audience to accept the "over-emphatic" screen acting of the silent era. The story then picks up with the Shelbys, those helpless, hand-wringing gentle folk who made Uncle Tom a privileged, happy slave and Eliza an educated inside maid. Massey's voice and a recorded music score of the late Erno Rapee ride the sound track.

The immediate questions which arise as to "Uncle Tom's Cabin" in this reissue form are (a) the quality of the film and (b) the entertainment and social implications of the theme. Though the prolog footage is brighter and sharper in grain than the original somewhat low-key photography, the film has stood the ravages of time well.

The editing seems competent with one glaring exception, the ridiculous feat of derring-do by the Quaker farmer on the Ohio side of the river. Besting Tarzan of the apes and Douglas Fairbanks of the magic carpet, this Quaker hangs by his legs and seizes Eliza and her child just at the brink of the falls. This is a yowl. There is no need for preserving this absurd rescue, as Eliza is almost across the river well before. The Quaker acrobat, worthy of the centre ring with Barnum & Bailey, spoils a certain plausible make-believe in the crossing.

Universal's scenario of 1926 projected Simon Legree into the final moments of the Confederacy and shows the arrival along the plantation road of a brigade of Yankee cavalry. They rescue the Negro wenches from Legree precisely as the hooded Klansmen in "Birth" rescue Lillian Gish from the Negro!—though not with the directorial skill and excitement achieved by Griffith.

Just how much booking and boxoffice potency remains in "Uncle Tom" is a matter of guess. Recent datings of "Birth" in such Northern spots as Philadelphia, Minneapolis and Baltimore (making "Birth of A Nation" a foreign art import from Dixie) may or may not imply that "Uncle Tom" can play Atlanta or Birmingham. Supposition would limit this reissue mostly to Northern exploitation situations.

Exploitation possibilities include arousal of history teachers, social science angles. The distributors have retained the N. Y. public relations firm headed by Ware Lynch (still known as Russell Birdwell Associates) to stir up the brethren.

Oldtimers in show business must have read the Broadway marquee signs "See Eliza Crossing the Ice." "Meet Saintly Eva! Fun loving Topsy" with memories of yesteryear show business, not forgetting the Duncan Sisters. There is not much surprise in the pop-eyed histrionics of Margarita Fischer's Eliza and the desperate sweetness of her curly-haired son (unbilled) and other characters. Actually many of the big-budget values of Universal's 1926 try for blockbuster still show. Especially memorable are the pantomimic achievements of a slave-trader played by Lucien Littiefield and the tobacco-chewing, leering villainy of George Siegmann, a truly plausible Legree, if sexual rather than economic motivations are assumed dominant. His death is actually an accidental fall. The Yankee soldiers do not hang him on the screen as they probably would have in reality.

Eva? She's as tubercular and as saintly as the stereotypic background of the role. Virginia Grey was Universal's candidate. Mona Ray played Topsy in cork (as did all the Negroes of Griffith's "Birth" nine years before).

The Civil War's start will be marked in 1961 as 100 years ago. This film is, in its hokey-pokey way, part of the background. It is a far fuller tale than the average of "exploitation" film today.

Land.

Night of the Blood Beast

At last — a pregnant man! Horrorific exploitioner. Should fare well. Coupled with "She Gods of Shark Reef."

Hollywood, Dec. 5.

American International Pictures release of a James H. Nicholson and Samuel Z. Arkoff Production. Stars Michael Emmet, Angela Greene, John Baer. Executive producer, Roger Corman. Produced by Gene Corman. Directed by Bernard L. Kowalski. Screenplay and story by Martin Varnof; camera, John Nicholaus; editor, Jodie Copelan; music supervision, Alexander Laszlo. Reviewed at the Vogue Theatre, Dec. 3, '58. Running time, **65 MINS.**

Major John Corcoran	Michael Emmet
Dr. Julie Benson	Angela Greene
Steve Dunlap	John Baer
Dave Randall	Ed Nelson
Dr. Alex Wyman	Tyler McVey
Donna Bixby	Georgianna Carter
The Creature	Rose Sturlin

It's finally happened—someone wrote a story about a pregnant man! Well, not exactly pregnant. Actually, he breeds embryos of outer space creatures while the parent monster is busy taking over the earth. The film is "Night of the Blood Beast," a respectfully suspenseful picture that is the better half of a new American International package. Sold with "She Gods of Shark Reef," pic lends itself to exploitation and should return ample rewards.

When Michael Emmet has disastrous trouble as the first earthman in space, he returns with a bound that results in no heart beat, pulse or pressure. "But," says Tyler McVey, head medico, "his tissues won't dissipate." It turns out a monster from a world destroyed by nuclear blasts gains entrance to the earth by returning with the spaceman, and it's his intention to save the earth from self-destruction. He uses the "dead" spaceman's body to breed the beasties, seen in all their glory through a fluoroscope. The monster generally is sympathetic, and for the most part it seems he truly is benevolent, but in the end the earthmen figure his sole motive is not to save the earth but to reestablish his own civilization down here. They hurl Molotov cocktails, aim their Very pistols, and the monster is burned to death while telling his opponents that they aren't ready for him.

Gene Corman produced in capable fashion, while Bernard L. Kowalski directed to the point of bringing adequate performances from everyone including Ross Sturlin as the creature. Best of the cast, which includes Emmet, McVey, Angela Greene, Ed Nelson and Georgianna Carter, is John Baer as a faithful member of the earth party.

Martin Varno scripted from his own story, and although the screenplay does fall into expected pitfalls, it is strong enough to sustain interest all the way. Technical credits are competent, from John Nicholaus Jr.'s photography to Jodie Copelan's editing, Alexander Laszlo's music supervision and Dan Haller's art direction. *Ron.*

The Hot Angel

Juve exploitation item. Some novel angles.

Hollywood, Dec. 5.

Paramount release of Stanley Kallis production. Stars Jackie Loughery, Edward Kemmer, Mason Alan Dinehart. Directed by Joe Parker; screenplay by Kallis; camera, Karl Struss; music, Richard Markowith; editors, Eda Warren and Leon Selditz. Previewed at the studio, Dec. 3, '58. Running time, **73 MINS.**

Mandy Wilson	Jackie Loughery
Chuck Lawson	Edward Kemmer
Joe Wilson	Mason Alan Dinehart
Judd Pfeifer	Emory Parnell
Van Richards	Lyle Talbot
Mick Pfeifer	Zon Teller
Lynn Conners	Heather Ames
Myrna	Steffi Sidney
Ray	John Nolan
Monk	Richard Stauffer
Liz	Kathi Thornton
Pilot	Harold Mallet

"The Hot Angel" is a low-budget feature about and for that category called teenagers. To its credit, the Stanley Kallis production for Paramount does not make its youthful criminals (delinquents seems much to mild a term) attractive. It even makes maturity an admirable and attractive quality. But is also has those exploitation values that seem to spell success for these features and it will undoubtedly do the usual flash business.

The picture, well directed by Joe Parker, even has something new for plot interest and exploitation. Instead of motorcycle or hot rod racing and "chicken" stunts, the teenagers this time are transferred to the sky. The "angle" of the title refers to light planes, and the "hot" to the fact that there is some action with the planes involved.

Mason Alan Dinehart plays the good teenager in Kallis' screenplay, a young man who has somehow fallen in with the black leather jacket and equally black-fingernail set, to the distress of his older sister, Jackie Loughery. She enlists the aid of pilot Edward Kemmer, a wartime friend of Dinehart's big brother, who was killed in action. Kemmer soon has Dinehart convinced that it is better to fly in a plane than just to attempt it from the seat of a motorcycle. There is some hocus-pocus about uranium mines and assorted skulduggery, but it's not too important, or, for that matter, too clear. The important story point is the boy's growth into something like manhood, and that point's made.

Kemmer and Miss Loughery handle the adult interest capably, and Dinehart makes a nice, husky juvenile, pretty brawny but also no square, in head-shape or anything else. Others important and interesting are Emory Parnell, Lyle Talbot, Zon Teller, Heatheames and Steffi Sidney.

Aerial photography by Elmer G. Dyer of the Grand Canyon is interesting, and Karl Struss handles ground camera work for maximum values. Richard Markowitz' musical score is notable, as these scores so often are on low budget pictures, economy apparently being the father of invention. *Powe.*

She-Gods of Shark Reef
(PATHECOLOR)

Weaker half of American International package.

Hollywood, Dec. 5.

American International Pictures release of a Ludwig H. Gerber production. Stars Don Durant, Lisa Montell, Bill Cord; features Jeanne Gerson, Carol Lindsay. Directed by Roger Corman. Screenplay by Robert Hill and Victor Stoloff; camera, Floyd Crosby; editor, Frank Sullivan; music, Ronald Stein. Reviewed at the Vogue Theatre, Dec. 3, '58. Running time, **63 MINS.**

Lee	Don Durant
Chris	Bill Cord
Mahia	Lisa Montell
Dua	Jeanne Gerson
Hula Dancer	Carol Lindsay

Completed a year and a half ago and just now released by American International, "She-Gods of Shark Reef" boasts fine color, rich red blood, capable underwater photography and very little story. It's being booked with "Night of the Blood Beast," and with promotion the package should do well.

Pic was lensed in Pathecolor in the Hawaiian Islands and tells the story of two American brothers, one escaping from the police, the other simply helping. They shipwreck near a Pacific island inhabited by pearl-diving femmes and are saved by the most luscious of them all, Lisa Montell. The good brother falls in love with the girl, saves her from death when the sharks are about to devour her and leaves the island with her to find happiness together. The bad brother goes the way of all bad brothers.

Don Durant and Bill Cord play the brothers in the Ludwig H. Gerber production. Both appear on the screen for the first time, and the credit for two performances that, if not highly professional, are at least believable, goes to director Roger Corman. Miss Montell makes a fetching native girl; acting well and looking better. Jeanne Gerson is sufficiently hard as the native leader, and Carol Lindsay does a whoppingly good hula.

Screenplay by Robert Hill and Victor Stoloff is full of broken English for the Polynesians and okay dialog for the Yanks, but there just isn't enough substance to the going-on. Cameraman Floyd Crosby did very well with the Pacific colors, and competent work also was done by film editor Frank Sullivan, sound editor, Robert Post and music supervisor Ronald Stein. Sylvia Sims warbles a pleasant tune, "Nearer My Love To You," behind the titles, with the Jack Lawrence-Frances Hall song likely to get some play from its Decca recording. *Ron.*

Murder by Contract

Suspenseful story of a paid killer's last assignment, suitable for program market.

Hollywood, Dec. 5.

Columbia Pictures release of Leon Chooluck production. Stars Vince Edwards; costars Phillip Pine, Herschel Bernardi; features Caprice Toriel, Michael Granger, Cathy Browne, Joseph Mell, Frances Osborne. Directed by Irving Lerner. Screenplay, Ben Simcoe; camera, Lucian Ballard; editor, Carlo Lodato; music, Perry Botkin. Previewed Dec. 5, '58. Running time, **80 MINS.**

Claude	Vince Edwards
Marc	Phillip Pine
George	Herschel Bernardi
Moon	Michael Granger
Billie Williams	Caprice Toriel

"Murder by Contract" is the story of a paid killer. The Leon Chooluck production has the benefit of mounting suspense, after a haphazard opening, and story is sufficiently interesting to make it a pretty fair entry for the program market.

Interest centers around Vince Edwards, an unemotional executioner who takes on a major assignment in Los Angeles after handling several eastern commitments with speed and dispatch. His victim here is a woman, who is to testify against his underworld employer. Events are given slick motivation in the Ben Simcoe screenplay, as two efforts fail to kill the woman who is surrounded by guards in her palatial home. His third attempt, after he finally gets to her inside her house and he chickens in a try to garrot her, leads to his own death by police gunfire.

Edwards is strongly cast as the killer and provides a quiet menace which pays off in audience attention. Direction by Irving Lerner is brisk as he persuasively guns his characters, several of whom are topnotch. Phillip Pine and Herschel Bernardi lend conviction as the killer's confederates, jittery because of the casualness with which he undertakes his assignment and who are killed after he learns they have been commissioned from above to rub him out after his two failures. Caprice Toriel, in briefly as the intended victim, nevertheless makes her work count, and Cathy Browne and Michael Granger likewise score in small roles.

A standout music score by Perry Botkin, using only a guitar which he plays to perfection, gives fine atmospheric backing, and editing by Carlo Lodato, via use of the clipped scene technique, is fast. Lucien Ballard's camera work is interesting and art direction by Jack Poplin is okay. *Whit.*

Maxime
(FRENCH)

Paris, Dec. 9.

Cocinor release of Raoul Ploquin production. Stars Michele Morgan, Charles Boyer, Arletty; features Felix Marten, Jacques Dufilho. Directed by Henri Verneuil. Screenplay, Henri Jeanson, Alfred Valentin from novel by Henri Duvernois; camera, Christian Matras; editor, Gabriel Rognier. At Biarritz, Paris. Running time, **125 MINS.**

Maxime	Charles Boyer
Jacqueline	Michele Morgan
Gazelle	Arletty
Hubert	Felix Marten
Flick	Jacques Dufilho
Liliane	Micheline Luccioni

Insouciant love drama, taking place in early 1914, has a bittersweet frank tang which could make this a good arty house bet. It is well acted and mounted and gives a frank look at age and love. It does not look to be too much of a general entry on its talkiness and length, but wise pruning and the Michele Morgan and Charles Boyer names could extend its overseas appeal.

An aging dandy, Boyer, is the factotum and arranger of female conquests for a brusque young millionaire, Felix Marten. Film concerns his job of softening up rich and haughty Michele Morgan, who has spurned Marten's advances. But love comes to Boyer and goes on even when she discovers he is destitute. But youth and money will be served, and he loses her to Marten when his age and her inherent female needs make her choose the young man.

This is a smooth, adroitly dialoged vehicle. It has knowing, telling shafts about age, love and manners of the time. Film deftly brings out its drama sans any mawkishness, self-pity or sentimentalizing. It is a frothy drama-comedy in the good French manner and thus should have possibilities abroad. Technically it is tops, with fine acting from such troupers as Boyer, Miss Morgan and Arletty playing rings around the younger members of the cast.

Mosk.

Der Nuernberger Prozess
(The Nuremberg Trial)
(GERMAN)

Berlin, Dec. 2.
Prisma release of Continent-Film production. Directed by Felix von Podmanitzky. Commentator, Jochen Willke. Based on a series of articles by Joe J. Heydecker and Johannes Leeb, published in "Muenchner Illustrierte." At Studio, Berlin. Running time, **90 MINS.**

This is a very interesting, important documentary film, particularly for young Germans who are not too familiar with their country's unholy (Hitler) past. An important reminder also for those who are apt to forget certain things too easily. Despite some technical deficiencies, the film recommends itself for export. Some of the scenes reportedly have never shown (at least not in this country) before.

Very objectively, film depicts via exceptionally authentic documentary material, the way of Nazism during its heydays up to its collapse. As the title reveals, it mainly dedicates itself to the sentencing of the Nazi war criminals at Nuremberg, the biggest trial the world has known. Woven in are newsreel shots of "history-making" speeches by the Nazi leaders (the "Fuehrer" himself, Goering, Goebbels, etc.).

Some very impressive footage is of Russian origin: The march of the defeated German Stalingrad army through the Soviet capital. Scenes of the Nazi tribunal against the men of the 20th of June, 1944, who plotted to overthrow the brutal Hitler regime. The most shocking scenes are in excerpts from Allied-made films about Hitler's hell camps, giving evidence of the incredible brutality.

This film can skip any polemics all scenes speak for themselves. Technically, "Trial" is not smooth all the way. Often it appears jumpy if not disorderly, but these flaws are secondary in view of the fact that this film has a praiseworthy honest and objective attitude. It has been declared particularly valuable by the West German classification board which means considerable tax relief.

Hans.

The Buccaneer
(VISTAVISION—COLOR)

Strong on production and names, including "supervisor" Cecil B. DeMille, but wordy, where action would have been preferred.

Paramount release of Henry Wilcoxon production as "supervised" by Cecil B. DeMille. Stars Yul Brynner, Charlton Heston, Claire Bloom, Charles Boyer, Inger Stevens; features Henry Hull, E. G. Marshall, Lorne Greene, Ted de Corsia, Douglas Dumbrille, Robert F. Simon, Jerry Hartleben, Fran Jeffries. Directed by Anthony Quinn. Screenplay, Jesse L. Lasky Jr. and Bernice Mosk, from screenplay by Harold Lamb, Edwin Justis Mayer and C. Gardner Sullivan, based on Jeanie Macpherson's adaptation of "Lafitte the Pirate" by Lyle Saxon; camera (Vista-Vision-Technicolor), Loyal Griggs; editor, Archie Marshek; music, Elmer Bernstein. Previewed at Paramount homeoffice, N.Y., Dec. 8, '58. Running time 121 **MINS.**

Jean Lafitte	Yul Brynner
Andrew Jackson	Charlton Heston
Bonnie Brown	Claire Bloom
Dominique You	Charles Boyer
Annette Claiborne	Inger Stevens
Ezra Peavey	Henry Hull
Gov. Claiborne	E. G. Marshall
Mercier	Lorne Greene
Capt. Rumbo	Ted de Corsia
Collector of Port	Douglas Dumbrille
Capt. Brown	Robert F. Simon
Scipio	Sir Lancelot
Cariba	Fran Jeffries
Deacon	John Dierkes
Sentry	Ken Miller
Pyke	George Mathews
Capt. McWilliams	Leslie E. Bradley
Gramby	Bruce Gordon
Commodore Patterson	Barry Kelley
Capt. Lockyer	Robert Warwick
Beluche	Steven Marlo
Whipple	James Todd
Miggs	Jerry Hartleben
Customs Inspector	Onslow Stevens
Marie Claiborne	Theodora Davitt
Lt. Shreve	Wally Richard
Wench	Iris Adrian
Creole Officer	James Seay
Tripes	Reginald Sheffield
Col. Butler	Stephen Chase
Woman	Julia Faye
Toro	Woodrow Strode
Capt. Flint	Paul Newlan
Mme. Hilaire	Norma Varden
Dragoon Captain	John Hubbard
Rocket Officer	Brad Johnson
Captain, Corinthian	Harry Shannon
Major	Henry Brandon
Girl at Spinet	Billie Lee Hart
Mouse	Ashley Cowen
Miguel	Julio de Diego
Orlando Corona	Manuel Rojas
Lobo	Syl Lamont
Horse-Face	Paul Wexler
Tina	Kathleen Freeman
Little Girl	Mimi Gibson
Chighizola	Leonard Graves
Junior Senator	Raymond Greenleaf
Capt. Bart	Frederick Ledebur
Major Reed	Judd Holdren
Lt. Rogers	Robin Hughes
Hans	Jack Kruschen
Naval Aide	Harlan Warde
Senior Senator	Charles Meredith
Tarsus	Mike Mazurki
Major Latour	Alberto Morin
Cato	Chester Jones
Pirates	Mickey Finn, Eric Alden, Jack Pennick, Frank Hagney

There's a winning combination of boxoffice values that suggests "The Buccaneer" is a likely success for the initial dates—thanks to names and a wham campaign. Romance is effectively brought in the Cecil B. DeMille-supervised production that focuses on the colorful historical character of Jean Lafitte. The names include Yul Brynner, Charlton Heston, Claire Bloom and Charles Boyer.

On the deficit side, and making "Buccaneer" a nervous entry, is a wordy script that lacks any large degree of excitement. While the property is bound to attract a wide audience at the start, the facts are that limited imagination in the presentation is showing and bound to be a detriment in the full commercial playoff.

It's a first-time-out for Henry Wilcoxon as producer, after several credits as associate to DeMille, with the latter now in the role of "supervisor." It marks the debut, too, for Anthony Quinn as director. DeMille appears in a prologue to cite chapter and verse anent the role Lafitte played in American history. And from there on in the audience is given an insight of the person of Lafitte who, by his own acknowledgement, is not the peg-legged pirate the on-looker might have hoped to see.

Instead, he's a gentlemanly type, indeed almost a suave cosmopolite equally at home at a governor's ball as he is at seafaring adventure. This may be historical accuracy on DeMille's part but it amounts to a letdown for the viewer who had come to expect a swashbuckler. A crossed-blades adventure in the DeMille tradition of spectacle would have been more desirable.

Continuity-wise, "Buccaneer" is a scrambled affair in the early reels. Under Quinn's direction, or due to a job of editing that invites criticism, one scene segues into the next in what amounts to a disconcerting sequence. Open to question, also, are the story angles in the Jesse Lasky Jr.-Bernice Mosk screenplay which derives from a previous "Buccaneer" scenario put out by DeMille more than 20 years ago and, in turn, from an adaptation of the original book by Lyle Saxon.

It's the War of 1812 against Britain and the battle arena in New Orleans. The action takes place on land except for the sinking of one ship, which is curiously underplayed, by a renegade buccaneer. For the audience this is little more than flash information, pictorially, and yet it amounts to a key point in the story. Lafitte, as played by Brynner, admits to responsibility for the massacre of the passengers. But it doesn't look at all like he was responsible, and his banishment from the States, to which he was loyal, hardly seems fitting.

Highpoint is the land battle between Andrew Jackson's forces and the British, with Jackson aided by Lafitte's personnel and ammunition. The British, like so many toy soldiers, go down in defeat as Lafitte rules the mast.

Inconsistencies in story content aside, there was a major effort in production. Some of the backgrounding by producer Wilcoxon is solid and effective. This certainly looks like the '12 battle in terms of authenticity of backdrops and costumes; and performances are in keeping with the proper times and places. Brynner is masterly as the pirate. Charlton Heston is a hard, firm Andrew Jackson, who, while mounted on horse, sees the wisdom of making a deal with the pirate Lafitte.

Claire Bloom is a fiery creation who alternately hates and loves Lafitte; Boyer is "light" as Lafitte's aide (a role basically inconsequential), and Inger Stevens is properly attractive as Lafitte's true love and daughter of the governor.

Competently working in featured roles are Henry Hull, an aide to Jackson; E. G. Marshall, as governor of New Orleans; Lorne Greene, Ted de Corsia, Douglas Dumbrille, Robert F. Simon and Jerry Hartleben. Hartleben particularly registers as an 11-year-old cabin boy.

Photography is standout, with Loyal Griggs behind the Technicolor-VistaVision camera, its plusses being especially noticeable in the fog-surrounded battle scene between the British and the Americans. Elmer Bernstein has contributed a meaningful musical background and other credits all are top notch.

Gene.

Tonka
(COLOR)

Good b.o. for this Disney pic in situations where "Old Yeller," etc., did well.

Hollywood, Dec. 12.

Buena Vista release of Walt Disney presentation. Stars Sal Mineo; costars Phil Carey and Jerome Courtland. Produced by James Pratt. Directed by Lewis R. Foster. Screenplay, Foster and Lillie Hayward; based on the book, "Comanche," by David Appel; camera (Technicolor), Loyal Griggs; music, Oliver Wallace; editor, H. Ellsworth Hoagland. Previewed at Academy Awards Theatre, Dec. 12, '58. Running time, **97 MINS**

White Bull .... Sal Mineo
Captain Keogh .... Philip Carey
Lieut. Nowlan .... Jerome Courtland
Strong Bear .... Rafael Campos
Yellow Bull .... H. M. Wynant
Prairie Flower .... Joy Page
Custer .... Britt Lomond
Captain Benteen .... Herbert Rudley
General Terry .... Sydney Smith
Sitting Bull .... John Wareagle
Cpl. Korn .... Gregg Martell
Ace .... Slim Pickins
Lt. Crittenden.............Robert Henry

Walt Disney has had remarkable success in parlaying the combination of a youngster and an animal friend into boxoffice success, i.e., "Old Yeller." His new picture, "Tonka," repeats the formula in a frontier setting with the climax of Custer's last stand at the battle of the Little Big Horn. It seems to be, on the face of it, strictly for the kids. But these Disney features have a way of pulling beyond their apparent strength, and with that in mind, "Tonka" should do better than "Old Yeller." "Tonka" is Disney's Christmas picture.

The screenplay is based on the story that the only survivor of the United States cavalry in its tangle with Sitting Bull's Sioux was a horse named Comanche. According to the screenplay by Lewis R. Foster and Lillie Hayward, based on David Appel's book, this horse was not only a U.S. calvary mount, but was originally an Indian pony named Tonka, which had been raised by a fledgling Teton Sioux brave.

Sal Mineo plays the Indian boy who captured and trained the stallion, which becomes Philip Carey's horse after it is taken by horse traders and sold to the Army. All finally meet on the plains of the Little Big Horn, where the fanatic glory-hunting Custer attacked the Sioux on the theory that his outmanned troops were more than a match for the Indians, one white-skin warrior being the equal of ten redskins. He learned the hard way.

The picture takes considerable time to set the background for the Indian boy, making clear his position in the tribe and the place and attitude of the Indian nations of the time. It also devotes space to his breaking of the horse and his training. It is probably somewhat romantic in its view of the Sioux, but seeing the whole thing through Indian eyes, and the eyes of an Indian youth, at that, gives the story a fresh approach. There are ignorance, vanity and cruelty on both sides and it is shown without excessive realism.

From the juvenile delinquents which he has essayed in the past, Mineo makes quite a leap to portray this clean-limbed young Indian, but he does it with ease and conviction. Philip Carey and Jerome Courtland, as U.S. Cavalry officers, present the more intelligent side of the American military while Britt Lomond, as Custer, strikingly illustrates the view that the only Good Indian etc. H. M. Wynant, as Mineo's Indian nemisis, Joy Page as his mother, and Rafael Campos as his Indian chum, are all good. Others in the cast who stand out include Herbert Rudley, Sydney Smith, John Wareagle, Gregg Martell, Slim Pickins and Robert Buzz Henry.

James Pratt's production values are excellent, and Lewis Forster's direction is clean and straight-forward. As with all Disney pictures, the research into such things as costumes and background is authentic and helpful. *Powe.*

The Last Blitzkrieg

Okay for the war market, where expectations aren't too great.

Hollywood, Dec. 12.

Columbia release of Sam Katzman production. Stars Van Johnson; costars Kerwin Mathews. Dick York; features Larry Storch, Lise Bourdin. Directed by Arthur Dreifuss; screenplay, Lou Morheim; camera, Ted Scaife; music, Hugo De Groot; editor, Lien d'Oliveyra. Previewed Dec. 11, '58. Running time, **85 MINS.**

Kroner .... Van Johnson
Wilitz .... Kerwin Mathews
Ludwig .... Dick York
Ennis .... Larry Storch
Belgian girl .... Lisa Bourdin
Steiner .... Leon Askin
Von Ruppel .... 'Han Bents v.d. Berg
Kirsch .... Robert Boon
Hoffner .... Ton van Duinhoven
Eindorf .... Gijsbert Tersteeg
Levin .... Montgomery Ford
Schwars .... Charles Rosenblum

"The Last Blitzkrieg" approaches World War II from an unorthodox angle in its story of a German High Command plan to sabotage the American war effort by infiltration behind the lines in France. Treatment of this Sam Katzman production—to be sold as an "A" for top billing—throws sympathy to the principal character, a German lieutenant, almost throughout its length, which may evoke certain criticism. Film has been given good production, however, and should do okay biz for its intended market.

Van Johnson stars in the Lou Morheim screenplay filmed entirely in Holland, offbeat casting with thesp playing the son of a high Nazi general picked to lead an English-speaking squad into Allied territory. Considerable stock footage is utilized for actual war scenes, and Arthur Dreifuss, who directs at good pace, has the benefit of some interesting types cast in Holland. Occasional Dutch landmarks likewise provide scenic interest to backdrop yarn's unfoldment.

Some fairly suspenseful action follows Johnson, who speaks perfect English as result of having lived in the U.S. before the war, as he and his squad undertake their assignment. Previously, he has briefed them in American mannerisms, so no suspicion can attach to them if the Americans become suspicious. He joins an outfit, claiming to be lost, and straightway starts his plan of demoralization by a series of incidents which leave the Americans hanging on the ropes but never out. There is a growing sense of his becoming disgusted with Nazi methods, and in the finale, after he has been discovered and made a prisoner, he turns the tide of battle for the American outfit by machine gunning and wiping out a company of Nazis before he dies.

Johnson acquits himself creditably and gets top backing by a competent cast headed by Kerwin Mathews, a sadistic member of his squad, and Dick York, an American sergeant who takes command of his outfit after his superiors are killed. Larry Storch as an American GI and Lise Bourdin in role of a Belgian girl are standouts in brief roles.

Technical departments are well executed, leading off with Ted Scaife's deft camera work. Hugo De Groot's music score, Lien d'Oliveyra's editing and Nico van Baarle's art direction also are an asset. *Whit.*

Der Veruntreute Himmel

(The Embezzled Heaven)
(GERMAN-COLOR)

Berlin, Dec. 9.

UFA release of Rhombus production. Stars Annie Rosar, Hans Holt, Victor de Kowa; features Vilma Degischer, Kai Fischer, Rudolf Vogel and Kurt Meisel. Directed by Ernst Marischka. Screenplay, Ernst Marischka, from novel by Franz Werfel; camera (Agfacolor), Bruno Mondi; music, Anton Profes. At Zoo Palast, Berlin. Running time, **105 MINS.**

Teta Linek .... Annie Rosar
Chaplain Seydel .... Hans Holt
Theo .... Victor de Kowa
Livia Argan .... Vilma Degischer
Leopold Argan .... Fred Liewehr
Mojmir .... Kurt Meisel
Mascha .... Kai Fischer
Kompert .... Rudolf Vogel
Frau Linek .... Lotte Lang
Frau Fleissig .... Jane Tilden

Franz Werfel's novel has not been exploited to best advantage but this is nevertheless the type of feature pic which carries strong boxoffice potential. Publicitywise, it can cash in on the fact that it brings many scenes shot inside the Vatican including some considerable footage of the late Pope Pius XII. It may sound strange but the latter's function in this film comes close to being that of a real supporting player.

Ernst Marischka has directed this with much sentiment and he wisely took advantage of the generous support granted him by the Catholic Church. Some may feel that he went too far with his sentiments. This applies to his numerous close-ups of pilgrims, the scenes around the dying aunt Teta with a chaplain giving her the extreme unction, etc.

The film's standout is the performance turned in by Annie Rosar who portrays the good-natured, naive, religious aunt Teta. Latter thinks that God will grant her a place in heaven if she sends all her earned money to her nephew so that latter can become a priest. There's no doubt that Marischka found Miss Rosar ideal for this role.

Another fine performance is contributed by Hans Holt as the chaplain Seydel to whom Miss Rosar unburdens her heart. Third impressive acting job is done by Kurt Meisel, her spoiled nephew who embezzles all her money.

Technically, the film benefits from beautiful Agfacolor photography. The Vatican scenes are particularly eye-filling. Other technical credits are satisfactory. *Hans.*

Les Grandes Familles

(The Big Families)
(FRENCH)

Paris, Dec. 9.

Cinedis release of Filmsonor-Intermondia production. Stars Jean Gabin, Pierre Brasseur, Bernard Blier; features Annie Ducaux, Francoise Christophe, Jean Desailly. Directed by Denys De La Patelliere. Screenplay, Michel Audiard, De La Patelliere from novel by Maurice Druon; camera, Louis Page; editor, Jacqueline Thiedot. At Paris, Paris. Running time, **95 MINS.**

Noel .... Jean Gabin
Lucien .... Pierre Brasseur
Simon .... Bernard Blier
Francois .... Jean Desailly
Adele .... Annie Ducaux
Jacqueline .... Francoise Christophe

Slickly mounted story of high finance skulduggery in one of France's top industrial families benefits from a roster of topnotch actors. However, it is somewhat talky and its fine points of observation on the French business, social and governmental scenes might be elusive in foreign marts. This looms mainly as a possible entry for special foreign situations on its good mounting and acting.

Jean Gabin's extraordinary presence lends weight and credulity to the pic in his portrait of a strong, rugged individualist, ruling his family and business (which include newspapers, sugar mills, etc.) with an iron hand. Pierre Brasseur is shrewd as the black sheep of the family who ends in a death struggle on the stock exchange with the hard-headed Gabin.

It is this battle which leads to the suicide of Gabin's son whom he is really giving only his first test under fire. High finance bits are somewhat confusing for those not initiated. But the family imbroglios are well done while fine acting all along the line, plus solid direction and good technical aspects, keep this looksee into high finance moving and palatable film fare. *Mosk.*

Une Balle Dans Le Canon

(A Slug In The Heater)
(FRENCH)

Paris, Dec. 9.

Corona release of Filmatec production. Stars Mijanou Bardot, Pierre Vaneck, Roger Hanin; features Paul Frankeur, Colette Duval. Directed by Charles Gerard, Michel Deville. Screenplay, Albert Simonin; camera, Claude Lecomte; editor, Bernard Lefevre. At Triomphe, Paris. Running time, **85 MINS.**

Brigitte .... Mijanou Bardot
Tony .... Pierre Vaneck
Dick .... Roger Hanin
Peper .... Paul Frankeur
Colette .... Colette Duval

Main reason for attention given this pic is that it is Mijanou Bardot's first starring role. She is Brigitte's kid sister. She is pert and pretty but completely lacks her big sister's perverse, promising attributes and emerges a fair ingenue without any signs of stardust or untoward possibilties of following in her sister's footsteps.

In this, two ex-paratroopers running a nightclub, go in for a holdup when gangsters put the squeeze on them for payments. Direction is amateurish, full of insipid love scenes and badly done sequences of violence. It only has Yank possibilities for dualer fare if the Bardot name can be exploited. *Mosk.*

Fanfare

(DUTCH)

Amsterdam, Dec 9.

Nederland release of Sapphire production. Directed by Bert Haanstra. Screenplay, Haanstra, Jan Blokker; music, Jan Mul; camera, Ed v.d. Ende. With Hans Kaart, Albert Mol, Bernard Droog, Andrea Domburg and Ton Lutz.

"Fanfare" may be one of the few Dutch pix that will get its feet on some little piece of ground outside of Holland, Belgium and the Scandinavia market. Though the international market will be limited only to arty houses, "Fanfare" has some comedy appeal. Sandy Mackendrick advised on the script and pointed out possibilities and limitations to director and coscripter Bert Haanstra.

This has a typical Dutch background, locale being the village of Giethoorn where traffic goes mainly by boat along the canals. Situation humor stems from competition between two brass bands which strive for a government subsidy. There's also some slight love interest between a village belle and the only police man in the village.

Bert Haanstra makes his bow as a feature film director, having gained kudos in the last 10 years with documentaries at international fests. His first try comes off very well. His handling of the actors, both pros and others, is good. At times, however, the mouthing of the dialog is awkward. Lensing is well done while the music of Jan Mull fits in well.

Saal.

The Solitary Child
(BRITISH)

Modest drama with little marquee value.

London, Dec. 9.

British Lion release of a Beaconsfield (Peter Rogers) production. Stars Philip Friend, Barbara Shelley. Directed by Gerald Thomas. Screenplay, Robert Dunbar, from Nina Bawden's novel; editor, Peter Boita; camera, Peter Hennessy. At Studio One, London. Running time, 64 MINS.

James Random	Philip Friend
Harriet	Barbara Shelley
Ann	Sarah Lawson
Jean	Rona Anderson
Maggie	Julia Lockwood
Mrs. Evans	Catherine Lacey
Cyril	Jack Watling
Mrs. Dennison	Violet Farebrother
Archie	John Fabian
Doctor	Frank Forsyth

The meaty plot of this modest drama needs a rather wider canvas than given in 64 minutes because its various characters are only portrayed sketchily here.

It's a story of suspicion and its impact on a family. Philip Friend, acquitted of the murder of his first wife, re-marries. His strange behavior arouses a suspicion in his new wife's mind that he may have been guilty. But suspicion also points to his teenage daughter and a local veterinary surgeon. Complications arise through an attractive spinster neighbor and a young man who had had an affair with the dead woman. The climax shows Friend's new wife nearly murdered.

Gerald Thomas's direction is tautly straightforward and Robert Dunbar's screenplay moves smoothly considering his lack of elbow room. Philip Friend aptly creates an air of mystery as the acquitted murderer, but the main burden of the drama falls on Barbara Shelley as his puzzled wife. Miss Shelley is an attractive and intelligent actress who promises to make her mark when given greater opportunities.

There are other capable performances by Sarah Lawson, Jack Watling and Rona Anderson. Julia Lockwood plays the title role of "The Solitary Child" and brings a melancholy feyness to a difficult role.

Rich.

Some Came Running
(COLOR; C'SCOPE)

Name-glittering, high-powered.

Hollywood, Dec. 19.

Metro release of Sol C. Siegel production. Stars Frank Sinatra, Dean Martin, Shirley MacLaine; costars Martha Hyer, Arthur Kennedy; features Nancy Gates, Leora Dana, Betty Lou Keim, Carmen Phillips, Steven Peck. Directed by Vincente Minnelli. Screenplay, John Patrick and Arthur Sheekman; based on the novel by James Jones; camera, William H. Daniels; music, Elmer Bernstein; editor, Adrienne Fazan. Previewed at the studio, Dec. 15, '58. Running time, 137 MINS.

Dave Hirsh	Frank Sinatra
Bama Dillert	Dean Martin
Ginny Moorhead	Shirley MacLaine
Gwen French	Martha Hyer
Frank Hirsh	Arthur Kennedy
Edith Barclay	Nancy Gates
Agnes Hirsh	Leora Dana
Dawn Hirsh	Betty Lou Keim
Rosalie	Carmen Phillips
Raymnd Lanchak	Steven Peck
Prof. French	Larry Gates
Jane Barclay	Connie Gilchrist
Smitty	Ned Wever
Wally Dennis	John Brennan

The only marquee problem on this one is: how are you going to get all those good names up there? "Some Came Running," despite some minor flaws, is certainly one of the most exciting pictures of the season, and with this cast to give it impetus, should make solid returns.

It is Sol C. Siegel's first personal production since his takeover at Metro. It has been brilliantly directed by Vincente Minnelli, with fine performances by Frank Sinatra and Dean Martin and a shattering one by Shirley MacLaine that could only have been surmised from her previous work.

The story is pure melodrama, despite the intention of the original author, James Jones, to invest it with greater stature. But the integrity with which the film is handled by all its contributors, lifts it at times to tragedy. Jones novel has been stripped to essentials in the screenplay by John Patrick and Arthur Sheekman, and those are presented in hard clean dialog and incisive situations.

Sinatra is an ex-serviceman and ex-novelist who returns to his home town, unwitting and unwilling, when he gets drunk in Chicago and is shipped back unconscious on a bus. Accompanying him is Miss MacLaine who is generally unwitting but never unwilling, a good-natured tart with no pretentions. Sinatra can't stand his brother, Arthur Kennedy, or the brother's wife, Leonra Dana, but he falls deeply in love with a friend of theirs, Martha Hyer. He meets a pal, Dean Martin, who becomes an ally, and he becomes involved in the personal life of his niece, Betty Lou Keim.

There have been mentions of "Peyton Place" in connection with "Some Came Running," and there are superficial resemblances. But the current picture is considerably more honest in its basic premise and therefore has more impact. The characters seem less stereotyped and the cast is—overall—far better. The plot has many convulutions, and some of them don't always get adequately explained. Some of the characters, too, are laid in with promises that are not fulfilled and remain unresolved and unexplained at the end.

The title, incidentally, is taken from St. Mark, and is construed to mean that some have come running to find the meaning of life, but are prevented from finding it by obsession with materialism.

Sinatra gives a top performance, sardonic and compassionate, full of touches both instinctive and technical. It is not easy, either, to play a man dying of a chronic illness and do it with grace and humor, and this Dean Martin does without faltering.

With her performance, Miss MacLaine moves into the front row of film actresses. She isn't conventionally pretty. Her hair looks like it was combed with an eggbeater. But it doesn't make any difference, because she elicits such empathy and humor that when she offers herself to Sinatra, she seems eminently worth taking.

Martha Hyer is another who comes into her own. Her playing of a frustrated woman unable to break lose until she is able to evaluate through tragedy, is contained playing of a high order. Arthur Kennedy makes a fine character study of the hypocritical brother, and Nancy Gates and Leora Dana are strong in support. Others in the large cast who contribute include Larry Gates, Betty Lou Keim, Carmen Phillips, Steven Peck, Connie Gilchrist, Ned Wever and John Brennan.

Minnelli, whose touch in "Gigi" was so deftly light, doesn't dodge an opportunity here for full-blooded action and emotion. His next-to-final sequence, a carnival setting photographed by William H. Daniels (with a new Panavision fast lens), aided by adroit editing by Adrienne Fazan, creates what is almost a ballet of jeopardy and terror. It may startle some—and it does seem a thrust of impressionism into realism—but it adds new depth to a basic plot turn as old as motion pictures.

The most impressive thing about Minnelli's direction is his ability to hold a concept of the picture as a whole. He does not hesitate (with the Patrick-Sheekman script) to cap violence with pathos, tragedy with humor, emphasizing and highlighting by contrast. The story never diffuses its intensity by the extraneous or diversionary.

Elmer Bernstein's score is one of his best, ranging from dissonance to the lyrical, and notably using the piano for exceptional effect. Other credits are first-rate, with a special mention for sound, by Franklin Milton. Too often on location shooting, with subsequent studio dubbing to correct deficiencies, you get the effect of two people talking in a windstorm in which all natural sound has been washed out. Milton preserves the natural sounds without sacrificing any dialog or dramatic effects.

Powe.

Rally 'Round the Flag, Boys
(COLOR; C'SCOPE)

Racy version of the best-selling novel.

Hollywood, Dec. 19.

Twentieth-Fox release of Leo McCarey production. Stars Paul Newman, Joanne Woodward, Joan Collins and Jack Carson. Directed by McCarey. Screenplay, Claude Binyon and McCarey; based on the novel by Max Shulman; camera (DeLuxe Color), Leon Shamroy; music, Cyril J. Mockridge; editor, Louis R. Loeffler. Previewed at the Westwod Village Theatre, Dec. 19, '58. Running time, 106 MINS.

Harry Bannerman	Paul Newman
Grace Bannerman	Joanne Woodward
Angela Hoffa	Joan Collins
Captain Hoxie	Jack Carson
Grady Metcalf	Dwayne Hickman
Comfort Goodpasture	Tuesday Weld
Col. Thorwald	Gale Gordon
Opie	Tom Gilson
Isaac Goodpasture	O. Z. Whitehead
Danny Bannerman	Ralph Osborn III
Peter	Stanley Livingston
George Melvin	Jon Lormer
Manning Thaw	Joseph Holland
Milton Evans	Burt Mustin
Waldo Pike	Percy Helton
Betty O'Shiel	Nora O'Mahony
Zack Crummitt	Richard Collier
Oscar Hoffa	Murvyn Vye

Somewhat slow and labored humor, "Rally 'Round the Flag, Boys," as filmed, is a bedroom farce of split-level thinking in split-level housing. Leo McCarey produced and directed the film version of Max Shulman's best-seller. It is unmistakably a McCarey picture. Some of the gags are as elaborate and as carefully timed as a dance sequence. The screenplay, by McCarey and Claude Binyon, picks out the married couple from the novel, elaborates some details, eliminates others.

The resultant plot is simple, Paul Newman and Joanne Woodward are the couple (two children), living in Fairfield County, Conn. They have, in the delicate phrase, drifted apart. Newman is all for drifting right back, but Miss Woodward is so busy organizing their town into a community as neat, tidy and efficient as their modern kitchen, she can't find the time.

Enter the Temptress, or third angle of triangle. She is Joan Collins.

McCarey handles story so there is never any slightest chance of anything coming to a real conclusion. The situations are real, but what happens within them is so far beyond reality as to preclude genuine belief. Marital infidelity —or the possibility of it— occupies considerable footage in the picture and accounts for most of the footwork on the part of the principals. But McCarey handles it to make infidelity so obviously hectic and wearisome that in the end it becomes a strong case for morality. Like most men trying to burn the candle at both ends, Newman winds up with nothing but a pair of scorched hands.

McCarey is working here with players, Newman, Miss Woodward and Miss Collins, who have done only incidental film comedy up to this one. They are called upon to slam into opening doors, swing from chandeliers, do the dropped pants bit (in Newman's case), takes and double-takes. Jack Carson, of course, is a past-master at the slow burn and volcanic reaction, and he more than holds his own.

Notable in the supporting cast are Dwayne Hickman as a "Wild One"-Brando delinquent, Tuesday Weld as his appropriate mate, and Tim Gilson as a Presley-Southern soldier. Also Gale Gordon, O. Z. Whitehead and Murvyn Vye.

Some of the lines are lost, inescapably, but it is a good screenplay job on a popular book.

The humor is carried over in the art direction, by Lyle R. Wheeler and Leland Fuller, and the music by Cyril Mockridge. It is also apparent in the set decoration by Walter M. Scott and Stuart A. Reiss. Sound, by Eugene Grossman and Harry M. Leonard, and editing by Louis R. Loeffler, are both good.

Powe.

Senior Prom
(SONGS)

Disk name tunefest; good b.o. prospects in teenage market.

Columbia release of a Harry Romm production. Stars Jill Corey, Paul Hampton, Jimmie Komack, Barbara Bostock; guest star, Ed Sullivan. Features Tom Laughlin, Frieda Inescort, Louis Prima and Keely Smith, with Sam Butera and The Witnesses. Directed by David Lowell Rich. Written by Hal Hackady; camera, Fred Jackman; editor, Al Clark; original songs, Don Gohman, Hal Hackady; music supervised and conducted by Morris Stoloff. Previewed N.Y., Nov. 21, '58. Running time, 82 MINS.

Gay Sherridan .... Jill Corey
Tom Harper .... Paul Hampton
Dog .... Jimmie Komack
Flip .... Barbara Bostock
Carter Breed III.......... Tom Laughlin
Mrs. Sherridan .... Frieda Inescort
Caroline .... Selene Walters
Carter Breed Sr.......... Francis De Sales
Girl with Holder............ Peggy Moffit
Louis Prima .... Himself
Keely Smith .... Herself
Sam Butera & The Witnesses..Themselves
Ed Sullivan .... Himself
Mitch Miller .... Himself
Connee Boswell................... Herself
Bob Crosby...................... Himself
Toni Arden........................ Herself
Freddy Martin & His Orchestra
Themselves
Jose Melis...................... Himself
Les Elgart...................... Himself

Primed for the teenage market is "Senior Prom," a disk name tuner which should do well in that field-Roster of principals for this Columbia release includes a flock of disk names. Among them are Jill Corey, Louis Prima & Keely Smith and Mitch Miller. But while presence of these platter stars more or less insures attention of the younger set, it's no guarantee of adult audiences.

With some 20 tunes spotted in this Harry Romm production, naturally there's a wealth of exploitation values to be tapped via disk jockey plays and record sales. More than half of the ditties are new numbers.

As written by Hal Hackady, script is no gem of originality for it's a conventional boy-meets-girl yarn with a campus background. Book, obviously, is merely an excuse on which to hang the film's countless tunes. Miss Corey is romantically inclined toward wealthy Tom Laughlin, a fellow collegian. However, after 82 minutes of footage she switches to the less affluent Paul Hampton. It's no surprise at the finale.

Miss Corey, who isn't particularly photogenic, handles four tunes on her own and duets a fifth with co-star Barbara Bostock. Some of her songs, cleffed by Don Gohman and scripter Hackady, are catchy—especially "One Year Older," which she sings after a birthday party. She does a punchy vocal of "Big Daddy," with music-lyrics by Lee Pockriss and Peter Udell.

Best of the musical melange is a lively sequence in which Louis Prima & Keely Smith do a terrific version of "That Old Black Magic." It's already making noise on the Capitol label. Paul Hampton, Miss Corey's vis-a-vis, is a personable lad who shows promise. In the past he's cut several minor platters for Columbia Records. Here he's heard to advantage on the title number, backed by the entire company.

Rounding out this tunefest are Jimmie Komack, Frieda Inescort, Ed Sullivan, Les Elgart, Jose Melis, Freddy Martin's band and the "Record Hall of Fame." Under latter heading are grouped Mitch Miller, Connee Boswell, Bob Crosby and Toni Arden. Komack and Miss Bostock do a couple zippy vocals and provide comic relief. Miss Inescort has little to do as Miss Corey's mother. Tom Laughlin registers as the rejected suitor.

Ed Sullivan, billed as appearing through "courtesy of CBS-TV," is seen briefly in his familiar emcee role. In view of the plethora of tunes and vocalists, director David Lowell Rich for the most part has coped nicely with the problem of getting his performers on and off camera. However, some scenes are reminiscent of oldtime musical shorts. Fred Jackman's lensing is competent as is editing of Al Clark. Carl Anderson's art direction and Morris Stoloff's musical supervision are good. *Gilb.*

Kvinnors Vantan
(Women Waiting)
(SWEDISH)

Paris, Dec. 16.

Svensk Film production and release. Stars Eva Dahlbeck, Maj-Britt Nilsson, Anita Bjork; features Gunnar Bjornstrand, Birger Malmsten. Written and directed by Ingmar Bergman; camera, Gunnar Fischer; editor, Oscar Rosander. At Pagode, Paris. Running time, 105 MINS.

Eva .... Eva Dahlbeck
Marta .... Maj-Britt Nilsson
Rakel .... Anita Bjork
Fredrik .... Gunnar Bjornstdand
Martin .... Birger Malmsten

This is the seventh film done by Swedish director-writer Ingmar Bergman to get specialized first-run booking here this season. Bergman now emerges as one of the most orginal film creators practicing in Europe today. Film bears his insight into female behavior, and his growing mastery of the visual and of narration. It is adult fare, with a good overall entertainment aspect, to make this of interest for Yank arty and some general cinema spots.

Four women, married to four brothers of a rich family, are waiting for their men at a vacation resort. The eldest suddenly confesses that she has lost all contact with her husband, and a young sister of one of them is planning to run off with a young man. The three others each tell the highlights of their lives with their men.

One is about a seduction in Paris. Another brutally exposes a husband's lack of prowess after the wife is seduced by another man, and a third is a witty, racy tale of a husband and wife, drifting apart, caught in an elevator and finding each other again after a first chance to really talk in years.

Pic is technically outstanding with the acting tops. Superior treatment makes sudsy material appear deep and dynamic. *Mosk.*

Bachelor of Hearts
(BRITISH-COLOR)

Light comedy about a German at Cambridge University, with only limited adolescent appeal.

London, Dec. 16.

Rank (Vivian A. Cox) production and release. Stars Hardy Kruger, Sylvia Syms, Ronald Lewis. Directed by Wolf Rilla. Screenplay, Leslie Bricusse and Frederic Raphael; camera, Geoffrey Unsworth; editor, Eric Boyd-Perkins; music, Hubert Clifford. At Rank private theatre, London. Running time, 94 MINS.

Wolf .... Hardy Kruger
Ann .... Sylvia Syms
Hugo .... Ronald Lewis
Adrian .... Jeremy Burnham
Jeremy .... Peter Myers
Conrad .... Philip Gilbert
Tom .... Charles Kay
Robin .... John Richardson
Virginia .... Gillian Vaughan
Lois .... Sandra Francis
Fiona .... Barbara Steele
Helene .... Catherine Feller
Vanessa .... Monica Stevenson
Bijou .... Pamela Barreaux
Aubrey Murdock .... Eric Barker
Dr. Butson .... Miles Malleson
Morgan .... Newton Blick
Mrs. Upcott .... Beatrice Varley
Shop Assistant .... Ronald Stevens
Lecturer .... Hugh Morton

"Bachelor of Hearts" is a switch on "A Yank At Oxford," and might have been more simply titled "A German at Cambridge." It is a facetious, rather embarrassing glimpse of life at Cambridge University. Since the screenplay was written by two ex-Cambridge students it must be assumed to be authentic. In which case, some rather adolescent malarkey appears to go on at the university. U.S. audiences are likely to be completely bewildered by the proceedings and there is little or no marquee value for this outside Europe.

The thin yarn has Hardy Kruger as a German student at Cambridge on an exchange scholarship system. At first treated with suspicion, he proves himself a good fellow, passes his exams and falls in love. But the story is only an excuse for some predictable situations and jokes. This might have been acceptable had there been more wit, but the wisecracks mostly depend on the young German's inability to understand the English idiom or the traditional behavior at the university.

Kruger, who made a big impression with his first British pic, "The One That Got Away," is less happy in this comedy. But he has a pleasant personality to make his slight love affair with Sylvia Syms acceptable. Miss Syms' talents as his girl friend are not overstrained. That dependable actor Ronald Lewis loyally struggles with his role as the leading light in the undergraduates' b r a s h aventures. Miles Malleson as a tutor and Eric Barker as a mathemathetics professor with a bent for jazz music bring some fun to the film. One of the funnier scenes involves Kruger in simultaneous dates with several girls, and the casting director has found a delectable bunch of young starlets to support him.

On the credit side of the film are well-handled sequences of a Jazz Club and the University rag, fine color photography by Geoffrey Unsworth and some brisk editing by Eric Boyd-Perkins. The university and the environments of Cambridge are wonderful to look at. *Rich.*

Good Day for a Hanging
(COLOR)

Western meller for programs, but somewhat above average,

Hollywood, Dec. 19.

Columbia release of Charles H. Schneer production. Stars Fred MacMurray and Maggie Hayes; costars Robert Vaughn and Joan Blackman. Directed by Nathan Juran. Screenplay, Daniel B. Ullman and Maurice Zimm; based on a story by John Reese; camera, Henry Freulich; editor, Jerome Thoms. Previewed at the studio, Dec. 19, '58. Running time, 85 MINS

Ben Cutler .... Fred MacMurray
Ruth Granger .... Maggie Hayes
The Kid .... Robert Vaughn
Laurie Cutler .... Joan Blackman
Paul Ridgely .... James Drury
Tallant Joslin .... Wendell Holmes
William Selby .... Edmon Ryan
Coley .... Stacy Harris
Molly Cain .... Kathryn Card
Marshal Hiram Cain......... Emile Meyer
George Fletcher .... Bing Russell
Landers .... Russell Thorson
Moore .... Denver Pyle
Avery .... Phil Chambers
Olson .... Howard McNear
Midge .... Rusty Swope
Matt Fletcher .... Harry Lauter
Frank .... Greg Barton
Pike .... Michael Garth

The title of "Good Day For A Hanging" is satiric in intent; there's no such thing, the Columbia picture seems to say. With this attitude, and attempting to explore the pre-event effects of a hanging on a small, frontier town, this film is somewhat offbeat in character. The Charles H. Schneer production is not altogether successful, but it is several notches above its modest budget class and will be a more than satisfactory entry in the double-bill market.

Fred MacMurray is the town's leading citizen who takes on the job as marshal, when that law officer is killed while leading a posse. The captured murderer is a young man, Robert Vaughn, who gains the town's sympathy and whose conviction makes MacMurray look like a blood-thirsty peace officer.

The audience will spot Vaugnn as a psychopath the first time he twitches across the screen, but it is easy to see how he could confuse those in the drama. There is "Method" in his madness, too, which makes him an unusually interesting young actor. MacMurray has a rather solid role, but invests it with authority and interest, and Miss Hayes is sympathetic. Miss Blackman, James Drury, Kathryn Card and the remainder of the cast are good.

The "Columbia color," as it's billed, has a tendency to be rather over-rouged, reducing the impact of what is essential a realistic melodrama. Black-and-white would have suited this picture better. Henry Freulich manages some interesting camera setups that enliven the action and Nathan Juran's direction manages to individualize the characters, but they do not build in importance for any strong impact. *Powe.*

La Tete Contre Les Murs
(Head Against the Walls)
(FRENCH)

Paris, Dec. 16.

Sirius release of Atica-Sirius-Elpenor production. Stars Pierre Brasseur, Anouk Aimee; features Jean-Pierre Mocky, Charles Aznavour, Jean Galland, Paul Meurisse. Directed by Georges Franju. Screenplay, J. P. Mocky from novel by Herve Bazin; camera, Eugen Shuftan; editor, Suzanne Sansberg. Preemed in Paris. Running time, 98 MINS.

Marbeau .... Pierre Brasseur
Emery .... Paul Meurisse
Francois .... Jean-Pierre Mocky
Sailor .... Charles Aznavour
Father .... Jean Galland
Stephanie .... Anouk Aimee

Jolting pic builds its story around an insane asylum. It clearly paints a sort of bedlam and looks into good and bad methods of treating mental illness and madness. These are the most striking segments of this offbeat pic which could make for good arty house chances abroad.

Premise hopes for the ameliorating of certain conditions in local sanatoriums. But director Georges Franju, a leading documentary filmmaker, in his first try on a feature film, leans heavily on painting the everyday ring of a mad house.

A disoriented youth, with a rich father, is sketched as he hunts for money among his friends in a rather amoral crowd dedicated to wild parties, rich older women, etc. After a run-in with his father, he's committed to a madhouse. Here the plight of sanity among the unbalanced is skilfully explored and underlined as he tries to escape.

Director Franju has given this some solid mounting and some grueling scenes. Though still more at home with documentary material than dramatic values, he emerges a new feature director with top possibilities. Pierre Brasseur is excellent as the old guard doctor while Jean-Pierre Mocky and Anouk Aimee register as the star-crossed, doomed lovers.

Singer Charles Aznavour is remarkable in his first acting stint. Technical credits are okay. *Mosk.*

Guns, Girls and Gangsters

Adequate dualer.

Hollywood, Dec. 23.
United Artists release of an Imperial Pictures production. Stars Mamie Van Doren; costars Gerald Mohr, Lee Van Cleef, Grant Richards; features Elaine Edwards, John Baer, Carlo Fiore, Paul Fix, W. Beal Wong. Produced by Robert E. Kent. Directed by Edward L. Cahn. Screenplay by Robert E. Kent; camera, Kenneth Peach; art director, William Glasgow; editor, Fred Feitshans; score, Emil Newman. Previewed Dec. 23, '58. Running time, 70 MINS.

"Guns, Girls and Gangsters" is an interesting chronicle of the blueprinting and near-carrying out of a $2,000,000 robbery. The crime comes much closer to perfection than does the film, but there is something to exploit about topliner Mamie Van Doren, though it's not her acting, and the United Artists release should manage to bring home some pennies of profit.

One of Edward Small's low-budgeters, the Imperial Pictures production will have tough sledding as a first-runner unless promoted by unrelenting penetration. As a dualer, it's more than adequate.

Producer Robert E. Kent screenplayed from a story by Paul Gangelin and Jerome Sackheim, lacing together the intricate detailing of the heist of an armored truck carrying bills from Las Vegas casinos to Los Angeles cashiers. Film unfolds in a semi-documentary vein that, had it been carried to its fullest, could have resulted in greater quality.

Miss Van Doren is a nitery singer with a husband in jail and a boy friend in hand. Comes along Gerald Mohr, released cellmate of the hubby, and the robbery plans begin to roll. The husband breaks out of jail at the last minute to upset all the plans, and just about everyone except the blonde charmer ends up dead.

Direction by Edward L. Cahn fails to bring a professional performance from Miss Van Doren, and Mohr seems entirely too smooth. Grant Richards, as the club owner, and Lee Van Cleef, as the husband, are very good, as are Elaine Edwards and John Baer as owners of a roadside motel where the crime takes place.

Technical credits — Kenneth Peach's photography, William Glasgow's art direction, Fred Feitshans' editing, Jack Solomon's sound and Emil Newman's score—are capable. Buddy Bregman and Stanley Styne penned a couple songs, both of which are fine for the film but neither of which will help sell the product. *Ron.*

The Square Peg
(BRITISH)

Reasonably amusing Army farce, with Norman Wisdom successfully playing a dual role.

London, Dec. 23.
Rank (Hugh Stewart) production and release. Stars Norman Wisdom. Directed by John Paddy Carstairs. Screenplay, Jack Davies; editor, Roger Cherrill; music, Philip Green; camera, Jack Cox. At Gaumont, London. Running time, 89 MINS.

Norman Pitkin, General Schreiber
.... Norman Wisdom
Leslie Cartland .... Honor Blackman
Mr. Grimsdale .... Edward Chapman
Sergeant Loder .... Campbell Singer
Gretchen .... Hattie Jacques
Henri Le Blanc .... Brian Worth
Captain Wharton......Terence Alexander
Colonel Layton .... John Warwick
General Hunt .... Arnold Bell
Jean-Claude .... Andre Maranne
Jogenkraut .... Victor Beaumont
Captain Ford .... Frank Williams
Medical Officer .... Eddie Leslie

The successful trio of producer Hugh Stewart, director John Paddy Carstairs and comedian Norman Wisdom has again teamed up in search of yocks. Set in the fairly safe field of Army slapstick, "The Square Peg" is a mildly amusing comedy with a number of hilarious situations among dullish patches. It should be a worthwhile booking for most family houses in U.K. Its success in the U.S. looks to depend on the drawing power of the star's name there.

"Peg" is interesting in that it continues the plan to get Wisdom away from his original "Gump" character in the ill-fitting suit and offer him a wider acting opportunity. He plays a dual role, a road-mender who gets drafted into the Pioneer Corps (Britain's army labor regiments) and a Nazi general whom he closely resembles. Wisdom plays the latter role straight, with only a hint of satire, and is very effective.

Yarn opens slowly with a lot of drawnout situations involving road-mender Wisdom in brushes with local Army officers. They decide that it's better to have him and his boss in the Army so they are drafted. From then on, the comedy pace quickens. In error they are dropped into enemy territory, and are captured with local resistance leaders. Wisdom saves the situation single-handed and escapes himself when about to face a firing squad.

Jack Davies' screenplay is custom-made for Wisdom, being genial rather than witty and offering the comic plenty of scope in such well-tried routines as learning to drill, use a bayonet and so on.

Carstairs' direction is uneven in pace but brings out the full possibilities of Wisdom, whose likeable personality as a little man striving to get ahead is given ample chance to shine. Remainder of the cast loyally fulfill their respective roles as chorus to the star. Among them, useful performances are given by Honor Blackman, as a comely femme officer, who's really a secret service agent; Edward Chapman, as the pompous boss of Wisdom; Campbell Singer, as a typical film farce sergeant and Hattie Jacques, as an outsize vamp.

Jack Cox's photography is okay, but Roger Cherrill's editing might have been brisker at the opening. *Rich.*

Un Drole de Dimanche
(What a Sunday)
(FRENCH)

Paris, Dec. 23.
CCFC release of J. J. Vital-CCFC production. Stars Danielle Darrieux, Bourvil; features Arletty, Cathia Caro, Jean Belmondo, Roger Hanin. Directed by Marc Allegret. Screenplay, Serge De Boissac, Pascal Jardin, Jean Marsan; camera, Jacques Natteau; editor, Suzanne De Troie. At Normandie, Paris. Running time, 90 MINS.

Catherine .... Danielle Darrieux
Jean ......4.................... Bourvil
Armier .... Arletty
Caroline .... Cathia Caro
Patrick .... Jean Belmondo
Sartori .... Roger Hanin

A pleasant pic, this is about a man who meets his wife in a bus after she had walked out on him five years before. Pic then recounts the high points of his affair and marriage in flashback and his winning her hand again. Skimpiness of characterizations and pedestrian direction hurt the film's dramatic punch. It is okay as a possible dualer or special spotting in foreign situations.

Bourvil, a gangling, timid comedian, has become a heavyweight actor here since winning a Venice Film Fest thesp award two years ago. He is engaging and warm as the nice guy who has no ambition except for the love for his wife. He masquerades as a success when she returns to him and she realizes she still loves him. Danielle Darrieux is fetching as the wife in spite of the sketchy role. Pic is technically good and agreeably mounted. Supporting players also help but the production remains a lightweight affair which is saved by knowing performances. *Mosk.*

Le Joueur
(The Gambler)
(FRENCH; COLOR)

Paris, Dec. 23.
Gaumont release of Franco London production. Stars Gerard Philipe, Liselotte Pulver, Bernard Blier; features Nadine Alari, Francoise Rosay, Jean Danet, Carette. Directed by Claude Autant-Lara. Screenplay, Jean Aurenche, Pierre Bost, Francois Boyer from novel by Feodor Dostoyevsky; camera (Eastmancolor), Jacques Natteau; editor, Madeleine Gug. At Colisee, Paris. Running time, 105 MINS.
Alevel .... Gerard Philipe
Pauline .... Liselotte Pulver
Blanche .... Nadine Alari
Zagoriensky .... Bernard Blier
Des Grieux .... Jean Danet
Grandmother .... Francoise Rosay
Muzjik .... Carette

This is another pic version of Dostoyevsky's "The Gambler," which was done in Hollywood back in 1948. This production is in color. This fact coupled with a solid cast makes an uneven tale a colorful entry which might be of offshore arty theatre interest.

Film has its bevy of Russians in the 19th Century Baden-Baden, wearing their souls on their sleeves and fighting over heritages with some ensuing suicide, deaths and a run of gambling fever. An aging general, waiting for an old want to die, is living it up in Baden-Baden on the expenses of a French adventurer, waiting for his payment. The general is engaged to a French coquette and his daughter is the Frenchman's mistress.

Into this comes their tutor, Gerard Philipe, a headstrong, overpassionate type, in love with the general's daughter. All this comes to a head when the old aunt arrives and loses her coin at the gambling table. The family is ruined but the tutor has a run of luck and wins a fortune only to be too late in saving the proud girl he loves from suicide.

Philipe has the intensity and dash for his role while the supporting cast is good, with Francoise Rosay outstanding as the old aunt. Remainder of cast is good, especially Liselotte Pulver's impassioned, headstrong girl. Technical qualities are fine with the garish color a plus. Some pruning of the early segments would make the tense scenes and dramatic climax even stronger. *Mosk.*

Antarctic Crossing
(BRITISH-COLOR)

Important, fascinating documentary on the Fuchs-Hillary Antarctic expedition; excellent prestige booking.

London, Dec. 23.
Rank release of a World Wide Pictures (James Carr) production. Camera, George Lowe, Derek Wright, others; editor, Dennis Gurney; music, Humphrey, Searle. Previewed at R. F. D. private theatre. Running time, 45 MINS.

Here is a fascinating documentary which will be a must for anyone who thrilled to the headlines concerning the exploits of Sir Vivian Fuchs and Sir Edmund Hillary and their teams in the recent Antarctic expedition. Beautifully photographed, with a taut commentary which never falls into the trap of hyperbole, it is a triumph for the cameramen who brought back about nine miles of color film and to the editor, Dennis Gurney, who brought the material down to 45 minutes playing time. The pic manages to cover most of the important events of the two-year expedition.

The achievement was obviously a tremendous one. Dangerous, monotonous, frustrating, but this is not conveyed as much as might be expected. The color photography robs the Antarctic of much of its harshness as can be seen when compared with the inset films of the Scott and Shackleton expeditions. The amazing colors of the Antarctic, beautiful to behold, somehow take away to some extent a feeling of bitter, freezing cold. The expedition's equipment, strong ship, modern tractors, up-to-date kitchen and well-stocked larder also contrast strongly with that used by the two previous explorers. This is by no way of detracting from either the gigantic enterprise or from this pictorial record of it. It is simply that the commentary is needed to remind the audience completely about the toughness of the job.

George Lowe who accompanied the Fuchs' expedition and Derek Wright who travelled with the Hillary party have done a standout piece of lensing. Artistically, it is excellent and technically superb especially considering that the job had no rehearsals or re-takes, and that for 18 months they were unable to check the result of their work. Women will be particularly interested in watching these hardy explorers fending for themselves as cooks, tailors, and "housewives."

Music by Humphrey Searle sets off the film, which is one to fill every audience with a sense of wonder and of pride that men are prepared to endure such discomfort, danger and grinding monotony not merely for a sense of adventure but because of the invaluable scientific results. *Rich.*